The Almanac of American Politics

2022

Members of Congress and Governors:
Their Profiles and Election Results,
Their Districts and States

Richard Cohen
Charlie Cook

Senior Authors
Louis Jacobson
Louis Peck
Jessica Taylor

Founding Author
Michael Barone

Columbia Books & Information Services
National Journal

ISBN-13: 978-1-952374-09-8 (paper)

ISBN-13: 978-1-952374-08-1 (hardback)

ISBN-13: 978-1-952374-12-8 (e-book)

THE ALMANAC OF AMERICAN POLITICS
2022

Chief Author	Richard Cohen
Co-author	Charlie Cook
Managing Editor	Alexandra Watkins
Editorial Director	Duncan Bell
Senior Authors	Louis Jacobson, Louis Peck, Jessica Taylor
Founding Author	Michael Barone
Senior Editors	John Bicknell, Judah Taylor
Data Editor	Dr. Emil Pitkin
Contributing Writers	Cam Joseph, Abby Livingston, Ally Mutnick, David Wasserman
Director of Research	Rob Oldham
Researchers	Madelena Goffredo, Jack Miller (researcher-writers); Mary Landers. Diana Oxner, Brent Peabody
Election Results	Dave Leip's Atlas of U.S. Presidential Elections (uselectionatlas.org)
District Maps	Polidata

Columbia Books & Information Services
President: Brittany Carter

About the Authors

Richard Cohen has been chief author of The Almanac of American Politics since 2015 and was co-author from 2001 through 2010. Rich has written about Congress for National Journal, Politico and Congressional Quarterly. Rich is the author of several books, including Washington at Work: Back Rooms and Clean Air, a case study of the 1990 Clean Air Act, and Rostenkowski: The Pursuit of Power and the End of the Old Politics. He co-authored The Partisan Divide, with former Reps. Tom Davis of Virginia and Martin Frost of Texas. Rich won the Everett McKinley Dirksen Award for distinguished reporting on Congress.

Charlie Cook is the Editor and Publisher of The Cook Political Report, a political analyst for the National Journal Group, and an analyst for NBC News. Over the years, Charlie has served as an Election Night analyst for CBS, CNN, and since 1996 on NBC News Election Night Decision Desk in New York. In 2010, Charlie was the co-recipient of the American Political Science Association's prestigious Carey McWilliams award to honor "a major journalistic contribution to our understanding of politics." In 2013, Charlie served as a Resident Fellow at the Institute of Politics at Harvard's Kennedy School of Government.

Louis Jacobson is the Senior Correspondent for PolitiFact. Since 2004, he has written a column on politics in the states, currently split among the Cook Political Report, Sabato's Crystal Ball, and U.S. News & World Report. Louis has handicapped political races since 2002, including races for Congress, governor, state legislature, other state offices, and the electoral college. Louis has served as deputy editor of Roll Call and as the founding editor of its legislative wire service, CongressNow. Earlier, he spent more than a decade as a reporter covering Congress, politics and lobbying for National Journal.

Louis Peck is politics editor for Bethesda magazine and a co-founder of Maryland Matters, which provides online coverage of politics and government in that state. Since 1978, Louis has been a Washington-based journalist who has written extensively on Congress and national politics. For nearly two decades, he was editor-in-chief of National Journal's CongressDaily. Earlier, Louis was editor of Campaigns and Elections magazine and a national political correspondent for the Washington bureau of Gannett newspapers, as well as collaborating on two books on campaign finance reform with the late Professor Herbert Alexander of the University of Southern California.

Jessica Taylor is the Senate and Governors Editor for the Cook Political Report. For more than 14 years, she has reported on and analyzed congressional and gubernatorial elections. Jessica previously served as a political reporter for NPR. She has been the campaign editor at The Hill and has reported for the NBC News Political Unit, Inside Elections, National Journal, The Hotline and Politico. She has served as an Election Night analyst for CBS and C-SPAN, and has appeared on MSNBC, Fox News and CNN. Jessica was an intern on the 2008 Almanac of American Politics and later served as Research Director for the 2010 edition.

Michael Barone is Senior Political Analyst for the Washington Examiner, a Resident Fellow at the American Enterprise Institute and a contributor to Fox News Channel. He was co-author of The Almanac of American Politics 1972-2016. He is also the author of Our Country: The Shaping of America from Roosevelt to Reagan, The New Americans: How the Melting Pot Can Work Again, and many other publications in the United States and several other countries. Mr. Barone received the Bradley Prize from the Lynde and Harry Bradley Foundation in 2010, the Barbara Olsen Award from The American Spectator in

2006 and the Carey McWilliams Award from the American Political Science Association in 1992.

Acknowledgements

The authors owe their customary debt of gratitude to many people and organizations that have made essential contributions to the 2022 edition of The Almanac of American Politics. Most notably, Michael Barone co-founded and authored the original 1972 Almanac. Since then, his insights and prodigious knowledge of American politics and government have been the heart and soul of this vital work. We are pleased to include his memories in this golden anniversary edition of the Almanac, which is a tribute to Michael's inspiration and remarkable longevity in political analysis. Charlie Cook and his staff at the Cook Political Report made significant contributions to this latest edition. The Brookings Institution graciously allowed usage of key figures from their report, "Vital Statistics on Congress." Dave Leip provided election and other data. Clark Benson, at Polidata, contributed updated congressional district maps. We are grateful to Brittany Carter, Matthew Barnes, Sami McPadden and the staff of Columbia Books and Information Services for their efforts in getting this book to press. Thanks also to Rob Oldham for skillfully assembling and leading our research team in their indispensable efforts. Beth Hahn, historical editor at the Senate Historical Office, gave vital research assistance. And we are grateful for the dozens of political experts in the states who commented on our writing and assisted in other ways.

As we celebrate 50 years of the Almanac, we are appreciative that John Fox Sullivan, the former president and publisher of National Journal, and David Bradley, the owner of National Journal's parent company, Atlantic Media, nurtured the Almanac for three decades. We are mindful of the many superb journalists and editorial managers who sustained "the bible" during that time and have pursued exemplary careers since then.

TABLE OF CONTENTS

GUIDE TO USAGE

The following guide explains the information sources used by The Almanac of American Politics. Major sources of information include the U.S. Census Bureau, the Center for Responsive Politics, The Cook Political Report and the Almanac's writers and researchers. The 2022 Almanac offers significant updates from the previous edition of the book, published in 2019. Figures released by the Census Bureau may vary slightly from those used by the Almanac due to different methods of data aggregation or tabulation. Percentages used in the book may not add up to 100% because of rounding.

Biography

This section lists the date each governor, senator, and representative were elected or appointed, the date and place of birth, academic degrees earned, religion, marital status, and, if applicable, spouse's name and number of children. Also provided is a brief outline of the subject's past elected offices, professional career and military service, and office addresses, telephone numbers, and websites. Committee and subcommittee assignments are current as of June 2021. (Note: On many committees, the chairman and ranking minority member are ex officio members of subcommittees. Leaders in the House typically do not serve on committees.)

Group Ratings

The congressional ratings by nine interest groups provide insight into a legislator's general ideology and the degree to which he or she reflects the group's point of view. Some organizations provided just one rating for 2019 and 2020, the two sessions of the 116th Congress

ADA: Americans for Democratic Action

Liberal: Since ADA's founding in 1947, the Annual Voting Records have served as the standard measure of political liberalism. Rating is calculated by combining 20 key votes on a wide range of social and economic issues, both domestic and international. Its analysis is based on roll call votes in 2019.

ACLU: American Civil Liberties Union

Pro-individual liberties: ACLU seeks to protect individuals from what it views as legal, executive, and congressional infringements on civil liberties. The ACLU compiles a combined score for each two-year Congress. (C = Combined)

AFL-CIO: American Federation of Labor Congress of Industrial Organizations

Liberal labor: The AFL-CIO is a federation of 56 unions representing some 12.5 million members that advocates for social and economic justice and improved working conditions through collective bargaining. Its analysis is based on roll call votes in 2019.

LCV: League of Conservation Voters

Environmental: Formed in 1970, LCV is the arm of the environmental movement that works to elect pro-environmental protection candidates to Congress. LCV ratings are based on key votes on energy, environment, and natural resources legislation. Its scores are annual.

COC: U.S. Chamber of Commerce

Pro-business: Founded in 1912, COC represents local, regional, and state chambers of commerce in addition to trade and professional organizations. It promotes free market policies and ranks members of Congress for key business votes. Its analysis is based on roll call votes in 2019.

HAFA: Heritage Action for America

Conservative: HAFA advocates for conservative policies, many of which are developed by its sister organization, the Heritage Foundation. Key votes in this rating encompass a broad range of conservative issues. It compiles a combined score for each two-year Congress. (C = Combined)

ACU: American Conservative Union

Conservative: Since 1971, ACU ratings have provided a means of gauging the conservatism of members of Congress on foreign policy, social, and budget issues. Its scores are annual.

CFG: Club for Growth

Pro-tax limitation: CFG supports limited government, lower taxes, and policies it deems favorable to economic growth. CFG's annual ratings are based on key votes on taxes, trade, and the economy. Its analysis is based on roll call votes in 2019.

FRC: Family Research Council

Social conservative: The FRC promotes traditional marriage and family and advocates for policies that uphold Judeo-Christian values. Its annual ratings are based on votes on abortion and family issues. It compiles a score annually for each member of Congress. Its analysis is based on roll call votes in 2019.

Almanac Vote Ratings

Emil Pitkin, CEO of GovPredict, has computed the Almanac congressional vote ratings for 2019-20. Almanac editors have selected a list of key congressional roll call votes and classified them as economic, social, or foreign policy-related. Within each issue area, a principal component analysis (PCA) is applied to the votes. PCA is a general statistical procedure that reduces a complex data set with many dimensions into its most descriptive constituent parts, called principle components. This blind statistical procedure found that the most salient, one-number summary of how a legislator voted across dozens of votes corresponds to the liberalism or conservatism of each Member of Congress. That one number is known as the score of the first principal component.

The Members of Congress have been ranked according to their score, and their scores are normalized to fit in the 0 to 100 range, both for the "conservative score" and for their "liberal score." The liberal score is simply 100 minus the conservative score, and vice versa. The composite score is an average of a member's three issue-based scores.

Only Members of Congress who participate in at least half of the votes in an issue area receive ratings. Absences are not scored, while abstentions are scored as a 0.5, with an aye vote scored as a 1 and a nay vote as a 0.

Key Votes

The key votes section presents the positions of Senators and House members on important issues. The following key votes, selected by the Almanac staff, took place during the 116th Congress (2019-2020). There are 12 votes in the Senate and 12 votes in the House, which are split among economic, foreign policy, and social issues. A member who was absent or declined to vote receives NV for "not voting." The letter P signifies a vote of "present." No listings are provided for members who were not in office at the time. Roll-call data were obtained from the Secretary of the Senate and the Clerk of the House.

Senate Votes

- *EPA clean energy rules:* (Senate Vote 324, S.J. Res. 153) Disapprove the Environmental Protection Agency's repeal of the Clean Power Plan. Oct. 17, 2019. Defeated 41-53. (R: 1-50; D: 40-2; I: 0-1)
- *U.S./Mex./Can. trade deal:* (Senate Vote 14, H.R. 5430) Approve the revised U.S. trade agreement with Mexico and Canada. Jan. 16, 2020. Passed 89-10. (R: 51-1; D: 37-8; I: 1-1)
- *Cut unemployment benefits:* (Senate Vote 75, H.R. 6201) Cut proposed sick pay and paid family leave and increase support of unemployment funds. March 18, 2020. Passed 50-48. (R: 48-2; D: 1-44; I: 0-2)
- *Shelton to Fed Reserve:* (Senate Vote 233) Invoke cloture to limit debate of the nomination of Judy Shelton as a member of the board of governors of the Federal Reserve System. Defeated 47-50. (R: 47-3; D: 0-45; I: 0-2)
- *Russia sanctions:* (Senate Vote 6, S.J.Res. 2) Invoke cloture to limit debate on a resolution disapproving the President's action on sanctions of Russia. Jan. 16, 2019. Defeated 57-42; 60 votes required. (R: 11-42; D: 45-0; I: 1-0)
- *Troops in Syria, Afghanistan:* (Senate Vote 14, S. 1) Express the sense of the Senate that the precipitous withdrawal of U.S. troops from Syria or Afghanistan could risk U.S. national security. Feb. 4, 2019. Passed 70-26. (R: 46-4; D: 23-21; I: 1-1)

- *Veto Arms sales to Saudis:* (Senate Vote 178, S.J. Res. 38) Disapprove export of military weapons to Saudi Arabia. June 20,2019. Passed 53-45. (R: 7-45; D: 44-0; I: 2-0)
- *Defense $$$, veto override:* (Senate Vote 291, H.R. 6395) Invoke cloture to limit debate of the President's veto of the defense spending bill. Jan. 1, 2021. Passed 80-12. (R: 40-5; D: 40-5; I: 1-1)
- *Barr as Attorney General:* (Senate Vote 24) Confirm William Barr as Attorney General. Feb. 14, 2019. Passed 54-45. (R: 51-1; D: 3-42; I: 0-2)
- *Spending at the border:* (Senate Vote 185, H.R. 3401) Approve supplemental appropriation in 2019 for humanitarian assistance and security at the southern border. June 26, 2019. Passed 84-8. (R: 50-2; D: 33-6; I: 1-0)
- *Coney Barrett to Sup. Ct.:* (Senate Vote 224) Confirm Amy Coney Barrett as a Justice of the Supreme Court. Oct. 26, 2020. Passed 52-48. (R: 52-1; D: 0-45; I: 0-2)
- *Electoral College objections:* (Senate Votes 1, 2) Object to certifying the Electoral College results from Arizona or Pennsylvania. Jan. 6-7, 2021. Defeated 6-93; 7-92. (R: 6-44; D: 0-46; I: 0-2; (R: 7-45; D: 0-46; I: 0-2)

House Votes

- *U.S./Mex./Can. trade deal:* (House Vote 701, H.R. 5430) Approve the revised U.S. trade agreement with Mexico and Canada. Dec. 19, 2019. Passed 385-41. (D: 193-38; R: 192-2; I: 0-1)
- *First Coronavirus response:* (House Vote 102, H.R. 6201) Approve the initial assistance for victims of the Coronavirus. March 14, 2020. Passed 363-40. (D: 223-0; R: 140-40)
- *HEROES Act:* (House Vote 109, H.R. 6800) Approve the HEROES Act, with extensive support in response to the Coronavirus. May 15, 2020. 208-199. (D: 207-14; R: 1-184; I: 0-1)
- *CASH Act:* (House Vote 252, H.R. 9501) Approve the CASH Act with recovery relief, including to taxpayers, in response to the Coronavirus. Dec. 28, 2020. Passed 275-134. (D: 231-2; R: 44-130; I: 0-2)
- *Russia sanctions:* (House Vote 42, H.J. Res. 30) Disapprove the President's action on sanctions of Russia. Jan. 17, 2019. Passed 362-53. (D: 226-0; R: 136-53)
- *Veto Arms sales to Saudis:* (House Vote 488, S.J. Res. 38) Disapprove export of military weapons to Saudi Arabia. July 17, 2019. Passed 237-190. (D: 232-9; R: 4-190; I: 1-0)
- *Troops in Syria:* (House Vote 560, H.J. Res. 77) Oppose the decision to end U.S. military operations against Kurdish forces in Syria. Oct. 16, 2019. Passed 354-60. (D: 225-0; R: 129-60)
- *Defense $$$, veto override:* (House Vote 253, H.R. 6395) Override the President's veto of the defense spending bill. Dec. 28, 2020. Passed 322-87. (D: 212-20; R: 109-66; I: 1-1)
- *Firearms background checks:* (House Vote 99, H.R. 8) Increase the scope of background checks of firearms sales. Feb. 27, 2019. 240-190. (D: 232-2; R: 8-188)
- *Spending at the border:* (House Vote 429, H.R. 3401) Approve supplemental appropriation in 2019 for humanitarian assistance and security at the southern border. June 27, 2019. Passed 305-102. (D: 129-95; R: 176-7)
- *Marijuana liberalized rules:* (House Vote 235, H.R. 3884) Decriminalize the manufacture, distribution or possession of marijuana. Dec. 4, 2020. Passed 228-164. (D: 222-6; R: 5-158; I: 1-0)
- *Electoral College objections:* (House Votes 10, 11) Object to certifying the Electoral College results from Arizona or Pennsylvania. Jan. 6-7, 2021. Defeated 121-303; 138-282. (D: 0-220; R: 121-83) (D: 0-218; R: 138-64)

NOTE: Freshman members of the House and Senate, because they took office in January 2021, do not have key votes (except for the January 2021 votes on objecting to Electoral College results), vote scores from the interest groups, or ratings from the Almanac for the 116th Congress (2019-2020).

Election Results

The most recent election results are listed for senators and governors. For House members, the results are from the 2020 primary and general elections, as well as any runoffs in 2020 or special elections held since November 2018. Candidates in primaries receiving less than 5% (before rounding) of the total vote and candidates in general election receiving less than 2% (before rounding) of the total were excluded. Election results were supplied by Secretary of State websites. Prior Winning Percentages: The incumbent's winning percentages in earlier elections.

Campaign Finance

Campaign finance data in the Almanac was sourced from the Federal Elections Commission (FEC) website. The FEC makes bulk campaign finance data available in several reports, however principally two were used for the purposes of the Almanac: Operating Expenditures and Independent Expenditures. The Operating Expenditures file was referenced to gather all spending activity for each candidate's principal campaign committee during the relevant election cycle; the Independent Expenditures file was referenced to gather all spending from outside groups attempting to influence an election result.

In the "Election Results" section of each Senator and Member profile, campaign finance data can be found in the 3 columns aligned to the right of each candidate election result. "Cand. Spent" provides the spending total for the principal campaign committee of the candidate during the election cycle in question. "Ind. Exp. Support" and "Ind. Exp. Oppose" both relate to the Intendent Expenditures file, which reports any spending from outside groups to impact an election outcome. The FEC requires that these filers indicate the relevant candidate, as well as whether they "support" or "oppose" the election of that candidate. "Outside groups" may include Super PACs, social welfare 501(c)(4) organizations, trade associations, unions, political parties, corporations, individuals or other groups. However, the monies may not account for all outside money spent in a race, as some outside spending is subject to different federal campaign finance disclosure rules.

The FEC Operating Expenses file for the 2019-2020 cycle was downloaded in May of 2021; the Independent Expenditures file for the 2019-2020 cycle was downloaded in May of 2021. These were mapped to the Candidate Master and Committee Master files, downloaded in May of 2021. Campaign finance data for 2020 special elections was downloaded from the FEC website in June 2021.

Demographics

Population: Figures are from the 2019 American Community Survey (ACS) one-year estimates reported by the U.S. Census Bureau.

Born in state: Percent of entire population of the district that was born in the state in which that district is located.

Race and ethnicity: Figures are from the 2019 ACS reported by the Census Bureau. As defined by the Census Bureau, race reflects individual respondents' perception of their racial identity. Latino origin is defined as an ethnicity. The Census Bureau initially reports data for whites, blacks, and other racial groups that include both Latinos and non-Latinos, but traditionally will follow this initial report with figures that breaks racial and ethnic data into results that are more useful for political analysis. As a result, this version of the Almanac uses the following definitions:

- *White* refers to people who describe their race as white and who say they are not of Latino ancestry or descent.
- *Black* refers to people who describe their race as black or African-American and who say they are not of Latino ancestry or descent.
- *Latino* refers to people who say they are of Latino or Hispanic ancestry, regardless of how they answer questions about their racial identity.
- *Asian* refers to people who describe their race as Asian and who say they are not of Latino ancestry or descent.
- *Two races* refer to people who choose more than one racial category (white, black, Asian, American Indian or Pacific Islander) to describe themselves. This does not include people who describe themselves as Latino.
- *Other* is comprised of the following groups: American Indian, Pacific Islander and those who report "Other".

- *American Indian* refers to people who describe their race as American Indian or Alaska Native and who say they are not of Latino ancestry or descent.
- *Pacific Islander* refers to people who describe their race as black or Native Hawaiian or "other Pacific Islander" and who say they are not of Latino ancestry or descent.

Education: H.S. grad or less refers to people who did not attend college. Some college refers to people who attended college but did not receive a diploma, or who received an associate's degree but not a bachelor's degree. College degree, 4 yr. refers to people who received a bachelor's degree but did not receive a graduate or professional degree after attending college. Post-grad study refers to people who received a graduate or professional degree. All groups are a percentage of people 25 years and older.

Veteran: This category includes both men and women in the civilian population who served in the U.S. military.

Active duty: This category refers to men and women currently employed in the U.S. armed forces.

Median income: This figure represents the median income (not the average income) for all households in the congressional district (or state) for 2019. The numbers in parentheses immediately below indicates where the district ranks among all 436 districts, with the richest district indicated by (1 of 436) and the poorest by (436 of 436).

Income: Each category represents the number of households in each district (or state) with a reported income that fell within that bracket in 2019. Poverty rate: This figure indicates the poverty rate computed by the Census Bureau for 2019 for each district using the definition outlined in the Office of Management and Budget's (OMB) Statistical Policy Directive 14.

Work: The Census Bureau asks all respondents over the age of 16 who are employed in the civilian workforce about their occupation and assigns each respondent to one of five occupation codes defined by the federal government.

- *White collar* refers to civilian workers assigned to the category titled "Management, Business, Science and Arts occupations."
- *Blue collar* refers to workers assigned to two categories: "Natural Resources, Construction and Maintenance occupations" and "Production, Transportation and Material Moving occupations."
- *Sales and service* refers to workers assigned to the final two categories: "Service occupations" and "Sales and Office occupations."
- *Govt. workers* refers to the percentage of respondents over the age of 16 who are employed in the civilian government workforce.

Language: This is percentage of households in the nation speaking a certain language as a percentage of people 5 years and older. The abbreviation other European refers to other Indo-European languages.

Place of Birth: The Census asks people if they are native or foreign born, and if they currently reside in the state in which they were born or if they were born in a different state.

Foreign-born Citizenship Status: This category shows the percentage of foreign-born residents in the U.S. who are citizens.

Region of Foreign Born: This category shows the regions of the world where foreign-born residents were born.

Abbreviations

ACLU	American Civil Liberties Union	HSOB	Hart Senate Office Building
ACU	American Conservative Union	I	Independent
ADA	Americans for Democratic Action	IAP	Independent American Party (NV)
AFDC	Aid to Families with Dependent Children	IC	Independent Conservative
		ID	Independent Democrat
AFL-CIO	American Federation of Labor and Congress of Industrial Organizations	IG	Independent Green
		Ind	Independence Party
		ITI	Information Technology Industry Council
AID	Agency for International Development	IVP	Independent Voters Party
ANWR	Arctic National Wildlife Refuge	LCV	League of Conservation Voters
BL	Better Life Party	LHOB	Longworth House Office Building
C	Conservative Party (NY		
CAFE	Corporate Average Fuel Economy	Lib	Libertarian Party
		Mod	Moderate Party
CAFTA	Central America Free Trade Agreement	NAFTA	North American Free Trade Agreement
CFG	Club for Growth	NARAL	NARAL Pro-Choice America
CHMN	Chairman	NL	Natural Law Party
CHOB	Cannon House Office Building	NP	Non-Partisan
CIA	Central Intelligence Agency	NPA	No Party Affiliation
CNP	Constitution Party	NRSC	National Republican Senatorial Committee
COC	United States Chamber of Commerce	NSA	National Security Agency
COLA	Cost of Living Adjustment	NTU	National Taxpayers Union
D	Democratic Party	PF	Peace and Freedom Party
DCCC	Democratic Congressional Campaign Committee	PNP	New Progressive Party (PR) (Spanish: Partido Nuevo Progresista)
DCS	District of Columbia Statehood	POP	Populist Party
DFL	Democratic-Farmer-Labor Party (MN)	PPD	Popular Democratic Party (PR) (Spanish: Partido Popular Democrático)
DLC	Democratic Leadership Council		
DNC	Democratic National Committee		
DSCC	Democratic Senatorial Campaign Committee	PRG	Progressive Party
		R	Republican Party
DSOB	Dirksen Senate Office Building	Ref	Reform Party
EMILY	EMILY's List (Early Money is Like Yeast)	RHOB	Rayburn House Office Building
		RMM	Ranking Minority Member
ERISA	Employee Retirement Income Security Act	RNC	Republican National Committee
		RSOB	Russell Senate Office Building
FEC	Federal Election Commission	RTL	Right-to-Life Party
FERC	Federal Energy Regulatory Commission	S	Capitol Building Room (Senate side)
FRC	Family Research Council	SOC	Socialist Party
GOP	Republican Party (Grand Old Party)	SW	Socialist Workers Party
		UAW	United Auto Workers
G	Green Party	UMJ	United States Marijuana Party
H	Capitol Building Room (House side)	WF	Working Families
HAFA	Heritage Action for America		

50 Years of the Almanac

By Michael Barone

This year marks the fiftieth anniversary of the publication of the first edition of The Almanac of American Politics. The idea for the book was in germination for a year and a half. My colleague on the Harvard Crimson, Grant Ujifusa, had the idea of publishing a guide to Congress—about each of its members, their states and districts, their voting records and prospects for reelection—for the students protesting the American military action in Cambodia in May 1970. He recruited me to write the text sections because he remembered that when we had been introduced and he said he was from Worland Wyoming, I replied that it was the western terminus of U.S. 16 (one summer afternoon I had made a list of the termini of all double-digit U.S. highways, and the eastern terminus of U.S. 16 was in downtown Detroit, my home town). No one else at Harvard knew anything about Worland and many had never heard of Wyoming, and so he decided I had the requisite knowledge to describe the demographics and politics of every state and congressional district. It soon became clear to us that a reference book useful for antiwar protesters would also be useful for citizens of all views and interests. We recruited another college colleague, Douglas Matthews, to write an introduction, and were fortunate to find a small publisher in Boston, Lovell Thompson, the proprietor of Gambit Inc., interested in publishing the book. We were fortunate in gaining blurbs from John Kenneth Galbraith and William F. Buckley Jr., and some notice in the media—an article in Time magazine, an appearance on the Today program—and a nomination for the National Book Award. In writing, I had the advantage of the latest technology—a Smith-Corona portable electric typewriter, purchased for $140 at Kmart; one of the brand new pocket calculators, purchased for $110; and NCR (No Carbon Required) paper to make copies of my drafts for co-authors and editors.

I thought at the time that the Almanac would make a few ripples in the political pond, then quietly sink to the bottom. Instead, it's still around, 50 years later, thanks to a series of publishers including Gambit Inc., E.P. Dutton, National Journal and now Columbia Books. In retrospect, I think it appeared at a propitious moment, just when the market for such a product was suddenly large enough for commercial viability but before anyone realized that. Congressional Quarterly could have produced such a book (and in time did publish a competitive volume), and National Journal could have (and in time published multiple volumes of the Almanac). Political junkies scattered across the country were always potential purchasers, but the commercial marketplace was probably proportionate to the square footage of Washington office buildings, which was expanding rapidly past a critical mass in the early 1970s, to house the lobbyists and industry representatives with vested interests in congressional action—or inaction. In correspondence with Grant, I used (and perhaps invented) the term "K Street" to describe this market; I don't recall having seen the term used before, but memory often plays tricks and I would be happy to learn who had coined the phrase earlier.

What were my sources for the Almanac text? The political journalism of the time, of course; this was the heyday of "the boys on the bus," talented pre-baby boom generation political reporters like David Broder, Johnny Apple and Jack Germond. I was a regular reader of the Washington Post and the New York Times, of the three weekly news magazines. For the specific politics of each state, Grant went down to Sheldon Cohen's out-of-town newsstand in Harvard Square and pre-purchased a month's worth of copies of a major newspaper from each of the 50 states, and periodically mailed them off to me in Detroit, where I was then living in an apartment with a view to the south of Canada. My perspective on the demographic and political history of the different states was shaped especially by three books, which I still recommend to young people who want to understand what America was like at the beginning of the post-World War II period. One was John Gunther's Inside U.S.A., a compulsively readable bestseller in its day, uneven in its coverage (Maryland and Delaware get about a page near the end, California leads off with three or four chapters) but full of insights. Another was the Texas-born Harvard professor V.O. Key's Southern Politics, with perceptive chapters on each state in the era of complex one-party Democratic politics. A third was the journalist Samuel Lubell's The Future of American Politics, based on the author's personal interviewing in middle-income swing constituencies like the one in which I had grown up in northwest Detroit. In addition, the historical material in Kevin Phillips's recently published The Emerging Republican Majority was very helpful.

But most of all I relied on data, or my interpretations thereof. I have always been fascinated by maps and election data. I had a copy of the 1961 World Almanac, which showed the vote for Kennedy and Nixon in 1960 for each county in the nation (fortunately there was little third-candidate vote that year outside Mississippi and Louisiana), and with a slide rule, I calculated the percentage for Kennedy in each county, and then in my Rand McNally Road Atlas colored in with magic marker the counties Kennedy carried or where he won 45 percent of the two-party vote. So it came naturally to me to overlay on top of maps election returns and demographic data. In writing descriptions of each congressional district for the Almanac, I drew heavily on the Congressional District Data Book that Richard Scammon caused to be created when he headed the Bureau of the Census in the early 1960s. The book provided data for income of each district (Illinois 10, in Chicago's North Shore suburbs, was the nation's highest-income district when it elected the 30-year-old Donald Rumsfeld in 1962) and for its percentage of (in the contemporary polite term) Negroes; but nothing for Hispanics, a term the Census Bureau didn't invent until 1970. The ethnic composition of districts was indicated by the numbers born in, or with parents born in, particular countries. Those numbers required some interpretation, however; the largest concentration of those with roots in Russia, for example, included Jews in the four large boroughs of New York City and the Volga German wheat farmers in North Dakota.

I was writing, mostly without realizing it, at a particularly unsettled time in American politics. The United States was in the often painful process of transition from a nation where political allegiance in many regions and states was determined by events and conflicts at various times in the past, toward a national politics dominated by relatively contemporary issues and attitudes. Large parts of the nation still voted as they fought in the Civil War. Kennedy's second best state in percentage terms in 1960 was Georgia, not because the (then almost entirely White) voters there agreed with Kennedy's generally liberal platform but because Sherman had marched through only 96 years before. Mountain counties in Kentucky and Tennessee, with some of the nation's lowest incomes, voted overwhelmingly Republican, just as they had stuck with the Union and fought against the Confederates 100 years before.

Less distant events also had continuing impact. The giant industrial metropolises of Pittsburgh and Cleveland and Detroit, and the smaller factory towns of Youngstown and Flint and Gary, and the iron mining Mesabi Range of Minnesota voted overwhelmingly Democratic, in fealty to the industrial unions which had won pitched battles against giant companies in the late 1930s; forgotten was the fact that these areas had been overwhelmingly Republican for years before. Ethnic conflict defined the politics of New England, with Yankee Republicans slowly becoming outnumbered by Irish Catholic Democrats (Italians were something of a wild card), so that John Fitzgerald Kennedy's 1952 narrow victory over Henry Cabot Lodge Jr., recalled the reverse result in the Senate election between their grandfathers in 1916.

All of this was complicated by the fact that the parties stood for different things in different parts of the country. Southern Democrats were almost unanimously opposed to civil rights bills, while Democrats outside the 11 states of the Confederacy were, with just a few exceptions (like West Virginia's Robert Byrd) in favor. There were more subtle differences between the different constituencies of a party that had always, from its beginning in Andrew Jackson's time, been a coalition of out-groups. Take the dominant constituencies at the 1960 Democratic National Convention, as identified by Theodore H. White in The Making of the President 1960: Southern governors, big city machine bosses and labor union leaders. By 1971, when the first Almanac appeared, these constituencies were on their way toward extinction. Republicans held the governorships of Kentucky, Tennessee and Virginia, and had recently won those in Arkansas, Florida and Oklahoma and won the popular vote in Georgia. The big city machines, with the expansion of government welfare programs and outmigration to suburbs, withered in importance, and the new rules of the national Democratic Party would result in the ouster from the next year's national convention of the most prominent boss, Richard J. Daley of Chicago. Labor leaders faded in importance as well, as union memberships had been declining since the middle 1950s while the public-sector union movement was still in its infancy. So was the voting bloc of high-education liberals, visible heretofore in the limited number of "reform" Democrats in central cities like New York and Chicago and in university towns, and now heavily represented in Democratic antiwar movements.

The Republican party of 50 years ago had its own divide, notwithstanding its generally less fissiparous nature since its founding in Abraham Lincoln's time and its continuing character as a party centered on a core constituency of people considered to be ordinary Americans but who are not by themselves a majority of the electorate. But Republican politicians, like Democrats, tended to adapt to local terrain. In midcentury America, journalists classified Republicans as liberals or conservatives, depending on whether they were inclined to accommodate or oppose New Deal policies and whether on foreign policy they were classified as internationalists or isolationists (though not all liberal Republicans were internationalists or all conservatives isolationists).

Playing a major role in these classifications was New York, then much more than now the mass media and journalistic center of the nation. New York was the most populous state in the nation, with 47 electoral votes in the 1930s and 1940s; in 1944, the five boroughs of New York City cast 7 percent, one out of every 14, of the nation's votes. New York was also, in every seriously contested presidential election for a century after the Civil War, a marginal and therefore target state politically, and so it produced more than its proportionate share of presidential and vice presidential candidates and influenced more than proportionately the political strategies and public policies of candidates of both political parties. In the 19th century, New York was narrowly divided between heavily Catholic and Democratic metro New York City and heavily Protestant and Republican Upstate New York. To this, the Ellis Island era from 1892 to 1924 added several million Jewish immigrants, who distrusted both major parties and tended to be more liberal on both economic and cultural issues than the core constituencies of either major party. This process was described by Samuel Lubell, who wrote about the "urban vote." Thus the incentives for New York, and for many national, politicians was to appeal to voters in the middle of the partisan spectrum with policies on the left of the ideological spectrum. The results were apparent in the political careers of Republicans from Theodore Roosevelt to Thomas Dewey and Nelson Rockefeller, and of Democrats from Al Smith and Robert Wagner to Franklin Roosevelt and Averell Harriman. In 1971 this framework was becoming obsolete. Nelson Rockefeller was still governor of New York, but the liberal New York City Mayor John Lindsay that year switched from the Republican to the Democratic Party, and New York was no longer marginal but leaned Democratic in close national elections.

The 1970s would produce more political surprises and upheavals that disproved political conventional wisdom but proved to be evanescent rather than permanent alterations of the political landscape. Voters in postwar America were in the habit of reelecting successful presidents of both parties with landslide majorities—Dwight Eisenhower with 57 percent in 1956, Lyndon Johnson with 61 percent in 1964 (pre-assassination polling suggests John Kennedy would have run just about as well if he had lived), Richard Nixon with 61 percent in 1972 and Ronald Reagan with 59 percent in 1984. But none of those Republicans carried with him Republican majorities in the House of Representatives, and the across-the-board Democratic landslide of 1964 had no lasting power, with Republicans winning House majorities outside the South in 1966 and 1968, which they otherwise failed to do between 1958 and 1980. In retrospect, the failure of any presidential candidate since 1984 to win more than 53 percent of the popular vote (and of any president to win more than 51 percent when he sought re-election) clarifies what these landslides meant (as does the failure of any presidential candidate between 1820 and 1920 to win such large percentages of the popular vote): the grateful response of an electorate with personal memories of the Great Depression and World War to incumbent presidents who seemed to have produced prosperity and peace.

This was only one way in which the ructions of electoral politics in the years around 1971 provided a poor guide of the half-century to come. The results of the most recent presidential election, in 1968, resembled those of 1960, with a close division between Democrats and Republicans. But the total number of votes for both were down, 2.9 million for Democrats and 2.3 million for Republicans (actually the same nominee, Richard Nixon), with 9.9 million for the formerly segregationist Alabama Governor George Wallace. That close election was followed by the landslide of 1972, then by the election of Democrat Jimmy Carter by a 50%-48% margin in 1976 and his 51%-41% defeat by Ronald Reagan in 1980. Huge numbers of votes switched between elections. Alabama, to start with alphabetical order, voted 14% Republican in 1968, 72% in 1972, 43% in 1976 and 61% in 1984.

As Democratic nominee in 1972, George McGovern carried only 89 of 435 congressional districts, while half the districts that voted for the Republican Nixon also elected Democratic congressmen. Outside the Northeast, Carter in 1976 carried only four states that voted for Joe Biden (the first senator to endorse his candidacy) 44 years later, his own and his running mate's home states plus, by narrow margins, Wisconsin and Hawaii. Carter carried every Southern state but Virginia (today the most Democratic Southern state) and Oklahoma in 1976 and lost every Southern state except West Virginia (today overwhelmingly Republican) and Georgia in 1980. Such wild swings in political preference were perhaps not surprising in a country that ended up rejecting four presidents in a row: Lyndon Johnson and Richard Nixon after landslide victories were forced to leave office, and Gerald Ford and Jimmy Carter were both defeated.

Amidst such upheavals, historic preferences were being overridden by contemporary concerns —many of which have been long forgotten. Consider the 1970 Senate races, the most recent such contests as I was writing the Almanac in 1971. With Southern states now featuring two-party contests and Northern states dealing with cross currents of issues from school busing to the Vietnam War, there were more seriously contested Senate races that year than in any other election year in American history, before or since. There were 19 by my count, and several others that still reverberate: among the losers in seriously contested races was future President George H.W. Bush, and among the losers in non-seriously contested races were Lenore Romney, Mitt Romney's mother, in Michigan and John McLaughlin, later the longtime host of the eponymous political talkfest, in Rhode Island. That there were so many seriously contested races was largely the work of the Nixon White House, which set out audaciously to reduce the Democrats' 57-43 Senate majority in a year when 25 Democratic seats and only 10 Republican seats were up for grabs. Republicans did make a net gain of two seats. But they fell short in seven other seriously contested races (in California, Florida, Indiana, Missouri, New Mexico, Texas and Wyoming)—enough if they had fallen to produce the 52-48 Republican majority that, contrary to almost all expectations, came into being in the 1980 election 10 years later.

In their 2004 book The Big Sort, journalist Bill Bishop and academic Robert Cushing noted that in the 1976 election only 26 percent of Americans lived in a "landslide" county, one carried by a presidential candidate by a margin of 20 percentage points or more. In 2004 that percentage nearly doubled, to 48 percent and, as Bishop noted later, it rose to 60 percent in 2016. His point, that geographic areas have become more monopartisan, is factually correct. But the inference some readers draw, that the politics of the 1970s was a time of bland consensus and neighborly friendliness, is an overstatement. What was actually happening in 1976 was that, as historic partisan allegiances were wearing thin, the two parties happened to nominate two candidates who came from and exemplified many of the values of their party's historic homelands. Gerald Ford was from Outstate Michigan, one of the birthplaces of the Republican Party in 1854, and was the House minority leader for almost a decade before becoming vice president and president. Jimmy Carter was from south Georgia, historically Democratic from the days of Andrew Jackson and the nation's second most Democratic state as recently as 1960 (and its most Democratic when Carter was the nominee). Carter temporarily halted his party's decline in the South; Ford temporarily stopped his party's decline in the lands of the New England diaspora (from Maine and Vermont to Ann Arbor Michigan and Marin County California). But those declines continued after Carter was defeated, carrying only six states and the District of Columbia, in 1980.

The 1980s were a calmer electoral era. Ronald Reagan was elected and reelected president, carrying 93 out of 100 possible states in 1980 and 1984. His vice president, George Bush, was elected in his own right in 1988 by a 53%-46% margin—a margin not exceeded since and the only time since the 1940s one party has won a third consecutive presidential election. It became conventional wisdom among journalists and political scientists that Republicans had a lock on the presidency and Democrats had a perpetual majority in Congress, or at least in the House of Representatives, since Republicans held majorities in the Senate after the 1980, 1982 and 1984 elections. A variety of explanations were offered for this state of affairs, persuasive in the short term but not without weaknesses (after all, one party or the other came close to winning a third consecutive presidential term in 1960 and 1968, and would again in 2000 and 2016). One reason for Republican ascendancy in presidential elections was the unpopularity of liberal policies that seemed to produce a near tripling of violent crime and welfare dependency in 1965-75, with rates remaining on a stubbornly high plateau thereafter. Reasons for Democratic ascendancy in House elections included their dominance in redistricting in the 1960, 1970 and 1980 census cycles, the residual power in committee positions of senior Southern Democrats from districts that were increasingly Republican at the presidential level the political adeptness of the young liberal Democrats elected in the 1970s, whose candidacies were inspired by opposition to the Vietnam war and enhanced by revulsion at the Watergate scandal.

All these factors seemed solidly in place as the 1990s began. But within two years the Republicans' lock on the presidency was broken and within four years the Democrats' hold on Congress was gone. Bill Clinton managed to win the 1992 Democratic presidential nomination from a party chastened by defeat in six of the previous seven presidential elections, by campaigning to end welfare as we know it and to reduce rather than excuse violent crime. As late as June he ran third in polls, behind the incumbent and behind independent businessman Ross Perot; then in July, on the Wednesday of the Democratic National Convention, Perot suddenly dropped out and virtually all his support moved to Clinton. Perot reappeared as a candidate in October and managed to win 19 percent of the popular vote. But by then Clinton was well ahead and managed to defeat an incumbent who, having achieved breathtaking foreign policy success, and 50 years after volunteering in World War II, seemed ready to retire.

Meanwhile, House Republican rebel Newt Gingrich, noting the retirement, death or defeat of both conservative Southern Democrats and the aging Vietnam/Watergate veterans, rallied conservative and moderate colleagues tired of serving in the minority and got 1994 Republican candidates to unanimously endorse a Contract With America. Republicans campaigned against Clinton's Democrats-only tax increase, against the gun control provisions in his crime bill and against Hillary Clinton's unsuccessful health insurance legislation. And so in 1994, for the first time in 42 years Americans elected a Republican House of Representatives, and in 1996, after Gingrich had successfully pressed Clinton to sign a welfare reform bill, Americans for the first time in 52 years reelected a previously elected Democratic president.

What has followed is a political era significantly different from the one before, the one in which the first edition of The Almanac of American Politics was written. Democrats won five of the next eight presidential elections, but while the Republicans' average popular vote margin from 1968 to 1988 was 10 percent, the Democrats' average popular vote margin from 1992 to 2020 has been just 4 percent. And that might overstate their advantage, given that the Electoral College majority in the last two elections has been decided by only 77,736 and 42,918 popular votes in three different states, notwithstanding Democrats' 2 percent and 4 percent margins in popular votes. Republicans have won majorities in the House of Representatives in 10 of the 14 congressional elections from 1994 to 2020, but while Democrats never won fewer than 243 House seats in the elections between 1958 and 1992, Republicans have only once, in 2014, won more than 243 House seats in the elections since 1946. So in 2021, it appears that Democrats have a less secure lock on the presidency than Republicans appeared to have in 1991, and that Republicans now have a weaker position in the House of Representatives than Democrats appeared to have at that time three decades ago. Historic partisan divisions have faded away, replaced by divisions based primarily on religion or degree of religiosity and moral values. Starting in the 1990s, accelerating in the late 2010s, voters with high education credentials have trended Democratic and voters with low education credentials have trended Republican. The split ticket voting common in 1952-1992 has given way to straight-ticket voting, to the point that in 2020 only 16 congressional districts voted for a congressman of one party and president of the other. The political scientists have gotten their way: sharp partisanship has resulted in the virtual extinction of conservative Democrats and liberal Republicans.

This perspective is consistent with the thesis of political scientist Sean Trende in his 2012 book The Lost Majority. Contrary to Samuel Lubell, John Gunther and Kevin Phillips, who all seemed to assume that Democrats had a natural political majority in the post-World War II decades, Trende argued that from the 1952 election—a contest that showed a sharp increase in turnout, from 49 million in the three elections in the 1940s to 62 million—Republicans tended to have an advantage in presidential, though not congressional elections: an Eisenhower majority, perhaps. (Another argument for continuity from Eisenhower to Reagan comes from Gene Keelson's 2016 book Reagan's 1968 Dress Rehearsal, which describes a surprisingly close and appreciative relationship between the two Republican presidents during Eisenhower's winter residence in California in the 1960s.)

Trende's view is that this Eisenhower majority was replaced, in fairly short order in the 1990s, by a more tenuous Clinton majority at the presidential level. Aiding that process was the sharp reductions in welfare dependency and violent crime effected by policies initiated by Wisconsin's Tommy Thompson and New York's Rudy Giuliani, imitated and adapted by many Republicans and some Democrats; few things hurt a party more than suddenly solving a problem it has won votes on for years. Ironically, when the Republicans and Democrats seemed to have solid locks on the executive and legislative branch, bipartisan compromises were often reached, and the impulse continued until the Clinton-Gingrich negotiations were precluded by the Monica Lewinsky scandal. Now that Democrats and Republicans have weaker holds on each branch, they are less ready for compromise, since it often seems that the next election may give them control of the presidency, Senate and House, which Republicans held in 2001, 2003-07 and 2017-19 and Democrats held in 1993-95, 2009-11 and now since the 2020 election.

In the 1950s there was a movement in the American Political Science Association, led by the preeminent political scientist of the time E. E. Schattschneider, to realign the two political parties, so that there would be one clearly liberal party and one clearly conservative party. (Schattschneider and most of his supportive colleagues probably hoped the clearly liberal party would usually win.) So much for liberal Republicans and conservative Democrats; voters would get a clear choice between two distinct alternatives, and the winning candidates would be in a position to convert the voters' choices into effective legislation. When I was preparing the first Almanac of American Politics for publication in 1971, Schattschneider died in March and his committee was long gone, but things were moving in their direction: Rockefeller had been booed at the 1964 Republican National Convention, and Daley and conservative Southern governors were about to be unseated at the 1972 Democratic National Convention. Today the prayers of the political scientists have been answered. We have one clearly liberal party, though it is not precisely clear exactly how liberal Biden is prepared to let it be, and we have one clearly conservative party, though the precise content of its conservatism is not precisely clear after Donald Trump's presidency. We have continuing close elections and bitter partisanship, much as the United States did in the 1870s and 1880s, and we have presidents widely seen as deficient in important respects.

How long will this situation stay in place? It's impossible to say before the fact, and often obvious after, but history suggests that the emergence of talented political strategists of a younger generation, political operators with no vested interest in things continuing as they have been, can at propitious times make a difference. Going back in history, the partisan deadlock of the 1870s and 1880s was broken in 1896 by the 36-year-old political entrepreneur William Jennings Bryan and by the responses of William McKinley, one of the youngest veterans of the Civil War (he was under fire at Antietam at age 19). Election year 1952 saw the triumph of Dwight Eisenhower, of the same generation as his two predecessors, but also the emergence of leaders of the young G.I. generation—Richard Nixon, John Kennedy, Henry Jackson, Hubert Humphrey, Barry Goldwater. Men who served in uniform during World War II won the presidency in every election from 1952 to 1988. Then they were replaced by creative baby boomers hoping to escape from threatened obscurity and tedium: Bill Clinton, whose successful run was just about over in Arkansas, and Newt Gingrich, always eager to avoid being a powerless backbencher in the House. Members of the baby boom generation now have won the presidency in every election from 1992 to 2020, if one includes Joe Biden, born in November 1942, two months before the Boom began according to the authors of Generations.

As it happens, after writing the first edition of the Almanac, I interviewed Biden by telephone in May 1972. The 29-year-old New Castle County Council member sketched out just how he would beat a beloved longtime incumbent that fall—an interview that helped me write many Biden Almanac profiles. But he was absent in that first edition 50 years ago, as was every member of Congress today. As for me, I was younger than any member of Congress 50 years ago and today am older than all but 31. Fifty years is a long time, but Congress goes on. And so does The Almanac of American Politics.

30 Years of Deepening Partisanship

By Charlie Cook

Introduction

The nature and dynamics that we see in American politics today bear little resemblance to what existed when Michael Barone, Grant Ujifusa and Douglas Matthews analyzed and meticulously detailed the political landscape 50 years ago in the first edition of the Almanac of American Politics. For that matter, it isn't much like what existed 30 years ago when the 11th edition was published in 1992.

Politics have never been static but for so many elements and forces to change in such a relatively short period of time is extraordinary, and for many, a bit disturbing. Things were hardly idyllic in 1972 when the first edition was published. It was just over halfway through the 44-year Cold War, the Vietnam War was nearing its final phases and the infamous Watergate burglary would occur in June of that year.

We have had partisanship for as long as we have had parties. Indeed, President George Washington warned of the danger of "factions" in his farewell address. Partisanship certainly existed in 1972 when that first edition was published. But the reality that existed in those first 20 years of the Almanac's publication looked far more like it had for the preceding 50 years than it has for the most recent 30 years.

What began in and after the 1992 campaign between President George H.W. Bush and Arkansas Gov. Bill Clinton, his Democratic challenger, in retrospect, has taken American politics on a very different course and to what many believe is a very distressing place.

Heading into that 1992 election, the Republican Party had prevailed in four of the five preceding presidential elections, the lone exception being Jimmy Carter's 1976 defeat of President Gerald Ford. Widening the lens to a longer timeframe, the GOP had prevailed in seven out of the 11 post-World War II elections, the only variations were John Kennedy's 1960 and Lyndon Johnson's 1964 victories.

While Republicans clearly had the upper hand in contests for the White House, Democrats were dominant in the battles for Congressional majorities. While Republican losses of two Senate and 19 House seats in President Eisenhower's first midterm election in 1954 were about average, they were enough to cost Republicans their majorities in both chambers. No one at the time knew that Democrats would go on to win House majorities in the next 20 consecutive elections, and in 23 of the 25 Post-World War II elections (the GOP won majorities in 1946 and 1952). On the Senate side, from 1954 on, Democrats won Senate majorities in 17 of those next 20 elections, (all but 1980, 1982 and 1984), as well as 20 out of 25 for the Post-War period (including the two prior exceptions, 19467 and 1952).

Deliberately or not, American voters had constructed their own separation of powers, perhaps not fully trusting either party enough with complete control of both the executive and legislative policymaking institutions, usually putting Republicans in the White House and Democrats in charge of Capitol Hill. The product of this period of mostly divided government was compromise and relatively centrist governing, a stark contrast with the paralysis that has become the norm of late.

In a conversation about politics at a cookout in the backyard of a Capitol Hill townhouse, someone asked the rhetorical question, "What will happen first, Democrats will elect a President or Republicans a Speaker?" Someone else suggested, "when one happens, the other will probably follow," with chuckles from all. What seemed so improbable is precisely what happened.

Clinton defeated Bush in 1992. Two years later came a Republican tsunami tidal wave, inspired and led by then Minority Whip Newt Gingrich. The GOP needed a 40-seat net gain in the House but picked up 52 seats, breaking that 40 year period of exile for the GOP in the House. Though Gingrich was both the war planner and commander-in-chief of this assault, the wave extended to the Senate sweeping Democrats out of control. Republicans needed a seven-seat net gain for a majority but won eight seats, unseating two incumbents and capturing six open seats while losing none of their own. The losses then inspired both Sens. Richard Shelby of Alabama and Ben Nighthorse Campbell of Colorado to switch from the Democratic to the Republican side of the aisle. Not only was a 40-year pattern broken, but things have not been the same since.

Clinton's 1992 victory and the subsequent 1994 midterm marked the first of four waves of unprecedented and escalating levels of partisanship. Upon taking office, the newly-minted, young president from Arkansas faced a level of animosity among Republicans far exceeding anything his three Democratic predecessors, John Kennedy, Lyndon Johnson and Jimmy Carter ever faced and was a central ingredient of what happened in 1994.

After eight years of Clinton and a galvanizing period of party politics, the photo-finish election in 2000, with then-Vice President Al Gore prevailing in the popular vote yet George W. Bush capturing the more relevant Electoral College vote, triggered a mirror-image explosion of partisanship. Only, this was among Democrats toward the new Texan president, who suddenly was the target of a level of vitriol that exceeded what the four previous Republicans, Eisenhower, Ford, his father or even Richard Nixon endured. The cycle reversed yet again eight years later when Barack Obama won, who in turn faced a fury that had an intensity far greater than what Clinton had faced. Four years later the fourth wave of escalation occurred when Donald Trump came out ahead in the electoral vote while Hillary Clinton, like Gore, won the popular vote. None of Trump's three predecessors faced the extraordinary levels of animosity or contempt from those in the opposite party that Trump did.

Central to this new trend was the declining level of support among opposition party members towards a president. As of their 100th day in office, both Eisenhower and Kennedy had Gallup job approval ratings in the sixties among those in the opposition party. Nixon, Carter, Reagan and George H.W. Bush had approval ratings in the forties among those in the other party. For Clinton, George W. Bush and Obama it was in the twenties and thirties. But for Trump, it was nine percent, for Biden 11 percent.

Tribalism had taken hold. Emory University political scientist Alan Abramowitz put the label of "negative partisanship" to describe partisans who loath the other party even more than they like their own.

Still, party members began sticking almost monolithically in opposition to presidents, presidential nominees and increasingly down-ballot candidates of the other party and just as single-mindedly supporting those of their own party. There seemed to be little or nothing that the other party or its elected officials and candidates can do right, and little or nothing wrong for those of their own party.

For many partisans in both parties, they could see no evil, hear no evil or speak no evil of those in their own party.

This partisan dynamic created high floors and low ceilings for each side. Such uniform support insured that a president, nominee or even candidates in some down-ballot contests in competitive states and districts would rarely if ever drop below a certain level no matter what, and equally monolithic opposition kept them from rising much beyond a certain point. There were two notable exceptions, just after the U.S. victory in the 1991 war in the Persian Gulf for George H.W. Bush and for a longer period after the September 11 attacks for his son, both temporarily cracking a usually impenetrable ceiling. Though the former ended up losing re-election and the latter a mammoth second midterm loss five years later, it required events of that rarity and magnitude for that ceiling to crack for even that time.

Electorally, the trading range of job approval and support levels has become relatively narrow. This means that nationally and in competitive states and districts, trailing candidates are rarely outside of striking range. A fortunate break or mistake by an opponent can easily change the trajectory and outcome of races.

This being the case and the parties being so evenly divided, it should not be surprising that for the first time in American history, in this 30-year period, four consecutive presidents have lost their parties' Senate and House majorities.

Today the US political process is taking on a decidedly more parliamentary-like quality, with the party affiliation of a candidate increasingly more important than the more traditional points of comparison like experience, relatability, performance in office and overall candidate quality. More voters are casting straight-ticket ballots from top to bottom, either all Democratic or all Republican. The old boast that "I vote the person, not the party," is far and away the exception rather than the norm.

This change in both the direction and practice of politics has now permeated the national level and is now expanding into state Capitols and state politics in many, though not yet all states and generally not down to the county and municipal levels.

In the new world order, if an opponent could not be defeated on Election Day, their rivals tried to remove them by other means. Congressional investigative fishing expeditions tried not just to embarrass an incumbent, but to develop evidence that could lead to criminal prosecution or impeachment. On the state level, recalls successfully removed California Democratic Gov. Gray Davis in 2003 and failed to remove Wisconsin Republican Gov. Scott Walker in 2012. At this writing, the current California Governor, Gavin Newsom, is fending off another effort. These were not frequently utilized tools for most in the past but more acceptable now.

There are now two competing "exit polls" employed by major news organizations to examine who voted how and why. With only about one-third of voters physically voting in person on Election Day, there are no longer traditional exit polls to look at who voted how and why. The two most widely followed Election Day polls are the Edison Research survey conducted for ABC, CBS, CNN and NBC, the other the Votecast poll conducted by the University of Chicago's National Opinion Research Center for the Associated Press, Fox News, National Public Radio and for PBS NewsHour. Both are multimodal, with interviewing methods used including in-person interviews, via telephone to both cell phones and landlines, online and even by mail.

Among Democrats in the Edison survey in 2020, Biden beat Trump by 88 points (94 to six percent) and by 91 points (95 to four percent) in the competing Votecast poll. Among Republicans, Trump beat Biden by 88 points (94 to six percent) in Edison's numbers, and by 83 percent (91 to eight percent) in the Votecast survey. These patterns were simply a continuation of what happened four years earlier, Biden prevailed in the Edison Research poll among Clinton voters by 93 points (96 to three percent) while those who backed Trump four years earlier did it again by 87 points (93 to six percent).

Straight-ticket voting has now manifested itself in a way unseen before. The 2016 election was the first time since U.S. Senators became directly elected in 1914 that every single winner in the 34 Senate races that year was from the same party that was winning that state in the presidential race. In 2020 it was almost as monolithic; GOP incumbent Susan Collins of Maine was the only winner of either party in the 35 Senate races to capture or hold a seat that the other party was winning on the presidential level.

According to the Pew Research Center, in 158 of the 176 Senate elections since 2012, the Senate race was won by the same party as carried that state in the presidential race that night or for midterm elections, two years earlier. For many years between a fifth and a half of all Senate delegations were split, a Democrat and a Republican, in 2021 it is just six.

On the House level, from 1956 through 1996, there were between 109 and 192 Congressional districts where the presidential and congressional results went opposite directions---ticket splitting was commonplace. By the time the vote was counted in 2012, it was down to 26, four years later it was 35 and after 2020 just 16.

Not that long ago, individual candidates, particularly an incumbent, could build a brand and be judged on their own merit, giving them strength to run ahead of the top of their ticket and be able to stand on their own. They often were able to withstand the undertow that frequently is created in a tough election year for one party. Now it is very hard for a candidate to run much ahead of the top of the ticket, a variation on the "we all hang together or we all hang separately".

What has happened is a combination of factors, starting out with ideological sorting. Conservative and moderate Democrats, mostly representing Southern and border states and districts, particularly those with large rural and small town populations, were plentiful when that 1972 edition of the Almanac was published, as were liberal and moderate Republicans, in the Northeast and particularly New England and on the West Coast, as well in suburbs around major Northern cities like Chicago. There were a fair number of those still around when the 1992 edition came out as well. But over time, these political unicorns eventually retired, resigned, lost re-election, switched parties or died in office, usually replaced by either a member of the opposite party or one of their own who was less moderate.

The same has happened in the rank-and-file electorate for each party. There are very few conservative or even moderate Democratic voters around today, just as there are few liberal or moderate Republican voters either. This is reflected in party primary results with Democrats nominating increasingly liberal candidates, Republicans increasingly conservative ones.

Over time, both major political parties became more ideologically coherent. What had been a center-left oriented Democratic Party became more of a liberal party, the center-right Republican Party became more of a conservative party.

Then there were external factors that increased that ideological intensity on both sides. The rise of political talk radio in the 1980s and 1990s, mostly on the conservative side and led by Rush Limbaugh, extended and amplified conservative messaging and was a major factor in building the Republican wave of 1994 that captured both the House and Senate for the first time in two generations. Then came the rise of cable television news networks with a considerable amount of more ideological and opinion programming, sometimes bordering on political food fights, but interspersed with more conventional, talented and objective journalists. But it was the opinion programming that fueled even more intensity, whether from CNN and MSNBC on the left or Fox News on the right, joined much later by One America and Newsmax networks with considerably more pure opinion and attitude than the other three. More and more voters, who eschew traditionally curated sources of news, rely instead on talk radio, the more ideological cable television news networks, internet websites and social media, where one's "friends" effectively act as editors and publishers; a great many attitudes are formed on the basis of often misleading and selectively reported news, without the scrubbing that took place in journalism not that many years ago.

Additionally, there is a form of political segregation that exists today. As author Bill Bishop described in his seminal 2008 book, The Big Sort, most Americans live, work and socialize with those who generally share the same ideological and partisan points of view, catering to this establishment of ideological and partisan silos and echo chambers that build the intensity of emotions among many at much higher levels than forty years ago. Gerrymandering has made this problem considerably worse, with the vast majority of districts designed to produce representatives of a certain party and ideology, while leaving very few competitive districts, ones most likely to produce more compromise-oriented members.

Taken together, each party nationally and to a large extent, in competitive states and districts, the level of monolithic opposition to them creates an almost impenetrable ceiling of support or approval, but the equally adamant support and approval among those in their own party creates a floor that is hard to fall beneath. Consequently, the days with the kinds of streaks of party control of either the Senate or the House, or the White House for that matter, are gone. Equally true, it makes it less likely that there will be landslide presidential election wins the way that Johnson enjoyed over Barry Goldwater in 1964, Johnson winning nationally by 23 points, carrying 44 states, Nixon beat George McGovern by the same, 23-point margin and a 49-state victory, or even Reagan's ten point lead over Carter in 1980, winning 45 states.

By comparison, in the four most recent presidential elections, the presidential victors, Obama beat John McCain by only seven points and carrying 28 states in 2008 and four points and 26 states four years later, Trump lost the general election vote by just over two percentage points but carried 30 states in 2016, Biden won the popular vote by four points and prevailed in 25 states, hardly the blowouts that Johnson, Nixon and Reagan enjoyed.

The 2020 Election

An inherent danger in trying to predict election outcomes is that it requires anticipating human behavior, knowing that intervening events might change the trajectory of a campaign and even the outcome of that election. The nomination and subsequent election of Donald Trump in 2016 is a case in point.

There was simply no historic precedent for Republicans to nominate or Americans to elect someone with no experience in local, state or Federal government, in either a civilian or military capacity, whether elected, appointed or simply employed. Prior to Trump, every presidential nominee in the GOP's 160-year history had been a current or former vice president, governor, Senator, Congressman, commanding general of the Army (Grant and Eisenhower) or cabinet member (Taft and Hoover), often someone who fit more than one of those categories. Trump met none of those tests, and yet, was nominated twice by the party and won one general election.

The party's nomination process had long been hierarchical. Some joked that the nomination usually went to whoever's turn it seemed to be to be the standard-bearer. As it became increasingly clear in 2015 and 2016 that none of the 13 current or former governors or senators running was going to win the Republican nomination and history was not going to repeat itself, that was a surprise, as was Trump's Electoral College victory, despite losing the national popular vote.

In this opening essay in the 2020 Almanac, written over a year before the election, the argument put forward was that President Trump was an underdog in his bid for a second term. Three factors were suggested to be important.

First, would a **"Trump Fatigue"** set in among the quintile of voters that neither loved nor loathed Trump, nor leaned much either way?

Second, what would be the state of the economy heading into the election? While presidential job approval has long been the best predictor of whether an incumbent president would be re-elected, it was no longer clear what drove that approval. Political scientists Lynn Vavreck, John Sides and Michael Tesler pointed out in their fascinating book, Identity Crisis, that from John F. Kennedy's presidency through that of George W. Bush, the best single predictor of whether a president would be re-elected was the job approval rating and that consumer confidence, specifically the University of Michigan's Index of Consumer Sentiment, was highly correlated with presidential approval. If people felt that the economy was good and/or improving, they were more likely to approve of the job the current president was doing; if they thought it bad or in decline, they were more likely to disapprove. But Vavreck, Sides and Tesler statistically found that during the presidencies of Donald Trump and Joe Biden, that relationship between consumer confidence and presidential approval collapsed, it just was not there anymore, and that identity politics and the culture wars had partially or even mostly supplanted the traditionally dominant role that the economy had long played.

At the time of the 2020 election, what would the state and direction of the economy be, and would it return as a major factor in whether Trump would be re-elected, or not? With the economy strong and improving, Republican pollsters at the time were privately saying that a less polarizing president would have a job approval of 60 percent or more. Trump could not even crack 50 percent. But it could be argued that, given his manner and often his behavior, did the strong economy prop him up, keep his approval ratings from dropping still lower, as other presidents had seen?

The third factor was **who Democrats would nominate**, whether the party offered voters someone who represented a greater or lesser risk than the incumbent, how acceptable was the alternative.

That essay pointed to two pearls of wisdom from conversations long before the campaign had taken shape. My Cook Political Report colleague Amy Walter pointed out that in 2019, while many Democratic voters, activists and donors had preferences for their party's presidential nomination, surprisingly few had strong attachments, few enthusiastically supported one specific candidate to the extent that if the nomination went elsewhere, they might not vote in the general election or even vote Republican, or for an independent or third party candidate.

The second comment was made by highly regarded Democratic pollster Geoff Garin. even before the 2018 midterm election. When it was suggested that electability was rarely a primary concern for voters in deciding who they would back for their nomination, Garin suggested that "unelectability" might.

Both Walter and Garin were, in essence, saying that Donald Trump was the unifying force in the Democratic Party. The search was less who they liked the most. They still might be reluctant to nominate a candidate who seemed to have a more difficult time beating Trump. For most Democrats, the most important thing was beating Trump, everything else secondary.

The Democratic Nomination

Democrats had an enormous field of 26 candidates, eclipsing even the 17 who sought the Republican presidential nomination four years earlier. The field was the most diverse in the 191-year history of the party. There were 16 candidates under 60 years of age, (Gabbard, Klobuchar, Buttigieg, Bennet, Yang, Delaney, Booker, Castro, Harris, Bullock, O'Rourke, Ryan, de Blasio, Gillibrand, Moulton, Swalwell), six women (Gabbard, Warren, Klobuchar, Harris, Gillibrand, Williamson) two African Americans (Booker, Patrick), another was half African American and half South Asian (Harris), one Latino (Castro), and one 38-year old gay man (Buttigieg). Comparing with the field of candidates in most past races, only 16 out of the 26 were straight white men and just seven were straight, white guys 60 or more years old. (Biden, Sanders, Bloomberg, Steyer, Sestak, Inslee, Hickenlooper).

There is little doubt that the Democratic Party had moved more to the left in the years since Bill Clinton was president and, for that matter, when Barack Obama was in the Oval Office.

Unlike many past Democratic nomination fights, the contest did not shape up as an establishment choice, an insider, versus another more anti-establishment option, an outsider. This was not going to be like former Vice President Walter Mondale in 1984 as the insider candidate and Sen. Gary Hart, the outsider or Hillary Clinton and Bernie Sanders in 2016.

In 2019 and 2020, the Democratic Party seemed to constitute two factions. One, of candidates and voters who, while left of center, were not overly so, not stridently ideological; this group made up perhaps 60 percent of the Democratic Party. The other was not only more progressive, but rather than just spend even more money or grow the size or cost of government even more than most liberals would, they sought fundamental, indeed systemic change. This group had even less deference to the concepts of capitalism and free enterprise and sought to significantly change the roles, limitations and reach of the public and private sectors, far more than other liberal Democratic nominees like Hubert Humphrey, George McGovern, Walter Mondale, Michael Dukakis, John Kerry, Barack Obama or Hillary Clinton had. This segment of the Democratic Party, making up about 40 percent of all Democrats, were more attuned to Bernie Sanders and Elizabeth Warren, saw Alexandria Ocasio Cortez and her fellow "Squad" members as the future of the party, and had little patience for Democrats who they saw as too cautious, too incremental, too likely to compromise or cave on their principles. While the 40 percent certainly wanted to drive Trump from the White House, that was just step one; step two was remaking the Federal government and American politics. The other 60 percent would have been content with just removing the former real estate developer who they held in such disdain.

The earliest phases of the 2020 Democratic nomination fight saw Sanders begin as the frontrunner for the left/progressive lane, then in the late Summer and early Fall of 2019, Warren overtook Sanders, then she stumbled or faded, with Sanders consolidating the left lane well before the Iowa Caucus and New Hampshire Primary were even held.

Meanwhile, the less ideological and more pragmatic 60 percent were split more among almost a dozen from the conventional wing, those perceived to be more moderate like Biden, Michael Bloomberg, Pete Buttigieg and Amy Klobuchar, earlier on Michael Bennet, Steve Bullock, John Delaney, Kirsten Gillibrand, John Hickenlooper, Beto O'Rourke, Tim Ryan, and to a certain extent, more conventional liberals like Cory Booker, Julian Castro, Bill deBlasio, Kamala Harris, Jay Inslee, and Eric Swalwell, who were short of the systemic change positioning and rhetoric of Sanders and Warren.

Joe Biden was almost universally known among Democratic voters before he even announced his candidacy, one reason why he led in many early national polls asking Democrats their preference for the nomination. Besides name recognition, he was positively associated with President Obama, who was revered in the party. That gave Biden a particularly good standing among African American Democrats who saw him as having been loyal to the first nominee of their race. And the longtime Senator and former vice president was generally well liked among party insiders.

And yet there was a resistance to nominating Biden among party insiders. Some of it was simply demographic. It was common to hear Democrats question nominating a 77-year old, straight white guy, someone who could have fit right into Howard Chandler Christy's famous, 20-by-30 foot painting of the signing of the Constitution hanging near the House chamber of the Capitol building.

While not quite one in three (32%) Democratic votes for president in 2020 would come from white men, the 34% share in 2016 was only slightly higher. Of the Democratic vote for Congress in the 2018 midterm election, 35% came from white men.

They wondered if, at 77, if he was too old, if he had lost a step or two over the years and for a party that was becoming more oriented toward youth and diversity, if nominating an older white guy was the best idea in the world. Biden also had a history of missteps and verbal miscues, and once called himself a "gaffe machine." There were the inevitable references to an incident of appropriating lines in his campaign speech from British Labour Party leader Neil Kinnock, resulting in his being forced out of his bid for the 1988 Democratic nomination. Finally, Biden had a reputation, both in the Senate and as a presidential candidate. as a less than stellar fundraiser.

After Biden's nomination and subsequent election, these doubts seem ill-placed if not frivolous. But his fourth place showing in the Iowa caucuses on February 3 and fifth place in the New Hampshire primary eight days later underscore the initial resistance there was to nominating him. His breakthrough February 29 win in South Carolina and dominance in the Super Tuesday primaries on March 3 illustrate both how much of a longshot Biden had been for the nomination and how fast the situation changed and how his nomination quickly became a fait accompli.

There had seemed to be two dynamics at work. First, establishment Democrats were confronted with what behaviorists call, "the paradox of choice," what Alvin Toppler, in his 1970 bestseller, "Future Shock," called "overchoice," they had too many options, some intriguing options. They could not decide. Also, many of these same Democrats were still traumatized by Clinton's 2016 shocking loss and Trump's win, and what they saw as the consequences of that Trump victory, making some paralyzed with fear that they would make a mistake again and re-elect him; fear of failure again prevented them from making a swift decision. Democrats had allowed the perfect to become the enemy of the good.

The realization that Sanders eclipsed Warren and consolidated the left, while the establishment seemed hopelessly indecisive and paralyzed into inaction. Along with the vagaries of the Democratic nomination rules that allow a candidate roll up a large advantage of delegates even with far less than majority support of primary voters soon dawned on both the party establishment and the media. Sanders was about to lock up the Democratic nomination. But what were his chances of beating Trump and winning a general election?

The General Election

Many observers have noted the coincidence, irony, or ironic coincidence of Joe Biden's 306 to 232 Electoral College victory over Donald Trump, precisely the same electoral vote then-President Trump defeated Hillary Clinton four years earlier. Biden's national popular vote margin was 7.1 million votes, 4.5 percentage points, Clinton's popular votes were a bit less than half as wide, 2.9 million votes and 2.1 percentage points.

Many people assume that incumbent presidents will win re-election and it is true that they do not often lose. Donald Trump is only the fourth president unseated in the last 88 years, joining Gerald Ford, Jimmy Carter and George H.W. Bush as the only incumbents to be defeated. But it does happen, and a president like Trump, who never had majority job approval rating in a major national poll, was more likely to lose than other presidents seeking re-election.

The results of the 2020 election, taken together, the Presidency, House and Senate, were a curious mix of the expected, of surprises, ending with the predicted outcome but by surprisingly narrow margins.

Less noticed was that in 2016, five states had margins of one-and-a-half percentage point or less, with Donald Trump carrying four of those five, Michigan, Pennsylvania, Wisconsin and Florida, totaling 75 Electoral votes. Hillary Clinton only won one state by that narrow margin, New Hampshire, with just four electoral votes. Trump got the breaks that year, winning the electoral votes of large states by tiny margins.

In 2020 there again were five states that were won by a point and a half or less, but this time, Biden won four out of five, Georgia, Arizona, Wisconsin and Pennsylvania, with 57 electoral votes. Trump carried just one, North Carolina, with 15 electoral votes; again, big states, small margins.

In terms of getting over the top, reaching the magic 270 electoral votes, in 2016, the presidency was effectively decided in three states, Michigan, Pennsylvania and Wisconsin. Trump carried Michigan, by two-tenths of one percent, fewer than 23,000 votes of almost five million cast. Trump won Pennsylvania by fewer than 45,000 votes of over six million and Wisconsin, just over 11,000 of almost three million cast. It seemed remarkable that 77,744 votes scattered over three states determined the presidency.

In 2020, it was three states that put Biden over the top instead. He won Georgia by fewer than 12,000 votes, Arizona by a bit over 10,000 votes and Wisconsin, by almost 21,000 votes. This time the White House turned on even fewer votes, 42,918 votes, scattered across three states, a number of votes roughly the equivalent of populations of Valdosta Georgia or Moline Illinois or Charlottesville Virginia or Conway Arkansas. Only Wisconsin was effectively a decider in both elections.

But it wasn't just the Presidency that was decided by photo-finishes in a very few locales. The Senate seat that gave Democrats their 50th seat, allowing Vice President Kamala Harris to break ties in their favor, was the regularly-scheduled Georgia Senate contest, in which Jon Ossoff beat GOP incumbent David Perdue by fewer than 55,000 votes.

The House had a similar story to tell, but with a somewhat different twist. Instead of gaining seats as was widely expected by pros in both parties, Democrats were barely able to cling to their majority, suffering a 12-seat loss.

This is what can be expected to happen in a nation as narrowly and bitterly divided as the United States is today, and not likely to change much anytime soon.

Expectations and Outcomes

In the Presidential race, there were actually no real surprises. In the final Cook Political Report ratings, 24 states were rated Leaning, Likely or Solid Biden, along with the District of Columbia, the First Congressional District of Maine and the Second District of Nebraska (Maine and Nebraska are the two states that divide their electoral votes). Biden won all 24 of those states plus D.C. and those two districts in Maine and Nebraska, a total of 290 Electoral College votes, 20 more than the 270 electoral votes required to win.

In those same ratings going into Election Day, another 20 states were given ratings of Lean, Likely or Solid Trump, along with Nebraska's First and Third Congressional districts. Trump won all 20 of those states and both Nebraska districts.

So, no surprises, no upsets in the states and districts that were expected to go to Biden or Trump. That left six states in the Toss Up column, Florida, Georgia, Iowa, North Carolina, Ohio and Texas, as well as the Second District of Maine. When all of the votes were counted, Trump won five out of the six Toss Up states (all but Georgia), plus Maine's Second District. No upsets, but Trump won almost all that had been expected to be close.

But Trump's near sweep of the Toss Up column was not the only surprise in the presidential race. Several of the states that Biden had been expected to carry with some room to spare, he did win, but by surprisingly small margins--Arizona, Pennsylvania and Wisconsin for example. Two of those three, Pennsylvania and Wisconsin, were the surprise states along with Michigan four years earlier. Almost across the board, the margins just moved a notch or two toward Trump. Biden receiving pretty much the vote polls were indicating, but the undecideds, and there were not many, broke to the right. In most cases, the moves did not change the outcome but did affect the margins, either Biden winning by a narrower margin or Trump winning by a slightly larger margin than expected.

2020 Senate Elections

Senate Republicans headed into the 2020 election in a high-risk situation. With the Senate split 53 Republicans to 47 Democrats, the GOP had 23 seats up and potentially at risk, almost double the 12 that Democrats would have on the ballot. Making matters a bit worse, three of the Republican seats had no incumbent, therefore no incumbency advantage, Democrats just one. Democrats would need at least a four seat net gain to win the Senate outright, though the combination of a three-seat gain and a White House victory would enable a Democratic vice president to break the tie.

The danger for Republicans was not just statistical, it was real. Going into Election Day, the final Cook Political Report Senate ratings, had 13 Senate seats rated Lean, Likely or Solid Democrat, including the seats of two GOP incumbents, Martha McSally (Arizona) and Cory Gardner (Colorado). Just 16 out of the 23 GOP-held seats were rated as Lean, Likely or Solid Republican, along with that of one Democratic incumbent, Doug Jones (Alabama).

That meant that there were seven Senate seats in the Toss Up column, and all held by Republican incumbents. The GOP was defending Susan Collins (Maine), Steve Daines (Montana), Joni Ernst (Iowa), Lindsay Graham (South Carolina), Thom Tillis (North Carolina).

In an unusual twist, there were also two Republican seats in Georgia, a state that has changed enormously in recent years, an influx of new residents from outside of the South and even the U.S. and the reliably-Republican small town and rural share of the vote shrinking, while the Democrat-trending suburbs and long-Democratic urban areas were gaining in their share of the electorate. One seat was held by elected incumbent David Perdue, seeking a second term, the other by Kelly Loeffler, appointed to the seat after the resignation of Johnny Isakson, who stepped down after almost three terms for health reasons. Under Georgia law, a majority of the vote is required to win a Senate seat, so a January 5 runoff was virtually inevitable in the special election, where under Georgia law, a special election is run as a "jungle primary, with all candidates, regardless of party affiliation, running in one contest. With 20 candidates ultimately running, including eight Democrats and six Republicans, it was a virtual impossibility that any candidate would receive 50 percent of the vote. The other Senate race was conducted under more conventional procedures with a primary and general election, but still the requirement of a majority to win. A Libertarian candidate on the November ballot siphoned off enough votes that Perdue came less than three-tenths of a percentage point from a majority, only to lose the January 5 runoff. There is good reason to believe that Trump's refusal to concede the election and the fallout from his criticism of two Georgia statewide officials, both Republicans, contributed to the dual Senate runoff losses for the party.

The Republican incumbents facing tough races had their own circumstances. Gardner in Colorado was a strong candidate with an equally impressive record but had the misfortune of representing a state that was growing more Democratic, while Trump at the top of the ticket was exacerbating that challenge, losing the state to Biden by almost 14 points. McSally's problem in Arizona was not just that the once quite Republican state was becoming increasingly competitive, but in her Senate bid two years earlier, before her appointment to fill the seat of the late John McCain, out of necessity she ran far to the right to win the primary. But she kept headed that way once she had secured the nomination, becoming well out of position and losing to Democrat Kyrsten Sinema by just over two percentage points, leaving her badly positioned for the general election in 2020. Montana's Daines was quite popular and the state very Republican but he was challenged by the most popular political figure in the state, Democratic Gov. Steve Bullock. Collins has long been an extremely popular figure in Maine, winning extraordinary numbers of not just independent voters but also many Democrats. The state is getting more competitive and partisanship is so powerful, making crossover votes far more difficult, made worse because Trump has been so unpopular in the heavily-populated and staunchly Democratic Portland area. Even with a strong brand, she was having to swim hard to avoid being pulled down in the political undertow.

Ernst had no particular problems in Iowa and the state definitely leans Republican, but the freshman had not yet sunk deep political roots and had quite squishy numbers. Tillis in North Carolina was in a state, like Arizona and Georgia, that was changing rapidly and becoming less Republican by the day. He had been caught in a squeeze between the more establishment-oriented, less ideological side of the GOP and the far more conservative, Trump-oriented flank. Tillis wound up having trouble being not moderate enough for the former nor pure enough for the latter.

Graham's problem was certainly not that South Carolina was not Republican or conservative enough. It certainly was, but it was his personal and political maneuvering that grated on quite a few voters--going in a short period of time from John McCain's closest friend in the Senate to Trump's closest buddy in the chamber. Following harsh and quite personal criticism of Trump during the 2016 presidential primaries, now they were joined at the hip. Sometimes he was a maverick putting himself above party like McCain; other times, he took among the most conservative positions of any GOP member in the Senate. Graham was increasingly perceived as overly opportunistic, even for a politician, often engaging in a political version of the sailing maneuver of tacking. When encountering headwinds, a sailor sets a course to the port (right) side, then turning to starboard (left), zig-zagging from one side to the other, avoiding heading straight into the wind. But in politics, it can leave voters and political leaders wondering who he is or even if he knows who he is.

With Trump's job approval numbers nationally languishing in the '40s, never reaching 50 percent in a single major national survey, handling the Coronavirus Pandemic in an unimpressive fashion and then, by all accounts, his poor performance in the September 29 presidential debate, some Republican Senators and strategists wondered if the party would be lucky to keep their losses down to just three or four seats.

When the November 3 election results were counted, Democrats had won all 13 of those races rated as Lean, Likely or Solid Democrat, including unseating incumbents Gardner and McSally, though one Democrat, Gary Peters in Michigan, ended up with a much closer race than expected. Republicans prevailed in all 16 of theirs, including unseating Jones in Alabama. Taken together, there were no upsets in the Senate.

But the seven Toss Up races were a different story, contributing to the view that something had changed in the final days of the campaign. All five that were decided on November 3 remained in Republican hands, meaning that the tight contests all broke in the same direction, giving Republicans a minimum of 50 seats and Democrats 48. But in the two that were settled in the January 5 Georgia runoffs, both fell to Democrats, with Ossoff beating Perdue and Raphael Warnock unseating Loeffler, bringing Democrats up to 50 seats. Once Harris was sworn in as Vice President on January 20, Democrats had a majority.

2020 House Elections

While the presidential and Senate contests ended with no real upsets but the Toss Up races breaking heavily toward Republicans, the House races were somewhat different. In the final Cook Political Report House ratings, 179 districts were rated as Lean, Likely or Solid Republican; the GOP won every one. There were 27 contests rated as Toss Ups; Republicans won every single one. Of the 229 seats that were rated as Lean, Likely or Solid Democrat, Republicans managed to pull off 13 upsets, Democrats holding onto only 216 of the 229 that they had been expected to win somewhat handily.

Basically, allocating vacant seats caused by deaths or resignations in reliably partisan districts, Democrats dropped 11 seats from 233 to 222 while Republicans **increased their ranks by 12**, the difference being the defeat of incumbent Justin Amash in Michigan's Third District. Amash had been elected and re-elected as a Republican but after a break with Trump, dropped his GOP status to become an independent, though not running in the general election, so a gain for Republicans but not a loss for Democrats. Interestingly, every district in which a Republican took a seat held by Democrats, the successful Republican was a woman, a minority, or both.

House Democrats had expected to expand their ranks, instead they just barely hung onto their majority. The gap between the two parties is the narrowest since the election in 2000, and the smallest margin for a Democratic majority since the Congress elected in 1942.

Wave or No Wave?

After the election, one of the most common discussion topics in political circles was whether there had been a wave; if there had been one, what happened to it; if not, why did it appear to happen; and whether this was another manifestation of shortcomings in polling in an era of cell phones, voice call and caller ID.

In this period of extreme partisanship and very little ticket-splitting, to a large extent, a party's fortunes rise and fall with the top of the ticket. 2016 was the first election since the direct election of Senators that every Senate seat was won by the same party that prevailed that night in the presidential race in that state. In 2020, as earlier noted, the party winning the state in the presidential race also won the Senate contest, except for Maine, where Susan Collins survived a tough race. Only four percent of House members are in districts that were not carried by their party in the presidential race.

A party heading into a presidential year with a White House incumbent who has never had a 50 percent job approval rating in any major national poll has to be a bit nervous, and most Republican elected officials and strategists were. When Trump at first denied the seriousness of the Coronavirus and then chronically mishandled it, that did nothing to create confidence. Once the country went into lockdown in mid-March, the U.S. economy went into a freefall for three months. While the downturn was not blamed on Trump--after all, the Coronavirus was a global problem that did not originate in the U.S., and wrecked economic havoc, Republicans were showing Trump's problems beginning to metastasize, just as it was in surveys done for Democrats and conducted independently, weighing down other Republicans on the ballot. Enthusiasm was waning among Republicans. Though there were few defections, very worrisome signs were appearing. But it wasn't just polling, it was what their elected officials in competitive states and districts were seeing and hearing every day, as well.

When the economy found its bottom in July and began showing signs of life, it seemed that things had stabilized for the GOP and there was a slight recovery in polls for both the president and his party. But that improvement stopped and began to reverse with his disastrous debate performance on September 29. With just five weeks to go before the election, and with early and mail voting already underway, Republican leaders and operatives were at DEFCON 1 status: the Department of Defense's top level of preparedness for war, anticipating the worst.

Political journalists cannot report what they are told off the record and have to be careful about what is said on background. But, consider these two very public statements to be representative of what leading Republicans were seeing and thinking. In a CNBC interview aired on October 9, just over a week after that debate, Sen. Ted Cruz confided to the interviewer how "volatile" that he felt the election was, then saying that the election had the "potential to be bloodbath of Watergate proportions." The next day, Ed Rollins, who had managed President Reagan's successful 1984 re-election campaign and in 2020 was running a pro-Trump superpac but was known to be candid to a fault, was quoted by a CNN reporter suggesting that the presidential race was "over." These statements were representative of what Republican and Democratic strategists were seeing and saying in private, not only from polls but also in their reports from field operatives on the ground in competitive states and districts, as well.

So what happened? Partisans on each side were going to stay on their own sides and vote straight party tickets already; that didn't change. And while the slice of voters who do not align or even lean to either party is fairly small, about five to 12 percent, pure independents as a rule do not like politics or politicians and do not trust either party. What happens is that heading into a big election, they often get more disappointed, angry or feel more threatened by one side than the other, swinging disproportionately toward one side. Most famously, that happened in the last few days of the 1980 presidential race, when the contest between President Jimmy Carter and Ronald Reagan was too close to call, then, after their first and only one-on-one debate, independents gave up on Carter and felt sufficiently comfortable with the former Hollywood actor. It was as if, as a group, they all stood and walked into the Reagan and Republican column, triggering a ten-point Reagan win, a GOP capture of the Senate for the first time in 26 years and the strongest gains the party had enjoyed in the House since 1966 and the second biggest jump in the post-World War II era.

With this movement in 2020 and the inevitable talk of a Democratic wave, that it appeared increasingly likely that Democrats, already holding a majority in the House, would probably expand that majority, that Democrats in the Senate, already having a good chance of winning a majority, but beginning to look like their very strong gains could be four, five or six seats.

Newton's Third Law of Action, that for every action in nature, there is an equal and opposite reaction, applies to mathematics and physics, not necessarily to politics. But sometimes movement can trigger something. Accompanying what appeared to be a Trump collapse with his acceptability to and viability among independent and swing voters--though certainly not within his base--which weighed down other GOP candidates on the ballot, it may well have triggered something.

Speculation of a Democratic wave prompted conversations about democratic socialism, embraced by Bernie Sanders and uber-progressive Rep. Alexandria Ocasio-Cortez, and disavowed but not terribly convincingly by Elizabeth Warren, is a phrase that is appealing to some young people but quite toxic among others of a certain age. Other hot topics include "Medicare for All," which was attractive to many in the Democratic base but seen as a trojan horse for single-payer among others who trust their private health insurance that is often employer provided, plus "Green New Deal," again popular with many loyal Democrats and progressives, but viewed with considerable suspicion among those who work in or are sympathetic with oil and gas, natural resources and mineral extraction and manufacturing as a recipe for killing jobs.

Talk during the Democratic primaries of decriminalizing illegal immigration and to "Abolish ICE" (the Immigration and Customs Enforcement agency), was disconcerting to some of these swing voters who were not sure that Trump's border wall was a good idea, but did not want open borders either. There had been a string of highly publicized allegations and acts of police abuse, and in some cases unjustified killing of minorities, particularly African Americans, with some cases, such as those of George Floyd in Minneapolis, Breonna Taylor in Louisville and two cases in Georgia, Rayshard Brooks in Atlanta and Ahmaud Arbery in Brunswick, garnered world-wide publicity and concern. Peaceful and perfectly legitimate daylight demonstrations sometimes turned into mob violence once the sun went down (probably not committed by many of the peaceful and legitimate protesters but by hooligans), also prompting more talk of "defunding the police," and "end policing" and concerns whether Democrats would be sufficiently attentive and address effectively law and order matters.

Some swing voters worried that "Pack the Supreme Court," a move that Biden and Harris refused in debates and interviews to disavow, and the move to end the filibuster indicated a willingness among Democrats and progressives to change the rules if they were not winning the game.

While some believed before the election that some of this talk could affect some swing voters, many pollsters and operatives in both parties now believe that this played a least some role in what happened.

Quite simply, some of those independent and swing voters may have gotten cold feet about giving Democrats all of the levers of power. While sufficient numbers of them might have decided that it was time for Trump to leave office, some may have shifted back. Even more, they may have been willing to give Biden the keys to the car, but they were not so sure they wanted to fill the tank with gas and supply a credit card with a high limit.

It was suggested to me in a mid-September conversation with a senior Republican member of the Senate that this was, in his opinion, the best argument Republicans had. He was not sure whether it would work, but they had no better case to make than push an argument that Democrats were not to be trusted with control of everything and that the Senate was the firewall to keep that from happening, in effect, conceding that Trump would probably lose and that it was unlikely that the GOP would take the House, but that the Senate was the only way to avoid one=party rule.

Little has been said here about polling. There is no question that polling has become problematic, it was true before the 2020 election and even before the 2016 election, though in that case, most polling outside of Michigan, Pennsylvania and Wisconsin was quite accurate, and that 2018 midterm election polling was incredibly accurate. Confusion of whether national polls would and could predict the outcome of an election that was determined by the Electoral College, not a national popular vote, fueled much of the talk that year of the failure of polling. Still there are growing challenges to the polling profession.

But talk of the "shy Trump voter," that some supporting Trump would lie to pollsters about their intention to support him, did not and still does not ring true to most pollsters and astute political analysts. Does anyone think that someone would have claimed that they were going to vote for Hillary Clinton when their plan was to actually vote for Donald Trump? Does anyone really believe that someone would say that they would vote for Joe Biden but actually vote for Trump? Or lie in either race, claiming to be undecided, when there was no bulge in the size of the undecided vote. There is a body of thought and indeed some research that suggests that there is a group of voters that are deeply mistrustful of institutions, of politics and indeed of society beyond their own family, friends and co-workers. This group is less likely to pick up a telephone, cooperate with any survey--whether on the phone or online--or complete an interview, and will largely fly under the radar. While those voters were not all Trump supporters, they disproportionately were, thus would be undersampled in most, if not all, polls. It was not that they did not subject themselves to interviews because they were Trump supporters, but that those who were not interviewed, for whatever reason, were disproportionately for Trump. This may or may not account for polling not being particularly off in the 2018 midterms. This could be a one-off situation that is significantly correlated with Trump more than overall partisanship or ideology.

Another theory is that there is a pool of voters who generally do not fit the profile of those likely to vote and indeed they do not often vote. Again, it is not as much about their own political views as much as their attitudes about politics and politicians. Some pollsters believe and have seen evidence that they find convincing that among those "low propensity voters," the ones that were more supportive of Trump ended up turning out in greater numbers than those who would have supported Biden had they voted. There is research that compared what various registered voters told pollsters before the election and, when voting records after the election were checked to see who really did vote (you cannot tell how they voted, but you can see if they did), that those who professed support or were leaning toward Trump ended up voting in higher numbers than other seemingly low propensity voters.

A lot of research has been underway and is continuing to get to the bottom of these questions. No one wants to get to the bottom of this dilemma more than pollsters and those who pay for and consume most polls.

So what should we learn from Trump's loss? A few weeks after the election, in a (Zoom) call with several people, a Republican Congressman was asked what he took from the results, Trump losing, but his party not taking a beating. His response, "don't be an asshole, and don't be a socialist." That is the most succinct, albeit profane, analysis of the election that I have heard yet. And probably not wrong.

Biden and Congress

When taking the measure of a new president, particularly in a political context, it is important to remember that the more time there is before an election, the less that public opinion polls matter.

Historically presidents have enjoyed the glow of a honeymoon early in their terms, enjoying unrealistically high approval ratings as Americans were willing to wish the best for a new Oval Office occupant, and the new president has not had much time to alienate or disappoint the public. But in time, the honeymoon is over, and the poll numbers return to earth and begin to settle into a pattern, reaching an equilibrium point, a pattern of rising with favorable news while falling with unfavorable developments.

As different in personality and style as Trump and Biden are, they share one thing in common --- serving as president at a time of hyper-partisanship and tribalism, with large blocks of Americans either automatically supportive or automatically opposed to them, almost regardless of what they say or do. The instinctive opposition by those in the other party effectively puts a ceiling on how high job approval can go, but the equally monolithic support among those in their own party creates a floor that a president can't drop below.

Partisanship has been a part of our political landscape almost as long as we have been a country, indeed President George Washington's farewell address featured a warning about the dangers of factions. But at various points in American history, even when it seemed to be so pernicious, it was nothing like we see today.

Something changed about 30 years ago, beginning around 1991 and 1992, and since that time, we have had four waves of escalating levels of extreme partisanship that has shaken the entire political process and helped produce four consecutive presidents losing control of both the Senate and the House during their White House tenures, a first in American history.

Arguably though, political polarization and partisanship are not the cause, but arguably the effect, of larger divisions in the United States, along economic, demographic, geographic, religious, social and cultural lines. These divisions are simply manifested through politics.

Bill Clinton faced a level of animosity from Republicans and conservatives that far exceeded what previous Democratic presidents like John Kennedy, Lyndon Johnson and Jimmy Carter saw. Then, after eight years of that, George W. Bush was confronted by an enmity from Democrats and liberals much greater than Eisenhower, Nixon, Ford, Reagan and his father had to endure. Still, eight years later, Barack Obama was greeted by a level of hatred far worse than Clinton had. Then, Donald Trump encountered a loathing far worse than George W. Bush or any previous Republican ever encountered.

Increasingly, in this era of political tribalism, a president of the other party can do little or nothing right, while a president of your own can do little or nothing wrong.

Most party members nowadays are willing to stick with a president who is a member of their tribe, almost no matter what. That was less true in the old days when Truman, Nixon, Carter and George H.W. Bush plunged into the '20s among all adults during their lowest periods in office. Johnson and Reagan dipped to 37 percent and Obama to 38 percent.

Conversely, when times were good, presidents could hit stratospherically high approval ratings. Truman, Kennedy, George H.W. Bush and George W. Bush hit 90 percent. The elder Bush hit 89 percent after the victory in the first Persian Gulf War, the latter 90 percent after the September 11 attacks. Eisenhower, Johnson, Ford, Carter and Clinton at times reached the 70's. Nixon, Reagan and Obama hit 67, 68 and 69 percent, respectively.

For Trump, the distance between his very lowest and very highest approval ratings was just 15 points. For Biden, as of early June 2021, only three points. This compares to the interval between lows and highs of anywhere from 31 to 65 points among their 12 Post-World War predecessors. There was just little variance in Trump's lows and highs. Given the partisanship today, we don't expect to see it with Biden either. The floors and ceilings are hard and almost impenetrable, with most variation accounted for by shifts among the more fluid independents.

Electorally speaking, under this new configuration of voting patterns, it would be very hard to see how a presidential candidate can win a general election by the margin and carry 44 states as Ronald Reagan did over Carter in 1980, or by 23 points as did both Lyndon Johnson (1964) and Richard Nixon in 1972, the former winning 44 states and the latter 49 states. In the most recent four presidential elections, Biden won 25 states, Obama 26 and 28 states in 2012 and 2008 respectively, and Trump 30 states in 2016. The widest popular vote margin in those four elections was Obama's seven point win over John McCain in 2008. In that election, Obama won not quite 53 percent of the vote, the highest of those last four elections. This is a different era.

Most assumed that, if elected, Biden would certainly be left-of-center as most Democrats are, just as most Republicans are right of center, but few thought Biden would be far left compared to many others in his party. Progressives such as those who supported Bernie Sanders or Elizabeth Warren for the 2020 Democratic nomination feared that Biden would be highly conventional and maybe even unimaginative, taking an incremental approach to his legislative agenda. Taking, they feared, baby steps on policy, needing to compromise with and accommodate Republicans from the beginning.

Conversely, more centrist Democrats were elated, at least ideologically speaking, that their party had dodged a bullet, they would get a cautious person in the White House, one unlikely to drive off a policy cliff, not commit the overreach that has contributed to the last four presidents losing control of both the House and Senate during their terms in the White House. While Republicans were disappointed to lose the White House and certain anticipated partisan battles, they did anticipate playing the loyal opposition to a president trying to reverse the Reagan Revolution of 40 years ago, an era of governing that has constrained Democratic presidents and at least theoretically been the North Star for Republicans in the office.

There were considerable arguments to support this theory that Biden would not try to reverse the entire direction of the Federal Government. By temperament, experience and circumstance, it seemed logical that Biden would take a more cautious and measured approach to governing, that he would be a very temperate president.

Some people, particularly some politicians, seem to always be spoiling for a fight, unwilling to or incapable of avoiding conflict. Others are aloof and distant, not prone to building and nurturing relationships. With the notable exception of his handling the Supreme Court nomination of Robert Bork as chairman of the Senate Judiciary Committee in 1987, that did not describe Biden. Widely seen both in the Senate and as Vice President as an affable figure, one always quick with a smile and a wisecrack, looking to make a deal, as a freshman at the young age of 30, showed that he was willing to deal with some of the oldest and most curmudgeonly conservatives in the Senate, like Mississippi's James Eastland, a Democrat but one who shared few ideological positions with Biden.

In terms of experience, having come to the Senate in January 1973, he arrived at a time that Congress, while never particularly speedy and efficient, got things done. From 1955 when Democrats captured majorities in both the House and Senate, holding control of the House for the next 40 years, majorities in the Senate for 34 out of the 40 years, all but the first six years of the Reagan Presidency. Prior to Bill Clinton's defeat of George H.W. Bush, Republicans had won the White House four of the most recent five elections (all except Carter's victory over Ford in 1976) leaving Republicans usually in control the executive branch, Democrats the legislative branch. American voters had found their own separation of powers, preferring divided government, with compromise the order of the day.

When Biden was first sworn into the Senate in January 1973, it was toward the end of an era. From 1960 through 1976, four presidents had occupied the Oval Office: Kennedy, Johnson, Nixon and Ford. All four had served as members of the House, in fact, Kennedy, Johnson and Nixon actually overlapped in the House, Ford was sworn into the House the day Johnson was leaving the chamber to be sworn into the Senate. Ford served in the House for 24 years, including 20 in the House GOP leadership. Three out of four had been members of the Senate, all but Ford. Johnson served in Senate Democratic leadership for ten of his 12 years. Three out of four had served as vice president, all but Kennedy. The presidents during that period, in varying degrees, were creatures of Capitol Hill, knowing the institution, process, the mores, and had relationships with other players built over decades in the Nation's Capital. With Carter's defeat of Ford in 1976, the U.S. entered a very different era, one of mostly governors, Reagan, Clinton, George W. Bush, and, to a certain extent, outsiders, with Trump the most outside of the outsiders. The major exception was George H.W. Bush, while he had only served in the House for four years, he was a vice president for eight years, CIA Director, UN Ambassador, RNC Chairman and, arguably while U.S. envoy to China, he was certainly no stranger to Washington, the institution and players, and an insider by any standard. The other partial exception was Obama, who while he had been a member of the Senate for four years when sworn into the Presidency, he was only a full-time member for two years, and a rather aloof one at that, angling to move on and out of that body from the first day, not looking to immerse himself or move up in that chamber. He spent the next two years running for President full-time.

Biden was more of a throwback to that earlier era. He had seen how the city and institutions were at least supposed to work and that relationships mattered. He had a good vantage point to watch the wheels coming off the bus. Presumably, he would seek to replicate that old approach, to the extent possible.

The final reason to expect a certain approach from Biden was the circumstances that seemed to exist the day after he won the election. Democrats had unexpectedly lost 11 seats in the House, in an election when there was much anticipation that they would expand their hold on the chamber, and they had only 48 seats in the Senate, fewer than they expected to have. They would gain narrow control only if they won both Senate runoffs slated for January 5, needing to go 2-0 in a state that had no statewide elected Democrats and last won Senate races in 1990 and 2000.

Biden could hope to beat the odds and win both Georgia Senate seats. But there was a far better chance that Democrats would lose at least one, if not both, and plan to have divided government, his party with a minority in the Senate, and a bare majority in the House. That being the case, it made no sense for the new president to do anything but try to construct new majorities for every single legislative proposal, to get majorities, if not 60 votes in the Senate, knowing that those against him on one vote might be allies on the next. Having two centrist Democrats, Joe Manchin (West Virginia) and Kyrsten Sinema (Arizona), would just make things more difficult. On some issues there was a chance to entice a Republican or two to back something, with Susan Collins (Maine), Lisa Murkowski (Alaska) and Mitt Romney (Utah) the three most likely to stray from the Republican line under the right circumstances.

Speaker Nancy Pelosi had a well-earned reputation for reading the minds of her members and skillfully managing both her members in highly competitive districts, some in districts that had voted for John McCain and Mitt Romney, if not for Donald Trump, but also keeping some of her more exotic members in check, to the extent possible. Still, there would be a limit to what Biden could ask of Pelosi.

There was considerable surprise to those expecting a cautious and incremental Biden agenda when he proposed the $1.9 trillion American Rescue Plan not even a month after President Trump signed his own $1.4 trillion deal, signaling what has turned out to be an attempt to reverse the Reagan Revolution of 40 years earlier.

Then came a much grander set of proposals, the first a $2.3 trillion American Jobs Plan of traditional public works projects like streets, highways, bridges, tunnels, mass transit, airports, water and sewer lines and broadband cable expansion into rural and inner city urban areas, essentially attempts to catch up on almost 30 years of chronic underfunding and having a good bit of support among Republicans. The only disagreements were over spending levels and how to finance it: increased taxes, user fees or deficit spending. The second, and a bit more difficult for Republicans to take, was a $1.8 trillion American Family Plan. Made up of what some called human infrastructure or soft infrastructure, that included child and elder care, expanded pre-school, free community college and tax cuts for lower income families.

Taken together, the Biden package was a series of measures that would attempt to expand the size and scope of Federal domestic spending that by some indices matched Lyndon Johnson's Great Society of the 1960s and Franklin Roosevelt's New Deal in the 1930s, something that was neither cautious or incremental and dwarfed efforts to expand domestic spending programs by Biden's most recent Democratic predecessors, Clinton and Obama. In fact, one close Obama advisor privately said that during their eight years in the White House, great efforts were made to keep program price tags "in the 'B's" (billions) and "below the 'T's" (trillions), a reticence that Biden obviously didn't have.

To some critics, it was not that the individual elements in the Biden proposals were particularly radical or even innovative. It was simply the size of it, a "go big or go home" approach throwing caution to the wind that took many aback, particularly compared with expectation.

It seems as if the Biden White House has been haunted by the ghosts of Obama's first term, what many Democrats see as a mistake made then. In combat, injuries are sustained, scars are created, both physical and psychological, often carried like baggage for the rest of a soldier's life. As politics has become more combative, scars of a different nature are created. From one political battle to another, scar tissue accumulates and thickens, animosity and distrust between the two sides builds and intensify, and is reinforced, again and again.

When a new president comes into office and puts together a team, it is often highly-populated with people who served in the administration of the previous president or two of the same party. Some have been less than others. Trump certainly didn't draw that much on veterans of the two Bush administrations or Reagan before that, but did some. Jimmy Carter may not have drawn much on Kennedy and Johnson administration veterans. In the case of Bill Clinton, it had been 12, not four or eight years since there had been a Democratic president, so a little less so. Also, Clinton reflected a certain degree of generational change, as did Obama to a little bit. A former vice president coming into the presidency will often rely even more on such veterans, particularly if they are coming straight into the presidency, as GHWB did, though there was a bit of housecleaning then as well.

To the extent that many key people did not come from that party's previous administration, they may well have come from Capitol Hill, where it was their job to deliver legislatively the agenda that the earlier president had proposed.

Veterans of these years of political warfare bring their experiences and animus with them to their next positions. It is human nature to be affected by your own experiences, lessons learned, scar tissue carried on.

For veterans of the Obama administration, particularly the White House and those there in their first two years, there are at least two major impressions that they brought from that experience.

Many have been convinced that valuable time was wasted attempting to gain Republican support for the Obama economic stimulus package, designed to jump-start the economy after the stock market collapse and the Great Recession had begun. There is a conviction among many that few Republicans were ever going to support the package, that the delay and what they saw as watering down elements of the package undercut its effectiveness, virtually for naught, as the $787 billion package passed the House 246 to 183, with no Republican support, then passing the Senate 60 to 38, with only three Republicans, Olympia Snowe and Susan Collins, both of Maine, and Arlen Specter of Pennsylvania casting yea votes. Senator Ted Kennedy, fighting cancer, was unable to make it to the Senate to vote.

As far as most Obama and congressional Democrats are concerned, most House and Senate Republicans then and now are unwilling or even incapable of negotiating in good faith, there is no point and valuable time wasted trying to win them over. Many forget that the economic growth in 2009 and over the next two years was exceedingly slow, Obama's job approval ratings were in caution to danger zone the entire time, his re-election a year out was not the foregone conclusion that many seem to remember it being.

The related conviction they have, in retrospect, was that the measure was too small, that the country was exceedingly slow coming out of that downturn because a larger and more aggressive package was not pushed through, a view that many economists now think is correct. It is true that economic downturns triggered by financial crises tend to be deeper than most other recessions and depressions and are more difficult to recover from. Calibrating the size of a package combating a severe economic crisis is an inexact science, and in that case, it was too small.

In 2021, Biden and his Congressional allies insisted many times that the danger was going too small, not too big. A very ambitious, extensive and expensive package was constructed and they seemed determined to get as much of it through as possible, despite the fact that the economy seemed to bottom out in July of the previous year, that while certainly fragile, things were getting better every month. Critics argued that as the economy improved, the size of the package should have contracted.

The earliest on the Democratic side to challenge the magnitude of the package was former Clinton Treasury Secretary Larry Summers, who professed no opposition to any of the individual elements within the proposal, insisting that many were very good ideas, but that the size of the spending package had a real danger of being inflationary, that demand could far exceed supply, that labor shortages and other price increases amounted to too much money injected into the economy at one time. Summers compared it to the 1960s, when President Johnson was trying to build a Great Society while trying to win a war in Vietnam, triggering horrific inflation. With inflation now under control since the 1990s, some feared a resurrection, while others thought that the inflation that had been seen was purely transitory and there was little danger of the economy overheating.

There are many theories as to why Biden surprised his friends and foes alike with a much more aggressive posture than expected. Some in the Biden camp argue that there is a new paradigm, that after the country was hit by the Coronavirus and as a result of Trump's policies, there is not only a greater tolerance for an expanded role for government, that there is more of an appetite for it. They argue that the changing demographics of the nation and generational change are driving this, as well.

Polling on this subject is inconclusive at best. One poll question that pollsters have utilized for decades asks respondents whether government should do more to address the country's problems or is government trying to do too much that would be better handled by individuals and businesses. Those numbers don't show much movement at all.

Others suggest that Biden is simply responding to his role as the leader of a party that is not only considerably more liberal than it was under Bill Clinton but also from when Barack Obama left office in 2017.

Another theory is simply the application of an argument made in 2012 by former Clinton White House chief of staff Rahm Emanuel, who told the Wall Street Journal that, "You never want a serious crisis to go to waste. And what I mean by that is an opportunity to do things that you think you could not do before." (There are some reports that Winston Churchill said it earlier but no firm record of that exists).

Biden's approach to his legislative agenda in his first five months in office certainly did not lack for ambition. To what extent it would be a template for the balance of his term is unknown, as is how aggressive his administration will be on the non-legislative side, on the promulgation and enforcement of regulations on issues like occupational safety and health, labor issues, the environment and taxes, other than setting rates. Would it be as aggressive as it was under Obama, or more so? Business certainly wasn't happy with many of the Clinton Administration's regulatory actions but looked nostalgically at those days with the more aggressive and, in their minds, hostile approach under Obama.

This raises the question of why Biden changed his approach, assuming that there was a change from the plan before the victories in Georgia. Did he do it because he could, or was there something else, or more?

Bordering on psychoanalysis is the suggestion that Biden's approach is reflective of his view of his place and life. At his first news conference in March 2021, just over two months after taking office when a reporter asked if he was going to run again, the President's response was that he was a big believer in "fate." Heading into his first year in office, Biden knew that he was 78 years old and would turn 82 just three weeks after the 2024 election. He knows that he had two brain aneurysms in 1988 (recovering completely from both). His first wife and daughter were killed and two sons badly injured in an automobile crash just before Christmas, right after he was first elected, and before even sworn into office. His older son Beau died of a brain tumor at age 46. Someone who has experienced all of that, and run for the office twice before, the first time 32 years before his eventual election, may simply believe that if he finally made it to the Oval Office and Resolute Desk, he should swing for the fences, do as much as possible when he can, that life may not give him other opportunities to do try it again.

On a related matter, many have wondered how is it that Biden, who had been so accident-prone and had such a propensity for verbosity and committing gaffes, managed to get through a primary nomination fight, general election and first months in office without replicating the problems that had plagued him throughout his political career. At least one close advisor to Biden believes that both the experience of his eight years as Vice President and the 2015 death of his son Beau infused him with a seriousness of purpose, a focus and discipline that had sometimes been previously lacking.

2022 Midterm Election

The margins on Capitol Hill could hardly be narrower or the stakes higher than in 2022. At 50-50, the Senate literally cannot be closer, Democrats only took control of the chamber by virtue of Jon Ossoff's narrow 54,944-vote win in the closer of the two January 5 runoff elections in Georgia. The Senate majority was effectively determined by a vote margin equivalent to the population of Casper Wyoming.

Democrats effectively clung to their House majority by virtue of 31,751 votes scattered across a half-dozen districts across the country; a number equivalent to the population of Walla Walla, Washington. The current House majority of fewer than a half dozen seats is the narrowest for either party since 2000 and the slimmest Democratic majority in the post-World War II era.

Midterm Election History and Patterns

Congressional midterm elections are almost always referenda on the incumbent president, even more so when a party bears full responsibility for governing, holding not only the White House but majorities in the House and Senate as well, giving little opportunity to shift any blame elsewhere.

In the House, the historical record is very clear. Since the end of the Civil War, the party holding the White House has lost House seats in 36 out of the 39 midterm elections. The exceptions were Franklin D. Roosevelt's first midterm election in 1934, Bill Clinton's second midterm in 1998 and George W. Bush's first midterm in 2002. In 1902, Teddy Roosevelt's first midterm, his GOP scored a net gain of nine seats; however, with the number of seats in the House that year expanded from 357 to 386 and the opposition Democrats picking up 25 seats, effectively the party in the White House lost seats.

As one might expect, the exceptions occurred in pretty exceptional circumstances. In 1934, in the wake of the 1929 stock market crash and the subsequent Great Depression, the electorate had still not forgiven the Republican Party for Herbert Hoover's presidency. That 1934 election was the third of four consecutive elections that voters punished Republicans with a net loss of seats in both the House and Senate. In 1998 it was a backlash against the impeachment and trial of Clinton that seemed to break the pattern. Americans generally believe in elections and see that as the appropriate vehicle to select and remove elected officials, which is why impeachment and recalls are rarely successful. Four years later in 2002, the midterm election was held just 14 months after 9/11, while George W. Bush's popularity was still sky high.

For elected presidents in the post-World War II era, the House average is a net loss of 22 seats, with little difference between the first midterm average of 20 seats and 23 seats lost for midterms in a second presidential term (It is better to average elected rather than all presidents. The circumstances around the death or resignation of presidents and ascension of vice president, as was the case with Harry Truman, Lyndon Johnson and Gerald Ford are not really analogous with others).

The historical record in the Senate is a little less conclusive. The President's party has lost seats in the upper chamber in 19 out of 26 midterm elections since the direct election of Senators began in 1914, that party losing ground in all but Franklin Roosevelt's first midterm in 1934, John F. Kennedy's only midterm in 1962, Richard Nixon's first midterm in 1970, Ronald Reagan first midterm in 1982, George W. Bush's first midterm in 2002 and Donald Trump's only midterm in 2018. The post-World War II average net Senate loss under elected president is three seats, but there is a huge difference between the first-term average loss of only one seat, but with second-terms presidents, the Senators elected when that president first won, the average loss was seven seats.

Reapportionment, Redistricting and the 2022 House Elections

At least half of the current Democratic margin in the House could be erased just by reapportionment, the decennial redistribution of seats after each Census. Six states will be gaining House seats and electoral votes for the coming decade with Texas picking up two seats, Colorado, Florida, Montana, North Carolina and Oregon gaining one seat each. Seven states will lose one seat each, California which will lose a seat for the first time since it became a state; Illinois, Michigan, New York, Ohio, Pennsylvania and West Virginia. States won by Trump will gain three seats at the expense of those that cast their ballots for Biden, hence the strong danger of reapportionment for Democrats.

Then there is redistricting. For the second decade in a row, Republicans will have the dominant hand in drawing districts in the 44 states with more than one district. David Wasserman, House Editor of the Cook Political Report, calculates that by virtue of their hold on state legislative chambers and governorships, the GOP will control the remapping process in 20 states with 187 districts, while Democrats will be able to draw the map in 8 states with 75 districts. Independent commissions will draw maps in 10 states with 121 districts, 6 states with 46 districts have split control.

Unfortunately, the national lockdown from the Coronavirus Pandemic came at the peak time when Census data were being collected. Extraordinary efforts had to be made by the Census Bureau to ensure that their data represented the best possible effort to reach all groups. As a result, the detailed data mapmakers need to draw Congressional and state legislative boundaries will not be delivered to the states until September 2021, meaning that most maps will not be completed until early 2022, injecting a great deal of uncertainty for all concerned. In some states, filing deadlines and primary elections may have to be delayed. In some cases, decisions by incumbents to seek re-election or not will be delayed. For non-incumbents, whether to throw their hats in the ring for open seat or challenger races will have to come later as well, injecting even more uncertainty.

Though reapportionment and redistricting are certainly important and could be the determinative factors in who controls the House after the next election, there are others that could be decisive as well.

President Biden's standing with voters at the time of the election and how each of the two parties is perceived at that point, incumbent retirements, candidate recruitment and whether either party is badly divided are critical, as well. In competitive states and districts, "exotic" candidates are chosen in party primaries, such as was the case in Senate races in Delaware and Nevada in 2010 and Indiana and Missouri in 2012. In those years, when GOP Senate primaries nominated Tea Party-backed Christine O'Donnell, Sharron Angle, Richard Mourdock and Todd Akin respectively, those choices ended up costing Republicans seats that they would likely have otherwise won. Both parties have risks in this area, Republicans with candidates coming out of the staunchly and dominant pro-Trump faction of the party could face a challenging situation in many suburban districts, particularly those that skew toward more highly educated voters. Democrats could face similar problems in swing, particularly suburban, districts if they nominate candidates from the most progressive elements of the party. Positions more akin to Alexandria Ocasio Cortez and "The Squad," Bernie Sanders and Elizabeth Warren, backing "democratic socialism" and utilizing rhetoric like "defund the police," or "end policing," or "Medicare for All" or advocating packing the Supreme Court, could trigger a backlash similar to what appears to have happened in the closing days of the 2020 campaign. Talk of a Democratic wave and concerns about giving Democrats all of the levers of power in Washington turned what seemed likely to be Democratic gains in the House to losses and limited Senate gains to the three seats that was the barest margin that would give them a majority there, as well as making Biden's margin in some states considerably narrower than anticipated.

Given the referendum nature of midterm elections, one unknowable factor is where Biden will stand with the electorate in the autumn of 2022. There is little relationship between a president's poll standing in the first year in office and how that party will fare in an election late in the following year. The closer an election is, the more relevant job approval poll ratings become. In the early summer of 2021, Biden's approval ratings were in the low-to-middle '50s after his first quarter in office; better than Trump's were, roughly in line with those of Clinton and George H.W. Bush, somewhat below the standing of George W. Bush, Barack Obama, Carter and Reagan. But at this early point, job approval ratings have little predictive value.

Put together, Democrats appear to face an uphill challenge to retain their majority. The micro-political factors at this point are seemingly working against them. Democrats' best hope is that the macro factors, the political climate, Biden's standing with voters and potential problems within the GOP will be more charitable for them than the structural factors.

2022 Senate Races

While Senate Democrats enter the 2022 cycle knowing that the curse of midterm elections is potentially hanging over their heads, Republicans have to contend with greater numerical exposure to potential losses.

One-third of the Senate is up every two years, but it matters which third of the Senate seats it is. The relative exposure that each party carries that cycle, determined in part by the partisan leanings of the states with Senate seats up and the number each party has at risk are important variables. One key factor that few observers appreciate is the importance of previous elections, particularly those six and

12 years earlier, most importantly after "wave years," when one party scored big gains over the other, creating more exposure six years later. Often, parties win seats that they might not otherwise carry, and as a result, six years later are very difficult to defend. This usually occurs in midterm elections and with greater frequency in recent years. Keep in mind that for the first time in American history, four consecutive presidents have lost majorities in both the Senate and the House, a reflection of the extreme levels of partisanship we are seeing today, and the volatility--even explosiveness--that can sometimes occur.

In Senate nomenclature, this 2022 group of Senate seats is known as Class III. With the exceptions of Arizona Democrat Mark Kelly and Raphael Warnock in Georgia, who both just won special elections, these seats last faced the electorate in 2016 and before that in 2010 and 2004. The GOP had scored a net gain of four seats in 2004 and six seats in 2010 (Obama's first midterm), with a net loss of just two seats in 2016, accounting for their greater exposure.

The partisan asymmetry flips in 2024, when Class I faces the voters, Democrats have 23 seats up then, Republicans 10, the consequences of Democrats scoring a net gain of six seats in 2006 (George W. Bush's second midterm) and two more seats in 2012, then lost just two in 2018 when this group was last up. That was Trump's midterm, when the national political environment favored Democrats.
There were ten Democratic seats up in states that Trump won two years earlier, five by 19 points or more, only one GOP seat was up in a state where Hillary Clinton had prevailed, an indication of a far greater level of serious Democratic exposure that year.

The partisan exposure differential flips yet again in 2026 with Class II up, Republicans having 20 seats up then, Democrats 13. Republicans enjoyed a nine seat gain in 2014 (Obama's second midterm) then lost just three in 2020, helping create the asymmetry.

Arithmetically speaking, the GOP exposure is not just limited to total number of seats up, but also that Republicans will be defending, at this writing, five open seats, while Democrats have none. Usually but not always, with no incumbency advantage, open seats are more difficult to defend, so the retirements of Roy Blunt (Missouri), Richard Burr (North Carolina) Rob Portman (Ohio), Richard Shelby (Alabama) and Pat Toomey (Pennsylvania) inject an element of uncertainty for the GOP.

Having said that, the overall Senate picture through the lens of which states are more or less likely to be competitive, the numbers are not nearly so lopsided in favor of Democrats. Using the Cook Political Report's Partisan Voting Index (PVI), that calculates, based on the two previous presidential elections, how much more Democrat or Republican a state or district votes than the country as a whole, Republicans only have four seats up in states where the GOP does not have a Republican PVI advantage of five points or more. Those are the open seats in North Carolina and Pennsylvania, as well as Florida, where Marco Rubio is widely expected to seek re-election, and Wisconsin, where it has been unclear whether Ron Johnson will seek a third term. If Johnson runs, he would be the only Republican running for reelection in a state that Trump lost. Republican open seats in both Alabama and Missouri, by this measurement, seem less at risk. Conversely, Democrats have three states, all with incumbents running again, Catherine Cortez Masto in Nevada, Kelly in Arizona and Warnock in Georgia, that are likely to be competitive. One more Democratic incumbent, Maggie Hassan in New Hampshire, with a slightly higher Democratic PVI, is expected to face a stiff challenge, particularly if GOP Gov. Chris Sununu takes her on.

With American politics increasingly parliamentary in nature, two-thirds of the electorate are partisans, with the vast majority of them rarely breaking ranks to vote for a candidate of the other side. Looking at the presidential voting patterns of a state is of strong predictive power, but more so in presidential than midterm elections. In 2016 and 2020, all but one Senate candidate from the presidential party prevailed. You can call it coattails or whatever you want, but the power is strong. In the 2018 midterm elections, by contrast, only 28 out of 35 Senate races were won by the same party that carried the state in the presidential election two years earlier. Seven candidates, all

Democrats, managed to win 2018 Senate races in states that Trump carried in 2016: Tammy Baldwin (Wisconsin), Sherrod Brown (Ohio), Bob Casey (Pennsylvania), Joe Manchin (West Virginia), Kyrsten Sinema (Arizona), Debbie Stabenow (Michigan) and Jon Tester (Montana). Conversely, three Democratic incumbents, Joe Donnelly (Indiana), Heidi Heitkamp (North Dakota) and Claire McCaskill (Missouri) lost re-election in Trump states while one GOP incumbent, Dean Heller (Nevada) lost in a Clinton state.

2021 and 2022 Governors Races

Currently, Republicans hold 27 governorships while Democrats have 23. The gubernatorial election cycle leaves only two governorships, New Jersey and Virginia, that are up in the first year of a presidential term; 36 are up in the midterm election year; three--Kentucky, Louisiana and Mississippi--are up in the year before a presidential election and 11 are up in presidential election years. Only two states, New Hampshire and Vermont, still have two-year terms.

The two gubernatorial elections in 2021--in New Jersey where Phil Murphy is seeking a second term, and the open seat in Virginia, where incumbents are not allowed to seek re-election--are both currently in Democratic hands. Murphy is strongly favored to win a second term in this staunchly Democratic state. Virginia, a once red Republican state, has become a purple swing state and is now edging more into the Democratic column. Currently, Republicans in Virginia hold no statewide offices. Former Democratic Gov. Terry McAuliffe is favored to win the general election. Interestingly, starting in 1977, Jimmy Carter's first year in office and Republican John Dalton's gubernatorial victory, the party holding the White House has lost every Virginia governor's race save one, in 2013, when McAuliffe won during Barack Obama's second term, a span of 11 elections.

In 2022 there are 20 Republican and 16 Democratic governorships up. As of the early summer of 2021, four Republican gubernatorial seats are open--Arizona, Arkansas, Maryland and Nebraska--while Democrats have three, in Hawaii, Oregon and Pennsylvania. The most competitive gubernatorial seats appear likely to be Democratic incumbent Laura Kelly in Kansas, in Pennsylvania, where another Democrat, Tom Wolf, has a two-term limit, and in Arizona where the Republican governor, Doug Ducey, cannot run for a third term. Republicans face an uphill challenge hanging onto the governorship in Maryland, an extremely Democratic state, yet Larry Hogan was not only elected and re-elected, but has consistently been among the three most popular governors in the nation.

Democrats are currently favored to hold both the Michigan and Wisconsin governorships, where Gretchen Whitmer and Tony Evers are seeking re-election, but both states can be expected to have competitive races. These industrial Midwest states are emblematic of the places that Democrats are having an increasingly difficult time nailing down, where the party's relationship with whites without a college degree has become more difficult. Democratic governors who could face competitive races are Janet Mills (Maine), Tim Walz (Minnesota) and Steve Sisolak (Nevada), while Republican governors whose races could become competitive are Brian Kemp (Georgia), Kim Reynolds (Iowa), Mike DeWine (Ohio), Henry McMaster (South Carolina) and Greg Abbott (Texas), with Abbott potentially facing a stiff Republican primary challenge as well.

Georgia Governor

Of the 36 governor's races in 2018, only the Florida and Wisconsin contests were narrower than the fight in Georgia between then-Secretary of State Brian Kemp (R), and former state House Minority Leader Stacey Abrams (D). All three were open seats. The 2022 Georgia contest is expected to be a rematch and very competitive, with Kemp now the incumbent. As this book went to press, Abrams had not officially announced her candidacy, but it appeared all but certain. As more move into the Peach State, particularly from non-Southern parts of the country, and the share of the electorate in rural and small-town Georgia shrinks, the shift from red Republican continues. This time, though, Democrats have to worry about the rebound that often hurts a party holding the White House in midterm elections, potentially mitigating a long-term trend. At the same time, it is unclear how much Trump's criticism of Kemp for not being supportive of the then-President's efforts to overturn the 2020 results will hurt Kemp among Republicans, either in a contested primary or with depressed general-election turnout, or both.

State Legislative Elections

Republicans now control 61 state legislative chambers, Democrats 37 chambers, the Alaskan House has a power sharing agreement between the two parties and Nebraska has a non-partisan, unicameral Senate. Republicans control the governorship and both state legislative chambers in 23 states, Democrats in 15, the rest, other than Nebraska, have split control.

Democrats have yet to climb back from devastating state legislative and gubernatorial losses in the two Obama midterm elections. The first, in 2010, leading into the 2011 redistricting, put the party at a huge disadvantage in the remapping that year for the next decade. In 2016, 2018 and 2020, cumulative modest gains had the cumulative effect of putting Democrats at state legislative and Congressional redistricting disadvantages for a second decade in a row.

Three states legislative chambers are up in 2021. The New Jersey House and Senate and the Virginia House have state legislative races slated. The Senate in Virginia, currently split between 21 Democrats and 19 Republicans, has its regularly scheduled elections in the year before presidential elections. Roughly 80 percent of state legislative seats nationally are up every two years, all but a handful of state House chambers have two-year terms. Most state Senates have four-year terms, so there is not the bulge of seats up in midterm years compared to presidential years, as there are in governorships.

Conclusion

It is easy to become disillusioned by this new tone and direction of American politics, but some of this is not particularly new. Pulitzer Prize-winning historian Joseph Ellis wrote in the Los Angeles Times in 2021 that "The enduring question is stunningly simple: Is national government "us" or "them?" On the "us" side of the question was George Washington, John Adams, Alexander Hamilton and John Marshall, who believed only collective power could embody and act in the public interest. Coming down on the "them" side was Thomas Jefferson, Samuel Adams, Patrick Henry and George Mason, who were suspicious of government and considered then central government an intrusive evil.

Over 230 years later, this debate remains vigorous and just as relevant. Pointing to the last line of the Pledge of Allegiance, "...with liberty and justice for all," Virginia state Sen. David Marsden has another interesting take on our differences today. Marsden, a Democrat, argues that while most every American believes in both liberty and justice, conservatives and Republicans tend to put a greater emphasis on liberty, liberals and Democrats on justice. It is an intriguing thought, that the conservative and Republican side put a premium on freedom, individual choice, self-reliance, that we are a meritocracy, that someone should be able to go as far as their talents, work ethic and ingenuity will take them, and enjoy the fruits of their accomplishments. That greater risk should have the potential for greater reward, and that those that are successful should be able to enjoy the fruits of that attainment.

Conversely, liberals and Democrats equate justice with fairness and equality, that society and government should seek to level the playing field and that there should be a social safety net for those less fortunate or successful. The common good, they argue, should sometimes be prioritized over individual choice.

It is as if the two sides not only see the role of government differently but to a certain extent, have differing value systems, not mutually exclusive, but putting much more weight on one than the other.

But what has become so destructive is more behavioral than structural. Process changes like open primaries and term limitations can only nibble at the edges of the problem at best. Redistricting reform, along the lines that Iowa has used for years would be more helpful, rank-choice voting has Maine has embraced also shows some potential.

There is a growing intolerance of anyone with a different point of view. Rather than agreeing to disagree or civilly discussing an issue, instead the other's motives, integrity and honesty or intellectual capacity come into question. Attacking the messenger rather than discussing the message has become the rule. Any news that does not align with pre-existing points of view is quickly labeled as biased by many, with little consideration that as undesirable as it may be to read or hear, there is a chance that it is right.

It is a failure of parents, educators, religious, community and other opinion leaders to teach a greater openness to ideas and tolerance of differences. There is little to discourage political arsonists determined to set political fires and fan flames, often manufacturing fights over symbolic rather than substantive issues, setting up proxy fights, all with the intention of dividing the country and marginalizing the opposition.

Sadly, many elected officials, their staff and political operatives have accumulated too many scars from previous political battles, often feeling that those in the opposition party are unwilling or even incapable of dealing in good faith and anxious to settle old scores, perpetuating the downward spiral.

But thinking about the crises and challenges that this country has faced over the last 230 years that began with revolution and survived slavery, the Civil War, Reconstruction, a Great Depression, two World and one Cold Wars, Vietnam, Watergate and 9/11 should teach us that this too will pass.

We should always be mindful of the unexpected. When British conservative Harold Macmillan was elected prime minister in 1957, a journalist asked him what most troubled him, what could derail his government. Macmillan was said to respond, "events, dear boy, events." That's what keeps politics so challenging, unanticipated events changing a trajectory in a way that no one did or could expect.

Once again, it is my honor to be associated with this Almanac tradition that I have found so valuable and cherished, since, as a high school senior in 1972, I bought the first edition in a hometown bookstore as soon as it came out.

The tradition and great work originated by Barone, Ujifusa and Matthews, now ably carried on by Rich Cohen and an incredibly talented group of researchers and writers and the great folks at Columbia Books is a unique and remarkable contribution to our understanding of both the details and the nuance of this constantly changing American politics.

The President: Joe Biden

By Louis Peck

President

Joseph R. Biden Jr. (D)

Elected 2020, term expires Jan. 2025, b. Nov 20, 1942; Scranton, PA; University of Delaware, B.A., 1965; Syracuse University College of Law, J.D., 1968; Roman Catholic; Widower (Neilia Hunter); Married (Jill Jacobs); 2 children (2 deceased); 5 grandchildren.

Elected Office: Member, New Castle County Council, 1970-1972; U.S. Senate, 1973-2009; Vice President, U.S., 2009-2017.

Professional Career: Attorney/Public Defender; Adjunct Professor, Widener University School of Law.

In 1974, a cocky 31-year-old Joe Biden – a year after entering the Senate -- gave a frank interview to Washingtonian magazine, asserting: "…I know I can be a good president…And my family still expects me to be there one of these days. With them behind me anything can happen." His sister, Valerie Biden Owens – who had run his first Senate campaign, and would manage all of his others -- was even less guarded: "Joey is going to be president someday. He was made to be in the White House. There is no one else who can lead the country. Just you wait and see."

It was an ambition that would require three tries over nearly half a century to realize. By the time he moved into the Oval Office in January 2021, Biden – sworn in as the sixth-youngest senator in history in January 1973 – had become the oldest person ever elected president. The Biden that the public witnessed during his first months in office – an avuncular figure who, in contrast to his immediate predecessor, was measured in what he shared publicly and the tone in which he shared it – had evolved considerably from a brash young senator prone to longwindedness, exaggeration and excessive familiarity. New York Times columnist Maureen Dowd, after observing Biden for more than three decades, concluded in 2020: "Biden's gaffes, logorrhea, puffery and handsiness are part of the messy package that is Uncle Joe. So are his empathy, sentimentality and loyalty."

In substance, Biden moved markedly left during the 2020 campaign – reportedly telling his erstwhile intraparty rival, Sen. Bernie Sanders, "I want to be the most progressive president since FDR." It was a far cry from the young Democrat first elected when Delaware was a reliably red state. "Those ADA [Americans for Democratic Action] ratings get us into so much trouble that a lot of us sit around thinking up ways to vote conservative just so we don't come out with a liberal rating," he told the Washingtonian in 1974. "When it comes to civil rights and civil liberties, I'm a liberal but that's it. I'm really quite conservative on most other issues. My wife said I was the most socially conservative man she had ever known." On economic issues, the president who would push for more than $6 trillion in pandemic relief, infrastructure and social spending in his first 100 days backed a budget freeze and a constitutional amendment to limit debt nearly four decades earlier.

"In the usual telling, Joseph Robinette Biden Jr. is a product of the Silent Generation, the cohort of cautious Americans born between the Great Depression and the end of the Second World War, who were too young to have fought overseas and too old to lead the counterculture," New Yorker writer Evan Osnos noted in a 2020 Biden biography. During his first presidential bid in the late 1980s, Biden summoned up memories of the civil rights revolution and opposition to the Vietnam War – proclaiming he was ready to take up where his generation's heroes had left off. There was more than a trace of hyperbole in his appeal to the Baby Boom generation: Born in 1942, he was at least four years too old to qualify as a Baby Boomer. He supported integration in Wilmington Delaware, but never joined the activists who journeyed to the Deep South on behalf of the cause -- despite implying he had. And while many Baby Boomers were protesting the Vietnam War in the 1960s, Biden was a quiet law student with a family. An episode in which he failed a course and was forced to repeat it after being found to have plagiarized a law review article helped lead to the premature end of his 1988 presidential bid.

Biden was born in Scranton Pennsylvania, the first of four children of a car dealership manager. The family moved to Delaware in 1953 when he was 10, settling in a suburb just north of Wilmington.

Biden attended Archmere Academy, a Catholic prep school, where he played football. (He is the second Catholic to be elected president, a first achieved by John F. Kennedy's 1960 election.) As was often highlighted during the 2020 campaign, Biden stuttered as a child – an affliction he largely overcame during high school, when he taught himself to deliver a speech to the school by reciting works ranging from the Declaration of Independence to the poetry of William Butler Yeats.

Ultimately, Biden's efforts earned him a reputation as a gifted political orator. Because of his stutter, however, reading aloud remained more awkward than speaking extemporaneously – which, in turn, left him gaffe-prone. Recalling Biden's experience as Barack Obama's vice-presidential running mate during the 2008 campaign, biographer Osnos related, "Sometimes he worked with speechwriters and then ignored the script, which would make him vulnerable to what members of Obama's campaign team called Joe Bombs -- the things he says but doesn't mean…and the things he means but shouldn't say." Before launching his bid for the 2020 presidential nomination, Biden faced an interviewer who suggested his political liabilities included being a "gaffe machine." According to CNN, Biden came back with a swipe aimed at President Donald Trump, acknowledging, "I am a gaffe machine, but my God what a wonderful thing compared to a guy who can't tell the truth."

Biden earned a bachelor's degree from the University of Delaware in 1965 and graduated from Syracuse University College of Law in 1968 -- ranking 76th in a class of 85. (He was the first Democratic presidential nominee lacking an Ivy League degree since Walter Mondale's 1984 candidacy.) Returning to Wilmington to practice law, it didn't take him long to enter the political arena: In 1970, he ran for a seat on the six-member New Castle County Council. Reflecting Delaware at large, most elected offices in New Castle County were then held by Republicans. A confident local GOP nominated an elementary school music teacher named Lawrence Messick -- who turned out to be no match for Biden's skills as a one-on-one campaigner, or the ability of Biden's sister/campaign manager to mobilize volunteers. Biden won, 55%-43%.

Just two years later, he sought the Senate seat occupied by Republican J. Caleb Boggs, a former governor. At 63 -- more than twice Biden's age – Boggs was a reluctant reelection candidate. He ran only after being persuaded by President Richard Nixon, to save the Delaware GOP from a potentially divisive primary. Biden avoided direct attacks on the well-liked Boggs, but played up his youth. His ads ended with the tagline, "He understands what is happening today." He ousted Boggs by 50%-49% -- a margin of just under 3,200 votes – as Nixon overwhelmed the Democratic presidential nominee, George McGovern, 60%-39%, in the state. Biden went on to win reelection to the Senate six times – most recently in 2008, when he ran simultaneously as Obama's ticket mate. He never won less than 58 percent in seeking reelection, usually taking more than 60 percent.

Biden was 29 when first elected, several weeks from the constitutional minimum age of 30 required for a senator, which he reached before being sworn in. The elation surrounding his historic victory was soon swept away by the first of several personal tragedies and trials that he faced in the ensuing decades. On the week before Christmas 1972, as Biden was on Capitol Hill assembling a staff, his wife – the former Neilia Hunter, whom he had married during law school – along with their three young children were driving home west of Wilmington after shopping for a Christmas tree. A tractor trailer broadsided the family station wagon, killing Neilia Biden and the couple's 13-month-old daughter, Naomi. Their sons, four-year-old Joseph – nicknamed Beau – and two-year-old Robert – known as Hunter – were seriously injured.

Biden took the Senate oath of office in his son's hospital room, as Beau lay nearby in traction. As a single parent, he considered resigning his seat but was persuaded to stay by several colleagues – including Majority Leader Mike Mansfield and Sens. Hubert Humphrey of Minnesota and Ted Kennedy of Massachusetts. Even before the election, Biden's youth, Irish Catholic background and future ambitions had prompted comparisons to the Kennedy clan – with his family tragedy adding another layer to the parallels.

Bidens' sister and brother-in-law moved into his home to help take care of the boys, and the senator began commuting to Washington from Wilmington by rail to see his sons in the morning and evening. On Capitol Hill, Biden initially was assigned to the Banking, Housing and Urban Affairs Committee as well as the Public Works Committee. By the mid-1970s, he left both for the two panels he would later chair: Judiciary and Foreign Relations. In 1977, Biden married Jill Jacobs – now-First Lady Jill Biden. The couple had a daughter, Ashley, in 1981. "Amtrak Joe" continued the daily commute – 80 minutes each way – throughout his 36-year Senate career, while becoming a key legislative ally of the intercity rail service. In 2011, the Wilmington Amtrak station was renamed in his honor.

As adults, Beau and Hunter Biden would both play roles in their father's political career, albeit in widely differing ways. Beau Biden, elected to two terms as Delaware's attorney general, became a trusted adviser to Joe Biden as well as his political heir apparent. Beau Biden was planning a run for governor when diagnosed in 2013 with an aggressive form of brain cancer; he died in 2015 at 46. The timing of this latest tragedy played into Joe Biden's decision to forgo a run for president in 2016. Hunter Biden—whose adult life was punctuated by struggles with drug and alcohol addiction – pursued a business career, joining the board of Burisma, a Ukrainian energy firm, in early 2014. The move coincided with his father becoming the Obama administration's point man on Ukraine after a pro-Western government took power. Five years later, Trump – spurred by unsupported claims that Joe Biden had sought to intervene on behalf of Burisma to help his son – allegedly threatened to withhold U.S. aid to pressure Ukraine's government to investigate his potential 2020 rival. Trump's ploy triggered the first of two impeachment trials. Hunter Biden later acknowledged poor judgment in taking the Burisma post while his father was vice president; both denied any wrongdoing.

The first Biden presidential campaign was launched in June 1987 and concluded in September. The disclosure of plagiarism on his law school paper was secondary to the central controversy that precipitated Biden's exit. A leaked video – whose release was later traced to the campaign manager of a Democratic presidential rival, Michael Dukakis – showed Biden mouthing a speech by British Labor Leader Neil Kinnock nearly word-for-word, without attribution. Biden's lack of originality was aggravated by exaggeration. Quoting Kinnock, Biden claimed he was "the first in his family ever to go to university"; he later acknowledged there were relatives on his mother's side who had done so. Further borrowing Kinnock's comments, Biden spoke of "my ancestors who worked in the coal mines of northeast Pennsylvania and would come up after 12 hours." In fact, there were no coal mining ancestors. (A 2021 Washington Post examination of census records found that Biden's great-grandfather and great-great-grandfather on his mother's side -- while not coal miners per se -- had worked, respectively, as a mining engineer and mining inspector.)

Initially, Biden blamed opposition research and the media for his demise, but later conceded he had been inadequately prepared for a presidential race. As he prepared to try again 20 years later, he issued a mea culpa for his earlier experience, telling an interviewer: "The bottom line was I made a mistake and it was born out of arrogance. I didn't deserve to be president." His premature exit from the 1988 race may have saved his life. In February -- just days before the Iowa caucuses and New Hampshire primary in which he would have been competing – the 45-year-old Biden underwent emergency surgery to repair a life-threatening brain aneurysm after suffering from severe headaches. More surgery was needed later to deal with blood clots in his lungs; he did not return to Capitol Hill until the fall of 1988.

His initial presidential campaign came several months after he had assumed the Judiciary Committee chairmanship – while coinciding with hearings on President Ronald Reagan's Supreme Court nomination of Robert Bork. The nomination of Bork, an influential conservative in legal circles, came as many liberals felt Reagan was seeking to load the federal bench with doctrinaire conservatives. Biden declined to join some in the party's left wing who characterized Bork as a radical ideologue, later writing in "Promises To Keep", his 2007 memoir: "If there was an argument to be made against Bork in the Senate, it would have to be made to Republicans and Democrats in the political center." He closely questioned Bork on the 1965 Griswold vs. Connecticut ruling, of which Bork had been critical. That decision, which ruled couples had to the right to use contraceptives to prevent unwanted pregnancies, led Biden to argue the Constitution protected a zone of personal privacy.

Pacing the hearings to Bork's disadvantage, Biden helped shift critical committee votes -- two conservative Democrats and a Republican – against the nomination, which was later defeated on the Senate floor. Mark Gitenstein, Biden's counsel at the time, years later told Politico that Biden's explicit goal was preserving the legal precedents of the liberal Warren Court. By defeating Bork and prompting Reagan to nominate the moderate Anthony Kennedy instead, Gitenstein contended Biden "shaped the court for 30 years, and it took 30 years to undo what he did." Alluding to the massive effort by Senate Republican Leader Mitch McConnell to install conservative jurists during the Trump administration, Gitenstein added, "They didn't win the Bork fight until the [Brett] Kavanaugh fight."

More than a quarter of a century prior to Kavanaugh, Biden took heat for his handling of another Supreme Court nomination hearing featuring allegations of sexual harassment. President George H.W. Bush's nominee, Clarence Thomas, appeared to be on his way to confirmation in 1991 when charges leaked out involving his behavior toward Anita Hill while she had worked for Thomas. Although Biden was accused of covering up this information, he had shared it with Democratic committee colleagues – who reportedly concurred that Hill's initial unwillingness to testify would make public airing of the allegations unfair to Thomas. Hill did later agree to testify, and Biden caught additional fire from Thomas opponents for not seeking to curtail sharp questioning of Hill by committee Republicans -- and not calling a witness said to be ready to back her testimony. Biden ultimately voted against confirming Thomas, now the high court's senior member.

After launching his bid for the 2020 presidential nomination, Biden attempted political damage control, telling ABC News in 2019: "Hill did not get treated well. I take responsibility for that." He also telephoned Hill in an effort to apologize. On a more personal note, Biden also apologized as he started his latest presidential bid for overly familiar and affectionate greetings of women over the years, as he faced complaints on this score. Saying that his style reflected an earlier era, he pledged to be "more mindful about respecting personal space in the future."

His comments reflected a continuing effort to demonstrate greater sensitivity to gender issues that had started soon after the Thomas hearings when he recruited two women to join the then-all male Judiciary Committee following the 1992 election -- including California Democrat Dianne Feinstein, who remains a panel member. He also was the initial sponsor of the Violence Against Women, which became law in 1994 and has since provided federal funding to combat sexual assault and domestic abuse. If Biden has labeled that measure his proudest legislative accomplishment, it was initially passed as part of what was arguably his most controversial accomplishment – the 1994 crime bill. That legislation – which encouraged mass incarceration through creation of a federal "three strikes" law and billions of dollars for construction of more prisons – became a lightning rod for progressives amid the push for criminal justice reform in recent years.

His decade as the senior Judiciary Committee Democrat placed Biden in the midst of a tension between the leftward movement of the national Democratic Party and the social conservatism with which he grew up – and that was widespread in Delaware for much of his Senate tenure. He has been raised to regard abortion as murder, and, as a senator, sought to strike a balance between his own beliefs and the rights and prerogatives of others. In his 2007 memoir, he wrote, "I still vote against partial birth abortion and federal funding, and I'd like to make it easier for scared young mothers to choose not to have an abortion, but I will also vote against a constitutional amendment that strips a woman of her right to make her own choice." He dropped his opposition to federal funding of abortions during the 2020 campaign.

On another hot-button social issue -- school busing to achieve racial integration --Biden was heckled by angry white suburbanites at a community meeting early in his first Senate term, and subsequently became a leading Democratic voice against compulsory busing. It produced a memorable moment in the first Democratic presidential debate of the 2020 campaign, when then-California Sen. Kamala Harris took on Biden for boasting he had worked early in his career with segregationist colleagues to find common ground. "You also worked with them to oppose busing," Harris told Biden. "You know, there was a little girl in California who was part of the second class to integrate her public schools, and she was bused to school every day…And that little girl was me." Biden decried a "mischaracterization" of his position," and many in the Biden inner circle were deeply angered by what they regarded as a calculated ambush. But Harris' performance did not stop Biden from tapping her as his running mate – underscoring his long-time persona as a political dealmaker willing to forgive and forget.

In fact, he appears to have seen Harris' aggressive debate style as a plus in the coming general election. Similarly, Biden's debate performance 12 years earlier had factored into Obama's selection of him as a running mate – despite a rocky experience early in the campaign. Biden launched his second presidential bid in January 2007, nearly 20 years after his first was cut short. On the day of his announcement, the New York Observer published a story in which he called Obama "the first mainstream African-American who's articulate and bright and clean and a nice-looking guy." Biden immediately expressed regret over this latest gaffe, but his campaign never gained traction: He dropped out in early 2008 after finishing fifth in the Iowa caucuses. Obama, with just four years in Washington, was attracted to Biden as a running mate due to the latter's contacts abroad as well as his connections on Capitol Hill. In accepting the vice-presidential slot, Biden insisted he be the "last guy in the room" when major decisions were made – a condition that Obama accepted, and reflecting a commitment Biden made to Harris 12 years later.

Biden's influence on the Obama administration was captured by the headline of an Atlantic story as he began his second term: "The Most Influential Vice President In History?" But he didn't get his way on some major foreign policy decisions. He was a dovish, though knowledgeable, voice in the debate over several risky foreign missions and entanglements – including opposition to the 2011 raid that killed Osama bin Laden. In the Senate, he spent a dozen years as the top Democrat on the Foreign Relations panel – which he chaired for four years prior to becoming vice president in 2009.

On Capitol Hill, Biden – known in the Obama White House as the "McConnell whisperer," according to a book by Washington Post journalist Bob Woodward – was detailed to handle major negotiations with the prickly Republican leader, whom Biden had known for more than a quarter of a century. In the "fiscal cliff" negotiations in late 2012, aimed at averting automatic budget cuts and tax hikes that could impair the nation's economic recovery, Biden succeeded in achieving the Obama administration's goal of a tax increase on the wealthiest Americans. But other elements of a tax cut enacted during the Bush administration a decade earlier remained in place, prompting grumbling by some congressional Democrats that Biden had conceded too much.

After traveling the country as he contemplated another campaign for president, Biden in October 2015 – less than five months after Beau Biden's death -- announced he would not run, leaving the 2016 Democratic field to Hillary Clinton and Sanders. "Unfortunately, I believe we're out of time, the time necessary to mount a winning campaign for the nomination," he said. He moved toward a 2020 run after Trump's much criticized remarks that there were "very fine people" on both sides of the confrontation between white supremacists and counterdemonstrators in Charlottesville in late 2017. "This guy is going to be so much worse than I thought he was," Biden told Osnos at the time. Viewed as the frontrunner after his entry into the race in April 2019, Biden faltered in the early primaries and caucuses – finishing fourth in Iowa, fifth in New Hampshire, and a distant second in Nevada. But he won a huge victory in the South Carolina primary, where the majority Black Democratic electorate remembered his service to the nation's first African-American president. That victory triggered a consolidation among centrist candidates fearful of the chances of Sanders' progressive candidacy in a race against Trump.

Biden carried 10 of 14 primaries on Super Tuesday in March and won eight more contests in the weeks that immediately followed. In early April, his remaining intraparty rival, Sanders, dropped out and endorsed him. And, despite a year encompassing a series of tumultuous events, Biden – largely due to the COVID-19 pandemic and Trump's mishandling of it – remained consistently ahead in poll matchups with the incumbent president in the 12 months prior to November 2020. Biden ousted Trump, 51%-47%, a 7 million vote margin, as he reconstructed the "Blue Wall" – Michigan, Pennsylvania and Wisconsin – that had enabled Trump to win an Electoral College victory four years earlier. And Biden flipped traditionally red Arizona and Georgia, the latter electing in January two Democratic senators who allowed his party to reclaim a narrow Senate majority. That gave him 306 Electoral votes to 232 for Trump.

Throughout the year, a political evolution that had taken place over Biden's 50 years in public life accelerated. Biden began the 2020 contest with the narrow goal of ending the divisive Trump presidency and restoring a prior status quo, often harkening back to his time in the Obama White House. But, after he took office, Biden revealed a stark change in both tone and substance as he moved to unite the disparate wings of the Democratic Party behind him. Appearing on a webcast with Sanders in April, Biden – alluding to the pandemic – declared: "When this crisis has receded, we can't just talk about, think about, building back to the way things were before. We need to build better for the future."

Forty years after Reagan declared, "Government is not the solution to our problem, government is the problem," Biden was betting that massive government intervention was necessary. "The politics of redistribution, which are at the heart of what Biden is proposing, could test decades of assumptions that Democrats should be afraid of being tagged as the party of big government," wrote Dan Balz, the Washington Post's chief correspondent. Noting the scope and expense of such programs proposed during Biden's first 100 days in office, Balz observed: "Biden had to wait nearly 50 years to achieve his dream of becoming president. In office, he is operating as if he has no time to spare."

The Vice President: Kamala Harris

Vice President

Kamala D. Harris (D)

Elected 2020, term expires Jan. 2025, 1st term, b. Oct 24, 1964; Oakland; Howard University (DC), Bach. Deg.; University of California Hastings College of Law, J.D; Baptist; Married (Douglas Emhoff).

Elected Office: District Attorney of San Francisco, 2004-2011; Attorney General, State of CA, 2011-2016; U.S. Senate 2017-2021.

Professional Career: Deputy District Attorney, Alameda County, 1990-1998; Chief, Career Criminal Division, Office of the San Francisco District Attorney, 1998-2000; Chief, Family and Children's Services Division, Office of the San Francisco City Attorney, 2000-2003.

Not long after she was first elected as San Francisco's district attorney in 2003, Kamala Harris raised money for a young Democratic state senator named Barack Obama, then embarking on a Senate campaign half a continent away in Illinois. Harris and Obama not only shared backgrounds as the children of multiracial marriages; they shared career paths to a significant degree. "With an Indian mother and a Jamaican father, Harris strikes some observers as a California version of Barack Obama," the Los Angeles Times wrote in October 2004, a month before Obama was elected senator. In 2016, Harris herself won election to the Senate. And in January 2019, she announced her presidential candidacy after two high-profile, buzz-filled years on Capitol Hill — mirroring the start of Obama's meteoric rise to the White House years earlier.

But Harris' presidential bid was over before the end of 2019 – as she struggled to define herself to Democratic voters. Notwithstanding this setback, she quickly became a leading option for the second spot on the ticket – with her prospects ascending as the presumptive presidential nominee, Joe Biden, pledged in the spring of 2020 to choose a female running mate, and later was pressed to select a woman of color. The election of the Biden-Harris ticket in November not only made her the highest-ranking woman elected official in the nation's history; she stepped into a role shaped by Biden to wield the broad influence he had enjoyed for eight years as Obama's vice president. And, as the governing partner of the oldest president ever elected, Harris – perhaps as early as 2024 – could be poised to become the nation's first woman and second Black chief executive.

It was only the latest in a career of firsts: Harris was the first Black and first woman elected as San Francisco's district attorney and later as state attorney general, and became the first woman of color chosen as senator from California. Nationwide, she was only the second African-American woman in history to serve in the Senate. Such milestones aside, Harris — born just months after passage of the Civil Rights Act of 1964 -- has at times appeared ambivalent about making racial issues central to her political persona. She targeted Black voters – particularly the Democratic Party's key bloc of African-American women – as she launched her presidential bid, and aggressively promoted several pieces of racial justice legislation to bolster her standing while being considered as Biden's running mate. But as she was getting ready to make her first Senate run, Harris told the Los Angeles Times in 2015, "I don't feel compelled to sing long ballads about my experiences with injustice."

Such experiences, however, were part of Harris' upbringing, even in the left-leaning Northern California of the 1960s and 1970s. Her parents met as graduate students at the University of California, Berkeley. In the early 1970s, Harris' elementary school was only the second in Berkeley to integrate by use of busing. This chapter of Harris' life came to the fore in the first debate among 2020 Democratic presidential contenders -- when she attacked Biden for boasting earlier that he had been able early in his Senate career to work with segregationist colleagues to find common ground. "You also worked with them to oppose busing," Harris said during the debate. "You know, there was a little girl in California who was part of the second class to integrate her public schools, and she was bused to school every day…And that little girl was me." Harris' poll numbers jumped following the debate. But Biden, who opposed compulsory school busing as a young lawmaker, was caught off-guard. And the episode -- angrily regarded by some Biden associates as a calculated ambush -- would complicate her prospects for selection as a running mate.

Harris attended a Hindu temple growing up; as an adult, she has identified as a Baptist. (In 2014, she married Los Angeles attorney Douglas Emhoff, who has been designated as the nation's first

"Second Gentleman." Emhoff is also the first Jewish spouse of a president or vice president.) Harris' parents divorced when she was five, and she and her younger sister, Maya Harris -- a senior policy adviser to Hillary Clinton's 2016 presidential bid and later chair of her older sister's 2020 White House bid -- visited their father, a Stanford University economics professor, on weekends. "The neighbors' kids were not allowed to play with us because we were Black," Kamala Harris recalled years later. "In Palo Alto. The home of Google."

Harris spent her high school years in Montreal, where her mother worked as a breast cancer researcher affiliated with McGill University. She earned her undergraduate degree at Howard University in Washington, the nation's oldest historically black college, before returning to the Bay Area to graduate from the University of California's Hastings College of Law. She took a job in the Alameda County district attorney's office, prosecuting crimes ranging from homicide and robbery to child sexual assault cases in Oakland. In 1998, she transferred to the San Francisco district attorney's office, before moving to the city attorney's office as head of its division on families and children.

In 2003, Harris challenged her former boss, San Francisco District Attorney Terence Hallinan, whose office had come under criticism for low conviction rates and an outdated administrative operation. Fighting for his political life, Hallinan sought to link Harris to Willie Brown, a colorful and controversial figure completing his final term as San Francisco's mayor. Harris dated Brown for a couple of years in the 1990s when he was speaker of the California Assembly; he had appointed her to state boards that added nearly $400,000 in compensation over five years to her annual salary, according to published reports. Harris and Brown stopped dating after he became mayor in 1996. Hallinan attacked Harris as part of "the old Willie Brown machine." In November 2003, Hallinan ran slightly ahead of Harris, 36%-34%, with the rest going to a third candidate. In a runoff a month later, Harris won 56%-44%.

Harris faced a political firestorm early in her first term, when, three days after the murder of a San Francisco police officer, Isaac Espinoza, she announced she would not seek the death penalty for the accused killer. Harris later conceded she had been "politically naive" to rule out the death penalty so soon after Espinoza's killing, but argued the killer's second-degree murder conviction and sentence of life without parole had justified her action. After winning praise for being among the first district attorneys in the nation to emphasize alternatives to incarceration for some drug-related offenses, Harris ran unopposed for a second term in 2007.

However, as she prepared to run for the open state attorney general seat in 2010, Harris published a book titled "Smart On Crime" that presaged problems she would face a decade later in attracting Black and progressive activists to her presidential bid. Harris voiced views that broke with progressives' criminal justice reform agenda while downplaying racial bias in policing. "There is a widely held notion that poor communities, particularly poor African-American and Latino communities, consider law enforcement the enemy. … In fact, the opposite is true. … I can state categorically that economically poor people want and support law enforcement," she wrote in the book. She adopted a markedly different tone in her January 2019 presidential announcement speech. "Too many unarmed Black men and women are killed in America," she declared. "Too many Black and Brown Americans are being locked up. Our criminal justice system needs drastic repair."

In the attorney general contest, Harris dealt with another controversy from her tenure as district attorney: The theft of cocaine by a technician in San Francisco's police crime lab forced her to drop drug charges in nearly 1,300 cases, and a judge accused her office of hiding damaging information about the technician. Harris denied the charge, but her Republican opponent, Los Angeles District Attorney Steve Cooley, used it against her — while also going after her handling of the Espinoza murder case. Final returns gave Harris a razor-thin victory, 46.1%-45.3%.

One of her high-profile accomplishments was brokering a $25 billion settlement with several large mortgage institutions for improper foreclosure practices during the Great Recession's housing market crash — which, according to her office, yielded $18 billion in mortgage relief for California homeowners. After the settlement, Harris created a task force to prosecute mortgage and foreclosure fraud. She was later dogged by criticism for failing to act against OneWest Bank — then headed by Steven Mnuchin, who would become Treasury secretary under President Donald Trump. The California Department of Justice found OneWest had participated in "widespread misconduct" in foreclosing on homes and recommended Harris file a civil enforcement action. In 2019, a Harris spokesman told CNBC that Harris had limited authority to go after OneWest at the time. "Unfortunately, the law was squarely on their side and they were shielded from state subpoenas because they're a federal bank," the spokesman said.

During the litigation of the housing market crash, Harris met her Delaware counterpart: Attorney General Beau Biden, Joe Biden's oldest son. That friendship with Beau Biden, who died of brain cancer in 2015, helped bring about a rapprochement of sorts between the older Biden and Harris in a series of conversations following their June 2019 debate clash. A Biden campaign statement after Harris was tapped as the vice-presidential running mate noted she and Beau Biden "grew close while fighting to take on the banking industry," adding: "Through her friendship with Beau, she got to know Joe Biden. From hearing about Kamala from Beau to seeing her fight for others directly, Joe has long been impressed by how tough Kamala is." For his part, Joe Biden said his late son had "enormous respect" for Harris and her work as California attorney general. "I thought a lot about that as I made this decision," he said of asking Harris to join the ticket. "There is no one's opinion I valued more than Beau's."

Meanwhile, Harris' ties to Obama grew tighter during her tenure as district attorney and later as attorney general. She was the first elected official in California to endorse Obama for the 2008 Democratic presidential nomination; Obama got her a prime-time speaking role at the 2012 Democratic National Convention. Midway through Obama's second term, Harris was considered as a replacement for U.S. Attorney General Eric Holder. But she was waging a reelection campaign, which she won by a 15-point margin, and then disavowed interest in moving to the Obama administration. When Sen. Barbara Boxer announced her retirement in January 2015, Harris jumped into the contest to succeed her.

Harris and Democratic Rep. Loretta Sanchez faced off in the 2016 general election under California's "blanket" primary system, in which the top two vote-getters in the first round advance to a runoff, regardless of party. Sanchez, seeking victory in a state that is nearly 40 percent Latino, entered the contest four months after Harris. After winning the endorsement of the state Democratic Party, Harris led the June first-round primary with 40 percent of the vote in a 34-candidate field. Sanchez finished a distant second, taking 19 percent. The runoff matchup had several intriguing aspects: Featuring two women who were minority group members, it also marked the first high-profile contest between two candidates of the same party since the adoption of the state's blanket primary six years earlier.

The candidates presented a contrast in style. Harris had been criticized as too cautious as attorney general, while Sanchez earned a shoot-from-the-hip reputation during a 20-year career in Congress. While there was little ideological daylight between the two, Sanchez sought to attract Republicans and independents. She collected endorsements from GOP officeholders and went on a conservative radio talk show to tout her record against "Islamic extremists." Sanchez also tried to peel away Democratic support by pointing to $6,000 in donations made by Trump, then the Republican presidential nominee, to Harris' 2014 attorney general reelection campaign. Harris gave the money to charity following disparaging remarks Trump made about Mexicans in 2015. When Sanchez sought to tie these donations to Harris' failure to open an investigation of Trump University after a 2010 federal class-action lawsuit against the company, Harris pointed to a $1.1 billion judgment her office had won against another large for-profit institution, Corinthian Colleges. Harris easily defeated Sanchez, 62%-38%.

Named to the Senate Intelligence panel, Harris raised her national profile after less than six months in office. Utilizing the rapid-fire, aggressive style of questioning honed as a prosecutor, she took on several high-ranking Trump administration officials who testified before the panel — most notably then-Attorney General Jeff Sessions, who became rattled during a grilling by Harris about his dealings with Russian officials on behalf of the Trump campaign. Amid GOP protests that Harris was not allowing Sessions to finish his answers, Intelligence Committee Chair Richard Burr intervened. "Sen. Harris, let him answer," Burr declared. A week earlier, Burr had cut off Harris' questioning of Deputy Attorney General Rod Rosenstein, saying she was not allowing Rosenstein to finish. It sparked suggestions of sexism. "Again, @SenKamalaHarris was doing her job," another committee member, Oregon Democrat Ron Wyden, asserted via Twitter. "She was interrupted for asking tough questions. I was not interrupted." Harris utilized the episode for fundraising purposes, telling potential donors via email: "Thank you for standing with me yesterday when the GOP tried to shut me down."

Harris -- needled by the Los Angeles Times as "unwilling to stake out a position on controversial issues" during her tenure as state attorney general -- worked to burnish her criminal justice reform credentials in the Senate, amid criticism from progressives for earlier sidestepping a stance on two sentencing reform ballot initiatives. One, in 2012, modified California's "three strikes" law for repeat offenders in cases of nonviolent offenses; the other, in 2014, reduced certain nonviolent felonies to misdemeanors. Both were approved by wide margins. Harris said she had remained neutral because her office prepared the title and summary seen by voters, although this had not kept several of her predecessors from taking sides in similar battles. In mid-2017, Harris teamed up with libertarian-leaning Kentucky Republican Sen. Rand Paul on legislation to encourage states to replace money-based bail systems with individualized risk assessments. "A lot of what we're talking about is disparities in terms of how Americans are treated in the criminal justice system because of their wealth," Harris said. A year later, she co-sponsored a bill to legalize marijuana — another issue on which she previously had avoided a clear position.

Harris also won points from progressives when, in early 2018, she was one of only three Senate Democrats to vote against a bipartisan immigration bill. It provided a path to citizenship for immigrants brought to the country illegally as children — called "Dreamers" — but Harris objected to the $25 billion allotted for border security. According to Politico, her move angered Minority Leader Charles Schumer and other Democrats looking to strike a long-elusive immigration deal with Trump. Harris later called for re-examining the Immigration and Custom Enforcement Agency "from the ground up," and, as a presidential contender, sought to put distance between herself and the Obama administration's record of deporting millions of undocumented aliens. (Among the first vice-presidential duties given her by Biden was a plan to reduce the number of Central American refugees seeking entry into the U.S.)

Harris launched her 2020 presidential bid to generally positive reviews, and with an Oakland rally that attracted more than 22,000; many party leaders viewed her as capable of reassembling the coalition that had brought Obama into office. But polls found many Democrats lacked a clear view of who she was and for what she stood. Amid mixed reviews of her criminal justice record, Harris' divided campaign organization – split between offices in Baltimore and the West Coast – waged lengthy internal debates over the degree to which her prosecutorial background should be emphasized or played down. In an election cycle in which the race for the party's presidential nomination largely broke down into centrist and progressive "lanes," Harris – like several other contenders – sought to straddle both camps. The result was the lack of a clear message: On more than one occasion, Harris appeared to embrace rival Bernie Sanders' "Medicare For All" government-run health plan – only to later say she did not support abolishing private health insurance.

After starting the campaign in the top tier of candidates, Harris dropped to single digits in several polls of early primary and caucus states. Her campaign bet heavily on a good showing early on in South Carolina's Democratic primary, with its Black majority electorate, to provide political momentum. But Biden remained strong in the South Carolina contest – which he later won overwhelmingly – and by early November 2019, the Harris campaign announced widespread staff layoffs and a refocusing on the first-in-the nation Iowa delegate caucuses. A month later, Harris ended her campaign – two months prior to the Iowa contest. "My campaign for president simply doesn't have the financial resources we need to continue," she said, as contributions dropped off sharply in the last quarter of 2019.

Harris endorsed Biden's candidacy in March 2020 as he was emerging as the presumptive nominee while continuing her efforts to appeal to the party's progressive wing on her handling of criminal justice issues. Following George Floyd's death in Minneapolis in May 2020, she was a leading sponsor of comprehensive policing reform legislation. Among other provisions, it barred no-knock warrants and chokeholds and carotid holds – the latter of which had been responsible for Floyd's death.

Following an extensive vetting process, Harris was unveiled as Biden's choice for a running mate in August 2020 from a field that – according to The New York Times – included three other finalists. The ascendancy of the Black Lives Matter movement, combined with Biden's earlier pledge to name a female running mate, had ratcheted up calls for a woman of color on the ticket. Two of the finalists –Michigan Gov. Gretchen Whitmer and Massachusetts Sen. Elizabeth Warren – were white, and Warren, like Biden, is in her 70s. Harris, who turned 56 in late 2020, brought not only racial but age diversity. The remaining finalist, former White House National Security Adviser Susan Rice, is Black, but had never sought elected office; that inexperience was seen as a major downside.

If the memory of Harris' attack on Biden in the first Democratic presidential debate lingered in the vetting, her abilities as a debater – as well as a pointed interrogator, exhibited in committee faceoffs with several Trump appointees – were seen as helping to bolster Democratic prospects in November. And, looking ahead to governing, Harris – despite overtures to the progressive wing in the runup to her presidential bid – was seen as more of a pragmatist and consensus-seeker in the Biden mode. The fact that Biden and Harris had known each other going back nearly a decade also came into play. Discussing Biden's priorities in selecting Harris, the campaign's co-chair, then-Louisiana Rep. Cedric Richmond, told The Washington Post, "A lot of his thought process was who shared his values, who he could work with, who could help him win and who could be ready on Day 1."

As a condition of accepting the vice-presidential role with Obama, Biden had demanded to serve as Obama's senior most adviser. As New York Magazine noted, "He has still never tired of reminding anyone who will listen that he was always 'the last guy in the room' for Obama's big decisions." In selecting Harris, Biden said, "I asked Kamala to be the last voice in the room." Whatever 2024 may bring, it seemed to ensure Harris would be the latest in a line of influential seconds-in-command going back to Vice President Walter Mondale nearly a half-century earlier. When Mondale was on his deathbed three months after Harris was sworn in, she was among a number of prominent political officeholders to call him – with Harris, according to the Associated Press, thanking Mondale for all he had done to change the office she now holds.

The United States of America

Population

Total	328,239,523
% change since 2010	6.12%
Land area (sq. miles)	3,531,905
Pop/ sq mi	92.94

Race and Ethnicity

White	72.%
Black	12.8%
Latino	18.4%
Mexican	11.3%
Puerto Rican	1.8%
Cuban	0.7%
Other Hispanic or Latino	4.6%
Asian	6.8%
Pacific Islander	0.4%
American Indian and Alaska Native	1.7%
Two or more races	3.4%
Other	5.%

Language

English only	78.%
Spanish	13.5%
Other European	3.7%
Asian	3.6%

Work

White Collar	39.9%
Sales and Service	38.1%
Blue Collar	22.%
Government	14.%

Place of Birth

Native	86.3%
Born in US	84.7%
State of residence	58.%
Different state	26.7%
Puerto Rico, U.S Islands or abroad to american parent	1.6%
Foreign Born	13.7%

Foreign-born Citizenship Status

Naturalized U.S citizen	51.6%
Not a U.S citizen	48.4%

Region of Foreign Born

Europe	10.4%
Asia	31.4%
Africa	5.5%
Oceania	0.7%
Latin America	50.3%
Northern America	1.8%

Education

H.S grad or less	38.3%
Some college	28.6%
College Degree, 4 yr	20.3%
Post grad	12.8%

Military

Veteran	6.9%
Active Duty	0.5%

Age Groups

Under 18	22.2%
18-34	23.1%
35-64	38.1%
Over 64	16.5%

18 years and over

Male	48.7%
Female	51.3%

65 years and over

Male	44.5%
Female	55.5%

Income

Median Income	65,712
Under $50,000	38.4%
$50,000-$99,999	30.2%
$100,000-$199,999	22.9%
$200,000 or more	8.5%
Poverty Rate	12.3%

Health Insurance

With health insurance coverage	90.8%

Public Assistance

Cash public assistance income	2.2%
Food stamp/SNAP benefits	10.7%

2020 Pres. Vote

Joe Biden (D)	81,286,358	(51%)
Donald Trump (R)	74,225,839	(47%)

2016 Pres. Vote

Hillary Clinton (D)	65,853,652	(48%)
Donald Trump (R)	62,985,134	(46%)
Gary Johnson (L)	4,489,235	(3%)

ALABAMA

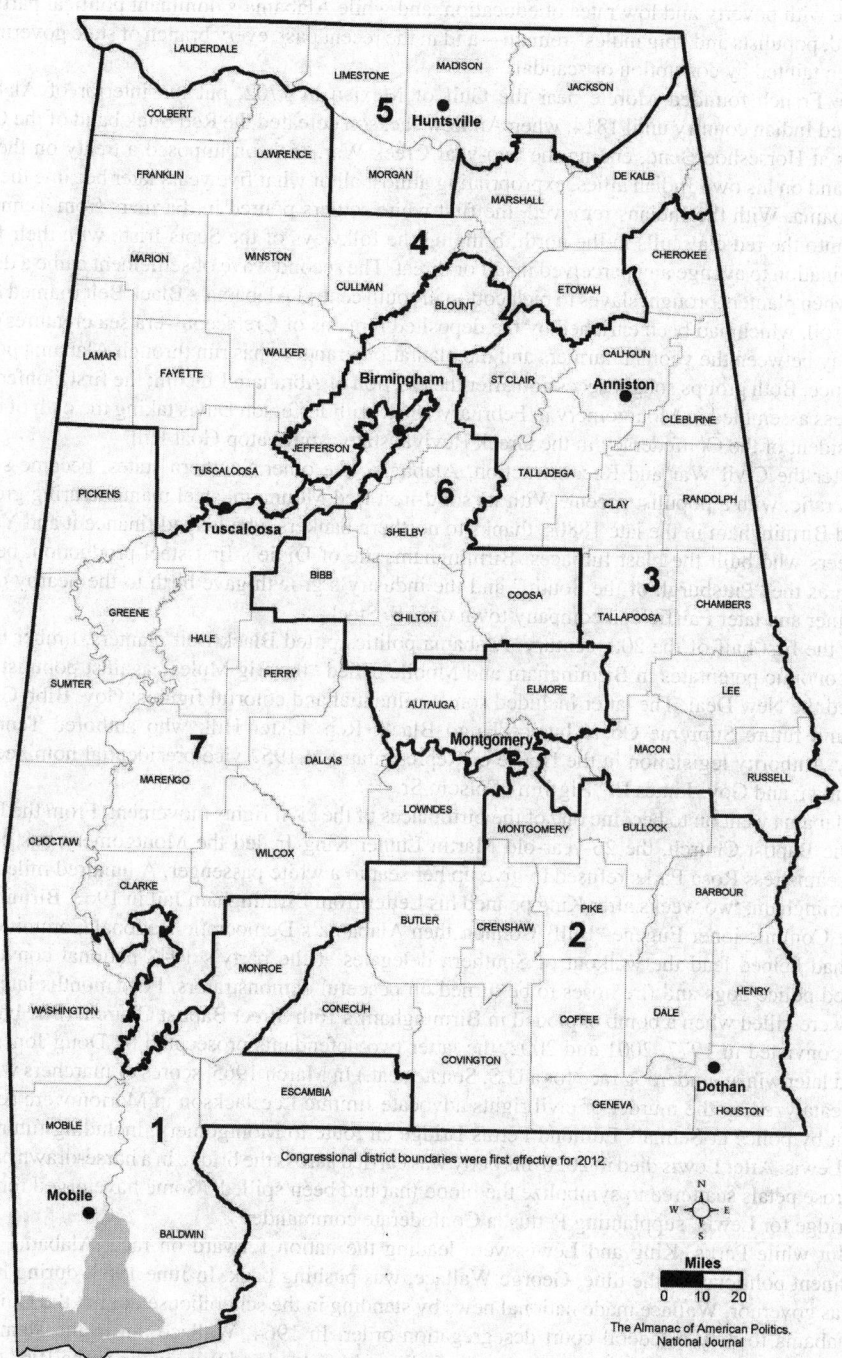

Congressional district boundaries were first effective for 2012.

Miles
0   10   20

The Almanac of American Politics.
National Journal

The past hangs over Alabama like its tall yellow pines: Refrains from decades-old civil rights struggles recur in the debate on gay marriage and Confederate memorials, and the state's manufacturing base has once again been built with the help of outsiders. The state continues to struggle with poverty and low rates of education, and while Alabama's dominant political party has changed, populists and "big mules" remain—and in the recent past, every branch of state government has been tainted by corruption or scandal.

The French founded Mobile near the Gulf of Mexico in 1702, but the interior of Alabama remained Indian country until 1814, when Andrew Jackson defeated the Red Stick band of the Creek Indians at Horseshoe Bend, ending the two-year Creek War. Jackson imposed a treaty on the Red Sticks and on his own Indian allies, expropriating almost all of what five years later became the state of Alabama. With the Indians removed, the first white settlers poured in. Farmers from Tennessee swept into the red clay hills in the north, bringing the folkways of the Scots-Irish, with their fierce determination to avenge any perceived insult or threat. The second wave of settlement came a decade later, when planters brought slaves to pick cotton in south central Alabama's Black Belt (named for its fertile soil, which had been enriched by the deposited remains of Cretaceous-era sea creatures). The interplay between the yeoman farmers and the plantation grandees has run through Alabama politics ever since. Both groups sought secession after the election of Abraham Lincoln; the first Confederate Congress assembled in Montgomery in February 1861, with Jefferson Davis taking the oath of office as president of the Confederacy in the Greek Revival state capitol atop Goat Hill.

After the Civil War and Reconstruction, Alabama, like other Southern states, became solidly Democratic, with a populist accent. With its solid-iron Red Mountain, steel manufacturing grew up around Birmingham in the late 1880s, thanks to northern bankers who helped finance it and Yankee engineers who built the blast furnaces. Birmingham, site of Dixie's first steel production, became known as the "Pittsburgh of the South," and the industry's growth gave birth to the nearby city of Bessemer and later Fairfield, a company town of U.S. Steel.

In the first half of the 20th century, Alabama politics pitted Black Belt planters, timber barons and economic potentates in Birmingham and Mobile called "the Big Mules" against populists who favored the New Deal. The latter included some influential and colorful figures: Gov. Bibb Graves; Sen. and future Supreme Court Justice Hugo Black; Rep. Lister Hill, who authored Tennessee Valley Authority legislation in the House of Representatives; 1952 vice presidential nominee John Sparkman; and Gov. James E. "Big Jim" Folsom Sr.

Alabama went on to become one of the birthplaces of the civil rights movement. From the Dexter Avenue Baptist Church, the 26-year-old Martin Luther King Jr. led the Montgomery bus boycott after seamstress Rosa Parks refused to give up her seat to a white passenger. A hundred miles north in Birmingham, two weeks after King penned his Letter from Birmingham Jail in 1963, Birmingham Police Commissioner Eugene "Bull" Connor, then Alabama's Democratic National Committeeman who had helped lead the walkout of Southern delegates at the party's 1948 national convention, ordered police dogs and fire hoses to be turned on peaceful demonstrators. Four months later, four girls were killed when a bomb exploded in Birmingham's 16th Street Baptist Church. (The bombers were convicted in 1977, 2001 and 2002, the latter two defendants prosecuted by Doug Jones, who would later win an underdog race for a U.S. Senate seat.) In March 1965, scores of marchers who had been catalyzed by the murder of civil rights advocate Jimmie Lee Jackson in Marion were severely beaten by police at Selma's Edmund Pettus Bridge en route to Montgomery, including future Rep. John Lewis. After Lewis died in 2020, his body was carried across the bridge in a horse-drawn caisson, with rose petals scattered to symbolize the blood that had been spilled. (Some have urged renaming the bridge for Lewis, supplanting Pettus, a Confederate commander.)

But while Parks, King and Lewis were leading the nation forward on race, Alabama's most prominent politician of the time, George Wallace, was pushing back. In June 1963, during his first term as governor, Wallace made national news by standing in the schoolhouse door at the University of Alabama to defy a federal court desegregation order. In 1964, Wallace ran in the Democratic presidential primaries and got strong support in Indiana, Maryland and Wisconsin. In the 1968 general election, running as a third-party candidate, he won 13.5 percent of the popular vote and carried five Southern states with 46 electoral votes. He ran in the Democratic primaries again in 1972 before being shot and partially paralyzed while campaigning in Laurel Maryland. He dominated Alabama politics, winning the governorship in 1962, running his wife to succeed him in 1966 (she died while in office), regaining the governorship in 1970 and 1974, then running and winning one last time in 1982. He spent the final years before his death in 1998 apologizing for his earlier acts. "The South has changed, and for the better," he said. After Wallace's death, Lewis forgave him in an op-ed.

Today, civil rights tourism is a major business. Not far from the state capitol, Montgomery boasts sculptor-architect Maya Lin's circular Civil Rights Memorial, Troy University's Rosa Parks Museum, the Dexter Parsonage, and a new national memorial to the victims of lynching. The Selma to Montgomery National Historic Trail runs along U.S. Highway 80, and the Alabama Civil Rights Museum Trail includes the Tuskegee Airmen National Historic Site and the 16th Street Baptist Church. The Alabama Department of Archives and History, which for decades promoted the Confederate cause, issued a "statement of recommitment" in June 2020 that acknowledged its past failures to "offer an honest assessment of the past."

Still, conflict over remembrance of the pre-civil rights era has spiked, as it has elsewhere in the South. In May 2017, Gov. Kay Ivey signed legislation to ban "relocation, removal, alteration, renaming or other disturbance" of longstanding memorials. And in 2020, amid national protests by African Americans against police brutality, President Donald Trump called for Wallace-style "law and order" and stoked fears of low-income housing coming to suburbia if he were to lose reelection.

Economically, Alabama lost ground during the Wallace years. While Atlanta was peacefully desegregating and beginning decades of white-collar growth, Birmingham was violently resisting the civil rights movement, only to see its blue-collar base in the steel industry shrink and its most talented residents of all races flee to calmer climes. Agriculture remains a significant industry, including the second-highest sales of broilers, the second-highest production of peanuts, and the third-highest percentage of timber acreage in the Lower 48. But where the state has really gained ground is in manufacturing.

Automobiles are now a major part of Alabama's economy. Mercedes opened its first U.S. assembly line in 1997 near Tuscaloosa, while Honda has a major plant in Lincoln, and Hyundai has one in Montgomery. These operations spawned dozens of supplier and subcontractor firms. A new, $1.6 billion joint facility for Toyota and Mazda in Huntsville is projected to build 300,000 vehicles annually, with production starting in 2021.

Aerospace has been another key to Alabama's economy. The Marshall Space Flight Center in Huntsville has attracted the United Launch Alliance, a joint venture between Boeing and Lockheed Martin to develop NASA's launch system for human flight, as well as its rocket-engine partner Blue Origin, founded by Amazon's Jeff Bezos. In conventional aviation, Airbus opened a plant in Mobile, producing A220 and A320 aircraft, while Lockheed Martin chose Courtland as the hub for its hypersonic programs. A new sector flocking to the state is technology, including data centers that require cheap and environmentally friendly sources of electricity—something that TVA hydropower provides in abundance. In 2018, Facebook announced a $750 million data center in Huntsville, while Google is building a $600 million data facility northeast of the city. Meanwhile, in a move that would have made the Big Mules proud, Senate Appropriations Chairman Richard Shelby used his clout to make Huntsville the home for 1,500 FBI personnel previously based in D.C. The economic growth around Huntsville boosted population in Madison County by 11 percent between 2010 and 2019, at a time when the state's overall population growth was 5.1 percent.

Manufacturing gains have been driven by weaker unionization than in the north, although Alabama does rank first among the former Confederate states with 8.5 percent of workers holding union cards in 2019. (Most members are public employees, including teachers in the politically potent Alabama Education Association.) In the spring of 2021, an Amazon warehouse in Bessemer became the center of the labor universe, as workers voted on whether to organize. President Joe Biden cheered on the unionization effort, but in the end, it fell short. Still, prosperity has largely eluded rural Alabama, where joblessness and grinding poverty persist. As the coronavirus pandemic began in April, six counties in the Black Belt reported Depression-like unemployment rates of 20% or more, and counties in the belt would soon account for eight of the nine worst infection counts in the state. Alabama has the fifth-lowest median income of any state, and the state ranked dead last in the 50-state rankings for math and reading as measured by the National Assessment of Educational Progress in 2019. "Our education system in this state sucks," opined then-Gov. Robert Bentley in 2016.

Alabama's prison system is also troubled; in 2019, a U.S. Department of Justice report demanded reforms to counter the violence, sexual abuse, drug trafficking and extortion in the state's prisons. While Ivey has closed some prisons and pursued new construction, the report had warned that "new facilities alone will not resolve the contributing factors to the overall unconstitutional conditions."

In the nearly 40 years since Wallace's name last appeared on the Democratic ballot line, the state has become solidly Republican. For a while, many of the talented state politicians remained Democrats who, along with their allies—the AEA, major black political associations and trial lawyers—could defeat less-experienced Republicans with regularity. But even these canny Democratic survivors were overcome amid a disciplined and relentless Republican offensive. The local Democratic machinery atrophied, and the party's longstanding control of the state legislature disappeared in 2010—the first GOP majorities in Montgomery since Reconstruction. Like other states in the South, Alabama has joined the front lines of the culture wars, enacting a series of abortion restrictions that have been set aside by courts. (As she signed one bill, Ivey acknowledged that the law was probably "unenforceable" but hoped it would push the issue forward.) The state was criticized in 2020 when Alabama Public Television declined to air an episode of the PBS children's show "Arthur" that included a same-sex wedding.

Power proved corrupting for Alabama Republicans. By 2016, the leaders of each of the three branches of state government—all Republicans—were mired in troubles of one kind or another. In the judicial branch, Roy Moore—chief justice of the Alabama Supreme Court who had in 2003 defied a federal judge's order to remove a 5,280-pound granite monument to the Ten Commandments that he had installed in his Montgomery courthouse, leading to his ouster—was once again removed from his position, this time for defying federal court orders on same-sex marriage.

In 2017, Moore proved too radioactive even for Alabama voters. In a special election to fill the Senate seat given up by U.S. Attorney General-designate Jeff Sessions, Moore, backed by the party's socially conservative base, defeated Rep. Mo Brooks and the appointed senator, Luther Strange, in the GOP primary and runoff. This gave Jones, the former prosecutor who had won the Democratic nomination, a surprising opening, and Moore's challenge intensified with revelations about past alleged sexual indiscretions with underage girls. Weak support among suburban voters, combined with a supercharged African-American turnout, enabled Jones to win narrowly. In 2020, however, Jones failed in his bid to win a full term, losing by 20 points to former Auburn football coach Tommy Tuberville (who had defeated Sessions, by then on the outs with Trump, to win the nomination). The difference between 2017 and 2020 was simple: In a presidential election year, the total two-party turnout rose by 74 percent from the special election, and while Jones outran Democratic presidential nominee Joe Biden in some of the state's more populated counties, and by about three points statewide, the Trump-energized electorate proved decisive. In the presidential race, Trump beat Biden by 25 points, a modest narrowing of his 28-point win in 2016. Biden's strongest improvements in red counties came in Shelby (suburban Birmingham), Madison (Huntsville), and Tuscaloosa, with Biden gains of nine, nine and five points, respectively. Biden also strengthened the Democratic edge in two populous blue counties—five points in Montgomery (Montgomery) and five points in Jefferson (Birmingham).

Population		Race and Ethnicity		Income	
Total	4,903,185	White	67.80%	Median Income	51,734
Land area (sq. miles)	50,645	Black	26.90%	State Income Rank	46 out of 50
Pop/ sq mi	96.81	Latino	4.50%	Poverty Rate	15.50%
Born in state	69.20%	Asian	1.80%	With health insurance	90.30%
		Two or more races	1.90%	Cash public assistance	1.40%
Age Groups		Other	2.00%	Food stamp/SNAP	15.0%
Under 18	22.10%				
18-34	22.40%	Education		Work	
35-64	38.20%	H.S grad or less	43.80%	White Collar	35.90%
Over 64	17.40%	Some college	29.80%	Sales and Service	36.80%
		College Degree, 4 yr	16.30%	Blue Collar	27.30%
Military		Post grad	10.00%	Government	16.20%
Veteran/ Active Duty	8.80%				

Presidential Politics

2020 Primary (D)	Biden (D)	286,649(63%)	Sanders (D)	75,035(17%)	Bloomberg (D)	52,874(12%)
	Warren (D)	25,923 (6%)				
2020 Pres. Vote	Trump (R)	1,441,170(62%)	Biden (D)	849,624(37%)		
2016 Pres. Vote	Trump (R)	1,318,255(62%)	Clinton (D)	729,547(34%)	Johnson (L)	44,467 (2%)

Alabama has been a reliably Republican state in presidential races since 1980. Jimmy Carter, a son of the South, in 1976 was the last Democratic nominee to carry Alabama, winning 60 of its 67 counties. But in 2015, a huge August rally at Ladd-Peebles Stadium outside of Mobile for Donald Trump's nascent bid for the 2016 GOP presidential nomination attracted some 30,000 boisterous supporters and signaled the candidate's unique appeal to many Republican voters who had become alienated from the party establishment and wanted more culture warrior and less economic conservatism. Populist GOP Sen. Jeff Sessions praised Trump's anti-immigration stance and was the first senator to endorse the New York real estate developer, who handily won the state's Super Tuesday primary with 43 percent. Trump's strong performance across the South made him all but impossible to catch in the GOP primaries. (Sessions would go on to be Trump's first attorney general, got fired after Trump turned on him and failed in his 2020 Senate comeback bid, showing how powerful Trump's pull was with the GOP base). In 2020, Joe Biden won the state's March 3 primary in dominant fashion with 63 percent of the vote to 17 percent for Bernie Sanders and 12 percent for Michael Bloomberg. The Super Tuesday victory came as part of Biden's sweep of the South that helped cement his nomination.

The general election was a foregone conclusion: Trump bested Biden 62%-37%, winning 54 of the state's 67 counties. Biden won 12 counties in the state's Black Belt, named for the rich dark soil that was once worked by cotton plantation slaves and sharecroppers. The region has a high share of African-American voters. He won Jefferson County (Birmingham), marking the fourth consecutive time that a Democratic presidential nominee carried the state's largest vote-producing county, and improved on Hillary Clinton's showing thee, as well as slightly shrinking Trump's big margins in growing, exurban Shelby and St. Clair counties. He also did better in Madison County, home to highly educated Huntsville, and Montgomery County, home to the state's capital, evidence that Trump's suburban problem carried even into the Deep South. But while Biden made some inroads with white suburbanites, the state's racially polarized nature and large share of deeply conservative, rural white voters meant he never had a shot—and in an election with presidential-level turnout, neither did Sen. Doug Jones, who had won a 2017 special election against a fatally flawed opponent.

Congressional Districts

117th Congress Lineup	1D 6R	**116th Congress Lineup**	1D 6R

In contrast to most of the South, Alabama has been losing House seats. As recently as 1960, it had nine. Since 1972, it has held steady at seven. Despite widespread expectation that it might drop another seat in 2022, the Census data showed that its seventh seat was not in serious jeopardy. But that left another issue for Alabama.

With the history of the Voting Rights Act—and the mathematics of a state with 27 percent black population—Democrats likely will seek the creation of a second African-American majority, in addition to the 7th District, which extends from the outskirts of Mobile to the western side of Montgomery and significant parts of Birmingham and Tuscaloosa. As David Wasserman wrote in the Cook Political Report, the 7th could be split into two districts: one "covering inner Birmingham and rural Black Belt counties," plus Tuscaloosa, and the other "stretching from Mobile to Montgomery to the Georgia border." That likely would leave Reps. Jerry Carl and Barry Moore, the first-term Republicans in the 1st and 2nd Districts, to compete in a "fair fight" in a heavily Republican district. To succeed in this redistricting strategy, with little influence in state government, Democrats likely would need friendly federal judges in the Deep South and, eventually, perhaps at the Supreme Court. "It may be a long shot, but the court fight is worth watching," Wasserman wrote.

Regardless of whether a second African-American/Democratic seat is created, the four remaining Republican-held seats--in the northern and eastern parts of Alabama—likely will remain relatively unchanged. One factor worth watching is whether the decision of Rep. Mo Brooks in the Huntsville-based 5th District to run for the open Senate seat in 2022 might shift parts of his district into the 4th—the only district that it borders—or even the 3rd. Those two districts are held by senior House Republicans—Robert Aderholt at Appropriations and Mike Rogers at Armed Services—whose House committee clout might tempt them to seek representation of parts of the huge aerospace interests in the current 5th. Although these alternative scenarios might warrant exploration, the course of least resistance likely will be to retain a version of the current redistricting plan, which has been in place for 30 years. In the past decade, Democrats have not been competitive in any of the six Republican-held districts.

Kay Ivey (R)

Assumed office in 2017, term expires 2023, 1st term; b. Oct. 15, 1944, Camden; Auburn U, B.S., 1967; Baptist; Single.

Elected Office: AL House, 1980-1982; AL Treasurer, 2002-2010; AL Lt. Governor, 2011-2017.

Professional Career: High School teacher; Assistant Vice President, Merchants National Bank/Regions Bank, 1970-1979; Consultant, American Bankers Association, 1979; Reading Clerk, Assistant Director, Alabama Development Office, 1982-1985; Director of Government Affairs, Alabama Commission on Higher Education, 1985-1998.

Office: 600 Dexter Avenue Montgomery, 36130; 334-242-7100; Fax: 334-353-0004; Website: alabama.gov

Lt. Gov.: Will Ainsworth (R) **Atty. Gen:** Steve Marshall (R) **Sec. of State:** John Merrill (R)
State Legislature: Senate: 7D, 26R, 2 vacancies **House:** 28D, 76R, 1V

Election Results

Election	Name (Party)	Vote (%)
2018 General	Kay Ivey (R)	1,022,457 (59%)
	Walt Maddox (D)	694,495 (40%)
2018 Primary	Kay Ivey (R)	331,739 (56%)
	Tommy Battle (R)	147,207 (25%)
	Scott Dawson (R)	79,546 (14%)
	Bill Hightower (R)	29,367 (5%)

Republican Kay Ivey became governor of Alabama in April 2017, ending a long, soap-opera-like sex scandal involving fellow Republican Robert Bentley, who resigned under the threat of impeachment. Ivey took office at age 72, becoming only the second woman to serve as governor of Alabama, after Lurleen Burns Wallace, the wife of four-time Gov. George Wallace. Bolstered by a strong economy and a lack of scandal, Ivey coasted to a term of her own in 2018 and continued to follow a strongly conservative path in office.

Ivey was raised on a family cattle farm in Camden, served as lieutenant governor at Alabama Girls State while in high school, and earned a degree from Auburn University in 1967. While a student, she helped the Wallace campaign organize on campus. She worked as a high school teacher, as assistant vice president of Merchants National Bank/Regions Bank, as a reading clerk in the state House, as assistant director of the Alabama Development Office, and as director of government affairs for the Alabama Commission on Higher Education. In 1982, she ran as a Democrat (as most Alabamians did at the time) for her first statewide office, state auditor, but lost.

Two decades later, Ivey began a more successful phase of her electoral career, as a Republican, a label that was becoming advantageous in the state. She was elected state treasurer in 2002 and 2006, then, after a brief flirtation with a gubernatorial bid in 2010, ran for lieutenant governor. Ivey's biggest albatross was her past leadership of the state's Prepaid Affordable College Tuition program, which closed in 2008 due to financial pressures. Still, she was able to narrowly defeat Democratic incumbent Jim Folsom Jr. to win the lieutenant governorship, and she was reelected in 2014 before being elevated to governor on Bentley's resignation.

Bentley's ethical problems were separate from, but occurred at roughly the same time as, serious troubles within the leadership of the other two branches of Alabama government, namely Republican House Speaker Mike Hubbard and state Supreme Court Justice Roy Moore. At her swearing-in, Ivey sought to turn the page, saying, "Today is a dark day in Alabama but also one of opportunity. Together we steady the ship of state and improve the image of the state. These are my two priorities as governor."

In 2017, she signed a bill to limit death-row inmate appeals and another to permit adoption organizations that are faith-based to deny the placement of children with gay parents. But Alabama's political scene that year was dominated by the open-seat Senate race that emerged when President Donald Trump named longtime Republican Sen. Jeff Sessions to be attorney general. Bentley had appointed state Attorney General Luther Strange to the seat, but Strange ended up losing the GOP nomination to Moore. Initially, Ivey said she would "hold judgment" until more facts came out about allegations against Moore of past sexual improprieties with underage girls. By mid-November, a few weeks before the election, she announced that she would vote for her fellow Republican over Democrat Doug Jones. But Jones won narrowly.

In 2018, Ivey turned her attention to her own election. She pursued a risk-averse strategy while tending to the GOP base. Ivey aired an ad in the primary touting her signing of a bill to protect historical monuments that featured two Confederate images. She also called for giving Trump the Nobel Peace Prize, citing his overtures to North Korea. (In a rare break with the president, Ivey warned that tariffs imposed by Trump threatened the state's $21.7 billion export economy.) In the June primary, Ivey easily defeated Huntsville Mayor Tommy Battle, preacher Scott Dawson, and several lesser-known candidates. In the general election, she easily defeated Tuscaloosa Mayor Walt Maddox.

A few months into her own term, Ivey signed an equal-pay act for gender and race, making Alabama the second-to-last state in the nation to enact such protections. She also spurned some Republicans by signing a bipartisan bill to raise state fuel taxes by 10 cents over three years to support work on roads and bridges. More often, though, Ivey pursued a strongly conservative agenda. She signed a bill in 2019 that would make abortion illegal, including in cases of rape and incest, with a 99-year prison sentence for doctors performing the procedure. She also signed legislation to require certain paroled sex offenders to undergo chemical castration.

In March 2020, Lt. Gov. Will Ainsworth publicly criticized Ivey's initial handling of the coronavirus pandemic as inadequate. (Ainsworth is a Republican but is elected separately from the governor; at about 37 years Ivey's junior, he is considered a strong candidate to succeed her if she declines to seek another term in 2022.) During a spike in cases in June, Ivey at first resisted expanding restrictions even as other Sun Belt states increased their own, referring to the pandemic as a "new normal." By July she relented, issuing a statewide mask order like ones that some other Republican governors had sought to avoid. By December 2020, Alabama's coronavirus case rate ranked in the top half of states, at more than double its early summer peak.

On the personal front, Ivey absorbed two blows in 2019. A recording of an Auburn campus radio show from 1967 surfaced in which she discussed participating in a Baptist Student Union skit in which she wore blackface. Though Ivey said she didn't recall the skit or the interview, she quickly offered her "heartfelt apologies" and said "the Alabama of today is a far cry from the Alabama of the 1960s. We have come a long way, for sure, but we still have a long way to go." In the meantime, Ivey was diagnosed with lung cancer, but she was declared cancer-free in January 2020.

Richard Shelby (R)

Elected 1986, term expires 2022, 6th term, b. May 06, 1934; Birmingham, AL; University of AL, B.A., 1957; University of AL School of Law, LL.B., 1963; Presbyterian; Married (Annette Nevin Shelby); 2 children; 2 grandchildren.

Elected Office: AL Senate, 1970-1978; U.S. House, 1979-1987.

Professional Career: Practicing attorney, 1963-1978; City Prosecutor, Tuscaloosa, 1963-1971; U.S Magistrate, 1966-1970; Special Assistant to AL Attorney General, 1969-1971.

DC Office: 304 RSOB 20510, 202-224-5744, Fax: 202-224-3416, shelby.senate.gov

State Offices: Birmingham, 205-731-1384; Huntsville, 256-772-0460; Mobile, 251-694-4164; Montgomery, 334-223-7303; Tuscaloosa, 205-759-5047.

Committees: *Appropriations (RMM)*: Ex Officio membership on all subcommittees. *Banking, Housing & Urban Affairs*: Financial Institutions & Consumer Protection; Housing, Transportation & Community Development; Securities, Insurance & Investment. *Environment & Public Works*: Chem Safety, Waste Mngmnt, Enviro Justice & Reg Oversight; Clean Air & Nuclear Safety; Transportation & Infrastructure. *Rules & Administration*.

Group Ratings

	ADA	ACLU	AFL-CIO	LCV	COC	HAFA	ACU	CFG	FRC
2020	-	0%	-	0%	-	64%	77%	-	-
2019	0%	C	21%	29%	75%	C	77%	43%	100%

Almanac Ratings 2019-2020

	Economy	Social	Foreign	Composite
Liberal	0%	0%	0%	0%
Conservative	100%	100%	100%	100%

Key Votes of the 116th Congress

1. EPA clean energy rules N	5. Russia sanctions N	9. Barr as Atty. General Y
2. U.S./Mex./Can. trade deal Y	6. Troops in SYR, AFG Y	10. Spending at the border Y
3. Cut unemployment benefits Y	7. Veto arms sales to Saudis N	11. Coney Barrett to Sup. Ct. Y
4. Shelton to Fed Reserve Y	8. Defense $$$, veto override Y	12. Electoral College objections N

Election Results

Election	Name (Party)	Vote (%)	Cand. Spent	Ind. Exp. Support	Ind. Exp. Oppose
2016 General	Richard Shelby (R)	1,335,104 (64%)	$11,473,078	$479,359	
	Ron Crumpton (D)	748,709 (36%)	$22,060		
2016 Primary	Richard Shelby (R)	505,586 (65%)			
	Jonathan McConnell (R)	214,770 (28%)			
	John Martin (R)	23,558 (3%)			

Prior winning percentages: 2016 (64%), 2010 (65%), 2004 (68%), 1998 (63%), 1992 (65%), 1986 (50%); House: 1984 (97%), 1982 (97%), 1980 (73%), 1978 (94%)

After nearly a third of a century in the Senate, Republican Richard Shelby, Alabama's senior senator, had the distinction of having chaired four standing committees. As chair of the Intelligence Committee, he tangled with the nation's spy chiefs. Later, heading the Banking, Housing and Urban Affairs panel in separate stints nearly a decade apart, Shelby battled against bank bailouts while resisting stiffer regulation of the nation's banking industry amid the 2008 financial crisis. Although Senate Republican Conference rules shuttled him to a lower-profile post chairing the Rules and Administration Committee at the end of 2016, he would realize his fourth—and most influential—chairmanship a little more than a year later, when the resignation of Mississippi Sen. Thad Cochran gave Shelby the Appropriations Committee gavel in April 2018.In February 2021, he announced that he will retire at the end of his term in 2022.

In the face of intense polarization on Capitol Hill, Shelby worked with his Democratic counterpart on that panel, Patrick Leahy of Vermont, to restore "regular order" to an annual appropriations process that had gone off-track in recent years—often resulting in the government being funded by short-term "continuing resolutions." Notwithstanding his longtime conservative credentials, Shelby at times was at odds with conservative hard-liners in his own party. In 2019, Shelby worked with the Trump White House and House Democrats to craft a $1.4 trillion package funding the government through September of that year and that pushed the deficit to record levels, over the protest of budget hawks. "We owe a lot of money, but until Congress and the American people decide to do something about entitlements, we could never balance the budget or rein in spending in a profound way on discretionary spending," Shelby told the Washington Post.

If there is a feat responsible for Shelby's political longevity in the heart of Dixie—where he has been elected to the Senate twice as a Democrat and four times as a Republican—it has been the steering federal funds to his home state from his perch on the Appropriations Committee. A half-dozen buildings that bear Shelby's name can be found on the campuses of the University of Alabama, Auburn University and the University of South Alabama.

In the 2016 Republican primary, facing his first significant political challenge since he was first elected to the Senate in 1986, Shelby emphasized the benefits of his seniority, while touting the prospect that he would soon ascend to the Appropriations Committee chairmanship. But Shelby had set his cap on chairing the Appropriations panel well before that. A former aide told the Washington Post that Shelby had long been "counting who had to lose, retire, or otherwise get out of the way to allow him to rise to the chairmanship of the Appropriations Committee."

On the surface, Shelby fits the mold of Southern politicians of another era, quick to backslap and recount political war stories during downtime on the Senate floor. During a 2018 meeting with President Donald Trump not long after becoming Appropriations chairman, Shelby—facing the task of telling the president the Senate would not give him the amount he requested for a southern-border wall—reportedly kept a difficult conversation amiable by opening with a long chat about college football, it was said. But Shelby is a tough negotiator, known for keeping his cards close to his chest and preserving his legislative options for as long as possible.

At 87, Shelby has honed his skills in a public career that goes back a half-century. He grew up the son of a steelworker in Birmingham, and, after earning both an undergraduate and law degree at the University of Alabama, he remained in Tuscaloosa and practiced law with future Democratic Rep. Walter Flowers—who was part of an informal group of conservative Democrats and Republicans who were instrumental in the 1974 impeachment of President Richard Nixon.

Shelby was elected to the state Senate in 1970 as a Democrat, and, when Flowers unsuccessfully ran for the Senate in 1978, Shelby sought his House seat. The critical contest was the Democratic runoff against Chris McNair, an African-American state legislator whose daughter was one of the four girls killed in the 1963 Birmingham church bombing. In a district that had the most black residents of any in the state, Shelby won 59%-41%. In the House, Shelby had a conservative voting record: He opposed the Voting Rights Act extension and making Martin Luther King Jr. Day a national holiday. He was part of a bloc of conservative Southern Democrats known as the "boll weevils" that was often allied with House Republicans.

Shelby ran for the Senate in 1986 and won a five-way Democratic primary with 51 percent of votes. In the general election, he took on Republican Sen. Jeremiah Denton, a retired admiral and former Vietnam prisoner of war who had been swept into office by President Ronald Reagan's landslide victory six years earlier. Shelby slammed Denton for voting to cut Social Security and owning two Mercedes-Benz cars. He won by a slim margin of 7,000 votes. As one of a half-dozen or so conservative Southern Democratic senators in the mid-1980s, Shelby at first attracted little notice. He was easily reelected in 1992, as Democrat Bill Clinton won the presidency but ran nearly 25 points behind Shelby in Alabama.

Soon after Clinton took office, Shelby broke ranks with the new administration. At a meeting with Vice President Al Gore, Shelby turned to the television cameras and criticized the Clinton program as "high on taxes, low on spending cuts." The administration retaliated, announcing a multimillion-dollar space facility would be in Texas instead of Alabama (although it eventually was built in Alabama). The more he defied Clinton, the better Shelby's favorability ratings were at home.

The day after Republicans regained control of the Senate in 1994, Shelby announced he was switching parties, increasing the GOP majority to 53 members. Republicans allowed him to keep his seniority on the Banking committee and gave him his coveted seats on Appropriations and its defense subcommittee. In an interview with CNN several years later, Shelby said he switched parties because of the Democratic Party's leftward shift and rejected the idea that he made the move to gain power. "What I did, didn't cause a political earthquake here," he said. "I just crossed the aisle and voted just like I've always been voting."

The switch paid dividends in 1997 when Shelby became chairman of the Intelligence Committee. One of his first acts was to scuttle Clinton's nomination of national security adviser Anthony Lake to be director of the CIA. By Sept. 11, 2001, the Senate was back in Democratic hands, but Shelby, as the ranking Republican on the committee, was an important player in the aftermath of the terrorist attacks. He had an adversarial posture toward the intelligence agencies during the Clinton and Bush presidencies. Soon after 9/11, Shelby stopped just short of calling for the resignation of then-CIA Director George Tenet. But Shelby was mostly supportive of the Bush administration's conduct in the "war on terrorism". Later, he was 1 of 10 senators to sign a letter calling for a plan "to eliminate the threat from Iraq." He led the call for the creation of a director of national intelligence, which was approved by Congress in 2004.

Republicans won back the Senate in the 2002 election, opening the way for Shelby, over the next decade and a half, to wield substantial influence over the nation's financial and housing industries during a time of crisis for both. He chaired the Banking Committee from 2003 to 2007 and 2015 to 2017. Shelby opposed the 2010 Dodd-Frank financial reforms. He believed the bill over-reached in setting rules for regional and smaller community banks. But he has exhibited a populist streak when it comes to Wall Street and the country's largest financial institutions. As far back as 1999, Shelby was the only Senate Republican to vote against a financial-services deregulation bill that repealed the Glass-Steagall Act, a Depression-era law that separated commercial and investment banking.

During the 2008 financial crisis, Shelby opposed the $700 billion rescue of the financial markets. Not long afterward, Shelby protested the massive government loan for the Big Three domestic automakers, calling them "dinosaurs." He threatened to filibuster. The bill did not pass the Senate, but President Barack Obama bailed out the auto industry anyway. Shelby later drew praise from the Troubled Asset Relief Program special inspector general, Neil Barofsky. In a 2012 book criticizing Congress and the Treasury Department for their handling of the issue, Barofsky singled out Shelby for being more interested in substance than many of his colleagues. Of one briefing with the senator, Barofsky wrote, "I probably covered more in fifteen minutes of rapid-fire questions and answers than in most hour-long meetings with other members of Congress."

As efforts to reform the nation's financial-regulatory system geared up in 2009, Shelby and the Democratic chairman of the Banking Committee, Sen. Christopher Dodd of Connecticut, agreed, at least in theory, on the creation of a consumer financial protection division or agency. But a sticking point surfaced over its structure. Dodd and Obama wanted the agency to be housed within the Federal Reserve and given more independence. But Shelby called for making it a division of the Federal Deposit Insurance Corp. After his substitute plan failed on the Senate floor, Shelby voted against it.

Returning to the Banking Committee as chairman in 2015, Shelby sought to overhaul Dodd-Frank. But after clearing the panel, Shelby's bill died. Democrats objected to Shelby's handling of the issue, and they were pleased that he was subject to term limits after the 2016 elections. Legislation loosening Dodd-Frank regulations on all but the largest banks was signed into law by Trump in May 2018.

Shelby has enjoyed a warmer relationship with his Appropriations Committee colleagues—most recently Leahy, and earlier, Democrat Barbara Mikulski of Maryland. In 2014, Mikulski agreed to boost spending for NASA's Space Launch System, a major project at the Marshall Space Flight Center in Huntsville. Critics have derided the SLS as a "rocket to nowhere," arguing its technology is outmoded and much more costly than using private-sector alternatives to propel heavy payloads into space. But Shelby and Mikulski, with her own home-state interest at the Goddard Space Flight Center, worked collaboratively to fund NASA programs. "He's a true partner," the avowedly liberal Mikulski said of Shelby at a hearing that year. Even after Mikulski's retirement, Shelby maintained robust support for space programs and the SLS rocket. In 2019, he sparred with new NASA Administrator Jim Bridenstine, then an Oklahoma congressman, after he showed openness to using commercial rockets instead of SLS to launch the moon mission Orion. Bridenstine subsequently was complimentary of the SLS.

Shelby forged a partnership with Leahy, another leading Senate liberal, after taking the Appropriations gavel in 2018. Trump had recently signed "omnibus" legislation in which the 12 annual appropriations bills funding departments and agencies were merged into one hastily passed measure totaling 2,200 pages. Trump called the process "ridiculous" and vowed not to sign such legislation again. But Shelby and Leahy shared longer-term concerns that the breakdown of the appropriations process had concentrated power to cut last-minute deals with congressional leaders at the expense of increasingly frustrated rank-and-file legislators. "We took a couple of trips together and we talked about it, and just said unless we get this back, the Senate is really screwed," Leahy told The New York Times. "We have to get back to doing it the regular way."

The upshot was that Shelby and Leahy persuaded their respective Senate party leaders to keep poison-pill "policy riders" off of appropriations bills. Democrats credited Shelby for holding up his part of the bargain—often to the consternation of his fellow Republicans seeking to advance pet causes and even when it meant Shelby had to vote against policy riders he personally supported. "If we're going to avoid another omnibus, and instead pass individual spending bills and send them to the president's desk, we have to work in a bipartisan fashion, which I'm going to try hard to do," Shelby told the Appropriations panel shortly after becoming chairman.

After a decade with few individual spending bills clearing the Senate floor, Shelby shepherded nine of the 12 annual appropriations measures to Senate passage on bipartisan votes in 2018. It was an accomplishment overshadowed by Trump's periodic threats to shut down the government over funding for a southern-border wall—an approach with which Shelby pointedly took issue. "Both sides, Democrats and Republicans, realize that shutting down the government, the specter of shutting down the government ... is not in anyone's political interests," Shelby told the Times. He backed a disaster bill in early 2019 that did not use military funding to pay for Trump's border wall.

While he boasts that he has biennially introduced a balanced-budget constitutional amendment, Shelby makes no apologies for the federal funds he has sought to direct to his home state. In 2020, he secured $1.1 billion for a new FBI center in Huntsville, which will welcome at least 1,500 staffers from the nation's capital, and possibly more in the coming years. When it came to earmarking, which has allowed individual lawmakers to tuck special provisions into spending bills, Shelby "made a kind of art form out of it," former GOP Rep. Jack Edwards of Alabama—a longtime member of the House Appropriations Committee—told the Mobile Press-Register.

Shelby bemoaned the Senate earmark ban. After it was adopted in November 2010, he complained it would hamper his long-term goal of securing $1 billion for science, engineering, and research projects at his state's colleges. Such efforts are one reason he has easily won reelection for three decades. Another is the massive campaign treasury that, until the 2016 primary, scared off competitive challengers—with lawyers and law firms the biggest single source of campaign contributions during Shelby's career, according to the Center for Responsive Politics. Despite his party switch, Shelby remained friendly with trial lawyers, who usually support Democrats in Alabama.

By the end of 2014, Shelby had amassed a campaign treasury of $18 million. He took hits that fall for directing only $17,000 to the National Republican Senatorial Committee while his party was seeking to recapture the Senate. But Shelby objected on principle to senators financing the NRSC and other campaigns, despite receiving the committee's assistance himself. After easily defeating a primary opponent in 2010 by more than 5-1, Shelby faced a credible threat in 2016 from former Marine Capt. Jonathan McConnell, an owner of a maritime security company. McConnell said Shelby was "too old" and had been in Washington for "too long," while taking aim at Shelby's role as an appropriator. "People are sick of his big spending ways," McConnell said. But, five days before the primary, the Tea Party Patriots Citizens Fund endorsed Shelby, citing his 2008 opposition to the TARP legislation. Groups ranging from the National Rifle Association to the National Right to Life Committee had earlier endorsed the incumbent. Shelby outspent McConnell 15-1 and defeated him 65%-28%. In November, Shelby won a sixth term 64%-36%.

Perhaps out of a lack of concern about electoral repercussions, Shelby did not hesitate to differ with Trump on issues ranging from the imposition of tariffs on steel and aluminum to the president's call for banning transgender people from serving in the military. According to Watergate journalist Carl Bernstein, Shelby was one of several senators who "expressed extreme contempt" for Trump. However, he voted to acquit Trump during the impeachment trial, saying on ABC's "This Week" that Trump was "human" and was "going to make mistakes of judgment and everything else" in asking Ukraine to investigate his eventual presidential rival, Joe Biden. But, when Trump later lost to Biden, Shelby accepted the results despite a push among his GOP Senate colleges to overturn the Electoral College vote.

Shelby's most visible split from Trump—as well as his home-state Republican Party—came in late 2017, when he withheld support from former Alabama Chief Justice Roy Moore, the controversial Republican nominee in the special Senate election to fill the seat vacated when Jeff Sessions became attorney general. Shelby called the allegations against Moore—involving sexual contact with teenage girls when Moore was in his 30s—"believable"; he opted to vote for a write-in candidate rather than for Moore. "I think Alabama deserves better," he said of Moore. "I think the image of anything matters," he told the Post. "It's not 1860. It's not 1900. It's not 1940. It's not 1964 or 1965. ... And Alabama in a lot of ways is on the cutting edge, on the cusp of a lot of good things." His comments likely helped Democrat Doug Jones pull off the upset against Moore.

After Sessions fell out of favor with Trump for recusing himself from the Russia investigation —and then sought to reclaim his Senate seat in 2020—Shelby became one of his former colleague's most influential backers. He circulated an "open letter to conservatives" endorsing Sessions' candidacy, pointing to his "character and his temperament," and calling him a "man of his word." Shelby tried to persuade Trump to remain neutral in the primary, but in a final act of revenge, the president enthusiastically supported the eventual winner, former Auburn football coach Tommy Tuberville.

Following Shelby's retirement announcement, Rep. Mo Brooks was the first major candidate in the field. He won the important endorsement of Trump, which was not surprising given the vocal support that Brooks gave to Trump's claims of fraud following the 2020 presidential election. Lynda Blanchard, who was Trump's Ambassador to Slovenia, also entered the contest; a multi-candidate primary seemed likely. The fact that Brooks got only 20 percent in the Republican primary when he ran in the 2017 special election for what had been Sessions's seat suggests that he does not have a lock on the nomination. For the Democrats, a repeat of their success in that special election seemed unlikely.

Tommy Tuberville (R)

Elected 2020, term expires 2026, 1st term, b. Sep 18, 1954; Camden, AR; Southern Arkansas University, B.S., 1976; Church of Christ; Married (Suzanne Fette); 2 children

Professional Career: Head Coach, University of Mississippi, 1995–1998; University of Auburn, 1999–2008; Texas Tech University, 2010–2012; University of Cincinnati, 2013–2016. Analyst, ESPN, 2017-2019.

DC Office: 142 RSOB 20510, 202-224-4124, Fax: 202-224-3149, tuberville.senate.gov

State Offices: Dothan, 334-547-7441; Mobile, 251-414-3083; Montgomery, 334-523-7424.

Committees: *Agriculture, Nutrition & Forestry*: Commodities, Risk Management & Trade; Conservation, Climate, Forestry & Natural Resources; Rural Development & Energy. *Armed Services*: Emerging Threats & Capabilities; Personnel; Strategic Forces. *Health, Education, Labor & Pensions*: Children & Families; Employment & Workplace Safety. *Veterans' Affairs*.

Election Results

Election	Name (Party)	Vote (%)		Cand. Spent	Ind. Exp. Support	Ind. Exp. Oppose
2020 General	Tommy Tuberville (R)	1,392,076	(60%)	$8,415,103	$1,406,277	$107,210
	Doug Jones (D)	920,478	(40%)	$31,015,172	$306,741	$1,848,388
2020 Primary	Tommy Tuberville (R)	239,616	(33%)			
	Jeff Sessions (R)	227,088	(32%)			
	Bradley Byrne (R)	178,627	(25%)			
	Roy Moore (R)	51,377	(7%)			

Tommy Tuberville, a longtime college football coach with no political experience, hitched himself to President Donald Trump and defeated Jeff Sessions in the 2020 Republican primary runoff with 61 percent of the vote—thwarting the former attorney general's quest for a return to the Senate. In what became an afterthought, his victory over the former senator set up Tuberville's perfunctory defeat of Democratic Sen. Doug Jones, who had won the seat in a special election in 2017 that set off shock waves on the national political scene. Sessions created the vacancy when he resigned to become Trump's attorney general.

Tuberville, an Arkansas native whose decade as coach at Auburn University was the only extended time that he lived in Alabama prior to his run for the Senate, ran a low-profile campaign and offered little insight into his Senate plans or policy hopes beyond his unwavering support for

Trump. Jones, meanwhile, ran a robust and well-financed campaign. But he collided with the reality that—other than his unique special election—no Democrat had won a Senate seat in Alabama since Howell Heflin was reelected in 1990. When Heflin retired, Sessions succeeded him. Tuberville is the only Republican who flipped a Democratic-held Senate seat in 2020.

Sessions had been widely popular in his home state: He was elected to his fourth term in 2014 with no opponent from either party. But he became the political victim of Trump's outrage after recusing himself from the Russia investigation. During his initial months in Trump's Cabinet, Sessions said he had no choice but to recuse himself from the probe, which Trump saw as the ultimate betrayal. Then, his deputy appointed former FBI Director Robert Mueller as a special counsel with a broad mandate to look into allegations that Trump and his campaign committed criminal violations with their Russian contacts during the 2016 campaign; the move would hang over all of Sessions' tenure. Mueller won the convictions of several senior officials in Trump's campaign, but he took no action against the president. Trump later pardoned many of those convicted.

Tuberville, grew up in Camden Arkansas, earned a bachelor's degree in education at Southern Arkansas University, where he not only majored in education but also was a letterman at free safety in football. Shortly after graduating from college, he went on to coach at Hermitage High School, spending the first two years as an assistant and the last two as the head coach. This paved the way for this first job coaching at the collegiate level, taking residency at Arkansas State University for four years as assistant coach.

In 1986, Tuberville began his long and successful tenure at the University of Miami. Beginning as a graduate assistant, he went on to become the Hurricanes' defensive coordinator in 1993. The Hurricanes won three AP national championships before he left, solidifying their place as one of the most storied programs in college football history. As the Hurricanes defensive coordinator, he coached future Hall of Fame inductees Ray Lewis and Warren Sapp, as well as Dwayne "The Rock" Johnson. Tuberville spent the 1994 season in College Station, Texas, as coach R.C. Slocum's defensive coordinator and finished with a 10-0-1 record.

Shortly after leaving the Hurricanes, Tuberville spent four seasons as head coach at the University of Mississippi before becoming the head coach of Auburn. Throughout his tenure, the Tigers made eight consecutive bowl appearances, including five New Year's Day bowl appearances, five SEC Western Division titles, one SEC Championship, and a 13-0 season in 2004. Tuberville received a number of accolades including AP Coach of the Year, Walter Camp Coach of the Year, Sporting News Coach of the Year and was inducted into the Arkansas Sports Hall of Fame.

In the years following his time at Auburn, Tuberville served as head coach for Texas Tech University as well as University of Cincinnati before announcing his retirement in 2016 and joining the ESPN broadcast staff, working beside broadcaster Mike Patrick.

Apart from his career in football, Tuberville had a brief spell as co-owner of a hedge fund. Tuberville entered into a 50-50 partnership with a former Lehman Brothers broker named John Stroud. Their ventures, which included TS Capital Management and TS Capital Partners— "T" for Tuberville and "S" for Stroud—turned out to be a financial fraud. While Stroud was sentenced to 10 years in prison, Tuberville was sued by investors, who accused him of fraud and violating his fiduciary duty to take care of their investments. Tuberville responded: "They sued me because I invested in it, and he used my name to get other people to put money in. There was nothing ever implicated by anyone that I'd done anything wrong." He later reached a private settlement in 2013.

Tuberville's failed investment career was seldom mentioned during his campaign for the Senate in 2020. He had two central campaign messages: his devout allegiance to Trump and the failures of his opponent. The seven-candidate Republican primary was wide open and required the winner to capture a majority of the vote. Tuberville and Sessions were the frontrunners, and won33and 32 percent of the vote, respectively.

In the primary runoff, with Trump unleashing harsh attacks on Sessions, the former senator struggled to keep up financially with Tuberville, who was bolstered by more than $5 million in spending by the conservative Club for Growth and the Trump-aligned America First Action super PAC. As described by Politico, support for Tuberville became "a mix of football obsession, the appeal of outsider status in Alabama politics and the 'winner' branding Trump has found a way to exploit." Tuberville prevailed 61%-39%—a stunning end to Sessions' once-storied career in Alabama politics.

Jones' 2017 victory was widely viewed as a fluke. A former U.S. attorney and onetime aide to Heflin, Jones was best known for his prosecution of Klu Klux Klan members after the horrific bombing in 1963 of a Birmingham church, which killed four young girls. The convictions earned him strong support among Alabama's African-American electorate. Roy Moore—a former chief justice of the state Supreme Court and an icon of social conservatives—won the primary runoff against Luther Strange, the state attorney general who had been appointed to fill Sessions' vacancy.

But Moore's campaign against Jones was sent reeling by allegations that he had repeatedly made sexual advances to four teenage women while in his 30s. With robust financial support from Democrats across the nation, Jones outspent his opponent in the special election by more than 4-1 and defeated Moore 50%-48%—with a margin of fewer than 22,000 votes; the turnout was roughly one-third lower than in a presidential election. In the 2020 GOP primary to oppose Jones, the discredited Moore got just 7percent of the vote.

The general election, in which Jones vastly outspent his Republican opponent, included ads that dismissed Tuberville for walking away from his Auburn coaching and spotlighted his financial failures. But few observers, either local or national, viewed the contest as competitive. Even Senate Democrats conceded that Jones faced daunting odds, especially with Trump at the top of the ticket. Tuberville, who largely ignored Jones and claimed that Trump would be reelected, was bolstered by deep support for Trump in Alabama—outside of African-American voters.

During the final weeks of the campaign, the Birmingham News reported, Tuberville "mostly avoided the media" and refused to debate Jones—despite demands by the incumbent. Pre-election polls showed that more than 70 percent of white voters supported Tuberville. Overall, he won 60%-40%.

Even before he could take office, the thin political and historical knowledge that Tuberville displayed during the campaign quickly became even more apparent. In an interview with the Alabama Daily News just days after his win, Tuberville misidentified the three branches of government as "the House, the Senate, and the executive." In the same interview, he claimed that World War II was fought "to free Europe of socialism," when it was instead a battle against fascism. Tuberville's driving force continued to be his fealty to Trump, as one of seven Republican senators to object to certification of the Electoral College votes for Pennsylvania and six who objected to the votes for Arizona; they, called for an electoral commission to investigate states where conservatives alleged, without evidence, that there was fraud. Their efforts, of course, failed.

Jerry Carl (R)

Elected 2020, 1st term, b. Jun 17, 1958; Mobile, AL; Lake City Community College, 1979; Southern Baptist; Married (Tina Carl); 3 children.

Elected Office: Commissioner, Mobile County, AL.

Professional Career: Founder, management group, 2013; Founder, lumber and timber company.

DC Office: 1330 LHOB 20515, 202-225-4931, Fax: 202-225-0562, carl.house.gov

State Offices: Mobile, 251-283-6280; Summerdale, 251-677-6630.

Committees: *Armed Services*: Military Personnel; Seapower & Projection Forces. *Natural Resources*: Indigenous Peoples of the United States; Water, Oceans & Wildlife.

Election Results

Election	Name (Party)	Vote (%)		Cand. Spent	Ind. Exp. Support	Ind. Exp. Oppose
2020 General	Jerry Carl (R)...............................	211,825	(64%)	$1,988,409	$128,272	$1,159,143
	James Averhart (D).......................	116,949	(36%)	$65,796		
2020 Primary	Jerry Carl (R)...............................	38,490	(39%)			
	Bill Hightower (R).........................	37,283	(37%)			
	Chris Pringle (R)...........................	19,126	(19%)			
2020 Primary	Jerry Carl (R)...............................	44,421	(52%)			
Runoff	Bill Hightower (R)........................	40,552	(48%)			

Jerry Carl, a successful businessman and a county commissioner, was elected in 2020 after winning a competitive Republican primary against an opponent who emphasized his conservative social views. Carl was endorsed in that contest by his predecessor, Rep. Bradley Byrne, an activist lawmaker who ran unsuccessfully in the Republican primary to challenge Democratic Sen. Doug Jones.

A native of Mobile, Carl built several local businesses during his entrepreneurial career. He started in 1989 with Stat Medical, a healthcare equipment firm, which expanded to seven locations before he sold the business to Rotech Medical; Carl remained as a regional manager. Later, he started local real estate and home health services firms. In 2009, he established Cricket and Butterfly, a company dedicated to buying and selling timber and timberland.

In 2012, Carl was elected to the Mobile County Commission. In that office, he was known as a fiscal hawk who called for pro-growth, job-creating policies. He said he consistently voted against tax increases and encouraged local economic opportunities. During his time on the commission, he said the county's unemployment rate fell from nearly 11 percent to 4 percent—before the COVID-19 pandemic struck in early 2020.

When Byrne in early 2019 announced his plan to run for the Senate, Carl said he wanted to continue Byrne's "conservative leadership" and get things done for Alabama and the nation. He centered his campaign on economic growth and additional healthcare choices for veterans, plus broader goals of standing with President Donald Trump and fighting for conservative principles. In the Republican primary, his chief opponent was Bill Hightower, who managed sales for a local industrial firm and served six years in the state Senate. Hightower ran in the 2018 Republican primary against Gov. Kay Ivey and finished a distant fourth, with 5 percent of the vote. Against Carl, Hightower highlighted his legislative experience, including proposals to ban the sale of fetal body parts and set term limits for state legislators. With each candidate well-financed and supported by local and national business groups, the contest became a battle of campaign ads and organization.

Hightower attacked Carl for supporting a local road project that would "benefit" real estate he owned. But WKRG, a Mobile television station, found that the county commission planned the highway in 2007, five years before Carl was elected to the commission. "Either Bill Hightower is intentionally lying to the voters for political gain, or he is completely confused" about the road project, Carl responded. In turn, Carl highlighted Hightower's failure to vote in the 2016 presidential primary and his earlier comment that he was "disgusted" by Trump. The national Club for Growth spent more than $1 million on ads that attacked Carl, which spurred local criticism of outside spending.

Voters were nearly evenly divided. In the first round of the primary, Carl received 39 percent of the vote to 38 percent for Hightower. In their July runoff, Carl prevailed, 52%-48%. In Mobile County, which cast half the total vote, Carl got 56 percent. Hightower led in four of the other five counties, but those tight margins could not overcome Carl's 5,050-vote advantage in Mobile.

In November, Carl defeated Democrat James Averhart, executive director of the Mobile chapter of the National Association for the Advancement of Colored People. After serving30 years as a Marine, Averhart was also president of a nonprofit group that worked with ex-offenders seeking to re-enter society.

In the House, he became the third House Republican from Alabama to get a seat on the Armed Services Committee. He also joined the Natural Resources Committee.

AL-1: Southwest Alabama   Cook Partisan Voting Index: R+16

Population		Race and Ethnicity		Income	
Total	717,438	White	66.90%	Median Income	$50,663
Land area (sq. miles)	6,067	Black	27.40%	District Income Rank	380
Pop/ sq mi	118.26	Latino	3.30%	Poverty Rate	15.40%
Born in State	68.10%	Asian	1.40%	With health insurance	89.80%
		Two or more races	2.10%	Cash public assistance	0.80%
Age Groups		Other	2.10%	Food stamp/SNAP	11.80%
Under 18	22.50%				
18-34	20.90%	**Education**		**Work**	
35-64	38.20%	H.S grad or less	45.40%	White Collar	35.20%
Over 64	18.30%	Some college	29.60%	Sales and Service	39.30%
		College Degree, 4 yr	16.10%	Blue Collar	25.60%
Military		Post grad	8.90%	Government	15.70%
Veteran/ Active Duty	9.60%				

2020 Pres. Vote	Trump	211,370	(64%)	Biden	117,135	(35%)		
2016 Pres. Vote	Trump	192,633	(63%)	Clinton	103,363	(34%)	Johnson	6,153	(2%)

Mobile Bay: Mobile, the port where the Tombigbee and Alabama rivers flow into the Gulf of Mexico, was a strategic point on the American frontier. Spanish after the Revolutionary War, it was wrested away by threats of war from Secretary of State John Quincy Adams. During the Civil War, it was one of the major Confederate ports. In 1864, Admiral David Farragut, while steaming into the harbor lashed to his ship's rigging, cried, "Damn the torpedoes! Full speed ahead." Today, Mobile is full of graceful signs of its turbulent past. Behind the docks and rail lines are downtown buildings and old houses with Spanish motifs, French accents or tropical Art Deco lines. Further inland are neighborhoods with spacious houses, often with double porches, overhung by huge live oaks graced with Spanish moss. Mobile is a Gulf Coast version of Charleston or a smaller, more comfortable New Orleans, with a taste for shellfish and spicy food and an even older Mardi Gras, which the locals have been celebrating since 1703. As befits a frontier city with a martial past, Mobile is bristling with arms: One of the city's proudest possessions is the battleship USS Alabama, moored at the head of Mobile Bay, with its guns aimed out toward the Gulf. In June 2018, the Clotilda, the last-known slave ship, was discovered in the Mobile River.

Mobile's economy was based originally on docks and shipyards, factories and terminals, but with a determination to impose touches of beauty on its hot, flat landscape. The continuing expansion of the container terminal serves Alabama's booming auto factories. Three recent developments have attracted more business to the port: expansion of the Panama Canal; the local assembly line by European aircraft manufacturer Airbus for its A320 airline and a second assembly line for a smaller Bombardier passenger jet; and the return of Carnival Cruise Lines, which was a boost for local tourism. In June 2020, state officials and the Army Corps of Engineers announced plans to widen and deepen the port.

In August 2005, Hurricane Katrina struck Mobile and its beaches with Category 4 intensity. On Dauphin Island, the 14-mile spit of land south of Mobile Bay, 300 homes were swept away, and a one-mile gash created a new island. Disaster struck the area again in 2010. After the explosion of BP's Deepwater Horizon offshore drilling rig, oil washed up on beaches and into Mobile Bay. Adecade later, the seafood industry was still struggling to recover.

Mobile is the focus of Alabama's 1st Congressional District, which extends north along the usually lazy Tombigbee and Alabama rivers, with their old forts and mansions. There are surviving backcountry settlements of blacks and Cajans (who may or may not be descended from Louisiana Cajuns) and Creek Indians. Once cotton fields, this is now timberland, a major contributor to Alabama's economy. East of Mobile Bay, along the shores of the Gulf of Mexico, are condominium communities in Baldwin County. The area hosts the annual National Shrimp Festival, and its glorious Gulf beaches are among the South's best. For years, this southern seaboard of the Confederacy has been among the most hawkish parts of America, and today it is solidly Republican in national elections. Donald Trump made early appearances here during his 2016 campaign and was well-received.

Barry Moore (R)

Elected 2020, 1st term, b. Sep 26, 1966; Enterprise, AL; Enterprise State Junior College Foundation, A.D.; Troy State University; Auburn University, B.S., 1992; Baptist; Married (Heather Hopper); 4 children.

Military Career: AL National Guard and Reserves, 1989-1995.

Elected Office: AL House, 2010-2018.

Professional Career: Founder, waste hauling company.

DC Office: 1504 LHOB 20515, 202-225-2901, barrymoore.house.gov

State Offices: Andalusia, 334-428-1129; Dothan, 334-547-6330; Wetumpka, 334-478-6330.

Committees: *Agriculture*: Conservation & Forestry; Livestock & Foreign Agriculture. *Veterans' Affairs*: Disability Assistance & Memorial Affairs; Economic Opportunity (RMM).

Election Results

Election	Name (Party)	Vote (%)		Cand. Spent	Ind. Exp. Support	Ind. Exp. Oppose
2020 General	Barry Moore (R)	197,996	(65%)	$648,653	$327,914	
	Phyllis Harvey-Hall (D)	105,286	(35%)	$49,673		
2020 Primary	Jeff Coleman (R)	39,804	(38%)			
	Barry Moore (R)	21,392	(20%)			
	Jessica Taylor (R)	20,789	(20%)			
	Troy King (R)	15,171	(15%)			
2020 Primary Runoff	Barry Moore (R)	52,248	(60%)			
	Jeff Coleman (R)	34,185	(40%)			

Barry Moore was elected to the House after he lost his challenge to Rep. Martha Roby for the Republican nomination in 2018. Although Moore's GOP primary opponent in 2020 outraised him by almost $2 million, Moore was bolstered by his claim that, in 2015, he was the first elected official in the nation to endorse Donald Trump's presidential campaign. Roby, who had been a rising star among House Republicans, retired after conservatives turned against her following her disavowal of Trump late in the 2016 campaign.

Moore grew up on a farm in Coffee County before getting an associate degree from Enterprise State Junior College and a bachelor's degree from Auburn University. At Auburn, he enlisted in the Alabama National Guard, where he became a member of the Army Ranger Challenge Team in the Reserve Officers' Training Corps program.

In 1998, Moore founded his company: Barry Moore Industries. After starting with a single garbage truck, the firm had robust growth. In 2018, the business assisted Tyndall Air Force Base in the Florida Panhandle to rebuild its facilities following devastation by Hurricane Michael.

Moore entered politics in 2010 when he won a seat in the state House. As chairman of the Military and Veteran Affairs Committee, he authored legislation that brought the "Red Tails" F-35 Fighter Squadron to an Air National Guard base in Montgomery. He also sponsored legislation that sought to protect military families in child custody cases, to secure in-state tuition programs for military families and veterans, and to protect the licensing of working spouses. Moore's political career was jeopardized in 2014 when he was indicted for perjury and making false statements to a grand jury that was investigating state House Speaker Mike Hubbard. A jury found Moore not guilty on all four counts. Hubbard was convicted in 2016 on multiple ethics charges of using his public office for personal gain.

In his 2018 challenge to Roby, Moore focused on her criticism of Trump during the 2016 presidential campaign. He placed third with 19 percent of the vote in the Republican primary, which Roby subsequently won in a runoff. (The runner-up, Bobby Bright, earlier served one term in the House as a Democrat, before he changed parties.) After Roby announced that she would not seek re-election in 2020, Moore reiterated his early support for Trump, which came during the then-New York businessman's first campaign rally, in Mobile. He also highlighted his view that, "Faith, family, finance, and freedom are the fundamentals that guide all aspects" of his life.

In the GOP primary, Moore and Jeff Coleman both described themselves as Trump loyalists. Coleman, the wealthy owner of a moving company, ran as an outsider like Trump, while Moore positioned himself as an experienced legislator who could get things done. Coleman led the first round of the primary with 38 percent to 20 percent for Moore; Jessica Taylor, who ran a faith-based office for Republican Gov. Bob Riley from 2008 to 2010, finished third, 603 votes behind Moore. In the runoff, Moore reversed the initial vote, defeating Coleman 60%-40%; Moore won 12 of the 15 counties. Coleman, with nearly $1 million in self-financing, out-spent Moore six-to-one. He suffered from a disclosure by the Alabama Political Reporter that his company paid $5 million to settle fraud charges that resulted from fixing weights during military shipments. Moore got a boost from more than $700,000 that the Club for Growth spent on his behalf during the campaign, plus support from the House Freedom Caucus.

In November, Moore defeated Democrat Phyllis Harvey-Hall, a longtime public school teacher.

AL-2: Southeast Alabama   Cook Partisan Voting Index: R+17

Population		Race and Ethnicity		Income	
Total	674,920	White	62.80%	Median Income	$50,494
Land area (sq. miles)	10,142	Black	32.20%	District Income Rank	381
Pop/ sq mi	66.55	Latino	3.90%	Poverty Rate	16.40%
Born in State	68.00%	Asian	1.30%	With health insurance	89.60%
		Two or more races	1.90%	Cash public assistance	1.30%
Age Groups		Other	1.70%	Food stamp/SNAP	13.70%
Under 18	22.50%				
18-34	22.60%	Education		Work	
35-64	37.00%	H.S grad or less	45.30%	White Collar	33.70%
Over 64	17.80%	Some college	31.20%	Sales and Service	39.50%
		College Degree, 4 yr	14.80%	Blue Collar	26.80%
Military		Post grad	8.70%	Government	19.50%
Veteran/ Active Duty	11.70%				

2020 Pres. Vote	Trump	195,965	(64%)	Biden	107,773	(35%)	
2016 Pres. Vote	Trump	185,504	(64%)	Clinton	94,300	(33%)	

Montgomery, Dothan: Thick green countryside blankets southern Alabama. Even in Montgomery, the stone and brick buildings of the downtown district do not mask the contours of the hills or hide the lush foliage. One can look downhill from the restored Greek Revival capitol toward Dexter Avenue King Memorial Baptist Church, where the young Martin Luther King Jr. was pastor in the 1950s, or out past the impressive Carolyn Blount Theatre, host of the Alabama Shakespeare Festival, toward new subdivisions and shopping malls, and easily imagine when this land was covered with cotton fields and pine trees, and a young Wilson Pickett was still performing in Baptist church choirs in Prattville. The atmosphere is especially rural in southeast Alabama's Wiregrass region, named for the stiff native grass. There is the fishing town of Eufaula, along the Chattahoochee River; the Army's Fort Rucker, home of Army aviation flight training; Maxwell-Gunter Air Force Base, which is the largest employer in the Montgomery area; and Enterprise, site of the Boll Weevil Monument that commemorates the insect that destroyed two-thirds of the cotton crop in 1915 and then spread throughout the South. In October 2019, Steven Reed was elected the first African-American mayor of Montgomery.

Timber is an important resource here, and peanuts replaced cotton as the main crop in the area surrounding Dothan, which calls itself the "peanut capital of the world." Each fall, Dothan holds the National Peanut Festival, the largest of its kind, to celebrate growers and the harvest season. A statue of peanut innovator George Washington Carver can be found here. Dothan also is the home of the expanded Wayne Farms chicken processing plant, which handles1.3 million chickens weekly.

The area's industrial diversification has been led by the automobile industry. Hyundai, the world's fifth-largest automaker, built its first U.S. assembly plant in southwest Montgomery County, with about 2,500 jobs and more than 400 robots to meet annual production capacity of 336,000 cars. The company calls the facility one of the most advanced in the North American auto industry, producing Sonata and Elantra sedans. In 2019, Hyundai announced plans to expand the plant to build the Santa Cruz pickup. Despite the economic growth, Montgomery's population continued to drop in recent years.

The 2nd Congressional District of Alabama covers 14 counties in the southeast corner of the state. It includes a thin link in the heart of Montgomery, but shares the surrounding metropolitan area with the 3rd and 7th districts to the east and west. The more heavily black precincts in west Montgomery, as well as mostly African-American Lowndes County, are part of the majority-minority 7th. The remaining Montgomery County precincts in the 2nd district vote heavily Republican, as do suburban Elmore and Autauga counties and Houston County in the Wiregrass region; each gave Donald Trump more than 70 percent of the vote in 2016 and again in 2020. These areas outvote the district's "Black Belt" counties, including Bullock, with a large black majority and the only Democratic county in the district, and Barbour on the Georgia border, which was George Wallace's home base. Like all of Alabama except for the 7th, this district is solidly Republican.

Mike Rogers (R)

Elected 2002, 10th term, b. Jul 16, 1958; Hammond, IN; Jacksonville State University, B.A., 1981; Jacksonville State University, M.P.A., 1984; Birmingham School of Law, J.D., 1991; Baptist; Married (Beth Rogers); 3 children.

Elected Office: Calhoun County Commission, 1986-1990; AL House, 1994-2002; Min. Leader, 1998-2000.

Professional Career: Practicing attorney, 1991-2002.

DC Office: 2184 RHOB 20515, 202-225-3261, Fax: 202-226-8485, mikerogers.house.gov

State Offices: Anniston, 256-236-5655; Opelika, 334-745-6221.

Committees: *Armed Services (RMM).*

Group Ratings

	ADA	ACLU	AFL-CIO	LCV	COC	HAFA	ACU	CFG	FRC
2020	**	11%	**	5%	-	88%	78%	**	-
2019	10%	C	26%	3%	77%	C	78%	75%	90%

Almanac Ratings 2019-2020

	Economy	Social	Foreign	Composite
Liberal	25%	23%	13%	21%
Conservative	75%	77%	87%	79%

Key Votes of the 116th Congress

1. U.S./Mex./Can. trade deal	Y	5. Russia sanctions	N
2. First Coronavirus response	N/A	6. Troops in Syria	Y
3. HEROES Act	N	7. Veto arms sales to Saudis	N
4. CASH Act	N	8. Defense $$$, veto override	Y

9. Firearms background checks	N
10. Spending at the border	Y
11. Marijuana liberalized rules	N
12. Electoral College objections	Y

Election Results

Election	Name (Party)	Vote (%)		Cand. Spent	Ind. Exp. Support	Ind. Exp. Oppose
2020 General	Mike Rogers (R)	217,384	(67%)	$1,010,619		$750
	Adia Winfrey (D)	104,595	(32%)	$31,616		

Prior winning percentages: 2018 (64%), 2016 (67%), 2014 (66%), 2012 (64%), 2010 (59%), 2008 (53%), 2006 (59%), 2004 (61%), 2002 (50%)

Mike Rogers, a senior House Republican, has been influential on national security and agriculture issues. In2021, he became the ranking minority member of the House Armed Services Committee, where he typically sought a bipartisan approach to defense policy—including his successful advocacy of creation of the Space Force.

Rogers is a fifth-generation resident of Calhoun County, the son of a textile worker and a fireman. At the age of 28, he was the first Republican elected to the county commission. In 1994, he won a seat in the Alabama House and, in his second term, became minority leader. Running for an open seat in the House in 2002, he had stiff competition from Democrat Joe Turnham Jr., who served three years as state party chairman. Rogers touted his working-class values, support from the National Rifle Association and backing of a constitutional amendment permitting prayer in public schools. Turnham did not risk bringing in national Democrats to campaign for him in the socially conservative district, while Rogers got frequent visits from national Republican leaders. The contrast in national party support was evident in Rogers's big fundraising advantage. He won, but only 50%-48%.

On the Armed Services Committee, Rogers sought to protect Anniston Army Depot as well as Maxwell-Gunter Air Force Base and Fort Benning just across the state line in Georgia. He is a leading Republican hawk on defense issues, including his call for increased attention to missile defense. After Sen. Dianne Feinstein of California said that current spending for nuclear weapons is "unsustainable," Rogers wrote that her comment shows a disregard for reality. "Nuclear weapons are not undermining other national security priorities—they are undergirding them." President Donald Trump later picked up on that theme.

Rogers has advocated space defense technology as a vital feature of American military strength, and took the lead when Congress created the Space Force as the sixth service branch of the military. He criticized Air Force leaders as "in denial" for their resistance to the plan. When Congress in 2019 approved the step, the creation of the first new military force since 1947, Rogers cited the collaboration of Democratic Rep. Jim Cooper of Tennessee and said that Congress had taken "an important step for our national security." With approval from Trump, the Space Force was placed under the Air Force.

Rogers has sought to enhance Alabama's role in domestic protection against terrorism. His district includes the Federal Emergency Management Agency's Center for Domestic Preparedness. Following the 2018 election, House Republican tapped him for the top slot on the Homeland Security Committee. Rogers narrowly lost to Rep. Mike McCaul of Texas in 2012, when he competed to fill a vacancy as chairman of the committee. He has been outspoken in describing security threats facing the nation. With the Islamic State, he said during a meeting in his district, "we can't put our head in the sand because all of us are tired of war."

After two years as the top Republican on Homeland Security, Rogers won a tough competition with Rep. Mike Turner of Ohio to replace the term-limited Mac Thornberry of Texas as the top Republican on Armed Services. Their clash was, in part, a battle of personalities between Rogers, "a prolific fundraiser with an affable Southern charm" and Turner's "more aggressive style," according to Defense One, a Washington-based news service. They also had differences on some issues, including Turner's opposition to the Space Force.

Rogers has shown populist leanings on economic issues. He bucked the Bush administration and won local praise by opposing a trade agreement with Morocco on the grounds that it would reduce local textile and apparel jobs. Following the 2016 election, he stirred discussion among House Republicans to revive the practice of legislative earmarks for members of Congress to direct federal spending to their constituents. House Speaker Paul Ryan objected and shut down that internal debate for the next two years. Still, Rogers mostly has been a reliable Republican vote. His Almanac vote ratings have placed him among conservative House Republicans.

Rogers has worked hard to entrench himself and raise money to discourage Democratic opposition in this ancestrally Democratic district, with a 25 percent African-American population. In 2018, he faced his first serious challenger in a decade: Mallory Hagan, an Opelika native and winner of the Miss America pageant in 2013, who later was a television news reporter in Columbus Georgia. Hagan mostly avoided discussion of Trump. Instead, she said in an interview that she sought to be a "role model and leader to young people."

In a pre-election editorial, which did not endorse either candidate, the Anniston Star described Rogers as "unresponsive" to local residents, but added that "his experience and ability to protect the district's interests" were "undeniable." Hagan raised nearly $500,000, but she had scant national party support and was outspent nearly 3-to-1. Rogers won, 64%-36%, and took 11 of the 13 counties, trailing only in Macon and neighboring Russell. In 2020, Rogers had an easy ride against Adia McClellan, a writer and professor of psychology who emphasized the need for empowerment of young people. She spent less than $50,000 and Rogers won, 67%-32%, leading in all but the two Black Belt counties.

Rogers occasionally has engaged in partisan volleys. When Democratic Rep. Ilhan Omar of Minnesota in 2019 described the September 2001 terror attacks as "some people did something," he wrote in Facebook that Omar was among "radical Democrats" who "devalue and degrade our great nation."

AL-3: Eastern Alabama   **Cook Partisan Voting Index: R+18**

Population		Race and Ethnicity		Income	
Total	717,896	White	68.90%	Median Income	$51,925
Land area (sq. miles)	7,544	Black	26.30%	District Income Rank	368
Pop/ sq mi	95.16	Latino	2.90%	Poverty Rate	15.00%
Born in State	64.20%	Asian	1.80%	With health insurance	91.50%
		Two or more races	1.70%	Cash public assistance	0.90%
Age Groups		Other	1.40%	Food stamp/SNAP	13.20%
Under 18	21.70%				
18-34	23.30%	**Education**		**Work**	
35-64	38.20%	H.S grad or less	45.80%	White Collar	35.10%
Over 64	16.70%	Some college	30.20%	Sales and Service	35.00%
		College Degree, 4 yr	13.60%	Blue Collar	29.90%
Military		Post grad	10.40%	Government	19.00%
Veteran/ Active Duty	9.00%				

2020 Pres. Vote	Trump	212,047	(65%)	Biden	109,506	(34%)		
2016 Pres. Vote	Trump	188,476	(65%)	Clinton	93,301	(32%)	Johnson	5,766	(2%)

Auburn, Anniston: The 3rd Congressional District of Alabama is centered geographically and philosophically in Lineville. The small town's progress from Ku Klux Klan country to an integrated community where the racial desegregation has echoed that of America's most integrated institution, the military. The local military presence is unmistakable: Calhoun County is home to Anniston Army Depot. Horseshoe Bend is where Andrew Jackson won a climactic battle against the Upper Creek Indians. Fort Mitchell, a 19th-century frontier military outpost, is the site of a national military cemetery sometimes referred to as the "Arlington of the South." Phenix City, across the Chattahoochee River from Georgia's Fort Benning, served as a "sin city" in the 1940s and 1950s, a place so sleazy that Gen. George Patton threatened to level it with his tanks. Today, the huge military installation plays a more constructive role in the local economy.

There are other places of distinction in the district: Tuskegee is the home of Booker T. Washington's Tuskegee University, training ground for the Tuskegee Airmen, the first black pilots trained to fly for the U.S. military. Auburn is the home of Auburn University and its renowned sports teams and veterinary school. Talladega is the site of the Alabama Institute for the Deaf and Blind and is perhaps America's most user-friendly city for people with disabilities. NASCAR fans know it as the home of a famed speedway and for the International Motorsports Hall of Fame—the Cooperstown of auto racing—where a $50 million "transformation" was completed in 2019, including a huge covered area with a giant video screen. In June 2020, the area gained a reminder of its sordid history when a large rope shaped like a noose was found in the garage of Bubba Wallace, an African-American driver.

This looks and feels like rural country, though few people here make a living off their farms. An economy once dependent on cotton mills is today more diverse, and interstates have brought in new businesses. The Honda assembly plant in Talladega County employed more than 4,500 workers, who built 352,000 minivans, SUVs and pick-up trucks in 2019.

Politically, this was long one of the heartlands of the conservative wing of the Democratic Party, with a large population of African-American descendants of slaves from plantations. Tuskegee's Macon County is the only remaining Democratic county in the district. St. Clair County, close to Birmingham and solidly Republican, has been among the fastest-growing in the state. Redistricting changes in 2012 boosted Republicans, and Democrats have had a more difficult time competing here. Donald Trump twice won the district with 65 percent of the vote.

Robert Aderholt (R)

Elected 1996, 13th term, b. Jul 22, 1965; Haleyville, AL; Birmingham-Southern College, B.A., 1987; Samford University Cumberland Law School, J.D., 1990; Methodist; Married (Caroline McDonald Aderholt); 2 children.

Professional Career: Haleyville Municipal Judge, 1992-1995; Assistant legal advisor, Gov. Fob James, 1995-1996.

DC Office: 1203 LHOB 20515, 202-225-4876, Fax: 202-225-5587, aderholt.house.gov

State Offices: Cullman, 256-734-6043; Gadsden, 256-546-0201; Jasper, 205-221-2310; Tuscumbia, 256-381-3450.

Committees: *Appropriations*: Agriculture, Rural Development, FDA & Related Agencies; Commerce, Justice, Science & Related Agencies (RMM); Defense.

Group Ratings

	ADA	ACLU	AFL-CIO	LCV	COC	HAFA	ACU	CFG	FRC
2020	**	10%	**	5%	-	77%	83%	**	-
2019	5%	C	33%	3%	81%	C	83%	62%	100%

Almanac Ratings 2019-2020

	Economy	Social	Foreign	Composite
Liberal	27%	16%	6%	17%
Conservative	73%	84%	94%	83%

Key Votes of the 116th Congress

1. U.S./Mex./Can. trade deal Y	5. Russia sanctions N	9. Firearms background checks N
2. First Coronavirus response Y	6. Troops in Syria Y	10. Spending at the border Y
3. HEROES Act N	7. Veto arms sales to Saudis N	11. Marijuana liberalized rules N/A
4. CASH Act Y	8. Defense $$$, veto override Y	12. Electoral College objections Y

Election Results

Election	Name (Party)	Vote (%)		Cand. Spent	Ind. Exp. Support	Ind. Exp. Oppose
2020 General	Robert Aderholt (R)	261,553	(82%)	$1,489,278		$750
	Rick Neighbors (D)	56,237	(18%)	$44,924		

Prior winning percentages: 2018 (80%), 2016 (99%), 2014 (99%), 2012 (74%), 2010 (100%), 2008 (75%), 2006 (70%), 2004 (75%), 2002 (87%), 2000 (61%), 1998 (56%), 1996 (50%)

Robert Aderholt, a Republican first elected in 1996, lost his bid in 2019 to become ranking minority member of the House Appropriations Committee. But, as the top Republican on the subcommittee that controls spending for NASA, he received a valuable consolation prize of robust funding for its vital facility in Huntsville, which employs many of his constituents. Aderholt remained an influential player on agriculture and defense spending and he viewed federal money for the state to be an essential part of his job.

Aderholt is from Winston County, the one ancestrally Republican county in north Alabama; it opposed secession in the Civil War and declared itself the Free State of Winston. His father was a circuit judge for more than 30 years; his wife's father was a state senator and state commissioner of agriculture and industry. In 1992, Aderholt was appointed Haleyville municipal judge. Three years later, he became a top aide to Republican Gov. Fob James.

With that pedigree, at age 31, he decided to run for Congress when 30-year veteran Rep. Tom Bevill, a Democrat and a pork-barrel spending appropriator, retired. As the Republican nominee, he faced state Sen. Bob Wilson Jr., who called himself a Democrat "in the Tom Bevill tradition." In this culturally conservative district, Aderholt emphasized social issues, opposing abortion rights, gun control, same-sex marriage and prohibitions on school prayer. "We want to go to Washington to deliver a message, and that is, don't mess with our traditional family values," he said. He attacked

Wilson for his support from labor unions and trial lawyers. Aderholt won 50%-48%. The outcome was a landmark in the Republican takeover of rural Southern districts.

Aderholt's voting record is generally conservative, and he was among the first House Republicans to join the Tea Party Caucus in 2010. His Almanac vote ratings have ranked him among GOP conservatives. Aderholt has often sided with labor and economic populists on trade issues, mainly because of local imperatives. He has supported quotas on steel imports and voted against normalizing trade relations with China. In another populist leaning, he was the only House member from Alabama in 2008 to vote against the $700 billion rescue of the financial markets. He cited the need for a more market-based approach.

Republican leaders put Aderholt on the Appropriations Committee, where he secured more highway and water projects money than most of his GOP colleagues. In the old-style Southern tradition, he worked his way up the ranks by learning how deals are made and trading favors. After Republicans assumed House control in 2011, he became chairman of the Homeland Security Subcommittee.

For six years, Aderholt chaired the Agriculture Appropriations Subcommittee, an area of interest for many of his constituents. He listed his priorities as "cutting edge" agricultural research, vibrant rural communities, nutrition for the most vulnerable, competitive markets in the global economy and the safest food and drug supply in the world. He also was mindful of agribusiness needs. When a federal advisory panel urged consideration of the environmental impact of nutrition plans, Aderholt criticized "politically motivated" steps such as taxes on certain foods that he said were at odds with sound science.

At Appropriations, he retained his interest in social issues. In June 2019, he won committee approval of a controversial provision to prohibit the Food and Drug Administration from approving research that involves gene-editing of human embryos. The previous year, the House approved an Aderholt rider to a spending bill that permitted adoption agencies to have separate standards for same-sex couples. In 2012, Aderholt added an amendment specifying that none of the funds provided to Immigration and Customs Enforcement could be used to pay for an abortion, except under limited circumstances.

Aderholt was positioned as the next Republican to lead the Appropriations Committee after Rep. Rodney Frelinghuysen of New Jersey in early 2018 announced his retirement. Rep. Kay Granger of Texas, who entered the House the same year as Aderholt, waged a hard-fought campaign. She benefited from the support of the largest state delegation in the House, plus pressure to increase the influence of women among House Republicans. Some Republicans contended that Aderholt suffered because another Alabaman, Richard Shelby, chaired the Senate Appropriations Committee.

In 2019, Aderholt became the ranking minority member of the Appropriations Subcommittee on Commerce, Justice, Science and Related Agencies, which includes NASA. He made clear his intentions when he took the assignment. "With my leadership on this subcommittee, I will work to ensure that North Alabama continues to lead as we return to the moon, put boots on Mars and travel into deep space," he said.

By December 2019, he had delivered benefits to the prime NASA facility in Huntsville, especially its objective of a heavy-lift rocket designed to carry astronauts into deep space. "Today is a significant day for Marshall Space Flight Center's continued leadership in our nation's focus on space," Aderholt said, as he described additional funding for four of its programs. "We have positioned Huntsville and all of North Alabama to play a vital role in our push to go back to the moon and on to Mars," he concluded.

When President-elect Donald Trump tapped Alabama Sen. Jeff Sessions for attorney general, Aderholt said that he would like to be appointed as his successor. "I would be someone who could hit the ground running," he told the Yellowhammer News. Although he didn't get the appointment, Aderholt, with his relatively young age, could have other opportunities for the Senate. In 2020, the attempted comeback by Sessions plus the unexpected campaign of Tommy Tuberville left little room for Aderholt, as Alabama Republicans vied to regain the seat that Sessions had relinquished. Then, when Shelby announced his retirement in February 2021, Aderholt voiced no immediate interest in running for his Senate seat.

AL-4: North-Central Alabama   Cook Partisan Voting Index: R+34

Population		Race and Ethnicity		Income	
Total	687,453	White	86.80%	Median Income	$47,531
Land area (sq. miles)	8,889	Black	7.40%	District Income Rank	401
Pop/ sq mi	77.34	Latino	6.90%	Poverty Rate	15.60%
Born in State	74.20%	Asian	0.50%	With health insurance	88.60%
		Two or more races	1.80%	Cash public assistance	1.50%
Age Groups		Other	3.60%	Food stamp/SNAP	13.70%
Under 18	22.50%				
18-34	20.20%	**Education**		**Work**	
35-64	38.60%	H.S grad or less	51.30%	White Collar	30.30%
Over 64	18.70%	Some college	31.20%	Sales and Service	34.60%
		College Degree, 4 yr	11.50%	Blue Collar	35.20%
Military		Post grad	6.10%	Government	13.80%
Veteran/ Active Duty	7.30%				

2020 Pres. Vote	Trump	260,573	(81%)	Biden	57,145	(18%)
2016 Pres. Vote	Trump	233,662	(80%)	Clinton	50,722	(17%)

Gadsden: The Appalachian Mountains' corduroy ridges, dividing the Atlantic coast from the interior, make up America's coal-and-steel industrial spine, from the black coal country of western Pennsylvania to the red hill country of northern Alabama. Here rose America's two premier steel cities, Pittsburgh and Birmingham. Around both, and for many miles in between, is countryside settled by feisty Scots-Irish farmers in the years between the Revolution and the Civil War. In valley land accessible to railroads, great steel factories were built in the 80 years after the Civil War, along with smaller factories that produced socks, tires, glass and chemicals, and that butchered chickens. Northern Alabama was solidly Democratic through the 1950s. It was populist on economics, conservative on cultural issues. Since then, the region has become firmly Republican even as it has benefited from massive federal public works programs.

Alabama's 4th Congressional District is a collection of small towns—Cullman, Jasper, Russellville, Fort Payne and Albertville. The last is the home of a military helicopter plant and other aerospace facilities. Sandwiched between Huntsville to the north and Birmingham to the south, the 4th District crosses the state and the Appalachian ridges, from the Georgia line to Mississippi. Decades of coal mining scarred 150 square miles of landscape, about one-fourth of which has been reclaimed, with pockets of jobs. Gritty Gadsden (pop. 35,000) the biggest city, is losing population, like many parts of this area. Its Goodyear tire plant, built in 1929, was the largest tire plant in the world, with more than 4,000 workers in the 1980s. In 2016, the company spent $30 million to expand the aging facility and its operations. But coronavirus became the death knell in April 2020, when the company announced a shutdown. The plant's most famous employee was activist Lilly Ledbetter, who waged a nine-year battle on behalf of equal pay for women. President Barack Obama in 2009 signed into law the Lilly Ledbetter Fair Pay Act extending the statute of limitations on equal-pay discrimination law suits. Other auto companies have moved into the area. In Gadsden, Motus Integrated Technologies manufactures interior parts. Japanese-based Yoruzu Automotive manufactures stamped parts for nearby auto companies, with 300 employees in Jasper.

The 4th is Alabama's premier Scots-Irish district, with the lowest African-American population percentage of the state's seven congressional districts. In 2016, the 80 percent for Donald Trump was his highest in the nation. Four years later, his vote increased to 81 percent and again was Trump's best nationwide.

Mo Brooks (R)

Elected 2010, 6th term, b. Apr 29, 1954; Charleston, SC; Duke University, B.A., 1975; University of AL School of Law, J.D., 1978; Christian Church; Married (Martha Brooks); 4 children; 8 grandchildren.

Elected Office: AL House, 1983-1992; Madison County Commissioner, 1996-2010.

Professional Career: Tuscaloosa County prosecutor, 1978-1980; Clerk, Circuit Ct. Judge John Snodgrass, 1980-1982; Madison County district Attorney, 1991-1993; AL special Assistant Attorney General, 1995-2002; practicing Attorney, 1993-2010.

DC Office: 2246 RHOB 20515, 202-225-4801, brooks.house.gov

State Offices: Decatur, 256-355-9400; Florence, 256-718-5155; Huntsville, 256-551-0190.

Committees: *Armed Services*: Cyber, Innovative Technologies & Information Systems; Strategic Forces. *Science, Space & Technology*: Space & Aeronautics.

Group Ratings

	ADA	ACLU	AFL-CIO	LCV	COC	HAFA	ACU	CFG	FRC
2020	**	19%	**	0%	-	100%	91%	**	-
2019	0%	C	19%	3%	71%	C	91%	89%	95%

Almanac Ratings 2019-2020

	Economy	Social	Foreign	Composite
Liberal	25%	8%	31%	22%
Conservative	75%	92%	69%	78%

Key Votes of the 116th Congress

1. U.S./Mex./Can. trade deal Y	5. Russia sanctions N	9. Firearms background checks N
2. First Coronavirus response Y	6. Troops in Syria N	10. Spending at the border N
3. HEROES Act N	7. Veto arms sales to Saudis N	11. Marijuana liberalized rules N
4. CASH Act N	8. Defense $$$, veto override Y	12. Electoral College objections Y

Election Results

Election	Name (Party)	Vote (%)	Cand. Spent	Ind. Exp. Support	Ind. Exp. Oppose
2020 General	Mo Brooks (R)............................	253,094 (96%)	$254,403	$4,489	$750
2020 Primary	Mo Brooks (R)............................	84,013 (75%)			
	Chris Lewis (R).................................	28,182 (25%)			

Prior winning percentages: 2018 (61%), 2016 (67%), 2014 (74%), 2012 (65%), 2010 (58%)

Mo Brooks, who in 2010 became the first Republican elected to the seat since 1868, has a boisterous style that has been accompanied by some legislative successes. A member of the maverick Freedom Caucus, he achieved celebrity status as the third candidate during the contentious Republican primary in 2017 for the special election to fill the remainder of the term of former Sen. Jeff Sessions. But his campaign left ill will among some Republicans. In January 2021, he gained renewed attention when he challenged the outcome of the usually routine count of the Electoral College votes, which declared that Joe Biden had won the presidential election. Two months later, he launched another bid for the Senate after Sen. Richard Shelby announced his retirement.

Brooks was born in Charleston, South Carolina. His father was raised "dirt poor" in Chattanooga Tennessee, and later worked as an electrical engineer. His mother grew up without electricity or indoor plumbing, and later taught high school economics and government in Huntsville. "Out of that poverty, my parents learned that you'd better work, and work hard," Brooks said. He studied economics and political science at Duke University and got his law degree from the University of Alabama. As one of 11 Republicans in the state House, the Alabama Taxpayers' Defense Fund gave him its No. 1 ranking for opposing tax increases. He served two years as district attorney, lost reelection, then in 1996 was elected to the Madison County Commission.

Brooks won his House seat in two hard-fought battles. In the Republican primary, he defeated first-term Rep. Parker Griffith, who had been elected as a Democrat but switched parties in December 2009. Brooks campaigned on the theme that the district "deserves a congressman who acts honorably." He defeated Griffith, 51%-33%. In the general election, he was opposed by Steve Raby, the longtime chief of staff to former Sen. Howell Heflin of Alabama. The Democrat shunned his party label, focusing almost exclusively on local issues. Brooks took on hot-button issues, declaring that he favored repealing the Affordable Care Act and deporting all illegal immigrants. He won, 58%-42%.

He made a quick impression. Within four months, he charged in a House speech that the United States is at "risk of insolvency and bankruptcy because the socialist members of this body choose to spend money that we do not have." Several months later, at a forum back home, Brooks said he supported any measure "short of shooting them" to force illegal immigrants back to their home countries. Latino lawmakers and groups condemned his remarks.

Brooks landed in an even bigger controversy in 2014. Asked by conservative radio host Laura Ingraham about a statement that the Republican Party was alienating non-white voters, Brooks responded: "This is a part of the war on whites that's being launched by the Democratic Party." Democrats blasted Brooks for playing the race card. He was unapologetic.

His committee assignments have matched up well with his district. On Science, Space and Technology, Brooks has been part of a bipartisan coalition that has sought to reshape space policy with a stepping-stone approach to exploration. That plan featured access by American astronauts on American rockets to an international space station, and envisioned long-term plans for planetary destinations such as Mars. On the Armed Services Committee, he said the United States should spend what it takes to fight terrorism. Following House passage in 2016 of the defense spending bill, he claimed credit for provisions that support Redstone Arsenal programs for military capability in space and small satellite technology development. He urged the Trump administration to base the Space Force at Redstone.

In what had been an entrenched Democratic district less than a decade ago, Brooks secured his House seat. In the 2012 primary, he again dispatched Griffith in the Republican primary, with 71 percent of the vote. He endorsed Ted Cruz and kept his distance from Donald Trump during the 2016 presidential primary. He used terms such as "serial adultery," "notorious flip-flopper" and "gutter mouth" to describe Trump and said he would never endorse him. After Trump won the nomination, Brooks said he was supporting the entire Republican ticket without mentioning Trump by name.

In May 2017, Brooks joined the campaign to succeed Sessions, after he quit the Senate to become Trump's attorney general. He stressed his support for Trump's "America First" agenda, though he criticized the president for his "public water-boarding" of Sessions in his management of the Justice Department. He described Senate Majority Leader Mitch McConnell as "head of the swamp" and said the Kentuckian has "got to go". Attacks on Brooks accomplished their objective of weakening the outsider candidate, who ran third with 20 percent of the vote in the July primary. In the subsequent runoff, former state Chief Justice Roy Moore and appointed Sen. Luther Strange faced each other, which led to Moore's nomination and his subsequent defeat by Democrat Doug Jones. Later that year, Brooks had surgery for prostate cancer.

Subsequently, Brooks faced Republican primary challengers. In 2018 Clayton Hinchman, an Iraq war veteran, criticized Brooks for his support of Cruz in 2016 and for insufficient funding for Redstone. Brooks won the primary, 61%-39%. In 2020, Chris Lewis, a retired Navy officer, sought the GOP nomination. He promised "a new vitality" for the district and "a real champion" for the military. In a curious twist, state House Speaker Al McCutcheon—a resident of the 5th Congressional District—endorsed Lewis. In a 43-second video tape, he said, "It is time to make a change" in representation. Brooks won this time, 75%-25%. The GOP contests might be a residue of the bitter Senate primary. McCutcheon's influence in the 2022 redistricting could prove problematic for Brooks.

In the weeks following Trump's 2020 defeat, Brooks delivered several speeches to the House in which he claimed—without direct evidence—that Trump had been the victim of voter fraud. On January 6, he joined Trump in speaking to the crowd behind the White House before many of them joined the protest at the Capitol that day. It was time to start "taking down names and kicking ass," he told the rally. Following the riot at the Capitol, he tweeted that the violence was "despicable, un-American and tears at the fabric of our great republic." Weeks later, Democratic Rep. Pramila Jayapal of Washington included Brooks among House members that the House Ethics Committee should investigate "for their involvement in instigating and aiding the deadly attack at the Capitol."

In March 2021, a month after Shelby's retirement announcement, Brooks declared his candidacy for the Senate. "I don't cut and run," he told supporters in Huntsville. :I stand strong when the going gets tough. In April, Trump endorsed him with a statement, "Few Republicans have as much courage and fight" as Brooks. Although Trump's support was expected to provide a big boost, Brooks faced lingering objections from his unsuccessful Senate bid in 2017.

AL-5: North Alabama   Cook Partisan Voting Index: R+17

Population		Race and Ethnicity		Income	
Total	735,858	White	75.00%	Median Income	$59,950
Land area (sq. miles)	3,677	Black	18.30%	District Income Rank	264
Pop/ sq mi	200.11	Latino	5.50%	Poverty Rate	13.20%
Born in State	59.20%	Asian	1.70%	With health insurance	90.70%
		Two or more races	2.60%	Cash public assistance	2.50%
Age Groups		Other	2.30%	Food stamp/SNAP	10.70%
Under 18	21.60%				
18-34	22.00%	**Education**		**Work**	
35-64	39.30%	H.S grad or less	37.80%	White Collar	40.40%
Over 64	17.10%	Some college	28.70%	Sales and Service	35.00%
		College Degree, 4 yr	20.90%	Blue Collar	24.60%
Military		Post grad	12.60%	Government	15.70%
Veteran/ Active Duty	9.90%				

2020 Pres. Vote	Trump	228,397	(62%)	Biden	129,813	(36%)			
2016 Pres. Vote	Trump	200,570	(64%)	Clinton	97,159	(31%)	Johnson	10,223	(3%)

Huntsville, Decatur: After the Soviets put up Sputnik in 1957, the Redstone Arsenal in Huntsville became the nation's foremost missile development center. Then a sleepy town huddled around a well-preserved, early-19th-century settlement, Huntsville grew to become the center of Alabama's northern tier. Residents are fond of referring to their hometown as "Rocket City." The first of the large U.S. ballistic missiles were developed here. On the grounds of Redstone, NASA built its Marshall Space Flight Center in the 1960s, and the Huntsville-Decatur area soon achieved high-tech critical mass. With leadership from Wernher von Braun and other German engineers, Redstone and Marshall built Explorer 1, the first American orbiting satellite; the Mercury-Redstone vehicle that boosted astronaut Alan Shepard into suborbital flight; and the Saturn V rocket that sent men to the moon. Later, Marshall produced Skylab and developed the space shuttle's main engines and solid-rocket boosters. The Obama administration, wary of large-scale space exploration programs funded entirely by the government, scuttled the Constellation program. Still, the Arsenal has more than 44,000 employees. In December 2019, the director of Marshall said that the arsenal would exceed 50,000 employees by 2025.

Huntsville has diversified its high-tech economy in recent years, and space-related jobs have evolved with a broader defense focus. In 2018, the Boeing facility won a $6.6 billion contract for missile-defense development and support. The FBI opened a terrorist explosive device analytical center at the Arsenal and planned more than 1,500 jobs by 2021, including relocations from the Washington D.C. area, with the strong support of Senate Appropriations Committee chairman Richard Shelby of Alabama. Over several decades, city leaders carefully cultivated Cummings Research Park, which is the second-largest research park in the nation and home to more than 300 companies, 26,000 employees and 13,000 students specializing in technology-based manufacturing, biotechnology and pharmaceutical firms that transform research into business opportunities. Blue-collar jobs also are increasing. At its engine production factory in Huntsville, Toyota expects to increase its workforce to 1,800 employees in 2021.

Huntsville, which has annexed land in Limestone and Morgan counties, in 2017 surpassed Mobile as the third-largest city in Alabama. Demographers predict that it will replace Birmingham as number one by 2024. Like high-tech centers in places like Cambridge, Austin and Silicon Valley, Huntsville has attracted many educated and motivated people who also are socially liberal. After a federal judge in 2015 ruled that same-sex marriages were legal in Alabama, the city became a destination wedding site for gays in the South.

The 5th Congressional District of Alabama takes in most of the space counties. For decades, most voters here were staunch New Deal Democrats, liberal on economics and not much interested in race issues. Sen. John Sparkman, who taught school and practiced law in Huntsville, was the party's vice presidential nominee in 1952. The district has voted Republican for president since 1980 but did not elect a Republican to Congress until 2010. Of the five counties in the district, Huntsville-based Madison County has nearly 60 percent of the voters.

Gary Palmer (R)

Elected 2014, 4th term, b. May 14, 1954; Hackleburg, AL; Northwest AL Junior College, Att., 1974; University of AL, B.S., 1977; Presbyterian; Married (Ann Cushing); 3 children.

Professional Career: Engineer, 1977-1989; Founder/President, AL Policy Institute (formerly AL Family Alliance), 1989-2013; Founding board member, State Policy Network, 1992-1998.

DC Office: 207 CHOB 20515, 202-225-4921, Fax: 202-225-2082, palmer.house.gov

State Offices: Birmingham, 205-968-1290; Clanton, 205-280-6846; Oneonta, 205-625-4160.

Committees: House Republican Policy Committee Chairman. *Select Committee on the Climate Crisis.*

Group Ratings

	ADA	ACLU	AFL-CIO	LCV	COC	HAFA	ACU	CFG	FRC
2020	**	15%	**	0%	-	87%	97%	**	-
2019	0%	C	19%	0%	66%	C	98%	100%	100%

Almanac Ratings 2019-2020

	Economy	Social	Foreign	Composite
Liberal	25%	5%	11%	14%
Conservative	75%	95%	89%	86%

Key Votes of the 116th Congress

1. U.S./Mex./Can. trade deal	Y	5. Russia sanctions	Y	9. Firearms background checks N
2. First Coronavirus response	Y	6. Troops in Syria	Y	10. Spending at the border	Y
3. HEROES Act	N	7. Veto arms sales to Saudis	N	11. Marijuana liberalized rules	N/A
4. CASH Act	N	8. Defense $$$, veto override	N	12. Electoral College objections Y

Election Results

Election	Name (Party)	Vote (%)	Cand. Spent	Ind. Exp. Support	Ind. Exp. Oppose
2020 General	Gary Palmer (R)............................	274,160 (97%)	$558,178	$49	$750

Prior winning percentages: 2018 (69%), 2016 (75%), 2014 (76%)

Republican Gary Palmer, elected in 2014 as a political outsider, allied with conservative and free-spirited Republicans. He later earned his party stripes and was twice selected to chair the Republican Policy Committee. In that leadership post, he has had a low public profile.

Palmer grew up on a small farm in Hackleburg Alabama. He was the first in his family to go to college, where he studied engineering. He started his career in the private sector before cofounding the Alabama Policy Institute in 1989. As president of the think tank with ties to the right-leaning American Legislative Exchange Council, Palmer engaged for years in state-level policy issues, including tax and regulatory affairs.

Following the retirement of Rep. Spencer Bachus, a former chairman of the House Financial Services Committee, there was a wide-open contest to succeed him. The path to victory focused on the party primary, which began with a seven-candidate field. Palmer came in second in the initial vote, trailing GOP state Rep. Paul DeMarco, 33%-19%. In the runoff, the Club for Growth weighed in for

Palmer after deeming DeMarco pro-tax. Palmer got the Club's endorsement, along with $250,000 for ads that helped him go on the offensive. He also won the backing of prominent national Republicans such as Indiana Gov. Mike Pence. Palmer won the runoff handily, 64%-36%. He didn't need to break a sweat to defeat Democrat Mark Lester, 76%-24%.

Palmer joined forces with several incoming GOP members who said they would not back John Boehner for another term as Speaker in 2015. He told a local audience: "I cannot in good conscience support John Boehner because I think he lost his legitimacy to lead" after bringing to the House floor bills that most Republican members opposed. Palmer later said he regretted making that pledge because it jeopardized his ability to land good committee assignments. But he had told Boehner before the election that he would need to keep his word to his constituents. As he later recounted his conversation with the Speaker, "not only would I lose their confidence, but I would lose his. I think he respected that." As he predicted, Palmer fell short on influential committee posts. In a delegation where each of the other five Republicans served on either the Appropriations or Armed Services committees, Palmer initially shifted among several less influential panels.. In January 2021, he gained a seat on the influential Energy and Commerce Committee—the first Alabama member to join the panel in more than 30 years, he said.

Palmer has remained a policy entrepreneur. Summarizing his first term, Palmer told a local reporter that he had become "one of the top policy thinkers in our [Republican] conference." He cited his participation with a handful of Budget Committee members who crafted a compromise on the annual budget resolution with Majority Leader Kevin McCarthy. He also contributed to the party's "Better Way" policy agenda, which included eliminating the Environmental Protection Agency's authority to regulate greenhouse gases.

During debate in April 2017 of their proposal to repeal the Affordable Care Act, House Republicans included a plan prepared by Palmer for a $15 billion federal high-risk pool for people with pre-existing conditions. The plan, which he termed "invisible risk-sharing," would give states a block grant with more flexibility to meet the needs of Medicaid-eligible beneficiaries.

Palmer occasionally distanced himself from Donald Trump. In October 2016, during the closing weeks of the presidential campaign, Palmer condemned as "offensive and inappropriate" the lewd remarks Trump made on a 2005 video recording. But he subsequently added that supporting Trump over Hillary Clinton "is not a difficult choice." A longtime friend of former Sen. Jeff Sessions, Palmer in August 2018 told Politico that there were other officials at the Justice Department who the then-attorney general was "not being well-served by." Trump ousted Sessions that November.

Following the 2018 election, Palmer successfully ran for the open position of Republican Policy Committee chairman against Rep. Dave Schweikert of Arizona, who had more seniority but had become the target of an ethics investigation. He cited his career-long experience as a problem-solver and in "developing and promoting sound policies." Palmer became the first Freedom Caucus member to take a GOP leadership position. After winning a second term as chairman, he said he was committed to building the committee "as a dependable in-house think tank for House Republicans."

In his district, Palmer's chief reelection concern has been a contest with a more "establishment" Republican candidate. In his three reelection campaigns, he got a free pass in the primary. Democrat Danner Kline, a craft-beer industry entrepreneur, opposed Palmer in 2018 and attacked Trump's character. Palmer outspent Kline 5-to-1 and won, 69%-31%.In 2020, he ran unopposed. Palmer was among the early group of Republicans listed as potential challengers to Democratic Sen. Doug Jones in 2020, though he did not take any steps toward a candidacy.

AL-6: Central Alabama   **Cook Partisan Voting Index: R+22**

Population		Race and Ethnicity		Income	
Total	699,605	White	78.60%	Median Income	$69,072
Land area (sq. miles)	4,171	Black	16.00%	District Income Rank	175
Pop/ sq mi	167.74	Latino	5.10%	Poverty Rate	9.50%
Born in State	72.30%	Asian	1.60%	With health insurance	92.80%
		Two or more races	1.70%	Cash public assistance	0.70%
Age Groups		Other	2.20%	Food stamp/SNAP	7.20%
Under 18	22.70%				
18-34	21.10%	**Education**		**Work**	
35-64	39.60%	H.S grad or less	32.80%	White Collar	45.30%
Over 64	16.50%	Some college	28.90%	Sales and Service	33.90%
		College Degree, 4 yr	23.90%	Blue Collar	20.90%
Military		Post grad	14.60%	Government	13.40%
Veteran/ Active Duty	7.40%				

2020 Pres. Vote	Trump	248,259	(67%)	Biden	117,545	(32%)		
2016 Pres. Vote	Trump	233,494	(70%)	Clinton	86,117	(26%)	Johnson	8,709	(3%)

Birmingham Suburbs, Shelby County: Birmingham, once one of America's booming industrial cities, was better known in the middle of the 20th century as a center of white resistance to the civil rights movement. Its prospects in the 21st century have been more hopeful. This is a new city by Southern standards. Before the Civil War, there was nothing here but a few creeks running below Red Mountain. But Red Mountain is almost pure iron ore. With the additional mining of coal, Birmingham —the self-styled Magic City—had by 1890 the South's largest steel mills. In the early 20th century, as the statue of Vulcan, the Roman god of fire and metalworking, looked out over the smokestack-filled valley, Birmingham seemed prosperous and the most progressive city in the South. But the worldwide overcapacity of steel and technological obsolescence at home sent the American steel industry into long-term decline starting in the 1950s.

Meanwhile, Birmingham's political leaders plotted to avoid desegregation. The city's violent reaction to the civil rights movement made a vivid impression on the rest of the country. Police Commissioner (and Democratic National Committeeman at the time) Bull Connor set dogs and fire hoses against peaceful demonstrators, and Ku Klux Klansmen bombed the 16th Street Baptist Church, killing four young girls in 1963. Those images haunted Birmingham for a generation. As the more civic-minded Atlanta became the new heart of the South, Birmingham suffered from uninspired business leadership and it downsized as a regional force.

In recent years, Birmingham has worked to improve race relations and develop a new economic base. Health care is a major industry. The city has some of the largest and most advanced medical care centers in the South and is renowned for its sports medicine facilities and specialists who tend to the ailments of famous athletes. While Atlanta's banks foundered and were acquired by outsiders, Birmingham became the largest Southern banking center outside Charlotte, North Carolina. But city leaders have worried that the viability of the downtown area and white movement to newer suburbs have continued the racial polarization.

Whites have been moving out of Birmingham's Jefferson County to Shelby County, which grew 44 percent in the 1990s, 36 percent in the next decade and 12 percent from 2010 to 2019—the fastest growth in the state. (The African-American population in Shelby has increased as well, though the county is about 83 percent white.) Jefferson County, once more Republican than most of Alabama, votes Democratic in close statewide elections; of the four largest counties in Alabama, Shelby is the most Republican. Metropolitan planners projected continuing large increases for Shelby, but little change for Jefferson, where physical expansion is limited by the hills and there has been virtually no growth in the past decade, even in prosperous neighborhoods. Shelby County played a vital role in a civil rights debate when it challenged the constitutionality of a provision of the Voting Rights Act that required most Southern states to report ballot changes to the Justice Department. In a landmark 2013 ruling, the U.S. Supreme Court agreed with Shelby County that it was no longer required to get "preclearance" of each voting change. Some congressional Democrats have advocated a statutory reversal of the ruling and have named their legislation in the memory of Rep. John Lewis of Georgia, the civil rights icon, who died in 2020.

The 6th Congressional District of Alabama is the suburban Birmingham-area district and strongly Republican. It includes Shelby County and more than half of Jefferson County, including prosperous Hoover with upscale estates and shopping malls, and stretches toward Tuscaloosa and Montgomery. Jefferson retains a slight majority of the district vote and Shelby has 30 percent. Overall, Jefferson remains nearly three times larger than Shelby. This has been one of the most Republican districts in the nation. Mitt Romney got 74 percent in 2012, his ninth-best in the nation. In his two contests, the vote for Donald Trump dipped to 70 percent and then to 67 percent in 2020.

Terri Sewell (D)

Elected 2010, 6th term, b. Jan 01, 1965; Huntsville, AL; Princeton University, A.B., 1986; Oxford University, M.A., 1988; Harvard University Law School, J.D., 1992; Protestant - Unspecified Christian; Divorced.

Professional Career: Clerk, U.S. District Court judge, 1993-1994; practicing Attorney, 1994-2010.

DC Office: 2201 RHOB 20515, 202-225-2665, Fax: 202-226-9567, sewell.house.gov

State Offices: Birmingham, 205-254-1960; Montgomery, 334-262-1919; Selma, 334-877-4414; Tuscaloosa, 205-752-5380.

Committees: *Ways & Means*: Health; Select Revenue Measures; Social Security.

Group Ratings

	ADA	ACLU	AFL-CIO	LCV	COC	HAFA	ACU	CFG	FRC
2020	**	74%	**	90%	-	0%	6%	**	-
2019	85%	C	100%	97%	68%	C	7%	12%	5%

Almanac Ratings 2019-2020

	Economy	Social	Foreign	Composite
Liberal	58%	60%	80%	66%
Conservative	42%	40%	20%	34%

Key Votes of the 116th Congress

1. U.S./Mex./Can. trade deal Y	5. Russia sanctions Y	9. Firearms background checks Y
2. First Coronavirus response Y	6. Troops in Syria Y	10. Spending at the border Y
3. HEROES Act Y	7. Veto arms sales to Saudis Y	11. Marijuana liberalized rules Y
4. CASH Act Y	8. Defense $$$, veto override Y	12. Electoral College objections N

Election Results

Election	Name (Party)	Vote (%)	Cand. Spent	Ind. Exp. Support	Ind. Exp. Oppose
2020 General	Terri Sewell (D).............................	225,742 (97%)	$1,684,227		$7,863

Prior winning percentages: 2016 (98%), 2014 (98%), 2012 (76%), 2010 (73%)

Long a rising star within the Democratic caucus, Sewell spent her first decade in the House quietly building seniority, securing prestigious committee assignments and gaining respect among her colleagues. Along the way, Sewell has shown a lifelong knack for making friends who become powerful political allies.

Sewell was born in Huntsville and raised in Selma, a hotbed of activity for the civil rights movement. She grew up near the famed Edmund Pettus Bridge, site of the 1965 Bloody Sunday clash between protest marchers and state troopers. Sewell's family offered shelter for wayward travelers making the march from Selma to Montgomery in 1965. Hailing from such a place, "you appreciate the significance of your elders' fight for voting rights and civil rights," said Sewell, who was two months old at the time of the march. Her mother, Nancy Sewell, was the first African-American woman elected to the Selma City Council. In the past, Sewell opposed renaming the Edmund Pettus Bridge, arguing the name should serve as a reminder of Bloody Sunday. But in the wake of George Floyd's killing, she told The Birmingham News that "the only person's name that should be on the bridge" is that of the late Rep. John Lewis of Georgia, one of the protestors beaten that day.

Sewell earned her undergraduate degree from Princeton University. During that time, she took part in a Big Sister program and drew inspiration from the mentor assigned to her, Michelle Robinson, later first lady Michelle Obama. While Sewell was writing her senior thesis at Princeton, she met former Democratic Rep. Shirley Chisholm of New York, the first African-American woman elected to Congress and a 1972 candidate for president, who was retired by then and teaching at Mount Holyoke College. "I don't know if anybody could ever follow in Shirley Chisholm's footsteps, but I can tell you that I was inspired by her whole life story," Sewell said.

Sewell later studied politics at Oxford University on a scholarship, earning a master's degree. A theater buff, she dabbled in drama while at Oxford, directing and starring in the play For Colored Girls Who Have Considered Suicide When the Rainbow is Enuf by Ntozake Shange, which also starred fellow Oxonian and future Obama and Biden adviser Susan Rice. Later, while earning her law degree from Harvard, Sewell was a classmate of future President Barack Obama.

After law school, Sewell clerked for a U.S. District Court judge in Birmingham. In 1994 she moved to New York City to work at the Davis, Polk & Wardwell law firm. There, she befriended a fellow associate, Tina Rutnik, who would be better known by her married name: Sen. Kirsten Gillibrand of New York. Sewell eventually returned home to Alabama to care for her ailing father, working as a bond lawyer and a partner in a Birmingham law firm.

When Democratic Rep. Artur Davis decided to leave the House to run for governor, House Democratic women brainstormed female recruits for the open seat. Gillibrand recruited her old friend. Sewell eventually jumped into the primary contest against eight other candidates. Sewell had lower name recognition than her rivals, but she made up for it by outraising the other candidates with both a local and national fundraising network that included the support of EMILY's List. She finished first in the Democratic primary with 37 percent of the vote. Jefferson County Commissioner Sheila Smoot snagged second place with 29 percent, setting up a runoff. Smoot got the endorsement of House Majority Whip James Clyburn. Sewell outspent her by nearly $1 million. In a relatively congenial runoff, Sewell won, 55%-45%. She has not faced a competitive contest since.

Once in Congress, she was elected freshman class president, and she spent her early years in Congress living in the Washington townhouse owned by Rep. Carolyn Maloney, a longtime boarding house for female members.

In the House, Sewell is more of a centrist than most of her Black Caucus colleagues. In 2019-2020, she was vice chair of the New Democrat Coalition—moderate House Democrats who work on job creation and innovation, often with business groups. In that role, Sewell pushed back against allegations from the then-chief of staff to freshman Rep. Alexandria Ocasio Cortez, that the New Democrats were comparable to "1940s Southern Democrats." Not one inclined to engage in controversy, Sewell nonetheless released a statement saying "to even insinuate that I, or any other member of the New Dems, would promote policies that are racist and hateful or ones that would negatively impact communities of color is deeply offensive and couldn't be further from the truth."

In 2013, then-Minority Whip Steny Hoyer of Maryland named Sewell as a chief deputy whip. With increased seniority, Sewell gained influential committee assignments. At Ways and Means, she brought a unique voice as an African-American woman with the perspective of underserved communities in the industrial and rural South. A longtime Intelligence Committee member, Sewell found herself at the center of the House investigation into Russian interference in the 2016 election.

More recently, Sewell was part of a movement of Black women to coalesce around former Vice President Joe Biden during the darkest moment of his presidential campaign—the winter of 2020—to deliver support and, eventually, the Democratic nomination. Six months later, Sewell was the focus of speculation that Biden might choose her as his vice presidential running mate.

Sewell likely will remain safe in redistricting, in any case. But she could become part of a Democratic strategy to seek a second district in Alabama with an African-American majority, or—at least—a district with African-American influence. That likely would require a division of her current district into two: a northern portion that would combine Tuscaloosa and large parts of Birmingham with rural Black Belt counties, and a southern portion that would stretch from the Mississippi border to the Georgia border and include a large part of Montgomery. Such a redistricting strategy almost certainly would require expansive use of the Voting Rights Act and the cooperation of federal judges.

AL-7: Central Alabama　　　　　　　　　　**Cook Partisan Voting Index:　D+19**

Population		Race and Ethnicity		Income	
Total	670,015	White	34.20%	Median Income	$38,023
Land area (sq. miles)	10,156	Black	62.60%	District Income Rank	433
Pop/ sq mi	65.97	Latino	3.70%	Poverty Rate	23.70%
Born in State	79.70%	Asian	1.20%	With health insurance	88.90%
		Two or more races	1.20%	Cash public assistance	2.10%
Age Groups		Other	0.80%	Food stamp/SNAP	21.50%
Under 18	21.60%				
18-34	26.10%	**Education**		**Work**	
35-64	35.30%	H.S grad or less	49.30%	White Collar	28.80%
Over 64	16.80%	Some college	29.10%	Sales and Service	41.80%
		College Degree, 4 yr	12.80%	Blue Collar	29.40%
Military		Post grad	8.70%	Government	16.90%
Veteran/ Active Duty	6.60%				

2020 Pres. Vote	Biden	210,707	(71%)	Trump	84,559	(28%)	
2016 Pres. Vote	Clinton	204,585	(69%)	Trump	83,916	(28%)	

Birmingham, Tuscaloosa, Parts of Montgomery: Alabama has learned to celebrate its Black heritage, building striking memorials to the civil rights movement in Montgomery and Birmingham, while acknowledging its history as ground zero of white resistance to the empowerment of Blacks in the 1950s and 1960s. Blacks first came here as slaves. The last slave ship to the United States, the Clotilde, docked in Mobile in 1859, where its cargo was then set free. Blacks were part of the great migration into the cotton lands after the Jacksonians swept the Indians out of the Southeast and sent them on their Trail of Tears to what is now Oklahoma. Today, Alabama's rural African Americans are still clustered in the Black Belt of fertile dark soil across the center of the state.

In Selma, founded by Alabama's one vice president, William Rufus King, Sheriff Jim Clark's troops beat up peaceful marchers on the Edmund Pettus Bridge in demonstrations that led to the march on Montgomery and the 1965 Voting Rights Act. Birmingham served as the nerve center of the civil rights movement, and downtown includes the 16th Street Baptist Church, the site of a 1963 bombing that killed four young Black girls and subsequently galvanized the movement. More recently, city leaders removed a Confederate monument in nearby Linn Park in the summer of 2020.

All 11 of Alabama's majority-Black counties are in the rich farm country of the Black Belt, but most Alabama Blacks now live in urban areas—one-quarter of them in metropolitan Birmingham.

After decades of decline, Birmingham pulled itself out of the spiral of abandoned neighborhoods, soaring joblessness and crime through the savvy use of public-private partnerships and other incentives. Numerous vacant and boarded up buildings have been supplanted by lofts and cafes for young professionals and empty-nesters, slowing migration to the suburbs. Crime zones like the Metropolitan Gardens public housing project were leveled and replaced with mixed-income apartments. The turnaround was slow, but by 2019, Birmingham saw 10,000 new jobs come to town.

The 7th Congressional District of Alabama, which was created in 1992, is a majority African-American district that sprawls from Birmingham and Tuscaloosa to the western Black precincts of Montgomery and nearly to Mobile County. Republican redistricting in 2011 made the 2nd and 3rd districts whiter and safer for the GOP, and further solidified the 7th for the Democrats.

The Alabama River flows on the district's eastern edge, while the Tombigbee River straddles the western border. The area is filled with old plantations and a thriving catfish industry. The district takes in part of Tuscaloosa, home of the University of Alabama, and nearby Vance, site of a Mercedes factory. Bessemer is the site of a giant Amazon warehouse where an attempt to establish a union in early 2021 failed by more than 2-to-1. Birmingham received an additional boost when President Barack Obama, in one of his final official actions, signed a proclamation designating the Birmingham Civil Rights District a national monument. This remains one of the poorest districts in the nation. Growth in Birmingham continues to be outpaced by other southern metro areas.

With its 63 percent African-American population, this is the only district in Alabama where Democrats have an expectation of victory. Biden got 71 percent here.

ALASKA

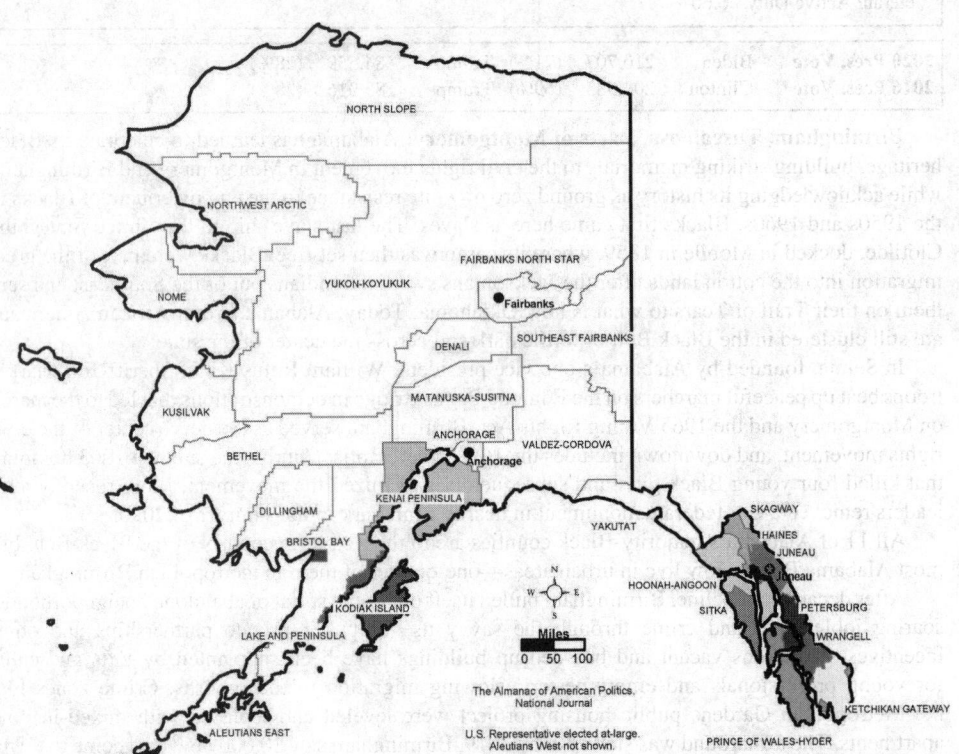

NORTH SLOPE

NORTHWEST ARCTIC

FAIRBANKS NORTH STAR

Fairbanks

YUKON-KOYUKUK

NOME

DENALI

SOUTHEAST FAIRBANKS

MATANUSKA-SUSITNA

KUSILVAK

ANCHORAGE

VALDEZ-CORDOVA

BETHEL

Anchorage

KENAI PENINSULA

DILLINGHAM

YAKUTAT

SKAGWAY

HAINES

JUNEAU

BRISTOL BAY

Juneau

KODIAK ISLAND

HOONAH-ANGOON

PETERSBURG

SITKA

LAKE AND PENINSULA

WRANGELL

Miles

0   50   100

KETCHIKAN GATEWAY

The Almanac of American Politics.
National Journal

ALEUTIANS EAST

U.S. Representative elected at-large.
Aleutians West not shown.

PRINCE OF WALES-HYDER

Alaska—far removed from the Lower 48, what Alaskans sometimes refer to as "Outside"—has a culture sometimes described as a blend of moralist and individualist. It is dependent on Washington for federal largesse, yet the relationship between Washington and Alaska is often fraught. Alaska at once depends on subsidies and special treatment and is resentful of what it considers Washington's heavy-handed intervention.

Secretary of State William Seward took advantage of an opportunity in 1867 to create an American Pacific empire by purchasing the region from Russia for $7.2 million. The Alaska territory owed much of its early growth to federal decisions. While the state burst into national consciousness with the Klondike Gold Rush of 1897, its largest city, Anchorage, had its beginnings in 1914 as the chief worksite for the federal government's Alaska Railroad, completed in 1923. Its famous sled dog race, the Iditarod, started in 1973 on a trail originally cleared and graded by the Army after Congress established the Alaska Road Commission in 1905. The race honors the 1925 emergency 20-team relay that delivered medicine from Nenana almost 700 miles to icebound Nome in 127 hours, saving hundreds of lives from a diphtheria outbreak. Alaska became strategic territory in World War II, when the Aleutian Islands of Attu and Kiska were invaded by a small force of Japanese, the only part of the United States occupied by a foreign enemy since the War of 1812. Alaska, with only 72,000 people when the war began, was connected to the states by the Army's Alcan Highway, completed in 1942; by 1943, there were 152,000 troops in the territory. Alaska is the only state facing Russia, across the Bering Strait and over the North Pole—you can see Russia from part of Alaska—and the state maintains a strategic geographic position. In the first half of 2020 alone, U.S. and Canadian forces intercepted Russian reconnaissance aircraft off Alaska on 10 occasions. The military is a major presence at Joint Base Elmendorf-Richardson near Anchorage and at Fort Wainwright and Eielson Air Force Base near Fairbanks, with interceptors for the national missile defense system not far to the south at Fort Greely. The state also has the highest per capita rate of military veterans in the nation.

The third least-populated state and the least densely populated, Alaska's 731,000 people amount to less than one-quarter of one percent of the nation's total; births fell in 2019 to their lowest level in 20 years, and in-migration dropped to its lowest level since 1988, during an oil bust. Alaska's land area is equal to one-fifth of the Lower 48. If superimposed on the continental United States, Alaska would stretch from Florida to California. The westernmost Aleutians are closer to Tokyo than to Juneau and farther west than Wellington, New Zealand. Many Alaskans have no access to state roads and are reachable only by boat, airplane, dog sleds and snow machines; its insularity enabled Blockbuster Video to last a decade longer than almost anywhere else before its final store closed in 2018.The rusted, green-and-white bus where Christopher McCandless starved to death in 1992 became a symbol of the Alaskan wilderness after Jon Krakauer told his story in Into the Wild it became such a popular destination that the state had to remove the bus by helicopter in 2020 it to prevent tourists from getting harmed looking for it.

About two-thirds of the population resides in Anchorage and the nearby Kenai Peninsula and Matanuska-Susitna ("Mat-Su") Valley. This plus the Fairbanks area, accounting for about one-eighth of the population, are the fastest-growing parts of Alaska. The Panhandle, with about one-tenth of the population, is the old Alaska, its towns settled by Russians and built up against steep mountains on inlets from the Pacific. This includes the state capital of Juneau, which is inaccessible by road— you have to ferry or fly in. The rest of the population lives in the rural "Bush" and the Aleutians, scattered in small towns, Native settlements and the wilderness. (Only in Alaska does the term "Bush Democrat" not refer to a cross-party supporter of the presidential dynasty.)

Alaska became a state in January 1959. While this technically ended federal dominance, Washington remains the largest landowner in Alaska, with roughly 60 percent of the state's total area under the supervision of more than a dozen federal agencies, including national parks, wildlife refuges, national forests, military bases and the North Slope National Petroleum Reserve. Alaskans continue to seek federal subsidies for intrastate air service, loan guarantees for the fishing industry and funding for the Alaska Railroad. The state's special needs, as longtime Sen. Ted Stevens used to argue, justify its special treatment. Sometimes the state and the federal government agree. In 2015, President Barack Obama acted to rename Mount McKinley, the nation's highest peak, "Denali," its ancestral name, and the state's two Republican senators successfully lobbied President Donald Trump not to change it back, as Trump had promised as a candidate. But such agreement is not always the case.

Alaska's forbidding terrain is responsible for some of its economic assets. In 1959, Alaska's economy depended on fishing and the military, and they continue to be important. For two decades, Alaska has reeled in the highest volume of fish of any state. Alaska has major mines producing gold, copper, coal and zinc, although the long-proposed Pebble Mine appeared to hit a surprising dead-end under the pro-resource Trump administration in 2020. The copper and gold mine had been controversial for its impact on the environment, including a major sockeye salmon fishery in the Bristol Bay region in Southwest Alaska. Both of Alaska's Republican senators concurred with the decision to shelve the proposal. Alaska has more aircraft per capita than any other state; private contractors provide much of the Postal Service's deliveries to the Bush. Tourism had become the No. 2 private employer, with cruise ships prowling the intra-coastal inlets amid glaciers and grizzlies and docking in Anchorage for side trips to Denali National Park and Preserve; warming of the Bering Sea has opened new ports of call. But the coronavirus devastated this sector—a 99 percent decline in trips during a year when the state had been expecting 1.4 million cruise tourists and $1 billion of economic impact. The pandemic also pushed Ravn Air Group, the state's largest rural airline, into bankruptcy.

Twelve Native corporations created by the Alaska Native Claims Settlement Act have proved to be successful, not only in providing dividend income, elderly benefits and scholarships and employment opportunities for Natives, but also in helping them preserve Native traditions and adapt to Alaska's market economy. One Alaska Native company, the Arctic Slope Regional Corporation, has aggressively sought drilling opportunities, fueled by $7.5 billion in federal contracts over 10 years, though other Alaska Native groups, such as the Gwich'in, worried about the potential environmental impact. Indeed, not all is rosy. Native villages in the Bush have little in the way of a private-sector economy; alcoholism and suicide rates remain high. Alaska has the highest rate of sexual assault of any state; about one-third of Alaska women have experienced sexual violence during their lives. Just 64 percent of Alaska Natives graduated from high school on time in 2016, almost 17 points below the rate for white students.

Still, something has transformed Alaska—something not fully envisioned by those who obtained statehood in 1959. Within a decade, Alaska's economy and public life were reshaped by the discovery of North Slope oil. It began suddenly, almost accidentally, as Arco chief executive Robert Anderson, after seven dry wells on Prudhoe Bay, decided to use a nearby drilling rig to make another try—and a natural gas flare shot 30 feet in the air. The North Slope oil field proved to be the greatest single strike in U.S. history.

It was not clear in 1968 who owned the oil or how it could be taken out. The Statehood Act of 1959 gave the state the right to choose its own public lands, but only after settling Native land claims. Because the Arctic Ocean ice broke up in late July back then, and for only six weeks, the only feasible way to get the oil out was a pipeline. Environmentalists opposed that option for fears —which proved unfounded—that it would destroy the delicate permafrost and interfere with caribou migrations. Congress passed the Alaska Natives Claims Settlement Act in 1971 and a pipeline bill in 1973, but the pipeline had to be built on stilts and wasn't opened until 1977. Then in 1980, after astute lobbying by environmentalists, Congress passed—over the objections of Alaska's two senators and Rep. Don Young—the Alaska National Interest Lands Conservation Act, which set aside 159 million acres as national parks, national monuments or wilderness: one-third of the state was kept from development. It has paid environmental dividends. Caribou had fallen to just 75,000 in 1976, before increasing to 500,000 in 2002 and settling in at 244,000 by 2018.

Oil provides most of Alaska's revenue—historically around 85 percent—and this enabled the state to abolish its income tax in 1980. (Alaska doesn't have a state sales tax, either.) In 1976, Alaskans approved a constitutional amendment to establish a Permanent Fund for petroleum revenues, and Republican Gov. Jay Hammond helped enact it. Each year, every qualified resident—man, woman and child—receives a dividend based on a five-year rolling average of the Permanent Fund's financial performance, which is now largely generated by stock, bond and real estate investments, rather than oil revenue. "The dividend has turned Alaska into a shivering paradox," Mark Oppenheimer wrote in Politico. "Despite its proud libertarian streak, they are the only Americans living the socialist dream of a guaranteed income." However, fluctuations in the oil markets have squeezed the state budget, and revenues have been used to fill budget holes; the $992 dividend in 2020 was the smallest since 2013.

For years, efforts to develop Alaska's energy resources beyond the North Slope were stymied, causing no end of friction. The state's congressional delegation, despite its relative seniority, was unable to overcome the opposition to oil drilling in the Arctic National Wildlife Refuge, east of Prudhoe Bay. Obama made moves to limit oil and gas drilling, but the Trump administration expanded exploration and drilling. The state's petro-fueled hayride has been hampered by the fluctuation in petroleum prices. Prior to the pandemic, Alaska was stuck with an unemployment rate of 5.8 percent at a time when the national rate was 3.5 percent. A longer-term challenge for the state is climate change. In spring 2019, Alaska's temperatures were six degrees warmer than the previous seasonal record, and July ended up as the state's warmest month ever, with Anchorage hitting an unprecedented 90 degrees. Arctic sea ice coverage plummeted, putting polar bears and walruses at risk, and the state experienced a lengthy wildfire season and vulnerability to leaf-eating insects. While global warming has had some positives locally, such as the emergence of newly ice-free paths for high-speed internet cables to be laid to Asia and Europe, the negative effects—from thawing permafrost to inundated coastal communities to declining fish stocks—have become worrisome. This has made big investors skittish: Wells Fargo, JPMorgan Chase, and Goldman Sachs have said they aren't directly funding Arctic oil and gas projects.

Alaska's congressional delegation has been notable for its longevity. Young won his House seat in a 1973 special election and, despite occasional turbulence, has been reelected ever since. Meanwhile, even though the state is about one-third non-white, the intense focus on the oil sector and its rural, gun-friendly nature has helped make Alaska Republican. It does, however, have a maverick streak: Bill Walker, an independent, won the governorship with a Democratic running mate in 2014, and a coalition of 17 Democrats, two independents and three Republicans forged a majority in the state House after the 2016 election. On the GOP side, Sen. Lisa Murkowski has been one of the most likely in her conference to break party ranks. Democrats were excited in 2020 about their chances of unseating Young and Sen. Dan Sullivan, but they fell short again, and while the presidential race was closer than usual, only Young had a winning margin not in the double digits. Showing their maverick streak, however, voters approved a ballot measure that will create open primaries, ranked-choice voting, and tighter campaign-finance disclosure rules.

Cook Partisan Voting Index: R+9

Population		Race and Ethnicity		Income	
Total	731,545	White	64.20%	Median Income	75,463
Land area (sq. miles)	570,641	Black	3.10%	State Income Rank	12 out of 50
Pop/ sq mi	1.28	Latino	7.20%	Poverty Rate	10.10%
Born in state	42.90%	Asian	8.40%	With health insurance	87.80%
		Two or more races	7.90%	Cash public assistance	6.00%
Age Groups		Other	18.90%	Food stamp/SNAP	10.3%
Under 18	24.60%				
18-34	25.40%	**Education**		**Work**	
35-64	37.70%	H.S grad or less	35.20%	White Collar	38.30%
Over 64	12.40%	Some college	34.70%	Sales and Service	36.90%
		College Degree, 4 yr	18.50%	Blue Collar	24.80%
Military		Post grad	11.70%	Government	23.60%
Veteran/ Active Duty	14.00%				

Presidential Politics

2020 Caucus (D)	Biden (D)	10,834(55%)	Sanders (D)	8,755(45%)			
2020 Primary (D)	Biden (D)	9,862(50%)	Sanders (D)	7,764(39%)	Warren (D)	1,402 (7%)	
2016 Caucus (D)	Sanders (D)	8,447(80%)	Clinton (D)	2,146(20%)			
2016 Caucus (R)	Cruz (R)	8,369(36%)	Trump (R)	7,740(34%)	Rubio (R)	3,488(15%)	
	Carson (R)	2,492(11%)					
2020 Pres. Vote	Trump (R)	189,951(53%)	Biden (D)	153,778(43%)			
2016 Pres. Vote	Trump (R)	163,387(51%)	Clinton (D)	116,454(37%)	Johnson (L)	18,725 (6%)	

Donald Trump carried the state by 53%-43%, a comfortable win in a state that has gone Democratic only once in its 60-year history. But Biden's share of the vote was the highest for a Democratic presidential candidate since Lyndon Johnson carried the state in his 1964 national landslide. Trump's 10-point 2020 win was narrower than his 14percentage point win in 2016, which matched Mitt Romney's 2012 margin.

While federal resources flow to the state, Alaska's voters also have a healthy suspicion of Washington, particularly when it comes to the federal government's oversight of the state's natural resources. Many Alaskans chafed at Obama administration environmental orders limiting oil and gas extraction. Trump went hard the other way, opening up the Arctic National Wildlife Refuge for drilling and relaxing hunting restrictions on federal lands.

While both parties traditionally held presidential caucuses in the state, Democrats switched to a primary in 2020. The election was originally scheduled for April 4.But in-person voting was canceled and mail voting was extended for six days in response to the first wave of the coronavirus pandemic. As a result, the primary was the first that concluded after Bernie Sanders suspended his campaign; Biden beat him, 49%-39%.

Alaska has traditionally been hospitable to third-party candidates: in 1992 Ross Perot won 28 percent here, his second-best showing in the country; and in 2000, Ralph Nader captured 10 percent of the vote, his best showing. In 2016, Libertarian nominee Gary Johnson won about 6 percent— up from 2 percent in 2012—and Green Party standard-bearer Jill Stein managed almost 2 percent. But as was true nationally, third-party support collapsed in Alaska in 2020. Libertarian nominee Jo Jorgensen managed just 2.5 percent and the Green Party didn't reach 1 percent. In 2020, voters narrowly passed a referendum to allow for ranked-choice voting, which could benefit third-party candidates in future elections.

When Alaska and Hawaii were admitted to the union in 1959, it was expected that Alaska would vote Democratic and Hawaii Republican. The opposite occurred. Rural areas in the northern and western regions of the state, including hundreds of tiny settlements of Native Alaskans, are the most Democratic, while Republicans are strongest in the Mat-Su Valley, containing the northern suburbs of Anchorage.

Neither Trump nor Biden made a 2019-2020 campaign stop in Alaska.

Congressional Districts

117th Congress Lineup	1R	116th Congress Lineup	1R

Mike Dunleavy (R)

Elected 2018, term expires 2022, 1st term; b. May 5, 1961, Scranton, PA; Misericordia University, B.A., 1983 ; University of Alaska Fairbanks, M.Ed., 1991; Catholic; Married (Rose); 3 children.

Elected Office: AK Senate, 2012-2018.

Professional Career: Educational consultant; Program Manager, Alaska Statewide Mentor Project; Director, K-12 Outreach, University of Alaska; Logging camp employee.

Office: 120 4th Street P.O. Box 110001, Juneau, 99801
Lt. Gov.: Kevin Meyer (R)
State Legislature: Senate: 7D, 13R **House:** 15D, 23R, 2I

Election Results

Election	Name (Party)	Vote (%)
2018 General	Mike Dunleavy (R)..	145,631 (51%)
	Mark Begich (D)..	125,739 (44%)
	Bill Walker (I)...	5,757 (2%)
2018 Primary	Mike Dunleavy (R)..	43,802 (62%)
	Mead Treadwell (R)..	22,780

In his first term as Alaska governor, Mike Dunleavy ruffled feathers with a fiscally conservative agenda, even prompting a recall attempt that remains active but has so far not succeeded. Dunleavy had entered office in 2018 by defeating former Democratic Sen. Mark Begich after the incumbent—independent Gov. Bill Walker—quit the three-way race just weeks before Election Day. Dunleavy's victory became the sole gubernatorial seat the Republicans were able to flip in the 2018 midterm election.

Dunleavy grew up in Scranton Pennsylvania. His father was a mailman and a World War II veteran; his mother was a city clerk. Dunleavy received his bachelor's degree at nearby Misericordia University, then settled in Alaska, attracted by its hunting and fishing. He earned a master's in education from the University of Alaska-Fairbanks and worked in education for most of his career. For a time, he was the only teacher in the small coastal town of Koyuk. "It's a tricky endeavor to be teaching multiple grade levels at one time in multiple subjects, and you have to be able to organize and do it the right way to get the outcomes that you want," Dunleavy told Alaska Public Media. He settled in Noorvik, a predominantly Inupiat village in the state's vast interior that was the home of his wife, Rose. In 2004, the family moved to Wasilla, later famous as the home of Gov. Sarah Palin, who was mayor of the city; Dunleavy served on the Matanuska-Susitna Borough school board, then ran successfully for state Senate in 2012.

In the legislature, Dunleavy chaired the chamber's Education Committee, State Affairs Committee and Labor and Commerce Committee, but his relationship with other lawmakers was sometimes fraught. He was kicked out of the majority caucus and stripped of his chairmanships after voting against the Republican budget, having sought deeper spending cuts. Dunleavy was the first majority senator in three decades not to see one of his own bills pass. "My goal wasn't to pass a lot of bills," Dunleavy told the Anchorage Daily News. "My goal was to go down there, and in many cases, ensure that certain things didn't happen to Alaskans, such as taxes." He announced his gubernatorial bid in July 2017, briefly dropped out for medical reasons, then returned to the race. He resigned from the legislature in January 2018 to focus on his campaign.

The state's big challenge during Walker's tenure was grappling with the falling price of oil, which had squeezed state finances. Walker acted to fill budget holes by capping the Permanent Fund dividend, an annual payout to all qualifying Alaskans funded by investment gains from state oil revenues. This drew the ire of a broad cross-section of Alaskans, ranging from anti-tax Republicans to lower-income Alaska Natives for whom the annual dividend was important for keeping families afloat. During the first half of 2017, the GOP Senate and the Democratic coalition-led House failed to agree on the scope of cuts and the possibility of new revenues. With a government shutdown looming, legislators and the governor agreed to a stopgap measure that combined an end to oil-industry tax credits with increased withdrawals from the state's Constitutional Budget Reserve. In the meantime, a burgeoning opioid addiction problem led to a spike in property crimes. By 2018, Walker's approval ratings were far under water.

Walker's prospects worsened further as a three-way contest developed. Walker had initially considered running as a Democrat, but Begich, a one-term U.S. senator and the scion of an Alaska political dynasty, effectively elbowed him out of the way. On the Republican side, Dunleavy won the August 2018 primary over former Lt. Gov. Mead Treadwell by a 2-to-1 margin, bolstered by an independent expenditure campaign partly funded by his brother Francis, a former high-ranking executive with JPMorgan Chase. While Walker pitched himself as someone willing to make tough financial decisions, both of his general-election opponents criticized his handling of the Permanent Fund dividend and the growth of crime on his watch. Dunleavy stuck to generalities about expanding the dividend and cutting the budget; in polls, he easily led the field, with Walker and Begich splitting the state's moderate-to-liberal vote.

Three weeks before Election Day, Walker decided to quit the race, throwing his support to Begich, who had supported Walker's earlier expansion of Medicaid. Walker's departure came just days after his Democratic lieutenant governor, Byron Mallott, resigned, citing inappropriate comments to a woman. This #metoo casualty robbed the Democrats of a leading politician of Alaska Native ancestry. On Election Day, Dunleavy defeated Begich, 51%-44%, with 2% for Walker, whose name remained on the ballot. Dunleavy had planned to take the oath of office in Noorvik, more than 1,000 miles from the state capital, but a dense fog kept him 43 miles away in Kotzebue. So in a hastily arranged ceremony, he was inaugurated in Kotzebue, as Walker stayed in Anchorage to handle the response to a 7.0-magnitude earthquake. Despite the uncooperative weather, Dunleavy became the first governor of a state to be sworn in above the Arctic Circle.

After taking office, Dunleavy proposed an increased dividend, paid for by more than $1 billion in budget cuts, hitting education—especially the University of Alaska system—especially hard, along with reductions to the low-income safety net. Dunleavy's budget positions were shaped by Donna Arduin, whom he hired as his budget director after working in the firm founded by Arthur Laffer, the supply-side economist. Dunleavy's proposals sparked opposition not only among Democrats and independents in the legislature but also among some Republicans, cementing the multi-partisan governing coalition in the House. Continuing budgetary strife led to dueling legislative sessions, with pro-Dunleavy legislators meeting in Wasilla as anti-Dunleavy legislators were meeting in the usual location, Juneau. Eventually some of his proposed cuts, including the one for higher education, were pared back. Separately, Dunleavy called for the resignation of almost 1,000 state employees, including many employed in jobs less senior than those targeted as political positions by previous governors. Dunleavy also disbanded a climate change task force that had been created by Walker.

By August, critics mobilized a recall effort. After more than enough signatures had been submitted, the petition was rejected following a ruling by Kevin Clarkson, the Dunleavy-appointed state attorney general. Supporters appealed, and two courts successively ruled in favor of the recall going forward. However, the effort's fate remained unclear, as supporters had not yet collected the new signature requirement by April 2021. Dunleavy also steadied the ship somewhat after hiring Ben Stevens, son of the late Sen. Ted Stevens, as his chief of staff.

Meanwhile, the partisan rancor left Republicans who had been siding with Democrats in trouble with their party's base, and in the 2020 state House primaries in August, six of those Republicans were defeated by challengers. Confusion continued to reign past the general election and into the new year. Despite a numerical Republican majority, control of the state House remained split; an agreement was struck to install a Republican speaker, a Democratic majority leader, and a mix of Republicans, Democrats and Independents as committee chairs. For most of the coronavirus pandemic, Alaska was able to keep infection rates low, thanks to its relative isolation and its robust efforts at testing and contact tracing. But the number of cases rose significantly as 2020 came to a close; by winter 2020 and spring 2021, Alaska ranked in the top quarter of the states in per capita coronavirus cases.

Lisa Murkowski (R)

Appointed 2002, term expires 2022, 3rd full term, b. May 22, 1957; Ketchikan, AK; Willamette University, 1977; Georgetown University, B.A., 1980; Willamette University College of Law, J.D., 1985; Roman Catholic; Married (Verne Martell); 2 children.

Elected Office: AK House, 1998-2002.

Professional Career: District Court Attorney, State of Alaska, District Court, 1986-1989; Attorney, 1989-1998.

DC Office: 522 HSOB 20510, 202-224-6665, Fax: 202-224-5301, murkowski.senate.gov

State Offices: Anchorage, 907-271-3735; Fairbanks, 907-456-0233; Juneau, 907-586-7277; Ketchikan, 907-225-6880; Soldotna, 907-262-4220; Wasilla, 907-376-7665.

Committees: *Appropriations*: Commerce, Justice, Science & Related Agencies; Department of Defense; Department of Homeland Security; Department of the Interior, Environment & Related Agencies (RMM); Energy & Water Development; Military Construction & Veteran Affairs & Related Agencies. *Energy & Natural Resources*: Energy; National Parks; Public Lands, Forests &

Mining. *Health, Education, Labor & Pensions*: Children & Families; Primary Health & Retirement Security. *Indian Affairs*.

Group Ratings

	ADA	ACLU	AFL-CIO	LCV	COC	HAFA	ACU	CFG	FRC
2020	-	58%	-	15%	-	46%	56%	-	-
2019	10%	C	26%	36%	95%	C	57%	19%	0%

Almanac Ratings 2019-2020

	Economy	Social	Foreign	Composite
Liberal	34%	34%	10%	26%
Conservative	66%	66%	90%	74%

Key Votes of the 116th Congress

1. EPA clean energy rules	N	5. Russia sanctions	N
2. U.S./Mex./Can. trade deal	Y	6. Troops in SYR, AFG	N/A
3. Cut unemployment benefits	N	7. Veto arms sales to Saudis	Y
4. Shelton to Fed Reserve	Y	8. Defense $$$, veto override	Y

9. Barr as Atty. General	Y
10. Spending at the border	Y
11. Coney Barrett to Sup. Ct.	Y
12. Electoral College objections	N

Election Results

Election	Name (Party)	Vote (%)		Cand. Spent	Ind. Exp. Support	Ind. Exp. Oppose
2016 General	Lisa Murkowski (R)	138,149	(44%)	$5,905,748	$147,178	
	Joe Miller (L)	90,825	(29%)	$727,527		
	Margaret Stock (I)	41,194	(13%)	$708,297		
	Ray Metcalfe (D)	36,200	(12%)	$12,355		
2016 Primary	Lisa Murkowski (R)	39,545	(72%)			
	Bob Lochner (R)	8,480	(15%)			
	Paul Kendall (R)	4,272	(8%)			
	Thomas Lamb (R)	2,996	(5%)			

Prior winning percentages: 2016 (44%), 2010 (39%), 2004 (49%)

As one of the few centrist senators in either party, Republican Lisa Murkowski has emerged as a powerful force in the narrowly divided chamber. With Donald Trump as president, there were few incentives for any senators—especially Republicans—to seek bipartisanship. Even Murkowski struggled to find options. But the new administration of Joe Biden, who explicitly advocated a bipartisan approach in working with Congress, seemed tailor-made for Murkowski. With a freedom that has been enhanced by narrow election victories, plus the hostility of many voters in her own party, she has enjoyed pursuing her own course. She has shown a shrewd sense of timing and understanding of Senate folkways. And, not incidentally, she has worked with her own party to score big gains for her home state.

As Congress struggled to wrap up its lame-duck business before Biden's inauguration in January 2021, Murkowski revealed how that consensus-building could work. She invited a cross-section of congressional deal-makers to dinner at her Capitol Hill home to discuss options to find common ground. That session led, days later, to a sweeping agreement by congressional leaders on both the year-end spending bill and much delayed (and stripped-down) economic relief for the millions of Americans suffering amid the coronavirus pandemic. That plan was enacted, despite the objections of Trump.

How far Murkowski could press her unique legislative model during the Biden presidency remained to be seen. Likewise, Murkowski faced reelection in 2022, where she seemed likely to seek validation of her consensus-seeking approach—despite the objections of many Republicans at home and in Washington. Another dimension of Murkowski's Senate role in 2021 was that Republicans term limits forced her to step down from her influential chairmanship of the Senate Energy and Natural Resources Committee, while leaving her no new top committee position, despite her extensive seniority.

Since the first Congress more than 230 years ago, there have been no less than 45 sons who followed their fathers into Senate service. To date, there has been only one woman to follow her dad: Murkowski, Alaska's senior senator, who was appointed in 2002 by her father, then-Gov. Frank

Murkowski, to fill the Senate vacancy created when he resigned to become governor. She's gone on to win three Senate elections without ever reaching 50 percent of the vote. Father and daughter have occupied not only the same Senate seat for 40 years, but also the same chairmanship: the Energy panel. Its legislative jurisdiction is crucial to their vast, sparsely populated home state, where more than 60 percent of the land is owned by the federal government and 90 percent of the state's revenues are derived from the oil industry.

Philosophically, Lisa Murkowski often has not been her father's daughter. If Frank Murkowski was largely a traditional conservative, his daughter has been more of a Republican moderate with a decidedly libertarian streak: She supports abortion rights, while her father was an abortion opponent, and she has been at odds with conservatives on issues ranging from gay rights to health care. Such independence has at times created political problems for her at home.

Murkowski has established a reputation for a willingness to reach across the but does hew to a hard line in terms of what she sees as the economic prerogatives of her home state, resisting efforts by the federal government to restrict Alaska's ability to access its energy resources. But if the late Republican Ted Stevens, a longtime Alaska senator, was known for berating colleagues on the Senate floor, the personable Murkowski is known more for her calm albeit steely resolve. "Channeling my inner #Hulk while meeting with the press," she once posted on her Instagram account, according to a profile in High Country News.

Murkowski, the first Alaska-born U.S. senator, was born in Ketchikan, at the southern end of Alaska's Panhandle, in 1957, two years before Alaska achieved statehood. The family moved up the Panhandle in the early 1960s to Wrangell, then known as the timber capital of Alaska, where Frank Murkowski—a native of Seattle, Washington—managed a bank. A decade later, the Murkowskis moved 900 miles further north, to Fairbanks, then reaping the economic benefits of construction of the Trans-Alaska pipeline, which opened in 1977.

Lisa Murkowski graduated from Georgetown University in 1980, the year her father was first elected to the Senate, and went on to earn a law degree from the Willamette University in Salem, Oregon, in 1985. She settled in Anchorage, serving as a district court attorney before going into private law practice. In 1998, Murkowski launched her political career. Motivated to run in part by concern about declines in two mainstays of the Alaskan economy—oil and timber—she was elected to the state House.

The independent streak that Murkowski has displayed throughout her political career was evident during her state legislative tenure. When Alaska faced a $1.1 billion budget shortfall in 2002, she found herself at odds with her father, then running for governor on a pledge of no new taxes. She won the fight and enactment of a bill making Alaska the state with the highest alcohol tax in the country. Some conservatives derisively referred to her and her allies as "RIMs"— "Republican Invertebrate Moderates." Facing a conservative challenger in the 2002 primary, Murkowski was renominated by a margin of just 57 votes. Nonetheless, she subsequently became the House majority leader.

She was not in that leadership position for long. After Alaskans elected her father to the governorship by a wide margin, Frank Murkowski compiled a long list of possible successors, saying he was looking for someone whose views on Alaska issues were in sync with his, had legislative experience and was young enough to serve many years. Among the candidates: then-state Sen. Ben Stevens, Ted Stevens' son, and a rising political star named Sarah Palin, the former mayor of Wasilla. In an interview more than a decade afterward, Frank Murkowski recalled putting the candidates' names on a spreadsheet to compare qualifications. At first, he wasn't particularly serious about his daughter as a potential appointee — but, as he studied the spreadsheet, she began moving up the list.

It was the only time in U.S. history that a governor had appointed his or her child to the Senate. "Lisa, who's your daddy?" read derisive bumper stickers at the time. In response, Murkowski sought to highlight her political differences with the man who had appointed her. "I haven't called him for counseling, and typically he doesn't offer," she said.

Still, Murkowski knew that, as she completed her father's term, critics would be watching to see if she were up to the job. In learning the ropes, Murkowski got significant help from Ted Stevens, one of Capitol Hill's most influential lawmakers. Murkowski pushed through a bill, with Stevens' help, that included federal loan guarantees for a 3,500-mile pipeline that would bring natural gas from the North Slope to the lower 48 states—a major venture for Alaska.

Nonetheless, as Murkowski entered the 2004 campaign, she was vulnerable. She turned back a challenge from the right, 58%-37%, in the primary, but in the general election, she faced a tough challenge against Tony Knowles. A Vietnam veteran and Yale University classmate and friend of President George W. Bush, Knowles had twice been elected mayor of Anchorage and twice won gubernatorial races. The nepotism issue loomed over the campaign. This strongly red state voted to give Bush a second term by a 25-point margin, helping Murkowski to eke out victory, 49%-46%.Frank Murkowski ended up paying the political price for the nepotism controversy. Seeking reelection in 2006, he finished third in a three-way primary, as Sarah Palin toppled him and went on to win the general election.

Following Ted Stevens' reelection defeat in 2008—eight days after his conviction on corruption charges for concealing gifts—Murkowski assumed a much larger role in the Senate on Alaska-centric issues. With Stevens gone, she succeeded him the Appropriations Committee, a critical post for a state so dependent on federal spending. Also, she joined the GOP leadership as a counsel to then-Minority Leader Mitch McConnell.

Murkowski continued to demonstrate her independent streak. She joined three other Republican senators to seek more civil liberties protections in the Patriot Act. And, after President Barack Obama took office in 2009, Murkowski was one of just five Senate Republicans to help pass into law the Matthew Shepard Act, expanding the federal hate crimes statute to cover a victim's sexual orientation and gender identity.

Murkowski's growing influence was not enough to stave off a vigorous primary challenge in 2010 from Joe Miller. A graduate of West Point and Yale Law School, the self-described "constitutional conservative" charged that Murkowski was a Washington insider who had abandoned Republican values by supporting abortion rights and higher taxes. His candidacy was backed by Palin, two years after her 2008 stint as the Republican vice presidential nominee. He narrowly prevailed, 51%-49%.

Murkowski conceded, and, for a time, appeared ready to move back to Alaska with her husband, Verne Martell, and their two sons. But after repeated urgings from friends and supporters, she announced seven weeks before the general election that she would pursue a long-shot write-in effort. Using the slogan "Let's Make History," she waged a spirited campaign, pointing to the considerable seniority that federally dependent Alaska would forsake if she lost. Miller's campaign suffered from numerous missteps. With the support of some Democrats, Murkowski won a three-way contest with 39 percent of the vote. Miller got 35 percent and the Democratic candidate, Scott McAdams, finished a distant third with 23 percent. She became only the second senator to win via write-in, matching an electoral feat that Strom Thurmond, as a Democrat, had accomplished in South Carolina more than a half-century earlier.

Murkowski's difficult victory appeared to accelerate her march to the political middle. In the 2010 lame-duck session, she was among just seven Republican senators to support the repeal of the military's "don't ask, don't tell policy." In 2013, she became the third GOP senator to voice support for same-sexmarriage. Two years later, Murkowski was the lead Republican on a bill designed to restore several provisions of the Voting Rights Act ruled unconstitutional by the Supreme Court. That stance reflected the strong support that Alaska Natives had given her in the 2010 write-in effort.

When Republicans regained control of the Senate in 2014, Murkowski began six years chairing not only the Energy and Natural Resources Committee but also the Appropriations Subcommittee on Interior, Environment and Related Agencies, adding to her leverage on home-state issues. She showed her independence on several fronts. In 2015, she was one of only seven GOP senators not to sign an open letter intended to undermine Obama's efforts to reach a nuclear deal with Iran. She was among a handful of Republicans to initially support holding hearings on Obama's 2016 nomination of Judge Merrick Garland to the fill the Supreme Court vacancy created by the death of Justice Antonin Scalia.

One source of repeated confrontation with the Obama administration was the state delegation's long-standing goal of opening the Alaska National Wildlife Refuge to oil and gas exploration—a popular idea in the state, but one that was rebuffed repeatedly in Washington. While the area is home toa wide array of wildlife, it also is thought to hold large oil and gas reserves. Murkowski was incensed when Obama in 2015 said he would ask Congress to designate 12 million of the refuge's19 million acres as wilderness. She blasted the move as "a stunning attack on our sovereignty." "The only thing more shocking than this reckless, short-sighted, last-minute gift to the extreme environmental agenda is that President Obama had the nerve to claim he is doing Alaska a favor," Murkowski said.

Finally, after Trump took office, she won approval of the proposal, sought for decades by Alaska Republicans, to permit oil and natural gas drilling in part of the Arctic National Wildlife Refuge. Working with McConnell and Trump, Murkowski included that legislative action as a rider to the GOP's big tax cut bill. Murkowski said, with understatement, "We have come to a good place." As it turned out, due to declining world demand for petroleum, drillers had less interest in the land than was earlier expected.

On the Energy and Natural Resources panel, Murkowski worked on comprehensive energy legislation with Maria Cantwell of Washington, the committee's ranking Democrat. But, after clearing the Senate in the spring of 2016 on an overwhelmingly bipartisan vote, their bill ran into a far more partisan counterpart from the Republican-controlled House. The legislation died in conference committee at the end of 2016. Four years later, that bill remained stalled, to Murkowski's great frustration. Working in 2019-20 with Sen. Joe Manchin of West Virginia, one of her partners in the efforts to strengthen the Senate's centrists and the new top Democrat on the Energy panel, their bill became the victim of Senate gridlock.

Murkowski entered the 2016 election in an unfamiliar position — heavily favored to win a third term. But, while far from a repeat of 2010, it was short of a cakewalk. Former Anchorage Mayor Dan Sullivan (no relation to Murkowski's junior colleague, GOP Sen. Dan Sullivan) filed to take on Murkowski but then dropped his bid. Murkowski, taking no chances, started earlier and spent more money, winning the primary with 72 percent of the vote. She benefitted from a split in the Democratic ranks: Democratic nominee Ray Metcalfe was a longtime critic of former Sen. Mark Begich, who returned the favor by endorsing independent candidate Margaret Stock. Miller, who ran again, this time on the Libertarian Party line in the general election, garnered 29 percent, second to Murkowski's victorious 44 percent.

During the campaign, Murkowski kept her distance from Republican presidential nominee Donald Trump. She never endorsed him, and, after a videotape surfaced of Trump making lewd comments about women, Murkowski called on him to step aside, saying he had "forfeited the right to be our party's nominee." After the election, Murkowski was conciliatory. "When they want to work with us to do good things for Alaska, we'll be working together," she told Alaska Public Media about Trump. "So yes, I can absolutely [work] with anyone."

In 2017, she made clear that cooperation would be on her terms. With Sens. Susan Collins of Maine and John McCain of Arizona, she was one of three Republican Senators who voted against —and defeated—the GOP proposal to repeal the Affordable Care Act. That came in the face of presidential tweets and angry party stalwarts in Washington and at home. "The Affordable Care Act remains a flawed law that I am committed to reforming," she said. "But to do that, the Senate must fully devote itself to an effort to improve the health care system in this country." The Alaska GOP chairman said local Republicans were unanimous in their unhappiness with Murkowski. Her vote, Murkowski told the Washington Post a year later, brought "an emotional outpouring that made it just —"intense" is the best word."

Murkowski also went her own way in September 2018, when she voted against Brett Kavanaugh's nomination to the Supreme Court. "We are dealing with issues right now that are bigger than a nominee," she told reporters, in an apparent reference to allegations of sexual assault against the nominee. "In my view, he's not the right man for the court at this time." In that case, Kavanaugh was confirmed and her vote proved less consequential—in the short term, at least. Palin tweeted: "Hey @LisaMurkowski—I can see 2022 from my house." Murkowski responded that she wasn't worried.

Two years later, on the eve of another election, Murkowski went a different direction on another Trump nominee to the Supreme Court. With Judge Amy Coney Barrett, she initially objected to Republicans' rushed handling of the nomination. But, again showing her independence, Murkowski decided that Barrett deserved confirmation and that she should not be a victim of the partisan conflicts. "My constitutional responsibility is to now look beyond process and to vote based on a solid evaluation of her qualifications and fitness of judicial temperament," Murkowski said. "It is clear that she is qualified by any objective standard."

That approach was notably similar to Murkowski's response in Trump's impeachment trial. She criticized all of the players: Trump's "shameful and wrong" conduct, House Democrats' "rushed" issuance of the charges, and Senate Republicans' "total coordination" with the Trump White House during the trial. The result, she told the Senate, was "congressional abdication."

"It is my hope that we have found the bottom," she said, "that both sides can look inward and reflect on the apparent willingness each has to destroy not just each other, but all of the institutions of our government." Oddly perhaps, she disagreed with Collins, her close ally, on the two nominations: Amid loud criticism from both sides, Collins had voted for Kavanaugh and against Barrett.

During Trump's campaign for reelection, she repeatedly criticized his tactics. She said his pre-election suggestion to delay the date of the vote "is not going to happen," that his predictions of election fraud were "not leadership" and that his attempts to tamper with postal delivery during the final weeks of the campaign were "inappropriate." For months, she publicly said she was "struggling" with her own vote; she ultimately did not reveal whom she had voted for. When Biden was determined to be the winner, she was among the first Republicans to congratulate him publicly and to urge Trump to cooperate with the transition.

In the Senate's second impeachment trial of Trump, she was one of seven Republicans who found him guilty. Trump's "course of conduct amounts to incitement of insurrection," Murkowski said. The Alaska Republican Party subsequently censured Murkowski and vowed to support another Republican in the 2022 primary. Coincidentally, Alaska election law has been changed so that the top four candidates in a primary will move to the general election, where ranked-choice voting will be used. Those procedural changes seem likely to weaken party primaries and, consequently, to benefit Murkowski.

Murkowski faced many questions about her future in the Senate, including her effectiveness in working with Biden as a dealmaker, her reelection prospects in 2022 and the possibility that she will be in line in a few years to chair the Appropriations Committee—a position once held by Ted Stevens. Even with her continuing independence, she had achieved results on which her powerful predecessors from Alaska had fallen short.

Dan Sullivan (R)

Elected 2014, term expires 2026, 2nd term, b. Nov 13, 1964; Fairview Park, OH; Harvard University, B.A., 1987; Georgetown University Law Center, J.D., 1993; Georgetown University Law Center, M.S., 1993; Roman Catholic; Married (Julie Fate); 3 children.

Military Career: U.S. Marine Corps and Reserves 1993-pres. (Afghanistan)

Professional Career: Law clerk, U.S Court of Appeals for the Ninth Circuit, 1997-1998; Law clerk, AK Supreme Court, 1998-1999; Assistant Secretary of State for Economic, Energy, and Business Affairs, U.S Department of State, 2006-2009; AK Attorney General, 2009-2010; Commissioner, AK Department of Natural Resources, 2010-2013.

DC Office: 302 HSOB 20510, 202-224-3004, Fax: 202-224-6501, sullivan.senate.gov
State Offices: Anchorage, 907-271-5915; Fairbanks, 907-456-0261; Juneau, 907-586-7277; Ketchikan, 907-225-6880; Soldotna, 907-283-4000; Wasilla, 907-357-9956.

Committees: *Armed Services*: Airland; Readiness & Management Support (RMM); Strategic Forces. *Commerce, Science & Transportation*: Communications, Media & Broadband; Oceans, Fisheries, Climate Change & Manufacturing (RMM); Surface Transportation, Maritime Freight & Ports; Tourism, Trade & Export Promotion. *Environment & Public Works*: Chem Safety, Waste Mngmnt, Enviro Justice & Reg Oversight; Fisheries, Water, and Wildlife; Transportation & Infrastructure. *Veterans' Affairs*.

Group Ratings

	ADA	ACLU	AFL-CIO	LCV	COC	HAFA	ACU	CFG	FRC
2020	-	23%	-	8%	-	64%	79%	-	-
2019	0%	C	21%	14%	95%	C	81%	36%	100%

Almanac Ratings 2019-2020

	Economy	Social	Foreign	Composite
Liberal	0%	0%	6%	2%
Conservative	100%	100%	94%	98%

Key Votes of the 116th Congress

1. EPA clean energy rules	N	5. Russia sanctions	N	9. Barr as Atty. General	Y
2. U.S./Mex./Can. trade deal	Y	6. Troops in SYR, AFG	Y	10. Spending at the border	Y
3. Cut unemployment benefits	Y	7. Veto arms sales to Saudis	N	11. Coney Barrett to Sup. Ct.	Y
4. Shelton to Fed Reserve	Y	8. Defense $$$, veto override	Y	12. Electoral College objections	N

Election Results

Election	Name (Party)	Vote (%)		Cand. Spent	Ind. Exp. Support	Ind. Exp. Oppose
2020 General	Dan Sullivan (R)............................	191,112	(54%)	$9,513,023	$144,976	$14,224,213
	Al Gross (I).....................................	146,068	(41%)	$19,904,724	$4,075,971	$8,761,025
	John Howe (AI)....................................	17,407	(5%)			
2020 Primary	Dan Sullivan (R)............................	65,257	(100%)			

Prior winning percentages: 2014 (48%)

Dan Sullivan, the junior senator from Alaska, has mostly been a party loyalist focused on issues of interest to himself and his constituents, especially military topics. Like other Alaskans in Congress, he has shown occasional independence, especially when it comes to home-state priorities. After narrowly defeating the Democratic incumbent in 2014, Sullivan appeared relatively safe heading into his first reelection campaign. His challenger—well-funded and with a stronger Alaskan pedigree than Sullivan—tightened their contest. But, like many other Senate Republicans in 2020,Sullivan won comfortably — by double digits.

Sullivan grew up in Fairview Park, Ohio, in a prominent family. His paternal grandfather started a business just after World War II that has employed more than 10,000 workers in the manufacture of commercial and residential paints, coatings and sealants. Sullivan's father later ran and grew the firm. Sullivan chose a different course. He got a bachelor's degree in economics from Harvard University and earned a joint law and foreign service degree from Georgetown University. At Georgetown, he met Julie Fate, a staffer for then-Sen. Ted Stevens and part of a prominent Alaska Native family. They married in Fairbanks.

Sullivan enlisted in the Marine Corps and was commissioned a second lieutenant. He then moved to Alaska, where he clerked for a federal appeals court judge and for the chief justice of the state Supreme Court. After spending a couple of years in the Anchorage office of the Seattle-based Perkins Coie law firm, he left Alaska for what he said was good reason. Sullivan told the Anchorage Daily News during the Senate campaign: "9/11 happened and that changed everything." He spent more than two years on a White House fellowship with President George W. Bush, working for the National Security Council and the National Economic Council. After Condoleezza Rice left the White House and became secretary of State, Sullivan joined her as assistant secretary of State for economic, energy and business affairs.

After he returned to Alaska in early 2009Sullivan was appointed state attorney general by Gov. Sarah Palin a month before she resigned. Palin's successor, Republican Sean Parnell, chose Sullivan to head the Department of Natural Resources. Until his election in 2014, Sullivan was sometimes referred to in his home state as the "other" Dan Sullivan — so was not to confuse him with former Anchorage Mayor Dan Sullivan, a Republican and a native of Alaska who now serves on the influential Alaska Regulatory Commission. Foes of the Senate candidate sometimes derided him as "Ohio Dan," an allusion to his early years and a continuing debate over precisely how long he resided in Alaska. In his first campaign for office, he faced Mark Begich, another former Anchorage mayor, who is part of a prominent Alaska political family. In 2008, Begich narrowly defeated Stevens, a legendary Alaskan who had served in the Senate for 40 years. Begich became the first Alaska Democrat elected to Congress since 1974.

In the GOP primary, Sullivan faced Lt. Gov. Mead Treadwell and Fairbanks attorney Joe Miller, a tea party favorite who had defeated Sen. Lisa Murkowski in the 2010 primary but lost to her in the general. Treadwell sought to depict Sullivan as a carpetbagger — "I've got a jar of mayonnaise in my refrigerator that's been there longer than Dan Sullivan's been in Alaska," Treadwell gibed to Politico. Palin endorsed Miller. The prospect of the GOP retaking Senate control prompted national conservative groups—including the Club for Growth and U.S. Chamber of Commerce—to support Sullivan, a political newcomer, as the best candidate to defeat Begich. Sullivan won the primary with 40 percent, to 32 percent for Miller and 25 percent for Treadwell.

As a Democrat from a deep-red state, Begich worked to show his independence from President Barack Obama and his congressional colleagues. He was one of only four Senate Democrats to vote against a bill ending tax breaks for oil companies and opposed a ban on so-called earmark spending — a device that Stevens had used to steer appropriations to his huge, sparsely populated state. Democrats raised the carpetbagger theme throughout the election. In his carefully managed campaign, Sullivan's overriding goal was to tie Begich to Obama, who was deeply unpopular in Alaska. The bitter battle consumed $61 million, making it the most expensive race in Alaska history. Republicans had a superior ground game and Sullivan eked out a 48%-46% victory.

During the campaign, Begich sought to appear nonpartisan by running an ad that featured the image of Murkowski and touted their close relationship in the small community of veteran Alaska politicians. The often fiercely independent Murkowski told Begich to stop using her image and made clear that she supported Sullivan. Nonetheless, in the Senate, Sullivan and Murkowski have differed on both policy and political matters. Sullivan, unlike Murkowski, endorsed Donald Trump after he emerged as the Republican presidential nominee in 2016. After the release of the "Access Hollywood" tape containing lewd comments about women, Sullivan urged that Trump be replaced by his running mate, Mike Pence, a leading social conservative. During his campaigns, Sullivan had staked out positions at odds with Murkowski on abortion and same-sex marriage, saying he opposed both.

On the Armed Services Committee, Sullivan has approached defense issues from a hawkish perspective. During a committee hearing in 2015, he accused Obama of holding an "almost delusional view of the world environment" after the president suggested in his State of the Union address that the shadow of crisis had passed on various threats, from ISIS's advance to Russia's aggression and Iran's nuclear program. In 2016, when ISIS forces killed a Navy SEAL who was advising Kurdish forces in Iraq, an Obama spokesman told reporters that the SEAL had not been on a combat mission. "The White House continues to diminish the service and sacrifice of our troops serving in Iraq, Syria, Afghanistan and elsewhere by peddling the fiction that they are not engaged in combat," snapped Sullivan, who has been called up for three tours of duty as Marine reservist, including a six-week stint in Afghanistan in 2013.

Sullivan, the only current senator serving in the military reserves, was promoted in 2018 to the rank of colonel in the Marine Corps Forces Reserve, though the constitutional separation of powers forced him to give up command of a California-based reserve unit after he became a senator. While his military experience was a significant political asset in his campaign for the Senate, Sullivan contended it had given him a legislative edge as well. "Having firsthand experience, being able to talk about just how incredible Alaska is for military training, I think, gives me a lot of credibility as a senator to make the case to not only my fellow senators but to senior administration officials," he told Alaska Public Media.

In the reorganization of the Armed Services panel after the death in 2018 of Sen. John McCain, Sullivan became chairman of the Readiness Subcommittee. He focused on the role that Alaska plays as the military "rebalances" its attention to the Pacific Ocean, including the importance of its installations. In the defense spending bill that Congress enacted that year, he won approval of six Polar-class icebreakers for the Coast Guard and a provision requiring the Pentagon to update its "Arctic strategy." In 2020, Sullivan worked with Democratic Sen. Maria Cantwell of Washington to secure additional funding for the icebreakers. The vessels were initially to be based in Seattle, but Sullivan urged the Coast Guard to base at least some of them in Alaska.

As he continued to urge a military commitment to the Arctic, Sullivan warned of the growing threat of Russia, which has based many more ships in the region. In the defense spending bill that was enacted in December 2020, he secured provisions for a new Ted Stevens Center for Arctic Security Studies, new facilities in Alaska for Pentagon operations and communications, plus modernization of the radar warning system across the Arctic. "We've seen Russia push all-in on controlling the Arctic," Sullivan said. "Without persistent U.S. presence in the Arctic, we risk leaving an opening for these types of aggressive actions to continue."

Sullivan's other committee assignments have enabled him to look out for Alaskan interests, as well. On both the Commerce, Science and Transportation Committee and the Environment and Public Works Committee, Sullivan has chaired subcommittees that have jurisdiction over fisheries. About 60 percent of the seafood caught in the United States comes from Alaskan waters. With Sen. Sheldon Whitehouse, Democrat of Rhode Island, he won enactment in 2018 of the "Save Our Seas" bill to address the problem of plastic trash in oceans.

In December 2020, Sullivan teamed up again with Cantwell, the senior Democrat on the Commerce committee, and with Sen. Brian Schatz of Hawaii to enact a bill to improve and modernize the management of the National Oceanic and Atmospheric Administration's commissioned officer corps. The corps maintains aircraft and shipping fleets to advance various maritime interests, many of them in the Pacific Ocean.

Despite his reservations about Trump during the campaign, Sullivan approved the president's actions on behalf of Alaska. "In terms of a federal government that is finally working to help grow Alaska's economy, we are making significant progress," he said in a February 2018 speech to the state Legislature, citing oil exploration in the Arctic Refuge and construction of a natural gas pipeline from the North Slope.

Sullivan broke with Trump on his tariff increases on imports, especially for steel and aluminum. "I do worry about retaliation," he said in a March 2018 interview with Alaska Public Media. "We're a huge exporter, particularly of fish and natural resource products." He also took issue with the Trump administration's court challenges to key parts of the Affordable Care Act. In September 2020, Sullivan was one of five GOP senators—all of whom were in tight reelection campaigns—who joined Senate Democrats in seeking to block funds to support that litigation.

In the 2020 campaign, his chief opponent was Al Gross, an Alaska Native whose father, a Democrat, once served as the state's attorney general. Gross, an orthopedic surgeon, met his wife—a pediatrician—at the University of Washington Medical School. They gave up their medical practices in 2013 to return to school to get masters' degrees in public health and seek to improve and decrease the cost of health care. As a first-time candidate in 2020, Gross was a successful fundraiser. He outspent Sullivan, $20 million to $10 million; in addition, outside groups spent nearly that total on the contest. As often is the case in Alaska, Gross sought to run as an independent, in a bid to keep his distance from national Democrats, though a local judge required him to be listed on the ballot as a Democrat.

Senate Democrats hoped that the late-breaking Alaska contest could work to their benefit. The flood of Democratic money "suggests that the race is tightening," the Anchorage Daily News reported in mid-October. In its review of the contest in October, the Cook Political Report wrote, "Public and private polling now shows this race tightening, though Sullivan still retains an advantage." Because of the state's far-flung voting network, it took more than a week to count enough votes for Sullivan to emerge as the clear winner, 54%-41%. Sullivan narrowly outpaced Trump, who defeated Biden in Alaska, 53%-43%.

Days after his victory, Sullivan found himself in an unusual spat while in the Senate. As he was addressing the chamber, Democratic Sen. Sherrod Brown of Ohio asked Sullivan to "please wear a mask," in part to protect staff seated nearby from the novel coronavirus. Sullivan, whose mask was on the desk in front of him, responded, "I don't wear a mask when I'm speaking. ...I don't need your instruction."

Don Young (R)

Elected 1973, 24th full term, b. Jun 09, 1933; Meridian, CA; Yuba Junior College, A.A., 1952; CA State University, Chico, B.A., 1958; Episcopalian; Married (Anne Garland Walton); 2 children; 14 grandchildren; 1 great-grandchild.

Military Career: U.S. Army 1955-1957

Elected Office: Fort Yukon City Council, 1960-1964; Fort Yukon Mayor, 1964-1968; AK House, 1966-1970; AK Senate, 1970-1973.

Professional Career: School teacher, Fort Yukon, 1960-1968; Riverboat captain, 1968-1972.

DC Office: 2314 RHOB 20515, 202-225-5765, Fax: 202-225-0425, donyoung.house.gov

State Offices: Anchorage, 907-271-5978; Fairbanks, 907-456-0210.

Committees: *Natural Resources*: Indigenous Peoples of the United States (RMM); Water, Oceans & Wildlife. *Transportation & Infrastructure*: Aviation; Highways & Transit.

Group Ratings

	ADA	ACLU	AFL-CIO	LCV	COC	HAFA	ACU	CFG	FRC
2020	**	26%	**	33%	-	69%	73%	**	-
2019	10%	C	55%	19%	91%	C	73%	59%	86%

Almanac Ratings 2019-2020

	Economy	Social	Foreign	Composite
Liberal	42%	43%	15%	34%
Conservative	58%	57%	85%	66%

Key Votes of the 116th Congress

1. U.S./Mex./Can. trade deal	Y	5. Russia sanctions	N
2. First Coronavirus response	N/A	6. Troops in Syria	Y
3. HEROES Act	N	7. Veto arms sales to Saudis	N
4. CASH Act	N/A	8. Defense $$$, veto override	Y

9. Firearms background checks	N
10. Spending at the border	N/A
11. Marijuana liberalized rules	Y
12. Electoral College objections	N

Election Results

Election	Name (Party)	Vote (%)		Cand. Spent	Ind. Exp. Support	Ind. Exp. Oppose
2020 General	Don Young (R).....................................	192,126	(54%)	$1,825,831	$51,197	$1,763,072
	Alyse Galvin (D)................................	159,856	(45%)	$5,103,911	$104,622	$1,656,829
2020 Primary	Don Young (R).....................................	51,972	(76%)			
	Thomas "John" Nelson (R)....................	12,344	(18%)			
	Geral Heikes (R)............................	3,954	(6%)			

Prior winning percentages: 2018 (53%), 2016 (50%), 2014 (51%), 2012 (64%), 2010 (69%), 2008 (50%), 2006 (57%), 2004 (71%), 2002 (75%), 2000 (70%), 1998 (63%), 1996 (59%), 1994 (57%), 1992 (47%), 1990 (52%), 1988 (63%), 1986 (57%), 1984 (55%), 1982 (71%), 1980 (74%), 1978 (55%), 1976 (71%), 1974 (54%), 1973 special (56%)

Don Young has been Alaska's congressman-at-large since 1973. He became the most-senior member of the House following the resignation in December 2017 of Democrat John Conyers of Michigan. In March 2019, he passed Speaker Joe Cannon, who retired in 1923 after 46 years, as the longest-serving Republican in the history of the House. Young's robust political career was nearly destroyed by an influence-peddling scandal in 2008. After having served six years each as a deal-making chairman of two House committees that are vital to his home state, he lost much of his internal clout, though he retained his frequently ornery manner.

Young grew up on his family's farm in the Sacramento Valley of California, served in the Army, and graduated from college. He had a thirst for adventure and the rugged outdoors: He remembers that The Call of the Wild by Jack London was a favorite book growing up. He moved to Alaska in 1959, the year that the vast, untamed U.S. territory became a state. Young worked in construction, fishing, trapping and gold prospecting. He taught elementary school to indigenous Alaskan children in Fort Yukon, population 700. After spring thaws, he worked as a tugboat captain on the Yukon. He is a licensed mariner, which, in his words, is definitely not a typical profession of "one of these smooth, namby-pamby politicians."

Young was elected mayor of Fort Yukon in 1964, to the state House in 1966, and to the state Senate in 1970. He ran for Congress in 1972. His opponent, incumbent Democrat Nick Begich, was killed in a plane crash in October, which also killed House Majority Leader Hale Boggs, and was reelected posthumously. Young won the March 1973 special election to succeed him. Young is not a free-market conservative and has voted with liberals on some cultural issues, but he is a consistent, fierce advocate for Alaska's interests. He is temperamental and salty-tongued. To critics who once proposed shifting money for Alaska bridges to Hurricane Katrina recovery efforts, he said, "They can kiss my ear."

Soon after taking his seat in the House, Young voted to build the Alaska oil pipeline. His aggressive pursuit of economic development for his state often conflicted with the environmental lobby and its interest in preserving wildlife. He called his critics a "self-centered bunch, the waffle-stomping, Harvard-graduating, intellectual idiots."

When Republicans controlled the House, Young occupied power positions that allowed him to work around his adversaries. He chaired the Resources Committee from 1995 to 2001 and the Transportation and Infrastructure Committee from 2001 to 2007. In each case, his tenure was ended by the House GOP term-limits rule for committee chairmen. He steered to House passage bills allowing oil drilling in the Arctic National Wildlife Refuge in 1995, 2001, and 2006, only to see them defeated or bottled up in the Senate. On the Resources Committee, his attempts to roll back environmental rulings, such as the one that barred logging in the Tongass National Forest, were frustrated in the 1990s by Democratic President Bill Clinton or by adverse votes cast by moderate Republicans. In 2000, he got Congress to pass the Conservation and Reinvestment Act to dedicate royalties from offshore oil and gas wells to state purchases of land.

On the Transportation and Infrastructure Committee, he led arguably the most bipartisan panel in the House because its chairmen traditionally larded bills to make sure every cooperating committee member received plenty of highway or mass transit projects for his or her district. In 2003, Young proposed a surface transportation bill with $375 billion in spending, financed with a gas tax increase. The Bush administration and House Republican leaders stoutly opposed any such hike. In 2005, he got the House to pass a $284 billion bill. There was harsh criticism of the bill's earmarks—special projects for certain lawmakers—particularly two bridges in Alaska. One was from Anchorage to largely uninhabited land across the Knik Arm at a cost of $230 million; the other, for $220 million, was from the town of Ketchikan (pop. 14,000) to the island of Gravina (pop. 50), whose airport could be reached by local ferry. They were derisively dubbed the "bridges to nowhere." In July, both chambers passed by near-unanimous votes a $286 billion bill with more than 6,300 earmarks.

That likely would have been the end of the earmark controversy, except that Hurricane Katrina struck the Gulf Coast in August 2005. Suddenly, there were demands that money be shifted from Alaska's "bridges to nowhere" to New Orleans and other parts of the devastated region. "That is the dumbest thing I ever heard," Young said. But criticism of earmarks and the bridges continued. Conservative Republicans as well as Democrats chimed in, and profligate spending, symbolized by the two spans, emerged as an issue in the 2006 election. The punch lines helped wipe out the Republican majorities that year.

For an incumbent with record seniority, Young has had a bumpy history with Alaska voters and has frequently drawn serious challengers. His acerbic personality has been accompanied by ethical problems. In 2007, a former Young aide pleaded guilty to accepting cash from disgraced lobbyist Jack Abramoff in exchange for inside government information. Records showed 120 contacts between Young and his staff with Abramoff and his clients. The next month, Rick Smith, an associate of Young's and a former lobbyist with the oil services firm VECO, a major Young contributor since 1989, pleaded guilty to bribing Alaska state legislators. In 2008, House Speaker Nancy Pelosi ordered an ethics investigation; the Justice Department conducted its own review. Following lengthy inquiries, no charges were lodged against Young.

That year, Republican Lt. Gov. Sean Parnell announced he would challenge Young in the primary. Parnell was endorsed by GOP Gov. Sarah Palin. Polls in summer 2008 showed Young trailing, but he professed to be unfazed. During a debate with Parnell, he said: "I've been accused of being arrogant, being a bully, and sometimes I'll plead to being both of those. Most of the time and every time I've done that is because I'm fighting for this state." Parnell spent $572,000, with strong support from the anti-tax Club for Growth. "We're tired of being the nation's symbol of excess and greed," Parnell said in a debate. Young beat Parnell by just 304 votes.

His battle was far from over. Former Alaska House Minority Leader Ethan Berkowitz, a Democrat, ran against him in the general election. Berkowitz was well funded, with $1.6 million, while Young's resources were depleted by legal fees and by the primary contest. Berkowitz framed the choice as one of style, contrasting his consensus-building approach to Young's tendency to "bully and intimidate." He said he would seek earmarks if communities and citizens asked for them, but not for lobbyists. During a debate, tongue in cheek, Young called himself, "one of the nicest, kindest persons in the world." He added, "but when you mess with the state, you're messing with me." He defeated Berkowitz 50%-45%.

Ethics problems lingered for Young. In 2014, the House Ethics Committee rebuked him for "improperly accepting nearly $60,000 in hunting trips, rides on private planes and other gifts and failing to report them on his financial disclosure forms." The gifts dated back to 2001. Young repaid the donors of the gifts, plus his campaign account. "I've been under a cloud all my life," Young told reporters in Juneau. "It's sort of like living in Juneau. It rains on you all the time. You don't even notice it."

He has remained an active legislator. He introduced a sweeping bill—with long odds of passage and designed to make a political point—that would have required the Obama administration to review and justify every regulation implemented in the past 20 years. In 2017, he won enactment of a bill to expand a hydroelectric project in the Kodiak Island National Wildlife Refuge, plus a resolution to nullify an Obama administration regulation to restrict hunting in Alaska's wildlife refuges. Democrats and environmentalists opposed the hunting measure. His Almanac vote ratings on social issues have placed him near the center of the House.

Young has remained as feisty and vocal as ever. In a 2013 radio interview in Alaska, he referred to Latino immigrants as "wetbacks." Other Republicans swiftly condemned him, and Young apologized for what he acknowledged was an "insensitive" term. Speaking out against gun control in early 2018, he said that the Jews could have resisted the Holocaust more effectively if they had owned firearms. The litany continued in April 2019, when he shoved a reporter, Melanie Zanona of Politico, while she was trying to interview another House member in the Capitol. Later that day, Young apologized to her. In 2020, months after he dismissed concerns about the coronavirus as overblown, he tested positive for COVID-19. "I am feeling strong, following proper protocols, working from home in Alaska, and ask for privacy at this time," he tweeted in November.

In 2018, Democrats were enthusiastic about Alyce Galvin, an education activist and campaign novice who opposed the Trump administration. She outspent Young, $1.9 million to $1.3 million. He was reelected, 53%-46%.Galvin ran again in 2020 and spent more than $5 million, which nearly tripled the spending by Young. It hardly made a difference. This time, he won, 54%-45%.

At age 85 when he set the longevity record for House Republicans, Young had no plans to retire. "Not to run, as long as you enjoy what you're doing and you're, frankly, good at it, why would you quit? Most people retire because they don't like their jobs," he told the Anchorage Daily News in 2018. His real enthusiasm is no longer legislation, he said in an earlier interview, but "helping people that have problems." With the retirement in 2020 of Rep. Jim Sensenbrenner, the Wisconsin Republican, Young was the only House member who served prior to 1980. The record longevity of 59 years in Congress—held by Rep. John Dingell of Michigan, who retired in 2014—seemed secure.

ARIZONA

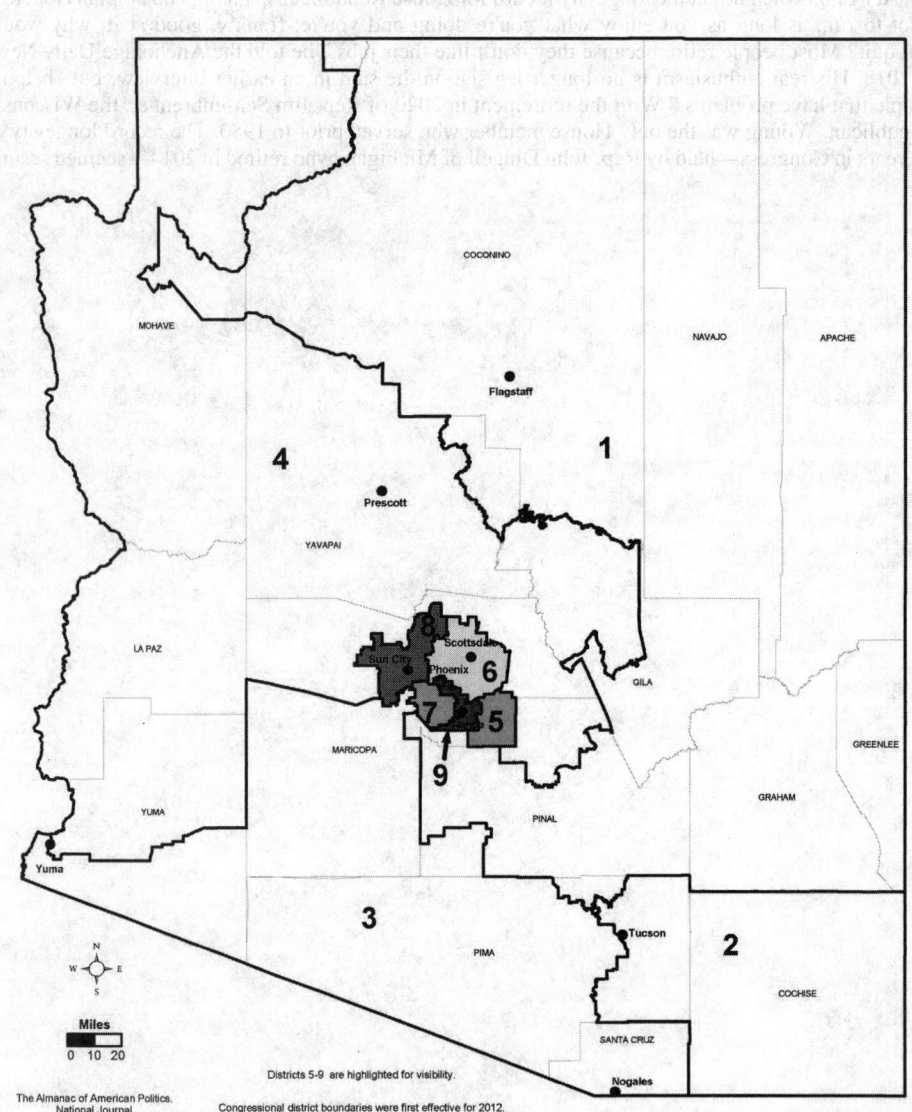

Districts 5-9 are highlighted for visibility.

The Almanac of American Politics.
National Journal

Congressional district boundaries were first effective for 2012.

From the beginning of the 2020 election cycle, Arizona was a clear battleground state—and one of the nation's most important. Even though Arizona had voted Democratic for president only once since 1948, Hillary Clinton in 2016 came about 3.5 points short of defeating Donald Trump in the state, fueling Democrats' hopes of flipping it. In 2020, both President Donald Trump and former Vice President Joe Biden contested Arizona aggressively, with Biden ultimately able to turn the state blue on the strength of a strong showing among Latinos and suburbanites in the most populous county, Maricopa. Indeed, the turning point on Election Night turned out to be Fox News' (arguably premature) call of Arizona for Biden, which enraged Trump. Adding insult to injury, Democrat Mark Kelly ousted appointed Republican Sen. Martha McSally by a slightly bigger margin.

Arizona is at the intersection of some of America's most urgent demographic and political trends —migration from colder states to the Sun Belt, the impact of immigration, and the increase in Hispanic influence on politics. Yet, while Arizona has changed rapidly in recent decades, it is also home to the Hopi Indians, who have lived as shepherds on the plateaus east of the Grand Canyon for more than 900 years—the oldest continuous community in the United States. The Hopi have spurned Christianity since 1680, when they killed the local Franciscan priests and burned their churches. Their land disputes with the more numerous Navajo have dragged on for centuries. Today, Arizona has 21 federally recognized Native American tribes who collectively control more than a quarter of the state's land.

Beyond the Native American population, Arizona, with its rugged desert, mountains and forests, was sparsely populated when the United States obtained it as part of the treaty that ended the Mexican War in 1848 (and another chunk a few years later to provide land for a southern route for a transcontinental railroad). Arizona was made a separate territory in 1863 after some locals tried to join the Confederacy. Nearly half a century later, in 1912, it became the 48th state. Back then, few imagined that Arizona would transcend its frontier roots. For decades it relied on the five Cs, memorialized in the state seal. The first C was copper, which was locally mined and encases the dome of the state capitol. The second C was cattle; as late as the mid-1960s, a dozen or so cattle barons dominated the state legislature. The third C was cotton: The signature achievement of Carl Hayden, a Democratic senator from 1927 to 1969, was the Central Arizona Project, which brought irrigated cotton farms to the flatlands around Phoenix. The water also helped with the fourth C: citrus. The fifth C was climate: Dry, clear air drew visitors seeking its therapeutic benefits, though the scorching summer heat deterred permanent transplants for many years.

Then came air conditioning, which brought waves of retirees. In the years after World War II, Arizona became less dependent on federal largesse, except for its military bases and defense contracts. (The state counts two Air Force bases and a Marine air station, plus the huge Barry M. Goldwater Range, where many of America's pilots have trained.) Businessmen, lawyers, developers and water companies, notably the Salt River Project, built Arizona and fostered an environment that welcomed new technological ideas. Their political champion was Goldwater, a Phoenix City Council member, senator and the 1964 GOP presidential nominee who was the nation's most recognizable conservative for much of the 1950s and 1960s (and someone who today would be considered a libertarian, a strain of Republicanism with especially strong roots in the West). Later, Republican Sen. John McCain took up conservatism's mantle in Arizona; he died in 2018.

Arizona ranks second to California in production of vegetables, and it has significant uranium reserves (though in 2018, the U.S. Supreme Court upheld a ban on uranium mining near Grand Canyon National Park.) Still, Arizona's growth has long been based on high-tech and low taxes. Phoenix began attracting technology industries when Motorola built a research center for military electronics there in 1948. Other major employers followed, with both defense and commercial lines: Honeywell, Raytheon, Intel, Avnet and General Dynamics. Apple has cloud storage in Arizona; Nikola Motor Co. broke ground on a plant for zero-emissions vehicles; India-based Infosys is building an artificial intelligence facility; and Bill Gates is backing a 24,000-acre "smart city" complex near Phoenix. In 2020, Phoenix lured microchip maker Taiwan Semiconductor Manufacturing to build its first manufacturing plant in the United States, with a goal of opening in 2024. Meanwhile, the growth in finance jobs has recently outpaced that in the rest of the country.

The state is coming to grips with a changing climate, which includes a mix of rising temperatures, smaller snowpacks, reduced Colorado River flow and more frequent wildfires; since 1984, more than

2 percent of Arizona has burned per decade. In 2019, the Phoenix area set records for heat-related deaths for the fourth year in a row; officials are now spending money to bolster vegetated "cool corridors" to compensate for past decisions to pave over the desert. In 2020, the state's Republican-majority regulatory body voted to accelerate the timetable for utilities to secure their energy from carbon-free sources—half by 2035 and all by 2050. Currently, Arizona ranks third in installed solar capacity behind California and North Carolina, and it has the nation's largest nuclear power plant, the Palo Verde Nuclear Generating Station.

Arizona has been one of the nation's boom states, driven by the relocation of retirees from the Midwest and elsewhere. Its population nearly doubled from 3.7 million in 1990 to 7.3 million in 2019; its favorable real estate costs have induced a consistent stream of relocations, especially from California. The growth has centered on metro Phoenix, in places like the western exurb of Buckeye, which has grown about tenfold since 2000. In the meantime, Arizona has been a focal point for the battle over illegal immigration. The hilly Arizona desert in Cochise and Santa Cruz counties became a major entry point, and Joe Arpaio, the Maricopa County sheriff, made himself the embodiment of the get-tough approach for more than two decades until he lost office in 2016 (and failed in a 2020 comeback bid). In 2010, the legislature passed Senate Bill 1070, authorizing law enforcement officials to check the immigration status of people stopped for other reasons. President Barack Obama denounced the law, saying it encouraged racial profiling, and Hispanic organizations called for a boycott of the state. After some legal victories, critics of the law lost at the Supreme Court in 2012, and gradually the crisis atmosphere in the state ebbed. Trump's pursuit of a border wall energized his supporters, but it drew opposition not only from immigrant advocates but also environmentalists (for encroaching on sensitive habitats in the Organ Pipe Cactus National Monument) and members of the Tohono O'odham Nation, whose lands straddle the border.

For years, Democrats had expected Arizona's growing Latino population to nudge the state their way, and it did provide a strong basis for Democratic growth; Hillary Clinton improved on Obama's performance, and two years later Democrats flipped the secretary of state and education superintendent seats, picked up a corporation commission seat and made gains in the legislature. But Democratic gains were supercharged by shifts among white voters in the Phoenix suburbs who, like their peers in other states, had accelerated their movement towards the Democrats during the Trump era. One beneficiary was Democratic Rep. Kyrsten Sinema, who ran as a moderate and won an open Senate seat in 2018 over then–Rep. McSally. The blue shift really came to fruition in 2020, when Maricopa cast about three-fifths of the state's votes and handed Biden and Kelly victories. These wins were aided by the rightward shift of Arizona's Republican Party under Kelli Ward, "a pro-Trump zealot with a soft spot for conspiracy theories," in the words of the Atlantic. Many traditional Arizona Republicans presumably followed the lead of McCain's widow, Cindy, who endorsed Biden in the home stretch after enduring repeated barbs from Trump about her late husband.

Ultimately, Biden notched a victory of just over 10,000 votes, thanks to his turning Clinton's 44,000-vote deficit in Maricopa into a 45,000-vote edge. Biden also expanded the party's margin of victory by five points in the Democratic strongholds of Pima County (Tucson) and Coconino County (Flagstaff). Trump lavished attention on friendlier, more rural areas and made some marginal gains in redder regions such as Yuma County (Yuma) and Yavapai County (Prescott).In the Senate race, Kelly ran 44,000 votes ahead of Biden statewide, with more than half of that coming from Maricopa; by contrast, McSally. who had been appointed to the Senate after her loss to Sinema, ran 24,000 votes behind Trump. Underlining the state's leftward shift, voters also approved ballot measures to raise taxes on higher-income households and legalize recreational marijuana, though Democrats were unable to pick up either of the narrowly divided chambers of the legislature. After the election, Arizona's Republican state party continued to be a hotbed of Trump support, formally censuring Ducey, McCain, and Sen. Jeff Flake – the party's three most successful statewide candidates in the past decade – for insufficient loyalty to the president. "Arizona's urban vs. rural divide is deepening, just like the rest of the nation's," wrote Five Thirty Eight's Nathaniel Rakich. "But because Arizona is one of the most urbanized states in the country, that's a good trade for Democrats."

In May, the post–election reverberations continued as the Republican–controlled state Senate ordered an "audit" of all November 2020 votes in Maricopa County. The unprecedented action, which raised questions about GOP motivations and the inexperience of the group that was hired to perform the weeks–long count, was strongly opposed by state Democrats plus most officials in Maricopa, where Republicans largely retain control of county offices. Senate GOP leaders said that Trump had encouraged them and voiced his appreciation.

Population		Race and Ethnicity		Income	
Total	7,278,717	White	78.30%	Median Income	62,055
Land area (sq. miles)	113,594	Black	4.70%	State Income Rank	28 out of 50
Pop/ sq mi	64.08	Latino	31.70%	Poverty Rate	13.50%
Born in state	39.90%	Asian	4.60%	With health insurance	88.70%
		Two or more races	3.90%	Cash public assistance	1.50%
Age Groups		Other	9.80%	Food stamp/SNAP	12.5%
Under 18	22.50%				
18-34	23.30%	**Education**		**Work**	
35-64	36.10%	H.S grad or less	36.10%	White Collar	37.90%
Over 64	18.00%	Some college	33.70%	Sales and Service	41.40%
		College Degree, 4 yr	18.80%	Blue Collar	20.70%
Military		Post grad	11.30%	Government	13.60%
Veteran/ Active Duty	8.90%				

Presidential Politics

2020 Primary (D)	Biden (D)	268,029(44%)	Sanders (D)	200,456(33%)	Bloomberg (D)	58,788(10%)
	Warren (D)	35,537 (6%)				
2020 Pres. Vote	Biden (D)	1,672,143(49%)	Trump (R)	1,661,686(49%)		
2016 Pres. Vote	Trump (R)	1,252,401(48%)	Clinton (D)	1,161,167(45%)	Johnson (L)	106,327 (4%)

Arizona's fast-growing, rapidly diversifying population has made it competitive and raised Democrats' hopes that it could become a swing state for years to come. In 2020, Joe Biden become just the second Democrat since Harry Truman in 1948 to win the state.

Biden won Arizona by becoming the first Democrat in a generation to carry fast-growing Maricopa County, winning it by two percentage points. Barack Obama lost it by nine points in both 2008 and 2012, while Hillary Clinton had lost it by three. Maricopa contains more than 60 percent of Arizona's population, centered on metro Phoenix and its neighbors of Glendale, Mesa and Scottsdale, with booming suburbs and exurbs such as Surprise, Buckeye, Goodyear and Gilbert. Maricopa County has the fourth-largest population of any county in the nation, and from 2010 to 2019, greater Phoenix added more than 750,000 people, more than any U.S. metro area except Houston and Dallas. The county, like the state, once tilted Republican, but waves of new residents—Hispanics, college-educated white suburbanites, California ex-pats and retirees from the Midwest—have made it increasingly competitive in recent years.

Pima County, dominated by Tucson, the state's second largest city, is a Democratic stronghold that casts about one-sixth of the state's votes. Arizona's largely rural territory had been home to conservative ranchers and others who were once known as "Pinto" or "Goldwater" Democrats. Today it is strong GOP turf, except for Apache County with its tribal reservations; Coconino County, with Flagstaff and Northern Arizona University; and Santa Cruz County, where four of five residents are Hispanic. To prevail, a Democratic presidential candidate needs to battle a Republican close to a draw in Maricopa, score a big turnout in Pima, and hold down losses in the rest of the state. That was the formula Biden followed—as did Bill Clinton, the only other Democrat to carry the state, when he won in 1996.

Trump easily won the state's 2016 GOP primary, no surprise given how heated an issue immigration has been in Arizona for the past two decades. The state's 2020 Democratic primary was held on March 17, just as the coronavirus began wreaking havoc on elections; unlike other states that were forced to delay their primaries or push forward with low turnout, Arizona's heavily mail-voting electorate permitted the state to carry on largely without issues. Biden defeated Bernie Sanders 44%-33%, a closer result than other states that day and one that hinted at Biden's looming general-election problem with Hispanics.

Arizona's rapid growth and Trump's struggles with college-educated suburban voters made the general election competitive from the start. Biden, Trump and their allies combined to spend more than $50 million on TV ads in the Phoenix market, according to the Wesleyan Media Project, making it the most expensive media market in the nation during the campaign. It was the first time presidential campaigns invested heavily in the state in a generation.

Polls generally showed Biden with a slight lead in the state. But like other 2020 polls, they underestimated Trump's strength, and the election came down to the wire.

The Associated Press and Fox News called the state for Biden on election night. But other networks waited nine days, until the state had completed counting ballots and it was clear that Biden's lead would hold up. After numerous lawsuits from Trump and his allies were shot down by the courts, Biden won 49.4%-49.1%, winning by just over 10,000 votes—his narrowest margin of 2020.

Arizonans flocked to the polls in record numbers: Almost 3.4 million votes were cast in 2020, up from just 2.6 million in 2016 and 2.3 million in 2012. Turnout showed 70 percent of voting-age citizens casting ballots in 2020, up from 56 percent four years earlier. That was the second-largest surge in turnout, behind only Utah, according to a Bloomberg News analysis.

Biden undoubtedly benefited from the state's Hispanic growth, and a surge in Hispanic turnout. Trump made some inroads with Hispanic voters in the state: He lost Hispanics 61%-37%, according to exit polls, better than the 61%-31% split in 2016, and he ran ahead of his 2016 numbers in many of Phoenix's majority-Hispanic precincts. He also improved his performance in heavily Hispanic, more rural Santa Cruz and Yuma counties. But the Latino share of the vote jumped from 15 percent in 2016 to 19 percent in 2020.

Biden's biggest improvement came in white suburban areas filled with former McCain Republicans. (Biden made sure to highlight endorsements from Cindy McCain, the late senator's widow, as well as former GOP Sen. Jeff Flake). Biden won white college graduates in Arizona 53%-46%, according to exit polls, after Trump won them 50%-44% in 2016. Biden did much better than Clinton in areas like upscale Glendale and Mesa. Biden's 45,000-vote victory in Maricopa County made up four times his statewide margin of victory. Biden also benefited from a huge surge of Native American voters—tiny Apache County, which includes much of the Navajo reservation, saw turnout increase by 29 percent—and from improvements in Pima County, where his margin was nearly 100,000 votes, roughly 40,000 more than Clinton's lead four years earlier.

The state almost certainly will be a battleground once again in 2024.

Congressional Districts

117th Congress Lineup	5D 4R	116th Congress Lineup	5D 4R

Arizona has become a competitive battleground for House seats. Its nine-member delegation includes four relatively secure Republican districts, two solidly Democratic districts (with large Hispanic majorities), and three districts that started the past decade as "toss-ups," but are now held by Democrats. Those three districts are: the 1st, in the sprawling rural eastern part of the state; the 2nd, anchored in Tucson; and the 9th, in the university bastion of Tempe.

The outlines of the current map were drawn by the five-member Independent Redistricting Commission, which was created by a statewide referendum in 2000. It is composed of two Democrats, two Republicans and an ostensibly independent member picked by the other four. The commission's map resulted in a delegation of six Republican and two Democrats after the 2002 election, but it shifted to five Democrats and three Republicans in 2008. The GOP wave of 2010 restored Republicans to a 5-3 majority. When Arizona gained a seat from the 2010 census, Democrats emerged from a state dominated by a Republican governor and legislature with the map of their dreams and five of the state's nine House seats.

The map in 2012 infuriated Republicans: Not only did it maximize Democratic opportunities, it forced Republicans David Schweikert and Ben Quayle to run against each other even though the state gained a seat. Democrats won all three of the swing districts and have retained them since then, except for a four-year interlude in which Republican Martha McSally held the 2nd. Meanwhile, state Republicans challenged the redistricting commission, which approved its map for a second time.

The U.S. Supreme Court, in a 5-4 decision, ruled that Arizona voters had the authority to create a redistricting commission.

In the next redistricting cycle, Arizona had been widely expected to gain a tenth seat, replicating its pattern of increasing its delegation by at least one seat following each decennial count since 1960. But, with the apparent undercount of Latinos in border states, the state will retain nine seats. Still, that leave plenty of opportunity for each side to engage in creative map-drawing and legal strategy.

With Republicans in control of the governorship and legislature, they could seek other steps to limit the authority of the commission. Regardless of the procedures, the 2020 census gave Maricopa County about 60 percent of the state's population and enough residents to gain influence in an additional district—beyond the current five, which are held by three Republicans and two Democrats. The Latino population in both the state and the county slightly exceeds 30 percent. That makes a strong case for three Hispanic-majority districts. Of the current two, the 3rd District sprawls from Tucson to Yuma and includes suburbs southwest of Phoenix, and the 7th is entirely in Maricopa. With the retirement of Democratic Rep. Ann Kirkpatrick in the Tucson-based 2nd District, that could lead to a shift of many Latinos from the 3rd to the 2nd and make the 3rd more Maricopa-based while retaining a Hispanic majority.

At least one of the two remaining districts in mostly rural areas, including the Navajo and Hopi reservation plus the growing areas surrounding Flagstaff and Prescott, would be politically competitive. Depending on the quality of the candidates and their campaigns, it's a good bet that the 9-member delegation in the very competitive state will include at least three safe seats for each party —with as many as three "swing" seats, perhaps including two in Maricopa.

Doug Ducey (R)

Elected 2014, term expires 2023, 2nd term; b. Apr. 9, 1964, Toledo, OH; Arizona State U., B.S. 1986; Catholic; Married (Angela); 3 children.

Elected Office: AZ Treasurer, 2010-2014.

Professional Career: Beer Distributorship Marketing Coordinator, Hensley & Co., 1982-1986; Sales and Marketing Executive, Proctor & Gamble, 1986-1993; CEO and Chairman, Cold Stone Creamery, 1996-2007; Chairman, iMemories, 2008-2012.

Office: 1700 W. Washington St. Phoenix, 85007; 602-542-4331; Fax: 602-542-7601

Atty. Gen: Mark Brnovich (R) **Sec. of State:** Katie Hobbs (D)

State Legislature: Senate: 13D, 17R **House:** 29D, 31R

Election Results

Election	Name (Party)	Vote (%)
2018 General	Doug Ducey (R)	1,330,863 (56%)
	David Garcia (D)	994,341 (42%)
	Angel Torres (G)	50,962 (2%)
2018 Primary	Doug Ducey (R)	463,672 (71%)
	Ken Bennett (R)	191,775 (29%)

Republican Doug Ducey, a self-professed "conservative ice cream guy," won the governorship in 2014 and was reelected four years later. As Arizona has become an increasingly purple state, Ducey has walked a tightrope between the Donald Trump-allied wing of his party and more moderate, suburban voters who are increasingly open to voting Democratic.

Ducey grew up in Toledo Ohio and graduated from St. John's Jesuit High School in 1982. He drove west in his Datsun B210, leaving his recession-ravaged state to attend Arizona State University. He found his future in a Tempe ice cream store. After graduating with a degree in finance in 1986, and a brief stint in marketing at Procter & Gamble, Ducey joined up with the founder of Cold Stone Creamery and helped turn it into a global brand with more than 1,000 locations. He eventually became CEO. In 2007, at 43, Ducey helped engineer a merger with another Arizona franchising heavyweight, Kahala Corp. He got rich in the process, but that corporate marriage didn't work out, an experience Ducey described to Bloomberg Business as "incredibly frustrating and disappointing, but equally liberating all at once." Ducey took some time off, refocused, and became the lead investor and chairman of the board of iMemories, a friend's technology startup in Scottsdale, which helps people digitize their home movies and share them online.

Ducey made his first foray into elective politics in 2010 by seeking the state treasurer's post, vowing to utilize his business background to promote economic growth. That's not a core function of the state treasurer's office, and at the time many viewed his bid for the treasurer's job as a warm-up for a Senate or gubernatorial run. Nevertheless, his connections to the Phoenix business elite enabled Ducey to outraise and outspend his more politically credentialed GOP opponents; he handily won the primary and prevailed in the fall. As treasurer, Ducey laid the groundwork for higher office by leading a successful fight to defeat a 2012 ballot initiative that would have funded increased education spending by making a temporary one-cent sales tax increase permanent.

In 2014, he jumped into the spirited Republican contest to succeed Republican Gov. Jan Brewer. Ducey once again played up his business know-how, but this time he had plenty of backing from prominent conservatives, including Sen. Ted Cruz of Texas, former Alaska Gov. Sarah Palin, and Maricopa County Sheriff Joe Arpaio, an immigration hardliner who had supported one of Ducey's GOP primary rivals four years prior. He easily won the nomination and squared off against former Board of Regents member Fred DuVal, a centrist Democrat, in the general. Ducey pumped about $5 million of his own money into the campaign which, along with allied groups, resulted in more than $10 million being spent on his behalf in the election, compared with about $3 million spent by DuVal and his outside backers. Ducey won by nearly 12 percentage points and Arizonans extended their streak of electing governors not native to the state. (The last was Democrat Bruce Babbitt in 1982.)

Confronting a yawning state deficit, Ducey pushed through a budget that cut nearly $100 million in funding to higher education, borrowed more than $100 million from the state's rainy day fund and clawed back some $220 million in unspent agency funds. Ducey backed off a plan to prune non-classroom K-12 education spending and negotiated a deal with legislators giving schools more flexibility. To the chagrin of his more conservative backers, Ducey steered clear of some controversial topics, including Common Core education standards and adoptions by same-sex couples. In 2016, Ducey signed legislation that allows the state to withhold funding from local jurisdictions that pursue policies at odds with the state. Given Arizona's unified Republican government at the state level and the predominance of Democratic governance in many of the state's big cities, this law held the potential for sinking liberal policies.

In early 2018, teachers, wearing red and carrying the banner of #RedForEd, staged a walkout that closed 1,000 schools; they argued that Arizona's per-pupil expenditures in 2015 were lower than any state except Idaho and Utah. The strike ended after Ducey signed a bill to boost teacher pay 20 percent by 2020, plus $100 million for support staff. It wasn't all the teachers had asked for, but it was considered a victory. Boasting an approval rating that was positive but not wildly so, Ducey faced a GOP primary challenge from the right by former Secretary of State Ken Bennett. Bennett attacked Ducey for "caving" to the teachers, but the incumbent largely ignored his challenger and won, 71%-29%. In the general election, Ducey faced David Garcia, an Arizona State University professor who served as an Army infantryman and narrowly lost a 2014 race for state education superintendent. Garcia, a fourth-generation Mexican-American, took pains to boost turnout among younger, less-frequent Latino voters who had a stronger sense of ethnic nationality and a more progressive outlook. But Ducey, bolstered by a sizable fundraising advantage, portrayed Garcia as being too far to the left, and voters agreed. Ducey won 56%-42%, even as Kyrsten Sinema, a Democrat who kept her distance from Garcia, was winning a highly competitive Senate race. In populous Maricopa County, Ducey-Sinema voters were common: Ducey won, 56%-42%, while Sinema prevailed, 51%-49%.

In the first year of his second term, Ducey pursued a largely pragmatic agenda that featured some policy zig-zagging. He signed a law popular among free-market advocates that loosened restrictions on occupational licensing; repealed a 28-year-old law that barred HIV-AIDS instruction that "promotes a homosexual lifestyle"; agreed to continue accepting refugees despite having complained about the resettlement of Syrian refugees four years earlier; vetoed a GOP-backed bill that would have eased a tax hit related to the 2017 federal tax bill; and signed a measure tightening the parameters for carrying out the death penalty. That summer, a controversy emerged over Nike backing off production of a sneaker featuring the 1777 "Betsy Ross flag," following opposition by former pro quarterback Colin Kaepernick. Ducey initially said he would "withdraw all financial incentive dollars" for a pending Nike plant in Goodyear, tweeting, "Arizona's economy is doing just fine without Nike. We don't need to suck up to companies that consciously denigrate our nation's history." But within days, he reversed himself, tweeting, "Arizona is open for business, and we welcome @Nike to our state." In 2020, Ducey backed off a proposal to seek a constitutional amendment banning "sanctuary cities" that spurn cooperation with federal immigration enforcement; the decision, which was joined by GOP legislative leaders, followed opposition from Latino organizations and some business groups.

The coronavirus pandemic put Ducey in the national spotlight, as cases surged in metro Phoenix in the early summer. (By then, the virus had already begun to devastate the more remote Navajo Nation in northeastern Arizona.) Ducey allowed an early stay-at-home order to expire and initially kept localities from requiring masks; he later reversed the mask policy and tightened some reopening guidance for businesses. After a decline in infections in the fall, Arizona saw cases rise to record levels in early winter, ranking it among the top five states for cases and top 10 states for deaths in late December. Amid this surge in infections, Ducey tightened requirements for public events and threatened to close businesses that flouted guidelines. The moves fell short of what public-health advocates had sought, yet further irritated critics on the right who demanded a more aggressive reopening.

Ducey also attracted national notice for his role in affirming Joe Biden's victory in the presidential race. After the state voted for a Democratic presidential candidate for the first time since 1996, it fell to Ducey to certify Biden's win. This meant facing down the pro-Trump wing of his own party, which wanted him to help overturn the results, citing (debunked) allegations of electoral fraud. Ducey made clear that he would not block the election results and sparred with Trump-allied state party chair Kelli Ward and Reps. Paul Gosar and Andy Biggs. While he was signing the certification papers on live television, Ducey pointedly ignored a call on his cellphone from the White House. In April 2021, Ducey signed a bill to block federal restrictions against the Second Amendment in the state.

Ducey is term-limited in 2022, and some Republicans would like him to challenge newly elected Democratic Sen. Mark Kelly, whose term is up in 2022. His visits in Washington in early 2021 indicated that he was thinking about that option. The early contenders who announced for the seat included Republican state Treasurer Kimberly Yee and Democratic Secretary of State Katie Hobbs. Interest in that contest was roiled by the Republican-ordered "audit" of the November 2020 election count in Maricopa County. The state's political shifts seemed likely to make the race competitive.

Kyrsten Sinema (D)

Elected 2018, term expires 2024, 1st term, b. Jul 12, 1976; Tucson, AZ; Brigham Young University, B.A., 1995; Arizona State University, M.S.W., 1999; Arizona State University Law School, J.D., 2004; Arizona State University, Ph.D., 2012; None; Single.

Elected Office: AZ House, 2004-2010; AZ Senate, 2010-2012; U.S. house 2013-2019.

Professional Career: Social worker, 1995-2002; Practicing lawyer, 2005-present; Instructor, Center for Progressive Leadership, 2006-present.

DC Office: 317 HSOB 20510, 202-224-4521, sinema.senate.gov

State Offices: Phoenix, 602-598-7327.

Committees: *Banking, Housing & Urban Affairs*: Financial Institutions & Consumer Protection; National Security & International Trade & Finance; Securities, Insurance & Investment. *Commerce, Science & Transportation*: Aviation Safety, Operations & Innovations (Chmn); Communications, Media & Broadband; Space & Science; Tourism, Trade & Export Promotion. *Homeland Security & Government Affairs*: Emerging Threats & Spending Oversight; Government Operations & Border Management (Chmn). *Veterans' Affairs*.

Group Ratings (House)

	ADA	ACLU	AFL-CIO	LCV	COC	HAFA	ACU	CFG	FRC
2020	-	69%	-	62%	-	0%	15%	-	-
2019	65%	C	100%	71%	82%	C	15%	12%	0%

Almanac Ratings 2019-2020

	Economy	Social	Foreign	Composite
Liberal	48%	70%	22%	47%
Conservative	52%	30%	78%	53%

Key Votes of the 116th Congress (House)

1. EPA clean energy rules N	5. Russia sanctions Y	9. Barr as Atty. General Y
2. U.S./Mex./Can. trade deal Y	6. Troops in SYR, AFG Y	10. Spending at the border Y
3. Cut unemployment benefits Y	7. Veto arms sales to Saudis Y	11. Coney Barrett to Sup. Ct. N
4. Shelton to Fed Reserve N	8. Defense $$$, veto override Y	12. Electoral College objections N

Election Results

Election	Name (Party)	Vote (%)		Cand. Spent	Ind. Exp. Support	Ind. Exp. Oppose
2018 General	Kyrsten Sinema (D)............................ 1,191,100	(50%)	$24,309,295	$9,050,763	$24,740,811
	Martha McSally (R)....................... 1,135,200	(48%)	$20,514,746	$3,054,086	$25,569,266
	Angela Green (G)............................... 57,442	(2%)			
2018 Primary	Kyrsten Sinema (D)............................ 404,170	(79%)			
	Deedra Abboud (D)............................ 105,800	(21%)			

Prior winning percentages: 2018 (50%), House: 2016 (61%), 2014 (55%), 2012 (49%)

Kyrsten Sinema won a hard-fought race in 2018 to become the first openly bisexual senator in U.S. history, the first female senator from Arizona and the first Democrat to win a Senate race in the state in three decades. In her political career, she has transformed from Green Party-supporting activist to one of the more moderate, bipartisan members of Congress—a rare centrist in the narrowly divided Senate. What's been consistent throughout her life has been a singular drive that's taken her from an impoverished childhood to Congress.

Sinema grew up in Tucson. After her parents divorced, her mother married a teacher. When her stepfather lost his job, the family took shelter for two years in a former gas station on his parents' Florida property that she said lacked electricity and running water — a period she's described as homelessness, though some family members have said she's exaggerated how dire the living conditions were. The family relied on food donations from the close-knit Latter-day Saints community; her mother is Mormon. They eventually moved into a home but remained poor.

Those tough early years shaped her life—and play a key role in her political narrative. "For nearly three years, we lived in an old, abandoned gas station without running water or electricity," Sinema said in her Senate campaign launch video. "Sometimes, we didn't have enough food to eat, but we got by thanks to help from family, church and, sometimes, even the government."

At 16, Sinema graduated as her high school's valedictorian and went on to earn a bachelor's degree in social work from Brigham Young University. She also earned a master's degree in social work, a law degree and a doctorate in justice studies from Arizona State University — all while working full time. After graduating from BYU at 18, she became a social worker in a central Phoenix school district. Before her election to Congress, she worked as a lawyer, an adjunct professor at Arizona State, and an instructor at the Center for Progressive Leadership, a Washington-based institute that trains activists in progressive policies. Sinema is a fitness fiend: She has run more than 10 marathons, including the Boston Marathon, and is the first member of Congress to have completed a triathlon. She completed her third Ironman in New Zealand just two months after joining the Senate and also chaired the board of Women for Tri, which aims to increase the number of women in the competitions. She has taught spin classes to colleagues in the House gym and has recruited a bipartisan group to join her for boot-camp-like Solid core workout classes. Another congressional first for Sinema: She describes her religion as "none."

Sinema, who said a role model is Helen Keller, was motivated to enter politics to help people with backgrounds like hers. "I'm a Democrat today … because they taught me the best of both ideas: help each other when you're struggling but work very hard on your own," she told National Journal.

After serving as the state spokeswoman for the Green Party during Ralph Nader's 2000 presidential run and honing her political chops as an antiwar activist, she lost her first bid for the Arizona House running as an independent in 2002. She ran as a Democrat and won in 2004, serving there until 2010, when she was elected to the state Senate. As a liberal advocate in the state Legislature, she promoted LGBTQ rights and sponsored several bills aimed at reining in Maricopa County Sheriff Joe Arpaio's tough and sometimes extralegal crackdowns on undocumented immigrants. She worked with Republicans to pass legislation on human trafficking and other issues.

She ran in 2012 in a newly created U.S. House district in suburban Phoenix that was originally designed as a toss-up seat. She won the three-way Democratic primary with 41 percent of the vote. Her general election opponent was Vernon Parker, a former Paradise Valley mayor who served in both Bush administrations. They fought for the independent vote, each painting the other as extreme in attack ads. Sinema supported closing corporate tax loopholes and protecting payroll tax cuts for working families. Parker followed the national GOP playbook in vowing to repeal the Affordable Care Act and rein in runaway spending. Sinema won 49%-45%. It was her only competitive House race in a fast-growing district that leaned blue.

The former liberal firebrand joined the Blue Dog Coalition of centrist Democrats and bipartisan Problem Solvers Caucus and co-founded the United Solutions Caucus, a bipartisan House group seeking consensus policies. Sinema hewed close to the center during her time in the House, breaking occasionally with her party on fiscal issues and voting against keeping Nancy Pelosi as Democratic leader in 2015 and 2017. She occasionally criticized President Barack Obama and worked across the aisle with House Republicans, voting with them to repeal some parts of Obama care and the Dodd-Frank financial regulations. She also worked on legislation to protect victims of sexual violence on school campuses.

Sinema worked on housing and consumer issues on the House Financial Services Committee. The panel approved several of her proposals, including a 2016 measure to help law enforcement officials track down financial criminals who target seniors.

She tacked to the center on immigration, a hot-button issue in her home state, making some votes that infuriated Hispanic groups. In 2017, she was one of 24 House Democrats to vote for "Kate's Law," which would have guaranteed jail time for undocumented immigrants who reenter the U.S. after being deported and increased penalties for undocumented immigrants who had committed other crimes. She was one of only 11 Democrats who voted for GOP legislation that year that would have made it easier to deport immigrants suspected of having gang ties. She voted against House Republicans' more expansive immigration reform efforts.

She routinely ranked as one of the most conservative Democrats in the Almanac's annual vote ratings. "I'm just doing my thing," she told Roll Call in 2015. "I know my thing's a little bit different than other people, but I don't think there's anything wrong with that at all. And, you know what? I don't mind if some people like it or don't like it. That's OK."

Arizona operatives had long expected Sinema to run for statewide office. And she took the plunge in late 2017, announcing her bid to challenge Republican Sen. Jeff Flake. But Flake had emerged as one of President Donald Trump's most vocal critics and was facing a tough primary challenge from conservative iconoclast Kelli Ward, a former state senator who had put a scare into Sen. John McCain two years earlier. Flake admitted there was no way for him to win reelection and announced he would not seek another term just one month after Sinema launched her campaign.

Republican Rep. Martha McSally received strong encouragement from Senate Majority Leader Mitch McConnell and other establishment Republicans and soon entered the Senate contest. While McSally and Sinema had some commonalities—House members with impressive personal stories, long-held ambitions to run statewide and moderate profiles—McSally was hamstrung throughout the campaign by her need to ward off primary challengers. She spent much of the campaign pivoting to the right to defeat Ward and Arpaio, which allowed Sinema to dominate the center.

McSally was forced to fight on two fronts through the primary and navigate a state where the GOP base, strongly behind Trump, was distrustful of her former brand as a moderate and furious at its pair of senators — Flake and McCain — for regularly bucking the party. To shore up her base, McSally dropped her support for legislation to help undocumented immigrants who entered the United States as children and embraced Trump.

Sinema dominated the center with campaign ads touting her independence and bipartisan values. Those spots featured her talking about her tough upbringing and her work on education and veterans issues — including one memorable spot featuring her brother, a police officer and Marine veteran, touting her independence. She vowed to support new leadership in the Senate, a promise she broke soon after her election when Senate Minority Leader Chuck Schumer was reelected without opposition.

When McCain died from brain cancer days before the August primary, McSally, a former protege of the senator, stayed silent about his death, seemingly worried that her party's anti-McCain base would turn on her if she mourned him too vocally. Sinema heaped praise on McCain, embracing his maverick persona and praising his lifetime of service.

But Sinema's past offered McSally plenty of fodder. Her campaign unleashed some brutal ads spotlighting Sinema's past hard-line liberalism, including ads featuring her in a pink tutu protesting the war in Afghanistan. McSally's allies later unearthed a pair of 2011 videos of Sinema mocking her home state, calling its population "crazy" and joking it "is clearly the meth lab of democracy" because of its attempted crackdowns on immigrants.

McSally went too far in their one debate, accusing Sinema of treason—comments that drew rebukes in local media. Sinema earned the endorsement of the Arizona Republic, the state's largest paper, which almost always backs Republicans. McSally did little to steer back to the center, worried she would offend the state's conservative base. That allowed Sinema to position herself as the natural heir to Arizona's long line of maverick politicians, like McCain and Flake, rather than as a party-line Democrat.

The election in the GOP-leaning state tightened in the final month, with McSally leading a number of surveys. The Republican led on election night and for two days afterward, as Arizona's slow count of postal ballots dragged out the result. After Sinema took the lead, some national Republicans, including Trump, claimed voter fraud—without evidence.

The race was called in Sinema's favor by 55,900 votes. She ran well ahead of her state's gubernatorial nominee, liberal Democrat David Garcia, who struggled with fundraising against popular center-right Gov. Doug Ducey. Sinema and Garcia never endorsed one another. Sinema repeatedly name-checked McCain in her victory speech, as she positioned herself to assume his mantle of independent voting in the Senate.

But Sinema hadn't seen the last of McSally. Ducey appointed the failed candidate to the Senate after caretaker Sen. Jon Kyl resigned McCain's seat at the end of 2018, putting the old rivals in the same chamber. The two never developed a working rapport and old wounds would die hard. In McSally's campaign in the 2020 special election for the remainder of McCain's term, Sinema cut a brutal ad for Democratic nominee Mark Kelly. "Arizonans know that Martha McSally will say anything to get elected," Sinema said in the video. "Her false attacks against me were desperate and over the top. Now she's doing the same to Mark Kelly."

Sinema became part of a cohort of centrists in the Senate that proved vital to advancing legislation and helped set the tone for Democrats. She was one of three Democrats who crossed party lines to vote to confirm William Barr as attorney general in February 2019.

During Trump's first impeachment trial, she joined with fellow moderate Democrats Doug Jones of Alabama and Joe Manchin of West Virginia to criticize Democratic House managers' failure to seek formal negotiations with the White House over documents and witnesses. According to the New York Times, Sinema became a "wild card" on whether to convict Trump. Ultimately, she voted in favor of both articles of impeachment, saying in a subsequent statement, "Future presidents—of both parties—will use this case as a guide to avoid transparency and accountability to the American people. That should be gravely concerning to all of us."

Her lone-wolf approach irritated many Democrats. Sinema often skipped party lunches, telling Politico, "I'm not missing anything. I prefer happiness." She rarely agrees to interviews with newspapers or cable news.

During the COVID-19 pandemic, she began wearing colorful wigs on the Senate floor, including purple locks while holding a Bible for Sen. Mark Kelly's swearing-in ceremony after the 2020 elections. Her office told the Arizona Republic that the look—instead of her usual blonde tresses— was her way "to call attention to the need for all of us to stay home as much as possible and practice social distancing—which she is diligently practicing, including from her hair salon."

Sinema continued to demonstrate her independence. She drew ire from progressives for endorsing Rep. Joe Kennedy in his challenge to Massachusetts Sen. Ed Markey during their bitter 2020 primary. She said she would oppose the abolition of the filibuster if Democrats won back the majority, even supporting a resumption of the super-majority threshold to end filibusters of presidential nominees. She has taken a centrist view on environmental issues—voting to confirm David Bernhardt as Trump's Interior secretary and opposing efforts to weaken the Trump administration's efforts to relax regulations on the use of coal. The Arizona Democratic Party pushed for a resolution "advising" Sinema to follow the party's platform, but the proposal was tabled.

Early in the 2020 presidential campaign, she played coy on whether she would back the party's nominee regardless of whether he or she were a centrist or more far left, but she endorsed eventual nominee Joe Biden shortly after Super Tuesday. "Vice President Biden is authentic, genuine and has a track record of building bipartisan coalitions to achieve results," she said in a statement. "Not all candidates in this race represent those Arizona values. Joe Biden does." That middle of the road stance won her praise from former Republicans turned off by Trump. Arizona seemed to agree by voting for a Democrat for president for the first time in 24 years.

Still, as the state grows more blue with a younger, more diverse population, fellow Arizona lawmakers warned that her positions could soon be out of vogue. "She runs her own thing. It worked for her getting elected. In terms of effectiveness, we'll see," Democratic Rep. Raul Grijalva told Politico. "I would be more concerned about not reflecting where the demographics in Arizona are going." In another potential red flag, Sinema became a favorite of large pharmaceutical donors and the leading Senate recipient of drug-company contributions far ahead of her 2024 reelection, according to Kaiser Health News.

Mark Kelly (D)

Elected 2020, term expires 2022, 1st term, b. Feb 21, 1964; Orange, NJ; U.S. Naval Test Pilot School; U.S. Merchant Marine Academy, B.S., 1986; U.S. Naval Postgraduate School, M.S., 1994; Catholic; Married (Hon. Gabrielle Giffords); 2 children (2 from previous marriage)

Military Career: U.S. Navy officer.

Professional Career: NASA Astronaut, 1996-2011; Founder, Americans for Responsible Solutions.

DC Office: Suite B40B DSOB 20510, 202-224-2235, Fax: 202-228-2862, kelly.senate.gov

State Offices: Phoenix, 602-671-7901; Prescott, 928-420-7732; Tucson, 520-475-5177.

Committees: *Aging. Armed Services*: Airland; Emerging Threats & Capabilities (Chmn); Strategic Forces. *Energy & Natural Resources*: National Parks; Public Lands, Forests & Mining; Water & Power. *Environment & Public Works*: Chem Safety, Waste Mngmnt, Enviro Justice & Reg Oversight; Fisheries, Water, and Wildlife; Transportation & Infrastructure. *Joint Economic.*

Election Results

Election	Name (Party)	Vote (%)		Cand. Spent	Ind. Exp. Support	Ind. Exp. Oppose
2020 General	Mark Kelly (D)	1,716,467	(51%)	$99,641,306	$8,622,253	$41,677,633
	Martha McSally (R)	1,637,661	(49%)	$70,880,548	$1,388,439	$30,388,496
2020 Primary	Mark Kelly (D)	665,620	(100%)			

Mark Kelly, a former NASA astronaut and the husband of former-Rep. Gabby Giffords, was elected to the Senate in his first political campaign. His victory in the special election for the final two years of the term of the late Republican Sen. John McCain, who died in 2018 of brain cancer, required him to run for a full term in 2022 to remain in the Senate. Before she was grievously wounded by gunfire while meeting with constituents in January 2011, the popular Giffords had been widely expected to seek a Senate seat. Instead, she gave up her House seat, pursued extensive medical rehabilitation, and—with Kelly—became an outspoken advocate and organizational force for gun control.

Kelly defeated Martha McSally, the former House member whom Republican Gov. Doug Ducey appointed to fill McCain's seat after the 2018 election. McSally, who won three terms in the Tucson-based seat that Giffords earlier held, had been heralded by Republicans for her centrist appeal and experience as the first female Air Force fighter pilot to fly in combat. She gained the dubious distinction of losing, in consecutive cycles, Senate seats that had been controlled by Arizona Republicans for more than two decades. In 2018, she was narrowly defeated by then-Rep. Kyrsten Sinema in the contest for an open Senate seat.

Sinema and Kelly are the first pair of Democrats to hold Arizona's Senate seats concurrently since 1952. Democrat Ernest McFarland, the Senate majority leader, was defeated that year by Republican Barry Goldwater.

Kelly, the son of two police officers, grew up in New Jersey. He earned a bachelor's degree in marine engineering from the U.S. Merchant Marine Academy and a master's degree in aeronautical engineering from the U.S. Naval Postgraduate School before beginning his career in aviation. He made two deployments on the USS Midway during the first Gulf War and flew 39 combat missions during Operation Desert Storm.

In 1996, Kelly was selected to be an astronaut. He flew four missions as a space shuttle pilot, spending over 540 days in space. Scott Kelly, his identical twin brother, also was a naval aviator and an astronaut in space shuttle missions.

Mark Kelly left NASA and retired from the Navy in 2011 and cared for Giffords full time during her grueling recovery from the attempted assassination. She was shot in the head from point-blank range while attending an outdoor event in Tucson called "Congress on Your Corner." Six people were killed in the attack and 12 were wounded. Two years later, the couple launched an organization called Americans for Responsible Solutions. The nonprofit and its affiliated super PAC became prominent advocates for gun control by encouraging elected officials to "stand up for solutions to prevent gun violence and protect responsible gun ownership."

In 2016, their group merged with the Law Center to Prevent Gun Violence to create a new nonprofit organization called the Giffords Law Center, based in San Francisco. The mission of the public-interest organization has been to "fight for stronger gun laws, hold the gun lobby accountable, and support political candidates who stand for safer schools and communities."

Kelly launched his Senate campaign in February 2019 with intensive fund-raising, bolstered by support from donors to the Giffords advocacy groups. Although he ruled out contributions from corporate political action committees to his campaign, which he called "a mission for Arizona," the Arizona Republic reported that he accepted funds from individual business executives. A spokesman for the National Republican Senatorial Committee blasted Kelly, saying he was "talking out of both sides of his mouth."

Both the Kelly and McSally campaigns became fundraising powerhouses, with nearly $14 million and $8 million, respectively, in cash on hand at the end of 2019. The total of $170 million that the two candidates had spent on their contest was the second-largest total ever for a Senate election; at that time, the amount was exceeded only by the $205 million spent by candidates in that year's Senate election in South Carolina. In addition, more than $30 million had been spent in Arizona by the two parties and other outside groups—mostly on attack ads. Kelly and his allies considerably outspent McSally and her supporters.

Kelly showed impressive political skills for a rookie candidate. In March 2020, the Cook Political Report profiled him as "Democrats' best recruit" in their Senate contests and reported that he was leading McSally in public and private polls.

Some campaign observers noted that Kelly gave scant campaign attention to gun control. Occasionally, he mentioned that he was a gun owner and that he supported those "rights and traditions." Historically, Arizona has imposed few restrictions on firearms. "I'm going to focus on the things that both Arizonans need and issues where I feel like, based on my personal experience, I can really help," he said, according to The New York Times.

For her part, McSally called herself a "Second Amendment senator" and attacked the Giffords gun control group as a "very radical political organization." But, in search of a political balance, she sought to distance herself from President Donald Trump during the final weeks of the campaign. Asked by a reporter at an October 6 debate whether she was proud to support Trump, she responded that she had, publicly and privately, asked him to stop attacking McCain. "Quite frankly, it pisses me off when he does it," she said.

The outcome was closer than expected: Kelly won 51%-49%. Since he was competing in a special election to fill the rest of McCain's term, he was sworn in early on December 2, giving him seniority over other freshmen. One the morning of his ceremony, Giffords posted a photo of Kelly holding the Bible at her first congressional swearing in. The two also made a trip to the nearby U.S. Naval Academy to visit McCain's grave and lay a wreath before Kelly took the seat he once held. "He was a hero of mine when I was young, and we often don't get to meet our heroes," Kelly told the Arizona Republic. "It's also much less often that you eventually get to call them a friend and to be elected to his United States Senate seat; that—that's a very big deal for me."

Kelly won't have a lot of time to adjust to legislating, since he needs to run in 2022 for a full term. Gov. Ducey has been mentioned as a possible GOP challenger; given Trump's ire with him over certifying Arizona's electoral votes for Biden in the presidential election, he could face a tough road in a Republican primary. That could leave Republicans, instead, with a far-right and unelectable nominee, such as Arizona GOP Chairwoman Kelli Ward, who unsuccessfully challenged McCain and has moved the state party further to the right—and perhaps toward irrelevance.

Tom O'Halleran (D)

Elected 2016, 3rd term, b. Jan 24, 1946; Chicago, IL; Lewis University, Att., 1966; DePaul University, Att., 1993; Catholic; Married (Pat O'Halleran); 3 children; 3 grandchildren.

Elected Office: AZ House, 2001-2007; AZ Senate, 2007-2009.

Professional Career: Police officer, 1966-1979; Bond trader/business owner.

DC Office: 324 CHOB 20515, 202-225-3361, Fax: 202-225-3462, ohalleran.house.gov

State Offices: Casa Grande, 520-316-0839; Flagstaff, 928-286-5338; Tucson, 928-304-0131.

Committees: *Agriculture*: Conservation & Forestry; General Farm Commodities & Risk Management. *Energy & Commerce*: Communications & Technology; Energy; Environment & Climate Change; Oversight & Investigations.

Group Ratings

	ADA	ACLU	AFL-CIO	LCV	COC	HAFA	ACU	CFG	FRC
2020	**	73%	**	100%	-	0%	9%	**	-
2019	80%	C	100%	97%	64%	C	9%	12%	0%

Almanac Ratings 2019-2020

	Economy	Social	Foreign	Composite
Liberal	100%	53%	52%	69%
Conservative	0%	47%	48%	31%

Key Votes of the 116th Congress

1. U.S./Mex./Can. trade deal	Y	5. Russia sanctions	Y	9. Firearms background checks Y
2. First Coronavirus response	Y	6. Troops in Syria	Y	10. Spending at the border Y
3. HEROES Act	Y	7. Veto arms sales to Saudis	Y	11. Marijuana liberalized rules Y
4. CASH Act	Y	8. Defense $$$, veto override	Y	12. Electoral College objections N

Election Results

Election	Name (Party)	Vote (%)		Cand. Spent	Ind. Exp. Support	Ind. Exp. Oppose
2020 General	Tom O'Halleran (D)........................	188,469	(52%)	$3,856,689	$321,342	$1,038,443
	Tiffany Shedd (R)........................	176,709	(48%)	$1,578,719	$240,955	$2,331,026
2020 Primary	Tom O'Halleran (D)........................	47,083	(59%)			
	Eva Putzova (D)............................	33,248	(41%)			

Prior winning percentages: 2018 (54%), 2016 (51%)

Democrat Tom O'Halleran, a former Republican state legislator who switched parties to run for the House, in 2016won an open seat in Arizona. In this competitive district, he initially defeated an ethically flawed opponent and then placed his imprint on the district—pending the 2022 redistricting. O'Halleran, who has emphasized his independence and political centrism, became a leader of the House Blue Dog Coalition.

O'Halleran was born in Chicago. His father grew up on a dairy farm that his family lost during the Great Depression, and he worked in a steel foundry and later was a janitor. O'Halleran joined the Chicago Police Department in 1966,serving as an officer and later a sergeant in a special operations unit. He became a government bond trader and served on the Chicago Board of Trade's executive board of directors. After he retired and moved with his family to Arizona, O'Halleran became involved in local politics. He was elected as a Republican to the state House in 2000, where he chaired the Natural Resources and Agriculture Committee. In 2006, he was elected to the state Senate, where he chaired the Higher Education Committee, but was defeated in 2008.

Citing Republicans' inability to legislate on issues such as education, child welfare and water problems, O'Halleran became an independent in 2014 and ran again unsuccessfully that year for the state Senate. When Democratic Rep. Ann Kirkpatrick challenged Sen. John McCain, O'Halleran ran as a Democrat for the open House seat. Republicans nominated Paul Babeu, who got 31 percent of the vote in a six-candidate field. Babeu was well-known as the sheriff of Pinal County, where he was outspoken on illegal immigration. "I'm for enforcing the law, securing the border and protecting America. I don't feel our nation is more secure or more safe than it was eight years ago," Babeu said, referring to President Barack Obama. O'Halleran called for improved security at the border, with the best technology and experts.

The campaign was overwhelmed by charges against Babeu, stemming from reports of alleged abuses while he was headmaster of a private Massachusetts school for troubled children, which subsequently was shut down; a state investigation concluded that the school's disciplinary practices were abusive and in humane. The National Republican Congressional Committee decided to steer clear of the contest and spent no money in this competitive district. National Democratic groups and their allies spent $3 million, chiefly on ads attacking Babeu's personal history. O'Halleran won, 51%-43%. He led, 2-to-1, in Apache and Coconino counties.

Age 70 when he entered the House, O'Halleran sought bipartisanship and often kept his distance from national Democrats. In the Almanac vote ratings in 2017, he ranked as the fourth most-conservative Democrat. When Congress enacted bipartisan legislation in 2018 to reduce opioid addiction, the bill included his amendment that allowed states with high addiction rates to receive added Medicaid funds. O'Halleran was the chief House sponsor of a bill signed by Trump that improved the water supply on the White River for the White Mountain Apache Tribe.

When Democrats took control of the House in 2019, O'Halleran was a leader of the party's moderates. He became the policy co-chair of the Blue Dogs and pledged to be "the voice of common sense and thoughtful leadership." He was among the Democrats on the bipartisan Problem Solvers Caucus who agreed to support Nancy Pelosi for Speaker after she reached agreement with them on House rules changes for more open debate. To discourage government shutdowns, he said the Congressional Budget Office should issue daily reports of the economic impact, which would be designed to highlight the costs of gridlock.

With his seat on the Energy and Commerce Committee, O'Halleran worked on energy issues affecting his district. In September 2020, when the House approved a bill to promote clean energy, it included his program for grants to rural electric cooperatives. Another part of that measure was a plan that he prepared with Republican Rep. Markwayne Mullin of Oklahoma to increase funds for access to electricity in tribal communities.

O'Halleran's bids for reelection generated concern among House Democrats and their allies, who spent more than $3 million on his behalf in 2018 and another $2 million in 2020. In 2018, he was challenged by Wendy Rogers, a retired Air Force pilot and officer. The Arizona Republic, in endorsing O'Halleran, described Rogers as "another rock-throwing partisan." He won, 54%-46%. His lead of over 25,000 votes in Apache and Coconino counties was more than enough to cover the small lead by Rogers in Pinal and Pima counties.

In 2020, running against Tiffany Shedd, a farmer and small business attorney, O'Halleran won 51.6%-48.4%, the closest victory in his three contests. House Democrats fared poorly that year in rural battlegrounds such as his district. Shedd won five of the seven largest counties, but O'Halleran again was saved by his 2-to-1 majorities in Apache and Coconino. In a potential warning sign, O'Halleran was held to 59 percent of the vote in the primary by Eva Putzova, a native of Slovakia, who became an activist on environmental and immigration issues and was a member of the Flagstaff City Council.

Redistricting could become a key factor for O'Halleran. In his sprawling and competitive district, even a seemingly minor change could have a significant impact.

AZ-1: Northeast/Central Arizona   **Cook Partisan Voting Index: R+2**

Population		Race and Ethnicity		Income	
Total	782,088	White	64.20%	Median Income	$56,117
Land area (sq. miles)	55,040	Black	2.80%	District Income Rank	316
Pop/ sq mi	14.21	Latino	23.00%	Poverty Rate	18.00%
Born in State	52.40%	Asian	1.60%	With health insurance	86.90%
		Two or more races	3.70%	Cash public assistance	1.70%
Age Groups		Other	27.70%	Food stamp/SNAP	11.90%
Under 18	22.70%				
18-34	22.60%	**Education**		**Work**	
35-64	34.90%	H.S grad or less	37.80%	White Collar	35.50%
Over 64	19.80%	Some college	37.10%	Sales and Service	41.60%
		College Degree, 4 yr	14.90%	Blue Collar	23.00%
Military		Post grad	10.20%	Government	23.30%
Veteran/ Active Duty	8.70%				

2020 Pres. Vote	Biden	187,182	(50%)	Trump	180,673	(48%)		
2016 Pres. Vote	Trump	135,928	(47%)	Clinton	132,874	(46%)	Johnson	11,732 (4%)

Southern Phoenix, Navajo Nation, Flagstaff: Beyond Phoenix, Arizona is a vast state of stunning beauty: the awe-inspiring Grand Canyon, the subtle pastel hues of the Painted Desert, the sheer cliff walls of Canyon de Chelly, the majestic spires of Monument Valley, the still waters of Lake Powell, the mountainous pine forests around Flagstaff, and the rust-and-rose red rocks of Sedona. It also has man-made landmarks. The celebrated U.S. 66, now mostly superseded by Interstate 40, is dotted with old copper mining towns like Globe.

All of these places are in the 1st Congressional District in rural northeastern Arizona plus exurban sites between Phoenix and Tucson, the tenth largest district in the nation. It encompasses Flagstaff, with rapid growth at Northern Arizona University, a gateway to the Grand Canyon and a growing tourism and retirement mecca that has lured snowbirds with its climate and affordable housing. In Casa Grande, between Phoenix and Tucson, the long-delayed Phoenix Mart was scheduled to open in 2019as a 1.6-millionsquarefoot commercial complex over 585 acres that styles itself as "North America's most complete global product marketplace," designed to connect manufacturers, distributors, wholesalers and retailers. But the opening was delayed by an FBI investigation of overseas investors, plus unpaid bills and liens that had been placed on the property. Also in Casa Grande, Lucid Motors—with $1 billion invested by Saudi Arabia—moved ahead with a plant to manufacture 130,000 luxury electric vehicles annually by 2022, as a competitor to Tesla Motors. In December 2020, a company official said the facility would open in spring 2021.

The 1st is home to the nation's largest Indian population. A full 23 percent of its residents identify themselves as Native Americans, who slightly outnumber Hispanics in the district. Redistricting after the 2010 census united the Navajo and Hopi reservations in the same congressional district for the first time in the state's history. The two tribes, historic enemies, concluded they could wield more political clout together than apart. Other tribes with a presence here are the Fort Apache, San Carlos, Havasupai, Hualapai, Kaibab, Gila River and Zuni.

By far the largest is the Navajo Nation. Most of the Navajo are in Apache County and others are on parts of the reservation that extend into New Mexico and Utah. There are about 286,000 Navajo in the three states, of whom an estimated 73 percent speak the language, and many still practice the traditional Navajo lifestyle. They have a history of fiercely contested tribal elections and considerable social problems. Alcoholism and drug abuse are rampant, violent crime is a problem, and there is little economic development. After a failed $500 million effort to encourage the Navajo and Hopi to share land, the federal government decided to remove members of each tribe from the property of the other. Another local setback was the decision by utility companies, under pressure from environmentalists, to shut down in November 2019 a Navajo-owned power-generating plant, known as the Salt River Project; its use of coal was expensive and inefficient.

The 1st District was drawn to be competitive politically. With its diversity and huge size, it is one of the most difficult in the nation to manage. The district has leaned slightly Republican in recent presidential elections. Apache County, with its Navajo majority, is heavily Democratic. Flagstaff-based Coconino County has moved in that direction. South of Phoenix, Pinal County, which has the most voters, leans Republican, as does the sliver of Pima County included in the 1st.

Ann Kirkpatrick (D)

Elected 2018, 5th term, b. Mar 24, 1950; McNary, AZ; University of AZ, B.A., 1972; University of AZ James E. Rogers College of Law, J.D., 1979; Roman Catholic; Married (Roger Curley); 2 children.

Elected Office: AZ House, 2005-2007; U.S. House, 2009-2011, 2013-2017.

Professional Career: Attorney & Co-founder, Kirkpatrick & Harris, Law Firm; Business Law and Ethics Instructor, Coconino Community College; Coconino County Deputy County Attorney; Sedona City Attorney.

DC Office: 309 CHOB 20515, 202-225-2542

State Offices: Sierra Vista, 520-459-3115; Tucson, 520-881-3588.

Committees: *Agriculture*: Biotechnology, Horticulture & Research. *Appropriations*: Defense; Energy & Water Development & Related Agencies; Financial Services & General Government.

Almanac Ratings 2019-2020

	Economy	Social	Foreign	Composite
Liberal	52%	58%	54%	55%
Conservative	48%	42%	46%	45%

Key Votes of the 116th Congress

1. U.S./Mex./Can. trade deal	Y	5. Russia sanctions	Y	9. Firearms background checks	Y
2. First Coronavirus response	N/A	6. Troops in Syria	Y	10. Spending at the border	Y
3. HEROES Act	N/A	7. Veto arms sales to Saudis	Y	11. Marijuana liberalized rules	Y
4. CASH Act	Y	8. Defense $$$, veto override	Y	12. Electoral College objections	N

Election Results

Election	Name (Party)	Vote (%)		Cand. Spent	Ind. Exp. Support	Ind. Exp. Oppose
2020 General	Ann Kirkpatrick (D)	209,945	(55%)	$1,442,964	$1,935	
	Brandon Martin (R)	170,975	(45%)	$368,984	$2,595	$54
2020 Primary	Ann Kirkpatrick (D)	77,517	(76%)			
	Peter Quilter (D)	24,035	(24%)			

Prior winning percentages: 2018 (55%), 2014 (53%), 2012 (49%), 2008 (56%)

Few House members have had as many political and personal comebacks as Democrat Ann Kirkpatrick. She served two terms in Arizona's sprawling 1st District, losing reelection in 2010 and then a statewide challenge to Republican Sen. John McCain in 2016. In 2018, her third trip to the House, she faced a competitive Democratic primary, but had a relatively easy time in November. She replaced GOP Rep. Martha McSally, who twice ran unsuccessfully for the Senate. Fun fact: For each of her three arrivals in the House, Kirkpatrick won an open seat that had been held by a Republican. In March 2021, she announced that she won't seek reelection in 2022. For the first time, she will voluntarily end her service in Congress.

Kirkpatrick hails from the White Mountain Apache Nation reservation in eastern Arizona. After earning her bachelor's degree from the University of Arizona, she taught for two years in Tucson. She earned a law degree and worked as a prosecutor for the Coconino County Attorney's Office. In 2004, Kirkpatrick was elected to the state House from a district where two-thirds of the registered voters were Native Americans. She defeated the incumbent, who was a Navajo and political independent.

She made her first bid for the House in 2008 after GOP freshman Rep. Rick Renzi was the target of misconduct charges. (He opted not to seek reelection and was convicted in 2013 on charges related to a land deal that allegedly benefited one of his former business partners.) Kirkpatrick won a four-way Democratic primary with 47 percent of the vote, then soundly defeated GOP anti-tax activist Sydney Hay in November. In the House, she mostly supported President Barack Obama's agenda. Running for reelection, she was challenged by Republican Paul Gosar, a dentist and political newcomer. He attacked her support of the 2010 health care law and took a hard line on immigration. Kirkpatrick refused to distance herself from Obama, and she lost, 50%-44%.

After redistricting in 2012 made the 1st District more favorable to a Democrat but still competitive, Gosar decided to run in the GOP-friendly 4th District. In mounting her comeback, Kirkpatrick faced Republican Jonathan Paton, a former state legislator. She pulled out a 49%-45% win. In 2014, she survived a stiff challenge from state House Speaker Andy Tobin, who sought to make the campaign a referendum on Obama. In all those races, Kirkpatrick built a reputation as a relentless campaigner. Beyond television advertising, one of her largest campaign expenses was gasoline.

That led to Kirkpatrick's challenge to the iconic McCain. After he won his three-way primary with 51 percent of the vote, Kirkpatrick sought to tie McCain to GOP presidential nominee Donald Trump, while suggesting that he was no longer the outspoken independent he had once been. McCain renounced his endorsement of Trump a month before the election, following the release of the decade-old videotape in which Trump made lewd comments about women. Kirkpatrick lost 54%-41%.

When McSally's first Senate run two years later created an open seat to the south, Kirkpatrick made yet another comeback bid. Thanks to her early career in Tucson and a shared television market between the two districts, Kirkpatrick was the frontrunner among the seven Democratic candidates. In the primary, she described herself as "the most progressive candidate in this race who has a track record of getting things done." Former state Rep. Matt Heinz, her chief opponent, compared her to a "meth addict" in her eagerness to return to Congress and criticized her as an outsider with a centrist record. In 2016, Heinz—an emergency-room physician—lost to McSally, 57%-43%. Kirkpatrick, with the backing of the Democratic Congressional Campaign, won the primary 42%-30%.

Republicans initially were enthusiastic about their nominee, Lea Marquez-Peterson, a conservative Latina and chief executive of the Tucson Hispanic Chamber of Commerce. But Kirkpatrick's experience and the enthusiasm among Democrats for women candidates became obstacles for Republicans in this swing district. The National Republican Congressional Committee abandoned its funding of the contest in early October.

With her previous service, Kirkpatrick had an advantage in the large freshman class, resulting in a seat on the Appropriations Committee. In July 2020, she claimed credit for committee approval of accelerated construction of new security gates at Davis-Monthan Air Force Base.

A year into that term, Kirkpatrick announced she would take a leave of absence to treat alcoholism after a fall on a train platform. "I am taking this important step forward with the full expectation and desire to return to work stronger and healthier and to continue serving my beloved Arizona," she said in a statement. Eleven months later, she faced Republican Brandon Martin, who served as an intelligence operator in Afghanistan for the Army Reserve. Kirkpatrick took 58 percent of the vote in Tucson-based Pima County, which cast more than four-fifths of the vote, and won, 55%-45%—a once-unthinkable margin in what has been one of the most competitive districts in the country.

With her retirement and redistricting in 2022, her Tucson-area seat faced the prospect of a significant showdown.

AZ-2: Southeast Arizona   Cook Partisan Voting Index: D+2

Population		Race and Ethnicity		Income	
Total	733,197	White	81.80%	Median Income	$54,835
Land area (sq. miles)	7,838	Black	4.30%	District Income Rank	334
Pop/ sq mi	93.54	Latino	29.40%	Poverty Rate	13.10%
Born in State	37.40%	Asian	2.80%	With health insurance	91.60%
		Two or more races	4.80%	Cash public assistance	1.10%
Age Groups		Other	6.20%	Food stamp/SNAP	10.00%
Under 18	18.90%				
18-34	23.40%	Education		Work	
35-64	35.50%	H.S grad or less	30.20%	White Collar	41.00%
Over 64	22.30%	Some college	34.50%	Sales and Service	42.20%
		College Degree, 4 yr	20.50%	Blue Collar	16.90%
Military		Post grad	14.80%	Government	17.70%
Veteran/ Active Duty	13.90%				

2020 Pres. Vote	Biden	213,408	(54%)	Trump	171,803	(44%)			
2016 Pres. Vote	Clinton	156,676	(49%)	Trump	141,196	(44%)	Johnson	12,989	(4%)

Tucson Metro: Arizona's first frontier was just south of today's Tucson, where Franciscan friars built Mission San Xavier del Bac in the 18th century. To the east, the late-19th century mining towns of Tombstone and Bisbee sprang up on mountainsides, where miners dug up gold, silver and much of America's copper. In those wild and wicked mining days, the Earp brothers waged their famous gunfight against a gang of outlaws at the O.K. Corral in Tombstone. A 1957 movie starring Burt Lancaster and Kirk Douglas told that tale and helped put the city on the tourism map. Here the rebellion of the land-starved American Indian was quashed, when the Apache leader Geronimo surrendered in 1886.

In recent years, Cochise County became an active frontier again. After the Border Patrol reduced illegal crossings in California and Texas, Mexicans and others trying to enter the United States illegally began coming to Agua Prieta, just across the border from the town of Douglas. There they fanned out, crossed the border and used the area's numerous roads, mountain trails and ranch lands to get to Tucson and Phoenix. The Tucson sector became the Border Patrol's most active in both apprehensions and illegal drug seizures. Stepped-up border enforcement and a reduced flow of illegal immigrants have significantly decreased these metrics. But the bodies of many who didn't make it are still found in the mountains and desert. Drug trafficking remains active. Local law enforcement officials worry that legalization of marijuana in western states will increase business for illegal cartels, including more powerful drugs.

Tucson is Arizona's second metropolis. It is much smaller, poorer and politically more progressive than Phoenix. Tucson is a hip, high-tech city and home to the University of Arizona. In 2011, the city earned an unwanted international spotlight when a shooting in a grocery store parking lot left six people dead and shocked the country. Rep. Gabrielle Giffords was seriously injured in that incident and eventually resigned from Congress as a result of her injuries. Defense giant Raytheon Co. has a huge missile plant at Tucson International Airport, which is in the 3rd District. Davis-Monthan Air Force base near downtown is home to F-16 fighter jets and drone pilot training; with 11,000 service members, it contributes more than $1 billion a year to the area economy. In 2019, Regina Romero made history when she was sworn in as the city's first Latina mayor.

The 2nd Congressional District includes most of Tucson, except the Latino-dominated west and south sides. It also includes the eastern half of surrounding Pima County. Also here are southeastern Arizona high desert real estate, including all of mountainous Cochise County, the small, border-crossing town of Douglas, and the city of Sierra Vista near Fort Huachuca, the site of the Army Military Intelligence Center, where military interrogators are trained. The population of Sierra Vista-Douglas dropped 8 percent from 2010 to 2019, one of the largest decreases in the nation. Politically, the 2nd has been closely divided, voting for Arizona GOP favorite son John McCain by less than a percentage point in 2008. Donald Trump lost much of the swing vote in 2016, and Hillary Clinton won the district by five points. Joe Biden comfortably took the district, 54%-44%. He increased the Democratic majority in Pima from 54%-40% to 59%-40%.

Raul Grijalva (D)

Elected 2002, 10th term, b. Feb 19, 1948; Tucson, AZ; University of AZ, B.A., 1986; Roman Catholic; Married (Ramona Grijalva); 3 children.

Elected Office: Tucson Unified School District Governing Board, 1974-1986; Pima County Board of Supervisors, 1988-2002.

Professional Career: Assistant dean of Hispanic Affairs, University of AZ., 1987.

DC Office: 1511 LHOB 20515, 202-225-2435, Fax: 202-225-1541, grijalva.house.gov

State Offices: Avondale, 623-536-3388; Somerton, 928-343-7933; Tucson, 520-622-6788.

Committees: *Education & Labor*: Early Childhood, Elementary & Secondary Education; Higher Education & Workforce Investment. *Natural Resources (Chmn)*: Ex Officio membership on all subcommittees.

Group Ratings

	ADA	ACLU	AFL-CIO	LCV	COC	HAFA	ACU	CFG	FRC
2020	**	83%	**	100%	-	0%	4%	**	-
2019	95%	C	95%	97%	36%	C	4%	24%	0%

Almanac Ratings 2019-2020

	Economy	Social	Foreign	Composite
Liberal	100%	65%	96%	87%
Conservative	0%	35%	4%	13%

Key Votes of the 116th Congress

1. U.S./Mex./Can. trade deal	Y	5. Russia sanctions	Y	9. Firearms background checks	Y
2. First Coronavirus response	N/A	6. Troops in Syria	Y	10. Spending at the border	N
3. HEROES Act	Y	7. Veto arms sales to Saudis	Y	11. Marijuana liberalized rules	Y
4. CASH Act	Y	8. Defense $$$, veto override	Y	12. Electoral College objections	N

Election Results

Election	Name (Party)	Vote (%)		Cand. Spent	Ind. Exp. Support	Ind. Exp. Oppose
2020 General	Raul Grijalva (D)	174,243	(65%)	$633,845	$2,189	
	Daniel Wood (R)	95,594	(35%)	$34,910		$113
2020 Primary	Raul Grijalva (D)	63,282	(100%)			

Prior winning percentages: 2018 (64%), 2016 (99%), 2014 (56%), 2012 (58%), 2010 (50%), 2008 (63%), 2006 (61%), 2004 (62%), 2002 (59%)

Raul Grijalva, a Democrat first elected in 2002, chairs the Natural Resources Committee. As one of the most liberal committee chairmen, and the only Hispanic to head a major House panel, he has voiced his outspoken progressive views that often feature a border perspective. Following his frequent clashes with the Trump administration, whose officials launched unusual attacks against him, he showed early cooperation with President Joe Biden. Although he occasionally has had narrow reelections, Grijalva appears politically secure in his wide-ranging district.

Grijalva was born and grew up in Tucson, the son of a bracero, or guest worker, who emigrated from Mexico in 1945. He graduated from the University of Arizona and has deep roots in the immigrant community on the city's southwest side. He was director of El Pueblo Neighborhood Center and assistant dean for Hispanic student affairs at the university. In 1974, he was elected to the Tucson school board and served 12 years. In 1988, he was elected a Pima County supervisor and served 14 years. As supervisor, he backed an effort to extend medical and dental benefits to same-sex domestic partners of county employees and focused on affordable health care, family and children services, and economic growth. Developers and builders helped elect him to office, but his support for planned growth and impact fees later alienated them.

He won election to the House in a new seat created by redistricting. His chief opponent was state Sen. Elaine Richardson, who was endorsed by EMILY's List, which spent more than $500,000 on ads. Mocking his opponent's national funding, Grijalva created "Adelita's List," an allusion to the women who fought in the Mexican Revolution. He won the primary, 41%-21% and swept the general election in the heavily Democratic district.

In 2008, Grijalva was elected co-chair of the Progressive Caucus. In that position, he initially insisted that any health care overhaul include a government-run insurance option to compete with private insurers, but he later backed away from that demand. He espoused a "war tax" to finance military operations in Afghanistan, an effort he considered immoral. His Almanac vote rating has been among the most liberal in the House.

From his border district, Grijalva has focused consistently on immigration policy. He has co-sponsored bills to raise the number of low-skill visas from 5,000 to 400,000 and to allow legalization for some illegal immigrants, provided they pay a $500 civil fine. After Arizona state lawmakers passed an immigration bill in 2010 expanding law enforcement's powers to detain suspected immigrants, Grijalva took the unusual step of urging a boycott of his state, calling on sympathetic organizations to refrain from using Arizona as a convention site. He abandoned the boycott after a federal judge halted implementation of most of the immigration law, although the central provision was later upheld by the U.S. Supreme Court. He has encouraged Congress to find common ground on a bipartisan plan to approve immigration changes that he viewed as "low-hanging fruit."

His initial efforts on environmental and energy issues were at home. He worked to stop uranium mining in the Kaibab National Forest and on federal lands near the Grand Canyon, and he was behind efforts to create a Sonoran Desert conservation system. Grijalva sponsored legislation to protect parts of Pima and Santa Cruz counties from future mining claims, and he has supported the San Carlos Apache Tribe in battling copper-mining operations around its lands. Combining his interests in the environment and immigration, he has implored Homeland Security Department officials to take into account protecting native plants and species when building security checkpoints at the border.

On the Natural Resources Committee, where he became the top Democrat in 2015, Grijalva worked with party leaders in opposing Republican efforts to approve the Keystone XL pipeline. He urged environmentalists to view issues from the viewpoint of Hispanics and other minority groups. After Donald Trump became president, Grijalva filed a lawsuit with the Center for Biological Diversity to highlight the environmental hazards of an expanded border wall. In September 2017, he was arrested for disorderly conduct during a protest of immigration policy in front of Trump Tower in New York City.

In the House minority, Grijalva repeatedly clashed with Interior Secretary Ryan Zinke, a former House colleague, over the use of scientific data, management of public lands and what he called the "culture of corruption" at the department. In response to Grijalva's call on him to resign, Zinke said that it was hard for the chairman "to think straight from the bottom of the bottle." That swipe was a reference to news reports that Grijalva in 2015 reached a severance agreement with a former female aide over her claims of drunkenness and a hostile workplace. He later said the agreement prevented him from discussing the specifics. Zinke resigned in December 2018.

When he became chairman in 2019, Grijalva said "we're not going to waste time on" legislation that rips apart environmental laws. He promised more attention to climate change, which he said had been "scrubbed from the discussion." Grijalva continued his steadfast opposition to the border wall, which he approached from the multiple perspectives of immigration, environmental and Native American policy. More than a score of archeological and tribal sites in the Arizona desert were placed at risk by construction of the wall, he said.

Partisan tensions within the committee grew in the summer of 2020 when Rep. Louie Gohmert, a Texas Republican, tested positive for the coronavirus soon after he attended a committee meeting without wearing a mask. Days later, Grijalva went into quarantine and then tested positive. "Numerous Republican members routinely strut around the Capitol without a mask to selfishly make a political statement at the expense of their colleagues, staff, and their families," he said in a statement.

Despite the strongly Democratic lean of his district, Grijalva has faced reelection challenges. In 2010, Republican Ruth McClung, a 28-year-old physicist, voiced the slogan "Boycott Grijalva, not Arizona." She got help from tea party groups, along with a televised endorsement from Republican Sen. John McCain, and pulled nearly even in polls. But national Democrats raced to Grijalva's assistance with ads, and he eked out a 50%-44% victory. When the Arizona Republic reported in 2014 that Grijalva had missed 13 percent of the previous year's votes, giving him one of the worst attendance records in Congress, he shrugged it off. "I had perfect attendance in the fifth grade," he told the newspaper. "That didn't make me the smartest kid in the class."

In a 2014 challenge from conservative activist Gabriela Saucedo Mercer, he won with 56 percent. In Pima County, which cast nearly half the total vote, Grijalva led 61%-39%. But he trailed narrowly in Maricopa County and barely led in Yuma. He has been reelected easily since then, though those results showed the potential risk—and reward--that he faced with redistricting in 2022. With Arizona gaining a seat, one option that might satisfy both Grijalva and Democrats from Maricopa County would be to shift the Maricopa part of his district into a new district with a Latino majority. That would leave him with a district that extended along the border from its core in Tucson.

In the 2016 presidential campaign, Grijalva was the first member of Congress to endorse Bernie Sanders and he was a key ally when Sanders and Hillary Clinton sought to reconcile their differences on the Democratic platform. "The positions he has taken and the values he holds are ones I share," Grijalva told The New York Times.

In the 2020 campaign, Grijalva switched his endorsement to Sen. Elizabeth Warren, whom he described as "a bold, persistent, visionary leader who cares about working families." His switch from Sanders was notable if only because most other leaders of the Progressive Caucus remained supporters of the Vermont senator. Following the election, Grijalva said Biden needed to "go big" in addressing national problems and that climate change was a "common thread" affecting policies such as economic development, transportation, housing and agriculture. He called for a forward-looking policy "that's strong enough to weather the shocks we know are coming." Democrats, he added, were "on the right side of the science and public opinion."

AZ-3: Southwest Arizona

Cook Partisan Voting Index: D+13

Population		Race and Ethnicity		Income	
Total	801,531	White	74.50%	Median Income	$54,583
Land area (sq. miles)	15,689	Black	4.40%	District Income Rank	338
Pop/ sq mi	51.09	Latino	65.10%	Poverty Rate	16.90%
Born in State	47.70%	Asian	1.70%	With health insurance	85.40%
		Two or more races	4.80%	Cash public assistance	2.30%
Age Groups		Other	14.60%	Food stamp/SNAP	17.40%
Under 18	27.00%				
18-34	27.20%	**Education**		**Work**	
35-64	33.70%	H.S grad or less	51.30%	White Collar	26.60%
Over 64	12.10%	Some college	32.00%	Sales and Service	45.20%
		College Degree, 4 yr	10.60%	Blue Collar	28.10%
Military		Post grad	6.00%	Government	15.60%
Veteran/ Active Duty	6.80%				

2020 Pres. Vote	Biden	174,882	(63%)	Trump	99,539	(36%)		
2016 Pres. Vote	Clinton	130,466	(62%)	Trump	67,952	(32%)	Johnson	7,197	(3%)

Tucson West, Western Phoenix Exurbs, Yuma: Southern Arizona, although technically part of Mexico for hundreds of years, was never a home to Latin American civilization the way southern New Mexico has been. Here the hot desert land was inhabited mainly by Native American tribes such as the Apache and Cocopah. They kept their culture and language alive in the region until they were uprooted by English-speaking whites who came in on cavalry horses and in miners' wagons and railroad cars in the late 19th century. In 1854, the Gadsden Purchase—$10 million to Mexico for 30,000 square miles of desert—cleared the way for a southern transcontinental railroad. Today's Hispanic Arizonans are mostly descendants of later emigrants from Mexico, some of whom came over the border in the sleepier days before World War II, when the frontier was scarcely patrolled. Many more came in the 1980s to partake in the dazzling economic growth in the region. The continuing influx of mostly illegal immigrants has increased the national focus on this area.

The 3rd Congressional District is one of the state's two Hispanic-majority districts, with a population that is 65 percent Hispanic and 21 percent foreign-born. One of the two overwhelmingly Democratic districts in the state, it shares a 293-mile border with Mexico. The district is a collection of four distant communities connected by many square miles of uninhabited Sonoran desert.

One is centered in the suburb of Avondale, west of downtown Phoenix, the site of the Palo Verde Nuclear Generating Station, the nation's largest nuclear power plant and the only one not located by a large body of water. Nearby Buckeye, with inexpensive housing for workers in Maricopa County, in 2017 was the fifth fastest-growing city in the nation. A firm tied to Microsoft founder Bill Gates purchased more than 25,000 acres for at least $80 million, with the plan to build a solar-powered "smart" community west of Phoenix, near Buckeye. Since 2019, the city reportedly has approved several thousand home-building permits. The second community is the heavily Latino and mostly low-income west and south sides of Tucson, where the University of Arizona, the largest employer in southern Arizona, is located. The Tucson area includes a little more than 40 percent of the district's population, with 35 percent in the rapidly growing area of Maricopa County.

The third part of the district is the Mexican border town of Nogales, which is 95 percent Hispanic and located near many maquiladora plants. It is one of the busiest cargo terminals along the Mexican border, but it also has long been an entry point for the drug trade and the scene of many illegal border crossings in recent years. The twin smuggling tides—drugs and people—have inflicted damage on the fragile desert ecosystem. The fourth is Yuma, located on the California border at a Colorado River crossing in an irrigated agricultural valley that is often the hottest place in the nation. In winter, the Yuma area produces 90 percent of the nation's leafy green vegetables—including 500 million heads of lettuce—on more than 90,000 acres, with an estimated 30,000 Mexican workers crossing the border daily.

In the desert you find the Organ Pipe Cactus National Monument, the Sonoran Desert National Monument, the Tohono O'odham Indian Reservation, and the Barry M. Goldwater Air Force Range, the largest aerial gunnery range after Nevada's Nellis Air Force Range. Near Nogales, unique forms of wildlife are found in the Tumacacori Highlands, including endangered species such as the jaguar, peregrine falcon, Chiricahua leopard frog and the Mexican spotted owl. In October 2020, the Border Patrol reported nearly 10,000 "apprehensions" of Central American families and unaccompanied minors entering the country illegally in the Yuma area, which tripled the total in October 2019. When President Donald Trump visited Yuma in June 2020, 216 miles of wall had been built along the nearly 2,000-mile border since he took office, most of which replaced older barriers. In a 5-4 ruling in July 2020, the Supreme Court OK'd continued construction of the wall, while other courts ruled on legal challenges.

In 2016, Hillary Clinton defeated Donald Trump, 62%-32%. That margin was a few points higher than Barack Obama's local performance in 2012. Joe Biden took the district, 63%-36%.

Paul Gosar (R)

Elected 2010, 6th term, b. Nov 27, 1958; Rock Springs, WY; Creighton University, B.S., 1981; Creighton Boyne School of Dentistry, D.D.S., 1985; Roman Catholic; Married (Maude Gosar); 3 children.

Professional Career: Owner, dental practice.

DC Office: 2057 RHOB 20515, 202-225-2315, Fax: 202-226-9739, gosar.house.gov

State Offices: Gold Canyon, 480-882-2697; Kingman, 928-445-1683; Prescott, 928-445-1683.

Committees: *Natural Resources*: Energy & Mineral Resources; Oversight & Investigations (RMM). *Oversight & Reform*: National Security; Subcommittee on Environment.

Group Ratings

	ADA	ACLU	AFL-CIO	LCV	COC	HAFA	ACU	CFG	FRC
2020	**	18%	**	5%	-	96%	93%	**	-
2019	0%	C	17%	3%	52%	C	93%	100%	100%

Almanac Ratings 2019-2020

	Economy	Social	Foreign	Composite
Liberal	34%	11%	40%	29%
Conservative	66%	89%	60%	71%

Key Votes of the 116th Congress

1. U.S./Mex./Can. trade deal Y	5. Russia sanctions N	9. Firearms background checks N
2. First Coronavirus response N/A	6. Troops in Syria N	10. Spending at the border N
3. HEROES Act N	7. Veto arms sales to Saudis N	11. Marijuana liberalized rules N
4. CASH Act N	8. Defense $$$, veto override N	12. Electoral College objections Y

Election Results

Election	Name (Party)	Vote (%)		Cand. Spent	Ind. Exp. Support	Ind. Exp. Oppose
2020 General	Paul Gosar (R)	278,002	(70%)	$725,052	$40,357	$1,819
	Delina DiSanto (D)	120,484	(30%)	$73,537		
2020 Primary	Paul Gosar (R)	82,370	(63%)			
	Anne Marie Ward (R)	48,116	(37%)			

Prior winning percentages: 2018 (68%), 2016 (72%), 2014 (70%), 2012 (67%), 2010 (50%)

Republican Paul Gosar, first elected in 2010, survived two competitive elections. He then settled into the Republican-friendly 4th District and signed on with other party renegades in the House. With an interest in western and mining issues, his legislative record has been modest. His clashes with Republican leaders have been a factor in his failure to win prime GOP posts at the Natural Resources and Oversight committees. He has remained an occasional party maverick in Arizona. In April 2021, following objections from GOP leaders, Gosar and Rep. Marjorie Taylor Greene abandoned plans to create an America First Caucus.

Gosar grew up in Pinedale Wyoming. His father was often away working on rigs as a geologist, and an uncle, who was a dentist, stepped in as a role model during those absences. Gosar studied dentistry at Creighton University with the expectation that he would return to Wyoming to enter practice with his uncle. His father advised him to seek a more vibrant locale. After receiving his dental degree, Gosar settled in Flagstaff. Appealing to a local banker for financing to launch his practice, Gosar emphasized his frugality, vowing to eat nothing but peanut-butter-and-jelly sandwiches until his business was established.

When he challenged freshman Democratic Rep. Ann Kirkpatrick in 2010, Gosar sharply criticized her votes for President Barack Obama's agenda. He took a hard line on immigration. Kirkpatrick's ads highlighted her support for Obama's initiatives and cast Gosar as an irresponsible millionaire who was late paying business and property taxes 12 times. Gosar received help from the American Dental Association and other medical groups that opposed the 2010 health care law. The national GOP wave in high-growth areas helped to seal his 50%-44% victory.

On the Oversight and Government Reform Committee, he became one of the first House members to call on Attorney General Eric Holder to resign because of the failed "Operation Fast and Furious," a program that facilitated the sale of thousands of weapons to Mexican drug cartels. The House voted in 2012 to cite the attorney general for contempt of Congress. In 2014, Congress approved as part of its annual defense spending bill Gosar's proposal to swap 2,400 acres of Tonto forest land—which includes the San Carlos Apache reservation—to make way for a new $4 billion copper mine. In exchange, the Resolution Copper Co. gave up land scattered across the state.

On the Natural Resources Committee, Gosar has been the top Republican on the Energy and Mineral Resources Subcommittee. He chaired the Congressional Western Caucus, where he sought to protect the interests of western and rural communities, including their opposition to expansion of public lands without local input. In 2018, the House passed his bill to increase the transparency of the Western Area Power Administration, which delivers hydropower from federal facilities. He won House approval of his legislation to transfer federal and county lands in Cottonwood and elsewhere in Yavapai County.

In January 2015, Gosar was one of 25 House Republicans who opposed giving John Boehner another term as Speaker. Instead, he voted for Rep. Daniel Webster of Florida. "Our leadership in D.C. should be bold and determined," Gosar said. "We do not need more status quo." He became active in the House GOP's Freedom Caucus, which prepared conservative strategy and policy alternatives. In September, Boehner announced his resignation as Speaker under pressure from that faction. A month later, Gosar was one of nine House Republicans who voted against Paul Ryan as the new Speaker.

He eventually became a victim of his independence. In June 2020, when Republican leaders filled the vacancy for the top Republican on the Oversight panel, they passed over Gosar, who was the most senior GOP member of the panel, though he was not a formal contender for the post. Instead, they selected James Comer, a second-term member from Kentucky. In a similar scenario six months later, Gosar sought the top GOP slot at the Natural Resources panel. The winner was Bruce Westerman of Arkansas, who was junior to Gosar. The selection of Westerman also was unusual because that GOP committee post typically has gone to a westerner—a niche that Gosar has filled elsewhere.

Gosar has shown his independence at home. Faced with new redistricting lines in 2012, he ran in the more Republican-leaning 4th District. Pinal County Sheriff Paul Babeu, a strong foe of illegal immigration, initially was considered the frontrunner in the primary, but his momentum halted when a former boyfriend (and illegal immigrant) accused him of threatening deportation to keep their relationship quiet. That left Gosar with state Sen. Ron Gould of Lake Havasu City, one of the legislature's most conservative members, as his chief challenger in the GOP primary. Gould attacked Gosar as the only House Republican from Arizona to support the 2011 deal to raise the federal debt limit. Gosar won with 51 percent to Gould's 32 percent.

Ray Strauss, a local pastor, challenged Gosar in the 2016 primary. The contest gained added attention when Washington-based business groups spent $300,000 to run ads critical of Gosar. That group's biggest contributor was the Western Growers Association, an agri-business group that advocates immigration reform, in part to provide foreign workers to aid farmers. Gosar won the primary, 71%-29%, and he defeated a token Democratic challenger in November.

Gosar stirred the ire of some Arizona Republicans when, following the hospitalization of Sen. John McCain for brain cancer in 2017, his chief of staff texted that Gosar was interested in securing the appointment of Gov. Doug Ducey if McCain's seat became open. Ducey responded harshly: "To anyone who uses this as an opportunity to speculate or fan the rumor mill: Washington D.C.'s obsession with this when there is no issue to be discussed is disgraceful." Gosar further distanced himself from party regulars when he endorsed Kelli Ward in the 2018 GOP primary against Rep. Martha McSally for the seat of retiring Sen. Jeff Flake. "We cannot afford another establishment patsy who promises one thing and votes differently," Gosar said. McSally, as the Republican nominee, lost Senate races in 2018 and 2020.

During his otherwise uneventful reelection in 2018, six of Gosar's siblings ran an online ad opposing their brother's strongly conservative views and speaking out to "stand up for our good name." Gosar responded that they were "liberal Democrats who hate President Trump" and added, "you can't pick your family."

In 2020, Gosar again was challenged in the GOP primary. Anne Marie Ward, a businesswoman in Prescott, criticized his failure to support the agenda of President Donald Trump and for not attending impeachment-related hearings in the House. She also attacked Gosar for not residing in the district, according to the Payson Roundup, a political website in Arizona. A Gosar spokesman responded that Ward's charges were lies and that Trump had endorsed Gosar. Gosar won the primary, 63%-37%, and led in all seven counties. In the general election, he defeated Delina DiSanto, a registered nurse, 70%-30%.

Following the 2020 election—when Trump challenged the presidential results in several states, including Arizona—many conservatives in the state were unhappy that Ducey failed to respond to Trump's demands. Soon after they launched an effort to recall Ducey, Gosar voiced support for their campaign. In the House, he pursued "Make America Great Again" initiatives—often with the objections of the GOP rank-and-file.

AZ-4: Western Arizona   Cook Partisan Voting Index: R+22

Population		Race and Ethnicity		Income	
Total	825,763	White	87.80%	Median Income	$55,040
Land area (sq. miles)	33,199	Black	1.70%	District Income Rank	330
Pop/ sq mi	24.87	Latino	20.50%	Poverty Rate	12.20%
Born in State	28.80%	Asian	1.00%	With health insurance	91.20%
		Two or more races	3.20%	Cash public assistance	1.70%
Age Groups		Other	6.20%	Food stamp/SNAP	9.30%
Under 18	18.60%				
18-34	17.30%	**Education**		**Work**	
35-64	36.10%	H.S grad or less	40.50%	White Collar	31.50%
Over 64	28.00%	Some college	38.60%	Sales and Service	45.40%
		College Degree, 4 yr	13.30%	Blue Collar	23.10%
Military		Post grad	7.60%	Government	14.90%
Veteran/ Active Duty	13.50%				

2020 Pres. Vote	Trump	280,122	(68%)	Biden	126,024	(31%)		
2016 Pres. Vote	Trump	202,043	(67%)	Clinton	82,192	(27%)	Johnson	10,965	(4%)

Eastern Phoenix Exurbs, Prescott, Lake Havasu City: Beyond the cities of Phoenix and Tucson, much of Arizona looks as it did a century ago. Some places maintain a timeless western look, like Wickenburg, the oldest Arizona town north of Tucson. Others preserve antiquated ways of life, such as the polygamist community of Colorado City, just south of Utah. In some cases, nature and settlement juxtapose jarringly: The real London Bridge was transplanted to Lake Havasu City, a retirement community on the Colorado River and a popular spring break destination for college students.

The expansive 4th Congressional District stretches from the Hoover Dam and Lake Mead in the northwest corner of the state to the outskirts of Yuma, and it spans east to Prescott and beyond to the exurbs east of Phoenix in Pinal County. The district covers La Paz County, most of Mohave and Yavapai counties, and parts of Yuma, Gila and Pinal counties, along with a tiny slice of Maricopa. Its population center is in fast-growing Prescott, in the valley north of Phoenix, where Barry Goldwater announced his presidential campaign in 1964. Once a gold mining camp, Prescott has been home since 1888 to America's oldest annual rodeo and it retains the charming markers of an older city. The American Planning Association described the Yavapai County Courthouse Plaza as "a majestic, man-made urban forest in the heart of a historic commercial district."

The district's economy is fueled by tourism, with visitors coming to explore western folklore. Jerome, a mining town built improbably on hillside stilts, has been reborn as an artist colony. Bullhead City is home to the annual River Regatta, where participants take an eight-mile float down the Colorado. Its rapid growth has increased demands for additional water supply. Arizona highway planners have discussed upgrading Route 93 between Phoenix and Las Vegas to an interstate highway. The district is a retirement haven and a mecca for second homes. According to the Census Bureau, Lake Havasu City has become the "remarriage capital" of the nation; in this self-styled "party town," 42 percent of women and 41 percent of men have married at least twice. The area is infused with a cultural and political conservatism, placing it among the top 10 percent of Republican districts nationwide. On Labor Day weekend in 2020, local boaters held an aquatic parade to celebrate President Donald Trump. Trump won 67 percent of the vote in 2016 and 68 percent in 2020, by far his strongest district in Arizona in each case. "Socialism. Guns. Water. Those are some of the top issues for voters" (opposed, and in favor) in the 4th Congressional District, the Arizona Republic reported in September 2020.

Andy Biggs (R)

Elected 2016, 3rd term, b. Nov 07, 1958; Tucson, AZ; Brigham Young University, B.A., 1982; University of AZ Rogers College of Law, J.D., 1984; AZ State University, M.A., 1999; Mormon; Married (Cindy Biggs); 6 children.

Elected Office: AZ house, 2003-2011; AZ Senate, 2011-2016, Majority Leader, 2011-2012, Senate President, 2013-2016.

Professional Career: Practicing attorney.

DC Office: 1318 LHOB 20515, 202-225-2635, biggs.house.gov

State Offices: Mesa, 480-699-8239.

Committees: *Judiciary*: Crime, Terrorism & Homeland Security (RMM); Immigration & Citizenship. *Oversight & Reform*: Government Operations; Subcommittee on Civil Rights & Civil Liberties.

Group Ratings

	ADA	ACLU	AFL-CIO	LCV	COC	HAFA	ACU	CFG	FRC
2020	**	20%	**	0%	-	98%	96%	**	-
2019	0%	C	19%	0%	62%	C	95%	100%	100%

Almanac Ratings 2019-2020

	Economy	Social	Foreign	Composite
Liberal	25%	4%	41%	24%
Conservative	75%	96%	59%	76%

Key Votes of the 116th Congress

1. U.S./Mex./Can. trade deal Y	5. Russia sanctions N	9. Firearms background checks N
2. First Coronavirus response N	6. Troops in Syria N	10. Spending at the border N
3. HEROES Act N	7. Veto arms sales to Saudis N	11. Marijuana liberalized rules N
4. CASH Act N	8. Defense $$$, veto override N	12. Electoral College objections Y

Election Results

Election	Name (Party)	Vote (%)	Cand. Spent	Ind. Exp. Support	Ind. Exp. Oppose
2020 General	Andy Biggs (R)................................	262,414 (59%)	$1,142,682	$15,478	$750
	Joan Greene (D).............................	183,171 (41%)	$206,526	$3,013	
2020 Primary	Andy Biggs (R)................................	104,888 (100%)			

Prior winning percentages: 2018 (59%), 2016 (64%)

Andy Biggs, elected in 2016, became a conservative leader as chairman of the House Freedom Caucus and an outspoken defender of President Donald Trump from charges of wrongdoing. With his lengthy experience in state government, he sometimes clashed with state officials as he zealously promoted Trump's interests. After winning his House seat by 27 votes in a GOP primary, Biggs secured his political status at home.

A native of Tucson, Biggs got his undergraduate degree in Asian studies from Brigham Young University, his master's degree in political science from Arizona State University and a law degree from the University of Arizona. In 1993, he won $10 million in the Publishers Clearing House sweepstakes. After practicing law in Phoenix and then Gilbert, he was elected to the state House, where he served eight years. He moved to the Senate in 2010, and became majority leader and then president of the Senate. He was a hardliner on illegal immigration, and a conservative icon. Americans for Prosperity's Arizona Chapter named him a "Champion of the Taxpayer;" the Goldwater Institute tapped him as a "Friend of Liberty;" and the American Conservative Union gave him its "Conservative Excellence Award."

After Republican Rep. Matt Salmon announced his retirement, Biggs was the initial frontrunner among four candidates in the GOP primary. He survived the closest contest that determined a House election in 2016, when he defeated Christine Jones, a former legal counsel with GoDaddy, an internet domain company. Jones ran as an outsider who emphasized her business record, and contributed $1.9 million to her own campaign. Biggs, who was endorsed by Salmon, spent nearly $1 million on the campaign and received another $560,000 in support from the Club for Growth. Maricopa County Supervisor Don Stapley identified with the GOP establishment and advocated controls on federal spending.

Jones was the leader in the vote count on the evening of the Aug. 30 primary, and she delivered a victory speech. The recount showed that as many as 728 voters had gone to the wrong voting precinct and then cast a provisional ballot. When Superior Court Judge Joshua Rogers announced the official result, he conceded that many voters had been "disenfranchised." The official results of the primary showed that Biggs defeated Jones, 25,244 to 25,217. Each received 29.5 percent of the vote, while Stapley had 20.7 percent. In the pro forma general election, Biggs defeated Democrat Talia Fuentes, a single mother who had supported Bernie Sanders for president; he won, 64%-36%.

When House Republicans in 2017 passed their American Health Care Act, Biggs was among the few conservatives who voted against it. He called the proposal "an ill-considered, ill-defined, and an almost certainly ill-fated three-stage plan to completely repeal Obama care at an unspecified later date." He dismissed pressure from Trump and other party leaders. "I'm here to do a job and represent my constituents," he said. Biggs was more productive in other areas. He was the chief House sponsor of the "Right to Try" bill, signed by Trump, which makes it easier for patients with life-threatening conditions to use treatments that haven't received final Food and Drug Administration approval. He enacted a bill that extended to tribal areas the emergency Amber Alert system for missing children.

Biggs was an outspoken critic of Robert Mueller, the special counsel investigating Trump, and cosponsored a resolution that called for his removal. "Mueller's investigation is clearly careening far beyond the scope of his original charge," he wrote in USA Today. "His witch hunt must end." As Trump was pushed increasingly on the defensive, especially during the pandemic, Biggs defended the president and chastised apparent critics.

When he thought Trump's advisers on the coronavirus were sending conflicting messages, Biggs accused them of "causing panic" with the economy and called for shutting down their task force. When the House in April 2020 voted, 388-5, for an economic stimulus bill in response to the pandemic, he explained that he voted against the measure because its mandates "sanction abuse of the rights of Americans." When Rep. Liz Cheney of Wyoming, who chaired the House Republican Conference, defended the advice of federal medical expert Dr. Anthony Fauci, Biggs accused her of undermining House GOP election prospects.

His voice gained a wider audience in September 2019 when Biggs was selected to succeed Rep. Mark Meadows as chairman of the House Freedom Caucus. "We will stand with President Trump as he keeps his promises to the American people," Biggs said in response. Consistent with that pledge, he joined Trump allies in challenging the narrow election victory of Joe Biden in Arizona and criticizing, among others, Republican Gov. Doug Ducey for supporting the state's election procedures and for his advocacy of public-health steps to control the coronavirus. In response, Ducey's chief of staff tweeted that Biggs "should enjoy your time as a permanent resident of Crazytown." Intercept, the liberal website, reported that Biggs was actively involved in planning for the January 6 protests at the Capitol, which resulted in violence, five deaths and brief takeovers of the House and Senate chambers. His spokesman denied contact with or encouragement of the protesters.

In his two reelections, Biggs defeated Democrat Joan Greene, a marketing executive, by the same margin, 59%-41%. In early 2021, he said that he was considering a challenge to Sen. Mark Kelly in 2022.

AZ-5: Eastern Phoenix Suburbs   Cook Partisan Voting Index: R+11

Population		Race and Ethnicity		Income	
Total	849,917	White	82.90%	Median Income	$82,540
Land area (sq. miles)	293	Black	4.00%	District Income Rank	76
Pop/ sq mi	2,896.1	Latino	16.60%	Poverty Rate	6.50%
Born in State	37.80%	Asian	5.30%	With health insurance	92.50%
		Two or more races	3.90%	Cash public assistance	0.70%
Age Groups		Other	3.90%	Food stamp/SNAP	3.80%
Under 18	25.40%				
18-34	18.90%	**Education**		**Work**	
35-64	38.30%	H.S grad or less	26.30%	White Collar	45.40%
Over 64	17.30%	Some college	35.50%	Sales and Service	38.60%
		College Degree, 4 yr	25.30%	Blue Collar	16.00%
Military		Post grad	12.90%	Government	11.30%
Veteran/ Active Duty	8.80%				

2020 Pres. Vote	Trump	262,810	(56%)	Biden	195,270	(42%)			
2016 Pres. Vote	Trump	191,432	(56%)	Clinton	121,280	(36%)	Johnson	15,845	(5%)

Eastern Mesa, Gilbert: The city of Phoenix is exceedingly young. In the early 20th century, local people remembered when the Valley of the Sun—or the Valley, as most people say—was virtually empty, with a few parched settlements set above a dry riverbed. As late as 1950, only 107,000 people lived in Phoenix and 332,000 in all of Maricopa County. But the air conditioner and military technology transformed Phoenix into today's high-rise studded metropolis, with 1.7 million city dwellers. After a slowdown early in the new decade, following the collapse of the local housing market and the state's crackdowns on illegal immigration, Maricopa regained in 2017 its title as the fastest-growing county in the nation. The 4.5 million people in the county, as of 2019, were an 18 percent increase since 2010. Phoenix is not, as some people think, a giant retirement village, nor is it overrun by crooked land salesmen and fast-buck artists, though the area has attracted its share of each.

Maricopa's second-largest city is Mesa, south of the Salt River and east of Phoenix. It was founded by Mormons in 1878 on one square mile and was laid out Salt Lake City-style on broad streets with large lots. A gleaming white Mormon temple was built in 1927, one of the few in the United States then. In 1950, Mesa had 17,000 people, and more than half of its residents earned their living from farming, primarily citrus and cotton. In 2019, it had 518,000 people, more than Kansas City or Atlanta. A former Air Force base is the Phoenix-Mesa Gateway Airport, now a center for flight-training and testing; its joint customs-clearance center between the U.S. and Mexico is designed to speed cargo shipments. Valley Metro, the regional transit authority, opened in 2019 a 2-mile light-rail extension from Mesa to Gilbert, which has enhanced local economic development. Beyond Gilbert, the state Department of Water Resources approved in 2020 a plan to deliver more water from the Colorado River to Queen Creek, a growing exurban area.

The 5th Congressional District of Arizona is made up of Phoenix's East Valley suburbs: Mesa, Chandler, Gilbert and Queen Creek. Nicknamed the Silicon Desert, Chandler has become one of the fastest-growing tech centers in the country, with companies drawn to relatively cheap real estate and semiconductor chip maker Intel's longstanding presence. After it was forced to abandon plans to manufacture additional chips at its Fab 42 facility, Intel, the largest private employer in Arizona, redesigned its operations to produce microprocessors, with thousands of additional workers. In its largely hidden 1.3 million-square-foot data center in Mesa, which the Arizona Republic termed "The Fortress," Apple monitors the company's operations from its "global data command center."

The 5th has the highest median income in Arizona, though the district's cultural tone is resolutely middle class. Donald Trump won 56 percent of the vote here in each of his campaigns, compared with Mitt Romney's 64 percent in 2012.

David Schweikert (R)

Elected 2010, 6th term, b. Mar 03, 1962; Los Angeles, CA; Scottsdale Community College, A.A., 1985; AZ State University, B.S., 1988; AZ State University, M.B.A., 2005; Roman Catholic; Married (Joyce Schweikert); 1 child.

Elected Office: AZ House, 1989-1994; Treasurer, Maricopa County, 2004-2006.

Professional Career: Member, AZ State Board of Equalization, 1995-2003; Owner, Sheridan Equities & Sheridan Equities Holdings.

DC Office: 1526 LHOB 20515, 202-225-2190, Fax: 202-225-0096, schweikert.house.gov

State Offices: Scottsdale, 480-946-2411.

Committees: *Joint Economic. Ways & Means*: Health; Select Revenue Measures.

Group Ratings

	ADA	ACLU	AFL-CIO	LCV	COC	HAFA	ACU	CFG	FRC
2020	**	26%	**	14%	-	98%	96%	**	-
2019	0%	C	19%	14%	83%	C	98%	100%	91%

Almanac Ratings 2019-2020

	Economy	Social	Foreign	Composite
Liberal	25%	18%	45%	30%
Conservative	75%	82%	55%	70%

Key Votes of the 116th Congress

1. U.S./Mex./Can. trade deal	Y	5. Russia sanctions	Y	9. Firearms background checks N
2. First Coronavirus response	Y	6. Troops in Syria	Y	10. Spending at the border	Y
3. HEROES Act	N	7. Veto arms sales to Saudis	N	11. Marijuana liberalized rules	N
4. CASH Act	N	8. Defense $$$, veto override	N	12. Electoral College objections Y

Election Results

Election	Name (Party)	Vote (%)	Cand. Spent	Ind. Exp. Support	Ind. Exp. Oppose
2020 General	David Schweikert (R)	217,783 (52%)	$2,059,467	$244,355	$4,965,793
	Hiral Tipirneni (D)	199,644 (48%)	$6,665,671	$544,270	$3,074,009
2020 Primary	David Schweikert (R)	94,434 (100%)			

Prior winning percentages: 2018 (55%), 2016 (62%), 2014 (65%), 2012 (61%), 2010 (52%)

Republican David Schweikert, elected in 2010, is a wonkish fiscal conservative who has clashed with Republican leaders. Following his rehabilitation with a seat on the Ways and Means Committee, where he became more of a team player, Schweikert ran into new problems with ethics sanctions and tough reelection challenges in his once-safe seat. In 2020, he prevailed, despite being one of the most vulnerable House Republicans. ·

Schweikert was born in a Catholic home for unwed mothers in downtown Los Angeles; he was adopted and raised by a family in Arizona. As an undergraduate at Arizona State University, where he later got an MBA, Schweikert focused on finance and real estate. He acquired a real estate license at age 18, worked full-time while taking classes at night and graduated in six years.

Growing up in Scottsdale, he credits his early affinity for politics to former President Ronald Reagan. Schweikert ventured into the political arena at 26, when he lost a bid for the Arizona House. Two years later, he won an open seat in the Scottsdale area, and at the end of his freshman term, he became majority whip. He worked to pass legislation that laid the foundation for tax cuts, tort reform and charter schools, as well as a bill shortening the legislative session from 170 to 98 days. In 2004, he was elected Maricopa County treasurer. In that role, he managed a $4 billion budget, created a program to help low-income seniors pay their property taxes and corrected thousands of deed errors.

In 2008, Schweikert challenged Democratic Rep. Harry Mitchell, who had taken a GOP seat two years earlier. Schweikert lost by nine percentage points in an inhospitable year for Republicans. Two years later, their rematch told the larger tale of the 2010 election. Schweikert made Mitchell's vote for President Barack Obama's $787 billion economic stimulus bill a central theme, and his campaign signs called Mitchell a "lap dog" for liberal House Speaker Nancy Pelosi. Mitchell countered that he had been among the Democrats most likely to buck his party and he raised about twice as much money. Schweikert won convincingly, 52%-43%.

During his early months in the House, Schweikert told The Washington Post that he spent five hours a day as a member of the Financial Services Committee learning about government-sponsored mortgage giants Fannie Mae and Freddie Mac. That summer, he strongly opposed raising the federal debt ceiling. He accused Treasury Secretary Tim Geithner of having "his hair on fire....It's absolutely silly. We have plenty of cash flow to pay debt." He proposed a constitutional amendment that would force Congress to get approval from a majority of the states before increasing the debt limit.

After the 2010 census, the state's independent redistricting commission lumped Schweikert in a district with Rep. Ben Quayle, son of former Vice President Dan Quayle. The younger Quayle represented two-thirds of the new district. House GOP leaders lined up to support Quayle, whom they considered the more loyal Republican. Schweikert ran as a self-styled reformer. The acrimony peaked when Schweikert's campaign sent a mailer claiming that Quayle "goes both ways" on conservative issues. Quayle and his supporters, including Sen. John McCain, angrily accused Schweikert of sexual innuendo, a charge that the congressman denied. Schweikert prevailed, 51%-49%. The general-election race was a formality.

In 2013, Republican leaders took the rare step of booting Schweikert off Financial Services. His aides claimed that it resulted from his challenges to the leadership. Schweikert moved to the Science, Space and Technology Committee and quietly reestablished his party credentials. Following the 2016 election, Speaker Paul Ryan closed the book on his earlier transgressions by awarding Schweikert his seat on Ways and Means.

Instead of blocking legislation, as he and others had occasionally done in the past, he said the Republican-controlled Congress should work with President Donald Trump. He worked with others at Ways and Means to pass the party's American Health Care Act, which was designed to replace Obama care. He was an outspoken advocate of the tax cuts enacted in 2017. As he told the House, "Tax reform is fair to individuals. It is simpler....This is not a win for Republicans. It is a win for society."

Schweikert's ethics problems followed allegations from an Arizona Democrat that payments to his chief of staff for campaign work in 2014 exceeded House limits on outside income and that he misused official funds. Less than a month after the House Ethics Committee in June 2018created an investigative subcommittee to review their actions, the aide resigned.

That year, the inquiry spurred Democratic challengers to Schweikert's reelection. "The incumbent is reeling [and] has been shrouded in suspicion," the Arizona Republic wrote in an editorial prior to the August primary. Anita Malik, a tech executive who won the primary with 42 percent of the vote, attacked Schweikert's support for Trump's agenda, which she said "is not supporting the middle class." Unlike other House Democratic challengers in 2018, Malik was outspent 4-to-1. In what might have been a missed opportunity for Democrats, Schweikert prevailed, 55%-45%, his first reelection with less than 60 percent of the vote.

Following the election, Schweikert sought the chairmanship of the Republican Policy Committee. He lost to Rep. Gary Palmer of Alabama, another member of the conservative House Freedom Caucus, in what reportedly was a 130-63 vote. He reached out to the center by joining the House's bipartisan Climate Solutions Caucus. In October 2020, he joined a bipartisan group that filed a proposal that sought to develop new technology for removal of carbon dioxide from the atmosphere.

His legislative actions were disrupted when the House in July 2020 passed, without opposition, a resolution that reprimanded him on 11 counts, including failure to disclose loans and campaign contributions. Schweikert's efforts "to delay and impede the investigation were not only highly detrimental to the committee's work and reputation of the House, they were themselves sanctionable misconduct," the Ethics panel concluded. Schweikert admitted his violations and paid a $50,000 fine. He said he decided to settle the charges because the investigation was "time-consuming and extremely costly."

The election-eve reprimand encouraged Democrats. Their nominee, Hiral Tipernini, a former emergency-room physician, in 2018 held Rep. Debbie Lesko to 55 percent of the vote in her more Republican adjacent district. "Schweikert is up against a perfect storm," David Wasserman of the Cook Political Report wrote in August. Tipernini more than 3-to-1 and had more than $4 million in outside support. Despite top-of-the-ticket Democratic strength in Arizona, Schweikert again showed his survivor skills, 52%-48%.

AZ-6: Northeastern Phoenix Suburbs   Cook Partisan Voting Index: R+5

Population		Race and Ethnicity		Income	
Total	814,971	White	82.60%	Median Income	$76,615
Land area (sq. miles)	625	Black	3.00%	District Income Rank	114
Pop/ sq mi	1,303.81	Latino	17.90%	Poverty Rate	8.60%
Born in State	31.90%	Asian	5.70%	With health insurance	90.90%
		Two or more races	3.70%	Cash public assistance	1.20%
Age Groups		Other	4.90%	Food stamp/SNAP	5.10%
Under 18	19.00%				
18-34	21.10%	**Education**		**Work**	
35-64	39.90%	H.S grad or less	26.30%	White Collar	46.40%
Over 64	19.90%	Some college	30.10%	Sales and Service	39.10%
		College Degree, 4 yr	25.90%	Blue Collar	14.50%
Military		Post grad	17.60%	Government	8.70%
Veteran/ Active Duty	7.20%				

2020 Pres. Vote	Trump	222,166	(51%)	Biden	204,365	(47%)		
2016 Pres. Vote	Trump	177,332	(52%)	Clinton	143,571	(42%)	Johnson 13,891	(4%)

Scottsdale: Like Los Angeles and San Francisco, Phoenix is dotted with mountains that rise grandly from the valley and are preserved as undeveloped parkland. From the landmark Camelback Mountain, 1,800 feet above Phoenix and Paradise Valley, one can appreciate with comparable awe what the land was originally like and how impressively Phoenix has grown. Over the mountains, east of the affluent part of Phoenix and north of Tempe and the Salt River Indian Reservation, is Scottsdale, a city that grew from 130,000 in 1990 to 258,000 in 2017. Scottsdale is home to Frank Lloyd Wright's Taliesin West, the architect's onetime winter home and studio, which was beyond the reach of electricity and telephone lines when built in the McDowell Mountain foothills in the 1940s.

Today, the city boasts luxury shopping malls, resorts and the most expensive real estate market in Arizona. As part of what has been described as a biomedical corridor in north Phoenix, the Mayo Clinic plans to double by 2023 its local campus, with expanded clinics and a new patient tower. San Francisco-based McKesson Corp., a health care services firm, has a facility with more than 2,000 workers. Scottsdale touts its reputation as one of the most retiree-friendly cities in the country. With 24 percent of its residents 65 and older, it has the largest share among cities with 100,000 or more people. Only 4 percent are younger than five years old. The city has not been immune to the national culture. In June 2020, City Council member Guy Phillips organized a protest against local requirements to wear a mask; he then donned a face mask and mockingly said, "I can't breathe," the dying words of George Floyd, the victim of Minneapolis police. After Republican Gov. Doug Ducey called his comments "despicable," Phillips apologized.

The 6th Congressional District of Arizona includes the northern part of Phoenix, most of Scottsdale, plus Paradise Valley, Cave Creek and Carefree, so named in 1955 by developers who hoped to lure snowbird retirees. Of the five Arizona districts contained entirely in Maricopa County, the 6th has the most college graduates and is the only one that borders each of the other four. This has been an affluent and comfortably Republican district. It showed less support for Donald Trump, who won 52 percent of the vote in 2016 and 51 percent in 2020, only his fourth-best district in Arizona in each case, and a notable dip from the 60 percent that Mitt Romney took in 2012.

Ruben Gallego (D)

Elected 2014, 4th term, b. Nov 20, 1979; Chicago, IL; Harvard University, B.A.; Catholic; Married.

Military Career: U.S. Marine Corps 2000-2006 (Iraq)

Elected Office: AZ House, 2010-2014.

Professional Career: Public affairs consultant 2007-2008; Delegate, DNC 2008; Vice chair, AZ Democratic Party, 2009.

DC Office: 1131 LHOB 20515, 202-225-4065, rubengallego.house.gov

State Offices: Phoenix, 602-256-0551.

Committees: *Armed Services*: Intelligence & Special Operations (Chmn); Tactical Air & Land Forces. *Natural Resources*: Indigenous Peoples of the United States; National Parks, Forests & Public Lands. *Veterans' Affairs*: Economic Opportunity.

Group Ratings

	ADA	ACLU	AFL-CIO	LCV	COC	HAFA	ACU	CFG	FRC
2020	**	80%	**	100%	-	0%	4%	**	-
2019	90%	C	95%	97%	57%	C	4%	19%	0%

Almanac Ratings 2019-2020

	Economy	Social	Foreign	Composite
Liberal	100%	100%	60%	87%
Conservative	0%	0%	40%	13%

Key Votes of the 116th Congress

1. U.S./Mex./Can. trade deal Y	5. Russia sanctions	Y	9. Firearms background checks Y
2. First Coronavirus response Y	6. Troops in Syria	Y	10. Spending at the border N
3. HEROES Act Y	7. Veto arms sales to Saudis	Y	11. Marijuana liberalized rules Y
4. CASH Act Y	8. Defense $$$, veto override	Y	12. Electoral College objections N

Election Results

Election	Name (Party)	Vote (%)	Cand. Spent	Ind. Exp. Support	Ind. Exp. Oppose
2020 General	Ruben Gallego (D).......................	165,452	(77%)	$1,087,981	$6,091	
	Joshua Barnett (R).................................	50,226	(23%)	$15,342		$113
2020 Primary	Ruben Gallego (D)........................	56,037	(100%)			

Prior winning percentages: 2018 (86%), 2016 (75%), 2014 (75%)

Democrat Ruben Gallego, a first-generation American with an impressive bio, was easily elected in 2014. With his military and local political plus his engaging persona, he spent the Trump years as an outspoken critic of that administration and became a leader of ambitious Democrats in rapidly changing Arizona.

Gallego's life story is made for politics: a hardscrabble upbringing, a Harvard degree and military service in Iraq. Born in Chicago to Hispanic immigrant parents, Gallego and his family struggled after his father left home. He received his undergraduate degree in international relations. While attending Harvard, he enlisted in the Marine Corps. He served in Iraq as an assistant machine gunner and fought in more than 10 combat operations in urban areas; his best friend died in combat. That experience, including his anger over the quality of the troops' equipment, led him to become involved in politics and veterans issues.

Gallego was elected to the Arizona Senate in 2010, rising to assistant minority leader in 2012. When Democratic Rep. Ed Pastor retired, Gallego ran in this ultra-blue district, where the Democratic nominee was a shoo-in for the general. His chief primary rival was Mary Rose Wilcox, a Latina with high name recognition as a Maricopa County supervisor. Pastor endorsed Wilcox, who may have suffered because she was 30 years older than Gallego. Gallego combined a social media presence with aggressive door-to-door campaigning. In the five-candidate field, Gallego defeated Wilcox,

48%-36%. In November, he won without Republican opposition. He said that he hoped to serve his career in the House. "I'll be trying to work my way fast into leadership," he told a local reporter.

On the Armed Services Committee, he got off to a quick start. He opposed additional U.S. military action in Iraq, which he described as "a horrible sequel to a horrible movie." He cited the many men and women who died because of the decisions of officials in Washington and at the Pentagon, and said that additional steps to assist Iraq should not come at the risk of losing more American lives. Gallego joined a congressional caucus of lawmakers who had served in the military since 2001

He was a harsh critic of President Donald Trump. In reaction to Trump's order to federal troops to remove protestors near the White House in June 2020, Gallego seized on his military background and Armed Services Committee assignment to write a letter to Gen. Mark Milley, chairman of the Joint Chiefs of Staff: "General Milley: Do you intend to obey illegal orders from the President?" In 2021, Gallegos became chairman of the Armed Services Subcommittee on Intelligence and Special Operations, a new panel with jurisdiction over military intelligence and related topics.

Gallego was an outspoken proponent of replacing Democratic Leader Nancy Pelosi following House Democrats' poor performance in the 2016 election and was an early supporter of Rep. Tim Ryan of Ohio in his unsuccessful bid to replace Pelosi. Since then, Gallego frequently urged House Democrats to begin planning for a younger generation to lead their caucus.

Gallego initially backed then-Sen. Kamala Harris in her 2020 bid for the Democratic nomination. As for his own ambitions, Gallego voiced early interest in the November 2020 contest to complete McCain's Senate term. Gallego told reporters that he would have no trouble winning the Democratic nomination but conceded that Arizona's competitive general-election battleground posed challenges. He backed away, especially with the strong early fundraising among Democrats by Mark Kelly, who won the seat. Even so, Gallego remains one to watch for a statewide bid in the future.

AZ-7: Central and Western Phoenix

Cook Partisan Voting Index: D+24

Population		Race and Ethnicity		Income	
Total	853,856	White	72.90%	Median Income	$49,066
Land area (sq. miles)	205	Black	9.90%	District Income Rank	394
Pop/ sq mi	4,162.71	Latino	64.00%	Poverty Rate	23.10%
Born in State	49.40%	Asian	2.50%	With health insurance	79.50%
		Two or more races	3.40%	Cash public assistance	2.30%
Age Groups		Other	11.30%	Food stamp/SNAP	17.60%
Under 18	28.70%				
18-34	27.40%	**Education**		**Work**	
35-64	35.40%	H.S grad or less	57.60%	White Collar	24.60%
Over 64	8.50%	Some college	26.50%	Sales and Service	43.50%
		College Degree, 4 yr	11.00%	Blue Collar	31.90%
Military		Post grad	4.90%	Government	10.20%
Veteran/ Active Duty	4.00%				

2020 Pres. Vote	Biden	165,129	(73%)	Trump	55,436	(25%)		
2016 Pres. Vote	Clinton	117,958	(71%)	Trump	37,232	(22%)	Johnson	6,228	(4%)

Downtown Phoenix: Phoenix is a relatively new American metropolis. It has grown to a big city just in the past two generations. Yet it is also an ancient city, or built on top of one. The Arizona Canal, several miles north of downtown Phoenix, runs along the route of a canal built about 600 years ago by the Hohokam aboriginal people. They distributed irrigated water diverted from the Salt River in its wet moments to farmers in what today is called the Valley of the Sun, and they made sophisticated astronomical observations from the mountains that jut up from the desert. This society disappeared for reasons unknown less than half a century before the Spaniards arrived in North America.

Half a century ago, Phoenix spread six miles north, west and east of the downtown and only a few miles south. Downtown was its only office center and its main shopping area, and people blew fans over boxes of ice to cool off. Today, the old warehouse district continues to evolve into an innovation and technology center. The view from downtown Phoenix stretches toward office towers many miles to the north, northeast and northwest. With a 16 percent population increase from 2010 to 2019, Phoenix overtook Philadelphia as the fifth-largest in the nation. It is nearly 40 percent of even faster-growing Maricopa County.

The city opened its first light-rail transit line in 2008, connecting residents of the Tempe and Mesa suburbs to downtown Phoenix. In 2015, the city council approved a 35-year, $32 billion transportation plan for 40 more miles of light rail across the area, plus additional bus service, with financing from a sales tax hike. Public transportation ridership plummeted in 2020 because of the COVID-19 pandemic, but city planners and construction workers seized the opportunity of reduced auto traffic to accelerate light rail construction, which shares financing from the sales tax. Sky Harbor airport completed in 2020 a $600 million renovation of its international terminal, which it renamed for Sen. John McCain. In 2019, the city council approved a 20-year blueprint to double the size of the airport. At Grand Canyon University, a private Christian school in West Phoenix, on-campus enrollment was 23,000, with more than 85,000 online students.

The 7th Congressional District of Arizona is centered in downtown Phoenix. It covers the capitol, in a rundown neighborhood a couple miles to the west, and the airport, situated in an industrial corridor several miles east. It includes most of southern Phoenix, and its boundaries follow approximately the southern and western city limits. It stretches south into Guadalupe and northwest into parts of Glendale. Geographically, the district covers most of the land between South Mountain and Camelback Mountain. The district is 64 percent Hispanic, and its median income is the lowest in the state. Most of the immigrants originated in Mexico.

The local veterans' hospital became the unfortunate symbol of the failure of the Veterans Affairs Department's health system: delayed or inadequate care, fabricated records and flawed management. During a 2015 visit to the hospital, President Barack Obama said the care was "outstanding," but there was a need to restore "trust and confidence" in the VA. During campaign visits to Arizona, Donald Trump criticized the Phoenix hospital and promised improvements for veterans. "Nobody has been treated worse and there is no more corrupt group in terms of government than what's happening with the VA in Arizona. You're the poster child for everybody. And we're going to fix it, and we're going to take care of our vets, our greatest people," he told a June 2016 rally in Phoenix. As of October 2018, the hospital retained its one-star rating on a five-star scale. In 2020, the VA eliminated its star-rating system.

Politically, this is the most Democratic district in the state. Joe Biden won here, 73%-25%.

Debbie Lesko (R)

Elected 2018, 2nd full term, b. Nov. 14, 1958; Sheboygan, WI; University of WI - Madison, B.B.A.; Marquette University; Christian Church; Married (Joe Lesko); 3 children.

Elected Office: AZ House, 2009-2015; AZ Senate, 2015-2018

DC Office: 1113 LHOB 20515, 202-225-4576, Fax: 202-225-6328, lesko.house.gov

State Offices: Glendale, 623-776-7911.

Committees: *Energy & Commerce*: Consumer Protection & Commerce; Energy.

Group Ratings

	ADA	ACLU	AFL-CIO	LCV	COC	HAFA	ACU	CFG	FRC
2020	**	16%	**	0%	-	93%	93%	**	-
2019	0%	C	29%	3%	82%	C	95%	94%	100%

Almanac Ratings 2019-2020

	Economy	Social	Foreign	Composite
Liberal	25%	5%	4%	12%
Conservative	75%	95%	96%	88%

Key Votes of the 116th Congress

1. U.S./Mex./Can. trade deal Y	5. Russia sanctions N	9. Firearms background checks N
2. First Coronavirus response N	6. Troops in Syria N	10. Spending at the border Y
3. HEROES Act N	7. Veto arms sales to Saudis N	11. Marijuana liberalized rules N
4. CASH Act N	8. Defense $$$, veto override N	12. Electoral College objections Y

Election Results

Election	Name (Party)	Vote (%)	Cand. Spent	Ind. Exp. Support	Ind. Exp. Oppose
2020 General	Debbie Lesko (R)............................ 251,633	(60%)	$925,215	$17,157	$750
	Michael Muscato (D)..................... 170,816	(40%)	$376,325	$148	
2020 Primary	Debbie Lesko (R)............................ 105,630	(100%)			

Prior winning percentages: 2018 special (52%)

Republican Debbie Lesko struggled to win her seat in 2018 during a special election in April and then in November. Lesko, a conservative, faced primary opposition and well-financed Democratic challenges as she survived contests that were closer than expected in what has been a secure GOP seat. She became a reliable supporter of House GOP leaders and served on the defense team of President Donald Trump during his first impeachment trial. Lesko succeeded Republican Rep. Trent Franks, a fervent social conservative who resigned following reports that he offered to pay aides to serve as a surrogate mother for his child.

Lesko grew up near Sheboygan Wisconsin and graduated from the University of Wisconsin with a bachelor's in business administration. She moved to Arizona, ran a business in construction sales and became active in civic and political activities in Glendale. She was elected to the state House in 2008 for the first of three terms, while serving as Arizona chairwoman of the American Legislative Exchange Council. During four years in the state Senate, she chaired the Appropriations Committee and served as president pro tempore.

Soon after Franks quit, Lesko resigned from the Senate to launch her campaign. She took a hard line on immigration, emphasized support for Trump and was endorsed by former Gov. Jan Brewer. The special election, which drew 12 Republican and three Democratic contenders, became unexpectedly messy. Initially, Lesko's chief challenger was Steve Montenegro, a state senator who had been endorsed by Franks and Republican Sen. Ted Cruz of Texas. Phil Lovas, who was Arizona chairman for Trump in the 2016 campaign, charged Lesko with violating federal campaign law by using $50,000 from her state legislative campaign account. Lesko won with 35 percent of the vote; Lovas and Montenegro each got 24 percent.

The Democratic nominee was Hiral Tipernini, a former emergency-room physician who supported expanded healthcare coverage and protections for immigrants. The little-known Tipernini had virtually no national party backing. But she drew support from Emily's List and extensive grassroots financing and significantly outspent Lesko. Republicans sought to depict Tipernini as out of touch with the district. Her 52%-48% victory was unexpectedly close—another early signal of suburban unhappiness with Trump and congressional Republicans.

The November election for a two-year term was a rematch with Tipernini. Again, the Democrat outspent Lesko, by about $2 million to $1 million, but received little national party aid. Lesko opposed expansion of federal healthcare programs and said she was open to raising the eligibility age for recipients of Social Security. Tipernini said Medicare should be widely available as a public insurance option. Lesko ran ads calling Tipernini a "phony" doctor who had not practiced for a decade. This time, Lesko won, 55%-45%. Also on Election Day, 65 percent of Arizona voters approved a referendum that repealed an expanded school-voucher program that Lesko had helped to enact.

In the House, Lesko joined the conservative Freedom Caucus, where she was the only female member. The first legislation she filed would increase state autonomy in setting education policy. "Arizonans know their schools better than any bureaucrat," she said. She opposed the Democrats' revival of the Equal Right Amendment, which she said would lead to greater demand for abortions. As a defender of Trump during impeachment, she called the hearings "a total joke."

Republican leaders showed their trust in Lesko by giving her a seat on the House Rules Committee. In 2021, she exited that panel and joined Energy and Commerce. In a bipartisan move, Lesko co-chaired the Congressional Caucus for Women's Issues. A survivor of domestic violence, she supported renewal of the Violence Against Women Act, though she opposed provisions targeting transgender persons.

In 2020, Tipernini challenged Republican Rep. David Schweikert in a neighboring district. Democratic nominee Michael Muscato, an Arizona native, was a video engineer who lost his job during the pandemic. Lesko restored normalcy to her district, with a 60%-40% victory.

AZ-8: Western Phoenix Suburbs

Cook Partisan Voting Index: R+11

Population		Race and Ethnicity		Income	
Total	798,544	White	82.80%	Median Income	$73,632
Land area (sq. miles)	540	Black	5.10%	District Income Rank	138
Pop/ sq mi	1,479.72	Latino	21.60%	Poverty Rate	9.10%
Born in State	33.80%	Asian	3.80%	With health insurance	92.90%
		Two or more races	3.60%	Cash public assistance	1.20%
Age Groups		Other	4.70%	Food stamp/SNAP	6.10%
Under 18	21.60%				
18-34	19.10%	**Education**		**Work**	
35-64	37.00%	H.S grad or less	31.20%	White Collar	40.40%
Over 64	22.40%	Some college	37.30%	Sales and Service	40.80%
		College Degree, 4 yr	19.90%	Blue Collar	18.80%
Military		Post grad	11.60%	Government	13.80%
Veteran/ Active Duty	11.20%				

2020 Pres. Vote	Trump	251,443	(57%)	Biden	181,691	(41%)			
2016 Pres. Vote	Trump	190,163	(57%)	Clinton	120,992	(36%)	Johnson	12,712	(4%)

Glendale, Peoria: In 1938, when most of Phoenix's West Valley was barren, desert landscape, Flora Mae Statler paid 35 cents an acre to acquire land on the site of what became the city of Surprise. Statler chose the name, she later recalled, because she'd "be surprised if this town ever amounted to much." But the city got the last laugh on Statler: It has become one of the fastest-growing cities in Maricopa County.Since2000, its population more than quadrupled.

Once a haven for retirees looking for warmer climates, Surprise and Phoenix's surrounding western suburbs have been booming. Astride Grand Avenue, the only diagonal street in the rigorous grid of metro Phoenix, is the suburb of Glendale, not so long ago just a crossroads but now home to 252,000 people. The city is also the home of the Phoenix Coyotes hockey arena and State Farm Stadium, which has a retractable roof and capacity of more than 78,000. The stadium has hosted the Super Bowl, plus NCAA football and basketball championships. Tucked between Surprise and Glendale are Peoria, as middle-American as its namesake in Illinois, and Sun City, a huge retirement community that markets its affordability. Peoria has revived its older neighborhood as an historic area. The master-planned community of Anthem, 30 miles north of downtown, has about 22,000 residents.

All of these cities are part of the 8th Congressional District of Arizona, which covers Phoenix's West Valley. After a slow recovery from the housing bust and subsequent economic downturn in the mid-2000s, real estate values have been on the rise. The Desert Diamond Casino West Valley north of the stadium, operated by the Tohono O'odham Nation, stirred controversy over tribal rights; initially, the facility was licensed to operate only bingo-style games. A few miles beyond Glendale is Luke Air Force Base, which has the largest fighter training wing in the Air Force and the only active duty F-16 training base in the United States. It functions as the chief operational training base for pilots of the F-35A Lightning II fighter jets, many of which have been purchased by other nations.

This has been conservative territory, though Republican downturns in the suburbs have been apparent here. In 2020, President Donald Trump won this district, 57%-41%, compared with Mitt Romney's 62%-37% lead in the 2012 presidential election.

Greg Stanton (D)

Elected 2018, 2nd term, b. Mar 08, 1970; Phoenix, AZ; Marquette University, B.A., 1992; University of MI Law School, J.D., 1995; Catholic; Married (Nicole Stanton); 2 children.

Elected Office: Phoenix City Council, 2000-2009; AZ Deputy Attorney General 2009-2011; Phoenix Mayor, 2012-2018.

Professional Career: Attorney

DC Office: 128 CHOB 20515, 202-225-9888, stanton.house.gov

State Offices: Phoenix, 602-956-2463.

Committees: *Judiciary*: Courts, Intellectual Property & Internet. *Transportation & Infrastructure*: Aviation; Highways & Transit; Water Resources & Environment.

Almanac Ratings 2019-2020

	Economy	Social	Foreign	Composite
Liberal	100%	56%	80%	79%
Conservative	0%	44%	20%	21%

Key Votes of the 116th Congress

1. U.S./Mex./Can. trade deal Y	5. Russia sanctions Y	9. Firearms background checks Y
2. First Coronavirus response Y	6. Troops in Syria Y	10. Spending at the border Y
3. HEROES Act Y	7. Veto arms sales to Saudis Y	11. Marijuana liberalized rules Y
4. CASH Act Y	8. Defense $$$, veto override Y	12. Electoral College objections N

Election Results

Election	Name (Party)	Vote (%)	Cand. Spent	Ind. Exp. Support	Ind. Exp. Oppose
2020 General	Greg Stanton (D)	217,094 (62%)	$824,610	$683	
	Dave Giles (R)	135,180 (38%)	$99,574		$113
2020 Primary	Greg Stanton (D)	83,443 (100%)			

Prior winning percentages: 2018 (61%)

Democrat Greg Stanton barely worked up a sweat in the desert in 2018 when he won the seat vacated by Rep. Kyrsten Sinema when she ran successfully for the Senate. He has voiced standard-issue progressive views and has been comfortable with party leaders. His success in what was designed in the 2012 redistricting as a competitive seat is a prime example of suburbs moving toward Democrats.

Stanton, a Phoenix native, graduated from Marquette University and got his law degree from the University of Michigan. After practicing law in Phoenix for a few years, he was elected to the city council at age 30. In a review of his eight years on the council, which he departed in 2009, the Phoenix New Times concluded, "A cynical political watcher might say that Stanton often picked neighborhood interests over special interests, carefully measured each decision, and weighed its political ramification with an eye to someday making a bid for mayor."

After working two years as an Arizona deputy attorney general, Stanton in 2011 won his first term as mayor with 56 percent of the vote. A mix of Democrats and Republicans recently have held the position, which generally has operated with limited partisanship. Stanton claimed to have operated in that tradition by setting aside partisan politics.

In a profile in 2017, Governing magazine named him one of its "public officials of the year." Under Stanton, the publication wrote, "the city has taken significant steps in the direction of sustainability," including major expansion of light rail, bus service and bike lanes. During his years as mayor, Phoenix had major economic growth, including a big increase in tech jobs.

In announcing his bid for Congress, Stanton styled himself as "a progressive who gets things done." He criticized President Donald Trump for his reversal of President Barack Obama's policy on the Paris climate agreement, and embraced the enrollment of immigrants in the Deferred Action for Childhood Arrivals program. "There has never been a more consequential time in the fight to protect the middle class," he said. He was unopposed in the Democratic primary and he had no apparent worry about a prospective opponent.

His Republican challenger was Steve Ferrara, a surgeon who has used endovascular techniques that he developed while serving in the U.S. Navy, where he was chief medical officer. As a first-time candidate, his fundraising was competitive with Stanton. Ferrara criticized Stanton's record as mayor, but received little encouragement from national Republicans. Stanton won, 61%-39%.

In the House, Stanton kept busy with his committee work. On Transportation and Infrastructure, he secured numerous provisions for Arizona, including its tribal regions, in water resources and transportation legislation. Stanton was reelected, 62%-38%, against Dave Giles, an international business consultant. He was mentioned as a potential candidate for governor in 2022.

AZ-9: Central and Eastern Phoenix Suburbs   Cook Partisan Voting Index: D+9

Population		Race and Ethnicity		Income	
Total	818,850	White	75.10%	Median Income	$65,379
Land area (sq. miles)	165	Black	7.00%	District Income Rank	208
Pop/ sq mi	4,969.05	Latino	26.60%	Poverty Rate	13.90%
Born in State	39.70%	Asian	5.30%	With health insurance	87.90%
		Two or more races	3.80%	Cash public assistance	1.20%
Age Groups		Other	8.60%	Food stamp/SNAP	6.90%
Under 18	20.20%				
18-34	32.50%	**Education**		**Work**	
35-64	34.90%	H.S grad or less	27.50%	White Collar	45.30%
Over 64	12.20%	Some college	31.20%	Sales and Service	38.90%
		College Degree, 4 yr	26.00%	Blue Collar	15.80%
Military		Post grad	15.30%	Government	11.50%
Veteran/ Active Duty	6.20%				

2020 Pres. Vote	Biden	224,192	(60%)	Trump	137,694	(37%)			
2016 Pres. Vote	Clinton	155,158	(54%)	Trump	109,123	(38%)	Johnson	14,768	(5%)

Tempe, Western Mesa: As metropolitan Phoenix has expanded in the Valley of the Sun over the past half century, it has absorbed the crossroads towns that were once separate and distinct. One such town is Tempe, east of downtown Phoenix. It was founded in 1871 as Hayden's Ferry by the father of future Democratic Sen. Carl Hayden, who held that office from 1927 to 1969, and it was renamed in 1879 for an ancient Greek vale. Arrival of the railroad in 1887 was instrumental in that progress. The old agricultural town centered on Arizona State University, and both the town and the university have expanded greatly over the decades, while struggling to keep up with development and the financial costs of gentrification. The campus, which sits astride a rise with a fine view of much of metropolitan Phoenix, has an undergraduate enrollment of 54,000 students. Its online student enrollment is the largest in the nation. The research park on the campus has 51 business tenants with 6,700 employees; many of the firms are technology-based. ASU planned to open in 2021 a new campus in downtown Mesa, which will feature digital innovation.

Tempe is relatively affluent, with 196,000 people in 2019, up from 142,000 in 1990, which is slower growth than other Phoenix suburbs. The city has nine stations along the original 20-mile light rail system from the city, with a three-mile extension from downtown to the campus scheduled to open in 2021. Its Mill Avenue district across from the ASU campus is a pedestrian-friendly downtown featuring red brick sidewalks and turn-of-the-century buildings. The day before college football's Fiesta Bowl (now played in Glendale), Tempe hosts a parade and block party.

The 9th Congressional District of Arizona includes Tempe and parts of Scottsdale, Mesa, Chandler and Phoenix. It was drawn to be the only politically competitive district in the Phoenix area, but its demographic characteristics are favorable for Democrats. The district contains high shares of college graduates and high-income households. Hillary Clinton won the district in 2016, 54%-38%, a big boost for Democrats over the 51%-47% local win by President Barack Obama in 2012. Joe Biden added several more points to the Democratic vote with his 60%-37% win here. Outside of Arizona's two majority-minority districts, the 9th contains the largest concentration of Hispanics, at 27 percent, and its strongest Democratic performance. With Arizona gaining a seat from reapportionment in 2022, this area could become the core of a third Hispanic district.

ARKANSAS

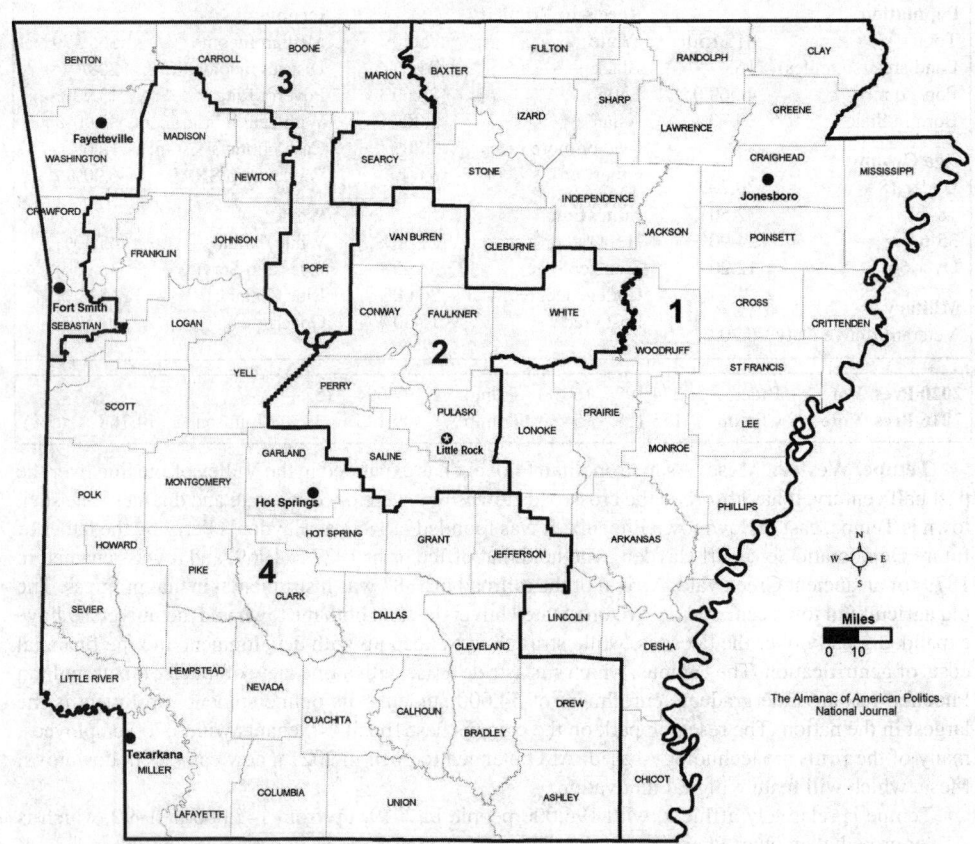

Congressional district boundaries were first effective for 2012.

Arkansas, the state that brought Bill and Hillary Clinton to national prominence, has turned decisively away from the party they led. In 2008, the state's governor, both senators and three of its four House members were Democrats. Today, the GOP controls everything. And in a state that's whiter, less affluent, older, more rural and with lower rates of college education than the national average—five key demographic factors in determining partisan leanings today—there's little chance that Democrats will be returning to influence in Arkansas anytime soon. In 2020, only one of the state's four Republican House members—French Hill—won by fewer than 30 points. GOP control of redistricting in Little Rock likely will seek to fix his problems.

Like Clinton, Arkansas began life without many advantages. It consists of the land left over when Louisiana and Missouri were carved out of the Louisiana Purchase and what is now Oklahoma was fenced off as Indian Territory. In area, it is the second-smallest state between the Mississippi River and the Pacific Ocean. In population, it is the smallest southern state except for Mississippi (the two are neck and neck) and, if you consider it southern, West Virginia. Arkansas was not blessed with great natural resources, with the exception of bauxite, once the main source of aluminum, and flame-retarding bromine. Its first two senators could not agree on how to pronounce the state's name, but since 1881, it has been illegal to call it ar-KAN-sas. Settled by poor farmers with large families, few slaves and little cash, Arkansas has had no major city like Atlanta, Dallas or even Memphis. Arkansas was settled more by Scots-Irish farmers than by grand plantation owners. It fought for the Confederacy, except for a few Union men in the northwest, and it followed other southern states in establishing government-enforced racial segregation. It is the birthplace of Pentecostal denominations like the Church of God in Christ, which had roots in late 1800s Little Rock, and the Assemblies of God, founded in Hot Springs in 1914 and now headquartered in Springfield Missouri.

In 1973, when Clinton was returning to the state from Yale Law School, the dominant figure in Arkansas, as far as most Americans knew, was Orval Faubus, governor from 1955 to 1967. Faubus had blocked desegregation of Little Rock's Central High School in 1957 until President Dwight Eisenhower sent in federal troops to enforce the court's order. And Arkansas was one of five states to vote for segregationist George Wallace for president in 1968. But Arkansas was evolving, culturally and economically, in ways that made Clinton's career possible. Faubus was succeeded by governors who repudiated his legacy: Republican Winthrop Rockefeller in 1966 and Democrat Dale Bumpers in 1970. Their politics made Clinton, then 28, a plausible candidate in the Republican-dominated 3rd Congressional District in 1974. He narrowly lost to the incumbent Republican but came to the attention of leading entrepreneurs in the northwest corner of Arkansas, none of whom had quite yet achieved national fame: Sam Walton, whose first Walmart had opened only a dozen years before; Don Tyson of chicken-producing Tyson Foods; and J.B. Hunt and his trucking firm. In less than two decades, Walton was America's richest man, and Clinton was president.

Arkansas still ranks low on many national indexes—its median household income is the nation's third-lowest and was largely flat even during the "good times" before the coronavirus hit. Roughly one-in-six residents live in poverty, and poverty rates for Black children hit nearly 45 percent in 2018. Rates of high school degrees are only slightly lower than in the U.S. as a whole, but only about one-in-five Arkansas residents have a bachelor's degree, well below the U.S. average. The incarceration rate in Arkansas was the country's fourth-highest in 2019, trailing only Louisiana, Oklahoma and Mississippi, according to the Sentencing Project. The dismal conditions in the state's prisons attracted national attention in 2020, as more than 2,300 inmates at Cummins Unit in southeast Arkansas contracted the coronavirus, a disproportionate number of them Black. That came 50 years after a judge had singled out Cummins for special criticism when describing the state's prison system as a "dark and evil world." A plea by inmates for greater protections from the virus was rejected in the courts, but amid the controversy, the head of the prison system announced her retirement.

Arkansas continues to lead the nation in rice production while ranking No. 4 in cotton and No. 2 in chickens. Livestock and poultry sales now account for about two-thirds of the state's agricultural sales; partly as a result, the state has taken great interest in the labeling terms used by makers of plant-based meat substitutes, though legal efforts to police such language have yet to see much success in court. Meanwhile, the agricultural export economy has made Arkansas vulnerable to tariffs imposed by the Trump administration; an analysis by JP Morgan ranked Arkansas the state with the fourth-highest risk from tariffs on Chinese imports. The state's poultry plants were also hit hard by the coronavirus, putting their heavily Hispanic workforce at risk.

Little Rock has become a vibrant regional center, with exurban growth spreading out past the Pulaski County line, and it has been attracting tourists thanks to the William J. Clinton Presidential Center, the nation's largest presidential library. Northwest Arkansas—led by Rogers, Fayetteville, Bentonville and Springdale—has boomed even more. Bentonville is where Walmart's headquarters are housed and where Sam Walton's daughter, Alice Walton, in 2011 opened the Crystal Bridges museum, with a magnificent collection of American art; Fayetteville is home to the University of Arkansas and the research and technology firms its presence has midwifed. Since 2010, the population of Benton County has grown by a full 25 percent and neighboring Washington County has grown by 17 percent. Both figures far exceed the growth rate of the state (3.3 percent) and Little Rock's Pulaski County (2.1 percent). The other region with significant growth is Craighead County (Jonesboro) in the northeast part of the state, which has grown by 14 percent during the past decade.

Left behind are the aging, shrinking rural regions of the state. Of the nation's 1,000 biggest declines in city and town population since 2010, no fewer than 92 were in Arkansas. The Hispanic population, at about 8 percent, is modest but growing, and since the 1980s, Arkansas has been home to the largest concentration of Marshall Islanders outside the Pacific islands, owing to historical labor ties to Tyson Foods. Still, "we need more migrants," Pam Willrodt, a demographer at the University of Arkansas-Little Rock, told the Arkansas Democrat-Gazette. "We need more young, vibrant people who will then start having more babies."

Politically, Arkansas was long solidly Democratic, with Republican pockets in the mountains of the northwest. For years, it produced Democratic politicians who accumulated great seniority and power in Washington: longtime House Ways and Means Chairman Wilbur Mills; Sens. John McClellan and J. William Fulbright, who represented the state for a total of 65 years from the 1940s to the 1970s; and Sens. Dale Bumpers and David Pryor, who served for a total of 42 years from the 1970s to the 1990s. Republicans won some gubernatorial races—Rockefeller in the 1960s, Frank White in 1980 (when he beat Clinton), and future presidential candidate Mike Huckabee in 1998 and 2002—and John Paul Hammerschmidt amassed influence in the House, serving from 1967 to 1993. Still, as late as the 1990s, Arkansas remained one of the most Democratic states in the South in presidential and congressional elections.

No longer. As throughout the Scots-Irish belt of America, which runs from western Pennsylvania southwest along the Appalachian chain and west to Texas, Arkansans turned sharply against Barack Obama and Hillary Clinton, who decided to run for the Senate in New York rather than returning to Arkansas after her husband vacated the White House. The Democrats' share of the Arkansas vote in the 2008, 2012 and 2016 presidential elections fell from 39 percent to 37 percent to less than 34 percent against Trump, who proved extraordinarily popular in rural areas. In 2020, Arkansas was one of just six states where Trump ran stronger in 2020 than 2016, and of these, it was the only solidly red state to show this pattern other than Utah, where third-party candidates had taken a quarter of the 2016 vote. Perhaps Hillary Clinton had a small, residual appeal in the state that Joe Biden did not?

Down ballot, the Arkansas GOP has been relentlessly ascendant. Today, the governor, both chambers of the legislature, both U.S. senators, all four U.S. House seats, and every elected state-level office is held by a Republican. The legislature has steered to the right, voting to cut taxes and passing a raft of socially conservative legislation, including a measure declaring that life begins at conception and a ban on most abortions after 12 weeks. Arkansas became the third state to receive approval from the Trump administration to impose work requirements for Medicaid recipients and the first to enact them, although the courts eventually overturned the policy. State government finances have been in good shape thanks to budget reforms instituted after the state defaulted on bonds in the 1930s (its bank balance in January 1933 was supposedly $4.80).

There is a residual strain of populism in Arkansas: Voters approved minimum wage hikes in 2014 and 2018. They also approved medical marijuana in 2016, though political and legal obstacles delayed its implementation until 2019. But Arkansas has followed a different course than such southern states as North Carolina, Georgia, and Virginia, where an influx of liberal-leaning outsiders in large metropolitan areas have turned these states various shades of purple and blue. Trump won Arkansas by 27 points in 2020, and no county switched its support from 2016. Biden's gains were mostly limited to the fast-growing northwestern part of the state: Compared to 2016, Biden narrowed the gap by a half-dozen points in both Benton County (Bentonville) and Washington County (Fayetteville). Even so, those counties still backed Trump by 27 points and four points, respectively.

Population		Race and Ethnicity		Income	
Total	3,017,804	White	76.70%	Median Income	48,952
Land area (sq. miles)	52,035	Black	15.50%	State Income Rank	48 out of 50
Pop/ sq mi	58.00	Latino	7.70%	Poverty Rate	16.20%
Born in state	60.50%	Asian	2.00%	With health insurance	90.90%
		Two or more races	2.80%	Cash public assistance	2.20%
Age Groups		Other	3.50%	Food stamp/SNAP	13.6%
Under 18	23.20%				
18-34	22.20%	Education		Work	
35-64	37.30%	H.S grad or less	47.40%	White Collar	33.90%
Over 64	17.40%	Some college	29.30%	Sales and Service	37.70%
		College Degree, 4 yr	15.10%	Blue Collar	28.40%
Military		Post grad	8.30%	Government	15.80%
Veteran/ Active Duty	8.20%				

Presidential Politics

2020 Primary (D)	Biden (D)	93,011(41%)	Sanders (D)	51,413(22%)	Bloomberg (D)	38,312(17%)	
	Warren (D)	22,970(10%)					
2020 Pres. Vote	Trump (R)	760,647(62%)	Biden (D)	423,932(35%)			
2016 Pres. Vote	Trump (R)	684,872(61%)	Clinton (D)	380,494(34%)	Johnson (L)	29,829 (3%)	

Like most southern states, Arkansas voted more Democratic than the nation as a whole in presidential elections from Reconstruction to 1960. Since then, it has done so only when Jimmy Carter and Bill Clinton were atop the Democratic ticket. In the past decade it has become one of the most reliably Republican states in the nation. In the past six elections, it has voted 51 and 54 percent for George W. Bush, 59 percent for John McCain, 61 percent for Mitt Romney, and 61 and 62 percent for Donald Trump. Between the presidential elections of 2000 and 2020, only in West Virginia has the Democratic percentage declined more precipitously than in Arkansas. In 1996, Bill Clinton carried all but nine of the state's 75 counties. In 2016, his wife, Hillary Clinton, won just eight. The Democratic base in presidential contests is Pulaski County (Little Rock), where more than a third of the residents are African-American. Jefferson County (Pine Bluff) also leans Democratic, as do the rural, heavily African-American counties along the Mississippi River on the state's eastern border. Northwest Arkansas, the Ozark Mountain region, is historically Republican and home to the corporate headquarters of Walmart in Bentonville.

In the 2016 GOP presidential primary, Trump edged out Texas Sen. Ted Cruz, 33%-31%, with 25% to Florida Sen. Marco Rubio. Joe Biden won the 2020 Democratic primary on March 3 by 41%-22% over Bernie Sanders, with Michael Bloomberg drawing 17% after investing heavily in the state. That contest came on Super Tuesday, when Biden's dominance across the South helped him cement his primary win. In the general election, Trump ran ahead of his 2016 numbers in much of the state, though Biden improved on Clinton's performance in the more urban and better-educated areas around Little Rock, Bentonville and Fayetteville.

Congressional Districts

117th Congress Lineup	4R	116th Congress Lineup	4R

During the 2011 redistricting, Democrats still held the governorship and both houses of the legislature in Arkansas, though they retained only one seat in the House delegation. Their efforts to secure the only surviving Democratic district fell flat when Democrat Mike Ross in the southern 4th District announced his retirement prior to the 2012 election. That gave Republicans control of all four House seats during the next decade. Only the 2nd District has been competitive since then.

This time, Republicans control all the levers in Arkansas, in addition to the entire congressional delegation. Presumably, their chief priority will be to shore up the 2nd District so it becomes nearly as secure for the GOP as the other three districts. Little Rock-based Pulaski County, the source of most of those Democrats, includes about half of the district's population. One option would be to remove heavily Democratic parts of Little Rock and add them to adjacent areas in either the 1st or the 4th District. In return, the 2nd District would gain a strongly Republican nearby area, such as Lonoke County or Grant County. The 1st District, which includes a string of heavily African-American rural counties along the Mississippi River, is the strongest Republican district in the state. It could easily absorb additional black voters and remain secure for the GOP.

Litigation appears to be the only option for Democrats to gain a district with black influence. As in the past, that likely would require an artful Democratic redrawing of the 1st and 2nd districts.

Asa Hutchinson (R)

Elected 2014, term expires 2023, 2nd term; b. Dec. 3, 1950, Bentonville; Bob Jones U., B.S. 1972; U of AR (Fayetteville), J.D. 1975; Christian; Married (Susan); 4 children.

Elected Office: Chairman, AR Republican Committee, 1990-95; U.S. House, 1996-2001.

Professional Career: Bentonville City Attorney, 1997-1978; U.S. Attorney, 1982-1985; Director, DEA, 2001-2003; Under Secretary for Border & Transportation Security, Department Homeland Security, 2003-2005.

Office: State Capitol Room 250, Little Rock, 72201; 501-682-2345; Fax: 501-682-1382

Lt. Gov.: Tim Griffin (R) **Atty. Gen:** Leslie Rutledge (R) **Sec. of State:** John Thurston (R)

State Legislature: Senate: 9D, 26R **House:** 24D, 76R

Election Results

Election	Name (Party)	Vote (%)
2018 General	Asa Hutchinson (R)	582,406 (65%)
	Jared Henderson (D)	283,218 (32%)
	Mark West (Lib)	25,885 (3%)
2018 Primary	Asa Hutchinson (R)	143,648 (70%)
	Jan Morgan (R)	62,757 (30%)

Prior winning percentage: 2014 (55%), House: 2000 (unopposed); 1998 (81%); 1996 (56%)

Republican Asa Hutchinson has governed as a pragmatic conservative in solidly Republican Arkansas. He won his second term as governor in 2018, improving from 55 percent of the vote in 2014 to 65 percent four years later—the highest percentage in Arkansas since the advent of four-year terms in 1986.

Hutchinson grew up on a farm in northwestern Arkansas, the state's Republican heartland, with his brother Tim, who later became a senator. Their parents also operated a Christian radio station and school. After graduating from Bob Jones University, Asa Hutchinson attended the University of Arkansas law school at the same time Bill Clinton started teaching there. He became U.S. attorney in western Arkansas and prosecuted Clinton's half-brother, Roger, for cocaine possession. He lost a longshot 1986 bid for the Senate against Democrat Dale Bumpers, then ran for attorney general in 1990 and lost again. He spent the next five years as the state GOP chairman.

Hutchinson easily won election to the House in 1996 to succeed his brother, who moved to the Senate. He combined a conservative voting record with a pleasant demeanor to become an important player in a short time. In 1998, he served as one of the House's impeachment managers against Clinton. When George W. Bush was elected president, he tapped Hutchinson to head the Drug

Enforcement Administration, then to be undersecretary for transportation and border security in the new Homeland Security Department. Hutchinson returned to Arkansas to run for governor in 2006, but he lost. After the 2012 mass shooting in Newtown, Connecticut, the National Rifle Association advocated allowing teachers and school security personnel to carry firearms and tapped Hutchinson to head a "multifaceted" education and training program "available to every school in America free of charge."

With Democratic Gov. Mike Beebe term-limited in 2014, Hutchinson prepared for another race. He faced former Rep. Mike Ross, who in 12 years in the House had been a Blue Dog Democrat with a moderate voting record, including a vote against the Affordable Care Act. Hutchinson took less ideological stands during the campaign than he had in the past. He backed a November ballot measure to increase the state minimum wage and to provide additional funding for early-childhood education, two proposals that Democrats nationally had favored. He also aired an ad targeting women that featured his school-age granddaughter, who helped him advocate a plan to put computer-science classes in every high school and to help women compete for high-tech jobs. Backed by $6.2 million from the Republican Governors Association aimed at tying Ross to President Barack Obama and other national Democrats, Hutchison prevailed, 55%-42%. Once in office—and leading the state's first unified Republican government since Reconstruction—Hutchinson succeeded in getting much of his agenda enacted, including a middle-class tax cut, scaled back from $100 million to $80 million.

A pair of legislative battles from his first two years stood out. One was the latest chapter in the fight over the state's "private option"—Beebe's creative way of getting a red state to accept Medicaid expansion under the Affordable Care Act, by applying federal funds for Medicaid-eligible residents toward securing them private health coverage. It was approved narrowly in 2013 and reauthorized even more narrowly in 2014. Facing fierce conservative opposition in the legislature, Hutchinson took a middle course, keeping the program in place through the end of 2016 and establishing a task force to draw up recommendations for a possible new direction after that. In April 2016, he used a line-item veto to keep the expansion alive.

The other conflict involved a religious freedom measure that blew up shortly after a similar bill in Indiana drew fire for allegedly enabling businesses to refuse to serve gays and lesbians. As in Indiana, disapproval from the business community, including home-state giant Walmart, was critical in forestalling the measure. Hutchinson rejected the first version he received from lawmakers. The legislature complied with his request for changes and Hutchinson signed the revised measure.

Hutchinson took a harder line on certain issues. He opposed the settlement of Syrian refugees in Arkansas, and criticized an Obama administration effort to pressure public schools to allow transgender students to use bathrooms and locker rooms for their chosen gender, calling it "offensive, intrusive and totally lacking in common sense." But he also signed a bipartisan criminal justice measure and backed agricultural sales to Cuba, even visiting the island nation after the Obama administration's reopening of ties.

In 2017, Hutchinson signed a $50 million tax cut for lower-income residents as well as a bill that tied higher education funding to performance-based metrics. He also signed a raft of bills designed to enact a voter-passed medical marijuana ballot measure that he had opposed, although some advocates criticized the implementation process as too slow. Hutchinson also signed a bipartisan measure of symbolic importance—one that separated what had been a joint holiday celebration of Martin Luther King Jr. and Confederate Gen. Robert E. Lee.

In 2018, Hutchinson leapt at the opportunity offered by the Trump administration to impose work requirements on many of the 285,000 beneficiaries of Arkansas' expanded Medicaid program. The requirements would eventually require able-bodied, childless adults between 19 and 49 to either work or perform 20 hours a week of volunteer service or vocational training. (The 645,000 beneficiaries in traditional Medicaid were not affected.) The policy was overturned in court in 2019, on the grounds that it was arbitrary and inconsistent with Medicaid's objectives; the rejection of Arkansas' policy was upheld on appeal the following year.

Given President Donald Trump's popularity in the state, Hutchinson had to tread carefully with his aggressive trade posture. About 350,000 jobs in Arkansas depend on trade, according to the World Trade Center Arkansas, and agricultural exports such as cotton, rice and soybeans were among the first to lose out in the trade skirmishes. Trade tensions eventually led China to pull the plug on a planned Sun Paper plant in Arkadelphia that would have produced cardboard box components, employing an estimated 2,000 people during construction and 1,000 in the timber industry.

In his bid for a second term, Hutchinson faced a primary challenge by television commentator Jan Morgan. Hutchinson represented the establishment wing of the GOP, while Morgan took a more Trumpist approach (though Trump himself endorsed Hutchinson shortly before the primary). Morgan charged that the incumbent hadn't cut taxes enough and that he was too soft on Second Amendment rights, but Hutchinson defeated Morgan, 70%-30%, and in the fall faced Democrat Jared Henderson. While Henderson cut an attractive young profile—he had previously headed Teach for America in Arkansas—he was a political novice and, more importantly, had the wrong party affiliation for the state. In the middle of the campaign, a nephew of the governor, state Sen. Jeremy Hutchinson, was indicted for conspiring to steal thousands of dollars in campaign contributions and falsifying documents to cover it up. (After the election, he pleaded guilty to various charges.) This didn't affect the governor's chances, and he ended up defeating Henderson, 66%-32%. Henderson won only seven counties—down from the 23 won by Ross in 2014.

After winning reelection, Hutchinson continued to juggle conservative initiatives and more centrist policies. He signed several strict abortion laws; one, later blocked in court, limited abortions to the first 18 weeks of pregnancy, while another would automatically ban abortion if the Supreme Court overturned Roe v. Wade. Hutchinson also signed legislation to end funding to "sanctuary cities" that don't work with federal immigration officials. Advocates for immigration were happier with Hutchinson's decision to sign bills allowing in-state tuition rates and access to nursing licenses for immigrants in the Deferred Action for Childhood Arrivals program, which covers people who were brought to the United States illegally as children. And despite taking fire from some in his party, the governor moved to continue refugee resettlement in the state at least through the end of 2020. Arkansas, he said, is "a welcoming state, and we want to be able to continue that."

Hutchinson also worked with legislative leaders to enact a hate-crimes law, seeking to end the state's status as one of just three without one. Hutchinson initially backed a hate-crimes bill after the 2019 mass shooting at a Walmart in El Paso, Texas, where the gunman reportedly targeted Hispanics. A measure didn't pass before the end of 2020, but the governor and legislators pledged to continue working on it. On the coronavirus, Hutchinson initially held off on strict behavioral measures, but during a summer spike in cases, he issued a statewide mask order. Meanwhile, voters approved a major policy priority for Hutchinson on Election Day, voting to continue a 0.5 percent sales tax dedicated to state and local highways, roads, and bridges that would have expired in 2023.

In 2021, Hutchinson signed a law that banned nearly all abortions except to save a mother's life. But he tangled with social conservatives over transgender policy. He vetoed a proposed ban on medical care for transgender youth, saying that the GOP doesn't need to "engage in every cultural battle." But the legislature overrode his veto. Hutchinson did, however, sign a bill to ban transgender women athletes from playing girls' and women's teams.

The state's gubernatorial term limit means that Hutchinson can't seek reelection in 2022. Former White House Press Secretary Sarah Huckabee Sanders is the frontrunner and has raised a significant amount of money; her father, Mike Huckabee, was governor from 1996 to 2007. Republican Attorney General Leslie Rutledge is also running, with Lt. Gov. Tim Griffin forgoing a gubernatorial bid to run for attorney general. Meanwhile, state Sen. Jim Hendren, who is Hutchinson's nephew and who had initially been considered a possible gubernatorial contender, switched his party affiliation from Republican to independent.

John Boozman (R)

Elected 2010, term expires 2022, 2nd term, b. Dec 10, 1950; Shreveport, LA; University of Arkansas, O.D., 1972; University of Arkansas Southern College of Optometry, O.D., 1977; Baptist; Married (Cathy Marley Boozman); 3 children; 2 grandchildren.

Elected Office: Rogers School Board, 1994-2001; U.S. House, 2001-2011; Assistant Whip, U.S. House, 2003-2011.

Professional Career: Co-Founder/Partner/Optometrist, Boozman-Hof Regional Eye Clinic, 1977-2001.

DC Office: 141 HSOB 20510, 202-224-4843, Fax: 202-228-1371, boozman.senate.gov

State Offices: El Dorado, 870-863-4641; Fort Smith, 479-573-0189; Jonesboro, 870-268-6925; Little Rock, 501-372-7153; Lowell, 479-725-0400; Mountain Home, 870-424-0129; Stuttgart, 870-672-6941.

Committees: *Agriculture, Nutrition & Forestry (RMM)*: Ex Officio membership on all subcommittees. *Appropriations*: Commerce, Justice, Science & Related Agencies; Department of Defense; Financial Services & General Government; Military Construction & Veteran Affairs & Related Agencies (RMM); State, Foreign Operations & Related Programs; Transportation, HUD & Related Agencies. *Environment & Public Works*: Clean Air & Nuclear Safety; Fisheries, Water, and Wildlife; Transportation & Infrastructure. *Veterans' Affairs*.

Group Ratings

	ADA	ACLU	AFL-CIO	LCV	COC	HAFA	ACU	CFG	FRC
2020	-	0%	-	15%	-	64%	85%	-	-
2019	5%	C	21%	21%	92%	C	86%	29%	100%

Almanac Ratings 2019-2020

	Economy	Social	Foreign	Composite
Liberal	0%	0%	0%	0%
Conservative	100%	100%	100%	100%

Key Votes of the 116th Congress

1. EPA clean energy rules	N	5. Russia sanctions	Y	9. Barr as Atty. General	Y
2. U.S./Mex./Can. trade deal	Y	6. Troops in SYR, AFG	Y	10. Spending at the border	Y
3. Cut unemployment benefits	Y	7. Veto arms sales to Saudis	N	11. Coney Barrett to Sup. Ct.	Y
4. Shelton to Fed Reserve	Y	8. Defense $$$, veto override	Y	12. Electoral College objections	N

Election Results

Election	Name (Party)	Vote (%)		Cand. Spent	Ind. Exp. Support	Ind. Exp. Oppose
2016 General	John Boozman (R)	661,984	(60%)	$4,097,463	$164,806	
	Conner Eldridge (D)	400,602	(36%)	$2,227,706		$29,991
	Frank Gilbert (L)	43,866	(4%)			
2016 Primary	John Boozman (R)	298,039	(77%)			
	Curtis Coleman (R)	91,795	(24%)			

Prior winning percentages: 2016 (60%), 2010 (58%), House: 2008 (79%), 2006 (62%), 2004 (59%), 2002 (99%), 2001 special (56%)

Republican John Boozman, Arkansas' senior senator, personifies his state's dramatic political shift from one of the last Democratic strongholds in the South to the bedrock of the Republican Party. When he won a special election to the House in 2001, he was the only Republican in the state's congressional delegation; it's now entirely controlled by the GOP. Like the state's junior senator, Tom Cotton, Boozman ousted a two-term Democratic incumbent by a wide margin to secure his seat in the chamber. His defeat of Blanche Lincoln in 2010 made him only the second Republican to represent Arkansas in the Senate since Reconstruction.

Today, he is the longest-serving member of Arkansas' six-person delegation. He is an amiable conservative, and his chief public criticism of President Donald Trump was on trade policy and other foreign-policy issues. Boozman has occasionally worked across the aisle, as he did during his five terms in the House. He had little trouble winning reelection in 2016, and he is not expected to face a serious challenge for a third Senate term.

In 2021, the seniority system gave Boozman an influential post. With the retirement of Sen. Pat Roberts of Kansas, Boozman became the senior Republican on the Agriculture, Nutrition and Forestry Committee—a significant assignment for a representative of a largely rural state. Although the 2018 farm bill does not expire until 2023, the committee planned to extend the child nutrition program and potentially to join the climate change debate by crafting ways for farmers to reduce their carbon emissions. Plus, the committee will prepare for its usual ide-ranging debate on agricultural support. Boozman has typically aligned with his fellow Southerners in support subsidies of certain crops, such as sugar and rice—as opposed to the grains that mostly consume the attention of farm interests from the Midwest. That's a contrast to Cotton, who has shown less interest in farm programs.

Boozman's stances on farm policy have reflected state and regional interests more than ideology. In 2012, he joined 34 colleagues in voting against the Senate version of the farm bill reauthorization; the opponents included many other Southerners who felt it did too little for farmers in their region, particularly rice and peanut growers. A year later, Boozman voted for a version of the farm bill that had been revised to the liking of Southern agricultural interests. He has aligned with Arkansas' rice and chicken producers and showed independence from some nationalists, including the Trump administration, by supporting the end of the trade embargo of Cuba. But he has been skeptical of the farm innovation urged by some Agriculture Committee members—including Chairwoman Debbie Stabenow of Michigan and Republican Mike Braun of Indiana—who would encourage agriculture producers to have access to environmentally friendly carbon credit markets. "How do we make sure that the benefit, the value, actually goes to the farmers and not the middlemen or corporations?" Boozman asked at a committee hearing in June 2020.

In February 2021, during a hearing on President Joe Biden's nomination of former Obama Agriculture Secretary Tom Vilsack to return in that capacity, Boozman praised his earlier tenure in that job when he "took the time to learn about and understand Southern agriculture." A week later, Boozman said he was "confident" he and Stabenow would "work together to address the many challenges our agricultural producers and rural America face."

Born in Shreveport Louisiana, Boozman grew up in Fort Smith, the second-largest city in Arkansas. He credits his upbringing—his father was an Air Force master sergeant and bomber during WWII—for his appreciation of issues that military families face. Boozman attended the University of Arkansas, where he played offensive guard on the football team. He left after completing his pre-optometry requirements and went on to graduate from the Southern College of Optometry in 1977. He opened a clinic in Rogers with his older brother, Fay Boozman, an ophthalmologist. John Boozman also raised polled Hereford cattle that were competitive in the show ring.

Boozman had his first experience in public office as a member of the Rogers Board of Education, a seat he won in 1994. Four years later, Fay Boozman—by then a member of the state Senate—unsuccessfully ran against Lincoln for an open Senate seat, as John Boozman got a taste of statewide politics working on his brother's campaign. Fay Boozman went on to serve for six years as director of the state health department under Gov. Mike Huckabee until his 2005 death in an accident on his farm. In 2001, John Boozman sought the 3rd District seat vacated by Republican Rep. Asa Hutchinson, who had left to lead the Drug Enforcement Administration and eventually became governor; Boozman had Huckabee's support in the special election. After emerging with a 57%-43% victory in the primary runoff, Boozman won the general election, 56%-42%.

During his early years in the House, Boozman exhibited his more conservative side in opposing President George W. Bush's immigration proposal, calling it amnesty for undocumented immigrants. A devout evangelical Christian—he co-chaired the 2017 National Prayer Breakfast in Washington—Boozman sponsored measures to display the Ten Commandments in the House and Senate chambers and sought to weaken restrictions on churches' political activities. Boozman created a dust-up in 2005 by sponsoring and then withdrawing a bill to increase the maximum workday for truckers to 16 hours. It was a move sought by Arkansas-based Walmart but lambasted by critics as a "sweatshop on wheels" that would have jeopardized safety.

In 2010, Boozman entered the Senate race against Lincoln, who was seeking a third term. The political dynamics in Arkansas had changed markedly; GOP presidential nominee John McCain had trounced Democratic nominee Barack Obama in 2008 in the state. Boozman had some vulnerabilities in an eight-candidate primary contest: He had backed Bush's controversial 2008 legislation to bail out the nation's financial institutions in the midst of the Great Recession—an issue that tea party supporters used against some Republicans in 2010. But, as the best-known candidate and having represented a district that was home to the largest concentration of the state's GOP voters, Boozman captured 53 percent of the primary vote, avoiding a runoff. His campaign manager in that contest was Sarah Huckabee Sanders—the daughter of the former governor, who later became a high-profile aide to Trump before returning home to run for governor in 2022.

Meanwhile, Lincoln's reelection bid was hampered by a spirited primary challenge from the left by Democratic Lt. Gov. Bill Halter, who not only made her drain her campaign war chest but also forced her into a runoff. She narrowly won, but the battle left her weakened. Like other Republican Senate candidates in 2010, Boozman sought to exploit the state's disenchantment with Obama by seeking to tie Lincoln to the White House. Lincoln tried to distance herself from Obama and stress the importance to the state of her position as chair of the Agriculture Committee. Senate Republican Leader Mitch McConnell gave Boozman a boost by promising him a seat on that panel if he won. Echoing an attack line used against Boozman in his first congressional campaign, Lincoln criticized him for supporting Social Security "privatization." Boozman countered that Lincoln was taking a card out of the old Democratic playbook by trying to scare seniors.

The race was no contest: Boozman swept to a 58%-37%win as part of the national GOP tide. Boozman got his promised seat on the Agriculture panel and his clout was enhanced a couple of years later when he was named to the Appropriations Committee.

Boozman has compiled a consistently conservative record. A staunch abortion opponent, he introduced a measure to require parental notification at least four days before a minor could have an abortion. He has supported efforts to withdraw federal funding to Planned Parenthood. In 2015, Boozman became chairman of the Appropriations Subcommittee on Financial Services and General Government and teamed up with fellow Republicans in attacking the Consumer Financial Protection Bureau—created in2010 as part of the Dodd-Frank financial reforms.

He was a reliable vote for Republican leaders on major legislation and presidential nominations during the Trump presidency, though Boozman occasionally went his own way. He made progress in his long pursuit of slowly peeling back the Cold War-era trade embargo of Cuba. He and Democratic Sen. Heidi Heitkamp of North Dakota secured passage in the 2018 farm bill of their proposal to allow farmers to use the Agriculture Department to promote their products in Cuba, the first measure related to Cuba to pass in almost two decades. His support for that legislation contrasted to some conservative opposition, including from Cotton, over the failure to include stricter House-passed work requirements for millions of Americans who use food stamps; those provisions were jettisoned after Senate Democrats refused to support the measure. With Democratic Sen. Michael Bennet of Colorado in May 2019, he filed a bill to lift restrictions on private financing of U.S. exports to Cuba.

On the environmental front, Boozman supported Trump's decisions to withdraw the U.S. from the Paris climate agreement and to kill the Obama-era plan for the Environmental Protection Agency to reduce carbon emissions at power plants, which Boozman said would drive up costs in Arkansas. Like others in his party, he said that he doubted the scientific consensus that humans are contributing to climate change.

While Arkansas' two senators generally vote in unison, they clashed on a crime bill in 2018. Boozman sided with party leadership and Trump on changing some federal sentencing laws through the "First Step Act," which Cotton excoriated in public and said was a "criminal leniency bill." Boozman joined 12 Republican senators in criticizing the Trump administration's "zero tolerance" immigration policy that led to the separation of migrant families at the southern border and sparked a national outcry. In January 2019, during a government shutdown triggered by Trump's demand for additional funds to build a wall along the border with Mexico, Boozman said that he opposed Trump's threat to build the wall without congressional approval. "I view it as a last resort," he said. "I'd like us to exhaust everything else first."

Like many Republicans, Boozman criticized Trump's use of tariffs. As the president challenged America's traditional allies, Boozman, a former member of the NATO Parliamentary Assembly, continued to stress the importance of the organization. Boozman took issue with Trump's refusal to criticize North Korean dictator Kim Jong Un, who told Trump during a February 2019 meeting in Vietnam that he was not familiar with the circumstances that led to the death of American student Otto Warmbier after he had been held captive by North Korea for more than a year. "I would disagree with the president. I wouldn't trust the leader of North Korea any further than I could throw him and he's a pretty big little guy," Boozman said.

As chairman of the Military Construction and Veterans Affairs Subcommittee before Democrats took the Senate after the 2020 elections, and subsequently the ranking member, Boozman cited his success in the December 2020 year-end omnibus spending bill in delivering funds to several military bases in Arkansas. He also cited progress with his long-standing priority to slash the growing number of suicides by military veterans. Three months earlier, Trump signed a bill that was sponsored by Boozman and Sen. Mark Warner of Virginia to increase mental health treatment options for veterans and increase access to VA mental health care in rural areas.

Boozman had emergency heart surgery in April 2014 after discovery of an aortic aneurysm, but he returned to Capitol Hill a couple of months later. Three years later, he underwent a successful follow-up procedure.

In 2016, at 65, he ran for a second term. His Democratic opponent, Conner Eldridge, was a quarter of a century younger and had served as U.S. attorney in Arkansas from 2010-2015 after working as a congressional aide and bank executive. Boozman criticized Eldridge as someone who would enable "a third term of Barack Obama." Eldridge distanced himself from Obama on issues like gun control while citing his record prosecuting child abusers and pornographers as U.S. attorney.

Eldridge was banking on the anti-incumbent mood in the 2016 elections. After release of a decade-old video in which then-Republican presidential candidate Trump made lewd comments about women, Boozman said the contest was a "race to the bottom of humanity," adding: "As a husband, father of three daughters, and grandfather of two precious little girls, if I ever heard anyone speak this way about them, they would be shopping for a new set of teeth." But Boozman never withdrew his support of Trump. And, during a debate a week after the video surfaced, he said he supported Trump because the next president would likely nominate several Supreme Court justices. Boozman won 60%-36%.

Looking ahead to the 2022 campaign, the candidacy of Huckabee Sanders created uncertainty in the open-seat contest for Arkansas governor. Boozman's connections to Huckabee Sanders and her father signaled that that alliance will continue. Although Democrats kept their options open in the contest for governor, they showed little interest in a big investment to challenge Boozman.

Tom Cotton (R)

Elected 2014, term expires 2026, 2nd term, b. May 13, 1977; Dardanelle, AR; Harvard University, A.B., 1999; Claremont Graduate University; Harvard University Law School, J.D., 2002; Methodist; Married (Anna Cotton); 2 children.

Military Career: Captain, U.S. Army 2004-2009 (Afghanistan, Iraq); United States Army Reserve, 2010-2013.

Elected Office: U.S. House, 2012-2014.

Professional Career: Clerk, U.S Court of Appeals, 2002-2003; Practicing attorney, 2003-2004; Management Consultant, McKinsey & Co., 2010-2011.

DC Office: 326 RSOB 20510, 202-224-2353, Fax: 202-228-0908, cotton.senate.gov

State Offices: El Dorado, 870-864-8582; Jonesboro, 870-933-6223; Little Rock, 501-223-9081; Springdale, 479-751-0879.

Committees: *Armed Services*: Airland (RMM); Seapower; Strategic Forces. *Intelligence*. *Joint Economic*. *Judiciary*: Competition Policy, Antitrust & Consumer Rights; Criminal Justice & Counterterrorism (RMM); Immigration, Citizenship & Border Security; Subcommittee on Intellectual Property.

Group Ratings

	ADA	ACLU	AFL-CIO	LCV	COC	HAFA	ACU	CFG	FRC
2020	-	8%	-	15%	-	85%	86%	-	-
2019	5%	C	11%	14%	75%	C	88%	64%	100%

Almanac Ratings 2019-2020

	Economy	Social	Foreign	Composite
Liberal	0%	0%	0%	0%
Conservative	100%	100%	100%	100%

Key Votes of the 116th Congress

1. EPA clean energy rules	N	5. Russia sanctions	Y	9. Barr as Atty. General	Y
2. U.S./Mex./Can. trade deal	Y	6. Troops in SYR, AFG	Y	10. Spending at the border	Y
3. Cut unemployment benefits	Y	7. Veto arms sales to Saudis	N	11. Coney Barrett to Sup. Ct.	Y
4. Shelton to Fed Reserve	Y	8. Defense $$$, veto override	N/A	12. Electoral College objections	N

Election Results

Election	Name (Party)	Vote (%)		Cand. Spent	Ind. Exp. Support	Ind. Exp. Oppose
2020 General	Tom Cotton (R)...............................	793,871	(67%)	$5,105,051	$2,320	$488
	Rick Dale Harrington Jr. (L)..................	399,390	(33%)	$62,540	$325	
2020 Primary	Tom Cotton (R)............................. Unopposed		(0%)			

Prior winning percentages: 2014 (57%), House: 2012 (60%)

Republican Tom Cotton of Arkansas, first elected in 2014, has made no secret of his interest in running for president in 2024. For the most part, Arkansas' junior senator carries the portfolio of former President Donald Trump, though with a more disciplined approach. Just months after being sworn in in 2015, he led an effort to undermine President Barack Iran nuclear deal with Iran. His populist views on immigration and his hawkish stances toward Iran and China found a perfect partner in Trump. Avowedly conservative with a prickly wit, Cotton has been unsparing in a body that values congeniality. In June 2020, he became the focus of an internal clash at The New York Times after the paper's opinions division published an op-ed in which Cotton called for using military force to quell nationwide protests against police brutality and racism. Many inside and outside the Times found it objectionable. Days after publication, the editorial page editor resigned.

A Harvard University-educated veteran of the wars in Iraq and Afghanistan, Cotton has had a meteoric political ascent: In 2014, he ousted Democratic Sen. Mark Pryor, a well-known name in Arkansas politics, after serving only one term in the House. Hardly a natural politician, he is more a cerebral, introverted, principled conservative than a back-slapper who enjoys mixing it up on the campaign trail. Still, Cotton's tough-minded views caught the attention of national groups when he sought an open House seat in 2012, earning endorsements from the anti-tax Club for Growth and the late Sen. John McCain of Arizona, who shared his hawkish views.

A sixth-generation Arkansan, Cotton grew up on his family's cattle farm in Dardanelle. Even at a young age, he made an impression with his serious demeanor. Friends remember him as a contrarian and admirer of Winston Churchill. He studied government at Harvard and later earned a degree from its law school. Cotton clerked for a federal appeals court judge and later worked at two law firms. He has said 9/11 caused him to reexamine his life. He enlisted in the Army in December 2004 and turned down an opportunity to join the Judge Advocate General's Corps, preferring to serve in combat.

Cotton was deployed to Baghdad in May 2006 as a platoon leader in the 101st Airborne Division, leading daily patrols through the city. His ferocity came through during his deployment when he wrote a letter to the New York Times, responding to a story the newspaper broke in 2006 about the Bush administration's program tracing financial transactions of people suspected of ties to terrorist organizations. "You may think you have done a public service," he wrote in his initial conflict with the Times, "but you have gravely endangered the lives of my soldiers and all other soldiers and innocent Iraqis here." He went on: "Next time I hear that familiar explosion—or next time I feel it—I will wonder whether we could have stopped that bomb had you not instructed terrorists how to evade our financial surveillance. By the time we return home, maybe you will be in your rightful place: not at the Pulitzer announcements, but behind bars."

Though the Times chose not to publish the letter, Cotton had copied PowerLine, a conservative blog, which did publish it. His words impressed some leading conservatives. Bill Kristol, the editor of the now-defunct neoconservative magazine the Weekly Standard, befriended Cotton and became his champion. In 2007, Cotton joined the Old Guard, the regiment that guards the Tomb of the Unknown Soldier at Arlington National Cemetery. The following year, he went to Afghanistan as an operations officer for a provincial construction team. After completing his military service, Cotton postponed pursuit of political office and joined McKinsey & Co., a high-powered management consulting firm.

When Democratic Rep. Mike Ross announced in 2011 that he would not seek reelection, Republicans saw an opportunity. Cotton decided it was the right time to take the plunge into politics. He won the GOP primary with 58 percent of the vote over Beth Anne Rankin, a onetime aide to former Gov. Mike Huckabee, and trounced Democratic state Rep. Gene Jeffress in the general election with 60 percent, becoming just the second Republican elected in the historically Democratic 4thDistrict.

In the House, Cotton compiled a conservative record and exhibited an uncompromising streak. He opposed an initial version of the 2014 farm bill, which he scorned as a "food stamp bill." He later backed a version that didn't contain food stamp programs. He opposed disaster relief for Hurricane Sandy victims. After the April 2013 Boston Marathon bombing, he blasted the Obama administration for "failing in its mission to stop terrorism before it reaches its targets in the United States." Cotton didn't spare his party's own anti-interventionist wing and, just months later, joined with another military veteran, then-Rep. Mike Pompeo of Kansas—who later served as director of the CIA and then secretary of State under Trump—to write an op-ed in the Washington Post urging fellow Republicans to support Obama's call for military intervention in Syria.

Pryor held the same seat that his father, onetime Gov. David Pryor, had occupied for three terms. Republicans hadn't even bothered to field a candidate against the younger Pryor when he won a second term in 2008. But, six years later, Arkansas' increasingly rightward shift, combined with Obama's deep unpopularity there, provided an opening for the GOP. Cotton, with his military background and strong conservative credentials, was seen as the party's best prospect to unseat Mark Pryor. Even though he was one of the most conservative Democrats in the Senate, Pryor was painted by Republicans as a liberal Obama ally. The GOP hammered him for backing the Affordable Care Act and the Obama administration's $787 billion economic stimulus bill.

Democrats' strategy was to paint Cotton as an extremist, driven by ideological convictions that put him at odds with most Arkansans. They highlighted his vote against lowering student loan interest rates—he was the only member of the state's delegation to oppose it—and his opposition to the farm bill. Cotton said hometown banks should finance student loans rather than the federal government. And he took aim at the food stamp component of the farm bill, demanding it include work requirements and drug testing. Democrats' effort to paint Cotton as too far to the right failed to make a dent in Arkansas' decade long rightward shift. Cotton won 57%-40%. His victory marked a milestone for Arkansas, the first time since Reconstruction that Republicans held every seat in its congressional delegation.

Cotton made an early impression on the Armed Services Committee when he grilled an Obama Defense Department official about Guantanamo Bay. Obama had promised to close the facility in Cuba, used to detain foreigners suspected of terrorism, during his 2008 campaign. But Cotton said, "The only problem with Guantanamo Bay is that there are too many empty cells."

Intending to head off what he saw as the White House negotiating a bad nuclear deal with Iran, Cotton spearheaded in March 2015 an "open letter to the leaders" of that country; it garnered widespread attention. It warned the Islamic republic's leaders that striking an agreement with Obama without congressional approval was nothing more than an executive agreement that could be short-lived—since it could be undone by a future president. (That proved to be the case soon after Trump was elected.) While Cotton persuaded46 of his Senate Republican colleagues—all but seven of them—to join him in signing the letter, officials of the Obama administration were infuriated, saying it was an inappropriate interference in the conduct of foreign policy. The Senate overwhelmingly approved a plan for congressional review of an agreement with Iran, although Obama ultimately rounded up enough supporters to block a super-majority needed to reject the deal.

Trump praised Cotton on Twitter before the 2016 Republican National Convention, fueling speculation that the Arkansan was on a short list of possible nominees for vice president. He was an in-demand speaker in Cleveland, including appearances before the delegations from Iowa, New Hampshire and South Carolina—states that would be the first to select delegates in the 2020 campaign. When Trump's candidacy hit the rocks in October after the release of the "Access Hollywood" tape—on which Trump can be heard bragging about sexual assault—Cotton was one of many Republicans who distanced themselves from the party's nominee. But he later walked it back, saying Trump had apologized and could "change his ways," reaffirming his endorsement of the soon-to-be president.

At times, Cotton's sharp tongue has made even some members of his own party uncomfortable. His support of legislation to rein in legal immigration rankled fellow Republican Sen. Lindsey Graham of South Carolina. Graham said his colleague had become "sort of the Steve King of the Senate," referring to the controversial House Republican from Iowa who would later be stripped of his committee seats after making racist comments in a New York Times interview. "The difference between Steve King and Lindsey Graham is that Steve King can actually win an election in Iowa," Cotton responded. "He didn't make it to the starting line and he didn't even make it off the kiddie table in the debates. "Later, in an op-ed piece in the Wall Street Journal, Cotton wrote that bipartisan criminal justice changes were a "jailbreak that would endanger communities."

Cotton's uncompromising attitude has been evident even when home-state economic interests were involved. When Obama restored diplomatic relations with Cuba in 2015, after more than a half-century, most of Arkansas' all-Republican congressional delegation—along with the state's GOP governor—welcomed the move, seeing the prospect of a new export market for the state's abundant rice crop. Cotton was the lone holdout in the delegation, joining other hard-line Republicans in opposition. He was slammed by journalists at home for avoiding the news media during the Senate's consideration of legislation to repeal the Affordable Care Act, which Cotton helped write as part of the 13-member group tasked with shaping the Senate's proposal. Despite the prominent role of senior Arkansas Sen. John Boozman and the support of the rest of the delegation for the final version of 2018 farm bill, Cotton opposed it and slammed the measure, like previous efforts, for lacking stringent requirements for recipients of food assistance.

Like many Republicans, Cotton questioned Trump's decision to impose steel and aluminum tariffs, including on allies. But that was an exception. Trump sided with Cotton over Secretary of State Rex Tillerson and Secretary of Defense Jim Mattis, his initial selections for those Cabinet posts, who had cautioned against pulling out of the Iran nuclear agreement. Cotton also urged Trump to replace Michael Flynn as national security adviser with Army Gen. H.R. McMaster, and he assisted Marine Corps Gen. John Kelly to snag a spot in the Cabinet, before Kelly became Trump's chief of staff.

After building a reputation as a derailer of ballyhooed bipartisan proposals, Cotton ended 2018 with a rare setback when he opposed final action on the criminal justice changes. That positioned him against an effort backed by Jared Kushner, a senior White House adviser and Trump's son-in-law, along with most Republicans in Congress.

When the novel coronavirus first struck American soil, Cotton was among the first political leaders to sound the alarm. With Rep. Liz Cheney of Wyoming, he defended concerns raised by medical experts and warned of the need for a serious national response, even in the face of resistance by many other Republicans. In interviews, "Cotton and Cheney made clear that their early focus on the virus made them outliers," the Washington Post reported in early April 2020. Rhetorically, he placed the blame largely on China and suggested steps to punish that nation.

Cotton was in the national spotlight in June of that year after he wrote an op-ed in the Times calling for the military to be deployed with "an overwhelming show of force to disperse, detain and ultimately deter lawbreakers" amid nationwide protests that came after white police officers killed unarmed Black men. Many reporters at the Times raised internal objections—consistent with concerns voiced by many readers and public officials—that Cotton's views were ill-advised as a matter of military tradition, should not have been published and jeopardized their relationships with sources.

Five days later, after extensive second-guessing and criticism of his handling of Cotton's piece, James Bennet—the brother of Democratic Sen. Michael Bennet of Colorado—apologized for publishing Cotton's op-ed and resigned as the chief of the editorial pages. Although Cotton largely became collateral damage in the incident, the depth of the protests highlighted the divisiveness of his views among a slice of public opinion. In response, Cotton said that his views had been mischaracterized with "false and offensive" attacks.

Cotton, meanwhile, offered unusual support for Trump in his reelection campaign. During the primary in Ohio that spring, he ran television ads that criticized Democratic presidential frontrunner Joe Biden as "weak on China" and described himself as standing with Trump to "keep America great." Political pundits said that Cotton was making an early move to position himself for the Republican presidential nomination in 2024. "Tom Cotton is indeed setting himself up to be the heir to Trumpism," Geoffrey Kabaservice, a scholar who has written widely about Republicans, told the Wall Street Journal in June 2020.

Cotton ran for reelection without facing a Democratic opponent. His main competition: Libertarian Party candidate Ricky Harrington, who spent $62,000 while Cotton spent $5.1 million. Cotton won 67%-33%. Notably, Harrington, a minister and former prison chaplain, won three counties—including Little Rock-based Pulaski County, which is the largest in the state. Much of the vote for Harrington likely came from solid Democrats.

Rick Crawford (R)

Elected 2010, 6th term, b. Jan 22, 1966; Homestead Air Force Base, FL; Southwest MO State University, Att., 1993; AR State University, Jonesboro, B.S., 1996; Baptist; Married (Stacy Crawford); 2 children.

Military Career: U.S. Army 1985-1989

Professional Career: News anchor; Agri-reporter; Marketing Manager, John Deere; Owner, AgWatch Network.

DC Office: 2422 RHOB 20515, 202-225-4076, Fax: 202-225-5602, crawford.house.gov

State Offices: Cabot, 501-843-3043; Dumas, 870-377-5571; Jonesboro, 870-203-0540; Mountain Home, 870-424-2075.

Committees: *Agriculture*: Biotechnology, Horticulture & Research; General Farm Commodities & Risk Management; Subcommittee Nutrition, Oversight & Department Operations. *Permanent Select on Intelligence*: Counterterrorism, Counterintelligence & Counterproliferation (RMM); Defense Intelligence & Warfighter Support. *Transportation & Infrastructure*: Highways & Transit; Railroads, Pipelines & Hazardous Materials (RMM).

Group Ratings

	ADA	ACLU	AFL-CIO	LCV	COC	HAFA	ACU	CFG	FRC
2020	**	10%	**	10%	-	93%	80%	**	-
2019	0%	C	26%	97%	72%	C	80%	80%	100%

Almanac Ratings 2019-2020

	Economy	Social	Foreign	Composite
Liberal	30%	19%	37%	29%
Conservative	70%	81%	63%	71%

Key Votes of the 116th Congress

1. U.S./Mex./Can. trade deal Y	5. Russia sanctions	Y	9. Firearms background checks N
2. First Coronavirus response Y	6. Troops in Syria	Y	10. Spending at the border	Y
3. HEROES Act	N	7. Veto arms sales to Saudis	N	11. Marijuana liberalized rules	N
4. CASH Act	Y	8. Defense $$$, veto override Y	12. Electoral College objections Y

Election Results

Election	Name (Party)	Vote (%)	Cand. Spent	Ind. Exp. Support	Ind. Exp. Oppose
2020 General	Rick Crawford (R)............................. 237,596 (100%)		$690,009		

Prior winning percentages: 2018 (69%), 2016 (76%), 2014 (63%), 2012 (56%), 2010 (52%)

First District Rep. Rick Crawford, who in 2010 became the first Republican since Reconstruction to win this eastern Arkansas district, has settled in and delivers federal payments and projects back home. A former news anchor and owner of an agricultural broadcasting business, he keeps an eye out for the region's cotton and rice farmers. Like the many Democrats who served this and similar rural southern districts in decades past, he is usually a loyalist who quietly produces farm and other legislation for party leaders. With his seniority, he has eyed the top Republican post on two House committees

Crawford was born in Florida on the former Homestead Air Force Base, where his father, a munitions expert, was stationed. Moving around a lot, he attended a dozen schools as a child. After graduating from high school in Hudson, New Hampshire, he enlisted in the Army, where he trained as a bomb-disposal technician, disabling suspected live explosives. Crawford became a sergeant, did a tour of duty in Pakistan, and later served on Secret Service details for Presidents Ronald Reagan and George H.W. Bush.

When his military service ended, he enrolled at Arkansas State University in Jonesboro to study agribusiness and economics. He competed on the college rodeo circuit until injuries forced him to quit. In 1994, he declared personal bankruptcy, but eventually found full-time employment in rodeo announcing. He worked some 100 shows a year before finishing his degree. Working the rodeo-broadcasting gigs helped Crawford land a news-anchor job in Jonesboro after graduation. His experience in agricultural broadcasting led to his own business, the AgWatch Network, a farm-news outlet that broadcasted on dozens of radio stations in the mid-South, as well as on television stations in Little Rock and Jonesboro.

When Crawford decided to challenge seven-term Democratic Rep. Marion Berry in 2010, national Republicans were skeptical, hoping for a more seasoned candidate. Crawford gained traction after Berry announced his retirement, making the district ripe for a GOP takeover. Crawford coasted to an easy primary victory and argued in the general election that Democrats had lost touch with the region's rural and small-town conservative voters. Democrat Chad Causey, Berry's former chief of staff, highlighted Crawford's personal bankruptcy and attacked him for not releasing his financial records. Crawford portrayed Causey as a Washington insider beholden to national Democrats. Former President Bill Clinton returned to Arkansas to help raise money for Causey, to no avail. Crawford won, 52%-44%.

In the House, Crawford sits on the Agriculture Committee, where he focuses on ways to protect farmers from overly burdensome regulations. He argued tariffs would help boost soybean exports (the Agricultural Counsel of Arkansas disagreed) along with bolstering the district's steel industry. Crawford took the lead among a bipartisan group of House members from Delta districts who opposed a move by the Obama administration to reverse a provision in the 2014 farm bill that shifted inspection of catfish imports from the Agriculture Department to the Food and Drug Administration. In 2020, he voiced his interest in filling the vacancy for the top Republican on the Agriculture Committee. But the position went to Rep. Glenn Thompson of Pennsylvania, who had more seniority.

On the Transportation and Infrastructure Committee, Crawford added a provision to the 2015 highway bill that permitted farm vehicles to use a three-mile stretch of the redesignated Interstate 555 near Jonesboro. As ranking Republican on the Railroads, Pipelines and Hazardous Materials Subcommittee, he has urged greater flexibility for rail companies to develop and utilize more technologies to increase efficiency. On that committee, his seniority has placed him in line to succeed Rep. Sam Graves of Missouri as the top Republican by 2024. Crawford is also a senior Republican on the Select Intelligence Committee.

Crawford supported President Donald Trump's tariffs on China, saying fears of a "trade war" were overblown. He voiced concern about the national security implications of Chinese investment in America, including three companies in his House district.

His inclination to seek bipartisan consensus occasionally has caused problems for Crawford with other Republicans. He has urged a more flexible approach on illegal immigration, arguing that immigrants are an important economic force. In 2017, he expressed concerns about the American Health Care Act, the GOP's failed plan to replace Obama care, citing problems with the process, but he eventually voted yes when the House passed the bill.

Crawford won his first reelection with 56 percent of the vote. In 2016, and again in 2020, Democrats failed to run a candidate against him. With a Republican-controlled legislature to protect the GOP during redistricting, Crawford appears to have become entrenched in what only a decade ago was a "Yellow Dog" Democratic district.

AR-1: Eastern Arkansas   Cook Partisan Voting Index: R+21

Population		Race and Ethnicity		Income	
Total	719,048	White	77.40%	Median Income	$43,193
Land area (sq. miles)	19,318	Black	17.60%	District Income Rank	425
Pop/ sq mi	37.22	Latino	3.40%	Poverty Rate	18.30%
Born in State	65.10%	Asian	0.50%	With health insurance	91.40%
		Two or more races	3.10%	Cash public assistance	2.10%
Age Groups		Other	1.50%	Food stamp/SNAP	14.30%
Under 18	22.70%				
18-34	20.90%	Education		Work	
35-64	38.10%	H.S grad or less	54.00%	White Collar	30.30%
Over 64	18.40%	Some college	29.80%	Sales and Service	36.90%
		College Degree, 4 yr	10.90%	Blue Collar	32.80%
Military		Post grad	5.30%	Government	16.70%
Veteran/ Active Duty	8.20%				

2020 Pres. Vote	Trump	187,640	(69%)	Biden	75,898	(28%)			
2016 Pres. Vote	Trump	169,438	(65%)	Clinton	78,688	(30%)	Johnson	5,489	(2%)

The Delta, Jonesboro: The Mississippi Delta, the flat, mucky, river-crossed lowland on both sides of the great river, was some of the country's first industrial farmland. Uncultivated for most of the 19th century, the Delta's big landowners eventually used machines to drain the muddy marshlands and persuaded poor blacks to move there to tend fields of cotton, rice and, later, soybeans. The results were bountiful agriculture and impoverished people. But the first minimum-wage and war-industry jobs up North drew young people out of the region, and the mechanical cotton picker idled many farm workers. In 2020, the Walton Family Foundation donated $20 million to help complete an 84-mile bike and pedestrian trail through the Delta.

This area remains poor by national standards. Education rates are low, unemployment is high and the district is among the bottom 5 percent in the nation in median income. Opioid addiction has become a problem, and the district ranked seventh in the country for opioid prescription rates.

Local rice farmers are among the biggest recipients of federal farm subsidies. In Stuttgart, Riceland Foods is a farmer-owned agricultural marketing cooperative and the world's largest miller and marketer of rice. The local rice fields also attract ducks, making Arkansas the most productive state for mallard hunters. In the small town of Gillett, a political highlight is the annual Coon Supper, where Govs. Bill Clinton and Mike Huckabee frequently mingled with guests.

The local economy is increasingly supported by manufacturing. The Jonesboro area has become a rail-car manufacturing center with the opening of a Southwest Steel Processing Co. facility in Newport. Several big auto parts plants operate in Marion, across the Mississippi River from Memphis. In 2018, Big River Steel announced an expansion of its flex mill facility in Blytheville, to produce high-grade electrical steel—increasingly in demand for hybrid and electric vehicles. In December 2020, U.S. Steel said it will complete its purchase of Big River.

The 1st Congressional District of Arkansas includes almost all the state's Delta lands and stretches west to the cool, green Ozarks. The largest city in the district is Jonesboro—heart of one of the fastest-growing areas in the state—where cheap labor and flat land have made it a hub for food-processing companies such as Nestle and Frito-Lay. Jonesboro native John Grisham makes a number of references to the city in his book A Painted House. For decades, the Delta was the most Democratic part of Arkansas. Some of the hill counties are ancestrally Republican. Craigshead County (Jonesboro) and Lonoke County near Little Rock are the largest in the district and both have become heavily Republican. Six rural counties along the Mississippi River voted for Joe Biden in 2020, but overall this was the strongest district in Arkansas for Donald Trump, with 69 percent of the vote.

French Hill (R)

Elected 2014, 4th term, b. Dec 05, 1956; Little Rock, AR; Vanderbilt University, B.S., 1979; Roman Catholic; Married (Martha Hill); 2 children.

Professional Career: Staff, U.S. Senate Committee on Banking, Housing & Urban Affairs, 1982-1984; Deputy Assistant, U.S. Treasury, 1989-1991; Special Assistant, Economic Policy Council, 1991-1993; Sr. advisor, Gov. Huckabee, 2008; Banker, Businessman.

DC Office: 1533 LHOB 20515, 202-225-2506, Fax: 202-225-5903, hill.house.gov

State Offices: Conway, 501-358-3481; Little Rock, 501-324-5941.

Committees: *Financial Services*: Housing, Community Development & Insurance (RMM); Investor Protection, Entrepreneurship & Capital Markets; Task Force on Financial Technology. *Joint Congressional Oversight Commission*.

Group Ratings

	ADA	ACLU	AFL-CIO	LCV	COC	HAFA	ACU	CFG	FRC
2020	**	17%	**	19%	-	77%	82%	**	-
2019	5%	C	33%	10%	94%	C	84%	68%	95%

Almanac Ratings 2019-2020

	Economy	Social	Foreign	Composite
Liberal	25%	38%	27%	30%
Conservative	75%	62%	73%	70%

Key Votes of the 116th Congress

1. U.S./Mex./Can. trade deal	Y	5. Russia sanctions	Y
2. First Coronavirus response	Y	6. Troops in Syria	Y
3. HEROES Act	N	7. Veto arms sales to Saudis	N
4. CASH Act	N	8. Defense $$$, veto override	Y

9. Firearms background checks	N
10. Spending at the border	Y
11. Marijuana liberalized rules	N
12. Electoral College objections	N

Election Results

Election	Name (Party)	Vote (%)		Cand. Spent	Ind. Exp. Support	Ind. Exp. Oppose
2020 General	French Hill (R)............................	184,093	(55%)	$3,199,777	$164,951	$2,488,159
	Joyce Elliott (D)...........................	148,410	(45%)	$3,422,332	$997,384	$1,764,775

Prior winning percentages: 2018 (52%), 2016 (58%), 2014 (52%)

Republican French Hill has faced competitive challenges in his Republican-leaning district. In the House, he has focused chiefly on his work on the Financial Service Committee, where Republicans have relied on his extensive private-sector experience in banking.

A ninth-generation Arkansan, Hill's career as an investment banker linked his business and policy interests. The son and grandson of commercial and investment bankers, he earned a bachelor's degree in economics from Vanderbilt University. He worked as a banking officer and senior financial analyst for Interfirst Bank in Dallas until 1982, when he moved to Washington as a legislative aide for Texas Republican Sen. John Tower, who was a senior member of the Banking Committee. When Tower retired two years later, Hill became director of the Dallas-based Mason Best Co.

After returning to Washington in 1989 as a deputy assistant Treasury secretary, he became a senior policy adviser for President George H.W. Bush and the Economic Policy Council. Hill resumed his career in investment banking as chairman of First Commerce Trust and First Commercial Investments. In 1999, he joined with other investors to form Delta Trust & Bank in Little Rock, serving as its chairman. In 2008, Hill served as senior adviser for former Arkansas Gov. Mike Huckabee's run for the White House. The Center for Responsive Politics has estimated his net worth at about $7 million.

Hill sought the open House seat when Rep. Tim Griffin ran successfully for lieutenant governor. Against two credible opponents in the primary, he campaigned on a platform of fiscal conservatism that he highlighted in ads promoting "old Blue," a dusty 1998 Volvo. He took some heat for failing to mention his other cars, including a BMW and Mercedes-Benz, but easily won the primary with 55 percent of the vote. Hill pushed for a reduction in the corporate income tax while opposing efforts to hike the minimum wage—a stance he modified when voters approved an effort to put the issue on the ballot. National Democrats were enthusiastic about former North Little Rock Mayor Patrick Henry Hays. But Hill had a heavy fundraising advantage and won with 52 percent of the vote, slightly underperforming the district's recent GOP vote.

On the Financial Services Committee, Hill sought changes in the 2010 Dodd-Frank banking law and worked to enhance the accountability of federal agencies that handle banking issues. He sponsored a measure to put the Federal Reserve in charge of enforcing the Volker Rule, part of Dodd-Frank that restricts a bank's ability to trade with its own money. The bill passed the House but was not taken up in the Senate, though some of the provisions he had pushed for easing regulation of community banks were included in the Economic Growth, Regulatory Relief, and Consumer Protection Act that President Donald Trump signed in May 2018.In 2017 Hill helped lead the charge on a change to the mortgage disclosure rule on title insurance by the Consumer Financial Protection Bureau, an agency he has often criticized. He is the ranking Republican on the National Security, International Development and Monetary Policy Subcommittee at Financial Services.

In April 2020, Minority Leader Kevin McCarthy named him to a bipartisan committee that was reviewing the Trump administration's handling of federal economic relief in response to the coronavirus. In an interview with Morning Consult, Hill said his focus would be, "Are you leveraging the fund in such a way that you can rapidly stabilize the economy, employment and pivot back to a growing economy?"

Representing the only district in Arkansas that is remotely competitive, Hill has been a regular target. In 2018, state Rep. Clarke Tucker hammered Hill over his vote to repeal Obama care, arguing that would weaken protections for people with preexisting conditions. Hill pushed back that Tucker was weak on immigration. He took the challenge seriously, bringing in Vice President Mike Pence to stump for him. Hill outspent Tucker by $1 million and won, 52%-46%.

Two years later, Democratic challenger Joyce Elliott, a liberal leader in the state Senate, increased grassroots enthusiasm and got support from national groups representing women and African-Americans. In their October debate, Hill said that Elliott's claim that he would deprive health insurance coverage to persons with pre-existing conditions was "a systematic falsehood." Elliott said Republican tax cuts were "an absolute giveaway to the richest people in this country." Elliott won 60 percent in Pulaski County, which cast half of the total vote. But Hill survived by winning at least 65 percent in each of the remaining six counties. That gave Hill a 55%-45% victory.

AR-2: Central Arkansas   Cook Partisan Voting Index: R+7

Population		Race and Ethnicity		Income	
Total	767,662	White	70.80%	Median Income	$53,600
Land area (sq. miles)	4,978	Black	23.30%	District Income Rank	351
Pop/ sq mi	154.21	Latino	5.40%	Poverty Rate	14.60%
Born in State	66.50%	Asian	1.60%	With health insurance	91.20%
		Two or more races	2.50%	Cash public assistance	2.70%
Age Groups		Other	1.90%	Food stamp/SNAP	10.10%
Under 18	22.90%				
18-34	23.20%	Education		Work	
35-64	37.20%	H.S grad or less	41.00%	White Collar	37.10%
Over 64	16.70%	Some college	29.50%	Sales and Service	38.60%
		College Degree, 4 yr	18.60%	Blue Collar	24.30%
Military		Post grad	10.90%	Government	17.50%
Veteran/ Active Duty	9.20%				

2020 Pres. Vote	Trump	177,053	(53%)	Biden	147,552	(44%)		
2016 Pres. Vote	Trump	160,782	(52%)	Clinton	127,883	(42%)	Johnson	8,630 (3%)

Little Rock, Pulaski: Little Rock has been the capital of Arkansas and its largest city for more than a century. The geographic center of an otherwise rural state, it is home to the presidential library of former Arkansas Gov. Bill Clinton. The city was harshly criticized for its role at the dawn of the civil rights movement. In September 1957, Democratic Gov. Orval Faubus sent in the National Guard to block a desegregation order at Central High School. President Dwight Eisenhower sent in U.S. troops and federalized the National Guard to enforce the order, and Little Rock became a synonym for bigotry around the world. Forty years later, the Little Rock Nine who integrated the high school returned for an anniversary commemoration with Clinton. "It was Little Rock that made racial equality a driving obsession in my life," Clinton said.

On the banks of the Arkansas River in Little Rock is the Clinton Presidential Center and Park, which opened in 2004.But the political influence of the Clintons in the city they once dominated has faded. Other than biographical details that she voiced at the Democratic convention in 2016, Hillary Clinton largely ignored her former home during her presidential campaign.

The 2nd Congressional District of Arkansas includes Little Rock and North Little Rock, an industrial suburb across the Arkansas River known informally for years as Dog Town. The district also takes in Saline (named for its early salt works) and Faulkner (named for fiddle player Sanford C. Faulkner, the original Arkansas Traveler) counties, which have grown rapidly. In 2020, Saline was the fourth fastest growing county in the state. With its large shipping facilities, Little Rock is a robust market for trade and international companies. Dassault Falcon Jet is the top manufacturing employer in the region. A plant in North Little Rock employs 500 people who make cosmetics for the L'Oreal and Maybelline cosmetics brands. And Canadian-based DBG chose Conway as its U.S. headquarters to make metal products for agriculture and heavy commercial vehicles.

This is the least conservative of the state's four districts, though it has a GOP lean. Pulaski County (Little Rock) is entirely in the 2nd District and includes just over half of the district's voters and is comfortably Democratic. The outlying areas, led by Faulkner and Saline, have become heavily Republican and outweigh the Pulaski vote. In2020, Donald Trump won 53 percent of the district vote —a dip from the 55 percent for Republican Mitt Romney in 2012. In redistricting, Republicans likely will seek to strengthen their performance in this district, which is far more competitive than the other three districts in Arkansas.

Steve Womack (R)

Elected 2010, 6th term, b. Feb 18, 1957; Russellville, AZ; AR Tech University, B.A., 1979; Southern Baptist; Married (Terri Williams Womack); 3 children; 2 grandchildren.

Military Career: AR Army National Guard 1979-2009

Elected Office: Rogers Mayor, 1998-2010.

Professional Career: Stn. Manager, KURM Radio, 1979-1990; Rogers Cty. Council, 1983-1984, 1997-1998; Executive officer, Army ROTC, University of AR, 1990-1996; Financial consultant, Merrill Lynch, 1996.

DC Office: 2412 RHOB 20515, 202-225-4301, Fax: 202-225-5713, womack.house.gov

State Offices: Fort Smith, 479-424-1146; Harrison, 870-741-6900; Rogers, 479-464-0446.

Committees: *Appropriations*: Defense; Financial Services & General Government (RMM); Transportation, HUD & Related Agencies.

Group Ratings

	ADA	ACLU	AFL-CIO	LCV	COC	HAFA	ACU	CFG	FRC
2020	**	16%	**	10%	-	77%	73%	**	-
2019	5%	C	33%	7%	87%	C	73%	66%	95%

Almanac Ratings 2019-2020

	Economy	Social	Foreign	Composite
Liberal	25%	16%	27%	23%
Conservative	75%	84%	73%	77%

Key Votes of the 116th Congress

1. U.S./Mex./Can. trade deal Y	5. Russia sanctions Y	9. Firearms background checks N
2. First Coronavirus response Y	6. Troops in Syria Y	10. Spending at the border Y
3. HEROES Act N	7. Veto arms sales to Saudis N	11. Marijuana liberalized rules N
4. CASH Act N	8. Defense $$$, veto override Y	12. Electoral College objections N

Election Results

Election	Name (Party)	Vote (%)		Cand. Spent	Ind. Exp. Support	Ind. Exp. Oppose
2020 General	Steve Womack (R)	214,960	(64%)	$992,172		$113
	Celeste Williams (D)	106,325	(32%)	$354,459	$113	
	Michael Kalagias (L)	12,977	(4%)			

Prior winning percentages: 2018 (65%), 2016 (77%), 2014 (79%), 2012 (76%), 2010 (72%)

Republican Steve Womack, first elected in 2010, has become an active Republican lawmaker with a knack for cutting deals and working on budget issues. During two years as chairman of the House Budget Committee, he faced the familiar fiscal gridlock on the panel. Weeks before the 2020 election, he took a senior GOP post on the Appropriations Committee.

Womack was born in Russellville Arkansas and spent a good portion of his childhood in Moberly Missouri. His father, a local radio broadcaster, introduced him to popular political figures in the region, including former Sens. Tom Eagleton and Stuart Symington and Gov. Warren Hearnes, all Missouri Democrats. "If I 'Dr. Phil' myself about what got me involved in public service, it's that I always admired political leaders," Womack said. After high school, Womack earned his bachelor's degree at Arkansas Tech. He and his father established KURM radio, which focused on community news, weather, the county fair, high school football and Little League baseball. Womack covered local politics for the station.

In 1990, as a member of the Army National Guard, Womack served as executive officer of the Army ROTC program at the University of Arkansas. In 2002, he led a peacekeeping task force of 500 troops in the Sinai Desert in Egypt. Womack was elected mayor of Rogers in 1998 and worked to turn the city into a shopping destination. He also had a reputation for tough enforcement of immigration laws. Local Hispanic leaders were incensed when Womack claimed a majority of crimes in the city were committed by illegal immigrants. In 2007, Womack directed city officials to cooperate with raids by federal immigration agents on a Northwest Arkansas Mexican restaurant chain. After Hispanic motorists filed a lawsuit charging racial profiling by Rogers and its police department, a settlement was reached without an award of damages or an admission of guilt; Womack formed a committee to build better relations with the immigrant community.

When then-Rep. John Boozman ran for the Senate in 2010, Womack topped a crowded field of Republicans, then won in November,72%-28%.

In the House, Womack established himself as firmly conservative and won a coveted slot on the Appropriations Committee as a freshman by arguing that being a mayor had taught him how to say "no." But he has been eager to say "yes" to local interests in their dealings with the federal government. With Rep. Jackie Speier, D-Calif., and others, he filed a bill to allow states to require Amazon and other out-of-state retailers to collect sales tax when they sell products over the internet, something that benefitted brick-and-mortar retailers such as Arkansas' Walmart, which already collect state sales taxes online. He joined with Rep. Jim Costa, another California Democrat, to create the Chicken Caucus. In 2018, Benton and Washington counties in the 3rd District reported chicken capacity of more than 50 million birds.

In 2017, Womack assumed the chairmanship of the Budget Committee. The position thrust him into unenviable fights over government funding and President Donald Trump's fiscal priorities. He defended Trump's budget, which included more spending on infrastructure and a border wall, while arguing that the 2017 tax cuts would boost the economy (and thus federal revenues). He also supported defense spending increases as critical to national security. Those budget projections were exceedingly optimistic. The Budget Committee passed a plan in June 2018 with cuts to entitlement program such as Medicare to balance the budget in nine years, but it was never brought to a vote on the House floor.

Womack co-chaired a Joint Select Committee on Budget and Appropriations Process Reform to seek bipartisan solutions to the budget process on Capitol Hill. Among the recommendations were to move from annual to biennial budgets. No major reforms came out of the committee, which disbanded amid partisan squabbling. "I am extremely disappointed in our failure and in my colleagues who lacked the 'political will' we have preached is so needed in Washington to vote out this good, bipartisan proposal," Womack said. Testifying before a House select committee in October 2019, he said Congress should "modernize our procedures" for determining how much to spend and how to reduce the budget deficit.

In October 2020, following the resignation from the House of Rep. Tom Graves of Georgia, Womack succeeded him as the top Republican on the Appropriations Subcommittee on Financial Services and General Government. He pledged to make "tough choices to chart a responsible fiscal path."

Womack, who earlier endorsed Sen. Marco Rubio of Florida for the presidential nomination, displayed his moderate credentials prior to the 2016 Republican convention when he advised Trump to select Ohio Gov. John Kasich as his running mate. "I think that would be the very best possible outcome for [Trump's] sake and for the sake of our party in terms of some sustainability, "he said in a local newspaper interview. Kasich subsequently became a harsh critic of Trump and endorsed Joe Biden in the 2020 presidential campaign.

Back home, Womack avoided a Republican primary and a Democratic challenger in his reelection bids until 2018. In the GOP primary, pastor Robb Ryerse ran to his left, supporting "Medicare for all" and an increase in the minimum wage, leading Womack to question whether Ryerse was even a true Republican; Womack won 84%-16%. In the general election he faced Democrat Josh Mahony, who attacked Womack on his opposition to immigration reform. Womack won reelection 65%-33%, carrying every county in the district. In 2020, Womack avoided a primary and faced Democrat Celeste Williams, a practicing nurse. In a similar outcome, Womack won, 64%-32%. He got 53 percent of the vote in Fayetteville-based Washington County and won at least 65 percent in the other counties.

AR-3: Northwest Arkansas   **Cook Partisan Voting Index: R+17**

Population		Race and Ethnicity		Income	
Total	829,149	White	83.80%	Median Income	$54,310
Land area (sq. miles)	5,401	Black	3.10%	District Income Rank	342
Pop/ sq mi	153.52	Latino	14.90%	Poverty Rate	14.60%
Born in State	48.70%	Asian	3.10%	With health insurance	89.50%
		Two or more races	3.50%	Cash public assistance	1.40%
Age Groups		Other	6.60%	Food stamp/SNAP	6.90%
Under 18	24.50%				
18-34	24.20%	**Education**		**Work**	
35-64	36.30%	H.S grad or less	43.50%	White Collar	36.40%
Over 64	15.10%	Some college	27.50%	Sales and Service	36.90%
		College Degree, 4 yr	18.60%	Blue Collar	26.70%
Military		Post grad	10.50%	Government	11.20%
Veteran/ Active Duty	7.70%				

2020 Pres. Vote	Trump	207,782	(62%)	Biden	118,141	(35%)			
2016 Pres. Vote	Trump	180,921	(62%)	Clinton	89,081	(31%)	Johnson	10,587	(4%)

Fayetteville, Fort Smith: The northwest corner of Arkansas has become one of America's boom areas, with major corporate headquarters and dozens of small factories, tourist attractions and retirement developments in the Ozarks. The area is the fastest growing in the state. Anchoring the local economy are three major employers: Walmart Stores, Tyson Foods, and J.B. Hunt Transport Services. The area has a rapidly growing population of Hispanics working at these companies in Springdale and Rogers. About 10,000 "climate refugees" from the Marshall Islands in the South Pacific moved here to escape the long-term risk of a rising ocean. This is also home to the University of Arkansas in Fayetteville, where young lawyers Bill Clinton and Hillary Rodham settled.

The friendly atmosphere, the prevalence of religious faith, and the natural backdrop of rounded green mountains and wide valleys in northwest Arkansas have contributed to the economic creativity. There have also been touches of genius. Sam Walton, who opened his first Walmart on the town square of Bentonville (it's now a small museum), had the inspiration to build a retail chain in tradition-minded small towns and rural areas, using sophisticated computerized management. It made him the richest man in America before he died in 1992, though he still drove a pickup truck and kept the corporate headquarters in a deliberately unglitzy building in Bentonville. That will soon change. In 2019,the company unveiled plans for an updated corporate headquarters in Bentonville, which would house 14,000 employees on a campus with the ambience of a "community." Construction of the roughly 350-acre site was tentatively scheduled for completion by 2025 and will consolidate smaller offices across the state into one main home office. Meanwhile, Walmart has reduced its growth of brick and mortar stores. During the final nine months of 2019, it added only three new stores to its 4,756 facilities. Other firms have flocked in, especially to do business with Walmart, the world's largest food retailer. Tyson Foods in Springdale is the world's leading chicken producer and processor. Local leaders have moved to diversify into professional services and tourism.

The 3rd Congressional District covers Northwest Arkansas, including Bentonville, Fayetteville and Springdale, plus Fort Smith on the Oklahoma line. For decades, this area was consistently the most Republican part of Arkansas since the Civil War. John Paul Hammerschmidt was elected to the House in 1966 as one of the first Republican congressmen from the South, and the district has not elected a Democrat since. He beat 28-year-old Bill Clinton in the Democratic year of 1974, although Clinton got an impressive 48 percent of the vote. That has evolved in recent years as the managerial class has become more bipartisan and rural areas in the eastern part of the state have become more solidly Republican. In each of his elections, Donald Trump won 62 percent, less than the 66 percent support for Mitt Romney in 2012 and only his third best among the four districts in Arkansas. As with other campus towns across the nation, Trump fared relatively poorly in Washington County (Fayetteville), with a lead of only four percentage points.

Bruce Westerman (R)

Elected 2014, 4th term, b. Nov 18, 1967; Hot Springs, AR; University of AR, B.S., 1990; Yale University, M.S., 2001; Southern Baptist; Married (Sharon French); 4 children.

Elected Office: AR House, 2010-2014, Minority Leader, 2012-2013, Majority Leader, 2013-2014.

Professional Career: Fountain Lake School Board, 2006-2010, President, 2009-2010; Engineer, forester, Mid-South Engineering; Deacon, Walnut Valley Baptist Church.

DC Office: 209 CHOB 20515, 202-225-3772, Fax: 202-225-1314, westerman.house.gov

State Offices: El Dorado, 870-864-8946; Hot Springs, 501-609-9796; Ozark, 479-667-0075; Pine Bluff, 870-536-8178.

Committees: *Natural Resources (RMM)*: Ex Officio membership on all subcommittees. *Transportation & Infrastructure*: Highways & Transit; Railroads, Pipelines & Hazardous Materials; Water Resources & Environment.

Group Ratings

	ADA	ACLU	AFL-CIO	LCV	COC	HAFA	ACU	CFG	FRC
2020	**	15%	**	10%	-	87%	90%	**	-
2019	5%	C	30%	3%	81%	C	90%	85%	100%

Almanac Ratings 2019-2020

	Economy	Social	Foreign	Composite
Liberal	25%	24%	27%	26%
Conservative	75%	76%	73%	74%

Key Votes of the 116th Congress

1. U.S./Mex./Can. trade deal Y	5. Russia sanctions Y	9. Firearms background checks N
2. First Coronavirus response Y	6. Troops in Syria Y	10. Spending at the border Y
3. HEROES Act N	7. Veto arms sales to Saudis N	11. Marijuana liberalized rules N
4. CASH Act N	8. Defense $$$, veto override N	12. Electoral College objections N

Election Results

Election	Name (Party)	Vote (%)		Cand. Spent	Ind. Exp. Support	Ind. Exp. Oppose
2020 General	Bruce Westerman (R)	191,617	(70%)	$1,108,801		
	William Hanson (D)	75,750	(28%)	$108,903		
	Frank Gilbert (L)	7,668	(3%)			

Prior winning percentages: 2018 (67%), 2016 (75%), 2014 (54%)

Republican Bruce Westerman has used his unique background in forestry to gain opportunities to influence policy in the House. Following the 2020 election, he was selected as ranking Republican on the Natural Resources Committee. With the active support of House Republican Leader Kevin McCarthy, he overcame two obstacles in his contest with Paul Gosar of Arizona: Westerman had less seniority in the House and on the committee, and he lacked the western roots that typically have been a prerequisite for the post. He was elected to the House in 2014 in the district that had been the home until 2012 of the most recent House Democrat from Arkansas.

Born in Hot Springs, Westerman earned his bachelor's degree in biological and agricultural engineering at the University of Arkansas, where he played for the Razorbacks football team. He completed his master's in forestry at Yale. He worked as a plant engineer for Riceland Foods and as an engineer and forester for Mid-South Engineering before being elected to the Arkansas House in 2010. When the GOP two years later took control of both chambers of the state legislature for the first time since Reconstruction, Westerman became House majority leader. He had a solid record as a conservative, voting to override a gubernatorial veto of a voter ID law and to approve a bill banning abortions after 20 weeks. He supported legislation expanding gun rights, setting dress codes in public schools, requiring that tests for driver's licenses be offered only in English, pushing for fiscal conservatism and opposing expansion of Medicaid under the Affordable Care Act.

The 4th District, with its strong Old South flavor, had elected just two Republicans since Reconstruction—now-Sen. Tom Cotton and Jay Dickey, a four-term congressman who lost in 2000 to Democrat Mike Ross after Dickey voted to impeach home-grown Bill Clinton, who remained popular in the district. In the 2014 primary, Westerman defeated energy businessman Tommy Moll 54%-46%. Westerman ran stronger in the southern part of the district, while Moll swept most of the northern counties. Westerman's 4,345-vote margin in Garland County accounted for his victory.

In the general election, James Lee Witt, who was the Federal Emergency Management Agency director in the Clinton administration, ran a vigorous, old-style campaign. Witt was one of the few prominent Democratic candidates in recent years who opposed gay marriage and abortion rights and supported gun rights. Despite a campaign visit from Clinton and outspending his opponent by $250,000, Witt could not overcome the GOP tide in the district. Westerman won easily, 54%-43%.

In the House, he joined the GOP whip team and served on the Budget Committee. On the Natural Resources Committee, Westerman used his academic background in forestry and took an interest in the 2.5 million acres of timber on public lands in his district. His Resilient Federal Forests Act, which set management policies on federally owned timber and would impose legal hurdles on litigants who seek to limit forestry plans, passed the House in both 2015 and 2017, but the Senate never considered it.

Some forest management tools he pushed for were included in the 2018 farm bill, but many were ultimately stripped during conference. In the wake of devastating forest fires in California in late 2018, Westerman—the only licensed forester in Congress—argued that the legislation was even more pressing. He introduced legislation that would authorize more firefighting tools for at-risk communities and more help to the Forest Service.

With his articulate presentation of Republican talking points on energy and the environment, including his acknowledgment that climate change posed serious challenges, Westerman was encouraged by House Republican leaders. His trademark legislation was the Trillion Tree Act, which was designed to plant more trees worldwide as a way to remove carbon emissions from the atmosphere, envisioned that 100 billion of those trees would be planted in the United States by 2050.

The projected envisioned planting 3.3 billion trees annually, compared with the estimate of 2.5 billion trees planted across the nation under the status quo. "We have tremendous opportunities with trees," Westerman told the Northwest Arkansas Democrat-Gazette. "They're more abundant, they're more economical and they're the best tool that we have to take existing atmospheric carbon out of the atmosphere."

Although his proposal was well-received by most Republicans, he was criticized by both the political left and right. "We must not lose focus on what the science tells us we must do to stabilize global temperatures and avoid catastrophic impacts," said Democrat Rep. Raul Grijalva of Arizona, chairman of the Natural Resources panel. "This will require a lot more than planting new trees." David McIntosh, president of the conservative Club for Growth, told The Washington Post, Westerman's proposal "will not make a single environmentalist vote for a Republican."

Westerman's informal leadership role became more timely following the House retirement of Republican Rep. Rob Bishop of Utah, who was term-limited as the top Republican on the Resources panel. Many Republicans were reluctant to give the post to the often outspoken Gosar, a Freedom Caucus activist. Westerman gave them the opportunity to show that "conservatives care about the environment," according to E&E News, which covers energy and environment issues. "I want to bring Republicans back to conservation," he told the publication. "There is a hunger to see Republicans taking a lead in more of those issues." He won the Resources post from a leadership panel controlled by McCarthy.

Westerman hasn't faced a serious challenge since he was first elected. In 2020, he defeated Democrat William Hanson, a lawyer and teacher, whose family had lived in the area for 150 years. Westerman won, by 70%-28%. Hanson carried Jefferson County (Pine Bluff), the lone Democratic holdout in the district.

AR-4: Western Arkansas

Cook Partisan Voting Index: R+20

Population		Race and Ethnicity		Income	
Total	701,945	White	74.00%	Median Income	$43,824
Land area (sq. miles)	22,338	Black	19.40%	District Income Rank	422
Pop/ sq mi	31.42	Latino	6.00%	Poverty Rate	17.80%
Born in State	63.30%	Asian	0.70%	With health insurance	91.50%
		Two or more races	1.90%	Cash public assistance	2.50%
Age Groups		Other	3.80%	Food stamp/SNAP	13.10%
Under 18	22.40%				
18-34	20.00%	**Education**		**Work**	
35-64	37.90%	H.S grad or less	51.90%	White Collar	30.40%
Over 64	19.80%	Some college	30.50%	Sales and Service	38.40%
		College Degree, 4 yr	11.80%	Blue Collar	31.20%
Military		Post grad	5.90%	Government	18.70%
Veteran/ Active Duty	7.90%				

2020 Pres. Vote	Trump	188,172	(68%)	Biden	82,341	(30%)	
2016 Pres. Vote	Trump	173,731	(64%)	Clinton	84,842	(31%)	

Hot Springs, Pine Bluff: West from the Delta flatlands along the Mississippi River, where the water-soaked fields produce America's largest rice crop, are small cities like Pine Bluff and El Dorado and the Ouachita Mountains. Southern Arkansas might well be called the northwest corner of the Deep South. It includes the state's largest African-American population in Pine Bluff, a reminder that parts of southern Arkansas near the Delta were once plantation country. There is also oil production, and the broiler-chicken industry looms large in these parts. The accent is clearly Arkansan: El Dorado, Nevada and Lafayette are all pronounced with long a's and accents on the penultimate syllable, and Ouachita, with a bow to the original French rendition of the Indian name, is WASH-i-taw.

The 4th Congressional District occupies much of the southern half of Arkansas, stretching from the eastern part of the state all the way west to Texarkana. Not far from the Texas border is the little railroad-crossing, county-seat town of Hope, where President Bill Clinton and his first White House chief of staff, Mack McLarty, were classmates in Miss Mary's kindergarten room and where former Gov. Mike Huckabee grew up a decade later. Hot Springs is the spa resort and gambling haven where Clinton's stepfather sold Buicks, his mother bet on the horses, and he excelled in high school. Established in1832, Hot Springs National Park is the oldest federal reserve in the country, predating Yellowstone by 40 years (though Hot Springs was not declared a national park until 1921).

To the east is Pine Bluff, now 77 percent black, where a century and a half ago Union soldiers withstood a Confederate attack on the fortified courthouse square. Despite the presence of several plants for poultry giant Tyson Foods, the region has taken hits to its economy and population. The metro region has seen the biggest decrease in population in the state since 2010.In Camden, Lockheed Martin relocated its production of the Tactical Missile System, including artillery rockets and launchers. The area got a tourism boost after voters in 2018 legalized casinos in Pope and Jefferson counties and in Hot Springs, where Oak lawn Racing and Gaming completed a $100 million expansion of its famed horse track, adding a luxury hotel, event space and casino.

The 4th includes territory in the Ozark National Forest to the northwest, including Madison, Johnson and Franklin counties. The district leans substantially Republican. In 2016 and 2020, Jefferson County (Pine Bluff), just south of Little Rock and 57 percent African-American, was the only county in the district that voted against Donald Trump, who took 68 percent of the overall vote.

CALIFORNIA

DEL NORTE

SISKIYOU

MODOC

HUMBOLDT

TRINITY

SHASTA

LASSEN

1

2

TEHAMA

PLUMAS

MENDOCINO

GLENN

BUTTE

SIERRA

COLUSA

NEVADA

LAKE

YUBA

PLACER

SUTTER

3

YOLO

EL DORADO

SONOMA

6

Sacramento

ALPINE

5

NAPA

SACRAMENTO

AMADOR

SOLANO

CALAVERAS

TUOLUMNE

MARIN

SAN JOAQUIN

9

Stockton

MONO

San Francisco

Oakland

ALAMEDA

SAN MATEO

10

San Jose

STANISLAUS

SANTA CLARA

MARIPOSA

SANTA CRUZ

16

SEE INSET for detail
on 11-15; 17-19.

MADERA

MERCED

SAN BENITO

Fresno

INYO

20

FRESNO

KINGS

22

MONTEREY

21

TULARE

23

Bakersfield

SAN LUIS OBISPO

KERN

8

24

VENTURA

SAN BERNARDINO

SANTA BARBARA

25

LOS ANGELES

26

Pasadena

Los Angeles

Riverside

Long Beach

36

RIVERSIDE

ORANGE

42

SEE INSET for detail
on 27-35; 37-41; 43-48.

49

50

52

San Diego

SAN DIEGO

IMPERIAL

51

53

Miles

0   20   40

The Almanac of American Politics.
National Journal

Congressional district boundaries were first effective for 2012.

Americans have long thought of California as the Golden State, but its political hue has become ever bluer in recent years. The 2020 election offered glimmers of hope to the nearly extinct state GOP; the party won back four of the seven House seats it lost in 2018, it saw voters choose the more conservative option on several ballot measures, and it laid the groundwork for recalling Democratic Gov. Gavin Newsom. Still, Democrats won the presidential race in California by a robust 29 points, maintained a four-to-one edge in congressional seats, and saw Sen. Kamala Harris sworn in as vice president.

California was initially a distant and dreamy land, then a shaper of culture and a promised land for millions of Americans and immigrants for many decades. America's most populous state remains in many ways a great success story. But in other ways, it has failed to fulfill its promise. It is the birthplace of much of the world's most advanced technology, yet it has plenty of poor neighborhoods. Among the states, California has attracted the largest number of immigrants from Mexico, Latin America and Asia, but has also seen a sizable exodus of citizens to other states. With one out of eight people in the United States, California is a demographic giant, which means that both its achievements and problems are the nation's. California's population is almost 40 million, far ahead of second-place Texas at 29.3 million. Metro Los Angeles has 13.2 million people, second only to metro New York City's 19.2 million. San Diego and Orange counties, with more than 3 million people each, are the nation's fifth and sixth most populous counties, and Riverside, with 2.1 million, rounds out the nation's top 10. California has more registered voters—22 million—than there are people living in 48 of the other 49 states. However, the state's decades-long run of rapid population growth has stalled in the past decade. Since the 2010 census, California has grown by a bit more than 6 percent, which wasn't enough to keep it from losing a seat in the post-2020 reapportionment. During the past decade, almost 1 million more Californians have left the state than have moved to it, which ranks as the second biggest net loss, after New York's. The spectacular success of high-tech companies, combined with anti-development sentiment, has sent housing prices soaring, driving out middle- and lower-income residents from coastal California. "There's a reason 130,000 more people leave than enter each year," wrote liberal columnist Ezra Klein, a California native, in 2021. "California is dominated by Democrats, but many of the people Democrats claim to care about most can't afford to live there." Some of those departing have brought their liberal values to red states such as Colorado, Texas, and Arizona—Texas Gov. Greg Abbott used the slogan "Don't California my Texas" in his 2018 reelection—but others left California precisely because of its political leanings, egged on by conservative-leaning Facebook groups and YouTube videos. Silicon Valley mainstays, sometimes citing high taxes, have decamped from the state, including Palantir Technologies (to Colorado) and both Hewlett Packard Enterprise and Oracle (to Texas), while Tesla founder Elon Musk personally relocated to Texas after establishing new operations there. Such centripetal trends may accelerate given the new appetite for remote work discovered during the coronavirus pandemic. Amid the pandemic, residential rents in San Francisco fell for the first time in years, and office vacancies multiplied, with tech titans trying to downsize their workspace holdings and some even adopting permanent work-from-home policies.

California is 36.5 percent white, almost four percentage points lower than in 2010 and the second-lowest of any state. Hispanics account for 39.4 percent, ranking California third behind New Mexico and Texas; in 2020, Hispanics for the first time accounted for a plurality of the freshmen accepted into the University of California system. Asians account for 15.5 percent, ranking second only to Hawaii; since 2014, Asians have been the largest racial group in Santa Clara County (San Jose), and Alameda County (Oakland) has since become plurality Asian. In California, almost 27 percent of residents are foreign born, and nearly a quarter of residents are native-born but have at least one immigrant parent. Among California's immigrants, 38 percent are Mexican, followed by Filipino, Chinese, Indian, and Vietnamese. Meanwhile, California's percentage of African Americans—6.5 percent—is roughly half the national average.

Change has been a constant in California's history, and it owes its preeminence not only to its natural advantages, including its vast geographic area and (usually) pleasant climate, but also to human ingenuity. California's economy has been transformed by one group of newcomers after another, and its politics are periodically transformed with the suddenness of an earthquake. In 1848, when California passed from Mexico to the United States by the Treaty of Guadalupe Hidalgo, it was sparsely populated, inhabited by a few thousand Indians and Mexicans and by a few hundred U.S. soldiers and adventurers of various kinds. Later that year, gold was found at Sutter's Mill, and the world rushed in. Within months, San Francisco became one of America's 25 largest cities. The big money in the Gold Rush was made not by the miners but by the grocers and dry-goods merchants and transportation entrepreneurs who provisioned them, such as the Big Four—Crocker, Hopkins, Huntington and Stanford—who built the Central and Southern Pacific Railroads. Many of the laborers were Chinese, and California whites, angry at low-wage competition and fearful of a wave of Asian immigrants, were the impetus behind the bluntly named Chinese Exclusion Act of 1882, which suspended legal Chinese immigration and was not fully repealed until 1965.

The railroads sold off vast chunks of the Central Valley to large farming operations and enticed settlers with low fares to newly created suburbs in the Los Angeles Basin. Engineers built giant aqueducts that stretched hundreds of miles, from Yosemite to San Francisco and from the Owens River to Los Angeles, bringing water essential to the cities' growth. Early 20th century California was affluent and cultured, containing abundant museums, libraries and universities such as Stanford and the University of California, Berkeley. It was America's window on the Pacific, alert to developments in China and Japan, Hawaii and the Philippines, and it was eager to extend America's economic reach and military strength. Yet, as author Carey McWilliams wrote, Southern California was an "island" separated from the rest of the country. That began to change in World War II, when it became one of the great defense-industry states, building ships and airplanes by the thousands. Millions of Americans came and millions stayed. The population rose from 7 million in 1940 to 17 million in 1963, when California passed New York as the nation's most populous state.

Map for Greater San Francisco

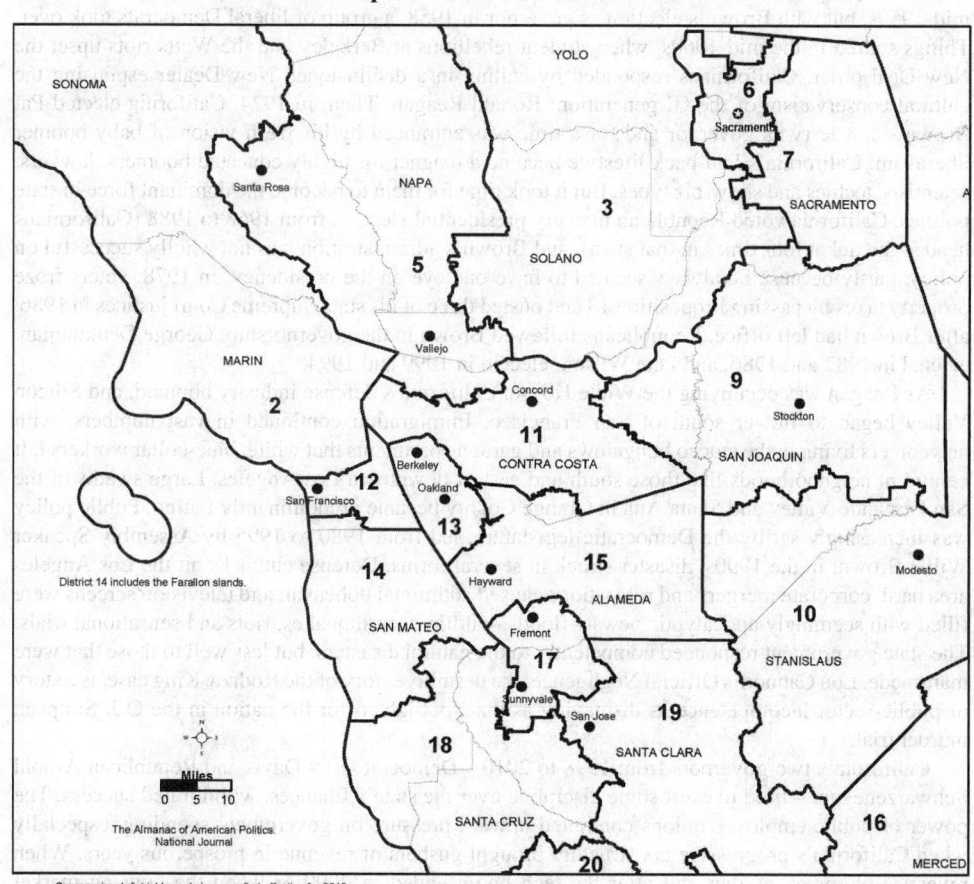

Congressional district boundaries were first effective for 2012.

The heads of the big units of government and business planned California's future—leaders such as President Franklin D. Roosevelt and industrial mogul Henry J. Kaiser, who constructed vast shipyards and steel and aluminum factories. Republican Gov. Earl Warren husbanded tax monies after the war to build schools and the freeways that did as much as Detroit's auto factories —if not more—to cement the automobile's place in American culture. Democratic Gov. Pat Brown added to the vast web of canals and aqueducts. But the real engine of growth was the little people who took advantage of this infrastructure and built a humming economy. When California's defense plants closed down after World War II, government and civic leaders imagined that hundreds of thousands would head back east. But in those days before universal air conditioning and thermal winter clothing, people had experienced a climate in which it was comfortable to be outdoors all year. They wanted to stay, and so, as urbanologist Jane Jacobs pointed out, they created one-eighth of all the new jobs in the nation in the late 1940s in metro Los Angeles. This growth, multiplied thousands of times over, helped make California a mega-state. Los Angeles County became what New York City was 100 years before: the great entry point in the United States, with some of the largest concentrations of Mexicans, Iranians, Samoans, Filipinos, Salvadorans, Armenians, Guatemalans, Koreans and Thais outside their native lands.

The demographic changes transformed California politically. Before the war, it was a Republican state with progressive leanings; most of the struggles for political power took place within the GOP. The in-rush of the GI generation, with its allegiance to the New Deal, and the building of auto and steel factories with unionized workforces, transformed California into a two-party state. These new migrants were middle- and working-class, family men and women enjoying a life in suburbs in the lovely California climate. Warren's progressive Republicans remained dominant through the mid-1950s, but with Brown's election as governor in 1958, a group of liberal Democrats took over. Things soured in the mid-1960s, when student rebellions at Berkeley and the Watts riots upset the New Deal order. Californians responded by calling in a disillusioned New Dealer espousing the cultural conservatism of the GI generation: Ronald Reagan. Then, in 1974, California elected Pat Brown's son Jerry as governor and for a time was entranced by his fresh vision of baby boomer liberalism. California's laid-back lifestyle became a magnet for highly educated boomers, lawyers, scientists, techies and show-biz types. But it took time for them to become the dominant force in state politics. California voted Republican in every presidential election from 1968 to 1988 (Californians headed the ticket four times in that span), and Brown's administration was not wholly successful on policy, partly because he always seemed to have one eye on the presidency. In 1978, voters froze property taxes by passing Proposition 13 and ousted three of his state Supreme Court justices in 1986, after Brown had left office. Republicans followed Brown in the governorship: George Deukmejian, elected in 1982 and 1986, and Pete Wilson, elected in 1990 and 1994.

As Reagan was occupying the White House, California's defense industry boomed, and Silicon Valley began to flower south of San Francisco. Immigration continued in vast numbers, with newcomers living in the stucco bungalows and garden apartments that white, blue-collar workers left behind in neighborhoods like those south and east of downtown Los Angeles. Large swaths of the San Fernando Valley and Santa Ana in Orange County became predominantly Latino. Public policy was increasingly set by the Democratic legislature, led from 1980 to 1995 by Assembly Speaker Willie Brown. In the 1990s, disaster struck in several forms. Defense cutbacks hit the Los Angeles area hard, corporate mergers and relocations caused additional upheaval, and television screens were filled with seemingly apocalyptic news—floods, wildfires, earthquakes, riots and sensational trials. The state government responded competently to the natural disasters, but less well to those that were man-made. Lou Cannon's Official Negligence, the definitive story of the Rodney King case, is a story of public-sector incompetence as dismaying as that spotlighted for the nation in the O.J. Simpson murder trial.

California's two governors from 1998 to 2010—Democrat Gray Davis and Republican Arnold Schwarzenegger—tried to exert some discipline over the state's finances, with limited success. The power of public employee unions continued upward pressure on government spending, especially when California's progressive tax structure brought gushers of revenue in prosperous years. When revenues plummet, as they did after the tech boom ended in 2000 or when the housing market crashed in 2007, the pressure is then to increase taxes. Davis was unable to hold spending down and was blamed for electricity blackouts. He was recalled, 55%-45%, and on the replacement ballot, Schwarzenegger finished first with 49 percent. In office, the ex-bodybuilder/actor sought a conservative shift via ballot measures, but voters rebuffed him, and his job ratings flagged. He turned things around by backing liberal measures like carbon emissions reduction legislation and bonds for a high-speed rail line, and it was enough to easily win him reelection in 2006.

Map for Greater Los Angeles

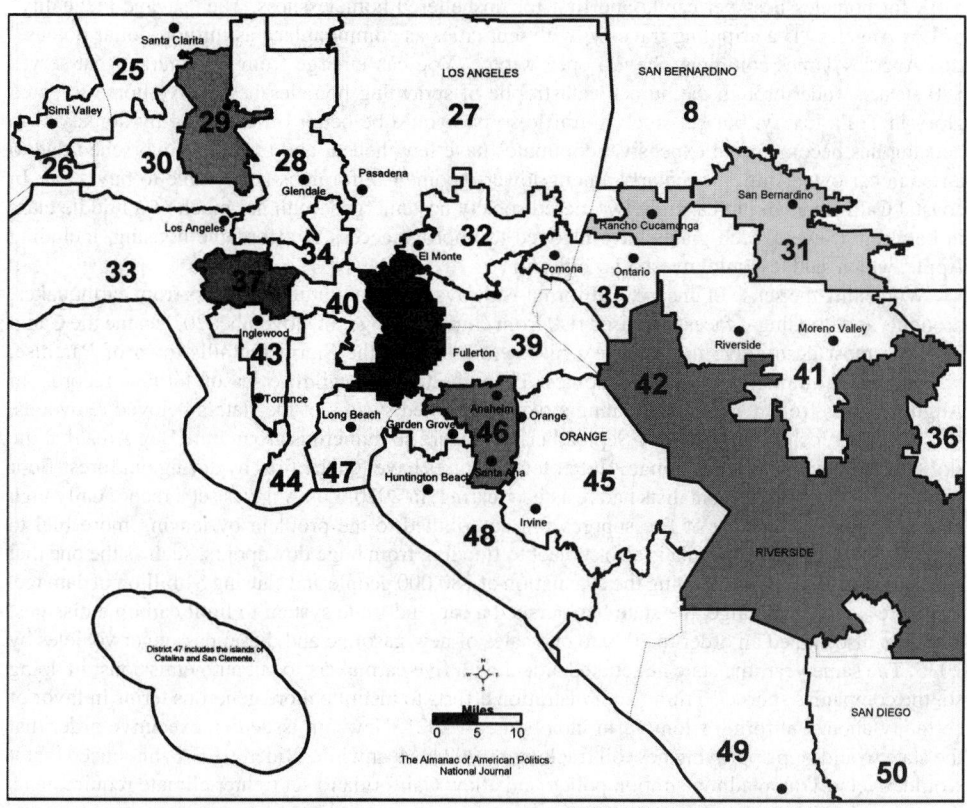

Congressional district boundaries were first effective for 2012.

Districts 29, 31, 37, 38, 42, and 46 are highlighted for visibility.

California's economy was slowing even before the housing market crashed in 2007. Corporate executives complained that high taxes, stringent regulations, complex land-use controls and high litigation risks hampered the economic recovery. Public employee unions' success in negotiating large pension benefits, combined with overall personnel costs and weakening economic conditions, led to some municipal bankruptcies, such as Vallejo in 2008 and Stockton and San Bernardino in 2012. But the Great Recession made things far worse. From the late 1990s to the housing bust of 2007, federal policies encouraging mortgages for borrowers of more modest means produced a housing and construction boom in the Inland Empire—the sprawling San Bernardino and Riverside counties east of Los Angeles—and in the Central Valley. Latinos moved out from central Los Angeles County and bought new houses with little or no down payment and hopes of windfall profits from seemingly endless home price increases. But the market crashed in 2007, and the Inland Empire and Central Valley saw some of the nation's highest foreclosure rates. For the next five years, California also had one of the nation's highest unemployment rates.

Seemingly adrift, California voters turned to a familiar face in 2010—Jerry Brown. Once mocked as the flaky "Governor Moonbeam," Brown gained ground-level experience as a two-term mayor of troubled Oakland and matured into a moderate technocrat who knew the inside game; crucially, he was at last undistracted by presidential ambitions. Task No. 1 was fixing the state's fiscal outlook; Brown made great strides, ultimately squeezing out an annual surplus that would have been unthinkable a few years earlier.

Yet even as California created the fifth-largest economy on the planet—bigger than the United Kingdom, France and India—poverty persisted, with almost one of every five Californians at or below the poverty line when adjusted for the cost of living. And the inequality gap was huge; White households in Los Angeles had a median net worth of $355,000, compared to just $4,000 for Black households, according to Federal Reserve data. African Americans account for 16 percent of all arrests and a quarter of the incarcerated population. California also ranked second to New York for homelessness per capita and first for unsheltered homelessness. The "savage inequality" of Los Angeles "is a crippling travesty, with tent cities as commonplace as million-dollar homes," Los Angeles Times columnist Steve Lopez wrote. "You can emerge from a restaurant that serves $80 steaks, wade through the human catastrophe of sprawling homelessness, drive home to gated glory in Tesla luxury, but get stuck in traffic so bad you'd be better off traveling by donkey." As housing has become more expensive, commutes have lengthened, and traffic has worsened due to a rise in car ownership, particularly among lower-income Californians newly able to buy a car. In coastal California, an increasingly two-tiered society has emerged, with not much of a middle class in between. (Several tech giants have pledged to improve access to affordable housing, including Apple, which said it would invest $2.5 billion.)

Worsening the sense of unease, California—always at risk of natural disasters from earthquakes, droughts and flooding—faces increased risk from climate change. In November 2018 came the Camp Fire, the most destructive in the state's history, destroying the Sierra foothills town of Paradise, killing 86 and gutting nearly 14,000 homes. Then, in 2020, the wildfire season hit new records. In August, blazes from a spate of lightning strikes consumed swaths of the state's beloved redwoods, sequoias, and Joshua trees, and by September, fires were so numerous around the Bay Area that the sky glowed an impenetrable orange. Hotter temperatures have fed the fires by drying out forest-floor kindling, which environmentalists had resisted clearing; in 2020, Los Angeles set a record daily high of 121 degrees. A history of fire suppression contributed to the problem by leaving more fuel to burn. Paradoxically, California is also subject to flooding from huge downpours, such as the one that pierced the Oroville Dam, forcing the evacuation of 180,000 people and causing $1 billion in damage. To address climate change, the state has pursued a cap-and-trade system to limit carbon emissions. Newsom also signed an order in 2020 to end sales of new gasoline and diesel passenger vehicles by 2035. The same year, the state negotiated a deal with five carmakers to cut auto emissions; in doing so, the companies spurned Trump administration efforts to institute more generous terms in favor of certainty about California's long-term intentions. In 2021, Newsom issued an executive order that the state would stop approving new oil fracking by 2024. Meanwhile, Biden's EPA announced that it would reverse Trump administration policy and allow California to set tighter climate requirements for cars and SUVs.

Key pillars of California's economy have faced reckonings in recent years. The #MeToo movement targeting sexual misconduct emerged in Hollywood, with a secondary appearance in Silicon Valley. And the role of companies like Facebook in enabling the spread of misinformation, along with general angst about the impact of social media on society, damaged the tech sector's reservoir of goodwill. Then in 2020 came the coronavirus. The state imposed some of the harshest mask and lockdown mandates. But the shutdowns hammered tourism and the virus prompted dangerous levels of hospitalizations, especially in southern California. In a Zoom summit of four former California governors convened by Newsom during the pandemic, Davis said the virus "dwarfs any problem the four of us had. There's no playbook. There's no precedent." Local governments have seen differing impacts. Jurisdictions dependent on big box retailers and cannabis for tax revenue have survived without much of a hitch; hotel and resort destinations have done poorly, though coastal and mountain locations with many short-term rentals have done better.

Politically, California was a key target in presidential elections in the decades after World War II. In Reagan's time, it went Republican in presidential elections while usually tilting Democratic in congressional and state contests. But starting in the early 1990s, it has become one of the bedrock Democratic states. The shift occurred slowly: While Bill Clinton carried California 46%-33% in 1992 and proceeded to lavish attention on the state, Republican Gov. Pete Wilson won reelection in 1994 by a 14-point margin while supporting Proposition 187, which barred state aid to illegal immigrants. But ever since, California's increasing Latino voter share has given Democrats enormous margins.

Two other voting blocs have helped make California solidly Democratic. One group consists of affluent, highly educated Whites living in lush corners of the big metropolitan areas, many with ties to the state's two resilient economic and cultural behemoths—Hollywood and Silicon Valley. These voters tend to be liberal on cultural issues such as abortion rights and same-sex marriage, more moderate on fiscal issues, and hostile to the religious conservatives who hold sway within the national Republican Party. They have been similarly repelled by the increasingly conservative edge of the state's vestigial GOP, while adapting just fine to the increasingly left-wing tilt of the state and national Democratic Party. In the Reagan years, affluent neighborhoods, except for the heavily Jewish west side of Los Angeles, usually cast large Republican majorities; since then, they have voted increasingly Democratic. This has helped Democrats maintain large majorities in California's House delegation and in both houses of the state legislature since 1996. Meanwhile, the second group bolstering Democratic fortunes is Asian Americans, who are a major population group in Orange County and the San Gabriel Valley. In 1992, they favored George H.W. Bush over Clinton, but by the 2016 election, they backed Hillary Clinton over Donald Trump, 70%-17%, and Joe Biden over Trump in 2020 by a similar margin. Asian voters have become an important factor in the lopsided margins by which Democrats carry the San Francisco Bay Area and Los Angeles County.

Once upon a time, people used to analyze California politics by distinguishing between Democratic Northern California and Republican Southern California. Today, the geographic divisions run on a different axis, between Democratic coastal California—all the counties that touch the ocean or San Francisco Bay—and Republican interior California. If interior California were a separate state, it would be competitive in presidential elections and would have 19 electoral votes. But coastal California, more than twice as populous as interior California, is dominant economically and politically. For the most part, since Prop 187, the state has been out of reach for Republicans. In 2016, California voted for Clinton by 30 points, up from Barack Obama's 23-point margin in 2012. No Republican has won statewide office since 2006, and for a while, Republican voter registration trailed "no party preference" registration. The withered state Republican Party has become pugnaciously conservative, and California helped birth such Trump-era mainstays as Breitbart News, Steve Bannon, Ben Shapiro, Stephen Miller, and Peter Thiel. Resistance to Trump, however, has been more broadly popular among Californians, especially on immigration and climate policy.

In 2020, Trump made tiny gains in some populous counties like Los Angeles, San Francisco, and Santa Clara, but the Democrats' winning margins in each of those counties remained massive; Biden, for his part, increased Democratic margins a bit in such ancestrally Republican counties as San Diego and Santa Barbara. After the Biden-Harris victory, Democrats drew heavily from California's talent pool to staff the new administration, including state Attorney General Xavier Becerra to head the Department of Health and Human Services, Berkeley professor Janet L. Yellen as Treasury secretary, and Alejandro Mayorkas to run the Department of Homeland Security. In addition, House Speaker Nancy Pelosi of San Francisco prepared to play a key role in shepherding the new president's agenda. Republicans, however, were able to celebrate a few victories: They flipped back four of the seven House seats that had changed hands in the 2018 midterms, including two in Orange County, even as Biden was winning the county by nine points and Democrats were flipping two state Senate seats in the county. (The House gains put Minority Leader Kevin McCarthy, a Republican from the Central Valley, in a position to retake the chamber in 2022.) Republicans could also take heart in the results of several key ballot measures, as voters chose not to repeal a ban on affirmative action, nixed rent control, turned down a chance to replace cash bail, and approved an easing of work restrictions on ride-share contractors. Then, in 2021, critics of Newsom managed to place a gubernatorial recall on the ballot, though the incumbent was favored to survive. Overall, California Democrats faced risks from becoming such a dominant party. "Because relatively little is demanded of them," wrote Bill Whalen, a fellow at Stanford University's Hoover Institution, "California's elected leaders have an easy time getting elected, but haven't yet mastered the part that comes after—leading."

Population		Race and Ethnicity		Income	
Total	39,512,223	White	59.40%	Median Income	80,440
Land area (sq. miles)	155,779	Black	5.80%	State Income Rank	5 out of 50
Pop/ sq mi	253.64	Latino	39.40%	Poverty Rate	11.80%
Born in state	56.10%	Asian	17.10%	With health insurance	92.30%
		Two or more races	5.00%	Cash public assistance	2.80%
Age Groups		Other	14.90%	Food stamp/SNAP	9.3%
Under 18	22.50%				
18-34	24.60%	**Education**		**Work**	
35-64	38.10%	H.S grad or less	36.60%	White Collar	40.70%
Over 64	14.80%	Some college	28.50%	Sales and Service	38.50%
		College Degree, 4 yr	21.90%	Blue Collar	20.90%
Military		Post grad	13.10%	Government	13.90%
Veteran/ Active Duty	5.30%				

Presidential Politics

2020 Primary (D)	Sanders (D)	2,080,846(36%)	Biden (D)	1,613,854(28%) Warren (D)	762,555(13%)
	Bloomberg (D)	701,803(12%)			
2020 Pres. Vote	Biden (D)	11,110,639(63%)	Trump (R)	6,006,518(34%)	
2016 Pres. Vote	Clinton (D)	8,753,792(62%)	Trump (R)	4,483,814(32%) Johnson (L)	478,500 (3%)
	Stein (G)	278,658 (2%)			

Since 1972, California has had substantially more electoral votes than any other state. That fact gave Republicans a near lock on the presidency in the 1970s and 1980s. Then, from 1992 to 2020, Democrats swept the state, giving them a structural advantage in the Electoral College. The state's vote for Democratic presidential candidates has grown from 46 percent in 1992 to 63 percent in 2020. President Donald Trump lost all 10 of the state's most populous counties in both 2016 and 2020, including Orange County, the one-time home of GOP conservatism in California. Biden received a higher percentage of votes than any presidential candidate since FDR won 67 percent in California in 1936; his 5.1 million-vote margin in the state made up a large chunk of his 7.1-million vote win in the national popular vote.

For years, California's June primary was a kingmaker. Nelson Rockefeller's presidential hopes dissolved when he lost to Barry Goldwater in the 1964 GOP contest. Robert Kennedy prevailed over Eugene McCarthy in the 1968 Democratic contest, but was assassinated by Sirhan Sirhan after delivering his victory speech at the Ambassador Hotel in Los Angeles. George McGovern edged out Hubert Humphrey in the 1972 Democratic primary and the state's delegation was decided by a pivotal credentials fight at the Democratic National Convention where McGovern prevailed, assuring him the nomination. The state lost its marquee status in four of the next five presidential elections when both parties' nominations were essentially clinched long before California voted, prompting officials to move its 1996 primary to late March. In 2008, California voted early on Super Tuesday; after reverting back to June in 2012 and 2016, it joined the Super Tuesday primary once again in 2020.

The state's June primary served as a moral victory for Bernie Sanders in 2016, when he took 46 percent of the vote and won a large chunk of delegates. But it was a pyrrhic victory for him in March 2020, when after Sanders invested a tremendous amount of time, money and energy into the state he beat Joe Biden by just eight points, 36%-28%, winning 225 delegates to 172 for Biden. That was far from enough, as Biden's lopsided wins in other Super Tuesday states made him the heavy favorite for the nomination, which he clinched a few weeks later. California's slow-counting vote system, which relies heavily on mail ballots, also undercut any momentum for Sanders, since it wasn't certain for days that he'd won.

In the general election, Biden won handily, but his coattails didn't help House Democrats. The GOP held seven districts Trump lost in 2016; Democrats won all seven seats in 2018, but four flipped back to the GOP in 2020 even as Biden carried those districts.

Congressional Districts

117th Congress Lineup	42D 11R	116th Congress Lineup	46D 7R

By the recent standards of House Republicans in California, the 2020 election was a resounding success. They won back four seats they had lost in 2018. Those winners were two Asian females, a Latino male and a Portuguese-American male.(They defeated three incumbents, two of whom were white males and one a Hispanic male, plus a challenger who was a white female.) Three of the four successful Republicans had extensive experience as elected officials; the fourth, who won a special election earlier in 2020, was a political novice at that time. Strikingly, the four Republicans won their two-candidate contests with a vote share between 50.05 and 51.1 percent. President Donald Trump lost each of their four districts in 2020, as he did in 2016. In short, they beat the odds. But they will hold their seats for at least two years—pending the potential challenges of redistricting and the perils of being prime Democratic targets in 2022. The three other Democrats who took GOP-held seats in 2018 won at least 53 percent of the vote in 2020.

Even with those GOP victories, Democrats retain 42-11 control of the California delegation, with the state losing one seat to reapportionment. That unique occurrence makes it difficult to predict which incumbent (or, potentially, incumbents) will take the fall when the new map is drawn. Given the state's ethnic diversity, there are no guarantees—not even for the seven white males who are the remaining Republicans in the delegation; Trump won each of their districts. The 11 House Republicans, for the most part, represent interior California. Only one serves a district on the Pacific Ocean: the Orange County-based 48th District. In short, 2022 could be another unusually competitive election for the California delegation. Another wild card is that, for the first time in the state's history, it lost a seat in the current reapportionment. Population changes suggest that Los Angeles County will suffer that loss. But many factors will come into play, including race, potential retirements in the state's aging delegation and likely Democratic attempts to target second-term Republican Rep. Mike Garcia.

California has a rich tradition of partisan gerrymandering and incumbent protection: Republicans drew the lines to their advantage in the 1940s and 1950s, Democrats in the 1960s, 1970s, and 1980s. Democratic Rep. Phillip Burton, the former godfather of the process, used to defend the drawing of safe seats by deviously arguing it was inhumane to make congressmen catch red-eye flights to Washington every week. In 2001, consultant Michael Berman, brother of then-Rep. Howard Berman, charged every incumbent Democrat $20,000 to draw a map that granted Democrats 33 and Republicans 20 safe seats.

Those customs were largely eliminated by two significant changes in the 2012 redistricting. Thanks to voter approval, 61%-39%, of a 2010 ballot proposition spearheaded by GOP Gov. Arnold Schwarzenegger, the state became a large laboratory for redistricting reform. The Democratic-dominated legislature was forced to cede power to a 14-member Citizens Redistricting Commission barred from taking into account any partisan data or where incumbents live. The other historical development was that, for the first time since it was admitted to the Union in 1850, California in 2012 did not gain House seats following the decennial census.

After months of tedious meetings and mountains of public testimony, the commission in August 2011 adopted a new map that radically—and more logically—rearranged the state's 53 seats. Under the 2001 Democratic map, mangled lines had produced a delegation so safe that just one House seat changed partisan hands one time in 10 years' worth of elections. Moreover, clever incumbent protection had delayed advancements in Latino representation; in 2010, Latinos were 38 percent of California's population, but held just nine of the state's 53 seats. The new map threw 27 incumbents into 13 districts and created 14 seats with no resident incumbent. It created three new or altered districts with functional majorities of Latino citizens.

The end result in 2012 was the most upheaval and loss of seniority California's delegation had ever seen. The state's new top-two jungle primary law meant that candidates of the same party advanced to the November election in eight districts. In addition to seven retirees (three Democrats, four Republicans) in 2012, several senior members lost reelection and 40-year Democratic veterans

George Miller and Henry Waxman retired in 2014. What incumbents viewed as seniority, many voters saw as entrenchment. Reformers got the burst of competition and new blood they wanted.

But there was nothing "nonpartisan" about the map the commission produced, and it has turned out to be much more beneficial for Democrats than the one the Democratic legislature passed in 2001. In 2014, spurred by then-House Majority Leader Kevin McCarthy of Bakersfield, Republicans waged a half-dozen competitive challenges. But every Democrat survived—a few by narrow margins. Despite a few more close contests in 2016, including the defeat of veteran Democratic Rep. Mike Honda by another Democrat in the 17th District, another cycle passed with no changes in party control. Then, in 2018, came the Republican deluge. They lost two seats in the Central Valley, one in L.A. County, and all four they held in substantial parts of Orange County.

As for the next round of redistricting, their success in 2018 showed that Republicans retained the ability to regain seats. But, as was the case in 2012, with almost any plan that is not drawn chiefly to protect incumbents, the state is so big and diverse that the consequences are unpredictable.

Gavin Newsom (D)

Elected 2018, term expires 2023, 1st term; b. Oct. 10, 1967, San Francisco; Santa Clara University, B.S.,1989; Roman Catholic; Married (Jennifer); 3 children.

Elected Office: Board Member, San Francisco Board of Supervisors, 1997-2003; Mayor, San Francisco, 2004-2010; CA Lt. Gov., 2011-2018.

Professional Career: Author; Founder, PlumpJack

Office: State Capitol Building Suite 1173, Sacramento, 95814; 916-445-2841; Fax: 916-558-3160
Lt. Gov.: Eleni Kounalakis (D) **Atty. Gen:** Rob Bonta (D) **Sec. of State:** Shirley Weber (D)
State Legislature: Senate: 28D, 10R, 2V **House:** 61D, 19R

Election Results

Election	Name (Party)	Vote (%)
2018 General	Gavin Newsom (D)	7,721,410 (62%)
	John H. Cox (R)	4,742,825 (38%)
2018 Primary	Gavin Newsom (D)	2,343,792 (34%)
	John H. Cox (R)	1,766,488 (25%)
	Antonio Villaraigosa (D)	926,394 (13%)
	Travis Allen (R)	658,798 (10%)
	John Chiang (D)	655,920 (9%)

Democrat Gavin Newsom easily won California's governorship in 2018, succeeding four-term Gov. Jerry Brown and completing a charmed rise in California politics, including stints as mayor of San Francisco and as lieutenant governor under Brown. Once a pro-business moderate, at least by San Francisco standards, Newsom moved leftward as the state evolved in the Trump era. But the pressures of the coronavirus pandemic, including a self-inflicted wound of attending a lavish, non-socially distanced dinner with a prominent lobbyist, increased pressure for his recall in 2021.

Newsom was born into an affluent and well-connected family in California. His father, William A. Newsom III, was childhood friends with the oil heirs Gordon and Paul Getty and was later tapped to administer Getty family trusts. Another childhood friend was John Burton, a future Democratic state lawmaker and congressman. Newsom's grandfather, William A. Newsom II, served as a campaign manager for Edmund G. (Pat) Brown, Jerry Brown's father and one of his predecessors as governor; the younger Brown appointed Newsom's father to a Superior Court judgeship and then to the state

Court of Appeals. Before becoming a judge, Newsom's father ran unsuccessfully for the state Senate; during the 1968 campaign, he stumped with Robert F. Kennedy just days before RFK was assassinated. But Newsom's parents separated when he was young, and he and his sister Hilary were mostly raised by their mother, Tessa, who sometimes held more than one job to support the family. Newsom's father died about a month after his son won the governorship. His mother died in 2002 after a long bout with cancer; the New Yorker reported that Newsom had helped assist in her suicide, a decision he said gave him PTSD.

Newsom has grappled with dyslexia—to this day, he uses an elaborate coping system involving handwritten notes and binders—but as a youngster he excelled at baseball and basketball. In high school, "he began applying hair gel and wearing blazers and business suits, a costume inspired by Remington Steele, the TV show that starred Pierce Brosnan as a con man who assumes the identity of a glamorous private detective," according to the New Yorker. After graduating from Santa Clara University, Newsom went into business, backed by a roster of investors that included members of the Getty family. He began with a wine store on San Francisco's Fillmore Street, but his holdings eventually expanded to include some two dozen enterprises, including bars, restaurants, hotels and wineries. (His sister now handles the businesses.) Newsom crossed over into politics when San Francisco Mayor Willie Brown named him to the city's Parking and Traffic Commission, and later to a vacant seat on the city's Board of Supervisors. The New Yorker described him as having "the air of a man who just sauntered off a yacht," while New York magazine said Newsom "looks more like a politician than any actor who's ever played one in a movie."

In 2003, Newsom ran for mayor of San Francisco and won. Some of his ideas were quirky, such as installing turbines under the Golden Gate Bridge to harness the tides, or his decision to deliver a state of the city address in a 7-1/2 hour YouTube monologue. "We were willing to try new things," Newsom recalled to San Francisco Chronicle columnist Heather Knight. He was able to erase a $483 million deficit in 2010 without calamitous closures, but the city's homeless problem—despite his efforts to replace cash assistance with housing and other services—proved stubborn. Another issue, however, drew national attention: His decision in 2004, years before it became mainstream, to order city clerks to approve same-sex marriages. After more than 4,000 couples took advantage of the new policy, the state Supreme Court struck it down, and many Democrats kept their distance from Newsom.

Newsom faced another challenge as mayor—his personal life. In 2007, he admitted an affair with a staffer, Ruby Rippey-Tourk, who was married to another top Newsom staffer and friend. He went into counseling for abusing alcohol, and his marriage to Kimberly Guilfoyle, a prosecutor-turned-television personality, fell apart. (Guilfoyle later became the girlfriend of Donald Trump Jr.; Newsom, for his part, married Jennifer Siebel in 2008, with whom he has had four children.) The affair didn't seem to hurt Newsom's political ambitions; he easily won reelection as mayor, and after an aborted gubernatorial campaign in 2010, he switched to the race for lieutenant governor and won, as Brown won his race to return to the governor's office. Newsom's eight years as lieutenant governor were largely quiet; the office's official duties are limited, though he took care to master the intricacies of the state budget. His relationship with Brown, despite the families' longstanding ties, was distant, even frosty. So it was not a surprise that Newsom began running for governor shortly after winning reelection, giving him more than three and a half years to prepare his bid to succeed Brown. In 2014, he published a book, Citizenville, in which he styled himself as a high-tech wonk.

In California's top-two primary, Newsom faced former Los Angeles Mayor and former Assembly Speaker Antonio Villaraigosa, as well as state Treasurer John Chiang, and former Superintendent of Public Instruction Delaine Eastin, all Democrats, plus Republican John Cox. Newsom ran ads attacking Cox, which were widely interpreted as an effort to boost the Republican's standing among GOP primary voters, which in turn would increase Newsom's chances of facing a Republican in the runoff rather than another Democrat. Villaraigosa, despite strong financial support from charter school advocates, underperformed in the primary, particularly among his putative base of Hispanic voters. Newsom finished first with 34 percent, followed by Cox with 25 percent, Villaraigosa with 13 percent, Republican Travis Allen with 10 percent, Chiang with 9 percent, and Eastin with 3 percent. Cox, who had lost multiple races in his home state of Illinois, was hobbled by his partisan affiliation, and an endorsement by Trump amounted to a kiss of death. Newsom defeated Cox, 62%-38%, which was the highest percentage ever for a Democrat in California. It was also the first time since 1887 that a Democratic governor succeeded a Democratic governor in California and, unlike Brown, Newsom won historically Republican Orange County.

Shortly after taking office, Newsom drastically downsized Brown's dream of a costly high-speed rail network, with the ironic exception of a corridor in the more Republican Central Valley.

(The project would continue to be plagued by technical problems during his governorship.) Despite employing negotiating tactics that sometimes irritated legislators, Newsom signed a number of progressive bills passed by the Democratic supermajority during his first year in office, including one limiting when police can fire on suspects, another to allow local jurisdictions to establish public banks, and a third to allow undocumented immigrants between 19 and 25 to obtain Medicaid coverage. Newsom also extended a moratorium on the death penalty; executions haven't been carried out in the state since 2006. In addition, Newsom approved two measures that would ultimately be overturned by voters in 2020—an expansion of rent control and a measure to increase labor mandates for contractors working for ride-share companies.

Newsom also sought to shape the future of the electric utility Pacific Gas & Electric, which was blamed for sparking wildfires due to downed power lines and eventually had to declare bankruptcy. Accusing the company of "more than two decades of mismanagement," Newsom eventually struck a deal to allow the utility to emerge from bankruptcy as long as it swallowed changes to its board, limits on shareholder dividends, and a plan for a state takeover if safety and accountability benchmarks weren't met. Meanwhile, Newsom engaged in an odd dance with Trump. While the state regularly filed lawsuits against the Trump administration, Newsom took care to cultivate a non-confrontational and respectful tone in public comments. As a result, Trump often refrained from the kind of public criticism that he directed at other Democratic governors.

Despite a two-month break in legislating due to the pandemic, Newsom and the legislature had a productive year. The governor signed bills to expand paid family leave to 6 million more employees, tighten accountability for police officers accused of misconduct, expand mental health parity in health care, empanel a task force to consider reparations for slavery, ban flavored tobacco, expand access to less-expensive generic drugs, curb administrative fees in the criminal justice system, increase the role of nurse-practitioners, tighten regulations on debt collectors, and require greater diversity on corporate boards. Political observers say Newsom genuinely enjoys being governor. During much of the coronavirus pandemic, he took a fairly aggressive approach typical of blue-state governors, though with inconstant results. By January 2021, the state ranked in the top 10 states for per capita cases.

Newsom's stop-start shutdown orders provoked irritation among Californians, and glitches in the processing of unemployment claims as the pandemic hit made matters worse. But Newsom made life worse for himself in November, when he attended a 50th birthday party for influential political operative Jason Kinney at the French Laundry, the celebrated Napa Valley restaurant. After ordering Californians to wear masks and stay home, photos emerged of Newsom and other guests without masks and observing minimal social distancing; while the governor acknowledged a lapse in judgment, the incident broke a dam of frustration over his administration's policies to restrain ordinary Californians' behavior during the pandemic. The episode turbo-charged an effort to recall Newsom that, due to California's generous recall rules, was approved for the ballot in 2021. (The rules remained the same as 2003, when Gov. Gray Davis was recalled and, on the same ballot, Arnold Schwarzenegger was elected as his successor; backers of Newsom's recall even got a court-ordered extension on signature gathering due to difficulty of circulating petitions during the pandemic.) Newsom was favored to survive a recall, given the Democrats' gains in the state than 2003 and the national GOP's tarnished reputation, but it could come amid a messy, and unpredictable, celebrity-driven campaign.

Dianne Feinstein (D)

Elected 1992, term expires 2024, 5th full term, b. Jun 22, 1933; San Francisco, CA; Stanford University, B.A., 1955; Jewish; Married (Richard C. Blum); 1 child; 3 stepchildren.

Elected Office: President, San Francisco Board of Supervisors, 1970-1971, 1974-1975, 1978; San Francisco Mayor, 1978-1988.

Professional Career: CA Women's Parole Board, 1960-1966; Director, Bank of CA, 1988-1989.

DC Office: 331 HSOB 20510, 202-224-3841, Fax: 202-228-3954, feinstein.senate.gov

State Offices: Fresno, 559-485-7430; Los Angeles, 310-914-7300; San Diego, 619-231-9712; San Francisco, 415-393-0707.

Committees: *Appropriations*: Agriculture, Rural Development, FDA & Related Agencies; Commerce, Justice, Science & Related Agencies; Department of Defense; Department of the Interior, Environment & Related Agencies; Energy & Water Development (Chmn); Transportation, HUD & Related Agencies. *Intelligence. Judiciary*: Constitution; Criminal Justice & Counterterrorism; Human Rights & the Law (Chmn); Immigration, Citizenship & Border Security. *Rules & Administration.*

Group Ratings

	ADA	ACLU	AFL-CIO	LCV	COC	HAFA	ACU	CFG	FRC
2020	-	85%	-	92%	-	0%	7%	-	-
2019	100%	C	100%	100%	65%	C	7%	0%	0%

Almanac Ratings 2019-2020

	Economy	Social	Foreign	Composite
Liberal	93%	93%	51%	79%
Conservative	7%	7%	49%	21%

Key Votes of the 116th Congress

1. EPA clean energy rules	Y	5. Russia sanctions	Y	9. Barr as Atty. General	N
2. U.S./Mex./Can. trade deal	Y	6. Troops in SYR, AFG	Y	10. Spending at the border	Y
3. Cut unemployment benefits	N	7. Veto arms sales to Saudis	Y	11. Coney Barrett to Sup. Ct.	N
4. Shelton to Fed Reserve	N	8. Defense $$$, veto override	Y	12. Electoral College objections	N

Election Results

Election	Name (Party)	Vote (%)		Cand. Spent	Ind. Exp. Support	Ind. Exp. Oppose
2018 General	Dianne Feinstein (D)...................... 6,019,422	(54%)	$17,612,064	$226,320		
	Kevin De Leon (D)....................... 5,093,942	(46%)	$2,457,537	$949,232		
2018 Primary	Dianne Feinstein (D)...................... 2,947,035	(44%)				
	Kevin De Leon (D)....................... 805,446	(12%)				

Prior winning percentages: 2018 (54%), 2012 (63%), 2006 (59%), 2000 (56%), 1994 (47%), 1992 special (54%)

Few people in American political life have witnessed—or made—as much history as Dianne Feinstein, California's senior senator. Her half-century in politics has made for a career not merely about the first woman to hold many high positions in office but that of a witness to violence and pandemic, a politician who tried to stop such miseries, and an effective legislator. At the same time, she was the dominant politico in the Golden State as it shifted from Reagan Republican country to the liberal bastion that it is today. Her pragmatic style can seem anachronistic, and her centrist tendencies now collide with a Democratic electorate that has shifted leftward.

First elected in a 1992 special election, Feinstein came to the Senate in a cycle known as the "Year of the Woman." She would go on to spend the next 30 years at the center of the most heated debates in American life, including over Supreme Court nominations, torture, intelligence gathering and gun policy. The campaign that initially sent Feinstein to Capitol Hill set precedent. Democrat Barbara Boxer was chosen the same year—marking the first time that a state had elected two female senators. The two campaigned together in 1992, with Feinstein at one point saying: "Just as Cagney had Lacey and Thelma had Louise, Dianne has Barbara and Barbara has Dianne." They served in California's delegation together for four terms. While Boxer retired in 2016, Feinstein—as the Senate's oldest member, at 85—ran for reelection two years later. She spent the past decade at the pinnacle of the Senate, serving as the top Democrat on two committees thanks to years of accumulated seniority. But whispers about her capacity to hold those roles given her age grew louder, and she has begun the process of handing off that power.

Feinstein has never been easy to pigeonhole: For many years, she backed the death penalty, while also being one of the Senate's most persistent advocates of gun control legislation. She has been a staunch defender of government surveillance programs and federal intelligence gathering agencies. But she rebuked the harsh interrogation techniques used on terrorism suspects after 9/11 and fought with the CIA over that issue.

Born Dianne Goldman, she grew up in San Francisco's lush Presidio Heights neighborhood. Her father, a prominent physician, was Jewish, while her mother belonged to the Russian Orthodox faith. Feinstein attended San Francisco's Convent of the Sacred Heart High School before converting to Judaism at 20.

She hoped to follow in her father's footsteps, but in her first semester at Stanford University, she got a "D" in genetics and decided she did not have the aptitude for medicine. However, she loved a class on American political thought. And she had an uncle active in local Democratic politics who is said to have fueled her interest in moving in that direction. Feinstein graduated with a degree in criminology and then, while on an internship, wrote a paper about post-conviction phases of the justice system. She sent the paper to Gov. Pat Brown, for whom her father was a personal physician. Despite Feinstein's youth—she was just 27—the governor appointed her to the California Women's Board of Terms and Parole.

In 1969, she won her first election, to the San Francisco County Board of Supervisors. However, she was defeated in bids for mayor in 1971 and 1975 and began to question her future in the city's polarized politics. "I was convinced I was not electable," she said years later. 1978 was a year of tumult for Feinstein and her city. On Nov. 18, hundreds of members of the Peoples Temple—a church once based in San Francisco—died after drinking poisoned Flavor Aid. Prior to the massacre, members assassinated San Francisco-area Rep. Leo Ryan, who had traveled to Jonestown Guyana to investigate on behalf of concerned relatives of church members. Less than two weeks later, Feinstein —who had lost her second husband, neurosurgeon Bertram Feinstein, to cancer just months earlier —was talking to reporters, openly contemplating leaving politics. Hours later, as president of the Board of Supervisors, she became the city's acting mayor after Mayor George Moscone and fellow Supervisor Harvey Milk were assassinated by former Supervisor Dan White. Feinstein discovered Milk's body and had to announce to the world what had happened.

Her steadiness and sense of command calmed the city, and she went on to win full mayoral terms in 1979 and 1983. The central crisis of her mayor ship was the AIDS epidemic, which acutely struck San Francisco's gay community. Nearly three decades later, she would describe that outbreak as "one of the most formative experiences of my time in public service." Many of the physicians at the time found her, the daughter of a doctor, to be strikingly receptive to their advocacy. "Unlike other politicians, Dianne never thought that HIV/AIDS was a result of bad behavior but rather a public health emergency," John Luce later said. Luce, one of the doctors who treated many of the first American AIDS patients at a San Francisco hospital, had a long alliance with Feinstein's father.

The other major headline of Feinstein's tenure as mayor involved the manhunt of serial killer Richard Ramirez, known as the "Night Stalker." Feinstein infuriated law enforcement officials when she revealed sensitive information about evidence in a 1985 news conference.

In 1984, Democratic presidential candidate Walter Mondale considered naming Feinstein as his running mate. But he passed her over for Geraldine Ferraro partly because of qualms about the business dealings of Feinstein's third husband, Richard Blum, to whom she has been married since 1980. Feinstein presided over the 1984 Democratic National Convention in San Francisco, while, ironically, Ferraro confronted questions about her own husband's business dealings. Blum's extensive assets helped place Feinstein among the wealthiest members of Congress—the third wealthiest senator, according to Roll Call compilation in 2018.They also have yielded periodic political headaches for her, in the form of allegations of conflicts of interest.

Ineligible for a third term as mayor, Feinstein left the city's politics in 1987 and ran for governor in 1990, buoyed by $3 million she and her husband lent to the effort. She won the Democratic primary 52%-41% but lost in the general election, 49%-46%, to Republican Pete Wilson. During that campaign, Feinstein—who had opposed the death penalty as a young member of the Board of Terms and Parole—said she had changed her mind and had come to believe capital punishment was a deterrent for certain types of crimes. She was booed at the 1990 Democratic State Convention over her stance but won points for a willingness to demonstrate her independence. Nearly three decades later, facing an aggressive challenge from the left, Feinstein said her position on the death penalty had changed again. "It became crystal clear to me that the risk of unequal application is high and its effect on deterrence is low," Feinstein said shortly before the 2018 Senate primary, adding that her change of heart had come "several years ago."

When Wilson appointed little-known state Sen. John Seymour to replace himself in the Senate, Feinstein announced for the 1992 special election to fill the remainder of the term. She defeated state Controller Gray Davis 58%-33% in a heated primary that soured her relationship with Davis, who went on to be elected governor in 1998. Seymour struggled throughout the campaign, shifting to support abortion rights and seeing his attacks on illegal immigration fall flat. Feinstein won 54%-38%.

Soon after arriving to the Senate, Feinstein was recruited as one of the first two women to serve on the Judiciary Committee by Chairman Joe Biden, who was smarting from criticism over his handling of Anita Hill during hearings over Clarence Thomas' Supreme Court nomination. That election of a record number of women to the Senate in 1992 was attributed in part to political backlash over the handling of Hill's sexual harassment accusations against Thomas.

Feinstein's approach to nominations to high court by one Republican president, George W. Bush, was partisan but courteous. After an interview with Supreme Court nominee John Roberts in July 2005, she called him "very impressive" but voted against confirmation out of concern he might overturn Roe v. Wade, which protects women's access to abortions. She also opposed Samuel Alito's confirmation in early 2006; Bush had nominated Alito after his initial choice of White House counsel Harriet Miers ran into trouble, prompting Feinstein to say, "I don't believe they would have attacked a man the way she was attacked."

But everything changed when Donald Trump became president. Feinstein became the Judiciary Committee's ranking member less than a month before he nominated federal appellate Judge Neil Gorsuch to a Supreme Court seat that had been vacant for nearly a year after the death of Justice Antonin Scalia—when Barack Obama was still president. In an interview with the San Francisco Chronicle before Gorsuch's confirmation hearings, she blasted Senate Republicans' refusal to grant federal Judge Merrick Garland, Obama's nominee for the vacancy, a hearing or vote throughout the last year of Obama's tenure as "appalling." "The humiliation that he went through," Feinstein said of Garland. "Asking people just to meet with him and getting turned down. ... Walking these halls day and night and getting the back of the Republican hand. Many of us haven't recovered from that." Feinstein also voiced concerns about the future of Roe v. Wade when Gorsuch came before the panel in March 2017. She called the 1973 decision "settled law," noting Trump's campaign promise to appoint anti-abortion judges. Although Gorsuch had not ruled directly on abortion, "his writings do raise questions," Feinstein said.

But it was Feinstein's handling of Trump's next Supreme Court nominee, federal Judge Brett Kavanaugh, that generated rancor from the president and Senate Republican leaders—as well as some quiet grumbling among her Democratic colleagues. Shortly after Trump nominated Kavanaugh in July 2018, Christine Blasey Ford approached her congresswoman, Democrat Anna Eshoo of California, with sexual assault allegations against Kavanaugh that dated to the early 1980s, when she and Kavanaugh were in high school. Blasey Ford initially insisted on confidentiality; her allegations were put in a letter that was forwarded to Feinstein in late July. The existence of the letter was first disclosed in mid-September by The Intercept shortly after Kavanaugh had gone through lengthy confirmation hearings. It was not until then that Feinstein provided the letter to other committee Democrats, who urged her to forward it to the FBI—which she did.

Feinstein denied that she or anyone in her office had leaked the letter and defended not having brought it to light sooner. "Let me be clear: I did not hide Dr. Ford's letter. ... She asked me to keep it confidential, and I kept it confidential," she told the Judiciary Committee. She also told reporters she had been "looking for a way to get it investigated by an outside investigator" without violating Blasey Ford's confidentiality. But several of her Democratic colleagues were said to be upset at what they regarded as clumsy handling of the matter from a political standpoint—even as Republican argued the letter was an eleventh-hour effort to derail Kavanaugh's nomination. "When Sen. Feinstein sat with Judge Kavanaugh for a long, long meeting, she had this letter," Trump told reporters. "Why didn't the Democrats bring it up then? Because they obstruct and because they resist." Then-Senate Majority Leader Mitch McConnell said Feinstein "decided to spring it at the end."

The letter prompted a follow-up and highly charged hearing at which Blasey Ford and Kavanaugh testified and after which Feinstein blasted Kavanaugh's "aggressive and belligerent" behavior. With several key senators undecided, Republican leaders agreed to a supplemental FBI investigation. It found no corroboration of the allegations by Blasey Ford or other women. Feinstein joined other Democrats in criticizing the scope of the FBI probe, which did not include interviews with Blasey Ford or Kavanaugh. "When he wasn't yelling and demeaning senators, he was making misleading statements that cast doubt on his overall trustworthiness," Feinstein said of Kavanaugh and his testimony at the follow-up hearing. "I don't think that would happen with FBI agents seated across the table." Kavanaugh was narrowly confirmed, with Trump using the controversy to fire up his base at rallies before the 2018 midterm elections. He targeted Feinstein, accusing her of "disgraceful behavior"; his supporters responded with chants of "lock her up"—the same war cry aimed at Hillary Clinton during Trump campaign rallies two years earlier.

It was the next high court confirmation hearing—of Trump nominee Amy Coney Barrett—that effectively ended Feinstein's time as the committee's top Democrat. Trump nominated Barrett to replace liberal icon Ruth Bader Ginsburg, who died in September 2020 in the thick of the presidential campaign. Democrats held out hope the Senate would respect the justice's dying wish—that the person who would win that election would nominate her successor. But that was extinguished when conservatives consolidated control of the court by confirming Barrett. While Barrett's testimony lacked the pyrotechnics of other Supreme Court hearings, the left was demoralized by her smooth confirmation. Liberals were shocked when Feinstein called that round "one of the best set of hearings that I've participated in." Her standing among liberals only became more tenuous when she hugged Judiciary Chairman Lindsey Graham, one of the most reviled Republicans among liberals. To make matters worse, neither senator wore a mask in the encounter despite the COVID-19 pandemic.

After the election of her former colleague Biden-and under pressure from many Democrats-Feinstein announced she would step down as the top Democrat on the Judiciary Committee, a decision that came amid questions over whether she was still in step with the liberal swing of her party and if her age—87—meant she could no longer handle such a role.

As for policy on Judiciary, Feinstein's first major legislative accomplishment came in 1994 and fit her tough-on-crime background: She sponsored a ban on the manufacture and sale of assault weapons, which President Bill Clinton signed into law. When Idaho Republican Larry Craig contended that her definition of assault weapons was not rigorous enough and challenged her knowledge of firearms, she stopped the argument in its tracks: "I know something about what firearms can do," Feinstein said, referring to the killings of Milk and Moscone. She pressed unsuccessfully for reauthorization of the assault weapons ban in 2004, when Congress was under GOP control.

As the Democratic Party's support for gun control waned—some blamed the assault weapons ban for the party's loss of the Senate and House in 1994—Feinstein had a harder time persuading colleagues to consider gun restrictions. The public mood changed after the December 2012 mass shooting of 26 children and teachers at an elementary school in Newtown Connecticut. Feinstein became the point person in the Democratic-controlled Senate for legislation even tougher than the 1994 law; it sought to ban assault weapons and high-capacity magazines. But Democratic leaders abandoned the proposal to focus on measures they hoped could draw more bipartisan support, such as expanding criminal background checks for gun purchases. After those proposals failed in the spring of 2013, Feinstein blamed the National Rifle Association for making colleagues afraid to vote on gun control legislation. In 2016, after the Orlando Florida nightclub shooting in which 50 people including the perpetrator were killed, Feinstein tried again, sponsoring a measure to deny the sale of firearms to those in the federal government's terrorist screening database. The proposal was defeated on a largely party-line vote.

As chairwoman of the Senate Rules and Administration Committee in early 2009, Feinstein managed Obama's swearing-in. That was another first for a woman, as was Feinstein's assumption of the Intelligence panel's gavel. The scale of Feinstein's work on the Judiciary and Intelligence committees has overshadowed her service on a committee that would otherwise define any other senator's career: Feinstein has served on the Senate Appropriations Committee since her freshman year. On that front, she has remained the top Democrat on the Energy and Water subcommittee, a key appointment for a senator representing a drought-plagued state.

Feinstein chaired the Intelligence Committee from 2009 until Republicans retook the Senate in 2015. During the Bush administration, she took issue with other Democrats who claimed the USA Patriot Act had led to violations of civil liberties. During Obama's second term, when former National Security Agency contractor Edward Snowden leaked details of the NSA's domestic surveillance efforts, she accused Snowden of treason while taking the agency to task for being unable to prevent him from accessing so much highly classified material. She also defended the NSA's far-reaching covert collection of Americans' phone records.

The latter episode caused her approval ratings in California to plummet. Feinstein shrugged it off, telling the Los Angeles Times, "Numbers go down, numbers go up. I don't think people understand" the NSA's work. But in spring 2015, as debate raged over reauthorizing the Patriot Act, she backed ending the NSA's bulk collection of phone records—putting her in league with most Democrats and libertarian-leaning Republicans. She again took a hard line after a San Bernardino shooting rampage in late 2015, as the Justice Department sought access to an iPhone used by one of the shooters. She pushed a draft bill to give law enforcement a "back door" to access encrypted data, putting her at odds with technology firms and civil libertarians. With Trump as president, Feinstein was among a minority of Senate Democrats who in early 2018 joined most Republicans to support renewal of a key provision—Section 702—of the Foreign Intelligence Surveillance Act, allowing the NSA to obtain communications of foreigners outside the United States without a warrant. Civil liberties advocates have complained it provided a loophole for warrantless surveillance of Americans.

Her actions on the Intelligence Committee turned confrontational after she questioned the rationale and effectiveness of waterboarding and other "enhanced interrogation techniques" on terrorist suspects after 9/11. She won nearly unanimous committee approval for an investigation into the CIA's interrogation tactics. In late 2012, it yielded a 6,700-page report. With the aim of making a 500-page "executive summary" public, the committee forwarded it to the White House for review.

To Feinstein's displeasure, the Obama White House turned the so-called torture report over to the target of the probe—the CIA—for review. Tensions spilled into public view in the spring of 2014 when media reports appeared in which the CIA accused Senate staffers working on the investigation of hacking into the agency's computers. Feinstein, in a Senate floor speech, said the CIA had removed classified documents from the committee staff's computers in the middle of the investigation. The CIA later apologized. In late 2014, the Intelligence Committee released the torture report, which slammed the "deeply flawed" Bush-era harsh interrogation methods used by the CIA on detainees. Vermont Sen. Patrick Leahy, who preceded Feinstein as the Judiciary panel's ranking Democrat, told Roll Call: "She was under enormous pressure to allow a cover-up. She didn't." Amazon Studios documented Feinstein's saga in a movie starring Annette Bening, who said her portrayal of the senator was in part inspired from her time living in San Francisco during Feinstein's tumultuous tenure as mayor.

In March 2018, amid her latest reelection campaign, Feinstein took heat from her left when she described Deputy CIA Director Gina Haspel—Trump's nominee to head the agency—as a "good deputy director." Haspel had supervised a secret CIA prison in Thailand where detainees were subjected to the methods criticized in the 2014 report. As Feinstein declined to take a position on the Haspel's nomination, her leading opponent for reelection, former state Senate President Kevin de León, goaded her, telling The Hill: "Having released a torture report, Feinstein knows better than most how morally and legally wrong torture is. This should be an easy call." A week before the floor vote, Feinstein announced she would oppose confirming Haspel as the CIA's first director, saying, "For the Senate to confirm someone so involved with the [interrogation] program to the highest position at the CIA would in effect tell the world that we approve of what happened, and I absolutely do not."

De León criticized Feinstein for giving Haspel the benefit of the doubt. The 2018 contest marked the first serious challenge Feinstein had confronted in a quarter of a century. Running for her first full term in the Republican-dominated year of 1994, she faced Rep. Michael Huffington, who spent $30 million of his own money. At the time, he was married to Arianna Huffington, who later founded HuffPost. Days before that election, it was revealed that Feinstein, despite earlier denials, had employed a woman whose work permit had expired. She won 47%-45%. In 2000, moderate GOP Rep. Tom Campbell challenged her. Feinstein greatly outspent him and won 56%-37%. In her 2006 and 2012, she defeated little-known opponents by of 59%-35% and 63%-37%, respectively.

When Feinstein announced for a fifth full term in October 2017, her political standing at home appeared tenuous. A month earlier, she encountered a firestorm after she called for "some patience" during Trump's presidency—while expressing hope the president would learn and change. Her comments spurred de León, term limited in the state Senate, into the race. That contest reflected the broader debate over the direction of the Democratic Party.

"We don't owe Trump patience. We owe Californians resistance," de León told the Los Angeles Times. Feinstein responded: "Resistance to me means doing the best I can to serve people in the way we do. ... Now, I don't rant and rail because I've got other ways of being constructive, and I think the majority of people want me to be constructive." De León promised to more strongly challenge Trump and his policies, and he found some help: After the 2016 election, the California Democratic Party structure became dominated by progressives who found de León's definition of resistance closer to their own. At the state party's February 2018 convention, de León defeated Feinstein 54%-37% —just short of the 60 percent needed for an endorsement. But, in June's nonpartisan "blanket" primary, Feinstein finished far ahead. She led de León 44%-12%—setting up a November runoff. Four Republican candidates trailed, all polling in single digits.

Feinstein lined up endorsements from the party establishment—notably Obama, Biden and House Democratic Leader Nancy Pelosi, a fellow San Franciscan. Feinstein's personal wealth also came into play: She gave her campaign $3.7 million and loaned it another $8 million. She spent nearly $17 million in the campaign, almost 10 times as much as de León. One-third of a century younger than Feinstein, de León didn't make age an issue. Instead, he called attention to her long tenure in office, saying she was out of touch. "It's time to have a voice that's reflective of today's California, not the California of a quarter-century ago," he told Vox.

Public polls showed Feinstein with a double-digit lead and indicated much of de León's support came from Republicans looking to cast a vote against the incumbent. She won 54%-46%, in what likely was her final campaign. At 85 when she began her current term, she was the oldest senator. Feinstein filed early paperwork in early 2021 in advance for a 2024 campaign. But a spokeswoman told Los Angeles magazine that the filing was routine compliance with fundraising laws and did not indicate any decision. Even so, some California Democrats seized on the revelation, plus her demotion at the Judiciary Committee, to demand that she retire, if not outright resign. She will likely continue to be a lightning rod as her party sorts through its generational and ideological divide.

Alex Padilla (D)

Appointed 2021, term expires 2022, 1st term, b. Mar 22, 1973; Pacoima, CA; Massachusetts Institute of Technology, B.S., 1994; Catholic; Married (Angela Padilla); 3 children

Elected Office: Member, Los Angeles City Council 1999-2001; President, Los Angeles City Council, 2001-2006; CA Senate, 2006-2014; CA Secretary of State, 2015-2021.

Professional Career: Engineer; Member, MIT Governing Board; President, National Association of Latino Elected and Appointed Officials.

DC Office: 112 HSOB 20510, 202-224-3553, Fax: 202-224-2200, padilla.senate.gov

State Offices: Fresno, 559-497-5109; Los Angeles, 310-231-4494; Sacramento, 916-448-2787; San Diego, 619-239-3884; San Francisco, 415-981-9369.

Committees: *Budget. Environment & Public Works*: Chem Safety, Waste Mngmnt, Enviro Justice & Reg Oversight; Clean Air & Nuclear Safety; Transportation & Infrastructure. *Homeland Security & Government Affairs*: Government Operations & Border Management; Investigations. *Judiciary*: Criminal Justice & Counterterrorism; Federal Courts, Oversight, Agency Action & Federal Rights; Immigration, Citizenship & Border Security (Chmn); Subcommittee on Intellectual Property. *Rules & Administration*.

For weeks, there had been widespread speculation that Democrat Alex Padilla— California's secretary of state and a longtime ally of Gov. Gavin Newsom—was Newsom's top choice to fill the final two years of Sen. Kamala Harris' term when she became vice president. But when Newsom— quarantined due to COVID-19—called via Zoom just before Christmas to offer him the appointment, Padilla seemed caught off guard.

"Can you imagine what your mom would be thinking now as I ask you if you want to be the next senator?" Newsom queried Padilla, the middle child of Mexican immigrants.

"You serious?" Padilla responded, losing his composure. He later told NPR: "I just couldn't help but immediately think of my parents and their journey. And like so many others…worked so hard, struggled, sacrificed, trying to achieve the American dream— less so for themselves, frankly, but for the next generation. And to think that a short-order cook and a housekeeper raised three children to all be public servants and one of them would be entering the United States Senate, it feels surreal sometimes."

Padilla's appointment was historic: He is the first Latino to represent California in the Senate in its170 years as a state. It also marked a rite of passage for a state whose population is now 40 percent Latino and that has shifted from swing state to deeply blue in the past quarter-century—a transformation set in motion by the backlash from an anti-immigrant ballot referendum, Proposition 187, in 1994.Intended to deny education, nonemergency health care and other public services to undocumented immigrants, Proposition 187 won at the ballot box but was blocked by court challenges. Padilla is part of a generation of Latinos that was drawn to political and civic engagement during that period. At the time, he joined a massive march against the referendum, carrying his nephew on his shoulders from East Los Angeles to City Hall downtown. "Before that, I wouldn't say I had ever dreamed of running for office, but I knew I'd have to do my part or our community would continue to be scapegoated," Padilla told the New York Times.

Just months prior to the vote on Proposition 187, Padilla had graduated from the Massachusetts Institute of Technology, an education he helped pay for with janitorial jobs and work-study positions; he returned to California to design satellite software for Hughes Aircraft. His decision to forsake rocket science for politics initially prompted consternation on the part of his parents, who had met in Los Angeles after emigrating separately from Mexico. He recalled to CalMatters their reaction: "Wait a minute, four years of MIT engineering school…for what?" But the political career arc of a man who had once aspired to be an aerospace engineer was described as "nothing short of meteoric" by the Los Angeles Times when, in 2001, Padilla was elected president of the Los Angeles City Council at 28.His ascent continued with election to the California Senate in 2006, then as state secretary of state in 2014.

Formally Alejandro Padilla, he grew up in northeast Los Angeles, in the San Fernando Valley neighborhood of Pacoima. He began his political career working in a field office of the state's senior senator, Democrat Dianne Feinstein—who years later publicly urged Newsom to appoint Padilla to fill Harris' seat—while also running a couple of state legislative campaigns. One of them was a bid for the California Assembly by Tony Cárdenas, now a member of the U.S. House. Padilla was a 26-year-old still living in his parents' house when, in 1999, he was elected to an open seat on the City Council with the backing of Los Angeles' Latino-dominated labor unions. During the campaign, Padilla emphasized better delivery of city services to a working-class district for which he believed they had long been denied: His first act was to push for safety improvements at a street crossing near the elementary school he had once attended.

By the time Padilla was elected president of the council two years later, he had moved out of his parents' home to his own place around the corner. His mother became a U.S. citizen two days after his election to the council, joining his father, who had taken the citizenship oath three years earlier. Padilla remains a San Fernando Valley resident, living with his wife and three children within a few miles of his father (his mother died in 2018), his sister and younger brother. The latter, Ackley Padilla, is chief of staff to the current Los Angeles City Council president, Nury Martinez. When Alex Padilla won that job two decades ago, he defeated a veteran council member with the help of five newly elected members. His backers included Eric Garcetti, who became council president when Padilla was elected to the California Senate—and who went on to become the city's mayor.

As council president, Padilla was acting mayor for four days after the 9/11 attacks, while then-Mayor James Hahn was grounded in Washington, D.C.—and amid speculation that the West Coast could be hit with attacks similar to those in New York and Washington. "It was a tough introduction to the spotlight, but the 28-year-old handled the moment with calm and grace," the Los Angeles Times observed when Padilla was appointed senator. On the council, Padilla had a knack for bringing "consensus and calm and peace," Harvey Englander, a longtime lobbyist and public affairs consultant, told CalMatters. "It's not that he didn't make waves, but he didn't make enemies."

Arriving in Sacramento after the 2006 elections—at 33, the youngest member of the state Senate—Padilla authored a smoke-free housing law and won approval of a bill requiring California restaurants to post calorie information on their menus. The most controversial bill of his eight-year state Senate tenure— signed into law in 2014—outlawed single-use plastic bags at grocery stores. Padilla took heat from both inside and outside his party: Conservatives derided it as another example of California playing "nanny state," while fellow Los Angeles Democrats worried the measure would harm a major plastic bag manufacturer in the city.

Toward the end of Padilla's first state Senate term, Newsom, then San Francisco's mayor, recruited him to chair his nascent 2010 campaign for governor. It was an effort by Newsom to make inroads into Southern California, and particularly its large Latino vote—but it also elevated Padilla's statewide profile. The Newsom-Padilla relationship dates to 2003, when Newsom was first running for mayor. Padilla helped him make contacts in Los Angeles, bolstering Newsom in a competitive race against a Latino candidate (Matt Gonzalez, then president of the San Francisco Board of Supervisors, running as the Green Party candidate). In 2010, faced with taking on former Gov. Jerry Brown in the Democratic primary for governor, Newsom backed out and successfully ran for lieutenant governor instead. In 2018, with Brown term-limited, Padilla gave Newsom an early endorsement for governor in a crowded primary field that included another prominent Latino politician, former Los Angeles Mayor Antonio Villaraigosa.

Barred by term limits from seeking reelection to the California Senate in 2014, Padilla ran for secretary of state, winning by 54%-46%—becoming the first Latino to hold that post. His victory was even stronger in 2018: 65%-35%. He became one of the first state officials to tangle with President Donald Trump, over unfounded allegations by Trump that millions of California ballots had been cast illegally in 2016. Citing privacy concerns, Padilla rejected requests from a Trump-created commission for access to detailed voter information. Perhaps his most notable achievement was his successful push for enactment of the Voter's Choice Act, allowing California counties to swap out neighborhood polling places for community voting centers on the condition they mail a ballot to every registered voter. A dozen counties opted to take advantage of the law prior to the 2020 pandemic, during which the practice of mailing ballots to all voters was utilized statewide.

Padilla vowed to register a million new California voters during his tenure—and ended up adding more than 4million. The surge in registration was largely the result of legislation he backed that automatically registers California residents when they obtain a driver's license. The program was beset by a number of errors when it debuted in 2019. But those problems were "quickly identified and quickly addressed," Padilla told NBC News, terming the program "an overwhelming success." As head of the National Association of State Election Directors, Padilla gained visibility in the nation's capital advocating for the kinds of reforms adopted in California. He also served as head of the National Association of Latino Elected and Appointed Officials.

Padilla arrived on Capitol Hill dogged by a controversy from his time as secretary of state. In an effort to increase voter turnout during the 2020 pandemic, his office awarded a $35 million contract to Washington-based SKDKnickerbocker, a strategic communications firm—one of whose principals, Anita Dunn, was a top official of President Joe Biden's campaign. While Republicans charged the contract was politically motivated, the state's Democratic controller, Betty Yee, questioned whether Padilla's office had the authority to spend the money. Yee contended the funding being tapped was intended for use by counties for pandemic-related election costs, to which Padilla countered that the SKDKnickerbocker effort was conducted "on behalf of counties," telling Yee in an email that "similar contracting on behalf of counties has been done previously" by his office and other agencies. A Padilla spokeswoman blamed the controversy on a "misinformation campaign."

Padilla's appointment to the Senate was a moment of elation for California's Latino community that came after months of intense lobbying—triggered by Biden's selection of Harris as his running mate in August 2020. The unrelenting pressure prompted Newsom at one point to complain of a "vexing decision" that he said he wouldn't wish even on his worst enemy. Biden's decision to nominate California Attorney General Xavier Becerra— a former House member—as Health and Human Services secretary left Padilla as the clear front-runner. But Newsom faced an organized effort lobbying to replace Harris, only the second Black woman to serve in the Senate, with another African-American woman. Another former San Francisco mayor, Willie Brown—also a former Assembly speaker—declared, "There's no way that Gavin Newsom should allow anyone other than a Black woman to fill the seat of Harris," while promoting Reps. Karen Bass and Barbara Lee for the appointment. And 150 of California's leading Democratic female donors took out full-page newspaper ads with an open letter urging Newsom to pick a woman of color.

Newsom's selection of Padilla left the Senate without a Black woman; Newsom sought to cushion the blow by selecting Assemblywoman Shirley Weber to succeed Padilla as secretary of state, the first Black woman to hold that post. Bass, former chair of the Congressional Black Caucus, issued a conciliatory statement on Padilla's appointment, saying, "After then-Senator Harris's historic election in 2016 as the first woman of color to represent California, we now have another historic barrier shattered." But other Black female office holders, notably San Francisco Mayor London Breed, were critical. Taisha Brown, chair of the state Democratic Party's Black Caucus, complained Newsom "has denied Black females representation in the United States Senate… at a time when Black women were critical in delivering the White House" to Democrats. While Brown said the governor "couldn't have picked a better person" in nominating Weber as secretary of state, she pointedly added: "It is not a substitution for the U.S. Senate seat."

Such bruised feelings were among the political challenges facing Padilla as he prepared to seek a full term in 2022. Given how rarely U.S. Senate seats come open in California, there was speculation that he might face a competitive primary—although the expected 2024 retirement of Feinstein, when she will be 91, could be a mitigating factor. While he has the advantage of having run twice statewide, Padilla did not have a federal campaign account prior to his appointment. According to CalMatters, he sent out a fundraising pitch less than two hours after Newsom named him—with the governor sending out a blast to his own email list seeking donations for Padilla. Meanwhile, Padilla repeatedly said his first order of business in the Senate would be "Covid, Covid, Covid"; the pandemic disproportionately hit the state's Latino population. By the late spring of 2021, Padilla appeared well positioned to win election in his own right the following year -- garnering the endorsement of 41 of California's 42 Democratic House members.

Doug LaMalfa (R)

Elected 2012, 5th term, b. Jul 02, 1960; Oroville, CA; Butte College, A.A., 1980; CA Polytechnic State University, San Luis Obispo, B.S., 1982; Evangelical; Married (Jill LaMalfa); 4 children.

Elected Office: CA Assembly, 2002-2008; CA Senate, 2010-2012.

Professional Career: Manager family rice farm.

DC Office: 322 CHOB 20515, 202-225-3076, lamalfa.house.gov

State Offices: Auburn, 530-878-5035; Chico, 530-343-1000; Redding, 530-223-5898.

Committees: *Agriculture*: Conservation & Forestry (RMM). *Transportation & Infrastructure*: Highways & Transit; Railroads, Pipelines & Hazardous Materials; Water Resources & Environment.

Group Ratings

	ADA	ACLU	AFL-CIO	LCV	COC	HAFA	ACU	CFG	FRC
2020	**	22%	**	5%	-	83%	87%	**	-
2019	0%	C	33%	7%	88%	C	88%	72%	100%

Almanac Ratings 2019-2020

	Economy	Social	Foreign	Composite
Liberal	25%	10%	11%	16%
Conservative	75%	90%	89%	84%

Key Votes of the 116th Congress

1. U.S./Mex./Can. trade deal Y	5. Russia sanctions Y	9. Firearms background checks N
2. First Coronavirus response Y	6. Troops in Syria Y	10. Spending at the border Y
3. HEROES Act N	7. Veto arms sales to Saudis N	11. Marijuana liberalized rules N
4. CASH Act N	8. Defense $$$, veto override N	12. Electoral College objections Y

Election Results

Election	Name (Party)	Vote (%)		Cand. Spent	Ind. Exp. Support	Ind. Exp. Oppose
2020 General	Doug LaMalfa (R).............................. 204,291	(57%)		$1,156,567	$2,237	$1,849
	Audrey Denney (D)........................... 154,466	(43%)		$2,464,622	$27,855	$27,422
2020 Primary	Doug LaMalfa (R)............................. 128,613	(55%)				

Prior winning percentages: 2018 (55%), 2016 (59%), 2014 (61%), 2012 (57%)

Republican Doug LaMalfa, elected in 2012 in this isolated district, has caused few ripples in Congress. His committee work has focused on local issues. Many of his interests have had bipartisan support, though he remains a strong conservative on social issues.

LaMalfa hails from what he calls "the real California," a wide swath of rural country north of Sacramento. A fourth-generation rice farmer from Richvale in Butte County, he was born in Oroville. He graduated with degrees in agriculture and business from California Polytechnic State University in San Luis Obispo. LaMalfa and his wife, Jill, operate in Richvale the farm his great-grandfather started in 1931.

He won election in 2002 to the state Assembly, where he spent six years, and was elected to the Senate in 2010. LaMalfa made his name in Sacramento by promoting agricultural interests and fighting new government spending and regulation. He sought unsuccessfully to freeze funding for the state's voter-approved high-speed rail project, citing its cost overruns. He opposed a state-level Dream Act proposal giving financial aid to children of illegal immigrants.

When he ran for Congress in 2012, LaMalfa came in first under California's all-party system, getting 38 percent of the vote. The second-highest vote getter was Democrat Jim Reed, an estate and tax attorney, with 25 percent. LaMalfa amassed five times more money than Reed, with the largest sums coming from agricultural interests. Critics highlighted the $4.7 million in federal agricultural subsidies he received for his family's rice farm. LaMalfa claimed the help was necessary for a small farm to comply with onerous regulations; rice farmers have long received sizable support. In his 57%-43% win, he won all 11 counties, but had only 51 percent in Butte, which had the largest turnout.

In the House, LaMalfa worked with neighboring Democratic Rep. John Garamendi to create a large new reservoir in Glenn and Colusa counties to serve Northern California, paid for mostly with state funding. It would be the largest reservoir built in California in four decades. In November 2018, the Trump administration approved a $450 million loan for the Sites Reservoir project, which will build a tunnel to the existing reservoir. He worked on a Republican bill to assure that metropolitan water districts would receive all available water from the reservoir, but the measure was opposed by Democrats.

On the farm bill that was enacted in 2018, LaMalfa took credit for provisions designed to prevent large fires in federal forests, including increased timber sales and accelerated salvage operations. As ranking Republican on the Conservation and Forestry Subcommittee, LaMalfa said in January 2020 that producers were using an "array of both voluntary and innovative conservation practices." In December 2020, he applauded final passage of the Water Resources Development Act, noting that it "empowers our local governments to take control of the construction phase on water projects."

On local issues, he joined a bipartisan group, including Democratic Rep. Jared Huffman, on a bill to assist local law enforcement agencies to eradicate illegal marijuana on public lands. He took credit for a $500,000 grant to Chico from the Small Community Air Service Development Program. The local airport said it would result in service to Los Angeles.

In 2014, LaMalfa was reelected, 61%-39%, over Heidi Hall, a conservation expert with the state's Department of Water Resources. LaMalfa increased his support in Butte County to 56 percent. In 2018, Democratic challenger Audrey Denney said LaMalfa "isn't doing his job," given the high tariffs that local farmers were suffering. Denney, who taught agriculture at California State University, Chico, and was a first-time candidate, matched LaMalfa in spending, with $1.1 million each. The Chico Enterprise-Record newspaper endorsed Denney and said LaMalfa was "a yes man for Trump." In his closest victory, LaMalfa won, 55%-45%. The challenger took the population centers of Butte and Nevada counties, which are closest to the Sacramento area, with 54 and 55 percent of the vote.

In 2020, Denney challenged in a rematch. With an endorsement from EMILY'S List, the Washington-based group that backs Democratic women who support abortion rights, Denney doubled LaMalfa's spending. The pandemic had shown that "the politics in Washington D.C. are stuck in such entrenched partisanship that they can't do their basic job, to provide relief to their citizens," Denney told the Union newspaper in Nevada County. LaMalfa improved his victory to 57%-43%; he lost Butte and Nevada by more narrow margins than in 2018.

CA-1: Northeast   **Cook Partisan Voting Index: R+11**

Population		Race and Ethnicity		Income	
Total	711,905	White	84.80%	Median Income	$61,433
Land area (sq. miles)	28,089	Black	1.60%	District Income Rank	240
Pop/ sq mi	25.34	Latino	15.30%	Poverty Rate	13.90%
Born in State	71.60%	Asian	3.00%	With health insurance	93.90%
		Two or more races	5.40%	Cash public assistance	3.10%
Age Groups		Other	5.20%	Food stamp/SNAP	10.00%
Under 18	20.30%				
18-34	21.90%	Education		Work	
35-64	36.60%	H.S grad or less	34.60%	White Collar	37.40%
Over 64	21.30%	Some college	39.60%	Sales and Service	40.70%
		College Degree, 4 yr	17.30%	Blue Collar	22.00%
Military		Post grad	8.50%	Government	20.10%
Veteran/ Active Duty	8.50%				

2020 Pres. Vote	Trump	203,646	(56%)	Biden	148,825	(41%)			
2016 Pres. Vote	Trump	176,358	(56%)	Clinton	114,727	(36%)	Johnson	14,110	(4%)
	Stein	7,501	(2%)						

Redding, Chico: Rising 14,000 feet over low foothills and the Central Valley, visible for 100 miles, is the snow-capped volcanic cone of Mount Shasta, one of a string of (supposedly) burnt-out volcanoes up and down the Pacific Coast. This is the far northern tier of California, where truck traffic on Interstate 5 is the only reminder of the choked metropolitan areas where most of the state's people live. This is lumber country mostly, where the mountains that rise on all sides—the Coast Range to the west, the Sierra Nevada to the east, the scattered mountains sealing off the Central Valley north of Redding—are thick with trees. It's rugged, flannel-shirt, two-lane-road country that was left behind economically when Los Angeles and San Francisco boomed after World War II. Since the 1980s, mostly young families have come here to raise their children in a small-town environment; retirees are looking for a calm atmosphere and low cost of living.

The 1st Congressional District of California is mountainous and mostly rural. It is the largest district in the state, with two major population areas. One is Redding in Shasta County, south of Mount Shasta, where increased high-altitude snowfall from Pacific Ocean moisture has allowed the Whitney Glacier to defy global warming trends by growing in the past century, the only glacier to do so and the longest glacier in the state. The second is farther south, at the edge of the Sierra foothills, around the Butte County communities of Paradise and Chico, home to a state university campus and Sierra Nevada Pale Ale, where the brewery is powered by a solar installation. Butte produces about 60 percent of the nation's almonds, with more than $6 billion in sales in 2019.

The area has suffered recent calamities. Following heavy rain and snow in 2017, the Oroville Dam, the tallest in the nation, developed a large hole that forced a shutdown of the spillway and resulted in $1.1 billion in repairs, including the equivalent of a new half-mile spillway. Despite initial objections, the Federal Emergency Management Agency in February 2020 paid an additional $170 million—as part of its total payment of $562 million. The incident resulted from poor design and maintenance; after it reopened in August 2019, officials were hopeful about the long-term prospects for the dam. In November 2018, the area surrounding Paradise in Butte County suffered the most devastating wildfire in California history, including the loss of 86 lives and more than 14,000 homes in what became known as the Camp fire. Officials were criticized for inadequate preparation, including the local evacuation plan. Pacific Gas and Electric was investigated for poor protection of its power equipment, which may have fueled what some called a "fire tornado." In September 2020, Butte County suffered more devastation from the North Complex fire in the Plumas National Forest, which was ignited by a lightning storm. The frequency raised fear about the area's long-term future.

The 1st District covers the northeast corner of California, sharing borders with Oregon and Nevada. Until 1980, the area elected rough-and-ready Democrats who pulled strings in Sacramento and Washington to build roads and dams. Since then, it has elected abstemious Republicans who have solidly conservative voting records and tend to local needs. The mountain areas, including Shasta County, have a stronger Republican lean. Butte and Nevada counties, which are on the southern border of the district, have nearly half of the population and lean Democratic. Donald Trump got 56 percent of the vote in each of his campaigns. In each case, this was his second-best district in the state, behind the Bakersfield-based 23rd District.

Jared Huffman (D)

Elected 2012, 5th term, b. Feb 18, 1964; Independence, MO; University of CA, Santa Barbara, B.A., 1986; Boston College Law School, J.S.D., 1990; Humanist; Married (Susan Huffman); 2 children.

Elected Office: Board member, Marin Municipal Water District, 1994- 2006; CA Assembly, 2006-2012.

Professional Career: Attorney, McCutchen, Doyle, Brown & Enersen, 1990-1992; Managing partner, Boyd, Huffman & Williams, 1992-1996; Managing partner, The Legal Solutions Group, 1996-2001; Sr. Attorney, Natural Resources Defense Cncl., 2001-2006.

DC Office: 1527 LHOB 20515, 202-225-5161, Fax: 202-225-5163, huffman.house.gov

State Offices: Eureka, 707-407-3585; Fort Bragg, 707-962-0933; Petaluma, 707-981-8967; San Rafael, 415-258-9657; Ukiah, 707-671-7449.

Committees: *Natural Resources*: Energy & Mineral Resources; Oversight & Investigations; Water, Oceans & Wildlife (Chmn). *Select Committee on the Climate Crisis. Transportation & Infrastructure*: Highways & Transit; Railroads, Pipelines & Hazardous Materials; Water Resources & Environment.

Group Ratings

	ADA	ACLU	AFL-CIO	LCV	COC	HAFA	ACU	CFG	FRC
2020	**	83%	**	100%	-	5%	5%	**	-
2019	100%	C	83%	100%	43%	C	5%	16%	5%

Almanac Ratings 2019-2020

	Economy	Social	Foreign	Composite
Liberal	58%	100%	57%	72%
Conservative	42%	0%	43%	28%

Key Votes of the 116th Congress

1. U.S./Mex./Can. trade deal N	5. Russia sanctions Y	9. Firearms background checks Y
2. First Coronavirus response Y	6. Troops in Syria Y	10. Spending at the border N
3. HEROES Act Y	7. Veto arms sales to Saudis Y	11. Marijuana liberalized rules Y
4. CASH Act Y	8. Defense $$$, veto override N	12. Electoral College objections N

Election Results

Election	Name (Party)	Vote (%)		Cand. Spent	Ind. Exp. Support	Ind. Exp. Oppose
2020 General	Jared Huffman (D)	294,435	(76%)	$523,100	$2,169	
	Dale Mensing (R)	94,320	(24%)	$20		$113
2020 Primary	Jared Huffman (D)	184,155	(68%)			
	Rachel Moniz (D)	20,609	(8%)			

Prior winning percentages: 2018 (77%), 2016 (77%), 2014 (75%), 2012 (71%)

Democrat Jared Huffman, first elected in 2012, has joined activist lawmakers in the California delegation and beyond. With his deep interest and expertise in resource issues, he has taken a leadership position at the Natural Resources Committee and has had policy impact with both partisan and bipartisan initiatives. With Democratic plans in 2021 to enact sweeping climate-change legislation, his chairmanship of the Water, Oceans and Wildlife Subcommittee positioned Huffman to be a leading proponent.

Huffman was born in President Harry Truman's hometown of Independence Missouri. He attended the University of California, Santa Barbara, on a volleyball scholarship, later becoming a three-time NCAA All-American. Huffman earned his law degree at Boston College and went to work on antitrust litigation at a San Francisco-based firm before opening his own practice. His interest in student athletics led to his work on Title IX cases, including a landmark case in which California State University agreed to guarantee gender equity in its men's and women's athletic programs.

In 1994, Huffman won a position on the board of the Marin Municipal Water District, which led to a job as a senior attorney on water and fisheries issues with the Natural Resources Defense Council. In 2006, he defeated a 14-year Marin County supervisor in the primary and was elected to the state Assembly, with a focus on environmental policy. During his three terms, he helped block efforts by Republican Gov. Arnold Schwarzenegger to construct a $356 million death row complex at San Quentin.

When he ran for the House in 2012, Huffman had the support of Democratic leaders and a celebrity endorsement from Mickey Hart, former drummer for the Grateful Dead. In California's jungle primary, eight Democrats split the progressive vote. Huffman finished first with 37 percent. In the general election, he defeated Republican Daniel Roberts, 71%-29%.

Huffman quickly showed his activist stripes on the Natural Resources panel, with an initial focus on his district's diverse interests—including fishing and forestry. The House approved his bill to add Mendocino public lands to the California Coastal National Monument, and he worked with Republican Jamie Herrera Beutler of Washington on their bill to sustain Pacific coast fishing communities by reducing interest rates for ground fish fishing boats.

On the Water subcommittee, which handles local projects that are vital to many lawmakers, Huffman said he has sought to tackle "the complex natural resource issues that we face in a constructive, problem-solving manner." He challenged what he described as "President Trump's radical agenda to expand dirty energy and undermine public health safeguards." In September 2019, the House passed Huffman's bill to ban drilling in Alaska's Arctic Natural Wildlife Refuge. The measure died in the Republican-controlled Senate.

In 2019, his seat on the Select Committee on the Climate Crisis gave Huffman an opportunity to work with other Democrats on the issue, though that panel lacked the authority to report legislation for House action. When the select committee issued its report in June 2020, he cited the need to address the economy, infrastructure and public health "if we are going to have a fighting chance to save our planet and build a more healthy, just, and resilient America."

Following the election of Joe Biden as president, Huffman said Democrats "expect to see new measures to protect land and water, reduce carbon emissions on public lands and waters, and work toward clean energy." On the Transportation and Infrastructure panel, he has filed a bill to replace the 18.4 cents-per-gallon federal tax on gasoline with a carbon tax, which might average about 50 cents per gallon and be designed to finance highway and transit improvements.

In 2017, Huffman said he was a humanist, or non-theist, and added, "I don't believe in God"— reportedly the second member of Congress ever to declare such a position. With Democratic Rep. Jamie Raskin of Maryland, he created the congressional Free thought Caucus. Its goals included "public policy formed on the basis of reason, science and moral values," and the promotion of the "secular character of our government by adhering to the strict constitutional principle of the separation of church and state." Huffman added that it was "preposterous" that witnesses were required to take an oath to God when they testify before congressional committees. Some panels have loosened the requirement, he said.

He has won reelection with minimal major-party opposition. Following the 2018 election, the Marin Independent Journal wrote that Huffman plans to be a "lifer" in the House and that his ambition is to chair the Natural Resources Committee. At his relatively young age, he is well on his way.

CA-2: Coastal North

Cook Partisan Voting Index: D+23

Population		Race and Ethnicity		Income	
Total	708,434	White	79.90%	Median Income	$80,051
Land area (sq. miles)	12,952	Black	1.80%	District Income Rank	91
Pop/ sq mi	54.7	Latino	18.20%	Poverty Rate	9.80%
Born in State	61.30%	Asian	3.90%	With health insurance	94.60%
		Two or more races	5.10%	Cash public assistance	2.00%
Age Groups		Other	9.20%	Food stamp/SNAP	6.10%
Under 18	19.20%				
18-34	18.80%	**Education**		**Work**	
35-64	39.60%	H.S grad or less	26.10%	White Collar	44.90%
Over 64	22.30%	Some college	31.30%	Sales and Service	38.90%
		College Degree, 4 yr	26.80%	Blue Collar	16.30%
Military		Post grad	15.90%	Government	14.20%
Veteran/ Active Duty	6.30%				

2020 Pres. Vote	Biden	294,489	(74%)	Trump	95,658	(24%)		
2016 Pres. Vote	Clinton	238,157	(68%)	Trump	80,545	(23%)	Johnson	12,239	(4%)
	Stein	12,778	(4%)					

Marin, Sonoma: The North Coast of California is unlike any other place in America. It is the only part of the lower 48 states first settled by Russians, who built Fort Ross in 1812. They sold it in 1841 to a Swiss pioneer named John Augustus Sutter; a Sutter employee's discovery of gold near Sacramento seven years later started the Gold Rush. It is the only part of the world with large numbers of redwood trees, shooting up hundreds of feet in the drizzly air. It is wet country, and for years it was one of America's prime lumbering areas. Coastal Eureka and smaller lumber towns are filled with filigreed Victorian houses and old mills, but also art galleries, hiking trails, pubs and waterfront hotels. The redwoods along the North Coast have survived recent widespread fires better than redwoods in the warmer, drier forests south of the Bay Area. The local seafood industry has suffered in recent years, due in part to warmer and more acidic ocean waters. With the decreased harvest, the price of Chinook salmon and Dungeness crab soared.

Humboldt County is known for its quality marijuana fields, and the local economy relies heavily on the product. One-third of licensed production in California is in Humboldt. The saturation of marijuana growers led to increased production and lower prices. In 2016, following state enactment of the Medical Marijuana Regulation and Safety Act, Humboldt passed its first law restricting commercial cannabis growing. In the following three years, the New Yorker reported in May 2019, prices dropped by more than half to below $1,000 per pound. In 2020, Forbes reported, wildfires forced hundreds of growers to evacuate their farms and reduce their harvest; as a result, prices increased.

Environmental groups have grown concerned about marijuana's impact on the region's salmon streams. The farms consume enormous amounts of water while also spilling pesticides, fertilizers and other products into the Eel and Klamath rivers, which historically have produced large salmon harvests. The problem has been compounded by California's extended drought and wildfires, plus the influx of young people who can get good pay and are eager to join in the harvest—typically from September to November. Some experts believe the weed industry in northern California eventually might rival the size of wine production. In Humboldt, that has moved the local industry toward "boutique" shops that cater to various tastes. In August 2019, a New York Times travel story described the "Lost Coast" in Humboldt as a largely road less shore that is "cold and foggy, even in summer, and just rough enough to keep all but the most intrepid day-trippers away."

The 2nd Congressional District of California runs from the Oregon border in the northwest corner of the state down through Marin County to San Francisco Bay. It includes all the coastal counties of Del Norte, Humboldt, Mendocino and Marin, which are connected by Highway 101, and inland Trinity County. The North Coast lumbering area, from Mendocino north, was once filled with rough-hewn working men, and was historically Democratic. Now the focus is on sustainable forestry and the area remains heavily Democratic, but with more socially liberal views. Del Norte and Trinity, the smallest in population, are Republican enclaves. The district takes in nearly half of Sonoma County, including Healdsburg, the Alexander Valley and Simi Winery, one of the oldest boutique wineries in the state. Nearly 40 percent of the voters are in upscale Marin, which identifies more with the Bay Area than with the North Coast. Joe Biden won Marin County in 2020 with a huge 82 percent of the vote. His overall 74%-24%, several percentage points higher than recent Democratic performance, made this area comparable to most Bay Area districts.

John Garamendi (D)

Elected 2009, 6th full term, b. Jan 24, 1945; Camp Blanding, FL; University of CA, Berkeley, B.A., 1966; Harvard Business School, M.B.A., 1970; Christian Church; Married (Patricia Wilkinson Garamendi); 6 children; 10 grandchildren.

Elected Office: CA Assembly, 1974-1976; CA Senate, 1976-1990; CA state ins. commissioner, 1991-1994, 2002-2006; CA Lt. Governor, 2007-2009.

Professional Career: U.S. Peace Corps, Ethiopia, 1966-1968; Deputy Secretary, U.S. Department of Interior, 1995-1998.

DC Office: 2368 RHOB 20515, 202-225-1880, Fax: 202-225-5914, garamendi.house.gov

State Offices: Davis, 530-753-5301; Fairfield, 707-438-1822.

Committees: *Armed Services*: Readiness (Chmn); Strategic Forces. *Transportation & Infrastructure*: Aviation; Economic Dev't, Public Buildings & Emergency Management; Highways & Transit; Water Resources & Environment.

Group Ratings

	ADA	ACLU	AFL-CIO	LCV	COC	HAFA	ACU	CFG	FRC
2020	**	80%	**	100%	-	0%	5%	**	-
2019	90%	C	100%	97%	63%	C	5%	12%	0%

Almanac Ratings 2019-2020

	Economy	Social	Foreign	Composite
Liberal	100%	100%	80%	94%
Conservative	0%	0%	20%	6%

Key Votes of the 116th Congress

1. U.S./Mex./Can. trade deal Y	5. Russia sanctions Y	9. Firearms background checks Y
2. First Coronavirus response Y	6. Troops in Syria Y	10. Spending at the border Y
3. HEROES Act Y	7. Veto arms sales to Saudis Y	11. Marijuana liberalized rules Y
4. CASH Act Y	8. Defense $$$, veto override Y	12. Electoral College objections N

Election Results

Election	Name (Party)	Vote (%)	Cand. Spent	Ind. Exp. Support	Ind. Exp. Oppose
2020 General	John Garamendi (D)	176,043 (55%)	$561,726	$2,053	
	Tamika Hamilton (R)	145,945 (45%)	$443,050		
2020 Primary	John Garamendi (D)	110,504 (59%)			

Prior winning percentages: 2018 (58%), 2016 (59%), 2014 (53%), 2012 (54%), 2010 (59%), 2009 special (53%)

John Garamendi is one of the House's most politically seasoned Democrats, with a public service career spanning more than 40 years. An active legislator, with committee interests in military and transportation issues, he has adjusted to redistricting changes in 2011 that made his district more competitive, but still safely Democratic. His experience has given him independence and an outspoken style, including his criticism of President Donald Trump.

Garamendi was raised on his family's cattle ranch in Calaveras County. At the University of California, Berkeley, he was an All-American offensive lineman in football and a competitive wrestler. After graduating, he joined the Peace Corps and served in Ethiopia, where his wife, Patti, also was a volunteer. The experience launched his career in public service. In 1974, he won his first campaign to the state Assembly. Two years later, he was elected to the state Senate, where he eventually became majority leader. During his career, he did two stints as the state's insurance commissioner and was President Bill Clinton's deputy secretary of Interior. He failed twice in bids to become governor of California. In the 2006 Democratic primary for lieutenant governor, Garamendi narrowly defeated Jackie Speier. He went on to beat Republican Tom McClintock. Garamendi was planning to seek an open seat for governor in 2010 when Ellen Tauscher resigned from the House to become President Barack Obama's undersecretary of State.

In the special election in September 2009, state Sen. Mark DeSaulnier was better-known locally and gained endorsements from prominent Democrats. Garamendi, who had higher name ID from his statewide campaigns, was endorsed by Clinton and former Vice President Al Gore. In the all-party primary, Garamendi prevailed among Democrats, with 26 percent to DeSaulnier's 18 percent. In the runoff, Republican attorney David Harmer, though competitive financially, faced an uphill battle in a suburban San Francisco district. Garamendi embraced Obama's agenda while Harmer opposed the president and his bailouts of the financial and auto industries. Garamendi won 53%-43%. DeSaulnier later was elected to the House from the adjacent 11th District.

In the House, Garamendi has been an ardent environmentalist. He was among the strongest critics of offshore oil drilling in the wake of the 2010 BP oil spill in the Gulf of Mexico, pressing to bar new federal drilling leases off the Pacific coast. He was outspoken in opposing Democratic Gov. Jerry Brown's plan to build two 35-mile tunnels to pipe Sierra Nevada snowmelt to San Joaquin Valley farms and Southern California cities. He called the proposal "a boondoggle" for the benefit of wealthy farmers and said it "wouldn't create a drop of new water for the state and would serve only to reignite the California water wars." Brown failed to gain final state and federal approval.

On Transportation and Infrastructure, as the ranking minority member of the Coast Guard and Maritime Transportation Subcommittee, Garamendi sought to enhance farm and manufacturing exports. He had some Republican support for his bill to support the maritime industry by requiring that a share of strategic energy exports be shipped on U.S.-flagged vessels—subsidies that critics have called boondoggles. But the GOP-controlled House did not act on the proposal. He helped win enactment in a water-resources bill of a measure to restore parts of the Lake Tahoe area. His Almanac vote ratings have placed him toward the center of the House in each of the three issue areas.

With his seniority on the Armed Services Committee, Garamendi chairs the Readiness Subcommittee. In February 2020, when Trump proposed taking $3.8 billion from military accounts to pay to build the wall on the southern border, Garamendi called it "grossly irresponsible" to "raid money that is necessary to support and defend our nation for his vanity wall." In the defense spending bill in 2020, he claimed credit for provisions to help the military reduce its greenhouse gas emissions, and address contamination and health risks at military installations. He also included steps to bolster the U.S. maritime fleet, a longtime interest.

Garamendi was a harsh critic of Trump. In broadcast interviews, he said Trump saw himself "as a dictator, as above the law," that "he has no empathy." In November 2019, he made an early endorsement of Joe Biden in the presidential campaign. "We have seen the most divisive president ever, ever in our history, really tearing us apart," Garamendi told CNN. "We got to end that. Joe Biden can do that better than any other person that is running for president."

California's independent redistricting commission in 2011 put Garamendi's residence in a district where 77 percent of voters were new to him, making him ripe for a GOP challenge. In the June 2012 primary, he got 51 percent of the vote, setting up a contest with Republican Kim Vann, a Colusa County supervisor. Vann refused to sign the Republicans' no-tax pledge and embraced popular provisions in Obama's health care law. The U.S. Chamber of Commerce spent $600,000 on her behalf. Garamendi won with 54 percent, precisely the district's vote for Obama. In the 2014 campaign, Assemblyman Dan Logue opposed a minimum-wage hike and comprehensive immigration reform. Garamendi supported both, plus high-speed rail for California. Garamendi had a fundraising advantage: $1.3 million to $800,000 and got 52.7 percent, his lowest reelection vote.

In 2020, Garamendi had an unexpectedly close contest with Tamika Hamilton, who served 14 years as a sergeant in the Air Force and was based at Travis Air Force Base. In her first political campaign, Hamilton cited the need for improved housing—both military and civilian. Although outspent, she was competitive with her $440,000. After Garamendi won the three-way primary with 59 percent, Hamilton held him to 55 percent in November. Hamilton took the five outlying counties, but Garamendi ran up the vote in the three suburban counties.

Depending on its new boundaries, Garamendi could find that redistricting poses new challenges. But this veteran politician has shown survivor skills and seems likely to end his career in the House on his terms.

CA-3: North Central   Cook Partisan Voting Index: D+5

Population		Race and Ethnicity		Income	
Total	755,811	White	68.70%	Median Income	$73,191
Land area (sq. miles)	6,184	Black	6.30%	District Income Rank	141
Pop/ sq mi	122.23	Latino	30.20%	Poverty Rate	12.80%
Born in State	63.70%	Asian	11.30%	With health insurance	94.40%
		Two or more races	6.60%	Cash public assistance	3.00%
Age Groups		Other	7.10%	Food stamp/SNAP	9.70%
Under 18	22.90%				
18-34	26.50%	Education		Work	
35-64	36.00%	H.S grad or less	37.70%	White Collar	34.50%
Over 64	14.80%	Some college	35.20%	Sales and Service	39.70%
		College Degree, 4 yr	17.00%	Blue Collar	25.70%
Military		Post grad	10.20%	Government	21.20%
Veteran/ Active Duty	9.20%				

2020 Pres. Vote	Biden	179,806	(55%)	Trump	139,735	(43%)			
2016 Pres. Vote	Clinton	138,882	(52%)	Trump	105,860	(40%)	Johnson	11,300	(4%)

Western Sacramento Suburbs, Solano: In California's Central Valley, north and west of Sacramento, are the farm counties of Colusa, Sutter and Yuba. Marysville, the county seat of Yuba County, sits on the east bank of the Feather River. This heavily agricultural region includes locally cultivated rice hybrids from Colusa County, the leading rice-producing county in the nation. Sutter County is the nation's largest producer of prunes and the third-largest producer of walnuts. The local farm economy has suffered in recent years and Colusa County has lost thousands of farm jobs with scant recovery. Passage of a state water bond plus approval of a federal loan have been steps toward construction of the giant Sites Reservoir in Colusa. In May 2020, during the coronavirus crisis, Sutter and Yuba officials defied the shutdown orders of Gov. Gavin Newsom and permitted some local businesses to reopen. Newsom said they were making "a big mistake." In December, 20 percent of Sutter's residents were testing positive for COVID-19, the highest in California; the situation was "dire," said the counties' health official.

Solano County, which is about midway between the Bay Area and Sacramento, has been thriving economically as an exurban commuter locale and styles itself as "a place of opportunity." The Yuba City area has one of the largest Sikh populations in the United States, with a temple that serves more than 20,000. The city refers to itself as "the mini-Punjab". Davis is home to a branch of the University of California, with an activist liberal faculty and student body. The university, with nearly 40,000 students, has been ranked the best in the world for its veterinary and forensic science programs.

The 3rd Congressional District of California includes Republican-leaning areas like Colusa, Sutter and Yuba counties, along with a large portion of more Democratic Lake County closer to the wine country. Solano and adjacent Yolo counties, which include about 40 and 25 percent of the district, respectively, are comfortably Democratic. To the west are Fairfield and Vacaville, on the outskirts of the Bay Area. Fairfield is home to Travis Air Force Base, which has more than 14,000 personnel and is home to the military's airlift and aerial refueling, including the KC-46A tanker. Politically, the rural counties have made the 3rd more competitive than most districts in northern California. In 2020, Joe Biden led in the district, 55%-43%.

Tom McClintock (R)

Elected 2008, 7th term, b. Jul 10, 1956; Bronxville, NY; University of CA, Los Angeles, B.S., 1978; Baptist; Married (Lori McClintock); 2 children.

Elected Office: CA Assembly, 1982-1992, 1996-2000; CA Senate, 2000-2008.

Professional Career: Newspaper columnist, journalist, public policy analyst.

DC Office: 2312 RHOB 20515, 202-225-2511, Fax: 202-225-5444, mcclintock.house.gov

State Offices: Roseville, 916-786-5560.

Committees: *Budget. Judiciary*: Constitution, Civil Rights & Civil Liberties; Immigration & Citizenship (RMM). *Natural Resources*: National Parks, Forests & Public Lands; Water, Oceans & Wildlife.

Group Ratings

	ADA	ACLU	AFL-CIO	LCV	COC	HAFA	ACU	CFG	FRC
2020	**	20%	**	0%	-	94%	99%	**	-
2019	0%	C	19%	3%	61%	C	99%	100%	91%

Almanac Ratings 2019-2020

	Economy	Social	Foreign	Composite
Liberal	25%	25%	8%	20%
Conservative	75%	75%	92%	80%

Key Votes of the 116th Congress

1. U.S./Mex./Can. trade deal	Y	5. Russia sanctions	N	9. Firearms background checks	N
2. First Coronavirus response	N	6. Troops in Syria	N	10. Spending at the border	Y
3. HEROES Act	N	7. Veto arms sales to Saudis	N	11. Marijuana liberalized rules	Y
4. CASH Act	N	8. Defense $$$, veto override	N	12. Electoral College objections	N

Election Results

Election	Name (Party)	Vote (%)		Cand. Spent	Ind. Exp. Support	Ind. Exp. Oppose
2020 General	Tom McClintock (R)	247,291	(56%)	$2,008,916	$813	$148,892
	Brynne Kennedy (D)	194,731	(44%)	$3,017,407	$7,545	$211,188
2020 Primary	Tom McClintock (R)	141,244	(51%)			

Prior winning percentages: 2018 (54%), 2016 (63%), 2014 (60%), 2012 (61%), 2010 (61%), 2008 (50%)

Republican Tom McClintock, who was first elected in 2008, has been a conservative leader in California for decades, actively espousing his limited-government views. In contrast to tea party and other junior House Republicans, he has spent most of his career in public office and he often deliberately pursues a separate course from the self-styled outsiders. His legislative accomplishments have been limited.

McClintock spent his early childhood in White Plains New York. After graduating from the University of California, Los Angeles, he worked briefly as a political columnist and a state Senate aide before winning a seat in the California Assembly at age 26. From his earliest days in the legislature, McClintock was perhaps its most vocal, if not the most effective, budget hawk, railing against tax increases and high spending under Democratic and Republican administrations alike. Supporters saw an eloquent champion of conservative ideas, a policy wonk with a penchant for quoting Abraham Lincoln.

McClintock tested the limits of his statewide appeal in an increasingly liberal California through a relentless but unsuccessful effort to win higher office. He ran for state controller in 1994 and again in 2002, narrowly losing each time. In 2006, he was defeated as his party's nominee for lieutenant governor, even as Republican Gov. Arnold Schwarzenegger sailed to reelection. No race elevated McClintock's profile in the state as much as his quixotic campaign for governor in the 2003 recall election. As star-struck Republicans backed Schwarzenegger, McClintock forged ahead, presenting himself as the true Republican. He finished with 13 percent.

Opportunity struck again for McClintock in 2008. He ran in an intense primary for an open seat against former Rep. Doug Ose, a Republican moderate who had held the neighboring district's seat. Ose, who also lived outside the district, attacked McClintock as a career politician and carpetbagger who had represented the Thousand Oaks area in southern California in the legislature. McClintock branded Ose as a liberal who had voted to raise taxes and earmarked millions of dollars for federal projects in his district. McClintock won the primary 54%-39%.In November, he faced Democrat Charlie Brown, a retired Air Force officer who renewed criticism of McClintock as an opportunist who didn't live in the district. His win was unexpectedly close, 50.2%-49.8%.

McClintock has been a faithful conservative vote, though occasionally nettlesome to GOP leaders. He promised to eschew spending earmarks for his district and called for the earmarking process to be abolished. He consistently filed amendments to slash funding, even when Republicans controlled the House. He joined Democratic Rep. Jared Huffman of California to pass an amendment to strike a provision that required U.S. military bases in Europe to burn anthracite coal from Pennsylvania. In September 2015, a few days before Speaker John Boehner resigned, McClintock quit the House Freedom Caucus because its tactics "thwarted vital conservative policy objectives and unwittingly become Nancy Pelosi's tactical ally."

On the Natural Resources Committee, McClintock chaired the Water and Power Subcommittee for four years. He complained that about half of the state's water supply is consumed to meet various environmental regulations. In 2017, he filed a bill to streamline the process for federal approval of dams. He praised the Trump administration for its October 2018 executive action to prioritize expanded water storage in California. From 2015 to 2018, he chaired the Federal Lands Subcommittee, which has jurisdiction over national forests and parks. The House passed his bill to speed emergency timber salvage as a tool to reduce fire hazards on federal lands.

McClintock was one of 13 Republicans to vote against House passage of the tax-cut bill in December 2017. He reversed course on the final deal after he was satisfied with changes that expanded the availability of the deduction for state and local taxes. In May 2018, he ran for chairman of the Republican Study Committee, the longtime forum for House conservatives. He lost to first-term Rep. Mike Johnson of Louisiana.

McClintock showed his libertarian instincts when he backed legislation to legalize marijuana. Current laws "are doing more harm than good," he told the San Francisco Chronicle in 2019. In the same interview, he dismissed impeachment charges against President Donald Trump. "I realize that the president is certainly ham-handed in a lot of the things he does. He is not a skilled diplomat," he said. But he saw no problem with Trump's requests to the president of Ukraine "even if they were cringe-worthy in the way they were worded." During the coronavirus, he objected to requirements that he wear a mask. "I consider masks much more effective at spreading panic and much less effective at stopping a virus," he said at a Judiciary Committee meeting in June 2020.

When House Democrats again impeached Trump in January 2021 for inciting violence at the Capitol, McClintock told the Los Angeles Times that they were trivializing the constitutional prerogative. "I cannot think of a more petty, vindictive and gratuitous act than to impeach an already defeated president a week before he is to leave office."

McClintock was challenged in the 2014 primary by a moderate Republican who criticized him as too conservative. Art Moore, a West Point graduate who worked on intelligence issues as a consultant, complained about gridlock and dysfunction in Washington and said competition was good for the GOP. McClintock took the primary, 56%-23%. In November, McClintock got 60 percent.

In 2018, he faced his first credible Democratic challenger. Jessica Morse, a political newcomer and former State Department aide, called McClintock "a career politician" who followed the party line. McClintock said Morse supported the liberal agenda, including "Medicare for all." Morse spent $3.7 million, twice as much as the incumbent. McClintock won, 54%-46%, the closest victory of his career. Two years later, he faced another well-financed first-time candidate: Brynne Kennedy, the founder of a successful software company. She outspent McClintock, $3 million to $2 million. He won, 56%-44%, taking all but two small counties.

The two latest contests suggested potential problems for McClintock, including redistricting uncertainties in the Sacramento area, which has four Democratic-held districts. In 2021, he became ranking minority member of the Immigration and Citizenship Subcommittee.

CA-4: East Central

Cook Partisan Voting Index: R+8

Population		Race and Ethnicity		Income	
Total	757,806	White	84.40%	Median Income	$86,374
Land area (sq. miles)	12,836	Black	1.70%	District Income Rank	68
Pop/ sq mi	59.04	Latino	13.10%	Poverty Rate	8.40%
Born in State	65.60%	Asian	5.90%	With health insurance	95.10%
		Two or more races	4.60%	Cash public assistance	1.70%
Age Groups		Other	3.30%	Food stamp/SNAP	5.80%
Under 18	20.50%				
18-34	17.00%	**Education**		**Work**	
35-64	40.40%	H.S grad or less	27.90%	White Collar	43.70%
Over 64	22.20%	Some college	36.70%	Sales and Service	39.20%
		College Degree, 4 yr	23.70%	Blue Collar	17.00%
Military		Post grad	11.50%	Government	16.70%
Veteran/ Active Duty	9.10%				

2020 Pres. Vote	Trump	240,869	(54%)	Biden	197,157	(44%)		
2016 Pres. Vote	Trump	190,924	(53%)	Clinton	138,790	(39%)	Johnson	17,650 (5%)

Northern Sacramento Suburbs, Madera: California sprang into existence with the Gold Rush of 1849. Statehood and the creation of the first 27 counties followed in 1850. The new state's first boom area was the Mother Lode Country in the foothills of the Sierra Nevada above Sacramento. Mining camps the size of Eastern cities grew up almost overnight in vacant valleys locked amid steep hills, with thousands of would-be millionaires gathered to find gold. Most of those who actually got rich did so by providing goods and services that catered to miners' needs. In Placerville, John Studebaker had a buggy shop, Philip Armour ran a butcher shop, and Mark Hopkins had a dry goods store. The biggest mine in California was in Grass Valley in 1857 and was worked for half a century. But long before that, most of the Mother Lode Country emptied out, leaving ghost towns and villages with hundreds of deserted houses, an antique vacation country left behind in time.

The area has been resurrected as a booming exurban and tourist mecca. Thousands of Californians —many of them families from smog-filled, middle-class suburbs of the Los Angeles Basin and the San Francisco Bay Area—went looking for a more pleasant, small-town, orderly environment and found it along fast-flowing creeks where the '49ers camped. Placer County, which includes Sacramento suburbs and part of the Mother Lode Country, grew 14 percent from 2010 to 2019, among the most rapid in California. It also ranks among its wealthiest counties, with a median household income nearly 20 percent above the state average. The Mother Lode "offers modern-day prospectors an intriguing pastiche of bed-and-breakfast inns, musty antique stores and such blink-and-you'll-miss-'em outposts as Volcano, Fiddletown, and Rough and Ready," USA Today reported.

Developers have begun work in Placers' Vineyards, a 5,230-acre master planned community projected to include more than 14,000 homes just west of Roseville, which will include commercial centers, business parks and schools. Critics fear continuing development will make Placer an extension of Sacramento. A swath of the district has a large elderly population. In Amador, Calaveras, and Tuolumne counties, senior citizens make up 25 percent of the population, twice the state average.

The 4th Congressional District of California takes in the Mother Lode counties of Mariposa and Tuolumne and a large share of Yosemite National Park. Placer County is the population center. With neighboring El Dorado County, it includes 70 percent of the district in the suburbs and exurbs east of Sacramento. Many residents are concentrated in Sacramento suburbs like Roseville, which has grown 19 percent since 2010. The 4th was Mitt Romney's third-best district in California, when he won 58%-40%. Donald Trump took the district, with 53 percent and then 54 percent.

Mike Thompson (D)

Elected 1998, 12th term, b. Jan 24, 1951; St. Helena, CA; CA State University, Chico, B.A., 1982; CA State University, Chico, M.A., 1996; Roman Catholic; Married (Janet Thompson); 2 children; 3 grandchildren.

Military Career: U.S. Army 1967-1973 (Vietnam)

Elected Office: CA Senate, 1990-1998.

Professional Career: Supervisor, Beringer Winery; CA Assembly fellow, 1982-1983; Chief of Staff, CA Assemblyman Lou Papan, 1984-1987; Chief of Staff, CA Assemblywoman Jackie Speier, 1987-1990; Owner, vineyard.

DC Office: 406 CHOB 20515, 202-225-3311, Fax: 202-225-4335, mikethompson.house.gov

State Offices: Napa, 707-226-9898; Santa Rosa, 707-542-7182; Vallejo, 707-645-1888.

Committees: *Joint Taxation. Ways & Means*: Health; Select Revenue Measures (Chmn).

Group Ratings

	ADA	ACLU	AFL-CIO	LCV	COC	HAFA	ACU	CFG	FRC
2020	**	79%	**	100%	-	0%	7%	**	-
2019	95%	C	100%	90%	66%	C	7%	13%	0%

Almanac Ratings 2019-2020

	Economy	Social	Foreign	Composite
Liberal	100%	100%	80%	94%
Conservative	0%	0%	20%	6%

Key Votes of the 116th Congress

1. U.S./Mex./Can. trade deal Y	5. Russia sanctions Y	9. Firearms background checks Y
2. First Coronavirus response Y	6. Troops in Syria Y	10. Spending at the border Y
3. HEROES Act Y	7. Veto arms sales to Saudis Y	11. Marijuana liberalized rules Y
4. CASH Act Y	8. Defense $$$, veto override Y	12. Electoral College objections N

Election Results

Election	Name (Party)	Vote (%)		Cand. Spent	Ind. Exp. Support	Ind. Exp. Oppose
2020 General	Mike Thompson (D)............................ 271,233	(76%)		$1,748,773	$2,166	
	Scott Giblin (R)..................................... 85,227	(24%)				$113
2020 Primary	Mike Thompson (D)........................... 146,980	(68%)				
	John Wesley Tyler (D)......................... 20,725	(10%)				

Prior winning percentages: 2018 (79%), 2016 (77%), 2014 (76%), 2012 (75%), 2010 (63%), 2008 (68%), 2006 (66%), 2004 (67%), 2002 (64%), 2000 (65%), 1998 (62%)

Democrat Mike Thompson, first elected in 1998, has a moderate voting record that has been among the least liberal of coastal Californians. As a senior member of the Ways and Means Committee, he chairs the Subcommittee on Select Revenue Measures, which is the starting point for tax legislation. Thompson, who watches out for the interests of the wine industry, is a trusted ally of Speaker Nancy Pelosi and a major fundraiser for his party.

Thompson grew up in the Napa Valley town of St. Helena, dropped out of high school, served in the Army in Vietnam, and earned a Purple Heart. Later, he got bachelor's and master's degrees from what is now California State University, Chico. He owned a vineyard and worked as a maintenance supervisor for Beringer, a big winery in the valley. From 1984 to 1990, he was chief of staff to two Assembly members from the Bay Area. In 1990, he was elected to the state Senate, where he chaired the Budget Committee.

In 1998, Thompson ran for the House seat of Republican Frank Riggs, who planned to challenge Democratic Sen. Barbara Boxer that year. Thompson faced weak opposition and had support from almost every interest group that matters in the district: unions, medical providers, vintners, oil and timber interests, environmental advocates, law enforcement groups and fishermen. His issue stands —opposition to oil drilling off the California coast, support of abortion rights and the death penalty —were broadly popular. He won the primary 78%-22% and the general election 62%-33%.

As an active member of Ways and Means, he has been a proponent for the wine industry and other rural interests in California. He enacted a tax break for landowners who place their land under conservation easements, a way to preserve farmland. As co-chairman of the Congressional Wine Caucus, he has battled with allies of beer and alcohol wholesalers over a bill giving states new power to restrict sales over the internet. In 2016, he introduced a bipartisan bill to reduce the excise tax on sparkling wine to the rate charged for still wine. The Republican tax bill that was enacted in 2017, which Thompson opposed, included his provision to increase access to tax credits for large wineries, plus beer and liquor distributors. On another local farm issue, Thompson filed with neighboring Democratic Rep. Jared Huffman a bill to strengthen criminal penalties for illegal marijuana farms.

As chairman of the Select Revenue Measures Subcommittee in 2019-20, Thompson filed bills affecting various economic sectors and tax benefits, including: removal of the cap on state and local tax deductions in high-tax states, expansion of renewable energy by promoting clean energy technologies, and reimbursement of insurance carriers that voluntarily pay business interruption claims tied to the coronavirus.

Thompson has joined both the centrist New Democrats and the Blue Dog Coalition. He has agreed with Republicans on the need to abolish the estate tax, which he said unfairly burdens family farms. In 2016, the House passed his Small Business Health Care Relief Act to provide protections for tax benefits under health reimbursement arrangements, despite conflicts with the Affordable Care Act. The measure became part of the 21st Century Cures Act, which was enacted that year.

He remains a reliable lieutenant for Pelosi. She tapped him to coordinate redistricting efforts for Democrats following the 2010 census. Following the deadly school massacre in Newtown Connecticut in December 2012, she named Thompson, a hunter and former chair of the Congressional Sportsmen's Caucus, to head a House Democratic task force to develop a response on gun issues. His proposals, which went nowhere in the Republican-controlled House, included steps to close the internet and gun-show loopholes in existing rules and expand background checks to all gun sales.

When Democrats regained House control in 2019, he said the American public "demanded action to help end the tragedy of gun violence…and we will deliver." On Feb. 27, the House passed its broadest gun-control measure in a quarter-century on a largely party-line vote. The bill died in the Republican-controlled Senate.

Thompson has been easily reelected and has been popular throughout the varied parts of his district. With Pelosi likely stepping down as Speaker by 2022, Thompson faces a decision on whether to retire with her or keep his influential committee niche.

CA-5: Wine Country   Cook Partisan Voting Index: D+22

Population		Race and Ethnicity		Income	
Total	726,072	White	62.50%	Median Income	$85,856
Land area (sq. miles)	1,731	Black	6.60%	District Income Rank	69
Pop/ sq mi	419.5	Latino	28.90%	Poverty Rate	7.80%
Born in State	61.30%	Asian	11.70%	With health insurance	94.10%
		Two or more races	5.60%	Cash public assistance	1.70%
Age Groups		Other	13.60%	Food stamp/SNAP	5.50%
Under 18	20.10%				
18-34	21.20%	**Education**		**Work**	
35-64	39.80%	H.S grad or less	33.00%	White Collar	38.50%
Over 64	18.90%	Some college	33.70%	Sales and Service	39.80%
		College Degree, 4 yr	20.90%	Blue Collar	21.80%
Military		Post grad	12.40%	Government	14.40%
Veteran/ Active Duty	5.80%				

2020 Pres. Vote	Biden	264,128	(72%)	Trump	92,096	(25%)			
2016 Pres. Vote	Clinton	210,950	(68%)	Trump	74,088	(24%)	Johnson	11,171	(4%)
	Stein	7,681	(3%)						

Sonoma, Napa: In sunny valleys sealed off from the Coast Range, some of the nation's premium wine grapes are grown on ridges. Three decades ago, there were only 20 wineries in Napa Valley. Today there are several hundred, with more just west of the ridges in Sonoma County. In Napa, more than 1,000 brands generate a total of about $50 billion in annual revenue. In January 2020, a financial expert told the Napa Valley Register that the area had become "over-supplied" and the market was trending toward premium labels. The tourism industry in Sonoma County has had double-digit annual increases, with more marketing of the region to foreign tourists, including boutique hotels and high-end wine tastings. In Napa, the emphasis has turned from the vineyards to bottling and tourism; in 2014, more than two-thirds of the grapes used for wine were from outside the county. Olive trees are also grown here. Santa Rosa, wine country's largest city, is increasingly upscale and laborers have become hard-pressed to find housing.

In October 2017, a horrendous wildfire was the most destructive ever to that time, with the loss of 3,000 homes in Santa Rosa and damage to the wineries—including from smoke. Devastating fires continued in wine country as the annual "new normal." The Kincade fire of 2019 evolved to the Lightning Complex fire of 2020. Wine country had become the "epicenter" of wildfires, the Los Angeles Times headlined in September 2020. In Sonoma, officials responded in 2019 to the largest homeless camps in county history. Experts have cited the climate change impact of dry heat as a major factor.

Vallejo is named for a Mexican general and early member of the California Senate. From 1853 to 1996, the city was the site of the giant Mare Island Naval Shipyard, where 41,000 people worked during World War II. After the shipyard closed, Vallejo filed for bankruptcy in 2008, a dire turn of events also blamed on the huge public employee salaries and pensions the city was paying—292 of 411 city workers earned more than $100,000 a year. Although it emerged from bankruptcy, the city retained huge pension costs. Since the crisis, Vallejo has become one of the hottest real-estate markets in the nation and a popular housing alternative for young professionals to the prohibitively expensive San Francisco. The Hub, a new art gallery and event space, attracts visitors. Commuters can take a one-hour ferry ride from the municipal marina to the Embarcadero, instead of the two-hour commute during rush hour. Sol Trans offers express bus service from Vallejo to the El Cerrito stop on BART's Red Line. Some of the shipyard's huge dry docks remain in operation for ship repair.

The 5th Congressional District includes all of Napa County and parts of Contra Costa, Lake, Vallejo-based Solano and Sonoma counties. Sonoma is the population center, with about 40 percent of the district, with another 20 percent each in Napa and Solano. All these areas are heavily Democratic, more akin to the Bay Area than to farm country, and the district is unlikely to be competitive any time soon. Joe Biden in 2020 took the district, 72%-25%. The Democratic vote in all of Sonoma increased to 75 percent from 70 percent for Hillary Clinton.

Doris Matsui (D)

Elected 2005, 8th full term, b. Sep 25, 1944; Poston, AZ; University of CA, Berkeley, B.A., 1966; Methodist; Widow (Robert Matsui); 1 child ; 2 grandchildren.

Professional Career: Transition team, President-elect Bill Clinton, 1992-1993; Deputy Assistant to the President, deputy Director of public liaison, White House, 1993-1998; Lobbyist, 1998-2005.

DC Office: 2311 RHOB 20515, 202-225-7163, Fax: 202-225-0566, matsui.house.gov

State Offices: Sacramento, 916-498-5600.

Committees: *Energy & Commerce*: Communications & Technology; Energy; Health. *Natural Resources*: Water, Oceans & Wildlife.

Group Ratings

	ADA	ACLU	AFL-CIO	LCV	COC	HAFA	ACU	CFG	FRC
2020	**	81%	**	100%	-	0%	2%	**	-
2019	95%	C	100%	97%	57%	C	2%	13%	0%

Almanac Ratings 2019-2020

	Economy	Social	Foreign	Composite
Liberal	100%	100%	80%	94%
Conservative	0%	0%	20%	6%

Key Votes of the 116th Congress

1. U.S./Mex./Can. trade deal Y	5. Russia sanctions Y	9. Firearms background checks Y
2. First Coronavirus response Y	6. Troops in Syria Y	10. Spending at the border Y
3. HEROES Act Y	7. Veto arms sales to Saudis Y	11. Marijuana liberalized rules Y
4. CASH Act Y	8. Defense $$$, veto override Y	12. Electoral College objections N

Election Results

Election	Name (Party)	Vote (%)	Cand. Spent	Ind. Exp. Support	Ind. Exp. Oppose
2020 General	Doris Matsui (D)	229,648 (73%)	$828,736	$2,166	
	Chris Bish (R)	83,466 (27%)	$43,398		$113
2020 Primary	Doris Matsui (D)	119,408 (70%)			
	Benjamin Emard (D)	13,253 (8%)			

Prior winning percentages: 2018 (80%), 2016 (75%), 2014 (73%), 2012 (75%), 2010 (72%), 2008 (74%), 2006 (71%), 2005 special (68%)

Democrat Doris Matsui, after winning a special election in 2005 to replace her late husband, Robert Matsui, has matched his legislative prowess with a choice seat on the Energy and Commerce Committee, where she has had an impact on health and communications policy. Although she does not attract much attention, she has been skillful in identifying issues and building coalitions to address them.

Matsui, who was born in a Japanese internment camp in Arizona, was a well-known political figure during her husband's career in Congress. She grew up in Dinuba in Fresno County and graduated from the University of California, Berkeley. In Sacramento, she chaired the board of the local public television station and participated in many civic organizations. After working on Bill Clinton's presidential campaign, she joined his transition team, then served as deputy director of public liaison, where she worked on economic and budget issues. When she left the White House in 1998, she became a senior adviser at a Washington law firm.

Robert Matsui, who was a senior member of the Ways and Means Committee, died of complications from a rare blood disorder in January 2005, after serving 13 terms. A few days after his memorial services, Doris Matsui announced that she would run in the special election. None of Matsui's 10 opponents in the nonpartisan contest had significant political experience or name recognition. She emphasized her support for local water projects and her opposition to President George W. Bush's proposal for personal retirement accounts in Social Security. Some called the contest a "coronation," but the lack of competition surely reflected the respect the Matsuis had won over the years. She won the all-party primary with 68 percent of the vote to 9 percent for the runner-up. Since then, she has not faced a competitive major-party challenger.

With her seat on Energy and Commerce, she has taken the initiative on telecommunications and consumer issues. In 2015, she filed a bill that would ban companies from charging more for faster internet access. After Trump administration officials at the Federal Communications Commission overturned what had become "net neutrality" rules, Matsui sought to revive the earlier policy and reiterated her calls for "the free and open internet."

As co-chair of the Congressional Spectrum Caucus, Matsui has proposed steps for the next generation of broadband networks and she has enacted measures to facilitate the auction of parts of the federal spectrum. With Republican Rep. Brett Guthrie of Kentucky, who also serves on Energy and Commerce, she enacted a bill in 2020that prohibited the use of federal funds to purchase telecommunications equipment from companies deemed national security threats and required the Federal Communications Commission to prepare a list of companies that posed such risks to telecom companies. The measure was directed at the Chinese telecom group Huawei, among others. With Guthrie, she also filed a bill that year to finance the Commerce Department's support for the deployment and use of 5G networks in the United States.

She has filed legislation to remove roadblocks to health care technology. In 2016, Congress enacted legislation she filed with Republican Rep. Mike Burgess of Texas: the Expanding Capacity for Health Outcomes (ECHO) Act, which was designed to use technology to provide expertise in community health centers and among other providers in underserved areas. Matsui has sought to expand the community-based mental health system, including her proposal for certified community behavioral health centers. During the coronavirus pandemic, she said one "silver lining" would be expansion of tele health opportunities.

Matsui co-chaired the Congressional Caucus on Women's Issues, where she helped to enact the Human Trafficking Prevention, Intervention, and Recovery Act of 2015.On environmental issues, she has co-chaired the Sustainable Energy and Environmental Coalition to address climate change.

Matsui sometimes invokes her family's experience in internment camps to warn of potential civil liberties abuses. Following the election of Donald Trump, she criticized his call for restrictions on immigration from Muslim-majority countries. "Casting a shadow on everyone, not just individuals doing these bad things, is not the American way," she told the Sacramento Bee. "We are a nation of immigrants inviting people from all over the world." In 2019, she called "unconscionable" a proposal from Trump to pay for the wall on the border with Mexico, in part, with funds set aside for flood protection in Sacramento. "These previously allocated funds should not be diverted to fulfill an unpopular campaign promise," Matsui said.

CA-6: Sacramento   Cook Partisan Voting Index: D+21

Population		Race and Ethnicity		Income	
Total	781,943	White	49.60%	Median Income	$64,687
Land area (sq. miles)	175	Black	11.80%	District Income Rank	212
Pop/ sq mi	4,467.22	Latino	29.90%	Poverty Rate	15.50%
Born in State	62.10%	Asian	15.20%	With health insurance	93.60%
		Two or more races	8.80%	Cash public assistance	5.00%
Age Groups		Other	14.60%	Food stamp/SNAP	13.20%
Under 18	24.90%				
18-34	26.70%	**Education**		**Work**	
35-64	35.40%	H.S grad or less	38.70%	White Collar	35.80%
Over 64	13.00%	Some college	31.70%	Sales and Service	42.30%
		College Degree, 4 yr	19.90%	Blue Collar	21.90%
Military		Post grad	9.80%	Government	20.50%
Veteran/ Active Duty	5.60%				

2020 Pres. Vote	Biden	225,218	(70%)	Trump	87,284	(27%)			
2016 Pres. Vote	Clinton	168,687	(68%)	Trump	59,549	(24%)	Johnson	9,354	(4%)
	Stein	4,975	(2%)						

Sacramento: Sacramento, capital of the nation's most populous state and a vibrant metropolis with its 43-mile light-rail system, is no longer just a small city with a lot of civil servants and a vegetable-packing economy. Sacramento started as a port on the sluggish waters of the Sacramento and American rivers. It was the destination of many overland migrants, the site of Sutter's Fort, where workers for John Augustus Sutter found the gold that set off the Gold Rush of 1848, and the western terminus of the Pony Express in 1860. This was the natural choice at the time to be California's capital, halfway between San Francisco Bay and the Mother Lode Country in the foothills of the Sierras, and in the middle of California's vast valley. It has the corporate home of the world's largest almond processing plant, and agriculture continues to be important in Sacramento, or Sacto, as some locals call it. A prime local concern: The confluence of the two rivers and a growing population have made the area a major flood hazard. More than $2 billion has been spent on levees and other steps to reduce risk, though doubts remain. Next to New Orleans, Sacramento is the most vulnerable city in the nation to a catastrophic flood, The Washington Post reported in 2017.

In the old days, government was not a big business. Just a few lobbyists hung out near the capital in saloons on K or J streets, the governor's mansion was a musty antique, and the summers' 100-plus degree days emptied out what there was of the city. Air conditioning long ago replaced awnings, and freeways and shopping malls have followed the city's growth east and north toward the Sierra foothills. Platoons of lobbyists, lawyers and consultants set up permanent shop. Today, more than 1,850 registered lobbyists prowl the halls of the capitol. In the first six months of 2019, they spent $187 million; the two largest spenders represented teachers and the petroleum industry. In 2017, the metro area's population of 2.7 million—an increase from about 800,000 in 1980—was about the same as metro Portland or San Antonio.

Most of the growth has been outside the city. Technology firms have moved east from Silicon Valley into the metro area, with Intel and Hewlett-Packard maintaining large campuses. Bay Area refugees have welcomed less expensive living standards. Local officials hope to make Sacramento the center for development of self-driving vehicles. In 2017, they created the Autonomous Transportation Open Standards Lab, a public-private consortium. Two years later, they announced plans for a Center for Future Mobility—with concepts such as remote "drivers" sitting at computers hundreds of miles away. Health care is another large business: In January 2020, the four largest companies—UC Davis Health, Kaiser Permanente, Sutter Health and Dignity Health—had about 25,000 employees in Sacramento. Prior to the pandemic in 2020, the state reported more than 80,000 employees in the Sacramento area.

The 6th Congressional District of California consists of the city of Sacramento, West Sacramento in Yolo County and parts of Sacramento County. The majority-minority district contains affluent neighborhoods and scattered low-income Latino and Black neighborhoods, plus new condominiums north of the American River and middle-class subdivisions south of downtown. Its ethnically diverse communities include, among others, Hmong refugees from Laos, Vietnamese, Russians and Ukrainians. In contrast to the 7th District, which is a politically mixed area, this is the solidly Democratic part of greater Sacramento. The Democratic presidential vote in the 6th increased from 68 percent in 2016 to 72 percent in 2020. In the entire county, the 440,000 voters for Biden were a 35 percent increase over the 326,000 votes for Hillary Clinton.

Ami Bera (D)

Elected 2012, 5th term, b. Mar 02, 1965; Los Angeles, CA; University of CA, Irvine, B.S., 1987; University of CA, Irvine, M.D., 1991; Unitarian; Married (Janine Bera); 1 child.

Professional Career: Professor, University of CA Davis, 2004-2012, Association dean, 2004-2008; Chief med. officer, Sacramento County Department of Health & Human Services, 1999-2004; Med. Director, Mercy Healthcare Sacramento, 1998-1999; MedClinic Med. Group, physician, 1999, Assistant med. Director, 1997-1998, chief of internal med. Department, 1996-1997.

DC Office: 1727 LHOB 20515, 202-225-5716, Fax: 202-226-1298, bera.house.gov

State Offices: Sacramento, 916-635-0505.

Committees: *Foreign Affairs*: Africa, Global Health & Global Human Rights; Asia, the Pacific, Central Asia, Nonproliferation (Chmn). *Science, Space & Technology*: Investigations & Oversight; Space & Aeronautics.

Group Ratings

	ADA	ACLU	AFL-CIO	LCV	COC	HAFA	ACU	CFG	FRC
2020	**	79%	**	100%	-	0%	5%	**	-
2019	90%	C	100%	97%	70%	C	6%	12%	0%

Almanac Ratings 2019-2020

	Economy	Social	Foreign	Composite
Liberal	100%	100%	80%	94%
Conservative	0%	0%	20%	6%

Key Votes of the 116th Congress

1. U.S./Mex./Can. trade deal	Y	5. Russia sanctions	Y	9. Firearms background checks	Y
2. First Coronavirus response	Y	6. Troops in Syria	Y	10. Spending at the border	Y
3. HEROES Act	Y	7. Veto arms sales to Saudis	Y	11. Marijuana liberalized rules	Y
4. CASH Act	Y	8. Defense $$$, veto override	Y	12. Electoral College objections	N

Election Results

Election	Name (Party)	Vote (%)		Cand. Spent	Ind. Exp. Support	Ind. Exp. Oppose
2020 General	Ami Bera (D)	217,416	(57%)	$779,333	$8,623	
	Buzz Patterson (R)	166,549	(43%)	$29,128		$113
2020 Primary	Ami Bera (D)	106,124	(50%)			
	Jeff Burdick (D)	15,114	(7%)			

Prior winning percentages: 2018 (55%), 2016 (51%), 2014 (50%), 2012 (52%)

Democrat Ami Bera, after winning three consecutive tight contests since he was elected in 2012, has rolled to two easy victories. A physician and medical administrator before he entered public office, he has been the rare Democrat in the large California delegation who occasionally has sought to separate himself from the party's mainstream. In 2020, he was an early supporter of Joe Biden for the Democratic presidential nomination and warned about the consequences if the party selected Bernie Sanders.

Bera was born in Hollywood, the son of parents who emigrated from India to the United States in the 1950s to attend college. His mother studied education and became a public elementary school teacher; his father paid for his engineering degree by ushering at Los Angeles Dodgers baseball games. The younger Bera excelled in science and math, and went to the University of California, Irvine, to study biology and then earn his medical degree.

After several years practicing internal medicine, Bera became the medical director of care management for Mercy Healthcare Sacramento. There, he discovered inefficiency and set about identifying "simple solutions" to reduce waste. He became the county's chief medical officer and realized that the managers were unprepared to meet the demands of the uninsured, which became a top priority for Bera. He said the Affordable Care Act "is not the direction I would have gone," but said the law offered a starting point to bring down spiraling costs.

In 2010, Bera challenged Rep. Dan Lungren, a Republican stalwart and former state attorney general. Bera was an impressive fundraiser, drawing donations from Indian Americans across the country. He accused Lungren of being out of touch with district voters, while the incumbent portrayed him as a rubber stamp for Nancy Pelosi's liberal agenda. Nearly $700,000 in late ads from GOP strategist Karl Rove's American Crossroads organization helped seal Lungren's win. In a second run in the post-redistricting district, which was three percentage points more Democratic, Bera benefited from a Sacramento Bee endorsement that said "Bera has matured, and Lungren has failed to meet local expectations." He won, 52%-48%.

Bera has been one of the California delegation's most moderate and politically attuned members. In 2014, he backed an unsuccessful version of the farm bill that cut $20 billion from the federal food stamp program. Bera was one of 28 House Democrats who voted in 2015 for presidential authority to make international trade deals, which caused heartburn for many Democrats. Angry leaders of organized labor said they would not back Bera for reelection, to which he responded that he would not succumb to "bullying" tactics or "special-interest" groups. In 2017, Bera became co-chairman with Republican Rep. Tom Reed of New York of the bipartisan Problem Solvers Caucus.

On the Foreign Affairs Committee, Bera worked to improve ties between India and Afghanistan. He accompanied President Barack Obama to India, where he praised the civilian nuclear agreement that was reached with Prime Minister Narenda Modi. In 2017, Bera became vice ranking member of the Foreign Affairs panel. Still, he continued to buck his party, as one of 18 Democrats in 2018 who voted for a proposal to support the Immigration and Customs Enforcement agency, though he said his support was reluctant and the Republican resolution was "a partisan gimmick." In 2019, he filed a bill to require that at least 70 percent of all ambassadors be members of the career Foreign Service. In 2021, Bera became chairman of the Asia, the Pacific, Central Asia and Nonproliferation Subcommittee.

Following the 2018 election, Bera remained noncommittal on whether he would support Pelosi for Speaker. With the Problems Solvers Caucus, he pushed for House rules changes. Pelosi eventually supported a modified version and Bera voted to return her as Speaker. His caution caused tension with many of his California colleagues, who have enthusiastically backed her. Following his early endorsement of Biden, he said support by Sanders of the "Medicare for All" proposal would force Democrats in competitive House district to "run away from the nominee" if Sanders were selected.

In his competitive district, Bera remained a top GOP campaign target. In 2014, he faced former Rep. Doug Ose, who served six years before abiding by his term-limits pledge to retire in 2004. This became the most expensive House campaign in the 2014 cycle. National Republican groups poured more than $6 million into the general election on Ose's behalf, while Democrats spent more than $5 million for Bera. In a contest that took several days to resolve, Bera eked out a win, 50.4%-49.6%.

In 2016, unions remained unhappy with Bera's support for Obama's Trans-Pacific Partnership trade deal, but they failed to find a primary challenger. Republicans cleared the field for Sacramento County Sheriff Scott Jones, who was attacked by Democrats over decade-old allegations that he sexually harassed a young woman who was a deputy sheriff, which he denied. Bera faced his own ethical problems after his 83-year-old father in May 2016 pleaded guilty to election fraud in the financing of his son's first two campaigns and was sentenced to a year in prison. Bera said his father made "a grave mistake" and prosecutors said that they had no evidence that he knew of his father's actions. Jones conceded 10 days following Election Day, after late-counted votes gave Bera a 51.2%-48.8% win.

Although Bera was easily reelected in 2020, he had an early stumble. At an October 2019 meeting of Democratic delegates in his district, he received 62 percent support—short of the 70 percent required for endorsement. Jeff Burdick, his only challenger, said the outcome showed support for his own more liberal views. But Bera easily prevailed in the all-party primary in March 2020, with 50 percent to 7 percent for Burdick. Two Republicans and a Green Party candidate split the remaining vote. Against Republican Buzz Patterson, whom he outspent $780,000 to $30,000, Bera won in November, 57%-43%.

CA-7: Sacramento

Cook Partisan Voting Index: D+5

Population		Race and Ethnicity		Income	
Total	756,668	White	60.40%	Median Income	$77,786
Land area (sq. miles)	549	Black	7.20%	District Income Rank	104
Pop/ sq mi	1,379.15	Latino	17.40%	Poverty Rate	10.10%
Born in State	60.80%	Asian	17.80%	With health insurance	95.10%
		Two or more races	7.60%	Cash public assistance	3.50%
Age Groups		Other	7.00%	Food stamp/SNAP	7.80%
Under 18	22.10%				
18-34	21.70%	**Education**		**Work**	
35-64	40.20%	H.S grad or less	29.70%	White Collar	41.60%
Over 64	15.90%	Some college	36.60%	Sales and Service	42.00%
		College Degree, 4 yr	22.20%	Blue Collar	16.40%
Military		Post grad	11.50%	Government	21.10%
Veteran/ Active Duty	6.80%				

2020 Pres. Vote	Biden	218,137	(56%)	Trump	164,052	(42%)		
2016 Pres. Vote	Clinton	159,066	(52%)	Trump	124,249	(40%) Johnson	14,747	(5%)

Eastern Sacramento Suburbs: Until recently, Sacramento was chiefly the metropolis of a fertile valley that produced a marvelous variety of crops: rice, plums, almonds, olives, asparagus, pears, hops, beans, celery, onions and potatoes, plus caviar-yielding sturgeon in pools of filtered water. The farmlands remain, and the capital city flourished as a center of government. Greater Sacramento has been one of the fastest-growing metro areas in the country. Almost all the growth was away from the floodplain of the Sacramento River, in the higher land east of the city that eventually turns into hills rising toward the Sierra Nevada.

Still, the county has a high rate of income inequality. Across the American River in Fair Oaks, Gov. Gavin Newsom moved his family into a $3.7 million mansion after he took office. In Arden-Arcade, pockets of poverty remain; the poverty rate of 22 percent in 2019 nearly doubled that of both Sacramento County and the state. California North state University, a private institution, planned to open in 2022 the first hospital in rapidly growing Elk Grove; a new medical center was expected to follow.

The 7th Congressional District of California includes suburban Sacramento and much of Sacramento County outside the mostly urban 6th District. All its residents are in Sacramento County. There is the old town of Folsom, where the Intel campus—the largest tech site in the area—had about 6,300 employees in 2020. Intel calls the research lab its "nerve center," where engineers develop its core intellectual property. The company's chips once dominated the market, but the decline in the share of personal computers and laptops in the world led Intel to shift some of its production to semiconductors. With its high pay scale for engineers, the prosperous company town has moved beyond the image singer Johnny Cash created in his song, Folsom Prison Blues—though, in his honor, the city opened the 2.5-mile Johnny Cash Trail, which runs along the prison property. The city of Sacramento historically has been Democratic.

Sacramento County, with its rapid growth, is no longer marginal. In the 2004 presidential race, Democrat John Kerry won the county over George W. Bush by just 1,118 votes. By 2020, the Democratic advantage had grown to 61%-36% for Joe Biden over Donald Trump. With the more conservative parts of the county in the 7th, Biden took the district, 56%-42%, a notable increase from Barack Obama's 51%-47% win over Mitt Romney in 2012.

Jay Obernolte (R)

Elected 2020, 1st term, b. Aug 18, 1970; Chicago, IL; CA Institute of Technology, B.S.; University of CA, Los Angeles, M.S.; Christian; Married (Heather Obernolte); 2 children.

Elected Office: CA State Assembly, 2014-2020; Mayor, City of Big Bear Lake.

Professional Career: Owner and technical director, video game development company.

DC Office: 1029 LHOB 20515, 202-225-5861, obernolte.house.gov

State Offices: Hesperia, 760-247-1815.

Committees: *Budget. Natural Resources*: Indigenous Peoples of the United States; National Parks, Forests & Public Lands. *Science, Space & Technology*: Investigations & Oversight (RMM).

Election Results

Election	Name (Party)	Vote (%)		Cand. Spent	Ind. Exp. Support	Ind. Exp. Oppose
2020 General	Jay Obernolte (R)............................	158,711	(56%)	$1,812,159	$365,006	$113
	Christine Bubser (D).....................	124,400	(44%)	$1,971,125	$11,771	
2020 Primary	Jay Obernolte (R)............................	50,677	(35%)			
	Tim Donnelly (R)............................	30,079	(21%)			

Jay Obernolte, who served six years in the California Assembly, was elected in one of the state's few House seats that are safely Republican. He largely wrapped up this contest when he led Republicans in the primary, defeating Tim Donnelly, an outspoken conservative who had lost two earlier challenges to Republican Rep. Paul Cook in this district. Obernolte became the successor to Cook, who gave up the seat and was elected to the San Bernardino County Board of Supervisors.

Obernolte got his bachelor's degree in computer engineering from California Institute of Technology. While in college, he started FarSight Studios, a video-game development company. After receiving a master's degree in artificial intelligence from UCLA, Obernolte grew his company, creating hundreds of jobs.

He began his public service in 2005 when he was elected to the board of directors of the Big Bear City Airport, utilizing his pilot's license and fifteen years of light aircraft flight experience. As a pilot, he volunteered with the Veterans Airlift Command to provide transportation for wounded and disabled veterans. Later, he served four years on the city council and was elected mayor of Big Bear Lake for another four years.

In 2014, he was easily elected to the state Assembly. Obernolte claimed passage of more bills than any other state lawmaker from the Inland Empire, even though he was in the minority party. To promote transparency and accountability for taxpayer dollars, he passed a bill that required the ballot summaries of tax and bond proposals to include estimates of how much they would increase taxes. Obernolte was instrumental in preventing the removal of the Veterans Home of California-Barstow from a state spending plan.

Two days after Cook announced his retirement in September 2019, Obernolte said he was asking voters to elect him to Congress to "stand up for the middleclass, cut government waste, balance the budget, defend our constitutional rights, protect our veterans and strengthen our national defense." Cook praised Obernolte's service in Sacramento and said there was nobody to "trust more to represent [their constituents] in Washington D.C." President Donald Trump tweeted his endorsement of Obernolte.

Obernolte faced a credible challenge from Donnelly, who had served four years in the Assembly before he ran unsuccessfully for governor in 2014, when he finished third in the first round of voting, and then twice against Cook. In 2018, after they were the top two among the five contenders in the first round of voting, Cook won Trump's endorsement and defeated Donnelly, 60%-40%. Donnelly has backed strong measures to stop illegal immigrants from Mexico, including his participation in the Minuteman Project that sponsored private patrols at the border.

In the March 2020 primary, the candidates made clear their contrasts. "We're two candidates, both Republicans, with two different styles," Donnelly said. "I go to Washington to pick a fight. I don't mind being the only 'no' vote because I believe most bills we don't need. I don't want to be a politician, I want to be a voice." He was endorsed by Republican Rep. Jim Jordan of Ohio, a leader of the House Freedom Caucus. Obernolte said a member of Congress needed to meet two criteria: knowing the responsibilities of a good representative and serving as the local voice when there is a dispute with the government.

With endorsements from Trump and House Republican Leader Kevin McCarthy of California, plus a more than 10-to-1 advantage in campaign spending, Obernolte got 35 percent of the total vote to 21 percent for Donnelly; Democrat Christine Bubser took 29 percent. Obernolte defeated Bubser in November, 56%-44%.

CA-8: High Desert   Cook Partisan Voting Index: R+8

Population		Race and Ethnicity		Income	
Total	723,311	White	73.90%	Median Income	$56,140
Land area (sq. miles)	32,867	Black	8.50%	District Income Rank	315
Pop/ sq mi	22.01	Latino	44.80%	Poverty Rate	16.60%
Born in State	65.90%	Asian	2.40%	With health insurance	90.60%
		Two or more races	5.30%	Cash public assistance	5.20%
Age Groups		Other	10.00%	Food stamp/SNAP	16.00%
Under 18	28.10%				
18-34	24.00%	**Education**		**Work**	
35-64	34.70%	H.S grad or less	46.60%	White Collar	29.90%
Over 64	13.20%	Some college	36.10%	Sales and Service	40.40%
		College Degree, 4 yr	10.90%	Blue Collar	29.70%
Military		Post grad	6.40%	Government	19.90%
Veteran/ Active Duty	10.00%				

2020 Pres. Vote	Trump	158,451	(54%)	Biden	127,769	(44%)		
2016 Pres. Vote	Trump	127,471	(54%)	Clinton	92,238	(39%)	Johnson	8,210	(4%)

San Bernardino County: The eastern High Desert of California runs along the Nevada border, with a huge swath of land uninhabited for dozens of miles. In the west are the towns of Apple Valley and Victorville, a high-growth area that was once home to cowboy stars Roy Rogers and Dale Evans. Other San Bernardino County cities and towns dot the landscape: the heavily Hispanic city of Adelanto; Hesperia, a wayside on the Mormon Trail; and Needles, where the fictional Joad family stops soon after entering California in The Grapes of Wrath. In Adelanto, not far from Victorville, a federal judge in April 2020 ordered the release of more than 250 immigrants who were illegally detained at the Immigration and Customs Enforcement processing center.

To the north, off Interstate 15 heading to Las Vegas, are Barstow and the military training center at Fort Irwin. In Victorville, which is at the entrance to the desert, a fierce wind in April 2018 resulted in a destructive invasion of tumbleweed. In April 2020, the California Debt Limit Allocation Committee approved the issuance of the remainder of a total of $600 million in tax-exempt bonds to finance train service from Victorville to Las Vegas, which will be operated by Virgin Trains USA; it plans to extend that service to the Los Angeles area. San Bernardino has the most land of any county in the nation, but more than 80 percent of it is publicly owned. In February 2019, the county OK'd the decision by private landowners to reject solar and wind farms on more than 1 million acres of private land of residents who objected to the project.

The 8th Congressional District of California covers Mono and Inyo counties, as well as the rural parts of San Bernardino County; more than 90 percent of the population is in San Bernardino. The 8th does not include the city of San Bernardino, which accounts for only 10 percent of the county's 2.2 million population. Its geography is vast. It sweeps in the sleepy Mojave Desert and mountains, Death Valley (where the International Dark-Sky Association laments the visibility of lights from Las Vegas), and Owens Valley, the source of Los Angeles' water supply and the site of the California "Water Wars" that became the inspiration for the movie Chinatown. In August 2020, Death Valley reached a temperature of 130 degrees, the hottest temperature ever measured on the planet. The district includes Mammoth Lakes and the Mammoth ski resort area in the Inyo National Forest, where more than 40 feet of snow fell during the winter of 2016-17. Despite pockets of Democratic support, this is strong Republican territory. In 2020, Donald Trump won the district, 54%-44%.

Jerry McNerney (D)

Elected 2006, 8th term, b. Jun 18, 1951; Albuquerque, NM; St. Joseph's Military Academy; U.S. Military Academy, Att., 1971; University of NM, B.S., 1973; University of NM, M.S., 1975; University of NM, Ph.D., 1981; Roman Catholic; Married (Mary McNerney); 3 children.

Professional Career: National security contractor, Sandia National Labs., 1979-1985; Engineer, U.S. Windpower Kenetech, 1985-1994; Energy consultant, 1994-1999; CEO, start-up wind turbine manufacturer, 2000-2006.

DC Office: 2265 RHOB 20515, 202-225-1947, Fax: 202-225-4060, mcnerney.house.gov

State Offices: Antioch, 925-754-0716; Stockton, 209-476-8552.

Committees: *Energy & Commerce*: Communications & Technology; Consumer Protection & Commerce; Energy. *Science, Space & Technology*: Energy.

Group Ratings

	ADA	ACLU	AFL-CIO	LCV	COC	HAFA	ACU	CFG	FRC
2020	**	80%	**	100%	-	0%	6%	**	-
2019	95%	C	100%	97%	63%	C	6%	12%	0%

Almanac Ratings 2019-2020

	Economy	Social	Foreign	Composite
Liberal	100%	100%	80%	94%
Conservative	0%	0%	20%	6%

Key Votes of the 116th Congress

1. U.S./Mex./Can. trade deal Y	5. Russia sanctions Y	9. Firearms background checks Y
2. First Coronavirus response Y	6. Troops in Syria Y	10. Spending at the border Y
3. HEROES Act Y	7. Veto arms sales to Saudis Y	11. Marijuana liberalized rules Y
4. CASH Act Y	8. Defense $$$, veto override Y	12. Electoral College objections N

Election Results

Election	Name (Party)	Vote (%)		Cand. Spent	Ind. Exp. Support	Ind. Exp. Oppose
2020 General	Jerry McNerney (D)	174,252	(58%)	$888,903	$873	
	Tony Amador (R)	128,358	(42%)	$74,640		$59
2020 Primary	Jerry McNerney (D)	86,556	(57%)			

Prior winning percentages: 2018 (57%), 2016 (57%), 2014 (52%), 2012 (56%), 2010 (48%), 2008 (55%), 2006 (53%)

Democrat Jerry McNerney has become relatively secure in what had been a Republican district —with help from his collegial style and the weakness of local Republicans. In 2020 when he won his eighth term, he reached his personal high share of the vote. He has been more moderate than most California Democrats and often seeks bipartisanship, though he has usually been a party loyalist.

McNerney's father was a union organizer in the 1930s and later worked for the U.S. Geological Survey in Albuquerque, where Jerry McNerney was born. Along with his twin brother, he was sent to a military boarding school in Hays Kansas, and later won an appointment to the U.S. Military Academy. He left West Point after two years in the late 1960s because he opposed the war in Vietnam. He transferred to the University of New Mexico, where he earned his bachelor's degree and a doctorate in differential geometry. He spent several years as a contractor for Sandia National Laboratories, working on national security programs. In 1985, he moved to the private sector with U.S. Wind power and later was chief executive of a wind turbine firm. McNerney claimed his work contributed to keeping 8.3 million tons of carbon dioxide out of the atmosphere.

In 2006, McNerney was an unlikely winner against Republican Rep. Richard Pombo, a local rancher in an area that was dubbed "Pombo Country." As chairman of the House Resources Committee, Pombo was leader of the property-rights movement backed by ranchers and farmers. McNerney was endorsed by the state party and by local organized labor and easily won the primary, though the Democratic Congressional Campaign Committee favored another candidate. In the general election, Pombo outspent McNerney by nearly 2-to-1. McNerney turned the election into a referendum on Pombo, who was hated by national environmental groups, which called him an "eco-thug" and "Wildlife Enemy No. 1." Bolstered by a strong anti-Republican tide, McNerney won 53%-47%.

In the House, McNerney established a moderate voting record. On the influential Energy and Commerce Committee, he won a provision regulating carbon emissions as part of a measure to encourage electric vehicle usage. He has turned his friendship with Republican Rep. Bob Latta of Ohio, a committee member, into productive bipartisanship. In 2018, they created a WiFi Caucus to "open a dialogue about appropriate policy solutions" related to the digital divide.

Following their creation of the Grid Innovation Caucus, McNerney and Latta won House approval in September 2020 of measures to require the Energy Department to create a pilot program to test the cyber security of products that might be used in the power grid or by electric utilities. A year earlier, McNerney won bipartisan support in an Energy and Commerce subcommittee of a bill to prepare for the storage of nuclear waste at Yucca Mountain in Nevada; the House did not take action. For years, Nevadans and foes of nuclear power have vehemently opposed similar measures for Yucca.

With his background as an engineer, McNerney has worked with scientists on a bill he filed to request the National Academies of Science to explore technologies in the emerging study of "geoengineering," which they hope can address the challenges of climate change. In 2020, he teamed with Rep. Michael Burgess of Texas, another Republican on Energy and Commerce, on a bill directing the Consumer Product Safety Commission to establish a pilot program to use artificial intelligence to protect consumers from unsafe products.

His history of tight reelection races has promoted his interest in issues that have been less partisan, McNerney said. "I have to be more moderate," he told the Modesto Bee in 2012. "If I alienate Republicans, I can't win. If I alienate Democrats, I can't win." Republicans came after him in 2010. David Harmer promised to shun earmarks, calling them "the gateway drug of federal spending." Democratic interest groups attacked Harmer for writing an op-ed column calling for the abolition of public education. After ballot-counting continued for days after the election, McNerney prevailed with 48 percent of the vote.

In 2012, McNerney's opponent was Ricky Gill, an ambitious 25-year-old Indian American hailed as a rising GOP star. Gill raised nearly $3 million, and the National Republican Congressional Committee spent another $2.5 million on his behalf. As a Lodi native, Gill had ties to the area. Gill described himself as a "different kind of Republican," holding moderate stances on immigration and education. McNerney called Gill a novice who was propped up by his wealthy parents' business ties. Benefitting from the strong showing in California of President Barack Obama, he won, 56%-44%.

Since then, McNerney has had an easier time running against lightly funded GOP challengers —including a perennial candidate whom he defeated three times. In 2020, he scored 58 percent of the vote, his high mark.

CA-9: Central Valley   Cook Partisan Voting Index: D+8

Population		Race and Ethnicity		Income	
Total	784,956	White	53.00%	Median Income	$72,237
Land area (sq. miles)	1,245	Black	9.50%	District Income Rank	147
Pop/ sq mi	630.34	Latino	38.40%	Poverty Rate	13.40%
Born in State	65.30%	Asian	16.30%	With health insurance	93.80%
		Two or more races	11.00%	Cash public assistance	3.50%
Age Groups		Other	10.20%	Food stamp/SNAP	13.80%
Under 18	26.30%				
18-34	23.00%	**Education**		**Work**	
35-64	36.60%	H.S grad or less	46.90%	White Collar	30.70%
Over 64	14.10%	Some college	30.50%	Sales and Service	40.00%
		College Degree, 4 yr	15.30%	Blue Collar	29.30%
Military		Post grad	7.20%	Government	14.80%
Veteran/ Active Duty	5.40%				

2020 Pres. Vote	Biden	180,096	(58%)	Trump	124,105	(40%)		
2016 Pres. Vote	Clinton	134,719	(56%)	Trump	90,484	(38%)	Johnson	8,518	(4%)

Stockton, San Joaquin: California is often defined by its cosmopolitan cities, its gorgeous Pacific coastline and its world-class vineyards. But beyond Beverly Hills and Nob Hill, there is another California that likes to get its hands dirty. This is an old part of the state, settled in the 1840s. When the Gold Rush fortune seekers departed, the land was left to a determined population of farmers. Crisscrossed with railroads and canals, the Central Valley became one of the world's greatest agricultural regions. The San Joaquin River channel was deepened to 37 feet, and Stockton today is the Central Valley's port. The rich land attracted immigrants from all over: Mexicans came up Route 99 and joined Germans from the Dakotas flocking to the town of Lodi. Italian and Yugoslavian immigrants brought their Old World crops. Yankees and Okies brought their distinct churches and beliefs. Recently, Southeast Asian refugees have crowded into the old streets of Stockton. The region endures the usual plagues of a farm economy, such as the availability of migrant workers at harvest time and chronic concerns about the water supply. With large use of chemicals and pesticides, air pollution in the San Joaquin Valley has been ranked as the worst in the nation, with high levels of cancer and asthma.

In recent decades, the Central Valley has also become a suburban zone. Because of the high cost of living in the San Francisco Bay Area, racial minorities have been moving to outlying suburbs. Workers with modest incomes bought lower-priced houses around Tracy and Stockton and commute to work on Interstate 580, past the windmills of Altamont. Stockton was a poster child for urban dysfunction. In 2012, facing close to $1 billion in long-term debt, Stockton became the biggest city in American history to declare bankruptcy. With a non-Hispanic white population of 21 percent, it has become the nation's most racially diverse large city.

To address endemic poverty, Stockton officials in 2018 launched a trial period for a universal basic income, in which 125 randomly selected residents received a $500 monthly guarantee. Michael Tubbs, the city's young African-American mayor, said in April 2020 that initial results of the program, which was extended to 2021, were positive. "Every century or so, we find a way to be more humane, more civilized, and extend the safety net," he told California Magazine—published for alumni of UC, Berkeley. In November 2020, Tubbs unexpectedly lost reelection to Republican challenger Kevin Lincoln, a military veteran.

The 9th Congressional District contains about two-thirds of San Joaquin County, plus an eastern slice of Contra Costa County and a southern nip of Sacramento County. It includes all of Stockton, plus Lodi, a town with a sizable Muslim community and a thriving downtown. The district takes in fast-growing Brentwood in Contra Costa County. Antioch, on the western end of the district, had become known as unsafe and uninteresting. But the high cost of living in most of the Bay Area, plus a new BART station at the terminus of the Yellow Line from Oakland, have created appeal for families seeking lower-priced housing. In 2019, Blacks and Latinos totaled 55 percent of the population in Antioch, which had grown 9 percent since 2010.The district is not overwhelmingly Democratic and could become competitive, especially with continued economic woes. After Hillary Clinton got 56 percent of the vote in 2016, Joe Biden won, 58%-40%.

Josh Harder (D)

Elected 2018, 2nd term, b. Aug 01, 1986; Turlock, CA; Stanford University, B.A., 2008; Harvard University Kennedy School of Government, M.P.P., 2014; Christian Church; Married (Pamela Harder).

Professional Career: Management Consultant, Bessemer Venture Partners.

DC Office: 131 CHOB 20515, 202-225-4540, harder.house.gov

State Offices: Modesto, 209-579-5458.

Committees: *Agriculture*: Biotechnology, Horticulture & Research; Livestock & Foreign Agriculture. *Appropriations*: Interior, Environment & Related Agencies; Labor, Health & Human Services, Education & Related Agencies.

Almanac Ratings 2019-2020

	Economy	Social	Foreign	Composite
Liberal	100%	100%	80%	94%
Conservative	0%	0%	20%	6%

Key Votes of the 116th Congress

1. U.S./Mex./Can. trade deal	Y	5. Russia sanctions	Y	9. Firearms background checks	Y
2. First Coronavirus response	Y	6. Troops in Syria	Y	10. Spending at the border	Y
3. HEROES Act	Y	7. Veto arms sales to Saudis	Y	11. Marijuana liberalized rules	Y
4. CASH Act	Y	8. Defense $$$, veto override	Y	12. Electoral College objections	N

Election Results

Election	Name (Party)	Vote (%)		Cand. Spent	Ind. Exp. Support	Ind. Exp. Oppose
2020 General	Josh Harder (D)..................................	166,865	(55%)	$3,793,080	$75,699	$691
	Ted Howze (R)...................................	135,629	(45%)	$1,969,486	$386	$15,613
2020 Primary	Josh Harder (D).................................	69,668	(44%)			

Prior winning percentages: 2018 (52%)

Democrat Josh Harder, elected in 2018 as a venture capitalist working in San Francisco, represents the district with the lowest median income in the Bay Area. Downplaying his high-finance connections, he sought to identify with the rural communities of his youth when he defeated Republican Rep. Jeff Denham and has centered his work in Congress on improving water quality and local business. He caught a lucky break in his first reelection campaign in 2020 when top Republican leaders disavowed and financially cut off his expected GOP opponent after learning about a trove of racist and Islamophobic posts on his social media accounts.

Growing up in Turlock in the Central Valley farming area, Harder interned while he was in high school for Denham, who was then a state senator. He graduated from Stanford University and got master's degrees in business administration and public policy from Harvard. After working for the Boston Consulting Group, where he advised businesses around the world, he joined the San Francisco-based Bessemer Venture Partners. He returned to the Bay Area as a vice president of the firm, where his clients were chiefly telecommunications firms.

When he launched his campaign for Congress, "Harder was reluctant to talk about his background in tech-investing, taking pains to stress the more home-grown parts of his biography," according to Recode, a website that covered the tech industry. Denham, an almond farmer elected in 2010, was eager to remind voters of that background, running ads that referred to Harder as "a shady San Francisco venture capitalist." Recode reported that Harder became the only former venture capitalist serving in the House.

The all-party primary featured six Democratic candidates—including beekeeper Michael Eggman, the challenger to Denham in 2014 and 2016, when he lost 52%-48%.In addition to Denham, the other Republican candidate was Ted Howze, a conservative veterinarian who styled himself as more loyal to President Donald Trump, especially on immigration issues. To the relief of House Democrats who feared that Howze would place second, which would have shut out Democrats in November, Harder got 17 percent of the total vote, trailed by Howze with 15 percent and Eggman with 10 percent. Denham led the field with 38 percent.(Howze returned as the 2020 GOP nominee.)

Harder was a prolific fundraiser, garnering ample support from his Bay Area network. With his nearly $7 million, he doubled the spending by Denham, who benefited from more than $2 million in spending by House Republican groups. Harder won, 52%-48%, in the only Northern California contest that took several days following the election to declare a winner. He led in both Stanislaus County and the less populous San Joaquin part of the district. Harder's victory left the GOP without any of the more than a dozen districts closest to San Francisco—a significant political shift since the 1990s.

In his first-term, Harder labored to further shed his corporate ties, introducing a bill that targeted PG&E for doling out bonuses to its executives while infrastructure failures led to blackouts. He also grilled Education Secretary Betsy DeVos over plans to eliminate federally funded literacy programs. In February 2020, he trotted out a taxidermized water rodent, called a nutria, onto the House floor to raise awareness about his bill to eradicate the invasive species, which is wreaking havoc on critical wetlands. The president signed his bill into law later that year.

Six candidates, three Democrats and three Republicans, competed in the top-two primary in March. Harder took first with 44%, followed by Howze with 34%—an unsurprising result given Howze's name ID from his 2018 run. Yet Howze's second run was neutered by a pair of Politico stories that revealed dozens of offensive posts on his personal social media accounts that compared the recipients of the Deferred Action for Childhood Arrivals program to pedophiles, called the Islamic prophet Muhammad a rapist, his religion "a death cult" and described the Black Lives Matter community as "political slaves" of the Democratic Party.

Howze claimed he did not write any of the posts and indicated someone else had access to his accounts and passwords, but provided no detail on who that was or why the posts remained live until the day he launched his first House campaign in 2018. Republicans were unconvinced. NRCC Chairman Tom Emmer yanked Howze from the committee's Young Guns program for top recruits. A few days later House Minority Leader Kevin McCarthy rescinded his endorsement.

National Republicans declined to run any TV ads for Howze in the fall, a death knell to his campaign which was poorly funded. Harder spent $3.8 million to Howze's $2 million and won 55%-45%, leading in both Stanislaus and San Joaquin counties. Most significantly, Harder finished with over $3.4 million in the bank, a hefty 2022 war chest. Following the election, he got a seat on the Appropriations Committee, a comfortable perch to deliver federal largesse to his district.

CA-10: Central Valley

Cook Partisan Voting Index: EVEN

Population		Race and Ethnicity		Income	
Total	764,859	White	76.70%	Median Income	$69,647
Land area (sq. miles)	1,819	Black	3.50%	District Income Rank	168
Pop/ sq mi	420.53	Latino	45.10%	Poverty Rate	11.80%
Born in State	68.30%	Asian	7.40%	With health insurance	93.40%
		Two or more races	5.20%	Cash public assistance	2.70%
Age Groups		Other	7.10%	Food stamp/SNAP	9.60%
Under 18	26.30%				
18-34	24.00%	**Education**		**Work**	
35-64	36.80%	H.S grad or less	48.10%	White Collar	27.70%
Over 64	12.90%	Some college	33.90%	Sales and Service	40.30%
		College Degree, 4 yr	13.10%	Blue Collar	32.10%
Military		Post grad	4.90%	Government	14.70%
Veteran/ Active Duty	4.80%				

2020 Pres. Vote	Biden	154,990	(50%)	Trump	146,084	(47%)		
2016 Pres. Vote	Clinton	116,335	(48%)	Trump	109,145	(45%)	Johnson	9,370	(4%)

Modesto, Stanislaus: The Central Valley of California is a miraculous landscape, an outdoor factory stretching as far as the eye can see. Nature created the vast flatlands, rimmed by mountains rising in the distant haze. In the 20th century, people disciplined the land with a remorseless mile-square grid of roads, the California Aqueduct, and dozens of arrow-straight canals. Pipes fitted with valves and gauges pump water, fertilizer and pesticides to the fields in measured quantities with industrial precision. The crops grow in carefully spaced rows. The rich soil and the irrigated water were too precious to waste on decorative fountains or flower gardens. Throughout history, farming here has been a business, not a way of life. In the 19th century, the U.S. government did not give the land to 160-acre homesteaders but rather sold it to large enterprises in thousands-of-acres parcels. Among the most famous local capitalists were the Gallo brothers, Ernest and Julio, who started a winery in Modesto in 1933 with virtually no money. It now covers more than 23,000 acres of vineyards and produces more than 86 million cases of wine each year.

In recent years, the Central Valley has become one of California's boom areas, not just for crops, but also for people. Middle-income workers in the San Francisco Bay Area drive east at the end of the day on Interstate 580 to modestly priced homes in Modesto, the town immortalized (when it was much smaller) in the 1973 film American Graffiti. Warehouses and factories have sprung up on land that for all its farming value is cheaper than industrial land in the Bay Area. But there have been costs: traffic has become a problem as the pace of life has become more hectic; and California's wildfires in the fall of 2020 produced the stretch of the worst air quality on record in the Central Valley, according to local air-pollution control. The over-pumping of groundwater has caused the valley to sink a half-inch each month, the Los Angeles Times reported.

Stanislaus County saw record farming revenues of $3.7 billion in 2016, with almonds the leading crop along with milk and walnuts. In fact, the state supplied over 80 percent of the world's almond supply in 2018, according to the California Almond Board, a local nonprofit. But farmers worry about the ever-present threat of water scarcity, made worse by the constant tension between growers and environmentalists. Some local residents and the Sierra Club of Stanislaus County have fiercely opposed plans to build a reservoir that would aid farmers in drier years because the project would inundate a scenic canyon.

The 10th Congressional District of California includes all of Stanislaus County and part of San Joaquin County, including Tracy, Ripon and the almond center of Manteca. Nearly three-fourths of the voters are in Stanislaus. It takes in Modesto, Oakdale and Riverbank. The political tradition here had been Democratic. In the 1960s, Democrats in Washington and Democratic Gov. Pat Brown built the irrigation canals and authorized the water subsidies. This area produced two House Democratic whips, John McFall in the mid-1970s and Tony Coelho in the 1980s. But the Central Valley grew to be more culturally conservative than other parts of the state. In recent decades, it has trended Republican, and even the Latinos here are less solidly Democratic than those in Los Angeles. Still, with a 43 percent Hispanic population, this has become one of the few political "swing" areas in California. In each of the past four presidential elections, Democrats have won the district by about three percentage points.

Mark DeSaulnier (D)

Elected 2014, 4th term, b. Mar 31, 1952; Lowell, MA; College of The Holy Cross, B.A., 1974; Harvard University John F. Kennedy School of Government, 2003; Roman Catholic; Divorced; 2 children.

Elected Office: Concord City Council, 1991-1994; Concord Mayor, 1993; Contra Costa County Board Supervisors, 1994-2006, chair, 1994; CA Assembly 2006-2008; CA Senate, 2008-2014.

Professional Career: Deputy probation officer; Warehouse worker; Hotel service; Restauranteur; Business owner; Fellow, JFK School of Gov't, Harvard University, 2003.

DC Office: 503 CHOB 20515, 202-225-2095, Fax: 202-225-5609, desaulnier.house.gov

State Offices: Richmond, 510-620-1000; Walnut Creek, 925-933-2660.

Committees: *Education & Labor*: Early Childhood, Elementary & Secondary Education; Health, Employment, Labor & Pensions (Chmn). *Oversight & Reform*: National Security; Subcommittee on Economic & Consumer Policy. *Rules*: Expedited Procedures. *Transportation & Infrastructure*: Aviation; Highways & Transit.

Group Ratings

	ADA	ACLU	AFL-CIO	LCV	COC	HAFA	ACU	CFG	FRC
2020	**	83%	**	95%	-	0%	1%	**	-
2019	100%	C	90%	100%	43%	C	2%	12%	0%

Almanac Ratings 2019-2020

	Economy	Social	Foreign	Composite
Liberal	59%	100%	100%	87%
Conservative	41%	0%	0%	13%

Key Votes of the 116th Congress

1. U.S./Mex./Can. trade deal	N	5. Russia sanctions	Y	9. Firearms background checks Y
2. First Coronavirus response	N/A	6. Troops in Syria	Y	10. Spending at the border N
3. HEROES Act	N/A	7. Veto arms sales to Saudis	Y	11. Marijuana liberalized rules Y
4. CASH Act	Y	8. Defense $$$, veto override	N	12. Electoral College objections N

Election Results

Election	Name (Party)	Vote (%)		Cand. Spent	Ind. Exp. Support	Ind. Exp. Oppose
2020 General	Mark DeSaulnier (D)............................	271,063	(73%)	$322,772	$2,166	
	Nisha Sharma (R)...............................	100,293	(27%)	$227,558		$113
2020 Primary	Mark DeSaulnier (D).........................	151,544	(71%)			

Prior winning percentages: 2018 (74%), 2016 (72%), 2014 (67%)

Democrat Mark DeSaulnier, elected to a solidly blue district in 2014, has shown his legislative experience and expertise. With particular interest in education and transportation policy, he gained new opportunities when Democrats took control of the House. But his life in the majority was interrupted when a combination of medical problems left him close to death and in a ventilator for four weeks. During the national confinement resulting from the coronavirus, his gradual recovery became an inspiration to many in Congress.

DeSaulnier is a veteran of California politics with blue-collar bona fides. He had been a trucker, probation officer and hotel worker before entering the restaurant business, eventually owning several Bay Area dining locales. He was elected to the Concord City Council in 1991, and he became mayor in 1993. In those years, he was a Republican. Gov. Pete Wilson appointed him to the influential state Air Resources Board. As he saw the GOP move to the right, DeSaulnier switched parties and became a Democrat. He was elected to the state Assembly in 2006 and the state Senate in 2008. He chaired the Transportation Committee in each chamber. With his partisan independence, he opposed proposals to revive California's troubled high-speed rail project, and he pledged to work with business groups to amend his corporate tax bill.

In 2014, when influential liberal leader George Miller announced his retirement after 40 years, DeSaulnier got his opening. He had lost a special election five years earlier to a better-known candidate, John Garamendi. This time, armed with the biggest war chest and a slew of endorsements, DeSaulnier quickly became the frontrunner. He used his day job in the state Senate to advance liberal priorities. That included a bill to adjust the state corporate tax rate according to the wage disparity in each firm, which fell short of the required two-thirds majority to pass. He proposed another bill to set up a pilot project to reform the state's gasoline tax so motorists pay based on mileage rather than by the gallon. That measure passed. DeSaulnier easily won election. He took 59 percent of the vote in the first round of voting, well ahead of 28 percent for Republican Tue Phan-Quang. In the general election, he won 67 percent. This was a relatively low-cost contest, with DeSaulnier spending $540,000.

After three years in the House, he enacted the first bill he introduced, which expanded the John Muir National Historic Site with 44 additional acres of donated land in Martinez. Muir, a conservationist, was the father of the national parks, although he has lately come under criticism from some on the left, including the Sierra Club, for derogatory comments about Blacks. He filed legislation to make the income from student Pell Grants tax-exempt for low-income recipients. In response to incidents in which law-enforcement agents had their firearms stolen from their cars, DeSaulnier proposed a bill that would require federal agents to store their guns in a locked box while they are in a car. He pursued other proposals to reduce gun violence, including the creation of an independent board to seek solutions. Following up on his call for "radical and immediate change" in Bay Area transportation, he joined with Sen. Dianne Feinstein to support a new bridge across the bay to southern San Francisco, plus an accompanying underwater rail tube.

DeSaulnier took several steps to call attention to the case of the Port Chicago 50, a group of African Americans who were found guilty of mutiny in 1944 when they refused to return to work following a huge munitions explosion during the loading of a ship at the Naval Magazine in Concord, which killed 320 people. The House-passed defense spending bill in May 2016 included his amendment to require that the Navy investigate their treatment at the time to determine if there was racial bias. Despite appeals from many lawmakers, President Barack Obama did not act on the issue.

In March 2019, DeSaulnier gained enactment of a bill addressing a long-fought local issue, when he added to a broader public lands bill his measure to transfer the title of the Contra Costa canal system from the federal Bureau of Reclamation to the county's water district so it could make safety and environmental improvements.

In 2016, DeSaulnier announced he had had six months of chemotherapy for a form of leukemia. He created the Congressional Cancer Survivors Caucus to seek additional research funds. In an interview with the San Francisco Chronicle in November 2019, he said he was treating the return of his illness with a newly available medication and that he had grown more focused on policy steps to help doctors treat patients who are in acute need. "The things that I'm actually really passionate about are people who are at risk, and how do you help them," he said.

In March 2020, his problems were exacerbated after DeSaulnier—a veteran marathoner—fell while running near the Capitol. With his immunity compromised by the cancer, his broken ribs led to pneumonia and his battle for life in an intensive care unit. His doctors said he had a 10 percent chance to survive. After nearly two months of hospitalization, he returned to his home in what the Chronicle described as "his second victory over death." Weakened and with a raspy voice, he released an 11-minute video in late May in which he discussed his experience. "Cancer was amazing enough, but I am so grateful every day," he said.

In 2021, DeSaulnier became chairman of the Education and Labor Subcommittee on Health, Employment, Labor and Pensions. He said that his experience as a restaurant owner had informed his advocacy of workers' rights.

CA-11: Outer East Bay   Cook Partisan Voting Index: D+24

Population		Race and Ethnicity		Income	
Total	765,504	White	54.00%	Median Income	$103,580
Land area (sq. miles)	494	Black	7.40%	District Income Rank	26
Pop/ sq mi	1,550.83	Latino	29.10%	Poverty Rate	8.70%
Born in State	52.30%	Asian	14.80%	With health insurance	94.00%
		Two or more races	6.40%	Cash public assistance	1.90%
Age Groups		Other	17.40%	Food stamp/SNAP	5.50%
Under 18	22.10%				
18-34	21.10%	Education		Work	
35-64	40.30%	H.S grad or less	28.90%	White Collar	45.00%
Over 64	16.60%	Some college	26.40%	Sales and Service	38.50%
		College Degree, 4 yr	26.40%	Blue Collar	16.50%
Military		Post grad	18.40%	Government	13.00%
Veteran/ Active Duty	4.30%				

2020 Pres. Vote	Biden	285,023	(74%)	Trump	90,513	(24%)			
2016 Pres. Vote	Clinton	223,559	(71%)	Trump	70,869	(23%)	Johnson	10,993	(4%)

Concord, Richmond: The maritime journey inward from the Pacific Ocean to the vast flatness of California's Central Valley passes through a wondrous variety of terrain. The traveler starts at the Golden Gate Bridge, with the lush green Presidio on one side and the bluffs of mountains in Marin County on the other. The journey continues through San Francisco Bay, through the narrow Carquinez Strait to Suisun Bay, with its sloughs and marshes and ships ready for scrap, and finally past the mountains, to the flat, fertile expanse of California's great interior. This journey was a familiar route to the first Americans in California, and it passes by much of the industrial base of the Bay Area. On the east side of Suisun Bay is Richmond, developed almost instantaneously during World War II when Henry J. Kaiser built a shipyard in its deep-water port and 91,000 people from all over the country were put to work building ships for the Pacific theater. What became known as Rosie the Riveter Memorial Park is now a national historical park.

In recent years, Richmond citizens have harbored doubts about safety at a Chevron refinery plant, the scene of frequent fires and explosions. After a 2012 fire at the plant, the federal Chemical Safety Board issued a report in 2015 that Chevron was responsible for the fire because it failed to respond when experts warned of defects at the site. In the 2014 election, Chevron fueled a backlash when it endorsed four candidates for the Richmond city council and spent more than $3 million on their behalf. All of them lost. A local political science professor said the result showed that "ordinary people can defeat huge corporate power." Chevron in 2018 agreed to pay $160 million for improvements at several sites nationally, including $20 million for safety projects in Richmond.

Following the settlement, local activists protested emissions from the refinery, which resulted in a high rate of respiratory illness among the mostly Black and Latino residents of Richmond. They also objected after the city council in 2019 OK'd a developer pouring concrete over contaminated soil in an area where it planned to build several thousand apartments. Richmond became a growth center. The city council approved construction of a large marijuana production complex, including 44 greenhouses. In 2019, the San Francisco Bay Ferry began service from a new terminal in Richmond to the Embarcadero across the Bay. Some community groups were fearful of gentrification. In another transportation milestone in East Bay, BART extended its service to Antioch. The new line is served by diesel trains, which use advanced biofuels.

The 11th District of California is entirely in Contra Costa County, including all of Richmond and Concord, which is the largest city in the county. About one-third of the county's voters are in adjoining districts. Interstate 680 running north-south provides a spine for businesses and shopping centers up and down the San Ramon Valley, from burgeoning Concord to Walnut Creek. The district also takes in the "Lamorinda" area of Lafayette, Moraga and Orinda. After the failure of multiple options for the site of the mostly unused Concord Naval Weapons Station—including a large housing project—local planners saw opportunities for large tech companies in Silicon Valley to cross to this East Bay area, Forbes reported in January 2020. The district is solidly Democratic, but culturally less liberal than San Francisco. Joe Biden got 74 percent of the vote in 2020, an increase from the 71 percent for Hillary Clinton.

Nancy Pelosi (D)

Elected 1987, 17th full term, b. Mar 26, 1940; Baltimore, MD; Trinity College, A.B., 1962; Roman Catholic; Married (Paul F. Pelosi); 5 children; 9 grandchildren.

Professional Career: CA Dem. Party, Northern Chairman, 1977-81, St. Chairman, 1981-1983; DSCC finance Chairman, 1985-1986; PR Executive, Ogilvy & Mather, 1986-1987.

DC Office: 1236 LHOB 20515, 202-225-4965, Fax: 202-225-8259, pelosi.house.gov

State Offices: San Francisco, 415-556-4862.

Democrats Speaker of the House.

Group Ratings

	ADA	ACLU	AFL-CIO	LCV	COC	HAFA	ACU	CFG	FRC
2020	**	82%	**	-	-	0%	3%	**	-
2019	N/A	C	100%	0%	39%	C	3%	23%	0%

Almanac Ratings 2019-2020

	Economy		Social		Foreign		Composite
Liberal	%		47%		%		%
Conservative	%		53%		%		%

Key Votes of the 116th Congress

1. U.S./Mex./Can. trade deal	Y	5. Russia sanctions	N/A	9. Firearms background checks Y
2. First Coronavirus response	Y	6. Troops in Syria	N/A	10. Spending at the border N/A
3. HEROES Act	Y	7. Veto arms sales to Saudis	N/A	11. Marijuana liberalized rules N/A
4. CASH Act	Y	8. Defense $$$, veto override	Y	12. Electoral College objections N

Election Results

Election	Name (Party)	Vote (%)	Cand. Spent	Ind. Exp. Support	Ind. Exp. Oppose
2020 General	Nancy Pelosi (D)	281,776 (78%)	$11,499,344	$3,483	$139,696
	Shahid Buttar (D)	81,174 (22%)	$1,718,335		
2020 Primary	Nancy Pelosi (D)	190,590 (74%)			
	Shahid Buttar (D)	33,344 (13%)			

Prior winning percentages: 2018 (87%), 2016 (81%), 2014 (83%), 2012 (85%), 2010 (80%), 2008 (72%), 2006 (80%), 2004 (83%), 2002 (80%), 2000 (84%), 1998 (86%), 1996 (84%), 1994 (82%), 1992 (83%), 1990 (77%), 1988 (76%), 1987 special (67%)

Nancy Pelosi, who regained in 2019 the gavel as Speaker of the House that she held from 2007 to 2011, also served for 12 years in the far less glamorous role of minority leader. Showing great patience and discipline in restoring Democratic control of the chamber and awaiting the election of a Democratic president, she led for two years a comfortable majority, though there were the customary clashes within the Democratic Caucus—notably between young liberals, who were mostly racial minorities, and the centrist "majority makers" who took swing districts, a large share of whom were women. Unexpectedly, the election of a Democratic president in 2020 was accompanied by a double-digit loss of House seats, which left her with a razor-thin majority.

The only woman to serve as Speaker, her accomplishments have been among the most productive for the House in the past century. The many cycles of her command have demonstrated that she has been one of the most polarizing figures in politics, even within her own party. Especially in her response to the complexities of the coronavirus, Pelosi was more in command than ever in negotiations with the Trump administration—with the unusual circumstance that she and President Donald Trump had developed a deep mutual enmity and had stopped communicating. She has understood, and deftly adjusted to, her own shortcomings, such as her limited ability to appeal beyond her enthusiastic political base. Perhaps her greatest skill, which she learned as the youngest of six children of the vaunted d'Alesandro family of Baltimore, has been the care and feeding of a partisan organization, including the two-way demands of political loyalty.

Detested by Republicans for her proudly liberal views and assertive style, Pelosi has been beloved in her party—even by her internal critics—for her legislative accomplishments as well as her fundraising and politicking, which continued unabated in her 80s. As Trump learned quickly and painfully after she returned as Speaker, Pelosi and her persistence should never be underestimated. Her longevity and her unapologetic control place her in the top ranks of influential House Speakers —with Joe Cannon and Sam Rayburn, whose legacies on Capitol Hill offer everyday reminders of their influence. And yet, that made it all the more remarkable that her own party forced her to an agreement that she would exit as Speaker by 2022, a timetable she had defiantly resisted before she realized that it was an offer she could not refuse if she wanted to remain as Speaker.

Elected to Congress in June 1987, she has the energy and shrewdness of one who has handled the most delicate of political chores, and the charm and unflappability of one who is the mother of five and grandmother of nine. During her most recent eight years as minority leader, Pelosi's public image receded while Republicans ran thousands of ads vilifying her in their successful campaign to retain control of the House. In 2018, voters—especially in the pivotal suburbs—no longer were swayed by the warnings of GOP strategists and candidates or presidential tweets that a return of Democratic control under Pelosi would be tantamount to the Apocalypse.

Democrats' dismal showings in the 2010 and 2014 midterm elections fueled speculation and some internal demands that it was time for her to step aside. But she has proven far too skilled at hauling in campaign funds. "I'm the one that brung everyone to the party by winning the House in the first place," she told The Washington Post during the 2016 cycle. "I could have walked away, but we built something and then we want to take it to the next step"—winning back control of the House. In 2018, with help from the rank and file, she delivered on her plea, well-known to fans of the old Oakland Raiders across the Bay from Pelosi's district: "Just win, baby."

Pelosi grew up on Albemarle Street in Baltimore's Little Italy, just east of downtown. Her father, Thomas D'Alesandro Jr., served in the House from 1939 to 1947 and was mayor of Baltimore for 12 years after that. Her mother, Annunciata D'Alesandro ("Big Nancy"), was an indefatigable political organizer, and her brother, Thomas, was mayor from 1967 to 1971. That period included her iconic photo as a college student at the White House, greeting President John Kennedy with her parents, which helped to seal her as a lifelong Kennedy loyalist. Pelosi says of her parents: "What I got from them was about economic fairness. That was the difference between Democrats and Republicans all those years ago." She graduated from Trinity University in Washington D.C., where she met her husband Paul. After marrying, they moved to his hometown of San Francisco. There he became a successful real estate investor, and she raised their children and got into local Democratic politics. Concerns about "economic fairness" aside, the couple eventually became extremely wealthy, with a home in San Francisco, a vineyard in the Napa Valley, a townhome in the Sierras, and a condominium in Washington. Their diversified investments ranked Pelosi seventh among the wealthiest members of Congress in 2018.

In the 1970s, Pelosi struck rough-hewn Rep. John Burton of California as just another stylish hostess in a city that had many of them. But she soon got Burton's attention and that of his older brother, Rep. Phillip Burton, the de facto liberal leader of the House, who lost his race for majority leader to Texas Democrat Jim Wright by one vote in 1976. That year, Pelosi returned east to run the Maryland campaign of presidential candidate Jerry Brown, then and later governor of California. In 1977, she became chairwoman of the Northern California Democratic Party, and four years later, she became chairwoman of the California Democratic Party. The positions required a considerable amount of diplomacy, including dealing with fractious regional antagonisms. Pelosi managed to remain on good terms with various warring Democrats and help the party hold majorities in the legislature.

Pelosi worked with Mayor Dianne Feinstein to land the 1984 Democratic National Convention for San Francisco. In 1985, she ran for Democratic National Chairman but lost to Paul Kirk. Before long, though, she had another opportunity. Phil Burton's widow, Sala Burton, was elected to succeed her husband after his death in 1983, but her health failed too. In 1987, as she was dying of cancer, she told her friends whom she wanted to succeed her: Nancy Pelosi.

This time, she ran. Her chief opponent in the Democratic primary was San Francisco Supervisor Harry Britt, who had succeeded Harvey Milk after he was assassinated. San Francisco's gay community at that time was not as mainstream as it has become, but Britt, who was gay, had a good record in office and Pelosi had to work hard to beat him, 35%-31%.

In her early years in Congress, Pelosi focused on important issues of local sensitivity. One was the Presidio. Burton had enacted a provision that transferred the Presidio from the military to the Interior Department. The problem was that it was so expensive to maintain, the cost threatened to exceed the National Park Service budget. Through several Congresses, Pelosi worked to get bipartisan support for a funding source, and in 1997 created the Presidio Trust.

Another sensitive issue was human rights, especially in China. After the Tiananmen Square massacre in 1989, Pelosi sponsored an amendment to give Chinese students the right to remain in the United States, but President George H.W. Bush vetoed it. In 1991, she became lead sponsor of the bill to make China's most-favored-nation status conditional on human rights reforms. The House overrode Bush's veto, but it was upheld in the Senate. She did all this at some political risk. Pelosi's position was by no means universally popular with Asian Americans in her district; many thought the United States should trade and negotiate quietly with China. Pelosi courted support from people on the opposite end of the ideological spectrum, especially religious conservatives in the Republican caucus who also wanted to remain vigilant on China's human rights record.

In addition to her seat on Appropriations, Pelosi became senior Democrat on the Intelligence Committee. Following the September 11 attacks, she joined in the committee's conclusion that, while the intelligence community did not have specific evidence in advance, it did have information that was relevant to the attacks.

Her move into the leadership was persistent, shrewd and well-organized. In 1997, as a member of the Ethics Committee, she doggedly pursued charges against Republican Speaker Newt Gingrich and worked with Minority Whip David Bonior in using scorched-earth tactics against him. In 1999, she launched a campaign for majority whip, anticipating Democrats would win a majority in 2000. Her opponent was Rep. Steny Hoyer. They were old acquaintances, having served as interns for Sen. Daniel Brewster of Maryland in the 1960s, but not confreres: there were considerable stylistic and ideological differences, plus apparent deep-seated antagonisms.

But in 2000, Republicans held onto their majority, and the race for majority whip was moot. Not for long, though. Michigan's Republican legislature, in drawing new congressional districts, put Bonior in a district that he could not win, and he decided to run for governor. He resigned as minority whip, and Pelosi was off and running against Hoyer. Some supporters played up her potential to become a celebrity— "a glamorous grandmother who knocks people off their feet," as then-Rep. Neil Abercrombie of Hawaii put it. With nearly unanimous support from the 32 California Democrats and from most women in the Democratic Caucus, Pelosi started with a strong base. In October 2001, she won by a convincing 118-95.

A major stepping-stone came in the fall of 2002, when she actively encouraged opponents of the resolution authorizing the use of force in Iraq, which Minority Leader Dick Gephardt had enthusiastically endorsed. Pelosi contended that supporters had not made the case for using force and that she had seen no evidence that Iraq "poses an imminent threat to our nation." To the surprise of many, her efforts helped win 126 Democratic votes against the resolution, while 81 backed Gephardt's position. The split signaled a transition in the caucus. Once Gephardt said he was stepping down after the disappointing 2002 election, Pelosi had all but locked up the support of a majority of the caucus. Harold Ford of Tennessee made a belated, quixotic bid designed to appeal to a combination of Blacks and New Democrats, but Pelosi won 177-29.

As the Democratic leader in the House, she brought a burst of energy—and favorable press coverage—to a party that badly needed both. She showed hands-on management in selecting members for committee vacancies and in developing a Democratic message criticizing the agenda of President George W. Bush. Pelosi declared Democrats would oppose the Republicans' Medicare prescription-drug bill. But 16 Democrats voted for the final deal in November 2003, providing the critical margin for passage. She was silent about the renegades, many of whom were responding to local pressures favoring the bill.

Pelosi traveled the country in 2004 raising money and boosting local candidates. If she became Speaker, Pelosi pledged, she would reform the House to give a greater voice to all members and to assure fairness. The three-seat loss in the November election that year turned out to be yet another disappointment for House Democrats. They emerged with a "Six for '06" program, including an increase in the minimum wage and approval of the remaining recommendations of the 9/11 Commission. Pelosi campaigned tirelessly across the country and was rewarded when Democrats gained 31 seats, enough for a Democratic majority, on Election Day.

As she assumed the office that put her second in line for the presidency, Pelosi said in January 2007, "This is an historic moment, for Congress, and for the women of this country. It is a moment for which we have waited more than 200 years. For our daughters and granddaughters, today we have broken the marble ceiling. To our daughters and granddaughters, the sky is the limit."

Beneath the velvet glove, Pelosi continued to operate with an iron fist. One of her key issues was reducing carbon dioxide emissions to curb global warming. So she announced the creation of a Select Committee on Energy Independence and Global Warming, to be headed by Energy and Commerce member Edward Markey of Massachusetts, a longtime ally. Energy and Commerce Chairman John Dingell of Michigan protested that he was being sidelined, but Pelosi had her way—not for the final time.

Pelosi and her Democratic leadership ran a tight ship and were largely successful, at least in the House. The Democrats' bill to expand the Children's Health Insurance Program was passed by both chambers, but Bush vetoed it. When gasoline hit $4 a gallon and public opinion began to favor more offshore oil drilling, Pelosi refused to allow a roll call vote. "I'm trying to save the planet," she said. But Democrats, too, were coming under pressure to act on gas prices, and Pelosi agreed to allow a vote on a bill that gave states a role in offshore drilling decisions.

Then, crisis struck, as the financial industry teetered on the verge of collapse, with the potential to send the United States into a second Great Depression. Treasury Secretary Henry Paulson and Federal Reserve Chairman Ben Bernanke confronted the House in September 2008 with a request for $700 billion to bail out big, failing financial firms. Pelosi, with Financial Services Committee Chairman Barney Frank of Massachusetts, decided to grant the request. But a few days later, it became clear that many Democrats were unwilling to vote for it. Pelosi announced she would bring Democrats along if 100 Republicans supported it as well. When the bill came to a vote on Sept. 29, it was defeated, and Republicans blamed Pelosi for speaking harshly about Bush administration economic policies. The Senate changed some of the terms of the bill, and it passed on Oct. 1. The House took up the Senate version and, with some vote switches prompted by Pelosi, passed it two days later.

In the November 2008 election, Democrats gained 21 House seats. With Barack Obama, the incoming Democratic president, Pelosi entered 2009 as the leader of 257 Democrats—the biggest majority a Speaker had enjoyed since Democrat Thomas Foley of Washington in 1993-94. Pelosi made it plain to the new Obama administration that she expected it to work through her and not make side deals with Democratic factions, much less Republicans. She presided over a record of legislative accomplishments that many consider the most impressive since the Great Society Congress of 1965-66.

The first order of business was Obama's massive economic stimulus bill. Pelosi largely delegated the specifics to Appropriations Chairman David Obey of Wisconsin. The $819 billion measure was passed without a single Republican vote. The size of the stimulus was reduced in the Senate, and Pelosi negotiated hard to get the final price tag to $787 billion.

On Iraq, Pelosi said she was unhappy with Obama's decision to leave 50,000 troops there and also with the Justice Department's decision not to prosecute Bush administration officials for approving enhanced interrogation techniques. She was embarrassed when the Central Intelligence Agency released documents indicating she had been present at a September 2002 briefing where waterboarding was discussed. In a tense press conference, she said, "in that or any other briefing, we were not and, I repeat, were not told that waterboarding or any of these other enhanced interrogation techniques were used"—only that they were legal.

Pelosi again pushed hard for legislation restricting carbon emissions, her signature issue. She quietly supported California Rep. Henry Waxman's shrewdly executed campaign to replace Dingell as chairman of Energy and Commerce, with prime jurisdiction over the issue. And she worked closely with Waxman and Markey on the contents of the bill, including Waxman's concessions to win over conservative Democrats. She even met with 11 Republican moderates to get their support. In late June, the bill passed, 219-212, with eight Republicans voting yes. But the Senate did not act.

The other major initiative for Pelosi was Obama's health care overhaul. But finding agreement on complex and far-reaching changes to the medical insurance system, including a proposal to let people opt into a federally sponsored plan, delayed the bill in committee. As Pelosi had feared, opposition to the bill gained momentum at town hall meetings across the country during the August recess, including many in Democratic districts. Lawmakers were more skittish about the legislation when they returned. Pelosi agreed to changes in the "public option" but refused to give in to pressure from conservative Democrats to drop it from the bill. And, in the 11th hour and to the dismay of abortion-rights supporters, she agreed to accept Michigan Rep. Bart Stupak's cosmetic amendment that included vague language some supporters claimed would bar coverage for abortions. The bill was passed 220-215 on Nov. 7, with 39 Democrats voting no and one Republican voting yes.

Then, in January 2010, Republican Scott Brown won the special Senate election in Massachusetts for the seat vacated by the death of Ted Kennedy. In his campaign, Brown had promised to be the 41st vote against the health care bill, denying Democrats the 60 votes they needed to stop a filibuster. The obstacles were great. But Pelosi characteristically braced for the fight. "We're in the majority," she told Obama. "We'll never have a better majority in your presidency in numbers than we've got right now. We can make this work."

Public opinion polls in early 2010 showed the public to be increasingly wary of the changes to the health care system. Pelosi agreed to drop a House-passed surtax on high-income earners, which was replaced by an excise tax on high-end insurance plans. She also got Stupak and other anti-abortion lawmakers to agree to changes to their provision that they had previously deemed unacceptable. On the day of the vote, March 21, Pelosi marched with fellow Democrats from their offices to the Capitol, while an angry crowd, held back by Capitol police, chanted "Kill the bill." Pelosi's attitude toward the anti-Obama health care forces was clear in a statement in January of that year: "We will go through the gate. If the gate is closed, we will go over the fence. If the fence is too high, we will pole vault in. If that doesn't work, we will parachute in. But we are going to get health care reform passed for the American people." The final roll call was 219-212, without a single Republican vote. The Senate acquiesced to the House changes and Obama signed the bill.

Its passage was the defining moment of Pelosi's initial speakership and showcased her skills at putting together complex legislation and rounding up reluctant votes, amid volatile public opinion. Polls around the country showed a large number of Democratic incumbents trailing their Republican challengers. In September, she hoped to send Democrats home to campaign on a high note by having them vote to extend the Bush-era income tax cuts except for upper income-earners of $200,000 or more. But when it became clear the votes weren't there, she moved to adjourn a week earlier than scheduled. Her ability to control a majority, after four years of doing so time and again, was in the hands of a restless electorate in November.

That fall, Pelosi campaigned for Democrats across the country, but she was more a liability than an asset in conservative-leaning districts. Democrats lost 63 seats, the most the party had lost since the 1938 election, and Republicans took majority control in January. Following the election, it was widely expected that Pelosi would relinquish her hold on her leadership position. But after two days of prayer and conversations, Pelosi announced she wanted to run for minority leader again. She could not stop North Carolina's conservative Heath Shuler from launching a quixotic challenge. Pelosi prevailed in the caucus vote 150-43. When asked to explain why she won, she said, "Because I'm an effective leader, because we got the job done on health care and Wall Street reform and consumer protection, the list goes on. Because they know that I'm the person that can attract the resources, both intellectual and otherwise, to take us to victory because I have done it before." Still, Pelosi began in January 2011 with 19 Democrats voting against her — the most defections that any party leader had suffered since 1913. Most of those votes were cast by the diminished corps of moderate "Blue Dog" Democrats.

Despite her furious fundraising, Pelosi and her lieutenants struggled to craft a path to the majority that would circumvent the twin Democratic demons of redistricting and demographic shifts in many large metropolitan areas. In many parts of the nation, from Pennsylvania and Ohio to Florida and

Texas, where Democrats once dominated the House delegations, her cultural liberalism and the relentless attacks of Republicans severely limited her appearances in public events on behalf of Democratic candidates or House members with whom she worked regularly at the Capitol. After two more elections, House Democrats in January 2015 held 188 seats, their smallest total since 1928.

At that point, Pelosi bowed to demands for new, younger faces in leadership. She appointed Rep. Ben Ray Luján of New Mexico, a Latino, to head the Democratic Congressional Campaign Committee. Later, she installed Eric Swalwell, a Bay Area upstart, as co-chair of the powerful Steering and Policy Committee along with longtime ally Rosa DeLauro of Connecticut. But her diminished influence was displayed in her inability to deliver the ranking member post on the Energy and Commerce Committee to her close friend and fellow Californian Anna Eshoo. New Jersey's Frank Pallone, working with Hoyer and other allies, beat out Eshoo for the job on a secret ballot after the 2014 election.

News reports revealed growing frustration among younger rank-and-file members with what they saw as the entrenchment of longtime, and aging, figures in leadership and top committee slots— mostly they were Pelosi allies. The 63 votes for 43-year-old Rep. Tim Ryan of Ohio in November 2016 when he challenged Pelosi for leader were a manifestation of economic populism and the desire for change, though she remained secure with a majority of the Caucus. She responded that "our values" continued to unify Democrats but continued tinkering with leadership ranks, including the creation of a new "vice ranking member" slot for a junior Democrat at each House committee.

In the minority, Pelosi's lingering legislative influence was both positive and negative. In March 2015, she worked with Speaker John Boehner in an impressive joint show of strength to win overwhelming House passage of a "doc fix" bill that solved longstanding problems with Medicare and other health care programs. Then, she had a showdown with Obama in June 2015 when she joined with rank-and-file Democrats who mostly opposed the expedited congressional procedures on the prospective Trans-Pacific Partnership agreement the president and his aides were negotiating with Asian allies and had become a centerpiece of his second-term agenda. In effect, Pelosi abandoned the lame-duck president for the Democrats' allies in organized labor. The result was a narrow defeat for her. In the 2016 election, Democrats regained only six seats. The bigger shock of Hillary Clinton losing to Donald Trump left House Democrats with an even weaker legislative hand. Eventually, however, the unpopularity of Trump and Democrats' rabid opposition to the Republican agenda led to big House gains in 2018. Pelosi was instrumental in achieving that success—especially with fundraising and candidate recruitment. She kept a lower profile in seeking to shape the campaign message.

Their initial breakthrough came in March 2018 when Democratic newcomer Conor Lamb won the vacant seat in the Pittsburgh suburbs and rural areas of southwest Pennsylvania—though Lamb emphasized during his campaign that he would not support Pelosi for a House leadership position. In his ads, the former Marine called it "a big lie" by Republicans that he would support Pelosi. Not least because of Lamb's success, that soon became a pattern for frontline Democratic candidates. Pelosi and her allies shrugged, at least for public consumption. "I think I'm worth the trouble," she told reporters, when asked about the continuing GOP attacks on Democrats who might be supporting her.

In her efforts to assist candidates across the country, Pelosi's actions fit a familiar pattern: closed-door events with the candidate and donors; very few public sessions; and minimal contact with local news media, except for occasional interviews with friendly reporters. For the most part, she stayed out of Trump's line of fire. And, compared to years earlier, her comments about Democrats' legislative plans were more generic.

Locking in the requisite 218 votes to become Speaker became an exhausting process that took nearly a month to resolve, with various Democrats voicing differing levels of commitment and seeking favors in exchange. She finally secured the requisite support only after submitting to the demands of some Democratic reformers that she agree to limit her tenure to four more years as the top House Democrat.

Her challenge was all the more difficult because many of the Democrats least willing to support her were elected in districts most likely to have competitive contests in 2020. In the January 2019 selection of the new Speaker, Pelosi received 220 votes—two more than a bare majority. Of the 15 Democrats who voted for another person or responded "present," 11 (including Lamb) were serving their first full term. Each of those 11 took a seat that previously was held by a Republican. For public consumption, she brushed off these concessions as largely a nuisance.

The next two years revealed growing legislative dysfunction—but demands for huge federal support in 2020 during the coronavirus pandemic. She controlled those negotiations with Treasury Secretary Steven Mnuchin—with their endless political, policy and financial complexities—and largely dictated the outcome, with scant opportunity for House members to second-guess her. In addition, during little more than a year, the House twice voted articles of impeachment against Trump on close to party-line votes. On the first set of charges, dealing with Trump's attempt to collect a political favor from the president of Ukraine, Pelosi was more cautious about proceeding than were many House Democrats.

Pelosi also became enmeshed in Democratic primaries. In an embarrassing setback, she backed Rep. Joe Kennedy in his failed September 2020 challenge to Sen. Ed Markey, Pelosi's erstwhile ally. But she successfully lined up against the progressive insurgent in the primary challenge in Massachusetts that same day to House Ways and Means Committee Chairman Richard Neal—a case in which the House outcome was more relevant to her immediate influence. The more jarring setbacks came in November when 12 Democratic incumbents (including three from California) were defeated —all but one of whom were freshmen. All Republican incumbents were reelected.

Back home, Pelosi has been overwhelmingly reelected—typically with more than 80 percent of the vote. In 2008, antiwar protester Cindy Sheehan ran against her as an independent. Pelosi refused to debate or acknowledge Sheehan, who wound up getting 16 percent of the vote.

As she moves toward the end of her congressional career, Pelosi will leave a legacy that is historic in ways that go far beyond her gender-based accomplishment.

CA-12: San Francisco

Cook Partisan Voting Index: D+38

Population		Race and Ethnicity		Income	
Total	779,824	White	46.90%	Median Income	$127,290
Land area (sq. miles)	39	Black	5.80%	District Income Rank	4
Pop/ sq mi	20,010.88	Latino	15.20%	Poverty Rate	9.50%
Born in State	39.50%	Asian	32.80%	With health insurance	96.10%
		Two or more races	5.90%	Cash public assistance	1.60%
Age Groups		Other	8.50%	Food stamp/SNAP	5.50%
Under 18	13.60%				
18-34	30.30%	**Education**		**Work**	
35-64	40.60%	H.S grad or less	22.40%	White Collar	61.80%
Over 64	15.60%	Some college	16.80%	Sales and Service	30.70%
		College Degree, 4 yr	35.90%	Blue Collar	7.50%
Military		Post grad	25.00%	Government	10.20%
Veteran/ Active Duty	2.80%				

2020 Pres. Vote	Biden	337,517	(86%)	Trump	46,574	(12%)			
2016 Pres. Vote	Clinton	309,221	(86%)	Trump	31,158	(9%)	Stein	8,881	(3%)
	Johnson	7,949	(2%)						

San Francisco: On Feb. 20, 1915, a crowd of 150,000 gathered on the grounds of the Panama-Pacific International Exposition to see the Spanish-Italian baroque-style structure built on reclaimed land in what was to become San Francisco's Marina district. The Exposition ostensibly celebrated the completion of the Panama Canal, but it was clearly intended to show off San Francisco's recovery from the 1906 earthquake. It also spotlighted the city as the central focus of America's efforts to open an economic door to the eastern part of the world, especially in light of the acquisition of Hawaii and the Philippines and of its interest in an open-door policy with China and trade with Japan. The Exposition established the physical style of San Francisco, encouraging the use of Mediterranean color, accent and detail that characterizes many of the post-Victorian houses and commercial structures in The City, as the San Francisco Examiner called it for years. On a sunny day, San Francisco can look almost tropical, with brown mountains baking in the sun and light shining off the pastel stucco buildings. When the clouds scud in from the Pacific, it can look sinister, full of dark corners where a private detective's partner might encounter unexpected temptations. The buildings can be majestic, like the monumental Beaux-Arts City Hall. The tawdry hotels of the Tenderloin District have become a gritty neighborhood with its own charms. The Crosstown Trail, a 17-mile hike, covers the entire city.

San Francisco grew from nothing to a major city in 1850, an instant product of the California Gold Rush. Within just a few years, culture was flourishing in the city, and San Francisco developed a parochial pride in the great writers who worked there—Jack London, Ambrose Bierce, Frank Norris—and in giving birth to the Arts and Crafts movement. Later, San Francisco newspaper scribe Herb Caen coined the term "beatnik" and wrote definitively about the hippies who thronged Haight-Ashbury in the 1960s. A decade later, the city was among the first to embrace the gay rights movement, in The Castro district. Gays lately have been moving to the suburbs and straights have been moving into the city. Over the years, the city's booming economy attracted talented newcomers, though its population is increasingly polarized between high-income and low-income. In a growing entertainment district in Mission Bay, the NBA's Warriors opened in 2019 their $500 million Chase Center, though no longer performing at a championship level—replacing their longtime home across the bay at the Oracle Center.

The income inequality ratio in San Francisco is especially high chiefly because the wealthy are really wealthy. Thanks to the flood of high-tech workers pouring in, many of whom commute daily to Silicon Valley on luxurious corporate buses ("Google buses"), the city's housing costs are so high that low-income people have become virtually precluded from living in most parts of the city. In early 2018, the median home-sale price was a mind-boggling $1.6 million, which had doubled in five years. Federal statisticians that year calculated the break point for low-income families in San Francisco, plus Marin and San Mateo counties, was $117,400. In a Brookings Institution study of economic inclusion that year, San Francisco ranked 84th among 100 regions in the United States. San Francisco has the lowest percentage of children, 13 percent, of any major city, raising questions about its post-modern future. Although it is proudly tolerant, San Francisco is one of California's whitest cities, with only about half as many Black residents as it had in 1970. The population on the west side is substantially Asian. Demographers projected that the gentrified city could regain its white-majority status. The commuter traffic, already heavy on the freeway and in rapid transit, has started to overwhelm the city's growing network of ferries.

In the past half-century, the city has elected a diverse group of mostly staunch liberal politicians, notably Vice President Kamala Harris. In 1978, Mayor George Moscone and the first openly gay supervisor, Harvey Milk were shot to death by Dan White, a former city supervisor, who was found guilty of the lesser crime of voluntary manslaughter. Over the next decade, the city's cultural liberalism was tempered by Democratic Mayor Dianne Feinstein, who vetoed a domestic partnership ordinance and opposed commercial rent control. In 1995, Willie Brown, ousted after 15 years as speaker of the state Assembly, was elected mayor. His political flair was always in evidence, but high taxes and an increasing homeless population drove out blue-collar families.

As his successor, Gavin Newsom in 2004 began issuing marriage licenses to same-sex couples. The state Supreme Court ordered him to stop and voided the marriages. In 2008, Newsom was vindicated when the same court declared the ban on same-sex marriage unconstitutional. That action was temporarily overturned later that year by the statewide Proposition 8, in a 52%-48% vote. The U.S. Supreme Court nullified that referendum in its seminal ruling in 2013, when it ruled that supporters of the ballot measure had no standing. After Newsom was elected lieutenant governor, City Administrator Ed Lee was appointed interim mayor. Lee, the first Asian American to serve in that office, subsequently won two four-year terms, though he died of a heart attack in 2017. With London Breed, an African American was elected mayor in a city with a 5 percent Black population.

The 12th Congressional District of California takes in most of the city and county of San Francisco, except the southwest corner, which is in the 14th District. It includes all the high-rise downtown area, the crowded and bustling Chinatown, Telegraph Hill, Nob Hill and Russian Hill, North Beach, Pacific Heights, and the Marina District (which does not have a very big marina). In the valleys are the Fillmore and Western Addition areas. The 12th also has Noe Valley; the Castro, still mainly gay; Haight-Ashbury, once the bedraggled center of hippie culture and now another gentrifying San Francisco neighborhood; and Potrero Hill, with its restored houses overlooking downtown. The Asian population of the district has grown to 33 percent, African Americans have dropped to 6 percent and Hispanics are 15 percent. Joe Biden won 86 percent of the vote in 2020, ranking the district fifth in the Cook PVI of the most Democratic districts in the nation.

Barbara Lee (D)

Elected 1998, 12th full term, b. Jul 16, 1946; El Paso, TX; Mills College, B.A., 1973; University of CA, Berkeley, M.S.W., 1975; Baptist; Divorced; 2 children; 5 grandchildren.

Elected Office: CA Assembly, 1991-1997; CA Senate, 1997-1998.

Professional Career: Chief of Staff, U.S. Rep. Ron Dellums, 1975-1987.

DC Office: 2470 RHOB 20515, 202-225-2661, Fax: 202-225-9817, lee.house.gov

State Offices: Oakland, 510-763-0370.

Committees: House Democratic Steering and Policy Committee Co-Chair. *Appropriations*: Agriculture, Rural Development, FDA & Related Agencies; Labor, Health & Human Services, Education & Related Agencies; State, Foreign Operations & Related Programs (Chmn). *Budget*.

Group Ratings

	ADA	ACLU	AFL-CIO	LCV	COC	HAFA	ACU	CFG	FRC
2020	**	88%	**	100%	-	0%	4%	**	-
2019	100%	C	90%	100%	42%	C	4%	12%	5%

Almanac Ratings 2019-2020

	Economy	Social	Foreign	Composite
Liberal	100%	100%	100%	100%
Conservative	0%	0%	0%	0%

Key Votes of the 116th Congress

1. U.S./Mex./Can. trade deal N	5. Russia sanctions Y	9. Firearms background checks Y
2. First Coronavirus response Y	6. Troops in Syria Y	10. Spending at the border N
3. HEROES Act Y	7. Veto arms sales to Saudis Y	11. Marijuana liberalized rules Y
4. CASH Act Y	8. Defense $$$, veto override N	12. Electoral College objections N

Election Results

Election	Name (Party)	Vote (%)		Cand. Spent	Ind. Exp. Support	Ind. Exp. Oppose
2020 General	Barbara Lee (D)	327,863	(90%)	$1,365,068	$3,166	
	Nikka Piterman (R)	34,955	(10%)	$6,380		$113
2020 Primary	Barbara Lee (D)	230,482	(93%)			

Prior winning percentages: 2018 (88%), 2016 (91%), 2014 (89%), 2012 (87%), 2010 (84%), 2008 (86%), 2006 (86%), 2004 (85%), 2002 (81%), 2000 (85%), 1998 (83%), 1998 special (67%)

Democrat Barbara Lee, who won a special election in 1998, is one of Congress' most liberal members and a close ally of Speaker Nancy Pelosi, who represents the district across San Francisco Bay. From her seat on the Appropriations Committee, Lee has sought to help the poor while condemning U.S. military involvement overseas and seeking to broaden diplomatic relations. She narrowly lost two bids for House leadership posts to other Democrats who are racial minorities. In 2021, she had her long-awaited elevation to chair an Appropriations subcommittee.

Lee spent her childhood in Texas and says her political thinking was shaped by her early exposure to race discrimination. While in labor with her, Lee's mother was at first denied treatment at an El Paso hospital. Lee attended a segregated school in that city until her parents sent their children to a Catholic school. In 1960, the family moved to Southern California, where Lee was the first Black cheerleader in her high school, a distinction she won after enlisting the help of the local chapter of the NAACP. In 2008, Lee authored a memoir, Renegade for Peace and Justice, in which she discussed her experiences as a single welfare mother raising two children while attending college and her early days of social advocacy. "In order to go the policy front, I had to do the personal," she said. Lee graduated from Mills College in Oakland and got a degree in social work at the University of California, Berkeley. She started a community mental health center in Berkeley and worked as a staffer for 12 years for Rep. Ron Dellums, who chaired the House Armed Services Committee. She was elected to the California Assembly in 1990 and to the Senate in 1996. After Dellums announced he was resigning, he endorsed Lee as his successor, and she won the special election with 67 percent of the vote. She has not faced a serious primary or general election challenge.

Lee agitates for a reduction in the nation's weapons stockpiles and sharp cuts in Pentagon spending. She was a founder of the Out of Iraq Caucus, a group of the most vocal antiwar House members. In 2008, the House passed, 399-24, her bill to prevent permanent U.S. military bases in Iraq or U.S. control of Iraqi oil. In January 2015, after President Barack Obama announced his plan to restore diplomatic relations with Cuba, the San Francisco Chronicle reported that she had a "gentlewoman's agreement" with Obama that she would become the ambassador to Havana. Lee denied the report and full-scale diplomatic relations were not restored, but she enthusiastically backed his efforts to lift the embargo and reach out to Cuba. She visited Cuba more than two dozen times and met senior officials to facilitate relatively minor agricultural and tourist dealings and to encourage more trust. When Fidel Castro died in November 2016, she extended her "deepest condolences," sparking widespread criticism.

Lee's consistent opposition to military action occasionally has made her a lonely voice. As most Democrats voted to authorize the Clinton administration to bomb Serbia in 1999, Lee was the only House member to oppose a resolution supporting U.S. troops. In September 2001, she was the only member of Congress to vote against the resolution authorizing the use of force in response to the terrorist attacks. "If we rush to launch a counterattack, we run too great a risk that women, children and other noncombatants will be caught in the crossfire," she said. Lee received threats of violence, and the Capitol police provided her with 24-hour protection.

In 2017, she made another bid to remove presidential authority to use military force against the Islamic State. This time, with a Republican in the White House, some conservative Republicans joined her—citing the need to safeguard the power of Congress to declare war. To the surprise of many, Lee was successful in an Appropriations Committee vote. But Speaker Paul Ryan used his parliamentary power to remove Lee's amendment before the spending bill reached the House floor.

In January 2020, after Democrats regained House control, Lee prevailed, 236-166, on a House vote to repeal the 2002 authorization for the use of force in Iraq—which was applied to other conflicts after Saddam Hussein had been ousted. She called the vote "a historic step to reassert our constitutional authority and stop our endless wars."

In July 2020, Lee achieved another long-term objective, when the House, on a 305-113 vote, passed legislation to remove five statues of Confederate leaders from the Capitol. "It's past time that we end the glorification of men who committed treason against the United States in a concerted effort to keep African Americans in chains," Lee said. Although the Republican-controlled Senate did not act on the measure, some of the statues subsequently were removed by the states that originally sponsored them. On another Capitol controversy, Lee said the January 2021 "attempted coup" demonstrated the "dangerous and violent white supremacy embedded in America's DNA."

In 2007, House Speaker Nancy Pelosi gave Lee a seat on Appropriations. As co-chair of the Progressive Caucus, Lee laid out an agenda with three priorities: economic justice and security; protection of civil rights and liberties; and promotion of global peace. As Republican criticism mounted over earmarked spending, Lee remained a staunch defender of the practice. "I'll tell them to come to my community and see what we can accomplish with whatever federal dollars we can get," she said in 2009.

After the 2008 election, Lee became chairwoman of the Congressional Black Caucus. She and other members lamented Obama's failure to pay more attention to minorities. Unlike many other Black Caucus members who backed Hillary Clinton in 2008, Lee was his early supporter, in large part because of Obama's opposition to the Iraq war.

In February 2019, Lee was an early co-chair of the presidential campaign of Kamala Harris, who launched her campaign with a rally in Oakland. Before Joe Biden selected Harris as his running mate, some California supporters of Bernie Sanders urged him to select Lee or Rep. Karen Bass, also from California. (Bass was on Biden's short list. Lee was not.)

Pursuing her longstanding ambition for a leadership post, Lee ran for vice chair of the Democratic Caucus following the 2016 election. Against Rep. Linda Sanchez from Los Angeles, Lee faced multiple obstacles: The party leadership already included Pelosi from the Bay Area and Rep. James Clyburn of South Carolina from the Black Caucus. Sanchez, at 47, was a generation younger and better connected to various Democratic factions. Sanchez won, 98-96.

Two years later, Lee ran for the vacant position of caucus chair—in the House majority, this time. Her opponent was Hakeem Jeffries of New York, a 48-year-old Democrat, also from the Black

Caucus. She lost, 123-113, with some residue of ill will. Lee said she was the victim, at 72, of age and sex discrimination—though each of the three top Democratic leaders was older than her and the Speaker was a woman. "That's something that women, especially women of color, African-American women, have to face," Lee said.

Pelosi named Lee as the third co-chair of the Democratic Steering and Policy Committee. At Appropriations, in 2021, Lee finally achieved her long-sought goal of chairing the Subcommittee on State, Foreign Operations and Related Programs.

CA-13: East Bay   **Cook Partisan Voting Index: D+40**

Population		Race and Ethnicity		Income	
Total	768,889	White	40.60%	Median Income	$91,514
Land area (sq. miles)	97	Black	17.50%	District Income Rank	51
Pop/ sq mi	7,943.89	Latino	22.30%	Poverty Rate	13.20%
Born in State	50.70%	Asian	20.70%	With health insurance	95.00%
		Two or more races	6.50%	Cash public assistance	3.20%
Age Groups		Other	14.60%	Food stamp/SNAP	7.20%
Under 18	18.30%				
18-34	28.60%	**Education**		**Work**	
35-64	38.30%	H.S grad or less	26.30%	White Collar	54.50%
Over 64	14.70%	Some college	20.00%	Sales and Service	31.50%
		College Degree, 4 yr	30.10%	Blue Collar	14.00%
Military		Post grad	23.70%	Government	15.50%
Veteran/ Active Duty	3.70%				

2020 Pres. Vote	Biden	335,474	(89%)	Trump	33,907	(9%)		
2016 Pres. Vote	Clinton	291,926	(87%)	Trump	22,743	(7%)	Stein	12,039	(4%)

Oakland, Berkeley: On the East Bay opposite San Francisco, Oakland and Berkeley stand today on one of the picturesque sites in America, overlooking the San Francisco-Oakland Bay Bridge and the Golden Gate Bridge and basking in the sunshine that is more common here than across the bay. Both cities host great institutions. In different ways they became museum pieces, antiques from a moment in the 1960s when both, especially Berkeley, gained identities that became hard to shake. But Oakland, in particular, has been transformed by the wealth that has made San Francisco accessible chiefly to the top income classes.

Berkeley was founded as a university town, named after the 18th-century Irish philosopher Bishop George Berkeley for his proclamation, "Westward the course of empire takes its way." Famous for years as the home of first-rate scholarship at the University of California, Berkeley became famous politically in the 1960s as ground zero of student rebellion. In 1969, students led protests at "People's Park," a lot owned by the university, and Republican Gov. Ronald Reagan sent in the National Guard to protect state property, an episode in which both sides relished the confrontation. Berkeley gave birth to a street culture that still exists. With its view of the bay, the campus is beautiful, and old buildings in the city are grand.

Oakland has a different history, centered on commerce. (Gertrude Stein was wrong: There is a there there.) It became the western terminus of the transcontinental railroad in 1870 and was connected by ferry to San Francisco. It has always had heavy industry, and its port today is the tenth-busiest in the country. The docks attracted young roustabouts like the writer Jack London, after whom a downtown square is named. With the Bay Area's largest Black community, Oakland spawned the Black Panthers, a militant organization that came to define late 1960s radicalism. "The Black Panthers were mostly young activists whose personal lives and oftentimes limited professional opportunities were defined by Oakland's increasingly impoverished landscape," wrote Peniel Joseph in his history of the Black Power movement, Waiting 'Til the Midnight Hour.

As mayor between his stints as governor, Jerry Brown irritated local factions by firing department heads and ignoring longstanding alliances, but he seemed to take seriously his mission of propelling Oakland to prominence. Crime rates dropped, and the local economy thrived. Many longtime residents, especially African Americans, complained about rising costs, and they moved to the outskirts. The city's Black population fell from 47 percent in 1980 to 24 percent in 2019. Still, the nationwide protests against police tactics in 2020 rang loudly here. Oakland agreed to remove police from local schools. Both Oakland and Berkeley cut millions of dollars from their police budgets.

Population in Oakland, after falling by 10,000 from 2000 to 2010, increased by 42,000 in the next nine years. Hispanics increased to 27 percent and Asians to 16 percent. Alameda County was Asian-plurality, with 32 percent. In a sign of income inequality in Oakland, both the poverty rate and per capita income were significantly above the state rates. The city agreed in 2020 to pay $33 million to victims of the horrific 2016 Ghost Ship fire that killed 36 persons at a warehouse in an entertainment district, which perversely put a spotlight on the bustling arts scene in Oakland.

The local sports scene was in turmoil. After winning the NBA championship three times in the previous four years at Oracle Arena in Oakland, the Golden State Warriors crossed the bay in 2019 to a new arena in San Francisco's Mission Bay. The NFL's Raiders, following the failure of lengthy discussions for a new stadium in Oakland, moved in 2020 to a publicly financed stadium in Las Vegas. The apparent good news was that, in December 2019, baseball's Athletics announced a deal with Alameda County in which they would build a stadium near Jack London Square and convert their home at the Oakland Coliseum into a "multi-sports facility" that would include affordable housing and parks. But subsequent delays resulting from an environmental review and the coronavirus raised doubts about the scheduled completion in 2023.

The 13th Congressional District of California consists of Oakland and Berkeley; the suburb of San Leandro, originally settled by Portuguese immigrants; and the island city of Alameda. It's the most Democratic district in California and, for decades, has been one of the most liberal in the nation. The 9 percent of the vote in 2020 for Donald Trump in the 13th,though two percentage points higher than in 2016, was his second-lowest in the nation—behind only the African-American majority district in Philadelphia.

Jackie Speier (D)

Elected 2008, 7th full term, b. May 14, 1950; San Francisco County, CA; University of CA, Davis, B.A., 1972; University of CA Hastings College of Law, J.D., 1976; Roman Catholic; Married (Barry Dennis); 2 children.

Elected Office: San Mateo County Board of Supervisors, 1980-1986; CA Assembly, 1986-1998; CA Senate, 1998-2006.

Professional Career: Staff aide, Rep. Leo Ryan, 1973-1978; Director, gov. affairs, Community Gatepath, 1996-1998; Director, gov. affairs, Electronic Arts, 1996-1998; Attorney, 2007-2008.

DC Office: 2465 RHOB 20515, 202-225-3531, Fax: 202-226-4183, speier.house.gov

State Offices: San Mateo, 650-342-0300.

Committees: *Armed Services*: Military Personnel (Chmn); Readiness. *Oversight & Reform*: National Security; Subcommittee on Economic & Consumer Policy. *Permanent Select on Intelligence*: Defense Intelligence & Warfighter Support; Strategic Technologies & Advanced Research (Chmn).

Group Ratings

	ADA	ACLU	AFL-CIO	LCV	COC	HAFA	ACU	CFG	FRC
2020	**	79%	**	100%	-	0%	4%	**	-
2019	95%	C	95%	93%	52%	C	4%	19%	0%

Almanac Ratings 2019-2020

	Economy	Social	Foreign	Composite
Liberal	100%	100%	52%	84%
Conservative	0%	0%	48%	16%

Key Votes of the 116th Congress

1. U.S./Mex./Can. trade deal Y	5. Russia sanctions Y	9. Firearms background checks Y
2. First Coronavirus response N/A	6. Troops in Syria N/A	10. Spending at the border N
3. HEROES Act Y	7. Veto arms sales to Saudis N/A	11. Marijuana liberalized rules Y
4. CASH Act Y	8. Defense $$$, veto override Y	12. Electoral College objections N

Election Results

Election	Name (Party)	Vote (%)	Cand. Spent	Ind. Exp. Support	Ind. Exp. Oppose
2020 General	Jackie Speier (D)	278,300 (79%)	$761,112	$2,166	
	Ran Petel (R)	72,705 (21%)			$59
2020 Primary	Jackie Speier (D)	158,158 (77%)			

Prior winning percentages: 2018 (79%), 2016 (81%), 2014 (77%), 2012 (79%), 2010 (76%), 2008 special (75%)

Jackie Speier, who won a special election in 2008, has become an influential House Democrat dealing with military and intelligence issues. She has become an outspoken advocate for gender equity and has taken a special interest in accountability for rapes and sexual assaults within the military and in society as a whole. She brought with her unique experiences as a young House aide. A committed liberal, she also has focused on consumer-protection issues.

Born in San Francisco's Sunset district, Speier graduated from the University of California, Davis, and got her law degree at UC Hastings College of the Law. While an undergraduate, she interned in Sacramento for Democratic Assemblyman Leo Ryan and later joined his staff after he was elected to Congress. In November 1978, Speier accompanied third-term Rep. Ryan to Jonestown Guyana to investigate claims that some of Ryan's constituents, who were members of a church called the Peoples Temple, were being held against their will by the Rev. Jim Jones of San Francisco. Some defectors from the church joined Ryan's entourage for the journey home, but the group made it only as far as the airport. Four assassins sent by Jones opened fire on the defenseless group. Ryan and four others, including two journalists, were killed. Speier was shot five times and left for dead on the airstrip, where she waited 15 hours before the Guyana police rescued her. In the meantime, Jones, back at his jungle camp, set in motion events that shocked the world. He forced his cult followers to commit "revolutionary suicide" by drinking poison-laced punch, which resulted in the deaths of more than 900 followers, some of them babies and children.

Once back in California, Speier underwent 10 surgeries, including skin grafts. Despite her injuries, she ran in the special election to succeed Ryan, gaining only 15 percent of the vote and finishing third among Democrats in the primary. She then went local to build her political career, starting on the San Mateo County Board of Supervisors and serving 20 years in the state legislature. Her pinnacle achievement was legislation protecting consumers' privacy from invasive practices by banks and insurance companies. In 2006, she unsuccessfully sought the nomination for lieutenant governor.

When Democratic Rep. Tom Lantos, chairman of the House Foreign Affairs Committee and the only Holocaust survivor to serve in Congress, announced his retirement in January 2008, he endorsed Speier as his successor. He died in February of complications from cancer. She won the all-party special election with 75 percent of the vote against four little-known opponents.

Immediately after she took her oath of office, she caused a ruckus when she launched a sharp partisan attack on President George W. Bush's handling of the war in Iraq. "History will not judge us kindly if we sacrifice four generations of Americans because of the folly of one," she declared. Her remarks triggered a volley of boos among Republican members on the House floor.

As a member of the Armed Services Committee, Speier regularly has spoken about military men and women who have been raped or sexually assaulted, and she has taken the lead in improving delivery of benefits to Bay Area veterans. As chairwoman of the committee's personnel panel, she has advocated steps such as free birth control and counseling for women in the military. Her objective, Speier said, was "to ensure that our government demonstrates the same level of commitment to our military personnel that they demonstrate by putting their lives on the line to defend our country." On the House Intelligence Committee, she said in 2017 that Rep. Devin Nunes of California, the chairman of the panel, should resign that post because he had shared sensitive information with White House officials. Nunes subsequently stepped aside as chairman for several months, pending an ethics investigation.

Speier expanded her focus on sexual assault to academia, where she has shined the spotlight on sexual harassers. She filed a bill to require universities to operate under greater transparency with respect to substantiated cases of sex discrimination. In 2014, she called on NFL Commissioner Roger Goodell to resign because of his handling of domestic-violence cases involving several of the league's players.

When the "me too" movement gained force in 2017, Speier took the lead in calling for accountability for members of Congress accused of sexual harassment. With Republican Rep. Barbara Comstock of Virginia, she described incidents that she and other women experienced as congressional aides—including, Speier said, some who had "their private parts grabbed on the House floor." She explicitly condemned the behavior of three members who subsequently resigned within weeks. In December 2018, Speier joined a bipartisan group that reached agreement to revise procedures for how sexual harassment allegations are handled in Congress, including a requirement that violators are personally liable for financial settlements. "Time is finally up for members of Congress who think that they can sexually harass and get away with it," she said.

In September 2020, Speier joined the four first-term Democratic women known as "The Squad" in filing a resolution urging policies that protect women in politics from violence or threats. "Each of my colleagues has experienced this form of weaponized sexism, whether it be death or rape threats, shootings, sexual harassment, verbal assaults, or worse," she said. Also that month, following an investigation with other House members of the murder of Vanessa Guillen at Fort Hood, Speier joined them on a bill to revise the Uniform Code of Military Justice; one change would make sexual harassment a crime.

Speier considered running for state attorney general in 2010 but opted to stay in the House. She has not faced a serious reelection challenge. She has published a memoir, Undaunted, including candid accounts of her personal and professional trials.

CA-14: San Francisco Peninsula   Cook Partisan Voting Index: D+28

Population		Race and Ethnicity		Income	
Total	742,980	White	43.60%	Median Income	$125,980
Land area (sq. miles)	260	Black	2.50%	District Income Rank	6
Pop/ sq mi	2,863.12	Latino	23.10%	Poverty Rate	6.60%
Born in State	45.20%	Asian	36.30%	With health insurance	95.50%
		Two or more races	5.30%	Cash public assistance	1.30%
Age Groups		Other	12.30%	Food stamp/SNAP	3.00%
Under 18	18.40%				
18-34	23.70%	**Education**		**Work**	
35-64	40.80%	H.S grad or less	26.90%	White Collar	50.10%
Over 64	17.10%	Some college	23.50%	Sales and Service	36.00%
		College Degree, 4 yr	28.70%	Blue Collar	13.80%
Military		Post grad	20.80%	Government	12.30%
Veteran/ Active Duty	3.50%				

2020 Pres. Vote	Biden	279,708	(78%)	Trump	73,798	(20%)		
2016 Pres. Vote	Clinton	229,008	(76%)	Trump	54,229	(18%)	Johnson	8,126	(3%)

San Mateo: The city of San Francisco sits at the tip of the San Francisco Peninsula on the California coast. This is geologically interesting country. The San Andreas Fault runs just east of the Coast Range, underneath the reservoirs that store San Francisco's water supply. To the west are green mountains running down to the ocean. To the east is a zone of flat land between the mountains and San Francisco Bay, an unbroken chain of suburbs and urban settlement, with light industry and salt flats along the bay front. Daly City and Pacifica on the ocean are a kind of extension of San Francisco's old working-class districts, with boxy houses on streets looking out on the ocean or the freeway. Today, these neighborhoods are home to many of the Bay Area's Asian immigrants. Pacific Islanders are prominent, too. A large concentration of Samoans is in Daly City, and San Bruno is home to a sizable Tongan community. A strip of Highway 1 that winds along the coastal cliffs south of Pacifica has passed through an area known as "Devil's Slide" for the mudslides that often follow heavy storms. A nearly one-mile tunnel now bypasses Devil's Slide.

On the bay side is South San Francisco, where Herb Boyer and Bob Swanson sketched on a napkin their plans for the first biotechnology company, Genentech. They bought space in an old warehouse on the waterfront near a Bethlehem Steel plant. The area is now one large biotech campus overlooking the bay, with lawns, parkways and earth-toned office complexes, the center of the industry. YouTube, started in 2005, is headquartered in San Bruno. Oracle, a computer software company, is based in a cluster of gleaming glass buildings in Redwood City. The exorbitant cost of real estate has imposed a premium on large employers. On the site of the former Bay Meadows racetrack near San Mateo, developers completed in 2018 the first phase of their 83-acre master-planned community. Stanford University opened in 2019 its Redwood City campus, four building complexes—at a cost of $500 million that were scheduled to house 2,700 employees and provide extensive amenities on 35 acres, five miles up El Camino Real. This is the first major expansion of the university from Leland Stanford's original "farm," as many refer to the main campus.

Between the Bay shore Freeway and Interstate 280 are middle-class suburbs that grew up to be cities with office complexes—Millbrae, Burlingame, San Mateo and San Carlos. The supply of new housing has not come close to keeping up with demand. From 2010 until 2015, only 3,844 new homes were built at the same time that 72,000 jobs were created, according to a report by a local business group. That a disproportionate share of those new homes were in the deluxe class helps explain why many workers have been forced to look elsewhere for a home. In San Mateo and San Francisco, households with up to $117,000 income were classified at the poverty level, in terms of their costs. A controversial proposal in Sacramento that was designed to increase housing supply died in September 2020 at the end of the legislative session. Agricultural production in San Mateo, which remains chiefly in floral and nursery crops, has dropped because of such factors as the paucity of labor, the high cost of land and the drought. The area has been the source of incredible athletic talent: Junipero Serra, an all-boys Catholic high school in San Mateo, enrolled both Tampa Bay Buccaneers (ex-Patriots) quarterback Tom Brady and former San Francisco Giants slugger Barry Bonds.

The 14th Congressional District of California consists of these northern peninsula suburbs plus the southwest corner of San Francisco, which has less than 20 percent of the district population. It takes in about 80 percent of affluent San Mateo County. The 14th is 36 percent Asian and 23 percent Hispanic. The economic orientation here was historically toward San Francisco, then later toward Silicon Valley. But now the district has its own burgeoning biotech industry, with income levels among the highest in the nation. It also has moved into the upper echelon of Democratic districts. Joe Biden won, 78%-20%, continuing a steady increase in recent elections.

Eric Swalwell (D)

Elected 2012, 5th term, b. Nov 16, 1980; Sac City, IA; University of MD - College Park, B.A., 2003; University of MD School of Law, J.D., 2006; Christian - Non-Denominational; Married (Brittany Ann Watts); 2 children.

Elected Office: Dublin City Council, 2010-2012.

Professional Career: Deputy District Attorney, Alameda County, 2006-2012.

DC Office: 407 CHOB 20515, 202-225-5065, Fax: 202-226-3805, swalwell.house.gov

State Offices: Castro Valley, 510-370-3322.

Committees: House Democratic Steering and Policy Committee Co-Chair. *Homeland Security*: Intelligence & Counterterrorism. *Judiciary*: Antitrust, Commercial & Administrative Law; Courts, Intellectual Property & Internet. *Permanent Select on Intelligence*.

Group Ratings

	ADA	ACLU	AFL-CIO	LCV	COC	HAFA	ACU	CFG	FRC
2020	**	78%	**	100%	-	0%	3%	**	-
2019	95%	C	100%	62%	70%	C	3%	13%	0%

Almanac Ratings 2019-2020

	Economy	Social	Foreign	Composite
Liberal	50%	54%	83%	63%
Conservative	50%	46%	17%	37%

Key Votes of the 116th Congress

1. U.S./Mex./Can. trade deal	Y	5. Russia sanctions	Y	9. Firearms background checks Y
2. First Coronavirus response	Y	6. Troops in Syria	Y	10. Spending at the border	N/A
3. HEROES Act	Y	7. Veto arms sales to Saudis	Y	11. Marijuana liberalized rules Y
4. CASH Act	Y	8. Defense $$$, veto override	Y	12. Electoral College objections N

Election Results

Election	Name (Party)	Vote (%)	Cand. Spent	Ind. Exp. Support	Ind. Exp. Oppose
2020 General	Eric Swalwell (D)................................ 242,991	(71%)	$2,142,248	$2,644	
	Alison Hayden (R).......................... 99,710	(29%)			$113
2020 Primary	Eric Swalwell (D)............................... 103,826	(59%)			
	Samantha Campbell (D).................. 17,286	(10%)			

Prior winning percentages: 2018 (73%), 2016 (74%), 2014 (70%), 2012 (52%)

Democrat Eric Swalwell, elected in 2012 when he defeated a Bay Area icon, quickly gained prominence with his focus on tech and intelligence issues, fresh thinking and a hyperactive media presence. He was a force during the Democrats' two impeachment cases against President Donald Trump. His 2020 presidential candidacy was quixotic and short-lived.

Born in Sac City Iowa, Swalwell grew up in Dublin California. He attended the University of Maryland, where he was bitten by the political bug and graduated with a bachelor's in government and politics and then a law degree. He got his start in politics as an unpaid intern on Capitol Hill, working for Rep. Ellen Tauscher, a Bay Area Democrat. To make ends meet, he worked two summer jobs around the Capitol, at the local gym and a restaurant, where he kept an eye out for members of Congress. After graduation, Swalwell returned to California and got a job as a prosecutor in the Alameda County district attorney's office, where he rose to the post of deputy district attorney. "I put a lot of bad guys away," he told voters on the campaign trail. In 2010, he ran successfully for city council in Dublin, an outer suburb of San Francisco.

Other prominent California Democrats had been patiently waiting for 40-year Rep. Pete Stark to retire, including former Obama administration official Ro Khanna. But when Khanna and others stepped aside as the 2012 election approached, Swalwell jumped the line. Much of the Democratic establishment backed Stark. Swalwell got support from a smattering of local officials, including Tauscher, who became a State Department official in the Obama administration. Swalwell pointedly competed in running races across the district, a series his campaign dubbed the "race for change." Beyond his hustle, Swalwell's campaign was largely fueled by Stark's own missteps.

Swalwell didn't promise to vote all that differently from Stark, but said he would at least listen intently as their congressman. His 52%-48% victory in the November runoff was an ironic way for Stark to exit: Four decades earlier, Stark had made much the same argument in unseating the previous octogenarian congressman.

In 2014, Stark and his allies warned that they planned to get even. Swalwell's chief challenger was Democratic state Senate Majority Leader Ellen Corbett. She attacked his inexperience and lack of Democratic credentials. Turning the tables, the incumbent claimed support from the party establishment and benefited from a huge fundraising advantage. Surprisingly, Corbett failed to survive the all-party primary. Swalwell got 49 percent of the total vote, and Corbett ran 430 votes behind Republican candidate Hugh Bussell. The general election became an afterthought, with Swalwell winning, 70%-30%. Since then, his Republican challengers have had scant financing or prospects in this district.

On the Intelligence Committee, Swalwell was the ranking Democrat on its CIA Subcommittee, which oversees the agency's policy, activities and budget. The House-passed intelligence authorization bill in 2016 included his proposal to keep Congress informed about foreign fighters traveling to terrorist safe havens. In 2017, Swalwell attacked Rep. Devin Nunes, a California Republican, for releasing a memo alleging illegal government surveillance of the Trump campaign in 2016, which Swalwell called "poisonous," and said that he should step down as committee chairman.

Nunes subsequently stepped aside for a few months during an Ethics Committee review. When House Republicans ended their investigation a year later, Swalwell said they sent "a bright green light to Russia to continue its interference at America's ballot boxes." In the majority, he chaired the Intelligence Modernization and Readiness Subcommittee.

After serving on the Judiciary Committee, Swalwell worked with Republicans on the Rapid DNA bill, which encouraged new technology for quick analysis of such evidence in police investigations. In 2018, when he mocked the National Rifle Association with a tweet that it would lose its "war" if it fought a government attempt to confiscate guns, the NRA ran a cover story about him in its magazine, which it titled, "Gas Bag in the House." He tweeted triumphantly that he was "living in the NRA's head."

Swalwell joined other junior House Democrats to create the Future Forum—chiefly to engage with millennials, especially on campuses. With his social-media skills, he became the Snapchat king of Congress. Pelosi gave him a political assignment to oversee Democratic outreach to young voters. She also appointed Swalwell to an insider post as co-chair of the Democratic Steering and Policy Committee. He made the most of these assignments and regular political stops during his weekly cross-country trips from his district to Washington.

In April 2019, when Swalwell became the 16th Democrat to enter the presidential campaign— with an announcement on The Late Show with Stephen Colbert—he had no major endorsements or approval in public-opinion polls. Other candidates already had staked out the California and youth votes. But, as Nathaniel Rakich wrote in 538, "there is one trump card in Swalwell's hand: He was born in Iowa," the home of the first-in-the-nation caucuses, where he had made at least 16 visits in the previous two years. If that was his strategy, it didn't work. Three months later, he threw in the towel, he said, with the need "to be honest about our own candidacy's viability." If he had created a lasting memory, it might have been at the first debate of Democratic candidates when he called on Joe Biden and others to "pass the torch" to a new generation of Democrats.

A year later, Swalwell recalled another reason why he ended his presidential campaign. As he wrote in his digital book about the first impeachment case against Trump, "it was hard to be away from Washington with so much coming to a boiling point there, when I was only one of three members of Congress to serve on both the Intelligence and Judiciary Committees." As it turned out, he had a larger public role in the second impeachment case against Trump when he was one of nine House managers for the Senate trial. During his presentation, he described video of the Capitol riot that had not been previously viewed by the public.

Swalwell received unwanted public attention in December 2020 when Axios reported that Chinese intelligence operatives had been interacting with him since before he was elected to Congress, with no indication of improper actions by Swalwell. In a subsequent interview, he told Politico that he had disclosed the contacts to congressional leaders and that the Chinese were "unsuccessful in whatever they were trying to do." Democrats dismissed Republican calls to strip Swalwell of his seat on the Intelligence Committee.

CA-15: Southern East Bay

Cook Partisan Voting Index: D+22

Population		Race and Ethnicity		Income	
Total	782,312	White	41.00%	Median Income	$125,018
Land area (sq. miles)	599	Black	4.90%	District Income Rank	7
Pop/ sq mi	1,305.05	Latino	21.50%	Poverty Rate	5.30%
Born in State	49.70%	Asian	37.10%	With health insurance	96.90%
		Two or more races	6.60%	Cash public assistance	2.40%
Age Groups		Other	10.30%	Food stamp/SNAP	3.70%
Under 18	22.80%				
18-34	20.40%	**Education**		**Work**	
35-64	42.50%	H.S grad or less	27.90%	White Collar	52.20%
Over 64	14.30%	Some college	24.20%	Sales and Service	32.80%
		College Degree, 4 yr	29.10%	Blue Collar	15.10%
Military		Post grad	18.90%	Government	11.90%
Veteran/ Active Duty	3.70%				

2020 Pres. Vote	Biden	255,427	(71%)	Trump	94,397	(26%)		
2016 Pres. Vote	Clinton	198,964	(69%)	Trump	68,808	(24%)	Johnson	10,604	(4%)

Hayward, Fremont: The East Bay is the workaday, unglamorous side of the San Francisco Bay Area—a narrow strip of land between the bay and the surprisingly high mountains that rise just to the east. The shoreline is not picturesque, with its closed-down Navy bases and its docks, airports and salt evaporators. In World War II, when the shipyards of Richmond were buzzing, the East Bay south of Oakland was still largely uninhabited farm fields. After the war, the area filled up, south along old Route 17: Hayward, with its California State University campus and seafood industry; Union City, with its rail yards; and Newark, with dozens of industrial plants ranging from salt processing to computer network servers. Hit hard by the dot-com bust at the turn of the century, the East Bay revived with biotech, construction and health care.

The national labs are a vital presence here. At Lawrence Livermore National Laboratory, the federal government conducts nuclear-warhead and energy research. In 2019, the lab began work on a next-generation supercomputer, with advanced capabilities for modeling, simulation and artificial intelligence. Also in Livermore is a part of the Albuquerque-based Sandia National Labs, which offers scientific and technological expertise on the nation's most challenging security issues. Since the 1980s, anti-nuclear protestors have gathered at Livermore to commemorate historical events and denounce nuclear weapons.

Underneath the East Bay is the Hayward Fault, not as famous as the San Andreas, but a branch of it that is just as dangerous. An earthquake there in 1868 registered about 7.0 on the Richter scale and destroyed downtown Hayward. Another rupture is overdue, and 7 million people in the region might be shaken significantly. In January 2018, an earthquake with a 4.4 magnitude struck underneath Berkeley. It was the biggest shake from the Hayward Fault since a 4.5 tremblor hit Fremont in 1981. Another major local hazard: Coastal land has been sinking in the Hayward area at a dangerous pace and faster than elsewhere along San Francisco Bay, according to academic researchers. Rising sea levels have compounded the threat.

The 15th Congressional District of California is made up of East Bay towns in southern Alameda County and part of Castro Valley. It includes a small slice of Contra Costa County near San Ramon. The majority-minority district is racially and ethnically mixed: 37 percent Asian, 22 percent Hispanic, and 5 percent Black. It includes Hayward, with its Hispanic and Asian populations that are two-thirds of the total for the city, and Union City, which has become more than 50 percent Asian. In 2020, Joe Biden got 71 percent of the vote, which was smaller than his vote in seven other Bay Area districts.

Jim Costa (D)

Elected 2004, 9th term, b. Apr 13, 1952; Fresno, CA; CA State University, Fresno, B.S., 1974; Roman Catholic; Single.

Elected Office: CA Assembly, 1978-1994; CA Senate, 1994-2002.

Professional Career: Consultant, 2002-2004.

DC Office: 2081 RHOB 20515, 202-225-3341, Fax: 202-225-9308, costa.house.gov

State Offices: Fresno, 559-495-1620; Merced, 209-384-1620.

Committees: *Agriculture*: Livestock & Foreign Agriculture (Chmn). *Foreign Affairs*: Europe, Energy, the Environment & Cyber. *Natural Resources*: Water, Oceans & Wildlife.

Group Ratings

	ADA	ACLU	AFL-CIO	LCV	COC	HAFA	ACU	CFG	FRC
2020	**	80%	**	100%	-	0%	15%	**	-
2019	80%	C	100%	79%	69%	C	16%	13%	0%

Almanac Ratings 2019-2020

	Economy	Social	Foreign	Composite
Liberal	51%	58%	80%	63%
Conservative	49%	42%	20%	37%

Key Votes of the 116th Congress

1. U.S./Mex./Can. trade deal	Y	5. Russia sanctions	Y	9. Firearms background checks	Y
2. First Coronavirus response	Y	6. Troops in Syria	Y	10. Spending at the border	Y
3. HEROES Act	Y	7. Veto arms sales to Saudis	Y	11. Marijuana liberalized rules	Y
4. CASH Act	Y	8. Defense $$$, veto override	Y	12. Electoral College objections	N

Election Results

Election	Name (Party)	Vote (%)		Cand. Spent	Ind. Exp. Support	Ind. Exp. Oppose
2020 General	Jim Costa (D)	128,690	(59%)	$1,954,115	$294,804	
	Kevin Cookingham (R)	88,039	(41%)	$317,131	$8,696	$113
2020 Primary	Jim Costa (D)	41,228	(38%)			
	Esmeralda Soria (D)	23,484	(21%)			
	Kimberly Elizabeth Williams (D)	6,458	(6%)			

Prior winning percentages: 2018 (58%), 2016 (58%), 2014 (51%), 2012 (57%), 2010 (52%), 2008 (74%), 2006 (unopposed), 2004 (53%)

Democrat Jim Costa, elected in 2004, is a third-generation farmer who concentrates on the agricultural issues that affect his district's rural residents, often going his own way from his party. In the 2020 election, Costa beat back a primary challenge from the left to keep his seat in Congress but lost out on a bid to chair the House Agriculture Committee.

Born in Fresno, he was raised on his family's dairy farm. He is the grandson of Portuguese immigrants who settled in the San Joaquin Valley near the turn of the 20th century. In 1978, Costa was elected to the state Assembly, where he was known as a moderate Democrat. In 2002, after he was forced to retire at age 50 because of term limits, Costa founded a consulting firm. Two years later, when Democratic Rep. Cal Dooley retired after 14 years, Costa entered the race with solid name recognition. In the March primary, he faced a bruising challenge from Lisa Quigley, Dooley's chief of staff who grew up in the Central Valley, but she hadn't lived in the district in nearly two decades. Costa questioned her residency and agricultural credentials. Quigley was endorsed by Dooley and national abortion rights groups, and she painted Costa as a special-interest lobbyist. Quigley ran ads mentioning Costa's 1986 arrest for soliciting a prostitute and a 1994 incident in which police found drug paraphernalia in his home. Costa shrugged off the attacks and won the primary by an unexpectedly large 73%-27%.

In the general election, the Republican nominee, state Sen. Roy Ashburn, ran a formidable campaign. He criticized Costa for supporting tax policies that he said hurt low-income families. But Costa's lengthy legislative record didn't readily lend itself to the "liberal" label. Costa won 53%-47%.

Costa sits on the Agriculture and Natural Resources committees, both important to his district. As a member of the House-Senate conference committee that completed the 2018 farm bill, Costa claimed credit for export incentives for California-grown commodities, technical assistance for fruit and vegetable growers and increased groundwater management. During the coronavirus pandemic, he led the effort to lobby for direct relief to farmers. Once Democratic Rep. Collin Peterson lost reelection in Minnesota in 2020, Costa entered the race to succeed him as Ag chairman. Costa lined up California farm interests and garnered a decent share of votes but lost to Democratic Rep. David Scott of Georgia, who was more senior. The final tally was 144-83. Costa remained chairman of the Livestock and Foreign Agriculture Subcommittee.

Local water supply has been a continuing preoccupation for Costa. He was among the final undecided votes in 2010 on President Barack Obama's health care overhaul. Republicans charged that he was given extra public water allocations for their region. Costa was one of 10 Democrats to vote for California GOP Rep. Devin Nunes' House-passed bill in 2012 to change California's system of water laws to benefit San Joaquin Valley farmers. In 2016, he helped to enact the sweeping water resources bill, with vital provisions that steered more water to the San Joaquin Delta. In 2018, the omnibus measure enacted for water development included Costa's bipartisan bill to increase water-storage capacity.

Costa did not face a significant reelection challenge until 2010. That year, Republican rancher Andy Vidak sought to blame Costa for the area's weak economy, running billboards depicting him as the pitchfork-holding "American Gothic" farmer with Speaker Nancy Pelosi at his side. Vidak surged in the polls, and in the closing weeks the race became a toss-up. Costa put in a month of heavy retail politicking and got last-minute help from the Democratic Congressional Campaign Committee. In a recount that dragged on for three weeks, Costa won 52%-48%. Vidak later became a state senator.

The 2012 redistricting gave Costa what seemed to be the favorable 16th District, though threes of it was new political territory for him. The 2014 election became a big surprise. In the first round of voting in June, Fresno County dairyman Johnny Tacherra easily led three other Republican candidates and moved into the general election with Costa. Tacherra worked the grassroots to show his connection to the drought-stricken district, and he painted the incumbent as out of touch. Costa outspent the challenger by nearly 5-to-1. When the initial votes were tallied, Tacherra shockingly held a narrow lead. But Costa prevailed just before Thanksgiving by 1,334 votes. Following that scare, Costa sided with Republicans on multiple House votes, including support of the Keystone XL pipeline and new restrictions on the president's regulatory authority.

In 2018, Costa faced Elizabeth Heng, the daughter of Cambodian refugees and a former aide to Republican Rep. Ed Royce of California. Heng criticized Costa as unproductive and said it was time for a change. But she was outspent by a 2-1 margin and the Democratic leanings of the district were too much for her to overcome. She lost 58%-42%. Costa worked with other moderate Democrats to secure her backing for rules changes before agreeing to vote for Nancy Pelosi for Speaker.

In 2020, Costa faced a credible primary threat from Fresno City Councilwoman Esmeralda Soria, who had the backing of some labor unions and the organized labor icon Dolores Huerta. Costa was dismissive of Soria, calling her "an ally of mine up until six months ago" and telling Politico "she is tired of waiting her turn," but took the threat seriously, running negative TV ads. Soria said Costa was not effective enough for working families and insufficiently supportive of the Democratic Party. Soria spent just $429,000 to Costa's $1.8 million. Even with three Democrats on the ballot, Costa took the first-place slot with 38 percent, advancing to the general with Republican Kevin Cookingham. In November, he won easily, 59%-41%.

In the huge California Democratic delegation, Costa is the most senior member from an inland district.

CA-16: Central Valley   **Cook Partisan Voting Index: D+9**

Population		Race and Ethnicity		Income	
Total	753,152	White	56.00%	Median Income	$50,401
Land area (sq. miles)	2,840	Black	5.30%	District Income Rank	383
Pop/ sq mi	265.24	Latino	62.10%	Poverty Rate	23.00%
Born in State	65.40%	Asian	9.30%	With health insurance	89.90%
		Two or more races	3.20%	Cash public assistance	7.90%
Age Groups		Other	26.20%	Food stamp/SNAP	23.70%
Under 18	29.60%				
18-34	26.30%	**Education**		**Work**	
35-64	33.10%	H.S grad or less	56.40%	White Collar	22.30%
Over 64	11.10%	Some college	30.40%	Sales and Service	40.40%
		College Degree, 4 yr	9.50%	Blue Collar	37.30%
Military		Post grad	3.70%	Government	17.00%
Veteran/ Active Duty	4.50%				

2020 Pres. Vote	Biden	129,458	(59%)	Trump	85,647	(39%)		
2016 Pres. Vote	Clinton	98,504	(57%)	Trump	61,813	(36%)	Johnson	5,546 (3%)

Merced, Part of Fresno: Under orders from the Spanish governor of California to explore what lay beyond the coastal mountains, army officer Gabriel Moraga became one of the first Europeans to behold the Central Valley, a fertile expanse teaming with wildlife—heron, antelope, elk and grizzly bear. He brought his soldiers through Pacheco Pass, which would become the main route for exporting the natural riches of the valley to the port cities springing up along the coast. During his travels in the early 1800s, Moraga bestowed Spanish names on the places and rivers he encountered. So the region he was inspired to call "Blessed Sacrament" became Sacramento. After one long and dusty day, he stumbled on a much-welcomed river, which he called Merced, or, "River of Our Lady of Mercy." Like much of the rest of the valley, Merced grew to be a hub of agriculture. Located north of

Fresno, its economy was long hitched to agribusiness. Harvest time attracted thousands of itinerant farmworkers from Mexico and elsewhere. Later, the region's affordable housing inspired new waves of migration. By 2017, Latinos had grown to 60 percent of the population in Merced.

The 16th District of California encompasses all of Merced County and takes in parts of Madera and Fresno counties. These parts of the San Joaquin Valley are 60 percent Hispanic and include much of the city of Fresno and its lower-income neighborhoods. The neighboring 22nd District includes more populous and suburban parts of Fresno County; much of the county's farmland is in the 21st. A bit more than a third of the population of the 16th is in Merced, where the per capita income is lower than in Fresno city and county and population growth in 2017 was the fastest in the state. Unemployment here in recent years was among the nation's highest. The 16th and the 21st Districts were tied with the highest poverty rates in the state. The University of California, Merced, the 10th university in the vast UC system, opened in 2005 and had 8,500 students in 2018, with plans for continued rapid growth. Uniquely in the UC system, a slight majority of the students are Latinos and an even larger share of them are the first in their family to attend college, though graduation rates are notably lower than elsewhere in the state. Highway 99 traverses the abundant farmland and connects most of the key cities and towns in the district, with their common agricultural and water interests: Livingston, Atwater, Merced, Chowchilla, Madera and down to Fresno. After the drought had become a new job crippler and major cutbacks in water supply forced many farmers to reduce their expenses or abandon their fields, the increased water supply since 2016 created a sudden turn around. These fiercely independent towns did not adapt easily to coronavirus restrictions. The Merced County sheriff mocked the state's stay-at-home orders, calling it "economic slaughter."

With its heavy concentration of Latinos and other immigrant groups, which respond to Voting Rights Act imperatives for fair Hispanic representation, Joe Biden won the 16thwith 59 percent in 2020—falling below 60 percent, as with all Democratic-held districts in the Central Valley. Voter turnout remains relatively low but saw a notable uptick in 2020.

Ro Khanna (D)

Elected 2016, 3rd term, b. Sep 13, 1976; Philadelphia, PA; University of Chicago, A.B., 1998; Yale University Law School, J.D., 2001; Hinduism; Married (Ritu Ahuja); 2 children.

Professional Career: Law Professor; Author; Deputy Assistant Secretary, United States Department of Commerce.

DC Office: 221 CHOB 20515, 202-225-2631

State Offices: Santa Clara, 408-436-2720.

Committees: *Agriculture*: Commodity Exchanges, Energy & Credit; Livestock & Foreign Agriculture. *Armed Services*: Cyber, Innovative Technologies & Information Systems; Strategic Forces. *Oversight & Reform*: Government Operations; Subcommittee on Environment (Chmn).

Group Ratings

	ADA	ACLU	AFL-CIO	LCV	COC	HAFA	ACU	CFG	FRC
2020	**	86%	**	100%	-	0%	4%	**	-
2019	95%	C	95%	97%	43%	C	4%	18%	0%

Almanac Ratings 2019-2020

	Economy	Social	Foreign	Composite
Liberal	100%	100%	96%	99%
Conservative	0%	0%	4%	1%

Key Votes of the 116th Congress

1. U.S./Mex./Can. trade deal	Y	5. Russia sanctions	Y	9. Firearms background checks	Y
2. First Coronavirus response	Y	6. Troops in Syria	Y	10. Spending at the border	N
3. HEROES Act	Y	7. Veto arms sales to Saudis	Y	11. Marijuana liberalized rules	Y
4. CASH Act	Y	8. Defense $$$, veto override	N	12. Electoral College objections	N

Election Results

Election	Name (Party)	Vote (%)		Cand. Spent	Ind. Exp. Support	Ind. Exp. Oppose
2020 General	Ro Khanna (D)	212,137	(71%)	$2,367,025	$10,612	$2,357
	Ritesh Tandon (R)	85,199	(29%)	$283,759		$113
2020 Primary	Ro Khanna (D)	107,638	(69%)			
	Stephen Forbes (D)	12,110	(8%)			

Prior winning percentages: 2018 (75%), 2016 (61%)

Democrat Ro Khanna, elected in 2016, was a patent lawyer in Silicon Valley who was elected to the House after failing in attempts to win two other Bay Area seats. He often advocates the views of the tech industry, though he occasionally has differed with them. As a self-styled reformer, he also has been willing to go his own way among House Democrats, which he initially revealed in his multiple challenges to veteran incumbents. He has shown his interest in policy issues, as a leader of the Progressive Caucus and with the presidential campaign of Bernie Sanders. Khanna is a first-generation Asian American, whose ancestors were victims of political prosecution.

Khanna was born in Philadelphia. Shortly before, his parents had emigrated from India to seek a better life for their children. His father was an electrical engineer and his mother was a substitute school teacher. Khanna's maternal grandfather had joined the independence movement in India led by Mahatma Gandhi and was imprisoned for several years for promoting human rights. Khanna got his bachelor's in economics from the University of Chicago and his law degree from Yale University. He was a volunteer in Barack Obama's successful bid for the state Senate in 1996.

Khanna worked for a law firm in the Silicon Valley, where he specialized in intellectual property issues and wrote the book Entrepreneurial Nation: Why Manufacturing is Still Key to America's Future. He taught economics at Stanford and law at Santa Clara University. He has shown interest in three separate Bay Area congressional districts. In 2004, he challenged Rep. Tom Lantos in the 2004 Democratic primary, with criticism for his support of the war in Iraq; Khanna got 20 percent of the vote. He was a deputy assistant secretary at the Commerce Department during Obama's first term as president. Gov. Jerry Brown appointed Khanna to the California Workforce Investment Board. He set his eyes on the seat held by Democratic Rep. Pete Stark of California in a district across the Bay from Lantos, but Eric Swalwell beat him to the punch by defeating Stark in 2012.

With a strong corps of campaign contributors, many of them Indian Americans, Khanna decided to take on Democratic Rep. Mike Honda in 2014 in an adjacent district. With a seat on the Appropriations Committee, Honda focused on funding for education programs. In their initial contest, Honda led Khanna in the primary 48%-28%. Republican candidates took the remaining votes. Honda was endorsed by major Democratic leaders, including Obama and Pelosi. Khanna, with endorsements from local technology leaders, styled himself as more tech-friendly and half Honda's age. Their November matchup was much closer, with Honda prevailing 51.8%-48.2%. Khanna outspent Honda $4.4 million to $3.4 million.

Undaunted, Khanna barely stopped campaigning and talked about broader economic issues, including automation. Honda was hindered by an investigation by the House Ethics Committee for his failure to keep his official House staff separate from his 2014 campaign. The case resulted in loss of political support, including the endorsements of Obama and some local tech leaders. Honda's campaign ran a negative ad in which a South Asian actor depicted Khanna taking a call from "Wall Street" on his cell phone. Khanna led the 2016 primary, 39.1%-37.4%. In the general election, support for Honda collapsed, which Khanna later attributed to "a frustration with Washington." In the Asian-majority district, control switched from Japanese to Indian heritage. Khanna won, 61%-39%.

In the House, Khanna served on the Armed Services Committee. He won approval of his amendment to the 2017 defense spending bill requiring a review of Pentagon procurement practices to encourage more transparency in its commercial acquisitions. A leader in seeking to end U.S. military involvement in the war in Yemen, he filed a measure with Rep. Matt Gaetz, a Republican ally of

President Donald Trump, to require congressional authorization of such support. In January 2020, the House approved a version of his plan.

In Khanna's work on tech issues, Trump signed in 2018 a bill he filed with Republican Rep. John Ratcliffe of Texas to modernize the technology of federal agencies, including their websites. Khanna said the tech industry needs to do a better job of dispersing "the concentration of economic opportunity," especially to minority groups and rural areas. He chairs the Environment Subcommittee at the Oversight and Reform Committee.

In 2019, he was vice chair of the Congressional Progressive Caucus. He and freshman Rep. Alexandria Ocasio-Cortez of New York were the only two Democrats to vote against the opening-day package of House rules changes; they objected to continuation of "pay as you go" budgeting, which Khanna tweeted was "terrible economics." He objected to Rep. Cheri Bustos, who chaired the Democratic Congressional Campaign Committee, about the DCCC's prohibition on hiring Democratic consultants who supported challengers to House incumbents—as he had done.

Khanna co-chaired the presidential campaign of Sen. Bernie Sanders and emphasized the importance for Democrats to embrace all party elements if they hoped to defeat Trump in 2020—in response to centrist Democrats who worried about the consequences of a liberal nominee. He opposed the Democratic party platform that year because it failed to support "Medicare for all." Universal health coverage must be a defining issue for Democrats, he insisted. Eventually, Khanna said he supported Joe Biden as "the bridge…to the next progressive era."

CA-17: South Bay   Cook Partisan Voting Index: D+24

Population		Race and Ethnicity		Income	
Total	790,519	White	27.60%	Median Income	$147,671
Land area (sq. miles)	185	Black	2.30%	District Income Rank	2
Pop/ sq mi	4,276.54	Latino	16.10%	Poverty Rate	5.10%
Born in State	37.50%	Asian	55.60%	With health insurance	96.90%
		Two or more races	4.70%	Cash public assistance	1.90%
Age Groups		Other	9.90%	Food stamp/SNAP	2.70%
Under 18	19.70%				
18-34	27.40%	**Education**		**Work**	
35-64	41.00%	H.S grad or less	21.20%	White Collar	62.10%
Over 64	11.90%	Some college	18.60%	Sales and Service	25.10%
		College Degree, 4 yr	30.40%	Blue Collar	12.80%
Military		Post grad	29.80%	Government	8.90%
Veteran/ Active Duty	3.10%				

2020 Pres. Vote	Biden	224,903	(72%)	Trump	79,260	(26%)		
2016 Pres. Vote	Clinton	184,151	(73%)	Trump	51,079	(20%)	Johnson	8,314	(3%)

San Jose suburbs, Central San Jose: A few decades ago, the broad valley of Santa Clara County around San Jose was mostly orchards and vineyards. Sheltered by mountains from the chilly ocean fogs, with soil incredibly fertile once it was irrigated, this valley produced peaches, plums, prunes, apricots and grapes and made San Jose the nation's biggest fruit-packing center. Today, subdivisions, shopping centers, office buildings—especially large tech companies—have replaced the orchards, and the population of the county exceeds 1.9 million. Real estate prices in Santa Clara County have been soaring. The average sales price for a single-family home, which reached $1 million in 2016, grew to $1,380,000in 2020. (For that latest median price, the median size home had about 1,700 square feet.)

Nearby Fremont in Alameda County has experienced economic rejuvenation. Tesla Motors converted a shuttered General Motors/Toyota plant, where it has been building high-end electric cars at what it describes as "one of the world's most advanced automotive plants," with more than 10,000 employees. Tesla CEO Elon Musk has had conflicts with Alameda officials about working conditions at its plant, including during the coronavirus. Irate because the compulsory shutdowns had jeopardized his production goal of 500,000 vehicles in 2020 at Tesla's only complete assembly line in the United States, Musk responded by moving some of the company's operations to facilities in Nevada and Texas. Fremont officials expect Tesla will remain. The city could become "the Detroit of the 21st century," gushed the newsletter California Planning & Development Report. Fremont is also home to the Little Kabul neighborhood, which may be the largest Afghan enclave in the western world.

In Cupertino, Apple is headquartered in its solar-powered Apple Park "spaceship," a $5 billion state-of-the-art building that houses some 12,000 employees on a 175-acre site. Part of that cost was for "base-isolation" technology, in which the foundation is separated from the earth by 692 "huge stainless steel saucers" that can shift up to four feet, making it less susceptible to earthquake damage. The hallways in the round building exceed one mile. In Sunnyvale, LinkedIn houses its "net zero energy" campus. Other companies that are based or plan large office space in Sunnyvale—strategically located behind San Jose and Palo Alto—include Google, Amazon, Facebook and another corporate campus for Apple.

The 17th Congressional District curves around the southern tip of San Francisco Bay and the Don Edwards National Wildlife Refuge—named for the long-time liberal member of the House Judiciary Committee. It consists of the city of Santa Clara and a northern wedge of Santa Clara County, with large numbers of Chinese, Vietnamese and Mexican immigrants. It is one of three districts that are based largely or entirely in Santa Clara, which is the sixth largest county in the state and the largest north of Los Angeles. In 2019, the county's population was 39 percent Asian, 31 percent white and 25 percent Hispanic. The district also takes in the northern part of San Jose, part of Fremont, Newark, Sunnyvale and Cupertino, where Steve Jobs started Apple in a garage in the 1970s. About one-fourth of the 17th is the southwest corner of Alameda County—chiefly, Fremont.

Both Cupertino and Milpitas are two-thirds Asian, and this growing population has become a political force. The 17th District as a whole is 56 percent (and climbing) Asian American, by far the largest percentage of any district in California. Its median household income of $147,671 was second in the nation. Joe Biden won this district, 72%-26%.

Anna Eshoo (D)

Elected 1992, 15th term, b. Dec 13, 1942; New Britain, CT; Canada College, A.A., 1975; University of San Francisco, Att., 1979; Roman Catholic; Divorced; 2 children.

Elected Office: San Mateo County Board of Supervisors, 1983-1992, President, 1986.

Professional Career: San Mateo County Dem. Party, 1980-1992; Speaker pro tempore, CA assembly speaker, 1981-1982.

DC Office: 202 CHOB 20515, 202-225-8104, Fax: 202-225-8890, eshoo.house.gov

State Offices: Palo Alto, 650-323-2984.

Committees: *Energy & Commerce*: Communications & Technology; Health (Chmn).

Group Ratings

	ADA	ACLU	AFL-CIO	LCV	COC	HAFA	ACU	CFG	FRC
2020	**	83%	**	100%	–	0%	4%	**	–
2019	95%	C	95%	93%	55%	C	4%	18%	0%

Almanac Ratings 2019-2020

	Economy	Social	Foreign	Composite
Liberal	100%	100%	80%	94%
Conservative	0%	0%	20%	6%

Key Votes of the 116th Congress

1. U.S./Mex./Can. trade deal Y	5. Russia sanctions Y	9. Firearms background checks Y
2. First Coronavirus response Y	6. Troops in Syria Y	10. Spending at the border Y
3. HEROES Act Y	7. Veto arms sales to Saudis Y	11. Marijuana liberalized rules Y
4. CASH Act Y	8. Defense $$$, veto override Y	12. Electoral College objections N

Election Results

Election	Name (Party)	Vote (%)		Cand. Spent	Ind. Exp. Support	Ind. Exp. Oppose
2020 General	Anna Eshoo (D)...................................	217,388	(63%)	$1,771,088	$2,053	$113
	Rishi Kumar (D)................................	126,751	(37%)			
2020 Primary	Anna Eshoo (D)............................	146,225	(62%)			
	Rishi Kumar (D).................................	38,826	(16%)			

Prior winning percentages: 2018 (75%), 2016 (71%), 2014 (68%), 2012 (71%), 2010 (69%), 2008 (70%), 2006 (71%), 2004 (70%), 2002 (68%), 2000 (70%), 1998 (69%), 1996 (65%), 1994 (61%), 1992 (57%)

Democrat Anna Eshoo, first elected in 1992, has had impressive accomplishments on the powerful Energy and Commerce Committee, especially on communications issues. In recent years, her career seemed to have peaked. Following the 2014 election, she sought the top Democratic slot on the committee, but lost to Frank Pallone of New Jersey. Then, she decided not to serve as ranking Democrat on any of the panel's subcommittees.

But Eshoo's enthusiasm was revived, at age 76,when Democrats regained House control. She became chairwoman of the Health Subcommittee—a vital position where she could offer informal advice and protect the interests of her close friend Nancy Pelosi, who returned as House Speaker. A few weeks before the 2018 election, Eshoo played an unexpected, though off-stage, role in the confirmation hearing of Brett Kavanaugh to the Supreme Court.

Born in Connecticut, Eshoo is the only member of Congress of Assyrian descent. Her father, a jeweler and an FDR Democrat, sparked her interest in politics at a young age by taking her to political rallies. The family moved to California. Eshoo married, had two children, and for a while was a stay-at-home mother working on a degree in English literature. She was active in civic groups, chaired the San Mateo County Democratic Party and in 1982 was elected to the San Mateo Board of Supervisors. In 1988, she ran for the House against Republican Rep. Tom Campbell. The two spent a total of $2.5 million, which was big bucks in those days. Campbell won 52%-46%. In 1992, Campbell ran for the Senate, and Eshoo sought the open seat. In the primary, she prevailed 40%-36% against Assemblyman Ted Lempert, who had strong backing from environmentalists. In the swing district, she had a tough contest against Republican Tom Huening, a San Mateo supervisor who was backed by Silicon Valley business leaders. Eshoo won by a convincing 57%-39%. She has not had a serious challenge for reelection.

Eshoo's voting record has been mostly liberal, with more parochial views on issues such as taxes that affect high-income earners in her district. She joined Republicans and her constituents' high-tech interests in votes on securities litigation and normalizing trade relations with China. But she sided with most Democrats in 2015 in opposing trade promotion authority for President Barack Obama, chiefly to conclude the Trans-Pacific Partnership.

From 2011 to 2016, Eshoo was the senior Democrat on the Energy and Commerce Subcommittee on Communications and Technology—a panel with obvious importance to her district. She has remained a strong supporter of net neutrality, the concept that broadband providers should be prohibited from blocking certain traffic or setting up tiered pathways for internet content. She argued in favor of ensuring that the FCC provide an adequate supply of spectrum that any company can use for free. Following the 2016 election, she voluntarily gave up the subcommittee post. "Senior members like myself must consider the best interest of our party and our need to develop leaders for the future. In other words, it's time to walk my talk," Eshoo said.

Even without the formal position, she retained interest in communications policy. In November 2019, she filed a bill, with Rep. Zoe Lofgren in her neighboring district, to create a Digital Privacy Agency to protect individual rights on social media. They said their proposal, which would not pre-empt state law, would result in "marked change" in how companies such as Facebook—a vital constituent of the two proponents—handle data collection and use. Eshoo proposed in May 2020 a bill to restrict micro-targeting of political advertising on social media, such as Facebook and Google. Such advertising, she said, "fractures our open democratic debate into millions of private, unchecked silos, allowing for the spread of false promises, polarizing lies, disinformation, fake news, and voter suppression."

In 2014, Eshoo sought unsuccessfully to replace Rep. Henry Waxman of California when he retired as the ranking Democrat on Energy and Commerce. Even with the active support of Pelosi, for whom Eshoo had been a valuable confidant since they first met at a Democratic event in the Bay Area in the early 1970s, that proved to be a step too far. Eshoo was stymied by multiple factors. Chief among them was that Pallone had more seniority. For some Democrats, the secret vote became an opportunity to express unhappiness with Pelosi and their deepening minority status in the House.

In September 2018, Eshoo played a cameo role in the Senate Judiciary Committee hearings on the nomination of Brett Kavanaugh to the Supreme Court. That resulted when Christine Blasey Ford, a constituent, contacted her during the summer to discuss Kavanaugh's alleged sexual attack of her when they were high school students outside of Washington D.C. during the mid-1980s. Following their meeting in Palo Alto, Eshoo suggested that Ford share the information with Sen. Dianne Feinstein of California, the senior Democrat on the Judiciary Committee. "At the end of the meeting, I told her I believed her," Eshoo said to the San Jose Mercury News. Ford sent the letter to Feinstein, who withheld the information for several weeks from other committee members and investigators, until it was leaked to reporters for The Washington Post. When Republicans objected to what they called an 11th-hour attack for which there was scant evidence, Eshoo defended Ford as "not a creature of Washington D.C." and said Kavanaugh's response was "totally disqualifying."

Eshoo returned to center stage in 2019 to fill the Democratic opening at the Health Subcommittee. "The 2018 midterm elections were won on the issue of health care and the American people now expect us to deliver," she said. She listed her priorities as strengthening of the Affordable Care Act, lower prices for prescription drugs and more funding for the National Institutes of Health. In 2020, she joined critics of the Trump administration for what she called its "dysfunctional approach" in responding to the coronavirus, especially in the development of a vaccine, although administration's vaccine partnership produced two options in record time.

Eshoo rankled many liberals with her unwillingness to hold hearings on "Medicare for all," which she opposed, and her preference to focus on what she called "consensus items" among Democrats. In December 2019, when the House on a mostly party-line vote passed a drug-pricing bill that was largely crafted by Pelosi, some liberals were unhappy with Eshoo's moderating influence on the details and their limited opportunity to offer amendments.

As congressional Democrats work with the Biden administration on healthcare policy, Eshoo likely will continue to assist her close friend Pelosi in finding common ground.

CA-18: Silicon Valley   Cook Partisan Voting Index: D+27

Population		Race and Ethnicity		Income	
Total	753,806	White	62.60%	Median Income	$149,375
Land area (sq. miles)	696	Black	2.40%	District Income Rank	1
Pop/ sq mi	1,082.87	Latino	15.80%	Poverty Rate	4.60%
Born in State	46.40%	Asian	24.40%	With health insurance	96.20%
		Two or more races	5.20%	Cash public assistance	1.10%
Age Groups		Other	5.40%	Food stamp/SNAP	2.50%
Under 18	22.80%				
18-34	20.30%	**Education**		**Work**	
35-64	40.80%	H.S grad or less	15.50%	White Collar	66.00%
Over 64	16.00%	Some college	18.60%	Sales and Service	25.20%
		College Degree, 4 yr	31.20%	Blue Collar	8.80%
Military		Post grad	34.60%	Government	9.20%
Veteran/ Active Duty	3.60%				

2020 Pres. Vote	Biden	294,545	(76%)	Trump	82,172	(21%)		
2016 Pres. Vote	Clinton	246,464	(73%)	Trump	67,842	(20%)	Johnson	13,894	(4%)

Western San Jose, Palo Alto: Silicon Valley is a place and a state of mind, an area that had no distinctive identity a half-century ago but that people all over the world today recognize and imitate. In the 1980s and 1990s, Silicon Valley emerged as the center of America's computer industry, a place where creative minds developed products that large corporations never thought would sell. Its beginnings can be traced back to 1939, when William Hewlett and David Packard started their electronics firm in a Palo Alto garage, or perhaps even to 1891, when Stanford University was founded on the estate of a California governor and senator. Not every aspect of the computer business is centered here, as Microsoft and IBM can attest. But the compact Silicon Valley is where most of the giants and much of the creativity of the technology business — as well as many dot-coms — have been based, and where they continue to grow in their pricey surroundings and generate extraordinary wealth.

How did Silicon Valley come to be where it is? One factor is Stanford, the students it attracts and produces, and its tradition of encouraging faculty members to pursue profit-making activity. Another key component is venture capital, widely available from innovation-minded old San Francisco money. A third ingredient is the presence of smart young innovators, attracted to the valley's pleasant climate. Sheltered by hills from coastal fogs and rains, Silicon Valley boasts mostly sunny weather with perceptible but gentle seasons, perfect for year-round outdoor sports. These communities were rustic but never poor, rural but not small-minded, country-like but still easily accessible to urban luxuries.

When the internet bubble burst in 2000, Silicon Valley fell on hard times. By one estimate, the area lost 220,000 jobs, nearly two-thirds of the 350,000 created during the dot-com boom. Stock prices plummeted and real estate prices did too. Billions of dollars in paper wealth disappeared, and technology exports from California fell. Subsequently, it had a strong revival. In 2017, the valley exceeded 1.6 million jobs, higher than in 2000. Housing prices have roared back and again are among the highest in the nation. Half the employees in the valley are foreign-born. But, even before the pandemic, the jobs market in the Valley had started to cool. In late 2020, the San Jose Mercury News reported that new local jobs postings were down 31 percent from a year earlier.

In Mountain View, Google planned to open in 2021 an ambitious new headquarters known as Charleston East. The Fast Company business website described the design as a "titanic metal circus tent" that will be covered by solar panels. Also underway for Google in Mountain View are additional office projects described as Bay View and Landings, plus a massive "village" campus that will feature 8,000 homes, ample retail space and 35 acres of public areas. The lack of housing for tech workers has been so dire that many live in recreational vehicles along the streets of Mountain View. Gov. Gavin Newsom has explored options for new housing in Silicon Valley and has looked to big tech companies for ideas—and financing.

The 18th Congressional District of California includes large portions of Silicon Valley, along with Palo Alto and Stanford University. It includes the southwest edge of San Jose and Menlo Park to the north. There are some ultra-wealthy enclaves here: Woodside, with its mansions in the hills, and Los Altos Hills, with its stark contemporary homes overlooking San Francisco Bay. The district takes in small San Jose-area cities such as Campbell, Los Gatos and the increasingly Asian—and very wealthy—Saratoga. To the west is a long stretch of hills and wilderness areas, with some camps and state parks but few homes or beaches; Route 1 overlooks the Pacific. About three-fourths of the district population is in Santa Clara County, with the remainder in southern San Mateo and northern Santa Cruz. The district's median household income of $149,375 ranked as the highest in the nation.

The area's political heritage is progressive, with a mix of environmental, dovish and culturally liberal. Through the 1980s, this was a center of moderate Republicanism. But that brand has become virtually extinct here, as in most of the nation. The GOP vote in the 18th dropped from 29 percent for Mitt Romney in 2012 to 21 percent for Donald Trump in 2020. The 76 percent for Joe Biden was his best in the three Santa Clara-based districts.

Zoe Lofgren (D)

Elected 1994, 14th term, b. Dec 21, 1947; San Mateo, CA; Stanford University, B.A., 1970; Santa Clara University Law School, J.D., 1975; Lutheran; Married (John Marshall Collins); 2 children.

Elected Office: Santa Clara Board of Supervisors, 1980-1994.

Professional Career: Staff Assistant, U.S. Rep. Don Edwards, 1970-1978; Practicing attorney, 1978-1980; Professor, University of Santa Clara School of Law, 1977-1980.

DC Office: 1401 LHOB 20515, 202-225-3072, Fax: 202-225-3336, zoelofgren.house.gov

State Offices: San Jose, 408-271-8700.

Committees: *Administration (Chmn). Joint Library. Joint Printing. Judiciary*: Courts, Intellectual Property & Internet; Immigration & Citizenship (Chmn). *Science, Space & Technology*: Space & Aeronautics. *Select Committee on the Modernization of Congress.*

Group Ratings

	ADA	ACLU	AFL-CIO	LCV	COC	HAFA	ACU	CFG	FRC
2020	**	87%	**	90%	-	0%	5%	**	-
2019	95%	C	95%	93%	54%	C	6%	19%	0%

Almanac Ratings 2019-2020

	Economy	Social	Foreign	Composite
Liberal	59%	100%	60%	73%
Conservative	41%	0%	40%	27%

Key Votes of the 116th Congress

1. U.S./Mex./Can. trade deal	Y	5. Russia sanctions	Y	9. Firearms background checks	Y
2. First Coronavirus response	Y	6. Troops in Syria	Y	10. Spending at the border	N
3. HEROES Act	N/A	7. Veto arms sales to Saudis	Y	11. Marijuana liberalized rules	Y
4. CASH Act	Y	8. Defense $$$, veto override	Y	12. Electoral College objections	N

Election Results

Election	Name (Party)	Vote (%)		Cand. Spent	Ind. Exp. Support	Ind. Exp. Oppose
2020 General	Zoe Lofgren (D)	224,385	(72%)	$1,547,708	$2,412	
	Justin Aguilera (R)	88,642	(28%)	$13,214		$113
2020 Primary	Zoe Lofgren (D)	104,456	(63%)			
	Ivan Torres (D)	18,916	(11%)			

Prior winning percentages: 2018 (74%), 2016 (74%), 2014 (67%), 2012 (67%), 2010 (68%), 2008 (71%), 2006 (73%), 2004 (71%), 2002 (67%), 2000 (72%), 1998 (73%), 1996 (66%), 1994 (65%)

Zoe Lofgren, a Democrat first elected in 1994, has been an active legislator on multiple issues, and a savvy player on issues inside the House and those with a broader impact. As chairwoman of the House Administration Committee, whose jurisdiction includes federal election laws in addition to management of the House, she was a reliable lieutenant of Speaker Nancy Pelosi. Although Lofgren had lost a bid to become the top Democrat on the Judiciary Committee, she remained busy on that panel, as the head of its pivotal Immigration Subcommittee and as a prime proponent of the impeachment of President Donald Trump.

Lofgren grew up in the Bay Area, where her father was a Teamsters truck driver and her mother worked for the Machinists Union. She graduated from Stanford University, then moved to Washington to work for Democratic Rep. Don Edwards while he was a leader on the Judiciary Committee that voted to impeach President Richard Nixon in 1974. She worked eight years as an aide to Edwards. Lofgren returned to California, where she specialized in immigration law. She served 14 years on the Santa Clara County Board of Supervisors. When Edwards retired, Lofgren ran for his House seat. Her chief Democratic opponent, former San Jose Mayor Tom McEnery, was better known. But Lofgren raised twice as much money, with support from liberal women's organizations and women in the California delegation. Lofgren won the primary 45%-42% and easily took the general election. She has had no trouble winning reelection.

Lofgren's voting record, while mostly liberal, includes bipartisan free-market positions that often are responsive to local businesses and law enforcement—and occasionally independent of Democratic dogma. Working with Republicans, she won expanded allotments of visas for tech-industry workers. She pushed for looser controls on encryption exports, securities litigation limitations and relaxation of trade restraints on supercomputers, all big Silicon Valley causes. When the House split 210-210 on a proposal to restrict government access to library records, Lofgren was the only House member to vote "present." She said the amendment went too far in preventing legitimate law enforcement searches. In 2020, when Congress debated extension of the foreign intelligence surveillance law, Lofgren took issue with Pelosi and other committee chairman as she sought to add restrictions on national security tactics.

As the top Democrat for many years on the Judiciary Subcommittee on Immigration, Lofgren has consistently advocated a major overhaul of immigration policy, but the politically charged issue bogged down. She was the chief sponsor of a new law to allow overseas military personnel and their spouses more time to file for permanent resident status through marriage. With Republican Rep. Robert Goodlatte of Virginia, the Judiciary Committee chairman, Lofgren criticized in 2015 the backlog of "green card" visa applications for talented foreign workers. In 2016, she filed with Democratic Sen. Patrick Leahy of Vermont the Refugee Protection Act, a proposal that reaffirmed the nation's commitment to refugees and strengthened safeguards for those seeking protection from persecution and violence.

She remained a leading Democratic advocate of legislation to provide citizenship to "dreamers," children who accompanied their parents as undocumented immigrants to the United States. She said that the measure was supported by many leaders in the private sector and had bipartisan backing in Congress. But, for a full decade starting in 2011, the legislation was stymied by either the Republican-controlled House or Trump.

Lofgren has had setbacks in seeking Democratic leadership positions. In 2003, she lost to James Clyburn of South Carolina in her bid for vice chair of the Democratic Caucus. Pelosi, also from the Bay Area, had just been elected minority leader and the Congressional Black Caucus pressed for one of its members to join the leadership.

In 2009, as chairwoman of the House Ethics Committee, she handled the politically sensitive inquiry of House Ways and Means Chairman Charles Rangel, and as questions were being raised about the connections of other senior Democrats to lobbyists. Lofgren's skills as a former staffer and law professor were tested by the politically combustible cases. Her panel subsequently found that no House members colluded with lobbyists. Rangel was afforded a trial but walked out in protest. Lofgren and the rest of the panel voted 9-1 to censure him—a decision Lofgren called "quite wrenching."

When Rep. John Conyers of Michigan resigned in December 2017 following revelations of sexual misconduct with House aides, Lofgren sought to replace him as the senior Democrat on the Judiciary Committee, citing her experience with the Nixon impeachment as a staffer and with the impeachment of Bill Clinton after she was elected to the House. Rep. Jerry Nadler of New York, who has two years more seniority, prevailed in the Democratic Caucus, reportedly on a 118-72 vote.

When Democrats regained the majority in 2019, Pelosi selected Lofgren to chair the House Administration Committee—a position viewed as the "mayor" of Capitol Hill and a vital spot to protect the interests of the House majority. On a bill that Pelosi designated as H.R. 1, Lofgren took command of the Democrats' package of reforms of voting rights, campaign finance laws and House ethics rules. The bill, she said, "ends the dominance of big money in our politics…[and] ensures public officials work in the public interest." Critics called it an incumbent-protection act. The House passed the bill on a nearly party-line vote, but it died without action in the Republican-controlled Senate. In 2020, her position gave her responsibility to manage the House's response to the coronavirus—including enforcement of social distancing and vaccination of House members. She objected when some Republicans sought to make enforcement "a political issue;" instead, she said, it was "a health issue."

Amid those many responsibilities, Lofgren's experience with impeachments of Presidents Nixon and Clinton made her a key Democratic strategist, especially during the first case against Trump. A profile in The New York Times described her as a "memory" and "a voice of restraint." Like Pelosi, Lofgren resisted initial pressure for action from many House Democrats in 2019, partly because of concern that the public was not sufficiently supportive. By the end of the year, when the Judiciary Committee submitted its charges, she said they were supported by the evidence.

Lofgren was one of seven Democrats who were House managers during the first Senate impeachment trial of Trump in early 2020. The Senate acquittal paralleled a comment she made during the House debate, when she referred to a House Republican from California who voted to impeach Nixon: "I've been waiting for Republican members here to have their Chuck Wiggins moment," she said.

CA-19: South Bay   Cook Partisan Voting Index: D+23

Population		Race and Ethnicity		Income	
Total	737,535	White	46.90%	Median Income	$107,240
Land area (sq. miles)	915	Black	2.80%	District Income Rank	20
Pop/ sq mi	805.75	Latino	39.00%	Poverty Rate	7.20%
Born in State	50.20%	Asian	31.00%	With health insurance	94.00%
		Two or more races	5.50%	Cash public assistance	1.60%
Age Groups		Other	13.80%	Food stamp/SNAP	5.40%
Under 18	22.00%				
18-34	24.60%	**Education**		**Work**	
35-64	39.20%	H.S grad or less	36.50%	White Collar	43.10%
Over 64	14.20%	Some college	26.40%	Sales and Service	37.00%
		College Degree, 4 yr	23.80%	Blue Collar	19.90%
Military		Post grad	13.40%	Government	11.90%
Veteran/ Active Duty	3.60%				

2020 Pres. Vote	Biden	228,232	(70%)	Trump	91,063	(28%)		
2016 Pres. Vote	Clinton	188,304	(72%)	Trump	55,489	(21%)	Johnson	8,620 (3%)

Southern San Jose: With more people than San Francisco, a tradition of high-tech innovation, and a professional sports team, San Jose finally has claims on national attention and respect. Yet San Jose does not register on the national consciousness as it should. At the southern end of San Francisco Bay, it remains in the shadow of the city on the Golden Gate. San Jose is quite different. It got its start as a farm-market town, with canneries and fruit-packing operations for the produce from the surrounding fertile plains. Farm labor icon Cesar Chavez settled with his family in the East San Jose barrio of Sal Si Puedes ("Get out if you can"). San Jose sits not on the bay but on the Southern Pacific rail line above the marshes and salt evaporators. Its major transportation arteries are the freeways — U.S. 101, Interstates 280, 680, and 880, California 87 — that encircle and bisect its revitalized downtown and the larger Bay Area.

Starting in the 1950s, San Jose grew in every direction, with developers hopscotching across the farmland and at times putting up subdivisions faster than the few city employees could update the street maps. Its population exceeds 1 million, not far below San Francisco and Oakland combined; it is growing faster than the other two and has more available land. Economically, San Jose has been sustained by everything from its traditional agriculture to manufacturing to the technology businesses that are centered in Silicon Valley towns just to the west and north, and are omnipresent here: an American city, 21st-century style. Santa Clara County not long ago had the highest median household income in the nation. Now, it is merely the highest in California. Only Los Angeles and San Diego are larger counties in California.

For many years, San Jose has been a focal point for immigration issues. It has Northern California's largest Mexican-American community, many of them farmworkers. Recent years have brought a diverse and substantial presence from Latin America and East and South Asia. In 2019, 53 percent of Santa Clara County residents speak a language other than English at home, mostly Spanish, Vietnamese or Chinese; 39 percent are foreign born. County voters in 2016 approved a half-cent increase in the sales tax for transportation projects.

In June 2020, BART took the significant step of opening a 10-mile extension from Fremont to the outskirts of San Jose—the first service into Santa Clara. The South Bay project took 30 years of planning, $2.3 billion and two years of final delay, the San Francisco Chronicle reported. BART plans to continue to downtown San Jose (with an innovative transportation hub) and the airport, though more years and dollars will be required.

The 19th Congressional District of California consists of substantial portions of San Jose, including much of the city's downtown area and the neighborhoods of Alum Rock and East Foothills. The district takes in eastern and southern parts of Santa Clara County, including Morgan Hill, a traditional farming town that has branched into technology. Near the southern edge of the district is Gilroy, which is 59percent Hispanic, the garlic capital of the world and home of the huge annual garlic festival. Politically, the district is solidly Democratic. Joe Biden got 70 percent of the vote in 2020, which was his lowest of the three Santa Clara-based districts. His 72.6 percent in Santa Clara was his fourth–highest county in California, trailing only San Francisco, Marin and Alameda (in that order), all in the north.

Jimmy Panetta (D)

Elected 2016, 3rd term, b. Oct 01, 1969; Washington, DC; Monterey Peninsula College, A.A., 1989; University of CA, Davis, B.A., 1991; Santa Clara University, J.D., 1996; Catholic; Married (Carrie Panetta); 2 children.

Military Career: U.S. Navy 2003-2011 (Afghanistan)

Elected Office: Monterey County Deputy District Attorney, 2010-2016.

Professional Career: Clerk, United States Department of State, 1992; Alameda County Deputy District Attorney, 1996-2010; Vice Chairman, Monterey Country Central Democratic Committee, 2012-2016.

DC Office: 212 CHOB 20515, 202-225-2861, Fax: 202-225-6791, panetta.house.gov
State Offices: Salinas, 831-424-2229; Santa Cruz, 831-429-1976.

Committees: *Agriculture*: Biotechnology, Horticulture & Research; Conservation & Forestry; Subcommittee Nutrition, Oversight & Department Operations. *Armed Services*: Intelligence & Special Operations; Strategic Forces. *Ways & Means*: Trade; Worker & Family Support.

Group Ratings

	ADA	ACLU	AFL-CIO	LCV	COC	HAFA	ACU	CFG	FRC
2020	**	78%	**	100%	-	0%	3%	**	-
2019	90%	C	95%	97%	56%	C	2%	18%	0%

Almanac Ratings 2019-2020

	Economy	Social	Foreign	Composite
Liberal	100%	100%	80%	94%
Conservative	0%	0%	20%	6%

Key Votes of the 116th Congress

1. U.S./Mex./Can. trade deal Y	5. Russia sanctions Y	9. Firearms background checks Y
2. First Coronavirus response Y	6. Troops in Syria Y	10. Spending at the border Y
3. HEROES Act Y	7. Veto arms sales to Saudis Y	11. Marijuana liberalized rules Y
4. CASH Act Y	8. Defense $$$, veto override Y	12. Electoral College objections N

Election Results

Election	Name (Party)	Vote (%)		Cand. Spent	Ind. Exp. Support	Ind. Exp. Oppose
2020 General	Jimmy Panetta (D)..............................	236,896	(77%)	$1,146,391	$8,583	
	Jeff Gorman (R).............................	71,658	(23%)	$81,003		$113
2020 Primary	Jimmy Panetta (D).......................	123,615	(66%)			
	Adam Bolaños Scow (D)......................	25,172	(14%)			

Prior winning percentages: 2018 (81%), 2016 (71%)

Democrat Jimmy Panetta, with three easy elections to the House since2016, has developed his own profile separate from his dad, Leon Panetta, a Washington insider for four decades. With a seat on the Ways and Means Committee, he took an active interest in revision of the U.S. trade agreement with Mexico and Canada—to enhance his legislative profile and to assist his large agricultural constituency. He made a point of pursuing bipartisanship.

The youngest of three sons of the former Defense Secretary and CIA Director, Panetta grew up in Carmel Valley. He got his bachelor's degree from the University of California, Davis, and his law degree from Santa Clara University. Growing up, he got up-close insight on Washington through the eyes of his father. Panetta began his legal career as a prosecutor for the Alameda County District Attorney. Later, he was appointed to the California Council on Criminal and Juvenile Justice, which provided guidance to the governor's office on criminal justice programs. In 2003, he was commissioned as an intelligence officer with the U.S. Navy Reserve. Four years later, he took a leave of absence from work and served with a special operations task force deployed to Afghanistan, as an intelligence officer with the Joint Special Operations Command. Before his election to Congress, he was deputy district attorney in Monterey County.

Panetta worked on missile and chemical weapons nonproliferation issues for the State Department and the Monterey Institute of International Studies. He also managed his family's large walnut farm in the area. His wife, Carrie McIntyre Panetta, was a Superior Court judge in Monterey County. His father, who chaired the Panetta Institute on Public Policy, held this seat for 16 years and chaired the House Budget Committee. "I am not afraid to pick up the phone and reach out to [my father] when necessary," Panetta told Politico. "But he also understands that...I'm the one who has to make the decision, despite what he may advise."

After Democrat Sam Farr—who held the seat for nearly 24 years after Leon Panetta resigned to join the Clinton White House—announced his retirement, Jimmy Panetta was the immediate frontrunner. His only major-party opponent was Republican Casey Lucius, a city councilwoman in Pacific Grove and a professor of national security at the Naval Postgraduate School. She was a strong conservative on most national security and economic issues, and had relatively liberal views on social issues. Lucius raised $420,000, compared with $1.4 million for Panetta. She probably never had a chance against the partisan lean and the iconic family name in this district. Panetta led the "top two" primary, 71%-20%, and took the general election, 71-29%.

In the House, Panetta initially positioned himself to address local issues. He proposed legislation to remove the cap on visas to victims of crime. In 2018, he introduced a bill to reverse a Trump administration decision to roll back regulations to sustain ocean and coastal resources. Later, he filed a bill to increase funds for affordable housing for farmworkers. During the coronavirus pandemic, he filed a bill with Republican Rep. Billy Long to compensate agricultural fairs across the nation and offset their large financial losses.

Panetta made a point of working with Republicans in the House. He visited the rural district of Rep. Rodney Davis of Illinois. "We have to be civil to each other to get things done," Panetta said. With Rep. Matt Gaetz of Florida, he proposed the "Warrior Act," to improve access for disabled veterans to athletic competition sponsored by the Defense Department. In February 2020, the House passed his bill to provide legal services to homeless veterans and veterans at risk of homelessness. His original cosponsors were four Republicans and one Democrat.

On Ways and Means, Panetta became actively involved in negotiations on the trade deal with Mexico and Canada. In September 2019, he voiced displeasure when he was not part of a smaller group of House Democrats who took the lead role in discussions. As a result, he insisted that Ways and Means members "ensure that we're able to do our job by getting the information...and just to let leadership know that we're here to work, not just to follow," he told Politico. Two weeks later, he joined four other committee Democrats—including Chairman Richard Neal—at a meeting in Mexico City with President Andres Obrador to discuss details, including protections for labor. In December, Panetta supported House passage of the deal, while emphasizing the benefits for farm interests in California and the addition of "the strongest and most progressive labor and environmental standards of any U.S. trade agreement."

After winning his first reelection without major-party opposition, Panetta breezed to a third term in 2020 against lightly funded challengers—one from each party. He got 66 percent against two opponents in the first round of voting and 77 percent in November against Republican Jeff Gorman, who chaired the Monterey County Republican Party.

CA-20: Central Coast   **Cook Partisan Voting Index: D+23**

Population		Race and Ethnicity		Income	
Total	741,838	White	58.20%	Median Income	$80,461
Land area (sq. miles)	4,874	Black	2.40%	District Income Rank	89
Pop/ sq mi	152.2	Latino	54.10%	Poverty Rate	12.70%
Born in State	58.50%	Asian	5.80%	With health insurance	91.50%
		Two or more races	4.50%	Cash public assistance	1.80%
Age Groups		Other	29.10%	Food stamp/SNAP	8.60%
Under 18	24.10%				
18-34	25.40%	**Education**		**Work**	
35-64	36.00%	H.S grad or less	42.90%	White Collar	33.90%
Over 64	14.60%	Some college	27.30%	Sales and Service	37.40%
		College Degree, 4 yr	17.50%	Blue Collar	28.60%
Military		Post grad	12.20%	Government	15.80%
Veteran/ Active Duty	5.60%				

2020 Pres. Vote	Biden	226,505	(73%)	Trump	77,969	(25%)		
2016 Pres. Vote	Clinton	180,499	(70%)	Trump	59,580	(23%)	Johnson	8,425	(3%)
	Stein	6,737	(3%)					

Monterey, Southern Santa Cruz: The California coast around Monterey Bay is for many a working definition of paradise. This kernel of California, site of the first state capital, still makes a fine living off the land and sea, as it has for 150 years. The inspiration for The Grapes of Wrath and many other John Steinbeck novels, the fields around Salinas provide much of the nation's lettuce and cauliflower. The area is often referred to as "the salad bowl of the world." Nearby, the farmlands around Castroville supply the country with its artichokes, and the vast greenhouses around Watsonville have been a popular supplier of roses. The fishing fleet and the 18 now-closed canneries of Monterey (the last sardines were canned in 1964) have generated a new industry. Once described by Steinbeck as "a poem, a stink, a grating noise, a quality of light, a tone, a habit, nostalgia, a dream," Cannery Row has been refurbished with upscale shops and hotels. The magnificent Monterey Bay Aquarium is one of California's top tourist destinations, and the National Marine Sanctuary holds more than 400 shipwrecks and ditched aircraft. The Monterey Bay area calls itself the world's language-learning capital, with the Defense Language Institute, Language Line Services, and Cal State Monterey Bay's School of World Languages and Cultures. This area was a magnet for the 1960s counterculture. The wealthy now entertain themselves with the annual Monterey Car Week, which sells many classic models. In 2018, a 1962 Ferrari sold for $44 million, a record for the event.

For many, the main attraction of the Monterey peninsula is the lush 17-Mile Drive along the Pacific Coast Highway, with Pebble Beach's golf courses, the Del Monte Lodge and Carmel, whose restrictive laws—no house numbers, no door-to-door mail delivery, no stoplights, no wearing of high-heeled shoes without permits—attempt to maintain the atmosphere of when it was an artists' colony. Monterey has suffered its own affordability gap. These days, top-flight buyers include many investors from China, some of whom initially spent time in the area for language training. Monterey County has been spending for its future. In 2016, voters approved—following two defeats in the previous decade —a sales tax increase to finance transportation improvements. In March 2020, voters in Monterey and Carmel approved another half-cent increase in the sales tax. With the hope to ease congestion on Highway 101, construction is underway on extension of Salinas Rail service to the Bay Area and Sacramento. In Santa Cruz, officials struggled to prevent erosion along the famed boardwalk.

The 20th Congressional District of California includes the entire coast of Monterey Bay and follows the stunning Big Sur coastline south along the steep slopes, taking in extensive wilderness areas and some of the most beautiful scenery in America. To the north along Monterey Bay, it runs past Watsonville to Santa Cruz. The district extends inland, into sunny valleys sheltered from ocean mists, and covers some of the nation's richest farmland. Most of the farmworkers are Latino, mainly Mexican. All of Monterey and San Benito counties are located here, and the district takes in most of Santa Cruz County and a small nip of Santa Clara. About half the population is in Monterey.

The gap between rich and poor in Monterey County is wide. It has thousands of homes valued at more than $1 million, but 13 percent of households live below the poverty line and 55 percent do not live in an English-speaking home. Monterey reportedly has the highest share of non-citizens of any county in the state. A half-century ago, this was a solidly Republican area, dominated politically by the landowners in Salinas and the townspeople who sympathized with them, plus retirees. An influx of young people, attracted less by the economy than by the atmosphere, moved these counties—like most of the California coast—nearly as far to the left as much of the Bay Area. In 2020, Joe Biden got a hefty 79 percent of the vote from Santa Cruz and 70 percent from Monterey. This district has climbed steadily to 54 percent Hispanic.

David Valadao (R)

Elected 2020, 4th term, b. Apr 14, 1977; Hanford, CA; College of the Sequoias, Att., 1998; Catholic; Married (Terra Valadao); 3 children.

Elected Office: Member, CA State Assembly, 2010-2012.

Professional Career: Managing Partner, dairy farm; Former Chair, Regional Leadership Council, Land O' Lakes, Inc.

DC Office: 1728 LHOB 20515, 202-225-4695, valadao.house.gov

State Offices: Bakersfield, 661-864-7736; Hanford, 559-460-6070.

Committees: *Appropriations*: Agriculture, Rural Development, FDA & Related Agencies; Military Construction, Veterans Affairs & Related Agencies.

Election Results

Election	Name (Party)	Vote (%)		Cand. Spent	Ind. Exp. Support	Ind. Exp. Oppose
2020 General	David Valadao (R)..........................	85,928	(50%)	$3,975,360	$238,456	$7,035,730
	TJ Cox (D)....................................	84,406	(50%)	$5,870,834	$431,064	$3,187,837
2020 Primary	David Valadao (R)........................	39,488	(50%)			

Republican David Valadao, a dairy farmer of Portuguese descent who served three House terms from California before he was defeated in 2018, reclaimed his seat in a rematch two years later with Democrat T.J. Cox. Like their first contest, Valadao's latest victory required more than two weeks of vote counts before a winner was declared. Valadao has shown skill and independence in addressing his district's agricultural and immigration demands. His tolerance earlier clashed with the hard line of President Donald Trump. In January 2021, he was 1 of 10 House Republicans who voted to impeach Trump—perhaps a necessary vote in this district.

Valadao's father emigrated to California from Portugal's Azores Islands and started a small dairy farm in Kings County in 1969. In 1992, Valadao and his brother became partners in the growing Valadao Dairy. He recalled riding in the car with his parents the day all three voted for the first time. He was 18 and a registered Republican; his parents, who became naturalized citizens, were Democrats, although they later switched parties.

Valadao worked on the family farm, which also grew grains as dairy feed stock and increased to more than 1,000 acres; he drove the tractor that carried feed for animals, and handled contracts and purchases. He was a part-time student at the College of the Sequoias but did not graduate. The single political science class he took "piqued my interest in politics, but I never considered running for office," he said.

His appetite for politics was whetted when he was elected regional leadership council chairman of Land O'Lakes, a member-owned agricultural cooperative. Valadao began traveling to Sacramento and Washington, where he spoke with elected officials and groups on issues affecting dairy farmers, such as his region's aging water infrastructure. "The more I got involved in dairy and agricultural issues, the more I saw how much of an importance government and policies play in our lives," he said.

In 2010, Valadao was elected to the state Assembly. He successfully sponsored legislation that eliminated millions of dollars in state funding to subsidize the production of corn-based ethanol. He also passed a bill that placed restrictions on people with criminal convictions who care for the elderly or disabled.

In 2012, running in a new House district created by redistricting, Valadao got an early fundraising advantage and finished first in the all-party primary, with 57 percent of the vote; Democrat John Hernandez came in second with 22 percent. As the head of the Central California Hispanic Chamber of Commerce, Hernandez hoped he could make inroads with Latino voters. But he suffered from not living in the district and as a first-time candidate. In his surprisingly comfortable 58%-42% victory, Valadao led by large margins in Fresno and Kings counties, while Hernandez won narrowly in more urban Kern County.

With help from House GOP leader Kevin McCarthy, who represents a neighboring district, Valadao gained a rare plum for a freshman: a seat on the Appropriations Committee, where he focused on securing funds for his district. He split with most Republicans on immigration legislation by cosponsoring in 2013 the Democrats' sweeping reform plan and speaking positively about the bipartisan bill that passed the Senate that spring. He was one of six House Republicans to vote against an amendment by GOP Rep. Steve King of Iowa that would give immigration authorities wider discretion to deport undocumented immigrants.

In 2014, Democrats actively promoted Amanda Renteria, a Latina who had been chief of staff to Democratic Sen. Debbie Stabenow of Michigan. In the June primary, she easily defeated Hernandez, but Valadao got 63 percent of the total vote. That diminished some of the enthusiasm for Renteria. Valadao had another 58%-42% victory, validating his bipartisan legislative approach.

Once again in 2016, Democrats were enthusiastic about their prospects. Their candidate, lawyer and businessman Emilio Huerta, had a magical name as the son of the iconic United Farmworkers co-founder Dolores Huerta. Valadao separated himself from the "divisive rhetoric" of Republican presidential nominee Trump and said he could not support Trump's candidacy. Huerta suffered from a big fundraising disparity, $2.8 million to $767,000, though he got more than $2 million in support from national Democratic groups.

The outcome was similar to Valadao's two previous victories. He won 57%-43%, with big leads in the rural parts of Fresno and Kings counties while trailing in Kern. Valadao helped himself at home with his work on legislation. McCarthy gave him a prominent role on behalf of a bill to increase local water flow and storage. Valadao pushed his bill to forgive the $375 million debt of Westland Water District, which gave the district time to complete its irrigation drainage plan, with new financing.

In the strongly Democratic 2018 cycle, Valadao's good fortune ran dry. Cox, a successful California businessman and a political newcomer, filed days before the deadline. Valadao's allies initially dismissed Cox as a "Washington insider...hand-picked" by House Democrats after Cox had "district-shopped" across California. Cox responded that Valadao—and Republicans—had failed to fix local problems, including immigration and water supply. Valadao said conservatives in the Freedom Caucus had stymied his efforts on immigration. In a contest that received little national attention, Cox won by 826 votes.

Valadao moved quickly to prepare for a rematch, with his campaign announcement in August 2019. He attacked Cox for pursuing "a radical liberal agenda that hurts our communities." In an apparent reference to Cox's personal business activity, Valadao said the district needed "a full-time representative." Cox responded by citing Valadao's limited accomplishments during his six years in Congress and cited Valadao's support for Trump.

In the March primary, Valadao scored an impressive lead over Cox, 50%-39%. The Fresno Bee, which endorsed Cox in their 2018 contest, switched to Valadao in the rematch. Describing Valadao as "open-minded" and "Valley born and bred," the editorial added that Valadao "knows how to work the halls of Congress" and cited a report that Cox owed $145,000 in unpaid taxes that pre-dated his election to Congress.

With his advantage on campaign spending, Cox narrowed the gap before the general election. Again, the contest was among the final House races that were resolved. This time, Valadao was the narrow winner, 50.5%-49.5%, a margin of more than 1,500 votes. In the vote count, Valadao reduced Cox's share of the vote in Kern County from 61 to 58 percent. And Valadao's base in Kings County delivered a larger share of the total vote.

In the House, he regained his seat on Appropriations. In voting to impeach Trump, Valadao called him "a driving force in the catastrophic events that took place on January 6 by encouraging masses of rioters to incite violence on elected officials, staff members and our representative democracy as a whole."

CA-21: Central Valley   Cook Partisan Voting Index: D+5

Population		Race and Ethnicity		Income	
Total	729,460	White	71.10%	Median Income	$46,037
Land area (sq. miles)	6,730	Black	2.90%	District Income Rank	413
Pop/ sq mi	108.39	Latino	75.30%	Poverty Rate	23.40%
Born in State	64.30%	Asian	3.20%	With health insurance	89.30%
		Two or more races	2.70%	Cash public assistance	5.00%
Age Groups		Other	20.10%	Food stamp/SNAP	19.60%
Under 18	30.60%				
18-34	27.30%	**Education**		**Work**	
35-64	32.80%	H.S grad or less	64.10%	White Collar	18.80%
Over 64	9.20%	Some college	25.30%	Sales and Service	35.60%
		College Degree, 4 yr	7.70%	Blue Collar	45.60%
Military		Post grad	3.00%	Government	14.70%
Veteran/ Active Duty	4.90%				

2020 Pres. Vote	Biden	93,560	(54%)	Trump	74,859	(44%)		
2016 Pres. Vote	Clinton	73,773	(55%)	Trump	52,972	(39%)	Johnson	4,029 (3%)

Southern Fresno Suburbs, Eastern Bakersfield: By car, California's Central Valley is a monotonous landscape: mile after mile of farmland with mile-square grid roads, intersected by railroads and canals, with an occasional cluster town. The land is hilly and gets more water near the Sierra Nevada mountains, and this is where the larger cities are. On the other side are the Westlands, where the land is flatter and the water scarcer. Its 600,000 acres are the nation's largest irrigation district. Here the land was always developed and sold in big plots; today, it has some of the world's largest farming operations. The land produces abundantly: alfalfa, cantaloupes, cotton, grapes, lima beans, olives, peaches, plums, raisins, sugar beets, tomatoes, walnuts, wheat. The landowners are a hardy and politically independent lot, but they have been happy to receive government help over the years, with money for crop price supports (in the case of cotton), agricultural research, irrigation systems and, most important, subsidized and plentiful water.

Landowners have fought hard against liberals' efforts to change their way of life, from Democratic Gov. Jerry Brown's encouragement of Cesar Chavez's United Farm Workers in the 1970s to congressional Democrats' enacting legislation to divert more water to the Sacramento delta and charge higher prices for it in the valley. From the other side, they have been stymied when conservatives in Congress have deadlocked on expansion of guest-worker programs pushed by valley farmers. In February 2020, the Westlands water district signed an agreement with the U.S. Interior Department for a permanent entitlement to annual water deliveries for irrigation. But the Los Angeles Times reported that there was no guarantee that sufficient water would be available, especially since the district will reportedly have a low priority. David Bernhardt, the secretary of Interior who arranged the deal, had been a lobbyist for the water district until 2016, the Associated Press reported.

This region is a major contributor to California's oil production, and Kern County has the most oil wells in the state. Census Bureau data have shown that the population growth in Kings County has been heavily Hispanic, poor and less likely to be married. Workers in the area's growing food-processing industry were often seasonal. Despite some increase in rainfall, the continuing shortfall of groundwater has been a warning that a turn around was not guaranteed.

The 21st Congressional District is rural, includes large portions of the Westlands Water District, and links communities with similar agricultural and water interests. It takes in all of heavily Hispanic Kings County and parts of Fresno and Kern counties. Fresno and Kern each have about one-third of the district's voters and Kings has one-fourth. The remainder are in a small corner of Tulare. The town of Delano is Chavez's old headquarters, and at the southeastern foot of the district is the Latino part of downtown Bakersfield. In August 2019, the city council in Delano agreed to become a sanctuary city, though it advised residents that undocumented migrants were not fully protected. The district has increased to 75 percent Hispanic, but Hispanic voter registration and turnout typically remain low. The district leans Democratic, with 54 percent for Joe Biden in 2020. But a local Republican can win with the right background and political appeal.

Devin Nunes (R)

Elected 2002, 10th term, b. Oct 01, 1973; Tulare County, CA; College of the Sequoias, A.A., 1993; CA State Polytechnic University, B.S., 1995; CA State Polytechnic University, M.S., 1996; Roman Catholic; Married (Elizabeth Tamariz Nunes); 3 children.

Elected Office: Col. of the Sequoias Governing Board, 1996-2002.

Professional Career: Appt. Director, USDA Rural Development, 2001.

DC Office: 1013 LHOB 20515, 202-225-2523, Fax: 202-225-3404, nunes.house.gov

State Offices: Clovis, 559-323-5235; Visalia, 559-733-3861.

Committees: *Joint Taxation. Permanent Select on Intelligence (RMM). Ways & Means*: Health; Health (RMM); Trade.

Group Ratings

	ADA	ACLU	AFL-CIO	LCV	COC	HAFA	ACU	CFG	FRC
2020	**	17%	**	10%	-	79%	84%	**	-
2019	0%	C	29%	0%	83%	C	84%	76%	95%

Almanac Ratings 2019-2020

	Economy	Social	Foreign	Composite
Liberal	25%	29%	27%	27%
Conservative	75%	71%	73%	73%

Key Votes of the 116th Congress

1. U.S./Mex./Can. trade deal Y	5. Russia sanctions Y	9. Firearms background checks N
2. First Coronavirus response Y	6. Troops in Syria Y	10. Spending at the border Y
3. HEROES Act N	7. Veto arms sales to Saudis N	11. Marijuana liberalized rules N
4. CASH Act N	8. Defense $$$, veto override N	12. Electoral College objections Y

Election Results

Election	Name (Party)	Vote (%)		Cand. Spent	Ind. Exp. Support	Ind. Exp. Oppose
2020 General	Devin Nunes (R)............................	170,888	(54%)	$20,391,261	$736	$36,470
	Phil Arballo (D).................................	144,251	(46%)	$5,064,160	$64,669	
2020 Primary	Devin Nunes (R).............................	94,686	(56%)			

Prior winning percentages: 2018 (52%), 2016 (68%), 2014 (72%), 2012 (62%), 2010 (100%), 2008 (68%), 2006 (67%), 2004 (73%), 2002 (70%)

Devin Nunes, a Republican first elected in 2002 at age 29, is an influential conservative with ambitions within and beyond the House. He has briefly toyed with running for the Senate and in 2016 he joined the Trump transition discussion of selection of Cabinet members. On the House Intelligence Committee, he plunged into controversy—including sharp conflict with Rep. Adam Schiff of California, the panel's top Democrat.

Following the election of President Donald Trump, Nunes encountered harsh criticism for his cooperation with Trump in the panel's investigation of alleged Russian influence in the 2016 presidential election. While his actions were reviewed by the House Ethics Committee for eight months, Nunes transferred control of that inquiry to other committee Republicans. He has remained active on the Ways and Means Committee and is in line to become its top Republican in 2023.

Nunes is the descendant of Portuguese immigrants from the Azores. His grandfather established the 600-acre-plus dairy farm that his parents ran when he was growing up in Tulare County. He graduated from California Polytechnic State University, San Luis Obispo, with degrees in agriculture, worked on the family farm, and married a local elementary schoolteacher whose family roots are also in Portugal. In 1998, at age 25, Nunes ran for the House in a neighboring district and finished second in the primary, 52%-48%. In 2000, he was the Tulare County campaign chairman for Republican Rep. Bill Thomas, who became the Ways and Means Committee chairman in 2001.

That year, with Thomas' help, Nunes was appointed California director of rural development for the U.S. Department of Agriculture. His immediate family sold its farm in 2006 and moved to Iowa, where they bought a dairy farm and resided, according to a profile of Nunes in Esquire in September 2018. Only his uncle Gerald retained a dairy farm in Tulare, Esquire reported. In October 2019, Nunes sued Esquire and reporter Ryan Lizza for defamation, including "injury to his good name and professional reputation." In August 2020, a federal judge in Iowa dismissed the lawsuit and its claim of false and defamatory statements.

When California's redistricting plan was unveiled in September 2001, a Fresno-area district was left without an incumbent, and Nunes moved quickly. He was supported by Thomas, whose deep-pocketed campaign contributors in the pharmaceutical and insurance industries helped Nunes. Nunes won the endorsement of the California Farm Bureau. He faced serious primary challenges from Jim Patterson, Fresno's conservative former mayor, who was backed by the anti-tax group Club for Growth, and California Assembly member Mike Briggs. All three promised to seek new water sources for farmers about to lose the San Joaquin River as a primary source after environmentalists successfully lobbied to restore the river. The candidates all called for tax cuts, fewer federal regulations and expanded guest-worker programs for immigrants. Nunes won with 37 percent of the vote to 33 percent for Patterson and 26 percent for Briggs. In November, Nunes won easily, 70%-26%.

Nunes has a mostly conservative voting record. In the Almanac vote ratings, he ash been near the center of House Republicans. Nunes can deliver a cutting sound bite, once comparing government spending with the actions of "a broke gambler who desperately keeps doubling down in a vain effort to break even." He said conservative Republicans who were blamed by many for shutting down part of the government in 2013 because they opposed the Affordable Care Act were "lemmings with suicide vests."

Legislatively, Nunes has dived into his district's most pressing issue: the use of water from the San Joaquin River. He clashed with supporters of alternatives to increase water flow over the Friant Dam so salmon could be returned to the parched lower reaches of the San Joaquin. Leaders of such projects were like "communist politburo members who collect big checks and do nothing," he said. When California's drought worsened, Nunes lashed out at the Obama administration for allying with "radical environmentalists" in preventing farmers from getting sufficient water for their crops. He got a bill through the House in 2012 to reshape California's water-rights system to deliver more San Joaquin water for farmers; Democrats condemned the move as a "water grab" and it did not move in the Senate, something Nunes attributed to California's Democratic senators for defending "their environmental wacko friends."

A member of Ways and Means, at the outset of the health care debate in 2009, Nunes joined his ally Paul Ryan in introducing a bill providing tax credits for people to buy insurance and ending the tax exemption for businesses providing workers with the benefit. Their strategy pre-empted other Republicans who preferred to take more time to craft a plan. Nunes later introduced his own bill in 2012 to create a voluntary pilot program in which Medicare and Medicaid recipients would be given a debit-style "Medi-choice" card to buy health insurance. Following the 2016 election, he joined Ryan in support of a border adjustment tax that would tax imports and invest in the domestic economy, and said opposition from some business groups was "a little offensive" given that other nations have comparable fees. The proposal failed to achieve sufficient Republican support to become part of their 2017 tax bill.

As Intelligence Committee chairman from 2015 to 2018, Nunes revamped the panel's subcommittees, forming new ones to concentrate on scrutinizing the CIA, as well as the NSA and cyber security. He initially was an advocate for intelligence agencies and kept a low profile, though he traveled widely. "My goal is to make sure we are getting our members out to every corner of the world," Nunes told McClatchy Newspapers when he took over as chairman. "You cannot conduct serious oversight work without getting on the ground and actually talking to the folks that are doing the work."

That changed with the election of Trump. Nunes had served on the executive committee of his presidential transition team, which advised on the selection of Cabinet members. He was among the first to recommend the selection of James Mattis for Defense secretary. From the House, he advocated fellow Rep. Mike Pompeo for director of the CIA.

Nunes initially voiced reluctance after the election to investigate ties between Russia and the Trump campaign. But, following the inauguration, he joined ranking Democrat Schiff in announcing that the Intelligence Committee would review Russian cyber-activity against the United States and its allies, plus the response of the intelligence community. He voiced concern about the leaking of Trump-related material to the news media. The leaking and his complaints about it led to a sharpening of partisan lines on the committee, which was a contrast to the bipartisan review of the election by the Senate Intelligence Committee.

Nunes got into trouble when he allegedly received classified information from a friendly source at the White House and then discussed the report with journalists, among others. He contended that there was surveillance of Trump and his associates at Trump Tower in New York City during the presidential transition. In March 2017, Nunes briefed Trump at the White House on his findings. When Democrats learned of his activities and voiced objections, Nunes initially apologized to the committee. Not satisfied, committee Democrats demanded that he recuse himself from the investigation. On April 6, the House Ethics Committee announced it would investigate Nunes for possible "unauthorized disclosures." On the same day, he said he would transfer control of the Intelligence Committee inquiry to other members, though he retained his chairmanship of the panel.

The bipartisan leaders of the Ethics Committee announced in a one-paragraph statement on Dec. 7 that, based on the conclusions of experts on intelligence classification, "the information that Rep. Nunes disclosed was not classified," and closed the case. Nunes said the allegations were "obviously frivolous and were rooted in politically motivated complaints against me by left-wing activist groups." Subsequently, several House Republicans charged that law-enforcement officials violated intelligence procedures in their review of alleged Russian interference in the election. In August 2018, MSNBC reported that Nunes said at a closed-door GOP fundraising event that House Republicans were "the only ones" to protect Trump from the investigation by special counsel Robert Mueller.

When Democrats regained House control in 2019, Nunes became the ranking minority member of the Intelligence panel. He defended Trump and criticized the Democrats' moves against him. He sought, for example, to undermine the credibility of their witnesses at committee hearings who described Trump's call for political assistance from the president of Ukraine, Volodymyr Zelensky. Nunes asked former National Security Council aide Alexander Vindman about his dealings with reporters and whether he knew the identity of the anonymous whistleblower who initially filed a complaint about Trump's phone call.

Although his defense of Trump had little impact in the mostly party-line impeachment debate and trial, his efforts gained the president's appreciation. In awarding Nunes the Medal of Freedom in a private White House event two weeks before he left office, Trump's action was based on his view that Nunes "pursued the Russia Hoax at great personal risk and never stopped standing up for the truth," according to a White House statement.

With Nunes having become a partisan lightning rod, he faced robust challenges to reelection in his comfortably Republican district. Nunes had never been held below 62 percent in his campaigns. In 2018, challenger Andrew Janz, a 34-year-old Trump critic and former deputy district attorney in Fresno County, called Nunes "a national security danger." He complained that the Democratic Congressional Campaign Committee gave him no support and refused to return his phone calls. "This became the most expensive House contest in 2018, with Nunes outspending Janz, $11.4 million to $9.1 million in a relatively cheap media market. After having led Janz, 58%-32% in the primary, Nunes won in November, 53%-47%. In 2020, Phil Arballo, who runs a financial business in Fresno and said Nunes had lost touch with his constituents, spent $5.1 million to the $20.4 million that Nunes spent. Nunes won, 54%-46%.

Nunes has retained his position as the number-two Republican on the Ways and Means Committee. With Rep. Kevin Brady term-limited as senior Republican on the panel and retiring, Nunes faced competition from Rep. Vern Buchanan of Florida to take the top GOP slot in 2023.

CA-22: Central Valley
Cook Partisan Voting Index: R+6

Population		Race and Ethnicity		Income	
Total	768,917	White	66.00%	Median Income	$66,532
Land area (sq. miles)	1,165	Black	3.20%	District Income Rank	199
Pop/ sq mi	659.95	Latino	50.60%	Poverty Rate	15.20%
Born in State	70.10%	Asian	8.40%	With health insurance	93.80%
		Two or more races	4.70%	Cash public assistance	4.00%
Age Groups		Other	17.70%	Food stamp/SNAP	15.00%
Under 18	28.70%				
18-34	24.10%	Education		Work	
35-64	34.60%	H.S grad or less	39.40%	White Collar	36.00%
Over 64	12.70%	Some college	36.10%	Sales and Service	36.90%
		College Degree, 4 yr	16.00%	Blue Collar	27.00%
Military		Post grad	8.60%	Government	18.60%
Veteran/ Active Duty	5.90%				

2020 Pres. Vote	Trump	163,584	(52%)	Biden	146,467	(46%)		
2016 Pres. Vote	Trump	125,089	(52%)	Clinton	102,292	(42%)	Johnson	8,628 (4%)

Eastern Fresno City and Suburbs: In California's Central Valley, between the flat Westlands and the Sierras, is Fresno, a city that is both agricultural and industrial, middle American and ethnically diverse. Although it began as a farm-market center, the city has long since grown out to the north, east and west from its downtown, and its economy has expanded to other sectors—construction, transportation and financial services. It is a creation of the Industrial Age and the Central Pacific Railroad. Historian Kevin Starr described the San Joaquin Valley, at the heart of the Central Valley, as "the most productive unnatural environment on Earth." Fresno's city fathers bred the local wine grape, developed the raisin industry and introduced the Smyrna fig. These are among the area's 300-plus crops, which include cotton, lima beans, nectarines, almonds, tomatoes, cantaloupes, plums, peaches and alfalfa.

Dairy is now the biggest commodity and Tulare County leads the nation in milk and dairy sales, with more than 600,000 cattle. Fresno surpassed both Tulare and neighboring Kern County as the largest agricultural producer in the United States, with more than $7.8 billion in value in 2019. Almonds have become the premium cash crop. Central Valley agriculture is industrial in its thoroughness and in its ownership by large corporations. The vineyards outside Fresno radiate in mechanical precision, with vines just 10 feet apart and exposed to the relentless summer sun: nothing romantic or quaint about it. Except for the disruption of the severe recession followed by drought, times have been good. The weak dollar boosted farm exports, large citrus groves benefited from losses in hurricane-plagued Florida and nuts found new export markets. Groundwater contamination has become a growing problem in Tulare, where it affects 99 percent of the drinking water.

Construction of the bullet train from San Francisco to Los Angeles began in the Central Valley, where the project was fiercely opposed by many local officials worried that it could attract too many people to the Fresno area, forcing residents out of single-family homes and into dense, urban communities. The original cost estimate of $6.4 billion for the 118 miles from Merced to Bakersfield proved wildly optimistic. Speaking to the legislature in 2019, Gov. Gavin Newsom said he had decided to kill the project, with the ironic exception of the Central Valley corridor.

The 22nd District covers a bit more than half of Fresno County and most of Tulare. Route 99, the old Farm-to-Market Corridor, runs through the district and leads to the Hispanic-majority city of Tulare. In the northern part of the district is Clovis, billed as the "gateway to the Sierras." The central area takes in the smaller city of Dinuba; Visalia is the district's largest whole city. It is a largely agricultural district that has been safely Republican. Fresno County is one of the most conservative urban centers in the nation. As was the case throughout California, Donald Trump under-performed in each of his campaigns. In Fresno, where Mitt Romney got 51 percent in 2012, Trump got 46 percent in 2016 and 45 percent in 2020. In Tulare, which is a bit more than one-third of the total, the Republican vote dropped from 58 percent to 53 percent each time.

Kevin McCarthy (R)

Elected 2006, 8th term, b. Jan 26, 1965; Bakersfield, CA; Bakersfield College, 1985; CA State University, Bakersfield, B.A., 1989; University of CA, Bakersfield, M.B.A., 1994; Baptist; Married (Judy McCarthy); 2 children.

Elected Office: Trustee, Kern Commissioner Col. Board, 2000-2002; CA Assembly, 2002-2007, Minority Leader, 2004-2006.

Professional Career: Owner, Kevin O's Deli, 1986-1987, Mesa Marin Batting Range, 1991-1992; Staff, U.S. Rep. Bill Thomas, 1987-2002.

DC Office: 2468 RHOB 20515, 202-225-2915, Fax: 202-225-2908, kevinmccarthy.house.gov

State Offices: Bakersfield, 661-327-3611.

House Minority Leader.

Group Ratings

	ADA	ACLU	AFL-CIO	LCV	COC	HAFA	ACU	CFG	FRC
2020	**	17%	**	14%	-	77%	85%	**	-
2019	5%	C	33%	3%	83%	C	86%	68%	95%

Almanac Ratings 2019-2020

	Economy	Social	Foreign	Composite
Liberal	25%	34%	27%	29%
Conservative	75%	66%	73%	71%

Key Votes of the 116th Congress

1. U.S./Mex./Can. trade deal	Y	5. Russia sanctions	Y	9. Firearms background checks	N
2. First Coronavirus response	Y	6. Troops in Syria	Y	10. Spending at the border	Y
3. HEROES Act	N	7. Veto arms sales to Saudis	N	11. Marijuana liberalized rules	N/A
4. CASH Act	N/A	8. Defense $$$, veto override	N/A	12. Electoral College objections	Y

Election Results

Election	Name (Party)	Vote (%)		Cand. Spent	Ind. Exp. Support	Ind. Exp. Oppose
2020 General	Kevin McCarthy (R)	190,222	(62%)	$22,490,934	$1,242	$23,796
	Kim Mangone (D)	115,896	(38%)	$1,664,433	$1,293	
2020 Primary	Kevin McCarthy (R)	107,897	(67%)			

Prior winning percentages: 2018 (64%), 2016 (69%), 2014 (75%), 2012 (73%), 2010 (99%), 2008 (100%), 2006 (71%)

Kevin McCarthy, a gregarious former Capitol Hill staffer elected in 2006, has combined hard work, the ability to reach across party factions and some survivor skills to step up as the House GOP leader. His disappointments include that he fell short in October 2015, when John Boehner unexpectedly announced his resignation as House Speaker and McCarthy was the heir apparent. Opposition from conservatives and self-induced errors led McCarthy to step aside for Paul Ryan, who served three years as Speaker. McCarthy had a more comfortable relationship with President Donald Trump than did Ryan, who seemed relieved to walk away from the ongoing chaos and their House setbacks.

This time, McCarthy had the support to become House Republican Leader. But in the transition from Ryan to McCarthy in 2018, Republicans lost 40 seats and relinquished House control for the first time since 2010. As is customary, the responsibility for that big midterm loss rested chiefly with the president. Trump's continuing appeal to his base of blue-collar, rural voters gave Democrats a large opening to gain seats in suburbs. They skillfully exploited those opportunities. The loss of seven GOP seats in California was a sharp indictment of McCarthy's limited home-state appeal and skills, especially his unwillingness to go his own way from Trump.

The results weakened McCarthy's base of House Republicans and left doubts about his long-term viability. Two years later, the election resulted in new shocks: Trump was the decisive loser, despite his refusal to accept the results. And House Republicans gained 14 seats in two years, leaving Democrats with a razor-thin majority and McCarthy—and his diverse flock—as the "loyal opposition," with the hope of taking back House control in 2022.

McCarthy grew up in Bakersfield, where his blue-collar family has lived for generations and often voted Democratic. He moved in the other direction. At 19, he won $5,000 in the state lottery and invested it in a deli, which helped pay for business school at Cal State, Bakersfield. In college, he was elected chairman of the California Young Republicans and later headed the national Young Republicans organization. After he sold the deli, he got a job in the local office of Rep. Bill Thomas, who was on his way to chairing the powerful Ways and Means Committee. McCarthy eventually became Thomas' district director and protégé. In 2000, he was elected to the Kern County Community College Board, and in 2002 he was elected to the Assembly. As Republican leader, McCarthy worked with Republican Gov. Arnold Schwarzenegger on the budget, workers' compensation issues and redistricting.

When Thomas announced his retirement in March 2006, just four days before the filing deadline, McCarthy was the obvious candidate to succeed him. He faced token Republican primary opposition. In November, he won 71%-29%.During that campaign, he raised more than $1 million and traveled the country for other Republican candidates. That attracted the attention of party leaders. After the election, he was chosen the freshman representative on the Republican Steering Committee, which makes committee assignments. He chaired the Platform Committee at the 2008 Republican National Convention, winning praise for uniting conservatives and moderates.

McCarthy landed a leadership position in 2009 when Minority Whip Eric Cantor of Virginia appointed him chief deputy. On the night of President Barack Obama's inauguration, he reportedly implored a gathering of leading GOP lawmakers and activists plotting strategy to be aggressive. "If you act like you're the minority, you're going to stay in the minority," McCarthy said, according to Robert Draper's 2012 book Do Not Ask What Good We Do: Inside the U.S. House of Representatives. "We've gotta challenge them on every single bill and challenge them on every single campaign."

In the next two years, McCarthy wore multiple hats. He was the head of recruiting for the National Republican Congressional Committee, in what became the highly successful 2010 election for the GOP. He traveled widely looking for candidates, identifying challengers to take on Democrats accustomed to weak opposition. Ultimately, Republicans had candidates in 430 of the 435 congressional districts, the highest number ever at that time. McCarthy kept in constant contact with the top contenders, often with quick cell phone calls while he was heading to meet other prospects. With Cantor and Ryan, he led the party's "Young Guns" program to spotlight and finance Republican challengers. Minority Leader John Boehner assigned McCarthy to draw up a document similar to the House Republicans' 1994 Contract with America. They kept their "Pledge to America" policy manifesto deliberately vague to deter Democratic attacks. Although it had less impact than the 1994 document, it sought to commit incoming and veteran Republicans to a single set of policies, such as extending the Bush-era tax cuts and repealing Obama's health care overhaul.

McCarthy was rewarded for his impressive efforts after Republicans won control of the House. He was the overwhelming choice for whip. In his new job, McCarthy employed a nice-guy approach in building trust. He mountain-biked with Republican members in the mornings and rounded up others in the evenings for group dinners. He encouraged lawmakers to hang around his whip office on the first floor of the Capitol and got acquainted with their families. "A conference united around policies creates better legislation than using intimidation," McCarthy told The New York Times.

McCarthy paid particular attention to the often-rambunctious tea party freshmen elected in 2010. He advised them to vote their consciences even if it meant disagreeing with the leadership. Sometimes the results were disastrous—especially for the whip, whose job is to assure the majority party prevails. When the leadership decided in April 2011 to back a continuing resolution to keep the federal government operating, 59 Republicans defected. And at the height of the "fiscal cliff" negotiations in December 2012, when the two parties struggled to agree on spending and tax cuts, Boehner's "Plan B" proposal was pulled from the floor when it became clear that it lacked sufficient Republican votes.

But there was little second-guessing of McCarthy after Cantor stepped down as majority leader following his unexpected 2014 primary defeat. With the support of friendly colleagues and the GOP's establishment wing, McCarthy geared up a campaign within hours to replace his fallen friend. Idaho maverick Raul Labrador, his only opponent, never stood a chance against McCarthy's formidable vote-counting operation.

In his new job, McCarthy laid out broad-based objectives that were designed to appeal across the board. When it came to specifics, he usually showed his allegiance to House conservatives. In early 2015, when Republicans gained more leverage from capturing Senate control, McCarthy helped create a working group of committee chairs to develop a Republican alternative to the Affordable Care Act. But they had scant workload or legislative success. They picked what many saw as an unwinnable fight with Obama over immigration policy. In another setback, the leadership jettisoned a planned vote on an anti-abortion bill after some Republican women lawmakers complained. With slight modifications, the House passed that bill a few months later.

The continuing Republican infighting that led to Boehner's September 2015 resignation as Speaker helped to stymie the move by McCarthy to take over as his successor. The conservative Freedom Caucus required that he meet a series of demands before several of its members would support him. When a partisan firestorm erupted after he claimed credit in a broadcast interview with Sean Hannity of Fox News for the hearings on the 2012 Benghazi terrorist attack, McCarthy proved to be unprepared to fill the big shoes. Eventually, he advised Ryan that he was the best hope for House Republicans. Still, McCarthy became a key lieutenant to his longtime ally and remained a major GOP fundraiser and advocate.

During those three years, until he inherited the wreckage as minority leader, McCarthy faced some rocky moments in seeking to manage the House. In 2018, a group of relatively centrist Republicans pressed to provide a pathway to some sort of legal status for immigrants who had entered the nation illegally. When Ryan opened the door by suggesting there was a "consensus sweet spot," McCarthy disagreed, siding with immigration hardliners who opposed any conciliatory action and tweeting a few weeks before the election, "Few things are more fundamental to a nation than a protected border."

Still, some conservatives remained reluctant to support McCarthy as the successor to Ryan. Rep. Jim Jordan of Ohio, a founder of the Freedom Caucus, entered the contest for party leader—in part to seek concessions on how McCarthy would manage the party. A further wrinkle was provided by Rep. Steve Scalise of Louisiana, the Republican whip. He told reporters he was interested in moving up the GOP leadership but that he wouldn't challenge McCarthy. His comments left the possibility that Scalise might run for the top party post if McCarthy had failed to secure the votes.

McCarthy was a prominent and unabashed ally when Donald Trump became a candidate and later president. He was a go-between in the more difficult relationship between Trump and Ryan. "As majority leader, my role is to keep a team together," he told The Washington Post. "I think it's been helpful." The Post described their relationship as "light on policy nitty-gritty but heavy on back-slapping, deal-making and personal rapport." During a celebratory lunch the day before his inauguration, Trump called him out, "There's my Kevin." This deference led GOP critics to describe McCarthy as a sycophant.

As it turned out, the House GOP setbacks in the election meant that no Republican would take the gavel. In the selection of the new minority leader, McCarthy defeated Jordan, 159-43. Even though McCarthy seemed in control of the downsized GOP Conference, the ambitions and animosities lingered.

As minority leader, McCarthy had a limited relationship with most Democrats, including Pelosi. But over the years he occasionally has sought to reach out. Facing partisan criticism of scant Republican participation at the 50th anniversary celebration of civil rights protests in Selma Alabama in 2015, he made a last-minute decision to join the festivities. In one of the few cases in which he engaged in bipartisan legislating, McCarthy in 2016 worked closely with his home-state Democratic Sen. Dianne Feinstein to ease the problems caused by California's crippling drought. They agreed on a California-focused piece of the water-resources bill, including expanded reservoir storage, financing of water recycling in the cities, and desalination projects. Obama signed the measure.

Leading his own party in the minority in 2019, McCarthy's paramount objective was unity—including with the Freedom Caucus. In an early move, he supported Jordan to become the ranking member of the Oversight committee. Little more than a year later, Jordan switched to fill the top Republican position on the Judiciary Committee after Georgia Rep. Doug Collins stepped down to run for the Senate.

By demanding support for his own objectives, Trump added to the challenges facing McCarthy. In December 2019, the House GOP's unanimous opposition to the first set of impeachment charges against the president was proof of that success, at least in the short term. Former Republican Rep. Tom Davis told The New York Times, with obvious skepticism, that House Republicans were operating "as an appendage of the Executive Branch."

The onset of the pandemic created new challenges for McCarthy, as Congress settled down to serious legislating for the first time since Democrats took House control. Once Congress gave speedy and bipartisan approval to an economic stimulus bill of about $3 trillion, he—like Senate Majority Leader Mitch McConnell—was reluctant to support additional spending largely aimed at benefitting Democratic constituencies. McCarthy also objected to Pelosi's decision to permit House members to vote by proxy on the House floor—without leaving their districts, in the interests of reducing health risks. Although Democrats made some concessions to McCarthy on the details of proxy voting, he was miffed that they decided to proceed unilaterally, in an action he said would "forever alter our democratic institution for the worse."

In preparing for the 2020 election, House Republicans issued a set of broad and Trump-friendly principles in their one-page "Commitment to American." That strategy included regular attacks on Democratic objectives as "defund, dismantle and destroy." An example of his deliberate approach to avoid stirring the pot was the decision by most Republicans to support the election of Margaret Taylor Greene of Georgia—despite earlier reservations about her conspiratorial advocacy.

With the surprising split decision of Trump's loss and House Republicans' double-digit seat gain, McCarthy and his cohorts found themselves during the post-election period in the odd position of embracing Trump's approach of challenging the election results as "fraud"—though not for the House election results.

The continuing reluctance of most Republicans to avoid challenging Trump, even after he had clearly lost, was shown in the January 7 vote by 138 House Republicans (with 64 opposed) to support the challenge to the presidential vote in Pennsylvania, after 121 challenged the vote in Arizona, during the usually routine count of the Electoral College votes—hours after the destructive insurrection in the Capitol. On January 13, only 10 House Republicans supported the second round of impeachment charges.

At home, after gliding to his first three reelection campaigns without major party opposition, McCarthy faced at least nominal opposition. In 2018, he was elected with 64 percent of the vote against little-known Democratic challenger Tatiana Matta. Although that contest was barely a nuisance, the outcome was symptomatic of the shellacking that House Republicans took that year in McCarthy's home state, when they lost half of their 14 seats in the delegation. In 2020, when the GOP regained four of those seats, he was held to 62 percent—his lowest-ever reelection—by Democratic political novice Kim Mangone, who spent an impressive $1.7 million.

Those results were a reminder of McCarthy's limitations at home—in contrast to other GOP leaders in years past who could rely on their dominance of home-state delegations, for example, in Ohio and Texas.

CA-23: Central Valley   Cook Partisan Voting Index: R+12

Population		Race and Ethnicity		Income	
Total	741,557	White	72.10%	Median Income	$63,550
Land area (sq. miles)	9,898	Black	6.80%	District Income Rank	219
Pop/ sq mi	74.92	Latino	40.70%	Poverty Rate	15.60%
Born in State	69.30%	Asian	5.00%	With health insurance	93.80%
		Two or more races	4.90%	Cash public assistance	4.80%
Age Groups		Other	11.10%	Food stamp/SNAP	15.00%
Under 18	26.20%				
18-34	23.60%	**Education**		**Work**	
35-64	36.20%	H.S grad or less	41.30%	White Collar	36.00%
Over 64	14.00%	Some college	36.60%	Sales and Service	37.00%
		College Degree, 4 yr	15.10%	Blue Collar	26.90%
Military		Post grad	7.00%	Government	21.80%
Veteran/ Active Duty	7.60%				

2020 Pres. Vote	Trump	176,413	(57%)	Biden	125,068	(40%)		
2016 Pres. Vote	Trump	142,351	(58%)	Clinton	88,314	(36%)	Johnson	9,850	(4%)

Central and Western Bakersfield and Suburbs: Bakersfield, near the southern end of California's Central Valley, has been the focus of great migrations four times: in the gold rush of 1885; in the boomlet that followed the discovery of oil in 1899; in the 1930s flight of Dust Bowl refugees from Oklahoma, Kansas and Texas; and in a flood of newcomers in the past two decades, when Bakersfield and Kern County grew more rapidly than California's biggest metro areas. The migration that made the deepest imprint was in the 1930s. The Okies drove across a thousand miles of brown landscape, then through the Tehachapi Pass, and found this vast green valley, with its irrigated fields and its eucalyptus-shaded towns—the richest farming country in the world. The story is told vividly in novelist John Steinbeck's The Grapes of Wrath and in Dan Morgan's Rising in the West, which explains how the Okies' descendants prospered in California.

People here are culturally conservative with little empathy for Los Angeles-style liberalism. More recently, Latinos have been coming in large numbers for farm work. The result is that the Central Valley, including Bakersfield, had both high population growth and high unemployment for a decade. Its 41 percent population increase from 2000 to 2010 placed Bakersfield among the top 10 fastest-growing cities in the nation; by 2019, it had grown by another 10 percent. Reduced oil prices during and following the recession, and the accompanying disincentive for drilling, became another hit to the Kern County economy, which is home to 66 percent of the oil production in California and produces more oil than any other county in the nation.

In recent years, the area has taken an "all of the above" approach to energy production. With new seismic technology, oil exploration firms have located additional oil deposits in Kern County. Kern had more than 5,000 wind turbines in 2019, the highest number for any county in the nation. In 2019, Amazon said it was planning to buy energy from a Kern County wind farm to power one of its cloud centers. Aera Energy announced plans for construction of what it contends will be the nation's largest solar-energy farm, spreading over 770 acres adjacent to the company's oil fields. But the project was delayed by financial problems. The area continued to suffer in 2018 from a less desirable mark: the poorest air quality of any city across the nation. More than 15 percent of the residents in the Bakersfield area suffer from asthma or some form of heart disease, a private study found.

The 23rd Congressional District includes about 80 percent of Kern County, with the remainder in rural Tulare and a northern tip of Los Angeles County. It includes much of downtown Bakersfield. The 23rd covers the southern part of the Sierras, including Sequoia National Forest and Lake Isabella. The southern end of the district in the Mojave Desert encompasses the sprawling Edwards Air Force Base, where Chuck Yeager flew the X-1 and where the Space Shuttle frequently landed. It recently has become the testing site for the B-21 Raider, the next-generation long-range strike bomber. The 23rd is 39 percent Hispanic. In 2020, as in the two previous presidential elections, this was the most Republican district in California. Donald Trump led Joe Biden, 57%-40%, a dip from 62 percent for Mitt Romney. Kern was no longer the most favorable Trump county in California, though with 54 percent of the vote, it was his best county with at least 100,000 voters.

Salud Carbajal (D)

Elected 2016, 3rd term, b. Nov 18, 1964; Moroleon, Mexico; University of CA, Santa Barbara, B.A., 1990; Fielding University, M.A., 1994; Catholic; Married (Gina Carbajal); 2 children.

Military Career: U.S. Marine Corps Reserves 1984-1992

Elected Office: Staff, County Supervisor Naomi Schwartz, 1993-2004; Member, Santa Barbara County Board of Supervisors, 2004-2016.

DC Office: 1431 LHOB 20515, 202-225-3601, Fax: 202-225-5632, carbajal.house.gov

State Offices: San Luis Obispo, 805-546-8348; Santa Barbara, 805-730-1710; Santa Maria, 805-730-1710.

Committees: *Agriculture*: Biotechnology, Horticulture & Research; General Farm Commodities & Risk Management; Subcommittee Nutrition, Oversight & Department Operations. *Armed Services*: Strategic Forces; Tactical Air & Land Forces. *Transportation & Infrastructure*: Coast Guard & Maritime Transportation (Chmn); Highways & Transit; Water Resources & Environment.

Group Ratings

	ADA	ACLU	AFL-CIO	LCV	COC	HAFA	ACU	CFG	FRC
2020	**	76%	**	100%	-	0%	3%	**	-
2019	90%	C	100%	97%	63%	C	3%	12%	0%

Almanac Ratings 2019-2020

	Economy	Social	Foreign	Composite
Liberal	100%	100%	80%	94%
Conservative	0%	0%	20%	6%

Key Votes of the 116th Congress

1. U.S./Mex./Can. trade deal	Y	5. Russia sanctions	Y	9. Firearms background checks	Y
2. First Coronavirus response	Y	6. Troops in Syria	Y	10. Spending at the border	Y
3. HEROES Act	Y	7. Veto arms sales to Saudis	Y	11. Marijuana liberalized rules	Y
4. CASH Act	Y	8. Defense $$$, veto override	Y	12. Electoral College objections	N

Election Results

Election	Name (Party)	Vote (%)		Cand. Spent	Ind. Exp. Support	Ind. Exp. Oppose
2020 General	Salud Carbajal (D)............................ 212,564	(59%)		$1,573,717	$62,183	
	Andy Caldwell (R)......................... 149,781	(41%)		$1,900,527		$113
2020 Primary	Salud Carbajal (D)....................... 139,973	(58%)				

Prior winning percentages: 2018 (59%), 2016 (53%)

Democrat Salud Carbajal, elected in 2016 in a contentious contest for an open seat, easily won a rematch two years later. He offered an innovative proposal that was designed to reduce gun violence. He occasionally reached out for bipartisanship, though he usually remained a party loyalist.

Carbajal was born in Mexico, and his family moved to a small mining town in Arizona when he was five. His father worked in a copper mine until it closed. One of eight children, he was the first in his family to graduate from college. He got his bachelor's in Iberian studies from the University of California, Santa Barbara, and a master's in organizational management from Fielding University. Carbajal was a member of the U.S. Marine Corps Reserve for eight years, including two years of active stateside duty during the Gulf War. He had several jobs on the public payroll, including chief of staff to a county supervisor and program director in the Santa Barbara Public Health Department. He served for 12 years on the Santa Barbara County Board of Supervisors, where he worked to improve local schools, protect the environment and advocate sustainable, clean energy sources.

When Rep. Lois Capps retired, she and Democratic Leader Nancy Pelosi were early supporters of Carbajal. Santa Barbara Mayor Helene Schneider, who backed Sen. Bernie Sanders in the presidential campaign, also ran. The chief Republican candidates were Assemblyman Katcho Achadjian and businessman Justin Fareed. In the "top two" primary, Carbajal and Fareed were the frontrunners with 33 percent and 21 percent. Fareed, who was an aide to Republican Rep. Ed Whitfield of Kentucky, accused Carbajal of being long on "political rhetoric and not actual solutions to the problems we're facing." Carbajal described himself as a public servant who crossed party lines. In September, he apologized after he referred to Lompoc, a military town that includes the Vandenberg base, as the "armpit" of Santa Barbara. The two national parties spent a total of nearly $4 million on the contest, which was closer than expected. Fareed took San Luis Obispo with 51.5 percent of the vote. Carbajal led in the more populous Santa Barbara with 57 percent, and won, 53%-47%.

On the Armed Services Committee, Carbajal won approval of an amendment to the defense spending bill in 2018, which directed the Pentagon to report on innovative ways to reduce water use and improve water sustainability on military bases. He worked to win a cyber security training complex at Camp San Luis Obispo. When the House in July 2020 passed the defense bill, he took credit for provisions to improve launch services at Vandenberg Air Force Base and technology-based military research partnerships with universities in his district.

On other local issues, Carbajal filed bills to bar oil and gas drilling off California's Central Coast and to encourage renewable energy in San Luis Obispo following the closing of the Diablo Canyon nuclear power plant. He supported the Green New Deal resolution as "very consistent with our Central Coast values." His Almanac vote ratings placed him among centrist Democrats.

Carbajal gained attention for legislation that he earlier filed to provide funds to states that implement restraining orders designed to prevent incidents of gun violence. Supporters said the proposal might have detected in advance some assailants' behavioral problems. Carbajal said the National Rifle Association, which opposed his bill, had become synonymous with "No Republican Action." With Sen. Dianne Feinstein, in an op-ed he co-authored for the Santa Barbara Independent, Carbajal noted that his sister, at age 12, killed herself with a firearm. They advocated federal legislation, based on the rules in many states, that gives law enforcement officials the authority to delay for 21 days gun sales to "dangerous individuals."

Carbajal faced well-financed challengers in his first two reelection campaigns, with similar outcomes. In a rematch in 2018, Carbajal spent $1.9 million to Fareed's $1.5 million. This time, Carbajal was not on a Democratic watch list and he won, 59%-41%.Two years later, the GOP challenger was Andy Caldwell, who was a longtime local conservative radio host and was described by the San Luis Obispo Tribune as "a pro-Trump, pro-oil, pro-'family unit' candidate." The candidate spending was comparable to 2018, as was the result. Carbajal again won, 59%-41%, with stronger performance in Santa Barbara County.

CA-24: Central Coast

Cook Partisan Voting Index: D+10

Population		Race and Ethnicity		Income	
Total	737,443	White	80.30%	Median Income	$76,308
Land area (sq. miles)	6,883	Black	2.00%	District Income Rank	118
Pop/ sq mi	107.13	Latino	37.00%	Poverty Rate	12.00%
Born in State	61.00%	Asian	5.00%	With health insurance	91.20%
		Two or more races	3.50%	Cash public assistance	2.30%
Age Groups		Other	9.20%	Food stamp/SNAP	6.50%
Under 18	20.10%				
18-34	28.00%	**Education**		**Work**	
35-64	34.10%	H.S grad or less	33.60%	White Collar	38.70%
Over 64	17.80%	Some college	30.80%	Sales and Service	39.30%
		College Degree, 4 yr	21.60%	Blue Collar	22.10%
Military		Post grad	14.10%	Government	16.30%
Veteran/ Active Duty	7.00%				

2020 Pres. Vote	Biden	221,831	(61%)	Trump	134,810	(37%)			
2016 Pres. Vote	Clinton	176,979	(56%)	Trump	113,887	(36%)	Johnson	13,426	(4%)
	Stein	6,733	(2%)						

Santa Barbara, San Luis Obispo: In a state where stunning coastal landscapes and charming small towns are a dime a dozen, Santa Barbara stands out as someplace special. It is a collection of red tile roofs and leafy live oaks, sheltered by towering mountains just above the sea. The impression is a bit misleading, for Santa Barbara has its problems. Most of its quaint white stucco buildings were put up not as part of 18th-century mission settlement, but after a 1925 earthquake leveled much of the town. The city has long been one of the nation's richest retirement communities, one comfortable with its high living costs and determined to preserve its pristine environment and serenity.

Both features came under threat spectacularly in 1969 when an underwater well ruptured, coating the beach with oil. Pictures of the slick in the channel, and of volunteers trying to wash oil off grounded birds, helped to launch the environmental movement, including limitations on off-shore drilling. The oil spill left a long-lasting residue in Santa Barbara's politics. This was once a mostly Republican community, uninterested in redistribution of wealth, but always concerned about the environment and having moderate-to-liberal impulses on cultural issues. Like most of coastal California, it has moved decisively to the left. In a city that is 2 percent Black, the Black Lives Matter movement in June 2020 won unanimous approval by the Santa Barbara City Council of a resolution declaring racism a public health crisis and condemning police brutality,

The largest towns in northern Santa Barbara County, as well as in San Luis Obispo, are pleasant, comfortable places, as untrendy as you can find in coastal California. The cost of rental housing in both counties has become unaffordable for many local workers. Farmers in Santa Barbara recently revived the planting of coffee beans, with initial success and—not surprisingly for California—plans to develop "specialty" brews. Much of the Santa Barbara coastline is occupied by Vandenberg Air Force Base, which was the site in December 1958 of the first U.S. test missile launch and now sends unmanned government and commercial satellites into polar orbit. In March 2019, the Defense Department used the base for a successful first-ever test of interceptor missiles in the missile defense system. In San Luis Obispo, PG&E is scheduled to complete by 2025 the shutdown of the Diablo Canyon nuclear power plant. The utility's decision in 2018 to decommission the plant, which was made largely for financial reasons, has generated second-guessing about potential options to finance and fuel the facility.

The 24th Congressional District of California includes all of San Luis Obispo and Santa Barbara counties. Santa Barbara is the larger of the two, and its 46 percent Latino population is twice that of its northern neighbor. Santa Maria is the largest city in Santa Barbara County. The city of Santa Barbara is only one-fifth of the population of its county. The 24th also brings in the rural northwest corner of Ventura County and a separate coastal part of Ventura to the south, and it encompasses much of the Los Padres National Forest. Politically, the district has shifted notably toward the Democrats. Joe Biden won the district, 61%-37%, more than twice the margin by which Barack Obama defeated Mitt Romney, 54%-43%. Closer to Los Angeles, Santa Barbara leans more heavily Democratic than does SLO.

Mike Garcia (R)

Elected 2020, 1st full term, b. Apr 24, 1976; Santa Clarita, CA; U.S. Naval Academy, B.S., 1998; Georgetown University, M.A., 1998; Not Known; Married (Rebecca Garcia); 2 children.

Military Career: Aviator, U.S. Navy, 1999-2012 (Iraq).

Professional Career: Chief Executive Officer, real estate group; Director/Vice President, Business Development, Raytheon, 2009-2018.

DC Office: 1535 LHOB 20515, 202-225-1956, Fax: 202-226-0683, mikegarcia.house.gov

State Offices: Palmdale, 661-839-0532; Santa Clarita, 661-568-4855; Simi Valley, 805-760-9090.

Committees: *Appropriations*: Commerce, Justice, Science & Related Agencies; Transportation, HUD & Related Agencies. *Science, Space & Technology*: Energy.

Election Results

Election	Name (Party)	Vote (%)		Cand. Spent	Ind. Exp. Support	Ind. Exp. Oppose
2020 General	Mike Garcia (R)	169,638	(50%)	$9,500,120	$1,365,038	$8,650,164
	Christy Smith (D)	169,305	(50%)	$5,714,413	$10,468	
2020 Primary	Mike Garcia (R)	37,381	(24%)			
	Steve Knight (R)	29,645	(19%)			

Republican Mike Garcia won both a special election in May 2020 and the general election six months later. Garcia's special election victory restored GOP control of a House seat that the party had held for 26 years and was one of the first significant contests that was primarily conducted via mail. The result marked Republican success with a first-time candidate who had an impressive military background, which had been a key element in several House Democratic victories in 2018. He replaced first-term Democratic Rep. Katie Hill, who resigned after reports—including photographs —of her extramarital affairs with aides reversed her meteoric political ascent.

Garcia is a first-generation citizen who spent his childhood in Santa Clarita after his mother and Los Angeles Police Department stepfather moved there when he turned six. Republican Rep. Buck McKeon nominated Garcia to attend the U.S. Naval Academy. At Annapolis, he obtained a bachelor's degree in political science, while also taking numerous engineering courses. He graduated in the top 3 percent of his class.

Garcia began his military service at flight school in Pensacola Florida. Praised as one of the most talented pilots in the Navy and one of its best leaders, Garcia saw combat operations during the first six months of Operation Iraqi Freedom in 2003. He participated in more than30 raids in the skies over Baghdad, Fallujah and Tikrit. Garcia, an F/A-18 pilot, was deployed on the USS Nimitz aircraft carrier. During 20 years of military service, Garcia accumulated more than 1,400 hours of operational flight time.

In 2009, he retired from active duty in the Navy and returned to California to work for the Raytheon Company while maintaining his role as a reservist instructor pilot. With Raytheon, Garcia said he spent 10years generating billions of dollars of revenue and creating hundreds of jobs in what later became his congressional district.

Hill, who had been a fresh voice for the district's rapidly changing demographics, resigned in November 2019 amid allegations of inappropriate relationships with staffers and the display of widely viewed "revenge porn" on the internet by her former husband in their bitter divorce case.In earlier announcing his candidacy, Garcia said, "I'm running because I don't want California politicians to bring the same policies of high taxes, out-of-control homelessness and lower wages to Congress.... If not me, who? If not today, when?"

Garcia had a relatively easy primary contest against Stephen Knight, who had held the House seat for four years before he was defeated by Hill. With another endorsement from former Rep. McKeon, who held this seat for 22 years, Garcia got 25 percent of the total vote to 17 percent for Knight. Democratic Assemblywoman Christy Smith—who centered her campaign on public education reform, plus more available and affordable health care—led the field with 36 percent; six Democratic candidates split 51 percent of the total vote.

Prior to the May 12 special election, each candidate spent more than $3 million and each national party spent more than $2 million on the contest, though Republicans were better organized on the ground. Garcia defeated Smith, 55%-45%. He took 54 percent of the vote in Los Angeles County, which cast three-fourths of the vote, and 57 percent in Ventura County. This win marked the first time the GOP flipped a Democratic seat in California in almost 22 years, when Republicans held 23 of the California delegation's 52 House seats.

Garcia quickly got to work. With Republican Rep. Pete Stauber of Minnesota he filed a policing-reform bill, called the JUSTICE Act. That measure was the House companion to the bill introduced by GOP Sen. Tim Scott of South Carolina. Garcia called for Congress to respond to "the horrific actions of the few [law enforcement officers who] have unfortunately cast a negative impression over all who stand watch along the thin blue line." The GOP alternative was defeated on a largely party-line vote.

Although Democrats had predicted that the larger turnout in November would reverse the earlier result, the 2020 general election contest was similar to Garcia's special election win. In their earlier primary campaign, Garcia got 24 percent of the total vote to 19 percent for Knight. Smith again faced off with Garcia, losing for a second time, though the outcome tightened to a margin of 333 votes. Republicans rewarded him with a seat on the Appropriations Committee.

CA-25: Northern LA Exurbs   Cook Partisan Voting Index: D+3

Population		Race and Ethnicity		Income	
Total	718,949	White	67.10%	Median Income	$84,670
Land area (sq. miles)	1,691	Black	10.10%	District Income Rank	72
Pop/ sq mi	425.29	Latino	40.00%	Poverty Rate	10.30%
Born in State	66.60%	Asian	8.60%	With health insurance	94.70%
		Two or more races	4.00%	Cash public assistance	2.40%
Age Groups		Other	10.10%	Food stamp/SNAP	7.50%
Under 18	25.50%				
18-34	21.80%	**Education**		**Work**	
35-64	40.20%	H.S grad or less	38.90%	White Collar	38.60%
Over 64	12.70%	Some college	32.90%	Sales and Service	40.20%
		College Degree, 4 yr	18.70%	Blue Collar	21.30%
Military		Post grad	9.50%	Government	15.40%
Veteran/ Active Duty	4.70%				

2020 Pres. Vote	Biden	188,421	(54%)	Trump	153,161	(44%)			
2016 Pres. Vote	Clinton	137,491	(50%)	Trump	119,249	(43%)	Johnson	9,969	(4%)

Santa Clarita, Palmdale: For decades, as the mild-temperature flatlands of the Los Angeles Basin and San Fernando Valley filled up with people, the rugged mountains and hot desert to the north in Los Angeles County remained mostly empty. In recent years, more people began moving north through Newhall Pass on Interstate 5 and northeast on Route 14 to the high desert country. Immediately north of the pass is Santa Clarita, the third-largest city in the county with more than 210,000 residents, and the Six Flags Magic Mountain theme park. Northeast on Route 14, past the former gold-mining center of Acton, the mountains stop at the San Andreas Fault and the desert stretches out low and flat. This is Antelope Valley, with huge aerospace plants and military bases around Palmdale and Lancaster, where more than 500,000 people live. Not far from upscale shopping centers, there has been a resurgence of specialty farm crops such as baby carrots, organic onions and parsnips. Access to health care has been a problem in Antelope Valley and the life expectancy of African Americans here has been four years shorter than in the rest of Los Angeles County.

The Air Force Plant 42 is home to many defense contractors, with projects that include the B-2 Stealth Bomber, the F-117 Stealth Fighter, and the F-35 Joint Strike Fighter. The RQ-170 Sentinel, a next-generation drone reportedly used in CIA operations, has been developed at Lockheed Martin's Skunk Works facility in Palmdale. Northrop Grumman is building an expected 100 of the next-generation B-21 Long-Range Strike Bombers, with close to half the work expected at Palmdale, in a contract of at least $80 billion and several thousand employees. The first B-21s are scheduled to enter service in the mid-2020s. In 2020, local officials pitched the Air Force to use Palmdale as the base for the new U.S. Space Command. The Trump administration tentatively decided to locate the operation in Huntsville Alabama.

In a welcome diversification, Santa Clarita has become a favorite alternative production site for Hollywood studios 30 miles to the south. In October 2019, a year after the state began to purchase land for a 63-mile high-desert freeway in the Mojave between Palmdale and Lancaster in San Bernardino County, state and local transportation agencies agreed to abandon the plan in a court settlement. The plan for the first new freeway in the L.A. area since the Century Freeway (the 105) opened in 1993 was criticized as a financial boondoggle and environmental disaster. Officials explored highway and transit options to use the available funds to address local needs, including a possible high-speed rail line through the desert to Las Vegas.

The 25th Congressional District of California includes all of the Santa Clarita Valley and the high desert parts of Los Angeles County. About one-fifth of the district is in Ventura County. The district extends to most of Simi Valley in Ventura, including the Ronald Reagan Presidential Library and Museum, which has become one of the most popular tourist attractions north of Los Angeles. Housed there are 55 million pages of presidential documents and a large piece of the Berlin Wall, which Reagan famously urged Soviet leader Mikhail Gorbachev to tear down. For the first time in a presidential library, this library added a three-dimensional holographic image of Reagan, which includes his facial features.

Politically, the district had been comfortably Republican. During the past decade, the influx of Latinos, which have grown to 40 percent of the 25th, and the extension of the L.A. psyche to this once-rural area have eliminated the GOP's voter-registration advantage and made this a competitive district. In a district where Mitt Romney led Barack Obama, 50%-48%, Joe Biden won comfortably in 2020, 54%-44%.

Julia Brownley (D)

Elected 2012, 5th term, b. Aug 28, 1952; Aiken, SC; Mount Vernon College, B.A., 1975; American University, M.B.A., 1979; Episcopalian; Divorced; 2 children.

Elected Office: CA Assembly, 2006-2012; Santa Monica Malibu School Board, 1994-2006.

Professional Career: Product Manager, Steelcase, 1984-1992; Sales Manager, Pitney Bowes, 1981-1984; Sales Manager, Burroughs Corporation, 1976-1981.

DC Office: 2262 RHOB 20515, 202-225-5811, Fax: 202-225-1100, juliabrownley.house.gov

State Offices: Oxnard, 805-379-1779; Thousand Oaks, 805-379-1779.

Committees: *Natural Resources. Select Committee on the Climate Crisis. Transportation & Infrastructure*: Aviation; Highways & Transit. *Veterans' Affairs*: Health (Chmn); Women Veterans Task Force (Chmn).

Group Ratings

	ADA	ACLU	AFL-CIO	LCV	COC	HAFA	ACU	CFG	FRC
2020	**	80%	**	100%	-	0%	4%	**	-
2019	90%	C	100%	97%	66%	C	4%	12%	0%

Almanac Ratings 2019-2020

	Economy	Social	Foreign	Composite
Liberal	100%	100%	54%	85%
Conservative	0%	0%	46%	15%

Key Votes of the 116th Congress

1. U.S./Mex./Can. trade deal	Y	5. Russia sanctions	Y	9. Firearms background checks	Y
2. First Coronavirus response	N/A	6. Troops in Syria	Y	10. Spending at the border	Y
3. HEROES Act	Y	7. Veto arms sales to Saudis	Y	11. Marijuana liberalized rules	Y
4. CASH Act	Y	8. Defense $$$, veto override	Y	12. Electoral College objections	N

Election Results

Election	Name (Party)	Vote (%)		Cand. Spent	Ind. Exp. Support	Ind. Exp. Oppose
2020 General	Julia Brownley (D)	208,856	(61%)	$992,518	$66,874	
	Ronda Kennedy (R)	135,877	(39%)	$59,451		$113
2020 Primary	Julia Brownley (D)	106,141	(56%)			
	Robert L. Salas (D)	12,717	(7%)			

Prior winning percentages: 2018 (62%), 2016 (60%), 2014 (51%), 2012 (53%)

Democrat Julia Brownley, elected in 2012, slowly established control of the Ventura County seat that had long been held by Republicans. She has carved out a niche on veterans' health issues and on shifting gender norms and has chaired the Veterans' Affairs Health Subcommittee.

Brownley grew up in Virginia in a Republican household. It wasn't until she went to Washington D.C.'s all-girls Mount Vernon College that she began to consider her personal politics. There, shaped by the emerging women's movement and the war in Vietnam, Brownley said she felt at home in the Democratic Party. After college, she pursued a career in marketing, earning a master's degree from American University and then working as a sales manager for several large companies. That career introduced her to her husband (they are divorced) and brought her to California.

Brownley's experiences with her children helped push her into politics. Her daughter, Hannah, suffered from dyslexia. Working with the school system to improve Hannah's education inspired Brownley to run for the Santa Monica-Malibu school board in 1994. She served on the board for 12 years and was its president. Frustrated with what she considered insufficient funding for the school district, Brownley in 2006 won a seat in the state Assembly. There, she chaired the Education Committee, advocating higher spending on the state's schools at every level.

In the contest for the open House seat, Brownley moved up the coast from Santa Monica and faced off in the primary against Linda Parks, a Republican-turned-independent hoping to win moderate votes. State Sen. Tony Strickland led the all-party primary with 44 percent, to 27 percent for Brownley and 18 percent for Parks. Strickland attacked Brownley for moving to the district. Contributions to Strickland from the U.S. Chamber of Commerce and other groups led Brownley to call him a captive of "Washington special interests." The Los Angeles Times endorsed her, saying the "ideologically rigid" Strickland lacked "real-world pragmatism." She won, 52.7%-47.3%. Strickland in 2014 lost to a Republican in the adjacent GOP-leaning 25th District.

Brownley initially had problems finding a comfort level with her new constituency. Her official bio listed that she served on a school board for 12 years, but it did not say where. She found a niche on the Veterans' Affairs Committee. In 2016, the House passed her bill to identify the best mental health and suicide-prevention program for at-risk women veterans. In 2018, Brownley organized a letter in which 83 House members wrote to the Veterans Affairs Department that it had an "obligation" to include gender-reassignment surgery in its coverage for veterans, stating that denial of the procedure was "unconscionable." She estimated there were 160,000 transgender veterans.

In the majority, she has been the number-two Democrat on the Veterans committee behind Mark Takano, also of California. Brownley in 2019 created and chaired the Women Veterans Task Force

—which she described as "the first organized effort dedicated to women veterans and the inequities that they endure." She led a bipartisan effort to make the motto of the Veterans Affairs Department gender neutral. In July 2020, she told a committee meeting that abortion services were "critical and necessary" to the health of veterans. At a hearing later that month, Brownley said medical catastrophes at some state-run veterans homes during the pandemic had shown that oversight needed to be "tightened up quite extensively."

She pursued her interest in education issues by calling for increased funding of bilingual programs. As co-chair of the House Dyslexia Caucus, she won enactment of the Research Excellence and Advancements for Dyslexia (READ) Act to require the National Science Foundation to spend at least $2.5 million annually for dyslexia research. In 2019, Brownley filed a bill to rewrite federal law to replace references to "husband" and "wife" with the term "spouse." Each gendered reference in the federal code "undermines and de-legitimizes same-sex couples," she said.

In 2014, Republican Assemblyman Jeff Gorell showcased his moderate voting record in Sacramento. Although Brownley was far better funded she won narrowly, 51.3%-48.7%. In the next cycle, the Democratic Congressional Campaign Committee included Brownley among the first 14 members of its Frontline program of vulnerable House Democrats. Perhaps that scared off potential challengers. Against Republican challenger Rafael Dagnesses, a real estate agent, Brownley won, 60%-40%.

Local Republican dynamics continued to deteriorate in 2018. The GOP talked up Antonio Sabato Jr., an actor who appeared on reality shows and was a model for Calvin Klein underwear. On a broadcast, he said he had been "blacklisted" in Hollywood because he was a supporter of President Donald Trump. Earlier, he said former President Barack Obama was "absolutely" a Muslim. That no longer was sound politics in this district. Brownley won, 62%-38%. Against Ronda Kennedy, an African-American Republican lawyer, the result in 2020 was similar—a 61%-39% victory for Brownley. Like all coastal Democrats in California, she has become entrenched.

CA-26: Southern Ventura   Cook Partisan Voting Index: D+10

Population		Race and Ethnicity		Income	
Total	725,535	White	81.10%	Median Income	$91,602
Land area (sq. miles)	939	Black	2.00%	District Income Rank	50
Pop/ sq mi	772.57	Latino	46.20%	Poverty Rate	8.10%
Born in State	59.50%	Asian	6.70%	With health insurance	89.90%
		Two or more races	4.60%	Cash public assistance	1.30%
Age Groups		Other	5.70%	Food stamp/SNAP	7.00%
Under 18	23.00%				
18-34	22.80%	**Education**		**Work**	
35-64	38.10%	H.S grad or less	35.10%	White Collar	36.30%
Over 64	16.20%	Some college	29.60%	Sales and Service	40.40%
		College Degree, 4 yr	22.10%	Blue Collar	23.20%
Military		Post grad	13.10%	Government	15.10%
Veteran/ Active Duty	6.10%				

2020 Pres. Vote	Biden	216,840	(61%)	Trump	128,914	(36%)	
2016 Pres. Vote	Clinton	169,083	(57%)	Trump	105,259	(36%)	Johnson 11,301 (4%)

Oxnard, Thousand Oaks: For many Americans, Simi Valley remains best known as the site of the 1992 trial where four Los Angeles police officers were acquitted for the beating of taxi driver Rodney King, who famously said, "People, I just want to say, can we all get along?" Granted, the incident took place during riots in South Los Angeles. The city of Simi Valley is a very different place than South L.A.—a product of the 1960s, the expansive postwar years when migrants from points across the United States moved west to Los Angeles and then spread beyond city and county limits to fill up the valleys between the mountains. In the valleys of Ventura County, northwest of Los Angeles, people built communities in what had been orange and lemon groves. Like California overall, the Ventura County population has trended socially liberal and economically conservative. To the south is upscale Thousand Oaks, the headquarters of biotechnology giant Amgen Inc. Farther west in Pleasant Valley is Camarillo, which is home to numerous technology firms.

The local economy has a strong export market, including pharmaceuticals, semiconductors and citrus fruit. In 2018, economists at California Lutheran University reported that the shortage of housing for farm workers, contributed to the high cost of living and stagnant economy in Ventura. The once-robust local farming, especially strawberries, has been reduced—a victim of imports, labor costs and drought. Port Hueneme, the only deep-water port along the Pacific coast between Los Angeles and San Francisco, is a large employer in Ventura County and does business around the world. In 2017, it was the first port in California certified as "Green Marine" by environmentalists. A low income, mostly Hispanic, community group in 2019 opposed a proposal to convert a nearby 34-acre lot into a storage facility for up to 5,000 imported cars. In September 2020, the Board of Supervisors increased restrictions on oil drilling in Ventura County.

In the inland valleys still farther west is Ojai, which remains a center for tourism. During the filming of the 1937 Frank Capra movie Lost Horizon, an aerial shot of the Ojai Valley was used to represent the mythical earthly paradise of Shangri-La. To the north in the foothills of wilderness areas here is the Santa Clara River Valley, with Santa Paula, Fillmore and Piru. The mountains are part of the large Santa Monica Mountains National Recreation Area. These places have suffered recent disasters: In November 2018, the Woolsey fire—destroying more than 1,600 structures—was the worst ever in Ventura and L.A., where it reached to Malibu. Also that month, a mass shooting at a bar in Thousand Oaks left 13 dead, including a police officer.

The 26th Congressional District covers80 percent of Ventura County, including its largest city, Oxnard. The district takes in Thousand Oaks and the Santa Clara River Valley. (Most of Simi Valley is in the 25th District.)The 26th juts into Porter Ranch, a thin slice of Los Angeles County to the west of Encino, but with only a few thousand voters. The 26th District leans Democratic, though it is more competitive than any Democratic-held district in L.A. County, other than the 25th. Joe Biden led Donald Trump, 61%-36%. He took the county overall, 59%-38%, which tripled the margin of Barack Obama's 52%-45% win over Mitt Romney in the county in 2012.

Judy Chu (D)

Elected 2009, 6th full term, b. Jul 07, 1953; Los Angeles, CA; University of CA, Santa Barbara, Att., 1973; University of CA, Los Angeles, B.A., 1974; CA School Professional Psychology, Los Angeles, M.A., 1977; CA School Professional Psychology, Los Angeles, Ph.D., 1979; Married (Michael Eng).

Elected Office: Garvey School Board, 1985-1988; Monterey Park City Council, 1988-2001; Mayor, Monterey Park; CA Assembly, 2001-2006; CA Board Of Equalization, 2006-2009, vice Chairman, 2009.

Professional Career: Professor, Los Angeles City College, Psychology Department, 1981-1988; E. Los Angeles College, Psychology Department, 1988-2001.

DC Office: 2423 RHOB 20515, 202-225-5464, Fax: 202-225-5467, chu.house.gov
State Offices: Claremont, 909-625-5394; Pasadena, 626-304-0110.

Committees: *Budget. Small Business*: Economic Growth, Tax & Capital Access; Oversight, Investigations & Regulations. *Ways & Means*: Health; Oversight; Worker & Family Support.

Group Ratings

	ADA	ACLU	AFL-CIO	LCV	COC	HAFA	ACU	CFG	FRC
2020	**	88%	**	100%	-	0%	4%	**	-
2019	95%	C	95%	97%	45%	C	4%	18%	0%

Almanac Ratings 2019-2020

	Economy	Social	Foreign	Composite
Liberal	100%	100%	96%	99%
Conservative	0%	0%	4%	1%

Key Votes of the 116th Congress

1. U.S./Mex./Can. trade deal	Y	5. Russia sanctions	Y	9. Firearms background checks	Y
2. First Coronavirus response	Y	6. Troops in Syria	Y	10. Spending at the border	N
3. HEROES Act	Y	7. Veto arms sales to Saudis	Y	11. Marijuana liberalized rules	Y
4. CASH Act	Y	8. Defense $$$, veto override	Y	12. Electoral College objections	N

Election Results

Election	Name (Party)	Vote (%)	Cand. Spent	Ind. Exp. Support	Ind. Exp. Oppose
2020 General	Judy Chu (D)..................................... 221,411	(70%)	$623,592	$1,915	
	Johnny Nalbandian (R)......................... 95,907	(30%)	$34,009		$113
2020 Primary	Judy Chu (D).................................... 117,724	(71%)			

Prior winning percentages: 2018 (79%), 2016 (67%), 2014 (59%), 2012 (64%), 2010 (71%), 2009 special (62%)

Democrat Judy Chu, who won a 2009 special election, became the first Chinese-American woman in the House. She is a strong liberal and has been a leader on women's and Asian-American issues. With her seat on the Ways and Means Committee, her interests include her many constituents in the motion picture industry and other creative entrepreneurs.

Chu grew up in Los Angeles as the daughter of an electrical technician who brought his wife from China under the War Brides Act. The family moved to the Bay Area when she was in junior high school. She graduated from the University of California, Los Angeles, got a Ph.D. in psychology, then taught for 13 years at East Los Angeles Community College. She served on the Garvey School District board for three years and was mayor of Monterey Park for 12 years. In 2000, Chu was elected to the California Assembly, where she focused on criminal justice and environmental issues. As chairwoman of the Appropriations Committee, she sponsored a tax amnesty program that brought in significant sums for the state. In 2006, she was elected to the state Board of Equalization, where she worked on closing tax loopholes.

After Rep. Hilda Solis was selected as President Barack Obama's Secretary of Labor, the contest for the Democratic nomination became a race between Chu and state Sen. Gil Cedillo, the leading Hispanic candidate. The special election was more nuanced than simply an ethnic showdown between an Asian and a Latino. Chu was endorsed by prominent Hispanics such as Los Angeles Mayor Antonio Villaraigosa and members of Solis' family. The Los Angeles County Labor Federation, which was impressed by Chu's support for farm workers, backed her, as did EMILY's List, the national advocacy group for pro-abortion rights Democratic women. Chu won the all-party primary with 32 percent, to 23 percent for Cedillo and 14 percent for Emanuel Pleitez, a 26-year-old financial analyst. In a runoff with Republican Betty Chu, a Monterey Park councilwoman who was Chu's distant cousin by marriage, the Democrat won, 62%-33%.

After her nephew, a lance corporal in the Marine Corps stationed in Afghanistan, committed suicide after being beaten up by his fellow Marines, Chu began introducing anti-hazing bills. In the fiscal 2017 defense spending bill, the House included her proposal to require the Defense Department to create a national database of military hazing incidents and submit an annual report on its efforts to end the practice. She founded and co-chaired the Creative Rights Caucus, which advocates increased copyright protections for creative artists. As co-chair of the Congressional Pro-Choice Caucus, Chu in 2020 proposed to codify the Supreme Court's Roe v. Wade ruling and to repeal the Hyde amendment prohibition of federal funding for abortions.

As chair of the Asian Pacific-American Caucus, Chu sponsored a House-passed resolution in 2012 to have the United States apologize for the anti-immigrant Chinese Exclusion Act of 1882.Her grandfather was forced to carry a certificate of U.S. residence for about 40 years. "It is for my grandfather, and for all Chinese Americans who were told for six decades by the U.S. government that the land of the free wasn't open to them, that we must pass this resolution," she said. When President Donald Trump took office, she voiced concern that discrimination against Muslims could parallel the Japanese internment camps during World War II. She filed a bill to increase mental health awareness among Asian Americans and to overcome the stigma. In 2017, she was arrested during a rally at the Capitol on behalf of young undocumented immigrants.

When Chu joined Ways and Means in 2017, ranking Democrat Richard Neal cited her experience on the Board of Equalization plus her commitment to tax fairness. She criticized Republicans' committee efforts to repeal and revise the Affordable Care Act. "This plan was rushed to committee, there has not been time for the Congressional Budget Office to release their analysis of how much this will cost or how many Americans will be covered," Chu said. With Democrats in House control, she worked with Neal to get access to Trump's tax returns. Even with her Ph.D. in psychology, Chu tweeted, she could not "fully capture how emotionally insecure our president is." In September 2020, she criticized the Small Business Administration for taking too long to publish coronavirus-relief forms in Asian languages. She also cited the "dire nature" of anti-Asian sentiment during the pandemic.

At home, Republican Jack Orswell, a small business owner and former FBI agent, challenged Chu in 2014 and got 41 percent of the vote. That was the only time Chu has been held below 60 percent in this safely Democratic district. A month after the election, the House Standards of Official Conduct (Ethics) Committee issued Chu a letter of reproval after concluding that she interfered with the panel's investigation of whether her House aides had performed campaign work. "The committee acknowledged that my intention was to ease the staff member's anxiety and that I expressed regret for this one moment of contact," Chu said. In February 2020, she filed a bill to make 30,000 acres of the San Gabriel Mountains federal wilderness lands. She called the mountains "a crown to the Los Angeles area."

CA-27: San Gabriel Foothills   **Cook Partisan Voting Index: D+18**

Population		Race and Ethnicity		Income	
Total	712,783	White	38.30%	Median Income	$90,792
Land area (sq. miles)	700	Black	3.90%	District Income Rank	54
Pop/ sq mi	1,018.41	Latino	27.80%	Poverty Rate	8.80%
Born in State	47.50%	Asian	39.30%	With health insurance	93.60%
		Two or more races	4.40%	Cash public assistance	1.60%
Age Groups		Other	14.00%	Food stamp/SNAP	4.00%
Under 18	18.60%				
18-34	22.60%	**Education**		**Work**	
35-64	41.00%	H.S grad or less	31.20%	White Collar	50.00%
Over 64	17.80%	Some college	23.00%	Sales and Service	37.20%
		College Degree, 4 yr	27.20%	Blue Collar	12.80%
Military		Post grad	18.70%	Government	15.40%
Veteran/ Active Duty	3.10%				

2020 Pres. Vote	Biden	226,666	(67%)	Trump	104,088	(31%)		
2016 Pres. Vote	Clinton	174,544	(66%)	Trump	74,984	(28%)	Johnson	7,862	(3%)
	Stein	5,717	(2%)					

Pasadena, Monterey Park: In the early part of the 20th century, when Los Angeles was growing rapidly and on its way to becoming one of America's major cities, its richest citizens settled not on the beach (too clammy and cold) or on the west side (too dusty and remote), but in communities they built at the base of the San Gabriel Mountains. Their snow-capped peaks, rising 10,000 feet above the city, are visible most of the year. The place to be was Pasadena, home of the Rose Bowl, Cal Tech and a baroque-domed city hall. Pasadena and South Pasadena have carefully preserved their bungalow neighborhoods, and Pasadena preserved and rebuilt the 80-year-old curving Colorado Boulevard Bridge over Arroyo Seco. With 15 percent of Pasadena living below the poverty level, city officials have sought to develop additional options for affordable housing. Nearby is luxurious San Marino, home of the Huntington Library, one of the world's great museums and scholarly institutions, with more than 150 acres of botanical gardens. Arcadia has the Santa Anita Park racetrack and the Los Angeles County Arboretum & Botanic Garden. Wealthy Chinese have invested in business opportunities in the area.

Parts of this area have significant Asian populations. Chinese and other Asians are 66 percent of the population in Monterey Park, which has been called America's first suburban Chinatown(the population is 4 percent white), and 62 percent in Rosemead. Young Asian Americans produced a YouTube rap video titled 626—the area code for much of the San Gabriel Valley—and it went viral. In 2018, the movie Crazy Rich Asians was a sensation that drew huge audiences in Asian-American neighborhoods. The Rose Bowl and the Tournament of Roses Parade annually yield spending that is a larger draw for L.A. than the Oscars. The 2021 parade was canceled for the first time since World War II. More painfully for local Asians, the coronavirus led to a local increase in anti-Asian hate crimes.

The 27th Congressional District includes much of the Pasadena area and other portions of Los Angeles County. It takes in San Marino and the San Gabriel foothills communities of Altadena, Glendora, Sierra Madre and San Antonio Heights, where vicious cycles of drought, fire, rain and mudslides have become familiar. Proposals to designate a large part of the San Gabriel Mountains as a national monument have drawn protests, especially from bikers, hunters and other recreational users. In September 2020, the Bobcat fire burned more than 100,000 acres north of Mount Wilson and was one of the worst ever in Los Angeles County. Also in the district are San Gabriel, Temple City and Claremont, dubbed "The City of Trees and Ph.D.'s" after its Claremont Colleges—plus the conservative-leaning Claremont Institute. The 27th has a small indentation of San Bernardino County, near Upland, which leans Republican, but it is barely 7percent of the district. The 27th is 39 percent Asian American, the second-highest of any California district, and 28 percent Hispanic. Politically, it is solidly Democratic, though not as strongly as some other L.A.-area districts. Joe Biden won the district, 67%-31%.

Adam Schiff (D)

Elected 2000, 11th term, b. Jun 22, 1960; Framingham, MA; Stanford University, B.A., 1982; Harvard University Law School, J.D., 1985; Jewish; Married (Eve Sanderson Schiff); 2 children.

Elected Office: CA Senate, 1996-2000.

Professional Career: Prosecutor, U.S. Attorney General Office, L.A., 1987- 93; Practicing attorney, 1986-1987, 1995-1996.

DC Office: 2269 RHOB 20515, 202-225-4176, Fax: 202-225-5828, schiff.house.gov

State Offices: Burbank, 818-450-2900; Los Angeles, 323-315-5555.

Committees: *Permanent Select on Intelligence (Chmn).*

Group Ratings

	ADA	ACLU	AFL-CIO	LCV	COC	HAFA	ACU	CFG	FRC
2020	**	79%	**	100%	-	0%	5%	**	-
2019	95%	C	100%	97%	56%	C	5%	12%	0%

Almanac Ratings 2019-2020

	Economy	Social	Foreign	Composite
Liberal	100%	100%	80%	94%
Conservative	0%	0%	20%	6%

Key Votes of the 116th Congress

1. U.S./Mex./Can. trade deal Y	5. Russia sanctions Y	9. Firearms background checks Y
2. First Coronavirus response Y	6. Troops in Syria Y	10. Spending at the border Y
3. HEROES Act Y	7. Veto arms sales to Saudis Y	11. Marijuana liberalized rules Y
4. CASH Act Y	8. Defense $$$, veto override Y	12. Electoral College objections N

Election Results

Election	Name (Party)	Vote (%)		Cand. Spent	Ind. Exp. Support	Ind. Exp. Oppose
2020 General	Adam Schiff (D)	244,271	(73%)	$9,062,143	$5,631	$1,326
	Eric Early (R)	91,928	(27%)	$3,843,054		$113
2020 Primary	Adam Schiff (D)	110,251	(60%)			
	Maebe A. Girl (D)	22,129	(12%)			

Prior winning percentages: 2018 (78%), 2016 (78%), 2014 (77%), 2012 (77%), 2010 (65%), 2008 (69%), 2006 (64%), 2004 (65%), 2002 (63%), 2000 (53%)

Adam Schiff, elected in 2000, is an active and ambitious Democrat who became a powerful voice on national security—and an outspoken critic of President Donald Trump—as chairman of the House Intelligence Committee. He demanded answers to allegations of misbehavior, including alleged encouragement of Russian interference in the 2016 election and his more recent demands for political assistance from the president of Ukraine, and took the high-profile role of House manager of its case during the first impeachment trial of Trump. His leadership has increased speculation about his future in or beyond the House, which Schiff has encouraged, though he hasn't found an immediate opportunity.

Schiff's father was a traveling salesman and later owned a lumberyard. Schiff grew up throughout the country, graduating from high school in Northern California. He went on to Stanford University and Harvard Law School. From 1987 to 1993, he worked in the U.S. attorney's office in Los Angeles. He ran for the California Assembly and lost three times. In 1996, he was elected to the state Senate. In his first two years, he enacted dozens of measures, including a bill guaranteeing up-to-date textbooks in classrooms and another reforming the child support system. Schiff also taught political science at Glendale Community College. In his 50s, he kept physically fit by participating in triathalons, which he described as "a real adventure" in an interview with the website www.goodinc.com.

In 2000, Schiff challenged Republican James Rogan, who was a Judiciary Committee leader and a persuasive voice in the 1998 impeachment case against President Bill Clinton, which centered on the president's lying under oath about an affair with a White House intern. The Schiff-Rogan race became a fundraising marathon, and was then the most expensive House race on record. The candidates raised more than $10 million combined, and much more was spent independently by Clinton's supporters as well as his detractors. Rogan branded his opponent as a traditional tax-and-spend liberal who would "run naked through the Treasury, spending everything he can." Schiff attacked Rogan for calling abortion a holocaust for the African-American community. Schiff won by an unexpectedly large 53%-44% vote, and has been easily reelected since.

In the House, Schiff joined the Blue Dog Coalition of moderate Democrats and has sometimes worked across party lines. Schiff served as co-chairman of the Congressional International Anti-Piracy Caucus, where he sponsored a bill to provide law enforcement and copyright holders with new tools to target websites based offshore that offer pirated music, movies and other counterfeit goods. Schiff stirred complaints from liberal constituents when he supported the resolution approving the use of force in Iraq in 2002 and for voting for the USA Patriot Act, the anti-terrorism law that gave new powers to law enforcement.

As the years passed, his views became more conventionally liberal. After the Supreme Court in the 2012 Citizens United case overturned a Montana law barring corporate spending in state elections, he worked with Harvard law professor Laurence Tribe to introduce a constitutional amendment to allow Congress and the states to impose limitations on independent campaign expenditures. After the fatal police shooting of an unarmed Black man in Ferguson Missouri in 2014, Schiff pushed Attorney General Eric Holder to help state and local law enforcement agencies acquire body-worn cameras. In the Almanac vote ratings in recent years, Schiff ranked consistently among the most liberal members of the House.

On foreign policy, Schiff has pressed for recognition of the Armenian genocide as the responsibility of the Ottoman Empire, a move Turkey adamantly opposes. His resolution was approved by the House Foreign Affairs Committee in 2007, but he agreed to postpone further action after a strong response from Turkey. Finally in 2019, amid bipartisan unhappiness with some of Turkey's current actions, the House passed Schiff's resolution recognizing the genocide, 405-11. Schiff has been concerned that major national security actions should not be left solely to a president's discretion. He has filed legislation to repeal the Authorization for Use of Military Force, which Congress passed after the 2001 attacks. He said it "was never intended to authorize a war without end, and it now poorly defines those who pose a threat to our country." When he offered an amendment based on the measure to the fiscal 2014 defense appropriations bill, it was defeated after Republicans said it was dangerous to set a specific timeline.

When the Islamic State (ISIS) terrorist group began capturing large swaths of territory in the Middle East in 2014, Schiff sought to call attention to the threat of Americans and Europeans carrying out attacks at home. Later, when Obama outlined a plan to deal with ISIS, Schiff became heavily involved in unsuccessful efforts to have Congress authorize the president's actions. "It's hard to explain the relative silence of my libertarian colleagues at a time when the president is about to announce a war effort that may take years," Schiff told The Washington Post. Schiff strongly objected to the Republican push to investigate the terrorist attacks on U.S. facilities in Benghazi Libya. He told Fox News that a select committee on the matter was "a colossal waste of time" and that his party should boycott it—something House leaders refused to do. He subsequently served on the select committee.

Democratic Leader Nancy Pelosi gave Schiff a significant national security niche when she named him the top Democrat on the House Intelligence Committee in 2015. He brought to the table new proposals on intelligence policy. He filed legislation to require greater transparency for the U.S. military drone program. He opposed paying ransoms to free Americans held by rebel groups, such as ISIS. He also advocated major changes in the National Security Agency's phone metadata surveillance program, which would require the government to request phone company records on a case-by-case basis.

Schiff used his Intelligence Committee post to criticize the failure of the Obama administration to sanction Russia for its computer hacking that he said had been designed to influence the 2016 election, and he demanded that Congress investigate. "They didn't just steal data, they weaponized it. They dumped it during an election with the specific intent of influencing the outcomes of that election and sowing discord in the United States," he said. Schiff voiced early warnings of Trump's use of "alternative facts," which he said "undermines his credibility" and is "a crisis waiting to happen." In March2017, he accused Republican Rep. Devin Nunes of California, the committee chairman, of working closely with Trump and said Nunes should step aside "from any further involvement in the Russia investigation." A week later, the House Ethics Committee began a review of Nunes's actions and he informally recused himself from the Russia inquiry.

During the review in 2017-18 by the Republican-controlled panel, Schiff pressed for a complete investigation. When the GOP majority balked, he often sought to hold them accountable. "All this has vaulted Schiff into the unlikely role of being the Democrats' leader not just on the investigation but on all things Trump and Russia," the Los Angeles Times reported in a July 2018 profile. "For many, he is the voice of reason, a steadying influence, the sober narrator in a time when chaos reigns."

After Nunes—who had regained his authority as chairman following the conclusion of the ethics inquiry—brought the formal investigation to what Schiff viewed as a premature conclusion in March 2018,he pursued his own review of Trump's actions. Following Trump's meeting with Russian President Vladimir Putin in Helsinki that July, Schiff called the president "the gravest threat to American democracy." Those counterattacks, in turn, increased his popularity among grassroots Democrats who were hostile to Trump.

After Democrats regained House control in the 2018 election, Pelosi appointed Schiff as Intelligence Committee chairman. As he pursued oversight of the Trump campaign and presidency and sought to "restore Congress as a co-equal branch of government," he said, he—like Pelosi—found himself resisting growing pressure in the Democratic Caucus to bring impeachment charges. By October, when House Democrats had reached consensus, he managed a tightly scheduled parade of witnesses of current and former State Department officials and other national security employees familiar with Trump's political demands on Ukraine President

Volodymyr Zelensky to investigate Joe Biden, then a Democratic presidential candidate. Schiff kept tight control, even when dealing with abusive tweets from Trump and with a group of House Republicans interrupting the committee's closed-door meeting in the Capitol.

Eventually, preparation of the impeachment resolution were handled by the Judiciary Committee and its chairman, Jerrold Nadler. But Schiff worked closely with Nadler and, when the time came, Pelosi appointed Schiff to lead the House managers for the Senate trial in January 2020. That proved to be a frustrating exercise for Schiff, as the Republican-controlled Senate refused his efforts to call witnesses. Invoking his experience as a prosecutor, Schiff closed the House's presentation to the Senate with a review of the case and what he viewed as the inevitable conclusion: "Do we really have any doubt about the facts here?" he asked the Senate. "No one is really making the argument Donald Trump would never do such a thing, because of course we know that he would, and of course we know that he did." Ultimately, he did not come close to securing the necessary two-thirds vote to convict, as only Republican Sen. Mitt Romney broke the party-line vote.

Schiff thought seriously about running for the open seat after Sen. Barbara Boxer in 2015 said she would not seek reelection. When he deferred to Kamala Harris and quietly announced that he would remain in the House, he kept the door open to "other challenges in the future." In 2017, he voiced interest in succeeding Dianne Feinstein whenever she departs the Senate. That option has remained unavailable. Meanwhile, Schiff spent time in Iowa and New Hampshire as he explored a bid for the 2020 Democratic presidential nomination. "My philosophy up to this point, which has suited me well, has been to focus on doing my current job as best I can and let the future take care of itself," he told a New York Times reporter following the 2020 election. That left the door open for other opportunities. He and his allies privately sought the appointment of Gov. Gavin Newsom to fill the Senate seat of Harris, but the position went to Alex Padilla.

CA-28: Northern Los Angeles

Cook Partisan Voting Index: D+23

Population		Race and Ethnicity		Income	
Total	693,299	White	67.20%	Median Income	$74,431
Land area (sq. miles)	218	Black	2.70%	District Income Rank	134
Pop/ sq mi	3,173.72	Latino	23.90%	Poverty Rate	12.60%
Born in State	38.10%	Asian	15.10%	With health insurance	91.10%
		Two or more races	4.80%	Cash public assistance	3.20%
Age Groups		Other	10.20%	Food stamp/SNAP	7.30%
Under 18	15.40%				
18-34	26.10%	**Education**		**Work**	
35-64	42.00%	H.S grad or less	28.00%	White Collar	52.00%
Over 64	16.40%	Some college	24.00%	Sales and Service	36.50%
		College Degree, 4 yr	31.80%	Blue Collar	11.50%
Military		Post grad	16.30%	Government	9.20%
Veteran/ Active Duty	2.40%				

2020 Pres. Vote	Biden	252,705	(71%)	Trump	97,112	(27%)			
2016 Pres. Vote	Clinton	208,645	(72%)	Trump	64,607	(22%)	Stein	7,433	(3%)
	Johnson	7,050	(2%)						

Westside and Hollywood: The Westside of Los Angeles is perhaps the most glamorous and flashiest concentration of affluence in the world. It is the heartland of one of America's most productive and creative industries and one of the nation's major exports, show business. The first moviemakers came here looking for a place to shoot silent films where the sunlight was more dependable than in Astoria Queens or Englewood New Jersey. They found it in Hollywood, a suburb just annexed by burgeoning Los Angeles when the first movie studio was built in 1911. In 1923 came the "Hollywood" sign (it said "Hollywoodland" then), overlooking the soon-famous intersection of Hollywood and Vine. By the 1930s, big studio lots were scattered around town, over the mountains in Burbank, or out toward the ocean in Westwood and Culver City. Miraculously, the studio bosses of that era—most of them Jewish immigrants with little ancestral experience of America—created a popular culture that was universally accessible and embodied the American spirit in a way that still rings true.

Beneath the Verdugo Mountains is Burbank, which Dr. David Burbank, a dentist, founded as a large ranch, on what is now a back lot of Warner Brothers. The city has become the "media capital of the world," including the headquarters for Warner Brothers, ABC Studios and Disney, plus many small entertainment and multimedia companies. The movie studios have been an integral part of the local economy. Warner Brothers remained the largest employer in Burbank, with 5,000 jobs in 2020, followed by Disney with 3,900. (NBC Studios moved to the huge Universal Studio complex in the San Fernando Valley.)The industry feared that coronavirus would slash revenues by more than $20 billion—from a combination of films not made and theaters that are empty or shut down, among other jarring results. To reduce congestion in a residential neighborhood that has resulted from more than 3 million annual tourists, Warner Brothers proposed in 2018 to build a tramway from its lot to the Hollywood sign. But a study in 2020 by the Los Angeles City Council revealed loud outcries, including from environmentalists. More middle-class is Glendale, north of downtown Los Angeles, site of Forest Lawn Cemetery and DreamWorks Animation. Glendale is a diverse city with a large concentration of Armenians, a politically influential community that has remained hostile to Turkey.

The 28th Congressional District, which is located between the San Fernando Valley and Pasadena, includes La Crescenta-Montrose and La Cañada Flintridge, home of NASA's Jet Propulsion Laboratory. The largest cities are Glendale and Burbank. Following 70 percent approval of a referendum in 2016, a new 14-gate terminal has been planned at the Hollywood Burbank Airport, though planners have wrestled with its estimated $1.2 billion cost, COVID-related delay and the tight urban space for the facility. South of the Hollywood Hills, West Hollywood has a large gay community. It is home to the Sunset Strip, a launching pad for many rock 'n' roll acts, including The Doors, Guns N' Roses and Led Zeppelin. This is a solidly Democratic district, with 24 percent Hispanic and 15 percent Asian population. Joe Biden got 71 percent of the vote in 2020—consistent with recent presidential results.

Tony Cárdenas (D)

Elected 2012, 5th term, b. Mar 31, 1963; Pacoima, CA; University of CA, Santa Barbara, B.S., 1986; Christian Church; Married (Norma Cárdenas); 4 children.

Elected Office: Los Angeles City Council, 2004-2012; CA Assembly, 1996-2002.

Professional Career: Real-estate broker, 1987-1996; Life ins. salesman, 1986-1987; Electrical engineer, Hewlett-Packard, 1986.

DC Office: 2438 RHOB 20515, 202-225-6131, Fax: 202-225-0819, cardenas.house.gov

State Offices: Panorama City, 818-221-3718.

Committees: *Energy & Commerce*: Communications & Technology; Consumer Protection & Commerce; Health.

Group Ratings

	ADA	ACLU	AFL-CIO	LCV	COC	HAFA	ACU	CFG	FRC
2020	**	81%	**	100%	-	0%	6%	**	-
2019	100%	C	90%	100%	52%	C	6%	13%	0%

Almanac Ratings 2019-2020

	Economy	Social	Foreign	Composite
Liberal	100%	100%	96%	99%
Conservative	0%	0%	4%	1%

Key Votes of the 116th Congress

1. U.S./Mex./Can. trade deal	N	5. Russia sanctions	Y	9. Firearms background checks	Y
2. First Coronavirus response	Y	6. Troops in Syria	Y	10. Spending at the border	N
3. HEROES Act	Y	7. Veto arms sales to Saudis	Y	11. Marijuana liberalized rules	Y
4. CASH Act	Y	8. Defense $$$, veto override	Y	12. Electoral College objections	N

Election Results

Election	Name (Party)	Vote (%)		Cand. Spent	Ind. Exp. Support	Ind. Exp. Oppose
2020 General	Tony Cárdenas (D)............................	119,420	(57%)	$1,284,237	$2,334	
	Angélica Dueñas (D)............................	91,524	(43%)	$72,341	$543	
2020 Primary	Tony Cárdenas (D)............................	56,984	(59%)			
	Angélica Dueñas (D)............................	22,423	(23%)			

Prior winning percentages: 2018 (81%), 2016 (75%), 2014 (75%), 2012 (74%)

Democrat Tony Cárdenas, elected in 2012, has been active on the House Energy and Commerce Committee and a leader of the Hispanic Caucus. He has been a player on issues that affect his district in the San Fernando Valley. In 2020, his ambitions for a Democratic leadership slot fell short. Cardenas got good news when a young woman dropped a lawsuit charging him with abusive behavior.

As the youngest of 11 children of Mexican immigrant parents, Cárdenas was born and raised in the Valley city of Pacoima, where his father was a self-employed gardener. He earned a bachelor's degree in electrical engineering from the University of California, Santa Barbara. He subsequently went to work for Hewlett-Packard but left just five months later. "There has to be something different for me," he remembered thinking.

He returned home to sell life insurance for a year, then sold real estate for five years before opening his own brokerage firm in the San Fernando Valley. During that time, the Valley had become more Latino—but, he observed, political representation did not mirror that change. One day, a friend suggested Cárdenas run for political office. He did, and in 1996 became the first Latino to represent the Valley in the state Assembly. Cárdenas worked to reform California's gang prevention and intervention programs. He increased funding for juvenile justice programs. Cárdenas says he became interested in gang-intervention programs after many of his childhood friends had run-ins with the law, lamenting, "they weren't exactly living a life that we had dreamed of."

In 2003, Cárdenas was elected to the Los Angeles City Council, where he continued to work on gang prevention. He sought additional opportunities for minority-owned businesses to compete for the city's bond underwriting work. He pushed for policies to fight human trafficking and prevent the mistreatment of animals.

When he decided to run for Congress in a redrawn district with no incumbent that was destined to elect a Latino, Cárdenas received 64 percent of the vote in the primary. His closest competitor was "No Party Preference" perennial candidate David Hernandez, who mocked Cárdenas for touting his Latino roots. Those attacks barely resonated in the Democratic district, and Cárdenas won in November 74%-26%.

Cárdenas has worn several hats in the House. He co-chaired two bipartisan groups: the Crime Prevention and Youth Development Caucus, and the Congressional Student-Athlete Protection Caucus. He helped create the Connecting the Americas Caucus, to strengthen business opportunities between the United States and Latin American nations. After Cardenas became chairman of BOLD PAC, the fundraising arm of the Congressional Hispanic Caucus, he increased its fundraising from $1 million in the 2014 campaign cycle to nearly $17 million in 2019-20.During that time, the Hispanic Caucus took seats in several states. Following the 2016 election, he won a Democratic leadership position for a member who had served less than three terms. He defeated Rep. Debbie Dingell of Michigan, 91-76.

On the Energy and Commerce Committee, Cárdenas was among the first House members to oppose the proposed merger of Comcast and Time Warner Cable, which he said would harm competition, raise costs and "eliminate good jobs in California." Following regulatory overview, the deal was scuttled. In 2017, he filed a bill to protect at-risk youth from termination of their Medicaid eligibility while they were prison inmates. The measure was enacted as part of the comprehensive legislation to combat opioid addiction. During the coronavirus pandemic, he led a bipartisan effort to increase Medicaid coverage for uninsured residents of U.S. territories in the Pacific.

In 2016, Cárdenas faced Democrat Richard Alarcon, a former member of the Los Angeles City Council. Alarcon raised only $70,000 to $1.7 million for Cardenas and was defeated, 75%-25%.

Cárdenas faced uncertain prospects after a woman filed a lawsuit charging him with drugging and fondling her while they were at a Los Angeles golf outing in 2007, when she was 16. When the allegations were referred to the House Ethics Committee, Cardenas said he would cooperate with the review. Following a court hearing in Los Angeles in July 2019, the woman dropped the lawsuit and said "I regret my decision" to hire her attorney, the Los Angeles Times reported. Following earlier demands by a few local Democrats that he should resign, Cárdenas responded, "The truth prevailed." His lawyers said he paid no money to resolve the case.

In 2020, Angelica Duenas—a community organizer and immigration-rights activist who actively supported Bernie Sanders in the 2016 and 2020 Democratic campaigns—challenged Cárdenas and was endorsed by Progressive Democrats of America. Cárdenas had support from Planned Parenthood and the Sierra Club, and he outspent Duenas, $1.3 million to $72,000. In November, he won, 57%-43%, a close result in a contest that received sparse coverage.

Before the November 2020 election, Cardenas announced his candidacy to succeed Rep. Ben Ray Lujan as assistant Speaker. Cardenas cited his success with BOLD PAC. Following the election, after Rep. Cheri Bustos decided not to seek reelection to chair the Democratic Congressional Campaign Committee, he switched to the contest to succeed her. In a brief but fiercely fought contest that focused partly on House Democrats' unexpected losses in November, including their poor performance with Latino voters in several key states, Cárdenas second-guessed Democratic strategy. Referring to the "defund the police" call from some Democrats, Cárdenas told CNN, "I think that slogans that your opponent uses more than you use them, at the end of the day, are probably not a smart way to communicate." He also called for more diversity at the DCCC. Cárdenas lost to Rep. Sean Mahoney of New York on a 119-107 vote in the Democratic Caucus, according to Roll Call, the Capitol Hill publication.

CA-29: Central San Fernando Valley   Cook Partisan Voting Index: D+27

Population		Race and Ethnicity		Income	
Total	717,659	White	58.20%	Median Income	$60,970
Land area (sq. miles)	92	Black	4.00%	District Income Rank	247
Pop/ sq mi	7,798.1	Latino	67.00%	Poverty Rate	15.90%
Born in State	47.70%	Asian	7.40%	With health insurance	87.10%
		Two or more races	3.40%	Cash public assistance	4.20%
Age Groups		Other	27.00%	Food stamp/SNAP	12.00%
Under 18	22.70%				
18-34	27.20%	**Education**		**Work**	
35-64	38.50%	H.S grad or less	52.30%	White Collar	29.40%
Over 64	11.50%	Some college	25.40%	Sales and Service	43.50%
		College Degree, 4 yr	17.40%	Blue Collar	27.20%
Military		Post grad	4.90%	Government	10.60%
Veteran/ Active Duty	2.40%				

2020 Pres. Vote	Biden	186,796	(74%)	Trump	59,671	(24%)		
2016 Pres. Vote	Clinton	152,517	(78%)	Trump	32,963	(17%)	Stein	4,863	(3%)
	Johnson	4,328	(2%)					

Van Nuys: A hiker looking north from the crest of the Santa Monica Mountains in 1912 would have seen a valley almost totally empty and barren, 20 miles long and 12 miles wide. Separated by the Cahuenga Pass from rapidly growing Los Angeles and Hollywood, the San Fernando Valley was bought up in massive tracts by civic leaders as they were urging city engineer William Mulholland to build a huge 250-mile aqueduct from the Owens Valley to bring water to Los Angeles and persuading the city in 1915 to annex 200 square miles of the Valley. In the years after World War II, this was modern suburbia, filled with Leave It to Beaver families. More recently, the San Fernando Valley has become postmodern urban. The driver topping the crest saw office towers looming out over slightly hazy air, shopping centers, occasional palm trees, stucco subdivisions, and the squat factory and warehouse buildings that once made Los Angeles County a top manufacturing locale.

Many of the big plants have closed and the Valley has changed. The 1950s white families with stay-at-home moms have been replaced by Latino families with parents juggling two jobs and trying to raise children who will have a better chance than they had. In Van Nuys, Canoga Park and Burbank, which was the industrial base, the GM plants were mostly shut down in the 1980s, and the last large factory, the Pratt and Whitney Rocketdyne plant, was sold to manufacturer GenCorp in 2012. The big factories have been supplanted by hundreds of small factories and multimedia plants. Despite soaring costs of housing, the economy in the Valley has strengthened, the Los Angeles Daily News reported in 2018. The information and technology sector has become a "catalyst," and there has been "a relative abundance" of good jobs, according to a report by local economic researchers.

The southern rim of the Valley, around the North Hollywood area, remains heavily Jewish and is attracting new families who often send their kids to religious schools. People with money cluster near the foot of the mountains around the Valley; those less well-off settle on the flatlands beyond. The L.A. Metro transit agency took steps in 2018 toward a new light-rail line that would run for nine miles through 14 stations in the Valley, mostly along Van Nuys Boulevard, and would open prior to the 2028 Olympics. This East San Fernando Light Rail Project would be the first significant public transit for the Valley and, officials expect, will spur nearby development. The busy Van Nuys airport, which is used chiefly for private planes and charters, has repaired its runways and taxiways and opened in 2019 a new hangar and office building. In 2019, a developer unveiled ambitious plans for a $1 billion residential and shopping complex at the end of Metro's Red Line, in North Hollywood: District NoHo is planned as a "true urban node," in planner-speak.

The 29th Congressional District of California consists of the eastern part of the San Fernando Valley in the city of Los Angeles. It includes affluent North Hollywood, as well as Van Nuys, North Hills and Panorama City. The southeast part of the district takes in the NoHo Arts District. Parts of the northern end of the Valley, including economically declining Pacoima and the small city of San Fernando, are in the district. Whiteman Airport and Los Angeles Valley College are also here. The District is 67 percent Hispanic and solidly Democratic. Joe Biden won 74 percent of the vote—an unusual urban California district where the Democratic vote dropped from the 78 percent that Hillary Clinton took in 2016.

Brad Sherman (D)

Elected 1996, 13th term, b. Oct 24, 1954; Los Angeles, CA; Orange Coast University, Att.; University of CA, Los Angeles, B.A., 1974; Harvard University Law School, J.D., 1979; Jewish; Married (Lisa Kaplan Sherman); 3 children.

Elected Office: CA Board of Equalization, 1990-1995, Chairman, 1991-1995.

Professional Career: Practicing attorney, Accountant, 1980-1990.

DC Office: 2181 RHOB 20515, 202-225-5911, Fax: 202-225-5879, sherman.house.gov

State Offices: Sherman Oaks, 818-501-9200.

Committees: *Communications Standards Commission. Financial Services*: Consumer Protection & Financial Institutions; Housing, Community Development & Insurance; Investor Protection, Entrepreneurship & Capital Markets (Chmn); Task Force on Artificial Intelligence. *Foreign Affairs*: Asia, the Pacific, Central Asia, Nonproliferation; Intern'l Dev't, Intern'l Orgs & Global Corporate Social Impact; Middle East, North Africa & Global Counterterrorism. *Science, Space & Technology*: Space & Aeronautics.

Group Ratings

	ADA	ACLU	AFL-CIO	LCV	COC	HAFA	ACU	CFG	FRC
2020	**	75%	**	100%	-	0%	7%	**	-
2019	90%	C	100%	93%	61%	C	7%	13%	0%

Almanac Ratings 2019-2020

	Economy	Social	Foreign	Composite
Liberal	100%	61%	92%	85%
Conservative	0%	39%	8%	15%

Key Votes of the 116th Congress

1. U.S./Mex./Can. trade deal Y	5. Russia sanctions Y	9. Firearms background checks Y
2. First Coronavirus response Y	6. Troops in Syria Y	10. Spending at the border N
3. HEROES Act Y	7. Veto arms sales to Saudis Y	11. Marijuana liberalized rules Y
4. CASH Act Y	8. Defense $$$, veto override Y	12. Electoral College objections N

Election Results

Election	Name (Party)	Vote (%)		Cand. Spent	Ind. Exp. Support	Ind. Exp. Oppose
2020 General	Brad Sherman (D)............................	240,038	(69%)	$546,337	$2,334	
	Mark Reed (R).................................	105,426	(31%)			$59
2020 Primary	Brad Sherman (D)............................	99,282	(58%)			
	Courtney "CJ" Berina (D).................	18,937	(11%)			

Prior winning percentages: 2018 (73%), 2016 (73%), 2014 (66%), 2012 (60%), 2010 (65%), 2008 (69%), 2006 (69%), 2004 (62%), 2002 (62%), 2000 (66%), 1998 (57%), 1996 (49%)

Brad Sherman, a Democrat first elected in 1996, has shown that he is a rough and ready political scrapper—in support of Israel and against Wall Street, for example. His reelection brawl in 2012 against more senior Democrat Howard Berman left lingering wounds within the party. Sherman remains outspoken, especially on foreign policy, and he was an early proponent of the impeachment of President Donald Trump. His career seemed to plateau when he lost a bid to chair the House Foreign Affairs Committee to a member with less seniority.

Sherman grew up in Monterey Park, in the San Gabriel Valley east of Los Angeles. He started working on Democratic campaigns at age 6, stuffing envelopes for Rep. George Brown. He set up his own stamp-wholesaling firm at age 14. He graduated with high honors from the University of California, Los Angeles, worked as an accountant, then went to Harvard Law School. He came back to the Los Angeles area to practice tax law, and represented the Philippines in its successful effort to seize the assets of deposed President Ferdinand Marcos.

In 1990, Sherman was elected from Los Angeles County to the state Board of Equalization, which is a sort of tax court. He was known as a stickler for detail, a "tax nerd," as one former staffer said, who used the office with a keen scent for political advantage. In the 1996 contest for an open seat, Sherman and his Republican opponent, businessman Rich Sybert, were self-financers; Sherman spent $578,000 of his own money. Both stressed their ideological moderation. Sherman campaigned against then-House Speaker Newt Gingrich and the Republican Congress, though he supported the death penalty, called for phasing out racial quotas and preferences, and favored tough measures on illegal immigration. Sybert stressed his independence from Gingrich as well as his support for abortion rights and environmental protection. Sherman won 49%-44%.

In the House, his voting record has been more moderate than those of most other Los Angeles County Democrats, and he has shown occasional independence from party leaders. One of the few certified public accountants in Congress, Sherman serves on the Financial Services Committee, where he has sought to unravel corporate accounting scandals. Sherman helped form the new Consumer Financial Protection Bureau as part of the 2010 Dodd-Frank financial overhaul law. But Rep. Barney Frank of Massachusetts accused him of overstating his role after Sherman boasted that he had "more to do with Dodd-Frank than anyone except Dodd and Frank."

Sherman faced his first serious opposition when redistricting following the 2010 census resulted in a bitter contest with Berman, a 30-year House veteran who had chaired the Foreign Affairs Committee. Berman had the backing of much of the state's Democratic establishment as well as the support of Hollywood elites for his work on anti-piracy legislation. But Berman was at a serious geographic disadvantage: The new 30th District covered twice as much of Sherman's old turf as Berman's base, which was in the new Hispanic-majority 29th District.

The final tab for the race was $16.3 million. Sherman went on the attack, depicting Berman as a Washington insider who didn't understand constituents' concerns. Berman highlighted his opponent's inability to get more than a handful of bills into law, while criticizing him for loaning his campaigns money and then charging interest, an allegation that Sherman heatedly denied. The acrimony peaked at an October debate when the two loudly bickered over immigration legislation, and Sherman threw his arm around his opponent's shoulders and demanded, "You want to get into this?" A sheriff's deputy and a debate organizer stepped between them to prevent an escalation. Berman sent out a YouTube video of the incident accusing Sherman of trying to start a fight, prompting Sherman to apologize. But it was too little, too late for Berman. Sherman won easily, 60%-40%.

Sherman soon paid the price when Democratic Leader Nancy Pelosi stymied his bid to become senior Democrat on the Foreign Affairs Committee, where he had been next in line among Democratic members behind Berman. In his committee work, Sherman often was assertive. As the top Democrat on the Asia and the Pacific Subcommittee, he strongly opposed President Barack Obama's deal with Iran on nuclear weapons, which he described as "preposterous." But he said Trump's efforts to decertify the deal could have dangerous consequences. When many Democrats boycotted the speech of Israeli Prime Minister Benjamin Netanyahu in 2015, Sherman said he was "honored" to serve on the escort committee that accompanied him into the House chamber.

In the majority, Sherman seemed to tamp down his foreign policy independence—publicly, at least. In June 2020, he joined most senior Democrats in urging Netanyahu not to follow through on his plan for Israel to annex parts of the West Bank controlled by the Palestinians. A month later, he led broad opposition to a proposal for an economic boycott of Israel. He also was a leading proponent of a bill to impose economic sanctions on Chinese leaders and financiers, which was enacted.

With Foreign Affairs chairman Eliot Engel having unexpectedly lost his Democratic primary in June, it appeared that Sherman was emphasizing reconciliation among Democrats as he prepared to seek the chairmanship. But, following the election, he again fell short of the top slot as he lost to Rep. Gregory Meeks, another New Yorker—dropping out of the contest after trailing in the vote of the leadership-dominated Democratic Steering Committee..

Sherman remains a senior member of the Financial Services Committee, where all three Democrats who outrank him already chair a House committee. His best option might be if House Democrats have new leaders before that panel's slot comes open. He chairs the Investor Protection, Entrepreneurship and Capital Markets Subcommittee.

Since 2012, he has had easy reelections at home. His hold on this district appears more secure than his approval in the Democratic Caucus.

CA-30: Southern and Western San Fernando Valley

Cook Partisan Voting Index: D+20

Population		Race and Ethnicity		Income	
Total	764,062	White	61.50%	Median Income	$89,460
Land area (sq. miles)	136	Black	4.50%	District Income Rank	59
Pop/ sq mi	5,620.58	Latino	29.30%	Poverty Rate	9.50%
Born in State	45.60%	Asian	12.40%	With health insurance	92.90%
		Two or more races	5.10%	Cash public assistance	1.60%
Age Groups		Other	16.40%	Food stamp/SNAP	4.30%
Under 18	18.80%				
18-34	23.20%	**Education**		**Work**	
35-64	41.90%	H.S grad or less	27.10%	White Collar	49.40%
Over 64	16.20%	Some college	27.70%	Sales and Service	37.00%
		College Degree, 4 yr	29.40%	Blue Collar	13.60%
Military		Post grad	15.80%	Government	9.00%
Veteran/ Active Duty	3.70%				

2020 Pres. Vote	Biden	258,910	(69%)	Trump	110,935	(29%)			
2016 Pres. Vote	Clinton	209,149	(69%)	Trump	77,701	(26%)	Johnson	8,278	(3%)
	Stein	6,244	(2%)						

The Valley, Reseda: In the early 20th century, when the movie business was young, the San Fernando Valley was a vast expanse of empty land that had been annexed to Los Angeles in 1915. Moviemakers, looking for filming sites for a western, drove past the vacant lots of Westwood, up narrow roads through the Santa Monica Mountains, and into the vast Valley, sheltered from ocean breezes and rain-bearing clouds by the mountains. This big bowl of land was transformed, first into 1950s suburbia, and then into a postmodern city of its own, economically vital and ethnically diverse. Even in its suburban years, the San Fernando Valley was not entirely residential. Big factories provided jobs. In those years, this was fast-growing, family-friendly territory.

Most of the big studios are not far away in Burbank, though Universal Studios—including NBC —comprise a motion-picture and entertainment complex and theme park in the Valley. In a not so family-friendly development, the Valley became a hub for the adult-film industry. After Los Angeles County voters approved a measure in 2012 that required actors to wear condoms in sex scenes to control the spread of sexually transmitted disease, some adult-movie producers moved studio operations out of the region. Other porn businesses diversified to new forms of technology and paraphernalia, and their headquarters remained in the area. The defeat of a similar statewide initiative in 2016 opened the door to the return of the porn industry in the Valley, which had suffered a 95 percent drop in permit requests. The coronavirus also affected the porn-making industry, where social distancing often is an alien concept. Performers sought innovative ways to do their work with limited production teams. Stat News, the health-news site, reported in May 2020 that public health experts found that longstanding testing techniques for porn stars offered useful tips for COVID testing.

Parts of the Valley have been unhappy to be linked with the city of Los Angeles, whose city council has imposed high taxes and irksome regulations. A secession movement arose, and the issue was put on the 2002 ballot. The Valley voted 51%-49% for it, with stronger support in the southern and western sections. But it failed to get the needed majority in all of Los Angeles to pass. Following the recession, the Valley's economy improved, thanks in part to a massive expansion in California's enterprise zone program. Nevertheless, many thousands of middle-class residents have relocated in recent years to less-costly places. The average sales price for homes in the Valley rose 4 percent to $740,000 in 2019. The Valley has been selected to host several events in the 2028 Olympics, including canoe, kayak, equestrian and shooting competitions.

The 30th Congressional District covers the western and southern parts of the San Fernando Valley within Los Angeles. Along its southern border, the 30th includes the upscale territory of Tarzana, Encino Los and Hidden Hills. In the center of the district are industrial Canoga Park, Winnetka and largely Hispanic Reseda. On the northern end are Granada Hills, where the San Fernando Valley's first oil well was drilled in 1916, and O'Melveny Park, one of the largest parks in Los Angeles. Also in the district is California State University, Northridge. Less than 1 percent of the 30th reaches into Ventura County. In a district that is 29 percent Hispanic and 12 percent Asian, Joe Biden led, 69%-29%, little changed from 2016.

Pete Aguilar (D)

Elected 2014, 4th term, b. Jun 19, 1979; Fontana, CA; University of Redlands, B.R.E., 2001; Roman Catholic; Married (Alisha Aguilar); 2 children.

Elected Office: Redlands City Council, 2006-2014; Mayor, Redlands, 2010-2014.

Professional Career: Business owner; Interim Director & deputy Director, Inland Empire regional office of the Gov., 2001.

DC Office: 109 CHOB 20515, 202-225-3201, Fax: 202-226-6962, aguilar.house.gov

State Offices: San Bernardino, 909-890-4445.

Committees: House Democratic Caucus Vice Chairman. *Administration*: Elections. *Appropriations*: Defense; Homeland Security; Transportation, HUD & Related Agencies.

Group Ratings

	ADA	ACLU	AFL-CIO	LCV	COC	HAFA	ACU	CFG	FRC
2020	**	81%	**	100%	-	0%	5%	**	-
2019	95%	C	95%	93%	56%	C	5%	18%	0%

Almanac Ratings 2019-2020

	Economy	Social	Foreign	Composite
Liberal	100%	100%	92%	98%
Conservative	0%	0%	8%	2%

Key Votes of the 116th Congress

1. U.S./Mex./Can. trade deal Y	5. Russia sanctions Y	9. Firearms background checks Y
2. First Coronavirus response Y	6. Troops in Syria Y	10. Spending at the border N
3. HEROES Act Y	7. Veto arms sales to Saudis Y	11. Marijuana liberalized rules Y
4. CASH Act Y	8. Defense $$$, veto override Y	12. Electoral College objections N

Election Results

Election	Name (Party)	Vote (%)		Cand. Spent	Ind. Exp. Support	Ind. Exp. Oppose
2020 General	Pete Aguilar (D).............................	175,315	(61%)	$1,427,539	$2,166	
	Agnes Gibboney (R)...........................	110,735	(39%)	$169,163		$113
2020 Primary	Pete Aguilar (D)................................	81,994	(62%)			

Prior winning percentages: 2018 (59%), 2016 (56%), 2014 (52%)

Democrat Pete Aguilar's 2014 win returned the 31st District seat to the Democrats, following turbulent local politics that gave the predominantly Hispanic district to Republicans in 2012. With his seat on the Appropriations Committee and selection as vice chairman of the Democratic Caucus, the youthful Aguilar was well-positioned for long-term influence.

Aguilar was born in Fontana and grew up in San Bernardino. He earned undergraduate degrees in government and business administration at the University of Redlands. One of his first jobs was at the San Bernardino County Courthouse cafeteria, where his blind grandfather was the operator. In 2001, Gov. Gray Davis appointed Aguilar as deputy director of the Inland Empire Regional Office of the Governor. In 2006, Aguilar was appointed to the Redlands City Council, making him the youngest-ever council member. He was elected mayor in 2010 by his fellow council members.

In 2012, he ran in this redrawn minority district. Four Democrats divided the vote in the all-party primary. Aguilar was the frontrunner among them with 23 percent of the total vote. But the two Republicans emerged at the top, with 27 and 25 percent. Rep. Gary Miller—who decided to run here for his eighth term, despite not having represented any of the district—won in November over fellow Republican Bob Dutton, 55%-45%.

Miller announced he would not seek reelection in 2014, and Aguilar again sought the seat. History almost repeated itself in the primary, as four Democrats faced off against three Republicans. GOP candidate Paul Chabot came in first with 27 percent; Aguilar had 17 percent and hung onto a 209-vote lead over Republican Leslie Gooch. This time, the four Democratic candidates in the primary got 53 percent of the total vote. Aguilar hammered Chabot for what he called his too-conservative views on education, immigration and heath care. Chabot, an Iraq war vet and Navy Reserve intelligence officer, focused on those experiences and how to combat terrorism. Aguilar won 52%-48%. Aguilar outspent Chabot, $2.2 million to $469,000. Republicans seem to have missed an opportunity by steering clear of this contest, to Chabot's dismay.

In the House, Aguilar criticized President Barack Obama's executive action on immigration reform as not good enough and demanded congressional action. With Republican support, he filed a bill in January 2018 to give a path to citizenship to students with Deferred Action for Childhood Arrivals (DACA) status. When Speaker Paul Ryan refused to schedule the bill, Aguilar took the unusual step of seeking to force a floor vote with a discharge petition. Although all Democrats signed, they fell two signatures short of the requisite majority of members to get House action. He was successful in adding to the 2018 defense spending bill his proposal to broaden the availability of grants in the Defense Department's cyber scholarship program. The broader bill was enacted in 2018.Aguilar has been a chief deputy whip in the Democratic Whip organization and a whip for the centrist New Democrat Coalition.

Early in the 2016 campaign cycle, the National Republican Congressional Committee placed Aguilar on its "Donkeys List" of vulnerable incumbents. Chabot, who had written an e-book about his 2014 campaign experience, decided to run again. He cited Aguilar's failure to improve the continuing weak local economy. Chabot referred to his opponent as "Agu-liar" and generated controversy when he issued "terrorist hunting permits" to campaign donors. Aguilar again had a big fundraising advantage, $2.9 million to $622,000, and national Republicans spent little money to back up their attacks on Aguilar. The higher presidential-year turnout provided a boost for Aguilar, who won 56%-44%. Aguilar, like most House Democrats, had an easier time in 2018. Republican Sean Flynn, an economics professor at Claremont College and author of the book Economics for Dummies, criticized the healthcare policies of both parties and advocated more choices for consumers. Flynn spent $1.3 million—more than his earlier opponents—to $2.4 million for Aguilar. But it didn't seem to help. Aguilar won, 59%-41% Against a lightly funded opponent in 2020, Aguilar got 61 percent.

Following the 2018 election, Aguilar ran for vice chairman of the Democratic Caucus. He said his moderate views would provide diversity of thought among party leaders. The only other contender was Katherine Clark of Massachusetts, who won the position. Two years later, when Clark moved up to fill the vacancy for assistant Speaker, Aguilar ran again for the number-two spot at the Caucus. This time, he had the advantage that no other Hispanics had been selected for a leadership post. He had the continued support of the centrist New Democrats.

CA-31: Southwestern San Bernardino

Cook Partisan Voting Index: D+9

Population		Race and Ethnicity		Income	
Total	753,576	White	60.50%	Median Income	$70,554
Land area (sq. miles)	218	Black	11.20%	District Income Rank	160
Pop/ sq mi	3,452.97	Latino	53.50%	Poverty Rate	12.30%
Born in State	65.90%	Asian	8.40%	With health insurance	91.30%
		Two or more races	5.20%	Cash public assistance	3.70%
Age Groups		Other	14.80%	Food stamp/SNAP	11.30%
Under 18	24.70%				
18-34	26.30%	**Education**		**Work**	
35-64	36.40%	H.S grad or less	42.30%	White Collar	34.30%
Over 64	12.40%	Some college	31.90%	Sales and Service	39.20%
		College Degree, 4 yr	15.70%	Blue Collar	26.40%
Military		Post grad	10.20%	Government	16.10%
Veteran/ Active Duty	5.20%				

2020 Pres. Vote	Biden	174,178	(59%)	Trump	115,221	(39%)		
2016 Pres. Vote	Clinton	131,966	(57%)	Trump	83,706	(36%)	Johnson	7,729	(3%)

Rancho Cucamonga: In the 1970s, as the coastal portions of the Los Angeles Basin became fully developed, and in the 1980s, as real estate values skyrocketed, people with modest incomes and young families increasingly moved east, from the high-cost, high-crime coast to the smoggier, hotter valleys inland. There was a lot of empty, low-priced land in what people began calling the Inland Empire, defined usually as San Bernardino and Riverside counties, and especially in the desert to the north and east of the passes through the mountains that rim the Basin. This was a high-growth area, with a population that expanded from 1.6 million in 1980 to nearly 4.7 million in 2019, when it was Hispanic-majority.

During the past two decades, there has been a boom in commercial real estate, especially warehouses to store merchandise offloaded at the port of Los Angeles-Long Beach. In 2019, the Inland Empire led the nation with 21 of the 100 largest warehouse-distribution center lease deals. Although some neighborhood groups complained that the buildings were an environmental blight, the uptick in construction attracted many Latinos, both citizens and immigrants. In 2020, Brightline —the nation's only privately run passenger rail line—explored the possibility of making Rancho Cucamonga a terminus for high-speed rail service from Las Vegas to the Los Angeles area. Elon Musk, chief executive of Tesla, was exploring the option of a nearly three-mile people-mover from the center of Riverside to its airport, which would be less costly than a rail line. San Bernardino has become the largest county in the nation for Latinos, with a population that is 54 percent Latino, an increase from 241,000 in 1980 to more than 1.2 million in 2019. The city of San Bernardino is 65 percent Latino.

In 2007 the housing bubble burst. The Inland Empire had one of the nation's highest foreclosure rates and housing values fell by half. Nowhere were the problems greater than in the city of San Bernardino, which was declared one of the weakest metropolitan areas in the country for job creation. The city was criticized for carrying inflated pension costs and high government salaries, with nearly one in four city employees earning more than $100,000 a year in 2010. Facing a $45.8 million budget shortfall, San Bernardino voted to declare bankruptcy in 2012. It emerged from bankruptcy in 2017, though it faced continuing budget constraints. In Rancho Cucamonga, economic growth shut down most of the orange groves. A few dozen firms in the airline and aircraft businesses eventually moved to the site of Norton Air Force Base, which closed in 1994.

The 31st Congressional District is the only district that is entirely within San Bernardino County; four other districts are partly in the county. This includes the cities of Colton, Loma Linda and Redlands along I-10,Rancho Cucamonga to the west and most of downtown San Bernardino. Rialto and Upland are split between this district and the more heavily Latino 35th to the south. The 31st was designed to comply with Voting Rights Act rules against racial discrimination. The district is 53 percent Hispanic and politically leans Democratic. Joe Biden got 59 percent of the vote, though the area has been competitive locally.

Grace Napolitano (D)

Elected 1998, 12th term, b. Dec 04, 1936; Brownsville, TX; TX Southmost College, Att.; Cerritos College, Att.; Roman Catholic; Widow; 5 children (5 from previous marriage); 14 grandchildren; 2 great-grandchildren.

Elected Office: Norwalk City Council, 1986-1992; Norwalk Mayor, 1990- 92; CA Assembly, 1992-1998.

Professional Career: Employee, Ford Motor Co., 1970-1992.

DC Office: 1610 LHOB 20515, 202-225-5256, Fax: 202-225-0027, napolitano.house.gov

State Offices: El Monte, 626-350-0150.

Committees: *Natural Resources*: Water, Oceans & Wildlife. *Transportation & Infrastructure*: Economic Dev't, Public Buildings & Emergency Management; Highways & Transit; Railroads, Pipelines & Hazardous Materials; Water Resources & Environment (Chmn).

Group Ratings

	ADA	ACLU	AFL-CIO	LCV	COC	HAFA	ACU	CFG	FRC
2020	**	79%	**	95%	-	0%	3%	**	-
2019	95%	C	95%	97%	48%	C	4%	18%	0%

Almanac Ratings 2019-2020

	Economy	Social	Foreign	Composite
Liberal	59%	100%	96%	85%
Conservative	41%	0%	4%	15%

Key Votes of the 116th Congress

1. U.S./Mex./Can. trade deal	Y	5. Russia sanctions	Y
2. First Coronavirus response	Y	6. Troops in Syria	Y
3. HEROES Act	N/A	7. Veto arms sales to Saudis	Y
4. CASH Act	Y	8. Defense $$$, veto override	Y

9. Firearms background checks Y
10. Spending at the border   N
11. Marijuana liberalized rules   Y
12. Electoral College objections N

Election Results

Election	Name (Party)	Vote (%)		Cand. Spent	Ind. Exp. Support	Ind. Exp. Oppose
2020 General	Grace Napolitano (D)...........................	172,942	(67%)	$235,849	$7,091	
	Joshua Scott (R)................................	86,818	(33%)	$14,071		$113
2020 Primary	Grace Napolitano (D)...........................	60,011	(52%)			
	Emanuel Gonzales (D)......................	14,475	(13%)			
	Meshal "Kash" Kashifalghita (D)...........	8,958	(8%)			

Prior winning percentages: 2018 (69%), 2016 (62%), 2014 (60%), 2012 (66%), 2010 (74%), 2008 (82%), 2006 (75%), 2004 (100%), 2002 (71%), 2000 (71%), 1998 (68%)

Grace Napolitano, a Democrat first elected in 1998, has concentrated on issues affecting lower-income Hispanics in her Southern California district, including jobs, water scarcity and mental health. Her committee assignments and seniority have given her the most clout on pork-barrel projects, on both land and water, of any California Democrat or member of the Hispanic Caucus. As one of the oldest members of the House, she has been considered a likely retiree for several years.

Napolitano grew up in the lower Rio Grande Valley of Texas, married at age 18, and eventually had five children. When she was 23, the family moved to California. She got a job as a secretary at Ford Motor Co. and stayed for 22 years. After her first husband died, she married Frank Napolitano, and in 1980, they started a pizzeria. She served on the Norwalk City Council from 1986 to 1992 and served one term as mayor, becoming the first Latino to hold the position. In 1992, she was elected to the California Assembly.

In 1998, she ran for Congress when 16-year Democratic Rep. Esteban Torres announced three days before the filing deadline that he was retiring. Torres' surprise move was designed to promote the election of Jamie Casso, his son-in-law and chief of staff, who immediately announced his candidacy. Napolitano was not deterred and got into the race. She criticized Casso for not living in the district, and he criticized a $180,000 loan she made to her campaign at an unusual 18 percent interest rate. Napolitano had the backing of national liberal women's organizations, including EMILY's List, plus the benefit of higher name recognition. The two candidates had few differences on major issues. Napolitano signed a pledge to serve only three terms. She won the primary by 618 votes, assuring her victory in November in the heavily Democratic district.

Napolitano, a former chairwoman of the Congressional Hispanic Caucus, has been more consensus-oriented on immigration legislation than some caucus members. She has been a longtime advocate on issues related to the mentally ill, an interest that was sparked by a report that one in three Hispanic girls contemplates suicide. "Mental health is treatable. But [the Latino community has] a stigma attached to it," Napolitano said. As chair of the Congressional Mental Health Caucus, she has written that most people who commit suicides use guns, and she advocated steps to reduce such incidents.

On the Natural Resources Committee, she chaired the panel's Water and Power Subcommittee from 2007 until 2011, with a focus on Southern California's acute need for more water. In hearings, she said that desalination research was critical to economic growth. In 2014, she unveiled her "Water in the 21st Century" bill, which provided $2 billion in loans and grants for water recycling, storm water capture and treatment, groundwater management and water infrastructure projects. After the 2014 election, despite her seniority, she stepped aside for Rep. Raul Grijalva of Arizona to become senior Democrat on the full committee.

On the Transportation and Infrastructure Committee, as the ranking Democrat on the Water Resources and Environment Subcommittee, Napolitano worked to fix "our nation's crumbling water infrastructure." She encouraged regulators to find ways to recycle water for irrigation use and groundwater replenishment and to assist local water agencies to find more ways to recapture water for their reservoirs. In 2018, she was part of the committee's bipartisan leadership that enacted new water-resource grants, which shifted funding to the states by requiring them to pay at least 80 percent of the costs for new projects.

As chairwoman of the subcommittee since 2019, she worked with other committee leaders to enact bipartisan legislation to authorize more than two dozen water infrastructure projects. The Water Resources Development Act of 2020 also released $10 billion in unspent harbor maintenance funding. The legislation is financed partly by the Harbor Maintenance Trust Fund, which includes fees from shippers. When Congress completed action on the bill in December 2020, Napolitano took credit for its "six-fold increase in funding"—to $175 million—for the ports of Los Angeles and Long Beach. Earlier that month, the Army Corps awarded her its annual gold medal for "significant contributions to Army engineering."

In 2003, Napolitano abandoned her earlier pledge to serve only three terms. She has not been seriously challenged for reelection. In 2012, she won with 66 percent of the vote in the redrawn 32nd District, in which more than 80 percent of voters were new to her. In her unusual campaign in 2016, Democratic Assemblyman Roger Hernandez finished second in the June all-party primary, then faced allegations of domestic violence from his ex-wife. In August, he formally ended his campaign, though he got 38 percent of the vote against Napolitano. In 2018, against Republican challenger Joshua Scott, a 25-year-old political newcomer and enthusiastic supporter of President Donald Trump who spent about $5,000, Napolitano won, 69%-31%. Two years later, after Scott more than doubled his spending, Napolitano won with 67 percent.

Napolitano's husband died of cancer in 2017. She reportedly recovered from a stroke the previous year. At 84 in January 2021, she was among the four oldest House members. In 2022, the uncertainties of redistricting might encourage her retirement. Her eventual successor almost certainly will be a Democrat, though the contest could be wide open. On his first full day in office in January 2021, President Joe Biden appointed Camille Touton, a longtime adviser to Napolitano on water policy, as deputy commissioner of the Bureau of Reclamation.

CA-32: Eastern L.A. Suburbs   Cook Partisan Voting Index: D+17

Population		Race and Ethnicity		Income	
Total	700,726	White	50.30%	Median Income	$71,136
Land area (sq. miles)	124	Black	2.60%	District Income Rank	156
Pop/ sq mi	5,640.55	Latino	61.00%	Poverty Rate	11.60%
Born in State	56.40%	Asian	19.20%	With health insurance	90.70%
		Two or more races	4.80%	Cash public assistance	3.10%
Age Groups		Other	23.00%	Food stamp/SNAP	9.50%
Under 18	20.90%				
18-34	24.10%	**Education**		**Work**	
35-64	39.50%	H.S grad or less	49.60%	White Collar	30.50%
Over 64	15.60%	Some college	28.00%	Sales and Service	42.50%
		College Degree, 4 yr	16.10%	Blue Collar	27.10%
Military		Post grad	6.30%	Government	13.50%
Veteran/ Active Duty	3.20%				

2020 Pres. Vote	Biden	184,978	(65%)	Trump	93,155	(33%)			
2016 Pres. Vote	Clinton	146,459	(66%)	Trump	60,921	(28%)	Johnson	5,996	(3%)
	Stein	4,678	(2%)						

Azusa, West Covina: It was the great route west to California in the first half of the 20th century: Passengers on the Santa Fe Railroad's Super Chief or motorists on U.S. 66, after hours and days in barren desert, would descend through Cajon Pass into the Los Angeles Basin, and come upon orange groves and exotic plants thriving beneath the 10,000-foot snow-capped San Gabriel Mountains. The railroad and highway ran through a line of towns built by Midwestern Protestants as independent communities. Foothills cities such as La Verne and San Dimas have horse trails and their own rodeos.

The small city of Irwindale, which has been concerned about the odor production of Sriracha hot sauce, resolved in 2018 its long-running legal dispute in which it had cited the Huy Fong Foods Co. as a public nuisance. The chili sauce has a devoted following. Bon Appetit has named it one of its favorite foods. In another environmental dispute, five companies that had been ruled responsible for contaminated groundwater in the San Gabriel Valley were ordered by a state water-quality agency to clean up the mess by 2027, at an estimated cost of $250 million.

After L.A. Metro opened an 11-mile light-rail "foothill" extension of the Gold Line from Pasadena to Azusa, the approval of a 2016 referendum to extend a sales tax increase for transit funding led Metro to plan the next extension of 9.1 miles from Glendora via San Dimas and LaVerne to Ponoma; construction was scheduled for completion by 2026.The extension will mark the first time the light-rail train will overlap with Metrolink's Los Angeles-to-San Bernardino commuter line. Metro delayed continuation to Montclair until "additional funding is secured."(In 2020, Metro name-changed its lines from colors to a letter—in this case, L.) The rail extension was one of 28 projects that Metro planned to complete prior to the Olympic games in 2028.

The 32nd District is 61 percent Hispanic and 19 percent Asian. The western parts of the compact 32nd—the areas closer to downtown Los Angeles—are heavily Latino: Covina, West Covina and Azusa all are Hispanic-majority cities. More than one-fourth of the population is foreign-born. In Baldwin Park, which is 75 percent Hispanic and 19 percent Asian, more than 80 percent of its population speaks a language other than English at home. Outlying areas to the east, such as La Verne and San Dimas, have lower poverty rates and higher household incomes. The heavily Hispanic composition of this district makes it safe Democratic territory. The demographic shifts that increased the Democratic margin to 66%-28% for Hillary Clinton in 2016 reversed in 2020, when increasing Latino unhappiness with Democrats reduced the victory for Joe Biden to 65%-33%.

Ted Lieu (D)

Elected 2014, 4th term, b. Mar 29, 1969; Taipei, Taiwan; Stanford University, B.A., 1991; Stanford University, B.S., 1991; Georgetown University Law Center, J.D., 1994; Roman Catholic; Married (Betty Lieu); 2 children.

Military Career: U.S. Air Force 1995-1999; U.S. Air Force Reserve 2000-pres.

Elected Office: Torrance City Council, 2002-2005; CA Assembly, 2005-2010. CA Senate, 2011-2014.

Professional Career: Clerk, U.S. Court of Appeals, 9th Circuit; Practicing attorney.

DC Office: 403 CHOB 20515, 202-225-3976, Fax: 202-225-4099, lieu.house.gov

State Offices: Los Angeles, 323-651-1040; Manhattan Beach, 310-321-7664.

Committees: *Foreign Affairs*: Asia, the Pacific, Central Asia, Nonproliferation; Middle East, North Africa & Global Counterterrorism. *Judiciary*: Courts, Intellectual Property & Internet; Crime, Terrorism & Homeland Security.

Group Ratings

	ADA	ACLU	AFL-CIO	LCV	COC	HAFA	ACU	CFG	FRC
2020	**	85%	**	95%	-	0%	4%	**	-
2019	90%	C	90%	93%	50%	C	4%	12%	0%

Almanac Ratings 2019-2020

	Economy	Social	Foreign	Composite
Liberal	49%	60%	97%	69%
Conservative	51%	40%	3%	31%

Key Votes of the 116th Congress

1. U.S./Mex./Can. trade deal	N	5. Russia sanctions	Y	9. Firearms background checks	Y
2. First Coronavirus response	Y	6. Troops in Syria	Y	10. Spending at the border	N
3. HEROES Act	N/A	7. Veto arms sales to Saudis	Y	11. Marijuana liberalized rules	Y
4. CASH Act	Y	8. Defense $$$, veto override	Y	12. Electoral College objections	N

Election Results

Election	Name (Party)	Vote (%)		Cand. Spent	Ind. Exp. Support	Ind. Exp. Oppose
2020 General	Ted Lieu (D)	257,094	(68%)	$879,885	$2,334	
	James Bradley (R)	123,334	(32%)	$73,185		$113
2020 Primary	Ted Lieu (D)	130,063	(61%)			
	Liz Barris (D)	15,180	(7%)			

Prior winning percentages: 2018 (70%), 2016 (66%), 2014 (59%)

Democrat Ted Lieu, elected in 2014 in one of the nation's richest and most liberal House districts, has pursued an activist approach, with both new liberal initiatives and occasional bipartisan action. He relentlessly tweaked President Donald Trump, both in the Judiciary Committee and on his Twitter feed, where he has nearly a million followers. He was selected to a Democratic leadership communications position. That background helps to explain how Lieu played a central role in preparing the second impeachment case against Trump, even while he and other House members were sheltering from rioters at the Capitol.

A Taiwanese American whose working-class family settled in Cleveland Ohio when he was a toddler, he got his bachelor's degree from Stanford University and a law degree from Georgetown. Lieu's early career centered on law and military service. After four years of active duty in the Air Force, including a posting in the JAG Corps, he divided his time between working in the private sector and serving on the Torrance City Council. In 2005, he won a special election to serve in the state Assembly, followed by election to the state Senate in 2010. He backed a successful bill allowing undocumented immigrants to take the bar exam, and called for a statewide referendum expressing opposition to the Citizens United campaign-finance ruling. On affirmative action, he staked out a more centrist position, opposing a bill that would have overturned the affirmative action ban at California state universities. That move drew criticism from Black and Latino lawmakers.

When liberal icon Henry Waxman announced his retirement in 2013 after 40 years, he set off a primary fight that attracted no fewer than 18 candidates. Along with Lieu, the best known were Republican Elan Carr, who served with the Army in Iraq and was a deputy in the L.A. District Attorney's office, former L.A. mayoral candidate Wendy Greuel, and self-help guru Marianne Williamson, an independent. Lieu leveraged his deep political ties to the district, his liberal voting record in Sacramento, and a lineup of top Democratic endorsements, including L.A. Mayor Eric Garcetti, as well as the Los Angeles Daily News. He underscored the need for more Asian-American representation in Congress. In the June primary, he came in second to Carr, 21%-19%; Greuel was third with 17 percent. That set Lieu up for an easy victory in a party stronghold, and his wealthy voters could help raise money for other Democrats. He won in November, 59%-41%.

Lieu was president of the Democrats' freshman class. He became the first House Democrat to announce opposition to the request by President Barack Obama to authorize the use of military force against the Islamic State. "I do not believe the administration has made the case that ISIL represents a direct, grave threat to our nation," he said. He joined several other junior House members in launching the bipartisan Post-9/11 Veterans Caucus. Noting that his district has one of the nation's largest populations of homeless veterans, plus a huge VA health care system, he emphasized the need for innovative solutions to the problems of returned service members. Lieu enacted a bill in 2016 to authorize leases for the VA's campus in West Los Angeles that would construct 1,200 units for homeless vets. In October 2019, the L.A. city council approved $24 million to create housing for the homeless on that VA campus.

Lieu voiced many concerns with Trump. With his seats on the Foreign Affairs and Judiciary committees, he filed a bill in 2017 with Sen. Edward Markey of Massachusetts to prevent the president from authorizing a nuclear first strike without a declaration of war by Congress. In October 2018, he played an audio tape on the House floor with the voices of crying migrant children who had been separated from their undocumented families at the border with Mexico. "This looks like kidnapping," he tweeted before he spoke. After the 2018 election, Lieu won a co-chair position on the Democratic leadership's Policy and Communications Committee.

As a communicator, he has been sensitive to anti-Asian bias, which was sparked during the coronavirus by Trump, among others. Lieu said that references to the "Wuhan virus" were racist and "an example of the myopia that allowed it to spread in the U.S." He was an outspoken critic of Trump's foreign policy. Lieu opposed arms sales to the United Arab Emirates as jeopardizing Israel's "qualitative military edge," even though Trump and Israeli Prime Minister Benjamin Netanyahu had agreed to the sale as an incentive for U.A.E. diplomatic relations with Israel. He said that State and Defense Department officials had "potential legal liability for aiding and abetting war crimes" with their support of arms sales to Saudi Arabia, which used the weapons in its war with Yemen.

Before the first impeachment case against Trump, Lieu pushed Democrats to support the charge that the president's refusal to permit executive branch officials to respond to congressional subpoenas or to testify at hearings was "unprecedented and illegal obstruction." He showed his quick ability to prepare a case when he took the lead with Reps. David Cicilline and Jamie Raskin as they drafted the second impeachment case while they were hiding in the Capitol amid the insurrection by pro-Trump rioters. The three Judiciary Committee members—led by Raskin, a constitutional law professor—wrote that Trump's actions amounted to "willfully inciting violence against the government of the United States." They were the lead sponsors of the impeachment resolution that the House passed on January 13, a week after the turmoil. Lieu was a House manager during the Senate trial.

In his first two reelection campaigns, Lieu was challenged by Kenneth Wright, a pediatric eye surgeon from South Bay, who described himself as a progressive Republican and told the Santa Monica Daily Press that Lieu was "a real bought-out politician." Lieu won 66 percent in 2016 and 70 percent in 2018, when Wright was outspent 6-to-1. In 2020, he faced corporate executive James Bradley, with a similar result, winning 68 percent.

CA-33: Coastal and Central L.A.   Cook Partisan Voting Index: D+19

Population		Race and Ethnicity		Income	
Total	703,908	White	71.40%	Median Income	$117,012
Land area (sq. miles)	289	Black	3.20%	District Income Rank	11
Pop/ sq mi	2,439.21	Latino	13.50%	Poverty Rate	7.70%
Born in State	46.20%	Asian	16.30%	With health insurance	96.00%
		Two or more races	5.70%	Cash public assistance	1.40%
Age Groups		Other	3.50%	Food stamp/SNAP	2.50%
Under 18	18.80%				
18-34	22.90%	**Education**		**Work**	
35-64	40.40%	H.S grad or less	12.80%	White Collar	65.10%
Over 64	18.10%	Some college	20.50%	Sales and Service	28.30%
		College Degree, 4 yr	39.40%	Blue Collar	6.60%
Military		Post grad	27.20%	Government	10.70%
Veteran/ Active Duty	3.90%				

2020 Pres. Vote	Biden	285,906	(69%)	Trump	120,287	(29%)		
2016 Pres. Vote	Clinton	239,982	(68%)	Trump	93,706	(26%)	Johnson	12,485	(4%)

Westside, Santa Monica: Showbiz still sets the tone for the Westside of Los Angeles. It remains tremendously profitable, and not just for the big conglomerate-owned studios. There are tens of thousands of entrepreneurs, actors, writers and craftsmen who are the best in the world at what they do and who tend to cluster on the Westside because so many others in the entertainment business work there. Not everyone is in show business, of course. The Westside is metro Los Angeles's biggest office center, with horrific traffic during the morning and evening rush hours. Most office workers can't afford to live in the limited and expensive neighborhoods nearby. The city's Purple Line subway (which has been renamed the D Line) is being extended to the Westside, a nine-mile extension from Wilshire/Western. Over the objections of Beverly Hills school district officials, the $5.6 billion project includes a tunnel underneath Beverly Hills High School. In May 2020, a local judge ruled that Metro's handling of the construction below the school "satisfied the obligation" under federal environmental laws. Construction broke ground in 2014 and completion has been tentatively set for 2025.

Beverly Hills and the Westside remain the locus of some of America's most expensive residential real estate, where people buy houses for millions of dollars, tear them down, and build new houses for many more millions. Rodeo Drive is one of the world's premier high-priced shopping areas. The L.A. City Council in 2015 imposed restrictions in 20 neighborhoods on what residents described as "mansionization," the building of mansion-like homes that are unusually large for their lots. In its annual review of the most expensive home sales in the United States, the Robb Report—which covers the global luxury market—found that six of the top 20 were in the Beverly Hill area; they were topped by the $165 million purchase by Amazon chief executive Jeff Bezos of the home that movie mogul Jack Warner built in the 1930s on a nine-acre estate.

Iranian Jews have poured in since the Islamic takeover in 1979 and include about 40,000 residents in Beverly Hills—from what had been an estimated 80,000 in Teheran. The old three-block Fairfax district has been home to many Russian Jewish immigrants and a number of corner delis. The closing of the Santa Monica airport, which had been scheduled for 2018, was delayed to 2028—conveniently, when L.A. will host the Olympics. The horrific Woolsey fire in November 2018, reportedly the worst ever in Los Angeles County, destroyed 475 homes, including entire neighborhoods, in Malibu. Rebuilding has been slowed by "restrictive zoning laws," Quartz reported in September 2020.

The 33rd Congressional District of California, the coastal district of Los Angeles, contains luxe Beverly Hills, Brentwood and parts of the Westside, which it shares with the 28th District. It takes in the campus of the University of California, Los Angeles and the J. Paul Getty Museum. Santa Monica is in the 33rd, as are the 21 miles of Malibu on the Pacific Ocean. It dips south to take in Marina del Rey and skirts along the ocean past Los Angeles International Airport to El Segundo— where the Los Angeles Times relocated its downtown office—plus Manhattan Beach and Redondo Beach. Its southernmost point is Rancho Palos Verdes, where, on cliffs overlooking the ocean, is famed architect Frank Lloyd Wright's Wayfarers Chapel, also known as "The Glass Church." With a racial composition that is more than two-thirds white, this is the least ethnically diverse House district in greater Los Angeles. But it is solid Democratic territory, though with a median household income that placed the district among the wealthiest 3 percent in the nation. Joe Biden in 2020 got 69 percent of the vote.

Jimmy Gomez (D)

Elected 2017, 2nd full term, b. Nov 25, 1974; Southern CA; University of CA, Los Angeles, B.A.; Harvard University John F. Kennedy School of Government, M.P.P.; Religion unknown; Married (Mary Hodge).

DC Office: 1530 LHOB 20515, 202-225-6235, Fax: 202-225-2202, gomez.house.gov

State Offices: Los Angeles, 213-481-1425.

Committees: *Oversight & Reform (VChmn)*: Subcommittee on Environment. *Ways & Means*: Health; Worker & Family Support.

Group Ratings

	ADA	ACLU	AFL-CIO	LCV	COC	HAFA	ACU	CFG	FRC
2020	**	83%	**	100%	-	0%	2%	**	-
2019	95%	C	95%	97%	45%	C	4%	24%	0%

Almanac Ratings 2019-2020

	Economy	Social	Foreign	Composite
Liberal	100%	100%	96%	99%
Conservative	0%	0%	4%	1%

Key Votes of the 116th Congress

1. U.S./Mex./Can. trade deal Y	5. Russia sanctions Y	9. Firearms background checks Y
2. First Coronavirus response Y	6. Troops in Syria Y	10. Spending at the border N
3. HEROES Act Y	7. Veto arms sales to Saudis Y	11. Marijuana liberalized rules Y
4. CASH Act Y	8. Defense $$$, veto override N	12. Electoral College objections N

Election Results

Election	Name (Party)	Vote (%)		Cand. Spent	Ind. Exp. Support	Ind. Exp. Oppose
2020 General	Jimmy Gomez (D)	108,792	(53%)	$1,314,606	$14,711	
	David Kim (D)	96,554	(47%)	$79,421	$10,000	$113
2020 Primary	Jimmy Gomez (D)	57,066	(52%)			
	David Kim (D)	23,055	(21%)			
	Frances Yasmeen Motiwalla (D)	14,961	(14%)			
	Keanakay Scott (D)	6,089	(6%)			

Prior winning percentages: 2018 (72%), 2017 special (60%)

Democrat Jimmy Gomez won the June 2017 special election against a leader of the local Korean-American community. He gained a seat on the Ways and Means Committee and became involved in Democratic Caucus activities. His narrow reelection in 2020 against another Korean American signaled that redistricting would influence his future.

Gomez was born and raised in southern California; his parents had immigrated from Mexico in the early 1970s. After graduating from high school, he worked 16 hours daily for several months at a fast-food restaurant and a local superstore. In search of a quality education, he enrolled in a community college and got his bachelor's degree at UCLA and then a master's in public policy from the John F. Kennedy School of Government at Harvard University.

He spent more than a decade working with local and federal officials at the Democratic National Committee and labor unions—most recently as political director of the United Nurses Associations of California. In the state Assembly, where he was first elected in 2012, Gomez styled himself as a progressive. He authored an expansion of California's paid family leave program to cover all workers who paid into it, which was enacted.

The House vacancy was created when Xavier Becerra resigned to fill the vacancy for attorney general of California, which was created when Kamala Harris was elected to the Senate. Becerra's resignation spurred a wide-open contest for his successor. The 24 candidates, who did not include a single Republican, featured several women and supporters of presidential candidate Sen. Bernie Sanders. None of them emerged from the pack. Nine candidates raised more than $100,000. They were led by Robert Lee Ahn, an attorney who worked in his family's real estate business and had been a member of the Los Angeles Planning Commission. He self-financed nearly one-third of the $1.7 million he spent. Gomez was supported by much of the local Democratic establishment, including Becerra. He spent $1.1 million and got more than $300,000 in campaign support from organized labor and Latino groups.

In the primary, Gomez got 25 percent of the vote and Ahn had 22 percent. No other candidate got more than 10 percent. The intra-party contest received less national attention than the four other special elections that were held in early 2017. Gomez won the runoff, 60%-40%, in a contest with a mere 43,000 voters.

Gomez quickly delivered on his promise to confront President Donald Trump and his policies. Referring to family separations at the border with Mexico, he tweeted that Trump's idea of helping California is "terrorizing and tearing families apart." In December 2018, he traveled to the border to investigate reports of illegal rejections of asylum seekers at ports of entry. He and Rep. Nanette Barragán spent the night in what he called a "cage," which was built by border agents and also enclosed refugee children and immigration activists.

When Gomez asked a Justice Department official whether personal data gathered during the census could be referred to law-enforcement agencies, a department lawyer advised in an internal email that they should not give him "too much" response, according to information revealed by a Freedom of Information Act request by The Washington Post. Gomez responded that the emails "prove that the Trump administration is using every tool at their disposal to vilify our immigrant communities." At a July 2020 hearing that focused on the counting of undocumented immigrants, Gomez said the inadequate responses of the director of the Census Bureau showed that "the political appointees of this administration" were making the key decisions in what might become the "worst census ever."

In 2019, Gomez joined Ways and Means, which he called "the frontline in the battle to protect our social safety net system." With Rep. Brad Schneider, he requested that the Internal Revenue Service review the tax-exempt status of the National Rifle Association, citing "self-dealing [and] looting of corporate assets" by NRA directors or members. With other Democrats, he filed a bill to relax requirements for eligibility for federal assistance for low-income beneficiaries. Gomez became vice chairman of the Future Forum, a group of young House Democrats who focused on issues facing young Americans.

After winning his first reelection without major-party opposition, Gomez in 2020 faced a competitive challenge in 2020 from David Kim, an immigration attorney and advocate of liberal proposals, such as "Medicare for All." Kim, a second-generation Korean American, was endorsed by former Democratic presidential candidates Marianne Williamson and Andrew Yang. He criticized Gomez for his large campaign contributions from corporate PACs and said Gomez had given "lip service" to public needs, especially affordable housing. Gomez outspent Kim, $1.3 million to $80,000, but won narrowly, 53%-47%, in a vote count that extended three weeks after Election Day. Kim had strong support in Korea town, which is about one-tenth of the district.

CA-34: Los Angeles   **Cook Partisan Voting Index: D+34**

Population		Race and Ethnicity		Income	
Total	730,042	White	34.70%	Median Income	$52,043
Land area (sq. miles)	48	Black	5.00%	District Income Rank	367
Pop/ sq mi	15,317.71	Latino	59.80%	Poverty Rate	22.10%
Born in State	43.50%	Asian	20.30%	With health insurance	83.40%
		Two or more races	3.80%	Cash public assistance	4.10%
Age Groups		Other	36.30%	Food stamp/SNAP	12.90%
Under 18	19.20%				
18-34	30.80%	Education		Work	
35-64	37.40%	H.S grad or less	50.30%	White Collar	35.10%
Over 64	12.70%	Some college	19.40%	Sales and Service	42.50%
		College Degree, 4 yr	21.70%	Blue Collar	22.40%
Military		Post grad	8.60%	Government	8.90%
Veteran/ Active Duty	2.00%				

2020 Pres. Vote	Biden	193,874	(81%)	Trump	40,552	(17%)		
2016 Pres. Vote	Clinton	154,259	(83%)	Trump	19,784	(11%)	Stein	6,129	(3%)

Downtown/Northeast L.A.: Downtown L.A. has been booming, with thousands of apartments, new hotels, shops and restaurants. Much of the financing has come from foreign investment. Although driving a few blocks can be a Manhattan-type nightmare, the area has become surprisingly pedestrian-friendly, with attractive plazas like the one around the Los Angeles Public Library. This is the heart of the nation's largest county, whose 10 million people are nearly twice as many as Chicago's shrinking Cook County. The New York City metro area exceeds by about 50 percent the population of the L.A. metro area (13.2 million), which includes Long Beach and Anaheim. L.A. is "a capital of commerce and high-energy cultural diversity [where] entire neighborhoods have risen from the dead," Los Angeles Times columnist Steve Lopez wrote in August 2018. But it also is a place where "savage inequality is a crippling travesty." Urban experts voiced concern that the pandemic-forced economic shutdown in these types of neighborhoods will accelerate gentrification. As the Times headlined in August 2020, "Coronavirus has turned once-bustling downtown L.A. into a ghost town. Can it recover?"

South of downtown is the garment district, with factories in nondescript buildings, an economically vibrant area that has helped make Los Angeles-Long Beach the largest manufacturing center in America, with 460,000 workers in 2020. The county's minimum-wage increase to $13.25 in 2018 caused some job loss in the Garment District, with factories moving across the border to Tijuana. The Los Angeles County Economic Development Corporation worried that it has become difficult to find workers with sufficient education and skill sets. As the host of the 2028 Olympics, L.A. will have new opportunities to showcase its strengths and short comings. A heat wave and minimal wind on Labor Day weekend in 2020 resulted in the worst smog levels since 1994.

Surrounding downtown Los Angeles and largely detached from it are ethnically diverse neighborhoods, many of them built in the mid-20th century. They have changed character with every new immigration flow. To the north is Lincoln Heights, one of the oldest neighborhoods in the city and a heavily Hispanic area centered on the busy shopping street of North Broadway. Highland Park and Eagle Rock, which were white middle-class enclaves 30 years ago, are now ethnically mixed and middle-class with large numbers of Latinos and Asians. Eagle Rock is the home of Occidental College, where former President Barack Obama attended his first two years of college. West of downtown is Pico Union, an entry point for new immigrants where Greeks, Mexicans and Central Americans co-mingle. Historic Filipinotown, known locally as Hi-Fi, was settled by Filipinos in the early 1900s and in recent years has become more of a polyglot. Further west toward (but not reaching) Beverly Hills is bustling and increasingly hip Koreatown, with boutique hotels, plus clubs and restaurants for a busy night life. "Despite the COVID-19 pandemic, Koreatown continues to be a hotbed of development," the Los Angeles Business Journal reported in September 2020.

These areas, plus Montecito Heights, Dodger Stadium and Elysian Park, are parts of California's 34th Congressional District. Just east of the Financial District, and on the other side of a maze of interstate highways, the district takes in Brooklyn Heights and Boyle Heights, once an entry neighborhood for Irish and Jewish immigrants and for the past 40 years predominantly Mexican American. This became a slow-growing district, as earlier newcomers moved out to middle-class neighborhoods and incoming immigrants spread more evenly around the Los Angeles Basin. The district is 60 percent Hispanic and 20 percent Asian. Politically, it is in the top 5 percent of Democratic districts in the nation. Joe Biden won 81 percent of the vote, topped in the L.A. area only by the adjacent 37th District.

Norma Torres (D)

Elected 2014, 4th term, b. Apr 04, 1965; Escuintla, Guatemala; Rio Hondo College, Att.; Mount San Antonio College, Att., 2000; National Labor College, B.A., 2012; Roman Catholic; Married (Louis Torres); 3 children.

Elected Office: Pomona City Council, 2000-2006; Pomona Mayor, 2006-2008; CA Assembly, 2008-2013; CA Senate, 2013-2014.

Professional Career: Emergency dispatcher; Sales rep..

DC Office: 2444 RHOB 20515, 202-225-6161, Fax: 202-225-8671, torres.house.gov

State Offices: Ontario, 909-481-6474.

Committees: *Appropriations*: Financial Services & General Government; State, Foreign Operations & Related Programs; Transportation, HUD & Related Agencies. *Rules*: Expedited Procedures; Rules & Organization of the House (Chmn).

Group Ratings

	ADA	ACLU	AFL-CIO	LCV	COC	HAFA	ACU	CFG	FRC
2020	**	81%	**	95%	-	0%	4%	**	-
2019	95%	C	95%	97%	51%	C	4%	18%	0%

Almanac Ratings 2019-2020

	Economy	Social	Foreign	Composite
Liberal	100%	66%	59%	75%
Conservative	0%	34%	41%	25%

Key Votes of the 116th Congress

1. U.S./Mex./Can. trade deal Y	5. Russia sanctions Y	9. Firearms background checks Y
2. First Coronavirus response Y	6. Troops in Syria Y	10. Spending at the border N
3. HEROES Act Y	7. Veto arms sales to Saudis Y	11. Marijuana liberalized rules Y
4. CASH Act Y	8. Defense $$$, veto override Y	12. Electoral College objections N

Election Results

Election	Name (Party)	Vote (%)		Cand. Spent	Ind. Exp. Support	Ind. Exp. Oppose
2020 General	Norma Torres (D)...............................	169,405	(69%)	$754,392	$5,632	
	Mike Cargile (R)............................	74,941	(31%)	$62,630		$113
2020 Primary	Norma Torres (D)...............................	70,813	(71%)			

Prior winning percentages: 2018 (69%), 2016 (72%), 2014 (63%)

Democrat Norma Torres, who won an open seat in 2014, has taken an interest in issues affecting her Central American homeland and her local ports. She has shown her cachet in the House by gaining seats on two of its prime committees: Appropriations and Rules. With longevity, she could become a very influential House member.

Torres was born in Guatemala but entered the United States at age 5, when her parents sent her to live with relatives in Whittier California, so she would be safe from that country's bloody civil war. Her interest in community safety led to work as a 911 dispatcher in Pomona, where she soon developed a deeper interest in public service. One episode was particularly profound: In 1994, while she was handling other calls, a fellow dispatcher put a frantic Spanish-speaking woman on hold because no one else could speak with her. When Torres finally picked up, she heard a domestic dispute escalate, resulting in the shooting death of an 11-year-old. Shaken, she led a successful fight to compel the police to hire more bilingual dispatchers. At age 47, she received her bachelor's degree in labor studies from the National Labor College, where she took online courses.

Torres became involved in broader community issues, especially union organizing and immigrants' rights. She was elected to the Pomona City Council in 2000 and was elected mayor in 2006. The following year, when she returned for the first time to her hometown in Guatemala, she was treated like a celebrity. In 2008, she won a seat in the state Assembly. She chaired the Housing and Community Development Committee, where she helped secure $2 billion for the "Keep Your Home" program to assist homeowners to avoid foreclosure. She wrote a law that modernized the 911 system by directing cell phone callers to their local police department during an emergency. After winning a 2013 special election to the state Senate, Torres championed a law to generate more revenue for programs that train and place doctors in medically underserved communities. To assist immigrants, she coauthored a measure that transferred $3 million to help unaccompanied minors fleeing Central America.

In 2014, Gloria Negrete McLeod decided not to seek reelection to the House and instead ran unsuccessfully for a seat on the San Bernardino County Board of Supervisors. In the all-party primary with five candidates, Torres benefited from a sizable cash advantage, name recognition and endorsements by major unions and liberal women's groups; she got 67 percent to Democrat Christina Gagnier's 15 percent. During the full campaign, she outspent Gagnier $423,000 to $84,000, and won 63%-37%.

During her first term, Torres used her Homeland Security Committee seat to oversee ports of entry at her district's Ontario International Airport and the inland port serving the maritime ports of Los Angeles and Long Beach. She told a reporter for the Inland Valley Daily Bulletin that she was surprised and dismayed by the pervasive partisanship, including in her committee work. "Homeland Security, you think 'that's life and death,'" she said. "But we're not able to work together on this issue." In 2017, she enacted a bill to strengthen sharing and coordination of cyber security information at the ports, following a malware attack at the Los Angeles port.

On international issues, Torres founded the bipartisan Central America Caucus to enhance understanding of the region, including immigration issues. She showed emotion during a House debate on restrictive immigration legislation in 2018 when she recounted her experience in crossing the border as a five-year-old. "I was welcomed here in a loving home. I was not put in a freezing cell," she said, with her voice breaking. "My parents had no choice. My mother died a couple years later. ... Let's help those who can't help themselves." In August 2020, in an op-ed for The Washington Post, she accused the Homeland Security Department of "betraying our values and failing its mandate," and advocated "a study of how best to dismantle the department."

Torres has occasionally been outspoken on domestic issues. In filing police reform legislation in June 2020, she cited her own experience as a dispatcher and said departments should continue investigations into officer misconduct, even if that officer resigns. A year earlier, during House debate of abortion legislation, she said, "it is tiring to hear from so many sex-starved males on this floor talk about a woman's right to choose." When a Republican member cited parliamentary practice and suggested that Torres withdraw her words from the permanent record, she agreed—though the video record remained.

In 2018, Democratic Leader Nancy Pelosi appointed Torres to fill a vacancy on the Rules Committee. Following the election, she was named to the Appropriations Committee, where she said her priorities included expansion of the Gold Line light rail in her district and modernization of the Ontario airport. Torres has been easily reelected against Republican challengers with scant financing.

CA-35: Inland Empire   Cook Partisan Voting Index: D+17

Population		Race and Ethnicity		Income	
Total	764,643	White	52.10%	Median Income	$73,069
Land area (sq. miles)	169	Black	5.30%	District Income Rank	143
Pop/ sq mi	4,527.73	Latino	71.20%	Poverty Rate	12.60%
Born in State	61.80%	Asian	7.40%	With health insurance	89.80%
		Two or more races	5.00%	Cash public assistance	3.00%
Age Groups		Other	30.30%	Food stamp/SNAP	12.20%
Under 18	25.80%				
18-34	26.80%	**Education**		**Work**	
35-64	36.90%	H.S grad or less	52.50%	White Collar	24.50%
Over 64	10.50%	Some college	29.30%	Sales and Service	40.60%
		College Degree, 4 yr	13.50%	Blue Collar	34.80%
Military		Post grad	4.80%	Government	12.50%
Veteran/ Active Duty	3.40%				

2020 Pres. Vote	Biden	166,339	(65%)	Trump	83,352	(33%)			
2016 Pres. Vote	Clinton	127,761	(67%)	Trump	50,824	(27%)	Johnson	5,069	(3%)

Fontana, Ontario: The gateway to the Los Angeles Basin for decades was San Bernardino. This was an agricultural zone until World War II, when Henry J. Kaiser built the West Coast's first major steel mill between the Santa Fe and Southern Pacific rail lines in Fontana, just west of San Bernardino. Today, these lands have largely filled up. The Inland Empire, as it is called, may be where the smog piles up against the mountains, but it also has an energetic small business economy, with lower real-estate costs than elsewhere in the Los Angeles Basin. After the large Kaiser steel mill closed in Fontana in 1994, new businesses moved in to supplant it. Earlier at this site, future California Gov. Arnold Schwarzenegger had a knock-down, drag-out fight with the enemy metal alloy machine in the 1991 blockbuster Terminator 2: Judgment Day.

Business growth has been spurred by huge distribution and warehouse centers that service overseas cargo from the Long Beach port. The recession hit hard in the Inland Empire, with home foreclosures among the highest in the nation and many residents fleeing the region. Jobs returned, with some help from the local California Steel plant that employed about 900 workers in 2020 and became the leading producer of flat rolled steel products in the western United States. Pomona remains the site of the county fairground and a motor speedway. Ontario established a fiber-optic broadband service that city official promote as one of the nation's first "giga-bit communities." Also contributing to the commercial growth is Ontario International Airport, which was transferred from control of Los Angeles International Airport in 2016 and was listed as the fastest-growing in the nation in 2018 and 2019, with service offered by nine airlines. FedEx, which completed in December 2020 its $100 million expansion at the airport, tripled its space for ground services. In October 2020, the city of Pomona replaced Southern California Edison as the local power utility and started to offer its own energy, with a greater share from renewable sources. Pomona used the power lines and infrastructure of its predecessor.

The 35th District is mostly in San Bernardino County, taking in heavily Hispanic areas in Fontana and Ontario. Ontario Mills is described as "California's largest outlet and retail value destination." Also here is part of Chino, a meatpacking area. This district covers Pomona Valley and the city of Pomona in Los Angeles County, though Pomona College is part of the Claremont Colleges a few miles away in the 27th District. The three largest cities—Fontana, Ontario and Pomona—are similar in size and each is about 70 percent Hispanic; the population in Fontana is a bit larger, as is household income. This is a safe Democratic district, though Hillary Clinton's 67%-27% win in 2016 shrunk to 65%-33% for Joe Biden.

Raul Ruiz (D)

Elected 2012, 5th term, b. Aug 25, 1972; Zacatecas, Mexico; University of CA, Los Angeles, B.S., 1994; Harvard University, M.P.P., 2001; Harvard University, M.D., 2001; Harvard University, M.PH, 2007; Seventh-Day Adventist; Married (Monica Ruiz); 2 children (twins).

Professional Career: Emergency physician, Eisenhower Med. Center, 2007-2013; Association dean, University of CA Riverside School of Med., 2011-2012.

DC Office: 2342 RHOB 20515, 202-225-5330, Fax: 202-225-1238, ruiz.house.gov

State Offices: Hemet, 951-765-2304; Palm Desert, 760-424-8888.

Committees: *Energy & Commerce*: Environment & Climate Change; Health; Oversight & Investigations. *Veterans' Affairs*: Disability Assistance & Memorial Affairs.

Group Ratings

	ADA	ACLU	AFL-CIO	LCV	COC	HAFA	ACU	CFG	FRC
2020	**	76%	**	100%	-	0%	8%	**	-
2019	90%	C	100%	97%	65%	C	10%	12%	0%

Almanac Ratings 2019-2020

	Economy	Social	Foreign	Composite
Liberal	100%	100%	80%	94%
Conservative	0%	0%	20%	6%

Key Votes of the 116th Congress

1. U.S./Mex./Can. trade deal	Y	5. Russia sanctions	Y	9. Firearms background checks Y
2. First Coronavirus response	Y	6. Troops in Syria	Y	10. Spending at the border	Y
3. HEROES Act	Y	7. Veto arms sales to Saudis	Y	11. Marijuana liberalized rules	Y
4. CASH Act	Y	8. Defense $$$, veto override Y	12. Electoral College objections N

Election Results

Election	Name (Party)	Vote (%)		Cand. Spent	Ind. Exp. Support	Ind. Exp. Oppose
2020 General	Raul Ruiz (D)	185,151	(60%)	$1,536,441	$9,233	
	Erin Cruz (R)	121,698	(40%)	$4,083		$113
2020 Primary	Raul Ruiz (D)	96,266	(61%)			

Prior winning percentages: 2018 (59%), 2016 (62%), 2014 (54%), 2012 (53%)

Democrat Raul Ruiz, an emergency room doctor, has turned his district safely Democratic after narrowly defeating a veteran Republican incumbent in 2012. He has pursued health care issues on the Energy and Commerce Committee, and has worked on environment and communications issues —including problems that are unique to the desert area of his district.

The son of farmworkers, Ruiz was born and raised in the Coachella Valley. He says he dreamed of being a doctor from a very young age. A family friend paid for Ruiz to apply to the University of California, Los Angeles, but he needed money for tuition. Ruiz went door-to-door in his hometown with a handmade contract, asking for contributions to his college fund in exchange for his future medical service to the community. He raised almost $2,000. After graduating from UCLA, Ruiz went to Harvard Medical School. As a student, he spent almost a year in Chiapas Mexico through a health and social justice organization, Partners in Health. "I came out of there realizing the tremendous nature of poverty and how real policies can actually affect human lives," he later told the Desert Sun newspaper. After graduating from Harvard with three degrees, including master's degrees in public policy and public health, Ruiz returned to the Coachella Valley and served in the emergency room of a nonprofit hospital.

Ruiz was the first Hispanic candidate to oppose Republican Rep. Mary Bono Mack since she won the seat of her late husband, musician Sonny Bono. She won the first round, 58%-42%. Ruiz got more than $1.1 million in support from the Democratic Congressional Campaign Committee. In the final weeks of the race, a local newspaper received an eight-page document from Bono Mack's campaign that outlined a Thanksgiving protest in which Ruiz was arrested and charged with two misdemeanors while attending Harvard. At issue was Ruiz's participation in the National Day of Mourning, an annual event at Plymouth Rock to publicize the suffering of Native Americans. Both charges were dropped in a deal that also discharged claims of police brutality. Ruiz characterized Bono Mack's efforts as desperate. Ruiz was endorsed by the Desert Sun, which said Bono Mack had gotten too comfortable in Congress. He won, 53%-47%.

On the Veterans' Affairs Committee, the former emergency room doctor took on problems with VA hospitals. He catalogued complaints of poor service and filed bills designed to reduce the claims backlog and to make it easier for veterans to use video conferencing for hearings before the Board of Veterans' Appeals. As the senior Democrat on the Natural Resources Subcommittee on Indian, Insular and Native American Affairs, he explored ways to improve health care and economic growth for Native Americans.

After he joined Energy and Commerce in 2017, Democratic leaders touted Ruiz for his bill to mandate benefits in limited-duration health insurance plans and to bar exclusion of individuals with pre-existing conditions. In 2018, he passed a bill to create a demonstration program for increased access to treatment of opioid use; his measure was wrapped into broader legislation that was enacted later that year. Ruiz also enacted his bill to expand broadband access for Native American tribes in the Coachella Valley.

Ruiz and Republican Rep. Brad Wenstrup of Ohio—another physician—formed a caucus that worked on behalf of veterans with ailments that likely were caused by burn pits used for waste and chemical disposal in Iraq and Afghanistan. The defense spending bill enacted in 2018 included their amendment to end the use of burn pits. In September 2020, Ruiz joined Sen. Kirsten Gillibrand in filing a bill to provide care for veterans who were victims of these pits; comedian Jon Stewart, who joined their announcement, had become an advocate for the cause.

The huge yearend spending bill in December 2020 included two provisions for which Ruiz took credit: the closing of a gap in Medicare coverage that forced some seniors to pay higher premiums, and $153 million for a project to address hazardous air quality that has resulted from decreased water levels in the Salton Sea, which is in his district.

In 2014, Ruiz was a top target of the National Republican Congressional Committee. He benefited from extensive media coverage of two airplane flights during which he provided emergency service to other passengers. Against Brian Nestande, a Republican Assemblyman and a former top aide to Bono Mack, Ruiz outspent $3.1 million to $1.3 million and won, 54%-46%.

Two years later, Ruiz showed interest in an open Senate seat, but deferred to two better-known Democrats, including Kamala Harris. The candidacy of Rep. Loretta Sanchez limited his opportunity to rally Latino support. Instead, he was opposed for reelection by Republican state Sen. Jeffrey Stone, the former mayor of Temecula. The outcome was a 62%-38% blowout for Ruiz. In 2018, Republican Kimberlin Brown Pelzer, a former television actress, criticized the National Republican Congressional Committee's "giving structure." Ruiz outspent her 3-to-1 and won, 59%-41%. Two years later, Ruiz outspent his opponent, 1.5 million to $4,100 and won 60 percent—strong evidence that he controls a once-secure Republican seat.

In 2021, Ruiz chaired the Congressional Hispanic Caucus.

CA-36: Eastern Riverside County   Cook Partisan Voting Index: D+4

Population		Race and Ethnicity		Income	
Total	755,764	White	71.20%	Median Income	$58,728
Land area (sq. miles)	5,913	Black	4.90%	District Income Rank	284
Pop/ sq mi	127.82	Latino	48.80%	Poverty Rate	15.50%
Born in State	56.40%	Asian	3.90%	With health insurance	91.60%
		Two or more races	3.50%	Cash public assistance	3.30%
Age Groups		Other	16.40%	Food stamp/SNAP	10.80%
Under 18	20.20%				
18-34	20.40%	Education		Work	
35-64	35.80%	H.S grad or less	43.50%	White Collar	30.70%
Over 64	23.50%	Some college	32.30%	Sales and Service	47.30%
		College Degree, 4 yr	15.10%	Blue Collar	22.00%
Military		Post grad	9.10%	Government	14.20%
Veteran/ Active Duty	7.30%				

2020 Pres. Vote	Biden	173,573	(56%)	Trump	131,304	(42%)			
2016 Pres. Vote	Clinton	123,795	(52%)	Trump	103,051	(43%)	Johnson	6,172	(3%)

Indio, Palm Springs: From the air a few decades ago, a night flight east from Los Angeles flew over the lights of homes of 10 million people and then into almost perfect darkness. The city then was a vast metropolis surrounded by almost uninhabited territory. Today, the sprinkled pattern of white lights has spread into the Inland Empire around Riverside and San Bernardino and has multiplied outward into the desert. Over the 10,000-foot-high San Jacinto Mountains, desert communities boomed: Palm Springs was once the lone winter resort for the stars but now is popular for its retro architecture and as a destination for gay couples. Reflecting a more youthful and open culture, including trendy hotels and clubs, it became in 2017 the first city in the nation in which all elected officials are LGBT: three gay men, a transgender woman and a bisexual woman. In 2020, the council chose Christy Holstege as mayor, which reportedly made her the first out bisexual mayor in the nation. Palm Springs is one of a string of communities along Highway 111 and Frank Sinatra and Bob Hope drives. The clean, dry, roomy desert, where the days are almost always crystal clear and the sky usually cloudless, generated nearly $8 billion in tourist revenue in 2018.Two presidents retired to the desert and its many golf courses here: Dwight Eisenhower wintered in Palm Desert, and Gerald Ford resided for 30 years in nearby Rancho Mirage.

The growth in the Coachella Valley has been chiefly in heavily Latino and fast-growing agricultural cities. The valley's nine cities extend from Palm Springs south and east to Coachella. Of its roughly 1 million acres, 700,000 have been designated for conservation, which keeps them mostly pristine. The area produces roughly 95 percent of the dates consumed in the U.S. The annual music and arts festival in Coachella, which began in 1999, has become the largest music festival in the world, with the most revenue. In 2019, it sold out each of its six days of performances during two weekends in April, with daily sales of 125,000. Tickets at $429 for the weekend sold out within one hour. A third weekend for the Stagecoach country music festival attracted 75,000 daily. The estimated impact for the local economy was $494 million. With its scenic location in the desert and a relatively short drive from Los Angeles, the events draw wide attention in the entertainment world.

The 36th District covers eastern Riverside County. Interstate 10 runs through the district, taking in Banning and Beaumont on the western side and stretching east to Blythe at the Arizona border. There are huge socioeconomic contrasts: Per capita income of $45,600 in Palm Springs is more than 60 percent higher than that of Indio and nearly three times Coachella. Officials in Indio, which is 64 percent Hispanic, unveiled in January 2020 plans for downtown revitalization, including more housing and entertainment. Joshua Tree National Park, with its high-desert sands, is a popular tourist spot here. The 36th is the largest and least urban of three congressional districts that are entirely within Riverside. Its Hispanic population has grown to 49 percent. This has been a politically competitive district, though Joe Biden's 56%-42% win continued a trend toward Democrats.

Karen Bass (D)

Elected 2010, 6th term, b. Oct 03, 1953; Los Angeles, CA; University of Southern CA School of Medicine; San Diego State University, 1973; CA State University - Dominguez Hills, B.S., 1990; Baptist; Divorced; 2 children (1 deceased); 4 stepchildren.

Elected Office: CA Assembly, 2005-2010, speaker, 2008-2010.

Professional Career: Physician's Assistant, Los Angeles County General Hosp.; Instructor, University of S. CA; Executive Director, Community Coalition, 1990-2004.

DC Office: 2059 RHOB 20515, 202-225-7084, Fax: 202-225-2422, bass.house.gov

State Offices: Los Angeles, 323-965-1422.

Committees: *Foreign Affairs*: Africa, Global Health & Global Human Rights (Chmn). *Judiciary*: Courts, Intellectual Property & Internet; Crime, Terrorism & Homeland Security.

Group Ratings

	ADA	ACLU	AFL-CIO	LCV	COC	HAFA	ACU	CFG	FRC
2020	**	83%	**	100%	-	0%	3%	**	-
2019	90%	C	95%	93%	44%	C	3%	19%	0%

Almanac Ratings 2019-2020

	Economy	Social	Foreign	Composite
Liberal	100%	56%	96%	84%
Conservative	0%	44%	4%	16%

Key Votes of the 116th Congress

1. U.S./Mex./Can. trade deal	Y	5. Russia sanctions	Y	9. Firearms background checks Y
2. First Coronavirus response	Y	6. Troops in Syria	Y	10. Spending at the border N
3. HEROES Act	Y	7. Veto arms sales to Saudis	Y	11. Marijuana liberalized rules Y
4. CASH Act	Y	8. Defense $$$, veto override	Y	12. Electoral College objections N

Election Results

Election	Name (Party)	Vote (%)	Cand. Spent	Ind. Exp. Support	Ind. Exp. Oppose
2020 General	Karen Bass (D)	254,916 (86%)	$1,255,347	$137	
	Errol Webber (R)	41,705 (14%)	$146,671		$113
2020 Primary	Karen Bass (D)	140,425 (88%)			

Prior winning percentages: 2018 (89%), 2016 (81%), 2014 (84%), 2012 (86%), 2010 (86%)

Karen Bass, elected in 2010, is a former California Assembly speaker and an influential House Democrat who emerged onto the national political scene when she was among the finalists Joe Biden considered as his running mate in 2020. She has shown impressive leadership skills, including on Africa-related legislation and on Democratic Party organization, and she gained several plum assignments when Democrats regained House control. Bass has drawn flattering comparisons to another speaker from California, Nancy Pelosi.

Bass was born and raised in Los Angeles. Her father was a letter carrier and her mother was a homemaker. Her father had moved to California from Texas after World War II; her mother was a Los Angeles native who learned to speak Spanish as a child. At age 14, Bass got involved in Democratic Sen. Robert F. Kennedy's 1968 presidential campaign by signing up her mother as a precinct captain and then doing all the neighborhood canvassing herself. At her high school in West Los Angeles, Bass joined her teachers in protests against the Vietnam War. She attended San Diego State University and stayed active in community organizing. Bass received a nursing certificate from the University of Southern California and a bachelor's degree from California State University, Dominguez Hills. "School wound up being rather secondary for me," she said. Bass served on a committee that investigated accusations of police abuses in Los Angeles.

In 1990, Bass founded the Community Coalition, a nonprofit that worked with African-American and Latino communities in South Los Angeles to combat drug use and gang violence by shutting down liquor stores and motels. The group campaigned against Proposition 187, which sought to deny public services to illegal immigrants, and Proposition 209, which prohibited affirmative action admissions policies in public universities. Bass served as executive director for 14 years.

Bass won election to the state Assembly in 2004. She sponsored several bills aimed at reforming the foster care system and expanding health insurance programs for children. In her first term in the term-limited Assembly, she was majority whip; in her second, she was majority leader; and in her third term, she became the first Black female speaker in any state legislature in the United States. Trying to balance California's budget in the midst of a fiscal crisis consumed much of her tenure. She negotiated budget compromises with Gov. Arnold Schwarzenegger that included cuts to education and social spending. Bass described her two years as speaker as "painful" and said, "I ran for office because I wanted to create, build, and expand programs, not tear them apart."

In 2010, when she ran for an open House seat, other prominent Democrats stayed out of the race, assuming Bass would easily win on turf she had represented in the Assembly. She won the Democratic primary with 86 percent of the vote. In the general election, she got 86 percent. She has not faced a serious reelection challenge.

Bass has taken on leadership assignments. On Foreign Affairs, as the senior Democrat on the Subcommittee on Africa, Global Health, Global Human Rights and International Organizations, her work has included successful efforts to extend the African Growth and Opportunity Act. During the Ebola crisis in 2014, she urged President Barack Obama to send U.S. troops to care for Ebola patients in west Africa. In 2018, Congress enacted a revised version of her bill to promote democracy and economic recovery in Zimbabwe.

At the same time she took over as Africa subcommittee chairman in 2019, Bass unexpectedly became chairwoman—in an interim status—of the Judiciary Subcommittee on Crime, Terrorism and Homeland Security. Rep. Sheila Jackson Lee of Texas stepped aside from that post (for what turned out to be two years), pending an Ethics Committee investigation of her handling of sexual-abuse claims by a former aide. Bass has maintained her advocacy of the poor and disadvantaged. She created the Congressional Caucus on Foster Youth and has filed several bills to improve foster care. The comprehensive bill enacted in 2018 to fight opioid addiction included a Bass provision to promote health insurance for former foster youth.

In addition to policy, Bass has pursued partisan interests. She co-chaired the Democratic Congressional Campaign Committee's Women LEAD program, charged with recruiting more female candidates. She has charged that Republican voter identification legislation was aimed at curtailing minorities' voting participation. "One of the darkest shadows of the past century is creeping into this one: one of our most basic rights—the right to vote, a right that we fought for and won—is under attack," she said.

Her previous platforms set the stage for Bass' increased prominence in 2019-20 as chairwoman of the Congressional Black Caucus, which grew to 55 members (including two senators) following the 2018 election. It turned out to be a busy time, including urban protests in response to multiple police actions that led many to believe that the nation remained divided by racial injustice. The death in July 2020 of the iconic Rep. John Lewis from pancreatic cancer marked a milestone for the civil rights movement in which he was a pioneer. Plus, President Donald Trump's hostility to improving race relations—real or in partisan terms—raised the stakes, including his bid for reelection, as did the pivotal role that African-American voters played in giving the Democratic nomination to Biden. The various tensions were compounded by the pandemic, which had a disproportionate impact nationally on African Americans.

Bass used her CBC platform to provide both rhetorical and policy leadership. With Pelosi's encouragement, she was instrumental in assembling House-passed legislation to offer national guidance for reform of police practices, which are set mostly at state and local levels. She also was mindful that many people—of all races, at home and abroad—looked to the CBC for guidance or inspiration, from an insider perspective. The death of Lewis placed the spotlight on changes in the CBC, in terms of both its leaders and its growing membership. In a sense, Bass summarized the role of the CBC when she became chairwoman in January 2019. The CBC, she said, "will exercise every ounce of our power and influence to continue the fight for justice."

As it turned out, the spotlight had only begun to shine on Bass. In the lengthy deliberations by Biden and his team over selection of his running mate, Bass received prominent attention. Why did that happen? One factor was that Biden stated publicly that he would select a woman as his running mate. Later, he said that he wanted to select a vice president who was a racial minority. Another insight might be that with Bass at age 67, she would be less likely to want to succeed Biden. "Now that the White House finally seems within reach, [Biden] does not want to be outshone, according to people who know him," The Atlantic speculated. One limitation, as that analysis noted, is that Bass does not fit among the "larger-than-life characters" who often are tapped for national office.

Ultimately, Bass had some downsides that were not a factor with Kamala Harris, the Californian whom Biden did select. Bass' praise of former Cuban President Fidel Castro would be "politically poisonous" in Florida, Politico wrote. Others noted that she was largely unknown to Biden, as well as to voters outside California.

Bass seemed to enjoy the spotlight and was content to return to her previous life, once Biden went with Harris. And the speculation likely was a plus for her prospects in the House, where a leadership shuffle was on the horizon and many colleagues—including Pelosi—had spoken positively about her. More than ever, her profile as an African-American woman from California would offer a large base in the Democratic Caucus.

CA-37: Los Angeles

Cook Partisan Voting Index: D+36

Population		Race and Ethnicity		Income	
Total	733,668	White	50.20%	Median Income	$69,573
Land area (sq. miles)	55	Black	21.90%	District Income Rank	170
Pop/ sq mi	13,276.66	Latino	40.00%	Poverty Rate	16.00%
Born in State	49.10%	Asian	9.20%	With health insurance	89.90%
		Two or more races	3.90%	Cash public assistance	3.80%
Age Groups		Other	14.80%	Food stamp/SNAP	10.40%
Under 18	18.70%				
18-34	30.40%	Education		Work	
35-64	38.00%	H.S grad or less	35.70%	White Collar	45.20%
Over 64	12.80%	Some college	24.10%	Sales and Service	39.10%
		College Degree, 4 yr	23.90%	Blue Collar	15.70%
Military		Post grad	16.30%	Government	12.00%
Veteran/ Active Duty	2.80%				

2020 Pres. Vote	Biden	275,573	(84%)	Trump	45,202	(14%)		
2016 Pres. Vote	Clinton	236,621	(85%)	Trump	26,608	(10%)	Stein	6,355	(2%)

Western L.A./South L.A., Culver City: Since the Los Angeles riots of 1992 and 1965, the city has had to live down its reputation as being inhospitable to African Americans, a problem exacerbated by racial tensions in the city's police department. This was the epicenter of L.A.'s two postwar riots, in the Watts district in 1965 and at the corner of Florence and Normandie in 1992. But by other measures, Blacks in Los Angeles have been doing better than those elsewhere in the United States. Job opportunities—up to and including the office of mayor for 20 years—have been relatively good. The long-simmering tension between the LAPD and the African-American community has been ameliorated by the region's changing demographics, with significant reduction in reported crime. Former Los Angeles Mayor Antonio Villaraigosa proudly noted that two-thirds of the city's police officers were non-white, as was nearly half the command staff. A less positive, though dramatic, side of the story has emerged. Partly due to the high cost of housing, Blacks fell from 17 percent of Los Angeles in the 1980s to 9 percent (of both the city and county) in 2017. Watts has become more than 70 percent Latino. The city ranked 40th out of 52 cities in the nation in terms of housing and income for the Blacks who have remained, L.A.-based urban-affairs scholar Joel Kotkin wrote.

The shortage of housing has been a spur to gentrification and rising prices. Baldwin Hills is a high-income, African-American neighborhood. Near View Park-Windsor Hills along Slauson Avenue are other comfortable Black-majority neighborhoods. Crenshaw, an Art Deco neighborhood built in the 1920s and 1930s, is the birthplace of West Coast hip hop music. In one of the more rundown sections of Crenshaw, former L.A. Lakers basketball star (and current Lakers executive) Magic Johnson built his multiplex theaters. The once desolate Culver City, which features sprawling studios and media businesses, has experienced an urban renaissance and is home to trendy new restaurants and a historically restored Culver Hotel. Local accessibility will benefit from the opening, delayed until late 2021, of an 8.5-mile light-rail line from Crenshaw to Los Angeles International Airport, at a $2 billion cost. In September 2020, the Los Angeles Times described the "new energy" in Leimert Park

These parts of Los Angeles are the heart of the 37th Congressional District, which is bisected by the Santa Monica Freeway. The district includes the University of Southern California, a private university with more than 43,000 students, and the adjacent Los Angeles Memorial Coliseum, which has hosted two Olympics, many famous concerts and speeches, and is the home of USC football. On 11 acres near Exposition Park, the scheduled completion date is late 2021 for the $1.5 billion museum of narrative art that will house the huge art collection of filmmaker George Lucas, who earlier sought to base the museum in Chicago. As described by Art News, Lucas "looks to change how a museum can be a part of society…an institution that places its audience at the core of everything it does." Its director described it as "the idea of how the mass image can expand art history in many ways."

Among the other cultural landmarks are the California Science Center, the Natural History Museum and the California African American Museum. The District is about 40 percent Latino and 22 percent Black. Even with that declining total, the 37th surpassed the 43rd districts for the highest share of Black residents in all of California. With its Democratic PVI of +37. it is one of the most Democratic districts in the nation and the strongest in L.A. Joe Biden got 84 percent of the local vote.

Linda Sánchez (D)

Elected 2002, 10th term, b. Jan 28, 1969; Orange, CA; University of CA, Berkeley, B.A., 1991; University of CA School of Law, Los Angeles (JD), J.D., 1995; Roman Catholic; Married (James M. Sullivan); 1 child ; 3 stepchildren.

Professional Career: Practicing attorney, 1995-1998; Executive Secretary treas. Of Orange County AFL-CIO, 2000-2002.

DC Office: 2329 RHOB 20515, 202-225-6676, Fax: 202-226-1012, lindasanchez.house.gov

State Offices: Norwalk, 562-860-5050.

Committees: *Ways & Means*: Select Revenue Measures; Social Security; Trade.

Group Ratings

	ADA	ACLU	AFL-CIO	LCV	COC	HAFA	ACU	CFG	FRC
2020	**	80%	**	95%	-	0%	4%	**	-
2019	95%	C	95%	97%	55%	C	4%	19%	0%

Almanac Ratings 2019-2020

	Economy	Social	Foreign	Composite
Liberal	100%	100%	92%	98%
Conservative	0%	0%	8%	2%

Key Votes of the 116th Congress

1. U.S./Mex./Can. trade deal	Y	5. Russia sanctions	Y
2. First Coronavirus response	Y	6. Troops in Syria	Y
3. HEROES Act	Y	7. Veto arms sales to Saudis	Y
4. CASH Act	Y	8. Defense $$$, veto override	Y

9. Firearms background checks Y
10. Spending at the border   N
11. Marijuana liberalized rules Y
12. Electoral College objections N

Election Results

Election	Name (Party)	Vote (%)		Cand. Spent	Ind. Exp. Support	Ind. Exp. Oppose
2020 General	Linda Sánchez (D)	190,467	(74%)	$971,556	$1,500	$750
	Michael Tolar (D)	65,739	(26%)			
2020 Primary	Linda Sánchez (D)	90,872	(78%)			
	Michael Tolar (D)	26,075	(22%)			

Prior winning percentages: 2018 (69%), 2016 (71%), 2014 (59%), 2012 (68%), 2010 (63%), 2008 (70%), 2006 (66%), 2004 (61%), 2002 (55%)

Linda Sánchez, first elected in 2002, provided a younger and outspoken voice in the Democratic leadership. Her hope to take a more prominent position crashed following the 2018 election when her husband, a business executive in Connecticut, was indicted for using tax payer funds to pay for personal expenses. Sanchez remained a member of the Ways and Means Committee, where she has been a defender of the Affordable Care Act. In January 2021, she said she would play an active role on immigration legislation.

Sanchez is one of the seven children of Mexican immigrant parents Ignacio Sánchez, a machinist, and Maria Macias, a bilingual education aide in an elementary school. Her parents met while trying to organize a union at a tire shop where they worked when they were young. She earned her bachelor's degree in Spanish literature at the University of California, Berkeley, and her law degree at the University of California, Los Angeles, working her way through school with jobs as a security guard, nanny and teacher's aide. She became a civil rights lawyer and was executive secretary-treasurer of the Orange County Federation of Labor. Her sister Loretta Sánchez served 20 years in the House before she ran unsuccessfully for the Senate in 2016. "She's definitely the more liberal one," Loretta said.

When the new district lines were unveiled after the 2000 census, Linda Sánchez was one of six Democrats who ran for the seat. Her most important asset was her sister's support. She tapped Loretta's extensive fundraising network, walked precincts with her, and appeared in a television commercial with her. These connections gave Linda Sánchez an advantage over her two chief opponents, who were better known when the race began: Assemblywoman Sally Havice and South Gate Councilman Hector De La Torre.

Sánchez's ties to labor helped her build a strong voter-turnout operation. She won the endorsement of then-House Minority Whip Nancy Pelosi of California. Her opponents charged that she was a political opportunist who abandoned her married name and residence to revive her Latina roots and run in the new district. She won the primary with 33 percent of the vote; De La Torre received 29 percent and Havice had 19 percent. In November, Republican Tim Escobar called her an inexperienced liberal extremist. Sánchez won 55%-41%, and she has been reelected easily since.

Sánchez has a strongly liberal voting record. In the Almanac vote ratings, her scores have ranked among the most liberal on economic issues. She has sponsored bills to end the Social Security Administration's policy of denying benefits to same-sex couples and to establish a federal definition of school bullying to protect vulnerable students, including those who have been targeted because of their sexual orientation.

When Democrats held the majority and George W. Bush was president, Sánchez chaired the Judiciary Subcommittee on Commercial and Administrative Law, where she held hearings to oversee allegations that his administration had initiated politically motivated firings of U.S. attorneys around the country. After senior White House political adviser Karl Rove refused to cooperate, Sánchez initiated a contempt of Congress action. Rove capitulated after Bush left office. As the top Democrat on the Ethics Committee, she was at the center of several thorny cases. Later, as co-founder of the House Trade Working Group, Sánchez pledged tougher review of proposed international trade deals that she feared would ship jobs overseas. She helped to lead opposition to the Trans-Pacific Partnership agreement.

Following the 2016 election, Sánchez was elected vice chair of the Democratic Caucus. She cited her background as a working mother in the contest with Rep. Barbara Lee, also of California, which she won 98-96.

Her ambitions were severely damaged when Sanchez said during a C-SPAN interview in October 2017 that "it's time to pass the torch to a new generation of leaders." At that point, when Democratic prospects for regaining control of the House seemed slim, she might have prevailed if Democrats had remained in the minority. The landscape for House Democrats, of course, changed when they gained 40 seats and Pelosi moved to reclaim her position as Speaker.

Two days after the 2018 election, Sanchez's leadership prospects were extinguished when her husband, James Sullivan, a lobbyist and former chairman of the Connecticut Municipal Electric Energy Cooperative, was indicted with other executives for diverting federal funds to cover his personal travel. The indictment was all the more perilous for Sánchez because she had attended related events as Sullivan's spouse, though she said she had received advice from the Ethics Committee. When the criminal action was disclosed, she withdrew from the contest for caucus chair. She joined a group of House Democratic dissidents who opposed Pelosi's bid for Speaker. When Pelosi agreed to serve no more than four more years as Speaker, Sanchez agreed with others to endorse her. But her prospects for moving up the political ladder had dimmed and her future was in question.

In January 2021, she sought to return to the arena as chair of the Immigration Task Force of the Hispanic Caucus. In response to President Joe Biden's call for comprehensive legislation, she also announced formation of "The Closers"—a group of six veteran House Democratic women, including four from California, "who have dedicated their careers to reforming our immigration system and who will see this through until we win."

CA-38: Eastern L.A. suburbs　　　　　　　　　　　　　Cook Partisan Voting Index: D+17

Population		Race and Ethnicity		Income	
Total	704,515	White	41.40%	Median Income	$79,573
Land area (sq. miles)	101	Black	4.80%	District Income Rank	97
Pop/ sq mi	6,943.77	Latino	61.50%	Poverty Rate	8.90%
Born in State	61.20%	Asian	16.10%	With health insurance	91.80%
		Two or more races	3.70%	Cash public assistance	2.50%
Age Groups		Other	34.00%	Food stamp/SNAP	6.80%
Under 18	21.40%				
18-34	24.50%	Education		Work	
35-64	38.40%	H.S grad or less	44.10%	White Collar	33.70%
Over 64	15.70%	Some college	31.00%	Sales and Service	42.50%
		College Degree, 4 yr	17.20%	Blue Collar	23.80%
Military		Post grad	7.70%	Government	14.60%
Veteran/ Active Duty	3.70%				

2020 Pres. Vote	Biden	207,000	(66%)	Trump	101,867	(32%)			
2016 Pres. Vote	Clinton	166,224	(67%)	Trump	68,033	(27%)	Johnson	6,730	(3%)
	Stein	5,055	(2%)						

Whittier, Norwalk: In the years just after World War II, much of southeast Los Angeles County was farmland—citrus groves and dairy farms. In the next two decades, housing subdivisions were built and new cities incorporated so that what had been a few towns separated by farmland became one continuous swath of suburbia. The towns were different in character. Whittier, founded by Midwestern Quakers, was the hometown of Richard Nixon, a young lawyer who was elected to Congress in 1946. Lakewood, just north of Long Beach, used to be an area of lima bean fields. Developers built it up so rapidly in the 1950s that Life magazine featured it as one of the first mass-produced suburbs.

Most of these communities are known as Gateway Cities in southeast Los Angeles County: Artesia, which Dutch and Portuguese dairy experts developed into a major dairy center for Southern California; Pico Rivera, which is 91 percent Hispanic; and La Mirada, named by Rand McNally Publishing founder Andrew McNally when he purchased 2,300 acres in the area in the late 1800s. After World War II, Montebello became a center of the large community of displaced Armenians. They built a monument to martyrs of the Armenian genocide. In the northern part of Montebello, a few miles from downtown Los Angeles, Southern California Gas Co. has a few dozen wells that produce oil and natural gas; as recently as the 1990s, some leaked onto nearby properties. In Norwalk, Southern California Edison operates the world's first hybrid battery and gas turbine power plants —a cleaner alternative during periods of peak demand. Officials of the L.A. Metro plan to extend their light-rail Green Line (now referred to as the C Line) from Norwalk to connect it with the transit station at LAX, which could become a commuter alternative to the crowded freeways and has been described as the "missing link" for regional transit.

The 38th Congressional District encompasses Whittier and some of the Gateway Cities in southeast Los Angeles County. It extends from outside Monterey Park nearly to Long Beach. It includes Norwalk, the district's largest city, which is 70 percent Hispanic, South El Monte and Montebello. Its small northern tip of Orange County amounts to 3 percent of the district. The 38th is 62 percent Hispanic and solidly Democratic. Joe Biden got 66 percent of the vote in 2020, which was virtually the same as the Democratic vote in the previous two presidential elections—contrary to the slippage of support among Latinos elsewhere.

Young Kim (R)

Elected 2020, 1st term, b. Oct 18, 1962; Incheon, South Korea; University of Southern CA, B.S., 1985; Christian - Non-Denominational; Married (Charles Kim); 4 children.

Elected Office: Assembly Member, CA State Assembly, District 65, 2014-2016.

Professional Career: Producer/Radio and Television Host, 1997-2011; Director of Community Relations and Asian Affairs, Representative Ed Royce.

DC Office: 1306 LHOB 20515, 202-225-4111, Fax: 202-225-1776, youngkim.house.gov

State Offices: Placentia, 714-984-2440.

Committees: *Foreign Affairs*: Africa, Global Health & Global Human Rights; Asia, the Pacific, Central Asia, Nonproliferation. *Science, Space & Technology*: Space & Aeronautics. *Small Business*: Economic Growth, Tax & Capital Access; Innovation, Entrepreneurship & Workforce Development (RMM).

Election Results

Election	Name (Party)	Vote (%)		Cand. Spent	Ind. Exp. Support	Ind. Exp. Oppose
2020 General	Young Kim (R)............................. 173,946	(51%)		$5,800,814	$16,117	$2,754,903
	Gil Cisneros (D)............................... 169,837	(49%)		$4,287,049	$1,252,091	$117,594
2020 Primary	Young Kim (R)............................. 83,941	(48%)				

Republican Young Kim won a rematch of the contest she lost to Democrat Gil Cisneros in 2018. Following her first campaign, Kim believed that she had won and joined the orientation for new House members at the Capitol the week after the election, only to learn that the delayed vote count flipped the outcome. Two years later, the vote tally was closer but the result became official more quickly.

As a former member of the California Assembly and a longtime congressional aide, Kim had a longer record than Cisneros, who financed his first run for Congress with some of the $266 million he won in the Mega Millions lottery. Her success on her second attempt resulted, in part, because Cisneros had compiled a record in Congress, including his vote for the impeachment of President Donald Trump, which Kim moved to turn against him.

Along with Michelle Steel, another experienced Republican in Orange County who defeated a freshman Democrat who had been new to politics, Kim offered hope for Republicans, who have struggled in California for many years. Prior to 2018, their two upscale districts with large and diverse minority populations had long been held by white male Republicans.

Kim, born in Inchon South Korea, departed Seoul as a teenager when her family moved to Guam and then to Hawaii. She got a bachelor's degree in business administration from the University of Southern California. After jobs as a financial analyst and with a clothing firm, she and her husband created their own company manufacturing women's clothing.

Kim, meanwhile, made contact with her local Republican Rep. Ed Royce soon after he was first elected in 1992. Her responsibilities with Royce, which included community liaison and director of Asian affairs, continued for 21 years. She also hosted a program on Korean-language radio. In 2014, Kim defeated an incumbent Democrat to win a seat in the California Assembly. She worked on legislation to protect victims of domestic violence. Two years later, she lost a rematch with her predecessor.

When Royce, who chaired the House Foreign Affairs Committee, announced his retirement in January 2018, he immediately endorsed Kim as his successor. That jungle primary became a wide-open contest with five Republicans and five Democrats. Kim, who was the early frontrunner, led the first round of voting with 21 percent of the vote, followed by the previously little-known Cisneros, who received 19 percent.

Cisneros, who self-financed more than $9 million of the $12 million of his campaign spending, voiced conventional themes—a call for new leadership" in Washington and criticism of Republican handling of health care. Kim, who spent nearly $3 million, embraced Republican themes. In addition, the two national parties spent more than $10 million on the contest.

At an October debate, Kim cited her three decades living in the area: "I look like the district, I talk like the district and I fit the district." But the national Democratic tide was enough to give Cisneros a 52%-48% victory. Kim and Cisneros nearly divided the vote in Orange and San Bernardino counties. His nearly 10,000-vote margin in Los Angeles County, which cast one-fourth of the total vote, put Cisneros over the top.

When Kim announced her second run in May 2019, she got the early endorsement of House Minority Leader Kevin McCarthy and the other Republicans in the California delegation. This time, both candidates cleared the field. In May 2020, when Congress expedited passage of $3 trillion for economic relief of COVID-19 restrictions, Kim attacked Cisneros for having "once again blindly fallen in line with his party leaders." She criticized Speaker Nancy Pelosi for her partisan handling of the measure and the failure to work across the aisle.

The rematch also featured a significant change in campaign spending: Kim slightly outspent Cisneros. And the incumbent financed less than 10 percent of his costs. With her victory, Kim led by about 10,000 votes in Orange County, which cast nearly two-thirds of the total. She managed to reduce the advantage for Cisneros in Los Angeles County to about 7,000 votes.

Her victory made Kim the third woman born in South Korea to join the incoming class of House freshman. The others are Steel, her longtime friend from Orange County whom Kim calls her "sister," and Marilyn Strickland, a Democrat from Washington.

CA-39: Northern Orange County

Cook Partisan Voting Index: D+3

Population		Race and Ethnicity		Income	
Total	717,176	White	51.90%	Median Income	$96,431
Land area (sq. miles)	204	Black	1.70%	District Income Rank	40
Pop/ sq mi	3,508.69	Latino	32.90%	Poverty Rate	7.40%
Born in State	54.20%	Asian	32.70%	With health insurance	93.10%
		Two or more races	3.80%	Cash public assistance	1.50%
Age Groups		Other	9.80%	Food stamp/SNAP	4.30%
Under 18	20.90%				
18-34	21.90%	**Education**		**Work**	
35-64	40.60%	H.S grad or less	28.10%	White Collar	44.60%
Over 64	16.60%	Some college	28.80%	Sales and Service	39.20%
		College Degree, 4 yr	28.40%	Blue Collar	16.20%
Military		Post grad	14.60%	Government	13.40%
Veteran/ Active Duty	4.20%				

2020 Pres. Vote	Biden	190,090	(54%)	Trump	154,439	(44%)			
2016 Pres. Vote	Clinton	140,231	(51%)	Trump	116,783	(43%)	Johnson	9,850	(4%)

Fullerton, Yorba Linda: During the Southern California land boom in the 1880s, Massachusetts grain merchants George and Edward Amerige headed west in search of new business opportunities. They went on a duck hunting trip near Anaheim and eventually opened a real estate business in the city. Through negotiations with railroad agent George Fullerton, the Ameriges eventually purchased 430 acres of land for $68,000 and allowed the railroad the right-of-way—provided, of course, that the railway's route include the new town they were developing. Local residents later voted to name the locale Fullerton, and it developed as a prime source of juicy Valencia oranges.

Today, the city is home to California State University, Fullerton, which enrolls about 41,000 students, with the largest business school in the state and a payroll of 4,000 faculty and staff. Nearby is affluent Yorba Linda, which has a median household income of $130,000 and is one of the wealthiest cities in the nation. Two Yorba Linda council members were recalled in 2016 following voter protests over a scheduled 380 percent increase in water rates over five years, which the council had approved unanimously; a third board member lost reelection, and a fourth did not seek another term. In 2018, the city—where the city council chooses its mayor for a one-year term from council members--selected as mayor 25-year-old Tara Campbell, who grew up locally and studied sports journalism at the University of Southern California. She staked her claim as the youngest female mayor in a city with a population of more than 30,000. Yorba Linda is the birthplace of President Richard Nixon and the site of his presidential library. In La Habra (which is Spanish for low mountain pass) Heights, in what was a very large ranch in the nineteenth century, the community rules have sought to retain a rural ambiance, including horse-back riding.

Only 40,000 people lived in Orange County in 1913 when Nixon was born; 3.2 million live there today, with a population that is 34 percent Hispanic and 22 percent Asian.

The 39th Congressional District of California is based in northern Orange County and includes the southeast corner of Los Angeles County and the southwest corner of San Bernardino County. About two-thirds of the voters are in Orange County. In San Bernardino, it includes part of Chino, which had been the site of a large youth prison. It also has large meatpacking plants, whose smell can carry across the valley on a windy day. Chino Hills, incorporated in 1991,is full of subdivisions for commuters who battle the heavy traffic on Interstate 5. In Los Angeles County, the 39th includes Diamond Bar, which is 58 percent Asian. The Orange County section takes in parts of Anaheim. Buena Park is a rapidly growing city that has become a center for Korean businesses as well as an entertainment destination—an Orange County version of Korea town in central L.A. The district is 33 percent Hispanic and 33 percent Asian. Politically, the 39th has included some of the few remaining areas of Los Angeles County that elect Republicans. That has been changing. Joe Biden led Donald Trump in the district, 54%-44%, and Biden ran even better in the L.A. County portion.

Lucille Roybal-Allard (D)

Elected 1992, 15th term, b. Jun 12, 1941; Boyle Heights, CA; CA State University, Los Angeles, B.A., 1965; Catholic; Married (Edward T. Allard III); 2 children; 2 stepchildren; 9 grandchildren.

Elected Office: CA Assembly, 1987-1992.

Professional Career: Community relations; Nonprofit Executive.

DC Office: 2083 RHOB 20515, 202-225-1766, Fax: 202-226-0350, roybal-allard.house.gov

State Offices: Commerce, 323-721-8790.

Committees: *Appropriations*: Homeland Security (Chmn); Labor, Health & Human Services, Education & Related Agencies.

Group Ratings

	ADA	ACLU	AFL-CIO	LCV	COC	HAFA	ACU	CFG	FRC
2020	**	81%	**	95%	-	0%	3%	**	-
2019	95%	C	95%	97%	48%	C	3%	18%	0%

Almanac Ratings 2019-2020

	Economy	Social	Foreign	Composite
Liberal	59%	100%	92%	84%
Conservative	41%	0%	8%	16%

Key Votes of the 116th Congress

1. U.S./Mex./Can. trade deal	Y	5. Russia sanctions	Y	9. Firearms background checks	Y
2. First Coronavirus response	Y	6. Troops in Syria	Y	10. Spending at the border	N
3. HEROES Act	N/A	7. Veto arms sales to Saudis	Y	11. Marijuana liberalized rules	Y
4. CASH Act	Y	8. Defense $$$, veto override	Y	12. Electoral College objections	N

Election Results

Election	Name (Party)	Vote (%)		Cand. Spent	Ind. Exp. Support	Ind. Exp. Oppose
2020 General	Lucille Roybal-Allard (D)	135,572	(73%)	$619,326	$2,334	
	Antonio Delgado (R)	50,809	(27%)	$95,840		$113
2020 Primary	Lucille Roybal-Allard (D)	38,837	(51%)			
	David John Sanchez (D)	10,256	(13%)			
	Anthony Felix Jr. (D)	9,473	(12%)			

Prior winning percentages: 2018 (77%), 2016 (71%), 2014 (61%), 2012 (59%), 2010 (77%), 2008 (77%), 2006 (77%), 2004 (75%), 2002 (74%), 2000 (85%), 1998 (87%), 1996 (82%), 1994 (82%), 1992 (63%)

Lucille Roybal-Allard, first elected in 1992, was the first Mexican-American woman to be elected to Congress. Immigration policy has been her continuing priority, along with social programs serving the poor. As chairwoman of the Appropriations Subcommittee on Homeland Security, she has been well-positioned to oversee that federal agency and its funding and to work on immigration issues—more constructively, when Joe Biden became president. Although she has maintained a low profile, her mark as the first Latina to chair an Appropriations subcommittee, with a vital policy niche, has elevated her stature in Congress and in the Hispanic community.

Roybal-Allard grew up in the Los Angeles area, the daughter of longtime Democratic Rep. Edward Roybal, who was the first Latino to serve on the Los Angeles City Council and became a founder of the Congressional Hispanic Caucus. She dreamed of a show business career as a teenager and later worked as a department store clerk and for nonprofit organizations. After raising a family—two of her children are lawyers—she followed her father into politics when she was 45 years old. She was elected to the California Assembly in 1986. Six years later he retired from the House, and she ran for the seat in a district that took in much of the territory he had represented for 30 years. Roybal-Allard won easily with 75 percent of the vote in the primary and 63 percent in the general election.

Roybal-Allard has compiled a solidly liberal voting record and was among the Hispanic lawmakers pushing President Barack Obama to act boldly on immigration reform. One session between lawmakers and Obama domestic policy adviser Cecilia Munoz grew so testy that Roybal-Allard walked out, The Washington Post reported in April 2012. She called Obama's reelection a mandate to focus on a comprehensive immigration overhaul. "The truth is that the facts are on our side, the majority of Americans are on our side and the momentum is on our side," she said at the time.

With Republican control of Congress and later the presidency, Roybal-Allard's role on immigration became increasingly defensive. When Republicans in 2015 sought to use the Homeland Security appropriations bill to restrict Obama's executive actions, she became more visible and vocal in what was becoming a fight against increased deportations of those in the country illegally. The Trump administration's overt actions to separate families at the border with Mexico in 2018 were "heartless" policy that was "tearing children from the loving arms of their undocumented parents," she protested. The Democratic takeover of the House significantly increased her leverage, though Trump's approach limited her options. When Biden entered the White House, she said "his plans for our country demonstrate his devotion to protecting and improving American lives and giving hope to all Americans for a better future and quality of life."

Roybal-Allard has a long history of advocacy for immigrants of all sorts. She was an original cosponsor in 2001 of the DREAM Act, which now would provide a path to citizenship for college or military-bound students and also protect that group from deportation. When Obama in 2014 posthumously gave the Presidential Medal of Freedom to her father, she recalled his success in working on bipartisan terms, including with Republican presidents, on behalf of undocumented immigrants. During Obama's final weeks in office, she requested that he issue a blanket pardon to the estimated 750,000 so-called dreamers. The official White House response was, "only Congress can create legal status for undocumented individuals."

On Appropriations, Roybal-Allard championed a new federal courthouse in Los Angeles. She got a bill signed into law to coordinate federal programs and research on underage drinking, and to fund a media campaign on its dangers. For California, she pushed for in-state college tuition rates for illegal immigrants. She filed legislation aimed at raising labor standards and protections for children of migrant farm workers to the same level as occupations outside of agriculture.

Taking over as subcommittee chairwoman, she faced struggles with both the right and left. In August 2019, when the Trump administration notified Congress of its plan to shift $271 million from other accounts to increased enforcement by the Immigration and Customs Enforcement agency, she urged Homeland Security officials to cooperate with Congress "to restore the partnership we once had in support of the department's many important missions." Separately, she said, "border security is more than physical barriers, and homeland security is more than border security." In July 2020, when liberal Democrats objected that her subcommittee bill needed more action to counter Trump administration actions, she said it "literally has everything in it that the advocates, the members, have told me over the years had to be in the bill."

Roybal-Allard isn't as close to Speaker Nancy Pelosi and her inner circle as other Democratic women from California, which sometimes has limited her leverage in the House. In 2006, Roybal-

Allard seconded the nomination of Steny Hoyer of Maryland for majority leader, in opposition to Pelosi's preferred candidate, John Murtha of Pennsylvania. Hoyer won the contest, so Roybal-Allard retained a friend in high places. She served with both Hoyer and Pelosi on Appropriations.

At home in 2012, under the state's all-party primary rules, Roybal-Allard faced a Democratic challenger, college instructor David Sanchez. He held her to 59 percent of the vote, her lowest ever. They faced each other again in 2014, when she won, 61%-39%. Sanchez did not report spending any campaign money in either contest. Since then, Roybal-Allard has not been seriously challenged and her victory margins have returned to the comfort zone. She will have this seat as long as she wants it.

At age 79 when Biden took office, she moved up three slots and became the fourth-ranked Democrat on the Appropriations Committee. With the prospect of redistricting challenges, she faced options on whether to continue beyond her father's 30 years in Congress.

CA-40: Eastern Los Angeles   Cook Partisan Voting Index: D+31

Population		Race and Ethnicity		Income	
Total	715,934	White	55.70%	Median Income	$51,774
Land area (sq. miles)	58	Black	5.10%	District Income Rank	371
Pop/ sq mi	12,410.02	Latino	89.20%	Poverty Rate	20.00%
Born in State	56.60%	Asian	1.90%	With health insurance	84.10%
		Two or more races	1.70%	Cash public assistance	4.60%
Age Groups		Other	35.60%	Food stamp/SNAP	16.90%
Under 18	28.40%				
18-34	26.30%	**Education**		**Work**	
35-64	36.10%	H.S grad or less	67.90%	White Collar	17.20%
Over 64	9.30%	Some college	22.00%	Sales and Service	45.00%
		College Degree, 4 yr	7.50%	Blue Collar	37.70%
Military		Post grad	2.60%	Government	9.40%
Veteran/ Active Duty	1.40%				

2020 Pres. Vote	Biden	156,662	(77%)	Trump	41,875	(21%)			
2016 Pres. Vote	Clinton	135,472	(82%)	Trump	21,077	(13%)	Stein	3,805	(2%)

Bell Gardens, Downey: East Los Angeles is a piece of Latin America transplanted to California. Hardworking immigrants from Mexico and Central and South America come to find affordable housing, doubling and tripling up with other families in places that are close enough to drive an old car to work in factories and warehouses south and east of downtown Los Angeles. The Gold Line extension of L.A.'s transit agency (now the L Line) made their commutes considerably easier by bringing light rail service to the area. This part of Los Angeles includes the 1940s working-class suburb of Huntington Park, with its shopping strip on the wide Pacific Boulevard, plus Bell Gardens, Downey and Maywood, all of which are now predominantly Latino. Each calls itself a "sanctuary city" for illegal immigrants, as do both the city and county of Los Angeles.

In the 1950s, the existence of an airplane production plant in Downey that built 13,000 airplanes for World War II led to what became the North American Rockwell company (purchased later by Boeing) and the early epicenter of space flight, including the Apollo program that sent men to the moon. In more cosmic terms, Downey is home to the world's oldest surviving McDonald's hamburgers site; it was started by Dick and Mac McDonald in 1953 and featured golden arches. Maywood, which is little more than one square mile, suffered from a municipal corruption scandal that forced it to lay off all but one of its employees in 2010 and has struggled to reorganize its governance. Somewhat more affluent Bellflower has made a comeback with multiple shopping centers.

These are communities in the 40th Congressional District of California, radiating south from East Los Angeles and downtown L.A. Bisecting much of the district is the concrete-lined Los Angeles River. Environmentalists have pushed the city for years to clean it up and return it to a more natural condition, with adjacent parkland and bicycle paths, while preserving its flood-control assets. In 2016, county voters overwhelmingly approved a $1 billion plan for a restoration that was designed to dig up the cement and restore the river along a 19-mile stretch between Vernon and Long Beach, and create an urban greenway from Glendale to downtown with additional land the city had purchased. With state aid of $100 million that the legislature approved in 2017 to initiate early improvements, local and state officials have continued to explore options. A local highlight is Paramount, where local businessmen Frank and Lawrence Zamboni invented refrigeration technology for the dairy industry and the Zamboni ice-resurfacing machine for skating rinks. Also in Paramount, the swap meet is a glorified flea market, with both new and used items. Operating daily since 1955, when Paramount was a dairy town, it has space for more than 800 vendors and a parking lot for 2,100 cars. It was forced to shut down by the coronavirus. But it reopened, with social distancing, in early June 2020.

With an 89 percent (and climbing) Latino population, and 41 percent foreign-born, the40th has become the most Hispanic district in California. Joe Biden's 77 percent fell short of the 82 percent vote for Hillary Clinton in 2016, but it remained the Democrats' fourth-best district in the L.A. area.

Mark Takano (D)

Elected 2012, 5th term, b. Dec 10, 1960; Riverside, CA; Harvard College, A.B., 1983; School of Education, University of CA, Riverside, M.F.A., 2010; Methodist; Single.

Elected Office: Board of Trustees, Riverside Commissioner Col. District, 1990-2012, President, 1992, 1997-198, 2005-2006.

Professional Career: Teacher, Rialto Unified School District, 1988-2013; Substitute teacher, Boston, 1984-1985.

DC Office: 420 CHOB 20515, 202-225-2305, Fax: 202-225-7018, takano.house.gov

State Offices: Riverside, 951-222-0203.

Committees: *Education & Labor*: Higher Education & Workforce Investment; Workforce Protections. *Veterans' Affairs (Chmn)*: Ex Officio membership on all subcommittees.

Group Ratings

	ADA	ACLU	AFL-CIO	LCV	COC	HAFA	ACU	CFG	FRC
2020	**	92%	**	100%	-	0%	4%	**	-
2019	95%	C	95%	97%	49%	C	4%	19%	0%

Almanac Ratings 2019-2020

	Economy	Social	Foreign	Composite
Liberal	100%	100%	92%	98%
Conservative	0%	0%	8%	2%

Key Votes of the 116th Congress

1. U.S./Mex./Can. trade deal	Y	5. Russia sanctions	Y
2. First Coronavirus response	Y	6. Troops in Syria	Y
3. HEROES Act	Y	7. Veto arms sales to Saudis	Y
4. CASH Act	Y	8. Defense $$$, veto override	Y

9. Firearms background checks	Y
10. Spending at the border	N
11. Marijuana liberalized rules	Y
12. Electoral College objections	N

Election Results

Election	Name (Party)	Vote (%)		Cand. Spent	Ind. Exp. Support	Ind. Exp. Oppose
2020 General	Mark Takano (D)...............................	168,126	(64%)	$950,548	$2,816	
	Aja Smith (R).....................................	94,447	(36%)	$655,557		$113
2020 Primary	Mark Takano (D)........................	58,723	(51%)			
	Grace Williams (D).......................	18,731	(16%)			

Prior winning percentages: 2018 (65%), 2016 (65%), 2014 (57%), 2012 (59%)

Mark Takano, a Democrat elected in 2012 after narrowly losing an election 20 years earlier, has begun to make an impact as a committee chairman—a position he called "the honor of my lifetime" following a long and winding quest for congressional influence. In his usually bipartisan work on veterans' issues, he has taken an interest in strengthening operations within the Veterans Affairs Department rather than pushing for health care options outside the VA.

In the majority, he used the influence of his chairmanship to pursue oversight of the Trump administration—which tended to be a search for headlines. Takano has brought his experience as an inner-city schoolteacher and his dexterity on social media. He is the first openly gay person of a racial minority—"gaysian," as he jokingly describes himself—to hold a seat in Congress.

Born and raised in Riverside, Takano grew up in a self-described "typical Japanese-American family" with a strong emphasis on education, self-reliance and public service. In his youth, he played junior football. He was fascinated by politics and remembers watching the televised Watergate hearings of the House Judiciary Committee, entranced by Democratic Rep. Barbara Jordan of Texas. He got his bachelor's in government from Harvard University. He was planning to go to law school but decided instead to try teaching, taking a job as a substitute teacher in the Boston area. He returned to school to get a teaching certificate and took a job as an English and social studies teacher at the Rialto Unified School District. In 1990, Takano was elected to the Riverside Community College District's Board of Trustees. He became the board's longest-serving member, with two terms as president.

Takano made a bid for an open House seat in 1992 but lost to Republican Ken Calvert in one of the closest elections in California history. In a 1994 rematch, Calvert defeated him by a double-digit margin in a strongly Republican year. Takano jokingly calls the ensuing time his "wilderness years," when he traveled to foreign countries while continuing to teach. In 2012, he ran in the all-party primary in the redrawn 41st District, which leaned Democratic. Republican John Tavaglione, a veteran Riverside County supervisor, got 45 percent of the vote to 37 percent for Takano. Tavaglione had worked with Democrats in Riverside County and took some moderate positions, declining to sign conservative activist Grover Norquist's "no new taxes" pledge. Takano ran as a populist, attacking lobbyists and oil and insurance companies. With the much higher turnout in November, Takano won 59%-41%.

Takano has cited his teaching experience in his work on the Education and Labor Committee. He worked with other House Democrats to form a Public Education Caucus, which protested the lack of public school experience for Education Secretary Betsy DeVos. In the minority, Takano made creative use of social media and his communications skills to score rhetorical points and attempt to influence Washington debates. He used a red pen to grade a letter that House Republicans had privately circulated among themselves about immigration. He gave the letter an "F," scrawled multiple comments in red, advised the GOP members to "See me after work," and posted the results on his Tumblr page.

On the Veterans' Affairs Committee, Takano spent six months as the acting ranking minority member after Democratic Rep. Corrine Brown of Florida was indicted and forced to step aside in July 2016. Then, he yielded the position to Rep. Tim Walz of Minnesota, who was more senior in the House. When Walz was elected governor, Takano was the obvious choice for committee chairman. He pledged to retain the panel's commitment to bipartisanship, rejected "ideological agendas" and said he would give the VA "the tools needed to meet these challenges head-on," referring to the shifting demographics among veterans. In 2018, he was the lead Democratic sponsor of a bill to extend sick-leave benefits to wounded warriors working in medical positions at the VA.

When he became chairman, Takano showed more interest in alleged improprieties by the Trump administration. His actions included claims that three patrons of President Donald Trump's Mar-a-Lago club were seeking special deals on behalf of the VA and his "disappointment" that VA steps to address veterans' suicides were "tepid" bureaucratic responses.

On other issues, Takano joined a delegation to Cuba in October 2017 that encouraged LGBT rights during meetings with officials. He criticized the decision of Trump to reinstate travel and trade restrictions on the island. "My sense is the Cubans are very much eager to cooperate in unprecedented ways," he told the Washington Blade. At home, he said Trump's policy to separate immigrant families at the border with Mexico "echoed my family's World War II internment," which had lasting damage. When Trump referred to the coronavirus as the "Chinese virus," Takano told The New York Times that he was fearful that, "mass blame and mass guilt get assigned to a group of people."

Takano has entrenched himself at home. In 2014, he faced Steve Adams, a Republican councilman from Riverside, who called himself "apolitical" and said an increase in the minimum wage would cost jobs. Takano outspent Adams more than 5-to-1, and won 57%-43%. When Aja Smith, an Air Force veteran and an African-American, waged a rematch against Takano in 2020, she said she had learned lessons from her campaign two years earlier. She increased her spending from about $43,000 to $656,000 and criticized Takano for not having served in the military. She also contrasted herself to Democratic women who were newcomers to the House, whom she said are "the face of an agenda that goes against Western values." She reduced Takano's vote from 65% to 64%.

CA-41: Inland Empire   Cook Partisan Voting Index: D+12

Population		Race and Ethnicity		Income	
Total	786,719	White	46.60%	Median Income	$69,984
Land area (sq. miles)	317	Black	9.10%	District Income Rank	163
Pop/ sq mi	2,485.37	Latino	62.70%	Poverty Rate	11.30%
Born in State	62.50%	Asian	6.70%	With health insurance	88.80%
		Two or more races	3.60%	Cash public assistance	3.40%
Age Groups		Other	34.00%	Food stamp/SNAP	10.70%
Under 18	26.80%				
18-34	28.00%	**Education**		**Work**	
35-64	35.50%	H.S grad or less	52.10%	White Collar	25.80%
Over 64	9.70%	Some college	30.40%	Sales and Service	41.00%
		College Degree, 4 yr	11.10%	Blue Collar	33.20%
Military		Post grad	6.50%	Government	13.90%
Veteran/ Active Duty	4.40%				

2020 Pres. Vote	Biden	164,574	(62%)	Trump	96,428	(36%)		
2016 Pres. Vote	Clinton	126,197	(61%)	Trump	68,526	(33%)	Johnson	6,847	(3%)
	Stein	4,219	(2%)					

Central and Western Riverside, Moreno Valley: Riverside was a sleepy town of 34,000 people, a couple hours' drive from Los Angeles, when Richard and Pat Nixon were married there in 1940 at the Mission Inn, built in 1876 and—with its bell towers, fountains and stained-glass windows —the setting for several Hollywood movies and an inspired setting for a wedding. Riverside was not much larger, with 46,000 people, when Ronald and Nancy Reagan spent their honeymoon at the Mission Inn a dozen years later. Riverside then was a citrus center, a market town amid orange groves, where the local agricultural college developed, among other things, the navel orange. Today the "historic" Mission Inn is again doing business, after being shuttered from 1985 to 1992, but Riverside has changed completely. The city has grown to 331,000 people. Riverside County has about 2.5 million people, nearly a quadrupling of its population since 1980. This has been a boom part of California, where modest-income families with jobs in the L.A. region found new houses in inexpensive developments and small businesses found steady markets.

The Great Recession halted that progress. Since then, the local economy has begun to turn around, though the area has struggled with economic development. Riverside, the fourth-largest county in California, had the largest population gain in the state in 2018. Ontario Ranch was the first "gigabit" community in southern California, with technologically "smart" and more affordable homes. The University of California, Riverside in 2017 graduated its first class of medical students, following a lengthy struggle to secure accreditation because of questions about the school's long-term funding. Riverside County has had a shortage of doctors. These inland areas offer inexpensive space for the sorting and packaging of huge shipments that arrived at the ports of Los Angeles and Long Beach. In June 2020, after extensive litigation, World Logistics Center gained approval from the Moreno Valley council for its proposed 40 million square foot industrial center on farmland; it reportedly would be the largest warehouse in the nation and create as many as 20,000 jobs. Other warehouses and distribution centers already employ tens of thousands of workers in Riverside and San Bernardino counties.

The 41st District includes western parts of Riverside County and all of Riverside city, and the towns of Moreno Valley and Perris. Of the three House districts in the county, this is the most urban and has the largest Hispanic population. Politically, it leans comfortably Democratic, but less so than Los Angeles or San Francisco urban districts. In 2020, Joe Biden defeated Donald Trump, 62%-36%, the same result as Barack Obama's victory over Mitt Romney in 2012.

Ken Calvert (R)

Elected 1992, 15th term, b. Jun 08, 1953; Corona, CA; Chaffey Community College, A.A., 1973; San Diego State University, B.A., 1975; Protestant; Divorced.

Professional Career: Restaurant owner, 1975-1980; Real estate broker, 1980-1992; Chairman, Riverside County Repub. Party, 1984-1988.

DC Office: 2205 RHOB 20515, 202-225-1986, Fax: 202-225-2004, calvert.house.gov

State Offices: Corona, 951-277-0042.

Committees: *Appropriations*: Defense (RMM); Energy & Water Development & Related Agencies.

Group Ratings

	ADA	ACLU	AFL-CIO	LCV	COC	HAFA	ACU	CFG	FRC
2020	**	14%	**	14%		77%	82%	**	-
2019	5%	C	38%	14%	94%	C	83%	64%	100%

Almanac Ratings 2019-2020

	Economy	Social	Foreign	Composite
Liberal	25%	31%	27%	28%
Conservative	75%	69%	73%	72%

Key Votes of the 116th Congress

1. U.S./Mex./Can. trade deal Y	5. Russia sanctions	Y	9. Firearms background checks N
2. First Coronavirus response Y	6. Troops in Syria	Y	10. Spending at the border Y
3. HEROES Act N	7. Veto arms sales to Saudis	N	11. Marijuana liberalized rules N/A
4. CASH Act Y	8. Defense $$$, veto override Y		12. Electoral College objections Y

Election Results

Election	Name (Party)	Vote (%)	Cand. Spent	Ind. Exp. Support	Ind. Exp. Oppose
2020 General	Ken Calvert (R)	210,274 (57%)	$1,743,070		$817
	Liam O'Mara (D)	157,773 (43%)	$131,677	$6,220	
2020 Primary	Ken Calvert (R)	97,781 (58%)			

Prior winning percentages: 2018 (57%), 2016 (59%), 2014 (66%), 2012 (61%), 2010 (56%), 2008 (51%), 2006 (60%), 2004 (62%), 2002 (64%), 2000 (74%), 1998 (56%), 1996 (55%), 1994 (55%), 1992 (47%)

Ken Calvert, a Republican first elected in 1992, has been an ally of GOP leaders and one of the few Californians in the party with persistent influence in Congress. He holds a plum spot on the Appropriations Committee, where he chaired a subcommittee that was at the center of frequent conflicts with Democrats. As ranking minority member of the Defense Subcommittee, he has continued its bipartisan tradition. Reaching three decades in the House, he is the fifth most-senior Republican.

Calvert grew up in Corona. While at San Diego State University, where he majored in economics, he was a congressional intern at the Senate Watergate hearings of 1973. Later, he ran the family restaurant back home and, in 1980, got into the commercial real estate business. In 1982, at age 29, he ran for Congress in a district that included almost all of Riverside County and lost a nine-candidate primary to Al McCandless by 868 votes. In 1992, he ran in a new district and won the GOP primary with 28 percent of the vote. His Democratic opponent was Mark Takano, a middle-school teacher who had the support of teachers' unions and Japanese Americans. Calvert beat Takano by 519 votes (Takano was elected to represent the neighboring 41st District in 2012.) Four decades after Calvert first ran, the booming Riverside County has three entire districts in Congress and a small corner of a fourth.

Soon after he was elected, Calvert ran into trouble at home when the Riverside Press-Enterprise reported that he had been stopped by police with a prostitute in his car. Calvert apologized and said he was upset because his wife had divorced him the month before and his father had recently committed suicide. His opponents in 1994 used the incident against him. Calvert survived the primary 51%-49%, with only an 884-vote margin, against business professor Joseph Khoury. Takano, running again in the general election, ran an ad that accused Calvert of "flagrant womanizing." But with the Republican tide that year, Calvert won 55%-38%.

Calvert has compiled a moderate-to-conservative voting record, with occasional bipartisanship. He broke with most GOP colleagues in 2008 by supporting housing finance legislation, citing his district's high foreclosure rate. He has been a major backer of E-Verify, an online system he helped enact that allows employers to confirm the immigration status of new hires. In 2018, he called for steps to make E-Verify mandatory for job seekers. He has regularly filed a bill to cut off funds to local governments that style themselves as "sanctuary cities" and resist federal efforts to deport undocumented immigrants who have been jailed.

After spending his early years on the Armed Services Committee, Calvert in 2007 snagged a coveted seat on Appropriations, where he aggressively sought spending earmarks for his district, though he lagged in seniority behind Republicans who had fewer years in the House but more committee tenure. He took over in 2013 the plum position as chairman of the Subcommittee on Interior and the Environment. He sought ways to strengthen domestic energy production on federal lands. Calvert has taken special interest in his constituents' demands for funds for wildfire fighting and prevention programs. To encourage the building of more infrastructure projects, he has backed legislation to streamline highway construction timelines.

In a clash with the Trump administration, Calvert worked with Democrats in 2018 to continue support for an Interior Department program to create a smart-phone app to provide early warning of an earthquake. In January 2020, the House Natural Resources Committee approved a bill that he filed with two House Democrats from the area that would create a new wildlife refuge in western Riverside County, in what he called a "commitment towards balancing natural resource conservation and future development."

In 2019, with Republicans in the minority, Calvert took the top GOP slot on the Defense Subcommittee. Promising to seek consensus, Calvert said that even with the boost in Pentagon spending during the Trump's first two years in office "we still have much more to do" to improve readiness of forces, upgrade equipment and respond to new challenges in cyber and in space. He also won a leadership appointment to the Select Intelligence Committee. When Congress cleared the huge spending bill in December 2020, he took credit for flood-control and water projects for his district, plus added steps to "rebuild our military" and build the wall on the southern border.

In 2003, Calvert abandoned his 1992 pledge to serve only 12 years in Congress. Campaign opponents have called into question his ethics. In 2006, the Los Angeles Times reported that he and his real estate partner had bought a four-acre tract for $550,000, then sold it less than a year later for $985,000, after Calvert secured an $8 million spending earmark for expansion of a nearby freeway interchange. Calvert denied wrongdoing, noting that it was not illegal for a member of Congress to make personal investments.

In 2008, Calvert had a close contest against Democrat Bill Hedrick, a Corona-Norco school board member who was poorly funded and had no national party help but benefited from Calvert's ethics problems. Calvert won by a little more than 6,000 votes, 51.2%-48.8%. Hedrick returned for a rematch in 2010. This time, he got help from the Democratic Congressional Campaign Committee, but they were two years late. In another strong Republican year, Calvert won 56%-44, outspending Hedrick, $1.5 million to $493,000.

In his secure Republican district during the past decade, Calvert has seen a steady decline in support. Against Tim Sheridan, a lawyer and official of the National Treasury Employees Union, Calvert got 66 percent in 2014 but was held to a 59%-41% win in a presidential year. In 2018, he was challenged by Julie Peacock, a high school teacher who called for more oversight of the Trump administration. She said Calvert was out of touch and called him a "murderer" because of his opposition to gun control. Peacock spent less than one-tenth of Calvert's $1.5 million, but held him to a 56%-44% win. Two years later against Liam O'Mara, a history professor and another campaign novice whom he outspent by more than 10-to-1, Calvert took 57 percent. Redistricting might give him an opportunity to meet some new voters.

CA-42: Inland Empire

Cook Partisan Voting Index: R+7

Population		Race and Ethnicity		Income	
Total	840,562	White	61.10%	Median Income	$90,651
Land area (sq. miles)	936	Black	6.20%	District Income Rank	55
Pop/ sq mi	898.07	Latino	41.70%	Poverty Rate	7.80%
Born in State	65.30%	Asian	9.50%	With health insurance	93.00%
		Two or more races	5.50%	Cash public assistance	2.20%
Age Groups		Other	17.70%	Food stamp/SNAP	4.70%
Under 18	26.70%				
18-34	22.40%	**Education**		**Work**	
35-64	38.60%	H.S grad or less	37.20%	White Collar	37.20%
Over 64	12.30%	Some college	36.30%	Sales and Service	40.50%
		College Degree, 4 yr	17.60%	Blue Collar	22.30%
Military		Post grad	9.00%	Government	17.40%
Veteran/ Active Duty	7.60%				

2020 Pres. Vote	Trump	198,259	(53%)	Biden	170,481	(45%)			
2016 Pres. Vote	Trump	143,175	(53%)	Clinton	111,103	(41%)	Johnson	9,587	(4%)

Corona, West Riverside: The fastest growth in the Los Angeles metropolitan area over the past 25 years has been in the Inland Empire, at the eastern end of the Los Angeles Basin. Mostly orange groves and dairy farms a few decades ago, this territory is now the site of personal upward mobility and ethnic and cultural diversity. The main ingredient of the growth has been small entrepreneurial businesses, many of them started by people with Asian or Latino immigrant backgrounds. One locale that has been strong is Murrieta. It doubled in population from 2000 to 2010, though growth has slowed since then. Its families are mostly young, with a 31 percent Hispanic share. To respond to the acute shortage of housing, the county board in 2017 approved plans for new villages in Nuevo, with more than 8,700 homes. By 2020, the comments from Nuevo on niche.com, a website that connects people to neighborhoods, were mixed. They ranged from "close-knit community" and "just love the country feel and great neighbors" to "a small area with not much to it" and "not a good place to raise a family."

Despite occasional tensions since World War II, this area has styled itself as a welcoming destination for legal immigrants. That mindset became more complex with the illegal immigration problems on the southern border. In 2014, local protesters surrounded and forced back three buses filled with immigration detainees who had been sent to Riverside County from Texas and were approaching a local Border Patrol station. The local mayor said the protesters were worried whether the town could safely house the detainees. The American Civil Liberties Union in 2019 filed a lawsuit against Corona after its police department stopped a driver for speeding and sent him to federal law enforcement officials for deportation, leaving behind his wife and three children, the Riverside Press-Enterprise reported in June 2019.In 2018, the city council in Murrieta went on the record seeking repeal of the California law permitting sanctuaries to protect undocumented immigrants. As recently as June 2020, the U.S. Supreme Court rejected an appeal from the Trump administration that sought a ruling on the constitutionality of sanctuary laws.

The 42nd Congressional District is based in Riverside County, which is the largest part of the Inland Empire. On the western side of Riverside, it takes in the towns of Corona, Norco, Murrieta, Lake Elsinore and the new city of Menifee. The 42nd is the largest land mass of the 21 House districts in the L.A. metro area. The district—one of three entirely in Riverside--includes the Republican core of the county, with a 42 percent Hispanic population. Donald Trump led Joe Biden, 53%-45%, one of seven districts in California where he had a majority of the vote.

Maxine Waters (D)

Elected 1990, 16th term, b. Aug 15, 1938; St. Louis, MO; CA State University, Los Angeles, B.A., 1970; Christian Church; Married (Amb. Sidney Williams); 2 children; 2 grandchildren.

Elected Office: CA Assembly, 1977-1991.

Professional Career: Head Start teacher, 1966; Deputy, City Councilman David Cunningham, 1973-1976.

DC Office: 2221 RHOB 20515, 202-225-2201, Fax: 202-225-7854, waters.house.gov

State Offices: Los Angeles, 323-757-8900.

Committees: *Financial Services (Chmn).*

Group Ratings

	ADA	ACLU	AFL-CIO	LCV	COC	HAFA	ACU	CFG	FRC
2020	**	79%	**	100%	-	0%	4%	**	-
2019	95%	C	95%	97%	54%	C	4%	18%	0%

Almanac Ratings 2019-2020

	Economy	Social	Foreign	Composite
Liberal	100%	100%	80%	94%
Conservative	0%	0%	20%	6%

Key Votes of the 116th Congress

1. U.S./Mex./Can. trade deal	Y	5. Russia sanctions	Y
2. First Coronavirus response	Y	6. Troops in Syria	Y
3. HEROES Act	Y	7. Veto arms sales to Saudis	Y
4. CASH Act	Y	8. Defense $$$, veto override	Y

9. Firearms background checks Y
10. Spending at the border   Y
11. Marijuana liberalized rules Y
12. Electoral College objections N

Election Results

Election	Name (Party)	Vote (%)		Cand. Spent	Ind. Exp. Support	Ind. Exp. Oppose
2020 General	Maxine Waters (D)	199,210	(72%)	$1,929,641	$46,613	$47,384
	Joe Collins (R)	78,688	(28%)	$9,792,809	$6,280	$113
2020 Primary	Maxine Waters (D)	100,468	(78%)			

Prior winning percentages: 2018 (78%), 2016 (76%), 2014 (71%), 2012 (71%), 2010 (79%), 2008 (83%), 2006 (84%), 2004 (81%), 2002 (78%), 2000 (87%), 1998 (89%), 1996 (86%), 1994 (78%), 1992 (83%), 1990 (79%)

Maxine Waters, a Democrat first elected in 1990, has chairs the Financial Services Committee. A harsh critic of big banks who has pressed for expanded aid for low-income groups, she and President Donald Trump directed harsh invective toward each other. With the gavel, she has been a forceful presence in pursuing what she views as inequality.

Waters grew up in St. Louis, one of 13 children. She has said, "I know all about welfare. I remember the social workers peeking in the refrigerator and under the beds." She moved to California in 1961, worked in a garment factory and raised two children. Waters got a sociology degree at California State University, Los Angeles, and became an assistant Head Start teacher after the Watts riot of 1965. She likes to call herself "The Organizer" and has shown the capacity to draw big supportive crowds to her protests over the years. She has held elected office since 1976, when she won a seat in the California Assembly. She helped pass legislation divesting state pension funds from apartheid South Africa, setting up a child abuse prevention training program, and prohibiting police strip searches for nonviolent offenses. When Democratic Rep. Augustus Hawkins retired in 1990 after 28 years in the House, Waters was the obvious choice for the seat and won it easily. Her husband, Sidney Williams, a former professional football player and Mercedes-Benz salesman, became President Bill Clinton's ambassador to the Bahamas.

Having grown up in poverty and under Jim Crow, Waters believes fervently in federal aid for the poor and for racial preferences to help Blacks overcome the legacies of slavery, segregation and discrimination. She has favored big reductions in defense spending in favor of domestic spending. She pushed for federal loan guarantees to cities for economic and infrastructure development. She has sponsored bills to repeal mandatory minimum sentences for drug crimes, and charges that the war on drugs has created "apartheid" in the United States.

On overseas issues, she voted against the Gulf War resolution in 1991 and was a staunch opponent a decade later of the Iraq war as well as the subsequent troop buildup in Afghanistan. Waters successfully sponsored an amendment to triple spending to erase the debts of poor nations, mostly in Africa.

Waters has brought an intensity bordering on fury to her work. Her anger is a political weapon she uses shrewdly to get both publicity and results. "I don't have time to be polite," Waters says. She hasn't been afraid to step on toes. When House Appropriations Chairman David Obey of Wisconsin sought to ban spending earmarks named after members in 2009, she heatedly confronted him over his refusal to fund her request for the Maxine Waters Employment Preparation Center. Obey eventually prevailed.

She was an occasional thorn in the side of President Barack Obama, starting with her endorsement of Hillary Clinton during the 2008 Democratic presidential primaries. She and other Congressional Black Caucus members held up a vote on the financial services overhaul in November 2009 because they said the administration wasn't addressing the needs of segments of the Black community. Waters repeatedly discussed the need to "educate" people advising Obama and encouraged him to fight harder when negotiating with the GOP on budget matters. "The Congressional Black Caucus loves the president, too. We're supportive of the president, but we're getting tired," she said in 2011. "The unemployment is unconscionable. We don't know what the strategy is."

On the Financial Services Committee, she has a long history of working to address housing issues. She took over as the senior Democrat in 2013, giving her a larger platform to push her pro-regulatory, pro-consumer agenda. In 2016, Congress enacted a bill that included her provision to expand the use of rental vouchers for Section 8 housing. Waters skillfully exploited divisions between pro-market Republicans and big businesses that benefit from corporate welfare, Politico reported in 2014. She had become "a sympathetic ally for corporate America," notably on extension of the Export-Import Bank, which makes loans to businesses — mostly big and already profitable —involved in trade. Her position has given her the opportunity to work with various interests, she said, "even if you've never worked with them before and even if you're never going to work with them again." She also retained her focus on broader economic conflicts, including income inequality. In 2014, she returned to her home town of St. Louis for the funeral of Michael Brown, whose shooting by police sparked riots in nearby Ferguson. She joined the community in "calling for justice."

With the gavel at Financial Services, Waters said she demanded accountability by public and private interests. "She is going to make a lot of powerful people uncomfortable," according to an analysis by the Vox website. Waters pursued extensive oversight, from the need for more housing to Trump's finances, including his business ties to Deutsche Bank. "I am not interested in simply having a fight," she told the Los Angeles Times. "But I won't let anybody run over me."

In an October 2019 hearing that was designed to explore Facebook's plan to create Libra, a digital currency, Waters told chief executive Mark Zuckerberg that he should first address his company's "many existing deficiencies and failures" and that the company's action had prompted "serious discussion about whether Facebook should be broken up."

During a hearing a year later with Health and Human Services Secretary Alex Azar, Waters bluntly described the Trump administration failures in addressing the coronavirus. Referring to the more than 200,000 deaths at that time, she asked, "Are you proud of the job you have done?" Referring to committee Democrats, she added, "we're very unhappy about what's going on."

Waters' personal finances have become the target of watchdogs. In 2005, the liberal-leaning Citizens for Responsibility and Ethics in Washington said members of her family had made more than $1 million in eight years doing business with companies, candidates and causes that she had helped in her official capacity. Her reply: "They do their business and I do mine."

The House Ethics Committee charged Waters with three counts of breaking House rules barring lawmakers from taking actions in their own financial interest. Hoping to seize political advantage, Republicans clamored to have her ethics trials held before the 2010 elections. Her trial was postponed until after Election Day when committee leaders cited the discovery of additional evidence. Waters contended the delay proved that the case against her was weak. "I have been denied basic due process," she said. In September 2012, the committee announced that Waters would not be charged with violating House rules.

During the ceremony to count the electoral votes for the 2016election, she sought unsuccessfully to get a senator to join her in objecting to certification of the vote and forcing debate about Trump's victory. "I don't honor him, I don't respect him and I don't want to be involved with him," she said in explaining her decision not to attend Trump's inauguration. In her frequent objections to his policies, Waters was an early advocate of impeachment and she said Trump should resign. On Twitter and at his political rallies, Trump responded by referring to her as "an extraordinarily low IQ person." Waters has remained a force to be reckoned with in L.A. politics and has been reelected without difficulty. The rising Hispanic percentage in her district has become the biggest threat to her career. But even with more than twice as many Hispanics than Blacks, she has had no trouble keeping this seat.

In 2018, she faced an unusual—though ineffectual—challenge from Omar Narvarro, a 29-year-old Republican activist and part-time salesman at a Target department store, who echoed some of Trump's rhetoric about Waters. Navarro spent $1 million, some of which he took as salary. He lost, 78%-22%.Navarro ran again in 2020, spent nearly $800,000 and finished third in the opening round of voting. In November, Waters faced Republican Joe Collins, a graduate of the Naval Academy who became a mechanic working on Navy aircraft. Collins ran ads with tough criticism of Waters that promoted himself as a better representative of the district. After spending nearly $10 million, Collins held Waters to 72 percent.

In April 2021, days before the verdict on the murder charges against local policeman Derek Chauvin for the death of George Floyd, she stirred a brief tempest when she told a Minneapolis group, "We've got to get more confrontational," if Chauvin was not found guilty. Claiming that she was inciting violence, Republicans forced a House vote to censure her. Their resolution lost on a party-line vote on the same afternoon that the jury found Chauvin guilty.

CA-43: Southern and Western L.A.   **Cook Partisan Voting Index: D+29**

Population		Race and Ethnicity		Income	
Total	748,092	White	43.30%	Median Income	$66,670
Land area (sq. miles)	72	Black	20.20%	District Income Rank	196
Pop/ sq mi	10,385.84	Latino	49.70%	Poverty Rate	14.40%
Born in State	53.50%	Asian	12.00%	With health insurance	89.40%
		Two or more races	4.80%	Cash public assistance	3.10%
Age Groups		Other	19.70%	Food stamp/SNAP	11.60%
Under 18	23.50%				
18-34	25.90%	**Education**		**Work**	
35-64	38.00%	H.S grad or less	43.90%	White Collar	33.80%
Over 64	12.60%	Some college	26.30%	Sales and Service	43.70%
		College Degree, 4 yr	20.80%	Blue Collar	22.50%
Military		Post grad	8.90%	Government	13.30%
Veteran/ Active Duty	3.60%				

2020 Pres. Vote	Biden	224,694	(77%)	Trump	61,138	(21%)		
2016 Pres. Vote	Clinton	183,434	(78%)	Trump	39,039	(17%)	Johnson	5,546	(2%)
	Stein	4,637	(2%)					

Inglewood, Torrance: In the years just after World War II, Los Angeles was the fastest-growing metropolitan area in America. LAX, today the world's third-busiest airport (behind Atlanta and Beijing), with eight central terminals, was then a small airfield amid open country. The mile-square grids east, north and south of the airport were just filling up with subdivisions. Inglewood, east of the airport around the Hollywood Park racetrack, attracted the young families of people who had moved to Los Angeles during the war—workers in the giant aircraft factories or in the small factories that every day were making California less dependent on goods from back East. In Hawthorne, near what has become the southeast corner of the airport, future celebrities were growing up—Sonny Bono, the Beach Boys and, during her early years, Marilyn Monroe. Gardena, east of Hawthorne, was known for its legal poker clubs and its Japanese-American residents, back from the wartime internment camps. Hawthorne had been home to a big Northrop Grumman plant.

The city council in 2003 officially renamed the community South Los Angeles in an effort to rid it of the "South Central" stigma of gang wars and race riots. In the days of residential segregation, much of this area was the home of Los Angeles' Black community, its numbers greatly expanded by migration from the South during and after the war. As the nation's focus on civil rights receded in the 1980s and 1990s, this part of Los Angeles continued to deal with racial tensions and chronic economic problems. An almost bankrupt Inglewood Unified School District was given $55 million as part of an emergency state takeover in 2012; six years later, the Los Angeles Times reported, the school district continued to face a budget crisis and buildings in disrepair. The coronavirus exacerbated the problem by reducing the availability of state funds.

Inglewood has a brighter future as the location of the lavish 300-acre stadium and shopping complex that opened in 2020 as the home for both the former St. Louis Rams and San Diego Chargers of the National Football League—albeit with no spectators because of pandemic restrictions. On what had been the home of Hollywood Park, the privately owned and multi-purpose stadium, with a price tag of perhaps $5 billion, has become a new model for NFL owners seeking to build ever-larger and more remunerative palaces. It spurred the already-underway gentrification of Inglewood, where the median value of a home increased 37 percent between January 2016 and June 2018 to a new sticker price of $542,000. By December 2020, the median sale price of a home purchase in Inglewood had skyrocketed to $712,000, according to the local realtors group. The opening of the 8.5 mile Crenshaw/LAX light-rail line (delayed until late 2021) plus extensive residential development have added to the makeover of Inglewood, where a return of white residents has begun.

Based in Hawthorne, Elon Musk's Space Exploration Technologies (Space X)in November 2020sent its first operational mission from Cape Canaveral in Florida to the International Space Station, with three Americans and one Japanese astronaut on board. Also in Hawthorne, Musk in 2018 unveiled his Boring Company's test transportation tunnel—1.4 miles under the Space X headquarters—which was designed as a prototype for harried L.A. freeway drivers. That company plans public use of self-driving cars in a loop tunnel system in Las Vegas.

The 43rd Congressional District covers much of this section of Los Angeles County, including Gardena, and the heavily Hispanic areas of Alondra Park, Hawthorne and Lawndale. It takes in part of Torrance, which is home to large Korean and Japanese communities and to the North American headquarters of Honda. On the northern end of the district is Inglewood and to the south is West Carson. At the Los Angeles International Airport, a $5 billion elevated train serving the airport area is scheduled to open in 2023 and reduce one source of local congestion. This is safe Democratic territory. Joe Biden got 77 percent of the district vote in 2020. The current district lines are 50 percent Hispanic and 20 percent Black. But the Black community wields more political clout.

Nanette Barragán (D)

Elected 2016, 3rd term, b. Sep 15, 1976; San Pedro, CA; University of CA, Los Angeles, B.A., 2000; University of Southern CA, J.D., 2005; Catholic; Single.

Elected Office: Hermosa Beach City Council, 2013-2015; Mayor Pro Tem, Hermosa Beach, 2015.

Professional Career: Practicing attorney.

DC Office: 1030 LHOB 20515, 202-225-8220, barragan.house.gov

State Offices: Carson, 310-831-1799; San Pedro, 310-831-1799; South Gate, 310-831-1799.

Committees: *Energy & Commerce*: Energy; Environment & Climate Change; Health. *Homeland Security*: Border Security, Facilitation & Operations (Chmn).

Group Ratings

	ADA	ACLU	AFL-CIO	LCV	COC	HAFA	ACU	CFG	FRC
2020	**	86%	**	100%	-	0%	4%	**	-
2019	100%	C	90%	100%	43%	C	4%	12%	0%

Almanac Ratings 2019-2020

	Economy	Social	Foreign	Composite
Liberal	100%	65%	97%	88%
Conservative	0%	35%	3%	12%

Key Votes of the 116th Congress

1. U.S./Mex./Can. trade deal N	5. Russia sanctions Y	9. Firearms background checks Y
2. First Coronavirus response Y	6. Troops in Syria Y	10. Spending at the border N
3. HEROES Act Y	7. Veto arms sales to Saudis Y	11. Marijuana liberalized rules Y
4. CASH Act Y	8. Defense $$$, veto override Y	12. Electoral College objections N

Election Results

Election	Name (Party)	Vote (%)	Cand. Spent	Ind. Exp. Support	Ind. Exp. Oppose
2020 General	Nanette Barragán (D).......................	139,661 (68%)	$433,279	$2,334	
	Analilia Joya (D)...............................	66,375 (32%)			
2020 Primary	Nanette Barragán (D).......................	57,033 (64%)			
	Analilia Joya (D)...............................	13,032 (15%)			
	Morris F. Griffin (D).............................	7,901 (9%)			

Prior winning percentages: 2018 (68%), 2016 (52%)

Democrat Nanette Barragán, elected in 2016 in a close contest with an African-American state senator, benefited from the support of activist Democratic women and her large Hispanic community. Building on her impressive professional background, she has taken the lead among junior House Democrats on the environment, where she has focused on the needs of her district, and on the conditions faced by immigrants and refugees at the southern border. Barragan has been reelected easily.

Barragán was the youngest of 11 children of undocumented immigrants from Mexico. She succeeded with what the Los Angeles Times described as "an up-from-the-bootstraps story" from the hardscrabble streets of Carson to graduate from UCLA and get a law degree from the University of Southern California. In the Clinton White House she worked on African-American outreach in the Office of Public Liaison. She was an extern for a California Supreme Court justice and later worked for the Los Angeles Legal Aid Foundation and the U.S. attorney's office. As a lawyer with Latham & Watkins, a top Los Angeles firm, she handled an immigration asylum case on behalf of a mother and child from Guatemala that lasted three years.

In 2012, Barragán took a leave from her law firm to work on the reelection campaign of President Barack Obama. A year later, she was elected to the Hermosa Beach City Council. She served barely a month as mayor before stepping down to run for Congress. She gained attention for working to impose a ban on oil drilling in Santa Monica Bay, where an oil company had planned to set up rigs.

When Rep. Janice Hahn retired for a successful run for the Los Angeles County Board of Supervisors, the frontrunners were Barragán and veteran state Sen. Isadore Hall III, an African American who was endorsed by much of the California Democratic establishment, including Gov. Jerry Brown. In the first round of voting, Hall led the 10-candidate field with 40 percent of the vote to 22 percent for Barragán. Each candidate raised about $1.9 million. Barragán got a big boost with nearly $700,000 in support from Women Vote!, a Super PAC created by EMILY'S List, the abortion-rights group. She won in November, 52%-48%, a margin of 7,835 votes.

Barragán was selected as an assistant whip and as one of three co-presidents of the Democrats' freshman class. She said she decided to attend the inauguration of President Donald Trump, while wearing a symbolic pink fleece hat, because "I want to show Donald Trump that immigrants have always added immeasurable value to our nation and we will not go away. We are here to stay."

Barragán pursued her interest in environmental issues. She chaired the environmental task forces of both the Hispanic Caucus and the Progressive Caucus. In 2019, she got a seat on the influential Energy and Commerce Committee, where she worked as a voice for communities "on the frontlines of the negative health impacts associated with climate change and environmental injustice." With Reps. Pramila Jayapal and Donald McEachin, who were first elected with her in 2016, Barragán organized the Climate and Environmental Justice Task Force. In June 2020, they urged the Trump administration to immediately withdraw an executive order that sought to expedite development projects by bypassing key environmental reviews.

On immigration, Barragán joined Rep. Jimmy Gomez in a visit to the U.S-Mexico border, where they sought to assist asylum seekers who were kept in a caged area by Border Patrol agents. She said denial of her requests for information and access were "intimidation tactics at its worst." In June 2020, she joined a congressional delegation that inspected an Immigration and Customs Enforcement detention facility in Georgia, where she said immigrant women complained unnecessary medical procedures were performed without their consent. "What I saw here were human rights abuses," she said, adding that facilities run by for-profit contracts lacked oversight or accountability.

In 2018, Barragán initially was challenged for reelection by Compton Mayor Aja Brown, who ended her campaign with an announcement that she was pregnant. But she remained on the ballot. Two years later, her challenger was Democrat Joya Analilia, a local school teacher of students with disabilities, who did not file campaign spending reports. In each case, Barragan won, 68%-32%.

CA-44: Southern L.A.

Cook Partisan Voting Index: D+32

Population		Race and Ethnicity		Income	
Total	717,140	White	45.80%	Median Income	$59,030
Land area (sq. miles)	79	Black	14.60%	District Income Rank	280
Pop/ sq mi	9,036.54	Latino	71.40%	Poverty Rate	14.40%
Born in State	58.40%	Asian	6.00%	With health insurance	87.10%
		Two or more races	3.80%	Cash public assistance	6.60%
Age Groups		Other	29.80%	Food stamp/SNAP	16.80%
Under 18	25.50%				
18-34	26.70%	Education		Work	
35-64	36.00%	H.S grad or less	59.30%	White Collar	21.20%
Over 64	11.70%	Some college	25.90%	Sales and Service	45.00%
		College Degree, 4 yr	11.30%	Blue Collar	33.70%
Military		Post grad	3.60%	Government	12.50%
Veteran/ Active Duty	3.00%				

2020 Pres. Vote	Biden	188,767	(78%)	Trump	46,174	(19%)			
2016 Pres. Vote	Clinton	164,251	(83%)	Trump	24,261	(12%)	Stein	4,213	(2%)

San Pedro, Compton: Just five days after President Lyndon Johnson signed the landmark Voting Rights Act into law, a police arrest gone wrong led to the explosion of the Watts riots. Six days later, 34 people were dead, more than 1,000 were injured and Los Angeles had a wound that would take years to heal. Still, the area has shown some recovery and retained a rich cultural heritage. In Compton, the Central Avenue entertainment district during the postwar years was filled with clubs and theaters hosting Ella Fitzgerald, Sarah Vaughan, Duke Ellington and Louis Armstrong.

Compton symbolizes many deep social problems: high crime rates, gang violence, drugs and poverty. The influential late 1980s rap group N.W.A. expressed the frustration of many city residents with the song Straight Outta Compton. That led to a full-length hit movie in 2015 with the same title, which told the story of the rappers. The Bloods and Crips street gangs have seen the rise of Hispanic counterparts. Blacks are disproportionately the victims, and they are most of the gang members. The once-dominant Blacks in Compton have been overtaken by Hispanics, 68 percent (and rising) to 29 percent (and falling). The Bloods and Crips eventually reached a truce, which contributed to a limited reduction in crime. At the same time, real estate prices in Compton soared, spurred partly by investors speculating on the long-term prospects.

But not all is well. A state audit in 2018 found that the Compton government mismanaged taxpayer funds. Two years later, the city continued to top the State Auditor's list of "fiscally challenged" cities—making Compton the most riskiest city in California for investors. Adding to the miseries of life in Compton, fire officials in September 2020 identified a nearby abandoned oil field as the possible source of a chemical spill that was causing gas-like odors throughout Los Angeles and Orange counties. Notable success stories: Serena and Venus Williams grew up in Compton before they became world-class tennis champions. Local gangs protected the sisters as their prominence grew. And rapper Kendrick Lamar in 2018 won a Pulitzer Prize for music.

The 44th Congressional District includes Carson, Compton, Willowbrook and Rancho Dominguez, plus the overwhelmingly Hispanic South Gate and Lynwood—96 percent and 88 percent Latino, respectively. The district stretches south to include coastal areas, including San Pedro and some of Long Beach, which are more middle-class in character. It shares some terminals in the massive ports of Los Angles and Long Beach. Similar to other coastal parts of Los Angeles, a 44 percent plurality of San Pedro is white. Life can be challenging in San Pedro, too. A huge butane explosion on the other side of the world in Lebanon raised local concerns because San Pedro has huge butane tanks similar to the Beirut tanks that were not properly maintained and caused devastation. Citizen groups in San Pedro have struggled for years to shut down their active tanks.

Overall, the district is 71 percent Hispanic and 15 percent Black. Politically, it is solidly Democratic. In 2020, Joe Biden got 78 percent of the vote here, a dip from the 83 percent for Hillary Clinton—but still the third highest Democratic vote among L.A. districts. Until 2012, the area south and west of downtown Los Angeles selected three African-Americans to the House. The changing demographics have left barely enough Blacks to influence the selection of two African-American members.

Katie Porter (D)

Elected 2018, 2nd term, b. Jan 03, 1974; Des Moines, IA; Yale University, B.A., 1996; Harvard University, J.D., 2001; Episcopalian; Divorced; 3 children.

Professional Career: Public Interest Attorney; Law Professor, University of California, Irvine.

DC Office: 1117 LHOB 20515, 202-225-5611, porter.house.gov

State Offices: Irvine, 949-668-6600.

Committees: *Natural Resources*: Energy & Mineral Resources; National Parks, Forests & Public Lands; Oversight & Investigations (Chmn). *Oversight & Reform*: Government Operations; Subcommittee on Economic & Consumer Policy.

Almanac Ratings 2019-2020

	Economy	Social	Foreign	Composite
Liberal	100%	63%	80%	81%
Conservative	0%	37%	20%	19%

Key Votes of the 116th Congress

1. U.S./Mex./Can. trade deal	Y	5. Russia sanctions	Y	9. Firearms background checks	Y
2. First Coronavirus response	Y	6. Troops in Syria	Y	10. Spending at the border	Y
3. HEROES Act	Y	7. Veto arms sales to Saudis	Y	11. Marijuana liberalized rules	Y
4. CASH Act	Y	8. Defense $$$, veto override	Y	12. Electoral College objections	N

Election Results

Election	Name (Party)	Vote (%)		Cand. Spent	Ind. Exp. Support	Ind. Exp. Oppose
2020 General	Katie Porter (D)	221,843	(53%)	$6,777,133	$2,828,103	
	Greg Raths (R)	193,096	(47%)	$1,230,681	$145,294	$15,613
2020 Primary	Katie Porter (D)	112,986	(51%)			

Prior winning percentages: 2018 (52%)

Democrat Katie Porter enjoyed a meteoric rise over the last four years from law professor to a star interrogator on the House Financial Services Committee, who grilled agency officials and CEOs with aplomb. After ousting a GOP incumbent in 2018 in a traditionally conservative seat in Orange County, Porter catapulted onto the national stage and honed a reputation as a consumer advocate who holds the powerful accountable. She has been rewarded by a legion of small-dollar donors who have helped her sail through her first reelection. Porter is frequently discussed as a candidate for statewide office.

Porter, who grew up in a farm town in Iowa, graduated from Yale University, where her undergraduate thesis focused on the effects of corporate farming on rural America. She got her law degree from Harvard University, where she became a protégé of professor (and later Sen.) Elizabeth Warren—an expert on the consumer impact of banking practices. They co-authored a book, The Law of Debtors and Creditors, and Porter was a frequent booster of Warren's 2020 presidential bid.

After teaching at the University of Iowa law school, Porter shifted to California where then-Attorney General Kamala Harris appointed her to monitor the state's share of a mortgage fraud settlement. At the University of California, Irvine, Porter was a bankruptcy law professor.

Porter was the first Democrat to challenge GOP Rep. Mimi Walters in the 2018 campaign. In her first campaign ad, both Warren and Harris introduced and praised her. Porter's chief Democratic opponent in the all-party primary was Dave Min—another professor at the Irvine law school and a financial policy expert. Their clash became nasty and personal. Min had previously worked for Sen. Chuck Schumer of New York, a frequent defender of Wall Street and big banks. Min ran ads attacking Porter for her backing from "Washington insiders," notably EMILY's List, the group that supports Democratic women who favor abortion rights.

The Democratic state convention endorsed Min by a single vote. According to the Huffington Post, several convention delegates said advocates of a Porter rival had spread rumors that Porter's sealed divorced records included information that might be politically damaging. That report suggested Min was the source of the rumors. In the June primary for second place behind Walters, Porter led Min, 20%-18%.

During her two terms in the House, Walters supported cutbacks in federal regulation, including repeal of the Affordable Care Act. As the only one of the four House Republicans from Orange County who voted for the sweeping tax-cut legislation in 2017, she enthusiastically embraced the measure, which had some adverse effects on well-off taxpayers in high-tax states. Walters cast Porter as too liberal, while Porter sought to link Walters to President Donald Trump's actions and his administration's repeal of consumer protections. The two candidates and their parties spent a total of more than $15 million on the contest, with a nearly even split. Porter won, 52%-48%.

Porter's seat on the Financial Services Committee gave her the opportunity to shape the national debate on banking issues and made her one of the most high-profile members of her freshman class. Armed with a whiteboard, Porter turned normally humdrum committee hearings into viral moments, schooling Housing and Urban Development Secretary Ben Carson on real estate acronyms and JPMorgan Chase CEO Jamie Dimon on the lives of working-class families. "I'll be happy to send you a copy of the textbook that I wrote," she said when the director of the Consumer Finance Protection Bureau could not explain the difference between an interest rate and an annual percentage rate. But perhaps her greatest impact on the committee came when she forced Robert Redfield, head of the Centers for Disease Control and Prevention, to issue a promise that all Americans could receive free COVID-19 testing. "He knew the law," Porter told Time magazine later. "He just didn't want to be accountable for using the law to better Americans' lives."

Porter's theatrical performances won her invites to appear on talk shows with Seth Meyers, Samantha Bee and Bill Maher. And her supporters rewarded her by padding her campaign account. Her fundraising was prolific; she brought in over $1 million for seven consecutive quarters. In the third quarter of 2020 she raised a staggering $5.2 million. Mission Viejo City Councilman Greg Raths beat out five other Republicans for a chance to take on Porter. Raths proved to be a lackluster candidate. He spent only$1.4 million and just a fraction of that on TV ads. To add insult, the Orange County Register reported that he paid former Trump campaign manager Corey Lewandowski and commentator Tomi Lahren to record videos for his campaign through a celebrity video service. Porter won 53%-47% and, more importantly, ended the cycle with over $10 million in the bank.

But other Democrats did not fare as well as Porter and their diminished House majority likely precluded her from being seriously considered for a job in the Biden administration or to fill the open state attorney general position. She also lost her slot on Financial Services after Democratic leadership declined to grant her a waiver to serve on three committees. She became chair of the Natural Resources Subcommittee on Oversight and Investigations. Many expect Porter to remain in the limelight and to put her considerable war chest to use, perhaps for a statewide election.

CA-45: Central Orange   Cook Partisan Voting Index: D+3

Population		Race and Ethnicity		Income	
Total	791,311	White	61.90%	Median Income	$115,427
Land area (sq. miles)	330	Black	1.80%	District Income Rank	13
Pop/ sq mi	2,395.08	Latino	18.20%	Poverty Rate	8.90%
Born in State	49.20%	Asian	26.20%	With health insurance	94.80%
		Two or more races	4.90%	Cash public assistance	1.30%
Age Groups		Other	5.10%	Food stamp/SNAP	2.60%
Under 18	20.90%				
18-34	23.40%	**Education**		**Work**	
35-64	39.90%	H.S grad or less	16.90%	White Collar	57.30%
Over 64	15.70%	Some college	26.50%	Sales and Service	33.10%
		College Degree, 4 yr	33.80%	Blue Collar	9.60%
Military		Post grad	22.80%	Government	12.50%
Veteran/ Active Duty	4.10%				

2020 Pres. Vote	Biden	228,624	(55%)	Trump	181,306	(43%)		
2016 Pres. Vote	Clinton	162,449	(49%)	Trump	144,713	(44%)	Johnson	13,200 (4%)

Irvine, Lake Forest: Orange County is the sixth most populous county in the United States, having grown steadily from 130,000 people in 1940 to nearly 2 million in 1980 and to 3.2 million in 2019. It is now a community with the patina of maturity, and in some respects, of an aging community fraying at the edges. In recent years, its economy has been constantly reshaped: Tourism remains key, but there is no single industry responsible for Orange County's prosperity. It was rocked by recession in 2008, when the hyperinflation of the local housing market abruptly burst and home values slid as much as 20 percent. Rapid moves by local governments to cut costs and attract new projects, such as alternative energy jobs, helped the county recover faster than other California counties.

The third-largest city in Orange County is Irvine. Irvine Ranch was purchased by Gold Rush merchant James Irvine from the Sepulveda and Yorba families. As Orange County grew, the Irvine family was sitting on some immensely valuable territory, the last large plot of vacant land in metro Los Angeles. In 1959, the Irvines donated a site for the University of California, Irvine, which has grown to 36,000 students and consistently places in the top ten for the U.S. News & World Report's ranking of public universities. In the 1970s, they sold the rest to developers. Irvine was born as a planned community, with eight-lane parkways, huge office parks, shopping malls and attractive subdivisions. It lured high-tech and high-growth businesses, highly educated and affluent people. The FBI reported in 2020 that it was the safest city in America among those with a population of over 250,000. About 42 percent are Asian, including large numbers of Koreans and Vietnamese, and the city is home to a Chinese-language library.

Republican since 1936, Orange County became a symbol of conservatism, first in California and then nationally. This was a solid base for Ronald Reagan in his campaigns for governor and president. In 1988, the district's 317,000-vote plurality for George H.W. Bush was his largest in any county in the nation. Orange County has become more diverse. The all white stereotype is thoroughly out of date. Nearly one-third of the county's residents were born in another country, and 46 percent speak a language other than English at home. Its majority-minority population in 2019 had grown to 34 percent Hispanic and 22 percent Asian, though only 2 percent Black. The GOP advantage has vanished—and not by a small amount. Hillary Clinton led Donald Trump in Orange County, 51%-43%, a margin of 103,000 votes. History was made again in 2019 when registered Democrats surpassed Republicans in Orange County for the first time since 1978. Their edge grew to over 45,000 by early 2021.

The 45th Congressional District is made up of central and southern Orange County. Its population center is Irvine, and it also takes in parts of Anaheim, Orange and Mission Viejo. It is 26 percent Asian and 18 percent Hispanic. This is one of three districts that are based entirely in Orange County, while three others are partly in the county. Its once strongly Republican lean has shifted. In a district that Mitt Romney won 55%-43% in 2012, Joe Biden flipped the result to 55%-43% for Democrats..

Lou Correa (D)

Elected 2016, 3rd term, b. Jan 24, 1958; Los Angeles, CA; CA State University (Fullerton), B.S., 1980; University of CA, Los Angeles, J.D., 1985; University of CA, Los Angeles, M.B.A., 1985; Catholic; Married (Esther Reynoso Correa); 4 children.

Elected Office: CA Assembly, 1998-2004; Orange County Board of Supervisors, 2005-2006; CA Senate, 2006-2014.

Professional Career: Investment banker/ real estate broker; California High Speed Rail Authority, 2015-2016.

DC Office: 1039 LHOB 20515, 202-225-2965, correa.house.gov

State Offices: Santa Ana, 714-621-0102.

Committees: *Agriculture*: Biotechnology, Horticulture & Research; Conservation & Forestry (RMM); Livestock & Foreign Agriculture. *Homeland Security*: Border Security, Facilitation & Operations; Oversight, Management & Accountability (Chmn). *Judiciary*: Crime, Terrorism & Homeland Security; Immigration & Citizenship.

Group Ratings

	ADA	ACLU	AFL-CIO	LCV	COC	HAFA	ACU	CFG	FRC
2020	**	83%	**	100%	-	0%	8%	**	-
2019	85%	C	95%	93%	71%	C	11%	24%	0%

Almanac Ratings 2019-2020

	Economy	Social	Foreign	Composite
Liberal	56%	100%	92%	83%
Conservative	44%	0%	8%	17%

Key Votes of the 116th Congress

1. U.S./Mex./Can. trade deal Y	5. Russia sanctions Y	9. Firearms background checks Y
2. First Coronavirus response Y	6. Troops in Syria Y	10. Spending at the border N
3. HEROES Act Y	7. Veto arms sales to Saudis Y	11. Marijuana liberalized rules Y
4. CASH Act Y	8. Defense $$$, veto override Y	12. Electoral College objections N

Election Results

Election	Name (Party)	Vote (%)		Cand. Spent	Ind. Exp. Support	Ind. Exp. Oppose
2020 General	Lou Correa (D)	157,803	(69%)	$569,350	$2,166	
	James Waters (R)	71,716	(31%)	$8,135		$113
2020 Primary	Lou Correa (D)	60,095	(58%)			
	Pablo Mendiolea (D)	9,257	(9%)			

Prior winning percentages: 2018 (69%), 2016 (70%)

Democrat Lou Correa, elected to an open seat in 2016, has a close connection to the Mexican-American immigrant community and a grass roots political style. He has taken his deal making approach to the handling of homeland security issues. A leader of the centrist Blue Dog Democrats, he was an early supporter within the Hispanic Caucus of the presidential campaign of Joe Biden—partly because of his commitment to advocate immigration legislation.

Correa was born in East Los Angeles. His grandfather and American-born father returned to Mexico to look for work. When he was a year old, his mother died in an automobile accident in Mexico. After spending five more years in Mexico, he returned with his father plus aunts and uncles to Anaheim, where they struggled in subsistence living in small apartments. "I had enough to eat, and I had a roof over me when I slept. That's all I really cared about," he told the Los Angeles Times. After graduating from Anaheim High School, he got his bachelor's at California State University, Fullerton, and then a law degree and MBA from UCLA. He worked as an attorney, investment banker and real estate broker.

The passage in 1994 of Proposition 187, which targeted illegal immigration, made Correa politically active. He ran for the state Assembly in 1996 and lost by 93 votes. Two years later, he easily defeated the Republican incumbent. After six years in the Assembly, he was elected to the Orange County Board of Supervisors and then eight years in the state Senate. In 2014, he narrowly lost a bid to return to the board. Correa styled himself as a political moderate, often to the annoyance of Democratic leaders. "A lot of politicians will wring their hands and put a wet finger in the air to get a feel for what he should do," former Senate Majority Leader Donn Perata told the Times. "Lou just intuitively knew." He was consistent in his advocacy of immigrants' rights and criticized President Barack Obama for his deportations.

When 10-term Democratic Rep. Loretta Sanchez decided to run for the Senate, Correa sought the open seat and was endorsed by Sanchez and many Democratic Party leaders. In the eight-candidate first round of voting, he got 42 percent. Runner-up with 15 percent was Garden Grove Mayor Bao Nguyen, who had fled Vietnam as a baby with his parents. Nguyen appealed to supporters of Sen. Bernie Sanders. Correa, who was an early supporter of Hillary Clinton for president, appealed chiefly to Latinos in this heavily Hispanic district. With a fundraising advantage of $920,000 to $270,000, he had another easy win in the general election, 70%-30%.

In the House, unlike many other Democrats, Correa attended the inauguration of President Donald Trump. "I'm going to D.C. to be at the table when decisions are made that affect my constituents. Either we are at the table or we are on the menu," he said. He went to work at the Homeland Security Committee, where he won House passage of bills that revised the management of acquisition activities and imposed tighter security standards on firearms controlled by the Homeland Security Department.

Following a visit to the border with Mexico in November 2018, Correa called for a "Marshall Plan" to stimulate the economies of nations in Central America and reduce poverty and violence in the region. Current policies at the border were "not working," he said. In 2019, he became chairman of the panel's Subcommittee on Transportation and Maritime Security. Later that year, the final version of the annual defense spending bill included his amendment that requires the secretary of Defense to send Congress an annual report on cyber attacks on Pentagon systems by Russia, China, Iran and North Korea.

With Republican Rep. Matt Gaetz of Florida, Correa introduced the "Sensible Enforcement of Cannabis Act" to prevent prosecution of persons using marijuana in states where it is permitted for legal or medical purposes. In September 2020, discussing legislation to decriminalize marijuana, he complained to Politico that Democratic leaders decided to "avoid this vote altogether."

Correa, who reinforced his centrist cred as communications co-chair of the Blue Dogs, the coalition of fiscally moderate Democrats, was among the Hispanic Caucus members who were early supporters of Biden. A prime factor in their decision, he said, was Biden's commitment to place a priority on immigration legislation. The new president delivered on that promise by unveiling his proposal within hours after he took his inaugural oath.

In his two reelections, Correa won, 69%-31%, against Republican challengers with little name ID or spending. In 2021, he chaired the Homeland Security Subcommittee on Oversight, Management and Accountability.

CA-46: Northern Orange

Cook Partisan Voting Index: D+16

Population		Race and Ethnicity		Income	
Total	734,651	White	50.70%	Median Income	$71,800
Land area (sq. miles)	72	Black	2.10%	District Income Rank	151
Pop/ sq mi	10,243.32	Latino	67.00%	Poverty Rate	12.60%
Born in State	54.20%	Asian	13.80%	With health insurance	87.50%
		Two or more races	2.70%	Cash public assistance	1.90%
Age Groups		Other	30.80%	Food stamp/SNAP	8.30%
Under 18	23.80%				
18-34	28.10%	**Education**		**Work**	
35-64	37.40%	H.S grad or less	54.10%	White Collar	27.90%
Over 64	10.70%	Some college	24.80%	Sales and Service	44.50%
		College Degree, 4 yr	14.50%	Blue Collar	27.70%
Military		Post grad	6.60%	Government	9.30%
Veteran/ Active Duty	2.70%				

2020 Pres. Vote	Biden	150,186	(64%)	Trump	78,247	(34%)		
2016 Pres. Vote	Clinton	119,762	(66%)	Trump	50,403	(28%)	Johnson	5,630	(3%)
	Stein	3,711	(2%)					

Santa Ana, Central and Western Anaheim: When Walt Disney began planning Disneyland in the late 1940s, he did not have to drive far from downtown Los Angeles before finding undeveloped land. Dairy farms and orange groves covered most of southeast Los Angeles County and adjacent Orange County, which had only 216,000 people in 1950. As Disneyland opened there in 1955 and became a great success, the area around it—a mass of flatland surrounded by mountains and sea —found itself directly in the path of the most explosively growing metropolitan area in the United States. With 3.2 million people, this has become the nation's sixth-largest county. Disneyland agreed with its hotel workers union to increase the minimum wage to $18 in 2021, though the increase combined with the shutdown and limited reopening resulting from the coronavirus to lead to a cutback of thousands of jobs.

Just as Orange County was once transformed by newcomers from Los Angeles County and the Midwest, so it is again being transformed by immigrants, from Mexico and other parts of Latin America, and from Vietnam, Taiwan, Korea and other parts of East Asia. The county seat of Santa Ana is a major arrival point for immigrants from Mexico and is 77 percent Hispanic, of whom nearly half have been counted as non-citizens. Other immigrants have moved farther out, like so many Southern Californians before them, working multiple jobs, commuting on freeways and living in stucco subdivisions. There are concentrations in various places—Latinos in Santa Ana and much of Anaheim plus Vietnamese in Garden Grove. Overall, the county has the third largest Asian population in the nation, behind Los Angeles and Santa Clara counties. These demographic changes have made for some political wobble. After the 1994 approval of Proposition 187, which sought to deny most social services to illegal immigrants, many more Latinos began voting, mostly Democratic. Santa Ana, which declared its community a "sanctuary city" in 2017, joined the state of California a year later contesting a suit by the Justice Department that challenged their action; several other cities in Orange County sided with the feds. The Supreme Court has turned down several opportunities to rule on the issue.

The 46th Congressional District covers central and western areas of Orange County. It takes in parts of Santa Ana, which is the second-largest city in Orange County, and Orange. It includes a significant portion of Anaheim, Orange County's largest city and 54 percent Hispanic. The district is the Democratic core of the county, with population that is 67 percent Hispanic and 14 percent Asian. The Democratic presidential vote increased from 58 percent in 2008 to 66 percent in 2016. In 2020, support for Joe Biden dipped to 64 percent.

Alan Lowenthal (D)

Elected 2012, 5th term, b. Mar 08, 1941; New York, NY; Hobart College, B.A., 1962; OH State University, M.A., 1965; OH State University, Ph.D., 1967; Jewish; Married (Deborah Malumed); 2 children; 1 grandchild.

Elected Office: Long Beach City Council, 1992-1998; CA Assembly, 1998-2004; CA Senate, 2004-2012.

Professional Career: Professor, CA. St. University Long Beach, 1969-1998.

DC Office: 108 CHOB 20515, 202-225-7924, Fax: 202-225-7926, lowenthal.house.gov

State Offices: Garden Grove, 714-243-4088; Long Beach, 562-436-3828.

Committees: *Natural Resources*: Energy & Mineral Resources (Chmn); Indigenous Peoples of the United States; Water, Oceans & Wildlife. *Transportation & Infrastructure*: Coast Guard & Maritime Transportation; Highways & Transit; Water Resources & Environment.

Group Ratings

	ADA	ACLU	AFL-CIO	LCV	COC	HAFA	ACU	CFG	FRC
2020	**	86%	**	100%	-	0%	3%	**	-
2019	100%	C	90%	100%	38%	C	3%	12%	0%

Almanac Ratings 2019-2020

	Economy	Social	Foreign	Composite
Liberal	100%	100%	100%	100%
Conservative	0%	0%	0%	0%

Key Votes of the 116th Congress

1. U.S./Mex./Can. trade deal	N	5. Russia sanctions	Y	9. Firearms background checks	Y
2. First Coronavirus response	Y	6. Troops in Syria	Y	10. Spending at the border	N
3. HEROES Act	Y	7. Veto arms sales to Saudis	Y	11. Marijuana liberalized rules	Y
4. CASH Act	Y	8. Defense $$$, veto override	Y	12. Electoral College objections	N

Election Results

Election	Name (Party)	Vote (%)		Cand. Spent	Ind. Exp. Support	Ind. Exp. Oppose
2020 General	Alan Lowenthal (D)..................... 197,028	(63%)		$594,334	$2,334	
	John Briscoe (R)................................ 114,371	(37%)		$27,252		$113
2020 Primary	Alan Lowenthal (D)..................... 72,759	(45%)				
	Peter Mathews (D)........................ 17,616	(11%)				
	Jalen Dupree McLeod (D).................... 13,955	(9%)				

Prior winning percentages: 2018 (65%), 2016 (64%), 2014 (56%), 2012 (57%)

Alan Lowenthal, a Democrat first elected in 2012, is a rare academician seeking to bring pragmatic problem-solving to Washington. As chairman of a subcommittee dealing with energy and mineral resource issues, he focused on sustainable and renewable energy development, including environmental issues in the oceans. His port district has made him familiar with freight and maritime issues. With lengthy experience at home and in Sacramento, he kept a low profile in the House but raised thoughtful ideas.

Lowenthal was born in New York City, grew up in Queens and went to high school on Long Island. Lowenthal studied psychology at Hobart College, where he got a bachelor's degree, and he continued his studies at Ohio State University, earning a master's and a doctorate. During his doctoral training, he had an internship in San Francisco and decided that he wanted to live in California. Lowenthal took a position at California State University, Long Beach, in 1969 as an assistant professor.

He became involved in local politics in 1989, when the misconduct of a Long Beach police officer led Lowenthal to seek reforms of the police department, including new procedures for citizen complaints. He joined Long Beach Area Citizens Involved, an umbrella group of community organizations trying to influence local government, and became the group's president. In 1992, he won a seat on the Long Beach City Council. He was elected to the state Assembly in 1998, and to the state Senate six years later. In the legislature, Lowenthal focused on reducing air pollution at California ports and protecting public health. "I wanted to make sure the community was livable and the port economically viable," he said.

Long Beach Councilman Gary DeLong, Lowenthal's opponent in 2012, ran as a moderate Republican who said he would not be bound by the decisions of the House Republican leadership. In this firmly Democratic district, Lowenthal did his best to tie DeLong to the GOP establishment. He seized on a comment DeLong made at a community event in which he said he had not seen scientific evidence that confirms the existence of climate change. DeLong had the edge in spending, $1.4 million to $1.2 million. Lowenthal won 57%-43%.

Lowenthal has styled himself as a behind-the-scenes operator. "I don't scream and yell," he told the Long Beach Post in 2018. "I just make it very clear where I am and what I am going to do." A long-time environmentalist, he has advocated upgraded technology to handle freight "in a way that reduces pollution and gets us off carbon." With Sen. Tom Udall, he filed in February 2020 what they called "landmark" legislation to "tackle the plastic waste pollution crisis." Their proposal focused especially on such waste in the ocean, which Lowenthal said is the equivalent of the contents of a garbage truck every minute. He sought cooperation from state and local lawmakers to achieve their objectives, including the phase-out of single-use plastic products and a nationwide beverage container refund program.

As chairman of the Natural Resources Subcommittee on Energy and Mineral Resources, Lowenthal focused on renewable energy development, especially on public lands. In 2019, he introduced a package of bills that would prevent drilling in the oceans around the United States. "We must make it clear, once and for all, that our coastlines will not pay the price of oil production greed and hubris," he said. Lowenthal has occasionally sought bipartisan opportunities, including his legislation with Republican Rep. Don Young of Alaska to provide funding for conservation of threatened species and habitat.

Lowenthal has worked on foreign policy issues. With Republican Rep. Steve Chabot of Ohio, he formed and co-chaired the Congressional Cambodia Caucus. Long Beach has the largest community of Cambodians outside that nation. In 2016, the House passed his resolution condemning the government of Cambodia for its physical attacks and other persecution of the opposition.

Lowenthal wrote an op-ed in May 2020 for The Washington Post with Rep. Rashida Tlaib —"a Jewish American from Queens and a Palestinian American from Detroit"—urging the Trump administration to release all funds appropriated by Congress to support the well-being of the Palestinians, especially for COVID-19 relief. Separately, the House in December 2019 passed his resolution on a virtually party-line vote that the conflict between Israel and the Palestinians should be resolved in "a negotiated two-state solution"—an implicit rebuke of the Trump administration's approach.

At home, Lowenthal's reelections have been two sets of rematches against Republicans: Andy Whallon, a former aeronautical engineer, and John Briscoe, a member of the Board of Trustees in the Ocean View school district. Since 2016, he has consistently won at least 60 percent of the vote. The combination of redistricting and turning age 80 might test his commitment to the House for another term.

CA-47: Coastal L.A./Inland Orange   **Cook Partisan Voting Index: D+14**

Population		Race and Ethnicity		Income	
Total	717,594	White	52.50%	Median Income	$72,493
Land area (sq. miles)	216	Black	6.90%	District Income Rank	146
Pop/ sq mi	3,318.97	Latino	36.00%	Poverty Rate	13.50%
Born in State	56.50%	Asian	23.40%	With health insurance	91.10%
		Two or more races	4.20%	Cash public assistance	2.90%
Age Groups		Other	12.90%	Food stamp/SNAP	9.10%
Under 18	21.10%				
18-34	24.00%	Education		Work	
35-64	40.20%	H.S grad or less	37.90%	White Collar	40.50%
Over 64	14.70%	Some college	28.00%	Sales and Service	39.90%
		College Degree, 4 yr	23.50%	Blue Collar	19.60%
Military		Post grad	10.70%	Government	14.10%
Veteran/ Active Duty	4.90%				

2020 Pres. Vote	Biden	203,636	(62%)	Trump	115,161	(35%)			
2016 Pres. Vote	Clinton	161,743	(62%)	Trump	80,162	(31%)	Johnson	9,260	(4%)
	Stein	5,690	(2%)						

Long Beach, Garden Grove: With 462,000 people, Long Beach would be a major metropolis almost anywhere but in Los Angeles County, where it seems just the largest of many suburbs. But it has an identity of its own. Founded as a beach resort in 1888, it soon became a port when Los Angeles civic leaders decided that if their town was to be a world-class city, it must have a world-class harbor. Since nature had not provided one, they built it where the Los Angeles River flows into the ocean at the western edge of Long Beach. By 1909, Los Angeles had annexed the harbor towns of San Pedro and Wilmington on the other side of the river. Over the next decades, the two cities persuaded the federal government to dredge channels and build a breakwater and turning basins. Long Beach was developing other businesses as well. It sprouted oil derricks in the 1920s and briefly became one of the nation's big oil producers. It was the site of major aircraft plants in the 1940s and beyond.

Since then, the Los Angeles-Long Beach port has become the nation's busiest cargo center, with huge steel-gray container ships pulling up to enormous automated loading facilities. The two ports in the complex compete with each other on business terms, but collaborate on many issues. The L.A. port is the larger, with 26 terminals and 86 cranes handling more than 31,000, 20-foot containers daily; it occupies 7,500 acres of land along 43 miles of waterfront. Long Beach, with 30,000 employees and 68 gantry cranes, handles the equivalent of 24,000 containers daily docked at 10 piers and 80 berths serving seven terminals. From there, nearly half the cargo leaves by rail in more than 40 daily trains along the high-speed, 20-mile Alameda Corridor to the large rail yards near downtown Los Angeles. Trucking accounts for a declining share of the $180 billion in annual cargo on 2,000 vessels through the port. These facilities handle about half the goods imported into the nation, and a smaller share of exports. More than 90 percent of the port shipments are to or from East Asia. Both ports have increased their use of robots to lower costs and increase efficiency.

The Queen Mary, converted into a floating hotel, has been a big tourist attraction in Long Beach. In 2017, the company that owns the ship unveiled plans for a $250 million renovation of the vessel, which was built in the 1930s.In 2019, the company announced that the plan, which includes a new island, was delayed for at least two years. The city will host several events during the 2028 Olympics, including water polo and sailing. The downsizing of manufacturing in Long Beach culminated with Boeing closing the plant where it built the C-17 military transport and selling the property, which is adjacent to the airport, for $200 million to an Australian property-development firm. The Long Beach plant had been the last aircraft-manufacturing facility in California. A replacement span for the Gerald Desmond Bridge from the port to the Long Beach freeway, which is wider and higher than the previous span, was opened in October 2020.In its winter 2020 issue, City Journal described middle-class Long Beach as "what much of Southern California once was: a gritty, blue-collar trade and manufacturing community."

The 47th Congressional District is centered on Long Beach, and takes in Signal Hill, where oil rigs are still pumping. Parts are in Orange County, including Los Alamitos and Cypress, which has a large Asian-American population and is the birthplace of golfing great Tiger Woods. Parts of Garden Grove and Westminster, founded as a Presbyterian temperance colony in 1870, are shared with the 48th District. Nearly two-thirds of the total vote is in Los Angeles County. Politically, it leans strongly Democratic. In 2020, Joe Biden led Donald Trump, 62%-35%.

Michelle Steel (R)

Elected 2020, 1st term, b. Jun 21, 1955; Seoul, South Korea; Pepperdine University, B.S.; University of Southern CA, M.B.A.; Christian - Non-Denominational; Married (Shawn Steel); 2 children.

Elected Office: Member, CA State Board of Equalization, 2007-2015; Member, Orange County Board of Supervisors, 2015-2021. Chair, Orange County Board of Supervisors, 2020-2021; Co-Chair, President's Advisory Commission on Asian Americans and Pacific Islanders, 2019-2021.

DC Office: 1113 LHOB 20515, 202-225-2415, steel.house.gov

State Offices: Huntington Beach, 714-960-6483.

Committees: *Education & Labor*: Early Childhood, Elementary & Secondary Education; Workforce Protections. *Joint Congressional-Executive Commission on China.*

Election Results

Election	Name (Party)	Vote (%)		Cand. Spent	Ind. Exp. Support	Ind. Exp. Oppose
2020 General	Michelle Steel (R)	201,738	(51%)	$5,864,062	$229,112	$10,275,023
	Harley Rouda (D)	193,362	(49%)	$6,769,043	$911,880	$2,876,370
2020 Primary	Michelle Steel (R)	74,418	(35%)			
	Brian Burley (R)	25,884	(12%)			

Michelle Steel, who was elected to the House in 2020 when she defeated first-term Democratic Rep. Harley Rouda, has challenged the widespread view that the California Republican Party is on its death bed. For several years, she was the highest-elected Republican to hold statewide office. Since then, she chaired the Board of Supervisors of Orange County, which is the third largest county in California and the sixth largest in the nation. Politics is the family business: Her husband, Shawn Steel, a personal-injury lawyer, chaired the California Republican Party. Since 2008, he has been his state's Republican National Committeeman.

The personal brand has been a trademark of this upscale coastal district. For 30 years, Republican Rep. Dana Rohrabacher held the seat and often marched to the beat of his own drum, with his motto, "fighting for freedom and having fun." But his shtick suffered a beating after he talked up his friendship with Russian President Vladimir Putin.

In the Republican-leaning district, Rohrabacher was ousted in 2018 by Rouda, a native of Columbus Ohio who built a successful law practice there and resettled in Orange County only a few years before he challenged Rohrabacher. He succeeded, with a campaign he self-financed with $6 million of his own funds. In the House, Rouda appeared to go his own way and left few tracks. Among the seven California Democrats who took Republican-held seats in 2018, he soon became the top GOP target for 2020.

Steel offered an appealing bio. Born in Seoul South Korea, her father was a diplomat who took the family to Japan. When he died, Steel's mother—who did not speak English—emigrated to the United States with Steel and her two younger sisters, according to the California Globe, a website of political news. She got her bachelor's degree in business from Pepperdine University and a master's in business administration from the University of Southern California.

Steel moved into politics after her mother's business ran into tax problems and received a bill from the state Board of Equalization which, according to Steel, her mother did not owe. Steel learned more about the board, an obscure state agency that is responsible for tax administration and collection. "I knew I needed to help those who couldn't help themselves, so I decided to run for public office," she told the Globe. In 2006, Steel was elected as one of five members of the board. She served eight years, until she was term-limited. "I stopped a lot of taxes! I did whatever I could," she said.

In 2014, Steel was elected as an Orange County supervisor. The board's responsibilities range from taxes and spending to traffic congestion and clean beaches. The five-member board selects its chair and vice-chair for one-year terms. In 2020, Steel began her second term as board chairwoman.

When Rohrabacher suggested that she challenge Rouda, Steel explored her options and discovered that two-thirds of her county board district was in her congressional district. Her campaign showed her proclivity to attract attention—both positive and negative. Early during the coronavirus pandemic, when Steel objected to an Orange County requirement for wearing masks, Rouda cited her failure to protect public health. When Steel attacked him for "politicizing" the pandemic, she apparently gained public support.

In the final weeks of the campaign, Rouda's campaign ran ads that accused Shawn Steel of selling access to Chinese officials and called Michelle Steel "the most corrupt politician in Orange County." As a familiar local figure, Steel apparently had built goodwill with voters. In a campaign in which each candidate spent more than $5 million, she won, 51%-49%, a spread of about 8,000 votes.

CA-48: Coastal Orange

Cook Partisan Voting Index: R+1

Population		Race and Ethnicity		Income	
Total	718,359	White	62.10%	Median Income	$100,604
Land area (sq. miles)	145	Black	1.40%	District Income Rank	34
Pop/ sq mi	4,938.19	Latino	21.50%	Poverty Rate	7.90%
Born in State	54.30%	Asian	19.60%	With health insurance	93.70%
		Two or more races	4.90%	Cash public assistance	1.30%
Age Groups		Other	12.10%	Food stamp/SNAP	4.20%
Under 18	20.20%				
18-34	21.60%	Education		Work	
35-64	40.20%	H.S grad or less	26.30%	White Collar	46.30%
Over 64	18.00%	Some college	29.10%	Sales and Service	39.10%
		College Degree, 4 yr	28.20%	Blue Collar	14.60%
Military		Post grad	16.40%	Government	10.00%
Veteran/ Active Duty	4.60%				

2020 Pres. Vote	Biden	199,791	(50%)	Trump	193,832	(48%)			
2016 Pres. Vote	Clinton	152,035	(48%)	Trump	146,595	(46%)	Johnson	13,127	(4%)

Huntington Beach, Costa Mesa: In the 1950s, when the Beach Boys were at Hawthorne High School in L.A., surfers would drive far down the coast to the vast expanse of Huntington Beach in Orange County to catch a wave. This was empty country then, vegetable fields and orange groves mainly, with nary a freeway or shopping center in sight. Today, the 42-mile shoreline of Orange County is pretty much filled in with pricey coastal resorts and other developments. Huntington Beach, a city of nearly 200,000, is a mixture of family subdivisions and garden apartments and home of the International Surfing Museum. Its eight miles of beach and self-depiction as Surf City make it a tourist draw in the summer. To counter the state's water crisis, Huntington Beach is scheduled to open in 2023 a desalination plant, with a daily capacity of 50 million gallons of drinking water. In August 2020, the Los Angeles Times said the managers of the $1 billion project "still cannot definitively say" who will be its customers.

To the north is Westminster, the center of a prominent Vietnamese-American community, with miles of shops in Little Saigon with Vietnamese names and its own Vietnamese-language daily newspaper—the only Vietnamese newspaper with audited circulation in the United States. Southeast along San Diego Freeway is Fountain Valley, the central focus of many Asian-owned technology businesses. Near the coast is Costa Mesa, site of South Coast Plaza's luxury stores and a grand performing arts center. Like other California cities, it has experienced a huge influx of Hispanic immigrants, and adapting has been rocky. The city council in Costa Mesa, which is 36 percent Hispanic, shut down a day-laborer center.

The 48th Congressional District takes in much of coastal Orange County and is anchored by Huntington Beach. It includes the ocean side cities of Laguna Beach, with its art galleries and cute shops, and Newport Beach, one of California's richest cities. Newport Beach was the setting for the popular teen drama, The O.C. With their entrepreneurial spirit, many of the Vietnamese communities compete with each other, for example, in celebrating Tet, the Lunar New Year.

Parts of Garden Grove and Santa Ana are in the district, as are Fountain Valley, Seal Beach and Leisure World, its large gated community for seniors. Politically, this district has leaned Republican. In the district, Mitt Romney led President Barack Obama in 2012, 55%-43%. That changed with President Donald Trump, who lost to Joe Biden, 50%-48%.

Mike Levin (D)

Elected 2018, 2nd term, b. Oct 20, 1978; Inglewood, CA; Duke Law School; Stanford University, B.A., 2001; Catholic; Married (Chrissy Levin); 2 children.

Professional Career: Attorney.

DC Office: 1626 LHOB 20515, 202-225-3906, mikelevin.house.gov

State Offices: Dana Point, 949-281-2449; Oceanside, 760-599-5000.

Committees: *Natural Resources*: Energy & Mineral Resources; Water, Oceans & Wildlife. *Select Committee on the Climate Crisis*. *Veterans' Affairs (VChmn)*: Economic Opportunity (Chmn); Health; Women Veterans Task Force.

Almanac Ratings 2019-2020

	Economy	Social	Foreign	Composite
Liberal	100%	100%	80%	94%
Conservative	0%	0%	20%	6%

Key Votes of the 116th Congress

1. U.S./Mex./Can. trade deal Y	5. Russia sanctions Y	9. Firearms background checks Y
2. First Coronavirus response Y	6. Troops in Syria Y	10. Spending at the border Y
3. HEROES Act Y	7. Veto arms sales to Saudis Y	11. Marijuana liberalized rules Y
4. CASH Act Y	8. Defense $$$, veto override Y	12. Electoral College objections N

Election Results

Election	Name (Party)	Vote (%)	Cand. Spent	Ind. Exp. Support	Ind. Exp. Oppose
2020 General	Mike Levin (D)............................. 205,349	(53%)	$3,514,578	$77,490	
	Brian Maryott (R)................................ 181,157	(47%)	$2,806,800		$113
2020 Primary	Mike Levin (D)............................. 125,639	(57%)			

Prior winning percentages: 2018 (56%)

Democrat Mike Levin, a lawyer who specialized in environmental and energy policy, parlayed his role as leader of the Orange County Democratic Party into a seat in Congress in 2018, joining a slew of political newcomers who turned Southern California blue. He has become a prominent voice on environmental issues and joined the Congressional Progressive Caucus. He replaced Republican Rep. Darrell Issa, former chairman of the House Oversight and Government Reform Committee, who retired after watching his district shift left.

Levin, a native of Orange County, was the son of a Mexican-American mother and a Jewish father in a family of refugees from Austria. He got his bachelor's degree from Stanford, where he was a classmate and became a friend of Chelsea Clinton, and his law degree from Duke University. After serving as executive director of Orange County Democrats, his interest in environmental law led him to join a company that developed technology to convert waste gas from landfills and wastewater plants into zero-emission electricity. He served on the board of the Center for Sustainable Energy.

Following Issa's unexpectedly narrow victory by1,621 votes in 2016, Levin launched his candidacy in March 2017. A fundraiser for Hillary Clinton's 2016 campaign, he decided to run while returning to California from New York City, where he spent election night in 2016. He described himself as "a political organizer" and he was endorsed by numerous liberal groups and House Democrats from California, plus local grassroots activists who had protested Issa.

In California's nonpartisan primary, Levin faced three other well-financed Democrats who had various shortcomings. Doug Applegate, a retired Marine Corps colonel and Issa's previously unknown challenger in 2016, had been accused of threatening his ex-wife, who obtained a restraining order against him. Sara Jacobs benefited as the only woman in the group and from $1 million in self-funding. But she received unfavorable media coverage for inflating her job descriptions as a State Department contractor during the Obama administration and as an aide in the 2016 Clinton campaign. Paul Kerr, a real-estate investor, contributed and loaned nearly $6 million to his campaign, but he suffered from political inexperience.

Levin led the Democrats in the primary, with 17 percent of the total vote, to 16 percent for Jacobs and 13 percent for Applegate. In 2020, Jacobs made a successful run for the nearby 53rd district. Levin is now serving in Congress with Issa, who ran to replace the embattled Republican Rep. Duncan Hunter in a more GOP-friendly district based in San Diego.

Republican Diane Harkey ran first overall in the primary, with 26 percent of the total vote, though the four Democrats received 51 percent of the combined vote. Harkey was politically experienced as a member of the state Board of Equalization, which manages tax collection, and as a former Assemblywoman. She described herself as a "tax-fighter" and mostly praised the policies of President Donald Trump, though she raised concerns about some of his style and tactics.

Levin had a big financial advantage, as he more than tripled Harkey's spending during the closing months of the campaign. He was lifted by the Democratic surge throughout southern California, where he had the most comfortable victory of the six Democratic newcomers who won House seats. In his 56%-44% victory, Levin had nearly 60 percent of the vote in San Diego portion of the district; Harkey led by about 5,000 votes in Orange County.

In the House, Levin joined the Hispanic Caucus and devoted much effort to advancing environmental priorities. In 2019, he marshalled four dozen Democratic colleagues to sign a letter denouncing the Environmental Protection Agency for "politically motivated attacks" on California after the agency accused San Francisco of violating the Clean Water Act. The House in the fall of 2020 passed a bill in which Levin drafted language. It created a federal research program that would remove nuclear waste from the San Onofre facility in his district. He took an interest in veterans' issues and in 2021 chaired the Veterans Affairs' Subcommittee on Economic Opportunity.

His first reelection was a quieter affair than in 2018. He had just one opponent in the primary and the general: Brian Maryott, a certified financial planner who gave his campaign nearly $900,000 through loans and personal contributions. He spent $2.8 million to Levin's $3.5 million but the race drew no outside spending on TV and neither party considered the contest to be especially competitive. Levin won 53%-47%. Maryott won the smaller Orange County portion, 56%-44%, but trailed Levin 56%-44% in the more populous San Diego County.

Levin's slice of southern California does not appear to be snapping back to its traditionally Republican roots. His neighboring Democratic freshmen colleagues in the region were not as fortunate. Two lost in 2020. But the prospect of California losing a seat in districting puts them all at risk in 2022.

CA-49: Northwest San Diego

Cook Partisan Voting Index: D+4

Population		Race and Ethnicity		Income	
Total	731,366	White	80.60%	Median Income	$100,037
Land area (sq. miles)	553	Black	2.30%	District Income Rank	36
Pop/ sq mi	1,322.35	Latino	27.80%	Poverty Rate	6.00%
Born in State	51.30%	Asian	6.90%	With health insurance	92.50%
		Two or more races	5.70%	Cash public assistance	1.20%
Age Groups		Other	4.50%	Food stamp/SNAP	3.20%
Under 18	22.50%				
18-34	22.50%	Education		Work	
35-64	38.60%	H.S grad or less	24.60%	White Collar	46.30%
Over 64	16.30%	Some college	28.30%	Sales and Service	38.70%
		College Degree, 4 yr	28.10%	Blue Collar	15.00%
Military		Post grad	19.10%	Government	11.50%
Veteran/ Active Duty	11.80%				

2020 Pres. Vote	Biden	217,061	(55%)	Trump	167,049	(43%)	
2016 Pres. Vote	Clinton	159,081	(50%)	Trump	135,576	(43%) Johnson	13,636　(4%)

Oceanside, Vista: The California coast between Los Angeles and San Diego has never entirely filled up with development—and never will as long as the Marine Corps retains custody of Camp Pendleton, the giant training base just south of the Orange-San Diego County line and the Corps' largest expeditionary training facility on the West Coast. The land along the coast and inland in northern San Diego County, usually referred to as North County, was largely empty territory a half-century ago—never fertile enough to produce a large farm community, never endowed with much manufacturing, never actively promoted as a retirement community.

But North County has been growing rapidly since then. Today more than 800,000 people live here, and who can blame them? This is one of America's most beautiful and comfortable environments, with ocean and mountain scenery, sunny and warm weather, and low crime. Just south of Camp Pendleton, the city of Oceanside approved an ordinance in 2018 that allows residents to grow and distribute medical cannabis. Amid dry but not desert landscape, there are miles of rolling hills, with occasional sagebrush-like bushes. It has attracted thousands of new migrants—many, but by no means all, retirees. The commercial value of the land and buildings at Camp Pendleton, with its 17 miles along the coast, is more than $1.7 billion.

Southern California Edison announced in 2013 the permanent shutdown of the San Onofre nuclear plant because of the financial costs and regulatory uncertainty of restarting a reactor following discovery of a radiation leak. The company began the decommissioning in 2018, which it estimated as a 20-year, $4.4 billion project. In return, homeowners in the area expected that their properties would appreciate several billion dollars in value. In Carlsbad, a $1 billion desalination plant opened in 2015, partly in response to the California water crisis, and has been meeting about 10 percent of the region's water demands.

The 49th Congressional District covers the southernmost coastal area of Orange County, including Laguna Niguel and the heavily Republican San Clemente. Known as the "Spanish Village by the Sea," San Clemente is where Richard Nixon retired to write his memoirs after resigning the presidency. Nixon purchased his 5.5-acre estate in 1969, reportedly for a bit less than $1 million, though the financing was complicated and later controversial. He sold it in 1980. In 2018, it was reported that the subsequent owner, the retired chief executive of Allergan pharmaceutical company, had reduced the listed price of the property to $63.5 million. Nearby, in Dana Point, a developer got county approval for a $330 million renovation of the old harbor that will include at least two new hotels and a sea lion and seal monitoring program. The district takes in parts of northern San Diego County and the North County, including Oceanside, Encinitas and Carlsbad, home of the La Costa resort and a big tourist destination. Much of the interior area is a mix of mountains and canyons, and lightly inhabited. About three-fourths of the voters in the 49th are in San Diego.

Politically, the district leaned Republican for decades, but it trended swiftly left in the last half of the past decade. Its traditionally conservative population did not take kindly to Donald Trump; Hillary Clinton led him, 50%-43% in 2016. Joe Biden beat Trump by an even larger margin in 2020, 55%-42%.

Darrell Issa (R)

Elected 2020, 10th term, b. Nov 01, 1953; Cleveland, OH; Kent State University, A.A., 1976; Siena Heights University, B.A., 1976; Christian - Non-Denominational; Separated; 1 child.

Military Career: Captain, U.S. Army, 1970–1972, 1976–1980.

Elected Office: U.S. House, 2001-2019.

Professional Career: CEO, auto security company.

DC Office: 2300 LHOB 20515, 202-225-5672, issa.house.gov

State Offices: San Marcos, 760-304-7575; Temecula, 760-304-7575.

Committees: *Foreign Affairs*: Africa, Global Health & Global Human Rights; Intern'l Dev't, Intern'l Orgs & Global Corporate Social Impact. *Judiciary*: Antitrust, Commercial & Administrative Law; Courts, Intellectual Property & Internet (RMM).

Election Results

Election	Name (Party)	Vote (%)		Cand. Spent	Ind. Exp. Support	Ind. Exp. Oppose
2020 General	Darrell Issa (R)	195,521	(54%)	$11,289,313	$62,831	$1,111,327
	Ammar Campa-Najjar (D)	166,869	(46%)	$6,219,892	$80,945	
2020 Primary	Darrell Issa (R)	47,036	(23%)			
	Carl DeMaio (R)	40,347	(20%)			
	Brian W. Jones (R)	21,495	(11%)			

Darrell Issa has returned to Congress after having served nine terms in an adjacent district. After he decided not to seek reelection in 2018, that seat flipped to Democratic Rep. Mike Levin. As chairman of the Oversight and Government Reform Committee from 2011 to 2015, Republican Issa made himself President Barack Obama's chief investigative nemesis. His aggressive, headline-grabbing pursuits of alleged waste, fraud and abuse in the administration made him a hero to conservatives and the scourge of liberals. Issa returned to Congress in a relatively safe Republican district, where six-term Rep. Duncan Hunter resigned in January 2020 after he pleaded guilty to federal corruption charges.

Issa grew up in a working-class section of Cleveland, the son of an X-ray technician. Hampered by dyslexia, he found academics difficult and dropped out of high school to join the Army. After his service, the military paid for him to finish school, and he graduated from Siena Heights University in Michigan. A brother's run-ins with the law for car theft spurred Issa's idea for his first business venture. He invested all his savings, some $7,000, in a car-alarm business in Cleveland, eventually taking it over with his wife, Kathy, and relocating the business to Vista California, north of San Diego.

Directed Electronics became the nation's largest manufacturer of vehicle security systems, including the popular Viper system, and earned them a fortune. Issa became active in the high-technology lobby, serving as chairman of the Consumer Electronics Association. In 2017, the Center for Responsive Politics ranked Issa as the wealthiest member of Congress, with an estimated net worth of about $330 million.

In the early 1990s, Issa turned to politics, contributing to Republicans and chairing the successful 1996 campaign to pass Proposition 209, which banned the use of racial quotas and preferences in California. In 1998, he sought the Republican nomination to challenge Sen. Barbara Boxer and spent

$9.8 million of his own money. He lost the primary 45%-40% to Matt Fong. In November 1999, when Rep. Ron Packard announced his retirement, 10 candidates ran in the Republican primary. This turned into a contest between Issa and state Sen. Bill Morrow. Morrow questioned Issa's business practices, and Issa raised questions about Morrow's honesty. On most issues, the candidates took similar positions. Issa spent $1.5 million of his own money on the primary and beat Morrow 46%-30%. In the fall, the Democratic nominee abandoned his campaign after getting little national party support and Issa won 61%-28%.

After the 2008 election, House Republican leaders chose Issa over several more senior Republicans as ranking member on the Oversight committee, with broad authority to investigate the federal government. As chairman in 2011, he began by accusing the Department of Homeland Security of letting political appointees interfere with Freedom of Information Act requests, and subsequently made a regular point of describing the Obama administration's refusal to release documents as inconsistent with its stated philosophy of openness. His committee issued a stinging report on the handling of the Deep water Horizon oil spill disaster in the Gulf of Mexico, accusing Obama and his administration of giving BP too much control over cleanup operations and compensation to affected Gulf Coast residents.

The "Fast and Furious" investigation dominated the committee's early agenda. The Bureau of Alcohol, Tobacco, Firearms and Explosives operation, which began in 2009, allowed guns to be shipped illegally into Mexico in an effort to track them to drug cartels. Two of the guns were found a year later at the scene of the killing of a U.S. Border Patrol agent in Arizona. Issa and other committee Republicans repeatedly pressed the administration to discuss who at the Justice Department was aware of the operation, as well as who authorized it. Justice officials, citing executive privilege, said releasing material Issa sought could jeopardize ongoing investigations. The spat became a hot topic for conservatives and conspiracy theories flourished, including one floated by Issa at a National Rifle Association convention that the Obama administration deliberately lost the guns to justify a push for renewal of a ban on so-called assault weapons.

In 2013,Issa conducted an extended review of the Internal Revenue Service's treatment of Tea Party political groups that had applied for tax-exempt status. Issa and his staff documented examples of the IRS treating conservative activists with a double standard compared to their liberal counterparts. After Lois Lerner, the head of the IRS division on tax-exempt organizations, was discovered to have "lost" tens of thousands of files in her office computer, Issa asked the Justice Department to investigate whether she had broken the law. Nearly a year later, the department concluded that there were not sufficient grounds on which to charge her.

In 2015, Issa became chairman of the Judiciary Subcommittee on Courts, Intellectual Property and Internet. He pursued, in particular, patent reform issues. Drawing on his experience as a patent holder (he has held 37), he had sponsored a bipartisan bill enacted in 2011 that gave federal district court judges hearing patent cases access to clerks trained in patent law. Issa pursued legislation to restrict "patent trolls" who obtain patents solely for the purpose of launching infringement suits to cash in on multibillion-dollar damage awards. But he ran into opposition from other conservatives, who feared that the proposal would stifle innovation and entrepreneurship.

With ambitions for statewide office, Issa in 2003 spent $1.7 million of his own money to get the signatures needed for a recall election of Democratic Gov. Gray Davis. His hopes of getting unified GOP support as a replacement candidate were dashed when Arnold Schwarzenegger joined the race. Issa tearfully announced that he would not run.

After that, he was reelected easily, until his political fortunes had an abrupt change in 2016. Democratic challenger Doug Applegate, a retired Marine Corps colonel and political neophyte, sought to take advantage of local voters' hostility to Republican presidential nominee Donald Trump. Applegate said Issa was "Trump before there was Trump. "Issa helped the Democrats make their case by introducing Trump at an enthusiastic rally in San Diego a few days before the June primary in California.

Issa was slow to respond to the challenge, even when he led the first round of voting by a mere 50%-45.5%. He was a "high-profile Trump booster in a rapidly changing, well-educated district where Trump is toxic," David Wasserman of the Cook Political Report wrote a month before the election. The Democratic Congressional Campaign Committee and its liberal allies spent $3.6 million, in addition to the $2.1 million that Applegate raised. The deep-pocketed Issa raised $2.9 million, but self-financed only $36,000 and had no national party assistance. Three weeks after the election, Issa was declared the winner, 50.3%-49.7%, a margin of 1,621 votes. Rather than face another tough challenge, Issa announced that he would not seek reelection in 2018. Late that year,

Trump nominated him to a senior position at the Commerce Department. But Democrats objected and the Senate failed to act.

Issa's retirement was short-lived. In September 2019, he announced his candidacy in the House district adjacent to his old seat; he emphasized a return to his actions as Oversight chairman, though Republicans no longer held House control. Hunter, a fellow Republican, was charged with using a quarter-million dollars in campaign funds for personal use. Issa said that while Hunter deserved his day in court, the House district "does deserve the ability to maintain this as a conservative district and quite frankly to have a member who can show up and take all of his committee assignments." Hunter resigned in January and was sentenced to 11 months in prison.

In the first round of voting, Issa's $7 million significantly outspent his opponents. He led Carl DeMaio, a Republican former San Diego City Council member who had become a proponent of statewide political reforms, with 23 percent of the total vote to 20 percent. Democrat Ammar Campa-Najjar, who got 37 percent of the vote, was making a second bid for the seat. In 2018, he lost to the already politically wounded Hunter, 52%-48%. In their November 2020 showdown, the district returned to normalcy—aside from the unusual circumstance of two major-party candidates of Arab descent. Although the outcome was a bit tighter than expected, Issa won, 54%-46%.

CA-50: Inland San Diego

Cook Partisan Voting Index: R+8

Population		Race and Ethnicity		Income	
Total	758,142	White	78.80%	Median Income	$78,346
Land area (sq. miles)	2,787	Black	2.70%	District Income Rank	102
Pop/ sq mi	271.99	Latino	32.20%	Poverty Rate	11.70%
Born in State	55.70%	Asian	5.90%	With health insurance	92.30%
		Two or more races	5.90%	Cash public assistance	2.40%
Age Groups		Other	6.80%	Food stamp/SNAP	7.20%
Under 18	23.80%				
18-34	22.50%	**Education**		**Work**	
35-64	38.00%	H.S grad or less	34.60%	White Collar	36.80%
Over 64	15.80%	Some college	34.50%	Sales and Service	41.20%
		College Degree, 4 yr	19.90%	Blue Collar	22.00%
Military		Post grad	11.00%	Government	12.60%
Veteran/ Active Duty	10.10%				

2020 Pres. Vote	Trump	195,430	(53%)	Biden	166,841	(45%)		
2016 Pres. Vote	Trump	159,822	(54%)	Clinton	115,864	(39%)	Johnson	12,240	(4%)

Escondido, El Cajon: San Diego began as a port, but today most metropolitan-area residents live out of sight of the sea, in hilltop neighborhoods that look out over distant ridges and freeways or in warm, sunny valleys amid the mountains that become dense and taller as one travels east from the Pacific Ocean. There is a discernible difference in attitudes and values between those who have settled inland and those who live nearer the ocean, part of the split between coastal California and interior California that has been at the heart of the state's political struggles and culture wars. Outside the city of San Diego, these groups in San Diego County have tended to identify as Republicans. Coastal residents tend to be more affluent, and those who settle inland are more likely to be culturally traditional, supportive of the military and dubious about the ability of government to help society's have-nots. Part of this can be explained by the area's large military presence. A 2019 report estimated that the Pentagon accounts for about $51 billion in annual spending in San Diego County, which is more than 20 percent of the local economy. That includes 143,000 civilians and active-duty military and 65 ships home-ported in San Diego, and two aircraft carriers based in Coronado. More than 240,000 veterans and military retirees have settled in the area.

North of San Diego on Interstate 15 is Escondido, a conservative city that is 51 percent Hispanic. Tensions between the Escondido political leadership and Latino activists have heightened in recent years, as the city council passed several tough ordinances cracking down on illegal immigration. In November 2018, participants in the long-running conflict clashed over the Justice Department's lawsuit against the California law supporting sanctuary cities. With a large turnout from newly enfranchised Hispanic voters, a liberal majority in 2018 elected a new mayor Paul McNamara, a retired Marine colonel.

The 50th Congressional District of California takes in much of the mountain and desert interior of San Diego County. The district includes a small slice of Riverside County, which is mostly in Temecula, the site of the largest wine-producing region in southern California. It touches neither the Pacific Ocean nor the border with Mexico, but it comes within a few miles of each. Eastern parts of the district are lightly inhabited. In the mountains is tiny Alpine and in the desert is the town of Borrego Springs, amid the giant Anza-Borrego Desert State Park. Politically, this district is solidly Republican. In 2020, this was the strongest California district for President Donald Trump south of Bakersfield. He led Joe Biden, 53%-45%.

Juan Vargas (D)

Elected 2012, 5th term, b. Mar 07, 1961; National City, CA; University of San Diego, B.A., 1983; Fordham University, 1987; Harvard University Law School, J.D., 1991; Roman Catholic; Married (Adrienne D'Ascoli); 2 children.

Elected Office: San Diego City Council, 1993-2000; CA Assembly, 2000-2006, Assistant Majority Leader, 2000; CA Senate, 2010-2012.

Professional Career: Practicing attorney, Luce, Forward, Hamilton, & Scripps; Vice President., external affairs, Safeco Ins., 2006-2008; Vice President., corporate legal, Liberty Mutual Group, 2008-2010.

DC Office: 2244 RHOB 20515, 202-225-8045, Fax: 202-225-2772, vargas.house.gov

State Offices: Chula Vista, 619-422-5963; El Centro, 760-312-9900.

Committees: *Financial Services*: Consumer Protection & Financial Institutions; Housing, Community Development & Insurance; Investor Protection, Entrepreneurship & Capital Markets. *Foreign Affairs*: Middle East, North Africa & Global Counterterrorism; West Hem, Civ Sec, Migration, & Intern'l Econ Policy.

Group Ratings

	ADA	ACLU	AFL-CIO	LCV	COC	HAFA	ACU	CFG	FRC
2020	**	81%	**	100%	-	0%	4%	**	-
2019	95%	C	100%	96%	51%	C	5%	24%	0%

Almanac Ratings 2019-2020

	Economy	Social	Foreign	Composite
Liberal	100%	100%	58%	86%
Conservative	0%	0%	42%	14%

Key Votes of the 116th Congress

1. U.S./Mex./Can. trade deal Y	5. Russia sanctions　Y	9.　Firearms background checks Y
2. First Coronavirus response Y	6. Troops in Syria　Y	10. Spending at the border　N
3. HEROES Act　Y	7. Veto arms sales to Saudis　Y	11. Marijuana liberalized rules　Y
4. CASH Act　Y	8. Defense $$$, veto override Y	12. Electoral College objections N

Election Results

Election	Name (Party)	Vote (%)		Cand. Spent	Ind. Exp. Support	Ind. Exp. Oppose
2020 General	Juan Vargas (D)	165,596	(68%)	$844,428	$2,193	
	Juan Hidalgo (R)	76,841	(32%)			$59
2020 Primary	Juan C. Vargas (D)	77,744	(71%)			

Prior winning percentages: 2018 (71%), 2016 (73%), 2014 (69%), 2012 (71%), 1992 (71%)

Democrat Juan Vargas, first elected in 2012, has taken control of the district that he first sought in 1996. In this border district, he has spent much of his time on immigration—seeking to deal pragmatically with real human needs, not simply a partisan clash. On the Financial Services

Committee, where he has personal expertise, he opposed in 2018 the rollback of the Dodd-Frank banking regulatory law. He has occasionally talked truth to the leaders of his own party.

Vargas was born in National City, just south of San Diego. He is the son of braceros, who were among the millions of legal Mexican immigrants brought to the U.S. for cheap labor. He grew up on a chicken ranch in an urbanized area. He considered entering the priesthood but said he was wary of going straight into a seminary. Instead, he graduated from the University of San Diego. After college, Vargas studied with the Jesuits, working with the poor, orphans and refugees in El Salvador and elsewhere. The Jesuits sent him to Fordham University, where he studied philosophy and earned a master's degree. At Harvard, he earned a law degree alongside a student named Barack Obama.

After law school, Vargas settled in San Diego and briefly worked at a large corporate law firm. He served on the City Council for seven years, then won election to the California Assembly, where he stayed for six years. In 2010, he won election to the state Senate, where he chaired the Banking and Financial Institutions Committee and advocated government support for children and the elderly. He sponsored a bill mandating the reporting of child abuse by athletic coaches in California. Between his stints in the legislature, he was an executive with two insurance companies.

Vargas ran three unsuccessful campaigns against Rep. Bob Filner in Democratic primaries. Filner stepped down in 2012 and was elected mayor of San Diego, but quickly faced allegations of sexual harassment and resigned under pressure. Running for the open House seat, Vargas and Latina Democrat Denise Moreno Ducheny competed in California's all-party primary. Vargas lavished attention on the Republican candidate, Michael Crimmins, to help him slide into second place. He refused to participate in a debate unless Crimmins was included. Meanwhile, Vargas hammered Ducheny for a previous drunken-driving arrest. Crimmins edged Ducheny 20%-15%. His defeat in the fall election was all but assured in the strongly Democratic district. It was a smart strategy. Vargas won 72%-28%. He has had no trouble with reelection.

Vargas has sought to provide a sympathetic ear to immigrants and refugees, no matter their circumstances. After protesters turned away busloads in Murrieta, he met with them the next day in El Centro in 2014. Carrying a Bible, Vargas prayed with them and told them they would be treated "fairly and with dignity." He did not promise they would remain in the United States. In 2016, he filed legislation that would require the military to inform recruits who are not citizens about the citizenship process while they are in training. While Donald Trump during his presidential campaign was promising to build a wall along the border with Mexico, Vargas told civic groups in his district that he wanted to build more bridges.

On two immigration issues in 2020, Vargas demonstrated his practical approach. With other House Democrats from California whose districts are near the border, he filed a bill in August that sought to address longstanding problems at the border related to the safety of drinking water. Designating the Environmental Protection Agency to work with government agencies from the local to the international levels in each nation, Vargas said, "is crucial to creating cost-effective projects with meaningful results" by addressing public health and environmental hazards. A month earlier, he took the lead with Hispanic Caucus chairman Rep. Joaquin Castro to demand that executives of private prisons that serve as detention centers for individuals who have illegally crossed the border give more attention to the spread of coronavirus. To confront the risk of accelerating transmission of the virus among detainees and facility staff, authorities needed to increase testing and enforce social distancing, Vargas and Castro wrote to the prison executives.

On the Financial Services Committee, Vargas worked with members who shared his interest in insurance issues. He cosponsored a bipartisan measure that conditioned trade agreements with the nations of the European Union on their rejection of the anti-Israel boycott, divestment and sanctions movement. That provision was enacted in 2015 as part of the measure that gave trade promotion authority to Obama. In 2018, the House passed a Vargas bill to require that the Government Accountability Office study how online marketplaces facilitate drug and sex trafficking and offer solutions to Congress.

Vargas remained hostile to Trump. When Trump met at the Capitol in June 2018 with House Republicans, Vargas joined four other House Democrats at the entrance and shouted at Trump, "Don't you have kids, Mr. President?" Trump ignored them. As the 2020 Democratic presidential nominating contest began, Vargas joined others in the Hispanic Caucus in voicing fear that Bernie Sanders could not defeat Trump in November. "In these districts we barely won [in 2018], if [Democratic incumbents] get labeled a socialist, and if our candidate is running as a democratic socialist, these guys would lose. There's no doubt in my mind." That was the result in many places, especially with many Hispanic voters, even without Sanders at the top of the ticket.

CA-51: San Diego to Nevada

Cook Partisan Voting Index: D+20

Population		Race and Ethnicity		Income	
Total	740,797	White	68.50%	Median Income	$52,471
Land area (sq. miles)	4,792	Black	6.60%	District Income Rank	363
Pop/ sq mi	154.6	Latino	71.30%	Poverty Rate	17.50%
Born in State	54.70%	Asian	7.70%	With health insurance	87.60%
		Two or more races	3.70%	Cash public assistance	3.60%
Age Groups		Other	13.50%	Food stamp/SNAP	14.30%
Under 18	24.90%				
18-34	27.10%	**Education**		**Work**	
35-64	35.60%	H.S grad or less	53.90%	White Collar	23.20%
Over 64	12.40%	Some college	30.40%	Sales and Service	50.00%
		College Degree, 4 yr	11.20%	Blue Collar	26.80%
Military		Post grad	4.50%	Government	16.10%
Veteran/ Active Duty	8.20%				

2020 Pres. Vote	Biden	166,351	(67%)	Trump	76,843	(31%)		
2016 Pres. Vote	Clinton	147,603	(71%)	Trump	46,825	(23%)	Johnson	5,714	(3%)
	Stein	4,065	(2%)					

Eastern Chula Vista, Imperial: Anchoring a corner of the continental United States, San Diego not so long ago was a small Navy town known for its good harbor and splendid weather. It is now a major metropolis of 1.4 million people and the center of a county of 3.3 million. To its occasional discomfort, it is also one of the largest cities directly on an international border, situated between countries with strikingly different economic conditions, political systems and cultural traditions. San Diego sits on the busiest border crossing in the world, and on a daily basis agents for the Border Patrol play a sometimes violent cat-and-mouse game with people trying to cross illegally. Apprehensions in the San Diego sector, which totaled 26,000 in 2015,jumped to 58,000 in 2019—the highest in a decade. At the San Ysidro port of entry, local agents in August 2018 seized what likely was a record total of 20,000 fentanyl pills—synthetic heroin—which had been stored inside a car panel.

Thousands of legal workers cross the border daily to reach the industrial zone on San Diego's southern edge, in Otay Mesa and San Ysidro and the industrial suburbs of Chula Vista and National City. Many children from Mexico cross daily to attend public and private schools. Latinos pour billions of dollars into the San Diego economy and are scattered in various parts of the city. Oddly, there is not much evidence of Mexican style in San Diego—less than in Los Angeles.

The thinly populated and agricultural Imperial County to the east has faced enormous economic adversity. Its unemployment rate has routinely remained the highest in California. The county is 85 percent Hispanic. Its salvation may lie in energy innovation. San Diego Gas & Electric, which has moved quickly to meet state requirements for the use of solar and wind power, reached about 40 percent renewable in 2020 and planned to be 100 percent clean-energy by 2035. Several investors have ambitious plans to draw lithium—used in electric car batteries—from the Salton Sea. A lithium geothermal power plant near the shallow lake was expected to open in 2023. A research report in March 2020 estimated that the Salton Sea could annually produce 600,000 tons of lithium, which would be eight times the production in 2019, Bloomberg News reported.

The 51st Congressional District of California covers California's entire border with Mexico, from the Arizona state line at Yuma to the southeast corner of the city of San Diego near Balboa Park, the eastern side of San Diego Bay, plus National City and Chula Vista. It includes the Salton Sea basin in the eastern desert and the Tijuana River National Estuarine Research Reserve on the western coast. About one-fourth of the vote is cast in Imperial County, with the remainder in San Diego County. The district is 71 percent Hispanic. The Democratic share of the presidential vote dropped to 67 percent in 2020 from 71 percent in 2016—another example of the Hispanic vote shifting toward Republicans.

Scott Peters (D)

Elected 2012, 5th term, b. Jun 17, 1958; Springfield, OH; Duke University, B.A., 1980; NY University Law School, J.D., 1984; Lutheran; Married (Lynn Gorguze); 2 children.

Elected Office: San Diego City Council, 2000-2008, President, 2006-2008.

Professional Career: Economist, U.S. Environmental Protection Agency, 1980-1981; Deputy Attorney, San Diego City, 1991-1996; Practicing attorney, 1984-1991, 1996-2000; CA Commission on Tax Policy in the New Economy, 2002-2003; CA Coastal Commission, 2002-2005; San Diego Unified Port District Commission, 2009-2012.

DC Office: 2338 RHOB 20515, 202-225-0508, scottpeters.house.gov

State Offices: San Diego, 858-455-5550.

Committees: *Budget. Energy & Commerce*: Energy; Environment & Climate Change; Oversight & Investigations. *Joint Economic*.

Group Ratings

	ADA	ACLU	AFL-CIO	LCV	COC	HAFA	ACU	CFG	FRC
2020	**	79%	**	100%	-	10%	8%	**	-
2019	85%	C	85%	97%	63%	C	9%	27%	0%

Almanac Ratings 2019-2020

	Economy	Social	Foreign	Composite
Liberal	100%	100%	80%	94%
Conservative	0%	0%	20%	6%

Key Votes of the 116th Congress

1. U.S./Mex./Can. trade deal Y	5. Russia sanctions Y	9. Firearms background checks Y
2. First Coronavirus response Y	6. Troops in Syria Y	10. Spending at the border Y
3. HEROES Act Y	7. Veto arms sales to Saudis Y	11. Marijuana liberalized rules Y
4. CASH Act Y	8. Defense $$$, veto override Y	12. Electoral College objections N

Election Results

Election	Name (Party)	Vote (%)		Cand. Spent	Ind. Exp. Support	Ind. Exp. Oppose
2020 General	Scott Peters (D)	244,145	(62%)	$1,644,829	$119,401	
	Jim DeBello (R)	152,350	(38%)	$245,125		$113
2020 Primary	Scott Peters (D)	111,897	(49%)			
	Nancy L. Casady (D)	36,422	(16%)			

Prior winning percentages: 2018 (64%), 2016 (57%), 2014 (52%), 2012 (51%)

Scott Peters, first elected in 2012, secured his seat after two costly and tight campaigns against experienced local Republicans. That success benefited from a centrist voting record and his occasional distancing from the liberal views of congressional Democrats from California. Since then, his district has followed the suburban march toward Democrats nationwide.

Peters is the son of a Lutheran minister who fought against redlining in Detroit in the 1960s. A threat against his family sparked a police chief to suggest his father take them out of town for a week. At age 14, while the family was briefly living in Chicago, Peters had his first taste of politics campaigning for Democrat George McGovern's unsuccessful 1972 presidential race. He studied political science and economics at Duke, taking a low-wage job cleaning pigeon cages for the psychology department to support himself. He graduated from New York University's law school.

His wife, Lynn Gorguze, forged a successful career in private equity, and her work brought them to San Diego in 1988. She is the daughter of a wealthy La Jolla industrialist who contributed to Republicans. For 2018, Roll Call ranked Peters as the 17th wealthiest member of Congress, with a net worth of $32 million. Peters had a wide-ranging, 16-year career as a lawyer handling environmental regulation, corporate taxes and litigation; served as a deputy county counsel; and opened a private practice before being elected to the city council in 2000. During two terms—the last three years as president—Peters worked on reducing sewage spills, redeveloping neighborhoods to make them more walkable, boosting jobs with support for a downtown ballpark and creating the city's first ethics commission.

In 2012, Peters endured a bruising primary battle against Lori Saldaña, a former state Assembly member. She drew support from a left-leaning coalition, but Peters snagged many Democratic endorsements. Despite outspending Saldaña 5-to-1, Peters eked out a victory by just 700 votes. Running against three-term Republican Rep. Brian Bilbray, Peters found himself on the defensive against GOP attacks that he underfunded public-employee pensions during his tenure on the council, something that had marred his unsuccessful race for city attorney in 2009. He accused Bilbray of talking as a moderate while voting as a conservative, and touted his own desire not to be bound by ideology. "I'm just not a purist. You set goals and you have to work with everyone to figure out how to get what you can," he said. Peters self-financed his campaign with more than $1 million and outspent the incumbent, $4.3 million to $2.8 million; he won 51%-49%.

His votes in the House, as shown by the Almanac vote ratings, have stamped him as a centrist. He tried to remain a political outsider by creating and publicizing his #FixCongressNow plan of broad changes in how Congress and elections operate, including five-day work weeks. He said Democrats "must move beyond economic fairness and now take the lead on creating an agenda for economic growth." His 2015 vote to give trade promotion authority to President Barack Obama infuriated the AFL-CIO, which denied him the support of organized labor in 2016. Peters lined up in favor of steps to combat climate change, protect seniors on Medicare and promote immigration reform.

With his seat on the Energy and Commerce Committee, Peters pursued bipartisan collaboration and economic development. In 2017, the House passed his bill to cut red tape in reviewing permits for hydropower projects and to give incentives for carbon-free investments. In 2017 and 2018, he led trade missions to the United Kingdom and Japan to promote San Diego. He became a vice chair of the centrist New Democrat Coalition in 2019. In September 2020, he spoke out against the possibility of House action to legalize marijuana. With the public suffering during the pandemic, Congress should focus on COVID-19 relief and deal with marijuana "later."

Peters faced a difficult reelection in 2014 against Republican Carl DeMaio, a former member of the city council who had narrowly lost a 2012 run for mayor of San Diego. DeMaio, who is openly gay, sought to move beyond traditional Republican support. In the first round, Peters got 42 percent of the vote with DeMaio at 36 percent, and three Republicans divided the remainder. That was a clear sign that Peters was vulnerable. DeMaio styled himself as a "next generation Republican," but Peters ran a tough ad campaign that focused on the challenger's sometimes abrasive style and hardline positions on the city council. DeMaio was put on the defensive by a former campaign aide's charges of sexual harassment and bribery. Peters outspent DeMaio, $4.5 million to $3.4 million, and the two candidates split another $7 million in national party money. Peters won 52%-48%. No charges were filed against DeMaio and the accuser later admitted that some of his charges were lies.

Since then, Peters has won easily. In January 2019, Peters filed papers to run for mayor in November 2020, when Republican incumbent Kevin Faulconer was term-limited. He subsequently abandoned that idea and won reelection to the House. In January 2020, Peters was among the members of Congress who endorsed former Mayor Mike Bloomberg—citing his skill in addressing big issues such as guns, climate and his prospect of defeating President Donald Trump. "I do believe we need an alternative to Sen. Sanders and Sen. Warren," Peters told Politico.

CA-52: Northern San Diego

Population		Race and Ethnicity		Income	
Total	767,151	White	66.40%	Median Income	$106,524
Land area (sq. miles)	267	Black	3.00%	District Income Rank	21
Pop/ sq mi	2,873.22	Latino	14.40%	Poverty Rate	8.10%
Born in State	42.60%	Asian	20.70%	With health insurance	95.40%
		Two or more races	6.10%	Cash public assistance	1.10%
Age Groups		Other	3.70%	Food stamp/SNAP	3.10%
Under 18	19.30%				
18-34	28.10%	**Education**		**Work**	
35-64	38.00%	H.S grad or less	14.70%	White Collar	60.80%
Over 64	14.60%	Some college	24.30%	Sales and Service	30.10%
		College Degree, 4 yr	34.90%	Blue Collar	9.00%
Military		Post grad	26.10%	Government	13.90%
Veteran/ Active Duty	11.10%				

2020 Pres. Vote	Biden	257,923	(63%)	Trump	139,172	(34%)		
2016 Pres. Vote	Clinton	191,325	(57%)	Trump	117,057	(35%)	Johnson	14,807	(4%)

La Jolla, Mission Bay: When the United States was dictating the terms of the Treaty of Guadalupe Hidalgo in 1848 after its successful war with Mexico, it made sure the southern boundary of its new California territory was just south of the port of San Diego. This is one of three splendid natural harbors on the Pacific Coast, and in 1914, the Marine Corps established a base on North Island. This was just the first of many military bases in San Diego, with its mild climate, deep harbor and plentiful land for aircraft maneuvers. Naval Base San Diego has been the major West Coast U.S. Navy base for more than 50 years, the second-largest Navy port behind Norfolk, and home to 143,000 active-duty personnel, with more than one-fourth of the nation's Marines. Also located here are about 240,000 veterans, and the retired aircraft carrier Midway. In July 2020, an explosion on the assault ship, U.S.S. Bonhomme Richard, caused several dozen injuries; the ship was later declared a total loss and would be scrapped.

The port and Navy base in the sheltered harbor remain the central focus of a rapidly growing metropolis that now stretches far inland and to the north. Downtown features post-modern buildings like the Horton Plaza amid a few well-preserved early-20th-century relics like the Spreckels Theatre. Across the harbor, on the sand spit that guards it against the ocean, is the white frame castle of the Hotel Del Coronado, with its dark wooden interior—the U.S.'s largest wooden structure, opened in 1888 and a favored resort of past American presidents. Work began in 2019 on a $400 million renovation of the Del, with completion scheduled by 2022. Already underway was construction of a $1.5 billion redevelopment on the city's waterfront, with an announcement in 2020 of a five-block Research and Development District. Confined in the port area that left scant space to expand and facing a host of local agencies, the airport authority announced in January 2020 plans to replace its 50-year-old terminal with a $3 billion terminal that would increase the gates from 19 to 30, plus a new taxiway to accompany the single runway, the San Diego Union-Tribune reported.

The coastal area is not all Navy. To the north, the Pacific waves pound against the beach beneath unique rock formations along the coast. Part of La Jolla is here, including the Scripps Institute of Oceanography. To the south are raffish Mission Beach; Ocean Beach, with its strong rip currents; and Point Loma, overlooking the entrance to the harbor. The weather—a sunny 70 degrees most of the time—lures tourists and new residents. San Diego is home to Comic-Con International, a four-day comic book and pop culture event that caps its attendance at 130,000 people annually.

The 52nd Congressional District includes much of the city of San Diego. It is one of two districts that are entirely within San Diego County. It runs along the west coast, taking in most of the city's Navy installations, ports and beaches. Inland and north of San Diego, it includes high-income Poway and most of La Jolla. Countywide the Democratic vote for president increased from 53 percent in 2012 to 60 percent in 2020. The Asian population of the 52nd exceeds the Hispanic community, 21 percent to 14 percent—a split that has been growing. Its median income is the highest of the five San Diego-based districts. Politically, it no longer is a competitive congressional battleground. Joe Biden defeated President Donald Trump, 63%-34%, a 29-point margin that was a huge spike from Barack Obama's six-point win over Mitt Romney in 2012.

Sara Jacobs (D)

Elected 2020, 1st term, b. Feb 01, 1989; Del Mar, CA; Columbia University, B.A.; Columbia University, M.A.; Jewish; Single.

Professional Career: Employee, Peacekeeping/Development, United Nations, 2011-2013; Employee, Innovation Unit, United Nations International Children's Emergency Fund, 2013-2014; Conflict and Stabilization Policy Officer, U.S. Department of State, 2014-2015; Policy Advisor, Hillary For America, 2015-2016; CEO, Project Connect, 2017; Founder/Chair, San Diego for Every Child: The Coalition to End Childhood Poverty.

DC Office: 1232 LHOB 20515, 202-225-2040, Fax: 202-225-2948, sarajacobs.house.gov

State Offices: San Diego, 619-280-5353.

Committees: *Armed Services*: Military Personnel; Seapower & Projection Forces. *Foreign Affairs*: Africa, Global Health & Global Human Rights; Intern'l Dev't, Intern'l Orgs & Global Corporate Social Impact.

Election Results

Election	Name (Party)	Vote (%)		Cand. Spent	Ind. Exp. Support	Ind. Exp. Oppose
2020 General	Sara Jacobs (D)	199,244	(60%)	$7,700,643	$2,079,753	$449,943
	Georgette Gómez (D)	135,614	(40%)	$1,617,887	$382,043	$704,283
2020 Primary	Sara Jacobs (D)	58,312	(29%)			
	Georgette Gómez (D)	39,962	(20%)			
	Janessa Goldbeck (D)	17,041	(9%)			

Sara Jacobs defeated another Democrat in 2020 to win an open seat in the suburbs of San Diego. Two years earlier, she ran in a nearby district and finished third in the nonpartisan primary. The common factor: Jacobs financed a large share of each campaign with millions of dollars she inherited as an heiress in one of the area's wealthiest families. Jacobs, who has been accused of inflating her bio, highlighted her charitable efforts to end childhood poverty. She succeeded Democrat Susan Davis, who retired after 20 years of working on local military issues.

A native of San Diego, Jacobs's grandfather, Irwin Jacobs, was the co-founder of Qualcomm, a large company based in that city that creates and manufactures wireless technology. She got a bachelor's degree and a master's in international relations from Columbia University. She worked for international organizations, including the United Nations, and for a contractor with the State Department.

During her campaign in 2018, Jacobs cited her State Department experience when she said that she had served as a policy adviser to the 2016 presidential campaign of former Secretary of State Hillary Clinton. But the San Diego Union-Tribune reported that Jacobs was "a junior employee working for a government contractor and federal regulations prohibited her from making policies." A campaign spokeswoman responded with a defense of Jacobs as "heavily involved in the policymaking process."

Among the 16 candidates in the primary, Jacobs ran third with 16 percent of the vote; she was the Democratic frontrunner in the San Diego County portion of the district. Democrat Mike Levin, who got 18 percent, later won the seat by defeating Republican Diane Harkey, who led the first round of voting. Jacobs spent $2.9 million in that contest, of which $2.1 million was self-financed. EMILY's List, the political action committee that supports Democratic women, spent $2.4 million on her behalf, which was based on a contribution that Jacobs's grandfather made to the PAC.

When Jacobs in 2020switched districts after Davis announced her retirement, she faced another wide-open primary—15 candidates, including 11 Democrats. In this contest, her $ 7.4million in spending was financed chiefly by her nearly $7 million contribution. Jacobs led the first round of voting with 29 percent of the vote. Running second, with 20 percent, was Georgette Gomez, president of the San Diego City Council.

The high finances of Jacobs posed a stark contrast to Gomez, who rose from poverty, as the daughter of undocumented immigrants, and became a community organizer and an environmental activist. "I am the only candidate in this race that actually has experience as a policymaker," Gomez told a reporter, in drawing one of her many contrasts to Jacobs. Gomez, who is openly LGBTQ, was backed by Latino and human-rights groups.

Ironically, when the two exchanged attacks about their personal tax returns, Gomez was placed on the defensive. Reporters discovered that she failed to report in a recent tax return her salary from the city council. Gomez blamed her accountant. After Jacobs released three years of her tax returns, which showed that her income was largely from capital gains, a spokeswoman said that Jacobs favored tax increases on the wealthy. Her grandfather financed a PAC that spent another $1.8 million on her behalf. Gomez spent $1.7 million in her campaign.

The Union-Tribune endorsed Jacobs as "extremely informed, not entitled," and cited the "immense gaps" between the candidates on issues, including that Gomez "didn't know much" about many foreign policy and domestic topics. "Jacobs has done her homework—and her taxes right—and Gomez hasn't," the editorial concluded. Jacobs won with about 60 percent of the vote.

In the House, Jacobs joined the Armed Services and Foreign Affairs committees. She was the freshman representative on the Democratic Steering and Policy Committee.

CA-53: San Diego   **Cook Partisan Voting Index: D+17**

Population		Race and Ethnicity		Income	
Total	782,599	White	62.70%	Median Income	$82,083
Land area (sq. miles)	135	Black	8.10%	District Income Rank	77
Pop/ sq mi	5,778.62	Latino	33.80%	Poverty Rate	9.90%
Born in State	52.90%	Asian	15.10%	With health insurance	92.80%
		Two or more races	6.10%	Cash public assistance	2.10%
Age Groups		Other	8.10%	Food stamp/SNAP	6.40%
Under 18	19.70%				
18-34	28.80%	**Education**		**Work**	
35-64	37.90%	H.S grad or less	26.80%	White Collar	46.20%
Over 64	13.50%	Some college	32.60%	Sales and Service	38.80%
		College Degree, 4 yr	26.00%	Blue Collar	15.00%
Military		Post grad	14.50%	Government	16.50%
Veteran/ Active Duty	10.60%				

2020 Pres. Vote	Biden	258,866	(67%)	Trump	119,398	(31%)		
2016 Pres. Vote	Clinton	200,237	(64%)	Trump	91,822	(29%)	Johnson	11,325	(4%)
	Stein	6,132	(2%)					

East San Diego, La Mesa: Often thought of as California's most conservative, straight-arrow city because of its long association with the U.S. Navy and the military, San Diego is now a multi-ethnic metropolis, with a population that is 30 percent Hispanic and 17 percent Asian; more than 40 percent of households speak a language other than English. In a sense, the city is returning to its roots. San Diego was a part of newly independent Mexico from the 1820s and did not join the United States until after the Mexican-American War. It sits directly across the border from the Tijuana metropolitan area, and roughly 300,000 people a day cross from one city to the other, including 70,000 vehicles and 20,000 pedestrians. The drive across the border at the San Ysidro port of entry, the busiest entry point in the Western Hemisphere, often takes as long as two hours. Regular users can move more quickly through the Ready Lane if they have the requisite electronic documents. The $741 million expansion completed in December 2019resulted in northbound capacity increased to 34 lanes, with the southbound I-5widened from five lanes to 10.Traffic was projected to increase another 87 percent by 2030.

San Diego has had a competitive and sometimes stormy political narrative. In 2012, 10-term Democratic Rep. Bob Filner was elected the city's first Democratic mayor in 20 years. But he quickly ran into ethical problems and survived only seven months before he resigned under pressure in the face of sexual harassment allegations by at least 18 women. Republican Kevin Faulconer, a former public relations executive, won a special election to complete Filner's term, then easily won a full term in 2016. Of all the Republican mayors in the nation, he led the largest city. After he stepped down in 2020, Faulconer became a prime candidate for governor. San Diego is projected to continue its rapid growth rate, with a nearly 50 percent increase by 2050. Most of that likely will come from Hispanics.

The 53rd Congressional District is geographically the smallest San Diego-area district, taking in the eastern edge of the city and points inland to include the suburbs of Lemon Grove and Spring Valley. It includes La Mesa and La Presa, which is 50 percent Hispanic, and extends about two miles short of the border with Mexico. The district has a number of parks, lakes and open space preserves. The zoo is among the 10 largest in the world. El Cajon has the nation's second-largest community of Chaldeans, Catholic Arabs from Iraq; some call the city, "Baghdad on the border." That Chaldean community has had conflicts with the church's international leadership over possible excommunication of local priests unless they recognized the authority in Baghdad.

Politically, this is a safe Democratic district. The Republican presidential vote fell from 36 percent in 2012 to 31percent in 2020.

COLORADO

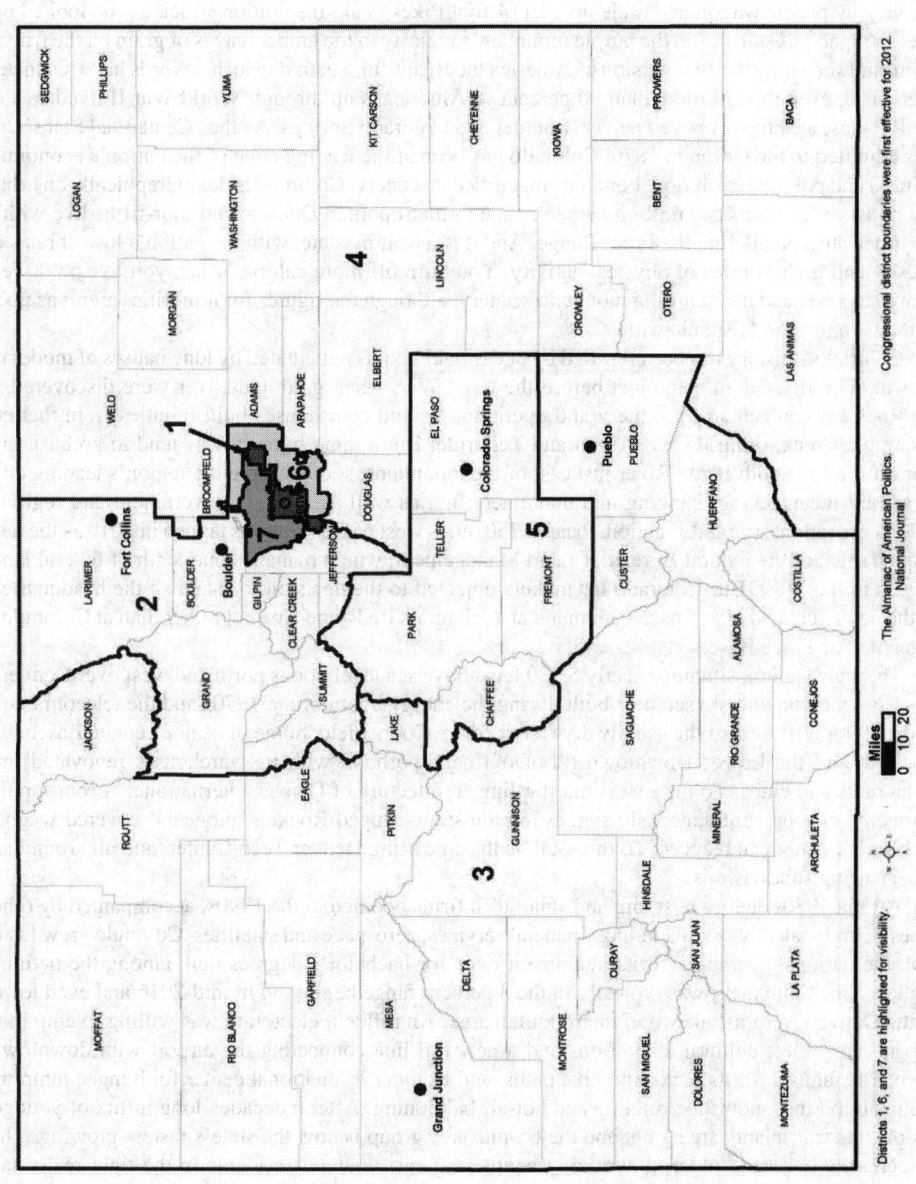

The Almanac of American Politics,
National Journal

Congressional district boundaries were first effective for 2012.

Colorado has been the kind of state Democrats point to when they dream of a future where their party is ascendant—fast-growing, well-educated, economically successful, tech-savvy, demographically diverse and beautifully situated. That future is now: In 2020, Joe Biden won the state by 13 points, an eight-point improvement over 2016, and former Gov. John Hickenlooper ousted GOP Sen. Cory Gardner by almost 10 points.

One summer day in 1893, Katherine Lee Bates, an English teacher at Colorado College, made her way by prairie wagon and mule up 14,114-foot Pikes Peak. Inspiration struck as she looked out over the spacious skies from the purple mountain's majesty to the amber waves of grain on the fruited plain, and she wrote the first version of America the Beautiful. Set to music, her words have resonated ever since, even though more than 90 percent of Americans up through World War II lived east of the Rockies, which rise above Denver, Boulder and Colorado Springs. As the "Centennial State" that was admitted to the Union in 1876, Colorado has been at the leading edge of the nation's economic, cultural and political evolution. For all its magnificent scenery, Colorado is demographically an urban state; just over half its 5.8 million people reside in metropolitan Denver, and four-fifths live within the urban strip paralleling the Front Range. And it is a healthy state, with the nation's lowest rates of obesity and highest rates of physical activity. You burn off more calories when you live 5,000 feet above sea level and near alluring mountain scenery, although the figures for minorities aren't as good as they are for non-Hispanic whites.

Colorado's history has been typified by occasional booms punctuated by long pauses of moderate growth. The first boom came just before the Civil War, when gold and silver were discovered in the Rockies; you can still see the grand opera houses and courthouses built in cities from that era —Cripple Creek, Central City, Aspen and Telluride. But mining boom towns tend to go bust, and Denver, on the South Platte River just east of the mountains, soon became the region's leading city, driven by meatpacking, banking and manufacturing, as well as by state government and regional federal operations. (Grand Junction, located 250 miles west of Denver, was tapped in 2019 as the new headquarters of the federal Bureau of Land Management, which manages one-tenth of federal land, mostly in the West. But Colorado lawmakers objected to the decision to establish the headquarters of the newly created U.S. Space Command at Alabama's Redstone Arsenal rather than at Colorado's Peterson Air Force Base.)

The state capitol, situated exactly 5,280 feet above sea level, looks north and west over Denver's busy downtown, with skyscrapers built during the energy boom of the 1970s and the telecom boom of the 1990s. Off toward the usually dry river bed are Coors Field, home of Major League Baseball's Rockies, and the Lower Downtown ("LoDo") neighborhood with its warehouses renovated into restaurants and clubs. To the east is the startling architecture of Denver International Airport on the plains, its canopy simultaneously suggesting the snow-capped Rockies, pioneers' covered wagons and Native American teepees. To the south is the sprawling Denver Tech Center, and all around are fast-growing subdivisions.

After a 1980s energy bust, big and small tech firms boomed in the 1990s, accompanied by other types of high-salary work, including financial services, aerospace and satellites. Colorado grew faster than the national average, and its attainment rates for bachelor's degrees rank among the nation's highest. Unemployment was typically in the 3 percent range beginning in mid-2016 and even lower in the Denver-Aurora-Lakewood metropolitan area. An affluent electorate was willing to chip in to expand amenities, cultural institutions and a new rail line connecting the airport with downtown. Denver is famous for its parks and bike paths, and Boulder is a national center for bungee jumping, mountain biking, snowshoe running and hot-air ballooning. After a decades-long influx of younger people, the transplants are aging, and the 65-plus age group is now the state's fastest-growing. This is increasingly pitting older, downsizing couples against younger residents in the tight real-estate market.

Prior to the coronavirus pandemic, tourists flocked in; the state regularly set yearly records for visitors over the past decade. Most strikingly, Coloradans voted to make their state the first jurisdiction in the world to fully license the manufacture, cultivation and sale of marijuana. While problems emerged, such as a difficulty in regulating "edibles," local jurisdictions have been thrilled with the new revenue, and the decision has been popular. Since legalization in 2014, consumers have bought more than $6 billion in marijuana products, which has generated more than $1 billion for government coffers. On the downside, Colorado has recently experienced an intense drought, harming agriculture and producing a spike in wildfires. Five of the 20 biggest wildfires in the state's history occurred in 2018, a worry for the 2.9 million people who live in Colorado's" wildland-urban interface."

Colorado has been reshaped politically by its successive waves of newcomers, who have increased the state's population from 1.7 million in 1960 to 5.8 million today. The conservative and booresterish Colorado of the 1960s was transformed in the 1970s by young liberal migrants who called for environmental protections and slow growth. Then in the 1990s, a new wave of migrants—tech-savvy, family-oriented cultural conservatives—moved Colorado's politics to the right. If the spirit of the 1970s newcomers was embodied by Boulder, with its pedestrian mall, outdoor sports shops and vegetarian restaurants, then the spirit of the 1990s was epitomized by religious conservatives in Colorado Springs, home of the Air Force Academy and Dr. James Dobson's Focus on the Family.

But the new century has been an era where affluent, educated urban and suburban Colorado is in ascendance, and that has enabled Democrats to consolidate their demographic gains. Colorado's Latino population now stands at 22 percent, the seventh-highest percentage of any state. The state also has one of the nation's youngest populations. Denver and Boulder attract young professionals imbued with progressive values, while the ski resorts—Telluride, Aspen, Vail, Crested Butte, Steamboat Springs—are inhabited by the wealthy and the people who wait on them in boutiques and restaurants, both demographics that lean Democratic. Today, some of the state's fastest-growing areas are on the northern edge of the Front Range; Loveland and Fort Collins, less than 20 miles from Wyoming, have each grown by 18 percent since the 2010 census and are turning bluer, matching the state. The state gained a congressional seat after the 2020 census.

Republicans remained competitive in some contests as late as 2014, including a stretch when the newly Democratic-controlled legislature enacted a gun control measure in the wake of a massacre at a movie theater in suburban Aurora; this prompted a Republican backlash in the 2014 midterms. But two years later, Hillary Clinton defeated Donald Trump by nearly five points, as the pro-Democratic tilt of suburban areas outweighed the migration of blue-collar areas toward Trump. The state GOP did itself no favors by turning increasingly to the right, alienating suburbanites. Democrats expanded their dominance during the 2018 midterms, as Rep. Jared Polis, a liberal Democrat, won the gubernatorial race, 53%-43%—a margin more than three times wider than that of his predecessor, Hickenlooper, four years earlier. Democrats in 2018 also flipped the attorney general, treasurer and secretary of state seats, as well as control of the state Senate and the 6th Congressional District.

The Republican bloodbath continued in 2020. Trump increased his vote haul in the state by 13 percent, but Biden increased his by 35 percent. While Biden flipped the blue-collar and heavily Hispanic Pueblo County (Pueblo), more crucial to his victory was his ability to harvest more Democratic votes in the already-blue areas of the Front Range. In seven Democratic counties stretching north from metro Denver past Fort Collins, Biden expanded on Clinton's raw vote totals by 32 percent. Biden cut Trump's winning margin in traditionally conservative El Paso County (Colorado Springs) from 22 points to 11. Meanwhile, Hickenlooper defeated Gardner, enabling the first Democratic sweep since 1941 of every Senate seat in Colorado, Arizona, Nevada, and New Mexico—a" tectonic remaking of the electoral battlefield," in the view of political analyst Ron Brownstein. Voters also passed several progressive ballot measures, including a family and medical leave plan, a Polis-backed tobacco tax hike, and reintroduction of gray wolves, while soundly rejecting restrictions on abortion.

Population		Race and Ethnicity		Income	
Total	5,758,736	White	83.70%	Median Income	77,127
Land area (sq. miles)	103,642	Black	4.20%	State Income Rank	9 out of 50
Pop/ sq mi	55.56	Latino	21.80%	Poverty Rate	9.30%
Born in state	42.20%	Asian	4.60%	With health insurance	92.00%
		Two or more races	4.00%	Cash public assistance	2.00%
Age Groups		Other	4.70%	Food stamp/SNAP	8.2%
Under 18	21.80%				
18-34	25.00%	Education		Work	
35-64	38.50%	H.S grad or less	28.60%	White Collar	45.10%
Over 64	14.70%	Some college	28.70%	Sales and Service	36.30%
		College Degree, 4 yr	26.60%	Blue Collar	18.60%
Military		Post grad	16.00%	Government	13.90%
Veteran/ Active Duty	8.90%				

Presidential Politics

2020 Primary (D)	Sanders (D)	355,293(37%)	Biden (D)	236,565(25%)	Bloomberg (D)	177,727(19%)	
	Warren (D)	168,695(18%)					
2016 Caucus (D)	Sanders (D)	72,846(59%)	Clinton (D)	49,789(40%)			
2020 Pres. Vote	Biden (D)	1,804,352(55%)	Trump (R)	1,364,607(42%)			
2016 Pres. Vote	Clinton (D)	1,338,870(48%)	Trump (R)	1,202,484(43%)	Johnson (L)	144,121 (5%)	

Colorado has transformed from a solidly Republican to fairly reliably Democratic state at the presidential level, and wasn't seriously contested in 2020—the first time since 2004 that it wasn't treated as a swing state. Joe Biden defeated Donald Trump 55%-42% on the strength of support from Hispanics and college-educated white voters. His coattails sunk the reelection chances of Republican Sen. Cory Gardner. Fast-growing metro Denver has pushed the state hard toward Democrats in the past two decades. In 2020, nearly the entire state shifted left, from metro Denver to the historically conservative, rural Western Slope. Biden ran ahead of Clinton in 52 of the state's 64 counties, including in every county that cast at least 15,000 votes. The biggest shifts were double-digit increases in Biden's margin of victory in Denver-area suburban Arapahoe and Jefferson counties. Trump still won the historic GOP bastions of exurban Douglas County and El Paso (Colorado Springs), but by smaller margins.

Between LBJ in 1964 and Barack Obama in 2008, the only Democrat to carry Colorado was Bill Clinton in 1992, and it's likely that independent candidate Ross Perot siphoned off enough GOP voters from George H.W. Bush to produce that outcome. But Democrats had Colorado in their sights when they selected Denver for their 2008 national convention site—Obama formally accepted the nomination in Mile High Stadium.

Colorado held an early March presidential primary from 1992 until 2000, which never attracted much national attention. In 2003, to save money, the legislature voted to eliminate the presidential primary and let the parties hold caucuses. The 2016 Republican and Democratic versions were both notable. Colorado GOP officials opted not to hold a typical presidential preference poll at their local caucuses, with the aim of sending uncommitted delegates to the party confab in Cleveland. But Texas Sen. Ted Cruz skillfully organized the subsequent congressional district conventions and the state convention and packed the delegation with his supporters, prompting Trump to complain that the Colorado GOP caucuses were "rigged." Vermont Sen. Bernie Sanders swamped Clinton in the Democratic caucuses, 59%-40%. In 2020, the state switched to a Super Tuesday primary, as Democratic officials pushed states to ditch the caucus system; Sanders defeated Biden 37%-25%.

Congressional Districts

117th Congress Lineup	4D 3R	116th Congress Lineup	4D 3R

For a state that has wrestled with the complications of divided government during recent redistricting, the dynamics of the 2022 remap in Colorado appear relatively straightforward: Democrats control state government. The state is gaining one seat. And the seven-member House delegation has been split since 2018 between four Democratic-held seats in the Denver metro area, including Boulder, and three large Republican-held seats in outlying areas to the east, south and west.

With the population growth mostly in the suburbs and exurbs of Denver, the logical solution is the creation of a new Democratic-leaning district in metro Denver. That area can be divided into five segments of comparable size: the counties of Denver, Arapahoe, Jefferson, the combination of Adams and Douglas, plus the more-distant combination of Boulder and Larimer. Of course, those starting points offer their own variables. For example, Denver is solidly Democratic, with slices that would be politically appealing appendages to any of the four other districts in the metro area, a step that Denver politicians likely would resist. And the politics of the suburban counties—all but one with double-digit growth since 2010, and each of them evolving to Democrats—cannot be confidently predicted to remain unchanged for the next decade. One other factor: Democratic clusters in the three current Republican-held districts, such as the skiing resorts on the Western Slope and largely blue-collar Pueblo, could become movable pieces that join the five nearby metro districts.

After the 2010 census, the two parties had a lengthy and bitter stalemate in the state legislature that forced the federal courts to intervene. A Denver district judge chose a Democratic plan for the sake of making the Republican-held 6th District south of Denver more "competitive." That map's biggest shift was to remove nearly all of heavily Republican Douglas County from the 6th District and replace it with increasingly Hispanic Aurora to the north, making the seat of GOP Rep. Mike Coffman seven percentage points less Republican. After three failed challenges in competitive contests, Democrats in 2018 finally defeated Coffman.

Jared Polis (D)

Elected 2018, term expires 2023, 1st term; b. May 12, 1975, Boulder, CO; Princeton University, B.A., 1996; Jewish; Married (Marlon Reis); 2 children.

Elected Office: Member, CO Board of Education, 2000-2007, Chair, 2004-2005; US House, 2009-2018.

Professional Career: Co-Founder, American Information Systems; Entrepreneur; Philanthropist.

Office: 136 State Capitol Denver, 80203-1792; 303-866-2471; Fax: 303-866-2003; Website: colorado.gov

Lt. Gov.: Dianne Primavera (D) **Atty. Gen:** Phil Weiser (D) **Sec. of State:** Jena Griswold (D)

State Legislature: Senate: 19D, 16R **House:** 40D, 24R, 1I

Election Results

Election	Name (Party)	Vote (%)
2018 General	Jared Polis (D)	1,348,888 (53%)
	Walker Stapleton (R)	1,080,801 (43%)
	Scott Helker (Lib)	69,519 (3%)
2018 Primary	Jared Polis (D)	283,340 (45%)
	Cary Kennedy (D)	157,396 (25%)
	Michael Johnston (D)	149,884 (24%)
	Donna Lynne (D)	46,382 (7%)

Jared Polis, a Democrat first elected to the House in 2008, won the Colorado governorship in 2018 by a double-digit margin, becoming the first openly gay man to be elected to each office. Leading a state that has turned increasingly blue, Polis enacted a lengthy, but pragmatic-minded, progressive agenda before being forced to grapple with the coronavirus pandemic.

Polis was born in Boulder but grew up in the San Diego suburb of La Jolla, with frequent vacations back in Colorado. His mother, a poet, and his father, an artist, were both politically active during the anti-war movement of the late 1960s. As a fifth-grader, and on his own volition, he addressed the La Jolla City Council to stop development in an urban canyon near his home; the mayor told the local paper that his argument swayed the vote to no. Initially preferring to go into politics immediately without attending college, Polis agreed with his parents to simply speed up the process: He graduated from high school in three years and applied successfully to Princeton at age 16, where he would earn a political science degree. As a student government official, Polis ran what he billed as the world's first fully online election (it was 1995) and joined with two sophomore friends to launch American Information Systems, an internet service provider. It was the first of 20 companies that Polis founded or co-founded. Soon afterward, Polis turned his parents' small greeting-card company, Blue Mountain Arts, into a website that at its height was the eighth most popular on the internet. He sold it for $780 million, then built Proflowers.com, which enabled customers to order fresh flowers directly from growers. In 2006, the flower service sold for $477 million. Along the way, at 25, he changed his name from Jared Polis Schutz to Jared Schutz Polis, to honor his grandmother, he said.

Financial security allowed Polis to focus on his political passions. In 2000, four years out of college, he was elected to the Colorado State Board of Education; he challenged an appointed incumbent, drove all over the state in a school bus, and spent $1.2 million, all of which broke the mold for the low-profile position. Polis won by 90 votes, outspending his opponent by more than 100 to 1. He served one six-year term and chaired the board for one year. Polis was most proud of his advancement of school choice through charter schools and his work improving accountability standards for schools. In part with his own money, he founded two innovative charter schools in Colorado, which helped new immigrants assimilate, especially with flexible day or evening programs, and teachers trained to help students learn English.

Political observers fully expected Polis to raise his political profile further, and he did. He became part of a "Gang of Four" consisting of Colorado multimillionaires, including QuarkXPress founder Tim Gill, medical device heiress Patricia Stryker and geophysicist and MicroMAX software creator Rutt Bridges. The group nurtured a web of liberal activist organizations and shrewdly framed and targeted issues such as same-sex marriage, ultimately reshaping the political landscape, including taking control of both legislative chambers in 2004.

When a House seat opened in 2008, he decided to run. In the Democratic primary, he outspent his two opponents by a 4-to-1 margin and won with 42 percent. At age 33, he breezed through the general election, 63%-34%. In the entire campaign, he spent $7 million, of which $6 million was his own. After that, he was not seriously challenged for the House seat, either in a primary or a general election. During his initial House campaign, Polis came out as gay.

In Washington, Democratic leaders gave Polis a seat on the Rules Committee, a tool of the majority leadership that controls the terms of debate for major bills on the House floor; despite the minority's institutional weakness, Polis was considered effective at getting floor consideration of Democratic amendments. He took many progressive positions but also defied the "Boulder liberal" stereotype at times. He was one of 22 Democrats in 2012 who voted for a plan that was based on the recommendations of President Barack Obama's Simpson-Bowles deficit-reduction commission. In 2015, he was one of 28 House Democrats who voted to give trade promotion authority to Obama, and he backed the Trans-Pacific Partnership.

In 2018, Gov. John Hickenlooper was term-limited, and Polis used sharp elbows to clear his way to the governorship. By the time he joined the Democratic primary field, it already included fellow Rep. Ed Perlmutter as well as several candidates with statewide experience. Within weeks of Polis' entry and the specter of a heavily self-funding primary opponent, Perlmutter dropped out. Former state Treasurer Cary Kennedy, backed by teachers' unions, initially gained establishment support, but an ad sponsored by an independent teachers' PAC that targeted Polis and former state Sen. Mike Johnston prompted a backlash against Kennedy. In the end, Polis, backed by $10 million of his own money, received 44 percent, Kennedy got 25 percent, Johnston got 24 percent, and Lt. Gov. Donna Lynne won 7 percent.

In the general election, he faced two-term state treasurer and Bush family member Walker Stapleton. Polis proposed taxpayer-funded universal pre-kindergarten; increased spending for teacher salaries and smaller class sizes; single-payer health care; an end to $1.6 billion in excise and corporate tax breaks; a phase-out of private prisons; an expansion of rural broadband; and 100 percent renewable energy by 2040. Stapleton countered that Polis' goals were unreasonably expensive and added that any shift away from oil and gas would imperil hundreds of thousands of jobs. But Polis had actually moved some distance toward the oil and gas industry over the previous few years. Polis moved left on gun control and targeted marijuana users and workers in the cannabis industry. His campaign spent more than $22 million, blowing away state records. He won the governorship 53%-43%—a margin more than three times bigger than Hickenlooper's four years earlier.

In his first year in office, Polis became the first governor to sign legislation capping co-payments for insulin, and he signed a bill that reduced industry influence on the Colorado Oil and Gas Conservation Commission while giving local governments greater say over oil and gas development. Polis signed a "red flag law" to enable the seizure of guns from people deemed by a court to be a threat, prompting many rural counties in the state to declare that they would not enforce it. He signed legislation to make it easier for transgender people to change their birth certificates as well as banning "gay conversion therapy" for minors; he also signed a measure to allow publicly traded companies to own marijuana businesses. In the meantime, Polis signed a bill to have Colorado join a multi-state compact that creates a workaround to the Electoral College; in 2020, voters narrowly backed a ballot measure that ratified his decision. The flurry of largely progressive legislation prompted some conservative leaders to seek to recall the governor, but they failed to secure enough signatures. A second recall effort in 2020 also failed. At the same time, Polis got some criticism from his left: Protesters calling for a full ban on fracking disrupted his 2020 State of the State address, leading to two dozen arrests.

In early 2020, Polis continued his legislative juggernaut. He signed a bill to abolish the death penalty and, amid police brutality protests, Polis signed a far-reaching bill to overhaul policing policy, including a ban on chokeholds and lifting "qualified immunity" protections for officers charged with wrongdoing. One policy disappointment for Polis was his inability to enact a public option for health insurance, an effort scuttled amid the coronavirus pandemic. In his efforts to handle the pandemic, Polis sought something of a middle path. From its earliest days, Polis worked in partnership with fellow Democratic governors in the West. But in April, he decided to lift stay-at-home orders earlier than other Democratic-led states and even some states with Republican governors, which led to a White House visit with President Donald Trump. By June, however, Polis ordered new closures for bars and nightclubs, and the following month, he signed an executive order mandating the wearing of face masks indoors. By winter, Colorado's case load had spiked far above its previous peak, as it had in most states; its per capita rate of positive tests ranked roughly in the middle of 50 states.

Michael Bennet (D)

Appointed 2009, term expires 2022, 2nd full term, b. Nov 28, 1964; New Delhi, India; Wesleyan University, B.A., 1987; Yale University Law School, J.D., 1993; Jewish; Married (Susan Daggett Bennet); 3 children.

Professional Career: Administrative Aide, OH Governor Richard Celeste, 1988-1990; Counsel to Deputy Attorney General, U.S Department of Justice, 1995-1997; Special Assistant, U.S. Attorney, State of CT, 1997; Managing Director, investment company, 1997-2003; Chief of Staff, Denver Mayor John Hickenlooper, 2003-2005; Superintendent, Denver Public Schools, 2005-2009.

DC Office: 261 RSOB 20510, 202-224-5852, Fax: 202-228-5097, bennet.senate.gov

State Offices: Alamosa, 719-587-0096; Colorado Springs, 719-328-1100; Denver, 303-455-7600; Durango, 970-259-1710; Fort Collins, 970-224-2200; Grand Junction, 970-241-6631; Pueblo, 719-542-7550.

Committees: *Agriculture, Nutrition & Forestry*: Conservation, Climate, Forestry & Natural Resources (Chmn); Food & Nutrition, Specialty Crops, Organics & Research; Rural Development &

Energy. *Finance*: Energy, Natural Resources & Infrastructure (Chmn); International Trade, Customs & Global Competitiveness; Social Security, Pensions & Family Policy. *Intelligence*.

Group Ratings

	ADA	ACLU	AFL-CIO	LCV	COC	HAFA	ACU	CFG	FRC
2020	-	77%	-	77%	-	10%	6%	-	-
2019	75%	C	94%	86%	70%	C	5%	17%	0%

Almanac Ratings 2019-2020

	Economy	Social	Foreign	Composite
Liberal	89%	89%	68%	82%
Conservative	11%	11%	32%	18%

Key Votes of the 116th Congress

1. EPA clean energy rules Y	5. Russia sanctions Y	9. Barr as Atty. General N
2. U.S./Mex./Can. trade deal Y	6. Troops in SYR, AFG Y	10. Spending at the border N/A
3. Cut unemployment benefits N	7. Veto arms sales to Saudis Y	11. Coney Barrett to Sup. Ct. N
4. Shelton to Fed Reserve N	8. Defense $$$, veto override Y	12. Electoral College objections N

Election Results

Election	Name (Party)	Vote (%)		Cand. Spent	Ind. Exp. Support	Ind. Exp. Oppose
2016 General	Michael Bennet (D).........................1,370,710	(50%)	$24,460,995	$1,277,047	$705,306
	Darryl Glenn (R)............................1,215,318	(44%)	$4,955,031	$2,987,974	$90,511
	Lily Tang Williams (L)..................99,277	(4%)	$6,810		
2016 Primary	Michael Bennet (D).........................Unopposed				

Prior winning percentages: 2016 (50%), 2010 (48%)

While raised in a family very much a part of the Washington establishment, Democrat Michael Bennet, Colorado's senior senator, reached Capitol Hill hardly by a straight line. If the start of his career—in law and politics—was in keeping with his background, Bennet moved west and made his fortune. After becoming a multimillionaire, he returned to politics, but then in a surprise move, he was named to head a large urban school district. In a second surprise, he was plucked from that post in 2009 for a vacant seat in the Senate, appointed over several better-known contenders. Since then, Bennet has been an affable, cerebral legislator ready to reach across party line and known for a low-key style—with rare exceptions. One—a fiery floor speech during a government shutdown in early 2019—went viral, fueling a long-shot presidential bid that ultimately failed to gain momentum.

In 2021, Bennet found himself teamed with a new junior colleague, Democrat John Hickenlooper. Rarely have the backgrounds of senators from the same state been so closely intertwined: Bennet has the same alma mater as and once worked for Hickenlooper, and, while they are longtime friends, they also have been political rivals. Hickenlooper was among those passed over when Bennet was appointed to the Senate. And, for several months in 2019, the two were presidential contenders from the same home base. Like Hickenlooper, a businessman who went on to serve two terms as governor, Bennet has been firmly in the mold of moderate Democrats in Colorado—a purple state with an increasingly blue hue. To keep his seat, Bennet has faced a couple bruising campaigns in which he was relentlessly attacked for supporting most major initiatives of President Barack Obama. Bennet has pursued an independent course on several high-profile issues, to the displeasure of his party's vocal progressive wing.

Bennet's lineage is intriguing: His father's family can trace itself to the arrival of the Mayflower, while his mother was born in the Jewish ghetto of Warsaw Poland, immigrating to the United States after being hidden from the Nazis during World War II. Bennet was born in 1964 in New Delhi India, where his father, Douglas Bennet, was an aide to Ambassador Chester Bowles. The elder Bennet, after working for such leading Democratic senators as Hubert Humphrey and Edmund Muskie, went on to become a top State Department official in the Carter and Clinton administrations as well as president of NPR. Michael Bennet attended private schools in Washington D.C. and was a Senate page in high school. A younger brother, James Bennet, is a former editorial page editor of the New York Times; when Michael Bennet announced his bid for president, James Bennet recused himself "from any work generated by the opinion desk related to the 2020 presidential election," according to a Times statement. (He resigned as editorial page editor several months after his brother's withdrawal from the race, amid an unrelated controversy.)

Michael Bennet is a third-generation graduate of Wesleyan University; his father later served as president of the school. At Yale Law School, he was editor-in-chief of the Yale Law Journal. He was an associate in Lloyd Cutler's influential law firm in Washington before moving to the Clinton administration's Justice Department, where he wrote speeches for Attorney General Janet Reno. Bennet's move west Earth justice came in 1997 when his wife, Susan Daggett, a natural resources lawyer, accepted a job with the Legal Defense Fund in Denver. Bennet went to work for an investment company headed by conservative billionaire Philip Anschutz. While Bennet had never read a balance sheet, Anschutz was impressed and hired him—while ordering Bennet to attend accounting school at night at his own expense.

Bennet landed such assignments as overseeing the consolidation of three separate entities into Regal Entertainment Group, one of the country's largest movie theater chains. After six years with Anschutz, during which he accumulated $12 million, Bennet returned to the public sector when Hickenlooper was elected Denver mayor and asked him to be his chief of staff. Bennet said he gave up millions in stock options to accept "an opportunity that wouldn't come around again." His accomplishments included a plan to balance the city's budget by cutting 10 percent — without laying off any workers. "I have referred to him as the second mayor, the hidden mayor," Hickenlooper told the Denver Post.

In 2005, the position of Denver Public Schools superintendent came open, and Bennet was among the top candidates—even though he had no experience in education, had attended private schools, and was sending his daughter to a private kindergarten. Selected to head a system of 73,000 students, three-quarters of whom were Latino or African-American, Bennet triggered controversy by moving to close a problem-plagued high school in the city's African-American community. But he instituted a plan to boost performance standards, while creating workshops to teach principals how to lead schools to reform. Proficiency in reading and math rose by 6 percent during Bennet's four-year tenure, according to the Washington-based Council of Great City Schools.

Bennet was Obama's on the short list to head the Department of Education in 2008. But—with very limited national political experience—he was not regarded as even a long shot for the Senate when Obama selected Colorado Sen. Ken Salazar to be his Interior secretary. Democratic Gov. Bill Ritter astonished just about everyone by naming Bennet to fill the remaining two years of Salazar's term. Ritter said he was impressed with Bennet's record of bringing diverse interests together to solve problems. Some leading Democrats were not happy. The Washington Post later recounted how now-Senate Democratic Leader Chuck Schumer of New York called Ritter at the time—and sarcastically thanked him for throwing away a seat on an unknown politician who could not win reelection.

Once sworn in, Bennet drew on his experience in Denver: He added more than half a dozen proposals as the Obama administration sought to replace the No Child Left Behind education law, such as tying new teacher licensing to performance and increasing the flexibility of school districts in spending federal money. His colleagues credited Bennet with moving both parties to the middle in that debate, finally leading to passage of a new law, the Every Student Succeeds Act, in late 2015. "He bridged the gap with the Republicans," the Health, Education, Labor and Pensions panel's ranking Democrat, Sen. Patty Murray of Washington, said.

Seeking election in 2010, Bennet faced a primary challenge from former state House Speaker Andrew Romanoff—another of the better-known names passed over for the Senate appointment. Targeting Bennet's work for Anschutz, Romanoff attacked the incumbent as a tool of Wall Street. While Romanoff surged in the closing days of the primary, Bennet hung on to win, 54%-46%. In November, Bennet faced Weld County District Attorney Ken Buck, who won the GOP nomination with the backing of tea party activists. Buck attacked Bennet for his vote for "Obamacare"—the Affordable Care Act. But Buck proved to be gaffe-prone, and Bennet made an issue of his decision as district attorney to not prosecute an accused rapist; Buck said at the time that a jury would likely conclude the victim's complaint was a case of "buyer's remorse." Bennet proved to be a strong fundraiser and saturated the airwaves portraying Buck as too extreme for Colorado voters; Buck had called for dismantling the Department of Education and opposed abortion in all circumstances. Bennet won 48%-46%. Four years later, Buck was elected to the House from Colorado's 4th District.

Returning to Capitol Hill, where the House had flipped to Republican control and the Senate had a decreased Democratic majority, Bennet looked for opportunities to reach across the aisle. He became part of a bipartisan "Gang of Eight" seeking ways to avoid the "fiscal cliff" looming at the end of 2012. However, the "fiscal cliff" solution ultimately adopted was largely the result of negotiations between the Obama White House and Senate Republican leaders; Bennet was one of three Senate

Democrats to oppose it. He said it "does not put in place a real process to reduce the debt down the road." Bennet's focus on this issue persisted: In November 2018, he unveiled a plan to replace the House and Senate budget committees with a "Joint Select Committee on Fiscal Responsibility," charged with reducing the national debt by an amount equal to at least 5 percent of the gross domestic product over a decade.

Shortly after the 2012 elections, Senate Majority Leader Harry Reid offered Bennet the chairmanship of the Democratic Senatorial Campaign Committee. It took Bennet three weeks to accept; he was concerned it would interfere with efforts to work across the aisle. For accepting the two-year post, Bennet was awarded a seat on the powerful Finance Committee. It turned out to be a disastrous election cycle for Democrats, who lost nine seats and control of the Senate. Despite the dismal showing, Bennet escaped second-guessing, as many in the party quietly blamed the Obama White House. Among the casualties was Bennet's Colorado colleague, Sen. Mark Udall, who ran a race similar to Bennet's in 2010 by stressing his opponent's "extreme" positions. In turn, Udall's victorious Republican opponent, Cory Gardner—upset about DSCC ads aimed at him—skewered Bennet as "the chief partisan of the United States Senate."

Notwithstanding such rocky beginnings, Bennet and Gardner—who was ousted by Hickenlooper in 2020—developed something of a bipartisan bromance. In their first two years serving together, they co-authored more than a dozen pieces of legislation—several specific to Colorado, but others national in scope. Bennet and Gardner found common ground on energy issues, agreeing on an "all of the above" approach favoring renewable sources while vowing to protect Colorado's liquid natural gas industry. They also were in accord on the Keystone XL pipeline: In early 2015, Bennet was among just eight Democrats to join an unsuccessful effort to override Obama's veto of the controversial project connecting Canada's oil sands fields with Gulf Coast refineries. The pipeline got the green light after the President Donald Trump took office two years later, although investors later backed away.

Bennet and Gardner were part of a bipartisan group of a half-dozen senators who worked on immigration reform—a response to Trump's September 2017 announcement that he planned to cancel the Deferred Action for Childhood Arrivals program initiated by Obama. A compromise proposal crafted by the group died after Trump declined to sign on. It was a follow-on to Bennet's participation in another "Gang of Eight" effort several years earlier. That resulted in a bipartisan immigration reform proposal that passed the Senate in 2013 but died after the House refused to take it up.

Gardner's upset victory over Udall emboldened national Republicans—who targeted Bennet as the one incumbent Democrat they had a chance of ousting in 2016. However, problems on the GOP side provided Bennet with a series of breaks. Republicans failed to attract a top-tier candidate. Former state Rep. Jon Keyser emerged as the choice of the GOP establishment, only to be removed from the ballot barely two months before the June primary after a number of the signatures on his nominating petition were deemed invalid. He was subsequently reinstated, but finished a distant fourth.

The nomination went to El Paso County Supervisor Darryl Glenn, an Air Force veteran who served in Iraq and Afghanistan and was endorsed by several conservative luminaries. But he ended up being outspent 4-1 by Bennet, who hammered away at a remark Glenn made during a primary debate; "it's not about reaching across the aisle" to compromise, Glenn had said. As he had six years earlier, Bennet suggested his opponent was too extreme for Colorado. Polls three weeks from the general election showed Bennet with a double-digit lead. It ended up being closer, with Bennet winning 50%-44%, his victory largely tracking Democratic presidential nominee Hillary Clinton's 48%-43% win in the state.

With Democrats out of power at both ends of Pennsylvania Avenue, Bennet found himself squeezed between home-state and national party pressures when Trump, in January 2017, nominated Denver-born federal Judge Neil Gorsuch to the Supreme Court. Some leading Democrats in Colorado pressed Bennet to back Gorsuch, while nationally, many Democrats remained enraged over the Republican-controlled Senate's refusal to consider Obama's nomination of another federal judge, Merrick Garland, for the vacancy—and were pushing for a filibuster. Bennet lobbied fellow Democrats to head off a filibuster fight: He argued to Schumer that, since Gorsuch would succeed the late conservative Justice Antonin Scalia, it wouldn't alter the balance of the court—and it was the next vacancy that would really matter. But Democratic leaders opted to filibuster, and then-Majority Leader Mitch McConnell, Republican of Kentucky, invoked the "nuclear option" effectively changing the rules to end filibusters of Supreme Court nominations.

Bennet sought to steer a middle course. As one of Gorsuch's home-state senators, he observed tradition and introduced the nominee to the Judiciary Committee, while voting to allow Gorsuch's nomination to go to the Senate floor—one of just four Democrats to do so. But, on the final vote, he opposed Gorsuch's confirmation. A visibly exasperated Bennet took a harder line 18 months later with the Supreme Court nomination of Brett Kavanaugh, castigating McConnell for how the process had been handled.

Bennet escalated his criticism in October 2020, when McConnell pushed the nomination of Amy Coney Barrett to the high court less than two weeks before Election Day-after blocking Garland for nine months leading up to the 2016 election. "The majority leader, more than any other actor, has transformed what used to be the overwhelming bipartisan confirmation of a qualified nominee—and a bipartisan ratification of the independence of the judiciary—into an entirely partisan exercise that has destroyed the Senate's constitutional responsibility to advise and consent and is now at risk of destroying the credibility of the Supreme Court and the lower courts as well," Bennett declared. But in his book on the causes of governmental dysfunction—"The Land of Flickering Lights," published while Bennet was running for president—he pointed the finger at his own party as well. He cited Reid's 2013 maneuver to do away with the filibuster for judicial nominations other than for the Supreme Court, which initially triggered the "nuclear option"; Bennet labeled his vote in favor of that move the biggest regret of his senatorial career.

When he broke with a majority of his Senate Democratic colleagues in voting to roll back rules imposed on smaller banks by the 2010 Dodd-Frank financial regulatory overhaul, Bennet bemoaned the breakdown of political discourse and compromise in a March 2018 op-ed in the Washington Post. "On issue after issue, voices on the left and right routinely decry modest concessions as a betrayal of principle. More often than not, that principle turns out to be little more than a tactic to garner media attention by casting small differences on policy as cataclysmic," he wrote. "Until this changes, we will struggle to make progress as both parties retreat to their corners instead of doing the unglamorous, vital work of governing."

Bennet adopted a far less professorial tone in the impassioned, apparently impromptu Senate floor speech in January 2019 that helped launch his presidential bid. When Texas Republican Ted Cruz, a hard-line conservative, sought to blame Democrats for prolonging federal employee furloughs during a standoff over funding the government, Bennet brought up a prior government shutdown in 2013 that had been precipitated by Cruz's effort to defund the Affordable Care Act. Bennet—his voice escalating to a yell—recalled that sections of his home state were ravaged by flooding at the time of that shutdown. "It was underwater," exclaimed Bennet. "People were killed. People's houses were destroyed. Their small businesses were ruined forever. And because of the senator from Texas, this government was shut down. For politics. That he surfed to a second-place finish in the Iowa caucuses." (Cruz in fact won the 2016 Iowa caucuses.)

This time, it was Bennet who sought to capitalize politically: His campaign purchased Facebook ads highlighting the speech—in which he also blasted Trump for shutting down the government to gain funding for the administration's proposed border wall—in early primary and caucus states in 2020. A portion of the speech became the most viewed C-SPAN video ever posted on Twitter, and 2,000 calls to Bennet's office in the 24 hours after the speech caused his office phone system to crash.

Bennet's presidential bid never attracted that type of attention after it was announced in May 2019. (The announcement was delayed for several weeks as Bennet underwent surgery for prostate cancer, from which he emerged with a clean bill of health.) By that time, he faced the daunting task of distinguishing himself from 20 other announced contenders in the Democratic primary field, including a half-dozen of his Senate colleagues.

Like several other moderates who hoped to benefit if Joe Biden stumbled, Bennet took issue with progressives' call for "Medicare for All" and questioned the electability of leading contenders from that wing of the party, fellow Sens. Bernie Sanders of Vermont and Elizabeth Warren of Massachusetts. Touting his bill to add a "robust public option" to the Affordable Care Act, Bennet told Politico in September 2019: "I worry a lot about Elizabeth running on 'Medicare for All,' Bernie's health care plan. If you went to a city council meeting in Denver and said, 'I've got a plan for health care for Denver and here's what we're gonna do: We're gonna make private insurance illegal and we're going to charge everybody a tax that's equivalent to 70 percent of all the revenue that Denver is going to collect over the next 10 years,' you would be ejected from the room. And that is 'Medicare for All.'" Stylistically, Bennet cast himself as the opposite of the volatile Trump. "If you elect me president, I promise you won't have to think about me for 2 weeks at a time," he tweeted.

However, after the first two Democratic primary debates, Bennet failed to meet the polling and fundraising qualifications for future such forums. His campaign officials boasted that Bennet spent more time in Iowa in September 2019 than any other candidate. But, with polls in the fall showing him mired at less 1 percent in Iowa, Bennet staked his prospects on the New Hampshire primary. It didn't work: He placed 10th among the Democratic field, with just 0.3 percent of the vote.

His withdrawal statement signaled that Bennet's presidential ambitions may not be over. "I feel nothing but joy tonight as we conclude this campaign and this chapter," he declared. "Tonight wasn't our night. But New Hampshire, you may see me once again." Several weeks later, he declared his intention to seek a reelection in 2022 at a Denver forum—albeit with a dig at the Senate and some of his colleagues. "There are a lot of reasons a person would not want to be in the United States Senate, but I feel very privileged to be there and have the opportunity to overcome what I feel is a group of people who have immobilized our exercise in self-governance," he said. "If I can have a role in the Senate in helping overcome that, then I think it's important to do that."

Bennet notched a significant legislative victory early in the Biden administration when a major expansion of the child tax credit -- which he had co-sponsored with Ohio Democrat Sherrod Brown two years earlier -- was included in the new president's $1.9 trillion stimulus package. Bennet, Brown, and a leading House advocate of the plan—Connecticut Democrat Rosa DeLauro—spent months lobbying Biden's inner circle to include it in the stimulus package. According to the Center on Budget and Policy Priorities, expanding the credit—to $3,600 annually for children under age six, and $3,000 for those six to 17—and making it refundable would cut the U.S. child poverty rate in half. The expanded credit contained in the stimulus package will expire in a year, but Bennet and Brown vowed to fight to make it permanent.

John Hickenlooper (D)

Elected 2020, term expires 2026, 1st term, b. Feb 07, 1952; Narberth, PA; Wesleyan University, B.A., 1974; Wesleyan University, M.A., 1980; Quaker; Married (Robin Pringle); 1 child (1 from previous marriage)

Elected Office: Mayor of Denver, 2003-2011; Chair, National Governors Association, 2014-2015; CO Governor, 2011-2019.

Professional Career: Geologist, petrolium company, 1981-1986; Co-Founder/Co-Owner, brewing company, 1987-2003.

DC Office: Suite B85 RSOB 20510, 202-224-5941, Fax: 202-224-6524

State Offices: Colorado Springs, 719-632-6706; Denver, 303-244-1628; Fort Collins, 970-484-3502; Grand Junction, 970-245-9553; Greeley, 970-352-5546.

Committees: *Commerce, Science & Transportation*: Aviation Safety, Operations & Innovations; Communications, Media & Broadband; Space & Science (Chmn); Tourism, Trade & Export Promotion. *Energy & Natural Resources*: Energy; Public Lands, Forests & Mining; Water & Power. *Health, Education, Labor & Pensions*: Children & Families; Employment & Workplace Safety (Chmn). *Small Business & Entrepreneurship*.

Election Results

Election	Name (Party)	Vote (%)		Cand. Spent	Ind. Exp. Support	Ind. Exp. Oppose
2020 General	John Hickenlooper (D)	1,731,114	(54%)	$41,674,067	$5,510,021	$18,219,711
	Cory Gardner (R)	1,429,492	(44%)	$26,573,417	$2,745,810	$10,659,153
2020 Primary	John Hickenlooper (D)	585,826	(59%)			
	Andrew Romanoff (D)	412,955	(41%)			

Democrat John Hickenlooper of Colorado, a former beer entrepreneur and two-term governor with a penchant for reaching across the aisle, reversed his earlier objections to serving in the Senate in 2020 and defeated Republican Sen. Cory Gardner. His circuitous route was complicated by his abbreviated bid for his party's presidential nomination in 2019. When that campaign aborted, Senate Democrats pressed Hickenlooper to seek the Senate seat. Other prominent Colorado Democrats already had entered the contest to face Gardner, a freshman who was widely viewed as vulnerable because of the state's accelerating leftward shift.

Though he suffered some lapses during his Senate campaign, Hickenlooper won both the primary and general elections with relative ease. He was elected governor of Colorado in 2010. During his first two years in office, his response to two major crises won him plaudits, and Esquire magazine named him one of its "Americans of the Year" in 2012, and he went on to win a tough reelection fight despite a strong GOP tide in 2014. In 2016, Hickenlooper was in the mix as a potential running mate for Hillary Clinton, but his past efforts to bridge partisan differences proved to be out of step with a highly polarized presidential campaign. In the summer of 2020, he was fined $2,750 after the Colorado Independent Ethics Commission ruled he had inappropriately accepted gifts as governor. He went on to win the Senate race, but it was closer than expected.

"Hick," as he's been known in Colorado newspaper headlines, grew up in the Philadelphia suburbs and was raised by a frugal, widowed mother. He is a descendant of Revolutionary War financier Robert Morris. "My great-grandparents were Quakers. And I tried to take that ethic into business. Quaker honesty, Quaker mindfulness, that effort to build community across differences," he told the Philadelphia Inquirer. He graduated from Wesleyan University, first studying English and then earning a master's degree in geology.

He moved to Colorado in 1981 and took a job in the oil industry. When oil prices fell later that decade, he was laid off. On a trip to the San Francisco Bay area, he stopped at a brewpub, then a rarity. He thought the concept might work in Denver, and in 1988, he opened the state's first brewpub, Wynkoop Brewery, in a warehouse district northwest of downtown. He ended up launching 14 restaurants, which spearheaded development of the Lower Downtown as an entertainment district. Since then, "LoDo" has been buzzing with activity.

Hickenlooper's business success got his friends talking about him running for mayor of Denver in 2003 to succeed term-limited incumbent Wellington Webb. Hickenlooper and city Auditor Don Mares were the top two finishers in a six-candidate field; their June 2003 runoff was noteworthy for its lack of vitriol. Hickenlooper refused to run negative ads (a policy he mostly continued in his Senate race, although independent groups sometimes did so on his behalf) and he campaigned against "the nonsense of government," including parking meter rates. One television ad showed Hickenlooper with a change-maker around his waist, thrusting quarters into meters. He also pledged to cut the city payroll by 4 percent. He beat Mares 65%-35%.

As mayor, Hickenlooper reached out to suburban officials and to Republican Gov. Bill Owens. In 2004, he got all 32 mayors in metro Denver to support a ballot proposition increasing sales taxes to raise $4.7 billion for a light-rail system. He also persuaded voters to approve the largest bond issue in the city's history, a permanent property tax increase and a tax increase for early childhood education. Hickenlooper took control of the city's troubled public schools and installed his chief of staff, Michael Bennet, now Colorado's senior senator, as superintendent, charging him with finding innovative ways to improve school performance. Hickenlooper's 2005 program to increase energy efficiency and decrease carbon emissions reduced energy use per passenger by 11 percent at Denver International Airport and increased recycling in the city by 69 percent.

In 2007, Hickenloooper won a second term as mayor. When Democrat Bill Ritter was elected governor, the two worked together to bring the 2008 Democratic National Convention to Denver—a memorable event for Democrats, when they sealed the presidential ticket of Barack Obama and Joe Biden. But they differed on other issues. Ritter favored restrictions on abortion rights, a position that put him at odds with many Democrats, and he favored limits on oil and gas drilling, which the business community opposed. Hickenlooper tended to take the opposite stands. In December 2008, when President Obama named Democratic Sen. Ken Salazar as his Interior secretary, it was widely expected that Ritter would appoint Hickenlooper to fill Salazar's Senate seat. Instead, Ritter appointed Bennet.

In January 2010, after Ritter said he would not seek a second term, Obama called Hickenlooper and asked him to run. A week later, he agreed. While he quickly won Ritter's endorsement, he also criticized Ritter's rulemaking process and said he was "coming from a very different place" on oil and gas issues, saying he wanted to cut red tape, not increase it. (Hickenlooper once went so far as to taste a newly created fracking fluid to demonstrate its safety.)

Despite Hickenlooper's popularity in the Denver media market, which covers much of the state, several Republicans seemed able to regain the office their party lost in 2006 in what became a successful year for Republicans across much of the nation. But one by one, the GOP's candidates imploded. The narrow primary winner, tea party-aligned businessman Daniel Maes, eventually became so hobbled by revelations about his past that former Rep. Tom Tancredo, who had run a quixotic presidential campaign in 2008 as a hardliner on immigration, announced a third-party bid. Blessed with not one but two flawed opponents, Hickenlooper won with 51 percent of the vote.

Hickenlooper used the story of his work in converting Colorado Springs' old Cheyenne Hotel into a successful brewpub as a metaphor for how the state could emerge from the recession. He created an economic-development initiative that came out with a report called "the Colorado Blueprint," which called for creating a business-friendly environment. He submitted a spending plan that made $570 million in cuts on top of those that Ritter had proposed—with spending on elementary education taking the biggest hit—while raising the state's general fund reserve from 2 percent to 4 percent.

An improved revenue forecast helped bring down the size of the education cuts, and Hickenlooper won positive marks for his willingness to broker differences between the Democratic-controlled Senate and the Republican-led House. The split between the chambers prevented bills on contentious issues such as gun rights and immigration from reaching his desk. But he was able to get through a measure creating state health care exchanges as part of Obama's new federal health care law. Polls showed him with strong approval ratings among both Republicans and Democrats, and even conservative columnist George Will hailed him as an example for the Democratic Party to follow.

Entering his second year, Hickenlooper called for substantially increasing spending for economic development and announced plans to follow neighboring New Mexico in creating a "spaceport" for commercial rockets. He got into a tussle with Republicans over a property tax break for seniors that cost the state $100 million a year. Hickenlooper said suspending the tax break would help avoid further cuts to schools, while Republicans countered that the state should instead reduce spending on Medicaid. When revenues were forecast to come in an estimated $231 million higher than previously expected, the governor boosted spending on schools. But Hickenlooper was unable to overcome Republican resistance to a bill allowing civil unions for same-sex couples.

Hickenlooper flew home from a trade mission to Mexico in 2012 to deal with the wildfires that were ravaging the state and be on the front lines, listening to rescue workers' requests. He subsequently called for more water storage and conservation to ease the effects of future droughts. His approval rating reached 60 percent, prompting some in Colorado political circles to begin wondering if he would be a future presidential candidate. Despite a foray to New Hampshire, Hickenlooper downplayed such talk, saying he didn't feel like he was the right type of person for the job. In 2012, he amicably separated from his wife of 10 years, author Helen Thorpe; their announcement included the guidance, "Please feel free to include both of us in social gatherings as we will not find it awkward." In 2016, Hickenlooper married Robin Pringle, 37, a vice president at a media company.

Hickenlooper won positive marks for his willingness to broker differences between the Democratic-controlled Senate and the Republican-led House. Although the chambers remained split on contentious issues such as gun rights and illegal immigration, he won approval of a measure creating state health care exchanges as part of Obama's new federal health care law. But he was unable to overcome Republican resistance to a bill allowing civil unions for same-sex couples.

Ironically, Democratic legislative gains in the 2012 election helped dim Hickenlooper's popularity, as lawmakers from his own party pushed him to the left. Hickenlooper took heat for signing gun control legislation after the movie theater massacre in Aurora. Hickenlooper reportedly told an audience of county sheriffs that he regretted signing the measures because of the uproar that followed and that he had not spoken to New York Mayor Michael Bloomberg—a staunch backer of gun control—about the bills, though he acknowledged later that the two had talked.

In 2014, former Rep. Bob Beauprez, the GOP's 2006 gubernatorial nominee, was a late entrant in the Republican primary to face Hickenlooper, but he won with 30 percent of the vote. By mid-September, polls showed the race tightening. Despite Democrats' dismal showing nationally and in Colorado, including then-Rep. Gardner's 48%-46% defeat of Democratic Sen. Mark Udall, Hickenlooper pulled off a 49%-46% victory. The win enabled him to continue as chairman of the National Governors Association.

By 2015, the state had completed its first year of voter-approved legalization of recreational marijuana. Hundreds of shops opened for recreational and medicinal sales, but the action also brought public-safety challenges and lower-than-expected tax revenues. Hickenlooper, who had opposed legalization from the beginning, said afterward that "if I could've waved a wand the day after the election, I would've reversed the election and said, 'This was a bad idea.'" Subsequently, the legalization has become popular, and Hickenlooper has come around on the issue, acknowledging in national media appearances that the scale of the problems may have been overstated initially. At Milken Institute's Global Conference in Los Angeles in 2016, he said, "If I had that magic wand now, I don't know if I would wave it," he said. "It's beginning to look like it might work." With the success of the marijuana rollout and unemployment below the national average, Hickenlooper saw his popularity rise again..

In the first two years of his second term, Hickenlooper continued to spar over fiscal policy with Republicans, who had taken back the Senate in 2014 while the Democrats retained the House. The two sides repeatedly butted heads over the scale of Medicaid spending and whether the state's Taxpayer Bill of Rights refund should remain sacrosanct. But some of the biggest fights were over energy policy. While environmentalists appreciated Hickenlooper's proposal to spend more than $100 million on bike infrastructure, they were unhappy about his continued support for fracking. In fact, there was widespread speculation that his energy views torpedoed his potential chances to become Hillary Clinton's vice presidential running mate in 2016 or to be tapped as Interior secretary had she won, with environmentalists, a key Democratic interest group, ready to wield a veto. Still, the governor supported Obama's emissions-curbing Clean Power Plan and opposed a lawsuit against it filed by Colorado's attorney general, Cynthia Coffman.

After the U.S. Supreme Court kept the Obama administration from implementing the plan until further judicial review was complete, Hickenlooper continued state efforts to prepare for its eventual enactment anyway. This drew fierce opposition from Republican lawmakers, who threatened to defund the work. A subsequent draft executive order by Hickenlooper pleased neither side—yet another sign that Hickenlooper's attempts at finding common ground were out of tune with the times. His past efforts to bridge partisan differences proved to be out of step with the highly polarized presidential campaign.

During his final two years as governor, Hickenlooper wrestled with his options. In the Senate, many Democrats viewed him as their best hope to defeat Gardner, who had shown political skills in his defeat of Udall in 2014 and moved into Senate Republican leadership. But Hickenlooper rejected that option for multiple reasons, including his publicly voiced disdain for serving as a legislator.

In March 2019, Hickenlooper announced that he was running for president. Pitching a centrist profile, he highlighted his support for tough environmental and gun-control legislation, plus his success in bringing "near-universal health care coverage" to his state. He centered his campaign on his ability to appeal to both the liberal Democrats and the white working-class voters who supported President Donald Trump in 2016. Despite his bipartisan dealmaker reputation, he failed to gain any real traction in the crowded field of Democrats running for president, consistently polling at zero percent. Being a "pragmatic progressive" and well-mannered 67-year-old white man who lacked Washington experience wasn't a strong enough argument to convince voters that he could defeat Trump in 2020.

In August of the same year, after extended discussion with Democratic Leader Chuck Schumer and others, he announced that he was running for the Senate. Several declared Democratic candidates withdrew and voiced support for Hickenlooper. That left him to face off against Andrew Romanoff, a former speaker of the state House who had lost a primary challenge in 2010 to Bennet and a 2014 challenge to a House Republican incumbent. Romanoff called for more radical change, advocating for the "Green New Deal" and "Medicare for All," while criticizing Hickenlooper as stuck in the "middle of the road."

Shortly before the primary vote, Hickenlooper was under fire for being cited for contempt for initially failing to appear before Colorado's Independent Ethics Commission in its review of a claim that he received private payments for travel while he was governor. He also came under fire for comments about race: He had said that "Black Lives Matter means that every life matters" at a forum on the Black Lives Matter movement. Concerns began to emerge that Hickenlooper was running a lackluster, gaffe-filled campaign. Despite these serious missteps, Hickenlooper ran strongly across the state and easily won the primary, 59%-41%.

Gardner, one of two Republican senators seeking reelection in a state that Trump lost in 2016, knew he faced an uphill challenge in increasingly blue Colorado. He struggled to show independence of Trump without alienating the Republican faithful. He highlighted his legislative accomplishments, including enactment of his Great American Outdoors Act, which increased funding for the growing needs of federal public lands, including national parks. The former National Republican Senatorial Committee chairman initially received lavish financial support from Republican committees, though that dried up during the final weeks of the campaign as the election handwriting was on the wall.

If there was any hope left, it disappeared after Gardner decided to support Amy Coney Barrett's Supreme Court nomination after the death of Justice Ruth Bader Ginsburg in September. Gardner did outrun Trump by 2 points, but Hickenlooper easily won, 53%-44%. Although Republican groups outspent Democrats on air, it was Hickenlooper who spent more than Gardner overall, $42 million to $27million.

Hickenlooper was teamed again with Bennet, whose strikingly similar backgrounds have made them allies in the past. But, as the Colorado Sun wrote, while "Bennet's intellectual curiosity and patience help him thrive on the minutiae and strategy of policymaking," that could be a frustrating transition for Hickenlooper. He might find a frustration with Washington, as have the six other former governors in the Senate at times—particularly since he was initially resistant to running.

Diana DeGette (D)

Elected 1996, 13th term, b. Jul 29, 1957; Tachikawa, Japan; CO College, B.A., 1979; NY University Law School, J.D., 1982; Presbyterian; Married (Lino Lipinsky); 2 children.

Elected Office: CO House, 1992-1996, Assistant Minority Leader, 1994-1995.

Professional Career: Practicing attorney, 1982-1996.

DC Office: 2111 RHOB 20515, 202-225-4431, Fax: 202-225-5657, degette.house.gov

State Offices: Denver, 303-844-4988.

Committees: *Energy & Commerce*: Energy; Environment & Climate Change; Oversight & Investigations (Chmn). *Natural Resources*: Energy & Mineral Resources; National Parks, Forests & Public Lands.

Group Ratings

	ADA	ACLU	AFL-CIO	LCV	COC	HAFA	ACU	CFG	FRC
2020	**	83%	**	100%	-	0%	3%	**	-
2019	95%	C	95%	97%	47%	C	3%	19%	0%

Almanac Ratings 2019-2020

	Economy	Social	Foreign	Composite
Liberal	100%	100%	96%	99%
Conservative	0%	0%	4%	1%

Key Votes of the 116th Congress

1. U.S./Mex./Can. trade deal Y	5. Russia sanctions Y	9. Firearms background checks Y
2. First Coronavirus response Y	6. Troops in Syria Y	10. Spending at the border N
3. HEROES Act Y	7. Veto arms sales to Saudis Y	11. Marijuana liberalized rules Y
4. CASH Act Y	8. Defense $$$, veto override Y	12. Electoral College objections N

Election Results

Election	Name (Party)	Vote (%)	Cand. Spent	Ind. Exp. Support	Ind. Exp. Oppose
2020 General	Diana DeGette (D)......................... 331,621	(74%)	$937,021	$1,010	
	Shane Bolling (R)................................ 105,955	(24%)	$13,346		$665
2020 Primary	Diana DeGette (D)......................... 187,341	(100%)			

Prior winning percentages: 2018 (74%), 2016 (68%), 2014 (66%), 2012 (68%), 2010 (67%), 2008 (72%), 2006 (80%), 2004 (74%), 2002 (66%), 2000 (69%), 1998 (67%), 1996 (57%)

Diana DeGette, first elected in 1996, is an energetic liberal and insider who has been among the House Democrats anxiously awaiting the chance to succeed the party's older, entrenched leaders. As chair of the Energy and Commerce Oversight Subcommittee, DeGette pursued numerous inquiries of the Trump administration. With her occasional success in the past with bipartisan legislation, DeGette insisted that Congress could "walk and chew gum"—enacting policy while investigating the president. During her quarter-century in the House, she has spent only six years in the majority.

DeGette is a fourth-generation resident of Denver, though she was born on a military base in Japan. She says that she was inspired at age 13 by the television show Storefront Lawyers to "crusade for justice," and decided she would be a public interest lawyer. She attended New York University's law school on a full scholarship, then returned to Denver to practice employment law. In 1992, at age 35, DeGette was elected to the Colorado House. Her signature accomplishment was the Bubble Bill, which was aimed at protecting women at abortion clinics by making it illegal for protesters to come within eight feet of a person entering or leaving a health care facility. The U.S. Supreme Court upheld the constitutionality of the law in a 6-3 decision. In 1995, when Rep. Patricia Schroeder, a pioneer of the feminist left, announced she was retiring, DeGette ran for the seat. Organizationally adept, legislatively creative and politically progressive, she proved a worthy successor to Schroeder.

In both the minority and the majority, she has achieved legislative successes. On Energy and Commerce she has focused on health care issues. She teamed with Republican Rep. Mike Castle of Delaware to expand funding for stem cell research. President George W. Bush opposed using federal tax money for such research, and in 2006 vetoed their bill. In 2009, President Barack Obama, using his executive powers, removed most federal restrictions on stem cell research. She wrote a book on the topic called Sex, Science, and Stem Cells.

DeGette secured key provisions giving the Food and Drug Administration the power to mandate product recalls and authorizing the FDA to establish a food-tracking system. Mandatory recall authority for the FDA became law in the Food Safety Modernization Act in 2011. During the health care overhaul debate in 2009 and 2010, DeGette helped to shape the final abortion provisions in the legislation. With Republican Energy and Commerce Chairman Fred Upton of Michigan, she launched an initiative in 2015 to reduce the time for getting "breakthrough drugs" into the hands of needy patients. in 2016, their 21st Century Cures bill was one of the few major bipartisan measures enacted during Obama's final year as president. DeGette called the legislation "a watershed moment in this country for biomedical research."

DeGette has been active on issues affecting Colorado and the West. After Colorado and Washington state in 2012 enacted laws legalizing marijuana, she filed legislation that barred the federal government from pre-empting such state laws. On Energy and Commerce, she has pushed to address climate change, including U.S.-led international funding of renewable energy production. In January 2020, she filed a bill to create the first national energy clean-air standard, which would require utilities to eliminate all carbon emissions by 2050.

DeGette has been active in House leadership politics, but has had setbacks. In 2001, she supported Maryland's Steny Hoyer in his unsuccessful bid for Democratic whip against California's Nancy Pelosi, who went on to become House Speaker. When Hoyer got the job as party whip in 2002, DeGette moved into the role of party strategist. When Democrats gained control of the House in 2007, she seriously considered running for whip against South Carolina's James Clyburn. She said she ultimately decided that it would have been disruptive to have another internal struggle. Clyburn made DeGette his chief deputy whip. A few days after the 2018 election, when Democrats regained the House majority, she declared her candidacy for whip. But DeGette again backed down when Clyburn reclaimed his post. With each of the top three Democratic leaders an octogenarian seemingly close to retirement, DeGette warned, "we need to have some transition planning."

As a hefty consolation prize, DeGette took over the Oversight Subcommittee, which has long been a prime investigative niche in Congress. In July 2020, she called in top executives from five pharmaceutical firms to inquire about their progress on a vaccine for COVID-19. Later, she led an effort by House Democrats to recommend confidence-building steps that those companies should take, with high ethical and scientific standards. On abortion policy, she remained a go-to player, working with Pelosi in 2020 to resist efforts by some liberal groups to repeal the Hyde amendment limitations on federal funding. They concluded that they were unlikely to prevail against the Republican-controlled Senate and President Donald Trump.

In December 2019, DeGette was entrusted with the responsibility to preside over the House debate on Trump's first impeachment. In the second impeachment trial of Trump in the Senate, DeGette was one of the nine House managers. Although she was not a member of the Judiciary Committee, she brought experience as a trial attorney in the private sector and as an expert in congressional oversight.

DeGette has faced limited campaign opposition. In 2002, Ramona Martinez, a 15-year member of the Denver City Council and a Democratic National Committeewoman, criticized her for having lost touch with the district. DeGette returned her family to Denver from the Maryland suburbs in 2001 and won impressively, 73%-27%.

Sixteen years later, she received a similar challenge. Saira Rao, a first-generation Indian American who had practiced law on Wall Street before settling in Denver and publishing children's books, said DeGette was not sufficiently active in her district and that it was time for a change. DeGette defended her record and said her seniority would benefit the district, especially if Democrats regained House control. Both candidates were well-funded. DeGette won, 68%-32%. "It really didn't turn out to be a very strong challenge, did it?" DeGette said to a reporter on primary night. Rao responded with Twitter attacks on journalists and other Democrats. In 2020, she won the Democratic primary without opposition and had her usual landslide in November.

CO-1: Denver Metro

Cook Partisan Voting Index: D+24

Population		Race and Ethnicity		Income	
Total	852,816	White	78.50%	Median Income	$77,507
Land area (sq. miles)	190	Black	7.80%	District Income Rank	105
Pop/ sq mi	4,497.5	Latino	27.10%	Poverty Rate	10.80%
Born in State	40.40%	Asian	3.40%	With health insurance	91.90%
		Two or more races	4.50%	Cash public assistance	1.50%
Age Groups		Other	5.80%	Food stamp/SNAP	6.40%
Under 18	19.50%				
18-34	29.90%	**Education**		**Work**	
35-64	38.00%	H.S grad or less	25.70%	White Collar	51.70%
Over 64	12.60%	Some college	22.30%	Sales and Service	33.40%
		College Degree, 4 yr	32.50%	Blue Collar	14.80%
Military		Post grad	19.60%	Government	11.50%
Veteran/ Active Duty	5.90%				

2020 Pres. Vote	Biden	357,845	(76%)	Trump	104,535	(22%)	
2016 Pres. Vote	Clinton	277,790	(69%)	Trump	93,486	(23%) Johnson	18,996 (5%)

Denver: Denver is serious about being the Mile High City: There are three markers on the granite steps of the gold-domed capitol that proclaim the elevation of 5,280 feet. Denver is situated a few miles from where the High Plains yield to the sharp peaks of the Front Range of the Rockies. With 727,000 people in 2017, a 21 percent increase since 2010, the city for a century has been the economic and cultural capital of the Rocky Mountain region. On top of its western heritage and early-20th-century elegance, Denver has developed an exuberant postmodern style. The National Western Stock Show held here every year and the LoDo entertainment district along the South Platte River evoke the Old West. The capitol, the spacious parks and the aspens that line the streets give the city a lush, burnished air, in contrast to the dry plains and stark peaks.

Amid its downtown grid are the skyscrapers of the 1970s energy boom and the 1990s tech boom, plus Coors Field, where Major League Baseball's Colorado Rockies play, the Elitch Gardens Theme and Water Park, and the Denver Museum of Nature & Science. Barack Obama claimed the Democratic presidential nomination at Mile High Stadium in 2008, with grand theatrics and expectations. Most of its neighborhoods have strong housing demand, including the African-American neighborhoods of northeastern Denver, filled with neat 1950s bungalows. The northwest quarter combines gentrified areas such as LoHi plus neighborhoods closer to downtown, with the Hispanic section nearby. To the south, Westwood has become a Mexican cultural district. More than three-quarters of the metro area's people now live in the suburbs, and Denver has disproportionate numbers of singles and cultural liberals who value an urban and physically active lifestyle.

Responding to the city's large Latino community, Denver Mayor Michael Hancock said following the 2016 election that the city's police officers would not cooperate with enforcement of federal immigration laws. In 2018, he refused to meet with President Donald Trump to discuss the status of the sanctuary city. "Denver doesn't violate federal law, and we won't be intimidated," Hancock tweeted.

Denver is the progressive heart of Colorado. The city has elected Hispanic and black mayors and is 30 percent Latino. In the early 1970s, Denver liberals were hostile to growth and boosterism. Since then, city leaders have argued that growth can produce more of the distinctiveness that people here appreciate. In May 2019, voters approved a city referendum that decriminalized "magic mushrooms," a drug that many use to cope with anxiety or depression. Palantir, a data analytics software company, relocated from Palo Alto, California, after its chief executive revolted against "the engineering elite" of Silicon Valley and sought Denver's good vibes on "how society should be organized or what justice requires."

The 1st Congressional District covers all of Denver and stretches northeast to include Denver International Airport. The district drops southwest to include suburban parts of Jefferson County, where Columbine High School was the location in 1999 of a mass shooting, when two teenage boys killed 13 people. More than 80 percent live in Denver, where the city is identical to the county. The 1st, which last elected a Republican in 1970 (when Colorado had only four House seats), recently has reinforced its solid Democratic lean. Not long ago, Democrats needed a huge turnout in Denver to win statewide. In 2016, Hillary Clinton's roughly 180,000 vote lead in Denver exceeded her statewide margin. Four years later, Joe Biden's 240,000 vote lead in the city was barely half of his statewide total. He took the district with 76 percent of the vote, an increase of seven percentage points since 2016.

Joe Neguse (D)

Elected 2018, 2nd term, b. May 13, 1984; Bakersfield, CA; University of CO, Boulder, B.S., 2005; University of CO, Boulder, J.D., 2009; Christian Church; Married (Andrea Neguse); 1 child.

Professional Career: Founder, New Era Colorado; Staff Assistant, CO Rep. Andrew Romanoff; Attorney, Snell and Wilner, 2009-2015; Executive Director , CO Department of Regulatory Agencies, 2015-2017

DC Office: 1419 LHOB 20515, 202-225-2161, neguse.house.gov

State Offices: Boulder, 303-335-1045; Fort Collins, 970-372-3971.

Committees: *Judiciary*: Antitrust, Commercial & Administrative Law; Courts, Intellectual Property & Internet; Immigration & Citizenship. *Natural Resources*: National Parks, Forests & Public Lands (Chmn). *Rules. Select Committee on the Climate Crisis.*

Almanac Ratings 2019-2020

	Economy	Social	Foreign	Composite
Liberal	100%	100%	96%	99%
Conservative	0%	0%	4%	1%

Key Votes of the 116th Congress

1. U.S./Mex./Can. trade deal	Y	5. Russia sanctions	Y	9. Firearms background checks Y
2. First Coronavirus response	Y	6. Troops in Syria	Y	10. Spending at the border	N
3. HEROES Act	Y	7. Veto arms sales to Saudis	Y	11. Marijuana liberalized rules	Y
4. CASH Act	Y	8. Defense $$$, veto override	Y	12. Electoral College objections N

Election Results

Election	Name (Party)	Vote (%)		Cand. Spent	Ind. Exp. Support	Ind. Exp. Oppose
2020 General	Joe Neguse (D)	316,925	(61%)	$506,321	$6,741	
	Charlie Winn (R)	182,547	(35%)	$96,481		$665
	Thom Atkinson (L)	13,657	(3%)			
2020 Primary	Joe Neguse (D)	168,393	(100%)			

Prior winning percentages: 2018 (60%)

Democrat Joe Neguse easily won his first term and took office as the state's first African American elected to Congress. He devoted much of his work to environmental and lands issues and served on the House's Select Committee on the Climate Crisis. He was one of the House's impeachment managers in the second Senate trial of former President Donald Trump. At home, he was politically secure.

Election to Congress, at age 34, marked the rapid political rise of the son of Eritrean refugees who were granted asylum in the United States after fleeing the East African nation. Neguse's youthful advance ironically became something of an American success story in which he found himself under attack for working too closely with establishment figures in the Denver area. He replaced Democrat Jared Polis, who was elected governor.

Neguse's parents separately fled Eritrea in 1980 and settled in Bakersfield California, where they were introduced to each other by mutual friends. When Joe was six, his family moved to Denver, where his parents worked in accounting and banking. He got his undergraduate and law degrees from the University of Colorado and was elected by voters to the university's board of regents.

After working for Colorado House Speaker Andrew Romanoff, Neguse co-founded New Era Colorado, a youth voter registration and mobilization nonprofit. He ran for secretary of state in 2014 and lost to Republican Wayne Williams, 47%-45%. Gov. John Hickenlooper appointed Neguse director of the Colorado Department of Regulatory Agencies, the state's consumer protection agency. He later joined Snell and Wilner, a Denver law firm.

Following Polis' long-expected decision to run for governor, Neguse was the Democratic frontrunner to succeed him. He took progressive views on issues such as single-payer health care and environmental protection. An outspoken critic of President Donald Trump and his immigration policies, Neguse cited his parents' experiences in seeking asylum in the United States from their war-torn nation. Contending that "the American dream" was under assault by Trump, he told the Fort Collins Coloradoan, "I think about my parents who immigrated to this country 35 years ago and how different their lives would be and my life would be if they tried to immigrate today."

He faced competition in the primary from Mark Williams, a former Air Force pilot who became a tech-industry executive. Neguse had a nearly 10-to-1 fundraising advantage over Williams. He was supported in the primary by many Democratic leaders, including former Vice President Joe Biden and House Minority Whip Steny Hoyer, plus several labor unions and the liberal-advocacy group Democracy for America.

Williams, a former chairman of Boulder County Democrats, embraced "citizen" campaigns and criticized Neguse's approach from "the world of old politics." When he announced his candidacy, Williams told a candidate forum in Boulder, "the knives came out pretty quick" from what he called the Democratic "old-boy network" in the Denver area. Neguse won the primary, 66%-34%, and led comfortably in each of the 10 counties. In November, he easily defeated Republican Peter Yu, a local businessman.

Neguse was one of three freshman Democrats to win a seat on the Democratic-created climate crisis select committee. In August 2019, he chaired the panel's hearing in Boulder during which state and local leaders described their roadmap for clean energy action, including large cuts in carbon emissions. In October, largely along party lines, the House passed his bill to protect 400,000 acres of public land in Colorado. With Republican Rep. John Curtis of Utah, Neguse announced plans to create a bipartisan wildfire caucus to increase awareness of fire management, especially in rural parts of the West.

He stepped up on other legislation. In May 2020, when the House passed the Democrats' Heroes Act for additional coronavirus relief, the measure included Neguse's provisions for direct aid to small cities plus increased funding for nutrition programs. In the lame-duck session following the election, Congress completed action on his measure creating a monument in Washington D.C. to honor suffragists and the 100th anniversary of the 19th Amendment extension of voting rights to women.

In the second impeachment trial of Trump, Neguse had the most speaking time of the nine House managers except for Rep. Jamie Raskin, who was the lead manager. He received plaudits as an impressive advocate as he urged Republicans to "rise to the occasion." The Los Angeles Times, which headlined him as "next-gen star," said that several Republican senators "complimented Neguse for his trial presentations, according to two people with knowledge of those conversations."

In 2020, Neguse won the Democratic primary without opposition and had a routine victory in November. His narrow setback in his earlier bid for statewide office suggests that the young Neguse will remain upwardly mobile. The Los Angeles Times profile said that Senate Democratic Leader Chuck Schumer considered Neguse as a challenger in the 2020 campaign against Colorado Republican Sen. Cory Gardner, but ultimately preferred John Hickenlooper.

CO-2: Northern Front Range **Cook Partisan Voting Index: D+12**

Population		Race and Ethnicity		Income	
Total	824,050	White	90.30%	Median Income	$87,585
Land area (sq. miles)	7,535	Black	1.00%	District Income Rank	64
Pop/ sq mi	109.36	Latino	11.00%	Poverty Rate	9.80%
Born in State	36.60%	Asian	3.60%	With health insurance	94.30%
		Two or more races	3.10%	Cash public assistance	1.20%
Age Groups		Other	2.10%	Food stamp/SNAP	4.10%
Under 18	19.20%				
18-34	26.40%	Education		Work	
35-64	38.80%	H.S grad or less	17.90%	White Collar	52.20%
Over 64	15.50%	Some college	25.20%	Sales and Service	33.50%
		College Degree, 4 yr	33.00%	Blue Collar	14.20%
Military		Post grad	23.90%	Government	15.60%
Veteran/ Active Duty	6.00%				

2020 Pres. Vote	Biden	338,261	(64%)	Trump	178,561	(34%)		
2016 Pres. Vote	Clinton	264,966	(56%)	Trump	164,769	(35%)	Johnson	24,820	(5%)

Fort Collins, Boulder: Nestled against the Front Range of the Rocky Mountains is Boulder, home of the 30,000-student University of Colorado, once billed by the city as "a combination of Lycra-clad athletes, New Age artists, and thoughtful intellectuals sipping cappuccinos." Boulder is one of the nation's leading centers for bungee jumping, mountain biking, snowshoeing, rock and ice climbing, downhill skiing, land surfing and hot-air ballooning. It has been called the nation's No. 1 town for outdoor sports by Outdoor magazine. Marathoners from around the world train in several camps here. All have come because of the setting. The streets of Boulder look up at craggy peaks rising to 14,000 feet from a mile-high plain stretching farther east than the eye can see.

The economics also have been appealing. Boulder has become a magnet for technology firms dissatisfied with the more congested Silicon Valley. In 2020, U.S. News ranked Boulder number-one in its list of the best places to live in the United States. According to Census Bureau data, 76 percent of the adult population in the city of Boulder are college graduates, the highest share in the nation; in Boulder County, 62 percent have graduated. Some of life's adversities have appeared in Boulder. In 2020, three of the largest fires in Colorado history consumed parts of Rocky Mountain forests north and west of Boulder, largely due to severe drought. From 2017 to 2019, Boulder city suffered small population losses each year. The mayor cited the high cost of housing plus the large share of aging residents.

The Fort Collins-Loveland area north of Boulder ranked fifth in the U.S. News survey. Fort Collins has faced some challenges. Demographic changes have widened the local income gap. Grassroots groups were displeased when the state Supreme Court in 2016 unanimously ruled that the Fort Collins moratorium on hydraulic fracking violated the state's authority to regulate oil and gas.

The 2nd Congressional District is centered in Boulder, though nearly one-third of the county is a liberal appendage of the 4th District. Interstate 70 charts a scenically awesome course through the mountains as it takes in Rocky Mountain acreage, and it is often congested with cars loaded with skis and snowboards. The district includes the old coal mining town of Central City, which describes itself as "the richest square mile on earth" and is home to multiple casinos. The lodges and resorts of Vail are farther west on Interstate 70. Once dependent on mining and agriculture, Vail evolved into an international resort city after the 10th Mountain Division ski troops were introduced to the Eagle River Valley in the 1940s. After World War II, a group of Army buddies returned and developed a ski resort, which has become a lush vacation destination.

Boulder County is a partisan hub for Democrats. Joe Biden got 77 percent in the county, nearly as much as his 80 percent in Denver, which cast twice as many votes. The remainder of the district is relatively balanced politically. Larimer County, with Fort Collins and Loveland, includes more than 40 percent of the voters in the district; once a swing county, it has been moving to the Democrats. Boulder has about 30 percent. Except for Vail-based Summit County, the rural counties to the west are more Republican; they have few voters. In the district, Biden got 64 percent, an increase of eight percentage points over the local vote for Hillary Clinton.

Lauren Boebert (R)

Elected 2020, 1st term, b. Dec 15, 1986; Orlando, FL; Christian - Non-Denominational; Married (Jayson Boebert); 4 children.

Professional Career: Owner, restaurant

DC Office: 1609 LHOB 20515, 202-225-4761, Fax: 202-225-4761, boebert.house.gov

State Offices: Durango, 970-317-6130; Grand Junction, 970-208-0460; Pueblo, 719-696-6970.

Committees: *Budget. Natural Resources*: Indigenous Peoples of the United States; Water, Oceans & Wildlife.

Election Results

Election	Name (Party)	Vote (%)		Cand. Spent	Ind. Exp. Support	Ind. Exp. Oppose
2020 General	Lauren Boebert (R)............................. 220,634	(51%)		$2,642,353	$485,992	$3,928,493
	Diane Mitsch Bush (D).................. 194,122	(45%)		$4,932,029	$146,937	$4,598,435
	John Ryan Keil (L)............................... 10,298	(2%)				
2020 Primary	Lauren Boebert (R)............................. 58,678	(55%)				
	Scott Tipton (R)........................... 48,805	(45%)				

Lauren Boebert, a gun-toting political novice, shocked the political world when she defeated Rep. Scott Tipton in the Republican primary, contending that he was not sufficiently conservative for his district. In November, she retained the seat for the GOP following a competitive contest. With her hardscrabble background, Boebert gained attention as the owner of a restaurant where she observed "open carry" practices with firearms. Tipton, who served five terms, did little campaigning prior to the primary and seemed as surprised as anyone by the outcome.

A native of the Orlando area in Florida, Boebert moved with her family to Colorado as a child. Her low-income parents received welfare payments and Boebert recounted standing in line for federal distribution of cheese. While in high school, she worked at a local McDonald's restaurant and eventually became a manager. She failed to complete school, she told the Durango Herald, because "I was a brand-new mom and I had to make hard decisions on successfully raising my child or getting to high school biology class."

In her hometown of Rifle, she opened a restaurant, Shooters Grill, where both staff and patrons were encouraged to carry guns. Early during the coronavirus pandemic in the spring of 2020, a county official cited the restaurant for operating in violation of public-health restrictions. The charge was dropped after the county relaxed its restrictions on restaurants.

While she was campaigning for Congress, Boebert said, she completed the required classes to receive a General Educational Development certificate, which many view as the equivalent of a high school diploma. "I wish that more members of Congress had the life experiences that I've had," she told the Herald. "I'm living the American dream." In challenging Tipton, she attacked his "politics as usual" and criticized him for cosponsoring a pandemic-relief bill that aided local governments. She called it the "Boulder relief" bill, referring to the upscale liberal bastion in Colorado.

Boebert won the Republican primary, 55%-45%. "Tipton had several hundred thousand dollars in the bank but his campaign chose to air very little media and to send very little mail," Dick Wadhams, the former state Republican chairman, wrote for Complete Colorado, a local website. "The campaign essentially ceded the field to Boebert." Tipton was the first member of Congress from Colorado to lose a primary since 1972.

Democrats nominated Diane Mitsch Bush, a former state representative and social science professor who resided in the ski resort town of Steamboat Springs. She challenged Tipton in 2018 and was defeated, 52%-44%. In an interview with the Aspen Daily News, Mitsch Bush said "Boebert is only interested in going to Congress to contribute to the partisan gridlock and to be a celebrity." Responding to Boebert's criticism that she was avoiding the public during the pandemic, Mitsch Bush added, "it's just not safe" to hold such events.

Mitsch Bush spent $5 million on the contest, which nearly doubled Boebert's spending. The two national parties combined for another $9 million. Boebert won, 51%-45%. Her 25,000-vote lead in Mesa County accounted for nearly all her winning margin. In the swing county of Pueblo, which virtually matched the turnout in Mesa, Mitsch Bush led by 204 votes.

In the House, Boebert got useful assignments to the Budget and Natural Resources committees.

CO-3: Western Slope   Cook Partisan Voting Index: R+6

Population		Race and Ethnicity		Income	
Total	756,569	White	89.50%	Median Income	$59,973
Land area (sq. miles)	49,732	Black	0.90%	District Income Rank	263
Pop/ sq mi	15.21	Latino	25.00%	Poverty Rate	13.60%
Born in State	48.40%	Asian	1.10%	With health insurance	90.10%
		Two or more races	2.70%	Cash public assistance	3.00%
Age Groups		Other	5.70%	Food stamp/SNAP	10.80%
Under 18	20.80%				
18-34	21.20%	**Education**		**Work**	
35-64	38.30%	H.S grad or less	34.60%	White Collar	37.20%
Over 64	19.60%	Some college	32.50%	Sales and Service	40.50%
		College Degree, 4 yr	22.20%	Blue Collar	22.20%
Military		Post grad	10.80%	Government	16.50%
Veteran/ Active Duty	8.60%				

2020 Pres. Vote	Trump	224,996	(52%)	Biden	200,886	(46%)		
2016 Pres. Vote	Trump	195,966	(52%)	Clinton	151,057	(40%)	Johnson	17,687	(5%)

Grand Junction, Pueblo: On a clear night from the air, they look like tiny mottled veins, thickest near Denver. These are the lights of the civilization Americans have built on the Western Slope of the Rockies in Colorado. The lights follow the trails of valley roads and mountainside switchbacks. The nodes mark the dozens of little towns built during mining boom years: the Gold Rush of the 1870s, the uranium boom of the 1950s, and the oil-shale boomlet of the 1970s. The Western Slope —everything west of the Front Range, with dozens of peaks over 14,000 feet—has always been an impediment to east-west movement. The miners who tracked gold and silver and lead ores also built Victorian towns with opera houses and gingerbread storefronts in Aspen and Telluride, in valleys and defiles scarcely accessible to the outside world. Many of these towns have been restored by ski resort operators and joined by dozens of new condominiums and shopping malls. Cries of overdevelopment have followed. Another peril: In recent years, rapid snow melt in the spring has exacerbated drought, which has led to devastating fires in the mountains.

Amid the tourism, development of gas deposits trapped beneath the Roan Plateau continued. In 2016, the U.S. Geological Survey increased by 40 times its estimate of natural gas reserves in the area's Piceance Basin, which would be the second largest in the nation behind the Marcellus Shale centered in Pennsylvania. A large share of the western Colorado reserves are on federal lands, where drilling companies planned to use hydraulic fracturing. Several counties in the area have reported large increases of new permits for drilling. In 2019, the Trump administration heralded the relocation of the headquarters of the Bureau of Land Management from Washington D.C. to Grand Junction, to the delight of many Coloradans and the dismay of national interest groups.

The political map of the Western Slope is as diverse as its history. Typically, the high-income areas, with lots of residents opposed to new oil and gas drilling, are the most Democratic, while more modest-income, working-class towns are the most Republican. A ribbon of counties along the Wasatch Range, from Wyoming on the northern border to New Mexico on the southern border, votes mostly Democratic. They include Aspen and the former coal mining centers of Crested Butte and Steamboat Springs, once Republican, today sporting ski lodges. Durango, an old frontier town, has moved in the same direction. Some areas are still heavily Republican and hostile to environmentalists and liberals generally: the rough-handed mining area around Grand Junction, the population center of the district, where piles of uranium tailings still crackle with radioactivity; and the northwest corner of the state, where people remember the oil shale boom with nostalgia.

The 3rd Congressional District of Colorado includes most of the Western Slope and occupies nearly half of Colorado. It extends east of the Front Range to include the industrial city of Pueblo.

There, on the banks of the Arkansas River, the Rockefellers built large steel factories before World War I to make barbed wire and rails. In 2016, the Army began to operate a $4.5 billion plant at the Pueblo Chemical Depot to destroy the largest remaining stockpile of chemical weapons: more than 780,000 shells with 2,600 tons of a mustard gas agent. The original target date for completion of 2020 was extended to 2023 after the Army reported setbacks due to concerns about worker safety. Pueblo County is the second-largest in the district and has been comfortably Democratic, with a 43 percent Hispanic population. In 2016, Donald Trump won Pueblo by 390 votes, with his blue-collar and rural appeal. In 2020, Joe Biden flipped Pueblo back to Democrats, by 2,500 votes. The 3rd has the lowest median income and education levels in the state. With the chief exception of the resort counties, the district has leaned increasingly Republican. After John McCain won here 50%-49% in 2008, Trump twice took the district with 52 percent.

Kenneth Buck (R)

Elected 2014, 4th term, b. Feb 16, 1959; Ossining, NY; Princeton University, A.B., 1981; University of WY, J.D., 1985; Wesleyan; Married (Perry Lynn); 2 children (2 from previous marriage).

Elected Office: Weld County, CO, DA 2005-2014.

Professional Career: Practicing attorney, 1987-2002; Staff, U.S. Committee to Investigate Cover Arms Transactions with Iran, 1986-1987.

DC Office: 2455 RHOB 20515, 202-225-4676, buck.house.gov

State Offices: Castle Rock, 720-639-9165; Greeley, 970-702-2136.

Committees: *Foreign Affairs*: Asia, the Pacific, Central Asia, Nonproliferation. *Judiciary*: Antitrust, Commercial & Administrative Law (RMM); Immigration & Citizenship.

Group Ratings

	ADA	ACLU	AFL-CIO	LCV	COC	HAFA	ACU	CFG	FRC
2020	**	17%	**	0%	-	100%	98%	**	-
2019	0%	C	16%	0%	56%	C	98%	100%	95%

Almanac Ratings 2019-2020

	Economy	Social	Foreign	Composite
Liberal	40%	4%	45%	30%
Conservative	60%	96%	55%	70%

Key Votes of the 116th Congress

1. U.S./Mex./Can. trade deal	Y	5. Russia sanctions	Y	9. Firearms background checks N
2. First Coronavirus response	N	6. Troops in Syria	Y	10. Spending at the border	N/A
3. HEROES Act	N	7. Veto arms sales to Saudis	N	11. Marijuana liberalized rules	N
4. CASH Act	N	8. Defense $$$, veto override	N	12. Electoral College objections N

Election Results

Election	Name (Party)	Vote (%)		Cand. Spent	Ind. Exp. Support	Ind. Exp. Oppose
2020 General	Kenneth Buck (R)	285,606	(60%)	$463,574	$725	$113
	Ike McCorkle (D)	173,945	(37%)	$196,776	$123	
	Bruce Griffith (L)	11,026	(2%)			
2020 Primary	Ken Buck (R)	109,230	(100%)			

Prior winning percentages: 2018 (61%), 2016 (64%), 2014 (65%)

Republican Kenneth Buck, with his political revival in 2014, became a Freedom Caucus member and an outspoken conservative critic of what he calls the Republican Party's loss of principles. He won the House seat after narrowly losing four years earlier a Senate contest to Democrat Michael

Bennet that many expected Buck would win. More recently, his two years as Colorado Republican chairman failed to halt the local GOP's downturn and resulted in questions about his conduct.

Buck cultivated his political chops early in his career. Fresh out of the University of Wyoming law school, he worked for then-Rep. Dick Cheney on the House's 1986-87 probe into the Iran-Contra scandal and later served as a trial attorney in the Justice Department. He returned to Colorado in the 1990s as chief of the Criminal Division in the U.S. Attorney's Office. In 2005, he successfully ran for Weld County district attorney and was reelected twice.

His political hopes crashed in 2010. In the GOP primary for a Senate seat, he attracted national attention by commenting that he would make a better candidate than his opponent, Lt. Gov. Jane Norton, because he didn't "wear heels." Buck won the primary, 52%-48%. Further damage was done when he compared homosexuality to alcoholism on Meet the Press. He lost to Bennet by less than two percentage points, prompting many Republicans to view Colorado as a squandered pickup opportunity.

Sporting a more professional image and emphasizing his career in law enforcement, Buck launched another shot at the Senate in 2014 against first-term Democratic Sen. Mark Udall. But when Rep. Cory Gardner threw his hat in the ring, Buck decided to step aside to compete instead for Gardner's open 4th District, where the turf is friendly for Republicans. GOP strategists were grateful to get a stronger Senate challenger. The softer-edged Gardner was relieved to avoid a competitive primary.

In the primary for Gardner's House seat, Buck's name recognition and conservative reputation gave him a big edge over three GOP opponents. He highlighted issues such as energy independence, touting his support for the Keystone XL pipeline. Boosted by endorsements from Gardner and other top Republicans, as well as the local newspaper, The Greeley Tribune, Buck topped the primary field with 44 percent. In the general election, Buck easily beat Vic Meyers, 65%-29%.

Buck was elected president of the Republican freshman class and said he would focus on problem-solving, not partisanship. But he maintained his blunt-spoken style. Criticizing President Barack Obama for abusing his executive authority, he said, "No more acting like King Barack." Buck faced the threat of insurrection from other freshmen after he was one of 34 Republicans who refused to support party leadership on a procedural vote on legislation to provide trade promotion authority to Obama.

In July 2018, the House passed Buck's bill to permit nonprofit status for mutual irrigation and ditch companies that reinvest revenue earned from non-member sources. When the Judiciary Committee was under Democratic control two years later and debated police reform, he proposed the restoration of qualified immunity for police officers accused of wrongdoing. He lost on a party-line vote. Also in 2020, Buck filed a separate report—which he called "The Third Way"—in response to Democrats' calls for antitrust action against Big Tech companies. While agreeing that they had engaged in anti-competitive practices, Buck warned against steps that might force those firms to divest their assets. In 2021, he became the ranking Republican on the Antitrust, Commercial and Administrative Law Subcommittee.

Buck continued to go his own way. He wrote a book, Drain the Swamp, in which he criticized the "bullying" tactics of House GOP leaders, including their fundraising obsession and "war on conservatives." With conservative Reps. Matt Gaetz of Florida and Tom Massie of Kentucky, who shared his outsider perspective, Buck was featured in The Swamp, a documentary on HBO in 2020 that sought to explain the dysfunction in Washington. In March 2020, he was one of three congressional Republicans who voted against the initial economic-relief bill in response to the coronavirus. "Since day one, Democrats have politicized the coronavirus," he said. "Throwing money at a problem without adequate forethought is not the answer."

Following Republican setbacks in Colorado in 2018, Buck agreed to serve as state party chairman. Two years later, he gave up his second hat—leaving Colorado Republicans in worse political shape, though he claimed credit for upgrading "a strong base" that would build for the future. His tenure raised charges of potential wrongdoing. In May 2020, the Denver Post reported that, according to an audio recording, Buck pressured a local GOP official to submit incorrect results in a party primary for the state Senate. Buck denied wrongdoing. Separately, the Post reported that a county Republican chairman filed a complaint with a local prosecutor that a Buck congressional aide committed election fraud in the organization of a party caucus. Buck had no comment.

Buck considered a bid for attorney general in 2018 to succeed Cynthia Coffman, who ran unsuccessfully for governor. Instead, he told a radio talk show, he decided to continue with "the job that I enjoy doing here in D.C." He has easily won reelection. In 2020, Democrats nominated Isaac McCorkle, a retired Marine officer who campaigned to "get big money out of politics." He was supported by Planned Parenthood and the Sierra Club. McCorkle was outspent by more than two-to-one, though finances don't have much impact in this district. Buck won, 60%-37%, and led in every county except for the small piece of Boulder.

CO-4: Eastern Colorado

Cook Partisan Voting Index: R+12

Population		Race and Ethnicity		Income	
Total	868,302	White	89.00%	Median Income	$83,609
Land area (sq. miles)	38,103	Black	1.60%	District Income Rank	75
Pop/ sq mi	22.79	Latino	22.40%	Poverty Rate	7.60%
Born in State	47.10%	Asian	2.20%	With health insurance	92.60%
		Two or more races	3.10%	Cash public assistance	2.40%
Age Groups		Other	3.90%	Food stamp/SNAP	6.50%
Under 18	24.50%				
18-34	21.50%	**Education**		**Work**	
35-64	39.90%	H.S grad or less	32.00%	White Collar	42.90%
Over 64	14.10%	Some college	30.80%	Sales and Service	34.30%
		College Degree, 4 yr	23.10%	Blue Collar	22.80%
Military		Post grad	14.10%	Government	14.50%
Veteran/ Active Duty	7.90%				

2020 Pres. Vote	Trump	276,309	(57%)	Biden	198,971	(41%)		
2016 Pres. Vote	Trump	230,945	(57%)	Clinton	137,784	(34%)	Johnson	20,104	(5%)

Weld, Douglas: The High Plains of eastern Colorado are dusty brown, gently rolling up toward the Rocky Mountains. The land is fertile, but dry. Rainfall is rare, the rivers are just a trickle most of the year, and in many places, groundwater is scarce. It is fine wheat country when irrigated, and one of the foremost beef cattle regions. But it has been squeezed in recent decades by declining prices for wheat, declining demand for beef and increased prices for water because of the high demand in Denver and along the Front Range. Bitter confrontations have erupted over who gets access to the South Platte River, leading to limitations on pumping from the basin. Local farmers have found that the value of their water rights to metro Denver far exceeds what they could hope to earn by farming. Their neighbors have condemned them for selling out and betraying a way of life. The free market that once made the High Plains the scene of farm protests has caused some of it to empty out and revert to untamed land, ready again for increasingly numerous buffalo, elk, deer and bighorn sheep.

This area stretches into the Denver exurbs, which have continued their rapid population growth. Until the 1970s, Douglas County was a sparsely populated patch of the High Plains just east of the Front Range. From 2000 to 2010, with a surge of telecom and aerospace companies, it grew 62 percent, making it the fastest-growing county in the state. From 2010 to 2019, it grew another 23 percent. In 2019, the county was the ninth wealthiest in the nation with a median income of $119,730. Activists have pressed for a more free-enterprise approach to governance. This is Patio Land, as writer David Brooks has described it: an area with a high-tech economy, highly educated families with relatively conservative cultural values and looking for a safe environment for children, with the serenity—if not the close personal ties—of a small town and the creativity of a metropolis. In 2020, U.S. News ranked Douglas as the second healthiest in the nation, between Denver and Colorado Springs.

Weld County, slightly smaller than Douglas, has grown even more rapidly—28 percent from 2010 to 2019. Greeley, the county seat, was best known for its beef production. But the growth of the University of Northern Colorado, where James Michener taught and wrote, has spurred local development. Oil production in Weld County has increased its antagonism to the liberal ethos in the Denver metro area. Because of decades-old practices on local water use, the pumping of wells also caused continuing problems for local farmers because of rising groundwater.

The 4th Congressional District covers much of the Eastern Plains and nearly the entire eastern half of the state, with a crescent that connects the growing exurbs north and south of Denver. To the north, it includes all of Weld County. To the south, the district includes two-thirds of Douglas. Each county includes about one-third of the district's population. Weld has a slightly larger share of Republican voters. Its large share of the land in Adams and Arapahoe counties is sparsely populated and stops short of the Denver exurbs. A small indentation of Boulder County is the Democratic outlier, with only about 13 percent of the district. The 4th is a solidly Republican district.

Doug Lamborn (R)

Elected 2006, 8th term, b. May 24, 1954; Leavenworth, KS; University of KS School of Journalism, B.S., 1978; University of KS School of Law, J.D., 1985; Christian Church; Married (Jeanie Lamborn); 5 children.

Elected Office: CO House, 1995-1999; CO Senate, 1998-2006.

Professional Career: Practicing attorney, 1987-2007.

DC Office: 2371 RHOB 20515, 202-225-4422, Fax: 202-226-2638, lamborn.house.gov

State Offices: Buena Vista, 719-520-0055; Colorado Springs, 719-520-0055.

Committees: *Armed Services*: Readiness (RMM); Strategic Forces; Strategic Forces; Tactical Air & Land Forces. *Natural Resources*: Energy & Mineral Resources; National Parks, Forests & Public Lands; National Parks, Forests & Public Lands.

Group Ratings

	ADA	ACLU	AFL-CIO	LCV	COC	HAFA	ACU	CFG	FRC
2020	**	17%	**	5%	-	94%	97%	**	-
2019	0%	C	25%	7%	80%	C	97%	94%	100%

Almanac Ratings 2019-2020

	Economy	Social	Foreign	Composite
Liberal	25%	4%	14%	15%
Conservative	75%	96%	86%	85%

Key Votes of the 116th Congress

1. U.S./Mex./Can. trade deal Y	5. Russia sanctions Y	9. Firearms background checks N
2. First Coronavirus response Y	6. Troops in Syria Y	10. Spending at the border Y
3. HEROES Act N	7. Veto arms sales to Saudis N	11. Marijuana liberalized rules N
4. CASH Act N	8. Defense $$$, veto override Y	12. Electoral College objections Y

Election Results

Election	Name (Party)	Vote (%)		Cand. Spent	Ind. Exp. Support	Ind. Exp. Oppose
2020 General	Doug Lamborn (R)................................	249,013	(58%)	$345,547	$9,853	
	Jillian Freeland (D)............................	161,600	(37%)	$176,914	$448	
	Ed Duffett (L)......................................	14,777	(3%)			
2020 Primary	Doug Lamborn (R)................................	104,302	(100%)			

Prior winning percentages: 2018 (57%), 2016 (62%), 2014 (60%), 2012 (65%), 2010 (66%), 2008 (60%), 2006 (60%)

Doug Lamborn, a conservative Republican first elected in 2006 and a fierce partisan, has been slow to shut down competitive challenges. An occasional maverick, he has been bypassed for prime posts despite his seniority, including his unsuccessful bid to take over as chairman of the Veterans' Affairs Committee. On the Armed Services Committee, he protects his district's extensive military facilities.

The son of a prison guard, Lamborn was born in Leavenworth Kansas. He studied journalism and earned a law degree at the University of Kansas. He said he voted for Jimmy Carter in 1976, but was then drawn to the Republican politics of Ronald Reagan in the 1980s. In 1987, Lamborn moved his family to Colorado Springs, where he practiced business and real estate law and became an avid mountain climber. In 1994, he was elected to the state House, and he was appointed in 1998 to a Senate seat. During 12 years in the legislature, Lamborn compiled a firmly conservative record on social and fiscal issues.

When Republican Joel Hefley retired and created an open seat in 2006, he endorsed Jeff Crank, a former aide. Lamborn won the backing of the anti-tax Club for Growth and the Colorado Christian Coalition. Crank won the delegate vote at the GOP convention, but Lamborn secured a place on the primary ballot and vowed never to raise taxes. The Christian Coalition sent a mailer suggesting Crank backed the "radical homosexual lobby." In the primary, absentee ballots flipped the results and Lamborn won by 892 votes, 27%-25%.

In November, Hefley accused Lamborn of running a "sleazy" primary and refused to endorse him. Democrat Jay Fawcett, an Air Force Academy graduate, purchased a newspaper ad featuring three dozen prominent local Republicans who declined to endorse their party's nominee. Despite October polls showing a dead heat, Lamborn won, 60%-40%.

Lamborn has maintained his conservative credentials. During the 2013 budget debate, Lamborn helped to prepare the proposal of the Republican Study Committee, which urged further large cuts in domestic programs. Later, he called for cuts in Social Security, Medicare and farm programs to pay for increased defense spending. He voiced concern that military cutbacks would affect personnel and missile programs in the Colorado Springs area.

His bid in 2016 for the Veterans' Affairs Committee chairmanship fell short in the leadership-controlled Republican Steering Committee, despite his ranking as the most senior GOP member of the committee. During Republican control of the House, he chaired the Natural Resources Subcommittee on Energy and Mineral Resources, where he supported more development of all forms of energy.

On the Armed Services Committee, Lamborn is ranking Republican on the Readiness Subcommittee. He has been an outspoken supporter of a Space Force and said Colorado Springs should remain "the epicenter of national security space." In addition to protecting local facilities, he has pledged to "make sure our brave men and women have some of the best training and equipping in the world." As a co-founder of the Missile Defense Caucus, he has advocated the development of new technology.

Back home, he has faced continuing problems. Lingering resentment over the 2006 primary led to a rematch with Crank in 2008. This time, Lamborn won 44%-30%. In 2014, he barely won the GOP primary, 53%-47%, over Bentley Rayburn, a retired Air Force general who complained that Lamborn was "out of touch" with local concerns about possible military base closings in the area. Similar criticisms were raised in the general election by Democratic foe Irving Halter, also a retired Air Force general. Halter raised $834,000 compared with only $490,000 for Lamborn, an unusual contrast for a veteran incumbent. Lamborn won 60%-40%.

His 2016 campaign suffered a self-imposed wound when Lamborn failed to take his opponent seriously. Calandra Vargas, a political neophyte, challenged him at the Republican convention. In a rousing speech that Vargas called "a statement on behalf of my generation," she "brought some of the crowd to its feet," the Colorado Springs Gazette reported. Vargas got 58 percent of the vote —just short of the 60 percent required to prevent a primary challenge. Lamborn won the primary, 68%-32%. In November, Lamborn won 62%-31% against Misty Plowright, a trans-gender Democrat who said her campaign was inspired by Bernie Sanders.

Lamborn suffered from additional self-inflicted wounds in 2018 when the state Supreme Court threw him off the ballot because he violated a state law that required state residents to collect signatures for his candidacy. A federal judge overturned the ruling and held that the residency requirement was "likely unconstitutional." In the primary, he faced state Sen. Owen Hill and El Paso County Commissioner Darryl Glenn. Hill described the two local officials as "counterfeit conservatives" and "swamp things." Lamborn won the primary with 52 percent; Glenn and Hill split the opposition vote with 20 and 18 percent, respectively. Against Democratic challengers who were political newcomers, he was held below 60 percent of the vote in both 2018 and 2020. Lamborn's modest victories could encourage more vigorous challengers.

CO-5: Central Colorado

Cook Partisan Voting Index: R+12

Population		Race and Ethnicity		Income	
Total	820,255	White	80.80%	Median Income	$71,244
Land area (sq. miles)	7,266	Black	6.00%	District Income Rank	153
Pop/ sq mi	112.89	Latino	16.70%	Poverty Rate	8.90%
Born in State	32.30%	Asian	2.60%	With health insurance	92.00%
		Two or more races	5.90%	Cash public assistance	2.50%
Age Groups		Other	4.80%	Food stamp/SNAP	8.80%
Under 18	22.40%				
18-34	25.80%	**Education**		**Work**	
35-64	36.90%	H.S grad or less	27.70%	White Collar	44.70%
Over 64	14.80%	Some college	34.60%	Sales and Service	38.40%
		College Degree, 4 yr	23.60%	Blue Collar	16.80%
Military		Post grad	14.20%	Government	15.80%
Veteran/ Active Duty	19.80%				

2020 Pres. Vote	Trump	241,369	(55%)	Biden	184,301	(42%)	Jorgensen	10,228	(2%)
2016 Pres. Vote	Trump	212,558	(57%)	Clinton	123,537	(33%)	Johnson	22,195	(6%)

Colorado Springs: In the center of Colorado, Pikes Peak, espied by Zebulon Pike in 1806, and Colorado Springs, with the Garden of the Gods and the Broadmoor hotel, have been tourist attractions for more than 100 years. In the second half of the 20th century, Colorado Springs, safe in the vastness of North America, became a great American military fortress. During the 1960s, the Pentagon constructed the North American Aerospace Defense Command more than 1,000 feet below Cheyenne Mountain, a fortified bunker theoretically able to survive a nuclear strike from a Soviet missile. The Pentagon, in part because of local traffic congestion, moved NORAD's surveillance operations to nearby Peterson Air Force Base, site of space-based defense research, with the option of a rapid return to secure Cheyenne Mountain in an emergency.

Other military installations dominate the landscape as well: the Army installation at Fort Carson; the Air Force Academy; and Schriever Air Force Base, named for Gen. Bernard A. Schriever, a pioneer in the development of ballistic missile programs. By some measures, this area has the biggest military footprint in the nation, with 40,000 active-duty troops and another 60,000 civilian jobs. In 2019, Colorado Springs became headquarters of the expanded U.S. Space Command. Local officials were hopeful that that the provisional status would become permanent.

Colorado Springs has built a high-tech, innovative economy. In 2019, El Paso County trailed Denver County by a few thousand residents as Colorado's largest. El Paso has the fastest growth rate for millennials of any county in the nation, according to a study by the Brookings Institution. One downside locally: The area must contend with occasional out-of-control fires that have become the bane of the West. Paradoxically perhaps, above-average precipitation has increased the growth of grasses, which can be a fuel for the fires.

Led by the arrival of James Dobson's Focus on the Family in 1994, Colorado Springs has been a center of conservative Christianity, the home of Colorado's young conservatism and the counterpoint to Denver's liberalism. This was the birthplace of Colorado's anti-tax initiatives and of Amendment 2, which in 1992 repealed the city's gay rights ordinances only to be later overturned by the U.S. Supreme Court. It is one of America's most Republican metropolitan areas. Following Dobson's exit in 2010, his organization reduced its payroll by nearly half from its peak employment of 1,400 workers, though it remained a powerful force in Colorado and beyond. The 5th Congressional District takes in Colorado Springs and all of El Paso County. It includes all or part of four rural counties: Park, Teller, Fremont and Chaffee. More than 85 percent of the district's voters are in El Paso. Along with the 4th District, it has been the strongest Republican district in Colorado. Still, its 55 percent for Donald Trump in 2020 had less impact than did the 76 percent vote for Joe Biden in the 1st District (Denver), when Biden won statewide 55%-42%.

Jason Crow (D)

Elected 2018, 2nd term, b. Mar 15, 1979; Beaver Dam, WI; University of WI - Madison, B.A., 2002; University of Denver, J.D., 2009; Christian - Non-Denominational; Married (Deserai Crow); 2 children.

Military Career: U.S. Army 2002-2006; CO Army National Guard 2006-2007 (Afghanistan & Iraq)

Professional Career: Holland and Hart, LLP, 2009-2018.

DC Office: 1229 LHOB 20515, 202-225-7882, crow.house.gov

State Offices: Aurora, 720-748-7514.

Committees: *Armed Services*: Cyber, Innovative Technologies & Information Systems; Readiness. *Permanent Select on Intelligence*: Defense Intelligence & Warfighter Support; Intelligence Modernization & Readiness. *Small Business*: Innovation, Entrepreneurship & Workforce Development (Chmn); Underserved, Agricultural & Rural Business Development.

Almanac Ratings 2019-2020

	Economy	Social	Foreign	Composite
Liberal	100%	100%	80%	94%
Conservative	0%	0%	20%	6%

Key Votes of the 116th Congress

1. U.S./Mex./Can. trade deal Y	5. Russia sanctions Y	9. Firearms background checks Y
2. First Coronavirus response Y	6. Troops in Syria Y	10. Spending at the border Y
3. HEROES Act Y	7. Veto arms sales to Saudis Y	11. Marijuana liberalized rules Y
4. CASH Act Y	8. Defense $$$, veto override Y	12. Electoral College objections N

Election Results

Election	Name (Party)	Vote (%)	Cand. Spent	Ind. Exp. Support	Ind. Exp. Oppose
2020 General	Jason Crow (D)............................ 250,314	(57%)	$2,857,672	$34,450	
	Steve House (R)............................ 175,192	(40%)	$1,210,472	$4,038	$665
	Norm Olsen (L)................................. 9,083	(2%)			
2020 Primary	Jason Crow (D)............................ 122,929	(100%)			

Prior winning percentages: 2018 (54%)

Democrat Jason Crow made an early mark as a freshman when he was one of the seven House managers in the first Senate impeachment trial of President Donald Trump, even though he had not served on the Judiciary Committee, which crafted the impeachment charges. Crow, who was a close adviser to Democratic leaders in Colorado, was elected in 2018 in his first bid for elected office. His chief committee assignment was Armed Services, where he worked across the aisle on several issues..

Crow, a native of Wisconsin, graduated from the University of Wisconsin and got his law degree from the University of Denver. As an infantry officer with the Army's 82nd Airborne Division, he led a platoon of paratroopers during the invasion of Iraq and received a Bronze Star. After attaining the rank of captain, he was assistant chief of staff with the Colorado Army National Guard.

Crow was a partner in the large Denver-based law firm of Holland and Hart, where his profile said that he "conducted internal investigations nationwide, responded to emergency events, and handled a wide-range of government inquiries." In political activities, he co-chaired the veterans affairs transition committee for Colorado Gov. John Hickenlooper and co-chaired Veterans for Mark Udall in his Senate campaign.

In the Democratic primary to select a challenger to Republican Rep. Mike Coffman, Crow faced Levi Tillerman, a technology adviser who was endorsed by Progressive Democrats of America and called for the impeachment of Trump. After House Democratic leaders endorsed Crow before the primary and urged Tillerman to withdraw, Tillerman released a recorded conversation and objected to the outside influence. Crow responded that he learned, including in the Army, "that it's better and more enduring to build than to tear down," the Denver Post reported; he added that President George

W. Bush made a mistake in going to war in Iraq. Crow spent $1 million in the primary, to $350,000 for Tillerman, and he won with 66 percent of the vote.

Coffman, who was a Marine Corps officer in both Iraq wars, was an active member of the Armed Services Committee. As his district shifted to a large Hispanic population, Coffman learned Spanish and spent time in immigrant neighborhoods. His three most recent reelection campaigns were close and costly contests against prominent Democratic state legislators. In the general election, Coffman distanced himself from President Donald Trump and cited his work in the House with bipartisan groups. Crow criticized his lack of leadership on immigration, among other issues. He called Coffman a career politician and noted in particular his support from the National Rifle Association. Crow won comfortably, 54%-43%.

In the House, with his seat on the Armed Services Committee, Crow collaborated with the growing cadre of military veterans in both parties. He gained his initial prominence when he joined six other first-term Democrats, with a military or national security background, who submitted an op-ed column to The Washington Post in September 2019 that made the case that Trump had committed impeachable offenses. These self-styled "security Democrats" urged the start of impeachment proceedings. The following day, Speaker Nancy Pelosi agreed to their request.

Crow's work on that piece, in showing his national security background plus his legal skills, led to his selection as an impeachment manager during the Senate trial. "One of the bigger dangers I feel like we face right now is that [Trump's] pretty egregious abuse of power and disregard for democratic norms and abuse of our institutions becomes normalized," he told a writer for 5280, a Denver-based magazine.

On another issue centered in the Judiciary Committee, Crow joined Democratic Rep. Sheila Jackson Lee in filing the Justice in Policing Act following the death of George Floyd in Minneapolis while being detained by police officers. Crow prepared the bill as part of a package of measures that sought to rebuild trust between communities and police departments.

On the Armed Services panel, he took credit for several provisions that were included in the final version of the annual defense spending bill that Congress approved in December 2020. They included a provision, offered with Republican Rep. Liz Cheney, to require that the president discuss with Congress any effort to withdraw troops from Afghanistan; with Republican Rep. Doug Lamborn, a call for a report by the Pentagon on the impact of water scarcity on military bases that has resulted from a warmer climate; and with Rep. Mike Turner, steps to assure voting rights for military members serving at diplomatic missions overseas. In 2021, he gained a seat on the Select Intelligence Committee.

At home, Republican Steve House, a health care consultant who had been Republican chairman in Colorado, challenged Crow's reelection bid. House called for less divisiveness in government and urged that the two parties stop "fighting over 2016." Crow more than doubled the spending by House and expanded his victory margin to 57%-40%. Pending redistricting, he has become secure in this formerly GOP-controlled district.

CO-6: Eastern and Southern Denver Suburbs

Cook Partisan Voting Index: D+6

Population		Race and Ethnicity		Income	
Total	828,201	White	73.20%	Median Income	$87,312
Land area (sq. miles)	475	Black	9.80%	District Income Rank	66
Pop/ sq mi	1,744.83	Latino	21.00%	Poverty Rate	6.60%
Born in State	40.30%	Asian	6.30%	With health insurance	91.50%
		Two or more races	4.40%	Cash public assistance	1.50%
Age Groups		Other	6.40%	Food stamp/SNAP	5.50%
Under 18	24.20%				
18-34	23.40%	**Education**		**Work**	
35-64	39.70%	H.S grad or less	27.50%	White Collar	44.30%
Over 64	12.80%	Some college	28.50%	Sales and Service	37.00%
		College Degree, 4 yr	27.20%	Blue Collar	18.70%
Military		Post grad	16.80%	Government	12.60%
Veteran/ Active Duty	8.10%				

2020 Pres. Vote	Biden	260,646	(58%)	Trump	175,733	(39%)		
2016 Pres. Vote	Clinton	191,099	(50%)	Trump	157,115	(41%)	Johnson	19,727	(5%)

Arapahoe County, Aurora: Two generations ago, most people in metropolitan Denver lived in the city itself. At the city limits, the tree-shaded sidewalks gave way to the empty High Plains. Today, more than three-quarters of metro Denver residents live outside the city, some in long-settled suburbs, some in large new subdivisions on rolling land with magnificent views of the Rocky Mountains. Littleton, originally a small, long-settled suburb just south of Denver, now extends to vast new tracts. Other areas that surround Denver were once quite rural but have grown into modern suburbs. To the east of the now-closed Stapleton Airport is Aurora; the area has developed as a hub for alternative energy firms, where new technologies can be studied for their commercial value. Just south of Littleton is fast-growing Douglas County and Highlands Ranch, whose 105,000 residents form one of the largest unincorporated communities in the nation.

Much of the growth in Arapahoe County, which includes many of the suburbs south and east of downtown Denver, has resulted from the many immigrants to the area. One in five are foreign-born, and 160 languages are spoken in the Aurora public schools. Its population increased 15 percent between 2010 and 2019. Hispanics make up 20 percent of the population, with 12 percent black and 7 percent Asian. Those increases led to social tensions in what had been mostly working-class white communities. The immigration policies of President Donald Trump raised concerns. In 2018, the Aurora City Council objected to including a citizenship question on the 2020 census form, though it opposed earlier calls to declare itself a sanctuary city. Solidly Republican until a few years ago, the county became a hard-fought political battleground in one of the most competitive states. Then, it quickly transitioned to Democratic-leaning. After Hillary Clinton took Arapahoe with 53 percent of the vote, Joe Biden won the county four years later with 61 percent.

Aurora, which is the largest city in Arapahoe, has been the site not only of innovation but also of unspeakable tragedy. At a July 2012 midnight showing of the movie The Dark Knight Rises, a mentally unstable gunman shot and killed 12 people and injured 58 others, an event that sparked an outpouring of public outrage and sympathy. In 2015, James Holmes was found guilty of the murders. That pain was compounded because nearby Littleton was the location of Columbine High School, which suffered in 1999 what had been the nation's worst school massacre when two teenagers killed 13 people and themselves. Columbine is in the 1st District.

The 6th Congressional District covers Aurora, Littleton and other south Denver suburbs. More than two-thirds of the district is in Arapahoe County, with small pieces in Adams and Douglas counties. The district has made a huge shift to Democrats. After Mitt Romney won the district in 2012, 59%-38%, Joe Biden won in 2020, 58%-39%.

Ed Perlmutter (D)

Elected 2006, 8th term, b. May 01, 1953; Denver, CO; University of CO, Boulder, B.A., 1975; University of CO School of Law, J.D., 1978; Protestant; Married (Deana M. Perlmutter); 3 children.

Elected Office: CO Senate, 1995-2003.

Professional Career: Practicing attorney, 1979-2006.

DC Office: 1226 LHOB 20515, 202-225-2645, Fax: 202-225-5278, perlmutter.house.gov

State Offices: Lakewood, 303-274-7944.

Committees: *Financial Services*: Consumer Protection & Financial Institutions (Chmn). *Rules*: Rules & Organization of the House. *Science, Space & Technology*: Investigations & Oversight; Space & Aeronautics. *Select Committee on the Modernization of Congress*.

Group Ratings

	ADA	ACLU	AFL-CIO	LCV	COC	HAFA	ACU	CFG	FRC
2020	**	76%	**	100%	-	0%	4%	**	-
2019	80%	C	100%	97%	68%	C	4%	12%	0%

Almanac Ratings 2019-2020

	Economy	Social	Foreign	Composite
Liberal	100%	100%	51%	84%
Conservative	0%	0%	49%	16%

Key Votes of the 116th Congress

1. U.S./Mex./Can. trade deal Y	5. Russia sanctions　　　　　Y	9. Firearms background checks Y
2. First Coronavirus response Y	6. Troops in Syria　　　　　Y	10. Spending at the border　　Y
3. HEROES Act　　　　　Y	7. Veto arms sales to Saudis Y	11. Marijuana liberalized rules Y
4. CASH Act　　　　　　Y	8. Defense $$$, veto override Y	12. Electoral College objections N

Election Results

Election	Name (Party)	Vote (%)		Cand. Spent	Ind. Exp. Support	Ind. Exp. Oppose
2020 General	Ed Perlmutter (D)	250,525	(59%)	$1,770,209	$458	
	Casper Stockham (R)	159,301	(38%)	$132,997	$15,145	$54
	Ken Biles (L)	11,510	(3%)			
2020 Primary	Ed Perlmutter (D)	125,880	(100%)			

Prior winning percentages: 2018 (60%), 2016 (55%), 2014 (55%), 2012 (54%), 2010 (53%), 2008 (64%), 2006 (55%)

Ed Perlmutter, first elected in 2006, has been the most centrist member of Colorado's congressional delegation and a self-described "business-oriented Democrat." He usually backs his party on major issues, but has sought out Republicans to work on financial, homeland security and energy matters. As was the case following the 2018 election in discussions among House Democrats about the future of Speaker Nancy Pelosi, he has skillfully turned apparent personal setbacks into opportunities to influence the Democratic mainstream.

Perlmutter grew up in Jefferson County, walking precincts with his father on Democratic campaigns. His family owned a concrete business. He attended the University of Colorado and earned a law degree in 1978, then went into private practice. In 1994, Perlmutter won election to the state Senate from a northern Jefferson County district that had not elected a Democrat in nearly 30 years. In the legislature, he gained a reputation as a mediator and served two years as Senate president pro tem. As chairman of the renewable energy caucus, he worked on legislation protecting consumer rights and promoting responsible growth.

In 2002, Perlmutter was considered the early frontrunner for the new 7th District seat. But he opted not to run, citing the time it would take away from his three daughters. The district elected Republican Bob Beauprez by just 121 votes. When Beauprez ran unsuccessfully for governor in 2006, Perlmutter entered the race. Against Peggy Lamm, a former state representative who had been the sister-in-law of former Democratic Gov. Richard Lamm, he won the primary 53%-38%. In the general, Republican Rick O'Donnell argued that Perlmutter's marriage to a Denver lobbyist for a D.C.-based lobbying firm would lead to conflicts of interest. (They later divorced and he remarried to a school teacher.) Beauprez's poor showing in the governor's race, and President George W. Bush's unpopularity worked against O'Donnell. Perlmutter won, 55%-42%.

In the House, Perlmutter has been a fairly consistent but not automatic Democratic vote. He chaired the centrist New Democrat Coalition's energy task force. In sync with local interests, he promoted an all-of-the-above energy policy, including incentives to lenders who create a market for energy-efficient buildings. He got a provision in the House-passed climate change bill in 2009 to benefit environmentally conscious banks, drawing criticism from Republicans when it was revealed that he was an investor in one of them. In 2015, he stuck with most House Democrats and opposed trade promotion authority for President Barack Obama.

On the Financial Services Committee, Perlmutter joined Republicans in adding protections for taxpayers to the government rescue of financial markets in 2008. Working with Republicans, he won House passage in 2018 of a bill to expand the Financial Crimes Enforcement Network to include terrorism. When centrist Democrats earlier that year joined House Republicans on a bill to loosen some restrictions in the 2010 Dodd-Frank law, Perlmutter surprisingly was not among them. Although he backed its regulatory relief for small banks and credit unions, he said, "we must continue to hold big banks accountable and protect consumers from another financial crisis."

In September 2019, Perlmutter won bipartisan House passage of his longtime legislation to give banking access to businesses that deal legally with marijuana, including in Colorado. "There's just so much cash that is generated by this business, we need to get it off the streets," he told Colorado Public Radio. In 2021, Perlmutter became chairman of the Consumer Protection and Financial Institutions Subcommittee at Financial Services.

In 2010, Aurora GOP Councilman Ryan Frazier, an African-American Navy veteran, attacked him for contributing to government overspending. Frazier couldn't keep pace financially with Perlmutter, who spent nearly $3 million and won with 53 percent of the vote. Perlmutter drew another formidable challenger two years later in Joe Coors, an heir to his family's brewing empire. Coors attacked Perlmutter's ex-wife's work as a lobbyist for California solar manufacturer Solyndra, which failed after getting significant federal help. Perlmutter fired back by accusing Coors of outsourcing jobs, which Coors denied. Perlmutter prevailed 54%-41%.

Following the 2016 election, he showed his independence with public support for Rep. Tim Ryan of Ohio in his unsuccessful challenge to Minority Leader Nancy Pelosi. "We need a change," he said. In April 2017, Perlmutter announced his candidacy to succeed term-limited Gov. John Hickenlooper in 2018. Three months later, he unexpectedly dropped out of the contest and decided to seek reelection. "I love this state," he told reporters. "But it takes time, it takes money, it takes energy, and putting all those together, I found looking deep down, it was going to be difficult." He acknowledged that he faced fundraising challenges against Jared Polis, his self-financing House Democratic colleague who won the contest.

In the House, Perlmutter continued his drumbeat for an overhaul of party leadership. When House Democrats met in late November to routinely select Pelosi as their choice for Speaker, he was among 32 caucus members who opposed her. He continued to work with renegades on an alternative, though none emerged.

Meanwhile, as Politico later reported, "Pelosi reached out privately to Perlmutter over the Thanksgiving break to kick-start talks, and the two decided to see if they could work out an agreement." Two weeks later, they reached a deal in which Pelosi agreed to serve no more than four additional years as party leader. "I am now convinced that generational change has started and will continue to accelerate," Perlmutter said. He added that Pelosi was "the best person to lead a very diverse and ambitious caucus."

Although House Democrats did not formalize her agreement, she acknowledged following the 2020 election that she likely would serve only one more term. For his part, Perlmutter voiced second thoughts about their deal. "Quite frankly, I was wrong," he told Colorado Matters. "I think Pelosi particularly has done an excellent job in leading our caucus."

For a Democrat who had decided in 2017 to quit elected office, his skills as a dealmaker positioned Perlmutter as a key player among party factions.

CO-7: Western and Northern Denver Suburbs   **Cook Partisan Voting Index: D+7**

Population		Race and Ethnicity		Income	
Total	808,543	White	85.40%	Median Income	$77,164
Land area (sq. miles)	342	Black	1.80%	District Income Rank	110
Pop/ sq mi	2,363.4	Latino	29.70%	Poverty Rate	8.50%
Born in State	50.90%	Asian	3.50%	With health insurance	91.40%
		Two or more races	4.50%	Cash public assistance	1.60%
Age Groups		Other	4.80%	Food stamp/SNAP	6.40%
Under 18	22.00%				
18-34	26.00%	**Education**		**Work**	
35-64	38.20%	H.S grad or less	35.80%	White Collar	40.40%
Over 64	13.90%	Some college	27.90%	Sales and Service	38.50%
		College Degree, 4 yr	23.90%	Blue Collar	21.10%
Military		Post grad	12.30%	Government	11.80%
Veteran/ Active Duty	7.00%				

2020 Pres. Vote	Biden	263,442	(60%)	Trump	163,104	(37%)	
2016 Pres. Vote	Clinton	192,637	(51%)	Trump	147,645	(39%) Johnson 20,592 (6%)

Jefferson County: West of Denver, on broad avenues running toward the mountains, the inner circle of suburbs comprise Jefferson County. Affluent in the south and more marginal near the Denver city limits, the politics of Jeffco has made it one of the nation's most competitive battlegrounds.

Its voters backed George W. Bush in 2000 and 2004, then supported Barack Obama in 2008 and 2012. National political campaigns have battle-tested their message here, and many political reporters flocked to the county in an attempt to get their fingers on the pulse of the nation. Jefferson is "one of the most important counties in the nation and symbolic in every way of the battle for the soul of the middle class," a local political observer told Governing.

To the west of the city is the town of Golden, with the old Colorado School of Mines and the Coors brewery. To the northwest are Arvada and Wheat Ridge, middle-income suburbs with an increasing number of Latinos. Farther north along Interstate 25 are rapidly growing Federal Heights, Thornton and Northglenn. Commerce City, with its large oil refinery, tripled its population from 2000 to 2019. In 2018, adjacent to Commerce City, the Interior Department opened the Rocky Mountain Arsenal National Wildlife Refuge. As state officials raised concerns about continued groundwater contamination, federal judges continued to review the safety of the refuge at what had been the site of a nuclear weapons plant, which shut down in 1989 and was cleaned up at a cost of $7 billion.

The 7th Congressional District covers the suburbs north and west of Denver, sweeping in Arvada, Lakewood, Thornton and Westminster, which are the district's largest cities. Within a few miles of downtown Denver, it takes in parks, lakes and recreational spots. Nearly two-thirds of the district is in Jefferson County, with southern and western slices of the county in the 1st and 2nd Districts. The remainder of the district population is in the western end of Adams County, extending just north of the airport. Adams, which is 41 percent Hispanic, has been projected as the fastest-growing county in Colorado between 2020 and 2040. Roughly two-thirds of both Arapahoe and Adams are in the 7th District.

Jefferson, which continued to lean to Republicans in down-ballot contests as recently as 2016, has shifted dramatically to the Democrats. After Hillary Clinton won Jeffco with 49 percent that year, Joe Biden took it with 60 percent in 2020. Pollsters and pundits might need to look elsewhere to test the pulse of swing voters.

CONNECTICUT

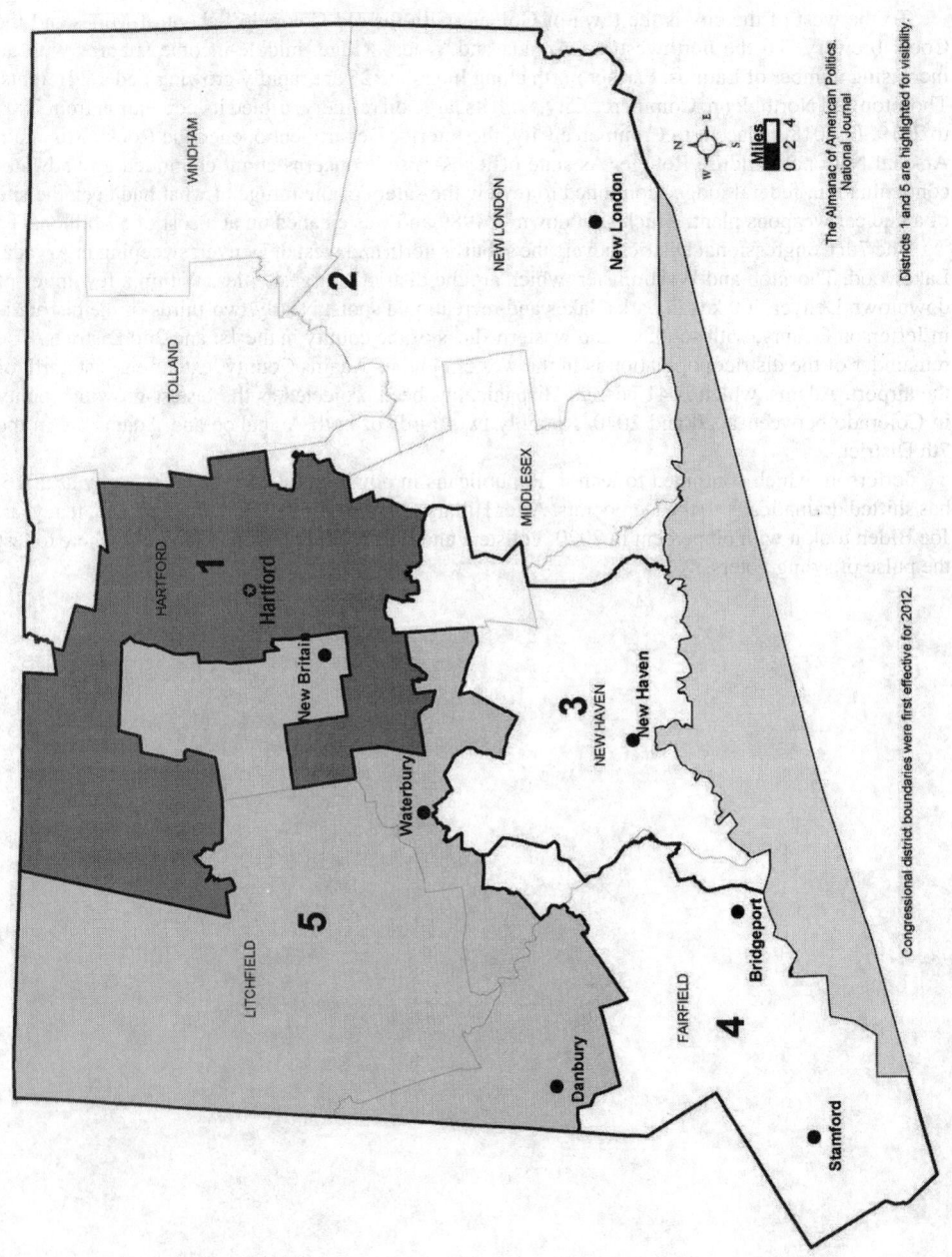

The Almanac of American Politics.
National Journal

Districts 1 and 5 are highlighted for visibility.

Congressional district boundaries were first effective for 2012.

Connecticut is in some respects America's highest achieving state, with one of the highest rates of bachelor's degrees, one of the top median incomes, and great accumulations of wealth—but it is also a state with a yawning gap between the rich and poor, visible in the contrast between hedge fund managers' estates in Greenwich and the slums of Bridgeport not far away. The home of Yale University is in the upper tier of states competitive in the global knowledge economy, but its economy back home has sputtered. Connecticut lost more in GDP than any state between 2007 and 2019; the number of employed residents never returned to its 2008 peak even before the coronavirus pandemic; and by 2019, home values had sunk to 20 percent below their pre-Great Recession levels. Due largely to outmigration to states like Florida, Connecticut has lost population each year for the better part of a decade, and the economic stagnation has created budgetary pressures.

Connecticut was founded by Puritans who considered Massachusetts too lenient, though they were also open to certain reforms. In 1784, Connecticut voted for gradual emancipation of the state's slaves, one of the first societies anywhere to do so. Across the state, 10 percent of residents are black, 17 percent Hispanic, and 5 percent are Asian American, while the city's capital and largest city, Hartford, is 22 percent foreign-born, peopled by immigrants from Cape Verde, the Middle East, Asia and the Caribbean. Native Americans have built a gaming empire—the Foxwoods Resort Casino, opened in 1992 and owned by the roughly 1,000-member Mashantucket Pequot tribe, and its big competitor, the Mohegan Sun, owned by the 1,700-member Mohegans—but profits have slumped with added competition, including an MGM casino in Springfield Massachusetts that opened in 2018. MGM has sued the federal Interior Department to block its competitors from opening casinos beyond tribal land.

Connecticut's accumulated affluence came not from any jackpot invention but from a knack for tinkering and making productive use of savings. Connecticut made clocks, hats, combs, cigars, silk thread, pins, matches, brass and furniture. Pez candy is still made in Orange, and the company that makes the Wiffle ball remains headquartered in Shelton. The quintessential Connecticut Yankee, Eli Whitney, was the inventor not only of the cotton gin but also of rifles with interchangeable parts, and Samuel Colt won a War Department contract to manufacture guns for the Mexican-American War. The state's longstanding gun connections caused tension following the 2012 massacre at Sandy Hook Elementary School in Newtown; in 2019, the U.S. Supreme Court green lighted a lawsuit by the victims' families against Remington Arms Co.

During the defense buildup of the 1980s, Connecticut produced Air Force jets and Army helicopters and, in the Electric Boat Shipyard in New London, nuclear submarines for the Navy, continuing a long seafaring tradition memorialized at Mystic Seaport. The sector is once again on an upswing, although tracking the players increasingly requires a scorecard. United Technologies, the parent of F-35 joint strike fighter engine-maker Pratt & Whitney, merged with Raytheon, forming Raytheon Technologies and relocating its headquarters from Farmington to the Boston suburbs. Helicopter maker Sikorsky, based in Stratford, is now a subsidiary of Lockheed Martin, while Electric Boat, with dozens of Virginia-class submarines on order and the next-generation Columbia-class sub in the works, is now part of General Dynamics. These companies already have increased their payrolls and they plan to expand by thousands more workers and create business for local subcontractors in the coming years—so much business that the state has scrambled to boost its workforce's waning base of manufacturing skills.

Connecticut has long been home to several of the nation's great insurance companies—its laws are unusually friendly to creditors and harsh to debtors—and hedge funds have sprouted in suburbs such as Greenwich on the fringes of New York City. This was not a recipe for job creation: Bridgewater, a roughly $150 billion hedge fund, employs only about 1,500 (very well-compensated) people. By contrast, the state's modestly sized central cities—New Haven, Hartford and Bridgeport—have been plagued by crime, depopulation and corruption. In 2018, the state agreed to pay off Hartford's debt so the city could avoid bankruptcy, a $550 million commitment over 20 years. (Surprisingly, the mayors of the state's largest cities are currently white men, with minority candidates having broken through only occasionally.)

Writing in The Atlantic, Derek Thompson dubbed Connecticut the Rorschach State. "Conservatives look at Connecticut and see a liberal dystopia, where high taxes have ruined the economy. Liberals, on the other hand, see a capitalist horror show, where the rich dwell in gilded mansions, ensconced in sylvan culs-de-sac, while nearby towns face rising poverty and bankruptcy." There's evidence to support both critiques. The state has among the highest tax burdens in the country, and the pension burden is set to grow from $1.5 billion in 2016 to $6 billion in 2032. Meanwhile, many of Connecticut's most affluent jurisdictions, despite styling themselves as liberal, have frozen out affordable housing: More than three dozen towns have used zoning to block any privately developed duplexes or apartments for the past two decades, often citing the need to preserve the jurisdiction's "character," ProPublica and the Connecticut Mirror reported.

Due to Connecticut's links to New York, the coronavirus hit the state early and hard, but there was a silver lining: Affluent New Yorkers flocked to second homes to work remotely, and the state used the opportunity to try to reverse longstanding gains by New York City and Boston at the expense of Connecticut's suburbs and small towns. "It took a global pandemic and a severe economic downturn to do what once seemed impossible: make the Connecticut suburbs cool again," The Wall Street Journal wrote.

For much of the 20th century, Connecticut politics was an ethnic struggle between Yankee Republicans and Catholic Democrats. Slowly, as Catholic birthrates exceeded those of Protestants, Democrats gained ground. For a long historical moment, the central cities and Catholic suburbs voted Democratic and the WASP-y suburbs and rural towns voted Republican. But those days are gone, due in large part to cultural issues. In 2005, the legislature legalized civil unions for same-sex couples, and in 2008, the state Supreme Court converted all these into same-sex marriages. As recently as 2006, Republicans (albeit moderate ones) held a majority of the state's five-member House delegation. Since 2009, all five seats have been Democratic. No Republican has won a Senate seat in Connecticut since maverick Lowell Weicker in 1982. Oddly, Connecticut did not have a Democratic governor for two decades, but that changed in 2010 with the election of Dannel Malloy, the longtime mayor of Stamford, who won two close races. He was succeeded in 2018 by fellow Democrat Ned Lamont, who led a full sweep of major state offices for his party.

Donald Trump has been toxic for his party in Connecticut: Joe Biden won the state by 20 points in 2020, a margin six points wider than Hillary Clinton's in 2016. Biden increased the Democratic vote total in the state by 20 percent above Clinton's level, while Trump increased his haul by just 6 percent. The shift can be seen most clearly in the affluent, historically Republican towns within commuting distance of New York City. In Darien, Mitt Romney won by 31 points in 2012, but Clinton won by 12 and Biden won by 23. In New Canaan, Romney won by 29, but Clinton won by 11 and Biden won by 20. And in Greenwich, Romney won by 11, but Clinton won by 18 and Biden won by 24. Whether Democrats can keep gaining ground in Connecticut or whether they've maxed out remains to be seen.

Population		Race and Ethnicity		Income	
Total	3,565,287	White	74.60%	Median Income	78,833
Land area (sq. miles)	4,842	Black	11.10%	State Income Rank	6 out of 50
Pop/ sq mi	736.27	Latino	16.90%	Poverty Rate	10.00%
Born in state	53.80%	Asian	5.60%	With health insurance	94.10%
		Two or more races	3.70%	Cash public assistance	3.00%
Age Groups		Other	5.90%	Food stamp/SNAP	12.4%
Under 18	20.40%				
18-34	22.10%	**Education**		**Work**	
35-64	40.00%	H.S grad or less	36.10%	White Collar	44.70%
Over 64	17.60%	Some college	24.10%	Sales and Service	37.90%
		College Degree, 4 yr	22.00%	Blue Collar	17.40%
Military		Post grad	17.80%	Government	13.30%
Veteran/ Active Duty	5.90%				

Presidential Politics

2020 Primary (D)	Biden (D)	224,500(85%)	Sanders (D)	30,512(12%)			
2020 Pres. Vote	Biden (D)	1,080,831(59%)	Trump (R)	715,311(39%)			
2016 Pres. Vote	Clinton (D)	897,572(55%)	Trump (R)	673,215(41%)	Johnson (L)	48,676 (3%)

In spite of its wealth, Connecticut has backed Democrats for decades. High taxes for the wealthy may not appeal in a state that has the sixth highest median income in the country. But liberal stands on cultural issues have long trumped economic concerns among the wealthy investment managers, attorneys and corporate leaders who commute into New York City from well-heeled "gold coast" towns of Greenwich, New Canaan and Westport in Fairfield County. (The Stamford area has the most millionaires per capita in the U.S., outside of Silicon Valley). And it may not have helped that Republicans' 2017 tax cut package also eliminated deductions for state and local taxes, a major hit to some of Connecticut's wealthiest earners. White ethnic voters here have remained more reliably Democratic than elsewhere in the country, while the state's sizable populations of Puerto Rican and Black voters are solidly Democratic.

In a state that was once a Republican bastion, the ever-increasing influence of Christian evangelicals in the GOP and Donald Trump's brand of populism have been anathema to these voters. In 2020, Joe Biden defeated Trump 59%-39%. Biden won a higher percentage of the state vote than any Democrat ever, save his running mate Barack Obama in 2008 and Lyndon Johnson in 1964. With the exception of George W. Bush's 44 percent in 2004 (the 9/11 attacks on Wall Street struck home), no Republican has topped 41 percent of the vote statewide since 1988.

It's easy to forget that from 1972 to 1988, Republican presidential candidates won the Nutmeg State, and that the state's congressional delegation was majority-Republican until 2006. In 1988, Democratic nominee Michael Dukakis won only one of the state's eight counties, Hartford. In 2020, Biden won six, losing only rural Litchfield and Windham. Democrats were not always the liberal party on social issues in Connecticut. Culturally conservative working-class Irish, Italian and Polish Catholics in Hartford, New Britain, New Haven, Bridgeport and New London were once the backbone of the party, while upscale WASPs often nominated socially liberal Republicans.

Connecticut's 2020 primary was originally scheduled for April 28, but was pushed back twice because of the coronavirus and eventually held on August 11, making it the final presidential primary of 2020 and landing one week before the delayed Democratic National Convention. Biden won, 85%-11%, over Bernie Sanders.

Congressional Districts

117th Congress Lineup	5D	116th Congress Lineup	5D

Connecticut has a bipartisan redistricting process. Two Republicans and two Democrats from each chamber of the legislature meet to draw the lines. If their map is approved by a two-thirds vote in both chambers, it becomes law. Otherwise, a ninth member is chosen by the other eight, and they try to reach consensus. Democrats retain complete control in Hartford, as was the case in 2011, when they controlled all five House seats. That could result in a similar scenario in which the commission deadlocks and the state Supreme Court intervenes, with the likelihood that it will adopt a version of the map sought by Democrats.

Since 2011, Democrats have retained their firm hold on all five districts. With the 5th District the most competitive, Democrats might seek to shift some of its Republican hill towns to the 4th District, which has become the strongest for Democrats. In return, the 5th could scoop up additional Democratic locales toward Hartford. The longtime Republican success in western Connecticut districts has been relegated to the distant past. As recently as 2006, the GOP had three of the five seats in the House delegation.

Ned Lamont (D)

Elected 2018, term expires 2023, 1st term; b. Jan. 3, 1954, Washington, DC; Harvard University, B.A., 1976; Yale University, M.B.A, 1980; Unknown; Married (Annie); 3 children.

Elected Office: Member, Greenwich Board of Selectmen, 1987-1989.

Professional Career: Managing Editor, Black River Tribune, 1976-1978; Teacher, 2004-2006; Founder & CEO, Lamont Digital; Professor, Connecticut State University, 2008-2018.

Office: State Capitol 210 Capitol Ave., Hartford, 06106; 860-566-4840; Fax: 860-524-7395; Website: ct.gov

Lt. Gov.: Susan Bysiewicz (D) **Atty. Gen:** William Tong (D) **Sec. of State:** Denise Merrill (D)

State Legislature: Senate: 22D, 14R **House:** 90D, 60R, 1I

Election Results

Election	Name (Party)	Vote (%)
2018 General	Ned Lamont (D)	694,510 (49%)
	Bob Stefanowski (R)	650,138 (46%)
	Oz Griebel (I)	54,741 (4%)
2018 Primary	Ned Lamont (D)	172,567 (81%)
	Joe Ganim (D)	39,976 (19%)

After two unsuccessful runs for statewide office, Democrat Ned Lamont won the Connecticut governorship in 2018, buoyed by voter dissatisfaction with President Donald Trump. It was the third consecutive time a Democrat had won the governorship by a narrow margin, and the first time since 1924 that an open seat was won by the party of the outgoing governor. In 2020, Lamont worked with fellow Democratic governors in New York and New Jersey to coordinate a response to the early regional explosion of coronavirus cases.

Lamont was a child of privilege—his great-grandfather, Thomas W. Lamont, was chairman of J.P. Morgan—but he later became an entrepreneur. Lamont attended Phillips Exeter Academy, earned his bachelor's degree from Harvard, and received an MBA from the Yale School of Management. After college, he founded a newspaper and eventually Lamont Digital Systems, a cable TV firm that, after rebranding as Campus Televideo, grew to serve 1 million college students nationally; he sold it in 2015. Lamont took some early steps toward politics, including a stint on the Greenwich board of selectmen in the 1980s.

In 2006, he ran for the Senate, challenging incumbent Democrat Joe Lieberman in the primary; Lamont ran from the left and took aim at Lieberman's support for the Iraq War, inspiring a wave of liberal activists in the process. Lamont won the primary, but the incumbent ran as an independent in the general election and prevailed in the three-way contest. In 2010, Lamont ran in the gubernatorial primary against former Stamford Mayor Dannel Malloy. Lamont led in early polls, but Malloy won the primary, 57%-43%. Malloy went on to serve two terms as governor, and when Lamont expressed early interest in succeeding him, his deep pockets kept most credible Democratic candidates out of the race.

The Republican primary was a five-way bruiser that included Danbury Mayor Mark Boughton, former UBS Chief Financial Officer Bob Stefanowski, former hedge fund chief David Stemerman, former Trumbull Selectman Tim Herbst, and tech entrepreneur Steve Obsitnik. Stefanowski, advocating a phase-out of the state's personal and corporate income taxes, finished first with 29 percent. In an election cycle in which the Democrats were mostly playing offense nationally, Connecticut was one state where Republicans had hopes, at least initially, of flipping a gubernatorial seat. But every GOP primary candidate ran a strongly conservative campaign and touted their support for Trump—a gift to Lamont, who successfully leveraged this rhetoric against Stefanowski in the general election.

Lamont defeated Stefanowski, 49%-46%, with Oz Griebel, a former Republican lawyer and business figure, taking 4% as an independent. The contest was close enough that Stefanowski was ahead until late-reported votes from the Democratic strongholds of New Haven, Hartford and Bridgeport were counted. Beyond those cities and their nearby suburbs, a key to Lamont's win was the New York City suburbs of Fairfield County, which Malloy had won by a hair's breadth in 2014 but which Lamont took by eight points. While Stefanowski increased the number of GOP votes in Fairfield County by 26 percent over 2014, Lamont increased his raw votes in Fairfield by even more, 46 percent.

Lamont racked up some achievements in his first year in office. "When the smoke cleared, Lamont had closed the shortfall, kept income taxes flat, grown the reserve, spared municipalities and social services from reductions, settled a long-running legal feud with Connecticut's hospitals, and averted a major nursing home strike," the Connecticut Mirror put it. "But to do it, there were painful trade-offs." Specifically, Lamont kicked the can down the road on pension payments, and he took heat from the left of his party for seeming to protect the wealthy over lower-income taxpayers. Lamont also failed in his initial attempts to enact several agenda items, including a public option for health insurance, highway tolls for trucks, a tax on sugary drinks, legalized sports betting, and marijuana legalization. However, he was able to enact several other priorities, including a $15 minimum wage, a family and medical leave program, and a plastic bag tax that, before it was suspended during the pandemic, was so effective in shaping consumer behavior that it collected just one-quarter of the revenue that had been projected.

The overwhelming story of 2020, however, was the pandemic. Two months in, Connecticut ranked third in the nation in per capita coronavirus deaths, behind only its neighbors New York and New Jersey, with which it cooperated on a coordinated regional response. (Lamont had bonded with New York Gov. Andrew Cuomo a year earlier, when they fished for steelhead trout on Lake Ontario.) Lamont took a pragmatic path, quickly ordering closures of schools and public spaces and, after it became clear that nursing homes were accounting for a majority of fatalities, firing the state's public health commissioner after clashing behind the scenes. The state was successful in keeping coronavirus cases and deaths low during the summer and early fall, earning Lamont approval from almost four of every five residents on his handling of the virus. But along with the rest of the country, Connecticut into the early winter saw a spike in cases that was even higher than its initial wave. Meanwhile, the billions of dollars in revenue lost during the pandemic-related recession complicated the state's already tenuous budget picture heading into 2021, though thanks to a 2017 bipartisan deal, Connecticut has a sizable rainy day fund.

Richard Blumenthal (D)

Elected 2010, term expires 2022, 2nd term, b. Feb 13, 1946; Brooklyn, NY; Harvard College, B.A., 1967; Cambridge University, 1968; Yale University Law School, J.D., 1973; Jewish; Married (Cynthia Allison Malkin); 4 children.

Military Career: Sergeant, U.S. Marine Corps Reserve 1970-1975.

Elected Office: CT House, 1984-1987; CT Senate, 1987-1990; CT Attorney General, 1991-2010.

Professional Career: Teacher, Washington D.C. Public Schools, 1968- 1969; Staff Assistant, White House Office of Economic Opportunity, 1969-1970; Clerk, Supreme Court Justice Harry Blackmun, 1974-1975; Administrative Assistant, Sen. Abraham Ribicoff, 1975-1976; U.S Attorney CT, 1977-1981; Practicing Attorney, 1981-1990.

DC Office: 706 HSOB 20510, 202-224-2823, Fax: 202-224-9673, blumenthal.senate.gov
State Offices: Bridgeport, 203-330-0598; Hartford, 860-258-6940.

Committees: *Aging. Armed Services*: Cybersecurity; Readiness & Management Support; Seapower. *Commerce, Science & Transportation*: Communications, Media & Broadband; Consumer Protection, Product Safety & Data Security (Chmn); Oceans, Fisheries, Climate Change & Manufacturing; Space & Science; Surface Transportation, Maritime Freight & Ports. *Judiciary*: Competition Policy,

Antitrust & Consumer Rights; Constitution (Chmn); Human Rights & the Law; Immigration, Citizenship & Border Security. *Veterans' Affairs.*

Group Ratings

	ADA	ACLU	AFL-CIO	LCV	COC	HAFA	ACU	CFG	FRC
2020	-	77%	-	92%	-	0%	3%	-	-
2019	95%	C	100%	100%	56%	C	3%	0%	0%

Almanac Ratings 2019-2020

	Economy	Social	Foreign	Composite
Liberal	97%	97%	95%	96%
Conservative	3%	3%	5%	4%

Key Votes of the 116th Congress

1. EPA clean energy rules	Y	5. Russia sanctions	Y	9. Barr as Atty. General	N
2. U.S./Mex./Can. trade deal	Y	6. Troops in SYR, AFG	Y	10. Spending at the border	Y
3. Cut unemployment benefits	N	7. Veto arms sales to Saudis	Y	11. Coney Barrett to Sup. Ct.	N
4. Shelton to Fed Reserve	N	8. Defense $$$, veto override	Y	12. Electoral College objections	N

Election Results

Election	Name (Party)	Vote (%)		Cand. Spent	Ind. Exp. Support	Ind. Exp. Oppose
2016 General	Richard Blumenthal (D)	1,008,714	(63%)	$6,794,120		
	Dan Carter (R)	552,621	(35%)	$244,556		
2016 Primary	Richard Blumenthal (D)	unopposed				

Prior winning percentages: 2016 (63%), 2010 (55%)

For 20 years, Democrat Richard Blumenthal was Connecticut's aggressive, media-savvy attorney general, focusing on one consumer protection issue after another and becoming the state's most popular elected official in the process. Blumenthal's political modus operandi has changed little since his election to the Senate in 2010: Much of his focus on Capitol Hill has been on acting as a consumer advocate in high-profile controversies ranging from transportation safety to TV blackouts by professional sports leagues to—most recently—Facebook's policies for handling user data and protecting individual privacy. It has remained a winning formula back home. "Blumenthal is his own brand after four decades in public life, a politician hard-wired for constant contact with public and press, pandemic or not," the Connecticut Mirror observed not long after the state's senior senator disclosed that he planned to stand for a third term in November 2022—three months prior to his 77th birthday.

Blumenthal's profile outside his home state grew significantly after he was reelected, thanks in large part to his status as perhaps President Donald Trump's least favorite senator. As a member of the Judiciary Committee, Blumenthal—five months into the Trump administration—led nearly 200 congressional Democrats in a lawsuit contending that the president, by retaining his global business empire, had violated the emoluments clause of the Constitution. That clause restricts federal officials from accepting payments or gifts from foreign states; the suit took aim at Trump-branded properties, including a hotel just blocks from Capitol Hill, playing host to foreign embassy events and visiting foreign officials. A district court ruled the plaintiffs had a cause of action against the president, but the suit was thwarted when the U.S. Court of Appeals for the D.C. Circuit—in a decision later upheld by the U.S. Supreme Court—ruled in early 2020 that the Democrats lacked legal standing to sue because they did not represent a majority of Congress.

But it was Blumenthal's outspoken opposition to his three Supreme Court nominees that seemed in particular to get under Trump's skin. Trump invariably responded by raising the same issue that has dogged Blumenthal since his first Senate run: comments earlier in his career suggesting that he had served in the Vietnam War when he had not. When Trump announced the nomination of federal Judge Amy Coney Barrett just weeks prior to the 2020 elections, Blumenthal tweeted that he would "refuse to treat this process as legitimate" and decline to meet with Barrett for the usual courtesy call Supreme Court nominees make to a Judiciary Committee member prior to confirmation hearings. Trump fired back: "Hanoi Dick, who lied for years by saying he was a war hero in Vietnam, and was never even there (Impeach him!), should not be entitled to a vote on anything of importance!" (Trump overlooked that senators cannot be impeached, although they can be expelled by a two-thirds vote of the chamber.)

Blumenthal faced far less confrontation with President Joe Biden in office—notwithstanding that he was among the first Senate Democrats to say he would oppose a waiver necessary for Biden's choice for Pentagon chief, retired Army Gen. Lloyd Austin. (Blumenthal complained it "would contravene the basic principle that there should be civilian control over a nonpolitical military," according to the Associated Press.) Blumenthal had few disagreements with Biden's old boss, President Barack Obama. A notable exception occurred when Blumenthal was at the forefront of the successful effort to override Obama's veto of a bill allowing families of 9/11 victims to sue Saudi Arabia in U.S. courts.

A closely divided Senate could impel Blumenthal—whose voting record placed him among the 10 most liberal members of the chamber, according to Almanac vote ratings, in 2017 and 2018—to reach across the political aisle with a more empathetic administration in place. Representing a state where gun violence has been a painful subject since a gunman killed 26 children and staff members at Newtown's Sandy Hook Elementary School in 2012, Blumenthal found common ground with a leading Trump ally: South Carolina Republican Lindsey Graham. Their compromise—announced in August 2019 shortly after back-to-back mass shootings in El Paso Texas and Dayton Ohio—called for a federal grant program to encourage states to enact "red flag" laws, enabling courts and law enforcement officials to act when gun owners show they are a threat to themselves or others. A year earlier, Blumenthal and Graham had failed to generate support for a plan to empower federal courts to seize guns from those who exhibit signs of violence—but, in the wake of the El Paso and Dayton shootings, Trump voiced support for several gun control measures, including the red flag initiative. The effort collapsed at the end of 2019 when Trump backed away.

Trump's animus toward Blumenthal appeared to stem, at least in part, out of their respective backgrounds as natives of New York's outer boroughs—Blumenthal was born in Brooklyn, Trump in Queens—with ties to rival camps in the often-cutthroat battles over Manhattan real estate. According to a Roll Call analysis of financial disclosure forms for 2018, Blumenthal, with a minimum net worth of $70 million, is among the 10 wealthiest members of Congress—largely by dint of marriage. Blumenthal's wife, Cynthia, is the daughter of real estate magnate Peter Malkin. Trump also made his name in New York real estate, often in competition with Malkin. The two had a feud involving the complex ownership structure of the iconic Empire State Building. Blumenthal's father, Martin, fled Nazi Germany in 1935 and became wealthy by trading commodities.

After graduating from Harvard University with a degree in political science, Blumenthal moved on to Yale Law School, where he edited the Yale Law Journal; Bill and Hillary Clinton were among his classmates. His post-college list of employers reads like a "Who's Who" of the Washington elite in the 1970s. They included Washington Post publisher Katharine Graham; future New York Sen. Daniel Patrick Moynihan, then a top adviser in the Nixon White House; and Supreme Court Justice Harry Blackmun, for whom Blumenthal clerked.

After a stint as a top aide to Sen. Abraham Ribicoff—who held the seat Blumenthal now occupies—President Jimmy Carter in 1977 appointed the 31-year-old Blumenthal as U.S. attorney for Connecticut. His career in elected office started with the Connecticut Assembly in 1984; he moved to the state Senate in 1987 before his successful run for attorney general in 1990. Blumenthal used the latter position to pursue lawsuits against health insurers and polluters as well as Big Tobacco and some of the nation's leading banks. Detractors derided him as "Sue 'Em All Blumenthal." Years later, when Republican Larry Kudlow—who went on to serve as Trump's chief economic adviser—flirted with opposing Blumenthal in 2016, he took aim at the incumbent's record as attorney general. "All these anti-business lawsuits never went anywhere," Kudlow told the Hartford Courant. "It was death by 1,000 press releases." Nevertheless, voters reelected Blumenthal four times, never with less than 59 percent of the vote.

Although unhesitant to take on powerful corporate targets, Blumenthal earned a reputation for caution when it came to his own political future. He resisted repeated entreaties to run for governor, a post occupied by Republicans during much of his tenure as attorney general. Just as Blumenthal finally seemed ready to take the plunge for higher office—eyeing a 2012 challenge to Democratic-turned-independent Sen. Joe Lieberman—an unexpected opening occurred. Veteran Democratic Sen. Chris Dodd, embattled over allegations that he had accepted political favors, announced his retirement in 2010. Blumenthal decided to run for Dodd's seat. At first, his Senate bid looked to be an electoral stroll in the park, given his popularity in a onetime swing state that had turned blue. But it was also the year that the tea party took flight, and the Republican nominee, Linda McMahon—who, with her husband, Vince McMahon, started World Wrestling Entertainment—harnessed an upswing in GOP voter energy to make it a real contest.

The first sign things were not going to be easy for Blumenthal was a New York Times report on the exaggeration of his military service. A member of the Marine Corps Reserve from 1970 to 1975, Blumenthal claimed on several occasions to have served in Vietnam, though he never was deployed. According to the Times, Blumenthal, after a series of deferments had run out, joined a reserve unit in Washington that conducted drills and focused on local projects such as fixing a campground and organizing a Toys for Tots drive. The McMahon campaign attacked him for distorting his record, putting a chink in his best asset: his image as a selfless crusader. Blumenthal apologized, but his wide lead in the polls was gone. Blumenthal's camp went after McMahon over sexism and use of steroids in professional wrestling, where McMahon had earned a fortune as WWE president. By the end of the campaign, she had spent more than $50 million—almost six times as much as Blumenthal—with most of it coming from her own pocket. But she "had persistent trouble winning over women voters, despite the fact she would have become the first female senator in the state's history," the Hartford Courant reported. "Some women were turned off by some of the racier images of WWE." Blumenthal scored a comfortable 55%-43% win.

In a touch of irony, Blumenthal found himself the ranking Democrat on the Veterans' Affairs Committee four years after arriving in the Senate. He teamed up with the chairman, Republican Johnny Isakson of Georgia, to sponsor a bill to overhaul the troubled Veterans Affairs Department—including provisions to facilitate the firing of problem employees while protecting whistleblowers and to expand mental health programs for veterans. A stripped-down version of the bill was adopted during the lame-duck session in 2016. Montana Sen. Jon Tester, who had more seniority than Blumenthal, then opted to take over as ranking Democrat. Since arriving on Capitol Hill, Blumenthal also has served on the Armed Services Committee, a politically important assignment in a state that is home to the New London Naval Submarine Base and the Electric Boat Shipyard in nearby Groton.

Blumenthal's consumer advocacy efforts during his first term were aimed largely at transportation safety. As a member of the Commerce, Science and Transportation Committee, he called for General Motors to create a compensation fund for victims of defective ignition switches. A year after the company announced it was setting up such a fund, Blumenthal called on Takata to establish a similar fund for victims of its ruptured air bags. Company officials rejected Blumenthal's request but later agreed to set up such a fund in early 2017 as part of a $1 billion settlement with the Justice Department. If Blumenthal's frequent jawboning didn't often translate into enacted legislation, he contended it helped prod the targeted industries to do the right thing. "One lesson to me is that legislation is only one lever to fight for benefits for the people of Connecticut. I can use my position to shine a light on problems," he told The Connecticut Mirror. In the spring of 2018, Blumenthal and liberal Massachusetts Sen. Ed Markey stalled legislation that would have removed regulatory obstacles to driverless-car development. Blumenthal insisted that any legislation include the ability to manually override self-driving cars.

Also in 2018, Blumenthal and Markey introduced a "privacy bill of rights" for users of such platforms as Facebook and Google. Their legislation followed revelations that Cambridge Analytica, a consulting firm with ties to the 2016 Trump campaign, had obtained data on as many as 87 million Facebook users without permission. A year later, Blumenthal continued his efforts to rein in Facebook by again reaching across the aisle. He teamed with Missouri Republican Josh Hawley— a hard-line conservative but, like Blumenthal, a former state attorney general— to send a letter to the Federal Trade Commission, characterizing a pending $5 billion settlement between Facebook and the federal government as a "bargain." They urged that long-term limits be placed on Facebook's collection and use of personal data. After the FTC announced the settlement, Blumenthal and Hawley introduced legislation in late 2019 to require Facebook and other large social media platforms to make it easier for users to move their data to another service. Facebook executives expressed support for the concept of data portability and promised to work with the bill's sponsors.

Trump's Twitter assault started just weeks into his presidency after Blumenthal, following a meeting with Supreme Court nominee Neil Gorsuch, told reporters that Gorsuch had characterized Trump's frequent criticisms of federal judges as "disheartening" and "demoralizing." Tweeted Trump: "Sen. Richard Blumenthal, who never fought in Vietnam when he said for years he had (major lie), now misrepresents what Judge Gorsuch told him?" Gorsuch later publicly acknowledged that Blumenthal—who joined most Senate Democrats in voting against Gorsuch's confirmation—had quoted him correctly.

The rhetorical siege escalated when another Trump nominee to the high court, Brett Kavanaugh, faced confirmation hearings in late 2018. Blumenthal asked whether Kavanaugh were familiar with

"Falsus in uno, falsus in omnibus"—a legal dictum that suggests jurors can deem a witness to lack credibility on all matters if he or she says one thing that is not true. "The core of why we're here, really, is credibility," Blumenthal said after Christine Blasey Ford alleged Kavanaugh had sexually assaulted her when they were in high school. Trump, joined by allies on Capitol Hill, counterattacked. "@SenBlumenthal lied for years about serving in Vietnam, which is all you need to know about his courage & honesty."

Prior to his 2016 reelection bid, Blumenthal came under pressure as one of the last Democratic holdouts on the Obama administration's nuclear agreement with Iran. (Trump later withdrew from the agreement, a move that Biden vowed to reverse.) Kudlow vowed to challenge Blumenthal if he voted for the deal, which Blumenthal ultimately agreed to support. But, after seven months of talking about taking on Blumenthal, Kudlow decided against running—which left Connecticut Republicans scrambling.

A month before the state GOP convention, conservative state Rep. Dan Carter entered the race; he was overwhelmingly nominated. But Carter was virtually unknown statewide, and Blumenthal outspent him 20-1, cruising to a 63%-35% victory. Few expected Blumenthal—an indefatigable campaigner who has never lost a race—to have a tougher time in 2022. "There is no discernible difference in Blumenthal's schedule from the start of an election cycle to the end," The Connecticut Mirror noted. "Blumenthal never has needed to gear up for a campaign. It's just what he does."

Chris Murphy (D)

Elected 2012, term expires 2024, 2nd term, b. Aug 03, 1973; White Plains, NY; Oxford University Exeter College, 1995; Williams College, B.A., 1996; University of Connecticut School of Law, J.D., 2002; Protestant; Married (Catherine Holahan Murphy); 2 children.

Elected Office: CT House, 1999-2003; CT Senate, 2003-2006; U.S. House, 2007-2013.

Professional Career: Campaign Manager, Charlotte Koskoff U.S. House Campaign, 1996; Southington CT Planning & Zoning Commission, 1997-1999; Practicing attorney, 2002-2006.

DC Office: 136 HSOB 20510, 202-224-4041, Fax: 202-224-9750, murphy.senate.gov

State Offices: Hartford, 860-549-8463.

Committees: *Appropriations*: Department of Homeland Security (Chmn); DOL, HHS & Education & Related Agencies; Legislative Branch; State, Foreign Operations & Related Programs; Transportation, HUD & Related Agencies. *Foreign Relations*: East Asia, the Pacific & International Cybersecurity Policy; Europe & Regional Security Cooperation; Near East, South Asia, Central Asia & Counterterrorism (Chmn); State Dept & USAID Mngmnt, Internat'l Ops & Internat'l Dev. *Health, Education, Labor & Pensions*: Children & Families; Primary Health & Retirement Security.

Group Ratings

	ADA	ACLU	AFL-CIO	LCV	COC	HAFA	ACU	CFG	FRC
2020	-	92%	-	85%	-	0%	2%	-	-
2019	100%	C	100%	100%	61%	C	2%	0%	0%

Almanac Ratings 2019-2020

	Economy	Social	Foreign	Composite
Liberal	97%	97%	69%	88%
Conservative	3%	3%	31%	12%

Key Votes of the 116th Congress

1. EPA clean energy rules	Y	5. Russia sanctions	Y	9. Barr as Atty. General	N
2. U.S./Mex./Can. trade deal	Y	6. Troops in SYR, AFG	N	10. Spending at the border	Y
3. Cut unemployment benefits	N	7. Veto arms sales to Saudis	Y	11. Coney Barrett to Sup. Ct.	N
4. Shelton to Fed Reserve	N	8. Defense $$$, veto override	Y	12. Electoral College objections	N

Election Results

Election	Name (Party)	Vote (%)	Cand. Spent	Ind. Exp. Support	Ind. Exp. Oppose
2018 General	Chris Murphy (D).................................	825,579 (60%)	$7,487,098	$5,513	
	Matthew Corey (R)...........................	545,717 (39%)	$185,883		
2018 Primary	Chris Murphy (D)...	(100%)			

Prior winning percentages: 2018 (60%), 2012 (55%); House: 2010 (54%), 2008 (59%), 2006 (56%)

By his own admission, Democrat Chris Murphy, Connecticut's junior senator, was first elected to that chamber in 2012 without a passionate purpose for being there. That changed just five weeks after Election Day, when a mass shooting took place at Sandy Hook Elementary School in Newtown, in the House district that Murphy had represented for three terms. He rushed to the school and remained with grieving parents until all the fatalities—20 children and six teachers and aides—were carried out. "There wasn't one issue that was driving me to get up every day and go to work. There is today," Murphy later told Politico. "This was something different … in part because my son just graduated from first grade. I'm the same age as all of these parents. I walked out of that tragedy feeling like I had just been handed my mission in public service."

Throughout his Senate tenure, Murphy has sought to move the needle on gun control, notably with a 15-hour filibuster in mid-2016 after the Orlando Florida nightclub shooting in which 50 people, including the gunman, died. But he can point to little more than the occasional incremental success; his repeated push for expanded, if not universal, background checks on gun ownership has been stymied by opposition from Capitol Hill's powerful gun lobby. He remains undeterred and has all but staked his legislative legacy on this issue. In his 2020 book, The Violence Inside Us: A Brief History Of An Ongoing American Tragedy, Murphy plaintively wrote: "I feel like if I don't get a bill done to address gun violence in this country by the time that I hang up my spikes, then I've failed. I've just fundamentally failed as a legislator. And that is a difference between being intellectually connected to issues and being emotionally connected to issues."

Nevertheless, his legislative legacy may be ultimately defined by a very different set of issues: the appropriate role for the United States in today's global power structure. His emergence as a leading Democratic voice on foreign policy prompted talk of a presidential bid—which he dismissed at the outset of the 2020 election cycle—and later speculation about Murphy as a potential secretary of state under President Joe Biden. "He's defining what a foreign policy would look like if Democrats take the White House," Ben Rhodes, President Barack Obama's deputy national security adviser, told the Connecticut Mirror 18 months prior to Biden's election. "You don't have a lot of national Democrats talking about foreign policy, and Murphy is filling that vacuum."

Murphy told Vox in 2020: "Not everything in domestic politics am I 100 percent sure about. But I am sure that we need a massive reorientation of America's place in the world." For Murphy, this includes avoiding long-term wars, while asserting Congress' power to restrain the president via the War Powers Act; directing additional investment toward the diplomatic rather than the military budget; and funding anti-corruption programs to weaken autocracies, including Russia, China and Saudi Arabia. Such views led to an up-and-down relationship with Obama on foreign policy and later to unrelenting criticism of the Trump administration. "Three and a half years of Donald Trump serving as the face of the United States have done incalculable damage to the country's standing in the world," Murphy declared in a June 2020 op-ed in Foreign Affairs magazine.

Such comments did not prevent Murphy—a self-described progressive who has frequently reached out to Republican colleagues on legislation— from seeking some common ground with Trump. In August 2019, after mass shootings in El Paso Texas and Dayton Ohio in which 33 were killed including the gunman in Ohio, Murphy teamed with two centrist senators, Republican Patrick Toomey of Pennsylvania and Democrat Joe Manchin of West Virginia to revive an effort to enact expanded background checks during gun purchases; Manchin and Toomey had pushed a similar proposal six years earlier after the Sandy Hook shootings. Trump initially expressed support in the wake of the El Paso and Dayton attacks, leading to conversations between the president and the three senators—and a difficult political balancing act for Murphy, who not long before had suggested that Trump "behaves like a child." Describing one phone conversation to Politico, Murphy acknowledged: "The president said a lot of things I deeply disagreed with. I tried my best to hold my tongue. I did my best to stay focused on finding common ground on guns." The effort collapsed when Trump backed away in late 2019, reportedly fearing blowback from his political base. It also became entangled in impeachment proceedings against Trump, in which Murphy would play a timely role.

Raised in the Hartford suburb of Wethersfield, Murphy has been in politics virtually his entire adult life. Soon after graduating from Williams College, he signed on as campaign manager for Democrat Charlotte Koskoff, who came within 1,600 votes of toppling then-Rep. Nancy Johnson. Two years later, Murphy ran for office himself, winning a seat in the state House when he was 25. He moved on to the state Senate in 2002, juggling state legislative duties with earning a law degree from the University of Connecticut.

In early 2005, he announced plans to challenge Johnson amid increasing skepticism about the U.S. invasion of Iraq two years earlier. "I got to Congress as somebody who had a mandate to try to untangle the United States from our unwise interventions in the Middle East," he told Vox a decade and a half later. Domestically, the debate focused on the Medicare prescription drug benefit that Johnson had helped design in 2003 while chairing the House Ways and Means Subcommittee on Health. Murphy contended that the program's enrollment deadlines penalized seniors and spotlighted drug industry contributions to Johnson. Johnson, who had served for nearly a quarter-century, outspent Murphy 2-1. But, as the Democrats rode a national wave to retake the House majority in 2006, Murphy won 56%-44%.

In the House, Murphy was a loyal Democrat, although he boasted of his role in Center Aisle Caucus, which he described as "one of the few places in the House where Republicans and Democrats are … getting together to try and talk about the importance of civility." While his district was home to many insurance industry employees, he backed a government-run public option to compete with private insurers during the 2009-10 debate over the Affordable Care Act. A decade later, as the 2020 presidential race loomed, Murphy floated a proposal to give individuals and businesses the option of buying into Medicare under the exchanges established by "Obamacare"—as an alternative to the "Medicare for All" approach pushed by Vermont Sen. Bernie Sanders and other progressives.

Beginning with his House tenure, Murphy has been an ardent advocate of "Buy America" requirements, introducing bills to require federal contracting officials to solicit information from businesses regarding how many U.S. jobs would be retained or created if their bid were chosen. Murphy later lauded the Trump administration for building support for Senate legislation to allow businesses and the public to examine the waivers federal agencies use to avoid Buy America requirements. Murphy first introduced the bill in January 2018 with Republican Sens. Lindsey Graham of South Carolina and Rob Portman of Ohio. While it did not move out of committee, Murphy told the Connecticut Post: "Trump is stronger on 'Buy America' than Obama. I wish that were not the case, but it's true. … I give him credit where credit is due."

Murphy announced his Senate bid in 2012 after four-term Sen. Joe Lieberman said he would not run again. Murphy faced a primary against former Connecticut Secretary of State Susan Bysiewicz, now the state's lieutenant governor. She ran a controversial TV ad seeking to link Murphy to Wall Street in the wake of the 2008 financial meltdown; it cited more than $700,000 in contributions to Murphy from Wall Street sources over a six-year period. But Bysiewicz found herself on the defensive after having to acknowledge the ad had overstated donations Murphy received from hedge funds. Murphy won the primary 2-1.

The general election turned out to be déjà vu. Linda McMahon, the former professional wrestling magnate who had lost the 2010 Senate race to Democratic Sen. Richard Blumenthal, was again the Republican nominee. And, like Blumenthal two years earlier, Murphy struggled despite being an odds-on favorite at the start of the campaign. He was tripped up over revelations that he missed mortgage payments and had been sued over failure to pay rent. Murphy blamed a busy schedule for the missed payments. As she had in 2010, McMahon tapped into her personal wealth, burning through nearly $50 million. Murphy targeted McMahon—later appointed by Trump to head the Small Business Administration—on issues affecting seniors, contending she would pose a threat to Social Security and Medicare. On Election Day, McMahon lost by the same 55%-43% margin by which she had come up short to Blumenthal.

As a member of the Health, Education, Labor and Pensions Committee, Murphy led the defense of the Affordable Care Act, also known as Obamacare, from Republican attacks. His willingness to perform that politically onerous task served him well with Democratic leaders: Murphy was given a coveted seat on the Appropriations Committee, the first Connecticut senator in almost 30 years to sit on that influential panel. (In 2021, with the Democrats back in the majority, Murphy assumed the chairmanship of a key Appropriations subcommittee with jurisdiction over homeland security spending).A major health policy bill that Murphy co-authored with Republican Sen. Bill Cassidy of Louisiana was signed into law by Obama at the end of 2016. Hailed as the first significant piece of mental health legislation in a decade, it was designed to strengthen insurance coverage for mental health treatment while providing grants to increase the number of psychiatrists and psychologists nationwide. A state report after the Sandy Hook school shooting found that the gunman, Adam Lanza, had gone untreated for both psychiatric and physical disorders.

While a number of his foreign policy stances stood in contrast to those of Lieberman, Murphy forged a relationship with one of Lieberman's closest Senate friends: Republican John McCain of Arizona. Toward the end of his first year in the Senate, Murphy accompanied McCain on a brief trip to Ukraine, highlighted by the two senators addressing a crowd of 500,000 protesting the pro-Russia government then in power. "I struck up a relationship with John that lasted for a long time," Murphy said in 2020 of McCain, who had died a couple of years earlier. "And I obviously acquired a passion for a policy area, U.S.-Ukraine relations, that stuck." After the 2016 presidential election, with a U.S.-friendly government in power in Ukraine, Murphy introduced legislation to penalize Russia over its incursion into Ukraine's Crimean Peninsula as well as interference in the U.S. election. Russia repaid the favor by denying Murphy, a member of the Foreign Relations Committee, a visa to visit as part of a congressional delegation in the summer of 2019.

Murphy visited Ukrainian President Volodymyr Zelensky in early September 2019 while his government was dealing with Trump's decision to freeze $400 million in security assistance. The meeting with Zelensky took place just prior to revelations that Trump, in a July 25 phone call to the Ukrainian president, had pressed him to investigate Biden and his son Hunter, who served on the board of a Ukrainian company. As allegations that Trump had withheld the security assistance to leverage political gain became the basis of impeachment proceedings, Murphy would later tell House impeachment investigators that he wanted to travel to Ukraine after learning of efforts by Trump personal attorney Rudy Giuliani to pressure Zelensky's government to investigate the Bidens. Murphy said he urged Zelensky to resist becoming "an actor in U.S. domestic politics," adding: "President Zelensky said he understood and represented to us that he had no desire to interfere in a U.S. election. I interpreted Zelensky's answer to my question as a concession of the premise of my question—that he was receiving improper overtures from Giuliani to interfere in the 2020 election."

At a press conference after release of a transcript of the July 25 phone call, Trump responded by charging that Murphy "literally threatened the president of Ukraine that if he doesn't do things right, they won't have Democrat support in Congress." Murphy denied threatening Zelensky, while saying he was not surprised by the president's attack—since Giuliani, in an earlier TV interview, had called for Murphy to be impeached. (In fact, senators cannot be impeached but can be removed by a two-thirds vote of their colleagues.)

Consistent with the stance that first impelled him to run for Congress, Murphy emerged as one of the Senate's most outspoken doves on U.S. involvement in the Middle East. He gained widespread attention during his first year in the chamber when he told Obama that he could not support the administration's plan to take military action against Syria. A year later, he came out against the Obama administration's efforts to train and arm Syrian rebels to fight ISIS. "I want ISIS defeated in Syria," Murphy said. "But too much can go wrong, for not enough possible gain, for the U.S. to increase our involvement in the Syrian civil war." At the end of 2018, when Trump ordered the withdrawal of 2,000 troops from Syria—a move widely criticized by both Democrats and Republicans—Murphy charged that Trump's action "was done in a ham-handed manner that makes us weaker in the world." But he again slammed the initial move to involve the U.S. military in Syria. "I thought this was a bad idea from the start," he said. "We should admit we have just prolonged [the war] instead of trying to end it."

Less than a week before Trump ordered the troop withdrawal from Syria, Murphy—a strong critic of the administration's close relationship with Saudi Arabia—joined with Sanders and conservative Republican Sen. Mike Lee of Utah to spearhead passage of a resolution withdrawing U.S. support for Saudi-backed forces at war in Yemen. It was a bipartisan rebuke to Trump—and marked the first time that the Senate, under the terms of the War Powers Act, had supported withdrawing forces from a war that Congress had not voted to approve. But Trump vetoed the measure and backers of the move lacked the two-thirds majority necessary to override his veto.

Notwithstanding their differences on Syria, Murphy provided key early support for Obama's nuclear agreement with Iran in 2015 when more senior Democrats on the Foreign Relations Committee were opposing it. Trump withdrew the United States from the deal, and yet another volley of hostile rhetoric was triggered in early 2020 after Murphy met with Iran's foreign minister during a conference in Germany. Trump accused Murphy of violating the Logan Act—a 220-year-old, never enforced statute barring unauthorized negotiations with foreign governments on the nation's behalf. Trump, who had previously criticized former Secretary of State John Kerry for meeting with Iranian officials, declared via Twitter: "Kerry& Murphy illegally violated the Logan Act. ... Must be dealt with strongly!" Murphy fired back at Trump on Twitter: "Iran restarted their nuclear program, fired at our troops, upped support for proxies. Your Iran policy is a disastrous failure." Murphy later asserted, "If Trump isn't going to talk to Iran, then someone should."

Murphy had no trouble winning reelection in 2018 after Connecticut Republicans failed to recruit a top-tier challenger—defeating Matthew Corey, a pro-Trump small businessman who had lost three previous bids for Congress, 59%-40%. Corey spent just $65,000 to Murphy's $7.8 million—who was often out of state campaigning for other candidates. His travels fueled speculation about a presidential bid, which Murphy shut down shortly after being sworn into a second term. "Let me be 100 percent clear: I am not running in 2020," he tweeted. Alluding to a half-dozen Democratic Senate colleagues getting ready to run, Murphy quipped, "At least two or three Democrats in the Senate need to stay behind to keep the fight going here!"

Asked by reporters whether he might make a future White House run, Murphy replied, "It's not something I would rule out." As one of the Senate's younger members—he turns 48 in 2021—he can afford to wait. He has maintained an active presence on TV cable talk shows, and, in an unguarded moment, acknowledged to The Washington Post in 2016 that he is a "big ball of political ambition." Added Murphy: "Everyone doing this job is fooling themselves if they don't admit that we are attracted to the show business element of it. We are all doing this in part because we enjoy being in front of the cameras."

John Larson (D)

Elected 1998, 12th term, b. Jul 22, 1948; Hartford, CT; Trinity College; Central CT State University, B.S., 1971; Catholic; Married (Leslie Best Larson); 3 children.

Elected Office: E. Hartford Board of Education, 1977-1979; E. Hartford Town Council, 1979-1983; CT Senate, 1986-1998, President pro-tem, 1990-1998.

Professional Career: H.S. teacher, 1972-1977; Ins. broker, 1977-1998; Sr. fellow, Yale Bush Center, 1995-1998.

DC Office: 1501 LHOB 20515, 202-225-2265, Fax: 202-225-1031, larson.house.gov

State Offices: Hartford, 860-278-8888.

Committees: *Ways & Means*: Select Revenue Measures; Social Security (Chmn).

Group Ratings

	ADA	ACLU	AFL-CIO	LCV	COC	HAFA	ACU	CFG	FRC
2020	**	80%	**	100%	-	0%	5%	**	-
2019	90%	C	100%	96%	58%	C	5%	12%	0%

Almanac Ratings 2019-2020

	Economy	Social	Foreign	Composite
Liberal	100%	63%	80%	81%
Conservative	0%	37%	20%	19%

Key Votes of the 116th Congress

1. U.S./Mex./Can. trade deal	Y	5. Russia sanctions	Y	9. Firearms background checks Y
2. First Coronavirus response	Y	6. Troops in Syria	Y	10. Spending at the border	Y
3. HEROES Act	Y	7. Veto arms sales to Saudis	Y	11. Marijuana liberalized rules	Y
4. CASH Act	Y	8. Defense $$$, veto override	Y	12. Electoral College objections	N

Election Results

Election	Name (Party)	Vote (%)		Cand. Spent	Ind. Exp. Support	Ind. Exp. Oppose
2020 General	John Larson (D)	222,668	(64%)	$1,030,681	$123	
	Mary Fay (R)	122,111	(35%)	$24,595		$113

Prior winning percentages: 2018 (64%), 2016 (64%), 2014 (62%), 2012 (70%), 2010 (60%), 2008 (72%), 2006 (74%), 2004 (73%), 2002 (67%), 2000 (72%), 1998 (58%)

Democrat John Larson, first elected in 1998, has been an influential figure among House Democrats and popular with colleagues. As a senior member of the tax-writing Ways and Means Committee and chairman of its Social Security Subcommittee, he pursued his expertise in the program. Once a leadership lieutenant of Speaker Nancy Pelosi, Larson became a cautious critic during the Democrats' long struggle in the minority.

One of eight children, Larson grew up in the Mayberry Village public-housing project in East Hartford, and is fond of saying that he is a "product of public housing, public education, and public service." His father was a fireman at Pratt & Whitney. His mother had a job at the state capitol and served on the town council. Speaking at the 2012 Democratic National Convention, he said that his mother had dementia and required round-the-clock care, paid for in part through her Social Security benefits. "Don't ever tell me or any American that's a handout," he said. "It's the insurance they paid for."

After graduating from Central Connecticut State University, Larson taught high school and coached athletics. In 1982, he was elected to the state Senate. Four years later, he became Senate president. He sponsored one of the nation's first family and medical leave laws, a prototype for the federal bill signed by President Bill Clinton in 1993.

Larson seemed headed for the governorship. But Comptroller Bill Curry in 1994 built an organization of unionists and liberal activists and beat him 55%-45% in the primary. When Democratic Rep. Barbara Kennelly ran for governor in 1998, Larson ran for her seat. In the primary, he won 46%-43% over Secretary of State Miles Rapoport. Against Republican Kevin O'Connor, a 31-year-old lawyer, Larson won 58%-41% and has not been seriously challenged since.

Larson's voting record places him near the center of his party. In the House minority, he worked with Republicans on legislation, especially with then-Ways and Means chairman Kevin Brady on a measure to make permanent a research and development tax credit. He has been co-chairman of the bipartisan Congressional Joint Strike Fighter Caucus, which backs the F-35, whose engines are made by Pratt & Whitney.

In 2003, Pelosi tapped Larson as senior Democrat on the House Administration Committee, the congressional housekeeping panel that handles office budgets and other perks of interest to colleagues. Among his legislative interests at the committee was campaign finance reform, including a proposal to allow the federal government to match funds raised by a candidate who agrees to limit contributions to $100 or less. In 2006, he was elected Democratic Caucus vice chairman. His competitors were Jan Schakowsky of Illinois and Joseph Crowley of New York. With Schakowsky's supporters, Larson prevailed on the second ballot, 116-87, over Crowley When Rahm Emanuel quit the House in 2008 to become chief of staff to President Barack Obama, Pelosi cleared the field for Larson to become caucus chairman.

Larson took on a number of leadership assignments, including dealing with party dissidents who complained that Pelosi's Iraq strategy was too accommodating to President George W. Bush and later coordinating the Democrats' strategy on energy policy. Some Democrats privately derided him as Pelosi's cheerleader, but he shrugged off such comments, saying his "bottom-up, member's member" approach differed from the imperious style of Emanuel, but was no less effective. After meeting the four-year limit in that post, Larson served as a mentor to younger members. He said he would welcome a return to party leadership, but that time might have passed. His voice grew more independent following the 2016 election when he joined critics of Pelosi for the failure of Democrats to regain House control. The Democratic Caucus needed "a frank discussion about what happened," he said.

Coincidentally, in 2017, Larson's close friend Rep. Richard Neal of Massachusetts—who had also shown independence of Pelosi—became the top Democrat at the Ways and Means Committee. Larson launched a bicameral Expand Social Security Caucus, with Bernie Sanders and Elizabeth Warren as co-chairs in the Senate. He filed the Social Security 2100 Act, which he said was designed to assure the long-term solvency of the program, with increased support for low-income beneficiaries and tax increases on higher earners. "I am committed to taking common-sense steps to expand benefits and to make the system solvent for the next 75 years and beyond," Larson said. When President Donald Trump proposed in 2020 a one-year deferral of Social Security withholding taxes in his plan to revive the economy that had been flattened by coronavirus, Larsen charged that he was "breaking his promise" not to touch the retirement program.

Larson was an outspoken foe of the tax cuts Republicans enacted in December 2017. He criticized the legislation for cutting taxes for the highest earners, while paradoxically complaining that it adversely affected high-income states such as Connecticut. In 2019, Larson was among the House Democrats assigned to negotiate the terms of a new trade agreement the Trump administration had reached with Mexico and Canada.

At home, Larson talked up his proposal for a massive "big dig" tunnel project that would replace the two interstate highways that bisect downtown Hartford and East Hartford, which would cost more than $10 billion and likely would take decades to build. "It's time for the Hartford region to think big again," he wrote. He said the project was about "economic vitality, growth for the region and creating livable communities." He called for a tax on carbon emissions to finance national transportation improvements.

"The choice is simple," Larson said about his proposed tunnels. "Think big again and make this happen." That approach defined his broader objectives.

CT-1: North-central Connecticut

Cook Partisan Voting Index: D+11

Population		Race and Ethnicity		Income	
Total	703,138	White	67.80%	Median Income	$75,502
Land area (sq. miles)	675	Black	15.30%	District Income Rank	123
Pop/ sq mi	1,040.99	Latino	17.20%	Poverty Rate	10.70%
Born in State	57.80%	Asian	5.60%	With health insurance	95.30%
		Two or more races	4.60%	Cash public assistance	3.80%
Age Groups		Other	6.70%	Food stamp/SNAP	12.60%
Under 18	20.60%				
18-34	21.80%	**Education**		**Work**	
35-64	39.80%	H.S grad or less	35.50%	White Collar	45.60%
Over 64	17.70%	Some college	25.90%	Sales and Service	38.00%
		College Degree, 4 yr	20.90%	Blue Collar	16.40%
Military		Post grad	17.70%	Government	15.00%
Veteran/ Active Duty	5.30%				

2020 Pres. Vote	Biden	229,220	(63%)	Trump	127,803	(35%)		
2016 Pres. Vote	Clinton	195,305	(59%)	Trump	119,395	(36%)	Johnson	9,468 (3%)

Hartford: The Puritans who founded Hartford certainly never expected, or even hoped, that Connecticut's Yankees would turn out to be shrewd businessmen. Yet this is exactly what happened. Mark Twain moved to Hartford in 1871 to become director of an insurance company, and in time became the Connecticut capital's most famous citizen. Some have departed, but Connecticut retains one of the largest concentrations of financial and insurance firms in the nation, mostly in the Hartford area. Its merchants wrote fire insurance, using the capital they had accumulated in the Napoleonic Wars to finance their ventures. Samuel Colt was instrumental in developing the state's armaments base; he conceived of the revolving-barrel pistol after watching the wheel of a ship spin while at sea. His gun factory, just south of downtown Hartford, became one of the nation's great arms plants. Thanks to the broad Connecticut River, Hartford became an inland seaport.

Despite their downsizing, insurance and armaments remain economic mainstays of Hartford. But many employers have moved out of Hartford itself, hastening the decline of this once rich city. Insurance industry employment dropped to 47,000 statewide in 2014, though it rebounded to 58,000 in 2020. Aetna, after abandoning plans to move to New York City, was purchased in 2018 by CVS, which committed to keep its insurance workforce of about 6,000 employees in Hartford for at least 10 years. Since the 1980s, the urban core has been filled with bedraggled, high-crime neighborhoods littered with abandoned buildings Where 177,000 people lived in 1950, there were about 122,100 residents in 2019. The population is 38 percent African-American and 44 percent Hispanic—mostly Puerto Rican. There have been signs of recovery. The University of Connecticut opened in 2017 a large downtown campus, inter-city train service has expanded, and new housing and retail facilities are under construction. Luke Bronin, a former Rhodes Scholar who served with the Navy in Afghanistan, has brought a youthful urgency as mayor. After Donald Trump was elected president, Bronin said that Hartford would remain a "sanctuary city" that would protect illegal immigrants. "We're not going to let our police force be commandeered by the federal government to target families that aren't posing any threat to anyone," he said in 2018. Also that month, Hartford avoided bankruptcy when the state took responsibility for payment of $700 million of city bonds.

Across the river is the Pratt & Whitney jet engine plant in East Hartford, cornerstone of Connecticut-based United Technologies. Though its operations have been shrunk by Pentagon spending cutbacks and its local workforce is less than one-fourth its size in 1980, it builds engines for more than 600 customers around the world. The areas west of Hartford are affluent suburbs and faring much better.

The 1st Congressional District of Connecticut is centered on Hartford. West Hartford has the most voters, though its population is only half the size of Hartford. The district is shaped like a lobster claw. The top half passes through Windsor. The claw then swings west across the northern border of the state, taking in small towns and part of Torrington. The bottom half of the district includes Bristol, site of the sprawling headquarters of ESPN, the multimedia network that has cut back several hundred jobs from its peak in 2017 of 4,000 local workers—in a worldwide force reduced from a peak of 8,000 to 6,000.

The Hartford area has long been more Democratic than the rest of Connecticut. The 2016 election produced a twist, when Hillary Clinton dropped below 60 percent in the 1st District and got a slightly larger vote in the upscale 4th District. In 2020, its vote returned to the 63 percent share that Barack Obama won in 2012, though it continued to trail the 4th as the most Democratic district in the state.

Joe Courtney (D)

Elected 2006, 8th term, b. Apr 06, 1953; West Hartford, CT; Tufts University, B.A., 1975; University of CT School of Law, J.D., 1978; Roman Catholic; Married (Audrey Courtney); 2 children.

Elected Office: CT House, 1987-1994.

Professional Career: Practicing attorney, 1978-2006; CT coordinator, John Edwards President campaign, 2004.

DC Office: 2332 RHOB 20515, 202-225-2076, Fax: 202-225-4977, courtney.house.gov

State Offices: Enfield, 860-741-6011; Norwich, 860-886-0139.

Committees: *Armed Services*: Readiness; Seapower & Projection Forces (Chmn). *Education & Labor*: Health, Employment, Labor & Pensions; Higher Education & Workforce Investment.

Group Ratings

	ADA	ACLU	AFL-CIO	LCV	COC	HAFA	ACU	CFG	FRC
2020	**	81%	**	100%	-	0%	3%	**	-
2019	90%	C	100%	93%	61%	C	3%	12%	0%

Almanac Ratings 2019-2020

	Economy	Social	Foreign	Composite
Liberal	100%	100%	80%	94%
Conservative	0%	0%	20%	6%

Key Votes of the 116th Congress

1. U.S./Mex./Can. trade deal Y	5. Russia sanctions Y	9. Firearms background checks Y
2. First Coronavirus response Y	6. Troops in Syria Y	10. Spending at the border Y
3. HEROES Act Y	7. Veto arms sales to Saudis Y	11. Marijuana liberalized rules Y
4. CASH Act Y	8. Defense $$$, veto override Y	12. Electoral College objections N

Election Results

Election	Name (Party)	Vote (%)		Cand. Spent	Ind. Exp. Support	Ind. Exp. Oppose
2020 General	Joe Courtney (D).............................	218,119	(59%)	$928,079	$123	
	Justin Anderson (R)............................	140,356	(38%)	$82,035		$113

Prior winning percentages: 2018 (62%), 2016 (63%), 2014 (62%), 2012 (68%), 2010 (60%), 2008 (66%), 2006 (50%)

Democrat Joe Courtney, elected in 2006, has tirelessly promoted issues that are important to him, chiefly defense and education. With his influence as chairman of the Armed Services Subcommittee on Seapower and Projection Forces, he has delivered huge local benefits as a guardian of General Dynamics' Electric Boat plant and the New London Naval Submarine Base. In 2020, he secured an agreement in the annual military spending bill to restore funding for construction of a second Virginia-class submarine, which President Donald Trump sought to eliminate in his proposed budget.

Courtney was raised in West Hartford. He studied at Tufts University, graduated from the University of Connecticut law school and went into private practice. In 1986, he won the first of four terms in the state House, where he served as chairman of the public health and human services committees. He ran unsuccessfully for lieutenant governor in 1998, then unsuccessfully in 2002 against Republican Rep. Rob Simmons, who won 54%-46%.

Courtney returned for a rematch in 2006. Democrats worked diligently to nationalize the race by exploiting voter anger over the Iraq war and GOP ethics scandals in Congress. Simmons touted his independence from the Bush administration on partial-birth abortion and same-sex marriage votes. He also highlighted his successful lobbying to keep the submarine base off the 2005 base-closing list. Courtney prevailed in the closest House race of the 2006 election, with a winning margin of 83 votes out of the more than 242,000 cast.

In the House, Courtney got a seat on Armed Services, where he effectively lobbied for the Navy's shipbuilding program at Groton. He worked with other Connecticut and Rhode Island lawmakers in 2007 to secure an extra $588 million in the defense appropriations bill for submarines, paving the way for the Navy to double its submarine production from one to two a year. That led to his nickname from colleagues: "Two Sub Joe."

Courtney took over as co-chair of the Congressional Shipbuilding Caucus and worked to prevent a one-year cut in submarine production in 2014 while protecting the appropriation for a "stretched" version of a Virginia-class sub with cruise-missile tubes, which was designed at the Electric Boat yard. He successfully lobbied the Pentagon to include in its Quadrennial Defense Review the need for a future fleet of as many as 55 submarines, up from the 48 called for in 2006.

In the 2014 defense spending bill, he secured as much as $3.5 billion for a "National Sea-Based Deterrence Fund" that would allow the Pentagon to finance a new class of submarines to be built in Groton. In 2015, as senior Democrat on the Seapower Subcommittee, he worked closely with Armed Services Committee Republicans to defeat an attempt by members of the House Appropriations Committee to restore annual funding for the new submarines. "We haven't seen this much work [at Electric Boat] since the late '80s and early '90s," Courtney told the Hartford Courant in 2016.

In June 2018, Courtney sought to accelerate a $1 billion down payment for the submarines, which he said would be more cost-effective. But the Appropriations Committee did not include the money in its defense spending bill. Courtney complained that Congress lacked a shipbuilding strategy that would permit it to "look at maritime issues in a logical way."

As the new chairman of the Seapower Subcommittee in 2019, with Democrats back in House control, he demanded a response. In December 2019, he got his intended result, when the Navy announced a $22 billion contract with Electric Boat, which included annual construction of two Virginia-class subs. The agreement "shows that we have a program that is locked in," Courtney said. That optimism unraveled two months later when President Donald Trump in his annual budget called for spending on only one new sub. In the annual military spending bill that Congress approved in December 2020, Courtney persuaded Congress to restore financing for two subs.

Representing a district that includes the University of Connecticut, Courtney has been the leading champion of below-market interest rates on federally backed college loans. With Sen. Elizabeth Warren of Massachusetts, he filed a bill in 2015 to permit a refinancing of student loans, which would save the average borrower $2,000 annually. With the growing call by Democrats to respond to the debt burden many college graduates carry, he and Warren filed in 2020 a new proposal that would permanently lock in lower rates on student loans.

During the 2009 health care debate, Courtney led House Democratic opposition to a proposed "Cadillac tax" on high-cost health insurance plans, which he said would harm millions in the middle class. During the next decade, Congress regularly agreed to defer imposition of what was described as an excise tax, which had never been collected. In July 2019, Courtney won House passage of a bill to repeal the tax entirely.

Unlike most Democrats elected in 2006, Courtney has had a much easier time keeping his office than he did in winning it, never receiving less than 60 percent in his next six campaigns. In 2018, he had a peculiar experience: Republican challenger Dan Postemski, an Iraq war veteran and perennial candidate, complained that the state and national GOP were giving him insufficient support and he shut down his campaign with a blunt "the hell with them" dismissal. "They were trying to make me a politician," he posted on Facebook. "They abandoned me, so I abandoned them." Postemski conceded the obvious: "No one's going to beat Joe Courtney." Courtney won, 62%-35%.

The 2020 campaign brought another peculiar twist. On the eve of the GOP primary, Thomas Gilmer, the Republican-endorsed candidate, was arrested after a violent clash with a former girlfriend. Justin Anderson, who served 30 years as an officer with the Army National Guard and 20 years as a state correctional officer, narrowly won the primary. In November, Courtney defeated him, 59%-38%, his closest victory since he was first elected. He remains secure.

CT-2: Eastern Connecticut   Cook Partisan Voting Index: D+2

Population		Race and Ethnicity		Income	
Total	701,590	White	86.20%	Median Income	$80,280
Land area (sq. miles)	1,988	Black	4.30%	District Income Rank	90
Pop/ sq mi	352.97	Latino	9.00%	Poverty Rate	7.50%
Born in State	55.10%	Asian	3.80%	With health insurance	96.00%
		Two or more races	3.00%	Cash public assistance	3.70%
Age Groups		Other	2.80%	Food stamp/SNAP	9.40%
Under 18	18.80%				
18-34	22.70%	**Education**		**Work**	
35-64	39.90%	H.S grad or less	35.70%	White Collar	43.80%
Over 64	18.60%	Some college	28.50%	Sales and Service	38.00%
		College Degree, 4 yr	20.30%	Blue Collar	18.30%
Military		Post grad	15.50%	Government	16.70%
Veteran/ Active Duty	9.90%				

2020 Pres. Vote	Biden	205,929	(54%)	Trump	164,480	(44%)	
2016 Pres. Vote	Clinton	165,799	(49%)	Trump	155,975	(46%) Johnson	13,080 (4%)

New London, Norwich: When Puritans from Massachusetts and England arrived in eastern Connecticut, the flinty hills were the home of small Indian tribes, whose numbers had been decimated by warfare and even more by disease. Factories quickly developed around mills in little villages on the fast-flowing Quinebaug and Shetucket rivers. Soon, New London and Norwich were among the 13 colonies' leading workshops and ports. The infamous plot of Connecticut native Benedict Arnold to deliver West Point in New York to the British was uncovered during the American Revolution, but his company did succeed in burning New London to the ground in 1781 and sacking Fort Griswold. The region's deep vein of human industriousness sustained it into the 20th century, when new technology took over in shaping the area. Four nuclear power plants were built here, more than in any other place in the nation. In Groton, the "Submarine Capital of the World" situated across the Thames River from New London, General Dynamics' Electric Boat company built its first submarines in 1915 and, later, nuclear subs.

The reductions in military spending following the end of the Cold War were painful for the region and the long-term survival of the facility was in doubt. But Congress provided a jolt of additional spending and the Navy chose Electric Boat to be the prime contractor for the new Virginia class of at least nine ballistic-missile submarines. In December 2019, the Navy announced a $22 billion contract with Electric Boat and its Virginia-based partner, Newport News Shipbuilding. The workforce at Groton and a related facility in Quonset Point, Rhode Island, which was 17,000 in 2019, was expected to peak at 20,000 in 2030. The shipyard, which is undergoing a nearly $1 billion expansion, also is planning construction of the larger, next-generation Columbia-class attack submarines. Nearby, construction is planned for a $100 million national Coast Guard museum on the New London downtown waterfront.

The area's economic base has relied heavily on entertainment, specifically gambling. The Foxwoods Resort Casino, built by the 650-member Mashantucket Pequot tribe, once was the largest casino in the Western Hemisphere. But its number of employees dropped from 10,500 to 5,000 in

March 2020, when the resort was shut down by the pandemic. In nearby Uncasville is the Mohegan Sun casino, with a slightly smaller payroll. Concerned about competition from a new MGM casino in Springfield Massachusetts, the two tribes won approval for a new casino across the border in East Windsor, Connecticut. MGM challenged the action as a violation of the tribes' earlier agreement with Connecticut and said that it would create illegal monopoly power.

The 2nd Congressional District includes most of the eastern half of the state, centering on the small cities of New London and Norwich and including mill towns and the University of Connecticut in Storrs. The district stretches west to the outskirts of Hartford and to antique-filled small towns like Essex and Old Lyme on Long Island Sound. For many years, this was a politically marginal district, with close battles between Yankee Republicans and Catholic Democrats. The 49%-46% margin for Hillary Clinton in 2016, which was 10 points less than Barack Obama's 56%-43% local win in 2012, made the 2nd District her lowest performance in the state. In 2020, Joe Biden restored the vote for Democrats to nearly its level in 2012.

Rosa DeLauro (D)

Elected 1990, 16th term, b. Mar 02, 1943; New Haven, CT; Queen Mary College - London School of Economics, 1963; Marymount College, B.A., 1964; Columbia University, M.A., 1966; Roman Catholic; Married (Stanley Greenberg); 3 children; 4 grandchildren.

Professional Career: Executive Assistant, New Haven Mayor Frank Logue, 1976-1977; Executive Assistant & develop. admin., City of New Haven, 1977-1979; Chief of Staff, U.S. Sen. Christopher Dodd, 1981-1987; Executive Director, Countdown '87, 1987-1988; Executive Director, EMILY's List, 1989-1990.

DC Office: 2413 RHOB 20515, 202-225-3661, Fax: 202-225-4890, delauro.house.gov

State Offices: Derby, 203-735-5005; Naugatuck, 203-729-0204; New Haven, 203-562-3718.

Committees: *Appropriations (Chmn)*: Ex Officio membership on all subcommittees.

Group Ratings

	ADA	ACLU	AFL-CIO	LCV	COC	HAFA	ACU	CFG	FRC
2020	**	81%	**	100%	-	0%	4%	**	-
2019	90%	C	100%	97%	52%	C	4%	13%	0%

Almanac Ratings 2019-2020

	Economy	Social	Foreign	Composite
Liberal	100%	100%	92%	98%
Conservative	0%	0%	8%	2%

Key Votes of the 116th Congress

1. U.S./Mex./Can. trade deal	Y	5. Russia sanctions	Y
2. First Coronavirus response	Y	6. Troops in Syria	Y
3. HEROES Act	Y	7. Veto arms sales to Saudis	Y
4. CASH Act	Y	8. Defense $$$, veto override	Y

9. Firearms background checks	Y
10. Spending at the border	N
11. Marijuana liberalized rules	Y
12. Electoral College objections	N

Election Results

Election	Name (Party)	Vote (%)		Cand. Spent	Ind. Exp. Support	Ind. Exp. Oppose
2020 General	Rosa DeLauro (D)............................	203,265	(59%)	$1,387,044	$175,623	
	Margaret Streicker (R)................	137,598	(40%)	$1,868,938		$135,413

Prior winning percentages: 2018 (65%), 2016 (69%), 2014 (67%), 2012 (75%), 2010 (64%), 2008 (77%), 2006 (76%), 2004 (72%), 2002 (66%), 2000 (72%), 1998 (71%), 1996 (71%), 1994 (68%), 1992 (66%), 1990 (52%)

Rosa DeLauro capped a long career as a Democratic activist by taking over in January 2021 as chair of the House Appropriations Committee. First elected in 1990, after serving in top staff positions on and off Capitol Hill, she has been an outspoken liberal and a party leader on health and food safety issues. As a confidant of Speaker Nancy Pelosi and a shrewd strategist with deep knowledge of program details and finances, DeLauro had a prime seat at the Democratic leadership table long before she took the Appropriations gavel.

DeLauro grew up in New Haven's Wooster Square and has been well-connected politically. Both of her parents were New Haven aldermen. Her mother, Luisa DeLauro, served 35 years, the longest tenure in New Haven history. In Wooster Square Park, a granite monument of a table, bench and two chairs honors the family's home as a social services center. Rosa DeLauro's husband, Stanley Greenberg, has been a pollster for many leading Democrats.

DeLauro has been in politics nearly all her life. She was a development administrator in New Haven in the 1970s, chief of staff to Democratic Sen. Christopher Dodd from 1980 to 1987, then spent a year working to stop U.S. military aid to Nicaraguan contras before she became director of EMILY's List, the women's campaign fundraising group that supports abortion rights. When the 3rd District seat opened in 1990, DeLauro prevailed 52%-48% over anti-tax and anti-abortion Republican state Sen. Tom Scott. She has not faced serious competition since 1992, when she won a rematch against Scott, 66%-34%. Her reelection in 2020 with 59 percent was her lowest vote since she was first elected.

DeLauro is one of the Democratic leadership's most vocal champions in debate. Pelosi in 2011 admiringly described her as "a force of nature." She is an active and ardent supporter of feminist causes. A cancer survivor, she sponsored the law to require that patients and doctors, not insurance companies, decide on 48-hour hospital stays for mastectomies. She lobbied for insurance coverage of early-detection tests for cervical cancer, and helped to enact "Johanna's Law" to increase awareness of gynecological cancers.

In 2009, the House passed her bill, the Lilly Ledbetter Fair Pay Act, which extended the statute of limitations for women alleging wage discrimination, reversing a Supreme Court decision. In March 2019, the House passed for the third time her Paycheck Fairness Act, which closed loopholes in the Equal Pay Act of 1963. "So many Americans are stuck in jobs that do not pay them enough to live on," DeLauro said. "It's not a partisan issue. It is a matter of right and wrong, and simple fairness." In response to the coronavirus pandemic, she introduced with Sen. Patty Murray a bill to guarantee paid sick leave to all workers. Democratic Rep. Lois Frankel called DeLauro the "Godmother of pay equity."

When Democrats regained House control in 2019, DeLauro took charge of the Appropriations Subcommittee on Labor, Health and Human Services and Education, a position she called "a dream come true." Serving as the House's chief spender on those programs was "my heart and soul," she told The Connecticut Post. She was outspoken in opposing cuts in education programs that were proposed by President Donald Trump. In 2017, DeLauro authored a book about her experiences in seeking to preserve the social safety net for the poor — The Least Among Us: Waging the Battle for the Vulnerable.

As a former chair of the Appropriations Subcommittee on Agriculture, Rural Development, Food and Drug Administration, DeLauro retained a keen interest in food safety, which she said should have the same priority as prescription drug and medical device safety. She said that the FDA was "badly broken" and faulted the Obama administration for not doing enough to address the problems. In 2018, she called for an investigation of the regulation of laboratory-grown meats.

In an often testy clash with President Barack Obama during his final two years in office, DeLauro was a leader among House Democrats in siding with unions to oppose the proposed Trans-Pacific Partnership trade agreement that the United States was negotiating with 11 nations. Despite the prospect of lower tariffs, her greater concern was that the deal would kill good-paying jobs. It was vital, she said, that "everyone who works hard and plays by the rules has a chance to succeed."

When Trump took office and withdrew the United States from the deal, and subsequently moved to revise the North American Free Trade Agreement with Mexico and Canada, DeLauro found herself in an unusual alliance. She supported Trump's revisions and was tapped by Pelosi to work in the House to resolve final details on enforcement of the revised agreement—DeLauro's first vote for a trade deal in more than 20 years.

As co-chair of the Steering and Policy Committee for many years, DeLauro was instrumental in advising on committee assignments for countless House Democrats. She has "an encyclopedic knowledge of members' committee aspirations," Pelosi said. In return, DeLauro remained an avid booster of Pelosi's continuation as the top House Democrat, despite growing restiveness in the Democratic Caucus. "You want the attributes of intellectual capacity, strategic acumen, compassion and core values. Add to that a spine of steel," DeLauro told The Connecticut Post.

In winning Democratic Caucus support for the Appropriations chairmanship, she was challenged by two other veteran members of the committee: Marcy Kaptur of Ohio, who withdrew prior to the Caucus vote, and Debbie Wasserman Schultz of Florida. The latter advocated increased openness and other reforms of the spending process. DeLauro—who reportedly won, 148-79—was endorsed by the leaders of many liberal groups and constituencies within the Democratic Party. As the committee chair, she succeeded Nita Lowey of New York, who retired.

The fact that those committee leaders—plus Pelosi, a former Appropriations member—have all been women offers useful insight into the evolution of the Democratic Caucus. Earlier in her career, DeLauro ran twice for chairwoman of the Democratic Caucus and suffered two painfully close setbacks. In 1998, she lost 108-97 to Martin Frost of Texas. In 2002, she lost 104-103 to Robert Menendez of New Jersey after an intense yearlong contest. In 2004, DeLauro led the drafting of the Democratic platform when John Kerry was nominated for president. She remained an influential voice in the national party on platform fights and other policy conflicts among Democrats, with her skillful blend of policy and politics.

At home, DeLauro faced a competitive reelection challenge in 2020 from Margaret Streicker, a real-estate developer making her first bid for elected office. She described herself as a business-oriented moderate who would not be a "blind follower" of President Donald Trump. Streicker outspent the incumbent, $1.9 million to $1.4 million. In her 59%-40% win, DeLauro led in the eight largest cities and towns in the district, though Streicker took 12 of the 25 communities.

Working closely with the Biden administration and a closely divided Congress, DeLauro moved quickly in 2021 on a new round of economic stimulus plus a reshaping of spending priorities. She was instrumental in increasing the amount of the child tax credit in that measure—which many Democrats cited as a historic social-policy measure. With the selection of DeLauro, Democrats from western New England chaired three powerful House committees. Richard Neal and Jim McGovern, both from Massachusetts, chaired the Ways and Means and Rules committees.

CT-3: South Central Connecticut   Cook Partisan Voting Index: D+8

Population		Race and Ethnicity		Income	
Total	717,989	White	71.50%	Median Income	$70,574
Land area (sq. miles)	470	Black	15.50%	District Income Rank	159
Pop/ sq mi	1,526.53	Latino	16.70%	Poverty Rate	10.80%
Born in State	59.80%	Asian	4.20%	With health insurance	94.50%
		Two or more races	3.20%	Cash public assistance	2.80%
Age Groups		Other	5.60%	Food stamp/SNAP	12.60%
Under 18	18.70%				
18-34	24.00%	**Education**		**Work**	
35-64	39.80%	H.S grad or less	40.70%	White Collar	42.60%
Over 64	17.60%	Some college	23.30%	Sales and Service	38.80%
		College Degree, 4 yr	19.00%	Blue Collar	18.60%
Military		Post grad	17.00%	Government	13.10%
Veteran/ Active Duty	5.20%				

2020 Pres. Vote	Biden	212,318	(60%)	Trump	137,581	(39%)		
2016 Pres. Vote	Clinton	179,832	(56%)	Trump	129,968	(40%)	Johnson	7,628	(2%)

New Haven: The New Haven Colony was founded in 1637 by a group of Puritan settlers who opted to bypass the Massachusetts Bay Colony after concluding the religious practices near Boston weren't strict enough. Their new colony was successful and grew rapidly. More than 150 years later, a young Yale graduate named Eli Whitney won an order from the young U.S. government to produce 10,000 muskets at $13.40 each. Whitney had invented the cotton gin six years earlier, which had embroiled him in a lengthy patent suit. He was determined to make a quick profit on the musket contract, so he set up a system of interchangeable parts and invented a milling machine and gauges: the birth of standardized American manufacturing. For the next 150 years or so, New Haven mass-produced rifles, clocks, locks, hardware and toys—anything its tinkerers and entrepreneurs could fashion. Today, few factories remain in New Haven. The factory that produced Winchester rifles and guns for 140 years closed in 2006. Southern Connecticut around New Haven discovered a new source of prosperity in scores of small technology and biomedical firms. Although the area's defense contracts are modest compared with those of the city's heyday, Stratford-based Sikorsky

Aircraft envisioned 8,000 employees and a doubling of its spending by 2032, chiefly on the King Stallion heavy-lift cargo helicopter for the Marine Corps. The company, whose prestige product is the presidential helicopter for the White House, has numerous deals overseas.

With significant crime rates and many neighborhoods scarred by abandoned homes, the population of New Haven has shrunk. In 2019, it had 130,000 people, down from 164,000 in 1950 but little-changed in the past 40 years. The city has roughly equal shares of Blacks, whites and Hispanics. Yale University, with its Gothic spires and red-brick halls, has always been the visual focus of New Haven and it has become its largest employer. In recent years, Yale provided 60 percent of the city's economic development. Local revival was sparked by a state development program that turned old retail and office buildings into residences and by $1 billion in investments by biotech firms. Racial minorities and immigrants have had an influential voice in New Haven. In 2020, the city council was one of several in Connecticut that officially declared racism a public health crisis.

The 3rd Congressional District covers the New Haven metropolitan area and extends to the outskirts of the former industrial cities of Bridgeport, Waterbury and Meriden. The suburb of Hamden has made it onto the CNN Money list of the 100 best places to live. Politically, the 3rd was once a marginal district, regularly changing partisan hands in the 1980s. It has become strongly Democratic, though with a recent twist. President Barack Obama got 63 percent of the vote in each of his campaigns. Hillary Clinton got only 56 percent in 2016, though Joe Biden split the difference with 60 percent of the vote in the 3rd District. By contrast, the Democratic presidential vote in the adjacent 4th District, which is more upscale, rose from 55 percent in 2012 to 64 percent in 2020.

Jim Himes (D)

Elected 2008, 7th term, b. Jul 05, 1966; Lima, Peru; Harvard University, B.A., 1988; Oxford University, M.Phil, 1990; Presbyterian; Married (Mary Himes); 2 children.

Elected Office: Greenwich Board of Estimate & Taxation, 2006-2007.

Professional Career: Financial analyst & Vice President., Goldman Sachs, 1990-2002; Chairman, Greenwich Housing Authority, 2003-2006; Vice President., Enterprise Community Partners, 2004-2008.

DC Office: 1227 LHOB 20515, 202-225-5541, Fax: 202-225-9629, himes.house.gov

State Offices: Bridgeport, 866-453-0028; Stamford, 203-353-9400.

Committees: *Financial Services*: Investor Protection, Entrepreneurship & Capital Markets; Nat'l Security, International Development & Monetary Policy (Chmn); Task Force on Financial Technology. *Permanent Select on Intelligence*: Defense Intelligence & Warfighter Support; Strategic Technologies & Advanced Research.

Group Ratings

	ADA	ACLU	AFL-CIO	LCV	COC	HAFA	ACU	CFG	FRC
2020	**	79%	**	100%	-	0%	6%	**	-
2019	90%	C	100%	97%	66%	C	7%	12%	0%

Almanac Ratings 2019-2020

	Economy	Social	Foreign	Composite
Liberal	100%	100%	80%	94%
Conservative	0%	0%	20%	6%

Key Votes of the 116th Congress

1. U.S./Mex./Can. trade deal Y	5. Russia sanctions Y	9. Firearms background checks Y
2. First Coronavirus response Y	6. Troops in Syria Y	10. Spending at the border Y
3. HEROES Act Y	7. Veto arms sales to Saudis Y	11. Marijuana liberalized rules Y
4. CASH Act Y	8. Defense $$$, veto override Y	12. Electoral College objections N

Election Results

Election	Name (Party)	Vote (%)		Cand. Spent	Ind. Exp. Support	Ind. Exp. Oppose
2020 General	Jim Himes (D).....................................	224,432	(62%)	$983,543	$123	
	Jonathan Riddle (R)............................	130,627	(36%)	$14,727		$113

Prior winning percentages: 2018 (61%), 2016 (60%), 2014 (54%), 2012 (60%), 2010 (53%), 2008 (51%)

Jim Himes, a Democrat elected in 2008, is a former investment banker who puts his understanding of Wall Street to use at the Financial Services Committee and in conversations with colleagues. Given the growing hostility of many Democrats to deep-pocket financiers, his influence in the Democratic Caucus has faced some limitations. Himes has asserted himself on other issues, such as guns and national security, and by using his seat on the Intelligence Committee as an early advocate to impeach President Donald Trump. Democrats' recapture of the House majority brought the arrival of numerous like-minded business-friendly colleagues to power their House majority.

Though he represents one of the wealthiest areas of the country, Himes grew up in different surroundings. Born in Lima Peru, he spent his early years in Peru and Colombia, where his father worked for the Ford Foundation. He speaks fluent Spanish and maintains a deep interest in Latin America. Himes earned his undergraduate degree from Harvard University and was a Rhodes Scholar at Oxford. Working for Goldman Sachs as a financial analyst on Sept. 11, 2001, he was at his office in Lower Manhattan and did volunteer work with ambulance crews. After 12 years with Goldman, he joined Enterprise Community Partners, a nonprofit dedicated to alleviating urban poverty.

Living in Greenwich, Himes chaired the town Democratic committee. He was a campaign volunteer in 2006 for Democrat Diane Farrell, who finished about 7,000 votes behind Rep. Christopher Shays, a moderate Republican who was a frequent Democratic target. The following April, he announced his own challenge against Shays. Himes set a torrid fundraising pace, aided in large measure by his Wall Street connections. He attempted to link Shays and the George W. Bush administration on the Iraq war. In 2008, the enthusiasm for Barack Obama provided a powerful final push that gave Himes a 51%-48% win. He comfortably took the district's urban centers and was competitive in the affluent suburbs.

Himes has taken a centrist approach in Congress, supporting major Democratic priorities but also asserting his independence. In 2012, he was one of 22 Democrats who supported a failed amendment to implement the recommendations of the Simpson-Bowles deficit reduction commission.

On the Financial Services Committee, when the panel took up what became the sweeping Dodd-Frank financial overhaul bill, he helped craft a provision regulating the complex financial instruments known as derivatives. Consumer advocates accused Himes and other centrist Democrats of watering down derivatives controls passed by the Senate in an effort to appease Wall Street. Himes argued that the bill took significant steps to crack down on abuses at investment firms. "He can explain things like derivatives and credit default swaps in plain English so [members] can have some degree of fluency in this, which is extremely helpful," fellow Connecticut Democrat Joe Courtney told the Connecticut Post.

Himes has worked on national security issues at the Select Intelligence Committee, and filed a bill that states that only Congress has the power to declare and wage war. Under Republican control, he said that the panel had become "not functional," in its failure to adequately investigate Russian interference in the 2016 election. When Democrats won House control, he voiced interest in chairing the Intelligence panel. But Rep. Adam Schiff of California had locked up that assignment. Instead, Himes became chairman of the Strategic Technologies and Advanced Research Subcommittee, which oversees new tools for intelligence collection.

In June 2019, breaking with Speaker Nancy Pelosi and Democratic leaders, he became the first House member from Connecticut to call for an impeachment inquiry of Trump. From the start of his presidency, Himes told the House, "this president has shown contempt for the truth, has attacked our institutions and has ignored the Constitution he swore to defend."

Following the 2014 election, Himes failed in his bid to be Pelosi's choice to chair the Democratic Congressional Campaign Committee. An anti-Wall Street activist praised Pelosi for "rejecting the Wall Street wing of the Democratic Party." After the 2016 election, he became chairman of the House's New Democrat Coalition, a self-described "fiscally responsible, moderate bloc of lawmakers."

He urged Democrats to remain mindful of the centrist voters whose support they would need to win House control. After Democrats regained House control, he told Business Insider that—despite news-media attention to the young firebrands—the result has been "a caucus that is more centrist, more pragmatic, maybe even slightly right shifted relative to when we were in the minority."

Himes has occasionally voiced his frustration with Congress, including its failure to deal with gun violence. Following the mass shooting in Las Vegas in 2017, Himes wrote that instead of responding to strong public support for action, "an impotent Congress will hold a moment of silence, and an uninterested president will order flags flown at half-mast and make a show of a somber visit to the scene of the latest crime."

Himes has become entrenched in what had been a solidly Republican seat. In 2010, Himes portrayed state Sen. Dan Debicella as an extremist and won 53%-47%. Debicella tried again in 2014, and Himes won 54%-46%. He got 71 percent in Bridgeport and Norwalk, which cast 21 percent of the total vote. Debicella's success with the upscale vote was not enough to overcome the urban support for Himes. In 2020, when Himes locked down the district with his best-ever 62 percent of the vote, he won all but three hill towns in the district.

CT-4: Southwest Connecticut   **Cook Partisan Voting Index: D+12**

Population		Race and Ethnicity		Income	
Total	737,733	White	72.30%	Median Income	$101,646
Land area (sq. miles)	461	Black	12.40%	District Income Rank	30
Pop/ sq mi	1,601.23	Latino	20.80%	Poverty Rate	9.60%
Born in State	42.00%	Asian	5.50%	With health insurance	90.80%
		Two or more races	3.60%	Cash public assistance	1.90%
Age Groups		Other	6.30%	Food stamp/SNAP	8.70%
Under 18	23.40%				
18-34	20.10%	**Education**		**Work**	
35-64	40.60%	H.S grad or less	29.20%	White Collar	50.00%
Over 64	15.80%	Some college	18.20%	Sales and Service	35.90%
		College Degree, 4 yr	29.00%	Blue Collar	14.10%
Military		Post grad	23.60%	Government	8.70%
Veteran/ Active Duty	3.80%				

2020 Pres. Vote	Biden	237,245	(64%)	Trump	127,566	(34%)		
2016 Pres. Vote	Clinton	195,494	(60%)	Trump	119,976	(37%)	Johnson	9,144 (3%)

Bridgeport, Stamford: No one in colonial America imagined that southern Connecticut would someday lodge one of the largest concentrations of wealth in the world. The soil was stony, the terrain unaccommodating and the harbors not as convenient as those in New York, Rhode Island and Massachusetts. For 200 years, this was the home of unnoticed Yankee farmers, sailors and tinkerers. After rich New Yorkers began taking the train north to country houses in Connecticut, in the 20th century Greenwich and other Yankee villages clustered around commuter railroad stations became the home of New York's elite.

Starting in the 1950s, New York City-based executives, eager to minimize their commutes and avoid New York's income taxes, moved their headquarters to Greenwich and farther into Fairfield County. Greenwich, sometimes referred to as "Wall Street by the Sea" for its proliferation of hedge fund offices and financial firms, is closest to New York and commands the highest commercial rents of all these places. But not all is well in the corporate suites: General Electric, which has been headquartered in Fairfield and has had its own problems, relocated its headquarters to Boston—in part, to escape high taxes. Many of the hedge funds and other corporate offices downsized after the financial crash in 2008 and the Great Recession. Real estate prices cooled and never fully recovered, even in Greenwich. But help came from an unexpected source: The coronavirus pandemic led many wealthy residents of New York City to escape its crowded streets and office buildings. Fairfield became a popular alternative. "Moves from New York City to Connecticut have more than doubled" from a year earlier, The Wall Street Journal reported in July 2020.

The 4th Congressional District is the wealthiest district in one of the nation's wealthiest states. The district covers most of the southwest corner of Connecticut along Long Island Sound, from industrial Bridgeport, now the state's largest city, to affluent Greenwich. The district's waterfront towns include bustling and pricey Stamford, woodsy Darien, modest Norwalk, artsy-craftsy Westport, and Fairfield. In low-income Bridgeport, some downtown revitalization accompanied the state-financed Harbor Yard sports complex. In 2019, a study by the Federal Reserve Bank found that the county was the metropolitan area with the highest income inequality in both 1980 and 2015.

Still, even wealthy sites have needs. In July 2019, a federal judge dismissed objections to the $1.1 billion project in Norwalk to replace the swing Walk Bridge, which was built in the 19th century to accommodate ships with tall masts. The Norwalk bridge is one of four movable bridges on the main rail line to New Haven, all in need of major repair and relocated tracks, especially with expected increased ridership in coming decades. Offshore, state officials selected Bridgeport as the staging area for a $900 million wind turbine project, which was expected to provide half of the state's wind power.

For many years, the heavily affluent suburbs outvoted Bridgeport and elected moderate-to-liberal Republicans such as Clare Boothe Luce, Lowell Weicker and Christopher Shays to Congress. But the influence of Christian conservatives in the national GOP repelled local Episcopalians and other mainline Protestants, and they have been increasingly voting Democratic. At the same time, the district has been diversifying. It has become only 62 percent non-Hispanic white, the lowest percentage in the state, with the largest share of Latinos. Joe Biden in 2020 got 64 percent, his best district in the state.

Jahana Hayes (D)

Elected 2018, 2nd term, b. Mar 08, 1973; Waterbury, CT; Naugatuck Valley Community College; Southern CT State University, B.S., 2005; University of Saint Joseph, M.A., 2012; Methodist; Married (Milford Hayes); 4 children.

Professional Career: High School History Teacher, 2004-2018.
DC Office: 1415 LHOB 20515, 202-225-4476
State Offices: Waterbury, 860-223-8412.

Committees: *Agriculture*: Livestock & Foreign Agriculture; Subcommittee Nutrition, Oversight & Department Operations (Chmn). *Education & Labor*: Civil Rights & Human Services; Early Childhood, Elementary & Secondary Education.

Almanac Ratings 2019-2020

	Economy	Social	Foreign	Composite
Liberal	100%	100%	80%	94%
Conservative	0%	0%	20%	6%

Key Votes of the 116th Congress

1. U.S./Mex./Can. trade deal Y	5. Russia sanctions Y	9. Firearms background checks Y
2. First Coronavirus response Y	6. Troops in Syria Y	10. Spending at the border Y
3. HEROES Act Y	7. Veto arms sales to Saudis Y	11. Marijuana liberalized rules Y
4. CASH Act Y	8. Defense $$$, veto override Y	12. Electoral College objections N

Election Results

Election	Name (Party)	Vote (%)		Cand. Spent	Ind. Exp. Support	Ind. Exp. Oppose
2020 General	Jahana Hayes (D).......................... 192,484	(55%)	$1,499,843	$5,105	$35,047
	David Sullivan (R)........................ 151,988	(43%)	$422,519	$20,138	$113

Prior winning percentages: 2018 (56%)

Democrat Jahana Hayes scored one of the big upsets of 2018 when she took this Democratic-leaning seat, chiefly by winning the primary against an opponent backed by the party establishment. Hayes, a first-time candidate, had been best-known for winning the national Teacher of the Year award in 2016. Embracing the policy goals of national progressive activists, she became the first

African-American Democrat to win a congressional seat in Connecticut. In contrast to some other House newcomers, Hayes kept a low profile as she sought to learn the ropes—including from influential home-state Democrats.

Hayes, a native of Waterbury, grew up in public housing. "Her family struggled with addiction, relied on public assistance and at one point lost their apartment," according to her campaign bio. For Hayes, the cycle of poverty intensified when she was pregnant at age 17 and became a single mother. With encouragement from friends, she enrolled in a local community college, got her bachelor's degree at Southern Connecticut State University, plus graduate degrees from the University of Saint Joseph and University of Bridgeport. She won plaudits as a social studies teacher at a high school in Waterbury. Meanwhile, she married a local police detective and became the mother of four children.

At the White House ceremony where she received her national award, Hayes was so enthusiastic that she continued clapping while President Barack Obama voiced his tribute to her. "You can't be great if you're not enthusiastic," Obama cheerfully ad libbed.

When Democratic Rep. Elizabeth Esty decided in April 2018 not to seek reelection following criticism of her handling of sexual-abuse charges against the top aide in her congressional office, local Democratic leaders rallied around Mary Glassman, a former town official. When Hayes expressed interest in running, they told her she had no chance of winning. Glassman narrowly got the endorsement of the Democratic convention, which was controlled by those leaders.

"People told me I had no chance and I had no business trying to do this," Hayes later said. She pressed ahead to the primary, with backing from national progressive groups, including teachers unions and supporters of Sen. Bernie Sanders's 2016 presidential campaign. Sen. Chris Murphy, who earlier held the House seat, privately encouraged and advised Hayes.

With campaign funds nearly equal to the amount raised by Glassman, Hayes ran ads in the relatively inexpensive market featuring Obama and her high school students. Her personal appeal clicked with the voters, as Hayes won the primary, 62%-38%. She ran strongly in the old urban areas of the district, with 80 percent of the vote in Waterbury, and at least 60 percent in each of the other cities: New Britain, Meriden and Danbury. Perhaps surprisingly, she also won many of the aristocratic country towns in Litchfield County.

In November, Republican Manny Santos, a native of Portugal, had a potentially appealing story as an immigrant, a Marine veteran and the former mayor of Meriden. But he had scant financing and received little attention from the national GOP in what has occasionally been a battleground district.

Hayes was one of three racial-minority women from the Northeast who in 2018 won House districts that had been held by white Democrats. The other two—Alexandria Ocasio-Cortez of New York and Ayanna Pressley of Massachusetts—defeated veteran incumbents in Democratic primaries. Running in more media-centered urban districts, they sought—and received—far more publicity than did Hayes, who was more of a team player for House Democrats. The contrasts were not only stylistic, but also reflected their very different districts. For her part, Hayes could not take reelection for granted.

Not surprisingly, the former school teacher was assigned to the Education and Labor Committee. She filed legislation to create a $1 billion program to encourage school buses that are powered by electricity. "It is absolutely essential that we invest in updating our national school bus fleet to protect our students and ecosystem," she testified on behalf of her bill.

With a few exceptions, Hayes did not seek attention. In a profile that was headlined, "Jahana Hayes quietly making a statement in Washington," the Connecticut Post described her as "one of the quieter members of a diverse, assertive and independent freshman class of House Democrats." In the news article, she said, "There's been a lot of attention that I don't think I was prepared for."

Behind closed doors, Hayes occasionally made her presence known, especially on topics that might affect her political fortune. When some House Democrats pressed to impeach President Donald Trump, Hayes joined a group of Democrats who urged caution, including a limited set of charges. "I do have concerns for where this is going," she told the Middletown Press in September 2019. "I represent a lot of people who did not vote for me and a lot of people who still don't support impeachment and I need to hear from them as well."

In her initial reelection bid, Hayes faced Republican David Sullivan, who had recently retired after 30 years as a federal prosecutor and ran as a "law and order" candidate who occasionally distanced himself from President Donald Trump. Hayes spent more than three times what Sullivan spent. The outcome was similar to Hayes' initial campaign. She won, 55%-43%. She had a double-digit lead in each of the eight largest cities and towns.

CT-5: Western and Central Connecticut

Cook Partisan Voting Index: D+2

Population		Race and Ethnicity		Income	
Total	704,837	White	75.50%	Median Income	$73,616
Land area (sq. miles)	1,248	Black	8.00%	District Income Rank	139
Pop/ sq mi	564.7	Latino	20.30%	Poverty Rate	11.40%
Born in State	54.60%	Asian	4.20%	With health insurance	94.00%
		Two or more races	4.10%	Cash public assistance	2.90%
Age Groups		Other	8.20%	Food stamp/SNAP	12.30%
Under 18	20.50%				
18-34	21.30%	**Education**		**Work**	
35-64	39.40%	H.S grad or less	39.10%	White Collar	41.60%
Over 64	18.70%	Some college	24.70%	Sales and Service	38.90%
		College Degree, 4 yr	20.80%	Blue Collar	19.60%
Military		Post grad	15.40%	Government	13.00%
Veteran/ Active Duty	5.30%				

2020 Pres. Vote	Biden	196,119	(55%)	Trump	157,881	(44%)		
2016 Pres. Vote	Clinton	161,142	(50%)	Trump	147,901	(46%)	Johnson	9,356 (3%)

Waterbury, Danbury, New Britain: Over the years, Connecticut's stony soil has become home to some of the most affluent people in the world. This is true in the hills of northwest Connecticut, distant from the interstates and from Connecticut's small urban capital of Hartford. In Litchfield County are exquisite Yankee towns like Washington and Kent, where Connecticut's ship owners once invested their accumulated capital in factories and mills. They now are considered the "anti-Hamptons," a weekend country-home mecca for ultra-rich New Yorkers seeking to avoid the glitz of Southampton and East Hampton. In towns that feature new money, Avon and Simsbury have become comfortable bedroom communities to Hartford.

Not far away are grittier parts, small industrial cities such as New Britain, America's ball-bearing capital for years; Meriden, which turned from making ivory combs, clocks and cutlery to producing electrical signaling equipment, biotech filters and nuclear instruments; and Waterbury, once the nation's largest producer of brass. Like many manufacturing centers, these towns have fallen on hard times, though there have been recovery efforts. Danbury, once the nation's leading producer of hats, has become a center for clean energy technology.

East of Danbury is the small town of Newtown, where gunman Adam Lanza shocked the nation and ignited debates—but little action—over gun control, care for the mentally ill and the marketing of violence to the young when he killed 26 people, 20 of them children, at Sandy Hook Elementary School, in 2012. The old building was demolished out of respect for the victims, and a new school opened in 2016.

In 2020, the social unrest across the nation found its way to some of these places. In Waterbury, protestors citing systemic racism beheaded a statue of Christopher Columbus outside of City Hall. A month later, in New Britain, protestors objected that another statue of Columbus was offensive to Native Americans and Latinos; local Italian Americans defended Columbus.

The 5th Congressional District of Connecticut covers much of the northwestern corner of the state, including the northern towns of Fairfield County. It has two arms that reach into the hills of central Connecticut—one to Democratic Meriden and the other to the affluent and Republican-leaning Farmington Valley suburbs of Hartford. It has been a Democratic-leaning district, but Republicans have become competitive here. After the margin for Hillary Clinton fell to 50%-46%, Joe Biden took a more comfortable 55%-44% win.

DELAWARE

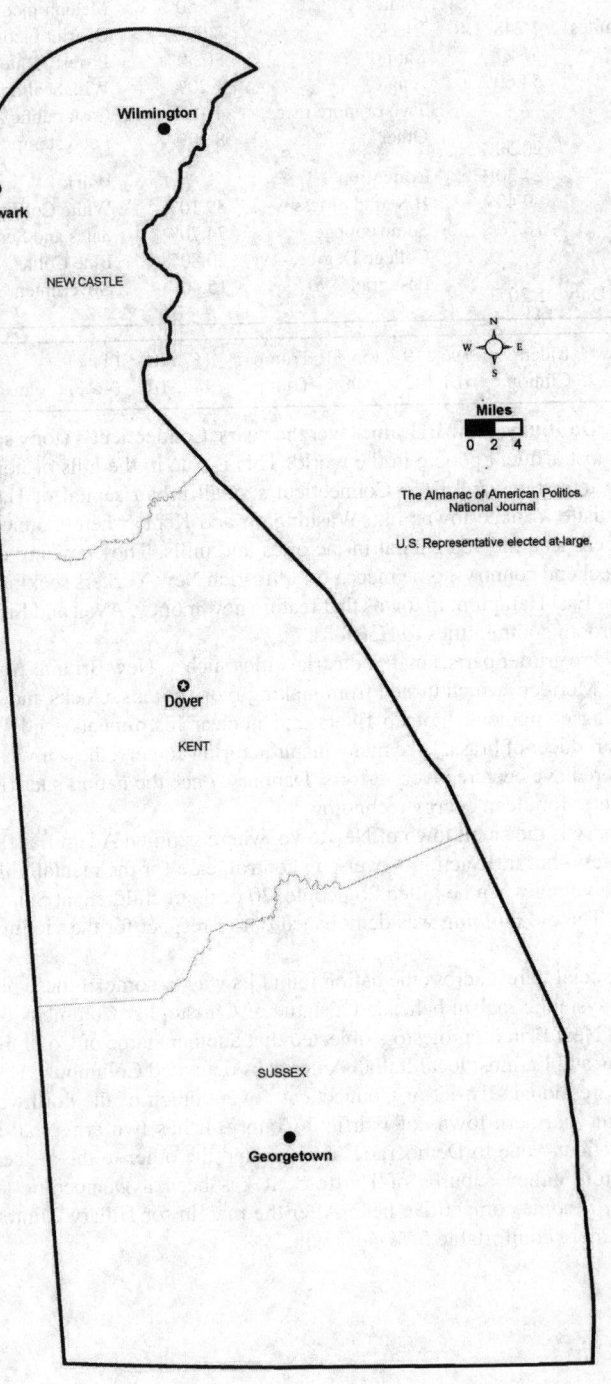

Wilmington

Newark

NEW CASTLE

N
W · E
S

Miles
0 2 4

The Almanac of American Politics.
National Journal

U.S. Representative elected at-large.

Dover

KENT

SUSSEX

Georgetown

When the media declared Joe Biden the president-elect on Nov. 7, Delaware celebrated the election of the state's first president. "That's right, the guy you saw eating breakfast at Kozy Korner diner, waiting in line at Pep Boys, shopping at Janssen's Market or bowing in prayer at St. Joseph on the Brandywine is about to be commander-in-chief," the News Journal, Delaware's leading newspaper, wrote. Biden's long-sought ascendancy to the White House coincides with the state's increasing turn toward the Democratic Party. In 2018, the last GOP-held statewide office fell to the Democrats, marking the first time in almost five decades that either party managed to hold every Delaware statewide office. And in 2020, Biden joined the party's nominees for governor, Senate, and House in clearing 58 percent of the vote.

On Dec. 7, 1787, 30 Delawareans met at the Golden Fleece Tavern in Dover and voted unanimously to ratify the Constitution. And thus, the second smallest state in area became, as it likes to boast, the First State. This small corner of America has a long history. The mouth of the Delaware River was explored by Henry Hudson, and the Dutch and Swedes built settlements on the west bank in the 1630s. But the three counties of Delaware owe their separate existence to the politics of the proprietors of William Penn's colony to the north and to Delawareans' determination—even before July 4, 1776—to declare independence not only from Britain but also from Pennsylvania. Well-preserved 18th century buildings line the streets of New Castle, the capital from 1704 to 1777; it is the home of the First State National Historical Park, a collection of vintage buildings dedicated by Obama in 2013, making Delaware the final state to secure a National Park Service unit.

Throughout most of its history, Delaware has been unusually affluent. Its income levels during the early 20th century were the nation's highest, and they remain close to the top today—Democratic dominance in the state is another indication that the Democratic Party has become the party of affluent suburbanites. The many members of the du Pont family maintain beautiful cobblestone mansions in its chateau country, and the charming Brandywine Valley, which spills across the 12-mile semicircular border with Pennsylvania, includes a trove of refined tourist attractions. The Mason-Dixon Line forms Delaware's western border with Maryland, and the state has both Northern and Southern heritages. It was still a slave state when the Civil War broke out, although 92 percent of its Blacks were free. Today, its population is 22 percent Black, well above the national average. On his train ride to Washington in January 2009, newly elected President Barack Obama, joined by native son Joe Biden, paid tribute to Delaware's Underground Railroad and diplomatically did not mention that Abraham Lincoln, during his 1861 train ride to Washington, decided not to risk a stop in slaveholding Delaware. It took until the Black Lives Matters protests in July 2020 for the state to remove its last whipping post from public display at the courthouse in Georgetown; until the practice was outlawed in 1972, whipping with a cat-o-nine-tails had been used on inmates, a disproportionate share of them Black.

Delaware's population grew by 18 percent in the 1990s, 15 percent from 2000 to 2010, 10 percent from 2010 to 2020. One reason has been a flow of retirees from Pennsylvania, Maryland and New Jersey; Delaware's percentage of senior citizens is tied for fifth in the nation. Another has been from immigrants employed in the beach-tourism industry (Biden has a home in Rehoboth Beach, a longtime summer haven for D.C.-area residents) and from Latino migrants working in 10 chicken plants downstate (which were hit hard during the coronavirus pandemic, first having to kill millions of birds during early public-health shutdowns, and then drawing criticism for inadequately protecting workers who returned to the production lines). The state is now 10 percent Hispanic, two points higher than neighboring Pennsylvania, and 4 percent Asian.

For much of the last two centuries, the central focus of Delaware's economy was the business started by Éleuthère Irénée du Pont, the practical-minded son of a dreamy, idealistic French immigrant. He built a gunpowder mill on the banks of Brandywine Creek in 1802—the first enterprise of the du Pont family. Over time it became one of America's great munitions and chemical companies. In the years on either side of World War II, DuPont prospered by bringing to the consumer and industrial markets new synthetics and plastics such as rayon, nylon, synthetic dyes, cellophane, Lucite, Teflon and Dacron: "Better Living Through Chemistry." At its peak, the company employed roughly one of every 10 workers in Delaware. But the company has undergone several rounds of belt-tightening, reducing its footprint in the state. The company temporarily merged with Dow Chemical, and after the merger ended in 2019, DuPont continued reassembling itself, with the goal of ultimately focusing more narrowly on electronics, advanced polymers, and construction.

Delaware has had an outsized impact on national policy. In the late 19th century, the state passed pioneering laws of incorporation, giving more flexibility and power to managers and owners. Most of the companies in the Fortune 500 and on the New York Stock Exchange and Nasdaq are incorporated in Delaware. Their legal births take place in a federal-style building near the capitol in Dover, which means that much of the nation's corporate law, especially on mergers and acquisitions, is made in Delaware's Chancery Court. Delaware also helped foster the credit card industry. In 1981, Republican Gov. Pete du Pont pushed through a law abolishing Delaware's usury laws and lowering its bank franchise tax. Inflation was high, and banks were looking for a state with no limit on interest rates to locate their credit card operations. MBNA Corp. moved there from Maryland in 1982, invented the affinity card in 1983, and became the nation's largest credit card issuer. Bank of America acquired MBNA in 2005. This turned Wilmington's downtown and waterfront prosperous, even as heavily minority neighborhoods of Wilmington remain desperately poor. One of Biden's few public visits during the coronavirus pandemic was to mark the death of George Floyd in Minneapolis; at the site of a recent Black Lives Matter protest, Biden called Floyd's death "an act of brutality so elemental it did more than deny one Black man in America his civil rights and human rights. It denied him of his very humanity and denied him of his life."

Delaware's state budget relies heavily on unconventional revenue streams that focus on out-of-state sources. Incorporation-related taxes account for an estimated 30 percent of the state's revenues, while something as mundane as repossession of unclaimed property accounts for 10 percent. The state also gets sizable revenues from turnpike tolls ($4 for just 11 miles on heavily trafficked I-95) and from the lottery and slot machines. Exporting taxes has allowed Delaware to be one of the five states with no sales tax, and its property taxes are among the nation's lowest. A bipartisan mix of governors has lowered the income tax several times. The state leaped at a new opportunity in 2018, when the U.S. Supreme Court allowed states to legalize sports betting; Delaware became the first state to allow it.

Democrats have gradually tightened their political control in the state. The state House turned Democratic in 2008, joining the state Senate and the governorship for unified governance. During this period, Delaware's Supreme Court abolished the death penalty, the state approved same-sex marriage and transgender rights, and Gov. Jack Markell signed a marijuana decriminalization bill. But Delaware elections are famously collegial, thanks to the state's small size. Historically, "the Delaware Way" has long prevailed—a habit of party establishments exerting tight control and minimizing ideological and personal conflicts. There's even a unique custom, dating back to 1792, of "Return Day." On the Thursday after an election, winning and losing candidates go to the Sussex County seat of Georgetown and ride together in carriages to receive the bipartisan cheers of the voters and, literally, bury a hatchet in a box of Lewes Beach sand.

Biden's presidential bid in 2020 drew unprecedented attention to the "Delaware Way," not all of it positive. On the upside, Biden regularly touted the approach as an antidote for the polarized politics of the Trump era, and said it was a course he aimed to follow. But critics across the ideological spectrum took potshots. The notion of cozy cronyism undergirded some of the Trump camp's attacks on Biden's family, notably his son Hunter, who had various entanglements with overseas interests. Meanwhile, some on Biden's left echoed the right's argument; The Nation wrote that "The Delaware Way looks a lot like what Gilded Age Tammany Hall politicians used to call legal graft." Biden's critics on the left also attacked his historically centrist policies as insufficient and said his willingness to work constructively with segregationist senators such as James Eastland and Herman Talmadge in the 1970s was distasteful. Back home, some Delawareans expressed exhaustion with least-common-denominator government. "For many, the Delaware Way has begun to symbolize the punches being pulled, the turfs being guarded, even in the face of daunting challenges in the state's struggling educational system or enduring poverty in some pockets," the Los Angeles Times wrote.

Inside the state, the highest-profile challenges to the Delaware Way came from progressives in Democratic primaries. In 2018, Kerri Evelyn Harris challenged Sen. Tom Carper, and in 2020, Jess Scarane challenged Sen. Chris Coons. But Carper won with 65 percent, Coons won with 73 percent, and both coasted to easy victories in their general elections. The strongest inroads came in down-ballot races in 2020, as diverse, progressive challengers defeated four targeted legislative incumbents in the primaries, including long-serving Senate President Pro Tem David McBride. But establishment Democrats largely maintained control of the state, thanks in part to the GOP's turn away from centrism and toward Trump. In 2020, favorite son Biden won by 19 points, a notably wider margin than Hillary Clinton's 11-point win in 2016. Biden flipped Kent County, in the state's midsection; Trump had won it by five points, but Biden won it by four. Biden even improved the Democratic showing in the conservative heartland of Sussex County, narrowing Trump's margin from 22 points in 2016 to 11 in 2020. The Delaware Way may be under unprecedented pressure today, but it appears to be more Democratic than ever.

Cook Partisan Voting Index: D+6

Population		Race and Ethnicity		Income	
Total	973,764	White	67.70%	Median Income	70,176
Land area (sq. miles)	1,949	Black	22.50%	State Income Rank	16 out of 50
Pop/ sq mi	499.74	Latino	9.60%	Poverty Rate	11.30%
Born in state	44.00%	Asian	4.70%	With health insurance	93.40%
		Two or more races	3.10%	Cash public assistance	2.80%
Age Groups		Other	2.80%	Food stamp/SNAP	12.1%
Under 18	20.90%				
18-34	21.80%	**Education**		**Work**	
35-64	38.00%	H.S grad or less	39.90%	White Collar	40.50%
Over 64	19.50%	Some college	26.90%	Sales and Service	38.90%
		College Degree, 4 yr	19.50%	Blue Collar	20.60%
Military		Post grad	13.70%	Government	15.60%
Veteran/ Active Duty	9.60%				

Presidential Politics

2020 Primary (D)	Biden (D)	81,954(89%)	Sanders (D)	6,878 (8%)			
2020 Pres. Vote	Biden (D)	296,268(59%)	Trump (R)	200,603(40%)			
2016 Pres. Vote	Clinton (D)	235,603(53%)	Trump (R)	185,127(42%)	Johnson (L)	14,757 (3%)

Delaware used to be a presidential bellwether. It mimicked the popular vote winner of every presidential election from 1952 to 2000, the longest winning streak of any state. But starting with the election of 2000, this relatively wealthy state began to vote significantly more Democratic than the national average. While Al Gore won the 2000 popular vote by about half a percentage point nationwide, he carried Delaware by 13 points. Lately, that Democratic margin has ranged from a high of 25 points in 2008 to a low of 7.5 points in 2016, with favorite son Joe Biden winning the state by 19 points in 2020. In a sense, tiny Delaware is two states: New Castle County and its suburbs dominate the state and nearly three out of five presidential votes are cast there. Like affluent parts of other major metropolitan areas, New Castle, which includes the state's largest city and Biden's hometown of Wilmington, with its majority African-American population, began tilting toward Democrats in the mid-1990s. It voted 2-to-1 or more for Obama in 2008 and 2012 and for Biden in 2020. Lower Delaware, the other part of the state, is made up of more rural Kent and Sussex counties, the latter of which is also home to the state's popular beach towns (including Rehoboth Beach, where the Bidens bought an oceanfront home in 2017). That area usually votes Republican. It backed President Donald Trump over Biden 53%-47%, after breaking for Trump 55%-40% against Hillary Clinton, though Biden carried Kent County 51%-47%. Most Delaware voters still see plenty of ads, because in the past three elections, all candidates have targeted Pennsylvania, and New Castle and Kent are in the Philadelphia media market. (Sussex is in the Salisbury Maryland market.)

The 2020 Democratic primary was initially scheduled for April 28 but delayed twice because of the coronavirus, eventually taking place July 7, long after Biden had locked up the nomination. Its favorite son won with 89 percent of the vote.

Congressional Districts

117th Congress Lineup	1D	116th Congress Lineup	1D

John Carney (D)

Elected 2016, term expires 2025, 2nd term; b. May. 20, 1956, Wilmington; Dartmouth College, BA 1978; Univ. Del. MPA 1987; Roman Catholic; Married (Tracey); 2 children.

Elected Office: DE Finance Secretary, 1997-2000; DE Lt. Governor, 2001-2009; US House, 2011-2017.

Professional Career: Staff, U.S. Senator Joe Biden, 1986-1989; Deputy Chief Administrative Officer, New Castle County, 1989-1994; Deputy Chief of Staff/Secretary of Finance, Gov. Tom Carper, 1994-1997; President/Chief Operating Officer, Transformative Technologies, LLC, 2009-2010.

Office: 150 Martin Luther King Jr. Blvd. 2nd Floor, Dover, 19901; 302-744-4101; Fax: 302-739-2775; Website: delaware.gov

Lt. Gov.: Bethany Hall-Long (D) **Atty. Gen:** Kathy Jennings (D)

State Legislature: Senate: 12D, 9R **House:** 26D, 15R

Election Results

Election	Name (Party)	Vote (%)
2020 General	John Carney (D)...	292,903 (59%)
	Julianne Murray (R)...	190,312 (39%)

Prior winning percentage: House: 2014 (64%), 2012 (59%), 2010 (57%)

John Carney, a former congressman, was elected governor of Delaware in 2016 and then reelected with ease in 2020.

Carney is the second of nine children born to two teachers and has lived in Wilmington for most of his life. He has been careful to stress his humble upbringing and the fact that he, his wife and their two children lived in a modest row house before the governor's mansion. Carney has spent nearly his entire adult life in public office, except for brief stints as president and chief operating officer of Transformative Technologies, a Delaware company, and as executive vice president of a wind farm start-up called DelaWind. After earning an English degree at Dartmouth College and a master's from the University of Delaware, Carney served as an aide to Joe Biden when the future president was serving in the Senate. In the 1990s, Carney became a top aide to then-Gov. Thomas Carper, including a stint as state secretary of finance from 1997 to 2000. That year, Carney won the first of two terms as lieutenant governor. Then in 2008, he lost a high-profile gubernatorial primary to Jack Markell, a former telecommunications executive, by just 1,700 votes.

Carney regrouped for 2010 and ran for the state's at-large House seat, which was being vacated by moderate Republican Michael Castle, who ran unsuccessfully for the Senate. Carney faced self-funding Republican Glen Urquhart, a Rehoboth Beach developer. Liberal Delawareans were skittish about Urquhart's conservative positions, which included repeal of the Affordable Care Act and abolition of the departments of Energy and Education. Carney won, 57%-41%, a rare Democratic takeover of a seat in that GOP-friendly year.

In the House, Carney followed the example of his predecessor Castle, a nine-term centrist Republican. But he continued to harbor gubernatorial ambitions, and he would have set them aside, at least temporarily, had Biden's son Beau—a rising star and the odds-on favorite to win the governorship had he run in 2016—not died of brain cancer in 2015. After the younger Biden's death, all attention turned to Carney. His prominence in the state and Delaware's weak Republican bench combined to make the 2016 gubernatorial contest arguably the least competitive in the nation. After some uncertainty about who the GOP would field as a candidate, state Sen. Colin Bonini jumped in. But Carney's fundraising edge was on the order of 20 to 1, and Markell's two terms were generally well-received, depriving Bonini of grist for campaign messaging. Carney won, 58%-39%, racking up a 2-to-1 margin in populous New Castle County.

Carney entered office with the prospect of a $385.6 million deficit, and he called for "shared sacrifice." It took five months of negotiations that stretched into overtime before the governor and legislators agreed on a budget in July 2017. In 2018, he signed a compromise bill to raise the minimum wage—eventually rising to $9.25. While this was short of the $10.25 sought by many Democrats, approval of the minimum wage bill enabled passage of an $816.3 million bond bill for transportation and school and university construction, an amount 40 percent higher than the previous year. Meanwhile, he enacted a ban on marriages for minors as well as one on gay-conversion therapy. Carney also signed a bill to guarantee state government workers 12 weeks of paid family leave.

In 2019, Carney signed legislation overhauling sentencing laws, including decreased penalties for nonviolent crimes. He signed a bill that added Delaware to a multi-state compact that would act as a work-around to the presidential Electoral College, as well as legislation to limit the use of single-use plastic bags. But Democratic-led efforts stalled on several other issues, including marijuana legalization, a $15 minimum wage, and several gun-control measures, including a proposed ban on semi-automatic weapons and limits on magazines to 15 rounds. The following year, during national protests against police brutality, Carney signed an executive order banning the Delaware State Police and the Capitol Police from using chokeholds. The coronavirus pandemic led to frequent sparring between Carney and Republicans over stay-at-home orders and restrictions on businesses and churches. For much of the year, Delaware's coronavirus case rate remained low, but it rose significantly in the fall of 2020, for a time cracking the list of 10 states with the highest number of positive tests per capita.

Despite these challenges, Carney's reelection in 2020 was never in serious doubt. In the Democratic primary, he easily defeated challenger David Lamar Williams, and in the general election Carney faced Julianne Murray, the winner of the six-way Republican primary. An attorney, Murray had sued Carney's administration over coronavirus restrictions, but she failed to get traction on the issue. Like every Republican gubernatorial nominee since 1988, she lost, in her case, 59%-39%. When the seat comes open in 2024, Democrats can expect to have a large field of potential candidates.

Tom Carper (D)

Elected 2000, term expires 2024, 4th term, b. Jan 23, 1947; Beckley, WV; Ohio State University, B.A., 1968; University of Delaware, M.B.A., 1975; Presbyterian; Married (Martha Ann Stacy Carper); 2 children.

Military Career: Naval Flight Officer, U.S. Navy 1968-1973 (Vietnam); Captain, U.S. Naval Reserves, 1973-1992.

Elected Office: DE Treasurer, 1976-1983; U.S. House, 1983-1993; DE Governor, 1993-2001; Chair, National Governors Association, 1998-1999.

Professional Career: Industrial Development Specialist, DE Division of Economic Development, 1975-1976, 1975-1976.

DC Office: 513 HSOB 20510, 202-224-2441, Fax: 202-228-2190, carper.senate.gov

State Offices: Dover, 302-674-3308; Georgetown, 302-856-7690; Wilmington, 302-573-6291.

Committees: *Environment & Public Works (Chmn)*: Ex Officio membership on all subcommittees. *Finance*: Energy, Natural Resources & Infrastructure; Health Care; International Trade, Customs & Global Competitiveness (Chmn). *Homeland Security & Government Affairs*: Government Operations & Border Management; Investigations.

Group Ratings

	ADA	ACLU	AFL-CIO	LCV	COC	HAFA	ACU	CFG	FRC
2020	-	85%	-	92%	-	18%	13%	-	-
2019	100%	C	84%	100%	45%	C	13%	34%	0%

Almanac Ratings 2019-2020

	Economy	Social	Foreign	Composite
Liberal	90%	90%	60%	70%
Conservative	10%	10%	40%	20%

Key Votes of the 116th Congress

1. EPA clean energy rules	Y	5. Russia sanctions	Y	9. Barr as Atty. General	N
2. U.S./Mex./Can. trade deal	Y	6. Troops in SYR, AFG	Y	10. Spending at the border	Y
3. Cut unemployment benefits	N	7. Veto arms sales to Saudis	Y	11. Coney Barrett to Sup. Ct.	N
4. Shelton to Fed Reserve	N	8. Defense $$$, veto override	Y	12. Electoral College objections	N

Election Results

Election	Name (Party)	Vote (%)		Cand. Spent	Ind. Exp. Support	Ind. Exp. Oppose
2018 General	Tom Carper (D)	217,385	(60%)	$2,798,144	$765,450	$1,230,346
	Robert Arlett (R)	137,127	(38%)	$238,002		
2018 Primary	Tom Carper (D)	53,635	(65%)			
	Kerri Evelyn Harris (D)	29,407	(35%)			

Prior winning percentages: 2018 (60%), 2012 (66%), 2006 (70%), 2000 (56%); Governor: 1996 (70%), 1992 (65%); House: 1990 (66%), 1988 (68%), 1986 (66%), 1984 (59%), 1982 (52%)

Democrat Tom Carper, Delaware's senior senator, is arguably the most successful politician in state history. He has won 14 statewide general elections, four more than his longtime Delaware congressional colleague, President Joe Biden; when his term ends in 2024, Carper will have held public office for an unbroken string of 48 years. Serving as state treasurer, at-large House member and governor before arriving in the Senate, Carper has earned a reputation as a centrist consensus-builder who is well-liked on both sides of the aisle.

He follows what insiders refer to as the "Delaware Way." That's the quiet, pragmatic manner of shaping public policy long practiced in a pocket-sized state that has the feel of an extended town—in which most of the key players know each other well and voters are accustomed to a retail politics that makes for first-name relationships with top elected officials. It's the political tradition that Biden embodied while representing Delaware in the Senate for more than a third of a century.

While it was Biden's close relationship with state's junior senator, Democrat Chris Coons, that received widespread attention before and after the 2020 presidential election, the duration and depth of the Biden-Carper friendship—and its potential role in Biden's legislative agenda—should not be overlooked. Notwithstanding the contrast in styles between the voluble Biden and lower-key Carper, the two have known each other for more than 40 years. Biden played a major part in persuading Carper to give up the politically secure treasurer's post to make a difficult House bid in 1982; they later served together for nearly two decades in the state's congressional delegation, often riding Amtrak together between Wilmington and Washington. Their wives are friends, and Carper also was close to Biden's late son, Beau, a two-term Delaware attorney general.

In 2018, when the Delaware Way collided with the sharp-edged tactics of the Democratic Party's ascendant progressive wing and Carper confronted a serious primary challenge, Joe Biden came to his aid with a televised endorsement. A year later, Carper was one of four senators to endorse Biden immediately after he announced for president.

The Democratic recapture of the Senate majority in early 2021 handed Carper the chairmanship of the Environment and Public Works Committee, positioning him as a leading advocate for two Biden priorities—rebuilding the nation's infrastructure and combating climate change. He worked closely with Gina McCarthy, the Biden White House's climate adviser, when she ran the Environmental Protection Agency under President Barack Obama. Carper's recent focus on environmental issues followed his longtime leading role on the Homeland Security and Governmental Affairs Committee, including two years as chairman. His work there underscored his image as a results-oriented legislator focused on important issues outside the political limelight—notably, his persistent efforts to put the Postal Service on sound financial footing.

Carper's decision to leverage his seniority to take Democrat's top slot on the Environment and Public Works panel in late 2016—succeeding retiring California Sen. Barbara Boxer—generated blowback from the party's progressive wing. The moderate Carper was a pronounced contrast to the liberal Boxer, and environmentalists were less than overjoyed—particularly given Carper's status as one of only eight Senate Democrats to vote to override Obama's veto of the Keystone XL pipeline project in 2015. Consistent with his consensus-oriented style, Carper had complained that the pipeline —which President Donald Trump later green-lighted, an action Biden vowed to reverse—"impeded our ability to work together and make progress even on issues that we're in agreement on. We need to address this issue and we need to move on."

But in his new role at the Environment and Public Works panel, Carper moved to underscore his pro-environment credentials, joining widespread Democratic criticism of Scott Pruitt, Trump's first choice to head the EPA. During Pruitt's 17-month tenure, Carper spearheaded Democratic criticism of the EPA administrator for rolling back Obama-era regulations and his lavish spending of public funds for personal amenities—the issue that forced Pruitt's resignation.

A decade earlier, Carper had co-authored legislation with Republican Lamar Alexander of Tennessee to limit emissions of sulfur dioxide, nitrous oxide, mercury and carbon dioxide; the pair also pushed for a bill to slash emissions from power plants. Such efforts made little headway, and Carper later supported Obama's efforts to accomplish similar aims through EPA regulations. When Pruitt appeared before the Environment and Public Works panel in early 2018, Carper lit into him over his attacks on Obama-era actions. I don't say this lightly: You repeatedly misrepresent the truth about Mr. Obama's record," Carper told Pruitt. "Stop doing it." Within months, Pruitt resigned under pressure.

When the Trump administration sought to roll back fuel-efficiency standards while challenging California's authority to regulate tailpipe emissions under the Clean Air Act in late 2019, Carper blasted a decision by several major automakers to support the move. "By aligning themselves with this administration's reckless and illegal proposal, these companies are actively challenging the rights of states to set their own emissions standards and tackle the climate crisis," Carper declared. (One of the automakers, General Motors, reversed its position after Biden's election.) After the Trump administration finalized the rollback, Carper highlighted analyses showing that it would increase deaths from air pollution and prodded the EPA to investigate the handling of the matter.

Carper grew up in Southside Virginia and attended Ohio State University on a Navy ROTC scholarship; he arrived in Delaware as a Navy ensign. After serving in Southeast Asia during the Vietnam War, in which he piloted submarine-hunting planes, Carper returned to earn his MBA at the University of Delaware. In 1976, at 29, Carper was elected as Delaware's treasurer.

Six years later, he challenged Republican incumbent Thomas Evans for the state's House seat. The race marked a rare detour from the Delaware Way; the New York Post labeled it "the nation's dirtiest campaign" that year. Evans had been politically damaged by an "association" with a young female lobbyist named Paula Parkinson, and Carper's marriage was dragged into the campaign. Carper won with 52 percent of the vote. Carper, who divorced and remarried not long after the 1982 election, denied charges of spousal abuse at the time. But, in an interview a decade and a half later, he admitted to having "slapped" his first wife once; the issue would resurface years later in the 2018 Senate contest.

Arriving on Capitol Hill, Carper joined then-Sen. Biden and veteran Republican Sen. William Roth in Delaware's delegation. After a decade in the House accumulating a moderate voting record—his strong support of a constitutional amendment requiring a balanced budget set him apart from many fellow Democrats—Carper in 1992 was party to what is still referred to as "The Swap" by Delaware insiders. Carper and Republican Gov. Michael Castle were friends who, despite differing partisan affiliations, were considered ideological twins. Castle was term-limited and ran for the House, while Carper ran to succeed Castle as governor and won with nearly two-thirds of the vote. As governor, he pursued an agenda that was more conservative than liberal: He reduced income tax rates by about 10 percent and signed a bill authorizing charter schools.

Barred from seeking a third term in 2000, Carper faced a possible interruption in a nearly quarter century of unbroken electoral success. Some thought Roth would retire after 30 years in the Senate and Castle would run to succeed him; Carper went so far as to say publicly that he would bow out of politics, at least temporarily, rather than run against his Republican friend. But Roth sought reelection and Castle shied away from a primary challenge to the incumbent. So, Carper ran for Senate.

Both Carper and Roth had high approval ratings and were familiar figures to voters. Roth had a legislative record that benefited many Delaware residents; as chairman of the Senate Finance Committee, he engineered the eponymous Roth IRA. His main problem was that he was 79 years old. Roth stayed in Washington and made only a few appearances in the state. In October, he fainted twice on the campaign trail, once in full view of cameras. Carper, then 53, was careful not to campaign negatively, but his slogan, "A Senator for Our Future," spotlighted the age gap. Carper won 56%-44%.

Headed back to Capitol Hill, Carper continued stuck to the middle of the road: in 2017, Almanac ratings scored him as the eighth least liberal Democrat. On the Senate Finance Committee during the Affordable Care Act debate early in the Obama administration, Carper bucked party liberals by opposing a government-run plan for those who could not afford private insurance. However, rather than attack the public option idea, he tried to broker a compromise he and other centrist Democrats could support. The public option was dropped from the final legislation, but Carper first sought to advance an alternative that would have allowed individual states to decide whether to offer a public option to compete with private insurers. More recently, he opposed the progressive wing's "Medicare for All" proposal.

On the Homeland Security panel, Carper enacted legislation beefing up protections against government payments to ineligible claimants of retiree or disability benefits and requiring audits to identify billions lost through waste and fraudulent claims. He also shepherded bills beefing up the government's cybersecurity. In the minority, he was on the forefront of flagging potential conflicts of interest posed by Trump's business interests. When the director of the Office of Government Ethics came under fire for suggesting that Trump should divest himself of his holdings while responding to a letter from Carper in early 2017, Carper issued a strongly worded defense of the director, Walter Shaub. "We as members of Congress should be focused on how our president-elect has no plan to resolve his massive conflicts of interest before assuming the highest office in our country," Carper said.

But the issue within the committee's jurisdiction with which Carper has been most identified is the perennial effort to rescue the ailing Postal Service. He worked with a fellow centrist, Republican Susan Collins of Maine, in 2006 to pass the first major revision of Postal Service operations since 1970. Delaware is a major center of the credit card industry, which accounts for about a quarter of mail sent through the Postal Service. As the service ran large deficits, Carper in 2012—with the Senate in Democratic control—engineered bipartisan passage of legislation with buyout and early retirement incentives and the option of reducing delivery to five days to save costs. But the bill stalled in the Republican-controlled House. Carper has kept pushing for reform: In 2018, he sought to attach his latest Postal Service modernization bill to annual spending legislation, but the move was blocked by Senate GOP leaders.

In the runup to the 2020 elections, Carper took aim at Postmaster General Louis DeJoy—a Trump fundraiser accused by Democrats of making changes to the Postal Service that would impede voting by mail during the COVID-19 pandemic. "Today, we're witnessing a new form of voter suppression right before our eyes. In the midst of a deadly pandemic, when Americans are even more reliant on regular and on-time deliveries, the United States Postal Service has abandoned one of its longstanding core values: to deliver every piece of mail to every home and business every day," Carper charged in an August 2020 op-ed in the Wilmington News Journal. He called for passage of legislation he had sponsored to block the postmaster general "from making any abrupt and sweeping changes that might harm service during this election season and for the duration of the coronavirus pandemic."

In a subsequent hearing before the Homeland Security panel, Carper stole the show as he unwittingly highlighted the frustration of many Americans in adapting to virtual communication during the pandemic. Carper struggled to unmute his microphone when his chance to question DeJoy came up, and, in frustration, he uttered "F---! F---! F---!" at an aide when it appeared he was about to be passed over. But Carper unknowingly had managed to get his microphone to work at that point, and a video of his outburst circulated around Capitol Hill—providing comic relief during a difficult year, albeit with a sprinkling of criticism. "Those who know me know that there are few things that get me more fired up than protecting the Postal Service! Carper later tweeted. Former Democratic Sen. Claire McCaskill of Missouri added: "Blooper aside, Tom Carper knows more about the postal service than any other U S Senator."

Seeking a fourth Senate term in 2018, Carper faced Kerri Evelyn Harris, a 38-year-old Air Force veteran and community organizer making her first run for public office, in a primary. Harris initially was seen as little threat. But in late June, the party's progressive wing scored a stunning upset when now-Rep. Alexandria Ocasio-Cortez ousted Joe Crowley, the chairman of the House Democratic Caucus, in New York. Operatives from the Ocasio-Cortez campaign and successful progressive candidates elsewhere descended on Delaware to aid Harris, and the New York-based Working Families Party mounted an independent expenditure campaign on her behalf. Contending Carper's consensus-oriented politics were no longer relevant in the polarized Trump era, Harris told the New York Times: "A warm smile, a firm handshake and a witty comment isn't doing it. Nice isn't getting the job done."

Despite the reliance of Delaware's economy on the financial services industry—which employs about 10 percent of the state's workforce—Harris went after Carper for a history of votes favored by the banking sector. Most recently, Carper and his Delaware colleague Coons split from a majority of Senate Democrats in 2018 to vote to roll back portions of the 2010 Dodd-Frank financial reforms. Recalling recent political history—Castle's upset in the 2010 Republican Senate primary by a lightly regarded tea party challenger—Carper left little to chance. He advertised heavily, outspending Harris 20-1. To assuage the party's left, he emphasized support for a $15 per hour minimum wage and decriminalization of marijuana. And, after being one of just four Senate Democrats to support Brett Kavanaugh's confirmation to the federal appeals court in 2006, he came out against Kavanaugh's 2018 Supreme Court nomination, terming the nominee a "profound disappointment" in his years on the bench. While giving Carper his toughest race since his initial election to the Senate, Harris lost by 30 percentage points.

In the general election, the president's son Donald Trump Jr. brought up the decades-old episode in which Carper had admitted to slapping his then-wife. The tweet was in apparent retaliation for a Carper tweet about the Office of Special Counsel citing first lady Melania Trump's spokeswoman for a Hatch Act violation. Carper's Republican opponent, Sussex County Councilman Rob Arlett—who had chaired Trump's Delaware campaign—accused Carper during a debate of having lied "for 19 years about that," adding, "There was a big cover-up." Carper responded: "Forty years ago, I made a mistake. I owned it. I didn't hide it. It was public knowledge." He told Arlett: "Every other year for 40 years, people like you, my friend, try to dredge this up, to make … political mischief for me. It doesn't work. … And you know what? It's not going to work this time either." In November, he defeated Arlett 60%-38%.

Carper—who will be 77 when his term ends—hinted that the 2018 election would be his last, quoting lyrics from the 1965 Rolling Stones hit "The Last Time," while telling the New York Times, "What we have now are a lot of forces from outside the state who don't think there's room for a centrist anymore." If the bare-knuckled nature of his latest campaign suggested that Delaware's longtime political modus operandi may be on its way out as well, the irony is that Carper's influence and effect within what has become a blue state have perhaps never been greater: At the outset of 2021, the First State's governor, at-large House member, and secretary of state, as well as its recently retired chief justice, were all onetime Carper aides.

Chris Coons (D)

Elected 2010, term expires 2026, 2nd full term, b. Sep 09, 1963; Greenwich, CT; University of Nairobi; Amherst College, B.A., 1985; Yale University Law School, J.D., 1992; Yale University Divinity School, M.A.R., 1992; Presbyterian; Married (Annie Lingenfelter); 3 children.

Elected Office: President, New Castle County Council, 2001-2005; County Executive, New Castle County, 2005-2010;

Professional Career: Practicing attorney, 1996-2004; Law Clerk, Judge Jane Richards Roth, U.S. 3rd Circuit Court of Appeals.

DC Office: 218 RSOB 20510, 202-224-5042, Fax: 202-228-3075, coons.senate.gov

State Offices: Dover, 302-736-5601; Wilmington, 302-573-6345.

Committees: *Appropriations*: Commerce, Justice, Science & Related Agencies; Energy & Water Development; Financial Services & General Government; Military Construction & Veteran Affairs & Related Agencies; State, Foreign Operations & Related Programs (Chmn); Transportation, HUD & Related Agencies. *Ethics (Chmn)*. *Foreign Relations*: Africa & Global Health Policy; East Asia, the Pacific & International Cybersecurity Policy; Europe & Regional Security Cooperation; Internat'l Dev Instit & Internat'l Econ, Energy & Environ Policy (Chmn). *Judiciary*: Human Rights & the Law; Immigration, Citizenship & Border Security; Privacy, Technology & the Law (Chmn); Subcommittee on Intellectual Property. *Small Business & Entrepreneurship*.

Group Ratings

	ADA	ACLU	AFL-CIO	LCV	COC	HAFA	ACU	CFG	FRC
2020	-	77%	-	92%	-	0%	4%	-	-
2019	90%	C	100%	100%	57%	C	3%	0%	0%

Almanac Ratings 2019-2020

	Economy	Social	Foreign	Composite
Liberal	94%	94%	77%	88%
Conservative	6%	6%	23%	12%

Key Votes of the 116th Congress

1. EPA clean energy rules	Y	5. Russia sanctions	Y	9. Barr as Atty. General	N
2. U.S./Mex./Can. trade deal	Y	6. Troops in SYR, AFG	Y	10. Spending at the border	Y
3. Cut unemployment benefits	N	7. Veto arms sales to Saudis	Y	11. Coney Barrett to Sup. Ct.	N
4. Shelton to Fed Reserve	N	8. Defense $$$, veto override	Y	12. Electoral College objections	N

Election Results

Election	Name (Party)	Vote (%)	Cand. Spent	Ind. Exp. Support	Ind. Exp. Oppose
2020 General	Chris Coons (D)..................................... 291,804	(59%)	$5,035,047	$1,123	
	Lauren Witzke (R)............................... 186,054	(38%)	$458,074		
2020 Primary	Chris Coons (D)........................... 87,332	(73%)			
	Jessica Scarane (D)................................ 32,547	(27%)			

Prior winning percentages: 2014 (56%), 2010 special (57%)

As vice president during the Obama administration, Joe Biden was known as the "McConnell whisperer" for his ability to negotiate with the often-prickly Senate Republican leader, Mitch McConnell. In turn, Democrat Chris Coons, Delaware's junior senator, has been dubbed the "Biden whisperer," as Coons—who holds the Senate seat Biden occupied for 36 years—has sought to emulate his predecessor's proclivity for bipartisan consensus. "Look, I'd be thrilled if at some point … people saw me as having the same level of passion and commitment to my core principles," Coons said of Biden as the former vice president launched his 2020 presidential bid. With Biden in the White House, Coons became a major conduit between 1600 Pennsylvania Ave. and Capitol Hill, as Biden sought to move his legislative agenda in a closely divided Senate.

Two decades apart in age, Biden and Coons have known each other since the mid-1980s—when Biden was beginning his third Senate term and Coons, stepson of a prominent Delaware businessman, was a recent college graduate. Coons also became close to Biden's late son, Beau Biden, when the two formed a Young Democrats' organization. While the younger Biden once appeared poised to succeed his father in the Senate, it is Coons who has emerged as Joe Biden's political heir—a centrist legislator who has become an influential member of the Judiciary and Foreign Relations committees, both panels that Biden once chaired. In the run-up to the 2020 election, Coons did not hide his interest in serving as Biden's secretary of State, with Coons supporters circulating talking points on why he should be appointed. He and another longtime Biden confidant, Antony Blinken, were the two finalists. "I need you in the Senate," Biden told Coons in a long conversation two weeks after Election Day, according to Politico. Meanwhile, Coons' overseas clout on Capitol Hill was enhanced when he became chairman of the Appropriations subcommittee with jurisdiction over foreign operations spending.

Coons' overtures to Republicans have generated blow-back from Democrats' progressive wing, including a left-wing primary challenge in 2020. And, by Coons' own admission, his bipartisan efforts were strained during Donald Trump's White House tenure, as he increasingly expressed sharp criticisms of the administration. Nonetheless, Coons' relationships and record—the most recent "bipartisan index" compiled by the Lugar Center deemed him the seventh most bipartisan Senate Democrat—will be invaluable to Biden. Notwithstanding Biden's reputation as bipartisan deal-maker while on Capitol Hill, the Senate is a very different place today: Two-thirds of current senators arrived after he left to become vice president in 2009, including 70 percent of the Republican Conference. Coons "has excellent relationships with a tremendous number of senators, including many Republicans," said Pennsylvania GOP Sen. Pat Toomey. "And I would include myself in that."

The depth of those ties is illustrated by an episode in April 2018. As the Foreign Relations Committee was voting on whether to send the nomination of Mike Pompeo to be secretary of State to the Senate floor, Coons changed his vote from "no" to "present." His action had no effect on the outcome, but it avoided the need for Coons' longtime Senate friend, Republican Johnny Isakson of Georgia, to rush back to Washington from a funeral in Atlanta. Such demonstrations of comity, once common in the Senate, have become rare in the hyper-partisan environment—so much so that the now-retired chairman of the Foreign Relations panel, Tennessee Republican Bob Corker, teared up while talking to reporters about Coons' gesture.

Born in Connecticut, Coons moved to Delaware as a child; bankruptcy wiped out much of his father's business success, and his parents divorced. His mother, Sally, a schoolteacher, remarried: Coons' stepfather, Robert Gore, played a key role in founding a highly successful family enterprise, Newark Delaware-based W.L. Gore and Associates. Holder of the patent for water-resistant Gore-Tex fabric, the firm is among the Top 200 privately held companies in the United States. While a student at Wilmington's elite Tower Hill School, Coons considered himself a Republican and volunteered for Ronald Reagan's 1980 presidential campaign. He became a Democrat as a student at Amherst College. Studying in Kenya for a semester, Coons said that observing his host family changed the way he thought about poverty and free markets. It led him to write a tongue-in-cheek column for the college newspaper titled, "Chris Coons: The Making of a Bearded Marxist," which would resurface as an issue in his initial Senate race.

After graduating with a dual major in chemistry and political science, Coons did relief work with a church group in South Africa. He also was issues director for the unsuccessful 1988 Senate campaign of Democrat S.B. Woo, then Delaware's lieutenant governor, before attending Yale Law School. He enrolled as well in Yale's Divinity School, graduating with a law degree and a Master of Arts in religion. In recent years, Coons, a Presbyterian, co-hosted the weekly Senate prayer breakfast with Oklahoma Republican James Lankford, also a frequent legislative collaborator. And, during the 2020 campaign, Coons worked with "Believers for Biden": "Joe knows the power of prayer, and I've seen him in moments of joy and triumph, of loss and despair turn to God for strength," he said during a virtual appearance at the Democratic National Convention.

After Yale, Coons worked in New York before returning to Delaware in 1996 as an in-house counsel for W.L. Gore when his stepfather was president. Coons' first run for office came in 2000, when he was elected president of the New Castle County Council. Four years later, he was elected county executive on an anti-corruption platform; his predecessor had been dogged by scandal. The experience foreshadowed his Capitol Hill modus operandi. "There were several people on County Council who were jerks and lied to me and promised me their vote to my face and stuck me in the back. And you know what? Those were Democrats," Coons recalled to Politico years later. "There were several people, who I expected nothing of them. … And they ended up helping me out of some jams. … Those were Republicans."

Coons was a distinct underdog when he first ran for Senate. But the biggest upset of the 2010 Republican primary season transformed him into the overwhelming favorite to win the final four years of Biden's term. "Chris Coons may turn out to be the luckiest politician in America this year," CNN declared. When Biden was elected vice president in 2008—simultaneously winning another Senate term—the assumption was that his son, then the state's attorney general, would run in the 2010 special election to succeed him. But Beau Biden, who died in May 2015, decided against it— preoccupied with a controversy affecting the attorney general's office and perhaps influenced by the widespread appraisal that the general election would be an uphill battle against moderate-to-liberal Republican Rep. Michael Castle, a former governor. Castle, elected statewide 12 times, was a heavy favorite despite Delaware's increasingly Democratic tilt. But in a year in which the tea party emerged as a major force, Castle lost the primary in a stunning upset to Christine O'Donnell, a conservative consultant defeated by Joe Biden two years earlier.

With Castle gone, Coons catapulted to a large lead in the polls. O'Donnell was put on the defensive by decade-old TV footage in which she claimed to have dabbled in witchcraft on Bill Maher's talk show "Politically Incorrect." Her attempt at damage control resulted in a widely ridiculed campaign ad in which she assured voters: "I am not a witch. I'm nothing you've heard. I am you." O'Donnell sought to shift the focus to Coons' record of raising taxes as county executive —but neither that nor attempts to target his "Bearded Marxist" essay gained much traction. "I am a clean-shaven capitalist," Coons quipped. He won 57%-40%.

With the Senate in Democratic control, Coons was named chairman of Foreign Relations Africa subcommittee in recognition of the time he spent on that continent. He struck up a friendship with Isakson, then the subcommittee's ranking Republican. The same month he voted "present" on the Foreign Relations Committee in deference to Isakson, he worked with two other Republicans, Lindsey Graham of South Carolina and Thom Tillis of North Carolina, to gain Judiciary Committee approval of a bill that would have protected special counsel Robert Mueller from being fired by Trump before completing an investigation of Russian interference in the 2016 elections. The move was stymied on the Senate floor by McConnell.

But it was another bipartisan initiative within the Judiciary panel—in which Coons and then-Sen. Jeff Flake of Arizona delayed a vote on Supreme Court nominee Brett Kavanaugh in late 2018 while the FBI looked into sexual assault allegations against him—that would elevate Coons' national profile. Coons and Flake, as Foreign Relations Committee colleagues, had forged a friendship during travel abroad. When Flake, a persistent GOP critic of Trump, announced in late 2017 that he would not seek reelection, Coons bemoaned the development in a New York Times op-ed piece. "We have opposed each other on nearly every vote for as long as we've served in the Senate," Coons wrote. "I may disagree with Mr. Flake on policy, but I consider him an honorable man, a loyal friend and a valued colleague. His retirement is deeply troubling to me because he represents a principled and patriotic Republican Party, one that has long championed strong American leadership around the world, and one I now fear is falling apart. That should scare all Americans. It sure scares me."

The meeting at which the Judiciary Committee was to vote on the Kavanaugh nomination produced high drama: While the committee marked time, Coons and Flake negotiated privately in an adjacent anteroom. Flake earlier in the day had said he would vote for Kavanaugh but wavered after being confronted in an elevator by survivors of sexual abuse—triggering the negotiations. What emerged was a gentleman's agreement under which Flake would vote to approve the nomination in committee—but not on the Senate floor without a delay to allow an FBI investigation into the allegations against Kavanaugh. Republican leaders, struggling to round up the votes needed to confirm Kavanaugh, had no choice but to accede to a weeklong delay.

Coons' effort delayed but did not derail the nomination: Kavanaugh was narrowly confirmed, with Flake voting yes. Coons joined all but one of his Democratic colleagues in voting no, while —immediately after the vote—criticizing the FBI's handling of the investigation he had triggered. A year later, a book on the Kavanaugh confirmation by two New York Times reporters disclosed Coons had written to FBI Director Christopher Wray at the time—complaining that several people who wanted to share information about Kavanaugh "have had difficulty reaching anybody who will collect their information." He also asked for "appropriate follow-up" with a Yale classmate of Kavanaugh's whose recollections might have buttressed a sexual assault allegation lodged by a former classmate, Deborah Ramirez. The follow-up apparently never occurred, and critics cited the Coons letter as evidence that the Ramirez accusation had been given short shrift—prompting calls from several Democratic presidential contenders for Kavanaugh's impeachment or an inquiry into the investigation that preceded his confirmation.

Winning a full Senate term in 2014 by 13 percentage points over Kevin Wade, an engineer, in a difficult year for Democrats, Coons emerged with what he described as a rekindled appetite for campaigning, along with an interest in one of the Senate's most partisan posts—chair of the Democratic Senatorial Campaign Committee—as the party began its quest to regain the Senate majority lost in the 2014 elections. But Coons withdrew from consideration, citing three teenagers at home and the travel demanded of the DSCC chair. Like the state's senior senator, Tom Carper, and, earlier, Biden, Coons commuted from Wilmington to Washington when Congress was in session. His emphasis on bipartisanship played a role: Coons "was concerned it would be harder to make real progress on some of his legislative priorities while running the DSCC," a spokesman explained. Senate Democratic leaders again eyed Coons for the post after the 2016 election, but Coons once more took a pass.

The 2016 campaign exacted a toll on Coons' bipartisan mien: In the fall of 2015, he lambasted Trump as "a thin-skinned reality-TV star" and "a Cheeto-faced, short-fingered vulgarian" during a Democratic rally in Delaware. A year later, it fell to the Yale Divinity School graduate to journey to New York and invite Trump to the January 2017 National Prayer Breakfast, of which Coons was co-chair. Coons avoided partisan issues during his 20-minute meeting with the president-elect; his campaign remarks did not come up. Coons expressed remorse to the Wilmington News Journal about the insults hurled at Trump a year earlier, saying he regretted "that one incident of my not keeping a measured tone in the campaign."

He refrained from taking further jabs at Trump's appearance, but Coons' criticism of the president's actions escalated as he became an increasing presence on TV. "The president's been a real challenge for me to find ways to work with. I'll tell you that praying for the president is probably one of the greatest spiritual challenges I've had to work through in my life." Coons told CBS' "Face the Nation" in late 2019. He opted for sarcasm over prayer as the presidential campaign shifted into high gear and Trump—via Twitter—derided Coons as a "very weak and pathetic Schumer puppet," alluding to Senate Democratic Leader Chuck Schumer. It came after a Coons appearance on "Fox News Sunday" in which he criticized Trump's handling of U.S.-China policy. Via Twitter, Coons responded, "Wow ... my first Trump slander. ... makes a boy feel all grown up... even if I am a puppet not a real boy.

After aggressively challenging Carper, a fellow centrist, in the 2018 primary, the party's progressive wing took on Coons in 2020. "He has repeatedly made compromises with Republicans at the expense of Delawareans," declared Jessica Scarane—a digital marketing firm official and member of the Democratic Socialists of America—in announcing her primary bid. Scarane targeted Coons for the January 2018 Senate vote in which he was among a half-dozen Democratic senators to vote to confirm Alex Azar as Trump's Health and Human Services secretary. "This is a man who has lobbied for Big Pharma and who is opposed to abortion rights," she told WHYY.

Scarane also cited an earlier confirmation vote by Coons that was a sore point among progressives. In March 2014, Coons was among seven Democrats whose votes helped derail President Barack Obama's nomination of Debo Adegbile to head the Justice Department's Civil Rights Division. Adegbile was controversial because of his participation in an appeal filed on behalf of Mumia Abu-Jamal, an internationally known prisoner convicted in the 1981 murder of Philadelphia police Officer Daniel Faulkner. Coons at the time said he was "was troubled by the idea of voting for an assistant attorney general for civil rights who would face such visceral opposition from law enforcement on his first day on the job." And while not blaming Adegbile, Coons complained that "the decades-long public campaign by others ... to elevate a heinous, cold-blooded killer to the status of a political prisoner and folk hero has ... shown great disrespect for law enforcement officers and families throughout our region." During the 2020 primary, Coons sought to mend fences on his left. "In the run-up to the [Senate] vote, I had asked Debo if he would call the widow of Dan Faulkner and express some regret about how the whole issue had ended up," Coons told the Washington Post. "And he would not. And I may have overreacted to that. I've had long conversations with the civil rights community [in Delaware] to say that I recognize that he would have been a great assistant attorney general for civil rights."

It was among several issues on which Coons endeavored to assuage progressives, much as Biden was doing on his way to the presidential nomination. It was a marked shift in tone from Coons' comments a couple years earlier, when he had criticized the party's progressive wing for "engaging in a relentless race to the left, with more and more outrageous proposals." He suggested positions taken by progressives, from abolishing the Immigration and Customs Enforcement agency to attacking energy companies, hampered opportunities for the Democrats to win back voters who had sent Trump to the White House. Forty percent of voters self-identify as pragmatic or moderate. We cannot abandon them, he asserted. Facing a primary opponent who endorsed "Medicare for All" and the "Green New Deal"—a loose roadmap toward reducing greenhouse gas emissions to a net of zero by 2050—Coons countered with a public health insurance option and pointed to legislation he sponsored to create a carbon tax. While we may have different approaches ... the basic goals of increasing wages, improving the access to quality health care and tackling climate change are goals that I share," he said in post-primary appeal to party progressives.

While the primary challenge to Carper two years earlier had received significant out-of-state assistance, progressive groups in 2020 generally turned their attention to candidates elsewhere more vulnerable than Coons. He outspent Scarane nearly 14-1 and had strong backing from Biden and nearly every Democratic elected official in Delaware. Coons easily won, 73%-27%. In the general election, he faced Lauren Witzke, a hard-line Trump supporter who upset the party's endorsed candidate in the Republican primary. Witzke, who admitted to having been a drug addict and pusher as recently as three years earlier, outdid Trump's anti-immigration initiatives by advocating a moratorium on all immigration into the United States. She promoted QAnon—a baseless conspiracy theory involving a "deep state" apparatus run by pedophiles—while telling Coons via Twitter, "I'm coming for your seat, Satanist." Coons was hardly bedeviled, winning 59%-38%.

Lisa Blunt Rochester (D)

Elected 2016, 3rd term, b. Feb 10, 1962; Philadelphia, PA; Padua Academy, 1980; Fairleigh Dickinson University, B.A., 1985; University of DE, M.A., 2003; Christian Church; Widow; 2 children.

Professional Career: Deputy Secretary, Delaware Department of Health and Social Services; Delaware Secretary of Labor, 1998-2001; Personnel Director, Delaware Office of Management and Budget, 2001-2004; Chief Executive, Metropolitan Wilmington Urban League, 2004-2007.

DC Office: 1519 LHOB 20515, 202-225-4165, bluntrochester.house.gov

State Offices: Georgetown, 302-858-4773; Wilmington, 302-830-2330.

Committees: *Energy & Commerce*: Energy; Environment & Climate Change; Health.

Group Ratings

	ADA	ACLU	AFL-CIO	LCV	COC	HAFA	ACU	CFG	FRC
2020	**	81%	**	95%	-	0%	3%	**	-
2019	95%	C	100%	97%	64%	C	4%	12%	0%

Almanac Ratings 2019-2020

	Economy	Social	Foreign	Composite
Liberal	100%	100%	80%	94%
Conservative	0%	0%	20%	6%

Key Votes of the 116th Congress

1. U.S./Mex./Can. trade deal Y	5. Russia sanctions Y	9. Firearms background checks Y
2. First Coronavirus response Y	6. Troops in Syria Y	10. Spending at the border Y
3. HEROES Act Y	7. Veto arms sales to Saudis Y	11. Marijuana liberalized rules Y
4. CASH Act Y	8. Defense $$$, veto override Y	12. Electoral College objections N

Election Results

Election	Name (Party)	Vote (%)		Cand. Spent	Ind. Exp. Support	Ind. Exp. Oppose
2020 General	Lisa Blunt Rochester (D)	281,382	(58%)	$999,409	$10,870	
	Lee Murphy (R)	196,392	(40%)	$120,526		$113

Prior winning percentages: 2018 (65%), 2016 (56%)

Democrat Lisa Blunt Rochester was elected in 2016 as the first woman and the first African American to represent Delaware in Congress. During her relatively quiet first two years, she spent more time than did most freshmen working to foster bipartisanship, which is valued in her home state. Then, with the success of Joe Biden, she took advantage of multiple opportunities to assist his presidential campaign and ultimately his move to the White House.

Blunt Rochester received many prime assignments and she often was near Biden's side at critical moments. But, even with her appealing persona and congressional credentials, she mostly avoided the public spotlight. She showed comfort with the Delaware Way of working as a team—with Biden and in the House, where she served on the Energy and Commerce Committee. Her actions seemed certain to advance her own quiet political ambitions, which could include a Senate seat before long.

Blunt Rochester was born in Philadelphia and moved with her family to Wilmington when she was a child. She has a political pedigree as a Democrat. Her father was president of the Wilmington City Council, where he served more than 20 years. Her sister was an aide to Biden in his Senate office, and state director for the Obama-Biden campaign. Blunt Rochester got her bachelor's in international relations from Fairleigh Dickinson University, and received a master's degree in urban affairs and public policy from the University of Delaware.

In 1987, she began her political career as an intern for then-Rep. Tom Carper, and recalls her experience as a case-worker dealing with constituent issues. In the close-knit style of Delaware, she continued with Carper when he was elected governor in 1992. She initially was a policy adviser and eventually served three years as secretary of labor in Carper's cabinet, where she focused on connecting employers to resources and jobseekers.

When Carper was elected to the Senate in 2000, Blunt Rochester joined the cabinet of new Democratic Gov. Ruth Ann Minner as personnel director. In that job her responsibilities included an investigation of the Delaware State Police for racial and sexual discrimination. She moved to the private sector as chief executive officer of the Metropolitan Wilmington Urban League, a public policy think tank.

There, she met her second husband, Charles Rochester, an engineer working in China. She moved to Shanghai after they married in 2006, writing a book, Thrive, that profiled women who reinvented themselves while living in a foreign country. She decided to write the book after nothing fell into place during her job search in China until she attended a 10-day meditation retreat in Hong Kong that helped her to clarify what she wanted from life. Blunt Rochester moved back to the United States when her husband was transferred to Boston. He died suddenly in 2014 after rupturing his Achilles tendon, and she returned to Delaware.

When John Carney ran for governor, Blunt Rochester was an early frontrunner to take the House seat. In the competitive six-candidate Democratic primary, she won with 44 percent of the vote. The runners-up were state Sen. Bryan Townsend and Iraq War veteran Sean Barney, who got 25 and 20 percent respectively. Blunt Rochester loaned her campaign $400,000 for the primary. Her net worth exceeded $5 million. In the general election against Republican Hans Reigle, Blunt Rochester criticized Donald Trump for supporting "hateful, racist and discriminatory" policies. Blunt Rochester won 56%-41%. She took 64 percent in New Castle County. Reigle won the two smaller counties.

In the Republican-controlled House during her first two years, Blunt Rochester often worked across the aisle. With Rep. Glenn Thompson of Pennsylvania, she wrote an op-ed calling for extension of the Family Violence Prevention and Services Act. She was one of eight House Democrats who voted to reopen the government in February 2018 following a brief shutdown and was the only Democratic cosponsor of a House-passed bill to extend disaster aid to homeowners in coastal areas.

Blunt Rochester was less favorably disposed to President Donald Trump. After visiting a detention facility for immigrant children in New York City, she described the experience as "painful and traumatic." She criticized as "deeply troubling" and "dangerous" reports in 2017 that Trump had shared with the Russian government highly classified information about terrorist threats.

On Energy and Commerce panel, she has dealt with an array of issues. When the committee crafted a wide-ranging health care bill in 2019, it included her proposal to offer increased information to teenagers to promote their "personal responsibility" on matters such as teen pregnancy and financial literacy. With Republican Rep. Cathy McMorris Rodgers, she filed a bill to reduce the risks of unsafe drinking water.

Not surprisingly, Blunt Rochester endorsed Biden's presidential bid at the start of his campaign in 2019. After he revived his prospects during the Super Tuesday primaries in March 2020, she became a national co-chair. She joined Biden at many events, in Washington and in Delaware. Following the death of George Floyd while he was being held by police in Minneapolis, she accompanied Biden to a meeting with community leaders at a Black church in Wilmington.

Biden named Blunt Rochester as one of four members of his search committee to review potential vice presidential running mates. Asked by a reporter whether she supported the selection of a racial minority for that spot, she cautiously responded that the review "needs to work its way out." In July, she accompanied Biden to a Capitol Hill meeting with Democratic leaders of the congressional women's caucus. Working mostly in the background, she had prime roles in planning for the presidential transition and for the inaugural ceremonies. She rarely sought, or received, extensive attention.

Blunt Rochester has been reelected easily. With Carper having hinted that he will retire in 2024, she seemed politically secure and well-positioned in incumbent-friendly Delaware.

DISTRICT OF COLUMBIA

The capital of the most powerful and affluent nation in history, Washington is a physically beautiful city of great achievements and astonishing contrasts that go back more than 200 years. In 1787, the Constitution's framers, familiar with contemporary London and Paris mobs and remembering how unruly crowds had threatened the Continental Congress in Philadelphia, gave the new federal government control over the 10-mile-square that came to be called the District of Columbia. The Residence Act of 1790 located the District on the Potomac River along the borders of Maryland and Virginia, though in 1848 the portion west of the Potomac was retroceded to Virginia on the grounds that the federal government would never need it. Over the years, Congress kept control of the District for its own advantage and, at times, out of distrust of the city's large African-American population. In the late 18th century, African Americans made up one-quarter of Washington's residents. The city was a refuge for free blacks before the Civil War and right after emancipation. Radical Republicans gave the District self-government in 1871, but the experiment ended three years later after Gov. Alexander Shepherd spent the city into bankruptcy. In the 20th century, Washington's growth spurts, starting with the New Deal and World War II, resulted in the development of large, mostly white suburbs in Virginia and Maryland. It was at this time that African Americans became a larger percentage of the city's population, reaching a majority in the 1960 census.

With the civil rights movement, the way that many District residents viewed their lack of voting rights began to change. In 1961, Congress amended the Constitution to give District residents the right to vote for president; in 1968, residents began voting for the school board; in 1971, they received a non-voting delegate in Congress; and in 1973, the District of Columbia Home Rule Act allowed the city to elect a mayor and a city council, though Congress retained control over the District's budget and the authority to review its legislation. For some time, self-government worked no better than it did in the 1870s. The Alexander Shepherd of modern times was the late Marion Barry, who held office for 16 years between 1978 and 1998. Under Barry, the District struggled. Neighborhoods fell into disarray and violent crime rates increased. Meanwhile, the size of local government soared to 51,000 employees. Barry nonetheless regularly won re-election. In January 1990, District police arrested him at a D.C. hotel for cocaine possession. After a six-month stint in prison, he returned to city government. Barry was elected to the city council in 1992 and won a fourth term as mayor in 1994.

At that time, the District was experiencing a dire fiscal crisis, and Congress stepped in. Republican House Speaker Newt Gingrich tasked Rep. Tom Davis, a Republican from northern Virginia, with the job of stabilizing the District's finances. Working closely with the District's elected delegate, Democrat Eleanor Holmes Norton, Davis set up a financial control board whose head, Anthony Williams, hacked away at the payroll and reformed management practices. In 1998, Barry chose not to run for a fifth term. Williams was elected mayor. The financial control board immediately relinquished power to Williams; in 2000, a court returned control of most District departments to the city.

Beginning with William's tenure, the District's population started rising, from 572,000 in 2000 to 705,000 in 2019, with a substantial portion of this increase coming from well-educated, unmarried young people: 59 percent of the D.C. adult population has at least a bachelor's degree-one of the highest percentages in the country.

With youth and population growth have come gentrification and an exceptionally high cost of living. The rental market has sprouted new bars and restaurants, rental bikes and bike lanes, food trucks and cupcake stores, dog parks and streetcar tracks. In southeast D.C., Nationals Park and other new developments are transforming neighborhoods along the Anacostia River, sometimes at the expense of longtime neighborhoods. According to the Institute of Metropolitan Opportunity, "Since 2000, the city of Washington, D.C. has experienced the strongest gentrification and displacement of any city in the country."

The city's black population peaked at 71 percent in 1970, as low-income black neighborhoods emptied out and middle-income blacks moved to majority-black suburbs, most notably Prince

George's County, Maryland. 2011 marked the first year in almost a half century that African Americans were not the majority in the District. As of 2019, 46 percent of the city was African American. The city's white population grew from 30 percent in 2000 to 37.5 percent in 2019. The west side of the District and the neighborhoods surrounding Capitol Hill are mostly white. African Americans are the majority in eastern D.C. neighborhoods, including Anacostia.

Adrian Fenty succeeded Williams as mayor in 2007. Fenty's biggest initiative was improving the floundering public schools. At Fenty's behest, the city council transferred control of the schools from an independent board of education to the mayor's office. His school superintendent, Michelle Rhee, closed non-performing and underused schools and negotiated a contract with the union that gave teachers the option of earning merit pay and Rhee the power to dismiss low-performing teachers. Rhee also encouraged the charter school movement. Charter school enrollments in the District rose from 25 percent in 2006 to 47 percent in 2018, among the highest in the nation. Charter school enrollment dropped for the first time in 2019 as the D.C. Public Charter School Board closed locations for poor academic and financial performance.

In 2010, Council President Vincent Gray harnessed African-American discontent with gentrification to defeat Fenty for the Democratic nomination. After he was elected, Gray found his administration derailed by a series of scandals, which set the stage for a grueling primary in 2014. Gray lost, 44%-32%, to Muriel Bowser, a councilwoman with close ties to Fenty. Bowser defeated David Catania, a Republican-turned-Independent councilman, in a contentious general election, 54%-34%. Bowser won re-election in 2018 with 76 percent of the vote.

Bowser has taken some risks as mayor, especially when it comes to the District's autonomy. In 2015, she defied the Republican-controlled Congress by allowing a voter-approved ballot measure that effectively legalized marijuana to take effect. Bowser also supported the Budget Autonomy Act, which passed by a citywide referendum in 2013. In 2020, Bowser dealt with the coronavirus pandemic by issuing a stay-at-home order in the spring and implementing travel restrictions. Black residents were disproportionately affected by the virus, making up 80 percent of the District's deaths. In the midst of the pandemic, D.C. was the sight of numerous Black Lives Matter protests, to which President Donald Trump responded harshly, including the movement of federal law-enforcement officers to the city's streets. Bowser objected and had the words "Black Lives Matter" painted on 16th Street, right by the White House. She signed police reform legislation but refused calls to defund law enforcement.

Bowser is a vocal proponent of D.C. statehood, which enjoys widespread support in the District. In 2020, the Democratic-controlled House voted on D.C. statehood for the first time since 1993, when it failed overwhelmingly. The measure passed, though it did not get a vote in the Republican-controlled Senate. In 2021, D.C. activists were hoping for a more positive outcome in the Senate, with its razor-thin Democratic control.

The federal government is the city's chief employer, and roughly 15 percent of the federal workforce is based in the metro area. The District's hospitality and tourism industries have prospered in recent years. A record-setting 22.8 million Americans visited the capital in 2019, spending nearly $6 billion on local transportation, hotels and restaurants. After ten consecutive years of growth, the industry took a hit in 2020 due to the pandemic.

The District has been the site of numerous famous political protests, including two high-profile incidents in 2020. In June, police and National Guard troops used tear gas to clear Black Lives Matter protestors in and surrounding Lafayette Park to make way for Trump's photo op in front of St. John's Church. In January 2021, Trump supporters descended on the District to object to the result of the presidential election. A violent mob breached the Capitol building and temporarily halted Congress' certification of the Electoral College vote. Five people, including a Capitol police officer, died during the riot.

Politically, the District supports Democratic candidates by overwhelming margins. Joe Biden received 92.1 percent against Trump, who was particularly loathed by District residents. His 4.1 percent of the vote in 2016 and 5.4 percent in 2020 were the lowest totals for a candidate since the District began voting for president in 1964 and the worst performance by a major-party presidential candidate in any state during that period.

Population		Race and Ethnicity		Income	
Total	705,749	White	42.50%	Median Income	92,266
Land area (sq. miles)	61	Black	45.40%	Poverty Rate	13.50%
Pop/ sq mi	11,560	Latino	11.30%	With health insurance	96.50%
Born in state	.37	Asian	5.40%	Cash public assistance	2.90%
		Two or more races	3.30%	Food stamp/SNAP	14.4%
Age Groups		Other	4.70%		
Under 18	18.10%			**Work**	
18-34	33.50%	**Education**		White Collar	67.80%
35-64	35.90%	H.S grad or less	24.00%	Sales and Service	26.20%
Over 64	12.40%	Some college	16.30%	Blue Collar	6.00%
		College Degree, 4 yr	25.70%	Government	24.90%
Military		Post grad	34.00%		
Veteran/ Active Duty	4.70%				

Presidential Politics

2020 Primary (D)	Biden (D)	84,093(76%)	Warren (D)	14,228(13%)	Sanders (D)	11,116(10%)	
2016 Conv. (R)	Rubio (R)	1,059(37%)	Kasich (R)	1,009(36%)	Trump (R)	391(14%)	
	Cruz (R)	351(12%)					
2020 Pres. Vote	Biden (D)	317,323(92%)	Trump (R)	18,586 (5%)			
2016 Pres. Vote	Clinton (D)	282,830(91%)	Trump (R)	12,723 (4%)			

Eleanor Holmes Norton (D)

Elected 1990, 16th term, b. Jun 13, 1937; Washington, DC; Antioch College, B.A., 1960; Yale University, M.A., 1963; Yale University Law School, J.D., 1964; Episcopalian; Divorced; 2 children.

Professional Career: Clerk, Judge A. Leon Higginbotham, 1964-1965; Assistant legal Director, ACLU, 1965-1970; Adjunct Assistant Professional, NY University Law School, 1970-1971; Staff, NY mayor, 1971-1974; Chair, NYC Human Rights Comm., 1970-1977; Chair, US Equal Empl. Oppor. Comm., 1977-1981; Sr. fellow, Urban Inst., 1981-1982; Professor, Georgetown University Law Center, 1982-1990.

DC Office: 2136 RHOB 20515, 202-225-8050, Fax: 202-225-3002, norton.house.gov

State Offices: Washington, 202-408-9041; Washington, 202-678-8900.

Committees: *Oversight & Reform*: Government Operations; Subcommittee on Civil Rights & Civil Liberties. *Transportation & Infrastructure*: Aviation; Economic Dev't, Public Buildings & Emergency Management; Highways & Transit; Water Resources & Environment.

Prior winning percentages: 2018 (87%), 2016 (89%), 2014 (97%), 2012 (89%), 2010 (89%), 2008 (92%), 2006 (100%), 2004 (91%), 2002 (93%), 2000 (90%), 1998 (90%), 1996 (90%), 1994 (89%), 1992 (85%), 1990 (62%)

Eleanor Holmes Norton is a Democrat who was elected delegate from the District of Columbia in 1990. The daughter of a District government employee and a schoolteacher, Norton graduated from Antioch College and got a law degree at Yale. She volunteered for the Student Nonviolent Coordinating Committee and traveled to Mississippi in 1963 to help register African-American voters. On June 11, she met with civil rights activist Medgar Evers, who tried to convince her to move to Jackson and work as a civil rights lawyer. Just hours after Evers dropped her off at a bus station, a white supremacist shot and killed him in his driveway. Norton worked for the American Civil Liberties Union and the New York City Commission on Human Rights, and was head of the Equal Employment Opportunity Commission in the Carter administration. Afterward, she taught law at Georgetown University. When the delegate seat came open in 1990, she edged past Council Member Betty Anne Kane, 39%-33%, in the primary. Norton has been re-elected easily since; in 2020, she won 86 percent. At age 85 for the 2022 election, she has not faced public pressure to retire.

Her relationship with congressional Republicans active on District matters has been mixed. She worked closely with former Republican Rep. Tom Davis of Virginia on several issues. In 1995, she collaborated with Davis and Speaker Newt Gingrich to create the fiscal control board that oversaw the District's financial recovery. In 1999, she and Davis passed a law providing in-state tuition for District students at colleges and universities in any state. But Norton has clashed with other Republicans seeking to impose restrictions on the District. When Republican Rep. Andy Harris of Maryland announced his intention to challenge a voter-approved ballot measure decriminalizing marijuana in 2014, Norton stated, "D.C. residents can rest assured that when a mandate comes directly from the people, they haven't seen a fight like the fight I'm preparing to make against Rep. Andy Harris and any other member of Congress who attempts to undo our democratic process."

Norton objected to President Barack Obama's 2011 budget deal with House Republicans because it kept a school voucher program in the District's budget. She also disagreed with Obama's opposition to a 2013 House bill to allow the District to tap local revenues for government operations. She was a vocal opponent of President Donald Trump. She continued her opposition to school voucher programs during his administration and slammed a push by Sen. Ted Cruz of Texas and Rep. Mark Meadows of North Carolina to give any D.C. resident a voucher to attend private school.

Norton has been frustrated in her attempts to secure full voting rights for D.C. in the House. During the 2000s, she fell short of a bipartisan deal securing the District a voting representative in Congress, with the agreement that Utah, which had just missed out on an additional House seat during the recent reapportionment would get one more seat. That passed the House in 2007 but the Senate failed to act; in 2009, it passed the Senate, but with a poison-pill amendment that would eliminate the district's strict gun control laws. In 2015, Norton introduced the New Columbia Admission Act, proposing to carve out a 51st state around the White House, Capitol, Supreme Court and National Mall. Norton rejected a Republican option to make the District a part of Maryland, saying residents of both jurisdictions opposed retrocession.

When Democrats took over the House in 2019, Norton's hand was strengthened. She regained her right to vote on House floor amendments, which Republicans had denied her and the territorial delegates. The fight for D.C. statehood had gained support in liberal circles. In 2020, Norton's bill granting the District statehood passed the House on a party-line vote. It was the first time the chamber had taken such a step. The Republican-controlled Senate did not take up the bill. In April 2021, the House again passed the bill making D.C. the 51st state. With a Democratic president and Senate (though narrowly), Norton voiced more optimism. But the Senate posed obstacles, including the stated opposition to the bill by Democratic Sen. Joe Manchin of West Virginia.

Norton has had successes on local issues, including the Southeast Federal Center Public-Private Development Act, which promoted development around the Washington Navy Yard. She sponsored a financial transparency act for D.C. judges that Obama signed into law in 2016. Norton's legislative agenda is not solely local. As the chair of the Transportation and Infrastructure Highways and Transit Subcommittee, she has advocated increased funding for roads and mass transit projects. That was a high priority of President Joe Biden, though committee chairman Rep. Peter DeFazio has taken the reins on that legislation. She has introduced a bill to dismantle the U.S. nuclear weapons program every year since 1994.

FLORIDA

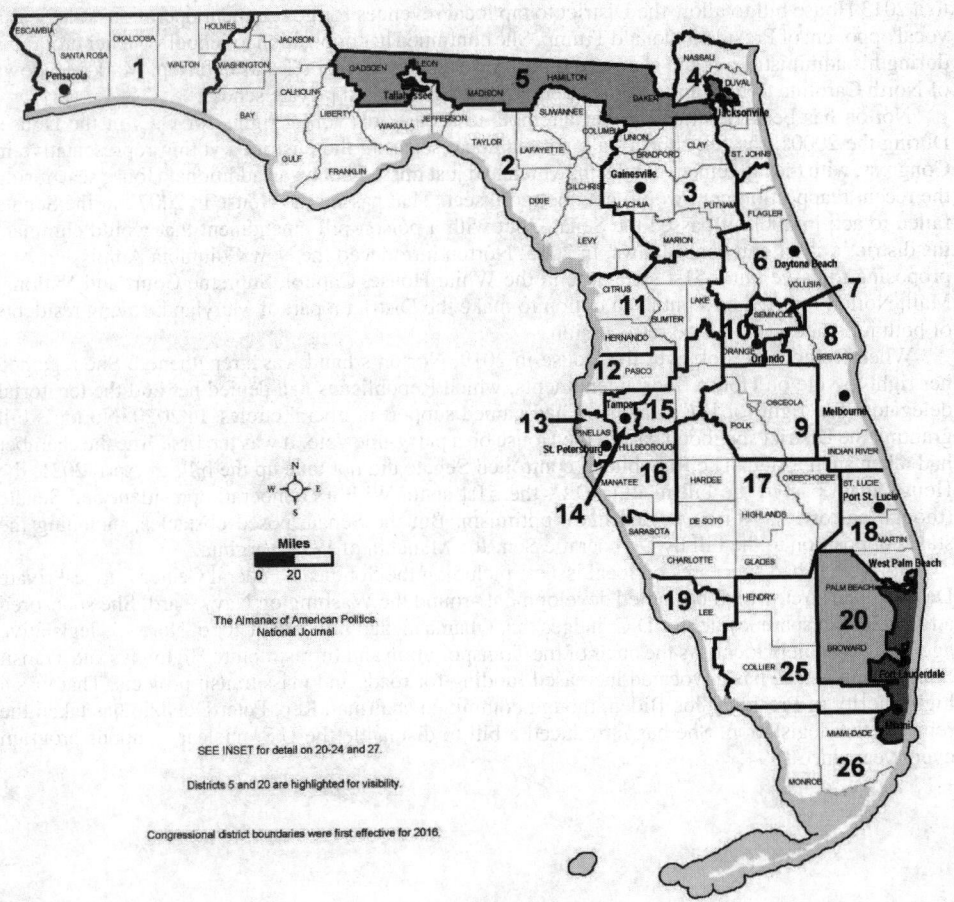

The Almanac of American Politics
National Journal

SEE INSET for detail on 20-24 and 27.

Districts 5 and 20 are highlighted for visibility.

Congressional district boundaries were first effective for 2016.

Since election night 2000, Florida has played host to some of the closest—and most closely watched—elections in the nation. The presidential races of 2012 and 2016, the gubernatorial races of 2010, 2014 and 2018, and the Senate race of 2018 were each decided by less than 1.2 percentage points. By that standard, the 2020 presidential race was a rout, with President Donald Trump winning by 3.4 percentage points. Trump's victory in his adopted home state underlined that, despite the state's near-constant demographic swirl, Florida has increasingly come up red.

More than 500 years ago, in March 1513, the Spanish conquistador Juan Ponce de León spied the coast of Florida. For the next 400 years, anyone sailing along Florida's 1,197 miles of coastline and 663 miles of beach would not have seen anything much different from what Ponce de Leon saw. But within the past century the state has been transformed, from a swampy, under-settled, mostly rural state of 1.5 million people (the smallest population in the South), to a metropolitan powerhouse of 21.7 million people that overtook New York as the third most populous state in 2014. The result is a heterogeneous nation-state, historically Southern, demographically Northeastern and Midwestern, and culturally, at least partly, Latin American. It has been economically vibrant for most of the past century, but vulnerable to sudden contractions, as in the mid-1920s when a hurricane abruptly ended the Miami real estate boom, and later during the Great Recession. But Florida has bounced back before, and it is growing again, with a population spike of 15 percent since 2010.

Florida is the only Atlantic Coast state that was not part of the colonial United States. In 1819, it was acquired from Spain, through the exertions of John Quincy Adams and Andrew Jackson. Adams thought that in foreign hands Florida could block the Gulf of Mexico and the Mississippi Valley, while Jackson saw it as a haven for runaway slaves and a launching pad for Indians to raid the farmers and planters of what was then the American Southwest. Florida was a minor agricultural state until the early 20th century, when its sunshine economy based on citrus production and tourism took hold. Florida's balmy winter climate inspired railroad barons Henry Flagler and Henry Plant to build grand resort hotels and accompanying rail lines (Flagler on the Atlantic coast and Plant on the Gulf), which not only brought vacationers to Florida but also helped transport Florida oranges north to urban markets. Later, auto entrepreneur Carl Fisher promoted tourism to Florida and construction of the Dixie Highway, which in the 1920s helped millions of visitors travel to the state, many of whom decided to stay. (Miami-Dade County voted in 2020 to rename Dixie Highway for abolitionist Harriet Tubman.) Miami, founded in 1896, boomed until the hurricane hit in 1926; in the 1930s, New Yorkers started retiring to art deco apartments in Miami Beach.

By the 1960s, retirees from further north were flocking to the state looking for year-round sunshine — driving down I-95 from the Northeast and ending up on the Atlantic coast, or down I-75 from the Midwest to reach the Gulf coast. Retirees joined agriculture and tourism as Florida's main economic drivers, but new industries, many related to the space program, also migrated to the state. In the 1980s and 1990s, the percentage of families with children as a share of Florida's population grew rapidly, lured by jobs and opportunities in communities that hadn't existed a generation earlier. The state's tourism sector, no longer dependent solely on beautiful beaches, was transformed as Orlando became the "Theme Park Capital of the World," starting, but hardly ending, with the Disney empire, which pre-pandemic had 70,000 employees to serve more than 20 million visitors annually. The cruise business exploded; Port Miami was the global leader for cruise travel, but Port Canaveral, about an hour's drive east from Orlando, and Port Everglades, outside of Fort Lauderdale, operate huge terminals as well. All told, the state economy grew to $1.1 trillion, which would rank as the world's 17th-largest economy.

Florida is an aerospace industry hub. Brevard County's Cape Canaveral Spaceport complex has launch pads operated not just by NASA but also Elon Musk's SpaceX, Jeff Bezos' Blue Origin, federal contractor United Launch Alliance, and a smattering of smaller startups. In May 2020, SpaceX carried out the first human launch in the United States in almost a decade, lifting a pair of astronauts to the International Space Station and boosting hopes for a space renaissance. Meanwhile, Brazilian manufacturer Embraer assembles executive jets in Melbourne, and added a new maintenance facility to its North American headquarters complex in Fort Lauderdale. European turboprop maker ATR relocated its North American operations to Miami Springs, and aerospace giant Northrop Grumman has invested heavily in its operations in Melbourne. The Florida Panhandle is home to several military installations, including Pensacola Naval Air Station and Eglin Air Force Base, which helped attract defense contractors, commercial aviation companies and industrial airparks to the region. Central Florida, meanwhile, is developing a high-tech corridor that runs from Tampa (home of the University of South Florida) through Orlando (the University of Central Florida) to the Space Coast and reaches up to Gainesville (the University of Florida).

But Florida's economy has also been built on construction and real estate, which suffered a serious slump during the Great Recession; the pain lasted longer in Florida than it did most other states. At the same time, one of the state's original economic pillars, the citrus industry, has been crippled by citrus greening disease, a bacterium known as canker, and Hurricane Irma in 2017, which felled between 50 and 90 percent of the crop in some areas. Much of the rest of Florida's agriculture sector has either remained stagnant or contracted; agriculture currently accounts for less than 1 percent of state economic output. The state had been forced to grapple with other natural threats. One is climate change, which is projected by some to raise sea level by one to four feet over the next century. It's also expected to promote the formation of hurricanes, worsening a longstanding risk for the state: Between 1986 and 2015, insured disaster losses in Florida amounted to $68.6 billion, the highest of any state. Environmental protection remains popular among Floridians, including Republicans; Trump initially moved to allow drilling off the coast, but reversed his position as the 2020 election approached.

Retirees continue to flock to Florida; more than one-fifth of the population is 65 or older, the nation's second-highest percentage, behind Maine. The fastest-growing retirement locale is The Villages in Sumter County, northwest of Orlando. It has grown by 40 percent since 2010, often growing faster than any metro area in the country; with 58 percent of its population over 65, it's the only majority-senior county in the nation. "The Villages represents the traditionalist side of a cultural and political war that began in the '60s and never really ended, an us-against-them battle over values between conservative Red America and progressive Blue America," Michael Grunwald, wrote in Politico, adding that when Trump "vows to make America great again, they sense that he means more like The Villages."

Yet Florida is also increasingly diverse, with 27 percent of the population Latino, up from 22 percent in 2010. For refugees from Cuba and Haiti and for immigrants from the Caribbean and Latin America, Florida has been a land of freedom from authoritarian and turbulent lands. The state's growth isn't fueled by births but rather by being continually replenished by people from other states, foreign countries and the U.S. territory of Puerto Rico. Today, only about one-third of Florida residents are natives. Miami has long been the economic and commercial capital of Latin America: You can fly nonstop from Miami to just about any major city in Central and South America, and both English and Spanish are common and Portuguese not unknown. Spurred by a weak economy and a debt crisis—and then by Hurricane Maria in 2017— large numbers of Puerto Ricans moved to Orlando and Osceola County, as have Venezuelans, Colombians and Dominicans; Mexicans are more prevalent in the state's verdant southwestern farmlands in Hendry, Collier and Hardee counties. (The Puerto Rican flow reversed somewhat as storm damage was repaired.) Along the Gulf Coast are a necklace of affluent communities. The Panhandle, the so-called Redneck Riviera around Pensacola and Panama City, is culturally Southern. State government is headquartered in Tallahassee, chosen because it was midway between the population centers of Jacksonville and Pensacola at a time when almost no one lived on the peninsula; Tallahassee and the university town of Gainesville are liberal bastions in a sea of conservatism.

Florida has a fragile civil society, and it can be chaotic and disorderly at times; the state has often ranked in the top 10 in violent crime. If Florida gives people more freedom and options than elsewhere, it also gives them more disruption than many anticipated. (Aggregating stories of weird crimes in Florida has become a cottage industry.) Florida has more gun permits than any other state, and it pioneered the right for citizens to carry concealed weapons in 1987. The state's "stand-your-ground" law, which allows Floridians to use deadly force when they believe their lives are threatened, became a focal point in the tragic 2012 shooting death of an unarmed black teenager, Trayvon Martin, in Sanford. Guns came to the fore again with the terrorism-inspired incident at the Pulse nightclub in Orlando in June 2016—at the time, the deadliest mass shooting in modern U.S. history, with 49 killed and 53 injured. Then, in February 2018, a teenaged former student went on a shooting rampage at Marjory Stoneman Douglas High School in Parkland that killed 17 and injured 17 others. Some of the school-age survivors touched off a national movement for gun control that bore partial fruit in

Tallahassee, as Republican Gov. Rick Scott within weeks signed gun-restriction legislation. A "red flag" law to take guns from people deemed a threat to themselves or others was used more than 3,500 times in its first year and a half on the books, an Associated Press analysis found, though rates varied widely by county.

Map for Greater Miami

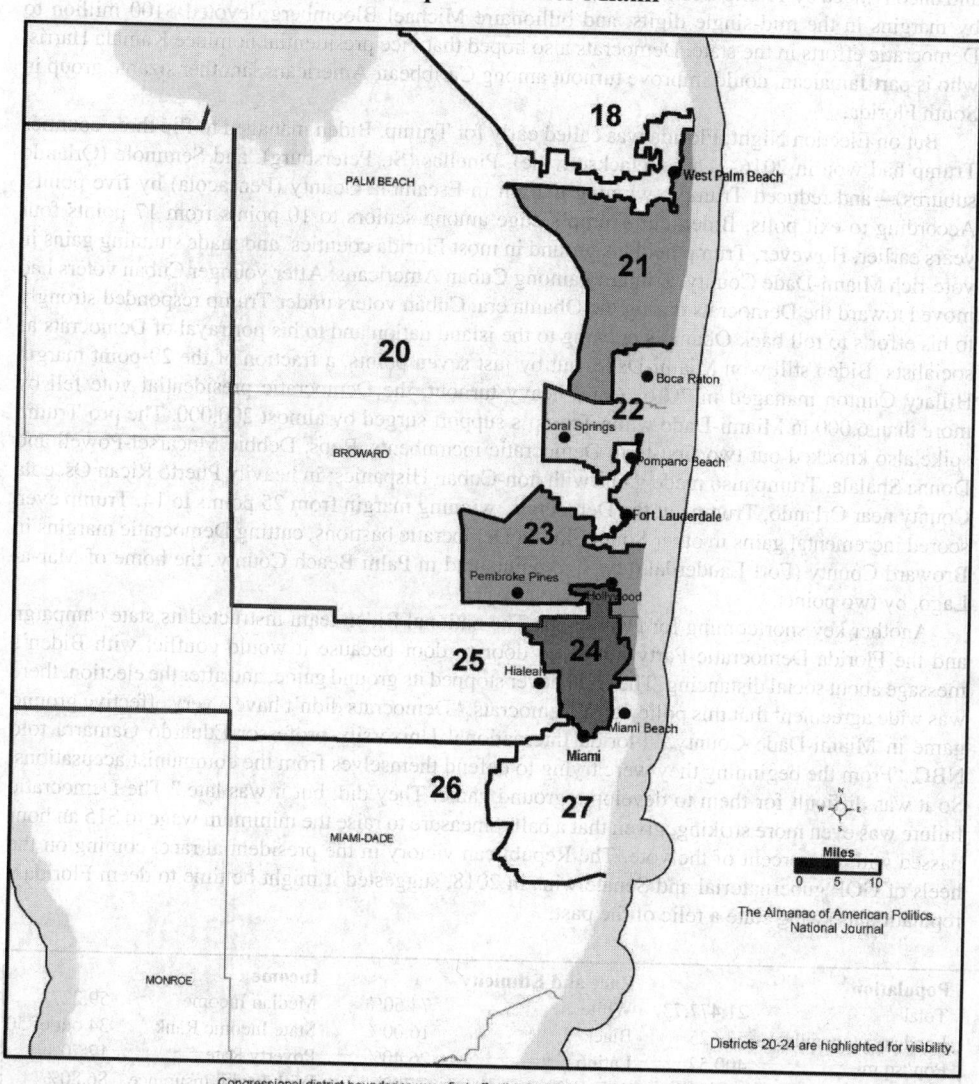

PALM BEACH

West Palm Beach

18

21

Boca Raton

20

BROWARD

22

Coral Springs

Pompano Beach

Fort Lauderdale

23

Pembroke Pines

Hollywood

24

25

Hialeah

Miami Beach

26

MIAMI-DADE

Miami

27

N

Miles
0   5   10

The Almanac of American Politics.
National Journal

MONROE

Districts 20-24 are highlighted for visibility.

Congressional district boundaries were first effective for 2016.

The coronavirus pandemic in 2020 devastated the Florida economy, as theme parks and cruises shuttered and fewer Americans felt comfortable traveling. In September 2020, six months into the pandemic, Florida chief economist Amy Baker testified that "tourism is going to take two to three years to recover, and it will be the longest-recovering sector that we have." The state also struggled with the health impacts of the virus, with Gov. Ron DeSantis, a Trump ally, favoring an aggressive reopening of the economy rather than the strict limits urged by public health experts and by officials in more urban areas. Despite the critics, by late December the state was beating the averages for cases and deaths per capita.

Politically, Republicans have had the upper hand in Florida since the 1990s, holding the governorship and the legislature. But the margins in key statewide races have often been close, and presidential candidates focus intently on the state. George W. Bush won it in 2000 and 2004, Barack

Obama won it in 2008 and 2012, and Trump won it in 2016. In 2020, Trump, by then officially a Florida resident, lavished attention on the state, including a brief flirtation with holding in-person Republican convention events in Jacksonville. (A spike in coronavirus cases scuttled that idea.) Biden also courted Floridians, including older voters who Democrats hoped were fearful of the coronavirus and unconvinced by Trump's efforts to fight it. For much of the race, polls showed Biden up in Florida by margins in the mid-single digits, and billionaire Michael Bloomberg devoted $100 million to Democratic efforts in the state. Democrats also hoped that vice presidential nominee Kamala Harris, who is part Jamaican, could improve turnout among Caribbean-Americans, another sizable group in South Florida.

But on Election Night, Florida was called early for Trump. Biden managed to flip three counties Trump had won in 2016—Duval (Jacksonville), Pinellas (St. Petersburg), and Seminole (Orlando suburbs)—and reduced Trump's winning margin in Escambia County (Pensacola) by five points. According to exit polls, Biden cut Trump's edge among seniors to 10 points from 17 points four years earlier. However, Trump held his ground in most Florida counties, and made stunning gains in vote-rich Miami-Dade County, primarily among Cuban Americans. After younger Cuban voters had moved toward the Democrats during the Obama era, Cuban voters under Trump responded strongly to his efforts to roll back Obama's opening to the island nation and to his portrayal of Democrats as socialists. Biden still won Miami-Dade, but by just seven points, a fraction of the 29-point margin Hillary Clinton managed in 2016. Amid heavy turnout, the Democratic presidential vote fell by more than 6,000 in Miami-Dade while Trump's support surged by almost 200,000. The pro-Trump spike also knocked out two first-term Democratic incumbents, Reps. Debbie Mucarsel-Powell and Donna Shalala. Trump also made gains with non-Cuban Hispanics; in heavily Puerto Rican Osceola County near Orlando, Trump cut the Democrats' winning margin from 25 points to 14. Trump even scored incremental gains in other South Florida Democratic bastions, cutting Democratic margins in Broward County (Fort Lauderdale) by five points and in Palm Beach County, the home of Mar-a-Lago, by two points.

Another key shortcoming for Democrats: The national Biden team instructed its state campaign and the Florida Democratic Party not to go door to door because it would conflict with Biden's message about social distancing. The GOP never stopped its ground game, and after the election, there was wide agreement that this policy cost Democrats. "Democrats didn't have a very effective ground game in Miami-Dade County," Florida International University professor Eduardo Gamarra told NBC. "From the beginning they were trying to defend themselves from the communist accusations. So it was difficult for them to develop a ground game. They did, but it was late." The Democratic failure was even more striking, given that a ballot measure to raise the minimum wage to $15 an hour passed with 61 percent of the vote. The Republican victory in the presidential race, coming on the heels of GOP gubernatorial and Senate wins in 2018, suggested it might be time to deem Florida's reputation as swing state a relic of the past.

Population		Race and Ethnicity		Income	
Total	21,477,737	White	74.50%	Median Income	59,227
Land area (sq. miles)	53,625	Black	16.00%	State Income Rank	34 out of 50
Pop/ sq mi	400.52	Latino	26.40%	Poverty Rate	12.70%
Born in state	35.80%	Asian	3.70%	With health insurance	86.80%
		Two or more races	2.90%	Cash public assistance	2.00%
Age Groups		Other	3.80%	Food stamp/SNAP	14.4%
Under 18	19.70%				
18-34	21.20%	Education		Work	
35-64	38.30%	H.S grad or less	40.00%	White Collar	36.50%
Over 64	20.90%	Some college	29.30%	Sales and Service	43.40%
		College Degree, 4 yr	19.30%	Blue Collar	20.10%
Military		Post grad	11.40%	Government	11.20%
Veteran/ Active Duty	8.60%				

Presidential Politics

2020 Primary (D)	Biden (D)	1,077,375(62%)	Sanders (D)	397,311(23%)	Bloomberg (D)	146,544 (8%)
2020 Pres. Vote	Trump (R)	5,668,731(51%)	Biden (D)	5,297,045(48%)		
2016 Pres. Vote	Trump (R)	4,617,886(49%)	Clinton (D)	4,504,975(47%)	Johnson (L)	207,043 (2%)

For the past three decades, Florida was both the largest and one of the most competitive battleground states in the country. With 29 electoral votes, the same number as New York, only California and Texas have more. Florida Democratic strategist Steven Schale, one of the state's savviest political observers, notes that from 1992 to 2016, more than 50 million votes have been cast in seven presidential elections and the two parties were separated by a miniscule 0.02 percent: Republican candidates having received a net 12,000 votes more than Democrats. But while both campaigns hotly contested Florida in 2020, Donald Trump won it by a shockingly comfortable margin, defeating Joe Biden 51.2%-47.9% with a margin of almost 372,000 votes. That's a landslide by Florida standards, the largest win for either party in a presidential election since 2004—and 7.6 points more Republican than the national popular vote, the farthest Florida's results have been from the national results since 1988. Joe Biden is the first person since John F. Kennedy to win the White House without carrying Florida.

Florida's presidential elections have been close for decades, but in reality the state has long leaned a bit more Republican than the nation as a whole. In every election since 1976, Florida's results have been more Republican than the national popular vote. And while the state will likely stay a battleground, it may not play the crucial role in future presidential contests that it has in past decades.

Trump's adopted home state was a top priority for both campaigns, a must-win for Trump and a virtual guarantee of victory for Biden. "You hold the key. If Florida goes blue, it's over," Biden said at a late October rally in Broward County.

It was both candidates' second-most-visited state, behind Pennsylvania; Trump made 16 campaign trips to Florida during the general election, while Biden was there eight times. The campaigns and their allies also spent more on Florida's expensive airwaves than on any other state, including a $100-million late investment from Michael Bloomberg to boost Biden in the state.

But while Biden and his allies outspent Trump in the state, Trump's campaign spent months targeting Florida's Hispanic voters—especially Cuban and Venezuelan Americans in South Florida. They hammered on the message that Biden was a socialist, tying him to his party's left wing and Latin American leftist dictators. The attacks did serious damage. Miami-Dade County shifted right by a whopping 22 points from 2016 to 2020, the largest swing in any populous county in the nation. Biden carried Miami-Dade by just 7 points and 85,000 votes, down from Clinton's 290,000-vote margin in the county. That shift alone accounted for more than three quarters of Trump's statewide improvement. Cubans weren't the only Hispanic population that shifted against Democrats, however —Biden won Osceola County, which is majority-Hispanic and heavily Puerto Rican, by just 14 percentage points after Clinton carried it by 25.

Biden actually did slightly better than Clinton in the areas around Tampa Bay, Jacksonville, and parts of the ruby-red panhandle, including Tallahassee, but it was far from enough.

Trump's win there was the first clear result on election night, sent some Democrats into panic mode and kept Biden from a quick knockout blow. But it also quickly became clear that Trump's win was powered by a huge swing in South Florida, a part of the U.S. unlike any other.

Biden's lack of a field operation in Florida due to the coronavirus pandemic, especially compared to Hillary Clinton's Miami machine, likely made a big difference as well.

Florida's presidential primary had not been crucial in determining a nomination between 1976, when Democrat Jimmy Carter defeated George Wallace and ended Wallace's career in national politics, and 2008, when Arizona Sen. John McCain defeated Mitt Romney, a victory that propelled him to success one week later on Super Tuesday. In 2016, Trump's comfortable win in the state forced home-state Sen. Marco Rubio from the race. In 2020, Florida's primary was held on March 17, two weeks after Biden's big Super Tuesday wins and just as it became clear exactly how big a threat the coronavirus would be. Biden dominated with a 62%-23% win over Bernie Sanders, carrying every county; along with Biden wins the same day in Illinois and Arizona, the result all but ended Sanders' already-flagging hopes for a comeback (he suspended his campaign two weeks later). The election was relatively uninterrupted because of Florida's heavy use of mail voting.

Florida might remain a swing state in the years to come, but it's unlikely to be the bellwether it has been unless presidential politics shifts once again in the coming years.

Congressional Districts

117th Congress Lineup	10D 16R 1V	116th Congress Lineup	13D 14R

Florida has gained congressional districts after every census since 1930, when it elected four House members. Its 17-seat gain since 1960 is more than any other state, including Texas, during those 60 years. With its one-seat gain in the latest reapportionment, it has surpassed New York. Heading into the 2022 redistricting, Florida's House delegation is 16 Republicans and 11 Democrats. A decade ago, by contrast, the count was 19 Republicans and six Democrats, which proved to be an unrealistic high point for the GOP.

As all sides prepared for the 2022 redistricting, two factors were the same as a decade ago: Republicans retain partisan control in Tallahassee and the state is gaining a seat. This time, they seem better positioned to retain all their incumbent seats. The GOP might seek to force a Democratic incumbent into a more competitive seat, most likely in the center of the state. Two tempting targets could be the districts of Reps. Stephanie Murphy and Charlie Crist; in each case, they were first elected in 2016, as beneficiaries of the mid-decade redistricting that gave them the opportunity to take control of long-time Republican seats. But that could jeopardize at least one of their own incumbents in that area. The safest GOP course likely would be to concede the 11 Democratic-held seats, entrench their most vulnerable incumbents and stake their claim to the additional district. Based on population growth and partisan shifts, the best GOP prospects for those new seats likely would be in growing Republican exurbs. Those could be in the north central part of the state or a strip across the southern part of Florida from the southern Gulf coast to the Treasure Coast north of Palm Beach County. Except for Jacksonville and Miami-Dade County, Republicans in the remainder of Florida have largely conceded districts in metro areas.

Following the 2010 census, Republican Gov. Rick Scott's narrow victory and big GOP margins in the legislature gave Republicans control of the redistricting process. But they consistently lost seats in the past decade—until 2020. Even in the 2012 redistricting, their growth opportunities were limited by two factors: Republicans' robust 19-6 edge following a banner year, and a voter-approved referendum in 2010 seeking to rein in the kind of gerrymandering that had created one of the strangest patchworks of districts in the country. Democrats made the most of their opportunities. Since 2012, they have held at least 10 of the 27 seats. With the court-ordered redistricting plan in 2016, they gained three seats—two in the Orlando area (with a boost from the influx of Puerto Ricans from the island) and one in St. Petersburg—though they lost one seat in south Florida. In 2018, they picked up two Hispanic-majority seats in Miami-Dade County. Combined with their loss of two seats outside the large metro areas, the delegation shifted to 14 Republicans and 13 Democrats—the Democrats' high point since 1990.

But the tide turned in 2020, when Republicans regained their two seats in Miami-Dade. As a result, Democrats hold a minority seat in north Florida, three seats in the Orlando area, two in Tampa-St. Petersburg and five in south Florida. Following the 2020 election, the Democratic delegation included four African Americans, one Latino and an Asian American; six of the 11 are women. (Democratic Rep. Alcee Hastings died in April 2021; his seat is a virtual lock to retain Democratic control.) Prior to the most recent election, all but one of the Republicans were white males. The exception, Mario Diaz-Balart, was the most senior of the GOP group. Their five current freshmen (three of whom took GOP open seats) include one African-American, two Latinos and two women.

Looming over the planning by the two parties are the activist reformers—with their continuing threat of voter initiatives and court review. Their Fair District movement had a significant impact in the past decade, starting with passage of the 2010 referendum. That action required legislators to draw compact districts conforming to county and city boundaries and prohibited them from considering partisan data or incumbent residences. The delayed impact resulted in the court-drawn map for the 2016 election that gave Democrats a net gain of two seats.

The recent history of redistricting in Florida suggests that neither party has been inclined to take the course of least resistance, and that citizens groups will assert their prerogatives. It's a safe bet that the state and federal courts will have additional opportunities for influence.

Ron DeSantis (R)

Elected 2018, term expires 2023, 1st term; b. Sept. 14, 1978, Jacksonville, FL; Yale University, B.A., 2001; Harvard Law School, J.D., 2005; Catholic; Married (Casey); 2 children.

Military Career: US Navy, 2004-2010 (Iraq); US Navy Reserves, 2010-pres.

Elected Office: US House, 2013-2018.

Professional Career: Military Prosecutor, United States Navy; Federal Prosecutor, U.S. Department of Justice; Lecturer, Law of War, Florida Coastal School of Law.

Office: 400 S. Monroe St. Tallahassee, 32399-0001; 850-488-7146; Fax: 850-487-0801

Lt. Gov.: Jeanette Núñez (R) **Atty. Gen:** Ashley Moody (R)

State Legislature: Senate: 17D, 23R **House:** 46D, 71R, 3I

Election Results

Election	Name (Party)	Vote (%)
2018 General	Ron DeSantis (R)	4,076,186 (50%)
	Andrew Gillum (D)	4,043,723 (49%)
2018 Primary	Ron DeSantis (R)	916,298 (57%)
	Adam Putnam (R)	592,518 (37%)

Prior winning percentage: House: 2016 (59%), 2014 (63%), 2012 (57%)

With the strong support of President Donald Trump, Republican Rep. Ron DeSantis won the Florida governorship in 2018 by just 32,000 votes out of more than 8 million cast. The victory rocketed DeSantis to national prominence just months after turning 40. After taking office, DeSantis won praise from all corners for an ideologically eclectic agenda, but his approval ratings fell as he took a more combative, Trump-aligned approach, particularly after the onset of the coronavirus pandemic.

DeSantis' father installed television ratings devices for Nielsen. A talented baseball player, DeSantis played on a team from Dunedin that made the final four of the 1991 Little League World Series. He went on to captain the squad at Yale, where he majored in history. To help pay for his studies, he held a variety of jobs, including collecting trash, moving furniture and coaching baseball clinics. He earned his law degree at Harvard and became a judge advocate general in the Navy, earning a Bronze Star and serving at Guantanamo Bay and in Iraq. His military service helped shape his views on national security, including a skepticism of nation-building. While there are a lot of "good people" in Iraq, he added that "getting involved in guerilla war doesn't play to our strengths." He remained a lieutenant commander in the Navy Reserve. In 2009, he married his wife, Casey, a former TV host in Jacksonville, who by all accounts has remained one of DeSantis' few close confidants.

DeSantis ran for office when the new 6th District unexpectedly had no incumbent following the 2012 redistricting. He had written a book, Dreams From Our Founding Fathers, a play off President Barack Obama's memoir, Dreams From My Father. Touting his military experience and strong conservative views, DeSantis easily defeated six rivals in the primary, winning 39 percent of the vote. In the general election, he faced Democrat Heather Beaven, a fellow Navy veteran. In the heavily Republican district DeSantis won, 57%-43%.

In the House, DeSantis forged ties to conservative Republicans, but also built bridges to the party's establishment. Unlike several other junior Republicans from Florida, he voted in January 2015 to give John Boehner another term as Speaker, despite pressure from constituents to oppose him; this helped enable DeSantis to secure the chairmanship of the Oversight and Government Reform Subcommittee on National Security. But DeSantis also helped found the Freedom Caucus, which would go on to cause headaches for Boehner and his team. Facing pressure from Majority Whip Steve Scalise to toe the party line, DeSantis quit his post on the Republican whip team. "Very few people got to know DeSantis," former GOP Rep. David Jolly told Politico. "Beyond his Freedom Caucus buddies, I don't really think he had many relationships at all." DeSantis didn't exactly deny that, saying, "I was not in Congress to necessarily socialize. I really wasn't there to necessarily make friends."

After Sen. Marco Rubio said he would run for president and forgo reelection to the Senate in 2016, DeSantis entered the race. His plan was to run as the conservative alternative, with extensive support from national advocacy groups such as the Club for Growth and Senate Conservatives Fund. But he faced steep challenges in gaining traction in the wide-open GOP primary, including low name ID outside his district and the greater diversity among Florida Republicans than within his constituency. As DeSantis was struggling, Rubio responded to pleas from party leaders to reclaim his seat days before the June filing deadline. After Rubio jumped back in, DeSantis quit the Senate race. DeSantis, with a large war chest, won the House primary, 61%-25%, over state Rep. Fred Costello, the second-place finisher in the 2012 primary that DeSantis had won. In November, DeSantis coasted to a 59%-41% victory.

Two years later, DeSantis sought higher office again—this time the governorship, which was coming open with the impending departure of term-limited Republican Gov. Rick Scott. Initially, the frontrunner for the GOP nomination was Adam Putnam, a former state legislator and congressman and, most recently, the twice-elected state agriculture secretary. Putnam, a familiar figure in the state who came from a prominent citrus family, had locked up most of the GOP establishment support and amassed a significant campaign treasury. But DeSantis gained ground, in part thanks to Trump, who on Twitter and in person made clear that DeSantis was his favorite. Trump-aligned conservative media figures followed with their support, as did GOP megadonor Sheldon Adelson. DeSantis ran a nationally focused campaign, making "121 appearances on Fox and Fox Business," which his campaign estimated would have cost $9.3 million to purchase, wrote veteran Florida political reporter Marc Caputo. DeSantis even aired a commercial in which he taught one of his children to build Trump's border wall using blocks and read The Art of the Deal to his infant. Despite being mocked outside of pro-Trump circles, the ad—and DeSantis' overall strategy—proved immensely popular among the GOP's base voters. DeSantis won, 57%-37%.

The Democratic primary was at least as interesting, with an equally unexpected result. The frontrunner for the nomination was former Rep. Gwen Graham, a moderate and the daughter of popular former Gov. and Sen. Bob Graham. Other candidates included former Miami Beach Mayor Philip Levine and a pair of deep-pocketed businessmen, Chris King and Jeff Greene. Tallahassee Mayor Andrew Gillum, despite his evident charisma and oratorical skills, attracted relatively little attention at first. Gillum—like DeSantis, 39 years old at the time of his nomination—was the fifth of seven children born to a bus driver and a construction laborer. At Florida A&M University, where he became the first in his family to earn a college degree, Gillum became a leader in student government and drove opposition to then-Gov. Jeb Bush's education policies. Gillum was elected to the Tallahassee City Commission at 23 and became mayor for four years. Gillum found success with a staunchly progressive agenda that was in tune with the Democrats' most likely voters. Gillum took 34 percent to Graham's 31 percent, Levine's 20, and Greene and King far behind. The twin victories by DeSantis and Gillum left nominees on the ideological ends of the spectrum in the nation's most populous swing state.

In the general election, DeSantis reaffirmed his conservative agenda. He advocated tax cuts and repeal of the Affordable Care Act, and said he would not have signed the gun control bill signed by Scott after the mass shooting at Marjory Stoneman Douglas High School in Parkland. Gillum stuck with his progressive agenda—so much so that Democratic Sen. Bill Nelson, a moderate engaged in an intense reelection battle against Scott, distanced himself from Gillum's policy agenda. Gillum maintained a modest but consistent lead in the polls, but DeSantis put together a narrow victory—so close that it was a week and a half before Gillum conceded. Gillum managed to secure about 90 percent of the votes that Hillary Clinton had won in the presidential year of 2016, and flipped Duval County (Jacksonville), Pinellas County (St. Petersburg), Seminole County (suburban Orlando) and St. Lucie County (Fort Pierce). DeSantis won, however, because Trump wasn't as unpopular in Florida as he was in other states, and because he over performed in Miami-Dade County after assiduously courting Hispanic voters—not just Cuban Americans but also Venezuelans and Central Americans who responded to the Republicans' labeling of Gillum as a socialist (an argument that would prove even more potent for Republicans in 2020). The transition between Scott and DeSantis proved awkward; shortly before leaving office, Scott announced appointments for some 84 positions, but a piqued DeSantis rescinded the 46 that required Senate approval.

In office, DeSantis worked with Republicans to undermine a statewide ballot measure that cleared the way for hundreds of thousands of ex-felons to be able to vote. A new law slowed the process, requiring ex-felons to pay all their outstanding fees before being allowed to vote. Critics called this a poll tax, but the U.S. Supreme Court in 2020 allowed the law to stand. DeSantis pleased conservatives by signing a bill restricting "sanctuary cities," and he cheered business interests by enacting an expansion of toll roads. But DeSantis also won applause from Democrats for spending big on Everglades restoration and for hiring a chief science officer with a portfolio that included sea-level rise. "DeSantis isn't sticking to one playbook," Emily L. Mahoney and Steve Contorno wrote in the Tampa Bay Times. "He plays hardball at times. He demanded lawmakers allow smokable medical marijuana. He surprised the state with his first veto: a bill that prohibited cities from banning plastic drinking straws."

But his second year in office proved to be less convivial. DeSantis openly feuded with Agriculture Commissioner Nikki Fried, the only statewide elected Democrat and a potential challenger in 2022, going so far as to cancel cabinet meetings, where Fried could have promoted a platform. On the heels of Black Lives Matter protests, DeSantis provoked his critics by proposing new penalties for public demonstrations that result in injuries and that would make it a crime to obstruct traffic during protests without a permit; it received backing from GOP leaders but was not enacted. DeSantis quietly signed one bill requiring parental consent for abortion and another to require some employers to use the E-Verify immigration database, although the latter included some exceptions for much of the agriculture industry. He also signed a measure to raise the bar for approving ballot measures; this irked Democrats, who had used ballot measures to enact policies they couldn't as a minority party.

DeSantis' sternest test was the coronavirus pandemic. The governor took a combative approach, and one usually aligned with priorities backed by Trump. DeSantis pushed for a quick reopening of the economy and called on Florida school districts to conduct five days of in-person teaching in the fall. In the summer, even as cases were rising, DeSantis touted the state as open for business; he courted the Republican National Convention and declared that professional wrestling was an "essential" business. (One notable success was the completion of the National Basketball Association's season, held in a "bubble" in Orlando and almost entirely free of the virus.) But local officials knocked DeSantis for restricting their ability to enforce coronavirus mandates locally, public health officials questioned his administration's handling of data on the virus, residents complained about a bumpy vaccine rollout, and gubernatorial approval ratings showed double-digit declines. One of the pandemic's most serious shortcomings was the state's dysfunctional unemployment insurance system, which was crafted during the Scott administration. "It's a shit sandwich, and it was designed that way by Scott," one DeSantis advisor told Politico. "It wasn't about saving money. It was about making it harder for people to get benefits or keep benefits so that the unemployment numbers were low to give the governor something to brag about." Ultimately, though, none of this tumult prevented Trump from achieving a historic victory in the state.

And by the end of 2020, Florida had relatively modest rates of cases and deaths, leading DeSantis to take a victory lap and easing coronavirus restrictions. He also pressed an aggressive agenda in 2021 that was expected to burnish his standing with the GOP base. He signed largely party-line measures to restrict voting drop boxes and mail balloting, as well as a law to increase penalties for public disorder crimes and provide civil liability protections for motorists who injure protesters.

DeSantis is one of several Florida Republicans with presidential ambitions, alongside Scott and Sen. Marco Rubio. Despite Florida Democrats' deep disappointments in 2020, several prospects explored a challenge. As of late spring, the frontrunners for the nomination were Fried and Rep. Charlie Crist, who served one term as a Republican governor before narrowly losing a bid as the Democratic nominee in 2014. But one who won't be on the list is Gillum. In March 2020, police found him on a bathroom floor in a Miami Beach hotel with a companion alongside prescription drugs and suspected crystal meth. Within days, Gillum had checked himself into rehab for treatment of alcoholism and depression and said he would step back from public life.

Marco Rubio (R)

Elected 2010, term expires 2022, 2nd term, b. May 28, 1971; Miami, FL; Tarkio College, Att., 1990; Santa Fe College, Att., 1991; University of Florida, B.S., 1993; University of Miami, J.D., 1996; Roman Catholic; Married (Jeanette Dousdebes); 4 children.

Elected Office: West Miami City Commissioner, 1998-2000; FL House, 2000-2008, Speaker, 2006-2008.

Professional Career: Practicing attorney, 1997-2010; Professor, FL Intl. University, 2009-2010.

DC Office: 284 RSOB 20510, 202-224-3041, Fax: 202-228-0285, rubio.senate.gov

State Offices: Jacksonville, 904-354-4300; Miami, 305-596-4224; Orlando, 407-254-2573; Palm Beach Gardens, 561-775-3360; Pensacola, 850-433-2603; Tallahassee, 850-599-9100; Tampa, 813-853-1099.

Committees: *Aging. Appropriations*: Department of the Interior, Environment & Related Agencies; DOL, HHS & Education & Related Agencies; Legislative Branch; Military Construction & Veteran Affairs & Related Agencies; State, Foreign Operations & Related Programs. *Foreign Relations*: Africa & Global Health Policy; State Dept & USAID Mngmnt, Internat'l Ops & Internat'l Dev; West Hem Crime Civ Sec Dem Rights & Women's Issues (RMM). *Intelligence. Small Business & Entrepreneurship*.

Group Ratings

	ADA	ACLU	AFL-CIO	LCV	COC	HAFA	ACU	CFG	FRC
2020	-	9%	-	15%	-	76%	89%	-	-
2019	10%	C	17%	7%	83%	C	91%	66%	100%

Almanac Ratings 2019-2020

	Economy	Social	Foreign	Composite
Liberal	0%	0%	0%	0%
Conservative	100%	100%	100%	100%

Key Votes of the 116th Congress

1. EPA clean energy rules	N	5. Russia sanctions	Y	9. Barr as Atty. General	Y
2. U.S./Mex./Can. trade deal	Y	6. Troops in SYR, AFG	Y	10. Spending at the border	Y
3. Cut unemployment benefits	Y	7. Veto arms sales to Saudis	N	11. Coney Barrett to Sup. Ct.	Y
4. Shelton to Fed Reserve	Y	8. Defense $$$, veto override	Y	12. Electoral College objections	N

Election Results

Election	Name (Party)	Vote (%)		Cand. Spent	Ind. Exp. Support	Ind. Exp. Oppose
2016 General	Marco Rubio (R)	4,835,191	(52%)	$21,152,492	$6,102,547	$6,894,783
	Patrick Murphy (D)	4,122,088	(44%)	$8,684,853	$5,145,141	$28,326,406
	Paul Stanton (L)	196,956	(2%)	$19,601		
2016 Primary	Marco Rubio (R)	1,029,830	(72%)			
	Carlos Beruff (R)	264,427	(19%)			

Prior winning percentages: 2016 (52%), 2010 (49%)

Marco Rubio, Florida's senior senator, has gone through a remarkable number of political transformations in his still-young political career. He had been: a conservative institutionalist in the Florida Legislature, a tea party darling in 2010, a rising national star promoted by establishment-minded party elders in the Senate, a key player on immigration reform efforts in 2013, a top-tier presidential candidate in 2015 and one of many candidates vanquished in embarrassing fashion by

Donald Trump in that campaign. In Rubio's second term in the Senate, he was mostly a party-line vote for his onetime primary rival, though he's held fast on the foreign policy issues closest to his heart.

Born in Miami, Rubio grew up in a working-class neighborhood near Little Havana. He was the third child of emigrants who left Cuba in 1956, before Fidel Castro came to power. Rubio has often described himself as the "son of exiles" who were forced out by Castro's regime, though he used that characterization less after facing media scrutiny over whether he had embellished the story. His father worked long days as a hotel bartender after immigrating to Miami, and his mother was a hotel maid with a second job at Kmart. The family moved to follow work; Rubio spent six years in Las Vegas while his parents worked in hotels before he returned to Miami for high school. At the encouragement of an aunt, he was baptized as a Mormon along with his mother and sister, only to convert back to Catholicism as a teenager.

Rubio was initially a Democrat, inspired by Massachusetts Sen. Ted Kennedy's famous "the dream shall never die" speech at the 1980 Democratic National Convention. But he soon joined his grandfather in becoming a staunch Reagan supporter. Rubio played football in high school, and despite his small stature, he earned a football scholarship to Tarkio College in Missouri. He returned to Florida after the school went bankrupt, spent a year at a junior college and then earned his bachelor's degree at the University of Florida. As an undergraduate, he worked for a couple leading Cuban-American GOP politicians from the Miami area, interning for Rep. Ileana Ros-Lehtinen and volunteering on Rep. Lincoln Díaz-Balart's first campaign.

In his last year at the University of Miami Law School, Rubio ran the Dade County operation for Republican Sen. Bob Dole's presidential campaign in 1996. There, he met future Florida Gov. Jeb Bush, who served as a mentor and ally until their relationship soured when both ran for president in 2016.

At 26, Rubio ousted a city commissioner in West Miami, a small, heavily Cuban town just south of Miami International Airport. He still lives there with his wife, Jeanette, a onetime Miami Dolphins cheerleader, and their four children. Rubio had been on the city commission only a year before running for the state House. Rubio quickly rose through the ranks in Tallahassee, becoming Florida House speaker in 2005 at 34, the youngest person and the first Hispanic-American to achieve that position. At a ceremony, Bush presented him with a sword, a symbolic passing of the conservative torch in the state.

Forced out of the state House by term limits, Rubio caught the tea party movement's lightning in its nascent days and used it to power his upstart Senate primary campaign against then-popular Republican Gov. Charlie Crist. The governor had been urged by leading national Republicans to run for the Senate, and he had huge cash and name recognition advantages. Rubio initially seemed ready to defer to Crist, telling the Tampa Bay Times in early 2009 that Crist was the "best candidate" for the job. But conservatives never trusted Crist, who is now a House Democratic member. His embrace of President Barack Obama's $787 billion economic stimulus bill—and his literal embrace of the president at a public event—infuriated many. Rubio announced his bid in May 2009 and received early support from then-Sen. Jim DeMint of South Carolina, a conservative stalwart who was backing insurgent GOP candidates, as well as quiet support from Bush and his allies. By the time Crist realized the conservative base was slipping away, it was too late. On the verge of losing the primary in the spring of 2010, Crist quit the Republican Party to run as an independent.

In the general election, Rubio faced Crist and the Democratic nominee, Rep. Kendrick Meek. Crist started with an early lead in the polls, but his support plummeted as he got caught in the crossfire from Rubio on the right and Meek on the left, both of whom painted Crist as an opportunist. Crist tried to become the de facto Democratic candidate, but Meek refused to drop out, denying Crist a matchup with Rubio. Tea party activists embraced Rubio's campaign and slogan "Reclaim America," but Rubio was careful not to come off as a firebrand, like some of the movement's other stars. He stressed fiscal responsibility, opposed abortion rights and took a more conservative position than Crist on immigration, supporting Arizona's crackdown on undocumented immigrants. Rubio won the race with 49 percent of the vote; Crist took 30 percent and Meek 20 percent.

In the Senate, Rubio's voting pattern initially kept the tea party happy. He was one of just eight senators to oppose the New Year's Day 2013 fiscal cliff deal. However, at party elders' urging, Rubio sought to offer his party a lifeline on immigration to bolster its low standing among Hispanic-Americans. He attempted to craft a compromise to the stalled DREAM Act aimed at helping undocumented immigrants brought to the U.S. as children. His alternative called for extending legal residency to immigrants bound for college or the military. The proposal came under sharp attack from the right, and he sought to characterize it as being less about immigration and more about humanitarian relief for a group facing deportation. But Rubio's political momentum ended in 2011 when Obama used his executive powers to put into place the major elements of Rubio's bill, leaving the senator grumbling that he deserved some of the credit.

With the 2012 presidential campaign looming, Rubio—after vowing to remain neutral during the primary season—endorsed former Massachusetts Gov. Mitt Romney and came to Romney's aid on immigration. Romney had Rubio on his running-mate shortlist before picking Wisconsin Rep. Paul Ryan. The speculation benefited the senator, elevating his national profile while leaving him a safe political distance from a candidate many conservatives considered inauthentic. Rubio introduced Romney at the Republican National Convention in Tampa. His speech drew widespread praise, with some pundits deeming it the best of the convention.

Buzz about a 2016 presidential run began after Obama's reelection. Rubio did little to tamp it down, giving several policy-oriented speeches, including one in which he mentioned the phrase "middle class" nearly three dozen times while discussing the need to close "the opportunity gap." As income inequality became an increasingly prominent issue, Rubio worked to come up with a conservative answer, focusing on college affordability. He was chosen to give the Republican response to Obama's State of the Union address in 2013. That didn't go well, as Rubio's dry-mouthed struggle through the first half of the speech and a frantic dive for a water bottle drew more attention than anything he said.

After hesitating, Rubio joined what became known as the "Gang of Eight" negotiations on immigration. The group produced a comprehensive bipartisan bill to tighten border security while creating an eventual path to citizenship for many undocumented immigrants. The legislation passed the Senate by a wide margin in 2013, but House GOP leaders refused to take it up. Rubio got some praise from donors and establishment figures but faced severe blowback from his former tea party allies. Right-wing radio turned on its onetime hero, and Rubio, who had been leading some early 2016 presidential polls, saw his stock plummet. He retreated to his original stance on immigration, telling a crowd at the 2015 Conservative Political Action Conference that he had learned voters would not approve a pathway to citizenship until it's "proven to them that future illegal immigration will be controlled"—and that immigration reform should be done in a piecemeal fashion, with border security first.

Rubio announced his presidential bid in April 2015, seeking to draw a contrast with both Bush and former Secretary of State Hillary Clinton, the Democratic front-runner. "This election is a generational choice about what kind of country we will be," Rubio said in his announcement speech. As the campaign heated up, he sought to further distance himself from his past immigration work.

Rubio finished third in the first-in-the-nation Iowa caucuses in early February 2016 and rolled into New Hampshire with a head of steam. But his campaign came apart on the debate stage a few days later, and he never recovered. As New Jersey Gov. Chris Christie badgered him for repeating a "memorized 25-second speech," Rubio lost his usual oratorical command, proving Christie's point by repeating talking points over and over. Rubio finished fifth in New Hampshire. He was steadier in later debates and finished second in two other early voting states, South Carolina and Nevada. But Rubio still trailed Trump and knew he needed to shake things up to prevail in his must-win home state primary. Rubio tried to match insults with the front-running Trump, a move he later said he regretted. After mocking Trump's appearance, skin tone and hand size, he moved to another body part: "You know what they say about guys with small hands," Rubio snickered. Trump, master of the snide nickname, later derided Rubio as "Little Marco" in a debate 10 days before their showdown in Florida.

Trump won that primary by a landslide, 46%-27%, carrying 66 of 67 counties. Some suggested the loss, which forced Rubio's withdrawal from the presidential race, was a byproduct of Rubio burning too many bridges at home. Others attributed Rubio's demise to failing to build on the optimistic, forward-looking persona that had gotten him elected to the Senate six years earlier. Rubio himself argued his downfall came from factors outside his control—an upbeat message at odds with the angry mood of many in the electorate. "America is in the middle of a real political storm, a real tsunami, and we should have seen this coming," Rubio told Real Clear Politics. "Look, people are angry, and people are very frustrated." But Rubio's series of strategic missteps, particularly on immigration, and his inability to go toe-to-toe with Christie, much less Trump, also were key factors in his loss.

Having grown frustrated with the body's often slow pace, Rubio swore time and again that he was done with the Senate even if his presidential campaign came up short: "I have only said like 10,000 times I will be a private citizen in January," he tweeted in May 2016. But by the end of June, he was a candidate for reelection—prodded both by fears among Republican leaders that the seat was in jeopardy without him in the race and by his own hope of remaining relevant on the national political scene. He promised to be a check on Trump should they both win: "We will need senators willing to encourage him in the right direction, and if necessary, stand up to him. I've proven a willingness to do both," he said as he announced his Senate run. Other top GOP candidates bowed out, and Rubio won the primary with 72 percent of the vote.

A victory in November wasn't a sure bet in a state where Clinton was ahead in many polls and national Democratic leaders had lined up behind two-term Rep. Patrick Murphy. Murphy, borrowing a page from some of Rubio's presidential rivals, raised the issue of the incumbent's high Senate absenteeism rate. The Democrat also sought to tie Rubio to Trump at every turn. But the 33-year-old Murphy was hit with media reports showing that he had overstated his résumé, and Rubio had a big edge in campaign spending: In the closing weeks of the campaign, as they concluded that Murphy had no path to victory, national Democratic groups pulled back on Florida ad buys to concentrate on less expensive media markets in other states. Rubio won 52%-44%, as Trump bested Clinton in the state 49%-48%. Exit polls showed Rubio, who had tepidly endorsed Trump just before the Republican convention in July, running several points ahead of Trump among women and independent voters while outdistancing Trump by double digits among Latinos.

Returning to Washington, Rubio refocused on the Foreign Relations Committee. With Trump entering the White House, Rubio signaled that he would continue calling for a more muscular, interventionist America. He teamed with Democratic Sen. Ed Markey of Massachusetts to urge the new president to strengthen the system of longstanding U.S. strategic alliances—notably NATO, the subject of several skeptical comments by Trump. "I'm prepared to be a senator that will encourage him to make the right decisions but also stand up to the bad decisions and the bad policies," Rubio said.

For a time, it appeared Rubio might derail the confirmation of Trump's first secretary of State, Rex Tillerson—a former Exxon Mobil chief executive known for his close relationship with Russian President Vladimir Putin. Rubio, who had characterized Putin as a "gangster" and "thug" during the presidential campaign, expressed "serious concerns" about Tillerson and grilled the nominee during hearings. Hours before the committee vote, Rubio backed away from a confrontation with his erstwhile rival for the White House and announced he'd back Tillerson.

That was not the only time Rubio threatened to take on Trump before backing down. He warned he might oppose Trump's pick to head NASA, Oklahoma Rep. Jim Bridenstine, because he wanted a nonpolitician to lead a program that is a major job creator in Florida's "Space Coast" region. Rubio relented after Bridenstine promised he'd run the agency in a nonpolitical way, casting the deciding vote for confirmation.

Rubio also backed Trump's trade war with China, after earlier criticizing Trump for not being aggressive enough. It was a new stance for Rubio, and in taking it, he took a Trumpian tone on Twitter: "Sadly #China is out-negotiating the administration & winning the trade talks right now," he wrote in May 2018. "This is #NotWinning." But Rubio went further than Trump in pushing against the country's human rights abuses too. Along with Republican Sen. Ted Cruz of Texas, Rubio has worked to punish China for its abuse of ethnic minorities; in return, China symbolically sanctioned the duo. Rubio's bill to require Trump to implement sanctions against the top Communist Party official in the region where more than a million Uyghur Muslims were being held in internment camps overwhelmingly passed the Senate and House and was signed into law. It also directed U.S. intelligence to compile a list of Chinese companies involved in building and maintaining the camp, a provision that the Chamber of Commerce opposed, worrying that it could punish companies doing legitimate business in Xinjiang.

But Rubio remained consistent on some key foreign policy priorities that have long driven his worldview, refusing to join other Republicans who defended Trump at all costs. He persuaded Trump to reverse Obama-era policies opening trade and travel with Cuba and played a role in pushing Trump toward more hard-line policies toward Venezuela. As a member of the Senate Intelligence Committee, Rubio defended special counsel Robert Mueller's investigation into whether Russia had colluded with Trump's 2016 presidential campaign. Rubio's campaign had been targeted by Russian agents during the 2016 primary, according to Mueller's probe. He's repeatedly voted for sanctions on Russia and introduced legislation that would automatically trigger sanctions on countries that the director of national intelligence determined had attempted to interfere in elections. In early 2019, Rubio was 1 of 11 GOP senators to break with Trump and vote with Democrats in an unsuccessful push to keep sanctions in place on an influential Russian oligarch with close ties to Putin.

In 2020, Rubio became acting chairman of the Intelligence Committee after North Carolina Sen. Richard Burr had to step aside amid an FBI investigation into his stock trades. Rubio was supportive of the panel's largely bipartisan investigation into Russia's interference in the 2016 election and its connections to Trump campaign, but he later claimed the report exonerated Trump, which it did not. He also didn't embrace some of the issues Trump wanted Republicans to focus on to distract from the 2020 election, namely an investigation into candidate Joe Biden's son Hunter. He also warned of Russian disinformation being disseminated leading up to the election. "I will say to you that I think it's pretty clear that the Russians are constantly pursuing narratives that they believe will drive conflict in our politics and divide us against each other," Rubio told Politico. He also pressed the White House on reports that Russia had offered bounties to Afghani militants in exchange for killing U.S. troops.

But Rubio co-opted some of Trump's rhetoric, calling for a "new nationalism" in a 2018 speech. And he continued to look for GOP-friendly policies to help low-income Americans and address his longtime concerns with income inequality. He worked with Ivanka Trump to develop paid family-leave legislation. He pushed Republicans to increase the expanded child tax credits for the working poor in the GOP's tax overhaul, threatening to vote against the bill if the credits weren't increased. He voted for the final package, which included large tax cuts for corporations and wealthy Americans after GOP leaders increased the tax credit to $1,400 from a proposed $1,100 per family. Rubio also introduced a bill in 2020 that would have permitted college athletes to be compensated when their names, images and likenesses are used for profit. It did not receive a vote.

During the COVID-19 pandemic, Rubio was one of the architects of the Paycheck Protection Program, which gave businesses money to keep paying employees. As the popular program was up for reauthorization, Rubio, who chaired the Small Business Committee, told Politico that new assistance should be "very targeted" to help businesses "survive and restart" and be particularly geared toward Black- and Hispanic-owned businesses, which data said were more likely to close.

After Trump's loss, Rubio quickly positioned himself for 2024: He didn't fully rebuke the outgoing president but he also began to chart a different path. Telling Axios that Republicans should rebrand themselves as champions of working-class voters instead of big business, he said, "The future of the party is based on a multiethnic, multiracial working-class coalition," and voters are "very suspicious, quite frankly dismissive of elites at every level. And obviously that's a powerful sentiment." He put that sentiment to use in opposing some of President Biden's Cabinet picks, tweeting that his nominees "went to Ivy League schools, have strong resumes, attend all the right conferences & will be polite & orderly caretakers of America's decline."

Rick Scott (R)

Elected 2018, term expires 2024, 1st term, b. Dec 01, 1952; Bloomington, IL; University of Missouri, B.S., 1975; Southern Methodist University Law School, J.D., 1978; Christian; Married (Ann Scott); 2 children; 6 grandchildren.

Military Career: U.S. Navy, 1970-1972.

Elected Office: FL Governor, 2011-2018.

Professional Career: Founder, Columbia Hospital Corporation, 1987-1997; Co-Founder, urgent-care medical chain; Founder, investment firm; Founder, online healthcare community; Attorney.

DC Office: 716 HSOB 20510, 202-224-5274, rickscott.senate.gov

State Offices: Tallahassee, 850-942-8415; Tampa, 813-225-7040.

Committees: National Republican Senatorial Committee Chairman. *Aging*. *Armed Services*: Airland; Emerging Threats & Capabilities; Seapower. *Budget*. *Commerce, Science & Transportation*: Communications, Media & Broadband; Space & Science; Surface Transportation, Maritime Freight & Ports; Tourism, Trade & Export Promotion (RMM). *Homeland Security & Government Affairs*: Emerging Threats & Spending Oversight; Investigations.

Almanac Ratings 2019-2020

	Economy	Social	Foreign	Composite
Liberal	47%	11%	1%	20%
Conservative	53%	89%	99%	80%

Key Votes of the 116th Congress

1. EPA clean energy rules	N	5. Russia sanctions	N	9. Barr as Atty. General	Y
2. U.S./Mex./Can. trade deal	Y	6. Troops in SYR, AFG	Y	10. Spending at the border	Y
3. Cut unemployment benefits	N/A	7. Veto arms sales to Saudis	N	11. Coney Barrett to Sup. Ct.	Y
4. Shelton to Fed Reserve	N/A	8. Defense $$$, veto override	Y	12. Electoral College objections	Y

Election Results

Election	Name (Party)	Vote (%)	Cand. Spent	Ind. Exp. Support	Ind. Exp. Oppose
2018 General	Rick Scott (R) 4,099,505	(50%)	$83,029,150	$554,877	$35,696,033
	Bill Nelson (D) 4,089,472	(50%)	$29,774,682	$19,150,229	$31,760,801
2018 Primary	Rick Scott (R) 1,456,187	(89%)			
	Roque De La Fuente (R) 187,209	(11%)			

Prior winning percentages: 2018 (50%), Governor: 2014 (48%), 2010 (49%)

Republican Rick Scott, a conservative former health care CEO, has used his huge personal fortune and hard-driving personality to grind out three straight statewide wins with less than 51 percent of the vote, proving to be a tough and resilient politician in America's ultimate swing state even as his aloof style has made him enemies in both parties. The former Florida governor, who moved to the Senate in 2019, is tasked winning back the GOP's Senate majority in 2022 as chairman of the National Republican Senatorial Committee.

Scott grew up in Kansas City Missouri, the son of a truck driver and a JCPenney clerk. He enlisted in the Navy after one year of community college. After his military service, Scott enrolled in the University of Missouri-Kansas City and, displaying an early entrepreneurial streak, financed his education by buying two doughnut shops and hiring his mother to manage them. After graduating, he earned a law degree from Southern Methodist University and joined a large firm, where he specialized in health care mergers and acquisitions.

In 1987, Scott put together a $6 billion bid to purchase HCA, a hospital company founded by the father and brother of former GOP Sen. Bill Frist of Tennessee. When that offer was rejected, he and Texas billionaire Richard Rainwater launched their own hospital company, Columbia, in 1988. That company expanded, buying dozens of hospitals in the next decade, and in 1994 Scott bought HCA on his second attempt.

By 1997, Columbia/HCA was the nation's largest health care company and its seventh largest employer, with 340 hospitals, $20 billion in revenue and 285,000 employees. But the FBI began investigating whether Columbia/HCA had overbilled Medicare and Medicaid, twice raiding the firm's hospitals. The board of directors ousted Scott, who wanted to fight the FBI's accusations rather than settling, shortly after the second raid. The firm pleaded guilty to several federal fraud charges in 2000 and 2002 and paid $1.7 billion in fines—the largest health care fraud fine in U.S. history at the time. Scott invoked his Fifth Amendment right against self-incrimination 75 times rather than answer questions during a related deposition— a spectacle that came to haunt his future campaigns. His business associates told the New York Times at the time that Scott was a brilliant and incisive businessman who was undone by his fatal flaws, including arrogance and aggressiveness that had permeated the company. Scott would later display both those traits in his political career.

Scott left Columbia/HCA with $10 million in cash and $300 million in stock and options. In rehabilitating his image, Scott maintained that he was never charged with wrongdoing. Scott later bought control of America's Health Network cable channel, and in 2001 he co-founded Solantic, which operates walk-in urgent care centers throughout Florida and specializes serving in patients without insurance. He moved to Naples in 2003.

As the national political conversation turned to health care during the early Obama years, Scott showed an increased interest in politics. In early 2009, he spent $5 million on TV ads attacking Democrats' health insurance reform proposals, particularly a provision creating a government-financed insurance option. A month after the Affordable Care Act became law in 2010, Scott launched his campaign for governor, immediately dropping another $5 million on ads.

The early GOP front-runner and establishment favorite was Attorney General Bill McCollum, a former House member and the 2000 GOP Senate nominee. Scott unveiled a catchy economic plan with seven steps to create 700,000 jobs in seven years by cutting corporate and property taxes, reducing public payroll, and streamlining government agencies. The two engaged in an intense TV ad war, with Scott painting McCollum as a tax-and-spend career politician and McCollum highlighting Columbia/HCA's Medicare fraud settlements. Scott spent nearly $50 million of his own money on the primary, edging McCollum, 46%-44%.

Scott's opponent in the general election was Florida Chief Financial Officer Alex Sink, a moderate former banker. The general election continued in an acrimonious vein, as Democratic ads revived the Columbia/HCA case and Republican ads painted Sink as a "Tallahassee insider" and a supporter of President Barack Obama, who was toxic in that year's midterm elections. Scott prevailed, 49%-48%, boosted by his huge campaign spending: $83 million, $73 million of which came from his own pocket. He carried Hispanics by a narrow margin and had a big lead among Cuban voters, according to exit polls.

Scott took a conservative approach, cutting the state budget by $1.3 billion and vetoing bills totaling a record $615 million, moves that thrilled tea party members but enraged some of the GOP lawmakers whose earmarks for local projects were axed. Scott took on teachers unions, signing education bills that expanded school voucher funding and increased charter school enrollment. He rejected $2.4 billion in federal transportation funds for a high-speed train line between Tampa and Orlando, claiming Florida taxpayers would have to pay for part of the project. The project had been in the works for years, and legislators from both parties criticized Scott's decision.

Scott enraged Democrats by requiring welfare recipients to take drug tests. The law proved popular with conservatives in other states but was struck down by a federal judge. Scott signed a bill cracking down on companies dealing with Cuba and Syria but infuriated many in the Cuban-American community by issuing a statement complaining that the law was unenforceable without support from the federal government. That earned a rebuke from Sen. Marco Rubio, who said Scott had undermined the new policy—one of many disputes between the two Florida Republicans over the years.

Scott shifted to the center as he prepared for reelection, looking to shed his tea party image and recast himself as an education champion. In 2014, he signed a record $77 billion budget that increased funding for public schools, universities, child protection services and the environment. After vetoing a bill in 2013 that would have allowed undocumented Florida residents to apply for a temporary driver's licenses, he signed legislation providing in-state college tuition to them in 2014, angering immigration hard-liners.

Scott's brash manner, combined with a sluggish economic recovery, kept his poll numbers low. The governor's vulnerability inspired former Republican Gov. Charlie Crist to make a comeback, this time as a Democrat. Crist scolded Scott for cutting education and restricting abortion, and he vowed to raise the minimum wage. Scott promised to pump money into education, environmental protection, airports and seaport infrastructure and to cut taxes by up to $1 billion while maintaining his focus on creating jobs.

Scott defeated Crist 48%-47%, bolstered by another GOP midterm wave. Scott once again spent a fortune, including more than $12 million in the race's closing days. Crist was better-funded than Sink but was still badly outspent. Scott didn't perform as strongly with Hispanic voters as he had before, losing the statewide Hispanic vote by a wide margin and narrowly losing the Cuban vote. But he spurred huge turnout in GOP-heavy communities.

Scott began his second term with a $1 billion state surplus, which he planned to use on increased education spending and tax cuts. He was criticized from all sides for waffling on Medicaid expansion. The governor had long opposed it, arguing the state would have to pick up more of the costs once the federal government reduced its subsidies. But he reversed course after Obama won the state a second time in 2012, saying his change of heart had come after his mother died in an intensive care unit in late 2012, calling it a "compassionate, commonsense step forward." But he didn't push the idea aggressively in the face of a hostile Republican-controlled Legislature. He reversed himself again in 2015. A Centers for Medicare and Medicaid Services decision not to renew a Medicaid waiver spurred state Senate Republicans to embrace Medicaid expansion, but the more conservative Florida House refused, leading to an intraparty budget impasse. Scott, after failing to persuade federal officials to extend the state's Medicaid waiver, announced he couldn't support Medicaid expansion.

Disasters, both natural and manmade, made their mark in 2016. Florida grappled with the threat of Zika virus. Scott declared a state of emergency, called for more federal assistance and offered free testing for pregnant women, who were at highest risk. Little noticed: Five years earlier, Scott and lawmakers had slashed the state's mosquito-control budget. In June, an ISIS-inspired gunman killed 49 and injured 53 before being killed by police in a shootout at Pulse, an LGBTQ nightclub in Orlando. That October, Hurricane Matthew wracked the Atlantic Coast, ending a decade without a significant hurricane in the state. Scott was praised for his response, though the courts rebuked him for refusing to extend the state's voter-registration deadline because of the storm.

The other big story of 2016, of course, was Donald Trump. Scott was officially neutral during the Florida primary, but he wrote an op-ed favorable to Trump in USA Today in early January— long before it was clear Trump would be the nominee. The move was a slight to Rubio, in the latest escalation of their tensions. After Trump won the Florida primary, Scott endorsed him. He was named national chairman of the pro-Trump Rebuilding America Now super PAC and worked hard to elect his fellow billionaire businessman. Trump carried Florida by a narrow margin.

Scott began the Trump presidency with close ties to the White House and a goal to stay in national politics by running against longtime Democratic Sen. Bill Nelson in 2018. The race would prove to be Scott's most challenging. Unlike in his first two victories, he ran with the wind in his face. He also faced a more popular opponent than in his previous two: Nelson's sunny personality contrasted with Scott's lack of charisma, though Nelson's popularity would prove relatively shallow as the campaign wore on.

Scott knew he was in for a tough fight from the beginning, while Nelson seemed much slower on the uptake. Nelson hadn't faced a tough election fight since his first Senate win in 2000, and he never fully seemed to grasp the workings of a modern campaign. He didn't hire a campaign manager until March 2018, months after Scott had put his team in place, and throughout the campaign seemed reluctant to go on the attack, to the chagrin of his Democratic allies.

As often happens in Florida, natural disasters played a major role in the campaign. Scott initially got positive headlines for his handling of Hurricane Irma, a major storm that hit the state in 2017. But he later faced questions on why he had not responded to pleas for help from a Hollywood Hills nursing home where 12 people died of heat-related causes and whether he had wasted taxpayers' money with unnecessary emergency contracts.

The storm that may have had the biggest political effect hit hundreds of miles off Florida's coast. Hurricane Maria devastated Puerto Rico in late 2017, killing roughly 3,000 people and forcing hundreds of thousands to flee the island, many resettling in Florida. Scott reached out to welcome the new residents and prove he was responding well to the crisis, even as the Trump administration bungled its response. He visited Puerto Rico eight times after the hurricane, courted Puerto Rican voters living in the state and rejected Trump's claim that the death count had been inflated by Democrats and local officials to make the president look bad. That fit the pattern of Scott's hard work with various Hispanic communities, which may have been the difference, as exit polls showed Scott won about 45 percent of the Hispanic vote, an increase over his 2014 performance and especially impressive considering how Trump had alienated those communities.

Gun violence pushed its way into the campaign. A shooting at Stoneman Douglas High School in Parkland in February 2018 left 17 students dead and had become the deadliest school shooting in U.S. history and the third mass shooting in Florida in as many years, after massacres at the Orlando nightclub and Fort Lauderdale airport. The rampage triggered massive protests and put huge pressure on the pro-gun Scott. It gave Nelson a chance to hammer Scott.

At a CNN town hall shortly after the shooting, Nelson attacked the governor for refusing to act on the issue and contrasted Scott's refusal to attend an event with students with Rubio's attendance. The two senators had a strong bipartisan friendship, and Rubio seemed happy to let Nelson draw that contrast. Scott responded by backing legislation that increased from 18 to 21 the minimum age at which one can buy a rifle and created three-day waiting periods for long-gun purchases. The law was the first new gun control measure in the state in two decades and gave Scott bipartisan credibility on the issue even as it angered some in his base. That was not Scott's only pivot to the center during the campaign: In a reversal, he split with Trump to oppose offshore drilling along Florida's coast. Until late in the campaign, he declined to appear with the president when Trump campaigned in the state.

Scott spent tens of millions on TV ads over the spring and summer—while Nelson was silent —and built a small but steady lead in public polling. National Democratic groups responded in midsummer, and Nelson went on the air not long after that. By mid-September, Nelson appeared to have reversed the tide of the race, pulling into a small lead in most public polls that held through Election Day.

Scott's campaign howled that the public polls were wrong. Election night proved it right. Scott emerged with a narrow win. But the contest ended in uncertainty as lawyers rushed in for a statewide recount. Just like in the 2000 presidential recount, legal fights centered around ballot-design problems in Democratic-heavy Broward County. Because of a flaw, the Senate race was not listed prominently on ballots. There was a significantly larger drop in Senate votes in Broward than anywhere else in the state, likely enough to have cost Nelson his seat. Nelson's attorneys subsequently battled the Broward result in the courts, but ran out of options after 12 days, and Nelson conceded.

Scott spent almost $64 million of his own money on the race and his campaign outspent Nelson 3-1, though national Democratic groups tightened that gap with more than $200 million. Scott's final margin of victory was just over 10,000 votes out of more than 8 million cast. He was the only GOP Senate candidate in a state Trump won by less than 18 percentage points to defeat a Democratic incumbent. His margin of victory was about 1 percentage point below Trump's, making him the only Republican Senate candidate in a competitive race who came close to Trump's 2016 percentage and showing that Florida remains deeply—if closely—divided along partisan lines.

During his first year in the Senate, Scott relied on his health care background, which led to Trump tasking the new senator, along with Louisiana's Bill Cassidy and Wyoming's John Barrasso, with finding an "Obamacare" replacement. But the quest didn't result in any identifiable plan, which would have been dead on arrival in the newly Democratic-controlled House anyway. Scott did introduce a bill that would have called for drug companies to charge no more than their counterparts in comparable countries, such as Canada and Great Britain, for drugs. When the COVID-19 pandemic hit in early 2020, Scott largely echoed and praised Trump: He blamed China, blasted the World Health Organization and rejected mask mandates and closing worship centers. "Do I believe that government should be telling us what to do? Do I believe government can tell us we don't have a right to worship? I don't believe they can," Scott said on CNN's "State of the Union."

Scott, never short on ambition, is viewed as a potential presidential candidate. Just ahead of the 2020 Iowa caucuses, Scott bought $19,000 worth of TV ads attacking Joe Biden and Democrats over Trump's first impeachment in the important political state; one former GOP consultant who'd worked for Scott told Politico it was "the starting gun for 2024." He's also tried to engender goodwill by inviting vulnerable GOP senators up in 2020 onto his private plane to fundraise across Florida. All that was a lead-up to his chairing the NRSC—a post that gives him access to major donors.

But he stirred controversy on Jan. 6, 2021, by voting against certifying the results of the presidential election in Pennsylvania even after Trump supporters overran the Capitol hoping to stop that vote. The Keystone State, which Biden won in 2020, is a key seat that Scott will have to defend in 2022. Scott was the only member of GOP leadership to vote against the certification of any state. Scott defended his decision, arguing that postal voting during a pandemic—of which the U.S. Supreme Court had already ruled in favor—was "in direct conflict with" the state's constitution. Just before Election Day, Scott had proposed the Verifiable, Orderly and Timely Elections Results Act to "establish uniform standards for vote-by-mail systems across the country" and require states during federal elections to count and report all ballots within 24 hours.

Scott's vote against certification, especially as other GOP senators withdrew their planned objections after the deadly insurrection, raised key questions about Scott's ability to draw big donors for the GOP's campaign arm: Major corporations, including Goldman Sachs and JPMorgan Chase, announced they were suspending political donations after the insurrection. Others, such as Marriott, said they wouldn't donate to lawmakers who voted against certification. The relief for Scott may be that only a fraction of the NRSC's fundraising comes from corporate PACs. In a video to donors, Scott shrugged off any friction: "I run a tight ship. I respect our donors. There are two things I don't do: I don't waste money, and I don't lose elections."

If Scott does run for president in 2024, that perfect record will be tested. He could have competition in the 2024 primary from two fellow Floridians: his successor, Gov. Ron DeSantis, and Rubio. (Or, even new Florida resident Trump.) He and DeSantis have a rocky relationship, and the transition between the two was acrimonious, with Scott making 70 last-minute appointments, many of which DeSantis rescinded. Scott criticized DeSantis over his handling of COVID-19, sending out daily charts showing the uptick in cases in Florida early in the pandemic and said the lack of communication from the DeSantis administration was "alarming."

Matt Gaetz (R)

Elected 2016, 3rd term, b. May 07, 1982; Hollywood, FL; FL State University, B.S., 2003; College of William and Mary - Marshall-Wythe Law School, J.D., 2007; Baptist.

Elected Office: FL House, 2010-2016.

Professional Career: Practicing attorney.

DC Office: 1721 LHOB 20515, 202-225-4136, Fax: 202-225-3414, gaetz.house.gov

State Offices: Fort Walton Beach, 850-479-1183; Pensacola, 850-479-1183.

Committees: *Armed Services*: Cyber, Innovative Technologies & Information Systems; Tactical Air & Land Forces. *Judiciary*: Antitrust, Commercial & Administrative Law; Courts, Intellectual Property & Internet.

Group Ratings

	ADA	ACLU	AFL-CIO	LCV	COC	HAFA	ACU	CFG	FRC
2020	**	21%	**	10%	-	98%	92%	**	-
2019	5%	C	24%	24%	60%	C	89%	83%	90%

Almanac Ratings 2019-2020

	Economy	Social	Foreign	Composite
Liberal	44%	20%	42%	36%
Conservative	56%	80%	58%	64%

Key Votes of the 116th Congress

1. U.S./Mex./Can. trade deal	Y	5. Russia sanctions	N/A	9. Firearms background checks N
2. First Coronavirus response	N/A	6. Troops in Syria	N	10. Spending at the border Y
3. HEROES Act	N	7. Veto arms sales to Saudis	N	11. Marijuana liberalized rules Y
4. CASH Act	N	8. Defense $$$, veto override	N	12. Electoral College objections Y

Election Results

Election	Name (Party)	Vote (%)		Cand. Spent	Ind. Exp. Support	Ind. Exp. Oppose
2020 General	Matt Gaetz (R)	283,352	(65%)	$4,383,837	$11,839	$22,220
	Phil Her (D)	149,172	(34%)	$2,125,081	$3,706	
2020 Primary	Matt Gaetz (R)	87,457	(81%)			
	John Mills (R)	10,383	(10%)			
	Greg Merk (R)	10,227	(10%)			

Prior winning percentages: 2018 (67%), 2016 (69%)

Republican Matt Gaetz, elected in 2016 to a solidly Republican open seat with an appeal to the military interests of his district, has been an outspoken public defender of former President Donald Trump. With his frequent television appearances, he became a celebrity with some audiences and less of a presence in legislative backrooms. Hot Takes, his regular podcast, and Firebrand, the book he published in 2020, were features of Gaetz's political brand. His criticism of other Republicans, as when he believed they did not fully support Trump, often had the intended result of generating controversy. Reports that he was being investigated for charges related to sex with a teenager raised uncertainty about his future.

A Florida native, Gaetz graduated from Florida State University and got his law degree from the College of William and Mary in Virginia. After briefly practicing law with a firm in Fort Walton Beach, he ran in 2010 for an open seat in the state House. He was unopposed that year and in his two reelections. He chaired the House Finance and Tax Committee, where he was an enthusiastic supporter of tax cuts. As a social conservative, he sought to expand the pro-gun "Stand Your Ground" law. The American Conservative Union gave him its "Defender of Liberty" award.

Before veteran Republican Rep. Jeff Miller announced his retirement, Gaetz had been planning to run for the seat in the state Senate that had been held by his influential father, Senate President Don Gaetz, who was retiring. After the two had a heart-to-heart talk, his father told the Pensacola News Journal, "Matt said he didn't like anything that was happening in Washington, and I said, 'Well, Matt, maybe you should go there and do something about it.'"

In the Republican primary, state Sen. Greg Evers led in an early poll and had higher favorability scores than Gaetz. Evers gained national attention when he raffled off a semi-automatic rifle among people in the district who "liked" his Facebook page. He explained that he was trying to highlight the importance of the right to bear arms during a time of rising terrorism. Gaetz drew attention when he said that the Black Lives Matter group was "a terrorist organization," and he criticized Evers for voting to expand Medicaid. Gaetz opposed cuts in the military, which were detrimental to the district and its large military installations. "When the Pentagon gets a cold, we get the flu," he said. Gaetz's advertising called him "the most conservative" candidate.

A late-filing candidate was Cris Dosev, a self-financing Pensacola businessman and political newcomer. Gaetz spent $1.1 million, which exceeded the total for his opponents. Gaetz won the seven-candidate primary with 36 percent of the vote to 22 percent for Evers and 21 percent for Dosev. In the general election, Steven Specht, an Air Force veteran, spent $54,000 and attracted scant public attention. Gaetz won, 69%-31%.

In the House, he got useful assignments on the Armed Services and Judiciary committees. With Democratic Rep. Seth Moulton of Massachusetts, Gaetz filed legislation to modify medical marijuana practices of the Veterans Affairs Department so that cannabis would be a more realistic treatment option for veterans, as an alternative to opioids and other addictive painkillers. The action was supported by the American Legion.

Gaetz became a tireless defender of Trump. In November 2017, he filed a House resolution to force special counsel Robert Mueller to resign because of his alleged conflicts of interest. Two months later, Gaetz sought to declassify a House Republican memo alleging investigative abuses by the FBI. That led Trump to make regular phone calls to Gaetz. "I think it's because I defend him on television," Gaetz told BuzzFeed. Asked by a reporter whether he might be gaining notoriety rather than star power, he responded, "What's the difference?" He added in the interview, "I was tired of the Democrats being the only team playing offense."

In July 2020, after Rep. Liz Cheney criticized Trump's decision to withdraw military forces from Germany and defended federal infectious-disease expert Anthony Fauci from criticism of some Trump allies, Gaetz responded that she should be removed as House Republican Conference chairwoman. "Liz Cheney has worked behind the scenes (and now in public) against @realDonaldTrump and his agenda. House Republicans deserve better as our Conference Chair," Gaetz tweeted.

Although there was no vote, Gaetz gained limited support. House Minority Leader Kevin McCarthy defended Cheney. "She does an amazing job," he told reporters. The Dispatch, a conservative website, headlined the incident, "A Preview of the Coming GOP Crackup." Gaetz's occasional social visits to Mar-A-Lago, Trump's resort in Palm Beach Florida, reinforced that Gaetz's activities had presidential support. In profiling Gaetz in September 2020, Vanity Fair wrote, "Gaetz, like Trump, sees politics as entertainment: if you can keep the people's attention, you can keep your power. ... That Gaetz is regularly knee-deep in the outrage cycle ... is by design."

After Cheney, who was reelected without opposition to chair the GOP Conference following the 2020 election, Gaetz confronted her again when she was 1 of 10 House Republicans to vote for the second impeachment charge against Trump. In late January, he took the unusual step of traveling to Wyoming, where he urged her defeat in the 2022 election. "We are in a battle for the soul of the Republican party, and I intend to win it," Gaetz told a rally at the state capitol. "You can help me break a corrupt system. You can send a representative who actually represents you." The following week, he brimmed with confidence as he forced a vote in the GOP Conference on whether to retain Cheney. But Cheney rallied support—including from McCarthy, who urged party unity—and easily prevailed, 145-61. Following the outcome, which was also viewed as a setback for Trump, Gaetz explained the outcome, "Tonight Liz Cheney was fighting on her home turf — Washington D.C."

Gaetz soon faced reports that he was being investigated for potential criminal violations of having paid for sex with a 17-year-old female—a violation of federal sex trafficking laws. He denied the charges, which were part of a broader investigation of his Florida political ally, though there also were reports that he had unsuccessfully urged Trump to grant him a pardon.

Gaetz has been reelected easily. In 2020, Democratic challenger Phil Ehr, a retired Navy commander, said that Gaetz's behavior in Congress had made him "extremely unpopular" in his district, according to a private survey. Her spent $2.1 million and lost, 65%-34%, a small reduction in support for Gaetz.

FL-1: Western Panhandle

Cook Partisan Voting Index: R+20

Population		Race and Ethnicity		Income	
Total	798,305	White	76.40%	Median Income	$58,358
Land area (sq. miles)	4,016	Black	12.90%	District Income Rank	286
Pop/ sq mi	198.77	Latino	6.90%	Poverty Rate	12.50%
Born in State	41.20%	Asian	2.40%	With health insurance	87.50%
		Two or more races	5.50%	Cash public assistance	1.50%
Age Groups		Other	2.80%	Food stamp/SNAP	10.20%
Under 18	21.40%				
18-34	23.80%	Education		Work	
35-64	37.50%	H.S grad or less	38.70%	White Collar	36.20%
Over 64	17.20%	Some college	34.50%	Sales and Service	43.00%
		College Degree, 4 yr	17.50%	Blue Collar	20.80%
Military		Post grad	9.50%	Government	14.70%
Veteran/ Active Duty	19.40%				

2020 Pres. Vote	Trump	292,019	(66%)	Biden	143,654	(32%)			
2016 Pres. Vote	Trump	256,609	(67%)	Clinton	107,063	(28%)	Johnson	12,770	(3%)

Pensacola, Fort Walton: The "Redneck Riviera" is the affectionate local name for the Gulf Coast beaches of Florida's Emerald Coast, stretching from Pensacola east to Destin. This has been military country since John Quincy Adams persuaded Spain to sell Florida to the United States in 1819, with the goal of gaining control of the port of Pensacola on the Gulf of Mexico. In October 1861, the Union defeated the Confederates in a battle to control Santa Rosa Island, the outermost spit of land protecting Pensacola Bay. In the 20th century, the Pensacola Naval Air Station was turned into the nation's first naval-aviation training base, giving birth to carrier aviation. About 17,000 people—more than half of them active-duty military—are employed at Eglin Air Force Base, which spreads over three counties. With approximately 100,000 square miles of airspace stretching over the Gulf to the Florida Keys, Eglin is considered the largest air base in the free world. It has been the Air Force center for the development, acquisition, testing, deployment and sustainment of all air-delivered weapons, including the F-35 Joint Strike Fighter. The naval air station in Pensacola received unwelcome attention in December 2019 when an Air Force trainee from Saudi Arabia, who was a visiting student, killed three sailors in a classroom building on the base before he was fatally shot by sheriff's deputies.

The western panhandle of Florida is culturally part of Dixie and lies closer to Houston than to Miami. A columnist for the Pensacola News Journal once recommended the creation of an independent commonwealth of West Florida. "We don't have much in common with the people inhabiting what I call peninsular Florida," wrote Jerry Maygarden. "I'm convinced that the further south you drive, the further north you get." As the South has become more prosperous, the shore has attracted vacationing and retiring southerners to its vast, fine-grained, white sand beaches and its pleasant, inlet-dotted bays. It has become a leading spring break destination for sometimes-rowdy college students and the site of an annual gay-focused Memorial Day weekend party with upwards of 200,000 visitors.

The economy in the Pensacola area has been strong. In 2018, a $46 million aerospace facility to maintain, repair and overhaul aircraft from around the world began operations at Pensacola Airport. In February 2020, officials announced that the project, nearing completion, will create 1,700 jobs. "I think that if you look around the country, Florida is doing more aviation and aerospace than anybody and we've got great momentum," said Pensacola Mayor Grover Robinson.

The 1st Congressional District of Florida runs from Pensacola, adjoining the Alabama border, through Fort Walton Beach and Destin to Santa Rosa Beach. It is so far west it is in the Central time zone. Inland, the 1st takes in rural Walton and Holmes counties. With 40 percent in Pensacola-based Escambia County, the district population has grown steadily. Young civilians, as well as military retirees, have settled here and raised education and quality-of-life issues. The region has long been culturally and economically conservative, with a strong pro-military bent. In 2016, Donald Trump had his best Florida showing in the district, with a 67%-28% win. Four years later, he took the district with 66 percent, which was one percentage point short of his best in the state--the neighboring 2nd District.

Neal Dunn (R)

Elected 2016, 3rd term, b. Feb 16, 1953; New Haven, CT; Washington and Lee University, B.S.; George Washington University Medical School, M.D.; Catholic; Married (Leah Dunn); 3 children; 3 grandchildren.

Military Career: U.S. Army 1989-2001

Professional Career: Urologist; Banker.

DC Office: 316 CHOB 20515, 202-225-5235, Fax: 202-225-5615, dunn.house.gov

State Offices: Panama City, 850-785-0812; Tallahassee, 850-891-8610.

Committees: *Energy & Commerce*: Consumer Protection & Commerce; Health; Oversight & Investigations.

Group Ratings

	ADA	ACLU	AFL-CIO	LCV	COC	HAFA	ACU	CFG	FRC
2020	**	14%	**	5%	-	86%	81%	**	-
2019	5%	C	40%	10%	87%	C	78%	69%	100%

Almanac Ratings 2019-2020

	Economy	Social	Foreign	Composite
Liberal	25%	21%	4%	17%
Conservative	75%	79%	96%	83%

Key Votes of the 116th Congress

1. U.S./Mex./Can. trade deal	Y	5. Russia sanctions	N	9. Firearms background checks N
2. First Coronavirus response	Y	6. Troops in Syria	N	10. Spending at the border	Y
3. HEROES Act	N	7. Veto arms sales to Saudis	N	11. Marijuana liberalized rules	N/A
4. CASH Act	N/A	8. Defense $$$, veto override	N/A	12. Electoral College objections Y

Election Results

Election	Name (Party)	Vote (%)	Cand. Spent	Ind. Exp. Support	Ind. Exp. Oppose
2020 General	Neal Dunn (R)	305,337 (98%)	$689,012	$18,299	
	Kim O'Connor (Write-in)	6,662 (2%)			

Prior winning percentages: 2018 (67%), 2016 (67%)

Neal Dunn, elected in 2016, is one of several House Republicans who have been physicians. He also served in the military—a combination that left him well-suited to chair the Veterans' Affairs Subcommittee on Health for a few months, until the GOP lost House control.

Dunn was born in Boston to a military family. Growing up, he was an Eagle Scout and active in rifle competitions. He received an Army ROTC scholarship at Washington & Lee University, where he got his bachelor's degree before earning his medical degree from George Washington University. He completed his residency at Walter Reed Army Medical Center and served as an attending urologist in the Army for 11 years, before moving to Panama City, where he had his medical practice for 25 years. Dunn became chief medical officer for the Advanced Urology Institute in North Florida. In 2014, Senate President Don Gaetz (the father of Dunn's colleague Matt Gaetz in the adjacent 1st District) appointed him to the Enterprise Florida Board of Directors. Dunn was founding chairman of Summit Bank in Panama City.

When redistricting created a new African-American plurality district from Tallahassee to Jacksonville, the district to the south became a strong Republican pickup opportunity. The two chief

GOP contenders were Dunn and Mary Thomas, a Tallahassee attorney. Because Panama City-based Bay County had 50 percent more Republicans than did the parts of Tallahassee-based Leon County in the district, Dunn had an advantage. Former U.S. Attorney Ken Sukhia, a third GOP candidate, also was from Leon and likely drew votes from Thomas. Dunn ran as an "unapologetic conservative Republican" whose top priority was to repeal the Affordable Care Act. That objective required, he said, lawmakers "who have represented patients, not bureaucrats."

Some conservatives criticized Dunn for having made campaign contributions to Florida Democratic Senator Bill Nelson and to former Gov. Charlie Crist, who was elected to the House in 2016 as a Democrat. Thomas was backed by the conservative Club for Growth, which spent $584,000 on her behalf and called Dunn "a liberal lobbyist." Dunn spent $2 million for his campaign, with Thomas and Sukhia spending $1.1 million and $207,000 respectively. Dunn defeated Thomas 41%-39%, a margin of 1,708 votes. Sukhia got 19 percent. Thomas won 11 of the 19 counties. Dunn won the two largest counties—easily in Bay County and oddly in Leon, which the three candidates split almost evenly. In the general election, Dunn faced Walt Dartland, a former Marine Corps major and state deputy attorney general, who called himself "pretty conservative in terms of fiscal policy." Dartland spent $130,000 and was competitive only in Leon County. Dunn won, 67%-30%.

In the House, Dunn's chief legislative work was on the Veterans' Affairs Committee. President Donald Trump signed a bill with two provisions proposed by Dunn. His Veterans Increased Choice for Transplanted Organs and Recovery (VICTOR) measure gave veterans more choices for organ transplants. His other provision, the Veterans Opioid Abuse Prevention Act, connected VA health care providers to a national network of state-based prescription drug monitoring programs. "As a doctor and a veteran, I have met heroes who need help, but aren't finding it at the VA. We can change that," Dunn said. Following a shuffling of committee assignments in May 2018, Dunn became chairman of the panel's Health Subcommittee. He promised to assist veterans who "return from war only to find they have to fight government bureaucracy." But he lost his gavel following the elections six months later.

In October 2018, Dunn took on a new workload after Hurricane Michael devastated parts of his district. He filed bills to assure education and retirement benefits for storm victims. And he successfully sought to expedite repairs at Tyndall Air Force Base.

In the minority, Dunn retained his senior GOP position on the Health Subcommittee at Veterans' Affairs. Teaming with Democratic Rep. Conor Lamb, vice chairman of the committee and a former Marine, they filed a bill to encourage veterans pursuing STEM (science, technology, engineering and math) careers. In February 2019, the House passed the bill, without opposition. After the Senate made minor changes, Trump signed the bill a year later. The legislation "eases the transition from active duty to civilian life, while keeping America at the forefront of the world's ever-growing technology arena," Dunn said.

Dunn has taken an interest in the unusual Supreme Court case in which Florida and Georgia have battled over water rights, including from the Apalachicola River. When a Circuit Court judge sided with Georgia in issuing his findings on the case, Dunn said the result was "very disappointing." He urged the Supreme Court to "ensure Florida gets its fair share of water," but Georgia prevailed again.

Dunn has had easy reelections. In 2018, he won the GOP nomination without opposition and defeated Democrat Bob Rackleff, 67%-33%. A former Leon County commissioner, Rackleff took 54 percent in Leon, which cast nearly one-fourth of the total vote. Dunn won the remaining counties. Two years later, Dunn had no major-party opposition. Redistricting can hardly improve his district, though he likely has little reason to worry. In 2021, he got a plum assignment with a seat on the Energy and Commerce Committee, where he joined an informal GOP "doc caucus."

FL-2: Central Panhandle   **Cook Partisan Voting Index: R+20**

Population		Race and Ethnicity		Income	
Total	720,777	White	81.20%	Median Income	$54,087
Land area (sq. miles)	8,614	Black	12.60%	District Income Rank	345
Pop/ sq mi	83.68	Latino	6.60%	Poverty Rate	13.60%
Born in State	51.80%	Asian	2.00%	With health insurance	88.20%
		Two or more races	2.50%	Cash public assistance	2.60%
Age Groups		Other	1.70%	Food stamp/SNAP	13.20%
Under 18	19.80%				
18-34	21.30%	**Education**		**Work**	
35-64	38.20%	H.S grad or less	44.50%	White Collar	37.00%
Over 64	20.70%	Some college	30.90%	Sales and Service	41.30%
		College Degree, 4 yr	14.50%	Blue Collar	21.60%
Military		Post grad	10.20%	Government	24.00%
Veteran/ Active Duty	11.90%				

2020 Pres. Vote	Trump	263,499	(67%)	Biden	125,747	(32%)		
2016 Pres. Vote	Trump	234,990	(66%)	Clinton	108,636	(30%)	Johnson	8,400	(2%)

Panama City, Parts of Tallahassee: Much of northern Florida is swampy lowlands. Along the 355-mile route across the northern tier of the state from Jacksonville on the Atlantic Coast to Pensacola on the Gulf of Mexico, there are occasional small towns—some of them from the 19th century—and lots of empty land. To outsiders, this is mostly fly-over or drive-through Florida. In a few decades, perhaps this area will become a modern version of central Florida from Orlando to Tampa, or south Florida from Palm Beach to Miami.

For now, there are only two urban centers along the northern tier. By Florida standards, each is small. Tallahassee, inland from the Gulf and relatively isolated, became the state capital when Florida's then-modest population lived mostly along the state's northern tier, placing it, more or less, at its center of gravity. Ralph Waldo Emerson, visiting Tallahassee at the time, called it a "grotesque place, rapidly settled by public officers, land speculators, and desperadoes." Until fairly recently, it remained little more than a Spanish-mossed county seat with a pair of universities and a handsome Creole capitol, which was built in 1845 and preserved opposite its 1977 skyscraper replacement. Since the 1980s, it has spread out and become a middling-sized city, with a sometimes fractious political and legal elite, bringing a taste of urbanized Florida to the state's north. Tallahassee, which remains a deeply segregated city, has not yet attained the critical mass of Sacramento, Austin or Albany—once small-town capitals of the other largest states in the nation. But, with increased development, perhaps it is on its way. There is plenty of room for physical growth and economic upgrade.

Panama City is a very different place. What was a popular spring break destination along the state's pretty and underappreciated northwest beaches has become a growing retirement and resort area. The opening of a nearby airport in 2010 spurred development, though the area has suffered several blows since. In 2015, Panama City officials voted to ban alcohol on the beach during each March. That resulted in a 41 percent decline in the city's revenue. Devastation struck in 2018 when the area was walloped by Hurricane Michael, the strongest storm ever to hit the Panhandle. In Panama City, 60 percent of the homes were destroyed, due partly to lax building codes. At Tyndall Air Force Base, 95 percent of the buildings no longer functioned. To local relief, Congress appropriated the following year more than $2 billion to rebuild Tyndall, with greater protection against storm surge and destructive winds. Civilian reconstruction has been slower.

The 2nd District of Florida, the largest in the state, is an amorphous area based in Panama City plus the parts of the Tallahassee area that are not in the 5th District. The drive from Panama City at the northwest tip to Inglis in the southeast is a Texas-sized 251 miles. Redistricting changes dropped the Black population in the new 2nd to 13 percent and created a solidly Republican district. As the Tallahassee Democrat aptly described in 2016, the odd configurations of the new district lines in that city lack "common sense." Gone are the Democratic parts of Tallahassee, though the state capitol remained. Included is the main campus of Florida State University, but not nearby Florida A&M. In their place are seven mostly rural and white counties that curve along the bend of the Gulf with mostly undeveloped beaches, much of which is state park land or wildlife areas. The district moves inland to the outskirts of Ocala and Gainesville. In 2020, Donald Trump's 67%-32% win was one percentage point better than four years earlier, resulting in his best district in the state.

Kat Cammack (R)

Elected 2020, 1st term, b. Feb 16, 1988; Denver, CO; Naval War College, M.A.; University of VA, 2009; Metropolitan State University of Denver, B.A., 2011; Christian; Married (Matt Harrison).

Professional Career: Campaign Manager, Ted Yoho for Congress, 2011-2018; Deputy Chief of Staff, Congressman Ted Yoho, 2013-2019; Co-Founder and Vice President, The Grit Foundation.

DC Office: 1626 LHOB 20515, 202-225-5744, Fax: 202-225-3973, cammack.house.gov

State Offices: Gainesville, 352-505-0838; Orange Park, 904-276-9626.

Committees: *Communications Standards Commission.* *Homeland Security*: Emergency Preparedness, Response & Recovery (RMM).

Election Results

Election	Name (Party)	Vote (%)		Cand. Spent	Ind. Exp. Support	Ind. Exp. Oppose
2020 General	Kat Cammack (R)............................	223,075	(57%)	$1,192,194	$373,248	
	Adam Christensen (D)........................	167,326	(43%)	$205,143	$16,676	$21
2020 Primary	Kat Cammack (R)............................	21,679	(25%)			
	Judson Sapp (R)................................	17,180	(20%)			
	Gavin Rollins (R)............................	13,118	(15%)			
	James St. George (R)........................	12,125	(14%)			
	Todd Chase (R)................................	8,165	(10%)			
	Ryan Chamberlin (R)........................	5,067	(6%)			

Republican Kat Cammack won an open House seat following a campaign in which she gained attention for outspoken comments and her conservative views. She won a competitive primary against nine opponents, including self-funding candidates who had local businesses and outspent her. Cammack succeeded Rep. Ted Yoho—known as a frequent iconoclast, who retired after four terms. Earlier, she had been Yoho's longtime deputy chief of staff, which gave her a head start in knowing local politics.

A native of Colorado, Cammack graduated from Metropolitan State University in Denver and got a master's degree in national defense and strategic studies from the Naval War College. With her husband, a Florida firefighter, she founded the nonprofit Grit Foundation, which supported local first responders.

She became active in politics after her family became homeless in 2011 following eviction from its cattle ranch, which she said was the result of the requirements of a federal housing program during the Obama administration. That led her to join the congressional campaign of Yoho, a local veterinarian making his first political bid and running as a political outsider. At age 24, she managed that campaign, in which Yoho unexpectedly won the GOP primary by 875 votes against 12-term Rep. Cliff Stearns in the solidly Republican district. As a top aide to Yoho, Cammack worked on economic development programs in the district and claimed credit for four new local clinics of the Veterans Affairs Department.

After Yoho announced his retirement in December 2019, having stirred doubts that he would comply with his initial term-limit pledge, Cammack cited him as a role model during her campaign. She ran ads that highlighted her support for gun rights, pro-life views on abortion and opposition to illegal immigration, and said that socialism was "the greatest threat to America." She described herself as part of the millennial generation of conservative women.

In the wide-open GOP primary, the biggest spenders were Judson Sapp, a railroad contractor who got 24 percent of the vote in a 2018 primary challenge to Yoho, and James St. George, a physician. Each spent more than $500,000, with a majority of their funds from personal loans. Cammack spent about $400,000 in the primary. She was endorsed by tea party groups and Sen. Rand Paul of Kentucky.

Cammack "managed to separate herself from the pack ... hosting chats with voters over Facebook," the Florida Politics website reported.

Cammack won the primary with 25 percent of the vote to 20 percent for Sapp. They were followed by Gavin Rollins, a Clay County commissioner, who got 15 percent, and St. George, with 14 percent. Cammack won five of the six counties. Sapp took Putnam County by one vote. In Alachua, her home county, Cammack got 28 percent.

In November, Cammack defeated Adam Christensen, a political newcomer. She won each of the counties, except for Alachua, which cast about one-third of the total vote. In each county, the leading vote-getter got at least 60 percent of the vote.

Cammack was assigned to the Agriculture Committee and Homeland Security, where she became ranking Republican on the Emergency Preparedness, Response and Recovery Subcommittee. Entering the House at age 33, she was its youngest Republican woman.

FL-3: North Florida   **Cook Partisan Voting Index: R+9**

Population		Race and Ethnicity		Income	
Total	758,939	White	74.70%	Median Income	$56,005
Land area (sq. miles)	7,306	Black	16.40%	District Income Rank	317
Pop/ sq mi	103.88	Latino	11.40%	Poverty Rate	15.60%
Born in State	49.70%	Asian	3.30%	With health insurance	88.80%
		Two or more races	3.40%	Cash public assistance	1.60%
Age Groups		Other	2.30%	Food stamp/SNAP	10.40%
Under 18	20.20%				
18-34	25.60%	Education		Work	
35-64	37.10%	H.S grad or less	38.20%	White Collar	40.40%
Over 64	17.10%	Some college	31.70%	Sales and Service	40.00%
		College Degree, 4 yr	17.40%	Blue Collar	19.50%
Military		Post grad	12.60%	Government	20.40%
Veteran/ Active Duty	11.10%				

2020 Pres. Vote	Trump	223,087	(56%)	Biden	170,433	(43%)		
2016 Pres. Vote	Trump	197,478	(56%)	Clinton	141,362	(40%)	Johnson 9,138	(3%)

Jacksonville Suburbs, Gainesville: The flat grasslands of central Florida, once bypassed by southbound tourists heading for the coastal resorts and cities, have become a prime growth area in this high-growth state. North Florida's economy once depended on farming, on tourists getting off the interstate and on state institutions, most notably the University of Florida in Gainesville. Then retirees began settling in places like the bluegrass country around Ocala, one of America's prime horse-breeding grounds, and the area began to share the development boom, growing more than 30 percent from 2000 to 2019. The Great Recession hit the region hard, with home foreclosures reaching record levels.

By 2014, Ocala-based Marion County led the state in economic growth. Ocala has become a distribution center in the heart of Florida. In October 2017, Forbes magazine ranked the Ocala area eighth in the nation for projected job growth. In addition to the university, the Gainesville area has added hundreds of manufacturing jobs since 2010. Gainesville has styled itself as "a new American city," which has addressed numerous social problems. With surrounding Alachua County, the area has promoted opportunities for tourists. In north-central Florida, including the rapidly growing outskirts of Jacksonville, voting patterns have solidified for the Republicans and have partly offset the movement toward Democrats in South Florida.

The 3rd Congressional District of Florida is a compact core of north Florida, with 85 percent of its population in three counties: all of Alachua, which includes Gainesville; all of Clay, which is chiefly Orange Park, Middleburg and other suburbs southwest of Jacksonville; and more than a third of Marion, which includes Ocala. With the exception of firmly Democratic Gainesville and its large state university campus, these areas are comfortably Republican.

What had been the third strongest Republican district in Florida before redistricting in 2016 slipped several notches. Donald Trump won 56 percent in each of his campaigns.

John Rutherford (R)

Elected 2016, 3rd term, b. Sep 02, 1952; Omaha, NE; FL Junior College, A.A., 1972; FL State University, B.S., 1974; Catholic; Married (Patricia Rutherford); 2 children; 6 grandchildren.

Elected Office: Sheriff, City of Jacksonville, 2003-2015.

DC Office: 1711 LHOB 20515, 202-225-2501, Fax: 202-225-2504, rutherford.house.gov

State Offices: Jacksonville, 904-831-5205.

Committees: *Appropriations*: Homeland Security; Military Construction, Veterans Affairs & Related Agencies; Transportation, HUD & Related Agencies. *Ethics*.

Group Ratings

	ADA	ACLU	AFL-CIO	LCV	COC	HAFA	ACU	CFG	FRC
2020	**	14%	**	14%	-	79%	71%	**	-
2019	10%	C	38%	17%	93%	C	73%	58%	100%

Almanac Ratings 2019-2020

	Economy	Social	Foreign	Composite
Liberal	41%	14%	6%	21%
Conservative	59%	86%	94%	79%

Key Votes of the 116th Congress

1. U.S./Mex./Can. trade deal Y	5. Russia sanctions N	9. Firearms background checks N
2. First Coronavirus response Y	6. Troops in Syria N	10. Spending at the border Y
3. HEROES Act N	7. Veto arms sales to Saudis N	11. Marijuana liberalized rules N
4. CASH Act Y	8. Defense $$$, veto override Y	12. Electoral College objections Y

Election Results

Election	Name (Party)	Vote (%)		Cand. Spent	Ind. Exp. Support	Ind. Exp. Oppose
2020 General	John Rutherford (R)	308,497	(61%)	$1,175,596	$156,465	
	Donna Deegan (D)	196,423	(39%)	$1,008,519	$21,510	
2020 Primary	John Rutherford (R)	80,101	(80%)			
	Erick Aguilar (R)	19,798	(20%)			

Prior winning percentages: 2018 (65%), 2016 (70%)

Republican John Rutherford, who was elected in 2016, has been a quiet insider who serves on the Appropriations Committee and highlights the funds that he directs to commercial and military projects in his district. He joined the committee midway through his first term. Of the three incoming Republicans from north Florida that year, Rutherford operated most closely as a leadership ally. Well-known locally as the sheriff, he easily won reelection in 2020 against his most competitive challenger.

Rutherford, who has lived in Jacksonville since he was six, earned an associate's degree in police administration from Florida Junior College and a bachelor's degree in criminology from Florida State University. He began his police career as a patrolman in 1974 and was the Jacksonville police department's director of corrections from 1995 until 2003. He was elected sheriff of Jacksonville in 2003 and stepped down 12 years later because of term limits.

As sheriff, Rutherford introduced several initiatives to reduce crime. In addition to greater community engagement, he focused on better treatment of the mentally ill to reduce their recidivism rate. By the end of his tenure, Jacksonville's violent crime rate was at a 40-year low. He also served as chairman of the Florida Sheriff's Association, where he advocated state legislation intended to reduce crime.

After eight-term Republican Rep. Ander Crenshaw announced his retirement, seven Republicans competed in the primary that was likely to determine the outcome. In addition to Rutherford, the best-known were state Rep. Lake Ray and Hans Tanzler, son of a former Jacksonville mayor. Tanzler challenged Rutherford's conservative credentials, including the former sheriff's opposition to the death penalty and his support for protecting illegal immigrants in Jacksonville. Rutherford charged that Tanzler was a "political insider" who had been an ally of former Republican Gov. turned Democrat Charlie Crist. Rutherford and Tanzler each spent a bit more than $800,000. Rutherford won with 39 percent to 20 percent for the quieter Ray and 19 percent for Tanzler; the vote was split evenly across the three counties. The general election was a breeze for Rutherford, who won 70%-28%.

In the House, Rutherford went to work on the Homeland Security Committee. The House passed his bill consolidating the more than $2 billion in leases and real estate costs of the more than 20 components of the Homeland Security Department. With Rep. Michael McCaul of Texas, chairman of the committee, Rutherford filed a bill to improve the efficiency of the department's acquisition programs. The House passed that bill in 2017, plus another Rutherford bill to permit the department to work on overseas counterterrorism task forces.

In 2018, Republican leaders selected Rutherford to fill a vacancy on the Appropriations Committee. His assignments include the Military Construction and Veterans' Affairs Subcommittee. That seat positioned him to look after the interests of Jacksonville's large Navy bases. Later in the year, he took credit for congressional approval of purchasing three additional littoral combat ships from the shipbuilding yard at Mayport.

With the House under Democratic control in 2019, Rutherford continued as an appropriator to secure funds for his district. He took credit for $20 million to the Jacksonville port to modernize 100 acres of a marine cargo terminal on an island in the harbor, plus $32 million for a support facility for a surveillance system at the naval air station.

The usually mild-mannered Rutherford triggered an angry response from Democratic Rep. Alexandria Ocasio-Cortez after he accused Democratic Rep. Pramila Jayapal of lying about a classified briefing to House members about the killing of Gen. Qassem Soleimani of Iran at the Baghdad airport in January 2020. "You and your squad of Ayatollah sympathizers are spreading propaganda that divides our nation," he told Jayapal. Ocasio-Cortez, whose freshman allies referred to themselves as the "squad," tweeted that Rutherford had shown his "racism."

At home, Rutherford faced his first well-financed Democratic opponent—Donna Deegan, who was a local TV news reporter for many years. In the incumbent's first debate with a Democrat, Deegan called him a "partisan" who attended "mask-less rallies" with supporters of President Donald Trump. When she charged that as sheriff Rutherford was known as an apologist for police shootings, he said that he "rejected the narrative that America is somehow a racist country." He added that Deegan's campaign backed petitions to legalize recreational marijuana and ban assault weapons. Each candidate spent a bit more than $1 million.

Rutherford won, 61%-39%. He got 58 percent in the Duval portion of the district and 64 percent in St. Johns County. That contrast might affect how Republicans in Tallahassee redraw the local lines during redistricting.

FL-4: Jacksonville area   **Cook Partisan Voting Index: R+14**

Population		Race and Ethnicity		Income	
Total	836,235	White	79.50%	Median Income	$77,026
Land area (sq. miles)	1,876	Black	9.90%	District Income Rank	111
Pop/ sq mi	445.76	Latino	8.70%	Poverty Rate	8.00%
Born in State	40.40%	Asian	4.60%	With health insurance	90.70%
		Two or more races	3.60%	Cash public assistance	1.60%
Age Groups		Other	2.40%	Food stamp/SNAP	5.80%
Under 18	21.20%				
18-34	22.10%	**Education**		**Work**	
35-64	39.40%	H.S grad or less	29.90%	White Collar	45.20%
Over 64	17.30%	Some college	28.20%	Sales and Service	39.00%
		College Degree, 4 yr	27.10%	Blue Collar	15.80%
Military		Post grad	14.80%	Government	10.80%
Veteran/ Active Duty	12.90%				

2020 Pres. Vote	Trump	305,934	(60%)	Biden	198,414	(39%)	
2016 Pres. Vote	Trump	261,828	(62%)	Clinton	143,674	(34%)	Johnson 12,473 (3%)

Parts of Jacksonville and Suburbs: With a metropolitan area of 1.6 million people, and continuing to grow, Jacksonville has overcome its reputation as Florida's overlooked city. Not long ago, it was considered a backwater, dominated by insurance companies and smelly paper mills. Jacksonville is now the largest city by land area in the contiguous 48 states, boasting a National Football League franchise and bold skyscrapers looming above the St. Johns River. Wide freeways sidestep primeval wetlands on their way to huge beachfront subdivisions.

Jacksonville's harbor has grown as a destination for cargo and cruise-line operations, with a total annual economic impact of more than $31 billion. It is the busiest container port in the state, though it substantially trails Savannah and Charleston to the north. The port has the second-largest volume of vehicle handling in the U.S. With Naval Station Mayport and Naval Air Station Jacksonville—two of the three largest metro-area employers—the city has a significant military employment base. Shipbuilding and repair provide more than 10,000 jobs in the area.

Business leaders have made the area into the "Silicon Valley of Logistics"—building on its land, air and sea transportation facilities. The Port Authority is dredging 11 miles of the river from 40 feet to 47 feet, with completion scheduled in 2022. In 2020, UPS proposed a $138 million expansion, in addition to the $196 million it recently spent at its ground hub, which has 2,500 workers. The Navy designated Mayport and San Diego as the bases for its new class of 52 littoral combat ships, which are faster and carry more weapons but with a smaller crew. Navy pilots fly overseas unmanned Triton drone systems from their computers at the naval air station. Mayport was selected by the Navy as the East Coast headquarters of its Triton drone operations.

The 4th District of Florida is centered in Jacksonville-based Duval County; a smaller piece of the county is in the strongly Democratic 5th District. It also is home to most of rapidly growing St. Johns County, which had a 39 percent population increase from 2010 to 2019 and has been rated as the healthiest and wealthiest in the state. The median household income of St. Johns is 50 percent higher than Florida as a whole. The county includes well-restored St. Augustine, founded by Spanish colonists as the oldest permanent European settlement in North America—42 years older than Jamestown Virginia. To the north is rapidly growing Nassau County, including a planned community of 3,200 homes in Yulee; the first phase was scheduled for completion in 2021.

The boosterish Jacksonville civic culture and significant military presence make the 4th a pro-business, pro-military and pro-Republican district. Despite the stronger statewide victory for President Donald Trump in 2020, his local support dropped. After having won Duval County by 6,000 votes against Hillary Clinton, he lost it by 19,000 to Joe Biden. The Democratic parts of Duval have mostly been carved into the 5th District. For a few weeks in 2020, Jacksonville became the alternative site to Charlotte to host the Republican National Convention, until party officials decided that the coronavirus made it impossible to permit any large gathering. In November, Trump won the district, 60%-39%, including 58 percent in its share of Duval.

Al Lawson (D)

Elected 2016, 3rd term, b. Sep 23, 1948; Midway, FL; University of FL, B.S., 1970; FL State University, M.S., 1973; Episcopalian; Married (Delores J. Brooks Lawson); 2 children; 2 grandchildren.

Elected Office: FL House, 1982-2000; FL Senate, 2000-2010, Minority Leader, 2008-2010.

Professional Career: Prof. Basketball player & coach, Florida State Univ.; President, Lawson & Assoc. Inc. .

DC Office: 1406 LHOB 20515, 202-225-0123, Fax: 202-225-2256, lawson.house.gov

State Offices: Jacksonville, 904-354-1652; Tallahassee, 850-558-9450.

Committees: *Agriculture*: Biotechnology, Horticulture & Research; General Farm Commodities & Risk Management; Subcommittee Nutrition, Oversight & Department Operations. *Financial Services*: Consumer Protection & Financial Institutions; Housing, Community Development & Insurance; Task Force on Financial Technology.

Group Ratings

	ADA	ACLU	AFL-CIO	LCV	COC	HAFA	ACU	CFG	FRC
2020	**	74%	**	100%	-	0%	8%	**	-
2019	80%	C	100%	97%	68%	C	9%	12%	0%

Almanac Ratings 2019-2020

	Economy	Social	Foreign	Composite
Liberal	100%	59%	56%	72%
Conservative	0%	41%	44%	28%

Key Votes of the 116th Congress

1. U.S./Mex./Can. trade deal	Y	5. Russia sanctions	Y	9. Firearms background checks	Y
2. First Coronavirus response	Y	6. Troops in Syria	N/A	10. Spending at the border	Y
3. HEROES Act	Y	7. Veto arms sales to Saudis	Y	11. Marijuana liberalized rules	Y
4. CASH Act	Y	8. Defense $$$, veto override	Y	12. Electoral College objections	N

Election Results

Election	Name (Party)	Vote (%)		Cand. Spent	Ind. Exp. Support	Ind. Exp. Oppose
2020 General	Al Lawson (D)	219,463	(65%)	$764,340	$481	
	Gary Adler (R)	117,510	(35%)	$151,833		$113
2020 Primary	Al Lawson (D)	52,823	(56%)			
	Albert Chester (D)	24,579	(26%)			
	LaShonda "LJ" Holloway (D)	17,378	(18%)			

Prior winning percentages: 2018 (67%), 2016 (64%)

Democrat Al Lawson, elected in 2016 under unusual circumstances in a district that had been radically altered in a mid-decade redistricting that benefited him, faced continuing campaign challenges. His legislative activities have focused on agriculture and financial issues facing low-income groups.

Lawson, a fourth-generation Floridian, was born in Midway. He worked his first job in the Gadsden Community tobacco fields at the age of 8. In high school, he was an accomplished athlete and went on to play basketball at Florida Agricultural and Mechanical University, where he was a team leader. He received his bachelor's degree in political science and a master's in public administration from Florida State University. He had a brief career in professional basketball. Lawson was elected to the Florida House in 1982 and served for 18 years before winning election in 2000 to the state Senate, where he served for another 10 years. He chaired the House Natural Resources Committee, authoring the Preservation 2000 law, which created the largest state-funded land acquisition program in the country.

Following his departure from the legislature, he became a lobbyist and insurance agent. Lawson had twice run for Congress. In 2010, he sought the Democratic nomination in the Tallahassee-based 2nd District, losing narrowly in the primary to seven-term Rep. Allen Boyd. Then he lost in the 2012 general to Republican Rep. Steve Southerland, who had defeated Boyd two years earlier.

In 2016, Lawson took on yet another incumbent. This time, it was the Democratic primary against Rep. Corinne Brown, a 12-term incumbent who had overcome numerous obstacles, but couldn't survive the combination of adverse redistricting and an indictment for corruption. Their radically redrawn district had two geographic poles: Brown's hometown of Jacksonville and Lawson's long-time base in Tallahassee and Gadsden. Brown focused on constituents in her House work and used the slogan "Corrine Delivers." She survived, despite a string of controversial comments and ethics issues. Eight weeks before the primary, a federal grand jury issued a 22-count indictment of Brown following a lengthy investigation into what prosecutors termed a phony educational charity that she and her chief of staff turned into a personal slush fund with $800,000 in solicitations.

Lawson won the primary, 48%-39%, with LaShonda Holloway getting 13 percent. Both Lawson and Brown ran well in their home areas. In Tallahassee-based Leon County plus adjoining Gadsden, Lawson won 76 percent of the 31,491 votes. In Jacksonville-based Duval County, Brown won 62 percent of the 39,888 votes cast. Those three counties, separated by 160 miles, cast 86 percent of the total votes. Lawson easily won the general election. In 2017, Brown was convicted on 18 felony counts and began to serve a five-year sentence. In April 2020, she was released to home confinement due to coronavirus fears.

In the House, Lawson was a member of the House-Senate conference committee that approved the final version of the 2018 farm bill. It included his legislation to increase federal support for historically black colleges and universities, with steps such as development of an agricultural work force and food security. The defense spending bill Congress enacted in 2018 included his provision to assist small startup businesses to commercialize their products.

With House Democrats in the majority in 2019, Lawson introduced with Sen. Elizabeth Warren legislation to extend food stamp benefits to low-income college students and reduce their work requirement. Many students had been forced "to make a choice between buying food or paying for books and housing," Lawson said. As a member of the Financial Services Committee, he won the panel's approval in 2019 of a bill that cracked down on how companies use credit reports in making hiring decisions. "An individual's history does not prove a person's ability to perform a job well," he said.

At home, Lawson was challenged in the August 2018 Democratic primary by Alvin Brown, the former mayor of Jacksonville. Brown criticized Lawson for his approval of President Donald Trump and for his support of Florida's "stand your ground" law that protects gun owners. "There's nothing wrong with being a moderate," Lawson responded. Each spent about $500,000. In a pattern similar to Lawson's victory in the 2016 primary, he trailed in Duval County, but had a 5-to-1 lead in Leon and Gadsden counties. Lawson won, 60%-40%.

In 2020, he faced another Jacksonville-based Democratic challenger. Albert Chester said Lawson had "no record of fighting against injustice and police brutality." Lawson, who had been endorsed by the Fraternal Order of Police, cited his support for steps to assure racial justice. Lawson defeated Chester, 56%-26%, with Holloway running again and getting 18 percent. Lawson got 73 percent of the total vote in Leon and Gadsden counties, but only 40 percent in Duval.

Lawson endorsed Joe Biden in May 2019. "Joe has a long history of doing what's right and not what's easy to advance the causes of America's working families," he said. "We need Joe's experience, common sense and decency in the White House."

FL-5: Northern Florida metro areas   **Cook Partisan Voting Index: D+12**

Population		Race and Ethnicity		Income	
Total	742,643	White	44.50%	Median Income	$43,667
Land area (sq. miles)	1,355	Black	47.10%	District Income Rank	424
Pop/ sq mi	548.06	Latino	9.70%	Poverty Rate	21.90%
Born in State	59.10%	Asian	2.40%	With health insurance	86.10%
		Two or more races	2.80%	Cash public assistance	4.40%
Age Groups		Other	3.20%	Food stamp/SNAP	19.90%
Under 18	22.10%				
18-34	28.20%	**Education**		**Work**	
35-64	36.10%	H.S grad or less	47.90%	White Collar	30.30%
Over 64	13.40%	Some college	31.80%	Sales and Service	45.30%
		College Degree, 4 yr	12.70%	Blue Collar	24.40%
Military		Post grad	7.60%	Government	17.80%
Veteran/ Active Duty	9.90%				

2020 Pres. Vote	Biden	214,889	(63%)	Trump	123,978	(36%)		
2016 Pres. Vote	Clinton	191,195	(61%)	Trump	111,891	(36%)	Johnson	5,997 (2%)

Downtown Jacksonville and Parts of Tallahassee: Before the Civil War, most of Florida was still an uncharted watery wilderness, festooned with exotic greenery, inhabited by unusual animals, a part of the United States so far out of the experience of most Americans as to seem foreign. As late as 1940, Florida had the smallest population of any state in the South, and most of the people here lived in classic Dixie rural counties with small courthouse towns. Civic affairs were run by the richest White men, and African Americans lived in poorly constructed, unpainted shotgun shacks propped up on blocks, with little money and no vote. This was a land of swamps, lakes and orange groves. The broad St. Johns River, one of the few North American rivers that flows (if only sluggishly) north, meanders through orange-grove country to the port of Jacksonville.

The city's planners have been eager to revitalize the downtown area, which is dominated by shipyards, warehouses and some office buildings. Especially with the major hurricane damage elsewhere in the state in recent years, officials have voiced growing concern about the threat of destruction if a major storm hits the extensive low-lying areas of the city. In 2018, Shad Khan, the billionaire businessman owner of the Jacksonville Jaguars football franchise, made sweeping development proposals for both the riverfront and the downtown area around the stadium. After a June 2020 deadline was reached without agreement, city officials kept open the possibility of resuming negotiations. Also in 2018, the Mayo Clinic announced plans for a new medical building on its 400-acre local campus. But the clinic said in April 2020 that construction had been delayed because Mayo faced budget problems.

Tallahassee, the seat of state government with many public-sector jobs, has been a source of discomfort for the state's Republican rulers. Its African-American population grew from about 25 percent in the 1990s to 35 percent in 2019. The city's liberal bent is fueled by its two big universities in the downtown area, Florida State and Florida A&M. This remains a government town, as promises from state leaders of a "new economy" have been mostly unfulfilled. Nearby Gadsden County, the state's only Black-majority county, is rural and heavily Democratic. The countryside around Tallahassee is distinctly Dixie and is more reminiscent of southern Georgia than of southern Florida. The landscape is marked by cotton fields, soft pine stands, catfish farms and small towns with big churches.

The 5th Congressional District is like a barbell that extends more than 160 miles from Jacksonville to Tallahassee. But the barbell is unequal. The Jacksonville-based Duval County territory has 403,000 residents, while the western end in Leon and Gadsden Counties has 206,000. The Jacksonville section of the district includes much of downtown and the large port, though it stops a few miles short of the Atlantic. The larger share of Duval County is the core of the solidly Republican 4th District. On the western end, the 5th includes about 50 percent of Leon; the more Republican section is in the 2nd District. The Leon County portion can show its weight in elections because its many government employees are more politically connected. Between the two ends of the barbell are five rural Republican counties, each with a population of less than 30,000.

The 5th is the only Democratic district north of Orlando. Its population is 47 percent African American and 10 percent Hispanic. It trails only two south Florida districts in its minority population. Joe Biden's 63%-36% win was his third best in the state behind those two other districts.

Michael Waltz (R)

Elected 2018, 2nd term, b. Jan 31, 1974; Boynton Beach, FL; VA Military Institute, B.A., 1996; Christian Church; Divorced; 1 child.

Military Career: U.S. Navy and Reserve 1996-2007 (Afghanistan)

Professional Career: U.S. Department of Defense, Program Manager, 2004-2007, Afghanistan Country Director, 2006-2007; Special Advisor to the Vice President for South Asia and Counterterrorism, 2007-2009; Fox News Contributor, 2016-2018; Chief Executive Officer, METIS Solutions, 2010-2018.

DC Office: 216 CHOB 20515, 202-225-2706, waltz.house.gov

State Offices: Deland, 386-279-0707; Palm Coast, 386-302-0442; Port Orange, 386-238-9711.

Committees: *Armed Services*: Intelligence & Special Operations; Strategic Forces. *Science, Space & Technology*: Research & Technology (RMM).

Almanac Ratings 2019-2020

	Economy	Social	Foreign	Composite
Liberal	38%	27%	27%	31%
Conservative	62%	73%	73%	69%

Key Votes of the 116th Congress

1. U.S./Mex./Can. trade deal	Y	5. Russia sanctions	Y	9. Firearms background checks	N
2. First Coronavirus response	N	6. Troops in Syria	Y	10. Spending at the border	Y
3. HEROES Act	N	7. Veto arms sales to Saudis	N	11. Marijuana liberalized rules	N
4. CASH Act	N	8. Defense $$$, veto override	Y	12. Electoral College objections	N

Election Results

Election	Name (Party)	Vote (%)		Cand. Spent	Ind. Exp. Support	Ind. Exp. Oppose
2020 General	Michael Waltz (R)	265,393	(61%)	$1,735,770	$50,328	
	Clint Curtis (D)	172,305	(39%)	$21,762		$54

Prior winning percentages: 2018 (56%)

Republican Michael Waltz, who was elected in 2018 after winning competitive primary and general-election contests, had extensive experience with military and national security issues as a Green Beret in the Army and as a top policy aide during the presidency of George W. Bush. In the House, he served on the Armed Services Committee and reached out for bipartisanship. But he caused some local dissent with his decision to join a legal brief in support of President Donald Trump following the 2020 election.

Waltz, a Florida native, graduated from the Virginia Military Institute. The first former Green Beret to serve in Congress, he commanded an Army Special Forces unit that had multiple deployments to Afghanistan and the Middle East, and joined with other Special Forces units in four provinces along the border with Pakistan. On one of those tours, he led the search for Bowe Bergdahl, an Army soldier who had deserted his unit and was held captive for five years by the Taliban.

While in the military, Waltz was director for Afghanistan policy at the Pentagon. As an adviser to Vice President Dick Cheney, he served as policy director for counterterrorism in the Bush White House. In the private sector, Waltz ran a defense and intelligence contracting firm and was a cofounder and partner of an international consulting firm that provided strategic advice to foreign governments and businesses. During most of that time, he was a think-tank fellow and a media commentator on military issues.

When Rep. Ron DeSantis decided to run for governor, Waltz moved into politics. "I will fight for you in Congress like I fought for you in combat," he said. Also seeking the Republican nomination were John Ward, a retired Navy intelligence officer, and former state representative Fred Costello. Waltz and Ward each spent more than $1 million in the primary—much of it self-financed in each case. Waltz called for expansion of the commercial space industry into Volusia County and reform of the Veterans Affairs Department. Ward, a business investor, emphasized changes in domestic programs and rollbacks of federal regulations. Waltz took the primary with 42 percent of the vote to 30 percent for Ward.

In the general election, Waltz faced Nancy Soderberg, who had a lengthy career in Washington as a foreign policy aide. She held senior positions on national security issues with Presidents Bill Clinton and Barack Obama. Subsequently, Soderberg directed the public service leadership program at the University of North Florida. The Orlando Sentinel reported that each candidate had thin ties to the district and each was accused of "carpetbagging" by opponents. Soderberg focused on the need for improved health care services and criticized Republican-enacted tax cuts. Like many House Democratic candidates in 2018, she outspent her opponent. Waltz said the outcome of the primaries showed that voters had little concern about where the candidates resided. "I wish I'd been here," Waltz told the Sentinel. "I'd been running around getting shot at the last few years."

With his victory, Waltz joined a growing number of Afghanistan and Iraq war veterans from both parties in the House, who occasionally have pressed for bipartisanship on national security issues. With a seat on the Armed Services panel, he got amendments to the annual defense spending bill in 2020 that sought to protect federally funded research from Chinese espionage by setting a federal requirement that researchers disclose foreign funding sources. In August 2019, he took issue with the decision by President Donald Trump to withdraw U.S. forces from Afghanistan. "Let's fight these wars in places like Kabul, [otherwise] it will follow us home," he said on FOX News. "I do not want to lose Americans fighting their way back in."

He looked for opportunities to join Democrats on other issues. With Rep. Stephanie Murphy, he filed a bill to require the federal government to send immediate notification to state and local agencies—and voters—when election and voter information systems have been hacked. With Rep.

Val Demings, also of Florida, Waltz proposed placing a statue of Florida educator Mary McLeod Bethune in the Capitol. He said that she would be the first black woman in American history to receive that honor. Waltz worked with Rep. Don Beyer of Virginia at the Science, Space and Technology Committee to show that the United States must invest in technology to deter overseas enemies from using "deep fake" systems that are a threat to artificial intelligence. In 2021, he became ranking Republican on that panel's Research and Technology Subcommittee.

Following the 2020 election, Waltz was one of 126 House Republicans who signed a legal brief urging the Supreme Court to review a case filed by the attorney general of Texas challenging the victory of Joe Biden in several states. That led the Sentinel, which had endorsed his reelection in a contest that received little attention, to "apologize" to its readers for having endorsed Waltz. "We had no idea, had no way of knowing at the time, that Waltz was not committed to democracy," the newspaper wrote. In the future, it added, editorial writers will ask candidates, especially Republicans, if they would support efforts "to overthrow a presidential election." Waltz responded that he had "shown my commitment" to the Constitution during his military service.

FL-6: Northeast Florida   Cook Partisan Voting Index: R+10

Population		Race and Ethnicity		Income	
Total	790,455	White	79.70%	Median Income	$55,281
Land area (sq. miles)	2,507	Black	10.90%	District Income Rank	325
Pop/ sq mi	315.31	Latino	13.40%	Poverty Rate	12.70%
Born in State	35.00%	Asian	1.90%	With health insurance	86.60%
		Two or more races	2.50%	Cash public assistance	1.30%
Age Groups		Other	5.00%	Food stamp/SNAP	11.10%
Under 18	17.70%				
18-34	18.20%	**Education**		**Work**	
35-64	38.10%	H.S grad or less	42.00%	White Collar	33.10%
Over 64	25.90%	Some college	33.30%	Sales and Service	45.40%
		College Degree, 4 yr	15.70%	Blue Collar	21.50%
Military		Post grad	9.10%	Government	10.30%
Veteran/ Active Duty	11.40%				

2020 Pres. Vote	Trump	263,645	(58%)	Biden	184,607	(41%)		
2016 Pres. Vote	Trump	215,940	(56%)	Clinton	151,453	(40%)	Johnson	8,694 (2%)

Daytona Beach: In 1513, Spanish explorer Juan Ponce de León headed to the New World, hoping to discover the Fountain of Youth. Instead, he found Ponte Vedra Beach, located just south of modern-day Jacksonville. A few decades later, Spanish colonists founded St. Augustine, the oldest permanent European settlement in North America. Less well-known is New Smyrna Beach. Another 75 miles down the Atlantic Coast, it was established in 1768 in an attempt by the British to colonize Florida with Greek settlers, whom they believed to be ideally suited to the warm climate. They were not, however, well suited for the brutal wilderness conditions. By 1777, many had abandoned the colony, walking and swimming back to St. Augustine. The area was a popular hideout for rum-runners during Prohibition, and today has become a popular vacation spot and quieter in many ways than nearby and better-known Daytona Beach.

The beaches in Daytona have been attracting sun-seekers for decades, although the city is best known for the Daytona 500 held each February at Daytona International Speedway. With the coronavirus shutting down the theme parks for much of 2020, the beaches at Daytona became a crowded alternative—often without social distancing. Further inland, northeast Florida still retains a taste of "Old Florida." DeLand has a small-town atmosphere centered on Stetson University. Most of Volusia County has managed to avoid the familiar pattern in Florida of miles of high-rise condominiums. Flagler and St. Johns, the two coastal counties between Jacksonville and Daytona Beach, were filled with cattle ranches a few decades ago. Both have grown rapidly since then. Between 2000 and 2010, the total population of the smaller Flagler nearly doubled; from 2010 to 2019, the 39 percent increase in St. Johns doubled the rate in Flagler.

The 6th District covers the Atlantic coast for nearly 90 miles, more than any other district in Florida, from just south of St. Augustine to the Canaveral National Seashore, which has offered splendid views of NASA lift-offs from the John F. Kennedy Space Center. Other Florida districts along the Gulf or in the Keys offer longer stretches of beachfront, but with fewer towns or people. About 70 percent of the population is concentrated in Volusia County, 20 percent in the northern beachfront counties (though most of St. Johns is in the 4th District), with the balance in rural Lake County. Donald Trump did well in the many blue-collar communities of Volusia, all of which is in the 6th. In 2020, the turnout in the county increased by 25 percent, with Trump's vote share growing from 54.8 percent to 56.4 percent and an increase of 30,000 votes. He took the district, 58%-41%.

Stephanie Murphy (D)

Elected 2016, 3rd term, b. Sep 16, 1978; Ho Chi Minh City, Vietnam; College of William and Mary, B.A., 2000; Georgetown University, M.S., 2004; Christian Church; Married (Sean Murphy); 2 children.

Professional Career: Foreign Affairs Specialist, U.S Dept. of Defense, 2004-2008; Businesswoman; Faculty/Instructor, Rollins College, 2014-2016.

DC Office: 1710 LHOB 20515, 202-225-4035, Fax: 202-226-0821, stephaniemurphy.house.gov

State Offices: Orlando, 888-205-5421; Sanford, 888-205-5421.

Committees: *Armed Services*: Intelligence & Special Operations; Tactical Air & Land Forces. *Ways & Means*: Trade; Worker & Family Support.

Group Ratings

	ADA	ACLU	AFL-CIO	LCV	COC	HAFA	ACU	CFG	FRC
2020	**	55%	**	95%	-	5%	6%	**	-
2019	80%	C	95%	97%	69%	C	7%	24%	0%

Almanac Ratings 2019-2020

	Economy	Social	Foreign	Composite
Liberal	51%	51%	46%	50%
Conservative	49%	49%	54%	50%

Key Votes of the 116th Congress

1. U.S./Mex./Can. trade deal Y	5. Russia sanctions Y	9. Firearms background checks Y
2. First Coronavirus response Y	6. Troops in Syria Y	10. Spending at the border Y
3. HEROES Act Y	7. Veto arms sales to Saudis Y	11. Marijuana liberalized rules Y
4. CASH Act Y	8. Defense $$$, veto override Y	12. Electoral College objections N

Election Results

Election	Name (Party)	Vote (%)		Cand. Spent	Ind. Exp. Support	Ind. Exp. Oppose
2020 General	Stephanie Murphy (D)	224,946	(55%)	$1,672,596	$142,115	$89,602
	Leo Valentín (R)	175,750	(43%)	$1,012,493	$88,304	$113

Prior winning percentages: 2018 (58%), 2016 (52%)

Democrat Stephanie Murphy, elected in 2016 when she narrowly defeated an influential House Republican, worked with centrist Democrats and across the political aisle. She has impressed many with her personal story as a refugee from Vietnam with a remarkably self-made life story in the American immigrant tradition. In the House, she became a leader of the junior Democrats.

At six months, Stephanie Dang fled Vietnam on a refugee boat with her family. After the small craft ran out of fuel and went adrift in the South China Sea, the group was rescued by the U.S. Navy, which provided supplies that aided in the boat reaching Malaysia and a refugee camp. The Lutheran Church helped the family to the United States, and they eventually settled in Virginia. She graduated in 2000 from the College of William and Mary. On Sept. 11, 2001, she was working at Deloitte Consulting in Washington. Motivated by a desire for public service, she quit that job to attend graduate school at the Georgetown University School of Foreign Service, where she got a master's degree.

As a national security specialist for the secretary of Defense, Murphy helped organize the rescue effort for victims of a 2004 tsunami in South Asia. Her work as chief of staff to a global strategic guidance planning effort won her a Defense Department Medal for Exceptional Civilian Service. Later, she was an executive at Sungate Capital, advising on investment decisions and implementing government affairs initiatives. After marrying Sean Murphy, whom she had met while working at Deloitte, they settled in Winter Park Florida, where his family had been politically active. She taught business and social entrepreneurship at Rollins College. As an advocate of LGBT rights, she spoke out for that community following the June 2016 terrorist attack at Pulse Nightclub in Orlando that killed 49.

Also in 2016, Murphy advised the Democratic Congressional Campaign Committee, which was looking for a challenger to Rep. John Mica, who had chaired the House Transportation and Infrastructure Committee. After failing to find a credible candidate, the DCCC recruited Murphy to run. She was mentored by several prominent Democratic women, including Nancy Pelosi. Murphy spent $1.1 million to $1.8 million for Mica, who had not faced a serious Democratic opponent since 2002 and was slow to take her candidacy seriously. She received $4.7 million in support from the DCCC and other party affiliates, and $3 million more from liberal groups. The National Republican Congressional Committee spent $1.7 million for Mica.

Murphy said Mica was out of touch with the district, and criticized his views on gun control, gay rights and women's issues. "He is a career politician who has been part of the problem," she said. Mica highlighted the many benefits, including significant transportation projects, that he had delivered to the district. Mica had given Donald Trump and his business legislative assistance in securing a $3 million annual lease at the Old Post Office Building on Pennsylvania Avenue in Washington as the site for his new Trump International Hotel. After Mica proudly acknowledged his role, the DCCC issued a statement alleging that "Mica has not only helped Trump line his own pockets, he's stood by Trump every step of the way, even after he was caught bragging about sexual assault."

Murphy became the giant killer, 51.5%-48.5%. Mica got 53 percent of the vote in Seminole County. But Murphy prevailed with 58 percent in Orange County.

In the House, Murphy filed a bill to end the 22-year restriction on the use of federal funds to conduct research to promote gun control; her measure was enacted as part of a spending bill. In October 2018, Time magazine placed her photo on the cover of a story about the gun debate. She became a leader of the bipartisan Problem Solvers Caucus, which prepared recommendations to change House procedures to encourage more open debate. Following the 2018 election, Pelosi agreed to some of those changes to secure support from Murphy and other moderate Democrats in her campaign for House Speaker.

In 2019, Murphy became a chair of two groups of House Democrats: the centrist Blue Dog Coalition and the Future Forum of young party members. "In this new era of divided government, we Democrats must introduce bold ideas and fight for our shared values, and we must also seek bipartisan cooperation," she said.

With the Blue Dogs, Murphy continued the group's focus on national security and fiscal responsibility, though the Republican tax cuts, entitlement spending, and the coronavirus had sent the federal deficit spiraling and left the budget hawks as a lonely group. Within the Democratic Caucus, they became a force in restraining some costly proposals. In an op-ed column in The Washington Post in April 2019, she objected that the "socialism" label had been attached to many Democrats: "For partisan reasons, [Republicans] seek to paint the entire Democratic Party as drifting toward socialism, when the philosophy is espoused by a small minority of members," she wrote. "I will continue to support … a market economy driven by the innovation of the private sector and constrained by guardrails constructed by a duly-elected government."

She clashed with Rep. Alexandria Ocasio-Cortez when the latter's chief of staff tweeted that the Blue Dogs "seem hell bent to do to black and brown people today what the old Southern Democrats did in the 40s." Murphy told the Orlando Sentinel that it was insulting and unprofessional "to have my colleagues question my motivations." In addition to her seat on the powerful Ways and Means Committee, Murphy showed her influence among House Democrats when she became a chief deputy whip in 2021.

At home, Murphy has been reelected handily with similar results against two credible Republican challengers. In 2018, Mike Miller, a state representative, called for lower taxes and a balanced budget. Murphy outspent him, $3.1 million to $1.1 million, and won 58%-42%, with 54 percent of the vote in Seminole. In 2020, Leo Valentin, a radiology doctor, offered himself as "part of a new generation of Republican leaders who will bring innovation and a fresh perspective to Congress." He spent $1 million and lost 55%-43%. Pending changes in redistricting, Murphy secured what had been a Republican district.

In January 2020, citing his work on climate change and gun control, Murphy became the second congressional Democrat to endorse Michael Bloomberg as "the best person to take on Donald Trump" and she became a national co-chair of his presidential campaign. In early 2021, she said that she was exploring a statewide race in 2022. In May, she abandoned her tentative plan to run for the Senate after Rep. Val Demings said that she was planning to challenge Sen. Marco Rubio.

FL-7: Northern Orlando Suburbs

Cook Partisan Voting Index: D+3

Population		Race and Ethnicity		Income	
Total	814,980	White	73.90%	Median Income	$66,748
Land area (sq. miles)	514	Black	11.60%	District Income Rank	195
Pop/ sq mi	1,586.86	Latino	26.70%	Poverty Rate	11.70%
Born in State	37.20%	Asian	5.10%	With health insurance	89.30%
		Two or more races	2.90%	Cash public assistance	1.70%
Age Groups		Other	6.50%	Food stamp/SNAP	10.00%
Under 18	19.50%				
18-34	27.60%	**Education**		**Work**	
35-64	38.10%	H.S grad or less	29.30%	White Collar	44.10%
Over 64	14.70%	Some college	29.50%	Sales and Service	39.90%
		College Degree, 4 yr	26.80%	Blue Collar	16.00%
Military		Post grad	14.30%	Government	8.40%
Veteran/ Active Duty	6.40%				

2020 Pres. Vote	Biden	226,505	(54%)	Trump	183,414	(44%)		
2016 Pres. Vote	Clinton	186,658	(51%)	Trump	160,178	(44%)	Johnson	11,551	(3%)

Seminole, Orange: For much of the 19th century, central Florida was a sparsely populated region at the southern frontier of the state. The native Timucua tribe had been driven to extinction by war and disease, and only a few towns of any size dotted the state's interior. Steamboats traveled up and down the St. Johns River to supply small trading centers that sprang up at the end of the navigable portions of that waterway on Lake Monroe and Lake Jesup (known for its many alligators) in what is now Seminole County. This state of affairs largely persisted until 1971, when Disney World opened in neighboring Orange County, setting off startling growth and development in the region. Tourism flourished and Seminole County became one of the primary beneficiaries of that explosive development. Its population shot up from 55,000 in 1960 to 472,000 in 2019. The once-quiet county became a collection of largely high-end suburbs with a median income of $66,768, a rapid increase from $57,010 in 2015. The area was hit hard by the housing collapse and recession, but has been rebounding. Work on the $2.3 billion reconstruction of a 21-mile stretch of Interstate 4 in Seminole and Orange counties, which will add express lanes through Orlando, was accelerated in 2020 because the pandemic reduced auto traffic. Work was underway to upgrade I-4 for 20 miles east and 20 miles west of Orlando.

The 7th Congressional District of Florida includes all of Seminole County, which supplies a bit more than 60 percent of the population, and one-fourth of Orlando-based Orange County. Seminole has been a key battleground county in one of the nation's key battleground states, and it has become a shifting bellwether. In 2018, The New York Times described Seminole as "a modern microcosm whose population most closely matches the nation's current mix." Bolstered by the explosion of young families, it has become a brighter spot for Democrats in Florida. In a county that Mitt Romney won 53%-46% when he lost the state in 2012, Joe Biden won 51%-48%, though he too lost the state. Biden was the first Democratic presidential nominee to win Seminole since Harry Truman in 1948. Likewise, in 2018, Democrats Bill Nelson and Andrew Gillum each had a two-point lead in Seminole, even though they lost statewide in their contests for the Senate and governor. From 2010 to 2019, the Hispanic population grew from 17 percent to 23 percent.

The redistricting in 2016 added the eastern side of Orlando, which had a significant Hispanic population. The district overall became 24 percent Hispanic and 10 percent Black. It had been 19 percent Hispanic and 9 percent Black. Of course, the next round of redistricting could shift those numbers again—up or down. In its current lines, Joe Biden took the district, 54%-44%--a marked improvement for Democrats from the 50%-50% presidential-election split in 2012.

Bill Posey (R)

Elected 2008, 7th term, b. Dec 18, 1947; Washington, DC; Brevard Community College, A.A., 1969; Stetson University, Att., 1978; Methodist; Married (Katie Ingram Posey); 2 children; 3 grandchildren.

Elected Office: Rockledge City Council, 1976-1986; FL House, 1992-2000; FL Senate, 2000-2008.

Professional Career: McDonnell Douglas Astronautics Co., 1966-1969; Crawford & Co./Gay & Taylor, 1970-1974; Founder, Posey & Co. Realtors, 1974-present.

DC Office: 2150 RHOB 20515, 202-225-3671, Fax: 202-225-3516, posey.house.gov

State Offices: Melbourne, 321-632-1776.

Committees: *Financial Services*: Consumer Protection & Financial Institutions; Housing, Community Development & Insurance. *Science, Space & Technology*: Space & Aeronautics.

Group Ratings

	ADA	ACLU	AFL-CIO	LCV	COC	HAFA	ACU	CFG	FRC
2020	**	24%	**	19%	-	95%	89%	**	-
2019	0%	C	29%	14%	83%	C	90%	77%	100%

Almanac Ratings 2019-2020

	Economy	Social	Foreign	Composite
Liberal	25%	10%	15%	17%
Conservative	75%	90%	85%	83%

Key Votes of the 116th Congress

1. U.S./Mex./Can. trade deal	Y	5. Russia sanctions	N	9. Firearms background checks	N
2. First Coronavirus response	Y	6. Troops in Syria	N	10. Spending at the border	Y
3. HEROES Act	N	7. Veto arms sales to Saudis	N	11. Marijuana liberalized rules	N
4. CASH Act	N	8. Defense $$$, veto override	N	12. Electoral College objections	Y

Election Results

Election	Name (Party)	Vote (%)		Cand. Spent	Ind. Exp. Support	Ind. Exp. Oppose
2020 General	Bill Posey (R)	282,093	(61%)	$1,115,846	$18,489	
	Jim Kennedy (D)	177,695	(39%)	$126,953	$5,100	
2020 Primary	Bill Posey (R)	54,861	(63%)			
	Scott Caine (R)	32,952	(38%)			

Prior winning percentages: 2018 (61%), 2016 (63%), 2014 (66%), 2012 (59%), 2010 (65%), 2008 (53%)

Bill Posey, a Republican first elected in 2008, has pursued his personal interest in finance issues and his district's interest in space issues, with high seniority in his committee assignments. He combines extensive experience in business and local government, with a penchant to shake up business-as-usual and an occasionally maverick approach. Entrenched in what has been a safe seat, redistricting or his age of 73 might be the chief factors leading him to step down.

Posey was born in Washington D.C. and moved several times because of his father's work in the aircraft business. His family landed in Brevard County in 1956. After graduating from high school, Posey took a job with McDonnell Douglas Astronautics at the Kennedy Space Center. He worked on the Apollo 11 Launch Team that in 1969 sent the first men to the moon, and he attended Brevard Community College at night. After Apollo 11, Posey was laid off and went into real estate as founder of Posey & Co. Realtors. Until an accident at an Orlando speedway in 2004 left him with spinal fractures, Posey had been an accomplished stock car racer. As the first member of his family to register as a Republican, Posey was elected to the Rockledge City Council in 1976 and served a decade. Later, he served eight years each in the state House and Senate. He authored legislation that set new standards for state government accountability.

In 2008, he ran for an open House seat. Other Republicans who had been interested in running fell in line. Democrats were unable to find a strong candidate. Posey faced Democrat Stephen Blythe, a Melbourne family physician, and made government accountability and immigration reform the central themes of his campaign. It was an amiable contest. The candidates expressed mutual admiration and said they would vote for each other if they could not vote for themselves. Posey outspent Blythe by almost 9-to-1 and won 53%-42% in a Democratic year.

On the Financial Services Committee, Posey got the results of every committee vote posted on its website within two days. He pushed a measure to require state governments to submit fiscal accounting reports as a condition of getting federal money. In 2018, he won enactment of his legislation to expand protections, including compensation, for American victims of international terrorism. Despite his seniority, he has not been the top Republican on a subcommittee.

On the Space, Science and Technology Committee, Posey has worked on behalf of the Kennedy Space Center and the Space Coast to find ways to live with NASA cutbacks. He won praise from the local Sunshine State News for using that seat "as a bully pulpit to push private space flight and jab the Obama administration for retreating from space exploration." In 2018, he spearheaded a letter of congressional support for a new mobile launcher that NASA was seeking. With Democratic Rep. Charlie Crist in May 2020, Posey filed the American Space Commerce Act, which gives incentive to American space firms to invest in and launch from the U.S. The domestic space launch industry, Posey said, faces "unfair trade practices from nations like China and Russia that heavily subsidize space launches."

His maverick instincts have extended to House leadership contests. In 2015, Posey voted for fellow Florida Rep. Daniel Webster for Speaker, instead of John Boehner. That October, he again joined the dissidents, as one of nine Republicans who voted for Webster when Paul Ryan was elected to succeed Boehner. In March 2020, he was the only original Republican cosponsor, with 138 House Democrats, of a resolution "condemning all forms of anti-Asian sentiment as related to COVID-19"—without citing President Donald Trump or anyone else.

In December 2020, Posey was one of 64 Republicans who voted against the omnibus spending bill, which included economic stimulus to respond to the coronavirus. Although he backed many portions of the bill, he said the "legislation should have taken place long ago on the House floor through spirited, transparent debate and votes on amendments from both sides of the aisle, not written behind closed doors by a handful of people. We must end the practice that allows a small number of people in a back room to rewrite the laws of this nation and spend trillions of dollars with no transparency or oversight."

At home, Posey has not faced a serious reelection threat from a Democrat. In 2020, he faced his first significant primary challenge. Scott Caine retired after 30 years in the Air Force—as a fighter pilot and later as a commander—and said it was time for "a fresh voice and new ideas." Citing Posey's support for the resolution on Asians, Caine criticized him in an ad for having "turned his back" on Trump. Posey responded that the charge was "laughable" and that he had Trump's endorsement.

Posey spent $1.1 million, four times the total by Caine, and won the August contest, 62%-38%, perhaps close enough to encourage a 2022 bid by Caine or another local Republican. In September, when the House passed the resolution on anti-Asian views, 243-164, Posey joined all but 14 Republicans in voting against the measure.

FL-8: Space Coast/Northern Treasure Coast

Cook Partisan Voting Index: R+12

Population		Race and Ethnicity		Income	
Total	780,036	White	82.80%	Median Income	$58,740
Land area (sq. miles)	1,752	Black	9.00%	District Income Rank	283
Pop/ sq mi	445.21	Latino	11.80%	Poverty Rate	9.50%
Born in State	31.60%	Asian	2.20%	With health insurance	88.90%
		Two or more races	3.80%	Cash public assistance	1.70%
Age Groups		Other	2.10%	Food stamp/SNAP	8.20%
Under 18	17.90%				
18-34	18.20%	**Education**		**Work**	
35-64	38.00%	H.S grad or less	36.00%	White Collar	38.60%
Over 64	25.90%	Some college	33.50%	Sales and Service	41.90%
		College Degree, 4 yr	19.20%	Blue Collar	19.50%
Military		Post grad	11.30%	Government	12.60%
Veteran/ Active Duty	14.00%				

2020 Pres. Vote	Trump	272,109	(58%)	Biden	189,808	(41%)		
2016 Pres. Vote	Trump	234,648	(58%)	Clinton	151,412	(37%)	Johnson	11,387 (3%)

Melbourne: When Cape Canaveral was chosen in the 1940s as the nation's rocket testing site, only 20,000 people lived in all of Brevard County, which stretches along 63 miles of the coast north and south of the cape. It was a quiet, winter-vacation spot that relied on fishing and citrus and its location on the sunny Atlantic coast. Rockets could be launched eastward so that spent parts fell into the ocean. In 2019, Brevard had 601,000 people, and its metropolitan area had the fastest-growing economy in the state. The county is mostly coastal communities and has no major city center. But it has a white-collar, service economy, knitted together by interest in the space program. The Kennedy Space Center attracts 1.7 million visitors annually. As with most tourist attractions, that total plunged in 2020 because of the coronavirus. When the Florida Public Service Commission announced in 1998 that the region needed a new area code, a space enthusiast suggested 321. The North American agency that assigns area codes agreed.

Local uncertainty grew following the retirement of the space shuttle fleet, a move that slashed thousands of aerospace jobs. Officials have sought alternatives. The large share of individuals affiliated with the space program led to a spurt in technological entrepreneurship in sectors as varied as aviation, synthetic materials and clean energy. Harris Corp., a Fortune 500 defense contractor based in Brevard, has 6,600 employees locally. In April 2019, Harris merged with Melbourne-based L3 Technologies, in a stock deal worth $33.5 billion, which Florida Today described as the largest-ever merger in the defense industry. Elon Musk's SpaceX company, which operates launch pads at Cape Canaveral Air Force Station and Kennedy Space Center, and a rocket refurbishing facility in Port Canaveral, had its maiden launch in 2018. In June 2019, the launch of Space X's Falcon Heavy, with a diverse payload of 24 satellites, added to the space community's hopes for the future.

Proximity to Disney World and Orlando spawned growth in the cruise-line business, which has soared beyond expectations. Port Canaveral has become the second-largest passenger port in the world, with its 4.5 million annual cruisers, trailing only Miami. Eco-tourism is another promising avenue for growth. The Merritt Island National Wildlife Refuge and Canaveral National Seashore draw wildlife aficionados to view their vast array of flora and fauna. In May 2020, National Geographic described the seashore as the largest natural beach on Florida's east coast; plus, the Indian River Lagoon is one of the most biologically diverse estuaries in North America.

The 8th Congressional District of Florida encompasses all of Brevard and Indian River counties, and makes a nip in the eastern end of Orange County. About 75 percent of the population resides in Brevard. Among the bigger towns are Cocoa Beach, Melbourne, Palm Bay and Vero Beach. The district has become safely Republican. In 2020, Donald Trump captured 58 percent in Brevard and 60 percent in Indian River—virtually no change for each from 2016. Overall, he won the district, 58%-41%. This was a rare district in Florida that had no change in the 2016 redistricting.

Darren Soto (D)

Elected 2016, 3rd term, b. Feb 25, 1978; Ringwood, NJ; Rutgers University, B.A., 2000; George WA University School of Law, J.D., 2004; Catholic; Married (Amanda Soto).

Elected Office: FL House, 2007-2012; FL Senate, 2012-2016, Deputy Minority Whip, 2012-2014.

DC Office: 1507 LHOB 20515, 202-225-9889, Fax: 202-225-9742, soto.house.gov

State Offices: Haines City, 202-600-0843; Kissimmee, 407-452-1171; Lake Wales, 202-600-0843; Orlando, 202-332-4476; Winter Haven, 202-615-1308.

Committees: *Energy & Commerce*: Communications & Technology; Consumer Protection & Commerce; Environment & Climate Change.

Group Ratings

	ADA	ACLU	AFL-CIO	LCV	COC	HAFA	ACU	CFG	FRC
2020	**	80%	**	100%	-	0%	3%	**	-
2019	90%	C	100%	97%	64%	C	2%	12%	0%

Almanac Ratings 2019-2020

	Economy	Social	Foreign	Composite
Liberal	100%	64%	92%	86%
Conservative	0%	36%	8%	14%

Key Votes of the 116th Congress

1. U.S./Mex./Can. trade deal	Y	5. Russia sanctions	Y
2. First Coronavirus response	Y	6. Troops in Syria	Y
3. HEROES Act	Y	7. Veto arms sales to Saudis	Y
4. CASH Act	Y	8. Defense $$$, veto override	Y

9. Firearms background checks Y
10. Spending at the border N
11. Marijuana liberalized rules Y
12. Electoral College objections N

Election Results

Election	Name (Party)	Vote (%)		Cand. Spent	Ind. Exp. Support	Ind. Exp. Oppose
2020 General	Darren Soto (D)	240,724	(56%)	$660,696	$10,457	
	Bill Olson (R)	188,889	(44%)	$399,486	$3,364	$113

Prior winning percentages: 2018 (58%), 2016 (57%)

Darren Soto, the first Puerto Rican elected to Congress from Florida, has prevailed in competitive primaries against his predecessor and his predecessor's wife. As was the case when he was a state legislator, he has styled himself as a coalition-builder who works across the aisle. Soto has kept a close interest in the struggling Caribbean island that many of his constituents exited in search of a better life.

He was one of three newly elected Orlando-area Democrats following a mid-decade redistricting in 2016: an African-American woman, a Vietnamese-American woman and a Latino man. Their districts cover 99 percent of Orange County, plus large parts of three surrounding counties in this rapidly growing metropolitan area.

Soto was born in New Jersey to a Puerto Rican father and an Italian-American mother. He worked in finance for Prudential Insurance while he attended Rutgers University, where he graduated with a bachelor's in economics, and got his law degree from George Washington University. Soto practiced as a commercial and civil rights attorney in central Florida. He joined the Young Democrats club in Orlando, where friends encouraged him to run for the state House. He was successful at age 28 and served there for six years, and then another four years in the Senate.

He passed legislation making it easier for immigrant children with deferred-action status to acquire a driver's license. Gov. Rick Scott vetoed the measure, sparking widespread protests. Soto helped to enact a bill that reduced from five years to one year the statute of limitations for banks to collect foreclosure debt. In 2014, he passed legislation giving the Florida Supreme Court authority to admit immigrant lawyers into the Florida Bar.

Soto sought the House seat when Rep. Alan Grayson ran unsuccessfully for the Senate. Dena Grayson, a biochemist who had a medical residency and a doctorate in molecular cell biology, married Grayson three months before the primary. Susanna Randolph, the wife of Orange County Tax Collector Scott Randolph, spent hundreds of thousands of dollars for negative ads against Soto. Soto highlighted his efforts in Tallahassee to deliver tens of millions to fight citrus disease in Polk County orchards. He spent $1.2 million for the campaign, nearly double each of his opponents. Soto won the primary with 36 percent of the vote; Randolph and Grayson each got 28 percent. In Osceola, Soto took 44 percent. He ran third with 26 percent in Polk, which had the smallest share of Hispanics. In the general, against Wayne Liebnitzky, a businessman and retired Navy aviation electrician, Soto won, 57%-43%.

In his first term, Soto claimed credit for several provisions that were in the final deal on the farm bill. They included farm-related technology to assist veterans with disabilities, the removal of algae from the list of excluded materials for biomass crop research, and codification of a research and development farm program between Israel and the United States. He enacted a bill to improve the protection of sharks by limiting the sale of billfish caught by U.S. fishing vessels.

He was a member of the bipartisan Problem Solvers Caucus that prepared revisions in House procedures and got Nancy Pelosi to agree to some of the changes when she was seeking support from Democrats to become Speaker in January 2019. "Our proposal is a progressive one, that each member should have reasonable input in Congress on behalf of their constituents," Soto told the Orlando Sentinel.

In the Democratic primary for reelection, he faced his predecessor, Alan Grayson. During a debate, Grayson criticized Soto's support for conservative legislation while he served in the legislature, plus his belated endorsement of progressive legislation in Congress. Soto responded, according to a report in Politico, that he would "give the district the dignity and respect it deserves." He was endorsed by Pelosi and former Vice President Joe Biden. Soto spent more than $1 million in the primary. Grayson spent $600,000 and, notably, left nearly $1 million in his account. Soto won, 66%-34%, and took more than two-thirds of the vote in both Osceola and Orange counties.

In 2019, Soto worked with Republican Rep. Mario Diaz-Balart, also of Florida, to grant temporary protected status eligibility to Venezuelan nationals living in the United States. In Florida alone, he said, "there are hundreds of thousands political-asylum seekers who face persecution and even death upon return to their country." Soto also took a bipartisan approach in working with Republican Rep. David Schweikert of Arizona to win House approval of their plan to improve the supply chain in the Food and Drug Administration's management of vaccines and other medical supplies during the coronavirus.

Following the devastation of Hurricane Maria in 2017, Soto traveled to Puerto Rico to organize a task force to advise local residents who were moving to central Florida. Later, he filed a bill to give statehood to Puerto Rico—an objective that he said is "about respecting democracy." In July 2019, as a member of the Energy and Commerce Committee, he won the panel's approval of his proposal to provide equal access to Medicaid for residents of Puerto Rico and the other territories. "Our plan ensures families have continued access to health care while immediately relieving financial pressures on the territories," Soto said. The House did not act on the plan, which was part of a broader health care measure. During the 2020 presidential campaign, in meeting with Puerto Rican groups, he said Biden would end "second-class citizenship" treatment on the island.

In 2020, Soto was reelected routinely—without a Grayson candidacy.

FL-9: Central Florida

Cook Partisan Voting Index: D+3

Population		Race and Ethnicity		Income	
Total	931,872	White	74.00%	Median Income	$54,878
Land area (sq. miles)	1,707	Black	13.10%	District Income Rank	333
Pop/ sq mi	545.76	Latino	44.00%	Poverty Rate	13.40%
Born in State	29.50%	Asian	3.00%	With health insurance	86.90%
		Two or more races	3.00%	Cash public assistance	2.10%
Age Groups		Other	6.90%	Food stamp/SNAP	14.10%
Under 18	23.50%				
18-34	22.20%	**Education**		**Work**	
35-64	38.00%	H.S grad or less	43.30%	White Collar	31.00%
Over 64	16.50%	Some college	31.00%	Sales and Service	45.30%
		College Degree, 4 yr	17.10%	Blue Collar	23.60%
Military		Post grad	8.60%	Government	11.20%
Veteran/ Active Duty	7.60%				

2020 Pres. Vote	Biden	232,318	(53%)	Trump	201,924	(46%)		
2016 Pres. Vote	Clinton	195,368	(54%)	Trump	149,352	(42%)	Johnson	7,899 (2%)

Orlando, Kissimmee: Orlando has become the area with the fastest-growing Puerto Rican population in the United States. Places like Azalea Park in Orange County, as well as Buenaventura Lakes (known as "BVL" to the locals) in neighboring Osceola County, have Puerto Rican-majority populations. One local real estate agent who specializes in the Puerto Rican homes market called BVL "a Puerto Rican Levittown," referring to the developments that sprung up after World War II , where the children of turn-of-the-century immigrants made their first moves into suburban life and the American middle class.

Businesses increasingly cater to this emerging "Little Puerto Rico." Non-Hispanic companies such as the supermarket chain Publix have sought to adapt, opening Sabor (Spanish for "taste") stores here, for example. Countless small businesses appealing to the burgeoning Hispanic population line streets. Goya foods located its central Florida distribution center in nearby Meadow Woods. In July 2020, when Goya President Robert Unanue said the U.S. was "blessed" to have President Donald Trump, the company discovered some of the plusses and minuses of political polarization. Government ethics experts said that First Daughter Ivanka Trump might have violated federal ethics law by posing with a can of Goya beans.

In 2019, 56 percent of the 376,000 residents in what had been the relatively empty and cheaper spaces of Osceola were Hispanic. From 2010 to 2019, the population of Osceola increased by 40 percent. At the same time, 33 percent of the 1.4 million in Orange were Hispanic; that county grew by 22 percent since 2010. The population of those two counties in 1960 was 19,000 and 263,000, respectively. The recent increase in Puerto Ricans has been driven, in part, by islanders escaping the economic collapse in their commonwealth as a result of its severe public debt. After Hurricane Maria devastated Puerto Rico in September 2017, Florida declared its own state of emergency and created disaster relief centers in Orlando and Miami. Islanders settled with family and friends, and many had no plans to return to Puerto Rico. With the help of a strong local economy, many were able to find jobs. But the social dislocation was extensive, including for long-term housing and local schools.

The 9th District of Florida represented a bow by both political and judicial voices in redistricting to the emerging political realities of central Florida. The Hispanic share of its population is 44 percent, and growing. Many Black neighborhoods in Orlando were shifted to the adjoining 10th District, which is based entirely in Orange County and is also heavily Democratic; Blacks are only 13 percent of the new 9th. In exchange, the district gained a large slice of eastern Polk County, which leans Republican. The district retains all of Osceola. The airport, which is split between the 9th and 10th districts, passed Miami in 2017 with the largest passenger load in Florida. It planned to open a new $2.7 billion terminal in 2022, with 15 gates and options for 120. In contrast to the existing terminal, passengers will not need a shuttle.

Many of the Hispanics in the 9th have slowly become eligible to vote. Many were too young, others chose not to register and some were not legally in the United States. (Puerto Ricans are immediately eligible to vote on the mainland). Consequently, it has taken time for their political power to catch up to their demographic influence. As happened on a larger scale in Miami-Dade, the 2020 election in Osceola featured a notable shift to President Donald Trump. After Hillary Clinton took the county with 61 percent of the vote, Joe Biden got 56 percent. Trump's total vote grew from 50,000 to 73,000. Biden took the district, 53%-46%.

Val Demings (D)

Elected 2016, 3rd term, b. Mar 12, 1957; Jacksonville, FL; Webster University, M.P.A.; Southern Police Institute; FL State University, B.S., 1979; African Methodist Episcopal; Married (Jerry L. Demings); 3 children; 5 grandchildren.

Professional Career: Social worker; Police officer; Commander of Special Operation, FLPD, 2003-2006; Police Chief, FLPD, 2007-2012.

DC Office: 217 CHOB 20515, 202-225-2176, Fax: 202-226-6559, demings.house.gov

State Offices: Orlando, 321-388-9808.

Committees: *Homeland Security*: Emergency Preparedness, Response & Recovery (Chmn). *Judiciary*: Antitrust, Commercial & Administrative Law; Crime, Terrorism & Homeland Security. *Permanent Select on Intelligence*: Counterterrorism, Counterintelligence & Counterproliferation; Intelligence Modernization & Readiness.

Group Ratings

	ADA	ACLU	AFL-CIO	LCV	COC	HAFA	ACU	CFG	FRC
2020	**	78%	**	100%	-	0%	3%	**	-
2019	90%	C	100%	97%	67%	C	2%	12%	0%

Almanac Ratings 2019-2020

	Economy	Social	Foreign	Composite
Liberal	100%	100%	80%	94%
Conservative	0%	0%	20%	6%

Key Votes of the 116th Congress

1. U.S./Mex./Can. trade deal Y	5. Russia sanctions Y	9. Firearms background checks Y
2. First Coronavirus response Y	6. Troops in Syria Y	10. Spending at the border Y
3. HEROES Act Y	7. Veto arms sales to Saudis Y	11. Marijuana liberalized rules Y
4. CASH Act Y	8. Defense $$$, veto override Y	12. Electoral College objections N

Election Results

Election	Name (Party)	Vote (%)		Cand. Spent	Ind. Exp. Support	Ind. Exp. Oppose
2020 General	Val Demings (D)................................	239,434	(64%)	$793,092	$117,411	
	Vennia Francois (R)........................	136,889	(36%)	$352,658	$264,250	$113

Prior winning percentages: 2016 (65%)

Val Demings unexpectedly had two star turns in 2019-20: as an impeachment manager when the House presented its case in the Senate trial of President Donald Trump, and as a finalist in Joe Biden's selection of his vice presidential running mate. The experiences left her well-positioned for political advancement, though the slender Democratic majority in the House worked against her taking an immediate position in the Biden administration. Demings had a background in police work that made her a prime Democratic recruit when she ran for the House in 2016. She likes to call herself a unifier. Her husband, Jerry Demings, was elected Orange County mayor, the first African American to hold that position. He earlier was Orlando police chief, the same position his wife later held.

Demings was born in Jacksonville, the youngest of seven children. Her mother was a maid and her father was a janitor. She got a bachelor's degree in criminology from Florida State University, the first in her family to graduate from college. She started as a social worker in Jacksonville, but set her sights on becoming a police officer. After moving to Orlando and enrolling in the police academy, where she was the class president, Demings served with the police department for 27 years, including four years as chief of police. She placed a priority on community engagement to address some of the root causes of violent crime.

In 2012, Demings ran in the old 10th District against first-term Republican Rep. Daniel Webster. With the narrow GOP leaning of the district at the time, she lost a close contest, 52%-48%. In that campaign, she was aided by more than $2 million from the political committee that then-New York City Mayor Michael Bloomberg created to support gun control.

Following the major changes in the 2016 redistricting, Webster wisely concluded that he could not win the revamped district and ran in an open seat in the 11th District to the west; the GOP largely conceded his old seat. Demings was elected in two relatively easy contests. In the four-candidate Democratic primary, she won 57 percent of the vote against credible opponents. State Sen. Geraldine Thompson, who was runner-up with 20 percent, criticized the national party for giving Demings a speaking slot at the Democratic national convention a month earlier. Bob Poe, the former state Democratic chairman, self-financed his campaign with $2 million; he got 17 percent. In one ad, he said Demings had condoned police brutality. Demings spent $1.5 million, and benefited from another $538,000 spent on her behalf by the Bloomberg Super PAC. In November, Demings defeated little-known Republican Thuy Lowe, 65%-35%.

On the Homeland Security Committee, Demings persuaded officials of the Homeland Security Department to revise their criteria so that Orlando became eligible for anti-terrorism grants. After gaining a seat on the Judiciary Committee in December 2017, she joined Jerry Nadler, the panel's ranking Democrat, on a resolution that proposed the censure of Trump after he referred to immigrants arriving in the United States from "shithole" countries. "We cannot allow racism and prejudice to become the basis for federal policy," Demings said. In 2019, Speaker Nancy Pelosi gave her a much-sought seat on the Intelligence Committee.

Her work on the Intelligence panel plus her role in the Judiciary Committee's impeachment hearings convinced Pelosi to select Demings as one of the Democrats' seven managers during the Senate trial. She was the only one who was not a lawyer. As a former police chief, Pelosi told reporters in January 2020, Demings "knows her way around a courtroom." As the Miami Herald reported after Pelosi introduced the group, Demings had shown notable independence from Democratic leaders. "She first called for Trump's removal from office a year before party leadership and is now agitating for [Senator Majority Leader Mitch] McConnell's recusal" from the trial. Citing the fact that McConnell had told reporters a month earlier, "I'm not an impartial juror." Demings said that statement was "in violation" of his constitutional oath of impartiality.

As part of the managers' opening argument to the Senate, Demings said Trump acted corruptly. "When it came down to choosing between the national interest of the country and his own personal interests, his reelection, President Trump chose himself," she said. She often described his actions from her law-enforcement background. Trump, she said, "used the power of his office to try to shake down—I will use that term because I am familiar with it—a foreign power to interfere into this year's election." Demings later told the Senate, "innocent people don't try to hide every document and witness, especially those that would clear them. … That's what guilty people do."

After the Senate voted that Trump was not guilty of the two impeachment articles, Demings said the result was "disappointing." But she was confident the House had effectively made its case. "Had we not proved our case, there is no way that [Utah Republican] Mitt Romney would have voted guilty against the president," she told National Public Radio in an interview.

The Biden campaign's review of Demings as a potential running mate followed Biden's earlier announcement that he would select an African-American woman for that position. Although she lacked the public familiarity and wide political experience of some of the other contenders, Washington Post columnist David Byler wrote, she would "bolster Biden's appeal as a working-class Democrat," plus she had the electoral appeal of representing the swing state of Florida. Byler also cited her experience in making the case for Trump's corruption.

Her experience as police chief may have worked against her, given that police violence was a theme of many of the protests for racial justice during 2020. And there had been reports of controversial actions involving the Orlando police department while Demings was chief. She had often defended actions by her department, even when serious charges were made.

The largely positive response to Demings led some observers—reportedly including Biden—to suggest she challenge Florida Sen. Marco Rubio for reelection in 2022. In June 2021, she announced her candidacy and criticized Rubio for relying on "tired talking points and backward solutions." Multiple Democrats lined up to run for Demings's seat, but prospects for succession could be affected by redistricting.

FL-10: Central Florida   **Cook Partisan Voting Index: D+12**

Population		Race and Ethnicity		Income	
Total	811,634	White	54.20%	Median Income	$61,737
Land area (sq. miles)	1,129	Black	29.50%	District Income Rank	235
Pop/ sq mi	718.69	Latino	28.50%	Poverty Rate	12.50%
Born in State	35.60%	Asian	5.20%	With health insurance	85.60%
		Two or more races	4.10%	Cash public assistance	2.10%
Age Groups		Other	7.10%	Food stamp/SNAP	13.70%
Under 18	23.20%				
18-34	25.30%	**Education**		**Work**	
35-64	39.60%	H.S grad or less	39.00%	White Collar	35.50%
Over 64	11.90%	Some college	28.40%	Sales and Service	45.70%
		College Degree, 4 yr	21.20%	Blue Collar	18.80%
Military		Post grad	11.40%	Government	8.40%
Veteran/ Active Duty	5.10%				

2020 Pres. Vote	Biden	236,868	(62%)	Trump	141,377	(37%)		
2016 Pres. Vote	Clinton	194,934	(61%)	Trump	110,062	(35%)	Johnson	7,205	(2%)

Downtown Orlando: Who would have supposed 60 years ago that the most popular tourist destination in the world would rise amid the swamps and orange groves of central Florida? The answer: Walt Disney, and just about no one else. In the mid-1960s, Disney looked at the map and decided that the intersection of Interstate 4 and Florida's Turnpike, the "crossroads of Florida," just a few miles southwest of Orlando, was the perfect place for the vast theme park he was planning. The spirit of the place was established by a man who never lived there but created something now taken for granted. Disney conceived the first theme park in Orange County, California, in 1955, but he perfected it in the 17,000 acres of Florida swamp that his associates stealthily snapped up and where Walt Disney World opened in 1971. With the invention of the theme park, Disney also pioneered sophisticated communications, utility and waste-disposal methods—all out of sight and underground.

Disney World is not just an engineering marvel. It required more than 60,000 "cast members" (employees) with know-how and earnest cheerfulness to entertain its 20.5 million visitors in 2017. The pandemic in 2020 was devastating for the park. As a prime example of the conflict between the economy and public health, Disney World struggled to accommodate its workers, its customers and its Florida host—with little success in 2020. When Disney World partially reopened in July, at a time when positive COVID-19 tests were surging locally, about 20,000 of what had been 77,000 employees were called back to work.

Disney is hardly the only site that has made Orlando one of the world's great tourist destinations. Other popular theme parks, including Sea World and Universal Studios, struggled with the coronavirus. Cape Canaveral is about 60 miles away from Disney World and Orlando The technology economy also has moved into Greater Orlando. Defense contractor Lockheed Martin opened in 2019 a new building at its "mission system and training" facility southwest of the city, with more than 8,000 employees in Orlando. In July 2020, Lockheed won a Pentagon contract for local work on the F-35 jet fighter. The University of Central Florida opened its main campus in east Orlando in 1963; since then, it has opened 13 colleges, with 72,000 students, including a new campus in downtown. Half the students are racial minorities. Downtown Orlando was the site of the horrific terrorist attack that killed 49 persons at the Pulse nightclub in 2016, which renewed calls for gun control. Continuing growth—of the downtown skyline and in the expanding metropolitan region—has spurred what might be uphill efforts to control the sprawl and congestion in one of the nation's booming areas. Privately financed passenger train service to Miami was scheduled to start in 2022, though Richard Branson and his struggling Virgin Group ended their affiliation.

The 10th Congressional District of Florida is entirely in Orange County, including the western portion of Orlando, with the enormous Disney complex near its southern border. Redistricting increased both its Black and Hispanic shares to 27 percent. The population gains, on top of citrus diseases and devastating frosts, downsized the acreage for the eponymous citrus that gave the county its name. The number of citrus acres in Orange County dropped from 9,155 in 1998 to 1,130 in 2018. The district retains some small Black rural settlements, such as lettuce-producing Zellwood and

Eatonville, a town depicted in the stories of Zora Neale Hurston, a preeminent novelist and folklorist. In 2020, Joe Biden took the district, 62%-37%.

Daniel Webster (R)

Elected 2010, 6th term, b. Apr 27, 1949; Charleston, WV; GA Institute of Technology, B.E.E., 1971; Baptist; Married (Sandy Jordan); 6 children; 14 grandchildren.

Elected Office: FL House, 1980-1998, speaker, 1996-1998; FL Senate, 1998-2008.

Professional Career: Owner, Webster Air Conditioning & Heating.

DC Office: 1210 LHOB 20515, 202-225-1002, Fax: 202-226-6559, webster.house.gov

State Offices: Brooksville, 352-241-9230; Inverness, 352-241-9204; Leesburg, 352-241-9220; The Villages, 352-383-3552.

Committees: *Natural Resources*: Water, Oceans & Wildlife. *Science, Space & Technology*: Space & Aeronautics. *Transportation & Infrastructure*: Economic Dev't, Public Buildings & Emergency Management (RMM); Water Resources & Environment.

Group Ratings

	ADA	ACLU	AFL-CIO	LCV	COC	HAFA	ACU	CFG	FRC
2020	**	21%	**	10%	-	94%	84%	**	-
2019	0%	C	29%	14%	75%	C	85%	78%	100%

Almanac Ratings 2019-2020

	Economy	Social	Foreign	Composite
Liberal	30%	16%	35%	27%
Conservative	70%	84%	65%	73%

Key Votes of the 116th Congress

1. U.S./Mex./Can. trade deal	Y	5. Russia sanctions Y	9. Firearms background checks N
2. First Coronavirus response	Y	6. Troops in Syria N/A	10. Spending at the border Y
3. HEROES Act	N	7. Veto arms sales to Saudis N	11. Marijuana liberalized rules N
4. CASH Act	N	8. Defense $$$, veto override Y	12. Electoral College objections Y

Election Results

Election	Name (Party)	Vote (%)		Cand. Spent	Ind. Exp. Support	Ind. Exp. Oppose
2020 General	Daniel Webster (R)	316,979	(67%)	$433,565	$10,060	
	Dana Cottrell (D)	158,094	(33%)	$59,564		

Prior winning percentages: 2018 (65%), 2016 (65%), 2014 (62%), 2012 (52%), 2010 (56%)

Republican Daniel Webster, a staunch and often activist conservative, prevailed in contentious elections in 2010 and 2012. He settled into the House with an insider's demeanor, then unexpectedly became the chief GOP challenger to Speaker John Boehner and, later, Paul Ryan in futile bids by House conservatives to register their unhappiness. Webster subsequently was stripped of his prime committee assignment, though he outlasted both Boehner and Ryan and wielded influence at his new committees. Further demonstrating his survival skills, he switched districts and became secure following the 2016 redistricting.

Webster was born in Charleston West Virginia and is distantly related to his 19th century namesake, considered one of the greatest senators and orators in history. His family moved to Florida when he was 7 years old because a doctor told them the climate would help cure young Daniel's sinus problems. He graduated from the Georgia Institute of Technology with a degree in electrical engineering and eventually took over his family's heating and air conditioning business in Orlando. He became politically active in 1979, when he led his church's effort to turn a house into a Sunday school, only to be refused a zoning exemption by the county commission.

Webster won a seat in the state House in 1980 and later became the first Republican speaker of the Florida House in 122 years. In 1998, he moved to the state Senate, where he pushed to ease gun regulations and restrict abortion rights, including his bill requiring women to get an ultrasound test and view the results before getting an abortion. He led legislative efforts to prolong the life of Terri Schiavo, a woman in a persistent vegetative state who became a national cause for conservatives.

With the backing of national Republicans, he challenged controversial Democratic Rep. Alan Grayson in 2010. Grayson had become a lightning rod for conservatives because of his harsh rhetoric. Webster and Republicans believed that Grayson was a poor fit for the more tempered politics of the swing Orlando-based district. Webster refused to debate Grayson, or to return his attacks in kind, saying, "We're taking the high road. I'm not getting down in the dirt with him." He focused his campaign on the size of the federal government and the passage of President Barack Obama's health care law. The voters turned out Grayson decisively, 56%-38%.

In the newly Republican-controlled House, Webster won a seat on the Rules Committee, a coveted position usually reserved for members whom leaders can trust to hew to the party line. He became the first member of the large freshman class to get a substantive bill through the House, with a measure aimed at limiting executive bonuses at companies that received financial industry bailout funds.

In 2012, Webster was initially considered a reelection shoo-in against Val Demings, the former Orlando police chief, but she outworked and outraised him. The Democrat accused Webster of using taxpayer money to create a "lobbyists' lounge" when he served in the legislature, a reference to his decision to spend about $100,000 for renovations to the speaker's office suite. He adamantly denied that the remodeling was done to serve lobbyists. The GOP tilt of the district proved decisive and Webster won, 52%-48%.

As Congress prepared to convene in January 2015, Webster surprised many on Capitol Hill by speaking out against Boehner and Republican management of the House. In previous weeks, he had quietly circulated to other Republicans a white paper that was titled "Widgets, Principles and Republicans." It concluded that "Congress is broken, the Republican brand is in trouble, and nothing can change unless congressional processes become less power- and self-preservation driven, and more open to rank-and-file members," the Orlando Sentinel reported. "A lot of people liked it," Webster later said. Webster agreed to enter his name for Speaker two hours before the vote. He was supported by 12 Republican lawmakers, which was fewer than the number who had told him they would support him, he said. Boehner won a bare majority and avoided what could have been a catastrophic second ballot.

With Boehner's allies outraged by his candidacy, Webster was stripped of his seat on the Rules Committee. But Boehner was feeling more pressure from conservatives. At the end of September, he stepped down as Speaker. Webster announced his candidacy to replace Boehner, though he attracted little support. After most House Republicans rallied behind Ryan, Webster got the votes of nine Republicans.

Webster regained status as a rank-and-file member. In August 2018, he won enactment of a bill to aid small businesses with cybersecurity. The following month, Congress passed his bipartisan bill to strengthen disaster preparedness for hospitals and long-term care facilities. In the minority in 2019, he became the deputy GOP leader at the Natural Resources Committee. At Transportation and Infrastructure, he is ranking Republican on the Economic Development, Public Buildings and Emergency Management Subcommittee.

At home, Webster encountered stormy waves in 2015 when the legislature's plan for redistricting turned his Orlando-based district into one that he said would be "impossible" for him to win. Unexpectedly, he was rescued when neighboring Rep. Rick Nugent announced that he would retire from his solidly Republican 11th District. But there was a catch: Nugent's chief of staff, Justin Grabelle, said he was running for his boss' seat, with the support of Nugent. Webster had little familiarity with the new district. But he had one big advantage: He was an incumbent and Grabelle was a first-time candidate. Webster raised more than twice as much money: $1 million to $360,000. He won, 60%-40%, including all five counties. Webster breezed to victory in November with 65 percent of the vote.

Since then, Webster has been easily reelected and has become a more conventional member. But there's no guarantee he will again be a big winner in redistricting.

FL-11: Gulf Coast, Central Florida

Cook Partisan Voting Index: R+18

Population			Race and Ethnicity		Income		
Total	813,112		White	86.50%	Median Income	$52,749	
Land area (sq. miles)	2,510		Black	7.40%	District Income Rank	361	
Pop/ sq mi	323.96		Latino	11.80%	Poverty Rate	12.50%	
Born in State	30.10%		Asian	1.50%	With health insurance	89.20%	
			Two or more races	2.50%	Cash public assistance	1.90%	
Age Groups			Other	2.20%	Food stamp/SNAP	10.60%	
Under 18	15.40%						
18-34	14.40%		**Education**		**Work**		
35-64	32.80%		H.S grad or less	42.70%	White Collar	32.50%	
Over 64	37.50%		Some college	33.90%	Sales and Service	46.70%	
			College Degree, 4 yr	14.20%	Blue Collar	20.90%	
Military			Post grad	9.30%	Government	11.30%	
Veteran/ Active Duty	14.30%						

2020 Pres. Vote	Trump	318,054	(65%)	Biden	164,285	(34%)		
2016 Pres. Vote	Trump	266,257	(64%)	Clinton	133,448	(32%)	Johnson	7,953 (2%)

Ocala, Tampa suburbs: Over the past quarter-century, Florida's urban areas have grown in almost every direction, occupying the high ground between the swamps that still take up much of the state's peninsula. The pattern of development is evident in counties to the north and east of St. Petersburg and Tampa, where subdivisions, trailer parks and Winn-Dixie supermarkets sprang up in what had been farms and sleepy little towns, with low brick buildings baking in the Florida sun. Drawn by the many inland lakes, greenery and the pleasant climate, retirees from the Midwest flocked here by traveling south on Interstate 75—a pattern distinct from the retirees who drove Interstate 95 from the Boston-Washington corridor to south Florida. The development here has been nothing short of astonishing; the population of Hernando County increased tenfold since 1970, while Citrus County increased nearly that much, though each county has slowed since 2010.

Instead, the rapid development has shifted to Sumter County, which contains large tracts of open land. That county's population has grown by 42 percent from 2010 to 2019—mostly a result of the massive retirement community known as The Villages, with more than 100 miles of golf cart paths and a population that reached 132,000 in 2020. The Census Bureau named the site the nation's fastest growing metropolitan statistical area from 2010 to 2019. And The Villages remains the fastest growing master planned community in the nation, with expansion into neighboring locales in Lake County. The median age in Sumter is 67 years, which makes it the only county in the nation that exceeds 65; of the total population, 58 percent are at least 65. The community does not permit residents younger than 19 years, nor young visitors for longer than a 30-day period. Golf carts are the vehicle of choice, with a total of more than 60,000.

Residents at The Villages are 90 percent white and they vote more than 2-to-1 for Republicans. The community, which Politico in 2018 described as "the most significant source of Republican optimism for many years to come," has become a popular story line for visiting journalists. But the area is not immune from political tensions. In June 2020, President Donald Trump retweeted a video of a golf-cart parade at The Villages in which one of his supporters yelled "white power." He deleted the tweet a few hours later. Later that year, the area had pockets of supporters with yard signs for Joe Biden.

The 11th Congressional District of Florida covers much of this rapidly growing area. It includes all of coastal Citrus and Hernando counties, where the beach areas are largely undeveloped, plus Sumter County. The federal government declared the Crystal River National Wildlife Refuge a restricted manatee refuge after tourists were observed chasing, riding and poking the gentle sea cows. The remaining 40 percent of the district is farther inland in Lake and Marion counties, in places like Inverness, Spring Hill and Brooksville. The five counties in the district have similar population totals. This was once politically marginal territory, but it has become solidly Republican. In 2020, Donald Trump took the district, 65%-34%.

Gus Bilirakis (R)

Elected 2006, 8th term, b. Feb 08, 1963; Gainesville, FL; St. Petersburg Junior College, 1983; University of FL, B.S., 1986; Stetson University College of Law, J.D., 1989; Greek Orthodox; Married (Eva Lialios Bilirakis); 4 children.

Elected Office: FL House, 1998-2006.

Professional Career: Intern, U.S. President Ronald Reagan, 1983; Intern, NRCC, 1984; Aide, U.S. Rep. Don Sundquist, 1985; Teacher, St. Petersburg College, 1997-2001; Practicing attorney, 1989-2006.

DC Office: 2227 RHOB 20515, 202-225-5755, Fax: 202-225-4085, bilirakis.house.gov

State Offices: New Port Richey, 727-232-2921; Tarpon Springs, 727-940-5860; Wesley Chapel, 813-501-4942.

Committees: *Energy & Commerce*: Communications & Technology; Consumer Protection & Commerce (RMM); Health.

Group Ratings

	ADA	ACLU	AFL-CIO	LCV	COC	HAFA	ACU	CFG	FRC
2020	**	15%	**	19%	-	83%	84%	**	-
2019	5%	C	32%	21%	94%	C	85%	67%	100%

Almanac Ratings 2019-2020

	Economy	Social	Foreign	Composite
Liberal	25%	34%	11%	24%
Conservative	75%	66%	89%	76%

Key Votes of the 116th Congress

1. U.S./Mex./Can. trade deal	Y	5. Russia sanctions	Y
2. First Coronavirus response	Y	6. Troops in Syria	Y
3. HEROES Act	N	7. Veto arms sales to Saudis	N
4. CASH Act	N/A	8. Defense $$$, veto override	N/A

9. Firearms background checks N
10. Spending at the border Y
11. Marijuana liberalized rules N
12. Electoral College objections N/A

Election Results

Election	Name (Party)	Vote (%)	Cand. Spent	Ind. Exp. Support	Ind. Exp. Oppose
2020 General	Gus Bilirakis (R)	284,941 (63%)	$1,415,990	$63,208	
	Kimberly Walker (D)	168,194 (37%)	$11,331		

Prior winning percentages: 2018 (58%), 2016 (69%), 2014 (100%), 2012 (64%), 2010 (71%), 2008 (63%), 2006 (56%)

Gus Bilirakis, a Republican first elected in 2006, came into office distancing himself from partisan fights and focusing on his legislative agenda. While gaining seniority, he sharpened his rhetorical edge. But that has not been enough for party leaders who look for more aggressive advocates to fill top committee positions. Bilirakis has been unsuccessful in two attempts to gain the top GOP slot on the House Veterans' Affairs Committee. On the Energy and Commerce Committee, his work on health care issues has played well at home.

Bilirakis remembers stuffing envelopes at age 7 for Republican Louis "Skip" Bafalis, who lost his 1970 bid for governor but was elected to five terms in Congress. As an undergraduate at the University of Florida, Bilirakis interned in the Reagan White House. He earned a law degree from Stetson University. He later was a probate lawyer and estate planner.

In 1998, Bilirakis was elected to the first of four terms in the Florida House. His career was closely tied to his father's. When 12-term Republican Rep. Michael Bilirakis decided to retire, his son drew nominal opposition for the GOP nomination. Gus Bilirakis was not shy about running on the family name and his Greek heritage. He appeared on the ballot as Gus Michael Bilirakis and raised money from many political action committees that supported his father, who served on the Energy and Commerce Committee.

Democrats recruited Phyllis Busansky, a former member of the Hillsborough County Commission and the first executive director of the state's welfare-to-work program. Bilirakis pointed to his credentials as a lawyer who specialized in elder law. HIs soft-spoken style contrasted with Busansky's assertive personality. She ran television ads portraying Bilirakis as a follower who relied on his father's reputation. President George W. Bush, Vice President Dick Cheney and Speaker Dennis Hastert all stumped for Bilirakis and helped him raise money. In a strongly Democratic year, he outspent Busansky $2.6 million to $1.4 million, and won 56%-44%.

In the House, Bilirakis has shown centrism. In 2008, he worked with Rep. Lloyd Doggett, a Texas Democrat, to win House passage of a "silver alert" bill to assist states in finding senior citizens who disappear. He was one of 10 Republicans in 2009 to support a bill to limit executive bonuses in financial companies receiving government bailout money. On other issues, he stuck more closely to Republican talking points. In 2010, he took the House floor on several occasions to denounce the Democrats' health care overhaul as a "government takeover." On the Foreign Affairs Committee, he followed his father's footsteps in standing up for Greek causes.

After Bilirakis joined Energy and Commerce in 2013, he struggled to find a partisan balance. Left-leaning groups attacked him for signing a pledge that he "opposes any legislation relating to climate change that includes a net increase in government revenue." When he worked with Democrats in 2014 to oppose soaring premium hikes for flood insurance coverage, Majority Whip Kevin McCarthy bounced him from his whip team. "I have no hard feelings at all, but I had to do what I had to do," Bilirakis told the Tampa Bay Times. In 2014, President Barack Obama signed his bill to promote travel by reauthorizing Brand USA, a public-private partnership that encourages tourists to visit the United States. Some conservatives had opposed the bill as excessive spending.

As vice chairman of the Veterans' Affairs Committee, Bilirakis worked on the 2014 law to overhaul the VA hospital system. That resulted, he said, in the opening of an outpatient clinic in New Port Richey. He enacted bills to offer alternative therapies to veterans. Following the 2016 election, he failed in his bid for chairman of the committee. Party leaders gave the post to the less senior but more outgoing Phil Roe of Tennessee. Roe retired four years later. Bilirakis, the next-senior Republican on Veterans' Affairs, again sought the top committee post. This time, GOP leaders gave the position to Rep. Mike Bost of Illinois, an outspoken former Marine who was eight years junior to Bilirakis. The Floridian gave up his seat on that panel and became chairman of the Republican Policy Committee Veterans' Affairs Task Force.

Bilirakis has remained comfortable with his bipartisan initiatives. With Democratic Rep. Kathy Castor, who holds a neighboring district and is a colleague on Energy and Commerce, they won approval of a measure to increase penalties for Medicare fraud. He also took charge of a provision to extend for two years the program for community health centers. In 2017-18, he had a centrist ranking among Republicans in the Almanac vote ratings.

In 2019, with Democratic Rep. Ted Deutch of Florida, Bilirakis filed a bill to assist local schools in identifying potential suicide incidents and other threats. The Lugar Center at Georgetown University ranked him as the most bipartisan House member from Florida. In response, he said, "I consider myself a workhorse, not a show horse—always seeking to work in a bipartisan manner to find areas of common ground on matters that will make a positive difference in the lives of the people I serve."

In a district that leans Republican, Bilirakis has not faced a serious reelection challenge. In 2018, he had his smallest victory margin since he was first elected, 58%-40%, against Democrat Chris Hunter. Hunter was a former FBI agent and federal prosecutor who pursued international fugitives until he quit his job with the Justice Department. "We're a better country than this," he told voters, in referring to the Trump administration. Hunter was endorsed by national environmental groups, but Democrats found superior opportunities elsewhere in Florida. Bilirakis had an easier time in 2020 against Kimberly Walker, a lightly funded military veteran. He won more comfortably, 63%-37%.

FL-12: Northern Tampa Suburbs   **Cook Partisan Voting Index: R+11**

Population		Race and Ethnicity		Income	
Total	811,308	White	86.30%	Median Income	$56,761
Land area (sq. miles)	884	Black	5.50%	District Income Rank	300
Pop/ sq mi	918.03	Latino	14.00%	Poverty Rate	11.00%
Born in State	33.70%	Asian	3.00%	With health insurance	87.70%
		Two or more races	3.50%	Cash public assistance	2.00%
Age Groups		Other	1.70%	Food stamp/SNAP	9.40%
Under 18	19.60%				
18-34	16.80%	**Education**		**Work**	
35-64	38.80%	H.S grad or less	40.60%	White Collar	41.40%
Over 64	24.50%	Some college	31.10%	Sales and Service	41.50%
		College Degree, 4 yr	18.40%	Blue Collar	17.00%
Military		Post grad	9.90%	Government	10.10%
Veteran/ Active Duty	10.30%				

2020 Pres. Vote	Trump	266,291	(58%)	Biden	188,631	(41%)		
2016 Pres. Vote	Trump	218,488	(57%)	Clinton	147,759	(39%)	Johnson	9,918	(3%)

Pasco, Pinellas: In 1873, turtle hunters discovered a large sponge bed off the coast of the Pinellas Peninsula. Soon, boats from Key West began harvesting the sponges, and shortly thereafter, trading outposts were set up at sites that grew into Tarpon Springs and Anclote. Anclote is now just a speck on the map, but Tarpon Springs is a busy city of 26,000. It boasts the highest share of Greek Americans of any place in the United States—descendants of the Greek sponge fishermen who began arriving in the early 1900s.

Over the years, Pasco County has become a classic bedroom community as development has moved up the once-empty coast. Population density remains low compared with other parts of Florida. There were plans to change this. Two big financial companies—St. Petersburg's Raymond James Financial and Baltimore's T. Rowe Price—purchased land in Pasco County and each planned to build large campuses for thousands of employees. But each abandoned its plans and built elsewhere. More positively, developers in 2018 opened a 16 million gallon clearwater lagoon in Wesley Chapel, with more than 2,000 homes. Medical tourism has become a growing industry for patients who travel for treatment they cannot receive in their home states or other nations. In September 2019, plans were unveiled for an 800-acre corporate business park in Pasco, with a cancer center and life sciences research building. Between 2010 and 2019, Pasco had robust growth of 19 percent.

The 12th Congressional District covers an area north and east of Tampa and St. Petersburg. In northern Pinellas County, that includes Republican locales of Tarpon Springs, Palm Harbor and Dunedin. Most of Pinellas is in the Democratic-leaning 13th District. Two-thirds of the district includes all of Pasco County. This area was largely undeveloped until the 1950s, but now hosts a string of towns along the Gulf of Mexico. Further inland, the district covers older settlements like Land O'Lakes, Dade City and Zephyrhills, established in 1911 as a retirement center for veterans of the Union Army in an area that remains on the edge of huge swamps.

As Florida retirements became more feasible for people with modest incomes in the 1970s and 1980s, the partisan balance locally shifted toward Democrats. In the 1990s, young arrivals with professional and technical backgrounds and partisan independence turned this into a competitive area. Republican-drawn redistricting and the modest minority populations have given the 12th District a secure Republican lean. In Pasco, the vote for President Donald Trump increased from 59 percent to 60 percent in his reelection, which gave him an additional 37,000 votes. He took the district, 58%-41%. Joe Biden increased the Democratic vote by 29,000.

Charlie Crist (D)

Elected 2016, 3rd term, b. Jul 24, 1956; Altoona, PA; Wake Forest University, Att.; FL State University, B.S., 1978; Cumberland School of Law, Stamford University, J.D., 1981; Methodist; Married (Carole Rome Crist); 2 stepchildren.

Elected Office: FL Senate, 1993-1999; FL Education Commissioner, 2001-2003; FL Attorney General, 2003-2007; FL Governor, 2007-2011.

Professional Career: Staff, United States Senator Connie Mack, 1988-1989; FL Deputy Secretary of Business and Prof. Reg., 1999-2001.

DC Office: 215 CHOB 20515, 202-225-5961, Fax: 202-225-9764, crist.house.gov

State Offices: Seminole, 727-318-6770; St. Petersburg, 727-318-6770; St. Petersburg, 727-318-6770.

Committees: *Appropriations*: Commerce, Justice, Science & Related Agencies; Defense; Military Construction, Veterans Affairs & Related Agencies. *Science, Space & Technology*: Environment; Space & Aeronautics.

Group Ratings

	ADA	ACLU	AFL-CIO	LCV	COC	HAFA	ACU	CFG	FRC
2020	**	74%	**	100%	-	0%	6%	**	-
2019	80%	C	100%	97%	69%	C	6%	12%	0%

Almanac Ratings 2019-2020

	Economy	Social	Foreign	Composite
Liberal	100%	58%	80%	80%
Conservative	0%	42%	20%	20%

Key Votes of the 116th Congress

1. U.S./Mex./Can. trade deal Y	5. Russia sanctions Y	9. Firearms background checks Y
2. First Coronavirus response Y	6. Troops in Syria Y	10. Spending at the border Y
3. HEROES Act Y	7. Veto arms sales to Saudis Y	11. Marijuana liberalized rules Y
4. CASH Act Y	8. Defense $$$, veto override Y	12. Electoral College objections N

Election Results

Election	Name (Party)	Vote (%)		Cand. Spent	Ind. Exp. Support	Ind. Exp. Oppose
2020 General	Charlie Crist (D)	215,405	(53%)	$4,180,136	$159,163	$197,797
	Anna Paulina Luna (R)	190,713	(47%)	$3,261,514	$222,476	$4,613

Prior winning percentages: 2018 (58%), House: 2016 (62%); Governor: 2006 (52%)

Charlie Crist was elected in 2016 to a seat that shifted to Democrats following a mid-decade court-ordered redistricting. Crist succeeded in his decade-long political odyssey from Republican governor for four years to independent to Democrat, and that included two statewide defeats. In the House, he received far less public attention, though he used his seat on the Appropriations Committee to benefit his district and call attention to timely issues.

Crist was born in Altoona Pennsylvania, where his grandfather, a Greek immigrant from Cyprus who arrived in America in 1912, ran a shoe-shine parlor. His family moved to Atlanta before his first birthday, when his father, who shortened the family name from Christodoulos to Crist, was accepted to medical school at Emory University. In 1960, the Crists settled in St. Petersburg. A nearby Greek community and a rising population of retirees made the location a nice fit for a young doctor hoping to build a practice. At 10, Charlie was campaigning for his father, who won a seat on the Pinellas County School Board. In high school, he was the starting quarterback and class president. After two years at Wake Forest University, he transferred to Florida State, where he was student body vice president and homecoming king. He earned his law degree at Cumberland School of Law in Alabama, then worked as general counsel for the minor league division of Major League Baseball.

After an unsuccessful run for the state Senate in 1986, Crist served as state director for Republican Sen. Connie Mack. He ran again for the state Senate and won, serving six years. In the legislature, he gained the nickname of "Chain Gang Charlie" for taking touch stances on crime. He gained a reputation as an ambitious, media-savvy pol, always sporting a healthy tan and blessed with retail campaigning skills. He ran statewide six times between 1998 and 2014, with three victories. In 1998, he challenged Democratic Sen. Bob Graham but lost, 62%-38%. In the next six years, he was elected state education commissioner, attorney general and then governor in 2006, when he succeeded term-limited Jeb Bush.

Crist brought to the governorship a folksy style and a bipartisan perspective that contrasted with Bush. The first issue he tackled was insurance. Seven hurricanes had slammed Florida in 2004 and 2005, and property-insurance rates had skyrocketed. Crist denounced insurance companies for being stingy about paying claims, and he expanded the state-owned Citizens Property Insurance until it became the largest wind insurer in Florida. Fiscally, Crist proved to be as conservative as Bush had been.

His job ratings were extraordinarily high, including among Democrats and independents. But Republicans didn't rate him as high as Bush. When a Senate seat opened in 2010, Crist said he would seek the GOP nomination. The National Republican Senatorial Committee immediately endorsed him over former Florida House Speaker Marco Rubio. But the conservative Rubio received support from local and national activists. Crist deepened the hostility of Republicans when he supported President Barack Obama's $787 billion economic stimulus bill. By the time Crist realized the conservative base was slipping away, it was too late. He lost the nomination, then quit the Republican Party and ran as an independent. He got caught in the crossfire between Rubio and Democratic Rep. Kendrick Meek, both of whom painted Crist as a political opportunist. Crist tried to appeal as the de facto Democratic candidate, but Meek refused to bow out. Rubio won with 49 percent of the vote to 30 percent for Crist and 20 percent for Meek.

Crist made another bid for governor in 2014—this time as a Democrat and with the enthusiastic support of Obama. Running against Gov. Rick Scott, who was seeking reelection, Crist adopted the Democratic playbook and criticized Scott for cutting education and restricting abortion; he vowed to raise the minimum wage. Scott blamed Crist for leaving the state in poor economic shape, and took credit for the subsequent economic turnaround. In a Republican year, Crist lost 48%-47%, a margin of 64,000 votes.

With two statewide losses, most politicians would have called it quits. But Crist gained a new opportunity when redistricting made the 13th District, with his home base of St. Petersburg, an inviting target. Crist secured the support of the Democratic Congressional Campaign Committee. He appeared to lock up the seat after Republican Rep. David Jolly said it would be "impossible" for a Republican to win the new seat. Jolly decided to run instead for the Senate after Rubio decided to run for president and not seek a second term.

That game plan changed in June 2016, a few days before the filing deadline, when Rubio opted to reclaim his Senate seat. Jolly stepped back to seek reelection to his House seat. He had made his bid even more uphill, with his poor-mouthing of campaign fundraising generally and the National Republican Congressional Committee specifically. The NRCC denied financial support to Jolly. With money he had raised for his Senate campaign, Jolly had a fundraising advantage, $3.9 million to $2 million. But Crist was bolstered by $2.6 million in support from the DCCC and other party adjuncts.

The contest turned out closer than most—including Jolly—had expected. Democrats sought to tie Donald Trump around Jolly's neck. Jolly described Crist as an "untrustworthy political opportunist." Crist won, 52%-48%. Without redistricting, he almost certainly would have lost.

As a freshman, Crist served on the Financial Services Committee and joined Democrats who sought to prevent a loosening of the 2010 Dodd-Frank banking regulations. "With this bill, members are being asked to again trust the very people who brought us to this financial crisis," he told the House. Crist had successful initiatives. In July 2018, the House passed a bill he sponsored with Republican Rep. Jeff Denham of California to install on-site medical waste treatment systems at VA facilities. He wrote an op-ed column for USA Today that called for restoration of voting rights to ex-felons in Florida. Voters approved that step in a November 2018 referendum. In 2019, the House passed his bill to create a program at the Justice Department to assist state and local governments to support courts that aid veterans accused of minor crimes.

Crist got a seat on Appropriations. He claimed credit for delivering $23 million of federal largesse to the Bus Rapid Transit line in Pinellas County. He had a moment in the spotlight at a committee hearing in April 2019 with Attorney General William Barr, asking about his handling of special counsel Robert Mueller's investigation of alleged Russian interference in the 2016 presidential election. Weeks later, it was revealed that Barr failed to inform the panel that he already had received written objections from Mueller. It was the "most consequential moment" in Crist's House career to that point, the Tampa Bay Times reported.

In 2018, Crist had an easy reelection, 58%-42%, against Republican George Buck, a poorly funded consultant on emergency management. Two years later, he had a tougher contest with Anna Paulina Luna, an Air Force veteran who criticized Congress for using economic-relief legislation to support "special interests" during the coronavirus. Luna, who spent nearly as much as Crist, lost 53%-47% and left open the option of another challenge. In May 2021, Crist announced that he was running again for governor in 2022, with a campaign theme of "Florida for all."

FL-13: St. Petersburg, Clearwater Cook Partisan Voting Index: EVEN

Population		Race and Ethnicity		Income	
Total	731,658	White	78.90%	Median Income	$56,612
Land area (sq. miles)	186	Black	12.10%	District Income Rank	305
Pop/ sq mi	3,933.01	Latino	10.80%	Poverty Rate	11.50%
Born in State	34.20%	Asian	3.50%	With health insurance	88.50%
		Two or more races	3.70%	Cash public assistance	2.50%
Age Groups		Other	1.80%	Food stamp/SNAP	8.90%
Under 18	15.50%				
18-34	20.10%	**Education**		**Work**	
35-64	40.30%	H.S grad or less	36.20%	White Collar	40.50%
Over 64	24.00%	Some college	30.80%	Sales and Service	43.50%
Military		College Degree, 4 yr	21.60%	Blue Collar	15.90%
Veteran/ Active Duty	10.10%	Post grad	11.40%	Government	10.10%

2020 Pres. Vote	Biden	211,530	(51%)	Trump	194,721	(47%)			
2016 Pres. Vote	Clinton	178,892	(49%)	Trump	167,348	(46%)	Johnson	10,022	(3%)

Pinellas County: When Spanish explorers arrived in what is now St. Petersburg some 500 years ago, they discovered an area covered by a primeval pine forest and teeming with bears, panthers, turkeys and bald eagles. They named the area "Punta Pinal" ("point of pines"), a name that has since been Anglicized into the Pinellas Peninsula. The area remained under-populated—only 50 families lived here when the Civil War broke out—until two events accelerated its development. First, the Orange Belt Railway connected the region to national markets in the 1880s. Second, Dr. W.C. Van Bibber, addressing the American Medical Society convention in 1885, named the peninsula the healthiest place on earth, setting off a stampede of interest. By 1897, the Belleview Hotel was built in Clearwater, and the area began its transition to a major tourist destination and, later, a retirement community.

The population of Pinellas County more than doubled in the 1920s, and did so once more in the 1950s. Mostly from the North and modestly affluent, the newcomers adapted easily to a place whose civic tone was set by the St. Petersburg Times (now the Tampa Bay Times) and its longtime owners, Nelson and Henrietta Poynter: sober, good-humored and supportive of clean government and civil rights. They brought Republican voting habits and presaged the political revolution that would take place in Florida. Democrats had a 56-point registration edge over Republicans here in 1940. By 1950, that edge was only six. In 1954, Pinellas County Republicans elected William Cramer to Congress, the first Republican from Florida since 1882. Until 2016, the House seat remained consistently in GOP hands.

In the 21st century, St. Petersburg has become a progressive community. The city has planned to be the first in Florida to rely 100 percent on renewable energy, though environmentalists complained that the utility companies have created obstacles in the move to solar power. Following many designs, a 26-acre Pier District, with a marine education center, opened in 2020—a short walk from downtown St. Petersburg. An additional eight-lane span across the Bay to Tampa was planned for 2024, which will replace one of the two current sections of the Howard Frankland Bridge. The population of Pinellas County grew 6 percent from 2010 to 2019, less than neighboring counties—chiefly because Pinellas has little open space.

The 13th Congressional District is located entirely within Pinellas County. Redistricting in 2016 made major shifts that benefited Democrats. It added about 100,000 people in the heavily African-American and Democratic precincts in south St. Petersburg that had been part of the Tampa-based 14th District. In return, the district lost Republican-leaning northern Pinellas, including the area surrounding Dunedin. The district retained the remainder of St. Petersburg plus Clearwater. It includes many of the beach communities on the barrier islands facing the Gulf of Mexico, including Belleair Beach down to Treasure Island. Inland, it incorporates the new subdivisions of Largo in the center of the peninsula. The Republican tilt faded and Pinellas County is now a swing area. In 2016, Donald Trump won the county by one percentage point. Four years later, Joe Biden took it by less than a half point, while turnout increased by 80,000 votes. Biden took the district, 51%-47%.

Kathy Castor (D)

Elected 2006, 8th term, b. Aug 20, 1966; Miami, FL; Emory University - Atlanta, B.A., 1988; FL State University School of Law, J.D., 1991; Presbyterian; Married (Bill Lewis); 2 children.

Elected Office: Hillsborough County Commissioner, 2002-2006.

Professional Career: Assistant General counsel, FL Department of Community Affairs, 1991-1994; Practicing attorney, 1994-2000.

DC Office: 2052 RHOB 20515, 202-225-3376, Fax: 202-225-5652, castor.house.gov

State Offices: Tampa, 813-871-2817.

Committees: *Energy & Commerce*: Consumer Protection & Commerce; Energy; Health. *Select Committee on the Climate Crisis (Chmn).*

Group Ratings

	ADA	ACLU	AFL-CIO	LCV	COC	HAFA	ACU	CFG	FRC
2020	**	79%	**	100%	-	0%	3%	**	-
2019	95%	C	100%	97%	59%	C	4%	12%	0%

Almanac Ratings 2019-2020

	Economy	Social	Foreign	Composite
Liberal	100%	100%	80%	94%
Conservative	0%	0%	20%	6%

Key Votes of the 116th Congress

1. U.S./Mex./Can. trade deal Y	5. Russia sanctions Y	9. Firearms background checks Y
2. First Coronavirus response Y	6. Troops in Syria Y	10. Spending at the border Y
3. HEROES Act Y	7. Veto arms sales to Saudis Y	11. Marijuana liberalized rules Y
4. CASH Act Y	8. Defense $$$, veto override Y	12. Electoral College objections N

Election Results

Election	Name (Party)	Vote (%)		Cand. Spent	Ind. Exp. Support	Ind. Exp. Oppose
2020 General	Kathy Castor (D)	224,240	(60%)	$1,014,136	$23,568	
	Christine Quinn (R)	147,896	(40%)	$246,221		$113

Prior winning percentages: 2016 (62%), 2014 (unopposed), 2012 (70%), 2010 (60%), 2008 (72%), 2006 (70%)

Kathy Castor, a Democrat first elected in 2006, has used her background as an environmental lawyer to assist local interests and to take a prominent role for Democrats in debates on climate policy. She has worked closely with Republicans to protect her district's sprawling MacDill Air Force Base. In 2019-20, as chair of the Select Committee on the Climate Crisis, she worked to prepare a broad legislative initiative for House Democrats. Although the panel had no legislative authority, Castor used that portfolio to work with top advisers to President Joe Biden on the new administration's plans. Castor continued to serve on the Energy and Commerce Committee, which has jurisdiction on environmental policy.

Castor studied political science at Emory University, earned her law degree from Florida State University and worked as a land-use attorney. Her parents were heavily involved in public service. Her father, Don Castor, sat on the Hillsborough County Court for two decades. Her mother, Betty Castor, served in the state Senate, as state education commissioner and as president of the University of South Florida. In 2004, Betty Castor was the Democratic nominee for Senate, but lost 49%-48% to Republican Mel Martinez. Kathy Castor ran unsuccessfully for the state Senate in 2000; two years later, she was elected to the Hillsborough County Commission.

In 2006, Kathy Castor ran for the open House seat, benefiting from the family name ID. In a district with a nearly 2-to-1 Democratic advantage, she faced four opponents in the primary. The most formidable was state Senate Minority Leader Les Miller, a veteran African-American legislator. With the support of EMILY's List, Castor raised nearly $1 million before the primary and outspent Miller 3-to-1. She won 54%-34%. In the general election, Castor campaigned for expanded health care for low-income families, stronger ethics and lobbying rules, and a rapid withdrawal of U.S. troops from Iraq. She won, 70%-30%.

Castor served on the House Ethics Committee, and chaired the subcommittee looking into California Democratic Rep. Maxine Waters' alleged efforts to help get federal bailout money for a bank in which her husband owned stock. Waters was cleared of wrongdoing in 2012. As a reward for her service on the Ethics panel, considered an undesirable posting, Castor got the seat on Energy and Commerce.

In 2009 Castor joined a group of liberals on the panel who insisted that any savings from a government-run insurance option in the Democrats' proposed health care overhaul should be used to increase subsidies for low-income persons. Also that year, she added an amendment to the climate-change bill to allow states to set rates for electricity generated from renewable energy under state incentive programs. In the Almanac's vote ratings, she has ranked among the liberal half of House Democrats.

Castor was a major player on offshore drilling following the 2010 BP oil spill in the Gulf of Mexico, prodding the company and the Obama administration for more research on the spill's impact. In 2012, she added a provision to a transportation bill directing that most fines collected under the Clean Water Act should go for Gulf clean-up instead of to the Treasury. In September 2017, she won House passage of her bipartisan bill to encourage private flood insurance policies in high-risk areas. The bill died in the Senate. Castor has avidly looked out for MacDill, headquarters of the U.S. Central Command and Special Operations Command. In the defense spending bill for 2019, she added a provision to protect families living at the base from mold contamination in their homes.

Castor, whose district has the third-highest number of Cuban Americans in the nation, embraced increased trade and travel to Cuba and was the first House member from Florida to support lifting travel restrictions. She praised President Barack Obama's decision to reopen diplomatic relations with Cuba. In March 2016, she accompanied him when he became the first president to visit the island since 1928. When the Trump administration tightened restrictions on Americans traveling to Cuba and prohibited dealings with some state-owned entities, she objected that the "backward policy" marked a "return to failed Cold War isolationist policies toward Cuba and the Cuban people."

When Democrats regained House control following the 2018 election, Speaker Nancy Pelosi tapped Castor to chair the updated version of the climate-change panel that worked with Energy and Commerce in 2009 to win House approval of major legislation. At the insistence of Energy and Commerce Chairman Frank Pallone of New Jersey, Castor's select committee was limited to studying the issues and making recommendations. It had no subpoena or legislative authority.

Castor took advantage of the opportunity. Facing pressure from national environmental activists who criticized her caution in failing to support the goals of their Green New Deal, Castor told the Tampa Bay Times, "I'm not going to rest until we make real progress." Local activists familiar with her record largely supported her. In its report in June 2020, the select committee called for reducing carbon dioxide emissions to zero by 2050 and proposed revival of the New Deal-era Civilian Conservation Corps to prepare for local action on climate change. "While local communities and states and businesses take climate action, what's been missing is the federal government," she told the Times. Later, she served on a task force that Biden created to prepare climate change action once he became president.

At home, Castor faced a tougher than usual reelection challenge in the Republican year of 2010 from Republican Mike Prendergast, a retired Army colonel. She narrowly outspent him and won with

60 percent of the vote, the lowest of her career. Even with additional Republican voters following the 2016 redistricting, her district has remained uncompetitive.

FL-14: Tampa   **Cook Partisan Voting Index: D+7**

Population		Race and Ethnicity		Income	
Total	831,508	White	68.60%	Median Income	$60,022
Land area (sq. miles)	265	Black	19.00%	District Income Rank	262
Pop/ sq mi	3,133.04	Latino	32.90%	Poverty Rate	14.50%
Born in State	39.00%	Asian	4.40%	With health insurance	87.10%
		Two or more races	4.10%	Cash public assistance	1.60%
Age Groups		Other	3.90%	Food stamp/SNAP	12.20%
Under 18	21.70%				
18-34	26.10%	**Education**		**Work**	
35-64	38.60%	H.S grad or less	36.70%	White Collar	41.00%
Over 64	13.50%	Some college	24.80%	Sales and Service	39.70%
		College Degree, 4 yr	23.50%	Blue Collar	19.30%
Military		Post grad	15.00%	Government	9.60%
Veteran/ Active Duty	7.00%				

2020 Pres. Vote	Biden	217,176	(57%)	Trump	158,027	(42%)		
2016 Pres. Vote	Clinton	188,870	(57%)	Trump	128,796	(39%)	Johnson	8,719	(3%)

Hillsborough County: Tampa's history goes back not much more than a century. Its industrial past can be traced to 1886, when Cuban cigar-makers from Key West settled in the city's Latin Quarter, called Ybor City. The city developed along the waterfront, with distinctive architectural touches like the 13 minarets on the Arabian-style Tampa Bay Hotel, built by railroad and real estate tycoon Henry B. Plant in the 1890s and now part of the University of Tampa. For a time, Tampa was Florida's only true industrial city, with a working-class, White population base. Today it has a diverse economy: a service sector, two universities and tourism, led by the Busch Gardens theme park. Tampa's subdivisions, condominiums, office towers and low-rise commercial buildings have spread inland across swamps and lowlands.

Since groundbreaking in 2018, growth has been booming in Water Street Tampa—a $3 billion, 16-block mega-development. The University of South Florida's College of Medicine and Heart Institute opened its doors in January 2020. The airport completed a $1 billion upgrade in 2018, including a 1.4-mile people-mover rail, and plans to open a new terminal in 2023. With a 20 percent increase from 2010 to 2019, Hillsborough has been one of the fastest growing areas in Florida.

Through its history, Tampa has remained a city of families and young people. Senior citizens account for only about 12 percent of the residents here, an unusually low percentage for Florida. It has been an important military center for much of its existence. During the Spanish-American War, when railroads were making their way down Florida's Atlantic Coast, Tampa was a major embarkation point for U.S. troops. MacDill Air Force Base, on the south side of the city and jutting into Tampa Bay, is the vital headquarters of Central Command, which ran the Persian Gulf War and the campaigns in Afghanistan and Iraq. It is also headquarters for Special Operations Command, and the coordinating center for international special operations forces.

The 14th Congressional District is centered on Tampa. With 57 percent of Hillsborough County, it includes most of the city of Tampa and its close-in suburbs, such as Town 'n' Country. The county population, which grew by 20 percent from 2010 to 2019, has increased at least 30 percent in nearly every decade since 1950; it is the fourth largest in Florida. In the 2016 redistricting, the 14th lost the heavily African-American and lower-income neighborhoods in St. Petersburg and gained new areas of northern Hillsborough. Even with the increased Republican vote, the district remained safely Democratic. The 14th includes a bit more than half of Hillsborough. The outlying, more Republican, areas are in the 15th and 16th districts. County-wide, Joe Biden added a percentage point and nearly 70,000 votes to the bare majority Hillary Clinton won four years earlier. He took the district, 57%-42%.

Scott Franklin (R)

Elected 2020, 1st term, b. Aug 23, 1964; Thomaston, GA; U.S. Naval Academy, B.S., 1986; Embry-Riddle Aeronautical University, M.B.A., 1994; Air Command and Staff College, 1997; University of PA Wharton School of Business, B.S., 2003; Presbyterian; Married (Amy Wood); 3 children.

Military Career: U.S. Navy, 1986-2000; Commander, U.S. Naval Reserve, 2000-2012.

Elected Office: Member, Lakeland City Commission, 2018-2021.

Professional Career: President/CEO, insurance agency, 2000-2020.

DC Office: 1517 LHOB 20515, 202-225-1252, Fax: 202-225-0585, franklin.house.gov

State Offices: Lakeland, 863-644-8215.

Committees: *Armed Services*: Cyber, Innovative Technologies & Information Systems; Intelligence & Special Operations. *Oversight & Reform*: Subcommittee on Civil Rights & Civil Liberties; Subcommittee on Economic & Consumer Policy.

Election Results

Election	Name (Party)	Vote (%)		Cand. Spent	Ind. Exp. Support	Ind. Exp. Oppose
2020 General	Scott Franklin (R)	216,374	(55%)	$1,637,333	$851,534	$293,577
	Alan Cohn (D)	174,297	(45%)	$2,296,036	$176,268	$377,124
2020 Primary	Scott Franklin (R)	30,736	(51%)			
	Ross Spano (R)	29,265	(49%)			

Republican Scott Franklin was elected to the House after defeating first-term Rep. Ross Spano in the GOP primary. The two candidates agreed on most issues. Spano had become vulnerable after a congressional ethics office found that he had violated federal election campaign law when he used personal loans to finance his 2018 campaign. Spano conceded the violation but said he was not familiar with the legal standard. In an unusual twist of incumbency, outspoken Florida Rep. Matt Gaetz actively backed Franklin during the primary—citing his concern that Spano would lose the seat to Democrats. Republican leaders and most House GOP members from Florida backed Spano.

A native of Georgia who grew up in Lakeland Florida, Franklin graduated from the U.S. Naval Academy and received his master's in business administration from Embry-Riddle Aeronautical University. During his 14 years of active service plus 12 years in the Naval Reserve, he was an aviator based on aircraft carriers—including combat operations in the Persian Gulf, Bosnia and Kosovo. In Lakeland, he was president of an insurance and risk-management agency. He was elected to the Lakeland City Commission in 2018.

Spano, a former state legislator, was outspent by his Democratic opponent in their 2018 contest for an open seat, which he won 53%-47%. Most of his victory margin came in rural Polk County. In that contest, Republican strategists "sounded the alarm" in mid-October and complained that Spano had not "raised enough money to define himself," according to the Cook Political Report. Democrat Kristen Carlson, executive director of the Florida Citrus Processors Association, spent a bit more than $2 million in the campaign—much less than many House Democratic candidates in battleground districts, but twice as much as Spano. In the final two weeks of the campaign, Speaker Paul Ryan's Congressional Leadership Fund spent $500,000 on Spano's behalf.

A month after he was elected, Spano's attorney wrote to the Federal Election Commission that he had loaned $167,000 to his campaign from personal loans he had received during a five-month period. Spano recognized that the finances "may have been in violation" of the Federal Election Campaign Act; his actions were based on faulty advice from his previous lawyer, according to the letter. In November 2019, the Office of Congressional Ethics unanimously ruled that there was "substantial reason to believe" that the loans were improper and said the House Ethics Committee should review the allegations. The committee subsequently referred the matter to the Justice Department for a criminal investigation.

Although prosecutors took no action prior to the August 2020 primary, Franklin told the Tampa Bay Times, "We can't go to Washington to fix problems if we elect people that we know have broken the law." In a taped message to Republican voters, Gaetz said, "Spano is so weakened by the Justice

Department corruption investigation that we can't count on him to defend President Trump against [Speaker Nancy] Pelosi and the liberals. … He's a drag. He's a drain."

Spano spent about $1 million in the primary—nearly twice the total of Franklin, who loaned his campaign $400,000. The conservative Club for Growth spent nearly $300,000 on behalf of Spano. Franklin won the primary, 51.2%-48.8%. His victory margin came entirely from Lakeland-based Polk County, where he got 62 percent of the vote. Spano led by smaller amounts in Lake and Hillsborough counties; Hillsborough, where Spano resided, cast nearly half the total vote.

In November, Franklin defeated Alan Cohn, a former local television reporter who had unsuccessfully challenged an earlier GOP incumbent in 2014. Franklin, who was outspent by Cohn, won, 55%-45%, and led in all three counties. Franklin's biggest margin was in Polk County, where he got 60 percent of the vote.

In the House, he got seats on the Armed Services and Oversight and Reform committees.

FL-15: Central Florida   **Cook Partisan Voting Index: R+6**

Population		Race and Ethnicity		Income	
Total	801,294	White	73.90%	Median Income	$57,496
Land area (sq. miles)	819	Black	14.10%	District Income Rank	295
Pop/ sq mi	978.97	Latino	23.80%	Poverty Rate	12.90%
Born in State	39.50%	Asian	3.20%	With health insurance	86.90%
		Two or more races	2.60%	Cash public assistance	2.10%
Age Groups		Other	6.20%	Food stamp/SNAP	11.90%
Under 18	21.60%				
18-34	22.30%	**Education**		**Work**	
35-64	39.50%	H.S grad or less	42.90%	White Collar	35.80%
Over 64	16.50%	Some college	31.40%	Sales and Service	41.10%
		College Degree, 4 yr	17.30%	Blue Collar	23.00%
Military		Post grad	8.50%	Government	9.60%
Veteran/ Active Duty	8.40%				

2020 Pres. Vote	Trump	213,736	(54%)	Biden	179,793	(45%)		
2016 Pres. Vote	Trump	177,634	(53%)	Clinton	144,226	(43%)	Johnson	8,906	(3%)

Tampa Suburbs, Lakeland: The heart of central Florida is Polk County, filled with lakes and small-to-medium-sized cities. Lakeland, with a population of 112,000, is the biggest city here and home to the corporate headquarters of the Publix chain of grocery stores, the largest employee-owned supermarket chain in the nation. With 225,000 employees and 1,264 store locations throughout the Southeast—two-thirds of them in Florida—Publix is the largest employer in the county. Its corporate headquarters in Lakeland planned to expand to more than 2,000 employees. Lakeland-area home prices historically made it one of the most affordable areas in the Sunshine State. In 2020, local real estate agents reported double-digit annual increases in sales, including a median sales price of $182,000. U.S. News and World Report in 2018 rated the Lakeland area ninth on its list of "Best Places People Are Moving to in the U.S."

This is the part of Florida that has been most dependent on agriculture. Strawberries, cattle and citrus are economic mainstays, although periodic freezes in recent years have persuaded some orange growers to move south or to switch to tomatoes. Polk has had a double-digit percentage drop in the number of farms and acreage in the past decade. In 2016, for the first time in 21 years, Polk no longer produced the most citrus in Florida. DeSoto has become the number-one county for oranges. But the total statewide yield dropped from more than 300 million boxes in 2005 (the start of the devastating greening bacteria) to 71 million boxes in 2019. Most of Florida's oranges are used to produce juice. Farmers fear the long-term loss of the state's nearly $1 billion annual strawberry harvest, due chiefly to labor costs and competition from Mexico. Proportionately, there have been more manufacturing jobs here than almost anywhere else in Florida (though still not very many). Some new businesses, including distribution centers, have taken advantage of cheap property values to build new plants in Lakeland. In Hillsborough, the Plant City area produces close to 90 percent of Florida's strawberry yield. At its annual Strawberry Festival in March, more than 500,000 patrons consume at least as many shortcakes. One of the few remnants of old Florida, this area has not become a major retiree haven.

The 15th Congressional District is a rural and suburban combo. About 35 percent of the district's population lives in agricultural Polk County, and 50 percent in the rapidly growing suburbs in Hillsborough County east of Tampa. Redistricting in 2016 had scant partisan impact. Overall, the district remains reliably Republican. In 2020, Trump won the district, 54%-45%.

Vern Buchanan (R)

Elected 2006, 8th term, b. May 08, 1951; Detroit, MI; Cleary University, B.B.A., 1975; University of Detroit, M.B.A., 1986; Baptist; Married (Sandy Harris Buchanan); 2 children.

Military Career: MI Air National Guard 1970-1976

Professional Career: Taekwondo instructor, 1971-1974; Marketing rep., Burroughs Corporation, 1975-1976; Founder, Vern Buchanan & Association, 1976-1978; Founder & CEO, American Speedy Printing Centers, 1976-1992; Founder & Chairman, Buchanan Automotive Group, 1992-2007; Founder & Chairman, Buchanan Enterprises, 1992-2007.

DC Office: 2427 RHOB 20515, 202-225-5015, Fax: 202-226-0828, buchanan.house.gov

State Offices: Bradenton, 941-747-9081; Sarasota, 941-951-6643.

Committees: *Ways & Means*: Health; Trade.

Group Ratings

	ADA	ACLU	AFL-CIO	LCV	COC	HAFA	ACU	CFG	FRC
2020	**	18%	**	33%	-	79%	72%	**	-
2019	15%	C	33%	31%	96%	C	73%	65%	100%

Almanac Ratings 2019-2020

	Economy	Social	Foreign	Composite
Liberal	38%	41%	39%	40%
Conservative	62%	59%	61%	60%

Key Votes of the 116th Congress

1. U.S./Mex./Can. trade deal Y	5. Russia sanctions Y	9. Firearms background checks Y
2. First Coronavirus response Y	6. Troops in Syria Y	10. Spending at the border Y
3. HEROES Act N	7. Veto arms sales to Saudis N	11. Marijuana liberalized rules N
4. CASH Act N	8. Defense $$$, veto override Y	12. Electoral College objections N

Election Results

Election	Name (Party)	Vote (%)		Cand. Spent	Ind. Exp. Support	Ind. Exp. Oppose
2020 General	Vern Buchanan (R)	269,001	(56%)	$3,394,315	$8,039	$44,873
	Margaret Good (D)	215,683	(45%)	$3,765,299	$8,705	

Prior winning percentages: 2018 (55%), 2016 (60%), 2014 (62%), 2012 (54%), 2010 (69%), 2008 (56%), 2006 50%)

Vern Buchanan, a Republican first elected in 2006, initially struggled politically with questionable business dealings and campaign finances. Since then, he has settled in as a senior member of the powerful Ways and Means Committee, though his work on the GOP's 2017 tax cuts exposed him to new political attacks. In the minority, he has been ranking Republican on the Trade Subcommittee. At home, Democrats continue to run well-financed challenges to him.

Buchanan grew up outside Detroit, the eldest of six children and the son of a factory foreman. He joined the Michigan Air National Guard and worked his way through college as a tae kwon do instructor. He earned a business degree at Cleary University and later an MBA at the University of Detroit. Buchanan founded American Speedy Printing Centers and made his fortune by selling 700 quick-printing franchises before his 40th birthday. In 1990, he moved his family to Florida, where he found new success as an automobile dealer with franchises throughout the Southeast. Buchanan has been among the wealthiest members of Congress. In 2018, the Center for Responsive Politics listed his estimated net worth of $157 million, the largest amount for House members at that time who were reelected in 2020. On Capitol Hill, he trailed only Democratic Sen. Mark Warner of Virginia, with $214 million.

Buchanan became active in Republican politics, serving as a top fundraiser for Gov. Jeb Bush and Sen. Mel Martinez. In 2002, he wanted to run for the House seat, but stepped aside for Secretary of State Katherine Harris, who had become a national figure for her role in the 2000 presidential vote recount. Buchanan got his chance in 2006, when Harris ran for the Senate. In the primary, he stressed his conservative credentials and spent more than $2 million of his own money. Buchanan won 32 percent of the vote in the five-way primary.

Democratic nominee Christine Jennings, who like Buchanan was a transplanted Midwesterner and a self-made business success, was a bank owner. National Democrats pummeled Buchanan for his business dealings. He characterized Jennings as a pro-tax liberal. This was the most expensive House race in 2006. Buchanan spent more than $8 million, including $5.5 million of his own money. Jennings spent $3 million, with about $2 million from her own pocket. Buchanan was certified the winner by 369 votes.

Entering the House, Buchanan softened his ideological positions. He was one of 19 Republicans who supported most of the Democrats' early legislative agenda when they took control in 2007. "I ran as a conservative, but I also ran as someone who is going to be independent," Buchanan told the Sarasota Herald-Tribune. On Ways and Means, he joined the bipartisan deal in 2015 to adjust Medicare payments to doctors and extend the Children's Health Insurance Program. Following the BP oil spill in 2010, he pushed for a moratorium on all deep-water drilling permits in the Gulf of Mexico. When the Trump administration in 2018 proposed to weaken offshore drilling regulations, Buchanan called the move "reckless and unacceptable."

By contrast, he took stances to the right on immigration and terrorism, calling for an English official-language law and using military tribunals instead of civilian courts to try terrorist suspects. The former car dealer voted against the bailout of Detroit automakers in 2008 because, he said, the companies "failed to develop viable restructuring proposals."

In 2011, Buchanan attracted unwanted attention. The Herald-Tribune reported that during the past year he had spent almost $1 million in campaign contributions on himself, companies he owned, or family members. Most of the money reportedly was used to repay campaign checks he wrote to himself in 2006. He steadfastly denied any wrongdoing, and maintained that the Federal Election Commission had exonerated him. But the Herald-Tribune unearthed FEC documents that found Buchanan to be "less than forthright and at times unbelievable." With ethics questions swirling in 2012, Democrat Keith Fitzgerald made Buchanan's integrity the main focus of his campaign. Then, over the summer, the Ethics Committee said it had ended its probe of Buchanan. In September his office announced that the Justice Department had concluded its investigation without charging him. Buchanan prevailed, 54%-46%.

Buchanan has grown more comfortable in the House as he moved into the elite ranks as a subcommittee chairman on Ways and Means. Starting in late 2015, he chaired three panels in three years: Human Resources, Oversight and Tax Policy. He was an enthusiastic proponent of the tax cuts enacted by Republicans in 2017, which he billed as "a little something extra in your paycheck." Those tax cuts became a source of embarrassment for Buchanan when his annual financial disclosure report to the House revealed that he purchased a yacht on the same day he voted for House passage of the legislation. A spokesman refused to discuss the personal impact for Buchanan, but said, "This isn't about Vern, it's about the tens of thousands of small businesses that have been unfairly penalized by high taxes."

In the House minority, Buchanan was one of only three Republicans who voted in May 2019 for a Democratic bill that sought to require the Trump administration to comply with the Paris climate agreement. In 2020, he called for Medicare coverage of the coronavirus vaccine for all seniors. With Rep. Kevin Brady term-limited in 2022 as the top Republican on Ways and Means and retiring, Buchanan said that he will seek to succeed him; presumably, that will result in a contest with Rep. Devin Nunes, the only committee Republican who is more senior, and perhaps with others.

At home, Democrats pounced on his finances. David Shapiro, his challenger in 2018, ran an ad claiming the tax law gave Buchanan "a tax handout of up to $2 million." Buchanan won, 55%-45%. In 2020, State Rep. Margaret Good, another Sarasota lawyer, had defeated Buchanan's son to win a Republican-held state House seat. Her message, according to the Florida Politics website, "focused on Buchanan being in Washington too long and casting votes to deny health care expansion while bailing out his own businesses." Good matched Buchanan's spending, with $3.8 million, but the outcome was virtually the same as two years earlier, 56%-44%. His best performance was in Manatee, where he took 60 percent of the vote.

FL-16: Central Gulf Coast

Cook Partisan Voting Index: R+7

Population		Race and Ethnicity		Income	
Total	873,875	White	82.20%	Median Income	$68,071
Land area (sq. miles)	875	Black	9.70%	District Income Rank	183
Pop/ sq mi	998.34	Latino	17.70%	Poverty Rate	9.70%
Born in State	31.60%	Asian	2.20%	With health insurance	87.70%
		Two or more races	2.30%	Cash public assistance	1.30%
Age Groups		Other	3.60%	Food stamp/SNAP	7.40%
Under 18	18.00%				
18-34	17.40%	Education		Work	
35-64	37.20%	H.S grad or less	37.40%	White Collar	36.90%
Over 64	27.50%	Some college	29.50%	Sales and Service	43.20%
		College Degree, 4 yr	19.90%	Blue Collar	19.90%
Military		Post grad	13.20%	Government	9.90%
Veteran/ Active Duty	10.00%				

2020 Pres. Vote	Trump	262,840	(53%)	Biden	223,366	(45%)			
2016 Pres. Vote	Trump	213,271	(53%)	Clinton	170,442	(43%)	Johnson	9,302	(2%)

Bradenton, North Sarasota: When the Ringling Brothers made a success of the circus they founded in the 1880s, they needed a place for performers and animals to rest during the winter months. They settled on Sarasota: just far enough north to be reachable by railroad and just far enough south to be semitropical so the elephants would stay healthy. John Ringling established the Ringling Museum of Art and a huge sculpture garden, and built his own Venetian palace, the Ca' d'Zan. Next door, his brother, Charles, built a pair of neoclassical revival mansions in pink Georgia marble, which are now part of New College of Florida. But this was still a sparsely populated area until just after World War II, when the balmy Gulf Coast attracted new settlers—affluent, well-educated Republicans from upper-crust suburbs in the North. The population exploded. Manatee and Sarasota counties grew from a combined 64,000 people in 1950 to 837,000 in 2019.

In May 2017, alas, the final curtain came down on the Ringling Brothers Circus (in a New York City performance) due to several factors, including a drop in ticket sales and protests by animal-rights groups. Otherwise, the pre-pandemic economy remained strong, including Sarasota's luxury indoor Mall at University. The bayfront area along the Intracoastal Waterway is lined with high-rises and is often clogged with traffic from Bradenton to Sarasota. In downtown, the $1 billion Quay waterfront district, including a new performing arts center, has been a major step.

Though some technology firms diversify the economy, the district as a whole remains reliant on tourists and well-off retirees: People 65 and older are 37 percent of the population in Sarasota, and 28 percent in Manatee, though the share of seniors has dropped in recent years. Now a center for sports tourism, Bradenton has a rowing facility that was a model for the Olympic Games in Tokyo. The 2017 World Rowing Championships and the 2018 World Sailing annual conference were both held in Sarasota. Reality check: Bradenton has become the opioid overdose capital of Florida, especially with fentanyl analogs. In 2020, the social dislocation from the pandemic led to a spike in cases. The area also suffered from an invasion of red tide algae on the beaches, which remained strong in 2020.

The 16th Congressional District of Florida includes all of Manatee and barely half of Sarasota. The district continues to include the pricey Longboat Key and Lido Key and the more casual Siesta Key. Besides all of Bradenton-based Manatee, the district swings north along the east coast of Tampa Bay to include the southern edge of Hillsborough. In both Sarasota and southern Hillsborough, Interstate 75 comes within a few miles of the Gulf of Mexico. West of 75, these areas are close to fully developed. East of 75, the lands had been mostly undeveloped until recent years. Some lower-cost subdivisions have opened in those areas. For many years, the 16th was heavily Republican, though voting results have grown closer. In 2020, Donald Trump got 58 percent in Manatee and 55 percent in Sarasota, which was virtually the same as his 2016 performance. He took the district, 53%-45%.

Greg Steube (R)

Elected 2018, 2nd term, b. May 19, 1978; Bradenton, FL; University of FL, B.S., 2001; University of FL Levin College of Law, J.D., 2003; Methodist; Married (Jennifer Mary Retzer); 1 child.

Military Career: U.S. Army 2004-2008 (Iraq)

Elected Office: FL House: 2010-2016; FL Senate: 2016-2018

Professional Career: Attorney, Becker & Poliakoff.

DC Office: 521 CHOB 20515, 202-225-5792, Fax: 202-225-3132, steube.house.gov

State Offices: Okeechobee, 941-575-9101; Punta Gorda, 941-575-9101.

Committees: *Foreign Affairs*: Africa, Global Health & Global Human Rights; Middle East, North Africa & Global Counterterrorism. *Judiciary*: Antitrust, Commercial & Administrative Law; Crime, Terrorism & Homeland Security.

Almanac Ratings 2019-2020

	Economy	Social	Foreign	Composite
Liberal	38%	13%	4%	19%
Conservative	62%	87%	96%	81%

Key Votes of the 116th Congress

1. U.S./Mex./Can. trade deal	Y	5. Russia sanctions	N	9. Firearms background checks	N
2. First Coronavirus response	N	6. Troops in Syria	N	10. Spending at the border	N/A
3. HEROES Act	N	7. Veto arms sales to Saudis	N	11. Marijuana liberalized rules	N
4. CASH Act	N	8. Defense $$$, veto override	N	12. Electoral College objections	Y

Election Results

Election	Name (Party)	Vote (%)		Cand. Spent	Ind. Exp. Support	Ind. Exp. Oppose
2020 General	Greg Steube (R)	266,514	(65%)	$416,301	$7,272	
	Allen Ellison (D)	140,487	(34%)	$67,945		

Prior winning percentages: 2018 (62%)

Republican Greg Steube, who has won easy elections to his safely Republican seat, is an outspoken conservative who is not afraid to voice his views. Occasionally, he can be an iconoclast, whether taking on executives with Big Tech companies or conservatives in the House. In his first term, he showed a keen sense of how to become an active player in Congress.

Steube grew up in rural Manatee County, where he had an early interest in ranching. His father, Brad Steube, was sheriff of Manatee County, which is in the adjacent 16th District. He got his bachelor's and law degrees from the University of Florida; as an undergraduate, he majored in beef cattle sciences. After enlisting in the Army following the September 2001 attacks, he served in the Judge Advocate General's Corps and was an infantry captain in Operation Iraqi Freedom. From 2011 to 2017, Steube was affiliated with Becker and Poliakoff, a large Florida-based law firm that has lobbied actively in Tallahassee.

In 2010, Steube cited his experience in agriculture and law to win a seat in the state House. He took credit for placing two constitutional amendments on Florida ballots in 2012, which provided tax breaks for low-income seniors and the surviving spouses of military veterans; each was approved by the voters. Term-limited in 2016, he won a seat in the state Senate, where he chaired the Judiciary Committee. He claimed to sponsor more pro-gun bills than any other member of the legislature.

When GOP Rep. Tom Rooney retired at age 48 after voicing unhappiness with how Republicans were running Washington, Steube was the early frontrunner to succeed him. He was endorsed by the state's largest organization of citrus growers, a large industry in the district, plus several national conservative groups, including the House Freedom Caucus. The Club for Growth spent nearly $800,000 on his behalf. Also running in the primary were Bill Akins, a businessman and Vietnam veteran, and state Rep. Julio Gonzalez, a surgeon who was endorsed by the U.S. Chamber of Commerce. In the legislature, both Steube and Gonzalez "have advanced conservative legislation, largely without success," the Sarasota Herald-Tribune reported.

Steube criticized Gonzalez for having endorsed Florida Sen. Marco Rubio against Donald Trump in the 2016 Republican presidential campaign. Gonzalez criticized Steube for exaggerating his military record and for running in a district in which he had not been a resident. Each spent a bit more than $500,000 in the primary; Akins spent less than one-tenth of that. Steube won with 62 percent of the vote, to 19 percent for Akins and 18 percent for Gonzalez.

Democrats nominated April Freeman, a film and television producer who had been the Democratic nominee in two earlier House campaigns. When she died suddenly of a heart attack four weeks after the primary, Democrats designated Allen Ellison, an adviser on economic development, to run in her place, though state law required that Freeman's name remain on the ballot. In this district, no Democratic candidate had much chance of winning. Steube easily defeated his dead opponent, 62%-38%.

Steube emphasized commitment to his conservative views. "The Tallahassee establishment was surprised when I actually followed up on my conservative campaign promises. I don't think the D.C. swamp will like it either," he said. In February 2019, he showed an early contrast of views with Rooney—a strong supporter of the North Atlantic Treaty Organization—when he was one of 22 Republicans who voted against a resolution supporting NATO. Calling that position a prerogative of Trump, Steube told the Herald-Tribune, "I support the Constitution and the Constitution gives the president that authority."

He showed additional independence when he decided not to join the Freedom Caucus, despite its campaign support for him. He did not want to be "pigeonholed," he said in the interview. "For a lot of people, if you're a member, they're just going to assume that's where you are on every single issue."

Steube had no trouble bringing attention to his conservative views. As a member of the House Judiciary Committee, he was an outspoken opponent of the impeachment of Trump. In 2019, he said he had 69 interviews on national television. Many of them dealt with impeachment; many were on FOX News. When the Judiciary Committee had a hearing with chief executives from the Big Tech companies, Steube objected that You Tube had censored his views in a video in which he promoted hydroxychloroquine as a treatment for coronavirus. And he told Facebook CEO Mark Zuckerberg, "It's fairly obvious that technology platforms have been stifling conservative news and opinions."

Steube filed a bill to amend the Controlled Substances Act to permit scientific research with marijuana to explore its positive health benefits. "I think it's time we remove the bureaucratic red tape that prevents us from thoroughly studying this substance," Steube said in September 2019. Six months later, the Veterans' Affairs Committee, where he was a member, approved his amendment to ensure that veterans have access to state-approved medical marijuana programs. The House took no action on the bill. In 2021, Steube moved from the veterans' panel to Foreign Affairs.

In 2020, he had a rematch with Ellison, who did not register his campaign committee with the Federal Election Commission. This time, Ellison got his name on the ballot. Steube improved his victory margin, 65%-34%.

FL-17: South Central Florida

Cook Partisan Voting Index: R+16

Population		Race and Ethnicity		Income	
Total	804,754	White	85.70%	Median Income	$53,693
Land area (sq. miles)	6,370	Black	7.60%	District Income Rank	350
Pop/ sq mi	126.34	Latino	16.80%	Poverty Rate	12.70%
Born in State	33.10%	Asian	1.30%	With health insurance	87.80%
		Two or more races	1.80%	Cash public assistance	1.70%
Age Groups		Other	3.60%	Food stamp/SNAP	10.30%
Under 18	16.60%				
18-34	15.80%	**Education**		**Work**	
35-64	34.70%	H.S grad or less	46.40%	White Collar	28.80%
Over 64	32.80%	Some college	30.50%	Sales and Service	46.50%
		College Degree, 4 yr	14.40%	Blue Collar	24.80%
Military		Post grad	8.60%	Government	13.30%
Veteran/ Active Duty	11.30%				

2020 Pres. Vote	Trump	267,579	(63%)	Biden	151,888	(36%)
2016 Pres. Vote	Trump	220,156	(62%)	Clinton	123,919	(35%)

Charlotte, South Sarasota, Okeechobee: The population of Charlotte County didn't reach 10,000 until the 1950s. But local histories assure us that the region was anything but quiet before then. In 1886, when railroads reached the convergence of the Peace River and Charlotte Harbor, the area was home to a small fishing center, a port that mostly shipped phosphate, and a few cattle ranches. But the exotic locale, pleasant climate and emerging sport of tarpon fishing encouraged developers to turn it into a destination for the wealthy. Elizabeth Colt, widow of gun-manufacturer Samuel Colt; John Wanamaker, of the eponymous Philadelphia department store; and other wealthy individuals began annual sojourns to winter in the semitropical paradise. But these riches existed uneasily alongside what remained of a frontier-like culture.

Today, Charlotte County is a very different place. The invention of air conditioning, advances in transportation and the surge of financially secure retirees conspired to drive rapid growth. The county's population roughly doubled each decade from the 1950s to the 1980s. Since then, the gains have slowed. From 2010 to 2019, the population grew from 160,000 to 189,000, an 18 percent gain; Port Charlotte, developed in the 1950s, has become the most populous locale. Punta Gorda maintains a small-town and small-business feel and has been regularly rated among the best places to retire by seniors groups. Of its population, 54 percent are 65 or older and 90 percent are White. In Charlotte Harbor, Allegiant Air planned to open in 2021 Sunseeker Resort, with projections of hundreds of thousands of guests annually. Inland is Babcock Ranch, the nation's first town that is entirely solar-powered—with 343,000 solar panels over 440 acres in a Florida Power & Light facility. The master-planned development of 18,000 acres gained its first residents in January 2018 and expects to grow to 50,000. In August 2020, population reached 1,545; Publix planned to build a local supermarket. With Florida's growing crises of destructive hurricanes and eroding shorelines, futurists view Babcock as an inland model that others will follow, especially with that state's continuing growth.

The 17th Congressional District of Florida has been based in Charlotte County, with lots of additional pieces. The district stretches from Sarasota and Charlotte counties on the Gulf coast north through the Big Cypress Swamp to Bartow in Polk County. The remainder of the population sprawls over five lightly populated and mostly rural counties, and includes Lake Okeechobee. The landscape, largely overlooked by most Floridians, remains dominated by cattle farms and others that produce citrus, tomatoes and vegetables. In 2019, DeSoto County narrowly edged Polk County in production of oranges, with 128 million boxes. Hurricane Irma devastated much of the crop the following year. Charlotte and Sarasota each have a bit more than one-fourth of the population. The 63 percent for Donald Trump in 2020 was his best Florida district south of Orlando.

Brian Mast (R)

Elected 2016, 3rd term, b. Jul 10, 1980; Grand Rapids, MI; Palm Beach Atlantic University, Att., 2002; American Military University, 2010; Harvard University, A.L.B., 2016; Christian Church; Married (Brianna Mast); 3 children.

Military Career: U.S. Army 2000-2012 (Afghanistan, WIA)

Professional Career: Analyst, National Nuclear Security Admin., 2011-2012; Explosive Specialist, U.S Dept. of Homeland Security, 2012-2015.

DC Office: 2182 RHOB 20515, 202-225-3026, Fax: 202-225-8398, mast.house.gov

State Offices: North Palm Beach, 561-530-7778; Port St Lucie, 772-336-2877; Stuart, 772-403-0900.

Committees: *Foreign Affairs*: Europe, Energy, the Environment & Cyber; Middle East, North Africa & Global Counterterrorism. *Transportation & Infrastructure*: Aviation; Water Resources & Environment.

Group Ratings

	ADA	ACLU	AFL-CIO	LCV	COC	HAFA	ACU	CFG	FRC
2020	**	27%	**	29%	-	79%	63%	**	-
2019	15%	C	38%	38%	85%	C	62%	78%	91%

Almanac Ratings 2019-2020

	Economy	Social	Foreign	Composite
Liberal	38%	40%	4%	28%
Conservative	62%	60%	96%	72%

Key Votes of the 116th Congress

1. U.S./Mex./Can. trade deal	Y	5. Russia sanctions	N/A
2. First Coronavirus response	Y	6. Troops in Syria	N
3. HEROES Act	N	7. Veto arms sales to Saudis	N
4. CASH Act	N	8. Defense $$$, veto override	N

9. Firearms background checks	Y
10. Spending at the border	Y
11. Marijuana liberalized rules	Y
12. Electoral College objections	Y

Election Results

Election	Name (Party)	Vote (%)		Cand. Spent	Ind. Exp. Support	Ind. Exp. Oppose
2020 General	Brian Mast (R)	253,286	(56%)	$5,194,563	$171,095	$87,721
	Pam Keith (D)	186,674	(42%)	$1,706,657	$215,920	$25,000
	K. W. Miller (I)	9,760	(2%)			
2020 Primary	Brian Mast (R)	62,121	(86%)			
	Nick Vessio (R)	10,081	(14%)			

Prior winning percentages: 2018 (54%), 2016 (54%)

Republican Brian Mast took an interest in environmental and firearms issues that were important to his constituents but sometimes separated him from other Republicans. An Army veteran who lost both legs while serving in Afghanistan, Mast initially gained a cachet on veterans' issues in Congress. He has prevailed in competitive reelections.

Mast was born in Grand Rapids Michigan. After graduating from high school there, he followed in his father's footsteps and enlisted in the Army. He served under the elite Joint Special Operations Command as a bomb disposal expert. This meant, he wrote in his campaign bio, "that life was always dangerous and very often deadly." His task was to detect and destroy improvised explosive devices. The final one he found along a roadside in Kandahar Afghanistan caused catastrophic injuries, including the loss of his legs below the knees, a portion of his forearm and a finger. He received numerous military honors.

As part of his recovery, Mast shared his expertise with the National Nuclear Security Administration's Office of Emergency Operations and the Bureau of Alcohol, Tobacco, Firearms and Explosives. Following his retirement from the Army, he worked in counter-terrorism and national defense as an explosives specialist for the Transportation Security Administration. He served as a volunteer for the Israel Defense Forces. In 2016, Mast graduated with a degree in economics from Harvard University's online program. Another distinctive characteristic is that he always wears shorts, he said, because his prosthetics legs rip through his pants.

While recovering from his injuries, Mast vowed to serve in Congress. In 2016, when Democrat Rep. Patrick Murphy ran for the Senate, he won the six-candidate Republican primary with 38 percent of the vote. The runner-up with 26 percent was Roberta Negron. As the wife of state Senate President Joe Negron, she had the support of many Florida Republican leaders. Democratic nominee Randy Perkins, who founded a lucrative debris-removal company in Florida following the devastation of Hurricane Andrew in 1992, self-financed most of his $10.8 million campaign. In a campaign debate, Perkins showed little subtlety. He asked Mast about the health insurance coverage he receives as a veteran, and why "the sacrifices and service you provided for this country make you capable of solving issues" facing Congress. Mast raised $2.8 million for his campaign and received more than $3.5 million from the Congressional Leadership Fund. He won, 54%-43%.

On the Transportation and Infrastructure Committee, Mast sought improvements in the water systems serving Lake Okeechobee, to prevent what he called a potential environmental disaster, especially from toxic algae. He pressed for expedited review of regulation of Lake Okeechobee and for the development of large-scale water filtration technology. His provision was included in the water resources bill that Congress enacted in 2018. Mast refused to endorse Florida Gov. Rick. Scott in his Senate bid that year until he endorsed his proposal. "I'm not going to support anyone who doesn't support our water," he said. Following the election of Ron DeSantis as governor, Mast chaired his transition advisory committee on environmental policy. He subsequently pressed the Army Corps of Engineers to issue tough standards for discharges from Okeechobee, in the face of strong opposition from U.S. Sugar. Mast also has a seat on the Foreign Affairs Committee.

In 2017, Mast enacted his bill to extend various veterans' programs. The following spring, White House officials said Mast was among those considered to serve as head of the Veterans Affairs Department. In 2020, the House passed the bill he filed with Democratic Rep. Kathleen Rice to eliminate gender-based references in the VA motto.

Following the shootings in 2018 that killed 17 persons at the high school in Parkland Florida, where Mast grew up, he announced support for a ban on some semi-automatic weapons. In 2019, he was one of eight House Republicans who voted for a bill to require background checks on all gun sales. The National Rifle Association switched Mast's "A" rating to an "F," which drew two challengers to him in the 2018 GOP primary. Mast won with 78 percent of the vote. In 2020, he advocated a referendum to amend the state constitution to ban so-called assault weapons. But his proposal failed to get enough signatures for ballot access.

In November 2018, Mast faced Lauren Baer, a former foreign policy adviser to President Barack Obama, who criticized Mast for his support of Trump administration policies. Each candidate spent several million dollars and had extensive party support. Mast won, 54%-46%. He got 53 percent in Palm Beach County, which cast nearly half the vote, and led by nearly 2-to-1 in Martin.

Two years later, his Democratic challenger was Pam Keith, a Black attorney who served 12 years in the military. She criticized Mast's Facebook comments with a friend about having sex with 15-year-old girls; he apologized. Mast outspent Keith, 3-to-1, and won, 56%-42%. In a district that has had a recent history of changes in party control, redistricting could have a significant impact on his political future.

FL-18: Palm Beach, Treasure Coast

Cook Partisan Voting Index: R+6

Population		Race and Ethnicity		Income	
Total	795,742	White	79.60%	Median Income	$68,744
Land area (sq. miles)	1,513	Black	12.80%	District Income Rank	178
Pop/ sq mi	526.09	Latino	17.50%	Poverty Rate	8.60%
Born in State	33.70%	Asian	2.30%	With health insurance	88.30%
		Two or more races	2.90%	Cash public assistance	2.50%
Age Groups		Other	2.40%	Food stamp/SNAP	8.60%
Under 18	18.30%				
18-34	18.00%	**Education**		**Work**	
35-64	37.40%	H.S grad or less	37.50%	White Collar	39.00%
Over 64	26.40%	Some college	30.20%	Sales and Service	42.90%
		College Degree, 4 yr	19.80%	Blue Collar	18.00%
Military		Post grad	12.50%	Government	10.50%
Veteran/ Active Duty	9.30%				

2020 Pres. Vote	Trump	244,705	(54%)	Biden	206,388	(45%)
2016 Pres. Vote	Trump	203,771	(53%)	Clinton	168,558	(44%)

Palm Beach Gardens, St. Lucie: Urban Florida has fanned far across the swamplands from its original nuclei in beachfront resort communities. Once, metro Palm Beach was a narrow stretch along Lake Worth; now it runs inland almost halfway to Lake Okeechobee, spreading out from its original locus around the posh Breakers Hotel. Old beach towns such as Hobe Sound have become the hub of affluent developments that extend north to Stuart in Martin County. Farther north, near the old town of Fort Pierce, are larger but more modest developments like Port St. Lucie, which had a population of only 330 in 1970. In 2020, it became the seventh largest city in Florida, with a population of 206,000, topping Cape Coral and Tallahassee. Of the 328,000 in St. Lucie County, the Hispanic share has grown to 20 percent.

Farther south, northern Palm Beach County is changing as well. The county, along with the state of Florida, subsidized the Scripps Research Institute's new center in Jupiter. That attracted several other biotechnology businesses to Jupiter. Mayor Todd Wodraska called the city "a biotechnology hub where important scientific advances are realized." More immediately, some local officials have voiced concern that agricultural runoff into Lake Okeechobee could create harmful discharges into the St. Lucie River. Instead, they have proposed redirecting the water to farmland south of the lake, with the possibility that sugar land in the Everglades would be taken by eminent domain or other government action.

The 18th Congressional District includes all of Martin County, with its affluent towns of Stuart and Hobe Sound, as well as all of more modest St. Lucie County. To the south, about 40 percent of the district's population resides in the northern precincts of Palm Beach County, including Palm Beach Gardens, an area filled with gated communities and home to the Professional Golfers' Association of America. Parts of north Palm Beach include less expensive real estate and home rentals, compared with other parts of the pricey county. A few miles east of the PGA's official home is Jupiter, where the largest concentration of PGA golfers resides amid lush greenery and plush mansions. At least 35 members of the PGA Tour, plus many retired stars, live in a 20-mile stretch along the Atlantic Ocean, just north of Palm Beach. Nearby, along the Intra-Coastal Waterway, the $150 million Harbourside Place entertainment complex includes the Woods Jupiter restaurant—a "family-friendly sports and dining club," owned by Tiger Woods. In December 2018, the PGA announced plans for a new headquarters in Frisco Texas, north of Plano, where it plans a mixed-use development with an initial investment exceeding $500 million. (No word yet on whether the pro golfers will abandon Jupiter.) Fun fact—American Horror Story: Freak Show, which starred Jessica Lange and Neil Patrick Harris, was set in Jupiter in 1952.

Donald Trump raised Republican performance here—and that's not because he sent his guests and employees to the voting precincts from his Mar-a-Lago estate, which is a few miles down Route 1, in the 21st District. In 2020, Trump won the 18th, 54%-45%, compared with Mitt Romney's 52%-48% local win over President Barack Obama in 2012.

Byron Donalds (R)

Elected 2020, 1st term, b. Oct 28, 1978; Brooklyn, NY; FL State University, B.S., 2002; Christian Church; Married (Erika Donalds); 3 children.

Elected Office: FL House, 2016-2020.

Professional Career: Assistant Vice President, Credit Manager, TIB Bank, 2006-2007; Portfolio Manager, financial services company; Financial Advisor, Wells Fargo Advisors.

DC Office: 523 CHOB 20515, 202-225-2536, donalds.house.gov

State Offices: Cape Coral, 239-599-6033; Naples, 239-252-6225.

Committees: *Budget. Oversight & Reform*: Subcommittee on Civil Rights & Civil Liberties; Subcommittee on Economic & Consumer Policy. *Small Business*: Economic Growth, Tax & Capital Access; Oversight, Investigations & Regulations.

Election Results

Election	Name (Party)	Vote (%)		Cand. Spent	Ind. Exp. Support	Ind. Exp. Oppose
2020 General	Byron Donalds (R)	272,440	(61%)			
	Cindy Banyai (D)	172,146	(39%)	$199,655		
2020 Primary	Byron Donalds (R)	23,492	(23%)			
	Dane Eagle (R)	22,715	(22%)			
	Casey Askar (R)	20,774	(20%)			
	William Figlesthaler (R)	19,075	(18%)			
	Randy Henderson (R)	7,858	(8%)			

Byron Donalds narrowly won a competitive primary against deep-pocketed opponents. In a Republican-controlled district that has had frequent turnover, he is the fourth Republican to win this seat in the past five elections. Donalds succeeded Francis Rooney, an occasional critic of President Donald Trump. With Burgess Owens of Utah, Donalds was one of two African-American Republican in the freshman class. He described himself as a "Trump-supporting ... politically incorrect Black man."

Donalds was born in Brooklyn New York and raised by his mother in a single-parent household. After attending Florida A&M University, he received a bachelor's degree in finance and marketing from Florida State University. He worked in the finance and insurance businesses in Florida and became a financial adviser in Naples. In 2016, he was elected to the first of two terms in the state House, where he chaired the Insurance and Banking Subcommittee, where he highlighted his work to prevent elder abuse in financial transactions.

Before serving in Tallahassee, he made his first bid for Congress in 2012. After Rep. Connie Mack IV gave up the seat that year for an unsuccessful challenge to Democratic Sen. Bill Nelson, Donalds finished fourth, with 14 percent, in the GOP primary. Trey Radel, who won the seat, had served less than a year when he resigned following his arrest on cocaine possession charges. Curt Clawson won a special election to fill the seat in 2014, but stepped down two years later after serving a full term. Then, Rooney was elected to two terms.

In 2020, Donalds highlighted his conservative views on economic issues, which were a factor in the more than $2.5 million that the Club for Growth spent during the primary on his behalf, which paid for many negative attacks on his opponents. He also was endorsed by the National Rifle Association, plus Rep. Jim Jordan and other members of the House Freedom Caucus. Like many Florida Republicans, Donalds sought to embrace environmental protection—especially for protection of local water resources.

According to the Florida Politics website, Trump allies reportedly gave Donalds quiet encouragement in the belief that "a young, black conservative would be able to help the president with minority outreach in the November election."

Donalds faced three strong contenders—including another state lawmaker and two self-funding businessmen. Dane Eagle had served four terms in the state House, where he was the GOP leader; earlier, he was deputy chief of staff to Gov. Charlie Crist, who was then a Republican. Casey Askar owned many fast-food franchises across the nation. William Figlesthaler had been a physician with a successful urology practice. Askar and Figlesthaler were the biggest spenders in the contest, with $7.6 million and $2.6 million, respectively. Each self-financed more than half the costs of his campaign. Donalds and Eagle each spent about $1 million.

Of the more than 100,000 votes that were cast for nine candidates in the primary, the four leading contenders were separated by fewer than 4,500 votes. Eagle led in Lee County, which was his base and cast nearly three-fourths of the total vote. Donalds led in his base of Collier County. A key factor in the outcome was that Donalds was the runner-up in Lee, but Eagle finished fourth in Collier. Donalds won the contest by 777 votes over Eagle, with Askar running third.

In November, Donalds easily defeated Democrat Cindy Banyai, a professor of American government at Florida Gulf Coast University and a consultant on housing for homeless families. He got seats on the Budget, Oversight and Reform, and Small Business committees.

FL-19: Southern Gulf Coast   **Cook Partisan Voting Index: R+12**

Population		Race and Ethnicity		Income	
Total	833,013	White	85.00%	Median Income	$67,598
Land area (sq. miles)	750	Black	7.80%	District Income Rank	186
Pop/ sq mi	1,110.14	Latino	20.50%	Poverty Rate	10.10%
Born in State	23.60%	Asian	1.90%	With health insurance	88.50%
		Two or more races	1.50%	Cash public assistance	1.30%
Age Groups		Other	3.80%	Food stamp/SNAP	6.00%
Under 18	16.00%				
18-34	16.40%	**Education**		**Work**	
35-64	35.00%	H.S grad or less	38.10%	White Collar	34.10%
Over 64	32.60%	Some college	28.00%	Sales and Service	46.60%
		College Degree, 4 yr	20.70%	Blue Collar	19.30%
Military		Post grad	13.10%	Government	10.10%
Veteran/ Active Duty	8.50%				

2020 Pres. Vote	Trump	272,764	(60%)	Biden	180,722	(39%)		
2016 Pres. Vote	Trump	227,096	(59%)	Clinton	143,001	(37%)	Johnson	8,014	(2%)

Fort Myers, Naples: Florida's Gulf Coast is at the edge of the tropics, a physical environment once teeming with disease and inhospitable to advanced civilization, but now evolved into a model for retirement living. One of the earliest White settlements here was Fort Myers, built in 1850 as an

Army post to pursue the Seminole Indians; in 1858, the last of the Seminole were driven out. For a century after that, this corner of Florida was mostly deserted, save for some small resort communities developed around wide, white-sand beaches with gentle breakers. The inlets and broad estuaries are perfect for boating, and the wetlands are graced with exotic birds. Thomas Edison had his winter home in Fort Myers, and tourists were drawn to beaches on nearby Sanibel and Captiva islands. But the local economy could not support many permanent residents. At the beginning of World War II, there were only 68,000 people living on the Gulf Coast from Bradenton south to Naples.

The climate and environment, and the fact that Florida has no state income or inheritance tax, attracted waves of affluent postwar suburbanites. Developers such as Barron Collier, who financed the building of Tamiami Trail across the soggy Everglades, were determined to avoid the high-rise canyons that line the Atlantic from Palm Beach to Miami. Their alternative was to construct low-rise, city-style developments. Environmental concerns remain a focus. The $1 billion Caloosahatchee River reservoir project in the Everglades, scheduled for completion in 2023, will be vital to local development.

The Great Recession hit this area hard in 2008, with the nation's largest number of housing foreclosures. Since 2012, business conditions have improved notably. From 2010 to 2019, the population of Lee County increased by 25 percent. Fort Myers and Naples have competed in surveys as the nation's best retirement spot. In a cautionary note, the Washington-based Economic Policy Institute in 2018 ranked the area from Naples to Marco Island as second in the nation for income inequality.

The 19th Congressional District occupies the southern half of the Gulf Coast below Tampa Bay. More than 30 percent of the residents here are over 65. The 19th includes almost all of Lee County and about half of the population of Collier County, including Naples and Marco Island. Over three-quarters of the district's residents live in Fort Myers, Cape Coral and Bonita Springs, and on Sanibel and Captiva. Only 27 percent were registered Democrats, the lowest share of any Florida congressional district. But Donald Trump's 59 percent of the vote in 2016 was a smaller share than he received in five other Florida districts. In both 2016 and 2020, Trump got 59 percent in Lee County and 62 percent in Collier. Turnout in each county increased by more than 20 percent in 2020. Trump took the district, 60%-39%.

FL-20 - VACANT (V)

DC Office: 2365 RHOB 20515, 202-225-1313, Fax: 202-225-1171, alceehastings.house.gov
State Offices: Tamarac, 954-733-2800; West Palm Beach, 561-461-6767.

The April 6, 2021, death of Democratic Rep. Alcee Hastings triggered a special election to fill the vacancy, which Democrats were virtually certain to win. Hastings died at 84, of pancreatic cancer, which had limited his activity during the final two years of his 15-term career. He was a historic figure in Broward County, as a racial pioneer and federal judge. In the House, he was a skillful insider, as a long-time member of the Rules Committee, which is instrumental in scheduling legislation. His career, as his obituary in South Florida Sun Sentinel headlined, featured "triumph, calamity and comeback."

Hastings, first elected in 1992, shrugged off an assortment of scandals, including his impeachment for bribery and perjury and subsequent conviction in a Senate trial, when he was a federal judge in the 1980s. Following his initial heated campaign for the House, he never faced a serious reelection challenge. He became a friendly and often candid figure with Democratic colleagues in the House and with his constituents.

Hastings had a wide-ranging upbringing in the segregated America of post-World War II. He grew up in a Black suburb of Orlando and moved as a child to Jersey City and New York, where his parents worked as domestic servants for a rich Jewish family. He attended a Rosenwald school in Altamonte Springs, one of hundreds established for Southern Blacks by Sears executive Julius Rosenwald. He graduated from Fisk University in Nashville and from Florida A&M law school in Tallahassee. From those beginnings, he made a rapid ascent, practicing law in Fort Lauderdale and finishing fourth in the five-candidate Democratic primary when he ran for the U.S. Senate in 1970, at age 34. He became a state judge in Broward County in 1977 and was confirmed as a federal judge in 1979.

Then his career took a sharp turn downward. He was charged with conspiring with a friend to take a $150,000 bribe and give two convicted swindlers light sentences. A Miami jury acquitted Hastings in 1983, but the friend was convicted. The U.S. Court of Appeals for the 11th Circuit called for impeachment in 1987 and referred the case to Congress. Hastings was impeached by the House on a vote of 413-3 and convicted by the Senate, 69-26. In the House, Democratic Rep. John Conyers of Michigan, a senior member of the Congressional Black Caucus, made the case for impeachment. As a footnote, during a 1997 investigation into the Federal Bureau of Investigation crime lab, the Department of Justice found that an agent falsely testified against Hastings.

After his removal from the bench, Hastings in 1990 ran an abortive campaign for governor, then lost in a primary for secretary of state. When a new African-American majority district was created in 1992, he led in the primary 28%-27%. In the October runoff, he faced Palm Beach County legislator Lois Frankel, who blasted Hastings for his record. He responded, "The bitch is a racist." Hastings was helped by a ruling from federal Judge Stanley Sporkin that his removal from office was invalid because the full Senate did not hear the charges. He won the runoff, 58%-42%, with voting closely following racial lines. He won the general election 59%-31%. (Twenty years later, when Frankel ran successfully in an adjacent district, Hastings endorsed her and offered praise.)

In the House, Hastings' voting record and his rhetoric were proudly liberal. Pro-Israel groups were among his most active campaign contributors, and he was a strong supporter of the Jewish state. In 2004, he was elected president of the Organization for Security and Cooperation in the pan-European Parliamentary Assembly . In 2006, the House passed his resolution condemning Iran for hosting a conference on Holocaust denial. However, he drew the attention of ethics investigators in 2010 over whether he exceeded foreign travel stipends. He told The Wall Street Journal that he was generous in giving money to people he encountered and said: "You are all concerned about nickels and dimes, and I'm not. You know, in a taxicab in Kazakhstan, I don't have time to get a receipt. I don't speak Kazakh." The investigation was dropped in 2011. In 2018, the Open Secrets website listed his negative net worth of more than $2 million, including many still unpaid bills related to his impeachment expenses.

As the number-two Democrat on the Rules Committee, his influential post gave him a hand in setting the terms of House action. Like other senior House members, he occasionally was creative in his use of House rules. He paraphrased an expression of Thomas Edison's: "There ain't no rule around here; we're trying to accomplish something." Taking an original stand, Hastings called for a commission to consider expanding the size of the House beyond 435 members. He said there were too many constituents in each district for lawmakers to serve them adequately.

Hastings continued to draw -and survive -attention for issues apart from legislating. In 2014, the House Ethics Committee dismissed charges of sexual harassment against him that had been brought by a Republican congressional aide, but added that his behavior had been "less than professional." In 2017, Roll Call reported that the federal Treasury paid $220,000 to the aide as part of that settlement. In June 2020, the Ethics Committee dropped an investigation of his allegedly improper relationship after he revealed that he was married to the staffer.

Hastings occasionally opened the door to retirement, though he retained his brash style. At a 2018 political rally in south Florida, the Sun Sentinel reported, Hastings said that a "crisis" would be if President Donald Trump fell into the Potomac River, but a "catastrophe" would be "if anybody saves his ass." In January 2019, Hastings said that he was being treated for pancreatic cancer.

FL-20: Western Broward and Palm Beach

Cook Partisan Voting Index:

Population		Race and Ethnicity		Income	
Total	802,463	White	38.40%	Median Income	$49,223
Land area (sq. miles)	2,427	Black	52.90%	District Income Rank	392
Pop/ sq mi	330.58	Latino	26.80%	Poverty Rate	17.00%
Born in State	42.50%	Asian	2.50%	With health insurance	80.90%
		Two or more races	3.60%	Cash public assistance	2.40%
Age Groups		Other	2.50%	Food stamp/SNAP	19.50%
Under 18	24.10%				
18-34	23.30%	**Education**		**Work**	
35-64	38.40%	H.S grad or less	51.40%	White Collar	26.90%
Over 64	14.10%	Some college	27.80%	Sales and Service	50.20%
		College Degree, 4 yr	14.00%	Blue Collar	22.90%
Military		Post grad	6.90%	Government	11.60%
Veteran/ Active Duty	4.30%				

2020 Pres. Vote	Biden	254,644	(77%)	Trump	72,815	(22%)
2016 Pres. Vote	Clinton	231,595	(80%)	Trump	52,250	(18%)

Parts of Fort Lauderdale and West Palm Beach: In the morning shadow of the high-rise condominiums that line the Atlantic Ocean, beyond the quiet waters that separate the barrier islands from the mainland, and a few blocks off old U.S. 1, are the African-American neighborhoods of South Florida's Gold Coast. They are clusters of older stucco homes and commercial storefronts, ranging from upper-middle-class enclaves to rundown slums. These neighborhoods, largely populated by the working poor and with relatively few seniors, are bypassed by most tourists.

To the west is a land of swamps and drainage canals, with some farms and citrus groves. Some people live in migrant worker camps, while others live in small towns around Lake Okeechobee. The water quality in the lake has raised alarms on both the southeast and southwest coasts of Florida. Sugar has been a big industry throughout this part of Florida. In 2008, the South Florida Water Management District approved Gov. Charlie Crist's proposal to buy much of the land owned by U.S. Sugar Corp. around Lake Okeechobee for $1.35 billion, with most farming originally scheduled for phase-out within seven years. That would allow water to pass over land from the lake, through the Everglades, to the Gulf of Mexico.

Following delays caused by the Great Recession and continuing resistance from sugar farmers, environmentalists sought its revival. In 2018, the state approved a $1.6 billion plan for a reservoir that will eventually cover 16,000 acres and will reduce discharges and toxic algae blooms. By 2020, progress had become real. Farmers in western Palm Beach County reported a 68 percent reduction in their runoff of harmful nutrients to the Everglades. Meanwhile, sugar production was booming. In 2017, growers in Palm Beach County reported the largest crop in their history—12.2 million tons; the county has accounted for about three-fourths of statewide production. The highly subsidized sugar industry in Florida has employed more than 14,000 workers, and sugar cane has remained the most valuable field crop in the state. At the Port of Palm Beach, much of the cargo is sugar-related, and the commerce is largely with Caribbean islands.

The 20th Congressional District of Florida gathers many of South Florida's Black neighborhoods in a geographically contrived, but demographically coherent, constituency. The body of the district is in the Everglades. The bulk of the district's population resides in the two arms that extend east from the Everglades. These arms surround most of the 21st and 22nd districts. The top arm moves through northern Palm Beach County, past high-income Wellington and into West Palm Beach and Palm Beach Lakes. The lower arm of the district reaches into Broward County to take in African-American areas in Fort Lauderdale, Lauderhill, North Lauderdale and Pompano Beach. The population in Broward is more than twice that in Palm Beach.

Overall, the population is 53 percent Black and 27 percent Hispanic, and surpassed the Dade County-based 24th District for the largest Black population, though the 24th had a larger minority population, including Hispanics. Joe Biden led here, 77%-22%, which made the 20th his best in the state, ahead of the 24th.

Lois Frankel (D)

Elected 2012, 5th term, b. May 16, 1948; New York, NY; Boston University, B.A., 1970; Georgetown University Law Center, J.D., 1973; Jewish; Divorced; 1 child.

Elected Office: FL House, 1986-1992, 1994-2002; Mayor, West Palm Beach, 2003-2011.

Professional Career: Law clerk, Hon. Judge David Norman, 1973-1974; Assistant public defender, West Palm Beach, 1974-1978; Practicing lawyer, 1978-2003.

DC Office: 2305 RHOB 20515, 202-225-9890, Fax: 202-225-1224, frankel.house.gov

State Offices: Boca Raton, 561-998-9045.

Committees: *Appropriations*: Energy & Water Development & Related Agencies; Labor, Health & Human Services, Education & Related Agencies; State, Foreign Operations & Related Programs. *Veterans' Affairs*: Health.

Group Ratings

	ADA	ACLU	AFL-CIO	LCV	COC	HAFA	ACU	CFG	FRC
2020	**	80%	**	100%	-	0%	4%	**	-
2019	90%	C	100%	96%	61%	C	5%	12%	0%

Almanac Ratings 2019-2020

	Economy	Social	Foreign	Composite
Liberal	100%	54%	53%	69%
Conservative	0%	46%	47%	31%

Key Votes of the 116th Congress

1. U.S./Mex./Can. trade deal	Y	5. Russia sanctions	Y
2. First Coronavirus response	Y	6. Troops in Syria	Y
3. HEROES Act	Y	7. Veto arms sales to Saudis	Y
4. CASH Act	Y	8. Defense $$$, veto override	Y

9. Firearms background checks N/A
10. Spending at the border Y
11. Marijuana liberalized rules Y
12. Electoral College objections N

Election Results

Election	Name (Party)	Vote (%)		Cand. Spent	Ind. Exp. Support	Ind. Exp. Oppose
2020 General	Lois Frankel (D)	237,925	(59%)	$1,022,427	$54,219	$17,456
	Laura Loomer (R)	157,612	(39%)	$2,251,391	$758,786	$113
2020 Primary	Lois Frankel (D)	75,504	(86%)			
	Guido Weiss (D)	12,308	(14%)			

Prior winning percentages: 2016 (63%), 2014 (58%), 2012 (55%)

Democrat Lois Frankel, elected in 2012 after decades in public office, has shown her skills in making alliances, including occasional interest in reaching across the aisle. In the majority for the first time and with a seat on the Appropriations Committee, Frankel has focused on delivering funds to local projects, with which she was very familiar.

Frankel was born in New York City and raised in Great Neck on Long Island. Her father was in manufacturing and her mother was a homemaker. Frankel studied psychology at Boston University with the intent of becoming a psychiatrist, but her career plans changed when she became involved in the social movements of the late 1960s. "I was a student activist, and I was involved in antiwar protesting and the women's liberation movement," Frankel told National Journal. "There were so many movements ... it was all bubbling." She has joked that she "majored in protests."

Frankel got her law degree from Georgetown University and spent a year as a law clerk before moving to West Palm Beach. She became a public defender and advocate for numerous social causes. Frankel won an open state House seat in 1986 and quickly rose to become the first woman minority leader in Florida. She wrote the state's first AIDS law, which ensured confidentiality in testing. She ran unsuccessfully against Alcee Hastings for a new majority-minority House seat in 1992; with race as a defining factor, she lost the Democratic primary in a runoff, 58%-42%.

After term limits forced Frankel to leave the Florida House, she thought about challenging Gov. Jeb Bush in 2002, but withdrew before the primary. After she was elected mayor of West Palm Beach in 2003, she compiled what the South Florida Sun-Sentinel described as an "impressive" record, though she angered several labor unions when the city laid off workers.

In 2012, Frankel challenged Republican firebrand Allen West. When West announced that he would run in the more GOP-friendly neighboring Treasure Coast district, Frankel faced a primary with Broward County Commissioner Kristin Jacobs. Frankel had the backing of party leaders, including Hastings, and got a rare visit from House Democratic Leader Nancy Pelosi eight days before the primary. She coasted to a 61%-39% win. In the general, Frankel attacked Republican nominee Adam Hasner for his support of Wisconsin Rep. Paul Ryan's budget plan to introduce vouchers into the Medicare program, and for his stance against abortion rights. The Miami Herald endorsed Frankel, citing her "longer familiarity" with the district. Its Democratic lean helped her pull out a 55%-45% win. Each candidate spent $3.4 million.

Arriving in the House minority, Frankel made alliances with conservative Republicans. On the Transportation and Infrastructure Committee, she served in 2014 on the House-Senate conference committee that reached a final agreement on a water resources bill; it included additional dredging for expansion of Port Everglades plus water conservation and supply in the Everglades swamps. She joined another public works deal in 2016 on a water resources bill that delivered $2 billion for restoration of the Everglades.

Frankel joined two south Florida colleagues among the 25 House Democrats who voted to disapprove of the Obama administration's agreement with Iran on its nuclear program. "It legitimizes Iran's nuclear program after 15 years and gives Iran access to billions of dollars without a commitment to cease its terrorist activity," she said. But, once the deal had been implemented, she opposed the move by President Donald Trump to withdraw. She said that such a step would "destabilize the region … and undermine American credibility around the world."

In 2017-18, Frankel co-chaired the bipartisan Congressional Women's Caucus. To dramatize the revelations of sexual harassment and other misconduct by powerful men in both the public and private sectors, she led an initiative for Democratic women to wear black at Trump's State of the Union address in 2018. She chaired a new political action committee that aided Democratic women running that year. Following the party's takeover of the House majority, Frankel warned that factional infighting "would turn us into the Republicans," referring to recent GOP internal schisms.

On the Appropriations Committee in 2019, she resumed her interest in delivering funds to local water projects. She claimed credit for $200 million for restoration of the Everglades and $29 million for the Army Corps of Engineers to start to deepen Port Everglades to facilitate use by larger ships.

When the state Supreme Court redistricting order in 2015 threw Frankel into the same district with Democratic Rep. Ted Deutch, Frankel made the logical choice to run in the Palm Beach County-based 21st District. That left Deutch to run in the Broward-based 22nd District, which was a bit less Democratic but included his home in Boca Raton. Each has easily won reelection. In 2020, Frankel faced Republican Laura Loomer, a conservative activist who outspent Frankel by nearly 2-to-1. Loomer's anti-Muslim views had led to social media prohibiting her access. Trump encouraged her on Twitter, saying she had "a great chance against a Pelosi puppet." Frankel said she did not want to give a platform to Loomer because of her "well-known track record of promoting bigotry." She won 59%-39%.

In March 2020, Frankel endorsed Joe Biden following his victory in the pivotal South Carolina primary. She said he would "have Israel's back … without making Israel a political football," as she suggested had been the case with Trump.

FL-21: Southern Palm Beach County

Cook Partisan Voting Index: D+8

Population		Race and Ethnicity		Income	
Total	786,566	White	74.40%	Median Income	$65,394
Land area (sq. miles)	261	Black	16.30%	District Income Rank	207
Pop/ sq mi	3,014.01	Latino	25.40%	Poverty Rate	10.40%
Born in State	26.70%	Asian	2.70%	With health insurance	84.90%
		Two or more races	2.80%	Cash public assistance	1.80%
Age Groups		Other	3.80%	Food stamp/SNAP	8.00%
Under 18	17.60%				
18-34	18.20%	**Education**		**Work**	
35-64	37.30%	H.S grad or less	35.00%	White Collar	37.80%
Over 64	26.90%	Some college	27.90%	Sales and Service	42.60%
		College Degree, 4 yr	22.20%	Blue Collar	19.60%
Military		Post grad	14.90%	Government	9.60%
Veteran/ Active Duty	6.30%				

2020 Pres. Vote	Biden	239,322	(58%)	Trump	169,556	(41%)
2016 Pres. Vote	Clinton	206,239	(58%)	Trump	137,490	(39%)

Palm Beach, Lake Worth: When the first millionaires came to Palm Beach in the 1920s to winter in their new mansions, there was virtually nothing man-made between Palm Beach and Miami. In 1920, Dade, Broward and Palm Beach counties boasted a mere 66,000 residents. By 1950, the combined population of the three counties had jumped to almost 700,000, and the beachfront areas had largely been incorporated and developed. But the interior regions of the counties, near where Florida's turnpike would soon be laid out, remained marshy, sparsely inhabited and ripe for development. As the coastal areas were filling up, the inland swamps were being drained, abetted by a sequence of canals and levees built by the state in response to flooding from a series of hurricanes in 1947.

More than 3.4 million people inhabited Broward and Palm Beach counties in 2019, an increase from 3.1 million in 2010. Palm Beach has 1.5 million. The Palm Beach area remains, as it has been since the 1920s, the precinct of the very rich. The top Rolls Royce dealer in the world is in Palm Beach. Wellington is an international site for equestrian events, including polo. Waterfront development has made downtown West Palm Beach a year-round urban center. Across the Intra-Coastal Waterway is Palm Beach, which includes President Donald Trump's Mar-a-Lago club hotel. As the winter White House for four years, the town received a tourism boost, though there were the inevitable inconveniences, especially in a densely populated area. Although revenue at Mar-a-Lago decreased during his presidency, the value of the property increased from $150 million to more than $160 million, according to Forbes magazine. Trump's decision in 2019 to shift his voting residence to Mar-a-Lago caused local controversy, as critics claimed that he agreed in purchasing the property in the early 1990s that it was a private club, which meant he could not claim a permanent residence.

The 21st District is entirely in Palm Beach County. Palm Beach is separate from the mainland and accessible on two bridges or by continuing south on South Ocean Boulevard. Farther on, Lake Worth, Boynton Beach and Delray Beach include narrow oceanfront locales; each of these cities sprawl several miles to the west. Delray Beach, the site in 1956 of a civil rights showdown over access to the beaches, now hosts international tennis events and has a large Haitian community. The district winds through a series of largely unincorporated residential communities to the west. Subdivisions extend far beyond the Florida Turnpike.

With the new lines, President Barack Obama in 2012 would have won, 60%-39%. Hillary Clinton took the district in 2016, 58%-39%. Joe Biden won, 58%-41%. That deduction signaled a problem for Democrats because they increasingly need to roll up their vote in south Florida to balance political challenges elsewhere in the state. With the growing disaster that Florida Democrats faced in 2020, Palm Beach County was a symptom. Hillary Clinton's 59 percent dropped to 58 percent for Joe Biden. With Trump's increased percentage, the more consequential number was the added 63,000 votes he won in the county.

Ted Deutch (D)

Elected 2010, 6th full term, b. May 07, 1966; Bethlehem, PA; University of MI, B.A., 1988; University of MI Law School, J.D., 1990; Jewish; Married (Jill Deutch); 3 children (twins).

Elected Office: FL Senate, 2006-2010.

Professional Career: Practicing attorney, 1991-2010.

DC Office: 2447 RHOB 20515, 202-225-3001, Fax: 202-225-5974, teddeutch.house.gov

State Offices: Boca Raton, 561-470-5440; Coral Springs, 954-255-8336; Margate, 954-972-6454.

Committees: *Ethics (Chmn). Foreign Affairs*: Europe, Energy, the Environment & Cyber; Middle East, North Africa & Global Counterterrorism (Chmn); West Hem, Civ Sec, Migration, & Intern'l Econ Policy. *Judiciary*: Antitrust, Commercial & Administrative Law; Courts, Intellectual Property & Internet.

Group Ratings

	ADA	ACLU	AFL-CIO	LCV	COC	HAFA	ACU	CFG	FRC
2020	**	80%	**	100%	-	0%	3%	**	-
2019	95%	C	100%	97%	67%	C	3%	13%	0%

Almanac Ratings 2019-2020

	Economy	Social	Foreign	Composite
Liberal	100%	100%	80%	94%
Conservative	0%	0%	20%	6%

Key Votes of the 116th Congress

1. U.S./Mex./Can. trade deal	Y	5. Russia sanctions	Y	9. Firearms background checks Y
2. First Coronavirus response	Y	6. Troops in Syria	Y	10. Spending at the border	Y
3. HEROES Act	Y	7. Veto arms sales to Saudis	Y	11. Marijuana liberalized rules	Y
4. CASH Act	Y	8. Defense $$$, veto override	Y	12. Electoral College objections N

Election Results

Election	Name (Party)	Vote (%)		Cand. Spent	Ind. Exp. Support	Ind. Exp. Oppose
2020 General	Ted Deutch (D)	235,764	(59%)	$1,294,760	$14,720	
	Jim Pruden (R)	166,553	(41%)	$346,986		$113

Prior winning percentages: 2018 (62%), 2016 (59%), 2014 (100%), 2012 (78%), 2010 (63%), 2010 special (62%)

Democrat Ted Deutch, who won a special election in 2010, has become an active legislator, with a knack for making bipartisan deals. On the Foreign Affairs Committee, as chairman of the subcommittee dealing with the Middle East, he remained largely supportive of Trump administration policy in that region. Deutch kept a low profile as chairman of the House Ethics Committee. In the district that was the site in 2018 of the mass shooting at the high school in Parkland, he became outspoken on behalf of gun-control measures.

Deutch has working-class roots in Bethlehem Pennsylvania, where his father ran a small painter-contracting company and his mother kept the books. His parents did not go to college and were determined that their five children would. He excelled in high school and was class president for four years. During that period, heart disease forced his father into early retirement and he spent a lot of time watching CNN. Deutch said that sitting next to his dad discussing what was unfolding on the news channel fueled his budding interest in current events. At the University of Michigan, Deutch got his bachelor's in political science and a law degree.

After law school, Deutch specialized in real estate law. That provided his initial entry to Washington, at a firm hired to sell off government assets from the savings and loan crisis. He moved to Boca Raton, where Ted's older brother, also a lawyer, hired him to handle his law firm's real estate business. Deutch got active in Florida politics. He worked on issues and raised money for Bill Clinton's two presidential campaigns. He also lobbied for pro-Israel causes. In 2006, he was elected to the Florida Senate. During three years in Tallahassee, he authored two signature measures: a bill putting a surcharge on tobacco products to help pay for smoking prevention programs and cancer research, and a bill barring the state from investing pension funds in any enterprise that aided Iran's effort to attain nuclear weapons or that abetted genocide in the Darfur region of Sudan.

When Democratic Rep. Robert Wexler resigned to head a Middle East think tank, Deutch announced for the seat. His liberal, pro-Israel politics appealed to the area's many Jewish retirees. Deutch faced minimal opposition in the Democratic primary, which was tantamount to election. In the general election, Republican Ed Lynch tried to make the election a referendum on the Obama administration and its health care bill. Deutch maintained that those changes would improve access to health care for people without insurance and for seniors. He won 62%-35%.

Deutch displayed a savvy legislative instinct, even when Republicans had House control. In 2017, he organized with Republican Rep. Carlos Curbelo of Florida the bipartisan Climate Solutions Caucus; Deutch said that the caucus was, in part, a reaction to the decision by President Donald Trump to withdraw the United States from the Paris climate agreement. Later, Deutch signed onto a bipartisan proposal to create a carbon tax. The legislation enacted in 2018 to respond to the opioid crisis included provisions cosponsored by Deutch to assist local communities and to crack down on individuals who receive kickbacks for improper patient referrals. He has drawn attention for campaign-finance reform proposals. His Democracy for All Amendment would overturn Supreme Court rulings that reduced restrictions on money in politics.

Deutch has been persistent on foreign policy conflicts. He got a provision in the 2012 Iran sanctions law that required companies to disclose to the Securities and Exchange Commission their business dealings with Iran. As ranking Democrat on the Middle East and North Africa Subcommittee, he became a go-to guy for his many Jewish constituents and the broader pro-Israel lobby in Washington. In 2014, he helped to write the Iran Threat Reduction Act, which imposed additional transparency and human rights requirements on Iran. He was outspoken after Secretary of State John Kerry concluded the agreement because, Deutch said, it failed to address "too many issues I have long raised as essential to any nuclear deal with Iran." In 2018, Congress enacted a bill he filed with Republican Rep. Ileana Ros-Lehtinen that codified a memorandum of understanding for $38 billion over 10 years in military assistance to Israel.

When Democrats won the House majority in 2018, Deutch became chairman of the Middle East Subcommittee. In August 2020, he was among the few congressional Democrats who praised Trump for facilitating the "historic announcement" of a peace agreement between Israel and the United Arab Emirates, which Deutch called an "incredibly significant development for regional stability." He attended the signing of the agreement at the White House the following month.

Also in 2019, Deutch became chairman of the House Ethics Committee. As the senior Democrat on that panel the two previous years, he worked closely with ranking Republican Rep. Kenny Marchant of Texas. They worked together on most issues before the committee. In four cases in 2019-20 involving allegations of criminal activity, Republicans Chris Collins and Duncan Hunter quit the House after they made guilty pleas in court, Republican Steve Watkins was defeated for reelection and Democrat Katie Hill resigned.

Following the 2018 shootings at Marjory Stoneman Douglas High School in his district, Deutch became an outspoken advocate for action on gun control. Following the 2018 election, he pushed for House action on two measures: universal background checks and a ban of "bump stocks," a firearm attachment that allows a gun to fire at a near-automatic rate, neither of which were relevant to the Parkland shooting. In April 2019, the House passed a bill to extend background checks for most firearm purchases. The Senate did not act on the measure. Deutch endorsed Michael Bloomberg for president in 2020, citing the former New York mayor's leadership on behalf of gun control.

Deutch has not faced a serious major-party challenge since he was first elected.

FL-22: Northern Broward, Boca Raton

Cook Partisan Voting Index: D+6

Population		Race and Ethnicity		Income	
Total	760,953	White	76.80%	Median Income	$69,452
Land area (sq. miles)	173	Black	15.10%	District Income Rank	171
Pop/ sq mi	4,401.63	Latino	23.20%	Poverty Rate	11.20%
Born in State	28.10%	Asian	3.50%	With health insurance	86.50%
		Two or more races	2.50%	Cash public assistance	1.60%
Age Groups		Other	2.10%	Food stamp/SNAP	6.90%
Under 18	17.50%				
18-34	19.40%	**Education**		**Work**	
35-64	40.60%	H.S grad or less	30.80%	White Collar	40.70%
Over 64	22.40%	Some college	27.60%	Sales and Service	42.80%
		College Degree, 4 yr	25.40%	Blue Collar	16.50%
Military		Post grad	16.20%	Government	8.80%
Veteran/ Active Duty	5.30%				

2020 Pres. Vote	Biden	236,393	(57%)	Trump	174,889	(42%)
2016 Pres. Vote	Clinton	202,357	(56%)	Trump	146,229	(41%)

Fort Lauderdale: The Marjory Stoneman Douglas High School in Parkland was added to the list of sites across the nation that have dealt with the excruciating experience of a mass shooting, with the accompanying horror and heartbreaking scenes. In February 2018, a teenage gunman who had attended the school, killed 17 persons with a semi-automatic rifle and was arrested nearby after a brief chase. Some in the community—students, family, teachers and local officials—responded with demands for gun control and organized the March for Our Lives, a rally in Washington the following month that attracted several hundred thousand participants. Their demands for a political movement shaped "a new kind of debate about gun violence," The Atlantic wrote. (Stoneman Douglas was a conservationist who helped preserve the Everglades.)

The towns and cities that now populate the western portions of Broward County, including Parkland, were generally incorporated during the late 1950s and early 1960s. This helped fuel yet another boom in Florida real estate, as people flocked to the new developments. It wasn't just retirees and developers who took an interest in the region. Westinghouse Electric Corp. initially invested in Coral Springs in the 1960s as a sort of "urban laboratory" for products such as central air conditioning, motion detecting lights, security systems and fully electric kitchens.

Downtown Fort Lauderdale, separated from the beach by miles of canals, is the site of the Museum of Art Fort Lauderdale, the Broward Center for the Performing Arts and the International Swimming Hall of Fame. Along with neighboring Wilton Manors, it became the home of choice for many gay people. In 2016, the Census Bureau reported that Fort Lauderdale had the highest percentage of same-sex couple households of any mid-sized or large city in the nation; Wilton Manors in November 2018 became the second locality in the nation—after Palm Springs, California—to elect an all-LGBTQ local government. In 2016, Port Everglades was the third-busiest port in the world for the number of passengers, behind Miami and Port Canaveral. In 2020, when the coronavirus shut down virtually the entire cruise industry, Port Everglades, which had grown to about 4,000 annual dockings, ambitiously unveiled plans for deeper and wider channels and a new logistics center, with a total cost of $1.6 billion. A less visible—or discussed—part of the cargo moving through Port Everglades was illegal.

The 22nd Congressional District includes the southeast corner of Palm Beach, chiefly Boca Raton, where the azure fountains and red-tiled roofs of the Boca Raton Resort & Club, which was opened in 1926, bespeak a vision of a holiday Florida. After moving through coastal parts of Pompano Beach and Fort Lauderdale, the district includes parts of upscale Plantation but loops around African-American precincts, placed in the 20th District. What was a Republican enclave until the 1990s has become a reliably Democratic district. Joe Biden took the new 22nd, 57%-42%, nearly the same as his vote in the 21st to the north.

Debbie Wasserman Schultz (D)

Elected 2004, 9th term, b. Sep 27, 1966; Forest Hills (Queens), NY; University of FL, B.A., 1988; University of FL, M.A., 1990; Jewish; Married (Steve Schultz); 3 children.

Elected Office: FL House, 1992-2000, Minority Leader pro tem., 1999-2000; FL Senate, 2000-2004.

Professional Career: Legislative aide, 1989-1992.

DC Office: 1114 LHOB 20515, 202-225-7931, Fax: 202-226-2052, wassermanschultz.house.gov

State Offices: Aventura, 305-936-5724; Sunrise, 954-845-1179.

Committees: *Appropriations*: Agriculture, Rural Development, FDA & Related Agencies; Energy & Water Development & Related Agencies; Military Construction, Veterans Affairs & Related Agencies (Chmn). *Oversight & Reform*: National Security; Subcommittee on Civil Rights & Civil Liberties.

Group Ratings

	ADA	ACLU	AFL-CIO	LCV	COC	HAFA	ACU	CFG	FRC
2020	**	76%	**	100%	-	0%	2%	**	-
2019	85%	C	100%	93%	57%	C	2%	12%	5%

Almanac Ratings 2019-2020

	Economy	Social	Foreign	Composite
Liberal	59%	66%	80%	69%
Conservative	41%	34%	20%	31%

Key Votes of the 116th Congress

1. U.S./Mex./Can. trade deal Y	5. Russia sanctions Y	9. Firearms background checks Y
2. First Coronavirus response Y	6. Troops in Syria Y	10. Spending at the border Y
3. HEROES Act Y	7. Veto arms sales to Saudis Y	11. Marijuana liberalized rules Y
4. CASH Act Y	8. Defense $$$, veto override Y	12. Electoral College objections N

Election Results

Election	Name (Party)	Vote (%)		Cand. Spent	Ind. Exp. Support	Ind. Exp. Oppose
2020 General	Debbie Wasserman Schultz (D)...........	221,239	(58%)	$1,641,069	$12,797	
	Carla Spalding (R).............................	158,874	(42%)	$917,022		$113
2020 Primary	Debbie Wasserman Schultz (D)...........	55,729	(72%)			
	Jen Perelman (D)..................................	21,631	(28%)			

Prior winning percentages: 2018 (59%), 2016 (57%), 2014 (63%), 2012 (63%), 2010 (60%), 2008 (77%), 2006 (100%), 2004 (70%)

Debbie Wasserman Schultz, a hard-charging Democrat elected in 2004, has suffered two notable setbacks, though she remains a significant force in the House and likely will have plenty of additional opportunities for influence. In 2016, after she was forced out as chair of the Democratic National Committee as the party convention convened in Philadelphia in the cross-fire between Hillary Clinton and Bernie Sanders. That led Wasserman Schultz in 2020 to challenge Rep. Rosa DeLauro—and the seniority system—to chair the Appropriations Committee. She was defeated soundly but retained her influence as an Appropriations subcommittee "cardinal."

Like many of her constituents, Wasserman Schultz was born in Queens. She grew up on Long Island, where she ran for student council every year and always lost. She got bachelor's and master's degrees from the University of Florida. State Rep. Peter Deutsch, a Democrat and former New Yorker from Broward County, gave her a summer job and then appointed her as his legislative aide. In 1992, he ran for the House and urged Wasserman Schultz to run for his seat in the legislature. She did, knocking on doors for six months and finishing far ahead of four opponents in the Democratic primary.

At age 26, she became the youngest woman elected to the state House. She served eight years there, including two as minority leader, followed by four in the state Senate. She called herself "a pragmatic liberal," and she sponsored a controversial law to require an equal number of men and women on state boards and a bill that failed to pass that would have required dry cleaners and some other businesses to charge the same prices for women as for men.

When Deutsch unsuccessfully ran in 2004 for the Democratic nomination for an open Senate seat, Wasserman Schultz again moved to replace him. She collected more than $1 million for what turned out to be a non-contest in the decisive Democratic primary because no one else filed to run. Against a Republican who attacked the "homosexual agenda" in the public schools, she won 70%-30%. For the next decade, she did not face a serious challenge, allowing her to channel campaign contributions to her colleagues from a wide spectrum of Democratic interests.

In the House, Wasserman Schultz has had a mostly liberal voting record, although she has been more centrist on foreign policy. She has been one of the Florida delegation's most ardent opponents of offshore oil drilling, declaring after the 2010 BP oil spill in the Gulf of Mexico that "our country needs to run on something other than oil."

Her move into the leadership began in 2006 when she was appointed co-chairwoman of the Democratic Congressional Campaign Committee's "Red to Blue" program. Working closely with DCCC Chairman Rahm Emanuel, she became a party spokeswoman and a mentor to Democratic recruits. When Democrats won House control that year, Majority Whip James Clyburn tapped her as a chief deputy whip. She snagged a seat on the Appropriations Committee and chaired the Legislative Branch Subcommittee. She took charge of the Capitol Visitors Center project, which was plagued by cost overruns, and extracted commitments on costs and completion dates.

Her success seemed all the more impressive when she announced in 2009 that for much of the previous year she had been battling breast cancer. Although her tumor was in the early stages, which would typically require surgery and radiation, she said that she elected to have a double mastectomy after learning that as an Ashkenazi Jew, she had a greater predisposition to recurrence. The mother of three school-aged children, Wasserman Schultz was diagnosed just after turning 40. "I didn't want it to define me," she told The New York Times of her illness.

The foreign policy pursuits of President Barack Obama forced Wasserman Schultz to navigate tricky terrain. As a longtime critic of the Cuban regime, she offered only limited and murky support when the president in December 2014 announced breakthrough initiatives to Cuba. When many House Democrats, including some Jewish members, protested the March 2015 speech to Congress by Israeli Prime Minister Benjamin Netanyahu, she carefully said, "Israel is an issue that should not be made partisan." In what became for many a test of party loyalty in September 2015, her decision to support Obama's nuclear deal with Iran led to strong objections from her many Jewish constituents and party contributors.

In 2011, Wasserman Schultz defeated former Ohio Gov. Ted Strickland to take the helm of the DNC, with Vice President Joe Biden citing "her tenacity, her strength, her fighting spirit, and her ability to overcome adversity." Vowing that the party would be "laser-focused on the economy" as it sought to reelect Obama, she was a ferocious Republican critic. She blasted House Budget Committee Chairman Paul Ryan's budget blueprint because it would "allow insurance companies to deny you coverage and drop you for pre-existing conditions"—a claim that the fact-checking website PolitiFact judged to be false.

Wasserman Schultz was frequently deployed in 2012 as a campaign surrogate for Obama, attending hundreds of events across the nation. But she developed a strained relationship with Obama campaign officials, who privately accused her of coming across as too partisan on television. Election Night's results served as her vindication: Not only did Obama win with substantial support from women and Jewish voters, two constituencies that Wasserman Schultz cultivated, he also captured Florida, a state where Republican Mitt Romney enjoyed a sizable lead in pre-election polls.

The most severe test of her mettle came during the 2016 Democratic presidential campaign showdown between Clinton and Sanders. She consistently denied criticisms that her actions as DNC chair had favored Clinton, whom Wasserman Schultz had strongly backed in the 2008 campaign. "I will be frank with you—if I was trying to rig the outcome of the primary, trust me, I could have," she told VICE News following the election. "There are so many things that we—not I—we could have done to enhance the campaign of one candidate over another." But amid the tensions at the July convention in Philadelphia, the demands by combative Sanders allies for a scalp—what she called a scapegoat for their own mistakes—left her and the Clinton forces little option if they wanted to have a harmonious week.

Later, in a book about the Democratic debacle in 2016, Donna Brazile, who became interim DNC chair prior to the election, wrote that "Debbie was not a good manager" and that she—with Obama and Clinton—had left the party deeply in debt. Wasserman Schultz also faced controversial, though inconclusive, inquiries from Justice Department and congressional investigators seeking details of DNC opposition research on Donald Trump plus alleged Russian hacking of DNC computers.

Following the convention, Wasserman Schultz turned her attention to a vigorous primary challenge from local law professor Tim Canova. As a Sanders backer, he had been criticizing her for months as insufficiently progressive and too responsive to special interests. Sanders endorsed Canova and signed a fundraising letter on his behalf, though he failed to make an expected personal appearance. Wasserman Schultz had several factors going her way: Canova's political inexperience; her lengthy and close relationship with constituents; persistence and energy; and support from many party leaders, including Obama and Clinton. Each candidate spent roughly $4 million. She won the primary, 57%-43%.

In the general election that was routine, Wasserman Schultz won, 57%-40%, against Republican Joseph Kaufman, a writer who had made two earlier challenges. In 2018, she faced both opponents again, in contests with a small fraction of the spending. This time, Canova ran as an independent in November and got 5 percent of vote. She defeated Kaufman, 58%-36%. Her victories in 2020 were even more routine. Her political career might have had one big missed opportunity. In March 2015, she ruled out a race for Marco Rubio's open Senate seat, in a contest that took unexpected twists before Rubio made a late return from his presidential bid and defeated a relatively weak Democratic challenger.

Declining the Senate option seemed to confirm that her political future was in the House. On the Appropriations Committee, she became top Democrat on the financial services subcommittee and then on the panel in charge of military construction and veterans affairs. When Democrats regained House control, she regained her post as an Appropriations "cardinal," this time with the military construction panel.

When Appropriations Chairwoman Nita Lowey in October 2019 announced her retirement, Wasserman Schultz launched an intensive yearlong campaign for the top spot. Her two opponents were Marcy Kaptur of Ohio and DeLauro, the two most senior Democrats on the committee. Little attention was given to the fact that all three were women—a striking statement of changing congressional demographics. As expected, Kaptur ran third on the first ballot and set up the final match-up.

Wasserman Schultz promised more dramatic change in Appropriations backroom deal-making, including greater transparency. In challenging the seniority system and emphasizing the need to address racial injustice, she won the support of some members of the Congressional Black Caucus, who traditionally have backed seniority. But DeLauro—a respected lawmaker and fierce defender of liberal programs, with close ties to Speaker Nancy Pelosi and the experience of having narrowly lost two leadership bids—had few weaknesses. And Wasserman's greater national experience at the DNC proved a mixed blessing, at best, especially after Biden's election added to Democrats' imperative for DeLauro's budget expertise and reduced the need for House Democrats to serve as party spokesmen. Likewise, Wasserman Schultz's Florida connection had less cachet after Biden was defeated in the state and Democrats lost two House seats.

Her defeat, reportedly on a 148-79 vote, left DeLauro in firm control of Appropriations. With eight Democrats senior to Wasserman Schultz on the panel, one factor that is likely to benefit her is that all but two of them were at least age 73 when DeLauro took the reins. The exceptions were Betty McCollum of Minnesota, 66, and Tim Ryan of Ohio, 47, though Ryan faced an uncertain future in home-state politics.

At age 54, Wasserman Schultz resumed her subcommittee work at Appropriations and could play the long game in a House where change has moved more quickly than in the past.

FL-23: Southern Broward, Coastal Dade   **Cook Partisan Voting Index: D+9**

Population		Race and Ethnicity		Income	
Total	762,858	White	72.00%	Median Income	$69,198
Land area (sq. miles)	169	Black	15.20%	District Income Rank	172
Pop/ sq mi	4,511.28	Latino	40.10%	Poverty Rate	9.70%
Born in State	33.50%	Asian	4.90%	With health insurance	88.50%
		Two or more races	3.50%	Cash public assistance	1.40%
Age Groups		Other	4.30%	Food stamp/SNAP	8.70%
Under 18	21.20%				
18-34	20.20%	**Education**		**Work**	
35-64	41.60%	H.S grad or less	30.80%	White Collar	42.80%
Over 64	17.00%	Some college	28.50%	Sales and Service	42.70%
		College Degree, 4 yr	25.10%	Blue Collar	14.40%
Military		Post grad	15.50%	Government	10.90%
Veteran/ Active Duty	4.20%				

2020 Pres. Vote	Biden	227,940	(58%)	Trump	161,029	(41%)
2016 Pres. Vote	Clinton	209,078	(62%)	Trump	120,967	(36%)

Hollywood: When Broward County was created in 1915, its name was to be "Everglades County," reflecting its largely agricultural character, save for a few fledgling beachfront communities like Fort Lauderdale. Development proceeded slowly. Instead, it was named for Napoleon Bonaparte Broward, a roguish riverboat captain who served as Florida governor early in the 20th century. Joseph Wesley Young dreamed of building a resort community by the sea and founded Hollywood in 1925. But a hurricane the following year devastated the infant town, people fled in droves, and Young's holdings were eventually auctioned off in 1930. But this prime beachfront real estate could not remain undeveloped for long, and by 1980, the population was exploding. Over time, these new residents increasingly came from the Northeast, and brought those Democratic politics. They were instrumental in transforming the state's Democratic Party from a rural, Southern party run by the so-called "Pork Chop Gang" of conservative senators into one more closely resembling its Northern counterparts, and eventually helped turn Florida into a swing state.

Today, Broward County is in the midst of another transformation. It is now a minority-majority county, with the non-Hispanic White share of the 2 million population dropping to 35 percent in 2019. Blacks and Latinos are 30 and 31 percent, respectively; each is a big increase since 2000. The most common countries of origin for these newcomers are Haiti, Jamaica and Colombia; one in three residents is foreign-born, but many of them are undocumented. Of all counties in the United States with a population of at least 1 million, only Riverside California has a smaller share of non-Hispanic White population. The Fort Lauderdale Airport, once a sleepy facility, is the third-busiest in Florida and is competing with Miami in its passenger load. Following $3 billion in improvements—including new gates and parking, and a runway over Federal Highway, Lauderdale airport officials worked on new plans to improve congestion at its four terminals.

The 23rd District of Florida includes much of southern Broward County. The district is anchored by coastal Hollywood, where huge high-rises house large numbers of retirees from the Northeast and new resorts attract vacationers. From there, the district moves inland, with a slight northwestern trajectory. It includes Davie, a former ranching town where the businesses lining downtown all have an "Old Western" motif. The western end of the district is new-growth suburbs, such as Southwest Ranches and Weston, which has many lakes and inlets and a large concentration of Venezuelan Americans. About 90 percent of the district's residents live in Broward, with the remainder occupying a string of barrier islands in northern Miami-Dade County, just north of Miami Beach. Located here are some of the upscale high-rises along Collins Avenue facing the ocean and Latino neighborhoods north of 88th Street.

While Broward gave Richard Nixon 72 percent of the vote in 1972, it was the second-strongest county in the state (behind only tiny Gadsden, near Tallahassee) for both Hillary Clinton and Joe Biden. Partly because of the growing Latino population, the vote in Broward dropped from 67 for Clinton to 65 percent for Biden. In Broward, President Donald Trump raised his vote by three percentage points and 72,000 votes from 2016 to 2020. The overall increase of 120,000 votes (15 per cent) grew the turnout in 2020 to above 75 percent—a record for the county. After Clinton won the district in 2016, 62%-36%, Biden's margin fell to 58%-41%.

Frederica Wilson (D)

Elected 2010, 6th term, b. Nov 05, 1942; Miami, FL; Fisk University, B.S., 1963; University of Miami, M.Ed., 1972; Episcopalian; Widow; 3 children; 5 grandchildren.

Elected Office: FL House, 1998-2002; FL Senate, 2002-2010.

Professional Career: Teacher; principal; Assistant principal.

DC Office: 2445 RHOB 20515, 202-225-4506, Fax: 202-226-0777, wilson.house.gov

State Offices: Hollywood, 954-921-3682; Miami Gardens, 305-690-5905; West Park, 954-989-2688.

Committees: *Education & Labor*: Early Childhood, Elementary & Secondary Education; Higher Education & Workforce Investment (Chmn). *Transportation & Infrastructure*: Highways & Transit; Water Resources & Environment.

Group Ratings

	ADA	ACLU	AFL-CIO	LCV	COC	HAFA	ACU	CFG	FRC
2020	**	80%	**	95%	-	0%	3%	**	-
2019	95%	C	100%	93%	51%	C	3%	13%	0%

Almanac Ratings 2019-2020

	Economy	Social	Foreign	Composite
Liberal	59%	61%	80%	67%
Conservative	41%	39%	20%	33%

Key Votes of the 116th Congress

1. U.S./Mex./Can. trade deal	Y	5. Russia sanctions	N/A
2. First Coronavirus response	Y	6. Troops in Syria	Y
3. HEROES Act	N/A	7. Veto arms sales to Saudis	Y
4. CASH Act	Y	8. Defense $$$, veto override	Y

9. Firearms background checks Y
10. Spending at the border N/A
11. Marijuana liberalized rules Y
12. Electoral College objections N

Election Results

Election	Name (Party)	Vote (%)		Cand. Spent	Ind. Exp. Support	Ind. Exp. Oppose
2020 General	Frederica Wilson (D)	218,825	(76%)	$319,411	$34,918	
	Lavern Spicer (R)	59,084	(20%)	$32,800		$113
	Christine Olivo (I)	11,703	(4%)	$31,011		
2020 Primary	Frederica Wilson (D)	68,505	(85%)			
	Sakinah Lehtola (D)	6,267	(8%)			
	Ricardo de La Fuente (D)	6,134	(8%)			

Prior winning percentages: 2016 (100%), 2014 (86%), 2012 (86%), 2010 (86%)

Democrat Frederica Wilson, elected in 2010, has compiled a solidly liberal voting record while speaking out on behalf of her low-income constituents, particularly Haitian Americans. She calls herself "a voice for the voiceless" and engaged in unusually harsh exchanges with President Donald Trump and his top officials.

Wilson's politics were inspired by her father, Thirlee Smith, a native of Timpson Texas, a town that in his day had an active chapter of the Ku Klux Klan. "He would sit me on his knee and tell me stories of what happened to him in Texas and how people were lynched," she recalled. In Miami, Smith ran a restaurant and a billiard hall, and became active in the civil rights movement, registering voters and pushing for sanitation workers' rights. The couple's three children were sensitized to acts of injustice at a young age. Once, in high school, Wilson spied a new kid in school being teased for wearing torn clothes. Wilson, who weighed about 70 pounds at the time, stepped into the circle of bullies and ordered them to leave the boy alone. She pursued a career in education and eventually politics.

Wilson graduated from Fisk University with a bachelor's degree in elementary education, and got her master's from the University of Miami. She worked as a teacher, then became an assistant educational coordinator for a Head Start program and later a principal. She served on the Miami-Dade County School Board. In 1984, she joined a campaign to lobby Congress to remove Haitian refugees from a local detention center. The Haitian women in particular, she said, "had no privacy at all, from guards, from visitors, from INS, from no one. When they would take a shower, they had no curtains. They were treating them like animals." The women were eventually released and allowed to remain in Miami.

Wilson was elected to the Florida House in 1998. After four years, she won a seat in the state Senate. In each chamber, she served as minority whip. In 2004, she led a sometimes bitter fight against Gov. Jeb Bush to scale back the use of standardized testing in schools, which she said had a negative impact on children. Wilson was known in the legislature for her trademark headgear of brightly colored, often rhinestone-studded hats, which were inspired by her grandmother, who wore similar hats as a cultural tradition in her native Bahamas. In July 2019, she told the Miami Herald, she decided to become more selective about wearing her hats after she had received a threatening phone message, "Everywhere you go, we're going to tell people to look for the hats."

When Democrat Kendrick Meek ran unsuccessfully for the Senate, Wilson ran for his House seat. In the nine-candidate Democratic primary, she won with 35 percent of the vote, helped by four candidates splitting Haitian voter support. In the fall, she won with 86 percent against an independent.

In the House, Wilson delivered a series of impassioned speeches following the death of black teenager Trayvon Martin, who in 2012 was shot in Sanford Florida by neighborhood watch volunteer George Zimmerman. Wilson said she was "tired of burying young black boys." Wilson founded the 5000 Role Models of Excellence Project, a local version of My Brother's Keeper, to assist at-risk young males. "There is this tension that never goes away between the police and especially black boys," she said.

In 2014, the Obama administration adopted Wilson's proposal for a family reunification program for Haitian immigrants. The action was part of the U.S. response to a devastating earthquake in Haiti in 2010 that left 1.5 million homeless. In May 2020, she filed a bill to suspend deportations to Haiti during the coronavirus pandemic.

After several violent hazing incidents at colleges, Wilson proposed denying federal aid to students who are punished by colleges or convicted for hazing. In 2019, she chaired the Education and Labor Subcommittee on Health, Employment, Labor and Pensions. Her objective, she said, was to "restore fairness to our economy." At a committee hearing that October, she told Education Secretary Betsy DeVos, "You are the most unpopular person in our government." Two years later, she became chairwoman of the Higher Education and Workforce Investment Subcommittee.

Wilson's conflicts with the Trump White House stemmed from her criticism in 2017 of the president's brief comments in a phone call with a widow prior to a ceremony at the Miami airport to receive the body of her husband, an Army sergeant from her district who had been killed on duty in Niger. When Trump's comments indicated, "I guess he knew what he was signing up for," the sergeant's pregnant widow "was rolled up almost in a fetal position, crying," Wilson recounted, adding to reporters, Trump "doesn't know how to be president." After presidential chief of staff John Kelly publicly criticized Wilson for grandstanding and as an example of "empty barrels making the most noise," she said that Kelly had "deeply tarnished" the stars that he had been awarded as a general in the Marines.

At home, Rudy Moise, a Haitian-American lawyer and doctor who finished second in the 2010 primary, returned for a rematch in 2012, and this time snagged a rare endorsement from a foreign leader, Haitian President Michel Martelly. Wilson countered with one from President Barack Obama and won with 66 percent. Since then, she has been reelected easily. In January 2020, after Kamala Harris withdrew from the campaign, Wilson endorsed Joe Biden for the presidential nomination. In August, she won the Democratic primary with 85 percent of the vote against two challengers.

FL-24: Northern Dade, Southern Broward   **Cook Partisan Voting Index: D+28**

Population		Race and Ethnicity		Income	
Total	754,731	White	43.30%	Median Income	$44,275
Land area (sq. miles)	106	Black	47.10%	District Income Rank	419
Pop/ sq mi	7,114.73	Latino	42.40%	Poverty Rate	17.80%
Born in State	41.50%	Asian	1.10%	With health insurance	80.30%
		Two or more races	2.50%	Cash public assistance	5.00%
Age Groups		Other	5.90%	Food stamp/SNAP	25.80%
Under 18	22.20%				
18-34	24.40%	**Education**		**Work**	
35-64	38.60%	H.S grad or less	53.40%	White Collar	26.90%
Over 64	14.70%	Some college	26.30%	Sales and Service	48.70%
		College Degree, 4 yr	12.90%	Blue Collar	24.40%
Military		Post grad	7.40%	Government	10.20%
Veteran/ Active Duty	2.90%				

2020 Pres. Vote	Biden	225,290	(75%)	Trump	71,622	(24%)
2016 Pres. Vote	Clinton	219,784	(82%)	Trump	40,817	(15%)

Liberty City, Miami Gardens: North from downtown, alongside Interstate 95, Miami's main north-south artery, is the largest African-American community in Florida. It stretches from the American Airlines Arena northwest to Overtown—originally called "Colored Town"—where racially restrictive covenants in the rest of Miami forced the city's original African-American laborers to reside. From there the community has spread through Allapattah and Liberty City to the brightly painted minarets and Moorish arches of the city of Opa-Locka, whose name is a shortened version of the Seminole name for the area. This has been a kind of frontierland in Miami, where hostilities between the city's Blacks and its Cuban-American majority have played out. Many of Miami's African Americans have resented the economic upward mobility and political strength of the Cubans. For the most part, Cuban Americans have been solidly Republican over the years. South Florida African Americans have remained largely Democratic, as has the growing Haitian-American community.

There is also tension between Cubans and Haitians in Little Haiti, exacerbated by federal policies that give refugee status to Cubans who reach U.S. shores, while Haitians are treated as any other immigrant group with potential for deportation. President Donald Trump increased that tension with his hostility toward Haitian immigrants (and toward most other immigrants) and their homeland. During a January 2018 meeting on immigration at the White House, he reportedly said, "Why do we need more Haitians? Take them out," and referred to "all these people from shithole countries." Even with their often desperate status in Miami, many of the Haitians feared returning to their homeland—which has been consumed by poverty, disease and violence for centuries. Especially for those with American-born children, who have citizenship, "the idea of uprooting preteens to live for the first time in a deeply impoverished country seems out of the question," the Los Angeles Times reported in January 2020. Later in the year, officials in Haiti complained that many Haitians deported from Florida tested positive for coronavirus.

The 24th Congressional District covers the historic heart of Miami's Black community. Located here are much of northeast Miami-Dade County, including Liberty City, which has suffered extensive crime and gun violence, Overtown and Opa-Locka. Miami Gardens, the third-largest city in Miami-Dade and 71 percent Black, has suffered numerous incidents of alleged police abuses, especially against Blacks. The county has explored a new elevated rail line through African-American neighborhoods along 27th Street, though reports in 2020 revealed second thoughts about the cost and disruption, plus revival of earlier options for an automated people mover or monorail. To the north are heavily Haitian-American towns like Golden Glades, El Portal, Ives Estates and North Miami Beach. The social gap between local Blacks and Hispanics grew in 2020 as the coronavirus disproportionately affected Black neighborhoods. There were more deaths and positive tests among Blacks, including young adults.

On the other side of the Broward County line, about 12 percent of the district resides in fast-growing Pembroke Pines. Redistricting dropped the district's Black population to 47 percent, while

Hispanics increased to 42 percent, though actual Hispanic voter registration and turnout is closer to 25 percent. The 24th has been among the top 10 most Democrats districts in the nation and the highest in the South. President Barack Obama in 2012 won 88 percent of the vote with the old lines. Hillary Clinton got 82 percent of the new district. In 2020, support for Joe Biden dropped to 75 percent, due to declining Latino support for Democrats. Consequently, the 24th was surpassed by the 20th as the Florida district with the strongest Democratic support.

Mario Diaz-Balart (R)

Elected 2002, 10th term, b. Sep 25, 1961; Fort Lauderdale, FL; University of South FL, Att., 1982; Roman Catholic; Married (Tia Diaz-Balart); 1 child.

Elected Office: FL House, 1988-1992, 2000-2002; FL Senate, 1992-2000.

Professional Career: A.A., Miami Mayor Xavier Suarez, 1985-1988; Public relations executive.

DC Office: 404 CHOB 20515, 202-225-4211, Fax: 202-225-8576, mariodiazbalart.house.gov

State Offices: Doral, 305-470-8555; Naples, 239-348-1620.

Committees: *Appropriations*: Defense; State, Foreign Operations & Related Programs; Transportation, HUD & Related Agencies (RMM).

Group Ratings

	ADA	ACLU	AFL-CIO	LCV	COC	HAFA	ACU	CFG	FRC
2020	**	29%	**	29%	-	54%	62%	**	-
2019	25%	C	52%	28%	94%	C	62%	50%	81%

Almanac Ratings 2019-2020

	Economy	Social	Foreign	Composite
Liberal	38%	45%	27%	37%
Conservative	62%	55%	73%	63%

Key Votes of the 116th Congress

1. U.S./Mex./Can. trade deal Y	5. Russia sanctions Y	9. Firearms background checks Y
2. First Coronavirus response Y	6. Troops in Syria Y	10. Spending at the border Y
3. HEROES Act N	7. Veto arms sales to Saudis N	11. Marijuana liberalized rules N
4. CASH Act Y	8. Defense $$$, veto override N	12. Electoral College objections Y

Election Results

Election	Name (Party)	Vote (%)	Cand. Spent	Ind. Exp. Support	Ind. Exp. Oppose
2020 General	Mario Díaz-Balart (R)	(0%)	$749,531	$1,000	

Prior winning percentages: 2018 (61%), 2016 (62%), 2014 (100%), 2012 (76%), 2010 (67%), 2008 (72%), 2006 (80%), 2004 (73%), 2002 (66%)

Mario Diaz-Balart, a Republican first elected in 2002, has been a pragmatic legislator who has sought to nudge his party closer to the political middle on immigration issues. On the Appropriations Committee, he has delivered large sums to projects back home. In 2020, he accurately forecast that Latino voters would shift to Republicans because of partisan contrasts on foreign policy.

The Diaz-Balart family history was intertwined with that of Fidel Castro and the rise of communism on the island nation of Cuba. Mario's father, Rafael Lincoln Diaz-Balart, was the majority leader in pre-revolution Cuba's House of Representatives. His uncle and grandfather also served in the Cuban House. The Diaz-Balarts fled Cuba in 1959, shortly after Castro took over and after their house was looted and burned while they were vacationing in Paris. His aunt was briefly Castro's wife and was the mother of the dictator's only recognized child. One of Mario's three older brothers is Lincoln Diaz-Balart, who served in the House from 1992 to 2010, then set up a consulting firm. Another brother, Jose, is an anchorman with Spanish-language Telemundo and an occasional anchor with NBC News, and Rafa is an international banker based in Miami.

Mario Diaz-Balart was born in the United States after the family had resettled. He dropped out of the University of South Florida at age 24 to work for former Miami Mayor Xavier Suarez, a Republican. In 1988, he was elected to the Florida House; four years later, at age 31, he became the youngest person elected to the state Senate. Diaz-Balart was chairman of the Senate Ways and Means Committee, where he was a budget hawk. His 1995 call for state agencies to cut spending by 25 percent earned him the nickname "The Slasher"—a moniker he wore with pride.

The eight-year term limit forced him from the Senate in 2000, so he again ran for the Florida House and was elected. No ordinary freshman, Diaz-Balart requested and received the chairmanship of the congressional redistricting committee. In the western Miami-Dade district he tailored for himself, Diaz-Balart coasted to victory over Democratic state Rep. Annie Betancourt, a former social worker and the widow of a Bay of Pigs veteran. With support from teachers and other unions, Diaz-Balart won 65%-35%.

Diaz-Balart's voting record has ranked him near the center of the House, according to Almanac vote ratings. With Republican leaders eager to diversify their caucus, he got a coveted seat on the Appropriations Committee. As chairman of the Subcommittee on Transportation, Housing and Urban Development, he worked with the Trump administration to deliver $20 million to Miami International Airport and more than $70 million for other local transportation projects. In the minority, he was ranking Republican on the transportation subcommittee. He has used his Appropriations seat to secure funding for the Everglades and consistently has opposed oil drilling off Florida's coast in the Gulf of Mexico.

Diaz-Balart organized the Congressional Hispanic Conference, a Republican alternative to the Democrats' Congressional Hispanic Caucus, and he has often engaged on immigration issues. After Republican Mitt Romney overwhelmingly lost the Hispanic vote to President Barack Obama in 2012, Diaz-Balart was among those urging support for a broad immigration reform bill, which he has called the "800-pound gorilla." Republicans "cannot pretend there are not millions of people in an underground society," he told the Orlando Sentinel. "We can no longer pretend that it's not affecting our ability to be competitive."

When House Republican leaders in 2014 declared the issue dead at the time, Diaz-Balart called the result "disappointing and highly unfortunate" and said it was "highly irresponsible not to deal with the issue." In 2018, he spearheaded an initiative by dissident Republicans to sign a discharge petition to force House votes on legislation to give legal status to undocumented immigrants; they fell short. In 2019, he worked with Democrats on House passage of a bill to permit Venezuelan immigrants to remain in the United States, without threat of deportation.

Diaz-Balart adamantly opposed the push by President Barack Obama to resume diplomatic relations with Cuba, and he has continued to resist tourist travel as an important revenue source for the Castro government. Diaz-Balart said Cuba had not met the terms set by Congress before the embargo could be lifted. When trade restrictions have been relaxed, he added, "the oppression worsens." With Sen. Marco Rubio of Florida, he pressed President Donald Trump to continue the crackdown and was mostly pleased with the results. As a leader of the bipartisan Congressional Taiwan Caucus, he urged increased U.S. dealings with the island nation.

In 2008, Diaz-Balart faced a serious challenge from Joe Garcia, the Miami-Dade County Democratic chairman and former executive director of the Cuban American National Foundation. Garcia opposed the restrictions on Cuba. Diaz-Balart won by a narrow 53%-47%. (Four years later, Garcia was elected in the 26th District, then lost his seat in 2014 after one term.)

After his close call, Diaz-Balart in 2010 sought and won his brother Lincoln's seat in a more Republican district when Lincoln retired from the House. With redistricting since then, he has returned to the new 25th district that extended across the Everglades and has been easily reelected. Diaz-Balart has remained in good shape politically.

Diaz-Balart kept his distance from the Trump campaign in 2016. With Trump in office, he largely sought to avoid public conflicts. "I literally did not read tweets," Diaz-Balart told the Miami Herald in 2018. "My job is to get things done." In 2020, he was more eager to support Trump. "People here understand socialism, probably better than most people in the country because they've experienced it or their relatives have experienced it," he told a business conference, the Herald reported.

FL-25: Southern Florida   **Cook Partisan Voting Index: R+8**

Population		Race and Ethnicity		Income	
Total	796,422	White	90.50%	Median Income	$56,270
Land area (sq. miles)	3,233	Black	4.10%	District Income Rank	311
Pop/ sq mi	246.36	Latino	76.00%	Poverty Rate	14.30%
Born in State	25.70%	Asian	1.10%	With health insurance	83.20%
		Two or more races	1.20%	Cash public assistance	3.50%
Age Groups		Other	3.00%	Food stamp/SNAP	21.90%
Under 18	19.60%				
18-34	20.60%	**Education**		**Work**	
35-64	40.80%	H.S grad or less	51.20%	White Collar	29.60%
Over 64	19.10%	Some college	21.90%	Sales and Service	42.60%
		College Degree, 4 yr	16.70%	Blue Collar	27.70%
Military		Post grad	10.20%	Government	7.40%
Veteran/ Active Duty	2.60%				

2020 Pres. Vote	Trump	197,678	(61%)	Biden	123,435	(38%)	
2016 Pres. Vote	Trump	131,320	(49%)	Clinton	126,668	(48%)	

Hialeah, Other Miami Suburbs: Cuban Americans have proved to be one of America's most dynamic immigrant groups over the past half-century, growing from 50,000 in 1960, the year after Fidel Castro took over Cuba, to well over 1 million today. They almost singlehandedly transformed Dade County from a place that John Kennedy won by 15 percent in 1960 to one that George H.W. Bush won by 11 percent in 1988. Over time, the Cuban-American neighborhoods centered along S.W. 8th Street— Calle Ocho—expanded west to the Florida Turnpike Extension in Fountainebleau and Sweetwater, and northwest to Hialeah. Starting in the 1980s, there was an influx of other Latinos, from Nicaragua, El Salvador, Venezuela and Colombia. In the process, new communities were built and old ones transformed.

The 25th Congressional District extends nearly across Florida but remains very much a creature of Miami-Dade, where two-thirds of its residents live. It includes many of the heavily Cuban neighborhoods west and northwest of Miami. To the west in the county, it takes in Doral, home to one of the nation's highest concentration of Venezuelan Americans. Some refer to Doral and its rapidly growing business center just beyond the Miami International Airport as "Doralzuela." In 2019, Venezuelans accounted for 17 percent of the residential real estate purchases in Miami-Dade by foreign buyers. Farther north, it includes parts of raffish Hialeah and nearby Miami Lakes, a planned town developed in the 1960s. With 96 percent of the residents Hispanic and 94 percent Spanish-speaking, Hialeah has the largest such concentration in the nation, and the smallest share of English-speaking residents; about 74 percent were foreign-born. Despite the pandemic, construction was set to begin in 2021 on plans by developers for a massive $4 billion American Dream Miami mega-mall that would pave over as many as 197 acres of wetlands between Interstate 75 and the Florida Turnpike.

The district continues west and north to Hendry County, one of Florida's largest producers of oranges. The farm town of Clewiston has made plans to upgrade its AirGlades Airport to a huge two-way commercial cargo center for both perishable and manufactured goods, with a new 11,000-foot runway. The facility, which opened in 1942 as part of the domestic military response to World War II, would not have commercial service. In 2018, the Federal Aviation Administration said the project met environmental standards. Developers hoped that financing would be resolved in 2020, with construction taking at least two more years. Construction began in 2020 of an accompanying facility for the Customs and Border Protection agency. The district sprawls across the Everglades to the edge of fast-growing Naples in Collier County. Residents of Collier County comprise nearly one-third of the district's population; most live in heavily Republican suburbs and exurbs of Naples a few miles from the Gulf of Mexico. The Big Cypress National Preserve, a huge swamp in the Everglades, was created by preservationists and established in 1974 as the first such preserve created in the United States. In January 2020, Gov. Ron DeSantis announced the purchase of an area in the Everglades where a company had received judicial approval of testing for oil and gas in 20,000 acres west of Miramar in the swamps. The state planned to use the area as public lands for recreation and Everglades restoration.

Of the three Republican-held districts based in Miami-Dade, the 25th has the most Hispanic voters and it has voted the most Republican, but not overwhelmingly so. That pattern has become more dramatic. The district's population is 76 percent Hispanic, 37 percent of whom report Cuban origins. Half the population is foreign-born. In a district that Mitt Romney took, 51%-49%, Donald Trump won in 2020, 61%-38%.

Carlos Gimenez (R)

Elected 2020, 1st term, b. Jan 17, 1954; Havana, Cuba; Barry University, B.A.; John F. Kennedy School of Government, Harvard University, 1993; Catholic; Married (Lourdes Portela); 3 children; 6 grandchildren.

Elected Office: Member, Miami-Dade Board of County Commissioners, 2004-2011; County Mayor, Miami-Dade County, FL, 2011-2020.

Professional Career: Chief Firefighter, Miami Fire-Rescue Department; Manager, City of Miami.

DC Office: 419 CHOB 20515, 202-225-2778, gimenez.house.gov

State Offices: Key West, 305-292-4485; Miami, 305-222-0160.

Committees: *Homeland Security*: Transportation & Maritime Security (RMM). *Science, Space & Technology*: Energy; Environment. *Transportation & Infrastructure*: Aviation; Economic Dev't; Public Buildings & Emergency Management; Highways & Transit.

Election Results

Election	Name (Party)	Vote (%)		Cand. Spent	Ind. Exp. Support	Ind. Exp. Oppose
2020 General	Carlos Gimenez (R)............................ 177,223	(52%)		$2,179,775	$1,037,564	$7,533,871
	Debbie Mucarsel-Powell (D)............... 165,407	(48%)		$7,052,891	$1,371,470	$8,697,651
2020 Primary	Carlos A. Giménez (R)......................... 29,480	(60%)				
	Omar Blanco (R)................................. 19,721	(40%)				

Republican Carlos Gimenez scored one of the most impressive victories in the 2020 congressional elections, as he ousted a House Democrat who had flipped the seat two years earlier. Gimenez deftly took advantage of the popularity he had built in Miami-Dade County during a career in the fire department and later as the top elected official, while seeking to transcend partisanship. With smart timing, he linked to the huge increase in local support for President Donald Trump, especially among Latinos. After having supported Hillary Clinton for president in 2016, he locked arms with Trump four years later.

Gimenez defeated first-term Democratic Rep. Debbie Mucarsel-Powell, an immigrant from Ecuador who became a medical-college administrator. Her initial successful campaign for Congress built on opposition to Trump and local concern that economic opportunities were disappearing. Following her defeat, she blamed the sharp turnaround, in part, on the failure of her party to disavow charges by Trump and other Republicans that linked national Democrats with socialism and "defunding the police."

Gimenez fled to Miami from Cuba with his family in 1960 following Fidel Castro's revolution. They settled in what became the activist Little Havana community, where the politics have evolved but the area has remained a hot zone on Latin American issues. He got a bachelor's degree in public administration from Barry University in Miami Shores. After 16 years as a fire-fighter with the Miami Fire-Rescue Department, he served 9 years as the department chief. That success led to his appointment as city manager in Miami, where he claimed credit for sound management and tax cuts.

In his first political campaign, Gimenez was elected in 2004 to the Miami-Dade County Commission. Following reelection, his big opportunity came in 2011 when he won a special election for Miami mayor after his predecessor was recalled because of unpopular fiscal decisions. Gimenez, while downplaying his Republican affiliation, then won two full terms in the nonpartisan office. Despite his support for Clinton, he quickly became an ally after Trump took office, reversing in February 2017 Miami's earlier status as a "sanctuary city" that was open to undocumented immigrants.

"Gimenez cast the policy as a mere return to county practice" four years earlier, the Miami Herald reported at the time. "After becoming the first big-city mayor to appease Trump, Gimenez drew weeks of protests." But the county commission backed his decision on a 9-to-3 vote. Three years later, Trump returned the favor. In January 2020, he endorsed the congressional bid by Gimenez hours after he made it official.

Later, at a campaign rally in south Florida on the eve of the GOP primary, Trump cited Gimenez—among other local officials—as "warriors" for their handling of the coronavirus pandemic. Gimenez "knew the power of Trump's favor," according to the Herald. Trump's support boosted Gimenez in his 60%-40% victory over Omar Blanco. Coincidentally, Blanco too was a local firefighter and served as president of the firefighters' union in Miami-Dade.

A month before he defeated Mucarsel-Powell, Gimenez described his own political strength. "The advantage that I have over my opponent is that I've run a large organization," he told the Herald. "I'll know what my constituents want and what they need. ... She came here from California and I guess that's why she is always agreeing with [House Speaker] Nancy Pelosi." Mucarsel-Powell had settled in Miami 20 years earlier. He added that local Latinos see that "Trump holds their values."

During a private conference call with House Democrats two days after the election, Mucarsel-Powell tearfully complained that divisions among Democrats had harmed her campaign, according to news reports. "If you have a problem, pick up the phone—don't tweet it out," she reportedly said, an apparent reference to liberal colleagues. In his campaign ads, Gimenez often cited the embrace of socialism and the "radical left" by leading national Democrats.

Gimenez won, 52%-48%, despite Mucarsel-Powell outspending him by more than 3-to-1. Of the more than $16 million in spending by the two parties and their allies, Gimenez had a slight advantage. He was bolstered by Trump taking his district, which the president lost by 16 percentage points in 2016. In the House, he got useful committee assignments for his district: Homeland Security; Science, Space and Technology; and Transportation and Infrastructure.

FL-26: Southern Florida

Cook Partisan Voting Index:　D+1

Population		Race and Ethnicity		Income	
Total	780,951	White	81.20%	Median Income	$65,584
Land area (sq. miles)	2,099	Black	11.20%	District Income Rank	205
Pop/ sq mi	372.12	Latino	72.40%	Poverty Rate	13.40%
Born in State	35.30%	Asian	1.40%	With health insurance	83.60%
Age Groups		Two or more races	2.30%	Cash public assistance	1.60%
Under 18	22.30%	Other	3.80%	Food stamp/SNAP	19.10%
18-34	21.00%				
35-64	41.10%	**Education**		**Work**	
Over 64	15.50%	H.S grad or less	45.60%	White Collar	32.90%
		Some college	25.80%	Sales and Service	43.70%
Military		College Degree, 4 yr	19.60%	Blue Collar	23.30%
Veteran/ Active Duty	3.60%	Post grad	8.90%	Government	11.20%

2020 Pres. Vote	Trump	184,019	(52%)	Biden	164,356	(47%)
2016 Pres. Vote	Clinton	164,252	(56%)	Trump	117,205	(40%)

Inland Dade, the Keys: At the tip of the Florida Keys, a string of islands connected to each other and to mainland Florida by U.S. 1, is Key West, the southernmost city in the continental United States. Over the years, Key West has attracted famous residents—Ernest Hemingway, Tennessee Williams, Jimmy Buffett—and a large gay population, many living in quaint clapboard bungalows called "conch houses." Along the way, U.S. 1 stretches 160 miles through small towns, parklands and beaches from Key Largo to Key West on a mostly two-lane highway, with several long causeways. With only a 25 percent Hispanic population, the Keys are a stark contrast to most of southern Florida.

In September 2017, Hurricane Irma scored a direct hit on the Keys. Many homes were not rebuilt. Jobs and tourist dollars suffered double-digit percentage drops. Long-term environmental threats from rising seas have led state officials to raise the height of some bridges. In June 2020, the Army Corps of Engineers released a draft plan for six miles of sea wall—with height ranging from one foot to 13 feet—that would be placed at the mouths of three waterways, to protect parts of the Miami-Dade County coastline. The project, with a cost of close to $5 billion, would be designed to protect more than10,000 homes and businesses. In another sign of environmental consciousness, Key West approved referenda in November 2020 that imposed limits on the size of cruise ships and the number of tourists that can disembark to 1,500 each day.

On the mainland, an influx of immigrants, first from Cuba and then from other Caribbean nations as well as Central and South America, has filled in the landscape of southern Miami-Dade. This immigration surge has created a multicultural pastiche of ethnicities. Tamiami is majority Cuban, but now boasts sizable Nicaraguan, Colombian, Dominican and Venezuelan communities. Homestead, where an Air Force Base and almost everything else were leveled by Hurricane Andrew in 1992, has since been redeveloped,

On the western and southern edges of Miami, close to the swamps, one can drive out on roads past the subdivisions and find strawberry, tomato and citrus farms. The trees thin out, and then the road just ends at the Everglades—an interconnected sea of wetlands that once covered 8.9 million acres. This was a coherent ecosystem, a "river of grass" in which water moved slowly down a gentle slope to the ocean. But the state's white settlers were intent on making the swampland more useful, and in 1948 Congress approved the construction of 1,720 miles of canals and levees to channel and drain the Everglades, making it possible to use the land for agriculture and housing. Floridians have had second thoughts about taming the Everglades. In 2008, the state proposed buying much of the land owned by U.S. Sugar Corp. around Lake Okeechobee for $1.35 billion, with farming to be phased out in seven years. Although timetables have been delayed by several years, most state officials say they are committed to the broad objectives. Congress in 2016 included $1.9 billion for Everglades restoration in a water resources bill. In 2017, the state approved $1.6 billion for a reservoir as part of the cleanup.

The 26th Congressional District combines Monroe County (whose residents are mostly on the Keys) with much of southern Miami-Dade County. The large majority of the residents live in mostly Hispanic neighborhoods on the western and southern edges of metropolitan Miami, close to the swamps. The district is 72 percent Hispanic, including 41 percent Cuban American. This has become volatile political territory. In 2016, Hillary Clinton carried the district 56%-40%. In 2020, Donald Trump flipped the district with a 52%-47% win.

Maria Salazar (R)

Elected 2020, 1st term, b. Nov 01, 1961; Miami, FL; University of Miami-Teacher's Certificate, B.A., 1983; Harvard University John F. Kennedy School of Government, M.P.A., 1995; Christian - Non-Denominational; Married (Jaime Court); 2 children.

Professional Career: Broadcast Journalist, Univision Communications Inc., 1983-1995, CNN, 1988-1990, NBC Telemundo, 1995-2004, CNN Latino Miami, 2013-2014, Mega TV, 2004-2017; Political Contributor, Fox News.

DC Office: 1616 LHOB 20515, 202-225-3931, salazar.house.gov

State Offices: Miami, 305-668-2285; Miami, 305-668-2285.

Committees: *Foreign Affairs*: Middle East, North Africa & Global Counterterrorism; West Hem, Civ Sec, Migration, & Intern'l Econ Policy. *Small Business*: Contracting & Infrastructure (RMM); Innovation, Entrepreneurship & Workforce Development; Underserved, Agricultural & Rural Business Development.

Election Results

Election	Name (Party)	Vote (%)	Cand. Spent	Ind. Exp. Support	Ind. Exp. Oppose
2020 General	Maria Salazar (R)..............................	176,141 (51%)	$3,539,257	$147,054	$113
	Donna Shalala (D)................................	166,758 (49%)	$3,818,578	$181,633	$203,050
2020 Primary	Maria Elvira Salazar (R)................	39,687 (79%)			
	Raymond Molina (R)......................	5,497 (11%)			
	Juan Fiol (R)..	5,018 (10%)			

Maria Salazar, well-known locally as a Spanish-language television news reporter, won a rematch against first-term Democratic Rep. Donna Shalala. Salazar rode the coattails of President Donald Trump, whose improved showing in Miami-Dade County was among his largest gains nationwide compared to the 2016 presidential election. She often was outspoken in advocating the views and interests of her community of Cuban-American exiles. Shalala, a former university president and a Cabinet secretary during the Clinton administration, struggled politically, as an aging persona who could not speak the Spanish language of most of her constituents.

Born in Miami's Little Havana to parents who fled Cuba following Fidel Castro's takeover and resided in Puerto Rico en route, Salazar got her bachelor's degree in communications from the University of Miami and later got a master's degree in public administration from Harvard University's John F. Kennedy School of Government.

She began her career in journalism as a local reporter with Univision. Later, she was an anchor for CNN Espanol and for Telemundo, where she spent time covering events in Central America. Her interviewees included Castro, Venezuelan President Nicholas Maduro and U.S. Presidents Bill Clinton and George W. Bush.

Her 2018 challenge to Shalala for an open House seat that had been held for 30 years by Republican Rep. Ileana Ros-Lehtinen was initially viewed as uphill, given that Hillary Clinton in 2016 won the district, 58%-39%. Salazar described Shalala as "not from here" and insisted on conducting debates in Spanish, with translation to English for Shalala, who regularly attacked Trump. Although polls showed the contest drawing closer in its final weeks, Shalala won, 52%-46%. The Miami Herald reported that Shalala conducted a "lackluster campaign."

In her second campaign, Salazar sought to turn the tables by voicing moderate views while accentuating her link to Trump, who she said sometimes used "insensitive words" about minorities. He tweeted that Salazar is "badly needed in Washington."

She sought the political center with her willingness to consider a ban on so-called assault weapons, a carbon tax and a path to legality for some groups of undocumented immigrants, positions that were largely consistent with those of Ros-Lehtinen. "I want to step into the center," Salazar told the editorial board of the Herald. "Whatever makes sense to the community, to the whole country, is what we need to do." She strongly criticized national Democrats such as Sen. Bernie Sanders for their praise for "socialist regimes" in Central America

In winning the contest by nearly 10,000 votes, Salazar surprised many political observers. Of the House Democratic incumbents who were defeated in 2020, Shalala was the only one who was rated on the eve of the election as a "likely" or "solid" winner by the three chief Washington-based pundits who follow House elections.

Along with Democratic Rep. Debbie Mucarsel-Powell in the neighboring district, who was first elected with Shalala and also was voted out after serving one term, the defeats of the two first-termers in south Florida were a stinging blow for local and national Democrats. The fact that Shalala was strong on policy expertise while Mucarsel-Powell was more of a community leader failed to rescue either in the face of the strong Republican tide in Miami-Dade in 2020. Both Shalala and Salazar spent about $3.8 million, though the national parties spent little here—in contrast to the adjacent contest.

Strikingly, the two House districts had nearly identical total votes of 343,000 and partisan splits of the vote. Likewise, both Salazar and Carlos Gimenez, the neighboring GOP winner, were longtime and popular local figures. Salazar took 51.4 percent, while Gimenez won with 51.7 percent. Biden ran about four percentage points stronger in Shalala's district than in the seat held by Mucarsel-Powell —making Salazar's victory all the more surprising.

FL-27: Miami   **Cook Partisan Voting Index: D+4**

Population		Race and Ethnicity		Income	
Total	750,653	White	85.60%	Median Income	$60,384
Land area (sq. miles)	209	Black	5.70%	District Income Rank	255
Pop/ sq mi	3,594.39	Latino	70.80%	Poverty Rate	14.80%
Born in State	28.30%	Asian	2.40%	With health insurance	86.10%
		Two or more races	2.10%	Cash public assistance	1.60%
Age Groups		Other	4.20%	Food stamp/SNAP	16.80%
Under 18	17.50%				
18-34	22.70%	**Education**		**Work**	
35-64	40.90%	H.S grad or less	36.50%	White Collar	42.60%
Over 64	18.90%	Some college	22.30%	Sales and Service	41.40%
		College Degree, 4 yr	24.10%	Blue Collar	16.10%
Military		Post grad	17.00%	Government	7.40%
Veteran/ Active Duty	1.90%				

2020 Pres. Vote	Biden	178,643	(51%)	Trump	167,420	(48%)
2016 Pres. Vote	Clinton	174,132	(58%)	Trump	115,815	(39%)

Coral Gables, Miami Beach: A century ago, Miami was a tiny tropical village where the Miami River emptied into Biscayne Bay. Today, it is a world-class city. The surrealistic high-rises of Brickell Boulevard, the winding lanes of Coral Gables and the shimmer of orange and pink neon signs in the hot night air. It lives on the cusp of two civilizations, North America and Latin America, with different traditions, styles and sensibilities converging in one place, with the strengths of each despite some frictions. In Miami, where it is easy to fly directly to any part of Latin America, top business and banking services are available to a sophisticated Spanish-speaking, and usually also English-speaking, clientele. Before the pandemic largely shut down cruises, the port was the busiest in the world.

Miami for decades has also been the locus of Cuban America, since the first refugees fled Fidel Castro in 1959. Increasing numbers of Cuban immigrants, implacably opposed to the totalitarian Castro, entered the voting stream as Republicans. Now, they are a dominant voice in a Latino majority in Miami-Dade County (as Dade County was renamed in 1997). But the Latino population has grown more diverse: Little Havana, centered on Calle Ocho (S.W. 8th Street), is home to many Nicaraguans, Hondurans and Peruvians. Many of these Latino immigrants rose in their adoptive society by going to school at Miami Dade College, the nation's largest community college, or to Florida International University, and then starting businesses or joining professions in Miami's vibrant economy.

The 27th Congressional District of Florida is one of Miami-Dade's three Hispanic-majority districts. It is 71 percent Hispanic, including 43 percent Cuban. The district follows Calle Ocho from Little Havana west to West Miami and Westchester. North of Miami International Airport, the district includes Miami Springs and parts of Hialeah. To the east, the district sweeps up many of metro Miami's high-income residential areas: Coral Gables, with luxurious streets laid out in the 1920s; and Cocoplum, a gated community of huge houses and boat docks for rich Cuban Americans. On the southern tip of Miami Beach is its world-famous South Beach, where luxurious art-deco hotels attract the glitziest celebrities of North America, Latin America and Europe.

Many of these places have become hot real estate for Latin Americans seeking safe investments, which often are made in cash. One topic of concern: With rising tides and less available space, the natural sand on the beaches has been disappearing. Some of it has been replaced by the Army Corps of Engineers, which uses scoops or hoses to move sand from the sea floor and pipe it back to the eroding beach. This is called "renourishment," though the substitute sand is not unlimited. A more immediate crisis struck in 2020 when the party life of Miami led to a soaring caseload of COVID-19 cases. During the summer, Florida accounted for 20 percent of all cases in the United States; within the state, a disproportionate share was in the Miami area.

For years, the district voted Republican, but there have been shifts here. Obama carried the district 53%-47% in 2012. Hillary Clinton's 58%-39% win over Donald Trump was boosted, in part, by redistricting in 2016. Four years later, when Joe Biden won 51%-48%, even Republicans were stunned by the much closer margin, which was driven by their rising support from Latinos.

GEORGIA

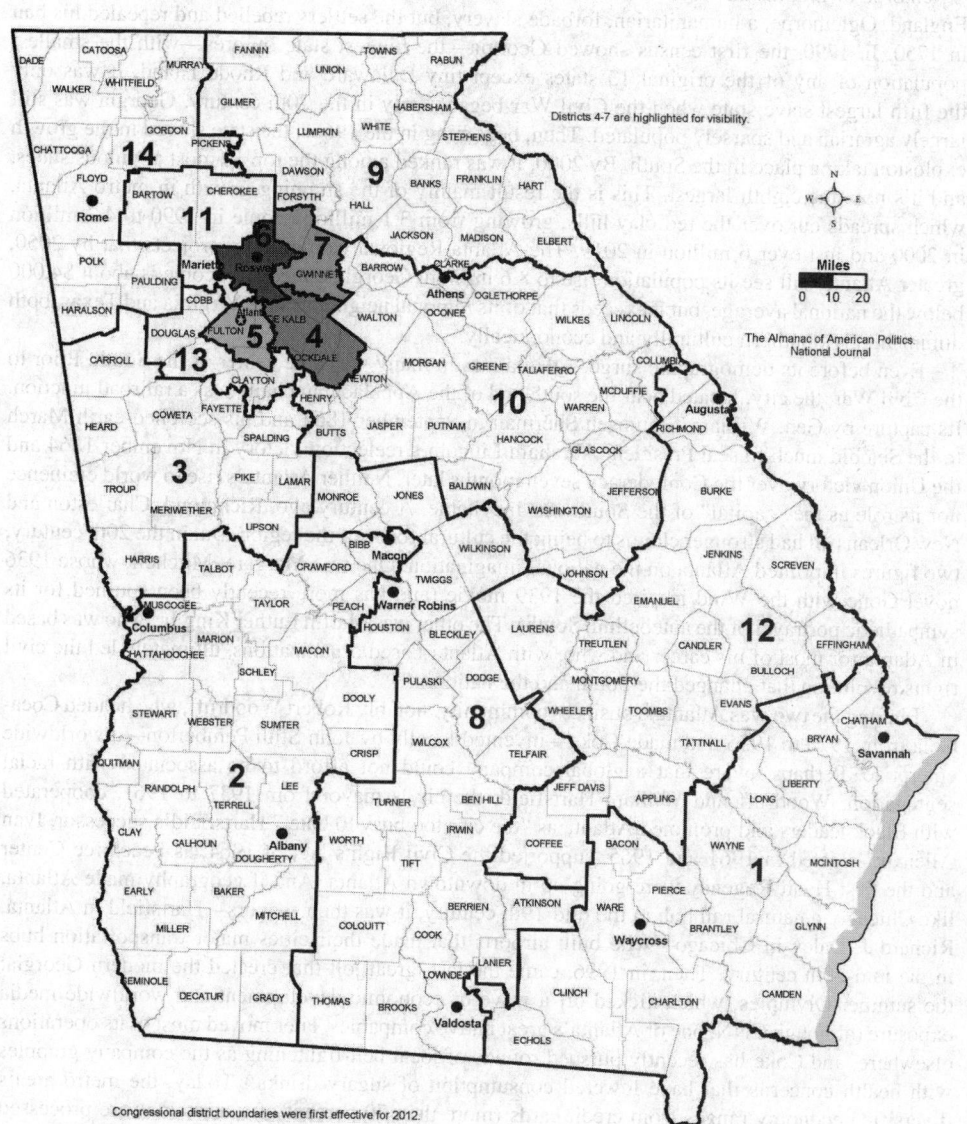

Districts 4-7 are highlighted for visibility.

The Almanac of American Politics
National Journal

Congressional district boundaries were first effective for 2012.

Georgia, once a Democratic bastion like the rest of the South, went heavily for Republicans over the past two decades in both federal and state races. But in 2020, Democrats surged not only to a victory in the presidential race but also in two Senate runoffs, a clear sign that changing views among suburban voters and the state's shifting demographics have turned Georgia into a highly competitive state.

Georgia was the last of the 13 colonies to be founded, by British soldier and politician James Oglethorpe in 1733 as an "asylum of the unfortunate," reserved for debtors and other outcasts from England. Oglethorpe, a humanitarian, forbade slavery, but the settlers rebelled and repealed his ban in 1750. In 1790, the first census showed Georgia—the biggest state by area—with the smallest population of any of the original 13 states except tiny Delaware and Rhode Island. It was only the fifth largest slave state when the Civil War began. Early in the 20th century, Georgia was still largely agrarian and sparsely populated. Then, beginning in the 1960s, the state shared in the growth explosion taking place in the South. By 2000, it was ranked among the top 10 most populous states, and it's now the eighth largest. This is the result mainly of the stunning growth in metro Atlanta, which spreads out over the red clay hills, growing from 3.1 million people in 1990 to 4.2 million in 2000 and just over 6 million in 2019. The Atlanta Regional Commission projects that by 2050, greater Atlanta will see its population rise to 8.6 million. Georgia's median income is about $4,000 below the national average, but it exceeds that of its regional neighbors save Virginia and Texas, both diminishingly Southern culturally and economically.

Even before its demographic surge, Atlanta was in many ways the center of the South. Prior to the Civil War, the city, located near the south end of the Appalachian chain, was a railroad junction. Its capture by Gen. William Tecumseh Sherman in September 1864 and his scorched-earth March to the Sea did much to seal President Abraham Lincoln's reelection victory in November 1864 and the Union victory over the Confederacy seven months later. Neither Atlanta's rise to world eminence nor its role as the "capital" of the South was inevitable. A century ago, Richmond, Charleston and New Orleans all had stronger claims to being the cultural focus of the region. But in the 20th century, two figures imprinted Atlanta on the national imagination. One was Margaret Mitchell, whose 1936 novel Gone with the Wind inspired the 1939 movie (and has more recently been spurned for its sympathetic portrayal of the antebellum South). The other was Martin Luther King Jr., who was based in Atlanta for most of his career and who, with Atlanta-based organizations, ultimately led the civil rights revolution that changed the South and the nation.

Linking the two was Atlanta's business community, notably Robert Woodruff, who headed Coca-Cola from 1923 to 1955 and made Coke—invented locally by John Stith Pemberton—a worldwide enterprise. Perhaps aware that a global company could not afford to be associated with racial segregation, Woodruff and William Hartsfield, the city's mayor from 1937 to 1961, cooperated with Black leaders and promoted Atlanta as "the city too busy to hate." Hartsfield's successor, Ivan Allen Jr., elected in 1961 and 1965, supported the Civil Rights Act of 1964, as Peachtree Center and the first Hyatt Regency were going up in downtown Atlanta. And if geography made Atlanta, like Chicago, a natural rail hub in the mid-19th century, it was their mayors—Hartsfield in Atlanta, Richard J. Daley in Chicago—who built airports that made their cities major transportation hubs in the mid-20th century. Then, in 1996, came the last, great jolt that created the modern Georgia: the summer Olympics, which kicked off a wave of economic development and worldwide media exposure (although CNN, one of Atlanta's great native companies, later moved most of its operations elsewhere, and Coke has recently pursued rounds of local belt-tightening as the company grapples with health concerns that have lowered consumption of sugary drinks.) Today, the metro area's diversified economy ranges from credit cards (more than 70 percent of transactions are processed in the Atlanta area, employing some 37,000 people) to television and film production, including such productions as Black Panther, The Walking Dead, and Ozark (in which Georgia stands in for Missouri). Georgia's film industry has remained strong, even as the state's $870 million tax-credit allowance has faced second-guessing by politicians, and as Hollywood contemplated a boycott after the state passed a "fetal heartbeat" law.

Today, Georgia is 31 percent Black, 10 percent Hispanic and 4 percent Asian. That's the third-highest African-American percentage of any state (behind Mississippi and Louisiana) and the second-lowest percentage of whites east of the Mississippi River (after Maryland). Seven of the nation's 10 counties with the fastest-growing Black populations are near Atlanta, according to the Pew Research Center. The state has seen faster Hispanic population growth than any of the 10 states with the largest Hispanic populations. Projections from the Atlanta Regional Commission find that the Atlanta area's white population is set to fall from 47.5 percent in 2015 to 31 percent in 2050. More than one of every 10 Georgians is foreign-born, up from 2.7 percent in 1990, and one-third of the foreign-born residents of Atlanta are undocumented, on the higher end of the major metro areas, according to Pew.

Metro Atlanta's population features wide pockets of prosperity, along with top-flight cultural institutions, a large millennial population and a vibrant LGBTQ community. African Americans have been moving to middle-class, suburban counties west and southeast of the city, while Hispanics have been clustering along Interstate 85 in Gwinnett County and Interstate 75 in Cobb County to the north. Gwinnett is home to hubs of Korean, Cuban, Indian, Vietnamese and Mexican residents, such as Duluth, where Asians account for more than a quarter of the population; non- white children account for three of every four students in Gwinnett's school system, up from one in five two decades ago, according to The Washington Post. The FX television show Atlanta, a popular and critical hit, has given the diverse region some national cultural cred. But in 2020, two incidents in Georgia helped fuel outrage not just locally but nationally: the killing of Ahmaud Arbery, a Black man in Brunswick, after three white men pursued him, thinking he was a break-in suspect, and the Atlanta police shooting of another Black man, Rayshard Brooks, who was shot while fleeing after he had fallen asleep in a Wendy's drive-through lane. Then, in March 2021, a white shooter killed eight people, including six Asian American women, in a rampage at massage parlors.

Meanwhile, Georgia's rural outstate regions have struggled. Georgia has the third-highest rate of uninsured residents in the nation, trailing only Texas and Oklahoma. This in turn has led to a rash of rural hospital closures. Nine counties, mostly in southern Georgia, lack practicing physicians, the president of the Georgia Alliance of Community Hospitals told the New Yorker, while 18 counties have no family-practice doctors, 32 have no internal-medicine doctors, and 76 counties have no ob-gyns. Georgia's increasingly efficient agriculture sector ranks high in the production of broilers, pecans, cotton, and peanuts (today's output would put Jimmy Carter's to shame) but many farmers were hit hard by Hurricanes Irma in 2017 and Michael in 2018, and Georgia farmers have been engaged in a long-running battle with Florida over water rights. In 2021, the justices unanimously handed Georgia a victory, rejecting Florida's claim that its northern neighbor has been using too much water.

Georgia cast the second-highest Democratic percentage for president in 1960, but in the next two elections, Georgia voters swung sharply, backing Barry Goldwater in 1964 and George Wallace in 1968. Statewide election contests were typically fought out in Democratic primaries that pitted Atlanta-supported moderates against rural-supported segregationists or conservatives, and the latter usually won. Then came change with the emergence of Carter, a former two-term state senator who was elected governor in 1970 with a rural base. After taking office, Carter proclaimed racial reconciliation and installed a portrait of King in the state capitol. Carter thus became one of the first politicians from the rural South to celebrate and honor the civil rights movement, and in the process, set himself on the road to being elected president in 1976. Carter was followed by a series of Democratic governors with connections to rural parts of the state—George Busbee, Joe Frank Harris, Zell Miller and Roy Barnes.

But countervailing political trends transformed Georgia, for a long historical moment, into a mostly Republican state. Affluent voters in metro Atlanta became generally Republican, while White voters outside metro Atlanta became Republican stalwarts; for years, Georgia's most prominent politician nationally was Republican Rep. Newt Gingrich. George W. Bush carried the state 55%-42% in 2000 and for the next three elections; Republican presidential nominees carried it with between 52 percent and 58 percent of the vote. With help from party switchers, Republicans captured the state Senate in 2002 and the state House in 2004 and have kept large majorities in both chambers. And the GOP has dominated statewide and federal races for the better part of two decades.

But the changing demographics and partisan trends in the Trump era changed everything. In 2016, Donald Trump won the state, but three metro counties that had supported Mitt Romney in 2012 shifted to Hillary Clinton—Gwinnett, with a 15-point swing, Cobb, with a 14-point swing, and Henry, with a seven-point swing. Clinton carried several other metro counties, including Fulton, Douglas,

Rockdale and DeKalb, by margins that were eight to 13 points higher than Barack Obama four years earlier. Then, in the 2018 midterms, Georgia was one of the nation's marquee battlegrounds, thanks to its gubernatorial race between Republican Brian Kemp, who ran as a Trump acolyte, and Democrat Stacey Abrams, an African-American former state House minority leader. After gubernatorial elections in 2010 and 2014 saw largely static turnout, the two nominees whipped their bases into gear in 2018. In the end, it wasn't enough for Abrams to win, but the GOP's gubernatorial margin continued to shrink—from 10 points in 2010 to eight points in 2014 to 1.4 points in 2018, or fewer than 55,000 votes. Continuing recent trends, the GOP cleaned up in rural areas, while Abrams trounced Kemp in the once-Republican Atlanta suburbs.

Such developments made it clear from the start of the 2020 campaign that Georgia would be a bona fide battleground state. After her close loss, Abrams continued to energize the grassroots and register voters, especially Black voters, who had accounted for a disproportionate share of the state's recent increases in the voting electorate. Abrams' effort ran up against Republican attempts to purge the rolls of inactive voters and other initiatives that critics, contrary to the record voter turnout, said made voting harder for minorities. The primary election on June 9, 2020, was notable for its long lines and general confusion at polling places, especially in urban locales; it was deemed a "complete meltdown" by the Atlanta Journal-Constitution and became a warning sign for the rest of the nation as officials grappled with the coronavirus pandemic's impact on election administration.

Both Trump and Biden campaigned in the state, as did Obama, even though it wasn't essential for Biden's electoral map. Biden also got help from Abrams and Atlanta Mayor Keisha Lance Bottoms, both of whom made his list of potential vice presidential picks. In the end, Biden turned Clinton's five-point deficit into a victory of fewer than 12,000 votes. While Trump increased his vote total by 18 percent in the state, Biden increased his by 32 percent over what Clinton achieved. Like Clinton, Biden won the nine core counties of the Atlanta area, but he prevailed by even bigger margins. Biden improved on Clinton's winning margins by 12 points in Gwinnett, 14 points in Cobb, 15 points in Rockdale, and 17 points in Henry, while also squeezing a few more points out of overwhelmingly Democratic Fulton and DeKalb counties. "If you jumped into a car at the state capitol, it would take nearly a half-hour's drive, in any direction, to find a precinct won by Trump," The Washington Post's Dave Weigel wrote. Trump increased his margins in Whiter, more rural parts of the state and flipped one county Clinton had won, Burke (Waynesboro) in east-central Georgia. However, "there simply weren't enough Republican votes in rural Georgia to make up for those Democratic gains," Weigel wrote.

Still, Biden's victory was narrow, and even after a hand-recount confirmed it, the margin was close enough to prompt Trump to try to strong-arm Republican Secretary of State Brad Raffensperger, Kemp, and other Georgia officials to "find" enough votes to put him over the top. Trump's obsession with losing the state may have contributed to the GOP's loss in the two Jan. 5 Senate runoffs, to Democrats Jon Ossoff and Raphael Warnock: Even when stumping for GOP Sens. David Perdue and Kelly Loeffler, Trump focused more on his own loss than the Senate runoff, on which Senate control depended. Warnock, a prominent Black pastor from King's Atlanta church, and his allies were able to supercharge Black turnout, including voters in rural areas far from Atlanta; Trump's support, for his part, dipped modestly in some of his strongest regions. The results suggested that while Georgia has not yet become a blue state—every non-federal statewide elected official remains in GOP hands—many of those statewide contests should be competitive in 2022, when Kemp faces reelection, and when Trump will no longer be on the ballot. A wild card will be whether the voting bill passed the GOP and signed by Kemp will change turnout patterns.

Population		Race and Ethnicity		Income	
Total	10,617,423	White	57.80%	Median Income	61,980
Land area (sq. miles)	57,513	Black	31.90%	State Income Rank	29 out of 50
Pop/ sq mi	184.61	Latino	9.80%	Poverty Rate	13.30%
Born in state	54.40%	Asian	4.90%	With health insurance	86.60%
		Two or more races	2.70%	Cash public assistance	1.40%
Age Groups		Other	3.50%	Food stamp/SNAP	14.5%
Under 18	23.60%				
18-34	23.30%	Education		Work	
35-64	38.70%	H.S grad or less	39.50%	White Collar	39.10%
Over 64	14.30%	Some college	28.00%	Sales and Service	37.00%
		College Degree, 4 yr	19.90%	Blue Collar	23.80%
Military		Post grad	12.60%	Government	14.00%
Veteran/ Active Duty	8.30%				

Presidential Politics

2020 Primary (D)	Biden (D)	922,177(85%)	Sanders (D)	101,668 (9%)			
2020 Pres. Vote	Biden (D)	2,473,633(49%)	Trump (R)	2,461,854(49%)			
2016 Pres. Vote	Trump (R)	2,089,104(51%)	Clinton (D)	1,877,963(46%)	Johnson (L)	125,306 (3%)	

Georgia's rapid demographic shifts have transformed it into a battleground, and in 2020 Joe Biden became the first Democrat since Bill Clinton in 1992 to carry the state, before it became the epicenter of President Donald Trump's false claims that the election had been rigged against him. The state once was part of the Solid South for Democrats and in 1976 native son Jimmy Carter carried all 159 of its counties; in 1980 it was one of just six states he carried.

Georgia's fast-growing non-White population and White suburbanites' hard shift against the GOP put the state in play in 2020. The state's population grew by almost 10 percent in the past decade, and a huge part of that population growth was driven by Blacks, Hispanics and Asian Americans. Georgia is on the cusp of becoming a majority-minority state: Its population was 48 percent non-White as of 2019, up from 44 percent in 2010.

The Peach State finally became ripe for Democrats in 2020, though even they were initially skeptical it would happen. Biden and his allies didn't start spending heavily on ads in the state until late in the campaign, and his first and only Georgia visit came in late October. But the state saw a massive surge in turnout from minority voters in November, especially among Hispanics and Asian Americans, and Atlanta's diverse and well-educated suburbs swung dramatically against Trump.

Trump led by more than 100,000 votes on election night and prematurely claimed victory. But a trove of votes remained from Atlanta and its inner suburbs. Biden pulled ahead by Friday morning, and in the final count led by more than 11,000 votes.

Biden's win was built in metro Atlanta. He netted almost 130,000 more votes than Hillary Clinton from Clayton, Fulton and DeKalb counties, the three which include parts of Atlanta. But the biggest swing came in Atlanta's suburban counties: Biden netted 160,000 more votes than Clinton from the six core suburban counties around Atlanta, and ran 10 points ahead of Clinton's numbers in eight counties in suburban and exurban Atlanta.

Trump wasn't willing to accept the results, however, claiming widespread voter fraud even after two separate recounts affirmed Biden's victory, pressuring the state's Republican secretary of state and governor to overturn the results and attacking them when they refused. The furious division he sowed within the GOP may have helped Democrats pull off victories in a pair of hotly contested Senate runoffs that gave them a tie in the Senate. Those results, and Stacey Abrams' near-miss in her bid for governor in 2018, indicate Biden's win wasn't a fluke and that Georgia will likely be a swing state in coming elections.

Georgians like their primary to play an important role in presidential politics. In 1992, Democratic Gov. Zell Miller scheduled it one week before Super Tuesday to help Democratic nominee Bill Clinton; his win gave Clinton momentum going into the large batch of Southern primaries one week later. In 2016, then-Georgia Secretary of State Brian Kemp (currently the governor) helped organize the "SEC primary," named after the South's college football powerhouse Southeastern Conference.

Six other southern states—Alabama, Arkansas, Oklahoma, Tennessee, Texas and Virginia—held presidential primaries March 1. Trump lost only Oklahoma and Texas. In Georgia, he defeated Florida Sen. Marco Rubio, 39%-24%. African-American voters dominate Georgia's Democratic primaries, and helped Clinton defeat Vermont Sen. Bernie Sanders, 71%-28% in 2016. In 2020, Georgia's primary was postponed because of the coronavirus until June 9, long after Biden had won the Democratic nomination. He defeated Sanders, who'd suspended his campaign, 85%-9%.

Congressional Districts

117th Congress Lineup	6D 8R	116th Congress Lineup	5D 9R

The good news for Georgia Republicans: Heading into redistricting, they retained firm control of state government, with congressional boundaries that appear relatively clean while having created four districts that are firmly controlled by minority voters. The bad news: As was clear in the presidential election in November 2020 and the subsequent two Senate runoffs, Georgia has become a 50-50 state. And, given the heavy concentration of Democratic voters in metro Atlanta, Republicans have shrinking options to make any of those five districts competitive in the 14-member House delegation.

In 2014 and 2016, Republicans got their way and the election results were not entirely accidental: 10 Republicans, all of them white and all of them first elected since 2010; four Democrats, all African American and all serving since at least 2006. But Democrats in 2018 scored a major gain with the Cobb County-based 6th District, which is 60 percent white and Republicans had comfortably held since it was created in 1992. Then, in 2020, Democrats added the adjacent Gwinnett County-based 7th District, where Republicans also held a lock since 1992 and which has rapidly become majority-minority. Including the Democrats' firm hold on the Macon-based 3rd District that shifted the delegation to eight Republicans and six Democrats. The GOP options are obvious: weaken the Democrats' grip on at least one of the suburban Cobb and Gwinnett districts. Prior to the 2020 election, the expectation had been that they would split those districts between the two parties. The numbers indicate that Republican mapmakers face a steep challenge.

In the eight counties surrounding Atlanta (Clayton, Cobb, DeKalb, Fulton, Gwinnett, Douglas, Henry and Rockdale), Joe Biden won by a hair less than 1.4 million votes. Jamming those voters into four strongly Democratic districts might be both a mathematical and geographic impossibility. In the presidential election, only one Georgia district gave Biden more than 300,000 votes (he got about 313,000 in the 5th District). In addition, he got roughly 280,000 in two other districts and close to 200,000 in the final two districts. If 300,000 is roughly the high-water mark for the number of Democrats in a district, that likely means Democrats, at a minimum, will have firm control in four districts and a good opportunity in a fifth district. The chief caveat is that Republicans might find a way to gerrymander at least one of those districts with Republican-held districts in the exurbs and beyond. But that, in turn, likely would endanger Republicans who have controlled those outlying districts. Indeed, Democrats might stake a strong claim to seven seats in the delegation, in what seems their inevitable court challenge.

In retrospect, Republicans were pressing their luck with their 10-4 advantage in the delegation—a dramatic shift from the Democrats' 9-1 control during most of the 1980s, when backbench Republican Newt Gingrich was plotting historic shifts. In reality, the true partisan balance in Georgia for nearly a half-century has been somewhere between those two ratios. Also of interest in redistricting will be how the new lines are drawn in metro Atlanta. With their redistricting pens, that might be one way in which Republicans create partisan mischief—especially in how they allocate minority voters and possibly make radical shifts in current districts.

Brian Kemp (R)

Elected 2018, term expires 2023, 1st term; b. Nov. 2, 1963, Athens; University of Georgia, B.S.; Christian; Married (Marty); 3 children.

Elected Office: GA Senate, 2003-2007; GA Secretary of State, 2010-2018.

Office: 206 Washington Street 111 State Capitol, Atlanta, 30334; 404-656-1776; Fax: 404-657-7332; Website: georgia.gov

Lt. Gov.: Geoff Duncan (R) **Atty. Gen:** Chris Carr (R) **Sec. of State:** Brad Raffensperger (R)

State Legislature: Senate: 21D, 35R **House:** 75D, 105R

Election Results

Election	Name (Party)	Vote (%)
2018 General	Brian Kemp (R)	1,978,408 (50%)
	Stacey Abrams (D)	1,923,685 (49%)
2018 Primary runoff	Brian Kemp (R)	406,703 (69%)
	Casey Cagle (R)	178,893 (31%)
2018 Primary	Casey Cagle (R)	236,987 (39%)
	Brian Kemp (R)	155,189 (26%)
	Hunter Hill (R)	111,464 (18%)
	Clay Tippins (R)	74,182 (12%)

Brian Kemp, Georgia's Republican governor, had a roller-coaster first two years in office. In 2018, Kemp narrowly defeated Democrat Stacey Abrams in an ideologically charged gubernatorial race, with strong support from President Donald Trump. When the coronavirus pandemic hit, Kemp faced criticism for reopening the state's economy quickly amid persistently high rates of cases. Then, when Trump narrowly lost the state in the presidential race, the president lashed out at Kemp and other top officials for certifying Joe Biden's presidential victory, even urging a GOP primary challenge to his onetime ally.

Growing up, Kemp worked on a farm near Athens. His ancestors include a Revolutionary War major, George Washington's postmaster general, and several state legislators. He graduated from the University of Georgia—the fourth generation in his family to do so—earning a bachelor's degree in agriculture. Kemp found financial success in homebuilding and real estate, although some of his ancillary investments in agriculture struggled. Frustrated in his interactions with local zoning rules, Kemp ran for the state Senate in 2002 and won in a strong Republican year. In 2006, he ran unsuccessfully for agriculture commissioner, but four years later, Gov. Sonny Perdue appointed him to the vacant secretary of state post. In that position, Kemp enacted a voter registration system that allowed voters to register online and by mobile app. But critics accused him of overzealously purging voters from the rolls. Kemp was also in office during a data breach of private information, including Social Security numbers that affected more than 6 million voters.

In 2017, Kemp became the first major Republican to announce a bid for governor, in anticipation of an open seat vacated by two-term Republican Gov. Nathan Deal. Of the candidates seeking the nomination, Lt. Gov. Casey Cagle had the most establishment support, although several other candidates ran as well—former state Sen. Hunter Hill, consulting firm executive Clay Tippins, and state Sen. Michael Williams. Each aggressively courted the Republican base, but Kemp was perhaps the most uncompromising. In one ad, he pointed a shotgun at a "young man" who was "interested in" one of his daughters. In another, he promised to personally "round up illegal criminals" using his pickup truck. Late in the primary campaign, Cagle miscalculated by attacking Hill in the hope of facing Kemp in a runoff. Cagle got what he wanted—he finished first in the primary with 39 percent, while Kemp finished second with 26 percent—but the two-man runoff only emphasized the base-vs.-establishment dynamic, and that ended up boosting Kemp. The coup de grace was Trump's tweeted endorsement of Kemp. He won, 70%-30%.

The Democratic primary was no less dramatic, pitting the "two Staceys." Stacey Abrams was born poor, but in a family with a strong educational drive. Abrams earned degrees from Spelman College, the University of Texas and Yale Law School, and she developed an interest in both politics and business. In 1992, she challenged then-Mayor Maynard Jackson over some of his policies at a town hall event; Jackson proceeded to hire her to work in the city's youth services office. Later, Abrams served as deputy city attorney. She also started a company that sold bottled water for babies, and another that handled payments for small businesses. In her spare time, Abrams wrote romance novels under a pen name. In 2006, Abrams won a seat in the state House; four years later, she was elected minority leader, the first woman to be chosen to lead a caucus in either chamber. Considered brainy, strategic, and charismatic, Abrams took charge of the shrunken Democratic ranks, at times shrewdly cooperating with the Republican majority. In the primary, Abrams faced Stacey Evans, who is white, grew up poor, raised by a single mother who moved the family in and around northern Georgia 16 times. Evans sought to recreate the old Georgia Democratic model of courting enough white moderates to put the party over the top. By contrast, Abrams—who had spearheaded a voter-mobilization group called the New Georgia Project—sought to energize less-frequent voters, many of them non-White. Democratic primary voters went hard for Abrams' approach; she defeated Evans, 76%-24%.

Despite some feints toward the center, the general election developed as a battle between clashing ideologies. The candidates divided sharply over expanding Medicaid, abortion, immigration, gun policy and marijuana legalization. Trump actively supported Kemp, including a rally in Macon days before the election. The closing weeks of the campaign were dominated by unsubstantiated allegations of voter fraud—an issue of special sensitivity to Kemp because he refused to step down as secretary of state as he was running for governor, with critics saying he was essentially overseeing his own election, although local election officials oversee balloting and counting. Democrats decried the state law that required an "exact match" in information on voting applications and other government databases, which affected an estimated 53,000 voters, many of them Black. When the votes were counted, the margin was close enough that Abrams refused to concede (and hadn't two years later). Kemp won by 55,000 votes out of 3.9 million cast, and he had only an 18,000-vote cushion above the threshold needed to avoid a runoff. Abrams made significant gains in once-Republican suburbs of Atlanta, but Kemp dominated in rural areas, enabling his victory.

In 2019, Kemp signed an overhaul of Georgia's election administration. While the measure was shepherded by Republicans, a number of its provisions had previously won Democratic support, including a ban on changing polling places 60 days before an election and a slower process for removing non-voters from registration lists. The measure also blocked county officials from rejecting absentee ballots due to mismatched signatures, and required the use of electronic voting machines that included a paper ballot. Kemp also signed a "fetal heartbeat" abortion bill, but it was blocked by a federal judge; the case continued on appeal.

The following year, Kemp signed hate crimes legislation that had stalled in previous legislative sessions. The debate came amid outrage over the killing of Ahmaud Arbery, a Black man pursued by three white men in Brunswick who said they thought he was a burglary suspect. "We witnessed a horrific, hate-filled act of violence," Kemp said during the legislative debate. "We saw injustice with our own eyes." As part of a legislative deal, language to consider police a protected class removed from the hate crimes bill but considered separately and passed. Also in 2020, Kemp won federal approval for a system to sell federally subsidized health insurance to Georgia residents through private brokers rather than a government-run website; he also won approval for a partial Medicaid expansion that included work requirements, even as other states were being forced by courts to abandon that approach.

But for Kemp, most of 2020 was dominated by the coronavirus pandemic. In April, he puzzled observers by saying he had been convinced to issue a shelter-in-place order only after learning that asymptomatic people can spread the disease, even though experts had been warning of that aspect of the disease for months. Then, later that month, Kemp reversed course, ending restrictions on many types of businesses, including gyms, tattoo parlors, and movie theaters. The move was opposed by public health specialists and local elected officials, and its speed and scope even raised Trump's eyebrows, with the president saying, "I was not happy with Brian Kemp. I will tell you that." In July, Kemp waged a court battle against Atlanta Mayor Keisha Lance Bottoms over the city's mask requirement; he backed down in August, which allowed the mandate to stay in place. The mask mandate did little to stem to the tide, however. By January 2021, Georgia ranked in the top 10 states nationally for most per capita cases, though the state ranked lower for coronavirus deaths.

After Trump lost Georgia in the 2020 election, he turned his ire on the state officials who refused to overturn the election results, including Kemp. Trump called the governor he had once endorsed a "clown" and a "fool," and he retweeted a call for Kemp to go to jail. Kemp countered that he "can only fight so much because I've got to follow the laws and the Constitution." Kemp added that Trump's attacks had prompted a wave of social media hatred against him and his family, including death threats. Kemp remained in the spotlight as the state's two Senate seats went to a Jan. 5 runoff. Kemp had appointed one of the GOP candidates, Kelly Loeffler, to the Senate, rebuffing Trump; the president had urged that a loyalist, Rep. Doug Collins, get the nod, but Kemp went with Loeffler, who was initially thought to be more electable as a suburban woman. The spurned Collins challenged Loeffler in the first round of voting but failed to make the runoff, and Loeffler, who had run to the right to make the initial cut, ultimately lost to Democrat Raphael Warnock. During the runoff, Trump continued to champion Collins—this time as a primary challenger to Kemp. Adding to the governor's headaches, Abrams was widely expected to run against Kemp in 2022, setting up another blockbuster contest in a state that had come to look increasingly purple.

In 2021, Georgia remained in the nation's political eye, as lawmakers passed, and Kemp signed, an election-law overhaul that Democrats decried, leading Major League Baseball to pull the All-Star Game from Atlanta. While some of the most controversial proposals didn't make the bill's final version, critics said that the ones that remained disproportionately harmed Black voters, and were unnecessary given the smooth election of 2020.

Jonathan Ossoff (D)

Elected 2021, term expires 2026, 1st term, b. Feb 16, 1987; Atlanta, GA; Georgetown University, B.S., 2009; London School of Economics, M.S., 2013; Jewish; Married (Alisha Kramer);

Professional Career: Deputy Communications Director, Hank Johnson for Congress, 2006-2007; Legislative Correspondent/ Systems Administrator, Office of Congressman Hank Johnson, 2007-2009; Campaign Manager, Committee to Re-Elect Congressman Hank Johnson, 2010; Senior Legislative Assistant/ Military Legislative Assistant, Office of Congressman Hank Johnson, 2009-2012; Managing Director/CEO, investigative television production company, 2013-2021.

DC Office: 455 RSOB 20510, 202-224-3521, Fax: 202-224-2575, ossoff.senate.gov

State Offices: Atlanta, 470-786-7800.

Committees: *Banking, Housing & Urban Affairs*: Economic Policy; Housing, Transportation & Community Development; National Security & International Trade & Finance. *Homeland Security & Government Affairs*: Emerging Threats & Spending Oversight; Government Operations & Border Management; Investigations (Chmn). *Judiciary*: Competition Policy, Antitrust & Consumer Rights; Constitution; Criminal Justice & Counterterrorism; Federal Courts, Oversight, Agency Action & Federal Rights; Privacy, Technology & the Law. *Rules & Administration*.

Election Results

Election	Name (Party)	Vote (%)	Cand. Spent	Ind. Exp. Support	Ind. Exp. Oppose
2020 General	Jonathan Ossoff (D)...................... 2,269,923	(51%)	$147,345,151	$21,679,376	$137,797,952
	David Perdue (R)............................. 2,214,979	(49%)	$88,564,495	$48,804,606	$63,793,891
2020 Primary	Jon Ossoff (D).................................. 626,819	(53%)			
	Teresa Tomlinson (D)..................... 187,416	(16%)			
	Sarah Riggs Amico (D)..................... 139,574	(12%)			
	Maya Dillard-Smith (D)................... 105,000	(9%)			

Elected at just 33, Jon Ossoff enters Congress as the youngest senator in nearly 50 years—a mark previously by a 30-year-old Joe Biden in 1973. Today, President Biden partially has Ossoff's runoff defeat of Republican Sen. David Perdue to thank for delivering a Democratic-controlled Senate. Ossoff, a documentary film executive, first rose to national political prominence in 2017 in a closely watched special House election in the Atlanta suburbs that marked the first measure of blowback to President Donald Trump. In what was then the most expensive House race ever, Ossoff fell short. Less than four years later, Ossoff came from behind to claim victory in the runoff, buoyed by an increasingly diverse electorate. Dual runoff victories on Jan. 5, 2021, made him and Democrat Raphael Warnock the first Democrats to win Senate seats in Georgia in 20 years; Ossoff also became the first Jewish senator from the state.

Ossoff grew up in the northwest Atlanta suburb of Northlake in DeKalb County, in a wealthy family whose father owned a legal-education company and whose mother, an Australian immigrant, helped recruit women to run for office in Georgia. While reading the memoir of civil rights icon John Lewis in high school, Ossoff wrote to the neighboring congressman and asked for an internship. Lewis was impressed and hired him. In 2006, then-DeKalb County Commissioner Hank Johnson was readying a primary challenge to controversial Democratic Rep. Cynthia McKinney. Ossoff became deputy communications director for Johnson's campaign, particularly focusing on emerging social media platforms. "He wanted to use blogs and this new thing that I'd never heard of, Facebook, and so I gave him license to do that," Johnson told the New York Times. "It immediately put my campaign on the map. It got my campaign national attention." After Johnson won, Ossoff worked part time in his Washington office as a legislative aide focusing on national security while attending Georgetown University's School of Foreign Service. One of his proudest accomplishments, Ossoff said, was writing a House resolution that Johnson sponsored calling for peace talks to resolve a conflict in northern Uganda. After working in Johnson's office for six years, Ossoff crossed the pond to attend the London School of Economics.

Ossoff had previously interned for Insight News, thanks to a meeting he had had when he was in high school with its founder, former BBC News journalist Ron McCullagh, at a dinner party his family attended while on vacation in France. McCullagh told the Times he "was completely blown away by his brightness, by his intelligence and by his knowledge." McCullagh hired the 26-year-old in 2013 as the Emmy, Peabody, and BAFTA-winning organization's CEO despite him having no journalism experience. Ossoff invested $250,000 of his own inheritance from his grandfather and changed the news group's name to Insight TWI, for "The World Investigates." Ossoff told the Washington Post he made the move because he admired the company and believed in its mission, but there was another reason too: "[I] had really seen enough of Congress in Washington to know that I didn't want to go back there and was really intrigued."

But the pull of Washington never fully left Ossoff. Four years later, he launched a run for Congress in Georgia's 6th District, vacated when GOP Rep. Tom Price resigned to be Trump's first Secretary of Health and Human Services. Democrats saw opportunity in the rapidly diversifying suburban district, which had voted for Mitt Romney in 2012 by 23 percentage points but had given Trump only a 1½-point margin of victory four years later. In the 18-candidate all-party field, Ossoff was one of five Democrats. Despite having never run for office, he quickly rose to the top of the pack with his impressive fundraising and a grassroots campaign—and with crucial endorsements from his former bosses and mentors, Lewis and Johnson. Republicans attacked Ossoff for living just outside the district, which he grew up in, and claimed he had embellished his role in Johnson's office. Nationwide, Democrats were energized at a chance to send a stinging rebuke to Trump and Republicans in a district once represented by former Speaker Newt Gingrich. In the April primary, Ossoff narrowly missed getting a majority of the vote, taking 48 percent of the vote. He advanced to a runoff against the second-place finisher, former Georgia Republican Secretary of State Karen Handel, who got 20 percent. Ossoff broke fundraising records, pulling in $23 million for the race, with over two-thirds coming from small-dollar donors. Republicans highlighted the out-of-state money pouring into the race, and Republican super PACs hammered Ossoff as an out-of-touch liberal who would be allied with House Minority Leader Nancy Pelosi if he won. That messaging helped Handel prevail in the July runoff, 52%-48%. The close race highlighted the rapid shifts in once-conservative Atlanta suburbs like Cobb County; the next year, Handel lost to Democrat Lucy McBath.

After his loss, Ossoff went back to his work at Insight TWI, focusing on the business side of the company, where he helped to vet story ideas and questions, set up interviews, and work with groups like the BBC and Al Jazeera English to commission documentary films. The company investigated and exposed crooked judges, human traffickers, war crimes, and bribery. Insight TWI's work exposing ISIS war crimes won particular acclaim. Its 2016 production for the BBC "Girls, Guns and ISIS" was described by The Sun as "hard hitting and unflinching." The 2018 follow up, "Face to Face with ISIS," won the One World Media Award. The award jury called the production "exemplary of popular journalism at its bravest, most insightful and empathetic."

After a Democratic wave swept Congress in 2018, Ossoff was pulled back into politics, and he challenged Perdue in 2020. He already had statewide name recognition and a massive fundraising email list thanks to his congressional run, which along with an ad cut by Lewis just months before his death, helped him to win the seven-way Democratic primary in June with 53 percent of the vote over several top-tier opponents. The race wasn't initially regarded as one of the top potential flips for Democrats, and for months Warnock's concurrent special election battle with Republican Sen. Kelly Loeffler overshadowed the looming Perdue-Ossoff fight. But both races became more competitive. Rising COVID-19 cases and related deaths as well as racial protests over the summer—sparked in part by the slayings in Georgia of two unarmed Black men, Ahmaud Arbery by white men in a truck and Rayshard Brooks by police—raised the temperature in the state.

Perdue at times appeared to bristle at facing his millennial opponent, who Republicans dismissed as a "trust fund socialist," despite the fact that Ossoff didn't agree with many progressive priorities, such as "Medicare for All." (He preferred a public option.) But Ossoff—who hadn't talked much about his work with Insight TWI during his House race—made fighting corruption a central focus of his campaign. That dovetailed with attacks on Trump, with whom Perdue had allied himself, and the president's strategy to fight the novel coronavirus, which was hitting Georgia hard. Later, the wealthy Perdue would come under fire for trading the highest number of stocks of any sitting senator, including shares of companies that had business before his committees and subcommittees. He would also be criticized for buying stocks right before the pandemic hit in companies that could stand to benefit, such as Pfizer. Perdue denied any wrongdoing, but the contrast benefited Ossoff. Perdue stumbled again just weeks before Election Day at a Trump rally when he mocked the name of Biden's running mate as "Kamala-mala-mala"—even though he was serving alongside California's Kamala Harris in the Senate.

Biden became the first Democratic presidential candidate to carry Georgia since 1992 that November, as Ossoff narrowly forced Perdue—who out-performed Trump by 780 votes and was the top Republican vote-getter statewide—into a runoff. Nationally, Democrats netted just one seat— far fewer than most analysts had projected, meaning the Senate would come down to Georgia—and Ossoff. This was the nightmare scenario for some Democrats, given that runoffs in Georgia were typically low-turnout affairs that benefited Republicans. And the GOP had a chef's-kiss message to motivate its base: a Republican Senate was needed as a check on a Democratic House and presidency. But Trump latched on to unfounded conspiracy theories that he had in fact won Georgia, and several other states, except for widespread voter fraud. Those claims were baseless, even as the president lashed out at not only Georgia Republican Secretary of State Brad Raffensperger for refusing to back him but also at GOP Gov. Brian Kemp when he certified the results. Trying to appeal to Trump voters they needed in the runoff, both Perdue and Loeffler called on Raffensperger to resign, though without giving a reason. Perdue largely ignored Ossoff throughout the runoff, skipping their only scheduled debate, and kept a closely guarded campaign schedule with few public appearances.

Ads overwhelmed the airwaves. Both Perdue and Loeffler were outspent by Democratic candidates, leaving GOP super PACs to try to make up the difference. But Trump's obsession with overturning the presidential election divided Republicans in the state. During two campaign stops there, including one on the eve of the election, Trump spent most of the time falsely claiming he won the election—and the state—and attacking Raffensperger and Kemp, rather than slamming Ossoff and Warnock. In the end, Republican fears were borne out. Despite the highest runoff turnout ever in the state—nearly 4.5 million, over 90 percent of the November turnout—it was Republican drop-off in heavy red areas such as North Georgia that was coupled with a huge Democratic turnout in heavily African American counties that sealed Perdue's fate. Ossoff prevailed 50.6%-49.4%, though he ran slightly behind Warnock. Underscoring their deep animosity, Perdue never called Ossoff to concede.

Raphael Warnock (D)

Elected 2021, term expires 2022, 1st term, b. Jul 23, 1969; Savannah, GA; Morehouse College, B.A., 1991; Union Theological Seminary, MDiv, MPhil, PhD; Baptist; Separated; 2 children.

Professional Career: Senior Pastor, Douglas Memorial Community Church of Baltimore; Youth Pastor/Assistant Pastor, Abyssinian Baptist Church of NYC; Senior Pastor, Ebenezer Baptist Church.

DC Office: Suite B40D DSOB 20510, 202-224-3643, Fax: 202-228-0724, warnock.senate.gov

State Offices: Atlanta, 770-694-7828.

Committees: *Aging. Agriculture, Nutrition & Forestry*: Commodities, Risk Management & Trade (Chmn); Food & Nutrition, Specialty Crops, Organics & Research; Livestock, Dairy, Poultry, Local Food Sys & Food Safety & Sec. *Banking, Housing & Urban Affairs*: Financial Institutions & Consumer Protection (Chmn); Housing, Transportation & Community Development; Securities, Insurance & Investment. *Commerce, Science & Transportation*: Aviation Safety, Operations & Innovations; Communications, Media & Broadband; Space & Science; Surface Transportation, Maritime Freight & Ports. *Joint Economic*.

Election Results

Election	Name (Party)	Vote (%)	Cand. Spent	Ind. Exp. Support	Ind. Exp. Oppose
2020 General	Raphael Warnock (D)...................... 2,289,113	(51%)	$95,592,379	$28,837,121	$79,277,838
	Kelly Loeffler (R)......................... 2,195,841	(49%)	$71,879,999	$25,644,492	$29,021,566

The Rev. Raphael Warnock already occupied an historic perch, spending over 15 years as the senior pastor of Ebenezer Baptist Church, where he preached from the same pulpit Martin Luther King Jr. once did. Now, Warnock has another line in history: He's the first Black senator from Georgia, a state both marred with the stain of the Civil War and a crucial pillar of the civil rights movement. In his defeat of appointed Republican Sen. Kelly Loeffler, Warnock became the first African-American Democrat elected to the Senate in the Deep South. And his January 2021 runoff win, alongside fellow Democrat Jon Ossoff, delivered Democrats their long-desired, albeit narrow, Senate majority.

The 11th of 12 children, Warnock was raised in public housing projects in Savannah Georgia, with the large family at times crammed into a four-bedroom apartment. Both Pentecostal pastors, his parents worked side jobs to make ends meet. His dad "worked on broken cars all week [and] worked on broken people on Sunday morning," Warnock told the Atlanta Journal-Constitution in 2005. So, perhaps Warnock's call to ministry was inevitable. After he delivered his first sermon at 11, he was nicknamed "The Rev." He took courses at Savannah State University while still in high school through the Upward Bound program to prepare for college. And he chose to attend the historically Black Morehouse College in Atlanta—which he paid for via loans and Pell Grants—in part because it was the alma mater of King, his hero.

Warnock's views shifted during college, away from his conservative Pentecostal upbringing and toward King's and the African-American Baptist tradition of civil rights. "It was the Baptists who preached a kind of Social Gospel that captured my attention and imagination," Warnock told the New York Times. Morehouse's campus pastor recommended Warnock for a summer internship at the historic Sixth Avenue Baptist Church in Birmingham, where he studied under pastor John Thomas Porter, a King mentee who had helped lead anti-segregation protests in the 1960s, and was ordained. After moving to New York City to attend Union Theological Seminary (from which he would eventually earn a master's degree in divinity, a master's of philosophy, and a doctorate), Warnock took a job as a youth pastor at Abyssinian Baptist Church, where former Harlem Democratic Rep. Adam Clayton Powell Jr. once preached. While at Abyssinian, Warnock would speak up against welfare work requirements that had been put in place by then-New York Mayor Rudy Giuliani, saying it was a "hoax" that pitted poor people "into competition with other poor people." Warnock served at Abyssinian for six years as youth pastor and four years as an assistant pastor before becoming senior pastor at Douglas Memorial Community Church in Baltimore.

In 2005, Warnock became Ebenezer's youngest pastor ever, returning him to his home state and to the footsteps of King. The downtown Atlanta church had long been one that married politics with the pulpit, and Warnock eagerly continued that tradition. Soon after Warnock arrived, the church organized a "Freedom Caravan," which transported Hurricane Katrina evacuees back to New Orleans to vote in a mayoral election. He worked with 2018 gubernatorial nominee Stacey Abrams's New Georgia Project to register minority voters in Georgia, expanding the drive into the pews. He eventually replaced Abrams as chair of the board of directors. "What I see in Raphael Warnock, every time we talk, every time we engage, is this belief that is core to him: that morality demands that he do good," Abrams told the Times.

In 2017, Warnock was arrested at the U.S. Capitol while protesting against Republican efforts to repeal the Affordable Care Act. In an interview with The Atlantic during his campaign, Warnock pointed to the Gospel of Luke. Jesus "says that he came to preach good news to the poor, and to set the captives free. ... I don't see how I could lift up that gospel on Sunday," he said, "and then fight to get rid of health care in the richest country in the world in the middle of a global pandemic on the floor of the United States Senate."

Warnock had thought about running for office before, particularly in 2016 against Republican Sen. Johnny Isakson. He consulted his congregation and ultimately demurred, but Warnock had a good relationship with Isakson that may have contributed to his hesitation. Just a few years later, when Isakson stepped down in late 2019 after being diagnosed with Parkinson's disease, Republican Gov. Brian Kemp chose a wealthy businesswoman to fill the seat: Loeffler. And as a civil war brewed on the Republican side, with Rep. Doug Collins jumping into the field to challenge the largely unknown and unvetted Loeffler from the right, Warnock sensed an opportunity. He announced his candidacy in January 2020 and was immediately endorsed by Abrams and the Democratic Senatorial Campaign Committee.

The special election was unique because all candidates would run on the same November ballot, regardless of party, and if no candidate got a majority, the race would head to a runoff—something that became a virtual certainty when 20 candidates qualified for the ballot. Most of the pre-November focus in the contest was on the bitter fight between Loeffler and Collins, with both angling for the pro-Trump vote. Collins, who had been one of the president's staunchest defenders during his first impeachment as ranking member of the House Judiciary Committee, believed he was the rightful heir to Isakson and felt snubbed, as did some in the White House, when Kemp bypassed him to appoint Loeffler. Kemp's choice seemed intended to appeal to suburban women, whom Republicans were losing badly in the age of Trump (and with whom Kemp had struggled during his 2018 narrow win over Abrams). Loeffler's husband, Jeffrey Sprecher, owned Intercontinental Exchange, the parent company of the New York Stock Exchange; she oversaw that company's cryptocurrency division and was also part owner of the WNBA's Atlanta Dream. Loeffler's net worth of over $500 million meant that she could self-fund a race too.

But with Collins in the race, Loeffler couldn't be the moderate, pragmatic businesswoman that likely most suited her views. Instead, she boasted of her 100 percent pro-Trump voting record, cozied up to QAnon-linked candidates like freshman Rep. Marjorie Taylor Greene of Georgia, and, in a bizarre series of ads, claimed she was "more conservative than Attila The Hun." Loeffler also came under scrutiny for selling about $20 million in stocks and buying shares in teleworking companies shortly after a Senate briefing on the COVID-19 threat. While her poor handling of that crisis seemed to harm her early on, she eventually would rebound, and Collins couldn't contend with the money she put into the race. There was some early worry among Democrats, too, who feared the presence of other Democrats in the race could stop Warnock from getting into the runoff. They pressured two other candidates—former U.S. Attorney Ed Tarver, who was also Black, and Matt Lieberman, the son of former vice presidential nominee and Connecticut Sen. Joe Lieberman—to drop out. Neither relented. But on Nov. 3, Warnock finished first, with 33 percent of the vote, and Loeffler took second with 26 percent. Collins was third with 20 percent, while Tarver and Lieberman finished far behind.

Republicans ran no negative ads against Warnock before November, but they believed they had a substantive opposition research trove to hit him with. The pastor anticipated the incoming volley, and his first runoff ad was a tongue-in-cheek look at the attacks to come, "hitting" Warnock for eating pizza with a fork and for stepping on a crack. "Raphael Warnock even hates puppies," the ad ominously intoned, before Warnock talked directly to camera: "I'm staying focused on what

Washington could do for you. … And by the way, I love puppies." Warnock's beagle would become a staple in his upbeat ads, standing in stark contrast to the negative barrage he was about to face.

With hours of sermons and public speeches under Warnock's belt, it's perhaps no surprise that his exegesis of scripture was central to the hits against him. To some, it went too far into attacks on the very core of the Black church and its rich civil rights foundation. It may have been a dog whistle to white conservative evangelicals but it also likely spurred even higher African-American turnout that led to victory. During one 2011 sermon, Warnock said that "nobody can serve God and the military," and GOP ads took the comment out of context. It was meant to expound upon Jesus's teaching in the Gospel of Matthew that "no one can serve two masters." Warnock pushed back against the anti-military characterization in an ad, noting his father had been a World War II veteran. Clips from 2008 of Warnock defending then-candidate Barack Obama's controversial pastor Jeremiah Wright also resurfaced. "We celebrate Rev. Wright in the same way we celebrate the truth-telling tradition of the Black church—which, when preachers tell the truth, very often it makes people uncomfortable," Obama told Fox News then.

Warnock's previous churches also became fodder: Abyssinian welcomed then-Cuban President Fidel Castro in 1995 (Warnock said was not involved), and there were allegations of abuse at a camp affiliated with his Baltimore church. The police had been investigating the claims, and Warnock was cited on obstruction charges. (Warnock said he was trying to make sure the teen camp counselors had legal representation.) At their only one-on-one debate, Loeffler called Warnock a "radical liberal" 13 times, pointed to his criticism of police officers, called his theology dangerous, and attacked him for supporting abortion rights. Loeffler denied her attacks were racially motivated, but Warnock retorted, "She's lied, not only on me, but about Jesus." Over 100 Black clergy signed a letter to Loeffler condemning her attacks on Warnock. "We call on you to cease and desist your false characterizations of Reverend Warnock as 'radical' or 'socialist,' when there is nothing in his background, writings or sermons that suggests those characterizations to be true, especially when taken in full context," they wrote.

Warnock's personal life also came under scrutiny. He and his wife had divorced earlier in 2020 after a brief marriage, and there were custody disputes over their two young children. The Journal-Constitution had reported early in the campaign that Ouleye Warnock claimed her estranged husband had run over her foot during a dispute; Raphael Warnock denied he had. and police found no damage to her foot. It wasn't until just weeks before the runoff, though, that body cam footage of that encounter surfaced on Fox News's "Tucker Carlson Tonight." "I've tried to keep the way that he acts under wraps for a long time and today he crossed the line," Ouleye Warnock told officers through tears. "So that is what is going on here. And he's a great actor. He is phenomenal at putting on a really good show." Loeffler said the woman's "voice deserved to be heard," and the National Republican Senatorial Committee quickly turned the video into an ad that ended with a phone number to a domestic violence hotline.

But all of Republicans' negative ads against Raphael Warnock couldn't counter their own Achilles's heel: the fact that Trump refused to acknowledge he had lost the election to Joe Biden and had spent two months claiming the November results in many states, including Georgia, were fraudulent. Loeffler and Republican Sen. David Perdue, fearful of losing the Trump base, backed the president's unsubstantiated allegations, even when he went on the attack against state GOP officials. Loeffler, especially, was in an uncomfortable position when Trump attacked Kemp for certifying the vote, given that he had appointed her. At his appearance in North Georgia on the eve of the election, Trump falsely claimed he had won the state and assailed Kemp—and Loeffler was silent. She then proclaimed that the following day she would vote to challenge the state's electoral votes in Congress —though she would eventually back off after Trump supporters stormed the Capitol in a riot that killed five and was incited by Trump.

In the end, turnout in the runoff was high—almost 90 percent of the November turnout. With more than 4 million votes, it was the biggest runoff in Georgia's history. However, turnout in Republican-heavy counties, especially in the northern part of the state, dipped substantially, while both Warnock and Ossoff, who was running against Perdue, drove up their victory margins in metro Atlanta, its suburbs and the Black Belt counties. Warnock prevailed 51.0%-49.0%, outrunning Ossoff. In his victory speech, he paid tribute to his mother: "The 82-year-old hands that used to pick somebody else's cotton went to the polls and picked her youngest son to be a United States senator." Warnock became just the 11th African-American to serve in the Senate, and he told CNN on the following day that, in context, his victory was "stunning" but showed that "in America anything is possible." Obama, just the fifth Black person to serve in the Senate, said the late Rep. John Lewis, a civil rights icon and a member Ebenezer, "is surely smiling down on his beloved Georgia this morning, as people across the state carried forward the baton that he and so many others passed down to them." Warnock said that he intended to continue serving and preaching at Ebenezer, but that could be tricky to juggle. Not only will he have to navigate his new role as senator, but he will need to run for a full term in 2022 in a seat Republicans were already making a top priority to regain.

Buddy Carter (R)

Elected 2014, 4th term, b. Sep 06, 1957; Port Wentworth, GA; Young Harris College, A.S., 1977; University of GA School of Pharmacy, B.S., 1980; Methodist; Married (Amy Coppage); 3 children; 3 grandchildren.

Elected Office: Pooler City Council, 1994-1995; Pooler Mayor, 1996-2004; GA House, 2005-2009; GA Senate, 2009-2014.

Professional Career: Pharmacist; Owner, Carter's Pharmacy Inc.

DC Office: 2432 RHOB 20515, 202-225-5831, Fax: 202-226-2269, buddycarter.house.gov

State Offices: Brunswick, 912-265-9010; Savannah, 912-352-0101.

Committees: *Budget. Energy & Commerce*: Communications & Technology; Environment & Climate Change; Health. *Select Committee on the Climate Crisis*.

Group Ratings

	ADA	ACLU	AFL-CIO	LCV	COC	HAFA	ACU	CFG	FRC
2020	**	20%	**	14%	-	87%	89%	**	-
2019	0%	C	24%	17%	77%	C	90%	90%	100%

Almanac Ratings 2019-2020

	Economy	Social	Foreign	Composite
Liberal	25%	14%	8%	16%
Conservative	75%	86%	92%	84%

Key Votes of the 116th Congress

1. U.S./Mex./Can. trade deal	Y	5. Russia sanctions	N	9. Firearms background checks	N
2. First Coronavirus response	Y	6. Troops in Syria	Y	10. Spending at the border	N/A
3. HEROES Act	N	7. Veto arms sales to Saudis	N	11. Marijuana liberalized rules	N/A
4. CASH Act	N	8. Defense $$$, veto override	Y	12. Electoral College objections	Y

Election Results

Election	Name (Party)	Vote (%)		Cand. Spent	Ind. Exp. Support	Ind. Exp. Oppose
2020 General	Buddy Carter (R)	189,457	(58%)	$1,366,017	$5,312	$750
	Joyce Griggs (D)	135,238	(42%)			
2020 Primary	Buddy Carter (R)	65,907	(82%)			
	Daniel Merritt (R)	13,154	(16%)			

Prior winning percentages: 2018 (58%), 2016 (100%), 2014 (61%)

First elected in 2014 after a fierce primary battle with a tea-party candidate, Republican Earl "Buddy" Carter usually aligns with the Main Street wing of the GOP. He has used his seat on the influential Energy and Commerce Committee to work on health care and prescription-drug issues, with which he had extensive private-sector experience.

A successful pharmacy owner, his campaign photo featured him behind the counter of his small-town drug store. Carter was spurred by his interest in local business issues to run for mayor of Pooler in 1996; he served eight years. He then won election to the state House in 2004 and moved to the state Senate in 2008, securing seats on the appropriations and health panels and eventually rising to deputy whip. The House seat opened when Rep. Jack Kingston made an unsuccessful Senate bid.

The 1st District is solidly Republican, but not as deep red as other parts of Georgia, thanks to the northern transplants who have settled there and the Democratic-leaning city of Savannah. That may have helped Carter in 2014, when he faced off in the primary against a well-funded challenger, surgeon Bob Johnson, who tried to outgun Carter from the right.

Johnson blasted Carter as a political insider and took aim at his ties to pharmacy groups, implying that Carter deliberately delayed the reporting of Medicaid reimbursements to his pharmacies. These positions helped Johnson win the backing of the Club for Growth. In the July runoff, Carter tied himself closely to Kingston, who also was on the runoff ballot, and he took aim at inflammatory comments by Johnson. The Club for Growth spent nearly $400,000 against Carter. However, Carter prevailed in the runoff, 54%-46%, then won the general election against an obscure Democratic candidate, 61%-39%. In 2020, he again demonstrated his aversion to the party's far right wing by opposing conservative firebrand Marjorie Taylor Greene in the Republican contest for an open seat. His efforts were unsuccessful, as Greene easily won the runoff.

Carter's selection to Energy and Commerce in 2017 gave him an opportunity to apply his drugstore knowledge to health care issues. Carter offered legislation to repeal the "gag clause" that permitted pharmacy benefit managers to bar pharmacists from informing customers about lower-priced options. Carter called it "a great day for patients" when President Donald Trump signed the bipartisan bill into law in October 2018. Also that month, Trump signed legislation designed to reduce opioid addiction, which included Carter's provisions to empower pharmacists with authority to reduce prescription sales from so-called pill mills. As the only pharmacist serving in Congress, he was a vocal supporter of vaccination during the COVID-19 pandemic and participated in Pfizer's vaccine trial. While he pushed for mask wearing on an individual level, he said the government should not mandate it.

Carter has also been attentive to local issues. He praised local leaders for their handling of racial justice protests after the February 2020 killing of Ahmaud Arbery, a 25-year-old Black man, in Brunswick. Arbery was shot by three white men who believed he was a criminal. In an interview with the Bryan County News, Carter said "Look, Black lives matter. I agree with that statement. I think they do matter, and I don't think there's any question about that." However, he also criticized the national Black Lives Matter group, calling it a "Marxist social movement." Carter has strongly supported a proposed spaceport in Camden County and attempted to facilitate the environmental review process by federal authorities. It raised eyebrows when a local news outlet discovered that Carter bought a $2 million property near the spaceport. Carter said he bought the land for recreational purposes only and was not required to disclose it under ethics rules.

Carter did not draw a Democratic challenger in his first reelection bid in 2016. In 2018 and 2020, however, he was challenged by Democrats Lisa Ring and Joyce Marie Griggs, respectively, and received 58 percent of the vote in each election. Carter, who represents Georgia's Atlantic coast, has taken moderate positions on climate change and offshore drilling. He says climate change is real but is skeptical of solutions that could harm the economy. He generally supports offshore oil drilling but has also pushed for state and local officials to weigh in on the issue. In April 2021, Carter said that he was exploring a run in what could be a crowded primary in 2022 to face freshman Sen. Raphael Warnock.

GA-1: Southeast Georgia   Cook Partisan Voting Index: **R+9**

Population		Race and Ethnicity		Income	
Total	749,949	White	62.10%	Median Income	$55,542
Land area (sq. miles)	7,983	Black	30.70%	District Income Rank	323
Pop/ sq mi	93.95	Latino	7.00%	Poverty Rate	14.80%
Born in State	54.00%	Asian	1.70%	With health insurance	85.40%
		Two or more races	2.80%	Cash public assistance	1.10%
Age Groups		Other	2.90%	Food stamp/SNAP	12.30%
Under 18	23.30%				
18-34	24.80%	**Education**		**Work**	
35-64	36.40%	H.S grad or less	41.60%	White Collar	33.50%
Over 64	15.70%	Some college	32.30%	Sales and Service	41.60%
		College Degree, 4 yr	16.50%	Blue Collar	24.90%
Military		Post grad	9.80%	Government	16.70%
Veteran/ Active Duty	14.00%				

2020 Pres. Vote	Trump	184,820	(55%)	Biden	143,608	(43%)		
2016 Pres. Vote	Trump	151,996	(56%)	Clinton	110,190	(41%)	Johnson	7,382 (3%)

Savannah, Brunswick: In Georgia, the focus is usually on Atlanta, but the state also has some urbane smaller cities with deep roots in the past. One is Savannah, the state's first capital, which by the 1830s was one of America's booming cotton ports. It languished after the Civil War and lived off paper mills and chemical plants for much of the 20th century, while impoverished Blacks on the islands a few miles offshore still spoke Gullah dialects. In the past few decades, houses and churches have been restored on a street grid laid out more than 200 years before.

Today, Savannah is one of the most graciously preserved cities in the country and a prime destination for tourists, who bolstered the local economy by nearly $3 billion annually before a dramatic slowdown during the COVID-19 pandemic. The population of the city is 54percent African American. The region has become a vibrant center for overseas trade. Savannah is the fourth-busiest port in the nation and has the busiest single terminal for container cargo in North America, which expedites fast distribution to customers. State and local officials have been deepening the port of Savannah to 47 feet and extending the channel of the Savannah River by seven miles, at a cost of nearly $1 billion, to attract the next generation of large container ships, which carry more cargo through the widened Panama Canal. Completion is scheduled for 2022. Local groups have sought to change the name of the Eugene Talmadge Bridge across the Savannah River; the former governor was an ardent segregationist. The renaming may be a moot point though as port officials say the 30-year-old bridge needs to be replaced within the next decade to accommodate larger ships. The cost would be about $1 billion.

The 1st Congressional District of Georgia covers the state's entire Atlantic coast, including all of Savannah. Also in the 1st are the Sea Islands, with a prospering resort economy and efforts to preserve the African-American Gullah culture and its eponymous West African-originated Creole language. Along the coast south of Savannah is the tiny, historic black settlement of Pin Point. Its citizens are mostly descendants of the first slaves in the area, and its most famous son is Supreme Court Justice Clarence Thomas.

The district has small cities, including Brunswick, a World War II shipbuilding center that has been revitalized as the gateway to the Sea Islands, and isolated Waycross, a railroad junction and gateway to the Okefenokee Swamp, the largest swamp in North America. In 2020, Brunswick came into the national spotlight after a 25-year-old black man, Ahmaud Arbery, was killed while jogging. His alleged killers were three White men who erroneously believed Arbery was a criminal. In the state's southeastern corner, Camden County officials have been attempting since 2012 to establish a private spaceport. However, the proposed launch trajectory passes over nearby Little Cumberland Island and the Federal Aviation Administration has not approved the project amid opposition from homeowners and environmental groups.

This was Democratic country for a century after Gen. William Tecumseh Sherman's troops marched through Georgia. Today it has become more firmly Republican. Donald Trump won the district with 55 percent of the vote in each of his elections. The only Democratic-leaning counties are Chatham, the home of Savannah – which had a Republican mayor from 2015 through 2019 – and Liberty, home of Hinesville.

Sanford Bishop (D)

Elected 1992, 15th term, b. Feb 04, 1947; Mobile, AL; Morehouse College, B.A., 1968; Emory University Law School, J.D., 1971; Baptist; Married (Vivian Creighton Bishop); 1 child; 1 grandchild.

Military Career: U.S. Army Reserve 1969-1971

Elected Office: GA House, 1977-1990; GA Senate, 1991-1992.

Professional Career: Primary partner Attorney, Bishop & Buckner, P.C., 1972-1992.

DC Office: 2407 RHOB 20515, 202-225-3631, Fax: 202-225-2203, bishop.house.gov

State Offices: Albany, 229-439-8067; Columbus, 706-320-9477; Macon, 478-803-2631.

Committees: *Agriculture*: General Farm Commodities & Risk Management; Livestock & Foreign Agriculture. *Appropriations*: Agriculture, Rural Development, FDA & Related Agencies (Chmn); Financial Services & General Government; Military Construction, Veterans Affairs & Related Agencies.

Group Ratings

	ADA	ACLU	AFL-CIO	LCV	COC	HAFA	ACU	CFG	FRC
2020	**	78%	**	100%	-	0%	23%	**	-
2019	90%	C	100%	93%	65%	C	24%	12%	0%

Almanac Ratings 2019-2020

	Economy	Social	Foreign	Composite
Liberal	100%	65%	80%	82%
Conservative	0%	35%	20%	18%

Key Votes of the 116th Congress

1. U.S./Mex./Can. trade deal	Y	5. Russia sanctions	Y	9. Firearms background checks Y
2. First Coronavirus response	Y	6. Troops in Syria	Y	10. Spending at the border	Y
3. HEROES Act	Y	7. Veto arms sales to Saudis	Y	11. Marijuana liberalized rules	Y
4. CASH Act	Y	8. Defense $$$, veto override	Y	12. Electoral College objections N

Election Results

Election	Name (Party)	Vote (%)		Cand. Spent	Ind. Exp. Support	Ind. Exp. Oppose
2020 General	Sanford Bishop (D)....................... 161,397	(59%)	$1,415,882	$9,774	
	Don Cole (R).................................... 111,620	(41%)	$160,374		
2020 Primary	Sanford Bishop (D)....................... 82,964	(100%)			

Prior winning percentages: 2018 (60%), 2016 (61%), 2014 (60%), 2012 (64%), 2010 (51%), 2008 (69%), 2006 (68%), 2004 (67%), 2002 (100%), 2000 (54%), 1998 (57%), 1996 (54%), 1994 (66%), 1992 (64%)

Sanford Bishop, first elected in 1992, has been among the most conservative members of the Congressional Black Caucus—and among House Democrats generally. With the Democratic takeover of the House in 2018, he became a subcommittee "cardinal" and a powerful lawmaker on agriculture spending. In 2020, he became the dean of Georgia's congressional delegation after Rep. John Lewis died.

Bishop grew up in Mobile Alabama, where his father was a college president. He went to Morehouse College in Atlanta, where he was student body president in 1968 and sang at Martin Luther King Jr.'s funeral. "I resolved, after his death, that I would try to follow in his footsteps," he told the Columbus Ledger-Enquirer years later. He went to Emory Law School, and then served in the Army. After a year in New York, he settled in Columbus to practice law. He was elected to the state House in 1976 at age 29. He served there until 1990, when he was elected to the Georgia Senate. In 1992, he ran for the House against Democratic Rep. Charles Hatcher, who was damaged by the House bank scandal that year; in addition, redistricting changes increased the African-American population of the district. Bishop defeated Hatcher in the runoff, 53%-47%, and won the general election 64%-36%.

Bishop has been up-front in separating himself from mainstream Democratic views, primarily on cultural issues. He joined the conservative Blue Dog Democrats and over the years has supported a balanced budget, school prayer, a ban on flag burning and a proposed constitutional amendment to prohibit same-sex marriage. For years he held an A+ rating from the National Rifle Association, but was downgraded to a C in the group's 2020 ratings. He was among the handful of Democrats who did not support the June 2016 House sit-in that protested inaction on gun-control legislation. Despite these deviations from Democratic orthodoxy, Bishop supports social welfare programs for low-income people, including food stamps and health care access under the Affordable Care Act.

With a seat on Appropriations, Bishop has worked to safeguard and deliver funds to an array of local interests. For four years, he was ranking Democrat on the Military Construction, Veterans Affairs and Related Agencies Subcommittee, where he defended the interests of his district's expansive military facilities. He worked with the Obama administration to strengthen the Department of Veterans Affairs. Throughout his career, Bishop has looked out for Georgia's peanut farmers. He worked with Republicans on the Freedom to Farm Act to fashion a "market-oriented, no-net cost" program for peanuts. On the 2008 farm bill, he helped design the peanut-rotation program, which he said encouraged "a cleaner, greener method of planting while ensuring an affordable and accessible supply to the markets that rely on U.S.-grown peanuts."

Bishop's clout on farm issues was enhanced when he switched in 2017 to ranking Democrat on the Agriculture Subcommittee. He became the subcommittee chairman after Democrats won the House in 2018. Although he expressed a willingness to work with Agriculture Secretary Sonny Perdue, the former Republican Georgia governor who Bishop served with in the state Senate, the two came into conflict over Trump administration policies, particularly the Agriculture Department's rule imposing work requirements on some food stamp recipients. Bishop particularly objected when the administration pushed ahead with the rule in the early days of the COVID-19 pandemic. However, it was eventually blocked by the federal courts.

Bishop, who was first elected to replace a scandal-tainted opponent, faced his own ethical issues in 2020. The Office of Congressional Ethics released a report in July that alleged Bishop improperly spent $90,000 in campaign and other official funds on personal expenses, mostly golf club fees and gasoline. Bishop acknowledged that errors were made by his campaign and said he was reimbursing many of the charges. However, the OCE report noted that Bishop was sloppy in his record keeping and that some of his justifications were not plausible. For example, he and his wife did not keep mileage logs for fuel costs, and he said golfing was akin to campaigning because it gave him the opportunity to "run into" supporters.

Bishop faced serious reelection competition in 2000 from Republican Dylan Glenn. The contest between two African Americans in a rural, then majority-white district was unprecedented, but race was not an issue in the campaign. Bishop largely ignored the challenger and ran on his record, while Glenn offered the perspective of a new generation focusing on economic growth. Bishop won 54%-46%.

In 2010, Republicans targeted him for what they called excessive fealty to Speaker Nancy Pelosi. His opponent was Mike Keown, a white state representative who highlighted Bishop's support of the Democrats' health care overhaul. He attacked Keown for lacking much of a political record and got a break when a strategist for Keown was indicted in a vote-buying case in Alabama. Bishop prevailed 51%-49%. Republican-led redistricting in 2012 strengthened Bishop and turned his seat into an African-American majority district, while reinforcing neighboring GOP Rep. Austin Scott. Since then, Bishop has not had a serious challenge. He faced Republican opponents in every election from 2012 to 2020 but always won with around 60 percent of the vote. In 2020, he was challenged by Don Cole, a pastor and former speechwriter for Secretary Perdue. Bishop won, 59%-41%.

After Democrats lost the House in 2010, Bishop refused to back Pelosi for minority leader. He warned that her leadership would make it difficult to recruit candidates in the South and Republican-leaning states. When they regained control in 2018, he moved quickly to support her for Speaker—and assure his own cachet in the new majority.

GA-2: Southwest Georgia

Cook Partisan Voting Index: D+4

Population		Race and Ethnicity		Income	
Total	671,831	White	41.60%	Median Income	$39,728
Land area (sq. miles)	9,626	Black	52.80%	District Income Rank	431
Pop/ sq mi	69.79	Latino	5.20%	Poverty Rate	23.90%
Born in State	71.80%	Asian	1.00%	With health insurance	85.40%
		Two or more races	2.00%	Cash public assistance	1.80%
Age Groups		Other	2.50%	Food stamp/SNAP	22.70%
Under 18	23.30%				
18-34	23.40%	Education		Work	
35-64	37.20%	H.S grad or less	48.60%	White Collar	29.00%
Over 64	16.10%	Some college	32.90%	Sales and Service	41.40%
		College Degree, 4 yr	10.40%	Blue Collar	29.60%
Military		Post grad	8.10%	Government	18.00%
Veteran/ Active Duty	10.90%				

2020 Pres. Vote	Biden	154,912	(56%)	Trump	120,780	(43%)	
2016 Pres. Vote	Clinton	136,456	(55%)	Trump	107,361	(43%)	

Columbus, Macon: The hub of central Georgia, Macon is a city proud of its restored houses and its Japanese cherry trees, which it shows off during its annual International Cherry Blossom Festival. It has been the home of music legends Otis Redding, James Brown, Little Richard and the Allman Brothers, and of the Harriet Tubman African-American Museum. Although businesses fled to the suburbs in the 1970s, downtown Macon has recently been revitalized thanks to the efforts of Mercer University. It now hosts a vibrant nightlife and high-rise apartments.

The long shadow of history is felt here. Before the Civil War, the southwest corner of Georgia was mostly plantation country. This is where the Confederate Army ran the Andersonville military prison. About 13,000 of the 45,000 Union soldiers confined there died, and they are remembered at the National Prisoner of War Museum at Andersonville. Today, the U.S. military is a strong presence in the Columbus area. Fort Benning, which spreads into Alabama, is the nation's fifth-largest military installation, home of the Army Infantry School and of the Army Armor School. Benning can now train as many as 17,000 at a time. In 2015, the base suffered a cutback of about 1,000 troops following force realignments. It retained about 11,000 military personnel and nearly as many civilians. Fort Benning will have its name changed in the near future as the 2020 defense authorization bill, passed over President Donald Trump's veto, provides for the renaming of bases with Confederate namesakes.

Much of the rest of this region is farmland. Cotton and peanuts are major crops, and pecans are also grown here. Near the Florida border is Cairo, birthplace of Black baseball pioneer Jackie Robinson. Albany has a civil rights museum and was the site of some of Martin Luther King Jr.'s protests in the 1960s. It was also an early hotspot for COVID-19 in 2020, which disproportionately affected the region's impoverished African-American communities. Even before the pandemic hit, the region's majority Black counties suffered from a lack of health care access and had some of the highest death rates in the country. Not far from Albany, between upland pine stands and bottomland habitats, is the Chickasawhatchee Swamp, one of the Southeast's largest freshwater swamps. Plains are the childhood home of President Jimmy Carter, who remained active and has said he wants to be buried in his front yard. In October 2018, Hurricane Michael became the worst hurricane to hit the area in more than a century; it caused more than $2.5 billion in damage to agriculture. Federal relief was not enacted until mid-2019 as it was tied to aid for Puerto Rico.

The 2nd Congressional District of Georgia covers the southwestern part of the state and includes counties that border Florida and Alabama. It is barely a Black-majority district and has a Democratic lean, though not nearly as strong as the three Black-majority districts in the Atlanta area. Joe Biden won the district in 2020 with 56 percent of the vote, nearly the same as Hillary Clinton's 2016 performance. Like Clinton, he won 11 of the district's 29 counties and had large margins in the population centers – Bibb County (Macon), Dougherty County (Albany), and Muskogee County (Columbus). Barack Obama received 59 percent in his 2012 victory over Mitt Romney.

Drew Ferguson (R)

Elected 2016, 3rd term, b. Nov 15, 1967; West Point, AL; University of GA, B.S., 1988; Medical College of GA, D.M.D., 1992; Catholic; Married (Elizabeth Ferguson); 4 children.

Elected Office: Mayor of West Point, GA, 2008-2016.

Professional Career: Practicing dentist, Medical College of GA, 1998-2016.

DC Office: 1032 LHOB 20515, 202-225-5901, Fax: 202-225-2515, ferguson.house.gov

State Offices: Newnan, 770-683-2033.

Committees: Republican Chief Deputy Whip. *Ways & Means*: Oversight; Select Revenue Measures; Trade.

Group Ratings

	ADA	ACLU	AFL-CIO	LCV	COC	HAFA	ACU	CFG	FRC
2020	**	15%	**	10%	-	88%	86%	**	-
2019	0%	C	29%	7%	85%	C	86%	76%	95%

Almanac Ratings 2019-2020

	Economy	Social	Foreign	Composite
Liberal	25%	12%	11%	16%
Conservative	75%	88%	89%	84%

Key Votes of the 116th Congress

1. U.S./Mex./Can. trade deal Y	5. Russia sanctions Y	9. Firearms background checks N
2. First Coronavirus response Y	6. Troops in Syria Y	10. Spending at the border Y
3. HEROES Act N	7. Veto arms sales to Saudis N	11. Marijuana liberalized rules N/A
4. CASH Act N	8. Defense $$$, veto override Y	12. Electoral College objections N

Election Results

Election	Name (Party)	Vote (%)		Cand. Spent	Ind. Exp. Support	Ind. Exp. Oppose
2020 General	Drew Ferguson (R)...............................	241,526	(65%)	$1,846,417	$7,236	$750
	Val Almonord (D).............................	129,792	(35%)	$29,512		
2020 Primary	Drew Ferguson (R)...............................	94,166	(100%)			

Prior winning percentages: 2018 (66%), 2016 (68%)

Ever since defeating a tea party challenger in his 2016 election, Drew Ferguson has been a firm ally of the Republican establishment. He moved quickly into House leadership as the GOP's chief deputy whip following the 2018 election and received a coveted slot on the Ways and Means Committee.

A native of West Point, Ferguson earned his bachelor's degree from the University of Georgia and his doctorate in dental medicine from the Medical College of Georgia. He established a family dental practice and joined the Medical College faculty. Meanwhile, his concern about the loss of local industrial jobs led him to participate actively in the civic and business life of West Point, which has a population of 4,000. In 2008, Ferguson was elected mayor. His crowning achievement was the opening of the massive Kia Motors plant in 2009, which employs thousands in the region.

Rep. Lynn Westmoreland's retirement in 2016 resulted in a seven-candidate Republican primary for his open seat. The best-known contender was state Sen. Mike Crane, who was viewed as the most conservative candidate, especially on social issues; he identified himself as close to Texas Sen. Ted Cruz, who made a campaign appearance. The Club for Growth endorsed Crane and spent more than $800,000 on his behalf. Ferguson highlighted his record as mayor of West Point, including the economic impact of the Kia auto plant. He won Westmoreland's endorsement, who said Ferguson was "a strong, conservative voice for hardworking Georgians" who could build political relationships. Ferguson led Crane in the May primary, 27%-26%, a margin of 93 votes.

In the runoff nine weeks later, Crane said he was "standing for liberty and freedom" against "a bunch of big government, big business, crony-capitalist types masquerading as true conservatives and now they have all lumped themselves together into one group." Ferguson responded that government requires coalition-building, rather than "going up there with a stick of dynamite and blowing it all up." The U.S. Chamber of Commerce spent more than $650,000 on his behalf. Crane's campaign spent about $500,000, almost half of Ferguson's fundraising. Ferguson prevailed 54%-46%. In the general election against Angela Pendley, a political neophyte, Ferguson won easily, 68%-32%.

With a boost from Westmoreland, who was an ally of House leaders, Ferguson quickly became a party insider. They identified him as one of several mainstream newcomers who defeated party outsiders in heavily Republican districts. Following the 2018 election, Rep. Patrick McHenry stepped down as chief deputy whip, and GOP Whip Steve Scalise named Ferguson as his successor. That position has become a stepping-stone to additional influence for other senior House Republicans.

Ferguson aligned with other Republican leaders in opposing Marjorie Taylor Greene in Georgia's open seat. After a Politico report revealed that Greene had made bigoted remarks about Blacks, Muslims, and Jews, Ferguson said she "shouldn't have a place in Congress" and endorsed her primary challenger, John Cowan. It was to little avail as Greene trounced Cowan in the runoff and then easily won the general election. He has also complimented House Republican Conference Chair Liz Cheney, despite criticism from some Republicans who saw her as insufficiently supportive of President Donald Trump.

His seat on Ways and Means was another sign that Ferguson is in the good graces of top Republican leaders. He has focused on trade policy and was one of four committee members who went to Canada to negotiate the revised trade agreement with Canada and Mexico. He also showcased his independence on trade issues in 2018 by opposing some of Trump's automobile tariffs, citing the impact they might have on the Kia plant in his district.

Ferguson has had no problem winning reelection; he received 66 and 65 percent of the vote against Democratic opponents in 2018 and 2020. His 2020 opponent was Val Almonord, an Army veteran and local union activist.

GA-3: Southern Atlanta Exurbs   Cook Partisan Voting Index: R+16

Population		Race and Ethnicity		Income	
Total	750,998	White	68.60%	Median Income	$66,614
Land area (sq. miles)	3,838	Black	25.40%	District Income Rank	198
Pop/ sq mi	195.66	Latino	6.00%	Poverty Rate	12.30%
Born in State	61.60%	Asian	2.10%	With health insurance	89.30%
		Two or more races	2.00%	Cash public assistance	1.20%
Age Groups		Other	1.90%	Food stamp/SNAP	11.30%
Under 18	23.70%				
18-34	21.40%	**Education**		**Work**	
35-64	39.10%	H.S grad or less	42.70%	White Collar	36.20%
Over 64	15.70%	Some college	31.30%	Sales and Service	35.90%
		College Degree, 4 yr	16.40%	Blue Collar	27.90%
Military		Post grad	9.70%	Government	13.80%
Veteran/ Active Duty	10.00%				

2020 Pres. Vote	Trump	235,751	(62%)	Biden	140,460	(37%)		
2016 Pres. Vote	Trump	200,624	(64%)	Clinton	102,155	(33%)	Johnson	9,085 (3%)

Newnan, Carrollton: South of Atlanta, Henry County has been among the fastest growing areas in the United States. In 1980 it was a rural community with 36,000 residents. Buoyed by its proximity to Hartsfield-Jackson International Airport and Interstate 75, the county became a logistics hub for businesses and a residence for Atlanta commuters. By 2019, the population was 235,000, a 550 percent increase over 40 years. The massive growth has made Henry a traffic nightmare, leading local officials to focus on road improvements and, potentially, public transit solutions.

West of Henry County is the old courthouse town of Fayetteville, whose Holliday-Dorsey-Fife House is thought to have inspired the columned architecture of Tara in Margaret Mitchell's classic Gone With the Wind. The surrounding area in Fayette County is engulfed by subdivisions spreading out from Atlanta. Sprawl has reached Newnan and Carrollton and extends farther south to Thomaston. Businesses are locating in these communities as well. Goodyear Tire and Rubber is building a massive facility in Newnan. Zinus, a South Korean mattress and furniture manufacturer, is locating its first US facility in McDonough and will create 800 jobs.

In the old textile town of West Point in Troup County, along the Alabama border, South Korean automaker Kia invested more than $1 billion for a local plant, its first North American facility, which opened in 2009. With its suppliers, the company said it brought more than 15,000 jobs to the region.

At the beginning of the COVID-19 pandemic, the Kia plant shut down twice (once for public health and again for supply chain issues), hurting its 2,700 workers and local companies that rely heavily on their business.

The 3rd Congressional District of Georgia takes in part of the Atlanta metro area, including southwest and central Henry County and Peachtree City, where many airline pilots live and use the city's famous golf cart paths that connect homes to businesses and shopping areas. It also extends into rural and exurban areas. Newnan is home of the African-American Museum and the adjacent Farmer Street Cemetery, believed to be the largest slave cemetery in the South. The district stretches south to include LaGrange and part of Columbus. Nearby is Warm Springs, where Franklin D. Roosevelt received extensive physical rehabilitation as president. Coweta is the population center of the district, followed by Fayette and Carroll counties.

The ancestral politics of this area was Democratic, but that is as much a part of history now as Tara. The 3rd is solidly Republican, but Democratic presidential candidates improved marginally over the decade. Romney's 66%-33% margin over Obama in 2012 shrunk to a 64%-33% win for Trump in 2016 and a 62%-37% win in 2020. Trump held or slightly improved Republican margins in rural counties but lost ground in south Atlanta and north Columbus counties.

Hank Johnson (D)

Elected 2006, 8th term, b. Oct 02, 1954; Washington, DC; Clark College, B.A., 1976; TX Southern University, Thurgood Marshall School of Law, J.D., 1979; Buddhism; Married (Mereda Davis Johnson); 2 children.

Elected Office: DeKalb County comm., 2001-2006.

Professional Career: Practicing attorney, 1980-2006; Association judge, DeKalb County magistrate court, 1989-2001.

DC Office: 2240 RHOB 20515, 202-225-1605, Fax: 202-226-0691, hankjohnson.house.gov

State Offices: Decatur, 770-987-2291.

Committees: *Judiciary*: Antitrust, Commercial & Administrative Law; Constitution, Civil Rights & Civil Liberties; Courts, Intellectual Property & Internet (Chmn). *Oversight & Reform*: National Security; Subcommittee on Economic & Consumer Policy. *Transportation & Infrastructure*: Aviation; Highways & Transit.

Group Ratings

	ADA	ACLU	AFL-CIO	LCV	COC	HAFA	ACU	CFG	FRC
2020	**	82%	**	100%	-	0%	3%	**	-
2019	95%	C	100%	97%	67%	C	3%	12%	0%

Key Votes of the 116th Congress

1. U.S./Mex./Can. trade deal Y	5. Russia sanctions Y	9. Firearms background checks Y
2. First Coronavirus response Y	6. Troops in Syria Y	10. Spending at the border Y
3. HEROES Act Y	7. Veto arms sales to Saudis Y	11. Marijuana liberalized rules Y
4. CASH Act Y	8. Defense $$$, veto override Y	12. Electoral College objections N

Election Results

Election	Name (Party)	Vote (%)		Cand. Spent	Ind. Exp. Support	Ind. Exp. Oppose
2020 General	Hank Johnson (D)............................	278,906	(80%)	$385,776	$951	
	Johsie Cruz (R).................................	69,393	(20%)	$10,670		$113
2020 Primary	Hank Johnson (D)........................	102,227	(68%)			
	Elaine Nietman (D)........................	27,376	(18%)			
	William Haston (D)...........................	19,829	(13%)			

Prior winning percentages: 2018 (79%), 2016 (76%), 2014 (100%), 2012 (74%), 2010 (75%), 2008 (100%), 2006 (75%)

Best known for his controversial, and often entertaining, remarks, Democrat Hank Johnson saw his major policy focus, law enforcement reform, gain traction in 2020 during a summer of racial justice protests. He also gained clout as chairman of the Judiciary Subcommittee on Courts, Intellectual Property and the Internet. Johnson is secure in his heavily Democratic seat, despite facing tough primary challenges in 2010 and 2014.

Johnson was born in Washington D.C., where his father was director of classifications and paroles for the Bureau of Prisons and his mother was a schoolteacher. He practiced law as a civil and criminal litigator and served 12 years as a magistrate judge in DeKalb County and then five years on the DeKalb County Commission. Although his immediate family members are Presbyterians, he has been a Buddhist since the 1970s; he and Democratic Sen. Mazie Hirono of Hawaii are the first practicing Buddhists in Congress. "If you could say what drives me, it's the middle ground, the middle way," he told The Atlanta Journal-Constitution in 2009, invoking a Buddhist principle. He is a member of the Congressional Free thought Caucus, which advocates secular government.

In 2006, Johnson ousted Democratic Rep. Cynthia McKinney in the primary. McKinney was a controversial incumbent whose own party lost patience with her. After McKinney led Johnson, 47%-44%, in the July primary, his fundraising suddenly picked up for the runoff, as donors, including former Democratic Gov. Roy Barnes, weighed in against McKinney. She responded by criticizing Johnson's past financial troubles, which included declaring bankruptcy in the late 1980s. In the runoff, turnout was up and Johnson easily won, 59%-41%. He breezed to victory in the general election.

In the House, Johnson has made eyebrow-raising statements that have landed him atop liberal as well as conservative blogs. After South Carolina Republican Rep. Joe Wilson shouted, "You lie!" at President Barack Obama in 2009 when he unveiled his health care plan to Congress, Johnson suggested that if the House took no disciplinary action against Wilson, "we'll have folks putting on white hoods and white uniforms again." Amid a series of incidents during 2015 in which African Americans had been shot by police, Johnson said, "It feels like open season on Black men in America." During President Donald Trump's 2019 impeachment hearing, he said Republican Rep. Matt Gaetz bringing up Hunter Biden's drug use was like the "pot calling the kettle black," a reference to Gaetz's 2008 arrest on suspicion of DUI. His most famous remark came in 2010 when he suggested during a committee hearing that the island of Guam "will become so overly populated that it will tip over and capsize." He later claimed that he was being metaphorical and referring to the island's "fragile ecosystem" and "stressed infrastructure."

His policy work has focused on consumer protection and law enforcement. In 2015, his Arbitration Fairness Act raised issues about practices that favor businesses over consumers, especially in mandatory arbitration cases without judicial oversight. He introduced bills to increase data privacy and protect consumers from identity theft, and he criticized Atlanta-based Equifax following reports of a huge data breach. On law enforcement reform, he has filed bipartisan legislation to restrict free Defense Department transfers of surplus military equipment to state and local agencies. "Militarizing America's main streets won't make us any safer, just more fearful and more reticent," Johnson said. In response to allegations of police malpractice, he introduced a bill to reform grand jury procedures, including the appointment of special prosecutors in the investigations of civilian deaths. Following the killing of George Floyd while being detained by Minneapolis police in 2020, he worked on a major Democratic police reform bill that would have addressed a number of issues, including use of force and qualified immunity. The bill passed the House but was not taken up by the Senate.

After winning reelection without a primary challenger in 2008, Johnson announced that he had battled hepatitis C, an incurable blood-borne liver disease, for more than a decade. Two Democrats lined up to challenge him in the 2010 primary. Johnson insisted his health was fine and unveiled an endorsement from Obama. He won the primary with 55 percent to 26 percent for former DeKalb County CEO Vernon Jones and 18 percent for former DeKalb County Commissioner Connie Stokes. Although he faced minor opposition in 2012, Johnson was challenged in 2014 by well-known DeKalb County Sheriff Tom Brown, who criticized Johnson's lack of accomplishments and mocked his comments about Guam. With another Obama endorsement, Johnson won 55%-45%. Since then, he has been unopposed in the Democratic primary or easily defeated weak challengers.

GA-4: Eastern Atlanta Suburbs   **Cook Partisan Voting Index: D+27**

Population		Race and Ethnicity		Income	
Total	782,142	White	27.30%	Median Income	$60,128
Land area (sq. miles)	497	Black	60.90%	District Income Rank	259
Pop/ sq mi	1,574.99	Latino	10.20%	Poverty Rate	11.20%
Born in State	48.40%	Asian	4.60%	With health insurance	82.90%
		Two or more races	2.50%	Cash public assistance	1.80%
Age Groups		Other	4.70%	Food stamp/SNAP	12.20%
Under 18	24.40%				
18-34	23.50%	**Education**		**Work**	
35-64	39.60%	H.S grad or less	38.70%	White Collar	35.20%
Over 64	12.50%	Some college	30.60%	Sales and Service	37.90%
		College Degree, 4 yr	18.80%	Blue Collar	26.90%
Military		Post grad	11.90%	Government	14.10%
Veteran/ Active Duty	7.50%				

2020 Pres. Vote	Biden	281,824	(79%)	Trump	72,283	(20%)		
2016 Pres. Vote	Clinton	224,907	(75%)	Trump	66,433	(22%)	Johnson	7,323 (2%)

DeKalb: In 1920, when Gutzon Borglum began sculpting Jefferson Davis, Robert E. Lee and Stonewall Jackson into the side of Stone Mountain—the largest single piece of sculpture in the world—the huge outcropping of granite was a day's drive into the country east of central Atlanta. Even when the memorial was completed in 1972, suburban development barely reached that far. But today, after some of the most explosive growth in the country, DeKalb (pronounced duh-KAB by locals) County is at the heart of the Atlanta metropolitan area. And the so-called "granddaddy" of Confederate monuments—located along the Stone Mountain Freeway, a few miles from the Interstate 285 Perimeter surrounding Atlanta—incongruously sits amid one of the most cosmopolitan and liberal constituencies in the South.

In 1962, the most recent attempt at a cross-burning by the Ku Klux Klan resulted in an armed clash with state police. In a sign of the times, most of the current visitors to Stone Mountain are African Americans, with many ignoring the Confederate history and enjoying the parkland as a recreational area. The city of Stone Mountain is nearly 80 percent black, and nearby Clarkston, a hub for international refugees since the 1990s, is known as the most diverse square mile in the country. Its 13,000 residents represent 40 nationalities and speak 60 languages.

South DeKalb County has been transformed from mostly rural territory in the 1970s into one of the nation's largest collections of middle-class African-American neighborhoods, rivaled only by Prince George's County Maryland. DeKalb's population grew 22 percent in the 1990s. Since 2010, it has resumed its growth, with an increase of 10 percent by 2019. It is now about 55 percent African American and 9 percent Latino.

The demographic changes have moved its politics to the left. DeKalb was a Republican county in the 1960s. Now, it is the second most heavily Democratic county in Georgia, following Clayton. Joe Biden won 83%-16% in 2020. As the county has evolved, south DeKalb has become much more African American and its property values have declined compared with north DeKalb, where affluent white communities formed their own cities over the last decade to gain autonomy. South DeKalb has recently joined the "cityhood" movement though. Stone crest was created in 2016 and advocates are pushing for the creation of Green haven, which would cover most of south DeKalb and become the second largest city in the state with nearly 300,000 residents. In east DeKalb, on the border with Gwinnett County, a $250 million Amazon fulfillment center will bring 1,000 jobs.

The 4th Congressional District includes about half of DeKalb County, with northern and western parts of DeKalb spilling into the neighboring 5th and 6th districts. The majority Black district takes in several communities in Gwinnett County to the north, all of Rockdale County, and close to half of more-rural Newton County. Slightly more than half the voters are in DeKalb. More than 20 percent are in Gwinnett and the rest are split evenly between Newton and Rockdale. Joe Biden slightly improved on Hillary Clinton's performance in the district in 2020, winning 79 percent of the vote to her 75 percent. This was despite enthusiastic support for Trump from local Democratic politician Vernon Jones, a speaker at the 2020 RNC.

Nikema Williams (D)

Elected 2020, 1st term, b. Jul 30, 1978; Smiths Station, AL; Talladega College, B.A.; Yale University; Methodist; Married (Leslie Williams); 1 child.

Elected Office: GA Senate, 2017-2021.

Professional Career: Campaign Manager, TJ Copeland, 2004-2006; Political Director, Young Democrats of Georgia, 2008; Public Policy Manager/Legislative Coordinator, Planned Parenthood of Georgia, 2008-2010; Deputy Director, Care in Action.

DC Office: 1406 LHOB 20515, 202-225-3801, nikemawilliams.house.gov

State Offices: Atlanta, 404-659-0116.

Committees: *Financial Services*: Diversity & Inclusion; Oversight & Investigations; Task Force on Financial Technology. *Select Committee on the Modernization of Congress. Transportation & Infrastructure*: Aviation; Highways & Transit.

Election Results

Election	Name (Party)	Vote (%)	Cand. Spent	Ind. Exp. Support	Ind. Exp. Oppose
2020 General	Nikema Williams (D)........................	301,857 (85%)	$393,784	$19,912	
	Angela Stanton-King (R)........................	52,646 (15%)	$298,414		$113

Following the death in July 2020 of iconic Rep. John Lewis, Nikema Williams, who chaired the state Democratic Party, was selected to replace him as the party's nominee. Respected for her efforts in the plan to turn Georgia blue, which attained national significance in 2020, Williams has a bright political future that could go beyond representing a safe House seat.

Lewis, a prominent civil rights activist in the 1960s, was a founding member of the Student Nonviolent Coordinating Committee and spoke at the 1963 March on Washington. In what became a seminal event in the enactment of the 1965 Voting Rights Act, he led peaceful demonstrators who were attacked by police while crossing the Edmund Pettus Bridge in Selma Alabama; he suffered serious head injuries. After 55 years, his casket was saluted by Alabama state patrolmen as his funeral procession crossed the same bridge.

Lewis was elected to Congress in 1986 to a seat previously held by civil rights activist Andrew Young and future Sen. Wyche Fowler. He was not seriously challenged during his 33-year House career. In December 2019, Lewis announced he had pancreatic cancer; he died seven months later. He received an elaborate sendoff, including ceremonies in the capitals of Alabama and Georgia, and at the U.S. Capitol. Former Presidents Bill Clinton, George W. Bush, and Barack Obama spoke at his funeral in Ebenezer Baptist Church. President Donald Trump, whom Lewis called "illegitimate," did not attend.

Three days after his death, the Georgia Democratic Party's executive committee chose Williams, 41, a state senator since 2017, to replace him on the November ballot. Since 2019, she had been chairwoman of the state Democratic Party, the first Black woman to hold the position. Williams held leadership positions in Planned Parenthood Southeast and the National Domestic Workers Alliance. She was born in rural Alabama, like Lewis, and moved to Georgia after graduating from Talladega College. Her husband earlier served as a Lewis aide.

Williams received nearly unanimous support from the executive committee, whose members included Atlanta Mayor Keisha Lance Bottoms and Stacey Abrams, the Democratic nominee for governor in 2018, who was a mentor to Williams. After winnowing the 131 applications for the seat to five finalists, the committee voted on the successor to Lewis. Running a distant second was state Rep. Park Cannon.

The vote to anoint Williams occurred shortly before the legal deadline to replace Lewis on the ballot. Some Georgia Democrats complained that the safe seat went to a well-connected—and young—party insider rather than a placeholder who could resign and set in motion a wide-open contest with no incumbent in 2021 or 2022. Michael Collins, a longtime aide to the late congressman, said Lewis would have preferred a "free and fair election" to replace him.

Executive committee members said the short timeline set by Georgia election law and the need to nominate a strong candidate forced their hand. When Gov. Brian Kemp called a special election to fill the seat for the final weeks of 2020, Williams declined to run. Seven candidates competed to serve what became a single month in the House. In November, Williams won the two-year term with 85 percent of the vote.

Williams cast herself as a worthy heir to Lewis' legacy of "good trouble," citing her 2018 arrest at a voting rights demonstration. As Democratic state chairwoman, she promoted Abrams' strategy of engaging unlikely voters through grassroots efforts and vocally opposing Republican policies. In retaining her party leadership post for the 2020 election, Williams saw her work come to fruition when Joe Biden narrowly won Georgia, the first time since 1992 that a Democrat had won the state in a presidential race.

Given Williams might be well positioned for a statewide run if Georgia continues to trend blue. Alternatively, she could follow Lewis with a long House career, depending partly on what redistricting holds for her district. She was elected president of the House's freshmen Democrats. She go seats on the Financial Services, and Transportation and Infrastructure committees.

GA-5: Atlanta Metro

Cook Partisan Voting Index: D+36

Population		Race and Ethnicity		Income	
Total	788,996	White	34.80%	Median Income	$60,247
Land area (sq. miles)	265	Black	55.40%	District Income Rank	256
Pop/ sq mi	2,978.35	Latino	6.80%	Poverty Rate	18.70%
Born in State	50.90%	Asian	5.20%	With health insurance	88.40%
		Two or more races	2.30%	Cash public assistance	1.60%
Age Groups		Other	2.30%	Food stamp/SNAP	15.10%
Under 18	19.90%				
18-34	31.50%	**Education**		**Work**	
35-64	36.20%	H.S grad or less	31.20%	White Collar	52.10%
Over 64	12.50%	Some college	21.50%	Sales and Service	33.60%
		College Degree, 4 yr	26.60%	Blue Collar	14.20%
Military		Post grad	20.80%	Government	13.60%
Veteran/ Active Duty	5.50%				

2020 Pres. Vote	Biden	313,084	(86%)	Trump	45,901	(13%)		
2016 Pres. Vote	Clinton	259,807	(85%)	Trump	36,384	(12%)	Johnson	9,564 (3%)

Atlanta: Venture out of the quiet of the Ebenezer Baptist Church or the shade of the Rev. Martin Luther King Jr.'s boyhood home two blocks away and into the steamy heat of the Georgia sun and one can see, a mile away, downtown Atlanta's atrium skyscrapers. They are evidence of the wealth and vibrant growth of the commercial capital of the South, the metropolis that has grown up where there was little more than a railroad junction at the time of the Civil War. But the human achievement that is downtown Atlanta is overshadowed by the revolution started in large part by a man who grew up on Auburn Avenue. Atlanta's white establishment during King's time, led by Mayors William Hartsfield and Ivan Allen and Coca-Cola's Robert Woodruff, deserve credit for abandoning segregation, but it was King and other civil rights leaders who took the risks that led them to do so. Atlanta's city fathers acted out of goodwill, but also with an eye for the economic growth of the city, having seen the damage that resulted in other Southern cities harmed by violent resistance—notably, Birmingham.

Today, Atlanta is the center of the nation's ninth-largest metropolitan area. From Auburn Avenue, it spreads into two dozen counties of northern Georgia. Its Hartsfield-Jackson Atlanta International Airport was the busiest in the world in 2019, with 110.5 million passengers. However, airport traffic dropped 18 percent in the first quarter of 2020 as travel slowed during the COVID-19 pandemic. The city's hospitality industry, previously valued at $12 billion, was also hit hard by the pandemic; experts say it will not recover until at least 2024. The public transit authority, MARTA, came under financial pressure when ridership plunged at the beginning of the pandemic and cut most of its bus routes. As a result, many low-income workers could not travel to work, leading community groups to sue for the resumption of service. Even before the pandemic hit, Atlanta had high levels of income inequality and its poor residents were under pressure from gentrification.

Atlanta has a vibrant business sector with office centers in downtown, Midtown and Buckhead to the north. Coca-Cola's skyscraper headquarters stands as a symbol of Atlanta's most successful worldwide business. The 16 Fortune 500 companies headquartered in metro Atlanta other than Coca-Cola include Home Depot, UPS, and Delta. A notable, and rare, corporate loss for the city came in 2019 when SunTrust moved to Charlotte after merging with BB&T. The city's burgeoning tech industry transitioned to online work and companies such as Microsoft, Mail Chimp, and Zillow all announced expansions. World-class universities—including Georgia Tech, Emory, and Morehouse —provide a fresh pool of talent for companies to draw from. One attraction for young graduates is the Atlanta Beltline, a 22-mile corridor which connects 45 in town neighborhoods. Companies with offices on the Beltline host nearly 19,000 jobs. The urban redevelopment project aims to bring in $10 billion in investment by 2030. There are plans for 5,600 units of affordable housing along the trail, but this has been a challenge.

Keisha Lance Bottoms was elected mayor in November 2017, becoming the second Black woman to lead Atlanta after Shirley Franklin. Bottoms faced a number of challenges during the 2020 racial justice protests, including rioting and the killing of Rayshard Brooks, a young Black man, by Atlanta police officers. After achieving national fame, she was briefly discussed as a running mate for Joe

Biden, who she endorsed early in the Democratic primary. She was not selected but Atlanta was instrumental to an appreciative Biden, who won Georgia in November.

The 5th Congressional District of Georgia includes much of the city of Atlanta, Forest Park and the smaller communities of Lake City and Morrow in Clayton County. High-end communities in the district include Republican-leaning Buckhead and more Democratic areas near Emory University and the Centers for Disease Control and Prevention. It is also home to Decatur, the seat of DeKalb County, which was named the best place to live in Georgia by the website Niche due to its "traditional small town atmosphere." Biden won 86 percent of the district's vote in the 2020 election, unsurprising after President Donald Trump called the district "horrible" in a 2017 spat with the late Rep. John Lewis.

Lucy McBath (D)

Elected 2018, 2nd term, b. Jun 01, 1960; Joliet, IL; VA State University, B.A., 1982; Christian Church; Married (Curtis McBath); 2 children (2 deceased).

Professional Career: Flight Attendant, Delta Airlines 1984-2014

DC Office: 1513 LHOB 20515, 202-225-4501, mcbath.house.gov

State Offices: Atlanta, 470-773-6330.

Committees: *Education & Labor*: Early Childhood, Elementary & Secondary Education; Health, Employment, Labor & Pensions. *Judiciary*: Antitrust, Commercial & Administrative Law; Crime, Terrorism & Homeland Security.

Almanac Ratings 2019-2020

	Economy	Social	Foreign	Composite
Liberal	51%	100%	80%	77%
Conservative	49%	0%	20%	23%

Key Votes of the 116th Congress

1. U.S./Mex./Can. trade deal	Y	5. Russia sanctions	Y	9. Firearms background checks	Y
2. First Coronavirus response	Y	6. Troops in Syria	Y	10. Spending at the border	Y
3. HEROES Act	Y	7. Veto arms sales to Saudis	Y	11. Marijuana liberalized rules	Y
4. CASH Act	Y	8. Defense $$$, veto override	Y	12. Electoral College objections	N

Election Results

Election	Name (Party)	Vote (%)		Cand. Spent	Ind. Exp. Support	Ind. Exp. Oppose
2020 General	Lucy McBath (D)	216,775	(55%)	$9,204,803	$405,513	$1,839,168
	Karen Handel (R)	180,329	(45%)	$2,976,825	$72,468	$4,776,282
2020 Primary	Lucy McBath (D)	90,660	(100%)			

Prior winning percentages: 2018 (51%)

A high-profile member of the 2018 Democratic freshman class, Lucy McBath has won back-to-back races in what used to be a solid Republican seat in the northern Atlanta suburbs. In Congress, she has been active on gun control, a personal issue for her following the death of her son in a 2012 shooting. Her district is at risk of being redrawn in the 2022 redistricting cycle given its rapid turn away from the Republican Party.

McBath grew up in Joliet Illinois. Her father, a dentist, was president of the state chapter of the NAACP. She graduated from Virginia State University. For nearly 30 years, she was a flight attendant for Delta Airlines. In 2012, her son, Jordan Davis, was killed by a man who complained about the music on his car radio while at a gas station in Florida. The assailant was convicted of first-degree murder. McBath became a national spokeswoman for two political advocacy groups: Every town for Gun Safety and Moms Demand Action for Gun Sense in America. In 2016, she spoke to the Democratic convention about gun violence.

Having planned to run for the Georgia Legislature in 2018, McBath decided to run for Congress following the killing of 17 people at a high school in Parkland Florida. "Championing for them in Washington is still championing for my child," she told The Washington Post. In the Democratic primary runoff, McBath faced Kevin Abel. He was a businessman who depicted McBath as a single-issue candidate working with national groups. Abel outspent her, but McBath was aided by gun-control groups. She won the runoff, 54%-46%.

In the general election, McBath faced Karen Handel, a well-known Republican who previously served as secretary of state. Handel was first elected in a 2017 special election against Democrat Jon Ossoff, who spent a record $31 million for his campaign. With a boost from House Speaker Paul Ryan's Congressional Leadership Fund, Handel won the special election, 52%-48%. The outcome was a dispiriting setback for Democrats. (Ossoff was elected to the Senate in January 2021, when he defeated Republican Sen. David Perdue.)

In her bid for a full term, Handel was far better-known than her challenger. She initially seemed safe and paid little attention to McBath. In addition to the personal story about her son, McBath cited her battle with breast cancer to argue for improved health care services, including expansion of Medicaid. Several factors gave her momentum during the final days of the campaign. Former New York City Mayor Michael Bloomberg, chief patron of the gun-control groups with which McBath was affiliated, spent $4 million on ads, more than doubling McBath's total spending. The Democratic Congressional Campaign Committee ran extensive ads in the closing days, as did Democratic women's groups. With a huge turnout that came close to the total vote in the district in the 2016 presidential contest, McBath won, 51%-49%. She was the first Democrat to win the district since the 1992 redistricting, when it was substantially redrawn.

As a member of the Judiciary Committee and vice chair of the Gun Violence Prevention Task Force, McBath played a major role in House Democrats' legislative efforts on gun control in 2019 (which were mostly symbolic given Republican control of the Senate and White House). She spoke about her son's death in the House's first hearing on gun violence since 2007 and pushed for the passage of legislation that would expand federal background checks. The background checks bill passed the House but was not taken up in the Senate. Although gun control is her signature issue, McBath saw more success in her work on legislation to assist veterans facing bankruptcy, which was signed into law by President Donald Trump in August 2019.

The 2020 race was a rematch with Handel, who accused McBath of being too far left for the district and of being insufficiently supportive of the police. The law-and-order message did not work, as the district had moved even further away from its Republican roots since the 2018 election. McBath expanded her margin of victory in 2020, winning 55%-45%. While McBath won only the DeKalb County portion of the district in 2018, she captured the DeKalb and Fulton portions in 2020 and lost the Cobb portion by only two percentage points.

Given the district's rapid Democratic shift at both the presidential and congressional levels, it will almost certainly be redrawn by Republican legislators in the upcoming redistricting cycle. They might try to combine Democratic areas in the 6th and 7th districts, creating a safe Democratic seat that McBath and Democrat Rep. Carolyn Bourdeaux would compete for in 2022.

GA-6: Northern Atlanta Suburbs

Cook Partisan Voting Index: D+1

Population		Race and Ethnicity		Income	
Total	742,932	White	66.70%	Median Income	$100,110
Land area (sq. miles)	299	Black	13.80%	District Income Rank	35
Pop/ sq mi	2,486.72	Latino	12.20%	Poverty Rate	6.70%
Born in State	34.70%	Asian	11.70%	With health insurance	91.70%
		Two or more races	3.30%	Cash public assistance	0.60%
Age Groups		Other	4.60%	Food stamp/SNAP	2.80%
Under 18	22.80%				
18-34	20.80%	**Education**		**Work**	
35-64	42.70%	H.S grad or less	16.60%	White Collar	60.00%
Over 64	13.60%	Some college	18.20%	Sales and Service	29.80%
		College Degree, 4 yr	38.10%	Blue Collar	10.20%
Military		Post grad	27.00%	Government	8.60%
Veteran/ Active Duty	5.40%				

2020 Pres. Vote	Biden	219,694	(55%)	Trump	175,065	(44%)		
2016 Pres. Vote	Trump	160,029	(48%)	Clinton	155,087	(47%)	Johnson	16,148	(5%)

Fulton, Cobb: In the red clay north of Atlanta, an almost wholly new metropolitan quarter has grown up over the past four decades. Affluent Atlanta has spread out past the Perimeter, the local name for Interstate 285, into territory that was once farms, small towns and modest factory cities. Where there were perhaps 100,000 people in the 1950s, there are more than 1 million today. Along the usually jammed Georgia 400 highway, in the fast-growing northern part of Fulton County, are the affluent suburbs of Sandy Springs, Roswell and Alpharetta, all business hubs as well as population centers. The increasingly diverse northern suburbs are changing politically as well. The district shifted from safely Republican to leaning Democratic in just four years.

Sandy Springs was incorporated in 2005. Affluent whites in the area pushed cityhood in order to split away from majority-Black Fulton County and gain more control over their tax dollars. This sparked the "cityhood movement" in northern Atlanta as other white communities, including Brookhaven and Dunwoody, also created their own cities. After its incorporation, Sandy Springs became an innovator in outsourcing basic government services to private industry. In 2019, the city brought most services in-house, citing the high prices of private-sector bidders.

Businesses have swarmed into northern Fulton County. Sandy Springs is home to Home Depot, the nation's second largest retailer. In 2018, Mercedes-Benz opened its new U.S. headquarters in Sandy Springs after moving from New Jersey. Perimeter Center is a major business district that exceeds downtown Atlanta in square footage. Commuters on Georgia 400 can see the district's famous King and Queen Towers as they approach the Perimeter. Developers are building a \$2 billion mixed-use project in Dunwoody for business, housing and entertainment. Further up 400 are Roswell, which has a charming downtown area, and Alpharetta, the self-styled "Technology City of the South."

The 6th Congressional District is based in the northern Atlanta suburbs. It includes the northern sections of DeKalb and Fulton counties and the eastern part of Cobb County. Nearly half the population is in Fulton.

The district had been safely Republican prior to Donald Trump. Mitt Romney and John McCain got 61 percent and 59 percent of the vote, respectively. Trump won by just one percentage point in 2016 and Democrats nearly flipped the seat in an early 2017 special election. The Democratic shift continued in 2020 as Joe Biden comfortably defeated Trump, 55%-44%. In just eight years, the North Fulton portion of the district went from giving Romney a 25-point victory to backing Biden by a 10-point margin. The Cobb and DeKalb portions saw similar shifts.

Carolyn Bourdeaux (D)

Elected 2020, 1st term, b. Jun 03, 1979; Roanoke, VA; Yale University, B.A., 1992; University of Southern CA, M.P.A., 1999; Syracuse University, Ph.D., 2003; Christian Church; Married (Jeff Skodnick); 1 child.

Professional Career: Associate professor, Georgia State University; Director, Georgia's Senate Budget and Evaluation Office, 2007-2010; Founder and Director, Andrew Young School's Center for State and Local Finance.

DC Office: 1319 LHOB 20515, 202-225-4272, Fax: 202-225-4696, bourdeaux.house.gov

State Offices: Lawrenceville, 770-232-3005.

Committees: *Small Business*: Economic Growth, Tax & Capital Access; Innovation, Entrepreneurship & Workforce Development. *Transportation & Infrastructure*: Highways & Transit; Water Resources & Environment.

Election Results

Election	Name (Party)	Vote (%)		Cand. Spent	Ind. Exp. Support	Ind. Exp. Oppose
2020 General	Carolyn Bourdeaux (D)	190,900	(51%)	$5,818,984	$222,526	$6,757,440
	Rich McCormick (R)	180,564	(49%)	$2,626,935	$1,706,604	$7,291,519
2020 Primary	Carolyn Bourdeaux (D)	44,710	(53%)			
	Brenda Lopez Romero (D)	10,497	(12%)			
	Nabilah Islam (D)	10,447	(12%)			
	Rashid Malik (D)	6,780	(8%)			
	John Eaves (D)	6,548	(8%)			
	Zahra Karinshak (D)	5,729	(7%)			

Carolyn Bourdeaux, the only Democrat in 2020 to flip a House seat with intact boundaries, was successful in her second run for the suburban Atlanta district. In 2018, she lost to Republican Rep. Rob Woodall by barely 400 votes. With Republicans in control of the Georgia legislature following the 2020 election, the district could be significantly changed by redistricting, putting Bourdeaux's political future in jeopardy.

Bourdeaux was born in Roanoke Virginia. She attended Yale for her bachelor's degree, the University of Southern California for her master's in public administration, and Syracuse University for her Ph.D. in public administration. After working as an aide to Sen. Ron Wyden of Oregon, she moved to Georgia and became a professor of public policy at Georgia State University.

With a leave of absence from 2007 to 2010, she directed the Georgia State Senate's budget office. Facing the Great Recession, the Republican-controlled legislature balanced the budget with spending cuts. Years, later, that made Bourdeaux the target of criticism from her Democratic opponents. In 2018, Bourdeaux was among six Democrats competing to oppose Woodall. First elected in 2010 with 67 percent of the vote, he was reelected three times with more than 60 percent. But Gwinnett County, which was a large share of his district, voted for Hillary Clinton in 2016—a signal that Woodall faced serious jeopardy in his reelection.

Bourdeaux and businessman David Kim were the frontrunners in the first round of the Democratic primary. In the runoff, Bourdeaux drew support from EMILY's List, which supports Democratic women who favor abortion rights, and from local elected officials, including Rep. Hank Johnson. Kim did not receive major endorsements, but self-financed his campaign. Bourdeaux narrowly prevailed, 52%-48%.

The general election initially stayed under the radar. Woodall barely campaigned, not releasing his first campaign ad until early November. With the Democratic surge in Gwinnett County, their contest became the closest House race in the nation. Woodall, who was outspent 2-1 by Bourdeaux, survived by 433 votes.

In early 2019, Woodall announced that he would not seek reelection, setting off a scramble to replace him. When Bourdeaux announced her candidacy, she was endorsed by the Democrats in the Georgia delegation. That did not discourage other Democrats. The leading contenders included two state legislators who were backed by prominent state Democrats, plus Nabilah Islam, who was endorsed by Rep. Alexandria Ocasio-Cortez of New York.

The Republican primary was similarly fractured. The chief contenders were state Sen. Renee Unterman and Rich McCormick, a physician and military veteran who was backed by national conservative leaders, including Rep. Jim Jordan of Ohio and Sen. Ted Cruz of Texas. Despite the competitive fields, both Bourdeaux and McCormick advanced from the initial primaries with the more than the 50 percent of the vote required to avoid runoffs.

Although McCormick did not distance himself from President Donald Trump, he branded himself as a "compassionate conservative"—a term famously coined by President George W. Bush, which sought to recognize the racial and ethnic diversity of McCormick's district. Bourdeaux pitched herself as a problem-solver who could work across partisan lines. She again outspent her opponent 2-to-1. McCormick made the contest closer than many observers had expected, but Bourdeaux won, 51%-49%.

With Republicans in full control of redistricting in Georgia, there was speculation that the legislature would combine Bourdeaux's district with the neighboring district of second-term Democratic Rep. Lucy McBath, creating one safe Democratic district and a second seat that likely would favor Republicans. That could force the two junior Democrats to run against each other in the 2022 primary.

GA-7: Northeastern Atlanta Suburbs   **Cook Partisan Voting Index: R+2**

Population		Race and Ethnicity		Income	
Total	844,773	White	51.30%	Median Income	$80,926
Land area (sq. miles)	393	Black	21.50%	District Income Rank	85
Pop/ sq mi	2,151.68	Latino	20.20%	Poverty Rate	8.20%
Born in State	36.40%	Asian	15.80%	With health insurance	85.60%
		Two or more races	3.10%	Cash public assistance	0.80%
Age Groups		Other	8.20%	Food stamp/SNAP	3.80%
Under 18	26.90%				
18-34	21.30%	**Education**		**Work**	
35-64	40.80%	H.S grad or less	29.80%	White Collar	43.40%
Over 64	10.80%	Some college	25.10%	Sales and Service	37.30%
		College Degree, 4 yr	29.40%	Blue Collar	19.30%
Military		Post grad	15.60%	Government	9.60%
Veteran/ Active Duty	4.80%				

2020 Pres. Vote	Biden	199,533	(53%)	Trump	174,869	(46%)	
2016 Pres. Vote	Trump	150,845	(51%)	Clinton	132,012	(44%)	Johnson 12,115 (4%)

Gwinnett, Forsyth: In the past two decades, greater Atlanta has grown out in every direction: south past the airport, west over the Chattahoochee River, north past Perimeter Center, and east and northeast past Stone Mountain. The outer suburbs north of Atlanta have grown—and changed —fastest of all. Gwinnett County combines mature neighborhoods of affluent professionals and entrepreneurs with closer-in communities near Interstate 85 that have attracted large numbers of Hispanics and middle-class Blacks. Farther out in Lawrenceville, Duluth and Buford, downtown Atlanta seems very far away, both physically—it is 20 to 40 miles, and more than an hour of rush-hour driving, to Peachtree Street—and in state of mind. For many, Atlanta is something off the highway on the way to Hartsfield-Jackson Atlanta International Airport.

The growth and its diversity here are hard to overstate. Gwinnett County's population grew 37 percent from 2000 to 2010, to more than 805,000. In the next nine years, it grew to nearly 940,000. Like other metro Atlanta counties, the non-Hispanic white population has been dropping in Gwinnett schools, while the overall student numbers soar. The school system boasts that its students speak more than 100 languages. About 26 percent of the county population is foreign-born. Overall, the minority population in the county has grown to 30 percent Black, 22 percent Hispanic and 13 percent Asian. Population projections for 2040 are close to 1.4 million, with less than 30 percent white.

Once a Republican stronghold due to white flight from Atlanta, Gwinnett County voted Democratic in the 2016 and 2020 presidential elections for the first time since 1976, when Georgia native Jimmy Carter was on the ballot. The county commission came under full Democratic control in the 2020 election, but voters have twice rejected sales tax hikes to expand transit options.

About 25 percent of the district's voters are in Forsyth County, the fastest growing and wealthiest county in Georgia. In a once-rural area where Blacks were terrorized and forced out in 1912, suburban housing and business development have been booming. Forsyth is expected to almost double in population by 2050, from 240,000 to 440,000, but it is far less diverse and far more Republican than Gwinnett.

The 7th Congressional District of Georgia comprises about 70 percent of Gwinnett County and 70 percent of Forsyth County. Its growth has far outpaced the state's other 13 congressional districts, and it now has nearly 850,000 residents. Trump's strong showing in Forsyth kept the district in the Republican column in 2016, 51%-44%. However, Joe Biden improved on Hillary Clinton's performance in both counties in 2020 and district went Democratic, 53%-46%.

Austin Scott (R)

Elected 2010, 6th term, b. Dec 10, 1969; Augusta, GA; Tiftarea Academy, Chula, GA, 1987; University of GA Terry College of Business, B.B.A., 1993; American College, 1995; Baptist; Married (Vivien Scott); 2 children.

Elected Office: GA House, 1997-2010.

Professional Career: Owner, Southern Group; Agent, Principal Financial Group, 1993-2010.

DC Office: 2417 RHOB 20515, 202-225-6531, Fax: 202-225-3013, austinscott.house.gov

State Offices: Tifton, 229-396-5175; Warner Robins, 478-971-1776.

Committees: *Agriculture*: Biotechnology, Horticulture & Research; Commodity Exchanges, Energy & Credit; General Farm Commodities & Risk Management (RMM). *Armed Services*: Intelligence & Special Operations; Readiness.

Group Ratings

	ADA	ACLU	AFL-CIO	LCV	COC	HAFA	ACU	CFG	FRC
2020	**	12%	**	10%	-	89%	87%	**	-
2019	10%	C	24%	7%	75%	C	87%	84%	100%

Almanac Ratings 2019-2020

	Economy	Social	Foreign	Composite
Liberal	25%	23%	11%	20%
Conservative	75%	77%	89%	80%

Key Votes of the 116th Congress

1. U.S./Mex./Can. trade deal Y	5. Russia sanctions Y	9. Firearms background checks N
2. First Coronavirus response Y	6. Troops in Syria Y	10. Spending at the border Y
3. HEROES Act N	7. Veto arms sales to Saudis N	11. Marijuana liberalized rules N/A
4. CASH Act N	8. Defense $$$, veto override Y	12. Electoral College objections N

Election Results

Election	Name (Party)	Vote (%)		Cand. Spent	Ind. Exp. Support	Ind. Exp. Oppose
2020 General	Austin Scott (R)	198,701	(65%)	$415,345	$6,665	$750
	Lindsay Holliday (D)	109,264	(35%)	$5,220		
2020 Primary	Austin Scott (R)	73,671	(90%)			
	Matt Gurtler (R)	29,426	(21%)			
	Vance Dean (R)	4,692	(6%)			

Prior winning percentages: 2016 (68%), 2014 (unopposed), 2012 (unopposed), 2010 (53%)

Republican Austin Scott, in the rural southern tradition, has been an active lawmaker on military and agriculture issues, both critical to his rural Georgia district. After defeating a Democratic incumbent in 2010 and then becoming politically secure at home, he has occasionally been blunt in criticizing various Republican factions.

Born in Augusta, Scott's father was an orthopedic surgeon and his mother was a teacher. He graduated from the University of Georgia with a degree in risk management and insurance. After college, he opened an insurance brokerage firm, which he operated for 17 years. Scott was elected to the state House in 1996 at age 26. In January 2009, he announced his candidacy for governor. But his campaign failed to gain traction, and he decided to challenge four-term Democratic Rep. Jim Marshall instead.

Marshall styled himself as a conservative Democrat and voted against President Barack Obama's health care law. But he was vulnerable in 2010 simply because he was a Democrat. Scott promised to reduce the deficit, and he attacked the incumbent for voting for Obama's $787 billion economic stimulus bill. Marshall, unlike most Democrats, was endorsed by the U.S. Chamber of Commerce and the National Rifle Association. Still, Scott won the seat, 53%-47%.

In the House, Scott was elected freshman class president and was regularly asked to explain his boisterous classmates' actions to the news media. They never intended to speak with a single voice, he replied in November 2011: "I think of us as a group of independent thinkers." A year later, he said their main job was "to play defense against what [President Barack Obama] was going to do. I think we were pretty effective at doing that." By 2018, he downplayed their influence. "We didn't come to take over the country," he said.

As a member of the Armed Services Committee, unlike many of the military's boosters on the panel, he has maintained that defense spending must be examined for budget cuts. But he has worked aggressively on behalf of his district, regardless of the administration in power. He opposed the Obama administration's request for another round of base closings, which could jeopardize Moody Air Force Base in Valdosta and Robins Air Force Base in Warner Robins. In 2018, Scott voiced serious concerns about the Trump administration's plan for a new Advanced Battle Management System that would replace the Joint Surveillance Target Attack Radar System (JSTARS), which has been based at Robins. That resulted in his unusual clash with Georgia Republican Sen. David Perdue, who advocated the proposal as a member of the Senate Armed Services Committee. After Congress rejected a plan backed by Scott for additional planes at Robins, Scott placed responsibility on Perdue and warned of potential dire consequences for Robins. "I do not believe you want to be an Air Force base without a flying mission when you go into a round of" base-closings.

On the Agriculture Committee, as chairman of the Commodity Exchanges, Energy, and Credit Subcommittee, Scott took on the financially complex and often risky derivatives markets and sought a bipartisan solution that struck a balance between market integrity and market access. In 2015, the House passed his bill to renew the Commodity Futures Trading Commission. Following the 2020 election, Scott made an unsuccessful bid to become the ranking Republican member on the committee. House Republican leaders instead selected Glenn Thompson of Pennsylvania. However, another Representative Scott from Georgia—Democrat David Scott from the Atlanta-based 13th District—was selected as committee chairman. Despite being from different parties and regions of the state, the two Scotts have a "cordial working relationship," according to the Atlanta Journal Constitution. Austin Scott became ranking Republican on the General Farm Commodities and Risk Management Subcommittee.

Scott has not been shy in criticizing his fellow Republicans, regardless of their faction or position of power. When Rep. Mark Meadows (who later became Trump's chief of staff) and other conservatives in the House Freedom Caucus stymied action to repeal the Affordable Care Act, Scott tweeted, "Mark Meadows betrayed Trump and America." Later, when GOP moderates—over the objections of party leaders—pushed a proposal to normalize the status of young illegal immigrants, Scott complained, "there ought to be discipline" for the mavericks. In 2019, Congress was gridlocked over a disaster relief bill that would have assisted farmers in his district who were slammed by Hurricane Michael in October 2018. Scott took aim at the Trump White House, claiming that Vice President Mike Pence was failing to deliver on a promise to help farmers and that the Office of Management and Budget did not support disaster aid.

Scott, who only reluctantly backed Trump in 2016, said, "there's a disconnect in what is actually coming out of the administration, and what the administration is telling us that they're going to do." While the disaster aid bill eventually passed, conservative Republicans slowed it though procedural maneuvers. Scott called the Republican obstructionists "clowns."

Scott's district was redrawn for the 2012 election to heavily favor the GOP. He faced Democratic opponents only in 2016 and 2020. He defeated James Harris, 68%-32%, in 2016 and beat Lindsay Holliday, 65%-35%, in 2020.

GA-8: South-Central Georgia

Population		Race and Ethnicity		Income	
Total	706,237	White	61.40%	Median Income	$50,745
Land area (sq. miles)	8,712	Black	31.40%	District Income Rank	379
Pop/ sq mi	81.07	Latino	6.90%	Poverty Rate	17.30%
Born in State	67.20%	Asian	1.70%	With health insurance	84.90%
		Two or more races	2.50%	Cash public assistance	1.30%
Age Groups		Other	3.10%	Food stamp/SNAP	15.10%
Under 18	23.30%				
18-34	23.20%	**Education**		**Work**	
35-64	37.10%	H.S grad or less	47.90%	White Collar	32.90%
Over 64	16.30%	Some college	29.40%	Sales and Service	39.80%
		College Degree, 4 yr	13.20%	Blue Collar	27.30%
Military		Post grad	9.50%	Government	20.50%
Veteran/ Active Duty	10.10%				

2020 Pres. Vote	Trump	195,733	(62%)	Biden	117,067	(37%)			
2016 Pres. Vote	Trump	168,193	(63%)	Clinton	91,360	(34%)	Johnson	5,961	(2%)

Warner Robins, Valdosta: South-central Georgia is a region of farm and forest lands and a collection of small, and some tiny, towns. Twiggs and Wilkinson counties have been among the world's major sources of kaolin, a clay used for china and ceramics. Scenes from Fried Green Tomatoes were filmed in Juliette, an old mill town that's too small for most maps. A former hardware store there became the film's Whistle Stop Café.

With its Air Logistics Center and testing and repair site for the F-22 Raptor, Robins Air Force Base and the surrounding city of Warner Robins have become a major presence. The sprawling base employed 24,000 people and had an economic impact of $3.4 billion in 2019. The Air Force is replacing the Joint Surveillance Target Attack Radar System (JSTARS) at Robins with the Advanced Battle Management System (ABMS). Although part of the ABMS mission is supposed to be based at Robins, members of Georgia's congressional delegation have become impatient with the Air Force for not giving them more information.

Twiggs County hosts the largest solar-power plant in the Southeast. Republicans on the state Public Service Commission support the project and have pushed Georgia Power to generate even more energy from solar. The industry could be a job creator in rural Georgia and a source of tax revenue for local governments.

In Pulaski County is Hawkinsville, founded on the banks of the Ocmulgee River and a winter home for harness horse training. Nearby is Tifton, home to the Georgia Museum of Agriculture. Georgia pecan farmers were hit hard by Hurricane Michael in 2018 and also struggled under President Donald Trump's trade policies. Farther south along Interstate 75 is Valdosta, a racially split city of 57,000 that has the most successful high school football program in the country. No team in the nation has won more games than the Valdosta High School Wildcats, who have a win-loss record of 929-234-34 since 1913.

The 8th Congressional District includes Monroe and Jones counties north of Macon in central Georgia and stretches all the way south to the Florida border; most of Macon is in the Democratic-leaning 2nd District. The 8th covers Berrien County, known for its turpentine and bell peppers, and it takes in most of Lowndes County, where Valdosta is located. The district is solidly Republican. Trump won 62 percent of the vote in 2020 and every county except Macon-based Bibb (although the 8th includes only the more Republican areas outside the city center).

Andrew Clyde (R)

Elected 2020, 1st term, b. Nov 22, 1963; Ontario, Canada; Bethel College, B.S.; University of Notre Dame, B.A., 1985; University of GA Terry College of Business, M.B.A., 1999; Baptist; Married (Jennifer Clyde); 4 children.

Military Career: Commander, U.S. Navy, 1985-2013 (Iraq, Kuwait).

Professional Career: Owner, Clyde Armory, Inc.

DC Office: 521 CHOB 20515, 202-225-9893, Fax: 202-226-1224, clyde.house.gov

State Offices: Gainesville, 470-768-6520.

Committees: *Homeland Security*: Border Security, Facilitation & Operations; Cybersecurity, Infrastructure Protection & Innovation. *Oversight & Reform*: Government Operations; Subcommittee on Economic & Consumer Policy.

Election Results

Election	Name (Party)	Vote (%)		Cand. Spent	Ind. Exp. Support	Ind. Exp. Oppose
2020 General	Andrew Clyde (R)	292,750	(79%)	$1,562,414	$60,426	$1,241,525
	Devin Pandy (D)	79,797	(21%)	$83,727		$50
2020 Primary	Andrew Clyde (R)	25,914	(19%)			
	Kevin Tanner (R)	22,187	(16%)			
	Paul Broun (R)	18,627	(13%)			
	John Wilkinson (R)	16,314	(12%)			
	Ethan Underwood (R)	12,117	(9%)			
2020 Primary	Andrew Clyde (R)	50,094	(56%)			
Runoff	Matt Gurtler (R)	38,865	(44%)			

Political newcomer Andrew Clyde won a contest to succeed Republican Rep. Doug Collins, who ran unsuccessfully in the special election for the Senate seat held by Republican Kelly Loeffler. In the tightly contested primary runoff, Georgia GOP leaders supported Clyde over Matt Gurtler, a young state representative who made powerful enemies while serving in the legislature. Given the strongly Republican tilt of northeast Georgia, Clyde was poised for a secure career in Congress.

Clyde, who was born in Ontario Canada, spent his young adult years in northern Indiana, where he attended Bethel College, a private Christian school. He received a commission in the U.S. Navy through the ROTC program at the University of Notre Dame, where he got his bachelor's degree. He spent 28 years in the Navy, including three combat deployments to Kuwait and Iraq. After completing his active military service, Clyde moved to Athens Georgia, where he got a master's degree at the University of Georgia. In 1991, he started the firearms store Clyde Armory, which grew into a national business that marketed to law enforcement officers.

Clyde's political career had an unlikely beginning in 2013, when the IRS confiscated $940,000 from his business. The IRS seized the money under civil asset forfeiture rules that were invoked when Clyde was suspected of avoiding taxes by making bank deposits just under $10,000. Instead, a 2017 review showed that Clyde was attempting to comply with an insurance limit on his deposits. But, under the law, the federal government was permitted to keep the money.

When Clyde challenged the IRS decision in court, he won. Later, he testified to Congress as part of a bipartisan effort to revise the law. Collins, with Democratic Rep. John Lewis of Georgia, sponsored the Clyde-Hirsch-Sowers RESPECT Act, which limited similar asset seizures to situations where prosecutors had probable cause to suspect criminal activity. In 2019, President Donald Trump signed the RESPECT Act into law, as part of a larger tax package. Clyde was invited to the signing ceremony.

With this political experience, Clyde joined nine other Republican candidates who ran to replace Collins, when he launched his campaign for the Senate. Featuring his background, Clyde highlighted his opposition to the IRS and put pictures of firearms on his campaign signs. His most formidable Republican opponent was Gurtler, 31, a state representative who earned the nickname Dr. No for voting against almost all major bills in the state legislature, including those supported by Republican leaders. Gurtler was endorsed by two members of Congress with anti-establishment bona fides—Sen. Rand Paul and Rep. Thomas Massie, both of Kentucky.

Gurtler competed for votes in the mountainous northern region with state Rep. Kevin Tanner, who operated more as a legislative insider. In the southern part of the district near Athens, Clyde's main competition was former Rep. Paul Broun, who was well known for his claim that the theory of evolution was "lies from the pits of hell" when he served in the House from 2007 to 2015; he left to run unsuccessfully for the Senate. In the primary, Clyde reached into his personal fortune, loaning himself nearly $750,000.

In the first round of the primary, Gurtler led the field with 21 percent of the vote. Clyde received almost 19 percent, narrowly leading Tanner and Broun for the second spot in the runoff. Gurtler's uncooperative behavior in the legislature backfired on him in the runoff, as many state Republican leaders lined up behind Clyde.

Although the conservative Club for Growth political action committee spent $1.1 million on his behalf, Gurtler faltered in the showdown against Clyde, 56%-44%. In this heavily Republican district, Clyde was elected with 79 percent of the vote against Democrat Devin Pandy, an Army veteran. In the House, he got seats on the Homeland Security, and Oversight and Reform Committees.

GA-9: Northeast Georgia

Cook Partisan Voting Index: R+30

Population		Race and Ethnicity		Income	
Total	771,168	White	87.40%	Median Income	$59,728
Land area (sq. miles)	5,211	Black	6.50%	District Income Rank	268
Pop/ sq mi	147.99	Latino	13.40%	Poverty Rate	13.00%
Born in State	59.00%	Asian	1.40%	With health insurance	84.80%
		Two or more races	2.10%	Cash public assistance	1.20%
Age Groups		Other	2.60%	Food stamp/SNAP	9.40%
Under 18	22.10%				
18-34	20.70%	**Education**		**Work**	
35-64	38.00%	H.S grad or less	47.10%	White Collar	33.30%
Over 64	19.10%	Some college	28.70%	Sales and Service	38.10%
		College Degree, 4 yr	15.10%	Blue Collar	28.60%
Military		Post grad	9.10%	Government	13.40%
Veteran/ Active Duty	8.20%				

2020 Pres. Vote	Trump	292,328	(76%)	Biden	85,106	(22%)			
2016 Pres. Vote	Trump	231,194	(77%)	Clinton	57,468	(19%)	Johnson	8,553	(3%)

Gainesville: Northeast Georgia is a land where the coastal plains and cotton fields yield to gently rolling hills and, near the North Carolina border, to the Appalachian Mountains. For most of its history, this was quiet, rural country, with courthouse towns and a few small cities, mostly forgotten by national elites, bypassed even by Union soldiers on their march to the sea. Today, it is undergoing a rush of change as the Atlanta metro area creeps north.

Agribusiness is a critical industry and has brought demographic change to Gainesville, the so-called "Poultry Capital of the World." Before the COVID-19 pandemic hit, Gainesville chicken plants were producing 30 million pounds of poultry per day, 15 percent of national production. Thousands of Central American immigrants have come to Gainesville for work in the industry. About 41 percent of Gainesville's population is Latino, earning a stretch of Atlanta Highway the nickname "Little Mexico." The rate of undocumented immigrants in the area, 12 percent in 2016, is the highest in the country. The Georgia Ports Authority is building a $90 million inland port in Gainesville, which will connect by rail to the harbor in Savannah. The port, set to open in 2021, was spearheaded by Nathan Deal, who represented northeast Georgia in Congress before serving as governor from 2011 to 2018.

Though the area was traditionally agrarian, interstate highways have brought it within easy range of Atlanta for leisure and business purposes. The area around Lake Sidney Lanier is filled with vacation houses and second homes. The popular Appalachian Trail starts (or ends) at Springer Mountain—a nearly 2,200-mile hike to (or from) Mount Katahdin in Maine. In Jackson County, the South Korean EV battery manufacturer SK Innovation is building a $1.7 billion plant that should bring 2,000 jobs to the area. It is one of the largest economic development projects in Georgia history and was secured by $300 million in state incentives.

The 9th Congressional District of Georgia covers the northeast corner of the state. Rural and mostly White, the district is anchored by Gainesville's Hall County, and includes the northern slice of fast-growing Forsyth and a small part of Athens-based Clarke County, the only part of the district that leans Democratic. It is the most Republican district in the state and one of the most conservative areas in the nation. Donald Trump took 76 percent in 2020. Even the increasingly diverse Hall County gave Trump 71 percent of the vote.

Jody Hice (R)

Elected 2014, 4th term, b. Apr 22, 1960; Atlanta, GA; Asbury College, B.A., 1982; Southwestern Baptist Theological Seminary, M.Div., 1986; Luther Rice Seminary and University, B.A., 1988; Southern Baptist; Married (Dee Hice); 2 children; 4 grandchildren.

Professional Career: Adjunct faculty, Luther Rice University; Pastor; Talk radio host, The Jody Hice Show.

DC Office: 409 CHOB 20515, 202-225-4101, hice.house.gov

State Offices: Milledgeville, 478-457-0007; Monroe, 770-207-1776; Thomson, 770-207-1776.

Committees: *Natural Resources*: National Parks, Forests & Public Lands; Oversight & Investigations. *Oversight & Reform*: Government Operations (RMM).

Group Ratings

	ADA	ACLU	AFL-CIO	LCV	COC	HAFA	ACU	CFG	FRC
2020	**	19%	**	0%	-	94%	98%	**	-
2019	0%	C	15%	0%	71%	C	98%	96%	100%

Almanac Ratings 2019-2020

	Economy	Social	Foreign	Composite
Liberal	25%	4%	31%	20%
Conservative	75%	96%	69%	80%

Key Votes of the 116th Congress

1. U.S./Mex./Can. trade deal	Y	5. Russia sanctions	Y
2. First Coronavirus response	N	6. Troops in Syria	N/A
3. HEROES Act	N	7. Veto arms sales to Saudis	N
4. CASH Act	N/A	8. Defense $$$, veto override	N/A

9. Firearms background checks N
10. Spending at the border   Y
11. Marijuana liberalized rules   N
12. Electoral College objections Y

Election Results

Election	Name (Party)	Vote (%)		Cand. Spent	Ind. Exp. Support	Ind. Exp. Oppose
2020 General	Jody Hice (R)............................	235,810	(62%)	$369,438	$8,761	$750
	Tabitha Johnson-Green (D)............	142,636	(38%)	$10,326		
2020 Primary	Jody Hice (R)..............................	93,506	(100%)			

Prior winning percentages: 2018 (63%), 2016 (100%), 2014 (67%)

Republican Jody Hice, who was elected in 2014 in his second bid for an open seat, has been a leader of the strongly conservative, and Trump-loyalist, House Freedom Caucus. Like most Freedom Caucus members, Hice has not endeared himself to Republican leaders and, thus, has struggled to gain clout in House committees.

Hice was born in Atlanta and grew up in Tucker Georgia. He graduated from Asbury College, earned his master's degree from Southwestern Seminary and his doctorate from Luther Rice University, a Christian college and seminary in Lithonia. He founded The Culture and Values Network and hosted The Jody Hice Show, a conservative talk radio program. A Baptist minister who served several churches in the metro Atlanta area, he argued in his 2012 book, It's Now or Never: A Call to Reclaim America, that supporters of abortion rights are worse than Adolf Hitler and that homosexuality causes shorter life spans as well as depression. He got his first taste of political battle in 2003 when he helped lead a campaign against a lawsuit by the American Civil Liberties Union seeking to remove a Ten Commandments display at the Barrow County courthouse. Five years later, he waged a successful effort against the Internal Revenue Service over whether politically active clergy can keep their tax-exempt status. In 2010, Hice was the close runner-up to Rob Woodall in the Republican primary for the neighboring 7th District.

When the seat opened in the 10th with incumbent Paul Broun's run for Senate, Hice jumped in and was among the best-known names in the GOP primary field of seven. The initial favorite was trucking company executive Mike Collins, who played up the achievements of his father, former Republican Rep. Mac Collins. Hice slammed Collins as an insider who was too close to Washington because of his father. Collins struck back, painting Hice as an extremist. He cited passages from Hice's book that argued against First Amendment protections for Muslims. Collins created his own vulnerability when he equivocated on whether Congress should raise the debt ceiling. Hice led the May primary by a hair, at 34 percent. In the July runoff, Hice had the advantage because he could unify the conservative vote. He defeated Collins, 54%-46%, and easily won in November.

Hice joined the Freedom Caucus, a conservative Republican faction that often opposes party leaders. The caucus originally formed in January 2015 over opposition to Speaker John Boehner. After Boehner stepped down in September, Hice was among a group of renegades who backed Rep. Daniel Webster of Florida as his successor. When it became clear that Rep. Paul Ryan had broad support among Republicans (including most Freedom Caucus members), Hice agreed to support him. In January 2019, Hice voted against Republican Leader Kevin McCarthy for Speaker, instead supporting Freedom Caucus founder, and McCarthy antagonist, Jim Jordan. Although the vote was symbolic (Nancy Pelosi was elected Speaker by Democratic majority in the House), it displeased Republican leaders who were hoping for more unity while in the minority. In 2019, Hice became the Freedom Caucus communications chairman and, true to his talk radio roots, began hosting a podcast where he interviewed fellow caucus members and conservative activists.

Hice closely allied himself with President Donald Trump, despite offering a belated and unenthusiastic endorsement of candidate Trump a month before the November 2016 election. "If you are struggling with who to vote for, just remember the platforms the parties are running on," he said. Once Trump became president, Hice and other Freedom Caucus members supported him in most policy and political battles, including Trump's 2019 impeachment and opposition to business shutdowns during the COVID-19 pandemic. Following the 2020 election, Hice amplified Trump's claims of voter fraud and was a leader in questioning the election result.

Although Hice's star quickly rose within the Freedom Caucus, he has seen less success on policy committees, where House leaders hold more sway. In January 2019, Republican leaders removed Hice from the Armed Services Committee, which he had joined in 2017 (his district includes parts of Augusta-based Fort Gordon). He lost his seat after voting against McCarthy for Speaker and opposing Republican-negotiated budget deals and other leadership priorities in 2017 and 2018. He tried to become ranking Republican on the Oversight and Reform Committee in 2020 but lost to Kentucky Rep. James Comer. Instead, he became ranking Republican on the Government Operations Subcommittee.

Hice has been safe at home. He defeated Democratic opponents in the 2018 and 2020 elections with more than 60 percent of the vote. In early 2021, he said that he will run in 2022 for Secretary of State in Georgia. The incumbent, Republican Brad Raffensperger, stood firm against President Donald Trump's claims of election fraud in 2020.

GA-10: East-Central Georgia

Cook Partisan Voting Index: R+13

Population		Race and Ethnicity		Income	
Total	757,807	White	67.40%	Median Income	$61,151
Land area (sq. miles)	7,096	Black	26.10%	District Income Rank	245
Pop/ sq mi	106.79	Latino	5.30%	Poverty Rate	13.60%
Born in State	64.20%	Asian	2.50%	With health insurance	88.10%
		Two or more races	2.60%	Cash public assistance	1.20%
Age Groups		Other	1.40%	Food stamp/SNAP	11.50%
Under 18	23.60%				
18-34	23.40%	**Education**		**Work**	
35-64	37.70%	H.S grad or less	42.70%	White Collar	38.70%
Over 64	15.20%	Some college	27.70%	Sales and Service	36.40%
		College Degree, 4 yr	17.60%	Blue Collar	24.80%
Military		Post grad	12.00%	Government	18.10%
Veteran/ Active Duty	7.20%				

2020 Pres. Vote	Trump	231,237	(60%)	Biden	151,194	(39%)		
2016 Pres. Vote	Trump	193,029	(61%)	Clinton	112,691	(36%)	Johnson	9,353 (3%)

Athens, Eastern Atlanta Exurbs: The north and south wings of Gen. William Tecumseh Sherman's Union Army converged at Milledgeville, wrote author E.L. Doctorow in his novel The March: "And then the town of Milledgeville, empty and quiet, sat in its dishevelment, gusts of wind flying paper and brush against the sides of buildings and the leavings of coal fires scuttering in the street." Baldwin County's Milledgeville was the capital of Georgia from 1804 to 1868, and it is where Georgia legislators decided in 1861 to secede from the Union. Sherman's Army occupied the town and burned the state penitentiary.

Central Georgia and its tragedies have served as inspiration for several great Southern writers. Alice Walker, author of The Color Purple, was born in Eatonton, and her writing draws on family oral histories of life in rural Georgia. Also from Eatonton was Joel Chandler Harris, a freed slave who used the character Uncle Remus to write old Southern stories with authentic folklore. Erskine Caldwell's scandalous best-seller, Tobacco Road, about an illiterate, Depression-racked farm family, was said to be influenced by his time living in the small town of Wrens in Jefferson County.

Today, the region's economy is dominated by small, high-tech manufacturing, Atlanta's urban sprawl, and the long reach of the University of Georgia in Athens, the first state-charted public university in the United States (although UGA was chartered in 1785, the University of North Carolina held the first classes in 1795). UGA faced controversy over its decision to bring students back during the height of the COVID-19 pandemic. Cases spiked and hundreds of faculty signed onto a letter criticizing the university. The community surrounding UGA was particularly vulnerable due to its high poverty and lack of health care access.

The 10th Congressional District runs from Barrow, Oglethorpe and Wilkes counties in the north to Baldwin, Washington and Jefferson counties in the south. Rapidly growing and affluent Columbia County—outside Augusta—is divided between this district and the 12th. The district takes parts of metro Atlanta, including portions of fast-growing Gwinnett and Henry counties, and the well-to-do Oconee County. With more than 300 miles of shoreline, the Lake Oconee area has gated communities and golf courses that beckon second-home buyers and retirees.

As the home of UGA, Clarke is the largest county in the district and has a solidly liberal base. While the district's rural counties mostly gave President Donald Trump huge margins, above and beyond those earned by Mitt Romney in 2012, Clarke voted for Joe Biden in 2020, 70%-28%. The county commission also removed a Confederate monument from downtown Athens and passed a resolution to "forever acknowledge Black Lives Matter." The district overall voted for Trump, 60%-39%.

Barry Loudermilk (R)

Elected 2014, 4th term, b. Dec 22, 1963; Riverdale, GA; Community College of the Air Force, A.A.S., 1987; Wayland Baptist University, B.S., 1992; Baptist; Married (Desiree Loudermilk); 3 children; 2 grandchildren.

Military Career: U.S. Air Force 1984-1992 (Operation Desert Storm)

Elected Office: GA House, 2005-2010; GA Senate, 2011-2013.

Professional Career: Chairman, GA Republican party, 2001-2004; Business owner.

DC Office: 422 CHOB 20515, 202-225-2931, Fax: 202-225-2944, loudermilk.house.gov

State Offices: Atlanta, 770-429-1776; Cartersville, 770-429-1776; Woodstock, 770-429-1776.

Committees: *Administration. Financial Services*: Consumer Protection & Financial Institutions; Oversight & Investigations; Task Force on Artificial Intelligence. *Joint Library. Joint Printing.*

Group Ratings

	ADA	ACLU	AFL-CIO	LCV	COC	HAFA	ACU	CFG	FRC
2020	**	18%	**	0%	-	98%	96%	**	-
2019	5%	C	24%	7%	79%	C	95%	84%	95%

Almanac Ratings 2019-2020

	Economy	Social	Foreign	Composite
Liberal	33%	32%	28%	31%
Conservative	67%	68%	72%	69%

Key Votes of the 116th Congress

1. U.S./Mex./Can. trade deal	Y	5. Russia sanctions	N/A	9. Firearms background checks N
2. First Coronavirus response	N	6. Troops in Syria	N	10. Spending at the border	Y
3. HEROES Act	N	7. Veto arms sales to Saudis	N	11. Marijuana liberalized rules	N/A
4. CASH Act	N	8. Defense $$$, veto override	N	12. Electoral College objections Y

Election Results

Election	Name (Party)	Vote (%)		Cand. Spent	Ind. Exp. Support	Ind. Exp. Oppose
2020 General	Barry Loudermilk (R)	245,259	(60%)	$629,901	$13,382	$950
	Dana Barrett (D)	160,623	(40%)	$390,557	$150	
2020 Primary	Barry Loudermilk (R)	86,050	(100%)			

Prior winning percentages: 2018 (62%), 2016 (67%), 2014 (100%)

Republican Barry Loudermilk was elected in 2014 with the support of tea party groups in a lively primary. Following several legislative battles and personal traumas, his rhetoric softened and he increased his search for political common ground. Still, he remained a loyal Republican and was a fierce defender of President Donald Trump during the House impeachment proceedings in 2019.

Loudermilk was born in Riverdale and got an associate degree in telecommunications technology from Air Force Community College and a bachelor of science in occupational education and information systems technology from Wayland Baptist University. After serving in the Air Force plus a stint in the cybersecurity business, he turned to politics. He chaired the Georgia Republican Party for four years. His decade as a state legislator included four years in the Senate, where he chaired the science and technology panel. He authored a book, And Then They Prayed, which features inspirational stories from American history.

The seat became open in 2014 when Republican incumbent Phil Gingrey ran for the Senate. Loudermilk and former Rep. Bob Barr were the top two vote-getters in the initial GOP primary, with 37 percent and 26 percent. In the runoff, Barr, a former federal prosecutor, four-term House member, and Libertarian presidential candidate in 2008, played up his conservative bona fides, including his role in the 1998 impeachment proceedings against President Bill Clinton. Loudermilk, taking a sharp anti-establishment turn, cited Barr's Washington experience as a liability. Loudermilk trounced Barr in the runoff, 66%-34%. Loudermilk won without opposition in November—which once was rare for a freshman.

When the House Republican Conference met in November to organize for the new Congress, Loudermilk was one of three members who cast what he called a "principled vote" against John Boehner for another term as Speaker. He told the Cherokee Tribune he was "probably punished" with his failure to get the committee assignment he had sought. After this initial dustup, Loudermilk moved closer to Republican leaders, despite criticism from right-wing talk radio hosts. When Boehner stepped down in October 2015, he voted for Paul Ryan as the next Speaker. In 2017, he dropped his membership in the anti-leadership Freedom Caucus, citing a lack of time, while increasing his activity with the more leadership-oriented Republican Study Committee. He received seats on Financial Services and House Administration, two committees where House leaders have interests.

Loudermilk survived an unusual array of life-threatening incidents: the May 2017 shooting at a congressional Republican baseball practice in Alexandria Virginia; an apparently random shooting in March 2018 while he and his wife were driving through the north Georgia mountains; plus train and car accidents that resulted in fatalities. Subsequently, he told the Atlanta Journal-Constitution, he sought a more civil approach to politics. He reached out for more bipartisanship on budget and banking issues. Still, Loudermilk maintained a partisan edge that shined through during the 2019 House impeachment of Trump, which he compared to Jesus Christ's persecution by Roman authorities (in fact, he said Jesus was treated more fairly than Trump).

In the 2020 general election, Loudermilk faced Dana Barrett, a local talk radio host, in a tougher-than-usual reelection bid. Barrett cut a moderate profile as a "socially liberal" but "fiscally responsible" Democrat. She also spent $390,000, more than half of Loudermilk's haul and far more than his previous Democratic opponents. Despite the tougher challenger, Loudermilk still won 60 percent of the vote, only a slight decline from his 62 percent in 2018.

GA-11: Northwestern Atlanta Suburbs   Cook Partisan Voting Index: R+12

Population		Race and Ethnicity		Income	
Total	782,704	White	71.20%	Median Income	$76,640
Land area (sq. miles)	1,071	Black	17.80%	District Income Rank	112
Pop/ sq mi	730.65	Latino	11.50%	Poverty Rate	9.00%
Born in State	45.50%	Asian	3.10%	With health insurance	87.10%
		Two or more races	2.40%	Cash public assistance	0.80%
Age Groups		Other	5.50%	Food stamp/SNAP	4.90%
Under 18	23.00%				
18-34	23.40%	**Education**		**Work**	
35-64	40.20%	H.S grad or less	29.80%	White Collar	46.00%
Over 64	13.30%	Some college	27.30%	Sales and Service	35.20%
		College Degree, 4 yr	27.70%	Blue Collar	18.80%
Military		Post grad	15.10%	Government	11.70%
Veteran/ Active Duty	6.70%				

2020 Pres. Vote	Trump	234,946	(57%)	Biden	171,611	(42%)		
2016 Pres. Vote	Trump	198,877	(60%)	Clinton	116,575	(35%)	Johnson	14,355	(4%)

Cherokee, Cobb: Marietta is one of Atlanta's largest suburbs and a hub for the aerospace industry. Its economic mainstay for many years was defense contractor Lockheed Martin. The assembly line shut down in 2011 after the F-22 was cut by the Obama administration. But layoffs at the Marietta plant were limited, chiefly because the Pentagon had ordered additional F-35 fighter jets, parts of which are built there. Prospects for Lockheed Martin and Marietta brightened in 2016, when the company won a contract for the C-130 Super Hercules airlift plane. In 2020, Lockheed received a $15 billion contract from the Air Force to work on the project through 2030. According to a 2020 PwC report, Georgia is the number one state for aerospace manufacturing. The industry employs more than 100,000 statewide and has an economic impact of nearly $60 billion.

Marietta is diverse compared to nearby counties: 31 percent is African American, and 16 percent is Hispanic. In 2017, the Atlanta Braves moved from downtown Atlanta to their new Truist Park (originally Sun Trust Park) in Cobb County, a short distance from the busy interchange of Interstates

75 and 285. The Braves fell one game short of the World Series in 2020, adding to Georgia's recent run of near misses in professional and college sports. Near Marietta is Kennesaw State University, the third largest university in Georgia.

North of the metro Atlanta core are outer-suburban and exurban communities in Cherokee and Bartow counties. Cherokee is fast growing; it saw a 21 percent increase from 2010 to 2019. Bartow County grew 32 percent from 2000 to 2010, though the growth slowed to 8 percent in the next nine years. Both counties are largely bedroom communities for Atlanta commuters, but businesses are locating there too. In 2019, Nippon Light Metal announced a $50 million facility in Adairsville.

The 11th Congressional District of Georgia is anchored by Marietta, the county seat and the largest city in Cobb, and takes in all of Bartow and Cherokee counties. Cobb's once solidly Republican vote has shifted—like many suburbs across the nation. After narrowly backing Hillary Clinton in 2016, it gave Joe Biden a 14-point victory in 2020. The district includes parts of northern Fulton County, which is more Republican than south Fulton but still narrowly backed Biden. Trump's share also declined in Cherokee and Bartow, but he still got around 70 percent in each. Overall, the district's 67 percent vote for Mitt Romney in 2012 slipped to 60 percent for Trump in 2016, then to 57 percent for Trump in 2020.

Rick Allen (R)

Elected 2014, 4th term, b. Nov 07, 1951; Augusta, GA; Auburn University School of Architecture and Fine Arts, B.S., 1973; Methodist; Married (Robin Reeve); 4 children; 12 grandchildren.

Professional Career: Founder, R.W. Allen & Associates, 1976.

DC Office: 2400 RHOB 20515, 202-225-2823, Fax: 202-225-3377, allen.house.gov

State Offices: Augusta, 706-228-1980; Dublin, 478-272-4030; Statesboro, 912-243-9452; Vidalia, 912-403-3311.

Committees: *Agriculture*: Conservation & Forestry; General Farm Commodities & Risk Management. *Education & Labor*: Early Childhood, Elementary & Secondary Education; Health, Employment, Labor & Pensions (RMM).

Group Ratings

	ADA	ACLU	AFL-CIO	LCV	COC	HAFA	ACU	CFG	FRC
2020	**	15%	**	0%	-	91%	89%	**	-
2019	5%	C	24%	7%	78%	C	88%	90%	100%

Almanac Ratings 2019-2020

	Economy	Social	Foreign	Composite
Liberal	27%	12%	4%	15%
Conservative	73%	88%	96%	85%

Key Votes of the 116th Congress

1. U.S./Mex./Can. trade deal	Y	5. Russia sanctions	N	9. Firearms background checks	N
2. First Coronavirus response	Y	6. Troops in Syria	N	10. Spending at the border	Y
3. HEROES Act	N	7. Veto arms sales to Saudis	N	11. Marijuana liberalized rules	N/A
4. CASH Act	N	8. Defense $$$, veto override	N	12. Electoral College objections	Y

Election Results

Election	Name (Party)	Vote (%)		Cand. Spent	Ind. Exp. Support	Ind. Exp. Oppose
2020 General	Rick Allen (R).................................	181,038	(58%)	$686,408	$5,649	$750
	Liz Johnson (D)................................	129,061	(42%)	$67,690		
2020 Primary	Rick W. Allen (R).............................	74,520	(100%)			

Prior winning percentages: 2018 (60%), 2016 (62%), 2014 (55%)

Republican Rick Allen was elected in 2014 when he defeated Georgia's only remaining white Democrat in the House. He has focused on agricultural and education issues in his committee work and been attentive to local stakeholders in his district. He is typically a leadership loyalist and makes few waves.

A native of Augusta, Allen graduated from Auburn University with a B.S. in building construction. After spending three years as a project manager with a local builder, he founded R.W. Allen & Associates, a construction company he has operated since 1976 in the Augusta and Athens areas. His experience as a small business owner and job creator, plus his inexperience in government office, formed the centerpiece of his congressional campaign.

Allen sought the Republican nomination in 2012 but finished second in the primary. Two years later, he spent nearly a million dollars of his own money and won the five-way primary with 54 percent of the vote. In the general election, Allen criticized Rep. John Barrow—one of the few remaining fiscally conservative Blue Dog Democrats in the House—for hewing too closely to President Barack Obama's agenda, while touting his own conservative credentials. Allen also highlighted his support for the Second Amendment, though Barrow boasted an A+ rating and endorsement from the National Rifle Association. With little daylight between the candidates on many issues, the Republican strategy focused on the national Democratic Party. Barrow outspent Allen $3.5 million to $2.5 million, but the nearly $4 million in national GOP assistance more than made up the difference. Allen won handily, 55%-45%.

Allen entered the House with more mainstream Republican views and style than other GOP newcomers. From his positions on the Agriculture Committee and the Education and Labor Committee, he has largely focused on policy work that affects his district. He has been attentive to the needs of Augusta-based Fort Gordon and its cyber security operations, working with other members of the Georgia delegation to direct more federal spending toward the base. He has also advocated nuclear power. His district includes Plant Vogtle, the only nuclear power plant under construction in the country. In a 2019 op-ed, he criticized presidential candidate Elizabeth Warren's plan to phase out nuclear power, saying it provides clean energy and creates thousands of jobs. In 2018, he worked in a more nationally oriented policy area by serving on the House-Senate conference committee that resolved final details of the farm bill.

Allen has faced pressure from the left and the right for his rhetoric and policy views. From the left, he was condemned by gay-rights advocates for delivering an opening prayer that referred harshly to the LBGT community at a closed-door meeting of the House Republican Conference. With his Main Street business views, Allen supported extension of the Export-Import Bank. That led to attack ads against him from Americans for Prosperity, an organization funded in party Charles Koch, which opposes corporate welfare. But tea party groups have failed to wage a significant primary challenge against him. On the Education and Labor Committee in 2021, he was ranking Republican on the Health, Employment, Labor and Pensions Subcommittee.

Allen has coasted to reelection since his initial win in 2014. Democratic challenger Patricia Carpenter McCracken made no "known appearances" to oppose Allen during the 2016 campaign, the Augusta Chronicle reported. Allen was reelected, 62%-38%. In 2018, Democrat Francis Johnson, former president of the Georgia NAACP, ran a more vigorous campaign and said he would seek to improve the quality of life in rural Georgia. Allen won, 59%-41%. In 2020, Allen defeated Liz Johnson, a Statesboro insurance agent and perennial Democratic candidate, by a 58%-42% margin.

GA-12: East Georgia

Cook Partisan Voting Index: R+9

Population		Race and Ethnicity		Income	
Total	732,810	White	58.10%	Median Income	$50,217
Land area (sq. miles)	8,185	Black	34.30%	District Income Rank	386
Pop/ sq mi	89.53	Latino	6.50%	Poverty Rate	18.30%
Born in State	66.60%	Asian	1.70%	With health insurance	86.70%
		Two or more races	3.40%	Cash public assistance	1.90%
Age Groups		Other	2.40%	Food stamp/SNAP	14.00%
Under 18	23.00%				
18-34	26.00%	**Education**		**Work**	
35-64	36.10%	H.S grad or less	49.30%	White Collar	32.60%
Over 64	15.00%	Some college	28.50%	Sales and Service	39.50%
		College Degree, 4 yr	13.80%	Blue Collar	27.90%
Military		Post grad	8.40%	Government	17.40%
Veteran/ Active Duty	11.40%				

2020 Pres. Vote	Trump	177,138	(56%)	Biden	136,639	(43%)		
2016 Pres. Vote	Trump	152,204	(57%)	Clinton	108,937	(41%)	Johnson	6,534 (2%)

Augusta: Upriver from Savannah is the city of Augusta. Founded in 1735 as a fur-trading post, it has been home since 1835 to the Medical College of Georgia, now part of Georgia Regents University, a public academic health center. It has become a manufacturing hub for big companies like Procter & Gamble, International Paper and Dart Container, and has gained prominence for military cyber operations. Many know the city best as the site of Augusta National Golf Club, a private club where the Masters Tournament is held every April, amid azaleas in bloom, reverence for its traditions by both players and spectators, and an annual economic impact in the tens of millions of dollars. The Masters was postponed in 2020 due to the COVID-19 pandemic. It ended up being held in November without spectators present, a blow to local businesses who hoped for a return to normalcy in 2021.

The 12th Congressional District takes in Augusta's Richmond County and part of neighboring Columbia County. They include half the total population for the district. Richmond is 58 percent African American, while Columbia is 19 percent. From 2010 to 2019, Columbia grew from 124,000 to 156,000, a 26 percent increase; Richmond had virtually no change at 200,000. In Augusta, the Fort Gordon Army base is home to 16,000 troops, 10,000 civilians and the Army Signal Corps. It has an annual economic impact of $2.4 billion. Fort Gordon's name will be changed in the near future as the 2020 defense authorization bill, passed over President Trump's veto, provides for the renaming of bases with Confederate namesakes. The base is the headquarters for the Army cyber command, which completed its move to a new $370 million headquarters in September 2020. Established in 2010, the cyber command works with other federal agencies to develop and field cyberspace capabilities, modernize networks and improve sensors and tools for defensive operations. Worldwide, it oversees 16,500 soldiers, civilians, and contract workers.

In Waynesboro, Georgia Power continues construction on its much-delayed Plant Vogtle, one of the last nuclear power plants under construction in the nation. The district includes Vidalia, home of the famous sweet onion, a state-owned brand harvested in only 20 counties, with help from guest workers.

In 2020, President Donald Trump won the district's vote, 56%-43. The two largest counties in the 12th went in different directions but both moved toward Democrats. Joe Biden won Richmond, 68%-31%, a three-point improvement on Hillary Clinton's 2016 performance. Trump won Columbia, 62%-36%, a five-point slide relative to his 2016 performance. Trump won the district's other 17 counties.

David Scott (D)

Elected 2002, 10th term, b. Jun 27, 1945; Aynor, SC; University of FL, B.A., 1967; University of PA Wharton School of Business Aresty Institute, M.B.A., 1969; Baptist; Married (Alfredia Aaron Scott); 2 children; 2 grandchildren.

Elected Office: GA House, 1975-1982; GA Senate, 1983-2002.

Professional Career: Founder & President, Dayn-Mark Advertising, 1979-2002.

DC Office: 225 CHOB 20515, 202-225-2939, Fax: 202-225-4628, davidscott.house.gov

State Offices: Jonesboro, 770-210-5073; Smyrna, 770-432-5405.

Committees: *Agriculture (Chmn)*: Ex Officio membership on all subcommittees. *Financial Services*: Consumer Protection & Financial Institutions; Investor Protection, Entrepreneurship & Capital Markets.

Group Ratings

	ADA	ACLU	AFL-CIO	LCV	COC	HAFA	ACU	CFG	FRC
2020	**	76%	**	100%	-	0%	12%	**	-
2019	85%	C	100%	97%	68%	C	12%	12%	100%

Almanac Ratings 2019-2020

	Economy	Social	Foreign	Composite
Liberal	100%	100%	80%	94%
Conservative	0%	0%	20%	6%

Key Votes of the 116th Congress

1. U.S./Mex./Can. trade deal	Y	5. Russia sanctions	Y	9. Firearms background checks Y
2. First Coronavirus response	Y	6. Troops in Syria	Y	10. Spending at the border	Y
3. HEROES Act	Y	7. Veto arms sales to Saudis	Y	11. Marijuana liberalized rules	Y
4. CASH Act	Y	8. Defense $$$, veto override	Y	12. Electoral College objections N

Election Results

Election	Name (Party)	Vote (%)		Cand. Spent	Ind. Exp. Support	Ind. Exp. Oppose
2020 General	David Scott (D)	279,045	(77%)	$1,507,494	$52,111	
	Becky Hites (R)	81,476	(23%)	$56,437		
2020 Primary	David Scott (D)	77,735	(53%)			
	Keisha Waites (D)	37,447	(26%)			
	Michael Owens (D)	19,415	(13%)			
	Jannquell Peters (D)	12,308	(8%)			

Prior winning percentages: 2018 (76%), 2016 (100%), 2014 (100%), 2012 (72%), 2010 (69%), 2008 (69%), 2006 (69%), 2004 (100%), 2002 (60%)

First elected in 2002, Democrat David Scott experienced highs and lows in 2020. He was nearly forced into a runoff in the Democratic primary after facing criticism for his bipartisan approach and centrist politics. Then he was selected to head the House Agriculture Committee after the election, becoming Georgia's only committee chair. Scott's political fortunes depend on the upcoming redistricting cycle and whether Democrats hold the House in 2022.

Born in rural South Carolina, Scott is the son of a minister and grandson of a deacon. During his middle-school years, his family moved to Scarsdale New York, where his parents took jobs as a chauffeur and housekeeper for a wealthy family. Scott was the only African American in his otherwise all-white school. He graduated from Florida A&M University and completed an internship at the Labor Department in Washington. There he met George Taylor, an authority in labor-management relations who encouraged him to apply to the prestigious Wharton School at the University of Pennsylvania, where Scott earned his MBA. He moved to Atlanta and in 1974 was elected to the Georgia House. In 1982, he won election to the state Senate, where he served for 20 years and chaired the Rules Committee. From 1979 to 2002, he owned Dayn-Mark Advertising, which creates and places radio, television and print ads. The firm has been operated by his wife and two daughters.

In 2002, Scott ran for the newly created 13th District, which was heavily Democratic. Four other Democrats ran, the best known of who was former state party Chairman David Worley, who nearly defeated Republican Rep. Newt Gingrich in 1990. If voters didn't know Scott as a state legislator, most knew of his campaign co-chairman: Henry Aaron, the Hall of Fame slugger and Atlanta-area icon, who was Scott's brother-in-law. Scott brought his advertising expertise, plastering the interstate highways with eye-catching billboards. His chief competitors, Worley and state Sen. Greg Hecht, both White, ran ads attacking each other. Scott won the primary with 54 percent of the vote. He won the general election, 60%-40%.

Since he first came to Congress, Scott has been a moderate voice in his party. As a freshman, Scott was one of seven Democrats to vote for final passage of President George W. Bush's tax cut, and one of 16 to vote for the prescription drug benefit under Medicare. He split with most of his party by voting for a constitutional amendment to ban same-sex marriage. In recent years, Scott has become a more reliable party vote, but he has had no reluctance to go his own way. In 2016, he urged President Barack Obama to "stop pussyfooting around, get a sense of urgency and declare war" on Islamic terrorism. He also rejected the calls of some Georgia Democrats to eliminate the Confederate statues on Stone Mountain. "Tell the Black man's struggle, how he overcame," he told The Atlanta Journal-Constitution. "We can't do that if we obliterate the Confederacy or the Civil War as if it didn't exist. It's a part of our history."

On the Financial Services Committee, Scott in 2009 initially opposed the bailout of the financial markets. After Chairman Barney Frank promised to address the Black Caucus' call for additional protections for homeowners facing foreclosure, Scott switched his vote to support the revised version. In 2018, he was part of the bipartisan coalition that eased the restrictions in the 2010 law.

Scott has served on the House Agriculture Committee since he was first elected. Following the 2020 elections, the Democratic Caucus selected him as the committee's first African-American chairman; his chief opponent was Jim Costa of California. He also became the first Black Georgian to head any House committee and the first Georgia Democrat to chair a House committee since John Flynt in the 1970s. Scott had spent years heading subcommittees and served as the number two Democrat to Collin Peterson, a moderate from Minnesota who was defeated in 2020. During the debate over the 2018 farm bill, he secured agriculture scholarships for historically Black colleges and universities and opposed work requirements for food stamps. Throughout the Trump administration, Scott worked well with Agriculture Secretary Sonny Perdue, who was his colleague in the Georgia State Senate. He even introduced Perdue at his Senate confirmation hearing. He had a similarly close relationship with Republican Senator Johnny Isakson, who Scott endorsed for reelection in 2016.

Scott's bipartisan approach caught up with him in 2020 as he struggled in the Democratic primary against three opponents, including former state Rep. Keisha Waites. Although none of his opponents raised significant funds, Scott got into hot water by skipping a debate where he was pilloried for being out of touch and cast as a Republican collaborator. He failed to hit 50 percent of the vote on election night and the Associated Press said he was headed to a runoff with Waites, who raised less than $1,000 but captured 25 percent of the vote. Ultimately, Scott barely passed the 50 percent mark and the AP reversed its call. As in previous years, he easily won the general election.

Still, the result was too close for comfort for an incumbent who usually received token opposition. The upcoming redistricting could significantly change the boundaries of his district in metro Atlanta and make Scott vulnerable to another primary challenge. Even with his new chairmanship (which will be lost if Republicans retake the House in 2022), the 75-year old Scott might seriously consider retirement.

GA-13: Southwestern Atlanta Exurbs

Population		Race and Ethnicity		Income	
Total	802,943	White	29.00%	Median Income	$66,203
Land area (sq. miles)	715	Black	61.60%	District Income Rank	203
Pop/ sq mi	1,123.08	Latino	11.90%	Poverty Rate	10.50%
Born in State	48.70%	Asian	2.70%	With health insurance	85.60%
		Two or more races	3.00%	Cash public assistance	1.90%
Age Groups		Other	3.70%	Food stamp/SNAP	13.00%
Under 18	26.30%				
18-34	23.80%	**Education**		**Work**	
35-64	39.00%	H.S grad or less	39.70%	White Collar	35.60%
Over 64	11.00%	Some college	30.60%	Sales and Service	38.90%
		College Degree, 4 yr	20.20%	Blue Collar	25.60%
Military		Post grad	9.40%	Government	13.30%
Veteran/ Active Duty	8.50%				

2020 Pres. Vote	Biden	277,932	(76%)	Trump	85,997	(23%)	
2016 Pres. Vote	Clinton	213,805	(71%)	Trump	80,086	(27%) Johnson	7,136 (2%)

Clayton, Cobb: In the 1960s, Atlanta's Blacks were clustered in ghetto neighborhoods on the south and west sides of the city. The north side and the suburbs in every direction were heavily White. Today, metro Atlanta's thriving Black middle class has moved outward in almost every direction in one of the nation's fastest-growing metro areas—to DeKalb County to the east, to Clayton directly south of the city, to southwest Fulton, and to Cobb and Douglas counties to the north and west. These substantial population shifts, however, have not broken longstanding patterns of racial segregation in metro Atlanta. As Blacks reached inner-suburban areas, Whites retreated into the outer-suburbs and exurbs, largely maintaining separate neighborhoods and schools.

Despite these systemic inequalities, south and west Atlanta have strong economic drivers. Before the COVID-19 pandemic, Hartsfield-Jackson Atlanta International Airport was the busiest in the world, with 110.5 million passengers arriving and departing in 2019. Unlike hubs in New York and Chicago, Atlanta has no major competition from nearby cities. Moreover, 80 percent of the U.S. population lives within a two-hour flight of the city, making it a hub for connecting flights. The "economic jewel of Georgia" contributes $35 billion to the economy and has made south Atlanta a logistics and warehousing hub. Local interests want to turn the area surrounding the airport into an "aerotropolis," that would include a corporate center, autonomous rapid-transit systems and a corridor of green trails. The planners aim to create the kind of development south of Atlanta that has taken place elsewhere in the metro area and in communities surrounding large airports across the nation. The Democratic-controlled city of Atlanta owns and operates Hartsfield-Jackson. The Republican-controlled state legislature proposed a state takeover in 2019, citing corruption and mismanagement concerns. The bill failed but could come back in future sessions.

Aside from the airport, the district is home to Trilith (formerly Pinewood) Studios, a famous movie production facility south of Atlanta that is expanding its operations after delivering *Avengers: End Game*—the highest grossing movie of all time. West of the city is the theme park Six Flags Over Georgia, which, along with its Marietta-based sister property, generated more than $370 million in economic impact in 2017 but saw business slow during the pandemic.

The 13th Congressional District of Georgia is a collection of suburban areas that have attracted Atlanta's African-American middle class. It includes most of Clayton County, which is 73 percent African American and 13 percent Latino. It was Clayton's heavily Democratic absentee ballots that gave Joe Biden a statewide lead over President Donald Trump (which Biden never lost) as Georgia tallied results for several days following the 2020 election. Additionally, the district takes in all of Douglas County, and parts of Cobb, Fulton, Fayette and Henry counties. Clayton, Cobb, Douglas and Fulton each have similar shares of the voters in the 13th. The airport is just across the district line in the 5th. The 13th is a majority-Black district and solidly Democratic. Biden won the district, 75%-23%.

Marjorie Greene (R)

Elected 2020, 1st term, b. May 27, 1974; Milledgeville, GA; University of GA, B.B.A.; Christian - Non-Denominational; Married (Perry Greene); 3 children.

Professional Career: Co-owner, construction company; Owner, gym franchise.

DC Office: 1023 LHOB 20515, 202-225-5211, greene.house.gov

State Offices: Dalton, 706-226-5320; Rome, 706-290-1776.

Election Results

Election	Name (Party)	Vote (%)		Cand. Spent	Ind. Exp. Support	Ind. Exp. Oppose
2020 General	Marjorie Greene (R)	229,827	(75%)	$2,257,469	$87,609	$65,441
	Kevin Van Ausdal (D)	77,798	(25%)	$82,912		
2020 Primary	Marjorie Greene (R)	43,892	(40%)			
	John Cowan (R)	22,862	(21%)			
	John Barge (R)	9,619	(9%)			
	Clayton Fuller (R)	7,433	(7%)			
	Bill Hembree (R)	6,988	(6%)			
	Kevin Cooke (R)	6,699	(6%)			
	Matt Laughridge (R)	6,220	(6%)			
2020 Primary Runoff	Marjorie Greene (R)	43,813	(57%)			
	John Cowan (R)	32,982	(43%)			

Businesswoman Marjorie Taylor Greene achieved national notoriety in 2020 and caused headaches for Republican leaders when she was elected to replace Republican Rep. Tom Graves, who retired after five terms. In contrast to her institutionally minded predecessor, Greene supported right-wing conspiracy theories and routinely made racist statements. Once she won the primary in her safely Republican district, House Republicans struggled with how to handle Greene, who developed an enthusiastic following among supporters of President Donald Trump. Once she was elected, they initially decided to move beyond her controversial past.

Greene, who was born in the central Georgia town of Milledgeville, grew up in the northern Atlanta suburbs where her father, Robert Taylor, started a residential housing construction company. At the University of Georgia, she graduated with a business degree. Her husband, Perry Greene, also graduated from UGA's business school. In 2002, they bought out Marjorie's father and took over the family company, which was renamed Taylor Commercial and focused on renovations across the Southeast. A fitness enthusiast, Greene also started, and later sold, a CrossFit gym.

Greene started to build a pro-Trump social media profile in 2017. She posted videos expressing support for conspiracy theories, including QAnon—which claimed that Trump was waging a secret war against a government ring of Satan-worshipping child pedophiles. She attended far-right conferences and served as a "correspondent" for the conspiracy news site, American Truth Seekers. Before she ran for Congress, many of her videos and online posts were deleted.

In June 2019, Greene announced she would challenge Democratic Rep. Lucy McBath in the northern Atlanta suburbs. But former Rep. Karen Handel regained the support of Georgia's Republican establishment, who saw Greene as a risky candidate in a swing district. Members of the conservative House Freedom Caucus persuaded Greene to switch to a solidly Republican seat in northwest Georgia after Graves announced his retirement.

Greene faced nine opponents (all men) in the Republican primary. She was endorsed by Rep. Jim Jordan of Ohio, the former Freedom Caucus chairman, and benefited from nearly $1 million in self-financing. One of her television ads featured Greene with a rifle telling "Antifa" to "stay the hell out of northwest Georgia." In another, she accused "nasty radical women" in Congress of "ripping our country apart." In the first round of the primary, she got 40 percent of the vote. Rome neurosurgeon John Cowan was runner-up with 21 percent, advancing with Greene to a runoff.

The runoff drew the national spotlight after Politico published a report on Greene's social media activities. Other journalists uncovered a number of her racist and anti-Semitic remarks. She dismissed the criticism as political correctness. House Republican leaders widely condemned Greene, but most of them stopped short of endorsing Cowan or helping to defeat her in the runoff—apparently concluding that her election was inevitable..

Cowan argued that Greene was "crazy" and claimed that her rhetoric would boost Democratic fundraising and harm other Republican candidates. Still, Greene won the runoff with 57 percent of the vote. In her victory speech, she castigated the Republican establishment, referred to House Speaker Nancy Pelosi as a "bitch," and expelled a reporter from the event. The next morning, Trump congratulated Greene, calling her a "future Republican star."

Media coverage of Greene escalated following the runoff. That led her to reverse her claim that the federal government was responsible for the September 11 attacks and to back away from QAnon. Still, Greene's fiery rhetoric and willingness to attack fellow Republicans kept her in the headlines. Following the runoff, her Democratic opponent, Kevin Van Ausdal, dropped out of the race —though his name remained on the ballot and he got 25 percent of the vote. The National Republican Congressional Committee showed its acceptance of Greene with a $5,000 donation to her campaign. Her Democratic opponent dropped out of the contest and GOP leaders acquiesced to her candidacy.

With tensions rising following the Capitol riot on January 6, CNN uncovered evidence that Greene had "liked" social media posts in 2018 and 2019, endorsing violence against Nancy Pelosi and federal law enforcement. This unleashed outrage in both parties, with many House Democrats calling for her expulsion and Mitch McConnell calling her views a "cancer" on the Republican Party. Greene apologized to her colleagues, saying she "was allowed to believe things that weren't true." When Republican Leader Kevin McCarthy declined to remove Greene from the Budget and Education and Labor Committees, the Democratic-controlled House voted to strip her of the assignments. Most Republicans condemned Greene but voted against removing her, saying committee decisions should remain within each party. Even without committees, Greene managed to stay in the headlines through dilatory procedural maneuvers and culture-war antics. Other House Members and her spokesman said that she was taking steps to organize an America First Caucus, though she denied the reports and abandoned the initiative.

Greene's has become a prodigious fundraiser and could make a statewide run. Many Georgia Republicans mostly see her as toxic (especially as the state becomes more competitive) and might try to weaken her electoral base in redistricting. In any case, Greene's support has remained firm among her northwest Georgia constituents, with many saying she is doing exactly what they elected her to do – stand-up and fight.

GA-14: Northwest Georgia

Cook Partisan Voting Index: R+28

Population		Race and Ethnicity		Income	
Total	732,133	White	84.60%	Median Income	$56,150
Land area (sq. miles)	3,623	Black	8.70%	District Income Rank	313
Pop/ sq mi	202.07	Latino	12.20%	Poverty Rate	11.70%
Born in State	58.70%	Asian	1.00%	With health insurance	86.30%
		Two or more races	3.30%	Cash public assistance	2.50%
Age Groups		Other	2.30%	Food stamp/SNAP	11.00%
Under 18	24.10%				
18-34	21.30%	**Education**		**Work**	
35-64	39.50%	H.S grad or less	52.10%	White Collar	28.30%
Over 64	15.00%	Some college	29.50%	Sales and Service	36.70%
		College Degree, 4 yr	10.80%	Blue Collar	35.10%
Military		Post grad	7.60%	Government	12.00%
Veteran/ Active Duty	7.10%				

2020 Pres. Vote	Trump	235,006	(73%)	Biden	80,969	(25%)	
2016 Pres. Vote	Trump	191,849	(75%)	Clinton	56,513	(22%)	Johnson 7,510 (3%)

Rome, Dalton: Northwest Georgia was the home of the Cherokee Nation before the tribe was sent west in the 1830s on the Trail of Tears. It has been manufacturing country for the past century. Hundreds of textile mills and dozens of carpet mills once clustered near the supply of cotton and along the railroad lines heading southwest at the base of the southern Appalachian chain. The late 19th-century boosters of the New South hailed factories as the vanguard of technological progress.

The plants produced a higher standard of living than did the farms on this stubborn land. But the mills put scant premium on education or the cultivation of civic virtues and did little to bring in higher-skilled work. All-white hiring practices maintained racial segregation in mostly white north Georgia.

Today, this area has developed a different kind of economy, as metro Atlanta has spread out along highways to the north and west. There are sprawling subdivisions in what once were mill towns. Floyd County is home to an auto parts manufacturing cluster. To the north in Dalton, the traditional craft of tufted bedspread handiwork was transformed into a carpet industry. About 85 percent of the nation's carpet is made within a 65-mile radius of Dalton, nicknamed "the Carpet Capital of the World." In recent years, recession and automation have reduced the workforce. The industry has also suffered from weaker demand as consumers turn toward hardwood and tile flooring. Still, the industry employed more than 50,000 workers in Georgia before the COVID-19 pandemic. Several Chinese companies that manufacture vinyl flooring announced investments in the area in 2020.

The debate over illegal immigration looms large in Dalton, which attracted a large community of Latino immigrants in the 1980s and 1990s as the carpet industry boomed. Whitfield County is one of seven Georgia counties that work with U.S. Immigration and Customs Enforcement to check the immigration status of detainees. The sheriff's office entered this partnership in 2008, citing rising crime in immigrant communities. At the same time, local business leaders have welcomed undocumented immigrants, who often work jobs that would otherwise go unfilled. As of 2019, Dalton was 46 percent Latino and 43 percent non-Hispanic White. Dalton State University is designated as a Hispanic-Serving Institution and has a 31 percent Latino student body.

The 14th Congressional District covers the northwest corner of Georgia, including Dalton-based Whitfield County. Chattanooga Tennessee's metro area has expanded across the state line into places like Chickamauga and LaFayette in Walker and Catoosa counties. It takes in Floyd County and its largest city, Rome, as well as Paulding County in exurban Atlanta. Fast-growing Paulding is the population center with about one-fourth of the voters, followed by Floyd and Whitfield. Politically, the 14th is among the strongest Republican districts in the nation. In 2020, President Donald Trump won 73 percent of the vote. The only county where he saw any notable decline compared to 2016 was Paulding, dropping from 69 percent to 64 percent.

HAWAII

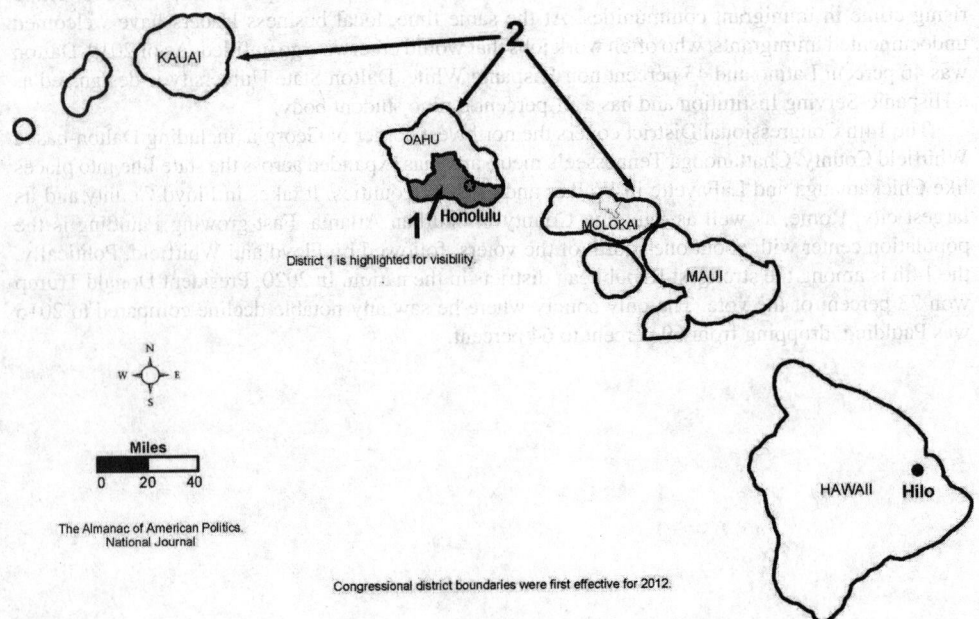

District 1 is highlighted for visibility.

Miles
0   20   40

The Almanac of American Politics.
National Journal

Congressional district boundaries were first effective for 2012.

America's state in the middle of the Pacific is geographically the most remote archipelago in the world, but it is hardly isolated. It has long been a crossroads of trade between the Asian and American continents, and it has been a vital military base for the United States since before the attack on Pearl Harbor in 1941. More recently, it produced a president, Barack Obama.

Thrust up from the ocean by volcanoes, Hawaii is geologically some of the youngest land on earth, and it continues to undergo transformations. Polynesians sailing double-hulled canoes from the Marquesas Islands nearly 2,000 miles away were the first humans to inhabit Hawaii roughly 1,600 years ago. Over time, several small kingdoms developed across the islands, each ruled by an ali'inui (a grand or great chief). The islands' isolation from the Western world ended when British Captain James Cook, on an exploration to find the Northwest Passage, landed on Kauai in 1778. Toward the end of the century, the most powerful ali'inui, Kamehameha, began a campaign of conquest, and by 1810, all the islands were united into one kingdom under his rule. With unification came foreign trade: Pacific fur traders who stopped off recognized that Hawaiian sandalwood would be popular in the markets of the Far East where it was prized for ornamental use and burning as incense. As king, Kamehameha controlled the harvesting of sandalwood, and by 1811 he was reaching deals with Boston maritime merchants whereby he would receive a hefty share of the profits from their sales. He died in 1819 and his memory is honored by a state holiday—King Kamehameha Day—every June 11.

One year later, two events occurred that would come to define the culture and economy of Hawaii. The first whaling ship arrived in 1820. So did missionaries, led by a New England Congregationalist, Reverend Hiram Bingham. Within a decade, more than a hundred ships were making annual stops in Honolulu, and it quickly became a thriving port. With the Gold Rush and California's admission to the union, shipping between San Francisco and Honolulu grew, strengthening ties to the United States. Mining companies in northern California began importing Hawaiian food and other supplies across the Pacific rather than waiting for them to make the difficult trip across the American interior. Meanwhile, the missionaries were converting native Hawaiians to Protestant Christianity. That was steady work after King Kamehameha's successor, Liholiho, abandoned the kapu system, the religiously inspired code of taboos that was used to guide and regulate people's lives. But the missionaries' greatest impact on the islands may have been economic, not spiritual. When they left their religious duties, they took up other avocations and some went into the sugar business. In 1851, after being released from their missionary work, Samuel Northrup Castle and Amos Starr Cooke formed a partnership, Castle & Cooke, which ended up investing heavily in sugar plantations that sprung up on the islands. Samuel Alexander and Henry Baldwin, both sons of missionaries, started the Haiku Sugar Co., which later become Alexander & Baldwin. Both these partnerships expanded into other commercial enterprises and both became members of the "Big Five" companies that built the sugar industry and associated businesses such as real estate, dominating Hawaii's economy for generations.

The boom in sugar required the importation of labor because a series of epidemics devastated the native population as it came into increasing contact with Westerners. Soon, contract workers from China and Japan were coming to Hawaii. American sugar interests helped elect King Kalakaua to the Hawaiian throne over the British-leaning Queen Emma in 1874. Kalakaua returned the favor and sought a trade agreement with the United States in 1876 that allowed the duty-free sale of Hawaiian sugar in the states. But American planters and businessmen eventually tired of the caprices of the royal family and in January 1893, with the help of the Marines, ousted Queen Liliuokalani from the Iolani Palace and called on the United States to annex Hawaii. President Grover Cleveland demurred, and Hawaii for five years was a republic until President William McKinley annexed it. This history has become a source of regret. An Onipa'a ceremony remembering Liliuokalani's overthrow was staged by John Waihee, the first governor of Native Hawaiian descent, in January 1993, with the American flag conspicuously absent. Later that year, Congress passed and President Bill Clinton signed an apology for the overthrow of Liliuokalani 100 years before. In 2009, Hawaii staged a commemoration, not a celebration, of the 50th anniversary of statehood.

The Japanese attack on Pearl Harbor led the United States to enter World War II, which brought a massive influx of U.S. armed forces to Hawaii. The population of the islands doubled to 858,000 by 1944, spurring greater demand for retail services and consumer products. After the war, the economy cooled as the nation demobilized, but with the Korean conflict in the early 1950s, there was another military build-up. The many sailors and troops who transited Hawaii on their way to the front lines, or who were stationed there, invariably shared its charms with family and friends when they returned home. By the 1960s, tourism had displaced sugar, pineapples and other agricultural products as Hawaii's leading industry. From statehood in 1959 to 1990, Hawaii's economic engine roared. Then it stumbled, as the end of the Cold War brought a decline in military spending and Japan experienced a "lost decade" that led vacationers to cut back their trips to Hawaii and real estate investors to stop bidding up properties in Oahu.

Hawaii also saw the demise of its plantation agriculture. Once, one-fifth of the sugar consumed in the United States came from Hawaii. Competition from lower-cost international producers and occasional environmental concerns closer to home changed all that. In 2016, the Hawaiian Commercial and Sugar Co. closed its doors after 180 years, marking a definitive end to the local sugar industry. By then, Del Monte had already picked its last pineapples on the islands. A disused Dole cannery was turned into a factory for processing Waialua-grown cacao, part of a boom let of artisanal chocolate in the state; only Hawaii among the 50 states has the right climate conditions for cacao cultivation. If such ventures succeed, they will join such specialty crops such as papayas, macadamia nuts, Kona coffee, genetically engineered seeds, and queen honey bees in a vastly reduced agriculture sector that today contributes only about one-half of 1 percent to the state GDP and less than 1 percent of its employment base.

During the Great Recession, real estate in Hawaii experienced a bad downturn; tourism slumped, then recovered. But the Great Recession proved to be mild compared to the economic wallop of the coronavirus pandemic. For much of the pandemic's first six months, Hawaii imposed the nation's strictest quarantine for out-of-state visitors: 14 days of isolation, sometimes enforced by one-entry-only hotel-room keycards, and occasionally by arrests. The quarantine was effective at keeping the virus out—Hawaii's per capita case rate consistently ranked among the nation's lowest, and the state consistently had a small enough number of cases to make contract tracing feasible.

But the public health successes came at the cost of profound economic hardship, especially for the state's crucial tourism industry. By late summer, one of every six jobs in Hawaii had disappeared, and by December, a quarter of businesses were closed, according to Yelp. "This is the most challenging time facing Hawaii since statehood," House Speaker Scott Saiki said. "It will not be easy to reopen Hawaii incrementally, while still ensuring public health and safety. "By the fall, the state softened the rules, allowing a recent negative test to suffice for entry, but even optimists knew a full economic recovery would be a long time coming. The challenge was that, as a state historically so susceptible to epidemics, Hawaii had little choice but to act decisively against the virus: There were no states nearby from which to borrow doctors or ICU capacity, The Atlantic noted, and the island of Kauai had just 15 ventilators.

As an archipelago, Hawaii is also unusually susceptible to environmental degradation, on land and in the water. Airliners' wheel housings are routinely inspected for the brown tree snakes that killed off most of the birds in Guam. Obama, who spent much of his youth in Hawaii, became the seventh president to preserve vast tracts of ocean that is home to rich and often endangered species; he expanded the protected area fourfold to more than half a million square miles, including bans on commercial fishing and other resource extraction while allowing recreational fishing, scientific study and traditional Hawaiian cultural practices. But Hawaii is losing much of its famed beachfront, including Waikiki Beach, where legendary Olympic athlete Duke Kahanamoku introduced longboard surfing more than a century ago; sea levels have already risen by six inches locally, and they are forecast to swell three feet by 2100. Spooked by this web of changes, Hawaii became the first state to pass legislation that implemented parts of the Paris climate accord.

Fair-weather Hawaii has one of the lowest energy usage rates per capita of any state, but because it has traditionally had to import petroleum, its energy costs are well above the national average. To reverse this pattern, the state has encouraged offshore wind and geothermal power, which have been controversial, as well as solar, which has been popular. Hawaiian Electric, a for-profit energy company, is trying to meet an aggressive state mandate to reach 100 percent renewable energy in its service areas by 2045.

The Kilauea volcano on the Big Island, which had begun to erupt virtually without pause in 1983, spewed forth one of its most disruptive lava flows in 2018, covering thousands of acre sand blanketing the island with potentially hazardous "vog," or sulfur-dioxide-infused volcanic fog. After two years of relative quiet, the volcano spewed lava again in December 2020. Meanwhile, in 2018, 50 inches of rain fell in a single day on Kauai, breaking a national record, and a rare hurricane, Lane, soaked parts of the Big Island with nearly 20 inches of rain.

Since 2016, Hawaii's population has shrunk by about 1.4 percent. "The old people aren't moving anywhere; they're staying," Jenjira Yahirun of the University of Hawaii told Honolulu Civil Beat. "The young people are leaving. That's the concern." Another persistent problem is homelessness, driven by the state's expensive housing market. On the upside, only about 4 percent of Hawaii residents lack health insurance, just 1 percentage point off the national low, and the state leads the nation in life expectancy at 82 years and has the lowest rate of depression in the U.S. For Native Hawaiians, the trends have been mixed. Native Hawaiians have 10 fewer years of healthy life than Caucasian residents do, but there are signs of a cultural renaissance. Use of the Hawaiian language has rebounded in recent decades thanks to 21 "immersion" schools, and younger Native Hawaiians have found a purpose in opposing construction of a new telescope on Mauna Kea, one of the culture's sacred sites.

Asian migrant laborers had long practiced traditions of hard work, family loyalty and group solidarity that found expression most vividly in the performance of the 442nd "Go for Broke" Regimental Combat Team, which was made up mostly of sons of Japanese immigrants and became the most decorated unit in U.S. military history. Once discriminated against, Japanese Americans today are neck and neck for the state's highest annual household incomes, alongside Filipinos. Meanwhile, the Yankee spirit has been evident in Hawaii's commercial success and in its attachment to the rule of Anglo-American law. The Hawaiian spirit is apparent in the vitality of the aloha ambience, the welcoming of others despite their differences, and a willingness to absorb the teachings of others while maintaining a certain Polynesian attitude toward life. During the tenure of President Donald Trump, the state took a leading role in challenging his immigration travel bans in court.

For decades, voting in Hawaii followed ethnic lines. Japanese Americans were the heart of the Democratic Party, along with Native Hawaiians; whites, with relatively high incomes, leaned Republican. Filipinos were heavily Democratic, with Chinese somewhat less so. Over the years the Democratic machine built a large government: About one-fifth of Hawaii's workers are government employees. Some suggest that this arrangement has favored seniority over competence, resulting in complacency and a lack of accountability. This came into sharp relief in 2018, when a state official mistakenly sent a text alert saying the state was under nuclear attack; reviews of the incident found that the employee had a history of performance problems that were never addressed, despite concerns among his co-workers.

Hawaii's political playing field has become particularly lopsided since former two-term Gov. Linda Lingle, a Republican, left office in 2010 and lost a seemingly competitive Senate race in 2012 by a 2-to-1 margin. In each state legislative chamber, the Republican caucus remains mired in the low single digits. In 2008, Hawaii gave native son Obama 72 percent of the vote, and in 2012, he got 70 percent. Hillary Clinton got 62 percent in 2016, and Joe Biden got 64 percent in 2020; due to support for third-party candidates in 2016, Biden's margin over Trump was slightly smaller than Clinton's in 2016, even though Biden added about 100,000 votes to her total. Regardless, Biden still won the state by 30 points, a wider margin than any state save Maryland, Massachusetts and Vermont. Hawaii seems poised to remain as blue as its waters.

Population		Race and Ethnicity		Income	
Total	1,415,872	White	24.10%	Median Income	83,102
Land area (sq. miles)	6,423	Black	1.90%	State Income Rank	4 out of 50
Pop/ sq mi	220.45	Latino	10.70%	Poverty Rate	9.30%
Born in state	52.30%	Asian	56.60%	With health insurance	95.80%
		Two or more races	22.40%	Cash public assistance	2.50%
Age Groups		Other	12.90%	Food stamp/SNAP	11.4%
Under 18	21.20%				
18-34	22.20%	Education		Work	
35-64	37.60%	H.S grad or less	35.00%	White Collar	36.10%
Over 64	19.00%	Some college	31.30%	Sales and Service	45.70%
		College Degree, 4 yr	22.10%	Blue Collar	18.10%
Military		Post grad	11.60%	Government	19.30%
Veteran/ Active Duty	12.50%				

Presidential Politics

2020 Caucus (D)	Biden (D)	21,215(61%)	Sanders (D)	12,337(35%)			
2020 Primary (D)	Biden (D)	19,593(56%)	Sanders (D)	10,777(31%)			
2016 Caucus (D)	Sanders (D)	23,521(70%)	Clinton (D)	10,126(30%)			
2016 Caucus (R)	Trump (R)	6,805(43%)	Cruz (R)	5,063(32%)	Rubio (R)	2,068(13%)	
	Kasich (R)	1,566(10%)					
2020 Pres. Vote	Biden (D)	366,130(64%)	Trump (R)	196,864(34%)			
2016 Pres. Vote	Clinton (D)	266,891(62%)	Trump (R)	128,847(30%)	Johnson (L)	15,954 (4%)	
	Stein (G)	12,737 (3%)					

Hawaii's voters have historically supported Democrats for the White House. Since the state began casting presidential ballots in 1960, the only Republican victories came in reelection landslides: Ronald Reagan's in 1984 and Richard Nixon's in 1972. Roughly two-thirds of Hawaii's votes come from Oahu; the other islands are even more Democratic-leaning than the most urban island in the archipelago. In 2020, Joe Biden defeated Donald Trump 64%-34%; Hillary Clinton won it 62%-30%in 2016. In 2008 and 2012, Hawaiians embraced their native son, Barack Obama, who won both times with more than 70 percent of the vote.

Hawaii traditionally chose presidential delegates by caucus, but like many former caucus states switched to a party-run primary in 2020 at the urging of the Democratic National Committee. It had the additional wrinkle of ranked-choice voting, where voters picked their top three choices. In 2020, the election was scheduled for April 4, but Hawaii was one of four states that day to postpone its primary in response to the coronavirus pandemic; in-person voting was canceled and the election was extended until May 22, long after Biden had secured the nomination. He beat Bernie Sanders 63%-37% after other candidates' votes were reallocated. Favorite daughter Tulsi Gabbard, who had dropped out and endorsed Biden in mid-March, took 4 percent and finished fourth, her best showing in any state (though she finished second and won two delegates in American Samoa, where she was born).

Congressional Districts

117th Congress Lineup	2D	116th Congress Lineup	2D

Hawaii has two congressional districts: The 1st includes urban Honolulu and extends westward to Pearl Harbor and the rural area beyond. The 2nd includes the rest of Oahu and the Neighbor Islands. The 1st District, the most heavily Asian district in the country, is the slightly less Democratic of the two and elected a Republican in 1986, 1988 and briefly in 2010, when Honolulu Councilman Charles Djou won an unusual special election against split Democratic opposition. In 2018, Djou renounced his membership in the Republican Party because of disagreements with President Donald Trump. The lower-income 2nd District has elected only Democrats since it was created in 1971.

Timing and ambition tend to overstep boundaries in Hawaii: In 2010, Democrat Colleen Hanabusa unseated Djou in the 1st District although she lived in the 2nd. In 2012, both major candidates for the open 2nd District lived in the 1st. When the 1st became open again in 2018, Ed Case was elected. A decade earlier, he served two terms in the 2nd District. Given the recent volatility, more changes in the House delegation seem possible. But it remains a heavy lift for Republicans to win a seat here. With virtually equal population in the two districts, shifts of the boundaries likely will be minimal.

David Ige (D)

Elected 2014, term expires 2022, 2nd term; b. Jan. 15, 1957, Honolulu; U of HI –Manoa, B.A., 1979; M.A., 1985; Buddhist; Married (Dawn); 3 children.

Elected Office: HI Senate 1994-2014; State House, 1985-1995.

Professional Career: Electronics engineer, Pacific Analysis Corp.; Senior Administrator, General Telephone & Electronics Hawaiian Telephone, 1981-1999; Project Manager, Pihana Pacific, LLC., 1999-2001; Vice President of Engineering for Net Enterprise, Inc., 2001-2002; Project Manager, R.A. Ige and Associates, Inc., 2003.

Office: Executive Chambers State Capitol, Honolulu, 96813; 808-586-0034; Fax: 808-586-0006; Website: hawaii.gov

Lt. Gov.: Josh Green (D)

State Legislature: Senate: 24D, 1R **House:** 46D, 5R

Election Results

Election	Name (Party)	Vote (%)
2018 General	David Ige (D)..	244,934 (63%)
	Andria Tupola (R)...	131,719 (34%)
	Jim Brewer (G)...	10,123 (3%)
2018 Primary	David Ige (D)..	124,572 (51%)
	Colleen Hanabusa (D)...	107,631 (44%)

Prior winning percentage: 2014 (49%)

After overcoming a strong primary challenge to win a second term, Democrat David Ige, Hawaii's second Japanese-American governor, found notable success keeping the coronavirus at bay but presided over an economy devastated by the virtual disappearance of tourism.

Ige serves in the 21st century, but his family history embodies a major story line of 20th century Hawaii. Born and raised in Pearl City, he was the fifth of six boys of Japanese-American parents who had settled in Hawaii a generation earlier, at a time when those of Japanese ancestry were widely discriminated against. His father, Tokio, won a Purple Heart and a Bronze Star during World War II while serving in the famous 100th Battalion, 442nd Regimental Combat Team of the U.S. Army, which was made up mostly of sons of Japanese immigrants. The veterans cultivated the educational institutions that trained the next generation of leaders, including Ige.

After studying engineering and business, Ige launched a successful career as an electrical engineer and project manager, working on information technology and telecommunications. Ige wasn't planning to enter politics, but in 1985 Democratic Gov. George Ariyoshi tapped Ige for a vacant state House seat after hearing recommendations from local activists in Pearl City. Ige wasn't a member of the Democratic Party when Ariyoshi reached out to him. He went on to win reelection four times, then advanced to the state Senate in 1994, all while continuing his regular employment.

Ige brought a novice's sensitivities to his new job and recoiled when he quickly came to understand that the legislative process is often an inside game where knowledge is not always shared and the public is often excluded from decision making. That led him to focus on improving communication with voters (and among his own colleagues) and their access to information. Drawing on his experience in the private sector, he often applied technology to the tasks of meeting his goals, posting draft legislation, hearing notices and budget documents online and setting up an electronic network to involve hundreds of high school students in the legislative process through a primitive form of videoconferencing. His years of committee work paid off when he rose to chair the state Senate Ways and Means Committee in 2009.

When Ige announced his gubernatorial bid in 2013, it was widely seen as a David-and-Goliath contest. Incumbent Democrat Neil Abercrombie outspent Ige by a more than 10-to-1 margin, and President Barack Obama, along with most other prominent Hawaii Democrats, endorsed him. What Abercrombie didn't expect was the voters' pushback against his confrontational style. Many Asian Americans were also unhappy with his decision to appoint Lt. Gov. Brian Schatz, rather than Rep. Colleen Hanabusa, to fill the seat of long-serving Sen. Dan Inouye after his death in 2012. And Abercrombie had pursued policies that alienated Hawaii's powerful public-sector unions. Ige won a shocker, defeating Abercrombie in the August primary by a staggering 67%-32% margin—the first time since 1962 that a sitting Hawaii governor had lost a primary. In the general, Ige comfortably defeated former Lt. Gov. "Duke" Aiona, the Republican nominee, and independent Mufi Hannemann.

In his first term, Ige broke with the tendency of most of his predecessors to govern as the ali'i nui (the term for a great or grand chief from Hawaii's early days) and began meeting every other week with the leaders of the state House of Representatives and Senate. He signed three bills restricting gun rights and grappled with the state's continuing challenges of homelessness, issuing an emergency proclamation to extend outreach efforts and urging greater investment in affordable housing. Ige signed the world's first ban on oxybenzone and octinoxate, two chemicals in sunscreen that have been blamed for harming coral, and he applauded efforts by the state attorney general's office to counter policies of the Trump administration on immigration and the environment. Ige's most far-reaching measures may have been those on energy: In 2018, he signed legislation to make the state carbon-neutral by 2045.

Just as Ige challenged Abercrombie in the 2014 Democratic primary, Ige himself received a primary challenge in 2018, from Hanabusa, a Yonsei—a fourth-generation American of Japanese descent whose grandfathers had been interned after Japan's attack on Pearl Harbor. In addition to two stints in the U.S. House, Hanabusa had spent 12 years in the state Senate, including a four-year run as state Senate president—the first woman to lead either chamber of the legislature. Hanabusa sought to portray Ige as an ineffectual leader, and fate initially intervened to make her case. In January 2018, a state employee mistakenly sent out a text alert that the state was under nuclear attack. It proved to be due to human error, but the mistake was not fully corrected for 38 minutes, and questions swirled about why Ige didn't act immediately after learning about it two minutes into the crisis. The incident undercut Ige's reputation for cool competence. By March, Hanabusa was leading in a Honolulu Star-Advertiser poll, 47%-27%, and was racking up endorsements. But fate intervened once again with a succession of natural disasters—flooding on Kauai and Oahu, and volcanic eruptions on the Big Island—that Ige was credited with handling much more effectively. Ige ended up defeating Hanabusa by seven points. The general election was anticlimactic, as Ige defeated Republican Andria Tupola, 63%-34%.

Not long into Ige's second term, an ongoing controversy flared again: The fate of the proposed $2 billion Thirty Meter Telescope project on the Big Island. The basketball-court-sized telescope was planned for Mauna Kea, a 14,000-foot mountain that is perhaps the best place in the world to study the skies—but is also located on land that Native Hawaiians consider sacred. After a series of Native Hawaiian-led protests and a protracted court battle, Ige said construction would begin in summer 2019. But protesters blocked access to the site, and polls showed public support for the telescope flagging. Ige withdrew an emergency proclamation and extended the timeline for construction. The telescope's fate remained unclear, with some hoping it would be built in the Canary Islands instead.

In early 2019, Ige signed legislation to decriminalize marijuana (while stopping short of legalizing it), as well as a bill to require vacation websites to collect taxes on rental properties and legislation to incrementally expand public preschool. The following year, he signed a measure to broaden paid family leave access and another to ban nondisclosure agreements relating to workplace sexual assaults. But several policies designed at lessening inequality, including a minimum wage hike and increased safety-net spending, withered as the state grappled with the economic impacts of the coronavirus. Well into the pandemic, Hawaii ranked among the states with the lowest rates of coronavirus infections, thanks to its isolation and the imposition for six months of a tough, 14-day quarantine restriction on visitors. But the tourism-based economy tanked. Amid the strains, some renewed the criticism that Ige had a rudderless governing style. The leadership void, Honolulu Civil Beat politics and opinion editor Chad Blair wrote in May 2020, "has forced others in government to step up and guide the state, including leaders in the state House and Senate, the congressional delegation, the lieutenant governor, county mayors and business executives."

With Ige term-limited, several potential Democratic candidates have emerged for 2022, led by popular Lt. Gov. Josh Green, an emergency room doctor who took a high-profile role in the coronavirus crisis. Other possible Democratic hopefuls include state Sen. Donovan Dela Cruz, Honolulu Mayor Kirk Caldwell, and former state Sen. Jill Tokuda. On the Republican side, Tupola may make a second bid for the office.

Brian Schatz (D)

Appointed 2012, term expires 2022, 1st full term, b. Oct 20, 1972; Ann Arbor, MI; School for International Training (Kenya), 1992; Pomona College, B.A., 1994; Jewish; Married (Linda Kwok Kai Yun); 2 children.

Elected Office: HI House, 1998-2006; HI Lt. Governor, 2010-2012.

Professional Career: CEO, Helping Hands HI, 2004-2010; Chairman, HI Democratic Party, 2008-2010.

DC Office: 722 HSOB 20510, 202-224-3934, Fax: 202-228-1153, schatz.senate.gov

State Offices: Honolulu, 808-523-2061.

Committees: *Appropriations*: Agriculture, Rural Development, FDA & Related Agencies; Commerce, Justice, Science & Related Agencies; Department of Defense; DOL, HHS & Education & Related Agencies; Military Construction & Veteran Affairs & Related Agencies; Transportation, HUD & Related Agencies (Chmn). *Commerce, Science & Transportation*: Communications, Media & Broadband; Consumer Protection, Product Safety & Data Security; Oceans, Fisheries, Climate Change & Manufacturing; Surface Transportation, Maritime Freight & Ports. *Ethics*. *Foreign Relations*: East Asia, the Pacific & International Cybersecurity Policy; Internat'l Dev Instit & Internat'l Econ, Energy & Environ Policy; State Dept & USAID Mngmnt, Internat'l Ops & Internat'l Dev. *Indian Affairs (Chmn)*.

Group Ratings

	ADA	ACLU	AFL-CIO	LCV	COC	HAFA	ACU	CFG	FRC
2020	-	92%	-	100%	-	0%	3%	-	-
2019	100%	C	100%	100%	45%	C	3%	0%	0%

Almanac Ratings 2019-2020

	Economy	Social	Foreign	Composite
Liberal	97%	97%	78%	91%
Conservative	3%	3%	22%	9%

Key Votes of the 116th Congress

1. EPA clean energy rules	Y	5. Russia sanctions	Y	9. Barr as Atty. General	N
2. U.S./Mex./Can. trade deal	N	6. Troops in SYR, AFG	N	10. Spending at the border	Y
3. Cut unemployment benefits	N	7. Veto arms sales to Saudis	Y	11. Coney Barrett to Sup. Ct.	N
4. Shelton to Fed Reserve	N	8. Defense $$$, veto override	Y	12. Electoral College objections	N

Election Results

Election	Name (Party)	Vote (%)		Cand. Spent	Ind. Exp. Support	Ind. Exp. Oppose
2016 General	Brian Schatz (D)	306,604	(74%)	$1,932,020		
	John Carroll (R)	92,653	(22%)	$54,517		
	Joy Allison (C)	9,103	(2%)			
2016 Primary	Brian Schatz (D)	162,905	(86%)			
	Makani Christensen (D)	11,899	(6%)			

Prior winning percentages: 2016 (74%), 2014 special (67%)

Democrat Brian Schatz's appointment to the Senate at the end of 2012 was at odds with the deathbed wishes of his predecessor, Daniel Inouye—long the state's most powerful and beloved political figure. In a letter to Gov. Neil Abercrombie before he died, Inouye—who had occupied the Senate seat for nearly a half-century—asked that Rep. Colleen Hanabusa be named his successor. Instead, Abercrombie named Schatz, his lieutenant governor. A former state legislator and state Democratic chair, Schatz was sworn in 10 days after Inouye's death—and, in 2014, narrowly held off Hanabusa in a primary battle for the remainder of Inouye's term. Since then, Schatz has been elected to a full six-year term and emerged as an outspoken, progressive voice in the Senate Democratic Caucus and on Twitter who crafts comprehensive legislative proposals on high-profile issues.

"I want Democrats in the Senate, Democrats running for Congress, to rally around an aggressive, progressive agenda," Schatz told New York magazine. "And it's not a gotcha, litmus test-style agenda, but one that, if we enact it, would be on a scale that is equal to the problems and has the ability to actually motivate voters." Democratic strategist Jim Manley, a longtime Senate leadership aide, told the magazine: "He's well-liked within the caucus; he's someone folks listen to. If given a chance, he has an opportunity to be a significant player in the Senate."

Schatz was born one of two identical twins in Ann Arbor Michigan. His twin brother, Stephen, ran a statewide partnership between the Hawaii Department of Education and the University of Hawaii aimed at achieving an increase in the number of college degrees. In the mid-1960s, while working in Detroit, his father, Irwin, a cardiologist, became aware of a decades-long study by the U.S. Public Health Service in Tuskegee Alabama in which poor Black sharecroppers with syphilis were left untreated so researchers could study the effects. A letter of protest he wrote to health officials helped trigger a public debate that led to new standards governing research on human subjects. When Brian Schatz was 2, his father accepted a job at the University of Hawaii. After graduating from the prestigious Punahou School—which Barack Obama also attended—Schatz went to Pomona College in California, studying abroad in Kenya before receiving his degree. He returned to Hawaii and worked as a community organizer, including heading a beach preservation group and later running a social services agency.

In 1998, Schatz, then 26, was elected to represent an urban Honolulu district in the Hawaii Legislature, where he served for eight years. In 2006, he was one of 10 candidates in the Democratic primary for an open congressional seat. Schatz finished sixth—losing to former Lt. Gov. Mazie Hirono, now Schatz's Senate colleague. The same year, Schatz founded a group urging Obama to run for president; he served as spokesman for the Obama campaign in Hawaii before being elected chairman of the state's Democratic Party in the spring of 2008. Two years later, he resigned and announced his candidacy for lieutenant governor. He ran with Abercrombie, a longtime member of Congress; they won by 17 percentage points in November. In office, Schatz worked on energy and climate issues and helped pass same-sex civil unions in the state. When the 88-year-old Inouye died six weeks after the November 2012 elections, the state Democratic Party—as required by law—sent Abercrombie three names from whom he would choose a replacement: Hanabusa, former congressional candidate Esther Kia'aina and Schatz. While Hanabusa was Inouye's choice, Abercrombie, who had a well-publicized rift with Inouye and much of the state's Democratic establishment, chose his ally, Schatz.

Schatz flew to Washington on Air Force One with President Obama, who had been spending Christmas in Hawaii, and was sworn in as the Senate faced crucial end-of-year votes, particularly on the "fiscal cliff" created by a combination of automatic tax increases and spending cuts. The timing made Schatz the state's senior senator by days. Hirono, elected in November 2012 to replace retiring Democratic Sen. Daniel Akaka, was to be sworn in January 3, 2013. The extra days of seniority also gave Schatz a boost over senators from other states who took office a few days later.

Hanabusa, after deciding to run in the 2014 Democratic primary for the remaining two years of Inouye's term, sought to depict Schatz—40 at the time of his appointment—as inexperienced. Abercrombie was said to have privately cited the 20-year age gap between Schatz and Hanabusa in making his choice, arguing that Schatz was in a position to serve longer and accumulate more seniority. Hanabusa was backed by the political networks of Inouye and Akaka and had financial support from EMILY's List, a national political action committee that backs Democratic women who favor abortion rights. Schatz lined up support from the national Democratic establishment, including Obama, then-Senate Majority Leader Harry Reid and progressive and environmental groups.

The contest broke along ethnic lines, as Hawaii's primaries often do, with Schatz winning among liberal white voters and Hanabusa, who is Japanese-American, performing well with Native

Hawaiians and Asian-Americans. The initial results of the August 9 primary, which came on the heels of a brutal tropical storm that prevented two precincts from voting, gave Schatz a 1,635-vote lead. State election officials said a makeup election would be held in areas affected by the storm the following Friday; Hanabusa unsuccessfully filed a legal challenge, contending those sections were insufficiently recovered to have voters cast ballots. After those precincts had voted, Schatz's lead stood at 1,769 votes out of a statewide total of more than 237,000 cast. He won 49%-48%. Schatz's victory in November was easy; so was his election to a full term in 2016. In both cases, he took about 70 percent of the vote, seemingly solidifying his place in the Senate for as long as he wants. Meanwhile, Schatz's onetime running mate, Abercrombie, lost a 2014 bid for renomination 66%-30%. His loss was fueled in part by having ignored the dying wishes of Inouye.

On Capitol Hill, Schatz maintained the abiding interest in environmental issues, particularly climate change that he demonstrated in state office. In 2015, his amendment to the Keystone XL pipeline bill put lawmakers on record on whether they believe "climate change is real and human activity significantly contributes" to it. The amendment, the first Senate vote on climate change in eight years, got 50 votes in favor, including five from Republicans. Schatz and Democratic Sen. Sheldon Whitehouse of Rhode Island introduced a proposed tax on carbon emissions they said would yield $2 trillion in revenue over 10 years.

They tried again in 2017, going so far as to appear before a conservative think tank, the American Enterprise Institute, to garner Republican support for their idea. "The idea is quite simple: Unleash markets to tackle climate change," Schatz said. "It establishes incentives that allow capital to flow and businesses to thrive when they can use clean energy, letting the free market compete and innovate and make profits." The AEI event was part of an effort to attract at least one Republican senator to co-sponsor the bill. But the legislation again died, with no GOP backers—and with Schatz shifting to attack mode. "The Republican Party is the only major political party on the planet that is explicitly dedicated to making climate change worse," he tweeted in spring 2018.

Later, Schatz introduced the Climate Change Financial Risk Act of 2019, which would have required the Federal Reserve to subject large banks to "stress tests" measuring how they could weather financial risks stemming from climate-induced disasters, such as floods and wildfires. In 2020, Schatz led a group of Democratic senators in putting out a 255-page report outlining the party's proposals to combat climate change, including spending billions to reduce the nation's carbon pollution to net-zero by 2050. "What we have now is the distinct possibility of a coalition that represents almost everybody except the Koch brothers trying to get this done," Schatz told the Atlantic.

Schatz's proclivity for sharp-tongued tweets was on display several months earlier, when President Donald Trump equated white nationalist groups—who had marched in a Charlottesville Virginia rally that turned violent and deadly—and counter-protesters. "As a Jew, as an American, as a human, words cannot express my disgust and disappointment," Schatz tweeted. "This is not my President." As protests against police brutality swept the country in the summer of 2020, Schatz helped lead a bipartisan bill that would have limited Pentagon transfers of military gear to local law enforcements; the bill earned 51 votes but didn't clear the 60-vote threshold to move forward. In 2019, Schatz introduced an amendment to abolish the Electoral College, but in the GOP-controlled Senate it went nowhere.

Schatz's appointment in 2012 coincided with the election of another progressive Democrat: Chris Murphy of Connecticut. As the two youngest senators at the time, Schatz and Murphy sponsored legislation aimed at college affordability by providing incentives to school administrators to lower costs. In 2018, Schatz unveiled a more ambitious plan. With a $95 billion price tag, it proposed matching grants to states that committed to providing debt-free education—covering tuition and all other expenses—for public university students. The measure was a follow-on to Vermont Sen. Bernie Sanders' call for free tuition at public colleges during his 2016 presidential bid. Schatz's proposal attracted the co-sponsorship of numerous Senate progressives eyeing the 2020 Democratic nomination for president. "It's essential that we have a plan for when we take power back," Schatz said. "We don't know when that will be, but we need to be ready to roll legislatively, and it's just a fact that campaigns are not equipped to prepare the kind of public policy that can be enacted."

Schatz also rolled out legislation in 2017 that would have enabled states to set up a "public option" for health insurance by expanding Medicaid and allowing any individual to buy in to it instead of purchasing private insurance. Schatz's plan was intended as a progressive, more incremental alternative to Sanders' "Medicare for All" proposal, which would give all Americans a government-operated insurance plan. Several of the Democratic presidential contenders who had sponsored Sanders' plan signed on to Schatz's bill as well. "With health care, somebody at some point decided that there was a bright line and that you had to pick sides," Schatz told the Atlantic. "Well, I reject that view. I think we should respect each other as colleagues, respect each other as progressives, enough to take all of these bills, and have hearings, and subject them to scrutiny."

Amid his increasing focus on high-profile national issues, Schatz has spent a great deal of time on issues related to Hawaii. He often reached across the political aisle to senators representing rural states with similar issues. In 2016, Schatz and Utah Republican Sen. Orrin Hatch passed a "telehealth" bill, intended to spur the use of videoconferencing to link teams of specialists to primary care providers in rural and underserved areas. Obama signed legislation by Schatz and Republican Sen. John Thune of South Dakota that was aimed at fostering greater federal involvement in tourism efforts by Native Hawaiian, Alaska Native and American Indian communities. In 2018, Schatz and Thune teamed up to pass a bill to improve the system for incoming missile alerts. It followed an incident during which, amid rising tensions with North Korea, an alert was mistakenly sent out in Hawaii—causing widespread panic before it was corrected after more than half an hour. Schatz and Thune again teamed up in 2020 to update liability protections for social media companies, proposing changes that would require them to disclose more about their content moderation, allow users to appeal decisions, and mandate tech companies issue quarterly reports of what content has been removed or limited.

Perhaps Schatz's biggest local impact has come not through legislation but in an executive order from Obama. In late spring of 2016, Schatz wrote to Obama, asking that the Papahanaumokuakea Marine National Monument, which surrounds the uninhabited Northwestern Hawaiian Islands, be quadrupled in size. The marine reserve, created by President George W. Bush, is home to 7,000 marine and terrestrial species, a quarter of which are found nowhere else on earth. Schatz asked Obama to increase the size of the protected area to nearly 583,000 square miles—an area greater than Alaska. Obama utilized his power under the 1906 Antiquities Act to make it the largest protected land or ocean conservation area on Earth.

Given his youth and base in a blue state, Schatz could be around Capitol Hill for a long time. In 2017, he was named one of three chief deputy whips, in part because of his strong fundraising. Unlike many of his fellow senators who ran for president in 2020, Schatz became a sounding board for colleagues, hoping to avoid "that whole stupid, unproductive, toxic debate" that followed the party's divisive 2016 presidential primary, he told Politico. If Schatz doesn't end up as a Senate Democratic leader, he could eventually chair the Appropriations panel—the same gavel once wielded by Inouye, the man whose deathbed wish sought to deter Schatz from Capitol Hill. After Democrats won back the Senate majority in 2021, Schatz became chairman of the Appropriations subcommittee on Transportation, Housing and Urban Development, which puts him in a key position to steer money to Hawaii for affordable housing, homelessness and public transit, all of which are pressing issues on the islands. Schatz also became chairman of the Indian Affairs Committee, a position that is crucial to Native Hawaiians.

Mazie Hirono (D)

Elected 2012, term expires 2024, 2nd term, b. Nov 03, 1947; Fukushima, Japan; University of Hawaii, Manoa, B.A., 1970; Georgetown University Law Center, J.D., 1978; Buddhism; Married (Leighton Kim Oshima); 1 stepchild.

Elected Office: U.S. House, 2006-2012; HI Lt. Governor, 1994-2002; HI House, 1980-1994.

Professional Career: HI Deputy Attorney General, 1978-1980; Practicing lawyer, 1984-1988.

DC Office: 713 HSOB 20510, 202-224-6361, Fax: 202-224-2126, hirono.senate.gov

State Offices: Honolulu, 808-522-8970.

Committees: *Armed Services*: Personnel; Readiness & Management Support; Seapower (Chmn). *Energy & Natural Resources*: Energy (Chmn); National Parks; Public Lands, Forests & Mining. *Judiciary*: Federal Courts, Oversight, Agency Action & Federal Rights; Immigration, Citizenship & Border Security; Privacy, Technology & the Law; Subcommittee on Intellectual Property. *Small Business & Entrepreneurship. Veterans' Affairs.*

Group Ratings

	ADA	ACLU	AFL-CIO	LCV	COC	HAFA	ACU	CFG	FRC
2020	-	92%	-	92%	-	0%	2%	-	-
2019	100%	C	100%	100%	46%	C	1%	0%	0%

Almanac Ratings 2019-2020

	Economy	Social	Foreign	Composite
Liberal	100%	100%	86%	95%
Conservative	0%	0%	15%	5%

Key Votes of the 116th Congress

1. EPA clean energy rules	Y	5. Russia sanctions	Y	9. Barr as Atty. General	N
2. U.S./Mex./Can. trade deal	Y	6. Troops in SYR, AFG	N	10. Spending at the border	N
3. Cut unemployment benefits	N	7. Veto arms sales to Saudis	Y	11. Coney Barrett to Sup. Ct.	N
4. Shelton to Fed Reserve	N	8. Defense $$$, veto override	Y	12. Electoral College objections	N

Election Results

Election	Name (Party)	Vote (%)		Cand. Spent	Ind. Exp. Support	Ind. Exp. Oppose
2018 General	Mazie K. Hirono (D)	276,316	(71%)	$2,518,141	$2,997	
	Ron Curtis (R)	112,035	(29%)			
2018 Primary	Mazie K. Hirono (D)	201,604	(100%)			

Prior winning percentages: 2018 (71%), 2012 (63%); House: 2010 (72%), 2008 (76%), 2006 (61%)

In her initial decade on Capitol Hill—which began in the House—Democrat Mazie Hirono, Hawaii's junior senator, was a low-profile legislator focused on matters of direct interest to her island state. That changed with Donald Trump. An immigrant, Hirono rebuked Trump and his immigration policies even before his surprise 2016 victory. During Trump's term, Hirono would describe the president as xenophobic and regularly call him a liar. Even with Trump out of office, Hirono could still become a leading voice against anti-immigrant and nationalistic views that remain pervasive among parts of the GOP.

Hirono has held state or federal office for almost four decades. First elected to the Senate in 2012, she became the chamber's first Asian-American woman and only its second nonwhite woman. Hirono is also the first senator born in Japan; she immigrated to Hawaii before her eighth birthday with her mother, Laura, who fled an abusive husband who drank and gambled frequently. As a child, she shared a bed in a boarding house with her mother and older brother, and at age 10 she went to work to help support the family. A sister died of pneumonia in Japan at age 2 because they did not have access to a hospital. It's an episode Hirono, choking back tears, recalled in a July 2017 floor speech during debate on repealing the Affordable Care Act. Her mother found work as a typesetter for a Japanese-language newspaper—minimum wage, no health insurance. "Growing up as a young girl in Hawaii, my greatest fear was that my mother would get sick. And, if she got sick, how were we going to pay for her care?" Hirono said during that speech. "And, if she didn't go to work, there would be no pay. I know what it's like to run out of money at the end of the month. That was my life as an immigrant here." Hirono's memoir, "Heart of Fire: An Immigrant Daughter's Story," about her mother and her childhood was published in April 2021.

Speaking only Japanese when she arrived, Hirono mastered English in public school and became a naturalized citizen in 1959, the year Hawaii became a state. As a college student, she worked in 1968 with at-risk youths; the experience transformed her into a political activist. After graduating from the University of Hawaii, Hirono was a staffer in the Hawaii Legislature and for several political campaigns before decamping for Washington. She earned a law degree from Georgetown University and returned to Honolulu to work for the Hawaii attorney general's office. She was elected to the state House in 1980 and served until 1994, when she was elected lieutenant governor. Hobbled by a bumpy relationship with her running mate, Gov. Ben Cayetano, Hirono barely won her party's nomination for governor in 2002, edging out then-state House Majority Leader Ed Case 41%-40%. Her general election campaign was undermined by Democratic Party scandals involving illegal campaign contributions. Despite the state's strongly Democratic tilt, Hirono lost to Republican Linda Lingle 52%-47%.

Hirono then formed a political action committee to assist Democratic women who backed abortion rights. She got her chance to return to elected office in 2006, when Case—then in his first stint in the U.S. House—unsuccessfully challenged veteran Sen. Daniel Akaka in the Democratic primary. Hirono ran for Case's open House seat and emerged atop a 10-candidate primary field. Brian Schatz, now Hawaii's senior senator, finished sixth. Hirono easily won the general election.

In yet another first, Hirono and Georgia Rep. Hank Johnson became the first Buddhists to serve in Congress. She amassed a liberal voting record in the House; her enthusiastic support of the Democratic agenda led the Hawaii Tribune-Herald to say, in endorsing her in 2008, "We wish she'd be a little more independent and less partisan." She was a staunch earmarker of funds for Hawaii; in fiscal 2010, she ranked third among House members in accumulating special-request spending items, according to the nonprofit Taxpayers for Common Sense.

When Akaka announced his retirement in 2012, Hirono was the early Democratic favorite to replace him, although she faced a primary challenge from the moderate Case. Meanwhile, Republicans landed their best possible candidate when Lingle agreed to run. In an unusual development, veteran Republican Rep. Don Young of Alaska, who served on the Transportation and Infrastructure Committee with Hirono, endorsed her in the Democratic primary. "While Mazie and I don't see eye to eye on everything, we've done something too many people in Washington refuse to cross the aisle and do: We've worked together," Young said, referring to their cooperation to preserve native Hawaiian and Native Alaskan education programs. Hirono defeated Case 57%-40%, setting up a another matchupwith Lingle.

Lingle campaigned on her record as a moderate governor and vowed not to be beholden to Senate GOP leaders. She ran an ad criticizing Hirono for not getting any of her own bills signed into law. Democrats eviscerated Lingle for her praise of Sarah Palin during a speech introducing the Alaska governor as the party's vice presidential nominee at the 2008 Republican National Convention. Lingle said she would vote for 2012 GOP presidential nominee Mitt Romney, which didn't play well in the state where President Barack Obama was born. Hirono argued that a vote for Lingle could put Republicans back in the Senate majority—threatening the influence of Sen. Daniel Inouye, the Appropriations Committee's top Democrat and an iconic figure in Hawaii. She defeated Lingle in a landslide, 63%-37%. In 2016, Hirono won reelection 71%-29%.

Inouye died six weeks after Election Day 2012; then-Gov. Neil Abercrombie appointed Schatz, his lieutenant governor, as Inouye's replacement. Schatz started his Senate service in late December of that year, and so Hirono became the state's junior senator by only days. Hirono was said to be unhappy at being leapfrogged by Schatz, and her allies sought to delay Schatz's swearing-in. But they were overruled by then-Majority Leader Harry Reid, who did not want a seat left vacant as a showdown on the "fiscal cliff" of expiring tax cuts and spending reductions was coming to a head. Initially maintaining her usual low profile, Hirono devoted significant effort to immigration issues. Reflecting the emergence of Filipino-Americans as her state's largest ethnic minority, Hirono worked to allow surviving Filipino veterans of World War II living in the United States to be joined by their children.

On the Judiciary Committee, Hirono played an active role in the panel's debate of immigration legislation in 2013. While most of her amendments dealt with issues specific to Hawaii, she championed a provision touching on what would later become a matter of intense controversy during the Trump administration: the separation of families seeking asylum along the U.S.-Mexico border. Her language—which cleared the panel on a party-line vote—required border agents to ask apprehended individuals whether they were traveling with spouses or children. The intent, Hirono said, was to ensure that families were not separated during the interrogation process, thereby making migrants "more vulnerable by returning them to dangerous places without their family members." The immigration bill passed the Senate with bipartisan support but was not taken up in the House.

In 2018, Hirono began posing two questions to Trump administration nominees: "Since you became a legal adult, have you ever made any unwanted requests for sexual favors or committed any verbal or physical harassment or assault of a sexual nature?" and "Have you ever faced discipline or entered into a settlement related to this kind of conduct?" Hirono told Newsweek: "I want nominees who come before me … to know that these questions are about to become normal. We all have a responsibility to take action to stop sexual harassment and assault and create lasting cultural change." She was saltier in off-air comments to NPR, while denying her line of questioning was rooted in partisanship. It was intended to vet judges on whether they "care about individual and civil rights,"

Hirono said. "If that's considered liberal, as opposed to what I call justice and fairness, as I am wont to say, f--- them!"

During the Judiciary Committee's confirmation hearings for Supreme Court nominee Brett Kavanaugh, she ingratiated herself with the left—as she took on both Kavanaugh and the Republicans pushing his confirmation in blunt, unvarnished terms. Hirono startled a September 2018 news conference when, amid allegations of sexual assault against Kavanaugh, she took aim at the broader issue of sexual misconduct. "Guess who is perpetuating all of these kinds of actions? It's the men in this country," she said. "And I just want to say to the men in this country: Just shut up and step up. Do the right thing for a change." She didn't mince words in an interview with the Washington Post when asked about Senate Republicans' treatment of Christine Blasey Ford, who had first raised sexual assault allegations against Kavanaugh. "They've extended a finger," Hirono said of the GOP, adding that she was being "very graphic in what I say," partly because of her advocacy for sexual assault victims early in her career. "I've been fighting these fights for a—" Hirono said, pausing a moment. "I was going to say a f---ing long time." Trump later mocked Hirono for her comments about men at the 2019 Conservative Political Action Conference, calling her a "crazy female senator."

Kavanaugh answered "no" to both of Hirono's standing questions before the Judiciary Committee. Hirono later said she was unaware at the time that Blasey Ford had written a confidential letter to the ranking Democrat on the committee, California Sen. Dianne Feinstein, containing allegations of decades-old sexual assault against Kavanaugh. When the letter surfaced, Republican leaders initially resisted Democratic demands for an FBI investigation—prompting Hirono to say Republicans were rushing to confirm Kavanaugh because the high court's "session is going to start in October and the president wants his guy there to, he hopes, help him evade criminal or civil proceedings." When then-Judiciary Chairman Chuck Grassley said he was doing everything possible to facilitate an appearance by Blasey Ford, Hirono retorted on ABC's "World News Tonight," "That's such bullshit. I can hardly stand it." ABC News bleeped out Hirono's profanity.

In May 2017, Hirono disclosed she had been diagnosed with late-stage kidney cancer. Her right kidney was removed, along with five inches of a rib to which the cancer had spread. She opted to undergo immunotherapy, requiring infusions every three weeks. Her emboldened rhetoric was on display during the Affordable Care Act debate two months later, when most Senate Republicans backed an unsuccessful effort to repeal Obamacare. Noting that, in the aftermath of her cancer diagnosis, she had heard from many GOP colleagues "who wrote me wonderful notes, sharing with me their own experience with major illness in their families or loved ones," Hirono—pounding her hand on her desk on the Senate floor—asked: "You showed me your care. You showed me your compassion. Where is that tonight?"

Toward the end of Trump's term, Hirono didn't turn down her rhetoric against the president or his allies in Congress. During a May 2019 Judiciary Committee hearing, Hirono excoriated Attorney General William Barr over his handling of the Justice Department investigation into Russian meddling in the 2016 election after special counsel Robert Mueller delivered his report. "Now we know more about your deep involvement in trying to cover up for Donald Trump," Hirono said. "Being attorney general... is a sacred trust. You have betrayed that trust. America deserves better. You should resign." On CNN,, she blasted Trump's first Senate impeachment trial, calling it "rigged" because witnesses weren't allowed. During an August 2020 Judiciary subcommittee hearing on Antifa, Hirono, who was the ranking member, sparred with Chairman Ted Cruz of Texas and objected to a witness from the Center for Security Policy, which has been labeled anti-Muslim. Walking out of the hearing, Hirono told Cruz, "I hope that we don't have to listen to any more of your rhetorical speeches."

During the COVID-19 pandemic, Hirono talked about the extra precautions cancer survivors like herself had to take to avoid the novel coronavirus. During relief bill talks, she voiced concerns over money going to large industries over smaller businesses that would be hit particularly hard in places like Hawaii, which relies heavily on tourism, and the low-income workers who would be affected. Hirono also told the Honolulu Civil Beat that one way she was staying occupied during quarantine was hand-making personalized cards to send to friends. In April 2021, the Senate overwhelmingly passed her resolution to strengthen federal enforcement of efforts to prevent hate crime targeted at Asian-Americans. Members of her community, Hirono said, "have often very invisible in our country; always seen as foreign, always seen as the other."

Ed Case (D)

Elected 2018, 4th full term, b. Sep 27, 1952; Hilo, HI; HI Preparatory School, 1970; Williams College, B.A., 1975; University of CA Hastings College of Law, J.D., 1981; Protestant; Married (Audrey Nakamura); 4 children.

Elected Office: HI House, 1994-2002, Majority Leader 1999-2001; U.S. House, 2002-2007.

Professional Career: Legislative Assistant, U.S. Rep. Spark Matsunaga; Partner and Attorney, Carlsmith Ball Law Firm.

DC Office: 2443 RHOB 20515, 202-225-2726, case.house.gov

State Offices: Honolulu, 808-650-6688.

Committees: *Appropriations*: Commerce, Justice, Science & Related Agencies; Legislative Branch; Military Construction, Veterans Affairs & Related Agencies. *Natural Resources*: Indigenous Peoples of the United States; National Parks, Forests & Public Lands; Water, Oceans & Wildlife.

Almanac Ratings 2019-2020

	Economy	Social	Foreign	Composite
Liberal	100%	100%	80%	94%
Conservative	0%	0%	20%	6%

Key Votes of the 116th Congress

1. U.S./Mex./Can. trade deal Y	5. Russia sanctions Y	9. Firearms background checks Y
2. First Coronavirus response Y	6. Troops in Syria Y	10. Spending at the border Y
3. HEROES Act Y	7. Veto arms sales to Saudis Y	11. Marijuana liberalized rules Y
4. CASH Act Y	8. Defense $$$, veto override Y	12. Electoral College objections N

Election Results

Election	Name (Party)	Vote (%)	Cand. Spent	Ind. Exp. Support	Ind. Exp. Oppose
2020 General	Ed Case (D)...	183,245 (72%)	$413,378	$2,473	
	Ron Curtis (R).....................................	71,188 (28%)	$12,285		$113
2020 Primary	Ed Case (D).......................................	131,802 (100%)			

Prior winning percentages: 2018 (73%), 2004 (63%), 2003 special (44%), 2002 special (51%)

Democrat Ed Case, in his return to the House, settled into his work as a member of the Appropriations Committee. As a Hawaiian, his chief interests were U.S. military operations in the Pacific and ocean research closer to home. He was elected in 2018 after having lost two Democratic primaries for Senate seats in the previous decade. His political career has been marked by a seemingly endless series of Democratic primaries and constant clashes with the Democratic machine, though it has weakened since the death of Sen. Daniel Inouye in 2012. Case earlier served two terms in the House, where he has the unusual distinction of having held each of the state's two districts.

A fourth-generation Hawaiian, Case graduated from Williams College in Massachusetts and Hastings Law School in San Francisco. He spent three years on Capitol Hill as an aide to Sen. Spark Matsunaga. He returned home to join a Honolulu law firm, where he specialized in land and commercial law. After earlier defeats, he was elected to the state House in 1994, where he was majority leader for two years.

In 2002, he lost the primary for governor to then-Lt. Gov. Mazie Hirono, 40.6%-39.2%; Hirono subsequently lost to Republican Laura Lingle. Unexpectedly, Case then ran for the House after longtime Democratic Rep. Patsy Mink died in September. In contests five weeks apart, he won two separate special elections for her seat. The first was to complete the final month of her term; the second was for the subsequent, nearly complete, two-year term. Each time, Case won a winner-take-all contest with more than three dozen candidates in the Outer Islands district. During the next four years in the House, he served in the minority and had a centrist voting record, which was a bit more conservative on foreign policy.

In his controversial challenge in 2006 to 82-year-old Sen. Daniel Akaka, who was strongly backed by Inouye, Case argued that Hawaii, with two octogenarian Senators, needed to prepare for the inevitable transition by electing a more youthful Democrat who could begin accumulating seniority. The transition eventually took place six years later, though without Case's imprint. Akaka had a limited legislative record, but he was revered in Hawaii for his gentleness and modesty. He won, 55%-45%. "The machine won," said Case.

He returned to the Islands to practice law. Soon, he had two opportunities to run for open seats in Congress. In 2010, he lost a special election for a House seat, where Democratic divisions led to an unusual Republican victory. In 2012, he entered the contest to succeed the retiring Akaka. Once again, his chief opponent in the Democratic primary was Hirono. This time, Hirono won, 58%-41%. After having lost four campaigns in the past decade, three of them statewide, Case became senior vice president of a group of Hawaiian hotels and said he likely had ended his political career.

Instead, circumstances took another twist. In 2018, on the final day before the filing deadline, he entered another House race for the open seat of Colleen Hanabusa, who lost the Democratic primary for governor. His policy priorities included ending partisan gridlock and maintaining U.S. ties in Asia. "I'm running again because we must do better, and I want to be part of the solution," Case said. This time, he cited his experience, in both Washington and the private sector. "I'm also running because our Hawaii needs proven effective leadership in Congress."

Two Democrats who were well-known locally got a head start in campaigning and fundraising: Lt. Gov. Doug Chin, who had been appointed the state's attorney general by Gov. David Ige, and state Sen. Donna Kim, who had been Senate president. Each of them outspent Case, who self-financed almost half the roughly $350,000 he spent on the primary. Running this time in the Honolulu-based district, Case benefited from his more extensive political experience and name recognition. He won with 39 percent of the vote to 25 percent for Chin and 18 percent for Kim. The general election here was an afterthought.

Entering the House with the large freshman class that had restored Democratic control, Case's previous service gave him an advantage in committee assignments. He chose Appropriations. In early 2019, he told a committee hearing that the United States faced a challenge from China as it sought to maintain "a free and open order in the Indo-Pacific region that guaranteed security, enhanced trade and development and promoted human rights." As he discussed Hawaii's vital role as "America's bridge to the East," he listed diplomatic, military and economic opportunities.

Serving on the Commerce, Justice, Science and Related Agencies Subcommittee, Case in 2020 cited the more than $100 million the full committee included for programs benefiting oceans and the atmosphere. He noted, in particular, support for the high-altitude Mauna Loa observatory on the island of Hawaii, which measures carbon dioxide levels in the atmosphere.

Unusually for Case, he was reelected in 2020 without a Democratic primary and with token Republican opposition. Although he was positioned for influence in the House, the rapid turnover —and internal challenges—among Hawaii's top leaders in recent years suggest that it might be premature to rule out another step in his political odyssey.

HI-1: Honolulu Metro   **Cook Partisan Voting Index: D+14**

Population		Race and Ethnicity		Income	
Total	720,786	White	16.80%	Median Income	$86,674
Land area (sq. miles)	209	Black	2.40%	District Income Rank	67
Pop/ sq mi	3,445.11	Latino	9.10%	Poverty Rate	7.60%
Born in State	52.40%	Asian	50.50%	With health insurance	96.30%
		Two or more races	20.30%	Cash public assistance	2.50%
Age Groups		Other	10.00%	Food stamp/SNAP	8.50%
Under 18	19.80%				
18-34	24.00%	**Education**		**Work**	
35-64	37.20%	H.S grad or less	32.60%	White Collar	38.40%
Over 64	19.10%	Some college	30.60%	Sales and Service	45.00%
		College Degree, 4 yr	24.00%	Blue Collar	16.60%
Military		Post grad	12.70%	Government	21.60%
Veteran/ Active Duty	13.10%				

2020 Pres. Vote	Biden	179,337	(64%)	Trump	96,924	(35%)			
2016 Pres. Vote	Clinton	132,009	(63%)	Trump	63,916	(31%)	Johnson	7,195	(3%)
	Stein	4,431	(2%)						

Honolulu: The landmarks for visitors to Honolulu are the Joint Base Pearl Harbor-Hickam military facility, the USS Arizona monument in Pearl Harbor, the downtown area, with its wondrously Victorian Iolani Palace, and, of course, Waikiki, with its 40-story hotels rising within a few feet of each other. This part of Hawaii is tightly packed with people living between the 3,000-foot Koolau Range and the beaches and harbor, where tropical bungalows and garden apartments house Hawaiians of all incomes. Behind New York, San Francisco and Los Angeles, Honolulu has been the densest metropolitan area in the nation. But local finances recently have resulted in reverse migration. From 2015 to 2018, more than 35,000 residents moved to the mainland to escape the high cost of living and tight quarters, The Wall Street Journal reported in 2019. The median list price of $630,000 for a house is more than twice the cost in the nation as a whole.

Hawaii's topography jams cars onto just a few freeways and avenues, where traffic slows during rush hour and the aloha spirit is sorely tested. But hope has been (slowly) on the way for relief of traffic congestion. The Honolulu Authority for Rapid Transportation is working on a 20-mile elevated rail line that will serve downtown and outlying communities, the largest public-works project in state history. By 2020, costs had increased to $10 billion from the $5.2 billion projection in 2012. Added costs have been financed by a surcharge on the excise tax and additional hotel taxes. The completion date has been delayed until at least 2026, amid fears that the system might need to be downsized to reduce costs.

Honolulu is key to the tourism industry, which has been the largest source of private capital for the local economy and was roaring prior to the coronavirus. During much of 2020, the strict quarantine forced officials to tell tourists to stay away. Instead of 30,000 visitors who arrived daily, the figure dropped below 10,000. Unemployment soared as many of the large hotels radically cut their workforce.

The 1st Congressional District of Hawaii is entirely in Honolulu, on Oahu. With little land left to develop on the southern part of the island, it has been growing less rapidly than the rest of the state. In 2020, several projects were underway to combat severe beach erosion at Waikiki, which is mostly man-made. Among them was the building of a 95-foot line of 10,000-pound bags of sand to hold the beach in place. Asians are 50 percent of the population in the 1st and 23 percent were foreign-born.

Kaiali'i Kahele (D)

Elected 2020, 1st term, b. Mar 28, 1974; Miloli'I, HI; HI Community College, Att.; University of HI at Hilo, Att.; University of HI, Manoa, B.A., 1998; Married (Maria Fe Day); 3 children.

Military Career: Lt. Colonel, Hawaii Air National Guard (Iraq, Afghanistan).

Elected Office: HI Senate, 2016-2020; Majority Whip, HI Senate, 2017-2018; Majority Floor Leader, HI Senate, 2018-2021.

Professional Career: Adjunct faculty member, University of Hawaii at Hilo; Commercial Airline Pilot, Hawaiian Airlines; Executive Director, non-profit organization.

DC Office: 1205 LHOB 20515, 202-225-4906, Fax: 202-225-4987, kahele.house.gov

State Offices: Hilo, 808-746-6220.

Committees: *Armed Services*: Readiness; Tactical Air & Land Forces. *Transportation & Infrastructure*: Aviation; Highways & Transit.

Election Results

Election	Name (Party)	Vote (%)	Cand. Spent	Ind. Exp. Support	Ind. Exp. Oppose
2020 General	Kaiali'i Kahele (D)............... 171,517	(63%)	$883,544	$290,886	
	Joe Akana (R)...................... 84,027	(31%)	$51,344		$113
	Michelle Tippens (L)............ 6,785	(2%)			
2020 Primary	Kai Kahele (D)...................... 100,841	(77%)			
	Brian Evans (D).................... 12,337	(9%)			
	Brenda Lee (D)..................... 10,694	(8%)			
	Noelle Famera (D)................ 7,992	(6%)			

Democrat Kai Kahele had what likely was the easiest ride to a House seat by any incoming freshman in 2020. In the crucial Democratic primary, none of his three opponents raised or spent any money for their campaign, according to their reports to the Federal Election Commission. The little-known Republican nominee had scant opportunity in a district that has not elected a Republican since Hawaii sent its first members to Congress in 1959.

Kahele succeeded Tulsi Gabbard, an often outspoken and independent Democrat who generated frequent conflict within the Hawaii delegation and in her rocky bid for the presidential nomination in 2020. Kahele announced his candidacy for the seat in January 2019, after Gabbard had voiced interest in running for president and nine months before she announced that she would not seek a fifth term.

Kahele's success was striking for a relative newcomer to politics. In February 2016, he was appointed by Gov. David Ige as state senator—his first public office—to succeed his father, Gil Kahele, who died three weeks earlier and had been appointed to the Senate in 2011.

Kahele, who is only the second native Hawaiian to serve in Congress since statehood, was born and raised in Hilo on the island of Hawaii. His family's heritage was from South Korea. He got a bachelor's degree in education from the University of Hawaii (Manoa).

In 1999, he joined the Air Force, where he has served with the air operations group based at Hickam Air Force Base in Honolulu. In July 2019, he was promoted to lieutenant colonel. Kahele logged more than 3,000 hours of flight time during the wars in Iraq and against terrorism, including 108 combat missions over Iraq and Afghanistan, starting in 2005. He received numerous military awards, including Air Medals for meritorious achievement. For a decade, he was a commercial pilot with Hawaiian Airlines, where he piloted the Airbus 330.

During his five years in the Senate, Kahele served as majority floor leader and chaired the Water and Land Committee. His legislative achievements included a law that established the Hilo Community Economic District, which was designed to promote investment. He enacted a bill that created an academic program for commercial aviation at the University of Hawaii (Hilo).

"Kai Kahele leads a charmed political life," the Honolulu Star-Advertiser wrote in a July 2020 profile. "Kahele is so confident of victory that he's effectively sitting out the campaign by volunteering for a COVID-relief assignment [in the National Guard], which prohibits him from participating in the campaign while on active duty. ...At 46, he's been a leading voice of a younger generation in the Legislature on land use issues, Native Hawaiian rights and higher education."

In announcing his candidacy, Kahele said, in an obvious reference to Gabbard, "We need teamwork. ...We need elected leaders working together, leaders who put the common interests of Hawaii's people ahead of their own." Later in 2019, he criticized Gabbard for frequently missing House votes and leaving her district "without a voice." He was endorsed by three former Hawaii governors before Gabbard announced her seemingly inevitable decision not to seek reelection.

In the Democratic primary, he got 66 percent of the vote. Each of his three opponents received less than 10 percent. ("Blank votes" finished second, with 14 percent.) The winner of the Republican primary, with one-fourth as many votes cast as in the Democratic primary, was Joe Akana, who had been an intelligence analyst with the Air Force and worked in the financial sector. He got 39 percent of the vote in the nine-candidate field. During the campaign, Akana spent $51,000. Kahele, who spent $900,000, breezed to a 63%-31% victory..

In the House, he got committee assignments that were well-suited to his interests: Armed Services, and Transportation and Infrastructure.

HI-2: Outer Oahu   Cook Partisan Voting Index: D+15

Population		Race and Ethnicity		Income	
Total	695,086	White	31.70%	Median Income	$79,985
Land area (sq. miles)	6,213	Black	1.40%	District Income Rank	94
Pop/ sq mi	111.87	Latino	12.30%	Poverty Rate	11.10%
Born in State	52.20%	Asian	26.40%	With health insurance	95.40%
		Two or more races	24.40%	Cash public assistance	2.50%
Age Groups		Other	16.10%	Food stamp/SNAP	12.50%
Under 18	22.60%				
18-34	20.50%	**Education**		**Work**	
35-64	38.00%	H.S grad or less	37.60%	White Collar	33.60%
Over 64	19.00%	Some college	32.00%	Sales and Service	46.50%
		College Degree, 4 yr	20.00%	Blue Collar	19.90%
Military		Post grad	10.40%	Government	16.80%
Veteran/ Active Duty	11.80%				

2020 Pres. Vote	Biden	186,793	(64%)	Trump	99,940	(34%)		
2016 Pres. Vote	Clinton	134,882	(61%)	Trump	64,931	(30%)	Johnson	8,759	(4%)
	Stein	8,306	(4%)					

Other Islands: The 2nd Congressional District encompasses each island in the Hawaii archipelago, including most of Oahu's acreage beyond the city of Honolulu. It takes in Wheeler Army Airfield and some farmlands north of Pearl Harbor, between two jagged chains of mountains that lift the island out of the sea. Over the mountains to the west on Oahu is the Leeward Coast—calm, sultry and lightly populated. Over the mountains to the northeast is the Windward Coast, with many prosperous subdivisions in and around Kaneohe and Kailua.

The 137 islands have distinct personalities. Hawaii, the Big Island, is the size of Connecticut and boasts huge cattle ranches; the active volcano Kilauea, which started erupting in 1983 and has not stopped since; and Mauna Kea, the highest mountain in the world if the count begins at its base far under the ocean. On the north shore, with heavy rainfall and tropical foliage, is the old port of Hilo and Hawaii's macadamia nut industry; this is a blue-collar Democratic area in a natural wonderland. On the Kona Coast, where there is little rainfall and the landscape is dominated by lava flows, there are retirement condominiums and a higher-income population.

Maui, favored more by North American than Asian tourists, has dozens of upscale resorts and idyllic beaches. In 2020, a public trust purchased more than 3,400 acres of the Kamehamenui Forest, which will protect a water aquifer and native forests. Kauai, much of which was devastated by Hurricane Iniki in 1992, is the least developed and most agricultural of the main islands. Parts of it have the nation's highest rainfall, while others seldom get wet. In 2020, the coronavirus led to a virtual shutdown of tourism. Furloughed workers pursued projects such as cleaning beaches and beautifying old villages.

Production of sugar and pineapples has virtually disappeared in Hawaii, chiefly a result of land costs and a higher return for other uses. In 2016, the remaining sugar mill laid off what remained of 650 employees. At one time, the state produced 20 percent of the sugar consumed in the United States. The largest pineapple plantation shut down in 2009.In 2016, President Barack Obama used his executive authority to create south and west of Hawaii the world's largest protected marine sanctuary, quadrupling the size of the existing refuge. Overall, the district is solidly Democratic. Hillary Clinton won, 61%-30%, slightly below her performance in the 1st District. Joe Biden won the 2nd District, 64%-34%, virtually the same as his vote in the mostly urban 1st District.

IDAHO

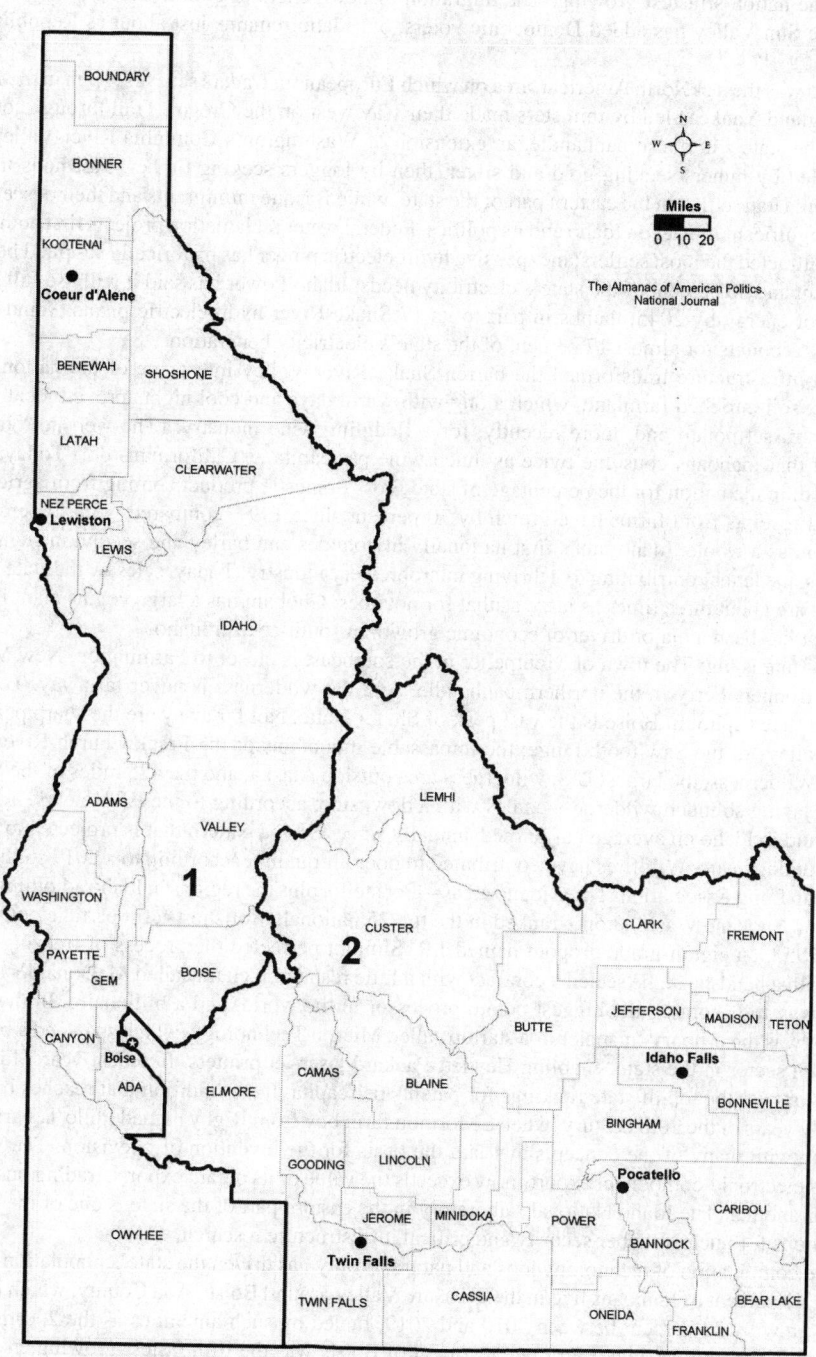

Miles
0 10 20

BOUNDARY

BONNER

KOOTENAI

Coeur d'Alene

BENEWAH

SHOSHONE

LATAH

CLEARWATER

NEZ PERCE

Lewiston

LEWIS

IDAHO

ADAMS

VALLEY

LEMHI

WASHINGTON

1

CUSTER

CLARK

FREMONT

PAYETTE

GEM

BOISE

2

JEFFERSON

MADISON

TETON

CANYON

Boise

BUTTE

ADA

ELMORE

CAMAS

BLAINE

Idaho Falls

BONNEVILLE

BINGHAM

GOODING

LINCOLN

OWYHEE

JEROME

MINIDOKA

Pocatello

POWER

CARIBOU

TWIN FALLS

Twin Falls

CASSIA

BANNOCK

BEAR LAKE

ONEIDA

FRANKLIN

Congressional district boundaries were first effective for 2012.

Tucked near the northwest edge of the continental United States, far from any major metro area, Idaho has seen its population grow by 81 percent since 1990, and its biggest city, Boise, has been among the nation's fastest-growing. The migration of newcomers to both livable Boise and resort areas like Sun Valley has added Democratic voters, but Idaho remains just about as Republican as ever.

Idaho was the last North American area on which European fur traders set eyes. Then in the 1840s, New England Yankees led by ministers made their way west on the Oregon Trail through southern Idaho. The state's northern panhandle, an extension of Washington's Columbia River Valley, was first settled by miners seeking gold and silver, then by loggers seeking timber. Mormons moving north from Utah settled in the eastern part of the state, while Basque immigrants and their descendants made a significant impact on Idaho and its politics. Federal water reclamation projects first authorized in 1894 attracted the most settlers; inexpensive hydroelectric power has historically supplied between 60 percent and 80 percent of the state's electricity needs. Idaho Power has said it will use fully clean sources of energy by 2045, thanks in part to its 17 Snake River hydroelectric plants. Wind power currently accounts for almost 17 percent of the state's electricity generation.

This infrastructure transformed the barren Snake River Valley into some of the nation's best volcanic, soil-enriched farmland, which along with warm days and cool nights proved ideal for the Burbank russet potato and, more recently, for a fledgling wine industry. (The website Vine Pair reported that Idahoans consume twice as much wine per capita as Californians do.) Today, Idaho ranks fifth in the nation for the percentage of state gross domestic product coming from agriculture, and total receipts from farms have grown by 70 percent since 1997, compared with 20 percent for the nation as a whole. Idaho ranks first nationally in potatoes and barley and second in sugar beets and hops, the latter contributing to a thriving microbrewery industry. Today, sales by the state's dairy industry are about three times as large as that for potatoes; Chobani has a large yogurt plant in Twin Falls that has been a major driver of economic growth in south-central Idaho.

The state is big: The town of Montpelier in the southeast is closer to Farmington, New Mexico, than to Bonners Ferry in the northern panhandle. And the wilderness is never far away. Towering over the state capitol in Boise is the vast peak of Shafer Butte. Not far away are the sharp peaks and broad valleys of the Saw tooth range; the impassable mountains of the Frank Church-River of No Return Wilderness, the largest U.S. wilderness area outside Alaska; and the 425 miles of the Salmon River. Having so much wilderness comes with a downside; according to the EPA, nearly 1 percent of the land in Idaho on average has burned annually since 1984, a pattern that is projected to worsen in the coming years. Wildfires have contributed to poor air quality, according to a 2019 study by the American Lung Association. Three Idaho areas—Pocatello, plus the regions in Idaho adjoining Logan Utah, and Spokane Washington—ranked in the top 25 nationally for short-term particle pollution.

In 1953, an eighth-grade dropout named J.R. Simplot perfected the process of freezing French fries; with a handshake, he sealed a contract with a little restaurant chain called McDonald's and was on his way to becoming the biggest potato processor in the world, and a billionaire. In the 1970s, Simplot was the primary financier of a startup called Micron Technology, which spawned a booming high-tech sector in the state, enabling Hewlett-Packard laser-jet printers. In recent years, Idaho has been at or near the top of state rankings for patents per capita. It's a tradition that reaches back into the early years of the 20th century, when a Mormon farm boy from Rigby named Philo T. Farnsworth came up with many of the concepts that laid the basis for the invention of television. The value of Idaho's electronic-component exports now exceeds the value of its potato exports, trading one type of chip for another. The Idaho National Laboratory in the eastern part of the state is one of the nation's major hubs for nuclear, cyber security and critical infrastructure research.

The combination of technology jobs and natural beauty has driven the state's population growth. Today, 41 percent of Idahoans live in the Treasure Valley around Boise; Ada County, which includes Boise, grew by 22 percent between 2010 and 2019, fueled by such amenities as the 200-mile-long Ridge to Rivers trail system. Meridian, just west of Boise, was the fifth fastest-growing city with at least 50,000 in population in the country, and Boise and Meridian have been joined by neighboring Nampa as cities of 100,000-plus population. Other areas have grown too, especially those attracting a wealthy clientele—Blaine County, which includes the resort of Sun Valley, and Teton County, a bedroom community for pricey Jackson Hole, Wyoming. In growth areas, traffic and high housing prices have followed the brewpubs and farm-to-table restaurants; in Boise, having the median income is sufficient to purchase just 13 percent of homes for sale, according to Realtor.com. But most of Idaho's counties have seen little population change in the past half-century. "All that massive growth you've heard about in Idaho has happened in the space of only a few hundred square miles, a tiny sliver of the state," longtime political observer Randy Stapilus has noted.

The number of Hispanic residents grew by almost 31 percent between 2010 and 2019, double the rate of the state overall. Idaho has welcomed not only Americans from other states but those from abroad, including refugees. The state has absorbed more than 20,000 refugees since the 1970s, mostly in Boise and Twin Falls—first Vietnamese and Cambodians, then Bosnians, and more recently refugees from Iraq, Afghanistan, Sudan, Congo, Eritrea, Nepal and Iran. In Twin Falls, just 17 miles from a World War II internment camp for Japanese Americans, this has periodically spawned controversy. But an anti-refugee ballot measure proposal in 2016 failed to secure enough signatures, despite fake Russian-controlled Facebook accounts trying to stir up an anti-refugee rally. The Mormon population may be a reason for the state's tolerant streak, due to its international missionary outreach: Idaho has the second highest percentage of Mormons of any state.

In its early years as a silver-producing state, Idaho backed populism and opposed the gold standard; from 1900 to 1960, it was politically marginal. It elected prominent national Democrats such as Sen. Frank Church, an intelligence watchdog and 1976 presidential candidate, and Gov. Cecil Andrus, Jimmy Carter's Interior secretary. But Idaho has become staunchly Republican: Since 1964, no Democratic presidential nominee has won more than 37 percent of the vote. Idahoans like to see themselves as pioneering entrepreneurs who, rather than seek federal help, want to get a bloated, bossy federal government off their backs. The U.S. government owns 63 percent of Idaho's land, and many Idahoans strongly oppose federal policies that block road building on one-third of national forestland, limit grazing on public lands, and breach Snake River dams to protect salmon (in the process, depriving potato farmers of water). Idaho has elected only Republicans to the governorship since 1994 and to the Senate since 1978. With one exception in 2008, the GOP has won every election for Idaho's two House seats since 1994. Gains of upscale professionals and minorities have been balanced by the influx of more conservative engineers and entrepreneurs who have come from California and all over for a fresh environment and a fresh start—and fewer cumbersome or expensive regulations.

Indeed, rural Idaho, amid population stagnation, has become redder than ever. The coronavirus pandemic exposed some fault lines in the state, as a vocal segment of rural conservatives rebelled against public-health restrictions imposed by the more pragmatic Republican governor, Brad Little. Despite its relative spaciousness, Idaho ranked in the top one-third of states for per-capita coronavirus cases by December 2020. For some Idaho Republicans, an 80 percent majority in both legislative chambers isn't enough; they have pushed to add a tie-breaking member to the state's bipartisan redistricting commission who would be appointed by Idaho's (exclusively Republican) statewide officials. And in May 2021, five rural counties in Oregon voted to join a conservative "greater Idaho" that wouldn't have to bow to liberal Portland.

Donald Trump easily won Idaho in 2020, by a margin similar to the one he had in 2016; the biggest difference between the two elections was the disappearance of the third-party candidates from 2016, Evan McMullin, Gary Johnson, and Jill Stein, who collectively took 12 percent of the vote, bolstered by McMullin's strength among Mormons. In 2020, Biden captured a decent share of 2016's third-party voters; he won 97,000 more votes in the state than Clinton had, compared to an increase of 145,000 votes for Trump, meaning Biden took 40 percent of the increases in the two-party vote, or well above the Democratic share statewide in either election. In Boise's Ada County, Biden narrowed Trump's margin of victory from nine points in 2016 to four in 2020. Biden also flipped Teton County, adjoining increasingly Democratic Jackson Hole, beating Trump by seven points after Clinton had lost it narrowly. Biden also expanded on Clinton's margins in Sun Valley's Blaine County, increasing the Democratic edge from 29 points to 37 points. Still, such changes were merely on the margins; overall, Trump assembled higher margins of victory in only four other states. And the 2020 contest involving Sen. Jim Risch showed that progressive Democrats remained unpopular in Idaho: Paulette Jordan lost by an even greater margin than she had in her gubernatorial race two years earlier, winning only 33 percent.

Population		Race and Ethnicity		Income	
Total	1,787,065	White	89.40%	Median Income	60,999
Land area (sq. miles)	82,643	Black	0.70%	State Income Rank	31 out of 50
Pop/ sq mi	21.62	Latino	12.80%	Poverty Rate	11.20%
Born in state	46.10%	Asian	2.50%	With health insurance	89.20%
		Two or more races	3.30%	Cash public assistance	2.30%
Age Groups		Other	5.20%	Food stamp/SNAP	11.3%
Under 18	25.10%				
18-34	22.40%	**Education**		**Work**	
35-64	36.20%	H.S grad or less	34.60%	White Collar	35.50%
Over 64	16.20%	Some college	36.60%	Sales and Service	39.40%
		College Degree, 4 yr	18.80%	Blue Collar	25.10%
Military		Post grad	9.90%	Government	14.30%
Veteran/ Active Duty	9.40%				

Presidential Politics

2020 Primary (D)	Biden (D)	53,151(49%)	Sanders (D)	46,114(42%)			
2016 Caucus (D)	Sanders (D)	18,640(78%)	Clinton (D)	5,065(21%)			
2020 Pres. Vote	Trump (R)	554,119(64%)	Biden (D)	287,021(33%)			
2016 Pres. Vote	Trump (R)	409,055(59%)	Clinton (D)	189,765(27%)	McMullin (I)	46,476 (7%)
	Johnson (L)	28,331 (4%)					

Idaho is one of the most Republican states in presidential politics. No Democratic nominee has come close to carrying it since the 1964 LBJ landslide, when the incumbent Democratic president narrowly defeated Barry Goldwater, 51%-49%. Donald Trump handily beat Hillary Clinton in 2016 59%-28%, with six third-party and independent candidates garnering 13 percent—the first time GOP nominee had failed to break 60 percent since Bob Dole won the state in 1996 with 52 percent of the vote. In 2020, Trump won 64%-33%, as the state's Mormon-heavy southeast came home to the Republican Party. The only pockets of Democratic strength are Ada County, home to the state capital and largest city, Boise, and small Blaine County, where the Sun Valley ski resort has attracted wealthy coastal liberals. But even in Ada, Democrats don't always win. Trump took the county twice, though his four-point win in 2020 was half his margin in 2016. Most of the remainder of the state, from the panhandle in the north to the industrial farms in the south, is Republican territory.

Idaho switched from a presidential caucus to a primary for the 2020 elections, and held its Democratic primary March 10. Bernie Sanders had won the 2016 caucus by a wide margin and looked to the state as one of his best hopes to reverse his fortunes after a rough Super Tuesday the week before. But as in other states, the switch from a caucus hurt him and Joe Biden won 49%-42%, carrying all but five counties as he won five of the six states holding elections that day to cement his frontrunner status.

Congressional Districts

117th Congress Lineup	2R	116th Congress Lineup	2R

Idaho has two congressional districts, which split Boise between them. It also has a six-member bipartisan reapportionment commission, which probably gives Democrats more of a role in the process than they deserve in a state where roughly four-fifths of state legislators are Republicans. Still, drawing a seat friendly to Democrats is a near-impossible task in Idaho and the commission's tradition has been to simply shift the Boise dividing line between the 1st and 2nd districts slightly west every 10 years to accommodate the 1st District's larger growth. In 2011, robust growth in northern Idaho and Boise's western suburbs forced the 1st District to shed about 58,000 residents. After a three-month stalemate, one Democratic commissioner folded and agreed to merely move the boundary three miles west. The shift subtly made the 1st District about a point more Republican, perhaps giving 2nd District Republican Mike Simpson a few more moderate primary voters. Simpson easily survived a conservative challenge in the 2014 primary.

The latest Census Bureau data on Idaho show that population growth has been strong across the state, though the 1st District would have to shift perhaps 20,000 of its residents to the 2nd District to achieve a new balance in 2022.More significantly, continued growth could position Idaho for the first time in its history to gain a third seat, perhaps in the next decade. That would generate significant jousting, including whether Boise should get its own seat or continue to influence two—or possibly all three—seats, with the other seats based in the north and the east.

Brad Little (R)

Elected 2018, term expires 2023, 1st term; b. Feb. 15, 1954, Emmett; University of Idaho, B.S., 1976; Episcopalian Married (Teresa); 2 children.

Elected Office: ID Senate, 2001-2009, President, 2009-2019; ID Lt. Gov., 2009-2019.

Professional Career: Owner and Partner, Little Land and Livestock Company; Operator, Little Enterprises, Inc.

Office: State Capitol PO Box 83720, Boise, 83720; 208-334-2100; Fax: 208-334-3454

Lt. Gov.: Janice McGeachin (R) **Atty. Gen:** Lawrence Wasden (R) **Sec. of State:** Lawerence Denney (R)

State Legislature: Senate: 7D, 28R **House:** 14D, 56R

Election Results

Election	Name (Party)	Vote (%)
2018 General	Brad Little (R)	361,661 (60%)
	Paulette Jordan (D)	231,081 (38%)
2018 Primary	Brad Little (R)	72,548 (38%)
	Raul Labrador (R)	63,478 (33%)
	Tommy Ahlquist (R)	51,008 (27%)

First-term Idaho Gov. Brad Little has steered a pragmatic course in his heavily Republican state, but that has prompted continuing attacks from the right wing of his party, including by his lieutenant governor, over his efforts to contain the coronavirus.

Little is a third-generation Idahoan whose grandfather emigrated from Scotland in 1894 and established a sheep operation that spanned across much of southwest Idaho; he became "Idaho's Sheep King," and it wasn't an exaggeration. His son carried on the business, and his grandson worked on the ranch while growing up and after graduating from the University of Idaho in 1977. Little served as president of the Idaho Wool Growers Association, chaired two committees of the American Sheep Industry Association, and chaired the Idaho Association of Commerce and Industry. But the family eventually sold the sheep operation and moved into the cattle business. They also opened some of their land as an off-road vehicle park.

The family's second business was politics. Little's father served in the state legislature and was a Republican National Committee member; as a youngster, Little helped his father campaign for Barry Goldwater in 1964. Four years later, he sat next to Ronald Reagan at the Republican National Convention. In 1972, Little became a delegate himself. In 2001, GOP Gov. Dirk Kempthorne appointed Little to a vacant state Senate seat, and he proceeded to win election four times. Then, in 2009, Little was appointed to the vacant lieutenant governorship and won the seat on his own in 2010 and 2014. When three-term Republican Gov. C.L. "Butch" Otter announced he would not be running again, Little jumped in and received Otter's endorsement.

Little was the establishment favorite, focusing on traditional Republican priorities such as low taxes and limited spending, but he faced two other major candidates in the free-spending, attack-ad-saturated2018 primary: Rep. Raul Labrador, a member of the House Freedom Caucus, and Tommy Ahlquist, a developer running as an outsider. Little got 38 percent, followed by Labrador with 33 percent and Ahlquist with 27 percent. Meanwhile, Idaho Democrats had a competitive primary between Paulette Jordan, a former state House member and former Coeur d'Alene Tribal Council official, and A.J. Balukoff, a businessman, Boise school board member and former gubernatorial candidate. Most Democratic officials backed Balukoff, a moderate, but Jordan ran an insurgent campaign—and a progressive one—that attracted attention and small-dollar donations from across the country. When the dust settled, Jordan defeated Balukoff, 58%-40%.

Little ran a largely orthodox Republican campaign, though he supported teacher pay raises and Idaho's version of the Common Core curriculum, while opposing efforts to implement school choice. While Little previously was critical of the Affordable Care Act, he said during the campaign that he would respect the results of a ballot measure to implement Medicaid expansion under that law; the ballot measure would eventually pass with greater than 60 percent of the vote. Despite the energy behind Jordan's gubernatorial bid in some quarters, some moderate Democratic voters abandoned her for Little. The Republican won, 60%-38%.

In his first year in office, Little expressed discomfort with some of the provisions of legislation to implement the Medicaid expansion, including a work requirement, but he ultimately signed them into law. (By January 2020, at least 60,000 of an estimated 91,000 eligible Idaho residents had secured coverage.) Little signed a bill expanding concealed carry to 18- to 20-year-olds in cities, but he vetoed one that would have set stricter requirements for ballot initiatives—a relief to Democrats, who had come to see ballot measures as their only viable tool for influencing policy in the GOP-dominated state. Liberals were also pleased by Little's renewal of the state's commitment to accept refugees, acknowledgement that climate change needed to be addressed, and recognition of Indigenous People's Day on what had been Columbus Day. And in 2020, Little signed legislation to raise starting pay for teachers. But Little spurned opposition from major Idaho employers—including Chobani, Clif Bar, HP and Micron—when he signed one bill that would ban transgender girls and women from female sports teams in the state, and another that would effectively prevent residents from changing their gender on birth certificates. Within months, a federal court had voided the birth certificate bill.

After the coronavirus hit, Little imposed a variety of restrictions on public gatherings that put him on a collision course with the most conservative Idahoans, including Ammon Bundy, who had once taken over a federal wildlife refuge in Oregon for 41 days, and Lt. Gov. Janice McGeachin. Tensions between Little and McGeachin, who were elected separately, got to the point where they were not on speaking terms. By fall, McGeachin appeared in a video in which she denounced the restrictions while holding a gun and a Bible. "We recognize that all of us are by nature, free and equal, and have certain inalienable rights," she said in the video, which elsewhere posited that the pandemic "may or may not be occurring." Little countered that the state was at "a crisis with our healthcare system" and needed to impose some restrictions. In April 2021, the legislature failed to override Little's veto of a bill that would have curbed the emergency powers he had used during the pandemic. Separately, that same month, Little finally signed a bill to make it harder to qualify initiatives for the ballot, enacting a priority of rural areas.

It was clear to observers that McGeachin was positioning herself as a possible primary challenger to Little in 2022; Labrador could make a second run as well. Either would pose a more severe test than whatever candidate the Democrats manage to come up with. Little also sparred with the more conservative wing of his party in the legislature; when he suggested that the legislature either delay its 2021 session or make it virtual, the idea got no traction from legislators.

Mike Crapo (R)

Elected 1998, term expires 2022, 4th term, b. May 20, 1951; Idaho Falls, ID; Brigham Young University, B.A., 1973; Harvard University Law School, J.D., 1977; Mormon; Married (Susan Diane Hasleton Crapo); 5 children; 8 grandchildren.

Elected Office: ID Senate, 1985-1992; President pro tempore, ID Senate, 1988-1992; U.S. House, 1993-1998.

Professional Career: Clerk, Judge James M. Carter, 1977-1978; Attorney.

DC Office: 239 DSOB 20510, 202-224-6142, Fax: 202-228-1375, crapo.senate.gov

State Offices: Boise, 208-334-1776; Coeur D'Alene, 208-664-5490; Idaho Falls, 208-522-9779; Lewiston, 208-743-1492; Pocatello, 208-236-6775; Twin Falls, 208-734-2515.

Committees: *Banking, Housing & Urban Affairs*: Housing, Transportation & Community Development; National Security & International Trade & Finance; Securities, Insurance & Investment. *Budget. Finance (RMM). Joint Taxation.*

Group Ratings

	ADA	ACLU	AFL-CIO	LCV	COC	HAFA	ACU	CFG	FRC
2020		17%	-	0%	-	61%	91%	-	-
2019	0%	C	21%	7%	90%	C	91%	42%	100%

Almanac Ratings 2019-2020

	Economy	Social	Foreign	Composite
Liberal	0%	0%	0%	0%
Conservative	100%	100%	100%	100%

Key Votes of the 116th Congress

1. EPA clean energy rules	N	5. Russia sanctions	N	9. Barr as Atty. General	Y
2. U.S./Mex./Can. trade deal	Y	6. Troops in SYR, AFG	Y	10. Spending at the border	Y
3. Cut unemployment benefits	Y	7. Veto arms sales to Saudis	N	11. Coney Barrett to Sup. Ct.	Y
4. Shelton to Fed Reserve	Y	8. Defense $$$, veto override	Y	12. Electoral College objections	N

Election Results

Election	Name (Party)	Vote (%)		Cand. Spent	Ind. Exp. Support	Ind. Exp. Oppose
2016 General	Mike Crapo (R)	449,017	(66%)	$6,461,442		
	Jerry Sturgill (D)	188,249	(28%)	$709,348		
	Ray Writz (C)	41,677	(6%)	$2,925		
2016 Primary	Mike Crapo (R)	Unopposed				

Prior winning percentages: 2016 (66%), 2010 (71%), 2004 (99%), 1998 (70%); House: 1996 (69%), 1994 (75%), 1992 (61%)

Mike Crapo, Idaho's senior senator, has become the top Republican on the powerful Senate Finance Committee. Although he has been a reliable partisan on key issues, he has shown an interest in bipartisanship during nearly three decades on Capitol Hill. He has worked with Sen. Ron Wyden of Oregon, his Democratic chairman of the Finance panel, on shared regional interests.

Crapo had previously wielded influence as chairman of the Banking, Housing and Urban Affairs Committee. In 2018, he led a bipartisan coalition that pared back the Dodd-Frank financial reforms and persuaded House Republicans and other critics of the law to agree to a less sweeping rewrite than many of them had sought. Crapo has continued in the Senate GOP leadership as chief deputy majority whip; for the past nine Congresses, he has helped GOP leader Mitch McConnell make committee assignments.

In 2011-12, the mild-mannered Crapo served as a member of the "Gang of Six"—a bipartisan group of senators who came up with a plan to reduce the federal deficit by $3.7 trillion over a decade, though they achieved scant success. More than a quarter of the deficit savings would have come from increased tax revenues, a move that was anathema to many conservatives.

"Mike's one of those guys that is a realist and understands that in legislation you don't get everything you want, but the good outweighs the bad," Sen. Jon Tester of Montana, a Democrat on the Banking panel who has negotiated with Crapo, told the Wall Street Journal. When he was Senate Democratic leader, Harry Reid singled out Crapo as one of three GOP senators who would make an "outstanding" Supreme Court justice.

His powerful Senate niche has represented a comeback from adversity. After a battle with cancer early in his Senate tenure, he was arrested in 2012 for drunken driving in suburban Virginia. The consumption of alcohol represented a violation of Crapo's Mormon faith, and Idahoans—nearly 25 percent of whom are Mormon—were bewildered. The Lewiston Morning Tribune ran an editorial headlined, "Is This Mike Crapo the Same Guy We Knew?" Crapo apologized, pleaded guilty to a misdemeanor, and, over a two-year period, held town halls in all of Idaho's 200 incorporated cities. That resulted in his political rehabilitation.

A fourth-generation Idahoan, Crapo was born and raised in Idaho Falls. His father ran the local post office, and his mother stayed home to care for the family's six children. The couple farmed 200 acres, growing potatoes and grain. After earning an undergraduate degree from Brigham Young University, Crapo graduated from Harvard Law School. In 1984, he was elected to the Idaho Senate at 33. Two years earlier, leukemia took the life of his older brother, Terry, who had been the state House majority leader and a rising star in Idaho politics. The brothers were close, and Mike Crapo followed his brother's path to the Legislature. He became Senate president pro tem in 1988.

Crapo ran for an open seat in the House in 1992on a platform of spending cuts, a balanced-budget amendment and the line-item veto. He won the primary by a margin better than 2-1. In the general election, "Cowboy Democrat" J.D. Williams, the state controller, ran on a "Put America First" platform on industrial policy and trade. Crapo won 61%-35%.

Crapo became a Republican freshman class leader and championed institutional reforms, advocating for more power for rank-and-file members to bring bills to the floor. Like many Republicans at that time, he favored strict budget rules to force tough decisions. He supported across-the-board discretionary spending cuts, excluding Social Security. Crapo opposed the North American Free Trade Agreement in 1993, but he later supported normalizing trade relations with China and Cuba.

Crapo faced a career choice in 1997. Republican Gov. Phil Batt retired, and GOP Sen. Dirk Kempthorne said he would run for governor. Crapo ran for Kempthorne's Senate seat the following year and was unopposed in the Republican primary. His opponent in the fall was trial lawyer Bill Mauk, a former Democratic state chairman. Despite its large Mormon population, Idaho had never elected a Mormon to the Senate—until Crapo. He won 70%-28%, carrying every county. He has been easily reelected ever since.

In the wake of the 2008 financial industry meltdown, Crapo worked on the Dodd-Frank financial reforms but was disappointed with the result. He expressed frustration that the bill did not revamp troubled mortgage giants Fannie Mae and Freddie Mac. He opposed the reform's creation of a Consumer Financial Protection Bureau and its requirement for commercial banks to spin off most of their derivatives-trading operations. At the same time, Crapo praised provisions in the 2010 law that required banks to hold more capital in reserve, saying this had helped "create a more stable protection against the need for taxpayer bailouts."

On some high-profile issues, Crapo has sided with the most conservative corners of the Senate. At the height of the 2008 recession, he was among a dozen Senate Republicans who voted against a Bush administration request to create the $700 billion Troubled Asset Relief Program aimed at shoring up troubled financial institutions. In 2013, he opposed the bipartisan immigration overhaul bill that cleared the Senate by a wide margin.

On other issues, Crapo has not allowed ideology to interfere with the search for consensus. Serving on the bipartisan Simpson-Bowles debt reduction commission in 2010, he endorsed the commission's plan, which called for tax increases, spending cuts and changes in entitlement programs. That put him at odds with House Republican son the panel. While calling the plan "flawed and incomplete," he joined a statement saying, "The time for action is now." Crapo voted in favor of the New Year's Day 2013 budget deal aimed at averting the so-called fiscal cliff of automatic tax increases and spending cuts. But he characterized it as a "missed opportunity to comprehensively address our nation's economic crisis."

In 2015 and 2016, Crapo counted seven bipartisan measures he sponsored that Obama signed into law. One of those had a personal dimension for him as a cancer survivor: He had his prostate removed in 2000 and underwent radiation treatment when the cancer recurred five years later. In 2016, Crapo attended a White House ceremony at which Obama signed a reauthorization of the Toxic Substances Control Act, which contained a provision known as "Trevor's Law." The bill, named for Trevor Schaefer of Boise—who survived a diagnosis of brain cancer at13—required the tracking of childhood and adult cancer clusters around the nation.

Crapo, who has been cancer-free for more than a decade, said his diagnosis had "accelerated and intensified" his interest in biomedical research, telling the Idaho Statesman, "Certainly, I believe when one gets the diagnosis that they have cancer, it's a gut-wrencher, and it's an attitude-changer in a lot of ways."

Meanwhile, Democratic challenger Jerry Sturgill was seeking to make a campaign issue in 2016 of Crapo's arrest for driving under the influence four years earlier. "The DUI revealed a long cover-up of personal behavior inconsistent with how Sen. Crapo had presented himself as a tee-totaling member of our church, one who had held high office," said Sturgill, a fellow Mormon—alluding to the fact that Crapo had become a bishop in the church when he was 31. On Dec. 23, 2012, Crapo drove across the Potomac River to Alexandria Virginia where he scored a 0.11 blood-alcohol level on a breathalyzer test after running a red light. The legal limit for driving in Virginia was 0.08. Crapo admitted to having had several shots of vodka, according to the police report. Two weeks later, Crapo pleaded guilty to a misdemeanor and received a $250 fine and 12-month suspension of his driver's license. "It was a poor choice to use alcohol to relieve stress—and one at odds with my personally held religious beliefs," he later said.

In an interview with the Idaho Statesman shortly before the 2016 election, Crapo said he had not had a drink since the episode, adding, "I do apologize again for that conduct, one of the worst times of my life, in terms of frankly being disappointed in myself and realizing that I disappointed my constituents." He said that he had worked "really hard" to recommit to his work and earn the support of his constituents, adding, "I think that I have made a strong case for that." The voters appeared to agree. Crapo defeated Sturgill 66%-28%.

In the presidential campaign, Crapo initially endorsed GOP nominee Donald Trump. He became one of the first Republicans to withdraw his endorsement after release of the decade-old tape on which Trump could be heard boasting about sexually assaulting women. Crapo said Trump's "disrespectful, profane and demeaning" comments made him unfit for the presidency and suggested Trump be replaced with vice presidential nominee Mike Pence. Two weeks before the election, Crapo acknowledged that that was not going to happen and restored his endorsement of Trump—citing the stakes in the coming election, particularly the prospect that the next president might nominate several Supreme Court justices. (Trump, indeed, appointed three—a third of the court.)

After Trump took office, Crapo's public comments were positive. "I've spent the last 14 months fighting for things that I think are good for the country," he told the state Legislature in February 2018. He praised the effects of Trump's tax cuts. "The economy has been growing at about 3.2 percent," Crapo told an Idaho reporter in July 2018. "We now have more jobs available than people seeking jobs."

On the Banking Committee, Sen. Richard Shelby of Alabama in 2017 was forced by internal GOP term limits to cede the gavel to Crapo—to the barely concealed delight of committee Democrats, who were on scratchy terms with Shelby. "We have a working relationship," the committee's senior Democrat, Sherrod Brown of Ohio, said of Crapo. "He's way more conservative than I am, but he's straightforward and honorable." Crapo sought common ground with Brown on cutbacks of Dodd-Frank banking regulations.

Those talks failed. But Crapo had success with a group of four relatively centrist Democrats on his committee—three of whom happened to be seeking reelection in 2018 in states that Trump had easily won in 2016.(Two of the three lost reelection, despite their bipartisan outreach.) After extensive negotiations, they agreed on a package reducing the number of banks subject to the increased scrutiny of the law and exempting smaller banks from some of the Dodd-Frank requirements. In March 2018, the Senate passed the bill, 67-31.That agreement largely pre-empted more sweeping changes sought by House Republicans. "It is a bipartisan compromise, the changes are commonsense, and it will allow financial institutions to better serve their customers and communities, while maintaining safety and soundness and important consumer protections," he said after Trump signed the bill.

On the Finance Committee, Crapo advocated for international trade deals. Although he supported a renegotiation of NAFTA with Canada and Mexico, he cautioned Trump to keep the existing deal in place in the meantime—not least because of his homestate's extensive commercial dealings with Canada. After a final deal was reached, he said in February 2020, "It is going to be a kind of improvement in our trade that we deserved in America." Crapo criticized Trump's extensive use of tariffs as a negotiating tactic, and he sought to narrow presidential discretion in trade negotiations.

In the closely divided Senate, Crapo has shown a continuing interest in bipartisan deals. With Democratic Sen. Amy Klobuchar of Minnesota, he won Senate passage in December 2020 of a bill to reduce unwanted rob calls by mandating the Federal Communications Commission to report to Congress on the effectiveness of its call-blocking programs. With Republican Tim Scott of South Carolina and Democrats Ben Cardin of Maryland and Michael Bennet of Colorado—all Finance Committee members—he filed a bill that month to provide Medicare coverage for screening tests that can detect multiple forms of cancer before symptoms develop.

Perhaps most significantly in terms of their leadership of the Finance Committee, Crapo and Wyden won Senate agreement to include in the huge year-end spending bill in 2020 their measure to extend a tax credit used to repair and upgrade short-line railroads, which are commercially vital in their neighboring states. In announcing the deal, the two veteran senators—who served together in the House in the 1990s—cited their "long-time partnership." Their collaboration is undoubtedly a topic of interest among tax lobbyists.

Jim Risch (R)

Elected 2008, term expires 2026, 3rd term, b. May 03, 1943; Milwaukee, WI; University of Wisconsin, Milwaukee, Att., 1963; University of Idaho, B.S., 1965; University of Idaho, Law School, J.D., 1968; Roman Catholic; Married (Vicki L. Choborda); 3 children; 7 grandchildren.

Elected Office: Ada County Prosecuting Attorney, 1970-1974; ID Senate, 1974-1989, 1995-2003, Majority Leader, 1976-1982, pres. pro temp., 1982-1989; ID Lt. Governor, 2003-2006, 2007-2009; ID Governor, 2006-2008.

Professional Career: Rancher; Sr. Partner, Risch Goss Insinger Gustavel, 1975-2008.

DC Office: 483 RSOB 20510, 202-224-2752, Fax: 202-224-2573, risch.senate.gov

State Offices: Boise, 208-342-7985; Coeur d'Alene, 208-667-6130; Idaho Falls, 208-523-5541; Lewiston, 208-743-0792; Pocatello, 208-236-6817; Twin Falls, 208-734-6780.

Committees: *Energy & Natural Resources*: Energy; Public Lands, Forests & Mining; Water & Power. *Ethics. Foreign Relations (RMM). Intelligence. Small Business & Entrepreneurship.*

Group Ratings

	ADA	ACLU	AFL-CIO	LCV	COC	HAFA	ACU	CFG	FRC
2020	-	17%	-	0%	-	87%	92%	-	-
2019	0%	C	11%	7%	78%	C	92%	79%	100%

Almanac Ratings 2019-2020

	Economy	Social	Foreign	Composite
Liberal	0%	0%	0%	0%
Conservative	100%	100%	100%	100%

Key Votes of the 116th Congress

1. EPA clean energy rules	N	5. Russia sanctions	N	9. Barr as Atty. General	Y
2. U.S./Mex./Can. trade deal	Y	6. Troops in SYR, AFG	Y	10. Spending at the border	Y
3. Cut unemployment benefits	Y	7. Veto arms sales to Saudis	N	11. Coney Barrett to Sup. Ct.	Y
4. Shelton to Fed Reserve	Y	8. Defense $$$, veto override	Y	12. Electoral College objections	N

Election Results

Election	Name (Party)	Vote (%)		Cand. Spent	Ind. Exp. Support	Ind. Exp. Oppose
2020 General	Jim Risch (R)................................	538,446	(63%)	$2,030,188	$1,375	$760
	Paulette Jordan (D)...........................	285,864	(33%)	$1,366,260		
	Natalie Fleming (I)..........................	25,329	(3%)			
2020 Primary	Jim Risch (R)................................	200,184	(100%)			

Prior winning percentages: 2014 (65%), 2008 (58%)

Republican James Risch has voiced blunt-spoken critiques of foreign policy. As chairman of the Foreign Relations Committee during the Trump administration, he occasionally disagreed with the president, though he usually sought to keep those conflicts private.

"If he feels the administration is making an error, he is assertive in pushing back," Sen. Mitt Romney, a committee member, told KTVB, a television station in Risch's hometown of Boise, in 2019. "I watched him in an interaction with the president, and the president didn't like the points of view that Republican senators were expressing. Sen. Risch was relentless and determined, and he succeeded in redirecting an important policy decision."

As the committee's top Republican, Risch has opportunities to deal directly with Democratic President Joe Biden, another former chairman of the Foreign Relations panel, who has often reached across the aisle. "There are very few senators with whom I vote the opposite way more frequently than Jim Risch, but he is responsive and listens, and I appreciate it," Democratic Sen. Chris Coons, another committee member and a Biden confidant, told KTVB.

Risch's record of public service in Idaho has spanned a half-century. Beginning as a local prosecutor, he went on to become a leader in the state Senate and lieutenant governor—and served a seven-month stint as the state's interim governor before his election to the Senate in 2008. Born in Milwaukee, he attended the University of Wisconsin at Milwaukee before transferring to the University of Idaho, where he earned a bachelor's degree in forestry. He became a successful rancher outside Boise and earned his law degree from the state university.

In 1970, when he was 27, Risch was elected Ada County prosecutor, a high-profile position in the state's capital and largest city, Boise. He went after the illicit drug trade so aggressively that his enemies tried to plant a bomb in his car. After that, Risch and his wife and political confidant, Vicki, put tape on the hood of their car every night so they could detect any tampering in the morning.

Risch has been a successful businessman and has been among the Senate's wealthiest members. His business interests have included a property management firm and joint ownership of 250 acres in the Boise area. The Center for Responsive Politics in 2018 listed his net worth as at least $16 million, including large parcels of land in the Boise area.

In 1974, Risch was elected to the Idaho Senate, where he would serve longer than anyone else in state history. He became majority leader after the 1976 election by defeating colleague Larry Craig—whom Risch would succeed in the U.S. Senate three decades later. After six years as majority leader, he spent another six years as Senate president pro tem.

Risch's political career hit a rough patch after he was defeated by a Democratic challenger in 1988. He ran again for the state Senate in 1994, but he lost in the GOP primary. A year later, he returned to that chamber when he was appointed to fill a vacancy. Less confrontational this time around, Risch moved back into the ranks of leadership as assistant Republican floor leader. In 2001, he had his eye on the vacant lieutenant governor's job. Gov. Dirk Kempthorne passed over Risch to appoint state Sen. Jack Riggs to the post. Risch defeated Riggs in the 2002 GOP primary 35%-28%; the rest of the vote was split among four other candidates.

After three years in the shadow of Kempthorne, Risch assumed the top job in 2006 when President George W. Bush tapped Kempthorne to be Interior secretary. Risch had just over half a year to serve in what he considered his dream job and was determined to make the most of it. Within two weeks of taking office, he ordered a reorganization of Idaho's Health and Welfare Department. He created the position of state drug czar to combat the spread of meth. Displeased that the Legislature failed to provide property tax relief during its regular session, Risch called the first special session in 14 years. The heavily Republican body passed bills cutting local property taxes by $260 million, raising the sales tax from 5 percent to 6 percent, and cutting state spending by $50 million. Voters overwhelmingly approved the tax changes.

In an odd twist, Risch returned to his previous post after his stint as governor. In November, Risch defeated former Democratic Rep. Larry LaRocco 58%-39% to become lieutenant governor. But another office soon became available: the Senate seat won by Craig, Risch's old rival. Craig was arrested in a Minneapolis airport men's room in 2007 after soliciting sex from an undercover police officer. He pleaded guilty to disorderly conduct. When Craig decided against seeking reelection in 2008, Risch had little competition for the Republican nomination. Once again, he faced LaRocco in the general election. Risch raised more than twice as much money as his opponent and cruised to victory by a margin of nearly 25 percentage points.

"I'm reputedly the most conservative member of the Senate," Risch told the Boise Metro Chamber of Commerce in 2016. Statistics back him up: Almanac ratings showed that his voting scores have been among the most conservative in the Senate. "I ran for this office as a deficit hawk, and now that I am here, I have moved even further in that direction," Risch told the Idaho Statesman. Risch's aggressive style has at times been a contrast to his more mild-mannered senior colleague, Republican Sen. Mike Crapo, although the two have similar voting records. "Crapo and I are very, very close—we're like brothers," Risch told the Idaho Statesman. "I mean, nobody votes the same more than we do: 99.9 percent of the time."

Risch made his initial imprint in the Senate as a critic of Obama's foreign policy. When the Foreign Relations panel sought to take up the New START arms control treaty with Russia in 2010, Risch tried to stop the vote: He cited new intelligence that he said he couldn't reveal in open session but which had led him to question Russia's intentions. And when the Democratic majority Senate approved the pact, Risch unsuccessfully demanded a delay, noting that Russian troops reportedly had stolen five U.S. Humvees used in military exercises.

After the Russian military supported rebels in eastern Ukraine in 2014, Risch urged the U.S. to provide weapons to the Ukrainian government. During testimony that year by Secretary of State John Kerry, Risch scolded the onetime Foreign Relations chairman. "I tell you, you can't help but get the impression our foreign policy is just spinning out of control. And we are losing control in virtually every area we are trying to do something in," Risch said.

In 2015, when Risch was one of 47 Senate Republicans to sign a letter to Iranian leaders warning that striking a nuclear agreement with the Obama White House without congressional approval could be short-lived, Kerry blasted the move as ignoring "200 years" of precedent in the conduct of foreign policy. Risch call Kerry's statement "absolute nonsense." He argued that senators had the right and responsibility to communicate with foreign officials. Such blunt talk has made Risch a frequent talking head. "He knocks out the television interviews. Risch is knowledgeable, engaging, quick on his feet and easy to understand," Idaho journalist Chuck Malloy said.

In the 2016 presidential campaign, Risch initially supported Sen. Marco Rubio, his ally on Foreign Relations. Like other congressional Republicans, Risch worked to define his relationship with eventual GOP nominee and President Donald Trump. After the 2016 election, his statement omitted mention of the winner. "Americans have clearly expressed their desire to move in the direction of our founders' vision of freedom from government intrusion and the opportunity for personal success," he said.

Risch did not always agree with Trump. But he sought to avoid public conflicts with him, he told KTVB in 2019. "The president and I have disagreements, but I have found the best way to try and have some influence is to keep it between he and I."

When members of Congress in both parties blasted Trump for his July 2018 meeting with Russian President Vladimir Putin in Helsinki, saying the president had been too deferential, Risch defended him. Although he voiced concern with some of Trump's rhetoric during a joint appearance with Putin, Risch told PBS "News Hour," "Even the president's enemies and his critics acknowledge that he has been tougher [with Russia] than anybody else." Risch said that Russia sought to influence the 2016 election, but that there was "no evidence of collusion" with Trump.

In the Mideast, Risch was friendly with Trump's allies. Publicly at least, he refused to hold Saudi leaders responsible for the slaying of journalist Jamal Khashoggi in the Saudi consulate in Istanbul. In July 2019, Risch resisted Senate calls for stiff sanctions on the Saudi royal family for their nation's human rights abuses—contending that Trump would veto such a measure. Instead, three Republicans joined the committee's Democrats, led by Sen. Bob Menendez, to vote for a stronger measure.

Risch has been a strong ally of Israel, praising that nation's moves in 2020 to establish diplomatic relations with the United Arab Emirates and Bahrain, among others. In a statement, he said that he had been "directly involved in encouraging" what he called a "historic breakthrough." The agreements, he added, had the potential "to propel the region into a new era."

Also that year, he stood with Menendez in clashing with Turkish President Recep Tayyip Erdogan over the proposed sale of F-35 fighter jets after Turkey had purchased a missile-defense system from Russia. The U.S. relationship with Turkey "has deteriorated dramatically in recent years and is quickly deteriorating further," Risch told Defense News. The Turkey-Russia arrangement "threatens the integrity of the NATO alliance," he added.

Risch has been blunt in criticizing China, including its crackdown on dissent in Hong Kong. In July 2020, he unveiled a bill that proposed "managed strategic competition" with China, voicing concern that tensions would harm trade between the two nations—and hurt Idaho farmers. "The relationship that we would hope to have would be with a developed country that acts like other developed countries," he told the Spokesman-Review.

On the domestic front, Risch has pushed to rein in the power of the Environmental Protection Agency, telling the Twin Falls Times-News in 2011 that he thought it was possible to have clean air and water "without sending out the Gestapo to enforce the thing." He has reached across the aisle to increase the roles of alternative energy sources, such as biomass and geothermal. He and Crapo joined with Democrats Ron Wyden and Jeff Merkley of Oregon to pass legislation that would have opened public lands to development of geothermal energy. The measure was part of a broader bipartisan energy bill that the Senate passed in 2016.

In 2014, Risch won a second term in the Senate nearly by 2-1. In 2020, he faced Paulette Jordan, who was seeking to become the first Native American woman in the Senate. But she might need to find another state, as Risch won 63%-33%, running nearly even with Trump in the state.

Dealing with Biden, who led Democrats on the Foreign Relations Committee in both the majority and minority, Risch has the opportunity for a constructive relationship—though he likely would not be as adverse to criticism as he was with Trump.

Russ Fulcher (R)

Elected 2018, 2nd term, b. Mar 09, 1962; Meridian, ID; Micron University; Boise State University, B.B.A., 1984; Boise State University, M.B.A., 1988; Protestant; Married (Kara Fulcher); 3 children.

Elected Office: ID Senate, 2005-2014.

Professional Career: Adjunct Professor, Boise State University, 2002-2003; Vice President, Preco Electronics.

DC Office: 1520 LHOB 20515, 202-225-6611, fulcher.house.gov

State Offices: Coeur d'Alene, 208-667-0127; Lewiston, 208-743-1388; Meridian, 208-888-3188.

Committees: *Education & Labor*: Civil Rights & Human Services (RMM); Higher Education & Workforce Investment. *Natural Resources*: National Parks, Forests & Public Lands (RMM); Water, Oceans & Wildlife.

Almanac Ratings 2019-2020

	Economy	Social	Foreign	Composite
Liberal	25%	10%	12%	16%
Conservative	75%	90%	88%	84%

Key Votes of the 116th Congress

1. U.S./Mex./Can. trade deal Y	5. Russia sanctions Y	9. Firearms background checks N	
2. First Coronavirus response N	6. Troops in Syria N	10. Spending at the border Y	
3. HEROES Act N	7. Veto arms sales to Saudis N	11. Marijuana liberalized rules N	
4. CASH Act N	8. Defense $$$, veto override N	12. Electoral College objections Y	

Election Results

Election	Name (Party)	Vote (%)		Cand. Spent	Ind. Exp. Support	Ind. Exp. Oppose
2020 General	Russ Fulcher (R)	310,736	(68%)	$378,525	$805	$750
	Rudy Soto (D)	131,380	(29%)	$305,469	$1,625	
	Joe Evans (L)	16,453	(4%)			
2020 Primary	Russ Fulcher (R)	93,879	(80%)			
	Nicholas Jones (R)	23,654	(20%)			

Prior winning percentages: 2018 (63%)

Republican Russ Fulcher, an outspoken conservative, easily won in 2018 the seat that was opened by Rep. Raul Labrador, who ran unsuccessfully in the GOP primary for Idaho governor. The victory revived his political career following Fulcher's loss to Gov. Butch Otter in the 2014 GOP primary. Fulcher's narrow defeat to Otter, who served three terms as governor, positioned him as the frontrunner after Labrador sought to move up the political ladder. Fulcher, like Labrador during his four terms in the House, was strongly supported by national conservative groups. The Idaho Press described his persona as "unwavering but amiable."

Fulcher grew up on a dairy farm in Meridian and received his bachelor's degree and a master's in business administration from Boise State University. He was a marketing executive and later handled international sales for Boise-based technology companies Micron Technology and Preco Electronics. Fulcher also was a commercial real estate broker, and he gained expertise in electrical engineering and energy policy.

He served 10 years in the state Senate, where he was chairman of the Republican Caucus. During that time, he criticized Otter for cooperating with the Obama administration to set up a health insurance exchange in Idaho as part of the Affordable Care Act. "Idaho became the administrator for a federal healthcare law that Idahoans do not want and cannot afford," said Fulcher, who joined other Republicans in the legislature to oppose the proposal. Later, Fulcher said the action resulted in a huge increase in the state's health insurance costs. In 2014, Fulcher lost the GOP primary to Otter, 51%-44%.

Running for Congress, Fulcher was endorsed by numerous conservative activists and interest groups, including the House Freedom Caucus and the Club for Growth, which described Fulcher as "the only conservative" in the contest. Also endorsing him was Labrador, who earlier backed Fulcher's challenge to Otter and said that Fulcher would continue his "fight for liberty" in Washington. (Fulcher had launched a second bid for governor, but switched his plans when Labrador decided to seek the office.) His chief opponent was 70-year-old trial lawyer David Leroy, who was the state's attorney general and lieutenant governor more than 30 years earlier and lost a Republican primary for Congress in 1994.

As a familiar figure in Idaho politics, Fulcher easily led the primary with 43 percent of the vote to 15 percent for Leroy and 14 percent for state Rep. Luke Malek, who said he voted for independent Evan McMullin in the 2016 presidential election. Fulcher won each of the 19 counties in the district. Fulcher raised more than $500,000 for the primary, in addition to a similar amount the Club for Growth spent on his behalf. Leroy led the other candidates in fundraising, with about $362,000.

Fulcher's success in November over Democrat Christina McNeil, a real estate agent and an advocate for immigrants, was never in doubt. A few days after the primary, Fulcher added some excitement to the contest when he suffered broken ribs and was hospitalized following a spill while riding a motorcycle.

In the House, Fulcher sided with the more partisan cadre of House Republicans. In October 2019, he joined about two dozen other members who disrupted a closed-door meeting of the House Intelligence Committee as it was holding a hearing related to impeachment charges against President Donald Trump. His aide said Fulcher objected to the secrecy of the hearing.

Taking the opposite side from Republican Rep. Mike Simpson, his Idaho colleague, Fulcher voted against bipartisan legislation to increase spending to buy and preserve national parks and other public lands. "Federal resources are stretched so thin," Fulcher said. Both Senators from Idaho also voted against the bill. He voted against the extension of the Foreign Intelligence Surveillance Act, citing the need for "a reasonable expectation of privacy," including for business records.

Seeking reelection in 2020, Fulcher was challenged by Democrat Rudy Soto, a military veteran and legislative director of the National Indian Gaming Association. In an editorial, the Idaho

Statesman endorsed Soto, while citing his advocacy of bipartisanship and problem solving, and criticized Fulcher as "among the representatives least likely to vote with or cosponsor legislation with members of the other party." Fulcher won, 68%-29%.

ID-1: Western Idaho

Cook Partisan Voting Index: R+22

Population		Race and Ethnicity		Income	
Total	934,826	White	88.70%	Median Income	$62,886
Land area (sq. miles)	39,418	Black	0.80%	District Income Rank	225
Pop/ sq mi	23.72	Latino	11.50%	Poverty Rate	9.40%
Born in State	41.40%	Asian	1.20%	With health insurance	89.10%
		Two or more races	3.60%	Cash public assistance	2.40%
Age Groups		Other	5.70%	Food stamp/SNAP	7.50%
Under 18	24.50%				
18-34	20.40%	**Education**		**Work**	
35-64	37.60%	H.S grad or less	35.10%	White Collar	34.80%
Over 64	17.50%	Some college	37.60%	Sales and Service	40.30%
		College Degree, 4 yr	18.00%	Blue Collar	24.90%
Military		Post grad	9.20%	Government	14.40%
Veteran/ Active Duty	10.40%				

2020 Pres. Vote	Trump	313,559	(67%)	Biden	140,452	(30%)			
2016 Pres. Vote	Trump	229,034	(64%)	Clinton	91,284	(25%)	McMullin	16,087	(5%)
	Johnson	14,916	(4%)						

Western Boise, Coeur D'Alene: The 1st Congressional District of Idaho stretches 479 miles from the Nevada border to Canada and includes the outskirts of Boise and all the panhandle. It encompasses two high-growth areas: the western suburbs of Boise and the Coeur d'Alene area in Kootenai County. Coeur d'Alene, which is in the mountains, is about 30 miles east of Spokane Washington. With 2,000 employees, its largest employer is the family-owned Hagadone Corp, a full-service digital marketing agency. Headquartered in an 18-story resort hotel on its name-sake lake, the company publishes more than 20 newspapers, has its own advertising agency, and offers hospitality and real estate services. In Coeur d'Alene, wealthy retirees from California account for much of the population growth.

To the south outside of Boise, commercial developers took over land in Nampa that not long ago grew wheat and alfalfa. The population nearly doubled in the 1990s, and it became Idaho's second-largest city. Since 2010, the boom in subdivisions has switched to nearby Meridian, which grew 48 percent from 2010 to 2019 and became the fastest-growing city in the state. With population exceeding 114,000, it surpassed Nampa and was the tenth fastest-growing city in the nation in 2017. "We all anticipated that Meridian would grow fast, but Meridian is fast even by Meridian standards," a local demographics planner told the Idaho Statesman in 2018.Closer-in Meridian is part of Boise-based Ada County, which is split between the state's two districts, with most of the city in the 2nd and the suburbs in the 1st.

The town of Star, a 30-minute drive west of Boise, might be the next "fastest-growing" place in the fastest-growing state. With a population of 10,500—which nearly doubled from 2010 to 2019 —Star has drawn many retirees to a place where not long ago ranchers drove their cattle, The Wall Street Journal reported in January 2020. But, alas, even this site faces traffic congestion at rush hour. Trevor Chadwick, who took over as mayor after defeating the incumbent with 73 percent of the vote, said, "managing growth is his priority," the Journal reported.

The growth in these once-rural areas has reinforced, rather than altered, the political landscape. Newcomers routinely say they moved to conservative Idaho to escape from city life, although some old-timers still worry that their communities might become new versions of San Jose or Orange County. Politically, the 1st District of Idaho is overwhelmingly Republican. Northern mining counties were once the district's Democratic base; now that base is the university town of Moscow in Latah County. In the three presidential elections since 2012, Latah was the larger of only two counties to vote for the Democratic presidential nominee each time—50%-46% in 2020. That year, the decrease in the third-party vote resulted in an increase of a few percentage points for both major parties. In the 1st, President Donald Trump led Joe Biden, 67%-30%.

Mike Simpson (R)

Elected 1998, 12th term, b. Sep 08, 1950; Burley,ID; UT State University, Att., 1972; WA University School of Dental Medicine, D.D.S., 1977; UT State University, B.S., 2002; Mormon; Married (Kathy Johnson Simpson).

Elected Office: Blackfoot City Council, 1980-1984; ID House, 1984-1998, speaker, 1993-1998.

Professional Career: Practicing dentist, 1977-1998.

DC Office: 2084 RHOB 20515, 202-225-5531, Fax: 202-225-8216, simpson.house.gov

State Offices: Boise, 208-334-1953; Idaho Falls, 208-523-6701; Twin Falls, 208-734-7219.

Committees: *Appropriations*: Energy & Water Development & Related Agencies (RMM); Interior, Environment & Related Agencies.

Group Ratings

	ADA	ACLU	AFL-CIO	LCV	COC	HAFA	ACU	CFG	FRC
2020	**	21%	**	19%	-	66%	75%	**	-
2019	15%	C	48%	21%	86%	C	75%	56%	86%

Almanac Ratings 2019-2020

	Economy	Social	Foreign	Composite
Liberal	25%	43%	33%	34%
Conservative	75%	57%	67%	66%

Key Votes of the 116th Congress

1. U.S./Mex./Can. trade deal Y	5. Russia sanctions Y	9. Firearms background checks N
2. First Coronavirus response Y	6. Troops in Syria Y	10. Spending at the border Y
3. HEROES Act N	7. Veto arms sales to Saudis N	11. Marijuana liberalized rules N
4. CASH Act N	8. Defense $$$, veto override Y	12. Electoral College objections N

Election Results

Election	Name (Party)	Vote (%)		Cand. Spent	Ind. Exp. Support	Ind. Exp. Oppose
2020 General	Mike Simpson (R)	250,669	(64%)	$934,441	$98,084	
	C. Aaron Swisher (D)	124,151	(32%)	$61,178		
	Idaho Sierra Law (L)	8,573	(2%)			
	Pro-Life (C)	7,940	(2%)			
2020 Primary	Mike Simpson (R)	68,675	(72%)			
	Kevin Rhoades (R)	26,724	(28%)			

Prior winning percentages: 2018 (61%), 2016 (63%), 2014 (61%), 2012 (65%), 2010 (69%), 2008 (71%), 2006 (62%), 2004 (71%), 2002 (68%), 2000 (71%), 1998 (53%)

Mike Simpson, an independent-minded and hardworking Republican first elected in 1998, has been an influential lawmaker regardless of which party controls the House. He has used his post on the Appropriations Committee to deliver huge federal benefits to his district and to enact sweeping federal lands and energy policies. He often reaches out to Democrats on economic and social issues. He easily defeated a primary challenge from the right in 2014.

Simpson grew up in Blackfoot, became a dentist, and joined his father's dental practice. He was elected to the city council in 1980 and to the state House in 1984. In 1993, he became speaker of the Idaho House while he maintained his dental practice. In the legislature, he was known as a moderate in a conservative chamber, affable and able to get differing sides together. When Republican Gov. Phil Batt announced he would retire in 1998, Simpson wanted to run, but GOP Sen. Dirk Kempthorne's decision to seek the office closed that option. Instead, he ran for the House when GOP Rep. Mike Crapo went for Kempthorne's Senate seat.

The election was hotly contested. In the Republican primary, state Rep. Mark Stubbs opposed nuclear programs at the Idaho National Laboratory, while Simpson wanted more work at the facility. Simpson refused to take a pledge to serve only three terms; the other candidates agreed to it. Term-limit advocates spent heavily against Simpson. Simpson ran ads against "out-of-state folk" interfering with Idaho's elections. He beat Stubbs 47%-41%.The Democratic nominee, Richard Stallings, emphasized his conservative voting record when he earlier served four terms in the House. Simpson won 53%-45%, losing Pocatello, Sun Valley and Boise, but winning just about everywhere else.

Simpson's open-mindedness led Esquire magazine in 2008 to call him one of the 10 best members of Congress, saying he "lives by the philosophy that democratic representation is a matter of finding not advantageous positions but common ground." He was one of just 16 House Republicans in March 2012 to back a budget plan along the lines of the bipartisan commission chaired by Alan Simpson (not related) and Erskine Bowles, and he led a bipartisan group of legislators urging budget negotiators to "go big" and look at raising taxes as well as cutting spending.

Simpson has wielded his influence on the Appropriations Committee to secure funding for the Bureau of Reclamation, the Army Corps of Engineers and the Idaho National Laboratory in his district. As a leading defender of appropriations earmarks, he disagreed when his friend Speaker John Boehner eliminated them, though Simpson supported greater transparency in the process. As chairman of the Energy and Water Development Subcommittee from 2013 to 2018, he promoted the Idaho Lab and other efforts to spur energy independence for the United States. In 2015, he played a key parliamentary role in breaking the deadlock on funding the Homeland Security Department, even though he did not serve on the subcommittee responsible for that bill.

In 2015, Simpson also gained a legacy victory when President Barack Obama signed the Saw tooth National Recreation Area and Jerry Peak Wilderness Additions Act, which included the Boulder-White Cloud Management Area designating 276,000 acres in central Idaho as wilderness, prohibiting development. He spent more than a decade negotiating the plan with numerous constituencies ranging from mountain bikers to environmentalists, only to run into opposition from fellow Idaho Republicans. Having earlier warned that he would "die trying" to make a deal, Simpson filed a scaled-down version to find common ground and to pre-empt potential unilateral action by Obama to declare the area a national monument. "The threat of a national monument, I think, convinced a lot of people it was better to have an Idaho solution than one imposed by Washington D.C.," Simpson said.

After easily winning reelection, he encountered problems in 2010, when his support for the rescue of the financial markets and other independent stances drew two primary opponents. They held Simpson to 58 percent. By 2014, Simpson's legislative rating from the conservative group Heritage Action was 45 percent. The anti-tax group Club for Growth spent more than $500,000 on behalf of Bryan Smith, who sought to portray Simpson as a Washington insider who was a captive of special interests. The U.S. Chamber of Commerce, the National Rifle Association, the National Association of Realtors and other groups responded by pouring in about $4 million on Simpson's behalf; that might have proved Smith's point, but it didn't help him electorally. Mitt Romney, a fellow Mormon, appeared in a Simpson ad. Smith ran ads criticizing Simpson as a "supporter of earmarks." In the primary, Simpson coasted to an easy 62%-38% victory. In November, Stallings again tried a comeback and lost 61%-39%. In the 2020 primary, challenger Kevin Rhoades said that Simpson was "not a real conservative." Simpson won, 72%-28%.

Despite the internal Republican schisms, Simpson appeared to be more influential and outspoken than ever. A month before the 2016 election, he stated that Donald Trump was "unfit to be president" and reiterated that he had never endorsed him. That view drew some support for Simpson at home. With Trump as president, Simpson remained an occasionally harsh critic. When Trump in the Oval Office publicly referred to "shithole" countries in the developing world, Simpson called his comment "stupid and irresponsible and childish." When Trump's clash with Congress over spending caused the government to shut down after the 2018 election, Simpson showed his impatience with the president. "It's very difficult to negotiate anything, because you don't know if he's going to stick with it," adding his unhappiness that countless Idahoans who were federal employees were unable to perform basic tasks.

Following the 2018 election, Simpson supported Kay Granger of Texas—who outranked him in seniority—as the new senior Republican on Appropriations. If she had been defeated, he said earlier, he would have run for the position. He might have other opportunities to fill the top slot.

Meanwhile, he continued to deliver for his constituents. The big spending bill enacted at the end of 2020 included several hefty allotments for the Idaho Lab, including $115 million for the Advanced

Small Modular Reactor program, $30 million for the National Reactor Innovation Center and $26 million for construction of the Sample Preparation Laboratory. Also in 2020, Simpson was the lead House Republican sponsor of the bipartisan bill that Congress enacted to pay for maintenance projects in national parks.

ID-2: Eastern Idaho

Cook Partisan Voting Index: R+15

Population		Race and Ethnicity		Income	
Total	852,239	White	90.10%	Median Income	$58,708
Land area (sq. miles)	43,225	Black	0.60%	District Income Rank	285
Pop/ sq mi	19.72	Latino	14.30%	Poverty Rate	13.10%
Born in State	51.20%	Asian	1.70%	With health insurance	89.20%
		Two or more races	3.00%	Cash public assistance	2.20%
Age Groups		Other	4.60%	Food stamp/SNAP	9.20%
Under 18	25.80%				
18-34	24.70%	Education		Work	
35-64	34.80%	H.S grad or less	33.90%	White Collar	36.30%
Over 64	14.60%	Some college	35.60%	Sales and Service	38.50%
		College Degree, 4 yr	19.80%	Blue Collar	25.20%
Military		Post grad	10.80%	Government	14.20%
Veteran/ Active Duty	8.40%				

2020 Pres. Vote	Trump	240,560	(60%)	Biden	146,569	(37%)	Jorgensen	8,093	(2%)
2016 Pres. Vote	Trump	180,021	(54%)	Clinton	98,481	(30%)	McMullin	30,389	(9%)
	Johnson	13,415	(4%)					

Eastern Boise, Idaho Falls: The 2nd District of Idaho, from Boise east to the Wyoming border, is one of America's most picturesque, with thick forests, mountain ranges, broad river valleys and vacant expanses. It was settled from the east by overland pioneers who stopped in Idaho to establish farms, and from the south by Mormons moving up from Utah to Franklin, Bear Lake and Caribou counties. It has one of the largest concentrations of Mormons among congressional districts.

On Interstate 15, Idaho Falls serves as the modern metropolis for a vast region stretching from West Yellowstone, Montana, to the Salmon River Mountains. Near Idaho Falls, on a windswept, desolate range is Idaho National Laboratory, known locally as "The Site." The Energy Department's leading laboratory for civilian nuclear energy research, development and demonstration, the facility covers 890 square miles and employs about 4,000 workers. It has helped to keep the area's economy stable, thanks in part to its work cleaning up Cold War-era nuclear plants. The Naval Nuclear Propulsion Program has launched a $1.6 billion facility at the lab to handle spent fuel.

The Lab's new cyber security research center examines emerging threats, with the goal of protecting the economy and public safety. Utah Associated Municipal Power Systems has begun work on a commercial nuclear reactor plant, which has been designed as a model for several nuclear power sites in the West; in August 2020, the Nuclear Regulatory Commission completed its technical review. In Twin Falls, Greek yogurt maker Chobani operates one of the largest yogurt-processing plants in the world and employs more than 700 people. Near Shoshone, developers planned to start construction in 2022 of one of the largest wind farms in the world.

To the west, amid the mountains, are Sun Valley and the nearby town of Ketchum. Sun Valley was established as a ski resort in 1936 by business mogul Averell Harriman before he began his political career. Ketchum attracted writer Ernest Hemingway in 1939, and various movie stars followed. In recent years, Blaine County has attracted rich expatriates from the East and West coasts, who have made it the most Democratic county in Idaho. Otherwise, the Idaho Falls area and the farmland along the Snake River have been among the most Republican areas in the nation.

The 2nd District of Idaho includes most of Boise, where high-tech businesses and tourism have fueled the economy. Boise is home to Micron Technology, which is a leading patent holder for digital memory and employs more than 6,000 people. The city has been among the fastest growing in the nation, though its growth relative to the rest of the state has slowed since 2010. Forbes ranked it number-two as the favorite location for young professionals in 2017. Donald Trump defeated Joe Biden here, 60%-37%, several points tighter than in the 1st District.

ILLINOIS

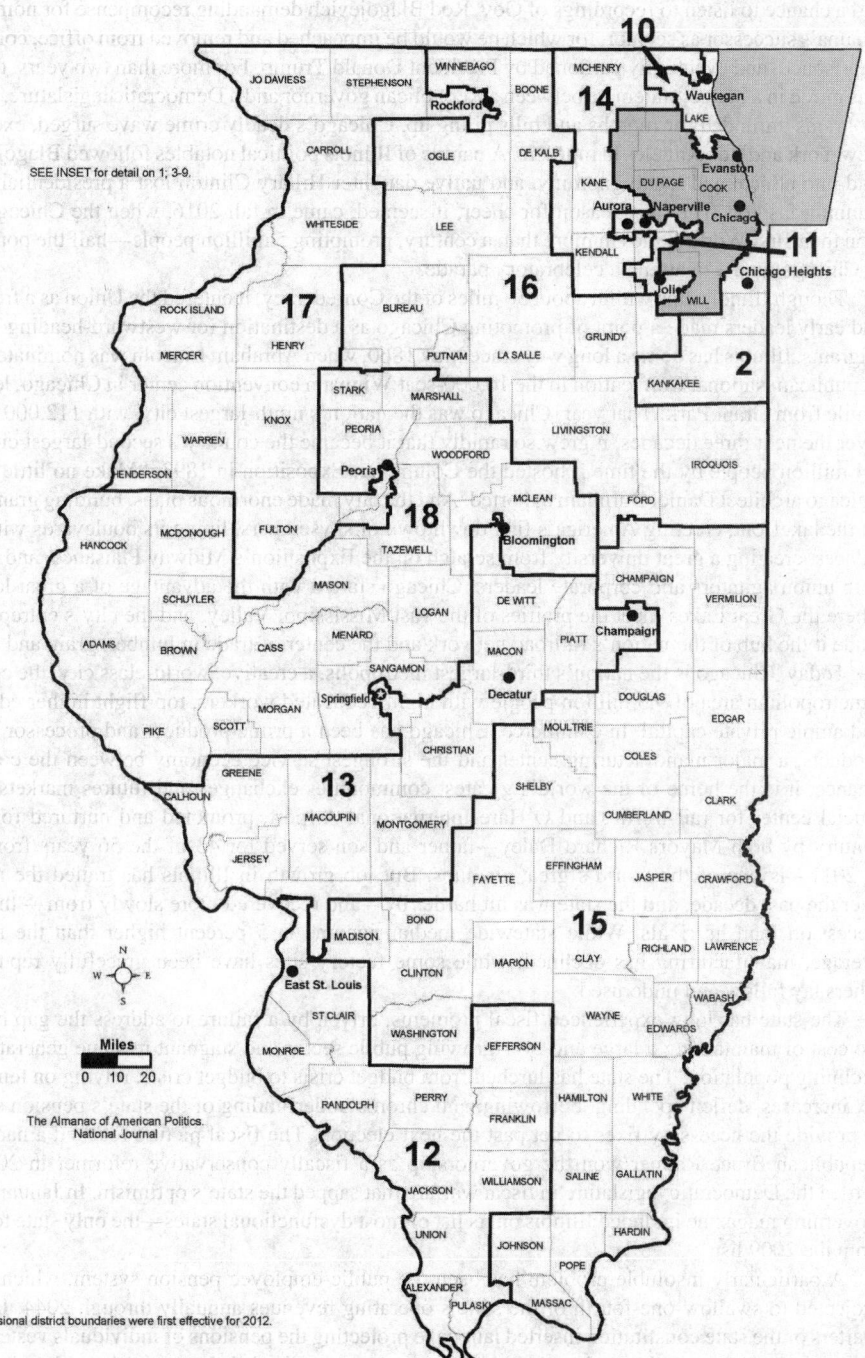

SEE INSET for detail on 1; 3-9.

The Almanac of American Politics.
National Journal

Congressional district boundaries were first effective for 2012.

For just over a decade, Illinois and the giant city that dominates it, Chicago, have experienced the best and the worst of times. On Election Night 2008, a million people thronged to Chicago's lakefront Grant Park to cheer Barack Obama, one of their own. Then, only a month later, the public had a chance to listen to recordings of Gov. Rod Blagojevich demanding recompense for nominating Obama's successor as senator, for which he would be impeached and removed from office, convicted, imprisoned, and eventually pardoned by President Donald Trump. For more than two years, the state was mired in a budget stalemate between a Republican governor and a Democratic legislature, leaving programs unfunded for months and bills piling up. Chicago's deadly crime wave surged, exceeding New York and Los Angeles in murders. A parade of Illinois political notables followed Blagojevich's lead into ethical and legal ignominy, and native daughter Hillary Clinton lost a presidential race in stunning fashion. The only reason for cheer, it seemed, came in fall 2016, when the Chicago Cubs won their first World Series in more than a century, prompting 5 million people—half the population of Chicago land—to attend a celebratory parade.

Though Illinois dips within about 50 miles of the Confederacy, it entered the Union as a free state, and early leaders made a point of promoting Chicago as a destination for westward-heading Yankee migrants. Illinois has come a long way since May 1860, when Abraham Lincoln was nominated at the Republican National Convention in the 10,000-seat Wigwam convention center in Chicago, less than a mile from Grant Park. That year, Chicago was the nation's ninth-largest city, with 112,000 people. Over the next three decades, it grew so rapidly that it became the country's second-largest city, with 1.4 million people by the time it hosted the Columbian Exposition in 1893. "Make no little plans," Chicago architect Daniel Burnham exhorted. And the city made enormous plans, building grand parks on the lakefront, erecting America's first downtown of skyscrapers, lining its boulevards with retail palaces, creating a great university from scratch on the Exposition's Midway Plaisance, and hosting both union agitators and corporate leaders. Chicago started with the advantage of a great location, where the Great Lakes meet the prairies of the vast Mississippi Valley, and the city's entrepreneurs made it the hub of the nation's railroad network and the center of trade in lumber, grain and meat.

Today, Chicago is the nation's third-largest metropolis, a creative, world-class city, the center of a metropolitan area of 9.5 million people with highly educated workers, top-flight higher education and ample private capital. In commerce, Chicago has been a prime producer and processor of food products, a major manufacturing center and the strongest service economy between the coasts. In finance, it is the home of the world's greatest commodities exchanges and futures markets. It is a crucial center for rail traffic, and O'Hare International Airport, promoted and nurtured for half a century by both Mayors Richard Daley—father and son served for 43 of the 56 years from 1955 to 2011—is one of the world's great air hubs. But job growth in Illinois has trailed the nation's over the past decade, and the state was hit harder by—and recovered more slowly from— the Great Recession than its rivals. While statewide median income is 5 percent higher than the national average, manufacturing has declined; while some factory sites have been gracefully repurposed, others lay fallow and underused.

The state has long experienced fiscal problems, driven by a failure to address the gap between the cost of maintaining a large and ever-growing public sector and stagnant revenue generated by a declining population. The state has lurched from budget crisis to budget crisis, relying on temporary tax increases, deficit spending, borrowing, and chronic underfunding of the state's pension systems to provide the necessary fixes to get past the next election. The fiscal picture reached a nadir after Republican Bruce Rauner won the governorship as a fiscally conservative reformer in 2014 and battled the Democratic legislature in fiscal warfare that sapped the state's optimism. In January 2018, Governing magazine included Illinois on its list of most dysfunctional states—the only state to repeat from the 2009 list.

A particularly insoluble problem has been the public-employee pension system, which is now projected to swallow one-fourth of the state's operating revenues annually through 2044. In 1970, drafters of the state constitution inserted language protecting the pensions of individuals vested under a state system from being reduced. But the state consistently failed to fund its obligations, and subsequent legislative revisions to increase benefits were popular with state employees and their unions even as they exacerbated the problem. A new law was enacted in 2010 that significantly curtailed benefits for new employees while not affecting pensions for those in the old system. In 2013, the legislature passed a fix that might have made a dent by reducing benefits served by the old system, but two years later the state Supreme Court—citing the constitutional provision—unanimously struck down the law. Illinois' unfunded pension liability is now $153 billion, and Fitch, Moody's and Standard & Poor's rate the state's credit barely above junk status.

Map for Greater Chicago

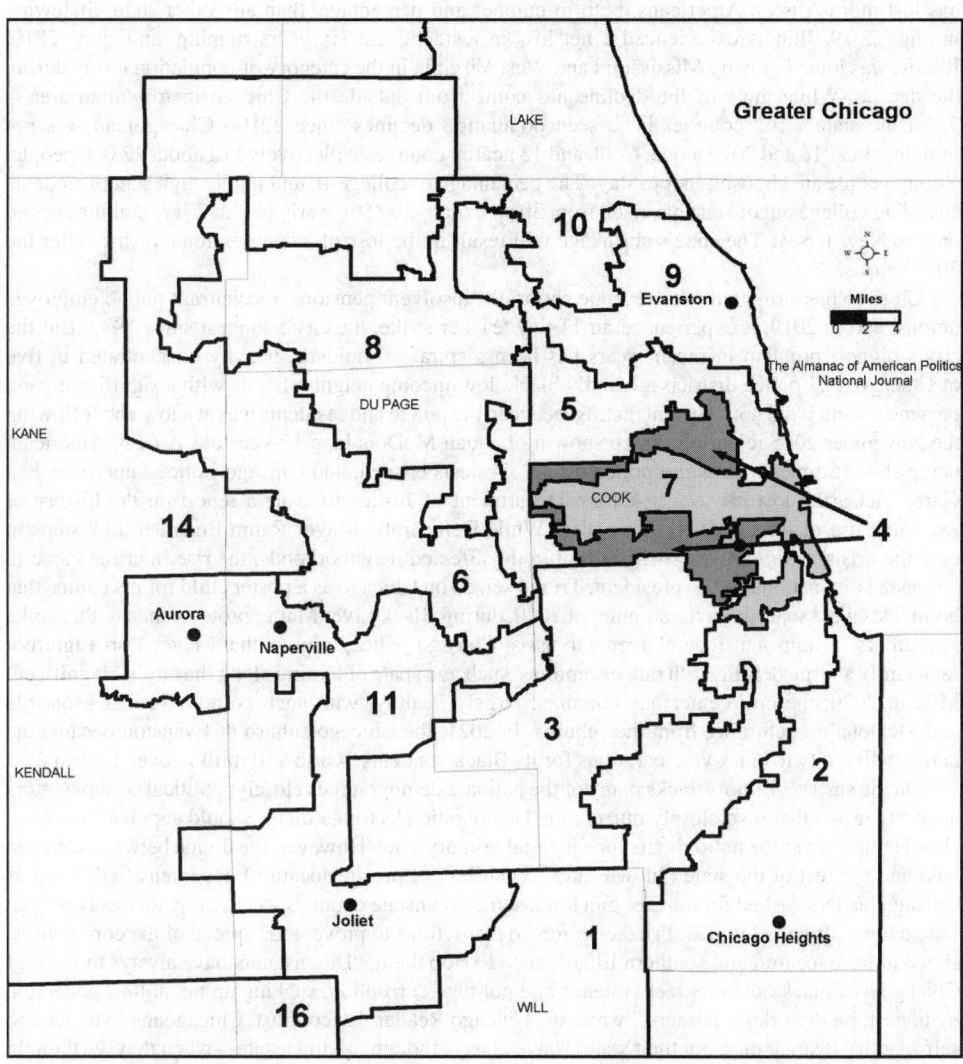

Congressional district boundaries were first effective for 2012.   Districts 4 and 7 are highlighted for visibility.

Waves of immigrants moved to Chicago—first Irish and German then Polish, Italian and Jewish in the Ellis Island years. Then, during the mid-20th century, Chicago became a mecca for African Americans as a primary destination for the migration of millions of Blacks who left the South. The shift in population was sweeping: Journalist Nicholas Lemann was moved to write his landmark book about the migration, The Promised Land, after hearing an announcement on a Chicago radio station about a reunion being held locally for a predominantly black high school class from Canton Mississippi. There was no point in holding the reunion in Mississippi; after graduating in 1955, virtually everyone had come north. Later, Chicago attracted hundreds of thousands of Hispanics. That shift can be seen in the Chicago neighborhood of Pilsen, the "Heart of Chicago" where Germans and Irish migrated in the 1860s and 1870s, followed later by Poles and Czechs. Now, bodegas and

Mexican bakeries line its lively South Side commercial center along 18th Street, reflecting the influx of Mexicans and, more recently, Guatemalans and Salvadorans.

Today, Cook County (which includes Chicago, plus such suburbs as Arlington Heights, Evanston, Skokie, and Des Plaines) is 24 percent African American, 26 percent Hispanic and 8 percent Asian. Since 2010, the number of Chicago-area residents born in Asia has risen by 60,000, even as the state has lost more African Americans, both in number and percentage, than any other state. Statewide through 2019, Illinois experienced a net loss in residents for six years running, and since 2010, Illinois was joined only by Mississippi and West Virginia in the category of population losers during the decade. While most of the decline has come from outside the Chicago metropolitan area— 93 of the state's 102 counties have seen population declines since 2010—Chicagoland was not immune. In 2018 and 2019 alone, Cook and 13 nearby counties collectively lost about 22,000 people. Young people are choosing not to stay: The percentage of college-bound public high school students attending college out of state has risen from 30 percent in 2002 to nearly half in 2017, ranking second only to New Jersey. The state's shrinkage will result in the loss of a congressional district after the 2020 census.

Chicago has struggled with revenue shortfalls, insolvent pensions, recalcitrant public employee unions, and in 2019, it experienced an 11-day teacher strike, the city's longest since 1987. But the city's biggest problem in recent years has been a spiral of violence, heavily concentrated in five of Chicago's 22 police districts—heavily black, low-income neighborhoods with a significant gang presence—and it did not help that distrust between the police and residents was at a low ebb following the November 2015 release of video showing Laquan McDonald, a 17-year-old African American, being shot 16 times by a white police officer. Protests ensued, and Chicago Police Superintendent Garry McCarthy lost his job. It led the Department of Justice to issue a report on the history of excessive use of force by Chicago police. While Democratic Mayor Rahm Emanuel took steps to ease the crisis and improve prospects within the affected neighborhoods, the rise in crime came to define the city nationally. As president, Trump seized on Chicago as a poster child for his claims that homicides were soaring. In the summer of 2020, during Black Lives Matter protests and another spike in murders, Trump sent federal agents to assist Chicago police, a move that Mayor Lori Lightfoot reluctantly accepted. Still, with rare exceptions, such as a spate of looting along the city's Magnificent Mile in 2020, the city center has remained largely healthy, with such corporations as Motorola and McDonald's returning from the suburbs. In 2021, the Chicago suburb of Evanston became the nation's first city to approve reparations for its Black residents, worth $10 million over 10 years.

On the surface, Illinois tracks many of the nation's demographics closely; political commentators have suggested that it so closely mirrors the Democratic electorate that it should supplant Iowa and New Hampshire as the nation's first presidential primary state. However, the divide between Chicago land and the rest of the state ("downstate," regardless of precise location) has intensified. Even as Chicago leaders wished for tougher gun laws, some downstate counties were voting themselves "gun sanctuaries." When Gov. J.B. Pritzker enforced restrictions to prevent the spread of the coronavirus, six counties in central and southern Illinois sued to stop them. "Downstaters have always thought of Chicago as a black hole of street violence and political corruption, sucking up tax dollars generated by honest, hard-working farmers," wrote the Chicago Reader. By contrast, Chicagoans (who tend to self-identify by their city, not their state) "have always thought of downstate—when they've thought of it at all—as an irrelevant agricultural appendage full of Baptists and gun owners who'd just love to turn Illinois into North Kentucky." Decades of deindustrialization and political polarization have only widened those gaps. "Without the Chicagoland area, Illinois would have fewer people than Connecticut," Stateline.org has noted.

Obama and Emanuel—who was succeeded in 2019 by Lightfoot, the city's first openly gay mayor and the first African-American woman to win the office—are just the most recent Illinois politicians to stand astride the national scene. Yet Illinois political history is rife with machine politics and cronyism. Since 2000, there have been nearly 900 public corruption convictions in Illinois, according to Chicago's WLS-TV, more than any other state. Even Lincoln was no stranger to the party machine of his day, which rallied thousands of Republicans to cheer him at his debates with Stephen Douglas in 1858 and packed the Wigwam for him in 1860. Machine politics continued in the 20th century, as politicians in a closely divided state competed for public jobs and as politicians of both parties courted the immigrants streaming into Chicago. Four Illinois governors in the past 50 years have gone to the pokey, and former Republican House Speaker Dennis Hastert was sentenced to 15 months in a blackmail case that revealed his past sexual abuse of young boys as a wrestling coach. In 2020 and 2021, the legislature's powerhouse since the early 1980s, House Speaker Michael Madigan, was ousted after prosecutors produced a flurry of indictments of the speaker's allies, related to a years-long influence scheme involving the utility ComEd. "Basically, we have one of the last old-school political machines in the country," Fritz Kaegi, Cook County's reformist assessor, told Politico. "Madigan's a lineal descendant of that tradition, and people don't think it works."

Politically, Illinois emerged from the Civil War as a solidly Republican state, with fast-growing Chicago and the northern counties settled by Yankees decisively outvoting the southern folk from Springfield south to Cairo (pronounced Kay-roe), which is closer to Mississippi than to Chicago. During the Depression, Chicago became reliably Democratic. In the decades that followed, the suburbs, wary of Chicago, became Republican (and developed machines of their own). For generations, downstate politicians offered an attractive balance to Chicago dominance— Democratic Sens. Alan Dixon and Paul Simon, and Republican Govs. Jim Edgar and George Ryan. But since 2002, suburban Cook has moved from purple to blue, the collar counties have shifted from red to blue, and downstate has moved from purple to red. On balance, this means the state has moved from purple to blue: In 2016, a moderate Republican from the Chicago suburbs, Mark Kirk, was unable to keep Democrat Tammy Duckworth from flipping his Senate seat, and Hillary Clinton won the state by a yawning 17 points. Two years later, Democrats won all of Illinois' statewide offices along with historic majorities in the legislature. Downstate, meanwhile, Democrats rooted in mining or manufacturing have all but disappeared, in favor of Republican dominance. Only six of the 41 Democratic state senators and nine of the 73 Democratic state representatives in 2021 will be from downstate, and none of them represent a rural district.

In the 2020 presidential race, Trump improved his showing slightly more than Joe Biden did over Clinton's performance, but it hardly mattered, as Biden won the state by 17 points. Biden flipped one county from red to blue: McLean (Bloomington), the home of Illinois State University and State Farm Insurance. But the most striking and significant shifts continued to occur in Chicagoland. In Cook and its five collar counties—DuPage, Kane, Lake, McHenry, and Will—Biden increased the collective Democratic vote total by 12 percent over its 2016 level and by 22 percent over what favorite son Obama achieved in 2012. In each of the collar counties, the number of Democratic votes increased by between 28 and 44 percent from 2012 to 2020. In turn, Republicans have lost their dominance of county elections in the collar counties; only McHenry remains a GOP stronghold at the local level. Illinois may have a shrinking population, but it's one that has become bluer than ever.

Population		Race and Ethnicity		Income	
Total	12,671,821	White	71.40%	Median Income	69,187
Land area (sq. miles)	55,519	Black	14.10%	State Income Rank	17 out of 50
Pop/ sq mi	228.24	Latino	17.50%	Poverty Rate	11.50%
Born in state	67.40%	Asian	6.60%	With health insurance	92.60%
		Two or more races	2.80%	Cash public assistance	2.00%
Age Groups		Other	6.10%	Food stamp/SNAP	13.3%
Under 18	22.20%				
18-34	22.90%	Education		Work	
35-64	38.60%	H.S grad or less	36.10%	White Collar	40.70%
Over 64	16.10%	Some college	28.20%	Sales and Service	37.30%
		College Degree, 4 yr	21.70%	Blue Collar	22.00%
Military		Post grad	14.10%	Government	12.40%
Veteran/ Active Duty	5.50%				

Presidential Politics

2020 Primary (D)	Biden (D)	986,661 (59%)	Sanders (D)	605,701 (36%)		
2020 Pres. Vote	Biden (D)	3,471,915 (57%)	Trump (R)	2,446,891 (40%)		
2016 Pres. Vote	Clinton (D)	3,090,729 (55%)	Trump (R)	2,146,015 (38%)	Johnson (L)	209,596 (4%)

For a century, Illinois was a political bellwether, voting only twice for losing presidential candidates between 1896 and 1996—in 1916 and 1976, when it went Republican while the nation went Democratic. It even sided with Dwight Eisenhower in 1952 and 1956, against native son Adlai Stevenson. But starting in the 1990s, Illinois has become significantly more Democratic than the nation. It voted 55 percent for Al Gore and John Kerry in 2000 and 2004 and gave home-stater Barack Obama 62 percent in 2008 and 58 percent in 2012. Hillary Clinton, who was born in Chicago, saw the Democratic percentage dip in 2016 when she bested Donald Trump in the state, 56%-39%; Joe Biden, lacking any hometown connections, won by a similar 57.5%-40.5%. But Illinois' internal politics have continued to shift. The state once pitted Democratic Chicago against its Republican suburbs, with the real fight downstate. Now, a long trend of suburban shifts left and rural shifts right has pushed the state as a whole toward Democrats but large swaths of rural territory out of their reach. As happened in other urban areas, Biden's margins shrunk a bit in Cook County, home to Chicago and 41 percent of the state's population. But he did even better than Clinton had in the five collar counties that make up Chicago's suburban core, outperforming both Clinton and Obama in DuPage, Kane, Lake, McHenry and Will counties.

Downstate Illinois is another story. Counties along the Mississippi River that traditionally voted Democratic sided with Trump in 2016 and 2020. Obama won 11 of the 18 Illinois counties along the Mississippi in 2008 and nine of them in 2012; in 2016 and 2020, Democrats won only three. The story's the same across the rest of the state: Outside of suburban and exurban Chicago, the only areas where Democrats haven't seen a plunge in support since the Obama era are around Peoria, Springfield and the college town of Champaign.

The Illinois primary was once a pivotal moment in presidential nominating contests — and after decades on the sidelines, it returned to importance in the last two presidential contests. In 2016, the state gave important boosts to both of the major parties' eventual standard-bearers. The Democratic contest was particularly close: Clinton edged Vermont Sen. Bernie Sanders, 51%-49%. After suffering an upset loss in the Michigan primary one week earlier, it was vital for Clinton to shut down Sanders' momentum in the industrial Midwest. On the Republican side, Trump defeated Texas Sen. Ted Cruz 39%-30% as he sought to knock out Cruz and John Kasich. In 2020, the Illinois primary fell just as Biden was looking to wrap up the nomination — and just as COVID-19 slammed into the U.S. The state plunged ahead with its March 17 primary, even as polling places in nursing homes and retirement centers had to be hastily moved and poll workers failed to turn up in droves, causing election-day delays. Turnout in the Democratic primary, unsurprisingly, dipped from 2.1 million voters in 2016 to 1.7 million in 2020, making Illinois one of the few states where Democratic primary turnout dropped in 2020. Biden won by 59%-36%, which along with wins in Arizona and Florida the same day helped cement his nomination.

Congressional Districts

117th Congress Lineup	13D 5R	116th Congress Lineup	13D 5R

Illinois, with its sluggish population growth, has lost at least one seat in all but one apportionment since 1930, when it had 27 seats. That pattern will continue in 2022, when the state downsizes to 17 seats. Democrats continue to have a strong hand—including firm control of the legislature and governorship, plus a 13-5 hold on the House delegation. Perhaps their biggest challenge will be finding enough Democratic voters to retain their 12 districts in the area surrounding Chicago. Republicans might be fortunate to hold their statewide losses to one district, including their one seat that has encircled Chicago land during the past decade.

The tensions facing Democrats are largely demographic. For the past two decades, they have held three districts in Chicago that are majority African American, though barely. And they continue to hold a single district that is largely Hispanic. But the Black and Latino populations are similar size in both Chicago and Cook County, which is about twice as large as the city alone: about 30 percent each in the city and 25 percent in the county. With the state's loss of one district forcing an increase in the population of each new district, that will force at least one of their African-American districts to drop below 50 percent—and could pose some jeopardy for the incumbents, at least in the primary. Alternatively, one of those aging incumbents—Bobby Rush or Danny Davis—could retire. The growing Latino population likely will increase pressure for two districts for their community— one based on the North side of Chicago, the other on the South side. Depending on how the lines are drawn, that could force one of the surviving white Democratic incumbents farther into the suburbs: Mike Quigley on the North side or first-termer Marie Newman on the South side.

As for the five remaining districts in "downstate," four of which are held by Republicans, at least one likely will be targeted for elimination. With his oddly-shaped district, Adam Kinzinger has seemed at serious risk. In addition to the district that Cheri Bustos holds in the northwest corner of Illinois, Democrats have been eager to draw a second district that would extend from East St. Louis and nearby areas along the Mississippi River to the university locales of Champaign-Urbana and Bloomington and blue-collar Decatur. That redesign could jeopardize Rep. Rodney Davis and force him to run against another GOP incumbent in one of the three adjacent districts. In Illinois, "Democrats are poised to enact another creative plan," wrote David Wasserman of the Cook Political Report.

Another potentially troublesome feature for local Democrats is that Illinois has been the site of some of the most creative gerrymandering in the nation during recent redistricting. "Democrats are poised to enact another creative plan," David Wasserman of the Cook Political Report wrote in April 2021. Depending on the dynamics among redistricting reformers or in the federal courts, that could create discomfort if Chicago pols engage in customary political chicanery. Or, they might find that they have drawn districts that have marginal Democratic control, which would be in jeopardy during a Republican political wave—especially in the exurbs of Chicago, where Democrats gained seats in the past decade.

J.B. Pritzker (D)

Elected 2018, term expires 2023, 1st term; b. Jan. 19, 1965, Atherton, CA; Duke University, B.A.; Northwestern University, J.D., 1993; Jewish; Married (M.K. Muenster); 2 children.

Professional Career: Co-Founder & Managing Partner, Pritzker Group.

Office: 207 State House Springfield, 62706; 217-782-0244; Fax: 217-524-4049

Lt. Gov.: Juliana Stratton (D) **Atty. Gen:** Kwame Raoul (D) **Sec. of State:** Jesse White (D)

State Legislature: Senate: 40D, 19R **House:** 74D, 44R

Election Results

Election	Name (Party)	Vote (%)
2018 General	J.B. Pritzker (D)	2,479,746 (54%)
	Bruce Rauner (R)	1,765,751 (39%)
	William McCann (C)	192,527 (4%)
	Grayson Jackson (Lib)	109,518 (2%)
2018 Primary	J.B. Pritzker (D)	597,756 (45%)
	Daniel K. Biss (D)	353,625 (27%)
	Chris Kennedy (D)	322,730 (24%)

Democratic venture capitalist J.B. Pritzker won the Illinois governorship in 2018 after spending a record $171.5 million from his own pocket to oust Republican Bruce Rauner, also a wealthy venture capitalist. In office, he worked with the Democratic-controlled legislature to implement an extensive progressive agenda and became one of the nation's most aggressive governors in combating the coronavirus, though with limited success.

Pritzker's family is one of America's wealthiest, estimated to be worth a collective $33.5 billion, stemming from a variety of holdings, including Hyatt hotels. The fortune was divided, at times acrimoniously, among various descendants beginning in the late 1990s. The share held by the governor's immediate family is now estimated to be $3.4 billion. That's more than Donald Trump, and Pritzker trails only Michael Bloomberg among those who have ever held elected office. (The Trump and Pritzker families engaged in a legal battle over New York real estate in the 1970s.)

Pritzker grew up in the Bay Area of California. His father, Donald, had moved to California to enter the hotel business with his brother Jay. One of his earliest memories was of door-knocking for Democratic candidates with his mother, Sue. "I grew up with parents who were very dedicated to social justice," he told the Chicago Jewish News during his run for governor. While the family found financial success, it also experienced tragedy: His father died at 39, when J.B. was 7, and his mother struggled with alcoholism until her death at 49, when J.B. was 17. In the decade between their deaths, family life was difficult.

Pritzker earned his undergraduate degree from Duke University and received a law degree from Northwestern University. He worked for a time in Washington for Democratic Sens. Terry Sanford of North Carolina and Alan Dixon of Illinois, meeting his wife, M.K., during this period; she was an aide to Sen. Tom Daschle of South Dakota. In 1990, they settled in Chicago, which was the extended family's longtime home. With his brother Anthony, Pritzker founded a private equity firm, the Pritzker Group, which among other things held a stake in SpaceX, the aerospace company founded by entrepreneur Elon Musk. (His other sibling, Penny, served as Commerce secretary in the Obama administration.) Pritzker also founded a digital incubator called 1871, named for the year of the great fire in Chicago. He chaired the Illinois Human Rights Commission and helped establish Northwestern's Center on Wrongful Convictions. In the political realm, he ran third in a House primary to Democrat Jan Schakowsky in 1998. Pritzker became a major Democratic donor, but his biggest leap into politics came when he challenged Rauner for governor.

Rauner had won in 2014 as a first-time candidate, touting a platform of economic reform and challenging the hidebound political culture of the state dominated by Chicago Democrats. While Rauner spent $22.5 million on his run, he also benefited from the support of billionaire patrons, including hedge fund executive Ken Griffin. In office, Rauner introduced a "turnaround agenda" more detailed than what he campaigned on; it included term limits, a right-to-work measure, tort reform, cuts in state medical spending, overhauls of workers' compensation and education funding, a property tax freeze, and pension system changes. Rauner sought to limit the power of private- and public-sector unions, as to make changes in workers' compensation.

Democrats and their key allies saw the turnaround agenda as an existential threat. But the irresistible force met the immovable object in Democratic House Speaker Mike Madigan, an old-style machine pol who had survived six governors with his immense powers intact. Madigan, a protégé of the late Chicago Mayor Richard J. Daley who got his first politically connected job as a young man operating a garbage truck, joined with Senate President John Cullerton to block Rauner's initiatives. So Rauner tried to leverage the state budget—minus K-12 funding, which was passed separately—to force the legislature to pass his agenda. Democrats were unmoved. For two years, a standoff between Rauner and the legislature turned Illinois into a fiscal laughingstock, unable to pay its bills. In 2016, Rauner dipped into his personal fortune, bolstered by donations from billionaires Griffin and Richard Uihlein, to try to mold a more amenable legislature, but their investment of more than $50 million produced gains of only four seats in the House and two in the Senate. Finally, in the summer of 2017, the legislature managed to enact a budget and a tax increase, after a narrow override of Rauner's veto. By fall 2017, the state's backlog of unpaid bills reached $16.7 billion.

Amid plunging approval ratings and the certainty of a tough reelection battle in a blue state, Rauner enacted some bills in collaboration with Democrats, including one that required the state to pay for abortions for poor women. But such efforts enraged conservative Republicans, and state Rep. Jeanne Ives ran an insurgent campaign to deny him renomination. Rauner barely won the GOP primary, 51.5%-48.5%. Meanwhile, Pritzker took 45 percent of the Democratic primary vote, defeating suburban Chicago state Sen. Daniel Biss and Chris Kennedy, a son of Robert F. Kennedy.

In the general election, the well-heeled nominees sparred over taxes, and Pritzker endorsed the $15 minimum wage that Rauner had vetoed, along with other progressive priorities. Pritzker dealt with a series of embarrassments—secret recordings of conversations with then-Gov. Rod Blagojevich about his possible interest in being appointed state treasurer or attorney general, and revelations about a $330,000 property tax break he secured by removing toilets from a mansion he owned, an action the Cook County inspector general called a "scheme to defraud." But none altered the arc of the race; Pritzker led Rauner from start to finish, eventually winning, 54%-39%, with candidates from the Conservative and Libertarian parties collectively taking 7%.

Once in office, Pritzker made good on many of his proposals. He signed a phased-in minimum wage hike to $15; a law that would continue allowing abortion if the U.S. Supreme Court were to overturn Roe v. Wade; a bill to implement sports betting; a $45 billion bipartisan infrastructure package that included funds for highways, bridges, railways, and universities; and a measure to consolidate 649 police and fire pension plans beyond Cook County into two plans. He also signed bills designed to fulfill an anti-Trump pledge on immigration, including providing immigrant children with strengthened guardianship protections. And Pritzker signed a bill legalizing marijuana, with 25 percent of the tax revenue going toward efforts to boost minority business ownership and 20 percent going to substance abuse treatment and mental health care. The bill also provided for expungement of smaller-scale marijuana convictions, and Pritzker pardoned more than 11,000 convicts.

In his January 2020 state of the state speech, Pritzker targeted the "scourge" of political corruption in the state. "It's no longer enough to sit idle while under-the-table deals, extortion and bribery persist," he said. "Protecting that culture or tolerating it is no longer acceptable." Within six months, he declared that Madigan, his partner on much of his agenda, "must resign" if allegations are proven about a years-long bribery scheme by the utility ComEd that ensnared several Madigan allies. (Madigan was eventually ousted in 2021.) But Pritzker's own toilets-in-mansion episode re-emerged in 2020 as federal prosecutors scrutinized property tax assessment records created during the tenure of Joe Berrios, the former Cook County Assessor and a Madigan ally.

Mostly, though, 2020 was dominated by the coronavirus. Pritzker issued a stay-at-home order in March, after just a handful of deaths had been detected in the state, making him one of the first governors to do so. He ordered a mask mandate effective May 1, followed by a limited reopening later that month. Such actions enabled Illinois to keep its positive-test rate relatively low during the summer, though it rose again in late fall before another decline in December. The state's death rate was among the highest. His actions on both the coronavirus pandemic and in dealing with police brutality protests made Pritzker a target of Trump. In a June conference call with governors, following a weekend in which protests turned violent, Trump urged governors to crack down, but Pritzker shot back that such a recommendation was "inflammatory" and that "the rhetoric coming out of the White House is making it worse." Trump responded, "I don't like your rhetoric very much, either, because I watched it with respect to the coronavirus. I think you could have done a much better job, frankly."

Pritzker suffered a loss on Election Day when a ballot measure he had proposed—and backed with tens of millions of his own dollars—was rejected by voters. The measure would have replaced the constitutional requirement for a flat income tax. Proponents and opponents combined to spend $128 million on the ballot initiative, which earned only 47 percent when it needed 60 percent to be enacted.

Pritzker is presumed to be running again in 2022, against a Republican field that could include Rep. Adam Kinzinger, Republican donor and Chicago Cubs co-owner Todd Ricketts, Chicago attorney Richard Porter, and possibly a state legislator or two. Pritzker's personal fortune and a solidly Democratic electorate will give him a leg up, but the right set of issues and a credible candidate could make it a race.

Dick Durbin (D)

Elected 1996, term expires 2026, 5th term, b. Nov 21, 1944; East St. Louis, IL; Georgetown University, B.S., 1966; Georgetown University Law Center, J.D., 1969; Roman Catholic; Married (Loretta Schaefer Durbin); 3 children (1 deceased); 3 grandchildren.

Elected Office: U.S. House, 1983-1997.

Professional Career: Staff, Lt. Governor Paul Simon, 1969-1972; Legal counsel, IL Senate Judiciary Committee, 1972-1982; Professor, Southern Illinois School of Medicine, 1978-1982.

DC Office: 711 HSOB 20510, 202-224-2152, Fax: 202-228-0400, durbin.senate.gov

State Offices: Carbondale, 618-351-1122; Chicago, 312-353-4952; Rock Island, 309-786-5173; Springfield, 217-492-4062.

Committees: Senate Majority Whip. *Agriculture, Nutrition & Forestry*: Commodities, Risk Management & Trade; Livestock, Dairy, Poultry, Local Food Sys & Food Safety & Sec; Rural Development & Energy. *Appropriations*: Department of Defense; DOL, HHS & Education & Related Agencies; Energy & Water Development; Financial Services & General Government; State, Foreign Operations & Related Programs; Transportation, HUD & Related Agencies. *Judiciary (Chmn)*.

Group Ratings

	ADA	ACLU	AFL-CIO	LCV	COC	HAFA	ACU	CFG	FRC
2020	-	92%	-	92%	-	0%	5%	-	-
2019	100%	C	100%	100%	60%	C	5%	0%	0%

Almanac Ratings 2019-2020

	Economy	Social	Foreign	Composite
Liberal	97%	97%	89%	94%
Conservative	3%	3%	11%	6%

Key Votes of the 116th Congress

1. EPA clean energy rules	Y	5. Russia sanctions	Y	9. Barr as Atty. General	N
2. U.S./Mex./Can. trade deal	Y	6. Troops in SYR, AFG	N	10. Spending at the border	Y
3. Cut unemployment benefits	N	7. Veto arms sales to Saudis	Y	11. Coney Barrett to Sup. Ct.	N
4. Shelton to Fed Reserve	N	8. Defense $$$, veto override	Y	12. Electoral College objections	N

Election Results

Election	Name (Party)	Vote (%)		Cand. Spent	Ind. Exp. Support	Ind. Exp. Oppose
2020 General	Dick Durbin (D)	3,278,930	(55%)	$8,646,464	$123	$77,000
	Mark Curran (R)	2,319,870	(39%)	$354,373		$113
	Willie Wilson (WWP)	294,428	(5%)	$1,234,081		
2020 Primary	Dick Durbin (D)	1,446,118	(100%)			

Prior winning percentages: 2014 (54%), 2008 (68%), 2002 (60%), 1996 (56%); House: 1994 (55%), 1992 (57%),1990 (66%), 1988 (69%), 1986 (68%), 1984 (61%), 1982 (50%

Democrat Dick Durbin, Illinois' senior senator, has spent nearly four decades on Capitol Hill as a key player— in both the House and the Senate. For more than a decade and a half, Durbin, as party whip, has been the No. 2 Senate Democrat. But in early 2015, when Democratic Leader Harry Reid retired, he backed Chuck Schumer— a hard-charging New Yorker who was No. 3 in the leadership structure—to take over. Although Durbin retained the whip's post without opposition, the turn of events ended his hope of climbing the leadership ladder any further. While continuing to round up votes for his party's positions and maintaining his status as a major player on bipartisan initiatives, Durbin toyed with running for governor in 2018—and ending his political career where it began, in the state capital of Springfield. Ultimately, he sought a fifth term in 2020, on the prospect that the campaign would both deny President Donald Trump a second term and return Senate Democrats to the majority.

Durbin's prescience paid off: Not only was he elevated to majority whip in 2021, but— after some debate within the Democratic Caucus— he claimed the chairmanship of the Senate Judiciary Committee as well. With the decision by 87-year-old California Sen. Dianne Feinstein to step down as the panel's top Democrat, Durbin became a full committee chair for the first time in nearly a quarter of a century in the Senate. He also became a key player in newly elected President Joe Biden's legislative push, which ranged from immigration reform to changes in the criminal justice system, both issues in which Durbin has long been involved. It also put Durbin at the center of vetting nominees for federal judicial vacancies, as Biden endeavored to mitigate the rightward shift of the judiciary under the Trump administration, which won confirmation of more than 220 nominees over four years— including three Supreme Court justices.

Durbin and Biden— himself a former Judiciary Committee chairman— were Senate colleagues for a dozen years. " We have to roll up our sleeves and get to work on undoing the damage of the last four years and protecting fundamental civil and human rights," Durbin told Politico. In an interview with The New York Times, he vowed to refocus the committee on strengthening voting rights and antitrust protections, while opposing the liability immunity that many Republicans were advocating for during the COVID-19 pandemic. At the same time, Durbin exhibited the pragmatic side that often has impelled him to reach across the aisle. He told NPR that, as chairman, he hoped he could help" restore the role of this committee in the new Congress on a bipartisan basis," adding, " The Senate Judiciary Committee, throughout our modern history, has always played a leadership role on issues of the moment. … It unfortunately, in the last few years, abandoned that role."

Now 76, Durbin— whose congressional tenure has spanned seven presidents— grew up in modest circumstances in East St. Louis. His father, a railroad night watchman, died of lung cancer when Durbin was 14— an event that later led to one of his most enduring legislative achievements. He graduated from Georgetown University and its law school while working as an intern for Illinois Democratic Sen. Paul Douglas, who held the seat Durbin now occupies. He returned home to join the staff of Lt. Gov. Paul Simon, who later became a senator. Durbin was a state Senate staff member for much of the 1970s, even serving as that chamber's parliamentarian— valuable training for someone who would later gain a reputation as an expert in U.S. Senate procedures. His first two tries for elected office, including a 1978 bid as Democrats' nominee for lieutenant governor, fell short. But in 1982, he was nominated to oppose GOP Rep. Paul Findley, among the few members of Congress to call for a more even-handed policy toward Palestinians. Durbin had no trouble raising money from well-heeled Israel supporters, and he narrowly ousted Findley from a central Illinois district.

In the House, Durbin won a seat on the Appropriations Committee, and, in 1993, became chair of the subcommittee with jurisdiction over the Food and Drug Administration. Years later, in the Senate, he enacted major reforms in the FDA's food safety inspection powers; President Barack Obama, in 2011, signed a Durbin-crafted bill allowing the FDA to issue mandatory recalls of food products. His centerpiece accomplishment in the House was the ban on smoking on domestic airline flights, enacted in 1988 and inspired by the death of his chain-smoking father. At the time, Durbin had little idea of its long-term societal impact. " I didn't realize it would make a difference in terms of whether you could smoke on a train, on a bus, in a building, in a restaurant, in a hospital," he said in a 2015 interview. He also pushed successfully to limit tobacco subsidies and give the FDA authority to regulate tobacco as a health hazard.

As a House member, Durbin rented a room in a Capitol Hill home owned by then-California Democratic Rep. George Miller; Schumer, then also a House member, was already a tenant. The Durbin-Schumer weekday roommate relationship continued after both had moved on to the Senate and become rivals for the leadership. The arrangement ended in 2014, when Miller retired from Congress and sold the town house— but not before inspiring a TV sitcom, " Alpha House." Finding himself in the minority after the 1994 elections, Durbin announced he would seek the Senate seat being relinquished in 1996 by his former boss, Simon. Durbin got more than twice as many votes as his primary opponent, future Gov. Pat Quinn, and comfortably won the general election with 56 percent of the vote.

Durbin's voting record places him in the Senate's left wing. " He's able to pull off the style of sounding like a moderate or compromiser when he often doesn't act like one," University of Illinois political scientist Brian Gaines observed. But Durbin has cautioned Democrats' progressive wing about pushing the party too far to the left. " We have to really appeal to that sensible center," Durbin said in a 2017 interview with a Chicago radio station. " It's a thin stripe now. It used to be a lot wider stripe, but it's an important and determining factor in most elections." He has not hesitated on several occasions to take on liberal orthodoxy; during negotiations on taxes and spending aimed at averting the "fiscal cliff" in late 2012, Durbin exhorted Democrats to support a deal that included cuts to entitlement programs. "My liberal friends who say, 'Don't touch it' (Medicare), they're crazy," Durbin said at the time. Earlier, he served on the bipartisan Simpson-Bowles deficit reduction commission that recommended raising the Medicare eligibility age.

On social issues, Durbin, a Catholic, favored restrictions on abortion while in the House but has opposed most such restrictions in the Senate— a shift that reportedly occurred after he met with victims of rape and incest. In 2004, the priest at his home church in Springfield said he wouldn't give Durbin communion as a consequence of his position. " Is that all this church is about, is one issue?" Durbin responded. " For bishops to announce that they are going to penalize Catholics on certain votes I think is … reaching too far." In February 2018, the bishop of Springfield reaffirmed the church's stance after Durbin voted against a Senate bill prohibiting abortion starting at 20 weeks after conception. " The determination continues that Sen. Durbin is not to be admitted to Holy Communion until he repents of this sin," the bishop, Thomas Paprocki, declared.

Durbin's position on another social issue has shifted as well: Initially a supporter of the death penalty, he told the State Journal Register in 2011 that the death penalty should be abolished except for " compelling exceptions" such as " terrorism and crimes of that nature." A decade later, as incoming Judiciary Committee chair, he teamed up with Massachusetts Democratic Rep. Ayanna Pressley—a progressive firebrand—to introduce legislation to permanently end federal capital punishment. The bill was a response to the Trump administration's resumption of federal executions in mid-2019 after a nearly two-decade hiatus.

Durbin's ascent in the Senate leadership ranks began in 2001, when he was named assistant floor leader. After Democratic Leader Tom Daschle lost his 2004 reelection bid, Reid succeeded him, and Durbin moved to secure Reid's old job as minority whip; he won by acclamation. His new position was but one significant development arising out of the 2004 election. He acquired a new junior colleague from Illinois: Obama. In an institution of sizable egos, many senators have had tense relationships with home-state colleagues— particularly when the two belong to the same party. But rather than chafing at Obama's quick rise and celebrity, Durbin urged him to run for president and later introduced the presidential nominee at the 2008 Democratic National Convention. Durbin did not join Obama at the massive 2008 election night celebration in Chicago's Grant Park because his 40-year-old daughter had died three days earlier, but he again introduced Obama at the 2012 convention.

Often described as the president's closest friend in the Senate during Obama's eight years in the White House, Durbin frequently appeared on talk shows to defend Obama's signature legislative achievement: the Affordable Care Act. In 2015, it was left to Durbin to line up Senate support for the Obama administration's nuclear agreement with Iran—a pact from which Trump later withdrew but which Biden has vowed to resurrect— after other members of the Democratic leadership came out against the deal or were slow to embrace it.

Before Obama became president, Durbin was chief sponsor of the DREAM Act, which aimed to provide a path to citizenship to those brought to the country illegally as children. In 2012, Obama issued an executive order— Deferred Action for Childhood Arrivals— to protect nearly 750,000 such immigrants when it became clear Congress would not act. When Trump announced plans to cancel Obama's DACA order in the fall of 2017, Durbin was part of a bipartisan group of a half-dozen senators who reached agreement on a legislative package pairing legal status for those covered by DACA with other immigration reforms and enhanced border security. But the effort was stymied when Trump told Durbin and South Carolina Republican Sen. Lindsey Graham during a White House meeting that he was not prepared to embrace the proposal.

The aftermath of the meeting produced a series of charges and countercharges. Durbin told CNN that the bipartisan group had been "sandbagged" after Trump earlier agreed to move ahead with comprehensive immigration reform that included DACA. He also confirmed reports that the president had referred to several African nations as "s---hole countries"— a remark that created a diplomatic firestorm. Trump, in a Reuters interview, declined "to get into what I said," adding, "I've lost all trust in Durbin." Trump later tweeted: " Senator Dicky Durbin totally misrepresented what was said at the DACA meeting. … Durbin blew DACA and is hurting our Military." Durbin and Graham kept trying, meeting with Trump's son-in-law and adviser, Jared Kushner, in mid-2019, hoping to use Trump's effort to make changes in the system for legal immigration as leverage to provide protection for those covered by DACA. But they made little headway. "I have no idea what will satisfy this president," Durbin told NPR. " I've been down this road so many times where he sets goals, we meet them with legislation, and he walks away from them."

However, Durbin and Trump were on the same page when Congress, at the end of 2018, overwhelmingly passed a criminal justice reform bill— an effort on which Durbin and Iowa Republican Chuck Grassley, then Judiciary Committee chair, had teamed up several years earlier.

Their initiative fell short in 2016 amid resistance from hard-line conservatives, but they vowed to try again. The bill, signed into law by Trump, boosted efforts at prisoner rehabilitation at federal facilities while granting judges more discretion in sentencing those convicted of drug-related offenses. " A breakthrough I' d never expect— the election of Donald Trump as president," Durbin told NBC News after the bill passed. " What does that have to do with this? He brought his son-in-law to town." While a coalition of liberal and conservative groups had pushed for a broader bill, Kushner initially committed the White House to a narrower proposal focused on prison reform. But Durbin and Grassley argued that an earlier version passed by the House didn't go far enough and ultimately reached a deal with the White House to include sentencing reforms in the final bill.

A Durbin-Grassley collaboration on drug prices was also in accord with an initiative supported by Trump. The two senators in August 2018 won Senate approval of funding to study and implement ads that would disclose the price of pharmaceuticals; it was like part of a plan advocated by Trump to lower drug costs. Durbin and Grassley attached an amendment to a version of the annual spending bill for the Department of Health and Human Services, but it was removed during a House-Senate conference committee. Durbin blamed House Republicans for capitulating to lobbying by the Pharmaceutical Research and Manufacturers of America. " We need transparency & it's time to put consumers ahead of Big Pharma," Durbin tweeted.

Perhaps the most high-profile episode of Durbin's Senate tenure came on the 2010 Dodd-Frank financial reform law. As part of Dodd-Frank, he engineered passage of what was widely referred to as the "Durbin amendment," giving the Federal Reserve authority to reduce the "swipe fees" that banks charge merchants for processing debit card transactions. It made Durbin a scourge of the banking industry, which mounted an extensive lobbying effort to get rid of the Durbin amendment. When legislation to repeal some provisions of Dodd-Frank— later signed by Trump— moved through Congress in mid-2017, Republican leaders of the House Financial Services Committee initially planned to include repeal of the Durbin amendment. But they backed off after counting votes. If leading banks are no fan of Durbin's, neither are groups pushing for tort reform. They have long accused him of defending the interests of the nation's trial lawyers and point to more than $6.5 million in campaign contributions, according to the Center for Responsive Politics, that Durbin has received from lawyers and law firms over the past three decades.

Durbin has not been hesitant to use his clout as a member of the Appropriations Committee to keep an eye out for another major player in the nation's financial marketplace: the Chicago-based commodities exchanges. He has opposed new fees on the exchanges and, at one point, worked behind the scenes to soften the effects of proposed controls on speculators in the oil futures market while gas prices soared.

In January 2013, Durbin became chair of Appropriations' Defense Subcommittee, and its ranking Democrat two years later. He utilized that position to fund production of electronic Navy warplanes manufactured at Boeing's St. Louis plant, just across the Mississippi River from Illinois. At the end of 2020, Durbin agreed to give up the chance to again control that subcommittee — and its control of $700 billion in annual military funding. It was a concession to more junior Democrats chafing at limited opportunities to move up the ladder: A rules change subsequently passed by the Democratic Caucus allowed Durbin to serve as both whip and Judiciary chair but required that he relinquish the Appropriations post. Rhode Island Democratic Sen. Sheldon Whitehouse— next in line to chair the Judiciary panel— unsuccessfully pushed an alternative barring the whip from serving as chair or ranking member of a full committee. "As I understand it, I am the object of his reform. For himself," Durbin quipped to Politico. Whitehouse had the backing of several progressive groups— who felt that Whitehouse, with his reputation as a political brawler, was more likely to adopt a confrontational stance toward Republicans.

If Durbin is regarded as more diplomatic amid his record of bipartisan outreach, his sharp-tongued side occasionally has surfaced. In 2015, when Obama's nomination of Loretta Lynch for attorney general faced a protracted delay by Senate Republicans, Durbin charged GOP leaders were putting Lynch at the " back of the bus," an allusion to historical bus segregation in the South. Then-Republican Sen. John McCain of Arizona demanded an apology for what he said was Durbin's effort to " suggest that racist tactics are being employed." Durbin refused to back down, saying he had thought " long and hard" before making his remarks.

In 2020, when Senate Republicans unveiled a proposal to encourage local police departments to adopt reforms, Democrats dismissed the plan— sponsored by Tim Scott of South Carolina, the Senate's only Black Republican— as lacking teeth; Durbin termed it a " a token, halfhearted approach." Scott, who had recently complained of being called a "token" in the GOP on issues of race, responded angrily on the Senate floor. He asserted that Durbin's comment, which came on the fifth anniversary of the massacre by a white supremacist of nine Black parishioners at a church in Scott's hometown of Charleston, " hurts the soul." Durbin privately apologized after Scott's floor speech. According to a spokeswoman, Durbin's comment was aimed at Majority Leader Mitch McConnell, whom Durbin feared would deny Democrats the chance to offer amendments to Scott's legislation — the product of negotiations among congressional Republicans and the Trump administration.

Durbin became majority whip in 2007after Democrats captured the Senate and he returned as minority whip in 2015 when the GOP regained control. For much of 2015 and 2016, Durbin claimed enough support to remain whip, even as Sen. Patty Murray of Washington declined to rule out a challenge to him. Schumer declined to take sides in the matter, further straining what had once been a close relationship. The turmoil was resolved a week after Election Day 2016: Durbin was unanimously reelected as whip, as Schumer crafted a new job— assistant Democratic leader— for Murray. In the wake of Trump's surprise election, Durbin declined to run for governor, telling the Chicago Tribune he had been approached by many Illinois constituents saying: " Stay in the Senate. We need you."

Durbin won reelection in 2002 and 2008 by 60 percent or more. While held to 54 percent in 2014, he still defeated his GOP opponent by double digits. In 2020, he won reelection 55%-39% over former Lake County Sheriff Mark Curran, a Democrat-turned-Republican who emphasized his opposition to state restrictions aimed at curbing the spread of COVID-19. Durbin told the Chicago Tribune that internal polling suggested a third candidate, independent Willie Wilson, would draw votes from him by attracting about 15 percent of the Black vote." His votes are my votes," Durbin said. " These are people who traditionally would support me, I believe." Durbin responded with ads touting the endorsements of Obama and vice presidential nominee Kamala Harris. Wilson, a wealthy food and medical glove distributor, drew 5 percent of the general election vote after spending $1.2 million of his own money. Durbin spent more than $8.6 million to just $354,000 by Curran, who received no assistance from the national GOP.

Curran campaigned as an enthusiastic backer of the president— while Wilson, after a quixotic bid for the 2016 Democratic presidential nomination, had voted for Trump. Durbin, meanwhile, used attacks on Trump to generate support. One TV spot called Trump "a big bully," while boasting Durbin had " brought him down to size." The ad depicted Trump shrinking to fit into the senator's palm— at which point Durbin is shown disposing of Trump with a flick of the wrist.

After the election, a bipartisan group of centrist lawmakers began meeting to break a months-long stalemate over another pandemic-related economic stimulus bill. The presence of Durbin—as a member of the Democratic leadership— at these sessions raised eyebrows. But it was Durbin's suggestion that the group abandon consideration of a long-term stimulus package and focus instead on an emergency plan to get the country through late winter that helped to jump-start the talks. Utah Republican Sen. Mitt Romney told the Washington Post that Durbin's comments had been a key " breakthrough." When the group of centrists first appeared publicly in early December 2020 with a $900 billion plan containing elements of what was ultimately signed into law, Durbin did not join them. Nonetheless, he urged that the legislation be brought to the Senate floor. "I'm not happy with a lot of these figures," he said. " But that's what it's all about in this world of the United States Congress: You come together, willing to sit down and listen to the other side and, if necessary, compromise."

Tammy Duckworth (D)

Elected 2016, term expires 2022, 1st term, b. Mar 12, 1968; Bangkok, Thailand; University of Hawaii, B.A., 1989; George Washington University Elliot School of International Affairs, M.A., 1992; Northern Illinois University; Capella University, Ph.D., 2015; Religion not stated; Married (Bryan Bowlsbey); 2 children.

Military Career: U.S. Army Reserve 1991-1996; Lt. Colonel, IL Army National Guard 1996-2014 (Iraq, WIA).

Elected Office: U.S. House, 2013-17.

Professional Career: Manager, Rotary International, Asia Pacific Region, 2003-2004; Director, IL Veterans Affairs Department, 2006-2009; Assistant Secretary, U.S Veterans Affairs Department, 2009-2011.

DC Office: 524 HSOB 20510, 202-224-2854, Fax: 202-228-0618

State Offices: Belleville, 618-722-7070; Carbondale, 618-677-7000; Chicago, 312-886-3506; Rock Island, 309-606-7060; Springfield, 217-528-6124.

Committees: *Armed Services*: Airland (Chmn); Readiness & Management Support; Strategic Forces. *Commerce, Science & Transportation*: Aviation Safety, Operations & Innovations; Communications, Media & Broadband; Surface Transportation, Maritime Freight & Ports; Tourism, Trade & Export Promotion. *Environment & Public Works*: Clean Air & Nuclear Safety; Fisheries, Water, and Wildlife (Chmn); Transportation & Infrastructure. *Small Business & Entrepreneurship*.

Group Ratings

	ADA	ACLU	AFL-CIO	LCV	COC	HAFA	ACU	CFG	FRC
2020	-	77%	-	92%	-	0%	4%	-	-
2019	95%	C	100%	100%	55%	C	4%	0%	0%

Almanac Ratings 2019-2020

	Economy	Social	Foreign	Composite
Liberal	97%	97%	76%	90%
Conservative	3%	3%	24%	10%

Key Votes of the 116th Congress

1. EPA clean energy rules Y	5. Russia sanctions Y	9. Barr as Atty. General N
2. U.S./Mex./Can. trade deal Y	6. Troops in SYR, AFG Y	10. Spending at the border Y
3. Cut unemployment benefits N	7. Veto arms sales to Saudis Y	11. Coney Barrett to Sup. Ct. N
4. Shelton to Fed Reserve N	8. Defense $$$, veto override Y	12. Electoral College objections N

Election Results

Election	Name (Party)	Vote (%)		Cand. Spent	Ind. Exp. Support	Ind. Exp. Oppose
2016 General	Tammy Duckworth (D)	3,012,940	(55%)	$9,000,361	$683,882	$2,061,868
	Mark Kirk (R)	2,184,692	(40%)	$10,513,124	$727,085	$62,499
	Kent McMillen (L)	175,988	(3%)			
	Scott Summers (G)	117,619	(2%)			
2016 Primary	Tammy Duckworth (D)	1,220,128	(64%)			
	Andrea Zopp (D)	455,729	(24%)			
	Napoleon Harris (D)	219,286	(12%)			

Prior winning percentages: 2016 (55%), House: 2014 (56%); 2012 (55%)

Democrat Tammy Duckworth, Illinois' junior senator, arrived in the Senate on the same day in 2016 as Vice President Kamala Harris, becoming only the second and third Asian-American women to serve in that chamber. Four years later, Harris is the country's first female vice president — and its first Black and South Asian one, too. But Duckworth was seriously vetted for that role, after reportedly impressing members of Joe Biden's vice presidential selection team in a series of interviews. Duckworth "was regarded by Biden advisers as among the candidates likeliest to help him achieve a smashing electoral victory in November," the New York Times reported, with an appeal to voters who had strayed in recent years and veterans—not traditionally a part of the Democratic coalition.

Starting with her first run for elected office a decade and a half earlier, Duckworth attracted widespread media attention as a female combat veteran who sacrificed much during her service. During the Iraq War, a rocket-propelled grenade struck the Army helicopter she had been piloting; she lost both legs and has used a wheelchair or prosthetic legs ever since. Duckworth's disability— and the manner in which she acquired it—appears to have had a liberating effect on both the tone and substance of her comments in public life, particularly those aimed at former President Donald Trump during his four years in office. At the outset of 2018, when Trump blamed Democrats for a government shutdown he said harmed the military, Duckworth lit into the president as "Cadet Bone Spurs"—a reference to the diagnosis that had enabled him to avoid military service during the Vietnam War. "I will not be lectured about what our military needs by a five-deferment draft dodger," Duckworth said on the Senate floor.

In both the Senate and the House— where she previously served two terms—Duckworth has been better known for her resume and rhetoric than her legislative accomplishments. The latter have been defined largely by personal experience, with a focus on veterans issues." I feel that I have a unique role to play, in terms of those who are in the Senate, to call out the president when he's not doing his job as commander in chief," Duckworth told the Atlantic in 2020.If Duckworth's vice presidential aspirations were possibly hindered by not being viewed as a leading voice on issues front and center during the 2020 campaign, what apparently eliminated her from consideration was her place of birth. While Biden's advisers were reported to believe she met the constitutional requirement that both the president and vice president be natural born citizens, they nervously recalled Trump questioning the eligibility of Texas Sen. Ted Cruz—born in Canada to a U.S.-born mother—when Trump and Cruz vied for the 2016 Republican presidential nomination. Biden campaign attorneys feared a court challenge, with a partisan judge in a swing state reaping legal and political havoc by throwing a Biden-Duckworth ticket off the ballot.

Born Ladda Tammy Duckworth in Bangkok Thailand, she spent much of her early life abroad because her American-born father, a Vietnam veteran, worked for the United Nations and at several international firms. The first Thai-American senator, Duckworth did not learn English until she was 8 and remains fluent in Thai and Indonesian. She lived in Indonesia as well as Singapore before her father moved the family to Hawaii after losing his job. Duckworth was 16 and took a series of low-paying jobs to help pay the bills, at one point selling flowers by the side of the road as the family lived in a low-rent hotel." Thank God for the food stamps, public education and Pell Grants that helped me finish high school and college," Duckworth said during a speech at the 2012 Democratic National Convention. She studied marine biology at the University of Hawaii and earned a master's degree in international affairs at George Washington University. Her interest in Southeast Asian history, culture and politics led to doctoral work at Northern Illinois University.

In 1990, Duckworth— whose family has a record of military service dating to the American Revolution— joined the Army ROTC at George Washington University, in part to acquire class credits." I just absolutely fell in love with the Army," she told The New York Times years later. " Because it was so hard in the Army, it didn't matter that I was a little Asian girl. It was all about, ' Can you shoot straight? Can you show leadership abilities?'" After moving to Illinois, Duckworth joined the Army National Guard, from which she retired as a lieutenant colonel in 2014. (Her husband, Bryan Bowlsbey, whom she met during ROTC training, served as a major in the Illinois National Guard unit; he is now an information technology consultant.)Although Duckworth later said she had opposed President George W. Bush's decision to invade Iraq, she felt it was her duty to complete her military service— and volunteered for deployment. She arrived in Iraq in March 2004, where she became one of the first women to fly combat missions.

The rocket-propelled grenade that hit her Black Hawk helicopter on Nov. 12, 2004, nearly killed her. Once her co-pilot landed the craft, a second helicopter crew, after evacuating the wounded, returned to retrieve what they thought was her corpse. " I am no hero," she told Vogue magazine in 2018. " The guy who carried me out of there? He's the hero." Duckworth's right arm was badly wounded; she lost nearly all of her right leg, and her left leg had to be amputated below the knee. She underwent numerous surgeries, and while recovering at Walter Reed National Military Medical Center outside Washington, met Sen. Barack Obama of Illinois, a member of the Veterans' Affairs Committee— who later asked her to testify. Illinois' other senator, Democratic Whip Dick Durbin, invited her to the 2005 State of the Union address and ultimately urged her to run for Congress. Then-Democratic Congressional Campaign Committee Chairman Rahm Emanuel— later White House chief of staff and then mayor of Chicago— was seeking veterans to run in 2006 and recruited Duckworth for a seat in Chicago's western suburbs being relinquished by veteran GOP Rep. Henry Hyde.

However, local Democrats lined up behind the party's 2004 nominee against Hyde, leading to a competitive primary that Duckworth won 44%-40%. Running in a traditionally Republican district, she pledged support for fiscal conservatism and punishments for immigrants who enter the country illegally. In November, she lost to Peter Roskam, 51%-49%. It was two years after the helicopter attack, and Duckworth later said she hadn't yet fully recovered from her wounds. Weeks after her defeat, she was named director of the Illinois Veterans Affairs Department. It was at times a bumpy experience, including a lawsuit that two employees filed against her, alleging workplace retaliation. The suit was settled out of court several months before her 2016 Senate bid.

Duckworth received a prominent speaking spot at the 2008 Democratic National Convention at which Obama was first nominated for president, beginning a string of featured convention appearances. At the virtual convention of 2020, she appeared just prior to Biden's acceptance speech, lacerating Trump as "a coward in chief who won't stand up to Vladimir Putin, read his daily intelligence briefings or even publicly admonish adversaries for reportedly putting bounties on our troops' heads." In 2009, she was named assistant secretary of Veterans Affairs for public and intergovernmental affairs. She left two years later to again run for Congress in a district in Chicago's northwestern suburbs that had been redrawn to be more favorable to Democrats. With another endorsement from Durbin, she easily won the March primary. Her November opponent was GOP Rep. Joe Walsh, elected in 2010 amid the national tea party wave. He had a reputation for outspokenness but also for politically damaging behavior. Redistricting left him with only a small piece of his old district, and Duckworth won with 55 percent of the vote.

Duckworth joined the House Armed Services Committee, where she filed a bill to extend maternity leave for servicewomen. Duckworth became a mother for the first time two weeks after being reelected by a 12-point margin in 2014. In early 2015, she scored a legislative victory when Obama signed the Clay Hunt Suicide Prevention for American Veterans Act— which improved mental health services for veterans—at a White House ceremony.

In March 2015, Duckworth announced a challenge to Republican Sen. Mark Kirk, who, in 2010, had narrowly won Obama's former Senate seat against a Democrat with political baggage. Several other Democrats in the Illinois House delegation took a pass on the Senate race, and Duckworth easily won the March 2016 primary with 64 percent of the vote. More than a quarter-century after the passage of the Americans With Disabilities Act, the Duckworth-Kirk race became the first Senate campaign in which both candidates used wheel chairs. Kirk had a near-fatal stroke a year into his Senate term, leaving him partially paralyzed. Politically, he began the 2016 election cycle as the most endangered Senate incumbent in the nation: He had to run during a presidential year in a state that had not cast its Electoral College votes for a Republican in nearly three decades.

Kirk struggled to raise money— Duckworth outraised him 2-1—and a series of verbal gaffes raised questions about whether the stroke had affected his behavior. In October, the Republican-leaning editorial page of the Chicago Tribune endorsed Duckworth, saying, "Our reluctant judgment is that, due to forces beyond his control, Kirk no longer can perform to the fullest the job of a U.S. senator." Less than two weeks before Election Day, Kirk placed the final nail in his candidacy: During a debate, Duckworth pointed to her father's family history of military service dating to the Revolutionary War. Kirk gibed, "I'd forgotten your parents came all the way from Thailand to serve George Washington." Democrats blasted the remark as racist, and Kirk initially refused to apologize. On Election Day, Duckworth won easily, 55%-40%. She goes into her first re-election in 2022 in a virtually unassailable position in what has become the most reliably Democratic state in the Midwest.

Fifteen months after being sworn in, Duckworth became the first sitting senator to give birth. The April 2018 arrival of her second daughter, which came nearly a month after Duckworth turned 50, was made possible by in vitro fertilization. Duckworth's Almanac voting score placed her among the dozen most liberal senators in her first year. But she has sought to distance herself from the party's progressive wing." I think that you can't win the White House without the Midwest," Duckworth told CNN. " And I don't think you can go too far to the left and still win the Midwest." Of "Medicare for All" pushed by a progressive Sen. Bernie Sanders of Vermont, Duckworth told the St. Louis Post-Dispatch, " I just don't think the Sanders proposal is achievable. ... For me, it is about realistically implementing something."

Duckworth moved to a seat on the Senate Armed Services Committee in 2019; a year later, she used Senate prerogatives to delay more than 1,100 military promotions in an effort to safeguard the promotion of Lt. Col. Alexander Vindman, a key witness in the inquiry that led to Trump's first impeachment. After Trump's acquittal by the Senate on charges that he withheld security assistance to Ukraine while trying to force that government to investigate Biden and his son Hunter, Vindman was ousted from his job at the White House's National Security Council amid public attacks by Trump. "This goes far beyond any single military officer. It is about protecting a merit-based system from political corruption and unlawful retaliation," Duckworth said of her "hold," which was dropped after written assurances that the Army and the Defense Department had approved Vindman's advancement to full colonel. Vindman announced his retirement from the military before the promotion list reached the White House, averting a potential partisan battle.

It was but one of a multitude of veterans and military issues in which Duckworth took aim at Trump. She called his desire to ban transgender individuals from the armed services "sickening" in view of his effort to avoid military service. " When I was bleeding to death in my Black Hawk helicopter after I was shot down, I didn't care if the American troops risking their lives to help save me were gay, straight, transgender, black, white or brown. All that mattered was they didn't leave me behind," she said.

In December 2020, Trump vetoed the annual Defense Department authorization bill, partly over a provision requiring renaming of military installations bearing the names of leaders of the Confederacy. " He cares more about preserving the legacy of dead traitors than he does about making sure that our troops get a pay raise, while we have soldiers and marines in harm's way right now, downrange?" Duckworth snapped. Congress overrode the veto.

" I can push back against Trump in a way others can't," Duckworth declared. That assertion was put to the test as she was under consideration for vice president: Her comments to CNN that Americans needed to " have a national dialogue" about whether statues of George Washington should be taken down generated a torrent of Republican criticism. Fox News commentator Tucker Carlson questioned her patriotism, employing nativistic language; Trump sent out video of Carlson's remarks via Twitter. " We live here," declared Carlson. " We have every right to fight to preserve our nation and our heritage and our culture."

Duckworth, in a New York Times op-ed, accused Carlson of putting words in her mouth. "I don't want George Washington's statue to be pulled down any more than I want the Purple Heart that he established to be ripped off my chest," she wrote, adding: " A little over 240 years ago, two of my ancestors put on the uniform of George Washington's Continental Army and marched into battle, willing to die if it meant bringing their fledgling nation inches closer to independence. … Even knowing how my tour in Iraq would turn out, even knowing that I'd lose both my legs in a battlefield just north of Baghdad… I would do it all over again. Because if there's anything that my ancestors' service taught me, it's the importance of protecting our founding values, including every American's right to speak out."

In April 2019, Duckworth returned to Iraq for the first time since the attack that nearly killed her, leading a bipartisan Senate delegation. Her travels took her over the area in which her helicopter had been shot down, yielding a mixture of déjà vu and closure. " When I was around other soldiers, I wanted to be another soldier," she told the Chicago Tribune. " To smell the hydraulic fluid and not be in a flight suit in the cockpit was … very weird. I just felt wrong." However, she added: "I've been waiting to leave Iraq on my terms for a long time. It bugged me I didn't leave under my own power. I was carried out of there. This time, I left on my own. … It felt empowering, like I took back the narrative."

Bobby Rush (D)

Elected 1992, 15th term, b. Nov 23, 1946; Albany, GA; Roosevelt University, B.A., 1973; University of IL, Chicago, Att., 1977; University of IL, Chicago, M.A., 1994; McCormick Theological Seminary, M.Th., 1998; Baptist; Married (Paulette Holloway); 7 children (1 deceased).

Military Career: U.S. Army 1963-1968

Elected Office: Chicago city alderman, 1983-1992; 2nd ward committeeman, 1984.

Professional Career: Member, Student Non-Violent Coord. Committee, 1966-1968; Co-founder, IL Black Panther Party, 1968; Med. clinic Director, 1970-1973; Ins. agent, 1978-1983.

DC Office: 2188 RHOB 20515, 202-225-4372, Fax: 202-226-0333, rush.house.gov

State Offices: Chicago, 773-779-2400.

Committees: *Agriculture*: Livestock & Foreign Agriculture; Subcommittee Nutrition, Oversight & Department Operations. *Energy & Commerce*: Consumer Protection & Commerce; Energy (Chmn).

Group Ratings

	ADA	ACLU	AFL-CIO	LCV	COC	HAFA	ACU	CFG	FRC
2020	**	81%	**	100%	-	0%	4%	**	-
2019	95%	C	100%	97%	64%	C	4%	12%	0%

Almanac Ratings 2019-2020

	Economy	Social	Foreign	Composite
Liberal	100%	100%	55%	85%
Conservative	0%	0%	45%	15%

Key Votes of the 116th Congress

1. U.S./Mex./Can. trade deal	Y	5. Russia sanctions	N/A	9. Firearms background checks	Y
2. First Coronavirus response	Y	6. Troops in Syria	N/A	10. Spending at the border	Y
3. HEROES Act	Y	7. Veto arms sales to Saudis	Y	11. Marijuana liberalized rules	Y
4. CASH Act	Y	8. Defense $$$, veto override	Y	12. Electoral College objections	N

Election Results

Election	Name (Party)	Vote (%)		Cand. Spent	Ind. Exp. Support	Ind. Exp. Oppose
2020 General	Bobby Rush (D)............................	239,943	(74%)	$488,092	$123	
	Philanise White (R)......................	85,027	(26%)	$1,860		$113
2020 Primary	Bobby Rush (D)............................	94,863	(72%)			
	Sarah Gad (D).............................	13,783	(10%)			
	Robert Emmons Jr. (D).................	13,628	(10%)			
	Ameena Matthews (D)...................	10,409	(8%)			

Prior winning percentages: 2018 (74%), 2016 (74%), 2014 (73%), 2012 (74%), 2010 (80%), 2008 (86%), 2006 (84%), 2004 (85%), 2002 (83%), 2000 (88%), 1998 (89%), 1996 (87%), 1994 (76%), 1992 (83%)

Once a Black Panther and prison inmate, Democrat Bobby Rush was elected in 1992 and has become a liberal elder statesman of Congress and Chicago's sharp-edged political scene. He will go down in history as the only politician ever to beat Barack Obama in an election.

Rush grew up on the North Side, a Boy Scout whose mother was a Republican precinct captain. While in the Army, he became involved in the Student Nonviolent Coordinating Committee in the South, then became disillusioned with the military and went AWOL in 1968 when Martin Luther King Jr. was assassinated. That year, he founded the Illinois Black Panthers, with its "Power to the People" slogan, and recruited Fred Hampton, who became chairman of the organization but was later killed by police in a 1969 raid. The next day, police raided Rush's family's apartment, but he wasn't there. Rush served six months in prison for illegal possession of firearms.

He has long battled Chicago's problematic police force, and during the Black Lives Matter protests in 2020 told VICE News that "the police department is probably more vicious now than they were even in the '60s." During his time with the Black Panthers, he ran a program providing free breakfasts to children and a medical clinic that developed the nation's first mass sickle cell anemia testing program. "I don't repudiate any of my involvement in the Panther party. It was part of my maturing," Rush later said.

In 1983, he was elected the 2nd Ward alderman on the Chicago City Council and was a strong supporter of Harold Washington, who became the city's first Black mayor. Rush earned master's degrees in political science and theological studies. Ordained as a Baptist minister, he founded a church in 2002 in the depressed Englewood community, but it struggled financially and closed. In 2017, a Cook County judge ordered him to pay $1.1 million on a delinquent bank loan and later arranged for garnishment of a share of Rush's congressional salary.

In 1992, Rush challenged Democratic Rep. Charles Hayes, an older-generation politician with a union background. Just before the primary, it was revealed that Hayes had 716 overdrafts at the House bank, a practice among lawmakers that blossomed into a national scandal. Rush won 42%-39%.

In the House, Rush has a liberal voting record. His rhetoric has softened some over the years, and his more deliberate style contrasts sharply with his days as a Panther, though he sometimes chafes at legislative compromises. He backed the 2010 health care overhaul law, but only after sending mixed signals because of his unhappiness over the removal of a provision to reimburse hospitals for indigent care.

He has devoted much of his time to the Energy and Commerce Committee, where he chairs the Energy Subcommittee. He's sought increased job opportunities for minorities throughout the energy industry. His Blue Collar to Green Collar Jobs Development Act of 2019 was approved by the committee, but never got a House floor vote. During a 2020 hearing, Rush got Dr. Anthony Fauci to say that he believed systemic racism was a contributing factor in why the coronavirus was killing African Americans at disproportionate rates.

In 2020, the House passed Rush's Emmett Till Ant lynching Act, which for the first time would make lynching a federal crime after 200 previous attempts failed in the past 118 years. But Republican Sen. Rand Paul of Kentucky blocked quick consideration in the Senate.

Rush waged a quixotic campaign in 1999 against Richard M. Daley, attacking the longtime mayor for allegedly tolerating police brutality, inadequate mass transit service, and cronyism. But Daley's popularity and the strength of the Chicago Democratic machine helped him defeat Rush in the primary, 72%-28%, with Daley winning nearly 45 percent of the African-American vote.

After that pounding, Rush found himself challenged in his own primary in 2000 by a little-known state senator named Barack Obama. Obama waged an aggressive campaign, saying at the time that Rush "exemplifies a politics that is reactive, that waits for crises to happen, then holds a press conference, and hasn't been particularly effective at building broad-based coalitions." Obama took fire for missing two months' worth of votes, including one on gun control. Rush was helped by an endorsement from President Bill Clinton and beat Obama 61%-30%.

During Obama's pitched battle with Hillary Clinton in the 2008 presidential primary, Rush endorsed Obama, calling it "one of the most difficult decisions I've had to make in politics." He backed Clinton in 2016. In 2020, he initially endorsed Kamala Harris for president, then supported Michael Bloomberg after she dropped out, becoming a campaign co-chairman. Rush said he supported the moderate billionaire's campaign came because it was " the clearest, the most focused, and the most reasonable voice for addressing the depressed state of the African-American economy." Rush was critical of Joe Biden during the primary, calling him "woefully ignorant" of the Black experience after Biden name-checked segregationist former senators during a speech.

Rush has had some other strange bedfellows. After Washington's death in 1987, Rush broke with Black activists who launched a splinter "Harold Washington Party," instead endorsing Democrats — some of them white candidates. In the 2015 mayoral election, Rush unexpectedly endorsed the reelection of Mayor Rahm Emanuel. Even more surprising: In 2019, Rush backed the brother of his old foe, Bill Daley, for mayor over a number of African-American candidates.

He endorsed Toni Preckwinkle over eventual Mayor Lori Lightfoot in the runoff of two African-American female candidates because of Lightfoot's record on policing issues , and warned Lightfoot voters about " the blood of the next young Black man or Black woman who is killed by the police" if she won. He later apologized, and a surprising turn of events made them allies: During the Black Lives Matter protests following George Floyd's death in summer 2020, police used Rush's district office without permission to nap, snack and lounge as nearby stores were being looted. Lightfoot and Rush held a joint press conference where they decried the cops' behavior— and Rush said he'd been wrong about the mayor, declaring it " the era of Lori Lightfoot."

Rush had a brush with cancer in 2008. He spent much of the year recovering from salivary gland cancer and surgery to remove a tumor near his jaw. The treatment left him with slurred speech, but doctors later declared him cancer-free. Following the death of his wife, Carolyn, in 2017, he married Paulette Holloway, a minister who has traveled the world as a missionary. In 2018, the House Ethics Committee sanctioned him with a reprove for having failed to pay rent on his campaign office for more than 24 years, which the panel ruled was a violation of the House's gift rules.

Perhaps the biggest threat facing Rush is that Chicago's rapidly declining African-American population will make it difficult to draw three Black-majority districts in the 2022 redistricting. There has been some talk that Rush or fellow septuagenarian Rep. Danny Davis might retire.

IL-1: Chicago   **Cook Partisan Voting Index: D+25**

Population		Race and Ethnicity		Income	
Total	711,039	White	42.00%	Median Income	$56,680
Land area (sq. miles)	258	Black	50.50%	District Income Rank	302
Pop/ sq mi	2,751.91	Latino	11.10%	Poverty Rate	16.00%
Born in State	76.80%	Asian	2.60%	With health insurance	91.80%
		Two or more races	2.10%	Cash public assistance	2.50%
Age Groups		Other	2.70%	Food stamp/SNAP	18.40%
Under 18	22.00%				
18-34	23.50%	**Education**		**Work**	
35-64	38.00%	H.S grad or less	36.60%	White Collar	37.20%
Over 64	16.70%	Some college	32.10%	Sales and Service	41.70%
		College Degree, 4 yr	18.70%	Blue Collar	21.10%
Military		Post grad	12.70%	Government	16.40%
Veteran/ Active Duty	5.10%				

2020 Pres. Vote	Biden	247,071	(74%)	Trump	82,475	(25%)
2016 Pres. Vote	Clinton	245,945	(75%)	Trump	69,913	(21%)

South Side, Southwest Suburbs: The South Side of Chicago has been home to a large urban Black community for nearly a century, which is one of the reasons the metro area has the third largest African-American population in the nation, after New York and Atlanta. A hundred years ago, there were just a few blocks where Black families from the South could settle. But the neighborhood grew rapidly with the first influx of blacks from the Mississippi Delta in the 1910s. By the 1920s, the South Side was well established as a center of black-owned businesses and of music, from blues to jazz. Politically, the South Side was heavily Republican throughout those years, and in 1928, the 1st District elected Republican Oscar De Priest, the first African American elected to the House in the 20th century.

The New Deal attracted African Americans to the Democratic Party, and Black Democrat Arthur Mitchell defeated De Priest in 1934. The South Side has been Democratic ever since, first as a part of the city's Democratic machine and later as the base for the city's Black political strength, powering Harold Washington's historic mayoral wins in the 1980s.

The 1st Congressional District of Illinois includes about half of Chicago's African-American community on the South Side. It also takes in several Black-majority Cook County suburbs and extends about 40 miles into conservative-leaning rural parts of Will County, more than an hour from downtown, which cover about 15 percent of the district. Overall, its gerrymandered voting population is 51 percent Black and 10 percent Hispanic. The 1st has a northern salient that extends to South 26th Street and includes the Gothic spires of the University of Chicago and the mansions of Kenwood, now an eclectic and racially integrated mix of well-to-do inhabitants. Kenwood, considered part of the greater Hyde Park community, was home to Barack Obama before he ran for president.

The Woodlawn neighborhood served as the setting for Lorraine Hansberry's 1959 play A Raisin in the Sun chronicling a Black family's challenges moving into what was then a largely white neighborhood. Bronzeville, which is partly in the district, was home to civil rights icons and artists including Ida B. Wells, Gwendolyn Brooks, Richard Wright, and, for a time, Louis Armstrong. In Englewood, thousands of homes have been built with federal support in recent years in hopes of creating a new Black middle-class community. But Englewood continued to struggle with high rates of poverty and violence in many neighborhoods that are both the cause and result of depopulation. Chicago's South and West sides have seen consistent population declines in recent years, as residents move to the suburbs or head to the South; Chicago's Black population has decreased by almost one-third since 1980, and more than 200,000 Black Chicagoans have left since 2000. Englewood alone has lost more than 56,000 residents since 2010, according to census estimates. That has exacerbated the region's problems, leading to closed schools, abandoned lots and food deserts. The coronavirus pandemic hit Chicago's Black community especially hard. Roughly 60 percent of Chicagoans who died of COVID-19 by late 2020 were Black, even though less than a third of the city's population is.

Chicago in recent years has experienced a crime wave. Murders peaked at 762 in 2016, which exceeded the combined total in the larger cities of New York and Los Angeles, and were pacing to be nearly that high in 2020, part of a nationwide increase in the homicide rate. Police shootings of black people, including the killing of teenager Laquan McDonald in 2014, have exacerbated tensions between police and residents. During the national Black Lives Matter protest following the police killing of Georg Floyd in Minneapolis, sporadic looting took place in some South Side communities. Later that summer, the police shooting of a black man in Englewood led to renewed protests, clashes with police and more than 100 arrests.

The 1st District is overwhelmingly Democratic. Joe Biden prevailed against Donald Trump, 74%-25%.

Robin Kelly (D)

Elected 2013, 4th full term, b. Apr 30, 1956; New York, NY; Bradley University, B.A., 1977; Bradley University, M.A., 1982; Northern IL University, Ph.D., 2004; Christian - Non-Denominational; Married (Nathaniel Horn); 2 children.

Elected Office: IL House, 2002-2007.

Professional Career: Director, minority student services and professional counselor, Bradley University, 1990-1992; Director, community affairs, Village of Matteson, IL, 1992-2006; Chief of Staff, IL Treas., 2007-2010; Chief admin. officer, Cook County Board President, 2010-2012.

DC Office: 2416 RHOB 20515, 202-225-0773, Fax: 202-225-4583, robinkelly.house.gov

State Offices: Chicago, 773-321-2001; Kankakee, 708-679-0078; Matteson, 708-679-0078.

Committees: *Energy & Commerce (VChmn)*: Communications & Technology; Consumer Protection & Commerce; Health. *Oversight & Reform*: Subcommittee on Civil Rights & Civil Liberties.

Group Ratings

	ADA	ACLU	AFL-CIO	LCV	COC	HAFA	ACU	CFG	FRC
2020	**	83%	**	100%	-	0%	4%	**	-
2019	90%	C	100%	97%	65%	C	4%	12%	0%

Almanac Ratings 2019-2020

	Economy	Social	Foreign	Composite
Liberal	100%	100%	80%	94%
Conservative	0%	0%	20%	6%

Key Votes of the 116th Congress

1. U.S./Mex./Can. trade deal Y	5. Russia sanctions Y	9. Firearms background checks Y
2. First Coronavirus response Y	6. Troops in Syria Y	10. Spending at the border Y
3. HEROES Act Y	7. Veto arms sales to Saudis Y	11. Marijuana liberalized rules Y
4. CASH Act Y	8. Defense $$$, veto override Y	12. Electoral College objections N

Election Results

Election	Name (Party)	Vote (%)		Cand. Spent	Ind. Exp. Support	Ind. Exp. Oppose
2020 General	Robin Kelly (D)	234,896	(79%)	$687,682	$990	
	Theresa Raborn (R)	63,142	(21%)			$113
2020 Primary	Robin Kelly (D)	94,767	(85%)			
	Marcus Lewis (D)	16,942	(15%)			

Prior winning percentages: 2018 (81%), 2016 (80%), 2014 (79%), 2013 special (71%)

Democrat Robin Kelly, who won a special election in 2013, has impressed Democrats with her clean-government appeal and ardent support for stronger gun-control laws. She developed a bipartisan partnership on information-technology issues. In 2021, she became vice-chair of the Energy and Commerce Committee, which gave her the opportunity to help manage the panel; her 2020 bid to join House leadership fell short.

Kelly grew up in New York and moved to Illinois to attend Bradley University in Peoria, where she graduated with a bachelor's degree in psychology and a master's degree in counseling and human development services. She earned a Ph.D. in political science from Northern Illinois University. After working at a youth shelter and a counseling center, she returned to Bradley to become director of minority student services. She then spent 14 years as director of community affairs in Matteson, a village on Chicago's South Side.

In 2002, Kelly won a seat in the Illinois House, where she served three terms and got to know then-state Sen. Barack Obama. The two have some friends in common, including Cheryl Whitaker, who chaired Kelly's first congressional run and whose husband was a regular golf partner of Obama. Kelly resigned in 2007 to become chief of staff to state Treasurer Alexi Giannoulias, who ran unsuccessfully in 2010 for the Senate. She ran to replace Giannoulias as treasurer, but lost to GOP state Sen. Dan Rutherford, 50%-45%. She became chief administrative officer to Cook County Board President Toni Preckwinkle (who later lost a bid to be mayor of Chicago).

The House seat became vacant in 2013 when Rep. Jesse Jackson Jr. resigned amid a criminal investigation and later served nearly two years in prison for personal use of $750,000 worth of campaign contributions. Kelly stepped forward for the special election and won the backing of local Democratic power brokers. " She is not a showboat," the Chicago Tribune said in supporting her candidacy. " She won't dazzle you with ebullience. She doesn't grandstand. She just works hard."

Kelly was endorsed by New York City Mayor Michael Bloomberg, whose super PAC ran ads lauding Kelly for backing universal background checks on purchases of firearms and a ban on some types of semi-automatic weapons. Those ads criticized Kelly's chief opponent in the primary, former Rep. Debbie Halvorson, who had the National Rifle Association's endorsement when she represented a suburban district based in Will County. Kelly won the primary, 50%-24%. " We not only won an election," Kelly said in her victory speech, " we took on the NRA, we gave a voice to the voiceless, and we put our communities on a brand new path to a brighter day."

As senior Democrat on the Oversight and Reform Subcommittee on Information Technology, Kelly's interests included improving cyber security, strengthening computer infrastructure and encouraging new technologies. With Republican Rep. Will Hurd of Texas, who chaired the subcommittee, Kelly authored The Internet of Things Cyber security Improvement Act, a bill that required all internet-connected government devices to meet minimal security standards. The House passed the bill in late 2020, as Hurd retired.

Kelly has retained her focus on tighter gun control and co-chairs the House Gun Violence Prevention Task Force. She has filed bills requiring the surgeon general to issue an annual report on the effects of gun violence on public health, and granting authority to the Consumer Product Safety Commission to regulate pistols, revolvers and other firearms as consumer products. When the NRA attacked her as " Assault Gun Kelly," she responded that she was not "anti-gun," but that she favored " common-sense" gun reform that respected " the right of every American to live free from the threat of gun violence."

Following her defeat in 2010, Kelly sought other opportunities to run statewide. She gave serious consideration to challenging the 2016 reelection of Republican Sen. Mark Kirk, who had narrowly defeated Giannoulias in 2010.But she deferred to Rep. Tammy Duckworth after Democratic power-brokers and the deep-pocketed EMILY's List, which supports Democratic women candidates who favor abortion rights, made it clear they preferred Duckworth. Kelly voiced early interest in challenging Republican Gov. Bruce Rauner in 2018. But that Democratic primary was dominated by deep-pocketed self-financers.

She turned her ambitions to leadership in the House. In 2020, she ran for Democratic Caucus Vice Chair and had the support of most of the Congressional Black Caucus. But she lost that race to Rep. Pete Aguilar of California, 148-82. Aguilar was supported by the Congressional Hispanic Caucus and the moderate New Democrat Coalition.

Redistricting options for 2022 could push Kelly farther south of Chicago. But Democrats are nearly certain to assure that she retains a safe district.

IL-2: Chicago   Cook Partisan Voting Index: D+28

Population		Race and Ethnicity		Income	
Total	685,695	White	37.90%	Median Income	$51,472
Land area (sq. miles)	1,081	Black	55.90%	District Income Rank	375
Pop/ sq mi	634.51	Latino	16.00%	Poverty Rate	17.10%
Born in State	77.30%	Asian	0.70%	With health insurance	91.10%
		Two or more races	2.30%	Cash public assistance	2.50%
Age Groups		Other	3.20%	Food stamp/SNAP	20.30%
Under 18	22.80%				
18-34	23.50%	Education		Work	
35-64	37.90%	H.S grad or less	41.50%	White Collar	29.50%
Over 64	15.70%	Some college	35.30%	Sales and Service	43.40%
		College Degree, 4 yr	14.70%	Blue Collar	27.10%
Military		Post grad	8.60%	Government	16.40%
Veteran/ Active Duty	5.80%				

2020 Pres. Vote	Biden	236,641	(77%)	Trump	64,872	(21%)
2016 Pres. Vote	Clinton	236,740	(77%)	Trump	58,026	(19%)

Southeast Chicago, Kankakee: Chicago is a great center of both commerce and industry. If the city's white-collar offices are heavily concentrated in the Loop, its blue-collar heavy industries are most visible on the far South Side. This part of Chicago, diminished in economic importance today, is historically significant. The remnants of its great hulking factories around Lake Calumet and the nearby rail yards have an undeniable majesty. Thomas Geoghegan wrote in his book, Which Side Are You On?, of the fights to win benefits for the workers of shuttered steel mills and of the decline of the labor movement in a place where it got much of its inspiration. This is where the Pullman strike of 1894 was broken by federal troops and where policemen killed 10 union supporters in the Little Steel strike of 1937.

For decades, those workplaces have been mostly empty buildings that suburbanites speed past on the Calumet and Dan Ryan expressways. There have been rumblings of a limited revival, but more failures than successes. In 2018, developers announced plans for an industrial complex on the site of a former Republic Steel mill in the Hegeswisch neighborhood, where Ford Motor Co. began building pickup trucks and SUVs. After temporarily shuttering the plant in 2020 because of the coronavirus pandemic and its impact on the auto industry, Ford had it running at full capacity by the end of the year. A plan to develop a neighborhood with as many as 20,000 homes was abandoned because of soil contamination on the site—another former steel mill.

The 2nd Congressional District of Illinois is a mix of the urban, majority African-American landscape of Chicago's old South Side industrial area and several Cook County suburbs to the south. In the city, the district includes Jackson Park on the lakeshore just to the south of the Museum of Science and Industry, where the Columbian Exposition of 1893 was held and where the Obama presidential library will be built, as part of the lakefront. To the south are South Shore, a once heavily Jewish neighborhood and now home to middle-class Blacks (rapper and quasi-2020 presidential candidate Kanye West grew up there), and the old industrial area around Lake Calumet.

Chicago's Black-majority South Side has steadily lost population over the last four decades, as people move to the suburbs or out of town entirely. Redistricters might be unable to preserve three Black-majority districts, though Democratic lawmakers will likely try to keep three Black-plurality districts, possibly by pushing the 2nd District further into the suburbs.

From its northern tip, the 2nd District extends more than 60 miles through eastern Will County and all of Kankakee County; combined, those two counties comprise about 24 percent of the district population. The district is one of the most Democratic in the nation. In 2020, Joe Biden won here, 77%-21%. The Chicago portion of the 2nd is overwhelmingly Black, though many African Americans, especially young parents fleeing Chicago public schools and crime, are moving into suburbs directly to the south—Harvey, Dolton, Markham, Matteson, Hazel Crest and Lynwood. Amazon planned to open a pair of warehouses in Matteson and Markham in 2020 that it said would employ 2,000 people. Farther south are economically revitalized Homewood and Flossmoor; high-income Olympia Fields; and the still vibrant Park Forest.

Marie Newman (D)

Elected 2020, 1st term, b. Apr 13, 1964; Chicago, IL; Marquette University, Att.; University of WI - Madison, B.A.; Catholic; Married (Jim Newman); 2 children.

Professional Career: Consultant, market research agency, 1988-1990; Associate Marketing Director, United Way Worldwide, 1990-1992; Senior Account Executive, Burson-Marsteller, 1992-1994; Account Director, marketing and communications firm, 1994-1995; Partner/Account Director, marketing and communications firm, 1995-1998; Chief Strategy Director, Magnani Continuum Marketing, 2000-2003; Director of Brand Development, Maddock Douglas, 2003-2005; Co-Founder/Chief Marketing Officer, Datatopia, 2013-2014; President, Marie Newman & Associates.

DC Office: 1022 LHOB 20515, 202-225-5701, newman.house.gov

State Offices: Chicago, 773-948-6223.

Committees: *Small Business*: Contracting & Infrastructure; Economic Growth, Tax & Capital Access; Innovation, Entrepreneurship & Workforce Development. *Transportation & Infrastructure*: Highways & Transit; Railroads, Pipelines & Hazardous Materials.

Election Results

Election	Name (Party)	Vote (%)		Cand. Spent	Ind. Exp. Support	Ind. Exp. Oppose
2020 General	Marie Newman (D)	172,997	(56%)	$3,045,624	$990,763	$12,089
	Mike Fricilone (R)	133,851	(44%)	$126,526		
2020 Primary	Marie Newman (D)	52,384	(47%)			
	Dan Lipinski (D)	49,568	(45%)			
	Rush Darwish (D)	6,351	(6%)			

Democrat Marie Newman was elected in 2020 after narrowly defeating eight-term Rep. Daniel Lipinski in their rematch in the Democratic primary. With her 47%-45% win, she reversed Lipinski's two percentage point victory in 2018. Newman criticized Lipinski's conservative voting record, especially on social issues, as out of step with his district, and offered herself as "a real Democrat with a real plan." She was endorsed in the primary by prominent liberal Democrats from the state and nation, and had the support of the Justice Democrats group that supported progressive challengers to Democratic incumbents across the nation. Although she breezed to victory in November, Newman faced potential jeopardy in redistricting from state Democratic leaders who had been close to Lipinski, plus Latinos seeking their own district on the South Side.

Newman was born in Evergreen Park on the Southwest side of Chicago and grew up in nearby Palos Park in a working-class family. After starting her college education at Marquette University, she switched to the University of Wisconsin, where she got her bachelor's degree in journalism and business.

After working for large advertising agencies, she opened her own consulting business in 2005. She first became politically active when she organized a national nonprofit program, "Team Up to Stop Bullying," after her daughter, who is transgender, encountered problems at school. In that capacity, Newman worked with state and federal legislators to make anti-bullying policies a priority and wrote a book providing solutions for parents and schools across the country.

Launching her first political campaign in 2018, Newman described herself as a "suburban mother" who supported "working families, healthcare for all and everybody's rights." She embraced Medicare for All, a $15 hourly minimum wage and Bernie Sanders-style progressive views. "I'm probably...(t)hat crazy lady from the Southwest suburbs that has the audacity to think she can actually represent her district in a proper way," she told a reporter during that campaign.

Lipinski was a low-profile lawmaker whose father, Bill, had held the seat for 22 years before handing it over to his son in a back-room deal and was close to longtime state House Speaker Mike Madigan, who was based in that House district. Newman ran the best organized and financed challenge the incumbent had faced. The support for Newman from Chicago-area Democratic Reps. Jan Schakowsky and Luis Gutierrez, plus progressive and women's groups, threw into question the customary support for incumbents by the Democratic Congressional Campaign Committee. After pressure from centrist House Blue Dogs, the DCCC endorsed Lipinski barely a week before the primary. Newman ran ahead in the Cook County suburbs and in Will County, but Lipinski's 5,000-vote lead in Chicago neighborhoods gave him a scant 2,100-vote victory.

In their 2020 contest, Newman benefited from her increased name ID, the larger turnout of a presidential primary, and the endorsements of Sens. Sanders and Elizabeth Warren; Chicago Mayor Lori Lightfoot said that Lipinski's social views were "on the wrong side of history." The Chicago Sun-Times, which had endorsed Lipinski in 2018, switched to Newman this time. Citing the shifting demographics of the district, the editorial called Lipinski "a reluctant Democrat" and said that Newman would be "a consistent fighter for better health care. "The challenger narrowly outspent the incumbent. Newman won by 2,800 votes—winning the Cook County suburbs by 3,500 votes and narrowing Lipinski's lead in the city to 2,400 votes.

In the general election, Republican Mike Fricilone, a salesman for an office furniture dealer and a member of the Will County Board since 2012, ran a surprisingly competitive campaign, even though he spent less than $100,000. He reached out to Lipinski supporters and criticized Newman as a "socialist." Newman won 56%-44%. In Will County, which cast one-sixth of the total vote, Fricilone took 54 percent. That outcome might have increased Newman's vulnerability to redistricting.

In the House, she was assigned to the Transportation and Infrastructure, and Small Business committees.

IL-3: Chicago   **Cook Partisan Voting Index: D+6**

Population		Race and Ethnicity		Income	
Total	702,503	White	77.30%	Median Income	$75,411
Land area (sq. miles)	237	Black	5.30%	District Income Rank	126
Pop/ sq mi	2,961.9	Latino	32.30%	Poverty Rate	9.00%
Born in State	69.80%	Asian	4.70%	With health insurance	91.00%
		Two or more races	2.60%	Cash public assistance	2.00%
Age Groups		Other	10.10%	Food stamp/SNAP	8.20%
Under 18	22.90%				
18-34	21.00%	**Education**		**Work**	
35-64	39.70%	H.S grad or less	41.10%	White Collar	36.80%
Over 64	16.40%	Some college	27.60%	Sales and Service	38.50%
		College Degree, 4 yr	20.30%	Blue Collar	24.70%
Military		Post grad	10.90%	Government	13.40%
Veteran/ Active Duty	3.90%				

2020 Pres. Vote	Biden	175,846	(55%)	Trump	135,941	(43%)		
2016 Pres. Vote	Clinton	157,273	(55%)	Trump	113,874	(40%)	Johnson	9,177	(3%)

Southwest Side, West Suburbs: A century ago, humorist Finley Peter Dunne's fictional Mr. Dooley pontificated on matters political in a saloon on Archery Road. This was Archer Avenue on the South Side of Chicago, one of the radial streets that cut across what was once open prairie near the Loop and along the Chicago River. Archer Avenue was one of the paths of outward migration and upward mobility for the children and grandchildren of Chicago's ethnic and cultural groups, and still is. Italians from the river wards along the Chicago Sanitary and Ship Canal moved west, the South Side Irish moved west and south along Cicero Avenue toward Oak Lawn, and the Bohemians (as they were called then; now Czechs) were heavily concentrated in the neat bungalows of industrial suburbs like Berwyn. Midway International Airport, Chicago's main airport from 1927 until O' Hare International Airport opened in 1955, has become a busy discount hub. It has renovated and expanded its congested terminals and parking lots, all squeezed into the heart of a busy commercial area on the Southwest Side. The facility has undergone a $323 million redevelopment, including a new and faster security pavilion. In January 2020, the airport abandoned its plan to expand its parking garage, citing high costs and lower demand.

The 3rd Congressional District of Illinois consists of much of this territory, crisscrossed by grid-pattern streets, the canal, the railroad lines and the switching yards so common in this, the center of the nation's rail network. It is part of Chicago's bungalow belt, where Poles cling to their heritage, with many weekend schools teaching Polish to local kids and adults. The Bridgeport neighborhood was the lifetime home of the late Mayor Richard J. Daley and the storied Irish stronghold that produced four other Chicago mayors. In recent years, Bridgeport has diversified, as Hispanics and Asians have moved in along with artists taking studio space in old warehouses. The neighborhood has reinvented itself as a commercial and entertainment destination, with a new maritime museum along the Chicago River. In 2019, officials unveiled a $45 million " advanced manufacturing center" at Richard J. Daley College, a two-year community college, with the hope that it will lead to the creation of 14,000 manufacturing jobs within a decade.

The 3rd includes the far southwest edge of Chicago, with its early 20th century, prairie-style houses in villages such as the mostly hite ethnic Oak Lawn; a few older, affluent suburbs like Western Springs; and middle-income towns like Palos Hills. An eastern slice of Will County includes the towns of Orland Park, Lockport and Lemont, home to the large campus of Argonne National Laboratory. The lab has become a research hub for batteries and energy storage, nicknamed " Lithium Valley" by its director.

The Hispanic population has grown to about 32 percent, the second largest Hispanic constituency in the state. African Americans are only 5 percent. The district has become decidedly more suburban than urban: In 2020, the vote was 30 percent city and nearly 60 percent in the Cook suburbs. Politically, this area is ancestrally Democratic, culturally conservative, multiethnic and viscerally patriotic. Of the seven congressional districts that include parts of Chicago, the 3rd has cast the highest percentages for Republican presidential candidates. It remains solidly Democratic, but it faces the risk of major shifts following redistricting in 2022. Joe Biden took the district, 55%-43%.

Chuy Garcia (D)

Elected 2018, 2nd term, b. Apr 12, 1956; Durango, Mexico; University of IL, Chicago, B.A., 1999; University of IL, Chicago, M.A., 2002; Catholic; Married (Evelyn Garcia); 3 children.

Elected Office: Chicago City Council, 1986-1993; IL Senate, 1993-1998; Cook County Board of Commissioners, 2010-2018.

DC Office: 530 CHOB 20515, 202-225-8203, chuygarcia.house.gov

State Offices: Chicago, 773-342-0774.

Committees: *Financial Services*: Nat'l Security, International Development & Monetary Policy; Oversight & Investigations. *Natural Resources (VChmn)*: Indigenous Peoples of the United States; Oversight & Investigations. *Transportation & Infrastructure*: Highways & Transit (Chmn); Railroads, Pipelines & Hazardous Materials.

Almanac Ratings 2019-2020

	Economy	Social	Foreign	Composite
Liberal	100%	100%	100%	100%
Conservative	0%	0%	0%	0%

Key Votes of the 116th Congress

1. U.S./Mex./Can. trade deal	N	5. Russia sanctions	Y	9. Firearms background checks Y
2. First Coronavirus response	Y	6. Troops in Syria	Y	10. Spending at the border N
3. HEROES Act	Y	7. Veto arms sales to Saudis	Y	11. Marijuana liberalized rules Y
4. CASH Act	Y	8. Defense $$$, veto override	N	12. Electoral College objections N

Election Results

Election	Name (Party)	Vote (%)		Cand. Spent	Ind. Exp. Support	Ind. Exp. Oppose
2020 General	Jesús Garcia (D)	187,219	(84%)	$819,961	$1,085	
	Jesus Solorio (R)	35,518	(16%)			$113
2020 Primary	Jesús "Chuy" García (D)		(100%)			

Prior winning percentages: 2018 (87%)

Freshman Democrat Jesus "Chuy" Garcia took his House seat after a long career in Chicago politics, where he has been a leader of the increasingly influential Latino community. He was best-known nationally for forcing Chicago Mayor Rahm Emanuel to a competitive runoff in his 2015 reelection. Garcia replaced veteran Rep. Luis Gutierrez, who retired in 2018 after 26 years. Garcia brought an even more progressive pedigree than Gutierrez, a longtime immigration reform leader. Rather than challenge his popularity, both Emanuel and Gutierrez supported Garcia in his easy primary victory in the heavily Democratic district.

Garcia was born in Mexico, and his father was a farmworker in several parts of the United States. Following his arrival in Chicago with his family as a 10-year-old, he graduated from the University of Illinois, Chicago, where he later received his master's degree in urban planning. His early activity in Chicago politics was with the successful 1983 mayoral campaign of Harold Washington, who tapped Garcia as his deputy water commissioner. He served six years as an alderman on the Chicago City Council (where he was a Washington ally in the fierce Council Wars), six years in the state Senate and seven years on the Cook County Board of Commissioners. In the latter position, he passed a measure ending the county's cooperation with the Immigration and Customs Enforcement agency.

Following his 1998 Senate reelection loss to an ally of then-Mayor Richard M. Daley, Garcia founded and became executive director of the community development organization Enlace Chicago, and he chaired the board of the Latino Policy forum. Garcia remained an ally of local political reformers and supported Sen. Bernie Sanders for the 2016 Democratic presidential nomination.

In his challenge to Emanuel in 2015, Garcia gained support from many African-American leaders who were unhappy with some of the mayor's policies, including his management of police and education. Backed by the large teachers' union, Garcia attacked Emanuel as "insensitive" in closing nearly 50 local schools. Most of the city's political establishment, including Latino leaders like Gutierrez, supported Emanuel, who won 56%-44% in the runoff, the first in the city's history.

After Gutierrez announced his retirement, several aldermen voiced interest in running for the seat, But Garcia's candidacy (plus endorsements from Gutierrez and Emanuel) convinced them otherwise. The primary became a formality, with Garcia winning 66%-22% over community activist Sol Flores.

Garcia is the first Mexican-American to represent Chicago's largest Hispanic community in Congress; Gutierrez is Puerto Rican. "The Southwest Side was ripe for change," Garcia told The Huffington Post following the primary. "The aspirations of the Mexican community for greater political empowerment would be an important ingredient in this election cycle."

In the House, Garcia got a seat on the Financial Services committee, where he emerged as a vocal critic of Big Tech. During an October 2019 hearing with Facebook CEO Mark Zuckerberg, Garcia warned the billionaire that "Facebook has operated as a shadow government with you as its head," and questioned whether Facebook's digital currency, Libra, should be regulated by the Securities and Exchange Commission. The following month, he introduced a bill to make it harder for tech companies to enter the financial services industry—regulations that drew praise from traditional banking institutions wary of the competition. He also has seats on the Natural Resources, and Transportation and Infrastructure committees.

He partnered with Democratic Sen. Elizabeth Warren on a bill to add scrutiny to bank mergers. When it came time for the 2020 election, Garcia again backed Sanders, campaigning hard for him in the primaries before helping Joe Biden woo Hispanic voters during the general election.

IL-4: Chicago   **Cook Partisan Voting Index: D+33**

Population		Race and Ethnicity		Income	
Total	676,674	White	58.10%	Median Income	$59,548
Land area (sq. miles)	52	Black	4.50%	District Income Rank	271
Pop/ sq mi	12,901.32	Latino	67.10%	Poverty Rate	12.90%
Born in State	53.70%	Asian	4.40%	With health insurance	84.80%
		Two or more races	3.40%	Cash public assistance	2.30%
Age Groups		Other	29.60%	Food stamp/SNAP	13.60%
Under 18	23.00%				
18-34	28.70%	**Education**		**Work**	
35-64	37.10%	H.S grad or less	51.50%	White Collar	32.90%
Over 64	11.30%	Some college	20.70%	Sales and Service	38.40%
		College Degree, 4 yr	18.20%	Blue Collar	28.70%
Military		Post grad	9.60%	Government	8.00%
Veteran/ Active Duty	2.20%				

2020 Pres. Vote	Biden	184,587	(81%)	Trump	39,629	(17%)		
2016 Pres. Vote	Clinton	172,367	(81%)	Trump	27,808	(13%)	Johnson	4,892	(2%)
	Stein	4,852	(2%)					

Parts of North and Southwest Sides: Just west of the Loop, the Chicago River splits into the North and South branches, both penetrating the heart of old neighborhoods where immigrants got their start. The South Branch is the guts of Chicago, the site of one of Western civilization's astonishing engineering feats. In 1900, the course of the river was reversed so that sewage flowed downstate through a canal rather than out into Lake Michigan. Just blocks away was Maxwell Street, then thronged with market stalls and long the arrival point for Chicago-bound Jews. Not far away in an Italian-American neighborhood on Halsted Street was Jane Addams' Hull House, the original settlement house, where social workers instructed new immigrants on adapting to American life. To the south were Pilsen, arrival neighborhood for the Bohemians (Czechs), and the Irish neighborhoods along Archer Avenue. To the north was Milwaukee Avenue, the main street of Polish Americans and Ukrainian Americans.

In recent decades, these areas have become arrival neighborhoods again, mostly for Chicago's wide variety of Hispanic immigrants. On the South Side, in the old river wards, is the heart of Chicago's Mexican-American community, extending west into Pilsen and into the once Bohemian suburb of Cicero, famous as a haven for Al Capone's mobsters in the 1920s. Beginning in the 1980s, Cicero became a transit point for Mexican immigrants. Its official census population is 81,000, of whom 90 percent are Hispanic. But town officials believe the actual number is significantly higher because of the influx of undocumented residents. Chicago has the largest Latino concentration north of Texas and Florida and between the two coasts. In 2019, Hispanics roughly equaled the rapidly shrinking Black population as Chicago's largest minority group, with 29 percent of the population, almost as large as the city's non-Hispanic White population.

The 4th Congressional District remains the only majority-Hispanic district in the Midwest. Given the community's rapid growth—more than 1.3 million Latinos live in Cook County—a second Hispanic-majority district might be created in the 2022 redistricting. With the South and West Side Mexican-American areas and the smaller North Side Puerto Rican communities separated by the West Side Black community, the solution has been the creation of one of the most bizarrely designed congressional districts in the country, shaped like a pair of earmuffs, with a thin line of territory stretching around the black-majority 7th District at the Cook-DuPage County line. Of the 70 percent of residents who are Hispanic, four-fifths are Mexican-American. The district is entirely in Cook County, with close to 75 percent of the votes cast in Chicago or Cicero.

On both the south and north sides, economic changes have led to social tensions. Historic Pilsen, whose manhole covers feature depictions of the Aztec calendar, has become "ground zero for gentrification," the Chicago Tribune wrote in April 2018. The district contains the rapidly gentrifying neighborhoods of Logan Square, famous for its boulevards and spacious mansions surrounding Milwaukee Avenue, and Humboldt Park, which includes the nation's only museum that focuses on Puerto Rican arts and culture. There, young professionals are moving in, with trendy restaurants, new condominiums and boutique shops locating alongside traditional Latin American taquerias and Hispanic churches. The Chicago Advocate referred to the area as the "Hipster Mecca of the Midwest."

The chief downside has been for the tenants—many of them Hispanic—who have been forced out by housing costs that have surged, with the price of an average home in Logan Square climbing from $218,000 in 2012 to $457,000 in 2020. Logan Square's population went from being two-thirds Hispanic and a quarter non-Hispanic White in 2000 to being 48 percent white and 42 percent Hispanic in 2018. Many Hispanic families have moved to Chicago's nearby inner suburbs. The 4th, which he won 81%-17%, was Joe Biden's second-best district in Illinois.

Mike Quigley (D)

Elected 2009, 6th full term, b. Oct 17, 1958; Indianapolis, IN; Roosevelt University, B.A., 1981; University of Chicago, M.P.P., 1985; Loyola University Law School, J.D., 1989; Christian - Non-Denominational; Married (Barbara Quigley); 2 children.

Elected Office: Cook County commissioner, 1998-2009.

Professional Career: Cook County aldermanic aide, 1983-1989; Adjunct Professional, Roosevelt University, 2006-2007; Adjunct Professional in political science, Loyola University Chicago, 2002-2009; Practicing attorney, 1990-present.

DC Office: 2458 RHOB 20515, 202-225-4061, Fax: 202-225-5603, quigley.house.gov

State Offices: Chicago, 773-267-5926; Chicago, 773-267-5926.

Committees: *Appropriations*: Financial Services & General Government (Chmn); Homeland Security; Transportation, HUD & Related Agencies. *Oversight & Reform*. *Permanent Select on Intelligence*: Counterterrorism, Counterintelligence & Counterproliferation; Defense Intelligence & Warfighter Support.

Group Ratings

	ADA	ACLU	AFL-CIO	LCV	COC	HAFA	ACU	CFG	FRC
2020	**	79%	**	100%	-	0%	3%	**	-
2019	95%	C	100%	97%	54%	C	3%	13%	0%

Almanac Ratings 2019-2020

	Economy	Social	Foreign	Composite
Liberal	100%	100%	60%	87%
Conservative	0%	0%	40%	13%

Key Votes of the 116th Congress

1. U.S./Mex./Can. trade deal	Y	5. Russia sanctions	Y	9. Firearms background checks	Y
2. First Coronavirus response	Y	6. Troops in Syria	Y	10. Spending at the border	N
3. HEROES Act	Y	7. Veto arms sales to Saudis	Y	11. Marijuana liberalized rules	Y
4. CASH Act	Y	8. Defense $$$, veto override	Y	12. Electoral College objections	N

Election Results

Election	Name (Party)	Vote (%)		Cand. Spent	Ind. Exp. Support	Ind. Exp. Oppose
2020 General	Mike Quigley (D)	255,661	(71%)	$557,174	$113	
	Tommy Hanson (R)	96,200	(27%)			$113
	Thomas Wilda (G)	9,408	(3%)			
2020 Primary	Mike Quigley (D)	97,865	(75%)			
	Brian Burns (D)	32,440	(25%)			

Prior winning percentages: 2018 (77%), 2016 (68%), 2014 (63%), 2012 (66%), 2010 (71%), 2009 special (69%)

Mike Quigley is a reform-minded Democrat who won a special election in 2009 and has built legislative influence in the district that had been held by Rahm Emanuel. He is both an avid hockey player— he has had more than 300 stitches to prove it— and an ex-political science professor whom The New York Times once called " the king of Chicago's public-policy nerds." In the House, he has become a force on the Appropriations and Intelligence committees, and played a key role in the House impeachment of President Donald Trump.

Quigley grew up in the working-class suburb of Carol Stream in DuPage County. He graduated from Roosevelt University, got a master's in public policy at the University of Chicago and his law degree from Loyola University of Chicago. He practiced criminal law and taught political science part-time at Loyola. He started his career in politics as an aide to Alderman Bernard Hansen and got involved in a community battle to stop the addition of lights for night games at Wrigley Field, which is in the heart of an old, gentrified neighborhood. He lost that fight and the Cubs started playing night games in 1988.

In 1998, Quigley was elected to the Cook County Board of Commissioners, where he became an independent voice and a frequent nemesis of machine politician and board President John Stroger. He pushed reforms such as ending patronage jobs at the Cook County Forest Preserve District, promoted environmental action, and sponsored a proposal to allow gay couples to register as domestic partners. In 2005, Quigley decided to challenge Stroger for board president, but later dropped out and backed Forrest Claypool, who lost to Stroger.

After President Barack Obama plucked Emanuel from the House to serve as his chief of staff, many candidates jumped into the wide-open Democratic primary. State Rep. Sara Feigenholtz was endorsed by EMILY's List, which supports abortion rights. Alderman Patrick O'Connor and state Rep. John Fritchey had local party machine support. Quigley ran a late ad comparing Feigenholtz to President Richard Nixon, saying she had resorted to unfair campaign charges. That may have extinguished any lingering friendship between Quigley and Feigenholtz, who had dated briefly years earlier. Quigley received key newspaper endorsements from the Chicago Sun-Times and Chicago Tribune, the latter praising him for an " outstanding record of independent, reform-minded performance in office." In a low-turnout event, Quigley won the primary with 20 percent of the vote to 17 percent for Fritchey and 15 percent for Feigenholtz. Quigley breezed to victory in the general election and hasn't faced real competition since.

In the House, Quigley has been a consistent Democratic vote but one who is unafraid to ruffle feathers. He was among the first Democrats in 2010 to call on Rep. Charles Rangel of New York to give up his Ways and Means Committee chairmanship while battling ethics problems. He cofounded the Congressional Transparency Caucus and introduced legislation requiring lobbyists to disclose the name of each executive branch official and each member of Congress and staffer with whom they meet.

He ran a persistent campaign to require Congressional Research Service reports to be made public. " Taxpayers have a stake in these reports, providing more than $100 million annually to support the work of the Congressional Research Service," he wrote in Time. He largely prevailed in the fiscal 2018 omnibus spending bill, which required that CRS publish on its website all non-confidential reports.

Quigley moved into the House hierarchy with a seat on the Appropriations Committee, where he was the only Illinois member from either party. In 2019, he became chairman of its Financial Services Subcommittee, whose spending domain includes White House operations. The subcommittee also oversees the post office. When Louis DeJoy, a major Trump donor, was put in charge of the U.S. Postal Service and immediately made changes that slowed down delivery times shortly before the 2020 election when many Americans were voting by mail, Quigley led the charge to reverse the changes. Under questioning from Quigley and other Democrats, DeJoy struggled to provide basic details, such as whether overtime had been limited for workers or how much it cost to mail a postcard.

On the Intelligence Committee, Quigley played a key support role in the impeachment of Trump. When Republicans shrugged off Trump's firing of career diplomat Marie Yovanovitch because she got a job as a professor afterwards, he shot back. " It's like a ' Hallmark' movie— you ended up at Georgetown, it's all OK," Quigley said sarcastically to Yovanovitch during the hearings, drawing laughs in the room and generating headlines.

Quigley has been active in calling for tighter gun-control laws. On two other issues of importance to his constituents, he has pushed for an extension of the visa waiver program to Poland, and for review by the Food and Drug Administration of its policy that bans gay and bisexual men from donating blood. In 2020, he introduced legislation to lift that ban. He has been a leader of the LGBT Equality Caucus. In late 2020, the House passed his Big Cat Public Safety Act with bipartisan support. The bill, which banned private ownership of large felines, got a jolt from the popular Netflix documentary series Tiger King, which spotlighted its effort.

Quigley has coasted to reelection. In 2018, as was the case eight years earlier, he toyed with the idea of running for an open seat for mayor, but decided not to join the crowded field in each case. With the Appropriations panel filled with aging Democrats who have more seniority but are getting close to retirement, Quigley likely will gain additional influence in the coming years.

IL-5: Chicago   **Cook Partisan Voting Index: D+22**

Population		Race and Ethnicity		Income	
Total	739,401	White	79.30%	Median Income	$94,144
Land area (sq. miles)	96	Black	3.00%	District Income Rank	45
Pop/ sq mi	7,725.43	Latino	21.90%	Poverty Rate	8.10%
Born in State	55.60%	Asian	7.00%	With health insurance	93.90%
		Two or more races	3.10%	Cash public assistance	1.20%
Age Groups		Other	7.60%	Food stamp/SNAP	5.80%
Under 18	19.60%				
18-34	28.70%	**Education**		**Work**	
35-64	38.80%	H.S grad or less	23.60%	White Collar	54.20%
Over 64	12.90%	Some college	19.70%	Sales and Service	32.20%
		College Degree, 4 yr	33.20%	Blue Collar	13.60%
Military		Post grad	23.60%	Government	8.90%
Veteran/ Active Duty	2.90%				

2020 Pres. Vote	Biden	267,654	(72%)	Trump	96,611	(26%)		
2016 Pres. Vote	Clinton	229,944	(70%)	Trump	78,074	(24%)	Johnson	12,645	(4%)

North Side, Cook Suburbs: Few places in America today have more ethnic and cultural variety than the North Side of Chicago. This has been the destination of one immigrant group after another. Its neighborhoods harbor all manner of successful, middle-class people. Wooden working men's cottages from the late 19th century give way to sturdy brick houses from the early 1900s, and then to the prairie bungalows of the 1920s and the white-shuttered, orange-brick colonials of the 1950s. Chicago was America's top immigrant destination for Poles, Lithuanians, Czechs, Slovaks, Ukrainians and Romanians. Something about the heavy, dull clouds of the long winters, the short, hot summers, and a climate suited to potatoes and cabbage and other hardy vegetables may have reminded them of Central and Eastern Europe, with the addition of the bustling Loop. In the 1980s, upwardly mobile immigrants from Mexico and Guatemala, Korea, and the Philippines moved in. The city is diverse but remains deeply segregated:

Family ties, webs of acquaintances that reach back to ancestral villages, have made the North Side of Chicago a natural port of entry for Eastern bloc migrants, even as other newcomers arrive with relationships extending to Latin America and Southeast Asia. The collapse of the Soviet Union encouraged new rounds of immigrants in the 1990s from Poland and Ukraine, joined by those from Pakistan, India and Bosnia. A couple of blocks from the Chicago River and the Kennedy Expressway is the grand old St. Stanislaus Kostka Church, an iconic center of the Polish community since the 19th century that now conducts masses in Spanish.

The 5th Congressional District covers an oddly shaped swath across Chicago's North Side and the city's western suburbs, running from the lakefront to, and including, O'Hare International Airport on the northwest side of the city, and dipping into western suburbs such as Elmhurst and affluent Hinsdale. It takes in the old Polish and Ukrainian neighborhoods and shops around Milwaukee Avenue, and the Italian neighborhoods running west on Grand Avenue. It also includes the gentrified Chicago neighborhoods of Old Town, where old houses and factories are being converted into upscale condominiums, often over the objections of preservationists. Nearby Lincoln Park is the second-richest neighborhood in Chicago (after the Gold Coast); it abounds with boutiques, clubs and restaurants and contains DePaul University, the nation's largest Catholic university. Those commercial activities have substantially reduced the residential population. Trendy Ravenswood, with large Victorian homes on tree-lined streets, has become a craft brewing and distilling hub.

The district is home to baseball's famed Wrigley Field, which opened in 1914 and is a protected landmark that has defied the tear-down trend in ballparks. The Friendly Confines finally rewarded the century-long heartbreak of its fans when the Cubs won the World Series in 2016. Just east of gentrified Wrigleyville is Boystown, the epicenter of Chicago's gay community; rainbow flags are present on most businesses. The 5th District contains the largest white population of the seven districts based in Chicago: The Hispanic share has increased modestly to 20 percent. A scant 3 percent is African-American, a historical remnant of redlining. While the 5th has some Republican-leaning western suburbs, it remains a solidly Democratic district. Joe Biden won, 72%-26%.

Sean Casten (D)

Elected 2018, 2nd term, b. Nov 23, 1971; Dublin, Ireland; Middlebury College, B.A., 1993; Dartmouth College, Hanover, M.S., 1998; Married (Kara Casten); 2 children.

Professional Career: President and Chief Executive Officer, Turbosteam Corporation, 2000-2007; Co-Founder, Recycled Energy Development LLC.

DC Office: 429 CHOB 20515, 202-225-4561, casten.house.gov

State Offices: West Chicago, 630-520-9450.

Committees: *Financial Services*: Consumer Protection & Financial Institutions; Investor Protection, Entrepreneurship & Capital Markets; Task Force on Artificial Intelligence. *Science, Space & Technology*: Energy; Environment; Investigations & Oversight. *Select Committee on the Climate Crisis.*

Almanac Ratings 2019-2020

	Economy	Social	Foreign	Composite
Liberal	100%	100%	80%	94%
Conservative	0%	0%	20%	6%

Key Votes of the 116th Congress

1. U.S./Mex./Can. trade deal	Y	5. Russia sanctions	Y	9. Firearms background checks	Y
2. First Coronavirus response	Y	6. Troops in Syria	Y	10. Spending at the border	Y
3. HEROES Act	Y	7. Veto arms sales to Saudis	Y	11. Marijuana liberalized rules	Y
4. CASH Act	Y	8. Defense $$$, veto override	Y	12. Electoral College objections	N

Election Results

Election	Name (Party)	Vote (%)		Cand. Spent	Ind. Exp. Support	Ind. Exp. Oppose
2020 General	Sean Casten (D)	213,777	(53%)	$5,410,742	$876	$35,671
	Jeanne Ives (R)	183,891	(45%)	$3,509,404	$573,000	$113
2020 Primary	Sean Casten (D)	82,909	(100%)			

Prior winning percentages: 2018 (54%)

Freshman Democrat Sean Casten, a political newcomer, was elected in a suburban district that Democratic redistricters designed as a Republican seat. A scientist and renewable energy entrepreneur, he has used his expertise to focus on climate change in Congress. Casten defeated Rep. Peter Roskam, who had been a House Republican leader and was a senior member of the Ways and Means Committee, where he had a prominent role in crafting the 2017 tax cuts. Casten defeated a flawed GOP candidate to retain the seat in 2020.

Born in Ireland to American parents and raised in New York, Casten majored in molecular biology at Middlebury College and got master's degrees in biochemical engineering and engineering management from Thayer School of Engineering at Dartmouth College. During his career working on clean-energy technologies, he was president of Massachusetts-based Turbostream Corp., which used energy-recycling techniques to reduce greenhouse gasses. With his father, Casten founded Illinois-based Recycled Energy Development, which sought ways to capture waste heat to generate electricity; the company was sold in 2016. He chaired the U.S. Combined Heat and Power Association and he worked with states in the Northeast on a plan that became the Regional Greenhouse Gas Initiative.

In 2018, Casten benefited from a crowded primary field with five female candidates, emerging as the winner with 30 percent of the vote. He ran hard against Roskam for helping craft the GOP tax cuts, slamming the law as an " immoral tax plan that is saddling our country with crippling debt and could force cuts to Social Security and Medicare." Roskam sought distance from President Donald Trump, even comparing Casten's blunt style to Trump's, while attacking him for some liberal positions— as well as his praise of sex columnist and LGBT advocate Dan Savage. Casten won, 54%-46%, against the entrenched incumbent, benefiting from a Democratic wave election and the suburbs' hard shift against the GOP during the Trump era.

In the House, Casten got seats on the Financial Services and Science, Space, and Technology committees. He joined the fiscally moderate New Democrats and co-chaired their Climate Change Task Force. Casten showed himself to have more of a progressive streak than other New Dems. He was one of the first swing-district Democrats to support an impeachment inquiry into Trump, after the release of Special Counsel Robert Mueller's report and before details were revealed about Trump's actions towards Ukraine, which Democrats said bolstered the case for impeachment. " Over two years into his presidency, we still do not know whether the president of the United States is beholden to foreign powers. This is a threat to our republic," Casten said, explaining his decision.

Casten gained more wiggle room in his Democratic-trending district than did other freshmen. And he benefited from his 2020 opponent, social conservative firebrand Jeanne Ives, a former state lawmaker who two years earlier nearly defeated Illinois Gov. Bruce Rauner in the GOP primary. Ives had a long history of controversial comments and stances on LGBT rights (she called gay marriage an attempt for gay and lesbian people to " weasel their way" into acceptability), immigration and abortion. After former establishment favorite and former Illinois Lt. Gov. Evelyn Sanguinetti dropped out of the contest and it became clear that Ives would win the GOP nomination, national Republican campaign groups largely gave up on defeating Casten.

Casten outspent Ives, $5.3 million to $3.1 million. Ives benefitted from almost $500,000 of outside spending, much of it from the House Freedom Caucus PAC. National Democrats were so confident Casten would win that they did not spend to help him.

Casten attacked Ives for opposing abortion rights and tied her to Trump, who was unpopular in the district. He got some crossover support: Former Illinois Republican Party Chairman Pat Brady, a Rauner ally, endorsed Casten and cut a TV ad for him. Ives sought to steer clear of her past controversies, focusing in her ads on taxes and government spending as well as her graduation from West Point. The final result was a bit closer than either party expected, with Casten winning 53%-45%. In DuPage, which cast about half of the vote, he took 55 percent. He won the other counties, except for his narrow loss in a sliver of Lake County. Democratic state lawmakers likely will move to shore up his district.

IL-6: West-Central Chicagoland   Cook Partisan Voting Index: D+3

Population		Race and Ethnicity		Income	
Total	710,626	White	82.00%	Median Income	$105,292
Land area (sq. miles)	379	Black	2.10%	District Income Rank	24
Pop/ sq mi	1,876.09	Latino	11.70%	Poverty Rate	4.60%
Born in State	65.70%	Asian	9.50%	With health insurance	95.60%
		Two or more races	3.00%	Cash public assistance	0.90%
Age Groups		Other	3.30%	Food stamp/SNAP	3.60%
Under 18	22.50%				
18-34	18.50%	**Education**		**Work**	
35-64	41.90%	H.S grad or less	21.80%	White Collar	52.10%
Over 64	17.20%	Some college	25.00%	Sales and Service	34.20%
		College Degree, 4 yr	32.00%	Blue Collar	13.70%
Military		Post grad	21.20%	Government	10.40%
Veteran/ Active Duty	4.50%				

2020 Pres. Vote	Biden	226,806	(55%)	Trump	174,829	(42%)			
2016 Pres. Vote	Clinton	177,549	(49%)	Trump	152,935	(42%)	Johnson	18,336	(5%)

DuPage, Kane: Most residents of Chicago land now live in the suburbs, and increasingly in the collar counties surrounding Cook County. DuPage County, west of Chicago, had 103,000 residents in 1940. In 2019, there were about 930,000, with new subdivisions still springing up at the western edges. This is no longer a one-trick county of bedroom suburbs. It has become an engine of economic growth, containing the Illinois Technology and Research Corridor, one of suburban Chicago's biggest employment hubs.

Nearby are graceful, old railroad-commuter towns like Hinsdale and Downers Grove, plus Barrington Hills, known for its country manors and large open areas protected by preservationists. Naperville, once a country village, is now an edge city with the third largest population in the state behind Chicago and Aurora, and a school district that is top-ranked in science. Wheaton is home to Cantigny Park, which was once the estate of Joseph Medill and his grandson, Col. Robert McCormick, longtime publishers of the Chicago Tribune. Wheaton College, known as the " evangelical Harvard," boasts Reverend Billy Graham among its alumni.

Politically, these suburbs were once rock-ribbed Republican. But in the 1990s, local voters began recoiling from the national party's cultural conservatism. After voting for Republicans in every presidential election in the 20th century, DuPage County has gone for Democrats in every presidential election starting in 2008. Joe Biden in 2020 carried it by 18 points, a stunning improvement over his former running mate and hometown hero Barack Obama's 1-point win in 2012; turnout increased by nearly 100,000 voters. In 2018, Republicans in DuPage had additional setbacks in state and local elections— a political tsunami that both carried and lifted Democrats—all women—" to unprecedented heights in county government," the Daily Herald reported. The once-rural county, now the second-largest in Illinois, has become more diverse; foreign-born residents make up 19 percent of the countywide population. That increase is part of the broader racial shifts across Chicago land, which is moving soon to majority-minority status.

The 6th Congressional District of Illinois forms a large C that encompasses a small wedge of Cook County and parts of the collar counties of Kane, McHenry and Lake; a bit more than half the population lives in DuPage, smaller parts of which have been grafted onto five other districts. It takes in towns including Barrington, Wheaton, Winfield, Downers Grove and parts of Naperville. The 6th was designed during the 2012 redistricting as a Republican vote-sink, with the solidly GOP Palatine in Cook, St. Charles in Kane, and Crystal Lake in McHenry. Despite those intentions, the Republican vote here slipped markedly in 2016 and continued to fall in 2020. What had been a 53%-45% lead for Mitt Romney in 2012 became a 49%-42% lead for Hillary Clinton and a 55%-42% mark for Joe Biden— a shift of 20 percentage points in less than a decade.

Danny Davis (D)

Elected 1996, 13th term, b. Sep 06, 1941; Parkdale, AR; AR Agricultural and Mechanical College, B.A., 1961; Chicago State University, M.A., 1968; Union Institute and University, Ph.D., 1977; Baptist; Married (Vera G. Davis); 2 children (1 deceased); 4 grandchildren (1 deceased).

Elected Office: Chicago city alderman, 1979-1990; Cook County commissioner, 1990-1996.

Professional Career: Teacher, Chicago Public Schls., 1962-1969; Health care planner, 1969-1979.

DC Office: 2159 RHOB 20515, 202-225-5006, Fax: 202-225-5641, davis.house.gov

State Offices: Chicago, 773-533-7520.

Committees: *Oversight & Reform*: Government Operations; Subcommittee on Civil Rights & Civil Liberties. *Ways & Means*: Trade; Worker & Family Support (Chmn).

Group Ratings

	ADA	ACLU	AFL-CIO	LCV	COC	HAFA	ACU	CFG	FRC
2020	**	83%	**	100%	-	0%	4%	**	-
2019	9%	C	100%	97%	55%	C	4%	12%	0%

Almanac Ratings 2019-2020

	Economy	Social	Foreign	Composite
Liberal	58%	100%	96%	85%
Conservative	42%	0%	4%	15%

Key Votes of the 116th Congress

1. U.S./Mex./Can. trade deal Y	5. Russia sanctions Y	9. Firearms background checks Y
2. First Coronavirus response Y	6. Troops in Syria Y	10. Spending at the border N
3. HEROES Act Y	7. Veto arms sales to Saudis Y	11. Marijuana liberalized rules Y
4. CASH Act Y	8. Defense $$$, veto override Y	12. Electoral College objections N

Election Results

Election	Name (Party)	Vote (%)		Cand. Spent	Ind. Exp. Support	Ind. Exp. Oppose
2020 General	Danny Davis (D).....................	249,383	(80%)	$274,360	$10	
	Craig Cameron (R)...................	41,390	(13%)			
	Tracy Jennings (I)....................	19,355	(6%)	$62,711		
2020 Primary	Danny K. Davis (D)................	79,813	(60%)			
	Kina Collins (D).....................	18,399	(14%)			
	Anthony Clark (D)..................	17,206	(13%)			
	Kristine Schanbacher (D).........	17,187	(13%)			

Prior winning percentages: 2018 (88%), 2016 (84%), 2014 (85%), 2012 (85%), 2010 (82%), 2008 (85%), 2006 (87%), 2004 (86%), 2002 (83%), 2000 (86%), 1998 (93%), 1996 (83%)

Danny Davis, a Democrat first elected in 1996 at age 55, is a staunch liberal who has waged two unsuccessful campaigns for Chicago mayor and twice flirted with running for president of the Cook County Board of Commissioners. His opportunities to seek other office likely have ended, however, and he might be close to retirement, though he has become a senior statesman in the Congressional Black Caucus and a subcommittee chairman at House Ways and Means.

Davis grew up on a cotton farm in Arkansas, graduated from college in that state, then moved to Chicago and worked as a teacher, assistant principal, and guidance counselor in Chicago public schools. For 10 years, he ran a community health project on the West Side. He was elected alderman in 1979, and supported Harold Washington, the city's first Black mayor, in his 1980s battles with White machine aldermen dubbed the "Council Wars."

Davis was elected a Cook County commissioner. in 1990, and in 1996 ran for an open House seat. His major opponents were 3rd Ward Alderman Dorothy Tillman, an ally of Chicago Mayor Richard M. Daley, and 28th Ward Alderman Ed Smith. Davis ran to the left, campaigning for a $7.60 minimum wage, affirmative action programs and a nationalized health care plan. He won with 33 percent and has not faced a serious challenge since, though that might be changing.

In the House, Davis has a liberal voting record but few major legislative accomplishments. He has pushed for tax incentives for businesses that create jobs in inner-city communities and distressed rural areas. He was a champion of organized labor as he worked with a bipartisan coalition that in 2006 enacted big changes in the Postal Service. Since then, congressional agreement on postal overhaul has remained elusive. When Trump appointed Louis DeJoy, a major donor, head of the USPS in 2020 and DeJoy implemented changes that slowed service ahead of the election, Davis said Trump was attempting to "gangster the Postal Service." DeJoy dropped some of his rushed changes.

His devotion to issues affecting the poor has won Davis respect, including from Republicans. With his wife, Vera, he supported in the mid-2000s a local program to increase the low rate of Black home ownership in his district by offering credit counseling and innovative forms of mortgage financing. With the view that everybody deserves a second chance, Davis has taken a deep interest in the problems of former convicts seeking to transition to the mainstream. He teamed on a bipartisan bill creating tax credits to encourage transitional housing and job training for former prisoners. That evolved into his Second Chance Act, which President George W. Bush signed into law in 2008.

Davis filed legislation to make available educational Pell Grants to prisoners At his urging, the Obama administration pursued it as a pilot program and Trump expanded it. Davis hoped to make the plan permanent and more widely available. On Ways and Means, Davis became chairman in 2019 of the renamed Worker and Family Support Subcommittee.

In 2006, Davis sought to become Cook County Board president after incumbent John Stroger suffered a serious stroke. But Democratic committeemen overwhelmingly supported Stroger's son, Todd, for the nomination. After the 2008 election, Davis campaigned publicly for the support of Democratic Gov. Rod Blagojevich to fill Obama's Senate seat. Blagojevich called Davis his top choice. Davis turned down what was bound to be a tainted appointment after Blagojevich was criminally charged and then convicted for trying to gain personally from his power to make the appointment.

Davis briefly ran for Chicago mayor in 2010, but bowed to pressure to unite the African-American vote and endorsed former Sen. Carol Moseley Braun. She finished fourth in the Democratic primary, which Rahm Emanuel won.

In late 2016, Davis' teen grandson was shot to death in a dispute over the possession of gym shoes. Davis called for the declaration of a "state of emergency" in high-crime areas of Chicago to address crime, violence, education, economic development and related problems. In 2018, he filed a bill aimed at reducing gun sales by placing national excise taxes on firearms and ammunition. Cook County has a similar tax.

In 2020, Davis won only 60 percent in the Democratic primary against three candidates who were each less than half his age. In an editorial, the Chicago Sun-Times endorsed one of his opponents, writing that "the people of the 7th Congressional District deserve a representative who will work for them with vigor." Though Davis was endorsed by the Democratic Socialists of America in 2008, the DSA and Justice Democrats backed high school teacher Anthony Clark, who finished third with 13 percent of the vote.

That outcome fueled rumors in Illinois political circles that Davis might retire as he also faces the disruption of redistricting..

IL-7: Chicago   Cook Partisan Voting Index: D+37

Population		Race and Ethnicity		Income	
Total	727,761	White	39.50%	Median Income	$64,312
Land area (sq. miles)	63	Black	42.50%	District Income Rank	214
Pop/ sq mi	11,640.45	Latino	17.30%	Poverty Rate	19.70%
Born in State	61.60%	Asian	7.80%	With health insurance	91.80%
		Two or more races	2.70%	Cash public assistance	2.90%
Age Groups		Other	7.60%	Food stamp/SNAP	19.30%
Under 18	19.90%				
18-34	30.00%	**Education**		**Work**	
35-64	36.30%	H.S grad or less	34.20%	White Collar	50.90%
Over 64	14.00%	Some college	20.90%	Sales and Service	33.80%
Military		College Degree, 4 yr	23.30%	Blue Collar	15.30%
Veteran/ Active Duty	3.20%	Post grad	21.60%	Government	11.60%

2020 Pres. Vote	Biden	274,336	(86%)	Trump	38,414	(12%)			
2016 Pres. Vote	Clinton	271,156	(87%)	Trump	28,523	(9%)	Johnson	6,759	(2%)

Downtown, West Side: An airplane passenger on a cloudless day can get a clear view of the biggest man-made cityscape between the Atlantic and Pacific oceans: Chicago's Loop. Its high rises and parks along Lake Michigan were built a century ago, and the downtown district was named in 1897 for the quadrilateral shape the elevated train forms around the city's center.

International School modernists built their most impressive collection of buildings here and along Lake Shore Drive in the years after World War II. The Loop now spreads beyond the elevated train, or the "El" as it's known locally. It reaches west beyond the financial exchanges to the 110-story Willis (formerly, and still known locally, as Sears) Tower— once the world's tallest building, now seventeenth and second in the United States behind Freedom Tower in New York City.

The Loop reaches north and stops at the Gold Coast, the wondrous shopping district along North Michigan Avenue. West of the Gold Coast is the River North neighborhood, which has become one of the city's most vibrant. In the South Loop, plans were underway for " The 78," a huge riverfront campus, with 10,000 residential units and a $250 million tech hub connected with the University of Illinois called the Discovery Partners Institute; the site name alludes to the fact that the city already had 77 official community areas.

This is the face Chicago likes to present to the world: giant structures rising where the prairies meet the great lake, a vast concentration of brains and muscle, the nerve center of the nation's commodities markets, and, most recently, a hive of political activity. President Barack Obama's high-rise headquarters in 2012 filled a 50,000-square foot floor at One Prudential Plaza; South Bend Indiana Mayor Pete Buttigieg's smaller presidential campaign headquarters were housed in the South

Loop in 2019, as well. Obama delivered his historic 2008 victory speech in front of 240,000 cheering onlookers in Grant Park. The 319-acre park includes several of the city's civic treasures, including the Art Institute, Millennium Park and Buckingham Fountain. The Loop was host to massive Black Lives Matter protests in 2020 that led to sometimes-violent clashes between police and protestors that had echoes of the 1968 Democratic National Convention. Widespread looting left much of the Magnificent Mile boarded up for weeks.

Not far west of the luxurious lakefront neighborhoods are the muscle and sinew of the city. Parts of the West Side began to gentrify in the 1990s. The United Center attracted commercial development, lower crime rates and higher land values to the West Loop. Former meatpacking buildings have been turned into art galleries. A massive new downtown dormitory houses students from nearby DePaul University, Roosevelt University and Columbia College.

The 7th Congressional District of Illinois contains the Loop, most of the North Michigan Avenue corridor, the Near North Side, and a few South Side neighborhoods. Its heart, demographically and spiritually, is the predominantly African-American West Side, parts of which remain more depopulated than the South Side. That includes the heavily Black communities of Austin, Garfield Park (home to the beautiful Garfield Park Conservatory) and Lawndale— areas long neglected by city leadership.

Like other minority neighborhoods in Chicago, the West Side has suffered from the recent surge in murders and other violence. The cycle of violence and shrinking neighborhoods has wracked the city's African-American community. The scheduled closure of Mercy Hospital on the city's near South Side was planned for spring 2021 but faced heavy protests in the middle of the coronavirus pandemic. A few blocks west of McCormick Place on the South Side is Chinatown, which has grown and largely avoided gentrification. The district is entirely in Cook County.

Just outside the city limits to the west, but in the district, is Oak Park, the boyhood home of writer Ernest Hemingway and the location of architect Frank Lloyd Wright's home and museum and many of his prairie-style houses. Farther out the Eisenhower Expressway are well-heeled River Forest; more modest Maywood, which is a Black-majority suburb; Broadview; and Hillside. African Americans now make up 43 percent of the district, with 17 percent Hispanic. Due to population loss, the district might need to expand further into the suburbs and dilute the African-American population a bit further. Joe Biden's 86%-12% win was his best district in Illinois; the district ranks sixth nationwide in its Democratic PVI, according to the Cook Political Report.

Raja Krishnamoorthi (D)

Elected 2016, 3rd term, b. Jul 19, 1973; New Delhi, IN; Princeton University, B.A., 1995; Harvard University, J.D., 2000; Hinduism; Married (Priya Krishnamoorthi); 2 children.

Professional Career: Clerk, U.S District Court N. IL, 2000-2002; Staff, Illinois Housing Development Auth., 2005-2007; IL Special Asst. Attorney General, 2006-2007; Deputy State Treasurer of IL, 2008-2009.

DC Office: 115 CHOB 20515, 202-225-3711, Fax: 202-225-7830

State Offices: Schaumburg, 847-413-1959.

Committees: *Oversight & Reform*: Select Investigative on the Coronavirus Crisis; Subcommittee on Economic & Consumer Policy (Chmn); Subcommittee on Environment. *Permanent Select on Intelligence*: Intelligence Modernization & Readiness; Strategic Technologies & Advanced Research.

Group Ratings

	ADA	ACLU	AFL-CIO	LCV	COC	HAFA	ACU	CFG	FRC
2020	**	79%	**	100%	-	0%	2%	**	-
2019	90%	C	100%	97%	68%	C	3%	12%	0%

Almanac Ratings 2019-2020

	Economy	Social	Foreign	Composite
Liberal	100%	100%	80%	94%
Conservative	0%	0%	20%	6%

Key Votes of the 116th Congress

1. U.S./Mex./Can. trade deal	Y	5. Russia sanctions	Y	9. Firearms background checks	Y
2. First Coronavirus response	Y	6. Troops in Syria	Y	10. Spending at the border	Y
3. HEROES Act	Y	7. Veto arms sales to Saudis	Y	11. Marijuana liberalized rules	Y
4. CASH Act	Y	8. Defense $$$, veto override	Y	12. Electoral College objections	N

Election Results

Election	Name (Party)	Vote (%)		Cand. Spent	Ind. Exp. Support	Ind. Exp. Oppose
2020 General	Raja Krishnamoorthi (D)......................	186,251	(73%)	$2,474,709	$873	
	Preston Nelson (L).........................	68,327	(27%)			
2020 Primary	Raja Krishnamoorthi (D)......................	51,829	(80%)			
	William Olson (D).................................	8,441	(13%)			
	Inam Hussain (D).............................	4,563	(7%)			

Prior winning percentages: 2018 (66%), 2016 (58%)

Raja Krishnamoorthi, elected on a second try in 2016, brought bipartisanship and a positive attitude to his work in the House. His domestic interests included education and solar energy. Following his loss in 2012 to more politically experienced Democrat Tammy Duckworth, who was then elected to the Senate, he has had no trouble securing his suburban seat.

Krishnamoorthi was born in India, came to the United States when he was three months old and was raised downstate in Peoria, where his father was a professor of engineering at Bradley University. He earned a bachelor's degree in mechanical engineering from Princeton University and got a law degree from Harvard. Following law school, Krishnamoorthi clerked for a federal judge in Chicago and later became a partner in the law firm of Kirkland & Ellis.

In 2004, he served as issues director for the Senate campaign of Barack Obama; the two had met at a Chicago reception for lawyers interested in civil rights, prior to Obama's unsuccessful campaign in 2000 for a House seat. In 2008, he was an adviser to Obama's presidential campaign. While practicing law, Krishnamoorthi served as a special assistant attorney general in the state's Public Integrity Unit. He was a member of the Illinois Housing Development Authority and the Illinois deputy treasurer, where he helped to manage the state's technology venture capital fund.

In the private sector, Krishnamoorthi was president of Sivananthan Labs and Episolar Inc., a group of small businesses that developed and sold national security and renewable energy products. He was co-founder of InSPIRE, a non-profit organization that provided training in solar technology to inner-city students and veterans, and a former vice chairman of the Illinois Innovation Council. He sought the Democratic nomination for state comptroller in 2010 but lost narrowly. When he first ran for the House two years later, Duckworth was actively supported by Democratic Sen. Richard Durbin and much of the state party establishment—though she had lost a previous campaign. Duckworth won the primary, 66%-34%.

In 2016, Krishnamoorthi had the easy win. In the Democratic primary, he benefited from a big fundraising advantage and his campaign experience, plus the large Asian—including Indian-American—population in the district. "Instead of buildings walls, we should be building bridges," was his campaign theme, an explicit contrast to Republican presidential nominee Donald Trump. With help from the active nationwide community of Democrats with an Indian heritage, Krishnamoorthi spent $2.6 million and defeated the more liberal state Sen. Michael Noland, who cited his support for a single-payer health care system, and Villa Park Village president Deborah Bullwinkel, winning the primary with 57 percent of the vote to 29 percent for Noland and 14 percent for Bullwinkel.

In the general, Republican Pete DiCianni, a member of the DuPage County Board and former mayor of Elmhurst, cited the "disappointing" loss of nearly $100 million in mutual funds from the state's college savings program while Krishnamoorthi was deputy treasurer. Krishnamoorthi won, 58%-42%, including 54 percent of the vote in DuPage. He won with 66 percent of the vote in 2018 against token opposition; in 2020 Republicans didn't nominate a candidate, and Krishnamoorthi took 73 percent of the vote against a Libertarian candidate.

On the Education and the Workforce Committee, Krishnamoorthi filed with Rep. Glenn Thompson of Pennsylvania, a senior Republican on the panel, a bill to expand career and technical education programs and respond to changing labor markets. The House passed the bill unanimously in 2017 and a modified version was enacted in 2018, with Krishnamoorthi standing directly behind President Donald Trump at the White House signing ceremony. "We desperately need some bipartisan victories right now," Krishnamoorthi told the Daily Herald.

Many of his views have been conventionally liberal, though Krishnamoorthi has added his background as a business entrepreneur and his bipartisan approach, and has emphasized his fiscal moderation. With Republican Rep. Ralph Norman of South Carolina, he created the Congressional Solar Caucus to encourage grassroots support for new technologies. Among his objectives, he said, was educating other lawmakers about the availability and declining cost of solar energy, plus the need for additional federal research and development. With Rep. Mike Gallagher of Wisconsin, a fellow Princeton grad, Krishnamoorthi formed the bipartisan Middle-Class Jobs Caucus.

Krishnamoorthi joined other Indian-American members of Congress in an informal "Samosa Caucus," a reference to an Indian snack. They encouraged Trump's efforts to collaborate with India, and he sought steps to facilitate visas for workers in the United States, an issue important to his district's immigrant communities. He filed bipartisan legislation to give more flexibility to holders of B-1 visas to switch jobs and gain exemptions. One goal, he said, was to ensure that "immigration laws match our country's high-tech workforce requirements."

A member of both the House Intelligence Committee and the Oversight and Reform Committee, Krishnamoorthi played a role in House Democrats' 2019 impeachment of Trump. As the member of Intelligence with the least seniority, he had the unenviable position of being the last of 13 Democrats to question witnesses. "I basically keep a running list of my questions and then I cross them off as they get asked," he told The Washington Post during the hearings.

IL-8: Chicago's Northwest Suburbs

Cook Partisan Voting Index: D+9

Population		Race and Ethnicity		Income	
Total	717,115	White	65.10%	Median Income	$77,991
Land area (sq. miles)	206	Black	6.40%	District Income Rank	103
Pop/ sq mi	3,489.27	Latino	28.00%	Poverty Rate	8.90%
Born in State	59.50%	Asian	13.50%	With health insurance	89.80%
		Two or more races	3.40%	Cash public assistance	1.50%
Age Groups		Other	11.40%	Food stamp/SNAP	9.30%
Under 18	23.70%				
18-34	23.20%	**Education**		**Work**	
35-64	39.40%	H.S grad or less	37.10%	White Collar	36.00%
Over 64	13.70%	Some college	27.80%	Sales and Service	37.40%
		College Degree, 4 yr	23.00%	Blue Collar	26.60%
Military		Post grad	12.00%	Government	7.50%
Veteran/ Active Duty	3.60%				

2020 Pres. Vote	Biden	171,821	(59%)	Trump	113,187	(39%)		
2016 Pres. Vote	Clinton	148,277	(58%)	Trump	92,892	(36%)	Johnson	9,851 (4%)

DuPage: Schaumburg has a long tradition as a center of America's major corporations. Sixty years ago, this suburb northwest of Chicago was farmland. Since then, Schaumburg— near the intersection of the Northwest Tollway and Interstate 290, and a few miles beyond O'Hare International Airport— became the headquarters of large companies such as Motorola and AT&T. Nearby Hoffman Estates is home to Sears' corporate headquarters. But those companies, and others that received huge tax breaks to build their campuses in Chicago's western suburbs, have relocated or downsized. Some of their abandoned suburban campuses have plans for redevelopment. In addition to subdivisions as far as the eye can see, Schaumburg has other attractions, including a performing arts center, an orchestra for young people and a traditional downtown district that it built from scratch.

Despite those attractions, the area recently has faced challenges. Some large companies have abandoned their suburban mindset, finding that large, isolated corporate campuses breed insularity and make it harder to recruit talent. Chicago Mayor Rahm Emanuel lured suburban businesses to relocate downtown with financial incentives. Motorola's mobile handset division, after being bought by Google, moved to Chicago's Merchandise Mart. AT&T decided to leave its suburban Hoffman Estates office and moved 500 employees to downtown Chicago. Financially beleaguered Sears stayed in Hoffman Estates, but its problems extend far beyond its corporate location. From 2006 through 2016, its annual revenues dropped by about half. In October 2018, Sears filed for bankruptcy; its sprawling campus has turned into a ghost town.

Since 2007, more than 50 companies have moved from these suburbs to downtown Chicago. Still, some of the facilities continue to prosper. Zurich North America, an insurance company, houses nearly 3,000. Sunstar, an oral-health care company, has a new corporate presence, with 400 employees. As Amazon's business boomed during the coronavirus pandemic, the company moved to hire 5,000 workers in the western suburbs, including Elgin and Schaumburg. The Chicago White Sox temporarily used the minor league Schaumburg Boomers' field as a training facility, Still, the vacancy rate for suburban Chicago offices has climbed for years, and during the pandemic hit 25 percent in late 2020, the highest in a decade.

The 8th Congressional District of Illinois is made up of Schaumburg and the more Democratic communities in Chicago's northwest suburbs, including Carol Stream in DuPage County and nearly majority Hispanic Elgin and Carpentersville in Kane County. About half the population of the 8th resides in the northwest corner of Cook County; most of the remainder are within jagged lines of northern DuPage, plus a few are in a small slice of Kane. It is one of the most Asian-American districts in the Midwest, at 13 percent of the population. Schaumburg has one of the nation's largest concentrations of Indian Americans, at 11 percent. Once-homogeneous DuPage County has seen an influx of immigrants, and more than a quarter of its residents now speak a first language other than English at home. The area lacks a regional identity, other than the " Northwest Suburbs."

In the past decade, like other parts of the Chicago suburbs, this area has moved toward the Democrats. Joe Biden won the 8th District, 59%-39%.

Jan Schakowsky (D)

Elected 1998, 12th term, b. May 26, 1944; Chicago, IL; University of IL, B.A., 1965; Jewish; Married (Robert Creamer); 3 children; 6 grandchildren.

Elected Office: IL House, 1990-1998.

Professional Career: Founder, National Consumers Unite, 1969-1973; Prog. Director, IL Public Action, 1976-1985; Executive Director, IL St. Cncl. of Sr. Citizens, 1985-1990.

DC Office: 2367 RHOB 20515, 202-225-2111, Fax: 202-226-6890, schakowsky.house.gov

State Offices: Chicago, 773-506-7100; Evanston, 847-328-3409; Glenview, 847-328-3409.

Committees: *Budget. Energy & Commerce*: Consumer Protection & Commerce (Chmn); Environment & Climate Change; Oversight & Investigations.

Group Ratings

	ADA	ACLU	AFL-CIO	LCV	COC	HAFA	ACU	CFG	FRC
2020	**	86%	**	95%	-	0%	3%	**	-
2019	95%	C	95%	97%	42%	C	3%	18%	0%

Almanac Ratings 2019-2020

	Economy	Social	Foreign	Composite
Liberal	100%	100%	96%	99%
Conservative	0%	0%	4%	1%

Key Votes of the 116th Congress

1. U.S./Mex./Can. trade deal	Y	5. Russia sanctions	Y	9. Firearms background checks	Y
2. First Coronavirus response	Y	6. Troops in Syria	Y	10. Spending at the border	N
3. HEROES Act	Y	7. Veto arms sales to Saudis	Y	11. Marijuana liberalized rules	Y
4. CASH Act	Y	8. Defense $$$, veto override	Y	12. Electoral College objections	N

Election Results

Election	Name (Party)	Vote (%)		Cand. Spent	Ind. Exp. Support	Ind. Exp. Oppose
2020 General	Jan Schakowsky (D)	262,045	(71%)	$1,238,495	$113	
	Sargis Sangari (R)	107,125	(29%)	$31,929		$113
2020 Primary	Jan Schakowsky (D)	127,467	(100%)			

Prior winning percentages: 2018 (74%), 2016 (67%), 2014 (66%), 2012 (66%), 2010 (66%), 2008 (75%), 2006 (75%), 2004 (76%), 2002 (70%), 2000 (76%), 1998 (75%)

Jan Schakowsky, a Democrat elected in 1998, is an outspoken progressive. She blends deep policy background with lengthy organizational experience, and has been a stalwart on Nancy Pelosi's Democratic leadership team who has occasionally pushed the Speaker to the left. As a senior member of the Energy and Commerce Committee, and chair of its Consumer Protection and Commerce Subcommittee, Schakowsky has been instrumental in setting the party's agenda on health and consumer issues.

Schakowsky grew up in Rogers Park and worked for two years as a teacher. In 1969, she formed National Consumers Unite to fight for date-of-freshness labels on dairy products and other food. Later she joined Illinois Public Action, a consumer group. In 1985, she became executive director of the Illinois State Council of Senior Citizens, where she organized the pivotal 1989 protest of Democratic Ways and Means Chairman Dan Rostenkowski's Medicare catastrophic health care law for seniors. Television news images of the powerful Rostenkowski fleeing an angry crowd of old people led Congress to repeal the benefit, which many said did not provide adequate coverage. In 1990, Schakowsky was elected to the state House from Evanston and Skokie, and later became Democratic floor leader.

With an open seat in 1998, her strategy was to run from the left—"I don't think I can be defined as too far left in a district like this," she said—and to build a volunteer organization. She raised $1.4 million, with help from the abortion-rights group EMILY's List, and hired a small army of student doorknockers. Her opponent was state Sen. Howard Carroll, who had the support of most Democratic ward committeemen and attacked Schakowsky for her opposition to the death penalty. Schakowsky's 1,500 workers, 250 of them from labor unions, helped her to a 45%-34% win. She easily won the general election and has been reelected without difficulty.

Her Almanac vote ratings have consistently been among the most liberal in the House. A close ally of Pelosi, Schakowsky has worked with Democratic leaders on electoral strategy, including leading a training program for political organizers and encouraging participation by women. She was an early supporter when Pelosi got her start in leadership, and was rewarded with a chief deputy whip post, which she holds to this day. As a major party fundraiser, she has drawn heavily from the traditional Democratic constituencies of lawyers, liberal women's interest groups and unions.

Schakowsky briefly considered a run for the Senate in 2004 but decided against it. In early 2006, she ran for vice chair of the Democratic Caucus and had Pelosi's support, but finished third. The contest occurred soon after her husband, Robert Creamer, the longtime head of Illinois Public Action Fund, pleaded guilty to bank fraud in a check-kiting scheme.

In 2008, she voiced interest in appointment to the remainder of President-elect Barack Obama's Senate term. She was an early backer of Obama for president, giving cover to other prominent Democratic women who may have wanted to back him but felt obliged to support New York Sen. Hillary Clinton.

Schakowsky calls herself a supporter of Israel, important in her Jewish-heavy district, but has been a critic of its policies towards the Palestinian people—helping to carve out a middle path for Democrats on the thorny issue. She fought to make sure the U.S. gave Israel its "iron dome" missile shield in 2010. But she's been critical of Israeli Prime Minister Benjamin Netanyahu: In what she called an "anguished" decision, she boycotted his 2015 speech to Congress. She spearheaded a 2019 letter from House Democrats that asked Israel to "reconsider" its unilateral annexation of parts of the West Bank. AIPAC, the pro-Israel lobby, opposed the letter. Amid increasing White supremacist attacks targeting both Jews and Muslims, she and Rep. Ilhan Omar coauthored a CNN op-ed saying that "whatever our differences, our two communities, Muslim and Jewish, must come together to confront the twin evils of anti-Semitic and Islamophobic violence."

Schakowsky's legislative work has centered on the Energy and Commerce Committee, where she chairs the Consumer Protection and Commerce Subcommittee and focuses on product safety, data privacy and security, and auto safety. She helped to enact in 2008 the child product safety bill, which increased regulations, and she has remained active on consumer issues. In 2009, she was a strong supporter of creating a federally run insurance option in the Democrats' health care bill. The public option provision ultimately was dropped because of opposition from party moderates.

She filed in 2016 the Medicare Fair Drug Pricing Act, which advanced her longstanding demand for transparency and accountability in prescription drug pricing, plus negotiation for the price of certain drugs covered by Medicare. In late 2020, she crafted the Online Consumer Protection Act, which would hold tech companies more accountable for third-party content posted on their sites.

Pelosi appointed Schakowsky to the Simpson-Bowles commission on the national debt in 2010, where she opposed ending federal economic stimulus funds and argued that safety-net spending should be exempt from budget cuts.

Schakowsky helped lead Democrats' negotiations in 2019 over the trade agreement with Mexico and Canada that replaced NAFTA. She successfully removed protections that would have benefited the pharmaceutical industry, which she said would have driven up medical and drug costs. Democrats were unsuccessful in removing provisions that benefitted tech companies, but Schakowsky voted for the agreement anyway—the first major trade agreement she supported in her 20-year career.

In 2018, Schakowsky stirred controversy among House Democrats when she actively backed Marie Newman in her Democratic primary challenge to Chicago-area pro-life Rep. Daniel Lipinski —an unusual step, especially with Schakowsky's leadership ties. Lipinski won, but lost his 2020 rematch.

During the coronavirus pandemic, Schakowsky introduced legislation to protect nursing-home workers, which included a requirement for two weeks of paid sick leave. With Democratic Sen. Elizabeth Warren, who Schakowsky endorsed for president, she filed a bill for the federal government to manufacture personal protective equipment, prescription drugs, and other medical supplies necessary to combat the COVID-19 pandemic.

IL-9: Chicago

Cook Partisan Voting Index: D+21

Population		Race and Ethnicity		Income	
Total	719,256	White	68.40%	Median Income	$78,569
Land area (sq. miles)	92	Black	9.50%	District Income Rank	101
Pop/ sq mi	7,830.77	Latino	11.20%	Poverty Rate	9.70%
Born in State	53.40%	Asian	14.70%	With health insurance	92.50%
		Two or more races	3.60%	Cash public assistance	1.70%
Age Groups		Other	3.70%	Food stamp/SNAP	8.50%
Under 18	20.80%				
18-34	22.00%	**Education**		**Work**	
35-64	39.00%	H.S grad or less	23.80%	White Collar	54.80%
Over 64	18.20%	Some college	20.40%	Sales and Service	32.90%
		College Degree, 4 yr	31.30%	Blue Collar	12.30%
Military		Post grad	24.40%	Government	9.80%
Veteran/ Active Duty	3.50%				

2020 Pres. Vote	Biden	269,588	(71%)	Trump	104,072	(27%)			
2016 Pres. Vote	Clinton	237,984	(69%)	Trump	84,527	(25%)	Johnson	11,494	(3%)

North Side, Northern Cook: "Make no little plans," architect Daniel Burnham once said, and he made no little plans for the Chicago lakefront. The glorious parks he designed are among America's urban jewels, and the row of high-rise apartment buildings—some austere works of masters of the International style, some in traditional styles evocative of some other place and time, some sleek Art Deco works of the 1920s and 1930s—is a splendid accompaniment. Beyond the lakefront is all the diversity of Chicago. In sturdy brick houses, with scarcely a shoehorn's space between them, or in stubby apartment buildings, are ethnic and racial groups of every sort, from Argentinians to Slavs, from Poles to Plains Indians.

Today, this part of Chicago has as much urban energy and lively diversity as any place in America. In what it describes as the largest capital improvement project in its history, the Chicago Transit Authority began construction in 2019 on rebuilding the Red Line, its busiest route, much of which was opened in 1925. The project includes modernizing the Purple Line from the North Side to Wilmette.

The lakefront has long been the most heavily Jewish part of Chicago. The local Jewish community, prominent for more than a century, has never been as much of a political force as it is in New York. Yet these voters' liberal impulses have been strong: the 19th century impulse to resist state authority and the imposition of cultural uniformity, and the 20th century impulse to strive for social justice. Chicago's North Side Jews have been a solidly Democratic voting bloc, involved with — but mostly keeping at arm's length— the old Democratic machine. They supported for mayor one of their own, Rahm Emanuel, but were disappointed when he fell short as a reformer, and broke hard for Lori Lightfoot in her 2019 victory, which made her Chicago's first black woman and first openly gay person to hold the office.

The 9th Congressional District of Illinois covers the north end of Chicago's lakefront, from just north of Diversey Harbor and the Lincoln Park Zoo up through Rogers Park, home of Loyola University-Chicago and the city's most diverse neighborhood— the only one on the North Side with many African-American residents— and Andersonville, historically Swedish and now home to the city's largest lesbian community. The district continues through the suburb of Evanston, founded by Methodists to promote temperance (a cause that never prospered in Chicago). Evanston, home to Northwestern University, long ago moved from Yankee Republicanism to postgraduate Democratic. In 2020, after Illinois legalized marijuana, Evanston's city council voted to use the tax revenue to pay for race-based reparations. The district spreads north and west through upscale suburbs like Wilmette, home to the only Baha'i Temple in the country— and one of only eight worldwide— and includes historically Jewish Skokie, home to the Illinois Holocaust Museum and Education Center, as well as Morton Grove, Niles, Des Plaines and parts of Glenview and Northbrook.

The district is entirely in Cook County, though two-thirds of its voters are outside of Chicago, and reaches west to incorporate once rock-solid Republican territory— Park Ridge, where Hillary Rodham in 1964 got her first taste of politics in high school as a "Goldwater girl"; the cluster of office buildings and interchanges in Rosemont, next to O' Hare International Airport; and parts of Arlington Heights, developed in the 1950s and 1960s on the Chicago & Northwestern commuter rail line. The 9th's population is 9 percent Black, 11 percent Hispanic, and 15 percent Asian, and is solidly Democratic, though less so than most of the other districts based in Chicago. Joe Biden won the district with 71 percent of the vote.

Brad Schneider (D)

Elected 2016, 4th term, b. Aug 20, 1961; Denver, CO; Northwestern University, B.S., 1983; Kellogg Graduate School of Management, Northwestern University, M.B.A., 1988; Jewish; Married (Julie Dann); 2 children.

Elected Office: U.S House, 2013-2015.

Professional Career: Strategic Mgmt Consultant & Founder, Cadence Consulting Group.

DC Office: 1432 LHOB 20515, 202-225-4835, Fax: 202-225-0837, schneider.house.gov

State Offices: Lincolnshire, 847-383-4870.

Committees: *Foreign Affairs*: Europe, Energy, the Environment & Cyber; Middle East, North Africa & Global Counterterrorism. *Ways & Means*: Health; Oversight.

Group Ratings

	ADA	ACLU	AFL-CIO	LCV	COC	HAFA	ACU	CFG	FRC
2020	**	79%	**	100%	-	0%	7%	**	-
2019	90%	C	100%	97%	67%	C	7%	13%	0%

Almanac Ratings 2019-2020

	Economy	Social	Foreign	Composite
Liberal	100%	100%	80%	94%
Conservative	0%	0%	20%	6%

Key Votes of the 116th Congress

1. U.S./Mex./Can. trade deal Y	5. Russia sanctions	Y	9. Firearms background checks Y
2. First Coronavirus response Y	6. Troops in Syria	Y	10. Spending at the border Y
3. HEROES Act Y	7. Veto arms sales to Saudis Y		11. Marijuana liberalized rules Y
4. CASH Act Y	8. Defense $$$, veto override Y		12. Electoral College objections N

Election Results

Election	Name (Party)	Vote (%)	Cand. Spent	Ind. Exp. Support	Ind. Exp. Oppose
2020 General	Brad Schneider (D)................................ 202,402	(64%)	$2,694,256	$873	
	Valerie Mukherjee (R)......................... 114,442	(36%)	$75,844		$113
2020 Primary	Brad Schneider (D)............................... 79,126	(100%)			

Prior winning percentages: 2018 (66%), 2016 (53%), 2012 (51%)

Democrat Brad Schneider, a business consultant who made a late career move to politics, regained his House seat in 2016 after a series of tough races against Republican Robert Dold. With the GOP's dramatic suburban decline, Schneider subsequently coasted to reelection..

Schneider was born and raised in Denver, where his parents were active Democrats. As a kid, he joined them to canvass for Hubert Humphrey's presidential campaign in 1968. Schneider went to Northwestern University, where he received a bachelor's degree in industrial engineering and a master's from the Kellogg Graduate School of Management. After spending a year in Israel working on a kibbutz, he returned to Chicago to take a corporate consulting job. Eventually, he became a consultant, working with small and mid-sized businesses. He worked for the Jewish United Fund and served as director of the Business and Professional People for the Business Interest, a local social-justice organization.

As part of their post-census redistricting in 2011, Democrats remade the 10th district into the most Democratic district represented by a Republican in the House, putting a bullseye on Dold's back in 2012. Schneider ran, and national Democrats saw him as a good fit in the district—his work within the Jewish community and moderate profile helped him in a district where Jewish voters and business-minded centrists often split their tickets. His chief opponent in the primary was Ilya Sheyman, a 25-year-old former community organizer who drew staunch support from liberal groups such as MoveOn.org. Schneider got the backing of the Democratic establishment and won the primary 47%-39%.

In the general, Schneider accused Dold of voting in lockstep with GOP leaders on major issues, including women's health and abortion rights. Dold called the charge misleading and cited his dissent from the leadership on such issues as the environment, education and gun control. But the Democratic tide in Illinois proved too much for him to overcome, and he lost 50.6%-49.4%.

Without President Barack Obama on the ticket in 2014, Republicans were enthusiastic about Dold's prospects. He stressed his moderate credentials while depicting Schneider as ineffective. This was one of the most expensive campaigns in the nation in 2014, drawing almost $19 million in total spending. This time, Dold won 51.3%-48.7%.

In 2016, Schneider made a comeback. Joining him in the primary was Highland Park Mayor Nancy Rotering, an attorney who had the support of EMILY's List, the political action committee that funds Democratic women who support abortion rights. As was the case in the 2012 primary, liberal activists griped about Schneider. But he prevailed 54%-46%, not all that impressive for a former House member. Dold moved quickly to disavow Donald Trump. Once again, both sides spent lavishly. Schneider regained the seat by the relatively comfortable 52.4%-47.6%. He cruised to reelection in 2018 and 2020 against poorly funded opponents.

Schneider carefully maintains his centrist profile: He's a member of the fiscally moderate Blue Dog Caucus and New Democrats, as well as the bipartisan Problem Solvers caucus.

As a House Foreign Affairs Committee member, Schneider filed a bipartisan bill to impose additional sanctions on Russia if it interfered with the 2018 election. He has been one of Israel's most vocal Democratic allies in Congress. But in 2020, he partnered with neighbor-district Rep. Jan

Schakowsky and others to pen a letter asking Israel not to unilaterally annex settlements in the West Bank, breaking with his normal allies at the American Israel Public Affairs Committee. The letter was signed by nearly 200 House Democrats.

He filed legislation to provide federal funding for communities—such as Zion, in his district—that store nuclear waste. In late 2020 he introduced legislation to close a loophole that allows some gun sales to gain approval without a background check if the FBI doesn't move fast enough, and he called for the National Rifle Association to lose its tax-exempt status. During the Trump impeachment, he encouraged House leaders to craft "very tightly defined" articles focused on Ukraine rather than "throwing the whole kitchen sink and try to overreach."

In 2019, Schneider got a seat on the Ways and Means Committee. He set a priority of removing restrictions on the state and local deduction for taxpayers, which Republicans included in their 2017 tax cuts; high-income, high-tax suburbanites, such as those in Schneider's district and other Democratic areas, have loudly opposed the loss of this tax break. Prospects for restoring the deductions seemed to dim when President Joe Biden proposed measures to increase taxes on the wealthy.

IL-10: Northern Chicagoland　　　　　　　　Cook Partisan Voting Index: D+14

Population		Race and Ethnicity		Income	
Total	706,189	White	68.80%	Median Income	$84,608
Land area (sq. miles)	300	Black	7.10%	District Income Rank	73
Pop/ sq mi	2,355.69	Latino	25.10%	Poverty Rate	7.80%
Born in State	57.60%	Asian	10.90%	With health insurance	91.20%
		Two or more races	3.00%	Cash public assistance	1.80%
Age Groups		Other	10.10%	Food stamp/SNAP	8.50%
Under 18	23.40%				
18-34	21.60%	Education		Work	
35-64	39.20%	H.S grad or less	31.50%	White Collar	42.60%
Over 64	15.80%	Some college	24.30%	Sales and Service	37.30%
		College Degree, 4 yr	25.40%	Blue Collar	20.10%
Military		Post grad	18.80%	Government	9.20%
Veteran/ Active Duty	6.60%				

2020 Pres. Vote	Biden	207,386	(64%)	Trump	109,732	(34%)	
2016 Pres. Vote	Clinton	178,872	(61%)	Trump	94,103	(32%) Johnson	11,681 (4%)

Lake, Northern Cook: Since 1855, when the Chicago & North Western opened the railroad line from downtown Chicago north along the lakeshore, the North Shore suburbs along Lake Michigan have been home to Chicago's elite. The North Shore starts in Evanston, goes north through Wilmette, Winnetka and Glencoe, and then leaves Cook County and crosses into the eastern Lake County towns of Highland Park and Lake Forest. Each burg has a slightly different personality, each is long established and mightily prosperous, and each exudes a patina of age. These are communities of affluent, well-educated people living in an environment whose natural beauty— the vistas over Lake Michigan, the gentle rolling terrain, and the old trees— is carefully disciplined. Corporate headquarters fit comfortably here, including Baxter Healthcare, Abbott Laboratories and Allstate Insurance. In January 2018, Caterpillar moved its corporate home to Deerfield from its longtime site in Peoria. The population of Lake County barely changed between 2010 and 2018, which was better than many other parts of Illinois.

The exceptions to the atmosphere of gracious high living are Waukegan and the nearby area around the Great Lakes Naval Training Center, where the median income is dramatically lower. The award-winning Years of Living Dangerously documentary on the National Geographic Channel in 2016 described the struggle in Waukegan as the area moved to clean up its coal-fueled power plant. In 2017, the Wallet Hub website ranked Waukegan last among 505 cities nationwide in the decrease in its local poverty rate. Farther north along the lake, the small community of Zion has struggled to recover from the shutdown in 1998 of the local nuclear power plant, which was caused by an operational error. Local leaders, unhappy that the radioactive spent fuel has not been removed, have sought federal aid in removing or storing the nuclear waste.

The 10th Congressional District of Illinois is the North Shore district. The district starts on the lakefront in Glencoe and runs north in a thin strip all the way to the blue-collar, majority-Hispanic city of Waukegan and on to the Wisconsin border. It moves inland to include most of Lake County and some Cook County suburbs west to Wheeling and parts of Mount Prospect. The district includes upscale Deerfield and much of Northbrook, plus Libertyville, near where the Adlai Stevensons, the governor and two-time presidential nominee and his son the former senator, owned a farm. Three-fourths of the district is in Lake, with the 6th and 14th Districts in the more Republican western corners of the county. Politically, the gerrymandered 10th leans Democratic, though it's more socially than fiscally liberal. It shifted further left in the Trump era. In 2020, Joe Biden won comfortably, 64%-34%. Democrats won control of the county board in 2018 for the first time in Lake's history; in 2020 they expanded to a 15-6 majority.

Bill Foster (D)

Elected 2012, 6th full term, b. Oct 07, 1955; Madison, WI; University of WI, B.A., 1976; Harvard University, Ph.D., 1983; Married (Aesook Byon); 2 children.

Elected Office: U.S. House, 2008-2010.

Professional Career: Scientist, Fermi National Accelerator Lab., 1990- 2006; Co-founder, Electronic Theatre Controls, 1975-2007.

DC Office: 2366 RHOB 20515, 202-225-3515, Fax: 202-225-9420, foster.house.gov

State Offices: Aurora, 630-585-7672; Joliet, 815-280-5876.

Committees: *Financial Services*: Consumer Protection & Financial Institutions; Investor Protection, Entrepreneurship & Capital Markets; Task Force on Artificial Intelligence (Chmn). *Science, Space & Technology*: Investigations & Oversight (Chmn); Research & Technology.

Group Ratings

	ADA	ACLU	AFL-CIO	LCV	COC	HAFA	ACU	CFG	FRC
2020	**	81%	**	100%	-	0%	6%	**	-
2019	90%	C	100%	97%	69%	C	7%	12%	0%

Almanac Ratings 2019-2020

	Economy	Social	Foreign	Composite
Liberal	100%	100%	80%	94%
Conservative	0%	0%	20%	6%

Key Votes of the 116th Congress

1. U.S./Mex./Can. trade deal Y	5. Russia sanctions Y	9. Firearms background checks Y
2. First Coronavirus response Y	6. Troops in Syria Y	10. Spending at the border Y
3. HEROES Act Y	7. Veto arms sales to Saudis Y	11. Marijuana liberalized rules Y
4. CASH Act Y	8. Defense $$$, veto override Y	12. Electoral College objections N

Election Results

Election	Name (Party)	Vote (%)		Cand. Spent	Ind. Exp. Support	Ind. Exp. Oppose
2020 General	Bill Foster (D)	194,557	(63%)	$1,143,470	$123	
	Rick Laib (R)	112,807	(37%)	$18,907		$113
2020 Primary	Bill Foster (D)	46,116	(59%)			
	Rachel Ventura (D)	32,422	(41%)			

Prior winning percentages: 2018 (64%), 2016 (60%), 2014 (53%), 2012 (59%), 2008 (58%), 2008 special (53%)

Democrat Bill Foster proudly styles himself as the only scientist in Congress with a Ph.D. He has a bipartisan lawmaking streak, and a congenial political style—unless he sees Republicans taking policy positions he believes conflict with scientific consensus. He showed his occasional independence following the 2018 election when he joined the small group of Democrats who forced concessions from Nancy Pelosi on the terms of her future as House Speaker.

Foster began life as a Washington insider. His parents met on Capitol Hill, where each worked for a senator. His father became a law professor at the University of Wisconsin, and Foster grew up in Madison, graduated from the university, and got his Ph.D. in physics from Harvard University. He was a physicist for 16 years at Fermilab, where he pursued groundbreaking research in elementary particle physics. Foster also ran a theater-lighting business with his younger brother that made each a multimillionaire.

He had not sought public office before volunteering in the 2006 campaign of Patrick Murphy, a Pennsylvania Democrat who ousted a House Republican incumbent. At age 51, Foster then spent five months working on Murphy's Capitol Hill staff. After former House Speaker Dennis Hastert resigned in 2007, Foster ran in the Democratic primary against the more liberal Jonathan Laesch, who had lost to Hastert in 2006. Foster won, 50%-43%. Against Republican Jim Oberweis, a successful dairy owner and fiery conservative who had lost numerous statewide campaigns, Foster was boosted by a 30-second endorsement from the Barack Obama presidential campaign. He won, 53%-47%. Foster was the first Democrat to represent the north-central Illinois district since the Great Depression.

In his first House stint, Foster served on the Financial Services Committee, where he supported most major Democratic priorities and helped to restore $62.5 million in funding for Fermilab. In the 2010 election, Foster did not mention his party affiliation and outspent Republican Randy Hultgren, $3.7 million to $1.6 million. But Hultgren won, 51%-45%.

Foster soon got another chance. During 2011 redistricting, Democrats carved out a new, Democratic-leaning district that moved closer to Chicagoland. Foster faced veteran Rep. Judy Biggert, a moderate Republican. Foster won convincingly with 59 percent.

Foster regained his seat on Financial Services, as well as a slot on the Science, Space and Technology Committee. He said he wanted to counter the "attacks" on science, including the National Science Foundation. He cited his background as a scientist when he voted for a chief priority for Obama: the deal with Iran to limit that nation's access to nuclear material that could be used for a weapon. "My support of this agreement is informed not just by trust but by science," said Foster, who added that he had attended 15 technical briefings. In 2021, he became chairman of the Investigations and Oversight Subcommittee at the Science panel.

When President Donald Trump said in a 2018 broadcast interview that climate-change scientists "have a very big political agenda." Foster responded that the comment was "an unfortunate example of the president's inability to understand the importance of science," especially when it's not "politically convenient." He was harshly critical of Trump's response to the coronavirus pandemic. "We've paid a heavy price for the scientific ignorance, embrace of fringe conspiracies, and overall incompetence that has defined the president's response to this pandemic from the very beginning," he said in a November 2020 statement after the U.S. surpassed 250,000 deaths.

Foster introduced bipartisan legislation in 2019 to improve security for government agencies' digital identity validation, teaming up with other members of the bipartisan Cybersecurity Caucus. He also co-chairs the Blockchain Caucus, a bipartisan group that focuses on issues such as the fast-growing cryptocurrency market and leans against regulation.

Following the 2018 election, Foster said he would not support Pelosi for Speaker unless she agreed to a transition plan to allow a new generation of leadership. "The top three positions in [House Democratic] leadership being stagnant for 16 years is simply an unfortunate situation for our party and our country," he told the Daily Herald. Initially, he set a limit of two years before Pelosi and other party leaders stepped down, and helped negotiate a deal in which Pelosi agreed to a maximum of four more years. The term limit, he said, was "the heart of the negotiation." Pelosi affirmed in late 2020 that the next Congress would be her final in leadership.

Foster ran for an open chairmanship of the House Financial Services subcommittee overseeing capital markets in 2019, but lost to Rep. Brad Sherman.

Back home, Foster faced a competitive contest in his Democratic-friendly district. In 2014, he was a national Republican target when he was challenged by state Rep. Darlene Senger, whom he outspent by more than 2-to-1. The Republican had small leads in DuPage and Cook counties, but Foster rolled up big margins in Will and Kane counties and won 53 percent of the vote. Since then, things have gotten easier as Foster's district has grown more Hispanic and Chicago's suburbs shifted more toward Democrats.

Foster's district might need to expand further into exurban Chicago as Democrats seek to maximize their advantage in the next redistricting, while drawing a map with one less district.

IL-11: Southwestern Chicagoland

Cook Partisan Voting Index: D+11

Population		Race and Ethnicity		Income	
Total	721,594	White	69.10%	Median Income	$81,598
Land area (sq. miles)	281	Black	11.50%	District Income Rank	80
Pop/ sq mi	2,568.41	Latino	28.10%	Poverty Rate	8.00%
Born in State	65.40%	Asian	7.90%	With health insurance	92.10%
		Two or more races	3.70%	Cash public assistance	1.70%
Age Groups		Other	7.80%	Food stamp/SNAP	10.30%
Under 18	24.50%				
18-34	22.40%	**Education**		**Work**	
35-64	40.30%	H.S grad or less	36.40%	White Collar	39.40%
Over 64	12.80%	Some college	26.20%	Sales and Service	36.70%
		College Degree, 4 yr	23.70%	Blue Collar	23.90%
Military		Post grad	13.90%	Government	10.30%
Veteran/ Active Duty	4.50%				

2020 Pres. Vote	Biden	195,557	(62%)	Trump	114,239	(36%)		
2016 Pres. Vote	Clinton	164,664	(58%)	Trump	99,087	(35%)	Johnson	11,728 (4%)

Aurora, Joliet: Joliet, known as the city of steel and stone, got its start in the mid-19th century as a melting pot of Irish, German, Slovakian, Slovenian, Polish, Croatian and Hungarian immigrants who built the canals and railroads that connected the city with the rest of the state, from the Great Lakes to the Mississippi River. It emerged as the state's largest transportation hub outside Chicago. Workers labored in the stone quarries and steel mill, which by the turn of the century became the economic engine of the manufacturing city. The rails remain relevant to daily life, with officials working to upgrade the safety of the several trains that pass through Aurora each day with freight cars filled with crude oil from North Dakota. The nickname for Aurora is the " city of lights." It was the first in the nation to use electricity to light an entire city.

Business developments in the area have been mixed. Caterpillar, which had downsized its local plant and shifted jobs to Mexico in recent years, laid off 800 workers in 2018 and 500 more in 2020. Butterball shut down its meatpacking plant, with a loss of 600 jobs. Both plants were in Montgomery, which is across the Fox River from Aurora. Joliet's prison, made famous in The Blues Brothers, shuttered in 2002, but reopened as a historical site. More encouraging has been Amazon's large fulfillment centers in Aurora and Joliet. Those sites confirm the prime transportation facilities of Chicago land, plus the plentiful supply of low-cost and less-skilled workers.

The 11th Congressional District takes in Chicago's western and southwest suburbs and exurbs, including Joliet in Will County, parts of Naperville in southern DuPage County, and Aurora in Kane County. About 28 percent of the district is Hispanic, with 11 percent Black and 8 percent Asian. Will County has nearly one-half of the district vote. It is the fastest-growing of the large suburban Chicago counties, jumping from a population of 502,000 in 2000 to 691,000 in 2019, as the number of Hispanic residents more than doubled and the number of Asian Americans nearly tripled. Aurora, the state's second most populous city with a long history of manufacturing, has grown by 54 percent in the last two decades, also thanks to a near doubling of Hispanics, who have become nearly half the total. The district's jigsaw-like boundaries run along the technology corridor in DuPage County, and straddle some large engineering facilities. The Argonne National Laboratory and Fermilab, another national laboratory, are just outside the district lines.

The district has trended solidly Democratic in an area that had been part of the Republican heartland not many years ago. Joe Biden took the district, 62%-36%.

Mike Bost (R)

Elected 2014, 4th term, b. Dec 30, 1960; Murphysboro; University of IL; University of IL, 1993; Southern Baptist; Married (Tracy Stanton Bost); 3 children; 11 grandchildren.

Military Career: U.S. Marine Corps, Electronic Specialist, Radar Repairman 1979-1982

Elected Office: IL House 1995-2015; Trustee, Murphysboro Township, 1993-1995; Treasurer, Murphysboro Township, 1989-1992; Jackson County Board, 1984-1988.

Professional Career: Cert., Firefighter II Academy, University, of IL, 1993.

DC Office: 1440 LHOB 20515, 202-225-5661, Fax: 202-225-0285, bost.house.gov

State Offices: Alton, 618-622-0766; Carbondale, 618-457-5787; Granite City, 618-622-0766; Mt. Vernon, 618-513-5294; O'Fallon, 618-622-0766.

Committees: *Transportation & Infrastructure*: Highways & Transit; Railroads, Pipelines & Hazardous Materials; Water Resources & Environment. *Veterans' Affairs (RMM)*: Ex Officio membership on all subcommittees.

Group Ratings

	ADA	ACLU	AFL-CIO	LCV	COC	HAFA	ACU	CFG	FRC
2020	**	21%	**	24%	-	72%	57%	**	-
2019	10%	C	50%	10%	95%	C	54%	61%	89%

Almanac Ratings 2019-2020

	Economy	Social	Foreign	Composite
Liberal	33%	40%	27%	34%
Conservative	67%	60%	73%	66%

Key Votes of the 116th Congress

1. U.S./Mex./Can. trade deal	Y	5. Russia sanctions	Y
2. First Coronavirus response	Y	6. Troops in Syria	Y
3. HEROES Act	N	7. Veto arms sales to Saudis	N
4. CASH Act	N	8. Defense $$$, veto override	Y

9. Firearms background checks N
10. Spending at the border Y
11. Marijuana liberalized rules N
12. Electoral College objections Y

Election Results

Election	Name (Party)	Vote (%)		Cand. Spent	Ind. Exp. Support	Ind. Exp. Oppose
2020 General	Mike Bost (R)	194,839	(60%)	$1,557,524	$45,425	
	Raymond Lenzi (D)	127,577	(40%)	$100,119		$10
2020 Primary	Mike Bost (R)	40,222	(100%)			

Prior winning percentages: 2018 (52%), 2016 (54%), 2014 (52%)

Republican Mike Bost, after settling into what had been a safe Democratic seat for decades, turned back a serious reelection challenge in 2018. At a time when the GOP has been wiped out in the suburbs, including in Illinois, the pugnacious lawmaker's continued success in a rural and blue-collar district foreshadowed his party's shift under Presidential Donald Trump.

Bost was born and raised in Murphysboro and enlisted in the Marine Corps upon graduating from high school. Following his service, he became a firefighter while working in the family trucking business. In 1989, he and his wife opened a beauty shop, the White House Salon, which they have continued to run. In his advocacy of smaller government and lower taxes, Bost often has cited his small business ownership as the formative experience that drove him into politics.

After several stints in local office, Bost was elected to the Illinois House in 1994, and later became Republican Caucus chairman. His work focused on sectors important to the region—especially coal and agriculture—and he became known for tangling with Democrats, who have controlled that chamber since 1996. He won national attention with an outburst on the House floor in 2012 as he protested the rules for a pension bill. After he tossed papers into the air and punched them, he cried out, "Let my people go!" Video of his tirade wound up on YouTube and went viral, attracting more than 430,000 views.

Armed with name recognition—"Meltdown Mike"—that he tried to spin to his advantage, Bost in 2014 challenged first-term Democratic Rep. Bill Enyart, a retired two-star general. Democrats had drawn the district for one of their own, but the region's growing divide over coal, plus rural and blue-collar White voters' trend away from Democrats, made it a top pickup priority for the GOP. Bost tried to make the best of his outspoken reputation. "If you want a person who goes and sits and does nothing and not argue on your behalf, then I'm not your guy," he told voters. The contest escalated into one of the most expensive House races in the country. Each party spent more than $4 million. Bost won by a surprisingly comfortable 52%-42%, the first Republican to represent St. Clair County since 1942. Enyart took the two largest counties, St. Clair and nearby Madison, but by relatively small margins. Bost won nine of the remaining 10 counties.

He made increasing the number of local jobs his chief priority. In response to the temporary closing of the local US Steel plant, he urged the Obama administration to enforce international trade laws against unfair practices of other nations. He worked on legislation to protect American companies from trade "dumping" by foreign competitors. As chairman of the Veterans' Affairs Subcommittee on Disability Assistance and Memorial Affairs in 2017, he won enactment of a bipartisan bill designed to reduce the time for appeals of veterans claims.

With several other House Republicans, Bost sought to change House rules to permit a return of spending earmarks, but was stymied by the opposition of Speaker Paul Ryan. In an interview with a St. Louis radio station, Bost objected to House Republicans who "would rather shut down government than govern." (Democrats moved to return earmarks after the 2020 elections).

He was a loyal Trump foot soldier, but along with other Illinois Republicans urged Trump not to commute disgraced former Illinois Gov. Rod Blagojevich's sentence and issued a statement expressing their disappointment when he did. He was critical of Illinois Gov. J.B. Pritzker's aggressive but largely ineffective response to the coronavirus pandemic, signing onto an April letter that called Pritzker's business restrictions "unreasonable and untenable" and later accusing Illinois Democrats of seeking federal COVID-19 relief money to cover up for years of "pre-existing financial mismanagement" of the state.

In 2018, Bost faced a serious challenge: Brendan Kelly, the prosecutor in St. Clair County and a former Navy officer with blue-collar roots. As Kelly cited his common ground with Trump on immigration and trade issues, Democrats pitched his appeal to Trump voters. At a rally for Bost in Carbondale a week before the election, Trump called Bost "a warrior" who has frequently sought his assistance. The St. Louis Post-Dispatch, which had previously endorsed Bost, backed Kelly—in part for his willingness to criticize his own party. Kelly outspent Bost $3.9 million to $2.8 million and the national parties spent an additional $4 million on the contest. Bost won 52%-45%, with strength outside the population centers.

In late 2020, Bost was chosen as ranking member on the House Veterans' Affairs Committee, an important slot for the veteran-heavy district. He also joined more than 100 other Republicans to back Texas' lawsuit that sought to upend Joe Biden's election wins in four states. In a statement to WSIL, he said he did so because "there have been concerns about irregularities in the 2020 presidential election."

Bost may not be out of the woods: Illinois is losing a congressional district, downstate Illinois has seen the steepest population decline, and the Democrats who control map-drawing hoped to erase at least one and perhaps two GOP House districts while drawing a new one for themselves outside of Chicagoland.

IL-12: Southwest Illinois

Cook Partisan Voting Index: R+9

Population		Race and Ethnicity		Income	
Total	679,002	White	77.80%	Median Income	$53,008
Land area (sq. miles)	5,008	Black	16.70%	District Income Rank	360
Pop/ sq mi	135.58	Latino	3.40%	Poverty Rate	14.50%
Born in State	67.30%	Asian	1.30%	With health insurance	93.20%
		Two or more races	3.00%	Cash public assistance	2.80%
Age Groups		Other	1.20%	Food stamp/SNAP	15.60%
Under 18	21.50%				
18-34	21.60%	**Education**		**Work**	
35-64	38.60%	H.S grad or less	40.40%	White Collar	34.30%
Over 64	18.10%	Some college	35.70%	Sales and Service	41.50%
		College Degree, 4 yr	14.50%	Blue Collar	24.20%
Military		Post grad	9.40%	Government	16.10%
Veteran/ Active Duty	11.20%				

2020 Pres. Vote	Trump	184,811	(56%)	Biden	137,911	(42%)		
2016 Pres. Vote	Trump	173,692	(54%)	Clinton	126,818	(40%)	Johnson	11,115	(4%)

East St. Louis, Carbondale: Their waters roiling together, the nation's two mightiest rivers, the Mississippi and Missouri, join at Hartford Illinois, where explorers Lewis and Clark spent five months preparing their team and collecting supplies for their journey westward. Just to the north is Alton, once a pro-slavery haven in the free state, where abolitionist Elijah Love joy's murder by a pro-slavery mob in 1837 made him a martyr and helped radicalize John Brown. To the south along the Mississippi is East St. Louis, situated on the Illinois side of the river, with a view of the Gateway Arch in the larger St. Louis on the Missouri side. It is a terminus for dozens of rail lines and highways that funnel into bridges over the river. Once a rail and stockyard center second only to Chicago, East St. Louis is now one of America's poorest and most troubled towns, a half-abandoned slum with one of the nation's highest crime rates and a rapidly declining tax base. After peaking at 82,000 in 1960, its population has shrunk to 26,000 and is 96 percent African American, with 33 percent living in poverty as of 2019.

South of East St. Louis and the industrial area around Belleville, the river counties are lightly inhabited. This was the site of the French Kaskaskia settlement that became Illinois's first capital in 1818, but repeated flooding turned it into an island and reduced its population to nine people and many more egrets. Farther south, the river abuts coal country and is not far from Carbondale, once a coal center and the home of Southern Illinois University, which has been struggling for years with shrinking enrollment.

The southern end of Illinois is sometimes known as Little Egypt, where the Ohio River meets the Mississippi: flat, fertile farmland, protected by giant constructed levees because it is susceptible to floods. The marshy landscape has created the Sinkhole Plain, with more than 10,000 sinkholes. There is more than a touch of Dixie here: The unofficial capital of Little Egypt, Cairo (pronounced KAY-roh), is a declining town closer to Memphis than to Chicago. The Shawnee National Forest has preserved Native American sites that are 10,000 years old.

The 12th District of Illinois covers all this Mississippi riverfront from Alton south to Cairo, with some inland territory as well. Slightly more than half its population is in the Metro East area in St. Clair and Madison counties. Combined, those two counties dipped from 539,000 in 2010 to 522,000 in 2019. The largest employer in Southern Illinois is Scott Air Force Base near Belleville, which has a workforce of 15,000 and is home of the U.S. Transportation Command, which directs troops and supply movements around the world.

The regional economy has struggled mightily, and it saw a brief reprieve when President Trump's hefty tariffs on steel imports drove up prices and production— which Trump celebrated with a visit to Granite City's US Steel plant that he used in 2020 campaign ads. But after hiring 800 workers locally in 2018, the company laid off that many in 2020, part of industry-wide layoffs triggered by falling prices and made worse by the coronavirus pandemic. The district was drawn to lean Democratic, but the party suffered a steep drop in support. In 2008, Barack Obama defeated John McCain, 55%-44%. In 2020, Donald Trump continued the huge turnaround, when he won the district, 56%-42%.

Rodney Davis (R)

Elected 2012, 5th term, b. Jan 05, 1970; Des Moines, IA; Millikin University, B.A., 1992; Roman Catholic; Married (Shannon Davis); 3 children.

Professional Career: Staff assistant, IL Secretary of State, 1992-1996; Projects Director, Rep. John Shimkus, 1997-2012; Executive Director, IL Republican Party, 2011.

DC Office: 1740 LHOB 20515, 202-225-2371, Fax: 202-226-0791, rodneydavis.house.gov

State Offices: Champaign, 217-403-4690; Decatur, 217-791-6224; Maryville, 618-205-8660; Normal, 309-252-8834; Springfield, 217-791-6224; Taylorville, 217-824-5117.

Committees: *Administration (RMM). Agriculture*: Biotechnology, Horticulture & Research; Commodity Exchanges, Energy & Credit; Livestock & Foreign Agriculture. *Joint Library. Joint Printing. Select Committee on the Modernization of Congress. Transportation & Infrastructure*: Economic Dev't, Public Buildings & Emergency Management; Highways & Transit (RMM); Railroads, Pipelines & Hazardous Materials; Railroads, Pipelines & Hazardous Materials.

Group Ratings

	ADA	ACLU	AFL-CIO	LCV	COC	HAFA	ACU	CFG	FRC
2020	**	26%	**	38%	-	72%	53%	**	-
2019	15%	C	57%	17%	94%	C	55%	54%	0%

Almanac Ratings 2019-2020

	Economy	Social	Foreign	Composite
Liberal	25%	45%	27%	33%
Conservative	75%	55%	73%	67%

Key Votes of the 116th Congress

1. U.S./Mex./Can. trade deal Y	5. Russia sanctions Y	9. Firearms background checks N
2. First Coronavirus response Y	6. Troops in Syria Y	10. Spending at the border Y
3. HEROES Act N	7. Veto arms sales to Saudis N	11. Marijuana liberalized rules N
4. CASH Act Y	8. Defense $$$, veto override Y	12. Electoral College objections N

Election Results

Election	Name (Party)	Vote (%)		Cand. Spent	Ind. Exp. Support	Ind. Exp. Oppose
2020 General	Rodney Davis (R)	181,373	(54%)	$4,905,544	$389,383	$6,473,831
	Betsy Dirksen Londrigan (D)	151,648	(46%)	$5,670,826	$62,215	$5,544,099
2020 Primary	Rodney Davis (R)	36,668	(100%)			

Prior winning percentages: 2018 (50%), 2016 (60%), 2014 (59%), 2012 (47%)

Republican Rodney Davis was first elected in a tight 2012 contest and has hung on in a series of competitive races— to the surprise of Democrats, including redistricters in Illinois, though his district is in their crosshairs once again. He has been an active and often bipartisan legislator and was an occasional critic of President Donald Trump and GOP policies.

Davis was born in Des Moines, Iowa, but moved to Taylorville Illinois when he was 7 years old and has never left the area. His parents opened a McDonald's franchise. He studied political science courses at Millikin University then went to work for Illinois Secretary of State George Ryan. At the time, Ryan's office was illegally selling government licenses, a massive fraud scheme that made Ryan Illinois' fourth governor in recent decades to land in jail. Davis was not implicated in the scheme.

Davis first ran for office at age 25, running for the Illinois legislature in 1996. He lost, then managed the first reelection bid of downstate Republican Rep. John Shimkus. Davis spent more than a decade on Shimkus' district office staff, except for a hiatus to run unsuccessfully for mayor of his hometown in 2000. He was Shimkus' project coordinator, securing local, federal and private funding for public works projects.

When Rep. Tim Johnson announced he was retiring from Congress shortly after winning his primary in 2012 in his redistricted seat, a small group of Illinois GOP leaders chose Davis to replace him on the ballot. Davis faced Democrat David Gill, an emergency room physician, left-wing activist and perennial candidate. Davis stressed the need to repeal President Barack Obama's health care reform law and to cut government spending, though he made an exception for federal Pell Grants (the district has several colleges and universities). Both candidates launched fierce negative attacks over the airwaves, prompting Johnson at one point to tell both of them to stop it. Davis eked out a victory by a margin of 1,002 votes—46.5%-46.2%. The national parties spent more than $6 million on the contest.

Davis has been busy on two committees: Agriculture, and Transportation and Infrastructure. As a freshman in 2014, he helped shape two major pieces of legislation, getting into the water resources bill language that permits the Army Corps of Engineers to cooperate with private businesses on waterway improvement projects and getting into the farm bill requirements that the Environmental Protection Administration give farmers a seat at the table when the agency considered new regulations that affect their industry.

Since 2019, he has been the senior Republican on the influential Highways and Transit Subcommittee. In 2021, he picked up a new leadership assignment, as ranking Republican on the House Administration Committee. Davis has shown occasional independence, as when he was one of 30 House Republicans who voted in 2016 to give illegal immigrant "dreamers" the right to join the military, and when he was among the minority of House Republicans who refused to support Texas' lawsuit that sought to overturn four states' election results to hand President Donald Trump another term. His Almanac vote ratings have placed him near the center of the House.

In 2014, Davis survived two significant challenges. In the Republican primary, his challenger was Erika Harold, a Harvard Law School graduate and 2003 Miss America who had tea party support; Davis won, 55%-41%. In the general election he faced Ann Callis, a former chief justice of the Madison County Court who broke with Democrats to paint the Affordable Care Act as "a disaster." She won the support of the Sierra Club, while Davis was backed by the United Mine Workers and the coal industry (Davis says climate change is real but opposes restrictions on the coal industry). Davis won by a robust 59%-41%.

Davis kept some distance from Trump during the 2016 election and after he settled into the White House. He criticized the tariffs that Trump imposed on imports as "devastating to our agricultural sector." He said the Trump administration should "absolutely not" separate children from their parents at the border. Shortly before the 2020 elections, Davis was one of 26 Republicans to back House Democrats' bill to increase funding for the Postal Service, which had become a flashpoint leading up to massive mail-in voting. Davis lectured his GOP colleagues on COVID-19 precautions, then days later he tested positive himself. He had few symptoms and quickly recovered.

Davis faced two tough challenges from Democrat Betsy Dirksen Londrigan, a close ally of Sen. Dick Durbin and a distant relative of the late Senate Minority Leader Everett Dirksen of Illinois. She said that Davis' support for repeal of the Affordable Care Act spurred her decision to run in 2018, and it became the focal point of the campaign. Davis won, 50.4%-49.6%, a margin of 2,058 votes, with Londrigan's strength in the district's university towns and her hometown of Springfield counterbalanced by his strength in rural areas.

In 2020, Davis ran on his bipartisan work on agriculture and transportation, while Londrigan once again focused on healthcare. The race was expensive: Londrigan edged Davis by $5.7 million to $4.9 million; Democratic outside groups edged the GOP by $6.5 million to $5,7 million. Davis, like other down-ticket Republicans, benefitted from Trump-driven rural turnout, winning 54.5%-45.5%.

Davis may have a bigger threat in his future: redistricting. Illinois is losing a district and Democrats might seek to erase two GOP districts and put Davis at the disadvantage by connecting the universities and other Democratic parts of his district with Democratic areas near St. Louis.

IL-13: West-Central Illinois

Cook Partisan Voting Index: R+4

Population		Race and Ethnicity		Income	
Total	698,830	White	80.90%	Median Income	$53,578
Land area (sq. miles)	5,794	Black	11.90%	District Income Rank	353
Pop/ sq mi	120.62	Latino	4.00%	Poverty Rate	17.90%
Born in State	73.70%	Asian	4.00%	With health insurance	95.40%
		Two or more races	2.50%	Cash public assistance	1.90%
Age Groups		Other	0.80%	Food stamp/SNAP	13.60%
Under 18	19.80%				
18-34	27.90%	Education		Work	
35-64	35.50%	H.S grad or less	38.40%	White Collar	40.50%
Over 64	16.60%	Some college	30.30%	Sales and Service	38.70%
		College Degree, 4 yr	18.20%	Blue Collar	20.80%
Military		Post grad	13.00%	Government	19.30%
Veteran/ Active Duty	7.30%				

2020 Pres. Vote	Trump	170,490	(50%)	Biden	158,905	(47%)			
2016 Pres. Vote	Trump	159,013	(49%)	Clinton	141,540	(44%)	Johnson	14,681	(5%)

St. Louis exurbs, Champaign: Springfield, the capital of Illinois, has changed rather little since its great moment in history— when it was home to Abraham Lincoln, railroad lawyer, elected to the House as a Whig opponent of the Mexican War and later, the 16th president of the United States. Today, beyond the suburban fringe, the prairie countryside outside Springfield is still mostly farmland with few towns, filled with large industrial farms producing soybeans and corn. Farming technology has changed vastly, but the patterns of cultivation, the contours of the land, even the shape of the ribbons of back country roads, cannot be entirely different from what Lincoln saw as a lawyer making his way from one county seat to another on the circuit.

Nor has downtown Springfield changed all that much, at least compared with booming Midwestern capitals such as Columbus, Indianapolis or even Des Moines. Lincoln's clapboard house is preserved in Springfield, and so is the courtroom where he argued cases before federal judges. The downtown block where Lincoln and his partner William Herndon kept their law offices is open for inspection, as is the state capitol built here in 1839. The governor's mansion downtown, built in 1855, is the third oldest continuously occupied residence in the country. Today, Springfield is known more for its dysfunction: a continuing loss of public jobs under governors of both parties; the dispiriting paralysis and debt of state government; and the corruption resulting in four of the state's past 10 governors being sentenced to jail time.

The 13th Congressional District contains prairie lands from Collinsville, just outside St. Louis, to Champaign-Urbana, a three-hour drive northeast. It includes much of Bloomington, birthplace of Vice President Adlai Stevenson, who served under Democrat Grover Cleveland, and the hometown of his grandson, Gov. Adlai Stevenson II, nominated by Democrats for president in 1952 and 1956. The largest of the towns in the district are anchored by the state's universities: the University of Illinois in Champaign-Urbana; Illinois State University in Bloomington-Normal; and Illinois Wesleyan University, also in Bloomington. Decatur is home to politically influential Archer Daniels Midland, one of the world's largest agricultural processors and a major champion of ethanol. Except for youthful Champaign, downstate has been suffering population losses.

As other universities either went online-only or had students back with few protections during the pandemic, the University of Illinois's flagship campus developed a cutting-edge COVID-19 saliva rapid test and ramped up to testing students every other day; the university had conducted 1 million tests by December 2020, more than 10 U.S. states, and largely kept on-campus cases under control even as the pandemic ravaged Illinois.

Politically, the district has been closely divided, with shrinking rural farm towns pulling farther right as the liberal academic population centers and government capital in Springfield continued to drift left in recent years. Trump narrowly carried the district in both of his campaigns, including 50%-47% in 2020.In 2018, J.B. Pritzker became the first Democratic candidate for governor to carry Champaign County since 1936.

Lauren Underwood (D)

Elected 2018, 2nd term, b. Oct 04, 1986; Mayfield Heights, OH; University of MI, B.S., 2008; Johns Hopkins University, M.S.N., 2009; Johns Hopkins University, M.PH, 2009; Christian Church; Single.

Professional Career: Government Affairs Fellow, American Association of Colleges of Nursing, 2009-2009; National Institutes of Health Fellow, 2008-2009; Research Nurse, Johns Hopkins University, 2009-2010; , U.S. Department of Health and Human Services, Policy Coordinator, 2010-2014, Senior Advisor 2014-2017; Adjunct Professor, Georgetown University School of Nursing & Health Studies, 2013-2018.

DC Office: 1118 LHOB 20515, 202-225-2976, underwood.house.gov

State Offices: West Chicago, 630-549-2190.

Committees: *Appropriations*: Agriculture, Rural Development, FDA & Related Agencies; Homeland Security. *Veterans' Affairs*: Health; Women Veterans Task Force.

Almanac Ratings 2019-2020

	Economy	Social	Foreign	Composite
Liberal	100%	100%	80%	94%
Conservative	0%	0%	20%	6%

Key Votes of the 116th Congress

1. U.S./Mex./Can. trade deal	Y	5. Russia sanctions	Y	9. Firearms background checks	Y
2. First Coronavirus response	Y	6. Troops in Syria	Y	10. Spending at the border	Y
3. HEROES Act	Y	7. Veto arms sales to Saudis	Y	11. Marijuana liberalized rules	Y
4. CASH Act	Y	8. Defense $$$, veto override	Y	12. Electoral College objections	N

Election Results

Election	Name (Party)	Vote (%)		Cand. Spent	Ind. Exp. Support	Ind. Exp. Oppose
2020 General	Lauren Underwood (D)................. 203,209	(51%)		$8,118,450	$270,023	$35,068
	Jim Oberweis (R)......................... 197,835	(49%)		$2,182,643	$208,168	$1,733,841
2020 Primary	Lauren Underwood (D).................... 77,707	(100%)				

Prior winning percentages: 2018 (53%)

Democrat Lauren Underwood pulled off an election win in 2018 in the most Republican-leaning district in Chicago's outer suburbs and held on in a nail-biter in 2020. A registered nurse who became an expert on health care policy, she built on her experiences in the Obama administration. She's one of only a handful of African-Americans to represent a heavily white district, and at age 32was the youngest Black woman ever elected to Congress. Underwood's gender and her health-policy expertise were more influential than race in her election wins.

Underwood is from Naperville, which is a few miles outside the 14th District. She graduated from the University of Michigan with a bachelor's of science in nursing, and got master's degrees in nursing and public health from Johns Hopkins University. As a special assistant to President Barack Obama, she advised communities on how to respond to disaster and public-health emergencies. In 2016, Obama appointed her as a senior adviser at the Health and Human Services Department, where she earlier worked on implementation of the Affordable Care Act. She advised local governments on steps to maximize cost-efficient care and taught nurses at Georgetown University.

Underwood returned home and challenged Republican Rep. Randy Hultgren, who hadn't faced a serious challenge in the GOP-leaning district. With her pre-existing heart condition, Underwood said that Hultgren's vote to repeal the Affordable Care Act spurred her to run for Congress. "The country needs new leaders who can put partisanship aside and make progress on the issues that matter to our community," she told the Chicago Sun-Times. In the Democratic primary, Underwood faced six other candidates—all of them white men. She won the primary with 57 percent of the vote.

Hultgren challenged Underwood's views on health policy and painted her as a bureaucrat pretending to be a nurse. The biggest difference between the them, he told the Sun-Times, was that she "helped engineer a federal takeover of the health care system in this country that left [residents of the 14th District] with higher health care costs, limited choice in their health care options and less control over their own health care."

Underwood's more than $4 million for the campaign doubled the spending by Hultgren, who national GOP strategists privately complained ran a lackluster campaign. House Democrats and their allies, including women's groups, spent more than $2 million on her behalf. In her 53%-47% victory, Underwood won all seven counties. In her victory speech, she quoted the late Rep. Shirley Chisholm of New York, Congress's first African American female representative, as she promised to be "unbought and unbossed."

Underwood told Bon Appetit magazine that she often gets stopped in the Capitol by policemen who assume she's not a member of Congress. "I think that is very much a function of being a young, Black woman in a space where there hasn't been someone like me—as young as I am and probably look—ever. Every week I get stopped and told I'm not supposed to be where I am," she said. She made friends with other Millennial members, including Rep. Alexandria Ocasio-Cortez, who called her "one of the straightest shooters in the freshman class" in a fundraising appeal. But unlike AOC and the Squad, Underwood avoided conflict with House Democratic leaders and was named one of six House first-term liaisons to leadership.

Underwood has showed legislative savvy, getting bills regulating insulin prices, setting standards for medical screenings of migrants entering the U.S., and securing $30 million for an electronic health records system for the Department of Homeland Security into broader packages that became law. She cofounded the Black Maternal Health Caucus.

She also displayed some fire: In a tense exchange on the Homeland Security Committee over Trump's refugee family separation policy, Underwood said "with five children dead and 5,000 separated from their families, this is intentional. It's a policy choice being made on purpose by this administration, and it's cruel and inhumane."

From the start of the 2020 campaign, Underwood was a top GOP target. But national Republicans were disappointed when dairy magnate, perennial candidate, conservative lightning rod and state Sen. Jim Oberweis emerged from a crowded eight-candidate primary as their nominee. Underwood, a favorite of both the establishment and grassroots activists, outspent the self-funding Oberweis $8.1 million to $2.2 million; neither got major outside spending, as both sides assumed she would win.

But the result was a surprise: Oberweis prematurely declared victory as he led by 20,000 votes election night. Underwood eventually won by 5,374 votes, a lead that withstood Oberweis' demand for a recount. Her win handed Oberweis his sixth loss in a federal race. Underwood ran slightly behind Biden in the district.

Democrats will undoubtedly try to shore up Underwood in redistricting, though the exurban terrain will pose challenges. She has a bright future in the Democratic caucus—if she can hold onto her seat.

IL-14: Northwestern Chicagoland   Cook Partisan Voting Index: R+2

Population		Race and Ethnicity		Income	
Total	727,525	White	86.10%	Median Income	$100,011
Land area (sq. miles)	1,598	Black	3.10%	District Income Rank	37
Pop/ sq mi	455.39	Latino	12.00%	Poverty Rate	4.30%
Born in State	72.30%	Asian	5.30%	With health insurance	94.90%
		Two or more races	2.50%	Cash public assistance	1.00%
Age Groups		Other	3.00%	Food stamp/SNAP	5.30%
Under 18	25.10%				
18-34	18.60%	**Education**		**Work**	
35-64	41.40%	H.S grad or less	28.40%	White Collar	44.30%
Over 64	14.80%	Some college	29.00%	Sales and Service	36.10%
		College Degree, 4 yr	27.30%	Blue Collar	19.60%
Military		Post grad	15.30%	Government	12.90%
Veteran/ Active Duty	5.60%				

2020 Pres. Vote	Biden	203,741	(50%)	Trump	193,889	(48%)		
2016 Pres. Vote	Trump	167,327	(48%)	Clinton	154,058	(44%)	Johnson	17,259 (5%)

McHenry, Kane: In the exurbs west of Chicago, the decade since the Great Recession has seen an economic slowdown exacerbated by the coronavirus-fueled recession. At the peak of the housing boom, Kendall County looked like the city's new suburban frontier. It was rated the fastest-growing large county in the nation by the Census Bureau in 2010. Its population more than doubled in the decade after 2000, as urban flight brought in families attracted by its affordable housing, good schools and low crime rates, all located near job centers in suburban DuPage and Kane counties. Farmland quickly transformed into new housing subdivisions. In effect, Kendall became a suburb of the suburbs. But the downside of the rapid growth became evident during the collapse of the housing finance market, when Kendall posted the highest foreclosure rate in the state.

Other nearby counties also haven't fared well: McHenry County's population shrank by 1,300 people from 2010-2019 after the population had boomed by 19 percent in the previous decade. The most common explanation is a combination of high taxes and fewer jobs. In McHenry, two-thirds of working residents commute to jobs in other counties. These problems have resulted partly from decades of dysfunctional state governance, leading Illinois to the highest unfunded pension liability and the worst credit rating in the nation.

The 14th District of Illinois arcs through seven counties in the suburbs of Chicago, including most of what have been solidly Republican Kendall and McHenry, and also Republican-leaning chunks of Kane and western Lake County, where small lake communities are surrounded by new suburbs like Wauconda, Deer Park and Volo. About 55 percent of the voting population resides in McHenry and Kane. Of all the Chicagoland districts, the 14th is the least ethnically diverse and least liberal, with a 86 percent white population. Huntley is the site of Del Webb's Sun City; with about 9,000 residents, it claims to be the largest retirement community in the Midwest. Batavia-based Fermilab, which describes itself as America's particle physics and accelerator laboratory and has 1,900 employees, received approval from the Energy Department to proceed with the design of a project that will generate an unprecedented stream of neutrinos, which are subatomic particles.

This is the most Republican district in the suburbs, though much of "downstate" has become notably more Republican than the 14th. Still, Democrats can run competitively here. Barack Obama narrowly carried it, under the present lines, with 50 percent of the vote in 2008. Donald Trump won here 48%-44% in 2016 but it flipped in 2020, when Joe Biden won, 50%-48%.

Mary Miller (R)

Elected 2020, 1st term, b. Aug 27, 1959; Naperville, IL; Northeastern IL University; Northeastern IL University; Northeastern IL University, B.S., 1981; Christian - Non-Denominational; Married (Mr. Chris Miller); 7 children; 16 grandchildren.

DC Office: 1529 LHOB 20515, 202-225-5271, Fax: 202-225-5880, marymiller.house.gov

State Offices: Danville, 217-703-6100; Effingham, 217-240-3155.

Committees: *Agriculture*: Conservation & Forestry; General Farm Commodities & Risk Management. *Education & Labor*: Early Childhood, Elementary & Secondary Education; Health, Employment, Labor & Pensions.

Election Results

Election	Name (Party)	Vote (%)		Cand. Spent	Ind. Exp. Support	Ind. Exp. Oppose
2020 General	Mary Miller (R)	244,947	(73%)	$565,024	$540,751	
	Erika Weaver (D)	88,559	(27%)	$21,757		
2020 Primary	Mary Miller (R)	48,129	(57%)			
	Darren Duncan (R)	18,309	(22%)			
	Kerry Wolff (R)	11,208	(13%)			
	Charles Ellington (R)	6,200	(7%)			

Republican Mary Miller, a political newcomer, won by large margins in both her primary and general election. Running on her background as a farmer and homeschool teacher, she embraced conservative principles in her heavily Republican district. Miller, who campaigned as a " true outsider" and proponent of term limits, won early support from leaders of House Republicans and the conservative Freedom Caucus. She replaced GOP Rep. John Shimkus, an active lawmaker who retired after 12 terms.

A native of Naperville in the suburbs west of Chicago, Miller got two bachelor's degrees from Eastern Illinois University— in business management and elementary education. With her husband, Chris, she ran their grain and cattle farm in Coles County. Miller has taught children in homeschools and religious schools at her local church. In 2018, Chris was elected to the state House.

After Shimkus announced his retirement, Miller launched her campaign on the themes of " faith, family and freedom." She cast herself as a citizen-politician who would serve only a few terms." Washington, D.C., won't change me. I am running to change Washington," she told the Chicago Tribune. With her emphasis on the need to reduce the federal debt, Miller included "real Social Security and Medicare reform," which she said should not reduce benefits to " anyone currently" receiving those benefits. She highlighted her political independence by citing her support of Jeanne Ives, who challenged Gov. Bruce Rauner in the competitive 2018 Republican primary.

The 2020Republican House primary, with four candidates, was a relatively low-key and inexpensive contest. Darren Duncan, Miller's chief opponent, also was a farmer and had held elected offices in Vermilion County. Each spent a bit more than $300,000 in the primary. In contrast to Miller's support from House GOP leaders, Duncan featured support from House Republicans outside of Illinois who were key players on agriculture issues— though Miller won the endorsement of the Illinois Farm Bureau. She also cited the backing she received from leaders of the House Freedom Caucus, which included nearly $500,000 in spending. "With their support, I have an opportunity to have a big impact before I even get to Congress," Miller said. Miller swamped Duncan, 57%-22%, in the primary. She ran strongly across the district.

In the general election, Democrat Erika Weaver rose from her background as a homeless mother with three small children and eventually graduated from the Loyola University Chicago School of Law, while commuting to classes from her home in southern Illinois. As a lawyer, she joined the public defender's office in Coles County. Weaver spent less than five percent of Miller's nearly $600,000 total and got about 27 percent of the vote. Weaver trailed badly in all counties— not exceeding 35 percent in any of them.

As the junior Republican serving the three House districts south of Peoria and with a district that lacks a major population center, Miller might draw a short straw in redistricting. But she has one potential advantage: Her district is so overwhelmingly Republican that it might remain a vote sink for downstate Illinois.

In the House, Miller got seats on the Agriculture, and Education and Labor committees.

IL-15: Eastern South-Central Illinois   **Cook Partisan Voting Index: R+26**

Population		Race and Ethnicity		Income	
Total	685,859	White	92.30%	Median Income	$56,268
Land area (sq. miles)	14,696	Black	4.70%	District Income Rank	312
Pop/ sq mi	46.67	Latino	2.80%	Poverty Rate	11.90%
Born in State	77.50%	Asian	0.70%	With health insurance	93.50%
		Two or more races	1.60%	Cash public assistance	2.40%
Age Groups		Other	0.60%	Food stamp/SNAP	13.00%
Under 18	22.00%				
18-34	19.80%	**Education**		**Work**	
35-64	38.90%	H.S grad or less	43.70%	White Collar	33.30%
Over 64	19.30%	Some college	35.40%	Sales and Service	36.70%
		College Degree, 4 yr	13.30%	Blue Collar	30.00%
Military		Post grad	7.60%	Government	15.40%
Veteran/ Active Duty	7.90%				

2020 Pres. Vote	Trump	246,927	(72%)	Biden	88,675	(26%)		
2016 Pres. Vote	Trump	226,606	(70%)	Clinton	78,573	(24%)	Johnson	12,468	(4%)

Metro St. Louis, Champaign County: Much of Southern Illinois is a land of prairies, flat, treeless stretches sloping imperceptibly down to the Ohio and Mississippi rivers. It was settled almost entirely from the south by farmers coming overland from Kentucky, such as Abraham Lincoln's ancestors, who settled in what was then the state capital of Vandalia. Just beyond the Ohio River, they found hilly terrain, some of which turned out to have vast coal deposits. As they traveled farther north, they must have been astonished, after miles of thick forest, to see the great American prairie stretch before them, a vast sea of empty land extending past the horizon. The black soil proved wondrously rich and the land was soon crisscrossed by rail lines taking their produce away and bringing in industrial products from St. Louis, Chicago and points east. This was the home turf of John L. Lewis, the imperious leader of the United Mine Workers, who during the middle of the 20th century was one of the most powerful and eloquent figures in American public life.

The local mining industry in recent years has become a shadow of its former self. In 1990, Illinois produced 62 million tons of coal and employed 10,000 workers in mining; by 2014, 4,500 workers produced 58 million tons. Employers and workers drew some hope—and a few jobs—from the campaign promises of Donald Trump to revive the production and burning of coal; in 2017, mining increased by 10percent, though jobs fell by 3 percent. In 2019, Illinois officials reached agreement with the owner of eight downstate coal-powered utilities to place a significant cap on their emissions, which will reduce the plants' reliance on coal.

The 15th Congressional District of Illinois, the largest geographically in the state, extends more than 250 miles up and down the Indiana border, and 150 miles across. Vermilion County and northern Champaign County are on the northern border of the district, which extends west to a few miles from East St. Louis and the Mississippi River. It covers all or part of 33 counties in the rich heartland of Southern Illinois. The old National Road (paralleled by Interstate 70), the traditional boundary between the part of downstate Illinois settled by southerners and the part settled by Yankees, traverses the district. Effingham, which straddles that line, is where corn and soybean fields give way to hills and valleys with orchards and woodlands. Racial diversity is limited here; in 2017, the district was 91 percent white.

The biggest voting blocs in the 15th are in Madison and Clinton counties (parts of the St. Louis metropolitan area), Coles County (home to Eastern Illinois University), plus Champaign and Vermilion counties. Politically, these prairie lands were the home of former House Speaker Joseph (Uncle Joe) Cannon, a Republican from the manufacturing city of Danville, which is the largest in the district. Danville's population of 30,479 fell 8 percent from 2010 to 2019.Traditional Democrats have become hard to find here. In his two campaigns, Trump won 70 percent and then 72 percent, and each county except for a slice of university-based Champaign. This is the most Republican district in Illinois—increasingly so since 2008, when John McCain got 55 percent—and among the top five percent nationwide.

Adam Kinzinger (R)

Elected 2010, 6th term, b. Feb 27, 1978; Kankakee; IL State University, B.A., 2000; IL State University, B.A., 2000; Christian Church; Single.

Military Career: U.S. Air Force 2003-2009; IL Air National Guard 29-pres. (Iraq).

Elected Office: McLean County Board, 1998-2003.

Professional Career: Partner, sales rep., STL Technology, 2000-2003.

DC Office: 2245 RHOB 20515, 202-225-3635, Fax: 202-225-3521, kinzinger.house.gov

State Offices: Ottawa, 815-431-9271; Rockford, 815-708-8032; Watseka, 815-432-0580.

Committees: *Energy & Commerce*: Communications & Technology; Energy. *Foreign Affairs*: Europe, Energy, the Environment & Cyber; Middle East, North Africa & Global Counterterrorism.

Group Ratings

	ADA	ACLU	AFL-CIO	LCV	COC	HAFA	ACU	CFG	FRC
2020	**	21%	**	29%	-	62%	58%	**	-
2019	10%	C	52%	14%	91%	C	59%	56%	86%

Almanac Ratings 2019-2020

	Economy	Social	Foreign	Composite
Liberal	34%	43%	39%	39%
Conservative	66%	57%	61%	61%

Key Votes of the 116th Congress

1. U.S./Mex./Can. trade deal	Y	5. Russia sanctions	Y	9. Firearms background checks	N
2. First Coronavirus response	Y	6. Troops in Syria	Y	10. Spending at the border	N/A
3. HEROES Act	N	7. Veto arms sales to Saudis	N	11. Marijuana liberalized rules	N
4. CASH Act	Y	8. Defense $$$, veto override	Y	12. Electoral College objections	N

Election Results

Election	Name (Party)	Vote (%)		Cand. Spent	Ind. Exp. Support	Ind. Exp. Oppose
2020 General	Adam Kinzinger (R)	218,839	(65%)	$1,466,643	$150,806	$113
	Dani Brzozowski (D)	119,313	(35%)	$426,392	$123	
2020 Primary	Adam Kinzinger (R)	45,296	(100%)			

Prior winning percentages: 2018 (59%), 2016 (100%), 2014 (71%), 2012 (62%), 2010 (57%)

Republican Adam Kinzinger, a former Air Force pilot, is a telegenic conservative who has racked up considerable experience in the military and political worlds. He remained in the good graces of House GOP leadership until he emerged as their most vocal critic of President Donald Trump.

Kinzinger was born in Kankakee, but spent the majority of his life in Bloomington. He attributed his interest in public service to his father, who ran a nonprofit homeless shelter, and his mother, a public school teacher. Wanting to stay near home, he got a bachelor's degree in political science from Illinois State University. In 1998, as a sophomore, he took seriously a joking suggestion that he run for the McLean County Board. He defeated an incumbent, and served five years. With the September 11 terrorist attacks, "that's when I basically woke up," he recalled. A month later, he joined the Air Force. He served three tours in Iraq and one in Afghanistan. In 2006 while in Milwaukee, he wrestled a man armed with a knife to the ground after witnessing that man slash his girlfriend's neck; she survived the assault.

In 2009, following his final tour in Iraq, Kinzinger campaigned for the district based in Will County. Touting his military service, he had important backing from local tea party activists and defeated four opponents in the Republican primary, with 64 percent of the vote. In the fall, he faced first-term Rep. Debbie Halvorson. She attacked Kinzinger's stance on free trade and depicted him as inexperienced. She ran a campaign ad with a senior citizen scolding, "Young man, you have no idea what you're doing." Kinzinger countered with endorsements from Mitt Romney and Sarah Palin, as well as the Chicago Sun-Times, which often backs Democrats. Kinzinger won convincingly, 57%-43%.

Democrats immediately put a target on his back in 2012, drawing him into the same district as 10-term Republican Rep. Don Manzullo, who was twice his age and had represented more of the new district. The race upended the traditional rules of seniority: Kinzinger won the endorsement of top House GOP leaders, while Manzullo played up his tea party support. Kinzinger touted his combat tours and hit Manzullo for voting to raise the debt limit 12 times in his career. Primary voters decided to go with youth over experience, and Kinzinger won 54%-46%. He has not faced serious opposition since.

GOP leaders put him on the whip team and gave him a choice seat on the Energy and Commerce Committee, where he has generally upheld business' interests. The House in 2012 passed his bill aimed at helping states streamline certification requirements for veterans with emergency medical technician training who want to continue as civilian EMTs. Time named him one of its "40 Under 40" young leaders.

Kinzinger has focused on multiple energy sources of interest to his constituents. He has been a major booster of nuclear energy that, he said, " will sustain our economic expansion and keep the lights on while we work to catch up with our international competition." In 2018, he enacted a bill with Democratic Rep. Mike Doyle of Pennsylvania to improve the " transparency, predictability and fairness" of the fee structure for nuclear regulation.

In recent years, Kinzinger became more outspoken in defending what used to be establishment GOP views, especially on national security— while he continued to serve in the Air National Guard, as a lieutenant colonel. In 2014, he criticized the Pentagon budget-cutting plan of Kentucky Sen. Rand Paul as " devastating for our party." In 2015, he filed a resolution to grant President Barack Obama full authority to wage war against the threat posed by the Islamic State. Following the 2016 Republican convention, he cited Trump's criticism of NATO and attacks on Muslims in his decision not to endorse his campaign for president. " Donald Trump is beginning to cross a lot of red lines of the unforgivable in politics. I'm not going to support Hillary, but in America we have the right to skip somebody," Kinzinger said on CNN.

While most other GOP critics became cheerleaders or bit their tongues, Kinzinger refused to be cowed, increasingly pushing back against Trump's foreign policy moves and conspiracy theorizing. He said that it was vital for the United States to call Russia to account for its actions to "mess around" with our election systems, and was among the first congressional Republicans to call for an independent counsel to investigate allegations of ties between Trump's campaign and Russia. He called a 2019 Trump tweet that warned of civil war " beyond repugnant," said his 2019 withdrawal of troops from Syria was " unbelievable," and criticized Trump's 2020 move to withdraw U.S. troops from Germany.

After the election, Kinzinger was the first House Republican not facing retirement who clearly stated that Trump had lost. Two days after the election, Kinzinger tweeted "STOP Spreading debunked misinformation. ... This is getting insane." In December, after Trump posted a 46-minute screed, Kinzinger replied " Time to delete your account."

" I think the long-term impact of this could be devastating," Kinzinger told Politico in explaining his vocal criticism. " That's why I decided to put this on the line. We've lost our moral authority to be outraged."

That criticism enraged Trump supporters, but it didn't seem to hurt Kinzinger's standing at home. He beat a pro-Trump primary challenger by a 2-to-1 margin in 2018, and didn't face a primary in 2020. In 2020, House GOP leaders put him on their China Task Force.

And it didn't seem to much affect his personal life, either. In early 2020, Kinzinger married Sofia Boza-Holman, who held multiple jobs in the Trump administration and was a staffer to former House Speaker John Boehner.

Following the election, Kinzinger firmly rejected House Republicans calls to investigate results of the Electoral College. " Congress does not have the power to overturn the will of the people, and any attempt to do so would create a constitutional crisis the likes of which we have not seen in our lifetimes," he said. " As difficult as it may be to accept political defeat, I would never act to subvert our system of self-governance, or the people who have spoken." He was 1 of 10 House Republicans who voted to impeach Trump following the riot at the Capitol. "There is no doubt in my mind that the President of the United States broke his oath of office and incited this insurrection. He used his position in the Executive to attack the Legislative." In response, the Republican Party in at least three counties in his district voted to censure Kinzinger, though the Winnebago County GOP responded only that it "strongly disagrees" with him.

Kinzinger's political future is unclear. It partly depends on what shape the post-Trump GOP and the Illinois redistricting map take. He could run for governor or senator in 2022, though he might find it difficult to survive a GOP primary.

IL-16: North-Central Illinois　　　　　　　**Cook Partisan Voting Index: R+10**

Population		Race and Ethnicity		Income	
Total	694,262	White	89.30%	Median Income	$62,868
Land area (sq. miles)	7,917	Black	3.80%	District Income Rank	226
Pop/ sq mi	87.69	Latino	10.60%	Poverty Rate	11.20%
Born in State	77.20%	Asian	1.60%	With health insurance	95.30%
		Two or more races	2.20%	Cash public assistance	1.90%
Age Groups		Other	3.00%	Food stamp/SNAP	11.00%
Under 18	21.40%				
18-34	21.20%	**Education**		**Work**	
35-64	38.50%	H.S grad or less	42.40%	White Collar	33.20%
Over 64	18.90%	Some college	34.10%	Sales and Service	36.70%
		College Degree, 4 yr	15.10%	Blue Collar	30.00%
Military		Post grad	8.30%	Government	12.40%
Veteran/ Active Duty	7.60%				

2020 Pres. Vote	Trump	196,237	(57%)	Biden	140,937	(41%)		
2016 Pres. Vote	Trump	173,068	(55%)	Clinton	119,529	(38%)	Johnson	15,073 (5%)

Rockford, Ottawa: Rockford, on the Rock River, was once a leading furniture and machine tool manufacturer. Its manufacturing base steadily declined after World War II, and it has struggled ever since— its population declined by 5 percent to 145,000 from 2010 to 2019, and it had slipped from Illinois' third- to fifth-largest city. Nearby DeKalb and Boone counties, which had boomed in the 2000s, have seen population growth flat-line in the past decade.

The region, like much of Illinois, has largely stagnated in the past decade. Chrysler's Belvidere plant, peaked at 5,400 workers when Chrysler shifted production of its Jeep Cherokee to the plant earlier this decade, but 1,400 were laid off in 2019 and the remaining employees were offered buyouts after the plant was temporarily shut down in early 2020.

The 16th Congressional District is where downstate Illinois begins, at least where it begins west of Chicago. The elongated district forms a crescent surrounding the exurbs of Chicago as it makes a long hook from the Wisconsin border on the north to the Indiana border on the east. It includes parts of Rockford, the population base of the district. Farther south, on bluffs above the Illinois River, are the factory towns of Ottawa, LaSalle, and Streator. On the eastern side of the district is DeKalb County, long the world's leading manufacturer of barbed wire. Dixon, to the west, is where Ronald Reagan grew up.

These mostly small towns traditionally were some of the most heavily Republican territory in the country, and were drawn as a GOP vote-sink by Democratic gerrymandering. Favorite son Barack Obama carried the district with 50 percent in 2008, Donald Trump won it by 55%-38% in 2016 and 57%-41% in 2020.

Cheri Bustos (D)

Elected 2012, 5th term, b. Oct 17, 1961; Springfield, IL; IL College - Jacksonville, Att., 1981; University of MD - College Park, B.A., 1983; University of IL - Springfield, M.A., 1985; Roman Catholic; Married (Gerry Bustos); 3 children; 2 grandchildren.

Elected Office: East Moline City Council, 2007-2011.

Professional Career: Vice President., Iowa Health Systems, 2008-2012; Sr. Director, Trinity Regional Health System, 2002-2008; Reporter, Quad-City Times, 1985-2002.

DC Office: 1233 LHOB 20515, 202-225-5905, Fax: 202-225-5396, bustos.house.gov

State Offices: Peoria, 309-966-1813; Rock Island, 309-786-3406; Rockford, 815-968-8011.

Committees: House Democratic Steering and Policy Committee Co-Chair. *Agriculture*: General Farm Commodities & Risk Management (Chmn). *Appropriations*: Defense; Energy & Water Development & Related Agencies; Labor, Health & Human Services, Education & Related Agencies.

Group Ratings

	ADA	ACLU	AFL-CIO	LCV	COC	HAFA	ACU	CFG	FRC
2020	**	70%	**	100%	-	0%	4%	**	-
2019	80%	C	100%	97%	69%	C	4%	12%	0%

Almanac Ratings 2019-2020

	Economy	Social	Foreign	Composite
Liberal	100%	60%	80%	80%
Conservative	0%	40%	20%	20%

Key Votes of the 116th Congress

1. U.S./Mex./Can. trade deal	Y	5. Russia sanctions	Y
2. First Coronavirus response	Y	6. Troops in Syria	Y
3. HEROES Act	Y	7. Veto arms sales to Saudis	Y
4. CASH Act	Y	8. Defense $$$, veto override	Y

9. Firearms background checks	Y
10. Spending at the border	Y
11. Marijuana liberalized rules	N
12. Electoral College objections	N

Election Results

Election	Name (Party)	Vote (%)	Cand. Spent	Ind. Exp. Support	Ind. Exp. Oppose
2020 General	Cheri Bustos (D)............................	156,011 (52%)	$5,234,158	$10,201	$479,036
	Esther Joy King (R)............................	143,863 (48%)	$1,931,207	$288,603	$1,044,115
2020 Primary	Cheri Bustos (D)............................	56,388 (100%)			

Prior winning percentages: 2018 (62%), 2016 (60%), 2014 (55%), 2012 (53%)

Democrat Cheri Bustos, first elected in 2012, has deep roots in Illinois politics— her father was a chief of staff for the late Democratic Sen. Alan Dixon. That has helped her survive in a Republican-trending district, though a rocky tenure running the Democratic Congressional Campaign Committee in the 2020 election cycle may have been a factor in her decision to retire in 2022.

Bustos grew up in the state capital of Springfield. Her mother was a social worker and preschool teacher, and her father was a journalist before entering government. Her first paid job was selling tacos and lemonade at the Illinois State Fair. She later babysat future Sen. Dick Durbin's kids as a teenager. After attending Illinois College, where she excelled at basketball and volleyball, Bustos graduated from the University of Maryland with a bachelor's degree in political science and history. She earned a master's degree in journalism at the University of Illinois and became a reporter for the Quad-City Times, where she had a 17-year career. Her husband, Gerry, is the Rock Island County sheriff.

After leaving journalism, Bustos went into public relations for regional health care providers, including as vice president of public relations and communications for Iowa Health System. Health insurance issues are a key concern for her: She lost her uninsured sister-in-law to cancer a few years ago, and her brother to cancer months later, after his insurance refused to cover the medication he needed.

She was elected to the City Council in East Moline, and served from 2007 to 2011. Democrats in Springfield had used redistricting to make the House district more Democratic for a challenge to freshman Republican Rep. Bobby Schilling, a former pizzeria owner; with Durbin's backing, Bustos ran for the seat and won the primary over two other candidates with 54 percent of the vote.

Her race in the fall against Schilling attracted more than $3 million each from party groups, in addition to the more than $2 million that each candidate raised. Bustos received an early endorsement from the abortion rights group EMILY's List and was backed by several labor unions. She won, 53%-47%.

Bustos concentrated, at first, on her committee work on agriculture and transportation issues. The former college athlete also emerged as a star shortstop on the congressional women's softball team. Her 2014 rematch against Schilling proved less competitive than their initial contest: She outspent him by $3.1 million to $1.1 million, and rolled to a 55%-45% win in the face of a GOP wave election.

Bustos served as one of three co-chairs of the Democratic Communications and Policy Committee for the 2018 election cycle, mentoring and campaigning with Rust Belt Democratic candidates. In December 2018, House Democrats chose her to defend Democrats' new majority as chair of the Democratic Congressional Campaign Committee. She also got a choice assignment on the Appropriations Committee. Bustos signaled she would hew close to the center when she was one of just six House Democrats to vote against federal marijuana decriminalization in late 2020.

Bustos' chairmanship at the DCCC got off to a rocky start, and she never fully recovered. She faced fury from Black and Hispanic colleagues for hiring a mostly white staff packed with loyalists; after months of tensions, many of them were let go in late July 2019, including her former chief of staff, who resigned as the DCCC's executive director. She also triggered an open war with progressives by formalizing a long-unofficial DCCC policy of refusing contracts to any strategists who also worked for candidates running against Democratic House incumbents—the move infuriated progressives and led to calls from Alexandria Ocasio-Cortez and others to boycott giving the committee donations.

Bustos seemed to get things back on track after that, aggressively recruiting candidates in historically Republican suburban seats they thought they could flip. The DCCC outraised the National Republican Congressional Committee $339 million to $271 million for the cycle, and Democrats thought they were on offense across the map, opting to spend heavily on takeover opportunities rather than shoring up their incumbents. Heading into Election Day, strategists in both parties expected Democrats to net as many as 10 House seats. Instead, they lost a dozen seats, a result that left Democrats barely clinging to the House majority. Bustos barely held onto her own seat, winning 52%-48%.

Bustos told colleagues that she was just as mad as they were during a post-election call. "I also want to say the thing we're all feeling: I'm furious. Something went wrong here across the entire political world," she said, pointing out that both Democratic and GOP polls had assumed Democrats would have a stronger election. She stepped down as DCCC chairwoman, though she got a plumb consolation prize when she was named co-chair of the Democrats' Steering and Policy Committee, which awards committee spots to House Democrats.

In April 2021, Bustos said that she was not seeking reelection in 2022. She faced the uncertainty of redistricting plus the likely end of her prospects in Democratic leadership. Her decision could result in significant realignment of the Democratic centers of her district.

IL-17: Northwest Illinois   **Cook Partisan Voting Index: R+2**

Population		Race and Ethnicity		Income	
Total	666,201	White	81.30%	Median Income	$50,346
Land area (sq. miles)	6,933	Black	12.40%	District Income Rank	384
Pop/ sq mi	96.09	Latino	9.60%	Poverty Rate	16.30%
Born in State	72.40%	Asian	1.00%	With health insurance	93.50%
		Two or more races	2.80%	Cash public assistance	2.60%
Age Groups		Other	2.60%	Food stamp/SNAP	19.10%
Under 18	22.00%				
18-34	20.90%	**Education**		**Work**	
35-64	38.00%	H.S grad or less	45.90%	White Collar	29.90%
Over 64	19.30%	Some college	33.90%	Sales and Service	41.20%
		College Degree, 4 yr	13.20%	Blue Collar	29.00%
Military		Post grad	7.00%	Government	12.80%
Veteran/ Active Duty	7.90%				

2020 Pres. Vote	Trump	150,764	(50%)	Biden	145,987	(48%)		
2016 Pres. Vote	Trump	136,017	(47%)	Clinton	133,999	(46%)	Johnson	13,457	(5%)

Moline, Rock Island: Illinois' western prairies are some of America's richest agricultural land. They were first settled by Yankees coming overland from northern Indiana and Ohio and upstate New York. After 1848, Germans left their homeland in search of better opportunities and settled in a place that in many ways resembled the flat, orderly plains of northern Germany. These migrants farmed quarter-sections and built small towns, with banks and stores, community churches and libraries. As farming expanded, so did the need for agricultural equipment. Entrepreneurs and investors built farm-machinery factories, and the Quad Cities of the Mississippi River— Davenport and Bettendorf in Iowa, Rock Island and Moline in Illinois— became the nation's largest agricultural equipment-manufacturing centers. John Deere, a blacksmith from Vermont, set up a " self-polishing plow" shop in 1837 in the small Rock River town of Grand Detour, Illinois. His company, now headquartered in Moline, ranked 84th on the 2019 Fortune 500 list of largest American corporations.

The U.S.-China trade war exacerbated by President Donald Trump slowed demand and led to layoffs at the company. The coronavirus pandemic forced even deeper cuts, but the company pivoted some production in 2020 to making 400,000 face shields for health care workers. From 2010 to 2019, Rock Island County, which includes Rock Island and Moline, saw its population shrink by almost 4 percent; tellingly, the population on the Iowa side of the river grew by more than 4 percent during that period. The good news on both sides: Construction of a new, higher-capacity bridge across the river was scheduled for completion in 2021.

Caterpillar was an iconic Peoria brand that provided 35,000 local jobs in the 1970s; by 2017 its local payroll has shrunk to 12,000 and the company announced it would move its corporate headquarters to the Chicago area. Peoria Mayor Jim Ardis told the Daily Herald the decision was " a punch in the gut." Another came when the company announced in 2020 that it would lay off 2,000 employees in Illinois.

The 17th Congressional District, drawn by Democrats, links the Illinois portion of the Quad Cities with arms extending to the Democratic-leaning parts of Peoria to the east and Rockford to the north. It takes in the hilly, almost mountainous country in the northwest corner of the state. The district is steeped in political history: Some 30 miles west of Rockford is Freeport, whose town square hosted 15,000 people to hear Abraham Lincoln and Stephen Douglas in one of their seven debates in 1858. Not far away, on a little river once navigable by Mississippi steamboats, is Galena, the home of Ulysses S. Grant.

The district contains some of the few parts of rural America carried by Barack Obama, who took the district 57%-41% in 2012.Like much of the territory along the upper Mississippi River, the area shifted hard toward the GOP under President Donald Trump, who narrowly carried the district in both 2016 and 2020.

Darin LaHood (R)

Elected 2015, 3rd full term, b. Jul 05, 1968; Peoria, IL; Loras College, B.A., 1990; John Marshall Law School, J.D., 1997; Catholic; Married (Kristen LaHood); 3 children.

Elected Office: IL Senate, 2011-2015.

Professional Career: Staff, U.S Rep. Charles Jeremy Lewis, 1990-1994; Cook County Prosecutor, 1997-1999; Tazewell County Prosecutor, 1999-2001; Prosecutor, NV U.S Attorney, 2001-2005; Adjunct Professor, University of Nevada- Las Vegas, 2003-2005.

DC Office: 1424 LHOB 20515, 202-225-6201, Fax: 202-225-9249, lahood.house.gov

State Offices: Bloomington, 309-205-9556; Jacksonville, 217-245-1431; Peoria, 309-671-7027; Springfield, 217-670-1653.

Committees: *Permanent Select on Intelligence*: Counterterrorism, Counterintelligence & Counterproliferation; Intelligence Modernization & Readiness. *Ways & Means*: Select Revenue Measures; Trade.

Group Ratings

	ADA	ACLU	AFL-CIO	LCV	COC	HAFA	ACU	CFG	FRC
2020	**	16%	**	14%	-	89%	82%	**	-
2019	0%	C	20%	7%	84%	C	83%	97%	100%

Almanac Ratings 2019-2020

	Economy	Social	Foreign	Composite
Liberal	30%	12%	27%	23%
Conservative	70%	88%	73%	77%

Key Votes of the 116th Congress

1. U.S./Mex./Can. trade deal Y	5. Russia sanctions Y	9. Firearms background checks N
2. First Coronavirus response Y	6. Troops in Syria Y	10. Spending at the border Y
3. HEROES Act N	7. Veto arms sales to Saudis N	11. Marijuana liberalized rules N
4. CASH Act N	8. Defense $$$, veto override Y	12. Electoral College objections N

Election Results

Election	Name (Party)	Vote (%)	Cand. Spent	Ind. Exp. Support	Ind. Exp. Oppose
2020 General	Darin LaHood (R)............................... 261,840	(70%)	$1,719,442	$204	
	George Petrilli (D).............................. 110,039	(30%)			
2020 Primary	Darin LaHood (R)................................ 59,542	(100%)			

Prior winning percentages: 2018 (67%), 2016 (72%), 2015 special (69%)

Republican Darin LaHood, who won a special election in 2015, has faced minimal competition in his campaigns. With his seat on the powerful Ways and Means Committee, he has restored stability to this traditionally GOP district.

LaHood, who has maintained a solidly conservative voting record both as a state senator and in Congress, is the son of former GOP Rep. Ray LaHood, a moderate member who served seven terms before he retired and became secretary of Transportation under President Barack Obama. Darin LaHood, a Peoria native, earned his bachelor's from Loras College and a law degree from John Marshall Law School. He spent nine years as a state and federal prosecutor, including with the U.S. attorney's office in Las Vegas, Nevada, where he was recognized for his "outstanding work in fighting terrorism." He returned home to join a law firm in Peoria and was elected to the state Senate in 2010. National Journal profiled him as "a media-shy, ethics-focused political scion," a welcome antithesis to his immediate predecessor, Republican Aaron Schock.

Elected to four terms, Schock drew more notice for his youth and buff physique until the focus shifted to his office-decorating tastes and lifestyle. An accumulation of well-publicized controversies involving his use of taxpayer money led him to announce his resignation in March 2015. Most notable was a Washington Post article about the lavish redecoration of his House office in the style of the popular television series Downton Abbey. He was indicted in 2016 on 24 counts, including wire fraud, false filings of tax returns and Federal Election Commission reports, and theft of government funds. Charges were dropped in 2020 after Schock agreed to pay fines.

Several prominent local Republicans stepped aside in apparent recognition of LaHood's strength and the desire of local Republicans to avoid more controversy. His sole primary opponent was little-known Mike Flynn, a libertarian political operative and a former editor of the Breitbart News conservative website. He criticized the LaHoods as a career politicians out of touch with the real world. LaHood won the Republican primary, 69%-28%. Democrat Rob Mellon, a high school history teacher and captain in the Army Reserve, raised little money or attention. LaHood won the general, 71%-29%.

LaHood settled into the House with serious purpose and little attention. In his first term, he helped to enact bills to support federal computer networking and information technology research; and to restore fish and wildlife restoration in the Great Lakes. In 2018, he joined the Ways and Means Committee. He urged the Trump administration to reach agreement on trade deals with China and Mexico, as urged by farmers and manufacturers in his district, though he defended Trump's broader trade war with China. " My district's farmers are hurt by tariffs, but they still side with the administration and the president on his tough trade negotiation stance," he told the Peoria Journal-Star in 2019. He co-chaired the U.S.-China Working Group and House GOP leaders in 2020 gave him a spot on their new China Task Force.

When Republicans controlled the House, he filed a bipartisan resolution calling for a Joint Committee on the Organization of Congress to consider possible reforms. Republican leaders ignored the proposal. When Democrats created a select committee in 2019, LaHood did not get a seat.

LaHood has been easily reelected. After distancing himself from some of President Donald Trump's controversial comments, he became a reliable supporter, serving as an Illinois campaign co-chairmen even as his father endorsed Joe Biden. One action with which he publicly disagreed was Trump's commutation of the sentence of former Illinois Democratic Gov. Rod Blagojevich. "As our state continues to grapple with political corruption, we shouldn't let those who breached the public trust off the hook," he said in a joint statement with other Illinois GOP lawmakers.

Following the 2020 election, he criticized comments that Trump made to his supporters prior to the riot at the Capitol. " Words matter," he said, while agreeing to certify the results of the Electoral College.

IL-18: West-Central Illinois   Cook Partisan Voting Index: R+15

Population		Race and Ethnicity		Income	
Total	702,289	White	90.30%	Median Income	$67,284
Land area (sq. miles)	10,516	Black	3.80%	District Income Rank	190
Pop/ sq mi	66.78	Latino	2.90%	Poverty Rate	10.20%
Born in State	78.20%	Asian	2.90%	With health insurance	95.30%
		Two or more races	2.30%	Cash public assistance	1.50%
Age Groups		Other	0.80%	Food stamp/SNAP	8.70%
Under 18	23.00%				
18-34	20.10%	**Education**		**Work**	
35-64	37.40%	H.S grad or less	35.80%	White Collar	42.40%
Over 64	19.50%	Some college	30.60%	Sales and Service	37.00%
		College Degree, 4 yr	21.70%	Blue Collar	20.70%
Military		Post grad	11.90%	Government	16.00%
Veteran/ Active Duty	7.30%				

2020 Pres. Vote	Trump	229,772	(61%)	Biden	138,466	(37%)			
2016 Pres. Vote	Trump	210,530	(60%)	Clinton	115,441	(33%)	Johnson	17,058	(5%)

Parts of Peoria and Springfield: Old vaudeville bookers, presented with a new act, used to ask, "Will it play in Peoria?" The implication was that if an act went over in this small city on the bluffs above the Illinois River, 154 miles from Chicago and 171 miles from St. Louis, it would go over just about anywhere. In the first half of the 20th century, Peoria seemed pretty typical of America. If its citizens were mostly of British or German descent, with a small percentage of African Americans, that was the image of ordinary America that prevailed into the 1960s. But Peoria's economy has changed, much as America's has changed. This has been a heavy manufacturing town, dominated by big plants that produce farm machinery and earth-moving equipment. Its biggest employer has long been Caterpillar, which was founded in 1910 with 12 employees. But like many smaller Midwest cities, Peoria declined steadily in the past half-century.

The Peoria area suffered terribly in the 1980s, as big farm-machinery plants laid off workers and some closed down. And the 2010s weren't much kinder. Caterpillar, an iconic Peoria brand that provided 35,000 local jobs in the 1970s, shrunk its local payroll to 12,000 after the company announced in 2019 it would move its corporate headquarters to the Chicago area. The town has been steadily losing population since the 1970s, and dipped by almost 5 percent from 2010 to 2019.

The 18th Congressional District of Illinois, variously configured, has been the Peoria district since the 1940s, and now includes nearly two-thirds of the city and its suburbs. Much of the downtown area and the Caterpillar campus in East Peoria, with six factory buildings along the Illinois River, are in the 17th District to the northwest. With all or parts of 10 counties, the 18th begins at Quincy along the Mississippi River and runs east through rich farmland to the suburbs of Peoria, Bloomington and Springfield. It includes the rural, Republican parts of McLean and Sangamon counties.

In addition to President Abraham Lincoln, who served one term in Congress, 1847-49, the 18th has been represented by two national Republican leaders: Everett McKinley Dirksen, who was the Senate Republican leader from 1959-69, and Robert Michel, House Republican leader from 1981-95. Neither ever served a day in the majority. It is the home of Eureka College, which Ronald Reagan attended, and Bradley University. Democrats drew the 18th as a heavily Republican district. In 2020, President Donald Trump won the district, 61%-37%. Overall, it has remained ethnically homogeneous, with a 91 percent white voting-age population.

INDIANA

South Bend
Elkhart
Gary
LAPORTE
ST JOSEPH
LAGRANGE
STEUBEN

1
LAKE
PORTER
ELKHART
NOBLE
DEKALB

STARKE
MARSHALL
KOSCIUSKO

WHITLEY
ALLEN

JASPER
PULASKI
FULTON
2
3
Fort Wayne

NEWTON
WABASH
HUNTINGTON
WELLS
ADAMS

WHITE
CASS
MIAMI

BENTON
CARROLL
Kokomo
GRANT
Marion

TIPPECANOE
HOWARD
BLACKFORD
JAY

WARREN
Lafayette
4
CLINTON
TIPTON
5
DELAWARE

FOUNTAIN
BOONE
HAMILTON
MADISON
Muncie
RANDOLPH

MONTGOMERY
HENRY
WAYNE

VERMILLION
HENDRICKS
Indianapolis
HANCOCK

PARKE
7
MARION
RUSH
FAYETTE
UNION

VIGO
PUTNAM
SHELBY
6

Terre Haute
CLAY
OWEN
MORGAN
JOHNSON
FRANKLIN

MONROE
BROWN
DECATUR

SULLIVAN
GREENE
Bloomington
BARTHOLOMEW
RIPLEY
DEARBORN

JENNINGS
OHIO

JACKSON
SWITZERLAND

LAWRENCE
9
JEFFERSON

KNOX
MARTIN
WASHINGTON
SCOTT

8
DAVIESS
ORANGE
CLARK

PIKE
DUBOIS
Jeffersonville

GIBSON
CRAWFORD
FLOYD

WARRICK
HARRISON

VANDERBURGH
PERRY

Evansville
POSEY
SPENCER

Miles
0 10 20

The Almanac of American Politics.
National Journal

Congressional district boundaries were first effective for 2012.

Indiana, a key manufacturing hub of the industrial Midwest and a major farm state, voted for Barack Obama in 2008 during a tough recession. But the state returned to its Republican roots with a vengeance, producing a near-total wipeout for Democrats in federal and statewide races. Even a promising Democrat like South Bend Mayor Pete Buttigieg decided that his electoral future lay in running for president rather than for any statewide office back home.

Indiana's name recalls its frontier past, when William Henry Harrison defeated Tecumseh's Indians at Tippecanoe in 1811. (Its nickname, "Hoosiers," was finally designated as official by the Government Printing Office in 2017.) In the 1940s, Indiana-raised journalist John Bartlow Martin wrote that Indiana was "the central place, the crossroads, the mean that is sometimes golden, sometimes only mean." Look no further than the map, with Indianapolis in the center and highways radiating at regular angles to all corners of the state.

This infrastructure enables Indiana to sit at the center of American manufacturing. Prior to the coronavirus pandemic, about 28 percent of Indiana's gross state product and 17 percent of its employment came from manufacturing; both percentages ranked first the nation. It has given the world canned pork and beans, tomato juice, Coca-Cola bottles, Coffee-Mate, Alka-Seltzer, and Crest toothpaste. It ranks first nationally in steel production, with giant, heavily automated steel mills on the south shore of Lake Michigan and mini-mills dotting the state, and it produces 85 percent of the nation's recreational vehicles, an industry centered on Elkhart. Indiana is a leading producer of engines, engine electrical equipment, and truck and bus bodies. American and Japanese auto companies—General Motors, Chrysler, Toyota, Subaru, Honda—have big plants in the state, as do many parts suppliers, such as Delphi. Leveraging its central location, Indiana has seen a boom in logistics, particularly warehousing. Indiana is also a major agriculture state, ranking first nationally in ducks; third in turkeys; fourth in eggs, soybeans, and hogs; fifth in corn (Indiana was the home of Orville Redenbacher); and sixth in watermelons.

The downside of Indiana's economy is that it is prone to sharp contraction when the economy is in decline. Auto-related manufacturing, in which Indiana ranks third nationally, was especially hard-hit by the Great Recession. It took until late 2016 for the statewide unemployment rate to drop to 4 percent, though by late 2018, Indiana had regained almost all the manufacturing jobs it had lost during the recession. There were big job gains in life sciences, a field in which Indiana has been a leader. Eli Lilly, founded in Indianapolis in 1876, spends billions annually on research and development and in 2019 announced a $400 million investment in facilities in Indianapolis. Other big life-science companies in the state are Roche Diagnostics, Beckman Coulter, Elanco Animal Health, and Corteva Agriscience, the agriculture division of DowDuPont. From Bloomington to Warsaw, Indiana is peppered with medical-device makers. Recently, tech firms—including Salesforce and Infosys—have established notable presences in Indianapolis.

Even so, Indiana's median income ranks below the national average, and it trails such Midwestern neighbors as Michigan, Ohio, Pennsylvania and Wisconsin. When President Donald Trump, who won Indiana overwhelmingly, imposed tariffs on steel and aluminum, it may have helped some steelmakers in the state, but it also raised prices for downstream manufacturers, including the RV sector, and hurt exporters like Columbus-based engine-maker Cummins Inc. and many farmers

One increasing source of economic activity in Indiana has been sports. Indiana's most famous venue opened in 1909—the Indianapolis Motor Speedway, where the Indy 500 is held every Memorial Day weekend, except in 2020, when the coronavirus delayed it until August. Today, Indianapolis—capital of the state that gave America such basketball icons as Larry Bird, Bobby Knight and the movie Hoosiers—has refashioned itself as a national sports center, with the NFL's Colts at Lucas Oil Stadium, the NBA's Pacers at Bankers Life Field house, a Triple-A baseball team that is regularly one of the top-drawing minor-league clubs, the NCAA headquarters, and a guarantee of hosting Final Four basketball every few years—including 2021, when it hosted most of the games in the men's tournament.

Culturally, Indiana is a lot like an earlier America. Its one major hub, Indianapolis, is only the nation's 33rd largest metro area, and 69 percent of the state's population resides elsewhere. The small-town ethos seeps into the songs of John Mellencamp, who is from Seymour. Except for the steel area around Gary—which is more a part of Chicagoland—Indiana has relatively few descendants from the 1840-1924 wave of immigration. Its population is 9 percent Black, 7 percent Hispanic and

2 percent Asian. In early 2015, Indiana played host to a high-profile, if brief, national battle between two big, longstanding constituencies within the state—its Christian conservatives and its pragmatic business class. These two camps battled over a religious-freedom law that critics said would make it possible for businesses to discriminate against gays and lesbians. After then-Gov. Mike Pence signed the law, it drew fire not only from liberals but also from much of the state's business establishment. The backlash pushed Pence and legislative leaders to scale back the measure, which in turn led to criticism from religious conservatives.

Indiana's politics were long shaped by a divide between Yankees from Ohio and New England, and "Butternuts," as they were called in the Civil War years, from Kentucky and the South. Most Yankees became Republicans, and most Butternuts became Democrats. Indiana was a crucial political target from the Civil War to the New Deal, a big reason why there were Hoosiers on 11 Republican and Democratic national tickets in the 16 elections between 1868 and 1928—more than any other state except New York. Ancestral partisan ties enabled Democrats to hold the governorship from 1988 to 2004 and to be competitive in state legislative elections. At the presidential level, however, Indiana's cultural conservatism and lack of a dovish tradition generally kept it in the Republican column. One reason for the Republican lean was that Indianapolis and the smaller factory towns were not as heavily Democratic as Chicago, Detroit or Cleveland, a trend reinforced by the 1970 consolidation of the city of Indianapolis and Marion County, which brought urban and suburban areas under the same jurisdictional umbrella.

For Democrats, 2008 was a high-water mark, when Obama won the state at a time of economic distress. Since then, Democratic prospects in the more culturally conservative Butternut regions have cratered, hampering the party's statewide prospects. In 2016, Trump, joined by Pence on the ticket, ran strong in Indiana. Channeling the bristling charisma of basketball icon Knight, who endorsed him days before the primary, Trump defeated Hillary Clinton by 19 points, almost twice Mitt Romney's margin in 2012. Democrats fared little better in 2018, when the big contest was over the seat held by Democratic Sen. Joe Donnelly. He had nabbed an open Senate seat in 2012 after Republican state Treasurer Richard Mourdock disastrously opined that pregnancy resulting from rape is part of God's plan. But despite a strong national environment for Democrats, Donnelly lost by six points. The weeks-apart deaths in 2019 of two Indiana political lions—liberal Democratic Sen. Birch Bayh and moderate Republican Sen. Richard Lugar—brought a political era to its metaphorical close.

In the 2020 presidential election, Joe Biden whittled down Trump's margin of victory in Indiana by three points, but the state was never seriously contested. Biden added one county to those won by Clinton, narrowly flipping Tippecanoe County (Lafayette). He also widened the Democratic edge in populous Marion County (Indianapolis) from 22 points to 30. But the Democrats' winning margin shrank by five points in Lake County, reflecting a shift in voters from the shrinking city of Gary to more rural precincts. And in Vigo County (Terre Haute), Trump won by 14 points, undermining the jurisdiction's mysterious pattern of following the national electoral tides; the county had voted for the losing presidential candidate only twice since the 1890s. Democrats also failed to capture the state's one competitive House district, the increasingly purple 5th District in the Indianapolis suburbs, when it was an open seat in 2020. In the one seemingly competitive statewide race, the GOP won the open seat for attorney general by double digits.

Population		Race and Ethnicity		Income	
Total	6,732,219	White	82.80%	Median Income	57,603
Land area (sq. miles)	35,826	Black	9.60%	State Income Rank	37 out of 50
Pop/ sq mi	187.91	Latino	7.20%	Poverty Rate	11.90%
Born in state	67.70%	Asian	3.10%	With health insurance	91.30%
		Two or more races	2.60%	Cash public assistance	1.60%
Age Groups		Other	2.50%	Food stamp/SNAP	11.5%
Under 18	23.30%				
18-34	23.00%	Education		Work	
35-64	37.60%	H.S grad or less	44.30%	White Collar	35.10%
Over 64	16.10%	Some college	28.70%	Sales and Service	36.60%
		College Degree, 4 yr	17.30%	Blue Collar	28.30%
Military		Post grad	9.70%	Government	11.20%
Veteran/ Active Duty	7.20%				

Presidential Politics

2020 Primary (D)	Biden (D)	380,836(76%)	Sanders (D)	67,688(14%)			
2020 Pres. Vote	Trump (R)	1,729,857(57%)	Biden (D)	1,242,498(41%)			
2016 Pres. Vote	Trump (R)	1,557,286(56%)	Clinton (D)	1,033,126(37%)	Johnson (L)	133,993 (5%)	

Indiana rarely generates much drama in the race for the White House. In 1968, Robert F. Kennedy upset Eugene McCarthy and Lyndon Johnson's stand-in, Gov. Roger Branigin, in the Democratic primary. In 2008, Barack Obama contested the primary and general election, and pulled off a shocking upset after opening 44 offices around the state for the general election and mobilizing 80,000 volunteers. Obama carried only 15 of Indiana's 92 counties in the fall, but he got a big vote out of Gary and Indianapolis, cut into traditional GOP margins in the Indianapolis suburbs and exurbs, won blue-collar counties such as Delaware (Muncie) and Madison (Anderson) and swept college towns to post a 50%-49% win over Arizona Republican Sen. John McCain. Since then, as before, it's been reliably Republican. In 2016, Donald Trump tapped Hoosier GOP Gov. Mike Pence as his running mate, and increased the Republican margin in the state, defeating Hillary Clinton in November, 57%-38%. Trump's vow to restore manufacturing jobs resonated in the state's blue-collar communities and he won all but four counties: Lake (Gary), Marion (Indianapolis), Monroe (Bloomington and Indiana University) and St. Joseph (South Bend and the University of Notre Dame). It was a similar story in 2020; Trump won 57%-41%, with Biden adding Tippecanoe County (Lafayette and Purdue University) to the Democratic column. Biden ran well ahead of Clinton's numbers in suburban Indianapolis's more college-educated areas, trimming more than 10 points off of Trump's 2016 margins in Hamilton and Boone Counties, and ran ahead of Clinton in the state's college towns and Fort Wayne. But he ran behind Clinton in industrial, blue-collar Lake County, and Trump further expanded his margins in southern Indiana along the Ohio River.

Indiana's May 2016 primaries served up plenty of excitement. Texas Sen. Ted Cruz said that winning Indiana was critical to the success of his GOP nomination bid. He got a reasonably clear shot at Trump after Ohio Gov. John Kasich stopped campaigning in the state. Pence half-heartedly endorsed the Texan. And Cruz announced that former Republican White House hopeful Carly Fiorina would be his running mate should he capture the nomination. Cruz dropped his gloves, called Trump a "pathological liar" and warned the country might "plunge into the abyss" if Trump won. Trump took up the challenge, suggesting that Cruz's father had been involved in assassinating President John F. Kennedy. His efforts were rewarded with a 53%-37% victory over Cruz, who won only five counties and announced the suspension of his campaign in his concession speech. The decisive win prompted Republican National Committee Chairman Reince Priebus to take to Twitter that night and declare that Trump was the party's "presumptive nominee." The next day, Kasich withdrew.

Four years later, there was little intrigue. The state's primary was pushed back to June 2 because of the coronavirus pandemic. Biden had already sewn up the Democratic nomination by then, and won 76%-14% over Bernie Sanders.

Congressional Districts

117th Congress Lineup	2D 7R	116th Congress Lineup	2D 7R

Indiana law provides that if the state House and Senate cannot agree on congressional redistricting, the decision goes to a five-member commission, with the tie-breaking member appointed by the governor. In 2011, Republicans had control of the process. They weakened the 2nd District for the Democrats. When Democratic Rep. Joe Donnelly in 2012 ran for the Senate, Republican Jackie Walorski took his House seat. That gave the GOP a 7-2 majority in the delegation, with Democrats retaining the 1st and 7th districts centered on Gary and Indianapolis. A look at the map shows that the nine districts seem to have been drawn logically and without many jagged lines. Not one district changed party control during the subsequent decade.

With Republicans retaining complete control of redistricting for 2022, they could seek to entrench their secure status quo. But some Republicans have explored an ambitious approach of making the 1st District more competitive by shifting it south from Lake County into rural areas, rather than continuing to move it east into suburban areas. Lake County, which lost 2 percent of its population from 2010 to 2019, includes about two-thirds of the 1st District. Republicans likely will seek to reinforce the 5th District in the suburbs of Indianapolis, which has become the most competitive district in the state. One option would be to shift elsewhere its heavily Democratic slice of Marion County, which is one-fourth of the district.

In 2001, when Democrats had the governorship and a majority of the state House, they drew a map that elected five Democrats and four Republicans as recently as 2008. Earlier iterations of the 2nd, 8th and 9th were the competitive districts that yielded swing seats. But the politics of those small-city and rural areas have changed considerable, as has the Republican takeover of state government.

Eric Holcomb (R)

Elected 2016, term expires 2025, 2nd term; b. May. 2, 1968, Indianapolis; Hanover College, BA; First Church of God; Married (Janet).

Military Career: U.S Navy, 1990-1996.

Elected Office: IN Lt. Governor 2016-2017.

Professional Career: Staff, U.S Rep. John Holstettler 1997-2000; Chief of Staff, U.S Sen. Dan Coats 2013-2015; Chair, IN Republican Party, 2010-2013.

Office: State House Room 206, Indianapolis, 46204; 317-232-4567; Fax: 317-232-3443
Lt. Gov.: Suzanne Crouch (R) **Atty. Gen:** Todd Rokita (R) **Sec. of State:** Holli Sullivan (R)
State Legislature: Senate: 10D, 40R **House:** 33D, 67R

Election Results

Election	Name (Party)	Vote (%)
2020 General	Eric Holcomb (R)	1,706,727 (57%)
	Woody Myers (D)	968,094 (32%)
	Donald Rainwater (L)	345,567 (11%)
Prior winning percentage: 2016 (51%)		

Eric Holcomb breezed to reelection as Indiana's governor in 2020, enlarging his margin of victory from six points in 2016, when he replaced vice presidential nominee Mike Pence on the ballot four months before Election Day, to 25 points four years later, even as a Libertarian challenger took 11 percent of the vote. Holcomb has governed in the pragmatic mold of his former boss, Republican Gov. Mitch Daniels, rather than following Pence's more ideologically charged approach.

Holcomb grew up in Indianapolis and earned a degree in American history from Hanover College, the same school Pence had graduated from nine years earlier. (The two governors belonged to the same fraternity but didn't overlap.) Holcomb served a six-year stint in the Navy in Jacksonville Florida and Lisbon Portugal, then got involved in Republican politics in Indiana. He lost a race for state representative, served as campaign manager and district director for Rep. John Hostettler, and worked in several positions, including deputy chief of staff, for Daniels. Holcomb was also director of Daniels' Aiming Higher PAC, which proved critical in electing a long-lasting Republican legislative supermajority. Holcomb spent two years chairing the Indiana Republican Party and later served as chief of staff to the state's Republican senator, Dan Coats. In 2015, he ran for the seat Coats was vacating, but after weak polling, Holcomb exited the race. Then Lt. Gov. Sue Ellspermann resigned and Pence nominated Holcomb as her successor. The legislature approved the appointment in March 2016.

Pence was set to run for a second term as governor in 2016 against Democrat John Gregg, the moderate former state House Speaker he had defeated narrowly in 2012. Then, in July, Trump tapped Pence as his running mate, and the gubernatorial contest was thrown into flux. Pence was already the official nominee for governor and, under party rules, it was up to the state party to choose a new nominee. Several well-known Republicans sought the nod, including Reps. Susan Brooks and Todd Rokita. Of these, Holcomb was the only one who had never won an election (though he has shot a basketball in a high school gym in all 92 counties in the state). On July 26, the party formally tapped Holcomb, following the lead of Pence, who had endorsed his No. 2.

The two campaigns had enough money to compete. Holcomb was bolstered by generous funding from the Republican Governors Association, while Gregg got a boost from Democratic spending intended primarily to help elect former Sen. Evan Bayh to Coats' Senate seat. But Gregg seemed to have the edge, with the Democrat up in polls by between four and 12 points as late as October. On Election Day, however, the Trump-led tide in the state was too much for Gregg to overcome. Holcomb won by a narrower margin than Trump's 19-point victory, but it was enough—51%-45%, close to Pence's winning margin in 2012.

Aided by a Republican-dominated legislature, Holcomb enacted many of his campaign proposals. In 2017, he expanded a pre-kindergarten pilot program to cover 20 counties; he signed a bill to make the state education superintendent an appointed post rather than an elected position beginning in 2024; he lowered reimbursement levels for electricity ratepayers who install solar or wind capacity; and he released a five-year, $4.7 billion road maintenance and construction plan that included the completion of Interstate 69 as well as maintenance, resurfacing or replacement of thousands of miles of roads and bridges. The funds will come from a 10-cent-a-gallon gas tax hike that is expected to collect $1.2 billion per year by 2025. Holcomb also signed a bill that allowed counties to establish needle exchanges, rather than having to wait for state approval. Needle exchanges were initially encouraged following some debate after a major HIV outbreak in Scott County in southern Indiana in 2015. The need has only intensified with the spread of opioid addiction; Indiana has above-average rates of overdose deaths.

In 2018, Holcomb pleased conservatives by signing a law that would require medical providers to report detailed information to the state if they treat women who experience complications from abortion. He made liberals and moderates happy when he signed a law ending occupational licensing restrictions on "dreamers," or immigrants who had been brought illegally into the United States when they were children. Meanwhile, Holcomb struck a deal with the operator of the Indiana Toll Road, a 156-mile long throughway that stretches across the northern part of the state from Illinois to Ohio, that allowed the operator to hike truck tolls by 35 percent in exchange for transferring $1 billion to the state for road work. About 80 percent of the proceeds were earmarked for expanding I-65 and I-70 by 2024, while much of the remainder was allocated to improving U.S. highways in the northern part of the state.

The following year, Holcomb signed a bill green lighting new casinos in Gary and Terre Haute and legalizing sports betting in the state; the latter change was enabled by the Indianapolis-based NCAA changing its policy of banning states with sports betting from hosting championship events. He also signed a hate-crimes bill, though one weaker than he had initially wanted; at the behest of conservative legislators, the measure did not explicitly include provisions on gender identity, gender, or age. In the budget he signed in April 2019, Holcomb approved teacher raises, but not as much as educators were seeking, and accepted a $70 million cut to additional funding intended to aid

Indiana's troubled Department of Child Services, which was facing a class-action lawsuit for failing to adequately protect more than 22,000 children. In what proved to be a fortuitous decision, the budget included $2 billion in cash reserves to protect against a future recession. Meanwhile, the state voluntarily withdrew its work requirement for Medicaid, after similar policies in other states had run into trouble in the courts.

As Holcomb prepared to run for reelection, Democrats coalesced in early 2020 around Woody Myers, who in 1985 had become the state's youngest and first African-American health commissioner, serving under both Republicans and Democrats. The state was soon confronted by the coronavirus pandemic, putting Holcomb in the spotlight. In some ways, he acted more quickly than other Republican governors, as in his early enactment of social-distancing measures and bans on gatherings of more than 10 people. Then, in July, Holcomb announced a statewide mask mandate. This prompted a fierce backlash from conservatives: By September, a poll showed a tight race between Holcomb and Myers, due to a little-known Libertarian candidate, Donald Rainwater, surging to 24 percent, seemingly an indication of unhappiness with the mask order. Soon after, Holcomb moved the state to the final stage in reopening, which allowed restaurants, bars, fitness centers and stores to operate at full capacity.

But despite his public-health background and his status as a Black candidate in a year when the pandemic and racial justice topped the national agenda, Myers never managed to gain traction against Holcomb. Bolstered by a massive fundraising advantage, Holcomb ultimately took 57 percent of the vote, easily besting Myers at 32 percent and Rainwater at 11 percent. (Rainwater got almost six times as many votes in Indiana as the Libertarian presidential candidate, and the second-highest percentage of the gubernatorial vote for any Libertarian candidate in U.S. history.) The number of votes for Myers plunged 22 percent below what Gregg had won four years earlier, and Biden outpolled the Democratic gubernatorial nominee by almost 275,000 votes statewide. In Marion County (Indianapolis), Biden ran more than 11 points ahead of Meyers. In the end, Holcomb entered his second term with undisputed strength.

Todd Young (R)

Elected 2016, term expires 2022, 1st term, b. Aug 24, 1972; Lancaster, PA; U.S. Naval Academy, B.S., 1995; University of Chicago's Graduate School of Business, M.B.A., 2000; University of London's Institute of U.S. Studies, M.A., 2001; Leipzig Graduate School of Management, 2001; Indiana University Law School, J.D., 2006; Christian Church; Married (Jennifer T. Young); 4 children.

Military Career: U.S. Navy 1990-1991; U.S. Marine Corps 1995-2000.

Elected Office: US House, 2011-2017.

Professional Career: Staff, Heritage Foundation, 2001; Legislative Assistant, Sen. Richard Lugar, 2001-2003; Adviser, Governor Mitch Daniels, 2004; Management consultant, 2004-2006; Deputy prosecutor, Orange County, 2007-2010.

DC Office: 185 DSOB 20510, 202-224-5623, young.senate.gov
State Offices: Evansville, 812-350-8956; Fort Wayne, 260-422-7397; Indianapolis, 812-288-3999; New Albany, 812-336-3000.

Committees: *Commerce, Science & Transportation*: Communications, Media & Broadband; Consumer Protection, Product Safety & Data Security; Oceans, Fisheries, Climate Change & Manufacturing; Space & Science; Surface Transportation, Maritime Freight & Ports. *Finance*: Health Care; International Trade, Customs & Global Competitiveness; Social Security, Pensions & Family Policy (RMM). *Foreign Relations*: Africa & Global Health Policy; Europe & Regional Security Cooperation; Internat'l Dev Instit & Internat'l Econ, Energy & Environ Policy; Near East, South Asia, Central Asia & Counterterrorism (RMM). *Small Business & Entrepreneurship*.

Group Ratings

	ADA	ACLU	AFL-CIO	LCV	COC	HAFA	ACU	CFG	FRC
2020	-	0%	-	15%	-	66%	80%	-	-
2019	5%	C	21%	29%	90%	C	81%	39%	100%

Almanac Ratings 2019-2020

	Economy	Social	Foreign	Composite
Liberal	0%	0%	20%	7%
Conservative	100%	100%	80%	93%

Key Votes of the 116th Congress

1. EPA clean energy rules	N	5. Russia sanctions	N	9. Barr as Atty. General	Y
2. U.S./Mex./Can. trade deal	Y	6. Troops in SYR, AFG	Y	10. Spending at the border	Y
3. Cut unemployment benefits	Y	7. Veto arms sales to Saudis	Y	11. Coney Barrett to Sup. Ct.	Y
4. Shelton to Fed Reserve	Y	8. Defense $$$, veto override	Y	12. Electoral College objections	N

Election Results

Election	Name (Party)	Vote (%)	Cand. Spent	Ind. Exp. Support	Ind. Exp. Oppose
2016 General	Todd Young (R)............................	1,423,991 (52%)	$15,194,428	$3,591,044	$16,862,554
	Evan Bayh (D)...............................	1,158,947 (42%)	$10,886,830	$388,888	$23,884,578
	Lucy Brenton (L)...........................	149,481 (6%)	$483		
2016 Primary	Todd Young (R)............................	661,136 (67%)			
	Marlin Stutzman (R)......................	324,429 (33%)			

Prior winning percentages: 2016 (52%), House: 2014 (62%); 2012 (55%); 2010 (52%)

Todd Young, Indiana's senior senator, was given the unenviable task of leading the National Republican Senatorial Committee during the 2020 cycle, defending nearly twice as many seats as Democrats on one of the most difficult maps for his party in years. On election night, what was expected to be an easy Democratic capture of the majority wasn't—and even moderate Sen. Susan Collins hung on in Maine, outperforming President Donald Trump by seven percentage points. Control of the chamber came down to Georgia, where two contests headed to January runoffs. Trump lost reelection but he kept dishonestly and baselessly insisting that the November election had been fraudulent and that he in fact had won. And then Republicans lost both Georgia seats—and the majority.

Campaigning amid the Trump tsunami was a feeling Young was not entirely unfamiliar with. He was one of just two new Republicans elected to the Senate in 2016 amid Trump's surprise White House win. But if Young was generally a loyal supporter of Trump during his first two years in the Senate—ratings by Five Thirty Eight showed Young voting in favor of the president's position nearly 93 percent of the time—his style became more akin to former Indiana GOP Sen. Richard Lugar, for whom Young once worked. In a third of a century on Capitol Hill, Lugar established a reputation as a pragmatic conservative who frequently reached across the political aisle. Likewise, Young described himself as an "independent-minded, center-right conservative Republican" in a 2018 interview with the South Bend Tribune. "But I went to Washington to get things done. Typically, that requires developing strong relationships with your Democratic colleagues." In fact, a think tank established by Lugar ranked Young among its top 10 senators in its 2017 "Bipartisan Index," which measures sponsorship of legislation with members of the other party.

For three decades, the Senate seat Young holds shifted from one Hoosier to another with close ties to one of two earlier senators, Democrat Birch Bayh or Republican Dan Quayle: Evan Bayh, Birch Bay's son and a former governor, and Dan Coats, who got his political start as a Quayle aide. Young falls within this tradition: His wife is a niece of former second lady Marilyn Quayle. And Young won in 2016 by thwarting Evan Bayh's comeback bid in one of that year's marquee Senate contests.

While Young was born in Lancaster Pennsylvania and spent his first 13 years outside Indiana, his family has ties to the Hoosier State stretching back five generations. Young went to high school in Hamilton County, a well-to-do suburb of Indianapolis, where his prowess as a soccer player helped his school's team win a state championship. He enlisted in the Navy after high school, and a year later received an appointment to the U.S. Naval Academy, where he also played on the soccer team. Upon graduation, he opted for service in the Marine Corps, where he worked with reconnaissance drones—including a stint fighting narcotics trafficking in the Caribbean.

Transferred to Chicago to oversee Marine recruiting, Young attended the University of Chicago's business school at night, earning an MBA. while becoming a fan of free-market economist Friedrich von Hayek. Young went on to the University of London's Institute for the Study of the Americas, where he received a second master's degree and wrote a thesis on the economic history of Midwestern agriculture. Moving to Washington, he worked at the conservative Heritage Foundation and as a legislative assistant to Lugar. In 2004, Young returned to Indiana to work on the gubernatorial campaign of Republican Mitch Daniels.

In January 2009, Young announced plans to run for the House of Representatives seat held by Democrat Baron Hill, who was first elected in 1998. Young narrowly won a three-way primary that included former Rep. Mike Sodrel—who had ousted Hill in 2004, only to see Hill regain the seat two years later. In the 2010 fall campaign, Young attacked Hill as a rubber stamp for the Obama administration. Hill, a former high school basketball star in a hoops-crazy state, emphasized his Hoosier roots and characterized Young as an out-of-touch lawyer who had spent much of his career outside Indiana. In a year in which House Democrats lost more than 60 seats nationwide, Young ousted Hill 52%-42%.

Young was awarded a prized seat on the Ways and Means Committee in 2013. The same year, he took over as lead sponsor of a key legislative initiative for Republican conservatives: the REINS Act, which would have given Congress oversight of federal regulations with economic effects exceeding $100 million. Unlike some of his more hard-line Class of 2010 colleagues, he supported the 2011 compromise to raise the debt limit, saying he wanted deeper spending cuts but that the measure "moves us in the right direction." Despite his desire to work with Democrats, Young at times utilized sharp rhetoric, once calling former Senate Democratic Leader Harry Reid "useless" and Reid's House counterpart, Nancy Pelosi, "an irrelevant cheerleader for lost-cause liberalism." He had a competitive reelection fight in 2012, defeating his Democratic opponent, Shelli Yoder, a former Miss Indiana who called for turning the region into a leader in clean energy, 55%-45%, but had little trouble winning a third term in 2014.

After his second stint in the Senate, Coats—who would go on to become Trump's first director of national intelligence—announced his retirement in March 2015. The state GOP establishment rallied around Young, and several other House Republicans opted to run for reelection after having eyed the Senate seat. But Rep. Marlin Stutzman, who had mounted a tea party-infused insurgency in the primary against Coats six years earlier, ran again. He charged that the "D.C. establishment" had selected Young "to play as their puppet."

Young's next hurdle was an effort by Indiana Democrats to have him thrown off the primary ballot for not having filed enough petition signatures in one congressional district. The national GOP came to Young's aid, and the state election commission rejected the ballot challenge. In the May primary, Young overwhelmed Stutzman, 67%-33%, and seemed poised to cruise to victory against the Democrats' candidate: Hill, his 2010 opponent. However, in July 2016, Evan Bayh—who earlier had turned aside entreaties to run again for the seat that he held from 1998 to 2010—was persuaded to change his mind, and Hill stepped aside. Early public opinion polls showed Bayh with a 20-point lead, and national Democrats saw him as a shoo-in. But it didn't take long for problems to surface for Bayh.

Unlike his father—author of the 25th and 26th amendments to the U.S. Constitution—the younger Bayh never appeared fully comfortable in the Senate. After forgoing reelection in 2010, he said he was fed up with congressional gridlock in an op-ed for The New York Times. Bayh said it was time for him to "contribute to society in another way." By the end of the campaign, Young—aided by nearly $29 million from independent groups—had succeeded in reframing Bayh's desire to contribute to society into a question of how much society had contributed to Bayh. The Democrat's net worth had increased six fold after he left the Senate, and he was put on the defensive by an Associated Press report disclosing he had had numerous conversations with headhunters and future corporate employers during his last year on Capitol Hill. The report noted Bayh was among a small group of Democrats who helped kill a tax increase on private equity gains, opposed by Apollo Global Management; he later went to work for Apollo, after initially having denied meeting with the group.

Bayh's ties to the state since leaving the Senate also came into question. His voter status had been classified as inactive. And, while asserting that he remained an Indiana resident, he was found to have rarely spent time at an Indianapolis condominium he owned—during a local television interview, he couldn't recall the correct address of the residence. Such stumbles were symptomatic of Bayh's apparent expectation that he could return to his old seat without major effort; he was unprepared for the rigors of a competitive campaign. Independent expenditure groups poured in $18 million in an effort to prop up his struggling candidacy. It wasn't enough: Young won 52%-42%.

Like his onetime boss Lugar, who took on Republican and Democratic presidents on foreign policy, Young challenged Trump on that front—particularly on the civil war in Yemen. In December 2018, he was among just seven Republicans to join with all Senate Democrats to support a resolution withdrawing U.S. support for Saudi-backed forces in Yemen. Young, a member of the Foreign Relations Committee, also authored legislation with the panel's ranking Democrat, Robert Menendez of New Jersey, to suspend U.S. arms sales to Saudi Arabia because of that country's efforts to prevent food and medical supplies from entering Yemen.

Earlier, Young had put a hold on Senate confirmation of Trump's choice for State Department legal adviser, which he lifted after Trump agreed to press the Saudis to lift their blockade of Yemeni ports—a tactic that had triggered concerns of widespread famine. "It offends my sensibilities—and I know it offends the sensibilities of all Americans—that there are countries in this day and age that are using food as a weapon of war," Young told USA Today in late 2018. "And it further offends my sensibilities … that the United States has partnered with these countries." In 2019, Young and Democratic Sen. Chris Murphy of Connecticut also worked to force a vote to terminate or restrict arms sales to Saudi Arabia.

On domestic issues, perhaps Young's most notable bipartisan legislative effort has been a bill authored with Sen. Elizabeth Warren of Massachusetts. The measure, which cleared the House and Senate at the end of 2018, required federal agencies to report in their budget requests whether they acted on recommendations by federal auditors and inspectors for cost reductions and program improvements. Young contended that $90 billion in savings could result if such recommendations were followed. "Let's face it: She's sort of emblematic of the left," Young told the South Bend Tribune: "I candidly wanted to send a message. I can work with anyone, anyone who wants to advance a good government agenda." Amid the coronavirus pandemic in 2020, Young reached across the aisle again, proposing with Colorado Democratic Sen. Michael Bennet the RESTART Act, which would build upon the Paycheck Protection Program by extending the timeframe businesses have to spend funds from eight to 16 weeks.

Young was selected as NRSC chairman for the 2020 cycle, without opposition for the highly partisan position. The task before him was daunting: defending 23 Republican seats to just 12 for Democrats. And Republicans running for reelection in states that Trump lost in 2016, including Cory Gardner in Colorado and Collins in Maine, had to walk a fine line, with the president's support cratering even more throughout their states. With the worsening pandemic and the absence of Trump's leadership on the issue, a cratering economy, and protests against racial injustice and police brutality that swept the country in the summer of 2020, Senate Republican prospects began to look even more dire. Even typically solid red states such as South Carolina, Kansas and Alaska became battlegrounds.

In April 2020, the NRSC circulated a memo advising candidates: "Don't defend Trump, other than the China Travel Ban—attack China." Predictably, it incensed Trump, and his advisers threatened to not support candidates who followed such advice. The NRSC later admitted it was "in artful in its wording" and was simply pressing Republicans to play offense on China, according to Politico. Young told reporters at the Capitol in May that working on the crisis could help boost incumbents. "Naturally our candidates have pivoted aggressively towards their official responsibilities. And I think that will be beneficial come November," Young said, according to Roll Call.

Throughout the late summer and fall, Republican messaging depicted the protests as violent, with the committee warning of an "angry mob" and the decimation of police budgets if Democrats were elected. But worries seeped up again in early October after Trump's disastrous debate performance and his subsequent COVID-19 diagnosis. But the death of liberal Supreme Court Justice Ruth Bader Ginsburg in late September gave Republicans an unexpected opening, and they quickly pushed through the confirmation of her replacement, conservative jurist Amy Coney Barrett. The renewed focus on the judiciary, a key issue for many Republican voters, was a gift.

Ultimately, even though polls showed Democrats were on path to win back the Senate on election night, Republicans emerged victorious in nearly every Senate battleground. Strategists credited the outcome not only to a surge in Trump voters that hadn't registered in polling but also a fear among suburban voters of a more progressive Democratic agenda. The GOP lost seats in Arizona and Colorado, but flipped back the Alabama seat they'd lost in a 2017 special election. That left Republicans with only one net loss, and Democrats two seats shy. Two seats were outstanding in Georgia, and those contests, headed to January runoffs, quickly took on outsize importance. If Republicans could hold just one seat, they would keep their narrow majority. But if Democrats flipped both, the Senate would be locked 50-50, giving Vice President Kamala Harris—and Democrats— a tiebreaker.

Young and national Republicans wanted to underscore that the races could be a firewall preventing Democrats from having unified control of the White House, House and Senate. But Trump myopically focused on his lie that the election was stolen from him and sought to overturn the results.

His unsubstantiated claims undercut and overpowered the GOP's checks-and-balances message in Georgia, where he had lost narrowly to Democrat Joe Biden and was fighting with top state officials —all Republicans. On a November call conference call, the Washington Post reported, Young said he was "assuming the worst but hoping for the best" regarding Trump's antics. On January 6, those fears would be realized: Both races in Georgia were called for Democrats—thanks to a surge in Black turnout and a dip in GOP voters compared to November—and a mob of Trump supports stormed the U.S. Capitol.

Mike Braun (R)

Elected 2018, term expires 2024, 1st term, b. Mar 24, 1954; Jasper, IN; Wabash College, B.A., 1976; Harvard University, M.B.A., 1978; Catholic; Married (Maureen Braun); 4 children.

Elected Office: IN House, 2014-2017.

Professional Career: Co-Founder, Crystal Farms, Inc., 1979; Founder/CEO, Meyer Distributing and Meyer Logistics.

DC Office: 374 RSOB 20510, 202-224-4814, braun.senate.gov

State Offices: Evansville, 317-822-8240; Fort Wayne, 260-427-2164; Hammond, 219-937-9650; Indianapolis, 317-822-8240; South Bend, 574-288-6302.

Committees: *Aging. Agriculture, Nutrition & Forestry*: Conservation, Climate, Forestry & Natural Resources; Food & Nutrition, Specialty Crops, Organics & Research (RMM); Rural Development & Energy. *Appropriations*: Agriculture, Rural Development, FDA & Related Agencies; Commerce, Justice, Science & Related Agencies; DOL, HHS & Education & Related Agencies; Legislative Branch (RMM); Transportation, HUD & Related Agencies. *Budget. Health, Education, Labor & Pensions*: Employment & Workplace Safety (RMM); Primary Health & Retirement Security.

Almanac Ratings 2019-2020

	Economy	Social	Foreign	Composite
Liberal	5%	11%	21%	12%
Conservative	95%	89%	79%	88%

Key Votes of the 116th Congress

1. EPA clean energy rules	N	5. Russia sanctions	N	9. Barr as Atty. General	Y
2. U.S./Mex./Can. trade deal	Y	6. Troops in SYR, AFG	Y	10. Spending at the border	Y
3. Cut unemployment benefits	Y	7. Veto arms sales to Saudis	N	11. Coney Barrett to Sup. Ct.	Y
4. Shelton to Fed Reserve	Y	8. Defense $$$, veto override	N	12. Electoral College objections	N

Election Results

Election	Name (Party)	Vote (%)		Cand. Spent	Ind. Exp. Support	Ind. Exp. Oppose
2018 General	Mike Braun (R)	1,158,000	(51%)	$19,149,604	$3,437,301	$30,910,945
	Joe Donnelly (D)	1,023,553	(45%)	$15,686,770	$10,720,943	$24,767,726
	Lucy Brenton (Lib)	100,942	(4%)			
2018 Primary	Mike Braun (R)	208,602	(41%)			
	Todd Rokita (R)	151,967	(30%)			
	Luke Messer (R)	146,131	(29%)			

Prior winning percentages: 2018 (51%)

One of the most talked-about—and arguably successful—TV ads of the 2018 midterm elections depicted Republican Mike Braun, now Indiana's junior senator, toting life-size cardboard cutouts of his two GOP Senate primary opponents, Reps. Luke Messer and Todd Rokita. In the cutouts, both House members are wearing navy suits, white shirts and red ties: It's what they wore during the first televised debate of the campaign, at which Braun appeared in a blue shirt wearing neither coat nor tie. In the ad, several voters say they can't tell Messer and Rokita apart and Braun, posing with the two cardboard candidates, asks the television audience, "Can you pick out the businessman in this lineup?" In a primary in which all three contenders ran as avid supporters of President Donald Trump, the ploy underscored Braun's contention that he most closely reflected the outsider profile of the businessman in the White House.

Braun won the nomination and, in November, ousted one-term Democratic Sen. Joe Donnelly in a red state that's only getting redder—as he derided the low-profile incumbent with Trumpian nicknames like "Sleepin' Joe" and "Mexico Joe." The latter was a reference to Donnelly having invested in a company run by his brother that created jobs in Mexico. Like Trump, Braun is not only a businessman, but a wealthy one: His holdings, pegged at between $35 million and $96 million in a disclosure form, placed him among the five wealthiest senators. Most of Braun's wealth is from an auto parts distribution firm he expanded over three decades. With 6,000 acres of land—mostly timber stands—spread over nine Indiana counties, Braun is among the state's largest private landowners. He poured nearly $11.6 million in personal loans into his campaign, more than half of that during the primary—which was key to his overtaking the House members initially considered the frontrunners.

Unlike Trump, Braun is considered frugal by family and friends; he scoffs at companies that operate with "extreme overhead and Taj Mahal corporate headquarters." He worked out of a trailer for years even after his business had become successful. He didn't buy a new vehicle until he was in his 50s. While Trump has faced multiple bankruptcies, Braun credits thriftiness with helping his business survive two recessions that killed off many competitors. "You live like you are going out of business every day and it makes you healthy," he told the Indianapolis Star.

"He is the most conservative, tightest guy I know," said his wife of 40 years, Maureen Braun.

Braun grew up in the Southern Indiana town of Jasper, where he still lives. After earning his undergraduate degree from Wabash College in Crawfordsville, he left the state to earn an MBA from Harvard Business School. Returning to Jasper, he sold kitchen cabinets for three years and co-founded Crystal Farms Inc.—now one of the largest turkey operations in the Midwest—before joining his father's business manufacturing truck bodies for farmers. The enterprise almost failed during the farm crisis of the early 1980s. Braun responded by redirecting the business toward selling truck accessories, later expanding it to include warehousing and shipping. Today, the firm, Meyer Distributing, employs more than 900 workers in 35 states. Before he joined the Senate, Braun's political experience comprised 10 years on the Jasper School Board and a three-year stint in the Indiana House of Representatives that began in 2015. His interest in the latter post appears to have been piqued by his younger brother, Steve Braun, who won a state legislative seat two years earlier from the Indianapolis suburbs.

Mike Braun resigned from the Indiana House in November 2017 to focus on his Senate bid. It was several months after Messer and Rokita entered the contest, which became one of the nastiest clashes that year. Messer and Rokita overlapped at Wabash College and, in the quarter of a century that followed, had seen each other as rivals as they climbed the political ladder: Rokita as Indiana secretary of state before his election to Congress and Messer as a member of the state Legislature before moving to Washington, where he became chairman of the House Republican Policy Committee. Their entry into the Senate race was preceded by months of jockeying in the competition to take on Donnelly —elected six years earlier largely because of self-inflicted wounds by his Republican opponent and viewed by many GOP strategists as the most vulnerable Senate Democrat in 2018.

In the end, Braun's primary victory was attributable to both his wealth, which allowed him to air TV ads before Messer and Rokita, and the wounds the two front running inflicted on each other. Rokita made issues both of Messer moving his family out of Indiana and to a home in the Washington suburbs and of a $240,000 annual contract for part-time legal work paid to Messer's wife. Messer accused Rokita of "spreading lies and half-truths," prompting a memo from the Rokita camp labeling Messer "unhinged" and a "ticking time bomb." They tried to outdo each other in fealty to Trump. Rokita was quick to point to 2016 comments by Messer suggesting Trump was not up to the job of being president, while Messer's camp highlighted Rokita calling Trump "vulgar if not profane" in an interview at the time.

Messer and Rokita continued to attack each other even as Braun gained ground; Braun did find himself being criticized for voting in Democratic primaries until 2012. Braun defended himself as a lifelong Republican while saying that, given longtime Democratic dominance in some Southern Indiana counties, he and other conservatives had little choice but to vote in Democratic primaries if they wanted a say in local government. In his final TV ad before the May primary, Braun sought to reinforce his shared background with Trump as businessman and political outsider, saying he was running because "President Trump paved the way." Braun won the primary with 41 percent of the vote, while Rokita and Messer finished with 30 percent and 29 percent, respectively.

In Donnelly, Braun faced a general election opponent widely labeled an "accidental senator." In 2011, after winning three terms in the House, he saw his district redrawn. Donnelly ran for the Senate. He started out as a long shot, but the seat became in play after tea party-backed state Treasurer Richard Mourdock toppled six-term Sen. Richard Lugar in the Republican primary. But Mourdock did himself in during the general election with incendiary comments and views, including his opposition to abortion in cases of rape. Donnelly—an abortion rights opponent who said the procedure should be permitted in cases of rape and incest—capitalized on Mourdock's missteps, winning 50%-44%.

In the Senate, Donnelly kept a low profile, crafting a centrist voting record and focusing on issues—such as improving care for veterans and combating opioid addiction—that didn't invite sharp partisan divisions. But his efforts at bipartisanship placed him on a political tightrope. Donnelly sought to inoculate himself from Republican voters' anger by emphasizing areas in which he agreed with the president. In one ad, he highlighted his support of Trump's proposed southern border wall. Another ad showed the president praising Donnelly during a bill-signing ceremony for "right to try" legislation he had sponsored that enabled patients with terminal illnesses to obtain unapproved drugs that might save their lives. For a time, it appeared Donnelly might pull off another unlikely upset. But Braun kept pumping in his own money—$2.7 million in loans just in the final month of the campaign—as he campaigned on a platform in lockstep with Trump, including support of the border wall and repeal of the Affordable Care Act, which Donnelly supported.

Braun steered clear of the media after debates and avoided mistakes. But it was the furor over Brett Kavanaugh's nomination to the Supreme Court in the closing weeks of the campaign that may have sealed the outcome. Donnelly was among the last senators to tip his hand—saying he had "deep reservations" about putting Trump's nominee on the high court because of allegations by Christine Blasey Ford. She said Kavanaugh had sexually assaulted her when they both were in high school. That conflict energized the Republican base while nationalizing the Senate contest in a state Trump had carried by 19 points. Trump visited the state three times during the final two weeks of the campaign, and, by the end, the contest ranked third among 2018 Senate races in independent expenditure funding—with $39 million going to prop up Donnelly and $28 million to boost Braun. Braun won, 51%-45%; Donnelly captured just eight counties, compared to 27 in 2012.

Braun pledged during the campaign to refuse a pension and serve no more than two terms before returning to the woods around Jasper, where he likes to hunt rabbits, doves and quail. His passion is said to be an annual quest for valuable morel mushrooms, which appear briefly each spring. As for his willingness to dig deep into his pocket in his hunt for a Senate seat—despite his frugal nature—Braun told the Star, "That's how big a deal I think it is that if guys like me don't step in, across the spectrum, that we're going to keep going down the trail where we were headed before Trump came along."

In the Senate, Braun was largely a staunch defender of Trump. He was especially outspoken during the president's first impeachment trial in early 2020, often racing to microphones before Democrats could. "I move a lot faster than Chuck Schumer—I can tell you that," he told Politico. Braun became a regular on the cable circuit and was usually eager to talk to journalists. He went further than many in his party during the trial. He not only denied that what Trump had done was wrong(he pressured Ukraine to investigate the Bidens by withholding congressionally approved military aid) but denied it even happened, despite concrete evidence. That stance won praise from Trump, who said he was a "big fixture on television and doing a great job."

Later, as the COVID-19 pandemic gripped the country, Braun echoed Trump by blaming China for the novel coronavirus' spread. And he criticized leading infectious disease experts—such as Dr. Anthony Fauci, the director of the National Institute of Allergy and Infectious Diseases—as pushing for too restrictive closure measures in the spring of 2020. " I never did like the idea that you treated the entirety of the country, and even counties within a state, the same way," Braun told Politico. Pointing to his family's experience in business, Braun told NPR that a "one-size-fits-all" shutdown approach was wrong. "I think we've got to do something that blends in a way that fits every county, every state due to its risk profile," he said.

But Braun occasionally took a different approach than Trump and the GOP, particularly on health care and climate change. During the pandemic, he said Republicans should focus on alerting the Affordable Care Act, instead of repealing it. "I think it does make it difficult for us to have credibility when that is still out there," he told the Washington Post about the Trump administration's push to get the Supreme Court to declare the Obama-era law unconstitutional. "To me, we shouldn't worry about that; we should be focusing on reforming the healthcare system itself and not paying attention to the ACA."

Along with Democratic Sen. Chris Coons of Delaware, Braun launched the bipartisan Senate Climate Solutions Caucus. After Trump attacked teenage climate activist Greta Thunberg when she was named Time magazine's 2019 Person of the Year, Braun said the criticism was uncalled for. "She's talking about an issue that she ought to be sincerely concerned about because if we don't, we'll pay a consequence for it. So yes, I admire her," he said. He added that if they have "no comment or view about climate," Republicans will continue to lose younger voters, pointing to concerns his own millennial children have about climate change. "I think there have been a lot of Republicans in the closet on climate." Braun and Coons told Politico they intend to lead a "large, bipartisan delegation" to the international climate summit scheduled in Glasgow Scotland in November 2021, hoping to recognize "climate as an emergency, as an existential crisis."

Braun also broke with Republicans on policing reform amid racial justice protests throughout the country in the summer of 2020. He filed a bill that would limit qualified police immunity, which often makes it difficult for victims of police brutality—many of whom are Black—to seek damages. Although "eliminating qualified immunity is a poison pill or a nonstarter," Braun told NPR, "there are more Republicans than what you might imagine that would be interested in a smart refinement of it. ...There is a sweet spot that we can hit. And if we don't do it, I think we're going to have more occurrences, as rare as they are."

Frank Mrvan (D)

Elected 2020, 1st term, b. Apr 16, 1969; Hammond, IN; Ball State University, B.A.; Christian; Married (Jane Mrvan); 2 children.

Professional Career: Trustee, North Township, Indiana

DC Office: 1607 LHOB 20515, 202-225-2461, Fax: 202-225-2493, mrvan.house.gov

State Offices: Merrillville, 219-795-1844.

Committees: *Education & Labor*: Civil Rights & Human Services; Health, Employment, Labor & Pensions. *Veterans' Affairs*: Health; Technology Modernization (Chmn).

Election Results

Election	Name (Party)	Vote (%)		Cand. Spent	Ind. Exp. Support	Ind. Exp. Oppose
2020 General	Frank Mrvan (D)	185,180	(57%)	$491,500	$129,576	$110,000
	Mark Leyva (R)	132,247	(40%)	$13,538		$531
	Michael Strauss (L)	9,521	(3%)			
2020 Primary	Frank J. Mrvan (D)	29,575	(33%)			
	Thomas McDermott Jr. (D)	25,426	(28%)			
	Jim Harper (D)	9,133	(10%)			
	Melissa Borom (D)	7,792	(9%)			
	Mara Candelaria Reardon (D)	6,997	(8%)			

Frank Mrvan narrowly won the Democratic primary, which was the ticket to victory in the longtime Democratic stronghold in northwest Indiana. In a battle of entrenched family dynasties, his chief opponent was Thomas McDermott Jr. Each had served for more than a decade as the chief executive of communities in neighboring parts of Lake County. Mrvan benefited from key endorsements from the United Steelworkers Union and retiring Rep. Pete Visclosky, a low-profile lawmaker who held the seat for 36 years and chaired the Appropriations Subcommittee on Defense. Visclosky held the record for the longest tenure of any House member from Indiana.

A native of Hammond, Mrvan got his bachelor's degree in journalism from Ball State University. He worked as a pharmaceutical sales representative and a licensed mortgage broker. In 2005, he was appointed as the trustee of North Township, which includes five communities and is the largest of the 11 townships in Lake County. The township is in the northwest corner of the county and includes one-third of its population. Mrvan's father, also Frank Mrvan, was first elected to the state Senate in 1978 and has held the seat since then—except for four years when he lost reelection.

McDermott, also a native of Hammond, has served as mayor of the city since 2004. He won the office by defeating the Republican incumbent. His father, Thomas McDermott Sr., earlier served eight years as Hammond mayor and was a Republican. A graduate of Purdue University and the University of Notre Dame Law School, McDermott was endorsed for the House seat by former Indiana Sen. Joe Donnelly and former South Bend Mayor Pete Buttigieg, a presidential candidate in 2020.

On the day Visclosky announced his retirement in November 2019, both Mrvan and McDermott announced their candidacies to succeed him. Mrvan emphasized his skills at bringing people together and his plan to continue his focus on the economy, including projects to assist the local region, the Northwest Indiana Times reported. "You have to be able to work with all communities," he said.

McDermott, by contrast, criticized the excessive partisanship in Congress, which had become "dysfunctional," he said. "I want to change the culture in Washington D.C." That news story described McDermott as the front-runner, given his earlier plan to challenge Visclosky in the 2020 Democratic primary. "I'm way ahead of the game as far as any other opponents that are going to run against me," he said.

Four months later, in a packed rally at a United Steelworkers hall, Visclosky announced his support of Mrvan. "I wanted someone who's a decent person, and he's a public servant without all the self-aggrandizement," Visclosky said. The head of the local steelworkers, which is the largest union in the region, said, "We're going to flex our muscles to win," the Chicago Tribune reported. In response, McDermott said that Visclosky was trying to control the outcome of the election. "Thankfully, it's up to the voters, not the political operatives," he added.

McDermott was the leading spender in the primary, with $630,000, which more than doubled Mrvan's spending. But Mrvan defeated McDermott, 33%-28%. Of the 10 other candidates, none received more than 10 percent of the vote. "We shocked the world," Mrvan said when the result became clear. Mrvan ran second in LaPorte and Porter counties but he took 37 percent of the vote in Lake County, which cast nearly four-fifths of the total vote.

In November, Mrvan got 57 percent of the vote against Republican Mark Leyva, a former carpenter and steelworker who lost seven challenges to Visclosky. He took Lake County with 61 percent, but lost Hammond—about one-fourth of the district vote—by less than 700 votes.

In the House, Mrvan joined the Education and Labor Committee, plus Veterans' Affairs.

IN-1: Northwest Indiana

Cook Partisan Voting Index: D+4

Population		Race and Ethnicity		Income	
Total	719,122	White	71.10%	Median Income	$61,104
Land area (sq. miles)	1,157	Black	18.50%	District Income Rank	246
Pop/ sq mi	621.53	Latino	16.30%	Poverty Rate	12.90%
Born in State	58.50%	Asian	1.50%	With health insurance	92.50%
		Two or more races	2.70%	Cash public assistance	1.30%
Age Groups		Other	6.30%	Food stamp/SNAP	10.40%
Under 18	22.80%				
18-34	21.10%	**Education**		**Work**	
35-64	39.20%	H.S grad or less	46.20%	White Collar	32.00%
Over 64	16.90%	Some college	30.60%	Sales and Service	39.10%
		College Degree, 4 yr	15.20%	Blue Collar	28.90%
Military		Post grad	8.00%	Government	10.40%
Veteran/ Active Duty	6.90%				

2020 Pres. Vote	Biden	177,630	(53%)	Trump	148,554	(45%)		
2016 Pres. Vote	Clinton	162,358	(53%)	Trump	124,638	(41%)	Johnson	13,287	(4%)

Gary, Hammond: At the southernmost shore of Lake Michigan is a part of America made by steel. In the northwest corner of Indiana, where the water highway of the Great Lakes comes closest to the rail highway of the transcontinental railroads, America's leading capitalists of a century ago identified an ideal site for manufacturing steel. On empty sand dunes, United States Steel, then the nation's largest corporation, founded the city of Gary in 1906 and named it for the company's chairman, Chicago Judge Elbert Gary. For nearly 70 years, the steel mills attracted a diverse and middle-class workforce, more like Chicago than the rest of Indiana: Irish, Poles, Czechs, Ukrainians and Blacks from the South.

Politics here has always been turbulent, from the long and unsuccessful steel strike of 1919 to the racially polarized politics of the 1960s and 1970s. The tone of public life—the clash between union stewards and management foremen, between African Americans and Eastern European ethnics, between the stalwarts of different factions vying for control of Gary's massive City Hall—was a clash of steel on steel. Steel brought sudden growth and sudden depression to northwest Indiana. The massive storefronts built on Gary's aptly named Broadway bear witness to the confidence and exuberance of the 1920s. The steel mills went cold during the Depression but were again thronged with workers during World War II. In the years afterward, their massiveness helped create the illusion that a robust economic life in the steel towns of Gary, Hammond and East Chicago would last forever.

The oil crunch of 1979 was the catalyst for change, reducing the demand for big cars, the primary customer for steel. Steel, which employed 70,000 workers in northwest Indiana in 1979, dropped to about 27,000 jobs in 1990. The decline accelerated to fewer than 12,000 jobs in 2017. Obsolete mills were closed, old mills modernized and new ones built that cut the number of man hours needed by two-thirds. Just-in-time methods were introduced, and management and highly skilled workers cooperated to engineer higher-quality, less-expensive steel to meet market demands. From 1991 to 2017, steel production in Indiana increased by 36 percent. Indiana remained the No. 1 steel-producing state, as it has been since 1980. Its tons were more than double the production of runner-up Ohio. The decision by President Donald Trump to impose a 25 percent tariff on steel imports added a few thousand industry jobs in northwest Indiana. But the turnaround was short-lived. In August 2020, ArcelorMittal, the largest steel-industry employer in the area, announced 877 layoffs. Adding to the pessimism, that company a month later cited its losses as it sold its Indiana plants to Ohio-based Cleveland-Cliffs, an iron-ore mining company.

In recent years, Gary has been largely in ruins. A 2012 Federal Reserve Bank of Chicago study categorized Gary as "overwhelmed" by the decline of manufacturing. The continuing white flight to the suburbs reduced the city's population from a peak of 178,000 in 1960 to 75,000 in 2018, of whom 80 percent are African American. More than one-third of them lived in poverty. In neighboring majority-White Hammond, with a slightly larger population, British Petroleum in early 2020 completed the $300 million expansion of its refinery, which resulted in no increase in the permanent workforce. In August, the company announced a 40 percent worldwide decrease in its petroleum production.

Indiana's 1st Congressional District stretches from Gary and Hammond along the Lake Michigan shoreline east to Michigan City. The 1st includes all of Lake and Porter counties, plus the western edge of LaPorte. About two-thirds of the vote in the 1st is in Lake County. Donald Trump's appeal to blue-collar workers and his promise to reduce subsidized imports struck a local chord. In 2016, Indianapolis-based Marion and Lake—the two largest counties in Indiana—each gave slightly less than 59 percent of the vote to Hillary Clinton. In 2020, Joe Biden got 64 percent in Marion, but his vote in Lake dropped to 57 percent. In LaPorte, Trump's vote increased from 50.6 percent to 52 percent. Overall, Biden took the district, 53%-45%--a big drop from the 61 percent that the ticket that he shared with Barack Obama won in 2012. As the slowest-growing district in Indiana since 2010, its boundaries will move further into strongly Republican country.

Jackie Walorski (R)

Elected 2012, 5th term, b. Aug 17, 1963; South Bend, IN; Liberty Baptist College, Att., 1983; Taylor University, B.A., 1985; Assembly of God; Married (Dean Swihart).

Elected Office: IN House, 2004-2010.

Professional Career: TV reporter, WSBT-TV, 1985-1989; Executive Director, St. Joseph County Humane Society, 1989-1991; Director of institutional advancement, Ancilla College, 1991-1996; Director of annual giving, IN University, 1997-1998; Founder, Impact Intl., 1999-2003.

DC Office: 419 CHOB 20515, 202-225-3915, Fax: 202-225-6798, walorski.house.gov

State Offices: Mishawaka, 574-204-2645; Rochester, 574-223-4373.

Committees: *Ethics (RMM). Ways & Means*: Oversight; Worker & Family Support (RMM).

Group Ratings

	ADA	ACLU	AFL-CIO	LCV	COC	HAFA	ACU	CFG	FRC
2020	**	21%	**	14%	-	84%	77%	**	-
2019	5%	C	33%	10%	98%	C	77%	72%	95%

Almanac Ratings 2019-2020

	Economy	Social	Foreign	Composite
Liberal	38%	30%	30%	33%
Conservative	62%	70%	70%	67%

Key Votes of the 116th Congress

1. U.S./Mex./Can. trade deal	Y	5. Russia sanctions	Y	9. Firearms background checks N
2. First Coronavirus response	Y	6. Troops in Syria	Y	10. Spending at the border N/A
3. HEROES Act	N	7. Veto arms sales to Saudis	N	11. Marijuana liberalized rules N
4. CASH Act	Y	8. Defense $$$, veto override	Y	12. Electoral College objections Y

Election Results

Election	Name (Party)	Vote (%)		Cand. Spent	Ind. Exp. Support	Ind. Exp. Oppose
2020 General	Jackie Walorski (R)	183,601	(61%)	$1,903,526	$1,355	
	Pat Hackett (D)	114,967	(39%)	$860,738		
2020 Primary	Jackie Walorski (R)	39,628	(79%)			
	Christopher Davis (R)	10,609	(21%)			

Prior winning percentages: 2018 (55%), 2016 (59%), 2014 (59%), 2012 (49%)

Republican Jackie Walorski was first elected in 2012 to what had been a political swing seat. After two close campaigns—one defeat and one victory—she eventually became entrenched at home and staked out her legislative niche with mainstream Republican views on most issues. With a seat on the Ways and Means Committee and in the minority party, she found opportunities to work with Democrats to assert influence in the House, including on health care and welfare issues.

Walorski grew up in a working-class family in South Bend, the granddaughter of Polish and German immigrants. Her father was a firefighter, and her mother worked at a hospital. She was the first in her family to attend college, graduating from Taylor University with a bachelor's degree in communications. She didn't become passionate about politics until she heard presidential candidate Ronald Reagan speak, recalling that he said Republicans "believed in smaller government and the power of individuals controlling their own destiny."

Walorski spent her first few years out of college working as a television reporter, then became an administrator for Ancilla College and Indiana University. In 1999, Walorski and her husband, Dean Swihart, volunteered as Christian missionaries in Romania. They were in Romania at the time of the Sept. 11, 2001, terrorist attacks, an experience that she said was life-changing. "We really did not know if we'd ever see our country or family again," she said. When the couple returned to Indiana, Walorski won a seat in the state House, where she served six years. She cosponsored the state's voter identification law and worked to establish the Indiana Economic Development Corporation as a public and private cooperative venture.

Walorski campaigned in tight races. In her 2010 challenge to Democratic Rep. Joe Donnelly, Walorski got more than $1 million in national party aid. Donnelly outspent her, $2 million to $1.3 million, and she lost 48%-47%, a margin of 2,538 votes. Two years later, when Donnelly ran successfully for the Senate, Walorski faced Democrat Brendan Mullen, an Army veteran of the Iraq war who campaigned as a pro-gun, anti-abortion rights moderate. The redrawn district's Republican tilt was instrumental in her close win, 49%-48%, a margin this time of 3,920 votes. Walorski was boosted by Mitt Romney's presidential bid and by Mike Pence's campaign for governor.

In the House, Walorski avoided the leadership and electoral ambitions of other junior Republicans from Indiana. As chair of the Nutrition Subcommittee of the Agriculture Committee, she held hearings on the food stamp program, including possible steps to better serve families and taxpayers. On the Armed Services and Veterans' Affairs committees, she worked with veterans' groups to encourage local business opportunities. In 2013, she enacted her proposal for whistleblower protections for victims of sexual assault in the military and a safe environment to report attacks.

With a seat on Ways and Means since 2017, Walorski has voiced concern over the impact of tariffs on auto parts. Though careful not to criticize directly President Donald Trump, she cited her "eyeball to eyeball" exchanges with Commerce Secretary Wilbur Ross. Following approval of the revised trade deal with Mexico and Canada, in April 2020, she cited the disruption caused by the pandemic to urge an extension of the transition period for the auto industry to comply with new rules of origin for their parts. Also on Ways and Means, Walorski and Democratic Rep. Danny Davis of Illinois—the senior members of the Worker and Family Support Subcommittee—pushed their bill to overhaul support by the states for child welfare services.

The sweeping legislation that Congress enacted in 2018 to reduce opioid addiction included her proposal to improve access to non-opioid pain treatments. Walorski sought permanent repeal of the tax on medical devices, which was part of the Affordable Care Act, though it was later suspended temporarily. She voiced concern that family separations at the border with Mexico "failed to live up to our American ideals;" she urged a solution for children with illegal status.

Politically, Walorski grew more secure, though she has faced competitive challengers. Her challenger in 2014 was Joe Bock, a global health professor at Notre Dame. Walorski attacked him for votes to increase his own pay as a member of the Missouri legislature in the 1980s and suggested that he was a carpetbagger. In a bad year for Democrats, the incumbent won 59%-38%.

Democrat Mel Hall, who had been a senior adviser to a large Washington-based law firm, spent more than $4 million against Walorski in 2018. He called her a "career politician" who refused to hold town meetings with constituents. Walorski's victory margin was reduced to 55%-45%. In 2020, she was challenged by South Bend attorney Patricia Hackett, who spent nearly $900,000. Walorski's 61 percent was the largest share of the vote she has received. Most impressively, she held Hackett to 51 percent of the vote in South Bend-based St. Joseph County, the Democratic heart of the district. Citing another local woman who scored a big victory in 2020 with her confirmation to the Supreme Court, South Bend Tribune columnist Jack Colwell wrote, Walorski "now has nearly the same job security as Amy Coney Barrett."

IN-2: North-Central Indiana

Cook Partisan Voting Index: R+13

Population		Race and Ethnicity		Income	
Total	721,469	White	84.70%	Median Income	$54,788
Land area (sq. miles)	3,959	Black	7.10%	District Income Rank	335
Pop/ sq mi	182.25	Latino	10.20%	Poverty Rate	12.40%
Born in State	69.20%	Asian	1.50%	With health insurance	88.90%
		Two or more races	3.00%	Cash public assistance	2.00%
Age Groups		Other	3.70%	Food stamp/SNAP	8.40%
Under 18	24.20%				
18-34	22.00%	**Education**		**Work**	
35-64	36.90%	H.S grad or less	49.80%	White Collar	31.40%
Over 64	16.80%	Some college	27.60%	Sales and Service	37.00%
		College Degree, 4 yr	14.30%	Blue Collar	31.70%
Military		Post grad	8.20%	Government	9.60%
Veteran/ Active Duty	6.90%				

2020 Pres. Vote	Trump	178,385	(59%)	Biden	116,794	(39%)		
2016 Pres. Vote	Trump	163,539	(58%)	Clinton	99,496	(36%)	Johnson	12,905 (5%)

South Bend, Elkhart: When the University of Notre Dame was founded in 1842, Catholics were still a rarity in most of America and certainly rare on the limestone-bottomed prairie of northern Indiana. This was still farm country and South Bend no more than a crossroads on the banks of the St. Joseph River. But by the 1920s, both the school and the town had grown. Notre Dame, thanks to its football team, the Fighting Irish, was the most famous Catholic university in the land, and South Bend was a significant industrial city, home of Studebaker, Bendix and dozens of other factories. In the past 50 years, Notre Dame has grown in size and reputation, but South Bend, like many Rust Belt cities, diminished in size and reputation. In the 1960s, Studebaker went out of business. In the early 1980s, there were massive factory layoffs.

But these high-profile job losses were accompanied by the much less visible creation of jobs in small factories throughout the region. The work in those facilities required more skill than did the old assembly lines, and the products had to be more responsive to just-in-time prime contractors or computer-inventory retailers. In recent years, many employers have had trouble filling job openings, and the economic base is more secure than when it depended on the fate of two or three big companies. Meanwhile, Notre Dame has led another transition, to a more technology-focused economy, including research centers for new processes and techniques.

In 2020, South Bend and Notre Dame drew added attention following the impressive performances of two rising national leaders. Former Mayor Pete Buttigeig attracted support in the presidential campaign for his youthful perspective and energy. When he dropped out of the contest on the eve of the Super Tuesday primaries, he immediately endorsed Joe Biden and became an outspoken supporter. Biden showed appreciation and, once elected, gave him the demanding job of Transportation secretary. As a law professor and then a federal judge, Amy Coney Barrett gained strong backing in conservative legal circles. Within hours of the death of Supreme Court Justice Ruth Bader Ginsburg in September 2020, she became the choice of leading conservatives. The decision by President Donald Trump to seek her Senate confirmation prior to the November election intensified the partisan climate. But Barrett largely steered clear of the controversy and won confirmation, albeit on a nearly party-line vote eight days before the election.

Elkhart County is a manufacturing hub, with creative ways to turn a profit and phenomenal employment increases. Local companies there make everything from pharmaceuticals to musical instruments. The county is best known as the manufacturing center for most of the nation's recreational vehicles. The local economy made an impressive turnaround, as joblessness in Elkhart dropped in a decade from nearly 20 percent to 2.4 percent in 2018. RV shipments from Elkhart were 321,000 in 2013, nearly double the total in 2009. Despite concerns about the impact of tariffs imposed by Trump on steel and aluminum, which added more than $2,000 to the cost of the average RV, manufacturing employment in Elkhart in 2018 had doubled to 72,000 from 37,000 a decade earlier. Despite initial local fears, the coronavirus sparked an economic boom for the RV industry. After sales had softened in 2018 and 2019, business turned strong as consumers sought travel opportunities in which they could sustain themselves. RVs were promoted as "a way to have the freedom to travel and experience an outdoor lifestyle while also controlling their environment." In late 2020, the industry forecast that it would sell a record 507,000 RVs in 2021.

The 2nd Congressional District of Indiana is centered on South Bend. This is a blue-collar and ethnic city. It has one of the nation's largest percentage of Hungarian Americans, plus a growing community of Mexican Americans. The Republican base of the district has been secured. Within boundaries that Barack Obama in 2008 took by 699 votes, Donald Trump in 2020 won the working-class district, 59%-39%.

Jim Banks (R)

Elected 2016, 3rd term, b. Jul 16, 1979; Columbia City, IN; IN University, Bloomington, B.A., 2004; Grace College, M.B.A., 2013; Evangelical; Married (Amanda Banks); 3 children.

Military Career: U.S. Navy Reserve 2012-pres. (Afghanistan)

Elected Office: IN Senate, 2010-2016.

DC Office: 1713 LHOB 20515, 202-225-4436, Fax: 202-226-9870, banks.house.gov

State Offices: Fort Wayne, 260-702-4750.

Committees: *Armed Services*: Cyber, Innovative Technologies & Information Systems (RMM); Seapower & Projection Forces. *Education & Labor*: Health, Employment, Labor & Pensions; Higher Education & Workforce Investment. *Veterans' Affairs*: Technology Modernization.

Group Ratings

	ADA	ACLU	AFL-CIO	LCV	COC	HAFA	ACU	CFG	FRC
2020	**	14%	**	5%	-	100%	95%	**	-
2019	0%	C	24%	3%	82%	C	94%	94%	95%

Almanac Ratings 2019-2020

	Economy	Social	Foreign	Composite
Liberal	25%	8%	27%	20%
Conservative	75%	92%	73%	80%

Key Votes of the 116th Congress

1. U.S./Mex./Can. trade deal	Y	5. Russia sanctions	Y	9. Firearms background checks	N
2. First Coronavirus response	N	6. Troops in Syria	Y	10. Spending at the border	Y
3. HEROES Act	N	7. Veto arms sales to Saudis	N	11. Marijuana liberalized rules	N
4. CASH Act	N	8. Defense $$$, veto override	Y	12. Electoral College objections	Y

Election Results

Election	Name (Party)	Vote (%)		Cand. Spent	Ind. Exp. Support	Ind. Exp. Oppose
2020 General	Jim Banks (R)	220,989	(68%)	$811,564	$24,287	
	Chip Coldiron (D)	104,762	(32%)	$82,819		
2020 Primary	Jim Banks (R)	64,574	(85%)			
	Chris Magiera (R)	11,200	(15%)			

Prior winning percentages: 2018 (65%), 2016 (70%)

Jim Banks was elected in 2016 to an open seat following a competitive primary contest in a traditionally Republican district. With extensive experience in the Navy Reserve plus support from national conservative groups, he emerged following the 2020 election as a leader of House conservatives. His position as chairman of the Republican Study Committee has become an influential platform for rising junior House Republicans.

Banks was born and continued to reside in Columbia City, not far from Fort Wayne. He graduated from Indiana University, where he was president of College Republicans, and got an MBA at Grace College and Seminary. He worked as a real estate broker with the Bradley Co. in Fort Wayne. Elected to the state Senate in 2010, where he claimed the most conservative record, he chaired the Veterans Affairs and the Military Committee. He invoked a state law to take a leave of absence in 2014, while he served for eight months at NATO headquarters in Afghanistan, where he assisted with equipment for the Afghans. He received the Defense Meritorious Service Medal for his military leadership. During that time, his wife, Amanda Banks, was appointed acting state senator.

When Rep. Marlin Stutzman announced that he was running for an open Senate seat in 2016, Banks staked out ground among conservative advocacy groups. His political consultant told Banks that he needed to become "less wonky" during the campaign, according to a story in GQ. Affiliates of the Club for Growth and the Senate Conservatives Fund spent more than $700,000 on his behalf. He won the primary with 34 percent to 32 percent for Kip Tom, a local farmer, and 25 percent for Elizabeth Brown, a veteran Fort Wayne elected official. David McIntosh, head of the Club for Growth who during the 1990s served in an earlier version of this district, made the election of Banks a top priority and took credit for playing a "pivotal role" in the victory. In the general, Banks defeated Tommy Schrader, a perennial Democratic candidate, 70%-23%.

On the Armed Services Committee, Banks said his objective was to "ensure our men and women in uniform receive the resources they need to protect our nation." In 2017, he filed a bill to authorize the use of force against the Islamic State in Iraq and Syria (ISIS). "The Constitution grants Congress the power of declaring war, and we need to take that obligation seriously," Banks said. "Rather than continuing to fight ISIS under an authorization passed by Congress in 2001 to fight al-Qaeda, it is time to pass a new authorization for the use of military force against ISIS."

Banks made other attempts to call for discipline in the nation's foreign policy. Following the friendly meeting in Helsinki in July 2018 between President Donald Trump and Russian President Vladimir Putin, he warned, "Russia is not our friend." Banks unsuccessfully urged Treasury Secretary Steve Mnuchin to cancel a visit to Saudi Arabia that October "until the world receives answers" about the apparent murder of journalist and activist Jamal Khashoggi, a1983 graduate of Indiana State University, at the Saudi embassy in Istanbul. In October 2019, he voted for a House-passed resolution that condemned President Donald Trump's withdrawal of U.S. troops from Syria. "I don't believe we can afford to turn our backs on this region," he said in an interview with National Public Radio. "If we see a resurgence of ISIS as many of us are worried and predict that we will, this will be a decision by this administration that we will live to very much regret."

As the top Republican on the Veterans Affairs Subcommittee on Technology Modernization, Banks reviewed the costly upgrade of veterans' medical records. The Defense Department, he found, maintains 10,000 information technology systems, many of which are "outdated and ill-managed, creating a self-imposed burden in the task of effective communications security."

Banks took the chairmanship of the Republican Study Committee, with a pledge to "promote a strong, principled legislative agenda that will limit government, strengthen our national defense, boost America's economy, preserve traditional values and balance our budget." Coincidentally, its chairmen since the 1990s have included three earlier House Members from Indiana: McIntosh, former Rep. Dan Burton and former Vice President Mike Pence.

Banks continued to distance himself from Trump, even before the former president left the White House. Trump's agenda was more popular than his personality, Banks said. Following the election, he was among the early Republicans who said publicly that the party was moving into its "post-Trump era."

The political challenge for Banks eased with his easy reelections. Democrat Courtney Tritch, who ran a marketing firm, spent nearly as much as the $1.1 million by Banks in 2018.The incumbent took all 12 counties and won, 65%-35%, including 56 percent of the vote in the population center of Allen County. In the 2020 Republican primary, local physician Chris Magiera self-financed his challenge with $290,000 and was defeated, 85%-15%. Prior to the May contest, Magiera challenged the "inflated statistical projections" of the COVID-19 threat.

IN-3: Northeast Indiana   **Cook Partisan Voting Index: R+19**

Population		Race and Ethnicity		Income	
Total	753,051	White	86.40%	Median Income	$57,288
Land area (sq. miles)	4,180	Black	6.10%	District Income Rank	297
Pop/ sq mi	180.14	Latino	6.30%	Poverty Rate	9.80%
Born in State	71.60%	Asian	2.70%	With health insurance	88.40%
		Two or more races	2.80%	Cash public assistance	1.70%
Age Groups		Other	2.10%	Food stamp/SNAP	7.60%
Under 18	25.30%				
18-34	22.00%	**Education**		**Work**	
35-64	36.80%	H.S grad or less	45.60%	White Collar	33.50%
Over 64	15.90%	Some college	29.90%	Sales and Service	33.50%
		College Degree, 4 yr	16.70%	Blue Collar	33.00%
Military		Post grad	7.80%	Government	9.00%
Veteran/ Active Duty	7.20%				

2020 Pres. Vote	Trump	211,169	(64%)	Biden	112,346	(34%)	Jorgensen	7,204	(2%)
2016 Pres. Vote	Trump	189,587	(64%)	Clinton	87,699	(30%)	Johnson	13,903	(5%)

Fort Wayne: The northeast corner of Indiana was first settled by people of New England Yankee stock, establishing orderly communities with public schools and colleges. They were joined by German immigrants, who built tidy farms and their own civic institutions. The one large city here, Fort Wayne, was built on the flat terrain along the Maumee River that flows to Toledo Ohio. It grew as a factory town, surging ahead and then falling back as large factories, often tied to the auto industry, opened and downsized over the years.

Manufacturing jobs in the Fort Wayne area dropped significantly in the 2000s. The local economy started to revive after a $150million biodiesel complex opened in Claypool, with the largest soybean processing plant in the United States. Following its $1.2 billion expansion for full-size pickup trucks, the local General Motors assembly plant kept busy with 4,700 workers on three shifts, plus overtime, and avoided the shutdown announcements that have affected other GM locales in recent years. Sweetwater, the largest online retailer for musical instruments, opened a new $50 million warehouse in February 2020.

In September 2020, Forbes enthusiastically described the future of downtown Fort Wayne as "an art-filled, nature-forward, food-diverse example of savvy redevelopment, poised to welcome the travelers of tomorrow." Three months earlier, after local law-enforcement officials used chemical agents in an attempt to disperse protesters, the American Civil Liberties Union was less impressed with the local scene. It filed a lawsuit in federal court to challenge the police actions. "Police must not respond to protesters speaking out against police brutality with yet more brutality," an ACLU lawyer said.

The 3rd Congressional District covers the northeastern part of the state and is centered on Fort Wayne. It is a diverse area, with a mix that includes a concentration of Amish, plus Central Americans, Bosnians, Somalis and the nation's largest number of Burmese refugees, with an increased refugee inflow following recent conflicts in that nation. This part of Indiana has been heavily Republican since the Civil War, though it has sometimes veered Democratic in times of economic distress.

The seat sometimes sends its representatives on to higher positions: Dan Quayle, elected here in 1976, was later a senator and vice president. Dan Coats, who succeeded Quayle in the Senate, was ambassador to Germany before winning a second term in the Senate in 2010and then became Director of National Intelligence. President Donald Trump ousted him in early 2020 following several independent public statements. In the 2008 and 2012 presidential elections, the 3rd was the most Republican district in Indiana. Trump got 64 percent in both of his campaigns, though this was only his third--best district in the state in 2020.

Jim Baird (R)

Elected 2018, 2nd term, b. Jun 04, 1945; Covington, IN; Purdue University, B.S., 1967; Purdue University, M.S., 1969; Purdue University, M.S., 1969; University of KY, Ph.D., 1975; Methodist; Married (Denise Baird); 3 children.

Military Career: US Army 1969-1971 (Vietnam)

Elected Office: Putnam County Board of Commissioners, 2006-2010; IN House, 2010-2018.

DC Office: 532 CHOB 20515, 202-225-5037, Fax: 202-226-0544, baird.house.gov

State Offices: Danville, 317-563-5567.

Committees: *Agriculture*: Biotechnology, Horticulture & Research (RMM); Livestock & Foreign Agriculture; Subcommittee Nutrition, Oversight & Department Operations. *Science, Space & Technology*: Energy; Research & Technology.

Almanac Ratings 2019-2020

	Economy	Social	Foreign	Composite
Liberal	33%	22%	12%	23%
Conservative	67%	78%	88%	77%

Key Votes of the 116th Congress

1. U.S./Mex./Can. trade deal	Y	5. Russia sanctions	Y	9. Firearms background checks N
2. First Coronavirus response	Y	6. Troops in Syria	N	10. Spending at the border	Y
3. HEROES Act	N	7. Veto arms sales to Saudis	N	11. Marijuana liberalized rules	N
4. CASH Act	Y	8. Defense $$$, veto override	Y	12. Electoral College objections	Y

Election Results

Election	Name (Party)	Vote (%)		Cand. Spent	Ind. Exp. Support	Ind. Exp. Oppose
2020 General	Jim Baird (R)	225,531	(67%)	$162,258	$17,457	
	Joe Mackey (D)	112,984	(33%)	$34,170		
2020 Primary	Jim Baird (R)	65,806	(100%)			

Prior winning percentages: 2018 (64%)

Republican freshman Jim Baird brought a combination of academic, business and political experience in the Indiana farm community to his surprising victory in an open district in 2018. Although Baird trailed significantly in fundraising, his chief opponent's support from outside political action committees may have backfired in the GOP primary. Baird succeeded Todd Rokita, who lost the GOP Senate primary to Mike Braun—the older brother of Steve Braun, who had been expected to defeat Baird.

Baird got his undergraduate and master's degrees in animal science from Purdue University and his Ph.D. from the University of Kentucky, where he specialized in nutrition for pigs. He served as a first lieutenant in the Army during the Vietnam War, where he lost an arm during combat. His suffered his injuries when his battalion was ambushed by Viet Cong forces while delivering cargo along a supply route. A lifelong resident of the district, Baird owned several businesses, including a family farm and a home healthcare agency. He was a livestock specialist with Purdue University's Cooperative Extension Service.

Following his service as a Putnam County commissioner, he was elected to the Indiana House for eight years. He worked on agriculture and veterans issues, and chaired the Health and Medicaid Subcommittee of House Ways and Means. He received an award for civility among the legislators.

In the contest to replace Rokita in the heavily Republican district, Steve Braun was well-connected, including his stint as head of the Workforce Development Department under then-Gov. Mike Pence. Braun was endorsed by the state Chamber of Commerce and the Farm Bureau. Diego Morales, another GOP candidate, also had been an aide to Pence in Indianapolis. Even with his lengthy time in office, Baird ran as an outsider, with his attacks on "career politicians" and calls for "a common-sense approach to fix the broken system in Washington." Compared to the $1.2 million Braun raised, Baird raised little more than $200,000 for the primary—most of which was from a personal loan. But he displayed a superior grassroots appeal.

The closing days of the campaign were marked by negative advertising from several outside political action committees. One of those late mailers criticized Baird's vote to increase the state's gasoline tax and said he had cost Hoosiers "an arm and a leg." Given his war injuries, that attack generated a sympathetic response for Baird from voters. "Disrespecting our wounded combat veterans crosses a line that Hoosiers will not tolerate," responded Baird, who earned a Bronze Star and two Purple Hearts in Vietnam.

Baird won the primary with 37 percent of the vote to 29 percent for Braun and 15 percent for Morales. The turnout of 80,000 voters, which likely was driven by local support for Rokita, was the largest of any district in Indiana in the primary. In this heavily Republican district, Baird easily defeated Democrat Tobi Beck, a woman Army veteran.

In the House, Baird was assigned to the Agriculture, and Science, Space and Technology committees. He continued his collegial approach and search for bipartisanship. With first-term Democratic Rep. Haley Stevens of Michigan, he filed a bill to encourage more education of young girls at an early age in the fields of science, technology, engineering and math. Stevens and Baird were the leaders of the Research and Technology Subcommittee of the Science panel. With Democratic Rep. Bill Foster of Illinois, Baird filed a bill to increase federal research and development programs that focus on industries of the future, such as artificial intelligence and advanced manufacturing.

In 2019, he called for an increase in legal immigration, citing the need for more workers in agriculture and the hospitality industry. "We don't have enough workers for some of these companies to expand like they would like to," Baird told the Lafayette Journal and Courier. In 2021, he became ranking Republican on the Agriculture Subcommittee on Biotechnology, Horticulture and Research, where he said that he would be "leveraging my expertise to pursue sound science and risk-based policy to benefit America's farmers."

Baird won reelection, 67%-33%, against Democrat Joe Mackey. Baird won all 16 counties. In Lafayette-based Tippecanoe, the only county where Baird got less than 64 percent of the vote, he won with 52 percent. Following the 2020 election, Baird was one of three House Republicans from the seven in the Indiana delegation who voted against certifying the Electoral College results in Arizona and Pennsylvania. "Concerns remain on how several states enacted new election rules without the consent from their state legislatures," he said.

IN-4: West-Central Indiana

Cook Partisan Voting Index: R+18

Population		Race and Ethnicity		Income	
Total	767,105	White	87.00%	Median Income	$60,119
Land area (sq. miles)	6,353	Black	4.60%	District Income Rank	260
Pop/ sq mi	120.76	Latino	6.30%	Poverty Rate	11.00%
Born in State	70.10%	Asian	3.30%	With health insurance	92.40%
		Two or more races	2.30%	Cash public assistance	1.10%
Age Groups		Other	2.80%	Food stamp/SNAP	6.20%
Under 18	22.50%				
18-34	25.60%	**Education**		**Work**	
35-64	36.40%	H.S grad or less	43.90%	White Collar	33.00%
Over 64	15.70%	Some college	29.50%	Sales and Service	36.40%
		College Degree, 4 yr	16.90%	Blue Collar	30.60%
Military		Post grad	9.70%	Government	14.10%
Veteran/ Active Duty	7.30%				

2020 Pres. Vote	Trump	220,013	(64%)	Biden	117,232	(34%)	Jorgensen	7,764 (2%)
2016 Pres. Vote	Trump	194,403	(64%)	Clinton	91,265	(30%)	Johnson	16,704 (6%)

Indianapolis Suburbs, Lafayette: The landscape of central and western Indiana is some of the most prosaic in the United States. It is mostly flat, with neat farms and towns of frame bungalows, looking mostly unchanged from many years ago. Across this landscape have run some of the nation's chief transportation arteries. The earliest was the old National Road, from Baltimore to St. Louis. The region was also crisscrossed by the great east-west rail lines carrying famed passenger trains like the Wabash Cannonball. Today, people bounce around the Midwest on commuter airlines from small city to hub. The landscape still looks rural, and there are some large farms, with more than 80 percent of agricultural income from corn and soybeans, and a small slice from hogs. The economy is more industrial, with small factories in crossroads and courthouse towns. President Donald Trump's trade war with China brought big cuts in soybeans exports and prices.

Tippecanoe County's Lafayette, where the main employer is Purdue University, has been growing and prosperous. It has benefited from a partnership between Toyota and longtime local auto manufacturer Subaru that helped the Lafayette plant's workforce grow to 6,000 people, making it the largest private employer in Tippecanoe. After spending $1.3 billion to expand the facility, Subaru added production of its Impreza and Ascent models, with about 400,000 vehicles annually. Subaru announced in February 2020 its plan to spend $140 million for another new local plant. Tippecanoe is the site for Subaru's only assembly line in the United States. In May 2019, Saab announced plans for a new manufacturing plant just west of the Purdue campus, where it expects to make fuselages for a new Boeing jet trainer.

Kokomo, which suffered from the collapse of local auto manufacturing, ranked third in the nation in its economic recovery since the Great Recession, according to a Bloomberg News study. Fiat-Chrysler, which has a large local plant, announced in January 2020 that it planned a $400 million expansion of its transmission plant to build a new four-cylinder engine, with improved fuel economy and reduced emissions..

Purdue Research Foundation and Browning Investments created the Purdue Research Foundation, with expected investment of more than $1 billion in West Lafayette. Its Convergence Center for Innovation and Collaboration is designed to encourage private companies to work together with campus groups and with other companies. Manufacturing in West Lafayette exceeds 19,000workers.

The 4th Congressional District covers much of west-central Indiana, including western parts of suburban Indianapolis. Each of the 16 counties usually votes Republican. Only Tippecanoe, which has about 20 percent of the voters, is competitive. Hendricks County in the Indianapolis suburbs is heavily Republican, with a slightly larger population than Tippecanoe. In 2020, Donald Trump repeated the 64 percent that he won four years earlier.

Victoria Spartz (R)

Elected 2020, 1st term, b. Oct 06, 1978; Nosivka, Ukraine; National University of Economics (Ukraine), B.S.; National University of Economics (Ukraine), M.B.A.; Kelley School of Business, M.A.; Havard University Business School; Eastern Orthodox; Married (Jason Spartz); 2 children.

Elected Office: IN Senate, 2017-2021.

Professional Career: CFO, IN Attorney General's Office; Partner, technology company; Adjunct Faculty, Kelley School of Business Indianapolis.

DC Office: 1523 LHOB 20515, 202-225-2276, spartz.house.gov

Committees: *Education & Labor*: Civil Rights & Human Services; Higher Education & Workforce Investment. *Judiciary*: Antitrust, Commercial & Administrative Law; Crime, Terrorism & Homeland Security; Immigration & Citizenship.

Election Results

Election	Name (Party)	Vote (%)		Cand. Spent	Ind. Exp. Support	Ind. Exp. Oppose
2020 General	Victoria Spartz (R)	208,212	(50%)	$2,998,613	$847,154	$5,538,870
	Christina Hale (D)	191,226	(46%)	$4,000,015	$16,422	$5,590,637
	Kenneth Tucker (L)	16,788	(4%)			
2020 Primary	Victoria Spartz (R)	34,526	(40%)			
	Beth Henderson (R)	15,343	(18%)			
	Micah Beckwith (R)	11,063	(13%)			
	Carl Brizzi (R)	5,619	(7%)			
	Kent W. Abernathy (R)	4,901	(6%)			
	Kelly Mitchell (R)	4,643	(5%)			

Republican Victoria Spartz won a competitive contest for an upscale suburban open seat, which had been viewed as a prime opportunity for a Democratic pick-up. Spartz, who is believed to be the first Republican woman elected to Congress after having immigrated to the United States, was born in the Ukraine and emphasized her conservative economic views. She succeeded Republican Susan Brooks, an influential lawmaker who retired after four terms.

Spartz received her bachelor and master's in business administration degrees from the National University of Economics in Kiev. Even before she left her homeland, Spartz had been critical of economic life in the former Soviet Union. As a college student, she met her husband, Jason, on a train in Europe; eventually, she agreed to marry him and return to his native Indiana. "I felt this is just a country of such wonderful opportunities and freedom," she told the Indianapolis Star.

In the United States, Spartz learned that her academic degrees had little professional value. She became a bank teller and got a master's in professional accounting from Indiana University. Spartz worked as a certified public accountant, became active in her husband's family business of real estate investment and development, and started her own financial firms. She served as chief financial officer for the state attorney general and was active politically as president of Hamilton County Republican Women.

In her initial campaign, Spartz ran successfully in a special election in 2017 for a seat in the state Senate. She won the nomination by defeating the candidate backed by her Senate predecessor. In the legislature, she described herself as "a limited government conservative" and worked on initiatives to reduce regulation.

Following the shooting of a teacher and a student at a local school, Spartz sparked controversy, the Star reported, when she opposed legislation to make it more difficult for individuals who had committed a violent crime as a juvenile to obtain a gun license. Her congressional bid was endorsed by the National Rifle Association.

The surprising decision to retire by Brooks, who headed campaign recruitment by House Republicans, led to a wide-open contest to succeed her, with 15 candidates in the Republican primary. Other leading contenders included Beth Henderson, who owned an adult learning firm, and Micah Beckwith, a pastor and small businessman.

Largely with self-financing, Spartz outspent her opponents. The Club for Growth, a political action committee of economic conservatives, backed her. Spartz won the primary with ease, getting 40 percent of the vote to 18 percent for Henderson and 13 percent for Beckwith. She had big leads in Hamilton and Marion counties, the chief population centers.

Democratic nominee Christina Hale, who was executive director of Kiwanis International, had served four years in the state House. She ran in 2016 for lieutenant governor on the Democratic ticket with John Gregg, who narrowly lost to Republican Eric Holcomb. In her bid for Congress, she won the Democratic primary with 41 percent of the vote against four opponents.

The House Democrats' success in 2018 in winning suburban districts led them to list the Indianapolis-area seat as one of their prime targets, even with its long history as a Republican bastion. Spartz's overseas background became a factor late in the campaign. The Congressional Leadership Fund, an arm of House GOP leaders, criticized Hale for "shameful anti-immigrant attacks" with Democratic ads that highlighted Spartz's prominent accent. Democrats responded that Spartz typically did not speak in her ads. Spartz defeated Hale, 50%-46%.

Hale won Marion County, with 63 percent of the vote. Spartz comfortably led elsewhere in the district, including 54 percent in Hamilton County, which cast nearly half of the total vote.

Spartz got seats on the Education and Labor, and Judiciary committees. During her first week in the House, she bucked a majority of House Republicans when she voted to certify the Electoral College results.

IN-5: Northern Indianapolis Metro

Cook Partisan Voting Index: R+5

Population		Race and Ethnicity		Income	
Total	791,257	White	84.30%	Median Income	$76,417
Land area (sq. miles)	1,925	Black	8.60%	District Income Rank	116
Pop/ sq mi	411.09	Latino	5.10%	Poverty Rate	8.10%
Born in State	64.10%	Asian	3.80%	With health insurance	93.30%
		Two or more races	2.30%	Cash public assistance	1.20%
Age Groups		Other	1.00%	Food stamp/SNAP	5.10%
Under 18	23.90%				
18-34	21.20%	**Education**		**Work**	
35-64	39.50%	H.S grad or less	27.70%	White Collar	49.90%
Over 64	15.30%	Some college	24.40%	Sales and Service	33.20%
		College Degree, 4 yr	29.60%	Blue Collar	17.00%
Military		Post grad	18.30%	Government	11.00%
Veteran/ Active Duty	6.80%				

2020 Pres. Vote	Trump	209,669	(50%)	Biden	200,376	(48%)			
2016 Pres. Vote	Trump	193,018	(52%)	Clinton	150,083	(41%)	Johnson	20,505	(6%)

Hamilton County: Indiana's most rapid growth has taken place in the suburban ring counties around Indianapolis, especially in Hamilton County, directly north of the city. This is affluent suburbia, with subdivisions full of spacious houses, shopping centers and office developments in what not too long ago were farm fields. Hamilton County's population increased from 82,000 in 1980 to 182,000 in 2000 and to 275,000 in 2010—a 50 percent jump in a decade, making it one of the fastest growing counties in the Midwest. The growth continued, and reached 338,000 in 2019. A group of business and civic leaders has developed a mass transit plan that could spur even greater growth.

Hamilton County has drawn many wealthy people from Indianapolis, where they had been concentrated on the north side of the city. Now, they're more likely to be in the former farm communities of Carmel, Fishers and Noblesville. Since the creation of its Midtown development in 2014, wealthy Carmel has attracted new businesses and condominiums. Hamilton has the highest median household income in Indiana and is the 35th richest county in the nation, with a population that is nearly 90 percent White. Hamilton is the most Republican of the large counties in Indiana and has been one of the most Republican in the nation. It voted 66%-32% for Mitt Romney in 2012. But the county's support for Donald Trump in 2020 dropped precipitously to 52%-46%, a common trend in high-income areas across the nation. In its post-election analysis in November 2020, the Indianapolis Star reported that Trump increased his 2016 vote in Hamilton by 14,000; Biden increased Hillary Clinton's total by 31,000 votes.

The 5th Congressional District is located in the center of the state and includes the northern Indianapolis suburbs. In addition to Hamilton County, which has increased to nearly 50 percent of the population, the 5th takes in all or part of seven other counties. Some, such as Grant and Tipton, are 2-to-1 Republican. The mostly upscale northern slice of Indianapolis's Marion County is the second largest part of the district and has become more than 60 percent Democratic; the remaining 70 percent of Marion is in the heavily Democratic 7th District. The district also includes increasingly Republican exurbs such as Madison County, with its county seat in Anderson, a manufacturing town. The overall makeup of this district is Republican. But the reduced support for Trump in Hamilton trimmed the Republican presidential vote in the district from 58 percent in 2012 to 53 percent in 2016 and 50 percent in 2020, ranking as the lowest of the state's seven Republican-held districts.

Greg Pence (R)

Elected 2018, 2nd term, b. Nov 04, 1956; Columbus, IN; Loyola University Chicago, B.A., 1981; Loyola University Chicago, M.B.A., 1986; Catholic; Married (Denice Pence); 4 children; 5 grandchildren.

Military Career: U.S. Marine Corps 1979-1984

Professional Career: President, Kiel Brothers Oil Company,1988-2004; Antique Mall owner.

DC Office: 222 CHOB 20515, 202-225-3021, pence.house.gov

State Offices: Columbus, 812-799-5230.

Committees: *Energy & Commerce*: Consumer Protection & Commerce; Energy.

Almanac Ratings 2019-2020

	Economy	Social	Foreign	Composite
Liberal	25%	17%	4%	16%
Conservative	75%	83%	96%	84%

Key Votes of the 116th Congress

1. U.S./Mex./Can. trade deal	Y	5. Russia sanctions	N	9. Firearms background checks N
2. First Coronavirus response	Y	6. Troops in Syria	N	10. Spending at the border	Y
3. HEROES Act	N	7. Veto arms sales to Saudis	N	11. Marijuana liberalized rules	N
4. CASH Act	Y	8. Defense $$$, veto override	N	12. Electoral College objections Y

Election Results

Election	Name (Party)	Vote (%)		Cand. Spent	Ind. Exp. Support	Ind. Exp. Oppose
2020 General	Greg Pence (R)	225,319	(69%)	$2,519,025	$1,750	
	Jeannine Lee Lake (D)	91,103	(28%)	$119,208		
	Tom Ferkinhoff (L)	11,791	(4%)			
2020 Primary	Greg Pence (R)	62,346	(84%)			
	Mike Campbell (R)	12,234	(16%)			

Prior winning percentages: 2018 (64%)

Freshman Republican Greg Pence rode his familiar name to an easy victory and then settled into a district that his younger brother, Vice President Mike Pence, held for 12 years before he was elected Indiana governor in 2012. With his minimal engagement at campaign events, in legislative sessions or with the news media, Greg Pence has used his close connections to influential political players to raise robust campaign funds and gain prominent endorsements. Pence has largely ignored his political opponents, including a self-funding Republican businessman who accused Pence of "running on nepotism." Following the reelection defeat of the Trump-Pence ticket in 2020, the less-known Pence had less political protection but his relevance also slipped.

After graduating from Loyola University of Chicago, where he later received a master's degree in business administration, Pence served as a lieutenant in the Marine Corps. He had a prominent business career in the Columbus Indiana area that took a separate route from his politically adept brother. Those marketplace experiences had a mixed record that left millions of dollars in fines and debt.

Following his father's path, Pence became president of the Kiel Brothers Oil Company, a local oil-supply business that developed a chain of more than 200 convenience stores in Indiana and surrounding areas. But the company faced financial difficulties after the state assessed an $8.4 million penalty for causing environmental damage with leaky storage tanks. Additional problems ensued when the price of oil collapsed in the years after Pence took control.

In 2004, "the chain announced it was filing for bankruptcy. Pence resigned that same day," the Indianapolis Star reported in a campaign profile of Pence. According to The New York Times, a Columbus bank—on which Pence had served as a director—later sued him for $3.8 million in debts he had guaranteed; Pence agreed "to settle for pennies on the dollar." A Pence campaign aide said the business problems resulted from major changes in the oil industry beyond his control.

When Republican Gov. Mitch Daniels took office in 2005, he gave Pence the number-two position with the Indiana Department of Environmental Management, the same agency that had fined his oil business for its spills and for failure to comply with safety regulations. Pence left that position after less than three months, "saying his work was finished," the Star reported. In recent years, Pence and his wife Denise owned two antique malls in southern Indiana.

In Pence's 2018 campaign, he raised more than $1.2 million prior to the primary. His chief opponent in that contest was Jonathan Lamb, a former commodities trader who became a successful local businessman and mostly self-financed his campaign with $450,000 in personal loans. Lamb, who said Pence was "unwilling to be transparent and upfront with the voters about his failure and share his business resume," also criticized his opponent's scant campaign appearances. "How can we educate the voters on what the true issues are if the perceived heir-apparent to the seat won't talk and grant interviews?" Lamb told the Star.

Like his brother Mike, Pence emphasized his conservative views on social issues. Even with his deep Washington connections, his campaign slogan styled him as an outsider, "Greg Pence will fight for Hoosier values, not D.C. values." His campaign website did not directly refer to the vice president, beyond the candidate's staunch support of "the Trump-Pence agenda."Pence defeated Lamb, 64%-24%. In the general election, Pence gave little attention to lightly funded Democrat Jeannine Lee Lake. He won, 64%-33%.

In the House, Pence got seats on the Foreign Affairs, and Transportation and Infrastructure committees. He left few tracks during his first term. He received limited public attention, beyond his connections to his more influential brother and to President Donald Trump. When the Foreign Affairs panel was among the House committees investigating the possible impeachment of Trump, Pence's chief of staff dismissed a press inquiry about whether his boss would recuse himself because of a potential conflict of interest.

Pence gravitated more toward the political side of Washington. In November 2019, Politico listed him among the members of Congress who were the most prolific spenders at Trump properties, including his hotel on Pennsylvania Avenue. Later, he was among nearly two dozen House members friendly to the Trump-Pence ticket who were designated as Congressional Captains by the presidential fundraising committee.

In his reelection campaign, Pence had a rematch with Lake. This time, she stirred more attention, including a report by ABC News that she used social media to accuse Pence of selling objects with offensive racial depictions at his antique malls. Lake described "awful objects degrading and dehumanizing Black people" and said, "it made me want to cry." A spokesman for Pence denied the accusation and added that he "is not engaged in the active management" of the mall. Neither Lake's accusations nor Pence's activities appeared to affect adversely his political fortunes. He widened his victory to 69%-28%. In Muncie-based Delaware County, Pence took 55 percent.

In 2021, Pence joined the Energy and Commerce Committee. "Especially during the COVID-19 pandemic, Energy and Commerce leads the way in Washington," Pence said, while citing the panel's work on health care, communications and energy issues.

IN-6: Southeast Indiana

Population		Race and Ethnicity		Income	
Total	720,190	White	92.60%	Median Income	$55,959
Land area (sq. miles)	6,207	Black	2.10%	District Income Rank	319
Pop/ sq mi	116.03	Latino	3.10%	Poverty Rate	12.80%
Born in State	70.80%	Asian	1.70%	With health insurance	92.10%
		Two or more races	2.40%	Cash public assistance	2.00%
Age Groups		Other	1.30%	Food stamp/SNAP	9.10%
Under 18	21.70%				
18-34	22.00%	Education		Work	
35-64	38.10%	H.S grad or less	49.20%	White Collar	34.00%
Over 64	18.00%	Some college	29.30%	Sales and Service	35.90%
		College Degree, 4 yr	13.90%	Blue Collar	30.10%
Military		Post grad	7.70%	Government	12.00%
Veteran/ Active Duty	8.10%				

2020 Pres. Vote	Trump	228,555	(69%)	Biden	96,584	(29%)		
2016 Pres. Vote	Trump	204,129	(67%)	Clinton	82,498	(27%)	Johnson	14,897 (5%)

Muncie: Muncie became famous as the "Middletown" where sociologists Robert and Helen Lynd lived and did research for their landmark report in 1924 and 1925. The Lynds were attracted to Muncie because it was typical of "every small city from Maine to California," as Life magazine put it. But it wasn't exactly. Muncie was a factory town in a country still almost 50 percent rural in the 1920s, and it was almost entirely Protestant and northern in a country that was one-fifth Catholic and one-third southern. Muncie was more typical in that it was culturally homogeneous but economically riven. In the 1920s, when General Motors opened a plant in Muncie, the city celebrated its common values and was loath to admit its economic disparities. In the 1930s, those differences were exposed when Muncie, like much of the industrial Midwest, was unionized, a process that sometimes led to violent clashes. Workers who were joining CIO unions and voting for Democrats fiercely opposed the business elite—local bankers, merchants, GM executives and the Ball family's glass company.

Muncie has remained a story of both sides of the American economic coin. "Local auto parts plants were in many ways the engine that drove the Muncie economy. At its peak in the 1950s, Warner Gear (later BorgWarner Automotive) employed more than 5,000 workers," the MuncieStar-Press wrote in a profile of its hometown in 2015. The BorgWarner plant closed in 2009. Earlier, the city was devastated in 2006 by the loss of a General Motors manual transmission plant. In 2018, the two largest employers in Muncie were Ball State University and the Indiana University hospital.

The area regained some of its manufacturing heft with the arrival of a foreign-owned automaker: The Honda plant in Greensburg employed 2,500 non-union workers who annually manufacture 250,000 cars, including the Insight, a gas-electric hybrid. The international trade policies of President Donald Trump became a big concern in this trade-dependent area. Columbus, hometown of former Vice President Mike Pence, has more than 40 overseas companies with local operations, with nearly 10,000 employees.

In other ways, recent incidents suggest that Muncie has become typical of Americana, for better or worse. In November 2019, Muncie Mayor Dennis Tyler was indicted on federal corruption charges, including his acceptance of illegal cash payments. As he had announced early that year, Tyler retired at the end of his term in December 2019. His trial was postponed to 2021. Separately, in the days following the 2020 election, protestors marched in downtown Muncie. The Star-Press reported that some gave onlookers "the impression they were trying to look like members of the Ku Klux Klan."

There is one constant in these environs: basketball. It is the civic religion here. Most of the nation's largest high school gyms are in Indiana. The Field house, in New Castle, near the Indiana Basketball Hall of Fame, is the largest of them all. Tiny Milan High School's 1954 state championship victory over Muncie Central was the basis for the 1986 movie Hoosiers.

The 6th Congressional District of Indiana covers most of the east-central and southeast parts of the state. It includes Muncie in the north as well as Richmond, founded by a major branch of American Quakers and home to their Earlham College. Batesville, to the south, is the site of the Batesville

Casket Co., which makes the coffins for U.S. military personnel who die in the line of duty. In 2020, the Trump Pence ticket got 69 percent of the district vote, its best showing in the state.

Andre Carson (D)

Elected 2008, 7th full term, b. Oct 16, 1974; Indianapolis, IN; Concordia University, B.S., 2003; IN Wesleyan University, M.A., 2005; Islam (Muslim); Married (Mariama Carson); 1 child.

Elected Office: Indianapolis/Marion City-County Council, 2007-2008.

Professional Career: Investigator, IN State Excise Police, 1996-2005; Investigator, IN Department of Homeland Security, 2006-2008.

DC Office: 2135 RHOB 20515, 202-225-4011, Fax: 202-225-5633, carson.house.gov

State Offices: Indianapolis, 317-283-6516.

Committees: *Permanent Select on Intelligence*: Counterterrorism, Counterintelligence & Counterproliferation (Chmn); Strategic Technologies & Advanced Research. *Transportation & Infrastructure*: Aviation; Railroads, Pipelines & Hazardous Materials.

Group Ratings

	ADA	ACLU	AFL-CIO	LCV	COC	HAFA	ACU	CFG	FRC
2020	**	79%	**	100%	-	0%	5%	**	-
2019	85%	C	100%	93%	60%	C	5%	12%	0%

Almanac Ratings 2019-2020

	Economy	Social	Foreign	Composite
Liberal	100%	100%	92%	98%
Conservative	0%	0%	8%	2%

Key Votes of the 116th Congress

1. U.S./Mex./Can. trade deal Y	5. Russia sanctions Y	9. Firearms background checks Y
2. First Coronavirus response Y	6. Troops in Syria Y	10. Spending at the border N
3. HEROES Act Y	7. Veto arms sales to Saudis Y	11. Marijuana liberalized rules Y
4. CASH Act Y	8. Defense $$$, veto override Y	12. Electoral College objections N

Election Results

Election	Name (Party)	Vote (%)	Cand. Spent	Ind. Exp. Support	Ind. Exp. Oppose
2020 General	Andre Carson (D)	176,422 (62%)	$866,881	$10	
	Susan Marie Smith (R)	106,146 (38%)	$58,842		
2020 Primary	André Carson (D)	62,117 (92%)			
	Pierre Quincy Pullins (D)	5,572 (8%)			

Prior winning percentages: 2018 (65%), 2016 (60%), 2014 (55%), 2012 (63%), 2010 (59%), 2008 (65%), 2008 special (54%)

Democrat André Carson of Indiana, an occasionally outspoken progressive active in the Congressional Black Caucus, used his seat on the House Intelligence Committee to make the case that President Donald Trump "betrayed America" and was "a major threat to our national security." As a Muslim, he was a sharp critic of the travel ban that Trump imposed on several majority-Muslim nations. Carson won his seat in a 2008 special election to succeed his grandmother, Julia Carson, who died in office. In his majority-white district, he has not been seriously challenged for reelection.

Originally interested in the priesthood, Carson converted to Islam and became the second Muslim elected to Congress. Carson also had an artistic side. He wrote poetry as a young man and performed as a rap artist under the name "Juggernaut." With a career in law enforcement in mind, he got a bachelor's degree in criminal justice management from Concordia University and a master's degree in business management from Indiana Wesleyan. Carson spent nine years as a plainclothes officer of the Indiana Excise Police, which enforces alcohol and tobacco laws. "I loved law enforcement," he told Esquire magazine in 2010. "But this job sure beats sitting and waiting for something bad to go down at three in the morning."

He recalled that his political interest began in 1984, at age 10, when he attended the Democratic convention in San Francisco and heard civil rights leader Jesse Jackson speak. Carson said his thinking was transformed by reading The Autobiography of Malcolm X, and he attended Nation of Islam leader Louis Farrakhan's Million Man March in 1995. In 2007, at age 32, he won a seat on the Indianapolis City-County Council, his first elected office.

After Julia Carson died in December 2007, her grandson faced significant opposition for the Democratic nomination in the special election to fill the remainder of her term. At the Democratic caucus, he won a bare majority with 223 of the 439 votes. Against Republican state Rep. Jon Elrod, a lawyer, Carson received extensive assistance from the Democratic Congressional Campaign Committee. He called for withdrawing U.S. troops from Iraq, endorsed tax cuts for working families, and said companies should have incentives to keep them from sending jobs overseas. He won, 54%-43%. Carson has faced minimal opposition since, including in the Democratic primary, though his vote in the general election has been relatively small compared with most other Black Caucus members.

In the House, his voting record has been mostly liberal. He has placed near the center of House Democrats in the Almanac vote ratings. He initially opposed the $700 billion bailout of financial markets in 2008, but switched his position after Barack Obama, then the Democratic presidential nominee, urged him to support it. Carson has been a senior whip for the Democratic whip organization.

As the first Muslim to get a seat on the Intelligence Committee, Carson's selection produced protests from some conservative activists. He has won committee approval of his amendments to increase the transparency of government efforts to counter violent extremism at home and abroad, calling it "critical that we maintain strong oversight of these programs to protect American privacy and civil rights. "During the 2016 campaign, Carson voiced concern about what he called Trump's anti-Muslim rhetoric. "That saying about 'Make America Great Again' is a form of meta-messaging to a certain segment, we're talking about our white brothers and sisters, largely blue collar," he said. When the Supreme Court in 2018 upheld a modified version of the travel ban in a 5-4 decision, Carson called it "a shameful sanctioning of discrimination."

Carson has chaired the Counterterrorism, Counterintelligence and Counter proliferation Subcommittee. Prior to House action on impeachment, he told Politico that Trump should be held accountable for "fanning the flames of Islam phobia, xenophobia and outright hatred. "During the panel's hearings during the House impeachment inquiry, he said Republican silence on the allegations was "deafening—because the more facts we learn, it becomes harder to defend the indefensible."

With the election in 2018 of two Muslim women to the House—Ilhan Omar of Minnesota and Rashida Tlaib of Michigan—Carson used the opportunity to spotlight Muslim culture. In May 2019, they hosted the first dinner on Capitol Hill that broke the daily fast during Ramadan. "This sacred time of fasting and sacrifice is a special opportunity for a diverse community of Muslims worldwide to grow closer to our faith and each other, and to reflect on our many blessings," he said. Earlier, when Omar's security was not adequately protected following criticism of her anti-Semitic statements, Carson said that House officials had been "slow to respond to death threats" against her.

In his district, which includes nearly three-fourths of Marion County, the 62 percent of the vote that Carson received in his 2020 reelection slightly trailed the 64 percent that Biden won countywide. In 2016, the 60 percent for Carson edged out the 59 percent that Clinton won in the county.

IN-7: Indianapolis

Population		Race and Ethnicity		Income	
Total	777,205	White	57.90%	Median Income	$46,118
Land area (sq. miles)	304	Black	30.70%	District Income Rank	412
Pop/ sq mi	2,557.94	Latino	11.50%	Poverty Rate	16.60%
Born in State	66.40%	Asian	4.20%	With health insurance	88.60%
		Two or more races	3.50%	Cash public assistance	2.60%
Age Groups		Other	3.60%	Food stamp/SNAP	13.50%
Under 18	25.50%				
18-34	26.30%	**Education**		**Work**	
35-64	35.90%	H.S grad or less	48.30%	White Collar	32.80%
Over 64	12.30%	Some college	26.80%	Sales and Service	39.20%
		College Degree, 4 yr	16.30%	Blue Collar	28.00%
Military		Post grad	8.60%	Government	9.40%
Veteran/ Active Duty	6.00%				

2020 Pres. Vote	Biden	177,925	(63%)	Trump	99,811	(35%)		
2016 Pres. Vote	Clinton	156,046	(58%)	Trump	95,656	(36%)	Johnson	12,689 (5%)

Indianapolis: Indianapolis, radiating outward from the soldiers and sailors statue in Monument Circle, is precisely at the center of Indiana and is the largest and most dominant city in the state. What residents once disparaged as "Nap Town" has become a thriving metropolis, including downtown. In 2020, home prices were rising and the median price exceeded $300,000 for the first time in more than a decade. The city is the political and governmental capital, industrial and financial hub, and the intellectual center of Indiana as well. It is symmetrically laid out: Just to the west of the circle is the state capitol, to the north is the American Legion headquarters, to the east is the City-County building, and to the south are the Circle Centre mall, Lucas Oil Stadium, home of the NFL's Indianapolis Colts, and the headquarters of the National Collegiate Athletic Association.

Indianapolis has fostered its niche as the nation's amateur sports capital, especially for basketball. It also is a popular place for religious conventions. Home to the iconic Indianapolis 500, the motorsports industry is a prominent local enterprise. In 2019, Hulman & Company—which had owned the Speedway since 1945—sold the business to the Detroit-based Penske Corp. Since 1951, drivers sponsored by the Penske family have 18 victories in the 500.

Many large companies are based in Indianapolis. Pharmaceutical giant Eli Lilly & Co. spent $400 million to expand its insulin manufacturing operations, including two insulin cartridge filling lines. FedEx has its second-largest airport hub here (behind Memphis), where it can sort 2 million packages each day; it plans a $1.5 billion expansion by 2025. State officials have promoted the city as a high-tech jobs center, which some have dubbed "Silicon Prairie." Less certain is the fate of old-line manufacturer Carrier. Shortly before he took office, President Donald Trump visited the Indianapolis plant to claim credit for a deal in which the company cut back its plan to send jobs to Mexico, which apparently saved about 800 jobs. But by 2018, Carrier had imposed new layoffs, with five production lines shrinking to three. Workers had growing fears of automation, in addition to the threat of cheaper foreign labor. In 2020, a two-week shutdown caused by the start of the coronavirus had the perverse effect of forcing Carrier employees to work seven-day weeks to meet demand, the Indianapolis Star reported.

Indiana's 7th Congressional District, which is entirely in Marion County, takes in most of Indianapolis. The more prosperous northern edge of the city is in the 5th District. In decades past, Indianapolis had robust political competition in local and national races. More recently, affluent young people have been moving to counties farther out. The median income has dropped in Marion County, especially in the 7th. It has become solidly Democratic. In 2020, Joe Biden took the district, 63%-35%--identical to the victory by Barack Obama in 2012 and an improvement over Hillary Clinton's 58%-36%. The District has the largest minority population in the state, though it remains 53 percent white. It is one of only two Democratic districts in the state; the other is the Gary-based 1st.

Larry Bucshon (R)

Elected 2010, 6th term, b. May 31, 1962; Taylorsville, IL; University of IL - Urbana, B.S., 1984; University of IL Medical School - Chicago, M.D., 1988; Lutheran; Married (Kathryn Bucshon); 4 children.

Military Career: U.S. Navy Reserve 1989-1998

Professional Career: Practicing cardiothoracic surgeon, 1995-1998; Ohio Valley HeartCare, 1998-2010, President, 2003-2010; Chief & Medical Director, St. Mary's Hospital.

DC Office: 2313 RHOB 20515, 202-225-4636, Fax: 202-225-3284, bucshon.house.gov

State Offices: Evansville, 812-465-6484; Jasper, 812-482-4255; Terre Haute, 812-232-0523; Vincennes, 855-519-1629.

Committees: *Energy & Commerce*: Consumer Protection & Commerce; Energy; Health.

Group Ratings

	ADA	ACLU	AFL-CIO	LCV	COC	HAFA	ACU	CFG	FRC
2020	**	21%	**	14%	-	83%	77%	**	-
2019	5%	C	40%	10%	85%	C	77%	81%	100%

Almanac Ratings 2019-2020

	Economy	Social	Foreign	Composite
Liberal	25%	28%	27%	27%
Conservative	75%	72%	73%	73%

Key Votes of the 116th Congress

1. U.S./Mex./Can. trade deal Y	5. Russia sanctions Y	9. Firearms background checks N
2. First Coronavirus response Y	6. Troops in Syria Y	10. Spending at the border Y
3. HEROES Act N	7. Veto arms sales to Saudis N	11. Marijuana liberalized rules N/A
4. CASH Act N	8. Defense $$$, veto override Y	12. Electoral College objections N

Election Results

Election	Name (Party)	Vote (%)	Cand. Spent	Ind. Exp. Support	Ind. Exp. Oppose
2020 General	Larry Bucshon (R)..............................	214,643 (67%)	$751,777	$8,790	
	E. Thomasina Marsili (D)......................	95,691 (30%)	$63,271		$1,962
	James Rodenberger (L).................	10,283 (3%)			
2020 Primary	Larry Bucshon (R)........................	51,343 (100%)			

Prior winning percentages: 2018 (65%), 2016 (64%), 2014 (60%), 2012 (53%), 2010 (57%)

Republican Larry Bucshon, elected in 2010, is well-positioned in the House as a physician and a member of the Energy and Commerce Committee. He used that combination to try to influence the national response to the coronavirus, often on a bipartisan basis.

Bucshon was raised in the rural town of Kincaid Illinois. As an undergraduate at the University of Illinois, his rightward shift solidified when he became enamored of President Ronald Reagan. In high school, Bucshon decided on a career in medicine, inspired by the surgeons he met at the hospital where his mother was a nurse. He got his medical degree at the University of Illinois at Chicago and completed a residency at the Medical College of Wisconsin, where he specialized in cardiothoracic surgery. Bucshon enlisted in the Navy Reserve, serving for nearly a decade. After three years in private practice in Wichita Kansas, he joined Ohio Valley HeartCare, a large cardiology and cardiovascular surgery practice in Evansville. In 2003, he became its president.

Bucshon ran when Democratic Rep. Brad Ellsworth unsuccessfully sought a Senate seat in 2010. Helped by the National Republican Congressional Committee, Bucshon prevailed over seven other candidates in the GOP primary, edging out tea party-backed Kristi Risk, 33%-29%.In the general, he faced state Rep. Trent Van Haaften, who fit the centrist mold of Ellsworth. Van Haaften was a prosecutor in rural Posey County who emphasized his law-and-order background, while Bucshon campaigned on curbing spending and repeal of the Democrats' Affordable Care Act. Bucshon won 57%-38%.

Bucshon actively opposed the excise tax on medical device equipment, as well as a Medicare cost-control board included in the new health care law. "I have been a practicing physician for over 15 years, and I don't think I have seen anything potentially more detrimental to seniors' health care than the Independent Payment Advisory Board," he said. But conservatives criticized his backing of the August 2011 increase in the debt limit, unlike other Indiana GOP freshmen.

In a 2018 profile , the Evansville Courier-Press described Bucshon as "a serious, sober minded —if unspectacular—legislator" who was in the middle of the House. A colleague said he was "a work horse, not a show horse." On Energy and Commerce, he joined in bipartisan support for the 2015 law establishing a permanent fix of Medicare reimbursement of doctor fees. He worked with Republican leaders on their priority legislation to treat opioid addiction. He criticized in November 2018 a proposal by President Donald Trump to limit prescription-drug prices; Bucshon called it a step toward "government price-fixing."

Bucshon worked with another physician with experience as an administrator, Democratic Rep. Ami Bera of California, to repeal a complex billing procedure imposed by Medicare officials. In October 2020, the two doctors called for a two-year freeze on cuts in Medicare reimbursement rates to encourage more complete coverage during the pandemic. Separately, Bucshon urged more-thorough testing to limit the spread of the coronavirus. "For decades, Republicans and Democrats in both the administration and in Congress have devoted inadequate attention and resources to critical pieces of our public health system," he wrote in the Indianapolis Star in July 2020. He cited legislation that he filed with Diana DeGette of Colorado, an Energy and Commerce Democrat, to establish a framework for oversight of diagnostic tests.

Also on Energy and Commerce, Bucshon worked on energy legislation to promote his district's large coal resources, and telecommunications priorities such as expanded broadband access. With Democratic Rep. Tony Cardenas of California, he proposed in 2020 a bill to grant $500 million to states and localities to expand recycling, especially plastics.

In 2012, tea party candidate Risk mounted another primary challenge but could not come close to competing financially, and the incumbent won 58%-42%. His Democratic challenger in the general election was broadcaster and former state Rep. Dave Crooks, who touted his own culturally and fiscally conservative views. Bucshon got help from conservative super PACs, notching a hardly overwhelming 53%-43% victory. Since then, Bucshon has become entrenched. In 2020, he was reelected, 67%-30% against Thomasina Marsili, an emergency medical technician and motivational speaker.

In what had been a competitive district, the Courier Press wrote following the 2020 election, "Democrats face challenges in any campaign against Bucshon."

IN-8: Southwest Indiana		**Cook Partisan Voting Index: R+19**	

Population		**Race and Ethnicity**		**Income**	
Total	716,924	White	91.20%	Median Income	$54,326
Land area (sq. miles)	7,255	Black	4.50%	District Income Rank	341
Pop/ sq mi	98.81	Latino	2.70%	Poverty Rate	12.30%
Born in State	75.50%	Asian	1.10%	With health insurance	92.00%
		Two or more races	2.10%	Cash public assistance	1.60%
Age Groups		Other	1.10%	Food stamp/SNAP	8.80%
Under 18	22.20%				
18-34	22.00%	**Education**		**Work**	
35-64	37.90%	H.S grad or less	47.30%	White Collar	31.30%
Over 64	18.00%	Some college	30.40%	Sales and Service	37.70%
		College Degree, 4 yr	14.50%	Blue Collar	31.10%
Military		Post grad	7.70%	Government	11.40%
Veteran/ Active Duty	8.10%				

2020 Pres. Vote	Trump	212,185	(65%)	Biden	108,025	(33%)			
2016 Pres. Vote	Trump	194,208	(64%)	Clinton	92,844	(31%)	Johnson	13,569	(5%)

Evansville, Terre Haute: "Evansville," wrote John Bartlow Martin in 1947, "is the capital of a tri-state area comprising the neglected tag ends of Indiana, Kentucky and Illinois." It was a factory town then, making car parts and refrigerators, drawing workers from Kentucky, Tennessee and the picturesque but not very fertile hills of Southern Indiana.

Evansville has become a headquarters for midsized companies that offer good-paying, skilled jobs. Car parts still get made here, though it is auto assembly that helps anchor the local manufacturing economy. Toyota in January 2020 announced plans to complete a $1.3 billion modernization of its plant, which has 7,000 workers in nearby Princeton, to meet consumer demand for its Highlander SUV. But the local Whirlpool refrigerator production plant closed in 2010, followed by the shuttering of its refrigeration product design center. In 2017, Alcoa reopened its aluminum smelter, increasing its workforce to 1,500.

In Vanderburgh County, Evansville is one of two major population centers of the 8th Congressional District, which covers Southwest Indiana. The other, in Vigo County, is Terre Haute, an old manufacturing town and the boyhood home of socialist Eugene Debs. It hosts a maximum-security penitentiary, which includes the only federal death chamber. In July 2020, the Trump administration carried out the first federal execution since 2003. By the end of the year, 10 inmates had died from lethal injections, the largest yearly total in at least a century. In August 2020, a local group announced plans to connect downtown Terre Haute to the Wabash River through design and art. Downstream, close to Evansville, is New Harmony, an early utopian community established by Welsh philanthropist and visionary Robert Owen.

Southern Indiana is ancestrally Democratic, just as northern Indiana is ancestrally Republican. The southern counties were hostile to the Union during the Civil War, and then in New Deal times workers in Evansville moved toward the Democrats. Vigo has been a swing county, which had voted for the winning presidential candidate in all but two elections since the 19th century; the 2020 election marked the third such switch, when Donald Trump won Vigo, 56%-42%. For decades, the result was a very close political balance, and this district was known as the "Bloody 8th" for its tight congressional races. At one point in the 1970s, it sent four different members to the House in four successive elections. In 1984, the state certified the Republican the winner by exactly 34 votes. The Democratic majority in the House investigated and overturned the result in a fight that left many Republicans bitter. As with other rural and blue-collar areas, the trend in presidential politics has been away from Democrats. In 2008, John McCain led Barack Obama, 51%-48%. In 2020, Trump swept Joe Biden, 65%-33%.

Trey Hollingsworth (R)

Elected 2016, 3rd term, b. Sep 12, 1983; Clinton, TN; Webb School; University of PA, B.S.E., 2004; Georgetown University, M.P.P., 2014; Christian Church; Married (Kelly Hollingsworth); 1 child.

Professional Career: Small Business Owner.

DC Office: 1641 LHOB 20515, 202-225-5315, Fax: 202-226-6866, hollingsworth.house.gov

State Offices: Franklin, 317-851-8710; Jeffersonville, 812-288-3999.

Committees: *Financial Services*: Investor Protection, Entrepreneurship & Capital Markets; Task Force on Artificial Intelligence.

Group Ratings

	ADA	ACLU	AFL-CIO	LCV	COC	HAFA	ACU	CFG	FRC
2020	**	27%	**	10%	-	87%	83%	**	-
2019	10%	C	26%	34%	89%	C	81%	90%	77%

Almanac Ratings 2019-2020

	Economy	Social	Foreign	Composite
Liberal	25%	40%	38%	35%
Conservative	75%	60%	62%	65%

Key Votes of the 116th Congress

1. U.S./Mex./Can. trade deal	Y	5. Russia sanctions	N	9. Firearms background checks	N
2. First Coronavirus response	Y	6. Troops in Syria	N	10. Spending at the border	Y
3. HEROES Act	N	7. Veto arms sales to Saudis	Y	11. Marijuana liberalized rules	N
4. CASH Act	N/A	8. Defense $$$, veto override	N/A	12. Electoral College objections	N

Election Results

Election	Name (Party)	Vote (%)		Cand. Spent	Ind. Exp. Support	Ind. Exp. Oppose
2020 General	Trey Hollingsworth (R)	222,057	(62%)	$526,562	$1,378	
	Andy Ruff (D)	122,566	(34%)	$134,997	$10	
	Tonya Millis (L)	14,415	(4%)	$6,071		
2020 Primary	Trey Hollingsworth (R)	62,962	(100%)			

Prior winning percentages: 2018 (57%), 2016 (54%)

Republican Trey Hollingsworth, elected in 2016, had no political experience and a limited connection to the 9th District, but he used ample self-financing to secure his seat. A few years later, he appeared to have become entrenched. In the House, Hollingsworth worked to roll back banking regulation as a member of the Financial Services Committee.

Hollingsworth was raised in Clinton Tennessee, a small city near Knoxville, which is about 230 miles from Indiana. He graduated from the University of Pennsylvania, with a degree in real estate, and later got a master's degree in public policy from Georgetown University. In the meantime, Hollingsworth became a managing partner and majority owner of his family's fast-growing Hollingsworth Capital Partners, which refurbished vacant factories—including some in Indiana. In 2008, he and a group of partners opened Alexin, an aluminum casting plant in Indiana. According to the Indianapolis Star, his company had filed legal papers in five other states that obligated him to live outside of Indiana to represent his business interests.

In September 2015, after then-Rep. Todd Young announced his campaign for the Senate, Hollingsworth moved from Tennessee to Jeffersonville Indiana. A month later, he announced his campaign for the open seat. In the hotly contested five-candidate primary, he spent heavily on campaign ads that touted his business acumen and outsider status. His challengers included Indiana Attorney General Greg Zoeller and state Sens. Erin Houchin and Brent Waltz. "Mr. Hollingsworth just moved here from Tennessee in the fall of last year trying to buy a congressional seat," Houchin said. Zoeller, who started the contest as the best-known candidate, called Hollingsworth a "political scam artist." Hollingsworth won the primary with 35 percent of the vote, to 25 percent for Houchin and 22 percent for Zoeller.

Democratic nominee Shelli Yoder was an Indiana native and a former Miss Indiana, who coincidentally lived in Tennessee for 10 years. According to the Star, which described her as "the quintessential Hoosier," Yoder attacked Hollingsworth for trying to buy the seat with "generic GOP talking points rather than an understanding of Southern Indiana." Hollingsworth attacked Yoder for supporting Hillary Clinton and her policies. He spent nearly $3.6 million for his campaign, of which $3.1 million was self-financed. His campaign report disclosed that his net worth exceeded $50 million. Hollingsworth prevailed, 54%-41%, with his anti-establishment message and business credentials. He won each of the 13 counties except for Monroe, which was Yoder's base and the Democratic stronghold.

Hollingsworth initially made few waves in the House. Fulfilling a campaign promise, his first legislation was a constitutional amendment to limit senators to two six-year terms and House members to four two-year terms. He also filed a bill to prohibit former members of Congress from seeking to work as lobbyists. On the Financial Services panel, he worked with other Republicans to ease the regulatory provisions of the Dodd-Frank financial services law, which was enacted in 2010 to address the banking crisis. That law's biggest failure, he said, was that "it institutionalized 'too big to fail,' instead of ending it." In 2018, Hollingsworth showed independence when he was one of six Republicans to vote against a House-passed resolution opposing a carbon tax.

As governors shut down much of the nation in early 2020 in response to the coronavirus, Hollingsworth was an early and vocal proponent for reopening. Contending that there was no "zero-harm choice" between sending people back to work or letting the economy continue to falter, he told CBS News in April that returning to work was "the lesser of these two evils." Later in the year, he objected that economic-relief legislation was being negotiated by a handful of congressional leaders. He said that increased deliberation would deliver a result "more reflective of what the American people want."

At home, Hollingsworth was attacked for failing to hold town-hall meetings and largely avoiding Monroe County, the Democratic bastion. According to critics, "he's unavailable back home [and] … unaccountable out in Washington, with a voting record that indicates he's more responsive to his donors than to his constituents," according to a pre-election report in a city-based magazine. The report cited supporters of Hollingsworth who credited him with "a more personal, individualized approach to connecting with constituents," especially in friendly territory.

In his first reelection bid, Hollingsworth faced Democratic challenger Liz Watson, an attorney from Bloomington and former labor-policy aide for Democrats at the House Education and the Workforce Committee, who was running her first campaign. She attacked Hollingsworth's out-of-state roots and his refusal to participate in campaign debates. With support from progressive and anti-gun groups, Watson outspent the incumbent, $2.5 million to $1.4 million. The outcome was similar to 2016: Watson took 69 percent in Monroe County. Hollingsworth won the remaining 12 counties and prevailed, 56%-44%. In 2020, Democrats appeared to have moved beyond this district. Andy Ruff, a former high school teacher and an academic adviser who served 20 years on the Bloomington City Council, spent less than $150,000 as their nominee. Hollingsworth scored his biggest win, 62%-34%. In Monroe, Ruff got 60 percent of the vote.

IN-9: South-Central Indiana

Cook Partisan Voting Index: R+15

Population		Race and Ethnicity		Income	
Total	765,896	White	90.70%	Median Income	$60,448
Land area (sq. miles)	4,487	Black	3.00%	District Income Rank	253
Pop/ sq mi	170.7	Latino	3.60%	Poverty Rate	11.50%
Born in State	63.80%	Asian	2.70%	With health insurance	93.40%
		Two or more races	2.30%	Cash public assistance	0.90%
Age Groups		Other	1.20%	Food stamp/SNAP	7.50%
Under 18	21.40%				
18-34	24.50%	**Education**		**Work**	
35-64	37.80%	H.S grad or less	42.40%	White Collar	35.50%
Over 64	16.40%	Some college	30.50%	Sales and Service	37.70%
Military		College Degree, 4 yr	17.00%	Blue Collar	26.90%
Veteran/ Active Duty	7.20%	Post grad	10.10%	Government	13.70%

2020 Pres. Vote	Trump	221,516	(61%)	Biden	135,586	(37%)			
2016 Pres. Vote	Trump	198,108	(60%)	Clinton	110,837	(34%)	Johnson	15,534	(5%)

Bloomington, Indianapolis Suburbs, Louisville Suburbs: The immense Ohio River is the largest tributary of the Mississippi. In Southern Indiana, it runs along the Indiana-Kentucky border and is an artery of commerce. Utilitarian barges replaced the old steamers, except for riverboat casinos. Along the river are towns like Corydon, which was the state capital from 1816 to 1825. Salem was the home of John Milton Hay, personal secretary to President Abraham Lincoln and later secretary of State in the William McKinley and Theodore Roosevelt administrations.

In 2018, Jeffersonville-based Jeff boat shut down its barge-manufacturing operations; a year later, the company auctioned its equipment. The city had not decided how to use the 65-acre site on the Ohio River. The company, which had employed more than 1,000, cited oversupply and a "very poor" outlook for new construction. The local shipyard opened in 1834. An affiliated company, which had nearly 4,000 employees in its barge-freight business, filed for bankruptcy in 2020. In Greenwood, which has a large business park that caters to contemporary shippers not far from the Indianapolis airport, Amazon and FedEx planned distribution centers that would employ nearly 2,000 workers.

In Indiana's 9th Congressional District, the largest city is Bloomington, where Indiana University and its 45,000 students are based. Bloomington, which has been rated second in the Milken Institute's index of best-performing cities for high-tech employment, has developed a technology park near the IU campus. TASUS Corp., which uses advanced robotics to manufacture automobile components, made a major investment in the development of a design and technical center. Other companies have been growing elsewhere in the Bloomington area. In September 2020, Catalent announced plans to spend $50 million to install a new high-speed vial filling line to respond to demand for coronavirus vaccines. In November, Italian-based Ferrero, which produces Tic Tac and Nutella brands, announced plans for its first chocolate factory in North America.

For 34 years, the 9th District was represented by Democrat Lee Hamilton, who chaired the House Foreign Affairs and Intelligence committees and retired in 1998. Like other parts of Indiana, the 9th has become comfortably Republican. In 2020, Bloomington-based Monroe County was the smallest of the five Indiana counties that voted for Joe Biden. That county's vote has been overwhelmed— especially by nearby Johnson and Morgan counties, which are growing Republican bastions in the suburbs of Indianapolis. The Louisville Kentucky suburbs in Clark and Floyd counties have trended Republican, though less strongly. Those four counties have a bit more than half of the population in the district. In 2020, Donald Trump took the district, 61%-37%.

IOWA

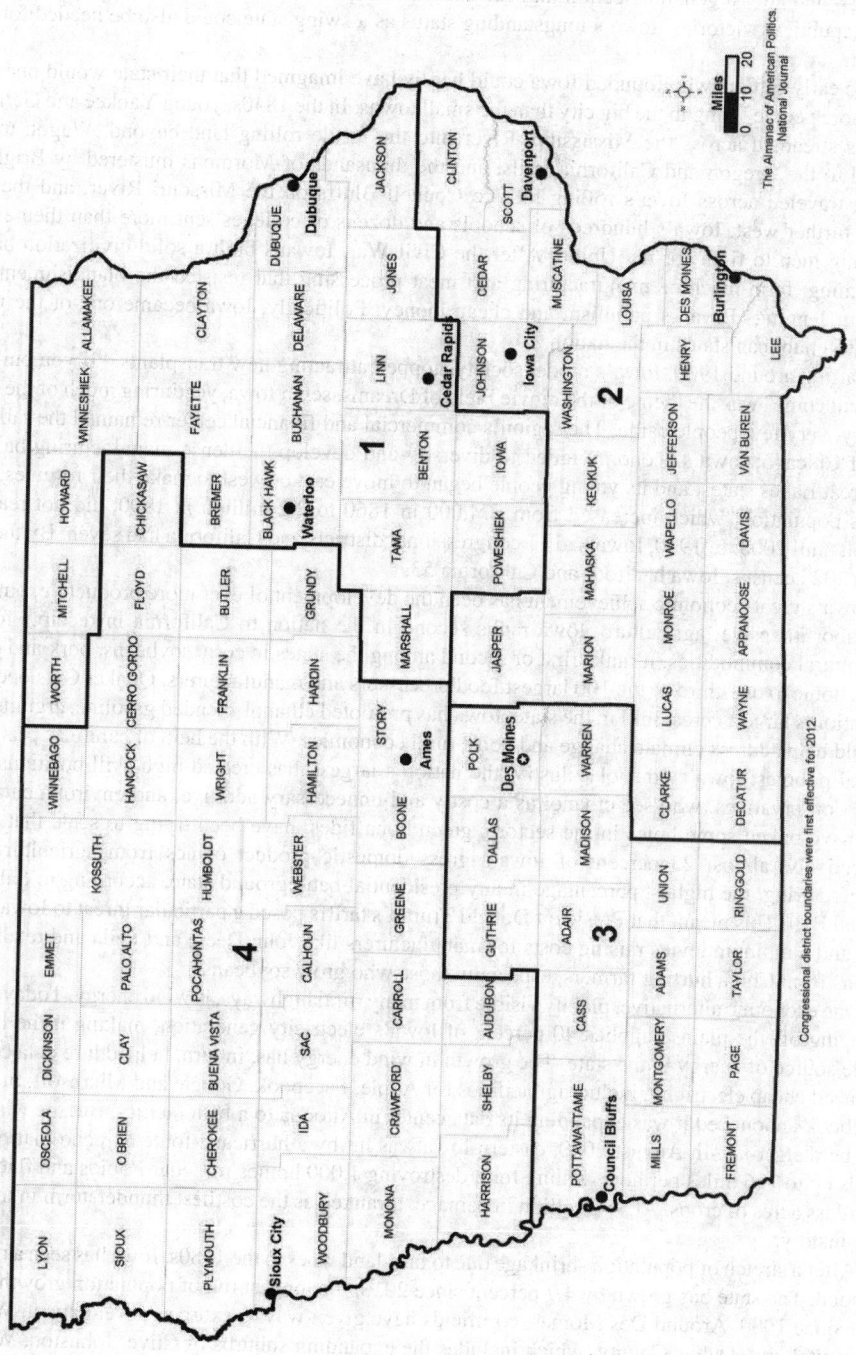

Miles
0 10 20

The Almanac of American Politics, National Journal

Congressional district boundaries were first effective for 2012.

Iowa holds a special place in American politics, thanks to its presidential caucuses, which are preceded by months of retail politicking on the snowy prairie. But after a disastrous election app malfunction in the 2020 Democratic caucuses, Iowa's primacy in the nominating contest is no longer assured—and after a general election that had seemed competitive between the parties yet ended in clear Republican victories, Iowa's longstanding status as a swing state could also be headed for the dustbin.

The early settlers who founded Iowa could hardly have imagined that their state would one day have more people living in the big city than the small towns. In the 1840s, young Yankee and German farmers streamed across the Mississippi River into the fertile rolling land beyond. Wagon trains headed to the Oregon and California trails, and the thousands of Mormons mustered by Brigham Young traveled across Iowa's rolling hills to Council Bluffs on the Missouri River, and then to points further west. Iowa's hundreds of schools and dozens of colleges sent more than their share of young men to fight for the Union. After the Civil War, Iowans built a solid civilization based on farming, farm-machine manufacturing and meat processing that resisted the blandishments of William Jennings Bryan's populism and cheap money. Politically, Iowa became one of the most solidly Republican states in the nation.

Starting around 1900, Iowa's model society stopped attracting new transplants. "If you build it, they will come" was the theme of the movie Field of Dreams, set in Iowa, yet during much of the 20th century, very few people came. The region's commercial and financial center remained the railroad hub of Chicago; Iowa's economy failed to diversify and develop the dense manufacturing base of the Great Lakes states, and its young people began to move east or west to make their fortunes. The state's population, which increased from 674,000 in 1860 to 2.2 million in 1900, did not reach 3 million until 2008. In 1900, Iowa had 11 congressional districts and California had seven. By the eve of the 2020 census, Iowa had four and California 53.

Iowa's great economic achievement has been the development of ever more productive, but also less labor-intensive, agriculture. Iowa ranks second in the nation to California in receipts for all agricultural commodities. It ranks first or second among the states in corn, soybeans, pork and eggs, and is home to one-third of the 100 largest food processors and manufacturers. Quaker Oats operates the nation's largest cereal mill in the state. Iowa has promoted ethanol-blended gasoline, arguing that it could help address climate change and boost rural economies. With the help of carefully protected federal policies, Iowa's ethanol industry, the nation's largest, has created high-skill positions. But fiscal conservatives, who see ethanol as a costly and unnecessary additive, and environmentalists, who have poked some holes in the sector's green bona fides, have been trying to scale that back. Collectively, almost 23 percent of Iowa's gross domestic product comes from agriculture and manufacturing, the highest percentage in any presidential battleground state, according to Sabato's Crystal Ball. This meant that President Donald Trump's tariffs posed a particular threat to Iowa, with steel and aluminum levies raising costs for manufacturers like John Deere and Pella and retaliatory actions from China hurting farmers, especially those who grow soybeans.

One economic alternative, plainly visible from many rural highways, is wind energy. Today, wind whipping off the plains supplies 40 percent of Iowa's electricity generation, making it the largest single source of energy in the state. The growth in wind energy has, in turn, helped lure data centers that need cheap electricity, including facilities for Apple, Facebook, Google and Microsoft; in 2019, Facebook announced it was expanding its data center in Altoona to a fifth facility. But the wind can also be dangerous. In August 2020, eastern Iowa was hit by a hurricane-force derecho that packed winds up to 126 miles per hour, killing four, destroying 1,000 homes in Cedar Rapids and flattening countless acres of crops. At $7.5 billion in damage, it ranked as the costliest thunderstorm in modern U.S. history.

After a stretch of population shrinkage due to farmland woes in the 1980s, Iowa has seen a modest rebound. The state has grown by 4.7 percent since 2010, the longest run of population growth in the state since 1900. Around Des Moines, cornfields have given way to exurban development. West of the capital city, Dallas County, which includes the expanding suburbs of Clive, Johnston, Waukee and West Des Moines, has grown by 40 percent since 2010. To the north, Ankeny, Altoona and Bondurant have been booming. Iowa City (home of the University of Iowa) and Ames (home of Iowa State) are also seeing significant population gains. Yet the ratio of housing costs to wages, a measure of affordability, remains the most favorable of any state, according to Moody's Analytics. Outside the metro areas, however, the picture is not so rosy. More than half of Iowa's population today is concentrated in just 10 of the state's 99 counties; more than two-thirds of counties in Iowa have gotten smaller since 2010, casualties of agricultural consolidation and mechanization. "Shrinking places were built to serve a late 19th to 20th-century economic system that doesn't exist," David Peters, associate professor of sociology at Iowa State University, told WBUR radio.

Iowa is 85 percent white, but Hispanics now account for more than 6 percent of the population, as Mexican immigrants have moved to smaller cities with meatpacking plants. (These plants became focuses of public health concern during the coronavirus pandemic.) Marshalltown, about an hour northeast of Des Moines, is now 31 percent Hispanic, and some 70 percent of kindergarten students there are minorities, ABC News reported. Indeed, over the past decade, Iowa's minority youth population has grown faster than older, white residents in 84 of 99 counties, according to Washington Post calculations. Jobs and small-town life have attracted refugees from eastern and central Africa as well as from Micronesia.

Voter turnout in Iowa is usually among the nation's highest, and the state has its distinctive political rituals, none more famous than its first-in-the-nation presidential caucuses. One, two, even three years beforehand, White House hopefuls have journeyed to the Iowa State Fair, held in August on the east side of Des Moines, to shake hands, eat a pork chop on a stick, and marvel at the famed butter cow sculpted out of 600 pounds of churned whole milk. (In 2020, the fair was canceled for the first time since World War II, due to the coronavirus.)

For much of the 20th century, Iowa was a culturally and politically counter-cyclical state, headed in the opposite direction of the rest of the nation. In the industrial New Deal era, it stayed mostly agricultural and Republican, even as Davenport and Des Moines radio announcer Ronald Reagan became an enthusiastic Roosevelt Democrat before heading to Hollywood. In the 1980s, when Reagan, by then a conservative Republican, was president and Iowa's economy was hit hard, anxiety became the dominant note of Iowa's politics, as voters sought protection from the vagaries of the market. In 1988, Iowa gave losing Democratic nominee Michael Dukakis his second highest vote percentage of any state. To a greater degree than other states, Iowa has a dovish streak on foreign policy, leavened by a desire for international trade. The Iowa delegation voted for the 1993 North American Free Trade Agreement, the 1999 normalization of trade relations with China (Mexicans eat lots of corn and the Chinese like pork), and the 2015 measure to give trade promotion authority to President Barack Obama.

Iowa voted twice for Democrat Bill Clinton, for Democrat Al Gore by just 4,144 votes in 2000, and for Republican George W. Bush by 10,059 votes in 2004. Iowa gave Obama a critical boost in its 2008 caucuses and then gave him its Electoral College votes in 2008 and 2012, before handing them to Trump in 2016. With Trump outperforming past Republican nominees among older, white, rural voters, no fewer than 31 counties—almost one of every three—flipped from Obama in 2012 to Trump in 2016. Meanwhile, the GOP also took control of the state Senate, allowing the party in 2017 to pass a raft of long-blocked conservative measures. During the 2018 midterms, the Democrats partially rebounded; they lost a competitive gubernatorial race by two points, but they flipped two GOP-held congressional seats and ousted the incumbent Republican state auditor.

Such incremental gains gave Democrats hope that they might be able to seriously contest the state in 2020. Despite the Democratic caucus debacle in February—which led party leaders to consider whether a more diverse state should lead the nominating pack in the future—there were strong signs that Iowa could be in play in November. In both June and September, J. Ann Selzer's gold-standard Iowa poll found that Joe Biden, who had finished a weak fourth in the caucuses, was in a dead heat with Trump; in the home stretch, Trump and his surrogates visited the state frequently, a sign that they were not overly confident of winning. But Trump ended up winning the state, 53%-45%, only slightly narrower than his 2016 margin, and the Obama counties that had flipped to Trump stayed with him in 2020. Biden made gains in urban and suburban areas, expanding the Democrats' margins in all six counties he won by between two and six percentage points. He also cut Trump's winning margin in Dallas County from 10 points to two. Meanwhile, in a hotly contested Senate race, GOP Sen. Joni Ernst won by seven points, despite a Libertarian candidate pulling almost 37,000 votes.

Republican candidates flipped two of the state's four House seats and held a third, while the GOP held both chambers of the legislature.

Between 2000 and 2016, Iowa was one of only three states to swing its support for president three times, joining Florida and Ohio. Now, all three states appear to be slipping away from Democrats, at least on the presidential level. "There's a lot of soul searching going on in Iowa right now," Sean Bagniewski, chairman of the Polk County Democrats, told Politico. "It looks pretty dire for the next couple of years."

Population		Race and Ethnicity		Income	
Total	3,155,070	White	89.90%	Median Income	61,691
Land area (sq. miles)	55,857	Black	4.10%	State Income Rank	30 out of 50
Pop/ sq mi	56.48	Latino	6.30%	Poverty Rate	11.20%
Born in state	69.70%	Asian	3.00%	With health insurance	95.00%
		Two or more races	2.20%	Cash public assistance	1.80%
Age Groups		Other	1.50%	Food stamp/SNAP	11.2%
Under 18	22.90%				
18-34	22.50%	Education		Work	
35-64	37.10%	H.S grad or less	38.30%	White Collar	37.80%
Over 64	17.50%	Some college	32.30%	Sales and Service	35.10%
		College Degree, 4 yr	19.80%	Blue Collar	27.10%
Military		Post grad	9.50%	Government	14.30%
Veteran/ Active Duty	7.70%				

Presidential Politics

2020 Caucus (D)	Sanders (D)	45,652(27%)	Buttigieg (D)	43,209(25%)	Warren (D)		34,909(20%)
	Biden (D)	23,605(14%)	Klobuchar (D)	21,100(12%)			
2016 Caucus (D)	Clinton (D)	70,047(50%)	Sanders (D)	69,692(50%)			
2016 Caucus (R)	Cruz (R)	51,666(28%)	Trump (R)	45,429(24%)	Rubio (R)		43,228(23%)
	Carson (R)	17,394 (9%)					
2020 Pres. Vote	Trump (R)	897,672(53%)	Biden (D)	759,061(45%)			
2016 Pres. Vote	Trump (R)	800,983(51%)	Clinton (D)	653,669(42%)	Johnson (L)		59,186 (4%)
	Bush (R)	(3%)					

Iowa has long played two crucial roles in the race for the presidency. For decades it has been a hotly contested swing state whose caucuses have kicked off the presidential primaries. But after a debacle of a 2020 Democratic caucus and a second straight general election where the presidential race wasn't that close, there are signs that Iowa's preeminence in presidential politics may be fading.

The caucuses were first scheduled early in the 1972 cycle by liberal Democrats who wanted more leverage for their views. They've often played a key role in both parties' nomination processes, helping frontrunners cement their status some years or launching dark-horse candidates into real contention. Democrats who owe a lot to the caucuses include George McGovern in 1972, Jimmy Carter in 1976 and Barack Obama in 2008; they also made household names out of Republicans Mike Huckabee in 2008 and Rick Santorum in 2012, though neither got much of a bounce. Iowa has also served as a key winnowing state, ending the campaigns of countless also-rans.

In 2008, both parties had candidates competing in the caucuses. Hillary Clinton led Democrats in initial polls, but her vote for the 2002 Iraq war resolution and her refusal to apologize for it hurt her with dovish Iowa Democrats. Obama out-organized her and won. His success in the heavily White state helped to convince African Americans that he could actually win (they flocked hard to him after the win) and turned him from insurgent into frontrunner. On the GOP side, Mitt Romney outspent all the other Republicans combined and had the most staffers. But Mike Huckabee quietly built a network of evangelical Christians and home-school parents and beat Romney, 34%-25%.

After being burned in 2008, Romney initially was hesitant to invest in the state in 2012, eschewing extensive campaigning until the final weeks before the caucus. He and Santorum each had 25 percent of the vote, but there was ambiguity about who actually won. The counting was done by the Iowa GOP, not state election officials, and they initially said Romney led by a few votes; it took 16 days for Santorum to be declared the winner by 34 votes, though results from eight precincts were still missing.

The botched contest undercut Santorum's momentum, helping Romney recover and eventually win the nomination. But his strong showing, like Huckabee's four years earlier, hinted that a sizable faction of the GOP base was dissatisfied with the party establishment and foreshadowed Donald Trump's rise four years later. For the first time, some Republicans clamored (unsuccessfully) for the end of Iowa's prominence. Democrats have since become even louder in pushing for its demise.

The 2016 caucuses marked Trump's electoral debut. He eschewed the painstaking retail organizing supposedly demanded by Iowans in favor of large, raucous rallies. While his chief rival, Ted Cruz, cultivated local evangelical leaders, Trump imported national evangelical figures such as Jerry Falwell Jr. to campaign with him and refused to participate in the final debate. Cruz's investment in organization helped the Texan claim a narrow 28%-24% victory over Trump, with Florida Sen. Marco Rubio a close third with 23 percent. Trump charged that Cruz "stole" the caucuses and committed "voter fraud" with a supposedly misleading direct mail piece, the first in a long series of Trump claims that elections he lost were rigged against him.

Clinton began her 2016 Iowa campaign with a huge lead in the polls over Vermont Sen. Bernie Sanders. But he gradually gained ground, capitalizing on the traditional dovish views and liberal sentiments of Iowa Democrats. In the closing days of the campaign she received the endorsement of the state's leading newspaper, The Des Moines Register. The Democratic caucus was at the time the closest in history: Clinton edged Sanders in "delegate equivalents" by a razor-thin 49.84%-49.59%.

The 2020 Democratic caucuses were even closer—and turned out to be an even bigger mess than Republicans' 2012 meltdown. Democrats sought to make the process more democratic, adding virtual caucuses to let people participate who were unable to attend the hours-long Saturday event in person, and agreed to release the raw vote totals for the first time, though the delegate-equivalent count churned out by a complex formula remained the official standard of victory. And they added a caucus reporting app, in what turned out to be a disastrous error. The app failed on election night, and local Democrats' backup plan fell apart. It took days for all the votes to be counted, and reporting errors marred faith that the final results were accurate. Iowa Democratic Party Chairman Troy Price resigned, but the national party deserved plenty of blame as well for forcing Iowa Democrats to use the new system.

Pete Buttigieg claimed victory on election night, and officially won the caucuses, determined by state delegate equivalents; he edged Sanders with 563 to 562, or 26.2%-26.1%, with Elizabeth Warren in third and Joe Biden a distant fourth. But in the raw-vote count, Sanders won 24.7%-21.3%. As had happened with Santorum in 2012, the drawn-out process undercut momentum for Buttigieg.

What's next for the Iowa caucuses remains to be seen. If they remain at the top of the calendar, it likely will be only after major changes to their byzantine structure. Numerous Democratic leaders have gone farther, calling for the state to lose its prized pole position in the nominating process.

Iowa might also be losing its swing-state status. In 2016, Trump bested Clinton, 51%-42%, the hardest shift toward the GOP of any 2012 swing state (Obama had won 52%-46% over Romney). Democrats hoped they could come back in 2020. With some polls showing the race competitive, both Biden and Trump spent money on Iowa ads. But 2020 looked much like 2016, with Trump winning 53%-45%. Iowa has followed a national pattern of rural and small-town America moving right as bigger cities and suburbs move left. Biden won just six of the state's 99 counties, down from the 38 Obama won in 2012. Obama won all 10 counties along the Mississippi River; Biden took just one. Greater Des Moines has become more Democratic, but much of the rest of the state is increasingly Republican.

Congressional Districts

117th Congress Lineup	1D 3R	116th Congress Lineup	3D 1R

Iowa's congressional district lines are drawn by the nonpartisan Legislative Services Bureau and then approved by the governor and legislature. But the process has not been entirely apolitical. The bureau is not supposed to take past voting patterns or a legislator's place of residence into account, and it has been even-handed in good Iowa fashion. But the governor and legislators can and do. As a result of the 2018 election, those influencers have remained chiefly Republican. And, in the often-competitive Iowa districts, the House delegation shifted from 3-to-1 Republican in 2017 to 3-to-1 Democratic in 2019 and then back to 3-to-1 Republican in 2021. The switches have taken place in three of the districts. Iowa's increasingly Republican tilt might encourage the GOP to try to lock down one of those seats.

In the current map, each of the four districts is based in one of the state's corners. That likely will continue to be a starting point, though such an approach offers plenty of opportunity for new options and partisan balances—including parochial questions such as which district would be the best fit for locales such as Cedar Rapids, Ames and Council Bluffs. The stability of retaining the current size of the delegation has become a rarity. In the six reapportionments between 1960 and 2010, Iowa lost a district four times—downsizing from eight seats to the current four.

With the one-seat loss following the 2010 census, the even-handed plan that was announced in 2011 resulted in a competitive contest in a Des Moines-based district between incumbents from each party. The one Iowa district that has been secure has been the GOP-held northwest 4th District.

Kim Reynolds (R)

Assumed office in 2017, term expires 2023, 1st full term; b. Aug. 4, 1959, St. Charles; Northwest Missouri State University, att. 1977-1980; Southeastern Community College, att.; Southwestern Community College, att. 1992-1995; Iowa State Univ., BA 2016.; United Methodist; Married (Kevin); 3 children.

Elected Office: IA Senate 2009-2011; IA Lt. Governor, 2011-2017; Clarke County Treasurer, 2001-2009.

Professional Career: Pharmacist assistant; Staff, Clarke County Treasurer.

Office: 1007 E. Grand Ave. Des Moines, 50319; 515-281-5211; Fax: 515-725-3527; Website: iowa.gov

Lt. Gov.: Adam Gregg (R) **Atty. Gen:** Tom Miller (D) **Sec. of State:** Paul Pate (R)

State Legislature: Senate: 18D, 32R **House:** 47D, 53R

Election Results

Election	Name (Party)	Vote (%)
2018 General	Kim Reynolds (R)	667,275 (50%)
	Fred Hubbell (D)	630,986 (48%)
2018 Primary	Kim Reynolds (R)	94,118 (100%)

Iowa Gov. Kim Reynolds, a Republican, was elevated from lieutenant governor in May 2017 when long-serving Gov. Terry Branstad was confirmed as U.S. ambassador to China. The following year, Reynolds won a term of her own, and she proceeded to spearhead liberal actions on racial justice but more conservative positions on abortion and measures to curb the spread of the coronavirus.

Reynolds hails from rural Iowa; she was born in Truro and raised in St. Charles. Her father worked at a John Deere factory, as did her grandfather and several other family members. Reynolds' father, unlike other family members, did not become a union member; he also farmed on the side. Reynolds attended Northwest Missouri State University, Southeastern Community College, and Southwestern Community College, but had not accumulated enough credits to graduate. She rectified that during her tenure as lieutenant governor, when she received a bachelor of liberal studies degree from Iowa State University. The speaker at the commencement ceremony was Sen. Joni Ernst, a longtime political ally of Reynolds.

While raising her young children, Reynolds worked as a part-time supermarket checker at a Hy-Vee. She also worked as a pharmacist's assistant and later as a motor vehicles clerk in the Clarke County treasurer's office. When the incumbent county treasurer declined to seek a new term,

Reynolds won the seat and was reelected three times. In 1998, she sought the GOP nomination for a state Senate special election. Despite securing the support of Branstad, she lost. Reynolds faced a personal crisis during this period when she was arrested in 1999 and 2000 for drunk driving. "Sitting in a jail cell that night, 'scared to death' because of alcoholism's grip on her psyche, Reynolds says she prayed, 'I can't do this on my own anymore. I need help,'" she told Politico's Tim Alberta. Reynolds reached 17 years of sobriety as she was running for governor.

In 2008, Reynolds won a seat in the state Senate. Two years later Branstad tapped her as his running mate. Having just survived a tough primary against Bob Vander Plaats, a strong social conservative, Branstad faced pressure to consolidate his party's support by choosing a running mate in Vander Plaats' mold. Instead, he settled on Reynolds, a more conventional economic conservative.

As lieutenant governor, Reynolds co-chaired the state advisory council on STEM education (science, technology, engineering and math). She also worked on trade promotion, making trips to China, South Korea, Germany, Brazil, Vietnam, the Philippines and Thailand. She considered but eventually declined a chance to run for the seat vacated by longtime Democratic Sen. Tom Harkin in 2014. Instead, it was Donald Trump who charted the course for Reynolds' political future when he tapped Branstad as ambassador to China. Branstad's nomination took longer than expected to surface in the Senate, so while Reynolds was widely seen as the governor-in-waiting, it was Branstad who presided over a landmark legislative session in early 2017. The previous fall, as Trump was winning the state, voters had also thrown out the Democratic majority in the state Senate, effectively removing the party's last defense against a conservative agenda. That enabled Branstad to sign a raft of laws on labor, liability, guns, abortion, and voting. After Branstad won confirmation for the China posting, Reynolds became the first woman to serve as Iowa's governor. She blocked a proposed rule to regulate guns in child-care facilities, and she grappled with Branstad's decision to have private companies run the state's Medicaid program, which had prompted widespread complaints about service delivery.

On the political front, Reynolds caught a break when an expected primary opponent, former Cedar Rapids Mayor Ron Corbett, fell short of enough signatures to qualify for the ballot. The Democrats saw their primary turn into a rout, as businessman Fred Hubbell won 56 percent in a six-way race. During the campaign, Reynolds touted the state's strong economy and fiscal situation, as well as a $2 billion cut in individual and corporate taxes she had signed. Hubbell, who spent millions of his own dollars on his candidacy, focused on health care, including Reynolds' handling of Medicaid, mental-health funding, and taxes, which he said the highest earners didn't pay enough of. Hubbell ran a strong race, but Reynolds pulled out a victory, 50%-48%, even as several other Midwestern states run by Republican governors—including Illinois, Kansas, Michigan, and Wisconsin—saw their governorships fall during the midterm Democratic surge. It was the narrowest victory for an Iowa governor since 1956. In some areas, a significant number of voters backed a Democrat for Congress yet stuck with Reynolds for governor; according to calculations by the Des Moines Register, the Democratic congressional candidates fared better than Hubbell did in 85 of the state's 99 counties.

After winning the election, Reynolds disappointed conservatives by not appealing a ruling that struck down a state law to ban abortions after a fetal heartbeat is detected. She also vetoed a bill that would have stopped Democratic attorney general Tom Miller from challenging Trump's policies, although Reynolds first obtained an agreement from Miller that he would voluntarily stop signing on to such lawsuits unless he had her consent. She signed a measure boosting K-12 education spending by about $90 million and another that legalized sports betting, but she vetoed a bill that would have eased the state's rules on medical marijuana. Reynolds signed a measure exempting Medicaid from having to cover gender reassignment surgery and cutting Planned Parenthood out of sex-education programs in the state.

After racial justice protests spread throughout the state and the nation in 2020, Reynolds signed bipartisan legislation to ban most police chokeholds and to increase scrutiny of officer-involved deaths. The bill took just a day to be introduced, debated and unanimously passed. The new law "is a loud and resounding signal from the people of Iowa and its leaders that we are ready and willing to act," Reynolds said at a signing ceremony attended by an array of legislators and activists. Reynolds also pursued other efforts to increase racial justice. In August, she signed an executive order that restored voting rights to tens of thousands of felons, after legislators rejected a constitutional amendment she had sought; the existing policy had blocked an estimated 10 percent of voting-age Black residents from voting. Reynolds said her own troubles with the law convinced her it was the right thing to do. "I am a firm believer that you can make a mistake but that shouldn't define you," she told the Associated Press. "Everybody deserves a second chance." In October, Reynolds said she would push in 2021 for the legislature to enact a state task force's recommendation that racial profiling be banned, and to track data to make sure that policy is enforced.

Reynolds' efforts to grapple with the coronavirus were rockier. It took her until November, after a large spike in cases, to issue a state mask mandate. Prior to that, she had dismissed such a mandate as a "feel-good" action, and she allowed businesses and schools freer rein for in-person operations than some other Republican governors. The September Iowa Poll found Reynolds' approval rating for handling the coronavirus had dropped by 15 points since June. After the surge in cases in November made Iowa among the nation's hardest-hit states, the per capita case rate fell significantly in December. Reynolds got good political news on Election Day, as Republicans cemented their hold on both legislative chambers, even though the Iowa House had been one of the national Democratic Party's biggest targets. The GOP effectively reversed the Democrats' 2018 gains in the state House. Reynolds is expected to seek another term in 2022, against an uncertain Democratic field. Reynolds was also voted vice chair of the Republican Governors Association.

In March 2021, Reynolds, despite strenuous objections from Democrats, signed a measure that reduced early voting by nine days and required mail ballots to be received by Election Day, rather than being postmarked by Election Day. The law also moved poll-closing times an hour earlier, banned election officials from sending out absentee voting forms unsolicited, and allowed voters to be removed from the active voter list if they fail to vote in a single general election. Reynolds also signed a measure legalizing the permit-less carrying of handguns and a bill that barred schools from requiring masks and curbed localities from issuing mask mandates that affect private property.

Chuck Grassley (R)

Elected 1980, term expires 2022, 7th term, b. Sep 17, 1933; New Hartford, IA; University of Northern Iowa, B.A., 1955; University of Northern Iowa, M.A., 1956; Baptist; Married (Barbara Ann Speicher Grassley); 5 children.

Elected Office: IA House, 1959-1974; U.S. House, 1975-1981.

Professional Career: Farmer; Sheet metal shearer, 1959-1961; Assembly line worker, 1961-1971; University Instructor.

DC Office: 135 HSOB 20510, 202-224-3744, Fax: 202-224-6020, grassley.senate.gov

State Offices: Cedar Rapids, 319-363-6832; Council Bluffs, 712-322-7103; Davenport, 563-322-4331; Des Moines, 515-288-1145; Sioux City, 712-233-1860; Waterloo, 319-232-6657.

Committees: *Agriculture, Nutrition & Forestry*: Commodities, Risk Management & Trade; Livestock, Dairy, Poultry, Local Food Sys & Food Safety & Sec; Rural Development & Energy. *Budget. Finance*: Health Care; International Trade, Customs & Global Competitiveness; Taxation & IRS Oversight. *Joint Taxation. Judiciary (RMM)*.

Group Ratings

	ADA	ACLU	AFL-CIO	LCV	COC	HAFA	ACU	CFG	FRC
2020	-	15%	-	8%	-	64%	83%	-	-
2019	0%	C	21%	7%	87%	C	84%	47%	100%

Almanac Ratings 2019-2020

	Economy	Social	Foreign	Composite
Liberal	6%	6%	0%	4%
Conservative	94%	94%	100%	96%

Key Votes of the 116th Congress

1. EPA clean energy rules	N	5. Russia sanctions	N	9. Barr as Atty. General	Y
2. U.S./Mex./Can. trade deal	Y	6. Troops in SYR, AFG	Y	10. Spending at the border	Y
3. Cut unemployment benefits	Y	7. Veto arms sales to Saudis	N	11. Coney Barrett to Sup. Ct.	Y
4. Shelton to Fed Reserve	N/A	8. Defense $$$, veto override	Y	12. Electoral College objections	N

Election Results

Election	Name (Party)	Vote (%)		Cand. Spent	Ind. Exp. Support	Ind. Exp. Oppose
2016 General	Chuck Grassley (R)............................ 926,007	(60%)	$10,306,743	$284,077	$37,897
	Patty Judge (D).................................... 549,460	(36%)	$2,189,617	$22,035	$80,410
	John Heiderscheit (L)....................... 41,794	(3%)			
2016 Primary	Chuck Grassley (R)....................... Unopposed				

Prior winning percentages: 2016 (60%), 2010 (64%), 2004 (70%), 1998 (68%), 1992 (70%), 1986 (66%), 1980 (54%); House: 1978 (75%), 1976 (57%), 1974 (51%)

One of the longest-serving senator sever, Chuck Grassley has shown he is equal parts cankerous and approachable. The conservative Iowan was responsible as Judiciary chairman for confirming the most federal judges ever in a two-year period, including two Supreme Court justices—reorienting the third branch of government. But, while acquiescing to President Donald Trump on judicial picks, he often bristled at what he said was the president's overreach, defending the separation of powers and the importance of the legislative branch being a check on the executive.

Grassley's legacy will be helping to reshape the federal judiciary, achieved first by: supporting then-Senate Majority Leader Mitch McConnell's decision to block President Barack Obama's nomination of Merrick Garland to the Supreme Court and curtailing the traditional deference to senators on lower court nominees. But Grassley has said the same panel that "reached the height of discord" during Brett Kavanaugh's confirmation to the Supreme Court also passed legislation responding to the opioid crisis, addressing elder abuse and reforming the juvenile justice system. And in a major bipartisan victory, Grassley teamed up with Sens. Dick Durbin, Democrat of Illinois, and Mike Lee, Republican of Utah, to pass the biggest changes to federal sentencing laws in a generation. The First Step Act addressed what are now acknowledged as missteps in tough-on-crime legislation that disproportionately affected communities of color. Summing up this legacy, Grassley tweeted at end of 2018: "To all the ppl who always disagree w my tweets bc I'm a Republican-what do u think of us passing bipartisan criminal justice reform that I've worked on for yrs???"

Perceptions of Grassley on Capitol Hill, where he has served for four decades and is the Senate's second oldest member at 87—California Democrat Dianne Feinstein is three months his senior—have evolved since his arrival in the chamber in 1981. His first election was facilitated by the Reagan presidential landslide, which brought a wave of reliable, often hard-line conservatives into the chamber. But virtually all of the Senate Republican Class of 1980 was gone within a term or two. Grassley not only survived but thrived. He transcended an initial image as a one-dimensional conservative and has been a dogged overseer of federal agencies, a hero to government whistleblowers, and an independent-minded deal-maker.

Grassley grew up on a farm in New Hartford. His parents were Democrats who switched to the Republican Party when Franklin D. Roosevelt ran for a third term in 1940. Grassley earned his bachelor's degree from the University of Northern Iowa and, while still in graduate school, ran for the Iowa House in 1956, losing by only 70-some votes. Two years later, he ran again and won at 25. While in the state Legislature, he worked as a sheet-metal shearer and on an assembly line. He won an open House seat in 1974, the hugely successful post-Watergate year for Democrats; he squeaked in with 51 percent of the vote. Six years later, he garnered 54 percent while ousting Democratic Sen. John Culver. A classmate of Massachusetts Sen. Ted Kennedy at Harvard University, Culver was among a group of influential liberals—notably George McGovern of South Dakota, Birch Bayh of Indiana and Frank Church of Idaho—that dominated the Senate during the 1960s and 1970s but was swept out of office in the 1980 wave.

Grassley has always been a committed fiscal conservative; he was among just eight senators to oppose the 2013 deal aimed at averting the so-called fiscal cliff because, he said, "Washington has a spending problem, not a taxing problem, and this deal doesn't do anything about the spending problem." He also is a steady conservative on social issues: He opposes abortion rights and most gun control initiatives. In 2013, he voted to block a compromise measure to expand background checks for gun owners after the mass shooting at Sandy Hook Elementary School in Newtown Connecticut, in which 28 were killed, including the perpetrator.

But he is a populist in the Midwestern agrarian tradition, suspicious of concentrations of both public and private power. He has made oversight of bloated, indifferent or corrupt government agencies a focal point of his Senate career. In the mid-1980s, his first major legislative achievement was passing the Federal False Claims Act, which imposed legal liability on those defrauding the government; he has said it has returned more than $59 billion to the federal Treasury. In 2015, Grassley blasted the Justice Department over its administration of civil asset forfeiture laws, a position that allied him with the American Civil Liberties Union.

Grassley has often used the Senate's oversight responsibilities to be a check on the White House—even when it's occupied by a member of his own party. A two-year dispute with Trump's Justice Department resulted in Grassley placing a hold on the nomination of William Evanina to head the National Counterintelligence and Security Center; in May 2020, Grassley relented after documents of the DOJ's probe into potential links between the Trump campaign and Russia were turned over. Grassley said in a statement that the executive branch "must recognize that it has an ongoing obligation to respond to congressional inquiries in a timely and reasonable manner."

Grassley was also very critical when Trump dismissed Michael Atkinson, the intelligence community inspector general, in the wake of the Ukraine scandal that resulted in Trump's first impeachment (he was acquitted in the GOP-controlled Senate) and blocked two of the president's nominees in retaliation. Along with Democratic Sen. Gary Peters of Michigan, Grassley sent a 665-word letter to the White House demanding an explanation. Grassley got backlash from some Republicans for challenging the president, but he had sent a similar missive in 2017 when the Justice Department claimed that only committee chairmen could make oversight requests. "It really isn't Grassley versus Obama or Grassley versus Trump or Grassley versus Bush or event going back to Reagan. It's Article I of the Constitution versus Article II of the Constitution," Grassley wrote. In the same vein, the senator has long been an advocate for whistleblowers, co-authoring the 1989 Whistleblowers Protection Act.

In the summer of 2020, Grassley warned Trump that his actions and laissez-faire attitude toward the coronavirus pandemic were leading him down the road to a likely loss, and he was particularly critical when the president couldn't answer a softball question from Fox News' Sean Hannity of what his second-term priorities would be. Urging Trump to campaign instead on his economic and judicial record, Grassley warned Trump in a tweet that "McKinley sat on his front porch and he didn't campaign and was elected president. So, it is possible for Biden to sit in his basement and not campaign and be elected President." Joe Biden campaigned virtually, from his basement, for much of 2020 because of the pandemic. Grassley was critical of Trump's push for a payroll tax cut in COVID relief packages. Along with GOP Sen. Ron Johnson of Wisconsin, Grassley led an investigation during the race into Biden's son Hunter and his ties to Ukraine; Democrats accused the duo of spreading Russian disinformation. However, when Trump suggested that the election be delayed because of the coronavirus pandemic, Grassley pushed back, telling CNN, "It doesn't matter what one individual in this country says. We are still a country based on the rule of law."

Grassley also has shown an inclination to challenge Wall Street. He attacked the Securities and Exchange Commission in 2011 for failing to detail how it handled nearly 20 referrals of suspicious trading at a major hedge fund. A year earlier, he was one of only four Republicans who voted for the Senate version of the Dodd-Frank financial reforms, although he voted against the final version of the bills. The same year, he was the only Republican to vote with Democrats on the Senate Agriculture Committee for sweeping reform of the derivatives market. He supported the government rescue of the financial industry in 2008, a vote for which he faced criticism from Iowa conservatives.

In February 2016, after the death of Justice Anton in Scalia gave Obama an opportunity to nominate a replacement for his Supreme Court seat, the Republican-controlled Senate took no action to fill the vacancy until after the presidential election. Although it was apparent that McConnell was the driving force, Democrats aimed the bulk of their rhetorical fire at the often independent-minded Grassley—hoping to force him to hold hearings on Obama's choice, Garland, a federal appeals court judge. But Grassley held firm.

Soon after, Trump took office and nominated another appeals court judge, Neil Gorsuch, for the opening. Republicans needed to "go nuclear" to confirm Gorsuch, removing the 60-vote threshold to OK Supreme Court nominees. Opposition to Gorsuch paled in comparison to the hostility aimed at Trump's next nominee, Kavanaugh, who replaced retired Justice Anthony Kennedy, widely viewed as having been the court's swing vote. Christine Blasey Ford, a professor at Palo Alto University, went public with allegations that Kavanaugh had sexually assaulted her at a party more than three decades earlier, when they were both in high school. Kavanaugh denied the charges. Democrats pushed for the FBI to investigate the matter, but Grassley disagreed that the bureau had any role to play and said committee staff were pursuing every lead that had been reported. Kavanaugh responded to Ford's claims in a raw, emotional manner, at times sneering at Democrats on the Judiciary panel. A last-minute deal hatched by Republican Jeff Flake and Democrat Chris Coons led to a favorable, party-line recommendation, but with the agreement that the FBI would conduct a limited investigation into some of the allegations against the nominee. Senators on the fence said the new probe did not change their minds about what they perceived to be a lack of evidence backing up Ford's claims, and Kavanaugh was confirmed 50-48.

For all the partisan rancor on the panel, Grassley refused to give up on a long-sought bipartisan agreement. In 2015, Grassley became interested in the public push for criminal justice reform, then being led by Durbin and Lee, and was ready to cash in any favor or good will to ensure passage. While the First Step Act was narrowed from the original Obama-era proposal, two persistent detractors impeded final passage: Jeff Sessions, who remained outspoken despite having left the Senate to become attorney general, and GOP Sen. Tom Cotton of Arkansas. Trump fired Sessions soon after the 2018 midterms. But Grassley was unable to woo Cotton, and therefore McConnell was uneasy about bringing a bill to the floor that might divide the GOP. Teaming up with Trump and his son-in-law, Jared Kushner, Grassley successfully turned the screws on McConnell. The legislation sailed through on 87-12 vote.

In Iowa, Grassley inherited an 80-acre farm in 1960 and has added to it over the years. It became a 750-acre estate that produced corn and soybeans and is managed by the senator's son Robin. In Washington, Grassley has exhibited a populist skepticism in debates over farm subsidies. He has argued that high payments to individual farmers put the entire agriculture program in political jeopardy. He was one of only 13 senators to vote against the 2018 farm bill. Grassley said the final legislation was too kind to wealthy farmers and offered subsidies to too many people who might not work directly on a farm. In 2020, after coronavirus outbreaks on hog farms had let pigs grow too large to be slaughtered for meat and after farmers had to kill them and dispose of the carcasses, Grassley asked the White House to provide mental health aid to the farmers and compensate them for the pigs that weren't used for meat.

In January 2019, Grassley gave up his Judiciary Committee gavel and resumed his chairmanship of the Finance Committee. The move placed him squarely in debates of fraught issues for his party. Grassley has been critical of Trump's use of tariffs, and the Iowa Republican signaled that he would review the law that the president has used to claim a national security threat to impose tariffs. In another potential blockbuster fight, Grassley said he would like to learn more about the law that would allow his panel access to Trump's tax returns, which the president had refused to release. Grassley used the committee to look out for the interests of his home state. Corn-based ethanol is an important product of Iowa's agribusiness, and Grassley has used his influence to win advantageous tax treatment of ethanol and wind energy, another major industry in the state. Grassley phased out a key tax credit for the wind industry that was set to end in 2020. Along with ranking Democrat Ron Wyden in 2019, Grassley proposed a bill to lower prescription drug prices, but it met resistance from Republicans, including McConnell, over a provision that would limit Medicare drug price increases to the rate of inflation.

In January 2016, Grassley set the record for the longest stretch in the Senate without missing a roll-call vote, a record that went back nearly a quarter-century to July 1993 when he was touring flood damage along the Mississippi River. The 27-year record of 8,927 consecutive roll-call votes was snapped in November 2020, though, when Grassley contracted COVID-19. "I'll be following my doctors' orders/CDC guidelines & continue to quarantine. I'm feeling good + will keep up on my work for the ppl of Iowa from home," he tweeted. Despite his age, Grassley experienced no symptoms. Outside of politics, he is known for his colorful use of Twitter and Instagram. A favorite target of his is the History Channel, which Grassley harangues on social media for programming he has said doesn't live up to the network's name. In one memorable September 2020 tweet, Grassley issued a note of sympathy: "If u lost ur pet pidgin/it's dead in front yard my Iowa farm JUST DISCOVERED.... Sorry for bad news."

Grassley is up for an eighth term in 2022, when he'll be 89—making him 95 at the end of his next term. In late 2020, he told the Washington Post that he still wakes up for runs at 4 a.m., still visits all 99 Iowa counties each year, and has "got a lot of work yet to get done for the people of Iowa." National Republican Senatorial Committee Chairman Rick Scott has said he wants him to run again. Grassley planned to make a decision by the middle of 2021. If the doesn't run again, Grassley's grandson Pat, an Iowa state representative who became House Speaker in 2019, has long been mentioned as a possible successors

Joni Ernst (R)

Elected 2014, term expires 2026, 2nd term, b. Jul 01, 1970; Red Oak, IA; IA State University, B.S., 1992; Columbus State University, M.P.A., 1995; Lutheran; Divorced; 1 child ; 2 stepchildren.

Military Career: U.S. Army Reserves 1992-2001; Iowa Army National Guard 2001-20015 (Iraq)

Elected Office: Montgomery County Auditor, 2005-2011. IA Senate, 2011-2014.

Professional Career: Auditor, Montgomery County IA, 2005-2011.

DC Office: 730 HSOB 20510, 202-224-3254, Fax: 202-224-9369, ernst.senate.gov

State Offices: Cedar Rapids, 319-365-4504; Council Bluffs, 712-352-1167; Davenport, 563-322-0677; Des Moines, 515-284-4574; Sioux City, 712-252-1550.

Committees: Senate Republican Conference Vice Chairman. *Agriculture, Nutrition & Forestry*: Food & Nutrition, Specialty Crops, Organics & Research; Livestock, Dairy, Poultry, Local Food Sys & Food Safety & Sec; Rural Development & Energy (RMM). *Armed Services*: Cybersecurity; Emerging Threats & Capabilities (RMM); Readiness & Management Support. *Environment & Public Works*: Chem Safety, Waste Mngmnt, Enviro Justice & Reg Oversight; Clean Air & Nuclear Safety; Fisheries, Water, and Wildlife. *Small Business & Entrepreneurship*.

Group Ratings

	ADA	ACLU	AFL-CIO	LCV	COC	HAFA	ACU	CFG	FRC
2020	-	15%	-	8%	-	64%	81%	-	-
2019	0%	C	21%	14%	93%	C	83%	45%	100%

Almanac Ratings 2019-2020

	Economy	Social	Foreign	Composite
Liberal	6%	6%	0%	4%
Conservative	94%	94%	100%	96%

Key Votes of the 116th Congress

1. EPA clean energy rules	N	5. Russia sanctions	N	9. Barr as Atty. General	Y
2. U.S./Mex./Can. trade deal	Y	6. Troops in SYR, AFG	Y	10. Spending at the border	Y
3. Cut unemployment benefits	Y	7. Veto arms sales to Saudis	N	11. Coney Barrett to Sup. Ct.	Y
4. Shelton to Fed Reserve	Y	8. Defense $$$, veto override	Y	12. Electoral College objections	N

Election Results

Election	Name (Party)	Vote (%)		Cand. Spent	Ind. Exp. Support	Ind. Exp. Oppose
2020 General	Joni Ernst (R)...............................	864,997	(52%)	$29,495,235	$10,551,628	$81,990,744
	Theresa Greenfield (D).......................	754,859	(45%)	$54,923,249	$24,942,351	$56,297,392
	Rick Stewart (L)................................	36,961	(2%)	$15,120		
2020 Primary	Joni Ernst (R)...............................	226,589	(99%)			

Prior winning percentages: 2014 (52%)

Joni Ernst is a woman of many firsts—the first woman elected to Congress from Iowa, the first female combat veteran elected to the Senate, and the first woman to serve in Senate Republican leadership in a decade. And after the junior senator survived her first reelection battle in a closely watched contest that became one of the expensive Senate races in history, she's likely poised to be an important voice in the chamber for many years to come.

Ernst's arrived in the Senate with an instant high profile after her 2014 victory. Less than a month after she was sworn in to the chamber, Republican leaders tapped her to give the GOP response to President Barack Obama's State of the Union address in 2015. She had a prominent speaking role at the 2016 Republican National Convention in Cleveland Ohio, where she was in high demand as a surrogate before state delegations.

However, in the mold of past senators who have arrived on Capitol Hill with a measure of celebrity but who strived to demonstrate a serious purpose, Ernst said her top priorities were representing her home state and acquiring legislative expertise. After meeting with Donald Trump in July 2016, amid speculation that she was under consideration to be his running mate, Ernst told Politico: "I made that very clear to him that I'm focused on Iowa. I feel that I have a lot more to do in the United States Senate. … I'm just getting started here." But a

run for national office by the 50-year-old can't be ruled out in the future.

Born and raised on a farm in rural Montgomery County in southwest Iowa, Ernst won scholarships to attend Iowa State University, where she majored in psychology; she later earned a master's degree in public administration from Georgia's Columbus State University. She joined the National Guard in 1993 and was deployed to Kuwait during the Iraq War a decade later; she highlighted her status as a veteran and her rank as a lieutenant colonel throughout the 2014 campaign, during which national security was high on voters' list of concerns. At the end of 2015, Ernst retired as a lieutenant colonel after 23 years in the Iowa National Guard, citing her Senate duties and family obligations.

Ernst was elected Montgomery County auditor in 2004, serving two terms before winning election to the state Senate in 2010, taking the seat left vacant by now-Gov. Kim Reynolds. After then-GOP Rep. Tom Latham opted against running for the seat of retiring Sen. Tom Harkin, Ernst became part of a five-way primary to replace the retiring five-term Democrat. Some establishment Republicans stood behind wealthy businessman Mark Jacobs after he indicated a willingness to pump several million dollars of his personal fortune into the race. But her "squeal" ad pushed Ernst to the front of the pack. "I grew up castrating hogs on an Iowa farm. So, when I get to Washington, I'll know how to cut pork. …Washington's full of big spenders, let's make them squeal," she said in a spot that went viral, placed her on the front pages of major newspapers and was the talk of cable TV. Buoyed by her newly found name recognition, she won the primary with 56 percent of the vote. Her success was also rooted in her knack for appealing to both the tea party and establishment wings of the GOP —best summarized by her endorsements from both2008 Republican vice presidential nominee Sarah Palin and the party's 2012 presidential nominee, Mitt Romney.

While Ernst waded through a GOP primary, Rep. Bruce Braley, a former trial lawyer first elected to the House in 2006, glided through his, as the Democratic Party ensured that the field was clear for the man expected to carry on the tradition of Iowa splitting its Senate delegation. But in a testament to Barley's hubris and the power of opposition research, Braley's effort was plagued by gaffes and missteps to such a degree that several political publications and handicappers later anointed his as the worst campaign of 2014. The most notable of those gaffes occurred at a private fundraiser of trial lawyers in Texas, where he was caught on tape deriding the prospect of veteran Sen. Chuck Grassley chairing the Judiciary Committee if the Republicans regained a Senate majority—characterizing Grassley as "a farmer from Iowa who never went to law school, never practiced law." Republican PAC America Rising recorded the clip and weaponized it in an ad campaign that blanketed the state. The comments were widely reported by local and national journalists and fueled the perception that Braley was an out-of-touch elitist, compared to Ernst's folksy image as a small-town Iowan.

Democrats counterattacked by portraying Ernst as a tea party member in the mold of Palin and former Minnesota Rep. Michele Bachmann. Then-Democratic National Committee Chairwoman Debbie Wasserman Schultz called Ernst "an onion of crazy." Braley and his allies hammered away at Ernst's calls to abolish the Education Department and the Environmental Protection Agency, her opposition to federal minimum wage laws, and her support for a "personhood" constitutional amendment to ban all abortions. Democrats griped about Ernst being the Teflon candidate of 2014, and she triumphed 52%-44%. Her election also presaged Trump's surprisingly strong showing in the state two years later and the continued collapse of the state's Democratic Party.

As an Iraq War veteran, Ernst has been a sought-after voice on veterans issues and has advocated a forceful foreign policy in line with the late Sen. John McCain, who campaigned extensively for her. On both the Armed Services and Homeland Security committees, Ernst focused on fighting terrorism and improving care for veterans.

In June 2015, an Ernst amendment to the defense spending bill, which would have allowed the Obama administration to sidestep the Iraqi government and directly arm Kurdish forces fighting the Islamic State terrorist group, was defeated 54-45. A handful of leading Democrats sided with Ernst, while a few fellow GOP conservatives voted against her. She joined a push by several senators from both parties for a new authorization for the use of military force against ISIS. Ernst took a more partisan tack in her speech to the Republican convention, blasting Obama's response to ISIS as "pathetic" and citing FBI reports of an ISIS presence in all 50 states. That speech, focused on military issues, was something of a contrast to her response to Obama's State of the Union address in early 2015, which was heavy on personal retrospective.

She authored a handful of bills that were signed into law by Obama. The Female Veterans Suicide Prevention Act authorized additional studies and treatment programs. Another law allowed the ashes of women who served in World War II to be buried in Arlington National Cemetery for the first time. In 2019, Ernst and Tennessee Republican Sen. Marsha Blackburn became the first Republican women to serve on the Senate Judiciary Committee. They were added after top Senate Republicans were chastised for the lack of women on the panel during the fierce Supreme Court confirmation hearings of Brett Kavanaugh, who was accused of sexual assault. In 2021, she left the Judiciary panel.

During the Trump presidency, Ernst mostly followed the well-worn path of politely criticizing the president and only on major Republican policies like support for free trade and a more robust foreign policy. She also broke with Trump over his decision to ban transgender people from serving in the military and, unlike many other Republicans, she pushed Trump to release his tax returns. When Trump used a vulgarity to describe Central American and African countries, Ernst said she didn't "appreciate the rhetoric" but that the president wasn't racist. And when Trump continued to disparage McCain, Ernst said at a March 2019 town hall that "what I can do is control what I say and do." She joined a handful of her colleagues in expressing concern over Trump's proposal to withdraw troops from Syria.

Like others in the Iowa delegation, she pushed back on EPA Administrator Scott Pruitt's efforts to undermine the Renewable Fuel Standard, a key policy for the powerful bio-fuels lobby in the state. Attacking the EPA was a major selling point for Ernst on the campaign trail and she wasted little time by leading the GOP's charge against the 2014 Clean Water Act, but Obama vetoed the GOP-led efforts to gut his administration's plan. The rule was later stayed in federal court and the Trump administration sought a replacement. In a nod to her campaign appeal to make Washington "squeal," Ernst sponsored bills aimed at gutting the federal bureaucracy and burnishing herself an image as a Washington outsider. Those proposals included cutting taxpayer money given to former presidents, nixing a tax write-off that members of Congress use for their time in Washington and even moving federal agencies from Washington.

In January 2019, affidavits from her divorce became public, revealing she alleged her husband had physically abused her. "I am a survivor," she said at a Cedar Falls town hall. "What I want people to understand is that I am the same person as I was last week. You just know more about what's inside of me now." In an interview with Bloomberg News, Ernst also revealed she had been raped in college. "I didn't want to share it with anybody, and in the era of #Me Too survivors, I always believed that every person is different, and they will confront their demons when they're ready. ... And I was not ready," Ernst said, noting she'd decided to open up only after the details of her divorce made news. Later in 2019, she accused Sen. Chuck Schumer, then the minority leader, of blocking her version of a bill authorizing the Violence Against Women Act to harm her reelection bid. Ernst's version would have reauthorized domestic violence grant programs and recognized sex trafficking as a form of sexual assault. Schumer criticized Ernst's bill for not barring people convicted of stalking or dating violence from obtaining a firearm.

As Ernst headed into her first reelection campaign though, Democrats were eager to portray her as a Trump lackey and pointed to her 91 percent voting record with the president. In July 2020, Ernst said on "Iowa Press" that Trump had shown early leadership on the coronavirus pandemic by shutting down travel from China, but she had criticized Obama for not showing "that same quick reactionary type of leadership" during the Ebola outbreak. Only four U.S. patients ever tested positive for the disease, while of millions contracted COVID-19, the disease caused by the novel coronavirus. While Ernst had also had a 57 percent approval rating in February 2019, by March 2020 it had slipped 10 points, according to Iowa pollster J. Ann Selzer. That gave Democrats further hope they could knock off Ernst.

Several Democrats vied for the chance to challenge Ernst, but commercial real estate executive Theresa Greenfield was the choice of the national party, earning the endorsement of the Democratic Senatorial Campaign Committee early in the race. Greenfield's only other attempt at elected office had come in 2018 when she ran for the 3rd District congressional seat, but she didn't qualify for the ballot after it was revealed her campaign manager had falsified signatures on her petition. Outside Democratic groups, such as Senate Majority PAC, spent early to try and damage Ernst's image in the state while boosting Greenfield's. The businesswoman had a compelling personal story she told in ads too: Her husband died on the job as a union electrician while she was caring for their young toddler and pregnant with their second child; she talked about how Social Security benefits are what saved her family and enabled her to rebuild her life, and she blasted Ernst for saying that lawmakers should discuss changing the entitlement program "behind closed doors." Greenfield would go on to win the four-way primary with nearly 48 percent of the vote.

Throughout the summer, the race became more and more competitive and became a key contest for Democrats hoping to win back control of the Senate. From the summer onward, Greenfield steadily outraised Ernst, and she turned the catchphrase that garnered acclaim for Ernst back on her. "Sen. Ernst told Iowans in 2014 she was going to be independent and different and she was going to 'make 'me squeal. The bottom line: Nobody's squealing except Iowans," Greenfield told the New York Times. She slammed Ernst for not curtailing federal spending, for accepting corporate PAC donations, and for voting to repeal the Affordable Care Act and its protections for preexisting conditions. Ernst tied Greenfield to national Democrats and positions unpopular in Iowa, such as the democratic socialist wing of the party and "defunding" the police. In debates, the disdain between the two women was palpable. But in their third and final debate, Ernst stumbled when asked what the break-even price for soybeans was, undercutting it by almost $5. (Greenfield had correctly answered a question about the price of corn). Greenfield and Democrats used the gaffe to underscore that Ernst was out of touch with Iowa, especially on agriculture, one of the most important issues in the state.

Nonetheless, the final poll from Selzer and the Des Moines Register showed Ernst jumping back into first, along with Trump, who widened his lead. On Election Day, that predicted surge was proved right when Ernst defeated Greenfield by 7 percentage points, 52%-45%. Greenfield's loss was a major blow to Democrats hoping to flip the Senate, but two Georgia runoffs later proved decisive. Ernst's race was the most expensive in Iowa history, topping $261.6 million; Democrats outspent Republican on ads by $39.7 million.

Ashley Hinson (R)

Elected 2020, 1st term, b. Jun 27, 1983; Des Moines, IA; University of Southern CA, B.A.; Christian Church; Married (Matthew Arenholz); 2 children.

Elected Office: IA House, 2017-2021.

Professional Career: Anchor/Reporter/Producer, KCRG-TV9, 2005-2015; Consulting Associate, 2016-2019.

DC Office: 1429 LHOB 20515, 202-225-2911, hinson.house.gov

State Offices: Cedar Rapids, 319-364-2288; Dubuque, 563-557-7789; Waterloo, 319-266-6925.

Committees: *Appropriations*: Homeland Security; Transportation, HUD & Related Agencies. *Budget*.

Election Results

Election	Name (Party)	Vote (%)		Cand. Spent	Ind. Exp. Support	Ind. Exp. Oppose
2020 General	Ashley Hinson (R)	212,088	(51%)	$5,022,294	$780,389	$4,087,678
	Abby Finkenauer (D)	201,347	(49%)	$5,816,365	$372,415	$4,816,939
2020 Primary	Ashley Hinson (R)	38,552	(78%)			
	Thomas Hansen (R)	10,845	(22%)			

Republican Ashley Hinson defeated first-term Rep. Abby Finkenauer of Iowa in one of the nation's most volatile swing districts. Her victory marked the third time in the past four elections that party control of the district flipped. A former television news reporter in Cedar Rapids who later served in the state House, Hinson likely benefited from the comfortable statewide victories by President Donald Trump and Sen. Joni Ernst.

A native of West Des Moines, Hinson got her bachelor's degree in broadcast journalism from the University of Southern California. Returning to Iowa, she spent more than a decade as a reporter and news anchor for KCRG-TV in Cedar Rapids, which boosted her name recognition in most of the 1st Congressional District. (She began some of her campaign ads, "I'm Ashley Hinson, you might know me from the morning news.")

Hinson launched her political career, she said, "because I got tired of talking about problems and instead wanted to work on solving those problems." She served four years in the state House, where she chaired the Transportation Committee and was vice chair of the Appropriations Committee. Local Republicans were impressed that she won two terms in her state House district, where Hillary Clinton led in the 2016 presidential race.

After Hinson declared her candidacy in May 2019, former Republican Rep. Rod Blum—who lost, 51%-46%, to Finkenauer in 2018—explored a return to the House.GOP Gov. Kim Reynolds endorsed Hinson in October 2019 and said that she would "do the hard work of building consensus," which signaled that Hinson had rallied party leaders. The governor's endorsement was intended, in part, to discourage other Republican candidates. Hinson won the GOP primary with 78 percent of the vote against Thomas Hansen, a cattle rancher.

Finkenauer, in her 2018 election, shared with Democratic Rep. Alexandria Ocasio-Cortez of New York the distinction of being the only women elected to the House before they turned 30. Emphasizing her blue-collar roots, Finkenauer criticized Hinson for supporting state legislation to roll back collective-bargaining rights for public employees. Hinson responded that Iowa policy previously "had gone in favor of labor unions. "

Hinson sought to link Finkenauer with national Democratic ideologues and leaders. "She has praised the Green New Deal, which would devastate Iowa farmers," including the bio-fuels industry, Hinson said. "Abby casts her vote with Nancy Pelosi 91 percent of the time. " Finkenauer agreed to only one debate, which was in early September.

In its editorial endorsement of Finkenauer, the Waterloo Telegraph Herald wrote that each candidate was "a strong, articulate woman who knows the issues and cares about Iowans." It praised the incumbent's ideas as "old-school Democratic" and said she had made "an impact" in Congress.

The two candidates spent about $10 million and the national parties and their allies spent another $10 million, with the funds split nearly evenly by the two sides.

Hinson won 51%-49%, a margin of a bit more than 10,000 votes. Finkenauer led by a total of about 20,000 votes in the three largest counties—Cedar Rapids-based Linn, Waterloo-based Black Hawk, and Dubuque. Together, they cast three-fifths of the total vote. Hinson won the remaining counties with larger majorities, mostly with at least 60 percent of the vote.

In the House, she got seats on the Appropriations—which is rare for a freshman—and Budget committees.

IA-1: Northeast Iowa   Cook Partisan Voting Index: R+4

Population		Race and Ethnicity		Income	
Total	774,014	White	90.50%	Median Income	$61,542
Land area (sq. miles)	12,049	Black	4.20%	District Income Rank	239
Pop/ sq mi	64.24	Latino	4.30%	Poverty Rate	11.60%
Born in State	73.40%	Asian	1.60%	With health insurance	95.80%
		Two or more races	2.30%	Cash public assistance	1.60%
Age Groups		Other	1.40%	Food stamp/SNAP	9.10%
Under 18	22.60%				
18-34	22.10%	Education		Work	
35-64	37.10%	H.S grad or less	40.40%	White Collar	35.30%
Over 64	18.40%	Some college	31.80%	Sales and Service	35.80%
		College Degree, 4 yr	19.00%	Blue Collar	28.90%
Military		Post grad	8.60%	Government	12.90%
Veteran/ Active Duty	7.80%				

2020 Pres. Vote	Trump	213,601	(51%)	Biden	199,259	(47%)		
2016 Pres. Vote	Trump	190,410	(48%)	Clinton	176,535	(45%)	Johnson	15,661 (4%)

Cedar Rapids, Dubuque, Waterloo: Northeast Iowa, along the Mississippi River and westward, has some of the loveliest landscape in America. Here the Mississippi flows past green bluffs, then broadens out in great quiet pools alongside picturesque towns. A century and a half ago, as settlers surged west of the Mississippi, Germans stopped at the river bluffs reminiscent of their native land and built neat farmhouses and substantial towns. Inland, on the rolling hills portrayed with surprisingly little exaggeration in the paintings of Iowa's Grant Wood, and in the more open territory to the west, New England Yankees and Midwesterners built their characteristic farmhouses, barns, town halls, church spires and small colleges. Railroad companies, headquartered in Chicago, extended their networks of steel rails over the plains and rivers.

Dubuque is a self-styled green city that has some large factories but is also proud of its waterfront-generated tourism. Local leaders cite their vision of a "Sustainable Dubuque," which allowed them to transform a rusting city in the 1980s into a successful place that rejuvenated urban life. In 2013, the program adopted a goal of 50 percent reduction in greenhouse gas emissions by 2030. As of 2019, it had achieved a 27 percent cut. Among the longstanding employers in Dubuque is John Deere, which employs about 2,000 people locally and has boosted its output of crawler products, a large and powerful tractor.

Southwest of Dubuque is Cedar Rapids, Iowa's second-largest city. It sports high-tech employers and contemporary office buildings. Unlike most of Iowa, its population boomed in the past two decades, and its per capita income rose. Both Cedar Rapids and Waterloo "built an internet infrastructure in the mid-1990s to draw technology companies to the area," then nurtured small technology companies, the Des Moines Register reported. The production of ethanol and other bio-fuels in Cedar Rapids contributed to its economic health. Although ethanol production slumped in recent years, C.R. continued to produce more ethanol than any other city in the world. Statewide, Iowa in 2020 produced about 30 percent of the nation's ethanol. Cedar Rapids remains the number-one corn-processing city in the world. Traditional industries remain a mainstay: Go down by the Cedar River and you can't miss the smell of cooking oats coming from the Quaker Oats and General Mills factories. In August 2020, Cedar Rapids was devastated by a derecho storm, with wind gusts up to 112 miles per hour. The storm removed 550,000 acres of crops from harvesting, the U.S. Department of Agriculture reported. "This is Iowa's Katrina," said a county supervisor, referring to the 2005 hurricane that levelled large parts of coastal Louisiana and Mississippi.

In rural Marshalltown, about midway from Cedar Rapids to Des Moines, Latino workers have filled a large share of the 2,700 jobs at the town's large meat-processing plant. In the town, where nearly one-third of the 27,000 residents are Latinos, Hispanic educational and cultural programs have flourished. In April 2020, 34 workers at the plant tested positive for COVID-19 in the plant's crowded working conditions.

The 1st Congressional District covers much of northeast Iowa, including the Mississippi riverfront and Cedar Rapids, Dubuque and Waterloo. Politically, this has become a swing district. Dubuque, heavily German Catholic, for years has been Iowa's most Democratic city, unless abortion rights are the issue. In 2012, President Barack Obama won 56%-42% and took 17 counties. In 2016, Donald Trump won the 1st, 49%-45%. He led in 18 of the 20 counties, losing only Cedar Rapids-based Linn and Waterloo-based Black Hawk. In his reelection bid, Trump improved to 51 percent.

Mariannette Miller-Meeks (R)

Elected 2020, 1st term, b. Sep 06, 1955; Herlong, CA; San Antonia Junior College; University of IA; TX Christian University, B.S.N., 1976; University of Southern CA, M.S., 1980; University of TX Health Science Center, San Antonia, M.S., 1980; University of MI, 1994; Roman Catholic; Married (Curt Meeks); 2 children.

Military Career: Operating and Ward Nurse, U.S Army, Walter Reed Army Hospital, 1976-1982; Medical Services, U.S. Army Reserves, 1983-2000; Lt. Colonel, U.S. Army.

Elected Office: Director, IA Department of Public Health, 2011-2013; IA Senate, 2019-2021.

Professional Career: Ophthalmologist; Councilor for IA American Academy of Ophthalmology, 2003-2009; President, Medical Staff, Ottumwa Regional Health Center.

DC Office: 1716 LHOB 20515, 202-225-6576, Fax: 202-226-0757, millermeeks.house.gov

State Offices: Davenport, 563-323-5988.

Committees: *Education & Labor*: Higher Education & Workforce Investment; Workforce Protections. *Homeland Security*: Emergency Preparedness, Response & Recovery; Transportation & Maritime Security. *Veterans' Affairs*: Disability Assistance & Memorial Affairs; Health.

Election Results

Election	Name (Party)	Vote (%)		Cand. Spent	Ind. Exp. Support	Ind. Exp. Oppose
2020 General	Mariannette Miller-Meeks (R)............. 196,964	(50%)		$1,675,552	$355,690	$7,486,506
	Rita Hart (D)................................ 196,958	(50%)		$4,024,304	$86,393	$6,481,579
2020 Primary	Mariannette Miller-Meeks (R)............... 23,052	(48%)				
	Bobby Schilling (R)....................... 17,582	(36%)				
	Steven Everly (R)................................ 2,806	(6%)				
	Rick Phillips (R)...................................... 2,444	(5%)				

Republican Mariannette Miller-Meeks won the closest House contest of 2020 and took the open seat of retiring Democratic Rep. Dave Loebsack. An ophthalmologist, she served 24 years in the U.S. Army. Later, she opened her medical practice in Ottumwa and taught at the University of Iowa. Miller-Meeks, who lost three challenges to Loebsack, defeated Rita Hart, who was the unsuccessful Democratic nominee for lieutenant governor in 2018.

A native of Her long California, in that state's rural northeast corner, Miller-Meeks got a bachelor's degree in nursing from Texas Christian University, a master's of science in education from the University of Southern California and her medical degree from the University of Texas (Houston). She decided to become a physician, she said, after recovering from severe burns that she and her brother suffered from a fire at home, when she was in high school.

After retiring from the Army as a lieutenant colonel and settling in Ottumwa, Miller-Meeks organized a program to recruit physicians to southeast Iowa. She was the first woman to serve as president of the Iowa Medical Society. From 2010 to 2013, she was the director of the Iowa Department of Public Health under Republican Gov. Terry Branstad.

In her unsuccessful challenges to Loebsack, Miller-Meeks lost 52%-47% in 2014, 51%-46% in 2010 and 57%-39% in 2008. She was elected in 2018 to the state Senate, where she chaired the Human Resources Committee for one year and was vice chair of the Veterans' Affairs Committee.

When Loebsack announced his retirement, Miller-Meeks was the frontrunner for the Republican nomination. She faced an unusual challenge in the GOP primary from former Rep. Bobby Schilling, who served two years in the Illinois district across the Mississippi River before switching his residence to Iowa's 2nd Congressional District; he lost his seat in 2012 to Democrat Cheri Bustos, who chaired the Democratic Congressional Campaign Committee in 2019-20. Miller-Meeks more than doubled Schilling's spending and won the primary, 48%-36%.

Hart, who earlier served in the state Senate and was a farmer and school teacher, was unopposed for the Democratic nomination for the congressional seat. During the campaign, Miller-Meeks described herself as a "pro-Trump conservative," though she occasionally went her own way on issues.

During their campaign debates, the candidates sparred over healthcare issues, Iowa Public Radio reported. Hart spotlighted Republican failure to offer a specific plan that would cover pre-existing conditions. Miller-Meeks denied that she wanted to repeal the Affordable Care Act and said that health care needed to be "affordable, portable, accessible…and it needs to be able to give us choice." She criticized Hart for her vote as a state senator in favor of a bill that would approve a Farm Bureau insurance plan that failed to cover pre-existing conditions.

Hart won editorial endorsements from newspapers in Des Moines, Quad Cities and Iowa City. Her campaign spending, which exceeded $4 million, more than doubled the spending by Miller-Meeks. The national parties spent more than $14 million on the contest, with a nearly even split.

The razor-thin outcome, which the state canvassing board certified as a six-vote victory for Miller-Meeks of more than 394,000 that were cast, resulted from her winning 20 of the 24 counties, taking at least two-thirds of the vote in nine of those counties. Hart led in the three largest counties: Scott, Clinton and University of Iowa-based Johnson, which she won 70%-30%. The victory by Miller-Meeks made her the third Republican woman in the six-member Iowa congressional delegation.

IA-2: Southeast Iowa   **Cook Partisan Voting Index: R+4**

Population		Race and Ethnicity		Income	
Total	782,989	White	88.60%	Median Income	$59,569
Land area (sq. miles)	12,262	Black	4.90%	District Income Rank	270
Pop/ sq mi	63.86	Latino	5.80%	Poverty Rate	12.90%
Born in State	66.80%	Asian	2.50%	With health insurance	94.00%
		Two or more races	2.60%	Cash public assistance	1.80%
Age Groups		Other	1.50%	Food stamp/SNAP	10.40%
Under 18	22.00%				
18-34	23.30%	**Education**		**Work**	
35-64	37.10%	H.S grad or less	39.80%	White Collar	37.50%
Over 64	17.70%	Some college	31.90%	Sales and Service	34.70%
		College Degree, 4 yr	17.50%	Blue Collar	27.90%
Military		Post grad	10.80%	Government	17.40%
Veteran/ Active Duty	8.10%				

2020 Pres. Vote	Trump	209,858	(51%)	Biden	193,437	(47%)			
2016 Pres. Vote	Trump	186,384	(49%)	Clinton	170,796	(44%)	Johnson	13,719	(4%)

Davenport, Iowa City: Southeast Iowa is a land of rolling hills and deep river valleys, of undulant farm fields and big skies, of prosperous small towns and grain elevators and factories. In the southeastern part of the state, one can find Iowa's contributions to the Quad Cities along the Mississippi River and the Illinois border. Bettendorf is where riverboat gambling was launched in the U.S. in 1991.Davenport, on the hills over the Mississippi, still has the look of the city where Ronald Reagan got his first radio job. Now, its largest employers are John Deere and the Rock Island Arsenal.

Other manufacturers in the area have had ups and downs. In May 2020, Procter & Gamble reversed an announcement two years earlier that it was cutting 500 jobs from its Iowa City plant, moving its hair care and body wash sections to West Virginia. Instead, it planned to keep many of those jobs in Iowa. In October 2019, Gov. Kim Reynolds announced investment in the educational technology sector in the corridor between Iowa City and Cedar Rapids. A study showed more than 3,100 employees in that sector already working locally. Iowa City, a university town dotted with trendy bookstores and vegetarian eateries, has been ranked among America's most gay-friendly cities. Its officials voted in 2017 to become a "sanctuary city," saying they wouldn't take steps to enforce federal immigration law.

Muscatine County, on the banks of the Mississippi River, has a legacy of abundant farm work in the area and, more recently, jobs at the Tyson Foods pork processing plant in nearby Columbus Junction. Hundreds of workers who perform grueling jobs at the plant have been Burmese refugees. Since a 2008 raid of an Iowa slaughterhouse, where nearly 400 immigrants were arrested, companies reported that they have become more careful about hiring only employees with legal papers.

The 2nd Congressional District covers the southeast quadrant of the state, with regularly shaped lines. Its population centers are Davenport and Iowa City. Politically, the district has been more progressive, thanks mostly to big Democratic majorities in Iowa City. In 2012, Barack Obama took the district, 56%-43%. But the next two elections brought a shift: Donald Trump won 49%-45% and then 51%-47% (the same outcomes each time, as in the neighboring 1st District).He won every county except for Iowa City-based Johnson and Davenport-based Scott, which are the two largest counties in the 2nd. Joe Biden took Johnson, 71%-27%.

Cindy Axne (D)

Elected 2018, 2nd term, b. Apr 20, 1965; Des Moines, IA; Drake University; University of IA, B.A., 1987; Northwestern University, M.B.A., 2002; Catholic; Married (John Axne); 2 children.

Professional Career: Chicago Tribune Media Group, 2000-2003; Administrator, IA Department of Administrative Services, 2005-2007, IA Department of Management, 2007-2010, IA Department of Natural Resources, 2010-2014; Principal, Axne Consulting Group, 2014-2016.

DC Office: 330 CHOB 20515, 202-225-5476, axne.house.gov

State Offices: Council Bluffs, 712-890-3117; Creston, 202-225-5476; Des Moines, 515-400-8180.

Committees: *Agriculture*: Commodity Exchanges, Energy & Credit; Livestock & Foreign Agriculture. *Financial Services*: Housing, Community Development & Insurance; Investor Protection, Entrepreneurship & Capital Markets.

Almanac Ratings 2019-2020

	Economy	Social	Foreign	Composite
Liberal	54%	48%	80%	61%
Conservative	46%	52%	20%	39%

Key Votes of the 116th Congress

1. U.S./Mex./Can. trade deal Y	5. Russia sanctions Y	9. Firearms background checks Y
2. First Coronavirus response Y	6. Troops in Syria Y	10. Spending at the border Y
3. HEROES Act N	7. Veto arms sales to Saudis Y	11. Marijuana liberalized rules Y
4. CASH Act Y	8. Defense $$$, veto override Y	12. Electoral College objections N

Election Results

Election	Name (Party)	Vote (%)		Cand. Spent	Ind. Exp. Support	Ind. Exp. Oppose
2020 General	Cindy Axne (D)	219,205	(49%)	$6,280,742	$6,405	$1,232,389
	David Young (R)	212,997	(48%)	$3,044,265	$31,508	$2,656,530
	Bryan Holder (L)	15,361	(3%)			
2020 Primary	Cindy Axne (D)	76,681	(99%)			

Prior winning percentages: 2018 (49%)

Democratic Rep. Cindy Axne secured a second term by beating former Republican Rep. David Young in a rematch, even as Donald Trump again narrowly carried the district. Axne represents the most urban of the state's four districts and it was Des Moines that powered her win, but in Congress she has become a forceful advocate for the rural parts of her district. She was the only one of Iowa's four House members to return for another term, as her three colleagues either retired, lost reelection or lost re-nomination.

Axne grew up in Des Moines and graduated from the University of Iowa with a degree in journalism. She got a masters' in business administration from the Kellogg School at Northwestern University. She worked on strategic planning for the Tribune Company in Chicago and started a digital-design business with her husband, John.

When their first son started kindergarten in Des Moines, Axne was outraged to learn that some local children did not have access to a full-day program. Complaining about the inequality, she organized an advocacy group and negotiated for nearly a year with school officials before gaining their agreement to make full-day kindergarten available to all local students. Later, she worked for nearly a decade with more than 20 Iowa state agencies under governors from both parties to assist in improving the delivery of services.

Axne's first campaign got a boost when Theresa Greenfield, a business executive, learned at the March 2018 filing deadline that her advisor had forged signatures that were required for all candidates. Her disqualification left Axne with two other contenders in the Democratic primary. Styling herself as a problem-solver, Axne easily won the primary over runner-up Eddie Mauro, 58%-26%.

In a district where the farm economy is vital, even in urban areas, Young found himself at odds with Trump over his trade war with China and the resulting tariffs on many crops. Still, Trump remained popular in many rural communities, including places where farmers were losing business. A former chief of staff to Iowa Sen. Chuck Grassley, Young had shown his political skills by gaining a seat on the House Appropriations Committee.

Like other successful House Democratic challengers in 2018, Axne was a strong fundraiser. She spent more than $4 million, which nearly doubled the spending by Young. In her 2-point victory, Axne got 56 percent in Polk County, which cast a bit more than half of the total vote. Axne rebuffed attempts by Senate Democrats to recruit her for a challenge against Republican Sen. Joni Ernst. (Ironically, the 2018 frontrunner for Axne's seat, Theresa Greenfield, disappointed Democrats as the challenger to Ernst.)

In her first term, Axne burnished her centrist credentials, joining the New Democrat Coalition and noting in a Des Moines Register column that she introduced a bipartisan bill with Ernst on the day the House voted Trump's impeachment. From her perch on the Agriculture Committee, she sponsored legislation to promote loan forgiveness for rural business and communities and publicly admonished Senate Majority Leader Mitch McConnell for delaying a vote on the revised trade deal with Mexico and Canada.

After Axne voted for the two articles of impeachment, Young hoped to take advantage of the local outrage by seeking a rematch. Part of his comeback plan was to turnout 2016 Trump voters who stayed home in 2018. Democrats saw presidential-level turnout in the midterms, while Republicans did not, he told Politico. "They may have peaked or are getting close to peaking, but Republicans have so much more room to grow."

Ultimately that was not the case. Axne spent a whopping $6.3 million to Young's $3.1 million. In TV ads, Democrats reprised a 2018 attack, warning that Young would gut protections for pre-existing conditions and an Axne spot warned that Young would ban all abortions, even in cases of rape and incest. Republicans tied Axne to Speaker Nancy Pelosi and accused her of failing to protect rural hospitals. By mid-October, GOP super PACs grew so pessimistic they stopped their ad buys supporting Young.

In the end, turnout exceeded both 2016 and 2012 and Axne won by about 6,200 votes. The midterms were not a ceiling for Democrats; Joe Biden lost to Trump by fewer than 1,000 votes in the district. After Republicans reclaimed the two other Democratic-held seats in Iowa, Axne became a top 2022 target. She is unlikely to be seriously affected by redistricting because Iowa starts, at least, as a nonpartisan process to draw the new districts and her Des Moines base is likely to remain whole. One potential opponent is GOP state Sen. Zach Nunn, who considered a 2020 bid but declined after Young jumped in the race.

IA-3: Southwest Iowa

Cook Partisan Voting Index: R+3

Population		Race and Ethnicity		Income	
Total	848,170	White	88.20%	Median Income	$67,681
Land area (sq. miles)	8,790	Black	5.20%	District Income Rank	185
Pop/ sq mi	96.5	Latino	7.20%	Poverty Rate	9.40%
Born in State	67.30%	Asian	3.70%	With health insurance	95.30%
		Two or more races	1.70%	Cash public assistance	1.80%
Age Groups		Other	1.20%	Food stamp/SNAP	10.20%
Under 18	24.40%				
18-34	22.20%	**Education**		**Work**	
35-64	38.20%	H.S grad or less	33.30%	White Collar	43.20%
Over 64	15.20%	Some college	31.50%	Sales and Service	34.80%
		College Degree, 4 yr	24.60%	Blue Collar	22.00%
Military		Post grad	10.60%	Government	12.50%
Veteran/ Active Duty	7.40%				

2020 Pres. Vote	Trump	224,726	(49%)	Biden	224,159	(49%)		
2016 Pres. Vote	Trump	192,960	(48%)	Clinton	178,937	(45%)	Johnson	16,693	(4%)

Des Moines, Council Bluffs: Iowa, which today seems very much in the middle of the country, was once part of the West. It was not only the home of sober farmers and pious burghers, but also the eastern terminus of the first transcontinental railroad, a way station for people in a hurry to get across the Great Plains to the Rockies and the Pacific Northwest. Those who stayed behind used the wealth accumulated by methodical husbandry of their fertile farmlands to implant firmly the glories of Western Civilization. One can feel that impulse today in Des Moines, looking across the river from downtown to the Victorian capitol, its gold dome above a Corinthian pediment. Terrace Hill, the beautifully restored governor's mansion, sits atop a rise overlooking the Raccoon River.

The city of Des Moines remains classically Middle American, even as it gains a livelier downtown and spreads into the countryside. The area has become a sanctuary for people looking for a family-friendly urban lifestyle. Insurance, agricultural supply, printing and financial service businesses have expanded in office centers downtown and at freeway interchanges. It has one of the nation's highest concentrations of financial services and insurance jobs. Principal Financial Group employs more than 6,400 people in the area and in April 2019 it bought Wells Fargo's retirement division for $1.2 billion. Kemin Industries, which makes nutritional ingredients, wrapped up a five-year expansion of its headquarters in 2017. More than 12,000 Bosnians have settled in Des Moines, many of whom work at meatpacking.

Des Moines and the southwest corner of Iowa make up the 3rd Congressional District. The second-most populous city here is Council Bluffs, home to the mansion of Gen. Grenville Dodge, who in 1859 lobbied Illinois lawyer Abraham Lincoln on the need for a transcontinental railroad. Lincoln got it through Congress in 1862, Dodge became its chief engineer, and Council Bluffs became its eastern terminus when it was completed in 1869. Surrounded by beef-grazing territory, Council Bluffs looks west across the Missouri River to Omaha, taking on the culturally more conservative tone of Nebraska. The area has developed an economically hip side with a dozen data centers owned by Microsoft, Amazon, Google and Facebook, at a total cost of more than $10 billion. Iowa has become an attractive place for these facilities because of its tax incentives, plenty of cheap land and access to high-speed fiber optics.

The small rural towns, where businesses have been struggling, were fertile ground in 2016 for Donald Trump, who won the 3rd district, 48%-45%. In October 2018, politics in the district shifted again. For the first time since 2012, registered Democrats outnumbered Republicans. Like other suburban districts that Democrats won in the midterms, the 3rd has become wealthier and more educated over the past decade, with the median household income jumping $15,000 from 2009 to 2019. In 2020, Trump carried the district by the slimmest of margins, less than half a percentage point —his weakest performance in Iowa's four districts. Joe Biden won Polk County by 15 percentage points, besting Hillary Clinton's 12-point margin. And he came within two percentage points of capturing neighboring Dallas County, which Clinton lost by 10 points.

Randy Feenstra (R)

Elected 2020, 1st term, b. Jan 14, 1969; Hull, IA; IA State University, M.P.A.; Dordt College, B.A., 1991; Protestant - Unspecified Christian; Married (Lynette Feenstra); 4 children.

Elected Office: Treasurer, Sioux County, 2006-2008; IA Senate, 2009-2021.

DC Office: 1440 LHOB 20515, 202-225-4426, Fax: 202-225-3193, feenstra.house.gov

State Offices: Fort Dodge, 515-302-7060; Sioux City, 712-224-4692.

Committees: *Agriculture*: Commodity Exchanges, Energy & Credit; Livestock & Foreign Agriculture. *Budget*. *Science, Space & Technology*: Energy; Environment.

Election Results

Election	Name (Party)	Vote (%)		Cand. Spent	Ind. Exp. Support	Ind. Exp. Oppose
2020 General	Randy Feenstra (R)........................ 237,369	(62%)	$1,979,066	$476,501	$113
	J. D. Scholten (D)............................... 144,761	(38%)	$2,968,322	$303	$3,000
2020 Primary	Randy Feenstra (R)........................ 37,329	(46%)			
	Steve King (R)................................. 29,366	(36%)			
	Jeremy Taylor (R)............................. 6,418	(8%)			
	Bret Richards (R)............................. 6,140	(8%)			

Republican Randy Feenstra, a state senator, was elected to the House in 2020 after he defeated controversial Rep. Steve King of Iowa in the GOP primary. His victory culminated a months long effort orchestrated by influential Republicans in Washington D.C. and Iowa who believed the nine-term incumbent's history of racist remarks reflected poorly on the party and jeopardized the solidly Republican seat. Several outside groups hammered home the same campaign message: King had lost his clout and could no longer effectively serve Iowa.

Feenstra grew up in Hull, a town of fewer than 3,000 residents. He graduated from Dordt University and received a master's degree from Iowa State. He worked for seven years as sales manager for the Foreign Candy Company before joining local government. He served as Hull city manager and then as Sioux County treasurer. In 2008, Feenstra was elected to a safely Republican open seat in the state Senate, with no competition in the GOP primary that year or during his two reelections.

During his congressional career, King sparked controversy with frequent comments that disparaged immigrants and the concept of multiculturalism. He frequently endorsed far right politicians from Europe and Canada who espoused white nationalist or anti-Semitic views.

In 2018, National Republican Congressional Committee Chairman Steve Stivers of Ohio publicly condemned King's comments and declared that the House GOP campaign arm would not support his reelection. King won, 50%-47%, against well-funded Democratic challenger J.D. Scholten, an embarrassing showing for King in a district that President Donald Trump won with 60 percent of the vote in 2016.

In response, Iowa Republicans decided to recruit a primary challenger. GOP Gov. Kim Reynolds said she would no longer endorse King. Feenstra entered the race in January 2019 with Reynolds allies on his campaign team.

The following day, King was quoted in a New York Times story posing a rhetorical question: "White nationalist, white supremacist, Western civilization—how did that language become offensive?" King later tried to backtrack, saying that he was a nationalist and a supporter of "western civilization's values." House Minority Leader Kevin McCarthy stripped King of his committee assignments, including his spot on the Agriculture Committee that was vital for his constituents.

Feenstra ran circles around King, spending nearly $1 million in the primary to King's $400,000, a paltry sum for an incumbent. King failed to run a single broadcast ad in the primary.

Feenstra was endorsed by a wide range of Republican supporters, including former Iowa Gov. Terry Branstad and Bob Van Der Plaats, an evangelical leader in the state. He was backed by a coalition of super PAC's that was run by a Reynolds ally and included the U.S. Chamber of Commerce, the Republican Main Street Partnership, the Republican Jewish Coalition and the National Right to Life Committee. In a rare rebuke of a colleague, five House Republicans donated to Feenstra.

Feenstra and his allies steered clear of directly criticizing King, wary of alienating his base and his deeply conservative supporters. Instead, they cast him as ineffective. The Chamber of Commerce broadcast an ad that slammed King for failing to achieve results for Iowa farmers. Feenstra won the primary, 44%-35%, with three other candidates splitting the remaining vote.

Scholten ran a second time, with a well-funded and populist campaign. But he had no chance to overcome a credible Republican in this district. Feenstra won with 62 percent of the vote, the only district in Iowa that was not competitive in 2020.

In the House, Feenstra was assigned to the Agriculture, Budget, and Science, Space and Technology committees.

IA-4: Northwest and Central Iowa   **Cook Partisan Voting Index: R+16**

Population		Race and Ethnicity		Income	
Total	749,897	White	92.50%	Median Income	$58,270
Land area (sq. miles)	22,757	Black	2.00%	District Income Rank	287
Pop/ sq mi	32.95	Latino	7.70%	Poverty Rate	11.00%
Born in State	71.70%	Asian	1.70%	With health insurance	94.80%
		Two or more races	2.10%	Cash public assistance	1.90%
Age Groups		Other	1.80%	Food stamp/SNAP	8.20%
Under 18	22.30%				
18-34	22.80%	Education		Work	
35-64	35.80%	H.S grad or less	40.60%	White Collar	34.40%
Over 64	19.10%	Some college	34.00%	Sales and Service	35.30%
		College Degree, 4 yr	17.50%	Blue Collar	30.20%
Military		Post grad	7.90%	Government	14.70%
Veteran/ Active Duty	7.50%				

2020 Pres. Vote	Trump	249,487	(63%)	Biden	142,206	(36%)		
2016 Pres. Vote	Trump	231,229	(60%)	Clinton	127,401	(33%)	Johnson	13,113	(3%)

Sioux City, Ames: Sioux City, one of the oldest market towns on the Great Plains, is nestled in the Loess Bluffs above the Missouri River. Sioux City has not grown much in the past half century. Its original economic base has become obsolete: The waterfront, once raucous with boatmen and stockyard workers, is now quiet. The stockyards, which employed thousands of people and slaughtered millions of hogs during their peak years in the 1920s, are shuttered. Downtown stores have been replaced by shopping malls at the edge of town, where people spend a day doing a season's shopping and then drive for hours to return to farm communities in one of four nearby states.

There are still plenty of hogs in western Iowa. Instead of meeting sellers in the markets in Sioux City, packers now contract directly with large farms and have built modern slaughterhouses nearby. Tyson Foods has facilities in Buena Vista and Crawford counties. Storm Lake, in Buena Vista County, is more than 60 percent non-White, attracting immigrants and refugees from Mexico and Central America, Asia and Africa to work in its factories with wages that have remained low and stagnant. More than one-third of Iowa's energy has been based on wind farming. It is second only to Texas in the amount of electricity generated by wind, despite objections from some farmers to the noise and the hazard to birds.

Western Iowa is small-town territory. It has some of the world's most productive soil and some of its most creative agricultural scientists and farmers. Ames, in Story County, is part of the growth zone around Des Moines. In May 2019, its 1.5 percent unemployment rate was the lowest in the country. In Winnebago County near the Minnesota border is Winnebago Industries, which manufactures motor homes and recreational vehicles on computer-controlled assembly lines with robotic equipment. The company has bounced back since the Great Recession by shifting its appeal from retirees to younger consumers, who often prefer less-gaudy vehicles. From its headquarters in Forest City, the company employs more than 2,100 workers.

The 4th Congressional District is Iowa's largest geographically, stretching from South Dakota nearly to Illinois. In 2020, Donald Trump won this 92 percent white district with 63 percent of the vote—his best in the state, by far.

KANSAS

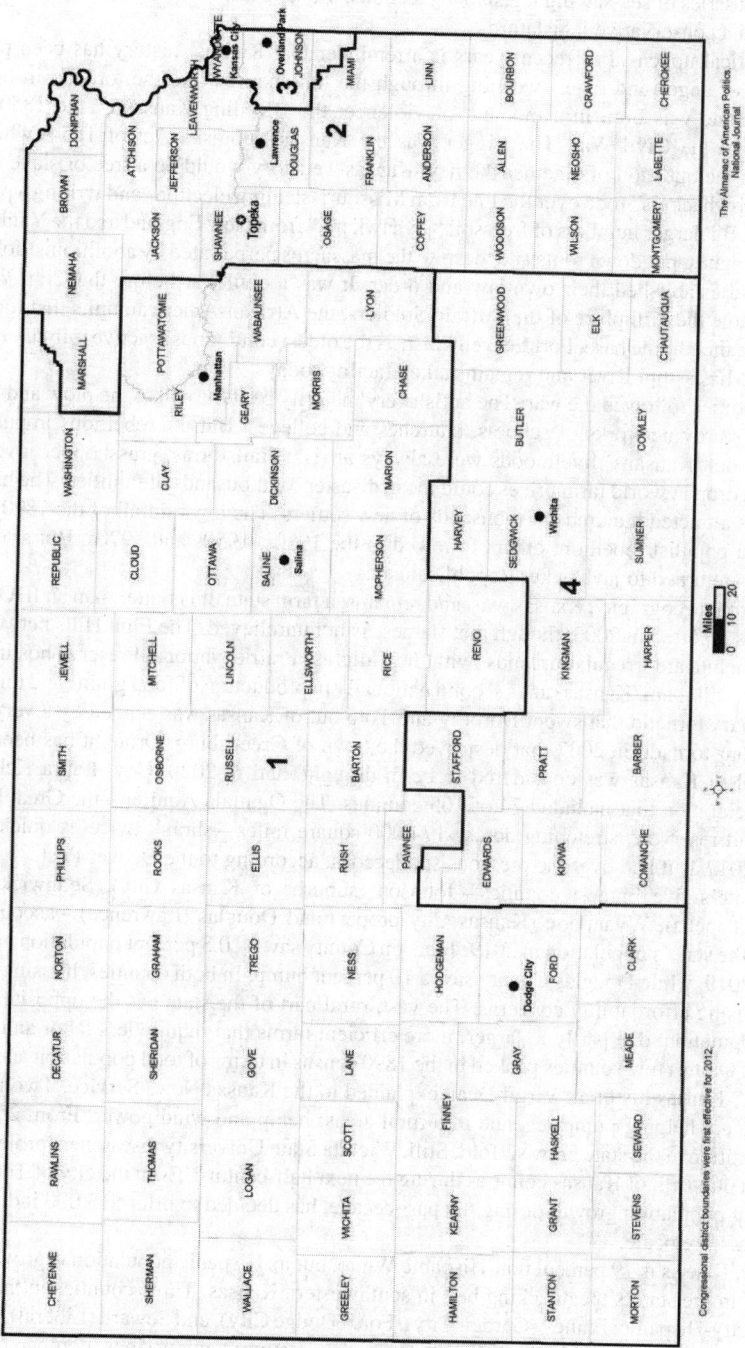

Congressional district boundaries were first effective for 2012.

Miles
0 10 20

Kansas is usually depicted as flat, average and uninteresting. It's not really, and in recent years its politics have been anything but. Conservatives have tried to turn the state into a small-government model for the nation and a place that pushed the envelope on policies on illegal immigration and voter fraud. After a series of see-sawing legislative elections, the state is now led by a moderate Democratic governor and a conservative legislature.

The political upheaval of recent years is a reminder that Kansas' history has been punctuated by episodes of anger and rage, sweeping through the tall sheaves like the tornado in the Wizard of Oz. The state was born in a moment of violence: the Bleeding Kansas of the 1850s that led proximately to the Civil War. The trigger was the Kansas-Nebraska Act of 1854, which left to local settlers the question of whether the new Kansas Territory would be a free or slave state. Pro-slavery "bushwhackers" rode over the line from Missouri, stealing elections and writing a pro-slavery constitution. But larger numbers of free-soil "jayhawkers," from New England and the Yankee-settled Great Lakes states, put down roots and, despite the massacres perpetrated by abolitionist John Brown, prevailed and established their own law and order. It was a civil war before the Civil War. Later, Kansas became the birthplace of the Buffalo Soldiers, the African-American units that fought in the Indian Wars; their home base, Fort Leavenworth, is the oldest continuously active military reservation west of the Mississippi River and remains a key facility today.

Calmer times followed the war: The antislavery majority bent the soil to the plow and built small towns with sturdy networks of schools, churches and colleges. But the rebellious impulse did not entirely die out. Kansans' livelihoods were always at risk: Hailstorms, grasshopper invasions, dry seasons or a drop in world farm prices could mean disaster for thousands of families. The high rainfall of the 1880s attracted hundreds of thousands of new settlers. The low rainfall of the 1890s produced a bust and a populist rebellion; others followed in the 1930s, 1950s and 1970s. But afterward, the state always returned to jayhawker Republicanism.

Owing to its geography, Kansas was, and remains, a farm state. It is flatter than an IHOP pancake, geographers reported in 2003, though that flatness is not unrelieved. The Flint Hills between Kansas City and Wichita are irregular uplands, with the Tallgrass Prairie National Preserve hosting bus trips where bison still roam. Kansas ranks second nationally in production of food grains and third in cattle. The imaginary tornado that swept Dorothy and Toto out of Kansas was echoed by a very real, 205-mile-per-hour tornado in 2007 that destroyed the town of Greensburg. Drought has been common; in 2018, all of Kansas was considered to be in drought, and in 2020, Gov. Laura Kelly issued a drought declaration that included 74 of 105 counties. The Ogallala Aquifer—the Great Plains' vast underground reservoir, stretching across 174,000 square miles—shrank twice as quickly between 2011 and 2017 as it had over the previous six decades, according to the Denver Post.

The state's five biggest counties—Johnson (suburbs of Kansas City), Sedgwick (Wichita), Shawnee (Topeka), Wyandotte (Kansas City proper) and Douglas (Lawrence)—accounted for 54 percent of the state's population in 2019; Johnson County saw a 10.3 percent population gain between 2010 and 2019, while Douglas County saw a 10 percent bump. In both counties, housing prices have shot up, raising affordability concerns. The vast, rural part of the state has the opposite problem: It has lost population, due partly to larger, more efficient farms that require less labor and fewer local suppliers. "Quite a few counties peaked in the 1890 census in terms of total population and have never recovered," Kansas historian Virgil Dean explained to the Kansas News Service. Two new sources of revenue are helping pump revenue into rural areas: hemp and wind power. From 2009 to 2018, wind generation in the state grew sixfold. Still, Wichita State University researchers project growth in fewer than one-fifth of Kansas counties during the next half-century. Even the city of Topeka, driven by stagnant population growth during the past decade, has decided to offer $15,000 inducements for newcomers to relocate.

Today, Kansas is 79 percent non-Hispanic White, but its Hispanic population is growing quickly, especially in the state's meatpacking belt in southwestern Kansas. Three counties in that region are now majority-Hispanic: Finney (Garden City), Ford (Dodge City), and Seward (Liberal). Despite this, by 2019, voters had elected just one Latino to the three county commissions, compared to 27 white commissioners, Kansas Public Radio noted. (Liberal is inaptly named; Donald Trump won 64 percent in Seward County.) The meatpacking plants became hotspots in the coronavirus pandemic, although they weren't the only reason rural Kansas was hit hard by the virus; the caseload was exacerbated by a flagging health infrastructure and a distrust of public-health measures. At one point in December 2020, Quinter in Gove County ranked as the nation's hardest-hit locale for the coronavirus. Yet in Gove County, where 88 percent voted for Trump, USA Today reported that "mask-wearing remains controversial ... and friendships are being strained as authorities struggle to persuade their neighbors to follow basic public health guidelines." In Dodge City, Mayor Joyce Warshaw resigned after being inundated with death threats following the city's issuance of a mask mandate.

Metropolitan Kansas City is the nation's second largest railroad hub, with a diverse economy that is by no means dependent on farming (though it does produce some of the nation's best barbecue). Wichita is the home base of Koch Industries, a conglomerate that started as an oil refining company and which later became a major force in politics; it has spent lavishly to promote the free-market credo of its owners, Charles Koch and his late brother, David. Their agenda was historically in tune with the GOP, but it has diverged during the Trump era: In 2020, Charles Koch wrote that he regretted his past partisanship for abetting divisiveness. "Boy, did we screw up! What a mess!" he wrote. Wichita has also been a leader in general aviation; Beechcraft, Cessna, Lear and Spirit have plants there, though the region was hit hard when Boeing left its 97-building operation in 2014 after more than eight decades. Oil and gas have a foothold in the state as well.

Kansas has long been reliably Republican in presidential elections and in most congressional contests; it has not elected a Democrat to the Senate since 1932. But state politics was dominated for 40 years by a coalition of Democrats and moderate Republicans, according to University of Kansas political scientist Burdett Loomis. That was the case under Republican Gov. Bill Graves, elected in 1994 and 1998, and Democratic Gov. Kathleen Sebelius, elected in 2002 and 2006. When she resigned to become President Barack Obama's secretary of Health and Human Services, she was succeeded by her lieutenant governor, Mark Parkinson, a former Republican state chairman who switched parties because of the rightward shift in the state GOP. Today, heirs of Alf Landon, Dwight Eisenhower (whose presidential library is in his hometown of Abilene) and longtime Sens. Bob Dole and Nancy Landon Kassebaum have been eclipsed by Republicans with harder-edged conservative views on fiscal and social issues.

In 2010, Sam Brownback, after 14 years in the Senate, was elected governor. Brownback turned the state rightward on social issues, and with Secretary of State Kris Kobach, enacted a requirement that voters show photo identification and proof of citizenship. But Brownback's signature initiative, signed in mid-2012, was a tax cut that removed 330,000 businesses from the tax rolls. Within months, he and the Koch-backed Americans for Prosperity targeted nine lawmakers for defeat in the August 2012 Republican primary; their candidates won, giving both chambers an even more solid conservative majority. The economic returns from the tax cuts were less than predicted, in part because spending continued to increase, and Standard & Poor's and Moody's slashed the state's credit rating. Throughout 2014, Brownback's approval ratings lagged. But in a solidly Republican year, he managed a narrow four-point win.

As Brownback's second term wore on, his approval ratings were among the worst of any governor in the nation. In the 2016 primaries, Brownback-aligned candidates lost a net of two dozen state House and Senate primaries to challengers backed by teachers' unions, roadbuilders and hospitals. In November, Kansas voted for Trump, 57%-36%, but Democrats gained seats in both state legislative chambers. In 2017, bipartisan majorities voted to expand Medicaid under the Affordable Care Act, but legislators fell short of overriding Brownback's veto. The legislature did override Brownback's veto of a bill to raise taxes by $1.2 billion, and spending continued to increase. In the 2018 Republican primary for governor, Kobach defeated the establishment choice, Jeff Colyer, who had been serving as governor since Brownback took a Trump administration post. The prospect of facing the polarizing Kobach energized Democrats, and state Sen. Laura Kelly went on to defeat Kobach, 48%-43%.

However, the 2020 elections brought disappointment to Democrats, despite some marginal gains. Joe Biden narrowed Trump's margin of victory in the state from 20 points in 2016 to 14 points in 2020, with Biden increasing the Democratic vote haul by 34 percent, compared to 15 percent for Trump. Biden flipped three counties that Trump had won in 2016: Riley (Manhattan), Shawnee, and most notably the populous and affluent Johnson, which Clinton had lost by three points but which Biden won by eight. Biden also improved on Clinton's performance by six points in Sedgwick County and seven points in Finney County. Sharice Davids, a lesbian Native American Democrat, also managed to hold her Johnson County-based House seat in 2020. However, Republican-turned-Democrat Barbara Bollier was unable to run much ahead of Biden in her seemingly competitive open-seat Senate race against Republican Rep. Roger Marshall, who won, 53%-42%. Equally frustrating for Democrats, the GOP maintained its supermajorities in both legislative chambers, even after a number of moderate GOP legislators were defeated by conservatives in the primary. As she prepared for reelection, Kelly girded for an even harder-line opposition than before.

Population		Race and Ethnicity		Income	
Total	2,913,314	White	83.60%	Median Income	62,087
Land area (sq. miles)	81,759	Black	5.70%	State Income Rank	27 out of 50
Pop/ sq mi	35.63	Latino	12.20%	Poverty Rate	11.40%
Born in state	59.20%	Asian	3.70%	With health insurance	90.80%
		Two or more races	3.70%	Cash public assistance	1.50%
Age Groups		Other	3.90%	Food stamp/SNAP	8.6%
Under 18	24.00%				
18-34	23.20%	Education		Work	
35-64	36.40%	H.S grad or less	34.50%	White Collar	40.00%
Over 64	16.40%	Some college	31.40%	Sales and Service	36.00%
		College Degree, 4 yr	21.60%	Blue Collar	24.10%
Military		Post grad	12.40%	Government	15.90%
Veteran/ Active Duty	8.40%				

Presidential Politics

2020 Caucus (D)	Biden (D)	110,041(77%)	Sanders (D)	33,142(23%)		
2020 Primary (D)	Biden (D)	102,829(70%)	Sanders (D)	26,555(18%)	Warren (D)	11,518 (8%)
2016 Caucus (D)	Sanders (D)	26,429(68%)	Clinton (D)	12,593(32%)		
2016 Caucus (R)	Cruz (R)	37,512(47%)	Trump (R)	18,443(23%)	Rubio (R)	13,295(17%)
	Kasich (R)	8,741(11%)				
2020 Pres. Vote	Trump (R)	771,406(56%)	Biden (D)	570,323(42%)		
2016 Pres. Vote	Trump (R)	671,018(57%)	Clinton (D)	427,005(36%)	Johnson (L)	55,406 (5%)
	Stein (G)	23,506 (2%)				

Except for 1964, when it narrowly favored Lyndon Johnson over Barry Goldwater, Kansas has voted Republican for president for three-fourths of a century. In the 105 counties, George W. Bush, Mitt Romney and Donald Trump in 2016 each lost only two: Wyandotte, which includes Kansas City and has a majority-minority population; and Douglas, which is home to the University of Kansas in Lawrence. John McCain in 2008 lost one more, by just over 200 votes, Crawford County, home to Pittsburg State University. But in 2020, Kansas' suburban territory swung hard against Trump, much like similar areas across the country; he lost five counties, with Biden adding Johnson (suburban Kansas City), Shawnee (Topeka) and Riley (Manhattan, and Kansas State University) to his column. Trump still won statewide by a solid 56%-42%--a bit tighter than his 57%-36% win in 2016.

Kansas held caucuses from 1996 through 2016, but Democrats switched to a party-run primary in 2020, part of their shift away from the caucus system. The contest occurred May 2, after Joe Biden had secured the nomination; he won 70%-18% over Bernie Sanders.

Congressional Districts

117th Congress Lineup	1D 3R	116th Congress Lineup	1D 3R

Redistricting in Kansas will have the new dynamic of a Democratic governor. But, after Kansas Democrats failed to break the GOP's two-thirds control of the state's two legislative chambers, Laura Kelly may have limited influence to protect Rep. Sharice Davids, the one Democrat in the House delegation from Kansas. Democrats will seek to revive their coalition with moderate Republicans in the capitol. Ambitious Democrats are mindful that the districts based in Topeka and Wichita have had competitive contests recently, though the GOP base has grown firmer, especially in Wichita. With the metro-area 3rd completely surrounded by the Topeka-based district, the GOP likely will need to make changes in the Wichita district as well. The biggest supply of Republican voters is in the sprawling 1st District. But stretching that district all the way from the Colorado border to close to the Missouri border might raise objections from numerous quarters.

The outcome of the most recent redistricting might be instructive. In spring 2012, a coalition of Democrats and moderate Republicans in the state Senate passed one redistricting plan and the conservative-dominated House passed another; they adjourned in May without reaching agreement. A federal court took the case, and a three-judge panel approved a map that moved Lawrence to the 2nd District and put Manhattan, home of Kansas State University, and Fort Riley into the 1st district. Those new boundaries were relevant at least as much for regional and business interests as for their partisan implications.

Laura Kelly (D)

Elected 2018, term expires 2023, 1st term; b. Jan. 24, 1950, New York, NY; Bradley University, B.S.; Indiana University, Bloomington, M.S.; Catholic; Married (Ted Daughety); 2 children.

Elected Office: KS Senate, 2005-2018.

Professional Career: Executive Director, Kansas Recreation and Park Association, 1988-2004; Recreation Therapist, Rockland Children's Psychiatric Center; Director, Recreation Therapy/Physical Education, National Jewish Hospital for Respiratory and Immune Diseases.

Office: 300 S.W. Tenth Ave. Suite 241-S, Topeka, 66612; 785-296-3232; Fax: 785-296-7973
Lt. Gov.: Lynn Rogers (D) **Atty. Gen:** Derek Schmidt (R) **Sec. of State:** Scott Schwab (R)
State Legislature: Senate: 11D, 28R, 1I **House:** 41D, 84R

Election Results

Election	Name (Party)	Vote (%)
2018 General	Laura Kelly (D)	506,509 (48%)
	Kris Kobach (R)	453,030 (43%)
	Greg Orman (I)	68,498 (6%)
2018 Primary	Laura Kelly (D)	80,377 (51%)
	Carl Brewer (D)	31,493 (20%)
	Joshua Svaty (D)	27,292 (18%)
	Arden Andersen (D)	13,161 (8%)

Laura Kelly was elected governor of Kansas in 2018, amid fatigue with the policies of the conservative Republicans who dominated state politics for the better part of a decade. Kelly won support from moderate Republicans who preferred her pragmatic approach to that of the GOP nominee, conservative Secretary of State Kris Kobach. But she faced fierce resistance from the conservative legislature on such issues as expanding Medicaid and implementing restrictions to curb the coronavirus pandemic.

Kelly was born in New York City but moved often as a child. Her family settled in Salina Kansas in the mid-1980s, then moved to Topeka. Kelly worked as an advocate for mental health services and patient care. For 19 years, she ran the Kansas Recreation and Park Association. Kathleen Sebelius, the future Democratic governor, tried to recruit her as a candidate in 1994; while Kelly turned her down, the two became longstanding allies. Initially an independent, Kelly became a Democrat. "It just became clear to me that the ideological arm of the Republican Party was really inflaming the culture wars, and I felt very uncomfortable with that, so I thought I needed to get off the fence and make a declaration," Kelly told the Wichita Eagle. She narrowly won a state Senate seat in 2004.

In the Senate, Kelly served for more than a decade in top committee positions overseeing health, budget and social-services policy. That gave her a front-row seat for some of the biggest battles during the governorship of Republican Sam Brownback. He pursued an ambitious conservative agenda, the centerpiece of which was the largest tax cut in Kansas history, trimming more than $1 billion in state revenue. This, coupled with continued increases in spending, produced a large and persistent budget gap that critics said hampered the state's economic growth. In 2017, President Donald Trump offered Brownback the post of ambassador-at-large for international religious freedom. For much of that year, Brownback awaited confirmation, producing an awkward situation in Topeka, as Lt. Gov. Jeff Colyer served as the heir apparent, but without the powers of the governorship. The differences between Brownback and Colyer—who were elected as a ticket in 2010—were often more stylistic than substantive, with both sharing an opposition to abortion and expansive government. After the Senate confirmed Brownback in January 2018, Colyer was sworn in as governor and immediately prepared for his election campaign.

While the GOP officially controlled both chambers, Colyer often faced off against an alliance of Democrats and moderate Republicans that had expanded its influence in the 2016 election. Colyer faced a primary challenge from Kobach, the two-term secretary of state who received national attention for his hard-line approaches to illegal immigration and voting access. While Colyer won most of the GOP establishment's support, Kobach parlayed Trump's backing in a late tweet into a victory, though his win was so narrow it took more than a week to officially call the race. The results of the GOP primary buoyed Democrats, who were more eager to face Kobach than Colyer. In the Democratic primary, Kelly faced former Wichita Mayor Carl Brewer and former state lawmaker and onetime agriculture secretary Josh Svaty. Kelly, the only woman in the race, pulled ahead by stressing Medicaid expansion—which Brownback, Colyer and Kobach had all opposed—and by advocating a steady-as-she-goes approach she billed as an antidote to Brownback. Kelly got 51 percent, ahead of Brewer with 20 percent and Svaty with 18 percent.

In the general election, Kobach grappled with an embarrassing episode in court, when a judge overseeing a voter-ID case struck down the law Kobach was defending, held him in contempt and ordered him to take remedial legal education. Kobach also tied himself to Trump, which alienated moderate Republicans. Kelly, powered by strong showings in suburban counties, won with 48 percent, to 43 percent for Kobach and 7 percent for third-party candidate Greg Orman. In 2013, Brownback had notched narrow wins in both Johnson County (Kansas City suburbs) and Sedgwick (Wichita), but Kelly took Johnson by 17 points and Sedgwick by six.

Shortly after taking office, Kelly overturned a Brownback order from 2015 that removed on-the-job discrimination protections for LGBT state employees; she expanded the rights further, to state contractors. She and Missouri Gov. Mike Parson, a Republican, signed twin measures that effectively barred cross-border poaching of companies from across the state line around Kansas City. Kelly also green lighted a comprehensive review of Kansas' economic and industrial future, the first major state-backed analysis of the type since the 1980s. Kelly signed a measure allowing the production of hemp, even as efforts to legalize medical marijuana languished. Working with Republicans, Kelly approved $90 million in new funding for schools, which they hoped would satisfy a long-running judicial challenge to the state's education funding system; the state Supreme Court later ruled that the change was satisfactory, although the justices promised continued oversight. Kelly also signed a $33 million increase in higher-education funding, which was designed to head off tuition increases.

The biggest fight—and one of the longest-running—was over expanding Medicaid. In 2019, the state House approved an expansion, but it failed to move beyond that. The following year, Kelly and Sen. Jim Denning, the Republican leader, reached a deal on an expansion. But Senate President Susan Wagle, who was running in the GOP primary for a U.S. Senate seat, blocked a vote until an anti-abortion constitutional amendment was voted on, a decision that three former Senate presidents, all of them Republican, criticized. The state House failed to approve the abortion amendment, leaving the Medicaid expansion in the lurch.

When the coronavirus hit, Kelly took an aggressive stance—one that prompted lots of GOP opposition. Kelly declared a state of emergency in March, well before the state had many cases; Kansas also became the first state in the nation to say it would shutter schools for the remainder of the 2019-20 academic year. Republicans in the legislature fought back, seeking to curb Kelly's emergency powers; in May, she vetoed one such measure, but in June, she approved a compromise version. In November, as cases were spiking, Kelly issued a statewide mask order, but it was blunted by opt-out provisions in the earlier bill curbing her powers. By late December, the state had the fifth-highest rate of cases per capita in the nation and ranked third in deaths per capita.

In the 2020 election, despite Democratic hopes for a breakthrough in the state, the GOP maintained its supermajorities in both chambers, portending an even more challenging 2021 for the governor. When Republican state Treasurer Jake LaTurner won a House race in 2020, Kelly named her lieutenant governor, Lynn Rogers, as the new treasurer and named her commerce secretary, David Toland, to be the new lieutenant governor. In April 2021, Kelly vetoed two high-profile bills — one that would have banned transgender students from girls' and women's school sports, and another that would have lowered the age for carry concealed weapons from 21 to 18. Kelly has indicated that she will seek another term, and she should be able to avoid a significant primary challenge. Kansas Republicans, meanwhile, have a deep bench of potential contenders.

Jerry Moran (R)

Elected 2010, term expires 2022, 2nd term, b. May 29, 1954; Great Bend, KS; Fort Hays State University, 1973; University of KS, B.S., 1976; University of KS, J.D., 1981; Methodist; Married (Robba Addison Moran); 2 children.

Elected Office: KS Senate, 1989-1997, Majority Leader, 1995-1996; U.S. House, 1997-2011.

Professional Career: Intern, Congressman Keith G. Sebelius, 1974; Operations Officer, Consolidated State Bank, 1975-1977; Mgr., Farmers State Bank & Trust Co., 1977-1978; Legislative Intern, KS House, 1980; Special Assistant Attorney General, Kansas, 1982-1985; Instructor, Ft. Hays St. University, 1986; Deputy Attorney, Rooks County, 1987-1995.

DC Office: 521 DSOB 20510, 202-224-6521, Fax: 202-228-6966
State Offices: Hays, 785-628-6401; Manhattan, 785-539-8973; Olathe, 913-393-0711; Pittsburg, 620-232-2286; Wichita, 316-269-9257.

Committees: *Appropriations*: Agriculture, Rural Development, FDA & Related Agencies; Commerce, Justice, Science & Related Agencies (RMM); Department of Defense; DOL, HHS & Education & Related Agencies; Financial Services & General Government; State, Foreign Operations & Related Programs. *Banking, Housing & Urban Affairs*: Financial Institutions & Consumer Protection; Housing, Transportation & Community Development; Securities, Insurance & Investment. *Commerce, Science & Transportation*: Aviation Safety, Operations & Innovations; Communications, Media & Broadband; Consumer Protection, Product Safety & Data Security; Space & Science. *Health, Education, Labor & Pensions*: Children & Families; Primary Health & Retirement Security. *Indian Affairs. Veterans' Affairs (RMM).*

Group Ratings

	ADA	ACLU	AFL-CIO	LCV	COC	HAFA	ACU	CFG	FRC
2020	-	38%	-	15%	-	57%	86%	-	-
2019	15%	C	22%	14%	92%	C	86%	32%	100%

Almanac Ratings 2019-2020

	Economy	Social	Foreign	Composite
Liberal	11%	11%	23%	15%
Conservative	89%	89%	77%	85%

Key Votes of the 116th Congress

1. EPA clean energy rules	N	5. Russia sanctions	Y	9. Barr as Atty. General	Y
2. U.S./Mex./Can. trade deal	Y	6. Troops in SYR, AFG	Y	10. Spending at the border	Y
3. Cut unemployment benefits	Y	7. Veto arms sales to Saudis	Y	11. Coney Barrett to Sup. Ct.	Y
4. Shelton to Fed Reserve	Y	8. Defense $$$, veto override	Y	12. Electoral College objections	N

Election Results

Election	Name (Party)	Vote (%)		Cand. Spent	Ind. Exp. Support	Ind. Exp. Oppose
2016 General	Jerry Moran (R)...................................	732,376	(62%)	$4,227,284	$529	
	Patrick Wiesner (D)...........................	379,740	(32%)	$34,939		
	Robert Garrard (L)........................	65,760	(6%)			
2016 Primary	Jerry Moran (R)................................	230,907	(79%)			
	D.J. Smith (R).................................	61,056	(21%)			

Prior winning percentages: 2016 (62%), 2010 (70%); House: 2008 (82%), 2006 (79%), 2004 (91%), 2002 (91%), 2000 (89%), 1998 (81%), 1996 (73%)

Kansas's senior senator, Jerry Moran, is a study in contradictions. He helped Republicans regain the majority in 2014 as the National Republican Senatorial Committee chairman. Still, during the Trump administration, Moran often sought distance from the president. And he has voiced reservations to the GOP party line at times, including the hard-line position of most of his colleagues on nominations to the Supreme Court and repeal of the Affordable Care Act. But as he approached his reelection bid in 2022, some of that apparent dissonance became more muted as he sought— and looked likely—to avoid a primary challenge thanks, ironically, to an early endorsement from the former president.

While accumulating a conservative voting record, Moran has demonstrated an independent streak during his more than two decades in Congress. Success in chairing a party's in-house campaign committee often boosts a lawmaker up the leadership ladder. Moran, once majority leader of the Kansas Senate, has downplayed any such aspirations on Capitol Hill. "I like my independence. The more that you are part of the leadership, the less flexibility you sometimes have in the positions you take," he told the Wichita Eagle. At the same time, in what has been something of a limitation, Moran has acquired a reputation for political caution. Some years ago, Moran's then-colleague, Pat Roberts —known for his pointed wit—stood before a gathering of Kansas Republicans and joked that he had only been invited because pop stars were unavailable. "Actually, both Jerry Moran and I received invitations, but he couldn't decide," Roberts was reported to have wisecracked.

Moran grew up the son of an oil-field worker in the tiny town of Plainville in the western plains of Kansas. In college, he interned for GOP Rep. Keith Sebelius, the father-in-law of future Democratic Gov. Kathleen Sebelius. The job gave Moran a close view of the 1974 impeachment hearings of President Richard Nixon. After graduating with a degree in economics from the University of Kansas, Moran worked as a banker before earning a law degree. In 1988, he won election to the state Senate, becoming majority leader in his last term. When Roberts ran for the U.S. Senate in 1996, Moran sought the open House seat. He won the primary with 76 percent of the vote, tantamount to election in a sprawling rural district as big as Illinois. Moran won reelection a half-dozen times in the "Big First," where he annually held town halls in each of the district's 69 counties.

Moran's independence—and caution—showed up occasionally during his House tenure. To the dismay of Speaker Dennis Hastert, Moran was one of 25 House Republicans who opposed the 2003 Republican-sponsored Medicare prescription drug bill. In a memoir, Hastert did not call out Moran by name, but he left little doubt about whom he was talking. "Some members had assured me that they would be with us, but when the crunch time came, they weren't," Hastert wrote. "One prairie state member, a fourth-term representative from a solidly Republican district, voted no, then ran and hid. I sent people to find him, they couldn't." Afterward, Moran said the bill did not do enough to lower prescription drug prices, adding that he favored a Democratic proposal to give federal officials negotiating authority to lower drug costs.

Moran ran for the Senate in 2010 when Republican Sam Brownback announced he would step aside to run for governor. Moran first had to get by fellow GOP Rep. Todd Tiahrt. The two waged a nasty and expensive primary race, costing nearly $7 million combined. Tiahrt sought to turn the contest into a referendum on who was more conservative, and the candidates battled over endorsements. Former Alaska Gov. Sarah Palin and former Pennsylvania Sen. Rick Santorum were in Tiahrt's camp, while Moran secured the backing of two outspoken Senate conservatives: Tom Coburn of Oklahoma and Jim DeMint of South Carolina. With the endorsement of most of the state's leading newspapers, Moran won 50%-45%, prevailing on the strength of his base in the state's most Republican district. He won the general election with 70 percent of the vote.

Moran was given a seat on the Appropriations Committee after he entered the Senate, while committing to efforts to ban "earmarks"—funds directed to a legislator's pet projects. Moran sought earmarked funding while in the House and took heat for it during the primary against Tiahrt. He was one of 26 senators in 2011 to oppose a bipartisan deal to raise the nation's debt limit, noting that the $21 billion in deficit reduction over the first year of the agreement would cover less than a week's worth of borrowing.

In 2012, Moran found himself in an awkward situation when a frail 89-year-old former GOP Sen. Bob Dole—who for nearly three decades had occupied the seat Moran now holds—showed up on the Senate floor in a wheelchair. Dole, whose right arm was badly damaged in World War II, engineered passage of the Americans with Disabilities Act in 1990; he returned to the Senate to lobby for an international treaty designed to encourage other nations to meet similar objectives. Moran, after having declared he supported the treaty and would be "standing up for the rights of those with disabilities," cast a key vote to block treaty ratification. He later said, "Foreign officials should not be put in a position to interfere with U.S. policymaking."

Moran has cited Kansas farmers in pushing to reopen trade with Cuba, another position that put him at odds with many in his party. In 2007, he won House approval of an amendment to ease restrictions on shipments of food and medicine to the island nation, only to see it removed from the legislation to avoid a veto by President George W. Bush. In the Senate, Moran inserted a provision into a 2012 appropriations bill to ease agricultural trade by allowing direct cash payments from Cuban buyers to U.S. institutions. It also was stripped out. In 2015, after President Barack Obama moved to normalize relations with Cuba, Moran said, "What we have been doing has not worked. ... because it's a unilateral sanction. When wheat, for example, is not sold to Cuba, it's not that they're not buying wheat, it's that wheat's being purchased from some other place: our competitors."

As chairman of the NRSC during the 2014 election cycle, Moran worked to avoid mistakes that had tripped up his party in the prior two cycles—nomination of poorly vetted, ideologically rigid candidates whose missteps had allowed several imperiled Democrats to survive. "We tried to get all aspects of our party—from tea party to the Chamber of Commerce—to sit in a room and decide on a candidate they could all agree on," he said. Republicans flipped nine seats and regained the Senate majority—a party goal that had previously proved elusive.

Despite his success in regaining the Senate majority, Moran faced the ire of conservative activists upset by his efforts to help Roberts withstand a primary challenge from Milton Wolf, a tea party-backed physician; they looked for a candidate to take on Moran in 2016. In the face of this threat, Moran appeared to tack right. Almanac vote ratings pegged him as the fifth most conservative member of the Senate in 2015.

Still, Moran has leaned to the center. Two days after the death of Supreme Court Justice Anton in Scalia in February 2016, as Senate Republican leaders made clear their opposition to replacing Scalia until after the presidential election, Moran said the Senate had an obligation to consider a nominee put forth by Obama, telling the Topeka Capital-Journal, "The Republican-led Senate, which I worked hard to secure, has a constitutional responsibility in the process of determining Supreme Court justices." Moran repeated his stance the following month in a meeting with 10 people in the town of Cimarron—after Obama had nominated federal Judge Merrick Garland. "I can't imagine the president has or will nominate somebody that meets my criteria, but I have my job to do," Moran said, according to the Garden City Telegram. He added, "I think the process ought to go forward."

Under sharp attack from conservative groups, Moran flipped: An aide said that he had examined Garland's record and that he was "unacceptable to serve," and that he was "committed to preventing" Obama from putting another jurist on the high court. However, when Supreme Court Justice Ruth Bader Ginsburg died in September 2020—far closer to the election than Scalia had—Moran supported pushing forward with hearings and the eventual confirmation of Amy Coney Barrett.

Moran's waffling on a Garland hearing spurred then-Rep. Mike Pompeo to open the door to a primary challenge in 2016, but after the senator changed his tune Pompeo—who later became Trump's first CIA director and second secretary of State—announced he wouldn't run. Wolf did not file either, leaving D.J. Smith, who took 6 percent against Roberts and Wolf in the 2014 Senate primary, as Moran's only intraparty challenger. Moran won the primary 4-1, and, in November, was reelected to a second term 62%-32% in a state that has not elected a Democrat to the Senate since 1932.

After Trump's election, congressional Republicans set repeal and replacement of "Obamacare" as their top legislative priority, but Moran was not convinced. "The Senate health care bill missed the mark for Kansas and therefore did not have my support," he tweeted in late June, which was a factor in the Senate's delay in taking up the bill. His chief concern, he said, was the need to protect people with preexisting conditions. He was responding to objections from constituents and Kansas hospitals. During a town hall meeting in early July in the small town of Palco, not far from his hometown, Moran lamented the failure of the two major parties to seek consensus. "Not one inch are we giving," the New York Times reported him as saying.

When he returned to the Capitol for additional back-room negotiations with Senate Republicans, led by then-Majority Leader Mitch McConnell, Moran remained steadfast, saying the proposal failed to address rising health care costs. After another week, Moran agreed to support a procedural vote to start debate of what he called "the full legislative process," though he continued to oppose the McConnell-led initiative as "bad policy." As it turned out, Sen. John McCain returned from his treatment for cancer and became the third Republican to object to the procedural step, killing the measure and taking the public heat for its demise. "Trying to do something with one party alone is a mistake," Moran said in a Kansas radio interview. Local health care advocates praised his responsiveness to their concerns.

Moran also showed his independence in voicing concern over Trump's tariffs, especially their adverse effects on Kansas farmers. "China is a problem," he told a meeting of farmers outside Manhattan in May 2018, the High Plains Journal reported. "They cheat. They misbehave. They don't follow the rules. But the solution is not a broad tariff battle. ... Don't isolate us and keep us out of the markets." He criticized Trump after the president met with Russian President Vladimir Putin in Helsinki in July 2018, saying he had missed an opportunity to "publicly condemn Russia for election interference or offer strong support for the NATO alliance." In January 2019, he was one of only 11 Republicans to vote to require Trump to enforce economic sanctions against a corporate ally of Putin; the measure failed. And in February 2020, along with seven other GOP senators, Moran also joined Democrats in a resolution to limit Trump's authority to order military action on Iran without congressional approval.

In recent years, Moran has turned his attention to various policy proposals that again showed his independence from the Trump administration. He criticized the president's controversial postmaster general, Louis DeJoy, writing a letter to him in August 2020 over mail delays. When he led the Senate Appropriations Commerce, Justice and Science subcommittee, he questioned Trump's "ambitious" timeline to return Americans to the moon by 2024, saying that would necessitate massive cuts to STEM education. "We will try to provide all the necessary funding to keep Artemis on track for a lunar landing on schedule, but it is and will remain a challenge," he told Politico, referring to NASA's lunar program. He also used that perch to target robocall health care scams targeting seniors. There were times Moran reached out to the White House for help, including when the government cancelled a contract with Wichita-based Spirit Aero Systems for 40,000 ventilators in September 2020, during the COVID-19 pandemic. Moran worked with Democratic partners on several bills, including one with Montana Sen. Jon Tester to protect GI Bill benefits during national emergencies and another with Connecticut Sen. Richard Blumenthal in the wake of the women's gymnastics sexual abuse scandal to hold Olympic committees and sports governing bodies legally responsible for failing to protect athletes. In 2021, Moran became the top Republican on the Veterans' Affairs Committee, which Tester chaired.

In the 2018 election for Kansas governor, Moran remained "the quiet observer" about Kris Kobach, the ultraconservative Republican nominee, the Salina Journal reported. When Sen. Roberts retired the next cycle, Moran stayed neutral in the primary, which featured Kobach, Rep. Roger Marshall and wealthy plumber Bob Hamilton. After Marshall won the primary, to the relief of national Republicans, Moran lined up behind him in what was a hotly contested general election in which the GOP congressman easily prevailed. Moran is up for reelection in 2022 and, somewhat surprisingly, received Trump's first Senate endorsement of the cycle shortly after the senator voted to acquit him in his second impeachment trial. "Senator Jerry Moran is doing a terrific job for the wonderful people of Kansas. Jerry has my Complete and Total Endorsement for his re-election in 2022!" the former president said in a February 2021 statement. That effectively ended any serious primary challenge Moran could face.

Roger Marshall (R)

Elected 2020, term expires 2026, 1st term, b. Aug 09, 1960; El Dorado, KS; Butler Community College, A.S., 1980; Kansas State University, B.S., 1982; University of Kansas, M.D., 1987; Christian Church; Married (Laina Marshall); 4 children; 2 grandchildren.

Military Career: Captain, U.S. Army Reserve, 1984-1991.

Elected Office: KS House, 2017-2021.

Professional Career: Obstetrician/Gynecologist, Great Bend Regional Hospital; Chairman, Board of Great Bend Regional Hospital; VP, Farmers Bank and Trust; District Governor, Rotary International.

DC Office: Suite B33 RSOB 20510, 202-224-4774, Fax: 202-224-3514

Committees: *Agriculture, Nutrition & Forestry*: Conservation, Climate, Forestry & Natural Resources (RMM); Food & Nutrition, Specialty Crops, Organics & Research; Livestock, Dairy, Poultry, Local Food Sys & Food Safety & Sec. *Energy & Natural Resources*: Energy; Water & Power. *Health, Education, Labor & Pensions*: Children & Families; Primary Health & Retirement Security. *Small Business & Entrepreneurship*.

Election Results

Election	Name (Party)	Vote (%)		Cand. Spent	Ind. Exp. Support	Ind. Exp. Oppose
2020 General	Roger Marshall (R)	727,962	(53%)	$7,147,704	$28,419	$50,750
	Barbara Bollier (D)	571,530	(42%)	$26,464,197	$1,011,016	$25,377,868
	Jason Buckley (L)	68,263	(5%)			
2020 Primary	Roger Marshall (R)	167,800	(40%)			
	Kris Kobach (R)	108,726	(26%)			
	Bob Hamilton (R)	77,952	(19%)			
	Dave Lindstrom (R)	27,451	(7%)			

Republican Roger Marshall was elected to the Senate in 2020 after hard-fought victories in both the GOP primary and the general election. Although Democrats had not won a Senate contest in Kansas since 1932, they had been hopeful about their prospects, given the ideological splits among Kansas Republicans and their own success in electing Laura Kelley as governor in 2018. Marshall, who worked on farm legislation during his two terms in the House, succeeded retiring Sen. Pat Roberts, whose combined House and Senate service totaled 40 years.

Born in El Dorado Kansas, Marshall worked on the family farm. He earned his bachelor's degree in biochemistry from Kansas State University and his medical degree from the University of Kansas. As an obstetrician-gynecologist in Great Bend, he delivered more than 5,000 babies and was chairman of the board of Great Bend Regional Hospital. He served seven years in the Army Reserve, where he was a captain and trained a mobile hospital support unit.

In the 2016, Marshall challenged GOP Rep. Tim Huelskamp, whose no-holds-barred conservatism had made him a leader of the House Freedom Caucus and an outspoken internal critic of Republican leadership during his three terms representing the 1st Congressional District. Even after he was stripped of his chief committee assignments in 2012, which reportedly was the first time in more than a century that the local representative did not have a seat on the Agriculture panel, he continued to go his own way. Marshall saw his opening.

With the district's many farmers engaged in the contest, endorsements had an effect. Perhaps the most significant from the Kansas Farm Bureau, which opposed an incumbent for the first time. The bureau's voice rippled through in the district, which is among the leading livestock producers in the nation. Long-ago local hero Bob Dole, then 92, tweeted his endorsement of Marshall. The U.S. Chamber of Commerce endorsed Marshall and spent about $400,000 on his behalf. The state chamber backed Huelskamp, who also benefited from more than $400,000 that the Club for Growth spent on his behalf. Marshall's $1.5 million in fundraising was competitive; $300,000 was self-financed.

Perhaps the most significant endorsement was one that Huelskamp failed to get—from then-House Speaker Paul Ryan, who remained neutral and refused the incumbent's request to promise him a return to the Agriculture Committee. Marshall won the August primary by an unexpectedly large margin: 14 percentage points.

Marshall got seats on the Agriculture Committee as well as the Science, Space and Technology Committee, where he was the ranking Republican on the Environment Subcommittee and advocated on behalf of the National Bio and Agro-Defense Facility in Manhattan Kansas. As a member of the House-Senate conference committee on the farm bill in 2018, he pushed for stricter requirements for food stamp recipients, though they weren't included in the final version of the bill. He secured an amendment helping wildfire victims in his district.

Marshall joined the House Republicans' "Doc Caucus" and pushed for repeal of the Affordable Care Act. During debate in 2017, he chaired the health care task force of the Republican Study Committee and faced backlash after telling the health care-news site STAT, "Just like Jesus said, 'The poor will always be with us.' There is a group of people that just don't want health care and aren't going to take care of themselves." He later sought to clarify, saying in a statement he was trying to say, "We cannot build a national health care policy around any one segment of the population." He voiced opposition to President Donald Trump's tariffs, citing harm to the farm and dairy industries in his district. Marshall told Breitbart News he supported a path to legalization for immigrants brought to the country illegally as children: "These kids are the American Dream, and they are conservatives."

In 2018, Marshall was reelected easily after Huelskamp decided not to seek a rematch. Initially, the Kansas Farm Bureau hesitated to endorse Marshall as he reportedly was seeking a seat on the Ways and Means Committee, in lieu of the Agriculture Committee. Such an idea gave its members "heartburn," the Farm Bureau said; eventually, Marshall chose to retain his assignment.

After Roberts announced his retirement in January 2019, Marshall delayed before entering the wide-open contest to succeed him. In addition to Roberts, other members from the "Big First" have used it as a steppingstone to the Senate, including Dole and the state's current senior senator, Jerry Moran. Senate Republican campaign strategists privately encouraged then-Secretary of State Mike Pompeo, who had served six years in the House from Kansas and had sent signals of his interest in returning to elected office. Pompeo ruled out his return to the campaign trail in Kansas, but national Republicans continued to hold out hope he would change his mind. Once the filing deadline passed, Marshall became the favorite of the GOP establishment—in Washington and at home— despite concerns with his lackluster fundraising and campaign style.

The GOP primary featured Marshall plus two other leading contenders: Bob Hamilton, who owned a plumbing company and self-financed more than 90 percent of his $4 million campaign, and former Secretary of State Kris Kobach, a conservative firebrand whose strong opposition to immigration and false alarms about voter fraud had been encouraged by Trump but divided Kansas Republicans. That became apparent in 2018, when he lost the contest for governor to Kelley, 48%-43%. Bowing to the pleas of then-Majority Leader Mitch McConnell, Trump remained neutral in the Senate primary. Marshall was endorsed by Roberts, the Kansas Farm Bureau, and anti-abortion groups. While the Club for Growth signaled early on it would oppose Marshall, Trump called the group's president, at the behest of McConnell, to ask that the group stop attacking the congressman for fear it could elevate Kobach. Meanwhile, a Democratic super PAC popped up to try and boost Kobach.

Even though Marshall had supported Ohio Gov. John Kasich in the 2016 Republican presidential primary, he hugged Trump during the Senate contest and took the primary by a surprisingly wide 40%-26% over Kobach; Hamilton trailed with 19 percent. Marshall swept the counties in his rural district and also led in the state's three largest counties: Johnson, Sedgwick and Shawnee.

By no means did Marshall's victory in the primary lock up the Senate seat. Democratic nominee Barbara Bollier, an anesthesiologist and a state senator, had switched from the GOP after the 2018 elections, in which she had supported Kelley. "Over time, it became clear to me that I really didn't have much in common with Republican leadership much anymore, and they had no interest in commonsense policies that would really serve the people of Kansas," she told voters.

Running as a centrist who decried political polarization, Bollier was the beneficiary of Democratic strength in the growing suburbs around Kansas City plus national Democrats' fundraising prowess. She criticized Marshall for supporting the attempts by Trump and congressional Republicans to repeal the Affordable Care Act and voiced alarm over the loss of health-care coverage that would result from failure to extend Medicaid coverage in states such as Kansas.

It's rare to have two doctors running against each other, and amid the COVID-19 pandemic each took vastly different approaches that showed how much the response to the novel coronavirus had been politicized. Bollier kept to socially distanced outdoor events. Marshall said he was taking the anti-malarial drug hydroxychloroquine that Trump touted to prevent the coronavirus, even as most medical professionals said it wasn't effective. Marshall also frequently held mask less events indoors. "I tell you what, if I walk into rural Kansas with a mask on, people look at me like I've got three eyes or something, right?" Marshall told the Washington Post.

In the end, Kansas returned to form and the national tide was too much for Bollier to overcome in a federal race. Marshall won 53%-42%, winning all but five mostly urban and suburban counties in the northeast corner of the state. Marshall got a seat on the Senate Agriculture Committee, plus the Energy and HELP panels.

Once in the Senate, Marshall kept his campaign promise to defend Trump, joining four other GOP senators in objecting to Electoral College votes from both Arizona and Pennsylvania, the latter vote coming after insurrectionists attacked the Capitol on January 6. In a statement afterward, Marshall said, "Joe Biden is the President-Elect and we must and will have a peaceful transition of power on January 20th." He said he was "sickened and angered" by the attack and that the rioters "should be prosecuted to the fullest extent." The next month, Marshall voted to acquit Trump in his second impeachment trial, in which Democrats sought to hold the former president responsible for inciting the insurrection. He got seat on the Agriculture, Energy and Natural Resources and HELP committees.

Tracey Mann (R)

Elected 2020, 1st term, b. Dec 17, 1976; Quinter, KS; KS State University, B.S.; Evangelical; Married (Audrey Haynes); 4 children.

Elected Office: KS Lt. Governor, 2018-2019.

Professional Career: Vice President/Director of Industrial Sales and Leasing, real estate company; President, real estate company.

DC Office: 522 CHOB 20515, 202-225-2715, mann.house.gov

State Offices: Dodge City, 620-682-7340; Manhattan, 785-370-7277.

Committees: *Agriculture*: General Farm Commodities & Risk Management; Livestock & Foreign Agriculture. *Veterans' Affairs*: Economic Opportunity; Oversight & Investigations (RMM).

Election Results

Election	Name (Party)	Vote (%)		Cand. Spent	Ind. Exp. Support	Ind. Exp. Oppose
2020 General	Tracey Mann (R)	208,229	(71%)	$1,124,379	$304,919	$105,463
	Kali Barnett (D)	84,393	(29%)	$653,433	$10	
2020 Primary	Tracey Mann (R)	65,373	(54%)			
	Bill Clifford (R)	39,914	(33%)			
	Jerry Molstad (R)	9,545	(8%)			

Republican Tracey Mann in 2020 was elected to the House in his solidly Republican district. His victory was driven by success in the GOP primary, after he earlier had lost two intra-party battles. Success in this district—sometimes called the "Big First"—has served as a springboard to the Senate for ambitious Republicans. The youthful Mann might pursue that option, assuming he can avoid the fratricide that has become common among Kansas Republicans in recent years. He took the seat of Roger Marshall, who was elected to the Senate.

Mann, a fifth-generation Kansan, grew up on the family's cattle farm in the small town of Quinter in the northwest part of the state. He got his bachelor's degree in agricultural economics at Kansas State University, where he was student body president. He caught the political bug when he was a Washington summer intern for then-Rep. Jerry Moran.

In 2010, Mann ran unsuccessfully for the office to which he was elected a decade later. In that bid, he finished third, with 14 percent of the vote, among six candidates in the Republican primary, which was won by Tim Huelskamp. News stories at the time reported that Mann joined other Republicans as "birthers" who questioned whether President Barack Obama was born in the United States. When asked about that incident years later, the Wichita Eagle reported, Mann said, "I had a football coach one time that says when you make a mistake, you don't make excuses and you move on. And I made some mistakes in that race, but I moved on."

His next political opportunity came in February 2018. When Jeff Colyer became governor after Sam Brownback stepped down to join the Trump administration, Colyer selected Mann to succeed him as lieutenant governor. Their ticket had an epic showdown in that year's Republican primary for governor, which Colyer lost by 343 votes to the more conservative Kris Kobach.

Two years later, when Marshall ran for the seat of retiring Sen. Pat Roberts, Mann was the early frontrunner in his second bid for the House seat. His chief opponent in the Republican primary was Bill Clifford, a member of the Finney County Commission and a former Air Force pilot. Their contest became bitter, the Emporia Gazette reported, when Clifford ran as "a conservative outsider" and attacked Mann for his "campaign of lies," including ads that attacked Clifford's assistance to Somali immigrants seeking work in the Garden City area.

With a campaign that was mostly self-financed, Clifford spent $1.2 million, which nearly tripled what Mann spent in the primary. Mann was endorsed by the Kansas Farm Bureau, Kansans for Life and the National Rifle Association. He defeated Clifford, 54%-33%, in the four-candidate contest. Mann was the frontrunner in each of the eight largest counties. In November, Mann easily clinched his victory against Kali Barnett, a teacher in Garden City.

The Republicans who have been elected to the Senate after serving in this House seat during the past half-century include Bob Dole, Roberts, Moran and Marshall. If Mann shows ambitions for the Senate, he might face competition from another young House Republican who joined him as an incoming freshman: Jake LaTurner, who had been elected statewide as Kansas Treasurer, was an early candidate for the open Senate seat in Kansas in 2020 before he switched to make a successful challenge to Republican Rep. Steve Watkins.

In the House, Mann got seats on the Agriculture (which is essential for this district) and Veterans' Affairs committees.

KS-1: Central and Western Kansas   Cook Partisan Voting Index: R+24

Population		Race and Ethnicity		Income	
Total	694,498	White	87.90%	Median Income	$55,188
Land area (sq. miles)	52,543	Black	2.80%	District Income Rank	329
Pop/ sq mi	13.22	Latino	16.40%	Poverty Rate	13.30%
Born in State	64.20%	Asian	1.60%	With health insurance	90.00%
		Two or more races	2.70%	Cash public assistance	1.30%
Age Groups		Other	5.10%	Food stamp/SNAP	5.90%
Under 18	23.50%				
18-34	24.80%	**Education**		**Work**	
35-64	34.30%	H.S grad or less	39.30%	White Collar	35.30%
Over 64	17.50%	Some college	34.60%	Sales and Service	36.90%
		College Degree, 4 yr	17.00%	Blue Collar	27.80%
Military		Post grad	9.10%	Government	18.90%
Veteran/ Active Duty	10.10%				

2020 Pres. Vote	Trump	207,727	(70%)	Biden	83,890	(28%)	Jorgensen	6,513	(2%)
2016 Pres. Vote	Trump	183,446	(69%)	Clinton	64,388	(24%)	Johnson	11,976	(5%)

Manhattan, Dodge City: "A prairie is not any old piece of flatland in the Midwest," wrote Kansas-born reporter Dennis Farney. "No, a prairie is wine-colored grass, dancing in the wind. A prairie is a sun-splashed hillside, bright with wild flowers. A prairie is a fleeting cloud shadow, the song of the meadowlark. It is the wild land that has never felt the slash of the plow." The prairie Farney described once covered almost all of Kansas and dipped into Oklahoma. Now only a little virgin prairie can still be found, in the Flint Hills region west and south of Topeka. At the Tall grass National Prairie Preserve, you can see 30 miles on a clear day and a waist-deep sea of grass waves in the wind as it did when traders and pioneers on the Santa Fe Trail passed through some 175 years ago. Farther west, near the 100th meridian, much of this western area was grazing land, first for buffalo, then for the cattle driven to Kansas railheads like Abilene and Dodge City in the 1870s and 1880s.

Today, the area's farm-dependent economy has undergone big change. Agricultural towns have seen a steep decline in population, while big meatpacking plants in Dodge City, Garden City and Liberal (the "Golden Triangle of meatpacking") have attracted large numbers of Hispanic immigrants, bringing with them a population boom. That evolution has even given way to a new "Latino-English" accent in the area, which is called the "Liberal sound," for the city whose Hispanic population had grown to 63 percent in 2019. Nearby Fort Dodge schools reported a spike to 79 percent. There are growing pockets of Burmese, Vietnamese and northern African immigrants in places such as Garden City, where 51 percent of residents are Latino. Some immigrants say they have been welcomed and have assimilated well. In June 2020, activists in Dodge City came together in support of the Black Lives Matter movement and against police brutality.

In Manhattan, the National Bio and Agro-Defense Facility has been a boost to Kansas State University and the local economy. The facility will be the prime animal disease research facility in the United States and will support research into animal-to-human diseases that threaten both the farm sector and public health. Working closely with the Departments of Homeland Security and Agriculture, it is scheduled to be operational by the end of 2022 and will replace the aging animal disease center on Plum Island at the eastern end of Long Island, New York.

The 1st Congressional District covers all of western and north-central Kansas. It extends more than 300 miles from the Colorado border to the outskirts of Topeka. While the area today is solidly Republican, it was not always so. Farmer uprisings handed the area to the Populists for much of the late 1800s, a Democrat represented southwest Kansas during the Great Depression and again in the late 1950s. The district includes Emporia, where progressive newspaper editor William Allen White published the once-famous Emporia Gazette; the paper is still run by the White family. The district contains 61 full counties and parts of two others. Their average population is about 12,000. By square miles, the district is the 13th largest in the nation. The 1st is in the top 5 percent of the most Republican districts nationwide. Donald Trump won 70 percent of the vote here in 2020, by far his best district in Kansas.

Jake LaTurner (R)

Elected 2020, 1st term, b. Feb 17, 1988; Galena, KS; Pittsburg State University, B.A., 2011; Catholic; Married (Suzanne LaTurner); 4 children.

Elected Office: KS Senate, 2013-2017; KS Treasurer, 2017-2021.

Professional Career: Staffmember, Office of Congressperson Lynn Jenkins.

DC Office: 1630 LHOB 20515, 202-225-6601, laturner.house.gov

State Offices: Pittsburg, 620-308-7450; Topeka, 785-205-5253.

Committees: *Homeland Security*: Cybersecurity, Infrastructure Protection & Innovation; Intelligence & Counterterrorism. *Oversight & Reform*: Government Operations. *Science, Space & Technology*: Research & Technology.

Election Results

Election	Name (Party)	Vote (%)		Cand. Spent	Ind. Exp. Support	Ind. Exp. Oppose
2020 General	Jake LaTurner (R)	185,464	(55%)	$1,578,713	$397,538	$142,712
	Michelle De La Isla (D)	136,650	(41%)	$1,831,669	$35,436	$248,450
	Robert Garrard (L)	14,201	(4%)			
2020 Primary	Jake LaTurner (R)	47,898	(49%)			
	Steve Watkins (R)	33,053	(34%)			
	Dennis Taylor (R)	16,512	(17%)			

Jake LaTurner was elected to the House after he defeated first-term Rep. Steve Watkins in the Republican primary and Topeka Mayor Michelle de la Isla in November. LaTurner, the state treasurer, had been a candidate for an open Senate seat in Kansas in 2020. But he switched plans following allegations that Watkins committed campaign-finance violations in 2018. Three weeks before the GOP primary, Watkins—whose local roots were questioned during his successful campaign—was charged with voter fraud after he voted in a local Kansas election and gave his address as the location of a postal service.

Raised in Galena Kansas, LaTurner got a bachelor's degree in political science at Pittsburg State University. In 2012, he was elected to the state Senate after defeating the Republican incumbent in the primary. Republican Gov. Sam Brownback appointed him as treasurer to fill a vacancy in April 2017. After winning a full term in 2018, the 30-year-old LaTurner said that he was the youngest elected statewide official in the nation. On that job, he claimed credit for a customer-service approach, including increased use of education savings accounts.

In January 2019, shortly after Sen. Pat Roberts said he would retire at the end of his term, LaTurner announced his candidacy to succeed him. Eight months later, he reversed course to run against Watkins, contending that the incumbent's legal problems could jeopardize Republican control of the House seat.

Watkins, who had graduated from the U.S. Military Academy and served in Afghanistan before becoming a Defense Department contractor, had not lived in Kansas for more than two decades before seeking the open House seat in 2018. According to news reports, he had two homes in Alaska but none in Kansas, and had expressed initial interest in seeking the Democratic nomination for the seat. In the seven-candidate Republican primary, which he won with 27 percent of the vote, Watkins outspent the field, with the benefit of personal loans of about $500,000. In November, he defeated Democrat Paul Davis, 48%-47%.

Once elected, questions about his finances and his professional background swirled around Watkins. Critics contended that his campaign loan was, in part, an illegal transfer from his family. Campaign-finance questions were raised about a super PAC that supported Watkins, which received large sums from his father. Probably the final straw was the July 2020 vote-fraud indictment by the Shawnee County district attorney, who also charged Watkins with giving false information. A Watkins aide contended that the prosecutor shared a political consultant with LaTurner and that the charges were politically motivated.

LaTurner attacked Watkins for "a distinct pattern of spinning lies and blaming others, rather than taking responsibility." With support from former Gov. Jeff Colyer, he added that Republicans "need to put our best foot forward" to retain the House seat. He was endorsed by the Kansas Farm Bureau and by groups that backed gun rights and opposed abortion.

LaTurner won the primary, 49%-34%, against Watkins, who outspent the other candidates. Dennis Taylor, who was the state's secretary of labor under Brownback, got 17 percent. LaTurner, who won all but two small counties, led Watkins, 44%-29%, in Topeka-based Shawnee County.

He defeated de la Isla, a Democrat, in the general election. A native of Puerto Rico, she was executive director of Habitat for Humanity in Topeka before she was elected in 2017 as the first Latina mayor of the city. She ran a well-financed campaign in a district where Democrats occasionally have been successful. Each candidate voiced customary partisan themes. In a campaign ad, LaTurner criticized de la Isla for her support of "defunding the police" based on her statement that the concept was "a very bad marketing term" that describes "what the city of Topeka has been doing as practice" while she was mayor.

LaTurner won, 55%-41%. De la Isla narrowly won Topeka-based Shawnee County and took about two-thirds of the vote in neighboring Douglas, which are the two largest counties in the district. LaTurner won all of the remaining counties, often with more than 70 percent of the vote.

KS-2: Eastern Kansas **Cook Partisan Voting Index: R+10**

Population		Race and Ethnicity		Income	
Total	715,881	White	86.40%	Median Income	$56,515
Land area (sq. miles)	14,143	Black	4.70%	District Income Rank	308
Pop/ sq mi	50.62	Latino	7.10%	Poverty Rate	12.30%
Born in State	64.30%	Asian	1.60%	With health insurance	92.10%
		Two or more races	4.20%	Cash public assistance	1.90%
Age Groups		Other	3.00%	Food stamp/SNAP	8.00%
Under 18	22.60%				
18-34	23.50%	**Education**		**Work**	
35-64	36.10%	H.S grad or less	37.80%	White Collar	37.10%
Over 64	17.70%	Some college	32.70%	Sales and Service	36.60%
		College Degree, 4 yr	18.70%	Blue Collar	26.30%
Military		Post grad	10.70%	Government	18.90%
Veteran/ Active Duty	8.60%				

2020 Pres. Vote	Trump	191,030	(56%)	Biden	140,303	(41%)	Jorgensen	8,024	(2%)
2016 Pres. Vote	Trump	165,002	(56%)	Clinton	110,597	(37%)	Johnson	13,250	(5%)
	Stein	6,811	(2%)						

Topeka, Kansas City Suburbs: The green plains of eastern Kansas have seen more than their share of American history. In 1827, on bluffs above the Missouri River, the Army built Fort Leavenworth, famous in later years for its war college and military prison and now the oldest U.S. fort west of the Mississippi River. In the 1850s, newly founded towns along the Kansas River and along the Missouri border were the centers of Bleeding Kansas, the name the state took after pro-slavery bushwhackers set up a state capital in tiny Lecompton and antislavery New Englanders established their stronghold down the river at Lawrence. These tensions bled into the Civil War; William Quantrill's infamous nighttime raid on pro-Union Lawrence in 1863 resulted in the burning to the ground of all but two businesses and the death of around 200 inhabitants.

Topeka, the antislavery and modern capital, today sits on a low bluff above the Kansas River. The city's system of legal segregation prompted the 1954 landmark case, Brown v. Board of Education, which unanimously concluded "separate but equal" is not equal. In November 2017, the city elected as its mayor Michelle de la Isla, a Latina and native of Puerto Rico. Topeka has had some success attracting corporate headquarters, including Hill's Pet Nutrition. There are more than 300 animal health companies in the corridor between Manhattan and Columbia Missouri. The population of Topeka declined 2 percent from 2010 to 2019, though its loss has not been as large as in western Kansas. The city offered incentives of up to $15,000 to new residents and offered to pay remote workers up to $10,000.

The area around Lawrence, where the University of Kansas is based, has grown steadily. Its economy has outperformed most of the state. Farther south of the cities, on the Missouri border, are the hills called "the Balkans," where Eastern European coal miners settled in towns such as Pittsburg and Girard. This area was once a center of American socialism: Clarence Darrow and Upton Sinclair made pilgrimages, and the local paper, Appeal to Reason, had a national circulation of 750,000.

These disparate areas, Topeka and Lawrence, Fort Leavenworth, the wheat-growing counties, and the Balkans—most of eastern Kansas except the Kansas City metropolitan area—make up the 2nd Congressional District. Topeka-based Shawnee County and Lawrence-based Douglas account for more than 40 percent of the population. In recent decades, Democrats have been competitive in state races here. For 20 of the years from 1970 to 1994, Democrats held the 2nd District seat. Republicans have held it for all but two years since. In 2016, Donald Trump won 56 percent of the vote in this district.

Sharice Davids (D)

Elected 2018, 2nd term, b. May 22, 1980; Frankfurt, Germany; Haskell Indian Nations University Board of Regents, Att.; Haskell Indian Nations University Board of Regents, Att.; Haskell Indian Nations University Board of Regents, Att.; University of KS, Att.; University of MO, B.A., 2007; Cornell University Law School, J.D., 2010; No religion; Single.

Professional Career: Mixed Martial Artist; Attorney, SNR Dentons, 2010-2012; Director, Community and Economic Development, Pine Ridge Indian Reservation; White House Fellow, 2016-2017

DC Office: 1541 LHOB 20515, 202-225-2865, davids.house.gov

State Offices: Overland Park, 913-621-0832.

Committees: *Joint Economic. Small Business*: Economic Growth, Tax & Capital Access (Chmn); Innovation, Entrepreneurship & Workforce Development; Oversight, Investigations & Regulations. *Transportation & Infrastructure (VChmn)*: Aviation; Economic Dev't, Public Buildings & Emergency Management; Highways & Transit.

Almanac Ratings 2019-2020

	Economy	Social	Foreign	Composite
Liberal	54%	100%	80%	78%
Conservative	46%	0%	20%	22%

Key Votes of the 116th Congress

1. U.S./Mex./Can. trade deal	Y	5. Russia sanctions	Y
2. First Coronavirus response	Y	6. Troops in Syria	Y
3. HEROES Act	N	7. Veto arms sales to Saudis	Y
4. CASH Act	Y	8. Defense $$$, veto override	Y

9. Firearms background checks Y
10. Spending at the border   Y
11. Marijuana liberalized rules Y
12. Electoral College objections N

Election Results

Election	Name (Party)	Vote (%)		Cand. Spent	Ind. Exp. Support	Ind. Exp. Oppose
2020 General	Sharice Davids (D)............................	220,049	(54%)	$5,173,590	$150,902	$20,000
	Amanda Adkins (R).......................	178,773	(44%)	$2,049,269	$397,094	$197,899
	Steve Hohe (L).................................	11,596	(3%)			
2020 Primary	Sharice Davids (D)............................	74,437	(100%)			

Prior winning percentages: 2018 (54%)

Democrat Sharice Davids, elected in 2018, won her first campaign with a profile that once would have been considered exotic in Kansas: a lesbian Native American who had competed professionally in mixed martial arts. A self-described "policy wonk," she sought a low profile in Congress after defeating GOP Rep. Kevin Yoder in 2018. Davids has benefited greatly from the deep hostility to President Donald Trump in suburban Kansas City, which transformed a battleground into a seemingly safe Democratic seat.

A native of Leavenworth, Davids graduated from the University of Missouri-Kansas City and got her law degree from Cornell University. She joined SNR Denton, an international law firm. A member of the Ho-Chunk Nation, a Native American tribe in Wisconsin, she worked with tribes on economic-development opportunities. On a reservation in South Dakota, she opened a coffee shop, which ultimately failed and resulted in a $20,000 court judgment against her.

In late 2016, during the final months of the Obama administration, Davids became a White House Fellow with the hope to remain if Hillary Clinton was elected president. Instead, she worked on the transition at the Transportation Department during the early days of the Trump administration. The anti-Trump anger that resulted, she said, gave her the incentive to challenge Yoder.

The wide-open Democratic primary attracted six candidates. In addition to Davids, the other leading contender was Brent Welder, who worked for Sen. Bernie Sanders in the 2016 Democratic presidential campaign and received help from his former boss on the campaign trail. Davids positioned herself as the centrist in the primary and was endorsed by the Kansas City Star, which cited her "unique array of life experiences" and willingness to seek compromise. Davids defeated Welder, 37%-34%.

Yoder criticized Davids for her vague responses to policy questions and in an unusual twist for a challenger, Davids responded cautiously to demands from Yoder for campaign debates, participating in just one. Davids campaigned on a pledge to "stand up for Kansas values, not for Donald Trump's values." Yoder sought to distance himself from Trump. He did not attend a Trump campaign rally in Kansas.

Each candidate spent more than $4 million in the contest. Including outside spending, the total exceeded $12 million, though House Republicans canceled more than $1 million of scheduling advertising a month before the election. The unpopularity in the district of Trump and Kris Kobach, the unsuccessful GOP nominee for governor, was too much for Yoder to overcome. As earlier polls had predicted, Davids won easily, 53%-44%. She took 52 percent of the vote in traditionally Republican Johnson County, which cast four-fifths of the total.

In Congress, Davids adopted a low-key approach, choosing judiciously when and how often to become active. A member of the House Transportation and Infrastructure Committee, Davids excoriated Boeing for paying its embattled CEO a $60-million exit package while it laid off 2,800 Kansas employees. She vocally opposed a Trump administration policy that would have limited adoption opportunities for LGBT families.

She focused largely on transportation, aviation and highway issues, declining to back progressive policy proposals such as the Green New Deal or Medicare for All. Her centrist streak drew the ire of progressives, including a former chief of staff for Rep. Alexandria Ocasio-Cortez, Saikat Chakrabarti, who accused Davids of enabling "a racist system" when she voted for a $4.6 billion border security bill. House Democrats' official Twitter account shot back with a tweet warning Chakrabarti to keep Davids' name out of his mouth. True to form, Davids ignored the controversy. Her spokeswoman issued a statement that Davids was focused wholly on "advocating for the infrastructure needs of our region."

Two Republicans battled to challenge Davids in 2020: Sara Hart Weir, a former president of the National Down Syndrome Society who had the support of Republican Rep. Cathy McMorris Rodgers of Washington, and Amanda Adkins, a former state GOP chairwoman and Brownback adviser. Adkins' benefitted from a super PAC, funded in large part by her father, that attacked Weir. She won the primary 31%-23%.

Facing Davids, Adkins tried to cast herself as above the partisan fray, while Davids yoked her to Brownback's education legacy. Davids vastly outspent Adkins, $5.2 million to $2 million. Adkins received no help on the air from national Republicans and lost 54%-44%. Davids again took 52 percent of the vote in Johnson County and more than doubled Adkins' vote in Kansas City-based Wyandotte.

Redistricting could pose a problem for Davids. State Senate President Susan Wagle indicated in October 2020 that Republicans would try to make Davids' district more challenging in the redraw and Democrats in 2020 were unable to break the GOP's veto-proof legislative majorities.

KS-3: Kansas City Metro   **Cook Partisan Voting Index: D+1**

Population		Race and Ethnicity		Income	
Total	779,860	White	79.00%	Median Income	$81,792
Land area (sq. miles)	757	Black	8.40%	District Income Rank	79
Pop/ sq mi	1,029.93	Latino	12.50%	Poverty Rate	8.60%
Born in State	44.40%	Asian	5.10%	With health insurance	91.30%
		Two or more races	3.50%	Cash public assistance	1.00%
Age Groups		Other	4.00%	Food stamp/SNAP	4.70%
Under 18	24.90%				
18-34	22.00%	**Education**		**Work**	
35-64	38.70%	H.S grad or less	25.80%	White Collar	49.00%
Over 64	14.50%	Some college	25.70%	Sales and Service	34.20%
Military		College Degree, 4 yr	30.10%	Blue Collar	16.80%
Veteran/ Active Duty	6.60%	Post grad	18.40%	Government	12.20%

2020 Pres. Vote	Biden	223,114	(54%)	Trump	179,583	(44%)	Jorgensen	8,542	(2%)
2016 Pres. Vote	Clinton	161,479	(47%)	Trump	157,304	(46%)	Johnson	17,127	(5%)

Johnson County: Though its central core is in Missouri, about 40 percent of metropolitan Kansas City's residents live west of the state line in Kansas. Some are in Kansas City, Kansas, or KCK as it is sometimes called, where the low-lying land near the Missouri River used to house one of the nation's largest stockyards. This is still a working-class town with lots of modest frame houses, new Latino neighborhoods that have surpassed in size the African-American community, and a Catholic ethnic neighborhood. Kansas City's Wyandotte County has lost 21,000 people since the 1970s, and is now majority-minority: 29 percent Hispanic and 23 percent Black. It is one of only four such counties in the state; the other three are in the southwestern corner, where farms and meatpacking plants have attracted immigrants from Mexico.

South of Kansas City and Wyandotte County is Johnson County, which has nearly tripled since 1970. It is more affluent and close to four times the size of Wyandotte. The newer neighborhoods are arrayed along the interstates, as subdivisions have replaced croplands. They have grown to the point that Overland Park, Olathe, Shawnee and Lenexa are among the largest cities in the state; Overland Park is the second-largest behind Wichita. Between 2013 and 2018, 7,200 apartments were built in the county. These towns became more than just residential neighborhoods over the past few decades. Sprint Nextel, which has been headquartered in Overland Park, in April 2018 merged with T-Mobile, the new majority owner. Sprint purchased its former campus. After Applebee's left Lenexa to cross the river in 2011, city officials responded by persuading Select Quote Senior Insurance Services to move from the Missouri side two years later. This swap was emblematic of a major problem for the region: Tax incentives are used by states to lure businesses across the tight state borders, producing a net wash in job creation, but a decrease in overall revenues for each state.

Johnson County, like Wyandotte (and the Missouri suburbs, too), has been diversifying demographically. In 1980, the county was 97 percent White. But the share of non-Hispanic Whites dropped to 79 percent of the population in 2019. Johnson, a one-time Republican bastion, was transformed during the Trump era. Joe Biden carried it by eight percentage points in 2020, four years after Trump won it by three points and eight years after Mitt Romney won it by 18 points.

The 3rd Congressional District consists of all of Johnson and Wyandotte counties, and a corner of rural Miami County. It has quickly turned into reliable Democratic turf. Biden carried the district 54%-44%, in a continuation of recent trends. In 2016 Hillary Clinton led Trump, 47%-46%, though Mitt Romney won, 54%-44% in 2012. Biden lost only deep red Miami County and slightly improved on Clinton's margin in Wyandotte, winning 65%-33%. Redistricting gives the GOP an opportunity to make the district more competitive again; splitting its two chief counties would be a start.

Ron Estes (R)

Elected 2017, 2nd full term, b. Jul 19, 1956; Topeka, KS; TN Technological University, B.S.; TN Technological University, M.B.A.; Lutheran; Married (Susan Oliver); 3 children.

Elected Office: Sedgwick County Treasurer, 2004-2010; KS Treasurer, 2010-2017.

Professional Career: Businessman; Farmer.

DC Office: 1524 LHOB 20515, 202-225-6216, Fax: 202-225-3489, estes.house.gov

State Offices: Wichita, 316-262-8992.

Committees: *Joint Economic. Ways & Means*: Select Revenue Measures; Social Security; Trade.

Group Ratings

	ADA	ACLU	AFL-CIO	LCV	COC	HAFA	ACU	CFG	FRC
2020	**	17%	**	0%	-	93%	88%	**	-
2019	0%	C	24%	14%	83%	C	87%	94%	95%

Almanac Ratings 2019-2020

	Economy	Social	Foreign	Composite
Liberal	25%	8%	6%	13%
Conservative	75%	92%	94%	87%

Key Votes of the 116th Congress

1. U.S./Mex./Can. trade deal	Y	5. Russia sanctions	N
2. First Coronavirus response	Y	6. Troops in Syria	N
3. HEROES Act	N	7. Veto arms sales to Saudis	N
4. CASH Act	N	8. Defense $$$, veto override	N

9. Firearms background checks	N
10. Spending at the border	Y
11. Marijuana liberalized rules	N
12. Electoral College objections	Y

Election Results

Election	Name (Party)	Vote (%)		Cand. Spent	Ind. Exp. Support	Ind. Exp. Oppose
2020 General	Ron Estes (R)	203,432	(64%)	$1,419,121	$7,870	$750
	Laura Lombard (D)	116,166	(36%)	$245,215		
2020 Primary	Ron Estes (R)	87,877	(100%)			

Prior winning percentages: 2018 (59%), 2017 special (52%)

Republican Ron Estes was elected in April 2017 to the seat vacated by Mike Pompeo, who became director of the Central Intelligence Agency and later secretary of State under President Donald Trump. Estes was a longtime businessman and elected official who ran a lackluster campaign in the special election. His victory was narrower than has been customary in this district for Republicans, who scrambled to avoid potential embarrassment during the final days before the vote. His subsequent victories were much more comfortable. With a seat on the Ways and Means Committee, he settled into an influential niche in the House.

Estes was born in Topeka, a fifth-generation Kansan. He got a bachelor's in civil engineering and then an MBA, both from Tennessee Technological University. He was a consultant and had management roles in several different industries, including aerospace, automotive, and oil and gas, where he implemented improved efficiencies with financial and other computer systems. He won his first elected office in 2004, as treasurer of Sedgwick County. In 2010, he was elected Kansas treasurer. In each position, he focused on improving efficiency, customer service and saving tax money. He became active in national associations for state treasurers and held several positions in the Republican Party, serving as the Kansas party's vice chairman.

After Pompeo resigned, each party selected its candidate at a small nominating convention. That limited their time and financial costs, but it also meant that the candidates had to persuade only a small number of party activists. The chief competitor to Estes was Alan Cobb, a coalitions director for Trump's national campaign and onetime aide to former Sen. Bob Dole. Estes won on the second ballot. At the Democratic selection meeting two days later, civil rights attorney James Thompson also won on the second ballot and quickly tried to cast the contest in national terms.

But the contest was slow to attract either local or national media attention. In the closing days, Republicans worried about the outcome. Trump and Vice President Mike Pence recorded robocalls urging Republicans to vote, and Texas Sen. Ted Cruz held an election eve rally. Democrats benefited from the hostility toward Trump among their supporters. In the early vote of more than 23,000 in Sedgwick County, Thompson got 61 percent. He raised $340,000, which was competitive with Estes' $400,000. In a district where Trump five months earlier led 60%-33%, Estes won 53%-46%. He narrowed the gap in Sedgwick so that he trailed by only 1,900 votes, which showed that Republicans were successful with Election Day turnout. The closer-than-usual outcome was a harbinger of Democratic success elsewhere in the state in 2018. Retrospectively, liberal activists second-guessed a missed opportunity.

In the House, Estes became the type of reliable Republican who gets rewarded with a seat on the tax-writing Ways and Means Committee. He expressed concern about Trump's tariffs on China, fearing they could hurt local business and farmers. "While I support President Trump's desire to negotiate a level playing field with our trade partners, we need a targeted approach that embraces free and fair trade over tariffs and protectionism," he said. Estes voiced support for the conservative Wichita-based Koch brothers after Trump attacked them on Twitter for not falling in line behind him. To respond to the economic slowdown caused by the coronavirus pandemic, he filed with Ways and Means Democratic Rep. John Larson a bill to give businesses an immediate tax write-off when they deducted their research and development expenses.

Thompson ran again in 2018. This time, Estes prevailed, 59%-41%, a more traditional Republican showing in the district. Unlike other Democrats who were successful in Kansas, Thompson ran a more ideological campaign, supporting Medicare for All and a $15 minimum wage. In July, he brought in Sen. Bernie Sanders and rising progressive star Alexandria Ocasio-Cortez. Estes allied himself with Trump, including support for the GOP tax cuts and a wall along the Mexican border.

In 2020, Estes biggest reelection concern was the fate in the Toledo-based district of freshman GOP Rep. Steve Watkins, who was indicted three weeks before the Republican primary on charges of voter fraud. In an unusual step, Estes publicly endorsed GOP challenger Jake LaTurner and warned Republicans not to "put this seat at risk by nominating a candidate charged with multiple felonies." LaTurner easily won the primary and retained the seat.

The rapid turnover in the Kansas delegation left Estes as its most senior House member after less than two terms. He showed every indication that he planned to remain in place for at least a few more years.

KS-4: South Central Kansas

Cook Partisan Voting Index: R+15

Population		Race and Ethnicity		Income	
Total	723,075	White	81.90%	Median Income	$58,119
Land area (sq. miles)	14,316	Black	6.70%	District Income Rank	288
Pop/ sq mi	50.51	Latino	12.90%	Poverty Rate	11.90%
Born in State	65.10%	Asian	3.40%	With health insurance	89.70%
		Two or more races	4.50%	Cash public assistance	2.00%
Age Groups		Other	3.50%	Food stamp/SNAP	9.40%
Under 18	25.10%				
18-34	22.30%	**Education**		**Work**	
35-64	36.60%	H.S grad or less	36.30%	White Collar	36.80%
Over 64	16.10%	Some college	33.60%	Sales and Service	36.60%
		College Degree, 4 yr	19.50%	Blue Collar	26.70%
Military		Post grad	10.50%	Government	14.40%
Veteran/ Active Duty	8.60%				

2020 Pres. Vote	Trump	193,066	(60%)	Biden	123,016	(38%)	Jorgensen 7,495	(2%)
2016 Pres. Vote	Trump	165,266	(60%)	Clinton	90,541	(33%)		

Wichita: With about 390,000 people, Wichita has been a Great Plains metropolis. It has been growing slowly, but it has fallen behind the size of Omaha and Tulsa—other regional centers in the Plains. It began as a farm market town and grew with local oil and gas discoveries in the 1920s. The aircraft business began in 1911 when Clyde Cessna first flew his plane from a farm in Kingman County and, five years later, moved his operations to north Wichita. The real impetus for the industry came during World War II and the years just afterward, when aircraft factories sprouted up on the Kansas prairie. Wichita suddenly became the nation's major producer of small aircraft. Workers poured in, many from neighboring Arkansas and Oklahoma, giving the city a taste of southern culture.

The September 11 attacks were a severe blow to the overall airline industry, with the loss of some 15,000 local jobs, from which the area has not fully recovered. Boeing, once the area's largest employer, shut down its local facilities in 2014; company officials cited cuts in the Pentagon budget and high overhead costs. In 2017, there were signs of a local rebound when Spirit Aero Systems announced a $1 billion factory bringing 1,000 jobs to build fuselages, plus engine and wing parts for Boeing 737 MAX planes.

But two disastrous 737 MAX crashes overseas led to shutdowns of service and new deliveries, plus two years of investigations into what went wrong. Spirit, the largest employer in Wichita, responded with layoffs of its 2,800 workers until the MAX was cleared for flight. In the self-styled "Air Capital of the World," the ripple effect led to job losses for twice that number.

Cargill Inc., the largest privately held corporation in the United States, is based in Wichita and includes 75 businesses. In 2019, Cargill began operation of its $90 million biodiesel plant in north Wichita, which was expected to produce 60 million gallons of fuel annually—connecting farmers to industrial customers. Koch Industries, owned by the politically active and conservative Koch family, which has been second only to Cargill as the nation's largest privately held company, employs about 60,000 in the United States and has revenues of $110 billion, much of it in agriculture and technology. At a time when the Kochs were battered politically for their well-financed conservative activism and shifting to a softer edge, their company was beloved at home as an employer and philanthropist. David Koch retired from the family business in 2018 due to health reasons and died a year later. His older brother Charles distanced their political network from the influence of President Donald Trump, doubling down on his free-market principles and philanthropy.

Kansas' 4th Congressional District covers wheat-growing areas to the east and west; two-thirds of its people are in Wichita and Sedgwick County. It occasionally votes Democratic in local and state contests, including for its first African-American mayor, Carl Brewer. He served two terms and was hailed as a consensus-builder when he stepped down in 2015. The 4th has been solidly Republican in federal elections. Donald Trump got 60 percent in both of his campaigns.

KENTUCKY

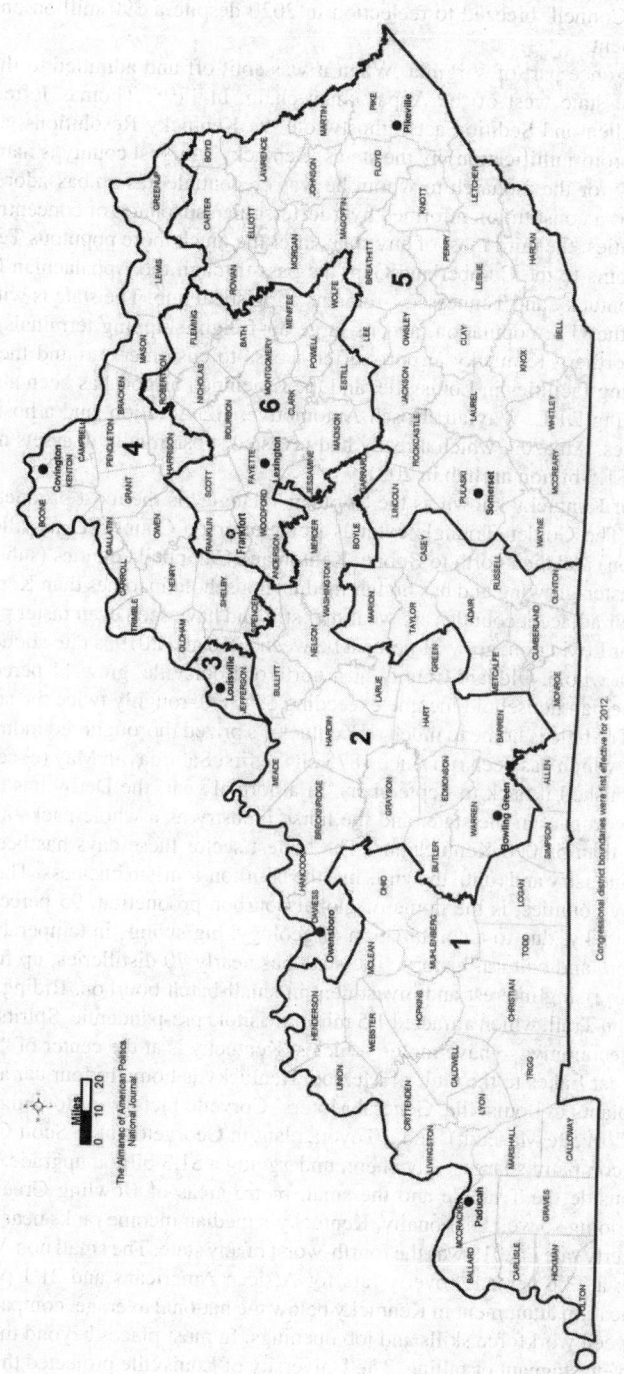

It took longer than it did in some other states, but over the past decade, Kentucky completed its transition from Democratic to Republican. While Kentucky has a Democratic governor, its other elected statewide offices are solidly Republican, and the state's political godfather, Senate Republican Leader Mitch McConnell, breezed to reelection in 2020 despite a $90 million onslaught from his Democratic opponent.

Kentucky was once part of Virginia. When it was split off and admitted to the union in 1792, it became the first state west of the Appalachian chain. In 1798, Thomas Jefferson, aroused by the Federalists' Alien and Sedition acts, ghostwrote the Kentucky Resolutions, a defense of self-governance (and proto-nullification) by the states. Kentucky's largest county is named for Jefferson, and its largest city for the monarch to whom he was credentialed as ambassador to France, Louis XVI. Kentucky has a constitution informed by a Jeffersonian suspicion of concentrating power. The state has 120 counties, the third most of any state, after the much more populous Texas and Georgia.

Kentucky—home to the Cumberland Gap, the pass through the Appalachian Mountains where Virginia meets Kentucky and Tennessee—remains a logistical hub. The state is within a day's drive of 65 percent of the U.S. population, and its large air-freight shipping terminals at the Louisville and Cincinnati-Northern Kentucky airports offer access to customers around the world. UPS has large and expanding facilities in Louisville, and the Cincinnati airport has been a magnet for major companies including DHL, Wayfair, Bosch Automotive, GE Aviation, and a host of lesser-known logistics companies. Amazon, which already had invested substantially in assets near the airport, is poised to open a $1.5 billion air hub in 2021.

The portion of Kentucky known as the "Golden Triangle" is the most productive and populous part of the state. The Golden Triangle extends from Jefferson County (Louisville) east to Fayette County (Lexington) and then north to Boone, Kenton and Campbell counties (suburban Cincinnati). The Triangle is faster-growing and has higher median household incomes than Kentucky as a whole, and several of their adjacent counties are wealthier still and have seen even faster population growth. Scott County, near Lexington, grew 21 percent between 2010 and 2019, a rate about five times higher than the state as a whole. Oldham County, just north of Louisville, grew 11 percent over the same period; it has a median household income exceeding $99,000, roughly twice the state average.

The Golden Triangle is home to much of Kentucky's prized thoroughbred industry, including the Kentucky Derby, which has been run since 1875 on the first Saturday in May (except for 2020, when the coronavirus pushed it back to September). In a normal year, the Derby has an estimated $400 million economic impact in the state, and the horse industry as a whole packs a $4 billion punch, employing more than 55,000 Kentuckians. The hottest sector these days has been the state's $8.5 billion distillery industry and (until the virus hit) the bourbon-tourism business. The Golden Triangle, with some nearby counties, is the home of global bourbon production: 95 percent of the liquor is produced in Kentucky, due to a combination of geology, big swings in temperature, soil favorable to corn production, and cultural history. The state has nearly 70 distilleries, up from fewer than 20 in 1999, thanks to rising interest and investment in small-batch bourbon. Riding this growth is the Kentucky Bourbon Trail, which attracted 1.5 million visitors pre-pandemic. Spirits have helped drive a healthy export economy; so have motor vehicles. Kentucky is at the center of "auto alley," which runs from the Great Lakes to the Gulf of Mexico. Kentucky is home to four car and truck assembly lines: two Ford plants in Louisville, General Motors' Corvette factory in Bowling Green (also home to the National Corvette Museum), and a Toyota plant in Georgetown, in Scott County just north of Lexington—the company's largest anywhere, undergoing a $1.3 billion upgrade.

However, outside the Triangle and the small metro areas of Bowling Green and Owensboro, Kentucky is not doing so well. Nationally, Kentucky's median income ranks near the bottom, and its 16.3 percent poverty rate in 2019 was the fourth-worst of any state. The small non-White communities fare even worse: a 23.6 percent poverty rate for African Americans and 21.1 percent for Latinos. With higher-education attainment in Kentucky below the national average, companies in the state see a mismatch between workforce skills and job openings. In most places beyond the Golden Triangle, population has been stagnant or falling. The University of Louisville projected that two-thirds of the state's counties will lose population between 2015 and 2040. In some rural counties, government jobs now account for two-thirds of all employment. One portion is in corrections: Even as prison populations have declined nationally in recent years, Kentucky saw its inmate population grow by more than 11 percent between 2008 and 2018. In some counties, long commutes to employment hubs are common.

One reason for the rural malaise has been the decline of coal, especially in the eastern part of the state, where the fuel was once king. The increasing popularity of horizontal hydraulic fracturing, or fracking, for low-cost natural gas has contributed significantly to the national slowdown in coal demand. Tougher federal regulations to protect water quality around mines, federal encouragement (at least before President Donald Trump) to shift away from coal, and greater industry sensitivity to the fuels used to generate electricity have exacerbated the downturn. Meanwhile, most coal seams in eastern Kentucky have been mined of their most accessible product, raising the cost of extraction; labor disputes have festered as well. In western Kentucky, production has not been as hard hit; the higher sulfur content of its coal once had difficulty coping with clean-air rules, but the installation of scrubbers at many power plants helped sustain the region's mines. Overall, though, coal-mining employment statewide fell from 16,600 in 2011 to 5,700 in 2019, and the presidentially appointed directors of the Tennessee Valley Authority spurned Trump in 2019, voting for a complete conversion of the Paradise Fossil Plant in western Kentucky, a major coal-fired facility, to natural gas. Some abandoned coal-mining territory in eastern Kentucky has become repurposed as habitat for wildlife, including elk.

Another declining product has been tobacco. For most of the last century, tens of thousands of Kentucky farmers grew at least a small crop of tobacco, but health concerns and evolving social mores gradually took their toll. (About a quarter of Kentuckians smoke, more than any other state but West Virginia, and the state leads the nation in lung cancer.) Leading politicians from both parties have eagerly endorsed efforts to expand hemp cultivation, which was legalized by the 2018 farm bill. Despite early progress, hemp backers were disappointed by the 2020 bankruptcy of GenCanna Global USA, the biggest player in the state's hemp sector.

As in other parts of Appalachia, substance abuse has spread. Kentucky ranks in the top 10 states for drug overdose death rates, and legislative efforts to curb the tide have proven ineffective. Andy Beshear, now the governor, filed several opioid-related lawsuits while he was serving as state attorney general, targeting companies such as Walgreens and Johnson & Johnson. Meanwhile, 54 Kentucky counties were among the 220 the Centers for Disease Control and Prevention determined to be most at risk of a major HIV outbreak, a consequence of the rise in injected drugs. The state, under then-Gov. Steve Beshear (the current governor's father), took advantage of health insurance expansion under the Affordable Care Act; the response was more enthusiastic than in almost any other state, with Kentucky's uninsured rate falling by more than half. The effect on health outcomes was murkier. Steve Beshear's successor as governor, Republican Matt Bevin, sought to tie the Medicaid expansion to work requirements, but the effort became snagged in the courts. After Andy Beshear defeated Bevin in 2019, the new governor pulled the plug on work requirements.

Kentucky long favored the Democratic Party, which can trace its ancestry back to Jefferson. The Bluegrass region and the western half of the state were slaveholding territory and voted Democratic. Louisville, with many German immigrants, was an anti-slavery town, and for years flirted with Republicans, but in the past century, the city and surrounding Jefferson County have been conspicuously more Democratic than the state as a whole. The eastern mountains were pro-Union and remain Republican, except for a few large counties where the United Mine Workers organized coal miners in the 1930s. But the national Democratic Party has moved to the left on social issues, including abortion and guns, while Kentucky has become known for Kim Davis, the elected Rowan County clerk who refused to sign same-sex marriage licenses, and for a $100 million Noah's Ark tourist attraction and Creation Museum built by Biblical literalists in Williamstown, between Cincinnati and Lexington. Kentucky has gone solidly Republican in the past six presidential elections.

For a while, state-level Democrats held on, thanks to incumbency and self-inflicted Republican mistakes. But the party's registration edge has eroded, and so has its ability to win statewide. In 2016, the GOP won control of the state House for the first time since 1920, joining the state Senate, which had been in Republican hands since 2000. The new GOP majority enacted a number of policies that conservatives had long awaited, including a right-to-work law, an end to prevailing wages on public construction jobs, and establishment of charter schools. A ban on abortions after a fetal heartbeat is detected ran into trouble in the courts, but language requiring patients to undergo and be shown the results of an ultrasound prior to having an abortion passed judicial muster. In the Trump era, Kentucky's demographics were a good fit for the Republican Party. Kentucky is the seventh-whitest state in the country at 85 percent, and only four states (Maine, Mississippi, Vermont and West Virginia) have a smaller Hispanic percentage. It's also among the top 10 rural states.

In March 2020, urban Kentucky became a flashpoint after police shot and killed Breonna Taylor, a Louisville EMT, during a raid on her home in an operation that targeted her former boyfriend. Protests ensued, intensifying and spreading following the death of George Floyd at the hands of police in Minneapolis. Grand jurors eventually declined to indict two of the officers involved in the Louisville raid, including the one determined to have shot Taylor, while one officer was indicted for firing rounds that put Taylor's neighbors in danger. The grand jury's decision further inflamed critics of the raid, as did the role played by state Attorney General Daniel Cameron, a McConnell protégé and African-American Republican; several jurors claimed he misled the public about their deliberations.

In the 2019 gubernatorial campaign, the younger Beshear ousted Bevin, but analysts attributed it less to warm feelings for Democrats and more to voters becoming irritated with Bevin's prickly approach to governance. Political analyst Perry Bacon Jr., a Kentucky native, noted that Beshear's father had won 92 counties in his initial 2007 gubernatorial run, but Andy Beshear had taken just 23 in his victory. Indeed, during the same election, Republicans won every other statewide elected office, including two, attorney general and secretary of state, that had been held by Democrats.

In the 2020 presidential race, Joe Biden took just 36 percent, with Trump maintaining the 62 percent share he notched in 2016. Biden, like Hillary Clinton four years earlier, won only two counties: Jefferson and Fayette. He did make marginal improvements in some of the state's growing areas. In each of the three northern Kentucky counties adjacent to Cincinnati, Biden narrowed Trump's margin by six points, although he still lost by between 18 and 36 points in each. Biden also narrowed Trump's winning margins by between three and nine points in Franklin (Frankfort), Warren (Bowling Green), Scott, and Oldham. But Trump's improvement in the state's vast rural areas was enough to negate these gains. In the Senate contest, McConnell fared four points worse than Trump, but still won, 58%-38%, confounding national Democratic small-dollar donors who thought they had a shot at toppling the Senate majority leader in a solidly red state.

Population			Race and Ethnicity		Income	
Total	4,467,673		White	86.70%	Median Income	52,295
Land area (sq. miles)	39,486		Black	8.10%	State Income Rank	44 out of 50
Pop/ sq mi	113.14		Latino	3.80%	Poverty Rate	16.30%
Born in state	68.30%		Asian	2.10%	With health insurance	93.60%
			Two or more races	2.30%	Cash public assistance	1.70%
Age Groups			Other	1.20%	Food stamp/SNAP	16.1%
Under 18	22.40%					
18-34	22.20%		Education		Work	
35-64	38.50%		H.S grad or less	46.00%	White Collar	36.20%
Over 64	16.90%		Some college	28.80%	Sales and Service	36.40%
			College Degree, 4 yr	14.90%	Blue Collar	27.40%
Military			Post grad	10.30%	Government	14.50%
Veteran/ Active Duty	7.60%					

Presidential Politics

2020 Primary (D)	Biden (D)	365,284(68%)	Sanders (D)	65,055(12%)		
2016 Caucus (R)	Trump (R)	82,493(36%)	Cruz (R)	72,503(32%)	Rubio (R)	37,579(16%)
	Kasich (R)	33,134(14%)				
2020 Pres. Vote	Trump (R)	1,326,646(62%)	Biden (D)	772,474(36%)		
2016 Pres. Vote	Trump (R)	1,202,971(63%)	Clinton (D)	628,854(33%)	Johnson (L)	53,752 (3%)

It has been 24 years since Democrats won Kentucky in a presidential election. In the intervening quarter-century, it's become one of the most reliably Republican states in the country. With two Southerners on their ticket, they carried the state in 1992 and 1996. In 2000, Al Gore from neighboring Tennessee was hobbled by stands hostile to tobacco, coal and guns, all staples of Kentucky culture.

George W. Bush carried the state, 57%-41%, that year, and Republicans have won by growing margins ever since. In 2012, Barack Obama carried only four of Kentucky's 120 counties, including those containing the state's two largest cities, Louisville and Lexington, and the state capital of Frankfort. He carried only one historically Democratic county in the eastern mountains. Even when losing by landslide margins, George McGovern carried seven mountain counties in 1972 and Walter Mondale carried 12 mountain counties in 1984.

The GOP trend has continued. Donald Trump won every coal country county in both 2016 and 2020 as he defeated Hillary Clinton by 63%-33 and beat Joe Biden by 62%-36%. In both elections, the Democratic nominee carried just two counties, Jefferson (Louisville) and Fayette (Lexington and the University of Kentucky). Democrats' policies toward combating global warming, the ongoing decline of the coal industry, Trump's promises to bring back coal, the region's conservative social values, and populist blue-collar voters' hard shift against Democrats, and antagonism toward the coasts have all remade Appalachia into one of the most solidly Republican areas of the country. And while the areas around Louisville and Lexington shifted left in 2020, much of the state's more rural territory continued its rightward drift. One illustration: Elliott County, a small coal county, went to Al Gore by nearly a 2-to-1 margin in 2000; in 2020, Trump won more than three quarters of its vote, seven points greater than his 2016 performance.

Congressional Districts

117th Congress Lineup	1D 5R	116th Congress Lineup	1D 5R

Republican majorities in both the state House and Senate easily exceed two-thirds control in Kentucky, where the legislature requires only a simple majority to override the governor's veto in most cases. So, the election of Democratic Gov. Andy Beshear in 2019 will have no direct effect on Republicans' control of redistricting. In the current House delegation, Republicans hold five of the six seats. Four of the GOP-held districts and Democratic-held 3rd district in Louisville's Jefferson County have not been competitive in federal contests during the past decade. The sole competitive seat has been the 6th District—the only one that does not border another state. Since 2012, Republican Rep. Andy Barr has survived competitive contests in that district. But Republicans have every reason to increase their party control in that district, by removing some of its politically marginal areas and adding nearby GOP-heavy counties.

Lexington-based Fayette County, the heart of the district, with about 40 percent of its population, leans Democratic. The next most-competitive county is Franklin County, which includes the state capital of Frankfort. Switching Franklin and adjacent Woodford County from the 6th and replacing them with counties from any of the three districts that border the 6th likely would make that district secure for Barr and other Republicans—while keeping Fayette County whole, or nearly so. The likely redrawing of the 6th will attract extensive attention, if only to see how counties compete to shift from—or remain in—their current districts. Those details will have significance in those local areas, though Republicans are nearly certain to hold the upper hand in making the decisions.

If Republicans get ambitious, they could pursue the option of dividing the Louisville-based 3rd District into two or three pieces to eliminate its Democratic control. But that likely would create anxiety among neighboring Republicans who worry about continuing control of their own districts.

Andy Beshear (D)

Elected 2019. term expires 2023, 1st term; b. Nov. 29, 1977, Louisville KY; Vanderbilt University, B.A., 2000; University of Virginia, J.D., 2003; Christian Church; Married (Brittany); 2 children.

Elected Office: Atty. Gen., 2016-19.

Professional Career: Partner, Stites and Harbison, Louisville KY.

Office: 700 Capitol Ave. Suite 100, Frankfort, 40601; 502-564-2611; Fax: 502-564-0437; Website: kentucky.gov

Lt. Gov.: Jacqueline Coleman (D); **Atty. Gen:** Daniel Cameron (R); **Sec. of State:** Michael Adams (R)

State Legislature: Senate: 8D, 30R House: 25D, 75R

Election Results

Election	Name (Party)	Vote (%)
2019 General	Andy Beshear (D)	709,577 (49%)
	Matt Bevin (R)	704,388 (49%)
2019 Primary	Andy Beshear (D)	149,438 (38%)
	Rocky Adkins (D)	125,970 (32%)
	Adam H. Edelin (D)	110,159 (28%)

Andy Beshear bucked Kentucky's increasingly Republican leanings in 2019, winning the governorship amid voters' irritation with Gov. Matt Bevin. In office, Beshear pursued a restoration of policies implemented by his father, two-term Gov. Steve Beshear, that were opposed by Bevin, including a Medicaid expansion.

The younger Beshear grew up as his father was climbing the political ladder in Kentucky, from state representative to attorney general to lieutenant governor between 1974 and 1987; the elder Beshear then had a long run with the Lexington-based law firm Stites& Harbison. Andy Beshear graduated from Vanderbilt University and earned his law degree from the University of Virginia. He worked for the law firm White & Case in Washington, then moved back to Kentucky to work as a litigator for Stites& Harbison. Andy Beshear announced in the run-up to the 2015 election that he would seek to succeed outgoing Democratic Attorney General Jack Conway. The announcement came as his father was finishing out his second term as governor, and critics saw some blurred lines in the record-breaking donations that flowed into his attorney general campaign from people who had ties to the governor or business with the state. Beshear won the race for attorney general, though despite a yawning disparity in war chests, it was close: The Republican nominee, Whitney Westerfield, came within about 2,000 votes of winning, and as a state senator, has remained a critic of Beshear.

In office, Beshear aggressively squared off against Bevin, who had won the governorship in the same election while articulating a reliably conservative agenda. The two clashed over cuts to higher education (the courts sided with Beshear), a reorganization of the state pension board, and Bevin's replacement of the University of Louisville board of trustees. After Republicans flipped the state House to GOP control in 2016 (for the first time since 1920) Bevin was able to push an even a stronger conservative agenda, including abortion limits, right-to-work, and charter schools.

By 2018, Kentucky politics had become dominated by two issues. One was Bevin's effort to enact work requirements for Medicaid recipients, a policy the Trump administration had allowed states to pursue. Bevin's initial plan was scrapped by a federal judge in June 2018, but state officials put together an alternate policy that received approval from the Trump administration in late 2018. The other issue involved the state's mess of a public pension system. Bevin pursued a plan that would have reduced guaranteed retirement benefits primarily for new teachers, as well as other government employees, to echo changes in most private retirement systems. Educators angrily protested: More than two dozen school districts closed due to sickouts, and districts across the state shut down a few days later as teachers rallied at the state capitol. Bevin called teachers "thugs" and had to apologize for suggesting that the teachers who had walked out on short notice likely exposed their students to sexual assaults and other perils. Meanwhile, Beshear sued to block the Bevin-backed pension plan that passed, and the state Supreme Court struck it down on procedural grounds. A special legislative session called by Bevin to pass a new law fizzled.

Bevin also skirmished with members of his own party, and the constant tensions helped wear down the governor's approval rating to among the worst in the country. Freshman state Rep. Robert Goforth announced a GOP primary challenge, blasting Bevin's style. Though Goforth was far less well-known than the governor, he took a strikingly high 39 percent of the primary vote, and two other minor candidates collectively took more than 8 percent. Meanwhile, in the Democratic primary, Beshear faced three rivals, including longtime state Rep. Rocky Adkins and former state Auditor Adam Edelen. Powered by his family name and his high-profile sparring with Bevin, Beshear won with almost 38 percent. Adkins, running as an old-fashioned Kentucky moderate, finished second with nearly 32 percent, thanks to a strong showing in his home base of eastern Kentucky. Edelen, the most progressive of the three, finished third with almost 28 percent. The Democratic candidates quickly presented a united front after the primary.

In the general, Beshear and Bevin continued to clash over teacher pensions and the Medicaid expansion; Beshear had chosen an educator, Jacqueline Coleman, as his running mate, while Bevin chose a physician, state Sen. Ralph Alvarado. Bevin attacked Beshear for his then-firm's representation of Purdue Pharma in a state lawsuit over opioids; the parties had settled for $24 million, a much smaller sum than subsequent lawsuits by states would secure. Beshear said he was not involved in the settlement negotiations, and he pointed to a string of pharmaceutical settlements he would later negotiate as attorney general. Bevin also reminded voters that one of Beshear's chief appointments as attorney general, Tim Longmeyer, was involved in kickbacks during his service for Steve Beshear; Longmeyer was eventually sentenced to 70 months in prison on federal bribery charges. Both Beshears said they had no knowledge of his actions. Beshear, for his part, worked to keep Bevin's history of unharnessed comments about teachers and other adversaries topmost in voters' minds, and with late polls showing a tight race, President Donald Trump came to the state to campaign for Bevin.

In a high-turnout election, Beshear eked out a victory by just over 5,000 votes, ousting an incumbent who had won by nine points four years earlier. (A Libertarian Party candidate won 28,000 votes, more than five times the margin of victory.) In his victory speech, Beshear said, "To our educators, this is your victory." Beshear won 23 counties, up from 14 won by Conway in Bevin's 2015 race. Beshear greatly expanded the winning Democratic margins in Jefferson County (Louisville) and Fayette County (Lexington), and flipped two counties adjoining Cincinnati, Kenton and Campbell, along with Warren (Bowling Green) and Scott (Georgetown). Beshear also cut Bevin's margin in Oldham County, north of Louisville, from 25 points to five. All told, Bevin won the vast majority of counties, but unlike many other contests in recent years, his strong showing in rural areas wasn't enough to secure a Republican victory. The race was close enough that Bevin took several days to concede, initially alleging "irregularities" in the vote count. On his way out the door Bevin issued more then 400 pardons, including one for a donor who had been convicted of homicide, and others for murderers and child rapists.

In office, Beshear ended Bevin's efforts to impose a work requirement for Medicaid and ensured that the expansion of Medicaid under his father would remain in place. He also restored voting rights for more than 140,000 ex-offenders and became the first Kentucky governor to appear at an annual pro-LGBTQ rally. In 2020, Beshear frequently sparred with his successor as attorney general, Daniel Cameron, a Republican and a protégé of Mitch McConnell, the Senate Republican leader. Beshear took issue with how Cameron handled a grand jury looking into the death of Breonna Taylor at the hands of Louisville police officers, a case that had become central in Black Lives Matter protests nationally. Beshear and Cameron also faced off in court over coronavirus-related restrictions. Beshear declared a state of emergency one day before New York Gov. Andrew Cuomo did and, at one point, irritated Kentucky's neighbors to the south by urging his constituents not to travel to Tennessee, terming that state's response to the virus insufficient (the two state's average daily case rates were nearly identical by January 2021). Beshear's daily press conferences early in the pandemic even made him something of a social media star. When Beshear issued a statewide mask mandate in July, Cameron sued, but the courts sided with Beshear. The most sustained criticism of Beshear's work on the pandemic has come from the legislature, though polls showed him with generally strong public support.

Beshear managed to work more cooperatively with another Republican statewide official, Secretary of State Michael Adams. In the run-up to a closely watched (and pandemic-delayed) June 23 primary, Beshear and Adams agreed to a significant expansion of mail balloting, and primary turnout ended up close to record-setting levels. "I think the election was pretty successful," Joshua A. Douglas, a University of Kentucky law professor who specializes in elections, told PolitiFact. In 2021, Beshear worked with Republicans to pass a bill that expanded voting access -- the only such legislation passed by a GOP-controlled legislature after Trump's repeated broadsides against early and mail balloting. On other issues, though, the GOP had its way: The legislature overrode most of Beshear's 27 vetoes, including measures to limit worker safety rules. The legislature also passed a constitutional amendment to preempt abortions in the state if Roe v. Wade is overturned; it is slated to go to the voters in 2022. However the remainder of Beshear's term plays out, he's likely to get a strong challenge in 2023 from one or more Kentucky Republicans, including Cameron, Agriculture Commissioner Ryan Quarles, and Rep. James Comer, who has kept his eye on the governor's office since losing to Bevin by 83 votes in the 2015 primary.

Mitch McConnell (R)

Elected 1984, term expires 2026, 7th term, b. Feb 20, 1942; Tuscumbia, AL; University of Louisville, B.A., 1964; University of Kentucky Law School, J.D., 1967; Baptist; Married (Elaine Chao); 3 children from previous marriage.

Military Career: United States Army Reserve, 1967.

Elected Office: Jefferson County Judge Executive, 1978-1985.

Professional Career: Intern, Senator John Sherman Cooper, 1964; Chief Legislative Assistant, U.S Sen. Marlow Cook, 1968-1970; Deputy Assistant, U.S Attorney General, 1974-1975.

DC Office: 317 RSOB 20510, 202-224-2541, Fax: 202-224-2499, mcconnell.senate.gov

State Offices: Bowling Green, 270-781-1673; Fort Wright, 859-578-0188; Lexington, 859-224-8286; London, 606-864-2026; Louisville, 502-582-6304; Paducah, 270-442-4554.

Committees: Senate Republican Leader. *Agriculture, Nutrition & Forestry*: Commodities, Risk Management & Trade; Food & Nutrition, Specialty Crops, Organics & Research; Rural Development & Energy. *Appropriations*: Agriculture, Rural Development, FDA & Related Agencies; Department of Defense; Department of the Interior, Environment & Related Agencies; Energy & Water Development; Military Construction & Veteran Affairs & Related Agencies; State, Foreign Operations & Related Programs. *Intelligence. Rules & Administration*.

Group Ratings

	ADA	ACLU	AFL-CIO	LCV	COC	HAFA	ACU	CFG	FRC
2020	-	15%	-	23%	-	64%	87%	-	-
2019	0%	C	21%	14%	82%	C	88%	29%	100%

Almanac Ratings 2019-2020

	Economy	Social	Foreign	Composite
Liberal	7%	7%	0%	5%
Conservative	93%	93%	100%	95%

Key Votes of the 116th Congress

1. EPA clean energy rules	N	5. Russia sanctions	N	9. Barr as Atty. General	Y
2. U.S./Mex./Can. trade deal	Y	6. Troops in SYR, AFG	Y	10. Spending at the border	Y
3. Cut unemployment benefits	Y	7. Veto arms sales to Saudis	N	11. Coney Barrett to Sup. Ct.	Y
4. Shelton to Fed Reserve	N	8. Defense $$$, veto override	Y	12. Electoral College objections	N

Election Results

Election	Name (Party)	Vote (%)		Cand. Spent	Ind. Exp. Support	Ind. Exp. Oppose
2020 General	Mitch McConnell (R)......................	1,233,315	(58%)	$62,992,734	$281,110	$11,997,558
	Amy McGrath (D)............................	816,257	(38%)	$95,751,731	$4,575,038	$13,044,675
	Brad Barron (L)....................................	85,386	(4%)	$16,514	$2,216,202	
2020 Primary	Mitch McConnell (R)......................	342,660	(83%)			
	Wesley Morgan (R)...........................	25,588	(6%)			

Prior winning percentages: 2014 (56%), 2008 (53%), 2002 (65%), 1996 (56%), 1990 (52%), 1984 (50%)

If many politicians gaze into the mirror and see a president, Republican Mitch McConnell has always seen a Senate majority leader staring back. It's a perch that Kentucky's senior senator occupied for six years and that he is single-mindedly focused on regaining—as his party vies in the 2022 midterm elections to erase the razor-thin Senate advantage the Democrats acquired in early 2021. Even though Joe Biden is a former Senate colleague with whom McConnell enjoyed a cordial relationship, the GOP leader has signaled that he would not grant the new White House occupant any victories. After realizing political gains from thwarting the previous Democratic president, Barack Obama, McConnell told Kentucky reporters in early 2021 that he would fight Biden's agenda "every step of the way."

McConnell's durability—he is the longest serving Republican leader in Senate history—can be attributed in significant part to his success in keeping united a caucus ranging from centrists to unyielding conservatives. In 2020, he became the second longest-serving Senate leader from any party—just two years behind the record holder, Democrat Mike Mansfield, who served from 1961 to 1977. McConnell has pointed to Mansfield as a role model, and there are parallels. McConnell is a restrained personality most comfortable operating outside the spotlight, with his power derived from mastery of the Senate's arcane procedures and his secretive strategizing; in the age of mass media, he is a dour presence on TV news shows. By the same token, McConnell—during the administration of President Donald Trump—came to be regarded as perhaps the most powerful majority leader since Mansfield's immediate predecessor, Lyndon B. Johnson.

If Johnson regularly resorted to arm-twisting, McConnell's power has stemmed more from an ability to quietly assess the members of his caucus and their needs. What does link the two—in the view of McConnell's numerous detractors—is a reputation for ruthlessness. Exhibit A has been McConnell's unprecedented refusal to consider Obama's Supreme Court nomination of Merrick Garland eight months prior to the 2016 election—only to later ramrod confirmation of Trump's nomination of Amy Coney Barrett two weeks prior to Election Day 2020. The latter was a capstone to McConnell's longstanding ambition to remake the federal judiciary in a more conservative image— as the Senate confirmed more than 200 jurists, including three Supreme Court justices and more than 50 appeals court judges, during Trump's four years. In late 2020, while telling the New York Times he regarded this as "the single most important accomplishment" of his career, McConnell compared himself to none other than Johnson. "At the risk of tooting my own horn, look at the majority leaders since LBJ and find another one who was able to do something as consequential as this," he declared.

In an interview a year earlier, McConnell called his thwarting of the Garland nomination to fill the vacancy left by the death of Justice Antonin Scalia "the most consequential thing I've ever done." It not only let Trump fill the seat with conservative Neil Gorsuch immediately after taking office it arguably helped Trump reach the White House by energizing conservative voters in 2016. The McConnell-Trump alliance—before it acrimoniously collapsed in the final days of Trump's term —underscored the maxim that "politics makes strange bedfellows." In contrast to Trump's Twitter tirades, McConnell always has chosen his words with care and calculation. ("The idea of an off-the-cuff comment is anathema to him," Louisville attorney John David Dyche wrote in a 2009 biography.) But the marriage of convenience proved mutually beneficial: When Trump was impeached for the first time in early 2020, McConnell maneuvered to ensure a quick acquittal. Seeking reelection back home, he benefited from the gratitude of Trump's base of conservative populists—who had viewed him warily as a creature of the Washington establishment.

However, the assault on the Capitol in early January 2021 by a pro-Trump mob prompted McConnell to condemn the outgoing president in terms that could have come from a Democrat— while, the New York Times reported, he privately concluded that Trump had committed impeachable offenses in inciting the mob. At the time, McConnell was said to believe that impeaching Trump would make it easier to purge him from the Republican Party. But, when a second Trump impeachment came to vote a month after the Capitol insurrection, McConnell voted no: He questioned the constitutionality of impeaching a president who already had left office. Experts said it was constitutional, and McConnell was widely viewed as having pulled back because Trump remained popular among GOP voters despite the insurrection—and a fear that a full-out assault on the former president could endanger chances of a restored Republican Senate majority. A similar calculus impelled McConnell in May 2021 to lead a successful filibuster to block creation of a bipartisan commission to investigate the January insurrection—going so far as to ask wavering senators to support the filibuster as a "personal favor" to him, according to CNN.As one former Trump administration official and Senate aide told the New Yorker, "His North Star is continuing as majority leader—it's really the only thing for him."

Addison Mitchell McConnell grew up in Alabama before his family moved to Louisville Kentucky. As a child, he overcame polio. In adulthood, he has developed a thick political skin. The walls of his Capitol office are decorated with cartoons in which he has been less than kindly depicted; he has boasted to audiences that opponents occasionally compare him to Darth Vader. The usually unflappable McConnell did object when House Speaker Nancy Pelosi derided him as "Moscow Mitch"—after he blocked election security legislation following intelligence agency findings of Russian interference in the 2016 presidential election. McConnell labeled the opprobrium as "McCarthyism", but that didn't deter a group of his lieutenants—under the Twitter handle of "Team Mitch"—from tweeting a "#MoscowMitch drink recipe."

McConnell has spent his entire adult life in politics. In between college at the University of Louisville and law school at the University of Kentucky, he was an intern for Kentucky Sen. John Sherman Cooper, then a friend of Mansfield and a member of what has become a critically endangered bloc in the Senate: moderate Republicans. In fact, McConnell began his career on the left wing of his party. Another biographer, journalist Alec MacGillis, noted in his 2014 book that McConnell supported abortion rights and labor unions—favoring collective bargaining for public employees— in the years before his election to the Senate. The young McConnell—who later said he admired Cooper for carrying out "his best judgment instead of pandering to the popular view"—watched up close as Cooper helped round up votes to break a filibuster of the 1964 Civil Rights Act. McConnell accompanied Cooper to the ceremony at which Johnson signed the measure—and even voted for Johnson that year.

After graduating from law school, McConnell became chief legislative assistant to Kentucky Sen. Marlow Cook and served in the Justice Department during the Ford administration. After moving back to Louisville, McConnell in 1977 was elected to the first of two terms as Jefferson County judge executive. In 1984, he took on Democratic Sen. Walter "Dee" Huddleston. McConnell ran an ad—conceived by Roger Ailes, later CEO of Fox News—that has become an enduring classic in political circles. It showed bloodhounds sniffing for Huddleston in vacation locales where the incumbent had collected speaking fees while the Senate was in session. McConnell won by about 5,000 votes out of 1.2 million cast. He emerged during his first term as an outspoken foe of campaign finance reform, with his stance a mix of principle—he argued money represented a form of free speech —and expediency. "I never would have been able to win my race if there had been a limit on the amount of money I could raise and spend," he wrote of his first Senate run in his 2016 autobiography, "The Long Game."

It was a marked shift from a Louisville Courier-Journal op-ed that McConnell wrote during the Watergate scandal—in which he called the influence of money in politics a "cancer" and advocated public funding of presidential elections. McConnell not only filibustered the 2002 McCain-Feingold campaign reform bill limiting certain kinds of donations, he later filed suit challenging its provisions. The Supreme Court upheld most of McCain-Feingold, but later removed many restraints on what corporations and large donors could spend to influence elections in its 2010 Citizens United decision; McConnell lauded that ruling as "an important step" in "restoring the First Amendment rights of these groups." A decade later, however, McConnell was decidedly unhappy when several large corporations utilized those rights to speak out against a controversial Georgia law on voter access enacted by the Republican-controlled state Legislature after Democrats won the state in the 2020 presidential election—and two concurrent Senate races. "My warning to corporate America is to stay out of politics," he said at a news conference, pointedly adding, "I'm not talking about political contributions."

In 1990, after winning a second term, McConnell ran for the chairmanship of the National Republican Senatorial Committee, the Senate GOP's campaign arm. He lost but won in his second try in 1996, serving in the post for the 1998 and 2000 election cycles. His acumen as a political strategist has been on display since: He has often shaped the party's message, repeating poll-tested phrases intended to sway public opinion. McConnell became Senate Republican whip after his third statewide election victory in 2002. He campaigned for months among his colleagues when the job opened, and his only opponent dropped out several days before the contest.

Shortly after McConnell's election as whip, Republican Leader Trent Lott of Mississippi came under a storm of criticism when he spoke favorably of Strom Thurmond's segregationist campaign for president in 1948 at an event honoring Thurmond's 100th birthday. McConnell was Lott's strongest public defender, threatening retaliation against Democrats if they moved to censure him. But, as the controversy showed no sign of abating, he privately recommended to Lott that he "step down as soon as possible." Ordinarily, McConnell might have been in line for the leader's position, but he did not challenge Tennessee's Bill Frist when—urged on by the Bush White House—Frist ran for Lott's post. Frist became Senate majority leader and McConnell majority whip and a key adviser to Frist, a former heart surgeon who was relatively unversed in Senate procedure. Frist retired in 2006 and Republicans lost their Senate majority that year; McConnell became minority leader.

McConnell stressed the importance of discipline to his GOP colleagues, preaching about how sticking together and playing "team ball" would give them greater leverage. Republicans learned that they crossed McConnell at their own peril. "There are few things more daunting in politics than the determined opposition of McConnell," the late Arizona GOP Sen. John McCain once observed. In his first two years as minority leader, which intersected with the end of George W. Bush's presidency, McConnell held 41 or more Republicans together to get his Democratic counterpart, Majority Leader Harry Reid, to meet his demands. In the process, Republicans conducted a record number of filibusters: The number of cloture motions filed during McConnell's first Congress as GOP leader was almost twice the previous high mark. It nearly doubled again in 2013-2014, just before Republicans retook the Senate majority.

But it was comments just before the 2010 midterm elections that exemplified what critics saw as McConnell's impede-at-all-costs approach. "The single most important thing we want to achieve is for President Obama to be a one-term president," he told National Journal—two years before Obama was due to run for a second term. McConnell complained that another part of the interview had been overlooked, in which he had said of incumbent president, "If he's willing to meet us halfway on some of the biggest issues, it's not inappropriate for us to do business with him." But, in his first one-on-one meeting with Obama a couple of months earlier, McConnell had expressed limited interest in finding common ground. A decade later, McConnell voiced a strikingly similar hard line toward Biden, not only a long-time colleague but, by all accounts, a personal friend as well. "One hundred percent of our focus is on stopping this new administration," McConnell declared in May 2021.

McConnell struck a couple of budget deals with the Obama White House after the 2010 elections —in which the Republicans gained six Senate seats, leaving Democrats far short of a filibuster-proof majority. The talks between the White House and Senate Republicans highlighted the McConnell-Biden relationship, developed during a quarter of a century as Senate colleagues. In 2011, negotiations stalled in a duel over raising the federal debt ceiling, prompting fears of a default with broad international consequences. McConnell met with then-Vice President Biden—known around the White House as "the McConnell Whisperer," according to Bob Woodward's book, "The Price of Politics"—to strike a deal. The debt ceiling talks turned out to be a prelude to the "fiscal cliff" negotiations in late 2012, aimed at averting automatic budget cuts and tax hikes that could impair the nation's economic recovery. By then, Obama had won a second term and Senate Democrats had added a couple seats to their majority. But talks between Obama and congressional Republicans aimed at avoiding the fiscal cliff had proved fruitless.

According to Politico, McConnell called Biden and got his voice mail. "Is there anyone over there who knows how to make a deal?" McConnell asked—his disdain for Obama's limited Capitol Hill experience apparent. Biden stepped in, setting in motion more than a dozen conversations that culminated in a New Year's Day 2013 agreement. While calling the deal "imperfect," McConnell said it was preferable to the large spending cuts that would have kicked in—while vowing not to accept tax hikes in future dealings with Democrats. Still, conservative activists were outraged that McConnell had given Obama his long-desired tax increase on the wealthy. As Biden left the vice presidency in early 2017, McConnell delivered an emotional Senate floor tribute, telling his former colleague, "You've been a real friend, you've been a trusted partner, and it's been an honor to serve with you." If such sentiments failed to translate into bipartisan cooperation as Biden assumed the presidency, McConnell—after the Electoral College had confirmed Biden's victory in 2020—unsuccessfully urged a handful of Senate Republicans not to join their House counterparts in objecting to the results, amid Trump's baseless claims of election fraud.

Before becoming Senate Republican leader, McConnell occupied the Senate floor desk at which Kentucky's most famous political figure, Henry Clay—"the Great Compromiser"—once sat. "Clay did not compromise in the sense of forsaking his principles," McConnell said in a 2006 speech. "Rather, his skill was to bring together disparate ideas and forge a consensus among his colleagues. That is a skill we could certainly use more of now." Eight years later, with McConnell poised to become majority leader, he vowed to break the gridlock that had settled over the chamber under Reid, the previous majority leader. McConnell pledged to allow both parties to offer amendments to legislation—even if it forced Republicans to take politically unpopular votes. "We'll just take our chances," he said in early 2016. "You know, we're big men and women. We're prepared to vote on proposals that are offered from both sides."

But in the summer of 2019, seven months into a new Congress in which the House had shifted to Democratic control while the Senate remained in Republican hands, a New York Times review found there had been only 18 Senate roll call votes on legislative amendments—as compared to anywhere from 34 to 231 amendment votes during the same period in 10 prior Congresses. Amid McConnell's focus on confirmation of conservatives to judgeships, he regularly declined to bring up bills that might divide his caucus or cause his members to cast difficult votes. "The Senate has deteriorated to the point where there is no debate whatsoever—he's dismantled the Senate brick by brick," Democratic Whip Dick Durbin told the New Yorker in early 2020.

In the early part of the 2016 presidential campaign, McConnell kept his distance from Trump. In May, he issued a perfunctory endorsement after it became clear Trump was on his way to the nomination—but, a month later, voiced concerns in a CNN interview that Trump's comments about Hispanic-Americans could hurt efforts to expand the GOP base, much as presidential candidate Barry Goldwater's vote against the 1964 Civil Right Act had alienated African-Americans a half-century earlier. And when the "Access Hollywood" tape, on which Trump can be heard boasting about sexually assaulting women, emerged during the fall campaign, McConnell termed the comments "repugnant and unacceptable in any circumstance."

He was more upbeat a month into Trump's presidency. "Back during the campaign, there were a lot of questions: 'Is Trump really a conservative?' ... But if you look at the steps that have been taken so far—looks good to me," McConnell said. By that time, Gorsuch had been nominated to the high court—and McConnell had begun coordinating in earnest with the incoming White House counsel, Don McGahn, to begin filling dozens of other federal court seats he had kept vacant during the final two years of Obama's presidency. Meanwhile, McConnell's wife, Elaine Chao, had been named Trump's Transportation secretary; she had been Labor secretary under President George W. Bush.

Still, the McConnell-Trump relationship got off to a rocky start: When Republican efforts to repeal the Affordable Care Act collapsed in the Senate six months into the new administration, the president teed off via his favorite social media platform. "Mitch, get back to work," Trump tweeted. McConnell, speaking to a Rotary Club in his home state a month later, said: "Our new president, of course, has not been in this line of work before. I think he had excessive expectations about how quickly things happen in the democratic process." McConnell also said he was "not a fan of tweeting," and that he'd "said that to him privately." That didn't stop Trump from responding with a tweet: "Can you believe that Mitch McConnell, who has screamed Repeal & Replace for 7 years, couldn't get it done." Asked by reporters whether McConnell should step down, Trump said, "If he doesn't get repeal and replace done, and if he doesn't get taxes done, meaning cuts and reform ... then you can ask me that question."

McConnell got a $1.5 trillion tax bill—one of the few major legislative accomplishments of Trump's presidency—passed at the end of 2017 on a party-line vote after a last-ditch effort to repeal the Affordable Care Act fell short. McConnell started the Trump presidency with a Republican caucus of 52, two fewer than the previous Congress. He faced a new Democratic counterpart, Minority Leader Chuck Schumer—who, taking a page from McConnell's playbook, held his caucus together in the face of efforts to do away with "Obamacare." And, after seven years of the mantra "repeal and replace," Republicans still had no consensus on a replacement. Three repeal options—crafted in closed, Republican-only sessions directed by McConnell's office—died on the Senate floor in July 2017; 13 Republicans voted against at least one of the three options, enough to sink all of them in the face of solid Democratic resistance. A fourth option, to replace the Affordable Care Act with block grants, died three months later. The tax bill did repeal the mandate that individuals purchase health care—which, McConnell boasted, "takes a big chunk" out of the Affordable Care Act.

Trump's tone toward McConnell was dramatically different a little more than a year later, after the bitter confirmation battle over the president's second Supreme Court nominee, Brett Kavanaugh. "He goes down as the greatest leader, in my opinion, in history," Trump told a Kentucky rally prior to the 2018 elections, adding: "There's nobody tougher, there's nobody smarter. He stared down the angry left-wing mob."

For McConnell, the Kavanaugh nomination fight had its seeds three decades earlier, when President Ronald Reagan nominated Robert Bork to the Supreme Court. Senate Democrats—with Biden, then chair of the Judiciary Committee, playing a key role—rejected Bork's nomination not because they felt he was unqualified but because they considered some of his conservative views out of the political mainstream. McConnell—who had served with Bork at the Justice Department —was infuriated. As Democrats in recent years railed at McConnell's win-at-all costs tactics on judicial nominations, he has laid the blame at their feet for their handling of the Bork nomination. In an October 1987 floor speech, McConnell complained: "It means for a majority of the Senate that we're going to make this decision on any basis we darn well please, and if we object as a matter of philosophical persuasion that the president is trying to move the court to the right or to the left, we'll just stand up and say that and vote accordingly." He added, "We may not be able to pick the nominee, but we can sure shoot 'em down."

The judicial nomination wars escalated early in the Obama administration when Republicans, under McConnell's leadership, insisted on confirming district court nominees individually— departing from the tradition of approving them in groups. McConnell slowed the judicial nomination process further after becoming majority leader toward the end of Obama's tenure in 2015—after Reid, two years earlier, had first invoked the "nuclear option" amid delays in confirming presidential appointments. The move changed Senate rules to prevent filibusters of executive branch appointments and judicial nominations below the Supreme Court level. McConnell all but telegraphed his future intentions that day in 2013. "You will regret this, and you may regret it a lot sooner than you think," he told Reid.

By most accounts, McConnell and Reid—another low-key figure who preferred operating behind the scenes—had the worst relationship of any two Senate leaders since such posts were formalized in the early 1900s. Schumer took over from Reid in early 2017, leading a 48-member minority in which many remained angry over the treatment of Garland. In April, with Schumer backing a filibuster of the Gorsuch nomination, all but three Democrats voted against ending debate—leaving it five votes short of the needed super-majority. McConnell then triggered a nuclear option: On a 52-48 party-line vote, the Senate changed its rules and dropped the 60-vote threshold for Supreme Court nominees—clearing the way for Gorsuch's confirmation. In April 2019, McConnell invoked the nuclear option again— reducing debate time for lower-level executive and judicial branch nominees from 30 hours to two. McConnell, after slowing the nomination process while Obama was in office, blamed Democrats' "historic obstruction" of Trump nominees for the rules change.

The filibuster changes affected only nominations, and McConnell—who frequently used legislative filibusters while in the minority—said after Gorsuch's nomination there were no plans to change that. Later in 2017, the issue played into the tensions between McConnell and Trump, as the president demanded that Senate Republicans, amid the failure of the Obamacare repeal, scrap the 60-vote threshold in legislative debates. McConnell replied that, even if he wanted to do so, support was lacking among Senate Republicans. During the 2020 campaign, Trump's filibuster stance was echoed by Democrats eager to facilitate passage of the party's agenda in the event of a Biden victory. When Democrats won a slim Senate majority in early 2021, McConnell—negotiating a power-sharing agreement—sought assurances that the legislative filibuster would remain; Schumer declined to provide such guarantees, but the issue became academic when at least two of 50 Democratic senators reiterated their opposition to eliminating the filibuster.

When Biden, also a longtime opponent of ending the filibuster, said in a March 2021 ABC News interview that he favored changing the rules to make them more difficult to conduct, it was followed by a threat of retribution from McConnell. "Let me say this very clearly for all 99 of my colleagues: Nobody serving in this chamber can even begin to imagine what a completely scorched-earth Senate would look like," he declared, warning: "The pendulum … would swing both ways. … As soon as Republicans wound up back in the saddle, we wouldn't just erase every liberal change that hurt the country. We'd strengthen America with all kinds of conservative policies with zero—zero—input from the other side."

While there were signs of an improving relationship between McConnell and Schumer in the wake of the confrontation over Gorsuch—in early 2018, they negotiated a deal to raise the debt ceiling while providing an additional $300 billon over two years for defense and domestic programs

—any budding collegiality was strained later in the year after the retirement of Supreme Court Justice Anthony Kennedy. It allowed Trump to make Kavanaugh his second Supreme Court appointment in less than two years. With control of the Senate at stake in the coming midterm elections, McConnell sought to keep the nomination on track for approval before Election Day—while resisting calls for an FBI investigation into sexual assault allegations, dating to high school, against Kavanaugh from Christine Blasey Ford. Schumer demanded an investigation, saying of McConnell on the Senate floor: "He slowed down a nomination to the Supreme Court for a year—and now a few days is too much. Give me a break." He later accused McConnell of telling "blatant falsehoods … day after day on this floor."

Scrambling to line up the votes needed for confirmation, McConnell agreed to an FBI investigation—and a weeklong delay in the process—after Arizona Republican Jeff Flake of Arizona said he would not consider voting for Kavanaugh without a probe. The FBI failed to corroborate allegations by Blasey Ford and other accusers, and Kavanaugh was confirmed on a 50-48 party-line vote. The furor over Kavanaugh created a backlash among conservatives, leading to defeat of Democrats in three red states in November and the Republican Senate majority growing to 53.

When liberal Supreme Court Justice Ruth Bader Ginsburg died six weeks before Election Day 2020, McConnell said the same evening that the Senate would move the fill the opening. It was no surprise: In May 2019, asked about the possibility of an election-year high court vacancy, McConnell had replied, "Oh, we'd fill it." Responding to criticism that he was applying a double-standard after blocking Garland's nomination in 2016, McConnell contended it was different—because the Senate and the White House were held by the same party, which had not been the case in the final year of the Obama presidency. McConnell lobbied Trump to appoint Coney Barrett—arguing that because she had already been through confirmation to the federal appeals court, she was the nominee best in a position to win confirmation in a tight timeframe.

With Democrats powerless to block Coney Barrett, McConnell—having presided over the remaking of the federal judiciary over a four-year period—once again blamed them for starting what had become a deeply politicized process. "I hope our colleague from New York is happy with what he has built. I hope he is happy with where his ingenuity has gotten the Senate," McConnell said of Schumer—with his back turned to Democrats in the chamber. Schumer—with polls showing Senate Democrats on the cusp of winning back the majority—vowed retribution. "I want to be very clear with my Republican colleagues. You may win this vote … but you will never, never get your credibility back," he said, facing Republicans on the Senate floor. "And the next time the American people give Democrats a majority in this chamber, you will have forfeited the right to tell us how to run that majority."

It was the culmination of a year that had started with Trump's first impeachment trial, as Schumer repeatedly demanded rules to facilitate the calling of witnesses. But McConnell, with several Senate Republicans—himself included—in competitive reelection fights, held his caucus together by warning that a protracted proceeding with witnesses would force endangered incumbents into tough votes. Ultimately, McConnell beat back the call for witnesses as well as the final impeachment vote—with only one Republican, Mitt Romney of Utah, joining 47 Democrats to vote to convict Trump on charges of abusing his office—far short of the two-thirds needed. At the outset of the trial, McConnell enraged the Democrats by promising "total coordination" with the White House; he told reporters that he was "not at all impartial." While Trump had been accused of withholding aid to the government of Ukraine to force the announcement of an investigation into Biden, McConnell—unlike some Republican colleagues who condemned Trump's actions while stopping short of voting for impeachment—repeatedly declined to offer an opinion of the president's conduct.

But a year later, before Trump's second impeachment trial after the Capitol insurrection on January 6, 2021, McConnell pointed the finger at the outgoing president. "The mob was fed lies," he declared. "They were provoked by the president and other powerful people, and they tried to use fear and violence to stop a specific proceeding of the first branch of the federal government that they did not like"—the counting of the Electoral College votes that would formalize Biden's win. McConnell's vote against convicting Trump in the second trial on the grounds that Trump was already out of office was seen by Democrats as another instance of his trying to have it both ways: It was McConnell who had pushed back the proceeding until after Trump had left office, arguing there was insufficient time to conduct a "fair or serious trial" before Biden was sworn in. At the same time, he ramped up his criticism of Trump: "There's no question—none—that President Trump is practically and morally responsible for provoking the events of the day. … The leader of the free world cannot spend weeks thundering that shadowy forces are stealing our country and then feign surprise when people believe him and do reckless things."

Nonetheless, in a February 2021 Fox News interview—not long after the trial concluded—McConnell was asked if he would support Trump if he were the 2024 Republican presidential nominee, and without hesitation he replied, "Absolutely." His response came despite Trump condemning McConnell as a "dour, sullen and unsmiling political hack" after the second trial. "McConnell's dedication to business as usual, status quo policies, together with his lack of political insight, wisdom, skill, and personality, has rapidly driven him from majority leader to minority leader, and it will only get worse," Trump said. Privately, McConnell was reported to have told associates he hoped never to speak to Trump again and blamed the latter's modus operandi for driving women and suburban voters from the GOP—costing Republicans both Congress and the presidency in just four years. McConnell had publicly expressed similar concerns after the 2018 elections. "The party has to be bigger than white men who didn't graduate from college," McConnell told the New York Times, referring to Trump's core base and adding, "That's not a sustainable position, politically, if you want to be a competitive party."

In Kentucky, McConnell has long been the de facto boss of the state GOP, but his grip was challenged—even before the emergence of Trump—with the rise of the party's tea party wing. When Republican Sen. Jim Bunning retired—under pressure from his senior colleague—in 2010, McConnell's choice to replace him was Kentucky Secretary of State Trey Grayson. But also running was Rand Paul, son of Texas Rep. Ron Paul—a onetime Libertarian Party presidential candidate. With tea party support, Rand Paul trounced Grayson in the primary and went on to win in November. Confronted with a difficult bid for another term in 2014, McConnell reached out to Paul and endorsed his unsuccessful bid for the 2016 Republican presidential nomination.

In his fifth reelection bid in 2014, McConnell faced a serious primary threat from Matt Bevin, a wealthy businessman favored by tea party forces. But Bevin was an inexperienced candidate who made numerous errors and McConnell crushed him 60%-35%. (Bevin, after having declined to endorse McConnell in the general election, got McConnell's support after narrowly winning the Republican gubernatorial nomination; he went on to win a term as governor, losing reelection.) In the 2014 general election, McConnell faced Democrat Alison Lundergan Grimes, Kentucky's 34-year-old secretary of state. The daughter of a former state representative and onetime state party chair, she was seen as a credible opponent but committed several errors, notably refusing to answer a question about whether she had voted for Obama in 2012. It was widely viewed as an opportunistic effort to keep the president, highly unpopular in Kentucky, at a distance. McConnell relentlessly tied her to Obama; he won, 56%-41%.

In 2020, McConnell's Democratic opponent was Amy McGrath, a retired Marine fighter pilot who found herself squeezed by forces on both her left and right. McGrath had to thread the needle between attacking McConnell and sidestepping Trump—who Kentucky polling showed to be far more popular than the state's senior senator. And, in the wake of the Black Lives Matter movement, McGrath struggled to fend off a June primary challenge from state Rep. Charles Booker, an African-American with support from prominent progressives; she barely won, 45%-43%. Aided by McConnell's national status as a Democratic bete noire, McGrath raised an astonishing $94 million, $23 million more than the incumbent—making it the 10th most expensive Senate race in history. But, after trailing McConnell by just 5 percentage points in a Quinnipiac poll in August, McGrath fell behind by 10 points in September. McConnell ended up winning by 58%-38%.

In prior reelection races, McConnell had spirited competition from former Louisville Mayor Harvey Sloane in 1990, future Gov. Steve Beshear in 1996, and Lois Combs Weinberg, daughter of a former governor, in 2002. Sloane and Beshear held McConnell to 52 percent and 55 percent, respectively. McConnell did better against Weinberg, winning with 65 percent. In 2008, Democrats recruited Bruce Lunsford, a multimillionaire hospital and nursing home operator. Lunsford spent more than $7 million of his own money and ran a string of negative ads—one a takeoff on McConnell's bloodhound ad of a quarter of a century earlier. McConnell won with 53 percent.

Legislation that cleared the Republican-controlled Kentucky Legislature in the spring of 2021—over the veto of Democratic Gov. Andy Beshear—prompted speculation about whether McConnell, who turned 79 in early 2021, would serve out his latest term. Under the new law—said to have been pushed quietly by McConnell—the governor, rather than being free to name anyone to fill a Senate vacancy, would have to choose from among three names proposed by the political party of the senator who left office. The measure was informally dubbed the "Daniel Cameron Election Bill": Cameron, the state attorney general, is considered by many to be McConnell's protégé and his choice as an eventual successor.

Rand Paul (R)

Elected 2010, term expires 2022, 2nd term, b. Jan 07, 1963; Pittsburgh, PA; Baylor University, 1984; Duke University, M.D., 1988; Presbyterian; Married (Kelley Paul); 3 children.

Professional Career: Ophthalmologist, 1993-2010; Founder, S. KY Lions Eye Clinic, 1995.

DC Office: 167 RSOB 20510, 202-224-4343, Fax: 202-228-6917, paul.senate.gov

State Offices: Bowling Green, 270-782-8303; Louisville, 502-582-5341.

Committees: *Foreign Relations*: Africa & Global Health Policy; Internat'l Dev Instit & Internat'l Econ, Energy & Environ Policy; Near East, South Asia, Central Asia & Counterterrorism; State Dept & USAID Mngmnt, Internat'l Ops & Internat'l Dev. *Health, Education, Labor & Pensions*: Employment & Workplace Safety; Primary Health & Retirement Security. *Homeland Security & Government Affairs*: Emerging Threats & Spending Oversight (RMM); Investigations. *Small Business & Entrepreneurship (RMM)*.

Group Ratings

	ADA	ACLU	AFL-CIO	LCV	COC	HAFA	ACU	CFG	FRC
2020	-	60%	-	8%	-	82%	97%	-	-
2019	30%	C	0%	0%	81%	C	96%	96%	100%

Almanac Ratings 2019-2020

	Economy	Social	Foreign	Composite
Liberal	19%	19%	56%	31%
Conservative	82%	82%	44%	69%

Key Votes of the 116th Congress

1. EPA clean energy rules	N	5. Russia sanctions	N	9. Barr as Atty. General	N
2. U.S./Mex./Can. trade deal	Y	6. Troops in SYR, AFG	N	10. Spending at the border	N
3. Cut unemployment benefits	Y	7. Veto arms sales to Saudis	Y	11. Coney Barrett to Sup. Ct.	Y
4. Shelton to Fed Reserve	Y	8. Defense $$$, veto override	N	12. Electoral College objections	N

Election Results

Election	Name (Party)	Vote (%)		Cand. Spent	Ind. Exp. Support	Ind. Exp. Oppose
2016 General	Rand Paul (R)	1,090,177	(57%)	$5,994,444	$83,795	
	Jim Gray (D)	813,246	(43%)	$4,665,712	$337,895	$563,868
2016 Primary	Rand Paul (R)	169,180	(85%)			
	James Gould (R)	16,611	(8%)			
	Stephen Slaughter (R)	13,728	(7%)			

Prior winning percentages: 2016 (57%), 2010 (56%)

Republican Rand Paul's timing was propitious when he launched his first run for elected office just over a decade ago. He had gained political experience working on his father's 2008 presidential campaign, but he was still an ophthalmologist with a limited statewide profile when he announced a Senate bid in 2009. Paul, however, waded in just in time to catch the rising tide of the tea party, enabling him to upset the Kentucky Republican establishment and win election as the state's junior senator. Less than four years later, some polls showed him leading the crowded field of prospects for the GOP presidential nomination, with a Time magazine cover anointing him "The Most Interesting Man in Politics."

But by the time the first delegates to the party's nominating convention had been chosen in early 2016, Paul's bid for the presidency had come crashing down. Despite his status as a political outsider —solidified by his tactics on Capitol Hill—Paul found himself eclipsed by an outsider with more celebrity: Donald Trump. Salvaging reelection to a second Senate term, Paul returned to Capitol Hill for a surprising third act in his political career: occasional golfing partner and frequent defender of Trump, whom Paul had derided as a "delusional narcissist and an orange-faced windbag" during their presidential campaign rivalry. In mid-2018, as Trump's conciliatory stance toward Russian President Vladimir Putin generated bipartisan criticism on Capitol Hill, Paul stood virtually alone in defending the president's posture toward a nation widely blamed for meddling in the 2016 presidential election to help Trump. When Trump faced his first impeachment trial in early 2020, Paul threatened to play hardball while defending him.

Paradoxically, vote rankings compiled by FiveThirtyEight pegged Paul as the GOP senator who second least often voted with Trump. Much of this stemmed from Paul's libertarian leanings. The appeal of his noninterventionist—critics would say neo-isolationist—foreign policy views fell flat during his presidential bid, amid the rise of the Islamic State terrorist group and escalating terror attacks abroad. Nevertheless, Paul continues to leverage Senate procedures to force showdowns on a host of domestic and foreign issues—sometimes delaying votes on key bills and visibly irritating his GOP colleagues. His outlier role has made for a sometimes-strained relationship with his fellow Kentuckian, Senate Republican Leader Mitch McConnell.

Paul inherited his ideological outlook from his father, former Texas Rep. Ron Paul, the Libertarian Party's White House candidate in 1988 and a contender for the Republican presidential nominations in 2008 and 2012. Born in Pittsburgh, Rand Paul was raised in Lake Jackson Texas, where his father had set up an obstetrics practice. Paul and his father have denied he was named after author Ayn Rand, whose advocacy of laissez-faire capitalism made her popular in libertarian circles. Named Randal at birth, he was known as Randy growing up and switched to Rand as an adult. Paul followed his father's footsteps and became a physician. He attended Baylor University but did not earn an undergraduate degree. He received a high score on the entrance exam to Duke University School of Medicine and was admitted. After graduating, Paul moved to Bowling Green Kentucky, near his wife's hometown, and opened an ophthalmology practice. Foreshadowing his political career, Paul took an outsider stance in medicine: Unhappy with the American Board of Ophthalmology, which had long certified practitioners of that specialty, he mounted an unsuccessful effort to create a rival certification board.

After Republican Sen. Jim Bunning announced his retirement in July 2009, Paul declared his candidacy. The favorite for the nomination was Kentucky Secretary of State Trey Grayson, who had the backing of McConnell, de facto boss of the state GOP. But Paul had access to his father's devoted network of contributors, who embraced his views that agencies such as the Environmental Protection Agency and the Education Department should be abolished and the powers of the Federal Reserve curbed. Foreshadowing criticism that would later confront his presidential bid, Paul faced ads saying he was weak on national security. Nonetheless, boosted by the accelerating tea party movement, he easily won the primary, 59%-35%. McConnell made a point of appearing at a victory rally for Paul, who went on to vote for McConnell for Senate GOP leader after earlier declining to say whether he would do so.

The Democratic nominee, state Attorney General Jack Conway, hammered Paul for having voiced opposition in principle to the 1964 Civil Rights Act as government interference with private business. Conway also seized on Paul's support for raising the Social Security retirement age and his opposing federal involvement in drug enforcement. But Paul had little trouble winning in a state that had trended increasingly red; it finished 56%-44%. Upon arriving in the Senate, Paul established a Tea Party Caucus, and, in January 2012, made national news when he refused a pat-down from the Transportation Security Administration at a Tennessee airport.

Paul's philosophical aversion to governmental mandates on individual behavior later received high-profile attention during the COVID-19 pandemic. He was the first senator to test positive, after learning two people at a fundraiser he had attended had tested positive for the novel coronavirus. Between being tested and receiving the results, Paul did not self-quarantine: He showed up in the Senate, dining with colleagues and using senators' private gym. Several colleagues were incensed upon learning that Paul had continued to circulate when he knew he might be infected, the New York Times reported. Paul—who a week earlier had voted against a multibillion-dollar coronavirus rescue bill because it would contribute to the national debt—offered no apologies. "For those who want to criticize me for lack of quarantine, realize that if the rules on testing had been followed to a "T," I would never have been tested and would still be walking around the halls of the Capitol," he said. Paul stirred further controversy in May 2021 for saying he would refuse a coronavirus vaccination, citing antibodies he contended he had developed from his bout with COVID-19 a year earlier.

In the ensuing months, Paul used his perch on the Senate Health, Education, Labor and Pensions Committee to become one of the few legislators to directly challenge the nation's top infectious disease expert, Dr. Anthony Fauci. Amid Fauci's warnings of serious consequences if pandemic-related restrictions were lifted too early, Paul told Politico: "There's a spectrum of everything. And I think he's on the overly cautious end of the spectrum." Added Paul: "If we're overly cautious and we wait until all infectious disease goes away … we'll wait forever and the country is going to be destroyed." His comments came after a May 2020 hearing at which Paul told Fauci, the longtime director of the National Institute of Allergy and Infectious Diseases, that he was not "the end all" of decision-making. Fauci's patience wore thin at a hearing four months later, when he repeatedly challenged claims by Paul. "No, you misconstrued that, Senator, and you've done that repetitively in the past," Fauci shot back at one point, asking for more time to respond "because this happens with Sen. Rand all the time."

On the civil liberties front, Paul has battled the USA Patriot Act, passed after 9/11. Not long after taking office, he sought to block extension of the law and tried again in May 2015—a month after announcing his presidential bid. Paul conducted an eleventh-hour filibuster to delay another Patriot Act reauthorization, objecting to bulk collection of phone records. His tactics not only led to a brief lapse in some government surveillance powers, they also forced then-Majority Leader McConnell to swallow House-passed changes in the statute that he opposed. McConnell, who had sought to build a relationship with Paul—going so far as to embrace his presidential bid—was irritated. Taking aim at Paul, McConnell blasted those who he said were spreading disinformation about the Patriot Act. The party's 2008 presidential nominee, Arizona Sen. John McCain—who earlier had labeled Paul a "wackobird"—suggested the Kentucky senator was putting his political ambitions above national security.

Rand Paul was unrepentant. "Little by little, we've allowed our freedom to slip away," he declared. Several days earlier, he blamed fellow Republicans for the growth of ISIS. "ISIS exists and grew stronger because of the hawks in our party who gave arms indiscriminately, and most of those arms were snatched up by ISIS," he said on MSNBC.

With Trump in the White House, Paul's philosophical bent complicated efforts to repeal the Affordable Care Act. After three GOP-crafted options to jettison "Obamacare" failed in July 2017, Republican leaders tried again a couple of months later—with a plan to replace the Affordable Care Act with block grants to states. The effort was abandoned when it became clear a handful of Republicans would not vote for it, Paul among them. While some other GOP dissenters felt the bill went too far, Paul contended it did not go far enough in getting the government out of the private insurance market. Although the final alternative—sponsored by Republican Bill Cassidy of Louisiana and South Carolina Republican Lindsey Graham—would have allowed states to apply for waivers to get rid of most aspects of Obamacare, Paul didn't trust the federal government to grant such waivers.

"I've already spent the better part of the year arguing with an army of bureaucrats and lawyers in the administration trying to get them to do something President Trump and I AGREE should be done —loosening up the rules on joining group plans," Paul wrote in a Fox News op-ed. In October 2018, Trump issued an executive order—on which he and Paul had collaborated—to expand availability of less expensive insurance across state lines; Paul hailed the move as "the biggest free-market reform of health care in a generation." Earlier, the president had unsuccessfully prodded Paul—gently, by Trump standards—to back the Graham-Cassidy legislation. "Rand Paul is a friend of mine but he is such a negative force when it comes to fixing healthcare. Graham-Cassidy Bill is GREAT! Ends Ocare!" Trump tweeted.

Earlier in 2018, Paul threatened to block Trump's nomination of Brett Kavanaugh to the Supreme Court over a ruling Kavanaugh, as a federal appeals court judge, had made in favor of the bulk collection of phone records—the same issue over which Paul filibustered the Patriot Act reauthorization. "Kavanaugh's position is basically that national security trumps privacy. And he said it very strongly and explicitly," Paul told Politico. But after meeting with Kavanaugh, Paul dropped his objections—because no one will "ever completely agree with a nominee" and nominees "must be judged on the totality of their views, character, and opinions." A similar scenario played out when Trump nominated Mike Pompeo as secretary of State. Paul vowed to do "whatever it takes" to block the nomination, citing Pompeo's support for military intervention in Iraq, Iran, Syria and Afghanistan. Paul, a Foreign Relations Committee member, changed his mind just before the panel voted—saying Trump had assured him Pompeo believed the Iraq War had been a mistake and that it was time for U.S. troops to leave Afghanistan.

But Paul's opposition to U.S. involvement in foreign conflicts prompted him to part company with Trump and Pompeo in June 2019: He was one of only seven Republican senators to oppose the administration's attempt to bypass a congressional hold on $8 billion in arms sales to Saudi Arabia and the United Arab Emirates. A resolution of disapproval cleared both the Senate and House but was vetoed by Trump. Meanwhile, Paul was among 12 Republicans to join Senate Democrats in disapproving of another Trump emergency declaration—this one aimed at bypassing Congress to secure funds for a wall along the U.S.-Mexico border. "We may want more money for border security, but Congress didn't authorize it," Paul said. "If we take away those checks and balances, it's a dangerous thing."

Notwithstanding such differences, Paul and Trump shared a deep suspicion toward the Washington establishment in general and the intelligence community in particular. Paul, echoing the president's calls for an end to the investigation into the 2016 Trump campaign's possible ties to Russia, told a conservative gathering that Trump's stance matched what he'd been saying for a decade: "We've allowed too much power to gravitate to these intelligence agencies." When Trump, in Helsinki in July 2018, appeared to take Putin's word over that of U.S. intelligence agencies regarding Russian election interference, Paul was a lonely defender of the president's position. "The hatred for the president is so intense that partisans would rather risk war than give diplomacy a chance," Paul said in a floor speech, describing Trump's critics as "unhinged" and "crazy."

When Trump faced impeachment in early 2020 on charges he had withheld aid from Ukraine to pressure that nation's government to announce an investigation into a prospective Democratic rival, Joe Biden, Paul vowed to force tough votes on a handful of Republicans contemplating backing Democrats' demands to call witnesses. Paul threatened to insist on votes to call Biden's son Hunter—who had served on the board of a Ukrainian energy firm—as well as the whistleblower who had first revealed the Ukraine scandal. Neither was a witness that moderate GOP senators were eager to call for fear of political blowback. "If you vote against Hunter Biden, you're voting to lose your election, basically. Seriously. That's what it is," Paul told Politico, in remarks aimed at wavering Republicans. "If you don't want to vote and you think you're going to have to vote against Hunter Biden, you should just vote against witnesses, period." Paul's tactics were consistent with efforts by McConnell to keep the slim GOP majority united against calling witnesses and bring the impeachment trial to a swift end.

But Paul again ran afoul of McConnell when he sought to pose a question during the trial. Paul's query referred to a person purported by conservative media to be the initial whistleblower in the case, along with an acquaintance who worked for the House Intelligence Committee. But Chief Justice John Roberts, presiding over the trial, declined to read Paul's question—prompting Paul to hold a news conference in which he read aloud the question with the name of alleged whistleblower. "I don't know who the whistleblower is," Paul acknowledged, while contending: "My question is not about the whistleblower. My question is about two people who are friends who worked together … who have been overheard talking about impeaching the president years in advance of a process that then was created to get the impeachment process going." In Senate floor comments, McConnell scolded Paul, declaring: "We've been respectful of the chief justice's unique position in reading our questions. And I want to be able to continue to assure him that that level of consideration for him will continue."

Later in 2020, Paul found himself dealing with Black Lives Matter protesters—enraged in part by the police killing of Breonna Taylor in Kentucky's largest municipality, Louisville. Surrounded by protesters after he left Trump's White House speech accepting nomination to a second term, Paul tweeted he had been "attacked by an angry mob" and thanked police for "literally saving our lives from a crazed mob." A video of the encounter showed no attack on Paul, who the next day on Fox News, alleged—without evidence—that the demonstrators had been paid to stir up trouble in downtown Washington. The demonstrators were calling for Paul to say Taylor's name; Paul called that ironic because, three months after her death, he had introduced legislation to end no-knock raids—such as the one in which police shot her multiple times—after talking with Taylor's family.

During the same month the no-knock legislation was introduced, Paul found himself in a heated Senate floor exchange with two Black colleagues—New Jersey Sen. Cory Booker and then-California Sen. Kamala Harris—after his objections stalled long-sought federal anti-lynching legislation. The bill had passed the House 410-4 and had the backing of 99 senators. But, since it was being considered under unanimous consent rules, Paul was blocking passage—arguing the wording of the bill could "cheapen the meaning of lynching by defining it so broadly as to include a minor bruise or abrasion." Booker, who had collaborated in the past with Paul on criminal justice reform issues, noted the debate was taking place on the same day as the funeral for George Floyd, a Black man who died in Minneapolis after a white police officer knelt on his neck for more than nine minutes. "If this bill passed today, what that would mean for America? … It would speak volumes for the racial pain and the hurt of generations," an emotional Booker declared. Paul's objections blocked the bill from becoming law; according to the New York Times, he had supported the legislation as written a year earlier and did not explain why his position had changed.

Paul's 2016 bid for the presidency ended days after the first-in-the-nation Iowa caucuses. He dropped out days after finishing fifth with 5 percent of the vote, less than a quarter of his father's 21.5 percent showing in Iowa four years earlier. While running for president, Paul stayed on the ballot for reelection to the Senate. He faced a legal obstacle: Kentucky law prohibited candidates from appearing on the ballot for two offices in the same election. To get around this, the Kentucky Republican Party scheduled a presidential caucus in March 2016 separate from the state's May primary. Paul agreed to provide $250,000 to help cover the increased cost.

Democrats nominated Lexington Mayor Jim Gray, who brought personal money and a business background to the race. Gray had been elected twice as an openly gay candidate in a state where a county clerk had recently garnered international attention for going to jail rather than issuing marriage licenses to same-sex couples. But Gray's sexuality was not his biggest political obstacle, according to backers: It was his association with President Barack Obama, who was highly unpopular in Kentucky. Gray acknowledged he had voted for Obama; Paul won 57%-43%. Paul planned to seek a third term in 2022 and entered the contest as the solid favorite.

In November 2017, Paul made national headlines after a bizarre episode at his Kentucky home. He was on a riding lawn mower when he was tackled by a neighbor—a fellow physician named Rene Boucher; Paul suffered broken ribs and excess fluid around his lungs that caused a bout with pneumonia. Boucher pleaded guilty to felony assault and got 30 days in jail. A jury later awarded Paul more than $580,000 in a lawsuit he brought against Boucher, who said he had attacked Paul because the senator had been stacking yard trimmings along their shared property line. Nearly two years after the attack, Paul underwent surgery to remove part of a damaged lung. Boucher said in court documents he had simply lost his temper, denying suggestions from the Paul camp that the attack had been motivated by politics.

Not long after his return to Capitol Hill after the assault, Paul in early 2018 delayed passage for several hours of a bipartisan agreement providing an additional $300 billon over two years for defense and domestic programs. "We have Republicans hand-in-hand with Democrats offering us trillion-dollar deficits," Paul told the Senate. "I want people to feel uncomfortable." Indeed, several of Paul's colleagues appeared exasperated by late night House and Senate sessions made necessary by Paul's ephemeral protest. Republican Rep. Charlie Dent of Pennsylvania quipped: "When Rand Paul pulls a stunt like this, it [is] easy to understand why it's difficult to be Rand Paul's next-door neighbor."

James Comer (R)

Elected 2016, 3rd term, b. Aug 19, 1972; Carthage, TN; Western KY University, B.S., 1993; Baptist; Married (Tamera Jo); 3 children.

Elected Office: Chairman, Monroe County Republican Party, 1993-1995; Delegate, Republican National Convention, 1996; KY House, 2001-2012; Commissioner, KY Department of Agriculture, 2012-2015.

Professional Career: Businessman; Farmer.

DC Office: 1037 LHOB 20515, 202-225-3115, Fax: 202-225-3547

State Offices: Madisonville, 270-487-9509; Paducah, 270-408-1865; Tompkinsville, 270-487-9509.

Committees: *Education & Labor*: Higher Education & Workforce Investment. *Oversight & Reform* (RMM).

Group Ratings

	ADA	ACLU	AFL-CIO	LCV	COC	HAFA	ACU	CFG	FRC
2020	**	21%	**	10%	-	90%	87%	**	-
2019	5%	C	24%	7%	84%	C	91%	95%	91%

Almanac Ratings 2019-2020

	Economy	Social	Foreign	Composite
Liberal	25%	25%	35%	29%
Conservative	75%	75%	65%	71%

Key Votes of the 116th Congress

1. U.S./Mex./Can. trade deal Y	5. Russia sanctions N	9. Firearms background checks N
2. First Coronavirus response Y	6. Troops in Syria N	10. Spending at the border Y
3. HEROES Act N	7. Veto arms sales to Saudis N	11. Marijuana liberalized rules N
4. CASH Act Y	8. Defense $$$, veto override N	12. Electoral College objections N

Election Results

Election	Name (Party)	Vote (%)	Cand. Spent	Ind. Exp. Support	Ind. Exp. Oppose
2020 General	James Comer (R)................................ 246,329	(75%)	$267,615	$8,599	$750
	James Rhodes (D)......................... 82,141	(25%)			

Prior winning percentages: 2018 (69%), 2016 (73%)

James Comer, who breezed to election in 2016 as a consolation prize of sorts following his 83-vote loss to Matt Bevin in the Republican primary for governor the year before, had an unusually rapid ascent to the top GOP slot on the House Oversight and Reform Committee. He quickly took advantage of the opportunities in the high-profile post. Comer earlier showed his legislative chops by scoring a big win for Kentucky farmers. He has positioned himself for another statewide run, as a House ally of Senate Minority Leader Mitch McConnell.

Comer grew up in rural Monroe County. He had dreamed of becoming a farmer. After graduating from Western Kentucky University, he borrowed $120,000 from a community bank to purchase his first farm and began his business. It became one of the largest farming operations in south central Kentucky. He had other interests in insurance and restaurant businesses. Comer also started young in politics, winning his first election to the state House at age 28. He served 11 years in what was then the Democratic-controlled House, where he claimed good bipartisan relationships and kept his distance from Republican "party bosses."

In 2011, Comer was elected to a four-year term as Kentucky commissioner of agriculture, the only Republican who won statewide that year. He supported legalizing the production of industrial hemp as a potential cash crop for Kentucky farmers. In his 2015 face-off for governor, Comer ran against the more outspoken conservative Bevin, who had taken on McConnell in the Republican primary in 2014. "I've fought corruption. I've made government more efficient. ... I've passed legislation," Comer said in a pre-primary interview with the Lexington Herald-Leader. In the official recanvass of the primary, Bevin prevailed by 83 votes.

When 11-term Republican Rep. Ed Whitfield announced his retirement, Comer was the early frontrunner and was not seriously threatened. His chief GOP challenger was Mike Pape, who gained local political connections during his many years as Whitfield's district director. Pape raised $420,000 to the $1 million Comer raised for the campaign. The U.S. Chamber of Commerce spent another $100,000 on behalf of Comer. He won the four-candidate primary with 61 percent of the vote to 23 percent for Pape. Comer won the general election, 73%-27%.

In the House, his chief committee assignment was Agriculture, where he brought firsthand experience. The first bill he filed was to loosen regulations on hemp by reclassifying it from a controlled substance to an agricultural crop. Liberal Democrats, including Reps. Jared Polis of Colorado and Earl Blumenauer of Oregon, joined Comer in holding press conferences and other events on his proposal. "We've proven it's not a drug," Comer said. He told reporters that McConnell had kept in touch with Kentucky farmers and was persuasive with "the handful of members who still cringe when I come up to talk to them about hemp," which some users lit up as an alternative to marijuana. The House did not include his proposal to legalize hemp when it passed the 2018 farm bill. But with Comer serving on the House-Senate conference committee that crafted the final deal on the bill, it included the provision, which he called "a significant win."

His opportunity to take the top GOP position at the Oversight committee resulted from a rapid turnover in the high command. After Rep. Jim Jordan of Ohio relinquished the slot in January 2020 and became senior Republican at the Judiciary Committee, his close ally Mark Meadows of North Carolina replaced him at the Oversight panel. But Meadows had an unusually brief stint, as he accelerated his earlier plan to retire from the House when President Donald Trump in March tapped him as White House chief of staff. Because the House had a curtailed legislative schedule due to the coronavirus, it took three more months before GOP leadership scheduled a meeting to select a successor to Meadows. Comer defeated Reps. Jody Hice of Georgia and freshman Mark Green of Tennessee.

When he took the GOP reins at the panel, Comer pledged to "take my obligation to pursue legitimate waste, fraud and abuse in government very seriously." He moved quickly to take command. Responding to topics in the news, he criticized Democrats—on and off Capitol Hill—for offenses ranging from inaction to excessive action. Citing their criticism of the Trump administration's management of ventilators for hospitals, Comer said House Democrats "will stop at nothing to politicize this pandemic." He attacked Washington D.C. Mayor Muriel Bowser and "radical city leaders" who want to "erase history" by questioning longstanding statuary in the nation's capital.

Comer became an outspoken defender of Trump, especially on the eve of—and following—the presidential election, when he joined the president in accusing Democrats of trying to "steal the election" with their expanded use of voting by mail. With the transition to President Joe Biden, Comer promised vigorous oversight—though Democrats retained their House control and gavels, albeit narrowly. In May, Comer opened the door to a potentially significant bipartisan deal when he filed a postal reform bill with Democratic Rep. Carolyn Maloney, the committee chairwoman.

At home, Comer twice won easy reelection, taking all 35 counties in each contest. He had no primary opposition. Prior to Bevin's announcement in January 2019 that he would seek reelection, Comer said he would have run if there was a vacancy. But he had "no interest" in making another run against Bevin, who subsequently was defeated by Democrat Andy Beshear. At age 48, Comer should have plenty of other opportunities to run statewide. He likely will benefit from his enhanced exposure at the Oversight panel. In 2021, he played a constructive role in working with Oversight committee Democrats to approve the bipartisan Postal Service Reform Act, which sought to break a long-standing deadlock.

KY-1: Western Kentucky

Cook Partisan Voting Index: R+26

Population		Race and Ethnicity		Income	
Total	717,704	White	88.70%	Median Income	$46,999
Land area (sq. miles)	12,080	Black	7.00%	District Income Rank	406
Pop/ sq mi	59.42	Latino	3.10%	Poverty Rate	17.70%
Born in State	68.00%	Asian	0.60%	With health insurance	92.70%
		Two or more races	2.30%	Cash public assistance	1.40%
Age Groups		Other	1.40%	Food stamp/SNAP	13.30%
Under 18	21.70%				
18-34	21.60%	**Education**		**Work**	
35-64	37.60%	H.S grad or less	53.90%	White Collar	29.80%
Over 64	19.00%	Some college	29.10%	Sales and Service	36.50%
		College Degree, 4 yr	10.10%	Blue Collar	33.70%
Military		Post grad	7.10%	Government	14.80%
Veteran/ Active Duty	9.40%				

2020 Pres. Vote	Trump	244,122	(73%)	Biden	85,228	(26%)			
2016 Pres. Vote	Trump	224,657	(72%)	Clinton	74,179	(24%)	Johnson	6,920	(2%)

Paducah: The point where the Ohio River flows into the Mississippi—the intersection Huckleberry Finn and Jim missed in the fog—must have struck early settlers as a site for a great city. But no Pittsburgh or St. Louis grew up on the fertile black soil. Instead, the Kentucky land west of the dammed-up Tennessee and Cumberland rivers, bought from the Chickasaw Indians by Gen. Andrew Jackson and Gov. Isaac Shelby in 1818—the Jackson Purchase—was settled by farmers, mostly from the South. This was one area of Kentucky where public sentiment clearly favored the Confederacy during the Civil War. A group of delegates from western Kentucky and western Tennessee gathered in Mayfield in 1861 and are believed to have voted to join together into a single state in the Confederacy. The movement was stopped by Tennessee's eventual decision to secede from the Union. To the east of the Jackson Purchase are the dwindling coalfields and the Pennyrile (after pennyroyal, a common variety of local wild mint), a land of low hills and small farms.

The 1st Congressional District of Kentucky is made up of the Jackson Purchase and much of the Pennyrile. There is a distinctive Southern atmosphere here—in the crops that are grown, in the historically low wages, and in the fact that the big city with the most influence locally is Nashville, not Louisville. Especially in the four counties that border the Mississippi River, St. Louis and New Orleans are their frame of reference. Paducah, on the Ohio River, has reinvented a large area with an artist relocation program in the Lowertown Arts District, which has reversed the deteriorating neighborhood. The sprawling Army base at Fort Campbell is home to the 101st Airborne Division, the only air assault division in the world, which deployed multiple times during the Iraq and Afghanistan conflicts. Including its facilities in Tennessee, the base had 30,500 troops in 2020, making it the third largest in the Army. Industrial hemp, which is used as a fuel and fiber, has gained a foothold in the Paducah area. In some areas, it has replaced tobacco as a better investment. Some call Kentucky the "hemp capital of the world." After Congress legalized hemp, as part of the farm bill in 2018, Walmart was among the major companies that entered the market.

The Jackson Purchase and the Pennyrile are ancestrally Democratic. Paducah was the home of Alben Barkley, who was Senate majority leader for 10 years and Harry Truman's vice president. This part of the state never elected a Republican to Congress until 1994. But the Republican voting pattern has become firmly established in national elections. With its 72%-24% win for Donald Trump over Hillary Clinton, the 1st joined the 5th as the two strongest Republican districts in Kentucky. They also are the two most rural in the state and are among the lowest 10 percent of districts nationwide in their median income.

Brett Guthrie (R)

Elected 2008, 7th term, b. Feb 18, 1964; Florence, AL; U.S. Military Academy, B.S., 1987; Yale University, M.P.A., 1997; Church of Christ; Married (Elizabeth Clemons); 3 children.

Military Career: U.S. Army 1987-1990; U.S. Army Reserve 199-22

Elected Office: KY Senate, 1998-2008.

Professional Career: Vice President., Trace Die Cast, 2001-2008.

DC Office: 2434 RHOB 20515, 202-225-3501, Fax: 202-226-2019, guthrie.house.gov

State Offices: Bowling Green, 270-842-9896; Owensboro, 270-842-9896; Radcliff, 270-842-9896.

Committees: *Energy & Commerce*: Communications & Technology; Consumer Protection & Commerce; Health (RMM).

Group Ratings

	ADA	ACLU	AFL-CIO	LCV	COC	HAFA	ACU	CFG	FRC
2020	**	19%	**	14%	-	78%	82%	**	-
2019	5%	C	33%	10%	94%	C	82%	71%	100%

Almanac Ratings 2019-2020

	Economy	Social	Foreign	Composite
Liberal	25%	26%	27%	26%
Conservative	75%	74%	73%	74%

Key Votes of the 116th Congress

1. U.S./Mex./Can. trade deal Y	5. Russia sanctions Y	9. Firearms background checks N
2. First Coronavirus response Y	6. Troops in Syria Y	10. Spending at the border Y
3. HEROES Act N	7. Veto arms sales to Saudis N	11. Marijuana liberalized rules N
4. CASH Act N	8. Defense $$$, veto override Y	12. Electoral College objections N

Election Results

Election	Name (Party)	Vote (%)		Cand. Spent	Ind. Exp. Support	Ind. Exp. Oppose
2020 General	Brett Guthrie (R)................................	255,735	(71%)	$10,318,261	$9,286	$750
	Hank Linderman (D)...........................	94,643	(26%)	$63,043		
	Robert Lee Perry (L)...........................	7,588	(2%)	$7,747		
2020 Primary	Brett Guthrie (R)................................	65,313	(89%)			
	Kathleen Free (R)................................	8,380	(11%)			

Prior winning percentages: 2018 (68%), 2016 (100%), 2014 (69%), 2012 (64%), 2010 (68%), 2008 (53%)

Republican Brett Guthrie, elected in 2008, has a military and business background that plays well with constituents, plus a reputation as a loyal party vote that endears him to party leaders. With his plum seat on the Energy and Commerce Committee, he has enacted numerous health care bills and sought to protect the state's coal and oil industries. With the GOP in the House minority, he has shown skill in working across the aisle.

A graduate of West Point, Guthrie served 14 years in the Army, first in the Reserve, then as a field artillery officer with the 101st Airborne Division at Fort Campbell. After his discharge, Guthrie joined the family business in Bowling Green, Trace Die Cast Inc., a leading supplier of aluminum castings for the automobile industry. His father started the business with five employees in the 1980s. In 1998, Guthrie was elected to the state Senate, where he became chairman of the Transportation Committee, helping the state develop its highway budget. Republicans expected him to join their leadership, but Guthrie set his sights on Congress.

When the seat was open in 2008, Guthrie had no opposition for the Republican nomination. The Democratic nominee was state Sen. David Boswell, a 30-year veteran of Kentucky politics. He ran as a conservative Democrat, and the two contenders were virtually indistinguishable on the issues. Both opposed abortion rights and supported gun ownership, and both spoke out against the massive bailout for the financial industry that Congress passed that fall. Guthrie emphasized his military background to the district's large active and retired military population. The Democratic Congressional Campaign Committee ran an ad claiming that Trace Die Cast had sent jobs to Mexico. Guthrie had a war chest of nearly $1.3 million compared with Boswell's $917,000. He won 53%-47%. Since then, he has been reelected with at least 64 percent of the vote.

In the House, Guthrie has taken a softer line in criticizing the Environmental Protection Agency than other Republicans on Energy and Commerce, telling the Owensboro Messenger-Inquirer that the agency needed to strike a better balance between regulation and the economy. "I've been to Mexico City and Beijing," he said. "I don't want to have to wear a mask when I go outside. But I want regulations that don't put companies out of business and cost my district $60,000-a-year jobs." In 2016, the House passed the bill he authored with Energy and Commerce Democratic Rep. Kathy Castor of Florida to give companies in the concrete masonry industry more flexibility to research and promote their products.

Guthrie has had responsibilities at multiple House subcommittees. As vice chairman of the Health Subcommittee, when the GOP was in the majority, he focused on steps to replace Obamacare with "patient-centered health care solutions" and to make the Medicaid program more effective. He failed to achieve those big goals but has taken several incremental steps. In 2018, he enacted bills to update the Missing Children's Assistance Act, facilitate in-home health services for Medicaid beneficiaries, provide legal protections for sports medicine professionals who cross state lines and create a public health infrastructure to aide patients with Alzheimer's disease and related dementia. In November 2020, the House passed a bill Guthrie cosponsored with Democratic Rep. Doris Matsui of California that authorized the Food and Drug Administration to require generic-drug manufacturers to update their labels with safety problems.

In the minority, as ranking Republican on the Oversight and Investigations Subcommittee, he joined senior committee Democrats in October 2020 in a bipartisan call for stronger cybersecurity protections by companies developing vaccines to combat the coronavirus. Also that year, he was the chief GOP sponsor of a bipartisan measure to protect American consumers from counterfeit medical devices.

In 2020, when Rep. Greg Walden was term-limited as the senior Republican on Energy and Commerce, Guthrie initially considered seeking the top position. But he deferred to two members more senior to him—including Rep. Cathy McMorris Rodgers of Washington, who won the post. In the subsequent rotation of subcommittee assignments, Guthrie became the ranking member of the influential Health Subcommittee.

On the Education and the Workforce Committee, Guthrie chaired the Higher Education and the Workforce Subcommittee. In 2018, the House passed a bill he filed with Democratic Rep. Suzanne Bonamici of Oregon to expand financial-aid counseling, especially for student-loan recipients.

Guthrie, who during the 2016 campaign urged Donald Trump to work with Congress "in a positive way," said following a June 2018 meeting at the White House to discuss concerns about family separation of immigrants at the southern border, "we cannot continue to allow this to happen." Following the 2020 election, Guthrie did not join the 126 House Republicans who filed a brief supporting an unlikely move by the Texas attorney general to challenge the certification of presidential electors in four other states.

KY-2: Central Kentucky

Cook Partisan Voting Index: R+22

Population		Race and Ethnicity		Income	
Total	774,897	White	89.10%	Median Income	$53,496
Land area (sq. miles)	7,177	Black	5.20%	District Income Rank	355
Pop/ sq mi	107.96	Latino	3.40%	Poverty Rate	14.80%
Born in State	70.70%	Asian	2.10%	With health insurance	94.20%
		Two or more races	2.50%	Cash public assistance	1.10%
Age Groups		Other	1.10%	Food stamp/SNAP	10.20%
Under 18	23.20%				
18-34	22.20%	**Education**		**Work**	
35-64	38.20%	H.S grad or less	47.40%	White Collar	33.00%
Over 64	16.30%	Some college	30.70%	Sales and Service	35.70%
		College Degree, 4 yr	13.10%	Blue Collar	31.30%
Military		Post grad	8.80%	Government	14.50%
Veteran/ Active Duty	9.90%				

2020 Pres. Vote	Trump	246,865	(68%)	Biden	111,859	(31%)		
2016 Pres. Vote	Trump	219,152	(68%)	Clinton	89,563	(28%)	Johnson	9,269	(3%)

Louisville Suburbs, Bowling Green, Elizabethtown: In the 1770s and 1780s, Americans began settling the limestone-soil country of central Kentucky, staking out towns like Bardstown and Elizabethtown and starting academies and colleges. They were well-settled when Stephen Foster wrote My Old Kentucky Home, just before the Civil War. The war tore deeply here. This part of Kentucky gave birth to Abraham Lincoln, and during the conflict it lost thousands of soldiers, both Union and Confederate. Today, the area hosts several Kentucky landmarks: Fort Knox, the nation's gold depository; some of the nation's largest bourbon distilleries; and Mammoth Cave, the world's largest accessible cavern, which is near Bowling Green. In the small town of Bardstown, site of My Old Kentucky Home State Park, the annual Kentucky Bourbon Festival draws more than 50,000 visitors to the weeklong event. In 2019, Jim Beam, which has operated in Kentucky since 1795 though it became a subsidiary of a Japanese beverage company, expanded its distillery in Clermont. The upgrade enhanced the "visitors' experience," which catered to the growth in bourbon tourism.

The 2nd Congressional District of Kentucky consists of much of the territory south and southwest of Louisville, starting with Spencer County and heading south to Bowling Green. That city is the headquarters of apparel giant Fruit of the Loom, and it has a bustling General Motors Corvette assembly plant, the only place in the world where the sleek sports cars have been produced since 1981. In 2017, GM spent $430 million to upgrade the Bowling Green assembly plant, which added a second shift in 2019. The company produced 20,368 cars during the 2020 model year, a 50 percent cut from its plan, due chiefly to the coronavirus. The base price for its most popular model was $60,000, though the flashier Stingray goes for about $105,000. The National Corvette Museum is across the street from the plant.

The district jogs west along the Ohio River to Owensboro, a port with warehouses that receive aluminum alloys to make lightweight engine parts. The aluminum industry in 2018 had 20,000 workers in Kentucky, which led the nation. Also in Owensboro is the Bluegrass Music Hall of Fame. The city, which has become a banking center, had a notable achievement in 2020. As of July, among the 389 metropolitan areas tracked by the Bureau of Labor Statistics, only Owensboro had not increased its unemployment rate (4.2 percent) during the pandemic. Officials cited the city's production of consumer staples such as bourbon, tobacco and Kimberly-Clark toilet paper, plus its location as a regional distribution hub. Owensboro still tries to preserve the feeling of "Old Kentucky," and hosts an annual international barbecue festival where mutton, a throwback to Welsh shepherds who settled in western Kentucky, remains a favorite.

Much of the district is rural and small-town country. For decades, it favored Democrats. In the 1990s, voters moved to the Republican Party, which better matched their conservative cultural leanings.

John Yarmuth (D)

Elected 2006, 8th term, b. Nov 04, 1947; Louisville, KY; Yale University, B.A., 1969; Georgetown University Law Center, Att., 1972; Jewish; Married (Catherine Yarmuth); 1 child.

Professional Career: Stockbroker, 1969-1971; Sr. aide, U.S. Sen. Marlow Cook, 1971-1975; Publisher, Louisville Today magazine, 1976-1982; Assistant Vice President. of university relations, University of Louisville, 1983-1986; Vice President., Caretenders, 1986-1990; Owner, columnist, & Executive editor, Louisville Eccentric Observer, 1990-2002; Co-host, Yarmuth & Ziegler, 2003; Commentator, Hot Button, 2004-2005.

DC Office: 402 CHOB 20515, 202-225-5401, Fax: 202-225-5776, yarmuth.house.gov

State Offices: Louisville, 502-582-5129; Louisville, 502-933-5863.

Committees: *Budget (Chmn)*. *Education & Labor*: Early Childhood, Elementary & Secondary Education; Workforce Protections.

Group Ratings

	ADA	ACLU	AFL-CIO	LCV	COC	HAFA	ACU	CFG	FRC
2020	**	83%	**	100%	-	0%	3%	**	-
2019	95%	C	100%	93%	59%	C	3%	12%	0%

Almanac Ratings 2019-2020

	Economy	Social	Foreign	Composite
Liberal	100%	100%	56%	86%
Conservative	0%	0%	44%	14%

Key Votes of the 116th Congress

1. U.S./Mex./Can. trade deal Y	5. Russia sanctions Y	9. Firearms background checks Y
2. First Coronavirus response Y	6. Troops in Syria Y	10. Spending at the border Y
3. HEROES Act Y	7. Veto arms sales to Saudis Y	11. Marijuana liberalized rules Y
4. CASH Act Y	8. Defense $$$, veto override Y	12. Electoral College objections N

Election Results

Election	Name (Party)	Vote (%)		Cand. Spent	Ind. Exp. Support	Ind. Exp. Oppose
2020 General	John Yarmuth (D)........................	230,672	(63%)	$571,221	$3,176	
	Rhonda Palazzo (R).....................	137,425	(37%)	$38,324		$113

Prior winning percentages: 2018 (62%), 2016 (64%), 2014 (64%), 2012 (64%), 2010 (55%), 2008 (59%), 2006 (51%)

Democrat John Yarmuth, who was first elected in 2006, is a former journalist who has enjoyed rebuking Republicans, especially home-state colleague Mitch McConnell, the Senate Republican leader. As chairman of the House Budget Committee, he has become a top party spokesman on fiscal issues, though he presides over a congressional budget process that has lost much of its discipline. With the Democrats' razor-thin majority in the House in 2021, he faced the imperative of coordinating with budget officials in the Biden administration as well as House Democratic leaders.

Yarmuth hails from a wealthy Louisville family. His father, Stanley Yarmuth, founded National Industries, a conglomerate that started as a used car business; his maternal grandfather, Samuel Klein, ran the Bank of Louisville. After graduating from Yale University, he worked briefly as a stockbroker and then as an aide to Republican Sen. Marlow Cook. Yarmuth attended two years of law school but didn't finish his degree.

He founded Louisville Today magazine and served as publisher from 1976 until 1982. He ran unsuccessfully for Louisville alderman in 1975, and for county commissioner in 1981. He worked in public relations from 1983 to 1990 for the University of Louisville and for a health care company. Unhappy with the policies of President Ronald Reagan, Yarmuth switched his party affiliation to Democrat in 1985. In 1990, he founded the Louisville Eccentric Observer, a free newsweekly popularly known as LEO, and for the next 15 years penned a column called "Hot Coals" that promoted his mostly liberal views. He also did televised political commentary.

In 2006, five-term Republican Rep. Anne Northup was vulnerable in the district. The Democratic Congressional Campaign Committee touted attorney Andrew Horne, an Iraq war veteran. But Yarmuth raised more money and proved a more formidable candidate than Horne, winning the four-way primary 54%-32%. He called for an immediate pullout of troops from Iraq and referred to Northup as a "rubber stamp" for President George W. Bush. Northup campaigned on Republican tax cuts and her work for the district. She unleashed an advertising offensive that blasted Yarmuth for his liberal writings, saying he supported removing the phrase "under God" from the Pledge of Allegiance and legalizing marijuana.

Northup raised $3.4 million to Yarmuth's $2.3 million, which included $700,000 of his own money. With a boost from the national tide against Republicans, Yarmuth won, 51%-48%. In 2008, Northup returned for a rematch after losing a primary contest for governor. She criticized Yarmuth for supporting the $700 billion bailout for the financial markets. Even though Northup raised more money, Yarmuth won more easily, 59%-41%. He has become entrenched in the seat.

Yarmuth told Esquire magazine in 2010 that he had trouble adjusting to elected office: "I never had to compromise on my opinion in the column. Suddenly you have to swallow all sorts of compromises, and that's not easy at all." With his journalism background, he joined a "messaging" group that advised Speaker Nancy Pelosi and other Democratic leaders on media strategy. He snared a seat on the Ways and Means Committee, but lost it after Republicans regained control of the House in 2011.

He has frequently jabbed at McConnell, with whom he has clashed since the 1970s. "Mitch McConnell will always do what's in Mitch McConnell's best interest," he has said. Yarmuth reveals an occasional independence that is somewhat unusual among the tightly disciplined senior House Democrats. After the House passed the fiscal-cliff budget compromise, he praised House Speaker John Boehner for being "courageous" in sending the Senate-passed deal to the House floor. He told Roll Call that enacting the Affordable Care Act in 2010 was the right thing to do policy-wise, but "big picture, politically, it probably wasn't worth it." He told a Louisville radio station after the Senate made changes to the bill, "We couldn't really go to the average American citizen and say, 'Here's what it means to you.'"

In naming Yarmuth as the top Democrat on the Budget Committee after the 2016 election, Pelosi said he "will represent our values in the budget debate, is a master at communicating to the public and has been a leader in advocating the use of social media." Yarmuth described his role: "Budgets are statements of our values, and the Budget Committee provides us the opportunity to show the American people the sharp contrasts between Democratic values and those of Republicans in the House and White House." As committee chairman following the 2018 election, he sought to turn the panel into a national forum on a host of causes.

Unusually for a Budget chairman, Yarmuth in 2019 failed to push for committee action on an annual budget resolution to set spending and revenue targets. With Republican control of the Senate and White House, there was scant likelihood of reaching a final agreement. Instead, working with Pelosi and leaders of other House committees, he prepared what became a bipartisan two-year deal that was enacted with spending caps—the Bipartisan Budget Act of 2019. Democrats gained support from most of their party's liberals because failure to approve new spending caps would have resulted in cuts in both domestic and defense spending.

"Passing bipartisan legislation to raise the caps and enact a realistic budget has been the most important accomplishment of this Congress," Yarmuth said in February 2020. Later in the year, he joined other House Democratic in unveiling the Congressional Power of the Purse Act, which imposed new requirements for executive branch transparency and compliance with congressional spending targets. For 2021, Yarmuth said, House Democrats planned to return to the traditional congressional budget—if only to give Senate Democrats the opportunity to take advantage of the procedural tools provided by its reconciliation process..

At home, following the violence that rocked his city following the police shooting of Breonna Taylor in March 2020, Yarmuth voiced his support for the Black Lives Matter movement. During a march in downtown Louisville with protestors, he cited progress in Congress, with "discussions about how we truly can take concrete steps to try to make this a much more fair, just and equitable nation." In September, he told another group of protesters that he was their ally in seeking a "public safety system that views Black people not as threats but neighbors to serve and protect."

KY-3: Louisville Metro

Cook Partisan Voting Index: D+8

Population		Race and Ethnicity		Income	
Total	742,543	White	70.90%	Median Income	$57,546
Land area (sq. miles)	319	Black	23.00%	District Income Rank	294
Pop/ sq mi	2,325.24	Latino	6.10%	Poverty Rate	14.40%
Born in State	66.30%	Asian	2.80%	With health insurance	94.00%
		Two or more races	2.40%	Cash public assistance	2.10%
Age Groups		Other	0.90%	Food stamp/SNAP	9.30%
Under 18	21.90%				
18-34	23.50%	Education		Work	
35-64	38.00%	H.S grad or less	35.80%	White Collar	40.00%
Over 64	16.70%	Some college	29.70%	Sales and Service	36.30%
		College Degree, 4 yr	20.70%	Blue Collar	23.70%
Military		Post grad	13.70%	Government	10.80%
Veteran/ Active Duty	7.10%				

2020 Pres. Vote	Biden	221,843	(60%)	Trump	141,027	(38%)		
2016 Pres. Vote	Clinton	186,549	(55%)	Trump	135,714	(40%)	Johnson	9,854	(3%)

Louisville: At the falls of the Ohio River, George Rogers Clark founded one of America's first inland metropolises in 1778: the river port and industrial city of Louisville. It is heavily influenced by the Cavalier culture that the second sons of big landowners from England brought to Virginia in the 17th century—and their heirs brought over the Appalachians to the valleys of Kentucky in the 18th century. When Kentucky decided not to secede from the union in 1861, the decision was not unanimous. The culture of tidewater Virginia is still evident in the Louisville lawn party. Mint juleps are served on the verandas of mansions, especially (but not only) during Kentucky Derby week in May; horse racing is a preoccupation throughout the year.

With 618,000 residents in 2019, Louisville is Kentucky's largest city. Another 150,000 reside in the remaining parts of Jefferson County. Its economy is in many ways "pre-postindustrial:" It produces cigarettes and whiskey, GE appliances (since 1907) and Ford automobiles (since 1969). Louisville is the headquarters of Humana health services; the long-term health care facility operator Signature HealthCARE; and several fast-food companies, including Yum! Brands, which owns KFC, Pizza Hut and Taco Bell. Muhammad Ali, born in Louisville as Cassius Marcellus Clay, has been memorialized by the Muhammad Ali Center, with its interactive exhibits. The Derby usually has an annual economic impact of $400 million. Because of the coronavirus, the Derby in 2020 was run in Louisville in September, without any spectators.

Louisville was the scene of a bitter and sometimes violent battle for racial justice following the shooting death in March 2020 of Breonna Taylor, during a police raid on her apartment. Police were searching for Kenneth Walker, her former boyfriend, who was inside the apartment and the target of a criminal investigation. Taylor was the innocent victim in crossfire between the police and Walker, which took place following the police entry under disputed circumstances. Taylor, like Walker, was African American. Two months later, seven persons were killed during a night of continuing protests by activists who demanded accountability for police. City officials contended that the additional deaths resulted from gunfire within the crowd and that police were not responsible. Meanwhile, Louisville Mayor Greg Fischer sought to assure protestors that police procedures had been revised to prevent a recurrence of the Taylor killing. The charges that were filed against Walker following that incident were later dropped.

But tensions remained high as the city awaited the results of an investigation by Attorney General Daniel Cameron of the shooting of Taylor. In September, following the completion of Cameron's inquiry, a grand jury brought charges of wanton endangerment against Brett Hankinson, one of the three police officers who were at Taylor's apartment. But Hankinson was cleared of responsibility for Taylor's death. No charges were brought against Jonathan Mattingly, who fired the fatal shot, according to the investigators. As the case moved to a series of lawsuits—with charges and counter-charges between Walker and the police—protests continued and racial tensions remained high.

The 3rd Congressional District of Kentucky includes all but a handful of precincts in Jefferson County. The large African-American population, which is 21 percent of the overall district, resides chiefly in the West End of Louisville. A low-income white population is along the strip highway that leads to Fort Knox. West Buechel, southeast of the city, has one of the highest concentrations of Yugoslavian Americans in the United States, many of whom were Bosnian refugees. The suburbs to the east tend to be affluent. Small, elite neighborhoods—Mockingbird Valley, Glenview and Ten Broeck—are nestled in the hills above the Ohio River.

The district, like Louisville, has long been an odd duck in Kentucky politics. Many of its burghers were Germans and Pennsylvanians who made the river town a Republican and anti-slavery island in a secessionist and pro-slavery sea. That tradition helps explain how Republican Mitch McConnell won election as Jefferson County judge-executive in 1977 and 1981, when the state was electing Democrats to most other offices. Since the 1990s, Louisville has trended toward Democrats, even as the rest of Kentucky trended Republican. In both 2016 and 2020, Jefferson was one of only two counties to vote Democratic, 54%-41% for Hillary Clinton and 59%-39% for Joe Biden.

Thomas Massie (R)

Elected 2012, 5th term, b. Jan 13, 1971; Huntington, WV; MA Institute of Technology, B.S., 1993; MA Institute of Technology, M.M.E., 1996; Methodist; Married (Rhonda Massie); 4 children.

Elected Office: Judge Executive, Lewis County KY, 2010-2012;

Professional Career: Founder, Chairman, & chief tech. officer, SensAble Technologies, 1993-2003; Farmer, 2003-present.

DC Office: 2453 RHOB 20515, 202-225-3465, Fax: 202-225-0003, massie.house.gov

State Offices: Ashland, 606-324-9898; Crescent Springs, 859-426-0080; LaGrange, 502-265-9119.

Committees: *Judiciary*: Courts, Intellectual Property & Internet; Crime, Terrorism & Homeland Security. *Transportation & Infrastructure*: Aviation; Economic Dev't, Public Buildings & Emergency Management; Highways & Transit.

Group Ratings

	ADA	ACLU	AFL-CIO	LCV	COC	HAFA	ACU	CFG	FRC
2020	**	36%	**	0%	-	92%	90%	**	-
2019	15%	C	5%	3%	41%	C	91%	94%	91%

Almanac Ratings 2019-2020

	Economy	Social	Foreign	Composite
Liberal	25%	13%	47%	29%
Conservative	75%	87%	53%	71%

Key Votes of the 116th Congress

1. U.S./Mex./Can. trade deal	N	5. Russia sanctions	N/A	9. Firearms background checks	N
2. First Coronavirus response	N/A	6. Troops in Syria	N	10. Spending at the border	N
3. HEROES Act	N	7. Veto arms sales to Saudis	Y	11. Marijuana liberalized rules	N
4. CASH Act	N	8. Defense $$$, veto override	N	12. Electoral College objections	N

Election Results

Election	Name (Party)	Vote (%)		Cand. Spent	Ind. Exp. Support	Ind. Exp. Oppose
2020 General	Thomas Massie (R)........................	256,613	(67%)	$1,541,200	$413,873	$133,250
	Alexandra Owensby (D).....................	125,896	(33%)	$99,363	$2,600	
2020 Primary	Thomas Massie (R)........................	68,591	(81%)			
	Todd McMurtry (R)........................	16,092	(19%)			

Prior winning percentages: 2018 (62%), 2016 (71%), 2014 (68%), 2012 (62%)

Republican Thomas Massie, first elected in 2012 as a political outsider, has remained an iconoclast. He has been a constant thorn to Republican leaders, who have bypassed him for chairmanships, and a free spirit who often goes his own way in House votes. He has been instrumental in starting up and leading groups of conservative activists in the House, including the Second Amendment Caucus. In 2020, Massie easily defeated a challenger in the GOP primary who initially received encouragement from senior Republicans.

Massie has an impressive scientific background. He was raised in Vanceburg Kentucky and got his bachelor's degree and master's in engineering at the Massachusetts Institute of Technology. While at MIT, Massie was part of a group that invented the Phantom, a device enabling users to interact with objects in cyberspace through touch. To market the product, he and his wife, Rhonda (his high school sweetheart and also an MIT student), started the firm SensAble Technologies, which raised more than $32 million of venture capital, created 70 jobs, and obtained 29 patents. Massie left SensAble Technologies in 2003 and returned to Kentucky with his family to run a farm, where he built a timber-frame house that runs on solar energy and is powered by a used Tesla car battery. He got interested in politics after learning about a proposed new tax in rural Lewis County. In 2010, he was elected the county's judge-executive.

When he ran for an open House seat in 2012, Massie described himself as a "conservative with conviction and common sense." He campaigned on his business background and won the vital support of tea party activists. He had backed tea party favorite Rand Paul in his 2010 Senate race. Paul appeared in a TV ad for Massie. Massie won the primary, with 45 percent of the vote. His two chief opponents split the establishment vote. In this solidly Republican district, Massie easily won in November.

He showed his rebellious streak on his first House vote in 2013, when he opposed John Boehner for a new term as House Speaker. Massie occasionally crossed the aisle to work with Democrats, especially on civil liberties issues where the wings of both parties came together in opposition to Big Government. In 2015, the House passed a bill he cosponsored with Democratic Rep. Zoe Lofgren of California to require that the National Security Agency seek a judicial warrant before it could spy on U.S. citizens in its online surveillance.

In profiling him as "Democrats' new go-to Republican," Buzzfeed quoted Massie: "Here's the difference between a partisan and an ideologue: An ideologue reads the bill, every word, period and section; a partisan reads the whip recommendation." (He's proudly the former.) His Almanac vote ratings placed him near the center of the House, especially on economic and foreign policy issues. On most social issues, he remained a solid conservative vote.

Massie has worked with other conservatives to channel their opposition to GOP leaders. The House leadership, he said, had become "a significant source of the dysfunction" in the chamber. He has been consistent, and increasingly lonely, in his independence. After Boehner resigned in 2015, Massie was one of nine Republicans who voted against Paul Ryan as the new Speaker. In 2019, he was one of six Republicans to vote against GOP Leader Kevin McCarthy in the House vote for Speaker. Party leaders have responded accordingly. During his first term, Massie chaired the Technology Subcommittee, a logical assignment for his background. Since then, he has no longer been the senior Republican on that subcommittee, or any other. On two occasions in 2020, when there was an opening for the top Republican on the Oversight and Reform Committee, GOP leaders twice bypassed Massie—once to select a junior Kentuckian, James Comer.

Massie worked with other members to organize the conservative Freedom Caucus as a way to strengthen their legislative leverage. He later dropped out of the group because he refused to comply with its requirements for membership. In 2016, he revived the Second Amendment Caucus and became its chairman. During the next two years, he filed bills to reduce from 21 to 18 the minimum age for handgun sales, allow persons with concealed-carry permits in their home state to carry in Washington D.C., and repeal gun-free zones around schools. The solution to school shootings, he said, was to add more armed guards or allow teachers to be armed. None of the proposals was considered by the Republican-controlled House.

In 2020, Massie triggered a series of events that highlighted GOP unhappiness and his success —by his terms, at least. In late March, the House prepared its first economic relief bill in response to the coronavirus. At that early point of social distancing for most of the nation, House leaders of both parties were desperate to avoid any action that would force members to travel to the Capitol. But Massie insisted that approval of a $2.2 trillion bill warranted a roll-call vote under the Constitution and House rules. The leaders got their quorum and passed the bill, by voice vote. Many members who complained they were inconvenienced—and perhaps placed at risk—were livid. President Donald Trump tweeted that Massie was a "third-rate Grandstander."

Two months later, that incident seemed tailor-made for Todd McMurtry, a lawyer who challenged Massie as ineffective in his first serious primary contest. Rep. Liz Cheney, who chaired the House

Republican Conference, wrote a contribution to the challenger—a highly unusual action. As it turned out, foes revealed that McMurtry had made hostile racial comments years earlier. An embarrassed Cheney sought—and received—a refund. McMurtry spent $383,000. Massie responded by spending $1.3 million. He benefited from more than $500,000 of support from the Freedom Caucus and the conservative Club for Growth. Massie won, 81%-19%, with at least a 3-to-1 lead in each of the 20 counties.

As Massie revealingly told The Washington Post a few weeks after his campaign success, "What I'm doing up here is looking for the one weakness in the Death Star—but sometimes I wind up in the trash compactor."

KY-4: Northern Kentucky

Cook Partisan Voting Index: R+19

Population		Race and Ethnicity		Income	
Total	761,936	White	91.90%	Median Income	$66,327
Land area (sq. miles)	4,382	Black	3.20%	District Income Rank	201
Pop/ sq mi	173.87	Latino	3.40%	Poverty Rate	11.40%
Born in State	59.90%	Asian	1.60%	With health insurance	94.00%
		Two or more races	2.10%	Cash public assistance	1.30%
Age Groups		Other	1.20%	Food stamp/SNAP	7.60%
Under 18	23.40%				
18-34	20.80%	**Education**		**Work**	
35-64	39.70%	H.S grad or less	41.40%	White Collar	39.60%
Over 64	16.20%	Some college	29.60%	Sales and Service	34.40%
Military		College Degree, 4 yr	18.10%	Blue Collar	26.00%
Veteran/ Active Duty	7.40%	Post grad	10.90%	Government	12.10%

2020 Pres. Vote	Trump	250,481	(65%)	Biden	129,335	(33%)			
2016 Pres. Vote	Trump	219,749	(65%)	Clinton	98,664	(29%)	Johnson	11,693	(4%)

Cincinnati and Louisville Suburbs: Along the Ohio River are some very different parts of Kentucky. Ashland, near the West Virginia border, is industrial, the former home of Ashland Inc.; the river here is bound in by tight hills that hold smoke and soot in the air. In the low-income area surrounding Ashland, investors planned a $1.7 billion aluminum rolling mill; a lawsuit over ownership of the company, which had delayed the project, was settled in 2020. Farther down the river, the country is more bucolic. This is where Eliza fled across the ice floes in Harriet Beecher Stowe's Uncle Tom's Cabin. But metropolitan growth obtrudes. Oldham County, just upriver from Louisville, has some of Kentucky's oldest homes, and is by far the most affluent county in the state.

The three Northern Kentucky counties across the river from Cincinnati—Campbell, Kenton and Boone—are named for pioneers, but are now urban and suburban. Following Jefferson (Louisville) and Fayette (Lexington), Kenton and Boone are the largest counties in Kentucky. Overlooking the suspension bridge built by John Roebling are new buildings on the Covington waterfront. Newport, with its panoramic view of the Cincinnati skyline plus its nightlife, has become a regional hot spot. New subdivisions are rising on the hills in Boone County, above the river, near the Cincinnati/ Northern Kentucky International Airport.

The fastest-growing major freight airport in the nation, CVG (an acronym for Covington, its home) ranks fourth in the nation for its volume of cargo. In competition with Memphis-based FedEx and Louisville-based United Parcel Service, Amazon planned to complete in 2021 a $1.5 billion international hub at the airport, which will be home for its fleet of at least 80 planes, with more than 2,000 workers and additional expansion plans. Amazon chief executive Jeff Bezos said its operation at CVG was a "big part" of Amazon Prime's move from two-day to one-day shipping. CVG is also one of three global hubs for DHL Cargo.

The 4th Congressional District of Kentucky is the northernmost district in the state. It covers 12 counties and 280 miles along the Ohio River and also lightly populated counties just inland. Economically, it runs the gamut from coal mining towns to rich suburbs. The region's clout in state government has been understated because the political focus is more on Cincinnati than on Louisville or Lexington. The three northern Kentucky counties across the river from Cincinnati, which have grown to a bit more than half the district's votes, are heavily Republican. This is a solidly

Republican district, though the 65%-29% support for Trump in 2016 ranked only fourth among the five Republican-held districts in Kentucky.

Hal Rogers (R)

Elected 1980, 21st term, b. Dec 31, 1937; Barrier, KY; Western KY University, Att., 1957; University of KY, B.A., 1962; University of KY College of Law, J.D., 1964; Baptist; Married (Cynthia Doyle Rogers); 3 children (from a previous marriage).

Military Career: U.S. Army National Guard 1956-1963

Professional Career: Practicing attorney, 1964-1969; Pulaski-Rockcastle Commonwealth's Attorney, 1969-1980.

DC Office: 2406 RHOB 20515, 202-225-4601, Fax: 202-225-0940, halrogers.house.gov

State Offices: Hazard, 606-439-0794; Prestonsburg, 606-886-0844; Somerset, 800-632-8588.

Committees: *Appropriations*: Defense; State, Foreign Operations & Related Programs (RMM).

Group Ratings

	ADA	ACLU	AFL-CIO	LCV	COC	HAFA	ACU	CFG	FRC
2020	**	19%	**	10%	-	77%	80%	**	-
2019	5%	C	33%	7%	94%	C	80%	66%	100%

Almanac Ratings 2019-2020

	Economy	Social	Foreign	Composite
Liberal	25%	17%	27%	23%
Conservative	75%	83%	73%	77%

Key Votes of the 116th Congress

1. U.S./Mex./Can. trade deal Y	5. Russia sanctions Y	9. Firearms background checks N
2. First Coronavirus response Y	6. Troops in Syria Y	10. Spending at the border Y
3. HEROES Act N	7. Veto arms sales to Saudis N	11. Marijuana liberalized rules N
4. CASH Act Y	8. Defense $$$, veto override Y	12. Electoral College objections Y

Election Results

Election	Name (Party)	Vote (%)		Cand. Spent	Ind. Exp. Support	Ind. Exp. Oppose
2020 General	Hal Rogers (R)	250,914	(84%)	$719,512	$9,548	$750
	Matthew Best (D)	47,056	(16%)			
2020 Primary	Hal Rogers (R)	76,575	(91%)			
	Gerardo Serrano (R)	7,436	(9%)			

Prior winning percentages: 2018 (79%), 2016 (100%), 2014 (78%), 2012 (78%), 2010 (77%), 2008 (84%), 2006 (74%), 2004 (100%), 2002 (78%), 2000 (74%), 1998 (78%), 1996 (100%), 1994 (79%), 1992 (55%), 1990 (100%), 1988 (100%), 1986 (100%), 1984 (76%), 1982 (65%), 1980 (68%)

Harold Rogers, a Republican first elected in 1980 and tied for the second most-senior member of the House, served six years as chairman of the House Appropriations Committee until he was term-limited in 2016. He chaired several subcommittees and remains an old-school dealmaker. In the days before—and since--the ban on earmarks, he not only defended them but boasted about the prodigious sums he steered back home to his needy constituents. In the minority, Rogers has been ranking member of the State and Foreign Operations Subcommittee, where he has taken a hard line on China. At 83, he is beloved in his rural district.

Rogers grew up in Wayne County, graduated from the University of Kentucky, served in the National Guard, then practiced law in Somerset before buying the Citizens National Bank in Somerset. In 1969, at age 34, he was elected Pulaski-Rockcastle commonwealth attorney. In 1979, he was the unsuccessful Republican nominee for lieutenant governor. The following year, when there was an open House seat, Rogers was one of 11 Republicans in the primary. He got the nomination with 23 percent of the vote and easily won in November.

His toughest race came in 1992, when redistricting combined two districts in eastern Kentucky. At first, his likely opponent was Rep. Chris Perkins, a Democrat and the son of Rep. Carl Perkins, who had chaired the Education and Labor Committee. Together, the Perkinses had held the seat for 44 years. But Perkins unexpectedly retired, just before it was revealed that he had 514 overdrafts at the House bank. Rogers instead faced state Sen. John Doug Hays of Pike County. Rogers won with 55 percent. Since then, he has been reelected with at least 74 percent of the vote.

His voting record is mostly, but not always, conservative. His district has long been hungry for federal aid, and Rogers often has found it difficult to maintain a conservative record on spending issues. He has argued that the federal-state partnership helped to close the gap between the impoverished area and the rest of the country.

During Republicans' initial 12 years in the House majority, Rogers chaired the Commerce, Justice, State Subcommittee starting in 1995, took over the Transportation Subcommittee in 2001, and became chairman in 2003 of the newly created Homeland Security Subcommittee. He helped to increase Kentucky to the fourth-highest state in transportation funding per capita. "The rate of return on highway spending far exceeds most other investments and is a proven engine," Rogers once wrote when he was criticized for his earmarked spending. The Hal Rogers Parkway crosses the Daniel Boone National Forest from London to Hazard.

Rogers rose to chairman of Appropriations in 2011. He took over just as most House Republicans, especially the 87 freshmen elected in 2010, were determined to end earmarking. Despite his work over the years funding projects at home, he succumbed to the moratorium on earmarks that Speaker John Boehner decreed. In 2012, Rogers touted his success as a born-again foe of wasteful spending. "We've cut the spending Congress does for three years now, which has not happened since World War II," he said. Nondiscretionary spending continued to rise unabated.

Part of the reason for Rogers' continuing clout is his ability to work with Democrats. "He's very approachable," senior committee Democrat Marcy Kaptur of Ohio said. "He's a matter-of-fact sort of gentleman—I mean, he doesn't spend a lot of time on wasted words, he's terse—but I think very effective." Another source of his influence has been the inability of recent congressional majorities to pass individual appropriations bills. That led to massive omnibus spending bills, something that enabled Republicans to make policy via "riders" crafted in backroom deals on the omnibus legislation.

When President Barack Obama in November 2014 issued an executive order protecting some illegal immigrants, many conservatives vowed to overturn it. But Rogers warned against using the issue to provoke another spending-bill confrontation. "I just don't think it's very smart, wise or prudent to talk about a shutdown scenario," he said. That enraged conservative activists. National Review ran an article headlined "Hal Rogers, Obama Republican." In that instance, Rogers prevailed.

In his final year as committee chairman, Rogers sought to deliver a parting gift to his constituents: Legislation to provide $1 billion for mine reclamation projects to revitalize coal communities in his district and nearby areas. The tight budget plus limited congressional action during the presidential year thwarted that goal and resulted in a status quo extension of federal spending.

In 2017, Rogers became chairman of the State and Foreign Operations Subcommittee at Appropriations. That was an unusual rebuke of an influential and senior House Republican. As McClatchy News earlier reported, Rogers wanted to chair the Defense Subcommittee. Instead, that position went to Kay Granger of Texas. Two years later, Granger unexpectedly became the senior Republican on the full committee. That gave Rogers a new opportunity at the Defense Subcommittee, with the GOP in the minority. Instead, he retained the top post on the Foreign Operations Subcommittee and Ken Calvert of California took the defense slot. In 2020, he helped to craft tough terms, including exposure of Chinese censorship and propaganda, and steps to counter "Beijing's debt-trap diplomacy through well-funded, open and transparent U.S. development."

He continues to deliver federal largesse to his district and state. With help from home-state Sen. Mitch McConnell, Rogers took credit in 2020 for eight new C-130 aircraft to the Kentucky Air National Guard. "I started working to secure federal funding for these essential military transport aircraft several years ago," he said.

KY-5: Eastern Kentucky

Cook Partisan Voting Index: R+33

Population		Race and Ethnicity		Income	
Total	689,793	White	96.40%	Median Income	$35,636
Land area (sq. miles)	11,235	Black	1.20%	District Income Rank	435
Pop/ sq mi	61.4	Latino	1.40%	Poverty Rate	25.00%
Born in State	77.70%	Asian	0.60%	With health insurance	92.60%
		Two or more races	1.40%	Cash public assistance	3.50%
Age Groups		Other	0.50%	Food stamp/SNAP	22.00%
Under 18	22.10%				
18-34	20.20%	**Education**		**Work**	
35-64	39.50%	H.S grad or less	60.80%	White Collar	31.00%
Over 64	18.20%	Some college	25.40%	Sales and Service	40.10%
		College Degree, 4 yr	7.50%	Blue Collar	28.90%
Military		Post grad	6.30%	Government	17.30%
Veteran/ Active Duty	5.40%				

2020 Pres. Vote	Trump	241,712	(80%)	Biden	56,153	(19%)
2016 Pres. Vote	Trump	221,558	(80%)	Clinton	48,628	(18%)

Somerset, Pikesville: Mountainous eastern Kentucky has been a unique place since Daniel Boone came through the Cumberland Gap in 1775. Scots-Irish pioneers followed him, bringing their assertive egalitarianism, loyalty to family and community, and passionate willingness to defend honor by feuds or violence. Most inhabitants of the mountains today are descendants of the Ulster Protestant and Border Scot families who settled there in the two or three generations after Boone. In the 2010 census, 0 percent of the population of Elliott, Magoffin and Menifee counties reported being foreign-born. This was never slave territory—hardly any Blacks have ever lived in these mountains. The local economic populism was well-suited to President Donald Trump. Social conservatism remains vocal in many of these places. In 2015, Rowan County Clerk Kim Davis received national attention when she was jailed for refusing to issue marriage licenses to same-sex couples.

Early in the 20th century, vast seams of coal were discovered under the Kentucky mountains and a new economy sprang up, bringing a new politics. Coal mining was harsh and deadly work. Mine accidents, black lung disease and simple exhaustion killed tens of thousands of miners, while low wages and company stores kept them poor. Then, John L. Lewis' United Mine Workers came in, and open warfare followed, with both mine operators and union organizers willing to use violence. The union mostly won in eastern Kentucky. In the War on Poverty, President Lyndon Johnson brought attention to this and other parts of Appalachia. He launched his "war" in the town of Inez in these mountains. A half-century later, high-school graduation rates and life expectancy remained low.

Some of these areas have some of the grimmest working conditions in the nation. The number of miners in eastern Kentucky fell from 14,000 in 2009 to below 4,000 in 2016. The strong rhetorical support from Trump, along with more favorable regulations, gave hope to many in the coal fields for the first time in decades. Jobs in the mines grew by 6 percent in 2017. Three years later, production had plummeted. The federal Energy Information Administration reported that coal production in eastern Kentucky declined by nearly 50 percent from the first six months of 2019 to the first six months of 2020. The number of local miners had dropped below 3,400 in mid-2019. One result has been social dysfunction. A research report in 2018 found that this district had the nation's second-highest opioid-prescription rate, according to the Harvard School of Public Health. Keeping hope alive in these places can be difficult. In 2019, the Justice Department's plans to build in Letcher County a $450 million prison were withdrawn, following local opposition. Plans by a lithium battery maker to build a new factory in Pikeville were "suspended" in 2019.

The 5th Congressional District of Kentucky includes much of the territory east of the Pottsville Escarpment, which separates the Cumberland Plateau and most of the eastern mountains from the rest of the state. It includes a few counties in the eastern Pennyrile region: small towns like Somerset, Monticello and Mount Vernon. And it takes in the mountains to the east, including Corbin, where Colonel Harland Sanders first served his fried chicken with 11 herbs and spices, birthing fast-food franchise KFC. The northeast section of the district is coal country. Few highways go through the mountains; only a handful of towns have a population over 10,000. Overall, this district is heavily

Republican, among the top 1 percent in the nation: The 80 percent of the vote for Trump was his second best performance in the nation in 2020. The district is the second-poorest in the nation in median household income. The poorest is New York's 15th District (South Bronx), which has voted the most Democratic in the nation.

Andy Barr (R)

Elected 2012, 5th term, b. Jul 24, 1973; Lexington, KY; University of VA, B.A., 1996; University of KY College of Law, J.D., 2001; Episcopalian; Widower (Eleanor Carol Leavell); 2 children.

Professional Career: Legislative Assistant, U.S. Rep. Jim Talent, 1996-1998; Instructor, Morehead St. University; Attorney, KY gov.'s office, 2004-2007; Practicing attorney, 2008-2012.

DC Office: 2430 RHOB 20515, 202-225-4706, Fax: 202-225-2122, barr.house.gov

State Offices: Lexington, 859-219-1366.

Committees: *Financial Services*: Consumer Protection & Financial Institutions; Nat'l Security, International Development & Monetary Policy (RMM). *Foreign Affairs*: Asia, the Pacific, Central Asia, Nonproliferation.

Group Ratings

	ADA	ACLU	AFL-CIO	LCV	COC	HAFA	ACU	CFG	FRC
2020	**	18%	**	10%	-	89%	79%	**	-
2019	5%	C	29%	10%	93%	C	81%	79%	95%

Almanac Ratings 2019-2020

	Economy	Social	Foreign	Composite
Liberal	25%	34%	27%	29%
Conservative	75%	66%	73%	71%

Key Votes of the 116th Congress

1. U.S./Mex./Can. trade deal	Y	5. Russia sanctions	Y	9. Firearms background checks N
2. First Coronavirus response	Y	6. Troops in Syria	Y	10. Spending at the border	Y
3. HEROES Act	N	7. Veto arms sales to Saudis	N	11. Marijuana liberalized rules	N
4. CASH Act	N/A	8. Defense $$$, veto override	N/A	12. Electoral College objections	N

Election Results

Election	Name (Party)	Vote (%)		Cand. Spent	Ind. Exp. Support	Ind. Exp. Oppose
2020 General	Andy Barr (R)	216,948	(57%)	$4,415,706	$15,815	$250,045
	Josh Hicks (D)	155,011	(41%)	$3,149,087	$19,000	
2020 Primary	Andy Barr (R)	62,706	(91%)			
	Chuck Eddy (R)	3,636	(5%)			

Prior winning percentages: 2018 (51%), 2016 (61%), 2014 (60%), 2012 (51%)

Republican Andy Barr, after winning two highly competitive contests, secured this swing seat. The youthful Barr seems well-placed for further political influence, in his House committee work and perhaps an eventual statewide bid. The redistricting for 2022 likely will affect the partisan direction of this district, with the Republican-controlled legislature seeking to provide additional GOP support to protect Barr—or his potential successor.

Barr grew up in Lexington and graduated from the University of Virginia with a bachelor's degree in government and philosophy. After two years as a legislative assistant for Republican Rep. Jim Talent of Missouri, Barr returned home to earn a law degree from the University of Kentucky. He practiced law and taught constitutional and administrative law as a part-time instructor at Morehead State University. Barr served as a deputy general counsel to former Kentucky Gov. Ernie Fletcher.

In his 2010 challenge to Democratic Rep. Ben Chandler, Barr distanced himself from Fletcher, whose tenure was marred by scandal over political hiring of state employees. Chandler won by 647 votes. Barr decided against a recount and conceded 10 days after the election. Barr got an earlier start in his 2012 rematch, though Chandler got help from redistricting. Barr attacked the policies of President Barack Obama—especially on coal, an important issue to the district—and used a picture of his own baby daughter on a campaign mailer that called Chandler a "pro-abortion extremist." Chandler brought up Barr's guilty plea to possession of a fake ID when he was 19. Barr responded with an ad calling the incident a "dumb mistake" by a teenager and blasting his rival as a "desperate politician scared of losing." He got fundraising help from outside Republican groups that helped put him over the top. He won, 51%-47%, leading in all but the two largest counties—Fayette (Lexington) and Franklin (Frankfort).

Barr has been active on the Financial Services Committee. In 2015, he filed legislation that would streamline financial regulations, especially affecting community banks and credit unions, which often are important in rural communities. In 2017, Barr joined other committee Republicans in enacting a partial rollback of the 2010 Dodd-Frank banking regulations. The law, he said, had been bad for Kentucky, with the closing of credit unions and small banks. "Dodd-Frank regulations clogged the plumbing of our economy, especially in rural and underserved communities," he told the Banking Committee of the state House. As chairman of the Subcommittee on Monetary Policy and Trade, he conducted oversight of the Federal Reserve System to encourage a stable monetary policy. He filed a bill to require "greater transparency and accountability" by the Fed in setting monetary policy.

In 2020, House Republican Leader Kevin McCarthy appointed Barr to the GOP's China Task Force, to coordinate the GOP's legislative strategy on the growing competitor. In its September report, the group called for "bold, achievable" action to protect U.S. economic, technological, and military interests. Barr said the report provided a "roadmap" for what he hoped will be bipartisan initiatives. Among its proposals was Barr's measure to place sanctions on Chinese banks responsible for failure to enforce international sanctions against North Korea.

Also in 2020, the House passed Barr's bill to create an independent private group that would issue a single set of nationwide rules for medication use and racetrack safety for thoroughbred horses. The bill, which was filed in the Senate by Majority Leader Mitch McConnell of Kentucky, would "increase the popularity, public confidence, and international competitiveness of the sport," Barr said. It passed the House and Senate on voice votes and was one of the final bills enacted in 2020.

After two relatively easy reelections, in which Barr took at least 60 percent of the vote and won all counties in the district, he had a high-profile showdown in 2018 with Naval Academy graduate Amy McGrath, the first female Marine to pilot an F-18 fighter in Afghanistan and a political newcomer. McGrath emphasized her military service and said it was time for a new political voice. She took positions on gun control, for example, that were more progressive than customary in the district. Barr tied himself closely to McConnell and President Donald Trump This was one of the most expensive campaigns in the nation, with McGrath outspending Barr, $8.4 million to $5.7 million and the national parties spending another $7 million. Barr won 51%-48%, a margin of nearly 10,000 votes. He again led in all counties except Fayette and Franklin.

In 2020, Lexington attorney Josh Hicks challenged Barr. Hicks criticized Trump's and other Republicans' response to the coronavirus pandemic and attacked Barr for the GOP's handling of the Affordable Care Act. Barr defended the "lifeline" that Congress had provided during the pandemic. Although Hicks spent $3 million on the contest, to $4.4 million for Barr, he attracted little national party financial support or attention. Barr won, 57%-41%, and took all but Fayette County, where he narrowed the Democratic lead to 53%-45%.

In June 2020, Barr's wife, Carol, died suddenly of a heart condition. In his eulogy at her funeral, Barr told his two young daughters, "Here's the deal: Whenever we see a heart, we will see Mommy." She had been the executive director of the Henry Clay Center for Statesmanship in Lexington and for more than a decade was a professional health care representative for Pfizer Inc., the pharmaceutical company.

KY-6: Bluegrass Country

Cook Partisan Voting Index: R+8

Population		Race and Ethnicity		Income	
Total	780,800	White	83.90%	Median Income	$55,613
Land area (sq. miles)	4,293	Black	8.90%	District Income Rank	322
Pop/ sq mi	181.89	Latino	4.90%	Poverty Rate	15.20%
Born in State	67.80%	Asian	2.00%	With health insurance	93.80%
		Two or more races	3.20%	Cash public assistance	1.30%
Age Groups		Other	2.10%	Food stamp/SNAP	10.00%
Under 18	22.20%				
18-34	25.10%	**Education**		**Work**	
35-64	37.60%	H.S grad or less	38.40%	White Collar	40.40%
Over 64	15.20%	Some college	28.30%	Sales and Service	36.50%
		College Degree, 4 yr	18.90%	Blue Collar	23.10%
Military		Post grad	14.40%	Government	18.50%
Veteran/ Active Duty	6.60%				

2020 Pres. Vote	Trump	202,439	(54%)	Biden	168,056	(44%)			
2016 Pres. Vote	Trump	182,141	(55%)	Clinton	131,271	(39%)	Johnson	11,074	(3%)

Lexington: With its white picket fences, horse farms and small towns, the rolling plateau of bluegrass in central Kentucky is the part of interior America longest settled by English speakers: Lexington was founded in 1775. Tobacco farming started here in the 1770s, horse racing in 1787, and the Reverend Elijah Craig is often credited with inventing bourbon distilling in 1789 (though many rivals have also affixed stakes to that claim). Tobacco, whiskey and racehorses remained the staples of the economy for six generations, until 1956, when IBM built its typewriter plant in Lexington. The personal computer eventually outclassed the typewriter, and the big employer here became Lexmark International, an IBM spinoff, now under the control of a Chinese consortium. From 2018 to 2020, local employment dropped from 2,300 to 1,400. Another mainstay is the Toyota plant in Georgetown, a town with early-19th-century houses and lush countryside just one county north of the city. This is the largest Toyota plant in the nation, with 8,200 workers. At full capacity, they produced 550,000 vehicles, including the company's top-selling Camry and its new Lexus ES 350 model. The company planned to start production in 2020 of a new Lexus hybrid, with up to 100,000 new cars annually.

Lexington, which includes all of Fayette County, grew nearly 10 percent between 2010 and 2019, as its well-educated, young populace continued to attract business. Another 30 percent increase is projected by 2040, while two-thirds of the counties in Kentucky are projected to lose population. Jim Gray, an openly gay construction executive, served two terms as mayor before stepping down in 2018. He unsuccessfully challenged Sen. Rand Paul in 2016, then lost the Democratic primary for a House seat. His sexual orientation was not an issue in his campaigns. Also here is the University of Kentucky, where basketball mania is featured at Rupp Arena (and some faculty have lobbied for a name change). This is the second-largest metropolitan area in the state, after Louisville-Jefferson County. Fayette was the only other county in Kentucky that Joe Biden won in 2020, as was the case with Hillary Clinton four years earlier.

The 6th Congressional District of Kentucky includes Lexington and the surrounding counties. Lexington casts about 40 percent of its votes. It is the only district in Kentucky that does not border another state. To the northwest is the state capital of Frankfort, platted during the War for Independence by Gen. James Wilkinson. This was traditionally a swing area of the state.

LOUISIANA

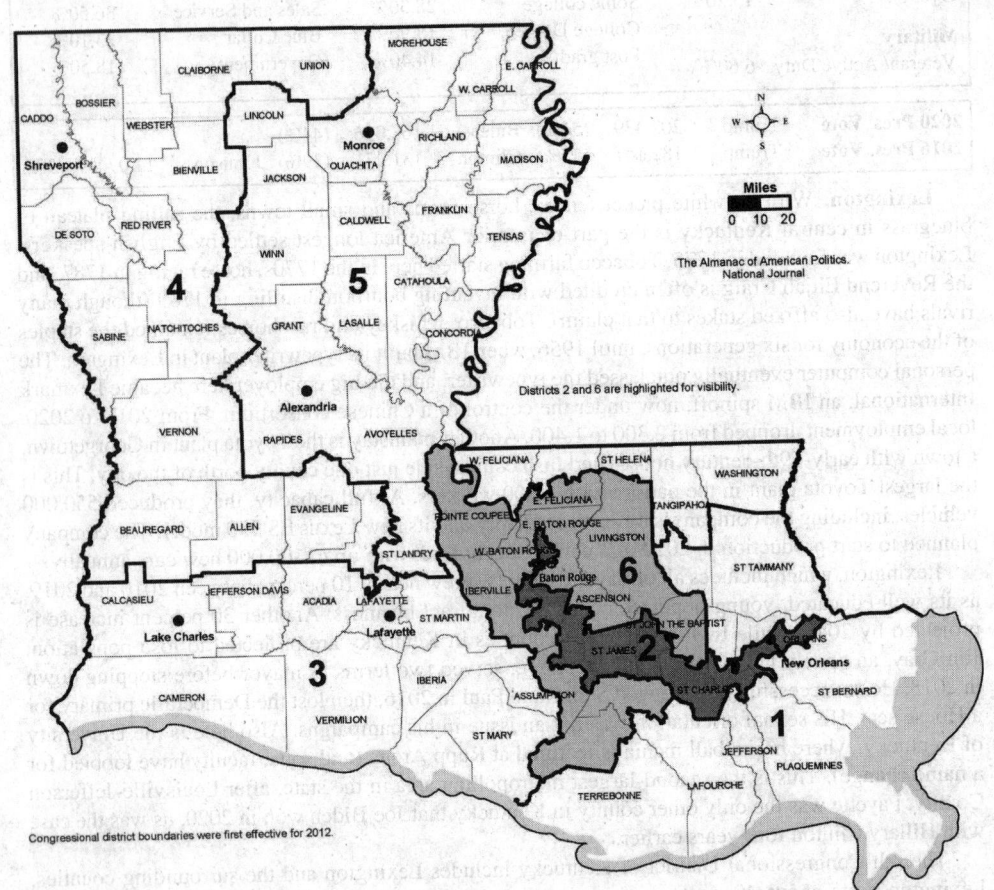

Districts 2 and 6 are highlighted for visibility.

The Almanac of American Politics.
National Journal

Congressional district boundaries were first effective for 2012.

Louisiana has always been a divided state politically, but that divide has changed in recent years. "If you looked around and saw oak trees and Spanish moss, you knew you were in a Democratic and Catholic part of the state," Democratic strategist Trey Ourso told Jonathan Martin of The New York Times. "If you saw pine trees, you were in a more Protestant and Republican area." But that is no longer the case. Much like the nation as a whole, Republicans dominate in Louisiana's outlying areas, while Democrats run up the score in cities. But unlike in some other states, the suburbs still lean Republican, and that has generally meant Republican control.

In the decade between 2000 and 2010, Louisiana—ravaged repeatedly by hurricanes—ranked third to last of any state in population growth. But since 2010, Louisiana's population has increased a bit more than 2.7 percent, and a striking 12 percent in Orleans Parish—Louisiana's singular, and singularly resilient, urban gem, New Orleans. The population also rose 11 percent in St. Tammany Parish, a suburban area north of New Orleans and Lake Pontchartrain. The comeback hasn't been perfect, but at least t's a comeback.

In 1718, the French founded New Orleans on a ridge formed by deposits of silt and declared the Mississippi Valley the colony of Louisiana. It was transferred to Spain in 1763 as part of the settlement of the Seven Years War, which France lost. After France took possession again under Napoleon Bonaparte, President Thomas Jefferson sought to buy the city in 1802. When Napoleon offered to sell the entire Louisiana Territory, Jefferson's envoys quickly and eagerly agreed—almost doubling the land area of the young republic. Its large French and small Spanish population had been ruled under European civil law rather than English common law. When Louisiana was admitted as a state in 1812, it included territory well to the north of the city that would soon be overrun by Americans heading west. The state's boundaries were rounded out with the acquisition of West Florida, the land north of Lake Pontchartrain heading west to Baton Rouge. With its large sugar and cotton slave plantations, Louisiana boomed, and by the outbreak of the Civil War, New Orleans was the nation's sixth largest city—the only substantial city in the Confederate South.

Louisiana has remained distinctive and exotic ever since. It is divided between a Catholic Cajun south, a Baptist Protestant north, and idiosyncratic New Orleans. Its population is 32 percent Black, the second-highest of any state; it was Black Louisianans who developed American jazz. (The state is 5 percent Hispanic and 2 percent Asian.) Louisiana's economy has always been based on the export of agricultural products and raw materials—sugar, rice and cotton in the 19th century, and oil, gas and their petrochemical derivatives in the 20th and 21st centuries. Its most talented politician was Huey Long, who as a young Public Service Commission chairman championed a severance tax on oil and who, in less than a single term each as governor (1928-32) and senator (1932-35), left an imprint on the state's public life and imposed an organization on its politics that faded into history only a generation ago. Long's genius was not that he promised to tax the rich to help the poor—hundreds of idealists and demagogues in America have done that—but that to an amazing extent he delivered, often by strong-arming or worse. He built a new skyscraper capitol, a new Louisiana State University, Mississippi River bridges in New Orleans and Baton Rouge, and more miles of roads than any other state but rich New York and huge Texas. He also built a national following and, by 1935, was planning to run for president on a platform of "Share the wealth, every man a king." That year, Long was assassinated at age 42 in the hallway of the capitol he built. According to legend, bullet holes can still be seen in the marble walls.

Long's impact was lasting, and not just in the literary character he inspired—Willie Stark of Robert Penn Warren's All the King's Men. The Long threat may have moved President Franklin D. Roosevelt to embrace the liberal programs—the Wagner Act, Social Security, and steeply graduated income taxes—of the Second New Deal. For Louisiana, Long delivered a political structure that revolved around him even after he was dead—and a class of political leaders who, lacking his talents, treated the state as Long's incompetent doctors had treated his fatal wound, leaving Louisiana with neither a fully developed economy nor a fully competent public sector. The Long experience strengthened Louisiana's already strong predispositions—tolerance of corruption, no interest in abstract reform, and a taste for colorful extremists regardless of their short-term means or long-term ends. This has persisted. The website FiveThirtyEight in 2015 tallied the number of public officials with federal corruption convictions in each state. On a per capita basis, Louisiana ranked first. In

2017, Jeffrey Sallet, the outgoing head of the FBI's New Orleans Division, told the Times-Picayune that "the corruption in this state is at an extremely unacceptable level."

This has not helped create a vibrant economy. Louisiana has chronically suffered low incomes, low workforce participation, and low levels of education, with income disparities greater than almost anywhere else in the United States. In 2019, Louisiana ranked second in the country for poverty at nearly 20 percent, and more than one in four children were below the poverty line. Median family income ranked fourth from the bottom, exceeding only Mississippi, West Virginia, and Arkansas. The United Health Foundation ranks Louisiana the second-worst state for cigarette smoking, high cholesterol, and depression; fourth-worst for teen pregnancies; and dead last for exercise and fruit- and vegetable consumption. Obesity and the prevalence of chronic diseases kept Louisiana above average for per capita deaths during most of the coronavirus pandemic. Meanwhile, Louisiana and Oklahoma have recently traded between themselves for the lead in the incarceration rate, and the Violence Policy Center determined that Louisiana ranked second nationally for the frequency of men murdering women. (During the Trump administration, Louisiana prisons agreed to house immigrants detained at the border when more liberal states refused to do so.)

Louisiana momentarily prospered when oil prices spiked upward in 1973 and 1979, then jobs and people flowed out in the 1980s as it failed to develop a diverse economy similar to that of its similarly oil-rich neighbor, Texas. This has made a huge difference over time. Metro New Orleans in 1940 had a population of 564,000; it was about the same size then as metro Houston (610,000) and metro Dallas (624,000). But in 2004, just before Hurricane Katrina struck, metro Houston had 5.1 million people, metro Dallas 5.8 million, and New Orleans 1.3 million. By 2019, metro Houston had more than 7 million and metro Dallas had 7.6 million, while metro New Orleans remained around 1.3 million.

Hurricane Katrina, by far the costliest on record, slammed the Gulf Coast on August 29, 2005, and for several weeks, New Orleans and Louisiana dominated the national spotlight. More than 80 percent of the city was flooded after the federally built floodwalls failed, and hundreds of thousands of residents abandoned their homes for higher ground. All told, Katrina was responsible for some 1,800 deaths and at least $108 billion in property damage, including $10 billion for damage to energy infrastructure. New Orleans mostly withstood the initial winds and storm surge. Then the levees broke, submerging much of the city. Katrina (with another powerful storm, Rita, less than a month later) also laid bare the state's political and economic frailties. New Orleans Mayor Ray Nagin seemed incapable of coping with the disaster and was later convicted of bribery charges. By July 2006, Louisiana's population had declined by 250,000 (mostly in the New Orleans area), although many people eventually returned, as did tourists. In April 2010, disaster struck Louisiana again when BP's Deepwater Horizon oil rig exploded, killing 11 workers and spewing an estimated 4 million barrels of oil into the Gulf of Mexico. Meanwhile, a second, slower leak known as the Taylor oil spill has dumped thousands of gallons a day since Hurricane Ivan in 2004.

Despite its risks, offshore drilling has been a major element of Louisiana's economy since the 1940s. The state has 125,000 miles of pipeline, said to be enough to encircle the planet five times. The resumption of offshore drilling in 2011 and the increasing use of fracking—the extraction of natural gas by hydraulic fracturing—in the Haynesville shale in northwest Louisiana touched off a recovery, with billion-dollar investments in refineries, gas-to-liquid facilities, and liquefied natural gas export terminals. The oil-price slump that began around 2014 only hastened the shift of the industry's center of gravity, as companies such as ConocoPhillips and Marathon moved their focus away from oil-drilling platforms in the gulf toward the state's shale resources further north. The chemical business, closely related to the petroleum industry, continued to show life: Formosa Petrochemical Corp. is developing a 2,400-acre site on the Mississippi River in St. James Parish for a planned $9.4 billion chemical complex, while Shintech is expanding an ethylene plant nearby. But these and other plants have attracted opposition from some local residents and environmentalists who say it will only worsen the unhealthy impacts on the low-income, heavily minority area that has become known as "Cancer Alley." Meanwhile, tourism-dependent New Orleans was hit hard by the coronavirus.

In recent years, Louisiana has suffered a bewildering succession of natural disasters. In 2016, Baton Rouge experienced severe flooding. The following year, parts of Louisiana, along with much of southeastern Texas, was soaked by Hurricane Harvey and its 22 inches of rain. In 2019, heavy precipitation in the Midwest forced the opening of Mississippi River spillways, upsetting the sensitive chemistry of Louisiana's fisheries. And in 2020, Hurricane Laura slammed into Lake Charles with gusts up to 132 miles per hour. Every storm is a reminder of Louisiana's precariousness in a time of climate change. Since 1932, Louisiana has lost a Delaware-sized chunk of land to encroaching water, due to a combination of rising sea levels, industrial intrusions, and reductions in Mississippi River sediment caused by upstream dams. Brett Anderson of the Times-Picayune wrote that if maps of the state rendered wetlands as water and counted only solid "walkable" ground as land, then the very shape of Louisiana—its iconic "boot"—would appear "as if it came out on the wrong side of a battle with a lawnmower's blades." A 2020 study led by a Tulane University geologist concluded that if sea levels were to rise by six to nine millimeters per year, the state's wetlands could be overtaken by ocean water within 50 years. To prevent this, the state is embarking on a 50-year, $50 billion master plan drawn up by a state panel. The plan, which will be updated every five years, is funded in part by settlement money from the BP oil spill. A key part of the effort will be diversions of the Mississippi River to increase the sediment flowing to wetlands. In the meantime, coastal parishes are seeking to negotiate deals with oil-drilling companies to compensate for past industrial damage; the first agreement was signed with Freeport-McMoRan in 2019 and totaled $100 million.

For more than a century after the Civil War, Louisiana was solidly Democratic, with political divides expressed in Democratic primaries. There were splits between the Cajun Catholic parishes, which cast about 30 percent of the state's votes, and Protestant parishes north of Baton Rouge, which cast about 45 percent. Another division was by income. Low-income voters of both races tended to support Huey Long and his populist successors; higher-income voters often opposed them. So for a long time, Louisiana politics were a struggle between reformist and conservative forces on one side and roguish populists on the other, a struggle waged in lavishly financed campaigns with grandiloquent rhetoric. Louisiana voted for Bill Clinton in 1992 and 1996—the only state in the Deep South to do so—but has since voted increasingly Republican. And Republican presidential performance in Louisiana has barely wavered: 57 percent in 2004, followed by 59 percent in 2008 and 58 percent in 2012, 2016, and 2020. The only Democrat with statewide success recently is Gov. John Bel Edwards, a West Point graduate who defeated scandal-tarred Republican Sen. David Vitter in 2015. In office, Edwards signed up 480,000 people for Medicaid expansion under the Affordable Care Act and enacted a bipartisan criminal justice bill. He won a tough reelection bid in 2019, by about two points.

In 2020, Donald Trump scored a winning margin of 19 points, roughly matching his 2016 performance. Joe Biden won the same 10 parishes Hillary Clinton carried in 2016, which was less than half as many as Edwards had won in his 2019 gubernatorial reelection. Still, many of the populous parishes shifted to Biden by a couple points, including Orleans, Caddo (Shreveport), and East Baton Rouge (Baton Rouge), which continued its leftward drift in the Trump era. Trump's winning margins also shrank by six points in Lafayette Parish (Lafayette) and seven points in St. Tammany. Traditionally Republican Jefferson Parish, which includes the New Orleans suburbs of Kenner and Gretna, illustrates both the promise and the limits for Democratic gains in Louisiana. The minority population has grown in recent years, including an influx of Hispanics and Vietnamese-Americans; in his reelection bid, Edwards won the parish by 14 points. But in the presidential race, Trump defeated Biden in the parish by double digits. Given the state's racially polarized voting patterns and its 59 percent white population, no one is expecting Louisiana's Republican leanings to weaken any time soon.

Population		Race and Ethnicity		Income	
Total	4,648,794	White	61.80%	Median Income	51,073
Land area (sq. miles)	43,204	Black	32.40%	State Income Rank	47 out of 50
Pop/ sq mi	107.60	Latino	5.40%	Poverty Rate	19.00%
Born in state	77.60%	Asian	2.10%	With health insurance	91.10%
		Two or more races	2.00%	Cash public assistance	1.80%
Age Groups		Other	2.00%	Food stamp/SNAP	16.0%
Under 18	23.30%				
18-34	22.90%	Education		Work	
35-64	37.80%	H.S grad or less	47.90%	White Collar	35.40%
Over 64	16.00%	Some college	27.00%	Sales and Service	40.70%
		College Degree, 4 yr	16.00%	Blue Collar	23.90%
Military		Post grad	8.90%	Government	15.30%
Veteran/ Active Duty	7.10%				

Presidential Politics

2020 Primary (D)	Biden (D)	212,555(80%)	Sanders (D)	19,859 (7%)
2020 Pres. Vote	Trump (R)	1,255,776(58%)	Biden (D)	856,034(40%)
2016 Pres. Vote	Trump (R)	1,178,638(58%)	Clinton (D)	780,154(38%)

Not many general election presidential campaign ads are going to be taped in Cajun any time soon. In the past five races, Louisiana voted for the Republican nominees by 57 percent, 59 percent, 58 percent, 58 percent and—surprise!—58 percent. The vote in President Donald Trump's victory over Joe Biden, who received 40 percent, was remarkably similar to the regional results in the state four and eight years earlier: Biden, Hillary Clinton and President Barack Obama all won Orleans Parish (New Orleans) with more than 80 percent; won metro Baton Rouge by single digits and carried the Parish that includes Shreveport; and the GOP nominee dominated in most of the rest of the state.

Louisiana has rarely played a significant role in presidential primaries and caucuses. In 2016, Trump narrowly defeated Ted Cruz 41%-38% on March 5, but Cruz managed to wrangle 10 additional delegates in the post-primary selection process. Trump threatened a lawsuit but never followed through. In the Democratic primary, Clinton trounced Vermont Sen. Bernie Sanders, 71%-23%. Louisiana's 2020 primary was supposed to be held April 4, but state officials moved it all the way back to July 11 because of the coronavirus, making the state the second to last to vote. Biden, who'd already won the nomination, won with 80% of the vote.

Congressional Districts

117th Congress Lineup	1D 5R	116th Congress Lineup	1D 5R

Following the 2002 redistricting in Louisiana, five of the seven districts elected House members from each party at some point in the elections from 2002 to 2010. Those politics have changed. The exodus from Louisiana after Hurricane Katrina led to the drop to six House seats after the 2010 census. As recently as 1992, the state had eight seats. Demographically, the 2nd District, centered in New Orleans, suffered the greatest population loss by far. Its Black-majority district now extends to parts of Baton Rouge. The latest round of redistricting eliminated a district in Cajun country. With Republican population centers in the New Orleans suburbs, Baton Rouge, the Bayous, Shreveport and the northeast corner, creating a second Democratic or Black-majority district would require creative gerrymandering, though breaking up the 2nd could create opportunities for them.

In a state that is 32 percent Black, the adjacent 4th and 5th Districts in northern Louisiana have 34 percent and 36 percent black population, respectively, which are widely dispersed in small cities and rural areas. Democratic Governor John Bel Edwards will face pressure from state and national Democrats to create a 2nd district that would be competitive for Democrats—which most likely would include the African-American portions of Baton Rouge and rural areas to the north where Black communities predominate. That could pose serious jeopardy for Rep. Julia Letlow, who won the special election in the 5th District in March 2021. Edwards has remained open to the possibility, which could become part of bargaining in the capitol on other issues. Still, as David Wasserman wrote in the Cook Political Report, "Republicans are optimistic the conservative Fifth Circuit [federal Court of Appeals] won't overturn the status quo." Both parties likely will want to delay action until after the November 2021 legislative elections.

John Bel Edwards (D)

Elected 2015, term expires 2023, 2nd term; b. Sep. 16, 1966, Amite; United States Military Academy, B.S 1988; Louisiana State University Law School, J.D 1999; Roman Catholic; Married (Donna); 3 children.

Military Career: U.S Army, 1988-1996.

Elected Office: LA House, 2007-2015.

Professional Career: Attorney, Edwards & Associates.

Office: PO Box 94004 Baton Rouge, 70804-9004; 225-342-7015; Fax: 225-342-7099
Lt. Gov.: Billy Nungesser (R) **Atty. Gen:** Jeff Landry (R) **Sec. of State:** Kyle Ardoin (R)
State Legislature: Senate: 14D, 25R **House:** 39D, 62R, 4I

Election Results

Election	Name (Party)	Vote (%)
2019 General	John Bel Edwards (D)...	774,498 (51%)
	Eddie Rispone (R)...	734,286 (49%)
2019 Primary	John Bel Edwards (D)...	625,970 (47%)
	Eddie Rispone (R)...	368,319 (27%)
	Ralph Abraham (R)...	317,149 (24%)

John Bel Edwards, the only Democrat currently serving as a statewide elected official in Louisiana, won a hard-fought reelection contest in 2019, overcoming the active opposition of President Donald Trump. In office, he has enacted an eclectic mix of measures, ranging from an expansion of Medicaid under the Affordable Care Act to criminal justice reform to one of the nation's most restrictive abortion laws.

Edwards was one of eight children born into a law-enforcement and political family in Amite, a town of roughly 4,000 residents 48 miles northeast of Baton Rouge in Tangipahoa Parish. His great-grandfather was the parish sheriff, and his grandfather, Frank Edwards, was a state legislator. His father, Frank Edwards Jr., also served as sheriff, as well as an appointee of then-Gov. Edwin Edwards (no relation). Edwards Jr. was succeeded as sheriff by his son—Jon Bel's brother, Daniel Edwards. Another brother, Frank Edwards III, serves as police chief of nearby Independence, while a sister-in-law, Blair Edwards, is a district court judge. The family had such deep political roots that it was inducted collectively into the Louisiana Political Hall of Fame. ("Bel" is his middle name—a family name going back generations—and he is often called "John Bel.")

In high school, Edwards captained the football team and was named valedictorian. He attended West Point, graduating with a bachelor's degree in engineering, then served for eight years as an airborne ranger. He later earned his law degree from Louisiana State University and became an attorney in private practice in Amite, eschewing criminal cases because of his brother's service as sheriff. In 2007, Edwards was elected to the state House and became a key player in the Democratic caucus; he used his position as a megaphone to criticize then-Gov. Bobby Jindal and served in the chamber until he was elected governor.

When Edwards decided to run for governor, he was far from well-known around the state, and he was a Democrat, a toxic label for recent statewide candidates in Louisiana. He gained some traction, though, by running against Jindal's record in office, including a projected $1.4 billion budget deficit. Edwards also pledged to raise the minimum wage and expand Medicaid, which Jindal had steadfastly refused to do. At the same time, Edwards blurred distinctions with Republicans on social issues, supporting gun rights and opposing abortion. A Catholic, Edwards ran an ad spotlighting how his family had ruled out an abortion after learning that their unborn daughter had spina bifida. She thrived and was married during Edwards' first year as governor. "I don't like being pigeonholed," he later told the Catholic magazine America. "There are people who say, 'You're pro-life on abortion, so that makes you conservative, but you're for the Medicaid expansion. That makes you liberal.' But it's the exact same Catholic Christian faith, at least as I understand it, that pushes me into both of those positions."

In Louisiana's all-party primary, Edwards faced three prominent Republicans: Public Service Commissioner Scott Angelle; Lt. Gov. Jay Dardenne; and Sen. David Vitter. Most observers had assumed that Vitter's 2007 prostitution scandal was settled business following his easy reelection to the Senate in 2010, but Dardenne and Angelle raised the issue, and it gained traction. On Election Day, Edwards, facing minimal Democratic opposition, took 40 percent of the vote, as Vitter barely qualified for the Nov. 21 runoff with 23 percent. Angelle and Dardenne split the Republican anti-Vitter vote with 19 percent and 15 percent, respectively. Edwards and his allies kept up the drumbeat on Vitter's past behavior, and Dardenne endorsed Edwards after the primary. (After Edwards won, he tapped Dardenne for a senior post.) Edwards won the runoff, 56%-44%—the biggest Democratic gubernatorial victory in the state since 1991's "Vote for the crook, it's important" race between the ethically challenged Edwin Edwards and White supremacist David Duke.

The newly elected governor quickly fulfilled his promise to expand Medicaid, and he worked with legislators to enact a temporary sales tax, a cigarette tax hike, and corporate income tax changes. Edwards pleased social conservatives by signing several bills on abortion, including one in 2018 that banned the procedure after 15 weeks, punishable by prison for the medical practitioner—the most stringent law in the nation, along with one enacted in neighboring Mississippi. But the laws were blocked in the courts. On criminal justice, Edwards signed a package of 10 bills in 2017 that curbed mandatory minimum sentences, overhauled drug sentencing, expanded alternatives to incarceration, and limited the most serious sentences for juveniles. The changes made an impact in their first year, as Louisiana fell from the top ranking in incarceration rate for the first time in years.

He also won plaudits for his handling of two crises early in his tenure. One was racial strife in Baton Rouge in 2016, which was sparked by the police killing of Alton Sterling, an African-American man, and continued with days of protests, and culminated almost two weeks later with the ambush murders of three law enforcement officers. (A few months earlier, Edwards had signed the nation's first "Blue Lives Matter" law, making the killings of police a hate crime.) The other crisis involved flooding in 2016—in the northern part of the state in March, and in the southern tier in August, the latter causing an estimated $8.7 billion in damage.

Edwards faced other challenges. After issuing an executive order protecting LGBT state employees, Edwards sparred with Republican Attorney General Jeff Landry over its implementation. Landry refused to sign dozens of legal contracts for the state as long as they contained the protections. In December 2016, Edwards' order was overturned in court. The two continued to spar as Edwards' term progressed—over an Edwards-supported delay in executions due to a lack of lethal injection chemicals, and over Landry's decision to join a lawsuit seeking to overturn the Affordable Care Act.

A side effect of Edwards' efforts on criminal justice was to bring Edwards closer to the Trump administration, which had pursued a federal criminal justice overhaul that was eventually enacted in late 2018. Edwards joined a criminal justice summit at Trump's golf club in Bedminster New Jersey, and he became the only Democratic elected official to attend a White House state dinner with French President Emmanuel Macron. Edwards returned the favor by inviting Trump to visit the state penitentiary at Angola to see the laws' impact in person. But Edwards' campaign for a second term in 2019 put him on a collision course with Trump.

In the 2019 election, Edwards faced off against two top-tier Republicans, Rep. Ralph Abraham and deep-pocketed construction magnate Eddie Rispone. Abraham was "a no-nonsense, grandfatherly physician," wrote Tyler Bridges of the Baton Rouge Advocate; Abraham had grown up on a farm, worked as a veterinarian, and served in the National Guard before becoming a doctor. Rispone had grown up poor, worked his way through LSU, then became rich as an electrical contractor; he was able to kickstart his fledgling campaign with a $10.5 million loan. Trump didn't take sides in the Abraham-Rispone face-off; Abraham began the race ahead of Rispone in the polls, but that changed once Rispone began airing a blizzard of negative ads. One charged that Abraham had voted with Democratic House Speaker Nancy Pelosi "more than 300 times." The charge was misleading—most of the votes were routine and mirrored by most other Republicans—but effective. Rispone also attacked Abraham's attendance record in the House, a charge that was better supported. Ultimately, Edwards fell short of a first-round knockout, winning 46.6 percent; Rispone advanced to the runoff, winning 27.4 percent to Abraham's 23.6 percent.

The runoff laid bare Rispone's lack of experience and polish as a candidate; he never fully succeeded in making peace with Abraham, and he skipped several key campaign events. Rispone leaned heavily on Trump, who campaigned for him in person; the president may have hoped to score a win as the House's impeachment inquiry was accelerating. But Edwards' record made it hard for either Rispone or Trump to dismiss him as a "far-left governor," as Trump put it in a campaign rally in Bossier City. Indeed, Edwards touted his cross-party interactions with Trump. Edwards needed to accomplish three things to win, Bridges wrote. One was to increase Black turnout from its modest levels in the first round; the second was to effectively parry Rispone's attempts to nationalize the race, by keeping the focus on Louisiana issues; and the third was to pick off a sliver of disaffected Abraham voters. In the end, Edwards managed to do all three. While his margin of victory was diminished from what it was in 2015—down from 12 points to two—his reelection came in a more polarized political environment, against an opponent with less baggage, and with a president of the opposite party trying to unseat him. Rispone managed to improve on Vitter's 2015 performance in many parts of the state, both in rural areas and in Caddo Parish (Shreveport) and Lafayette Parish (Lafayette), where he chalked up gains of between four and 14 points. However, Edwards owed his victory to substantial gains around New Orleans; the incumbent increased his raw-vote total by 40 percent in Orleans Parish (New Orleans) and by 45 percent in the traditionally Republican suburbs of Jefferson Parish. Edwards also managed to repeat his wide margins in East Baton Rouge Parish (Baton Rouge), which was Rispone's home base.

At the start of Edwards' second term, Democrats and a group of Republican defectors banded together to choose Clay Schexnayder as House speaker. While the governor and the speaker were not always in accord, they were able to enact bills to ease the carrying of guns into houses of worship and to overhaul how litigation over car accidents is handled. (Edwards vetoed a measure to tighten laws for trespassing unmarked property lines around critical infrastructure, which he said would unfairly quash First Amendment protest rights.) But Edwards' biggest challenge in 2020 came with the coronavirus pandemic. New Orleans became an early hot spot due to infections that had spread during Mardi Gras; on March 23, Edwards issued a stay-at-home order, earlier than any state but California, Illinois, and New York. After initial misgivings, he also imposed a statewide mask order and other business restrictions, eventually extending them. Such policies drew a strong Republican counterattack, led by Landry, his longstanding rival in the attorney general's office.

Bill Cassidy (R)

Elected 2014, term expires 2026, 2nd term, b. Sep 28, 1957; Highland Park, IL; Louisiana State University, B.S., 1979; Louisiana State University Medical School, M.D., 1983; Christian; Married (Laura Layden Cassidy); 3 children.

Elected Office: LA Senate, 2006-2008; U.S. House, 2009-2015; Assistant Whip, House Republican Conference.

Professional Career: Physician; Co-founder, Greater Baton Rouge Community Clinic, 1998; Doctor, Earl K. Long Hospital, LSU; Associate Professor of Medicine, Earl K. Long Hospital, LSU.

DC Office: 520 HSOB 20510, 202-224-5824, Fax: 202-224-9735, cassidy.senate.gov

State Offices: Alexandria, 318-448-7176; Baton Rouge, 225-929-7711; Lafayette, 337-261-1400; Lake Charles, 337-493-5398; Metairie, 504-838-0130; Monroe, 318-324-2111; Shreveport, 318-798-3215.

Committees: *Energy & Natural Resources*: Energy; Public Lands, Forests & Mining. *Finance*: Fiscal Responsibility & Economic Growth (RMM); Health Care; Social Security, Pensions & Family Policy. *Health, Education, Labor & Pensions*: Children & Families (RMM); Primary Health & Retirement Security. *Joint Economic. Veterans' Affairs.*

Group Ratings

	ADA	ACLU	AFL-CIO	LCV	COC	HAFA	ACU	CFG	FRC
2020	-	15%	-	0%	-	83%	83%	-	-
2019	0%	C	12%	7%	84%	C	83%	66%	100%

Almanac Ratings 2019-2020

	Economy	Social	Foreign	Composite
Liberal	0%	0%	0%	0%
Conservative	100%	100%	100%	100%

Key Votes of the 116th Congress

1. EPA clean energy rules	N	5. Russia sanctions	N	9. Barr as Atty. General	Y
2. U.S./Mex./Can. trade deal	Y	6. Troops in SYR, AFG	Y	10. Spending at the border	Y
3. Cut unemployment benefits	Y	7. Veto arms sales to Saudis	N	11. Coney Barrett to Sup. Ct.	Y
4. Shelton to Fed Reserve	Y	8. Defense $$$, veto override	Y	12. Electoral College objections	N

Election Results

Election	Name (Party)	Vote (%)		Cand. Spent	Ind. Exp. Support	Ind. Exp. Oppose
2020 General	Bill Cassidy (R)............................... 1,228,908	(59%)	$8,867,735	$808,122	
	Adrian Perkins (D)........................ 394,049	(19%)	$2,807,611	$9,000	

Prior winning percentages: 2014 (56%), House: 2012 (79%), 2010 (66%), 2008 (48%)

A physician, Bill Cassidy has become an important voice within the GOP on health care. But Louisiana's senior senator also became a surprising voice against President Donald Trump after the deadly insurrection at the U.S. Capitol on January 6, 2021. Cassidy was one of just seven Republican senators to vote to convict the former president for inciting the violence the day Electoral College votes were being counted. He explained his decision in a two-sentence statement: "Our Constitution and our country is more important than any one person. I voted to convict President Trump because he is guilty."

At the outset of the trial, the Louisianan wasn't on any watch lists of possible GOP crossovers. While Cassidy had never been a close ally of Trump, he was usually a loyal Republican foot soldier. After the former president's lawyers gave a rambling, somewhat incoherent opening statement, Cassidy said they did a "terrible" and "disorganized" job, while House Democratic managers gave a "focused" and "organized" presentation. He maintained throughout the trial he was keeping an open mind as a juror, and during the final vote, it became clear he had done just that.

Predictably, the reaction to Cassidy's vote was swift among Louisiana Republicans, and the state party soon voted unanimously to censure him. However, he had just won reelection in 2020 with 59 percent and wouldn't face voters again until 2026, when the state's all-party primary system should inoculate him from any primary threats. In an op-ed in the Advocate, Cassidy defended his vote, writing, "I have no illusions that this is a popular decision. I made this decision because Americans should not be fed lies about 'massive election fraud.' Police should not be left to the mercy of a mob. Mobs should not be inflamed to disrupt the peaceful transfer of power."

William Morgan Cassidy was born in Highland Park Illinois but grew up in Baton Rouge Louisiana, the son of a life insurance salesman. He attended Louisiana State University as an undergraduate and earned a degree from LSU's medical school. During a medical residency in Los Angeles, Cassidy met his wife, Laura, also a physician. The New Orleans Times-Picayune has described Laura Cassidy as his "most trusted political adviser." She founded Louisiana Key Academy, a public charter school specializing the instruction of in children with dyslexic symptoms, after one of their daughters was diagnosed with dyslexia.

In 1990, the gastroenterologist returned to Baton Rouge and joined the faculty of LSU's medical school. Bill Cassidy also began a nearly 25-year stint treating patients at LSU's Earl K. Long Hospital, part of Louisiana's charity hospital system devoted to caring for uninsured patients. His wife eventually became chief of surgery at Earl K. Long. He continued working there on a part-time basis after his election to the House in 2008, until the hospital closed in 2013. He co-founded the

Greater Baton Rouge Community Clinic, which provides free dental and health care to the working uninsured.

In a Times-Picayune profile, Cassidy said his family struggled financially at times when he was growing up, citing that as a major reason he had focused on caring for needier people rather than working in a more traditional private practice. Several former colleagues at Earl K. Long expressed surprise at his strong opposition to Obamacare and wondered privately if his opposition were motivated by politics. Cassidy brushed aside such suggestions, saying that after witnessing government-run health care up close, he had concluded that the private insurance market is better equipped to provide medical coverage. "I believe my hospital system was one in which the government had all the power, not the patient," he said of his experience there.

Cassidy had a defining moment after Hurricane Katrina hit in 2005. He created a makeshift field hospital in an abandoned Kmart store with the help of several other physicians. In a PBS documentary, he recalled entering the store after the storm to discover grease covering the floor, no electricity and no working phone lines. In two days, he and the others transformed the space to be ready to receive patients. He later said the experience played a major role in his decision to run for office.

In December 2006, Cassidy won a special election to the state Senate as a Republican, though like many Louisiana GOP politicians, he had previously been a Democrat and even contributed to the 2002 campaign of Sen. Mary Landrieu, whom he would oust in 2014. When GOP Rep. Richard Baker resigned, Cassidy passed up the opportunity to compete in the 2008 special election. After Democratic state Rep. Don Cazayoux narrowly defeated GOP social conservative Woody Jenkins, Cassidy vowed to retake the 6th District for the Republicans. In that campaign, Cassidy described himself as a "pro-life, pro-gun rights" social conservative, while highlighting his state Senate record of voting against spending bills and cutting taxes for businesses and parents with children in private schools. Cazayoux ran an ad criticizing Cassidy for supporting creation of private savings accounts in Social Security.

Cassidy defeated Cazayoux 48%-40% . He twice coasted to reelection. In the House, Cassidy had a plum seat on the Energy and Commerce Committee, which has significant jurisdiction over health care, and was called upon to publicly criticize the Obama administration on that issue. Saying that the government needed to get out of the way of patients, he supported providing incentives for preventive care along with creating health savings accounts. While a reliably conservative voter, Cassidy parted ways with his party on a few issues. In 2010, when Democrats controlled the House, Cassidy was one of four Republicans on the Agriculture Committee to vote to end the ban on U.S. travel to Cuba and ease regulations on sale of agricultural exports to the island. He backed Democratic bills to extend unemployment benefits and praised the Teach for America program that established a post-Katrina presence in Louisiana.

Cassidy's record led Louisiana Republicans to deem him the most formidable potential challenger to Landrieu, the last Senate Democrat from the Deep South at the time. Landrieu had been elected in 1996 by a mere 5,000 votes out of more than 1.7 million cast and survived reelection in 2002 and 2008 with just 52 percent of the vote each time. Over the course of Landrieu's career, Louisiana slipped politically and demographically away from the Democrats, accelerated by the departure of an estimated 125,000 Democratic voters after Katrina.

Given aspects of Cassidy's political past, his candidacy initially aroused suspicions among conservative groups about whether he was truly one of them; the Senate Conservatives Fund endorsed tea party-aligned Rob Maness, a retired Air Force colonel. Cassidy responded by moving to the right. He repudiated his earlier support of the Troubled Asset Relief Program created to prop up financial institutions in 2008 and accepted the backing of Americans for Prosperity, a conservative group affiliated with the Koch brothers, which spent more than $3 million on ads attacking Landrieu. Cassidy also disputed whether climate change was occurring, claiming during one debate—inaccurately—that "global temperatures have not risen in 15 years." Still, Landrieu drew just 42 percent of the vote in an eight-candidate first-round election in November. Cassidy was just behind with 41 percent; Maness ran a distant third at 14 percent.

With the GOP having won enough seats in November to take over the Senate, the national import of the Landrieu-Cassidy December runoff was diminished. But with the chance to expand the new GOP majority, conservative groups spent an estimated $5.65 million in ads . With President Barack Obama's approval rating in the state at just 39 percent, TV ads backing Cassidy "came down to four words: Mary Landrieu, Barack Obama," as Jason Berry, a New Orleans writer, put it. Cassidy rolled to an easy victory, 56%-44%, with exit polls showing only 18 percent of white voters backing Landrieu. His victory left Louisiana without a Democrat elected statewide for the first time since 1876. That changed the next year when Democrats recaptured the governorship.

Despite his background as a physician, Cassidy was initially shut out of the Senate Republicans' efforts to craft their own health care bill. He found an audience by tying his repeal goals to the promise that it would fulfill the "Jimmy Kimmel test," named after the late-night comedian's emotional plea to preserve the Affordable Care Act's provisions protecting people with preexisting conditions. One of four former physicians in the Senate, all of whom are Republicans, Cassidy had been critical of the House's repeal efforts and defended the Congressional Budget Office against attacks that it was unrealistically estimating how many people would lose insurance. In turn, he floated a policy that would allow states to decide what to do about keeping Obamacare, a move that conservatives balked at and Democratic members thought was still too conservative. After speculation that he might break with the party on how to repeal Obamacare, Cassidy voted for all three of the plans put forward for a vote, including the last-ditch "skinny repeal" proposal that failed in dramatic fashion when Sen. John McCain of Arizona joined fellow GOP Sens. Susan Collins of Maine and Lisa Murkowski of Alaska in opposition.

Cassidy, however, was adamant his party not give up, and he partnered with GOP Sen. Lindsey Graham of South Carolina to offer a health care repeal plan that allowed states three options, including to continue running Obamacare as is. Their bill garnered little support as it came at a time when Republicans had decided to use the budget reconciliation process to ram through a repeal without the need of a single Democratic vote. But the Louisianan's legislation sparked the interest of many of his colleagues. Graham-Cassidy, as it became known, would have converted much of Obamacare's funding to block grants for states to set up their own programs along with fundamentally changing Medicaid by establishing a cap per enrollee. Most controversially, the block grant approach would have allowed states to vary premiums for people with preexisting conditions. Cassidy defended the proposal, but the preexisting conditions part of the bill led to the same public outcry that doomed the other proposals.

Even after repeal efforts failed, Cassidy returned to health care in 2018 by proposing eight ideas to reduce the cost of care. Perhaps his greatest legislative achievements have been health care-related. To address the opioid crisis, Trump signed bipartisan legislation with several provisions Cassidy had authored in 2018. Cassidy also partnered with Democratic Sen. Chris Murphy of Connecticut to strengthen laws requiring parity for mental and physical health care while providing grants to increase the limited supply of psychologists and psychiatrists across the country. Obama signed that measure as part of the 21st Century Cures Act in late 2016. He has worked on health-care issues as a member of both the HELP and Finance committees.

During the COVID-19 pandemic, Cassidy often weighed in on the balance between public health and the struggling economy. Worried that Trump wasn't taking the virus seriously, he sought to talk with Vice President Mike Pence instead, suggesting a national "immunity registry" to collect data from blood testing to determine when individuals could safely return to work. "The answer to when our nation can reopen is complex," he wrote a May 2020 op-ed in RealClearPolitics. "A one-size-fits-all solution likely will not work" and community spread, age and medical history should be weighed. In August of that year, Cassidy tested positive for the virus but quickly recovered, and the next month he and Democrat Tina Smith of Minnesota introduced a bill to boost national coronavirus testing and contact tracing by providing incentives to states to form regional coalitions. He also worked with Democrat Bob Menendez of New Jersey to propose $500 billion in federal relief for states.

Like the rest of his state's delegation, Cassidy had been an ardent advocate for the oil and gas industry. Both he and the rest of the Republicans in the delegation backed the Trump administration's proposal in early 2018 to open both coasts to more offshore drilling. Cassidy worked with Louisiana Rep. Steve Scalise to give more revenue from offshore drilling to Gulf Coast states as part of the tax bill that Republicans enacted in 2017.

Unlike other Republicans from Louisiana, Cassidy announced his public support for a 2018 ballot initiative to amend the state's Constitution to require unanimous jury verdicts in criminal cases. The amendment, which was backed by then-Democratic Rep. Cedric Richmond, passed overwhelmingly. According to the Times-Picayune, Louisiana had been the only state in which a 12-person jury verdict of 11-1 or 10-2 could result in a life sentence in prison without the possibility of parole, a 120-year-old practice that undermined the presence of African-American jurors. In 2020, he secured $30 million in federal funds for Louisiana to improve its victim services and juvenile justice programs.

In 2020, Cassidy easily won reelection with 59 percent of the vote against Louisiana's typically wide-open field of candidates. Democrat Adrian Perkins, the mayor of Shreveport, was runner-up with 19 percent. He spent $2.7 million to $10.7 million for Cassidy.

John Kennedy (R)

Elected 2016, term expires 2022, 1st term, b. Nov 21, 1951; Centreville, MS; Vanderbilt University, B.A., 1973; University of Virginia School of Law, J.D., 1977; Oxford University, B.CL, 1979; Methodist; Married (Rebecca Stulb Kennedy); 1 child.

Elected Office: LA Treasurer, 1999-2016.

Professional Career: Special Counsel and Cabinet Secretary, Governor Buddy Roemer, 1988-1992; Secretary, LA Department of Revenue, 1996-1999; Practicing attorney; Adjunct Professor, Louisiana State University.

DC Office: 416 RSOB 20510, 202-224-4623, Fax: 202-228-0447, kennedy.senate.gov

State Offices: Baton Rouge, 225-926-8033; Lafayette, 337-269-5980; Monroe, 318-361-1489; New Orleans, 504-581-6190; Shreveport, 318-670-5192.

Committees: *Appropriations*: Commerce, Justice, Science & Related Agencies; Department of Homeland Security; DOL, HHS & Education & Related Agencies; Energy & Water Development (RMM); Financial Services & General Government; Transportation, HUD & Related Agencies. *Banking, Housing & Urban Affairs*: Economic Policy (RMM); National Security & International Trade & Finance; Securities, Insurance & Investment. *Budget. Judiciary*: Criminal Justice & Counterterrorism; Federal Courts, Oversight, Agency Action & Federal Rights (RMM); Human Rights & the Law; Immigration, Citizenship & Border Security; Privacy, Technology & the Law. *Small Business & Entrepreneurship*.

Group Ratings

	ADA	ACLU	AFL-CIO	LCV	COC	HAFA	ACU	CFG	FRC
2020	-	23%	-	0%	-	89%	84%	-	-
2019	5%	C	12%	7%	73%	C	81%	76%	100%

Almanac Ratings 2019-2020

	Economy	Social	Foreign	Composite
Liberal	6%	6%	0%	4%
Conservative	94%	94%	100%	96%

Key Votes of the 116th Congress

1. EPA clean energy rules	N	5. Russia sanctions	Y	9. Barr as Atty. General	Y
2. U.S./Mex./Can. trade deal	Y	6. Troops in SYR, AFG	N	10. Spending at the border	Y
3. Cut unemployment benefits	Y	7. Veto arms sales to Saudis	N	11. Coney Barrett to Sup. Ct.	Y
4. Shelton to Fed Reserve	Y	8. Defense $$$, veto override	N	12. Electoral College objections	Y

Election Results

Election	Name (Party)	Vote (%)		Cand. Spent	Ind. Exp. Support	Ind. Exp. Oppose
2016 General	John Kennedy (R)	536,191	(61%)	$8,886,736	$744,378	$733,207
	Foster Campbell (D)	347,816	(39%)	$8,258,670	$313,915	$978,864
2016 Primary	John Kennedy (R)	482,591	(25%)			
	Foster Campbell (D)	337,833	(18%)			
	Charles Boustany (R)	298,008	(15%)			
	Caroline Fayard (D)	240,917	(13%)			
	John Fleming (R)	204,026	(11%)			

Prior winning percentages: 2016 (61%)

John Kennedy entered the Senate, after two failed tries in 12 years, often forcing double takes and hurried queries to confirm he was not a northeast Kennedy. Soon, Louisiana's junior senator was holding court with a throng of journalists or on television, as he quipped in his Southern drawl about just about everything. He called Sen. John McCain "tough as a boiled owl," mused that President Donald Trump's judicial picks don't belong on the bench just because they watched "My Cousin

Vinny," suggested that if Trump tweeted a little less it would "not cause brain damage" and declared a White House meeting successful "because no one called anybody an ignorant slut or anything."

Kennedy's folksy fashion found a receptive audience in a town dominated by spin. His approach belied that he is one of the most educated members in the Senate, boasting five degrees, including a triple major as an undergraduate at Vanderbilt University and a pair of law degrees — from the University of Virginia and Oxford University. His legal expertise was on full display when he flummoxed a Trump judicial pick nominee, a showing that went viral and led to the nominee's withdrawal.

Kennedy has a reliably conservative voting record, going so far as to join 12 of his colleagues who voted against the bipartisan criminal justice overhaul in 2018. He has occasionally been critical of the president, especially on Russia-related issues.

Back home, Kennedy has been widely viewed as a potential candidate for governor. But in December 2018, he opted against challenging Democratic Gov. John Bel Edwards, telling Politico the Senate is "where I think I can do the most good."

Born in Centreville, Mississippi he grew up in Zachary in Louisiana's East Baton Rouge Parish. He later taught as an adjunct professor at Louisiana State University's law school.

Kennedy worked for a New Orleans law firm until he was named as special counsel to Gov. Buddy Roemer, a former member of Congress elected as a reformer. Kennedy remained with Roemer throughout his four years and helped win legislative approval of the state's first significant campaign finance regulations.

As Roemer's attorney, Kennedy defended the veto of a restrictive abortion bill that would have made the procedure illegal in cases of rape or incest. He has campaigned as an opponent of Roe v. Wade and has said that becoming a father influenced his thinking. Such shifts on policy, as well as his 2007 party switch, have provided fodder for opponents — notwithstanding that many influential Louisiana politicians have changed parties, as the onetime Democratic stronghold became a reliably red state.

After losing his first election — a race for state attorney general in 1991 — Kennedy returned to private law practice until he was named secretary of the Louisiana Department of Revenue in 1996 by Gov. Mike Foster, a Republican. Kennedy remained a Democrat and in 1999 made the first of five successful runs for state treasurer. He was re-elected as a Democrat in 2003 with no opposition but switched to the GOP in 2007 before winning a third term, again with no opponent. As treasurer, he was a bipartisan gadfly, criticizing the budget practices of the state's past three governors — two Democrats and a Republican.

Kennedy's first ran for Senate in 2004 as a Democrat. On economic issues, he positioned himself to the left of his chief Democratic rival, Rep. Chris John, in the state's "jungle" primary. Kennedy criticized the tax cuts enacted by President George W. Bush and supported increasing the minimum wage. He took conservative positions supporting gun rights and opposing same-sex marriage and abortion. In the November vote, Rep. David Vitter won 51 percent of the vote, avoiding a runoff and becoming Louisiana's first Republican senator in 120 years. John was second with 29 percent; Kennedy trailed with 15 percent. For Kennedy's next Senate bid in 2008, he was a Republican. His 2007 switch followed a political courtship by Vitter, aided by Bush's chief political strategist, Karl Rove.

Sen. Mary Landrieu was regarded as the most vulnerable Senate Democrat up for re-election in 2008. Kennedy was not the first choice of national GOP strategists, but he emerged after Rep. Richard Baker and Secretary of State Jay Dardenne declined to run. Landrieu outspent Kennedy by more than 2-1, while characterizing him as a "confused politician" who had mismanaged the Treasurer's Office. Kennedy stumbled by praising Oklahoma GOP Rep. Tom Coburn for blocking a farm disaster relief bill that Landrieu had pushed after hurricanes Gustav and Ike hit the state in 2008. Landrieu picked up endorsements from GOP officials in the New Orleans area as well as former GOP Gov. David Treen and defeated Kennedy 52%-46%.

Kennedy remained secure as treasurer, winning a fourth term in 2011 with no opposition and a fifth in 2015. With Vitter running for governor that year, Kennedy set himself up for a 2016 Senate race — spending heavily on TV commercials in his re-election campaign for treasurer, despite the absence of serious opposition. After his upset loss to Edwards in the governor's race, Vitter announced he would not seek re-election to the Senate. Twenty-four candidates filed for the open seat, with the leading Republican contenders including Kennedy and Reps. Charles Boustany and John Fleming. The latter, a founding member of the tea party-aligned House Freedom Caucus, had the backing of the Senate Conservatives Fund and the Club for Growth.

In a year in which Trump and Democratic Sen. Bernie Sanders shocked the political establishment with their outsider campaigns for president, Kennedy found success in his populist appeal too. While hailing Trump as a "change agent," Kennedy said in one ad, "You can't fix stupid, but you can vote it out." He echoed Trump's hard line on international trade agreements and President Barack Obama's signature health care law, beginning one commercial by saying, "I mean no disrespect, but Obamacare sucks."

The contest received limited national attention until August — when one candidate, former Ku Klux Klan leader David Duke, said he was "100 percent" behind Trump's agenda. As Trump bobbled a question about whether he disavowed Duke's support, Kennedy used the final televised debate before the first round of voting in November to condemn Duke as "a convicted liar and convicted felon," alluding to Duke's 2002 conviction on tax fraud. Kennedy focused most of his attention on keeping Boustany and Fleming out of the runoff. Barred by law from transferring money raised for his state treasurer campaigns into his Senate campaign account, Kennedy donated $2.4 million to the ESA Fund, a super PAC that spent nearly $2 million on ads attacking those two House members.

In the first round, Kennedy finished first with 25 percent of the vote. Democrat Foster Campbell, a longtime member of the state's elected Public Service Commission supported by Edwards, finished second with 18 percent. Boustany was third with 15 percent, followed by Democrat Caroline Fayard — a New Orleans attorney supported by Landrieu — with 13 percent, and Fleming with 11 percent. Duke finished a distant seventh at 3 percent. Given Trump's 20 percentage point win in Louisiana and the state's increasingly Republican complexion, Kennedy entered the second round as a clear favorite. But in the month before the Dec. 10 runoff, Campbell outraised him, $2.5 million to $1.6 million — fueled by Democrats around the country stunned by Trump's upset victory.

As Campbell benefited from donations outside the state, he emphasized his anti-abortion stance, attacking Kennedy for supporting abortion rights while a Democrat. But Kennedy overwhelmed him, 61%-39%.

Kennedy has compiled a mostly conservative voting record with a few twists. He and Lindsey Graham of South Carolina were the only Republicans to side with Democrats to save a landmark regulation that restricted banks and credit card companies from imposing mandatory arbitration on their customers; Vice President Mike Pence broke the tie and the rule was repealed.

Steve Scalise (R)

Elected 2008, 7th full term, b. Oct 06, 1965; New Orleans, LA; LA State University, B.S., 1989; LA State University, B.S., 1989; Catholic; Married (Jennifer Letulle Scalise); 2 children.

Elected Office: LA House, 1996-2007, LA Senate, 2008.

Professional Career: Systems engineer, Diamond Data Systems, eVenture Technologies.

DC Office: 2049 RHOB 20515, 202-225-3015, Fax: 202-226-0386, scalise.house.gov

State Offices: Hammond, 985-340-2185; Houma, 985-879-2300; Mandeville, 985-893-9064; Metairie, 504-837-1259.

Committees: House Minority Whip. *Energy & Commerce*: Communications & Technology.

Group Ratings

	ADA	ACLU	AFL-CIO	LCV	COC	HAFA	ACU	CFG	FRC
2020	**	17%	**	14%	-	86%	93%	**	-
2019	5%	C	33%	0%	73%	C	94%	72%	100%

Almanac Ratings 2019-2020

	Economy	Social	Foreign	Composite
Liberal	25%	20%	27%	24%
Conservative	75%	80%	73%	76%

Key Votes of the 116th Congress

1. U.S./Mex./Can. trade deal	Y	5. Russia sanctions	Y	9. Firearms background checks	N
2. First Coronavirus response	Y	6. Troops in Syria	Y	10. Spending at the border	Y
3. HEROES Act	N	7. Veto arms sales to Saudis	N	11. Marijuana liberalized rules	N
4. CASH Act	N	8. Defense $$$, veto override	N	12. Electoral College objections	Y

Election Results

Election	Name (Party)	Vote (%)	Cand. Spent	Ind. Exp. Support	Ind. Exp. Oppose
2020 General	Steve Scalise (R)............................	270,330 (72%)	$20,395,377	$3,746	$1,539
	Lee Ann Dugas (D)...........................	94,730 (25%)			
	Howard Kearney (L)........................	9,309 (2%)			

Prior winning percentages: 2018 (72%), 2016 (75%), 2014 (78%), 2012 (67%), 2010 (79%), 2008 (66%), 2008 special (75%)

Republican Steve Scalise, who won a special election in 2008, vaulted to House majority whip six years later through a blend of staunch conservatism, Cajun charm and unexpected opportunity. Now the second-ranking House Republican leader, and the top Southerner, he has been at the center of conflicts and tensions within the GOP. Their double-digit gain of seats in 2020, even as President Donald Trump lost reelection, postponed immediate change. He survived grievous gunshot wounds that he suffered in 2017 at an early-morning practice session of the congressional Republican baseball team.

A native of New Orleans, Scalise grew up in Metairie. When his parents gave their son a battery-powered microphone, he played town crier on his neighborhood street, decorating his bicycle in red, white and blue and calling people to the polls—the start of a political career. He majored in computer science at Louisiana State University, where he was twice elected speaker of the student assembly. After college, he settled in Jefferson Parish as a systems engineer. In 1995, at age 30, he was elected to the state House, where he served 12 years before winning a state Senate seat in 2007. He pushed legislation to give incentives to the motion picture industry to produce films in Louisiana, and he helped pass a bill that made it the first state to bar cities from suing gun manufacturers for the actions of criminals. Scalise had considered running for the open seat in the 1st District in 1999 and 2004 but deferred to David Vitter and then to Bobby Jindal; those two were elected to statewide office and then departed public life, leaving Scalise as the last man standing.

In the special election to replace Jindal, who was elected governor, the key contest was the Republican runoff between Scalise and state Rep. Tim Burns of St. Tammany. Burns cited Scalise's opposition to a bill banning smoking in restaurants and tried to tie him to special interests. Scalise called for limits on "out-of-control spending" and said he had "the experience to hit the ground running from Day One." Scalise won 58%-42%, capturing 83 percent of the Jefferson Parish vote. Against Democrat Gilda Reed, a college instructor and political neophyte, Scalise won 75%-23%.

When Scalise ran for his first full term, Democrat Jim Harlan, a venture capitalist, sank $1.8 million of his own money into the race and was not shy about throwing mud. In one television ad, he tried to tie Scalise to a local scandal involving the abuse of tax credits by the Louisiana Institute of Film Technology; Scalise had sponsored the tax credit program in the legislature. Scalise cited his opponent's support of presidential candidate Barack Obama as evidence that Harlan was too liberal for the district. Scalise rolled to a 66%-34% win. Since then, he has coasted to reelection.

Scalise is an ardent Republican with a sharp rhetorical edge. He railed against what he called Obama's "radical agenda." On the Energy and Commerce Committee, he called for more energy production, including offshore drilling. After the massive BP oil spill in the Gulf of Mexico in 2010, he shepherded colleagues to the region to see the disaster for themselves and was incensed by Obama's moratorium on offshore drilling, calling it "reckless." He later guided through the House and into law the 2012 RESTORE Act, which called for at least 80 percent of fines collected from BP and other parties to be sent directly to areas affected by the disaster.

Before joining the leadership, Scalise showed an occasional willingness to cross it. But he also paid his dues as a rank-and-file member. He opposed the 2011 compromise on raising the debt limit and joined most other Louisiana Republicans in refusing to support a relief bill for Hurricane Sandy in January 2013 because it didn't have offsetting cuts in spending. He was instrumental in passage of the January 2016 bill to eliminate the Affordable Care Act and end government funding for Planned Parenthood. That bill was sent to Obama, who quickly vetoed it.

Scalise has been known for his sense of humor and he is friendly with many Democrats. They include former 2nd District Rep. Cedric Richmond, an old friend from their days in Baton Rouge and now a top aide to President Joe Biden. They have worked closely to assure coastal restoration funds for Louisiana. "Steve is an example of how things used to work in Congress," said Republican Rep. Patrick McHenry of North Carolina, a close Scalise ally. "You'd battle it out and afterwards you can sit down and be friendly with one another."

When Ohio Republican Jim Jordan stepped down as chairman of the Republican Study Committee following the 2012 election, Georgia Republican Tom Graves won the endorsement of the group's founders and past chairmen and was set to take his place. But Scalise, who had been managing communications for the group, jumped in and demanded a more democratic method to choose the leader. "From the beginning, I felt like this ought to be a member-driven organization, and the members should decide who's the next chairman," he told National Journal. Scalise said he won the secret ballot "with votes to spare." That was a vital step in his move up the House GOP leadership ladder.

His next big step came in June 2014. Within hours of Virginia Republican Eric Cantor's shocking primary defeat, Scalise mobilized his bid to join the leadership. Kevin McCarthy of California, who had been whip, faced token opposition to replacing Cantor as majority leader. It helped that as RSC chairman, Scalise had a built-in base of support; it also helped that many Southern Republicans were anxious to see one of their own in a high-ranking post. Plus, as a result of McCarthy's national leadership of Young Republicans, they had been friends since long before either was elected to Congress "He's ... open and direct and he likes it when you're open and direct back to him," Rep. Kevin Brady of Texas, who chaired the House Ways and Means Committee, told the Times-Picayune.

Scalise faced an unexpected challenge in 2014 when a Louisiana liberal blogger reported that Scalise had spoken to a group of White supremacists and neo-Nazis in 2002, six years before he was elected to Congress. After a storm of criticism, he expressed his regrets about the appearance and said he had been there to seek support for a tax proposal. He distanced himself from the local group, saying he "wholeheartedly condemned" its views; House GOP leaders as well as other Republicans backed him. A key—and credible—defender was his friend Richmond, his Democratic colleague from New Orleans.

As part of a damage-control effort, Scalise then spent months meeting with the Congressional Black Caucus and civil rights leaders. Other liberal groups seized on the opportunity to try to depict Republicans as racists. Scalise later called it "a painful time" and "the ugly side of politics," and told Politico that he would be "forever grateful" to Richmond for coming to his defense. Not everyone welcomed Scalise's denials of decade-old connections to the supremacist group. Former Ku Klux Klan leader David Duke, who ran for the 1st District seat in 1999, called Scalise a "sell-out." Duke threatened to challenge him in the 2016 election, but backed off. In July 2020, with House Republicans split, Scalise voted to remove Confederate statues from the Capitol.

The House Republican leadership team remained rocky, notably when Boehner resigned under pressure in October 2015. After McCarthy became the early frontrunner to move up, Scalise quickly showed his intentions with a letter to House Republicans that he would seek to replace McCarthy. But McCarthy lacked sufficient support to become Speaker, and Republicans eventually turned to Rep. Paul Ryan. That left McCarthy in place, with no opportunity for Scalise.

Scalise's future was placed in serious question in early June 2017 when he was shot and severely wounded during early-morning practice for the congressional baseball game by a Democratic partisan from Belleville Illinois who had posted social-media attacks on Trump and congressional Republicans. Scalise was rushed to a Washington hospital with internal wounds that his surgeon later said had left him at "imminent risk of death." Following multiple surgeries, Scalise's condition slowly improved. He walked onto the House floor in late September, leaning heavily on two canes, and to resounding cheers. "The last three and a half months have been a pretty challenging time for me and my family," he told the House. The overwhelming support has "given us the strength to get through all of this." Following months more of intensive medical treatment and physical therapy, in which he essentially learned to walk again, Scalise settled back into his leadership responsibilities— including extensive travel. With some limitations, he returned to the baseball team in 2019.

The health of House Republicans was less robust. In addition to their failure to salvage the GOP majority, Scalise and McCarthy found themselves in a struggle, between themselves and with other House Republicans, for the succession to Speaker Paul Ryan, who retired in 2018. Scalise said he supported McCarthy for Speaker and hoped to replace him as majority leader. But that raised various questions, including the depth of GOP support for McCarthy, Scalise's ultimate intentions, the election outcome and what would become the new dynamics for the Republican minority. As it turned out, Republicans selected McCarthy over Jim Jordan of Ohio for minority leader, and Scalise became minority whip without opposition.

Scalise maintained his partisan edge. In October 2019, he joined a conservative coterie who stormed into a meeting in the Capitol of the House Intelligence Committee. The House GOP's positive results in the 2020 election deferred their seemingly endless internal conflicts. He remained an ally in Trump's claims of election fraud that November. If recent history is any guide, Scalise before long will have an opportunity for a top leadership post—either in the majority or minority. His more enthusiastic following, especially among conservatives, could serve him well.

LA-1: New Orleans Suburbs, Southeast Louisiana

Cook Partisan Voting Index: R+22

Population		Race and Ethnicity		Income	
Total	799,917	White	79.40%	Median Income	$61,431
Land area (sq. miles)	4,030	Black	14.00%	District Income Rank	241
Pop/ sq mi	198.48	Latino	8.90%	Poverty Rate	14.40%
Born in State	73.20%	Asian	2.20%	With health insurance	92.00%
		Two or more races	2.30%	Cash public assistance	1.40%
Age Groups		Other	2.00%	Food stamp/SNAP	9.50%
Under 18	22.90%				
18-34	21.10%	**Education**		**Work**	
35-64	38.60%	H.S grad or less	40.40%	White Collar	39.90%
Over 64	17.40%	Some college	27.40%	Sales and Service	40.00%
		College Degree, 4 yr	20.30%	Blue Collar	20.10%
Military		Post grad	12.00%	Government	12.60%
Veteran/ Active Duty	6.60%				

2020 Pres. Vote	Trump	267,164	(68%)	Biden	118,446	(30%)			
2016 Pres. Vote	Trump	244,906	(69%)	Clinton	95,170	(27%)	Johnson	9,742	(3%)

St. Tammany Parish: Founded in 1718 and the nation's sixth-largest city at the outbreak of the Civil War, New Orleans is ancient for an American metropolis. It is still closely girded by the peculiar wilderness of the mushy Delta lands of the sluggish Mississippi River. For decades, you could climb a levee overlooking the Mississippi and see an expanse of water with untidy clumps of trees and disorganized-looking, seemingly abandoned docks—what Mark Twain had in his mind's eye while writing Life on the Mississippi in the 1870s. For decades, the river funneled the products of half a continent down to a single port with an international heritage and flair. The New Orleans metropolitan area has lived off that geography and history, with an inward-looking elite preoccupied with who is in which Mardi Gras krewe and interested more in the genealogy of old families than in the geography of the Oil Patch.

That mighty river and its Delta deepened the catastrophe after Hurricane Katrina struck with Category 3 force on Aug. 29, 2005, and devastated many of the area's subdivisions and streetscapes. The city's population plummeted, housing stock was destroyed, some levees were breached, and others were no longer reliable. In Plaquemines and St. Bernard parishes, many people fled the high winds and floodwaters. Some have returned. By 2019, the recovery of St. Bernard's population of 46,000 yielded an increase of about 10,000 since 2010, but the total remained down 30 percent since 2000.

Louisiana's southern coast experienced yet more turmoil with the man-made disaster known as the BP Deepwater Horizon oil spill. The rig exploded on April 20, 2010, and spewed more than 200 million gallons of crude oil into the Gulf of Mexico over three months. Once the flow was finally stemmed in July, the hardest part was yet to come: cleaning up from the largest marine oil spill in U.S. history, one that caused extensive damage to wildlife and habitats, not to mention Louisiana's coastal economy. About 600 miles of shoreline were affected.

The Katrina and BP nightmares exacerbated an ongoing disaster in the Mississippi River Delta. Coastal erosion in the bayous has caused continuing losses in the wetlands, which some experts estimate is the size of a football field for every hour. In 2017, the legislature took a significant step when it ratified a state agency's coastal master plan, which envisioned a massive restoration. The plan included 124 projects to protect or restore up to 800 square miles of new land, will build and raise levee systems across the state, and raise or relocate homes and businesses that remain threatened by storm surges and the rise in sea level. The projected 50-year cost could exceed $50 billion, though it was expected to add 10,000 jobs. Some of that money will come from the $9 billion the state received from the BP litigation. The oil industry, whose royalties will finance some of the improvements, has been forced to prepare its own response. The rising coastline has placed at risk the huge and complex infrastructure of pipelines, refineries, tank farms and ports. By no means are they shutting down. In September 2019, the Federal Energy Regulatory Commission gave the go-ahead to construction of an $8.5 billion liquefied natural gas facility and export terminal along the Mississippi River in Plaquemines Parish. Scheduled to open in 2023, the facility would be the second LNG terminal in Louisiana.

The 1st Congressional District of Louisiana stretches from suburban St. Tammany Parish north of New Orleans to Houma in Terrebonne Parish. The district takes in the vast suburb of Metairie in Jefferson Parish as well as part of western New Orleans. Metairie has remained an attractive place for new businesses, though it faced uncertainties from the unique mix of the local economy with its new and younger citizenry, plus depopulation. Most people in the 1st District live in Jefferson and St. Tammany parishes. Jefferson, of which about 60 percent is in the 1st, had 432,000 residents in 2017 —down 23,000 from 2000. In St. Tammany, which was spared from the worst effects, the population has increased from 191,000 to 255,000 during that time.

The 14 percent African-American population in the 1st is the lowest of any Louisiana district, and the 9 percent Hispanic is the highest in the state. Even with its setbacks, this is a comfortable, well-educated and heavily Republican district. In 2020, Donald Trump won 68 percent of the vote, now only his second-best district in the state, behind the 3rd District. Perhaps the most significant result was that he took suburban Jefferson by only 55%-44%. In his successful reelection in 2019, Democratic Gov. John Bel Edwards took Jefferson 57%-43%—which might offer insight into its future.

Troy Carter (D)

Elected 2021, 1st term; b. Oct. 26, 1963, New Orleans, LA; Xavier University of LA, B.A.; Baptist; Married (Melanie); 2 children.

Elected Office: LA House, 1992-1994; Member, New Orleans City Council, 1994-2002; LA Senate, 2016-2021.

Professional Career: President, News and Brews, LLC, 1996-2003; Adjunct Instructor of Political Science, Xavier University of LA; Executive Assistant, Mayor Sidney Barthelemy; President, Commonwealth Properties, LLC; President/CEO, Policy and Planning Partners, LLC.

DC Office: 506 CHOB, 20515, 202-225-6636, troycarter.house.gov

Committees: *Small Business. Transportation & Infrastructure.*

Election Results

Election	Name (Party)	Vote (%)		Cand. Spent	Ind. Exp. Support	Ind. Exp. Oppose
2021 General	Troy Carter (D)	48,511	(55%)			
	Karen Peterson (R)	39,295	(45%)			
2021 Primary	Troy Carter (D)	34,396	(36%)			
	Karen Peterson (D)	21,670	(23%)			
	Gary Chambers (D)	20,151	(21%)			
	Claston Bernard (R)	9,237	(10%)			

Democrat Troy Carter won a special-election runoff on April 24, 2021, to fill the seat of Democratic Rep. Cedric Richmond, who resigned in January after having served five terms. Richmond became a senior adviser to President Joe Biden and director of the White House office of public engagement. Carter, a state senator with extensive experience in government and politics in the New Orleans area, defeated Karen Carter Peterson (no relation), who also served in the state senate. Carter was endorsed by Richmond. Peterson had the support of national liberal Democrat and progressive groups, which spent more than $1 million on her campaign.

Carter, a native of New Orleans, got a bachelor's degree in business administration and political science from Xavier University in New Orleans. Following college, he became a top aide to New Orleans Mayor Sidney Barthelemy. In 1991, Carter was elected to the state House. After winning reelection to that seat, he ran successfully in 1994 for the city council of New Orleans, where his district included the French Quarter. In 2002, Carter was defeated in a bid for mayor in a contest that ultimately was won by Ray Nagin.

Carter ran unsuccessfully for Congress in 2006, when Rep. Bill Jefferson was facing ethics charges that eventually led to his criminal conviction. During more than a decade in the private sector, Carter was the founder and president of a company that operated three gourmet coffee houses in New Orleans. In 2015, he was elected to the state Senate, where he served as Minority Leader and chairman of the Labor and Industrial Relations Committee.

When Redmond, who had been a close adviser to Biden during his presidential campaign, announced, decided to take a White House position, Carter quickly won his support and embraced his relatively moderate political positions. With Peterson, who was the other leading contender, the contest became "a fight between the competing wings of the Democratic Party," the Associated Press reported. "Peterson has planted herself firmly in the progressive camp, with their endorsements reflecting that divide."

As expected, none of the 15 candidates received the required majority to win the first round of voting on March 20. But, given the national support for Peterson—who had chaired the Louisiana Democratic Party—Peterson surprisingly only narrowly survived for the runoff. Carter led the initial vote with 36 percent of the vote to 23 percent for Peterson and 21 percent for Gary Chambers, a social justice advocate and community organizer based in Baton Rouge. Chambers said that he endorsed Peterson because of her more progressive views.

In the runoff with Peterson, Carter styled himself as a more effective lawmaker. Voters "need to send someone to Washington who can build bridges, not walls, that can establish relationships that mean something, not kick rocks because you don't get your way, not spew lies because you're losing," he said during a debate.

Peterson called for a "complete restructuring" of police practices. "This system wasn't built to protect Black and brown people. We can't just reform the police. We need to reimagine public safety," she said during the debate with Carter. Her supporters included voting-rights advocate Stacey Abrams of Georgia, Rep. Alexandria Ocasio-Cortez of New York and New Orleans Mayor LaToya Cantrell. Carter had endorsements from House Majority Whip James Clyburn of South Carolina and all African-American Democrats serving in the state Senate.

Carter out-spent Peterson, $1.3 million to $965.000. But Peterson was bolstered by more than $1.8 million in support from EMILY's List, which backs Democratic women who support abortion rights. In his 55%-45% victory, Carter took 53 percent in Orleans Parish, which cast a bit more than half of the total vote, and 67 percent in Jefferson Parish, which had nearly one-fifth of the vote. He and Peterson split the remaining eight parishes. Peterson took 65 percent in East Baton Rouge Parish, which had the third-largest turnout.

Commenting on the outcome, national Democratic strategist James Carville—a New Orleans resident—told the New Orleans Advocate that the low turnout and Peterson's financial advantage should have helped her. Instead, Carville said, "Voters voted against wokeness. They just did. Woke did very, very poorly."

LA-2: New Orleans Metro, Parts of Baton Rouge

Cook Partisan Voting Index:

Population		Race and Ethnicity		Income	
Total	788,021	White	31.40%	Median Income	$44,124
Land area (sq. miles)	1,268	Black	61.50%	District Income Rank	420
Pop/ sq mi	621.23	Latino	6.60%	Poverty Rate	21.60%
Born in State	77.40%	Asian	2.60%	With health insurance	89.90%
		Two or more races	1.90%	Cash public assistance	1.80%
Age Groups		Other	2.60%	Food stamp/SNAP	18.40%
Under 18	22.30%				
18-34	24.00%	**Education**		**Work**	
35-64	38.50%	H.S grad or less	46.70%	White Collar	34.40%
Over 64	15.30%	Some college	27.70%	Sales and Service	43.60%
		College Degree, 4 yr	15.50%	Blue Collar	22.00%
Military		Post grad	10.10%	Government	14.90%
Veteran/ Active Duty	6.00%				

2020 Pres. Vote	Biden	259,909	(75%)	Trump	78,732	(23%)
2016 Pres. Vote	Clinton	247,491	(75%)	Trump	73,779	(22%)

Orleans Parish: Established by the French and ruled by the Spanish from 1763 for almost 40 years, New Orleans was a Creole city—part French, a bit Spanish, more than a touch Caribbean—when the American flag was raised over what is now Jackson Square in 1803. The statue of Andrew Jackson still seems an intrusion in a square set off by the French Market, the Cabildo, the Presbytere, the Pontalba apartments, and St. Louis Cathedral. New Orleans was one of the six largest American cities from 1820 until the Civil War and the only sizable city in the Deep South. It was urbanized, yet poor, with yellow fever epidemics late in the 19th century, even as it was installing electric lights. It had a riot in which Italian immigrants were massacred, even as it was laying streetcar tracks and telephone lines. It also was one of the most corrupt American cities during Reconstruction and the Gilded Age, when its votes were regularly bid for and bought. Like other Southern cities, it became rigidly segregated after 1890.

For a time during the 1970s oil boom, New Orleans seemed to be a fast-growing Sun Belt city. It suffered economically through the 1980s, when it lost substantial port business—oil to Houston and Latin American trade to Miami. By the 1990s, New Orleans was humming again. Crime rates fell and no longer depressed tourism. Incomes went up, and home ownership increased, among African Americans as well as Whites. The downtown Superdome hosted the 1988 Republican convention.

Then, Hurricane Katrina made landfall early on a Monday morning, August 29, 2005. A nightmarish scene unfolded at the Superdome, the shelter of last resort for more than 20,000 people, many of whom had fled the rising water without food, drinking water or medicine. Conditions worsened when the storm ripped two holes in the roof. A few days later, city officials began to load people on buses for transport to cities better positioned to provide services. The breach of the city's levees led to a surge that churned through the low-income 9th Ward, while the French Quarter, on higher ground, was largely untouched by the floodwaters. Still, 80 percent of New Orleans flooded.

New Orleans was in for a very long recovery. Thousands of government trailers became semi-permanent homes. City residents who had fled the floodwaters only slowly trickled back. It took years to restore regular utility service. By 2017, the city's population was 390,000, 15 percent less than in 2000, but more than 80 percent larger than in 2006, showing an impressive recovery from the storm in many—but not all—parts of the city. Post-recession wages and median household income in the city and suburbs were also on the rise. Still, those increases have slowed. New Orleans was a relatively poor city before the hurricane and remains so.

The city's post-hurricane recovery and transition suffered when a second disaster struck in April 2010. BP's Deepwater Horizon offshore rig exploded and spewed oil into the Gulf of Mexico at an estimated rate of 60,000 barrels a day. A federally mandated moratorium on offshore drilling was lifted in October 2010 under pressure from local and state officials and the congressional delegation. The fragile regional economy took another serious blow when the 5,000 jobs at the Avondale shipyard in 2010 were all but eliminated.

With its unique character and characters, New Orleans remained a popular tourist destination. In the French Quarter—the Vieux Carré as it was originally called—are the 19th-century row houses decked out in their island pastels and ornate wrought-iron railings. At street level are restaurants, art galleries, and jazz and blues clubs, and the narrow sidewalks fill up nightly with diners, revelers, and patrons of the tiny voodoo establishments found only in New Orleans. Its storied restaurants serve a cuisine all New Orleans' own—spicy, rich and unaffected by trends in low-fat food.

Upriver from the Quarter is the Central Business District, with its skyscrapers and the Superdome, and the Garden District, with the graceful intact homes of the rich early American settlers lining St. Charles Avenue. A total of 18.5 million tourists visited New Orleans in 2018—breaking the pre-Katrina record set in 2004—and they spent a record-breaking $9.1 billion. Positive business reports included: the purchase of Avondale by two industrial-development firms that projected 2,000 transportation-related jobs; commercial use of the Avondale waterfront in 2019 for the first time in five years; completion of a new 35-gate terminal at the Louis Armstrong airport; and new petrochemical and chemical manufacturing plants outside the city with more than 2,500 jobs.

Much to the relief of locals, the city's revamped $14.5 billion flood control system worked. In the Ninth Ward, the large influx of Vietnamese immigrants, many of whom work at sea, offered a sense of community—albeit, with continuation of the stark economic inequality in that area. Still, amid the optimism, few would guarantee that the improvements across the city would survive the next disaster. In 2017, City Lab reported, many New Orleans neighborhoods "suffered Katrina-level floods … from a basic rainstorm." Other elements of the pre-Katrina reality remained: In 2019, 24 percent of the city lived in poverty and the city had the second-worst inequality in the nation, behind only Atlanta. More bad news arrived in March 2020, when New Orleans became one of the nation's first coronavirus hot spots, largely as a result of Mardi Gras festivities, with a disproportionate impact on African-Americans and a devastating impact on tourism.

The 2nd Congressional District of Louisiana includes much of the city of New Orleans. It contains nearly half of Jefferson Parish, most of Orleans Parish, and all or part of eight other parishes between New Orleans and Baton Rouge. More than 100,000 residents in largely Black neighborhoods on Baton Rouge's north side were added in the 2012 redistricting to make up for the downsizing in New Orleans. By including most of the heavily Black precincts in south Louisiana, the 2nd is 61 percent African American and one of the most Democratic districts in the South. Both Hillary Clinton and Joe Biden took 75 percent of the vote.

Clay Higgins (R)

Elected 2016, 3rd term, b. Aug 24, 1961; New Orleans, LA; LA State University, Att., 1983; LA State University, Att., 1990; Christian - Non-Denominational; Married (Becca Higgins); 4 children (1 deceased).

Military Career: U.S. Army 1979-1985; LA National Guard 1979-1985

Elected Office: Sheriff, St. Landry Parish, 2008-2016.

DC Office: 424 CHOB 20515, 202-225-2031, Fax: 202-225-5724, clayhiggins.house.gov

State Offices: Lafayette, 337-703-6105; Lake Charles, 337-656-2833.

Committees: *Homeland Security*: Border Security, Facilitation & Operations (RMM); Emergency Preparedness, Response & Recovery. *Oversight & Reform*: National Security; Subcommittee on Civil Rights & Civil Liberties.

Group Ratings

	ADA	ACLU	AFL-CIO	LCV	COC	HAFA	ACU	CFG	FRC
2020	**	24%	**	10%	-	92%	88%	**	-
2019	0%	C	20%	3%	69%	C	87%	96%	100%

Almanac Ratings 2019-2020

	Economy	Social	Foreign	Composite
Liberal	25%	9%	34%	23%
Conservative	75%	91%	66%	77%

Key Votes of the 116th Congress

1. U.S./Mex./Can. trade deal	Y	5. Russia sanctions	N	9. Firearms background checks	N
2. First Coronavirus response	Y	6. Troops in Syria	Y	10. Spending at the border	Y
3. HEROES Act	N	7. Veto arms sales to Saudis	N	11. Marijuana liberalized rules	N/A
4. CASH Act	Y	8. Defense $$$, veto override	N	12. Electoral College objections	Y

Election Results

Election	Name (Party)	Vote (%)		Cand. Spent	Ind. Exp. Support	Ind. Exp. Oppose
2020 General	Clay Higgins (R)	230,480	(68%)	$727,081	$22	$750
	Braylon Harris (D)	60,852	(18%)	$14,507		
	Rob Anderson (R)	39,423	(12%)	$45,276		
	Brandon Leleux (L)	9,365	(3%)			

Prior winning percentages: 2018 (58%), 2016 (56%)

Republican Clay Higgins, who unexpectedly won the open seat in 2016 against a veteran state elected official, has displayed elements of President Donald Trump's outsider and outspoken appeal. Higgins, a former captain and spokesman for the St. Landry Parish sheriff's office and political newcomer, has had some eccentric moments in the House. Two months before the 2020 election, Higgins had a conflict with Facebook, in which his threatening post was removed.

Higgins attended Louisiana State University and had several jobs, including as a police officer and manager of an automobile dealership. His personal life had some sketchy details, including an ex-wife claiming that Higgins owed more than $100,000 in child support. Before his run for Congress, he had gained local attention with "Crime Stopper" videos that he narrated. In a 2015 profile, The Washington Post described him as a "muscled Army veteran and hardened street cop who rarely cracks a smile [who might be] the most irresistibly intimidating man in America."

Known as the "Cajun John Wayne," his authentic style with a touch of empathy gained something of a cult following in the bayous and on YouTube. Many of the suspects, he later said, turned themselves in in response to the message of redemption from "Uncle Clay." Higgins resigned from the sheriff's office in February 2016, citing an unspecified "matter of principle" that apparently related to an order he was unwilling to follow. That led to calls for him to run for Congress.

Running for the open seat, the 12 candidates in the wide-open field included eight Republicans and two Democrats. The best-known Republican was Scott Angelle, chairman of the state Public Service Commission. Angelle had switched parties after he finished third in the nine-candidate contest for governor in 2015, and ran especially well in his native Cajun country. In the all-party House election in November, Angelle led Higgins, 29%-27%. Angelle had a big lead in St. Charles, Higgins's tea-party style ran well in the rural areas, and they split Lafayette. In the December runoff, Angelle highlighted his endorsement by the National Rifle Association and the Louisiana Sheriffs Association. A super PAC organized by friends of Higgins used the Trump-like slogan, "Make Louisiana Great Again." But with Higgins' background in "reality TV," the facts occasionally were muddled. Angelle spent $1.8 million to $380,000 for Higgins. Higgins won the runoff, 56%-44%, with a geographic split that was similar to the first round of voting.

In the House, Higgins described his agenda in standard Republican terms of "smaller government, less bureaucracy, free markets, a strong national defense and securing America's sovereign borders." He focused his work on the Homeland Security Committee, where he said that every border is "a sacred gateway we must protect." As ranking Republican on the panel's Border Security Subcommittee, he said, "the national security and humanitarian crisis on our southern border" is a significant challenge facing the nation. His chief focus would be providing front-line resources with the resources that they need, including modern technology, he added.

The Louisiana-based Advocate newspaper reported that Higgins had become "a reliable vote for the party's leadership," with a mostly low-key profile. His unguarded style resulted in occasional headlines. When he joined a congressional delegation to the site of the Auschwitz death camp in Poland, he prepared a five-minute video—taken, in part, inside a gas chamber—during which he argued that the military must be "invincible." Subsequently, the Auschwitz Memorial site responded to his film with a tweet, "There should be mournful silence. It's not a stage."

In September 2020, he created conflict with a Facebook post that accompanied a photo of armed Black militia members at a protest in Louisville. If they showed up in Louisiana, he wrote, "I wouldn't even spill my beer. I'd drop any 10 of you where you stand." After the post had been removed by Facebook, Democratic Rep. Cedric Richmond of Louisiana said the comments were "disappointing, but not surprising." Richmond added, "My colleague still has not learned that words have consequences, especially when they come from supposed leaders."

In his first reelection, Higgins faced six challengers, including Republican Josh Guillory, a local attorney. Rudy Giuliani, who was Trump's legal adviser, endorsed Guillory and planned a local event. Guillory had hired as his fundraiser Jennifer LeBlanc—the "new girlfriend" of the former New York City mayor, who months earlier had worked for Higgins—Politico reported. National and state GOP officials reportedly were surprised and unhappy. Days later, Trump met with Higgins and endorsed him. Higgins spent nearly $900,000 in his campaign to $300,000 for Guillory. He won with 56 percent of the vote. Guillory finished third with 13 percent. In 2020, Higgins was reelected uneventfully, with 68 percent of the vote.

LA-3: Southwest Louisiana

Cook Partisan Voting Index: R+21

Population		Race and Ethnicity		Income	
Total	785,101	White	69.80%	Median Income	$51,504
Land area (sq. miles)	6,983	Black	25.00%	District Income Rank	373
Pop/ sq mi	112.43	Latino	4.20%	Poverty Rate	19.50%
Born in State	82.60%	Asian	1.50%	With health insurance	92.40%
		Two or more races	2.10%	Cash public assistance	1.00%
Age Groups		Other	1.60%	Food stamp/SNAP	14.00%
Under 18	24.60%				
18-34	22.60%	Education		Work	
35-64	37.60%	H.S grad or less	51.00%	White Collar	35.10%
Over 64	15.10%	Some college	25.70%	Sales and Service	38.70%
		College Degree, 4 yr	16.20%	Blue Collar	26.10%
Military		Post grad	7.20%	Government	13.10%
Veteran/ Active Duty	6.60%				

2020 Pres. Vote	Trump	242,739	(68%)	Biden	107,447	(30%)
2016 Pres. Vote	Trump	231,017	(67%)	Clinton	100,241	(29%)

Lafayette, Lake Charles: More than 200 years ago, French-speaking settlers in Canada were forced to leave their land of Acadie, which the British had taken over and renamed Nova Scotia. They made their way to the wetlands of southern Louisiana, called Acadiana. Here, without much notice, they built steep-roofed houses to slough off nonexistent snow and adapted French cuisine to the crawfish and muskrats they found in abundance in the pelican-tended swamps. They are the Cajuns, and the heart of their adopted homeland is around Lafayette, just west of the Atchafalaya Basin, where Mississippi River waters pour through bayous and canals. Cajun French has survived decades of efforts to eliminate it. Cajun music—and its Black-influenced variant, zydeco—are popular here and nationally; spicy Cajun cooking attracts food lovers, who learn its secrets and then carry them home, in understated form.

Cajun country has thrived, thanks to the oil and gas that are plentiful on land and just offshore in the Gulf of Mexico. Oil rigs are common, and every once in a while, the swampy foliage parts to reveal a giant refinery or petrochemical plant. In southern Louisiana, "some 125 projects valued at $32 billion among 12 industries have begun construction or plan to begin construction in 2019," according to an August 2019 story in 1012 Business Report, a Louisiana publication. In a triumphant claim, the report added, "Louisiana appears to be beating the pants off Texas in pure investment dollars."

West of Lafayette, the economy in Lake Charles has been booming, with petrochemicals and engineering, plus construction jobs related to the natural-gas boom. The robust 28 percent job growth in the area between 2013 and 2018 was the strongest in the nation. Cajun country has thrived over the decades, thanks to the oil and gas that are plentiful on land and just offshore in the Gulf of

Mexico. In December 2019, the San Diego Union-Tribune reported, San Diego-based Sempra Energy opened a second liquefied natural gas terminal to export fuel across the globe, in addition to the $10 billion LNG processing unit that already was operating off the coast of Cameron Parish. The daily production of natural gas was enough energy to power 8.5 million homes for a day, the Houston Chronicle reported. But the challenge of everyday life continued. In September 2020, Hurricane Laura caused epic damage—the third calamitous hurricane in 15 years. In that same Cameron Parish, the devastation has been a factor in its nearly 30 percent decline in population—from almost 10,000 in 2000 to below 7,000 in 2019. Another consequence has been the loss of more coastal wetlands plus beach erosion along the barrier islands.

The 3rd Congressional District, following the 2011 redistricting, absorbed much of what had been a second district in the bayous. It covers the southern coast from the Texas border east to St. Mary Parish, plus much of Cajun country. The population centers are Lafayette Parish and Lake Charles-based Calcasieu Parish, which have about 30 percent and 25 percent of the district's population, respectively. Iberia Parish, the next largest, has less than 10 percent of the population. The 3rd District remains very conservative. Donald Trump won 68 percent of the vote in 2020, his best district in Louisiana.

Mike Johnson (R)

Elected 2016, 3rd term, b. Jan 30, 1972; Shreveport, LA; LA State University, B.S., 1995; LA State University Law School, J.D., 1998; Southern Baptist; Married (Kelly Lary Johnson); 4 children.

Elected Office: LA House, 2015-2016.

Professional Career: Practicing attorney; Talk radio host/columnist.

DC Office: 418 CHOB 20515, 202-225-2777, Fax: 202-225-8039, mikejohnson.house.gov

State Offices: Bossier City, 318-840-0309; Leesville, 337-423-4232; Natchitoches, 318-951-4316.

Committees: House Republican Conference Vice Chairman. *Armed Services*: Cyber, Innovative Technologies & Information Systems; Readiness. *Judiciary*: Antitrust, Commercial & Administrative Law; Constitution, Civil Rights & Civil Liberties (RMM); Courts, Intellectual Property & Internet.

Group Ratings

	ADA	ACLU	AFL-CIO	LCV	COC	HAFA	ACU	CFG	FRC
2020	**	18%	**	0%	-	91%	91%	**	-
2019	5%	C	25%	3%	72%	C	91%	96%	100%

Almanac Ratings 2019-2020

	Economy	Social	Foreign	Composite
Liberal	25%	22%	33%	27%
Conservative	75%	78%	67%	73%

Key Votes of the 116th Congress

1. U.S./Mex./Can. trade deal	Y	5. Russia sanctions	N/A	9. Firearms background checks	N
2. First Coronavirus response	Y	6. Troops in Syria	Y	10. Spending at the border	N/A
3. HEROES Act	N	7. Veto arms sales to Saudis	N	11. Marijuana liberalized rules	N/A
4. CASH Act	N	8. Defense $$$, veto override	Y	12. Electoral College objections	Y

Election Results

Election	Name (Party)	Vote (%)	Cand. Spent	Ind. Exp. Support	Ind. Exp. Oppose
2020 General	Mike Johnson (R)............................... 185,265	(60%)	$1,127,474	$22	$750
	Kenny Houston (D)............................ 78,157	(25%)	$30,823		
	Ryan Trundle (D).............................. 23,813	(8%)	$13,343		
	Ben Gibson (R)................................. 19,343	(6%)			

Prior winning percentages: 2018 (64%), 2016 (65%)

Republican Mike Johnson, elected in 2016 to an open seat, has shown his social conservatism and his skill at working with a cross-section of House Republicans. As chairman of the Republican Study Committee, he defended President Donald Trump against impeachment charges in his first Senate trial and helped lead the challenges against the outcome of the 2020 presidential election. Earlier, Johnson disagreed with Trump on proposed changes to the Affordable Care Act. In 2021, he took over as vice chairman of the House Republican Conference.

Johnson is a native of Shreveport. His father, a local firefighter, was critically burned and disabled in the line of duty. Johnson got his bachelor's in business administration and a law degree at Louisiana State University. In private practice, he advocated conservative constitutional principles. He was elected to the state House in 2015, where he enacted a bill that prohibited a "dismemberment" procedure for second-trimester abortions. Johnson stirred controversy as the chief sponsor of a religious freedom proposal that would have prohibited local governments from imposing fines or revoking tax benefits from a business based on its owner's views on marriage His measure was supported by the conservative Family Research Council, but opposed by business groups. A House committee defeated Johnson's bill. But Gov. Bobby Jindal then issued an executive order with similar provisions.

When the U.S. House seat opened, several Republicans competed in the contest. Other leading contenders were Shreveport cardiologist Trey Baucum and Shreveport City Council member Oliver Jenkins. An Associated Press report described the contest as "something of an anomaly, a race that's almost downright genteel." In the first round of voting, Johnson got 25 percent of the vote; Bracum and Jenkins trailed with 18 and 16 percent. Johnson led the Republican field in 11 of the 15 parishes, including the population centers of Shreveport-based Caddo and Bossier.

Democrat Marshall Jones was the frontrunner with 28 percent. In the relatively amiable runoff, Johnson consolidated the Republican vote, while Jones had little upside. Johnson won, 65%-35%. Each candidate was pro-gun and anti-abortion. The only parish that was close was Caddo, where Johnson took 52 percent of the vote. Johnson's $1 million in spending doubled the total for Jones. "I guess I wasn't able to distinguish myself from the national Democratic party," Jones said following his defeat.

In the House, Johnson won passage in 2017 of his bill that he said was designed to close a loophole in pornography laws by protecting children from the use of sexual images. The strict penalties would include a mandatory minimum prison sentence of 15 years. Johnson called the bill "a common-sense approach to better protect children from depraved sexual predators." Some liberals criticized the measure as overly broad and warned that it would criminalize "sexting" on phones, especially among teenagers. The House passed the legislation, 368-51.

In an unusual collaboration, Johnson worked with Louisiana Attorney General Jeff Landry on guidelines to clarify and promote religious expression in that state's public schools. The measure was designed to protect the rights of students to "live out their faith on campus," Johnson said. Despite opposition by law professors and civil libertarians, the legislature passed in 2018 a bill based on Johnson's proposal.

Johnson was at odds with Trump on the GOP proposal to repeal and revise the Affordable Care Act. He later said Republicans "fumbled" that effort and "squandered" the first several months of legislative action after Trump took office. Johnson also raised questions about Trump's policy of separating children from their families when they are detained at the border after illegally entering the country. "We must secure our borders, uphold our laws and keep families together—and we can," he said in a 2018 statement. "Our legal system and our immigration policies always seek a proper balance between justice and compassion."

Following the 2018 election, Johnson was elected to chair the Republican Study Committee. He said he would collaborate with the Freedom Caucus and use his platform for "moving our cause forward … [and] helping shape the future of the conservative movement." He defeated six-term

Rep. Tom McClintock of California, a long-time conservative leader. "My driving force is to get Republicans to work together, to bring the family together, so to speak," he told the Daily Beast. That became apparent when Johnson, as a Judiciary Committee member, became an outspoken defender of Trump during his initial impeachment trial. He called the Democrats' case a "charade" and the committee review "a lopsided and unfair process." His work on that case increased his contacts with Trump, including flights on Air Force One. When Trump challenged the results of the 2020 election, Johnson played a leading role in preparing the legal papers on behalf of congressional Republicans, which proved unsuccessful.

He gained another useful post as ranking Republican on the Judiciary Subcommittee on the Constitution, Civil Rights and Civil Liberties. During a May 2019 hearing, he led opposition to a Democratic effort to remove the deadline for ratifying the Equal Rights Amendment, which he said "would mean the end of laws that protect the sanctity of every human life." In September 2020, he was an enthusiastic proponent of Supreme Court nominee Amy Comey Barrett, whom he said had been a friend since high school in Shreveport. She had "all the qualities that America needs and deserves in a Supreme Court justice," Johnson wrote prior to Trump selecting her for the Court.

In 2021, Johnson got a seat on the Armed Services Committee, in addition to his leadership position as vice chairman of the House Republican Conference.

LA-4: Northwest Louisiana   Cook Partisan Voting Index: R+14

Population		Race and Ethnicity		Income	
Total	737,674	White	60.80%	Median Income	$44,580
Land area (sq. miles)	12,435	Black	33.90%	District Income Rank	418
Pop/ sq mi	59.32	Latino	4.40%	Poverty Rate	22.50%
Born in State	74.10%	Asian	1.00%	With health insurance	90.90%
		Two or more races	2.50%	Cash public assistance	4.00%
Age Groups		Other	1.70%	Food stamp/SNAP	16.90%
Under 18	23.40%				
18-34	22.20%	**Education**		**Work**	
35-64	37.10%	H.S grad or less	52.80%	White Collar	31.10%
Over 64	17.40%	Some college	27.90%	Sales and Service	42.60%
		College Degree, 4 yr	12.10%	Blue Collar	26.30%
Military		Post grad	7.20%	Government	17.90%
Veteran/ Active Duty	10.60%				

2020 Pres. Vote	Trump	201,820	(61%)	Biden	121,498	(37%)
2016 Pres. Vote	Trump	192,977	(61%)	Clinton	116,599	(37%)

Shreveport, Bossier City: Northwestern Louisiana, south of Little Rock and east of Dallas, is part of the Deep South. Unlike in New Orleans, most people here are Protestants, not Catholics. They are often tradition-minded, with names that are English or Scottish, not French. The tone is set not by wide-open Bourbon Street but by smaller Shreveport, which could be just another East Texas oil-patch town, albeit one that has its own, comparatively sedate, Mardi Gras. The countryside is agricultural, though there are some vestiges of large riverfront plantations. Roots here go back a long way. Natchitoches is the oldest town in Louisiana, founded by Louis Antoine Juchereau de St. Denis in 1714, and Shreveport was founded in the 1830s.

Natural gas was discovered in 1870. The nation's first gas pipeline was built from Caddo Field to Shreveport in 1908. However, it wasn't economical to drill until gas prices soared in 2000. Fracking at the Haynesville shale formation, which extends to east Texas, accounts for nearly 10 percent of the nation's natural gas production. That is the second-largest in the nation behind the Marcellus formation in Pennsylvania, where the deposits are shallower and thus cheaper to access. Oil fueled much of the region's economic growth in the 20th century. Riverboat gambling and the Port of Caddo-Bossier supplement the local economy. Benteler Steel and Tube, which operates a billion-dollar steel mill at the port, produces steel pipes for transporting oil and gas. Shreveport officials pursued options for their downtown Cross Bayou, including a possible sports complex. Local planners continued to advocate the long-discussed Interstate 69, which might bypass Shreveport en route from south Texas to Michigan. Barksdale Air Force Base in Bossier City is home of the Global Strike Command, which combined the nation's land-based nuclear missiles and long-range nuclear bombers under single leadership. In May 2020, the Command opened an innovation hub outside of the base to connect with inventors in business and academia.

Since 2010, the area has become a tale of two cities. Shreveport has been among the slowest-growing mid-sized cities in the nation, hovering around 200,000 since 1990 but dropping 7 percent to 187,000 from 2010 to 2019. Bossier City has grown 10 percent to 68,200 during the past decade. The Black population of Shreveport is 57 percent, compared with 28 percent in Bossier City, which has a lower poverty rate. Shreveport was the slowest-growing of the 515 cities in the nation, Wallet Hub reported in October 2019.

The 4th Congressional District of Louisiana drops down the western side of the state to the bayous. Nearly half the population is in Caddo Parish and suburban Bossier Parish east of Shreveport. The rest is scattered in rural areas. The district overall is 34 percent African American and it has had the lowest Republican support in the past three presidential elections of the five Republican-held districts in Louisiana. Joe Biden in 2020 won Caddo with 53 percent of the vote. But Donald Trump took 70 percent in Bossier and 61 percent overall, showing that the 4th is solidly Republican.

Julia Letlow (R)

Elected 2021, 1st term; Presbyterian; Widow, 2 children.

Professional Career: Director of Education and Patient Safety, Tulane University School of Medicine; Director of External Affairs and Strategic Communications, University of Louisiana at Monroe.

DC Office: 1408 LHOB- 20515, 202-225-8490, letlow.house.gov

State Offices: Alexandria, 318-319-6465; Amite, 985-284-5200; Monroe, 318-570-6440.

Committees: *Agriculture. Education & Labor*: Early Childhood, Elementary & Secondary Education; Higher Education & Workforce Investment.

Election Results

Election	Name (Party)	Vote (%)		Cand. Spent	Ind. Exp. Support	Ind. Exp. Oppose
2021 Special	Julia Letlow (R)	67,203	(65%)	$833,492		
	Sandra "Candy" Christophe (D)	28,255	(27%)	$126,522		
	Chad Conerly (R)	5,497	(5%)	$53,968		

Republican Julia Letlow of Louisiana, won a special election on March 20, 2021, to take the House seat to which her husband, Luke Letlow, had been elected. He died, at age 41, while hospitalized and being treated for COVID-19, on Dec. 29, 2020, five days before he was scheduled to join the House. Julia Letlow, who was making her first bid for public office, had a largely unencumbered victory in the strongly Republican district. She was elected less than three months after the death of her husband, who had faced a more competitive contest to win the seat in a runoff in early December.

Julia Letlow, a native of Monroe, got her bachelor's and master's degrees in speech communication from the University of Louisiana at Monroe. After earning her Ph.D. in communication at the University of South Florida, she returned to ULM to serve as the ombudsperson and special projects coordinator for the Provost and Vice President of Academic Affairs. She eventually became the executive director of external affairs and strategic communications for the University. Earlier, she held several administrative positions at the Tulane University School of Medicine in New Orleans. She and Luke had two young children.

In announcing her candidacy, Letlow said that she and her husband were a team and that she felt the need to carry on his work in Congress. "I am running to continue the mission Luke started -- to stand up for our Christian values, to fight for our rural agricultural communities, and to deliver real results to move our state forward," she said in a statement.

Running against 11 other candidates, Letlow won 65 percent of the vote. Candy Christophe, a Democrat, was the runner-up, with 27 percent. Letlow won 11 of the 12 parishes in the district and narrowly lost the remaining parish to Christophe, a clinical social worker and counselor. Letlow spent $837,000 to $126,000 for Christophe; Letlow's spending more than quadrupled the total reported by all of the other candidates combined. The brief campaign was uneventful and somber, given the sudden death of Luke Letlow, who had generated some excitement in his earlier victory.

Luke Letlow was a native of Start Louisiana, an unincorporated community in rural Richland Parish, where he continued to reside with his family. He got a bachelor's degree in computer information systems at Louisiana Tech University, where he was president of College Republicans. He was an aide to three House Republicans from Louisiana, including Rep. Ralph Abraham, who held the seat for three terms. With Gov. Bobby Jindal, Letlow served as director of intergovernmental affairs. In the private sector, he was director of government and community affairs for QEP Resources, an energy company based in Colorado.

When Abraham, a rural doctor, ran for Congress in 2014, Luke Letlow returned to Louisiana to serve as his campaign manager. Following that success, he transitioned to his boss's chief of staff. In 2019, Abraham ran for governor and finished third, with 24 percent of the vote, in the first round of voting; Democratic Gov. John Bel Edwards ultimately was reelected.

Following that defeat, when Abraham said he would honor his pledge to limit his service to three terms, Luke Letlow joined a field of nine candidates seeking his seat. He led the first round of voting with 33 percent to 17 percent for state Rep. Lance Harris, who edged out Candy Christophe by 428 votes to take the runner-up slot.

In their only debate during the month prior to the runoff vote, Harris described his success as a local businessman and said that Letlow was a political insider who spent most of his career working for other politicians. According to the (Monroe) News-Star, Harris criticized Letlow for "trying to take credit for things you haven't done." Letlow responded that he was "proud of his public service and questioned Harris's portrayal as an outsider as a three-term elected legislator" in Baton Rouge, where he chaired the House Republican delegation. Abraham actively supported his protégé during the campaign.

Luke Letlow won the December 5 runoff, 62%-38%. He won 23 of the 24 parishes, losing only the largest parish, Alexandria-based Rapides, which was Harris's base. Harris won that parish with 59 percent of the vote, a lead of about 3,000 votes. In Monroe-based Ouachita Parish, the second-largest in the district, Letlow got 70 percent, a lead of nearly 6,000 votes. Letlow's spending of more than $1 million exceeded the total of the other eight candidates in the contest.

Perhaps the biggest political threat that Julia Letlow faces is the hope of some Louisiana Democrats, with the support of Gov. Edwards, to draw a second congressional district in Louisiana with a majority of Black voters. Her district has the second largest share of African Americans, behind the New Orleans-based 2nd Congressional District. If Democrats are successful in creating a second African-American district, perhaps with judicial assistance, that might leave Letlow with the difficult option of facing Republican Rep. Mike Johnson, who likely would retain his larger base in neighboring Shreveport.

LA-5: Northeast Louisiana

Cook Partisan Voting Index: R+17

Population		Race and Ethnicity		Income	
Total	734,377	White	60.60%	Median Income	$41,257
Land area (sq. miles)	14,453	Black	35.10%	District Income Rank	429
Pop/ sq mi	50.81	Latino	2.70%	Poverty Rate	23.40%
Born in State	79.90%	Asian	0.80%	With health insurance	90.90%
		Two or more races	1.90%	Cash public assistance	1.60%
Age Groups		Other	1.60%	Food stamp/SNAP	18.70%
Under 18	23.40%				
18-34	22.20%	**Education**		**Work**	
35-64	38.10%	H.S grad or less	55.40%	White Collar	30.40%
Over 64	16.30%	Some college	26.40%	Sales and Service	43.30%
		College Degree, 4 yr	11.70%	Blue Collar	26.30%
Military		Post grad	6.50%	Government	17.80%
Veteran/ Active Duty	6.80%				

2020 Pres. Vote	Trump	215,066	(64%)	Biden	113,685	(34%)	
2016 Pres. Vote	Trump	205,258	(64%)	Clinton	110,259	(34%)	

Monroe, Alexandria: Northeast Louisiana is perhaps the least known part of the state. Along the Mississippi River and the Red River and their dozens of tributaries, it was plantation country before the Civil War, and there are African-American majorities today in many parishes. Away from the rivers, in the hill country, small farmers scratched out a living on land connected to parish courthouses by dusty lanes. Such was Winn Parish, where Huey Long, the transformative figure in modern Louisiana politics, was born in 1893 and from which he began his meteoric political career. Elected governor in 1928 and senator in 1930, he was a national figure when he was assassinated in 1935 in the new high-rise capitol he had built in Baton Rouge.

The 5th Congressional District of Louisiana contains much of this country, from the hills of Winn Parish to the several small Black-majority parishes along the Mississippi. About 35 percent of the population is African American. In this largely rural district, poverty is rampant. Along the river, the health of residents in Concordia is ranked among the "sickest" in the nation. The median income is in the bottom 2 percent of the nation. The biggest urban areas here are Monroe in the north and Alexandria to the south; each has slightly fewer than 50,000 people and is majority-Black. Monroe, in Ouachita Parish, is heavily Protestant. Alexandria, in Rapides Parish, sits at the northern extension of Cajun, Catholic Louisiana. The district also includes a few parishes east of the Mississippi River and on the outskirts of Baton Rouge.

This is one of the largest row-crop farming districts in the nation, including cotton, rice, corn and soybeans. Local farmers were battered by President Donald Trump's trade war, which stopped soybean sales in China, creating what one producer termed "the worst agricultural crisis to hit Louisiana" in a half-century. Even with Trump's bailouts of farmers and the limited trade deal with China in January 2020, Louisiana soybean farmers expected continuing damage from the sales that they already have lost, continuation of U.S. tariffs and the uncertain future about Chinese "commitments." Prior to the trade conflict, China purchased 60 percent of the soybeans produced in Louisiana. "When your No. 1 leaves, we [Louisiana] are impacted a little disproportionately as an export market," a farm bureau executive told the Lafayette Daily Advertiser. Soybeans are the state's second-largest crop, behind sugar cane. The area is a prime source of pine timber. After the federal government stunned local officials in 2010 by determining that the Red River's levees were no longer certified, officials in Rapides Parish used federal disaster relief funds and completed the repairs in 2017. Consistent with his strong showing in other rural districts across the nation, Donald Trump twice won this district with the same result, 64%-34%.

Garret Graves (R)

Elected 2014, 4th term, b. Jan 31, 1972; Baton Rouge, LA; AL University; LA Tech University, Att., 1995; American University, Att., 1996; Roman Catholic; Married (Carissa Graves); 3 children.

Professional Career: Staff, U.S. Sen. John Breaux; Staff, U.S. Rep. Billy Tauzin; Staff, U.S. Sen. David Vitter; Chairman, Coastal Protection & Restoration Authority of LA; Vice Chairman, Gulf Coast Ecosystem Restoration Task Force, U.S. EPA.

DC Office: 2402 RHOB 20515, 202-225-3901, Fax: 202-225-7313, garretgraves.house.gov

State Offices: Baton Rouge, 225-442-1731; Livingston, 225-686-4413; Thibodaux, 985-448-4103.

Committees: *Natural Resources*: Energy & Mineral Resources; Water, Oceans & Wildlife. *Select Committee on the Climate Crisis (RMM). Transportation & Infrastructure*: Aviation (RMM); Water Resources & Environment.

Group Ratings

	ADA	ACLU	AFL-CIO	LCV	COC	HAFA	ACU	CFG	FRC
2020	**	20%	**	5%	-	93%	87%	**	-
2019	10%	C	30%	17%	85%	C	89%	77%	100%

Almanac Ratings 2019-2020

	Economy	Social	Foreign	Composite
Liberal	25%	12%	27%	22%
Conservative	75%	88%	73%	78%

Key Votes of the 116th Congress

1. U.S./Mex./Can. trade deal	Y	5. Russia sanctions	Y	9. Firearms background checks	N
2. First Coronavirus response	Y	6. Troops in Syria	Y	10. Spending at the border	Y
3. HEROES Act	N	7. Veto arms sales to Saudis	N	11. Marijuana liberalized rules	N/A
4. CASH Act	N	8. Defense $$$, veto override	Y	12. Electoral College objections	Y

Election Results

Election	Name (Party)	Vote (%)		Cand. Spent	Ind. Exp. Support	Ind. Exp. Oppose
2020 General	Garret Graves (R)	265,706	(71%)	$1,374,188	$89,072	$750
	Dartanyon Williams (D)	95,541	(26%)	$96,381		
	Shannon Sloan (L)	9,732	(3%)			

Prior winning percentages: 2018 (70%), 2016 (63%), 2014 (62%)

Republican Garret Graves, who was elected in 2014 against the celebrated 87-year-old former governor and ex-federal convict Edwin Edwards, quickly became a player and made an impact in the House, especially on energy and environment issues. His substantial background on resource issues as a Louisiana official and as a Capitol Hill aide gave him influence from the start. Graves has signaled his interest in a possible statewide office.

Graves, a native of Baton Rouge, is an experienced politician and policy wonk, even though he is serving in his first elected office. He left home for Washington in his early 20s and began his political career as an intern for Democratic Sen. John Breaux. After a couple of months, he joined the office of GOP Rep. Billy Tauzin and worked his way up the ladder. He also worked for the House Energy and Commerce Committee, which Tauzin chaired, and later for Sen. David Vitter. All represented Louisiana.

In 2008, newly elected Gov. Bobby Jindal selected Graves to chair the Louisiana Coastal Protection and Restoration Authority and serve as his coastal adviser. Graves won praise for a $50 billion, 50-year master plan to promote coastal restoration and improve hurricane protection, as well as for coordinating the state's response to the 2010 Deepwater Horizon oil spill in the Gulf of Mexico. He was Jindal's point man in a Southeast Louisiana Flood Protection Authority-East lawsuit against more than 100 oil and gas companies, which alleged that decades of drilling and extraction had contributed to wetlands destruction. He said that he was responsible for $18 billion in projects to improve the economic, environmental and community resilience of the state.

After Republican Rep. Bill Cassidy ran successfully for the Senate, Graves stepped down from his state job and dove into the open-seat contest. In the all-party primary, he faced 11 other candidates, including eight Republicans. His best-known opponent was Democrat Edwards, who had been governor for 16 years and served eight years in federal prison on corruption charges. In the first round of voting in November, Edwards took 30 percent of the vote and Graves had 27 percent.

The colorful past exploits of Edwards vastly increased national attention on the contest, though he had been out of public office since 1996. He ran as a self-described New Deal Democrat and "old relic" who unabashedly favored government spending to help the district. Graves supported free-market principles and reduced government, and called for a halt to welfare in favor of incentivized hard work. He strove to convince voters that his familiarity with Washington would be a benefit but that he was not a "Washington insider." He outspent Edwards, $1.5 million to $400,000. No surprise, in this overwhelmingly Republican district, Graves won the runoff, 62%-38%.

With seats on the Natural Resources, and Transportation and Infrastructure committees, both of which are important to his district, Graves brought unusually broad experience in dealing with resource issues. His willingness to address climate change and its potential problems quickly gave him opportunities among House Republicans.

In 2016, Graves passed amendments to accelerate $150 million in projects in Louisiana, especially in areas that had suffered extensive flood damage a few months earlier. "We've been waiting decades for the Corps to build projects designed to fix [the Louisiana coast], but all we get is lip service about how it's 'still being considered.' Meanwhile, the coast continues to disappear and our communities become increasingly vulnerable," he said. He criticized Gov. John Bel Edwards for failing to deliver aid to flood victims—many of whom were constituents of Graves.

On the Water Resources and Environment Subcommittee, which he chaired in 2017-18, Graves was instrumental in the enactment of legislation in 2018 to authorize new water projects. The measure included $500 million in credit to Louisiana for coastal restoration and other water-related projects. "We've got to stop the stupidity of spending billions of dollars after disasters instead of millions before," Graves said. To combat coastal erosion, he pressed vigorously to maintain the revenue-sharing arrangement that Louisiana has with oil and gas companies.

Climbing the ladder of influence on the Transportation panel, Graves serves as top Republican on the Aviation Subcommittee. "I am excited about the opportunity to be on the front lines helping to modernize our technology and aviation system," he said, though he added—a bit defensively—"we are not backing off" interest in water priorities for Louisiana and the nation. In the 2020 water resources bill, he delivered a financial benefit for his home state when the committee approved his proposal for a significant reduction of the $100 million that Louisiana pays annually for its share of financing of strengthened levees in New Orleans that are being built on a delayed schedule following Hurricane Katrina in 2005.

When Democrats created a Select Committee on the Climate Crisis in 2019, Minority Leader Kevin McCarthy named Graves as the senior Republican. As a response to the Democrats' lengthy report, McCarthy and Graves submitted climate-related proposals that focused on promoting technology—with the goal of making the nation more competitive. The proposals included no new taxes or regulatory standards. "Democrats like sticks and we like carrots," Graves told the Washington Post.

In far less dramatic campaigns than his first contest, Graves has easily won reelection. Stating that he had no interest in challenging Democratic Gov. John Bel Edwards in 2019, Graves "was thought to be looking beyond 2019 for a possible gubernatorial run," WWL-TV of New Orleans reported in December 2018. In 2020, Graves was reelected without major-party opposition.

LA-6: Baton Rouge area

Cook Partisan Voting Index: R+18

Population		Race and Ethnicity		Income	
Total	803,704	White	68.50%	Median Income	$65,549
Land area (sq. miles)	4,034	Black	25.20%	District Income Rank	206
Pop/ sq mi	199.24	Latino	5.20%	Poverty Rate	13.60%
Born in State	78.30%	Asian	2.30%	With health insurance	90.40%
		Two or more races	1.40%	Cash public assistance	1.10%
Age Groups		Other	2.60%	Food stamp/SNAP	9.40%
Under 18	23.40%				
18-34	25.50%	**Education**		**Work**	
35-64	36.80%	H.S grad or less	42.70%	White Collar	39.20%
Over 64	14.40%	Some college	27.10%	Sales and Service	37.20%
		College Degree, 4 yr	19.90%	Blue Collar	23.60%
Military		Post grad	10.30%	Government	16.10%
Veteran/ Active Duty	5.80%				

2020 Pres. Vote	Trump	250,255	(64%)	Biden	135,049	(34%)	
2016 Pres. Vote	Trump	230,701	(65%)	Clinton	110,394	(31%) Johnson	8,531 (2%)

Baton Rouge: Baton Rouge sits on a cultural fault line in Louisiana, the boundary between the French-speaking, Catholic Cajun country and the heavily Baptist region to the north. Historically, it was part of the Florida Parishes, the territory east of the Mississippi River and north of Lake Pontchartrain that was not included in the Louisiana Purchase in 1803. It still belonged to Spain, until the locals rebelled and declared their own Republic of West Florida in 1810. Then it quickly became part of Louisiana and the United States.

Today, Baton Rouge is the center of a metropolitan area of about 800,000 people. It sits on the east bank of the Mississippi and is the largest inland deep-water port located on the river. In September 2020, the Army Corps of Engineers said it had begun dredging the river south of Baton Rouge to deepen the ship channel from 45 feet to 50 feet—chiefly to accommodate larger ships that now use the widened Panama Canal; projected completion is in 2024. More than 50 percent of the nation's corn and soybean exports to foreign market are shipped through this stretch of the mighty river.

Local features are the old Gothic-style capitol, where Huey Long took office, and the three-story Art Deco capitol, which he had built and where he died at the hands of an assassin in 1935. Also here is Louisiana State University, another Long legacy. The region benefits from the research productivity of LSU's main campus and has been called the "Creative Capital of the South," because of its success in creating public-private partnerships in high-growth sectors.

"Environmental racism" is a growing concern for the many low-income African Americans who reside along the Mississippi River and suffer the effects of its huge petro-chemical plants. With new facilities perhaps doubling the toxic hazards along what some describe as "cancer alley," local citizens' groups have fought back, according to a Pro Publica report in November 2019. The 85-mile stretch between Baton Rouge and New Orleans, which includes about 150 fossil fuel and petrochemical plants, includes seven of the 10 census tracts with the highest cancer risk in the nation, Rolling Stone reported in October 2019.

The 6th Congressional District of Louisiana includes the majority of residents in East and West Baton Rouge parishes. The 6th surrounds both north and south of the 2nd District—and the Mississippi River—from Baton Rouge to New Orleans; in some places, the river is the boundary between the two districts. The 6th District extends south to Thibodeaux and parts of the Bayous. Researchers revealed in 2018 that they had discovered the site of a mass grave in Thibodeaux, which likely resulted from a racial massacre in 1887 when a mob of white men killed at least 30 Blacks who worked at a sugar plantation. The burial site was not recorded at the time, though the researchers benefited from more than a century of informal oral histories. In 2016, writer John DeSantis published a book, Thibodeaux Massacre, with an account of the incident. With Baton Rouge's Black neighborhoods largely in the New Orleans-based 2nd District, the 6th's Black population is 25 percent, which places the district solidly in the GOP camp. In 2020, President Donald Trump won the district, 64%-35%.

MAINE

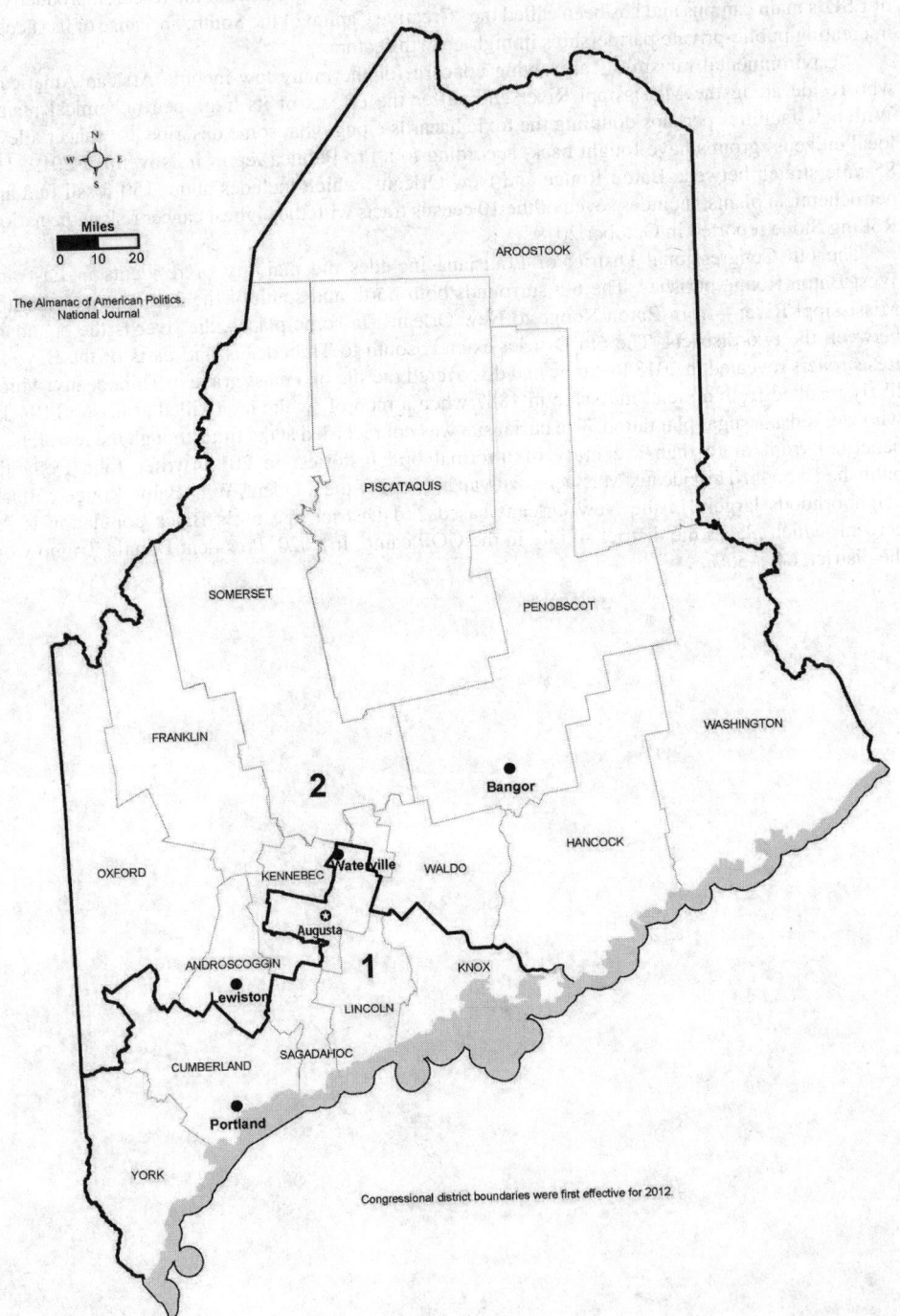

The Almanac of American Politics.
National Journal

Miles
0   10   20

Congressional district boundaries were first effective for 2012.

Voters in Maine, never a party-regimented bunch, seem comfortable with ticket-splitting these days. In 2020, Maine voters gave Joe Biden a wide edge in the presidential race, but for the second straight election, Donald Trump won an electoral vote from the state's 2nd Congressional District, even as the same district was reelecting Democratic Rep. Jared Golden. Meanwhile, voters returned Republican Susan Collins to the Senate—the only successful Senate candidate in a state where the other party won the presidential vote.

The phrase "up in Maine" conveys some of the state's distinctive personality— ornery, contrary-minded, almost bullheaded, and rough-hewn. In the far northeast corner of the United States, Maine is the state geographically closest to Europe, but it was not heavily settled until the mid-19th century, by people moving from its south and west, not the usual direction of American migrations. Maine grew in a rush, and then mostly stopped. There were 600,000 people there in 1860, but the population dipped after the Civil War— many soldiers did not return— and it did not top 1 million until the 1970s. In the urbanizing and rapidly changing country of the early 20th century, Maine was famous for its pointed firs, hardy moose and steady habits, with a few dozen small factory towns and paper-mill hamlets, yet nothing like a major metropolis.

Today, Maine is the Whitest state in the nation, but it " was actually much more racially diverse in the 19th century," historian Kate McMahon told Maine Public. As shipbuilding turned from wood to steel, many jobs held by Black residents who were working as coopers, a relatively well-paid job, were phased out; finding employment in other, growing manufacturing sectors was difficult. In 1912, the state razed every home in the interracial community of Malaga Island, and in the 1920s, the KKK rose in influence; many African Americans left. Today, only 1.4 percent of Maine residents are Black, but one of the few signs of population growth in the state comes from immigrants, many of them asylum seekers from Africa. Between 2011 and 2016, three-quarters of the population growth in the state's largest city, Portland, came from foreign-born residents; they have provided economic dynamism, but city officials have also expressed concern about over-taxed resources.

Despite the Yankee work ethic, Maine has repeatedly found itself at the bottom of various assessments of economic drivers. In the Maine Economic Growth Council's 2019 analysis, the state received " red flags" for low rankings on research and development expenditures, reading and math scores, the cost of health care, and transportation infrastructure. The state's tax code is archaic, with a relatively high corporate tax rate. But the biggest challenge facing Maine is demographic: The state is old. It recently passed Florida as the state with the largest percentage of residents over 65, and about a third of physicians in the state are older than 60. Overall population growth in the state has been just 1.7 percent since 2010, and government projections suggest that just one of every five localities will grow in population by 2034.

All this has put a crimp in economic development. Maine's GDP, when adjusted for inflation, was only 8.8 percent higher in 2019 than it was in 2007, prior to the Great Recession; that's far behind the nation's 22 percent growth over the same period. The median household income is about $7,000 below the national average—much closer to West Virginia than to neighboring New Hampshire.

A big part of the reason has been the shrinking of the state's blue-collar job base. Over the past 30 years, Maine has lost jobs in shoe manufacturing, chicken processing, papermaking, and leather processing. Scratching small Maine boiling potatoes out of the soil of sprawling Aroostook County has gotten harder, even more now that some high schools in northern Maine no longer shut down at the end of September for "harvest break" so farmers can pull their dwindling crop from the ground before it freezes. Timber has also struggled, falling from 14.1 million tons of harvest in 2014 to 11.8 million tons in 2018. The following year, a 130-year-old pulp mill in Old Town got a new lease on life when a major Chinese company, Nine Dragons Paper, purchased it, seeking U.S. pulp for cardboard boxes and packing material. The state's once prominent cod fishery has struggled due to overfishing, environmental factors, and regulatory restrictions, recording the smallest revenues in more than half a century. And while it has a long-term contract to build 21 Arleigh Burke-class Navy destroyers, Bath Iron Works, once the state's largest private employer, now trails Maine Health, Hannaford supermarkets and Walmart.

Gains have come in call centers, health care to serve the state's aging population, and tourism, which in "Vacationland" employed one-sixth of the state workforce in 2019 and generated $6.5 billion for the economy. But the sector was hit hard by the coronavirus pandemic, which canceled cruise ship stops and put a damper on visits to Acadia National Park and Bar Harbor. In 2020, cannabis beat out potatoes, milk, hay, and blueberries in agricultural sales. Lobster—an iconic Maine species—has had a roller-coaster ride. As waters further south have warmed, Maine's have remained below the 70 degrees lobsters need to thrive. Sales to China soared as its middle class came to view the crustacean as a dining status symbol; the lobster's red hue was considered particularly auspicious. But Trump's trade actions against China inspired counter-tariffs, resulting in a sudden plunge of purchases from China; Canada picked up many of those sales. Eventually, the U.S. struck deals with Europe and China, but the industry suffered again in 2020 as restaurants took a nosedive due to coronavirus-related lockdowns. Maine ranks high in air and water quality, and it has set a goal of 100 percent renewable energy by 2050. But the warming waters have kept whales away (or killed them) and, indirectly, hurt tourism.

In politics, Maine has a reputation for quirkiness. Until 1958, it held state elections in September, a date originally chosen because it followed the state's early harvest. Starting in 1840, long before the advent of public opinion polls, the election results were taken as a gauge of national sentiment—hence the saying, "As Maine goes, so goes the nation." In reality, Maine didn't vote like the rest of the country most of the time. In 1936, only Maine and Vermont voted for Republican Alf Landon over Democrat Franklin D. Roosevelt, prompting Roosevelt's campaign manager to wisecrack, "As Maine goes, so goes Vermont." Maine was known for its flinty Yankee Republicanism and for Prohibition; it banned liquor in 1851, after which other states enacted "Maine laws." Since voting four times against FDR, it has given its statewide electoral votes to the loser in the close presidential elections of 1948, 1960, 1968, 1976, 2000, 2004 and 2016—a record equaled by no other state.

Maine cast the nation's highest percentages for third-party presidential candidate Ross Perot—30 percent in 1992 and 14 percent in 1996. In 1974, it elected independent James Longley, a former Republican, as governor; in 1994 and 1998, it elected independent Angus King, a former Democrat, as governor. In 2010, it came close to electing independent Eliot Cutler as governor. The winner was Republican Paul LePage, an outspoken conservative who eked out a victory with 38 percent to Cutler's 36 percent. Perhaps tiring of seeing officials elected by pluralities, voters in 2016 approved via ballot measure a system of ranked-choice voting, in which last-place finishers' second-choice votes are reallocated to the remaining candidates until one candidate reaches 50 percent. Republicans fought the system, but the courts upheld it, and ranked-choice voting was used in party primaries and in federal elections for the first time in 2018.

The state's allocation of electoral votes by congressional district, a rule it shares with Nebraska, has made Maine, and especially its 2nd District, aggressively contested terrain. Trump saw promise in the 2nd district's heavily white, working-class electorate, and in 2016, the district swung heavily in his direction. He won nine counties in the state, eight more than Mitt Romney had won four years earlier. Then, in the 2018 midterms, Maine shifted back, electing Democrat Janet Mills as governor, thanks to fatigue with LePage's cantankerous tenure. In addition, the 2nd District ousted incumbent GOP Rep. Bruce Poliquin, thanks to an edge in ranked-choice votes for Golden, the Democrat.

The 2020 election produced a delicately balanced result. Biden won the state again for the Democrats, tripling Hillary Clinton's three-point margin in 2016, flipping Kennebec County (Augusta), and expanding the Democratic margins in York County (adjoining southern New Hampshire), Cumberland County (Portland), and Hancock County (Bar Harbor) by between six and 10 points. Yet Trump repeated his victory in the 2nd to gain one electoral vote, and Collins won the closely watched Senate race by a surprisingly large nine-point margin, losing only two counties and outrunning Trump by almost 57,000 votes. Meanwhile, in the 2nd District, Golden was reelected by six points even as Trump was winning the district by eight. Once more, Maine had managed to confound the nation's political patterns.

Population		Race and Ethnicity		Income	
Total	1,344,212	White	94.00%	Median Income	58,924
Land area (sq. miles)	30,843	Black	1.60%	State Income Rank	35 out of 50
Pop/ sq mi	43.58	Latino	1.70%	Poverty Rate	10.90%
Born in state	61.60%	Asian	1.70%	With health insurance	92.00%
		Two or more races	2.10%	Cash public assistance	2.40%
Age Groups		Other	1.10%	Food stamp/SNAP	15.3%
Under 18	18.30%				
18-34	20.10%	**Education**		**Work**	
35-64	40.20%	H.S grad or less	38.20%	White Collar	40.10%
Over 64	21.30%	Some college	28.60%	Sales and Service	37.80%
		College Degree, 4 yr	20.80%	Blue Collar	22.20%
Military		Post grad	12.40%	Government	13.80%
Veteran/ Active Duty	9.10%				

Presidential Politics

2020 Primary (D)	Biden (D)	68,729(34%)	Sanders (D)	66,826(33%)	Warren (D)	32,055(16%)	
	Bloomberg (D)	24,294(12%)					
2016 Caucus (D)	Sanders (D)	2,231(64%)	Clinton (D)	1,232(36%)			
2016 Caucus (R)	Cruz (R)	8,550(46%)	Trump (R)	6,070(33%)	Kasich (R)	2,270(12%)	
	Rubio (R)	1,492 (8%)					
2020 Pres. Vote	Biden (D)	435,072(53%)	Trump (R)	360,770(44%)			
2016 Pres. Vote	Clinton (D)	357,735(48%)	Trump (R)	335,593(45%)	Johnson (L)	38,105 (5%)	
	Stein (G)	14,251 (2%)					

Maine is one of only two states that voted against Franklin Roosevelt in all four of his elections (Vermont was the other). However, since 1992, Maine has voted for a Democratic presidential candidate eight straight times. In 2020, Joe Biden defeated Donald Trump 53%-44%, but the Republican still managed to win one of the state's four Electoral College votes, as he had in 2016. That's because Maine, like Nebraska, allocates one electoral vote to the winner of each of its two congressional districts. The statewide winner receives the other two. The 1st District, which includes Portland and Augusta, is the more liberal of the two. Biden took the 1st with 60 percent. The 2nd District is home to old mill towns, covers the vast rural interior of the state and includes Bangor and Lewiston. The voters of this economically depressed region were drawn to Trump, just like they were to the blunt and combative former GOP Gov. Paul LePage. Overall, Trump carried the 2nd District 52%-45%, not far from his 51%-41% margin in 2016. Biden won seven of the eight counties along the Atlantic coast; Trump won seven of the eight inland counties.

Maine held its first-ever presidential primary in March 1996, hoping to attract the candidates' early attention. That tactic didn't work, and the state abolished its presidential primary for 2004. In 2016, Republicans held their caucus on March 5, a Saturday, and the Democrats caucused the next day. Texas Sen. Ted Cruz bested Trump, 46%-33%, even though LePage had endorsed the New Yorker. Vermont Sen. Bernie Sanders defeated Clinton 64%-36% in state delegates allocated by the caucuses. In 2020, the state switched back to a primary, held on Super Tuesday March 3. Biden edged Sanders 34%-33%, a major upset and one of many disappointing Super Tuesday results for Sanders that turned him from frontrunner into underdog. Sanders was heavily favored after his 2016 showing, but as in other states that abandoned their caucuses, he saw his support dip.

Congressional Districts

117th Congress Lineup	2D	116th Congress Lineup	2D

Maine has had a bipartisan advisory commission that draws up a redistricting plan, which the legislature and governor can consider, but a state statute stipulated that redistricting must be approved by a two-thirds vote in the legislature and delayed until the third year after the census. In practice, that did not make much difference. Since Maine lost its third congressional district following the 1960 census, the lines between the largely rural northern district and the Portland-based southern district have shifted only slightly. Those procedures might change this time, with Democrats in firm control of state government and seeking ways to strengthen their hand in the Republican-leaning 2nd District.

In 2011, two citizens brought a lawsuit in federal court arguing that the timetable violated the Constitution because it left in place for one election districts that were not of equal population. Although the census showed the two districts' populations differed by only 8,669 people, the court ordered adoption of a new plan. The advisory commission voted 8-7 to submit the Democratic plan with minimal shifts. Harsh words were exchanged, but when the legislature met, it adopted the Democratic plan with only three dissenting votes and Gov. Paul LePage signed it into law. Then the 2nd District in 2014 elected the state's first Republican to the House in 20 years.

Now, a shift of perhaps 10,000 persons from the 1st to the 2nd will make them equal in size. Democrats could strengthen their base in the 2nd, by shifting a few Democratic towns from what has become their secure 1st, especially with the increased national stakes in redistricting.

Janet Mills (D)

Elected 2018, term expires 2023, 1st term; b. Dec. 30, 1947, Farmington; Colby College, Att.; University of Massachusetts, B.A.; University of Maine, J.D.; Unknown; Widow; 5 stepchildren.

Elected Office: ME House, 2002-2008; ME Attorney General, 2009-2011, 2013-2018.

Professional Career: District Attorney, Franklin & Oxford Counties, 1980-1995; Attorney.

Office: One State House Station Augusta, 04333-0001; 207-287-3531; Fax: 207-287-1034

State Legislature: Senate: 21D, 14R **House:** 88D, 56R, 5I, 1O, 1V

Election Results

Election	Name (Party)	Vote (%)
2018 General	Janet Mills (D)	320,962 (51%)
	Shawn Moody (R)	272,311 (43%)
	Teresea Hayes (I)	37,268 (6%)
2018 Primary	Janet Mills (D)	63,384 (54%)
	Adam Cote (D)	53,866 (46%)

Maine voters in 2018 chose Democrat Janet Mills, a long-serving attorney general and state legislator, to move past the eight-year tenure of Republican Gov. Paul LePage, who was known for his consistent conservatism and, perhaps even more so, for his irascible statements. Once in office, Mills and the Democratic legislature enacted a lengthy and mostly liberal agenda, but LePage lurked in the wings for an expected 2022 challenge.

Mills grew up in rural Aroostook County, the granddaughter of farmers who grew the region's signature potato crop. Her political roots ran deep. Mills' grandfather served two terms in the state Senate and her father, S. Peter Mills Jr., was the Republican floor leader in the state House and later served as a U.S. attorney. Her father supported Rep. Margaret Chase Smith's run for the Senate, forging lifelong bonds between the two families. One day during her 1948 Senate campaign, Smith stopped by the Mills house and held the future governor, then just six months old, on her lap, reporter Colin Woodard wrote. Smith "was a woman of both grit and integrity who held high public office with grace and vision," Mills said in 2009. "She held her ground and didn't take any grief from anyone, even from presidents and foreign leaders." Smith served in the Senate from 1949 to 1973, becoming the first woman to serve in both chambers. Mills emulated Smith's trailblazing accomplishments, becoming the state's first woman to serve as a criminal prosecutor, a district attorney, attorney general, and now as governor. She co-founded the Maine Women's Lobby, which worked on behalf of battered women.

At 14, Mills underwent surgery for scoliosis that kept her in a body cast for most of the year. She received her bachelor's degree from the University of Massachusetts-Boston and her law degree from the University of Maine. During her university years, she told Woodard, she was shaped by the broader cultural tumult, which "encouraged my somewhat rebellious nature" and pushed her to become a Democrat. She spent the Watergate summer of 1974 interning in the American Civil Liberties Union's Washington office, and then at the Center for Law and Social Policy the following summer. Mills prosecuted criminal cases, including murders, for the attorney general's office, then was appointed—and was later reelected four times—to the post of district attorney for Androscoggin, Franklin and Oxford counties. Mills survived allegations of drug use and abuse of office; they were never substantiated and she called them politically motivated. In 1994 Mills lost a primary for the 2nd Congressional District (she lost to future Democratic Gov. John Baldacci) but in 2002 won a state House seat formerly held by her father. In 2008, the legislature named her attorney general—Maine's system for filling this post is unique—and she remained in the job until she won the governorship, except for 2011 and 2012, when the GOP controlled the levers of appointment.

In this position, Mills had regular run-ins with LePage, a larger-than-life character in a small state. LePage was the oldest son of 18 children in a poverty-stricken, dysfunctional family; at times he slept in hallways, cars and even a strip joint. He became general manager of Marden's Surplus and Salvage, a Maine-based discount store chain, in 1996, then served as a city council member and mayor of Waterville. When LePage entered the 2010 governor's race, he led a seven-candidate Republican field with 37 percent and eked out a victory in the three-way general election with 38 percent; he would win a second term in 2014 by a more comfortable 48%-43% margin. In office, LePage pursued both fiscally and socially conservative policies, but he had a knack for irritating residents with his off-the-cuff remarks, often in a racial context. In his second term, LePage revealed that he'd been keeping a three-ring binder with mug shots of drug dealers, 90 percent of whom, he said, were Black or Hispanic, something official statistics called into question. Mills refused to represent LePage's positions several times, including when he sought to appeal a ruling on cuts to Medicaid benefits, in a case involving aid to asylum seekers, and a case about the closure of a Washington County correctional facility.

Sensing opportunity to ride a backlash against LePage, Maine Democrats flocked to the gubernatorial primary in 2018. They included veteran and attorney Adam Cote, activist and attorney Betsy Sweet, and former House speaker and family therapist Mark Eves. Mills and Cote were considered the more moderate candidates in the field. Generally, though, the candidates overlapped on many issues. The primary was decided using the ranked-choice voting system that residents had implemented through a ballot measure. In the initial voting, Mills got 33 percent, followed by Cote with 28 percent, Sweet with 16 percent, and Eves with 14 percent. After the lower-finishing candidates' votes were reassigned to the voter's second-choice candidates, Mills crossed the 50 percent threshold and was declared the winner eight days after the election. On the Republican side, businessman Shawn Moody won with an outright majority in the initial vote. Moody, an independent until 2017, was an entrepreneur who built a chain of collision-repair centers. Moody styled himself a candidate who would carry on LePage's policies in a less-confrontational style. But Mills benefited from an energized Democratic electorate, and she leveraged her past battles with LePage to draw a clear contrast. On Election Day, Mills received 51 percent, defeating Moody with 43 percent and state Treasurer Teresa Hayes with 6 percent.

Building on record surpluses from the strong economy, Mills had a productively progressive legislative year in 2019. On her first day, she ordered state officials to implement the long-delayed Medicaid expansion under the Affordable Care Act, which had been approved by voters in 2017 but blocked by LePage. She also scuttled LePage's proposed Medicaid work requirement. Mills signed legislation that legalized medically assisted suicide, allowed nurse practitioners and physician assistants to perform abortions, ended philosophical opt-outs for vaccinations, banned Styrofoam to-go containers, replaced Columbus Day with Indigenous Peoples' Day, and prohibited schools from using Native American mascots. She also strengthened the state's renewable energy requirements for electricity generation and approved a block grant program to increase solar infrastructure. She was even invited to speak at the United Nations about the state's response to climate change. Even with all that, Mills took heat from her left for cutting deals with Republicans on gun policy and paid time off, and for resisting tax increases. Meanwhile, her efforts to secure bond measures for broadband expansion and conservation came to naught. In 2020, her veto of a measure to allow sports betting in the state was upheld by the legislature.

In 2020, the coronavirus pandemic overshadowed everything else. Mills instituted emergency powers and eventually a mask mandate, and during the summer, she mandated a 72-hour quarantine requirement for travelers from every state except New Hampshire, Vermont, Connecticut, New Jersey and New York, a blow to the state's vital tourism industry. Mills' aggressive approach on the virus drew complaints from Republicans and from Maine's more rural areas. President Donald Trump amplified these during a visit to the state, where he was greeted by LePage. "You have a governor that doesn't know what she's doing, and she's like a dictator," Trump said. But the virus' potential to spread came into clear focus in August, when a 62-person wedding in East Millinocket was shown to result in at least 123 infections, reaching as far as a jail complex 200 miles to the south. In all, though, Maine wasn't hit as hard as most states in 2020, ending the year in the bottom 10 states for per capita cases.

LePage, who had taken a summer job bartending in Boothbay Harbor, appears likely to run against Mills in 2022.

Susan Collins (R)

Elected 1996, term expires 2026, 5th term, b. Dec 07, 1952; Caribou, ME; St. Lawrence University, B.A., 1975; Roman Catholic; Married (Thomas Daffron).

Professional Career: Legislative Aide, Senator Bill Cohen, 1975-1987; Staff Director, Senate Subcommittee on Oversight Government Management, 1981-1987; Commissioner, MA Department of Professional & Financial Regulation, 1987-1992; New England Regional Director, U.S. Small Business Administration, 1992-1993; Executive Director, Center for Family Business, Husson College, 1994-1996.

DC Office: 413 DSOB 20510, 202-224-2523, Fax: 202-224-2693, collins.senate.gov

State Offices: Augusta, 207-622-8414; Bangor, 207-945-0417; Biddeford, 207-283-1101; Caribou, 207-493-7873; Lewiston, 207-784-6969; Portland, 207-780-3575.

Committees: *Aging. Appropriations*: Agriculture, Rural Development, FDA & Related Agencies; Commerce, Justice, Science & Related Agencies; Department of Defense; Energy & Water Development; Military Construction & Veteran Affairs & Related Agencies; Transportation, HUD & Related Agencies (RMM). *Health, Education, Labor & Pensions*: Children & Families; Primary Health & Retirement Security (RMM). *Intelligence*.

Group Ratings

	ADA	ACLU	AFL-CIO	LCV	COC	HAFA	ACU	CFG	FRC
2020	-	38%	-	46%	-	18%	43%	-	-
2019	50%	C	58%	64%	95%	C	44%	17%	33%

Almanac Ratings 2019-2020

	Economy	Social	Foreign	Composite
Liberal	34%	34%	9%	26%
Conservative	66%	66%	91%	74%

Key Votes of the 116th Congress

1. EPA clean energy rules	Y	5. Russia sanctions	Y	9. Barr as Atty. General	Y
2. U.S./Mex./Can. trade deal	Y	6. Troops in SYR, AFG	Y	10. Spending at the border	Y
3. Cut unemployment benefits	N	7. Veto arms sales to Saudis	Y	11. Coney Barrett to Sup. Ct.	N
4. Shelton to Fed Reserve	N	8. Defense $$$, veto override	Y	12. Electoral College objections	N

Election Results

Election	Name (Party)	Vote (%)	Cand. Spent	Ind. Exp. Support	Ind. Exp. Oppose
2020 General	Susan Collins (R)........................	417,645 (51%)	$27,662,329	$8,442,908	$50,111,875
	Sara Gideon (D)............................	347,223 (42%)	$54,200,870	$13,813,773	$41,861,609
2020 Primary	Susan Collins (R)........................	87,375 (99%)			

Prior winning percentages: 2014 (68%), 2008 (61%), 2002 (58%), 1996 (49%)

When Republican Susan Collins, Maine's senior senator, won reelection in November 2020, she returned to Capitol Hill with her already considerable influence as a swing vote poised to reach its zenith. Shortly after her victory, she received a call from a former Senate colleague: incoming President Joe Biden, for whom Collins' backing could be crucial in the Senate's narrow partisan divide. She also received a call from another Joe: West Virginia Sen. Joe Manchin, who, like Collins, is one of the chamber's few remaining centrists. According to Politico, Manchin, a Democrat who had crossed party lines to endorse Collins for reelection, asked her: "What can we do next? How can we work together?" The answer was not long in coming, as Collins and Manchin—in a harbinger of what lay in store in the new Congress—were at the center of a bipartisan group of senators who, during a lame duck session, helped break the months-long stalemate over a second round of economic stimulus in response to the COVID-19 pandemic.

A member of a nearly extinct breed on the Hill, the moderate Republican, Collins had herself appeared headed for political extinction until the very end of the 2020 election cycle. Her approval ratings at home, the second highest of any senator in the country at the outset of her fourth term in 2015, had sunk to the lowest of any member of the Senate by the end of 2019—the backwash of her crucial vote for President Donald Trump's Supreme Court nomination of Brett Kavanaugh a year earlier. For months, Collins' Democratic opponent, Maine House Speaker Sara Gideon, ran 4-5 percentage points ahead in the polls. Buttressed by a flood of out-of-state contributions, Gideon outraised the incumbent by more than 2-1. Even many Republican strategists were quietly writing off the contest—deemed the most negative 2020 Senate race in the nation by the Wesleyan Media Project—until the very end.

But on Election Day, Collins came out on top 51%-42%. While short of her double-digit victory margins in prior races, she ran 7 points ahead of Trump as Biden cruised to an easy win in Maine. Postmortems attributed her come-from-behind win in large measure to a quarter of a century of delivering constituent services and bringing home the bacon in the small state. "Collins ran a back-to-the-basics campaign, wielding her incumbency advantages while defining the much less well-known Gideon negatively," Amy Fried, chair of the University of Maine's political science department, wrote in Talking Points Memo. Although Gideon relentlessly sought to tie Collins to Democrats' leading betesnoire—Trump and Senate GOP Leader Mitch McConnell—the Bangor Daily News observed: "Her comeback was buoyed by split-ticket voters who rebuked deep nationalization of the election and had lingering goodwill for Collins dating back to before her party's takeover by [Trump], whom she backed at times, bucked at others and contorted to avoid."

Collins declined repeatedly to say whether she would vote for Trump in 2020. It was a marked shift from her very public refusal in 2016, in a Washington Post op-ed column, to cast her ballot for him; she wrote in the name of then-House Speaker Paul Ryan instead. The next year, she was one of just three Republicans to join Senate Democrats in blocking Trump's efforts to repeal the Affordable Care Act. While she was literally greeted with applause at the airport in Bangor Maine afterward, her support of Kavanaugh, who was accused of sexual assault, in late 2018 released waves of pent-up anger and frustration from the left. Although vote rankings by Five Thirty Eight showed her less supportive of Trump than any other Senate Republican, detractors complained Collins exhibited independence primarily on occasions when the White House and Senate GOP leadership didn't need her vote. As The New York Times put it shortly before Election Day 2020: "She has become a national punchline among liberals for what they see as her toothless tut-tutting of President Trump, whom she is invariably 'concerned' about."

Collins was unfavorably compared to her professed role model, the late Maine Sen. Margaret Chase Smith, who stood up to the demagoguery of her fellow Republican Wisconsin Sen. Joseph McCarthy in the 1950s. "I've had so many Margaret Chase Smith moments," Collins retorted to the Times, citing her Affordable Care Act vote as well as opposing Trump's diversion of funds to build his trademark wall on the southern border. She vehemently rebuked criticism that she had changed during her years in office—and some independent observers agreed that what actually had shifted was the political terrain beneath her in an era of ever-intensifying partisan polarization. "It's not that Collins has changed," Mark Brewer, another University of Maine political science professor, told the Washington Post. "The political environment has changed around her."

The only congressional Republican from New England, Collins in January 2021 became the longest serving Republican woman in Senate history—surpassing a record previously held by Smith. (Collins occupies the Senate seat Smith once held and sits at the same Senate floor desk that Smith used.) Throughout the 2020 campaign, Collins told audiences, "With your help, when I'm reelected, a year later I become the chairman of the Senate Appropriations Committee." That depended on several pieces falling into place—including the retirement of the committee's senior Republican, 86-year-old Richard Shelby of Alabama in 2022, as well as the GOP regaining the Senate majority that it lost in the 2020 elections. In February 2021, Shelby announced his exit plan.

Collins grew up in Caribou, about as far northeast as you can get in the continental United States —and closer to the capitals of the Canadian provinces of New Brunswick and Quebec than to Maine's capital, Augusta. Her family has been in the lumber business since 1844 and active politically as well: Collins' father, grandfather, and great-grandfather served in the Maine Legislature. Both parents were mayors of Caribou, and her mother chaired the board of trustees of the University of Maine System.

In an insular state where residents lacking multigenerational roots often are referred to as being "from away," Collins in the closing weeks of the 2020 race depicted Gideon as an outsider—a message reinforced in ads for the Collins campaign by a popular retired TV sportscaster. "I grew up in Caribou; I've lived in Bangor for 26 years. My family's been in Maine for generations. She's been in Maine for about 15 years. … That's a big difference in our knowledge of the state," Collins told Politico, alluding to Gideon growing up in Rhode Island. Fried wrote in Talking Points Memo: "Something else that made Gideon seem 'other' was her parentage, which included a father who immigrated from India. The Collins campaign certainly never raised this. But the issue showed up in social media posts with comments about Gideon's skin color." The latest census figures show Maine's population as nearly 95 percent white.

Collins' got her first taste of Washington as a high school senior, when she visited the capital as part of a Senate youth program. Smith, then the Senate's only woman, spent nearly two hours talking with her. Another role model was William Cohen, her Senate predecessor and her boss for more than a decade. She interned for Cohen during the summer of 1974, when, as a freshman member of the House Judiciary Committee, he and several other Republicans voted to impeach President Richard Nixon. Cohen hired Collins a year later when she graduated from St. Lawrence University. Cohen moved to the Senate in 1978, and Collins spent six years as staff director of a Governmental Affairs Committee subpanel that Cohen chaired. As senator, Collins would find herself running the full committee: Before stepping down in 2013 because of internal Republican term limits, she spent a decade as chair or ranking member of the now-renamed Homeland Security and Governmental Affairs Committee.

In 1986, Collins returned to Maine to run the state's Department of Professional and Financial Regulation, later serving as regional administrator of the federal Small Business Administration. In 1994, after winning the Republican gubernatorial nomination, she ran third in a three-way general contest won by independent Angus King—now her Senate colleague. Two years later, Cohen announced his retirement. Collins played up her similarities to Cohen and then-GOP Sen. Olympia Snowe. While calling for a balanced-budget amendment and a line-item veto, Collins pledged to serve no more than two terms—a promise she broke in 2008 when she successfully sought a third term.

Collins was opposed by former Democratic Gov. Joseph Brennan. He criticized Collins for supporting repeal of the 1994 assault weapons ban. At the time, there were more gun owners per capita in Maine than any state except Alaska, and gun control was anathema in much of the state's rural areas, where Collins had grown up. But restrictions on firearms were more popular in the state's urban areas to the south, which Brennan had represented as a House member. Brennan cut into Collins' lead with his attacks on her gun stance—but she outraised him significantly and won 49%-44%.

After the 2012 Newton Connecticut shooting in which 28 people, including the gunman, died, Collins voted against a proposed assault weapons ban but became one of only four Republicans to break with her party and support a measure to expand background checks during firearms purchases. After that proposal and similar ones failed to gain passage, Collins in mid-2016—after the Orlando Florida nightclub shooting in which 50 people were killed, including the gunman—sought to broker a compromise. Her bill received solid Democratic support and peeled off seven of her GOP colleagues. But while it survived a procedural vote, it failed to advance. The gun control issue was emblematic of a broader evolution for Collins: While initially more conservative than her Maine colleague,

Snowe, she eventually eclipsed Snowe in the frequency with which she broke with her party. In 2017, Almanac rankings put Collins with the third least conservative voting record in the GOP caucus.

Early in President Barack Obama's first term, she provided a key vote to pass a $787 billion economic stimulus package—a measure on which then-Vice President Biden was the administration's point man—after using her leverage to insist that more than $100 billion be shaved from the original price tag. In 2010, she supported another law enacted in response to the 2008 financial crisis—the Dodd-Frank financial reforms—opposed by most Republicans. (In early 2018, Collins joined all Senate Republicans and a number of centrist Democrats in voting for a Trump-backed bill to roll back portions of Dodd-Frank.) At the end of Obama's first term, in the debate over extending middle-income tax cuts enacted early in George W. Bush's presidency, Collins was the only Senate Republican to support a surtax on millionaires. "They can afford to pay more to help with our deficit, and that's an area where I differ with many in our party," she said. On social issues, she was the only Republican on the Armed Services Committee to vote to repeal the ban on openly gay troops in the military in 2010.

Collins contemplated a run for governor in 2018, but ultimately decided to remain on Capitol Hill. There were questions about her ability to win a primary election for the open gubernatorial seat—in part because of her vote several months earlier that helped block repeal of the Affordable Care Act. Ironically, Obama's attempts to win Collins' support for passage of the law in 2010 had been fruitless, despite months of wooing. She expressed disdain for what she saw as a token effort to include a few Republican ideas in a largely Democratic-written measure. Explaining her vote years later to block its repeal, Collins said: "These problems require a bipartisan solution. The Democrats made a big mistake when they passed the ACA without a single Republican vote. I don't want to see Republicans make the same mistake."

Collins got behind the $1.5 trillion GOP tax law enacted along party lines at the end of 2017. It repealed a key ACA provision mandating that individuals carry health insurance or pay a penalty. Collins, while never particularly supportive of the individual mandate, was nonetheless concerned about the repeal's effects on the cost and availability of insurance. She received public assurances from McConnell that he would support passage of a couple of bills before the end of 2017 to mitigate any damage. But McConnell couldn't assure passage in the House—where Ryan, under conservative pressure, signaled he was not a party to the deal. Collins faced criticism from many who had praised her stance on the ACA months earlier; they said she had been duped. She responded with complaints that key provisions she had won using her leverage—such as increased medical deductions and deductibility for some state and local taxes—had been largely ignored. "I think I got more in this tax bill than any other member of the Senate," she declared.

While Collins had never voted against a Supreme Court nominee from presidents of either party, Senate GOP leaders were uncertain how she would come down on Kavanaugh's nomination until she gave a 45-minute floor speech on Oct. 5, 2018. Her support ensured Kavanaugh's confirmation the next day on a 50-48 vote. Collins, who had supported an FBI investigation into the allegations of sexual assault against Kavanaugh by Christine Blasey Ford, said after reviewing the FBI's findings that Ford's claims could not be corroborated. She also said that a two-hour meeting with Kavanaugh, along with a follow-up phone call and review of his opinions, had convinced her that he would not overturn Roe v. Wade. "Protecting this right [to abortion] is important to me," Collins said. "His views on honoring precedent would preclude attempts to do by stealth that which one has committed not to do overtly."

Coming amid the #MeToo movement, Collins' decision triggered a furious reaction among abortion rights advocates and liberal groups—which had spent hundreds of thousands of dollars on TV ads in Maine to push Collins to oppose Kavanaugh. Within days, a crowdfunding effort began that ultimately raised more than $4 million toward an effort to oust her in 2020. Several potential Democratic challengers quickly emerged, including Gideon and Susan Rice, a former ambassador to the United Nations who, while not a Maine resident, had a summer home and family ties there. But Rice, now head of the White House Domestic Policy Council under Biden, backed out of a possible challenge several months after the Kavanaugh debate.

Collins announced her reelection bid in late 2019, only to be faced with another politically fraught issue—the first Senate impeachment trial of Trump. Collins said the actions that had brought on the House-passed articles of impeachment—Trump's call to Ukrainian President Volodymyr Zelensky, during which he pushed for an investigation of Biden and the latter's son Hunter—had been "improper and demonstrated very poor judgment." But she voted to acquit the president, saying there had been "conflicting evidence in the record" about Trump's motivations.

Collins contended she was applying the same standard she used in opposing the impeachment of a Democratic president, Bill Clinton, more than two decades earlier. "I, too, was furious at President Clinton and felt that he had lied under oath, but it didn't reach the constitutional test of high crimes and misdemeanors and was not sufficient to overturn an election and throw him out of office," she told the New York Times. With regard to Trump, Collins told CBS News, "I believe that the president has learned from this case"—an assertion jumped on by critics after Trump denied his actions had been wrong and defended his approach to Zelensky as a "perfect phone call." Collins later walked back the statement, saying it had been "aspirational" and that she should have used "hope" instead of "believe." Trump was later impeached a second time, near the close of his term in January 2021, after he incited a mob that stormed the U.S. Capitol and left five people dead. This time, Collins was among seven Republicans to vote to convict Trump of the charges. She faced an effort by some Maine Republicans to censure her for her action, but the move was defeated, 41-19, by members of the state Republican Committee.

Polling indicated that Collins was vulnerable to a challenge from the right in the 2020 Republican primary had she voted to convict Trump in the first impeachment; she ended up unopposed for renomination. Collins acknowledged to the Times that running as an independent "crossed my mind"—but quickly added that she couldn't easily abandon "the New England brand of Republicanism." Former Gov. Paul LePage, a Trump-style personality with whom Collins had an uneasy relationship, endorsed her for reelection in 2019—as Collins relied more on the Republican base. The evangelical Christian Civic League of Maine for the first time supported Collins, a longtime backer of abortion and gay rights—telling members her reelection was needed to maintain Republican control of the Senate. Conversely, groups that in the past had embraced her—such as Planned Parenthood and the Human Rights Campaign—fell in behind Gideon for similar reasons. "We are fighting for our lives, and the only way to advance LGBTQ equality through the Senate is to install a new pro-equality majority leader and replace Mitch McConnell," said Alphonso David, president of the Human Rights Campaign.

Spending in the 2020 Maine Senate race ended up at nearly $205 million, making it the sixth most expensive Senate contest ever, according to the Center for Responsive Politics. A report by Ad Impact calculated that $202 per voter was spent on TV, radio and digital ads—second nationally to Montana in 2020 on a population-adjusted basis. Gideon—who won the July primary with 72 percent against two opponents—spent nearly $60 million compared to almost $30 million for Collins. Another $113 million poured in from outside groups, with $28 million of that coming from the Senate Majority PAC. The latter super PAC has close ties to the Senate Democratic leadership, and Collins' come-from-behind victory created potential complications for Democratic Leader Chuck Schumer of New York in wooing Collins' vote in the 50-50 Senate. Responding to a question during the impeachment debate regarding Schumer, Collins snapped to Politico: "I don't think he's really very interested in doing anything but trying to defeat me by telling lies to the people of Maine. And you can quote me on that."

The death of Supreme Court Justice Ruth Bader Ginsburg weeks before Election Day created another possible political landmine, by reminding voters of Collins' unpopular decision to support Kavanaugh. But Collins quickly announced she opposed filling the vacancy so close to the Election Day and later became the only GOP senator to vote against Trump's nomination of Amy Coney Barrett—her first vote ever against a high court nominee. My vote does not reflect any conclusion that I have reached about Judge Barrett's qualifications to serve on the Supreme Court," Collins said. "What I have concentrated on is being fair and consistent, and I do not think it is fair nor consistent to have a Senate confirmation vote prior to the election. An irritated Trump told an interviewer that Collins had been "very badly hurt" by her stance. But the episode may have boosted her at home among potential ticket-splitting voters by giving her the chance to highlight her independence.

"This is the first campaign I've ever been involved in where my opponent has attacked my integrity and distorted and outright lied about my record," Collins charged during one of five debates with Gideon. Indeed, her previous reelection bids were cakewalks by comparison. In 2002, she was challenged by former state Senate Majority Leader Chellie Pingree, who now represents the state's 1st Congressional District; Collins won with 58 percent of the vote in that race. In 2008, Democrat Rep. Tom Allen vacated the 1st District seat to take on Collins. Allen made the Iraq War a central issue; Collins voted for the 2002 resolution authorizing the war and later opposed a Democratic attempt to set a timetable for troop withdrawal. But Collins won with 61 percent. In 2014, she defeated an underfunded opponent, Shenna Bellows, a former director of the Maine chapter of the American Civil Liberties Union, with 68 percent. She beat Gideon by 9 points, with total spending of nearly $200 million.

At 68, Collins now has at least six more years to make progress toward the Senate record for consecutive floor votes, a streak that goes back to the beginning of her tenure. As of January 2021, her streak had reached 7,554 – third on the all-time list—despite a 2007 ankle fracture she suffered while racing to the Senate floor and a second broken ankle she got from a fall on ice in 2016. Collins has said the streak was inspired by Chase Smith, who maintained a similar streak for 13 years until surgery forced her to end it.

Angus King (I)

Elected 2012, term expires 2024, 2nd term, b. Mar 31, 1944; Alexandria, VA; Dartmouth College, A.B., 1966; University of Virginia Law School, J.D., 1969; Episcopalian; Married (Mary J. Herman); 5 children; 5 grandchildren.

Elected Office: ME Governor, 1995-2003.

Professional Career: Practicing attorney, 1969-1983, 2003-present; Chief counsel, Sen. William Hathaway, U.S Senate Subcommittee on Alcoholism & Narcotics, 1972-1975; Host, ME Public Television's MaineWatch, 1975-1993; VP, General counsel, Swift River/Hafslund, 1983-1989; Founder, President, Northeast Energy Management, 1989-1994; Partner, Independence Wind, 2007-2012.

DC Office: 133 HSOB 20510, 202-224-5344, Fax: 202-224-1946, king.senate.gov

State Offices: Augusta, 207-622-8292; Bangor, 207-945-8000; Presque Isle, 207-764-5124; Scarborough, 207-883-1588.

Committees: *Armed Services*: Airland; Seapower; Strategic Forces (Chmn). *Energy & Natural Resources*: Energy; National Parks (Chmn); Public Lands, Forests & Mining. *Intelligence. Rules & Administration.*

Group Ratings

	ADA	ACLU	AFL-CIO	LCV	COC	HAFA	ACU	CFG	FRC
2020	-	69%	-	77%	-	0%	7%	-	-
2019	85%	C	100%	93%	76%	C	6%	11%	0%

Almanac Ratings 2019-2020

	Economy	Social	Foreign	Composite
Liberal	76%	76%	30%	61%
Conservative	24%	24%	70%	39%

Key Votes of the 116th Congress

1. EPA clean energy rules	Y	5. Russia sanctions	Y	9. Barr as Atty. General	N
2. U.S./Mex./Can. trade deal	Y	6. Troops in SYR, AFG	Y	10. Spending at the border	Y
3. Cut unemployment benefits	N	7. Veto arms sales to Saudis	Y	11. Coney Barrett to Sup. Ct.	N
4. Shelton to Fed Reserve	N	8. Defense $$$, veto override	Y	12. Electoral College objections	N

Election Results

Election	Name (Party)	Vote (%)		Cand. Spent	Ind. Exp. Support	Ind. Exp. Oppose
2018 General	Angus King (I)	344,575	(54%)	$4,908,730		$963,993
	Eric Brakey (R)	223,502	(35%)	$1,171,899	$834,317	
	Zak Ringelstein (D)	66,268	(10%)	$373,232		

Prior winning percentages: 2018 (54%), 2012 (53%), Governor: 1998 (59%), 1994 (35%)

Residents of this state in the nation's northeastern tip, with its rocky and sometimes remote terrain, have often demonstrated an independent streak— and, when it comes to politics, Angus King, Maine's junior senator, is Exhibit No. 1. Originally a Democrat, King came to believe that " sometimes the best thing the government can do is get out of the way." He entered the 1994 governor's race as an independent and blasted the government for what he said was meddling in business. After two terms as Maine's chief executive, King left politics for a decade— only to emerge as a candidate for an open Senate seat in 2012, decrying the legislative gridlock in Congress. He again ran as independent, refusing to say with which party he would caucus if elected. When he won, King announced he would join the Democratic Caucus, a choice that did not surprise those who had watched his political progression in recent years.

King easily won a second Senate term in 2018 with the de facto support of Maine's Democratic Party, and in 2020 continued his recent practice of endorsing Democratic presidential nominees by backing Joe Biden. Shortly after Biden's election, King was reportedly considered for appointment as director of national intelligence— a post created after 9/11 to coordinate among federal intelligence agencies. King, a member of the Senate Armed Services and Intelligence committees, did not get the job in part because of political considerations. With the Senate closely divided along partisan lines, it would have triggered a special election to fill King's seat in an often-unpredictable state— two years prior to the expiration of King's term.

King's emergence as a contender for the post underscored his focus on national security issues in recent years, particularly cybersecurity. King served as co-chair of the bipartisan Cyberspace Solarium Commission, created by 2018 legislation to " develop a consensus on a strategic approach to defending the United States … against cyberattacks of significant consequences." Shortly after the commission's report was released in 2020, King told Axios: " I probably have sat through … 25 hearings over the last seven and a half years on both [the] Intelligence and Armed Services [committees] where it's been made crystal clear that we don't have a policy that causes our adversaries to calculate the risk of their actions. We are a cheap date."

While recent vote rankings have pegged King as more conservative than all but a handful his colleagues in the Democratic Caucus, his criticisms of President Donald Trump became increasingly sharp during Trump's presidency. "The problem is the president feels that he is the state, you know, like Louis the XIV, ' I am the state.' So, criticism of him is treason against the United States," King gibed on CNN in late 2019—after Trump had repeatedly described a whistleblower complaint that led to his first impeachment as treasonous. In the spring of 2020, during a testy phone call with Vice President Mike Pence, King termed the federal government's failure to provide widespread testing for the novel coronavirus that causes COVID-19 " a dereliction of duty." Trump fired back the next day, calling King " worse than any Democrat." That was a couple of months after King joined fellow members of the Democratic Caucus in voting to convict Trump on two articles of impeachment.

King was raised in the Washington suburb of Alexandria Virginia, but he has spent most of his adult life " Down East." After attending Dartmouth College and University of Virginia Law School, he moved to Maine to work for a legal assistance organization and then became an aide to Maine Sen. William Hathaway, a Democrat. When King was 29, physicians discovered he had an aggressive form of skin cancer during a routine checkup, which he said he would not have scheduled if it weren't free through his insurance. Years later, he reacted angrily to a report that opponents of the Obama administration's health insurance overhaul were urging college students not to sign up for insurance under the Affordable Care Act, suggesting those dispensing such advice were "guilty of murder." King told the Bangor Daily News: " The reason I feel so strongly about this is that if someone had given me that advice when I was 25, I wouldn't be here." In the Senate, he has repeatedly voted to block Republican efforts to repeal Obamacare.

After leaving Hathaway's office, King returned to Maine to practice law and start an energy conservation business. He sold the latter for $20 million in 1994, just before running for governor— a race in which he invested $750,000 of his own money. For nearly two decades, he hosted a Maine public television program, making him a well-known figure statewide. He dropped his longtime Democratic Party affiliation before announcing for governor. " I didn't feel comfortable with the Democrats on the taxation/regulation side. I didn't feel comfortable with the Republicans on the social issue side, on abortion and those kinds of things," King told CBS' "60 Minutes" more than a quarter of a century later. "So, I said, 'Hell, I think I'm going to take a path up the middle.'"

King blasted high taxes during the campaign and edged out former Democratic Gov. Joseph Brennan, 35%-34%. Running a distant third was the Republican nominee, now-Sen. Susan Collins. As governor, King cut the state budget and its workforce. He shortened waiting periods for environmental permits, but he signed a bill imposing tight controls on paper mills' dioxin discharges into waterways— and celebrated by jumping fully clothed into the Kennebec River. Reelected in 1998 with 59 percent of the vote, he signed legislation to use state financial leverage to negotiate lower prescription drug prices for Mainers without Medicaid or private insurance. Perhaps his best-known initiative was to provide middle school students with laptops— then a precedent-setting idea

Barred from seeking another gubernatorial term in 2002, there was speculation King would challenge Collins for her Senate seat— but he left politics. He embarked on a six-month, 15,000-mile road trip through 33 states, as he, his wife and two of his children lived in a 40-foot recreational vehicle. It produced a book: " Governor's Travels: How I Left Politics, Learned to Back Up a Bus, and Found America." Today, his favored mode of transportation on visits to constituents is often a Harley-Davidson motorcycle.

For nearly a decade, King practiced law and worked for a mergers-and-acquisitions advisory firm while forming a wind-energy company. His reentry into politics was almost by accident. Republican Olympia Snowe, a leading Senate moderate, had been expected to seek a fourth term— but she announced her retirement in February 2012, decrying a partisan climate that made passing legislation daunting. King stepped in, vowing to continue where Snowe had left off. " I can be a broker for common sense," he asserted. His campaign headquarters prominently featured two photographs side by side: one of Ronald Reagan and the other of Robert Kennedy. However, the widespread speculation was that King would caucus with Democrats, having revealed he would support President Barack Obama for reelection. As governor, he endorsed Republican George W. Bush in 2000 but has since backed Democratic presidential nominees.

National Democrats did little to support their 2012 Senate nominee, state Sen. Cynthia Dill, figuring that King would win and end up in their camp. The National Republican Senatorial Committee broadcast ads accusing King of using political connections to win a "sketchy" federal loan guarantee for his wind-energy firm— of which he divested himself before the election— to build an industrial wind farm. While the ad barrage caused some tightening of the race, King won, capturing 53 percent of the vote to 31 percent for the Republican nominee, Maine Secretary of State Charlie Summers, and Dill's 13 percent.

King was supportive of Obama's second-term agenda. He voted to sustain Obama's veto of the Keystone XL pipeline and helped provide the votes needed to derail a Republican-sponsored resolution to block the Iran nuclear agreement. According to his Almanac vote rankings, King has allied with members of the Democrats' moderate wing, which is significantly to the left of the GOP's most centrist members, including his senior colleague, Collins. King has argued it is not he, but rather the political landscape, that has shifted. "I've agreed more with the Democrats in part because the Republican Party has moved so far to the right," King said during an interview in late 2013. "When I was an independent in Maine 20 years ago as governor, the Republican Party was a different party." During a "60 Minutes" appearance in early 2021, King observed: " My Republican friends are… going to say, ' He's really a Democrat, come on.' What I say to that is that the Republicans haven't given me much to vote for lately."

Others contended King's floor votes told only part of the story. " If you look at who is working behind the scenes trying to find compromise, I think he is much more in that bipartisan school than are most of the Democrats and the Republicans," said Colby College government professor Sandy Maisel. Announcing for reelection in 2018, King told reporters: " I had to choose which side to caucus with, but caucusing doesn't mean I've joined the Democratic Party. … Almost every bill that I work on is bipartisan because that's the only way things are going to get done." Independents are compelled to join one of the two caucuses to sit on Senate committees.

Upon his arrival in the Senate, King co-founded the Former Governors Caucus to bring together the Senate's former governors " to chart pragmatic approaches to solutions," as his website put it. Shortly before launching his 2018 reelection bid, King teamed with Republican Sen. Mike Rounds of South Dakota— another former governor— in an effort to achieve a long-elusive legislative consensus on immigration overhaul. Their bill— containing a path to citizenship for children brought to the country illegally as children and providing the Trump administration with $25 billion for border security— won the support of all but three Democrats but only eight Republicans. It fell a half-dozen votes short of the supermajority needed to advance the measure.

At the end of 2017, King lashed out at Senate Republicans for the tightly controlled process they used to consider a tax bill that Trump later hailed as one of his signature achievements. " There were at least 15 or 20 Democrats that were anxious to do tax reform … and there was never a chance," King told CNN. He was blunter on the Senate floor: " It's the worst process I think I have ever seen in a public body. The Bangor City Council would not amend the leash law using this process. We are talking about one of the most important bills any of us will ever vote on that has had zero hearings before the United States Senate." At one point, it appeared King's motion to send the bill back to committee, with instructions to make it deficit-neutral, might succeed: Three GOP senators considered voting with King. But the Republican skeptics backed down after the Senate parliamentarian determined the trigger mechanism would run afoul of Senate rules. It made for some tense moments on the floor, as Texas Sen. John Cornyn, then the Republican whip, was heard loudly telling King that his motion— which failed on a 52-48 vote— was " designed to kill the bill."

As a member of the Energy and Natural Resources Committee, King teamed with the then-Chair Lisa Murkowski, Republican of Alaska, to establish the Senate Arctic Caucus. At the end of 2019, he joined Murkowski to introduce legislation to require strategic planning for a greater U.S. Arctic naval presence—which the legislators noted has lagged behind that of Russia and China. King's involvement reflected Maine's interest in becoming a gateway to the Northwest Passage —increasingly navigable due to climate change—and reaping economic benefits from trade and shipping. Pointing a finger at legislative dysfunction as a roadblock to U.S. Arctic policy, King lamented Senate failure to ratify the Law of the Sea Treaty, which established principles and limits on the ocean area that nations may claim. "There's an attitude in the Senate among some people that treaties are an abrogation of U.S. sovereignty," he told the Bangor Daily News. "I'm puzzled by that. It puts us on the sidelines."

Such comments bespoke a broader frustration. More than halfway into his first term, he complained during an NPR interview: "About…two-thirds of the senators have been here eight years or less. Most of us have never seen the place work. We're like a football team that's lost every game for the past five years. We don't know how to win. …On the big issues, the controversial issues, we're just stymied." But two years later, in declaring for reelection, King sounded a note of guarded optimism. He spoke of building relationships on both sides of the aisle, saying the Capitol Hill environment was not as bleak as it might appear. "It's not back to what it was in the '70s, it's not what it should be," King told the Portland Press Herald. "But I can tell you there are little, tender shoots of bipartisan cooperation, and that is what we are trying to encourage."

In spring 2014, when Republicans had a good chance to retake the Senate majority, King created a stir when he said he might caucus with the GOP if he felt the interests of his constituents would be served. But, after the Republicans regained Senate control that November, King stuck with the Democrats. " I think it is in Maine's interest to have a senator in each camp," he said, alluding to his senior colleague, Collins.

King endorsed Collins for reelection in 2014—a year in which she was heavily favored against an underfunded Democrat. Terming Collins a " model senator," he added, "I think she's one of the Senate's MVPs— smart, tough and always willing to listen." But, in 2020, as national Democrats went all-out to oust Collins, King made no endorsement— sidestepping questions about whom he favored. King's wife, Mary Herman—a consultant who works for the Maine Department of Education — endorsed Collins' Democratic opponent, Sara Gideon, in a video that made no mention of her marriage. Immediately after Collins' win, King and Collins were part of a small group of centrist senators who worked successfully to break a months-long stalemate on a $900 billion COVID-19 relief bill.

King underwent surgery in June 2015 after being diagnosed with early-stage prostate cancer, but he said it would not affect his plans to seek a second term. He received follow-up treatments for a recurrence in early 2020, noting that— including his youthful bout with skin cancer—he had now dodged cancer three times.

Then-Maine Gov. Paul LePage, a conservative Republican ineligible to seek reelection, suggested in early 2015 that he might challenge King's bid for a second term before ultimately deciding he wouldn't run. Trump—to whom LePage was often likened in both style and substance— sought to coax LePage into the race. But LePage endorsed state Sen. Eric Brakey, a libertarian-leaning Republican who had spearheaded a successful push in Maine to allow carrying of concealed firearms without a permit. Zak Ringelstein, founder of an education technology startup, was unopposed for the Democratic nomination— after state Democratic Party officials sought to discourage him from running. On Election Day 2018, the results were similar to six years earlier: King won 54 percent of the vote, Brakey got 35 percent and Ringelstein took 10 percent. Asked before the balloting whether this would be his last campaign, King— who will be 80 in 2024—replied, " I suspect so."

Chellie Pingree (D)

Elected 2008, 7th term, b. Apr 02, 1955; Minneapolis, MN; University of Southern ME, Att., 1973; College of the Atlantic, B.A., 1979; Lutheran; Divorced; 3 children; 2 grandchildren.

Elected Office: ME Senate, 1992-2000, Majority Leader, 1996-2000.

Professional Career: Farmer, 1977-1980; Founder & President, N. Island Designs Co., 1981-1992; President & CEO, Common Cause, 2003-2007.

DC Office: 2162 RHOB 20515, 202-225-6116, Fax: 202-225-5590, pingree.house.gov

State Offices: Portland, 207-774-5019; Waterville, 207-873-5713.

Committees: *Agriculture*: Biotechnology, Horticulture & Research; Conservation & Forestry. *Appropriations*: Agriculture, Rural Development, FDA & Related Agencies; Interior, Environment & Related Agencies (Chmn); Military Construction, Veterans Affairs & Related Agencies.

Group Ratings

	ADA	ACLU	AFL-CIO	LCV	COC	HAFA	ACU	CFG	FRC
2020	**	84%	**	100%	-	0%	4%	**	-
2019	100%	C	95%	97%	65%	C	5%	6%	0%

Almanac Ratings 2019-2020

	Economy	Social	Foreign	Composite
Liberal	100%	100%	82%	94%
Conservative	0%	0%	18%	6%

Key Votes of the 116th Congress

1. U.S./Mex./Can. trade deal N	5. Russia sanctions Y	9. Firearms background checks Y
2. First Coronavirus response N/A	6. Troops in Syria Y	10. Spending at the border Y
3. HEROES Act Y	7. Veto arms sales to Saudis Y	11. Marijuana liberalized rules Y
4. CASH Act Y	8. Defense $$$, veto override Y	12. Electoral College objections N

Election Results

Election	Name (Party)	Vote (%)		Cand. Spent	Ind. Exp. Support	Ind. Exp. Oppose
2020 General	Chellie Pingree (D)	271,004	(62%)	$233,309	$1,018	
	Jay Allen (R)	165,008	(38%)	$72,542		$54
2020 Primary	Chellie Pingree (D)	102,773	(100%)			

Prior winning percentages: 2018 (59%), 2016 (58%), 2014 (58%), 2012 (62%), 2010 (57%), 2008 (55%)

Chellie Pingree, elected in 2008, is a blunt-talking staunch liberal with a long career in public service. Pingree has paid close attention to state issues, from ships to seafood and farming and chided the Trump administration when its policies hurt Maine industries. Her decision to turn down opportunities for statewide bids indicates she is comfortable with her influence on the House Appropriations Committee, where she became a "cardinal" in 2021— chairwoman of the Interior Subcommittee.

Pingree grew up in Minnesota, the granddaughter of Scandinavian immigrants who worked as dairy farmers. Her parents moved to Minneapolis, where her father was an accountant and her mother a nurse. The city's anti-war activism during the Vietnam era had a profound influence on Pingree, and she left high school early for alternative education programs on the East Coast. At one program in Worcester Massachusetts, she met her future husband and followed him to Maine, where they settled on remote North Haven Island in Penobscot Bay. As disciples of the "back to the land" movement, they lived for years in a cabin without running water or electricity and made their living as organic farmers. Although the couple later divorced, Pingree thrived on the island, starting a successful business that sells knitting kits. She started her political career in local offices on the island, including serving as tax assessor.

In 1991, Pingree ran for an open seat in the state Senate. She went door-to-door in the traditionally Republican district in Knox County and won. Pingree rose to majority leader in 1996. As leader, she fought reluctant colleagues and a challenge from pharmaceutical companies and passed a law for Maine to negotiate prescription drug prices, the first such law in the country.

In 2002, Pingree challenged Republican Sen. Susan Collins, who won 58%-42%. Shortly after her loss, she became president of Common Cause, the government and campaign watchdog group. She took the reins just after the successful push to overhaul the nation's campaign finance law, though much of her time was spent defending the new rules against constitutional challenges that ultimately threw out some of the reforms. Pingree also led Common Cause in opposing media consolidation in the hands of a few companies.

She left Common Cause in 2007 to run for the House seat that Democrat Tom Allen gave up to run another sacrificial campaign against Collins. Although she had complained for years about the influence of money in politics, Pingree had no trouble raising far more of it than any of her five Democratic rivals. She mostly eschewed money from political action committees but enjoyed the backing of EMILY's List, which funds women candidates who support abortion rights. Pingree won the primary with 44 percent of the vote. In the general election, she more than tripled the fundraising of state Sen. Charles Summers and won, 55%-45%.

In the House, Pingree has been a loyal and usually liberal Democrat. She has used her seat on Appropriations to look after her region's defense interests. In 2019, she added to her portfolio a seat on the subcommittee that handles military construction projects, which enhanced that leverage. She has taken a strong interest in environmental issues, helping to form the House Sustainable Energy and Environmental Coalition and introducing a bill to force BP to pay royalties on the oil from its massive spill in the Gulf of Mexico in 2010. Pingree has been a vocal supporter of the "Green New Deal" in the progressive agenda.

With her continuing interest in agriculture, Pingree joined other Democrats in opposing the initial GOP-written version of the 2018 farm bill, but she took credit for provisions in the final version of the measure that doubled research funds for organic farming and created a national pilot program to increase access to healthy foods for low-income families. During Trump's tenure, Pingree was outspoken about the harm of his policies in her district, specifically proposed cuts to the Agriculture Department's budget and delays in compensating lobstermen hurt by the trade war. She also sounded the alarm that an underfunded Postal Service was shipping dead chicks to Maine farmers. Along with the three other members of Maine's delegation, Pingree successfully lobbied to end European Union tariffs on the state's lobsters.

Taking over the Interior Subcommittee in 2021, Pingree said that she would fight to undo the Trump administration's "enormous damage to our environment and....efforts to mitigate the climate crisis." In terms of Maine-based needs covered by her subcommittee, she cited "funding for Maine's tribes, environmental preservation programs, our cultural economy, and our forests."

She faced a competitive reelection campaign in 2010 against alternative energy company owner Dean Scontras, who got support from tea party activists. The Maine Republican Party ran ads accusing Pingree of taking trips on the corporate jet of her fiancée, hedge-fund billionaire Donald Sussman. She had a relatively easy 57%-43% win. Her subsequent marriage to Sussman, a major donor to Democratic super PACs, increased Pingree's access to big political contributors plus her own donations to other Democrats. It created some controversy when he bought a controlling interest in newspapers in Portland and Augusta. Those questions disappeared in 2015 when they filed for divorce. Pingree does not typically face serious challengers in her bids for reelection. She won 62%-38% in 2020 against Republican Army veteran Jay Allen, her highest vote-share since 2012.

Pingree often clashed with Republican Gov. Paul LePage on his call for cuts in Medicaid spending and she thought seriously about running to succeed him in 2018, when he was term-limited. But she decided not to, she said, because she had "so much more work to be done" in Congress— and perhaps mindful of the risk of another statewide loss. As it turned out, Democrats that year scored big gains in both Augusta and the House. Pingree, and her daughter Hannah, a former state House speaker, were mentioned as potential 2020 challengers to Collins. Both passed— probably wisely.

ME-1: Southern Maine

Population		Race and Ethnicity		Income	
Total	686,731	White	93.60%	Median Income	$67,392
Land area (sq. miles)	3,286	Black	2.10%	District Income Rank	189
Pop/ sq mi	209.02	Latino	1.90%	Poverty Rate	8.90%
Born in State	55.20%	Asian	1.50%	With health insurance	93.40%
		Two or more races	1.90%	Cash public assistance	2.00%
Age Groups		Other	0.90%	Food stamp/SNAP	9.00%
Under 18	18.10%				
18-34	20.70%	**Education**		**Work**	
35-64	40.10%	H.S grad or less	33.30%	White Collar	43.90%
Over 64	21.00%	Some college	26.10%	Sales and Service	36.40%
		College Degree, 4 yr	24.80%	Blue Collar	19.60%
Military		Post grad	15.70%	Government	13.40%
Veteran/ Active Duty	8.20%				

2020 Pres. Vote	Biden	266,376	(60%)	Trump	164,045	(37%)			
2016 Pres. Vote	Clinton	212,860	(54%)	Trump	154,399	(39%)	Johnson	18,593	(5%)

Portland: The 1st District of Maine stretches from southernmost Kittery and nearby Kennebunkport to the craggy-shored, ancestrally Republican counties to the east. It extends halfway up the Atlantic coast to Canada. The historic center is Portland, Maine's largest city, home to the yuppies and lawyers who have revived and renovated its downtown landmarks. Portland's antique charm, mostly booming economy, and tolerant lifestyle have made it a haven for the LGBT community. The more than 100-year-old L.L. Bean is not far away in Freeport. Old mill towns like Biddeford and Sanford have been redeveloped. There is an ongoing attempt to turn Portland into a local tech hub; Northeastern University planned to open a research institute focused on artificial intelligence.

The area has a strong defense presence. Base-closing rounds have spared the Portsmouth Naval Shipyard at Kittery, the nation's oldest continually operating naval shipyard. With a younger workforce that has grown above 6,000, the future of the yard has improved with billions of dollars in long-term federal contracts to repair and upgrade nuclear-powered submarines. Still, the shipyard's future has always been a topic of worried discussion for locals. It was hit by a coronavirus outbreak in fall 2020, prompting state officials to investigate. Up the coast at Bath Iron Works, with 5,500 workers, job cutbacks once loomed because of downsizing of the fleet and competition with the lower-cost shipyard in Pascagoula Mississippi. Management at Bath has sought more efficiencies. But in 2020, it lost out on a $936 million contract to build an Arleigh Burke-class destroyer to its Pascagoula rival. That loss happened while Bath was enduring its first strike in 20 years, a standoff that lasted 63 days until the shipbuilders, upset with the company's continued use of subcontractors, approved a three-year deal with the help of a federal mediator. Since the Brunswick Naval Air Station closed in 2011, more than 80 businesses and 800 jobs have moved into industrial and commercial space at the overhauled Brunswick Landing.

Portland and several other coastal towns in southern Maine are in the 1st Congressional District. The district includes the five coastal counties from York to Knox, and most of inland Augusta-based Kennebec. About 40 percent of the population is in Portland-based Cumberland. The 1st also takes in several remote islands off the coast, where people enjoy a lifestyle more reminiscent of the Alaska wilderness, shuttling to the mainland on ferries and Cessna aircraft. Lobsters are more than a tradition here; they're an economic necessity. In 2016, the 5,900 licensed lobstermen and women in the state hauled in an estimated 131 million pounds, with a seventh-consecutive record harvest and a recovery from what had been virtually giveaway prices. But the haul in 2017 dropped to 110 million pounds — the smallest since 2011 and a warning that climate change and warmer temperatures in the Gulf of Maine have reduced the lobster population. President Donald Trump's trade war further kneecapped the industry. The state's lobster trade with China dropped 50 percent from 2018 to 2019, prompting the Agriculture Department to dole out $50 million to fishermen in 2020. But the state's lobstermen scored a coup that summer when the European Union ended tariffs on imports of U.S. lobster, a status Canada had already enjoyed for years.

While most attention in 2020 focused on the battle for the electoral vote in the 2nd District, Joe Biden easily won the 1st, 60%-37%, carrying every county.

Jared Golden (D)

Elected 2018, 2nd term, b. Jul 25, 1982; Leed, ME; University of ME (Farmington), Att., 2002; Bates College, B.A., 2011; Married (Isobel Golden).

Military Career: US Marine Corps 2002-2006; US Marine Corps Reserves 2008-2009 (Afghanistan & Iraq)

Elected Office: ME House, 2014-2018.

Professional Career: Professional Staff Member, U.S. Senate Committee on Homeland Security and Governmental Affairs, 2011-2013; Legislative Assistant, U.S. Sen. Susan M. Collins, 2013-2013.

DC Office: 1223 LHOB 20515, 202-225-6306, Fax: 202-225-2943, golden.house.gov

State Offices: Bangor, 207-249-7400; Caribou, 207-492-6009; Lewiston, 207-241-6767.

Committees: *Armed Services*: Readiness; Seapower & Projection Forces. *Small Business*: Contracting & Infrastructure; Underserved, Agricultural & Rural Business Development (Chmn).

Almanac Ratings 2019-2020

	Economy	Social	Foreign	Composite
Liberal	54%	47%	82%	61%
Conservative	46%	53%	18%	39%

Key Votes of the 116th Congress

1. U.S./Mex./Can. trade deal	N	5. Russia sanctions	Y
2. First Coronavirus response	Y	6. Troops in Syria	Y
3. HEROES Act	N	7. Veto arms sales to Saudis	Y
4. CASH Act	Y	8. Defense $$$, veto override	Y

9. Firearms background checks N
10. Spending at the border Y
11. Marijuana liberalized rules Y
12. Electoral College objections N

Election Results

Election	Name (Party)	Vote (%)	Cand. Spent	Ind. Exp. Support	Ind. Exp. Oppose
2020 General	Jared Golden (D)...........................	197,974 (53%)	$5,598,876	$1,327,076	$1,716,750
	Dale Crafts (R).............................	175,228 (47%)	$1,287,962	$118,319	$734,960
2020 Primary	Jared Golden (D)...........................	57,718 (100%)			

Prior winning percentages: 2018 (51%)

Democrat Jared Golden made history in the 2018 election when he became the first candidate elected to Congress as the result of "ranked choice" voting, which voters approved for state and federal elections in a referendum in 2016. That procedure gave him his victory even though he trailed incumbent Republican Rep. Bruce Poliquin in the initial tabulation of the vote. Golden won outright in 2020 thanks to a lackluster campaign run by his GOP opponent. A member with a strong independent streak, Golden often flouts the party line but he remains one of the most endangered House Democrats in a Trump-won district.

Golden, a native of Lewiston, grew up on a golf course owned by his parents. He enlisted in the Marine Corps months after the September 2001 attacks and served in Iraq and Afghanistan. He was part of the failed attempt in 2004 to capture Osama bin Laden near the border with Pakistan. Following the end of his active duty, Golden was diagnosed with post-traumatic stress syndrome.

Returning to Maine, Golden worked in several short-term jobs and got his bachelor's degree in politics at Bates University. He joined the staff of Maine Republican Sen. Susan Collins at the Homeland Security and Government Affairs Committee. After taking a job as an aide to Democrats at the state House in Augusta, Golden was elected to the House in 2014. He worked on veterans' issues during his two terms and was the Democratic whip. Golden has touted his time on Collins's staff to burnish his bipartisan credentials. He notably declared his neutrality during her 2020 reelection contest.

When he announced his challenge to Poliquin, Golden said that Washington D.C. was "rigged" and that the political status quo demanded change. Doing his two terms, Poliquin was the only Republican from New England in the House. He struggled to define his role and was widely criticized at home when he voted for the GOP bill to repeal the Affordable Care Act. His vulnerability drew four Democratic candidates. The biggest spender in the primary was Lucas St. Clair, a conservationist. In the initial vote count, Golden led St. Clair, 46%-39%. Once the votes for the two trailing candidates were reallocated, Golden won 54%-46%.

Golden invoked many of the standard national Democratic themes against Poliquin, but with a decidedly populist streak. He vowed to "take power back from the special interests" and create middle-class jobs that pay respectable wages with real benefits." Poliquin, who distanced himself from President Donald Trump, characterized Golden as too liberal for the district. Each candidate spent more than $4 million— a huge sum in this rural, low-cost district. The national parties and other outside groups spent another $5 million, split between the two candidates. Following the ranked-choice calculations, Golden won, 50.5%-49.5%, a margin of about 3,000 votes. Not surprisingly, Poliquin challenged the outcome. But his gripes following the election had less impact than they might have had prior to the outcome. Golden's win was historic in another way: Before Poliquin's setback, no incumbent had lost this district in 100 years.

In Congress, Golden frequently broke ranks to side with Republicans. He was one of only five Democrats to vote against Nancy Pelosi for Speaker in both 2019 and in 2021, and one of only two Democrats to vote against a 2019 bill that mandated federal criminal background checks on all gun sales. And true to form, Golden was the only House Democrat in December 2019 to vote for one article of impeachment against Donald Trump but not the other, charging Trump with an abuse of power but not obstruction of Congress. It was a decision that garnered backlash from across the ideological spectrum. Following the January 2021 Capitol riot, Golden joined the unanimous House Democrats in voting to impeach Trump .

After Poliquin decided against a 2020 rematch, GOP recruiters struggled to land a solid candidate. The primary was a three-way affair among former state Sen. Eric Brakey, who lost a 2018 Senate race against Maine independent Angus King by nearly 20 points; Adrienne Bennett, a former aide to ex-Gov. Paul LePage; and former state Rep. Dale Crafts, who nabbed LePage's endorsement. Brakey was a decent fundraiser but he was plagued by the resurfacing of footage of him dancing in his underwear for a coconut water commercial he taped in 2011. Crafts, a successful businessman who was paralyzed in a motorcycle accident at age 25, had a compelling personal story. He beat Bennett 59%-41% after Brakey's votes were redistributed in ranked-choice.

Crafts, a staunch ally of Trump, said he was motivated to enter the race by Democrats' impeachment push. After supporting Medicare for All in his 2018 run, Golden backed away from that proposal in 2020, according to the Bangor Daily News, and supported the public option backed by Joe Biden. Crafts ran ads saying Golden backed " a government takeover of health care." Crafts proved to be a poor fundraiser, spending less than $1.3 million to Golden's $5.3 million and Republican outside groups declined to bail him out— they went virtually dark on the air by mid-October.

Golden won 53%-47%, carrying vote-rich Penobscot County, home to Bangor, and Androscoggin County, which includes Lewiston. He remains a top GOP target in 2022, though he might get a boost from redistricting..

ME-2: Northern and Central Maine

Population		Race and Ethnicity		Income	
Total	657,481	White	94.40%	Median Income	$51,202
Land area (sq. miles)	27,557	Black	1.10%	District Income Rank	377
Pop/ sq mi	23.86	Latino	1.50%	Poverty Rate	13.00%
Born in State	68.30%	Asian	0.80%	With health insurance	90.50%
		Two or more races	2.30%	Cash public assistance	2.80%
Age Groups		Other	1.40%	Food stamp/SNAP	15.70%
Under 18	18.60%				
18-34	19.50%	**Education**		**Work**	
35-64	40.30%	H.S grad or less	43.30%	White Collar	35.50%
Over 64	21.60%	Some college	31.30%	Sales and Service	39.30%
		College Degree, 4 yr	16.50%	Blue Collar	25.10%
Military		Post grad	9.00%	Government	14.20%
Veteran/ Active Duty	10.10%				

2020 Pres. Vote	Trump	196,725	(52%)	Biden	168,696	(45%)			
2016 Pres. Vote	Trump	181,194	(51%)	Clinton	144,875	(41%)	Johnson	19,512	(6%)

Lewiston, Bangor: The 2nd District of Maine is heavily forested, rough-hewn and enormous. Covering more than 85 percent of the state, it is larger than the states of New Hampshire, Vermont and Massachusetts combined. The population is not evenly distributed. There are several different Maines represented here: The bays of coastal Maine, with their small fishing towns; the potato fields of far northern Aroostook County; and the mill towns on the fast-running rivers and streams of western Maine. Some valleys have more moose than people. The district includes the heavily Democratic mill town of Lewiston and also Eastport. At Belfast on Penobscot Bay, art galleries and boutiques have replaced fish-processing plants. This was one of America's frontiers in the 1850s, when Bangor, on the Penobscot River, was the lumber capital of the world. Lewiston, the largest city in the district, has become home to more than 7,000 refugees from Somalia and elsewhere in east Africa. The immigrants have helped revive the city, while adding complex social dynamics, such as dozens of languages in the Lewiston schools. In 2019, the first Somali-American was elected to its city council.

These parts of Maine have had economic troubles, losing 22,000 jobs to neighboring Canada and other foreign markets with the free-trade agreements in the 1990s. Logging, long the largest industry in Maine, has suffered job cutbacks as big paper companies sell off acreage and shut down mills. A once-thriving sardine-canning industry ended with the closing of the last cannery in 2010. Washington County's sandy soil produces more than 90 percent of the nation's wild blueberry crop, but the growers were one of many causalities of President Donald Trump's trade war. China imposed a 70 percent tariff on the crop in retaliation and the industry was largely denied federal bailout money. Although potato production is less than half what it was in 1960, some encouraging developments have included the creation of the new high-yield Caribou Russet brand and state regulatory approval in 2017 of three new genetically engineered potatoes. A major controversy in Presque Isle: Starting in 2019, the high school no longer closed for three weeks in September so teenagers can harvest the potato crop in what has become a highly mechanized operation. Another local drama: Residents and environmental groups filed lawsuits and crafted a ballot initiative to block a $950 million power-transmission line connecting New England and Quebec. They were not successful. In the North Woods, fishing for wild and native brook trout (in waters that have never been stocked) has become a $300 million annual business.

Politically, the district is iconoclastic and permanently enamored of neither major political party. The old 2nd was presidential candidate Ross Perot's strongest district in the nation, with 33 percent in 1992 and 16 percent in 1996. Trump made multiple appearances here during his 2016 and 2020 campaign, with appeals to its blue-collar and trade-protectionist voters. In 2016, he handily won its electoral vote, 51%-41%, marking the first time the state's two districts split in a presidential election. It happened again in 2020, though Trump won the 2nd by a slightly smaller margin 52%-45%.

MARYLAND

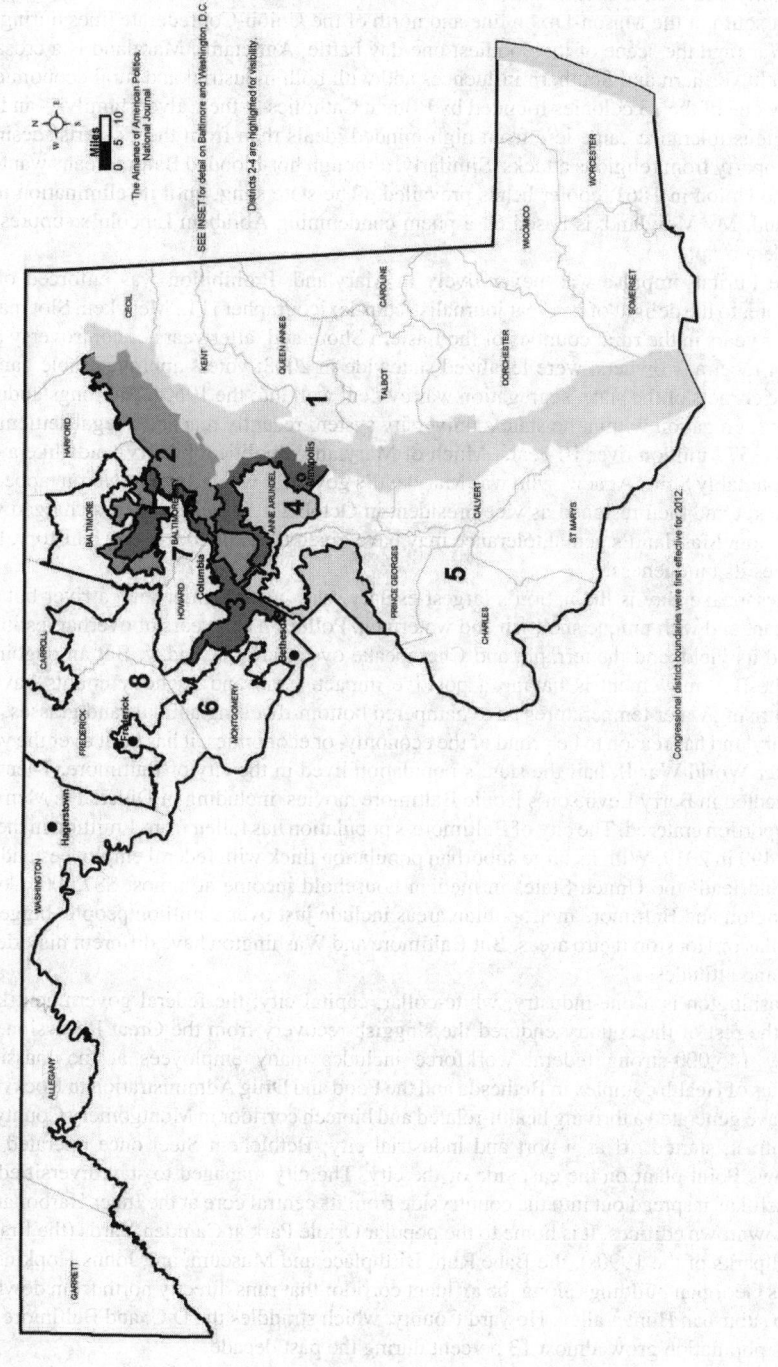

Maryland, one of the nation's most Democratic states, serves as a microcosm of the trends shaping today's Democratic Party: continuing lopsided support in ethnically and racially diverse urban areas, growing Democratic success with affluent, suburban voters and government employees, and a waning of the party's influence in rural areas.

Just south of the Mason-Dixon line and north of the Union-Confederate lines during most of the Civil War (and the scene of its bloodiest one-day battle, Antietam), Maryland is a crossroads state, with both Northern and Southern influences and with both industrial and rural economies. This was the only one of the 13 colonies founded by Roman Catholics— the Calvert family— and its embrace of religious tolerance came less from high-minded ideals than from the Calverts' desire to protect their property from religious attacks. Similarly, although hot-blooded Baltimoreans wanted to secede from the Union in 1861, cooler heads prevailed. (The state song, until its elimination in 2021, was Maryland, My Maryland, is based on a poem condemning Abraham Lincoln's suppression of pro-Confederate rioters.)

The Puritan impulse was never lively in Maryland. Prohibition was enforced only laxly in Baltimore, to the delight of its great journalist-cum-lexicographer H.L. Mencken. Slot machines were legal for years in the rural counties of the Eastern Shore and, after years of controversy and over the pleas of racetrack owners, were legalized statewide in 2008; voters approved table games in 2012. In some corners of the state, segregation was evident well into the 1960s, and longstanding efforts to remedy segregation within the state's university system recently reached a legal settlement in 2021, totaling $577 million over 10 years. Much of Maryland's political history reads like a chronicle of rogues, notably Spiro Agnew, who was Maryland's governor when Richard Nixon tapped him for his 1968 ticket and then resigned as vice president in October 1973 when he was charged with income tax evasion. Maryland's genial tolerance may have given it a little too savory a history, but this state cherishes its uniqueness.

Chesapeake Bay is the nation's largest estuary, with water saltier than a river but fresher than the ocean, and with unique shellfish and watermen. Pollution and years of overharvesting drastically reduced its yield, and the terrapin and Chesapeake oyster are rare today. But an ongoing statewide Save-the-Bay movement is having a positive impact. Crab and anchovy counts have improved, though rising water temperatures have hampered bottom-dwelling animals and grasses.

Maryland has reason to be proud of the economy, or economies, it has built over the years. During and after World War II, half the state's population lived in the city of Baltimore. Then, in a pattern documented in Barry Levinson's iconic Baltimore movies, including of Diner, Tin Men and Avalon, the proportion cratered. The city of Baltimore's population has fallen from 1 million in the early 1950s to 593,490 in 2019. With its large suburban population thick with federal employees and contractors, Maryland leads the United States in median household income at almost $87,000. Combined, the Washington and Baltimore metropolitan areas include just over 9 million people, bigger than either the Dallas or Houston metro areas. But Baltimore and Washington have different histories, economic bases, and attitudes.

Washington is a one-industry, white-collar, capital city; the federal government kept it going while the rest of the country endured the sluggish recovery from the Great Recession. Maryland's roughly 145,000-strong federal workforce includes many employees at the massive National Institutes of Health complex in Bethesda and the Food and Drug Administration in Rockville; these, in turn, have generated a thriving health-related and biotech corridor in Montgomery County. Baltimore, by contrast, started off as a port and industrial city; Bethlehem Steel once operated the massive Sparrows Point plant on the east side of the city. The city managed to stay diversified and largely successful as it spread out into the countryside from its central core at the Inner Harbor and its solidly built downtown edifices. It is home to the popular Oriole Park at Camden Yards (the first of the new-old ballparks of the 1990s), the Babe Ruth Birthplace and Museum, and Johns Hopkins University, with its Georgian buildings along the affluent corridor that runs directly north from downtown all the way to suburban Hunt Valley. Howard County, which straddles the D.C. and Baltimore metro areas, saw its population grow almost 13 percent during the past decade.

In recent years, however, the city of Baltimore has been known for its more dystopic elements, painstakingly (and prophetically) chronicled by the celebrated HBO dramatic series The Wire. In Maryland, more than 70 percent of prison inmates are Black, more than twice the percentage of

Black residents in the state and the highest African-American incarceration rate of any state in the country, according to the Justice Policy Institute. Amid a scourge of drugs and crime in Baltimore between 2011 and 2014, the city paid the staggering sum of $5.7 million for harms inflicted by police, with more than 100 victims winning court judgments, the Baltimore Sun revealed. The situation exploded in 2015, when Baltimore resident Freddie Gray, 25, died of spinal injuries after being taken into police custody. Rioting, particularly in the impoverished Sandtown-Winchester neighborhood, ensued. A curfew was imposed, and eventually charges were filed against six police officers. None were convicted. In August 2016, the Department of Justice released a report critical of the city's aggressive policing strategy against quality-of-life crimes. Gray's death shattered residents' trust in the police, and amid shifting political and law-enforcement leadership, the police seemed to retreat; as a result, violent crime surged, with Black residents accounting for most of the victims. In 2017, Baltimore " recorded 342 murders— its highest per-capita rate ever, more than double Chicago's, far higher than any other city of 500,000 or more residents and, astonishingly, a larger absolute number of killings than in New York, a city 14 times as populous," wrote Baltimore-based journalist Alec MacGillis. The city set a new murder record in 2019, before seeing the number fall slightly in 2020. Turnover in the mayor's office has not helped. Sheila Dixon resigned in a plea agreement with prosecutors in 2010. Her successor, Stephanie Rawlings-Blake, was damaged by the fallout from Gray's death and declined to seek another term. And her successor, Catherine Pugh, resigned amid a scandal involving insider deals to purchase a children's book she wrote.

In this context, it's hard to believe that, historically, most of Maryland's successful statewide politicians once came from Baltimore, including two mayors who won the governorship, William Donald Schaefer and Martin O'Malley. For three decades, Maryland's senators lived in Baltimore and commuted to Washington. Baltimore has a long Democratic tradition and most of its voters are registered Democrats. Until 2014, when Republican Larry Hogan won the first of his two terms, Democrats had yielded the governorship only once since 1966 — from 2002 to 2006, when Republican Bob Ehrlich served. In the state's House delegation, Democrats outnumber Republicans 7-to-1, an even more extreme discrepancy than voting patterns would suggest, thanks to an aggressive gerrymander. Maryland's strong Democratic preferences have enabled its members of Congress to wield influence, though often quietly, by the likes of Sens. Paul Sarbanes, Barbara Mikulski, Ben Cardin, and Chris Van Hollen. In the House, Majority Leader Steny Hoyer serves as the No. 2 to Speaker Nancy Pelosi, whose father, Thomas D'Alesandro, was a congressman from, and mayor of, Baltimore; the rivalry between Pelosi and Hoyer began when they were interns in the office of Sen. Daniel Brewster of Maryland. Baltimore-based Rep. Elijah Cummings died in 2019 following a distinguished career as a civil-rights advocate and chair of the House Committee on Oversight and Reform. (Another fixture in Maryland politics died in 2021: Thomas V. Mike Miller Jr., who served as state Senate president between 1987 and 2019.)

For many years, Maryland was a marginal state in national politics; it voted Republican for president as recently as 1988. But demographic and geographic shifts have made it solidly Democratic. While the state was 80 percent White in 1970, Maryland now ranks fourth-highest nationally for its Black population at 31 percent. Many Blacks in Maryland, especially in Prince George's County, are college-educated and economically upscale, although the coronavirus pandemic has demonstrated that even affluence doesn't prevent disproportionately negative health outcomes for African Americans. Meanwhile, the percentage of foreign-born residents in Maryland trailed the national average until around 2005 but now surpasses the nation as a whole, at 15 percent. In Montgomery County, an inner-ring suburb that saw its population grow by about 8 percent over the past decade, non-Hispanic Whites now account for less than 43 percent of the population. Hispanics account for 20 percent of the county's population and Asian-Americans account for 16 percent; almost one-third of county residents are immigrants.

In the 1980s, Montgomery and Prince George's weren't more Democratic than the rest of the state and were sometimes less so. But during a generation in which Republicans have backed smaller government and taken conservative cultural stands, Montgomery and Prince George's counties have become overwhelmingly Democratic and have cast a larger shadow statewide. In 2020, Montgomery and Prince George's cast 32 percent of the state's two-party presidential vote in the state, well above the combined 22 percent cast by Baltimore city and county. Another 16 percent was cast in the

Baltimore satellite counties of Anne Arundel and Howard, while 30 percent was cast elsewhere in the state. Once-rural and predominantly white Charles County is now 50 percent Black and has become Democratic as well.

Map for Greater Washington-Baltimore

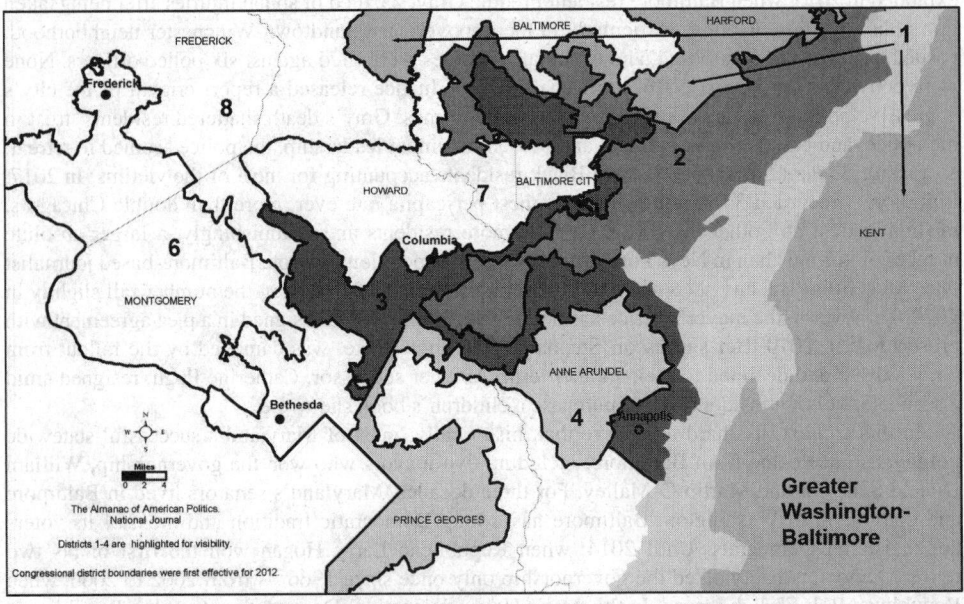

Such transformations have pushed Maryland to the left. In 2012, Maryland voters approved in-state college tuition for children of undocumented immigrants and measures in favor of same-sex marriage. Hogan's governorship curbed the most progressive impulses of the legislature's wide Democratic majority, but he's been among the nation's most moderate Republicans, protecting the state's Affordable Care Act insurance exchange and regularly taking issue with statements and policies from President Donald Trump. His approach produced high approval ratings and a 55%-44% reelection victory in 2018 despite a strong Democratic environment nationally; Hogan poached an estimated one-third of Democrats statewide. But Hogan aside, Democrats have maintained a yawning edge in the state. In the 2020 presidential race, Joe Biden won the state by 33 points, up seven points from Hillary Clinton's then-record margin in 2016. Biden flipped three counties Trump won in 2016: Frederick (Frederick), Kent (Chestertown), and Talbot (Easton). Biden also expanded the winning Democratic margins by between five and 13 points in Montgomery, Charles, Howard, Anne Arundel, and Baltimore counties. Unless Maryland Republicans manage to clone Hogan, the GOP will face a distinctly uphill battle to remain competitive in the state.

Population		Race and Ethnicity		Income	
Total	6,045,680	White	54.50%	Median Income	86,738
Land area (sq. miles)	9,707	Black	30.30%	State Income Rank	1 out of 50
Pop/ sq mi	622.80	Latino	10.60%	Poverty Rate	9.00%
Born in state	47.40%	Asian	7.70%	With health insurance	94.00%
		Two or more races	3.40%	Cash public assistance	2.20%
Age Groups		Other	5.40%	Food stamp/SNAP	10.9%
Under 18	22.00%				
18-34	22.40%	**Education**		**Work**	
35-64	39.70%	H.S grad or less	34.20%	White Collar	48.00%
Over 64	15.90%	Some college	24.90%	Sales and Service	35.10%
		College Degree, 4 yr	21.80%	Blue Collar	16.90%
Military		Post grad	19.10%	Government	21.70%
Veteran/ Active Duty	8.20%				

Presidential Politics

2020 Primary (D)	Biden (D)	879,753(84%)	Sanders (D)	81,939 (8%)	
2020 Pres. Vote	Biden (D)	1,985,023(65%)	Trump (R)	976,414(32%)	
2016 Pres. Vote	Clinton (D)	1,677,928(60%)	Trump (R)	943,169(34%) Johnson (L)	79,605 (3%)

In the eight presidential elections since 1992, Maryland's Democratic percentages consistently ranked high among the states— second in 1992, sixth in 1996, fourth in 2000 and 2004, fifth in 2008 and 2012, third in 2016 and 2020. Only Massachusetts and Vermont gave a higher percentage to Joe Biden, who won the state 65%-32% over Donald Trump. Two regions drove Biden's dominance: the close-in suburbs of Washington D.C., and Baltimore. Montgomery and Prince George's counties, which run the spectrum of wealthy white suburbs to working-class African-American communities, gave remarkable 79 and 89 percent of their respective votes to Biden. In Baltimore city, Biden won about 87 percent. The suburbs of Baltimore County gave Biden 62 percent of its votes; Howard County, which is exurban D.C. and Baltimore, gave 71 percent to Biden. In the state's rural Eastern Shore and western Appalachian regions, Trump won a solid majority.

Maryland's 2020 primary was originally scheduled for April 28, but was pushed back because of the coronavirus and held on June 2, long after the Democratic nomination was decided. Joe Biden won the race with 84 percent of the vote.

Congressional Districts

117th Congress Lineup	7D 1R	**116th Congress Lineup**	7D 1R

The long-running Maryland redistricting saga became the focus of Supreme Court review—more than seven years after the state approved the congressional map. In June 2019, the justices ruled, 5-4, that federal courts had no authority to rule on so-called partisan gerrymander cases. The case, one of several redistricting claims that has drawn its attention in recent years, resulted from a ruling by a three-judge court in November 2018 that held unconstitutional the drawing of the 6th District in the western part of the state. That court had ordered a new map to be drawn for the 2020 election. Republican Gov. Larry Hogan has continued to call for changes in the state's handling of redistricting, which opens the door to other options to reverse the Democrats' revision of the lines for the 6th from what had been a safely Republican district to a safely Democratic district. Hogan also wants to break up the blatant gerrymander of several districts in the Baltimore area, though he has limited direct influence with the Democratic-controlled legislature.

Democrats in Maryland have controlled redistricting since 2000 and have used their power to maximum advantage. Going into the 2002 election, the delegation was divided 4-4 between the two parties. After the boundaries were changed, the suburban Baltimore 2nd District became inhospitable for Republicans, as did the Montgomery County-centered 8th district. That left only two Republican districts, the 1st and the 6th. In 2011, Gov. Martin O'Malley and Democratic legislators made the 1st District more Republican by adding GOP precincts in suburban Baltimore and heavily Republican areas in Carroll County, which had been in the 6th. Republican Andy Harris ended up with a very safe seat, which covered the Eastern Shore and areas north of Baltimore. At the same time, they made the 6th District in western Maryland far less Republican, chiefly by adding a large chunk of heavily Democratic Montgomery County and subtracting much of Frederick County. These moves made the adjacent 8th District less Democratic, but not enough to put their party in peril. As intended, Republican Rep. Roscoe Bartlett lost in the newly drawn 6th. To maintain two Black-majority districts— the 4th in metro Washington and the 7th in metro Baltimore— the redistricters drew convoluted lines that have been featured among the nation's most gerrymandered districts.

When Hogan decried the partisanship and created an independent redistricting commission, the legislature responded with an alternative that was more form than substance, including a requirement that five neighboring states revise their redistricting procedures. Hogan, whose approach has received broad public approval, vetoed the plan in 2017 as "phony." He has said he will use his leverage to force some changes. That could enhance GOP prospects for one or perhaps two additional seats that will be competitive, at least, including the western Maryland district. But it also could make the 1st District more competitive for Harris, who has had chilly dealings with Hogan and other Maryland GOP leaders.

Larry Hogan (R)

Elected 2014, term expires 2023, 2nd term; b. May. 25, 1956, Landover; FL St. U., B.A. 1978; Catholic; Married (Yumi); 3 children.

Professional Career: Founder, Hogan Companies, 1985-present; Realtor, Murphy Hogan Commercial Real Estate Services, 1999-2003; MD Secretary of Appointments, Office of Governor, 2003-2007; Founder, Change Maryland, 2011.

Office: 100 State Circle Annapolis, 21401; 410-974-3901; Fax: 401-974-3275; Website: maryland.gov

Lt. Gov.: Boyd Rutherford (R) **Atty. Gen:** Brian Frosh (D)

State Legislature: Senate: 32D, 15R **House:** 99D, 42R

Election Results

Election	Name (Party)	Vote (%)
2018 General	Larry Hogan (R)..	1,275,644 (55%)
	Ben Jealous (D)..	1,002,639 (44%)
2018 Primary	Larry Hogan (R)..	210,935 (100%)

Prior winning percentage: 2014 (51%)

Throughout the spring and summer of 2020, Republican Larry Hogan enjoyed a wave of media exposure that other potential presidential aspirants could only envy. As chair of the National Governors Association when the COVID-19 pandemic exploded, Hogan was omnipresent on the TV talk show circuit and the beneficiary of a succession of laudatory print and online profiles: His advocacy of a consistent and coherent national strategy contrasted with the mixed messaging coming from the White House of President Donald Trump. "I pushed back very hard when there was no testing program and there was no availability of basic supplies," Hogan later recalled to the Washington Post. " There were a few times the president bristled when I wasn't saying everything was great. One time the president said on a call, 'You're not being very nice to me.' I said, ' No, Mr. President, I'm always nice. I'm just telling you what the governors see.'"

The famously thin-skinned Trump may have been recalling that Hogan, a year earlier, had toyed with the idea of challenging him for the Republican presidential nomination. Ultimately, Hogan opted to defer such ambitions. But, as he completed his year-long term as NGA chair, Hogan stepped up his criticism of Trump on COVID-19 as well as other fronts— one of the handful of prominent Republicans willing to do so. " There's no question in my mind that [Trump] was responsible for inciting this riotous mob," he asserted on CNN following the January 2021 storming of the Capitol. As the first GOP governor to win reelection in solidly blue Maryland since the 1950s, Hogan has sought to position himself as a steady, pragmatic antithesis of Trump: Facing the Democratic-dominated legislature during his 2019 State of the State address, he touted Maryland as a national model, declaring, " a divided government does not have to be a divisive government. ... We found a way to disagree without being disagreeable."

For many leading Democrats, the portrait of recent life in Annapolis has tended to be less rosy. They have criticized Hogan for alternately ignoring or attacking them— recalling occasions such as in 2019 when, after the legislature declined to go along with a Hogan plan aimed at crime in Baltimore, the governor snapped, "This seems to be like the most pro-criminal group of legislators I've ever seen." Some have likened Hogan to tough-talking ex-New Jersey Gov. Chris Christie, a one-time mentor to whom Hogan still talks frequently. For his part, Hogan has attributed the blunter aspects of his modus operandi to an enervating battle with non-Hodgkin's lymphoma in 2015, six months into his first term. "It changed me as a person and the way I look at life and what's important. And maybe that's one of the reasons I'm not afraid to stand up and say what I think," Hogan told National Public Radio in 2020. " Cancer is pretty scary. Nothing else really is going to scare me away from anything." Hogan remained cancer-free at the five-year milestone of his diagnosis, and his political health during that period has been excellent as well, with polls regularly putting his approval rating at or above 70 percent.

Throughout his two terms, Hogan's policy agenda has remained tightly focused on pocketbook issues. After blasting his immediate predecessor, Democrat Martin O' Malley, for "40 consecutive tax increases" over eight years, Hogan has boasted of holding the line on further hikes, although many of his tax cut proposals have gone nowhere. Noting that polling has found Maryland voters view the amount of taxes they pay as 'too high,' Goucher College political scientist Mileah Kromer added, "When they look at this moderate Republican governor, [they see] a check on the Democratic legislature – and also a check on increasing taxes."

Hogan, a successful real estate broker, is the first Maryland governor in the modern political era without prior experience in elected office, buttressing his claims to not being a career politician. But such self-depictions underplay the degree to which he grew up immersed in politics. As a teenager in Prince George's County, he spent weekends on Capitol Hill where his father, Larry Hogan Sr., served in the House. The elder Hogan achieved national attention in 1974 as the only Republican on the Judiciary Committee to vote for all three articles of impeachment against President Richard Nixon. In 2016, after announcing he would neither endorse nor vote for Trump, the governor wrote in his father's name for president, six months before the elder Hogan's death at 88.

By the time of the Nixon impeachment proceedings, the younger Hogan was in Florida, where he had moved with his mother following his parents' divorce. He graduated from Florida State University before returning to the Washington area to work as a congressional staffer. The elder Hogan was elected Prince George's County executive in 1978, and the younger Hogan was hired as his intergovernmental liaison. He took time out to run in a 1981 special election when his father's former congressional seat came open, finishing second in a 12-way Republican primary for the seat ultimately won by Democrat Steny Hoyer, now House majority leader. In 1992, Hogan made a second bid for Congress, challenging Hoyer after the latter's district was redrawn. Hoyer was reelected, but by the narrowest margin of his career, 53%-44%.

Hogan's real estate firm foundered in the wake of a series of bank failures in the early 1990s. After declaring personal bankruptcy in 1994, he rebuilt the Annapolis-based business. In 2002, he helped Rep. Robert Ehrlich become the first Republican elected governor since Spiro Agnew in 1966. Hogan took a leave from his business to serve as Ehrlich's secretary of appointments. After Ehrlich was ousted by O' Malley in 2006, Hogan contemplated running in 2010 before stepping aside for an unsuccessful comeback bid by Ehrlich. A year later, Hogan began laying the foundation for a 2014 gubernatorial run by founding Change Maryland, an anti-tax group.

He won a four-way Republican primary with 43 percent, but started the general election behind in the polls by double digits. The collapse of the Democratic nominee, Lt. Gov. Anthony Brown, was largely attributed to what was seen in party circles as one of the most poorly run campaigns in recent state history. Brown did little to define himself, confidently assuming that the huge Democratic edge in state voter registration would sweep him into office. In a difficult year for Democrats nationwide, tepid turnout in Democratic bastions such as Baltimore and the Washington D.C. suburbs proved insufficient to make up for landslide Hogan margins elsewhere. Hogan won, 51%-47%. (Brown staged a comeback in 2016 by winning a seat in Congress.)

In 2018, former NAACP national president Ben Jealous won an eight-way race for his party's nomination. Jealous emerged with his campaign treasury drained while Hogan, unchallenged for renomination, was flush with cash, ultimately outspending Jealous 3-1. The Republican Governors Association also spent $3 million. In his first bid for elected office, Jealous' political inexperience surfaced during several incidents, and he made little effort to expand his base beyond party progressives. Hogan won, 55%-44%, with polling showing Hogan capturing nearly one-third of the Black vote against the former civil rights leader.

Prior to the COVID-19 pandemic, economically troubled Baltimore, the state's largest city, yielded the biggest crisis of Hogan's tenure. In April 2015, rioting broke out following the death of a Black man, Freddie Gray, while in police custody. Hogan later complained that Baltimore Mayor

Stephanie Rawlings-Blake, a Democrat, failed to return his phone calls for two hours as the rioting spread. According to Washingtonian magazine, when he did reach her, Hogan told her he had two draft executive orders in front of him, one saying he was declaring a state of emergency and deploying the National Guard "at the request of the mayor of Baltimore," the other that he was doing so on his own authority. "But either way, we're coming in," Hogan told Rawlings-Blake, adding, "she calls back in 14 minutes and she says, ' Since you have a gun to my head and since you are going to do it anyway, I guess I'll ask you to come in.'"

Hogan's often scratchy relations with Democratic legislative leaders have generally been most intense when the General Assembly sought to curtail gubernatorial prerogatives. In 2016, Hogan compared the legislators to college students on spring break. " They come here for a few weeks. They start breaking up the furniture and throwing beer bottles off the balcony," he said.

In the face of Democratic supermajorities in the legislature, Hogan has had limited success on some fronts. In 2020, the legislature passed an overhaul of the state's public school system, at a cost of $4 billion a year when fully implemented, based on the recommendations of a commission headed by former University of Maryland System Chancellor William "Brit" Kirwan. Hogan derided it as the " Kirwan Tax Hike Commission" and vetoed the bill. He then revived the " Change Maryland" organization to underwrite a media campaign, but the legislature overrode the veto anyway.

Hogan has increasingly sought to compromise or pre-empt Democratic moves, particularly on environmental initiatives. During the 2014 campaign, Hogan favored hydraulic fracturing, or "fracking," to tap into natural gas reserves in western Maryland. Three years later he announced he would support a permanent ban even before legislation reached his desk. In 2016, Hogan vetoed legislation requiring that 25 percent of Maryland's energy come from renewable sources by 2020; the veto was overridden. In 2019, he allowed a bill mandating 50 percent renewable energy standard by 2030 to become law without his signature.

As Hogan emerged as spokesman for the nation's governors after the COVID-19 pandemic hit, he won Democratic praise for his response in Maryland. Hogan issued a statewide stay-at-home order at the end of March 2020, while sternly rebuking those who defied restrictions and reinforcing those warnings with arrests and fines. Maryland became the second state to close its schools. Hogan's order followed minutes after a similar one in Ohio. The early blowback came largely from conservatives within his own party: Three Republican state legislators filed suit charging that Hogan's actions violated their constitutional rights. Eventually, tensions with Democrats reemerged, as Hogan, in late summer 2020 and again in early 2021, prodded local jurisdictions to reopen schools, a move resisted by leaders of several large counties hard hit by the pandemic even as the Centers for Disease Control and Prevention endorsed school reopenings.

Early in the pandemic, Hogan had purchased 500,000 COVID-19 test kits from a South Korean firm, with an assist from his Korean-born wife, Yumi, who as the first Korean first lady in U.S. history had become something of an icon in her native country. After weeks of negotiations, the tests were flown to Baltimore and secured at an undisclosed location by the Maryland National Guard. Hogan later acknowledged fearing the federal government might try to seize them. An irritated Trump, upon learning of Hogan's gambit, told a White House briefing that Hogan " didn't really understand the federal testing capacity" and " needed more knowledge."

Declared Hogan: " The [Trump] administration made it clear over and over again they want the states to take the lead, and we have to go out and do it ourselves, and that'??s exactly what we did." But the initial public relations coup Hogan scored with the nearly $9.5 million purchase later dissolved amid controversy. Questions from state legislators about whether other supplies necessary to utilize the tests had been obtained, and if the tests had actually been deployed, went unanswered for weeks. Seven months after they were delivered, a Washington Post investigation revealed that the test kits had turned out to be flawed and had been quietly swapped out for a similar number of replacements at the cost of another $2.5 million, a development Hogan had failed to disclose.

A month after winning reelection in 2018, Hogan spoke to a Washington right-of-center think tank critical of Trump. He made a trip to Iowa, where the first delegates to the 2020 Republican National Convention would be chosen. After telling the Associated Press that he was not interested in a " kamikaze mission," he announced in June 2019 he would not mount a primary challenge to Trump. "I'm not going to say I won't run in the future," Hogan told the Baltimore Sun, as he published a memoir entitled, Still Standing: Surviving Cancer, Riots, a Global Pandemic and the Toxic Politics that Divide America.

The term-limited governor threw cold water on speculation that he might run for a Senate seat. " I have no interest in the Senate," Hogan told the Sun, while adding, " I want to have a future in the Republican Party. More importantly, I want the Republican Party to have a future. I believe in a bigger tent." Hogan later told The Washington Post he won't decide about a 2024 presidential run until after his second term ends in January 2023. " There's going to be a fight for the soul of the Republican Party," he said. " There are an awful lot of people in one lane fighting to take on the mantle of Donald Trump. I would argue that I'm one of the leading voices on the other side to say that we've got to move in a completely different direction."

In light of the state's 2-1 Democratic registration advantage, Democrats see Hogan's impending departure from Annapolis as a prime opportunity to reclaim the governorship. Four-term state Comptroller Peter Franchot announced his bid in early 2020, and as many as 10 other Democrats either had announced or were mulling a run, including two former Obama administration Cabinet members.

Ben Cardin (D)

Elected 2006, term expires 2024, 3rd term, b. Oct 05, 1943; Baltimore, MD; University of Pittsburgh, B.A., 1964; University of Maryland School of Law, J.D., 1967; Jewish; Married (Myrna Edelman Cardin); 2 children (1 deceased); 2 grandchildren.

Elected Office: MD House, 1966-1986, Speaker, 1979-1986; Ways & Means Committee, MD, 1974-1979; U.S. House, 1987-2006.

Professional Career: Practicing attorney, 1967-1986; Chairman, MD Legal Services Corporation, 1988-1995.

DC Office: 509 HSOB 20510, 202-224-4524, Fax: 202-224-1651, cardin.senate.gov
State Offices: Baltimore, 410-962-4436; Bowie, 301-860-0414; Cumberland, 301-777-2957; Rockville, 301-762-2974; Salisbury, 410-546-4250.

Committees: *Environment & Public Works*: Clean Air & Nuclear Safety; Fisheries, Water, and Wildlife; Transportation & Infrastructure (Chmn). *Finance*: Health Care; International Trade, Customs & Global Competitiveness; Taxation & IRS Oversight. *Foreign Relations*: Europe & Regional Security Cooperation; Internat'l Dev Instit & Internat'l Econ, Energy & Environ Policy; State Dept & USAID Mngmnt, Internat'l Ops & Internat'l Dev (Chmn); West Hem Crime Civ Sec Dem Rights & Women's Issues. *Small Business & Entrepreneurship (Chmn).*

Group Ratings

	ADA	ACLU	AFL-CIO	LCV	COC	HAFA	ACU	CFG	FRC
2020	-	77%	-	92%	-	0%	4%	-	-
2019	90%	C	100%	100%	50%	C	4%	0%	0%

Almanac Ratings 2019-2020

	Economy	Social	Foreign	Composite
Liberal	97%	97%	77%	90%
Conservative	3%	3%	23%	10%

Key Votes of the 116th Congress

1. EPA clean energy rules	Y	5. Russia sanctions	Y	9. Barr as Atty. General	N
2. U.S./Mex./Can. trade deal	Y	6. Troops in SYR, AFG	N	10. Spending at the border	Y
3. Cut unemployment benefits	N	7. Veto arms sales to Saudis	Y	11. Coney Barrett to Sup. Ct.	N
4. Shelton to Fed Reserve	N	8. Defense $$$, veto override	Y	12. Electoral College objections	N

Election Results

Election	Name (Party)	Vote (%)	Cand. Spent	Ind. Exp. Support	Ind. Exp. Oppose
2018 General	Ben Cardin (D)................................. 1,491,614	(65%)	$3,433,679	$3,763	$29,650
	Tony Campbell (R)........................ 697,017	(30%)	$215,795		
	Neal Simon (I)...................................... 85,964	(4%)	$2,059,835	$341,008	
2018 Primary	Ben Cardin (D)................................. 477,441	(80%)			
	Chelsea Manning (D)..................... 34,611	(6%)			

Prior winning percentages: 2018 (65%), 2012 (56%), 2006 (55%); House: 2004 (63%), 2002 (66%), 2000 (76%), 1998 (78%), 1996 (67%), 1994 (71%), 1992 (74%), 1990 (70%), 1988 (73%), 1986 (79%)

In March 2020, as the onset of the COVID-19 pandemic impelled Congress to respond with a massive economic relief package, among the legislative pieces to come together most expeditiously was a loan initiative— the Paycheck Protection Program— aimed at preserving small businesses and keeping their employees working. The speed exhibited in creating the program— which would disburse more than half a trillion dollars in federally guaranteed loans during the subsequent four months— was largely attributable to the ease with which Democrat Ben Cardin, Maryland's senior senator, has worked across the aisle throughout half-century in elected office.

Cardin and Florida Republican Marco Rubio had been colleagues on the Foreign Relations Committee for nearly a decade, frequently collaborating on legislation. "We really became soulmates on a lot of human rights issues," Cardin told the Washington Post. "It's a trust relationship." As the pandemic took hold, they found themselves leading the Small Business Committee— with Cardin as ranking Democrat and Rubio as chairman, the latter a post Cardin would assume in January 2021 with his party back in the Senate majority. "Almost immediately we had a meeting of the minds that we wanted to have money go out quickly, with minimal underwriting," Cardin said in describing his conversations with Rubio, even as partisan battles were waged around them on other parts of what ultimately emerged as the Coronavirus Aid, Relief and Economic Security Act.

While Almanac vote ratings put Cardin firmly on the liberal end of the Senate Democratic Caucus, his low-key, agreeable personality has enabled him to work effectively with many Republicans. He has demonstrated an abiding interest in the nitty-gritty of crafting legislation on a multitude of foreign and domestic policy fronts while generally shunning partisan sound bites. However, Cardin frequently flashed a sharp tongue during President Donald Trump's years in office, and he used his senior position on the Foreign Relations panel— including a temporary stint as the committee's ranking Democrat— to take on the Trump administration. "Equating our country with an authoritarian, murderous regime is outrageous and reprehensible, even for Mr. Trump," Cardin snapped after Trump at one point appeared to put abuses by Russian President Vladimir Putin on the same plane as some past actions by the United States. At the same time, Cardin continued to pursue bipartisanship, sponsoring with five Republican and four Democratic colleagues a law that sanctioned Russia over its interference in the 2016 elections.

In late 2020, Senate Democratic Leader Chuck Schumer turned to Cardin to moderate a dispute within the caucus over its internal rules— a task Schumer had delegated to Cardin on prior occasions. In this instance, younger Democrats were restive over the amount of power concentrated in more senior colleagues. Among both generations, Cardin has been regarded as a fair broker: While now 77—and having not entered the Senate until he was 63—Cardin was once a boy wonder of Maryland politics.

The son and nephew of state legislators, Cardin grew up in the Jewish neighborhoods of northwest Baltimore: The area and era of his youth were depicted in Barry Levinson's 1982 movie "Diner." He was elected to the state's House of Delegates at 23—in 1966, six months before graduating from the University of Maryland School of Law— and was chosen as speaker in 1978, when he was 35. Just as in Washington, Cardin had a reputation as a consensus-builder in Annapolis.

After achieving the top job in the House of Delegates, Cardin seemed to want to move from the first floor of the state House to the second— where the governor's office is. But when Democrat Barbara Mikulski left her House seat to run for the Senate in 1986, Cardin jumped into the race to replace her and was easily elected. He obtained a seat on the tax-writing Ways and Means Committee, where he remained a productive legislator even after the Democrats were relegated to the minority after the 1994 election.

Another of Cardin's long-term bipartisan partnerships— with Rob Portman of Ohio— goes back to when they served on Ways and Means. They co-sponsored the 1998 Internal Revenue Service reform law, and in 2001, when Congress enacted the Bush administration's tax cuts, it included their provision to increase the limits for IRA and 401(k) contributions. Two decades later, Cardin and Portman continue to collaborate on this issue as Finance Committee members. In 2019, citing the lack of retirement savings by nearly half of Americans older than 55, they introduced legislation to expand access to retirement accounts. Although the bill did not advance, Cardin and Portman planned to renew their effort in 2021.

As a House member, Cardin continued to eye the governorship and twice considered giving up his seat to run for it. But Senate seats don't often open in Maryland— and so when Sen. Paul Sarbanes decided to retire in 2006 after three decades in the seat, Cardin didn't hesitate. He began as the front-runner, even if his earnest, somewhat bland demeanor raised questions about his viability as a statewide candidate. His leading primary opponent was former Democratic Rep. Kweisi Mfume, a charismatic figure who had left the House a decade earlier to head the national NAACP. Mfume and Cardin were friends, but Mfume and other Black leaders warned that the state Democratic establishment's support for Cardin could breed resentment among Black voters— who constitute about 40 percent of registered Democrats in Maryland. Cardin heavily outspent Mfume and won 44%-41%, with the vote breaking largely along racial lines. The GOP nominee was Lt. Gov. Michael Steele, Maryland's first Black statewide officeholder and later chair of the Republican National Committee. Democrats, including Mfume— who has since returned to the House— coalesced around Cardin, who won 54%-44%.

Cardin was named to the Foreign Relations Committee upon his arrival in the Senate; during his first two years, it was chaired by then-Sen. Joe Biden. Perhaps the highest profile period of Cardin's Senate tenure came during his three years as the Foreign Relations panel's ranking member— a perch he assumed in early 2015 when New Jersey Democrat Bob Menendez stepped down after being indicted on corruption charges. (Menendez's 2018 reinstatement as ranking Democrat came after his trial ended in a hung jury and the Justice Department opted not to retry the case.) The initial portion of Cardin's ranking member stint coincided with the final two years of Barack Obama's presidency — putting in place a Democrat more supportive of the Obama administration's foreign policy than Menendez had been. Menendez, a Cuban-American, was resistant to engaging with Cuba; Cardin supported Obama's 2014 move to restore diplomatic ties with the island nation.

Like Menendez, Cardin opposed the Iran nuclear agreement the Obama administration negotiated in 2015. However, Cardin gave Obama a quiet boost by not announcing his opposition until it had become clear the White House had sufficient votes to block a Senate resolution disapproving the deal. When Trump announced in mid-2018 he was withdrawing from the agreement, Cardin— despite his original position— criticized the move. " By breaking the deal, President Trump has breathed air into Tehran's inevitable argument to the international community: We kept our end of the deal, but America is not good for its word and cannot be trusted," he told Vanity Fair. In early 2020, when Trump ordered the drone strike that killed Iranian Maj. Gen. Qassem Soleimani in Baghdad, Cardin blasted the move as a " provocative act taken without congressional consultation or authorization," adding, " This president has unfailingly raised tensions with Iran." He said Trump " should stop the provocations and allow diplomacy to take root."

As a former co-chair of the U.S. arm of the Commission on Security and Cooperation in Europe, which monitors international human rights issues, Cardin has long focused on such matters. His outspoken concern about the Trump administration being overly cozy with the Putin regime was not the first time he had taken on Russia. " My name is well-known in Russia, some places better than in Maryland," Cardin once quipped. One of his major legislative successes came with the 2012 passage of a bill that normalized trade relations with Russia after nearly 40 years— but also required the United States to freeze the assets of, and deny visas to, Russians implicated in human rights abuses. It was titled the Magnitsky Act for a lawyer who died while in the custody of Russian authorities; the roster of sanctioned people it authorized became known informally as the "Cardin List."

Just before leaving office, Obama signed legislation containing a related measure: the Global Magnitsky Act, co-authored by Cardin and Arizona Republican John McCain. It gave the president authority to apply sanctions to human rights transgressions by nations other than Russia. In late 2018, Cardin— along with Menendez and then-Foreign Relations Chairman Bob Corker of Tennessee — requested that Trump determine and sanction those responsible for the slaying of Washington Post columnist Jamal Khashoggi, murdered inside the Saudi consulate in Istanbul. When the Trump administration indicated it would decline to make such a determination, Cardin reacted with outrage, noting the law required action within 120 days after the chair and ranking member of the Foreign

Relations panel filed a request. In late 2019, Cardin— again teaming with Rubio— successfully co-authored a bill to apply this approach to Hong Kong. It required the secretary of State to annually certify Hong Kong's autonomy in order to justify special treatment afforded under a 1992 U.S. law and provided for sanctions on those involved in the suppression of internationally recognized rights in the onetime British colony.

Legislation introduced by Cardin and Rubio after Russian interfered in the 2016 U.S. elections expanded the original Magnitsky Act. It included new mandatory sanctions against Russia, while making it difficult for Trump to reverse existing sanctions via executive action. The Cardin plan was wrapped into broader legislation that passed Congress by a veto-proof majority. Trump signed it but called some provisions " clearly unconstitutional" and served notice he chose not to enforce them. In January 2018, the Trump administration published a lengthy list comprised of leading Russian business and political figures but stopped short of imposing sanctions— contending the legislation was already accomplishing its aim. Under pressure from Capitol Hill, the administration unveiled sanctions against Russia a couple of months later. It did little to mollify Cardin, who complained that " the almost purposeful foot-dragging by the Trump administration has sent a clear signal to Vladimir Putin that he can continue his destabilizing behavior against the United States."

Cardin also has pushed repeatedly for global anti-corruption legislation, requiring the State Department to compile an annual report rating countries worldwide on efforts to combat corruption. A version of the bill—co-sponsored with Indiana Republican Todd Young— passed the Senate unanimously at the end of 2019; Cardin and Young reintroduced it in 2021.

Cardin, a staunch supporter of Israel, took heat from some progressives in his party— as well as civil liberties advocates—f or a bill introduced in 2017 taking aim at the Boycott, Divestment and Sanctions movement. The legislation sought to bar Americans from supporting requests by foreign nations to boycott a country friendly to the United States. Advocates said it was intended only to protect U.S. companies facing pressure from interests abroad to boycott Israel over its treatment of the Palestinians— but critics blasted the proposal as an unconstitutional restriction on free speech. Cardin revised a section of the original bill aimed at companies that joined in boycotts of Israel, but the American Civil Liberties Union argued it still allowed for criminal financial penalties that violated First Amendment rights. Behind-the-scenes lobbying by Cardin to attach the measure to a spending bill at the end of 2018 fell short.

In 2020, Cardin declined to sign a letter circulated by three fellow Senate Democrats— including his junior in-state colleague, Chris Van Hollen— warning the Israeli government against a unilateral move to annex the West Bank area it has long occupied. While telling the Jewish Insider that he would " encourage [Israel] to try to preserve" advancement of a two-state solution in the region, Cardin added: " I don't think it is helpful for us to sow dissension in the United States as it relates to the support for Israel. I think we have to show that even when we disagree with the policies of the government that the relationship between the United States and Israel must remain strong."

Before joining the Finance Committee in 2011, Cardin fought successfully to include pediatric dental care as an essential benefit under the Affordable Care Act. The effort was prompted by the death of a Maryland child who had a brain infection that started as untreated tooth decay; it became the basis of a campaign ad that ran in the weeks leading up to the 2012 Democratic primary, as Cardin sought a second term. In it, a young girl recounts the episode and praises Cardin, ending with the line, " He's my friend Ben—I hope he's your friend, too." Other ads in the widely noticed " My Friend Ben" series showed the incumbent helping load bags onto an airplane and hauling in oysters with Maryland watermen as narrators highlighted his efforts to land funds to expand the Baltimore-Washington International Airport and restore the Chesapeake Bay. (Cardin also serves on the Environment and Public Works Committee.) The ads were an apparent attempt to compensate for Cardin's low-key modus operandi, which had left many Maryland voters with a hazy image of what he had accomplished in his first term.

As it turned out, Cardin had little to worry about: He turned back a primary challenge from a Black state senator by nearly 5-1 and won the general with 56 percent of the vote, as the opposition split between the Republican nominee and a self-financed independent. A similar scenario played out when Cardin ran again in 2018. The Republican nominee was Tony Campbell, a political science teacher who ran a thinly funded campaign supportive of Trump— who polls showed to be highly unpopular in Maryland. The more visible challenge came from independent candidate Neal Simon, a wealthy investment firm executive who spent more than $1.1 million from his own pocket and advertised extensively on TV. Simon differed little from Cardin on major policy issues, but he derided the incumbent as " part of the problem" of increasing gridlock on Capitol Hill. " He follows party leaders who are contributing to the partisan brawl that we're all so tired of watching," Simon declared.

Cardin responded by highlighting his efforts across the aisle. Simon ended up realizing a tiny return on his investment: He got 4 percent of the vote. Cardin captured 65 percent of the vote; Campbell got 30 percent. At age 81 when he faces reelection in November 2024, many in Maryland expect that he will retire.

When the pandemic hit in early 2020, Cardin and Rubio— working with Maine Republican Susan Collins and New Hampshire Democrat Jeanne Shaheen— reached accord in days on what would become the popular Paycheck Protection Program. Cardin preferred a direct federal lending effort, fearing many minority-owned businesses lacked adequate access to private financial institutions. But, with the Republicans then in the majority, he conceded to GOP insistence that the program be administered by private banks with a Small Business Administration guarantee. Cardin did successfully push to expand eligibility for nonprofit enterprises under PPP— as well as to bolster the preexisting Economic Injury Disaster Loan direct-lending program with an additional $50 billion, as the latter ran low on funding.

While PPP operations were not without controversy, by the time the first round of payments ended in August 2020, more than 5.2 million loans totaling $525 billion— nearly 70 percent of them for $50,000 or less— had gone out to eligible businesses; the loans were forgivable for enterprises that spent a majority of the money to maintain employment and salaries at pre-pandemic levels. Another $284 billion in PPP funding was included in a follow-up economic stimulus package passed at the end of 2020. " I was amazed at how it just caught on and it became the centerpiece of ... the CARES Act," Cardin told the Washington Post. " It really became the driving force."

Chris Van Hollen (D)

Elected 2016, term expires 2022, 1st term, b. Jan 10, 1959; Karachi, Pakistan; Swarthmore College, B.A., 1982; John F. Kennedy School of Government, Harvard University, M.P.P., 1985; Georgetown University, J.D., 1990; Episcopalian; Married (Katherine Wilkens Van Hollen); 3 children.

Elected Office: MD House, 1991-1995; MD Senate, 1995-2003; U.S House, 2003-2017.

Professional Career: Practicing attorney; Legislative Assistant, U.S Sen. Charles Mathias, 1985-1987; Staff, U.S Senate Foreign Relations Committee, 1987-1989; Sr. Legislative advisor, Governor William Donald Schaefer, 1989-1991.

DC Office: 110 HSOB 20510, 202-224-4654, Fax: 202-228-0629, vanhollen.senate.gov
State Offices: Annapolis, 410-263-1325; Baltimore, 667-212-4610; Cambridge, 410-221-2074; Hagerstown, 301-797-2826; Largo, 301-322-6560; Rockville, 301-545-1500.

Committees: *Appropriations*: Commerce, Justice, Science & Related Agencies; Department of the Interior, Environment & Related Agencies; Financial Services & General Government (Chmn); State, Foreign Operations & Related Programs; Transportation, HUD & Related Agencies. *Banking, Housing & Urban Affairs*: Economic Policy; Financial Institutions & Consumer Protection; Housing, Transportation & Community Development. *Budget*. *Foreign Relations*: Africa & Global Health Policy (Chmn); Europe & Regional Security Cooperation; Near East, South Asia, Central Asia & Counterterrorism.

Group Ratings

	ADA	ACLU	AFL-CIO	LCV	COC	HAFA	ACU	CFG	FRC
2020	-	92%	-	92%	-	0%	4%	-	-
2019	100%	C	95%	100%	41%	C	4%	5%	0%

Almanac Ratings 2019-2020

	Economy	Social	Foreign	Composite
Liberal	100%	100%	89%	96%
Conservative	0%	0%	11%	4%

Key Votes of the 116th Congress

1. EPA clean energy rules Y	5. Russia sanctions Y	9. Barr as Atty. General N
2. U.S./Mex./Can. trade deal Y	6. Troops in SYR, AFG N	10. Spending at the border N
3. Cut unemployment benefits N	7. Veto arms sales to Saudis Y	11. Coney Barrett to Sup. Ct. N
4. Shelton to Fed Reserve N	8. Defense $$$, veto override N	12. Electoral College objections N

Election Results

Election	Name (Party)	Vote (%)		Cand. Spent	Ind. Exp. Support	Ind. Exp. Oppose
2016 General	Chris Van Hollen (D)...................... 1,659,907	(61%)		$32,177,603	$1,758,111	
	Kathy Szeliga (R)............................. 972,557	(36%)		$1,510,202	$462,219	
	Margaret Flowers (G)........................... 89,970	(3%)		$90,437		
2016 Primary	Chris Van Hollen (D)....................... 470,320	(53%)				
	Donna Edwards (D)............................ 343,620	(39%)				

Prior winning percentages: 2016 (61%), House: 2014 (60%); 2012 (63%); 2010 (73%); 2008 (75%); 2006(77%); 2004 (75%); 2002 (52%)

Beneath an exterior of Boy Scout-like politeness, Democrat Chris Van Hollen is widely credited with possessing both the intellectual curiosity of a policy wonk and the savvy of a master political strategist. The latter attribute was front and center in late 2016 when Van Hollen was tapped to chair the Democratic Senatorial Campaign Committee— a full six weeks before he was sworn in as Maryland's new junior senator. Van Hollen had headed the House Democrats' campaign arm a decade earlier, and then-Senate Minority Leader Chuck Schumer was looking for an experienced hand to run the DSCC during an election cycle in which Senate Democrats would be defending three times as many seats as their Republican counterparts. Schumer was not finding a lot of takers for the assignment among veteran members of his caucus; Van Hollen accepted the job, vowing "to hold the blue line."

In the end, he accomplished just that. Democrats occupied 47 Senate seats as Congress convened in 2019, down only one from the beginning of the prior Congress after confronting what Van Hollen described as the " toughest political map any one party has faced in 60 years." His performance won him praise from colleagues— but immediately after the election, Van Hollen made clear he was not interested in reprising his role at the DSCC for another two years. " There are lots of [policy] issues … that I really want to focus on and turn my attention to in an even bigger way," he told Bethesda Magazine in early 2019.

Van Hollen moved quickly to craft comprehensive legislation— ranging from a 10-year, $400 billion plan for dealing with long-term unemployment to updated versions of proposals from earlier in his career to combat climate change— in order to influence the policy debate among Democratic presidential contenders. A majority of the Democratic aspirants, including now-President Joe Biden, embraced Van Hollen's proposal to fully fund Title I of federal education law; aimed at the nation's highest-need schools, it had been underfunded by a total of $350 billion over a period of 12 years, he complained. "I've been putting this bill in for a very long time. The good news is that it's finally catching fire," Van Hollen said after the 2020 elections. With the White House and Senate back in Democratic control, he plunged into meetings with White House aides as he sought the new administration's support for several policy initiatives.

Although Van Hollen arrived in the Senate well after Biden's 2009 departure from the chamber, he can point to ties to the new president dating back more than 30 years— when Van Hollen was a Senate Foreign Relations Committee staffer and Biden was in his second decade serving on that panel. Fast forward to 2011, when Van Hollen— as ranking Democrat on the House Budget Committee— worked closely with then-Vice President Biden, the Obama administration's point man on budget issues. At the time, the Budget Committee was chaired by a fellow policy wonk, Wisconsin Republican Paul Ryan, with whom Van Hollen regularly sparred. So, when Ryan was selected as the GOP's 2012 vice presidential nominee, Van Hollen was recruited to play Ryan in mock debates to prepare Biden for a televised encounter. Van Hollen spent several days with Biden in what he described as a " Delaware boot camp" that deepened their relationship. "Rarely do you get the opportunity to beat the hell out of the vice president of the United States and be thanked for it at the end of the day," Van Hollen quipped to Maryland Matters years later.

Van Hollen's acceptance of the job running the Senate Democratic campaign committee that nobody else wanted did yield some longer-term benefits— including a coveted appointment to the Appropriations Committee at the outset of his Senate tenure, followed by a seat at the table at weekly strategy sessions of the Senate Democratic leadership. It was the latest example of Van Hollen — whose three decades in elected office include the Maryland General Assembly as well as both houses of Congress— quickly climbing the leadership ladder. Elected to the state Senate in 1994 by ousting an incumbent well-liked by Annapolis insiders, he moved to mend fences with the Senate president and found himself vice chair of an influential committee. Arriving in the House after the 2002 election, he was chair of the Democratic Congressional Campaign Committee by the beginning of his third term and assistant to House Speaker Nancy Pelosi by the start of his fourth. In fact, until he announced his Senate bid in early 2015, many thought he was on track to one day succeed Pelosi. "He could have been speaker of the House, if he stuck around," said one friend from across the aisle, former GOP Rep. Tom Davis of Virginia.

Throughout his career in elected office, Van Hollen has taken calculated risks to move up— and seen them pay off. "Chris has an exquisite sense of timing and opportunity," said Democratic Rep. Gerry Connolly of Virginia, who has known Van Hollen since they were young Senate aides. "Even when conventional wisdom told him not to, his instincts were better, his timing was superior." A penchant for risk-taking was evident in Van Hollen when he was young, while his father served as ambassador to Sri Lanka. Family members tell stories of a teenage Van Hollen who insisted on riding atop jeeps during excursions into the jungle, only to have to scramble inside on occasions when the vehicle was charged by elephants. Van Hollen was born in Pakistan while his father was a Foreign Service officer there; his mother later served as chief of the South Asia division of the State Department's Bureau of Intelligence and Research. While his father's family roots were in Baltimore, Van Hollen largely grew up abroad before returning to the United States to attend boarding school and then Swarthmore College.

After earning a master's degree in public policy from Harvard University's John F. Kennedy School of Government in 1985, Van Hollen went to work for Maryland Sen. Charles Mathias, a liberal Republican who held the seat Van Hollen now occupies. He soon moved to the Foreign Relations Committee staff; after a hazardous trip along the Turkey-Iraq border, he co-authored a report confirming Iraq's use of chemical weapons against its Kurdish minority. Van Hollen seemed headed for a career in the family business of diplomacy but left the committee in 1989 for a job in Maryland's federal affairs office— a move aimed at positioning himself to run for office. In 1990, he was elected to the state House of Delegates on a slate pledged to work to codify Roe v. Wade. In 1994, Van Hollen mounted a primary challenge against the state senator on whose slate he had been elected just four years earlier. His move created some blowback in local political circles, but it paid off: Van Hollen won the primary 3-1, thanks to his well-executed campaign and the incumbent's missteps.

In 2002, Van Hollen gambled again—giving up a safe state Senate seat for an uphill run for Congress. Initially, the odds-on favorite for the Democratic nomination in Maryland's 8th District was a scion of the Kennedy dynasty: state Del. Mark Shriver, son of Sargent and Eunice Kennedy Shriver. But Van Hollen— bolstered by grassroots progressive groups with whom he had been allied on environmental and gun control issues and the endorsement of the Washington Post— defeated Shriver in the primary 44%-41%. He then had only eight weeks to campaign against eight-term Rep. Connie Morella, a liberal Republican. The congenial Morella ran negative ads for the first time, but Van Hollen chose not to directly aim his fire at the popular incumbent. Instead, he argued that Morella's vote with the GOP to organize the House kept in power a conservative majority out of sync with most district voters. Aided by a new redistricting plan, Van Hollen won 52%-47%, and was never seriously challenged in six reelection bids.

Notwithstanding his avowed liberalism and his leadership role at the DCCC, Van Hollen's genial personality enabled him to work across the aisle on House legislation, much as he later did with regularity in the Senate. At the outset of his second House term, he was selected by Illinois Rep. Rahm Emanuel, then chair of the DCCC, to manage candidate recruitment. When the Democrats captured the House majority in 2006 and Emanuel moved up to chair the Democratic Caucus, newly installed Speaker Pelosi exhibited her confidence in Van Hollen by naming him to head the DCCC. When House Democrats expanded their majority in November 2008, Van Hollen and the DCCC got much of the credit— although he was undoubtedly aided by the unpopularity of outgoing President George W. Bush and a cratering economy. Pelosi persuaded him to stay on for a second term as DCCC chair and sweetened the offer by giving him a newly created leadership post: assistant to the speaker. In that role and from a perch on the powerful Ways and Means Committee, he remained active on policy issues amid his DCCC duties.

In April 2009, Van Hollen introduced a cap-and-dividend bill on climate change, as an alternative to the Democrats' cap-and-trade legislation. More than a decade later, Van Hollen has doggedly continued to push this approach in the Senate, which would put a carbon tax on coal, oil and gas producers and distribute the money to regular citizens. He has contended that, by returning the revenues derived from controlling climate change to households, " it addresses the major concern of the critics of doing something— which is that the cost will go up to the American consumer." A related measure that Van Hollen also first proposed in 2009 called for a "Green Bank" to encourage private investment in clean energy projects. A similar mechanism, now dubbed the "clean energy accelerator," was included in legislation passed by the House in 2020. In an interview in early 2021, Van Hollen was optimistic about its future prospects, contending that it "fits nicely within the infrastructure modernization effort" that numbered among the Biden administration's policy priorities.

But in 2009, Van Hollen— donning his political strategy hat— privately urged House action be postponed on climate change, presciently fearing that tackling it on the heels of health care reform would create a backlash among many voters. While the House Democratic leadership guided a cap-and-trade bill to passage that year, it died in the Senate. During the Affordable Care Act debate, Van Hollen successfully co-sponsored an amendment allowing dependents up to age 26 to stay on their parents' health insurance— which became a major talking point for Democrats defending the bill. During the 2009-2010 election cycle, Van Hollen warned of " a very tough campaign season" when polls showed many Democratic incumbents trailing little-known challengers. In the run-up to Election Day 2010, he cut off DCCC funds to nine incumbents who could not be saved, while sending $12 million into districts where Democrats might still be able to win. Even so, Democrats lost 63 seats amid the nationwide tea party revolt— the largest loss either party had experienced in the House since 1948. Van Hollen's own fortunes were not adversely affected: In 2011, he gained the plum assignment as ranking Democrat on the Budget Committee, even though he had not previously served on that panel.

His interest in the Senate predated his rise in the House leadership. When Sen. Paul Sarbanes announced his retirement in early 2005, Van Hollen seriously thought about running. He backed down when it became clear that state Democratic leaders were coalescing around Van Hollen's current in-state senior colleague, Ben Cardin. In March 2015, when Democrat Barbara Mikulski decided to retire after 30 years in the Senate, Van Hollen entered the contest within days and picked up the support of much of the party leadership.

For perhaps the first time in his career, Van Hollen began a race for higher office as the front-runner: He was a heavy favorite over his major primary rival, Rep. Donna Edwards, who suffered from a rocky relationship with the state party establishment and many of her colleagues in the Congressional Black Caucus. Van Hollen reported a 12-1 financial advantage at the end of 2015. But Maryland is called " America in miniature" thanks to its varied geography, and its 2016 Senate Democratic primary became a microcosm of that year's Hillary Clinton vs. Bernie Sanders battle for the party's presidential nomination. As Sanders surged amid anti-incumbent sentiment, so did Edwards: She was viewed as the outsider and Van Hollen perceived as an insider, even if there were few policy differences between them. Polls showed Edwards with a large lead among Black voters in a primary electorate estimated to be 40 percent African American. Edwards' fundraising disadvantage was offset by nearly $3 million spent by a super PAC tied to EMILY'sList—an investment fueled by the fact that, with Mikulski retiring, a loss by Edwards threatened to leave the Maryland congressional delegation without a woman for the first time in four decades.

Two weeks before the primary, polls showed the race to be tight. The late momentum shifted to Van Hollen when Edwards overplayed her hand. It went back to 2010 legislation— the DISCLOSE Act— that Van Hollen had authored to mitigate the Supreme Court's Citizens United v. FEC ruling overturning restrictions on corporate involvement in campaign advertising. (A decade later, Van Hollen continues to cite the DISCLOSE Act— now part of a broader Democratic reform package— as a legislative priority.) Edwards criticized Van Hollen for exempting the National Rifle Association from the bill— a suggestion he was soft on the NRA. Van Hollen, citing his gun control advocacy dating to his state legislative days, reacted angrily. To facilitate House passage of the DISCLOSE Act (it later failed to clear the Senate), several membership-based organizations— including the Sierra Club and labor unions, as well as the NRA— had been exempted; President Barack Obama backed that move at the time. The controversy escalated when a pro-Edwards super PAC echoed her criticism of Van Hollen in an ad that contained footage of Obama. The White House called the ad misleading, putting Edwards on the defensive.

Van Hollen won 53%-39%. Edwards carried the Black-majority jurisdictions of Baltimore and Prince George's County, her home base. Van Hollen won 21 of the state's 22 remaining counties. Republicans nominated Kathy Szeliga, minority whip of the House of Delegates. She characterized Van Hollen as a career politician while tying herself to the state's popular Republican governor, Larry Hogan—and seeking to downplay her conservative voting record in a blue state. On Election Day, Van Hollen came out on top, 61%-36. Van Hollen plans to seek reelection in 2022, and Hogan is widely seen as the only Republican who could give him a competitive race: A Washington Post-University of Maryland poll in late 2019 give Hogan an 8-point lead in a hypothetical matchup. But Hogan has shown little to no interest in a Senate run, and he is widely believed to be focusing on a bid for his party's 2024 presidential nomination. Maryland has not had a Republican senator since Van Hollen's onetime boss, Mathias, retired in 1987.

When Van Hollen accepted the DSCC job shortly after his 2016 win, he leveraged it into the only Democratic vacancy on the Appropriations Committee— the seat that had been held by Mikulski. The committee plays a key role in determining annual funding for several agencies headquartered or with a large presence in Maryland, including the FDA, NASA and the National Institutes of Health. The state is home to nearly 146,000 federal civilian employees, fourth most in the nation.

As the offspring of two career diplomats, Van Hollen— named to a seat on the Foreign Relations Committee in early 2021—has long been active legislatively on numerous foreign policy fronts, often in partnership with Republican colleagues. In July 2020, Trump signed legislation sponsored by Van Hollen and Republican Pat Toomey of Pennsylvania to impose mandatory sanctions on individuals as well as banks and other entities complicit in China's violation of its 1984 agreement with Great Britain on the sovereignty of Hong Kong. One provision gave Congress the ability to override a president's decision to waive or end sanctions via a joint resolution of disapproval. " He didn't want to do it, but we had a veto override number on this," Van Hollen said of Trump signing of the bill. Not long before leaving office, Trump signed another Van Hollen bill aimed at China— this one sponsored with a fellow Banking Committee member, Republican John Kennedy of Louisiana. It could result in more than 250 Chinese firms being barred from U.S. stock exchanges if China continues its long-standing resistance to allowing overseas inspections of its companies' audits.

In another collaboration with Toomey, Van Hollen attached a measure to ratchet up pressure on North Korea to the Defense Department bill in 2019; it called for mandatory sanctions against foreign banks and companies involved in illicit financial transactions on behalf of that nation. A bipartisan effort by Van Hollen and Republican Marco Rubio of Florida to attach sanctions against Russia to the same bill—building on a 2017 measure shepherded by Cardin and Rubio—was less successful. The DETER Act was aimed at penalizing Russia for interfering in the 2016 elections; it mandated sanctions if the director of national intelligence determined there had been Russian interference within a month of an election. Van Hollen's repeated attempts to have the measure considered were blocked, as he pointed the finger at then-Senate Majority Leader Mitch McConnell. " When you get behind closed doors, it's not that anyone says they are opposed to it; they just won't engage," Van Hollen told the Atlantic. " McConnell would like to see this defeated without any of his fingerprints on it, but his fingerprints are there because he has refused to engage."

Van Hollen's ability to deftly balance his dual roles as bipartisan collaborator and hard-nosed partisan was highlighted when, in late 2019, he and South Carolina Republican Lindsey Graham— usually one of Trump's most outspoken backers— emerged as two of Congress' fiercest critics of Trump's decision to back Turkey's invasion of Syria, which involved taking on Kurdish militias that had aided American forces in that region. Van Hollen and Graham produced legislation threatening economic sanctions against Turkey. Such collaboration didn't later deter Van Hollen— in one of several fundraising appeals on behalf of 2020 Democratic Senate nominees—from labeling Graham, who was facing a competitive reelection race, as a "loyal sycophant" for Trump. Declared Van Hollen, " As chairman of the Senate Judiciary Committee, Lindsey Graham has sought to place the interests of Donald Trump above the rule of law over and over again."

Andy Harris (R)

Elected 2010, 6th term, b. Jan 25, 1957; Brooklyn, NY; University of PA, Att., 1975; Johns Hopkins University, B.S., 1977; Johns Hopkins University, M.D., 1980; Johns Hopkins University Bloomburg School of Hygiene and Public Health, M.H.S., 1995; Roman Catholic; Married (Sylvia Harris); 5 children; 6 grandchildren.

Military Career: U.S. Naval Reserve Medical Corps 1988-2001 (Operation Desert Storm)

Elected Office: MD Senate, 1998-2010, Minority whip.

Professional Career: Anesthesiologist, Johns Hopkins Hosp., 1980- 2010; Association Professional, Johns Hopkins Med. School, 1984-2010.

DC Office: 2334 RHOB 20515, 202-225-5311, harris.house.gov
State Offices: Bel Air, 410-588-5670; Chester, 410-643-5425; Salisbury, 443-944-8624.
Committees: *Appropriations*: Agriculture, Rural Development, FDA & Related Agencies; Labor, Health & Human Services, Education & Related Agencies.

Group Ratings

	ADA	ACLU	AFL-CIO	LCV	COC	HAFA	ACU	CFG	FRC
2020	**	17%	**	0%	-	93%	95%	**	-
2019	0%	C	14%	0%	68%	C	95%	94%	100%

Almanac Ratings 2019-2020

	Economy	Social	Foreign	Composite
Liberal	38%	4%	4%	16%
Conservative	62%	96%	96%	84%

Key Votes of the 116th Congress

1. U.S./Mex./Can. trade deal Y	5. Russia sanctions N	9. Firearms background checks N
2. First Coronavirus response Y	6. Troops in Syria N	10. Spending at the border Y
3. HEROES Act N	7. Veto arms sales to Saudis N	11. Marijuana liberalized rules N
4. CASH Act N	8. Defense $$$, veto override N	12. Electoral College objections Y

Election Results

Election	Name (Party)	Vote (%)		Cand. Spent	Ind. Exp. Support	Ind. Exp. Oppose
2020 General	Andy Harris (R)	250,901	(63%)	$768,484	$658	
	Mia Mason (D)	143,877	(36%)		$3,000	
2020 Primary	Andy Harris (R)	72,265	(82%)			
	Jorge Delgado (R)	16,281	(18%)			

Prior winning percentages: 2018 (60%), 2016 (67%), 2014 (71%), 2012 (63%), 2010 (54%)

Andy Harris, elected in 2010, is the lone Republican in Maryland's congressional delegation. He has juggled working with his Terrapin State colleagues on local matters with his fervently conservative views and support for former President Donald Trump. His growing number of critics could create problems for him following the 2022 redistricting, which likely will give him a more competitive district.

Harris, a Johns Hopkins University anesthesiologist and professor, was born in Brooklyn New York to immigrants from Eastern Europe. His father, a Hungarian anti-communist activist, had been jailed in a Siberian gulag for more than a year for his political views before meeting Harris' mother, who had fled Ukraine, at a displaced persons camp in Austria. Harris credits his parents' escape from communism and the spirited dinner-table conversations they encouraged among their four sons with fostering his fiercely held beliefs in the ills of big government and the sanctity of the private sector. After Harris completed his medical studies at Johns Hopkins, he began to practice and teach there.

Harris was elected to the state Senate to represent Baltimore County in 1998. In Annapolis, he was one of the most conservative members, and he served as Senate minority whip. In 2008, he challenged Rep. Wayne Gilchrest, a moderate Republican, in a bloody primary. When Harris defeated him,

Gilchrest refused to concede and then endorsed Frank Kratovil, the Democratic nominee. Kratovil continued Gilchrest's strategy of portraying Harris as too far right for the district and won by fewer than 3,000 votes.

In a rematch in 2010, Harris cast Kratovil as a puppet of President Barack Obama in a year when anti-incumbent feeling was rampant. After his first bid, Harris began to practice medicine a few days a week on the Eastern Shore, which helped deflect the criticism that he was running in an area where he had spent little time. Kratovil attacked Harris for his support of a conservative proposal to replace the income tax with a national sales tax. The first-termer was swept away by the Republican tide, 54%-42%.

Harris said the "proudest moment" of his first few months in office was voting for the House-passed omnibus spending bill that cut $61 billion for fiscal 2011. In 2013, he infuriated Maryland Democrats by joining 66 Republicans in voting against $9.7 billion in relief from Hurricane Sandy, which had battered parts of the Eastern Shore. He explained he wanted the bill to strengthen the National Flood Insurance Program instead of writing "another blank check." Following the 2016 election, Harris was defeated by Rep. Mark Walker of North Carolina for chairman of the Republican Study Committee. He had the support of conservative activists in the House Freedom Caucus.

On behalf of Trump in July 2020, he unsuccessfully sought to remove the Democrats' block on the border wall with Mexico. In October, he was the only House Member who voted "present" on a resolution to condemn the QAnon conspiracy movement. "Congress shouldn't be wasting our last day of work before the one-month election vacation on useless resolutions," he said in a statement about the measure, which passed on a 371-18 vote.

At home, Harris sought to help the Eastern Shore by introducing a bill in 2011 authorizing federal money to study oxygen-starved "dead zones" in Chesapeake Bay and the Gulf of Mexico that drive away fish. Harris has gone his own way on other regional issues. He infuriated residents of the District of Columbia when he sought to use congressional authority to stifle Washington's 2014 referendum legalizing sales of marijuana. On the Appropriations Committee, he has sought to roll back D.C. policies on needle-exchange programs, assisted suicide. waste and psychedelic mushrooms. Some of his opponents have suggested a boycott of the Eastern Shore. "The fact is the Constitution gives Congress the ultimate oversight about what happens in the federal district," Harris responded.

Despite the hostility toward Trump by most Maryland politicians, including Republican Gov. Larry Hogan, Harris remained supportive. He generated local blowback when he joined House Republicans who backed Trump's claims that the 2020 election had been fraudulent. Hogan described the January 2021 riot at the Capitol "a heinous and violent assault" and assigned blame to Trump. Harris defended the president and dismissed critics who called for his resignation. He added that he and other Republicans had "legitimate constitutional concerns" about the election. Peter Jensen, an editorial writer for the Baltimore Sun, wrote, "If Mr. Harris won't leave office willingly, his deplorable actions should not go unchecked. Even before the next election in 2022, decency demands there be a penalty."

In this district that became solidly Republican after the 2012 redistricting, Harris has not faced a serious reelection challenge. In 2015, he voiced interest in running for the Senate seat of retiring Democrat Barbara Mikulski. The Democratic lean of the state and his Appropriations Committee membership mitigated against the uphill challenge. Instead, he had three opponents in the Republican primary, including former state Delegate Michael Smigiel, a libertarian who had support from groups unhappy with Harris on marijuana in D.C. Harris won the primary with an impressive 78 percent to 11 percent for Smigiel. In 2018, Democrat Jesse Colvin, a small business owner and former Army ranger, ran against Trump and said that "Congress is broken." He spent $1.8 million, nearly matching the incumbent. In a Democratic year, Harris won 63%-36% and took 10 of the 12 counties.

Hogan might find common ground with Democrats who want to make Harris' district more competitive in redistricting, in exchange for making at least one Democratic-held district more competitive. Heather Mizeur, who served eight years in the state House of Delegates and ran third in the Democratic primary for governor in 2014, said following the January riot at the Capitol that she would challenge Harris in 2022. Changes in his district lines might give her an opportunity against Harris. He might also face a primary from a credible GOP opponent.

MD-1: Eastern Maryland   **Cook Partisan Voting Index: R+14**

Population		Race and Ethnicity		Income	
Total	737,341	White	81.80%	Median Income	$80,022
Land area (sq. miles)	3,977	Black	12.40%	District Income Rank	92
Pop/ sq mi	185.4	Latino	4.60%	Poverty Rate	9.40%
Born in State	61.90%	Asian	2.20%	With health insurance	95.90%
		Two or more races	2.30%	Cash public assistance	1.90%
Age Groups		Other	1.30%	Food stamp/SNAP	9.50%
Under 18	20.90%				
18-34	20.40%	**Education**		**Work**	
35-64	39.40%	H.S grad or less	39.00%	White Collar	43.00%
Over 64	19.40%	Some college	27.90%	Sales and Service	37.00%
		College Degree, 4 yr	19.10%	Blue Collar	20.00%
Military		Post grad	14.00%	Government	19.20%
Veteran/ Active Duty	8.80%				

2020 Pres. Vote	Trump	236,906	(58%)	Biden	157,430	(39%)		
2016 Pres. Vote	Trump	225,249	(61%)	Clinton	121,840	(33%)	Johnson	12,919 (4%)

Eastern Shore: Chesapeake Bay is technically not a bay but an estuary. It was the central focus of the most thickly settled of the 13 colonies and today remains a central focus for much of modern Maryland. The first British here were amazed at the Chesapeake's oysters, terrapins, crabs and rockfish. This was an estuary civilization in colonial days, with every little hamlet tied together by the highways of bays and creeks and inlets off the Chesapeake. The streets and docks of Chestertown, Oxford, St. Michaels and Cambridge still look something like they did when George Washington slept there. In post-colonial times, when most Americans were caught up in the romance of westward movement, these estuaries and peninsulas were mostly forgotten, located too far off the main lines of railroads and highways. In the 160 years between 1790 and 1950, the Eastern Shore counties of Maryland only doubled in population.

Since then, much of the Chesapeake has changed beyond recognition. The area has grown vigorously, with second-home buyers, retirees and commuters crossing the Chesapeake Bay Bridge. Now, this is a land of genteel estates fronting the water and of Frank Perdue's thriving chicken empire around Salisbury. The 4.3 billion (with a b) pounds of chicken meat produced from 608 million broiler chickens in 2019 on the DelMarVa peninsula doubled the total in 1987; the $3.4 billion value tripled during that time. With limited federal or state regulations, one result has been an increase in the stench from air pollution. The annual total of 750,000 tons of chicken manure is used mostly for nutrients on farm fields. Salisbury also has become a growth area for working-class commuters. A banking-industry study rated the city as having the most affordable housing in Maryland.

Easton has a Waterfowl Festival and quaint St. Michaels has an OysterFest, as do other towns on that part of the three-state DelMarVa peninsula. The Assateague Island National Seashore, with its famous wild ponies, annually attracts more than 2 million visitors and supports a $100 million tourism business. That is separate from the crowded beaches and boardwalks up the coast in Ocean City. Away from the shore, in Harford County, where the population more than tripled since 1960 and the supply of farm land has been cut sharply, demands for new housing and school rooms have accelerated.

Even more threatening is pollution. In 2010, the Chesapeake Bay Foundation settled a lawsuit against the Environmental Protection Agency to enforce limits on pollution entering the bay, especially with regulations on developers and farmers. In a 2020 report, the foundation gave a D+ grade to the health of the bay, a slight improvement from the D- a year earlier, which resulted chiefly from the Trump administration's rollback of environmental regulations plus increased storm runoff. The health of the bay's oysters resulted in large harvests in recent years.

The 1st Congressional District of Maryland includes all nine counties of the Eastern Shore. At the top of the bay, it takes in parts of the northern Baltimore suburbs of Harford, Baltimore and Carroll counties. Nearly half the votes are cast on the west side of the bay and to the north along the Susquehanna River, chiefly in the solidly Republican suburbs of Harford. The Republican precincts in these outer Baltimore suburbs maximize Democratic performance in neighboring districts. This is the only district in Maryland where Republicans hold a voter registration edge, and the only one that presidential nominee Donald Trump carried—with 61 percent of the vote in 2016 and 58 percent in 2020.

Dutch Ruppersberger (D)

Elected 2002, 10th term, b. Jan 31, 1946; Baltimore, MD; Baltimore City College; University of MD - College Park, B.A., 1967; University of Baltimore School of Law, J.D., 1970; Methodist; Married (Kay Murphy Ruppersberger); 2 children; 3 grandchildren.

Elected Office: Baltimore County Council, 1986-1994; Baltimore County Executive, 1994-2002.

Professional Career: Clerk, Judge Kenneth C. Proctor, 1970-1972; Assistant state Attorney, Baltimore County, 1972-1980; Partner, Ruppersberger, Clark & Mister, 1980-1994.

DC Office: 2206 RHOB 20515, 202-225-3061, Fax: 202-225-3094, ruppersberger.house.gov

State Offices: Timonium, 410-628-2701.

Committees: *Appropriations*: Commerce, Justice, Science & Related Agencies; Defense; Homeland Security.

Group Ratings

	ADA	ACLU	AFL-CIO	LCV	COC	HAFA	ACU	CFG	FRC
2020	**	79%	**	100%	-	0%	9%	**	-
2019	90%	C	100%	97%	65%	C	10%	12%	0%

Almanac Ratings 2019-2020

	Economy	Social	Foreign	Composite
Liberal	100%	100%	80%	94%
Conservative	0%	0%	20%	6%

Key Votes of the 116th Congress

1. U.S./Mex./Can. trade deal Y	5. Russia sanctions Y	9. Firearms background checks Y
2. First Coronavirus response Y	6. Troops in Syria Y	10. Spending at the border Y
3. HEROES Act Y	7. Veto arms sales to Saudis Y	11. Marijuana liberalized rules Y
4. CASH Act Y	8. Defense $$$, veto override Y	12. Electoral College objections N

Election Results

Election	Name (Party)	Vote (%)		Cand. Spent	Ind. Exp. Support	Ind. Exp. Oppose
2020 General	Dutch Ruppersberger (D)	224,836	(68%)	$893,818	$9,010	
	Johnny Ray Salling (R)	106,355	(32%)	$64,971		
2020 Primary	Dutch Ruppersberger (D)	82,167	(73%)			
	Michael Feldman (D)	20,222	(18%)			
	Jake Pretot (D)	9,780	(9%)			

Prior winning percentages: 2018 (66%), 2016 (62%), 2014 (61%), 2012 (66%), 2010 (64%), 2008 (72%), 2006(69%), 2004 (67%), 2002 (54%)

Dutch Ruppersberger, elected in 2002, has retained his focus on national security issues. With his base at the Appropriations Committee, he has continued his bipartisan approach to intelligence issues on behalf of a district that he calls " the cybersecurity capital of the world." His gerrymandered district lines, which were largely drawn for him, are at risk during the upcoming Maryland redistricting.

Charles Albert Ruppersberger grew up in Baltimore, attended the University of Maryland and graduated from the University of Baltimore School of Law. Working as a Baltimore County assistant state's attorney, Ruppersberger had a near-fatal car accident in 1975 while investigating a drug-trafficking case. When he asked his doctors at the University of Maryland's Shock Trauma Center how he could thank them, he said, they urged him to run for office so he could fund their facility.

In 1986, he won a seat on the Baltimore County Council and made good on his promise to help the hospital. In 1994, he was elected Baltimore County executive.

Barred from seeking a third term in 2002, Ruppersberger seriously considered running for governor. But he was dissuaded by state party leaders who felt he was politically vulnerable following a controversy over county redevelopment. Instead, he took advantage of a favorable House district when Democrats redrew the congressional map. Against investment banker Osman Bengur, who spent more than $500,000 of his own money. Ruppersberger won the primary, 50%-36%. In the fall, he faced Helen Delich Bentley, who served in the House for a decade until she ran, unsuccessfully, for governor in 1994. Both candidates supported additional dredging of shipping channels in Chesapeake Bay and increased port security. Ruppersberger won, 54%-46%. His popular-vote margin was largely in the small part of the district in Baltimore city.

In the House, his Almanac vote ratings have been the least liberal among Maryland Democrats. With the help of Baltimore native Nancy Pelosi, he was appointed to the Intelligence Committee, where he called for expanded oversight of intelligence agencies and for shifting resources from the Iraq war to terrorist "safe havens" in Afghanistan. Working with Chairman Mike Rogers, a Michigan Republican and former FBI agent, Ruppersberger sought to repair the panel's reputation for partisan infighting. "We both focus more on the teamwork," Ruppersberger told The Washington Post. The two men traveled together to foreign hot spots and sat together at classified White House briefings.

Ruppersberger did not hesitate to criticize President Barack Obama and his administration. In 2009, he said that he had not been adequately consulted on the White House's plan to buy and launch spy satellites. With Rogers, Ruppersberger signed a report that defended the Pentagon and the Central Intelligence Agency for their handling of the attacks in 2012 on the U.S. diplomatic compound in Benghazi Libya. Even after he left the committee, he remained an advocate of the intelligence legislation enacted in 2015 to end the National Security Agency's bulk collection of telephone and email data. The House-passed defense spending bill in 2016 included his provision to create a unified command for cyber operations, based at Fort Meade.

After leaving the Intelligence Committee in 2015, Ruppersberger retained his interest in steps to strengthen cybersecurity, an area that he said had been neglected under Obama. Prompted by concern about the potential sale of shipping operations at the Port of Baltimore to the United Arab Emirates, Ruppersberger helped to enact port security legislation.

Returning to the Appropriations Committee, where he focused on national security funding, he raised concerns about the Trump administration's handling of intelligence. In May 2018, the committee approved his amendment to enforce sanctions on the Chinese telecommunications firm ZTE; the Trump administration later lifted the ban. In June, he wrote an op-ed with Republican Rep. Mike McCaul, plus Sens. Chris Coons and Marco Rubio, urging that national security policies " transcend party lines" and that the administration learn from past examples of government working in unison to " form a coherent national security strategy." He said he had "nightmares" after Defense Secretary James Mattis resigned in December 2018. The following month, he wrote that President Donald Trump needed to " stop tweeting and start leading." In another op-ed for The Hill that he co-authored with Rogers, they wrote, "The key to good intelligence is … no politics." The fact that this point bears repeating is "alarming," they added.

With his interest in local governance, he launched the Municipal Finance Caucus to assist the financing of infrastructure. In 2018, he filed a bill to restore a tax break for refunding of municipal debt, which had been eliminated by the Republican-passed tax bill. In September 2020, he filed legislation to give a $225 monthly bonus to personnel— medical and non-medical— on the front line of the fight against the coronavirus; that is the same amount that troops receive when serving in combat zones.

Ruppersberger has been reelected easily. His early statewide ambitions dimmed when he passed up opportunities for vacant seats for governor and the Senate, which were won by other Democrats. The next round of redistricting might create sufficient change or pose enough of a reelection challenge to encourage him to retire in November 2022, when he will be 76.

MD-2: Baltimore Metro

Cook Partisan Voting Index: D+13

Population		Race and Ethnicity		Income	
Total	750,702	White	50.90%	Median Income	$73,004
Land area (sq. miles)	349	Black	36.90%	District Income Rank	144
Pop/ sq mi	2,151.75	Latino	7.70%	Poverty Rate	11.90%
Born in State	61.30%	Asian	5.30%	With health insurance	94.00%
		Two or more races	3.50%	Cash public assistance	2.70%
Age Groups		Other	3.30%	Food stamp/SNAP	13.10%
Under 18	22.60%				
18-34	24.10%	**Education**		**Work**	
35-64	38.60%	H.S grad or less	38.80%	White Collar	43.00%
Over 64	14.70%	Some college	28.40%	Sales and Service	38.20%
Military		College Degree, 4 yr	18.90%	Blue Collar	18.80%
Veteran/ Active Duty	9.00%	Post grad	14.00%	Government	20.50%

2020 Pres. Vote	Biden	225,433	(65%)	Trump	110,901	(32%)		
2016 Pres. Vote	Clinton	193,237	(59%)	Trump	114,460	(35%)	Johnson	8,990 (3%)

Parts of Baltimore County: The spokes of Baltimore's avenues spread out in all directions from the Inner Harbor, connecting the central city with the suburbs, where most residents of metropolitan Baltimore live. The streets reach east to Dundalk and Essex, industrial suburbs where the tone of life was set for years by the giant Sparrows Point steel mill, long the biggest in the country, but which was shuttered in 2012. Northeastward, they extend to charming Havre de Grace and the oldest lighthouse in continuous use on the East Coast, as well as to modest working-class suburbs in Harford County. In an arc north of downtown are middle-income towns from Randallstown to Owings Mills. A couple of miles northwest of the Baltimore County seat of Towson is Timonium, the site of the annual Maryland State Fair.

The 2nd Congressional District of Maryland is an irregularly shaped hodgepodge that includes much of this territory. Most of the district is not far from Chesapeake Bay, including the terminal for the huge Port of Baltimore, which has been rated as the most efficient container port in the nation. In 2019, it employed more than 15,000 workers and moved 858,000 cars and small trucks—the most in the nation. With the widening of the Panama Canal, Baltimore and Norfolk Virginia were the only East Coast ports wide and deep enough for post-Panamax cargo ships. A huge redevelopment has been underway to revive Sparrows Point as the Tradepoint Atlantic industrial park and international trade hub, with many commercial distribution centers, including Amazon, FedEx and Under Armour. The global logistics center operates over 3,300 acres, with port, rail and highway service. Inland, Towson officials in 2020 reported $700 million in development underway that was transforming this once sleepy part of suburbia.

With its short distance from Washington D.C., the Baltimore area has become a convenient locale for military work. The Aberdeen Proving Ground tests a wide variety of military weapons. The Baltimore Sun has described it as the local "economic lifeblood," with more than 20,000 government and contractor jobs. Down the Baltimore-Washington Parkway is Fort Meade, the sprawling Army post that houses the National Security Agency and supports more than 125,000 jobs in 1,500 buildings. It has evolved from an army base to a cybersecurity center, which houses more than 115 federal agencies, including the nation's cyber defense operations and the Defense Information Systems Agency.

Like the arms of a Maryland crab, the district angles inland to include some Baltimore County suburbs, residential neighborhoods in northeast Baltimore, an industrial pocket in far southeast Baltimore and a dip south of Baltimore along Interstate 95 to include the NSA headquarters. At that point, the district crosses the Harbor Tunnel to capture the row houses of Brooklyn and Curtis Bay, whose residents are mainly descendants of German and East European immigrants who moved there to work on the docks and in the factories along the Patapsco River and the harbor. About 60 percent of the district's population is in Baltimore County, where Vice President Spiro Agnew got his start as a Democrat before he became county executive and then governor; a bit less than 10 percent is in Baltimore city, and much of the remainder in Harford County. About one-third of its population is African American. This is a comfortably Democratic district, with some Republican enclaves. Joe Biden got 65 percent of the vote, an increase from the 59 percent for Hillary Clinton.

John Sarbanes (D)

Elected 2006, 8th term, b. May 22, 1962; Baltimore, MD; Princeton University Woodrow Wilson School of Public and International Affairs, B.A., 1984; Harvard University, J.D., 1988; Greek Orthodox; Married (Dina Sarbanes); 3 children.

Professional Career: Clerk, Judge Fred Motz, 1988-1989; Practicing attorney, Venable LLP, 1989-2006; Special Assistant MD Schls. Superintendent, 1998-2005.

DC Office: 2370 RHOB 20515, 202-225-4016, Fax: 202-225-9219, sarbanes.house.gov

State Offices: Annapolis, 410-295-1679; Towson, 410-832-8890.

Committees: *Energy & Commerce*: Environment & Climate Change; Health. *Oversight & Reform*: Government Operations.

Group Ratings

	ADA	ACLU	AFL-CIO	LCV	COC	HAFA	ACU	CFG	FRC
2020	**	81%	**	100%	-	0%	2%	**	-
2019	95%	C	100%	97%	57%	C	2%	12%	0%

Almanac Ratings 2019-2020

	Economy	Social	Foreign	Composite
Liberal	100%	100%	80%	94%
Conservative	0%	0%	20%	6%

Key Votes of the 116th Congress

1. U.S./Mex./Can. trade deal	Y	5. Russia sanctions	Y	9. Firearms background checks	Y
2. First Coronavirus response	Y	6. Troops in Syria	Y	10. Spending at the border	Y
3. HEROES Act	Y	7. Veto arms sales to Saudis	Y	11. Marijuana liberalized rules	Y
4. CASH Act	Y	8. Defense $$$, veto override	Y	12. Electoral College objections	N

Election Results

Election	Name (Party)	Vote (%)		Cand. Spent	Ind. Exp. Support	Ind. Exp. Oppose
2020 General	John Sarbanes (D)	260,358	(70%)	$429,719	$9,123	
	Charles Anthony (R)	112,117	(30%)	$1,294		$113
2020 Primary	John Sarbanes (D)	110,457	(83%)			
	Joseph C. Ardito (D)	17,877	(13%)			

Prior winning percentages: 2018 (69%), 2016 (63%), 2014 (60%), 2012 (67%), 2010 (61%), 2008 (70%), 2006 (64%)

Democrat John Sarbanes, elected in 2006, has been a prominent advocate of Democratic government-reform proposals and has been an ally of Nancy Pelosi, the former Baltimorean. On the Energy and Commerce Committee, he has worked on issues ranging from health care to campaign finance reform. He remains young enough to fulfill his ambition to follow his father's path from the House to the Senate, where he chaired the Banking Committee.

Sarbanes graduated from Princeton University and Harvard Law School, following the academic route taken by his dad, Paul Sarbanes, Following his retirement in 2006 after 36 years in Congress, his father died in 2020. The younger Sarbanes returned to Baltimore to clerk for a federal District Court judge, then joined the Venable law firm, where he chaired the health care practice and represented nonprofit hospitals and senior-living providers. He spent seven years as special assistant to the Maryland superintendent of schools, serving as liaison to Baltimore schools.

In his 2006 campaign, Sarbanes enjoyed a considerable advantage because of his name recognition. But the primary race was no cakewalk. When Democratic Rep. Ben Cardin left the House to run for the Senate seat of the senior Sarbanes, eight candidates filed for the primary. Contenders included veteran state Sen. Paula Hollinger and former Baltimore Health Commissioner Peter Beilenson. Sarbanes issued lengthy, detailed proposals on health care and education, which he called his top two legislative priorities. Beilenson emphasized his experience managing a large government budget. Hollinger was endorsed by the teachers' union, and had been an active state lawmaker. Sarbanes, who had a small fundraising advantage, won the Democratic primary with 32 percent to 25 percent for Beilenson and 21 percent for Hollinger. In the general election, Republican John White got little attention in a Democratic year. Sarbanes won, 64%-34%.

In the House, Sarbanes has a staunchly liberal voting record. In 2010, he got a provision in an auto safety bill to fund research into new technologies to prevent drunk-driving accidents. He urged the Federal Trade Commission in 2011 to take action against Pfizer for what he described as its attempts to keep consumers away from generic versions of its successful anti-cholesterol drug Lipitor. On Energy and Commerce, he called for the regulation of Facebook because of its failure to protect personal data. " They have a tremendous amount of power," he said in 2018. "It's one of the largest data brokerage firms in the world, vacuuming up data on 2 billion people every single day."

In 2016, Sarbanes took the lead on legislation that sought to address opioid addiction, which had become a major problem in Baltimore. The House passed his bill to train doctors to prescribe overdose-reversal drugs when they prescribe pain medication and other opiates. His approach, he said, was to bring together medical professionals, behavioral health experts and law enforcement with local, state and federal officials to improve addiction treatment and expand prevention services. Serving on the House-Senate conference committee that crafted the final details of the 21st Century Cures Act, Sarbanes pushed for the $1 billion that was approved to expand treatment programs. In 2018, the House passed a bill he cosponsored to permit the forgiveness of student loans for recipients who become professionals dealing with substance abuse.

Like his father, Sarbanes has been an outspoken advocate of Greece and its Hellenic values. In 2018, he added a provision to the annual defense spending bill that prevented the U.S. transfer of F-35 fighter jets to Turkey, pending a report by the Pentagon to Congress. When House Republicans shot down his proposal to create a national climate change service, he attacked their " reckless political stunt of climate change denial."

He has advocated legislative solutions to clean up pollution in Chesapeake Bay. In October 2020, he hailed the bipartisan increase to $92 million in annual spending, which included several provisions for conservation and cleanup in the watershed. He called the measure " tremendously important… to ensure that [the bay] remains an environmental treasure and an economic driver for years to come.

Sarbanes has been the lead sponsor of Democrats' " Government for the People" campaign finance plan that would give contributors tax credits for donations and create a fund to match small donations to "grassroots" candidates who refuse political action committee money. The plan would reinvigorate democracy, he wrote, by " empowering a more diverse pool of candidates who would have the resources to run, compete and win." In 2019, that proposal evolved into H.R. 1, a package that became the initial major legislation offered by House Democrats when they regained the majority. As chairman of the House Democracy Reform Task Force, Sarbanes worked closely with Pelosi to add voting rights, ethics reforms, donor disclosures and restrictions on gerrymandering. The House passed the measure on a party-line vote. With Pelosi, he disputed claims by President Donald Trump and other Republicans during the 2020 presidential campaign that mailed ballots favored Democrats. Given voter support, he told reporters, "I'm not sure why the president would want to get sideways with the broad public in terms of that priority."

Democrats passed a similar version in March 2021, though the measure continued to increase in size and with little public discussion of details. With Democratic control of the Senate and the White House increasing the prospects for enactment, reform advocates increasingly argued among themselves about the scope of the package— including whether to include such measures as statehood for the District of Columbia and expansion of the Voting Rights Act, or to handle those issues separately.

Sarbanes has been reelected easily. He says he drives home to Towson every night. Perhaps he will seek to succeed Cardin in the Senate, just as he did in the House— though Cardin, who will be 81 when his term expires in 2024, has shown no signs of retiring; in 2024, Sarbanes will be 62.

MD-3: Baltimore Metro

Cook Partisan Voting Index: D+16

Population		Race and Ethnicity		Income	
Total	779,502	White	61.70%	Median Income	$94,736
Land area (sq. miles)	304	Black	23.50%	District Income Rank	44
Pop/ sq mi	2,562.97	Latino	9.40%	Poverty Rate	7.70%
Born in State	49.00%	Asian	7.40%	With health insurance	95.20%
		Two or more races	4.10%	Cash public assistance	1.80%
Age Groups		Other	3.30%	Food stamp/SNAP	7.50%
Under 18	22.70%				
18-34	24.20%	**Education**		**Work**	
35-64	38.30%	H.S grad or less	25.70%	White Collar	56.00%
Over 64	14.80%	Some college	22.10%	Sales and Service	32.20%
		College Degree, 4 yr	26.90%	Blue Collar	11.80%
Military		Post grad	25.30%	Government	19.80%
Veteran/ Active Duty	8.80%				

2020 Pres. Vote	Biden	263,027	(68%)	Trump	112,328	(29%)		
2016 Pres. Vote	Clinton	221,842	(62%)	Trump	113,318	(32%)	Johnson	12,324 (3%)

Annapolis: Downtown Baltimore, one of America's major urban centers since the Revolution, has been viewed as one of America's star cities. Its Inner Harbor redevelopment, with a spectacular, multilevel aquarium on the water, and its ballpark at Camden Yards are national models. The local cuisine— crab cakes and steamed crabs spiced a certain way— is known well beyond the Chesapeake Bay watershed. In 2009, about half the city became a National Heritage Area, a designation that boosted tourism and economic development. The minority neighborhoods of Baltimore have had terrible urban problems— high crime, controversial policing, abandoned neighborhoods, poor schools— but the greater Baltimore area that has grown far beyond the city and county lines has fared better and retains a distinctive character. In Annapolis, the marble-halled Statehouse, built in 1772, is where the Continental Congress ratified the Treaty of Paris that ended the Revolutionary War and is the oldest state capitol in continuous use. In 2017, workers quietly removed from the lawn the statue of Maryland native Chief Justice Roger Taney, who wrote the pro-slavery Dred Scott decision. The home of the U.S. Naval Academy, including the cemetery where Sen. John McCain was buried in 2018, Annapolis is both a waterman's and yachter's port.

The 3rd District of Maryland consists of three oddly disjointed pieces of geography that extend from the Inner Harbor area. As it scoops up parts of Baltimore city, Baltimore County, Anne Arundel County, Howard County and a small slice of Montgomery County, the 3rd has been a prime contender for the most-gerrymandered district in the nation. According to the Washington Post's Wonkblog, this is the "Praying Mantis" district. From a distance, it seems like an ink spot. But there is a rationale to what some might consider its absurdity. Its boundaries were designed by Democrats with politics in mind: The 3rd borders the majority-Black 7th District on three sides. One spoke extends northeast and takes in Black city neighborhoods; another extends north and west from the city to the Baltimore County seat of Towson and the suburbs of Pikesville and Owings Mills. The last crooked spoke extends south to Glen Burnie and the Baltimore-Washington International Thurgood Marshall Airport, where it splits into two tangents: One goes south to Anne Arundel County and all of Annapolis, and the other heads west to Columbia in Howard County, plus rural Olney and Calverton in Montgomery County. About a third of the district's population resides in Anne Arundel, which is the least Democratic portion, and another quarter is in Baltimore city.

In Baltimore's revived Locust Point industrial neighborhood on the waterfront is the iconic orange Domino Sugars sign glowing from the refinery plant's rooftop— now powered by LED lights. The plant has continued to refine 6.5 million pounds of raw sugar a day, but other industrial land along the water is being redeveloped into upscale residential and commercial properties. The district includes the fabled restaurants and bars of Little Italy and Fell's Point. A water wheel, with solar and water power, periodically removes tons of trash and debris from the Inner Harbor. Port Covington, waterfront property in south Baltimore, is the site of a new development of apartments and offices, including the headquarters for Under Armour and its more than 10,000 employees; the pandemic delayed its scheduled opening until 2022. The solidly Democratic 3rd voted for Joe Biden, 68%-29%.

Anthony Brown (D)

Elected 2016, 3rd term, b. Nov 21, 1961; Huntington, NY; U.S. Military Academy at West Point, Att.; Harvard College, B.A., 1984; Harvard University Law School, J.D., 1992; Roman Catholic; Married (Karmen Bailey Walker Brown); 2 children; 1 stepchild.

Military Career: U.S. Army 1984-1989; U.S. Army Reserves 1989-2014 (Iraq)

Elected Office: Maryland Assembly, 1999-2007; Lt. Governor, 2007-2015; MD House of Delegates; Majority Whip.

Professional Career: Mbr., Board of Governors; Council of State Gov't Toll Fellow.

DC Office: 1323 LHOB 20515, 202-225-8699, anthonybrown.house.gov

State Offices: Annapolis, 410-266-3249; Largo, 301-458-2600.

Committees: *Armed Services*: Seapower & Projection Forces; Tactical Air & Land Forces. *Transportation & Infrastructure*: Aviation; Coast Guard & Maritime Transportation; Highways & Transit. *Veterans' Affairs*: Economic Opportunity; Technology Modernization.

Group Ratings

	ADA	ACLU	AFL-CIO	LCV	COC	HAFA	ACU	CFG	FRC
2020	**	79%	**	95%	-	0%	6%	**	-
2019	95%	C	95%	97%	56%	C	7%	6%	0%

Almanac Ratings 2019-2020

	Economy	Social	Foreign	Composite
Liberal	100%	66%	96%	88%
Conservative	0%	34%	4%	12%

Key Votes of the 116th Congress

1. U.S./Mex./Can. trade deal N	5. Russia sanctions Y	9. Firearms background checks Y
2. First Coronavirus response Y	6. Troops in Syria Y	10. Spending at the border N
3. HEROES Act Y	7. Veto arms sales to Saudis Y	11. Marijuana liberalized rules Y
4. CASH Act Y	8. Defense $$$, veto override Y	12. Electoral College objections N

Election Results

Election	Name (Party)	Vote (%)		Cand. Spent	Ind. Exp. Support	Ind. Exp. Oppose
2020 General	Anthony Brown (D)	282,119	(80%)	$456,053	$7,023	
	George McDermott (R)	71,671	(20%)			
2020 Primary	Anthony G. Brown (D)	110,232	(78%)			
	Shelia Bryant (D)	26,735	(19%)			

Prior winning percentages: 2018 (78%), 2016 (74%)

Anthony Brown of Maryland, elected to the House in 2016, settled into his seat on the Armed Services Committee, where he brought his extensive military background and worked on issues affecting his many constituents who are active-duty or veterans, plus others who work for Pentagon contractors. Following his lengthy service in Annapolis, he has kept the door open to another run for governor after his unsuccessful bid in 2014.

Brown is a native of Huntington New York, where his father was a native of Jamaica and worked as a physician on Long Island. He got his bachelor's and law degrees from Harvard University. He joined the Army ROTC program and was commissioned after college as a second lieutenant and served as a helicopter pilot and aviation officer in Germany. Later, in the Army Reserve, he was a lieutenant colonel in the Judge Advocate General's Corps. Following law school, where he was a classmate of Barack Obama, Brown moved to Maryland and clerked for the chief judge of the U.S. Court of Appeals for the Armed Forces. He remained a colonel in the Reserve.

In 1998, he was elected to the first of four terms in the Maryland House of Delegates and served as majority whip. In 2004, he was deployed to Iraq, where he was a senior consultant to the Iraqi Ministry of Displacement and Migration and worked on refugee problems; he earned the Bronze Star. He was elected lieutenant governor in 2006 as the running mate of Martin O' Malley and served two terms in that office. He won the Democratic nomination to run for governor in overwhelmingly Democratic Maryland in 2014, but lost to Republican Larry Hogan, 51%-47% after what many considered a lackluster campaign. He would be one of six defeated gubernatorial candidates who became members of his freshman class in the House.

When Rep. Donna Edwards ran for the Senate, Brown was the early favorite to succeed her and won endorsements from key local Democratic officials. He ran on a campaign of "redemption" following his setback in 2014, and described himself as a " workhorse, not a show horse." His chief opponent was Glenn Ivey, a former prosecutor in Prince George's County. His wife, Jolene Ivey, a former state delegate, ran for lieutenant governor on the ticket opposing Brown in the close Democratic primary for governor in 2014.

Brown, who loaned himself nearly $400,000 shortly before the primary, won the April primary, 42%-34%. State Del. Joseline Pena-Melnuk, who ran as the " progressive fighter," was third with 19 percent. In the general election that was a foregone conclusion in this district, Brown defeated businessman George McDermott, 74%-21%. He has not faced serious major-party opposition in his reelections.

On the Armed Services panel, Brown organized a defense and aerospace consortium of local businesses, plus academicians, with an interest in military policy to advise him on national security issues, including the aging workforce. " There has to be a public-private partnership," he told Defense News in 2019. The consortium could also be useful in organizing data security workshops for small businesses struggling to meet government requirements, Brown said. Earlier, he filed legislation, which he called the National Security Workforce Act, to provide incentives for businesses that include workforce development in their bids for defense programs. During committee debate on the military spending bill in 2018, he offered a proposal to retain the Defense Information Systems Agency as part of a reorganization of the Pentagon. His proposal was defeated on a party-line vote.

Brown maintained an interest in Pentagon operations. During the protests across the nation following the death of George Floyd in police custody in Minneapolis, he took the lead in a June 2020 congressional letter to secretary of Defense Mark Esper that criticized what he called the secretary's hostile rhetoric and added, " United States citizens are not the enemy and our military should not plan or execute attacks against them." Later that year, he criticized the Pentagon for failure to follow up on congressional requirements for more diversity among military forces. In a statement to The Hill, he criticized the Trump administration for " trying to slow-walk this progress— from defending the racist legacy of the Confederacy to ordering an end to race and sex discrimination trainings in the military."

Serving on the Ethics panel, Brown was assigned to a subcommittee to investigate the indictment on insider-trading charges against Republican Rep. Chris Collins of New York.   That assignment ended when Collins pleaded guilty in October 2019 to federal charges.

Asked in a June 2019 interview about another run for governor when the seat is open in 2022, Brown told Maryland Matters that he would " put my skills and ability to the highest use on behalf of Marylanders" and that " I learned a lot about Maryland" in his 2014 campaign.

MD-4: Eastern D.C. Suburbs   Cook Partisan Voting Index: D+29

Population		Race and Ethnicity		Income	
Total	758,795	White	28.50%	Median Income	$88,207
Land area (sq. miles)	298	Black	52.40%	District Income Rank	63
Pop/ sq mi	2,547.92	Latino	17.50%	Poverty Rate	7.70%
Born in State	30.90%	Asian	3.00%	With health insurance	90.20%
		Two or more races	3.10%	Cash public assistance	1.50%
Age Groups		Other	13.00%	Food stamp/SNAP	8.50%
Under 18	23.20%				
18-34	22.20%	**Education**		**Work**	
35-64	40.40%	H.S grad or less	38.30%	White Collar	41.30%
Over 64	14.10%	Some college	26.20%	Sales and Service	38.00%
		College Degree, 4 yr	20.50%	Blue Collar	20.70%
Military		Post grad	15.10%	Government	23.20%
Veteran/ Active Duty	8.80%				

2020 Pres. Vote	Biden	286,724	(79%)	Trump	69,533	(19%)
2016 Pres. Vote	Clinton	256,575	(77%)	Trump	63,390	(19%)

Prince George's County: In 1696, the proprietors of the colony of Maryland created a new county between the Potomac and Patuxent rivers and named it after the husband of the heir to the throne, Prince George of Denmark. During its 300 years, Prince George's County has not often won national fame, though it might now. With a population that is nearly two-thirds African American, Prince George's is the home of America's largest Black middle class. It is the wealthiest county with a majority Black population, and continues fast-growing with an increase in total population from 802,000 in 2000 to 909,000 in 2019.

Historically, Prince George's was tobacco country, dotted by slave plantations and pretty much controlled by its white property owners. A hundred years after the Civil War, the population grew as middle-class Blacks moved out of neighboring Washington D.C. into modest suburbs at the county's edge and affluent subdivisions farther to the east. Its African-American population increased from 14 percent in 1970, to 37 percent in 1980, to 64 percent in 2019. The county continues to grow, with working-class Black and Hispanic residents leaving gentrified Washington for more affordable housing and better schools across the border. More than 100,000 are current or former federal employees. As the Hispanic population has climbed above 20 percent, there has been some pushback from Black groups over jobs, plus new schools and public facilities in immigrant neighborhoods, including Largo and Langley Park.

With office and shopping mall development, Prince George's County has become commercially vibrant. On the edge of the Potomac River is the National Harbor development area, where the MGM casino opened in 2016; two years later, it accounted for nearly half of the state's casino revenues. The Washington Redskins play at FedEx Field in nearby Landover, with tentative plans to move to a more luxurious stadium elsewhere in the region. After years of litigation to protect its nickname, owner Dan Snyder in 2020 unilaterally modified the team's name to the Washington Football Team, pending a decision on a new name. Prince George's County is affluent by national standards. Its median household income of $84,920 easily tops the national median of about $62,843 and is nearly double the national median for Black households. Nearly 33 percent of the county population over 25 holds an undergraduate degree, which is slightly higher than the national average.

The 4th Congressional District of Maryland includes most of Prince George's County inside the Capital Beltway that rings Washington, and a GOP-leaning eastern salient into relatively rural central Anne Arundel County, including Severna Park. This is a safely Democratic seat; Joe Biden carried Prince George's by an extraordinary 89%-9% in 2020, the largest margin in the state. On certain social issues, however, the district is more conservative: While a 2012 referendum legalizing same-sex marriage in Maryland passed statewide with 52 percent of the vote, it narrowly failed in Prince George's County. The district's biggest employer is the federal government. Suitland, just across the D.C. border, is the home of the Census Bureau. Local and state officials have tried to lure the FBI; President Donald Trump, at least temporarily, blocked plans to move the bureau from its longtime downtown Washington headquarters.

Steny Hoyer (D)

Elected 1981, 20th full term, b. Jun 14, 1939; New York, NY; University of MD - College Park, B.S., 1963; Georgetown University Law Center, J.D., 1966; Baptist; Widower (Judith Pickett); 3 children; 3 grandchildren; 2 great-grandchildren.

Elected Office: MD Senate, 1966-1979, President, 1975-1978.

Professional Career: Practicing attorney, 1966-1980; MD Board of Higher Ed., 1978-1981.

DC Office: 1705 LHOB 20515, 202-225-4131, Fax: 202-225-4300, hoyer.house.gov

State Offices: Greenbelt, 301-474-0119; White Plains, 301-843-1577.

Committees: House Majority Leader.

Group Ratings

	ADA	ACLU	AFL-CIO	LCV	COC	HAFA	ACU	CFG	FRC
2020	**	79%	**	100%	-	0%	6%	**	-
2019	90%	C	100%	97%	58%	C	6%	12%	0%

Almanac Ratings 2019-2020

	Economy	Social	Foreign	Composite
Liberal	100%	100%	80%	94%
Conservative	0%	0%	20%	6%

Key Votes of the 116th Congress

1. U.S./Mex./Can. trade deal Y	5. Russia sanctions Y	9. Firearms background checks Y
2. First Coronavirus response Y	6. Troops in Syria Y	10. Spending at the border Y
3. HEROES Act Y	7. Veto arms sales to Saudis Y	11. Marijuana liberalized rules Y
4. CASH Act Y	8. Defense $$$, veto override Y	12. Electoral College objections N

Election Results

Election	Name (Party)	Vote (%)		Cand. Spent	Ind. Exp. Support	Ind. Exp. Oppose
2020 General	Steny Hoyer (D)	274,210	(69%)	$3,119,444	$4,013	
	Chris Palombi (R)	123,525	(31%)	$40,405		$113
2020 Primary	Steny Hoyer (D)	96,664	(64%)			
	Mckayla Wilkes (D)	40,105	(27%)			

Prior winning percentages: 2018 (70%), 2016 (67%), 2014 (64%), 2012 (69%), 2010 (64%), 2008 (74%), 2006 (83%), 2004 (69%), 2002(69%), 2000 (65%), 1998 (65%), 1996 (56.9%), 1994 (58.8%), 1992 (53%), 1990 (81%), 1988 (79%), 1986 (81.9%), 1984 (72%), 1982 (80%); 1981 special (56%)

Democrat Steny Hoyer, elected in 1981, is the longest-serving Democrat in the House. He is the majority leader and de facto leader of his party's moderate wing in the House, and he is at heart a bipartisan deal-cutter despite his role as a public critic of Republicans. He has remained part of the aging and entrenched Democratic leadership that regained House control in 2018, despite growing calls for generational transition.

Hoyer is of Danish descent. His first name, he says, was his parents' adaptation of the Danish name Steen. He grew up in New York City, but moved from place to place with his mother and stepfather, who was in the Air Force and, when Steny was in high school, was transferred from Florida to Andrews Air Force Base in Maryland. Hoyer graduated from the University of Maryland, where in 1959 he listened to Democratic presidential candidate John F. Kennedy deliver a campaign speech that inspired him to switch his major from public relations to political science. While working on his law degree at Georgetown University, Hoyer interned one summer with Maryland Sen. Daniel Brewster. Another intern in Brewster's office that summer was Nancy D' Alesandro, daughter of the former mayor of Baltimore and now House Speaker Nancy Pelosi.

In 1966, just after graduating from law school, Hoyer was elected to the Maryland Senate at age 27. He was Senate president from 1975 to 1978, the youngest person to hold that post in Maryland history. In 1978, he ran for lieutenant governor on a losing ticket. In 1981, after Rep. Gladys Spellman was incapacitated by a heart attack, the 5th District seat was declared vacant. Hoyer won the special election, edging out Spellman's husband and several other Democrats in the primary and beating a well-financed Republican in the general. Only three Republican members have more seniority in the House. Sen. Patrick Leahy of Vermont is the only congressional Democrat who has served longer.

Hoyer was also a fast riser in Congress. He excelled at constituent service and won a seat on the Appropriations Committee, where he worked with Republicans and became a champion for the Washington metro area. He has been an advocate of more spending for education and other social programs, and better pay and benefits for federal workers. He was the chief House sponsor of the Americans with Disabilities Act of 1990, which outlawed discrimination against people with disabilities. He counts that as his greatest legislative achievement, along with the 2002 federal election reform known as the Help America Vote Act. On Sept. 11, 2001, it was Hoyer's idea to have lawmakers gather in front of the Capitol in a show of unity. The group spontaneously sang " God Bless America," an image captured vividly on television on a dark day in U.S. history.

His voting record is relatively moderate among Democrats. He broke with the party by supporting the balanced budget amendment in 1995. He has backed many of the free-trade initiatives that organized labor opposed, including the North American Free Trade Agreement, though in 2015 he voted against expedited action on the Trans-Pacific Partnership. In 2002, he voted to authorize military action in Iraq and later complained that President George W. Bush "under-resourced" the war. He is a former chairman of the Helsinki Commission, and has remained a champion of human rights around the world.

Hoyer won his first leadership post in 1989 as chairman of the Democratic Caucus. When he tried to move up to the job of majority whip in 1991, he lost, 160-109, to David Bonior of Michigan. In 2001, Bonior, faced with unfavorable redistricting changes at home, decided to run for governor. Both Hoyer and Pelosi sought to replace him as minority whip. Hoyer argued that he had greater experience in leadership positions and could do a better job of unifying the caucus. With her stronger base among women and in her adopted state of California, Pelosi won 118-95.

When Pelosi ran to succeed Dick Gephardt as minority leader in 2002, Hoyer ran to succeed her as minority whip. He collected commitments for months and was elected unanimously. In that position, it was his job to be partisan, and he often was. As Hoyer conceded in 2010, as he was being criticized by Republicans, "I think both parties have acted defensively in some respects when they were in the majority." In the pivotal 2006 campaign, Hoyer worked closely with Illinois Rep. Rahm Emanuel, who chaired the committee to elect a Democratic majority. Many of the freshmen subsequently credited the help Hoyer provided, especially those from swing districts where liberal Democratic leaders were not always welcome.

When it came time to elect leaders to the new Democratic-controlled House, Hoyer had to fight for majority leader against Pennsylvania Rep. John Murtha, who was a close ally of incoming Speaker Pelosi. In spite of their years working together, Pelosi and Hoyer still viewed each other with suspicion. Hoyer had little choice but to speak positively about his longstanding relationship with her — he called her a "favorite daughter" of Maryland— and their success in largely unifying an often-unruly party. But Hoyer prevailed 149-86, a powerful endorsement of him for majority leader and a restraint on Pelosi. Hoyer won the support of many California Democrats who had been unified behind Pelosi and of numerous prospective committee chairmen who doubted Murtha's ability to do the job.

As majority leader, Hoyer assumed responsibility for determining the floor schedule, helping guide Democratic initiatives to passage, and holding weekly press briefings. He described his recipe for holding together what had historically been a fractious caucus this way: " First of all, work very hard on communications, find out what people can do and can't do. Secondly, put together a consensus that, while it may not be the first choice of everybody, it is a choice they can live with." And for the most part, the record justified his boast that House Democrats during their four years in the majority were "the most unified the Democratic Party has been in over half a century."

He actively pushed a " Make It in America" package of Democratic bills to boost U.S. manufacturers, with several becoming law. In early 2009, working with Pelosi, Hoyer steered to passage the $787 billion economic stimulus legislation, the first major initiative of the Obama administration. Only 11 House Democrats voted against it, and every Republican opposed it. He had a hand in the Democrats' successful efforts to increase the hourly minimum wage and in adoption of most of the 9/11 commission's homeland security and intelligence-reform recommendations. When Democrats lost their majority in 2010 in a historic 63-seat setback, Pelosi returned to minority leader and Hoyer to whip. Hoyer came out in favor of same-sex marriage in 2012, shortly before his daughter, Stefany Hoyer Hemmer, announced publicly that she is a lesbian.

More inclined to defer to committee chairs and hew to regular order than Pelosi, he supported doing away with term limits for committee leaders, which the Republicans imposed when they were in the majority. At his urging, Pelosi agreed to their repeal in late 2008. "I am not for term limits for chairmen," Hoyer said. " It puts intellect on hold."

Hoyer has fine political instincts, works hard and can speak in an old-fashioned, patriotic style that can be genuinely moving. With Democrats returned to the minority, he drew criticism from some conservatives for his rhetoric on the GOP's hardline stance on "fiscal cliff" budget negotiations shortly after the December 2012 school massacre in Newtown Connecticut. "It's somewhat like taking your child hostage and saying to somebody else, 'I'm going to shoot my child if you don't do what I want done,'" Hoyer said of Republicans. When John Boehner stepped down as Speaker in 2015, Hoyer called it "a bad day for the House" and praised him as a "positive legislator."

Over the years, Hoyer has remained unable to edge out Pelosi in the leadership. As Democrats' prospects to regain majority control dimmed, speculation occasionally swirled that Pelosi would give up her party post and Hoyer would become her successor. But she continued to stay on. Some Democrats believe that one reason Pelosi did not walk away is that she did not want Hoyer to take the top spot. Their lengthy reign has frustrated the ambitions of junior House Democrats.

Hoyer again got the better of Pelosi in November 2014 in the internal jockeying among House Democrats to succeed California's Henry Waxman as ranking member on the Energy and Commerce Committee. Pelosi lobbied on behalf of her close friend, fellow Californian Anna Eshoo, while Hoyer backed New Jersey's Frank Pallone. Hoyer's ability to count votes is "unmatched," a grateful Pallone said. "Hoyer, he's a shark who never sleeps. ... He's a shark with a killer disposition," Missouri Democrat Emanuel Cleaver, a senior Black Caucus member, told Politico.

In a parallel of sorts to the 2006 election, Hoyer played an active role in the 2018 campaign, which resulted in the Democrats' return to House control. As a candidate recruiter, he worked with national and local party groups to identify preferred candidates in battleground districts. That led to complaints by some contenders, as when Hoyer was recorded on tape urging Levi Tillerman of Colorado to step aside for Jason Crow, an Army veteran and the favorite of the party establishment, who ultimately defeated Tillerman and Republican Rep. Mike Coffman. For Democrats, Hoyer told reporters, the objective was "making sure that we have a Democrat that can win in districts that are tough."

With Democratic candidates often distancing themselves from Pelosi during the 2018 campaign, Hoyer took the opportunity to advise many of them and appear at campaign events. He revived his "Make It in America" theme and cited the success of centrist Democratic Rep. Conor Lamb, the special election winner in a Pennsylvania district that Donald Trump won in 2016. Hoyer sometimes was more open than was Pelosi to negotiating with Trump, as with the dispute over the border wall with Mexico. On other occasions, he could be a harsh critic of Trump. He attacked some of his language as "racist" and said that Trump's July 2018 meeting in Helsinki with Russian president Vladimir Putin was "treasonous."

Once again, Democratic victory created tension for Hoyer with Pelosi following the 2018 election. When she agreed to term limits for Democratic leaders in order to secure the final votes she needed to assure she would become Speaker, Hoyer objected to formalizing the agreement or to extending it beyond Pelosi. " She's not negotiating for me," Hoyer told reporters. He also found himself in something of a squeeze when Rep. James Clyburn of South Carolina, the third-ranking Democratic leader, suggested that he was considering a move up the leadership ladder. In any case, the top three leaders—now octogenarians— regained the leadership positions they had held in the majority a decade earlier.

As the chief advocate for centrist Democrats among party leaders, he worked closely with many to assure they were comfortable with the handling of the first impeachment case against Trump plus other challenging issues—especially for the large freshman class in 2019-20. " One of the reasons we've had success over the years," he told Maryland Matters in November 2019, is that "Nancy and I could reach across the breadth of the caucus." He took the lead in July 2020 in passing a House resolution to remove Confederate statues from the Capitol— including that of Chief Justice Roger Taney, a Maryland native, who wrote the Dred Scott decision supporting slavery.

When the coronavirus cut back the time members spent in the Capitol, Hoyer showed his parliamentary skill in working out the sometimes arcane details that permitted "proxy" voting on the House floor and "virtual" meetings of committees. In describing the rules change, he told The Washington Post in May 2020, " That one big step is to make sure Congress can act."

In his district, Hoyer has pushed for funding Chesapeake Bay cleanup. He has worked shrewdly to maintain and increase jobs at the Goddard Space Flight Center in Greenbelt, at Naval Air Station Patuxent River, and at the Naval Surface Warfare Center at Indian Head. He sponsored bills allowing more federal employees to work four-day weeks, granting eight weeks of paid parental leave, and raising the government contribution to employees' health care premiums. He kept his hand in other Maryland political campaigns, and usually but not always prevailed.

The last time Hoyer had serious competition in a general election was 1992, the first election after his district was reconfigured to extend beyond Prince George's County. He has won easily since, and has gained the loyalty of African-American voters in Democratic primaries. That could offer him security in the Maryland redistricting wars. Still, the endgame for his leadership ambitions and tenure in the House remained to be determined.

MD-5: Southern Maryland   **Cook Partisan Voting Index: D+16**

Population		Race and Ethnicity		Income	
Total	756,743	White	46.80%	Median Income	$101,298
Land area (sq. miles)	1,481	Black	39.20%	District Income Rank	31
Pop/ sq mi	510.88	Latino	10.40%	Poverty Rate	6.60%
Born in State	39.90%	Asian	4.10%	With health insurance	95.20%
		Two or more races	3.90%	Cash public assistance	1.40%
Age Groups		Other	6.10%	Food stamp/SNAP	6.20%
Under 18	22.00%				
18-34	22.70%	Education		Work	
35-64	40.60%	H.S grad or less	36.60%	White Collar	45.30%
Over 64	14.60%	Some college	29.00%	Sales and Service	34.80%
		College Degree, 4 yr	19.20%	Blue Collar	19.80%
Military		Post grad	15.10%	Government	29.00%
Veteran/ Active Duty	11.10%				

2020 Pres. Vote	Biden	276,896	(68%)	Trump	119,771	(30%)		
2016 Pres. Vote	Clinton	225,989	(63%)	Trump	115,869	(32%)	Johnson	9,375	(3%)

Prince George's County: Southern Maryland was established as a colony of the British Lords Baltimore, who were seeking a refuge for English Catholics in the New World. The Lords Baltimore, first George and then Cecil Calvert, founded St. Mary's in 1634, not long after the founding of Jamestown and Plymouth. Maryland became one of the two great Chesapeake tobacco colonies, with plantation houses on every inlet off the broad Potomac and Patuxent rivers. For years, the towns of southern Maryland grew slowly, and even today many of their residents are directly descended from the old families. The region was never Puritan country. Liquor flowed even during Prohibition, and for years, Maryland law specifically allowed slot machines. But tobacco farming is nearing an end.

The area's economic base has owed much to government installations: the Civil War Point Lookout prisoner-of-war camp; the Navy's Patuxent River complex, which started as a center for aircraft testing and where many astronauts began their training; and the Naval Air Warfare Center. Metro Washington and Baltimore have been spreading into southern Maryland. Charles and St. Mary's counties have continued with their rapid growth—11 and 8 percent, respectively, from 2010 to 2019. Charles County has become the new home of many African-American families fleeing crime and troubled schools in Prince George's County. Today, the county is 50 percent Black and most of its schoolchildren are Black. Its median household income rose to $100,000 in 2019, thanks in part to many two-government-employee families. The economy in St. Mary's has been bolstered by about 20,000 employees at the Patuxent River facility. Chesapeake Bay is vital to the local economy. St. Mary's has become a site for restoration of oyster beds, with increased use of aquaculture along the inlets. The cultivation helps to clean the bay.

But the growth in southern Maryland has caused nightmarish congestion. According to a Bloomberg News study in 2019, commuters from this area to Washington waste more time and money getting to work than any other group of commuters in the nation. Local advocates have demanded attention to a local study that called for an 18 mile, $2 billion light-rail system that would connect to the D.C. Metro system.

The 5th Congressional District of Maryland comprises all of Calvert, Charles and St. Mary's counties, plus most of Prince George's County outside the Capital Beltway and a small part of southern Anne Arundel County. Prince George's, with about 40 percent of the population, and Charles, with 20 percent, are the largest and heavily Democratic counties in the district. The three smaller ones lean Republican. The district takes in College Park, home of the University of Maryland, and nearby Hyattsville, Greenbelt, Beltsville and Bowie. On the bay, it stops just short of Annapolis. Whites in the rural areas have trended Republican, but African Americans— both new suburbanites and descendants of old southern Maryland families— make up 39 percent of the district's population. The district has been a Democratic stronghold for decades. Even with its Republican clusters, Joe Biden increased the Democratic vote to 68 percent from the 63 percent for Hillary Clinton four years earlier.

David Trone (D)

Elected 2018, 2nd term, b. Sep 21, 1955; Cheverly, MD; Furman University, B.A., 1977; University of PA Wharton School of Business, M.B.A., 1985; Lutheran; Married (June Trone); 4 children.

Professional Career: Founder & Owner, Total Wine & More.

DC Office: 1213 LHOB 20515, 202-225-2721, trone.house.gov

State Offices: Gaithersburg, 301-926-0300.

Committees: *Appropriations*: Commerce, Justice, Science & Related Agencies; Military Construction, Veterans Affairs & Related Agencies; Transportation, HUD & Related Agencies. *Joint Economic. Veterans' Affairs*: Disability Assistance & Memorial Affairs; Economic Opportunity.

Almanac Ratings 2019-2020

	Economy	Social	Foreign	Composite
Liberal	100%	100%	80%	94%
Conservative	0%	0%	20%	6%

Key Votes of the 116th Congress

1. U.S./Mex./Can. trade deal Y	5. Russia sanctions	Y	9. Firearms background checks Y
2. First Coronavirus response Y	6. Troops in Syria	Y	10. Spending at the border Y
3. HEROES Act Y	7. Veto arms sales to Saudis	Y	11. Marijuana liberalized rules Y
4. CASH Act Y	8. Defense $$$, veto override Y		12. Electoral College objections N

Election Results

Election	Name (Party)	Vote (%)		Cand. Spent	Ind. Exp. Support	Ind. Exp. Oppose
2020 General	David Trone (D)...............................	215,540	(59%)	$3,094,297		
	Neil Parrott (R)....................................	143,599	(39%)	$322,158		$88
2020 Primary	David Trone (D).................................	65,655	(72%)			
	Maxwell Bero (D)............................	25,037	(28%)			

Prior winning percentages: 2018 (59%)

Democrat David Trone spent a record amount—mostly his own money—to win his House seat. For the co-owner of a large chain of wine and beverage stores, the victory marked his first success in campaign politics. In 2016, he spent nearly as much of his own money to seek the open seat in an adjacent Maryland district. That initial appeal as a political outsider fell short in the Democratic primary to Jamie Raskin. With his victory on his second attempt, his deep pockets assured that he would be a competitive candidate.

Trone grew up on a farm in Pennsylvania. He graduated from Furman University and got his master's in business administration from the Wharton School at the University of Pennsylvania. His father lost the family farm to financial difficulties. But Trone went into business at a soda and beer store his mother took over after his parents separated. In 1984, he converted that store into Beer World, a large retail shop. That was the start of a multi-state beverage empire that Trone developed with his brother Robert, and eventually rebranded as Total Wine and More. As co-owners of the largest private wine retailer in the nation, with nearly 200 stores, they became very wealthy.

In 2016, Trone sought the Democratic nomination in the heavily Democratic 8th District, when Chris Van Hollen gave up the seat in his successful run for the Senate. His opponents were Raskin, a law professor and state legislator, and Kathleen Matthews, who spent many years as a broadcast-news reporter and anchor. Spending more than $13 million of his own money to craft his outsider appeal, Trone's self-financing became a major controversy in the campaign. Raskin won the primary with 34 percent of the vote to 27 percent for Trone and 24 percent for Matthews; he breezed to election in November.

When Rep. John Delaney, another wealthy financier from the Washington suburbs , decided to retire, Trone's second try had several similarities—including his self-financing, a leading opponent who served in the legislature and a district that was nearly as Democratic. This time, Trone was well-known in the urban core of the district, though he needed to get acquainted in the more-sprawling rural areas. His campaign message was familiar. In addition to his opposition to the Trump administration, he called for increased funding for the National Institutes of Health and local transportation projects.

In the eight-candidate Democratic primary, Trone's chief opponent was state Delegate Aruna Miller, an immigrant from India as a child. With her progressive agenda, she focused on expanded health care services. She criticized Trone for living in the adjacent district, in addition to his self-financing. With nearly $1.5 million she raised, plus the support of some unions and environmental groups, Miller had the resources to be competitive. Trone raised $12 million for the primary—$11.5 million from his own pocket.

Compared to Raskin in 2016, Miller's legislative record and her political appeal were more limited. In the primary results, Miller led Trone by 1,126 votes in Montgomery County, which cast nearly two-thirds of the total vote. But Trone swept nearly half the total vote in the four outlying counties, where he had a lead of more than 6,700 votes over Miller. That gave Trone a 40%-31% victory.

In November, Trone faced Amie Hoeber, onetime head of Army research and development at the Pentagon. Hoeber also self-financed, though with far less money than Trone. Hoeber was not positioned to seriously threaten in this Democratic district. During the fall campaign, Trone was sidelined by kidney surgery, which resulted in a loss of weight and hair. Several million more dollars of largely self-financed advertising—more than $18 million for the cycle-helped him to maintain an active campaign.

In the House, Trone founded the bipartisan Freshmen Working Group on Addiction, which included more than 60 members. One of the group's initiatives was a bill he filed with Republican Rep. John Joyce to require the Homeland Security Department to send Congress an annual report on the security of the medical-supply chain, especially with the sort of personal protective equipment that became in high demand during the coronavirus pandemic. "Why do we have all the N-95 masks being made in China? That's crazy," he told the Pittsburgh Post-Gazette in September 2020.

He was easily reelected in 2020, self-financing $3 million of the $3.1 million that he spent. He spent some of that money to become better-known among Democrats across Maryland as he considered the possibility of running for governor in 2022. Even if he stays in the House, Republicans might seek to restore their strength in this western Maryland district.

In January 2021, as a measure of appreciation for his financial support to their party, Democratic leaders named Trone to the Appropriations Committee. Citing the pandemic and the worsening addiction and mental health crisis, he called for "smart, long-term investments that live up to our American values and build our country back better."

In May 2021, Trone announced that he will seek reelection in 2022, ruling out a bid for governor. Still, he faced uncertainty in redistricting, given the call by Gov. Larry Hogan to end the gerrymander of the state's districts and an opportunity for competitive contests.

MD-6: Western Maryland

Cook Partisan Voting Index: D+8

Population		Race and Ethnicity		Income	
Total	769,046	White	66.30%	Median Income	$88,592
Land area (sq. miles)	1,950	Black	14.30%	District Income Rank	61
Pop/ sq mi	394.33	Latino	13.10%	Poverty Rate	8.30%
Born in State	42.90%	Asian	11.80%	With health insurance	94.20%
		Two or more races	4.20%	Cash public assistance	2.60%
Age Groups		Other	3.40%	Food stamp/SNAP	10.60%
Under 18	22.30%				
18-34	21.10%	Education		Work	
35-64	41.40%	H.S grad or less	33.40%	White Collar	48.40%
Over 64	15.30%	Some college	23.40%	Sales and Service	35.40%
		College Degree, 4 yr	22.70%	Blue Collar	16.20%
Military		Post grad	20.60%	Government	19.60%
Veteran/ Active Duty	6.40%				

2020 Pres. Vote	Biden	227,214	(60%)	Trump	140,735	(37%)		
2016 Pres. Vote	Clinton	189,512	(55%)	Trump	134,827	(39%)	Johnson	10,691	(3%)

D.C. Exurbs: One of America's first frontiers was western Maryland, where the Appalachian ridges that cross the state diagonally from northeast to southwest cut through long sloping fields. The land was settled by Pennsylvania Dutch and Scots-Irish hill people, not Chesapeake Bay tobacco growers. Maryland is where the 19th century's great paths to the interior were staked out: the National Road; the nation's first combined freight and passenger railroad, the Baltimore & Ohio, which crossed the wide valleys of bounteous farms and climbed over the Catoctin Mountains; and the Chesapeake and Ohio Canal, which began operating in 1828, primarily to haul coal from western Maryland to the port of Georgetown in Washington. Towns grew up with narrow streets of row houses amid cornfields, pastureland and ancient mountains.

Across this placid land moved vast armies during the Civil War. In Frederick, city officials paid the Confederates $200,000 not to burn the town, and near Sharpsburg, blue- and-gray-clad soldiers fought the Battle of Antietam on the bloodiest day in American military history. The battle is now commemorated with an annual illumination of 23,000 candles on the battlefield. A century later, without munitions, President Lyndon Johnson unveiled a different kind of War— on Poverty — on the steps of City Hall in Cumberland, near the coal-laced hills of Appalachia. Poverty fell here in the 1970s, but conditions worsened in the 1980s with the closure of several large factories. Frederick and Washington counties have seen large increases in Hispanics since 2000. The quickly diversifying population has created tensions: Frederick in 2010 became the first county in Maryland to declare English its official language, as county officials struggled to deal with a rise in illegal immigration. But the growing political influence of Hispanic migrants, plus farm operators who needed the workers, won a repeal of the language measure in 2015. Montgomery County officials, by contrast, said they will not honor federal requests to detain immigrants. In far western Garrett County, the adverse impact of hydraulic fracking on local tourism led local groups to urge Gov. Larry Hogan to issue a fracking ban, which he did in 2018. That area is on the edge of the Marcellus Shale formation.

The 6th Congressional District stretches nearly 200 miles from Republican-leaning western Maryland along the West Virginia border to the Washington D.C. suburbs. Instead of crossing Republican pockets east to Harford County as in the past, Democratic redistricters in 2011 dropped the district south from Frederick into Montgomery County. There, it scoops up heavily Democratic Washington suburbs, including most of affluent Potomac, multicultural Gaithersburg and fast-growing Germantown. Half the district's population lives in suburban Washington. The district has the highest concentration of Asian Americans in the state (12 percent); Hispanics make up 13 percent of its population. With the district transformed into a Democratic-leaning bellwether, President Barack Obama in 2012 and Hillary Clinton each won 55 percent of the vote. Joe Biden got 60 percent, even though President Donald Trump won two-thirds of the vote in the three western counties; they cast about 30 percent of the vote. If redistricters drew a new map close to the version that was used before 2012, which extended east along the Pennsylvania border   through the hunt country of the northern parts of Baltimore and Harford counties and eliminated most— if not all— of Montgomery County, it likely would be a comfortably Republican district.

Kweisi Mfume (D)

Elected 2020, 6th full term, b. Oct 24, 1948; Baltimore, MD; Morgan State University, B.S., 1976; Johns Hopkins University, M.A., 1984; Not Known; Married (Tiffany McMillan); 5 children.

Elected Office: Member, Baltimore City Council, 1978-1986; U.S. House, 1986-1996;.

Professional Career: President and CEO of the NAACP, 1996-2004; Principal Partner, The Mfume Group, LLC, 2009; Executive Director, National Medical Association, 2010-2011; Member, National Advisory Council of the NIMHD, 2011-2014; Principal Investigator, Health Policy Research Consortium, 2013-2018; Chief Health Equity Officer/Board Member, technology consulting company, 2015-2018; Vice Chairman of the Board, Research!America.

DC Office: 2263 RHOB 20515, 202-225-4741, Fax: 202-225-3178, mfume.house.gov

State Offices: Baltimore, 410-685-9199; Catonsville, 410-818-2120; Ellicott City, 443-364-5413.

Committees: *Education & Labor*: Civil Rights & Human Services. *Oversight & Reform*: National Security; Subcommittee on Civil Rights & Civil Liberties. *Small Business (VChmn)*: Contracting & Infrastructure (Chmn); Oversight, Investigations & Regulations.

Election Results

Election	Name (Party)	Vote (%)		Cand. Spent	Ind. Exp. Support	Ind. Exp. Oppose
2020 General	Kweisi Mfume (D)	237,084	(72%)	$716,289	$9,000	
	Kimberly Klacik (R)	92,825	(28%)	$7,484,802	$66,000	
2020 Primary	Kweisi Mfume (D)	113,061	(74%)			
	Maya Rockeymoore Cummings (D)	15,208	(10%)			
	Jill P. Carter (D)	13,237	(9%)			

Democrat Kweisi Mfume won a special election in April 2020 to fill the vacancy caused by the November 2019 death of Elijah Cummings, who chaired the House Oversight and Reform Committee. Mfume's victory marked an unusual return to Congress after a 24-year absence, following his resignation in February 1996 to become president of the NAACP. When he returned to the House, only 41 members remained who served with him earlier. Another odd circumstance is that Mfume has been both the predecessor and successor to Cummings and that, in each case, the transition was marked by a special election. The widely respected Cummings died in October 2019 following a series of medical problems, while he was one of several House committee chairmen preparing the case for the impeachment of President Donald Trump.

Mfume, whose name ("Conquering Son of Kings") has echoes of the Black Power movement in the 1960s, has a personal history that was touched by the problems of the Black underclass and a life story that shows how it can be overcome. His original name was Frizzell Gray. He was age 16 when his mother died, at which point he dropped out of school, held low-paying jobs and fathered five sons out of wedlock.

Then, he had what he called an "epiphany" on a Baltimore street corner, took control of his life and moved it in another direction. He adopted his African name, studied radio broadcasting, eventually graduating from Morgan State University, and was elected to the Baltimore City Council, at 30. Later, he got a master's degree in international studies from Johns Hopkins University.

On the council, he was a political critic of the longtime mayor, William Donald Schaefer. But he also was a stern critic of drug use and destructive behavior. In 1986, when Rep. Parren Mitchell retired, Mfume sought the House seat and won 44 percent in the crucial Democratic primary, to 23 percent for Clarence Mitchell III, the retiring incumbent's nephew.

Mfume moved from demanding Black power to emphasizing the need for individual self-discipline. He sponsored several laws, including to require the government to use "under-utilized" minority-owned banks and hire more lower-income workers, and to count only actual income toward determining public housing rents. Following the 1992 election, he was selected chairman of the Congressional Black Caucus, which he used as a springboard for national influence. At that time, he became chairman of the Africa Subcommittee of the Foreign Affairs Committee. During the first two years of Bill Clinton's presidency, Mfume and the Black Caucus were important forces, though the Caucus was split on issues such as aid to Somalia and the 1994 crime bill.

Following the 1994 election, in which Democrats lost House control for the first time in 40 years and had a shake-up of their leadership, Mfume ran for chairman of the Democratic Caucus against Vic Fazio of California and lost 149-57. In March 1995, he was appointed head of the Black Caucus task force to preserve affirmative action.

Mfume's career took an unexpected shift when he quit the House to take over the NAACP, an influential part of the civil rights community that was suffering organizational and financial problems. He unexpectedly departed the organization in 2004 after poor performance reviews and an employee's threat to sue the NAACP and Mfume for sexual harassment, which he later acknowledged. In response to subsequent news reports, he told the Baltimore Sun, "sometimes, strong-willed leaders have differences of opinion." Despite his initial denials that he had been forced out of the job, he eventually acknowledged that was the case. He took on other positions, including executive director of the National Medical Association and chairman of the board of Morgan State, his alma mater.

In 2006, he was an early frontrunner for the seat of retiring Sen. Paul Sarbanes. Mfume had a good personal relationship with then-Rep. Ben Cardin, the other leading contender. But Black leaders warned that the state Democratic establishment's support for Cardin would breed resentment among African-American voters. Cardin outspent Mfume nearly 4-to-1, though Mfume's compelling life story connected with many voters. Mfume more than doubled Cardin's vote in the city of Baltimore; Cardin nearly made up the difference in Baltimore County. Mfume also had a huge lead in Black-majority Prince George's County and won Charles County. Cardin took the remaining counties and won the primary, 44%-41%. Cardin won comfortably in November and has not been seriously challenged since.

Following the death of Cummings, a field of 24 Democrats ran in the primary to succeed him. In addition to Mfume, the most prominent contenders included state Senator Jill Carter and Maya Rockeymoore Cummings, who had chaired the state Democratic party and sought to run on her husband's legacy. A quarter-century later, Mfume's vote for the crime bill— with some harsh provisions— led Carter to criticize the measure's "mass incarceration."

The abbreviated primary campaign of less than three months, which was interrupted by the winter holidays, resulted in modest spending by most candidates. That was a boost for Mfume, whose high name identification was a legacy of his lengthy political career and his continuing presence in Baltimore and in the news media.

Mfume won the February primary with 40 percent, to 17 percent for Cummings and 16 percent for Carter. Mfume had big leads in Baltimore city and county. Terri Hill, a state senator who represented the suburban area, narrowly led Cummings and Mfume in Howard County, but she trailed badly elsewhere. Cummings suffered from family discord. Two daughters of her late husband from his first marriage supported another candidate, who had been a House aide to their father. Mfume swamped his opponents in the April special election and in the subsequent contests for a full term. Against Cummings and Carter, among others, Mfume got 74 percent of the vote in the June primary, with most voting by mail.

An unusual feature of both general election campaigns is that Republican nominee Kimberly Klacik had become a fundraising dynamo among national conservatives who ran ads lamenting dire social conditions in Baltimore. Running against Mfume in November, she spent about $5 million of the $7.4 million she raised during the cycle. Her lavish spending had little impact. Mfume won with 72 percent of the vote, comparable to the 70 to 80 percent share Cummings typically won. Klacik got 29 percent. In the April special election, which had a lower turnout, Mfume defeated Klacik, 74%-25%.

MD-7: Baltimore Metro   **Cook Partisan Voting Index: D+27**

Population		Race and Ethnicity		Income	
Total	717,158	White	35.70%	Median Income	$63,082
Land area (sq. miles)	488	Black	52.50%	District Income Rank	222
Pop/ sq mi	1,469.5	Latino	4.00%	Poverty Rate	14.30%
Born in State	61.00%	Asian	7.50%	With health insurance	94.90%
		Two or more races	2.60%	Cash public assistance	4.10%
Age Groups		Other	1.80%	Food stamp/SNAP	17.30%
Under 18	20.40%				
18-34	23.70%	**Education**		**Work**	
35-64	39.70%	H.S grad or less	36.10%	White Collar	49.80%
Over 64	16.40%	Some college	23.80%	Sales and Service	35.70%
		College Degree, 4 yr	22.00%	Blue Collar	14.50%
Military		Post grad	18.10%	Government	20.40%
Veteran/ Active Duty	6.00%				

2020 Pres. Vote	Biden	261,237	(78%)	Trump	66,703	(20%)			
2016 Pres. Vote	Clinton	233,796	(74%)	Trump	63,444	(20%)	Johnson	7,795	(3%)

Western and Northern Baltimore: At the junction of North and South, Baltimore is a product of both European immigration and the migration of African Americans from the South. Its Black community has a rich history. The Afro-American newspaper has been published there for more than 100 years, and there was once a Black symphony orchestra. Eubie Blake, one of the founders of ragtime music, grew up in Baltimore and has a museum in his honor on Charles Street. Jazz great Billie Holiday; Cab Calloway, the 1930s and 1940s big band leader; and Thurgood Marshall, the country's first African-American Supreme Court justice, all had roots in Baltimore. Near downtown on the west side are the childhood home of slugger Babe Ruth and the home of writer H.L. Mencken. Baltimore has been a Black-majority city since the late 1970s.

In the 1990s, the city was hit by a crime wave, with open drug markets on both the west and east sides. The city's gritty side was vividly depicted in HBO's acclaimed crime drama, The Wire. In a 2016 report, the Baltimore City Paper found that 85 percent of the more than 2,500 murder victims in Baltimore during the previous decade were African-American males, and 87 percent of them were killed by people using firearms. In 2019, the city broke its own record in the United States for the most murders per capita in a year. The city has lost 7 percent of its population since 2000, and is down more than a third from its peak in 1950.

Community anger exploded in April 2015 following the death of Freddie Gray, a young Black man who had suffered serious injuries in a police wagon after being been arrested. The initial response was a series of marches and peaceful protests throughout the west side of the city, especially the Sandtown-Winchester neighborhood. The response turned violent as demonstrators smashed storefront windows, threw rocks at police and damaged their cruisers as officers made dozens of arrests. Mayor Stephanie Rawlings-Blake was slow to increase security before she imposed a curfew for several nights. Gov. Larry Hogan declared a state of emergency and sent in 3,000 National Guard troops following a request from the mayor. Their presence generally restored order. Subsequently, six Baltimore police officers were indicted for their role in the death of Gray. The first trial resulted in a hung jury and the next three trials produced acquittals of three police officers.

In the local aftermath, Hogan and Rawlings-Blake unveiled a plan to demolish about 4,000 abandoned properties and make available $600 million, mostly state-financed, to encourage redevelopment in the Sandtown-Winchester area. But the position of Baltimore mayor has had more than its own share of criminal violations. In 2018, Mayor Catherine Pugh complained that crime remained too high and she fired the police commissioner. But the successor lasted only four months and he pleaded guilty in December for failing to file federal income taxes for three years. In March 2019, Pugh stepped down—at first, temporarily— when she faced problems with her health plus ethics allegations about her hefty income from book sales. Ultimately, she was convicted on fraud charges and imprisoned in June 2020. In November 2020, Brandon Scott— a native of a "tough" Baltimore neighborhood of Park Heights— narrowly defeated Sharon Pratt Dixon, who had been mayor a decade earlier but pleaded guilty to embezzlement and quit after three years as part of a plea deal, though she was not imprisoned.

Maryland's 7th Congressional District includes most of Baltimore's west side, plus the heavily African-American suburbs west of the city and extending to Catonsville along the old Baltimore National Pike. It includes much of suburban Howard County. About 40 percent of the district's votes are cast in Baltimore city's precincts, largely north of Pratt Street and including Charles Village, which is home to Johns Hopkins University. Baltimore County and Howard County each cast about 30 percent. Howard County is quite a different area. It grew 32 percent in the 1990s, and another 30 percent since then. Its largest community, Columbia, is a planned town that attracts a culturally liberal population that tends to vote Democratic. In July 2016, Ellicott City was devastated by a "1,000-year flood" that ravaged much of its historic downtown. In a tragic repetition, the city was rocked by flooding in May 2018 that caused further destruction. State and local officials explored alternatives for rebuilding. Preservationists opposed the tear-down of 10 vulnerable buildings.

Jamie Raskin (D)

Elected 2016, 3rd term, b. Dec 13, 1962; Washington, DC; Harvard College, B.A., 1983; Harvard University Law School, J.D., 1987; Married (Sarah Raskin); 2 children (1 deceased).

Elected Office: MD Senate, 2007-2016, Majority Whip, 2012-2016.

Professional Career: Law Professor, American University, 1990-2017; MA Asst. Attorney General, 1987-1989.

DC Office: 412 CHOB 20515, 202-225-5341, raskin.house.gov

State Offices: Rockville, 301-354-1000.

Committees: *Administration. Joint Printing. Judiciary*: Antitrust, Commercial & Administrative Law; Constitution, Civil Rights & Civil Liberties. *Oversight & Reform*: Government Operations; Select Investigative on the Coronavirus Crisis; Subcommittee on Civil Rights & Civil Liberties (Chmn). *Rules*: Expedited Procedures (Chmn).

Group Ratings

	ADA	ACLU	AFL-CIO	LCV	COC	HAFA	ACU	CFG	FRC
2020	**	87%	**	100%	-	0%	4%	**	-
2019	100%	C	90%	100%	41%	C	5%	12%	0%

Almanac Ratings 2019-2020

	Economy	Social	Foreign	Composite
Liberal	100%	100%	100%	100%
Conservative	0%	0%	0%	0%

Key Votes of the 116th Congress

1. U.S./Mex./Can. trade deal N	5. Russia sanctions	Y	9. Firearms background checks Y
2. First Coronavirus response Y	6. Troops in Syria	Y	10. Spending at the border N
3. HEROES Act Y	7. Veto arms sales to Saudis	Y	11. Marijuana liberalized rules Y
4. CASH Act Y	8. Defense $$$, veto override	Y	12. Electoral College objections N

Election Results

Election	Name (Party)	Vote (%)		Cand. Spent	Ind. Exp. Support	Ind. Exp. Oppose
2020 General	Jamie Raskin (D)	274,716	(68%)	$725,139	$123	
	Gregory Coll (R)	127,157	(32%)	$19,534		$113
2020 Primary	Jamie Raskin (D)	111,894	(87%)			
	Marcia H. Morgan (D)	10,236	(8%)			

Prior winning percentages: 2018 (68%), 2016 (61%)

Democrat Jamie Raskin was elected in 2016. In a district that is several miles from the Capitol, he has been familiar with Congress as a law professor and one-time House staffer, and as a veteran Maryland state legislator. His impressive collection of assignments positioned him at the center of the House's challenges to President Donald Trump— especially his role as the lead manager in the second impeachment trial the House pursued against President Donald Trump in January 2021. Raskin managed to skillfully blend his often-riveting constitutional-law expertise with the practical politics of the House and Senate. He initially prepared that case at a time of great personal distress — days following the suicide of his son.

A native of Washington D.C., Raskin got his bachelor's and law degrees from Harvard University, where he was editor of the law review. During college, he was an intern for the House Judiciary Committee. He joined American University's Washington College of Law as a faculty member, specializing in constitutional law. He has written widely about legal topics, including From 2001 to 2005, he chaired the Maryland Higher Education Labor Relations Board.

In 2006, he ran for the state Senate and defeated the 32-year incumbent in the Democratic primary. He served as majority whip and spent much of his time building legislative coalitions, which passed proposals such as mandatory minimums for drug sentencing, strict gun control with background checks, and environmental standards for state agencies and institutions to follow in their purchasing and other operations. His wife, Sarah Bloom Raskin, was deputy secretary of the Treasury during the Obama administration.

After Democratic Rep. Chris Van Hollen decided to run for the Senate, Raskin was the early frontrunner for the seat. But the Democratic primary became unexpectedly competitive and very expensive. Raskin ran as the progressive candidate with a grassroots network among the many liberal activists in the Washington suburbs.

His two chief opponents were both political neophytes in the district, though each had a well-known profile. Kathleen Matthews spent many years as a broadcast-news reporter and anchor, and before that with Marriott as a public-relations executive. David Trone launched the Total Wine and More retail stores as a family business, which made him very wealthy. Matthews used her close connections to the Democratic establishment— abetted by her husband, Chris Matthews, the veteran broadcast pundit and writer— to raise $2.7 million, including $600,000 in self-financing. Trone raised a record sum for a congressional primary: $13.4 million, all but $7,000 of which came from his own pocket. Raskin raised $2.5 million.

Raskin won the April primary, with 34 percent of the vote to 27 percent for Trone and 24 percent for Matthews. The general election gained scant attention, with little-known Republican Dan Cox raising $73,000, and losing 60%-34%. (Trone self-financed a similar sum in 2018 to win election to an open seat in the adjacent 6th District.)

With limited legislative opportunities in the minority, Raskin spent much of his first two years supporting Democratic candidates seeking House seats in 2018. His Democracy Summer project sent student interns to work for challengers in battleground districts. Following that election, he won a Democratic Caucus leadership post representing recently elected lawmakers and giving them more input with leadership. Raskin organized monthly meetings of that group.

In the majority, Raskin gained four committee assignments, an unusually large total under House rules. Speaker Nancy Pelosi named him to the Rules and House Administration committees, both of which are "arms of the leadership." He remained a member of the Judiciary and Oversight and Reform committees. On the latter, he chaired the Civil Rights and Civil Liberties Subcommittee, he said, " at a time when our most precious values are under attack." At Judiciary, he became vice chairman of the Constitution, Civil Rights and Civil Liberties Subcommittee, whose similar domain has more of a legislative focus.

Raskin's multiple assignments had common threads: committee work to which he brought his expertise in constitutional law, plus leadership assignments that emphasized his partisan activism and insider knowledge. That unusual combination of skills and interests gave Raskin a wide-ranging presence. In his spare time, he wrote the lyrics for a proposed new state song for Maryland, which has been designed to replace the tune that is sympathetic to the Confederacy, including its reference to Abraham Lincoln as a "tyrant."

Although he cautioned that impeachment resolutions from other House Democrats were premature, Raskin told an interviewer even before Trump took office that the president's personal finances— specifically, a gift or payment from a foreign government— could become an impeachable offense. In November 2019, as the House Judiciary Committee began to prepare its first impeachment charges against Trump for his attempt to convince the president of Ukraine to do a political favor,

Raskin described the incident as " the most impeachable thing an American president has ever done." In that case, he helped prepare some of the Democrats' formal arguments and became a frequent talking head on broadcast interviews and elsewhere. But he was not selected to serve on the team of managers during the Senate trial. In July 2020, when the Judiciary Committee approved a bill that set limits on the use of presidential clemency, Raskin won approval on a party-line vote of his amendment that a president could not issue a pardon to himself.

His opportunity to become an impeachment-trial manager unexpectedly arose when rioters stormed the Capitol on January 6, 2021. While House members were sheltering in a secure location near the Capitol, Raskin had initial discussions with Reps. David Cicilline and Ted Lieu, two other members of the Judiciary Committee, about making that day's incident the focus of a new impeachment charge. They circulated their proposal more widely and, within hours, they prepared the formal resolution that contended Trump had incited the crowd that subsequently breached the Capitol and engaged in violent and seditious actions. Democratic leaders decided to proceed. A week later, without committee hearings or a vote, the House approved the impeachment measure on a 232-197 vote.

When Pelosi subsequently told Raskin that she wanted him to lead the House managers at the Senate trial, he initially rejected her request—citing the trauma in his personal life following the New Year's Eve suicide of his only son, Tommy. But when Pelosi insisted, Raskin later said, "I don't know if you've ever tried to say no to Speaker Pelosi about anything." Preparing for the trial was daunting on its own terms, if only because— in contrast to the first Trump impeachment trial— there was not another House committee [the Intelligence Committee] that worked with the Judiciary Committee to prepare the evidence, the time period was compressed, and members of Congress uniquely were witnesses to the traumatic events before they became jurors.

On Feb. 9, the opening day of the Senate trial, Raskin delivered a riveting speech that cited his personal ordeal. After showing the Senate a 13-minute video with segments of the violence and other horrors committed by the rioters, he concluded, " If that's not an impeachable offense, then there's no such thing." In a trial in which it was widely conceded that the Democrats' team of managers had the better of the argument against Trump's lawyers, Raskin voiced satisfaction about the 57-43 Senate vote, which was 10 votes short of the required two-thirds to convict. " We left it totally out there on the floor of the U.S. Senate and every senator knew exactly what happened," he said on the day following the Senate vote.

With his House focus on constitutional challenges, Raskin hoped to eventually resume his classroom teaching. But, he said in a November 2018 interview with Bethesda Magazine, "I don't think it would be responsible for me to be teaching—even though it is acceptable within the rules of Congress—as long as Donald Trump is president. Once we get through the continuing crisis of the republic we' re living through now, then I could contemplate it." His dealings with Trump likely provided additional teaching materials for his classes.

MD-8: Northern D.C. Suburbs   **Cook Partisan Voting Index: D+17**

Population		Race and Ethnicity		Income	
Total	776,393	White	63.50%	Median Income	$109,016
Land area (sq. miles)	860	Black	12.70%	District Income Rank	17
Pop/ sq mi	902.94	Latino	17.70%	Poverty Rate	6.80%
Born in State	33.60%	Asian	9.50%	With health insurance	92.60%
		Two or more races	3.50%	Cash public assistance	1.40%
Age Groups		Other	10.80%	Food stamp/SNAP	5.30%
Under 18	22.20%				
18-34	20.10%	**Education**		**Work**	
35-64	39.80%	H.S grad or less	26.70%	White Collar	56.60%
Over 64	17.90%	Some college	18.90%	Sales and Service	29.90%
		College Degree, 4 yr	24.70%	Blue Collar	13.40%
Military		Post grad	29.60%	Government	21.90%
Veteran/ Active Duty	6.40%				

2020 Pres. Vote	Biden	287,062	(69%)	Trump	119,537	(29%)		
2016 Pres. Vote	Clinton	235,137	(63%)	Trump	112,612	(30%)	Johnson	11,143 (3%)

Montgomery County, Frederick: Colonial farmers once rolled barrels of tobacco to the port of Georgetown in Maryland, along an old road that is today the commercial spine of one of America's most affluent and best-educated areas. Wisconsin Avenue begins at the Potomac River in Washington D.C., traverses the city, and then becomes Rockville Pike after it passes over the Capital Beltway in Montgomery County. The foundation of the economy here is the federal government, with its huge facilities and ongoing construction projects — Walter Reed National Military Medical Center (which merged with Bethesda Naval Hospital), the National Institutes of Health and the Food and Drug Administration. Montgomery is a center of America's biotech industry, the home of firms such as Human Genome Sciences which, with the Human Genome Project, pioneered the study of the human genetic code. Defense contractor Lockheed Martin, with 4,700 employees, is the only manufacturing company among the county's top 10 employers. Marriott International, which has scheduled completion for 2022 of its corporate headquarters a few miles south to downtown Bethesda, employs 5,500.

From the 1960s through the 1980s, Montgomery County ranked at or near the top among counties nationwide in income and education. Downtown Bethesda remains a glitzy and popular entertainment and dining destination with expanding high-rise apartment buildings. Its increased urban development and taller office building have diminished the suburban or small-town ambiance. The county gradually became a magnet for legal immigrants attracted by the region's strong and stable economy. Today, Montgomery has a diverse population and has been overtaken in affluence regionally by other suburban counties in the metropolitan area. Along with its very upscale neighborhoods, Montgomery now has large Latino communities in areas from Wheaton northwest to Rockville. The county's population in 2017, which had grown 9 percent since 2010 and surpassed 1 million, was 20 percent African American, 20 percent Hispanic and 16 percent Asian. Even with those shifts, the median population has aged from 34 to 39 and real estate prices have soared 40 percent beyond inflation since the 1990s.

Still, the county has the nation's second-highest percentage of adults with graduate degrees, and it is thoroughly liberal on cultural issues and loyal to the Democratic Party. Montgomery County provided the margin of victory for the 2012 referendum legalizing same-sex marriage in Maryland. In 2014, the county passed legislation creating partial public financing of local elections. Perhaps its most unique precinct is Leisure World in Silver Spring, with its 8,500-plus senior citizens and an extraordinarily high voter-turnout rate, mostly Democrats.

The 8th Congressional District of Maryland includes much of the heavily populated parts of Montgomery County (Bethesda, Rockville, Silver Spring and pricey Potomac). Two-thirds of the voters reside in Montgomery, with the remainder split nearly evenly between Frederick and Carroll counties. To assist Democrats in the 6th District, which now includes 40 percent of Montgomery, it now extends beyond the Washington suburbs to include rural Republican precincts from Frederick and Carroll counties. The presidential retreat of Camp David, where Jimmy Carter brokered the Israeli-Egyptian peace accords, is outside the small town of Thurmont, though Presidents Barack Obama and Donald Trump each had less interest in the quiet, rural facility than their recent predecessors. The district is reliably Democratic but it's not as overwhelmingly liberal as it was during the previous decade. Joe Biden in 2020 won here 69%-29%.

MASSACHUSETTS

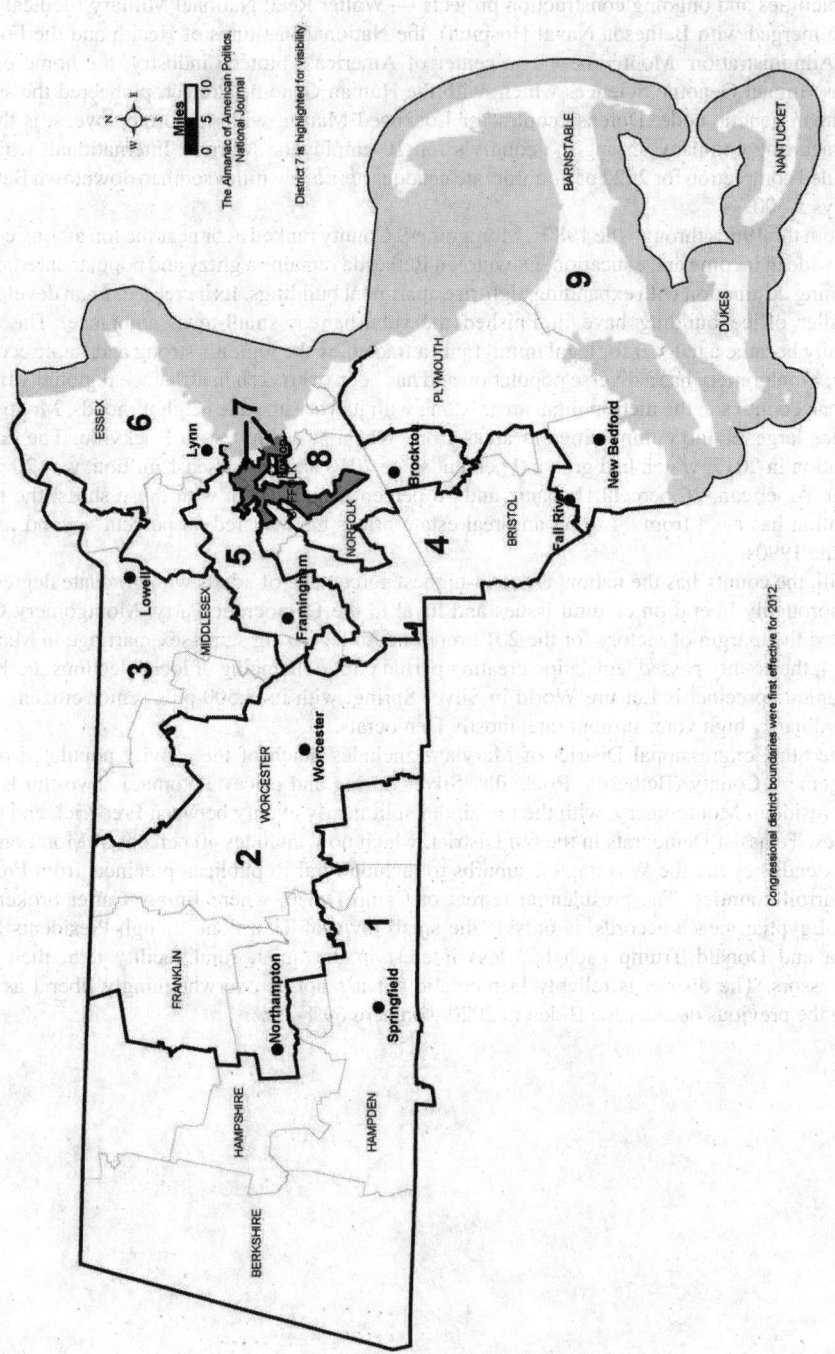

Massachusetts, an affluent, highly educated state at the top of its economic game, is one of the nation's bluest states, though it defies pigeonholing. Between 2016 and 2020, the winning Democratic presidential margin in the Bay State increased from an already wide 27 points to a whopping 34 points— yet in the midterm election in the interim, many of the same voters pulled the lever for a Republican governor, Charlie Baker, who won by a 2-to-1 margin.

The Puritan leader John Winthrop wrote that Massachusetts would be "as a city upon a hill"— an example to the entire world. For 150 years, New England was partial to learning, but the Puritans' austere creed was also insular and hostile to outsiders, sending merchants and fishing boats out to sea but keeping the world at bay. After the American Revolution, the wars between royal Britain and revolutionary and Napoleonic France enabled New England ship owners to cross enemy lines to become the world's leading merchants. They made vast profits and invested the money in textile mills, then railroads, then coal mines and steel mills, providing much of the capital that made industrial America.

Massachusetts remade the country in other ways. Intellectually, New England flowered in the 19th century, more than 200 years after Plymouth Rock. Writers from Boston and Cambridge, Concord and Salem— Ralph Waldo Emerson, Henry Wadsworth Longfellow, Henry David Thoreau, John Greenleaf Whittier and Nathaniel Hawthorne— created an American literature and popularized an American philosophy. There was a surge of New England Yankee influence across the continent, and beyond. By the 1820s, Boston whaling merchants and New England missionaries were planting their flag in the Sandwich Islands (Hawaii). By the 1850s, Yankees were in Iowa, Kansas and Oregon's Willamette Valley, and by the 1870s, in Los Angeles. They helped found the Republican Party and did much to start— and win— the Civil War. They planted their economic system and their values, articulated in the McGuffey Readers, across the continent.

In the meantime, Massachusetts itself and Boston, the "Hub of the Universe," were being remade. The Irish potato famine of the 1840s sent Catholic immigrants across the Atlantic, and many came to Boston, looking for work in the mills, docks and factories. Yankee Protestants had seen Catholics as their great political and cultural enemy since the 17th century and many felt that their commonwealth was under siege. As Catholics became a majority, first in Boston and then statewide, Protestants feared that the Irish would use their political clout to ladle out government jobs and benefits to their own. The Irish encountered such bigotry and rejection by the Yankees that even as successful an Irish Catholic as Joseph Kennedy abandoned Boston for New York in 1927. Sometimes the stakes of the culture war between Yankee Republicans and Irish Democrats were concrete— control of patronage, command of the Boston Police Department— but often they were symbolic.

Massachusetts' Irish and Catholic percentages rose slowly over the years. Yankees had smaller families, moved west, intermarried with people of immigrant stock and lost their Yankee identity. The Irish were likelier to stay put, raise large families and maintain their identity. Slowly but surely, Massachusetts moved from being one of the most Republican states to one of the most Democratic. The predominance of the textile mills meant that for a century beginning in the 1820s, Massachusetts imported low-skill labor and exported high-skill people. As textile mills began moving south in the 1920s, Massachusetts started exporting low-skill people as well.

The Kennedys occupied a unique place in Massachusetts politics. Rose Kennedy was the daughter of John "Honey Fitz" Fitzgerald, who was elected to Congress at age 32 and served as mayor of Boston in 1906-07 and 1910-14. Her husband, Joseph Kennedy, was chairman of the Securities and Exchange Commission in the 1930s and ambassador to the Court of St. James's from 1937 to 1940. Catholic and uncommonly rich, he was a shrewd and ruthless political operator. Their only residence in Massachusetts after 1927 was their summer home in Hyannis Port. In 1946, Joseph Kennedy moved his oldest surviving son, John, to Boston, and helped steer his election to the House that year, to the Senate in 1952, and to the presidency in 1960. With their elegant manners and charm, the Kennedys were like royalty to the Irish Catholics of Massachusetts. And Catholics across the country, 78 percent of whom voted for John Kennedy, greeted the Democrat's election in 1960 with great pride. Joseph and John Kennedy were, on many issues, conservative or skeptical of liberal government intervention. But JFK's administration was increasingly identified, even before its tragic end in Dallas, as liberal. His example and that of his brother, Edward Kennedy, who was elected to the Senate in 1962 at age

30 and served 46 years, moved Massachusetts Catholics to the left. At the same time, the leftward direction of the state's elite campuses in the 1960s influenced Massachusetts Protestants.

In the 1970s and 1980s, Massachusetts had the most liberal governance and outlook on national politics of any state in the country. It was the only state to vote for George McGovern in 1972, although it voted twice for Ronald Reagan, the son of an Irish Catholic. In the early 1990s, the 1980s "Massachusetts Miracle" turned into a curse; the state's tech, real estate and defense economy sagged, and the state government essentially went bankrupt. In 1990, when liberal Gov. Michael Dukakis retired, voters embraced tax cuts and elected patrician Republican William Weld in his place. Four different Republicans, fiscally conservative and socially moderate, would hold the governorship for the next 16 years. The last of those four, Mitt Romney, provided the biggest policy innovation— the health care plan passed by the legislature in 2006 that required all residents to buy health insurance, levied taxes on employers who did not provide it, and subsidized policies for low-wage earners. Romney's plan became the model for the national health care legislation passed by Congress and signed by President Barack Obama in 2010. But as he prepared to run for the GOP presidential nomination in 2008 (the first of his two presidential bids) Romney turned rightward, alienating voters back home. Democrat Deval Patrick succeeded him, becoming the state's first African-American governor in 2006. But the old model succeeded once again for Republicans in 2014 as Baker, the cabinet secretary for governors Weld and Paul Cellucci, won the governorship.

Massachusetts' population has grown by 7.4 percent since 2010, and the Boston metro area has increased 6.7 percent over the same period, though the Hub recently dropped just out of the nation's 10 biggest metro areas. The statewide population is 7 percent Black, 12.4 percent Hispanic and 6.7 percent Asian, with significant immigration, some from Ireland but also from Brazil and elsewhere; Massachusetts now ranks seventh nationally in the percentage of its population that was born in another country. The state's median income ranks second in the country, almost one-third higher than the U.S. as a whole— and that surely had something to do with the state's No. 1 national rankings in bachelor's and advanced degrees.

Manufacturing jobs have been replaced, and then some, by those in technology, health sciences, health care and financial services. The Massachusetts tech sector now has twice as many workers as the state's second-biggest, finance. In Boston and Cambridge, the life sciences are sizzling, and Amazon, Wayfair, and other companies have been hiring machines; gentrification continues apace. After initial not-in-my-backyard concerns, work was underway on an 800-megawatt wind farm located 15 miles off the coast of Martha's Vineyard that would be operated from the old "Moby-Dick" whaling town of New Bedford. (The timeline was recently pushed back for regulatory reasons.) Tech-related work is growing so quickly that by 2025, the state's colleges and universities may not be able to churn out enough qualified workers, according to the Massachusetts Department of Higher Education. The tech growth has had another impact: a high cost of living. The listings service Property Club found that Boston is the third-most expensive city in the world to rent a home, trailing only New York and San Francisco. (The tech industry also— unknowingly— prompted a crisis at the beginning of the coronavirus pandemic, when a biotech industry conference in late February 2020 became a super spreader event, linked to an estimated 300,000 cases nationwide.)

With its educated electorate, Democratic leanings and moderate Republican governors, cultural liberalism gradually prevailed over conservative Catholic social views in the state. Weld was one of America's first politicians to endorse gay rights, and after the legislature declined to endorse same-sex marriage, the courts in 2004 declared that same-sex couples had the right to marry. In 2016, the legislature passed, and Baker signed into law, a measure to expand existing protections for transgender people to include public bathrooms, locker rooms and showers. After critics put the issue on the 2018 ballot, the voters upheld the protections overwhelmingly, 68%-32%. In November 2016, voters opted to legalize marijuana for recreational use, despite opposition from Baker, Boston Mayor Marty Walsh and Cardinal Sean O'Malley; two years later, cannabis shops opened in Leicester and Northampton, becoming the first recreational stores on the East Coast. The state has been a leader in pursuing progressive ends through the court system, suing ride-share companies over labor policies, oil companies over climate change, and drug makers over the opioid crisis.

At the same time, the advent of the #Me-too movement peeled back a stark hypocrisy: a legislature dominated by progressives, yet with a retrograde culture toward women. In 2017, aides, lobbyists, activists and legislators told the Boston Globe about "situations where they were propositioned by men, including lawmakers, who could make or break their careers; where those men pressed up against them, touched their legs, massaged their shoulders, tried to kiss them, grabbed their behinds, chased them around offices, or demanded sex." Meanwhile, racial tensions, which had flared over school integration in the 1960s and 1970s, never went away. The number of schools in the state with at least 90 percent students of color has grown by more than a third, according to the Center for Education and Civil Rights. Studies have shown that in both the state's tech sector and its legislature, Blacks and Hispanics are underrepresented. But in 2020, a year when racial justice protests flared, Baker worked with minority legislators and advocacy groups to enact a major police reform bill, including a system to decertify officers shown to have committed misconduct, a ban on the use of chokeholds, and curbs on "no-knock" warrants.

At the ballot box, the state's leanings are liberal. After giving between 60 percent and 62 percent of the statewide vote to every Democratic presidential candidate between 1996 and 2016, Joe Biden increased that share to 66 percent in 2020. In fact, no county in Massachusetts gave Biden less than 55 percent of the vote. In a sign of the state's growing diversity, Ayanna Pressley in 2018 became the first Black woman from Massachusetts elected to the House. The state has also elected a growing number of prominent women, including Sen. Elizabeth Warren, Reps. Pressley and Katherine Clark, Attorney General Maura Healey, and state Senate President Karen Spilka. Meanwhile, in a landmark Senate election battle in 2020, incumbent Ed Markey held off primary rival Joseph P. Kennedy III to win the nomination; it was the first time a Kennedy had ever lost in Massachusetts.

Population		Race and Ethnicity		Income	
Total	6,892,503	White	77.00%	Median Income	85,843
Land area (sq. miles)	7,800	Black	7.90%	State Income Rank	2 out of 50
Pop/ sq mi	883.65	Latino	12.40%	Poverty Rate	9.40%
Born in state	59.40%	Asian	8.00%	With health insurance	97.00%
		Two or more races	3.60%	Cash public assistance	2.80%
Age Groups		Other	4.60%	Food stamp/SNAP	12.3%
Under 18	19.60%				
18-34	24.40%	**Education**		**Work**	
35-64	38.90%	H.S grad or less	32.60%	White Collar	48.40%
Over 64	17.00%	Some college	22.40%	Sales and Service	35.50%
		College Degree, 4 yr	24.70%	Blue Collar	16.20%
Military		Post grad	20.30%	Government	12.60%
Veteran/ Active Duty	5.10%				

Presidential Politics

2020 Primary (D)	Biden (D)	473,861(34%)	Sanders (D)	376,990(27%)	Warren (D)	303,864(21%)
	Bloomberg (D)	166,200(12%)				
2020 Pres. Vote	Biden (D)	2,382,202(66%)	Trump (R)	1,167,202(32%)		
2016 Pres. Vote	Clinton (D)	1,995,196(60%)	Trump (R)	1,090,893(33%)	Johnson (L)	138,018 (4%)

Massachusetts has been a solidly Democratic state in the past nine presidential elections. Joe Biden defeated Donald Trump in the 2020 race, 66%-32%, the most lopsided win since Lyndon Johnson's 1964 landslide. Biden won all 14 counties in the state—and carried every one by a wider margin than Hillary Clinton had in 2016.

What is striking about Massachusetts is how many serious presidential candidates it has produced over the past four decades: Ted Kennedy in 1980, Michael Dukakis in 1988, Paul Tsongas in 1992, John Kerry in 2004, Mitt Romney in 2008 and 2012 and Elizabeth Warren in 2020. Only California and Texas, with much larger populations, have produced more legitimate contenders over that period. Bay State hopefuls benefit from the first-in-the-nation primary status of New Hampshire, where most of the residents receive Boston television newscasts influenced by the hyper-political culture of that city.

Massachusetts has long held its primary on Super Tuesday, the same day as voters in multiple Southern states cast their ballots. Its 2016 results gave important previews of how both parties' nominating contests were going to unfold. On the Democratic side, Clinton's narrow 50%-49% win over Vermont Sen. Bernie Sanders showed both Clinton's continued struggles and the limits of Sanders' appeal. On the Republican side, Trump won a near landslide victory, capturing 49 percent of the vote, a higher percentage than he won in conservative states like Alabama and Arkansas on the same day. Ohio Gov. John Kasich finished second with 18 percent.

The 2020 primary was held on March 3. Heading into Super Tuesday, it was clear that favorite daughter Elizabeth Warren was in trouble—she'd underperformed in New Hampshire's primary and badly needed a strong showing not just at home but elsewhere to stay in the race. Sanders, smelling blood and hoping to build on his strong 2016 showing, campaigned in both Springfield and Boston in the race's closing days. But Joe Biden pulled off a surprise, beating Sanders 34%-27% as part of a huge week that turned him from underdog into the heavy favorite for the nomination. Warren finished in third with 21 percent of the vote, and dropped out of the race a few days later.

Congressional Districts

117th Congress Lineup	9D	116th Congress Lineup	9D

For many years, Massachusetts— the home of the original gerrymander— had some of the most convoluted congressional district boundaries in the nation. It also had a habit of electing moderate Republicans from suburban enclaves. Both practices have largely disappeared. The number of House seats fell from 14 in 1960 to 10 in 1992 and then to nine following the 2010 census; that most recent redistricting] gave the state legislature a chance to smooth the lines. Because all the seats had been held by Democrats, it meant a Democratic loss. With the retirement of the 1st District's John Olver, the elimination of the western-most district resulted in shifts to the west for two Democrats who subsequently have become House committee chairmen: Springfield-based Richard Neal absorbed the heavily Democratic Berkshires, and Worcester-based Jim McGovern no longer extended east to Fall River. Since then, Republicans have had one opportunity: They lost a close challenge in 2012 in the 6th District against an ethically scarred incumbent. That outcome continued the state's streak of not having elected a Republican to the House since 1994.

For 2022, with no change in the total of nine, districts in the west and southeast will need to take modest numbers of residents from districts in the Boston suburbs. Republican Gov. Charlie Baker could seek to enhance GOP prospects in the 6th and 9th, in the northeast and southeast corners. But GOP opportunities are limited and the party has no leverage in the legislature.

Charlie Baker (R)

Elected 2014, term expires 2023, 2nd term; b. Nov. 13, 1956, Elmira, NY; Harvard U., B.A. 1979; Northwestern U., M.B.A. 1986; Protestant; Married (Lauren); 3 children.

Elected Office: Swampscott Board of Selectmen, 2004-2009.

Professional Career: Founder, Pioneer Institute for Public Policy Research, 1988-1991; State Health Undersecretary, 1991-1992; MA Secretary of Health & Human Services, 1992-1994; State Administrations & Finance Secretary, 1994-1998; CEO, Harvard Vanguard Medical Associates, 1998-1999; Entrepreneur, 2011-2014.

Office: Massachusetts State House Room 280, Boston, 02133; 617-725-4005; Fax: 617-727-9725; Website: mass.gov

Lt. Gov.: Karyn Polito (R) **Atty. Gen:** Maura Healey (D) **Sec. of State:** William F. Galvin (D)

State Legislature: Senate: 34D, 6R **House:** 127D, 32R, 1I

Election Results

Election	Name (Party)	Vote (%)
2018 General	Charlie Baker (R)	1,781,341 (67%)
	Jay Gonzalez (D)	885,770 (33%)
2018 Primary	Charlie Baker (R)	174,126 (64%)
	Scott Lively (R)	98,421 (36%)

Prior winning percentage: 2014 (48%)

Charlie Baker, a moderate Republican, was easily reelected to the Massachusetts governorship in 2018 and is considering running for what would be an unprecedented third consecutive term. He has governed as a socially liberal, fiscally conservative Republican, like GOP predecessors who have served as governor for all but eight years since 1991. Baker has frequently ranked as the most popular governor in the nation— often more popular among Massachusetts Democrats than among the state's dwindling, increasingly conservative Republican Party.

Baker was born in Elmira New York to a family steeped in politics and public service. His great-grandfather was a federal prosecutor and state assemblyman; his grandfather was a prominent Newburyport politician; his father Charles was a well-connected conservative Republican who had worked for Republican Presidents Richard Nixon and Ronald Reagan. His mother was a liberal Democrat, leading to political arguments at the dinner table in Needham, where Baker mostly grew up and went to public schools. Baker earned a bachelor's degree in English from Harvard University, riding the bench for the basketball team (he's six-foot-six). He then received an MBA from the Kellogg Graduate School of Management at Northwestern University. (In the interim, Baker worked on the unsuccessful 1980 presidential campaign of former Texas Gov. John Connally.) He married the daughter of a Fortune 500 CEO and delved into policy work as the first executive director of the Pioneer Institute, a conservative think tank in Boston, created in part by Baker's father.

In 1992, at 36, Baker began his career in public service when GOP Gov. William Weld appointed him secretary of Health and Human Services, heading up the largest department in state government. Baker, showing efficiency and diligence, was elevated in 1994 to be secretary of Administration and Finance, putting him in charge of the state's budget. Weld's successor, Paul Cellucci, kept Baker in that post, where, among other things, he was the original architect of the financial plan for the Big Dig, the Boston tunnel project plagued by delays and cost overruns. When Baker left government, he became CEO of Harvard Pilgrim Health Care, a nonprofit health benefits organization, from 1999 to 2009. In 2004, Baker was elected to the Board of Selectmen in his hometown of Swampscott, an old fishing town on the North Shore of Boston, where the city skyline can be seen in the distance.

In his first run for governor in 2010, Baker took on Gov. Deval Patrick, who was seeking a second term. Baker promised no new taxes, and he was agnostic on human-caused climate change, a view that offended many environmentalists. Baker came off to some as distant, and he expressed some views that put him at odds with the state's Democratic-leaning electorate. He came to understand too late in the campaign that Massachusetts is "not an angry state," Baker later acknowledged to the Boston Globe. Baker's task in the election was complicated by the presence of a third candidate, former state Treasurer Tim Cahill, who left the Democratic Party to run as an independent. This effectively split the base of the state's fiscally conservative and moderate voters that Baker needed to rally to have any hopes of winning. On Election Day, Patrick defeated Baker, 48%-42% with Cahill capturing 8%.

When he mounted a second campaign for governor in 2014, Baker had morphed into a more genial, and female-voter-friendly, contender. Facing Democratic nominee Martha Coakley, Baker cast himself as a fiscally responsible businessman, able to use his private-sector fiscal skills to heal what he called a poorly run Democratic administration. He emphasized his liberal take on social issues such as abortion and gay marriage. After stumbling with female voters in 2010, Baker chose a woman, Karyn Polito, as his running mate. The "new" Baker tweeted out messages from Red Sox games and spoke easily about his openly gay brother. While Coakley accused Baker of being weak on gender issues, the strategy did not stick. On Election Day, Baker won by two points, carrying Worcester County, with its classic New England small towns; Essex County, with its Merrimack Valley mill towns and North Shore affluent Boston exurbs; and Norfolk County, with its mix of upper-income Boston exurbs and coastal towns of the South Shore populated by upper-middle-class Irish Catholics.

Baker chose an eclectic cabinet— traditional pro-business Republicans and a few Democrats, even some who disagreed with positions he had taken during the campaign. True to his roots as a budgeter, Baker signed a plan in early 2015 that offered early retirement to state employees to reduce the workforce by up to 5,000 jobs. The Massachusetts General Court approved the proposal, a down payment on Baker's efforts to close the budget deficit.

At times Baker took right-of-center stances, as when he joined with more conservative Republican governors in 2015 to urge caution about resettling any more Syrian refugees. Baker also defied teachers' unions by pushing for a ballot measure to expand charter schools; in 2016, voters rejected it by a wide margin. He opposed a 2016 ballot measure to legalize marijuana, but the voters passed it, and Baker signed implementing legislation. Initially, Baker was noncommittal about a bill to protect transgender rights, prompting a pro-LGBTQ audience to boo him off a stage. But three months later, in July 2016, he switched and signed the transgender law. (Critics of the law worked to place a repeal measure on the 2018 ballot; it failed.) Baker signed a law aimed at achieving equal pay for women by barring employers from requiring applicants to provide their salary history. He helped engineer a deal to bring General Electric's headquarters from Connecticut to Boston, though GE later downsized its presence. He also invested significant political capital in the fight against opioid abuse.

In November 2017, Baker signed a law that made Massachusetts the first state to ban the firearm attachments known as bump stocks following the mass-shooting in Las Vegas that utilized the devices to deadly effect. The following year, he signed a measure overturning an archaic 1845 law banning abortion, safeguarding abortion rights in the event the U.S. Supreme Court were to overturn Roe v. Wade. Baker also signed legislation to enact automatic voter registration, to raise the minimum wage to $15 by 2023, to implement paid leave, to allow judges to order gun confiscation if an individual is deemed a danger to themselves or others, and to expand access to medication-based treatment for opioid addicts in jails and emergency rooms. Perhaps more popular than Baker's policies, however, was his low-key, bipartisan approach— welcome in an increasingly polarized nation— as well as his decision not to vote for his party's presidential nominee, Donald Trump. (He said he left his ballot blank rather than voting for Hillary Clinton.) While Baker occasionally cooperated with the Trump White House, such as on opioid policy, he frequently criticized the president's comments and his policies on health care and immigration. In June 2018, he backed off sending National Guard troops to the U.S.-Mexico border to protest the administration's policy of separating minors from their migrant parents.

In the 2018 GOP primary, Baker faced Scott Lively, a Trump-aligned pastor with a record of preaching against LGBTQ rights. Though Lively was vastly underfunded and got little attention, he secured 36 percent of the primary vote. With Baker's popularity among the broader electorate. sky high, every prominent Democratic official took a pass on the race, leaving a final Democratic primary matchup between Jay Gonzalez, who had served as budget chief for Gov. Deval Patrick, and environmentalist Robert K. Massie IV. Gonzalez won the nomination and proceeded to advocate a 4 percent surtax on income over $1 million and the taxation of university endowments. But the general election was never competitive, as voters seemed satisfied with the economy, with Baker's efforts to distance himself from Trump, and with his ability to check excesses from a legislature dominated by Democrats. Baker won every county as he prevailed, 67%-33%.

In 2019, Baker signed a bill to ban gay-conversion therapy, and issued an executive order— and later signed legislation— to curb access to e-cigarettes. The following year, he signed a measure to allow any voter to cast ballots by mail and another to officially recognize the Juneteenth holiday that commemorates the day that enslaved African Americans in Texas learned of their freedom. For much of the year, Baker pursued a far-reaching, 179-page health care proposal that would have curbed surprise medical billing, placed downward pressure on prescription drug prices, and required hospitals and insurers to boost primary and behavioral health care by 30 percent over three years. Ultimately, in January 2021, he signed a stripped-down bill that mandated coverage of telehealth services, expanded the use of certain types of nurses, and increased disclosures on medical bills. The same month, he vetoed a climate change bill that would have made the state carbon-neutral by 2050; he said the bill would harm the fragile economy. Baker added that he supported the bill's goals but differed on implementation; further rounds of skirmishing on the issue were expected. Perhaps the biggest surprise, given his longstanding support for abortion rights, was Baker's veto of a bill that would have allowed 16- and 17-year olds to secure an abortion without parental consent and would have permitted certain late-term abortions.

When the coronavirus pandemic arrived in the U.S., Baker took an early and aggressive posture, establishing what was perhaps the largest army of contract tracers in any state and joining a regional compact of states that would coordinate their responses to the virus. He also signed a bill, which was later extended, to block eviction and foreclosure proceedings for those affected by the virus or the resulting economic downturn. In May, Baker issued a mask mandate, and in August, he tightened restrictions on gathering amid an uptick in cases. Despite these moves, Massachusetts was consistently among the worst states in both infection and death rates throughout the pandemic. With few obvious benefits from the mandates, Baker's restrictions outraged many Massachusetts Republicans. By then, the state party apparatus was controlled by Trump-allied conservatives, and if Baker were to seek a third term as governor in 2022—a strong possibility— he might be faced with another primary challenge. Despite this, Baker continued to distance himself from the Trump wing of the party; in 2020, he again said he left his presidential vote blank.

If Baker decides against seeking a third term, or even if he does run again, the Democrats should have a large field of potential candidates, including Attorney General Maura Healey, former Rep. Joe Kennedy, Somerville Mayor Joe Curtatone, former state Sen. Ben Downing, and Harvard professor Danielle Allen. On the Republican side, Lt. Gov. Karyn Polito and former state Rep. Geoff Diehl are potential successors. Still, the state's Democratic lean would make it tough for any Republican other than Baker to win the governorship in 2022.

Elizabeth Warren (D)

Elected 2012, term expires 2024, 2nd term, b. Jun 22, 1949; Oklahoma City, OK; George Washington University, 1968; University of Houston, B.A., 1970; Rutgers University, J.D., 1976; Methodist; Married (Bruce H. Mann); 2 children; 3 grandchildren.

Professional Career: Professor, University of TX, 1981-1987; Professor, University of PA Law School, 1987-1995; Professor, Harvard Law School, 1992-2013; Chair, Congressional Oversight Panel for the Troubled Asset Relief Program, 2008-2010; Assistant to the President & Special Advisor to Treasury Secretary, 2010-2011.

DC Office: 309 HSOB 20510, 202-224-4543, Fax: 202-228-2072, warren.senate.gov

State Offices: Boston, 617-565-3170; Springfield, 413-788-2690.

Committees: Senate Democratic Conference Vice Chairman. *Aging. Armed Services*: Emerging Threats & Capabilities; Personnel; Strategic Forces. *Banking, Housing & Urban Affairs*: Economic Policy (Chmn); Financial Institutions & Consumer Protection; Securities, Insurance & Investment. *Finance*: Fiscal Responsibility & Economic Growth (Chmn); Health Care; Taxation & IRS Oversight.

Group Ratings

	ADA	ACLU	AFL-CIO	LCV	COC	HAFA	ACU	CFG	FRC
2020	-	91%	-	62%	-	0%	4%	-	-
2019	75%	C	100%	79%	52%	C	4%	20%	0%

Almanac Ratings 2019-2020

	Economy	Social	Foreign	Composite
Liberal	97%	97%	100%	98%
Conservative	3%	3%	0%	2%

Key Votes of the 116th Congress

1. EPA clean energy rules	Y	5. Russia sanctions	Y	9. Barr as Atty. General	N
2. U.S./Mex./Can. trade deal	Y	6. Troops in SYR, AFG	N	10. Spending at the border	N/A
3. Cut unemployment benefits	N	7. Veto arms sales to Saudis	Y	11. Coney Barrett to Sup. Ct.	N
4. Shelton to Fed Reserve	N	8. Defense $$$, veto override	N	12. Electoral College objections	N

Election Results

Election	Name (Party)	Vote (%)		Cand. Spent	Ind. Exp. Support	Ind. Exp. Oppose
2018 General	Elizabeth Warren (D)......................	1,633,371	(60%)	$17,185,436	$91	$1,281,120
	Geoff Diehl (R).............................	979,210	(36%)	$4,314,231		
	Shiva Ayyadurai (I)........................	91,710	(3%)	$5,014,779		
2018 Primary	Elizabeth Warren (D)......................	591,038	(100%)			

Prior winning percentages: 2018 (60%), 2012 (54%)

Democrat Elizabeth Warren, Massachusetts' senior senator, occupies the seat held for nearly half a century by the late Ted Kennedy. Just as the traditional liberal wing of the Democratic Party long looked to Kennedy for leadership and inspiration, progressives working to push the party to the left have looked to Warren since her 2012 election to the Senate. " She has been a lot more effective than most in communicating an anti-Wall Street message that has been part of the Democratic Party for 80 years," Charles Geisst, a Manhattan College professor who specializes in Wall Street history, told Politico. In 2020, Warren sought the Democratic presidential nomination, and, just as Kennedy had four decades earlier, came up short. But the parallels between the former Harvard Law School professor and her predecessor don't end there. Just as Kennedy remained in the Senate as a key player long after his presidential run, Warren— already one of the most influential figures on Capitol Hill thanks to a sharp tongue, deft use of social media and a large fundraising base— returned for the 2021-22 congressional session with her clout enhanced.

"I'll always be an outsider," Warren told the Washington Post in 2015. "That's how I understand the world." But she emerged as an insider in the 2020 campaign, becoming an informal economic adviser to now-President Joe Biden after trading swipes with him during the crowded contest for the presidential nomination. While Warren was not tapped as his vice presidential running mate— she was among four finalists, according to the New York Times—Biden did embrace several of her policy proposals. Among them: her plan for easing the nation's bankruptcy laws, the issue that first brought Warren to public prominence and produced a faceoff with then-Sen. Biden at a 2005 hearing. Some wondered whether Warren's relationship with the new president would turn out to be long-term alliance or short-term détente: She was a thorn in President Barack Obama's side for much of his second term, even after he helped launch her political career by naming her a special adviser at the Treasury Department in 2010. But, this time around, she enjoyed an embedded influence, thanks in part to several protégés and former aides in key Biden administration posts.

In 2015, when then-Vice President Biden was considering a run for the Democratic presidential nomination, he sounded out Warren about being his running mate— even though they did not know each other well at the time. Biden ultimately declined to seek the presidency in 2016, just as Warren had earlier passed on the same contest. Soon after Warren first arrived on Capitol Hill in early 2013, progressive groups began a " draft Warren" effort to entice her into the contest as an alternative to Hillary Clinton. In ruling herself out then, Warren opened the way for the insurgent progressive candidacy of Vermont Sen. Bernie Sanders. Sanders fell short, but he redefined the Democratic Party's platform and left Warren somewhat in his shadow— and some wondering whether she had missed her moment. The presence of both Sanders and Warren in the 2020 primary not only complicated the contest but also strained the once-friendly relationship between the Democratic Party's two most prominent progressives: Warren was even caught on a hot mic after one debate accusing Sanders of calling her a "liar."

While Sanders is a self-described democratic socialist who at times has decried capitalism, Warren cast herself as focused on reforming the economic status quo as she prepared for the 2020 presidential race. " I am a capitalist," she told CNBC in mid-2018. " I believe in markets. What I don't believe in is theft; what I don't believe in is cheating." She campaigned—albeit unsuccessfully— as the "unity candidate," a bridge between Sanders' followers and the centrist lane of the party as represented by Biden.

Born Elizabeth Herring, she grew up in Oklahoma City where her teenage years were marred by her father's heart attack. His lost pay as a maintenance worker and the ensuing medical bills imperiled the family. Warren and her mother went to work; then known as "Betsy," she waited tables as a 13-year-old at her aunt's Mexican restaurant. Her three older brothers played a bit role in her presidential campaign—only one of them a Democrat, as Warren would note to audiences. The three appeared in a campaign video as part of an effort to underscore the modest and conservative roots of a candidate largely known as a professor at an elite liberal university prior to her entry into politics. (Her oldest brother, a 20-year Air Force veteran, died of complications from COVID-19 shortly after the end of Warren's presidential bid.)

In high school, Warren was a champion debater— so good, in fact, she won a scholarship to George Washington University; she completed a bachelor's degree at the University of Houston. She married her high school sweetheart, Jim Warren, at 19, had two children, taught elementary school, earned a law degree from Rutgers University and went through a divorce— earning an appreciation for working mothers. She developed a specialty in bankruptcy law as a member of the law faculty at three universities before arriving at Harvard in the mid-1990s. Along the way, she married Bruce Mann, a fellow law professor.

As recently as 1996, Warren was a Republican: She said the families she met during her research into bankruptcy changed her views. " These were hard-working middle-class families who by and large had lost jobs, gotten sick, had family breakups, and that's what was driving them over the edge financially. It changed my vision," Warren said during a 2007 speech. Shortly after announcing her presidential candidacy, she told Five Thirty Eight, "I've been working on one central question for 30 years: 'What's going wrong with working families across this country, why is America's middle class getting hollowed out?'" Warren used her academic expertise and ability to communicate complicated policy issues to frame the broader political debate and emerged as a leading advocate for consumer interests, as she became an increasing presence on the TV talk show circuit. She co-authored a couple of general audience books on consumer finance with her daughter, Amelia Warren Tyagi. The second, " All Your Worth: The Ultimate Lifetime Money Plan,' made the New York Times best-seller list in 2005.

Their first book, " The Two-Income Trap," published a couple of years earlier, notably declared, "Senators like Joe Biden should not be allowed to sell out women in the morning and be heralded as their friend in the evening." At the time, Warren was leading a fight against legislation that made it harder for consumers to file for bankruptcy— a measure pushed by the credit card industry, a major employer in Biden's home state of Delaware. The two dueled when Warren appeared as a witness before the Senate Judiciary Committee. Biden, his voice rising, told Warren: " Your problem with credit card companies is usury rates from your position. It is not about the bankruptcy bill." Responded Warren, " But, Senator, if you are not going to fix that problem, you can't take away the last shred of protection from these families." Biden ended the exchange by paying tribute to Warren's debating skills. "I got it, OK," he said with a laugh. " You are very good, Professor."

In 2008, then-Senate Majority Leader Harry Reid named Warren to chair the congressional oversight panel for the $700 billion Troubled Asset Relief Program enacted after the financial crash. A year earlier, Warren had written an article in which she proposed a " Financial Product Safety Commission" modeled on the Consumer Product Safety Commission created in the early 1970s. Her idea was incorporated into the 2010 Dodd-Frank financial reform law as an agency within the Treasury Department, and Warren was hired by the Obama White House to design and launch the Consumer Financial Protection Bureau. But her barbed criticisms over the years made her persona non grata to much of the nation's financial industry. With Senate Republicans vowing to block her appointment, Obama instead nominated former Ohio Attorney General Richard Cordray as the bureau's first director.

During the debate on Dodd-Frank, Warren successfully pushed to insulate the CFPB from political pressures. " My second choice is no agency at all and plenty of blood and teeth left on the floor," she told HuffPost at the time. As enacted, the CFPB received funding from the Federal Reserve rather than Congress— with its director appointed to a five-year term, subject to removal only for " inefficiency, neglect of duty, or malfeasance in office." In mid-2020, the Supreme Court ruled that the latter provision violated the Constitution's separation of powers principle, but otherwise left the agency intact.

While Warren didn't get to be the CFPB's first director, her visibility during her year in the Obama administration prompted Massachusetts Democrats to encourage her to challenge Republican Sen. Scott Brown. Not long after leaving her advisory post at the Treasury Department in late 2011, Warren announced her candidacy. She became a national sensation after a speech she gave, in which she exhorted wealthy Americans to recognize the debt they owe to the community and " pay forward for the next kid who comes along," went viral. Warren became a "Doonesbury" cartoon heroine and got a prime-time speaking slot at the 2012 Democratic National Convention.

Brown had shocked Democrats by winning the January 2010 special election to succeed Kennedy. Along with compiling a centrist voting record, he possessed an Everyman persona and pointedly referred to his opponent as "Professor Warren" to drive a wedge between her and rank-and-file voters.

In turn, she frequently asserted a vote for Brown was a vote for a GOP Senate majority, a sentiment that resonated with the blue state's electorate. Warren won 54%-46% to become the first woman to represent Massachusetts in the Senate— but not until Brown had attacked her for claiming Cherokee ancestry. It was an issue that would dog her for years to come, with Donald Trump— as a candidate in 2016 and later as president— repeatedly taunting her as "Pocahontas." Brown's backers said her claim was a ruse to exploit affirmative action plans at schools at which Warren had been hired. In late 2018, shortly before Warren easily won reelection against state Rep. Geoff Diehl, who had co-chaired Trump's campaign in the state, a Boston Globe investigation found no evidence that her claims of a Native American background had played a role in her hiring at four law schools, including Harvard's.

Before being sworn-in, Warren sought a seat on the Senate Banking, Housing and Urban Affairs Committee. Financial industry executives openly crusaded against the idea, but her liberal allies pushed back and she was named to the panel. After her presidential run, she added a slot on the influential Finance Committee— with its jurisdiction over taxes— to her résumé. At her first Banking panel hearing in early 2013, she pressured federal regulators to take legal action against more of the nation's largest financial institutions. "They can break the law and drag in billions in profits and then turn around and settle, paying out of those profits," she complained. She pressed the Securities and Exchange Commission to seek admission of guilt from corporations found to have violated the law rather than allowing them to pay a fine without admitting guilt— and claimed part of the credit when the policy was changed to do so.

Strains between Warren and the Obama White House became evident in early 2015 when Antonio Weiss, nominated to be Treasury undersecretary for domestic finance, withdrew his name. He had drawn Warren's fierce opposition: She felt his role as a Wall Street investment banker made him unsuited for implementing the Dodd-Frank law. That skirmish turned out to be a preview of the battle over Obama's pursuit of the Trans-Pacific Partnership. Just as the Senate was about to vote on a bill giving Obama "fast-track" authority to expedite negotiation of the trade accord, Warren warned that, if Democrats lost the White House in 2016, " a Republican president could easily use a future trade deal to override our domestic financial rules." Obama called Warren " absolutely wrong" and appeared to question her motives. " The truth of the matter is that Elizabeth is, you know, a politician like everybody else," he said. Warren also found herself again at odds with Biden when, in 2016, she voted against the 21st Century Cures Act, which contained the then-vice president's plan for a cancer cure " moonshot." Warren charged the broadly supported bill— that she helped to write— had turned into a giveaway to the pharmaceutical industry.

Four months after Obama left office, Warren criticized him for being out of touch with average voters, telling the Guardian: " President Obama, like many others in both parties, talks about a set of big national statistics that look shiny and great but increasingly have giant blind spots. … The Republicans have clearly thrown their lot in with the rich and the powerful, but so have a lot of Democrats." Such statements reflected the view from the Democratic Party's left wing that Obama had spent insufficient capital on income equality issues. Those tensions also nourished early Warren-for-president talk.

At the liberal Netroots Nation conference in summer 2014, she brought the crowd to its feet with angry denunciations of big business. A draft-Warren movement ramped up; by January 2015, MoveOn.org and Democracy for America had collected nearly 250,000 signatures in an online petition urging her to run. After months of batting away questions in less than definitive terms, Warren in March 2015 said, " I am not running, and I am not going to run." But Warren had succeeded in defining the battle lines of the 2016 Democratic contest: Clinton, preparing to launch her second presidential bid, privately solicited ideas from Warren in late 2014—and her rhetoric on the campaign trail often sounded much like Warren's. Warren stayed out of the 2016 primary battle, endorsing Clinton only after Sanders was preparing to drop out. Her failure to endorse Sanders angered many of his backers—as would her declining to do so after she left the race in 2020 and the contest became a head-to-head between Biden and Sanders. As Warren addressed the 2016 Democratic National Convention, Sanders supporters chanted, " We trusted you! We trusted you!"

Warren's rising influence on the party was solidified in late 2014 when she joined Senate Democratic leadership. In 2016, she was promoted to vice chairwoman of the Senate Democratic Caucus. But Warren's leadership role did not keep her from triggering a contentious intraparty battle: In March 2018, she publicly chastised 16 Democrats— most of them moderates, and some of whom were in tough reelection battles— after they voted to support legislation authored by Senate Republicans to roll back some Dodd-Frank provisions. A Warren fundraising email criticizing them led to a rancorous caucus meeting. Efforts by Sen. Chuck Schumer of New York, the caucus' leader, afterward did little to persuade Warren to lower the temperature. " This is what I said I was going to do," Warren told Schumer, according to Politico. " This is why I ran for the Senate."

In 2017, Warren took a seat on the Armed Services Committee, as she sought to highlight her attention to national security issues in advance of a presidential bid; In late 2018, she delivered a speech questioning " unsustainable and ill-advised military commitments" around the globe. Shortly thereafter, Warren became the first major candidate to enter the Democratic presidential race by announcing an exploratory committee. But the enthusiasm that surrounded the effort to draft her into the race in 2016 wasn't there. For the early part of the campaign, her poll numbers remained mired in the single digits and fundraising lagged. And while she had shown an ability to get under Trump's skin as a surrogate for Clinton four years earlier— deriding him as a " small, insecure money grubber" on the stump and a " thin-skinned bully who thinks humiliating women at 3 a.m. qualifies him to be president"— many Democrats felt she made a major tactical error in her engaging him as she prepared to roll out her candidacy.

Amid his taunts of " Pocahontas," Trump challenged Warren to DNA test, saying he would pay $1 million to a charity of her choice if the test proved her to be Native American; she accepted. When the issue initially arose in 2012, Warren cited family lore that she had ancestors from Cherokee and Delaware tribes on her mother's side. The results of the DNA test, released in October 2018, found " strong evidence" that she had a Native American ancestor 6 to 10 generations in the past. Seizing on the worst-case scenario, Republicans noted a native ancestor 10 generations back would make her as little as 1/1024 American Indian— and Trump, ignoring his promised charitable donation, continued to mock her. Meanwhile, Warren found herself caught in a revival of the sensitive debate over racial science and the extent to which DNA should govern racial and ethnic identity. In an effort to put the controversy behind her, she apologized after the secretary of the Cherokee Nation said she had made " a mockery out of DNA tests" while " dishonoring legitimate tribal governments and their citizens, whose ancestors are well documented and whose heritage is proven."

The campaign began to find its footing as 2019 progressed with Warren playing to her strength as a policy wonk. " I have a plan for that," became her mantra, as her website featured more than 80 detailed plans— ranging from breaking up large technology companies to providing universal childcare. To underwrite these plans, she rolled out 15 tax proposals aimed at wealthy Americans, including an annual 2 percent tax on household wealth of more than $50 million and 3 percent on billionaires' wealth. Warren's campaign fundraising quadrupled from $6 million during the first quarter of 2019 to $24.6 million in the third quarter, and, by October, one poll showed her as the national frontrunner among Democrats—7 percentage points ahead of Biden and 13 points ahead of Sanders. She drew huge crowds, including one estimated at 20,000 in New York's Washington Square Park.

But it was a plan by Sanders, not Warren—" Medicare for All"— that derailed her momentum in late 2019. Warren had embraced the health care proposal a year before launching her presidential bid, but— as she peaked in the polls— she came under fire for refusing to acknowledge what Sanders had conceded: Middle-class taxes would need to rise to pay for it. Attempting to defuse the controversy, Warren released another plan relying on tax increases on the wealthy and corporations to underwrite Medicare for All, avoiding middle-class tax hikes. But the attacks from Biden and other centrist candidates in the race only intensified, as they cited economists' arguments that the bulk of the tax increases she was proposing would be passed on to workers. " She is making it up. There is no way," Biden said of Warren's plan on PBS. (She suggested Biden was " running in the wrong presidential primary.") Warren went a step further, offering a "transition plan" that would have enabled individuals to participate in an optional government-run plan— while efforts proceeded to enact a mandatory Medicare for All" system by her third year in the White House.

In the end, Warren's efforts to compromise attracted little support in the centrist wing of the party, but they did anger progressives. Her numbers in national surveys dropped sharply, as did her showing in polls in the key early contests in Iowa and New Hampshire. The Boston Globe put it this way at the beginning of 2020: " While some pundits worry Warren is too liberal to win the general election — given her embrace of Medicare for All and public battles with Wall Street and billionaires— to the smaller group of liberal activists who have spent years trying to push the party to the left, she's been judged as just not liberal enough." The "electability" question hounded Warren as well as other female contenders in the 2020 race, amid voter concerns about defeating Trump, who had beaten the party's first female nominee four years earlier. Warren's post-debate accusations of dishonesty against Sanders were sparked by a comment she said Sanders had made at a private dinner a year earlier: that a woman could not defeat Trump. Sanders denied having said that.

While some Warren staffers had feared that going on the attack in debates could create a sexist backlash, her tumble in the polls appeared to have a liberating effect of sorts: Her evisceration of former New York Mayor Mike Bloomberg during a February debate all but ended his candidacy. "I'd like to talk about who we're running against— a billionaire who calls women ' fat broads' and 'horse-faced lesbians.' And no, I'm not talking about Donald Trump. I'm talking about Mayor Bloomberg," Warren said, demanding Bloomberg release women who had taken legal action after accusing him of such comments from non-disclosure settlement agreements. The episode helped Warren recapture some of her earlier momentum: Her campaign raised $30 million in February 2020. But it was not enough. Despite the endorsement of the Des Moines Register, she finished third in the Iowa caucuses and fourth in the New Hampshire primary. On Super Tuesday in March, she failed to finish in the top two in any contest, placing third in her home state behind both Biden and Sanders. Days later, she dropped out.

Warren was the last of Biden's major primary opponents to endorse him, waiting until mid-April. But immediately after withdrawing, when asked on MSNBC whether she would accept an offer to be his running mate, she did not hesitate to say yes. Biden seriously considered Warren for two key reasons: Her presence on the ticket would gin up progressive enthusiasm and her debate performances underscored her effectiveness in the attack dog role that vice presidential candidates are often assigned. But two other major considerations led to her being passing over. With Biden in his late 70s, Warren, at 71, did not provide generational diversity. And, while Biden had pledged to select a woman as his running mate, he fell under pressure to select a woman of color amid nationwide protests against police violence and racial injustice. There were also concerns that her selection could imperil Democrats' hopes for Senate majority because Massachusetts' Republican governor would appoint her successor pending a special election.

But, even before Warren's endorsement of Biden, her influence was in evidence as he sought to reach out to the party's progressive wing. Not only did Biden endorse Warren's bankruptcy plan, a move that effectively repudiated his support of the restrictive plan adopted by Congress a decade and a half earlier, he also embraced Warren's proposals for forgiving student loan debt and increasing Social Security payments. "I always said I would throw a parade if people adopted my plans," Warren told the Boston Globe in early 2021, asserting, "There's a lot of indication in fact— think about it — they already have." There were points of conflict: Shortly after taking office, Biden dismissed a plan by Warren and Schumer to forgive $50,000 in student loan debt, endorsing instead a proposal for $10,000 in forgiveness. But Warren did not seem eager to revert to the type of sharp intraparty criticism that had characterized her earlier years. As she told the Globe, "I hope we never get there."

Ed Markey (D)

Elected 2013, term expires 2026, 2nd full term, b. Jul 11, 1946; Malden, MA; Boston College, B.A., 1968; Boston College Law School, J.D., 1972; Roman Catholic; Married (Susan Blumenthal).

Military Career: U.S. Army Reserve, 1968-1973.

Elected Office: MA House, 1973-1976; U.S. House, 1976-2013.

Professional Career: Attorney.

DC Office: 255 DSOB 20510, 202-224-2742, Fax: 202-224-8525, markey.senate.gov

State Offices: Boston, 617-565-8519; Fall River, 508-677-0523; Springfield, 413-785-4610.

Committees: *Commerce, Science & Transportation*: Communications, Media & Broadband; Consumer Protection, Product Safety & Data Security; Oceans, Fisheries, Climate Change & Manufacturing; Space & Science; Surface Transportation, Maritime Freight & Ports. *Environment & Public Works*: Chem Safety, Waste Mngmnt, Enviro Justice & Reg Oversight; Clean Air & Nuclear Safety (Chmn); Fisheries, Water, and Wildlife. *Foreign Relations*: East Asia, the Pacific & International Cybersecurity Policy (Chmn); Near East, South Asia, Central Asia & Counterterrorism; State Dept & USAID Mngmnt, Internat'l Ops & Internat'l Dev; West Hem Crime Civ Sec Dem Rights & Women's Issues. *Small Business & Entrepreneurship*.

Group Ratings

	ADA	ACLU	AFL-CIO	LCV	COC	HAFA	ACU	CFG	FRC
2020	-	85%	-	77%	-	0%	4%	-	-
2019	100%	C	95%	100%	27%	C	4%	14%	0%

Almanac Ratings 2019-2020

	Economy	Social	Foreign	Composite
Liberal	100%	100%	96%	99%
Conservative	0%	0%	4%	1%

Key Votes of the 116th Congress

1. EPA clean energy rules	Y	5. Russia sanctions	Y	9. Barr as Atty. General	N
2. U.S./Mex./Can. trade deal	N	6. Troops in SYR, AFG	N	10. Spending at the border	N
3. Cut unemployment benefits	N	7. Veto arms sales to Saudis	Y	11. Coney Barrett to Sup. Ct.	N
4. Shelton to Fed Reserve	N	8. Defense $$$, veto override	N	12. Electoral College objections	N

Election Results

Election	Name (Party)	Vote (%)		Cand. Spent	Ind. Exp. Support	Ind. Exp. Oppose
2020 General	Ed Markey (D)	2,357,809	(66%)	$15,310,905	$4,014,216	$1,148,979
	Kevin O'Connor (R)	1,177,765	(33%)	$881,309		$113
2020 Primary	Ed Markey (D)	782,694	(55%)			
	Joe Kennedy III (D)	629,359	(45%)			

Prior winning percentages: 2014 (62%), 2013 special (55%), House: 2012(71%), 2010 (66%), 2008 (71%), 2006 (100%), 2004 (74%), 2002 (100%), 2000 (100%), 1998 (71%), 1996 (70%), 1994 (64%), 1992 (62%), 1990 (100%), 1988 (100%), 1986 (100%), 1984 (71%), 1982 (78%), 1980 (100%), 1978 (85%), 1976 (77%)

Never had a House member with so much seniority as Massachusetts' Ed Markey— nearly 37 years' worth— traded it in to become a freshman senator. As extraordinary as that June 2013 special election was, it all appeared nearly over for Markey in September 2019: Rep. Joe Kennedy, scion of a political dynasty, announced a primary challenge to the Bay State's junior senator, and polls showed the 38-year-old with a double-digit lead. Many thought Markey might retire rather than risk his first defeat in a political career that stretches back nearly a half-century.

Not only did Markey, 74, stay and fight, he also deftly recast himself as an insurgent— a role he had played during his early years in politics. His positioning was buttressed by a legion of youthful supporters drawn to Markey by an issue with which he long had been associated: combating climate change. And his association with New York Rep. Alexandria Ocasio-Cortez— an iconic progressive figure with whom Markey had co-authored the " Green New Deal"— would prove crucial. Meanwhile, Markey emphasized his working-class roots while pursuing the risky course of taking swipes at the Kennedy clan on their home turf, as to suggest that his opponent's candidacy was motivated largely by a sense of entitlement. His strategy worked: Markey turned the race around and won the September 2020 primary by nearly 11 percentage points, becoming the first candidate ever to defeat a member of the Kennedy family in a Massachusetts election. It broke a streak of more than 30 primary and general election victories dating to 1946, when Kennedy's great-uncle, future President John F. Kennedy, won a Boston-area House seat.

Four years before Markey took his seat in the Senate, the September 2009 death of Sen. Ted Kennedy, another of Joe Kennedy's great-uncles, opened that seat after five decades. Markey was seen as an early frontrunner but passed on the special election to fill the slot. Democrat had the House majority, and Markey, besides being third in line for the powerful chairmanship of the Energy and Commerce Committee, was also chairing a special panel tasked with laying the groundwork for legislation to curb climate change. All that soon changed: House Democrats lost the majority in the 2010 elections, with no clear prospect of regaining it in the near term, and a highly visible Senate slot became significantly more appealing. At the time, Markey had little way of foreseeing the election of President Donald Trump and the resulting backlash that would return House Democrats to the majority in 2019. If he had chosen to remain put, he would almost certainly today be chairing the Energy and Commerce panel— where for years he exercised substantial influence over telecommunications and technology policy, as well as environmental issues.

Instead, with Senate Democrats relegated to the minority for years after Markey's arrival, he largely operated at the margins in that chamber— in the shadow of his state's senior senator, Democrat Elizabeth Warren, a leader of the party's progressive wing and a 2020 presidential contender. In fact, it was noted on occasion that, of the six Democrats who have been elected to the Senate from Massachusetts since World War II— John and Ted Kennedy, John Kerry and Paul Tsongas, Warren and Markey— only Markey had never sought the presidency. An unspoken but implicit premise of Joe Kennedy's run against Markey was that he would fit more into the national leadership mold of the other five.

Markey's victory over Kennedy not only allowed the incumbent to introduce himself statewide to many voters unfamiliar with his record it also rebranded him as a progressive crusader, like Warren. " The time to be timid is past. The age of incrementalism is over," Markey said in his victory speech on primary night. (Warren, who once taught Kennedy at Harvard Law School, endorsed Markey before Kennedy entered the contest— but, apart from an emailed fundraising appeal for Markey, largely kept her distance from the contest.)

Markey had eyed a Senate bid as far back as 1984, when, as a four-term House member, he briefly jumped into the Democratic primary for the opening created by Tsongas' retirement. Amid a bumpy reception, he reassessed his position, withdrew from the Senate contest and was reelected to the House. The winner of the Senate seat that year was then-Lt. Gov. Kerry, who held on to it until President Barack Obama nominated him to be secretary of State in 2012. Even as he accumulated seniority and influence in the House, Markey had continued to harbor senatorial aspirations— and hoped that the seat might come open in 2004 if Kerry, then the Democratic presidential nominee, won the White House. Finally, with Kerry poised to move to Obama's Cabinet, Markey saw his opportunity and went for it.

Markey grew up in the Boston suburb of Malden, where his father was a milkman. He graduated from Boston College and was elected to the state House at 26, soon after earning a degree from Boston College's law school. He moved to an open congressional seat four years later, winning a 12-candidate primary with 22 percent of the vote. Markey broke out of the crowded field with a TV ad that remains a mini-classic in political circles: It played off an episode in which state House leaders removed the furniture from Markey's office to retaliate for a court reform bill he had pushed over their objections. The ad shows a desk in the hallway of the Statehouse, as Markey declares:" The bosses may tell me where to sit. Nobody tells me where to stand." (In his 2020 race against Kennedy, Markey included that footage in a new ad that felt like the trailer for a Scorsese film— and went viral.)

In winning in 1976, Markey favored school prayer and advocated constitutional amendments to end school busing and ban abortion— positions geared to a socially conservative Catholic population in his district. He disavowed these positions before his brief 1984 Senate bid, but the timing of those reversals became a liability during that short-lived campaign. In recent decades, he has sidestepped questions about his change of position, telling The Boston Globe in 2013: " For 30 years, I have taken the progressive position, the liberal position, on each and every issue. I just evolved."

In his run for the Senate seat in 2013, Markey was the establishment favorite and the more traditional liberal in a primary against Rep. Stephen Lynch, whose district includes working-class neighborhoods in and around South Boston. As a onetime iron worker, Lynch enjoyed substantial labor union support. But Markey's 3-1 cash advantage helped him prevail, 57%-43%. Markey's GOP opponent in the special general election was businessman Gabriel Gomez, a former Navy SEAL. Gomez campaigned as a political outsider, declaring in one TV ad: " Markey is everything that's wrong with Congress: 37 years of pay raises, bounced checks, taking millions from people he regulates." But Markey outspent Gomez by nearly 4-1 and won 55%-45%. He was easily reelected to a full six-year term in the 2014 general election, defeating his little-known opponent, local selectman Brian Herr, 59%-36%.

Markey's arrival in the Senate was not the most auspicious: Two months after his swearing-in, when the Foreign Relations Committee voted to authorize Obama's use of force against Syria, Markey voted "present" while most other committee Democrats voted in support. Markey said he was concerned about the " unintended consequences" of a U.S. military attack, which never occurred — but critics saw it as an attempt to sidestep a tough issue. Boston magazine afterward captured the widespread reaction with a headline: " Ed Markey Annoys Literally Everyone by Voting 'Present' on Syrian Resolution." Markey's decision to straddle the issue may have been related to his House vote a decade earlier in favor of the 2002 resolution authorizing the war in Iraq, a decision about which he later expressed strong regret.

In 2020, Kennedy sought to highlight Markey's onetime support of the Iraq War— as well as his opposition to abortion and school busing early in his career— as the two dueled over which one was more progressive. Progressive Punch, a nonpartisan but liberal website, found little daylight between them: Markey had a 99 percent lifetime voting score to 97 percent for Kennedy. For 2017, Almanac vote rankings had Markey as the seventh most liberal senator, scoring just behind a fellow New Englander: Democrat Richard Blumenthal of Connecticut who, like Markey, is a media-savvy political veteran who arrived in the Senate late in his career. As members of the Commerce, Science and Transportation Committee, Markey and Blumenthal have teamed up on several consumer issues. In the process, Markey continued to deploy the barbed rhetoric that has long endeared him to consumer advocates and environmentalists— even if his propensity for sardonic acronyms (he has gibed that GOP stands for "Gutting Our Privacy" and FDA for "Fostering Drug Addiction") often elicits groans from political insiders and the media.

In 2018, Markey and Blumenthal utilized procedural maneuvers to block passage of legislation to remove regulatory obstacles to development of self-driving cars— citing safety concerns. The same year, they combined forces on another high-profile consumer issue—a digital " privacy bill of rights." They introduced the legislation after revelations that Cambridge Analytica, a consulting firm with ties to Trump's 2016 presidential campaign, had obtained data on as many as 87 million Facebook users without permission; Markey accused the social media giant of " privacy malpractice."

In the House, Markey left his most lasting effect on telecommunications and information technology policy— while often working with Republicans to come up with innovative initiatives. His proposals were frequently inclined toward deregulation, but consumer advocates regarded him as a friend— blaming the skyrocketing cable TV bills of recent years not on Markey's legislation but on the failure of the industry to produce the level of competition originally promised. When his Massachusetts colleague, House Speaker Tip O'Neill, first assigned him a coveted seat on the Energy and Commerce Committee, Markey— impressed by the high-tech boom around suburban Boston's Route 128—joined the panel's Telecommunications Subcommittee. In early 1987, Markey became subcommittee chair. It was a couple of years after a court ordered the breakup of the old " Ma Bell" monopoly, setting in motion a transformation of the nation's telecommunications industry.

In 1992, Markey crafted a cable TV regulation bill with enough support to override President George H.W. Bush's veto. The measure helped establish today's satellite TV industry. Markey lost the gavel of the Telecommunications Subcommittee when Republicans captured the House majority in 1994 but continued to exert influence as its ranking Democrat. He was a major player in passage of the landmark Telecommunications Act of 1996. The law, co-authored with Texas GOP Rep. Jack Fields, helped prod cable firms to build the broadband networks integral to the flow of information and images over today's internet. "Google, Hulu, YouTube — none of it was possible before the 1996 Telecom Act," Markey told The Boston Globe years later. "It required broadband in order to make the business models possible."

Fast forward more than two decades, and a high point of Markey's Senate tenure came in May 2018 when— in what he trumpeted as " the most important vote we're going to have in this generation on the internet"— he led a successful effort to reverse the Trump administration's repeal of Obama-era " net neutrality" rules, which required internet service providers give equal treatment and access to all traffic on the internet. Markey persuaded three Senate Republicans to join Democrats in a vote to reinstate the 2015 regulations. His measure died in the House, then under Republican control. In early 2021, President Joe Biden made changes at the Federal Communications Commission with an eye toward reviving net neutrality rules.

Markey's other major legislative interest— energy and the environment— became his priority after Democrats regained the House after the 2006 elections. House Speaker Nancy Pelosi chose Markey to chair the Select Committee on Energy Independence and Global Warming. It was an attempt to get around Michigan Rep. John Dingell, who as chair of the Energy and Commerce Committee and a representative of an auto-manufacturing-dependent district, had resisted efforts to toughen motor vehicle emission standards. When Dingell objected to the select committee, Pelosi announced it would not have authority to propose legislation— but she gave Markey free rein to hold hearings and make the case for a far-reaching bill to curb climate change.

After the 2008 elections, Dingell was ousted as head of the Energy and Commerce Committee, and Markey became chair of the panel's Energy and Environment Subcommittee while retaining the select committee gavel. It gave Pelosi the players she needed to pass legislation to achieve Democrats' goal of an 85 percent cut in greenhouse gas emissions by 2050. Markey worked with the energy and manufacturing industries to gain support— or at least to reduce their opposition. After intense negotiations, the bill passed the House 219-212 in June 2009. But the Senate never took it up, and the issue subsequently made little headway on Capitol Hill. Markey told Boston magazine the bill's failure to become law was the "top" disappointment of his career.

A decade later, in early 2019, Markey again captured headlines as lead Senate sponsor of a non-binding resolution for a " Green New Deal" pushed by the Democrats' newly emboldened progressive wing. The resolution, which urged a "10-year national mobilization effort" to achieve "net-zero greenhouse gas emissions" worldwide by 2050, was co-sponsored by six Senate Democrats seeking the party's presidential nomination, including Warren. But its aspirations not only were criticized by conservatives as extreme: Some liberals complained it involved no concrete steps to combat global warming. In an interview with Yale Environment 360, Markey responded: " This resolution has generated more debate about climate change in three weeks than we've had in the last nine years. And that's a good thing." It was also a good thing politically for Markey: It forged a partnership between him and Ocasio-Cortez, its chief House sponsor, who hadn't yet been born when Markey was first elected to Congress. She endorsed Markey early and appeared alone in a TV ad that the Markey campaign spent nearly a half-million dollars to air prior to the September 2020 primary against Kennedy.

While established environmental advocacy groups such as the League of Conservation Voters and the Sierra Club quickly lined up behind Markey, Ocasio-Cortez's support galvanized more youthful backers such as the Sunrise Movement. Markey was greeted enthusiastically by thousands of cheering young people at Boston's "Climate Strike" just days after Kennedy entered the race; many of them turned their attention to reelecting Markey after their favored contenders in the Democratic presidential contest, Warren and Vermont Sen. Bernie Sanders, fell short. It evoked memories of four decades earlier— when anti-nuclear activists threatened to collect enough signatures to put Markey up for the vice presidential nomination at the 1980 Democratic National Convention if convention organizers didn't grant him a prime-time speaking slot. The ploy gave the 34-year-old Markey, already a prominent critic of nuclear power, 10 minutes to make the case to a national audience to shut down nuclear reactors and increase solar energy.

While Kennedy maintained the lead in public opinion polls throughout much of his yearlong Senate bid, his campaign faced challenges from the outset. There was anger in Democratic circles that he was diverting money and effort to oust a fellow liberal as the party was seeking to oust Trump and capture the Senate majority. At one early debate, Kennedy, who as recently as late 2018 was disavowing any plans to take on Markey, struggled to explain why he was doing so. Globe columnist Scot Lehigh wrote: " One suspects what JPK III really wanted to say was this: Because I'm younger and more energetic— and besides, do you really think Markey spends weekends in that modest house in Malden rather than his million-dollar manse in Chevy Chase, Md.?"

Kennedy hoped to make an issue of the amount of time the incumbent spent in the state—a question that had long dogged Markey. In fact, a Boston Globe examination of travel records found that Markey had spent less time at home during the previous two years than other members of the congressional delegation— including Warren, who was running for president throughout 2019. But Kennedy's plan to crisscross Massachusetts— to underscore that he would be a " constant presence" in the state— was blunted by the coronavirus pandemic. At one point, the Kennedy campaign sent a memo to the media suggesting Markey was so unfamiliar with the state that he had left three towns off his website. But it produced an embarrassing gaffe for Kennedy when it turned out that the three towns in question had been wiped off the map more than 80 years earlier to make way for a huge reservoir in central Massachusetts. For his part, Markey used the modest house in Malden— owned by his father until the latter's death in 2001—to jab at Kennedy. " Welcome to the compound," he quipped to a visiting reporter, alluding to the Kennedys' large Cape Cod homestead.

The Markey campaign ran a digital ad that opened with a shot of Kennedy on a fancy-looking boat, to the tune of Hall and Oates' " Rich Girl." It focused on a debate moment in which Markey told his opponent to " tell your father"— a former congressman— not to give money to a pro-Kennedy super PAC that was running negative ads. It proved too much for Markey's onetime ally, Pelosi, who — without being asked— endorsed Kennedy shortly after Markey's attacks. Kennedy had been a loyalist at a time when other young House members were suggesting it was time for the 80-year-old Pelosi to step aside. But she also appeared to be upset at Markey's jabs at the Kennedy family, as she noted her longstanding ties to them— going back to when her father, longtime Baltimore Mayor Thomas D'Alesandro, had run JFK's campaign for president in Maryland in 1960. The silver lining for Markey was that Pelosi's rebuke underscored his narrative that he was the insurgent, with Kennedy being the establishment candidate.

" Markey went from tired old incumbent to progressive, insurgent firebrand in about three months. ... He stole Kennedy's change message," Mark Horan, a political consultant who had worked with

Markey previously but was not involved in the 2020 campaign, told the Boston Globe. " He should have done it earlier but it worked." Kennedy finally went on the attack, charging Markey with failing to show leadership on key issues to Black Americans and other communities of color. But even among some Kennedy supporters, it was considered too little, too late. While jabbing at the Kennedy wealth, Markey kept up in terms of fundraising: he and Kennedy each spent close to $14 million. In addition, Markey declined to embrace the "People's Pledge" to discourage outside spending, a shift from his position in prior races. Two pro-Markey super PACs spent $4.5 million, topping the nearly $4.3 million spent by the pro-Kennedy super PAC, according to the nonpartisan Center for Responsive Politics. Markey defeated Kennedy 55.4%-44.5% and went on to score a 66%-33% November win over attorney Kevin O' Connor, a political novice, to keep the Senate seat to which he had so long aspired.

Richard Neal (D)

Elected 1988, 17th term, b. Feb 14, 1949; Worcester, MA; American International College, B.A., 1972; University of Hartford Barney School of Business, M.P.A., 1976; University of MA, Att., 1982; Roman Catholic; Married (Maureen Conway Neal); 4 children.

Elected Office: Springfield City Council, 1978-1983; Springfield Mayor, 1984-1988.

Professional Career: Staff Assistant, Springfield Mayor William C. Sullivan, 1973-1978; H.S. & college teacher, 1978-1983.

DC Office: 2309 RHOB 20515, 202-225-5601, Fax: 202-225-8112, neal.house.gov

State Offices: Pittsfield, 413-442-0946; Springfield, 413-785-0325.

Committees: *Joint Taxation (Chmn). Ways & Means (Chmn).*

Group Ratings

	ADA	ACLU	AFL-CIO	LCV	COC	HAFA	ACU	CFG	FRC
2020	**	81%	**	100%	-	0%	7%	**	-
2019	95%	C	100%	97%	63%	C	7%	12%	0%

Almanac Ratings 2019-2020

	Economy	Social	Foreign	Composite
Liberal	100%	100%	80%	94%
Conservative	0%	0%	20%	6%

Key Votes of the 116th Congress

1. U.S./Mex./Can. trade deal	Y	5. Russia sanctions		9. Firearms background checks Y
2. First Coronavirus response	Y	6. Troops in Syria	Y	10. Spending at the border	Y
3. HEROES Act	Y	7. Veto arms sales to Saudis	Y	11. Marijuana liberalized rules	Y
4. CASH Act	Y	8. Defense $$$, veto override	Y	12. Electoral College objections N

Election Results

Election	Name (Party)	Vote (%)		Cand. Spent	Ind. Exp. Support	Ind. Exp. Oppose
2020 General	Richard Neal (D)	275,376	(97%)	$6,336,578	$605,782	$755,176
2020 Primary	Richard Neal (D)	84,092	(59%)			
	Alex Morse (D)	59,110	(41%)			

Prior winning percentages: 2016 (73%), 2014 (74%), 2012 (78%), 2010 (57%), 2008 (76%), 2006(77%), 2004 (77%), 2002 (77%), 2000 (95%), 1998 (99%), 1996 (72%), 1994 (59%), 1992 (53%), 1990 (68%), 1988 (80%),

Democrat Richard Neal, first elected in 1988, has become one of his party's leaders on economic policy as chairman of the tax-writing House Ways and Means Committee. His active agenda, including on health care and retirement security, has been a blend of steps for the middle class, lower-income groups and some business interests. Although he has a history of finding common ground with

Republicans, immediate prospects for bipartisanship have been limited. Neal asserted his authority to review the tax returns of President Donald Trump, but with little progress while Trump remained in office. The Boston Globe profiled Neal as " the insider's insider, a veteran relationship-builder on Capitol Hill, a quiet dealmaker." In 2020, he comfortably won a contentious primary against a more liberal challenger.

Neal grew up in Springfield amid the racial tensions of the 1960s. His parents died when he was a teenager, and Neal and his younger sisters received monthly Social Security survivor benefits while being raised by their grandmother and aunt. He graduated from American International College and earned a master's degree in public administration from the University of Hartford. In Springfield, he worked for the mayor; while teaching high school and college history, he was elected to the City Council in 1978. As mayor from 1984 to 1988, Neal worked to rehabilitate the downtown area and revitalize neighborhoods.

His congressional predecessor, 36-year incumbent Edward Boland, chairman of the House Intelligence Committee and a longtime pal of Democratic Speaker Tip O' Neill, essentially bequeathed him the House seat. Boland announced his retirement just before the filing deadline— and after Neal had traveled the district for a year. Unopposed in the Democratic primary, Neal won the general election with 80 percent of the vote.

Neal has a generally liberal voting record, but has favored enough moderate initiatives to separate himself from more-liberal Massachusetts colleagues. He voted for the 1996 welfare overhaul and supported both the North American Free Trade Agreement and normalization of trade relations with China, although organized labor opposed the pacts. In 2015, he opposed trade promotion authority for the president— a virtually mandatory position for a senior Democrat in the House.

Neal brings an old-style interest in bipartisanship that is less familiar to many junior Democrats in the House. "I think of him as someone who remembers he's a Democrat but harkens back to the old days where we were able to work across the aisle together," Janice Mays, a former Democratic staff director at Ways and Means, told the Globe. His move to the top post was a long grind. When Charles Rangel of New York was forced to step down as committee chairman in 2010 while battling ethics problems, Neal vigorously pushed for the job, arguing that the party needed to shelve seniority in favor of having a better spokesman. With Democrats back in the House minority, he contended he would be a more business-friendly alternative to Sander Levin of Michigan and could work more closely with Republicans to get bills passed. He won a 23-22 vote of the Democratic Steering Committee. But he lost to Levin in the full caucus, 109-78. Six years later, the 85-year-old Levin cut back his responsibilities. Rep. Xavier Becerra of California quickly voiced interest in replacing Levin. The following day, Becerra unexpectedly accepted an offer by Gov. Jerry Brown to fill the vacancy as attorney general of California. Neal fulfilled his ambition without a challenge from another Democrat. Two years later, he became chairman.

Neal has encouraged Democratic advocates of change. Following the 2016 election, he said "it's time for the Democratic Party to start thinking about a reset. .... The people who voted for Donald Trump, they used to be our people." Even with his independent streak, he remained loyal to Democratic Leader Nancy Pelosi when Rep. Tim Ryan of Ohio challenged her— not surprising, given his influential niche.

Neal has a longstanding interest in retirement security, especially for the middle class, and has filed a bipartisan bill that would set guidelines for insurance companies and other investment firms to advise their account-holders. He worked with the Obama administration on a bill to require employers who do not sponsor retirement plans for their workers to automatically enroll them in individual retirement accounts funded by payroll deductions, unless an employee opts out. More recently, he proposed an innovative plan to create a Treasury Department office that would issue bonds to finance loans to pension plans in a "critical and declining" status. He has urged reform of the tax code, which he has said is " creaking under its own weight;" as chairman, he began by reviewing the Republican-passed tax cuts of 2017. He took the lead for House Democrats on a proposal to clamp down on companies that incorporate in Bermuda and other offshore havens to avoid U.S. taxes.

On health care, Neal has sought to assure that pre-existing conditions were covered under Obama care. But he clashed with liberals by delaying action on a long-sought bill to restrict the medical practice of " surprise billing." At the end of 2019, both Democrats and Republicans had worked out an agreement to limit such billing practice. But the deal fell apart, Buzz Feed reported. " And people on both sides of the aisle are pointing their finger at one member for tanking the momentum." Neal unexpectedly released the vague outline of a proposal that " came out of the blue at the end," said a senior House Republican working on the issue. " It is crucial that we get this right," Neal said, in a statement with Rep. Kevin Brady, senior Republican on Ways and Means. He added that his panel didn't have time to review the tentative agreement.

A year later, Neal and Brady reached a final agreement on the issue with other congressional players, as Neal prevailed on his demand to include arbitration if insurers and health care providers were unable to reach agreement on reimbursement rates. His approach, he said, was " the sound consumer position."

Neal occasionally gets out front on an issue. In February 2021, when congressional Democrats were working on the terms of a COVID relief bill with the Biden administration, he took the lead in advocating a tax credit of up to $3,600 for each child in a family with annual income up to $150,000. " This is how the tax code is supposed to work for those who need it most," he told reporters.

As Ways and Means chairman, Neal shared with the chairman of the Senate Finance Committee the unique authority to review the returns of all taxpayers. In April 2019, he formally requested that the Internal Revenue Service provide him Trump's tax filings during the past six years. Unlike previous presidents, Trump consistently objected to such review. In July 2020, the Supreme Court in a related case held that a federal judge should further review requests for Trump's records, with Chief Justice John Roberts ruling for a cautious approach before opening a president's tax records. " The president's unique constitutional position means that Congress may not look to him as a 'case study' for general legislation," Roberts wrote.

On local issues, Neal has focused on the economic problems of Springfield. He secured funds for renovation of its Union Station, and more than $100 million for high-speed rail service in the region. With the large number of former Puerto Ricans living in his district, he took a special interest in the slow recovery from the devastation of the island that resulted from Hurricane Maria in 2017. In 2018, he demanded that the Trump administration assure funds for " infrastructure that supports utility services critical to health care delivery."

Neal had serious primary challenges in 1990 and 1992, but won by healthy margins. He faced a contest in 2010 with Republican business executive Thomas Wesley, who spent only $144,000 to $2.2 million for the incumbent. Neal was held to 57 percent of the vote. Otherwise, he did not face another serious contest. In 2018, he had a primary challenge from Tahirah Amatul-Wadud, a political newcomer who was hoping to join the nationwide Democratic insurgency against veteran incumbents. Amatul-Wadud spent $150,000—5 percent of Neal's total for the cycle— and lost, 71%-29%; she took 12 of the small hill towns in the sprawling district, but got only 24 percent in Springfield.

In 2020, he faced a well-financed Democratic challenger with political credentials. Alex Morse, a progressive and openly gay candidate, was the mayor of Holyoke— a formerly industrial city that had experienced hard economic times. Their campaign became nasty when students of Morse, who taught a course at the University of Massachusetts, complained to the campus newspaper that he used his position for " romantic or sexual gain" with students. Morse wrote that he was sorry for his " unacceptable behavior for anyone with institutional power." Neal denied that he fomented the conflict, though the state Democratic Party said it assisted the students in preparing the charges. When it came to campaign issues, most voters seemed to believe that Neal— especially as Ways and Means chairman, and with Pelosi's endorsement— had served the district well. Morse emphasized the need to change the status quo. Neal outspent Morse, $6 million to $2.1 million; outside groups spent an additional $3 million. Neal won, 59%-41%, with 52 percent in Morse's home city of Holyoke.

No matter how thin the Democratic majorities, Neal had the gavel for what he hoped would be a long and productive tenure at Ways and Means.

MA-1: Western Massachusetts

Population		Race and Ethnicity		Income	
Total	723,831	White	83.80%	Median Income	$61,559
Land area (sq. miles)	2,350	Black	6.60%	District Income Rank	238
Pop/ sq mi	307.98	Latino	19.30%	Poverty Rate	12.30%
Born in State	65.90%	Asian	2.20%	With health insurance	96.80%
		Two or more races	3.60%	Cash public assistance	4.40%
Age Groups		Other	3.80%	Food stamp/SNAP	18.30%
Under 18	20.40%				
18-34	22.20%	**Education**		**Work**	
35-64	38.50%	H.S grad or less	42.50%	White Collar	39.00%
Over 64	18.70%	Some college	26.70%	Sales and Service	39.30%
		College Degree, 4 yr	17.80%	Blue Collar	21.70%
Military		Post grad	13.10%	Government	14.70%
Veteran/ Active Duty	6.50%				

2020 Pres. Vote	Biden	224,939	(61%)	Trump	135,655	(37%)		
2016 Pres. Vote	Clinton	194,036	(56%)	Trump	123,953	(36%)	Johnson	14,550 (4%)

Springfield, Pittsfield: The stony hills and green mountains of western Massachusetts, which so inspired Henry David Thoreau in the 1840s, look a lot like they did 300 years ago. This was the frontier in the 17th century, where Puritan preachers founded towns in the wilderness, farmed the rocky soil and preached against declension. It remained Yankee New England's western frontier for nearly 200 years. In the 19th century, the area was the home of writers and artists. Edith Wharton lived grandly on her estate in Lenox. Herman Melville struck up a friendship with Nathaniel Hawthorne after purchasing a farm near Hawthorne's Pittsfield home, not far from where the Boston Symphony plays at the Tangle wood Festival each summer. As the 20th century progressed, much of western Massachusetts returned to its bucolic state. Few giant factories remain along the wide Connecticut River or the country streams. An exception is the Crane & Co. paper mill along the Housatonic River in Dalton, which since 1879 has been the only company to print money for the U.S. Treasury. The currency-production and stationery operations of the company have been sold to different companies. In each case, production remained at the Dalton plant. Tourism and vacation homes have been bustling in the Berkshires, but the day-to-day economy has not recovered from factory shutdowns.

Springfield is the largest city in western Massachusetts and the fourth-largest in New England, far from Boston in mindset and distance but with its own historical cachet. It is the site of the armory where unhappy farmers mounted Shays' Rebellion in 1786-87. It is where basketball was invented and where the Webster's unabridged dictionaries were edited and published. Founded by Puritans in the 17th century, Springfield has become home to immigrants from a dozen countries who have worked their way up here. Hispanics and African Americans, respectively, account for 45 percent and 21 percent of the population; the poverty rate of 27 percent contrasts with 9 percent statewide.

Springfield's downtown has emptied and its tax base has shrunk in recent decades. Business leaders have tried to revive it, in part with the expansion of the Basketball Hall of Fame. The firearms manufacturer Smith & Wesson and MassMutual insurance are headquartered in Springfield. But the once-robust city has suffered from corruption and serious crime, and in 2004 was forced to submit to state control in a financial bailout. Other than tourism and academia, the economy in much of the area has remained stagnant. The 2018 opening of the MGM casino on 14 acres in what had been the down-and-out South End of Springfield created rare hope, though initial revenues were not encouraging; first-year revenues were more than 30 percent below the $400 million projection, which undoubtedly was worsened by the pandemic. Springfield has shown other signs of life, including a $95 million rehab of the downtown train station, which has expanded service to New Haven. Local rail advocates want to increase east-west service to Boston, with the hope of drawing western Massachusetts— with its much lower living costs— into the booming Boston-area economy. A $100 million factory in East Springfield started by building rail cars for the Boston-area transit system, and added Philadelphia and Los Angeles. Concerns that the Chinese-government ownership might be forbidden were resolved by congressional action in 2019.

For many years, western Massachusetts was a heartland of the Republican Party— flinty, thrifty and chilly, just like the area's most famous politician, Calvin Coolidge. Frederick Gillett overlapped with President Coolidge for part of his six years as Speaker of the House. The area now contains some of the most liberal precincts of the United States. Progressive MSNBC host Rachel Maddow began as a broadcaster here and still has a home with her partner, Susan Mikula. "We kind of forget we're gay," Mikula told New York magazine. "We live in western Mass and New York, and it's very accommodating." Alice's Restaurant in Great Barrington was immortalized by folk singer Arlo Guthrie in his anti-war song of the same name.

The 1st District in western Massachusetts includes Springfield and the old mill towns Chicopee and Holyoke along the river, plus Dalton and once-industrial Pittsfield in the Berkshires. As recently as 1991, liberal Republican Silvio Conte for three decades represented much of this area in Congress. Not anymore. The district votes consistently Democratic, though the local orneriness reduced the Democratic presidential vote to 56 percent in 2016 and 61 percent in 2020.

Jim McGovern (D)

Elected 1996, 13th term, b. Nov 20, 1959; Worcester, MA; American University, B.A., 1981; American University, M.P.A., 1984; Roman Catholic; Married (Lisa Murray McGovern); 2 children.

Professional Career: Aide, U.S. Sen. George McGovern, 1981-1984; Sr. aide, U.S. Rep. Joseph Moakley, 1982-1996.

DC Office: 408 CHOB 20515, 202-225-6101, Fax: 202-225-5759, mcgovern.house.gov

State Offices: Leominster, 978-466-3552; Northampton, 413-341-8700; Worcester, 508-831-7356.

Committees: *Agriculture*: Subcommittee Nutrition, Oversight & Department Operations. *Rules (Chmn)*: Ex Officio membership on all subcommittees.

Group Ratings

	ADA	ACLU	AFL-CIO	LCV	COC	HAFA	ACU	CFG	FRC
2020	**	86%	**	100%	-	0%	3%	**	-
2019	100%	C	90%	100%	40%	C	3%	12%	0%

Almanac Ratings 2019-2020

	Economy	Social	Foreign	Composite
Liberal	100%	100%	92%	98%
Conservative	0%	0%	8%	2%

Key Votes of the 116th Congress

1. U.S./Mex./Can. trade deal	N	5. Russia sanctions	Y	9. Firearms background checks	Y
2. First Coronavirus response	Y	6. Troops in Syria	Y	10. Spending at the border	N
3. HEROES Act	Y	7. Veto arms sales to Saudis	Y	11. Marijuana liberalized rules	Y
4. CASH Act	Y	8. Defense $$$, veto override	N	12. Electoral College objections	N

Election Results

Election	Name (Party)	Vote (%)		Cand. Spent	Ind. Exp. Support	Ind. Exp. Oppose
2020 General	Jim McGovern (D)	249,854	(65%)	$849,060	$123	
	Tracy Lovvorn (R)	132,220	(35%)	$19,364		$113
2020 Primary	Jim McGovern (D)	121,645	(99%)			

Prior winning percentages: 2018 (67%), 2016 (98%), 2014 (72%), 2012 (76%), 2010 (57%), 2008 (75%), 2006(78%), 2004 (67%), 2002 (77%), 2000 (77%), 1998 (57%), 1996 (53%)

Jim McGovern, a liberal Democrat first elected in 1996, has been a savvy insider and active progressive on such causes as international human rights and ending hunger. As chairman of the

House Rules Committee, he gained influence on virtually all issues and access to other power centers. Demands on his parliamentary skills grew following the outbreak of the coronavirus, when House members sought to limit their time in the Capitol while continuing to vote on House business and participate in virtual committee hearings. With his long apprenticeship, McGovern had an opportunity for a lengthy reign— assuming he and others can satisfy the often-conflicting demands of Democratic factions.

McGovern grew up in Worcester, where his parents owned a liquor store. He attended American University in Washington and, while in graduate school, worked in South Dakota Sen. George McGovern's office. He ran McGovern's quixotic 1984 campaign in the Massachusetts presidential primary, where the senator finished third with 21 percent of the vote, and nominated him that year at the Democratic convention in San Francisco. Although not related by blood, Jim McGovern called George " my inspiration, my mentor, my dearest friend." He was an aide in Boston-area Rep. Joe Moakley's office and became chief of staff just as Moakley ascended to chairman of the Rules Committee. McGovern was the chief investigator in a 1989 review of the murders of six Jesuits and two lay women in El Salvador, which led to a cutoff of U.S. aid to the country.

In 1994, McGovern ran for the House and lost in the Democratic primary, 38%-30%. In 1996, he ran again, this time with no primary opposition. In the general election, Republican Rep. Peter Blute stressed his independence from then-Speaker Newt Gingrich and attacked McGovern for liberal stands on abortion rights and Cuba. McGovern ran a humorous spot that asked, " If you wouldn't vote for Newt, why would you ever vote for Blute?" At age 36, McGovern won, 53%-45%.

With deft maneuvers reflecting his Capitol Hill experience, McGovern positioned himself as a power broker in the Democratic caucus. In 2001, the dying Moakley asked Democratic Leader Dick Gephardt to help McGovern get a seat on Rules, which schedules most legislation for the House floor. McGovern got a commitment for the next available Democratic seat, with added seniority benefits.

On Rules, McGovern started with the advantage of being well-versed in House procedures. With the GOP in the majority, he showed a sharp partisan edge as he pursued parliamentary maneuvers that led to cries of outrage from House Republicans. When Louise Slaughter of New York died in March 2018, McGovern replaced her in the top Democratic post on Rules. His longstanding goals for House operations, he said, were increased public confidence in the House and more open debate, though he opposed Republican use of what he called " gotcha" amendments.

His foreign policy interests have been far-ranging. For years, McGovern was a party leader on Iraq war policy, though his influence has been mostly rhetorical. He sponsored an unsuccessful 2007 bill to withdraw U.S. troops from Iraq in six months. He turned his attention to Afghanistan, and in 2011 nearly succeeded in getting the House to pass a resolution aimed at accelerating troop withdrawals. McGovern was the House sponsor of a measure signed into law in 2012 that imposed a visa ban and asset freeze on suspected Russian human rights abusers. Russian President Vladimir Putin protested it was an intrusion into his country's affairs and retaliated by halting U.S. adoptions of Russian children, prompting McGovern to call Putin a "bully." But on the Cuba Working Group, McGovern welcomed the 2014 announcement by President Barack Obama to open the diplomatic door to Cuba as " a historic, long-overdue day." When he joined the congressional delegation that accompanied Obama to Cuba in 2016, it was at least his sixteenth visit since he was a college student in 1979. Following the apparent murder in 2018 of Saudi journalist Jamal Khashoggi, he sponsored a bipartisan bill to halt military sales and aid to Saudi Arabia. President Donald Trump signed McGovern's bill to require the State Department to punish Chinese officials who interfere with the rights of Americans seeking access to Tibet.

McGovern pushed for a government-run public option in the 2010 health care overhaul bill, though it was dropped under pressure from Democratic moderates. Since the Supreme Court's 2010 Citizens United decision, he has introduced bills aimed at diminishing the influence of money in politics. During the official counting of the electoral votes for the 2016 election, he cited reports of Russian interference in the election in his unsuccessful challenge to the proceeding. He refused " to sit quietly when our democratic institutions are under attack," he tweeted.

As chairman of the Congressional Hunger Center, McGovern has pushed for more spending on international nutrition and for less support of biofuels, which he says have driven up food costs. He has scheduled regular events to publicize his cause, sometimes with Republican allies, including " End Hunger Now" speeches. On the House Agriculture Committee, he branded GOP efforts to cut domestic funding for food stamps " unconscionable" and " immoral." With then-Rep. Marcia Fudge, he wrote an opinion column for The Hill in January 2020, in which they criticized a Trump administration regulation that supposedly would " literally take food off the tables of American families who are already struggling to get by."

When the pandemic struck, Congress faced a crisis similar to hypotheticals that arose following September 2001. In that earlier case, there were concerns of how and whether the House or Senate could act— in the event of an attack on Congress, perhaps a direct hit by an aircraft— if the resulting deaths meant that it no longer had a quorum to conduct business. In 2020, the members remained alive. But many were fearful of returning to the Capitol or they were unable to do so. Facing the demand for quick legislative action on coronavirus relief, McGovern worked with Pelosi and other House leaders on ways to conduct business without a quorum present in the Capitol. They rejected the option of permitting members to vote from their remote locations. Instead, they expanded the concept of " proxy voting," which historically has been a common device in congressional committees. The problem with remote voting, according to a report from McGovern's Rules Committee staff, was that it created logistical challenges, including cyber-security for lawmakers hundreds, or thousands, of miles away. It likely would require changes in House rules and could raise constitutional challenges. Even though proxy voting also required a rules change, it was " the best of the options available" under existing circumstances and " has a basis in parliamentary tradition," without raising security or technology concerns, according to the staff report. Republicans objected, but Democrats used their majority control to permit members to give colleagues their proxy to vote on a case-by-case basis.

As for committee hearings, which were largely shut down once the coronavirus struck, McGovern acknowledged that conducting " virtual hearings" would require a rule change. Instead, he suggested that committees operate informally with video hook-ups and refer to those sessions as briefings, roundtables or something similar.

Although Republicans held his seat a quarter century ago, they have all but given up on it. McGovern has run unopposed in seven of the past 11 elections, though he was held to 57 percent in the anti-Democratic environment of 2010. In 2020, GOP challenger Tracy Lovvorn, a physical therapist, spoke positively about QAnon conspiracy theories. She lost, 65%-35%.

Like other old-school Democrats, McGovern has been comfortable in setting long-term strategies and waiting until they have the votes to act. In discussing his role as committee chairman, McGovern recounted to the Springfield Republican newspaper that Moakley decades earlier counseled him, " learn the names of every member of the House and be patient because some day you can be chairman of the Rules Committee." Moakley, in particular, urged him not to " do anything stupid like run for the Senate" and to remember, " good waiters get good tips." With Reps. Richard Neal and Katherine Clark in adjacent districts serving as chairman of the Ways and Means Committee and assistant speaker, Massachusetts was positioned for influence.

MA-2: West Central Massachusetts   Cook Partisan Voting Index: D+10

Population		Race and Ethnicity		Income	
Total	759,750	White	83.10%	Median Income	$77,375
Land area (sq. miles)	1,628	Black	5.20%	District Income Rank	107
Pop/ sq mi	466.68	Latino	10.40%	Poverty Rate	9.50%
Born in State	62.60%	Asian	6.00%	With health insurance	97.30%
		Two or more races	3.30%	Cash public assistance	2.80%
Age Groups		Other	2.50%	Food stamp/SNAP	13.00%
Under 18	19.10%				
18-34	24.90%	**Education**		**Work**	
35-64	39.30%	H.S grad or less	33.50%	White Collar	45.40%
Over 64	16.70%	Some college	25.80%	Sales and Service	35.70%
		College Degree, 4 yr	22.70%	Blue Collar	18.90%
Military		Post grad	18.00%	Government	15.20%
Veteran/ Active Duty	5.80%				

2020 Pres. Vote	Biden	240,547	(61%)	Trump	140,377	(36%)		
2016 Pres. Vote	Clinton	197,492	(55%)	Trump	129,437	(36%) Johnson	17,743	(5%)

Worcester: For more than 200 years, Worcester has been one of the nation's centers of tinkering, contriving and inventing, even though it is one of the few active industrial cities not located on a river, lake or seacoast. In the past, its biggest industries were valentine-making, wire-making, textiles, grinding wheels and envelopes. It is where the birth control pill was invented and where Worcester native and Clark University professor Robert Goddard shot off experimental rockets before relieved locals saw him off to New Mexico.

In the 1970s and 1980s, electronics and computer firms sprouted along Interstate 495—the circumferential highway 20 miles east of Worcester— just as they had earlier around Route 128, closer to Boston. The high-tech boom brought prosperity, labor shortages, new residents and higher housing prices to central Massachusetts. Since then, Worcester's ingenious entrepreneurs and skilled labor force hustled. Local leaders set up a Biotechnology Research Institute to draw on the city's nine colleges and institutions of higher learning to steer the city back on course. "Worcester is booming," as a secondary market to crowded and expensive Boston, National Public Radio reported in October 2018. The area has gained the accoutrements of urban modernity, including service by major airlines and relocation of the top minor league franchise of the Boston Red Sox— for which Worcester opened in May 2021 a new $90 million stadium, with cost overruns expected. The stadium was named Polar Park, with the sponsorship of the local Polar Beverages company.

Just as Worcester's economy has changed, so has its face, with big increases in Asians and Hispanics, mainly from Puerto Rico. The area has also attracted Hmong, Vietnamese, Albanians and Africans, many of whom fled the civil war in Liberia. The second-largest city in New England, Worcester's population has increased 8 percent since 2000. The city population is 55 percent non-Hispanic White, though the non-whites are younger and their numbers are growing faster. In September 2019, the University of Massachusetts medical school announced plans to open on its Worcester campus a community-based out-patient clinic for military veterans.

The concentration of colleges and universities in the area west of Worcester brings together a critical mass of scholars and graduate students. The University of Massachusetts in Amherst is the largest, as it has expanded on former farmland. Also nearby are Amherst College and Smith College in Northampton. The precarious financial future of avant garde Hampshire College appeared to have been resolved by the announcement in April 2020 of a five-year fundraising campaign, which might include private use of its property in a former apple orchard. Noted abolitionist Thomas Wentworth Higginson, pastor of the Free Church in Worcester during the 1850s and a secret funder of John Brown, also became a literary mentor to a young Emily Dickinson, who lived quietly most of her life in Amherst.

The 2nd Congressional District includes Worcester and part of the Pioneer Valley. The population includes 10 percent Hispanics, and 6 percent Asians and 5 percent Blacks. To the north, it takes in Connecticut River towns such as Deerfield to the Vermont border. To the west is socially leftist Northampton. The district extends east to Leominster, a western outpost of the Boston suburbs, plus the intersection of 495 and the Massachusetts Turnpike that takes commuters into Boston. Many of the small rural towns west of Worcester vote Republican. But the district overall is firmly Democratic. Joe Biden won the district with 61 percent.

Lori Trahan (D)

Elected 2018, 2nd term, b. Oct 27, 1973; Lowell, MA; Georgetown University, B.S., 1995; Catholic; Married (David Trahan); 2 children; 3 stepchildren.

Professional Career: Chief of Staff, U.S. Rep. Marty Meehan, 1995-2005; ChoiceStream, 2005-2011.

DC Office: 1616 LHOB 20515, 202-225-3411, trahan.house.gov

State Offices: Lowell, 978-459-0101.

Committees: *Energy & Commerce*: Consumer Protection & Commerce; Health; Oversight & Investigations. *Natural Resources*: National Parks, Forests & Public Lands.

Almanac Ratings 2019-2020

	Economy	Social	Foreign	Composite
Liberal	100%	100%	92%	98%
Conservative	0%	0%	8%	2%

Key Votes of the 116th Congress

1. U.S./Mex./Can. trade deal	Y	5. Russia sanctions	Y
2. First Coronavirus response	Y	6. Troops in Syria	Y
3. HEROES Act	Y	7. Veto arms sales to Saudis	Y
4. CASH Act	Y	8. Defense $$$, veto override	Y

9. Firearms background checks	Y
10. Spending at the border	N
11. Marijuana liberalized rules	Y
12. Electoral College objections	N

Election Results

Election	Name (Party)	Vote (%)	Cand. Spent	Ind. Exp. Support	Ind. Exp. Oppose
2020 General	Lori Trahan (D)............................ 286,896	(98%)		$863	
2020 Primary	Lori Trahan (D)................................ 115,142	(99%)			

Prior winning percentages: 2018 (62%)

Lori Trahan, who won her seat in 2018 after a very narrow victory in the Democratic primary, escaped unharmed by an ethics investigation of her financing of that campaign and was reelected two years later without opposition from any declared candidate. With her experience in local and congressional politics, including serving as a top aide in Washington for a member who held the same seat, Trahan led a popular initiative to prevent minor league baseball teams from shutting down their local operations.

Trahan— who grew up in what she called a " hardscrabble, working-class" neighborhood in Lowell— graduated from Georgetown University, where she majored in international relations and was a leader of the volleyball team; she later attended Harvard Business School. She worked nearly a decade as an aide to Democratic Rep. Marty Meehan and served as his chief of staff; Meehan, who resigned in 2007, became president of the University of Massachusetts. She served two years as deputy treasurer of Massachusetts. In the private sector, she worked for a Boston-area advertising firm and was chief executive for five years of the Concire Leadership Institute, which provides strategic consulting to businesses.

After Nikki Tsongas, successor to Meehan and the widow of former Sen. Paul Tsongas, announced her retirement, the Democratic primary to succeed her became wide open. Trahan emphasized her local roots and the need for more women in Washington. "Better decisions are made when women are at the table," she told the Lowell Sun. The early frontrunner and best-financed candidate was Daniel Koh, who was chief of staff to then-Boston Mayor Marty Walsh, who later became secretary of Labor in the Biden administration; Walsh campaigned actively on behalf of Koh, whose parents were Lebanese and Korean. Other leading candidates included Rufus Gifford, a former ambassador to Denmark who had been finance director for President Barack Obama's 2012 reelection campaign, plus state lawmakers Barbara L'Italien and Juana Matias.

With the large field, each candidate had time to respond to only two questions at a typical campaign forum. In its endorsement of Trahan, the Boston Globe cited her " granular understanding of what she hopes to accomplish in Washington." In the unusually tight outcome, Trahan had 22 percent of the vote, with a 145-vote lead over Koh. L'Italien, Matias and Gifford trailed the leaders, with 15 percent each. Trahan's narrow lead in the election-night results had minor changes in the recount. Of the district's 37 cities and towns, Koh and Trahan led in 13 and 12, respectively. Trahan took 34 percent in Lowell and also led in several nearby towns. Koh— who spent $3.1 million, more than twice what Trahan spent in the primary— lacked a sizable local base.

Matias, a state representative who was born in the Dominican Republic, took 70 per cent of the vote in Lawrence, the second-largest city in the district, but that was the only place in which she ran first. L'Italien, who served 12 years in the legislature and was endorsed by teachers unions, ran relatively well across the district but failed to capture a single town. Gifford took upscale Concord and benefited from nearly $160,000 in spending by gay-rights groups. In November, Trahan defeated Rick Green, the wealthy owner of an online auto parts business. He founded the Massachusetts Fiscal Alliance, a conservative group that published scorecards on state legislators.

After she took office, Trahan faced a post mortem review of her contentious primary. Following a complaint brought by a conservative group in Massachusetts, the Office of Congressional Ethics reported to the House Ethics Committee that Trahan's husband was the " true source" of $274,000 in later campaign funds for her campaign, which would be a violation of campaign spending limits. Trahan conceded that she " deeply regrets and takes responsibility for" campaign-financing mistakes, but insisted that the money met the legal requirements for having been under her control, consistent with her marital arrangement. In July 2020, the Ethics Committee unanimously ruled that the late campaign funds were under her personal control and dismissed the ethics charges. Trahan said the "baseless accusations were just politics.'

Working with Republican Rep. David McKinley of West Virginia, Trahan created and co-chaired the bipartisan Save Minor League Baseball Task Force, which responded to shutdown plans by teams from Lowell and potentially dozens of other baseball franchises. " We will make perfectly clear that Congress is prepared to defend our communities," Trahan said. " Congress must have a voice in this conversation." In January 2020, Trahan and McKinley filed a resolution urging Major League Baseball to regain its affiliation with its minor-league teams. Later that year, the Spinners announced that they would not be an affiliate of the Boston Red Sox in 2021.

Given her narrow Democratic primary victory in 2018, Trahan faced a great risk that a Democratic challenger might seek to consolidate the opposition to her. But none of them ran. Koh moved to Washington as a top aide to now-Secretary Walsh.

MA-3: North Central Massachusetts   Cook Partisan Voting Index: D+12

Population		Race and Ethnicity		Income	
Total	771,723	White	74.00%	Median Income	$81,879
Land area (sq. miles)	758	Black	4.10%	District Income Rank	78
Pop/ sq mi	1,018.29	Latino	21.30%	Poverty Rate	8.10%
Born in State	59.50%	Asian	7.40%	With health insurance	96.30%
		Two or more races	2.70%	Cash public assistance	4.80%
Age Groups		Other	11.80%	Food stamp/SNAP	12.00%
Under 18	21.30%				
18-34	22.80%	**Education**		**Work**	
35-64	40.90%	H.S grad or less	37.10%	White Collar	42.40%
Over 64	15.00%	Some college	24.50%	Sales and Service	37.30%
Military		College Degree, 4 yr	22.10%	Blue Collar	20.30%
Veteran/ Active Duty	5.00%	Post grad	16.30%	Government	11.70%

2020 Pres. Vote	Biden	243,303	(63%)	Trump	132,757	(34%)			
2016 Pres. Vote	Clinton	202,952	(57%)	Trump	123,347	(35%)	Johnson	17,580	(5%)

Lowell, Lawrence: When Massachusetts was a kind of maritime republic in the 19th century, with its farmers struggling to scratch out a living from the stony soil, a few clever Yankees used their profits from the sea trade to try to tame the rapidly flowing Merrimack River and build cotton-spinning mills. Creating the cities of Lowell and Lawrence, they built model dormitories and recreation programs for their female workers. This was the center of America's textile industry for more than a century, long after the maritime industry faded. But in the 1920s, the price of labor rose and newly built mills in the Carolinas, much closer to the cotton supply, decimated the local industry that Lawrence and Lowell built. Many residents waited forlornly for an upturn in the local economy.

It came eventually, from an unexpected source. The high-tech industry drove the growth, beginning in the 1960s around the Massachusetts Institute of Technology, then moving out to the Route 128 ring road and eventually to Interstate 495, which passes through once-distant Lowell and Lawrence. Wang, headquartered in Lowell, grew spectacularly, and Democratic Sen. Paul Tsongas — the local kid who made it big before his early death to cancer— spearheaded a historic restoration of the old mill area. This was the Massachusetts miracle of the 1980s. Then came the bust: Sales of Wang's word processors and minicomputers slumped as businesses purchased personal computers and linked them together in networks.

But Lowell revived again. New immigrants provided vitality and entrepreneurial creativity. Cambodians owned many small businesses and are more than 30,000 of the local population, making Lowell second only to Long Beach California as a U.S. home for transplanted Cambodians, who fled their homeland following the brutal " killing fields" of the 1970s. Their experience in Lowell has helped preserve Cambodian heritage and culture. Some monks conceived a Khmer monument on the Merrimack River to honor local Cambodians; unveiled in 2017, the seven-foot stone structure featured a mother with her three young children. Old mills have been converted to artists' lofts and upscale condos. Lawrence, which is 81 percent Hispanic and 41 percent foreign-born (with both figures increasing), became a prime target of the Trump administration as a sanctuary city. In a March

2018 speech across the state line in Manchester, President Donald Trump singled out Lawrence as a cause for the opioid crisis in New Hampshire, though local officials disagreed. In July 2019, a local church became a sanctuary center for undocumented immigrants.

The 3rd Congressional District of Massachusetts includes Lowell, Lawrence and the high-tech corridor along 1-495. The district includes tony suburbs near the Revolutionary War battleground of Concord, where the Minutemen stood their ground in 1775; rural and old mill towns that never revived in hills along the New Hampshire state line; and small towns west of Lowell. Except for Lowell and Lawrence, the district is ancestrally Yankee Republican. It is culturally liberal, with pockets of big wealth as well as new office parks where young families sought to live the American dream; it trended Democratic in the early 1970s. Back then, this area produced two Democratic candidates who would later run for president after having succeeded each other in the Senate: Tsongas and John Kerry. Although it occasionally went Republican in statewide elections, that has become a distant memory. In February 2019, Sen. Elizabeth Warren launched her presidential campaign in Lawrence, citing its historical significance as the site in 1912 of a labor strike by women working at a local mill. As with other suburban areas across the nation, Joe Biden's 63 percent of the vote was a notable increase from the 57 percent that voted for President Barack Obama in 2012 and Hillary Clinton.

Jake Auchincloss (D)

Elected 2020, 1st term, b. Jan 29, 1988; Newton, MA; Harvard University, B.A., 2010; MA Institute of Technology, M.B.A., 2016; Jewish; Married (Michelle Auchincloss).

Military Career: Captain, U.S. Marine Corps, 2010-2015.

Elected Office: City Councilor-at-Large, City of Newton, 2016-2020.

Professional Career: Managing Director, MIT $100K Entrepreneurship Competition, 2014-2016; Project Manager, pet walking service company, 2016-2018; Manager, New Ventures Team, Liberty Mutual Insurance, 2018-2019.

DC Office: 1524 LHOB 20515, 202-225-5931, Fax: 202-225-0182, auchincloss.house.gov

State Offices: Attleboro, 508-431-1110; Newton, 617-332-3333.

Committees: *Financial Services*: Diversity & Inclusion; Nat'l Security, International Development & Monetary Policy; Task Force on Artificial Intelligence. *Transportation & Infrastructure*: Highways & Transit; Railroads, Pipelines & Hazardous Materials.

Election Results

Election	Name (Party)	Vote (%)	Cand. Spent	Ind. Exp. Support	Ind. Exp. Oppose
2020 General	Jake Auchincloss (D)	251,102 (61%)	$2,146,524	$558,945	$443,323
	Julie Hall (R)	160,474 (39%)	$126,300		$113
2020 Primary	Jake Auchincloss (D)	35,361 (22%)			
	Jesse Mermell (D)	33,216 (21%)			
	Becky Grossman (D)	28,578 (18%)			
	Natalia Linos (D)	18,364 (12%)			
	Ihssane Leckey (D)	17,539 (11%)			
	Alan Khazei (D)	14,440 (9%)			

Jake Auchincloss was elected to the House following his narrow victory in the nine-candidate Democratic primary, when he pursued the less-traveled parts of his district while several more liberal women split the vote in the upscale Boston suburbs. The surprising outcome fueled second-guessing about the strategic failures among progressive candidates and the groups that supported them. Auchincloss—a distant cousin of former first lady Jacqueline Kennedy Onassis—succeeded Joe Kennedy, grandson of the late Sen. Robert F. Kennedy, who lost his Democratic primary challenge to Sen. Ed Markey.

A native of Boston, Auchincloss got his bachelor's degree from Harvard and a master's of business administration in finance from the Sloan School of Management at the Massachusetts Institute of Technology. He served five years as a captain with the Marine Corps, commanding infantry forces in Afghanistan and working with a reconnaissance unit in Panama that sought to reduce the flow of illegal drugs from Colombia. His experience with the Marines, he later said, "deeply informed my commitment to ending the forever wars overseas."

In the private sector, Auchincloss worked with a cybersecurity firm where he sought to protect small businesses from online threats and he managed new products with Liberty Mutual Insurance to promote environmentally friendly transportation. He was elected to Newton City Council, where he chaired the transportation and public safety committee.

After Kennedy's decision to open his House seat, Auchincloss launched his candidacy with a commitment to "service and opportunity," with support for the Green New Deal and guaranteed health care for all Americans. Despite his Democratic ancestry, he was the target of second-guessing because he registered as a Republican for a short time while he was working with the state GOP to elect Gov. Charlie Baker. An opponent said that affiliation and some of his social-media comments years earlier "contradict any Democratic values he claims to have."

Several other experienced Democrats entered the contest, including Jesse Mermell, a leader of Planned Parenthood who was a former Brookline Select Board member and adviser to former Democratic Gov. Deval Patrick; Becky Grossman, another member of the Newton City Council; Ihsanne Leckey, an expert on public finance who worked on Wall Street regulatory issues for the Federal Reserve; and Alan Khazei, the wealthy cofounder of the City Year project, a national service program, who earlier made two unsuccessful runs for the Democratic nomination for U.S. Senate seats.

Each of those candidates plus Auchincloss spent more than $1 million in the primary contest. Oddly, eight of the nine candidates were from Newton or Brookline, which include fewer than one-third of the district's Democratic voters; some of them devoted a disproportionate share of their attention to the many political activists in those communities. A political action committee affiliated with EMILY'S List, the national group that supports Democratic women who favor abortion rights, spent more than $650,000 in efforts to defeat Auchincloss and Khazei, the most of any outside group; but it did not support an alternative in the contest.

Auchincloss got a boost when the Boston Globe endorsed him in an editorial that cited his "depth of experience and perspective that are valuable assets as Congress navigates crises in public health and the economy," and said that none of his opponents "have as much promise as Auchincloss." The editorial praised him for seeking support in the less-wealthy parts of the district, noting that he "seems most prepared to represent all his constituents."

He won the primary with 22 percent of the vote, to 21 percent for Mermell and 18 percent for Grossman. Mermell got the most votes in each of the four largest locales—Newton, Brookline, Needham and Wellesley, all of which are contiguous; Auchincloss ran second in three of those communities. He ran first in 25 of the remaining 30 cities and towns, where Mermell often trailed far behind; she lost by 2,145 votes.

In the aftermath of the primary, the Globe reported that "frustrated Democratic activists" pointed to the outcome as a rationale for ranked-choice voting, which permits voters to rank their preferred choice and acts as a sort of simultaneous runoff. In November, Auchincloss got 61 percent of the vote against Republican Julie Hall, a former Attleboro city councilor and a retired Air Force colonel who served as a medical officer.

MA-4: Western Boston Suburbs

Cook Partisan Voting Index: D+13

Population		Race and Ethnicity		Income	
Total	765,466	White	83.70%	Median Income	$104,857
Land area (sq. miles)	668	Black	3.50%	District Income Rank	25
Pop/ sq mi	1,145.44	Latino	5.00%	Poverty Rate	6.60%
Born in State	58.40%	Asian	7.20%	With health insurance	97.80%
		Two or more races	3.30%	Cash public assistance	1.90%
Age Groups		Other	2.30%	Food stamp/SNAP	7.60%
Under 18	21.30%				
18-34	21.30%	Education		Work	
35-64	40.70%	H.S grad or less	27.50%	White Collar	54.70%
Over 64	16.70%	Some college	20.50%	Sales and Service	30.80%
		College Degree, 4 yr	26.20%	Blue Collar	14.50%
Military		Post grad	25.80%	Government	11.60%
Veteran/ Active Duty	5.20%				

2020 Pres. Vote	Biden	276,820	(64%)	Trump	144,654	(34%)			
2016 Pres. Vote	Clinton	225,976	(58%)	Trump	133,705	(34%)	Johnson	17,360	(5%)

Brookline, Bristol County: The political transformation of Massachusetts is nowhere better illustrated than in the Boston suburbs of Newton and Brookline. These were Yankee enclaves a century ago, with avenues built to resemble the sweep of Haussmann's Grand Boulevards in Paris. Brookline was where the country club (the very first one) was established in 1882, and where Joseph Kennedy, an Irish Catholic 20-something banker seeking respectability moved his family in 1914. Brookline and Newton then were solidly Republican, the base of such leading politicians as Christian Herter, the governor of Massachusetts and U.S. secretary of State in the 1950s. As late as 1960, Brookline, Newton and adjacent wards of Boston were electing a Republican to Congress.

Then came the transformation, personified by the election in 1962 of Michael Dukakis at age 29 to the General Court (the legislature). As Massachusetts' university-educated classes became more liberal, as Jewish populations of Brookline and Newton grew, and as young, liberal-minded families refurbished the graceful old houses, these towns became Democratic bastions. The towns continue to diversify. Brookline is now 17 percent Asian, and nearly half of its school students are non-white. A local public school teachers Mandarin in kindergarten. With a median price of $1.6 million, Brookline had the most expensive homes in the state. At its town meeting in November 2019, Brookline voted to prohibit oil and gas connections in construction of new or renovated housing. Not far behind was Newton, at $1.5 million. In a sign of the business development in these suburbs, NBC Universal located in Needham its $125 million media center, with six televisions studios and easy access across the region.

The 4th Congressional District of Massachusetts starts with Brookline and Newton at its northern tip. Anchoring the district, they account for about a fifth of its population. About 40 miles away at the southern end of this modern-day gerrymandered district are the Bristol County cities of Freetown, Somerset and part of Fall River. Much of the port in Fall River has been rebuilt, chiefly for non-commercial purposes, including Heritage State Park and the boardwalk along the water. The northern and southern ends of the districts are very different sociologically and economically— affluent Boston suburbs suffered relatively little in the recession, the old textile-mill town of Fall River quite a lot. Connecting them is a corridor with a variety of towns— Foxborough with its Patriots football stadium; Sharon with its Orthodox Jews; Dover, the home of some old-time Boston Brahmins; and Wellesley with its college and high-income residents. At the northwest corner of the district, Hopkinton is 26 miles, 385 yards from downtown Boston. Politically, these areas historically were mostly Republican but in recent decades they have been, like most of middle-income Massachusetts, Democratic. Joe Biden got 64 percent of the vote, seven and six percentage points higher than President Barack Obama in 2012 and Hillary Clinton in 2016.

Katherine Clark (D)

Elected 2013, 4th full term, b. Jul 17, 1963; New Haven, CT; Saint Lawrence University, B.A., 1985; Cornell University Law School, J.D., 1989; Harvard University John F. Kennedy School of Government, M.P.A., 1997; Protestant - Unspecified Christian; Married (Rodney Dowell); 3 children.

Elected Office: MA House, 2008-2011; MA Senate, 2011-2013.

Professional Career: Clerk, Hon. Alfred Arraj, 1990-1991; Prosecutor, Colorado Attorney General office, 1991-1993; General counsel, MA Office of Child Care Svcs.; Policy Division Chief, MA Attorney General.

DC Office: 2448 RHOB 20515, 202-225-2836, Fax: 202-226-0092, katherineclark.house.gov

State Offices: Framingham, 508-319-9757; Malden, 617-354-0292.

Committees: House Assistant Speaker. *Appropriations*: Labor, Health & Human Services, Education & Related Agencies; Legislative Branch; Transportation, HUD & Related Agencies.

Group Ratings

	ADA	ACLU	AFL-CIO	LCV	COC	HAFA	ACU	CFG	FRC
2020	**	83%	**	100%	-	0%	3%	**	-
2019	90%	C	100%	97%	54%	C	3%	12%	0%

Almanac Ratings 2019-2020

	Economy	Social	Foreign	Composite
Liberal	100%	65%	92%	86%
Conservative	0%	35%	8%	14%

Key Votes of the 116th Congress

1. U.S./Mex./Can. trade deal Y	5. Russia sanctions Y	9. Firearms background checks Y
2. First Coronavirus response Y	6. Troops in Syria Y	10. Spending at the border N
3. HEROES Act Y	7. Veto arms sales to Saudis Y	11. Marijuana liberalized rules Y
4. CASH Act Y	8. Defense $$$, veto override Y	12. Electoral College objections N

Election Results

Election	Name (Party)	Vote (%)		Cand. Spent	Ind. Exp. Support	Ind. Exp. Oppose
2020 General	Katherine Clark (D)	294,427	(74%)	$1,204,446	$1,123	
	Caroline Colarusso (R)	101,351	(26%)	$149,680		$113
2020 Primary	Katherine Clark (D)	162,768	(99%)			

Prior winning percentages: 2018 (76%), 2016 (99%), 2014 (71%), 2013 special (66%)

Democrat Katherine Clark won a 2013 special election when previous Rep. Edward Markey, in turn, won a special election six months earlier to fill the Senate seat of John Kerry, who had become secretary of State. With her policymaking experience in state government and legislative savvy, plus her eagerness to work with on the party's message, she has become a fast-rising member of the Democratic Caucus—most recently, as assistant speaker—and could join the next team of Democratic leaders..

Clark was born and raised in New Haven Connecticut and graduated from St. Lawrence University, where she majored in history. She got her law degree at Cornell University before moving to Chicago and California to practice law. In 1995, Clark relocated to Massachusetts to earn a master's in public administration from Harvard's Kennedy School of Government. She then worked as general counsel for the Massachusetts Office of Child Care Services and as policy chief for Attorney General Martha Coakley. She was elected to the state House in 2008 and two years later to the state Senate, where she chaired the Judiciary Committee.

Markey had represented the 5th District since 1976, and his promotion set off a scramble for the safe Democratic seat. In the Democratic primary, Clark competed against six candidates, including Middlesex County Sheriff Peter Koutoujin, and three other state lawmakers. Her early start gave her an edge financially and in the polls. Clark focused her campaign on issues that appealed to her party's base, including equal pay for women and abortion rights.

Clark weaved the stories of her grandmother, a machinist during World War II, and her mother, who was discouraged from pursuing engineering as a young girl, into her TV ads. And she discussed her husband and three young sons to repeatedly make the point that "women's issues are family issues." Clark received a fundraising boost from the abortion-rights group EMILY's List, which proved a boon in a race where progressive and labor endorsements were fractured. She prevailed in the primary with 32 percent of the vote, to 22 percent for Koutoujin. Only Clark showed strength across the district. She won easily in the December general election.

Clark made her first splash when she played a crucial role in organizing what became an unprecedented sit-in on the House floor in June 2016 by Democrats who wanted more gun-control, following the terrorist shooting attack at Pulse night club in Orlando Florida. As she described to Time, Clark told Rep. John Lewis of Georgia that the typical moment of silence in the House was not a sufficient response.

"I wanted to do something to keep gun violence in the forefront of not only the American people but, more specifically, members of Congress and [Lewis] suggested, in his words, that we do something dramatic, and he suggested having a sit-in, and it really went from there," recalled Clark, who had tried civil rights cases in private practice. "When you have John Lewis, such an icon of the civil rights fight for justice, you know that good things are going to happen." Lewis told Time that Clark should be credited for the sit-in idea. The House sit-in, which was designed to force the hand of Speaker Paul Ryan, had little impact. It brought Capitol Hill to a pause for two days, but yielded no legislative action.

In 2017, she gained additional influence with a seat on the Appropriations Committee. Clark is a member of a tight-knit clique of Democratic women who took office in 2013. Known as "the Pink Ladies," they include Cheri Bustos of Illinois, Julia Brownley of California, Lois Frankel of Florida, Annie Kuster of New Hampshire and Grace Meng of New York.

Legislatively, Clark pursued her career interests in child-care issues. Her June 2020 initiative was pegged to the difficulties that many families faced during the pandemic, with most children at home because schools were shut down for many months. The proposal was designed to revitalize child-care providers—most of whom are women—with loan repayments and grants for renovations. Those services were at a "breaking point," she said, as "parents and providers face an impossible situation in which neither has the resources to get back to work safely."

Following the 2018 election, Clark entered Democratic leadership as caucus vice chair. She had built loyalties that year as the recruitment vice chair of the Democratic Congressional Campaign Committee, amid its successful midterms. Clark was often among the first House members that candidates met during their successful campaigns.

That success positioned her to run for assistant speaker, a relatively new position that Speaker Nancy Pelosi created that lacks a specific portfolio. When Clark launched her bid, she wrote to House Democrats, "effective leadership is not about individual ambition … but collective good." Rep. Tony Cardenas was an early contender for the position, but he withdrew to seek another leadership slot. Her only opponent was Rep. David Cicilline, another New Englander. Clark won, reportedly by a vote of 135-92. Her success positioned her well for the expected transition of House Democratic leaders —with each of the top three at least age 80.

At home, Clark has been reelected without significant opposition and seems entrenched.

MA-5: Northern and Western Boston Suburbs   Cook Partisan Voting Index: D+23

Population		Race and Ethnicity		Income	
Total	768,043	White	73.80%	Median Income	$106,311
Land area (sq. miles)	265	Black	5.60%	District Income Rank	22
Pop/ sq mi	2,897.4	Latino	10.00%	Poverty Rate	7.70%
Born in State	50.20%	Asian	13.40%	With health insurance	97.40%
		Two or more races	3.20%	Cash public assistance	1.40%
Age Groups		Other	4.00%	Food stamp/SNAP	5.70%
Under 18	19.70%				
18-34	25.90%	**Education**		**Work**	
35-64	38.50%	H.S grad or less	23.30%	White Collar	60.20%
Over 64	16.10%	Some college	16.60%	Sales and Service	29.40%
		College Degree, 4 yr	28.40%	Blue Collar	10.40%
Military		Post grad	31.70%	Government	10.70%
Veteran/ Active Duty	3.40%				

2020 Pres. Vote	Biden	304,072	(74%)	Trump	97,562	(24%)			
2016 Pres. Vote	Clinton	258,908	(68%)	Trump	95,922	(25%)	Johnson	13,712	(4%)

Northern and Western Suburbs: The Yankee Protestants and Irish Catholics who settled Massachusetts arrived by boat, the Yankees to a cold, stony land with a few Indians, the Irish to a crowded city with Yankees who seemed no more welcoming. The Yankees whose ancestors once farmed the soil had, by the early 20th century, founded suburbs filled with solid brick and white frame houses. As the years went on, their local public schools emptied as young people with children moved out, and attendance at mainline Protestant churches fell. The Irish, for decades heavily concentrated in the crowded wards of Boston, started moving out to the suburbs after World War II. There were other ethnic groups here and there (Jews, Italians, French Canadians), but the major conflict— fought out in neighborhood playgrounds, in school committee meetings, and not least in political campaigns — was between Protestant Yankee Republicans and Catholic Irish Democrats. These days, much of the local conflict is among the university towns— Cambridge as the epicenter of Harvard University; Medford, home of Tufts University; and Waltham, home of Brandeis University.

The 5th Congressional District of Massachusetts is made up of northern and western Boston suburbs, where vestiges of the cultural conflict can still be seen. Geographically, the district forms an arc around Boston, starting with the clapboard beach towns of Winthrop and Revere just beyond Logan Airport, going north as far as working-class Woburn (where Charles Goodyear developed the art of vulcanizing rubber) and encompassing Natick and Framingham, the headquarters town of Staples and TJX (T.J. Maxx, Marshalls, HomeGoods). Framingham has become diverse culturally, with 67 languages spoken in the public schools. MassBay Community College selected a site in downtown Framingham for its new $60 million campus, including a health science center.

Boston Business Journal reported in August 2019 that Greater Boston has " cemented itself as the global epicenter of life sciences research," with only the San Francisco area as a competitor. The area has benefited from the availability of venture capital to support innovation, plenty of talent plus professional clusters at prime sites. When Waltham-based Raytheon purchased United Technologies of Hartford, that was another highlight for the Massachusetts economy— the largest-ever merger in the military aerospace business. The long-delayed and over-budget Green Line rapid-transit extension of more than four miles to Medford was scheduled for completion in late 2021, with six new stations.

The 5th extends south to take in Ashland, Holliston and Sherborn, and west to take in most of Sudbury and Wayland. Sudbury is home to the historic Longfellow's Wayside Inn, which was renamed after Henry Wadsworth Longfellow's 1863 book Tales of a Wayside Inn made it a sight-seeing attraction. In Lexington, minutemen fired the shots heard ' round the world in 1775. The district reaches into Cambridge to include the main Harvard campus north of the Charles River, but Massachusetts Institute of Technology is across the line in the 7th District. In the 2020 presidential campaign, as in 2016, this was the second strongest Democratic-performing district in Massachusetts, behind only the 7th District. Joe Biden got 74 percent of the vote, compared to the 68 percent for Hillary Clinton.

Seth Moulton (D)

Elected 2014, 4th term, b. Oct 24, 1978; Salem, MA; Phillips Academy, M.P.A., 1997; Harvard University, B.S., 2001; Harvard Business School, M.B.A., 2011; Harvard University John F. Kennedy School of Government, M.P.A., 2011; Christian - Non-Denominational; Married (Liz Boardman); 1 child.

Military Career: U.S. Marine Corps 2002-2008 (Iraq)

Professional Career: Railway managing director, 2011-2012; Health care company president, 2012-2013.

DC Office: 1127 LHOB 20515, 202-225-8020, Fax: 202-225-5915, moulton.house.gov

State Offices: Salem, 978-531-1669.

Committees: *Armed Services*: Cyber, Innovative Technologies & Information Systems; Strategic Forces. *Budget. Transportation & Infrastructure*: Highways & Transit (RMM); Railroads, Pipelines & Hazardous Materials.

Group Ratings

	ADA	ACLU	AFL-CIO	LCV	COC	HAFA	ACU	CFG	FRC
2020	**	66%	**	100%	-	0%	4%	**	-
2019	75%	C	100%	93%	69%	C	4%	13%	0%

Almanac Ratings 2019-2020

	Economy	Social	Foreign	Composite
Liberal	100%	63%	80%	81%
Conservative	0%	37%	20%	19%

Key Votes of the 116th Congress

1. U.S./Mex./Can. trade deal Y	5. Russia sanctions Y	9. Firearms background checks Y
2. First Coronavirus response Y	6. Troops in Syria Y	10. Spending at the border N/A
3. HEROES Act Y	7. Veto arms sales to Saudis Y	11. Marijuana liberalized rules Y
4. CASH Act Y	8. Defense $$$, veto override Y	12. Electoral College objections N

Election Results

Election	Name (Party)	Vote (%)		Cand. Spent	Ind. Exp. Support	Ind. Exp. Oppose
2020 General	Seth Moulton (D)	286,377	(65%)	$1,199,956	$13,524	
	John Paul Moran (R)	150,695	(34%)	$297,008		$113
2020 Primary	Seth Moulton (D)	124,928	(78%)			
	Jamie Zahlaway Belsito (D)	19,492	(12%)			
	Angus McQuilken (D)	15,478	(10%)			

Prior winning percentages: 2018 (65%), 2016 (98%), 2014 (55%)

Democrat Seth Moulton, a former Marine Corps captain and Iraq War veteran, was elected in 2014. With unusual candor, he was outspoken in demanding accountability and change among House Democrats. His actions placed him at the forefront of Democrats seeking a post-Nancy Pelosi generation of leadership— an objective he continued to pursue even after Pelosi prevailed over her critics following the 2018 election. He has brought a similar bluntness to his legislative focus, chiefly on military issues. In 2019, he used that platform for an abbreviated run for president.

Moulton was born in Salem and grew up in Marblehead, the eldest of three siblings. He attended Phillips Academy Andover, an elite boarding school. He got his bachelor's degree in physics from Harvard University, delivering the Undergraduate English Oration at his commencement in which he focused on the importance of service. He joined the Marine Corps, graduated from Officer Candidate School as a 2nd lieutenant and was among the first soldiers to enter Baghdad at the beginning of the Iraq War. He served four tours of duty, and in 2008, at age 29, he was a special liaison with tribal leaders in southern Iraq at the request of Gen. David Petraeus. He left the Marines with the rank of captain. He later earned his MBA and master's in public policy from Harvard.

He decided to get involved in politics while still in the Marines. " I actually remember the moment," he told The Atlantic. "It was after a difficult day in Najaf in 2004. A young marine in my platoon said, 'sir, you should run for Congress someday. So this s— doesn't happen again.'" He considered running as an independent candidate in 2012 against embattled Democratic Rep. John Tierney, but decided against it. A close ally of Pelosi, Tierney was under fire because his wife, Patrice, had pleaded guilty to helping her brother file false tax returns. He eked out a 48%-47% victory against Republican Richard Tisei, whose résumé— he is gay and a fiscal conservative who vocally opposed the social policy of his party— made him an ideal challenger. Tisei ran again in 2014 and appeared well-positioned to take Tierney out.

Republican plans were foiled when Moulton challenged Tierney in the Democratic primary, secured the Boston Globe's endorsement, and won the nomination 51%-41%. Without the baggage of Tierney, Moulton ran as a progressive Democrat and cast Tisei, who was first elected to the state legislature in 1984, as a political insider. Moulton won endorsements from Petraeus, retired Army Gen. Stanley McChrystal and former New York City Mayor Michael Bloomberg. He outspent Tisei $3.3 million to $2 million and won 55%-41%. Each candidate was aided by millions of dollars from his national party and outside groups.

Moulton immediately began drawing attention for his unusual-for-a-Democrat resume. He vowed not to be a typical congressman, saying he told his former Marine buddies to watch him closely. "I've asked a few guys in particular to in fact speak up and call me out if I become quote-unquote ' one of them,'" he told Politico.

Following a bumpy transition to the House when Tierney refused to talk to him, Moulton got a seat on the Armed Services Committee. He made multiple trips to the Middle East, to visit with troops and understand the fight against the Islamic State. He has been outspoken on the need to have a plan to win the peace in Iraq and the Middle East. In 2016, he criticized President Barack Obama's refusal to say that American troops deployed to Iraq were on a combat mission. He focused on improving veterans' health care. Obama signed his Faster Care for Veterans Act, which enabled vets to use their phones or computers to schedule medical appointments. With Republican Rep. Matt Gaetz of Florida in 2018, he filed a bill to make it easier for the Veterans Affairs Department to offer marijuana as a medical treatment. Moulton kept up the criticism with President Donald Trump and his advisers who " use lies to manipulate what Americans think, to pit us against one another, and to pervert our democracy to attain power," he wrote in an op-ed. Concerned about Trump's early refugee and immigration bans, he joined a bipartisan group of House members who were military veterans to urge exceptions for people who risked their lives to aid U.S. forces.

Following the 2016 election, he demanded with other junior House Democrats a deeper review of the party's failures and discussion of new directions. In a post-election Tweet, Moulton wrote, " In the Marines, my job was clear: ' You are responsible for everything your platoon does or fails to do.' We need that in Congress." The lengthy discussions within the Democratic Caucus resulted in some sharing of authority with the rank-and-file, though no changes in specific leadership posts. He became vice chairman of the informal Bipartisan Working Group.

In 2018, Moulton continued his public and private drumbeat for what he described as " a new generation of leadership." Some of the incoming freshmen— mostly, military veterans— whom Moulton had helped finance with his political action committee and personally supported during their campaigns had pledged that they would not support Pelosi. But the efforts by Moulton and others suffered from their failure to find a challenger— a problem that was abetted by the accommodations that Pelosi and her supporters made to her critics. "We' re all united behind her, but we're a stronger party because of these reforms," Moulton told the Globe.

When Democrats reorganized the Armed Services Committee in 2019, they eliminated the Oversight and Investigation Subcommittee, on which Moulton had been the top Democrat. They cited a House rule limiting the number of subcommittees, though that might have been a convenient way for Pelosi to send him a message. In 2021, each of the seven Democratic subcommittee chairmen was more senior than Moulton on the committee.

In April 2019, he launched his campaign for president with a call for a new generation of leaders and more centrist policies, plus an attempt to position himself as the most knowledgeable about the Pentagon. He was delayed, he said, because of the birth of his first child. But young candidates already had entered the contest— including Pete Buttigieg, Rep. Tulsi Gabbard and former Rep. Beto O'Rourke. He didn't qualify for the early debates, though he made a point of criticizing Sen. Elizabeth Warren of his home state for her campaign proposals that were too costly. When he ended his campaign in August, he spoke positively about Joe Biden.

At home, Moulton's longstanding clashes with Pelosi led some Democrats to consider a primary challenge to him in 2020. They backed down when he decided to seek reelection. He had two opponents, both of whom criticized his opposition to Pelosi, though they did not pose a serious threat. Moulton won the primary with 80 percent of the vote.

MA-6: North Shore   **Cook Partisan Voting Index: D+10**

Population		Race and Ethnicity		Income	
Total	770,998	White	84.90%	Median Income	$97,115
Land area (sq. miles)	527	Black	4.10%	District Income Rank	39
Pop/ sq mi	1,463.58	Latino	10.50%	Poverty Rate	6.60%
Born in State	67.70%	Asian	4.50%	With health insurance	97.70%
		Two or more races	2.60%	Cash public assistance	2.20%
Age Groups		Other	3.90%	Food stamp/SNAP	7.60%
Under 18	20.20%				
18-34	19.80%	Education		Work	
35-64	41.00%	H.S grad or less	30.50%	White Collar	50.20%
Over 64	19.10%	Some college	22.10%	Sales and Service	35.40%
Military		College Degree, 4 yr	27.90%	Blue Collar	14.30%
Veteran/ Active Duty	5.80%	Post grad	19.50%	Government	12.60%

2020 Pres. Vote	Biden	279,782	(62%)	Trump	159,252	(35%)		
2016 Pres. Vote	Clinton	224,858	(55%)	Trump	153,244	(38%)	Johnson	18,124	(4%)

Lynn, Salem: The North Shore of Massachusetts Bay has often been at the leading edge of the nation's economy. In 1640, the Saugus Iron Works was built here—the beginning of American heavy industry. When Europe's great powers were convulsed in international war from 1792 to 1815, American ship owners suddenly became the richest in the world, and traders from Boston and Salem accumulated the capital needed to build textile mills and railroads and to finance much of the American Industrial Revolution. From the small port of Salem, ships left for China, bringing back porcelain and artifacts. Salem had the nation's first millionaire, Elias Hasket Derby. In 1900, it was the richest city per capita in the nation.

Today, the North Shore is no longer economically vital and is more competitive politically than elsewhere in the Boston area. From Boston Harbor north to the mouth of the Merrimack River, it is a collection of ethnic factory towns from Lynn to Peabody (once one of the world's great leather producers, with more than 100 tanneries) to the former shipbuilding Newburyport. There are a few high-income enclaves, such as Marblehead with its yachts. Coastal towns include artsy Rockport and the fishing center of Gloucester. In Salem, the witch trials are the town's most famous legacy, and local officials have capitalized with Halloween festivities that contribute to Salem's $100 million annual tourism industry.

The 6th Congressional District includes the North Shore from Saugus and Lynn northward to the New Hampshire line, plus towns and cities inland west to Tewksbury and Bedford. The district is mostly based in Essex County, but includes part of Middlesex County. The General Electric jet engine plant, the largest employer in Lynn, has seen its payroll drop from a peak of 13,000 in 1985 to 2,600 jobs in April 2020, though the company has been hiring machinists. It produces helicopter engines for the Black Hawk troop transport and jet engines for the F-18 Super Hornet fighter. Because most of its work is for military contracts, the Lynn plant was largely spared GE's cuts in aircraft employees early during the pandemic. For local officials, revival of the port, with residential housing, has been a priority. The state ended its subsidy for a seasonal commuter ferry from Lynn to Boston, which had struggled financially. Plans for the arrival in 2020 of luxury-yacht stops by Ritz Carlton, which planned to call at the Salem port, were delayed by the pandemic plus construction problems at the shipyard in Spain.

While the district is the site of the original gerrymander—named after Elbridge Gerry, who served two terms as governor before winning election as vice president with President James Madison— the current boundaries are hardly grotesque by contemporary standards. The district's high-income Yankee towns historically were liberal Republican, while the old mill towns of Lynn, Salem, Peabody and Merrimac were Irish working-class Democratic. The 6th has leaned Democratic since the 1960s, although it twice elected a Republican in the 1990s. Joe Biden led 62%-35%, which was his lowest among Boston-based districts, but higher than districts in western and southeast Massachusetts.

Ayanna Pressley (D)

Elected 2018, 2nd term, b. Feb 03, 1974; Cincinnati, OH; Boston University, Att., 1994; Baptist; Married (Conan Harris Pressley); 1 stepchild.

Elected Office: Boston City Counsel, 2010-2018

Professional Career: Political Director & Scheduler, U.S. Sen. John F. Kerry; Social Security Liaison, U.S. Rep. Joseph P. Kennedy.

DC Office: 1108 LHOB 20515, 202-225-5111, pressley.house.gov

State Offices: Boston, 617-850-0040.

Committees: *Financial Services*: Consumer Protection & Financial Institutions; Task Force on Artificial Intelligence. *Oversight & Reform*: Subcommittee on Civil Rights & Civil Liberties; Subcommittee on Economic & Consumer Policy.

Almanac Ratings 2019-2020

	Economy	Social	Foreign	Composite
Liberal	100%	100%	57%	86%
Conservative	0%	0%	43%	14%

Key Votes of the 116th Congress

1. U.S./Mex./Can. trade deal	N	5. Russia sanctions	Y	9. Firearms background checks	Y
2. First Coronavirus response	Y	6. Troops in Syria	Y	10. Spending at the border	N
3. HEROES Act	Y	7. Veto arms sales to Saudis	Y	11. Marijuana liberalized rules	Y
4. CASH Act	Y	8. Defense $$$, veto override	N	12. Electoral College objections	N

Election Results

Election	Name (Party)	Vote (%)		Cand. Spent	Ind. Exp. Support	Ind. Exp. Oppose
2020 General	Ayanna Pressley (D)	267,362	(87%)	$2,205,425	$33,692	$4,387
	Roy Owens, Sr. (I)	38,675	(13%)			
2020 Primary	Ayanna Pressley (D)	142,108	(99%)			

Ayanna Pressley, the first African American elected to the House from Massachusetts, comfortably moved into the national spotlight and talked up her policy interests. After her victory in the 2018 Democratic primary over 10-term Rep. Michael Capuano, who had been a close ally of Nancy Pelosi, Pressley occasionally clashed with the Speaker. Her membership in the Squad, a group of four women who were racial minorities and first elected to the House in 2018, became an occasional flash point— though Pressley sometimes disagreed with the other three. She is widely viewed as having an interest in the Senate, a realistic possibility given that her home-state senators are both in their 70s.

Pressley, who served nine years on the Boston City Council, successfully shaped her challenge to Capuano as a battle of generations and ethnicity in the rapidly changing Boston area. With Rep. Joe Crowley of New York, Capuano was the only Democratic incumbent who lost a primary in 2018. In contrast to Crowley, who chaired the House Democratic Caucus and did not take challenger Alexandria Ocasio-Cortez seriously until the closing days of their campaign, Pressley and Capuano battled openly for months and both spent most of the money they had raised. Her 58%-41% victory in the primary showed that voters agreed with her that "change can't wait." The turnout of more than 102,000 voters was more than three times the total in the New York contest.

Pressley, a native of Chicago, attended Boston University but did not graduate— in part because she needed to work to support her mother. She was a Boston-based aide to Rep. Joe Kennedy II (who held the House seat prior to Capuano) and had several positions, including political director, with

Sen. John Kerry. In 2009, she was elected as one of four at-large members of the Boston City Council. In each of her three victories, she got the most votes of the city-wide councilors.

On the council, she took credit for the establishment of the Committee on Healthy Women, Families and Communities, which took up her interest in issues that especially affect women and girls. Pressley pressed successfully to create 75 new liquor licenses, which she said created hundreds of new jobs, especially in lower-income parts of Boston.

Against Capuano, Pressley argued for a more assertive Democratic agenda— including the abolition of the Immigration and Customs Enforcement agency and more aggressive congressional action to limit or remove President Donald Trump. The Boston Globe, which endorsed her in an editorial, reported that her work with Kerry spurred Pressley's ambition for a seat in Congress.

Capuano styled himself as a strong liberal on most issues, including his support for a single-payer health care system and broad immigration reform. He received more endorsements than Pressley. Among them were Boston Mayor Marty Walsh and many congressional Democrats, including members of the Congressional Black Caucus. Rep. John Lewis, the Georgia Democrat and civil rights icon, made a local appearance for Capuano and praised his ability to get things done. Massachusetts Attorney General Maura Healey endorsed Pressley. Capuano spent $2.6 million on the contest, to $1.1 million for Pressley.

Pressley's victory was based entirely on her support in Boston, which cast 62 percent of the total vote and gave her a 17,700 vote lead. District-wide, she led by about 17,600 votes. Pressley also had a big edge in Cambridge, which cast 10 percent of the vote. Capuano led in his home town of Somerville and nearby Chelsea by slim margins. After the outcome was clear, Capuano told supporters, "Ayanna Pressley is going to be a good congresswoman." The only other African American from Massachusetts to serve in Congress was Edward Brooke, a Republican, who served 12 years in the Senate.

In the House, she served on the Financial Services Committee and took an interest in financial and urban issues and instances of racial injustice. With Rep. Alma Adams, she filed a bill to cancel student-loan debt in response to the coronavirus. She joined Reps. Chuy Garcia and Mark Takano in creating a Future of Transportation Caucus in the House, whose goals include the promotion of multi-modal options such as cycling, rapid transit and other steps to reduce large sources of carbon emissions.

Following the May 2019 death in police custody of George Floyd in Minneapolis, she filed with Reps. Karen Bass, Barbara Lee and Ilhan Omar a resolution that condemned police brutality and racial injustice. " For too long, Black and Brown bodies have been profiled, surveilled, policed, lynched, choked, brutalized and murdered at the hands of police officers," Pressley said. That proposal was an early step that led to House passage of police reform legislation.

In the 2020 presidential campaign, Pressley was an early supporter of Sen. Elizabeth Warren, while the three other members of the Squad endorsed Sen. Bernie Sanders. Aside from the fact that Warren is her home-state senator, Pressley was impressed by Warren's range of policy interests. "Pressley, who has been in elected public office for a decade and is the eldest member of the Squad, has also been, like Warren, a progressive institutionalist, working to bring change within the system," according to a Vanity Fair profile of Pressley in June 2020.

After Pelosi in an interview with New York Times columnist Maureen Dowd said the Squad "didn't have any following" in the House and separately warned Democrats, "do not tweet about our members and expect us to think that that is just OK," Pressley told the Washington Post that Pelosi's comments were "demoralizing." She added, "I am worried about the signal that it sends to people I speak to and for, who sent me here with a mandate."

At home in 2020, Pressley had no Democratic primary opponents and, for the second consecutive election, faced no Republican in her solidly Democratic district. As for her future, Avi Green, who was a political adviser to her years ago, told Vanity Fair, "There's no question [that] in Massachusetts, a common game is to think, What will Ayanna do next?"

MA-7: Boston area   Cook Partisan Voting Index: **D+35**

Population		Race and Ethnicity		Income	
Total	819,035	White	49.50%	Median Income	$75,461
Land area (sq. miles)	63	Black	25.40%	District Income Rank	125
Pop/ sq mi	13,069.01	Latino	22.40%	Poverty Rate	17.00%
Born in State	41.40%	Asian	10.70%	With health insurance	95.20%
		Two or more races	8.40%	Cash public assistance	3.20%
Age Groups		Other	5.90%	Food stamp/SNAP	16.90%
Under 18	17.00%				
18-34	38.10%	**Education**		**Work**	
35-64	33.50%	H.S grad or less	34.50%	White Collar	49.90%
Over 64	11.40%	Some college	18.30%	Sales and Service	38.20%
		College Degree, 4 yr	24.40%	Blue Collar	11.90%
Military		Post grad	22.70%	Government	11.30%
Veteran/ Active Duty	2.10%				

2020 Pres. Vote	Biden	276,091	(85%)	Trump	43,074	(13%)	
2016 Pres. Vote	Clinton	254,037	(83%)	Trump	36,018	(12%) Johnson	7,045 (2%)

Somerville, Cambridge: Boston, the most political of cities, has often been the focal point of essential moments in American history. On its streets, originally laid out as narrow 17th century cowpaths with many that still survive, Samuel Adams and Paul Revere plotted revolution, the abolitionist movement helped ignite the Civil War, and various Kennedys opened their campaign headquarters. Today's Boston is different from the Boston of John F. Kennedy's era. Then it was a gray city with no new buildings and dust on every windowsill. The sky was dark with pollution, and the air was thick with ancient Yankee and Irish animosity. The old office buildings were full of Brahmins seeking safe investments for their antique family fortunes. The government was full of Irishmen, scampering after good patronage jobs and regaling one another with political war stories. These days, that Boston is mostly gone— and memories are fading.

The new skyscrapers are full of well-educated venture capitalists, lawyers and management consultants, many working for high-tech and bio-tech companies radiating from Cambridge out into the countryside. Greater Boston may well have a larger concentration of graduate students and post-graduate hangers-on than any other major American city, and this graduate student community's world is centered in Cambridge, home of Harvard University. Boston's neighborhoods, full of large Irish families— and 95 percent white— when the city reached its peak population of 801,000 in 1950, are now different, with young singles in rowhouse apartments, professionals in waterfront apartment towers and African Americans in old triple-deckers. Most of those real-estate costs have soared. From 2010 to 2019, Boston had a growth spurt of 12 percent to 693,000 people; it is 25 percent African American and 20 percent Hispanic.

One of its premier civic events, the fabled Boston Marathon, was the scene of a national tragedy in 2013 when terrorists detonated two bombs near the finish line, killing three people and injuring more than 170 others. The 2015 jury verdict that convicted killer Dzhokhar Tsarnaev and gave him the death penalty riveted the city.

The 7th Congressional District includes most of Boston, although the State House and many of the historic sites in the North End are in the neighboring 8th District. Harvard Square and much of Cambridge are in the 5th District. But the Massachusetts Institute of Technology is in the 7th, as is the expanding Harvard campus across the Charles River in Allston, helping make it a booming technology center. The surrounding Allston Yards have become hot real estate for research centers, commercial development and new housing. The Encore Boston Harbor, a $2.6 billion casino on the Mystic River in Everett, opened in June 2019—the largest private-sector development ever in the Boston area— with Wynn Resorts, the owner, planning to use its 11 additional nearby acres.

The 7th takes in Somerville, economically revived Chelsea and many Boston neighborhoods— newly upscale and diverse East Boston around Logan Airport, Brighton and the Back Bay, Fenway, Mattapan, Mission Hill and the South End. It also includes Randolph, where minorities are a majority; and Dorchester, a neighborhood with large numbers of working-class Black, Latino, Caribbean Americans and Asian Americans. The Rev. Martin Luther King Jr. lived in Dorchester while he was earning his doctorate at Boston University. As the state's first minority-majority district, it has grown to 25 percent Black, 22 percent Hispanic and 11 percent Asian. The 7th is among the most Democratic districts in the nation. Joe Biden won here with 85 percent of the vote. Tip O' Neill, who ably meshed Town and Gown and was the most recent Speaker to leave the powerful position on his own terms and with a secure majority, represented a version of this district from 1953 to 1987.

Stephen Lynch (D)

Elected 2001, 10th full term, b. Mar 31, 1955; Boston, MA; Wentworth Institute of Technology, B.S., 1988; Boston College Law School, J.D., 1991; Harvard University John F. Kennedy School of Government, M.P.A., 1999; Roman Catholic; Married (Margaret Shaughnessy Lynch); 1 child.

Elected Office: MA House, 1995-1996; MA Senate, 1997-2001.

Professional Career: Structural ironworker, 1973-1991; Practicing attorney, 1991-2001.

DC Office: 2109 RHOB 20515, 202-225-8273, Fax: 202-225-3984, lynch.house.gov

State Offices: Boston, 617-428-2000; Brockton, 508-586-5555; Quincy, 617-657-6305.

Committees: *Financial Services*: Diversity & Inclusion; Nat'l Security, International Development & Monetary Policy; Task Force on Financial Technology (Chmn). *Oversight & Reform*: Government Operations; National Security (Chmn). *Transportation & Infrastructure*: Aviation; Highways & Transit.

Group Ratings

	ADA	ACLU	AFL-CIO	LCV	COC	HAFA	ACU	CFG	FRC
2020	**	79%	**	100%	-	0%	9%	**	-
2019	85%	C	100%	97%	59%	C	10%	12%	0%

Almanac Ratings 2019-2020

	Economy	Social	Foreign	Composite
Liberal	100%	100%	52%	84%
Conservative	0%	0%	48%	16%

Key Votes of the 116th Congress

1. U.S./Mex./Can. trade deal	Y	5. Russia sanctions	Y	9. Firearms background checks Y
2. First Coronavirus response	Y	6. Troops in Syria	Y	10. Spending at the border	Y
3. HEROES Act	Y	7. Veto arms sales to Saudis	Y	11. Marijuana liberalized rules	Y
4. CASH Act	Y	8. Defense $$$, veto override	Y	12. Electoral College objections N

Election Results

Election	Name (Party)	Vote (%)		Cand. Spent	Ind. Exp. Support	Ind. Exp. Oppose
2020 General	Stephen Lynch (D)...............................	310,940	(81%)	$948,650	$4,916	$35,325
	Jonathan Lott (I).................................	72,060	(19%)			
2020 Primary	Stephen F. Lynch (D)...........................	111,542	(66%)			
	Robbie Goldstein (D)............................	56,219	(34%)			

Prior winning percentages: 2016 (72%), 2014 (77%), 2012 (71%), 2010 (68%), 2008 (76%), 2006 (72%), 2004 (73%), 2002 (71%), 2001 special (65%)

Democrat Stephen Lynch, who won a special election in 2001 to succeed the late Joe Moakley, is an ironworker-turned-lawyer who is less liberal than his Massachusetts Democratic colleagues, but no less ambitious. He lost to Ed Markey in the primary for the 2013 special election for the Senate seat vacated when John Kerry became secretary of State. In 2019, following the death of Rep. Elijah Cummings, Lynch ran for the opening as chairman of the House Oversight and Reform Committee.

But he failed to get much support in the Democratic Steering and Policy Committee and dropped out before the Caucus voted.

Lynch grew up in Boston's housing projects and followed the old ethnic precepts of hard work, family loyalty and personal determination. After graduating from South Boston High School, he joined his father as a full-time ironworker while attending the Wentworth Institute of Technology, where he got a bachelor's degree in construction management. He became the youngest president of the 2,000-member Local 7 of the International Association of Iron Workers. He worked at several large plants that he later said suffered job losses as a result of unfair foreign trade practices. After a fall on the job cut short that career, he graduated from Boston College Law School and opened a legal practice representing working people. In 1994, he was elected to the state House. Fourteen months later, he won a special election for a seat in the state Senate.

Lynch built a political base in South Boston and had strong union ties, advantages when he pursued the seat after Moakley died. He became the frontrunner, though he stumbled after the Boston Globe revealed his student loan defaults from years earlier, plus a tax lien that was resolved in 1998. Three other state senators opposed Lynch. The strongest among them was Cheryl Jacques, who was openly gay and had support from EMILY's List and other national feminist groups that criticized Lynch's opposition to abortion rights. Lynch bested Jacques, 39%-29%. In the anti-climactic general election, he defeated another state senator, Jo Ann Sprague, 66%-33%.

In the House, Lynch's views have been right of center in the Democratic Caucus, and he has had the most conservative voting record in the Massachusetts delegation, especially on cultural issues. "That's like being called the slowest of the Kenyans in the marathon," he quipped to the Boston Herald. He was one of three Massachusetts House members to vote for the Iraq War resolution. He moderated his stance on abortion when he ran for the Senate in 2013, saying he believes it is a constitutionally protected right and that as a senator he would oppose anti-abortion Supreme Court nominees.

On the Oversight committee, Lynch chairs the Subcommittee on National Security, where he investigated Fort Hood in Texas, where there had been in 2020 at least nine deaths under " unusual circumstances." Separately, in September 2020, Lynch voiced concern about the security of Afghanistan following reports that the Trump administration was withdrawing U.S. troops from that country, without a guarantee that women would be protected from Taliban militants. At a hearing, he criticized U.S. special representative Zalmay Khalilzad for failing to make the protection of women "a priority" in negotiations with the Taliban. Also on the committee, Lynch has taken an interest in helping the financially strapped Postal Service, where his mother was a clerk. An opponent of privatization, he filed a bipartisan resolution in 2018 with 200 cosponsors supporting the Postal Service as an independent federal agency.

His occasional departures from the party line have mostly been tolerated by the leadership, but Lynch went too far for them in opposing the final health care overhaul bill in 2010. He cited the Senate's decision to strip an antitrust exemption for insurance companies and the elimination of the government-run public option to compete with private insurers. " In the end, we allowed the insurance companies to prevail," he said. In July 2017, he called the law "unsustainable." During a 2015 broadcast interview in Boston, he said Nancy Pelosi should step aside as House Democratic Leader. "Nancy Pelosi is not going to lead the Democrats back into the majority," he said. Despite continuing to call for change, he signed on to support Pelosi for Speaker when Democrats regained control in the 2018 election and her critics had "several days of productive conversation" with Pelosi, including her "reassurances" of support for working-class priorities.

That history likely was an obstacle for Lynch when he sought the Oversight chairmanship following the death of Cummings in October 2019. At what was a critical time for the House's handling of the first impeachment case against President Donald Trump, Lynch said he was prepared to continue the panel's investigations of Trump. But he finished third in the vote of the leadership-controlled steering committee; he withdrew before the Caucus selected Carolyn Maloney in a contest with Gerald Connolly. Maloney was senior to Lynch, though Connolly was not, which could be a factor for Lynch if there is another internal contest.

In the 2013 contest for Kerry's seat, running against Democratic Rep. Ed Markey, Lynch said, "I think what the Senate could use—it's such an elite club—is someone to bring the concerns of the average American people to the U.S. Senate, so they're not so insulated." Markey won the primary, 57%-42%. Lynch led with 56 percent in Norfolk County and 62 percent in Plymouth County, both parts of his district.

Lynch has been reelected without great difficulty. His opposition to the health care bill prompted a primary challenge from the left in 2010 from Mac D' Alessandro, a former regional political director for the Service Employees International Union. D' Alessandro drew support from MoveOn.org and other progressive groups. Lynch stressed his independence, outraised his opponent by more than 2-to-1, and won handily, 66%-34%. In the 2020 primary, Lynch got 66 percent against Robbie Goldstein, an infectious disease specialist at Massachusetts General Hospital.

MA-8: Southern Boston suburbs   **Cook Partisan Voting Index: D+14**

Population		Race and Ethnicity		Income	
Total	765,516	White	74.70%	Median Income	$100,690
Land area (sq. miles)	326	Black	11.40%	District Income Rank	33
Pop/ sq mi	2,345.55	Latino	6.10%	Poverty Rate	7.80%
Born in State	62.10%	Asian	8.30%	With health insurance	97.90%
		Two or more races	2.70%	Cash public assistance	2.40%
Age Groups		Other	2.90%	Food stamp/SNAP	9.70%
Under 18	18.60%				
18-34	24.40%	**Education**		**Work**	
35-64	39.70%	H.S grad or less	29.80%	White Collar	51.90%
Over 64	17.20%	Some college	20.90%	Sales and Service	34.60%
		College Degree, 4 yr	28.20%	Blue Collar	13.60%
Military		Post grad	21.00%	Government	13.30%
Veteran/ Active Duty	5.30%				

2020 Pres. Vote	Biden	283,426	(66%)	Trump	137,738	(32%)			
2016 Pres. Vote	Clinton	231,356	(60%)	Trump	131,624	(34%)	Johnson	15,395	(4%)

Downtown Boston, Quincy, Brockton: The Irish remain the dominant political tribe here, even as parts of South Boston, long the center of Irish Boston, have gentrified. Southie's influence endures in the memory of two Irish Democrats who represented the area for all but two years from the Great Depression to the start of the 21st century. The first was John McCormack, an old-style, backroom dealmaker who served as House Speaker during the 1960s. The second was Joe Moakley, a close pal of Speaker Tip O'Neill, who chaired the influential Rules Committee before Democrats lost the House majority in 1994.

The 8th Congressional District of Massachusetts has evolved from a mostly blue-collar district in the Boston area. It takes in South Boston as well as Beacon Hill, the Massachusetts State House, and is a living museum with many of the historic sites in Boston. They include the Paul Revere House; Faneuil Hall and a statue of revolutionary patriot Samuel Adams; the Old State House and the site of the Boston Massacre; the John F. Kennedy Presidential Library and Museum, plus the Edward M. Kennedy Institute for the United States Senate at Columbia Point.

Completion of the high-dollar Big Dig highway project, with a tunnel under Boston Harbor, spurred economic development in the Financial District and along the waterfront in the port, including office buildings, hotels, condominiums, the John Joseph Moakley Courthouse and a huge convention center. The booming Seaport area in the once deteriorating docks continued to transform the city, with new homes for companies ranging from Amazon to Mass Mutual insurance company, and the port has thrived with commuter ferries and mega-cruise ships. In a back-to-the-future note, seafood processing thrived because of shipments from nearby Logan Airport. But the Seaport has created new complications. Planners who worried about the impact of climate change abandoned the idea of a costly sea wall to protect the city, in favor of waterfront parks and elevation of flood-prone areas. Multibillion dollar options for a mile-long rail connection between North Station and South Station— first proposed more than a century ago— remained under discussion; the proposal would link Boston's subways to commuter rail. General Electric Co., which earlier moved its corporate headquarters from Connecticut and unveiled plans for a campus along the Fort Point Channel in Southie, reversed itself in 2019 as it downsized and returned $87 million in incentives to the state. The urban changes have reduced some of the parochialism but have priced many of the working class from their neighborhoods. Residents of East Boston resisted the gentrification that has overtaken South Boston. The annual St. Patrick's Day parade in Southie preceded by a rowdy political breakfast and roast remains a must-attend for state politicians.

On the South Shore, the district takes in Brockton, a once-bustling shoe manufacturing town that has suffered from extensive gun violence and has become minority-majority. Also in the district are blue-collar locales of Quincy (not to be confused with the Quincy Market in downtown Boston), the "city of presidents" as the birthplace of the two Presidents Adams, and Braintree, where a 1920 armed robbery and slaying of a shoe factory paymaster and his guard led to the trial and execution of two Italian immigrants blamed for the killings, Nicola Sacco and Bartolomeo Vanzetti, which became one of the most controversial legal disputes in American history. The 8th remains securely Democratic. Joe Biden won 66%-32%.

Bill Keating (D)

Elected 2010, 6th term, b. Sep 06, 1952; Norwood, MA; Boston College, B.A., 1974; Boston College, M.B.A., 1982; Suffolk University School of Law, J.D., 1985; Roman Catholic; Married (Tevis Keating); 2 children.

Elected Office: MA House, 1977-1984; MA Senate, 1985-1998; Norfolk County District Attorney, 1999-2010.

Professional Career: Practicing attorney, 1999-2010.

DC Office: 2351 RHOB 20515, 202-225-3111, Fax: 202-225-5658, keating.house.gov

State Offices: Hyannis, 508-771-6868; New Bedford, 508-999-6462; Plymouth, 508-746-9000.

Committees: *Armed Services*: Cyber, Innovative Technologies & Information Systems; Intelligence & Special Operations. *Foreign Affairs*: Europe, Energy, the Environment & Cyber (Chmn); Middle East, North Africa & Global Counterterrorism.

Group Ratings

	ADA	ACLU	AFL-CIO	LCV	COC	HAFA	ACU	CFG	FRC
2020	**	79%	**	95%	-	0%	4%	**	-
2019	90%	C	100%	97%	61%	C	5%	17%	0%

Almanac Ratings 2019-2020

	Economy	Social	Foreign	Composite
Liberal	100%	100%	56%	86%
Conservative	0%	0%	44%	14%

Key Votes of the 116th Congress

1. U.S./Mex./Can. trade deal	Y	5. Russia sanctions	Y	9. Firearms background checks Y
2. First Coronavirus response	Y	6. Troops in Syria	Y	10. Spending at the border	Y
3. HEROES Act	Y	7. Veto arms sales to Saudis	Y	11. Marijuana liberalized rules	Y
4. CASH Act	Y	8. Defense $$$, veto override	Y	12. Electoral College objections N

Election Results

Election	Name (Party)	Vote (%)		Cand. Spent	Ind. Exp. Support	Ind. Exp. Oppose
2020 General	Bill Keating (D)	260,262	(61%)	$494,669	$10	
	Helen Brady (R)	154,261	(36%)	$25,167		
	Michael Manley (I)	9,717	(2%)			
2020 Primary	Bill Keating (D)	125,608	(99%)			

Prior winning percentages: 2018 (59%), 2016 (56%), 2014 (55%), 2012 (55%), 2010 (47%)

Democrat William Keating, elected in 2010, is a former prosecutor who has put his experience to work on terrorism and overseas issues, often in bipartisan ways on the Foreign Affairs Committee. He also has sought to resolve maritime conflicts in Massachusetts' coastal areas.

A Massachusetts native and life-long public official, Keating followed the path of his father, a police officer and later a veterans' services agent. Keating put himself through Boston College by working at a post office. In 1977, at the age of 24, he was elected to the Massachusetts House. In 1985, Keating was elected to the state Senate, eventually becoming chairman of the Judiciary Committee and then the Committee on Taxation. He got his law degree from Suffolk University while serving in the legislature. As district attorney for Norfolk County, he became the first in the state to win a murder conviction in the absence of a victim's body by using DNA evidence. He set up facilities for veterans suffering from post-traumatic stress disorder. And he helped create the Norfolk Advocates for Children, an organization for children who have been victimized by sexual assault.

Keating ran for an open seat in a district that had been in Democratic hands for nearly a half-century, though it is relatively marginal for Massachusetts. It gave Republican Scott Brown 60 percent of the vote in the 2010 special election to fill the seat of the late Democratic Sen. Edward Kennedy. Tea party-backed Republican Jeff Perry, a member of the state House, campaigned for smaller government and less spending. Keating sought to paint Perry, a police officer, as having a "troubled relationship with the truth," pointing to a case in the 1990s in which an officer under Perry's command was involved in illegal strip searches of teenage girls. Perry said he did not know about the searches at the time. Keating had a slight edge in candidate spending, $1.5 million to $1.2 million, and in spending by outside groups. In a rare, though unimpressive, triumph in an otherwise dismal election for Democrats in 2010, he won 47%-42%.

In the House, Keating became a persistent inquisitor of Homeland Security Department officials, with an interest in failings in perimeter safety at airports. He challenged the Transportation Security Administration on its overly aggressive searches of passengers, and said the agency's approach was like " locking all the doors on your house but leaving the windows open." In 2016 and again in 2017, the House passed his bill to force TSA to enhance how it protects airport access points and the perimeters of the nation's airports, and to update its risk assessment for aviation security. The Senate did not act on the measure.

On the Foreign Affairs Committee, Keating sought bipartisanship in dealing with the world's trouble spots. With other senior members of the panel, Keating filed in 2015 a bipartisan anti-terrorism bill to coordinate U.S. efforts to protect historic sites around the world from attacks by the Islamic State and others, and to restrict imports of cultural property illegally trafficked from Syria. Following the apparent murder in 2018 of Saudi journalist Jamal Khashoggi at the Saudi embassy in Turkey, Keating called for a halt of arms sales to Saudi Arabia— a step that would affect defense contractors in Massachusetts. "We're not a country founded on arms sales," he said. As chairman of the Subcommittee on Europe, Eurasia, Energy and the Environment, he has sought to strengthen the alliance with Europe—" rather than threaten it as the Trump administration seems intent on doing"— and defend against threats posed by Russia and China. With Rep. Adam Kinzinger, the senior Republican on his subcommittee, Keating filed a bill in March 2019 that sought to promote global energy security for the United States and Europe. In March 2020, he proposed strengthening sanctions against Russia for the misinformation it communicated about coronavirus.

Long before the Nuclear Regulatory Commission decided in 2015 to shut down the Pilgrim nuclear power plant in Plymouth, Keating had raised concerns about its licensing. He has filed a bill to ease longstanding friction between federal and local officials in the management of the ocean area in the Monomoy Refuge off Nantucket. When Democrats regained House control in 2019, environmentalists grew more amenable to reaching a deal. But the House failed to act during the next two years.

At home, Keating has faced more competition for reelection than has any other current representative from Massachusetts. He had a big financial advantage over his two rivals in 2012 and won comfortably with 59 percent of the vote. His 2014 contest was tighter. GOP attorney John Chapman, a first-time candidate, raised $1 million, to $1.4 million for the incumbent. Keating won 55%-45%, with the benefit of big margins in New Bedford and Fall River. In 2018, he faced Peter Tedeschi, whose family had owned a chain of 200 local food stores. Tedeschi outspent Keating, $856,000 to $570,000, and said he would limit himself to three terms— in contrast to the " career politician." Keating emphasized the need for oversight of the Trump administration. In a bad year for Republicans in the Northeast, he won, 59%-41%. Against Helen Brady, who worked 32 years in the business office of the Boston Symphony Orchestra, Keating in 2020 won with 61 percent of the vote— his best-ever performance. He won every city and town.

MA-9: Southeast Massachusetts

Cook Partisan Voting Index: D+6

Population		Race and Ethnicity		Income	
Total	748,141	White	87.90%	Median Income	$77,167
Land area (sq. miles)	1,215	Black	3.70%	District Income Rank	109
Pop/ sq mi	615.89	Latino	6.00%	Poverty Rate	8.90%
Born in State	68.30%	Asian	1.50%	With health insurance	96.70%
		Two or more races	2.60%	Cash public assistance	2.30%
Age Groups		Other	4.50%	Food stamp/SNAP	10.00%
Under 18	19.10%				
18-34	19.40%	**Education**		**Work**	
35-64	38.80%	H.S grad or less	35.00%	White Collar	38.40%
Over 64	22.80%	Some college	27.10%	Sales and Service	39.60%
		College Degree, 4 yr	23.70%	Blue Collar	22.00%
Military		Post grad	14.10%	Government	12.90%
Veteran/ Active Duty	7.40%				

2020 Pres. Vote	Biden	253,222	(58%)	Trump	176,133	(40%)		
2016 Pres. Vote	Clinton	205,581	(52%)	Trump	163,643	(41%)	Johnson	16,509	(4%)

Cape Cod, Fall River: The South Shore of Massachusetts Bay, from Boston southward to Plymouth and then to Cape Cod, is Massachusetts's oldest settled territory. The Pilgrims landed here at Plymouth Rock in 1620. This stony land was farmed by John Adams' father. Daniel Webster lived in the South Shore town of Marshfield, today a high-income suburb of Boston.

The Kennedys spent their summers at Hyannis Port on the Cape. As a senator in the 1950s, John F. Kennedy left a lasting legacy by helping to create the 40-mile Cape Cod National Seashore, which preserved much of the beauty, including large sand dunes. Provincetown, at the tip of the Cape, is still a fishing port and also one of the major gay vacation areas in the country. Famed writers Norman Mailer, Eugene O' Neill and Tennessee Williams all spent time in Provincetown. The islands of Martha's Vineyard and Nantucket, rich whaling ports in the early 19th century, are favored summer resorts for the liberal rich of Boston, New York and Washington. In 2019, the Obamas purchased for nearly $15 million an oceanfront property on 29 acres of Martha's Vineyard. The Cape has filled with year-round retirees who enjoy the beauty and quiet pace.

Cape Cod Bay supports cranberry growers, who annually produce more than $100 million from more than 13,000 acres of bogs. Growers have coped with over-supply and in 2018 requested that the Agriculture Department authorize destruction of a large share of their crop. That year, they destroyed more than 240 million pounds of the berries. With the warming of ocean waters, lobsters have moved north and the local harvest of crustaceans has been decimated— reductions of as much as 90 percent since the late 1990s.

The 9th Congressional District of Massachusetts follows the South Shore from Rockland to the Cape and extends west to the famous whaling seaport of New Bedford and to parts of coastal Fall River, both of which have large Hispanic populations. It includes the two tony islands, where the glitterati generated a " not in my backyard" fury to proposed windmill farms in the nearby channel waters. Vineyard Wind moved ahead on a new farm with 84 turbines 15 miles south of the Vineyard, though it said in early 2020 that its estimated completion in 2022 was too optimistic. This would be the largest offshore wind-power project in the nation and could power close to one-third of all residences in Massachusetts. Safety fears and financial factors led to the closing in May 2019 of the Pilgrim nuclear power plant in Plymouth. In November 2020, the Boston Globe reported, a " nascent plan to build new bridges over the Cape Cod Canal has generated mostly enthusiasm up and down the peninsula." They would replace the nearby Bourne and Sagamore bridges, which provide the only access from the mainland to the Cape, but have deteriorated since they were built in the 1930s.

Politically, the South Shore and the Cape were Republican decades ago. But they have shifted and this district leans Democratic. Joe Biden won 58 percent of the vote, which was six percentage points higher than Hillary Clinton. The district remains the most competitive in Massachusetts.

MICHIGAN

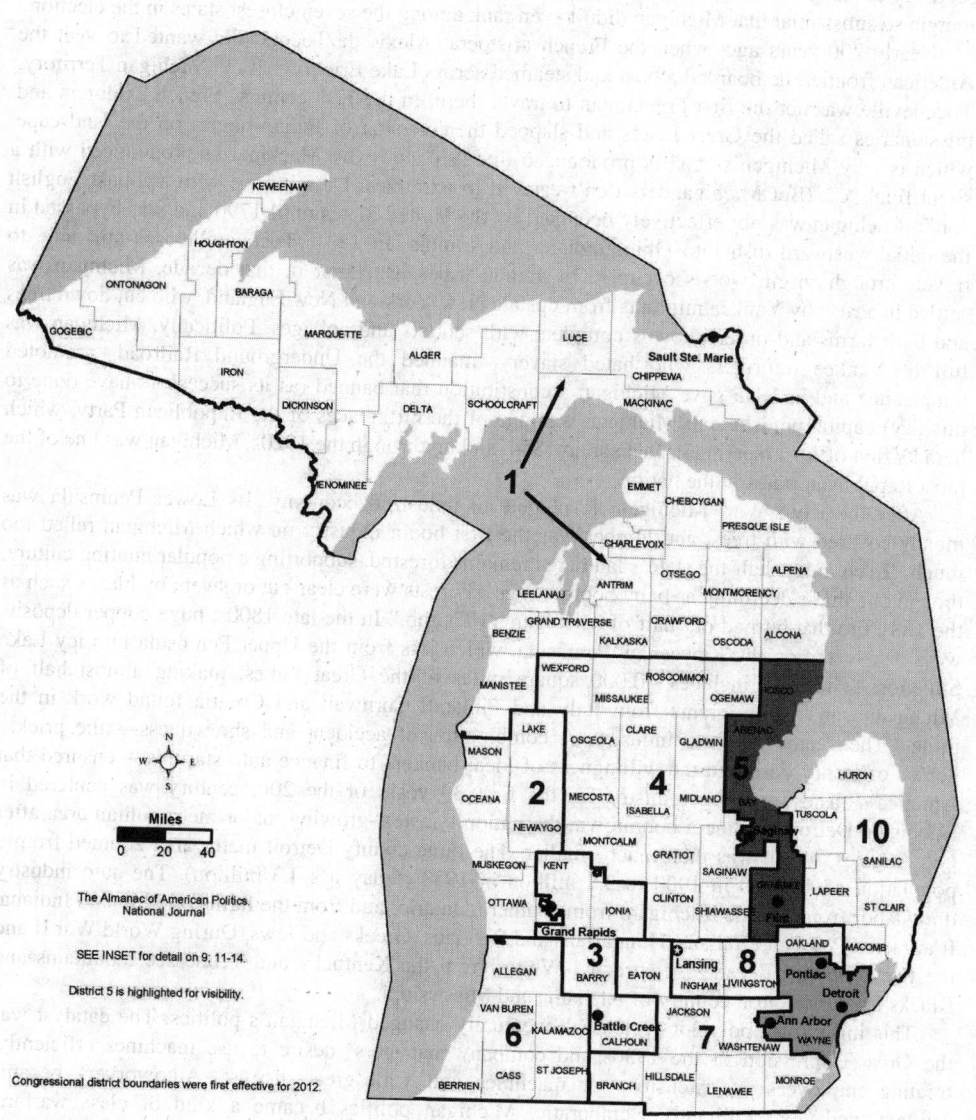

The Almanac of American Politics.
National Journal

SEE INSET for detail on 9; 11-14.

District 5 is highlighted for visibility.

Congressional district boundaries were first effective for 2012.

Michigan, though politically competitive in down-ballot races, hadn't voted Republican for president since 1988—until 2016, when Donald Trump won it by 10,704 votes. It was one of the three states, along with Pennsylvania and Wisconsin that enabled him to win the presidency by a healthy Electoral College margin, buoyed by a surge in blue-collar voters in declining industrial areas and apparent indifference from the Hillary Clinton campaign. But the state swung back, first in the 2018 midterm elections, when the Democrats flipped the offices of governor, attorney general and secretary of state, and then in 2020, when Joe Biden defeated Trump in the state by 154,188 votes, a margin so substantial that Michigan didn't even rank among the seven closest states in the election.

Nearly 200 years ago, when the French aristocrat Alexis de Tocqueville wanted to visit the American frontier, he boarded a boat and steamed across Lake Erie to visit the Michigan Territory. Tocqueville was not the first Frenchman to travel there. In the 17th century, French explorers and missionaries sailed the Great Lakes and slapped their version of Indian names on the landscape, which is why Michigan's "ch" is pronounced like "sh" and why Mackinac is pronounced with a silent final "c". (But Michiganders don't carry it to extremes: Detroit ends with a robust English "oit".) Michigan was not effectively occupied by the United States until 1796 and was bypassed in the initial westward rush into Ohio, Indiana and Illinois. In 1831, Tocqueville was still able to travel through virgin woods occupied by Indian tribes. But later in that decade, Michigan was settled in a rush by Yankee migrants from upstate New York and New England, who cut down trees and built farms and orderly towns complete with schools and colleges. Politically, Michigan was full of Yankee reformers who hated slavery, manned the Underground Railroad, promoted temperance and in 1855 gave Michigan a constitution that banned (as its successors have done to this day) capital punishment. Michigan was one of the birthplaces of the Republican Party, which held its first official meeting in Jackson in 1854, and up through the 1920s, Michigan was one of the most Republican states in the nation.

After the Civil War, Michigan developed an industrial economy. Its Lower Peninsula was mostly covered with trees, and lumber was the first boom industry on which Michigan relied too much. (Even today, half the state's land area remains forested, supporting a popular hunting culture, though one that's declining as baby boomers age.) Forests were clear-cut or swept by blazes such as the 1881 fire that burned out half of Michigan's" Thumb." In the late 1800s, huge copper deposits were discovered on the Keweenaw Peninsula, which juts from the Upper Peninsula into icy Lake Superior. (The state includes 40,000 square miles of the Great Lakes, making almost half of Michigan water.) Immigrants from Italy and Finland, Cornwall and Croatia found work in the mines. Then came the auto industry. A combination of accident and shrewdness— the prickly genius of Henry Ford and the willingness of local bankers to finance auto startups— ensured that America's fastest-growing industry for the first 30 years of the 20th century was centered in Michigan. Detroit became a boomtown, the nation's fastest-growing major metropolitan area after Los Angeles, which was then much smaller. The three-county Detroit metro area zoomed from a population of 426,000 in 1900 to 2.2 million in 1930 (today it's 4.3 million). The auto industry drew labor from outside Michigan, from southern Ontario, and from the farms of Ohio and Indiana. It attracted Poles and Italians, Hungarians and Belgians, Greeks and Jews. During World War II and the two following decades, it attracted Whites from the Kentucky and Tennessee mountains and Blacks from the cotton country of Alabama and Mississippi.

This influx of a polyglot proletariat eventually changed Michigan's politics. The catalyst was the Great Depression of the 1930s and company managers' desire to use machines efficiently, treating employees as extensions of machines and with great distrust. Autoworkers became militant, and more militantly Democratic. Michigan politics became a kind of class warfare, conducted with a bitterness that split families and neighbors. The unions mostly won, because autoworkers and post-1900 immigrants were larger in number and produced more children than did outstate Yankees or management. With continuing growth, though, economic issues turned less bitter. Republican George Romney, the former American Motors president elected governor in 1962, and his successor, William Milliken, accepted the social welfare policies endorsed by the UAW leadership and the Democrats. Michigan supported one of the nation's most distinguished and extensive higher-education systems, built state parks and recreation areas, and pioneered efforts to end racial discrimination.

Michigan grew faster than the nation as a whole from 1910 to 1970, and successive censuses and reapportionments increased its House delegation from 12 to 19. But by 2012 its House delegation had fallen back to 14, and it will decline by one more in 2022. Since 2010, the state's has grown by a sluggish 2 percent. A key turning point may have been changes in the domestic auto industry. After the UAW's strike against General Motors in 1970, the union won its central demand: "30 and out," retirement after 30 years on the assembly line. That, in turn, led to demands for costlier retiree health benefits on top of those negotiated for active workers. The assumption was that the Big Three— General Motors, Ford, and Chrysler— would continue to dominate the U.S. auto market as they had for decades and would be able to afford top-shelf benefits. The reality turned out to be different: Foreign competitors began producing better and cheaper cars that were more responsive to changes in gas prices and consumer preferences, first in Europe and Japan and then in nonunion plants in the United States. In the city of Detroit, the population fell from 1.8 million in 1950 to 713,000 in 2010 and 670,031 in 2019. Starting with riots in 1967, crime rates in Detroit remained intolerably high for 25 years, and much of the city simply vanished— houses were abandoned or burned down, commercial frontage had nearly 100 percent vacancy rates, and the downtown was a beleaguered fortress surrounded by vacant square miles. Detroit's crumbling architecture helped give birth to a subgenre of photography called "ruin porn."

Map for Greater Detroit

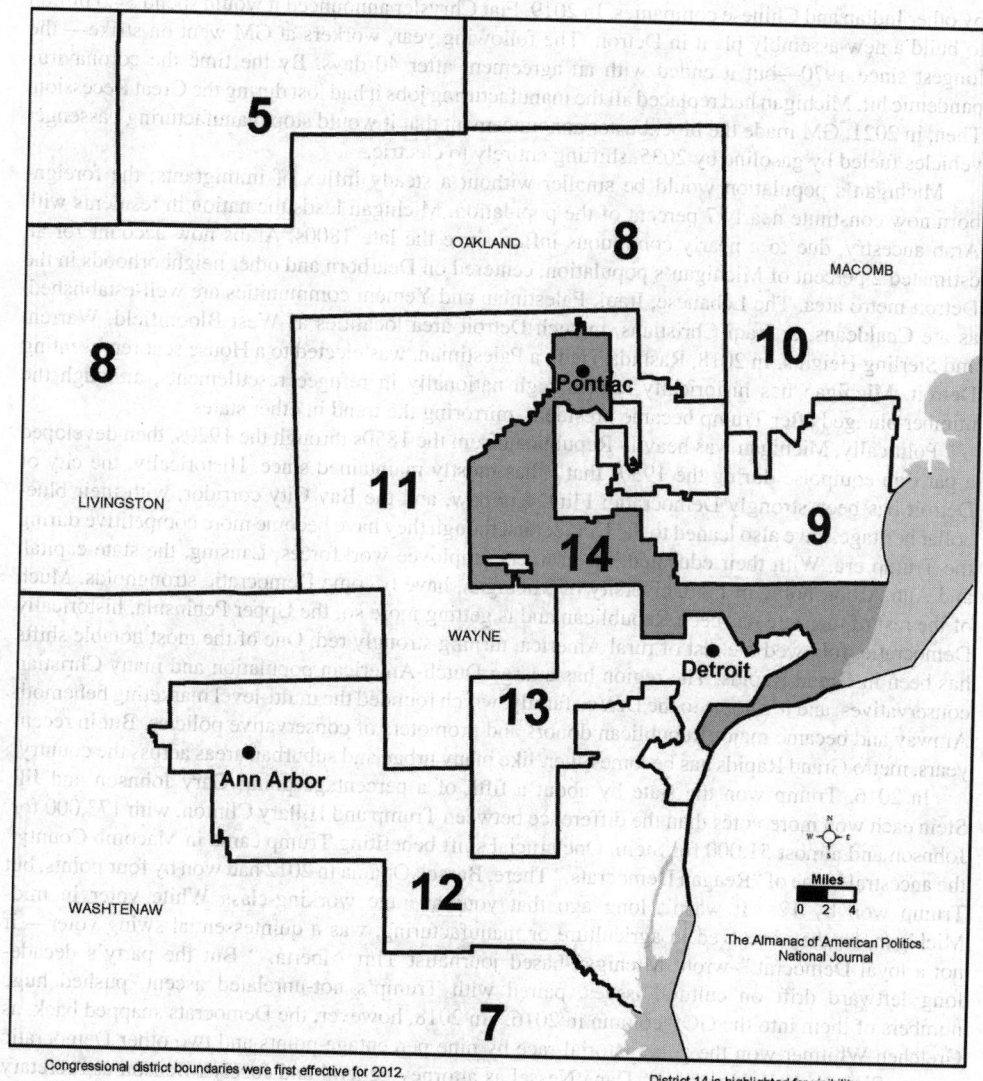

The Almanac of American Politics.
National Journal

Congressional district boundaries were first effective for 2012.

District 14 is highlighted for visibility.

Detroit began rebounding in the 1990s. Crime and welfare rolls were down, new sports stadiums and even some new housing were built downtown, and old theaters were refurbished. The decade that began in 2000 paused this comeback, as the Big Three, desperate to generate cash to pay huge costs for workers' and retirees' benefits, squeezed their subcontractors into bankruptcy, and GM and Chrysler followed in 2009; Ford managed to stay afloat only by mortgaging almost all its assets in 2007. But Michigan recovered along with the rest of the nation: After the Great Recession, the Big Three resumed making profits, and GM and Chrysler began buying back government-owned stock. After spending several years in the biggest municipal bankruptcy in the history of North America, Detroit struck a "grand bargain" with the state's GOP leadership in 2018—the final financial restrictions were lifted, leaving the city entirely free of such oversight for the first time since the 1970s. Over time, the auto industry became more high-tech, with fewer unionized workers and higher skill requirements. Just-in-time production methods encouraged subcontractors to stay in Michigan near big assembly plants, and the state boasted the nation's highest per capita concentration of engineers. In 2017, the Detroit area welcomed its first new vehicle assembly plant in a quarter century, to build off-road vehicles for the Indian company Mahindra Group; this followed local automotive-sector investments by other Indian and Chinese companies. In 2019, Fiat Chrysler announced it would spend $4.5 billion to build a new assembly plant in Detroit. The following year, workers at GM went on strike— the longest since 1970—but it ended with an agreement after 40 days. By the time the coronavirus pandemic hit, Michigan had replaced all the manufacturing jobs it had lost during the Great Recession. Then, in 2021, GM made the blockbuster announcement that it would stop manufacturing passenger vehicles fueled by gasoline by 2035, shifting entirely to electric.

Michigan's population would be smaller without a steady influx of immigrants; the foreign-born now constitute nearly 7 percent of the population. Michigan leads the nation in residents with Arab ancestry, due to a nearly continuous influx since the late 1800s. Arabs now account for an estimated 2 percent of Michigan's population, centered on Dearborn and other neighborhoods in the Detroit metro area. The Lebanese, Iraqi, Palestinian and Yemeni communities are well-established, as are Chaldeans, or Iraqi Christians, in such Detroit-area localities as West Bloomfield, Warren, and Sterling Heights. In 2018, Rashida Tlaib, a Palestinian, was elected to a House seat representing Detroit. Michigan has historically ranked high nationally in refugee resettlements, although the number plunged after Trump became president, mirroring the trend in other states.

Politically, Michigan was heavily Republican from the 1850s through the 1920s, then developed a partisan equipoise during the 1930s that it has mostly maintained since. Historically, the city of Detroit has been strongly Democratic; Flint, Saginaw, and the Bay City corridor, with their blue-collar heritage, have also leaned to the Democrats, though they have become more competitive during the Trump era. With their educated, government-employee workforces, Lansing, the state capital, and Ann Arbor, home of the University of Michigan, have become Democratic strongholds. Much of the rest of the state has been Republican and is getting more so; the Upper Peninsula, historically Democratic, followed the rest of rural America, turning strongly red. One of the most notable shifts has been in Grand Rapids. The region has a large Dutch-American population and many Christian conservatives, and it's home to the DeVos family, which founded the multi-level marketing behemoth Amway and became major Republican donors and promoters of conservative policies. But in recent years, metro Grand Rapids has become bluer, like many urban and suburban areas across the country.

In 2016, Trump won the state by about a fifth of a percentage point; Gary Johnson and Jill Stein each won more votes than the difference between Trump and Hillary Clinton, with 173,000 for Johnson and almost 51,000 for Stein. One crucial shift benefiting Trump came in Macomb County, the ancestral home of "Reagan Democrats." There, Barack Obama in 2012 had won by four points, but Trump won by 12. "It wasn't long ago that your average working-class White voter in mid-Michigan, be they involved in agriculture or manufacturing, was a quintessential swing voter— if not a loyal Democrat," wrote Michigan-based journalist Tim Alberta. " But the party's decade-long leftward drift on cultural issues, paired with Trump's not-unrelated ascent, pushed huge numbers of them into the GOP column in 2016." In 2018, however, the Democrats snapped back, as Gretchen Whitmer won the gubernatorial race by nine percentage points and two other Democratic women flipped statewide offices: Dana Nessel as attorney general and Jocelyn Benson as secretary of state. Democrats also seized two formerly Republican congressional seats.

For obvious reasons, Michigan was a major target for both the Trump and Biden campaigns, though consistent polling leads for Biden led the Trump campaign to periodically ease off its investments in the state. Biden ended up increasing the number of Democratic votes by 24 percent over what Clinton received four years earlier, while Trump increased his votes by just 16 percent. Biden flipped Kent County (Grand Rapids), Leelanau County (adjoining Traverse City), and Saginaw County, and he increased the winning Democratic margins by between 5 and 7 points in Washtenaw County (Ann Arbor), Ingham County (Lansing), Kalamazoo County and Marquette County in the Upper Peninsula. Crucial to Biden's victory was his success in the affluent Detroit suburb of Oakland County: He won it by 14 points and 91,078 votes. Biden wasn't able to flip Macomb County, but he cut Trump's winning margin there from 12 points to eight. While Biden ended up with a relatively comfortable victory, Trump targeted Michigan as a state where he sought to reverse the result, strong-arming local election officials and pressuring legislative leaders (unsuccessfully) to adopt the GOP Electoral College slate. These efforts alienated retiring Rep. Paul Mitchell, who quit the GOP in protest, much as fellow Rep. Justin Amash left the party in 2019. When Trump faced his second impeachment in 2021, Amash's successor, freshman Rep. Peter Meijer, became one of a handful of House Republicans to vote for Trump's impeachment. The Republicans' main consolation in 2020 was the party's ability to maintain control of the legislature, ensuring at least another two years of divided government in a closely divided state.

Population		Race and Ethnicity		Income	
Total	9,986,857	White	78.20%	Median Income	59,584
Land area (sq. miles)	56,539	Black	13.70%	State Income Rank	32 out of 50
Pop/ sq mi	176.64	Latino	5.30%	Poverty Rate	13.00%
Born in state	76.20%	Asian	4.00%	With health insurance	94.20%
		Two or more races	3.00%	Cash public assistance	2.20%
Age Groups		Other	1.70%	Food stamp/SNAP	14.9%
Under 18	21.50%				
18-34	22.50%	**Education**		**Work**	
35-64	38.30%	H.S grad or less	37.80%	White Collar	37.70%
Over 64	17.70%	Some college	32.20%	Sales and Service	37.30%
Military		College Degree, 4 yr	18.20%	Blue Collar	25.00%
Veteran/ Active Duty	6.70%	Post grad	11.90%	Government	11.00%

Presidential Politics

2020 Primary (D)	Biden (D)	840,360(53%)	Sanders (D)	576,926(36%)		
2020 Pres. Vote	Biden (D)	2,804,045(51%)	Trump (R)	2,649,864(48%)		
2016 Pres. Vote	Clinton (D)	2,268,839(47%)	Trump (R)	2,279,543(47%)	Johnson (L)	172,136 (4%)

Starting in 1992, Michigan voted for the Democratic presidential nominee in six consecutive elections and became a cornerstone in the so-called "blue wall" that gave Democrats an edge in winning 270 Electoral College votes. By 2008, Michigan gave Barack Obama a 16-percentage point margin over John McCain, more than double the Democrat's national advantage. In affluent suburban Oakland County, where whites once voted heavily Republican, voters shifted to Democrats on cultural issues in 1996 and haven't deviated from that course. When Donald Trump smashed through the blue wall and defeated Hillary Clinton in 2016, he won Michigan by 10,704 votes out of 4.8 million cast— a shocking upset not predicted by the polls and fueled by his winning blue-collar counties that had long eluded Republicans.

s

Exhibit "A" was Trump's victory in Macomb County, home to the Reagan Democrats. In 2012, Obama won Macomb by 16,103 votes. Trump defeated Clinton in Macomb by 48,348. Trump also won Saginaw, Bay and Monroe, and came within 1,200 votes of winning Muskegon, all blue-collar counties. Clinton carried white-collar Oakland by 1,000 votes more than Obama did in 2012. But in Wayne County, with heavily Democratic Detroit, Clinton's vote trailed Obama's by some 76,000, suggesting an enthusiasm gap in African-American precincts. Meanwhile, Trump tallied 15,000 votes more than Mitt Romney garnered in 2012, mostly in the western Wayne suburbs of Detroit. With such a narrow defeat, many factors could have caused Clinton's loss. Some Democrats blamed unions for not getting out their Democratic vote. Others blamed Clinton's national team for poor organization.

Democrats weren't going to make the same mistakes in 2020. They spent heavily on Michigan, and even as polls showed Joe Biden with a comfortable lead, they didn't cut back on their advertising. That turned out to be necessary, as for the second consecutive election polls underestimated Trump. He led on election night. But Biden pulled ahead the next day as more mail ballots were counted, eventually winning 51%-48%.

Biden's campaign pushed heavy turnout in much of metro Detroit, winning by much larger margins in tony Oakland County and Washtenaw County, home of Ann Arbor and the University of Michigan. He also turned out a lot more Black voters: While the margins didn't shift that much in Wayne County, home of Detroit, 100,000 more people voted, more than a 10 percent increase from the previous election. Biden also won long-Republican Kent County in Western Michigan, where college-educated white voters around Grand Rapids recoiled from Trump. Biden cut hard into Trump's margins around Traverse City, and narrowly flipped back blue-collar Saginaw County. Trump still carried Macomb and other ancestrally blue-collar Democratic counties, but Biden improved on the edges across most of the state.

That wasn't the end of the contest. At Trump's urging, Republicans claimed for weeks that there were enough irregularities to show that the election was stolen from him. They briefly refused to certify Wayne County's results before relenting. Multiple investigations by state GOP legislators, including a hearing with Trump attorney Rudy Giuliani, turned up no evidence of serious fraud. GOP lawmakers certified Michigan for Biden without incident.

The 2016 Democratic primary was, likewise, a rude awakening for Clinton and an embarrassment for the handful of pre-primary polls that showed her with a comfortable double-digit lead over Vermont Sen. Bernie Sanders, who took a stunning 50%-48% victory. Trump's anti-trade rhetoric played well among GOP primary voters and he defeated Texas Sen. Ted Cruz, 37%-25%.

Four years later, Sanders went all-in on Michigan to try to recharge his flagging campaign, canceling events in other states to focus on its March 10 primary a week after a disappointing Super Tuesday result. But Biden drubbed him 53%-36%, winning every county in the state. Biden's strong win further showed that Sanders' 2016 performance with White blue-collar workers was more about Clinton's weaknesses with those voters, and was a major step toward Sanders suspending his campaign a few weeks later.

Congressional Districts

117th Congress Lineup	7D 7R	116th Congress Lineup	7D 7R

For the fifth consecutive decade, Michigan is losing at least one House seat. A total of five states share that distinction, though the population in Michigan has been smaller than in the other four. In 1950, Detroit had five entire congressional districts; today, it falls short of enough population for one. But the loss of clout isn't exclusive to that city. In 1960, the Upper Peninsula had sufficient residents for 74 percent of a district; that has dropped to less than half a district. In contrast to the redistricting in 2011, when Republicans had complete control in Lansing, Democrats now have a stake— with Gov. Gretchen Whitmer— though Republicans retain both chambers of the legislature. More significantly, voters in 2018 approved a referendum that placed congressional redistricting under the control of a nominally nonpartisan commission— subject to possible court challenges.

Regardless of the procedures, the numbers remain relevant in redistricting. Following their gain of two suburban seats in 2018, Democrats control seven districts— six in the metro Detroit area and the other based in Flint and Saginaw. Republicans also hold seven seats— all of them largely outside the metro area, though one includes a big part of Macomb County. With the population change in Detroit continuing to lag the increases in Grand Rapids and elsewhere outside the metro area, the seven current Democratic-held districts will need to pick up Republican-leaning areas. That raises the question of whether Detroit will retain its two districts with African-American majorities, extending farther into the suburbs; alternatively, Detroit could have one super-district and the city would take the short straw for the state's loss of a district. If the commission acts on a truly nonpartisan basis, one option could be the creation of a "fair fight," which would match one incumbent from each party in an area near the geographic divide.

Whatever the choices, the Michigan delegation— which had been stable for a while until 2018 — likely is facing additional change and unpredictability.

Gretchen Whitmer (D)

Elected 2018, term expires 2023, 1st term; b. Aug. 23, 1971, Lansing; Michigan State University, B.A., 1998, J.D., 1993; Christian; Married (Marc Mallory) 2 children.

Elected Office: MI House, 2001-2006; MI Senate, 2006-2015, Minority Leader, 2011-2015; Ingham County Prosecutor, 2016.

Professional Career: Associate Attorney, Dickinson Wright, PLLC, 1998-2000; Lecturer, Gender and the Law, MI State University, 2015; Policy Maker in Residence, Towsley Foundation, Gerald R. Ford School of Public Policy, University of MI, 2015-2016.

Office: PO Box 30013 Lansing, 48909; 517-373-3400; Fax: 517-335-6863; Website: michigan.gov
Lt. Gov.: Garlin Gilchrist (D) **Atty. Gen:** Dana Nessel (D) **Sec. of State:** Jocelyn Benson (D)
State Legislature: Senate: 16D, 22R **House:** 52D, 58R

Election Results

Election	Name (Party)	Vote (%)
2018 General	Gretchen Whitmer (D)	2,266,193 (53%)
	Bill Schuette (R)	1,859,534 (44%)
2018 Primary	Gretchen Whitmer (D)	588,436 (52%)
	Abdul El-Sayed (D)	342,179 (30%)
	Shri Thanedar (D)	200,645 (18%)

Democrat Gretchen Whitmer, riding a blue wave of dissatisfaction with President Donald Trump and with outgoing GOP Gov. Rick Snyder, won the Michigan governorship in 2018. But she faced a challenging first two years in office, battling regularly with a Republican legislative majority and becoming the target of attacks from Trump and from militant opponents of the closures she ordered to combat the coronavirus. Whitmer even became the target of a foiled kidnapping plot. In the process, though, Whitmer gained national notoriety, becoming a finalist for Joe Biden's vice presidential slot.

Whitmer was raised as one of three children in Grand Rapids and East Lansing. Her father served as chief of the state Commerce Department in a Republican administration and later as CEO of Blue Cross Blue Shield; her mother, a Democrat, was a senior lawyer in the state attorney general's office. They divorced when she was young. Whitmer earned a bachelor's degree from Michigan State University and has spoken of her early desire to become a television sports correspondent. But after taking a political internship in Lansing, she changed her career focus and enrolled in law school at Michigan State. Less than three years after earning her law degree, Whitmer won a state House seat, prevailing in an expensive primary by just 281 votes. She served six years in the House, then won a state Senate seat, rising to become the chamber's minority leader for her final four years—the first woman to lead a Senate party caucus in Michigan.

As a legislator, Whitmer leveraged her oratorical skills and procedural knowledge to become an effective critic of Snyder and the GOP legislature, waging war against right-to-work legislation and other Republican priorities. In 2013, Whitmer announced in an emotional floor speech that she had been raped in college. She told her story during debate over legislation to require abortion insurance to be purchased separately from private health plans. Only four of 48 senators at the time were women, and Whitmer decided that someone had to make a compelling case against the measure. "I think you need to see the face of the women that you are impacting by this vote today," she said. "I think you need to think of the girls that we're raising and what kind of a state we want to be where you would put your approval on something this extreme." The speech attracted national attention, but the bill passed on a near-party-line vote. "It didn't change a damn thing," Whitmer told Michigan-based journalist Tim Alberta. "The next morning, I was about as depressed as I've ever been, because I've just laid my soul bare."

Whitmer considered a run for attorney general in 2010, but decided against it. Four years later, facing Senate term limits, she considered a gubernatorial bid, but once again opted against a run. In 2018, Whitmer saw her opening, with Snyder term-limited. This timing was fortuitous: 2018 proved to be a much friendlier year for a Democrat to run than either 2010 or 2014. Whitmer became the first Democrat to announce a candidacy, a tactic observers later credited with keeping a number of major Michigan Democrats out of the primary, including Sen. Gary Peters and Rep. Dan Kildee. From the start, Michigan Democrats were optimistic about their chances: In addition to the burst of Democratic enthusiasm in the Trump era, they expected to ride a backlash against Snyder. He had won in 2010 on his first foray into electoral politics, styling himself as "one tough nerd," a pragmatist who was able to rise above political gridlock. But his second term was overwhelmed by a drinking-water crisis in Flint.

In the Democratic primary, Whitmer was the establishment candidate, as well as the only woman in the race, although her roots outside Detroit meant that political bigwigs from the state's biggest metro area took longer to come to her side. Whitmer had vastly more political experience than either of her challengers—Abdul El-Sayed, a 33-year-old former city of Detroit health director, and Shri Thanedar, a deep-pocketed entrepreneur from Ann Arbor. Both positioned themselves as insurgents and attacked from her left. Late in the primary campaign, Sen. Bernie Sanders and future Rep. Alexandria Ocasio-Cortez, two of the party's biggest names on the left, came to the state to campaign for El-Sayed. But primary voters concluded that Whitmer was plenty progressive. She supported a $15 minimum wage, legalized marijuana, and universal preschool, and they liked her focus on nuts-and-bolts issues such as highway funding, which was encapsulated in her campaign slogan, "Fix The Damn Roads." Whitmer took 52 percent of the primary vote, besting El-Sayed with 30 percent and Thanedar with 18 percent. To ease any residual friction with progressives and Detroit Democrats, Whitmer tapped as her running mate Garlin Gilchrist, an African American who had served as director of innovation and emerging technology for the city of Detroit.

The Republicans also had a competitive primary, with two main contenders: Bill Schuette, who had served two terms as attorney general, and outgoing Lt. Gov. Brian Calley. Snyder, who had clashed with Schuette over prosecutions in the Flint crisis, backed Calley. But Trump backed Schuette and recorded a robocall on his behalf. Schuette took 51 percent, Calley got 25 percent, state Sen. Patrick Colbeck got 13 percent and obstetrician Jim Hines won 11 percent. The strains between Snyder and Schuette permeated the general election, with Snyder all but ignoring the GOP nominee. Schuette attacked Whitmer over her handling of early complaints about sexual misconduct by Larry Nassar, the gymnastics doctor at Michigan State University who would subsequently be convicted of serial sexual molestation and child pornography. But in the end, the overall political environment drowned out other concerns, and Whitmer won, 53%-44%. She took roughly twice as many counties as Hillary Clinton had in the presidential race two years earlier, flipping Kent (Grand Rapids), Eaton (suburban Lansing), Bay (Bay City), Saginaw (Saginaw) and, perhaps most importantly, the working-class Detroit suburbs of Macomb. Following Schuette's loss, Republicans legislators sought to handcuff Whitmer and other incoming Democrats by curbing the executive branch's powers. But after a national backlash, Snyder vetoed the measures.

In her first year in office, Whitmer notched some victories, including a bipartisan compromise on a long-simmering issue, the state's no-fault auto insurance system, which had left Michigan with some of the nation's highest rates for motorists. Whitmer also used executive action to ban flavored vaping products, though her efforts were overturned in court. But Whitmer suffered disappointments as well. She and the legislature fought endless battles over the state budget, and the issue that had been a centerpiece of her campaign, fixing the roads, crumbled amid opposition (including among Democrats) to her proposal to hike the gasoline tax by 45 cents per gallon. In 2020, Whitmer buoyed environmentalists and frustrated energy interests by moving to shut down an oil pipeline in the Straits of Mackinac that had been operating under a state easement for the past 67 years.

For Whitmer, 2020 was dominated by a cascade of challenges prompted by the coronavirus pandemic. Driven by an early surge of cases in the state, Whitmer took an aggressive stance, becoming a fixture on television and issuing limits on in-person shopping, the use of recreational boats, and many types of travel within the state. She imposed these policies under what many saw as dubious interpretations of executive powers that became targets of legal attack by the GOP-controlled legislature. She dismissed as a "failed attempt at humor" an instance when her husband sought to violate the restrictions. Her moves also sparked armed protests outside—and even inside—the state capitol. The restrictions didn't help Michigan much compared with other states; it consistently ranked in the top half of cases and death rates. Amid the pandemic, Whitmer also had to deal with another crisis, the collapse of two dams that resulted in the flooding of Midland, producing a spate of lawsuits against the state. Trump and his allies in the conservative media elevated Whitmer as a villain of the pandemic; the president referred to her as "the woman in Michigan" and as "'Half' Whitmer," and he urged his Twitter followers to "liberate Michigan." Tensions reached a crescendo in October, when federal and state officials announced charges against 13 men for allegedly planning to kidnap Whitmer. "Have one person go to her house. Knock on the door and when she answers it just cap her," said one encrypted group chat message released by the FBI.

Biden's consideration of Whitmer as a possible running mate fed a Republican narrative that she was prioritizing political ambition, though in the end, her sudden national prominence may have torpedoed any chance she'd had of being tapped by Biden. Either way, polls generally showed that Michigan residents preferred her performance to Trump's, and on Election Day, the president lost the state that had been so crucial to his 2016 victory. Still, Whitmer suffered a disappointment on Election Day when the GOP managed to keep control in both legislative chambers, ensuring two more years of divided government. Whitmer is presumed to be running for a second term in 2022, with the Republican field possibly including a variety of state legislators, members of Congress, and two-time Senate candidate John James.

Debbie Stabenow (D)

Elected 2000, term expires 2024, 4th term, b. Apr 29, 1950; Gladwin, MI; MI State University, B.A., 1972; MI State University, M.S.W., 1975; Methodist; Divorced; 2 children; 4 grandchildren.

Elected Office: Ingham County Commissioner, 1975-1978, Chair, 1976-1978; MI House, 1979-1991; MI Senate, 1991-1994; U.S. House, 1997-2001.

Professional Career: Social worker; Consultant & co-founder, MI Leadership Institute, 1995-1996.

DC Office: 731 HSOB 20510, 202-224-4822, Fax: 202-228-0325, stabenow.senate.gov

State Offices: Detroit, 313-961-4330; East Lansing, 517-203-1760; Flint, 810-720-4172; Grand Rapids, 616-975-0052; Marquette, 906-228-8756; Traverse City, 231-929-1031.

Committees: Senate Democratic Policy & Communications Committee Chairman. *Agriculture, Nutrition & Forestry (Chmn)*: Ex Officio membership on all subcommittees. *Budget. Environment & Public Works*: Clean Air & Nuclear Safety; Fisheries, Water, and Wildlife; Transportation & Infrastructure. *Finance*: Health Care (Chmn); International Trade, Customs & Global Competitiveness; Taxation & IRS Oversight. *Joint Taxation*.

Group Ratings

	ADA	ACLU	AFL-CIO	LCV	COC	HAFA	ACU	CFG	FRC
2020	-	77%	-	92%	-	0%	7%	-	-
2019	95%	C	100%	100%	50%	C	7%	0%	0%

Almanac Ratings 2019-2020

	Economy	Social	Foreign	Composite
Liberal	100%	100%	88%	96%
Conservative	0%	0%	12%	4%

Key Votes of the 116th Congress

1. EPA clean energy rules	Y	5. Russia sanctions	Y
2. U.S./Mex./Can. trade deal	Y	6. Troops in SYR, AFG	Y
3. Cut unemployment benefits	N	7. Veto arms sales to Saudis	Y
4. Shelton to Fed Reserve	N	8. Defense $$$, veto override	Y

9. Barr as Atty. General	N
10. Spending at the border	Y
11. Coney Barrett to Sup. Ct.	N
12. Electoral College objections	N

Election Results

Election	Name (Party)	Vote (%)	Cand. Spent	Ind. Exp. Support	Ind. Exp. Oppose
2018 General	Debbie Stabenow (D)..................... 2,214,478	(52%)	$14,614,819	$642,212	$642,910
	John James (R)............................... 1,938,818	(46%)	$11,426,822	$3,682,335	
2018 Primary	Debbie Stabenow (D)..................... 1,045,450	(100%)			

Prior winning percentages: 2018 (52%), 2012 (59%), 2006 (57%), 2000 (49%); House: 1998 (57%), 1996 (54%)

As chair of the Democratic Policy and Communications Committee, Debbie Stabenow ranks No. 4 in her party's Senate leadership. But Michigan's senior senator is also known for reaching across the political aisle—particularly on the Agriculture Committee, of which she reclaimed the gavel in 2021 after earlier chairing the panel from 2011 to 2015. She developed a collegial relationship with her longtime Republican counterpart on the committee, Pat Roberts of Kansas—and as debate began in 2017 on the latest five-year reauthorization of federal agricultural and nutrition programs, Stabenow and Roberts agreed to partner on the "farm bill." The upshot was that the $867 billion measure signed by President Donald Trump at the end of 2018 not only cleared the Senate on an overwhelmingly bipartisan vote but won over House counterparts during protracted conference committee deliberations. "It goes to the question of, 'Do you want to govern?'" Stabenow told McClatchy's Washington D.C. bureau. "Do you want to solve problems and get things done?"

In reassuming the helm of a committee on which the fault lines are often more regional than partisan, Stabenow signaled she would continue this collaborative approach as Arkansas Sen. John Boozman took over as the panel's top Republican as Roberts retired. Although the current farm bill does not expire until the end of the fiscal year ending in 2023, Stabenow said the committee would get a start on the next iteration—by assessing which pilot programs created in the 2018 legislation should become permanent, while reevaluating the current safety net for farmers. More immediately, the committee was poised to play a role in a major priority of President Joe Biden: combating climate change. Stabenow has teamed with Republicans Mike Braun of Indiana and Lindsey Graham of South Carolina on legislation to set up a program that would enable agricultural interests to receive credits for reducing carbon emissions. "We can provide voluntary, producer-led opportunities for our farmers and foresters that will allow them to continue to cut down their emissions and create new sources of income from the adoption of practices that store more carbon in soil and trees," Stabenow said.

In Michigan, Stabenow has been one of the more enduring figures in state politics throughout her more than 40 years in elected office: Her warm, personable demeanor often causes opponents to underestimate her political toughness. "For nearly four decades, Republicans have sneered at Debbie Stabenow. ... Then she beats them, every time," then-Detroit Metro Times columnist Jack Lessenberry wrote in 2012—when Stabenow captured 61 of the state's 83 counties to win a third Senate term by 20 percentage points. But once reliably blue Michigan has taken on a purple hue; in 2016, Trump became the first Republican presidential nominee to win the state in nearly three decades. Two years later, Stabenow found herself in a reelection battle more competitive than first expected—holding on to win by a little more than 6 percentage points over a political novice embraced by Trump.

Born Deborah Ann Greer, she grew up in the small northern Michigan town of Clare—where her family ran an Oldsmobile dealership. But her political base has long been the state capital, Lansing, and surrounding Ingham County, home to Michigan State University. She holds bachelor's and master's degrees in social work from the latter. Initially, she counseled students in public schools and made extra money singing folk songs in coffeehouses while volunteering for George McGovern's anti-Vietnam War presidential bid in 1972. Stabenow was first elected to office at 24, when, angered by the Ingham County Board of Commissioners' closing of a nursing home, she ran for the board in 1974; she beat an incumbent who had referred to her as "that young broad." She was elected to the Michigan House four years later and to the state Senate in 1990. Stabenow ran for governor in 1994, but the state Democratic establishment lined up behind former Rep. Howard Wolpe, who won the primary with 35 percent of the vote; Stabenow placed second with 30 percent. She became Wolpe's running mate, but the ticket lost in November.

Undaunted, Stabenow soon ran for Congress in a district that included Democratic Ingham County and heavily Republican Livingston County. She won 54 percent of the vote in 1996 to oust freshman Republican Rep. Dick Chrysler. In 2000, she challenged first-term Republican Sen. Spencer Abraham in what turned out to be one of that year's key Senate races. Abraham used his campaign's financial advantage to run ads attacking Stabenow as a free-spending liberal favoring increased bureaucracy and higher taxes. Stabenow hoarded her money for an October ad buy. She was down by 17 percentage points in mid-October polls but answered Abraham's charges by citing her House votes for a balanced budget and ending the marriage penalty in the tax code—while attacking the incumbent as beholden to corporations and special interests. Stabenow won 49%-48%, helping Democrats gain a 50-50 split of the Senate—and becoming the first woman to represent Michigan in that chamber.

Soon after Stabenow was sworn in, Senate Democrats moved to strengthen her grip on the seat: Capitalizing on a central issue of her election campaign, they named Stabenow head of a task force on prescription drugs. She organized bus trips to Canada to purchase drugs at lower prices for seniors and pressed for measures allowing reimportation of U.S. drugs from that country. Stabenow has remained active on this issue: In late 2018, Trump signed Stabenow-authored legislation prohibiting Medicare drug plans from including "gag clauses" in their contracts with pharmacies. Such clauses had been used to bar pharmacists from telling patients that, in some instances, they could purchase a drug at a price lower than the co-pay required by insurance.

Stabenow has been among the most loyal of Democrats, particularly on economic and social issues. But she joined other Rust Belt Democrats in challenging the international trade agenda put forth by Democratic President Barack Obama and his Republican predecessor, George W. Bush. In 2015, when Obama sought expedited authority to negotiate a 12-nation Pacific trade deal, Stabenow not only voted against it but also joined Ohio Republican Rob Portman to propose an amendment that would have required the administration to seek enforceable currency manipulation standards in such a deal. The amendment, which did not pass, was supported by the Michigan-based Big Three automakers.

Stabenow sought to bait Trump, who had campaigned on putting "America First," into embracing legislation she has introduced perennially since 2012 that would provide tax incentives to companies that return jobs to the United States while eliminating tax breaks to those firms shifting jobs overseas. "Republicans have refused to stop the loss of jobs to countries like Mexico and China by opposing the passage of my Bring Jobs Home Act," Stabenow complained in 2020. Although many of her colleagues had been critical a couple of years earlier when Trump—after slapping tariffs on steel and aluminum imports—threatened to impose tariffs on autos, Stabenow was at first supportive. However, in a September 2018 radio interview, she complained the administration was "just basically shooting in all directions and creating instability in terms of decisions that need to be made."

In early 2020, Stabenow doubled down by requesting a Government Accountability Office review of the $28 billion bailout for farmers hurt by foreign retaliation in the trade war triggered by Trump's tariffs. Stabenow had previously contended that the program had provided more funds to Southern states that had voted for the president and favored large agricultural firms over small farms. The GAO subsequently found the average payment to agricultural producers in Georgia— home state of Trump's Agriculture secretary, Sonny Perdue—were more than double the national average. Discussing her priorities for the next farm bill, Stabenow decried "the ad hoc payments, the chaos and the trade policy [and] the ... unfair way in which payments were distributed in some areas." She added, "We need to get back to something that is consistent, that is based on risk management, that allows our farmers to have confidence in the fairness of the system and stability in the system."

Stabenow was more upbeat in 2018 when Trump announced the U.S.-Mexico-Canada Agreement to supplant the North American Free Trade Agreement. "I've said from the beginning that, given NAFTA's importance to our economy in Michigan, a modernization is long overdue," she said. "I'm encouraged that there have been positive steps forward." She complained that NAFTA had "created a race to the bottom with jobs going to companies paying the lowest wages and countries with the lowest standard of living." In January 2020, Stabenow voted for the USMCA when it passed the Senate overwhelmingly, although she complained the Trump administration had initially "refused to include strong protections" for workers. "My Democratic colleagues and I held strong, and secured changes in the agreement that now include strong enforcement tools," she said in a statement. "Without these strong provisions, this agreement would have just been NAFTA all over again with all of its flaws."

When Stabenow first found herself in line to chair the Agriculture Committee in 2011, the farm industry's alarm bells went off. Many of the industry's leaders viewed her as an urban liberal interested mainly in two of her state's best-known products: automobiles and cherries. By the time a new farm bill was passed in early 2014, much of the agriculture industry had taken a political U-turn —and Stabenow was praised for balancing competing interests in what is one of the most lobbied pieces of legislation on Capitol Hill. "Past farm bills pit regions against regions. I said that we were going to support all of agriculture," Stabenow told The New York Times after the bill's passage.

Traditionally, farm bills have favored crops like corn and wheat that receive large subsidies. While such crops continued to benefit heavily in the 2014 rewrite overseen by Stabenow, subsidies for these commodities were cut by about 30 percent over 10 years. Although still a relatively small part of the overall bill, funding for specialty crops like fruits, vegetables and nuts—apples, blueberries and cherries are mainstays of Michigan agriculture—increased sharply. "This is not your father's farm bill," Stabenow said, pointing to savings—notably the elimination of a $5 billion-a-year, much-criticized subsidy that paid farmers whether or not they grew crops. The legislation took nearly three years to pull off, as she had to navigate regional differences. Stabenow was credited with dealing with such conflicts without allowing them to spill into public view. The House-Senate conference report on the bill contained some concessions to Southern growers from the House version, but most provisions originated in the Senate, making it very much Stabenow's handiwork.

Facing a Senate with a narrow 52-48 GOP majority at the beginning of 2017, Roberts and Stabenow opted for a farm bill draft that did not depart dramatically from the 2014 law. Their gambit worked, and the Senate passed the bill easily in June 2018. The House version squeaked through by two votes, with no Democrats voting for it. House and Senate negotiators clashed over some of the same regional issues as during the previous bill: Stabenow told the Detroit News she and Roberts had resisted House efforts to "skew" subsidies toward Southern crops like cotton and peanuts at the expense of major Midwestern crops like corn. For Michigan, Stabenow came away with expanded crop insurance for fruits, vegetables, hops and barley; greater supports for dairy, the state's agricultural mainstay; and a federal office to advocate for urban farms in cities like Detroit.

The biggest dispute involved the $70 billion annual Supplemental Nutrition Assistance Program, formerly known as food stamps, which helps more than 40 million people buy groceries. The House bill sought to expand work requirements for recipients with children older than 6; such a move would cause 1.2 million people each month to lose eligibility, according to congressional estimates. The Senate version did not contain such changes, with Roberts and Stabenow instead proposing rules to combat fraud. In the final deal on the bill in November 2018, the Senate view prevailed. Upon reassuming the chairmanship in 2021, Stabenow said that a priority would be to expand access to SNAP as the committee moved to respond to the COVID-19 pandemic.

Six years earlier, Roberts and Stabenow worked together to forge a compromise on labeling genetically modified food that was signed into law by Obama. They were less successful on a 2015 reauthorization of the school meals program. While they crafted a compromise that largely maintained the child nutrition standards that first lady Michelle Obama had adopted as a signature issue, it failed to become law despite clearing their committee unanimously. As a result, the law currently on the books—the Healthy, Hunger Free Kids Act of 2010—is now five years overdue for reauthorization; Stabenow said she and Boozman "both feel strongly" that the matter needs to be addressed in 2021-2022.

During her first term, Stabenow was selected as secretary of the Democratic Conference. It gave her a voice at leadership meetings, though her impact was limited. Some senior Democrats quietly discussed replacing her after the 2006 elections, in which she handily defeated Oakland County Sheriff Mike Bouchard, 57%-41%. After her reelection, a deal was reached in which Stabenow got a seat on the influential Finance Committee and became chair of the Democratic Steering and Outreach Committee while being replaced as caucus secretary. In 2011, she became vice chair of what is now the Democratic Policy and Communications Committee. She was elevated to chair it in 2017, when Sen. Chuck Schumer became Democratic leader.

Seeking a third term in 2012 against former Rep. Pete Hoekstra, Stabenow was targeted by what was arguably the most controversial TV ad of that election cycle: It featured an Asian woman bicycling through a rice paddy and thanking "Sen. Debbie Spend-It-Now" in broken English for sending U.S. jobs to China. Republicans and Democrats alike attacked Hoekstra for playing on racial stereotypes. He never recovered, and Stabenow bettered her 2006 performance, winning with 59 percent of the vote.

In 2018, Stabenow faced John James, a West Point graduate and Iraq War veteran who Trump called "SPECTACULAR!" on Twitter adding, "Rarely have I seen a candidate with such great potential. West Point graduate, successful businessman and a African American leader." James—head of a family-owned business who described himself as a "pro-life, pro-Second Amendment, pro-business conservative"—was largely unknown before the contest. He repeatedly attacked Stabenow as out of touch and ineffective, saying, "You aren't going to get results from a 43-year career politician." Stabenow had a substantial financial edge, which allowed her to buy TV ads first. James' TV effort got off to a bumpy start; his first ad, which showed him in a school setting, had a bulletin board in the background containing an image that appeared to be a swastika. James said it was unintentional and apologized.

James' paid TV ads never mentioned he was the Republican nominee, although one spot appealed to African American voters to leave the Democratic Party and "have a seat at both tables." That appeal had limited effect, as Stabenow garnered more than 95 percent of the Black vote on Election Day, according to the Detroit News. Trump kept up a steady stream of tweets attacking Stabenow as an "automatic far left vote" and a "Schumer Puppet." While James at times tried to put some distance between himself and Trump—who had a favorability rating of 37 percent statewide in a September Detroit News poll—he asked the president on Fox News to visit the state to campaign for him a week before the election.

Trump, who had taken Michigan by less than half a percentage point in 2016, didn't visit; on Election Day, Stabenow won 52%-46%. She captured only 15 of 83 counties, less than a quarter of the number she had captured six years earlier. Two years later, James made another Senate bid, this time against Stabenow's junior colleague, Gary Peters, in 2020. He lost again.

Gary Peters (D)

Elected 2014, term expires 2026, 2nd term, b. Dec 01, 1958; Pontiac, MI; Alma College, B.A., 1980; University of Detroit, M.B.A., 1984; Wayne State University Law School, J.D., 1989; MI State University, M.A., 2007; Episcopalian; Married (Colleen Ochoa); 3 children.

Military Career: U.S. Navy Reserve 1993-2000 (Iraq); 2001-2005

Elected Office: Rochester Hills City Council, 1991-1993; MI Senate, 1995-2002; U.S. House, 2009-2015.

Professional Career: Assistant VP, Merrill Lynch, 1980-1989; VP, UBS/Paine Webber, 1989-2003; CAO, MI bureau of investments, 2003; Commissioner, MI Lottery Bureau, 2003-2007; Professor, Central MI University, 2007-2008.

DC Office: 724 HSOB 20510, 202-224-6221, Fax: 202-224-7387, peters.senate.gov
State Offices: Detroit, 313-226-6020; Grand Rapids, 616-233-9150; Lansing, 517-377-1508; Marquette, 906-226-4554; Rochester, 248-608-8040; Saginaw, 989-754-0112; Traverse City, 231-947-7773.

Committees: Senate Democratic Senatorial Campaign Committee Chairman. *Armed Services*: Airland; Emerging Threats & Capabilities; Seapower. *Commerce, Science & Transportation*: Communications, Media & Broadband; Oceans, Fisheries, Climate Change & Manufacturing; Space & Science; Surface Transportation, Maritime Freight & Ports (Chmn). *Homeland Security & Government Affairs (Chmn)*: Ex Officio membership on all subcommittees.

Group Ratings

	ADA	ACLU	AFL-CIO	LCV	COC	HAFA	ACU	CFG	FRC
2020	-	85%	-	92%	-	0%	7%	-	-
2019	95%	C	100%	100%	51%	C	7%	0%	0%

Almanac Ratings 2019-2020

	Economy	Social	Foreign	Composite
Liberal	94%	94%	80%	89%
Conservative	6%	6%	20%	11%

Key Votes of the 116th Congress

1. EPA clean energy rules Y	5. Russia sanctions Y	9. Barr as Atty. General N
2. U.S./Mex./Can. trade deal Y	6. Troops in SYR, AFG Y	10. Spending at the border Y
3. Cut unemployment benefits N	7. Veto arms sales to Saudis Y	11. Coney Barrett to Sup. Ct. N
4. Shelton to Fed Reserve N	8. Defense $$$, veto override Y	12. Electoral College objections N

Election Results

Election	Name (Party)	Vote (%)	Cand. Spent	Ind. Exp. Support	Ind. Exp. Oppose
2020 General	Gary Peters (D)............................ 2,734,568	(50%)	$50,133,724	$11,594,807	$39,519,254
	John James (R).............................. 2,642,233	(48%)	$45,920,045	$6,714,627	$38,057,408
2020 Primary	Gary Peters (D)............................. 1,180,780	(100%)			

Prior winning percentages: 2014 (55%), House: 2012 (82%), 2010 (50%), 2008 (52%)

Throughout his first term, Michigan's low-key junior senator, Democrat Gary Peters, was among the least visible members of his caucus. That was poised to change when Peters returned to Capitol Hill after a grueling 2020 battle to win reelection in a once-blue state now shaded purple. Democrats' new Senate majority elevated Peters to chairman of the Homeland Security and Governmental Affairs Committee, on which he had served two years as ranking Democrat. Meanwhile, Peters was named to head the Democratic Senatorial Campaign Committee for the 2021-2022 cycle— handing him the challenge of protecting and expanding Democrats' narrow majority during an off-year election, in which the party in power historically faces difficult odds.

Peters has been winning elections for three decades— including three tough House races before moving to the Senate. "He's battle tested and he's a workhorse," former Michigan Gov. James Blanchard told CBS News after Peters was named to the DSCC post. " The Democrats are lucky to get him to do it." Nonetheless, Peters was an unusual choice in several respects. He is known neither as a seasoned political strategist nor as a relentless fundraiser; in fact, was he outraised during the first half of 2020 by his Republican challenger, John James, before eking out victory. The Detroit Free Press said Peters " carries himself like a college professor … who is more likely to be heard describing the intricate details of policy in a committee hearing than engaging in political bombast."

Although he travels around the Wolverine State on a Harley-Davidson Dyna Super Glide, Peters is often referred to as wonkish. He has earned degrees from four colleges and universities in Michigan, and, in the Senate, he often has focused on issues that can be described only as, well, wonkish. In short, it's not the type of stuff that captures a lot of headlines either in Washington or at home: In January 2019, a poll conducted by a Michigan-based survey firm found 36 percent of likely voters had never heard of him four years into his first term. " Many in Washington probably couldn't even pick him out of a lineup," Politico wrote in a story published a year earlier. During the 2020 campaign, James regularly derided Peters as an "invisible" senator, declaring at one rally, "Nobody knows him."

Peters' supporters say his effectiveness has been unfairly assessed, pointing to the May 2020 "Bipartisan Index" published by Georgetown University's Lugar Center, which ranked him as the third most bipartisan Senate Democrat. "In this session of Congress, I have passed more legislation through the U.S. Senate than any other senator, either Democratic or Republican," Peters boasted to MLive.com. According to GovTrack.us, 10 freestanding bills sponsored by Peters became law in 2019 and 2020. By and large, they were narrow measures tweaking the operations of federal agencies and programs, while sometimes touching on issues literally out of this world— such as the Promoting Research and Observations of Space Weather to Improve the Forecasting of Tomorrow Act. With Detroit-based General Motors staking its future on electric vehicles, Peters won passage of the Charging Helps Agencies Realize General Efficiencies Act to clarify that federal agencies could use charge cards for such vehicles at commercial charging stations.

As chair of the Homeland Security panel, Peters faced more immediate, higher-profile matters: After supporters of then-President Donald Trump stormed the Capitol in January 2021, Peters vowed to probe security and intelligence failures. " We have very broad jurisdiction to investigate anything that the federal government touches, and we're going to need to have that kind of comprehensive investigation," Peters told the Detroit News. He indicated other committee priorities would include oversight of the government's response to the COVID-19 pandemic, as well as cybersecurity in the wake of Russian attacks on computer networks of the federal government and private firms.

Peters' family roots in suburban Oakland County go back five generations. He grew up in Pontiac, the son of a public-school teacher and a nursing home aide. After graduating from Alma College in central Michigan, he spent more than two decades working as a financial adviser for investment firms. During that time, he earned an MBA from the University of Detroit Mercy and a law degree from Wayne State University in Detroit. Peters enlisted in the U.S. Navy Reserve, becoming a lieutenant commander and serving in the Persian Gulf as part of the operation enforcing a no-fly zone after the 1991 Gulf War. He left the Navy Reserve in 2000, but reenlisted after 9/11 and served for another four years. He serves on the Senate Armed Services Committee.

His political career began with his 1991 election to the Rochester Hills City Council; he followed that by winning a Michigan state Senate seat in 1994. There, he led an effort to ban oil drilling in the Great Lakes. Forced out of the Legislature by term limits, Peters mounted a short-lived 2002 candidacy for governor before running for state attorney general. He lost that race—his only electoral defeat— by just 5,200 votes. He spent nearly five years as the state's lottery commissioner, earning another degree on the side at Michigan State University—a master's in philosophy with a focus on the ethics of development. In 2008, Peters challenged veteran Republican Rep. Joe Knollenberg, winning with 52 percent of the vote.

Peters has described himself as a centrist who is pro-business and socially liberal; Almanac vote rankings put him in the middle of the Senate Democratic Caucus. In the House— and later in the Senate— Peters backed his party on most major votes but showed occasional independence. In his first House term, he was put on the 2010 conference committee that drafted the final version of the Dodd-Frank financial reform law. In 2018, Peters split from a majority of Senate Democrats to support Republican-sponsored legislation—signed by Trump—to roll back some provisions of Dodd-Frank. He and the 16 other Democratic supporters of the measure took heat from the party's progressive wing. As key reasons for his vote, Peters cited the regulatory relief that the bill provided to credit unions and to a provision he had attached making it easier for young workers who had defaulted on student loans to work out restructured payment plans and repair negative credit reports.

After Peters won reelection 50%-47% in 2010, a tough year for Democrats nationally, Michigan lost a congressional seat during reapportionment. The new map carved up Peters' district, confronting him with a tough choice in 2012: challenge longtime Democratic Rep. Sander Levin in another Detroit suburban district or go up against freshman Democratic Rep. Hansen Clarke, an African American, in a majority-Black district. Peters had ties to the latter district from his state Senate days, and he won the primary and general elections easily.

Peters benefited from political serendipity in 2014: In a year in which little went wrong for Senate Republicans in most battleground races, little went right for them in Michigan. Six-term Sen. Carl Levin announced his retirement in March 2013, and Peters had the Democratic nomination locked up in weeks. When the eventual Republican nominee, former Michigan Secretary of State Terri Lynn Land, announced in late spring, her candidacy was met with a lack of enthusiasm among party leaders, who had spent months trying to recruit another candidate.

While emphasizing job creation and other middle-class concerns, Peters was aided by a humorous TV campaign spot seeking to highlight his everyman persona. "I wouldn't call him cheap, but our washing machine is older than the kids," his wife, Colleen Ochoa Peters, said during the 30-second spot. "It still works," he responds, as his daughter holds up a ragged sweatshirt and shoes with holes he wore frequently. The ad ends with Gary Peters, sporting the worn attire, saying, "I approved this message because my family did this ad for free." In contrast, Land launched her TV effort with what may have been the oddest ad of the 2014 election cycle. In it, she declared: " Congressman Gary Peters and his buddies want you to believe I'm waging a war on women. Really? Think about that for a moment." In the rest of the 12 seconds of the ad, Land silently sips coffee, shakes her head and looks at her watch. Peters won 55%-41%, becoming the sole Democrat to capture an open Senate seat in 2014.

When President Barack Obama appeared at a Detroit rally for Peters three days before Election Day, Peters stressed the president's bailout of the auto industry several years earlier. A little more than two years later, on his final day in office, Obama left Peters with a farewell present: He designated the site of a former General Motors plant in Ypsilanti as a proving ground for driverless cars, 1 of 10 such sites in the nation. Peters, one of the project's leading advocates, was elated, declaring, " We cannot lose being at the center of this activity for the auto industry."

Peters has persisted on this issue— arguing not just Michigan's economy but also Americas leadership in technology is at stake. In 2018, on the Commerce, Science and Transportation Committee, he teamed with Republican Sen. John Thune, then the panel's chair, on a bill establishing federal standards for self-driving cars. The measure gradually waived traditional standards, such as steering wheels and brake pedals, for up to 80,000 vehicles per manufacturer. But several Democrats, citing safety concerns, objected to action by the Senate, and the bill stalled. With automakers contending that existing standards assuming a human driver have hindered the rollout of self-driving vehicles, Peters in late 2020 expressed hope that President Joe Biden—with his commitment to electric vehicles and clean energy— could break the legislative logjam. " It is the future of the auto industry. We face significant competition from Asian and European companies and manufacturers," Peters told a panel discussion. "We have to make sure we win this race."

On the Homeland Security Committee in 2019-20, Peters was opposite the panel's chair, Wisconsin Republican Ron Johnson— a fervent Trump defender with whom Peters had a scratchy relationship. During a hearing after the 2020 elections on Trump's baseless claims of widespread voter fraud, a shouting match erupted when Johnson accused Peters of lying on an unrelated matter. In turn, Peters charged Johnson with providing a platform for "conspiracy theories and lies," declaring, "Giving them more oxygen is a grave threat to the future of our democracy." When Peters assumed the chairmanship, internal GOP term limits made Ohio Sen. Rob Portman   the ranking member. Peters, saying he had a good working relationship with Portman, told the Detroit News he aimed to restore the panel's "bipartisan and nonpartisan record." He added: " That was strained in the last few months under Chairman Johnson. ... We're going to return the focus of the committee back to where it needs to be, which is making sure the homeland is secure."

In early 2018, Detroit Mayor Mike Duggan and several union leaders led a quiet effort to coax Peters to run for governor. Their move was prompted by concern over the prospects of the leading Democratic contender, Gretchen Whitmer. Peters declined to run for the job, which Whitmer went on to win. The same year, Peters' Senate colleague, Democrat Debbie Stabenow, was reelected by a narrower-than-anticipated 6.5-point margin over James— a Black Iraq War veteran who ran a warehouse and logistics business that his father started in suburban Detroit after leaving segregated Mississippi in the 1960s. In June 2019, James announced he would make another Senate bid.

Peters and James won their primaries unopposed. Heading into the fall, Peters was one of only two Democratic senators running in states that Trump had won in 2016. By October, Peters' lead was down to single digits in what had become one of the nation's nastiest races; two surveys less than a month before Election Day showed his edge over James within the polls' margin of error. James, a 39-year-old West Point graduate, was a compelling stump speaker, and his aggressive fundraising helped finance a barrage of ads hammering Peters as an ineffective career politician. In Washington, Democratic strategists grew nervous about a potential upset costing them the Senate majority, while in Michigan, some Democrats were openly critical of the Peters campaign. "What he hasn't done for the last six years is be visible and personable," Ed Sarpolus, a longtime Democratic pollster and consultant, told the New York Times. Referring to Peters' effective "washing machine" ad of six years earlier, Sarpolus asked: "What happened to his family in his ads? You've got to tell your story, but he's not shown any of that this year."

But James came under increasing scrutiny and criticism as he sought to thread the needle on demonstrating independence from Trump without offending him or his base. While calling for repeal and replacement of the Affordable Care Act, James said he opposed any insurance plan that did not include one of the underpinnings of "Obamacare"— coverage of preexisting conditions. Peters' campaign ads accused James of trying to have it both ways, as James sidestepped questions about the Trump administration's efforts to persuade the Supreme Court to rule Obamacare unconstitutional. The emergence of the Black Lives Matter movement proved to be particular challenge for James. "I didn't see the George Floyd video— I felt it," James told the Times, recalling his emotions watching footage of a Black man die as a white Minneapolis police officer pressed his knee on his neck. "We don't have enough people making decisions who feel the consequences of their actions." But James avoided offering any criticism of Trump, who had defended white supremacists while spreading racist content via social media.

On Election Day, exit polls showed Peters capturing 90 percent of the Black vote to narrowly win a second term, 49.9%-48.2%. With a margin of 92,000 votes, he ran behind Biden, who captured Michigan by about 155,000 votes. The Associated Press called the contest for Peters a day after the polls closed, but James refused to concede until the results were certified by the Board of State Canvassers three weeks later. Following Trump's lead, James repeatedly questioned how the vote count had been handled in Democratic-dominated Wayne County—metropolitan Detroit— without offering any evidence of wrongdoing. According to the Center for Responsive Politics, the contest was the eighth most expensive Senate race ever. After initially trailing James in fundraising, Peters overtook the challenger— $50.1 million to $45.9 million. In addition, more than $96.6 million was spent by independent expenditure groups. About $34.7 million of this came from the Senate Majority PAC, a super PAC with close ties to the Senate Democratic leadership.

The month before Election Day, Peters gained national attention when he discussed with Elle magazine his first wife's life-saving abortion in the 1980s—becoming the first sitting senator to go public about a personal experience with the procedure. His then-wife, Heidi, was four months pregnant when her water broke, leaving the baby with no chance of survival. But the hospital to which she had gone refused to allow an abortion, and she and Peters were told to go home and wait for a miscarriage. But her health deteriorated, and she was warned she could die of a uterine infection — at which point the couple found a hospital that agreed to perform the abortion. Peters said he went public because Trump had nominated federal Judge Amy Coney Barrett, who had ruled against abortion rights in lower court decisions, to the Supreme Court. But it also came amid his close race against James, a hard-line abortion opponent who in 2018 had compared the procedure to genocide. Peters told Elle: "It's important for folks to understand that these things happen to folks every day. I've always considered myself pro-choice and believe women should be able to make these decisions themselves, but when you live it in real life, you realize the significant impact it can have on a family."

John Bergman (R)

Elected 2016, 3rd term, b. Feb 02, 1947; Shakopee, MN; Gustavus Adolphus College; University of West FL, M.B.A., 1975; Lutheran; Married (Cindy Bergman); 5 children; 8 grandchildren.

Military Career: U.S. Marine Corps 1969-1975; RI National Guard 1975-1978; U.S. Marine Corps Reserve 1978-2003; U.S. Marine Corps 2003-2009 (Vietnam)

Professional Career: Commercial pilot; Business owner.

DC Office: 414 CHOB 20515, 202-225-4735, Fax: 202-225-4710, bergman.house.gov

State Offices: Marquette, 906-273-2227; Traverse City, 231-944-7633.

Committees: *Armed Services*: Readiness; Seapower & Projection Forces. *Veterans' Affairs*: Health (RMM); Oversight & Investigations; Women Veterans Task Force.

Group Ratings

	ADA	ACLU	AFL-CIO	LCV	COC	HAFA	ACU	CFG	FRC
2020	**	12%	**	14%	-	77%	76%	**	-
2019	5%	C	45%	17%	94%	C	76%	66%	100%

Almanac Ratings 2019-2020

	Economy	Social	Foreign	Composite
Liberal	41%	17%	5%	21%
Conservative	59%	83%	95%	79%

Key Votes of the 116th Congress

1. U.S./Mex./Can. trade deal Y	5. Russia sanctions Y	9. Firearms background checks N
2. First Coronavirus response Y	6. Troops in Syria N	10. Spending at the border Y
3. HEROES Act N	7. Veto arms sales to Saudis N	11. Marijuana liberalized rules N
4. CASH Act Y	8. Defense $$$, veto override Y	12. Electoral College objections Y

Election Results

Election	Name (Party)	Vote (%)		Cand. Spent	Ind. Exp. Support	Ind. Exp. Oppose
2020 General	John Bergman (R)................................	256,581	(62%)	$1,649,264	$87,481	
	Dana Ferguson (D)............................	153,328	(37%)	$293,416	$10	
2020 Primary	Jack Bergman (R)............................	100,716	(100%)			

Prior winning percentages: 2018 (56%), 2016 (55%)

Republican Jack Bergman, first elected in 2016, has become entrenched after twice winning by double-digit margins against well-financed opponents in what Democrats had considered an opportunity. A retired three-star Marine Corps lieutenant general, Bergman benefited from his party label in what recently had been a swing district. He helped to resolve a longstanding local issue.

A native of Minnesota, Bergman said his ancestors worked in the iron mines of the Upper Peninsula as far back as the 1800s. He got his bachelor's from Gustavus Adolphus College in St. Peter Minnesota, and an MBA from the University of West Florida. During more than 25 years in the military, he served as commanding general of the Marine Forces Reserve in Louisiana. He retired as a lieutenant general in 2009. Bergman also was a pilot for Northwest Airlines and built a business that sold surgical equipment. Although he had no previous experience as a political candidate, he had served on the advisory council for Louisiana Republican Gov. Bobby Jindal. He resided in Waters meet, a small town in the Ottawa National Forest, at the far western end of the U.P. He ran for a seat in the Michigan state House in 2012, but narrowly lost in the Republican primary.

When Republican Rep. Dan Benishek retired in 2016, Bergman ran as the outsider candidate in the Republican primary against two local political figures: state Sen. Tom Casperson from the U.P., who was a vocal advocate of more wolf hunting, and former state Sen. Jason Allen of Traverse City, who had been an official of the Michigan Veterans Affairs Agency. Bergman benefited from spending more than $270,000 of his own money in the primary campaign. He won with 39 percent of the vote to 32 percent for Casperson and 29 percent for Allen. Lon Johnson, who had chaired the Michigan Democratic Party, easily won the Democratic nomination.

The general election was well-financed, with each nominee getting more than $2 million of support from national party groups. Johnson emphasized his status as a political outsider against party official Johnson, whose wife Julianna Smoot was national deputy campaign manager for President Barack Obama in 2012. With neither candidate especially well-known in this sprawling district, the unexpectedly large 22-point victory for Donald Trump in the presidential contest likely provided coattails for Bergman. He took the House contest, 55%-40%.

In the House, Bergman made progress on a local priority by including authorization to replace the 50-year-old lock at Sault Ste. Marie among the water projects that Congress approved in October 2018. Bergman called the new lock the number-one issue of his first term. The start of construction was announced, not coincidentally, one month before the 2020 election.

On the Veterans' Affairs Committee, Bergman was a leading proponent of a bill to expedite medical coverage for veterans from private doctors and hospitals; Trump signed in 2018 this overhaul of the Veterans Choice Program. In addition to serving as the ranking Republican on the Oversight and Investigations Subcommittee of the veterans' panel, he has a seat on the Armed Services Committee —appropriate, he said, for the highest-ranking combat veteran ever elected to Congress. He urged Selfridge Air Force Base, which is not far from Detroit, as a home for new F-35 fighter jets.

In 2018, Bergman faced Democratic challenger Matt Morgan, who became the nominee by securing more than 30,000 write-in votes in the August primary after he had been denied ballot access because of a filing problem. Morgan, who styled himself as a progressive Marine veteran, had campaign help from filmmaker Michael Moore, a progressive icon in Michigan. Morgan, who complained that he received scant support from national Democrats, called for expanded Medicare coverage and repeal of the 2001 authorization for the use of military force as a justification for continued military engagements. Each candidate spent about $1.4 million. Bergman won, 56%-44%, and took all but two of the 32 counties.

The Detroit News endorsed Bergman for reelection in 2020, citing his bipartisan accomplishments—notably, the funding of the Soo Locks—and his "welcome voice of reason and responsibility." He easily won his third term against a lightly funded challenger.

MI-1: Northern Michigan

Cook Partisan Voting Index: R+12

Population		Race and Ethnicity		Income	
Total	697,102	White	92.20%	Median Income	$51,553
Land area (sq. miles)	4,140	Black	1.40%	District Income Rank	372
Pop/ sq mi	168.36	Latino	1.90%	Poverty Rate	11.70%
Born in State	78.10%	Asian	0.70%	With health insurance	93.30%
		Two or more races	2.70%	Cash public assistance	2.50%
Age Groups		Other	3.00%	Food stamp/SNAP	10.40%
Under 18	18.20%				
18-34	19.10%	**Education**		**Work**	
35-64	38.50%	H.S grad or less	39.90%	White Collar	32.80%
Over 64	24.20%	Some college	33.90%	Sales and Service	40.70%
Military		College Degree, 4 yr	16.60%	Blue Collar	26.50%
Veteran/ Active Duty	9.80%	Post grad	9.60%	Government	14.50%

2020 Pres. Vote	Trump	244,489	(58%)	Biden	171,370	(41%)		
2016 Pres. Vote	Trump	210,816	(58%)	Clinton	133,239	(36%)	Johnson	13,785 (4%)

Upper Peninsula: Michigan's Upper Peninsula, commonly known as the U.P., is a land apart. Surrounded on three sides by frigid Lakes Superior, Huron and Michigan, there are places here that have some of the coldest climates in settled parts of North America. These storms can be cruel. The "gales of November" have caught hundreds of vessels by surprise and sent them to the bottom of the lake, including the SS Edmund Fitzgerald, whose loss was memorialized in a Gordon Lightfoot ballad.

With ground too frozen and stony and a growing season too short for most crops, the peninsula was considered a poor consolation prize when much of it was appended to the Michigan Territory in 1836 in exchange for the incipient state giving up its claim to Toledo and its surrounding areas. The mineral veins of the Keweenaw Peninsula eventually produced more than 13 billion pounds of copper, while the Marquette, Menominee and Gogebic iron ranges produced more than 1 billion tons of iron ore. Immigrants flocked here to work the mines. Pluralities of residents were Finns, who must have found this cold land with its lakes and hills much like home. By the early 1900s, the U.P. had become a northern industrial belt with a workforce disposed to radical ideas and union movements.

A major strike in 1913-14 and falling ore prices after World War I accelerated the copper decline. Other industries have taken root. The region's natural beauty—90 percent of the U.P. is forested—has made tourism a leading economic driver in all seasons. Skiers can take advantage of the average 200 inches of annual snowfall at several mountain resorts. In summer, there are abundant outdoor opportunities, including mountain biking and surfing. Population of the U.P. peaked at 332,000 in 1920. In 2016, there were 311,000 "Yoopers," as the locals call themselves, many of whom harbor a strong sense of place. From 2010 to 2016, 14 of the 15 counties lost population. During a local political rally in 2018, President Donald Trump endorsed the proposed 1,200-foot Soo Locks Modernization Project in the St. Lawrence Seaway. "The Soo Locks are going to hell," he said. "And we're going to get them fixed up." In September 2020, the Army Corps of Engineers signed a $110 million contract to reinforce the walls and deepen the channel of the locks, with completion scheduled for 2023.

The 1st Congressional District of Michigan includes the Upper Peninsula and 16 1/2 northern counties in the Lower Peninsula. Almost half the people live in the U.P. Marquette, with 20,800 people, is the largest city in the district. Mackinac Island, home to a resort area where almost all cars are banned, lies just east of the breathtaking Mackinac Bridge, which connects the two peninsulas. (Even UPS delivers packages by bicycle, though the October 2019 visit by Vice President Mike Pence included a motorcade of eight vehicles.) On the Lower Peninsula, along Lake Michigan, are affluent resort areas around Petoskey and Charlevoix, long summer places for people from Chicago (this is Ernest Hemingway's "Up in Michigan"). At the start of the pandemic in early 2020, the locals were not as welcoming as usual of the city folks, largely due to fear that they were carrying the coronavirus —though it was a booming year for local real estate. The Traverse City area accounts for more than 70 percent of tart cherry production in the United States and the weeklong cherry festival attracts hundreds of thousands of visitors each summer.

Politically, the U.P. has a lengthy Democratic tradition, but it has moved toward Republicans in recent years. When Trump twice took the mostly blue-collar and low-income district—58%-41%, in 2020—it became clear that the partisan shifts were deep-seated. Marquette is the only remaining Democratic county in the 1st.

Bill Huizenga (R)

Elected 2010, 6th term, b. Jan 31, 1969; Zeeland, MI; Calvin College, B.A., 1991; Christian Reformed Church; Married (Natalie Huizenga); 5 children.

Elected Office: MI House, 2003-2008.

Professional Career: Realtor, 1991-1996; Aide, Rep. Pete Hoekstra, 1997-2002; Admin., Zeeland Christian Schls., 2009-2010; Co-owner, Huizenga Gravel, 1999-present.

DC Office: 2232 RHOB 20515, 202-225-4401, Fax: 202-226-0779, huizenga.house.gov

State Offices: Grand Haven, 616-414-5516; Grandville, 616-570-0917.

Committees: *Financial Services*: Housing, Community Development & Insurance; Investor Protection, Entrepreneurship & Capital Markets (RMM).

Group Ratings

	ADA	ACLU	AFL-CIO	LCV	COC	HAFA	ACU	CFG	FRC
2020	**	17%	**	29%	-	91%	89%	**	-
2019	10%	C	29%	0%	81%	C	90%	90%	100%

Almanac Ratings 2019-2020

	Economy	Social	Foreign	Composite
Liberal	41%	26%	27%	32%
Conservative	59%	74%	73%	68%

Key Votes of the 116th Congress

1. U.S./Mex./Can. trade deal Y	5. Russia sanctions Y	9. Firearms background checks N
2. First Coronavirus response Y	6. Troops in Syria Y	10. Spending at the border Y
3. HEROES Act N	7. Veto arms sales to Saudis N	11. Marijuana liberalized rules N
4. CASH Act N	8. Defense $$$, veto override Y	12. Electoral College objections N

Election Results

Election	Name (Party)	Vote (%)		Cand. Spent	Ind. Exp. Support	Ind. Exp. Oppose
2020 General	Bill Huizenga (R)	238,711	(59%)	$1,900,444	$6,610	
	Bryan Berghoef (D)	154,122	(38%)	$449,076	$19	
2020 Primary	Bill Huizenga (R)	88,258	(100%)			

Prior winning percentages: 2018 (55%), 2016 (63%), 2014 (64%), 2012 (61%), 2010 (65%)

Republican Bill Huizenga, elected in 2010, has upheld the rock-solid conservatism of his western Michigan district. When Republicans controlled the House, he was a key player in the overhaul of federal regulation of banks and other financial service firms. He failed in a bid to become the top Republican on the Financial Services Committee.

Huizenga grew up in Zeeland. His grandparents were farmers who started a gravel business by selling the leftover sand and stone that was lying around the farm. In high school, Huizenga was an inattentive student who ultimately transferred to vocational school. His instructors told him he had academic potential and advised him to go to college. Between his freshman and sophomore years, he made his first real estate investment: With money saved from working in his father's gravel pit, he became the junior stakeholder in a 19-unit housing development.

After college, he worked for a local real estate firm and took over as co-owner in the family business, Huizenga Gravel. As a business owner, he says, he gained a firm understanding of the regulatory, tax and compliance issues that small businesses face. His friend, Republican Rep. Pete Hoekstra, offered him a job in his district office. After serving as Hoekstra's director of public policy, Huizenga won a seat in the Michigan House, where he was chairman of the Commerce Committee.

When Hoekstra ran unsuccessfully for Michigan governor, the real contest for his heavily Republican district was the GOP primary. In the seven-way race, Huizenga touted his conservative credentials, including his support for replacing the income tax with a 23 percent sales tax and creating private Social Security accounts. Jay Riemersma, also of Zeeland, the former regional director for the Family Research Council, ran as an anti-abortion and fiscal conservative. He attacked Huizenga for voting for a state business tax in 2007. Huizenga eked out a victory with a better campaign organization, built largely on the many contacts he made with local political and business leaders. He prevailed by just 663 votes out of about 106,000 cast. In the general election, he faced nominal Democratic opposition.

Huizenga enacted a bill in 2012 giving taxpayers and businesses who submit information to the Consumer Financial Protection Bureau the same confidentiality protection that other financial regulators are required to provide. For two years, Huizenga chaired the Financial Services Subcommittee on Monetary Policy and Trade, where he used his oversight of the Federal Reserve Board to promote more transparent discussion of monetary policy. In 2015, the House passed his Mortgage Choice Act, which he said was designed to remove "technicalities" in qualification requirements for lower and middle-income homeowners. With other House conservatives, he questioned the organization of the Export-Import Bank and prevented it from conducting business for several months. With strong support for the bank in the business community, Huizenga and its other opponents ultimately lost their battle.

In 2017-18, Huizenga chaired the Capital Markets, Securities and Investment Subcommittee, where he spearheaded several House-passed bills during those two years to loosen the Dodd-Frank regimen of financial regulation, though he voiced disappointment that the House mostly deferred to the more limited Senate-passed versions. In February 2017, he enacted his bill that repealed regulations by the Securities and Exchange Commission that required mining and oil and gas companies to disclose payments they make to foreign governments.

Huizenga did not always agree with President Donald Trump. He opposed splitting immigrant families at the border with Mexico and joined Democrats at a press conference to describe his objections, including the denial of his attempt to visit a detention center in western Michigan. In 2018, he said Trump's tariffs on steel and aluminum failed to achieve "the desired outcome" and that imports did not pose the claimed risk to the United States. Early that year, he took issue with Trump's proposal for deep cuts in the Great Lakes Restoration Initiative and said that Congress ultimately would decide on that funding.

Huizenga, who had consistently won reelection with more than 60 percent of the vote, was held to a 55%-43% reelection in 2018 by Democratic challenger Rob Davidson, an emergency-room doctor who favored "Medicare for all" and objected to Huizenga's vote to repeal the Affordable Care Act. Huizenga outspent Davidson, $2.2 million to $1.3 million. Davidson took 53 percent of the vote in Muskegon and the vote was virtually even in Kent. Huizenga took 62 percent and led by 32,000 votes in Ottawa, the largest county, which accounted for nearly his entire victory margin.

The House Ethics Committee announced in November 2019 that it was investigating possible campaign finance violations by Huizenga. The panel had no additional details during the next year. In May 2020, Democratic challenger Bryan Berghoef, a pastor of the Holland United Church of Christ, criticized the incumbent's support for Trump. Referring to the ethics investigation, he wrote that voters deserved "someone who will fight for a political system that's less centered on big money and more focused on people." Huizenga won more routinely, 59%-38%.

Following the 2018 election, Huizenga competed for the open Republican position atop the Financial Services Committee. He was defeated by Rep. Patrick McHenry of North Carolina, who had more seniority plus experience in GOP leadership. Huizenga retained the top GOP slot on the renamed Investor Protection, Entrepreneurship and Capital Markets Subcommittee. He likely will have other opportunities to assert his influence.

MI-2: West-Central Michigan

Cook Partisan Voting Index: R+9

Population		Race and Ethnicity		Income	
Total	746,998	White	84.80%	Median Income	$59,356
Land area (sq. miles)	3,281	Black	6.20%	District Income Rank	277
Pop/ sq mi	227.66	Latino	9.60%	Poverty Rate	10.50%
Born in State	78.70%	Asian	2.30%	With health insurance	94.80%
		Two or more races	3.50%	Cash public assistance	1.80%
Age Groups		Other	3.20%	Food stamp/SNAP	9.70%
Under 18	23.30%				
18-34	23.60%	**Education**		**Work**	
35-64	36.50%	H.S grad or less	39.50%	White Collar	32.80%
Over 64	16.50%	Some college	33.00%	Sales and Service	36.90%
		College Degree, 4 yr	18.70%	Blue Collar	30.30%
Military		Post grad	8.80%	Government	8.70%
Veteran/ Active Duty	7.00%				

2020 Pres. Vote	Trump	225,382	(55%)	Biden	177,070	(43%)			
2016 Pres. Vote	Trump	193,201	(55%)	Clinton	132,467	(38%)	Johnson	15,127	(4%)

Holland, Muskegon: When the glaciers receded from Michigan some 16,000 years ago, they left behind piles of boulders, sand and clay. Over time, the lake winds eroded the boulders, while waves ground up glacial drift deposited in the lake and washed it ashore. The end result is a lakeshore that today is home to the largest collection of freshwater dunes in the world, located in several parks along the western rim of the state.

In the late 19th century, the river ports on this shoreline were choked with logs and full of lumbermen from Norway and Sweden, Ireland and Scotland, Quebec and New England. During the timber boom, the shoreline was the locus of the country's largest migration from the Netherlands and today still has the nation's largest concentration of Dutch Americans. Although wooden shoes are now seen only at the Tulip Festival in the town of Holland, conscientious Dutch work habits have produced many highly skilled workers. This is a busy manufacturing area, with products ranging from baby food at Gerber in Fremont to office furniture at Herman Miller in Zeeland and Haworth in Holland. In 2018, like 2017, Wallet Hub cited Holland as the best small city in America to start a small business, based on factors such as local costs and services. Away from the shore is fruit-growing country, with some of the nation's largest cherry orchards to the north and blueberry patches to the south. Since 2014, blueberry production has slowed, due to high costs.

The 2nd Congressional District of Michigan occupies four counties on the Lake Michigan shoreline, plus a tier of inland counties. It stretches from the old lumber port of Ludington south to Holland. About a fifth of the district's residents live in an arc of suburbs surrounding Grand Rapids in western Kent County. The economy in western Michigan has diversified and has had the strongest growth in the state. Holland-based Ottawa, the most populous county in the district, grew 28 percent from 2000 to 2019. The more industrial Muskegon grew only 2 percent during that period. In 2017, Muskegon showed hopes of a business renaissance, which local leaders described as a "post-industrial revival," led by young entrepreneurs who welcome the relatively cheap land and lower labor costs.

For years, the socially conservative Dutch-American voters have been strongly Republican and fast-growing. The chief exception to Republican voting patterns comes from the old industrial centers in Muskegon County. In 2008 and 2012, the 2nd was the most Republican district in the state. President Donald Trump's lead of 55%-43% in 2020 ranked only fifth highest. The largest factor has been the shift toward Democrats in the suburbs of Grand Rapids. Muskegon, by contrast, has been shifting to Republicans.

Peter Meijer (R)

Elected 2020, 1st term, b. Jan 10, 1988; Grand Rapids, MI; U.S. Military Academy; University of the District of Columbia, B.A., 2012; NY University, M.B.A., 2017; Christian Church; Married (Gabriella Meijer).

Military Career: U.S. Army Reserves, 2008-2016; Advisor/Sergeant, U.S. Army, 2010-2011 (Iraq).

Professional Career: Regional Safety Advisor/Acting Deputy Director, International NGO Safety Organization, 2013-2015; Analyst, Olympia Development of Michigan.

DC Office: 1508 LHOB 20515, 202-225-3831, Fax: 202-225-5144, meijer.house.gov

State Offices: Grand Rapids, 616-451-8383.

Committees: *Foreign Affairs*: Europe, Energy, the Environment & Cyber. *Homeland Security*: Intelligence & Counterterrorism; Oversight, Management & Accountability (RMM). *Science, Space & Technology*: Energy; Research & Technology.

Election Results

Election	Name (Party)	Vote (%)		Cand. Spent	Ind. Exp. Support	Ind. Exp. Oppose
2020 General	Peter Meijer (R)	213,649	(53%)	$3,204,199	$519,137	$3,435,615
	Hillary Scholten (D)	189,769	(47%)	$3,805,661	$15,879	$2,725,407
2020 Primary	Peter Meijer (R)	47,273	(50%)			
	Lynn Afendoulis (R)	24,579	(26%)			
	Tom Norton (R)	14,913	(16%)			

Peter Meijer retained Republican control of a district that had been a GOP stronghold but has grown increasingly competitive. Meijer, an heir to a wealthy Grand Rapids family that owned a supermarket business with more than 200 locations in the Midwest, served with the military in Iraq and worked with international-relief organizations before entering his first political campaign. In a district where national Democrats sought to exploit suburban unhappiness with President Donald Trump, Meijer defeated Democrat Hillary Scholten, another Grand Rapids native, who had worked on immigration issues in Washington for the Obama administration.

Meijer replaced Rep. Justin Amash, a free-spirit conservative whose five-term career became rocky when he grew estranged from Trump and dropped his party affiliation in 2019 to become an independent. Amash, who voted to impeach Trump, explored a third-party bid for president but did not take serious steps to become a candidate. When he later abandoned the option to retain his House seat as an independent, that was an apparent boost for Meijer.

Meijer, a Grand Rapids native, spent a year as a student at the U.S. Military Academy before transferring to Columbia University, where he received his bachelor's degree. He later got a master's in business administration at New York University. After leaving West Point, he enlisted in the Army Reserve and served as a noncommissioned officer in Iraq, where he conducted intelligence operations. During that service, he led a mission that captured enemy forces who had killed American soldiers.

After graduating from Columbia, Meijer joined Team Rubicon, a disaster-aid organization of military veterans. Those activities included humanitarian efforts in South Sudan to assist refugees, and relief assistance following natural disasters in areas ranging from the Philippines to New York, following Superstorm Sandy in 2012. He joined an organization that assisted relief efforts in Afghanistan. On his return to Grand Rapids, he worked for a real estate company.

Given his family wealth, the Detroit News reported, "Peter Meijer never had to work a day in his life. But he did." The 30-page financial disclosure report he filed with the House included a trust fund with a value exceeding $50 million. "He has grappled with his privilege his entire life," the News added.

Meijer, who announced his House campaign after Amash split from the GOP, cited the need for recent military veterans to serve in Congress. Four other candidates entered the primary, undaunted by his self-funding plus support from national and state party leaders. His chief opponent, state Rep. Lynn Afendoulis, cited her own political experience and attacked Meijer's work with a political action committee that supported military veterans in both parties. "I'm not going to try to apologize for trying to get more veterans into office," he responded. Meijer won the primary with 50 percent of the vote, to 26 percent for Afendoulis.

Scholten, who won the Democratic nomination without opposition, had served four years as an attorney adviser for the Justice Department's Board of Immigration Appeals. When Trump took office, she returned to Grand Rapids as an attorney for the Michigan Immigrant Rights Center. She cited her lack of political experience as a benefit in working with constituents who held various viewpoints and in seeking common ground in Congress. "West Michigan is ready for change," she added.

Although both candidates called for civility, Scholten raised questions about Meijer's finances and he cited her campaign support from "Hollywood liberals" and House Speaker Nancy Pelosi. Each spent more than $3 million, with Meijer financing nearly half of his campaign account. Meijer won, 53%-47%. In Kent County, which cast two-thirds of the total vote, Scholten led by fewer than 3,000 votes. Meijer ran up double-digit leads in the four outlying counties.

In the House, Meijer got attention when he was one of 10 Republicans—and the only first-termer —who voted for the second impeachment of Trump. Meijer subsequently said he and other family members had prepared for possible threats to their personal safety. At least two Republican county organizations in his district censured his vote, though the GOP organization in Grand Rapids was split in half.

MI-3: West-Central Michigan   Cook Partisan Voting Index: R+5

Population		Race and Ethnicity		Income	
Total	752,287	White	82.80%	Median Income	$64,919
Land area (sq. miles)	2,629	Black	8.30%	District Income Rank	211
Pop/ sq mi	286.18	Latino	8.00%	Poverty Rate	12.20%
Born in State	78.50%	Asian	2.10%	With health insurance	93.70%
		Two or more races	4.40%	Cash public assistance	2.10%
Age Groups		Other	2.40%	Food stamp/SNAP	9.20%
Under 18	23.20%				
18-34	23.50%	**Education**		**Work**	
35-64	37.80%	H.S grad or less	36.10%	White Collar	36.10%
Over 64	15.40%	Some college	31.80%	Sales and Service	36.10%
		College Degree, 4 yr	20.90%	Blue Collar	27.70%
Military		Post grad	11.10%	Government	8.60%
Veteran/ Active Duty	6.30%				

2020 Pres. Vote	Trump	207,752	(51%)	Biden	194,585	(47%)	
2016 Pres. Vote	Trump	180,341	(51%)	Clinton	147,335	(42%) Johnson	15,803 (5%)

Grand Rapids Metro: Grand Rapids is Michigan's second-largest city and the center of its most prosperous metropolitan area. It grew as a center for turning the hardwood forests of northern Michigan into furniture. By the early 20th century, Grand Rapids was the leading furniture manufacturer in the nation. The Great Depression knocked the bottom out of the residential furniture market, and many manufacturers moved to North Carolina, where labor was cheaper. So Grand Rapids reinvented itself. It went into office furniture, and today three of the nation's largest office furniture manufacturers—Steelcase, Haworth and Herman Miller—are in its metropolitan area. Of the area jobs, 20 percent were in manufacturing, making it the metro area with the most manufacturing jobs in the nation in 2020.

It also capitalized on a knack for sales. Rich DeVos and Jay Van Andel started Amway, the direct sales empire, which has had about 90 percent of its sales abroad. With nearly $10 billion in revenues in 2019, Amway was the largest direct-selling company in the world for the seventh consecutive year; China has been its largest market. DeVos's son Dick later ran the business and was the unsuccessful Republican nominee for governor of Michigan in 2006. Dick's wife, Betsy DeVos, became active in state and national Republican politics and the charter-school movement before she became Education secretary for President Donald Trump. The family members have been major charitable donors and Republican contributors for decades. The Grand Rapids area has been a center for machine tools, Hush Puppies shoes, and Bissell carpet sweepers. The metropolitan area was the nation's number-one mid-sized metro market for economic growth in 2019, according to a business-data firm.

Politically, the Grand Rapids area has been the center of Michigan Republicanism for much of the past century; cultural conservatism and a belief in market economics run deep among the descendants of the pious Dutch immigrants who settled in western Michigan in the 1870s. It has also produced national Republican leaders. The conversion of Sen. Arthur Vandenberg from isolationism to internationalism during World War II provided key support for the foreign policies of Franklin D. Roosevelt and Harry Truman; he chaired the Senate Foreign Relations Committee in 1947-48. Another was Gerald Ford, who rose to House Republican leader in 1965, vice president in 1973, and then president after Richard Nixon resigned in 1974.

The 3rd Congressional District of Michigan has three distinct parts. The first is the city of Grand Rapids itself, which constitutes about 25 percent of the population and has become heavily Democratic. The second includes most of the remainder of Kent, Ionia and Barry counties, and a small portion of Montcalm County. This part of the district, which includes a majority of its residents, is heavily Republican. The third part of the district is Calhoun County, which tends to vote close to the national average and is centered on Battle Creek, where sanitarium operator W.K. Kellogg invented corn flakes as a health food. The local economy is weaker than in Grand Rapids and the school system suffers from structural inequities, according to studies. The net result is a district that has leaned Republican; President Donald Trump won 51%-47% in 2020. But those dynamics are changing. Kent County had a big shift from 48%-45% for Trump in 2016 to 52%-46% for Joe Biden in 2020.

John Moolenaar (R)

Elected 2014, 4th term, b. May 08, 1961; Midland, MI; Hope College, B.S., 1983; Harvard University, M.P.A., 1989; Christian - Non-Denominational; Married (Amy Moolenaar); 6 children.

Elected Office: Midland MI City Council, 1997-2000; MI House, 2003-2008; MI Senate, 2011-2014.

Professional Career: Chemist, Dow Chemical; Director, Middle MI Development Corporation Small Business Cntr.; School admin., Midland Academy of Advanced & Creative Studies.

DC Office: 117 CHOB 20515, 202-225-3561, Fax: 202-225-9679, moolenaar.house.gov

State Offices: Cadillac, 231-942-5070; Midland, 989-631-2552.

Committees: *Appropriations*: Agriculture, Rural Development, FDA & Related Agencies; Labor, Health & Human Services, Education & Related Agencies.

Group Ratings

	ADA	ACLU	AFL-CIO	LCV	COC	HAFA	ACU	CFG	FRC
2020	**	19%	**	19%	-	86%	76%	**	-
2019	5%	C	29%	14%	91%	C	76%	76%	100%

Almanac Ratings 2019-2020

	Economy	Social	Foreign	Composite
Liberal	38%	26%	27%	31%
Conservative	62%	74%	73%	69%

Key Votes of the 116th Congress

1. U.S./Mex./Can. trade deal	Y	5. Russia sanctions	Y
2. First Coronavirus response	Y	6. Troops in Syria	Y
3. HEROES Act	N	7. Veto arms sales to Saudis	N
4. CASH Act	N	8. Defense $$$, veto override	Y

9. Firearms background checks N
10. Spending at the border   Y
11. Marijuana liberalized rules N
12. Electoral College objections N

Election Results

Election	Name (Party)	Vote (%)		Cand. Spent	Ind. Exp. Support	Ind. Exp. Oppose
2020 General	John Moolenaar (R)	242,621	(65%)	$1,159,207	$8,852	
	Jerry Hilliard (D)	120,802	(32%)	$23,012		
2020 Primary	John Moolenaar (R)	97,653	(100%)			

Prior winning percentages: 2018 (63%), 2016 (62%), 2014 (57%)

Republican John Moolenaar was elected in 2014, with a boost from his conservative credentials and endorsements. With his seat on the Appropriations Committee, he has focused on funding for Michigan. Much of his focus has been on water: the relatively tame Great Lakes, contamination in Flint, plus the devastation of floods.

Born in Midland, Moolenaar earned his bachelor's in chemistry from Hope College in Holland Michigan. He got his master's in public administration from Harvard. He was a chemist and director of business development for MITECH+ and Dow Chemical, where he helped develop new product markets. He was an administrator at the Midland Academy of Advanced and Creative Studies. In 2002, Moolenar was elected to the state House. Later in the Senate, he chaired the Veterans, Military Affairs and Homeland Security Committee, and was vice chair of the Appropriations Committee. A Democratic foe sought to recall Moolenaar in 2011 because he voted for a bill allowing taxation of public employee pensions, but the petition did not attract enough signatures.

The retirement of Rep. Dave Camp, who chaired the House Ways and Means Committee, led to a battle among three GOP primary contenders: Moolenaar, businessman Paul Mitchell, and software consultant Peter Konetchy. Mitchell vastly outspent his opponents, dumping $3.6 million of his own money—several times what Moolenaar and Konetchy had raised, combined—into his campaign to finance an aggressive TV ad blitz. He attacked Moolenaar as insufficiently conservative, accusing the state lawmaker in an ad of enabling the Affordable Care Act by voting to expand Medicaid.

Moolenaar turned Mitchell's campaign cash advantage against him, saying in a GOP primary debate that "quite frankly, I don't think this seat is up for sale." He had key Republican endorsements, including from Camp. Moolenaar questioned Mitchell's conservative credentials, including his contribution to the 2006 campaign of Democratic Sen. Debbie Stabenow. Moolenaar won the nomination with 52 percent of the vote, to 36 percent for Mitchell and 11 percent for Konetchy. He scored especially well in his base of Midland, where he got 67 percent. In the general, Moolenaar's conservative views prevailed against Democrat John Holmes, 57%-39%; he led in 14 of the 15 counties. (In 2016, Mitchell was elected in an open-seat contest in the nearby 10th District in Michigan's "thumb," then retired after two terms.)

During his first term, Moolenaar won House passage of his bill to designate the National Institute of Standards and Technology in the Commerce Department to serve as the president's principal adviser on standards for technological competitiveness and innovation ability. The effect of the legislation, he said, was to "provide small manufacturers like those here in Michigan with the expertise and advice they need when investing in new technologies." He worked with Democratic Rep. Dan Kildee in 2016 to provide $170 million to fix the badly contaminated drinking water system in Flint

As a new member of Appropriations in 2017, Moolenaar worked to deliver for his home state—even if that meant challenging the Trump administration. When President Donald Trump proposed in his first budget to slash funds for clean-up in the Great Lakes Restoration Initiative, Moolenar pushed for a cut-free $300 million during committee debate. He emphasized the importance of environmental assistance, especially for local tourism. He worked with others in the Michigan delegation for replacement of the Soo Locks at Sault Ste. Marie and to deliver $97 million to Michigan State University for its Facility for Rare Isotope Beams, which assembled the most powerful radioactive beam facility in the world.

The Great Lakes initiative became a continuing priority for Moolenaar. With other Republicans in the Michigan delegation, he successfully lobbied Trump to reverse his proposed budget cut during a 20-minute drive in Grand Rapids from the airport to the site of a rally in March 2019. "It's rare that you have concentrated time like that," Moolenaar told the Detroit News. They emphasized the importance of the funds in presidential-election battleground states.

In July 2020, Moolenaar heralded Trump's support—following another personal plea--for more than $43 million in emergency aid for flood relief to the Midland area. "I asked Trump to help speed up the process and cut through the red tape," he wrote in the News. Even though the formal request came from Democratic Gov. Gretchen Whitmer, Trump said that he was acting in response to Moolenaar.

He has been reelected easily, without opposition in the GOP primary.

MI-4: Central Michigan   Cook Partisan Voting Index: R+14

Population		Race and Ethnicity		Income	
Total	702,887	White	93.70%	Median Income	$54,166
Land area (sq. miles)	8,458	Black	1.80%	District Income Rank	343
Pop/ sq mi	83.11	Latino	3.50%	Poverty Rate	13.50%
Born in State	85.10%	Asian	1.00%	With health insurance	93.50%
		Two or more races	2.10%	Cash public assistance	3.00%
Age Groups		Other	1.30%	Food stamp/SNAP	11.40%
Under 18	20.40%				
18-34	22.20%	Education		Work	
35-64	37.90%	H.S grad or less	43.50%	White Collar	33.30%
Over 64	19.70%	Some college	33.20%	Sales and Service	39.10%
		College Degree, 4 yr	14.30%	Blue Collar	27.50%
Military		Post grad	9.10%	Government	14.00%
Veteran/ Active Duty	8.30%				

| 2020 Pres. Vote | Trump | 234,441 | (61%) | Biden | 142,630 | (37%) | | | |
| 2016 Pres. Vote | Trump | 195,303 | (59%) | Clinton | 113,817 | (35%) | Johnson | 14,062 | (4%) |

Midland: Flat and treeless for miles, the central reaches of Michigan's Lower Peninsula are farm country, exposed to bitter winds and snowdrifts in winter and shining sun for precious weeks in summer. Like the steppes of Eastern Europe, these are farmlands that produce hearty crops: potatoes, navy beans, sugar beets. The cities here are often small factory towns, with neat, tree-lined streets that end at bare fields. Midland in 1891 was a declining lumber town when Herbert Dow perfected an electrolytic process to extract chemicals from northern Michigan's extensive brine wells. That was the start of Dow Chemical, still headquartered in this now upscale town and today a large producer of pesticides and agricultural biotech products.

In 2015, Dow merged with another chemical giant; the resulting DowDuPont company retained a major local presence. Also that year, Dow completed its acquisition of Corning, a silicon-based materials company. With a cutback of about 700 jobs in the latter transaction, the company retained more than 5,000 jobs in the Midland area. Worries about local employment continued. "Employees are concerned" about the prospects of creating three separate unnamed companies from the new business, the president of the United Steelworkers local told the Detroit News in 2017. Some worried whether the Midland area had enough skilled workers. Poverty has increased and population has decreased in many rural parts of Michigan. Concerns about Dow's future were reinforced in July 2020 when the company announced a six percent cutback in its workforce. Some of the corporate problems were attributed to the slowdown resulting from the coronavirus.

The Midland area was further devastated by historic flooding in May 2020. The downfalls caused breaches in two privately owned dams, which forced thousands of Midland residents to abandon their homes—actions that were further complicated by the pandemic. Some of the floodwaters damaged Dow's industrial site. Gov. Gretchen Whitmer said that returning to normal in Midland would be a "Herculean" challenge, with close to 1,000 homes suffering major damage. The dams had suffered from years of deferred maintenance and negligence—yet another instance of harm resulting from aging infrastructure in Michigan.

The 4th Congressional District of Michigan, geographically the state's second-largest, includes much of this territory north of Lansing and Grand Rapids and west of Flint and Saginaw. Two-thirds of its populace lives in rural areas. It stretches north up the highways, barely venturing outside U.S. 131 to the west and Interstate 75 to the east. The rolling country around Houghton Lake was once lumber country and is now a retirement and resort area, with condominiums and knotty-pine cottages clustered around icy green lakes. This is historically Republican territory, having sent only one Democrat to Congress since it was created in 1912. President Donald Trump in 2020 won, 61%-37%. That was triple the spread of Michigan native Mitt Romney's lead, 53%-45%, over President Barack Obama in 2012.

Dan Kildee (D)

Elected 2012, 5th term, b. Aug 11, 1958; Flint, MI; Central MI University, B.S.; University of MI, Flint, Att., 1982; Roman Catholic; Married (Jennifer Kildee); 3 children; 2 grandchildren.

Elected Office: Flint MI Board of Education, 1977-1985; Genesee County Board of Commissioners, 1985-1997; Genesee County Treasurer, 1997-2009.

Professional Career: Youth specialist, Whaley Children's Center, 1976-1985; Founder, Genesee County Land Bank; Co-founder & CEO, Center For Comm. Progress, 2009-2012.

DC Office: 203 CHOB 20515, 202-225-3611, Fax: 202-225-6393, dankildee.house.gov

State Offices: Flint, 810-238-8627.

Committees: *Science, Space & Technology*: Environment. *Ways & Means*: Trade; Worker & Family Support.

Group Ratings

	ADA	ACLU	AFL-CIO	LCV	COC	HAFA	ACU	CFG	FRC
2020	**	86%	**	100%	-	0%	3%	**	-
2019	95%	C	100%	97%	61%	C	3%	12%	0%

Almanac Ratings 2019-2020

	Economy	Social	Foreign	Composite
Liberal	100%	100%	82%	94%
Conservative	0%	0%	18%	6%

Key Votes of the 116th Congress

1. U.S./Mex./Can. trade deal	Y	5. Russia sanctions	Y
2. First Coronavirus response	Y	6. Troops in Syria	Y
3. HEROES Act	Y	7. Veto arms sales to Saudis	Y
4. CASH Act	Y	8. Defense $$$, veto override	Y

9. Firearms background checks Y
10. Spending at the border   Y
11. Marijuana liberalized rules   Y
12. Electoral College objections N

Election Results

Election	Name (Party)	Vote (%)		Cand. Spent	Ind. Exp. Support	Ind. Exp. Oppose
2020 General	Dan Kildee (D).....................................	196,599	(54%)	$1,046,085	$2,162	
	Tim Kelly (R).....................................	150,772	(42%)	$65,694	$297	$224
	Kathy Goodwin (Working Class)..............	8,180	(2%)			
2020 Primary	Dan Kildee (D).....................................	91,288	(100%)			

Prior winning percentages: 2018 (60%), 2016 (61%), 2014 (57%), 2012 (65%)

Democrat Dan Kildee, elected in 2012, initially was a quiet and usually reliable party loyalist, who focused chiefly on local issues. He took the lead in securing a congressional response to the contaminated water crisis in his Flint-based district. As a member of the House Ways and Means Committee, he has played more of a leadership role, while promoting his working-class style.

Kildee grew up in a close-knit neighborhood in Flint. There were six children in his family, and so many in the neighborhood that they formed their own football team, the Genesee Jets. He carried that athleticism into high school and became captain of the hockey team. But his real interest was in hanging out at Democratic headquarters. He worked on his uncle Dale's campaigns for the state legislature and for Congress, distributing yard signs and doing other tasks.

After high school, Kildee enrolled at the University of Michigan's Flint campus and worked part-time at a treatment facility for emotionally disturbed children. That job became full-time and Kildee dropped out of college, although decades later, he earned a bachelor's degree in administration at Central Michigan University. At age 19, Kildee was elected to the Flint Board of Education. "I'd go to visit the schools and I'd quite literally get asked for a hall pass," he said. Kildee was a commissioner in Genesee County for 12 years before becoming county treasurer for another 12 years, during which time he founded a local land bank. His method for tackling abandoned properties—getting rid of them—brought him national attention. Though he took "a commonsense approach to urban planning in an age of decline," others viewed it as "a radically un-American idea that embraces defeat and limited horizons," according to a 2010 profile of Kildee in Slate. Since then, officials in Detroit have used a version of Kildee's land bank to assist with their huge surplus of properties.

When Dale Kildee announced his retirement after 36 years in the House, his nephew was instantly a strong contender, given his family name and years of public service. Kildee won the primary unopposed. He had little trouble dispatching Republican former state Rep. Jim Slezak in the general, 65%-31%.

On the Financial Services Committee, Kildee focused on cleaning up blight in Flint. He eventually got $100 million in federal funds for local demolition. With a bipartisan group of House members, he filed a resolution seeking to prevent any threat to the Great Lakes from a proposed Canadian nuclear waste site. When it became clear that the Flint water crisis would require a congressional response, the Senate took the lead and overwhelmingly approved emergency assistance. In the House, Republican leaders deferred action to await broader legislation on water projects, partly due to fear that many conservatives would object to the Flint aid. Kildee complained about the delay but didn't burn bridges. Teaming with Republican Rep. John Moolenaar of the neighboring district, they put together with Speaker Paul Ryan and other House leaders a bipartisan backroom deal for $170 million.

On a more recent local issue, Kildee took the lead in cleaning up PFAs, cancer-causing chemicals that had become a problem at the former Wurtsmith Air Force Base in Oscoda, which is part of his district. When it became apparent that the chemicals had become a widespread problem for military officials, he put together a group of House members that won Appropriations Committee approval in July 2020 of $200 million to address the issue.

His success opened other doors for Kildee. He made known his interest in running in 2018 for the open seat for governor, though he was reluctant to join a Democratic primary contest. In May 2017, he said he would run for reelection and focus on the challenges posed by Republicans. After Democrats regained House control, he joined the Ways and Means Committee, where his chief priorities have been fair international trade deals and strengthening Social Security. After his earlier interest in an elected leadership position, he was tapped as a chief deputy whip for the Democratic leadership.

Kildee has been reelected easily. But he has voiced ongoing worries about the perception of Democrats in middle America. With Democratic Reps. Tim Ryan of Ohio and John Yarmuth of Kentucky, he helped to form in 2017 the People's House Project, a progressive group that operated separately from the party's coastal elites. "This has to be a movement with a lot of hands rolling in the same direction," he told Vox, adding that the group would go "straight into the heartland with an economic message."

After co-chairing a task force of the Democratic Congressional Campaign Committee to encourage participation of other members during the successful 2018 campaign for Democrats, he sought other opportunities to advocate party interests. He has worked "to ensure that [Democratic] priorities and concerns are addressed" in legislation, according to Michigan Advance, which reports on progressive issues. "One really important principle is to never try to tell a member of Congress what's good for their district, because they know better than anyone," Kildee said. "I see people make that mistake a lot, and it's one that I think is a fatal mistake for a person in leadership."

With Michigan losing a seat in reapportionment, he faces some risk with the future of his district, especially with its population downsizing and the continuing exodus of blue-collar white voters to the Republican Party.

MI-5: East-Central Michigan

Population		Race and Ethnicity		Income	
Total	672,466	White	77.20%	Median Income	$47,655
Land area (sq. miles)	2,349	Black	17.50%	District Income Rank	400
Pop/ sq mi	286.31	Latino	5.10%	Poverty Rate	17.40%
Born in State	84.30%	Asian	1.00%	With health insurance	94.70%
		Two or more races	3.40%	Cash public assistance	2.70%
Age Groups		Other	1.00%	Food stamp/SNAP	19.90%
Under 18	21.60%				
18-34	20.30%	**Education**		**Work**	
35-64	38.90%	H.S grad or less	42.50%	White Collar	31.10%
Over 64	19.10%	Some college	37.30%	Sales and Service	40.70%
		College Degree, 4 yr	13.10%	Blue Collar	28.20%
Military		Post grad	7.10%	Government	9.50%
Veteran/ Active Duty	8.10%				

2020 Pres. Vote	Biden	189,245	(51%)	Trump	173,179	(47%)		
2016 Pres. Vote	Clinton	162,982	(49%)	Trump	148,953	(45%)	Johnson 10,880	(3%)

Flint, Bay City: The flat plains south of Saginaw Bay, the inlet of Lake Huron that separates Michigan's Thumb (people really call it that) from the mitten of the Lower Peninsula, was once one of America's top industrial areas. Some 130 years ago, it was the nation's premier lumber country, with huge stands of virgin trees feeding 36 sawmills in Bay City. When the trees were gone, farmers took over, and the land was sown with beans and sugar beets. Then, a century ago, came the automobile. Flint, a small town on a minor branch of the Saginaw River, was the home base of W.C. Durant, the investor who merged several young auto firms to form General Motors in 1908. GM put its Chevrolet and Buick factories in Flint and its power steering facility in Saginaw, chosen because it was already a center of precision machinery manufacturing.

From 1910 through the 1950s, Flint grew lustily as it built Chevys and Buicks. Miners from the east Kentucky coal fields, mountain folk from eastern Tennessee and farmers from the Black Belt of Alabama found their way to Flint. Before long, southern accents were common in an area settled by New England Yankees. Labor strife followed industrialization. In January 1937, Flint was the scene of the great sit-down strike that began when workers noticed GM preparing to move the dies that were used to stamp cars out of its plant—a potential prelude to a move to the South— and ended with GM recognizing the United Auto Workers as the bargaining agent for its workers.

Economic disaster struck with the energy crisis of the 1970s. Imports, especially from Japan, that were higher quality and lower price than American cars, took an increasing share of the market. In 1979, GM employed more than 70,000 workers in its Flint plants. Eventually, GM closed 13 of its 15 factories, and by the late 2000s, the GM payroll had fallen below 12,000. By 2010, more than 40 percent of Flint households were in poverty, and many skilled workers had fled what Forbes magazine called one of "America's fastest-dying cities." Michael Moore, the left-wing filmmaker, has used his hometown of Flint as the locale for much of his work about rust-belt hardships.

There have been some flickering signs of hope. Since General Motors emerged from bankruptcy in 2010, it has kept open a Flint engine plant and added a third shift at its truck assembly facility, which is the oldest GM factory in the nation. In 2018, GM turned its old Chevrolet plant into an automotive research facility with the local Kettering University. In October 2020, GM said it would spend $32 million on its plant in Flint to upgrade production of heavy pick-up trucks. Still, the departure of wealth and capital resulted in deep-seated poverty and economic decline that made Flint the third-worst city in the nation (behind Detroit and Birmingham Alabama) to live in, a Wall Street data service concluded in 2017. The economic dynamism of Michigan moved west to Grand Rapids.

In 2015, a new crisis hit Flint: the belated discovery of lead contamination in its drinking water system. The local government had turned to the Flint River as its water source while it was building a new pipeline to Lake Huron. A lawsuit revealed that the Environmental Quality Department had failed to treat the river with an anti-corrosive agent, which resulted in severe health risks. In his 2016 state of the state address, Republican Gov. Rick Snyder accepted part of the blame. "I'm sorry, and

I will fix it," he said. "Government failed you at the federal, state and local level. We need to make sure this never happens again in any Michigan city."

By 2018, a degree of normalcy had returned. Lead levels in the water had declined and the distribution of free water bottles ended. Criminal charges of manslaughter were brought against five state officials and a federal judge ordered the state to pay $87 million to localities to replace water lines. In August 2020, the state said it would pay $600 million to victims of the tainted water, especially the families of school children. On the positive side, Bloomberg News reported in May 2019 that the water crisis "failed to stanch the purpose and pride of the city's small business community," which had begun to improve Flint's economic development.

The 5th Congressional District includes Flint and surrounding Genesee County—which are about 60 percent of the district—Saginaw and eastern Saginaw County, Bay City and most of Bay County, and rural areas along Lake Huron. Flint, evenly divided between the parties during the sit-down strikes, had become 57 percent African American and heavily Democratic, Saginaw and Bay City somewhat less so. But Joe Biden fared poorly in this low-income, 77 percent White district. His lead of 51%-47% in 2020 was a big drop from 2012, when President Barack Obama won 62%-38%. The Democratic presidential vote in Genesee fell from 63 percent to 54 percent in eight years. In Saginaw County, which Democrats traditionally took by double digits, Biden won 49.4%-49.1%.

Fred Upton (R)

Elected 1986, 18th term, b. Apr 23, 1953; St. Joseph, MI; Shatluck School, 1971; University of MI, B.A., 1975; Congregationalist; Married (Amey Rulon-Miller Upton); 2 children.

Professional Career: Project Coordinator, U.S. Rep. David Stockman, 1975-1980; Legislative affairs, O.M.B., 1981-1983, Director, 1984-1985.

DC Office: 2183 RHOB 20515, 202-225-3761, Fax: 202-225-4986, upton.house.gov

State Offices: Kalamazoo, 269-385-0039; St. Joseph, 269-982-1986.

Committees: *Energy & Commerce*: Consumer Protection & Commerce; Energy (RMM); Health.

Group Ratings

	ADA	ACLU	AFL-CIO	LCV	COC	HAFA	ACU	CFG	FRC
2020	**	33%	**	62%	-	51%	68%	**	
2019	20%	C	57%	45%	99%	C	69%	46%	64%

Almanac Ratings 2019-2020

	Economy	Social	Foreign	Composite
Liberal	42%	45%	46%	45%
Conservative	58%	55%	54%	55%

Key Votes of the 116th Congress

1. U.S./Mex./Can. trade deal Y	5. Russia sanctions Y	9. Firearms background checks Y
2. First Coronavirus response Y	6. Troops in Syria Y	10. Spending at the border Y
3. HEROES Act N	7. Veto arms sales to Saudis N	11. Marijuana liberalized rules N
4. CASH Act Y	8. Defense $$$, veto override Y	12. Electoral College objections N

Election Results

Election	Name (Party)	Vote (%)		Cand. Spent	Ind. Exp. Support	Ind. Exp. Oppose
2020 General	Fred Upton (R)................................	211,496	(56%)	$3,557,046	$797,201	$547,348
	Jon Hoadley (D).............................	152,085	(40%)	$3,438,445	$68,643	$1,337,331
	Jeff DePoy (L).................................	10,399	(3%)			
2020 Primary	Fred Upton (R)................................	53,495	(63%)			
	Elena Oelke (R).............................	31,884	(37%)			

Prior winning percentages: 2018 (50%), 2016 (59%), 2014 (56%), 2012 (55%), 2010 (62%), 2008 (59%), 2006 (61%), 2004 (65%), 2002 (69%), 2000 (67.9%), 1998 (70%), 1996 (68%), 1994 (74%), 1992 (62%), 1990 (58%), 1988 (71%), 1986 (62%)

Fred Upton, an affable Republican first elected in 1986, chaired the House Energy and Commerce Committee for six years. Upton's voting record has been unusually moderate for a senior House Republican, though he has regularly aligned with business. He also sought to create a nonpartisan niche and grew uncomfortable in the GOP throughout the Trump era, voting to impeach the president in January 2021. It's possible, perhaps likely, that he intends for this term to be his last.

The grandson of one of the founders of Whirlpool, Upton grew up in St. Joseph. He attended the University of Michigan and worked for David Stockman—then a brash conservative icon—first on Stockman's congressional staff, then at the White House in the Office of Management and Budget from 1981 to 1985. Upton returned home and ran in the 1986 Republican primary against Rep. Mark Siljander, a conservative and evangelical Christian, and won 55%-45%, going on to win the seat handily in the general election.

Upton's family fortune puts him in the upper echelon among members of Congress in wealth, but he has a regular-guy image. He is well known for insisting that everyone, from reporters to staffers to fellow lawmakers, call him "Fred," and says he personally reads and signs all of his legislative mail. He is a devoted Chicago Cubs fan, rarely missing an Opening Day at Wrigley Field.

Early in his House career, Upton was a leader of the moderate Republicans' Tuesday Group, where he was outspoken about the need to find middle ground. He freely exercised his independence when his party controlled the House from 1995 to 2006, and he occasionally caused heartburn for GOP leaders. He sought, with limited success, to raise taxes by reversing some of the Bush-era tax cuts. He backed increases in the minimum wage, and increased funding for Amtrak and Democratic measures to expand government medical insurance for poor children.

In his committee work, Upton has been more of a party regular. When he chaired the Telecommunications Subcommittee, he supported a bill to allow regional telephone companies to provide broadband service more easily, and he pushed for larger fines against broadcasters for indecent programming. Taking the helm of Energy and Commerce in 2011, he confidently predicted that "a significant number of Democrats" would join his party's efforts to overturn President Barack Obama's 2010 health care law, which he dismissed as "a massive new government program that does real and lasting damage." It turned out, though, that the repeated repeal votes never drew more than a handful of Democrats in support.

Many of Upton's other initiatives as chairman got through the House on largely party-line votes and were left for dead in the Democratic-controlled Senate. They included legislation to overturn the Environmental Protection Agency's authority to regulate greenhouse gas emissions. Another bill overturned the Federal Communications Commission's net neutrality rules designed to prevent internet providers from creating tiered pricing structures. On the investigative front, his panel dug into the Obama administration's loan guarantees to the failed solar company Solyndra Corp.

Upton's efforts delighted fellow Republicans. But the Sierra Club and other environmental groups began running ads against him at home. And some Michiganders wondered what had happened to the politician who had championed legislation to ban incandescent light bulbs as part of the 2007 energy bill, and then voted four years later to undo the measure.

With Republicans in control of the Senate in 2015, Upton expressed hope that some of his efforts to block federal environmental regulations could at least clear Congress, if not get signed into law. But the Senate failed to act on most of those initiatives. Instead, he had an unexpectedly productive two years in enacting major bipartisan legislation. He worked with Democratic Rep. Diana DeGette of Colorado to accelerate innovative medical treatments and devices. Their 21st Century Cures Act easily passed the House. It picked up additional health-policy initiatives in the Senate — including funds to fight opioid addiction and to research cures for cancer — and was enacted after the 2016 election. Upton worked with Rep. Frank Pallone of New Jersey, the senior Democrat on Energy and Commerce, to overhaul the outdated chemical safety law. That measure, too, had overwhelming bipartisan support.

Upton has been an election target from both the left and right. In 2010, former state Rep. Jack Hoogendyk ran against him in the GOP primary, criticizing Upton for voting for the bailout of the financial industry. Upton vastly outspent Hoogendyk and won 57%-43%, not a robust outcome for a longtime incumbent. Hoogendyk came back for another challenge in 2012. Upton took him more seriously this time, conducting outreach to tea party groups and winning with ease, 67%-33%. His Democratic opponent that year was Mike O'Brien, a former Marine and office furniture company manager making his first run for elective office, who blasted Upton's support for the Republican spending plan. The $294,000 that O'Brien raised was no match for Upton's $4.7 million. Upton won, 55%-43%.

In 2014, Upton drew a better-funded Democratic challenger—Paul Clements, a Western Michigan University political scientist who was dismayed by Upton's reversal on climate change. Clements received help from Harvard law professor Lawrence Lessig's Mayday political action committee, which spent more than $2 million to portray Upton as a captive of oil and drug companies. Upton denied the allegations and responded that he continued to work on a bipartisan basis to steer clear of the Washington dysfunction. Upton spent $3.9 million to $800,000 for Clements and won, 56%-40%. Clements ran again in 2016, with help from Lessig's network, but his appeal faded. Upton won more comfortably, 59%-36%.

During the 2016 campaign, Upton remained neutral on Donald Trump and the presidential campaign. Upton said Trump should consider "stepping away from the ticket" following the early October release of the 2005 video with Trump's lewd comments about women. "It's a new low. It's outrageous. ... I urge him to think about our country over his own candidacy." After Trump was elected and issued executive orders with travel bans for refugees and immigrants, Upton criticized the plan for creating "real confusion" for travelers and those who enforce the laws. When House Republicans took up their bill to revise the Affordable Care Act, he objected that the proposal did not guarantee continued coverage of pre-existing conditions. In negotiations with House GOP leaders and later with Trump, he agreed to join the party ranks after they added funding designed to assure such coverage. That deal was essential in securing a bare majority for House passage of the bill.

After being term-limited as committee chairman, Upton settled in at the Energy Subcommittee as chairman in 2016 and, in 2019, as the ranking Republican. As a member of the bipartisan Climate Solutions Caucus, he urged "an economically realistic and pragmatic approach" to addressing climate change. He said Trump's decision to withdraw from the 2015 Paris climate agreement was "a mistake." He opposed the farm bill in 2018 because of work requirements that other Republicans imposed on food-stamp recipients. In 2020, he was one of just three Republicans to vote for Democrats' policing reform bill, a stance he took after voicing support for the Black Lives Matter movement in the wake of the death of George Floyd.

At home, Upton openly discussed a challenge in 2018 to Democratic Sen. Debbie Stabenow. In addition to the daunting prospects he faced in a hostile partisan climate, he feared he might not win the GOP nomination. Those challenges became apparent that year in his reelection, which he won by the narrowest margin of his career, 50%-46%. Democratic nominee Matthew Longjohn, the former national health officer for the YMCA, sought to hold Upton accountable for supporting House repeal of the Affordable Care Act. Republican research uncovered that Longjohn, who had a medical degree, was not licensed to practice medicine. Upton outspent Longjohn, $3.6 million to $1.5 million, and won five of the six counties—though he lost Kalamazoo, 55%-42%.

In an unexpected twist, Democrats following the election criticized then-former Vice President Joe Biden for praising Upton as "one of the finest guys I've ever worked with," as he cited his work on medical research during an October event sponsored by local business groups. Local Democrats complained about the timing, including GOP ads that excerpted his praise. Biden subsequently dismissed the attack on his bipartisanship: "Forgive me, Father, for I have sinned," he mocked to a Washington audience.

Though Upton voted against the first impeachment of Trump in December 2019, he grew disillusioned toward the end of his presidency. He demanded an apology from Trump when he insulted the late Rep. John Dingell at a campaign rally and urged him to accept his loss in the 2020 election. Then he was one of 10 Republicans to vote to impeach Trump after the Jan. 6 riots. Congress must "send a clear message that our country cannot and will not tolerate any effort by any president to impede the peaceful transfer of power," he said. Republican county leaders in his district responded by censuring Upton.

In the 2020 campaign, national Democrats offered little support to state Rep. Jon Hoadley. Each candidate spent over $3 million, but Upton won easily 56%-40%. With Michigan losing a seat in the 2022 redistricting, Upton might choose to retire on a high note.

MI-6: Southwest Michigan

Cook Partisan Voting Index: R+5

Population		Race and Ethnicity		Income	
Total	721,508	White	84.80%	Median Income	$56,520
Land area (sq. miles)	3,547	Black	8.50%	District Income Rank	307
Pop/ sq mi	203.43	Latino	6.50%	Poverty Rate	13.90%
Born in State	68.70%	Asian	1.50%	With health insurance	93.20%
		Two or more races	3.70%	Cash public assistance	2.10%
Age Groups		Other	1.40%	Food stamp/SNAP	9.40%
Under 18	22.20%				
18-34	22.80%	Education		Work	
35-64	37.20%	H.S grad or less	38.90%	White Collar	34.70%
Over 64	17.80%	Some college	32.50%	Sales and Service	37.60%
		College Degree, 4 yr	17.70%	Blue Collar	27.70%
Military		Post grad	10.80%	Government	10.60%
Veteran/ Active Duty	6.30%				

2020 Pres. Vote	Trump	197,508	(51%)	Biden	180,139	(47%)			
2016 Pres. Vote	Trump	170,320	(51%)	Clinton	142,293	(43%)	Johnson	14,034	(4%)

Kalamazoo: The southwest corner of Michigan was settled by New England Yankees and Upstate New Yorkers in the 1830s and 1840s. They built small towns with schools, churches and colleges; supported temperance; and opposed capital punishment. And in 1854, they joined the newly formed Republican Party. There are towns in southwest Michigan that still recall proudly their past as termini of the Underground Railroad, and there are Black families whose ancestors made their way north out of slavery to freedom. Later, big industries transformed some of the small towns into significant cities. Kalamazoo, started by Dutch Americans who introduced celery to this country, became the home of Upjohn pharmaceuticals, which is now part of Pfizer. That made this region a hub for production of the coronavirus vaccine. In July 2018, Pfizer announced plans for a sterile drug manufacturing facility in Portage, which will start production by 2024.

Predominantly Black and struggling Benton Harbor and predominantly white and prosperous St. Joseph are small towns that sit across from each other where the St. Joseph River empties into Lake Michigan. In 2015, a columnist for the local newspaper described the contrasts in their school systems as a "sad tale of educational apartheid." Benton Harbor had been known as the headquarters for Whirlpool. But Whirlpool closed its plant in 2010, and many other local companies and famous industrial names such as Gibson Guitars have moved out of the area, taking their thousands of jobs. Entergy Corp. in 2018 sold its nuclear power plant in Covert Township to the owner of another nuclear plant; the facility remained on schedule for shutdown in 2022.

In 2017, the Kalamazoo City Commission created a $500 million "foundation for excellence" that will encourage nonprofit groups to support local development. An investment loan program by another Kalamazoo foundation recently financed a new multi-use building with affordable housing and 24-hour childcare. To the southwest, Midwest Energy is investing $18 million to build an industrial park in Cassopolis that could create 1,000 jobs. Michigan's southwest corner is heavily influenced by Chicago, which is much closer than is Detroit; people here watch Chicago television and root for the Cubs or White Sox rather than the Detroit Tigers.

The 6th Congressional District occupies the southwest corner of Michigan. It takes in five counties and most of a sixth. Kalamazoo is the largest, with nearly 40 percent of the population. The counties in the far southwest of the state—Cass, Berrien and Van Buren—are part of the so-called "cabinet counties," named, respectively, for Andrew Jackson's secretary of War, attorney general, and vice president (only Cass was from Michigan). For many decades, this was arch-Republican territory. Since the 1990s, while continuing with Republican representation, the district, in particular Kalamazoo, trended toward the Democrats. Barack Obama took 53 percent in 2008. But the district swung back. Hillary Clinton trailed Donald Trump, 51%-43%. Joe Biden narrowed that slightly, but lost 51%-47%.

Tim Walberg (R)

Elected 2010, 8th term, b. Apr 12, 1951; Chicago, IL; Western IL University, Att.; Taylor University, B.S.; Wheaton College, M.A.; Moody Bible Institute, Att.; Fort Wayne Bible College, B.R.E., 1975; Protestant - Unspecified Christian; Married (Susan Walberg); 3 children; 2 grandchildren.

Elected Office: MI House, 1983-1998; U.S. House, 2007-2009.

Professional Career: Minister, 1973-1982; President, Warren Reuther Center, 1999-2000; Div. Manager, Moody Bible Inst., 2000-2005.

DC Office: 2266 RHOB 20515, 202-225-6276, Fax: 202-225-6281, walberg.house.gov

State Offices: Jackson, 517-780-9075.

Committees: *Education & Labor*: Health, Employment, Labor & Pensions. *Energy & Commerce*: Communications & Technology; Energy.

Group Ratings

	ADA	ACLU	AFL-CIO	LCV	COC	HAFA	ACU	CFG	FRC
2020	**	17%	**	5%	-	82%	90%	**	-
2019	5%	C	38%	10%	89%	C	91%	81%	100%

Almanac Ratings 2019-2020

	Economy	Social	Foreign	Composite
Liberal	38%	7%	12%	19%
Conservative	62%	93%	88%	81%

Key Votes of the 116th Congress

1. U.S./Mex./Can. trade deal	Y	5. Russia sanctions	Y
2. First Coronavirus response	Y	6. Troops in Syria	N
3. HEROES Act	N	7. Veto arms sales to Saudis	N
4. CASH Act	N	8. Defense $$$, veto override	Y

9. Firearms background checks N
10. Spending at the border Y
11. Marijuana liberalized rules N
12. Electoral College objections Y

Election Results

Election	Name (Party)	Vote (%)		Cand. Spent	Ind. Exp. Support	Ind. Exp. Oppose
2020 General	Tim Walberg (R)	227,524	(59%)	$1,702,345	$8,411	$224
	Gretchen Driskell (D)	159,743	(41%)	$1,944,876		
2020 Primary	Tim Walberg (R)	84,397	(100%)			

Prior winning percentages: 2018 (54%), 2016 (55%), 2014 (54%), 2012 (53%), 2010 (50%), 2006 (50%)

Republican Tim Walberg, first elected in 2006, is an ardent social and fiscal conservative who has become a political survivor occasionally willing to seek the political center. After having narrowly lost his first reelection bid and then reclaimed the seat in 2010 in another close election, he relied on his conservative base and a penchant for rematches to become entrenched with a slightly increasing electoral majority. Following GOP losses elsewhere in 2018, his Republican-held district survived as the closest to the outskirts of Metro Detroit.

Walberg was born in Chicago, growing up on the city's South Side. He worked in a steel mill to get through college and got his bachelor's degree from Fort Wayne Bible College and a master's from Wheaton College. He was a minister for 10 years before running for office in 1982, when he won a seat in the Michigan House by beating a moderate GOP incumbent. In his 16 years as a state legislator, Walberg had a reputation as a tireless advocate for gun rights and an opponent of abortion rights. He belonged to a group dubbed the "No" caucus for its unflinching opposition to tax hikes and increased spending. When term limits ended his tenure in 1998, he became president of a conservative education foundation and a division manager for the Moody Bible Institute of Chicago.

Walberg ran for this seat in 2004, when it was open. He placed third in a GOP primary field crowded with other conservatives; moderate Joe Schwarz won the primary with 28 percent of the vote and went on to win the general election. Two years later, Walberg again challenged the GOP incumbent. He ran on a record of having never once voted for a tax increase in the legislature. The anti-tax Club for Growth poured $500,000 into attacking Schwarz. The national GOP backed the incumbent, and Schwarz had a spending advantage of 2-to-1. Walberg prevailed 53%-47%, and went on to defeat a weak Democratic opponent, 50%-46%.

In 2008, Democrats nominated Mark Schauer, the Michigan Senate's minority leader and a former community organizer. Schauer focused on the economy and secured an endorsement from Republican Schwarz. The Club for Growth again spent heavily for Walberg, but Schauer had strong union support and won narrowly in a Democratic year, 49%-46%.

Walberg came back for a rematch in 2010 in a much more favorable climate for his party. In August, he won a three-way Republican primary with 57 percent of the vote. In the general election, Walberg and his allies attacked Schauer for his vote for President Barack Obama's $787 billion economic stimulus, saying he was part of the problem of deficit spending in Washington. Schauer and his backers portrayed Walberg as too far right for the district, highlighting his support for creating private accounts in Social Security. They spotlighted a September radio interview in which Walberg said he didn't know whether Obama is an American citizen. By day's end, he reversed course and acknowledged that Obama is "certainly an American citizen." Outside groups and national parties showered more than $7 million on the race. Walberg regained the seat, 50%-45%.

Walberg has had a solidly conservative voting record and takes a special interest in challenging labor unions seeking additional rights. As chairman of the Education and the Workforce Subcommittee on Workforce Protections, he argued that the Obama administration's proposal giving home-care workers minimum wage and overtime protections would result in reduced hours for workers and higher costs for taxpayers. In 2014, the House passed Walberg's Senior Executive Service Accountability Act, which made it easier for federal agencies to suspend or fire their top managers for sufficient cause.

In 2017, he took over as chairman of the Health, Education, Labor and Pensions Subcommittee at Education and the Workforce. He gained a seat on the Energy and Commerce Committee, which gave him an additional niche to restore what he called "patient-centered health care." Walberg collaborated with Democratic Rep. Debbie Dingell, who represented a neighboring district and served with him on Energy and Commerce, to enact a bill that clarified the review standard at the Federal Energy Regulatory Commission for energy-related mergers. He and Dingell also filed two provisions that became part of the comprehensive opioid-fighting measure that was enacted in 2018. In 2020, he organized labor's efforts to get approval by the National Labor Relations Board of telephone elections for union contests during the pandemic.

In the strong Republican year of 2014, against Democrat Pam Byrnes who spent $1.4 million but had little outside assistance, Walberg won 54%-41%. In 2016, he faced Gretchen Driskell, who was mayor of Saline for 14 years and then served in the state House. In her broadcast ads, she labeled Walberg as "Trade Deal Tim" because of his support for international trade agreements; Walberg responded that he was "a free and fair trader" and that he opposed the Trans-Pacific Partnership. Driskell evidently was hoping to benefit from coattails in the presidential campaign. But it turned out that Hillary Clinton performed poorly in this district and elsewhere in Michigan; Driskell lost badly, 55%-40%.

Driskell ran again in 2018, a more favorable climate for Democrats. She made an interesting twist by appealing to supporters of President Donald Trump with her claim that she was, like him, "a vote for change." She outspent Walberg, $2.7 million to $2.2 million. Walberg won surprisingly easily, 54%-46%, and took every county except Washtenaw and Eaton.

In 2020, he had a third contest with Driskell. With a turnout increase of 92,000 voters—and perhaps the benefit of greater enthusiasm in a presidential election or some voters deciding that they had enough with this matchup—Walberg increased his vote to 59 percent, the highest he has received in his seven victories. Perhaps Driskell is hoping for a better map in redistricting.

MI-7: Southern Michigan

Population		Race and Ethnicity		Income	
Total	710,064	White	90.90%	Median Income	$61,379
Land area (sq. miles)	4,228	Black	4.00%	District Income Rank	242
Pop/ sq mi	167.95	Latino	4.50%	Poverty Rate	10.90%
Born in State	73.70%	Asian	1.20%	With health insurance	94.50%
		Two or more races	3.00%	Cash public assistance	1.90%
Age Groups		Other	0.90%	Food stamp/SNAP	10.10%
Under 18	20.90%				
18-34	20.10%	**Education**		**Work**	
35-64	39.80%	H.S grad or less	40.40%	White Collar	35.90%
Over 64	19.10%	Some college	32.90%	Sales and Service	35.20%
Military		College Degree, 4 yr	16.80%	Blue Collar	29.00%
Veteran/ Active Duty	7.30%	Post grad	9.90%	Government	13.10%

2020 Pres. Vote	Trump	224,598	(57%)	Biden	164,944	(42%)			
2016 Pres. Vote	Trump	189,677	(55%)	Clinton	131,552	(38%)	Johnson	14,136	(4%)

Jackson, Monroe: The small cities and towns nestled in and around southern Michigan's Irish Hills, near where the major glaciers stopped their southward crawl in the last ice age, have been incubators of innovation since they were settled by Yankees from New England close to two centuries ago. Hillsdale, a picture-book old town south of Jackson, is home to Hillsdale College, founded a decade before the Republican Party by abolitionists and other likeminded people. Numerous mid-level officials in the Trump administration were Hillsdale graduates. Jackson, an old industrial town named for a founder of the Democratic Party and site of Michigan's first prison, is one of five towns that claim to have been the birthplace of the Republican Party in 1854. Today, Jackson is a city in decline, with population loss and the highest poverty rate in Michigan.

The area has had some positive developments. General Motors completed in 2016 a $583 million retooling and expansion project at its Lansing Delta Township assembly plant, which was opened in 2006 and is GM's newest plant in the United States. That assembly plant, which has been described as a technological pioneer, has about 2,500 workers. In February 2020, GM announced it was adding 800 workers—and a third shift—to build Chevrolet Traverse and Buick Enclave SUV's. In 2018, the Supreme Court dismissed an appeal by an anti-nuclear group that sought to block a construction license for the Fermi 3 nuclear reactor near Monroe, which had been certified by the Nuclear Regulatory Commission.

The 7th Congressional District takes in six counties in southern Michigan plus parts of another. The district includes three of the so-called "cabinet counties," named for members of President Andrew Jackson's administration (Jackson presided over Michigan's admission to the Union): Branch County, named for Jackson's secretary of the Navy; Eaton County, for his first secretary of War; and Jackson County, for the president himself. The district includes the outer townships of Washtenaw County, which lean Republican; more than two-thirds of Washtenaw is in the Democratic 12th District. The 7th historically has leaned Republican, though not overwhelmingly so. In the past 100 years, the congressional district for the region has tended to elect Democrats only in presidential wave years: in 1912, 1932, 1964 and 2008.

As with other Republican-held districts in Michigan, it had a big boost in Republican presidential support in 2016. Donald Trump won, 55%-38%, compared with the 51%-48% edge for Mitt Romney in 2012. Trump's edge narrowed a bit in 2020 to 57%-42%. But that remained a significant shift for this district to the GOP.

Elissa Slotkin (D)

Elected 2018, 2nd term, b. Jul 10, 1976; Holly, MI; Columbia University School of International and Public Affairs, M.A.; Cornell University, B.A., 1998; Jewish; Married (Dave Slotkin); 2 stepchildren.

Professional Career: Central Intelligence Agency, Political Analyst, 2003-2004, Intelligence Briefer, 2004-2005; Special Assistant, Office of the Director of National Intelligence, 2005-2006; Director for Iraq Policy, National Security Council, 2007-2009; Senior Advisor on Iraq Policy, U.S. Department of State, 2009-2011; Assistant Secretary of Defense for International Security Affairs, 2014-2017.

DC Office: 1531 LHOB 20515, 202-225-4872, slotkin.house.gov

State Offices: Lansing, 517-993-0510.

Committees: *Armed Services*: Cyber, Innovative Technologies & Information Systems; Readiness. *Homeland Security*: Cybersecurity, Infrastructure Protection & Innovation; Intelligence & Counterterrorism (Chmn). *Veterans' Affairs*: Disability Assistance & Memorial Affairs.

Almanac Ratings 2019-2020

	Economy	Social	Foreign	Composite
Liberal	100%	51%	80%	77%
Conservative	0%	49%	20%	23%

Key Votes of the 116th Congress

1. U.S./Mex./Can. trade deal	Y	5. Russia sanctions	Y	9. Firearms background checks Y
2. First Coronavirus response	Y	6. Troops in Syria	Y	10. Spending at the border	Y
3. HEROES Act	Y	7. Veto arms sales to Saudis	Y	11. Marijuana liberalized rules	Y
4. CASH Act	Y	8. Defense $$$, veto override	Y	12. Electoral College objections N

Election Results

Election	Name (Party)	Vote (%)	Cand. Spent	Ind. Exp. Support	Ind. Exp. Oppose
2020 General	Elissa Slotkin (D)	217,922 (51%)	$7,497,514	$177,604	$162,875
	Paul Junge (R)	202,525 (47%)	$1,887,137	$10,212	$880,816
2020 Primary	Elissa Slotkin (D)	90,570 (100%)			

Prior winning percentages: 2018 (51%)

Democrat Elissa Slotkin, elected in 2018, remained a junior member of the House, but few members carry as much say on national security issues. She brought to Congress impressive portfolio on intelligence and national security during both Democratic and Republican administrations. Her extended assignments in Iraq were followed by policy positions at the White House and Pentagon. She managed to hang on in her Republican-leaning district to win a second term even as many of her classmates lost reelection in comparable districts elsewhere.

In the House, she has been part of a clique of Democratic women newcomers who previously served in national security roles. When they speak in that space, their elders have listened. Slotkin's campaigns have combined robust fundraising with strong support from voters in the university core of her district.

Slotkin grew up in Michigan in a prominent family: Her grandfather's meatpacking company, Hygrade Food Products, was the hot dog vendor at Detroit Tigers games. The product was so popular, the company began selling them in grocery stores and came up with a name: Ball Park Franks. But she resided elsewhere after she left for college until shortly before her campaign for Congress. She graduated from Cornell University and earned a master's degree from the School of International and Public Affairs at Columbia University.

Slotkin decided on a career in intelligence when, amid her first week as a graduate student in New York City, she lived through the devastating attacks a few miles away in September 2001. "That terrible day changed the trajectory of my life," Slotkin later said. "I decided that after graduate school, I would join the intelligence community and work to prevent future terrorist attacks." She joined the

Central Intelligence Agency as a Middle East analyst and was deployed to Iraq for three tours over five years. During that period, Slotkin had national security and intelligence assignments at the Bush and Obama White House and State Departments and personally briefed both presidents.

Under President Barack Obama, her senior posts at the Defense Department included principal adviser to the undersecretary of Defense on security strategy and policy issues, plus acting assistant secretary for international security affairs. She worked on international negotiations in the fight against ISIS and the response to aggression by Russia.

In early 2017, she decided to run for Congress after she saw a televised report of Republican Rep. Mike Bishop smiling at a White House ceremony that celebrated House repeal of the Affordable Care Act. "In the military, this is called dereliction of duty," she told a local reporter. "We decided to fire him that day." In the Democratic primary, she got 71 percent of the vote against Chris Smith, a criminal justice professor at Michigan State University, who ran as the more progressive candidate but raised far less campaign money than did Slotkin.

Slotkin spent a total of about $7.4 million, which doubled the spending by Bishop. Including funds from the two national parties, spending on the contest exceeded $15 million. Her extended campaign allowed Slotkin to define the terms of the debate and overcome what David Wasserman of the Cook Political Report described as her most glaring vulnerability: the "carpet-bagging elitist" label. When Bishop predictably defined her as an outsider, the Detroit News reported in describing Slotkin's victory, she "seized on the issue of health care to make headway" in advocating change.

Slotkin rolled up more than a 2-to-1 margin in Ingham County, with its many university and state employees. Even though that vote was barely one-third of the district total and Bishop easily carried the two other suburban counties, her overwhelming support in Ingham gave Slotkin a comfortable 51%-47% victory.

Slotkin was the first Democrat elected in this district since Debbie Stabenow gave up the seat when she successfully ran for the Senate in 2000. She got seats on the Armed Services and Homeland Security committees. Most notably, she joined with six other freshmen with national security backgrounds in 2019 to pen an op-ed in The Washington Post calling for Trump's first impeachment.

Slotkin's reelection campaign became a pivotal test of the popularity of the Democratic takeover of the House and the new Democratic control in Michigan. Her 2020 campaign showed she was no one-hit wonder. She again won, even as down-ballot Democrats lost elsewhere around the country. Cautious in nature, she avoided liberal slogans like "Abolish ICE" and "Defund the Police" in favor of a more localized campaign. But that approach became more difficult as controversies exploded in her area of expertise involving President Donald Trump.

The outcome was similar to her initial victory: Against Republican challenger Paul Junge, she got 67 percent and led by 52,000 votes in Ingham—which cast one-third of the total. That was more than enough to overcome Junge's leads of 18 and nine percentage points in Livingston and Oakland counties, respectively; she again won 51%-47%. With Michigan losing a seat in 2022, her district's position at the geographic dividing line between the two parties likely will be perilous in redistricting.

MI-8: South-Central Michigan

Cook Partisan Voting Index: R+4

Population		Race and Ethnicity		Income	
Total	740,750	White	85.10%	Median Income	$74,841
Land area (sq. miles)	1,503	Black	6.10%	District Income Rank	131
Pop/ sq mi	492.79	Latino	5.20%	Poverty Rate	9.60%
Born in State	74.30%	Asian	5.10%	With health insurance	95.60%
		Two or more races	2.80%	Cash public assistance	2.50%
Age Groups		Other	0.90%	Food stamp/SNAP	7.30%
Under 18	20.50%				
18-34	24.60%	**Education**		**Work**	
35-64	39.20%	H.S grad or less	26.90%	White Collar	45.70%
Over 64	15.80%	Some college	30.90%	Sales and Service	37.00%
		College Degree, 4 yr	25.20%	Blue Collar	17.30%
Military		Post grad	17.00%	Government	14.50%
Veteran/ Active Duty	6.00%				

2020 Pres. Vote	Trump	215,649	(50%)	Biden	212,085	(49%)		
2016 Pres. Vote	Trump	189,891	(50%)	Clinton	164,436	(44%)	Johnson 15,205	(4%)

Detroit Exurbs, Lansing: Lansing is Michigan's state capital, chosen in 1847 because of its geographic position halfway between Lake Huron and Lake Michigan—and away from the border with Canada and the threat of invasion by British forces. It is a pleasant city with more than its share of amenities. It has a beautifully restored capitol, a fine state history museum, and is neighbor to Michigan State University in East Lansing, founded in 1855 as America's first land-grant college.

Its Oldsmobile plant stimulated growth in the first half of the 20th century, and state government did the same in the second half. Two GM assembly plants have operated in the Lansing area. At the Grand River plant, which suffered cutbacks, GM said in 2018 that it would spend $175 million to prepare for production of two new models. In 2020, the company announced it will move some production to its Lansing Delta Township plant, which included an additional investment of more than $100 million. GM also announced in 2020 that both plants will move toward solar energy. As public employee unions have grown in membership and strength, Lansing, like other state capitals, has become heavily Democratic, as are East Lansing and surrounding Ingham County. East Lansing voters approved in 2016 the legalization of marijuana on private property, but not on the Michigan State campus. Four years later, a marijuana company Bazonzoes Provisioning Center, opened its headquarters in Lansing. Otherwise, the university continued to grow and the Lansing area diversified, with about 10,000 employees working at several large insurance companies.

Just east of Ingham is quite another part of Michigan, Livingston County. Forty years ago it was mostly rural, known mainly for its many lakes. Then, subdivisions, schools and shopping malls sprouted up. Most of these people are conservatives, happy to leave behind the urban problems of Detroit, unhappy about high taxes, and hewing to traditional religious faiths. They have made Livingston one of Michigan's fastest-growing counties—its population rose 20 percent from 2000 to 2017—and, historically, one of its most Republican. But in 2020, Democrats ran almost even with their Republican rivals there in statewide campaigns.

The 8th Congressional District of Michigan includes exurban Ingham and Livingston counties and the northern, more rural parts of Oakland County north of Detroit, which has slightly more than one-third of the district vote. In past years, the two outlying counties more-or-less canceled each other out politically, with Oakland casting the tie-breaker. In 2016, Donald Trump took the district, 50%-43%. But the heavily Democratic trend and turnout in Ingham nearly matched the GOP leads in Livingston and Oakland, and narrowed the overall difference to less than one percentage point in Trump's favor.

Andy Levin (D)

Elected 2018, 2nd term, b. Aug 10, 1960; Berkley, MI; Williams College, B.A., 1983; University of MI, M.A., 1990; Harvard University Law School, J.D., 1994; Jewish; Married (Mary Freeman); 4 children.

Professional Career: Staff Attorney, Commission on the Future of Worker-Management Relations, 1994-1995; Chief Workforce Officer, State of Michigan, 2007-2010; Deputy Director, MI Department of Energy, Labor & Economic Growth, 2007-2011; Founder & Managing Partner, Levin Energy Partners, 2011-2018.

DC Office: 228 CHOB 20515, 202-225-4961, andylevin.house.gov

State Offices: Warren, 586-498-7122.

Committees: *Education & Labor*: Early Childhood, Elementary & Secondary Education; Health, Employment, Labor & Pensions. *Foreign Affairs*: Asia, the Pacific, Central Asia, Nonproliferation; West Hem, Civ Sec, Migration, & Intern'l Econ Policy.

Almanac Ratings 2019-2020

	Economy	Social	Foreign	Composite
Liberal	100%	100%	100%	100%
Conservative	0%	0%	0%	0%

Key Votes of the 116th Congress

1. U.S./Mex./Can. trade deal N	5. Russia sanctions Y	9. Firearms background checks Y
2. First Coronavirus response Y	6. Troops in Syria Y	10. Spending at the border N
3. HEROES Act Y	7. Veto arms sales to Saudis Y	11. Marijuana liberalized rules Y
4. CASH Act Y	8. Defense $$$, veto override Y	12. Electoral College objections N

Election Results

Election	Name (Party)	Vote (%)		Cand. Spent	Ind. Exp. Support	Ind. Exp. Oppose
2020 General	Andy Levin (D).............................	230,318	(58%)	$695,646	$14,880	
	Charles Langworthy (R)....................	153,296	(38%)		$400	$170
	Andrea Kirby (Working Class)...............	8,970	(2%)			
2020 Primary	Andy Levin (D)................................	103,202	(100%)			

Prior winning percentages: 2018 (60%)

Freshman Democrat Andy Levin had a mostly smooth ride as he succeeded his father, Sander Levin, who retired after holding the seat for 36 years. Carl Levin, his uncle, served 36 years as a senator from Michigan. The heir—who was not shy about reminding voters of his family connections —had spent much of his career dealing with public policy, both within and outside government. His election to the House was his first successful political bid.

Although he styled himself as a conventional Democrat, Levin occasionally straddled his approach. "Andy is hard to pigeonhole. He is a successful entrepreneur, but also an equally successful union organizer," according to his campaign bio. "He has been at the forefront of progressive causes for decades – while also building highly effective programs within government." That might reflect the political shifts among some of his Macomb County constituents, who occasionally have been described as "Reagan Democrats."

Levin's family roots in the Detroit area date to the 1890s, though his father's career also gave him a presence in Washington. After graduating from Williams College and getting a master's from the University of Michigan and his law degree from Harvard University, Levin spent his early professional years as an activist on environmental issues and international human rights in places ranging from China to Haiti. He was an assistant director of organizing for the national AFL-CIO and a staff attorney for the Commission on the Future of Worker-Management Relations during the Clinton administration.

After an unsuccessful campaign for the Michigan Senate in 2006, Levin worked for Democratic Gov. Jennifer Granholm as deputy director of the state's Department of Energy Labor and Economic Growth. In 2011, he created a Detroit-based business, Levin Energy Partners, which developed public-private partnerships to achieve clean-energy solutions.

Days after his father announced his retirement, Levin launched his candidacy for Congress. Democrats needed to refocus with "a new approach to politics," he said. "More progressive. More practical. Less partisan." The election of President Donald Trump in 2016, including his narrow victory in Michigan, was "the culmination of 40 years of trickle-down economics facilitated by 60 years of divide and conquer politics." He called for building "a movement for economic and social justice."

In the Democratic primary, Levin's chief challenger was Ellen Lipton, who served six years as a state representative before she was term-limited. Lipton, who lost a bid for the state Senate in 2014, told the Detroit Free Press that she approached politics with her training as a mediator in mind: "to do more listening than talking." Levin appealed to progressive voters with his embrace of "Medicare for all" and an expansion of Social Security. The Detroit News, in endorsing Lipton, cited her work in Lansing on issues such as stem cell research and criminal justice reform. Both Levin and Lipton spent a bit more than $1 million in the primary.

Levin led the primary with 53 percent of the vote to 42 percent for Lipton; Martin Brook, who had served as president of the Bloomfield Hills School Board of Education, got 5 percent. In Macomb County, which cast nearly three-fifths of the vote, Levin took 56 percent. Lipton led Levin by a few hundred votes in Oakland County.

In November, Levin defeated political newcomer Candius Stearns—a health care insurance agent who criticized the "outrageous" cost to consumers of the Affordable Care Act. His 60%-37% victory continued a tradition among Michigan Democrats of keeping House seats within their family for many decades: Reps. Debbie Dingell and Dan Kildee succeeded their husband and uncle, respectively.

In the House, Levin showed his father's interest in the details of international trade agreements. On the revision of the U.S. trade deal with Mexico and Canada, he joined other Democrats in pushing for higher wages for Mexican workers. He said it would take a new Democratic president to add tougher language on climate policy. On the annual defense spending bill in July 2020, Levin won House approval of his measure to prevent the use of PFA's, a cancer-causing chemical that is found in foam, until the Defense secretary completes approval of Pentagon regulations. With his seat on the Education and Labor Committee, he filed with Sen. Elizabeth Warren a bill to create a federal public health workforce to put unemployed Americans back to work in their communities. On the Foreign Affairs Committee, he advocated steps to promote democracy.

Levin won reelection with 58 percent of the vote against a low-profile challenger. Following the 2020 election, the Biden transition team reportedly gave him serious consideration for the position of Labor secretary. House Democrats' razor-thin majority and the risk that Republicans could win his seat in a special election worked against his prospects.

MI-9: Northern Detroit Suburbs   **Cook Partisan Voting Index: D+4**

Population		Race and Ethnicity		Income	
Total	718,223	White	76.60%	Median Income	$62,943
Land area (sq. miles)	184	Black	13.90%	District Income Rank	224
Pop/ sq mi	3,912.1	Latino	2.60%	Poverty Rate	9.30%
Born in State	76.20%	Asian	5.40%	With health insurance	94.40%
		Two or more races	3.30%	Cash public assistance	1.70%
Age Groups		Other	0.90%	Food stamp/SNAP	9.70%
Under 18	19.30%				
18-34	23.90%	Education		Work	
35-64	39.50%	H.S grad or less	37.90%	White Collar	38.70%
Over 64	17.30%	Some college	30.80%	Sales and Service	37.80%
		College Degree, 4 yr	19.30%	Blue Collar	23.50%
Military		Post grad	12.10%	Government	8.40%
Veteran/ Active Duty	5.80%				

2020 Pres. Vote	Biden	229,258	(56%)	Trump	175,081	(43%)		
2016 Pres. Vote	Clinton	183,085	(51%)	Trump	155,597	(44%)	Johnson 12,101	(3%)

Southern Macomb, Eastern Oakland: The flat expanse of land just north of Eight Mile Road, Detroit's northern city limit, was mostly vacant in the years just after World War II. A string of suburbs in Oakland County ran along Woodward Avenue from the Detroit city limits to the National Shrine of the Little Flower Catholic Church in Royal Oak, where Father Charles Coughlin in the 1930s made his radio broadcasts opposing Franklin D. Roosevelt and denouncing bankers and Jews. In the 1950s and 1960s, Woodward was one of America's greatest cruising highways, where teenagers drove big Detroit cars up and down the eight lanes and where the lights were timed at 42 miles per hour. Since 1994, the annual Woodward Dream Cruise of old cars has commemorated that era with a celebration drawing more than 1 million spectators. To the east, in Macomb County, was some industrial development along rail lines, but this too was mostly empty land in the 1950s.

Then, Polish Americans began migrating out Van Dyke Avenue from Hamtramck to Warren. Italian Americans headed out Gratiot Avenue from Detroit's east side to Roseville and Clinton Township. Belgian Americans from the Mack corridor moved out farther to St. Clair Shores. Today, half of metro Detroit's population is north of Eight Mile, as African Americans and other minorities have joined Whites in moving to the suburbs. In 2019, 14 percent of both Oakland and Macomb County residents were Black.

The 9th Congressional District covers this suburban territory, with about two-thirds of its population in Macomb County. On the more heavily Democratic Oakland County side are Royal Oak and Ferndale, which have been economically revitalized, attracting singles and gays as well as traditional families. The Macomb side includes its more Democratic neighborhoods in the southern part of the county: Warren and much of Sterling Heights, site of the General Motors Technical Center, a big Fiat Chrysler plant, and the M-1 tank plant, which helps make metro Detroit a major defense manufacturer. GM has improved its local battery lab as the company increases its production of electric vehicles. Chrysler has spent a billion dollars at its Warren plant to upgrade manufacturing of Ram trucks and Wagoneer SUVs.

Farther east are the blue-collar communities of the southern portion of Macomb: Eastpointe (formerly known as East Detroit, it voted to change its name to make it sound less like Detroit and more like tony Grosse Pointe); Roseville; St. Clair Shores; Clinton Township; and Mount Clemens. Overall, the district is Democratic, although not overwhelmingly so. Between 2007 and 2016, more than 20,000 refugees from Iraq and Syria settled in this area. Those numbers dropped sharply during the Trump administration. In 2020, Joe Biden won the district, 56%-43%, an improvement of five percentage points for Democrats. Donald Trump took Macomb, 53%-45%, a Democratic increase of three points; nearly half of Macomb—its far more Republican portion—is in the 10th District. Michael Taylor, the Republican mayor of Sterling Heights, in March 2020 endorsed Biden as "the candidate who can appeal to moderates and Republicans like me who don't want to see four more years of President Trump." Sterling Heights, the fourth largest city in Michigan, is divided between the 9th and 10th Districts.

Political experts in Macomb have cited parallels between "Reagan Democrats" and "Trump Democrats," especially in each president's embrace by working-class white voters.

Lisa McClain (R)

Elected 2020, 1st term, b. Apr 07, 1966; Stockbridge, MI; Lansing Community College, Assc. Deg.; Northwood University, B.B.A.; Roman Catholic; Married (Mike McClain); 3 children.

Professional Career: District Manager, American Express Financial Advisors Inc./IDS Life Insurance Company, 1987-1997; Senior Vice President, securities brokerage firm, 1997-1999; Advisor, Senior Vice President, President, financial company.

DC Office: 218 CHOB 20515, 202-225-2106, Fax: 202-226-1169, mcclain.house.gov

State Offices: Washington, 586-697-9300.

Committees: *Armed Services*: Military Personnel; Readiness. *Education & Labor*: Civil Rights & Human Services; Higher Education & Workforce Investment.

Election Results

Election	Name (Party)	Vote (%)		Cand. Spent	Ind. Exp. Support	Ind. Exp. Oppose
2020 General	Lisa McClain (R)	271,607	(66%)	$2,135,170	$124,072	$801,095
	Kimberly Bizon (D)	138,179	(34%)	$36,285	$10	
2020 Primary	Lisa McClain (R)	50,927	(42%)			
	Shane Hernandez (R)	44,526	(36%)			
	Doug Slocum (R)	26,750	(22%)			

Lisa McClain, a successful financial executive making her first bid for political office, was elected as the only Republican in a House seat in at least part of the Detroit metro area. In the Michigan delegation with five Democratic women, she is the first Republican woman since Candice Miller gave up the same seat in 2016. McClain succeeded Republican Paul Mitchell, who retired after two terms and voiced objections about how President Donald Trump performed his job.

A Michigan native, McClain got a bachelor's degree in business administration from Northwood University. She spent a decade as a district manager for Ameriprise, which was a division of American Express. In 1998, she helped to launch the Hantz Group, a Michigan-based financial services company, and became one of the first employees. As senior vice president of the firm, which grew to more than 700 employees, she managed more than $7 billion in assets.

In announcing her candidacy, McClain cited her "real-life business, leadership and people experience" and said that she would run as a "conservative outsider"—a theme that she believed would resonate in a district where Trump won 64 percent in the 2016 election. She was endorsed by Maggie's List, a national political action committee that seeks to elect fiscally conservative women. McClain also was supported by the Susan B. Anthony List, which backs pro-life candidates.

The early frontrunner in the GOP contest was Shane Hernandez, a state representative who chaired the House Appropriations Committee, while citing his father's background as a low-income migrant worker. He was supported by the conservative Club for Growth, which spent $1.6 million on his behalf—including an ad that criticized McClain because she "didn't give a dime to help President Trump against Hillary."

Retiring Rep. Mitchell endorsed Hernandez as "the only conservative" in the contest. In an ad, he criticized attacks from McClain and her supporters—including a McClain ad contending that Hernandez was late in supporting Trump in 2016 and that he worked with Democratic Gov. Gretchen Whitmer on the state budget.

McClain was the biggest spender in the primary, with $1.6 million, most of which she self-financed. She won the GOP contest with 42 percent of the vote and led in four of the six counties; she took 47 percent in Macomb County, which cast nearly half the total vote. Hernandez, who led in St. Clair and Sanilac counties, got 36 percent. Doug Slocum, a retired brigadier general in the Air Force and the former commander of Selfridge Air National Guard base, got the remaining 22 percent.

In a post-primary interview with the Detroit News, McClain explained her success, "I think that outsider sells." In its editorial endorsement, the News wrote, "McClain's conservative priorities seem well aligned with those of the district." The newspaper had endorsed Hernandez in the primary.

In November, McClain defeated Democrat Kimberly Bizon, an online marketing director and environmental activist for "international climate reality," with 66 percent of the vote. Her support was a few percentage points more than Mitchell received during his two successful campaigns. She took more than 60 percent in each of the six counties.

In the House, McClain got seats on the Armed Services, and Education and Labor committees. She joined the majority of House Republicans in voting for Congress to investigate the Electoral College results in Arizona and Pennsylvania. In reviewing the presidential vote, she said, Congress has "the authority to voice concerns, raised by their respective constituents, with an election."

MI-10: Detroit Northern Exurbs, "The Thumb"

Cook Partisan Voting Index: R+18

Population		Race and Ethnicity		Income	
Total	721,753	White	91.90%	Median Income	$67,472
Land area (sq. miles)	419	Black	3.20%	District Income Rank	187
Pop/ sq mi	1,721.49	Latino	3.40%	Poverty Rate	8.10%
Born in State	83.30%	Asian	1.70%	With health insurance	94.50%
		Two or more races	2.00%	Cash public assistance	2.20%
Age Groups		Other	1.20%	Food stamp/SNAP	8.10%
Under 18	21.00%				
18-34	19.00%	**Education**		**Work**	
35-64	40.70%	H.S grad or less	39.50%	White Collar	38.30%
Over 64	19.30%	Some college	35.70%	Sales and Service	35.00%
		College Degree, 4 yr	15.60%	Blue Collar	26.60%
Military		Post grad	9.30%	Government	10.50%
Veteran/ Active Duty	7.70%				

2020 Pres. Vote	Trump	273,904	(64%)	Biden	146,869	(34%)		
2016 Pres. Vote	Trump	228,190	(64%)	Clinton	113,045	(32%)	Johnson	11,997	(3%)

Macomb, St. Clair: Macomb County, just northeast of Detroit, has been one of the nation's most closely watched political battlegrounds, a place where it once seemed the electoral fate of Michigan and even the entire country might be determined. It owes much of that to its reputation as blue-collar suburbia. These suburbanites were often from the east side of Detroit and were typically Catholic, at least modestly well-off, and ancestrally Democratic. They accepted the New Deal as part of their natural heritage. In 1960, Macomb County was the most Democratic major suburban county in the nation, voting 63 percent for the first Catholic president, John F. Kennedy.

But these Democrats resented the efforts of Detroit politicians to tax them to pay for welfare programs and were fearful of the city's crime problem. From 1980 to 1992, no Democratic presidential candidate got more than 40 percent of the vote in Macomb. In 1996, after great effort and with the advice of pollster Stan Greenberg, who had studied Macomb closely, Bill Clinton carried the county by a solid 50%-39%. The 54 percent vote for Donald Trump in 2016 suggested that Macomb had gone back to the future.

"There are, in a sense, two Macombs," Zack Stanton wrote in Politico in 2017. "The county is bisected at the waist by M-59 (roughly speaking, 20 Mile Road). To the north are the traditionally Republican areas of the county ('the sticks,' as Kid Rock called it in 'Trucker Anthem'), once a largely rural area dotted with small towns, which has undergone massive growth during the last two decades thanks to an influx of sprawling upper middle-class subdivisions. The southern half of the county is its traditionally Democratic portion—denser, poorer, working-class, and, by and large, built in the mid-20th century and heavily reliant on manufacturing."

Lately, central and northern Macomb County have been filling up with fast-growing and expensive subdivisions that are more conservative than the affluent parts of Oakland County. More people hold white-collar jobs than blue-collar jobs these days, and there is far less work in auto plants than during earlier generations. But the recovery has been relatively strong. In 2019, Macomb had 874,000 people, compared with 185,000 residents in 1950. Those seeking optimism about the future of Macomb can point to Ford and Fiat Chrysler each spending more than $1 billion on their assembly plants in Sterling Heights. To the north, St. Clair County, which has become busy with commercial development, styles itself as the gateway to Lake Huron. The tip of the Thumb has more than 20 wind farms—the most in Michigan.

The 10th Congressional District of Michigan centers on the northern tier of Macomb, and encompasses nearly half of the county's population. M-59 is much of the east-west dividing line between the 9th and 10th Districts. The 10th includes Lapeer County and most of Michigan's Thumb, which probably was created by geological formations several hundred thousand years ago. The second-largest county is St. Clair, with Port Huron and its Blue Water Bridge to Sarnia in Canada; Students for a Democratic Society drafted its famous Port Huron Statement just north of there in Lakeport in 1962, setting the stage for the counterculture movement. The Thumb has long been very Republican. Slightly more than half the voters are in Macomb. In 2020, Trump increased GOP support to 64%-34%; as in 2016, that made the 10th the most Republican district in the state. That margin was a remarkable shift from John McCain's 50%-48% tight lead over Obama in 2008. Trump's strong performance in Macomb reinforced the parallels between "Reagan Democrats" and "Trump Democrats," especially in each president's embrace of economic change and hope.

Haley Stevens (D)

Elected 2018, 2nd term, b. Jun 24, 1983; Oakland County, MI; American University, B.A., 2005; American University, M.A., 2007; Christian Church; Married.

Professional Career: Chief of Staff, Presidential Task Force on the Auto Industry.

DC Office: 227 CHOB 20515, 202-225-8171, stevens.house.gov
State Offices: Livonia, 734-853-3040.

Committees: *Education & Labor*: Health, Employment, Labor & Pensions; Workforce Protections. *Science, Space & Technology*: Energy; Research & Technology (Chmn).

Almanac Ratings 2019-2020

	Economy	Social	Foreign	Composite
Liberal	100%	100%	80%	94%
Conservative	0%	0%	20%	6%

Key Votes of the 116th Congress

1. U.S./Mex./Can. trade deal Y	5. Russia sanctions Y	9. Firearms background checks Y
2. First Coronavirus response Y	6. Troops in Syria Y	10. Spending at the border Y
3. HEROES Act Y	7. Veto arms sales to Saudis Y	11. Marijuana liberalized rules Y
4. CASH Act Y	8. Defense $$$, veto override Y	12. Electoral College objections N

Election Results

Election	Name (Party)	Vote (%)	Cand. Spent	Ind. Exp. Support	Ind. Exp. Oppose
2020 General	Haley Stevens (D)............................ 226,128	(50%)	$6,034,086	$98,635	$2,369,469
	Eric Esshaki (R).............................. 215,405	(48%)	$1,268,569	$260,129	$1,166,025
2020 Primary	Haley Stevens (D).......................... 105,251	(100%)			

Prior winning percentages: 2018 (52%)

Democrat Haley Stevens won a suburban seat that Republicans had held for decades. Stevens—who had scant professional time in Michigan after leaving for college—emphasized her work during the Obama administration in helping rescue the auto industry, plus her private-sector experience in promoting the tech economy. In the House, she took an interest in education and science issues. She narrowly won reelection.

Stevens, a native of Oakland County, got her bachelor's degree in political science and a master's degree in social policy and philosophy, both from American University in Washington D.C. After working for Hillary Clinton and then for Barack Obama in the 2008 presidential campaign, she joined the new Obama administration as chief of staff for the White House auto task force that oversaw the bailout of General Motors and Chrysler, which she said resulted in the rescue of 200,000 Michigan jobs. Later, she was a policy adviser on advanced manufacturing at the Economic Development Administration.

Outside government, Stevens developed an export-assistance program for Bloomberg Philanthropies in Louisville Kentucky. With the Chicago-based Digital Manufacturing and Design Innovation Institute, she helped create an online certification program for digital manufacturing.

Stevens returned home in early 2017 and launched her campaign prior to Republican Rep. David Trott's decision to retire. She said her objective was to promote Michigan's tech economy and "world-class" workforce. "I have inarguably one of the most profound backgrounds in manufacturing of anyone running for Congress in the country," she told Crain's Detroit Business. Other contenders in the wide-open Democratic primary included Tim Greimel, the former state House Democratic leader, who was endorsed by the United Auto Workers and prominent local Democratic officials. Fayrouz Saad, who worked on immigration issues for Detroit Mayor Mike Duggan and was a Homeland Security Department official during the Obama administration, was backed by national progressive groups and highlighted her background as a Muslim woman.

Many Democrats believed Stevens would be their strongest candidate in the general election, David Wasserman of the Cook Political Report wrote prior to the primary. "But she's struggled to break out because the presence of another female candidate [Saad] ... has kept EMILY's List on the sidelines" — a reference to the pro-abortion rights group that supports Democratic women. Stevens won the primary with 27 percent of the vote. Greimel was runner-up with 22 percent; Saad got 19 percent.

Lena Epstein, the Republican nominee, was co-owner of a family business that produced automotive and industrial lubricants. In 2016, she co-chaired Donald Trump's successful presidential campaign in Michigan. In its editorial endorsing Stevens, the Detroit Free Press praised her "encyclopedic" knowledge of manufacturing issues in Michigan and criticized Epstein as "ill-prepared for elective office." Stevens, who outspent Epstein by a wide margin and received more than $1 million in support from House Democratic groups, won 52%-45%.

In the House, Stevens enacted her bipartisan bill to encourage more teaching of STEM (science, technology, education and math) topics, especially to young girls. "Women and girls everywhere need to know that they can succeed in the STEM fields, and that our country and our economy won't succeed without them," she said. As chairwoman of the Research and Technology Subcommittee of the Science, Space and Technology panel, she also won committee approval of a bill to combat sexual harassment in science.

In her swing district, Stevens got some coattails in 2020 from the improved local performance of the Democratic presidential ticket. Running against Eric Esshaki, a first-time candidate, Stevens also benefited from what Wasserman described as "a GOP recruitment failure" in the contest. Stevens spent $6 million, nearly five times what Esshaki spent, and was endorsed by the Chamber of Commerce of the United States—which typically has backed Republicans in competitive contests. Her 50%-48% victory was narrower than her first election.

In the Democratic presidential primary, Stevens initially supported former New York City Mayor Michael Bloomberg. After he dropped out, Stevens endorsed Joe Biden, citing his support for the auto industry in 2009, when it "was on its back."

MI-11: Central Detroit Suburbs

Cook Partisan Voting Index: R+2

Population		Race and Ethnicity		Income	
Total	735,677	White	80.60%	Median Income	$88,253
Land area (sq. miles)	403	Black	4.90%	District Income Rank	62
Pop/ sq mi	1,824.55	Latino	4.40%	Poverty Rate	5.70%
Born in State	68.90%	Asian	11.20%	With health insurance	96.20%
		Two or more races	2.80%	Cash public assistance	0.90%
Age Groups		Other	0.60%	Food stamp/SNAP	4.10%
Under 18	21.10%				
18-34	19.80%	**Education**		**Work**	
35-64	41.50%	H.S grad or less	22.60%	White Collar	53.40%
Over 64	17.70%	Some college	28.30%	Sales and Service	32.10%
Military		College Degree, 4 yr	27.80%	Blue Collar	14.40%
Veteran/ Active Duty	5.20%	Post grad	21.30%	Government	8.90%

2020 Pres. Vote	Biden	237,696	(51%)	Trump	216,799	(47%)		
2016 Pres. Vote	Trump	194,245	(49%)	Clinton	177,143	(45%)	Johnson	14,960	(4%)

Southern Oakland, Western Wayne: While Detroit has struggled with seemingly endemic urban decay, many of its suburbs have shown more resilience than the city that spawned them—and a more youthful adaptability to economic change. Sixty years ago, Livonia had 18,000 people. By 2019, it had a population of 94,000. Ford announced in December 2019 its plan to spend $1.5 billion at two factories in the Detroit area that will build new models of pickup trucks, SUVs, and electric and autonomous vehicles. The money will be split between Ford's plants in Wayne and Dearborn. Ford's F-150 is the largest-selling vehicle in the United States.

Novi, in Oakland County, is a high-income suburb that grew 29 percent between 2000 and 2019. Its Asian-American population was 24 percent in 2019, and it has been nicknamed "Little Tokyo." Many of these newcomers have work visas and participate in research and development, as Japanese automotive suppliers increasingly build their products in the United States; the city has adapted by offering multilingual instruction in its hospitals, workplaces and schools. Novi had plans for a $50 million, mixed-use Asian village that would feature the first local dedicated retail, restaurant and entertainment area. But groundbreaking, which had been planned for 2019, was stalled by several factors, including the pandemic. "We haven't made progress and there is an evolution of plans that is not loyal to the original vision," Justin Fischer, a member of the Novi City Council, said in September 2020, according to Hometown Life. "I am inclined to let the agreement lapse."

In partnership with Fiat-Chrysler, Google has built Waymo—a self-drive development center in Novi. In January 2019, Waymo announced its plan to build a 200,000-square-foot manufacturing center by 2024. Waymo said the Detroit-based plant will be the first factory dedicated to mass production of autonomous vehicles. Uber also has a research and testing facility. Oakland County has styled itself as the center for autonomous vehicles.

The 11th Congressional District of Michigan covers several suburbs west and northwest of Detroit. About three-fifths of the district is in southern Oakland County, including Troy, Birmingham and Novi, plus Bloomfield Hills and Waterford to the north; the remainder is in western Wayne County, with Northville and Plymouth plus Livonia. The district is 11 percent Asian, which is the largest minority group in the 80 percent white district. Livonia had been closely divided between the two major parties. An influx of affluent residents into this part of Wayne County has helped give the 11th District the highest per capita income and the lowest poverty rate of any district in Michigan. Strikingly, the upscale 11th had little change from 2012 to the 2016 presidential contest, which Donald Trump won 49%-45%. But the 2020 election was a significant turnaround: Joe Biden won the district, 52%-47%. The change resulted from an increase of about 60,000 Democratic votes during the four years, compared to an increase of only 22,000 Republicans.

Debbie Dingell (D)

Elected 2014, 4th term, b. Nov 23, 1953; Detroit, MI; Convent of the Sacred Heart, Grosse Pointe, MI; Georgetown University, B.S., 1975; Georgetown University, M.S., 1996; Roman Catholic; Widow; 4 children.

Elected Office: Wayne State U. Board of Governors, 2007-2014.

Professional Career: President, sr. Executive public affairs, GM Foundation; Founder, Chairman, Nat'l Women's Health Resource Cntr. & the Children's Inn, Nat'l Inst. of Health; Co-host, Detroit public TV show "Am I Right."

DC Office: 116 CHOB 20515, 202-225-4071, Fax: 202-226-0371, debbiedingell.house.gov

State Offices: Dearborn, 313-278-2936; Ypsilanti, 734-481-1100.

Committees: *Energy & Commerce*: Consumer Protection & Commerce; Environment & Climate Change; Health. *Natural Resources*: Energy & Mineral Resources; National Parks, Forests & Public Lands; Water, Oceans & Wildlife.

Group Ratings

	ADA	ACLU	AFL-CIO	LCV	COC	HAFA	ACU	CFG	FRC
2020	**	85%	**	100%	-	0%	2%	**	-
2019	85%	C	100%	97%	53%	C	2%	12%	0%

Almanac Ratings 2019-2020

	Economy	Social	Foreign	Composite
Liberal	100%	63%	81%	82%
Conservative	0%	37%	19%	18%

Key Votes of the 116th Congress

1. U.S./Mex./Can. trade deal Y	5. Russia sanctions Y	9. Firearms background checks Y
2. First Coronavirus response Y	6. Troops in Syria Y	10. Spending at the border N
3. HEROES Act Y	7. Veto arms sales to Saudis Y	11. Marijuana liberalized rules Y
4. CASH Act Y	8. Defense $$$, veto override Y	12. Electoral College objections N

Election Results

Election	Name (Party)	Vote (%)		Cand. Spent	Ind. Exp. Support	Ind. Exp. Oppose
2020 General	Debbie Dingell (D)	254,957	(66%)	$1,335,007	$7,394	
	Jeff Jones (R)	117,719	(31%)	$6,475		$224
	Gary Walkowicz (Working Class)	11,147	(3%)			
2020 Primary	Debbie Dingell (D)	103,953	(81%)			
	Solomon Rajput (D)	24,497	(19%)			

Prior winning percentages: 2018 (68%), 2016 (64%), 2014 (65%)

Democrat Debbie Dingell, elected in 2014, has been a longtime power player and the widow of Rep. John Dingell, the Dean of the House who retired after a record 59 years and died in 2019 after several illnesses. Her succession constituted a historic level of political continuity and she became the first wife of a sitting member to take a seat while the spouse remained alive. She has created her own niche: less cantankerous and more of a team player than her husband, but willing to hold Democrats accountable. She has served as one of three co-chairs of the Democrats' policy and communications arm.

During the long era that her husband was a powerful member of Congress, Debbie Dingell was a well-known figure in her own right following their marriage in 1981, the year John Dingell became chairman of the Energy and Commerce Committee. She grew up in a family with close ties to General Motors. Her grandfather cofounded Fisher Body, an early and important GM acquisition. After completing college at Georgetown, she joined GM as a lobbyist in 1977. That year, she met her future husband. After they married, she gave up her lobbying but remained a senior executive of GM until 2009, managing its public affairs operation and heading the GM Foundation.

As an influential operative, Dingell developed an extensive network with a hand in high-stakes political activities. A member of the Democratic National Committee, she ran Al Gore's Michigan campaign in 2000 and took on the same role for John Kerry four years later. She promoted women's health issues and Michigan economic development through her work with foundations.

Dingell decided against a run for the Senate when Democratic Sen. Carl Levin announced he would retire in 2014. When her husband said he would retire as Congress' longest-serving member, she became his likely successor in the solidly blue district where close ties to GM help rather than hurt. Remarkably, with her husband and his father John Dingell Sr., a Dingell family member has represented the Detroit area in the House non-stop since 1933.

Dingell won the primary with 78 percent of the vote against token opposition. Against Republican Terry Bowman, a Ford autoworker whom she outspent 38-to-1, Dingell coasted to a 65%-31% victory in November. After her win, she said, "I am more interested in finding solutions than looking for fights."

As a junior member in the minority party, Dingell wielded an unusual range of influence. She was named a senior whip, vice chair of the seniors' task force for the Democratic Caucus, and co-chair of a Democratic Congressional Campaign Committee project to recruit more women candidates. A few days before the 2016 election, she said one of the "worst things" with the Affordable Care Act is that Democrats passed it without any Republican votes. Two days after the election, she wrote in an op-ed in The Washington Post that she had repeatedly warned Democratic officials that they were taking her state for granted. "I was the crazy one. I predicted that Hillary Clinton was in trouble in Michigan during the Democratic primary. ... I noted that we could see a Trump presidency."

Dingell has set some distinctive policy viewpoints, occasionally with a personal nuance. She criticized GM when it announced in late 2018 its plan to cut more than 14,000 jobs, and she warned that she would oppose international trade modifications favored by the company if GM shifted more jobs overseas. "They'll never, ever get my support on anything," she said on CNN. With her seat on Energy and Commerce, where she has deep familiarity with its history, practices and tensions, Dingell has been a prime sponsor of legislation to speed the development of self-driving vehicles. Across the board, she emphasized the need for bipartisanship and compromise.

She was a founder and co-chair of the Medicare for All Caucus. (John Dingell Sr. filed the original bill that led to the creation of Medicare.), Citing physical threats she experienced from her father when she was a child, Dingell has filed bipartisan bills to restrict access to firearms by domestic abusers and stalkers. In December 2020, the House passed her bipartisan bill to eliminate restrictions on scientific research of medical marijuana. "We can empower the researchers who will educate the public about any and all potential benefits and risks of marijuana use," she said.

As a co-chair of the leadership's Democratic Policy and Communications Committee, Dingell has cautioned, "we have to listen to the working men and women and show them we are going to deliver on issues that matter to them." Prior to the 2020 election, she warned Democrats not to take for granted encouraging polls for Joe Biden. "There are some very complicated issues that Trump is playing to divide this country," she told The Atlantic in July.

Following the election, when GM withdrew from litigation challenging stricter fuel-economy standards in California, Dingell said the company "did the right thing." She said other automakers should follow its example of supporting a single national program that "delivers on the twin goals of giving the industry certainty while reducing greenhouse gas emissions."

MI-12: Southern Detroit Suburbs   Cook Partisan Voting Index: D+13

Population		Race and Ethnicity		Income	
Total	704,912	White	77.60%	Median Income	$62,253
Land area (sq. miles)	185	Black	11.30%	District Income Rank	229
Pop/ sq mi	3,813.43	Latino	6.20%	Poverty Rate	15.20%
Born in State	68.90%	Asian	5.50%	With health insurance	95.60%
		Two or more races	3.60%	Cash public assistance	1.80%
Age Groups		Other	2.10%	Food stamp/SNAP	9.80%
Under 18	20.50%				
18-34	27.80%	**Education**		**Work**	
35-64	36.10%	H.S grad or less	35.80%	White Collar	43.20%
Over 64	15.50%	Some college	29.40%	Sales and Service	34.50%
		College Degree, 4 yr	17.60%	Blue Collar	22.40%
Military		Post grad	17.30%	Government	15.20%
Veteran/ Active Duty	6.30%				

2020 Pres. Vote	Biden	251,772	(64%)	Trump	134,889	(34%)		
2016 Pres. Vote	Clinton	205,953	(60%)	Trump	116,719	(34%)	Johnson	10,293	(3%)

Ann Arbor: The American-made automobile may be a vanishing breed elsewhere, but it still reigns supreme in Dearborn, the home of Ford Motor Co.'s headquarters. At the far eastern edge of Dearborn is Ford's famous River Rouge complex, which initially produced anti-submarine ships for use in World War I and which at one point contained almost all the equipment needed to manufacture an automobile from raw materials through finished product.

The 12th District of Michigan covers southern and central Wayne County and is a predominantly White, blue-collar district centered on Dearborn. South of Dearborn, the district swings around heavily African-American Romulus and Inkster (which are in the 13th District), taking in several working-class Detroit suburbs known collectively as the "Downriver" area: Taylor; Southgate; Woodhaven, the site of another big Ford plant; and Flat Rock, home to a joint Ford-Mazda facility and one of the few Japanese auto plants in Michigan. When Ford initially announced its plan to spend $200 million at its manufacturing and innovation center in Flat Rock, its focus was on electric cars. That later shifted to autonomous vehicles, including an entirely new model; work on the cheaper electrics shifted to Mexico.

Ford has made long-term commitments to Dearborn, with an upgrade of its headquarters campus plus large office space on the west side of town. In November 2020, it unveiled a site plans to move up to 5,000 of its workers to a new campus in Detroit's Corktown neighborhood, which includes that city's train station that has been abandoned since 1988. The $740 million plan for what Bill Ford described as an "innovation hub" calls for four buildings on a 30-acre site. One project could be a self-driving corridor from Detroit to Ann Arbor. Also in Dearborn is the Arab American Museum, which provides an overview of Detroit's large and diverse Arab population. The district takes in Ypsilanti, where the Transportation Department established the American Center for Mobility, a driverless car testing facility at GM's abandoned Willow Run plant.

Also in the 12th is two-thirds of Washtenaw County, which centers on the University of Michigan and Ann Arbor, one of the nation's largest university towns. It is oriented to the university but also is home to auto executives and young families who like a town with plenty of bookstores, coffeehouses and liberal neighbors. The university has created a large pharmaceutical research center —with 2,200 employees—on a campus that it purchased from Pfizer. Ann Arbor has become a rapidly growing business center that has been ranked among the most innovative cities in the nation. In 2017, Google's Ad Words unit, which operates the company's "pay-per-click" advertising method, its main revenue source, opened its long-delayed corporate campus near the university, with 450 employees. A downside is that Washtenaw has become economically and racially segregated with rampant inequality across the county, according to a study by a national network of local governments.

The district is Democratic territory. In 2016, Hillary Clinton won 60 percent of the vote against Donald Trump. Joe Biden increased that to 64 percent, with an increase of 45,000 Democratic votes. The Washtenaw County portion includes about 40 percent of the district and the university center is its center of Democratic activism, with an overwhelming partisan vote. The remainder is in Wayne County.

Rashida Tlaib (D)

Elected 2018, 2nd term, b. Jul 24, 1976; Detroit, MI; Wayne State University, B.A., 1998; Western MI University, J.D., 2004; Muslim; Married (Fayez Tlaib); 2 children.

Elected Office: MI House, 2008-2015.

Professional Career: Assistant, MI State Rep. Steve Tobocman; Social Worker

DC Office: 1628 LHOB 20515, 202-225-5126, tlaib.house.gov

State Offices: River Rouge, 313-203-7540.

Committees: *Financial Services*: Diversity & Inclusion; Oversight & Investigations. *Natural Resources*: National Parks, Forests & Public Lands. *Oversight & Reform*: Subcommittee on Civil Rights & Civil Liberties; Subcommittee on Environment.

Almanac Ratings 2019-2020

	Economy	Social	Foreign	Composite
Liberal	100%	65%	57%	74%
Conservative	0%	35%	43%	26%

Key Votes of the 116th Congress

1. U.S./Mex./Can. trade deal	N	5. Russia sanctions	Y	9. Firearms background checks Y
2. First Coronavirus response	Y	6. Troops in Syria	Y	10. Spending at the border	N
3. HEROES Act	Y	7. Veto arms sales to Saudis	Y	11. Marijuana liberalized rules	Y
4. CASH Act	Y	8. Defense $$$, veto override	N	12. Electoral College objections N/A

Election Results

Election	Name (Party)	Vote (%)		Cand. Spent	Ind. Exp. Support	Ind. Exp. Oppose
2020 General	Rashida Tlaib (D)	223,205	(78%)	$3,948,858	$94,933	$18,077
	David Dudenhoefer (R)	53,311	(19%)			$224
2020 Primary	Rashida Tlaib (D)	71,703	(66%)			
	Brenda Jones (D)	36,493	(34%)			

Prior winning percentages: 2018 (85%)

Democrat Rashida Tlaib was one of the first two Muslim women elected to the House in 2018 and the second Palestinian-American. After a narrow victory in the Democratic primary when she was first elected, she easily won a rematch in 2020. Tlaib brought a distinctive voice on Arab causes in the Middle East and backed a strongly progressive agenda on domestic issues.

Tlaib was born in Detroit to parents who had lived in the Middle East prior to their emigration. Her father was born in a Palestinian neighborhood of Jerusalem and worked on a Ford assembly line in Detroit; her mother had resided near Ramallah in the West Bank. Tlaib got a bachelor's degree from Wayne State University and law degree from the Thomas Cooley Law School of Western Michigan University. She served six years as a state representative before she was term-limited in 2014; that year, she lost a Democratic primary for the state Senate.

In the legislature, where she was the senior Democrat on the Appropriations Committee, she focused on environmental and public-health concerns, plus funding for education. She "demonstrated a propensity for crossing establishment forces on both sides," the Detroit Free Press reported. Subsequently, she served as an advocate and community organizer with the Sugar Law Center for Economic and Social Justice, where she worked on local and national issues, including bigotry against Muslims. She protested a speech by Donald Trump in Detroit during the 2016 campaign and was removed from the site.

When Rep. John Conyers, the former House Judiciary Committee chairman, announced his resignation in December 2017 following charges of sexual harassment of congressional aides, attention immediately focused on his great nephew, state Sen. Ian Conyers. The former congressman later endorsed his son, John Conyers III, though he failed to get enough signatures to qualify for the ballot. During the campaign, Tlaib emphasized her heritage to protest harsh treatment of immigrants and to demand justice for Palestinians in the Middle East, including support for a "one-state solution" with Israel. Her chief opponent was Brenda Jones, president of the Detroit City Council, with a long history as a community activist. Jones was backed by the United Auto Workers and other unions and Detroit Mayor Mike Duggan.

Tlaib won the Democratic primary by 900 votes, with 31 percent to 30 percent for Jones and 14 percent for Bill Wild, the Westland mayor. Three other candidates split the remainder of the nearly 90,000 votes. Tlaib spent a bit more than $1 million in the primary, which was roughly the total of the remaining Democratic candidates.

Tlaib's victory was accompanied by a concurrent special election for the remaining two months of Conyers' final term, following the November election. Because two candidates for the two-year term did not file for the special election and most of their support shifted to Jones, she had a 1,648-vote victory in the primary for the special election. Jones served the final month in the lame-duck session of 2018.

In the House, Tlaib was in the vanguard of liberal activists in the freshman class. On the day she took her House oath, she gained wide attention for her profane reference to President Donald Trump and call for his impeachment at a partisan gathering. Tlaib occasionally voiced unhappiness with the caution by many Democrats and the limited steps by party leaders. "They put us in photos when they want to show our party is diverse. However, when we ask to be at the table, or speak up about issues that impact who we are, what we fight for & why we ran in the first place, we are ignored," she tweeted in April 2019.

Tlaib quickly bonded with Ilhan Omar of Minnesota as the initial Muslim women elected to the House. The Israeli government initially banned both of them from traveling to Israel, where Tlaib had planned to visit her family on the West Bank and to emphasize the rights of Palestinians. Although the Israelis eventually reversed their decision, she cited the "deep-rooted racism within Israel" and the "oppressive conditions meant to humiliate me," and she did not reschedule her travel. In December 2019, Tlaib met with immigrant Mexican families in Tijuana and cited the need to adopt "a humane immigration and asylum process."

With Omar, plus Reps. Alexandria Ocasio-Cortez and Ayanna Pressley, Tlaib organized "The Squad"—four progressive minority women who were elected in 2018. They pressed an agenda that emphasized their diversity, including their call for a universal guaranteed income and the elimination of the Immigration and Customs Enforcement agency. They described themselves as "the future of the Democratic Party."

In 2020, Tlaib again faced Jones in the Democratic primary, but without other candidates. Jones, who remained president of the Detroit City Council, was endorsed by numerous city officials plus the other candidates who had run in the 2018 primary. Tlaib spent nearly $4 million, more than 15 times the amount spent by Jones. This time, she won comfortably, 66%-34%. She said the victory was a mandate for "an unapologetic fighter who will take on the status quo."

When Joe Biden on the day he became president reversed Trump's travel ban from some Muslim-majority and African countries, Tlaib praised his "great step," and added that there was "much more work to do to combat racism, xenophobia and Islamophobia."

MI-13: Detroit Metro

Cook Partisan Voting Index: D+29

Population		Race and Ethnicity		Income	
Total	672,291	White	38.50%	Median Income	$39,005
Land area (sq. miles)	186	Black	54.10%	District Income Rank	432
Pop/ sq mi	3,619.72	Latino	7.70%	Poverty Rate	26.10%
Born in State	77.40%	Asian	1.20%	With health insurance	91.30%
		Two or more races	2.40%	Cash public assistance	3.20%
Age Groups		Other	3.70%	Food stamp/SNAP	26.10%
Under 18	24.60%				
18-34	24.90%	**Education**		**Work**	
35-64	36.00%	H.S grad or less	51.40%	White Collar	26.40%
Over 64	14.30%	Some college	32.70%	Sales and Service	43.40%
		College Degree, 4 yr	9.80%	Blue Collar	30.30%
Military		Post grad	6.10%	Government	8.90%
Veteran/ Active Duty	5.30%				

2020 Pres. Vote	Biden	229,535	(79%)	Trump	58,162	(20%)
2016 Pres. Vote	Clinton	209,105	(78%)	Trump	48,111	(18%)

West areas: Detroit's early auto factories—Packard, Hudson, Ford Highland Park, Dodge Main, Briggs, Ford River Rouge, Cadillac, Kelsey-Hayes, Chrysler, Plymouth, DeSoto—were built between 1905 and 1925 about five miles from the city's center and at what was then the edge of urban development. Almost instantly, the flat farmlands all around were platted in streets arranged in a grid and built up with wooden bungalows and brick prairie-style houses. Detroit's neighborhoods filled up with factory workers and civil servants, professionals and maintenance men, corner-store owners and management personnel, Catholics and Protestants and Jews: a middle-class melting pot. With one exception: Detroit in those days had few Blacks. They did not begin in earnest their great migration here from the South until around 1940, when defense plants began hiring African Americans in large numbers. In 1910, Blacks made up 1 percent of Detroit's population; in 1970, the share had risen to 44 percent. Today, Detroit is 78 percent black.

The history of the city is one of conflict and uplift, inspiration and tragedy. The wartime mixture of Appalachian whites and Deep South Blacks proved volatile. During the war years, Blacks were restricted to a few severely overcrowded neighborhoods like the Black Bottom, most of it now covered by the Chrysler Freeway; Whites opposed any attempt to expand Black neighborhoods, sometimes with violent measures. This tinderbox erupted in June 1943 after a fight started on a beach on Belle Isle. Rumors spread among Blacks that a White man had thrown a Black woman and her baby off a bridge, while a competing rumor spread among Whites that a White woman had been raped and murdered on the bridge. The ensuing race riot lasted three days and resulted in 34 deaths. After 1945, when African Americans began moving outward, real estate agents played on racial fears.

In the 1950s, whole square miles of Detroit changed racial composition in a matter of months. The 1960s started with hope that the civil rights movement, encouraged by Walter Reuther's United Auto Workers union, would improve matters. In fact, many Black Detroiters found good jobs and made good incomes. Then came the riots of July 1967, followed by extensive White flight and steep increases in crime. Detroit's first African-American mayor, Democrat Coleman Young, pressured major employers like the Big Three auto companies to build facilities in Detroit and raised taxes to expand city services. But economic conditions continued to deteriorate and violent crime became a part of everyday life. Crime reduced the value of much residential real estate to near zero, and the city's population fell from 1.7 million in 1960 to 675,000 in 2019.

Despite some salutary trends, the city remained largely blighted. In March 2013, Republican Gov. Rick Snyder declared the city in a state of financial emergency, and he appointed an emergency manager to try to steer it to fiscal stability. In December 2014, Detroit emerged from bankruptcy. But that transition marked only the start of the long-term revival of the city under Mayor Mike Duggan (who was elected as the city's first white mayor in a half-century) and a rapidly changed population. All financial controls ended in 2018..

The 13th Congressional District of Michigan covers much of the western half of the city. Republican redistricters had dual objectives: Maintain two black majority districts even though there are barely enough Blacks to achieve those numbers and there are not enough residents in Detroit for one district, and maximize Republican strength in the neighboring suburban districts. The 13th, based entirely in Wayne County, stretches from Highland Park to the east side of downtown Detroit. New housing and some gentrification in downtown have attracted professionals, and more are on the way. Still, deep-seated poverty remains.

One salient to the southwest takes in parts of "Mexicantown," with its growing Hispanic population, as well as the cities of Ecorse, River Rouge and Melvindale. Another swings south through white-majority neighborhoods, such as Dearborn Heights, Garden City and Westland. It takes in heavily African-American Inkster and Romulus, which is the home of Detroit's Metro Airport. Overall, the district is about 55 percent African American and one of the most strongly Democratic in the country. Joe Biden got 79 percent in 2020, a slight dip from the vote for President Barack Obama in 2012.

Brenda Lawrence (D)

Elected 2014, 4th term, b. Oct 18, 1954; Detroit, MI; University of Detroit Mercy, Att., 1972; Central MI University, B.A., 2005; Christian; Married (McArthur Lawrence); 2 children; 1 grandchild.

Elected Office: Southfield Board of Education, 1992-1996; Southfield City Council, 1997-2001, President, 1999; Southfield Mayor, 2002-2015.

Professional Career: Manager, USPS.

DC Office: 2463 RHOB 20515, 202-225-5802, Fax: 202-226-2356, lawrence.house.gov

State Offices: Southfield, 248-356-2052.

Committees: *Appropriations (VChmn)*: Commerce, Justice, Science & Related Agencies; Financial Services & General Government; Labor, Health & Human Services, Education & Related Agencies. *Oversight & Reform*: Government Operations.

Group Ratings

	ADA	ACLU	AFL-CIO	LCV	COC	HAFA	ACU	CFG	FRC
2020	**	78%	**	100%	-	0%	3%	**	-
2019	75%	C	100%	90%	58%	C	3%	12%	0%

Almanac Ratings 2019-2020

	Economy	Social	Foreign	Composite
Liberal	100%	100%	50%	84%
Conservative	0%	0%	50%	16%

Key Votes of the 116th Congress

1. U.S./Mex./Can. trade deal Y	5. Russia sanctions Y	9. Firearms background checks Y
2. First Coronavirus response Y	6. Troops in Syria Y	10. Spending at the border N
3. HEROES Act Y	7. Veto arms sales to Saudis Y	11. Marijuana liberalized rules Y
4. CASH Act Y	8. Defense $$$, veto override Y	12. Electoral College objections N

Election Results

Election	Name (Party)	Vote (%)		Cand. Spent	Ind. Exp. Support	Ind. Exp. Oppose
2020 General	Brenda Lawrence (D)	271,370	(79%)	$633,210	$234	
	Robert Patrick (R)	62,664	(18%)	$41,915		$224
2020 Primary	Brenda Lawrence (D)	127,006	(93%)			
	Terrance Morrison (D)	9,264	(7%)			

Prior winning percentages: 2018 (81%), 2016 (79%), 2014 (78%)

Democrat Brenda Lawrence was elected in 2014, with lengthy political experience. With a seat on the Appropriations Committee and as a co-chair of the Democratic Women's Caucus, she used her insider skills to address the needs of her low-income district.

Lawrence was born and raised in Detroit, earned a bachelor's degree in public administration from Central Michigan University, and started her career in the U.S. Postal Service, where she was a manager and worked for more than 30 years. As her children went through the public school system in Southfield, she was drawn to education issues and was elected to the school board. Later, she won a seat on the city council and was elected mayor in 2001. As the city's first African American or woman to hold that post, she was reelected three times. She underscored Southfield's resilience as a corporate hub that held up well despite the economic collapse of Detroit.

Lawrence's long tenure as mayor was slow to translate to other political victories. She fell short in her run for Oakland County executive in 2008, and then for lieutenant governor in 2010 with gubernatorial candidate Virg Bernero. In 2012, she made her first bid for the House, running against two sitting House Democrats: Reps. Gary Peters and Hansen Clarke. That primary became a contentious debate over race. Clarke, a biracial candidate, came under criticism amid questions over whether he was truly "Black." That skirmishing gave Peters a chance to stay above the fray, and he won the primary handily.

Lawrence got another chance in 2014 when Peters ran successfully for the Senate. State Rep. Rudy Hobbs, who was endorsed by Detroit Mayor Mike Duggan, was the early Democratic frontrunner. Lawrence gained an edge with endorsements from unions and local business groups. Lawrence made the best of her ground operation and won the primary by 2,391 votes. This time, she got 36 percent to 32 percent for Hobbs and 31 percent for Clarke, who sought a comeback. The general election in the heavily Democratic district was a formality.

In the House, Lawrence styled herself as a strong advocate for improved roads, bridges and regional transit. "My goal is to help make 8 Mile a major thoroughfare that is the 50-yard line of the congressional district that I represent, not a line that demarcates the haves and the have-nots," she wrote in the Detroit Free Press. Lawrence doggedly pursued more details of the Flint water crisis. In 2018, she worked with a bipartisan group of House members that urged the Environmental Protection Agency to lower the acceptable levels of toxins in the local water. She pursued her longtime interest in solving the Postal Service's financial problems. Also in 2018, she lambasted a Trump administration task force for recommendations that were "not a serious effort to help the Postal Service address its long-term future."

On the women's caucus, she moved into the leadership of that group, which has gained influence with its growing size. With the vital support of Nancy Pelosi, Lawrence was elected co-chair following the 2018 election. The alliance between Lawrence and Pelosi—and the latter's desire to assert control through her allies—caused some internal friction. In February 2020, members of the caucus wore white, in honor of the suffragette movement, when President Donald Trump delivered his State of the Union message in the Capitol. "To an administration that has closed its eyes to women, we will be seen," Lawrence said.

At the Appropriations Committee, Lawrence was elected in January 2021 as vice-chair—an important coordinating role on the spending panel. She also had seats on three subcommittees that handle pieces of domestic spending.

Lawrence's reelections have been uneventful, with perfunctory opposition. Although she likely will survive redistricting in 2022, a combination of factors could pose complications—including Michigan's loss of a House seat, the stagnant population in her district, and the junior Democrats seeking to entrench themselves in suburban districts.

MI-14: Detroit Metro   **Cook Partisan Voting Index: D+29**

Population		Race and Ethnicity		Income	
Total	689,939	White	34.10%	Median Income	$50,438
Land area (sq. miles)	25,028	Black	55.90%	District Income Rank	382
Pop/ sq mi	27.57	Latino	4.70%	Poverty Rate	19.30%
Born in State	71.80%	Asian	5.70%	With health insurance	93.40%
		Two or more races	2.50%	Cash public assistance	2.00%
Age Groups		Other	1.80%	Food stamp/SNAP	19.90%
Under 18	23.50%				
18-34	23.80%	**Education**		**Work**	
35-64	36.50%	H.S grad or less	36.00%	White Collar	39.30%
Over 64	16.10%	Some college	29.00%	Sales and Service	38.60%
		College Degree, 4 yr	19.20%	Blue Collar	22.10%
Military		Post grad	15.80%	Government	9.60%
Veteran/ Active Duty	4.30%				

2020 Pres. Vote	Biden	276,847	(79%)	Trump	68,031	(20%)
2016 Pres. Vote	Clinton	252,387	(79%)	Trump	58,179	(18%)

North and East areas: Few central cities in America were as vibrant in the 20th century as Detroit, the nation's fourth-largest during the middle decades, then in a class shared or surpassed only by New York, Chicago, Philadelphia and Los Angeles. Few have been as diminished as Detroit, which ranked in 2019 as the nation's 24th-largest city, just behind Nashville and ahead of Oklahoma City, both of which continue to grow. This was America's first automobile city, not just because it manufactured so many cars but also because it was built to automobile scale. Detroit started the 20th century, with fewer than half a million people and extending no farther than four or five miles from the site where the French built Fort Pontchartrain on the Detroit River in 1701. As the Motor City boomed, it grew outward along wide avenues and, starting in the 1950s, along freeways. Metro Detroit eventually expanded to 4 million people, each generation moving out in all directions, leaving behind the previous generation's neighborhoods and civic institutions.

Today, large parts of Detroit are literally empty. Formerly iconic buildings in the downtown area have been demolished, and others are all but vacant, while officials struggle to create new population centers and reestablish a business district. On the positive side, GM bought, for $72 million, the 70-story Renaissance Center, built in the 1970s for $350 million, and the company moved several thousand employees there. Quicken moved more than 10,000 employees from the suburbs to downtown and restored some of the landmark buildings in the city. At the site of the former J.L. Hudson department store, in a development spearheaded by Quicken founder Dan Gilbert, completion was scheduled for 2023 on a $1 billion skyscraper, which they term "a city within a city." Ford has begun work on an innovation campus with 5,000 employees at the once-grand but long-shuttered train station. But beyond these well-policed enclaves lie acres of vacant lots and half-empty blocks.

Some critics worried that the focus on a relatively small area of downtown ignored large parts of Detroit that remained poor and neglected. In 2019, the FBI ranked the violent crime rate of the city highest in the nation. In his "one Detroit" campaign, Mayor Mike Duggan was reelected in 2017 with 72 percent of the vote over state Sen. Coleman Young II, son of the former four-term mayor. He had legitimate claims for having promoted the turnaround, but the city still struggled to provide routine services such as trash pick-up.

The 14th Congressional District of Michigan is an amalgamation of heavily minority areas in metro Detroit. Its serpentine shape shows the difficulty of maintaining majority-minority districts as African Americans increasingly move out of compact neighborhoods in inner cities. The district takes in Hamtramck and the Grosse Pointes, both white majority areas, and also the northern neighborhoods of Wayne County, which became heavily African American following the flight of whites in the 1970s and 1980s. It includes the newest frontiers of African-American migration in southern Oakland County. Southfield was 0.1 percent black in the 1970 census and 69 percent black in 2019, while Oak Park went from being 0.2 percent black to 56 percent in the same period.

To the north and east, the district takes in majority-black Pontiac, which has removed most of the blight from its downtown and made an impressive comeback, with billions of dollars of investments in its new economic hub. GM, which once had eight plants in Pontiac but retained only two, closed its global propulsion center and shifted workers to its technical center in Warren, where it focuses on autonomous cars. Amazon became a new force in Pontiac, with work underway on joint distribution and fulfillment centers at the site of the former Silverdome. In Hamtramck, GM used its old assembly plant as the production site starting in late 2021 for its electric vehicles. The district is 56 percent African American and is overwhelmingly Democratic. It is split almost evenly between Wayne and Oakland counties, with their separate political networks. Joe Biden got 80 percent, the same as in the neighboring 13th District.

MINNESOTA

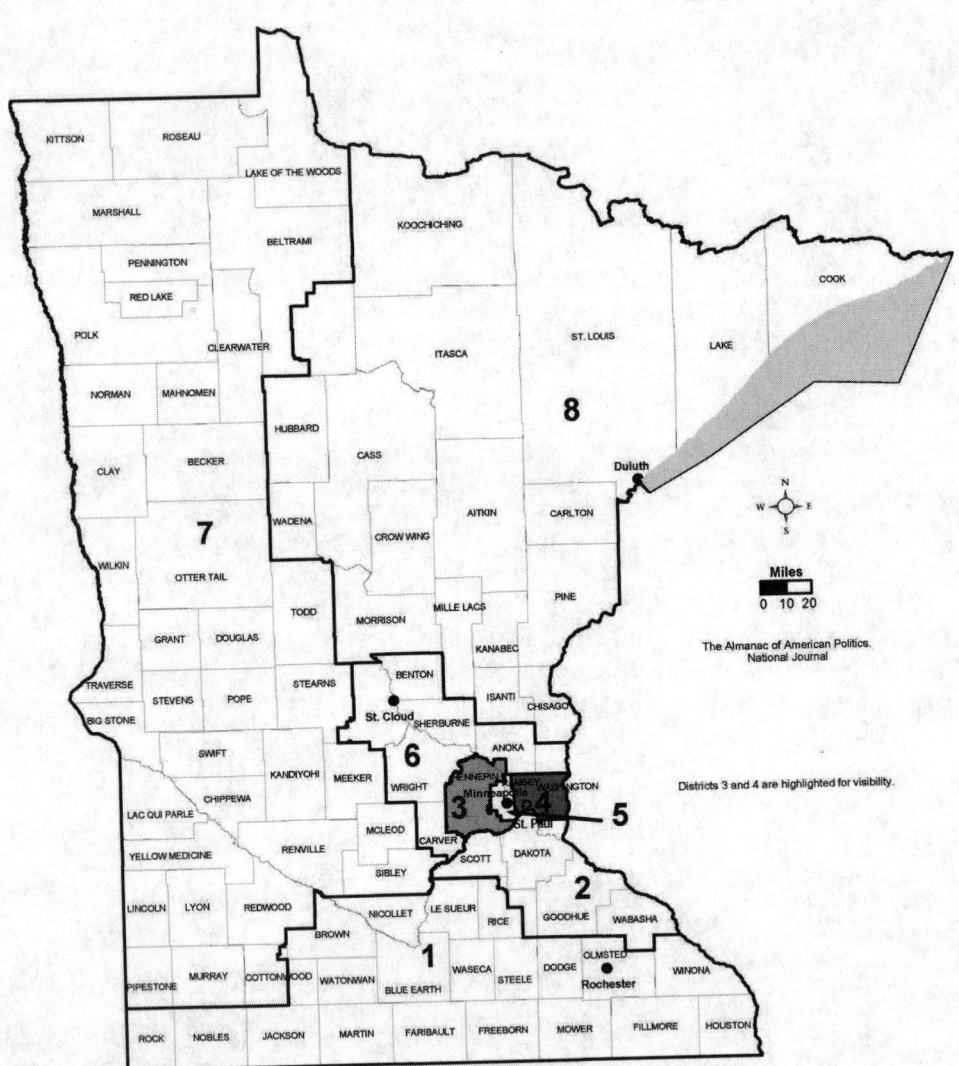

The Almanac of American Politics.
National Journal

Districts 3 and 4 are highlighted for visibility.

Congressional district boundaries were first effective for 2012.

Minnesota hasn't voted Republican for president since Richard Nixon's landslide in 1972. (The quirk of having native son Walter Mondale on the ballot against Ronald Reagan in 1984 kept it from going Republican that year.) In 2016, the state's Democratic-Farmer-Labor Party got a scare —Minnesota was the state Hillary Clinton won with the narrowest margin save New Hampshire— but in 2020, despite President Donald Trump's concerted effort to win the state, Joe Biden prevailed by a solid seven-point margin.

Minnesota began as the node of the transcontinental railroads that linked the winter wheat fields of the northern prairies to the great grain-milling center of Minneapolis and to the bustling Pacific ports of Puget Sound. The far northern states were ignored by most Yankee migrants, who headed straight west into Iowa, Nebraska and Kansas. But others saw opportunity in Minnesota's icy lakes and ferocious winters. James J. Hill, builder of the Great Northern Railroad, once said, "You can't interest me in any proposition in any place where it doesn't snow." He and other entrepreneurs, operating out of Minneapolis and St. Paul—already twin cities by 1860—worked to attract Norwegian, Swedish, and German migrants who would find the terrain and climate congenial. (One can get lutefisk—smelly, lye-soaked cod—around Christmastime in Minneapolis restaurants.) By 1890, the Twin Cities were the nerve center of a sprawling and rich agricultural empire stretching west from Minnesota through the Dakotas into Montana and beyond.

On the whole, Minnesota remained quietly prosperous. It has been innovative: It's the birthplace of Scotch tape and the Post-It note, Betty Crocker, Target, and the Mall of America; it produced the seminal musical talent Bob Dylan; and it's where the late artist Prince produced his wonderfully inventive musical oeuvre. Minnesota's median income is 14 percent above the national average and ranks 13th-highest of any state. It is tied for the nation's ninth highest rate of bachelor's degree attainment. Minnesota is home to the world-renowned health care provider, the Mayo Clinic, which has helped spawn research in the biosciences and medical devices. Companies such as 3M Drug Delivery Systems, Abbott Laboratories, and R&D Systems (Bio-Techne) have made advances in medical genomics and stem-cell research.

Minnesota's naturally cold climate and bountiful water supplies (it's the land of "10,000 lakes") has made it an attractive locale for data centers that need to stay cool as inexpensively as possible. Such companies as United Health Care, Century Link, Cologix and Databank have opened or expanded data center operations in the state in recent years, and Google has announced a plan to partner with Minneapolis-based Xcel Energy to build a $600 million data center run by wind power in a soon-to-be-phased-out coal-burning facility northwest of the Twin Cities. Minnesota ranks eighth in installed wind-energy capacity, and it meets 21 percent of its electricity needs from renewable energy. Agriculture and livestock remain staples of the state's economy; Minnesota is among the nation's top producers of corn, sugar beets, soybeans, oilseeds, oats, hogs, and turkeys, and it ranks fourth in the nation in ethanol production. But farm bankruptcies have been rising due to low prices, driven in part by higher efficiencies that have outstripped demand. The coronavirus hit the state's meatpacking industry, and later in 2020, longtime Democratic Rep. Collin Peterson was ousted by Republican Michelle Fischbach, depriving Minnesota farmers of his chairmanship of the House Agriculture Committee.

Meanwhile, the mining and lumber operations in the lightly populated north of the state are struggling. Even though 85 percent of the iron ore used in American steel comes from six taconite plants in Minnesota, the number of mining and logging workers statewide fell from almost 9,000 in 1998 to 6,600 prior to the coronavirus pandemic. While the state's Twin Cities-based medical technology sector has generally been supportive of free trade, the Iron Range industries in the north welcomed President Donald Trump's tariffs on steel and aluminum. Meanwhile, pressure to revive resource extraction through new projects has become a wedge issue for the state's Democratic-Farmer-Labor Party, pitting rural hardhats against urban environmentalists. In 2018, Republicans flipped two Democratic-held open House seats, one in the north that includes the Iron Range and the other a heavily rural district along the state's southern tier; these gains were evened out by two Twin Cities seats that flipped to the Democrats. Several mining projects in the north hang in the balance, including two sought by Antofagasta and PolyMet near the federally protected Boundary Waters area that adjoins the Canadian border. In rallies in Duluth, Trump strongly backed an expansion of mining, but Biden's victory could put a damper on progress for those projects.

Minnesota has more social connectedness than any other large state, political scientist Robert Putnam wrote in the book Bowling Alone, and this spirit of civic participation is echoed in everything from hockey to party precinct caucuses and conventions. The Twin Cities boast of having more museums than any other city but Chicago and Washington; the Minnesota Historical Society was founded in 1849, nine years before statehood. Beyond the Twin Cities, you can visit the Spam Museum in Austin, the Judy Garland Museum in Grand Rapids, and the Laura Ingalls Wilder Museum in Walnut Grove, near the banks of Plum Creek.

Today, Minnesota is 79 percent White, making it among the whitest states in the Midwest. But minority populations have been growing from a small base. Today, Minnesota is 6.4 percent Black, 5.6 percent Hispanic and 4.9 percent Asian. Overall, though, Minnesota's population has grown only modestly—7.6 percent since 2010—and the state came close to losing a seat during the 2020 congressional reapportionment. The increases have come almost exclusively from the Twin Cities metro area, with has grown 9.2 percent since 2010. The population is aging, too, leaving the minority and foreign-born share of Minnesota's population increasingly important for the state's economic future. Minnesota has the largest Somali population on the continent (Ilhan Omar became the first Somali native in Congress in 2018, representing the Minneapolis-based district) and the state has large Hmong and Vietnamese communities. Almost 9 percent of Minnesota residents are immigrants, and about one of every five children in the state has at least one immigrant parent. This has created some tensions. In 2010 the Justice Department indicted Somali immigrants in Minneapolis for allegedly raising money for the Islamist militant group Al-Shabaab; in 2017, White supremacists bombed a mosque in Bloomington. After Trump issued an executive order tightening immigration, Minnesota became one of the first states to sue. At one rally in Minneapolis, Trump bragged about his immigration policies and called Omar "a disgrace." At another rally in Bemidji, located in a county that had acted to curb refugee resettlement, Trump said that electing Biden would "flood" the state with Somalis and turn the state into a "refugee camp."

The question of race in Minnesota became urgent in 2020 with the death of George Floyd, a 46-year-old Black man, in police custody, a spark that forced a national reckoning with police brutality and racial and economic inequality. Floyd, after being arrested for allegedly passing a counterfeit $20 bill in a store in Minneapolis, died after eight minutes and 46 seconds under the knee of a White police officer. When footage of his death surfaced, the Twin Cities erupted in riots, with more than 100 buildings burned and many more looted; especially hard-hit were a five-mile stretch of Lake Street in Minneapolis and a three-mile stretch of University Avenue in St. Paul. The prosecution of the officers was removed from the jurisdiction of Hennepin County Attorney Mike Freeman to Attorney General Keith Ellison, a Black Muslim with a long record of progressive activism, and the Minneapolis city council sought to institute major reforms of the police department. One officer, Derek Chauvin, was convicted of murder charges, while three other officers – one Black and one Hmong – faced lesser charges. Just days before the Chauvin verdict was announced, another Black man, Daunte Wright, was killed by a white police officer in Brooklyn Center. Floyd's death ripped open a long-overlooked pattern of racial inequality in both the Twin Cities and Minnesota that had been obscured by prosperity and liberal pieties. A 2019 analysis by the Minneapolis Star-Tribune found that Minnesota had the third-widest gap in poverty in the nation between whites (7%) and Blacks (32%); the gap for unemployment was the nation's third-biggest; the gap for fourth-grade reading scores was the second-widest, and the gap for homeownership was the nation's third-widest. Research by the University of Minnesota's Mapping Prejudice project found numerous places within the Twin Cities where decades of racial real estate covenants produced isolated hot spots of poverty, including one near the intersection where Floyd was killed. Other Black neighborhoods were decimated by construction of the interstate highway system: One in every eight African Americans in St. Paul lost a home to the construction of I-94, according to the Minnesota Historical Society.

Minnesota's Scandinavian immigrants drew on their traditions of cooperative activity and bureaucratic socialism. The Farmer-Labor Party elected senators in the 1920s and came to dominate state politics. Hurt by ties to communists, they lost power in 1938, but Minnesota was still a New Deal state, and by 1944 the bedraggled local Democrats merged with the anti-communist faction of Farmer-Laborites to form the Democratic-Farmer-Labor Party. Hubert Humphrey's DFL—civic-minded, closely tied to labor unions, backed by many farmers and shorn of communists—attracted dozens of talented politicians, and for a long historical moment, Minnesota's Republican Party was barely an afterthought. By the 1990s, the DFL had begun to weaken as well, enabling former professional wrestler and suburban mayor Jesse Ventura to win the governorship as an independent in 1998. In 2002, the Twin Cities exurbs—the area just outside the Hennepin (Minneapolis) and Ramsey (St. Paul) core—went heavily Republican, helping Tim Pawlenty win the first of two terms as governor. Eventually, though, the DFL regained the upper hand, led by Sen. Amy Klobuchar and a steady stream of Democrats in statewide elected positions.

Trump's narrow loss in Minnesota in 2016 seemed to pose an existential threat for the DFL, as a half-dozen predominantly rural counties shifted their margins toward the GOP by between 20 and 36 percentage points. But the DFL's salvation was its continued edge in the Twin Cities region, which offered Minnesota more Democratic-leaning urban and suburban voters than neighboring states such as Iowa or Wisconsin. In the 2018 midterm elections, Rep. Tim Walz won the governorship by 12 points and fellow DFL candidates Klobuchar and Tina Smith won Senate races by double-digit margins.

In 2020, both the Trump and Biden campaigns considered Minnesota a battleground state and made campaign visits. But Biden ended up winning the state with relative ease, aided by the absence of a major third-party candidate on the presidential ballot. (In 2016, Minnesotans had cast a higher share of votes for third parties than voters in any state but Alaska and New Mexico.) Biden increased the number of Democratic presidential votes by 26 percent over Clinton's total in 2016, while Trump increased his own by just 12 percent. Biden flipped four Trump-won counties—Winona (Winona), Nicollet and Blue Earth (Mankato), and Clay (Morehead)—and improved the Democrats' winning margins by 10 points in Olmsted County (Rochester), by four points in St. Louis County (Duluth), and by between seven and 10 points in each of the four main Twin Cities metro counties: Hennepin, Ramsey, Washington, and Dakota. The DFL's main disappointment was its failure to capture the narrowly divided state Senate, despite a big spending edge. The failure may have owed something to two pro-marijuana parties running candidates, as well as Republican success in spotlighting Democratic calls to "defund the police." Still, despite Trump's close call in 2016, his significant setback in 2020 signaled that as long as Trumpism defines the Republican Party, the GOP will likely face an uphill climb in Minnesota.

Population		Race and Ethnicity		Income	
Total	5,639,632	White	82.10%	Median Income	74,593
Land area (sq. miles)	79,627	Black	6.60%	State Income Rank	13 out of 50
Pop/ sq mi	70.83	Latino	5.60%	Poverty Rate	9.00%
Born in state	67.70%	Asian	5.90%	With health insurance	95.10%
		Two or more races	3.30%	Cash public assistance	3.00%
Age Groups		Other	2.90%	Food stamp/SNAP	8.6%
Under 18	23.10%				
18-34	22.20%	**Education**		**Work**	
35-64	38.40%	H.S grad or less	30.80%	White Collar	42.80%
Over 64	16.30%	Some college	31.90%	Sales and Service	35.40%
		College Degree, 4 yr	24.50%	Blue Collar	21.80%
Military		Post grad	12.70%	Government	12.60%
Veteran/ Active Duty	6.50%				

Presidential Politics

2020 Primary (D)	Biden (D)	287,553(39%)	Sanders (D)	222,431(30%)	Warren (D)	114,674(15%)	
	Bloomberg (D)	61,882 (8%)	Klobuchar (D)	41,530 (6%)			
2016 Caucus (D)	Sanders (D)	126,229(61%)	Clinton (D)	78,381(38%)			
2016 Caucus (R)	Rubio (R)	41,397(36%)	Cruz (R)	33,181(29%)	Trump (R)	24,473(21%)	
	Carson (R)	8,422 (7%)	Kasich (R)	6,565 (6%)			
2020 Pres. Vote	Biden (D)	1,717,077(52%)	Trump (R)	1,484,065(45%)			
2016 Pres. Vote	Clinton (D)	1,367,825(46%)	Trump (R)	1,323,232(45%)	Johnson (L)	112,984 (4%)	

Minnesota has the longest consecutive streak of voting Democratic for president of any state, though it's become more competitive in recent elections. The last time Minnesota voted for the

Republican nominee was in 1972, and even then it gave Richard Nixon his lowest winning percentage margin over George McGovern. Before 1932 and the New Deal, the state voted Republican in every presidential race except 1912, when it supported Republican-turned-Bull Moose candidate Teddy Roosevelt. Barack Obama won the state handily in 2008 and 2012, and few thought it would be a battleground in 2016. But with few minority voters and large swaths of rural territory, the Democratic bastion was a competitive contest and Hillary Clinton defeated Donald Trump just 46%-45%.

In 2016, Trump won all but nine of the state's 87 counties: the two largest vote producers, Hennepin and Ramsey, home to Minneapolis and St. Paul, respectively; Dakota and Washington, two Democratic suburban counties outside the Twin Cities; four counties on the Iron Range; and Olmsted County, home to the Mayo Clinic and the University of Minnesota at Rochester. The Democratic-Farmer-Labor Party base, formerly prairie populists, Scandinavian farmers and blue-collar workers from industrial communities, is now more likely to be the cultural liberals who cluster in comfortable neighborhoods in Minneapolis and St. Paul. Of the 33 counties that voted for Obama in either 2008 or 2012 and then voted for Trump in 2016, Biden won back just four of those. While Trump's campaign repeatedly touted Minnesota as an opportunity to go on offense in 2020, neither they nor Biden's team spent any real money on the state, and Biden prevailed, 52%-45%.

Like the rest of the country, even as rural Minnesota shifted right, the Twin Cities and their suburbs continued to move left: Hennepin County moved left by 8 points, and every county it bordered shifted left by at least four points. Biden won Olmsted County by 10 points more than Clinton had.

In 2016, Florida Sen. Marco Rubio defeated Texas Sen. Ted Cruz 36%-29% in the GOP caucuses, making Minnesota the only state Rubio carried. In the Democratic contest, Vermont Sen. Bernie Sanders defeated Clinton 62%-38% and swept all eight congressional districts. With bipartisan support, Minnesota adopted a presidential primary for 2020. It was a top Super Tuesday priority for Sanders, who campaigned there ahead of the vote. But home-state favorite Sen. Amy Klobuchar's decision to drop out and endorse Biden just one day before the election helped him win, 39%-30%, one of several big victories that night that catapulted him back to frontrunner status.

Congressional Districts

117th Congress Lineup	4D 4R	116th Congress Lineup	5D 3R

Once-placid Minnesota had been set as the site for redistricting chaos. It was the only state that started 2021 with divided-party control of its legislature. Democrat Tim Walz, the governor, prefers to downplay partisanship. The House delegation had four new members—two from each party—who in 2018 took seats that had been held by the other party. And a fifth seat switched parties in 2020. Perhaps the overriding factor was that Minnesota was expected to lose a seat in reapportionment, its first cutback since 1962. Instead, the state narrowly escaped the worst consequences when, according to the overall state population data that the Census Bureau released in April 2021, Minnesota won the 435th House seat and will retain its eight-seat delegation.

Still, the scenario seems custom-made for a court review—and perhaps a court drawing of the map, from the start. No matter who holds the redistricting pen, a few governing points remain relevant. Of the eight current districts, two are urban (the Twin Cities), two are suburban and one is exurban; the remaining three are mostly rural and sprawling — to the north, west and south. Those seats now divide evenly between the two parties—with Republicans holding the exurban and rural districts, and the Democrats holding the four metro seats.

Two decades ago, four of the state's eight seats were rural. At that time, Democrats held at least two of the rural seats and Republicans ran well in the suburbs. Just as the partisan lines have changed, the population shifts within Minnesota continue to be away from those rural areas. That seemingly will shift the three rural districts closer to the metro area. Historically, safely Democratic Minneapolis and St. Paul have dominated their own districts — with some suburban appendages. That very likely will continue. Perhaps the most dicey decisions will deal with how the three other districts in the metro area manage the often delicate balance between the metro and rural areas.

In short, this will not be Minnesota Nice. But it came very close to a far worse scenario if the state's House delegation had been downsized.

Tim Walz (D)

Elected 2018, term expires 2023, 1st term; b. Apr 06, 1964, West Point, NE; Saint Mary's University of Minnesota; Chadron State College (NE), B.S., 1989; Minnesota State University, Mankato, M.S., 2001; Lutheran; Married (Gwen Whipple Walz); 2 children.

Military Career: U.S Army National Guard, 1981-2005.

Elected Office: US House, 2007-2018.

Professional Career: Teacher, Pine Ridge Indian Reservation, SD, 1984; Teacher, People's Republic of China, 1989-1990; Founder, Educational Travel Adventures, 1991-2006; H.S. teacher, 1989-2006.

Office: 130 State Capitol 75 Rev. Dr. Martin Luther King Jr. Blvd., St. Paul, 55155; 651-201-3400; Fax: 651-797-1850; Website: state.mn.us

Lt. Gov.: Peggy Flanagan (D) **Atty. Gen:** Keith Ellison (D) **Sec. of State:** Steve Simon (D)

State Legislature: Senate: 32D, 35R **House:** 75D, 59R

Election Results

Election	Name (Party)	Vote (%)
2018 General	Tim Walz (D)..	1,393,096 (54%)
	Jeff Johnson (R)...	1,097,705 (42%)
	Chris Wright (LMNP)...	68,667 (3%)
2018 Primary	Tim Walz (D)..	242,832 (42%)
	Erin Murphy (D)...	186,969 (32%)
	Lori Swanson (D)..	143,517 (25%)

Prior winning percentage: House: 2016 (50%), 2014 (54%), 2012 (58%), 2010 (49%), 2008 (63%), 2006 (53%)

Former congressman Tim Walz was elected governor of Minnesota in 2018, becoming the first Minnesota Democrat to succeed a Democratic governor who had served a full eight years. During his first two years, he was faced with the twin challenges of the coronavirus pandemic and the death of George Floyd while in the custody of the Minneapolis police, which was followed by several nights of widespread rioting.

Walz grew up in Nebraska and joined the Army National Guard when he was 17. When he retired from the Guard 24 years later, in 2005, he held the rank of command sergeant major. Walz earned his teaching degree in Nebraska, taught school in China for a year through a Harvard University program, and later established an educational travel company that helped high school students study in China. He and his wife moved to Minnesota in 1996 to take teaching jobs in Mankato. There, he taught high school geography and coached the football team to two state championships.

Walz got into politics relatively late in life—he was 42 when he ran for Congress. In 2004, President George W. Bush made an appearance in the area as part of his reelection campaign. Walz took two students to the event, where Bush campaign staffers demanded to know whether he supported the president and barred the students from entering after discovering one had a sticker for Democratic candidate John Kerry. Walz suggested it might be bad PR for the Bush campaign to bar an Army veteran, and he and the students were allowed in. Walz said the experience sparked his interest in politics, first as a volunteer for the Kerry campaign and then as a congressional candidate.

In 2006, Walz challenged six-term Republican Rep. Gil Gutknecht, an affable conservative who was not considered especially vulnerable. The district had sent Republicans to Washington for 102 of the previous 114 years. Walz was not a polished campaigner, but he struck a chord with his opposition to declining middle-class wages and tax cuts for high earners, as well as Congress' failure to hold Bush accountable on the Iraq war. He supported abortion rights and opposed a ban on same-sex marriage. Walz ran as a political outsider and painted Gutknecht as too closely tied to Bush. His military experience and football coaching gave an aura of authenticity to his campaign that made him harder to attack. Walz won, 53%-47%, and became the highest-ranking enlisted soldier ever to serve in Congress.

Walz assembled a mostly centrist voting record. He opposed the creation of the Troubled Asset Relief Program to assist the financial services industry because he said it didn't do enough to protect homeowners from foreclosure. His championing of gun owners' rights earned him the National Rifle Association's endorsement. He voted for the Keystone XL pipeline. But he backed most of President Barack Obama's chief initiatives, including the health care overhaul and the cap-and-trade bill to reduce carbon emissions. Walz was heavily involved in veterans' issues, including suicide prevention and improving the treatment of traumatic brain injuries; in 2017, he took the senior Democratic post on the Veterans' Affairs Committee. Walz faced competitive reelections in 2010, 2014, and 2016. In 2018, when Walz ran for governor, his 2016 opponent, Republican Jim Hagedorn, succeeded him.

In his race to succeed Democratic Gov. Mark Dayton, Walz did not have the Democratic field to himself. In the Democratic-Farmer-Labor convention, Walz faced state Rep. Erin Murphy and state Auditor Rebecca Otto. Murphy won the party's endorsement, likely because Walz's voting record, attuned to his rural district, clashed with the agenda preferred by the party's more progressive activists from the Twin Cities. But the party convention is non-binding, and Walz soldiered on to the August primary, where he won 42 percent, outpacing Murphy with 32 percent and, as a late entrant, Attorney General Lori Swanson with 25 percent. Walz balanced his ticket by naming as his running mate state Rep. Peggy Flanagan, who had represented a district in the Twin Cities metro area and who had headed the Children's Defense Fund in the state; Flanagan was also a member of the White Earth Band of Ojibwe.

The Republicans also had a contested primary, pitting former two-term Gov. Tim Pawlenty against Jeff Johnson, a commissioner in Hennepin County, which includes Minneapolis and its suburbs. National Republicans and their business allies saw Pawlenty as a strong contender and sent substantial funding his way, but Johnson, who had failed to oust Dayton in 2014, found success by lashing himself to Trump. Johnson won the state convention endorsement (Pawlenty had skipped the convention, irking some party regulars), then prevailed over Pawlenty in the primary, 53%-44%. The general election was never particularly competitive. Walz had a war chest roughly double Johnson's, and it was bolstered by substantial support from the Alliance for a Better Minnesota, a pro-Democratic group that ran ads hitting Johnson over health care. Johnson called for lower taxes and less regulation, while Walz focused on education, leveraging his former profession, and health care. Johnson accused Walz of being soft on immigration enforcement, while Walz said he saw little in Johnson's record to suggest an ability to work across party lines.

Walz won, 58%-42%, securing more votes than any other gubernatorial candidate in the state's history, and even collecting 25,000 more votes than Hillary Clinton had won in the presidential race two years earlier. Johnson, by contrast, fell about 225,000 votes short of Trump's total in 2016. Walz won 21 counties, more than double the nine Clinton had won. He flipped Anoka County, a GOP-leaning Twin Cities suburb, as well as several counties in his old southern-tier district and a few in northern and western Minnesota; Walz's positions on the environment, which were to the right of Twin Cities liberals, may have helped in those regions. Equally important for Walz, Democrats took over the state House from the GOP. The state Senate, which had only one seat up in the election, remained narrowly in GOP hands.

Walz's first official act in office was to create a diversity commission, which included not just familiar categories of racial, ethnic and gender diversity but geographic as well, a nod to more rural parts of the state. Walz was unable to enact several of his priorities, including a gasoline tax hike to fund roads, an option to buy into the state-run Minnesota Care health plan, and a plan to end fossil-fuel electricity by 2050. But he was able to hammer out a number of policy achievements with Republican legislators, including an additional $275 million for roads and bridges, more money for opioid treatment and prevention, new regulations on pharmacy benefit managers, restoration of a state corrections ombudsman's office, and a middle-income tax cut. Walz and legislative leaders declined to move ahead on several other issues, including outlawing gay conversion therapy, a ban on wolf hunting, a phase-out of suspected carcinogen trichloroethylene, a state pre-emption bill that would have eliminated the Twin Cities' $15 minimum wage, and measures on gun control, abortion, paid family leave, and recreational marijuana. Walz also walked a tightrope between environmentalists and business groups on several large mining projects and a pipeline known as Line 3.

In 2020, the combination of the pandemic, Floyd's death, and election year sparring soured relations between the governor and other leading officials. On the coronavirus, Walz took emergency powers, renewed them several times, and issued a mask mandate, all of which sparked friction with Republicans; cases spiked heavily in the fall, but then fell back to a low level by early 2021. After

Floyd's death prompted riots in the Twin Cities, Walz called in the National Guard but rejected offers of federal military assistance. Walz and Minneapolis Mayor Jacob Frey pointed fingers at each other, alleging shortcomings in responding to the violence and looting; Senate Majority Leader Paul Gazelka, a Republican, blamed Walz for a "failure in leadership." Two months after Floyd's death, Walz signed a policing overhaul bill that had passed the legislature by wide margins. It banned neck restraints and "warrior-style training" for officers, strengthened tools to investigate officer-involved killings, and heightened reporting requirements for officer misconduct. To craft the final bill, other provisions were kept out, including an easing of ex-felon voting rights and requirements that officers live where they serve. "This is only the beginning," Walz said in signing the measure. "The work does not end today."

In the 2020 election, control of the Democratic House and the Republican Senate was at stake; both parties focused their messaging on Walz, with Democrats seeking to leverage his relatively high approval ratings and Republicans saying they needed to keep the Democrats from gaining total control over state government. Ultimately, voters decided to keep government divided, as GOP legislative candidates generally outran Trump, who was losing the state by seven points. The state's split in partisan control—an unusual outcome nationally in the current era of partisan polarization—means that Minnesota's once-a-decade redistricting process may eventually fall to the courts. Walz's 2021 budget proposal tilts left, proposing several tax increases and ensuring continued partisan battles. Walz is expected to run for another term in 2022. Mike Murphy, the Republican mayor of Lexington, has already said he's running; other GOP candidates are expected to fill out the field.

Amy Klobuchar (D)

Elected 2006, term expires 2024, 3rd term, b. May 25, 1960; Plymouth, MN; Yale University, B.A., 1982; University of Chicago, J.D., 1985; Congregationalist; Married (John Bessler); 1 child.

Elected Office: Hennepin County Attorney, 1998-2006.

Professional Career: Practicing attorney, 1985-1998.

DC Office: 425 DSOB 20510, 202-224-3244, Fax: 202-228-2186, klobuchar.senate.gov

State Offices: Minneapolis, 612-727-5220; Moorhead, 218-287-2219; Rochester, 507-288-5321; Virginia, 218-741-9690.

Committees: Senate Democratic Steering Committee Chairman. *Agriculture, Nutrition & Forestry*: Conservation, Climate, Forestry & Natural Resources; Food & Nutrition, Specialty Crops, Organics & Research; Rural Development & Energy. *Commerce, Science & Transportation*: Communications, Media & Broadband; Consumer Protection, Product Safety & Data Security; Surface Transportation, Maritime Freight & Ports; Tourism, Trade & Export Promotion. *Joint Economic. Judiciary*: Competition Policy, Antitrust & Consumer Rights (Chmn); Criminal Justice & Counterterrorism; Immigration, Citizenship & Border Security; Privacy, Technology & the Law. *Rules & Administration (Chmn)*.

Group Ratings

	ADA	ACLU	AFL-CIO	LCV	COC	HAFA	ACU	CFG	FRC
2020	-	77%	-	62%	-	12%	5%	-	-
2019	80%	C	94%	79%	32%	C	5%	26%	0%

Almanac Ratings 2019-2020

	Economy	Social	Foreign	Composite
Liberal	97%	97%	51%	82%
Conservative	3%	3%	49%	18%

Key Votes of the 116th Congress

1. EPA clean energy rules	Y	5. Russia sanctions	Y	9. Barr as Atty. General	N		
2. U.S./Mex./Can. trade deal	Y	6. Troops in SYR, AFG	N	10. Spending at the border	N/A		
3. Cut unemployment benefits	N	7. Veto arms sales to Saudis	Y	11. Coney Barrett to Sup. Ct.	N		
4. Shelton to Fed Reserve	N	8. Defense $$$, veto override	Y	12. Electoral College objections	N		

Election Results

Election	Name (Party)	Vote (%)		Cand. Spent	Ind. Exp. Support	Ind. Exp. Oppose
2018 General	Amy Klobuchar (D)	1,566,174	(60%)	$9,022,199	$62,915	
	Jim Newberger (R)	940,437	(36%)	$231,131	$15,697	$101
	Dennis Schuller (LMNP)	66,236	(3%)			
2018 Primary	Amy Klobuchar (D)	557,306	(96%)			

Prior winning percentages: 2018 (60%), 2012 (65%), 2006 (58%)

When Democrat Amy Klobuchar, Minnesota's senior senator, declared for her party's presidential nomination in February 2019, she presented a marked contrast to three female Democratic colleagues—California's Kamala Harris, Massachusetts' Elizabeth Warren and New York's Kirsten Gillibrand—who had entered the race just weeks earlier. Unlike the solidly blue coastal states of the other women, who had aligned themselves with the party's progressive wing, Klobuchar's Midwestern home had become a political battleground—and the policy stances she espoused were decidedly centrist. Klobuchar believed that such distinctions would clear a path to the nomination: She had demonstrated cross-party appeal in a Rust Belt state that Donald Trump came within 2 percentage points of carrying in 2016, putting her in a stronger position than her intraparty rivals to compete elsewhere in the Midwest, where narrow Trump victories had unexpectedly put him in the White House. "I have won big time, every time," Klobuchar boasted in Iowa in early 2020, listing the Minnesota counties and congressional districts she had won—and that Trump had won as well.

But Klobuchar's sales pitch proved to have its limits as she confronted the diversity of the national Democratic electorate. Joe Biden, the front-running centrist whom Klobuchar hoped to dislodge in the congested nomination race, faltered in the early going. But his campaign was resuscitated by a win in South Carolina, where a majority of the party's primary voters were Black. Klobuchar, having overwhelmingly won three Senate terms in a state whose population is only 7 percent Black and 6 percent Latino, struggled to connect with minority-heavy electorates in Nevada and South Carolina. Falling short, she dropped out and endorsed Biden—who, weeks later, pledged to select a woman as his running mate. Coupled with her ideological rapport with Biden, Klobuchar's appeal in the Midwest battleground again emerged as a selling point for placing her on the ticket. "She's our best bet to get disaffected white, blue-collar Democrats who voted for Trump in 2016 back into the Democratic column," former Pennsylvania Gov. Ed Rendell told the New York Times in May 2020.

However, race would again intervene in Klobuchar's political fortunes: The Black Lives Matter movement was ignited by a tragedy in her hometown. The death of George Floyd, an unarmed Black man, at the hands of a white Minneapolis police officer, brought renewed attention to Klobuchar's strained relations with the local Black community as chief prosecuting attorney in Minneapolis nearly two decades earlier. Klobuchar had faced criticism for failing to prosecute several cases in which the police were accused of using excessive force against Black suspects. She joined other Minnesota elected officials in urging federal and local prosecutors to conduct a full investigation into Floyd's death, while mounting a major outreach effort to African-American leaders and organizations nationally. But, in a tacit acknowledgement that circumstances had all but removed her prospects to become Biden's running mate, she called him and asked her name be removed from consideration —while urging that a woman of color be chosen.

With Biden in the White House and her former Senate colleagues, Kamala Harris, installed as vice president, Klobuchar returned to Capitol Hill to complete the third term to which she was elected in 2018—her influence enhanced by Senate Democrats' newly acquired majority. She assumed the chair of the Rules and Administration Committee as well as that of Judiciary Subcommittee on Antitrust, Competition Policy and Consumer Rights— using the former gavel to seek to advance a sweeping election reform bill, while pledging to employ the latter to rein in the nation's giant technology firms. Klobuchar underscored her commitment on that front with the spring 2021 publication of a book entitled: "Antitrust: Taking on Monopoly Power from the Gilded Age to the Digital Age." In a speech earlier in the year, she declared: "While we've seen this enormous change in our economy, we really are not as sophisticated as the companies that we should be regulating. We need to start by working to strengthen antitrust enforcement and making it more effective."

Her new positions presented her with potential opportunities to answer critics who suggest that Klobuchar has taken an overly incremental approach to legislating. In the past, she has sometimes been dinged for not taking on the difficult issues associated with her Senate forebears from Minnesota —ranging from Hubert Humphrey and Eugene McCarthy to Walter Mondale and Paul Wellstone. To be sure, the latter served at a time when Minnesota was a progressive bastion, prior to turning its current shade of purple. And her supporters note that Klobuchar can claim one of the top legislative records in the frequently gridlocked Senate, even if her emphasis has been on legislative proposals with a prospect of near-term passage as opposed to serving as idealistic goalposts in the party's next platform. In 2019, the Center for Effective Lawmaking—a project of Vanderbilt University and the University of Virginia—rated Klobuchar the fifth most effective senator overall and the most effective Democrat in the chamber.

I tend not to be a spear-thrower, Klobuchar told the Minneapolis Star Tribune at the outset of her second term. To some people, that means I'm being overly careful. I am careful with how I say things. ... I don't complain about the state of things. I don't do it in my speeches, and I don't do it one-on-one. I try to look for solutions. In 2018, Klobuchar told the MinnPost the constant of her Senate tenure has been that she "works in the middle," adding, "I'm willing to stand my ground and find common ground." In doing so, she has regularly sought to reach across the aisle—Republican John Hoeven from neighboring North Dakota is a good friend, as was the late Arizona Sen. John McCain—to the point that some home-state liberals have taken pokes at her as "the last moderate Republican in Minnesota."

She was born in the Minneapolis suburb of Plymouth, the daughter of longtime Star Tribune columnist Jim Klobuchar— who died at age 93 in May 2021. On her father's side, she is descended from Slovenian immigrants who settled in northern Minnesota's Iron Range; her grandfather worked in the iron mines along with many others of Eastern European ancestry. Growing up, Klobuchar helped her father recover from alcoholism, a battle both later documented in memoirs. It was an experience to which Klobuchar publicly referred in fall 2018, when, as a member of the Senate Judiciary Committee, she earned widespread praise for her handling of a testy exchange with Supreme Court nominee Brett Kavanaugh during a nationally televised hearing.

Klobuchar graduated from Yale University, spending summers pounding stakes into the ground for the Minnesota Highway Department. Her thesis, on the machinations behind the building of Minneapolis' Hubert H. Humphrey Metrodome, was later published as a book titled "Uncovering the Dome." As an undergraduate, Klobuchar interned for then-Vice President Mondale, and, after earning a law degree from the University of Chicago, worked with the 1984 presidential nominee at a Minneapolis law firm. Klobuchar has characterized Mondale as "an incredibly important mentor" who "encouraged me to believe that someday I could actually run for office."

That goal was realized in 1998 when Klobuchar was elected Hennepin County attorney, serving two terms. She was credited with securing nearly 300 homicide convictions, while aggressively prosecuting lesser offenses such as vandalism and often seeking longer-than-recommended sentences. The latter prosecutions were done with the goal of curbing more serious crimes—but the results were criticized for a disproportionate effect on poor and minority communities. In an interview with The Washington Post in early 2019, Klobuchar said she had targeted repeat offenders, adding: "When I first came into the office, the major thing I heard from the African American community, bar none, was that there were a bunch of their kids that were killed by gangsters. We prosecuted those cases and got results for our community."

Floyd's death brought attention to the fact that, as the chief prosecutor for Minnesota's most populous county, Klobuchar had declined to file charges in more than two dozen instances involving individuals killed in encounters with the police. She instead sent those cases to a grand jury, an option numerous law enforcement experts contend favors the police. Klobuchar said this practice was followed "in every jurisdiction in the state" while she was in office but expressed regret following Floyd's death. "I think that was wrong now," she told MSNBC. "I think it would have been much better if I took the responsibility and looked at the cases and made the decision myself." Controversy surrounding Klobuchar's management of the county attorney's office also resurfaced just before the launch of her presidential bid. During her first Senate campaign, the head of the union representing many workers in her office wrote a letter opposing her, citing her "shameful treatment of her employees." At the time, Klobuchar contended the letter was backlash over salary negotiations.

Her tenure as county attorney was not the only controversy regarding her management style to emerge during her presidential candidacy: Multiple media stories presented a picture different from her "Minnesotanice" public persona. (Her 2015 memoir was titled "The Senator Next Door".) LegiStorm found that, during Klobuchar's first decade on Capitol Hill, her office had the highest rate of staff turnover of any in the Senate. HuffPost reported that several potential hires declined to sign on with her presidential campaign owing to her reputation as a difficult boss. Some former employees portrayed her as not only demanding but demeaning, prone to throwing office objects in the direction of aides and sending derisive emails at all hours. "I love our staff, Klobuchar responded in an interview with Politico. "And yes, I can be tough. And yes, I can push people. ... I have, I'd say, high expectations for myself. I have high expectations for the people who work for me. But I have high expectations for this country, and that's what we need.

Klobuchar launched her initial Senate bid in 2006 after Democrat Mark Dayton (later the state's governor) announced he would not seek re-election. She won the endorsement of the Democratic-Farmer-Labor Party after several prominent figures announced they would not run. In the general election, she faced Republican Rep. Mark Kennedy, who sought to distance himself from the Iraq War and President George W. Bush: It did him little good in what turned out to be a strong Democratic year. Klobuchar slammed Kennedy as a "rubberstamp" for Bush and touted her record as a prosecutor, even as Kennedy sought to highlight an increasing rate of violent crime in Minneapolis. Klobuchar consistently led in the polls and won on Election Day, 58%-38%, to become the first woman elected to represent Minnesota in the Senate.

In her first reelection bid in 2012, she trounced GOP state Rep. Kurt Bills, 65%-31%. It was the most lop-sided win by a Minnesota Senate candidate in nearly four decades, as Klobuchar carried all but two of the state's 87 counties. Her 2018 opponent, state Rep. Jim Newberger, tied himself closely to Trump. Klobuchar's victory, 60%-36%, was tighter than it was in 2012, but she carried 42 counties Trump had taken two years earlier—winning 51 counties in all. Part of this record of success has been attributed to constituent service: She visits each of the state's counties at least once a year. Her former in-state colleague Al Franken once wisecracked to a Minneapolis audience: "Amy wanted to be with us tonight, but she discovered there was one county in Minnesota where her popularity was below 70 percent. So, she's up there pumping gas and cleaning windshields."

Klobuchar's Senate assignments include the Commerce, Science and Transportation Committee, where a major focus of her work has been consumer protection. Shortly after she was first elected, a 6-year-old sustained serious injuries from a swimming pool drain in a Minneapolis suburb. Klobuchar sponsored a bill, ultimately signed into law, banning swimming pool covers that fail to meet entrapment safety standards and requiring automatic drain shutoffs. The next year, after disclosures about lead in children's toys made in China, Klobuchar sponsored provisions in a child safety bill— which also became law—that bans lead in children's products and requires that toys contain batch numbers to make recalls easier. It prompted some Minnesota Republicans to pin a derisive nickname —"Senator of Small Things"—on her. Asked about this in an interview shortly before her presidential launch, Klobuchar bristled, telling the New York Times: "Not for a minute do I view these as small things. They're big things for the people whose kids' lives were saved."

There has been griping from the left as well: LGBTQ activists complained she should have been quicker to support ending the military's "don't ask, don't tell" ban on openly gay service members, and environmentalists were angered at her efforts to remove Minnesota wolves from the federal endangered species list. At the same time, Klobuchar has a lifetime score of 92 percent from the League of Conservation Voters, and, in early 2019, co-sponsored the "Green New Deal," a nonbinding resolution pushed by the party's progressive wing urging a "10-year national mobilization effort" to achieve net-zero greenhouse gas emissions.

But Klobuchar didn't join her party's left wing in calling for tuition-free four-year college, instead favoring free community college. And unlike most of her Senate colleagues competing for the 2020 Democratic nomination, she declined to sign on to the "Medicare for All" legislation sponsored by Vermont Sen. Bernie Sanders. Klobuchar told the New York Times the proposal should be considered, but she advocated a "sensible transition," such as the option of voluntarily buying into the program. She has focused her health care efforts on bringing drug prices down. Working with Republican Chuck Grassley of Iowa, Klobuchar has pushed to allow importation of less expensive prescription drugs from Canada and to let the federal government negotiate for cheaper drug prices under Medicare Part D.

On the presidential campaign trail, she frequently boasted of the number of bills she had passed and of her cross-party collaborations. According to Klobuchar, two dozen bills on which she was the lead Democrat—ranging from increasing funding for the nation's water infrastructure to improving telephone service in rural areas—were signed into law during the first two years of the Trump administration. Among the bills signed by Trump at the end of 2018—after months of House-Senate negotiations—was a measure dealing with sexual harassment. The lead Senate sponsors were Klobuchar, then the ranking member on the Rules Committee, and the panel's chair at the time, Missouri Republican Roy Blunt. The law holds members of Congress liable for harassment and retaliation for claims of harassment, while requiring them to reimburse the federal government for settlements in such cases.

A year earlier, Klobuchar had taken over sponsorship of a sexual harassment bill drafted by Franken, before he resigned amid allegations of improper sexual advances. That legislation—which proposed grants to help train law enforcement personnel to better handle sexual assault victims—was prompted by the rape of a University of Minnesota student. The late 2017 episode culminating in the resignation of Franken—a onetime "Saturday Night Live" mainstay who served with Klobuchar for nearly nine years—was particularly awkward for her. Franken enjoyed support among progressives in Minnesota and nationally who often viewed Klobuchar skeptically; many of them felt Franken had been forced out prematurely.

When the initial allegations against Franken surfaced, Klobuchar condemned his behavior and called for an Ethics Committee investigation. But several weeks later, as more allegations emerged, more than half of Senate Democrats called for his resignation, but Klobuchar refrained. "I felt I was in a different role as his colleague, that I'm someone that has worked with him for a long time. There's a lot of trust there, and I felt it was best to handle it in that way," she told CNN after Franken said he would resign. Several months later, Klobuchar was quoted by Newsweek as disputing Franken had been forced out; she contended he had made his own choice after concluding the allegations would have made it difficult to do his job. Appointed—and later elected—to succeed Franken was Democrat Tina Smith, a centrist in the Klobuchar mold. The two reportedly have become close friends, with Klobuchar temporarily living at Smith's Washington apartment in early 2020 as her husband, University of Baltimore law professor John Bessler, recovered from COVID-19.

During the 2020 campaign, Klobuchar was hit with criticism from opposing contenders—particularly Pete Buttigieg, former mayor of South Bend Indiana—about her record of support for Trump's judicial nominees. For her part, Klobuchar did little to hide her disdain for Buttigieg—who later became Biden's Transportation secretary—as he emerged as an unexpectedly strong Midwestern rival for the "centrist lane" in the nomination battle. In an interview with the New York Times, Klobuchar questioned whether a woman with Buttigieg's limited electoral experience as mayor of a 100,000-person city would be taken seriously as a presidential candidate. When Buttigieg took aim at her on judicial nominees in a February 2020 debate, Klobuchar fired back, "I wish everyone was as perfect as you, Pete, but let me tell you what it's like to be in the arena"—arena being a favorite expression of hers for experience in Washington. She continued: "You have not been in the arena doing that work. You've memorized a bunch of talking points and a bunch of things."

In fact, Klobuchar's voting record showed her to be more supportive of Trump's judicial nominees during the first half of his term than other senators competing for the Democratic presidential nomination: In 2017 and 2018, Klobuchar voted 64 percent of the time for Trump's choices, according to an analysis by the MinnPost. By comparison, Gillibrand, Harris, Sanders, Warren and New Jersey Sen. Cory Booker voted for Trump's judicial nominees between 46 and 51 percent of the time. But Klobuchar was part of the solid bloc of Democrats who supported a filibuster to stymie the Supreme Court nomination of Neil Gorsuch in early 2017. And it was her role trying to block the confirmation of Trump's next high court nominee, Kavanaugh, that boosted her national profile.

At a Judiciary Committee hearing on allegations of sexual assault against Kavanaugh by Christine BlaseyFord—charges Kavanaugh denied—Klobuchar sought to probe whether Kavanaugh had experienced memory loss because of alcohol use. Noting her father's alcoholism, she referred to Kavanaugh's written testimony acknowledging that he had occasionally had too many drinks.

"Was there ever a time when you drank so much that you couldn't remember what happened, or part of what happened the night before?" Klobuchar asked.

Kavanaugh replied: "You're asking about, you know, blackout. I don't know. Have you?"

The onetime prosecutor pressed. "Could you answer the question, judge? So … that's not happened? Is that your answer?"

Kavanaugh came back at her. "Yeah, and I'm curious if you have," he responded.

"I have no drinking problem, judge," Klobuchar replied.

"Yeah, nor do I." Kavanaugh said.

Klobuchar ended the exchange: "OK, thank you."

After a break, Kavanaugh apologized: "This is a tough process. I'm sorry about that." Klobuchar accepted the apology. Her decision to end the testy exchange without grandstanding, and by letting Kavanaugh's performance speak for itself, won her widespread praise for persistence and a quiet toughness.

Speculation about Klobuchar as a presidential candidate had accelerated after her landslide reelection win in 2012. During the 2014 election cycle, she traveled to a dozen states, raising campaign funds for Democrats. During that period, she made four trips to Iowa. She hoped such proximity would give her an early advantage in a presidential bid. "I can see Iowa from my porch!" Klobuchar wisecracked to an Iowa delegation breakfast at the 2012 Democratic National Convention —a riff on a Saturday Night Live joke that parodied former Alaska Gov. Sarah Palin's statement about her state's proximity to Russia.

Klobuchar spent more than 70 days campaigning in Iowa in the first year of her candidacy, visiting all 99 counties and deploying the bulk of her staff to the state. But she struggled to generate voter enthusiasm. Part of her inability to break through there was attributed to the other centrist candidates, notably Buttigieg. She also appeared hampered at times by the same factor that dogged other female candidates: reluctance to nominate a woman, as many voters recalled the fate of Democratic nominee Hillary Clinton four years earlier. When the Iowa caucuses were held in early February 2020, Klobuchar finished fifth.

But Biden's anemic performance in Iowa—he finished fourth—gave Klobuchar an opening to surge in the New Hampshire primary a week later. In a pre-primary debate, she was deemed the hands-down winner. She got in another dig at Buttigieg—"We have a newcomer in the White House, and look where it got us"—while winning audience cheers for her closing statement. "There is a complete lack of empathy in this guy in the White House right now, and I will bring that to you," she vowed, adding: "I do not have the biggest name up on this stage. I don't have the biggest bank account. But I have a record of fighting for people. Her closing was quickly turned into a campaign ad, and one tracking poll showed her voter support shooting up from 6 percent prior to the debate. When the polls closed, she had finished with 20 percent—pulling twice as many votes as either Warren, who's from neighboring Massachusetts, or Biden. Amid "Klomentum" buzz, her campaign raised $12 million in a little over a week after the debate—more than she raised during the final three months of 2019.

But New Hampshire's voter demographics more resembled those of Minnesota than the primary states next on the calendar—jurisdictions in which Klobuchar lacked the organization needed to capitalize on her resurgence. She finished sixth in Nevada and again in South Carolina—drawing just 1 percent of the Black vote in the latter, as Biden was the choice of half the voters. She dropped out before the Super Tuesday primaries the following week, and immediately endorsed Biden (along with Buttigieg)—in a bid to slow the momentum of Sanders on the left. Her move bespoke her concern— expressed in debates throughout the campaign—that Sanders would lose badly to Trump, particularly in the Midwest.

"Bernie and I work together all the time," Klobuchar said during the pre-primary debate in New Hampshire. But, she added, "…I think we are not going to be able to out-divide the divider-in-chief. And I think we need someone to head up this ticket that actually brings people with her instead of shutting them out."

Tina Smith (D)

Appointed 2018, term expires 2026, 1st full term, b. Mar 04, 1958; Albuquerque, NM; Stanford University, B.A., 1980; Dartmouth College Tuck School of Business, M.B.A. 1984; Religion not stated; Married (Archie Smith); 2 children.

Elected Office: MN Lt. Governor, 2015-2017.

Professional Career: Campaign Manager, Ted Mondale for Governor, 1998; Principal, MacWilliams Cosrove Smith Robinson, 1992-1998; Campaign Manager, Walter Mondale for Senate, 2002; VP of External Affairs/Senior Manager, Planned Parenthood of MN, ND, SD, 2003-2006; Chief of Staff, Minneapolis Mayor R.T. Rybak, 2006-2010; Chief of Staff, MN Governor Mark Dayton, 2011-2014 .

DC Office: 720 HSOB 20510, 202-224-5641, Fax: 202-224-0044, smith.senate.gov

State Offices: Duluth, 218-722-2390; Moorhead, 218-284-8721; Rochester, 507-288-2003; Saint Paul, 651-221-1016.

Committees: *Agriculture, Nutrition & Forestry*: Commodities, Risk Management & Trade; Livestock, Dairy, Poultry, Local Food Sys & Food Safety & Sec; Rural Development & Energy (Chmn). *Banking, Housing & Urban Affairs*: Economic Policy; Housing, Transportation & Community Development (Chmn); Securities, Insurance & Investment. *Health, Education, Labor & Pensions*: Children & Families; Employment & Workplace Safety. *Indian Affairs*.

Group Ratings

	ADA	ACLU	AFL-CIO	LCV	COC	HAFA	ACU	CFG	FRC
2020	-	77%	-	92%	-	0%	3%	-	-

Almanac Ratings 2019-2020

	Economy	Social	Foreign	Composite
Liberal	82%	70%	93%	82%
Conservative	18%	30%	7%	18%

Key Votes of the 116th Congress

1. EPA clean energy rules	N/A	5. Russia sanctions	Y	9. Barr as Atty. General	N
2. U.S./Mex./Can. trade deal	Y	6. Troops in SYR, AFG	N	10. Spending at the border	Y
3. Cut unemployment benefits	N	7. Veto arms sales to Saudis	Y	11. Coney Barrett to Sup. Ct.	N
4. Shelton to Fed Reserve	N	8. Defense $$$, veto override	Y	12. Electoral College objections	N

Election Results

Election	Name (Party)	Vote (%)		Cand. Spent	Ind. Exp. Support	Ind. Exp. Oppose
2020 General	Tina Smith (D)	1,566,522	(49%)	$17,240,981	$796,261	$299,050
	Jason Lewis (R)	1,398,145	(44%)	$6,872,857	$599,064	$139,065
2020 Primary	Tina Smith (D)	497,498	(87%)			
	Paula Overby (D)	30,497	(5%)			
2018 Special	Tina Smith (DFL)	1,370,540	(53%)			
	Katrina Housley (R)	1,095,777	(42%)			
	Sarah Wellington (LMNP)	95,614	(4%)			
2018 Primary	Tina Smith (DFL)	433,705	(76%)			
	Richard Painter (DFL)	78,193	(14%)			

Prior winning percentages: 2018 (53%)

After spending much of her political career as a behind-the-scenes staffer and operative, Democrat Tina Smith suddenly—and quite unexpectedly—found herself in the spotlight at the outset of 2018. The resignation of Democrat Al Franken, amid allegations of improper sexual advances toward several women, led to the appointment of Smith as Minnesota's junior senator after three years as lieutenant governor. The latter post was Smith's first experience in elected office, and she was little-known when she entered the Senate, facing a special election in less than a year. She went on to comfortably win the remaining two years of Franken's term in a state that President Donald Trump lost by less than 2 percentage points in 2016, and then was elected to a full Senate term in 2020 as Democrat Joe Biden captured the state—and the White House.

Smith and the state's senior senator, Democrat Amy Klobuchar, are nearly Minnesota twins: The women, a couple of years apart in age, have become close while earning reputations as low-key politicians intent on consensus-building. Just as Klobuchar boasted of her outreach across the aisle during her unsuccessful bid for their party's 2020 presidential nomination, Smith likewise highlighted her bipartisan efforts on the campaign trail in a state that has become an electoral battleground. During her time as chief of staff to Minneapolis Mayor R.T. Rybak and then to Gov. Mark Dayton—who appointed her to the Senate—Smith was nicknamed the "velvet hammer" because of her ability to prod disparate interests into agreement without creating rancor. Smith "deserves a lot of credit for things that I've gotten credit for," Rybak told the MinnPost, adding, "She's just kind of wired to find common ground."

Both Smith and Klobuchar also claim the late Vice President Walter Mondale as a political mentor. Born Christine Flint in Albuquerque New Mexico, Smith grew up in Santa Fe—where she owns a second home. Her husband of more than 30 years, Archie Smith, is an investor who has specialized in medical device stocks: His career came into play in an attack ad during the 2018 Senate race. Tina Smith earned a bachelor's degree from Stanford University and an MBA from the Tuck School of Business at Dartmouth College before moving to Minnesota to work at General Mills as a marketing executive. She later formed her own marketing and public relations firm.

Smith in 1998 managed the unsuccessful gubernatorial bid of Ted Mondale, Walter Mondale's son. Just before Election Day 2002, Democratic Sen. Paul Wellstone died in a plane crash, and Walter Mondale was nominated as a last-minute replacement. Smith ran Mondale's brief bid, which he lost to Republican Norm Coleman. Smith then served as vice president of public affairs for Planned Parenthood of Minnesota, North Dakota and South Dakota before becoming Rybak's chief of staff in 2005. Two years later, when the Interstate 35 bridge that crosses the Mississippi River in Minneapolis collapsed, killing 13 people, it was left to Smith to navigate the difficult relationship between the offices of Democrat Rybak and Republican Gov. Tim Pawlenty. "Tina was the one, more than anybody, who pulled those two offices together and had them acting almost as one," Rybak later recalled.

In 2010, Smith managed Dayton's successful gubernatorial campaign before becoming his chief of staff. "When we wanted something to happen in the governor's office, frankly, I'd go to Tina, not to Mark" Dayton, Duluth-based labor leader Alan Netland later told the Minneapolis Star-Tribune. As Dayton prepared to seek reelection in 2014, his lieutenant governor, Yvonne Prettner Solon, announced she would not run again, and Dayton moved to replace her with his close adviser: Smith. Minnesota's lieutenant governorship had traditionally been a dead-end job. Smith redefined it: She often served as the administration's public face, while also continuing in her accustomed behind-the-scenes role, including representing Dayton in budget negotiations with state legislative leaders. With Dayton barred from seeking a third term, there was speculation he was setting Smith up to run in his stead. But she decided in 2016 not to seek the governorship and appeared headed back to private life —until Franken became a casualty of the accelerating #MeToo movement.

At the outset of 2017, Franken—once a comic mainstay of NBC's "Saturday Night Live"—was riding high amid buzz as a potential presidential candidate. But, in November 2017, radio anchor Leeann Tweeden alleged Franken forcibly kissed her in 2006, two years before his initial run for Senate; a posed photo emerged showing Franken pretending to grab at her breasts while she slept on a flight. Franken, while saying he did not remember the incident in the same manner as Tweeden, issued a public apology. As other women came forward with similar allegations, his Democratic colleagues grew increasingly uncomfortable. When, in early December, yet another allegation against Franken surfaced, it quickly triggered calls for his resignation from more than half of the Senate Democratic Caucus. A day later, Franken announced he would resign.

Smith was sworn in to the Senate on January 3, 2018. Her status as Franken's successor initially required something of a political tightrope act: In Minnesota, there were many who not only missed Franken's outspoken progressive advocacy but who also felt that he had not gotten a fair chance to defend himself. In March, during a podcast interview with Politico, she went out of her way to avoid mentioning Franken's name, opting instead to focus on the economic implications of the #MeToo movement. When the publication sent out a summary of the podcast with a headline identifying her as "Franken's replacement," she bristled—tweeting, "Hi there, @politico—the name is Tina Smith, and I'm a U.S. Senator for the great state of Minnesota." Steven Schier, a retired politics professor at Carleton College, observed to the MinnPost soon after Smith's appointment: "If someone wants to enter the U.S. Senate, it's hard to imagine more complicated and challenging circumstances than [Smith] has faced. Up against an immediate re-election, she is dealing with the Franken fallout and she's having to learn a new job."

Smith focused on matters at home with the special election coming up fast. She was assigned to the Agriculture Committee, where Klobuchar already was a member. The five-year farm bill debate allowed Smith to visibly advocate for rural Minnesota. Among her bragging points: a provision with grants to establish broadband service in remote, low-income rural areas. Smith's floor votes have put her in the ideological middle of the Senate Democratic Conference—with Klobuchar. Both have opposed "Medicare for All," a touchstone of the Democratic Party's left wing. In a rare contrast, Smith in her 2020 Senate campaign voiced opposition to another policy mainstay of progressives— the "Green New Deal," which Klobuchar embraced in advance of her presidential bid. Nonetheless, the League of Conservation Voters gave Smith a 98 percent voting score for her first three years on Capitol Hill.

Representing a state where Trump ran strongly in 2016, Smith avoided directly attacking the president during her first year in office. "I think that it is up to the voters of this country to decide whether he is fit for office," Smith told Politico. "I strongly disagree with him on almost everything. But I also believe that my state didn't send me to Washington, D.C., or any of us to Washington, D.C., to just throw bombs and fight." Likewise in 2020, she approached Trump's first impeachment trial with restraint. "I don't think Donald Trump should be president, but that's a very different question from whether I think that he should be removed from office because he's committed impeachable offenses," she told the MinnPost shortly before the trial got underway. But she later joined all Democrats in voting to convict Trump of charges that he had sought to leverage foreign aid to Ukraine for personal political gain.

State Sen. Karin Housley easily won the GOP nomination to fill the remainder of Franken's term in 2018, setting up Minnesota's first all-woman Senate race. Housley appeared at a rally with Trump in Rochester during the general election campaign but vowed not to be a "rubberstamp" for the president's policies— while deriding Smith as a "political insider" and "career politician." Housley's husband was considered a major asset to her campaign: Phil Housley is an NHL Hall of Fame defenseman widely regarded as the best player ever produced by hockey-loving Minnesota.

Karin Housley, meanwhile, took aim at Smith's spouse. In one of the more negative ads of the 2018 election cycle, her campaign accused Smith of profiting from the opioid crisis via her husband's ownership of stock in Abbott Laboratories, the original marketer of OxyContin. The 30-second spot, in which actors depicting the Smiths are shown drinking champagne on a beach, was called misleading by independent fact checkers. Smith's husband had bought between $250,000 and $500,000 worth of stock in Minnesota-based St. Jude Medical, which Abbott Laboratories had taken over—nearly a decade and a half after Abbott had stopped marketing OxyContin. Smith, whose campaign literature asserted she was "standing up to Big Pharma"—her first Senate bill sought to increase consumer access to less expensive generic drugs—fired back. She accused Housley of siding with the pharmaceutical industry by voting against legislation—which passed the Minnesota Senate in mid-2018—to impose millions of dollars in fees on the drug companies to address the opioid crisis.

Smith defeated Housley 53%-42% and, upon her return to Capitol Hill, continued her focus on bringing down high pharmaceutical costs. In mid-2019, she teamed with Republican Sen. Kevin Cramer of North Dakota to introduce legislation for grants to states to provide cost-free insulin to uninsured and underinsured people on a short-term basis. It was a response to the death of a Minnesotan who had self-rationed insulin because of its rocketing price. While the bill was not enacted, Smith did work with another GOP colleague—Bill Cassidy of Louisiana—on a proposal to lower insulin prices that did become law. Smith spent time prior to college working on the Trans-Alaska pipeline, which helped her to bond with Alaska GOP Sen. Lisa Murkowski of Alaska. A bill authored by the pair to expand telemedicine services for mental health treatment was included in broader legislation on opioid addiction signed into law.

As Smith faced her second statewide race, Housley announced in July 2019 that she would not make a second run. A month later, former one-term Rep. Jason Lewis declared for the Senate. Lewis, known for provocative statements during an earlier career as a conservative radio talk show host, aligned himself closely with Trump. Smith started the contest as a clear favorite, but with Trump on the ballot and his campaign targeting the state, the Senate contest was poised to be competitive. Polling showed Smith still with relatively low name recognition. "Nobody even knows who the hell she is!" Trump declared at a rally in the state late in the campaign. Lewis, however, was up against history: A Minnesota Republican had not won a Senate seat since Coleman's 2002 victory.

Lewis attacked Minnesota's response to the COVID-19 pandemic, belittling mask mandates and social distancing. He echoed the president's law-and-order messaging, particularly after the unrest that followed the death of George Floyd, an unarmed Black man, while in police custody in Minneapolis. "We don't have a problem with too many police; we have a problem with too little police," Lewis declared during a debate with Smith after running an ad seeking to tie Smith to the "defund the police" effort backed by some progressives. "I do not want to defund the police, and I've said that consistently," responded Smith, adding that the months since Floyd's death had "laid bare inequities in our policing and in our courts." She called for "commonsense reforms to bring more accountability, transparency and justice to policing."

Ultimately, the national GOP failed to steer any independent expenditure funds to Minnesota, although the U.S. Chamber of Commerce and conservative Citizens United spent $490,000 and $435,500, respectively, on Lewis' behalf. Smith got a boost from nearly $890,000 in independent expenditures by the Democratic Senatorial Campaign Committee. Smith's 48.8%-43.5% victory was much narrower than it had been two years earlier, and her nearly 170,000-vote edge was about 60,000 behind that of Biden.

Jim Hagedorn (R)

Elected 2018, 2nd term, b. Aug 04, 1962; Blue Earth, MN; George Mason University, B.A., 1992; Lutheran; Single.

Professional Career: Legislative Assistant, U.S. Rep. Arlan Strangeland, 1984-1991; U.S. Department of the Treasury, Director for Legislative and Public Affairs for the Financial Management Service, 1991 to 1998, Congressional Affairs Officer, Bureau of Engraving & Printing.

DC Office: 325 CHOB 20515, 202-225-2472, hagedorn.house.gov

State Offices: Mankato, 507-323-6090; Rochester, 507-323-6090.

Committees: *Agriculture*: Biotechnology, Horticulture & Research; Livestock & Foreign Agriculture. *Small Business*: Contracting & Infrastructure; Oversight, Investigations & Regulations; Underserved, Agricultural & Rural Business Development (RMM).

Almanac Ratings 2019-2020

	Economy	Social	Foreign	Composite
Liberal	30%	8%	27%	22%
Conservative	70%	92%	73%	78%

Key Votes of the 116th Congress

1. U.S./Mex./Can. trade deal	Y	5. Russia sanctions	Y	9. Firearms background checks N
2. First Coronavirus response	Y	6. Troops in Syria	Y	10. Spending at the border	Y
3. HEROES Act	N	7. Veto arms sales to Saudis	N	11. Marijuana liberalized rules	N
4. CASH Act	N/A	8. Defense $$$, veto override	N/A	12. Electoral College objections Y

Election Results

Election	Name (Party)	Vote (%)		Cand. Spent	Ind. Exp. Support	Ind. Exp. Oppose
2020 General	Jim Hagedorn (R)............................	179,234	(49%)	$2,298,384	$44,690	$6,334,726
	Dan Feehan (D)................................	167,890	(46%)	$4,863,052	$116,389	$4,189,674
	Bill Rood (LC)................................	21,448	(6%)			

Prior winning percentages: 2018 (50%)

Republican Jim Hagedorn was elected in 2018 in his third consecutive campaign for the district along the southern tier of Minnesota. After narrowly losing his challenge two years earlier to Democratic Rep. Tim Walz, he won an even more slender victory for the open seat, when Walz ran successfully for governor. In his close rematch, Hagedorn criticized Walz for his handling of the coronavirus. Tom Hagedorn, his father, served four terms in the House representing a similar area, until he lost reelection in 1982 to Democrat Tim Penny and remained in Washington as a lobbyist.

Hagedorn was raised in Washington and on the family farm near Truman Minnesota, while his father served in Congress. He graduated from George Mason University and worked for Rep. Arlan Stangeland, another Minnesota Republican. At the Treasury Department, he was director for legislative and public affairs for the Financial Management Service, and congressional affairs officer for the Bureau of Engraving and Printing. He claimed credit for the decision—which was approved in legislation—to start electronic funds transfer for hundreds of millions of annual federal payments. In his campaign bio, he said he stopped a Bush administration plan in 2005 to merge the federal currency and coin agencies, which Hagedorn said would have cost taxpayers $500 million.

In 2010, he lost his initial bid for the House seat in the Republican primary. In two challenges as the GOP nominee against Walz, who outspent him more than 4-to-1 in each campaign, Hagedorn criticized the influx of immigrants and refugees, including to the 1st District. In 2016, Hagedorn closely linked himself to the presidential campaign of Donald Trump, though he received scant support from House Republicans. He lost that contest by fewer than 2,600 votes.

Hagedorn's seeming inevitability in 2018 ran into some stumbling blocks in his GOP-leaning district. State Sen. Carla Nelson challenged him in the Republican primary. She cited her record in elected office, including support from the National Rifle Association, and criticized Hagedorn for having settled in the nation's capital. Hagedorn responded that Nelson was raised in Iowa and that he had the support of local Republican leaders. With the advantage of greater name recognition, he prevailed, 60%-32%.

Democratic nominee Dan Feehan, a former Army Ranger in Iraq, shared with Hagedorn an extended residency in the Washington area, where he was a deputy assistant secretary of Defense, handling readiness issues. With his youthful energy and more than twice as much campaign spending as Hagedorn, Feehan appealed for bipartisanship, including the need for health care and immigration reform. Republicans criticized Feehan's affiliation with the Washington-based Center for a New American Security, which they described as a liberal think tank—though James Mattis, Trump's first Defense secretary, had served on its board. Although Trump's tariffs on farm products had become problematic in this district, Hagedorn backed the president.

In its editorial endorsing Feehan, the Winona Daily News praised him as "the candidate who values compromise," and cited Hagedorn for "fearmongering" on immigration and "parroting the rhetoric from Trump's campaign rallies and tweets." This time, Hagedorn finished on the upside of a narrow outcome—with a lead of 1,315 of 291,000 that were cast. Feehan led in the two largest counties: Rochester-based Olmstead and Mankato-based Blue Earth. Hagedorn showed broader strength across the district, taking 16 of the 21 counties. This was one of only three House districts that switched to Republicans in 2018—two of them in Minnesota.

He joined the other Republicans in the Minnesota delegation in criticizing Walz for showing insufficient concern for coronavirus-related restrictions in rural areas. Instead of "more over-the-top arbitrary decrees," Hagedorn said in November 2020, "Walz should do the right thing and give up emergency powers." In 2021, Hagedorn became ranking Republican on the Small Business Subcommittee on Underserved, Agricultural and Rural Business Development.

In September 2020, Hagedorn became the target of an ethics complaint filed by a Democratic attorney in Minnesota, who cited a news report that raised questions of whether an aide benefited financially in handling Hagedorn's newsletters. A second complaint ensued from a report that Hagedorn had failed to pay rent on office space used by his campaign. The allegations were reported by Politico and Minnesota Reformer, a nonprofit news organization. Hagedorn responded that he fired the aide when he learned of the newsletter conflict.

His rematch with Feehan in 2020 had some similarities to his initial contest, including that Feehan doubled Hagedorn's spending and that the two national parties spent another $10 million on the race, which was split about evenly. With a boost from Trump's strength in the district, Hagedorn increased his victory to 11,344 votes, 48.6%-45.6%. Feehan won five of the seven largest counties, including a 54%-41% lead in Olmsted, which cast nearly one-fourth of the vote, but Hagedorn prevailed again with big leads in rural areas. Despite Feehan's charge that Hagedorn's office management was "disgraceful," the ethics complaints apparently had little impact on the contest.

MN-1: Southern Minnesota

Cook Partisan Voting Index: R+8

Population		Race and Ethnicity		Income	
Total	679,003	White	89.10%	Median Income	$66,330
Land area (sq. miles)	11,974	Black	3.10%	District Income Rank	200
Pop/ sq mi	56.71	Latino	6.80%	Poverty Rate	9.30%
Born in State	68.10%	Asian	3.00%	With health insurance	93.80%
		Two or more races	2.50%	Cash public assistance	2.30%
Age Groups		Other	2.30%	Food stamp/SNAP	6.10%
Under 18	23.20%				
18-34	22.40%	**Education**		**Work**	
35-64	36.40%	H.S grad or less	35.80%	White Collar	38.20%
Over 64	17.80%	Some college	33.10%	Sales and Service	35.30%
		College Degree, 4 yr	19.70%	Blue Collar	26.60%
Military		Post grad	11.40%	Government	11.40%
Veteran/ Active Duty	7.30%				

2020 Pres. Vote	Trump	202,121	(54%)	Biden	164,139	(44%)		
2016 Pres. Vote	Trump	181,647	(53%)	Clinton	130,831	(38%)	Johnson	13,881 (4%)
	McMullin	6,915	(2%)					

Rochester: The Mississippi River flows majestically southeast from Minneapolis and St. Paul, cutting through rolling hills and, where it widens, forming calm lakes. This far north, the westward tide of Yankee migrants thinned out; most settlers following the railroads on the flood plains west of the river after the Civil War were Germans and Scandinavians, bringing their families to a terrain much like the Rhineland and to the rolling uplands beyond, which resemble the northern European plain.

A little to the west is Rochester, home to the renowned Mayo Clinic, founded in 1863 when English-born physician William Mayo set up a practice to examine inductees into the Union Army. Today, 1.3 million people annually visit Mayo clinics in three states (Arizona and Florida, in addition to Minnesota) for cancer treatment and other illnesses. With more than 35,000 people employed in Rochester, that city is prosperous and has been the fastest-growing metropolitan area in Minnesota. The growth will continue, with Mayo's $6 billion plan for a high-tech medical center that will compete for what has been called the "global medical tourism industry" for health and wellness, with 22 projects planned by Mayo over two decades—plus a $250 million redevelopment of the riverfront area—in what officials style as their "warm, hospitable" community. Mayo and community leaders worried about the impact for employees and patients of President Donald Trump's executive orders to limit immigration and refugees. (Nearly 30 percent of doctors and surgeons in the United States are immigrants.) At least one of those projects was halted when a developer in September 2020 cited the pandemic to explain why it abandoned plans to expand a cancer center, with a 32-floor facility at Mayo.

In Mower County, Austin is the headquarters of the Hormel meatpacking firm, which produces "miracle meat" Spam, Hormel chili and Dinty Moore stew. This was the southern locus of the 1862 Dakota Uprising, which resulted in the simultaneous hangings of 38 Dakota warriors at Mankato. Many of the bodies were dug up at night by doctors—including William Mayo—for use in medical research. To the north is Le Sueur, where Minnesota Valley Canning Co., later renamed Green Giant, was founded; a 55-foot statue of the iconic giant is a feature in Blue Earth. The farther west you go, the more frequently you find communities with a German heritage. Many small towns in southern Minnesota are now filling up with Hispanic farmworkers. The Somali communities in Rochester and Faribault—a small town to the west—each exceed 4,000, of the more than 50,000 Somalis statewide. Still, the overall minority population in the area remains small.

The 1st Congressional District of Minnesota includes most of the state's two southern tiers of counties. It stretches over 250 miles, from the South Dakota border to the Wisconsin border. This historically was a political borderland, with Civil War Republicans in the east and Farmer-Laborites more common in the west, but the traditions have been upended. Rochester had long been a Republican stronghold, but like many Northern white-collar areas, it has trended Democratic. With its tradition of staunch unionism, Austin has remained solidly Democratic-Farmer-Labor. To the west, the population-losing farm counties between Mankato and the South Dakota border now vote solidly Republican. This is one of three mostly rural districts in Minnesota that have moved to the Republicans. In the 1st, it went from 49 percent for Barack Obama in 2012 to 38 percent for Hillary Clinton. Joe Biden recovered some of that loss, when he got 44 percent in 2020, chiefly with his increase in Rochester-based Olmsted County from 46 to 54 percent.

Angie Craig (DFL)

Elected 2018, 2nd term, b. Feb 14, 1972; W. Helena, AR; University of Memphis, B.A., 1994; Lutheran; Married (Cheryl Greene); 4 children.

Professional Career: Executive, St. Jude Medical; Newspaper Reporter.

DC Office: 1523 LHOB 20515, 202-225-2271, craig.house.gov

State Offices: Burnsville, 651-846-2120.

Committees: *Agriculture*: Commodity Exchanges, Energy & Credit; General Farm Commodities & Risk Management; Livestock & Foreign Agriculture. *Energy & Commerce*: Communications & Technology; Consumer Protection & Commerce; Health. *Small Business*: Oversight, Investigations & Regulations.

Almanac Ratings 2019-2020

	Economy	Social	Foreign	Composite
Liberal	100%	58%	80%	80%
Conservative	0%	42%	20%	20%

Key Votes of the 116th Congress

1. U.S./Mex./Can. trade deal Y	5. Russia sanctions Y	9. Firearms background checks Y
2. First Coronavirus response Y	6. Troops in Syria Y	10. Spending at the border Y
3. HEROES Act Y	7. Veto arms sales to Saudis Y	11. Marijuana liberalized rules Y
4. CASH Act Y	8. Defense $$$, veto override Y	12. Electoral College objections N

Election Results

Election	Name (Party)	Vote (%)		Cand. Spent	Ind. Exp. Support	Ind. Exp. Oppose
2020 General	Angie Craig (DFL)	204,534	(48%)	$5,075,865	$71,517	$29,000
	Tyler Kistner (R)	194,954	(46%)	$2,929,241	$78,518	$418,752
	Adam Weeks (LM)	24,751	(6%)			

Prior winning percentages: 2018 (53%)

Democrat Angie Craig won a rematch in 2018 against Republican Rep. Jason Lewis, who narrowly defeated her two years earlier when they competed for an open seat. In this swing district, Craig rode the national surge of political and financial support for Democratic women running in suburban areas. Craig was the only House first-termer who reversed a setback two years earlier against the same opponent. Even with her productive legislative work, her campaign for a second term became unexpectedly tight, following a move late in the campaign to delay the election until February.

Craig has a compelling life story. She was raised by her single mother in a trailer park in Arkansas and graduated from the University of Memphis. As a lesbian, before gay marriages were recognized, she won a major legal battle in 2000 when a judge in Tennessee gave her custody of her child, with her then-partner as the adoptive parent. Years later, Craig married her wife in Minnesota and they have four children.

She became a top executive of two medical-device companies, which are part of a major industry in the Twin Cities area. During a decade with St. Paul-based St. Jude Medical Foundation, which specialized in cardiovascular technology, Craig supervised communications and directed the company's political action committee, which contributed chiefly to Republicans. She stepped down as senior vice president of global human resources.

Running in 2016 against Lewis, who had built a devoted audience for more than two decades as a nationally syndicated conservative radio talk show host based in the Twin Cities area, Democrats seized on his countless incendiary comments and said many were racist or sexist. Lewis happily modeled himself after Donald Trump. Craig was a superior fundraiser, with $4 million (including nearly $1 million of self-financing) to $1 million for Lewis. Each party and its allies spent about $3 million for its candidate. Defying expectations and benefiting from Trump's lead in the district, Lewis won, 47%-45%. Craig suffered from the 8 percent that went to a liberal-leaning independent candidate.

In her 2018 campaign, Craig defeated Jeff Erdmann at the DFL district convention. Erdmann, a high school civics teacher who styled himself as a working-class candidate and criticized Craig's millions of dollars in campaign spending, withdrew before the primary. In contrast to her 2016 contest against Lewis, Craig gave less attention to Trump and focused more on the incumbent's votes in Congress — including the large tax cuts, which she described as "trickle-down economics," and repeal of the Affordable Care Act. "I never talk about the president," Craig told the Minnesota Post. "We've got to tell people what we're going to fight for." Lewis responded that he had sought bipartisanship, including on criminal justice reform "Lots of good things come to a halt if we don't prevail," he told the Post.

National news organizations, such as CNN and BuzzFeed, recycled some of Lewis' earlier provocative remarks from his radio talk show, including his defense of men who inappropriately touch women. Craig grew more eager to contend that such comments, plus Lewis's support for the confirmation of Brett Kavanaugh to the Supreme Court, did not represent "Minnesota values." Like other leading House Democratic challengers, Craig had a big fundraising advantage. House Republican campaign strategists acknowledged weeks before the election that the party was reducing its financial support for him. Craig's 53%-47% win confirmed that assessment.

In the House, Craig sought bipartisanship. Soon after the coronavirus caused a national upheaval, she became one of four House members—two Democrats, two Republicans—who were founding members of the Congressional Supply Chain Caucus, which sought to strengthen the national and international supplies of medications, medical devices and other essential products. She criticized the lack of coordination among the states and between the federal government and the private sector.

"As a new Member of Congress who spent more than two decades working for medical manufacturing companies that relied heavily on supply chain management," she wrote in April for the Star Tribune, "I know we would never have stood by as different divisions bid against one another to get the components necessary to complete their work." In subsequent months, she worked with others to make clear in legislation that businesses that had received a loan from the Payroll Protection Program could receive a second payment.

In her reelection campaign, an unusual scenario was triggered when Adam Weeks, the nominee of the Legal Marijuana Now Party, unexpectedly died in September. That triggered a state law requiring an election delay to designate a successor if a "major party" candidate died within 79 days of the election. The Marijuana Now Party barely met the 5 percent threshold in a contest for state auditor in 2018. On October 9, a federal judge circumvented the requirement, citing the "overwhelming importance" of the congressional vote in November and the need for the public to have "uninterrupted representation" in Congress.

Even that rescue failed to resolve Craig's electoral problems. Tyler Kistner, her Republican challenger, had recently retired from nine years as a Marine, where he commanded a special operations unit, with four overseas tours. He criticized Craig for voting consistently with Speaker Nancy Pelosi and "90 percent with Ilhan Omar," the outspoken first-term Democrat from the Minneapolis district. Kistner spent $3 million (to $4.7 million for Craig), which gave him sufficient funds to be competitive. Craig fell short of the seven percentage point lead that Joe Biden had in the district over Trump. She won, 48.2%-45.9%, with 5.8% going to the deceased Weeks.

Following the election, Craig was one of five Democratic women who got seats on the influential Energy and Commerce Committee. She said the selection was "an enormous privilege" and that she planned to devote her attention to steps to strengthen the Affordable Care Act and reduce the cost of prescription drugs. The uncertainty of redistricting seemed likely to demand some of her attention prior to the 2022 election. Of the four House Democrats from Minnesota, she had the weakest base.

MN-2: Twin Cities

Cook Partisan Voting Index: EVEN

Population		Race and Ethnicity		Income	
Total	717,698	White	82.70%	Median Income	$90,531
Land area (sq. miles)	2,438	Black	5.70%	District Income Rank	56
Pop/ sq mi	294.39	Latino	6.50%	Poverty Rate	5.90%
Born in State	67.30%	Asian	5.00%	With health insurance	96.10%
		Two or more races	3.60%	Cash public assistance	2.00%
Age Groups		Other	3.00%	Food stamp/SNAP	4.80%
Under 18	24.50%				
18-34	20.80%	**Education**		**Work**	
35-64	40.40%	H.S grad or less	26.80%	White Collar	43.80%
Over 64	14.40%	Some college	32.50%	Sales and Service	36.50%
		College Degree, 4 yr	27.30%	Blue Collar	19.80%
Military		Post grad	13.40%	Government	11.80%
Veteran/ Active Duty	6.20%				

2020 Pres. Vote	Biden	226,589	(52%)	Trump	197,005	(45%)		
2016 Pres. Vote	Trump	176,088	(46%)	Clinton	171,396	(45%)	Johnson 16,565	(4%)

South Suburbs: Driving south from the Twin Cities, one encounter big-box stores, catering to the youngish families that live nearby in new housing developments and who work in managerial, business and technical careers. Many come from elsewhere, attracted by Minnesota's strong economy and pleasant living (provided they can tolerate its cold winters). They have turned places such as Eagan, Lakeville, Apple Valley, Mendota Heights and Burnsville in Dakota County into fast-growing suburbs. The upscale suburban Scott County has grown an impressive 67 percent since 2000. Dakota, which with 429,000 remains nearly triple the size of Scott, has grown 21 percent during that time. (Minneapolis-based Hennepin, which is a bit more than twice the size of Dakota and Scott combined, has grown 12 percent since 2000. St. Paul-based Ramsey is virtually the same size as the two suburban counties; it has grown by 6 percent since 2000.) In recent years, these suburban areas have begun to see an influx of lower-income residents, attracted by the good schools and low crime rates.

This area has been attractive to the corporate world. In Eagan, across the Mississippi River from the MSP airport, several prominent businesses filled the space after Lockheed Martin closed its plant in 2013. The Minnesota Vikings of the NFL relocated their training camp, and added a conference center and a practice stadium. It is part of the Viking Lakes neighborhood. Across the river, south of St. Paul, Cottage Grove is the home of 3M, a "global innovation company" that operates with nearly 800 employees in 35 buildings in an area that extends 1,750 acres along the river. Lakeville, with its 100 miles of trails and many lakes, has been ranked in Money magazine's "50 best places to live." Drive farther south on Interstate 35 and U.S. 52—a little farther every year—and suddenly you are in farm country. Northfield is the home of Carleton College and its late professor-turned-liberal-senator, Paul Wellstone, who died with his wife in an airplane crash while campaigning for reelection in 2002.

These suburbs and hamlets make up the 2nd Congressional District of Minnesota. Like several districts in the state, this has become a battleground. Dakota County, just south of St. Paul, casts about 60 percent of the votes in the district; historically, Dakota was marginally Democratic, although today it is more of a swing county. Neighboring Scott County has the highest median income in the state, is rapidly growing and has become less solidly Republican than in the Reagan years; Scott casts about one-third as many votes as Dakota. In 2016, Donald Trump won this district by one percentage point —a bit more than 4,000 votes. Joe Biden turned the table and won the district, 52%-45%, a lead of more than 29,000 votes.

Dean Phillips (DFL)

Elected 2018, 2nd term, b. Jan 20, 1969; St. Paul, MN; Brown University, B.A., 1991; University of MN, M.B.A., 2000; Jewish; Divorced; 2 children.

Professional Career: President & Chief Executive Officer, Phillips Distilling Company, 1993-2012; Co-Founder, Penny's Coffee.

DC Office: 1305 LHOB 20515, 202-225-2871, Fax: 202-225-6351, phillips.house.gov

State Offices: Minnetonka, 952-563-4593.

Committees: *Ethics. Foreign Affairs*: Africa, Global Health & Global Human Rights; Europe, Energy, the Environment & Cyber. *Select Committee on the Modernization of Congress. Small Business*: Innovation, Entrepreneurship & Workforce Development; Oversight, Investigations & Regulations (Chmn).

Almanac Ratings 2019-2020

	Economy	Social	Foreign	Composite
Liberal	100%	100%	80%	94%
Conservative	0%	0%	20%	6%

Key Votes of the 116th Congress

1. U.S./Mex./Can. trade deal Y	5. Russia sanctions Y	9. Firearms background checks Y
2. First Coronavirus response Y	6. Troops in Syria Y	10. Spending at the border Y
3. HEROES Act Y	7. Veto arms sales to Saudis Y	11. Marijuana liberalized rules Y
4. CASH Act Y	8. Defense $$$, veto override Y	12. Electoral College objections N

Election Results

Election	Name (Party)	Vote (%)		Cand. Spent	Ind. Exp. Support	Ind. Exp. Oppose
2020 General	Dean Phillips (DFL).........................	246,666	(56%)	$1,991,212	$59,703	$20,000
	Kendall Qualls (R).........................	196,625	(44%)	$1,724,224	$44,211	$40,243
2020 Primary	Dean Phillips (DFL)............................	73,011	(91%)			
	Cole Young (DFL).........................	7,443	(9%)			

Prior winning percentages: 2018 (56%)

Freshman Democrat Dean Phillips, a businessman and heir of a prominent Minnesota family, was elected to a seat in the Minneapolis suburbs that Republicans had held since 1960. In his first bid for elected office, he rode the Democratic surge in upscale suburbs across the nation. He defeated Rep. Erik Paulsen, an active lawmaker and self-styled moderate on the tax-writing Ways and Means Committee. Phillips, one of three House Democratic newcomers in the Twin Cities area, became comfortable with aspects of his new job. But he struggled with some problems, including what he viewed as excessive legislative control by congressional leaders and occasional clashes with Democratic Rep. Ilhan Omar in the neighboring Minneapolis district.

Phillips grew up in Minnesota. His father, an Army captain, was killed in Vietnam when Phillips was six months old. His mother remarried the owner of the locally based Phillips Distilling Co. He graduated from Brown University and got his master's in business administration from the University of Minnesota. After working a few years with a start-up cycling business, he joined Phillips Distilling and eventually became president. He was proudest, he later said, of the new Prairie Vodka his team created, with a co-op of three family-owned organic corn growers in Minnesota.

Phillips also became familiar with his family legacy, including the close relationship that his great-grandfather had with Hubert Humphrey, the former senator from Minnesota and vice president. As Phillips described in an August 2019 profile of him by the Jewish Insider, "Hubert Humphrey gave my great-grandparents this [personally inscribed] phone in 1967 ... and the notion was that my great-grandfather could use that phone to call Hubert Humphrey when necessary." In that interview, he also described how his Jewish great-grandparents told him of their parents fleeing persecution and "horrid anti-Semitism" in Europe to find refuge in the United States.

Phillips left the distilling firm and helped to start a gelato business that became the largest gelato brand in the nation. During his business career, he participated in numerous community-service projects, including a global youth-empowerment initiative. The Phillips family has had many philanthropic legacies in Minnesota. "I am a fiscally responsible, socially inclusive and, yes, fortunate man ... with a strong, independent voice of reason, a focus on new ideas, and a commitment to principled and courageous leadership," he wrote on his campaign website. Abigail Van Buren, also known as the advice columnist Dear Abby, was his grandmother.

In what had been a safely Republican district, Paulsen focused on tax and trade issues and he fit comfortably with GOP moderates. During the 2016 presidential campaign, he objected to many actions of Donald Trump and said, "I will not be voting for him." Paulsen faced a well-funded reelection challenge that year and won, 57%-43%.

As he launched his challenge to Paulsen, Phillips said, "Congress needs a new generation of leaders willing to place principles over party." Paulsen's vote in May 2017 for the House GOP bill to repeal the Affordable Care Act "really ended my time on the bench," he told the Minnesota Post. Potential challengers for the DFL nomination largely stepped aside. In responding to campaign charges, Paulsen sought to distance himself from Trump. He ran an ad citing his environmental credentials, as an opponent of mining near the wilderness area in northern Minnesota. Republican ads attacked Phillips for his alleged failure to provide adequate health insurance coverage to his employees and cited an $89 interest charge for a late property tax payment. Phillips sought to downplay his wealth. He loaned his campaign $1.3 million, of which he repaid himself $500,000. Each candidate spent more than $5 million. \Phillips won, 56%-44%. In Hennepin County, which cast more than 80 percent of the vote, he took 57 percent. The two candidates split the two other counties, with smaller margins.

Phillips encountered unexpected early turmoil when he demanded that Omar apologize for public comments that he and many others viewed as anti-Semitic, according to news reports in March 2019. That led House Democrats to offer a resolution condemning anti-Semitism; in response, some of the junior Democrats rallied to Omar's defense. Democrats watered down their resolution, making more general references to hate speech.

With Phillips and Omar representing adjoining districts that included most of Hennepin County, the incident created personal awkwardness. In a March 2019 profile of the two freshmen for Politico, Tim Alberta wrote that the large group of freshman Democrats "are dangerously close to entering into their own fratricidal conflict." In that story, Ken Martin, chairman of the Minnesota Democratic-Farmer-Labor Party, said that the Phillips and Omar districts couldn't be more different. "They're neighboring, but don't have a lot of similarities," Martin said, according to the profile.

In early 2020, at the start of the coronavirus pandemic, Phillips was quoted in various news stories voicing frustration with the limited role that most House Members—especially freshmen—played in crafting trillions of dollars of economic stimulus legislation. "I'm frustrated, I'm dismayed, I'm disgusted," he told Politico in a separate story in April 2020. "And I speak for a lot of us when I say that."

Phillips worked with various Republicans in filing bipartisan proposals, including a bill the House passed in May 2020, which Phillips filed with Republican Rep. Chip Roy of Texas. That measure relaxed repayment deadlines and other rules with the Paycheck Protection Program. Still, his frustration continued. In October 2020, he co-authored a column in the (Sioux Falls) Argus Leader with freshman Republican Rep. Dusty Johnston of South Dakota, describing how they compiled a "comprehensive COVID-19 relief framework" that was supported by all 50 members—25 Democrats, 25 Republicans—of their Problem Solvers Caucus, which they urged the House to approve. As they wrote, their effort "demonstrated that a little friendship and a lot of trust can still go a long ways in a deeply divided Congress." Congress two months later approved a separate relief bill.

In a reelection contest in which Phillips spent $2 million and his Republican challenger spent $1.7 million, Phillips defeated Republican Kendall Qualls, an African-American business executive, 56%-44%.

MN-3: Twin Cities   **Cook Partisan Voting Index: D+6**

Population		Race and Ethnicity		Income	
Total	730,214	White	77.30%	Median Income	$98,877
Land area (sq. miles)	527	Black	8.30%	District Income Rank	38
Pop/ sq mi	1,385.47	Latino	4.00%	Poverty Rate	5.20%
Born in State	62.40%	Asian	8.80%	With health insurance	96.90%
		Two or more races	3.90%	Cash public assistance	2.20%
Age Groups		Other	1.60%	Food stamp/SNAP	4.50%
Under 18	23.50%				
18-34	18.80%	**Education**		**Work**	
35-64	41.60%	H.S grad or less	21.80%	White Collar	50.70%
Over 64	15.90%	Some college	28.00%	Sales and Service	33.60%
		College Degree, 4 yr	32.90%	Blue Collar	15.60%
Military		Post grad	17.20%	Government	9.10%
Veteran/ Active Duty	5.20%				

2020 Pres. Vote	Biden	265,552	(58%)	Trump	178,221	(39%)		
2016 Pres. Vote	Clinton	201,833	(50%)	Trump	164,259	(41%)	Johnson	16,012	(4%)
	McMullin	8,348	(2%)					

West Suburbs: Over the past half century, Minnesota's two-headed metropolis has spread out from the neat streets inside the city limits of Minneapolis and St. Paul into the countryside all around. People have sorted themselves out geographically. In the lower lands along the Mississippi and Minnesota rivers, where rail lines fan out from the Twin Cities, are the blue-collar suburbs, with modest houses and warehouses and factories near the tracks. Inland, around the lakes Minnesota is so proud of, in subdivisions with curved streets hugging the hills, are more affluent neighborhoods, quiet and unflashy in the Minnesota way but comfortable whether blanketed with snow or with a nearby lake glinting in the summer sun.

At the freeway interchanges, some of the Twin Cities' innovations can be seen—South dale shopping center in Edina, the first enclosed mall; huge indoor water parks; and the giant Mall of America in Bloomington, with its 5.4 million square feet, 520-plus stores, 85 eating options, 13 movie theaters, 25 rides, and more than 11,000 year-round employees. Pre-pandemic, the mall attracted more than 40 million people annually. Phase Two, with another 3 million square feet, has appealed to upscale patrons who travel a greater distance. To the west is Eden Prairie, with its 17 lakes, which Money magazine has named the best medium-sized U.S. city. For years, this was a high-growth area. That trend slowed in the 2010 census when 26 suburbs in the Twin Cities area lost population. But the metro area had an 8 percent increase from 2010 to 2017, including many cities in the 3rd District. Work began in 2018 on the 14.5 mile extension of the Southwest Light Rail Project from Eden Prairie to Target Field, the downtown Minneapolis home of baseball's Minnesota Twins. Completion remained on-track for 2023, the Minnesota Post reported.

The 3rd Congressional District of Minnesota consists mostly of the Hennepin County suburbs of the Twin Cities. Anoka and Carver counties each cover a bit less than 10 percent of the district. On the north side of the district is working-class Brooklyn Park, long a Democratic-Farmer-Labor Party stronghold, where professional wrestler-turned-governor Jesse Ventura began his political career as mayor. On the south is middle-income Bloomington. To the west are Edina, Plymouth, Wayzata and other towns around Lake Minnetonka, all traditionally Republican. The 3rd has been the home of Minnesota's traditional Republican establishment. As has been the case in many Northern suburban districts, that political class has moved substantially toward the Democrats in recent years.

For many years, the district had been close to evenly matched in presidential contests. That has quickly become a distant memory in the 3rd, where Barack Obama led Mitt Romney, 50%-49%, in 2012. Four years later, Hillary Clinton led, 50%-41%. Joe Biden increased that advantage to 58%-39%. Among the striking aspects is that in the neighboring 2nd District, Biden increased the Democratic advantage in that district to "only" seven percentage points. What accounted for the contrast between the two districts? One factor could be the double-digit advantage the 3rd has in the share of residents with at least an undergraduate degree. What might be more remarkable is that the vote in the 3rd District (with modestly different boundaries) for Bob Dole in 1996 was his second best of the state's eight districts, behind only the rural 7th.

Betty McCollum (DFL)

Elected 2000, 11th term, b. Jul 12, 1954; Minneapolis, MN; Saint Catherine University, B.S., 1986; Roman Catholic; Divorced; 2 children.

Elected Office: N. State Paul City Council, 1986-1992; MN House, 1992-2000.

Professional Career: Teacher; Retail Sales & Management.

DC Office: 2256 RHOB 20515, 202-225-6631, Fax: 202-225-1968, mccollum.house.gov

State Offices: St. Paul, 651-224-9191.

Committees: *Appropriations:* Agriculture, Rural Development, FDA & Related Agencies; Defense (Chmn); Interior, Environment & Related Agencies. *Natural Resources:* Energy & Mineral Resources; Indigenous Peoples of the United States.

Group Ratings

	ADA	ACLU	AFL-CIO	LCV	COC	HAFA	ACU	CFG	FRC
2020	**	86%	**	100%	-	0%	3%	**	-
2019	90%	C	100%	97%	54%	C	3%	12%	0%

Almanac Ratings 2019-2020

	Economy	Social	Foreign	Composite
Liberal	100%	100%	92%	98%
Conservative	0%	0%	8%	2%

Key Votes of the 116th Congress

1. U.S./Mex./Can. trade deal	Y	5. Russia sanctions Y	9. Firearms background checks Y
2. First Coronavirus response	Y	6. Troops in Syria Y	10. Spending at the border N
3. HEROES Act	Y	7. Veto arms sales to Saudis Y	11. Marijuana liberalized rules Y
4. CASH Act	Y	8. Defense $$$, veto override Y	12. Electoral College objections N

Election Results

Election	Name (Party)	Vote (%)		Cand. Spent	Ind. Exp. Support	Ind. Exp. Oppose
2020 General	Betty McCollum (DFL)	245,813	(63%)	$731,905	$3,131	
	Gene Rechtzigel (R)	112,730	(29%)			$113
	Susan Sindt (LC)	29,537	(8%)			
2020 Primary	Betty McCollum (DFL)	80,048	(84%)			
	Alberder Gillespie (DFL)	6,327	(7%)			

Prior winning percentages: 2018 (66%), 2016 (58%), 2014 (61%), 2012 (62%), 2010 (59%), 2008 (68%), 2006 (70%), 2004 (58%), 2002 (62%), 2000 (48%)

Democrat Betty McCollum, first elected in 2000, has been an assertive voice as a senior member of the Appropriations Committee, where she has kept a low profile and has been an ally of Speaker Nancy Pelosi, whom she calls a mentor. Several retirements and a shuffling of assignments following the 2020 election left McCollum as chairwoman of the subcommittee in charge of spending for the Defense Department—one of the most powerful niches in Congress.

McCollum grew up in North St. Paul and graduated from the College of St. Catherine. She was a substitute social studies teacher while working as a retail sales manager at a Sears department store and raising two children. After her daughter suffered a fractured skull in a fall from a slide in a city park, McCollum worked with local officials to add sand to soften the area around the slide. She ran for the North St. Paul City Council and was elected on her second try. In 1992, she was elected to the state House after defeating incumbents in both the primary and general elections.

When the congressional seat opened, McCollum was endorsed by the Democratic-Farmer-Labor Party. She faced three opponents in the primary. With the DFL's backing, McCollum won 50 percent to 23 percent for state Sen. Steve Novak. Republicans nominated state Sen. Linda Runbeck, a vigorously anti-abortion candidate. McCollum opposed cutting taxes before Congress paid down the national debt. Runbeck, who took conservative positions on health care and education, attacked McCollum and her Democratic allies for running "hateful, vicious attack ads." Former Ramsey County prosecutor Tom Foley, a longtime DFLer, ran on Gov. Jesse Ventura's Independence Party. Once again, McCollum won unexpectedly easily, 48%-31%, with 21 percent for Foley.

McCollum has a staunchly liberal voting record. Her Almanac vote ratings have ranked her among the most liberal 10 percent of the House. As chair of the Appropriations Interior-Environment Subcommittee in 2019-20, she had jurisdiction over one of her longtime interests: funding for Indian tribes across the nation, especially for school construction. She sought to limit cutbacks at the Environmental Protection Agency and the National Park Service, including spending for the National Mall.

"I don't make headlines," she told the Pioneer Press. "A lot of stuff I work on is not visible to the public." McCollum has advocated major changes in Appropriations operations, including the reinstatement of "earmarks" for specific projects rather than continued control by the executive branch. Minnesota Attorney General Keith Ellison, who served 12 years in the House with McCollum, told the Star-Tribune in January 2019, "It's a small group of people [who Pelosi takes into her confidence] and Betty is one of those people."

As she prepared to take over as Appropriations "cardinal" for the Pentagon, she sought to assure that large community of interests that she supported a "strong national defense," including the "training, tools and support" required for the more than 2 million servicewomen and men. She has had a consistent liberal voting record, according to Almanac ratings, including a tight approach to Pentagon spending. Even before she became subcommittee chair, McCollum earlier was successful in ending military support for NASCAR, a passion in the Republican-dominated South. "The Defense Department said it didn't have anything that could be cut. Seven million dollars to sponsor a car and we're cutting cops, we're cutting teachers, we're cutting programs for homeless vets?" she told The New York Times. The move triggered hate mail and angry blog posts, but the Army joined the Navy and Marine Corps in abandoning the sponsorships.

In 2018, she appeared to shut down an attempt by Dan Snyder, owner of the Washington franchise in the NFL, to arrange a land swap to win approval for a new football stadium on federal parkland. "That's not something the federal government should be condoning, encouraging or be a part of," she told The Washington Post.

McCollum has generated controversy in opposing U.S. support for Israel. The Minnesota Post headlined her as "one of the strongest critics of Israeli policy in Congress," in an August 2019 profile. Earlier that year, she filed a bill to prohibit the use of U.S. military funding by Israel to detain Palestinian children. In a speech the previous year, she accused Israel of practicing "apartheid" in dealing with Palestine. In 2006, she was one of 37 House Members who voted against a bill that imposed U.S. sanctions on the Palestinian Authority.

In February 2020, McCollum described the powerful American Israel Public Affairs Committee as a "hate group" after it ran a Facebook ad that claimed she was among a group of congressional Democrats who were a more "sinister threat" to Israel than was the Islamic State. "I hope Democrats understand what is at stake and will take a stand because working to advance peace, human rights and justice is not sinister—it is righteous," she said in a statement. AIPAC issued an apology and removed the ad. McCollum has taken a broad interest in overseas issues. Encouraging lawmakers to view the World Bank more positively, she founded a caucus advocating more dialogue with the global financier. In 2018, she won enactment of her proposal for increased funds to combat global tuberculosis, malaria and AIDS, especially among children.

McCollum has highlighted splits among Minnesotans, including Democrats, with her consistent efforts to restrict most copper-nickel mining in the national forest near Minnesota's Boundary Waters Canoe Area Wilderness. In 2019, she objected to a proposal by the Trump administration to renew mineral leases at the site.

McCollum has not faced serious major-party opposition to reelection.

MN-4: Twin Cities   **Cook Partisan Voting Index: D+16**

Population		Race and Ethnicity		Income	
Total	719,873	White	70.10%	Median Income	$75,665
Land area (sq. miles)	332	Black	10.80%	District Income Rank	122
Pop/ sq mi	2,165.1	Latino	6.70%	Poverty Rate	10.70%
Born in State	61.70%	Asian	12.90%	With health insurance	94.80%
		Two or more races	4.20%	Cash public assistance	3.70%
Age Groups		Other	2.00%	Food stamp/SNAP	9.70%
Under 18	23.40%				
18-34	24.30%	**Education**		**Work**	
35-64	37.20%	H.S grad or less	28.90%	White Collar	45.90%
Over 64	15.10%	Some college	26.30%	Sales and Service	36.30%
		College Degree, 4 yr	27.80%	Blue Collar	17.90%
Military		Post grad	16.90%	Government	13.20%
Veteran/ Active Duty	5.30%				

2020 Pres. Vote	Biden	273,197	(67%)	Trump	123,295	(30%)	
2016 Pres. Vote	Clinton	223,803	(61%)	Trump	111,163	(30%) Johnson	13,513 (4%)

St. Paul: Above the Mississippi River bluffs stand St. Paul's two most distinctive landmarks: the Minnesota state capitol and Archbishop John Ireland's Cathedral of St. Paul. The city's origins are more colorful than its pious name and status as state capital might imply. Its original name was "Pig's Eye," after the tavern set up by the first European settler in the area, Pierre "Pig's Eye" Parrant. The area was settled mainly by Catholic Irish and German immigrants in the 1850s, as opposed to the Protestant Swedes and Yankees who settled Minneapolis. St. Paul became a major transportation hub, a railroad center and river port, while Minneapolis, upriver at the Falls of St. Anthony, became the nation's largest grain milling center. Both industries stoked the ire of farmers in the Dakotas who were forced to deal with them to make a living. With the large curve in the river, St. Paul borders a longer stretch of the Mississippi than any other city.

Beyond the cathedral is Summit Avenue, on which capitalists like the Great Northern Railway's James J. Hill built grandiose Romanesque houses. Along with Monument Avenue in Richmond and Meridian Street in Indianapolis, (two other state capitals) it remains one of America's grand 19th century residential boulevards. The parallel Grand Avenue is home to a pleasant commercial strip with a walkable, urban feel. The Minnesota state fairgrounds are in nearby Falcon Heights.

The area has become home to Hmong immigrants, some of whom were recruited by the Central Intelligence Agency during the Vietnam War and resettled here after Laos fell to the communists in 1975. In 2019, the Asian population was 15 percent of Ramsey County, with a growth of more than 18,000 persons since 2010, while the white population has barely grown at all during those years; in St. Paul, which is slightly more than half of the county, Asians are 19 percent of the population. More than 30,000 in the county spoke Hmong. A spacious indoor marketplace on St. Paul's east side called Hmong Village caters to their shopping. Ramsey County grew 8 percent from 2010 to 2019, a notable increase from the previous decade. In the downtown area, a dramatic change underway near the curve along the riverfront envisions four new office buildings, including downtown's first new skyscraper in 30 years.

The rioting that was centered in Minneapolis following the death in May 2020 of George Floyd while he was in police custody caused extensive damage elsewhere in the Twin Cities. That included St. Paul, chiefly 3.5 miles of University Avenue, "stopping just short of the State Capitol," the Star-Tribune reported.

Minnesota's 4th Congressional District is based in St. Paul. Even before the Democratic-Farmer-Labor Party was formed in 1944, St. Paul was a firmly Democratic part of Minnesota. The 4th includes all of Ramsey County, which hasn't voted for a Republican presidential candidate since it narrowly went for Calvin Coolidge in 1924. To the north, it takes in two-thirds of Washington County, which is more evenly balanced politically. To the east are the St. Croix River and Wisconsin. The 67 percent for Joe Biden in 2020 narrowly led Hennepin as his best in the state and was an improvement over the 61 percent that Hillary Clinton attracted—though not so Democratic as the 5th District to the west.

Ilhan Omar (DFL)

Elected 2018, 2nd term, b. Oct 04, 1982; Mogadishu, Somalia; University of MN; ND State University, B.A., 2011; Muslim; Married (Ahmed Hirsi); 3 children.

Elected Office: MN House, 2012-2018

Professional Career: Community Health Educator, University of Minnesota & MN Department of Education; Senior Policy Aide, Minneapolis City Council.

DC Office: 1517 LHOB 20515, 202-225-4755, omar.house.gov

State Offices: Minneapolis, 612-333-1272.

Committees: *Education & Labor*: Higher Education & Workforce Investment; Workforce Protections. *Foreign Affairs*: Africa, Global Health & Global Human Rights; Intern'l Dev't, Intern'l Orgs & Global Corporate Social Impact.

Almanac Ratings 2019-2020

	Economy	Social	Foreign	Composite
Liberal	100%	100%	81%	94%
Conservative	0%	0%	19%	6%

Key Votes of the 116th Congress

1. U.S./Mex./Can. trade deal N	5. Russia sanctions Y	9. Firearms background checks Y	
2. First Coronavirus response Y	6. Troops in Syria N/A	10. Spending at the border N	
3. HEROES Act Y	7. Veto arms sales to Saudis Y	11. Marijuana liberalized rules Y	
4. CASH Act Y	8. Defense $$$, veto override N	12. Electoral College objections N	

Election Results

Election	Name (Party)	Vote (%)		Cand. Spent	Ind. Exp. Support	Ind. Exp. Oppose
2020 General	Ilhan Omar (DFL).......................	255,924	(64%)	$5,151,645	$250,435	$2,451,251
	Lacy Johnson (R)...........................	102,878	(26%)	$11,904,425	$8,985	$113
	Michael Moore (LM)...................	37,979	(10%)			
2020 Primary	Ilhan Omar (DFL).......................	103,535	(58%)			
	Antone Melton-Meaux (DFL).......	68,524	(39%)			

Prior winning percentages: 2018 (78%)

Democrat Ilhan Omar was elected in 2018 with one of the most unlikely congressional profiles. She easily defeated Democratic primary opponents with more political experience and became one of several incoming women from minority groups who won House seats as relative newcomers to politics. With Rep. Rashida Tlaib of Michigan, she was one of the first two Muslim women elected to the House. She frequently stirred controversy, to the discomfort of some Democrats. Seeking reelection, she again showed impressive support in a competitive primary.

After escaping the capital of Mogadishu during the Somalia civil war in 1991, when she was eight years old, Omar lived with her family in a Kenyan camp of 30,000 refugees for four years before immigrating to the United States; her mother had died earlier. Referring to her grandfather's position as director of Somalia's National Marine Transport, Omar was quoted in a 2016 profile of her in the Minneapolis City Pages, "You go from knowing a life of certainty and joy to one where everything is uncertain."

Settling in Minneapolis, which has attracted a large Somali community, Omar developed an interest in politics while she was in high school and became an interpreter for her grandfather at local meetings. After graduating from North Dakota State University, she used her background in nutrition and public health issues to work with community groups and political figures. In 2016, she defeated a longtime Democratic representative to win a seat in the state House.

Following Rep. Keith Ellison's move to create an open House seat in his successful run for attorney general, the early party frontrunner was Margaret Kelliher, a former state House speaker who narrowly lost the Democratic-Farmer-Labor nomination for governor to Mark Dayton in 2010.

In an editorial that endorsed Kelliher to succeed Ellison, the Minneapolis Star Tribune noted Omar's "compelling life story," but said her "accomplishments are lean," with "apparent overstatement on her campaign website." Opponents publicly questioned her personal life, including potential fraud in her marriage and an affair with her highly compensated political consultant. Omar, who was endorsed by Minneapolis Mayor Jacob Frey and other local political leaders, described herself as "the bold, progressive voice we need" and "an organizer."

In an early sign of shifting local politics, Omar won the non-binding endorsement of the DFL convention; Kelliher did not compete. The showdown was "a tug-of-war not over ideology, but between old guard and new guard," the Minnesota Post reported. When Ellison spoke to the convention and asked how many of the delegates participated in the 2006 convention that nominated him, "perhaps a dozen" of the roughly 200 participants raised their hand.

The primary became a contest between "a consensus-oriented dealmaker" and the activists of "the multicultural left," Steven Scheier, a political science professor at Carleton College, told the Post. Omar and Kelliher were the biggest spenders in the six-candidate primary contest, with a bit more than $500,000 each. With a large turnout of 135,000 voters, Omar won with 48 percent of the vote to 30 percent for Kelliher. Patricia Torres Ray, a Latina who had served 12 years in the state Senate, got 13 percent. Omar's rapid political rise was a striking success for Somali immigrants.

Soon after taking office, Omar became the center of controversy for multiple instances of remarks that many House Democrats condemned as anti-Semitic. In March, the House responded by passing a resolution, with virtually unanimous support, that condemned all forms of hate; Democratic leaders diluted an earlier version that focused more specifically on Omar's comments. Speaker Nancy Pelosi was slow to defend Omar when she was widely criticized for referring to the September 2001 attacks on the United States as "some people did something."

Omar's series of comments created tensions among Democrats in the Minnesota delegation—including Rep. Dean Phillips, who is Jewish, in the suburban Hennepin County district. Trump managed to unite House Democrats when he later said that Omar and three other first-term women who were racial minorities—known in the House as the Squad—should "go back" to "the totally broken and crime-infested places from which they came." Omar was the only one of the four who was not born in the United States.

In June 2019, Omar filed a bill to cancel all of the estimated $1.6 trillion in student loan debt. "I stand before you on behalf of 45 million Americans," she said, in unveiling her proposal, "people who have dreams of opening up a business or have dreams of public service, but are held back by a mountain of debt." Her chief cosponsors were Sen. Bernie Sanders and Rep. Pramila Jayapal, a leader of the Progressive Caucus. They proposed paying for their plan with a one-half percent tax on all stock transactions. In October, she endorsed Sanders for president, as the leader of a "working-class movement" who was "the best candidate to take on Donald Trump."

Serving on the Foreign Affairs Committee, Omar showed interest in various international topics. The sponsor of a resolution to support the "Boycott, Divestment and Sanctions" movement against Israel, she was one of 17 House members who voted in July 2019 against a resolution condemning the movement. She added that Israel should "accept the dismantling of its Zionist apartheid regime." In February 2020, she introduced a package of seven bills she described as her "Pathway to Peace" foreign-policy proposals. They included limits on U.S. economic sanctions, a requirement that U.S. security aid could be used only in nations that protected human rights and a global agreement on migration. In what some described as a "surprise move," she backed extension of the international arms embargo against Iran—which has been urged by Israel.

Running for reelection, Omar faced Antone Melton-Meaux, an attorney who founded a mediation practice. He emphasized his consensus-seeking approach. With implicit contrasts to Omar, the Star Tribune wrote in its editorial endorsement that he brought "a different sensibility to this race, one grounded in helping resolve disputes to move forward — a skill this country is much in need of" and that he was "the kind of leader who could unite a fractured district." Omar spent $5.7 million to $4.7 million for Melton-Meaux, who received substantial funds from pro-Israel interests. She won 58%-39%. In the general election, Republican Lacy Johnson spent the astounding sum of $12.1 million, mostly on self-promotional advertising, which had little impact. Omar won in November, 64%-26%. In a district where Joe Biden got 80 percent, Omar never had cause for concern.

MN-5: Twin Cities   **Cook Partisan Voting Index: D+29**

Population		Race and Ethnicity		Income	
Total	724,373	White	67.20%	Median Income	$68,709
Land area (sq. miles)	136	Black	16.70%	District Income Rank	179
Pop/ sq mi	5,339.62	Latino	9.90%	Poverty Rate	13.70%
Born in State	56.90%	Asian	5.60%	With health insurance	93.60%
		Two or more races	4.80%	Cash public assistance	4.60%
Age Groups		Other	5.60%	Food stamp/SNAP	10.90%
Under 18	20.40%				
18-34	30.40%	**Education**		**Work**	
35-64	35.70%	H.S grad or less	25.30%	White Collar	50.60%
Over 64	13.60%	Some college	26.40%	Sales and Service	35.40%
		College Degree, 4 yr	30.70%	Blue Collar	14.00%
Military		Post grad	17.60%	Government	12.20%
Veteran/ Active Duty	4.60%				

2020 Pres. Vote	Biden	328,766	(80%)	Trump	72,323	(18%)			
2016 Pres. Vote	Clinton	273,402	(73%)	Trump	68,535	(18%)	Johnson	12,558	(3%)
	Stein	7,522	(2%)						

Minneapolis: From almost nowhere in Minneapolis today can you see the geographic feature that created the city: the Falls of St. Anthony, where rapids still course beneath low downtown bridges. In olden days, every riverboat had to stop here—these are the only significant waterfalls on the upper Mississippi River—and the waterpower generated by the falls was the energy source first for the pioneers' grist mills and then for the giant grain mills that processed northern Great Plains wheat into food for the United States. By 1890, Minneapolis and St. Paul made up one of America's largest urban areas, living mainly off grain. Today, grain is still important to Minneapolis; after all, the headquarters for General Mills is located in nearby Golden Valley. But Minneapolis is also a center of high technology, banking and finance.

As it turned out, claims of racial progress in Minneapolis masked huge inequities. That became dramatically clear in May 2020, when tensions boiled to the surface after George Floyd died when Derek Chauvin, a local police officer, held Floyd on the ground with a knee in his back that choked, and then killed, Floyd while he was in police custody. The videotape of that incident and the insufficient explanation by civilian and police officers in Minneapolis triggered explosions of violence in that city and elsewhere across the nation. In retrospect, the incident in Minneapolis triggered a smoldering rage in many urban areas across the nation about racial inequality that had become a part of American life. The subsequent looting caused damage in more than 1,500 locations in Minneapolis and St. Paul, including dozens of buildings that burned to the ground, the Star-Tribune reported. All four police officers who were part of the incident were fired by the department. Chauvin was charged with second-degree murder and the other three faced charges of aiding and abetting Chauvin's action. In April 2021, a jury quickly found Chauvin guilty of murder plus lesser charges. The city council of Minneapolis responded to public protests by defunding the police department and creating a new department of community safety and violence prevention—over the objection of Mayor Jacob Frey. But, following weeks of adverse public reaction, the council had second thoughts and revised explanations about their decision. The police department changed some of its practices, including abolition of the chokehold. .

The city of Minneapolis and a few of its older suburbs make up the 5th Congressional District. In the southwest corner are the affluent neighborhoods around Lake Calhoun and Lake Harriet, long built-up and proudly maintained. Not far away are Minneapolis' skywalk-laced downtown skyscrapers and the museum quarter on the hill above Hennepin Avenue. Straddling the Mississippi is the University of Minnesota, which has fostered the area's cutting-edge biotechnology research and medical innovations, and nearby Dinkytown, a student area where Robert Zimmerman discovered folk music and reinvented himself as Bob Dylan. Left-leaning in its politics, the area is a product of Minneapolis's unique brand of liberalism, which is drawn from the Yankee tradition of clean government, the Scandinavian tradition of cooperative enterprise, and the industrial-labor tradition of economic redistribution. In 2017, the city became one of the first in the nation to set a $15 minimum wage. Economic growth has accelerated in recent years. The population increase of 47,000 between 2010 and 2019 signaled what likely will be the largest for Minneapolis in any decade since 1950, when the city peaked at 522,000, which remains nearly 100,000 more than the current figure. The city's development plan for 2040 envisioned an increased supply of affordable housing and more population density around transit stations.

Most of the 5th District has been low on the income scale. Except for a small section of Anoka County near Coon Rapids, the entire district is in Hennepin. Many of the working-class neighborhoods of small frame houses and ample parks are now kept up by new immigrants, and 37 percent of the district is nonwhite, the highest percentage in the state. To the northeast, behind the railroad and warehouse district along the Mississippi, are many Hmong from Laos. Hennepin County is also home to increasingly influential African immigrants, including many Somalis, and Brooklyn Center has a large concentration of Liberians. The Jewish community here has increased with immigrants from the former Soviet Union. The resulting district is the most heavily Democratic in the state. Joe Biden won the district, 80%-18%, notably higher than the 73 percent who voted for both Hillary Clinton and President Barack Obama in the two previous elections.

Thomas Emmer (R)

Elected 2014, 4th term, b. Mar 03, 1961; South Bend, IN; Saint Thomas Academy; Boston College, Att., 1980; University of AK, Fairbanks, B.A., 1984; William Mitchell College of Law, J.D., 1988; Roman Catholic; Married (Jacqueline Samuel Emmer); 7 children.

Elected Office: Independence City Council, 1995-2002; Delano City Council, 2003-2004; MN House, 2004-2010 (Deputy Minority Leader, 2007-2008).

Professional Career: Attorney; radio talk show host.

DC Office: 315 CHOB 20515, 202-225-2331, Fax: 202-225-6475, emmer.house.gov

State Offices: Otsego, 763-241-6848.

Committees: National Republican Congressional Committee Chairman. *Financial Services*: Investor Protection, Entrepreneurship & Capital Markets; Nat'l Security, International Development & Monetary Policy; Oversight & Investigations (RMM); Task Force on Financial Technology.

Group Ratings

	ADA	ACLU	AFL-CIO	LCV	COC	HAFA	ACU	CFG	FRC
2020	**	28%	**	10%	-	92%	82%	**	-
2019	0%	C	29%	7%	78%	C	83%	87%	90%

Almanac Ratings 2019-2020

	Economy	Social	Foreign	Composite
Liberal	33%	30%	30%	31%
Conservative	67%	70%	70%	69%

Key Votes of the 116th Congress

1. U.S./Mex./Can. trade deal	Y	5. Russia sanctions	Y	9. Firearms background checks	N
2. First Coronavirus response	N	6. Troops in Syria	Y	10. Spending at the border	N/A
3. HEROES Act	N	7. Veto arms sales to Saudis	N	11. Marijuana liberalized rules	N
4. CASH Act	N	8. Defense $$$, veto override	N	12. Electoral College objections	N

Election Results

Election	Name (Party)	Vote (%)		Cand. Spent	Ind. Exp. Support	Ind. Exp. Oppose
2020 General	Thomas Emmer (R)	270,901	(66%)	$1,604,362	$9,586	
	Tawnja Zahradka (D)	140,853	(34%)	$47,048	$627	
2020 Primary	Tom Emmer (R)	30,654	(87%)			
	Patrick Munro (R)	4,518	(13%)			

Prior winning percentages: 2018 (61%), 2016 (66%), 2014 (56%)

Republican Tom Emmer, elected in 2014, is a former talk-show host and an ardent conservative. He settled in comfortably and sought far less attention than his predecessor, Michele Bachmann, the tea party leader and one-time presidential contender. Emmer's occasional cooperation with party leaders was rewarded following the 2018 election with the challenging assignment to chair the National Republican Congressional Committee.

Emmer was born in South Bend Indiana, where his father was completing a degree at Notre Dame, and grew up in Edina. He got his bachelor's degree in political science at the University of Alaska, and his law degree from William Mitchell College. His great-grandfather founded a lumber business in Minneapolis that his family continued to run, under the name of Viking Forest Products. Emmer practiced law at his own firm and served on the city councils of Independence and Delano before winning election to the state House. His GOP colleagues voted him deputy majority leader.

In 2010, Emmer easily won the Republican nomination for governor and challenged Democrat Mark Dayton. He staked out a very conservative platform for his blue-leaning state. Along with calls to cut spending and taxes and to promote socially conservative values, he proposed a constitutional amendment requiring a supermajority in the legislature to approve any federal law before it could take effect in the state. The national Republican wave was not quite strong enough to lift him over Dayton, who won by 8,770 votes of the 2.1 million cast. Emmer subsequently launched a radio talk show in the Twin Cities.

After Bachmann announced her retirement in 2013, Emmer was the immediate frontrunner. He coasted to his primary victory with 73 percent of the vote in a low-turnout race. In the general election, which was not seriously contested, Emmer had close to a 10-to-1 fundraising advantage. He won, 56%-38%, and took all eight counties.

Emmer quickly showed that he intended to be a player in Congress, with a willingness to cross party lines. He helped organize an effort by freshmen House Republicans to send a letter to President Barack Obama with their support for approval of the Trans-Pacific Partnership. In 2016, he joined the bipartisan congressional delegation that accompanied Obama to Cuba. Citing the potential market for agricultural exports from Minnesota, he called for lifting the U.S. trade embargo on Cuba. On the Financial Services Committee, Emmer in 2016 won House passage of his bill to reduce the regulatory requirements imposed by the Financial Stability Oversight Council, which the Dodd-Frank law created in 2010. In May 2018, when broader changes were made to Dodd-Frank, that bill included Emmer's provision to adjust disclosure requirements on home mortgages, especially for smaller lending institutions.

Emmer disagreed with conservatives who opposed funding the Homeland Security Department to increase their leverage over immigration policy, and warned in 2015 that a government shutdown was a bad idea. "Two wrongs don't make a right," he said. The leader of the Minnesota Tea Party Alliance responded that he was "very disappointed" by his early votes. Emmer defended what he called his incremental approach, and seemed to make a pointed and informed jab at Bachmann, his erstwhile ally, about how to succeed in Congress. "If you want to go out there and make a lot of noise, maybe you're going to get people from all across the country to send you a lot of money, and that's great because then you can increase your own brand. But you'll never change the inside of the building," he told the St. Cloud Times.

After serving in 2017-18 as one of two deputy chairs of the NRCC, where he focused on its future operations, Emmer was unopposed for chairman following the 2018 election. He minimized the implications of the party's 40-seat House loss in 2018. "There's a narrative that people are trying to build out there that somehow there's been this shift, this political realignment, in the suburbs," he said in an interview with National Journal. "That's not true. It isn't there." He said that Republicans needed to do a better job with independent voters in highlighting their economic success. Emmer had an early clash with Rep. Elise Stefanik of New York and others who said that House Republicans needed to be more aggressive in seeking women candidates, particularly because they stood a better chance of wooing back affluent suburban voters turned off by Trump. He said it would be "a mistake" for the NRCC to take sides in GOP primaries. Stefanik tweeted in response: "NEWSFLASH…I wasn't asking for permission." Their public spat was a rocky start to what ultimately turned into a great partnership. Emmer and House Majority Leader Kevin McCarthy joined forces with Stefanik to encourage more women to run—a strategy that was highly successful: The number of Republican congresswomen grew from 13 to 30.

Initially, GOP prospects looked bleak. Republicans grappled with recruitment holes in key districts and massive cycle-long fundraising gap with the Democrats. The adoption of WinRed, the

GOP's online fundraising clearinghouse, helped reduce the funding disparity. Still, Emmer came under fire for its adversarial posture after staffers mocked the height of a Democratic incumbent and the wife of another. "Our communications team has a direct mandate from me and Leader McCarthy to be ruthless," Emmer told Politico.

Even as polls showed Republicans trailing in key districts and many in the party predicted the GOP would sink deeper into the minority, Emmer remained optimistic and urged his candidates to brand Democrats as radical "socialists" who planned to "defund the police." Emmer never shied away from Trump, but many GOP challengers distanced themselves as needed, particularly on tone. It worked; Republicans gained back a dozen seats in the midterms, leaving Democrats with a five-seat majority when the new Congress convened. Historical records that show double-digit losses by the party controlling the White House during its first mid-term, plus the optimistic outlook for Republicans in redistricting, indicate that Emmer is a good bet to be celebrating on Election Night in November 2022.

MN-6: Twin Cities Exurbs   Cook Partisan Voting Index: R+14

Population		Race and Ethnicity		Income	
Total	729,029	White	88.90%	Median Income	$84,159
Land area (sq. miles)	2,882	Black	4.10%	District Income Rank	74
Pop/ sq mi	252.94	Latino	3.40%	Poverty Rate	6.30%
Born in State	76.10%	Asian	2.60%	With health insurance	96.10%
		Two or more races	2.60%	Cash public assistance	2.40%
Age Groups		Other	1.70%	Food stamp/SNAP	5.60%
Under 18	25.30%				
18-34	21.40%	**Education**		**Work**	
35-64	39.80%	H.S grad or less	32.30%	White Collar	40.00%
Over 64	13.40%	Some college	35.20%	Sales and Service	34.60%
		College Degree, 4 yr	23.10%	Blue Collar	25.50%
Military		Post grad	9.40%	Government	12.30%
Veteran/ Active Duty	6.80%				

2020 Pres. Vote	Trump	251,056	(59%)	Biden	165,370	(39%)		
2016 Pres. Vote	Trump	218,546	(59%)	Clinton	123,329	(33%)	Johnson	15,314 (4%)

St. Cloud: The earliest settlers of Minneapolis and St. Paul lived within walking distance of the mills and factories and rail yards where they worked. As the first streetcars and then automobiles allowed them to live farther from their jobs, they spread out in the Twin Cities and then all around the lake-strewn countryside. The flatlands are bleak here when the winter sun struggles to pierce gray clouds, but even so, the creativity and productivity of Minnesotans have turned the countryside into some of the nation's most pleasant suburbs. Taking maximum advantage of their lakes, they refurbished old towns and farmhouses and built comfortable homes in new subdivisions.

The 6th Congressional District of Minnesota is a suburban and exurban area north and west of St. Paul and Minneapolis. It includes a mix of upscale and working-class suburbs in Anoka County, which has about one-third of the voters. More distant, up the Mississippi River, are Wright, Sherburne and Benton counties, which have nearly doubled from a combined total of 141,000 people in 1990 to 276,000 in 2019. Electrolux Co., which has been headquartered in St. Cloud since the 1940s, shut down its local plant for good in the fall of 2019 to consolidate its freezer operations in Anderson South Carolina. Some 760 employees were laid off. But in a hopeful trend, manufacturing employment has grown each year since the Great Recession, though overall levels have yet to recover. In 2018, the Catholic Diocese of St. Cloud declared bankruptcy to facilitate its payment of sex-abuse claims against clergy members.

The district includes the eastern half of St. Cloud-based Stearns County, a heavily German-Catholic area and a stronghold of anti-abortion sentiment. The city is 75 percent white, but its demographics have changed. The 1990s brought an influx of Vietnamese, Chinese and Japanese immigrants. Since they first arrived in 2000, more than 10,000 Somalis have moved in and started businesses or worked at local meat-processing plants. Many of them have settled in St. Cloud from elsewhere in the United States after learning of the tight-knit local Somali community. As a group, they are disproportionately young and many have struggled economically. Federal and local investigators have reviewed charges that Somalis in the public schools of St. Cloud have suffered civil rights violations, and there have been allegations of bullying of young Somalis. Business leaders have sought to educate local citizens about the Somali culture. In 2017, the city council rejected on a 6-to-1 vote a resolution to call for an end, at least temporarily, to resettlement of refugees in St. Cloud. But the defeat motivated some residents to join or form anti-immigration community groups, according to The New York Times. The anti-Muslim fear mongering is driven, in part, by these groups, local radio hosts and xenophobic digital media that warns that nonwhite and non-Christian newcomers pose a cultural threat.

The district is solidly Republican. Donald Trump got an overwhelming 58%-33% win, his second-largest Minnesota margin. In 2020, it dropped a bit to 59%-39%.

Michelle Fischbach (R)

Elected 2020, 1st term, b. Nov 03, 1965; Woodbury, MN; College of St. Benedict, 1986; St. Cloud State College, B.A., 1989; William Mitchell College of Law, J.D., 2010; Catholic; Married (Scott Fischbach); 2 children.

Elected Office: MN Senate, 1996-2018; President, MN Senate, 2017-2018; Lt. Governor, State of MN, 2018-2019.

DC Office: 1237 LHOB 20515, 202-225-2165, Fax: 202-225-1593, fischbach.house.gov

State Offices: Moorhead, 218-422-2090; Willmar, 320-403-6100.

Committees: *Agriculture*: Biotechnology, Horticulture & Research; Commodity Exchanges, Energy & Credit (RMM). *Judiciary*: Antitrust, Commercial & Administrative Law; Constitution, Civil Rights & Civil Liberties; Courts, Intellectual Property & Internet. *Rules*: Expedited Procedures (RMM).

Election Results

Election	Name (Party)	Vote (%)		Cand. Spent	Ind. Exp. Support	Ind. Exp. Oppose
2020 General	Michelle Fischbach (R)................ 194,066	(53%)		$2,584,108	$302,870	$5,025,046
	Collin Peterson (D)..................... 144,840	(40%)		$2,875,648	$637,195	$7,971,819
	Slater Johnson (LM)............................. 17,710	(5%)				
2020 Primary	Michelle Fischbach (R).................. 26,359	(59%)				
	Dave Hughes (R)..................................... 9,948	(22%)				
	Noel Collis (R)....................................... 6,747	(15%)				

Republican Michelle Fischbach in 2020 defeated Rep. Colin Peterson, who had defied repeated attempts to oust him from the most GOP-leaning seat held by a House Democrat. Fischbach, a former legislative leader and lieutenant governor, brought sufficient experience to leave scant opportunity for Peterson to survive what became a double-digit defeat. Peterson, who served 15 terms and was a founding member of the Blue Dogs, chaired the House Agriculture Committee and was one of the few surviving white Democrats from a rural district.

Fischhbach, who grew up in a suburb of the Twin Cities, got her bachelor's degree in political science from St. Cloud University. More than 20 years later, she got a law degree from William Mitchell School of Law in St. Paul. In 1995, she was elected to the city council in rural Paynesville. A year later, she won a special election for a seat in the state Senate.

During 22 years in the Senate, she was a Republican leader. In 2010, when the GOP took control, she became Senate president, the first woman to hold that position. She retained that influential post for four of the next eight years, while Democrat Mark Dayton was governor. "Few Republicans know the rules and procedures better than Fischbach," the Minnesota Post wrote in a profile. She also chaired the Higher Education Committee. During most of that time, her husband Scott was executive director of the state's largest anti-abortion group.

Fischbach unexpectedly became enmeshed in controversy in December 2017, when Dayton appointed Lt. Gov. Tina Smith to fill the Senate vacancy created by Al Franken, who had resigned. Under the state constitution, the Senate president was automatically promoted to lieutenant governor.

Fischbach resisted the move, not least because the GOP would lose its Senate majority. "I feel a commitment and a real kinship with the people in my district," she said.

After a series of rulings and court battles, in which Fischbach cited precedents that she could perform both jobs, she quit the Senate at the end of its annual session in May 2018 and became lieutenant governor. She ran for a full term on a ticket with former Gov. Tim Pawlenty. They were unexpectedly defeated in the Republican primary.

In her challenge to Peterson, Fischbach said Minnesotans deserved a representative "who will fight for their values in Washington and support President Trump's agenda—not the socialist agenda of Nancy Pelosi." She added that it was time for "new blood and new ideas."

In a district where Donald Trump got 61 percent of the vote in 2016, she said Peterson voted against Trump's agenda more than 75 percent of the time. Fischbach was soon endorsed by House Minority Leader Kevin McCarthy and other senior Republicans. She easily won both the Republican convention and primary.

Peterson, who had been held below 55 percent of the vote during his previous three reelections, retained the active support of the Minnesota Farm Bureau. He cited the fact that he was one of two Democrats who voted against the House impeachment of Trump.

In an October 2020 interview with the Minneapolis Star Tribune, he said, "I'm not going to change." He mentioned a recent phone call with Pelosi in which he told her that the solution for his reelection was, "What we need to do is have you come up here and tell them I'm a completely soulless S.O.B."

In a contest in which each candidate spent more than $2 million and the two parties spent a combined total of more than $13 million, the die was cast. Peterson won only five counties, all of which were in the rural northwest corner of the state. Fischbach ran strongly in the parts of the district that bordered on the Twin Cities metropolitan area. In a district that Trump won by more than 100,000 votes, Peterson managed to slice the GOP lead in half. That wasn't nearly enough. Fischbach won, 53%-40%.

In the House, Fischbach got an impressive array of assignments to the Agriculture, Judiciary and Rules committees.

MN-7: Western Minnesota   Cook Partisan Voting Index: R+17

Population		Race and Ethnicity		Income	
Total	668,096	White	90.40%	Median Income	$60,932
Land area (sq. miles)	33,429	Black	1.60%	District Income Rank	248
Pop/ sq mi	19.99	Latino	5.20%	Poverty Rate	10.40%
Born in State	71.80%	Asian	1.00%	With health insurance	94.50%
		Two or more races	2.10%	Cash public assistance	3.30%
Age Groups		Other	5.00%	Food stamp/SNAP	8.30%
Under 18	23.60%				
18-34	19.80%	**Education**		**Work**	
35-64	36.50%	H.S grad or less	38.90%	White Collar	35.30%
Over 64	20.10%	Some college	37.70%	Sales and Service	35.50%
		College Degree, 4 yr	16.80%	Blue Collar	29.20%
Military		Post grad	6.60%	Government	15.40%
Veteran/ Active Duty	7.50%				

2020 Pres. Vote	Trump	234,753	(64%)	Biden	126,528	(34%)		
2016 Pres. Vote	Trump	208,215	(61%)	Clinton	104,566	(31%)	Johnson	12,523	(4%)

Moorhead: The fabled Mississippi River begins modestly in Minnesota's Itasca State Park, 2,552 miles from the Gulf of Mexico. At that point, it can be crossed by foot on stepping-stones. The country in which the river begins has made its own contributions to American literature. More than a century ago, Sinclair Lewis grew up in the town of Sauk Centre, which provided grist for his critical but affectionate portrayals of small-town America in Main Street and Babbitt. In those years, this seemingly placid country was seething with rage, as WASP nationalists banned German from schools, renamed sauerkraut "liberty cabbage," and boycotted German-American businesses. This was also once prime logging country. Although that industry is in long-term decline here, Bemidji is still home to giant statues of Paul Bunyan and Babe the Blue Ox.

On the North Dakota border is Moorhead, the largest city in the district (pop. 43,652), which has gained prominence as the site—with Fargo, across the Red River—of a planned 30-mile flood-diversion project that has been designed to prevent a recurrence of the devastating floods of 1997 and 2009, and has been projected to cost $2.75 billion. The two states have designed the dam so the new channel would flow mostly through North Dakota. In October 2020, upstream landowners who have opposed the project signaled a willingness to enter talks that might end years of litigation, the Fargo Forum reported. The Minnesota Department of Natural Resources has issued a crucial permit for the project.

This is great farming country, the start of the wheat fields that sweep across the Dakotas and into Montana. Even today, farmers toil against the elements to make a profitable living, although many acres have been taken out of production by the federal Conservation Reserve Program. Farmers have turned to corn and soybeans, which have more markets and uses. This area is the nation's leading producer of sugar beets and a leading supplier of turkeys. In 2019, wet fields followed by an early frost left about one-third of the crop in the ground—one of the worst harvests in memory. The trade war with China left soybean farmers in similarly dire straits as they sought other overseas markets.

The 7th Congressional District of Minnesota covers almost all the western part of the state. Its southeastern corner extends to 30 miles from Minneapolis. From the Canadian border to the southern end of the district is roughly a 400-mile drive. It takes in the wheat-farming plains adjoining North Dakota as well as exurban German Catholic areas, with their farm villages named for saints. This has been the fourth most productive farm district in the nation.

In a benchmark of cultural change, DFL Rep. Coya Knutson was defeated for reelection in this district in 1958 when her husband, Andy, issued a plaintive statement urging her to come home from Washington and make his breakfast again. Knutson, who was not on good terms with the DFL, was the only incumbent Democrat to lose in that heavily Democratic year; they divorced shortly thereafter. More recently, the 7th has had a new distinction: In Donald Trump's two campaigns, this was the most Republican district in the nation that elected a Democrat. \In 2020, Trump took the district, 64%-34%, which became too steep of an obstacle for the local Democrat to overcome.

Pete Stauber (R)

Elected 2018, 2nd term, b. May 10, 1966; Duluth, MN; Lake Superior State University, B.S., 1988; Catholic; Married (Jodi Stauber); 4 children.

Elected Office: Hermantown City Council, 2001-2005, 2011-2013; Saint Louis County Commissioner, 2013-2018.

Professional Career: Area Commander, Duluth Police Department, 1995-2017; Player, Detroit Red Wings NHL Hockey Team.

DC Office: 126 CHOB 20515, 202-225-6211, stauber.house.gov

State Offices: Brainerd, 218-355-0862; Cambridge, 763-552-3359; Chisholm, 218-355-0726; Hermantown, 218-481-6396.

Committees: *Natural Resources*: Energy & Mineral Resources (RMM). *Small Business*: Contracting & Infrastructure; Underserved, Agricultural & Rural Business Development. *Transportation & Infrastructure*: Aviation; Highways & Transit; Railroads, Pipelines & Hazardous Materials.

Almanac Ratings 2019-2020

	Economy	Social	Foreign	Composite
Liberal	42%	40%	27%	37%
Conservative	58%	60%	73%	63%

Key Votes of the 116th Congress

1. U.S./Mex./Can. trade deal	Y	5. Russia sanctions	Y	9. Firearms background checks	N
2. First Coronavirus response	Y	6. Troops in Syria	Y	10. Spending at the border	Y
3. HEROES Act	N	7. Veto arms sales to Saudis	N	11. Marijuana liberalized rules	N
4. CASH Act	Y	8. Defense $$$, veto override	Y	12. Electoral College objections	N

Election Results

Election	Name (Party)	Vote (%)		Cand. Spent	Ind. Exp. Support	Ind. Exp. Oppose
2020 General	Pete Stauber (R)............................ 223,432	(57%)		$3,022,615	$13,212	$3,488
	Quinn Nystrom (D)...................... 147,853	(38%)		$1,592,954	$5,080	
	Judith Schwartzbacker (LM)......... 22,190	(6%)				
2020 Primary	Pete Stauber (R).............................. 39,060	(94%)				
	Harry Robb Welty (R)............................ 2,606	(6%)				

Prior winning percentages: 2018 (51%)

Republican Pete Stauber was a notable exception to the Democratic wave in the 2018 election: He replaced a Democratic member of the House, Rick Nolan. Stauber benefited from the shifting politics of Minnesota and the popularity of President Donald Trump in rural America. As a former elite hockey player and longtime police officer who had become active in local government, he mirrored the values of the Northland. In the House, he passed several bipartisan bills.

A native of Duluth, Stauber became well-known for his hockey exploits in high school and at Lake Superior State University, where his team was the national collegiate champion. A highlight of that experience—and the spur to his political career—came when President Ronald Reagan hosted the team at the White House. Stauber played three years of minor-league hockey in the Detroit Red Wings organization, chiefly for Adirondack in the East Coast Hockey League. He and his five brothers owned a summer hockey camp and a sporting-goods store in Duluth.

With his bachelor's degree in criminal justice, Stauber joined the Duluth Police Department, where he became an area commander and served 22 years. While an officer, he was shot twice in separate incidents and was president of the local law-enforcement union. He entered politics as a city council member for eight years in suburban Hermantown (population, 9,604). In 2012, he was elected to the Duluth-based St. Louis County Commission.

When Nolan retired, after barely surviving two narrow reelections, Stauber quickly became the consensus choice of local Republicans. He embraced the district's abundant natural resources, which often have been politically controversial. "I'm the only candidate who will make the following statement: I support iron ore and precious metal mining," he told the International Falls Journal newspaper. The Obama administration had imposed a moratorium on mining in the local Boundary Waters wilderness area. Under Trump, local iron production got a boost from his increased tariffs on steel imports; he also lifted some restrictions on mining in the Boundary Waters region.

Democratic nominee Joe Radinovich, previously a state representative and Nolan's campaign manager, separated himself from Stauber on some issues. He criticized the tax cut congressional Republicans enacted in 2017 and defended tax increases he supported when he was in the legislature. Citing tragedies in his family that resulted from firearms incidents, Radinovich said he backed stronger background checks on gun sales. Responding to campaign ads that cited a criminal charge that filed against him for marijuana use when he was a teenager, which subsequently was dropped, he said during a debate, "I've made mistakes in my life and I think that makes me more human."

In an inexpensive media market, the contest drew large expenditures from outside groups, plus comparable spending from the two candidates. The Democratic Congressional Campaign Committee cut back its support in October, following polls that showed Stauber with a comfortable lead. Stauber won 51%-45%, though Radinovich took 57 percent of the vote in Duluth-based St. Louis County, which cast one-third of the vote.

In the Democratic-controlled House, he worked across the aisle to enact legislation—notably, with other freshmen. With Rep. Angie Craig, he discovered that they shared not only their home state but also that each has a child with special education needs. Among their efforts was passage of a bill to require full funding of the Individuals with Disabilities Education Act. Craig sponsored his bill to revise requirements to determine the size standards for small business. With Rep. Jared Golden, who represents a rural district of Maine, Stauber filed a bill to establish a grant program to fund high-speed broadband service to small businesses in rural areas.

Stauber cited Olympics hockey coach Herb Brooks on his approach: "The name on the front of the jersey means more than the name on the back," he told the Minnesota Post. "If we all worked on the House floor with jerseys that said USA on the front, no name or label on the back, we could move mountains."

When it came to local mining, Stauber usually stayed on his side of the aisle. Referring to mining, he told a local audience, "I am tired of the Iron Range having to endure these attacks on our way of life," according to Minnesota Public Radio. "This is not just a playground for a few. This is our home." On mining in Boundary Waters, he clashed especially with Rep. Betty McCollum, who represents St. Paul and is an influential member of the Appropriations Committee.

Seeking reelection, Stauber was challenged by Quinn Nystrom, who was a national advocate on behalf of diabetes patients such as herself. She focused on health care, including lower prescription drug prices. Nystrom spent $1.6 million to Stauber's $2.6 million. In its endorsement of Stauber, the Bemidji Pioneer cited "his willingness to work with Democrats." Nystrom led by nearly 5,000 votes in Duluth-based St. Louis County. Stauber had double-digit leads in most of the remaining counties and won, 57%-38%. He became the first Republican to win reelection in this district since 1946.

MN-8: Northeastern Minnesota   **Cook Partisan Voting Index: R+10**

Population		Race and Ethnicity		Income	
Total	671,346	White	92.50%	Median Income	$61,659
Land area (sq. miles)	27,908	Black	1.10%	District Income Rank	236
Pop/ sq mi	24.06	Latino	1.90%	Poverty Rate	10.60%
Born in State	78.50%	Asian	0.80%	With health insurance	94.90%
		Two or more races	2.70%	Cash public assistance	3.20%
Age Groups		Other	2.80%	Food stamp/SNAP	8.40%
Under 18	20.80%				
18-34	19.10%	**Education**		**Work**	
35-64	38.90%	H.S grad or less	38.10%	White Collar	34.70%
Over 64	21.20%	Some college	37.20%	Sales and Service	36.80%
		College Degree, 4 yr	16.20%	Blue Collar	28.50%
Military		Post grad	8.40%	Government	16.70%
Veteran/ Active Duty	8.90%				

2020 Pres. Vote	Trump	225,291	(56%)	Biden	166,936	(42%)			
2016 Pres. Vote	Trump	194,779	(54%)	Clinton	138,665	(38%)	Johnson	12,618	(4%)

Duluth, Northern Twin Cities: In the 1860s, prospectors in Minnesota's Arrowhead region, northwest of Lake Superior in the low hills of the Mesabi Range, happened upon one of the nation's largest veins of iron ore. They moved on, looking for gold. But in the 1880s, Duluth banker George Stone and Philadelphia financier Charlemagne Tower started mining the Iron Range. Rail lines were built southward to the port of Duluth to carry the ore, plus abundant grains, to freighters for shipment across the Great Lakes. With its signature aerial lift bridge traversing its shipping channel, Duluth is nestled on dramatic bluffs over the often-frozen waters of Lake Superior—one of the most beautiful settings for a city in North America, though also one of the most isolated. Its city plan was drawn up by architect Daniel Burnham, who also planned Chicago, and its splendid turn-of-the-century buildings still celebrate the triumph of technology and civilization over wilderness and the elements.

For most of the 20th century, about 100,000 people lived on the Iron Range and another 100,000 in Duluth, most of them descendants of America's 1880-1924 wave of immigration: Italians, Poles, Serbs, Croats, Swedes, Finns and Eastern European Jews. In this punishing environment, they built solid houses with reliable central heating. The work was hard, the hours long and the pay low. The churches were the main community institutions. Even after living conditions improved vastly in the booming growth following World War II, periods of economic distress persisted. More efficient iron mines and steel mills needed fewer workers. Many in the industry welcomed the tariffs that President Donald Trump imposed on steel imports. At a political rally in Duluth in June 2018, Trump said that winning Minnesota in the 2020 presidential election would be "really, really easy." But the reality proved otherwise. The number of active state mining leases fell from 461 in October 2019 to 191 a year later, the Star-Tribune reported. That resulted after AngloGold, one of the world's largest gold mining companies, abandoned operations in Minnesota.

The port still ships large quantities of grain. Rising commodity prices brought new mining companies to the area to explore extraction of copper, nickel and other nonferrous metals. The airport terminal in Duluth was dedicated to longtime Democratic Rep. Jim Oberstar, who chaired the Transportation and Infrastructure Committee, from which he steered much of the financing for the project. The terminal has spurred resorts for adventure tourists. The new sports competition included the winter ultra-marathon, a 135-mile endurance contest of walking, running, cycling and skiing from International Falls to Tower.

The 8th Congressional District of Minnesota includes Duluth and the Iron Range, plus much of the state's north woods and lake country to the west and south. Duluth-based St. Louis County is the largest in the district, with about 30 percent of the voters. The population in the county and Duluth has remained flat for three decades. The district extends south to the boundaries of the Twin Cities metro area, to Isanti and Chisago counties, where young families are building new homes in pleasant old lakeside towns. Those fast-growing exurban and largely Republican counties have become an increasingly dominant part of the district, even as the Duluth area remains Democratic. From 1946 through 2008, the district elected only two congressmen, both Democrats. Oberstar had worked for the first, John Blatnik, who chaired the same committee. Issues like gun control and environmental regulation have sometimes moved those areas toward the Republicans. As with the two other rural districts in Minnesota that surround the Twin Cities metro area on three sides, the 2016 election brought a huge shift. In a district that President Barack Obama in 2012 took, 52%-46%, Donald Trump won 54%-38%. Contrary to Trump's boast, winning Minnesota was not easy for him. Even in this district, his margin shrank in 2020 when he won, 56%-42%.

MISSISSIPPI

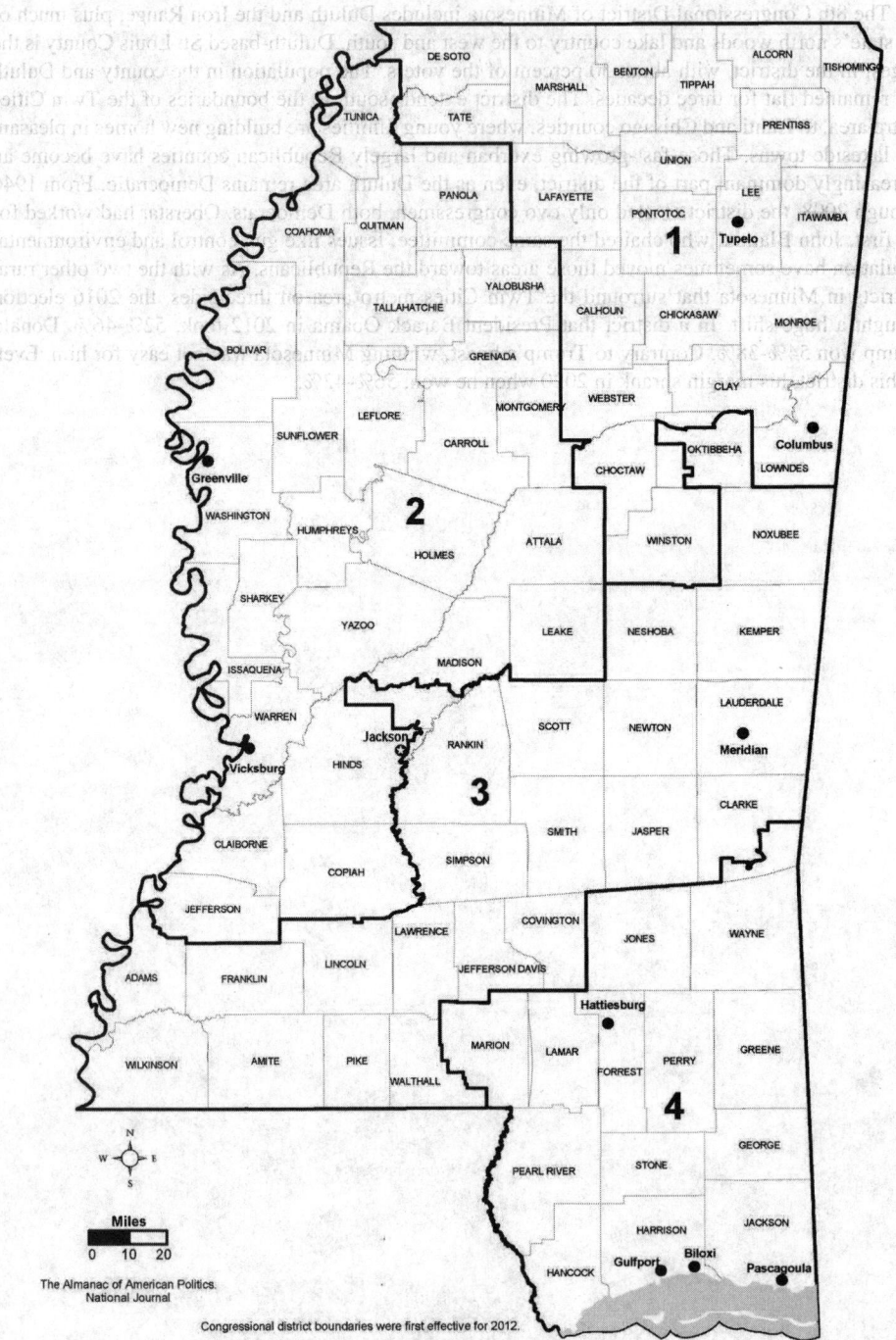

The Almanac of American Politics.
National Journal

Congressional district boundaries were first effective for 2012.

Symbolically, 2020 was a watershed year for Mississippi, as lawmakers voted to replace the state's Confederate-inspired flag, and voters, by a 3-to-1 margin, approved a new one featuring a magnolia flower. But in the state's presidential and Senate contests, the state's racially polarized voting patterns continued unabated: By double-digit margins, Donald Trump once again won the state and Sen. Cindy Hyde-Smith easily won her first full term.

This green land was settled in a rush in Jacksonian America, mostly by small farmers heading west from Georgia and south from Tennessee, and also by a few big planters who made, and sometimes lost, vast fortunes, built grand mansions, brought thousands of slaves in ship holds and coffles, and sent their sons to fight in the Civil War. For a century afterward, as planters and engineers drained the Delta lands, Mississippi—with its racial segregation, subsistence farmers, sharecroppers and low wages—lived apart from most of America. William Faulkner's Mississippi never knew giant factories, the rushes of immigration, or the burgeoning of the suburbs that characterized much of 20th-century America. Mississippi never developed great cities: Its two commercial hubs, Memphis and New Orleans, lie just outside its borders.

But if Mississippi did not thrive in commerce, it did produce great art. Mississippi gave us the blues (from the impoverished Mississippi Delta south of Memphis) and Elvis Presley (who was born in Tupelo). It produced writers like Faulkner, Eudora Welty, Walker Percy and Shelby Foote. The state with a historically low literacy rate has produced an inordinate number of Pulitzer Prize winners for literature. These authors' works were informed by a sense of the tragic that is less evident in other parts of America, where life is a triumphant sales pitch or a labor-saving invention. For years, no other state had such a painful contrast between image and reality, between an ideal sincerely strived for and the tawdry facts of everyday life. Gracious trees on the lawns of antebellum mansions and golden-haired women in white dresses on the veranda, alongside Black servants and retainers: This was once the ideal, at least for some. Behind the ideal stood loose-jointed frame houses and unpainted back-country stores, shotgun shacks without plumbing, and poor White crossroads. As author David Sansing wrote, "We at one time have the scent of magnolias and the smell of burning crosses."

Mississippi still ranks low on many quality-of-life scales. It has the nation's worst-performing health care system as rated by the Commonwealth Fund, and its schools placed in the bottom five in the nation according to Education Week. Still, the gulf between Mississippi and the rest of the country has narrowed. In recent years, the state has done particularly well in vaccinating its children, and it has cut teenage births significantly. Per capita income in Mississippi was 36 percent of the national average in 1940. But it had risen to 67 percent in 1990 and to about 70 percent today—still well below average but, given its lower cost of living, a level recognizably American. Nearly every classroom in the state is air conditioned and wired for the internet. And belatedly, the state is making some gains in K-12 education. In 2019, Mississippi made the biggest improvements of any state for fourth-grade reading and math, and for the first time, it met or exceeded national averages for fourth-grade reading and math. Some praised legislation from 2013 that required third-graders to pass a reading test before being promoted to fourth grade, and that provided funding to train teachers in scientific reading techniques. The state has also expanded school choice options. And it has recently begun to enhance its limited access to broadband, especially in rural areas. In 2019, then-Gov. Phil Bryant signed legislation promoted by Democratic Public Service Commissioner Brandon Presley (a distant cousin of Elvis) that lifted decades-old barriers that had kept electric cooperatives from offering broadband service; since passage, multiple co-ops have begun expanding the state's networks.

In 1940, Mississippi had an economy based on low-wage, subsistence, or sharecropper agriculture and a system of racial segregation often enforced by violence. The economy once depended on cotton, but no longer: In the mid-20th century, mechanization spawned a mass migration of African Americans from Mississippi to northern industrial cities like Chicago, profoundly changing both. Manufacturing jobs have declined in Mississippi as elsewhere, though northeast Mississippi around Tupelo remains the center of the nation's upholstered furniture industry, and the state ranks in the top 10 for automotive manufacturing jobs, including a Nissan plant in Canton, just north of Jackson, a Toyota plant in Tupelo, a Yokohama Tire facility in West Point, a Continental Tire plant near Jackson, and Cooper Tire & Rubber plants in Clarksdale and Tupelo. Near Gulfport is the nation's largest rocket engine test complex, NASA's Stennis Space Center, where SpaceX tested its next-generation rocket engines. Three companies build unmanned aerial systems in the state, many sold to the military and CIA: Aurora Flight Sciences, Northrop Grumman Unmanned Systems, and Stark Aerospace. The Gulf Coast has big military installations, with Air Force intelligence units and the Navy's Seabees, and the huge Ingalls shipyard is in Pascagoula. Then there is gambling. Mississippi approved it in 1990, and big companies have built casinos in economically struggling Tunica County south of Memphis, on riverboats on the Mississippi River, and on the Gulf Coast. Gambling has reached more than $2 billion a year in direct revenues, but Mississippi casinos have been threatened by the expansion of gambling in neighboring states (and in 2020 by the coronavirus). Overall, the state has fallen from third to seventh nationally in casino gaming revenue since 2007.

Statewide, Mississippi's population has fallen slightly since 2010, with rural areas shrinking the fastest. But scattered growth could be found in urban and suburban areas. DeSoto County (Memphis suburbs) saw its population grow 14 percent between 2010 and 2019, while two suburban counties near Jackson—Rankin and Madison—grew by 9 percent and 11 percent, respectively. On the coast, Harrison (Gulfport-Biloxi) grew 11 percent and Hancock County (Bay St. Louis) grew 8 percent. Lafayette County, home to Oxford and the University of Mississippi, grew 14 percent. Sociologist MimmoParisi of Mississippi State University has pegged the low growth rate statewide to the decline in teenage births and the fact that Mississippi is not a magnet for Hispanics: At 3 percent, Mississippi has the fourth-smallest percentage of Hispanics in the nation, though in August 2019, federal officials detained 680 undocumented immigrants, most of them Hispanic, in a wave of raids at Mississippi food-processing plants.

Race has hardly disappeared as an issue—it still hovers over everyday interactions in Mississippi to a degree it doesn't in most other places—but in some ways, an older generation would be astonished by contemporary race relations. Blacks make up 38 percent of the population, the highest of any state, but 40 years ago, none held public office in Mississippi. In recent years, voters have elected many Black officials, most of them in local or school board posts, including Black mayors in Vicksburg, Jackson, Hattiesburg, Greenville and Natchez. At times, more than a quarter of the legislature has been African-American, a national high, and perhaps spurred by memories of the franchise denied, Black turnout rates in Mississippi have exceeded White turnout in some recent elections. After four decades, prosecutors hunted down and tried Ku Klux Klan members who had killed civil rights activists in the 1960s. Former Republican Gov. Haley Barbour signed bills authorizing a civil rights curriculum in public schools and a civil rights museum in Jackson, which opened in 2017. The Jackson airport is named for the assassinated civil rights leader Medgar Evers. In 2013, Mississippi belatedly ratified the 13th amendment to the U.S. Constitution, which abolished slavery in 1865. And in 2020, Mississippi both eliminated its Confederate-linked flag and got rid of an electoral-college-like system for electing the governor, which had been instituted as a way to dilute Black voting power. One persistent problem, however, has been the state's prison system. In 2020, after a spate of killings and a statewide lockdown, Rep. Bennie Thompson joined with advocacy groups to petition the U.S. Justice Department to launch a civil rights investigation of the system, including the grim, century-old Parchman prison, which had been modeled on a slave plantation. The department agreed to a probe, and Republican Gov. Tate Reeves called the prison system a "catastrophe." Mississippi is also the only state to operate "restitution centers," where people are held until they pay off their court-ordered debts—what amounts to a debtor's prison.

Mississippi was once almost unanimously Democratic, although ready to support breakaway segregationist presidential candidates like Strom Thurmond in 1948 and George Wallace in 1968. Now it's reliably Republican, thanks to racially polarized voting. The GOP has held both Senate seats since John Stennis retired in 1988, and on the federal level, Democrats control only Thompson's Black-majority district stretching from the Delta to metro Jackson, which the party has held since 1986. A turning point in the state's shift from Democratic to Republican leadership came in 2003, when Haley Barbour, emphasizing his Yazoo City roots over his decades as a Washington powerbroker, unseated Democratic Gov. Ronnie Musgrove. Barbour was reelected in 2007, and by 2011 both chambers of the legislature had switched from Democratic to Republican. After Barbour, Mississippians elected Republican Phil Bryant as governor in 2011 and 2015, and gave Bryant's lieutenant governor, Tate Reeves, a promotion in 2019. In winning the governorship, Reeves defeated Attorney General Jim Hood, who had been the only remaining statewide elected Democrat, by five points. Mississippi's statewide offices are exclusively Republican for the first time since

Reconstruction, and both chambers of the legislature are controlled by a GOP supermajority. With this degree of political power, Mississippi has often sought to enact a cutting-edge conservative agenda. In 2016, Bryant signed legislation to allow guns to be carried in belt and shoulder holsters without a permit, and to let churches allow certain parishioners to carry concealed weapons on their premises. That same year, Bryant signed a law to allow government officials and businesses cite religious objections to refuse some services to same-sex couples, and in 2018, he signed a ban on abortion after 15 weeks of gestation. The courts, however, haven't always gone along, ruling the LGBT law and the abortion law unconstitutional. In May 2021, the Republican-dominated Supreme Court relied on a procedural technicality to strike down a medical marijuana initiative, which voters overwhelmingly approved in 2020; the ruling placed in doubt the state's entire ballot initiative process.

In 2020, Joe Biden narrowed President Donald Trump's statewide margin of victory, but only modestly, from 19 points in 2016 to a bit over 16 points four years later. Biden's gains were driven by improvements in four suburban counties: DeSoto shifted to the Democratic nominee by 10 points, Rankin by eight, Harrison by six, and Madison by four. Perhaps more representative of the state's political dynamics was the Senate race, a rerun of the 2018 special election between Smith, the Republican incumbent, and former congressman and U.S. Agriculture Secretary Mike Espy. Despite turnout that was 44 percent higher than the special election two years earlier, the candidates took virtually identical shares of the vote, with Smith coasting to victory by 10 percentage points. Espy, who is Black, failed to achieve the gains Biden saw in suburban areas. Voters did approve two medical marijuana ballot measures with greater than two-thirds of the vote, but in May 2021 the state supreme court struck down the state's ballot measure procedure on a technicality, effectively voiding the marijuana vote and other previously passed measures.

Population		Race and Ethnicity		Income	
Total	2,976,149	White	58.00%	Median Income	45,792
Land area (sq. miles)	46,923	Black	38.00%	State Income Rank	50 out of 50
Pop/ sq mi	63.43	Latino	3.00%	Poverty Rate	19.60%
Born in state	71.50%	Asian	1.40%	With health insurance	87.00%
		Two or more races	1.50%	Cash public assistance	1.80%
Age Groups		Other	1.50%	Food stamp/SNAP	17.3%
Under 18	23.50%				
18-34	22.30%	**Education**		**Work**	
35-64	37.80%	H.S grad or less	44.90%	White Collar	32.80%
Over 64	16.40%	Some college	32.80%	Sales and Service	38.60%
		College Degree, 4 yr	13.70%	Blue Collar	28.70%
Military		Post grad	8.60%	Government	17.70%
Veteran/ Active Duty	7.40%				

Presidential Politics

2020 Primary (D)	Biden (D)	222,160(81%)	Sanders (D)	40,657(15%)	
2020 Pres. Vote	Trump (R)	756,764(58%)	Biden (D)	539,398(41%)	
2016 Pres. Vote	Trump (R)	700,714(58%)	Clinton (D)	485,131(40%)	

Mississippi voted for Jimmy Carter in 1976 and came within 12,000 votes of doing so again in 1980. But starting in 1984, Democratic presidential nominees have won between only 37 and 44 percent here. The state's Delta region with its heavy African-American population hugs the Mississippi River and votes Democratic. The rest of the state, stretching from Tupelo in the north, to the suburban Jackson counties of Madison and Rankin, to Biloxi on the Gulf Coast, votes Republican. Mississippi followed its historical norm in 2020: President Donald Trump defeated Joe Biden, 58%-41%. The state has some of the most racially polarized voting patterns in the country: Exit polls found Trump winning 81 percent of white voters and just 5 percent of Black voters.

Mississippi has held a presidential primary in the second week of March since 1988. The 2016 GOP contest saw a record turnout of 416,270 votes, with Trump defeating Texas Sen. Ted Cruz, 47%-36%. On the Democratic side, African Americans accounted for more than 70 percent of the primary electorate, and their overwhelming support gave Hillary Clinton an 83%-17% victory over

Bernie Sanders. They flocked to Biden in 2020, giving him a dominant 81%-15% win over Sanders on March 10, a week after Biden's big Super Tuesday, and handed him 34 of the state's 36 delegates.

Congressional Districts

117th Congress Lineup	1D 3R	116th Congress Lineup	1D 3R

Redistricting in Mississippi has become relatively straightforward. Of its four districts, three typically have at least a 60 percent Republican vote in presidential elections and the 2nd District —with its African-American majority—has at least a 60 percent Democratic vote. With continuing GOP control of the governorship and legislature, Republicans have reason for confidence. And the African-American community likely will be wary of options to attempt to spread its strength over two districts in this racially polarized state with a 38 percent Black population. Adding to that challenge, the population of the 2nd has lagged behind the other three districts since 2010.

The dynamics following the 2010 census had an unusual procedural twist. Some Republicans were fearful that the Obama Justice Department would deny approval to any map that didn't create a second African-American seat. So they filed suit asking federal judges to step in, because any map drawn by a federal court did not need to win Justice Department sign-off. The end-around worked. When the legislature failed to meet its deadline, the court put its own proposal into place. The map made only minor changes. Mississippi has not had a competitive election for a House district during the past decade. That pattern likely will continue.

Tate Reeves (R)

Elected 2019. term expires 2023, 1st term; b. June 5, 1974, Rankin County MS; Millsaps College (MS), B.A.; Married (Elee); 3 children.

Elected Office: Treasurer, 2004-12; Lt. Gov., 2012-20.

Professional Career: Investment officer, Trustmark National Bank; assistant vice president, AmSouth.

Office: PO Box 139 Jackson, 39205; 601-359-3150; Fax: 601-359-3741

Lt. Gov.: Delbert Hosemann (R); **Atty. Gen:** Lynn Fitch (R); **Sec. of State:** Michael Watson (R)

State Legislature: Senate: 16D, 36R **House:** 46D, 75R, 1I.

Election Resuts:

Election 2019	Name (Party)	Vote (%)
General	Tate Reeves (R)	459,396 (52%)
	Jim Hood (D)	414,368 (47%)
2019 Primary Runoff	Tate Reeves (R)	177,270 (54%)
	Bill Waller (R)	149,413 (46%)
2019 Primary	Tate Reeves (R)	182,979 (49%)
	Bill Waller (R)	124,707 (33%)
	Robert Foster (R)	66,441 (18%)

Prior winning percentage: 2011 (61%)

Tate Reeves extended Mississippi Republicans' dominance of the governor's mansion in 2019 by defeating one of the state's few plausible Democratic statewide candidates, Attorney General Jim Hood, by a five-point margin. Reeves pursued a conservative agenda, but he also signed legislation to eliminate the nation's last remaining Confederate-linked state flag.

Reeves grew up in Florence, in the Rankin County suburbs of Jackson. His father, Terry, had grown up with 10 siblings in a two-bedroom house but founded a heating and air conditioning company in 1975; he turned the Pearl-based outfit into a multimillion-dollar business. Terry Reeves' success inspired his son to study finance at Millsaps College in Jackson. Reeves told the Jackson Clarion-Ledger in 2003 that his father "personifies the American dream of pulling yourself up by the bootstraps, building a successful business and giving back to the community." After graduation, he became a chartered financial analyst and worked for Park South Corp. and later at Trustmark National Bank, where he was a portfolio manager. Some of his work brought him into contact with the state treasurer's office. In 2003, at age 28, he joined a competitive Republican primary to become treasurer. "I had doubts about that first race," Arnie Hederman, a lobbyist and friend of Reeves told Mississippi Today. "He was young and had never run for anything." But Terry Reeves courted donors from his business network and gave generously himself, enabling his son's fledgling campaign to amass an impressive war chest of $600,000.

After winning the primary, the younger Reeves faced Democrat Gary Anderson, whose credentials included heading the Department of Finance and Administration and serving as deputy director of the Mississippi Development Authority. By 2003, Mississippi Democrats' chances of winning down-ballot state offices was dwindling, and Anderson faced the additional challenge of being Black in a state that had not elected a Black candidate to statewide office since Reconstruction. Reeves won by six points, becoming the state's first Republican treasurer. He won reelection in 2007, then in 2011 and 2015 ran successfully for lieutenant governor—a position of special influence in Mississippi because the officeholder appoints Senate committee chairs and assigns bills for committee review.

Reeves, in tune with his state, articulated a staunchly conservative agenda, including pro-gun, anti-abortion, and small-government positions; he proudly touted the 50 tax cuts he oversaw during his time at the helm of the Senate. With Gov. Phil Bryant term-limited in 2019, Reeves planned to run for governor, hoping to follow in the footsteps of Bryant, who had served as lieutenant governor under GOP Gov. Haley Barbour. But Reeves was not able to clear the GOP primary field; the three-way field included former state Supreme Court Chief Justice William Waller Jr., whose father had served as governor as a Democrat in the 1970s, as well as state Rep. Robert Foster. Reeves locked up most establishment support and benefited from a campaign-finance edge, but he wasn't able to dominate the race. Reeves did not have a politician's natural gifts, and as he climbed the ladder, he rubbed some figures in the state the wrong way; among the public, his approval ratings were lower than those of other Republicans in statewide office. This provided an opening for Waller, who pitched himself as a more pragmatic conservative than Reeves; Waller backed expanding Medicaid and hiking the gas tax to fund transportation infrastructure, positions at odds with Reeves'. Foster, meanwhile, challenged Reeves from the right; he attracted the most attention for his refusal to meet a female reporter alone, saying he followed the "Billy Graham rule." (Waller later said he abided by the rule as well.) Ultimately, Reeves fell just short of avoiding a runoff, winning almost 48 percent, with Waller taking 33 percent and Foster taking 18 percent. In the runoff, Reeves benefited from a significant cash advantage and a preference among GOP base voters for the more conservative nominee. He defeated Waller, 54%-46%.

In the general, Reeves faced Hood, who had parlayed conservative views on guns, abortion and the death penalty, a record of populist lawsuits against insurance and pharmaceutical companies, and a down-home, backslapping style into four terms as attorney general, at a time when Democratic candidates were facing longer and longer odds winning any statewide election in the deep South. Hood also helped successfully prosecute Edgar Ray Killen for the killings of civil rights activists James Chaney, Andrew Goodman, and Michael Schwerner in 1964, earning him goodwill among Black voters. Unlike Reeves, Hood supported a Medicaid expansion, and pushed for funding increases in education. Awkwardly, Hood's office had begun an investigation of Reeves in 2018 over allegations that the then-lieutenant governor had used undue influence in the construction of a road serving the subdivision where he lived; the probe continued into their head-to-head contest, with the office ultimately taking no action against Reeves. National handicappers considered the Reeves-Hood race competitive, though it was deemed the least competitive of the three red-state gubernatorial contests held that year. Reeves benefited from the backing of President Donald Trump, Vice President Mike Pence, and members of the Trump family; while Hood tried to distance himself from the national Democratic Party, Reeves was still able to paint him as too liberal for the state. Reeves won, 52%-47%, even as the Democrats flipped the Kentucky governorship and maintained the Louisiana governorship on Election Day.

For years, efforts to change the state's 126-year-old flag came to naught; a statewide vote in 2001 resoundingly backed the existing flag, with its connections to a racist era. But the mood changed in 2020 amid national racial justice protests; pressure by the NCAA and the Southeastern Conference proved particularly effective in the sports-loving state. After legislators moved inexorably toward changing the flag, Reeves signed legislation to remove it within 15 days and empower a panel to offer replacement designs featuring the phrase "In God We Trust." In explaining his decision, Reeves said "we as a family must show empathy. We must understand that all who want change are not attempting to erase history. And all who want the status quo are not mean-spirited or hateful." In the November election, voters easily approved a new design that featured a Magnolia flower.

Reeves' handling of the coronavirus pandemic was less sure-footed. His early attempts to communicate the state's position on local stay-at-home orders caused confusion. He tangled with Republican legislative leaders on how to spend federal relief funds; then an outbreak flared in the legislature during its June session. But Reeves pushed back against the notion promoted by some in Trump's orbit that the pandemic could be stopped through herd immunity in the absence of a vaccine. Reeves instituted a statewide mask order, a step that other Republican governors had sought to avoid. By January, Mississippi ranked near the median among states for cases per capita. However, the state ranked in the top five for coronavirus deaths per capita—a legacy of the state's widespread health challenges, its racial disparities, and its stressed hospital system.

Roger Wicker (R)

Elected 2007, term expires 2024, 2nd full term, b. Jul 05, 1951; Pontotoc, MS; University of MS, B.A., 1973; University of MS, J.D., 1975; Baptist; Married (Gayle Long Wicker); 3 children; 5 grandchildren.

Military Career: U.S. Air Force 1976-1998; U.S. Air Force Reserve 1980-2004

Elected Office: Tupelo City Judge Pro Tempore, 1986-1987; MS Senate, 1988-1994; U.S. House, 1995-2007.

Professional Career: Staff, U.S House Rules Committee, 1980-1982; Practicing attorney, 1982-1994; Lee County public defender, 1984-1987; Board Of Visitors, U.S Naval Academy, 2005.

DC Office: 555 DSOB 20510, 202-224-6253, Fax: 202-228-0378, wicker.senate.gov

State Offices: Gulfport, 228-871-7017; Hernando, 662-429-1002; Jackson, 601-965-4644; Tupelo, 662-844-5010.

Committees: *Armed Services*: Airland; Cybersecurity; Seapower. *Commerce, Science & Transportation (RMM)*: Ex Officio membership on all subcommittees. *Environment & Public Works*: Chem Safety, Waste Mngmnt, Enviro Justice & Reg Oversight (RMM); Clean Air & Nuclear Safety; Transportation & Infrastructure. *Rules & Administration*.

Group Ratings

	ADA	ACLU	AFL-CIO	LCV	COC	HAFA	ACU	CFG	FRC
2020	-	23%	-	15%	-	64%	84%	-	-
2019	5%	C	21%	7%	94%	C	84%	29%	100%

Almanac Ratings 2019-2020

	Economy	Social	Foreign	Composite
Liberal	6%	6%	0%	4%
Conservative	94%	94%	100%	96%

Key Votes of the 116th Congress

1. EPA clean energy rules	N	5. Russia sanctions	N	9. Barr as Atty. General	Y
2. U.S./Mex./Can. trade deal	Y	6. Troops in SYR, AFG	Y	10. Spending at the border	Y
3. Cut unemployment benefits	Y	7. Veto arms sales to Saudis	N	11. Coney Barrett to Sup. Ct.	Y
4. Shelton to Fed Reserve	Y	8. Defense $$$, veto override	Y	12. Electoral College objections	N

Election Results

Election	Name (Party)	Vote (%)		Cand. Spent	Ind. Exp. Support	Ind. Exp. Oppose
2018 General	Roger Wicker (R).................................	547,619	(59%)	$6,015,451	$278,125	$76,000
	David Baria (D)....................................	369,567	(40%)	$871,176	$1,501	
2018 Primary	Roger Wicker (R).................................	130,118	(83%)			
	Richard Boyanton (R).....................	27,052	(17%)			

Prior winning percentages: 2018 (59%), 2012 (57%), 2008 Special (55%), House: 2006 (66%), 2004 (79%), 2002 (71%), 2000 (70%), 1998 (67%), 1996 (68%), 1994 (63%)

As Mississippi's senior senator, Roger Wicker has become an influential GOP voice, particularly on tech and commerce issues, thanks in part to his close relationship with Senate Republican Leader Mitch McConnell. Their bond was strengthened after Wicker protected his party's close majority in 2016 as chairman of the National Republican Senatorial Committee despite a tough map. He has shown a desire to move beyond his state's deeply racist history by supporting Mississippi's removal of the Confederate emblem from its state flag.

Wicker was ap pointed in 2007 to fill the vacancy created by the resignation of Trent Lott, a powerful Mississippian who had served as both majority and minority leader but who stepped down from leadership after comments he made about Sen. Strom Thurmond's pro-segregation presidential campaign in 1948. Since then, Wicker has comfortably been elected three times in a state that has not elected a Democrat to the Senate since 1982, and he has compiled a very conservative record.

Wicker grew up in the North Mississippi town of Pontotoc. His father was a conservative Democrat, a state senator and a circuit judge. He attended public schools and as a teenager became interested in Republican politics. His career was intertwined with two Mississippians on Capitol Hill: Lott and Thad Cochran. He was a page in the House and campaigned door-to-door for Cochran in his first race for Congress. At the University of Mississippi, Wicker served in student government and earned bachelor's and law degrees. He spent four years in the Air Force Judge Advocate General's Corps.

Wicker worked for Lott on the House Rules Committee. After he returned to Mississippi, he served as the public defender in his wife's hometown of Tupelo. In 1987, he was elected to the state Senate, becoming the first Republican from North Mississippi elected to that chamber since Reconstruction. He helped draft a strict abortion law and was a leading advocate of government-sponsored vouchers for private school tuition.

In 1994, the longest-serving member of the House and chairman of the powerful Appropriations Committee, Democratic Rep. Jamie Whitten, retired, leaving big shoes to fill. Pent-up demand produced crowded primaries, attracting six Republicans and three Democrats. On the strength of support from Tupelo, Wicker finished first in the GOP primary and then easily won in the general election.

Wicker compiled a solidly conservative voting record in the House. He got a seat on Appropriations, an unusual prize for a freshman. In those days, appropriators retained an atmosphere of bipartisanship. Wicker worked quietly in subcommittees to secure funding for his low-income district, including Yalobusha River flood control and an interstate highway through DeSoto County. He delivered research dollars to Mississippi universities, and he worked with Lott to attract defense technology firms to the state. Citizens Against Government Waste gave him the dubious distinction of No. 1 earmarker in the House for securing $176 million in projects, most of it for his district. "I am a fiscal conservative, and I believe in keeping spending low," Wicker said later. "But once the national budget is set, I think it is only fair to fight for our fair share for Mississippi." He reluctantly supported the GOP's earmark ban in 2011.

In November 2007, Lott announced his resignation from the Senate. Wicker wanted the seat, but so did GOP Rep. Chip Pickering and Netscape founder James Barksdale. Gov. Haley Barbour appointed Wicker. Mississippi Democrats had not seriously contested a Senate race in 20 years, but with renewed hope, they nominated former Gov. Ronnie Musgrove, whom Barbour had ousted in 2003. It was a battle between old friends: Wicker and Musgrove had both been elected to the state Senate for the first time in 1987 and they roomed together in Jackson.

Musgrove criticized Wicker for his support of earmarks and called him a "poster child" for a moratorium on pork-barrel spending. Musgrove hinted at ethical misconduct, criticizing Wicker for securing a $6 million earmark, not sought by the Pentagon, for Aurora Flight Sciences to build drones in North Mississippi. Company executives had contributed $17,000 to his campaign and hired his former chief of staff to lobby for the project. Wicker said the effort was all about bringing high-paying jobs to Mississippi. Wicker outspent Musgrove, $6.2 million to $5.3 million, though the Democratic Senatorial Campaign Committee pumped in more than enough money to compensate. Wicker won 55%-45%.

In the Senate, Wicker has been particularly conservative on social issues. In 2015, he drew attention when he cast the lone "no" vote against Democratic Sen. Sheldon Whitehouse's amendment to get Republicans to acknowledge that climate change is occurring. Wicker called it a "gag" and said he agreed "with the more than 31,000 American scientists who do not believe the science on this matter is settled." After Congress voted in 2010 to repeal the "don't ask, don't tell" ban on openly gay service members, Wicker co-sponsored a bill forbidding same-sex marriages on military bases.

Wicker often has had a home-state focus. As chairman of the Armed Services Seapower Subcommittee, he secured funding in the 2016 defense spending bill for a new naval destroyer and a big-deck amphibious ship. Two years later, President Donald Trump signed into law Wicker's SHIPS Act, which declared the Navy's official policy to achieve a 355-ship fleet, many of which would be built in Mississippi. On the Commerce, Science and Transportation Committee, Wicker has sought more broadband access for rural areas and complained that the Federal Communications Commission was setting internet speed artificially high. He was the lead sponsor of a bill to extend a Safe Drinking Water Act program to assist public water systems in small and rural communities, which was enacted in 2015.

Wicker became chairman of the Commerce Committee in 2019. That year, he held hearings on violent and extremist online content and said he was "deeply disappointed" that Facebook CEO Mark Zuckerberg declined to testify. In 2020, Wicker helped lead a GOP push, heavily championed by Trump, to repeal Section 230 of the 1996 Communications Decency Act, which immunizes social media companies from legal liability for user content posted on their sites. He asked the White House to double funding for research into artificial intelligence and quantum information science fields. Amid privacy concerns after data breaches at large tech companies, Wicker introduced a bill that would set a nationwide standard for the handling of personal information online, including requiring companies to collect a minimum amount of personal data. The proposal would have superseded state laws, including a more lenient one in California. Wicker continued to press for increased and better broadband access, especially amid the pandemic. Social distancing to protect from the novel coronavirus "caused a huge uptick in the use of broadband," he said at a May 2020 hearing, adding, "One estimate shows that average broadband usage is up by 47 percent since the pandemic began." Wicker played a major role in hashing out the March 2020 $2.2 trillion CARES Act, particularly for aid to airlines that had been devastated by the cratering of travel early in the pandemic.

Even with his leadership role, Wicker distanced himself from Trump at times. Most notably, in March 2019, Wicker was one of 12 GOP senators who voted to overturn the president's declaration of a national emergency on the southern border, which was aimed at securing money for a border wall. Wicker worried that Trump's use of the national emergency law to bypass Congress could set a dangerous precedent. Elsewhere, Wicker criticized Trump on trade and foreign policy, including when Trump wanted to withdraw U.S. troops from Syria. He voted to certify Joe Biden's Electoral College win, the only Republican in the Mississippi congressional delegation to do so. But he voted to acquit Trump during his second impeachment—for inciting the Jan. 6 insurrection at the Capitol—siding with most Republicans in saying there was no precedent in convicting a former officeholder.

Wicker supported the 2020 decision to remove Confederate battle imagery from the Mississippi flag, the last state banner in the nation to display such an emblem. "It's a symbol that more and more represents a day in the past that we don't want to celebrate," Wicker said. It was a position he first announced in 2015 after the massacre at a Black church in Charleston South Carolina, noting his own Confederate ancestors but saying the old flag "should be put in a museum and replaced by one that is more unifying to all Mississippians." But he stopped short of backing efforts to rename military bases named for Confederate generals and remove Confederate statues from the Senate.

In 2012, Wicker defeated Albert Gore—a retired United Methodist minister and distant relative of the former vice president—who ran a bare-bones campaign, 57%-41%. In 2014, he helped Cochran survive an aggressive primary challenge from tea party-backed Chris McDaniel. In the runoff, Cochran narrowly edged McDaniel with outreach to African-American voters.

His assistance for Cochran aided his bid for the NRSC chairmanship. When seeking the post, one of his first calls was to Lott, who told him, "Golly, Roger, why would you want that job? It's the toughest job in the Senate leadership," Congressional Quarterly reported. As chairman during the 2016 campaign cycle, he faced a formidable task: Republicans were defending 24 seats, including nine in states that Barack Obama carried in either 2008 or 2012, while Democrats were defending 10. GOP incumbents lost only two seats: in Illinois and New Hampshire. Trump trailed in each state.

In 2018, Wicker prepared for McDaniel to try again to oust an incumbent. Unlike Cochran, who was slow to realize the serious challenge, Wicker built a $3.1 million war chest. He stashed the endorsements of some GOP leaders who backed McDaniel in 2014. The possible sequel was short-lived, as Trump endorsed Wicker. A few days later in March 2018, the aging Cochran announced his resignation; McDaniel ran for the vacant seat and trailed a distant third in the non-partisan primary. Wicker faced a long-shot challenge from Democratic state House Minority Leader David Baria, who tagged Wicker as "Roger the dodger" for refusing to debate him. The snub made little difference: Wicker won 59%-40%, and seems firmly ensconced in his seat for as long as he wants. As the number-two Republican on Armed Services, he can envision the prospect of heading a Senate panel that dispenses considerable largesse to his home state, especially its shipyard in Pascagoula.

Cindy Hyde-Smith (R)

Appointed 2018, term expires 2026, 1st full term, Brookhaven, MA; Copiah-Lincoln Community College, A.A., 1979; University of Southern Mississippi, 1981; Baptist; Married (Michael Smith); 1 child.

Elected Office: MS Senate, 1999-2011; MS Commissioner of Agriculture, 2012-2018.

Professional Career: Cattle Farmer; Congressional Affairs Consultant.

DC Office: 702 HSOB 20510, 202-224-5054, Fax: 202-224-5321, hydesmith.senate.gov

State Offices: Gulfport, 228-867-9710; Jackson, 601-965-4459; Oxford, 662-236-1018.

Committees: *Agriculture, Nutrition & Forestry*: Commodities, Risk Management & Trade; Conservation, Climate, Forestry & Natural Resources; Livestock, Dairy, Poultry, Local Food Sys & Food Safety & Sec (RMM). *Appropriations*: Agriculture, Rural Development, FDA & Related Agencies; Department of Homeland Security; Department of the Interior, Environment & Related Agencies; DOL, HHS & Education & Related Agencies; Energy & Water Development; Financial Services & General Government (RMM). *Energy & Natural Resources*: Energy; Public Lands, Forests & Mining; Water & Power (RMM). *Rules & Administration*.

Group Ratings

	ADA	ACLU	AFL-CIO	LCV	COC	HAFA	ACU	CFG	FRC
2020	-	0%	-	8%	-	6600%	76%	-	-

Almanac Ratings 2019-2020

	Economy	Social	Foreign	Composite
Liberal	36%	1%	1%	13%
Conservative	64%	99%	99%	87%

Key Votes of the 116th Congress

1. EPA clean energy rules	N	5. Russia sanctions	N	9. Barr as Atty. General	Y
2. U.S./Mex./Can. trade deal	Y	6. Troops in SYR, AFG	Y	10. Spending at the border	Y
3. Cut unemployment benefits	Y	7. Veto arms sales to Saudis	N	11. Coney Barrett to Sup. Ct.	Y
4. Shelton to Fed Reserve	Y	8. Defense $$$, veto override	Y	12. Electoral College objections	Y

Election Results

Election	Name (Party)	Vote (%)		Cand. Spent	Ind. Exp. Support	Ind. Exp. Oppose
2020 General	Cindy Hyde-Smith (R)..................	709,511	(54%)	$3,332,591	$25,455	$500,948
	Mike Espy (D).....................................	578,691	(44%)	$11,693,345	$208,034	$35,536
2020 Primary	Cindy Hyde-Smith (R)..................	235,463	(100%)			
2018 General	Cindy Hyde-Smith (R)..................	486,769	(54%)	$5,109,442	$3,132,460	$1,111,312
Runoff	Mike Espy (D).....................................	420,819	(46%)	$6,975,054	$2,440,281	$3,527,421
2018 General	Cindy Hyde-Smith (R)..................	389,995	(41%)			
	Mike Espy (D).....................................	386,742	(41%)			
	Chris McDaniel (R).............................	154,878	(16%)		$731,387	$973,737

Prior winning percentages: 2018 (54%)

Republican Cindy Hyde-Smith is the first woman ever elected to represent Mississippi in Congress, the 49th state to achieve that distinction, leaving Vermont as the only state that hasn't. Then the state's first female commissioner of agriculture and commerce, she was appointed in 2018 by Gov. Phil Bryant to fill the seat after the resignation of longtime GOP Sen. Thad Cochran, and she won a special election for the rest of the term the same year. In 2020, she was elected to a full six-year term. A former Democrat, Hyde-Smith has staked out a position as one of the most conservative women in the Senate.

Republicans were initially worried that Hyde-Smith would be slammed for switching parties in 2010. But it was instead an offhand comment about "attending a public hanging" that threatened to derail her first campaign, turning the race against former Agriculture Secretary Mike Espy, a Democrat, into a debate on race. The rhetoric, in a state that has seen some of the worst racial violence in the nation's history, was sharp. So was the significance: Espy would have been the first Black senator from Mississippi since Reconstruction. Nonetheless, Hyde-Smith defeated him in back-to-back elections.

In the Senate, Hyde-Smith has been a reliable Republican vote and was rarely critical of President Donald Trump. In 2018, s he literally wrapped his support around her campaign RV as she sought to discourage potential GOP spoilers who could have made a Democratic upset more likely. On January 6, 2021, she was one of just five Republican senators who objected to Joe Biden's Electoral College votes from Arizona and Pennsylvania, retaining her opposition to the latter even after the U.S. Capitol was sacked by Trump supporters seeking to overturn the presidential election.

Hyde-Smith was born in Brookhaven Mississippi but grew up east of there in Monticello. Her father, a truck driver, taught her how to drive a tractor when she was 7. Hyde-Smith recalls being a "major tomboy," riding horses and dirt bikes. According to The Washington Post, she met her future husband, Michael Smith, when a customer in her mother's beauty shop set them up on a blind date. She later attended Copiah-Lincoln Community College and graduated from the University of Southern Mississippi with degrees in criminal justice and political science. The couple live in Brookhaven, where Smith's family has raised beef cattle for four generations.

She began her career working for the American Cancer Society in Mississippi. Later, she was a lobbyist in Washington for the National Coalition on Health Care and the Southern Coalition for Safer Highways. She was elected in 1999 to the state Senate, where she worked on agricultural issues. As chairwoman of the Agriculture Committee for eight years, she passed legislation to protect farmers from eminent domain after a 2005 Supreme Court decision. In 2010, she switched parties to become a Republican, joining more than a dozen Mississippi officials who left the Democratic Party in a two-year span after Barack Obama's election as president. Building on her background as a farmer, Hyde-Smith ran and won her first statewide race to become commissioner of agriculture and commerce in 2011, taking 57 percent of the vote. She won reelection in 2015 with 61 percent.

Hyde-Smith was not among Republicans' top choices for a successor to Cochran, the chairman Appropriations Chairman who had been in poor health when he stepped down in March 2018. Although Trump reportedly said he would not endorse Hyde-Smith because of her Democratic past, Bryant tapped her for the temporary position. The other name that loomed was state senator and tea party conservative Chris McDaniel. McDaniel and his supporters were still incensed over what they felt was a stolen Senate seat after his 2014 primary challenge to Cochran fell just short. This time, McDaniel had the backing of Trump confidant Steve Bannon, who wanted him to primary Mississippi

Sen. Roger Wicker. But Trump endorsed Wicker shortly before McDaniel was expected to announce, leading McDaniel to decide that competing against Hyde-Smith was a better move.

Because it was a special election, there was no primary. So, it would be Hyde-Smith, Espy, McDaniel and little-known Democrat Tobey Bartee on the ballot. Hyde-Smith, the incumbent, carried the support of the National Republican Senatorial Committee and other outside groups aligned with the GOP leadership. The U.S. Chamber of Commerce committed to $750,000 in ads on her behalf. Hyde-Smith slammed McDaniel as a "liar" and refused to debate him saying, "My guys are saying that's like handing him a $200,000 campaign donation." McDaniel pushed back, but he lacked the fire he brought in 2014. In the first round of voting, Hyde-Smith led him 41%-16%. Espy had a surprisingly strong second-place finish, virtually even with Hyde-Smith.

Hyde-Smith appeared to have everything she needed to close out a victory. But on November 11, she was caught on tape telling a supporter, "If he invited me to a public hanging, I'd be on the front row." The clip was posted on Twitter and went viral. Soon Espy, the NAACP and Democrats demanded an apology for a remark that reminded many of racist lynchings and the worst of the state's history. Several large businesses and organizations, including Walmart, Major League Baseball and Pfizer, asked for Hyde-Smith to return their PAC donations.

In response, Hyde-Smith released a statement calling her words an "exaggerated expression of regard." But her entire record was under the microscope and reporters kept finding more threads to pull. In the following days, several revelations came to light: As a state senator, she proposed renaming a stretch of highway after Jefferson Davis. In a 2014 photo captioned "Mississippi history at its best!" she could be seen wearing a Confederate hat at Davis' homestead, and she had attended a private high school that appeared to open its doors just as a court order enforcing integration of public high schools in the state went into effect.

Those incidents gave Espy hope that he could pull off an upset. But the former Clinton Cabinet official was in a tough spot. Politically, he could not be too critical of Trump or express strongly liberal positions. He had to find a way to excite Black voters without alienating white moderates. Espy was also dogged by the fallout of his resignation as Agriculture secretary after he was accused of receiving improper gifts and indicted. He was later acquitted, but many voters remembered his messy exit. The Republican National Committee sent 100 staffers to Mississippi just before the runoff, and Trump campaigned with Hyde-Smith at two stops. She won 54%-46%.

Espy sought a rematch in 2020 when Hyde-Smith was vying for a full six-year term. She ran a low-key race, making few campaign appearances, perhaps having learned from the gaffes that plagued her prior race. She spent only $3.3 million for this campaign, compared to the $11.7 million Espy raised late, thanks to a massive online windfall after the September death of Supreme Court Justice Ruth Bader Ginsburg. But in the end, Hyde-Smith increased her victory margin to this time 54%-44%, a slight improvement over their previous contest.

In the Senate, Hyde-Smith kept Cochran's seat on Appropriations. Mississippi has long depended on its delegation to bring home federal dollars. In 2021, when the Democrats took control of the chamber, she became the ranking Republican on its Financial Services Subcommittee. She also took the ranking GOP post on the pork-laden Energy and Natural Resources Subcommittee on Water and Power. In the majority, she chaired the Agriculture Subcommittee on Livestock, Marketing and Agriculture Security. Addressing a growing concern at home, Hyde-Smith introduced legislation to respond to chronic wasting disease, a contagious and fatal neurological disease that affects white-tailed deer, which are common in the state. She proposed legislation to create a permanent disaster relief fund for the commercial fishing industry. In 2020, amid the coronavirus pandemic, Hyde-Smith introduced a bill that would require the Federal Emergency Management Agency to pay the full cost of any major disaster instead of using a cost-share system with states and localities. She introduced another bill with Republican John Barrasso of Wyoming and Democrat Michael Bennet of Colorado to provide financial assistance to rural hospitals.

Hyde-Smith also partnered with Wicker on a successful bill to make the home of civil rights icons Medgar and Myrlie Evers a national monument. Wicker had supported removing a Confederate emblem from the Mississippi state flag as early as 2015, but when the issue arose again in the summer of 2020, Hyde-Smith was more equivocating, saying in a statement, "Should the people of Mississippi and their elected leaders decide to begin the process of finding a more unifying banner that better represents all Mississippians and the progress we have made as a state, I would support that effort." The flag, indeed, was changed to a new one with a magnolia surrounded by the words "In God We Trust." Both Wicker and Hyde-Smith opposed removing Confederate statues from the Capitol.

Hyde-Smith also flexed her conservative muscles, blocking bills from Democrats that tried to implement gun background checks and to require campaigns to alert the FBI and the Federal Election

Commission about any foreign offers of election assistance. She introduced legislation to limit the sale of chemical abortion drugs.

Trent Kelly (R)

Elected 2015, 3rd full term, b. Mar 01, 1966; Union, MS; East Central Community College, A.A., 1986; University of MS Business School, B.A., 1989; University of MS Law School, J.D., 1994; Army War College, M.A., 2010; Methodist; Married (Sheila Kelly Hampton); 3 children.

Military Career: U.S. Army National Guard 1985-pres. (Iraq)

Elected Office: Tupelo City Prosecutor, 1999-2011; 1st Circuit Judicial District Attorney, 2012-2015.

Professional Career: Practicing attorney, 1995-1999.

DC Office: 1005 LHOB 20515, 202-225-4306, Fax: 202-225-3549, trentkelly.house.gov

State Offices: Columbus, 662-327-0748; Corinth, 662-687-1525; Eupora, 662-258-7240; Hernando, 662-449-3090; Tupelo, 662-841-8808.

Committees: *Agriculture*: Conservation & Forestry; Livestock & Foreign Agriculture. *Armed Services*: Intelligence & Special Operations (RMM); Seapower & Projection Forces. *Budget*. *Permanent Select on Intelligence*: Defense Intelligence & Warfighter Support; Intelligence Modernization & Readiness.

Group Ratings

	ADA	ACLU	AFL-CIO	LCV	COC	HAFA	ACU	CFG	FRC
2020	**	20%	**	5%	-	98%	86%	**	-
2019	5%	C	19%	7%	77%	C	84%	90%	100%

Almanac Ratings 2019-2020

	Economy	Social	Foreign	Composite
Liberal	25%	7%	4%	12%
Conservative	75%	93%	96%	88%

Key Votes of the 116th Congress

1. U.S./Mex./Can. trade deal	Y	5. Russia sanctions	N	9. Firearms background checks N
2. First Coronavirus response	N/A	6. Troops in Syria	N	10. Spending at the border Y
3. HEROES Act	N	7. Veto arms sales to Saudis	N	11. Marijuana liberalized rules N
4. CASH Act	N	8. Defense $$$, veto override	Y	12. Electoral College objections Y

Election Results

Election	Name (Party)	Vote (%)		Cand. Spent	Ind. Exp. Support	Ind. Exp. Oppose
2020 General	Trent Kelly (R)	228,787	(69%)	$779,255		
	Antonia Eliason (D)	104,008	(31%)	$17,672		
2020 Primary	Trent Kelly (R)	56,501	(100%)			

Prior winning percentages: 2018 (70%), 2016 (69%), 2015 special (70%)

Republican Trent Kelly, who won the seat in a special election in 2015, moved quickly to an influential position on the Armed Services Committee. He has taken advantage of his lengthy military experience to address the needs of military personnel.

Kelly graduated from the business school and law school at the University of Mississippi, then earned a master's degree in strategic studies from the U.S. Army War College. Kelly has been in the National Guard since the mid-1980s as an engineer. He served in Iraq during the Gulf War, then had two tours of duty during the Iraq War, where he commanded 670 troops. He received two Bronze Stars and numerous other military honors. In 2020, he was promoted to major general. He became Tupelo's city prosecutor in 1999, and held that position for 12 years before he was elected district attorney for seven rural counties in the northeast corner of the state.

After Rep. Alan Nunnelee died, 13 candidates filed for the special election. Of the 12 Republicans, not one was from DeSoto County, which is the population center of the district. That led to a wide-open contest, with none of the candidates posting big fundraising hauls. Mike Tagert, the northern Mississippi transportation commissioner, had the support of former Republican Gov. Haley Barbour. But Kelly received contributions from Nunnelee's campaign fund, assistance from the late congressman's former consultant and an aide, and an important endorsement from his widow, Tori. In the "jungle primary," Walter Zinn, the only Democrat, led with 17.4 percent, Kelly got 16.3 percent, and Tagert finished third with 12.7 percent. Given the Republican tilt of the district, it was no surprise that Kelly won the runoff with 70 percent of the vote.

In Kelly's first year, the House passed his bill to make it easier for Small Business Administration representatives to review contract requests from small businesses. The measure later was included in the House version of the annual defense spending bill. He chaired the Oversight and Investigations Subcommittee at Small Business, where he examined how the SBA and other federal agencies could operate programs that affect small businesses in a more cost-effective manner. In an interview with the Jackson Clarion-Ledger, Kelly said that what bothered him most about the House is, "there are so many opportunities where we as members like each other—we just disagree on policy."

In 2018, he cosponsored with Florida Democratic Rep. Al Lawson a bill to allow large prime contractors to take credit for subcontracting to smaller businesses, which passed the House. He developed a working relationship with neighboring Democratic Rep. Bennie Thompson, including their joint opposition to a Senate resolution to switch the regulation of catfish from the Agriculture Department to the Food and Drug Administration. Catfish farming is big business in Mississippi.

In 2017, Kelly achieved his goal of a seat on the Armed Services Committee. He quickly gained influence and leapfrogged more senior committee members, taking the top Republican position on the Military Personnel Subcommittee in 2019. On that panel, he cited his close cooperation with its chairwoman, Democratic Rep. Jackie Speier. In 2020, he claimed success in achieving his goals on the annual defense bill: better communication with military families, improved access to child care and health care improvements. In 2021, he became ranking Republican on the newly-organized Intelligence and Special Operations Subcommittee. He also gained plum assignments that year on the Budget and Select Intelligence committees.

Kelly won House passage in November 2019 of his bill to transfer the verification of service-disabled veteran-owned small businesses from the Veterans Affairs Department to the SBA. The bill, he said, marked a "significant step towards streamlining the two programs under one umbrella at the Small Business Administration and reduces red tape and confusion for veteran small business owners who wish to do business with the federal government." The Senate did not act on the bill. In April 2020, he announced a program with the Mississippi Department of Agriculture and Commerce to assist farmers struggling with labor shortages because of travel restrictions resulting from the coronavirus. The program signed up furloughed or unemployed members of local military units.

Kelly has remained a reliable GOP vote, though he told the Northeast Mississippi Daily Journal in 2018 that he'll "never be a guy who votes party lines on anything. I vote on the values I have." Kelly has won comfortable reelections. In 2018 he faced his most active Democratic challenger, Ole Miss biochemistry professor Randy Wadkins; Kelly won easily, 67%-32%. In 2020, he faced Antonia Eliason, a professor of international trade law at Ole Miss, who claimed to be the first Democratic Socialist to run for office in Mississippi. Kelly improved his performance to 69%-31%.

MS-1: Northeast Mississippi

Cook Partisan Voting Index: R+18

Population		Race and Ethnicity		Income	
Total	769,026	White	66.80%	Median Income	$50,243
Land area (sq. miles)	10,573	Black	29.00%	District Income Rank	385
Pop/ sq mi	72.74	Latino	3.30%	Poverty Rate	14.90%
Born in State	63.70%	Asian	1.10%	With health insurance	88.60%
		Two or more races	1.20%	Cash public assistance	1.10%
Age Groups		Other	1.90%	Food stamp/SNAP	10.00%
Under 18	23.40%				
18-34	22.30%	**Education**		**Work**	
35-64	38.40%	H.S grad or less	46.60%	White Collar	31.30%
Over 64	16.10%	Some college	32.00%	Sales and Service	35.80%
		College Degree, 4 yr	12.90%	Blue Collar	32.90%
Military		Post grad	8.50%	Government	14.40%
Veteran/ Active Duty	6.70%				

2020 Pres. Vote	Trump	222,345	(65%)	Biden	115,897	(34%)
2016 Pres. Vote	Trump	203,135	(65%)	Clinton	100,780	(32%)

Memphis area, Tupelo: The university town of Oxford—the "Jefferson" of William Faulkner's fictional Yoknapatawpha County—sits on a divide between the hill country of Mississippi and the flat farmlands of the Mississippi Delta. Named for Oxford England, it is home to the University of Mississippi, where violence broke out in 1962 when James Meredith became the school's first Black student. Ole Miss, as it is known, now houses Meredith's papers in its library. Under student pressure, the university in 2015 removed the state flag because it featured the Confederate battle flag within its design. In July 2020, at a reported cost of $1.2 million, the university moved a Confederate statute from a prominent spot on campus to a nearby cemetery. The words "Spiritual Genocide" had recently been sprayed on the monument.

To the west is the Delta, with a large African-American majority, and DeSoto County, just south of Memphis and Mississippi's fastest-growing county, with a nearly 15 percent increase from 2010 to 2019. That's all the more impressive in a state that had virtually no population change during that period. DeSoto has become a magnet for Memphis commuters looking for affordable housing, better schools and lower taxes across the state line. The median household income in DeSoto is about 50 percent higher than the state as a whole. DeSoto has become very aggressive in economic development and has taken business from Memphis. Some of the Old South remains in DeSoto. In January 2020, local supervisors declared the county a Second Amendment "safe haven," perhaps aimed at concerns about Washington, as there was no indication that state authorities were planning to infringe citizens' right to bear arms. East of Oxford is the hill country, which stretches to where the Tennessee River nicks the northeast corner of Tishomingo County. The Golden Triangle in the southeast corner has become a center for aerospace research, including work on unmanned air vehicle designs for surveillance and communications. In February 2020, the Tennessee Valley Authority awarded a contract to build a solar-energy facility in nearby Lowndes County.

The biggest town in the northeast corner is Tupelo, home to an upholstered furniture industry that has survived more prosperously than furniture centers elsewhere. Tupelo was the birthplace of Elvis Presley in 1935, and the family's two-room house is open to visitors. The town produces many Christian conservatives, the kind of townsfolk who were shocked by Presley's music and hip-swirling dance moves in the early days of rock 'n' roll. The American Family Association, a fundamentalist Christian organization that seeks to "transform American culture," is based there. The Tupelo region got a big economic boost when Toyota opened an assembly plant in nearby Blue Springs. Since 2011, the plant has manufactured more than 1.2 million Corollas, with 12 different models. In 2018 the company had a $170 million expansion that led to 6,700 total jobs. In 2019, the Tupelo Automobile Museum shut down, after auctioning 174 cars, many of them eclectic. Several suppliers have sprung up nearby. Clay County has become a tire-manufacturing center.

The 1st Congressional District of Mississippi includes Southaven (the district's biggest city), Oxford, Tupelo and most of the hill country. This once-conservative Democratic territory has become solidly Republican in national politics. With only rural Clay County voting for Joe Biden, President Donald Trump got 65 percent of the district vote—the same as in 2016.

Bennie Thompson (D)

Elected 1993, 14th full term, b. Jan 28, 1948; Bolton, MS; Tougaloo College, B.A., 1968; Jackson State University, M.S., 1972; Methodist; Married (London Johnson Thompson); 1 child ; 2 grandchildren.

Elected Office: Bolton Board of Aldermen, 1968-1972; Bolton Mayor, 1973-1980; Hinds County supervisor, 1980-1993.

DC Office: 2466 RHOB 20515, 202-225-5876, Fax: 202-225-5898, benniethompson.house.gov

State Offices: Bolton, 601-866-9003; Greenville, 662-335-9003; Greenwood, 662-455-9003; Jackson, 601-946-9003; Marks, 662-326-9003; Mound Bayou, 662-741-9003.

Committees: *Homeland Security (Chmn)*: Ex Officio membership on all subcommittees.

Group Ratings

	ADA	ACLU	AFL-CIO	LCV	COC	HAFA	ACU	CFG	FRC
2020	**	79%	**	100%	-	0%	8%	**	-
2019	90%	C	100%	86%	61%	C	8%	14%	0%

Almanac Ratings 2019-2020

	Economy	Social	Foreign	Composite
Liberal	58%	59%	53%	57%
Conservative	42%	41%	47%	43%

Key Votes of the 116th Congress

1. U.S./Mex./Can. trade deal Y	5. Russia sanctions	Y	9. Firearms background checks Y
2. First Coronavirus response Y	6. Troops in Syria	Y	10. Spending at the border Y
3. HEROES Act Y	7. Veto arms sales to Saudis	Y	11. Marijuana liberalized rules Y
4. CASH Act Y	8. Defense $$$, veto override	Y	12. Electoral College objections N

Election Results

Election	Name (Party)	Vote (%)		Cand. Spent	Ind. Exp. Support	Ind. Exp. Oppose
2020 General	Bennie Thompson (D)	196,224	(66%)	$1,527,577	$123	$183
	Brian Flowers (R)	101,010	(34%)	$14,332		$113
2020 Primary	Bennie Thompson (D)	97,921	(94%)			
	Sonia Rathburn (D)	6,256	(6%)			

Prior winning percentages: 2018 (72%), 2016 (67%), 2014 (68%), 2012 (67%), 2010 (62%), 2008 (69%), 2006 (64%), 2004 (58%), 2002 (55%), 2000 (65%), 1998 (71%), 1996 (60%), 1994 (54%), 1993 special (55%)

Bennie Thompson, first elected in 1993 and now the longest-serving African-American elected official in Mississippi, has been a liberal Democratic fixture in an otherwise deeply conservative Republican state. As chairman of the House Homeland Security Committee and a respected leader of the Congressional Black Caucus, he was an outspoken critic of President Donald Trump and his stringent immigration policies. Thompson defended Joe Biden from attacks during the 2020 campaign and was rewarded with the gavel to preside over the Democratic convention that summer.

Thompson grew up in Bolton, in Hinds County outside Jackson, graduated from Tougaloo College and got a master's degree from Jackson State University. He was elected alderman in Bolton in 1969, at age 21, and elected mayor four years later. A longtime volunteer firefighter, he got the first fire engine for Bolton and also a street named after the Rev. Martin Luther King Jr. In 1980, he became a Hinds County supervisor. A lifelong grassroots activist and labor organizer, he led voter-registration drives and successfully encouraged other African Americans to run for office. He organized associations of Mississippi Black mayors and supervisors.

After Democratic Rep. Mike Espy exited Congress to become President Bill Clinton's Agriculture secretary, Thompson ran for the seat. Among Democrats, he came out ahead of Henry Espy, the congressman's brother and mayor of Clarksdale, 28%-20%. Hayes Dent, an aide to Gov. Kirk Fordice, led Republicans with 34 percent. Voting in the runoff was largely along racial lines, and Thompson won 55%-45%, with his margin coming mostly from Hinds County. Mike Espy returned for unsuccessful Senate campaigns in 2018 and 2020.

Thompson has a staunchly liberal voting record. He initially made little attempt to win White votes in his district, making roughly as few concessions across the racial divide as White lawmakers had earlier made. In time, he moderated his votes and reached out to whites, including some of the district's large farmers. Still, he accused Republican Gov. Phil Bryant of refusing to go along with the health care plan of President Barack Obama "just because a Black man created it," Buzzfeed reported. In 2014, Thompson drew widespread attention for comments in an interview with a New Nation of Islam radio show in which he called Supreme Court Justice Clarence Thomas an "Uncle Tom" and accused Senate Republican Leader Mitch McConnell of being racist toward Obama. In 2020, Thompson was a leader, with Rep. Barbara Lee, of the successful call to remove Confederate statues from the Capitol.

At the Homeland Security Committee, Thompson has focused on the needs of first responders. He has been vocal about the threat of computer-based attacks and successfully pushed back in 2012 against Republican calls to scale back the Homeland Security Department's role in favor of defense and intelligence agencies. On a bipartisan basis, he worked to restructure the Federal Emergency Management Agency after its failures in the aftermath of Hurricane Katrina in 2005. Many House Republicans wanted it to become an independent agency. Thompson called for keeping it within the Homeland Security Department, but with the kind of autonomy the Coast Guard has. Despite tentative agreement in the committee, the deal foundered when Thompson demanded an additional $3 billion to spend on state and local communications capability.

As chairman in 2007, Thompson shepherded through the House the unfinished recommendations of the 9/11 commission. He enacted a requirement to screen all passenger jet and ship cargo. He won House passage of annual Homeland Security authorization bills, only to have the Senate ignore them. Back in the minority after Republicans regained control of the House, Thompson was named a vice chair of a House Democratic task force on gun violence formed after the 2012 school massacre in Newtown Connecticut. He regularly gets "F" ratings from the National Rifle Association. Thompson, an avid hunter, says the ratings don't reflect sportsmen's views.

Thompson was a vocal critic of Trump and his policies, especially at the border and with immigrants. "The president's desperate attempts to militarize our southern border and tease out unconstitutional immigration policy are nothing more than political stunts and must be called out as such," Thompson said. He clashed with Homeland Security Secretary Kirstjen Nielsen, as the government partially shut down when Congress and Trump disagreed about funding a border wall. "Your border security presentation submitted to Congress today is yet another example of the misinformation and outright lies the Trump administration has used to make the case for the president's boondoggle border wall," Thompson wrote to Nielsen. But he said that he "would not rule out a wall in certain instances."

After an inspector general report surfaced in January 2019 saying that child separations at the border had been even higher than first reported, Thompson and other Democratic chairmen said the document was "proof that the Trump administration secretly hatched a plan to separate thousands of vulnerable children from their parents and place them in federal custody in order to deter those seeking refuge in the United States."

A longtime friend of Majority Whip James Clyburn, Thompson joined his support for Joe Biden to become the Democratic nominee in 2020 following his victories on Super Tuesday. Thompson defended Biden against criticism that he had done business with segregationist southern Democrats during his early years in the Senate. "If he was able to work with [James] Eastland [of Mississippi], he's a great person," he told Politico. As chairman of the Democratic convention, which was almost entirely virtual, Thompson joined Democrats in attacking Trump for trying to suppress Black voters, especially by cutting funds for the Postal Service. "Trump doesn't believe Black Lives Matter but he knows Black votes do," Thompson tweeted. In April 2020, he proposed the creation of a high-level national commission to gain a "full accounting" of the nation's handling of the coronavirus.

Thompson has encountered occasional campaign opposition. In 2002, he was reelected 55%-43% against Republican challenger Clinton LeSueur, a consultant to the Yazoo Community Action Agency. State Rep. Chuck Espy, nephew of the former representative, challenged him in the 2006 primary, but Thompson prevailed 64%-35%. He has faced no serious challengers since then.

MS-2: Mississippi Delta   **Cook Partisan Voting Index: D+13**

Population		Race and Ethnicity		Income	
Total	692,452	White	30.60%	Median Income	$37,372
Land area (sq. miles)	15,552	Black	67.00%	District Income Rank	434
Pop/ sq mi	44.53	Latino	1.90%	Poverty Rate	25.90%
Born in State	84.60%	Asian	0.50%	With health insurance	85.70%
		Two or more races	1.00%	Cash public assistance	2.00%
Age Groups		Other	0.90%	Food stamp/SNAP	20.00%
Under 18	24.40%				
18-34	22.70%	**Education**		**Work**	
35-64	36.50%	H.S grad or less	49.30%	White Collar	28.30%
Over 64	16.10%	Some college	31.70%	Sales and Service	43.40%
		College Degree, 4 yr	11.60%	Blue Collar	28.30%
Military		Post grad	7.40%	Government	21.20%
Veteran/ Active Duty	5.00%				

2020 Pres. Vote	Biden	191,647	(64%)	Trump	105,472	(35%)
2016 Pres. Vote	Clinton	185,501	(64%)	Trump	102,159	(35%)

Jackson: "The Mississippi Delta," wrote native David Cohn, "begins in the lobby of the Peabody Hotel in Memphis and ends on Catfish Row in Vicksburg." For centuries, the flooding Mississippi and Yazoo rivers left their sediments here, producing a fertile, dark soil. In a bitter irony, what may well be America's richest agricultural land has been home for more than a century to many of its poorest people. Crisscrossed by rivers and famously disease-ridden, the Delta wasn't much settled until after the Civil War. Then, Reconstruction-era profit-seeking operators used late 19th century technology to drain the land, line the river with levees and build railroads on tracks above the rise of the river. Black sharecroppers and field hands worked here in conditions little better than bondage. From this episode of industrial farming came both great misery and great art: Clarksdale in Coahoma County, where Martin Luther King in 1958 held the first meeting of the Southern Christian Leadership Conference, was the real birthplace of blues music. Greenville on the Mississippi has produced writers of the caliber of Walker Percy and Shelby Foote. Yazoo City produced author Willie Morris and bluesman Skip James. Today, Vicksburg's antebellum mansions and battlefield monuments are popular tourist attractions. In Jackson, the Mississippi Civil Rights Museum is the only museum of its kind in the state.

Twentieth century technology changed life in the Delta. The mechanical cotton-picking machine, invented in 1944, came along just as Northern factories were seeking low-wage workers. The great exodus to Chicago and other Northern cities accelerated, and the Delta's population has been declining ever since. In the decade ending in 2010, each of the 16 counties in the Delta suffered a double-digit population loss. Income levels remain among the lowest in the nation, the teen pregnancy rate high and infant mortality at Third World levels. Yet there are signs of hope. Soybeans have become a big-dollar crop here and poultry farms have become a major enterprise. The Delta produces more than half of the nation's catfish, with a catch of 350 million pounds in 2018. To counter foreign production, catfish farmers have turned to promoting the health of their crop, as opposed to those raised in polluted areas of Vietnam. The industry has downsized its acreage and has become more efficient with increased use of aquaculture.

Not far from Memphis, Tunica County is one of the nation's poorest, its struggling economy dependent on the area's six casinos. At one time, there were 11 casinos in a business that was first licensed in 1992. But nearby competition caused revenues to plummet: from $1.7 billion in 2006 to half that in 2017. Just north of the affluent suburbs of Jackson, Nissan operates a 4,000-employee factory in Canton. The company expanded its production line for Altima sedans. The United Auto Workers has made several costly bids to unionize the plant. All have failed. In July 2020, NBC News reported that the pandemic was having a devastating impact on health conditions in the Delta, where medical care and public education already were limited. "Resistance to taking the disease seriously has only continued to grow," according to the report.

The 2nd Congressional District of Mississippi includes the entire Delta, with the Mississippi riverfront from Tunica almost to Natchez. It includes most of heavily African-American Jackson and surrounding Hinds County, except for the affluent Belhaven neighborhood. Nearly one-third of the population is in Hinds, which is 73 percent African American. This Black-majority district includes six counties in the east that are majority white and vote Republican, with about one-sixth of the total population. But the political tone of the district is set by the African-American neighborhoods in Jackson and the Delta counties. Since the district became Black majority in 1982, the 2nd has been the only Mississippi district to vote Democratic in presidential elections. Joe Biden got 64 percent of the vote—the same that voted for Hillary Clinton in 2016.

Michael Guest (R)

Elected 2018, 2nd term, b. Feb 04, 1970; Woodbury, NJ; MS State University, B.A., 1992; University of MS, J.D., 1995; Baptist; Married (Haley Guest); 2 children.

Elected Office: Madison and Rankin Counties, District Attorney, 2008-2018.

Professional Career: Madison and Rankin Counties, Assistant District Attorney, 1994-2008.

DC Office: 230 CHOB 20515, 202-225-5031, Fax: 202-225-5797, guest.house.gov

State Offices: Brandon, 769-241-6120; Meridian, 601-693-6681; Starkville, 662-324-0007.

Committees: *Ethics. Homeland Security*: Border Security, Facilitation & Operations; Intelligence & Counterterrorism. *Transportation & Infrastructure*: Economic Dev't, Public Buildings & Emergency Management; Highways & Transit.

Almanac Ratings 2019-2020

	Economy	Social	Foreign	Composite
Liberal	25%	7%	5%	13%
Conservative	75%	93%	95%	87%

Key Votes of the 116th Congress

1. U.S./Mex./Can. trade deal	Y	5. Russia sanctions	Y	9. Firearms background checks	N
2. First Coronavirus response	Y	6. Troops in Syria	N	10. Spending at the border	Y
3. HEROES Act	N	7. Veto arms sales to Saudis	N	11. Marijuana liberalized rules	N
4. CASH Act	N	8. Defense $$$, veto override	Y	12. Electoral College objections	Y

Election Results

Election	Name (Party)	Vote (%)		Cand. Spent	Ind. Exp. Support	Ind. Exp. Oppose
2020 General	Michael Guest (R)	221,064	(65%)	$513,618		
	Dot Benford (D)	120,782	(35%)			
2020 Primary	Michael Guest (R)	67,269	(90%)			
	James Tulp (R)	7,618	(10%)			

Prior winning percentages: 2018 (62%)

Freshman Republican Michael Guest was elected in 2018 following more than a decade as prosecutor for the two largest counties in his district. Although he was forced into a runoff to get the nomination in the comfortably Republican district, he led by nearly two-to-one margins in each round of the intra-party battle. Guest was widely supported by Mississippi's Republican establishment, including Gov. Phil Bryant. In 2020, he removed any lingering doubt about his support, when he swamped under-funded challengers in both the primary and general elections.

Guest graduated from Mississippi State University and got his law degree from the University of Mississippi. Following 12 years as assistant district attorney, he was elected in 2007 as district attorney for Madison and Rankin counties, which include about one-third of the voters in the district. He was a leader of local civic groups, including the Foundation for Rankin County Public Schools and Mississippi Crime Stoppers.

In the campaign, Guest said his top priority was improved enforcement along the Mexican border, including the construction of a wall to reduce illegal immigration and drugs. Handling complex cases as prosecutor "has taught me to always be prepared, the importance of standing on my principles, and how to work with others to accomplish what is right," he told the Jackson Free Press.

Whit Hughes, a health care development officer and Guest's chief opponent for the GOP nomination, was a former basketball star at Mississippi State University. He was closely connected to former Gov. Haley Barbour, as finance chairman in his successful 2003 campaign and then as deputy director of the Mississippi Development Authority. "Guest and Hughes did little to differentiate from each other on policy issues during the campaign," Mississippi Today reported.

The two leading candidates were also closely matched in fundraising, with a bit more than $500,000 each in their competition for the nomination. Guest benefited from his greater prominence in the two counties that are the core of the district. In the first round of voting in June, Guest got 45 percent to 22 percent for Hughes. Running third with 16 percent was Perry Parker, a businessman from the more rural part of the district and former international financier.

The runoff three weeks later had a similar pattern. In Rankin County, his home county, which cast 30 percent of the vote in the runoff, Guest took more than 80 percent of the total votes and led Hughes by nearly 10,000. In smaller Madison, Guest led by almost 2,000 votes. Overall, he won by nearly 15,000 votes—with a 65%-35% margin. In November, Guest easily defeated the Democratic nominee, state Rep. Michael "Big Country" Evans, 62%-37%.

On the Homeland Security Committee, Guest was the first freshman Republican in 2019 to gain House passage of his bill—a measure to identify and deter terrorists before they travel, by working with national intelligence agencies, state and local law enforcement, plus the private sector. The proposal was part of the Trump administration's national strategy to combat terrorist travel. The House passed the bill, 394-7. Following Senate approval, it was enacted in October.

In 2020, when there was widespread support in Congress to remove 11 statues in the Capitol of Confederate figures, Guest objected that these decisions should be left to the states—each of which has been authorized to designate two statues. The statues from Mississippi have been in the Capitol since 1931: James Zachariah George, a Confederate colonel, and Jefferson Davis, president of the Confederacy. "I would be opposed to the federal government ordering or dictating Mississippi to remove those statues," Guest said. "People who want to see those statues change, I encourage them to contact the governor's office, contact their local and state legislators and ask them to review that." Mississippi Sen. Cindy Hyde-Smith agreed with Guest and blocked Senate action on the House-passed measure.

Guest was opposed for the Republican nomination in 2020 by James Tulp, who advocated more aggressive action to stop illegal immigration. Guest won with 90 percent of the vote. He breezed to reelection in November against Dorothy Benford, 65%-35%. A perennial candidate, Benford did not file a campaign spending report with the Federal Election Commission.

MS-3: South Central Mississippi

Cook Partisan Voting Index: R+13

Population		Race and Ethnicity		Income	
Total	738,992	White	60.50%	Median Income	$49,863
Land area (sq. miles)	12,754	Black	35.40%	District Income Rank	389
Pop/ sq mi	57.94	Latino	2.40%	Poverty Rate	18.90%
Born in State	77.10%	Asian	1.20%	With health insurance	87.80%
		Two or more races	0.80%	Cash public assistance	1.30%
Age Groups		Other	2.10%	Food stamp/SNAP	12.00%
Under 18	23.10%				
18-34	22.50%	**Education**		**Work**	
35-64	37.80%	H.S grad or less	41.60%	White Collar	37.20%
Over 64	16.80%	Some college	31.90%	Sales and Service	36.20%
Military		College Degree, 4 yr	16.00%	Blue Collar	26.60%
Veteran/ Active Duty	7.10%	Post grad	10.60%	Government	18.70%

2020 Pres. Vote	Trump	210,891	(60%)	Biden	135,123	(39%)
2016 Pres. Vote	Trump	198,768	(61%)	Clinton	118,805	(37%)

Jackson Suburbs: The Neshoba County fair has been held every August since 1889 in the town of Philadelphia. What started as a farmer's picnic has become the traditional place where Mississippi politicians announce their candidacies, with the crowds watching to take their measure. Devotees call it "Mississippi's Giant House Party," and many stay the entire week. The crowds are also there to watch the races on the state's only legal horse track. The fair was canceled in 2020 because of the coronavirus—the only cancelation other than during World War II. But nationally, Philadelphia and Neshoba County are known for something less harmonious. There is no memorial, except engraved stones at two African-American churches, to mark the events of the summer of 1964, when three civil rights workers, two white and one Black, were murdered for the crime of urging Black American citizens to register to vote. It wasn't until June 2005 that a jury of nine whites and three blacks convicted Edgar Ray Killen, by then an 80-year-old preacher and sawmill operator, of manslaughter and sentenced him to three life sentences. In November 2014, President Barack Obama commemorated the 50th anniversary when he awarded a posthumous presidential Medal of Freedom to James Chaney, Andrew Goodman and Michael Schwerner.

The 3rd Congressional District of Mississippi includes the Jackson suburbs in Rankin County and south Madison County, which include one-third of the district population, plus the affluent neighborhoods of northeast Jackson in Hinds County. East and north of Jackson, subdivisions, shopping centers and office complexes have sprouted in the countryside. In 2018, the Jackson Clarion-Ledger reported that construction and new businesses were "hopeful signs of a coming rebirth" in downtown Jackson and was reaching "a tipping point" that could benefit the entire area. A year later, WLBT-TV reported that hundreds of millions of dollars had been invested on Capitol Street, "changing the look and feel of the downtown epicenter." Some of the construction was in buildings that had been vacant for decades.

From the Jackson suburbs, the 3rd stretches north to Starkville, home of Mississippi State University, and south almost to Laurel. In the southwest, which extends to the Louisiana border, it includes Natchez, where 668 antebellum mansions and other properties with live oaks sit atop bluffs overlooking the Mississippi River. Natchez, settled in 1716, two years before New Orleans, was ranked second by Lonely Planet in 2016 as the most exciting destination to visit in the United States. In the middle of the district are Neshoba County and Meridian. The district's political preference has become strongly Republican, even with its 35 percent Black population. In 2020, President Donald Trump won the district, 60-39%.That was only the third best performance for Trump of the four districts in Mississippi—a few percentage points behind the more rural districts. As recently as 2000, the 3rd performed the best for the GOP, though with a different redistricting map.

Steven Palazzo (R)

Elected 2010, 6th term, b. Feb 21, 1970; Gulfport, MS; University of Southern MS, B.B.A., 1994; University of Southern MS, M.S., 1996; Roman Catholic; Married (Lisa Palazzo); 3 children.

Military Career: U.S. Marine Corps Reserves 1988-1996; MS Army National Guard 2007-pres. (Gulf War)

Elected Office: MS House, 2007-2010.

Professional Career: FO, Biloxi Housing Authority; Owner, Palazzo & Co. PLLC.

DC Office: 2349 RHOB 20515, 202-225-5772, Fax: 202-225-7074, palazzo.house.gov

State Offices: Gulfport, 228-864-7670; Hattiesburg, 601-582-3246; Pascagoula, 228-202-8104.

Committees: *Appropriations*: Commerce, Justice, Science & Related Agencies; Homeland Security.

Group Ratings

	ADA	ACLU	AFL-CIO	LCV	COC	HAFA	ACU	CFG	FRC
2020	**	20%	**	10%	-	81%	82%	**	-
2019	0%	C	38%	7%	84%	C	81%	61%	100%

Almanac Ratings 2019-2020

	Economy	Social	Foreign	Composite
Liberal	33%	22%	14%	23%
Conservative	67%	78%	86%	77%

Key Votes of the 116th Congress

1. U.S./Mex./Can. trade deal Y	5. Russia sanctions Y	9. Firearms background checks N
2. First Coronavirus response N/A	6. Troops in Syria N	10. Spending at the border Y
3. HEROES Act N	7. Veto arms sales to Saudis N	11. Marijuana liberalized rules N
4. CASH Act N	8. Defense $$$, veto override Y	12. Electoral College objections Y

Election Results

Election	Name (Party)	Vote (%)	Cand. Spent	Ind. Exp. Support	Ind. Exp. Oppose
2020 General	Steven Palazzo (R).................................	255,971 (100%)	$780,925		
2020 Primary	Steven Palazzo (R).................................	54,318 (67%)			
	Robert Deming (R).................................	11,463 (14%)			
	Samuel Hickman (R).................................	7,981 (10%)			
	Carl Boyanton (R).................................	7,533 (9%)			

Prior winning percentages: 2018 (68%), 2016 (65%), 2014 (70%), 2012 (64%), 2010 (52%)

Republican Steven Palazzo, who unexpectedly won his seat in 2010, has styled himself as a firm conservative on fiscal and social issues, representing an area where Hurricane Katrina in 2005 caused severe damage and imposed huge costs. Since joining the Appropriations Committee, he has become more amenable to spending, though he has still struggled to balance that with his tea party inclinations and his constituents' conservative views. His electoral success in 2020 indicated he has locked down his district.

Born and raised in Gulfport, Palazzo enlisted in the Marine Corps. From 1988 to 1996, he was assigned to the 3rd Force Reconnaissance Company, gathering intelligence and taking tours of duty in Kuwait and Saudi Arabia during the Persian Gulf War. Following his full-time service, he joined the Mississippi Army National Guard and supported base operations at Camp Shelby for Operation Iraqi Freedom. Palazzo received his bachelor's and master's degrees in accounting from the University of Southern Mississippi. He worked in accounting positions at various firms, primarily in the construction industry. In 2001, he and his then-wife started the accounting practice Palazzo & Co., which grew into an international firm specializing in individual income tax returns for expatriates.

In 2007, Palazzo was elected to the state House. Two years later, he challenged veteran Blue Dog Democrat Gene Taylor. Taylor lost his home to Katrina, was in good stead with the National Rifle Association, had one of the most conservative voting records among House Democrats, and had opposed many of his party's major initiatives, including health care reform. But Taylor couldn't survive the pro-Republican environment of 2010. Palazzo portrayed him as an enabler of the Democratic agenda with his vote for Nancy Pelosi as House Speaker, which he said showed Taylor's support for a "liberal socialist agenda." Taylor touted his conservative positions and boasted that he voted for Republican John McCain for president in 2008. It wasn't enough, and Palazzo won 52%-47%.

In the House, Palazzo joined the Tea Party Caucus and the Republican Study Committee, calling for sharp reductions in spending. He opposed the New Year's Day 2013 budget deal aimed at averting the so-called fiscal cliff, saying it failed to cut enough. Palazzo found ways to protect defense spending, including funds to expand a National Guard facility in his district and for ship design and feasibility studies at Ingalls Shipbuilding in Pascagoula. Democrats and watchdog groups accused Palazzo of hypocrisy. He continued to pursue the military interests of his district, with shipbuilding and a provision to discourage downsizing at Keesler Air Force Base

Following the 2012 election, Palazzo was one of the 67 House Republicans who voted against the bill to provide $9.7 billion in government borrowing to pay claims from Super storm Sandy, which did considerable damage in the Northeast. He contended the measure should have made offsetting spending cuts. He drew attention because of the vast federal spending for his district following the devastation of Katrina. Most other GOP lawmakers from coastal areas backed the bill, prompting the Biloxi Sun Herald to say of Palazzo, "Seldom has a single vote in Congress appeared as cold-blooded and hard-headed." Aware of the political damage in his own hurricane-prone district, Palazzo backtracked and toured Sandy-stricken areas, then said he supported a larger aid bill.

In 2014, Palazzo survived an unusual re-election contest when Taylor switched parties and challenged him in the Republican primary. Having determined that it was "impossible" for a Democrat to win, Taylor offered himself as the candidate best-equipped to deliver for the 4th District. Palazzo barely avoided a run-off, winning 51%-43%.

But internal tensions remained as the new Congress convened. After more than one hour of a "man to man" conversation with John Boehner the evening before the vote, Palazzo decided that he was "willing to give the Speaker and his team a last chance to put us back on a conservative path for America." Two months later, Palazzo got a coveted seat on the Appropriations Committee and styled himself as an insider. "Serving as an appropriator is a privilege and a tremendous responsibility that I don't take lightly," he said.

Palazzo has continued to pursue his conservative agenda. In 2016, he filed a resolution to censure President Barack Obama for his executive order to restrict private gun sales. He voiced support when the Mississippi legislature went on record in opposition to the U.S. Supreme Court's recognition of same-sex marriages. He was a consistent supporter of President Donald Trump, including his 2020 post-election claims of vote fraud.

At home, the Sun Herald reported in early 2017 that Palazzo was dodging constituents and not publicizing his district events. In 2018, he faced conservative radio host Brian Rose in the GOP primary. Rose, an Air Force veteran, raised questions about Palazzo's military record, alleging he had sought special favors in getting assigned to Camp Shelby instead of going to Iraq. But Rose reported spending less than $20,000 and Palazzo brushed aside the accusations as he won, 70%-30.

In 2020, Palazzo faced three Republican primary opponents. The most experienced was Robert Deming, a city council member from Biloxi, who attacked Palazzo as not sufficiently conservative or supportive of Trump. Deming and Carl Boyanton each self-funded their campaign with more than $100,000. Endorsed by Trump, Palazzo won comfortably, with 67 percent of the vote to 14 percent for Deming, the runner-up.

Palazzo dealt with another headache in 2020 when the Washington-based Campaign Legal Center filed an ethics complaint charging that he misused campaign funds to finance his personal property and former business. In June, a Palazzo aide confirmed that the Office of Congressional Ethics was investigating the allegations.

MS-4: Southeast Mississippi   **Cook Partisan Voting Index: R+22**

Population		Race and Ethnicity		Income	
Total	775,679	White	71.50%	Median Income	$47,340
Land area (sq. miles)	8,044	Black	23.50%	District Income Rank	405
Pop/ sq mi	96.42	Latino	4.40%	Poverty Rate	19.40%
Born in State	62.30%	Asian	1.30%	With health insurance	85.90%
		Two or more races	2.70%	Cash public assistance	2.90%
Age Groups		Other	1.00%	Food stamp/SNAP	12.60%
Under 18	23.10%				
18-34	22.00%	**Education**		**Work**	
35-64	38.40%	H.S grad or less	42.70%	White Collar	33.60%
Over 64	16.40%	Some college	35.20%	Sales and Service	39.90%
		College Degree, 4 yr	14.00%	Blue Collar	26.50%
Military		Post grad	8.00%	Government	17.50%
Veteran/ Active Duty	10.60%				

2020 Pres. Vote	Trump	218,056	(68%)	Biden	96,731	(30%)
2016 Pres. Vote	Trump	196,652	(69%)	Clinton	80,045	(28%)

Gulfport/Biloxi, Hattiesburg: Coastal Mississippi has gone through several transformations in its history. French explorers founded Biloxi in 1699, before New Orleans or St. Louis, and made it the capital of an empire extending across the Rocky Mountains. Two hundred years later, rich people from New Orleans came to this section of the Gulf Coast in the summer to get away from yellow fever and to rest on Victorian verandas. Six American presidents have vacationed here. There is also a military flavor to the Gulf Coast. Biloxi's Keesler Air Force Base, one of the elite bases in the world, trains 28,000 aviators annually—with an average daily load of more than 2,700 students. Pascagoula, the largest military shipbuilder in the nation and the largest private employer in the state, is home to about 12,000 workers over 800 acres at the Huntington Ingalls Shipyard. Its gray, hangar-like buildings and skeletons of ships under construction loom over the landscape. "We manufacture war ships at Ingalls," Gov. Phil Bryant told CNBC in July 2019. "They build 70 percent of the combat vessels the Navy is sailing today." In June 2020, Ingalls got a $936 million contract to build a warship named for the late Sen. Thad Cochran, an Appropriations chairman who directed billions of dollars to the shipyard.

The region's economic growth was put on hold for several years after these coastal communities took a direct hit from Hurricane Katrina in August 2005. From Waveland to Pascagoula, about 80 miles were obliterated: Beachfront cottages, fishing villages, hotel casinos, oil-drilling platforms and refineries all were either cruelly swamped or swept away. The eye of the monster storm passed over the region, and in an instant, countless livelihoods were gone and property losses reached tens of billions of dollars. If there was a saving grace, many of the communities had a clean slate to start over, with more control over the building of high rises and strip malls that had begun to overwhelm more distinctive properties, especially in Biloxi. Condominium projects were more carefully managed, and shrimp boaters got docks for their boats and places to sell their catch.

Then, the Gulf suffered a setback with the massive BP oil spill in 2010. The huge fines from that recovery helped the state set more rigorous standards restore the coast and its facilities. In 2019-20, the new local hazard was a vast algae bloom that resulted from unusually heavy rainfall, and caused extensive damage to marine life and the seafood industry. In 2018, the Interior Department leased millions of acres off the Mississippi coast and nearby for new oil and gas development.

The heart of the 4th Congressional District is the three Gulf Coast counties—Harrison, Jackson and Hancock—which include nearly 40 percent of the population. The rest of the district's people live inland, in farm counties or around Hattiesburg and Laurel. It has long been Republican territory. A different configuration of the district gave President Richard Nixon his highest percentage of any congressional district in 1972. In 2020, the district gave 68 percent of the vote to President Donald Trump. The district, which has the smallest African-America population in Mississippi, has become the most Republican in the state.

MISSOURI

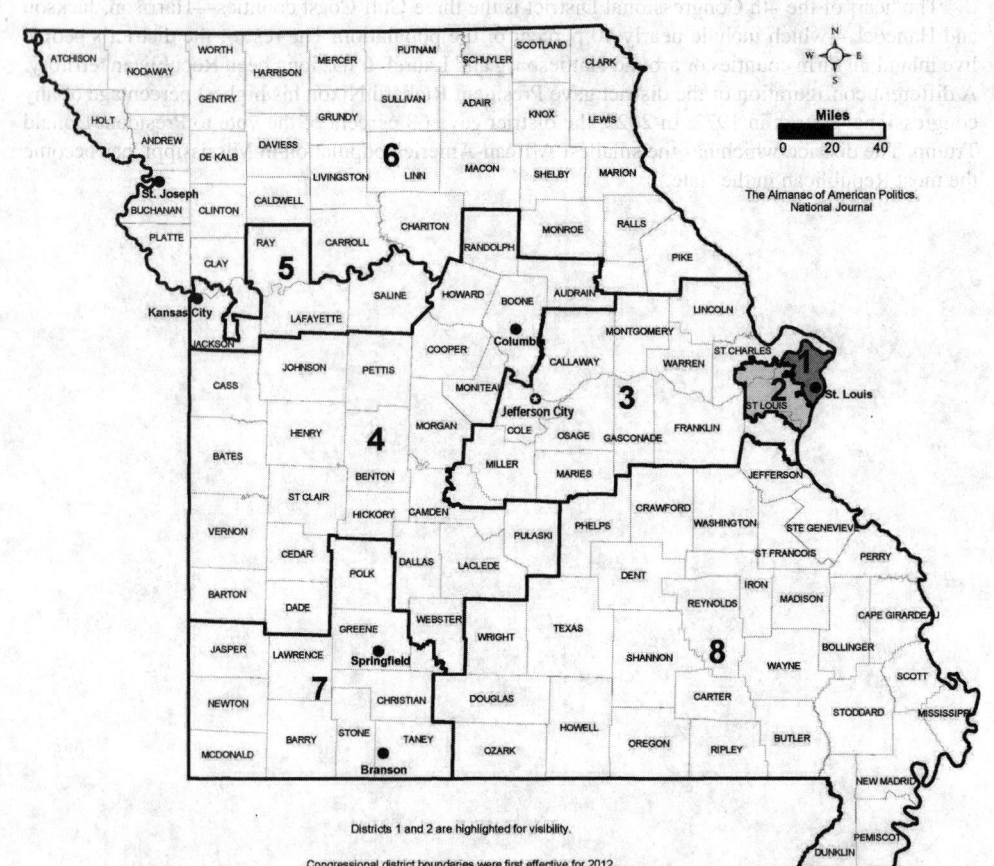

Districts 1 and 2 are highlighted for visibility.

Congressional district boundaries were first effective for 2012.

For a century, Missouri was one of America's political bellwether states. It voted for every presidential winner but one from 1904 to 2004. As recently as 2008, John McCain defeated Barack Obama by fewer than 4,000 votes in the state. But those days are gone. In 2012, Mitt Romney defeated Obama by 10 percentage points. Four years later, Donald Trump won by almost 19 points, inspiring a wave that swept Republicans into every statewide office on the ballot that year, four of them previously held by Democrats. In the 2018 midterms, Republican Josh Hawley defeated two-term Sen. Claire McCaskill, one of the last Missouri Democrats to have won statewide. Then in 2020, Trump won the state again, by the slightly narrower margin of 16 points.

The Gateway Arch, rising gracefully over the Mississippi River, is a worthy tribute to St. Louis and Missouri as the gateway to the American West, but it is no longer a gleaming symbol of vigor and prosperity. This land was part of France's thinly settled North American empire, acquired by the United States as part of the Louisiana Purchase of 1803. On May 14, 1804, at Thomas Jefferson's direction, Meriwether Lewis, William Clark and the Corps of Discovery set out from St. Louis on their expedition to the Pacific. St. Louis was then the one well-established city in America's interior, with an aristocracy of French merchants, a brawling bourgeoisie of Yankee and Southern frontiersmen and fur traders, and a proletariat of Black slaves. Statehood came in 1821, and for years thereafter the frontier democracy was a passage for westward expansion, captured in the paintings of George Caleb Bingham. West of St. Louis, new areas were settled: St. Joseph was the eastern terminus of the Pony Express; Westport, now part of Kansas City, was a starting point of the Oregon and California Trails; Independence, identified by Joseph Smith as the site of the Second Coming, was settled by Mormons who left after Gov. Lilburn Boggs ordered them "exterminated"; and Hannibal, on the Mississippi River, was where a boy named Sam Clemens engaged in pranks and watched the early steamboats he would later chronicle as Mark Twain.

Missouri was also a focus of the furious battle over slavery. It was the northernmost slave state in the 1850s, when Missouri ruffians rode across the border and killed antislavery settlers in the Kansas Territory. The state had its own bloody civil war in the hill counties along the Missouri River and in the southwest. After the war, in 1874, the Eads Bridge opened, one of the few spans on the Mississippi; St. Louis' Cupples Station was then the largest rail hub in the world. (It was razed in the 1960s to make way for the second Busch Stadium.) At the turn of the 20th century, Missouri was the fifth-largest state, and St. Louis was the fourth-largest city, site of the 1904 World's Fair and one of the few cities with two Major League Baseball teams, the Cardinals and the Browns. Missouri was also the national center of the mule trade (Harry Truman's father's line of work), an important business when half of Americans lived on farms and motorized tractors had not yet been invented.

After the 1900 census, Missouri had 16 congressional districts, twice the number it has now. In the 20th century, Americans increasingly headed toward the coasts. (Major league teams left too: baseball's Browns, who moved to Baltimore in 1954, and Kansas City's Athletics, who decamped to Oakland in 1968; football's Cardinals, who moved to Phoenix in 1988; and their NFL successor the Rams, who moved back to Los Angeles in 2016.) Missouri was the geographic center of the nation's population in the 2010 census: An imaginary, flat map of the United States population, if everyone weighed the same, would balance in Texas County. However, Missouri has seen below-average population growth since 1900, and today it is the 18th-largest state. Since the 2010 census, the state has grown just 2.8 percent. Inside its narrow 19th century boundaries, the city of St. Louis had 856,796 in 1950 and 622,000 people in 1970 but barely over 300,000 in 2019. St. Louis County, which does not include the city's population, has been pretty stable: 952,000 people in 1970 and 994,205 in 2019. The three counties around St. Louis County have grown—Franklin and Jefferson counties by about 2.5 percent since 2010 and St. Charles County by 11 percent. But one of the state's fastest-growing areas is the Lake of the Ozarks region in central and southwest Missouri, around the country music center of Branson. Taney County, which includes Branson, has grown almost 8 percent since 2010, fed (as viewers of the Netflix drama Ozark know) by an influx of modest-income retirees looking for traditional lifestyles and inexpensive recreation.

The St. Louis and Kansas City areas account for two-thirds of the state economy. Transportation manufacturing remains important, employing tens of thousands of workers at plants owned by Boeing, Ford, General Motors and the auto supply firms Yanfeng USA and TG Missouri, among others. In 2019, GM confirmed that it would invest $1.5 billion in an existing plant in Wentzville to produce midsize pickups; the move followed a state promise of $50 million in tax credits. St. Louis is home to Express Scripts, the second-largest pharmacy benefit manager in the country, as well as the investment firm Edward Jones and Enterprise Rent-A-Car. Gov. Mike Parson and his Kansas counterpart, Laura Kelly, agreed in 2019 to end poaching of businesses across their state's borders, while the Trump administration relocated two Agriculture Department research agencies to Kansas City. Still, Missouri's economy began lagging the nation's beginning in 1969, according to research by Lindenwood University economists Rik Hafer and William Rogers. Major companies native to the state—McDonnell Douglas, TWA, Ralston Purina, May Department Stores, Monsanto, Anheuser-Busch—have been acquired by outside competitors or multinationals or disappeared entirely. If the state's growth in gross domestic product had mirrored the national average over the past two decades, it would have been 30 percent bigger, representing $85 billion of lost economic activity, wrote St. Louis Post-Dispatch business columnist David Nicklaus.

Overall, the state is 79 percent White, 11 percent African American, 4 percent Hispanic and 2 percent Asian. Missouri has some tough immigration laws, even as it has attracted relatively few immigrants; barely 4 percent of residents are foreign-born. The existence of such a small minority population has profoundly shaped the state's political direction. Unlike more diverse states such as Colorado and Virginia, Missouri has not been pushed toward the Democrats by a growing minority population. Rural, conservative and largely White areas—with farms and small towns thick with churches and modest shopping centers and laced with man-made lakes and boat launches—have flexed their political muscle. Only one city outside the two big metro areas, Springfield, has a population in excess of 150,000, and in the state's rural heartland, life and politics seem not to have changed much over the past half-century. Missouri has permissive gun laws, including the right to carry a concealed weapon without a permit, and its one remaining abortion provider was almost shut down by the state Department of Health and Senior Services until a state hearing commission intervened.

Once-obscure Ferguson, a city of 20,500 in St. Louis County where two-thirds of the population is African American, attracted intense national attention when it was rocked by riots in 2014 following the shooting of an unarmed Black teenager, Michael Brown, by a White police officer who was later cleared of criminality by a Justice Department investigation. A St. Louis County grand jury had also previously declined to indict the officer. Brown's death became an inspiration for the Black Lives Matter movement, which led protests and marches in cities across the country (and which would gain wide sympathy in 2020 after Black Minneapolis resident George Floyd died in police custody). A Justice Department probe found that the Ferguson police department engaged in abusive policing. The Missouri legislature responded in 2015 by enacting a law to curb the use of traffic fines as a revenue stream to fill municipal coffers, a practice that disproportionately affected the poor and that had inflamed tensions. In 2020, Ferguson elected its first-ever Black mayor, Ella Jones, although another review of the case that year, by an elected Black prosecutor who had been critical of its initial handling, resulted in no charges for the police officer.

Historically, Missouri's political landscape was not just a mixture of urban and rural. Its Civil War political divisions still held, too, with Democrats dominant in the northeast and northwest and Republicans holding sway in the southwest and, to an extent, in the southeast. (This is the only state whose name is pronounced two ways, depending on where you're from. In metro St. Louis, they say "Mizuree." In the rest of the state it's "Mizuruh.") By 2000, however, these political patterns were fading. The large metro areas became even more Democratic, while the culturally conservative remainder of the state turned sharply Republican. For a while, the parties were in a state of balance: In the state's 10 contests for president, senator and governor between 2000 and 2008, only two were decided by wide margins. Since then, the balance has shifted to a strong GOP tilt, led by a relatively large contingent of evangelical voters and culminating in Trump's sweeping victory.

Today, the county-by-county map is a sea of red, with the Democratic presidential candidates in 2012, 2016, and 2020 winning only St. Louis city, St. Louis County, Jackson County (Kansas City), and Boone County (Columbia, home of the University of Missouri's largest campus). Equally worrisome for Democrats, seemingly strong statewide candidates—including Senate nominee Jason Kander in 2016, McCaskill in 2018, and Nicole Galloway, the state auditor and 2020 gubernatorial candidate—have consistently lost. In McCaskill's case, she was unable to make the kind of headway in suburban counties that Democrats in other states were doing in a strong Democratic election cycle, even as she lost her past support in more rural areas. In June 2021, Galloway—the only remaining statewide elected Democrat—said that she would not seek reelection nor any other office in 2022.

In 2020, Joe Biden made some marginal gains in Missouri; his vote total increased by 17 percent beyond what Hillary Clinton got in 2016, compared with less than an 8 percent increase for Trump. Biden expanded the Democratic margin of victory by three points in St. Louis City, by eight points in St. Louis County, by five points in Jackson County, and by seven points in Boone County. He also cut Trump's margins in outer portions of the two big metro areas, by eight points in St. Charles County near St. Louis, by nine points in Platte County (northwest of Kansas City), and by seven points in Clay County (north of Kansas City). Somewhat surprisingly, Biden also scored modest gains in a few more distant regions, paring Trump's margins in Greene County (Springfield) by seven points and Jasper County (Joplin) by five. Still, he lost solidly in all these places, and the concurrent race for governor showed what Missouri Democrats are up against: Galloway lost to Parson by essentially the same margins as Biden lost to Trump, even though the Democratic nominee for governor four years earlier, Chris Koster, had managed to run significantly ahead of Clinton.

The one silver lining for Missouri Democrats in recent elections has been an uncanny streak of progressive policy victories in ballot measures. In 2018, voters by a 2-to-1 margin rejected a right-to-work law; later that year, they legalized medical marijuana, raised the minimum wage to $12 by 2023, and approved an ethics and transparency measure that also overhauled the state's legislative redistricting process. Then, in 2020, voters approved a Medicaid expansion. But such wins for progressives have been the clear exceptions (and the GOP in 2020 successfully got voters to gut the redistricting measure, which tilts redistricting power back to the Republican-dominated legislature, and in 2021, Republican legislators refused to set aside any money for the Medicaid expansion). The old model for Democratic success in Missouri—a centrist approach that played well enough outside the big cities to put the party over the top when combined with a strong urban vote—is gone, likely for good.

Population		Race and Ethnicity		Income	
Total	6,137,428	White	81.80%	Median Income	57,409
Land area (sq. miles)	68,742	Black	11.50%	State Income Rank	38 out of 50
Pop/ sq mi	89.28	Latino	4.30%	Poverty Rate	12.90%
Born in state	65.90%	Asian	2.70%	With health insurance	90.00%
		Two or more races	2.80%	Cash public assistance	1.50%
Age Groups		Other	1.80%	Food stamp/SNAP	12.2%
Under 18	22.40%				
18-34	22.50%	Education		Work	
35-64	37.80%	H.S grad or less	40.40%	White Collar	38.40%
Over 64	17.20%	Some college	29.30%	Sales and Service	37.90%
		College Degree, 4 yr	18.40%	Blue Collar	23.60%
Military		Post grad	11.80%	Government	12.70%
Veteran/ Active Duty	8.50%				

Presidential Politics

2020 Primary (D)	Biden (D)	400,347(60%)	Sanders (D)	230,374(35%)			
2020 Pres. Vote	Trump (R)	1,718,736(57%)	Biden (D)	1,253,014(41%)			
2016 Pres. Vote	Trump (R)	1,594,511(57%)	Clinton (D)	1,071,068(38%)	Johnson (L)	97,359 (3%)	

From 1904 to 2004, Missouri went the same way as the nation in picking its president in all but one election, with the sole exception coming in 1956. Since 2000, Republican strength in the numerous rural counties outside the two big metros has made it more Republican than the nation, and in recent elections it hasn't even been close, ending Missouri's long run as a bellwether state.

In 2016, Donald Trump won 57%-38% over Hillary Clinton, who carried only the city of St. Louis and three of the state's 114 counties: Boone, home to the University of Missouri at Columbia; Jackson, Kansas City; and St. Louis County, the largest vote producer in the state. Joe Biden didn't do much better; Trump won by 57%-41% in 2020. The areas around St. Louis, Columbia, Kansas City and Springfield shifted left, while almost the entire rest of the state moved even further right.

Missouri provided two of the closest presidential primaries of the 2016 campaign. In the March 15 Republican primary, Trump edged Texas Sen. Ted Cruz by 1,965 votes out of more than 920,000 cast—essentially a 41%-41% tie—while on the Democratic side, Clinton squeaked out a 50%-49% victory over Vermont Sen. Bernie Sanders in which the margin was 1,574 votes out of some 630,000 cast. In 2020, Joe Biden crushed Sanders 60%-35%, making it one of a handful of solid wins that night that further cemented him as heavy favorite for the nomination one week after his Super Tuesday success. Biden carried every county in the state.

Congressional Districts

117th Congress Lineup	2D 6R	116th Congress Lineup	2D 6R

At first blush, prospects for redistricting in Missouri appear relatively straightforward. Following the 2012 redistricting, there has been no partisan change in the House delegation of six Republicans and two Democrats, with the Democrats based in the urban centers of St. Louis and Kansas City. Only the 2nd District of Rep. Ann Wagner in the St. Louis suburbs has been remotely competitive since then. With no change in the size of the delegation, plus GOP control of the governorship and the legislature, Republicans likely will seek to extend Wagner's district farther into the exurbs and exchange some parts of her district with the surrounding 3rd District of Rep. Blaine Leutkemeyer. Their two districts already share parts of Jefferson and St. Charles counties outside of St. Louis.

Other options exist if either party wants to be adventuresome. Wagner's district, instead, could become even more competitive by exchanging voters with the heavily Democratic 1st District of first-term Rep. Cori Bush in St. Louis city and county. Bush easily could sacrifice enough Democrats to threaten GOP control of Wagner's district without endangering her own prospects. But if that option is pursued, Democrats might then face jeopardy with the Kansas City-based 5th District of Democratic Rep. Emanuel Cleaver; a GOP-drawn map theoretically could place him at risk, though such a map would raise alarms among Republicans in the neighboring 4th or 6th District; each gave at least 63 percent of the vote to President Donald Trump in 2020.

For both parties, the course of least resistance might be keeping the 5th safely Democratic in a possible bargain over changes in the St. Louis area. That, in turn, would force both parties to be creative in identifying neighborhoods in the St. Louis area that have shifted in recent years or, at least as important, might change partisan direction in the next few years.

Mike Parson (R)

Assumed office in 2018, term expires 2025, 1st full term; b. Sept. 17, 1955, Wheatland; University of Maryland, Att.; University of Hawaii, Att.; Christian; Married (Teresa); 2 children.

Military Career: U.S Army, 1975-1981.

Elected Office: Polk County Sheriff, 1993-2005; MO House, 2005-2011; MO Senate, 2011-2017; MO Lt. Gov., 2017-2018.

Office: PO Box 720 Jefferson City, 65102-9500; 573-751-3222; Fax: 573-526-3291; Website: mo.gov

Lt. Gov.: Mike Kehoe (R) **Atty. Gen:** Eric Schmitt (R) **Sec. of State:** Jay Ashcroft (R)

State Legislature: Senate: 10D, 24R **House:** 46D, 114R, 3V

Election Results

Election	Name (Party)	Vote (%)
2020 General	Mike Parson (R)..	1,720,202 (57%)
	Nicole Galloway (D)..	1,225,771 (41%)

Mike Parson was elevated to the governorship of Missouri after onetime rising star Eric Greitens resigned the governorship after less than 18 months, under threat of impeachment due to a scandal in which he allegedly blackmailed a mistress using compromising photographs. Parson, a low-profile fixture in the legislature, contrasted sharply with Greitens, who had styled himself as a brash outsider. During Parson's bid for a term of his own in 2020, polls showed Democratic state Auditor Nicole Galloway within striking distance of ousting him. But in the end, the state's increasingly red hue enabled Parson to win by double digits.

Parson was raised on a farm in Wheatland and served for six years in the military police corps, including stints in Germany and Hawaii. He never earned a bachelor's degree, but he took night courses at the University of Maryland and the University of Hawaii during his Army service. Parson worked as a deputy in the Hickory County sheriff's office and then as a criminal investigator in the Polk County sheriff's office; he also bought a gas station, a farm and other real estate holdings. Parson served as the elected sheriff of Polk County from 1992 to 2004, when he won a seat in the state House and chaired the Rules Committee. He was elected to the state Senate in 2010, where he rose to majority whip. Parson's legislative achievements included an expansion of the state's castle doctrine, which ensures self-protection from intruders, and legislation that enshrined farming and ranching rights in the state constitution.

Parson initially sought the state's open gubernatorial seat in 2016, but facing a large field of GOP contenders, including Greitens, he switched to the lieutenant governor's race. In a strong Republican year, Parson won the general election, 55%-40%, against a Democratic candidate with a long Missouri pedigree—Russ Carnahan, a former congressman whose late father Mel had served as governor, whose mother Jean had served in the Senate, and whose sister Robin had served as Missouri's secretary of state. Parson won 112 of the state's 114 counties.

Greitens, a decorated Navy SEAL with stints in Afghanistan and Iraq, entered office as the first Republican governor to serve with GOP supermajorities in both of Missouri's legislative chambers. In office, the two men tended to be ideologically similar. But it wasn't long before the scandal made Greitens radioactive. The governor denied wrongdoing, but the allegations produced an indictment (the charges were eventually dropped) as well as a legislative investigation and the threat of impeachment. Greitens' aggressively anti-establishment style had already rubbed many of his fellow Republicans the wrong way, so GOP legislators were not reluctant to call for his resignation. Just a year and a half after taking office, Greitens resigned. Parson was reportedly herding cattle on his farm when he heard the news; upon taking office, he vowed a "fresh start" for the state.

After taking office, Parson signed legislation to ban marriages for 15-year-olds, a practice that had drawn the state negative attention nationally; under the new law, 16- and 17-year-olds could still marry, but only with the approval of at least one parent. The law also eliminated the statute of limitations for child abuse and for sexual offenses against minors. He signed a law that banned abortions after eight weeks, even in cases of rape or incest. Parson agreed to continue accepting refugees into the state, but he rebuffed calls by Black lawmakers to call a special session to consider legislation that would allow cities hard-hit by violence, including St. Louis, to tighten gun restrictions. By July 2020, as racial justice protests were underway nationwide, Parson did call a special session for violent crime, but with an agenda focused on supporting police rather than addressing use of force by law enforcement. Lawmakers ended up passing a bill to end St. Louis' residency requirement for police officers, which had hobbled staffing, and another to fund a witness protection program. Parson also became involved in the high-profile case of Mark and Patricia McCloskey, who drew weapons on Black Lives Matter protesters who were marching near their home in St. Louis. The couple became a conservative cause celebre, eventually speaking at the Republican National Convention, but they faced charges for unlawful use of weapons and tampering with physical evidence, to which they pled not guilty. Parson criticized the prosecution and told Fox News' Sean Hannity that "without a doubt" he would pardon them.

Meanwhile, Parson opposed a ballot initiative to expand Medicaid under the Affordable Care Act, calling it a "massive tax increase that Missourians cannot afford" in his 2020 State of the State address. A longtime ally of the governor, the Missouri Chamber of Commerce and Industry, broke ranks and supported the initiative. Despite Parson's decision to shift the timing of the vote from the general election in November to the lower-turnout primary in August, the measure narrowly passed. Like other Republican governors, Parson reopened the state relatively quickly and declined to impose a statewide mask mandate. In September, he and his wife tested positive for the virus. (Both recovered.) After a spike in cases during the fall, Missouri improved, falling to the bottom fifth of states for cases by January 2021.

Greitens, freshly cleared of any personal role in campaign-finance irregularities by the Missouri Ethics Commission in early 2020, considered challenging Parson in a primary before deciding against it. (Greitens eventually decided to run for an open Senate seat in 2022, as did McCloskey). In the general election, Parson faced Galloway, the only remaining Democrat elected statewide in Missouri. Galloway, a certified public accountant, was appointed in 2015 to the office of state auditor, a traditional stepping-stone to higher office in the state, following the suicide of Republican Auditor Tom Schweich. Galloway won a term of her own in 2018. On several issues, Galloway offered contrasts with Parson: She opposed the abortion law he had signed, backed the Medicaid initiative, and supported expanded background checks for gun sales. Galloway was considered the strongest possible Democratic candidate for the race, having carried several otherwise Republican counties in her 2018 run, including St. Charles County, near St. Louis. As Election Day neared, polls showed both the presidential and gubernatorial races narrowing, giving Democrats hope of an upset. But Parson's continuing support from President Donald Trump paid dividends, and in the end, he managed to win by 16 points, more than triple the margin Greitens had notched four years earlier. Compared with the 2016 gubernatorial race, Galloway lost ground in Jackson County (Kansas City) and Boone County (Columbia), while Parson expanded the GOP's winning margins in most counties, notably in St. Charles and Jefferson counties in metropolitan St. Louis. With continued overwhelming GOP control of both legislative chambers, Parson should have a relatively free hand to govern.

In 2021, Republican lawmakers dealt a blow to the voter-passed Medicaid expansion, refusing to set aside any money for it.

Roy Blunt (R)

Elected 2010, term expires 2022, 2nd term, b. Jan 10, 1950; Niangua, MO; Southwest Baptist University, B.A., 1970; Southwest Missouri State University, M.A., 1972; Baptist; Married (Abigail Blunt); 4 children; 6 grandchildren.

Elected Office: County Clerk/Chief Election Officer, Greene County, MO 1973-1985; MO Secretary of State, 1984-1993; U.S. House, 1997-2011; U.S. House Republican Chief Deputy Whip, 1999-2003; House Majority Whip, 2003-2007; Acting House Majority Leader, 2005-2006; House Minority Whip, 2007-2009; Vice Chair, Senate Republican Conference; Chair, Senate Rules Committee, 2015-2017, 2018-2021; Chair, Senate Republican Policy Committee.

Professional Career: H.S. Teacher, 1970-1973; Adjunct Instructor, Drury College, 1976-1982; President, SW Baptist University, 1993-1996.

DC Office: 260 RSOB 20510, 202-224-5721, Fax: 202-224-8149, blunt.senate.gov

State Offices: Cape Girardeau, 573-334-7044; Columbia, 573-442-8151; Kansas City, 816-471-7141; Springfield, 417-877-7814; St. Louis, 314-725-4484.

Committees: Senate Republican Policy Committee Chairman. *Appropriations*: Agriculture, Rural Development, FDA & Related Agencies; Department of Defense; Department of the Interior, Environment & Related Agencies; DOL, HHS & Education & Related Agencies (RMM); State, Foreign Operations & Related Programs; Transportation, HUD & Related Agencies. *Commerce, Science & Transportation*: Aviation Safety, Operations & Innovations; Communications, Media & Broadband; Consumer Protection, Product Safety & Data Security; Surface Transportation, Maritime Freight & Ports. *Intelligence. Rules & Administration (RMM)*.

Group Ratings

	ADA	ACLU	AFL-CIO	LCV	COC	HAFA	ACU	CFG	FRC
2020	-	15%		15%	-	61%	85%	-	-
2019	5%	C	21%	21%	96%	C	86%	29%	100%

Almanac Ratings 2019-2020

	Economy	Social	Foreign	Composite
Liberal	0%	0%	0%	0%
Conservative	100%	100%	100%	100%

Key Votes of the 116th Congress

1. EPA clean energy rules	N	5. Russia sanctions	N
2. U.S./Mex./Can. trade deal	Y	6. Troops in SYR, AFG	Y
3. Cut unemployment benefits	Y	7. Veto arms sales to Saudis	N
4. Shelton to Fed Reserve	Y	8. Defense $$$, veto override	Y

9. Barr as Atty. General   Y
10. Spending at the border   Y
11. Coney Barrett to Sup. Ct.   Y
12. Electoral College objections   N

Election Results

Election	Name (Party)	Vote (%)		Cand. Spent	Ind. Exp. Support	Ind. Exp. Oppose
2016 General	Roy Blunt (R)	1,378,458	(49%)	$13,690,121	$1,619,549	$15,738,323
	Jason Kander (D)	1,300,200	(46%)	$12,867,419	$6,305,759	$21,999,506
	Jonathan Dine (L)	67,738	(2%)			
2016 Primary	Roy Blunt (R)	481,444	(73%)			
	Kristi Nichols (R)	134,025	(20%)			

Prior winning percentages: 2016 (49%), 2010 (54%), House: 2008 (69%), 2006 (67%), 2004 (70%), 2002 (75%), 2000 (74%), 1998 (73%), 1996 (65%)

Republican Roy Blunt, Missouri's senior senator, is one of the few lawmakers who's risen to the leadership ranks in both chambers of Congress: He chairs the Republican Policy Committee, making him the No. 4 GOP senator. His decision to retire in 2022 could result in yet another shift in the dynamics within the Senate Republican Conference. In the last chapter of Blunt's five-decade political career, the consummate political insider and backroom deal-maker has served as a top lieutenant of Senate Republican Leader Mitch McConnell and as chairman of the Senate Rules and Administration Committee. He has also been a key player on the powerful Appropriations Committee and a loyal foot soldier for former President Donald Trump, though he split with Trump on some foreign policy and trade issues. Blunt barely survived a tough race in 2016, riding Trump's coattails and his state's strong shift toward the GOP to overcome questions about his family's lobbying work and his K Street ties.

Blunt grew up on a farm in Niangua, near Springfield in southwest Missouri. He graduated from Southwest Baptist University in 1970 and earned a master's degree there in 1972. He got his start in politics the same year, volunteering in the unsuccessful congressional campaign of Republican John Ashcroft—later governor, senator, and U.S. attorney general. In 1973, then-GOP Gov. Kit Bond named the 23-year-old Blunt as Greene County clerk. He lost a race for lieutenant governor in 1980. Four years later, he was elected Missouri secretary of state, becoming the first Republican to win that office in half a century. He served two terms and then ran for governor in 1992, narrowly losing the GOP primary. He spent four years as president of Southwest Baptist University before running in 1996 for an open House seat based in Springfield. He won with two-thirds of the vote and held the solidly Republican district for six more terms.

Blunt was one of 10 original members of then-Texas Gov. George W. Bush's presidential exploratory committee in 1999. That same year, House Majority Whip Tom DeLay, a Texas Republican, made him chief deputy whip, an important leadership stepping stone. Blunt had a reputation as a good listener with a light touch—Bush had described him as "a leader who knows how to raise his sights and lower his voice." Blunt's job was gin up support for bills for leadership. Blunt frequently met with lobbyists and organizing groups around issues like trade, taxes and energy, while raising substantial sums for GOP candidates. When DeLay replaced Majority Leader Dick Armey of Texas in 2002, Blunt took the whip post.

As whip, he met his toughest challenge in passing the 2003 bill to create a prescription drug benefit as part of Medicare. In a controversial vote in which the roll call was held open for three hours, he was able to persuade two Republicans to switch their votes. But there were rocky moments. In 2003, the House leadership was embarrassed by disclosures in The Washington Post that Blunt had quietly sought to insert into a homeland security bill a provision benefiting tobacco giant Philip Morris the previous year. At the time, Blunt was dating his future wife, then a Philip Morris lobbyist. Blunt's son Andrew, also a lobbyist, was working for Philip Morris in Missouri. Blunt defended the provision, dropped after other House leaders objected to it, as "good policy" aimed at curbing bootlegged cigarette sales. The flap came on the heels of another episode for which Blunt took heat: According to the Wall Street Journal, he was behind a last-minute effort to block a German-owned competitor of UPS—another client of his son's—from expanding in the United States.

In 2005, Blunt held two leadership posts: as acting majority leader and whip after DeLay was forced to step down when he was indicted on charges of violating election laws. Blunt ran to keep his new job as majority leader when DeLay announced he'd step down in early 2006; Blunt said he had the votes to prevail, but he faced a fierce challenge from John Boehner of Ohio. DeLay's controversies involving well-heeled lobbyists indirectly hurt Blunt, himself viewed as being cozy with K Street. Blunt led on the first ballot in the Republican Conference, coming within a half-dozen votes of the needed majority. On the second ballot, Boehner prevailed, 122-109. Blunt suffered the double indignity of losing his bid and looking like a whip who couldn't count votes.

Blunt remained majority whip and developed a smooth working relationship with Boehner. In September 2008, Boehner gave him the thankless task of negotiating the $700 billion financial bailout bill, which proved to be wildly unpopular with fellow Republicans. Blunt stepped down as whip to make way for his chief deputy, Rep. Eric Cantor of Virginia, after the 2008 elections. "Ten years of asking people to do things they don't want to do is a long time," Blunt told reporters.

Blunt had a conservative voting record, though he took occasional centrist votes on social issues. In 2006, he won passage of his Combat Meth Epidemic Act, the nation's first comprehensive approach to fighting the supply of methamphetamine. He sponsored a measure creating an internet database of federal spending, along with then-Sen. Barack Obama.

His path to the speakership blocked, Blunt saw an opportunity across the Capitol. In February 2009, Bond—who had helped launch Blunt's political career almost four decades earlier—announced he would not seek reelection, and Blunt geared up for a race to replace his mentor in the Senate. He scared off potentially competitive GOP challengers and won the primary over an underfunded tea party opponent, taking 71 percent of the vote. The state's rightward shift and a great midterm year for Republicans put Blunt in the driver's seat against Missouri Secretary of State Robin Carnahan, heir to a Democratic dynasty whose surname brought her instant name recognition. Blunt ran hard against the Affordable Care Act, a law that was toxic in that year for Democrats, and tied Carnahan to President Obama and Democratic policies unpopular with conservatives.

Carnahan tried to paint Blunt as the insider in the race. But her family ties made it a stretch for voters to see her as an outsider: Her father was a popular governor, her mother had served two years as an appointed U.S. senator and both her grandfather and brother served in the House. Carnahan sought to link Blunt to corruption, with one ad featuring a Fox News clip in which anchor Chris Wallace mentioned Blunt inserting the provision favorable to Philip Morris into the homeland security legislation. It mattered little to Missouri voters. Blunt won 54%-41%.

A tornado devastated the town of Joplin and killed 159 people just months after Blunt moved to the Senate; he pushed for a strong federal relief effort to help the battered community from his former House district. When Cantor, by then majority leader in the House, suggested that disaster relief aid should be offset with budget cuts, Blunt told Politico, "We need to prioritize spending, and this needs to be a priority."

Blunt didn't wait long to seek a Senate leadership position. In late 2011, he ran for vice chairman of the Republican Conference against Wisconsin Sen. Ron Johnson, another freshman, with the race portrayed as a battle between the establishment and tea party wings of the GOP. Despite Johnson's efforts to pitch himself as a fresh conservative face, Blunt prevailed in a secret ballot that reportedly went 25-22. His victory came shortly after Republican presidential aspirant Mitt Romney selected him as his primary liaison to win support from House and Senate lawmakers. Blunt's wife became one of the Romney campaign's "bundlers" to gather checks from other supporters. (Romney lost his presidential bid to Obama and later became a senator from Utah.)

An issue later that year was personal for Blunt: When Russian President Vladimir Putin announced in 2012 that he would ban U.S. adoptions of Russian children in retaliation for a law enabling the Obama administration to target Russian human rights violators, Blunt led an effort to persuade Putin to allow adoptions that had been completed. He told the story of how he and his wife had adopted a son born in a Russian orphanage in 2004.

When Republicans regained the majority after the 2014 elections, Blunt became chairman of the Appropriations subcommittee with jurisdiction over the Labor, Health and Human Services, and Education departments—giving him an influential voice in the allocation of a large portion of the federal government's domestic discretionary budget. Blunt led an unsuccessful effort to end Obama's program that gave legal protections to immigrants brought to the U.S. illegally as children and was among just five senators who opposed the nomination of Ash Carter as Defense secretary, accusing Obama of micromanaging the Pentagon without laying out a clear national security strategy to combat ISIS.

As he prepared for reelection in 2016, Blunt followed other Republican senators who veered to the right to preempt tea party primary challenges. Blunt remained the subject of grumbling among some conservative groups, although his Almanac vote ratings in 2015 pegged him as the fifth most conservative Senate Republican. In the GOP primary, he got 73 percent of the vote against three challengers.

But the real threat to his reelection was his coziness with lobbyists in a year in which voters in both parties were fed up with Washington insiders. Blunt's wife, Abigail, was the global head of governmental affairs for the Kraft Heinz Co., and had been a lobbyist for the Altria Group, the parent company of Philip Morris. Three of his adult sons were registered lobbyists, too. His oldest son, Matt, who was Missouri's governor from 2004 to 2008, was president of the American Automotive Policy Council, which represented the Big Three automakers. His son Andrew ran a Missouri-based lobbying firm, whose clients have included AT&T, American Airlines, MillerCoors and Motorola. He managed each of his father's Senate campaigns.

In the general election, Blunt faced Missouri Secretary of State Jason Kander, a politically talented 35-year-old former Army intelligence officer who emphasized his youth and service in Afghanistan while attacking Blunt's close ties with Washington and lobbyists.

Blunt's ads described Kander as "too liberal for Missouri," and he said the challenger shared the views of Hillary Clinton. Kander ran a widely viewed ad that showed him assembling a rifle while blindfolded and discussing his support for gun rights. The race remained close throughout the fall, with Kander gaining steadily in the polls. Blunt won 49%-46%, underperforming Trump by 16 percentage points. While Blunt may have been the epitome of the "swamp" that Trump spent his campaign attacking, Trump unquestionably helped him prevail.

As Senate Rules Committee chairman, Blunt officiated Trump's inauguration ceremony. That position also made him the top negotiator on overhauling Congress' notoriously weak sexual harassment payment policy. He negotiated a compromise that passed in late 2018 that required members to pay out of pocket for some settlements and court judgments instead of using taxpayer dollars.

Blunt occasionally criticized Trump but didn't often stand in his way. Blunt was one of many Republicans who criticized the Trump administration for separating migrant families at the U.S.-Mexico border, saying "separating families does not meet the standard of who we are as a country." He wasn't happy when Trump slapped trade sanctions on China but opposed other colleagues' efforts to push a bill undoing those sanctions. A member of the Senate Intelligence Committee, Blunt blasted Trump's foreign policy, warning that Russia and North Korea are bad actors that can't be trusted, and he publicly disagreed with Trump when the president claimed that Russia didn't meddle in the 2016 elections. But he canceled a hearing on a bipartisan bill to improve election cyber security, which he had claimed to support, in late 2018 after the Trump administration made clear that it opposed the bill.

While other Republicans broke with Trump for contradicting his own intelligence agents' assessment that Saudi Arabia's crown prince was behind the murder of journalist Jamal Khashoggi, a U.S. resident, Blunt defended Trump's stance. "The president's pretty different," Blunt said in early 2018, according to Roll Call. "And not necessarily in a bad way. He's getting a lot of things done."

When the novel coronavirus raised concerns about the health and safety of elderly members of Congress, Blunt said that testing would protect not only them but also the general public. But more senior congressional leaders rejected his suggestions for COVID-19 testing prior to the November 2020 elections.

Also wearing his hat as chairman of the Senate Rules Committee, Blunt rejected calls to remove Confederate statues from the Capitol. He cited the long-standing agreements that congressional officials had with leaders of the states on placement of those statues, indicating that each state had the authority to make such decisions. But Blunt joined the consensus that Confederate names and symbols should be removed from military bases—an action that was included in the military spending bill later in 2020.

In March 2021, Blunt announced that he would not seek reelection in 2022. He joined a large group of senators from the GOP's establishment wing who decided to step down during that cycle. His decision came after former Gov. Eric Greitens had made initial moves to challenge Blunt, while embracing Trump and his rhetoric. Likewise, Blunt found himself in growing disagreement with Josh Hawley, the junior senator from Missouri and a hard-line supporter of Trump. Missouri's red shift—and Democrats' limited bench strength—made the GOP the early favorite to hold the seat, though some Republicans worried about the prospect of a bloodbath in their primary and about the nomination possibly going to Greitens, who resigned under pressure as governor in 2018 amid a sex scandal and while facing hostility from other GOP officials. In addition to Greitens, state attorney general Eric Schmitt was an early GOP candidate for the seat. As multiple House members considered a bid, Rep. Vicky Hartzler was the first who entered the contest.

Josh Hawley (R)

Elected 2018, term expires 2024, 1st term, b. Dec 31, 1979; Springdale, AR, AZ; Stanford University, A.B., 2002; Yale Law School, J.D., 2006; Evangelical; Married (Erin Morrow); 2 children.

Elected Office: MO Attorney General 2016-2018.

Professional Career: Judicial Clerk, Judge Michael W. McConnell, 2006-2007; Judicial Clerk, Chief Justice of the United States John Roberts, United States Supreme Court, 2007-2008; Attorney, Hogan Lovells LLC, 2008-2011; Of Counsel, Becket Fund for Religious Liberty, 2011-2015; Founder/President, Missouri Liberty Project, 2014-2015; Associate Professor, University of Missouri School of Law.

DC Office: 212 RSOB 20510, 202-224-6154, hawley.senate.gov

Committees: *Armed Services*: Airland; Emerging Threats & Capabilities; Personnel; Seapower. *Homeland Security & Government Affairs*: Emerging Threats & Spending Oversight; Government Operations & Border Management. *Judiciary*: Competition Policy, Antitrust & Consumer Rights; Criminal Justice & Counterterrorism; Human Rights & the Law (RMM); Privacy, Technology & the Law. *Small Business & Entrepreneurship*.

Almanac Ratings 2019-2020

	Economy	Social	Foreign	Composite
Liberal	5%	11%	24%	13%
Conservative	95%	89%	76%	87%

Key Votes of the 116th Congress

1. EPA clean energy rules	N	5. Russia sanctions	Y	9. Barr as Atty. General	Y
2. U.S./Mex./Can. trade deal	Y	6. Troops in SYR, AFG	Y	10. Spending at the border	Y
3. Cut unemployment benefits	Y	7. Veto arms sales to Saudis	N	11. Coney Barrett to Sup. Ct.	Y
4. Shelton to Fed Reserve	Y	8. Defense $$$, veto override	N	12. Electoral College objections	Y

Election Results

Election	Name (Party)	Vote (%)		Cand. Spent	Ind. Exp. Support	Ind. Exp. Oppose
2018 General	Josh Hawley (R)	1,254,927	(51%)	$11,392,122	$1,666,100	$30,427,230
	Claire McCaskill (D)	1,112,935	(46%)	$36,808,683	$5,346,006	$40,544,816
2018 Primary	Josh Hawley (R)	389,006	(59%)			
	Tony Monetti (R)	64,718	(10%)			
	Austin Petersen (R)	54,810	(8%)			
	Kristi Nichols (R)	49,554	(8%)			
	Christina Smith (R)	34,948	(5%)			

Prior winning percentages: 2018 (51%)

Josh Hawley, elected in 2018, has become a fast-rising star in the Republican Party as a constitutional lawyer and staunch social conservative with clear ambitions for the 2024 GOP presidential nomination. But his role leading President Donald Trump's efforts to overturn the 2020 presidential election in Congress backfired, especially because he persisted even after Trump supporters stormed the Capitol on January 6, 2021. Hawley capitalized on Missouri's strong rightward shift to defeat battle-hardened incumbent Democrat Claire McCaskill in 2018 and become the youngest senator at 39.

Hawley was born in Springdale Arkansas. His family moved to Missouri when he was a child, and he grew up in Lexington, a small town east of Kansas City. His father was a banker and GOP activist who hosted George W. Bush while Bush was working on his father's 1988 presidential campaign. Hawley's mother was a schoolteacher. Despite being Presbyterian, his parents sent him to an all-boys Catholic school in Kansas City. Hawley went on to Stanford University, where he studied constitutional law and wrote for conservative campus publications. He interned in Washington at the conservative Heritage Foundation and connected with columnist George Will, who'd become a champion of Hawley's political career.

Hawley briefly taught high school in London after graduation before returning to the U.S. to attend Yale Law School, where he became president of the conservative Federalist Society. He clerked with a conservative appeals court judge in Colorado before landing a clerkship with Chief Justice John Roberts. There he met his wife, Erin, another Roberts clerk. During that time, he published a biography of President Theodore Roosevelt.

After a brief stint at a D.C. law firm, Hawley left to work for the Becket Fund for Religious Liberty, a nonprofit firm that works on First Amendment cases affecting faiths. There, he participated in Burwell v. Hobby Lobby, in which the Supreme Court ruled that some private companies did not need to follow Affordable Care Act requirements that their insurance plans cover birth control.

Hawley returned home in 2011 to teach at the University of Missouri's law school while keeping his job at Becket. He passed on a run for attorney general in 2012 but ran in 2016. He won by a huge margin and was the only statewide candidate to outpace Trump's 18-percentage point margin of victory in the state and became the state's first Republican attorney general in more than two decades.

Hawley promised during that campaign that he would stick around to do his job—he even ran an ad attacking "career politicians just climbing the ladder, using one office to get another." But state and national GOP leaders looking for a consensus candidate who could defeat McCaskill had other plans for him.

Republicans were desperate to avoid a replay of the 2012 campaign, in which a crowded field ——and some primary meddling by McCaskill—led to controversial Rep. Todd Akin, who self-immolated with his "legitimate rape" remarks, winning the nomination. Republican Rep. Ann Wagner had long been gearing up for a run, but her 2016 criticism of Trump made her a ripe target for a right-wing challenge, and she opted not to run. State and national Republicans turned their eyes to Hawley. Establishment-aligned Republicans, including Sen. Roy Blunt, former Sens. John Danforth and Kit Bond, former Ambassador to Belgium Sam Fox, and Senate Republican Leader Mitch McConnell, urged him to run. Even then-Vice President Mike Pence joined the effort, and Hawley launched his campaign just 10 months after being sworn in as attorney general.

Hawley at first kept Trump at arm's length, skipping an August visit from the president. His closeness to the anti-Trump Danforth had some right-wing Republicans threatening a primary. In response, Hawley met with people in Trump's orbit, including former campaign advisers David Bossie and Steve Bannon. He showed up the next time Trump visited the state—and was rewarded with a presidential endorsement. Hawley stuck to Trump for the rest of the race, and the president returned to Missouri six times to campaign for him.

As a contrast to McCaskill, who had been in politics for 36 years, Hawley was 2-years-old when she first ran for the state Legislature in 1982. He was lauded as an all-star recruit by Republicans who at the time appeared to be struggling to land strong candidates. As the race wore on, he went from hero to goat as McCaskill far outpaced him in fundraising—she ended up spending nearly $40 million to Hawley's $12 million, forcing Republican outside groups to make up the difference. Republican operatives grumbled about Hawley's work ethic as stories surfaced of him skipping GOP events, ignoring reporters—including right-wing radio hosts—and hitting the gym in the middle of workdays. Some also grew nervous he could repeat Akin's gaffe-fueled implosion when audio of him and pastors blaming human trafficking on the sexual revolution surfaced.

Whatever Hawley's missteps, they paled in comparison to then-Missouri Republican Gov. Eric Greitens, whose extramarital affair and alleged attempts to blackmail his mistress into keeping quiet threw the state party into chaos for the first half of 2018. Hawley initially said he didn't have the power to investigate Greitens, allowing Democrats to hammer him for protecting the scandal-plagued governor. Hawley later launched an investigation into Greitens' charity, infuriating the governor's remaining allies. Greitens resigned in June 2018.

McCaskill hammered Hawley on health care. As attorney general, he joined a multistate lawsuit to overturn the Affordable Care Act's requirement that insurance companies cover preexisting conditions, and McCaskill flayed him for that. Hawley responded with an ad saying his son had a preexisting condition and claiming that McCaskill was lying about his position, without saying how she was wrong.

Hawley bear-hugged Trump more than almost any other 2018 candidate. He defended the Trump administration's policy of separating immigrant and refugee families at the U.S.-Mexico border even as many other Republicans called on Trump to end the policy.

McCaskill had voted to confirm fewer Trump nominees than other red-state Democrats, including high-profile votes against Supreme Court nominees Brett Kavanaugh and Neil Gorsuch. Hawley and his allies hammered her in ads for those votes, painting her as an anti-Trump obstructionist. That argument got a huge boost in early October, when McCaskill voted against confirming Kavanaugh to the Supreme Court after an intense, polarizing battle.

McCaskill was caught between her base and wooing the conservative-leaning independents she needed to win the race. She faced blowback from liberals for an ad she ran in which a man said McCaskill wasn't "one of those crazy Democrats," and throughout the campaign she was dogged by questions about whether she were sufficiently supportive of the Black community in a state that's been roiled by racial tensions since 2014, when a white police officer shot to death an unarmed Black teenager, Michael Brown. She was caught on camera saying she "can give up a few votes in the Bootheel" in the state's rural southeast if she did well enough around St. Louis—a comment Hawley used in ads to argue McCaskill didn't care about rural Missouri.

Hawley faced one more crisis before Election Day. Reports surfaced that his political team had directed his government staff on what work to do and that government staff used personal email accounts in an apparent attempt to circumvent state sunshine laws. That wasn't enough to hurt him in the election but set off an investigation from Missouri's state auditor. In February 2020, Democrat Nicole Galloway, the auditor, concluded that Hawley may have misused state resources but that the evidence was inconclusive because Hawley and his staff frequently conducted state business on private email. Hawley attacked Galloway as politically biased because she was running for governor.

Hawley defeated McCaskill 51%-46 %, carrying 110 of the state's 114 counties. McCaskill was undone by rural Missouri's embrace of the GOP and Black voters' low turnout. In 2016, African-Americans made up 14 percent of the vote. In 2018, according to exit polls, they made up 8 percent.

While Hawley was a staunch champion of Trump on the campaign trail, he initially showed a bit of independence after being sworn in. Hawley was one of 11 GOP senators who bucked Trump and voted for a bill that would have overturned the Trump administration's decision to lift sanctions on a top Russian plutocrat close to Vladimir Putin. Hawley got a spot on the Senate Judiciary Committee, an assignment the legal expert had eagerly sought.

He moved to create his own version of Republican populism, which was largely styled on Trumpism. "His core belief is that middle-class Americans have been betrayed by elites on every level—political elites, cultural elites, financial elites," New York Times columnist David Brooks wrote in August 2020. "Corporate elites have concentrated so much power that they now crush the yeomen masses."

In economic terms, Hawley rejects the Republicans' long-standing free-market approach. "He rails against income inequality, condemns the policy deference afforded to corporations, and speaks warmly about the civic value of labor unions," the Atlantic wrote in November 2019. "He is totally comfortable citing statistics popular on the progressive left," including income disparity and wage stagnation.

Hawley has joined Democrats in railing against the power of Big Tech companies and arguing for antitrust action to restore competition to the marketplace. He has written a book, "The Tyranny of Big Tech," which was published in May 2021. "I want to draw attention to the robber barons of the modern era," Hawley said, describing the book. "This is the fight to recover America's populist democracy." Speaking to a conference sponsored by the Wall Street Journal in October 2020, he advocated an antitrust suit against Google and perhaps against Facebook. "Consumers ought to have more control over their data," he said.

Hawley has taken a hard-line approach on social issues and was critical of Trump's judicial picks for not sufficiently sharing religious and conservative values on issues such as abortion and the rights of gay and transgender people. In February 2019, he questioned the conservative views of Neomi Rao, a Trump nominee to the U.S. Court of Appeals for the D.C. Circuit, though he ultimately voted for her confirmation. Some conservative activists criticized his initial ambivalence.

During his first two years in the Senate, Hawley stirred the most attention—and criticism—when he led GOP efforts in Congress to oppose the certification of Pennsylvania's Electoral College votes for Joe Biden. He incorrectly contended that the state "failed to follow" its own election laws, and he also criticized the "unprecedented" interference in the election by Big Tech companies such as Facebook and Twitter without evidence. He pushed for a vote even after rioting Trump supporters in the Capitol delayed the certification process; the Senate defeated Hawley's motion 92-7, and the House defeated a similar motion 282-138. Separate objections to the vote for Arizona also were defeated. A widely circulated photo of Hawley taken that day showed him walking across the Capitol plaza, raising a clenched fist in apparent solidarity with Trump supporters—before they turned violent and deadly.

Hawley's objections to the Pennsylvania vote stirred widespread opposition. Simon and Schuster, which was scheduled to publish his book about Big Tech, cancelled those plans. The company said that it "cannot support Sen. Hawley after his role in what became a dangerous threat." Hawley threatened legal action, though he made a deal a few days later with Regnery, a conservative publisher, to issue his book. Former Sen. Danforth, who had been an enthusiastic advocate of Hawley in the Missouri Senate contest, said that support was "the worst mistake I ever made in my life." In response, Hawley repeated his earlier defense that congressional Democrats had raised similar objections to the results of previous elections and that he was responding to public demand for a review of the election results. Missourians "want Congress to take action to see that our elections at every level are free, fair, and secure. They have a right to be heard in Congress," he wrote.

Cori Bush (D)

Elected 2020, 1st term, b. Jul 21, 1976; St. Louis, MO; Harris-Stowe State University; Lutheran School of Nursing; Christian - Non-Denominational; Divorced; 2 children.

Professional Career: Registered Nurse, St. Louis University Hospital, 2008-2011; Nursing Supervisor, Hopewell Health Center, Inc.; Radio host.

DC Office: 563 CHOB 20515, 202-225-2406, Fax: 202-226-3717, bush.house.gov

State Offices: St. Louis, 314-955-9980.

Committees: *Judiciary*: Crime, Terrorism & Homeland Security. *Oversight & Reform*: Subcommittee on Economic & Consumer Policy; Subcommittee on Environment.

Election Results

Election	Name (Party)		Vote (%)	Cand. Spent	Ind. Exp. Support	Ind. Exp. Oppose
2020 General	Cori Bush (D)	249,087	(79%)	$1,323,350	$160,031	$20,849
	Anthony Rogers (R)	59,940	(19%)			
	Alex Furman (L)	6,766	(2%)			
2020 Primary	Cori Bush (D)	73,274	(49%)			
	Lacy Clay (D)	68,887	(46%)			
	Katherine Bruckner (D)	8,850	(6%)			

Cori Bush, a liberal activist and enthusiastic supporter of the Black Lives Matter movement, won the Democratic primary in 2020 against a 20-year incumbent in a rematch of their contest two years earlier. National liberal groups backed her as a prominent challenger seeking to place a more liberal stamp on a solidly Democratic district. She defeated Rep. William Lacy Clay, who had a prime legislative niche in setting the nation's housing policy. With his father, Bill Clay, they had represented the St. Louis district since 1969.

A native of St. Louis, Bush received her diploma as a registered nurse from the Lutheran School of Nursing and later became nursing supervisor at the Hopewell Health Center, both in St. Louis. As a medic, Bush treated victims of the street violence that resulted in August 2014, following a theft at a local convenience store in nearby Ferguson. Michael Brown, a Black teenager, was fatally shot by a white police officer during those events.

Bush turned to politics with the theme that, as a mother of two who earlier lived with them in a homeless shelter, "I understand the struggle of our communities because I've lived them myself." After serving as an active supporter of Sen. Bernie Sanders in the presidential primary in 2016, she launched her own campaign that year for the Democratic nomination for a Senate seat. She got 13 percent of the vote and finished second among four candidates in the contest that Jason Kander won with 70 percent; he lost that general election to Sen. Roy Blunt, 49%-46%.

In 2018, she challenged Clay with criticism that he and other local Democratic officials had failed to support the protests. "We've suffered while complacent leaders line their pockets with corporate contributions," she said, referring to Clay. Although Clay had been challenged in a redistricting-forced primary in 2012 by a White Democrat who represented a suburban district, his contest with Bush was the first serious challenge to Clay from another African American since he was first elected in 2000. Though outspent 4-to-1, she held Clay to a 57%-37% victory; she got 43 percent of the vote in the city of St. Louis, which cast two-fifths of the total vote, but trailed badly in outlying St. Louis County.

Following that setback, Bush was featured in a Netflix documentary film, Knock Down the House, that profiled insurgent challengers to House Democrats. As she continued her campaign efforts, she won the backing of national liberal groups. Justice Democrats, which was a prime supporter of Rep. Alexandria Ocasio-Cortez in her 2018 primary victory over Rep. Joe Crowley in New York, gave logistical support, though Ocasio-Cortez did not take sides in the Missouri contest.

Clay won endorsements from several Democratic allies, including the Progressive Caucus and Planned Parenthood. Members of the Congressional Black Caucus continued their practice of supporting incumbents, voicing objections when Sanders again endorsed Bush and joined her in online campaign events.

With more robust fundraising for the 2020 Democratic primary, Bush spent about $500,000, while Clay spent $1 million. Justice Democrats spent $150,000 on her behalf. Bush won, 49%-46%, with a more evenly balanced 51 percent of the vote in the city and 46 percent in the county. In her victory statement, Bush said her supporters had become a "mass movement united in demanding change, in demanding accountability, in demanding that our police, our government, our country recognize that Black lives do indeed matter."

Although three other House Democrats from urban areas were defeated by African-American challengers in primaries in 2018 and 2020, Clay became the first Black Caucus incumbent to lose such a contest. In the House, Bush got seats on the Judiciary and Oversight and Reform committees.

MO-1: St. Louis

Cook Partisan Voting Index: D+29

Population		Race and Ethnicity		Income	
Total	727,772	White	42.50%	Median Income	$50,163
Land area (sq. miles)	225	Black	49.00%	District Income Rank	387
Pop/ sq mi	3,229.38	Latino	3.60%	Poverty Rate	16.40%
Born in State	67.90%	Asian	3.50%	With health insurance	90.30%
		Two or more races	2.90%	Cash public assistance	1.90%
Age Groups		Other	2.10%	Food stamp/SNAP	15.60%
Under 18	21.70%				
18-34	26.80%	**Education**		**Work**	
35-64	36.80%	H.S grad or less	36.70%	White Collar	40.40%
Over 64	14.60%	Some college	29.60%	Sales and Service	40.20%
		College Degree, 4 yr	18.30%	Blue Collar	19.30%
Military		Post grad	15.20%	Government	10.50%
Veteran/ Active Duty	6.60%				

2020 Pres. Vote	Biden	257,909	(80%)	Trump	58,280	(18%)	
2016 Pres. Vote	Clinton	246,107	(77%)	Trump	60,136	(19%) Johnson	7,948 (3%)

St. Louis City, County: For a century or more, St. Louis seemed the center of America: the starting point for the Lewis and Clark expedition in 1804, the locus half a century later of the Dred Scott slavery case, and the site of the 1904 World's Fair, which introduced the hotdog and the ice cream cone and got 19 million people to Meet Me in St. Louis. Its 630-foot-high

Gateway Arch is just below the point where the waters of the Missouri flow into the Mississippi, about halfway between Lake Superior and New Orleans, between the Atlantic and the Pacific. This was the first major American city west of the Mississippi River and, for many years, Chicago's rival as the transportation hub of America. It was a heavily German city, with a Teutonic solidity and orderliness that distinguished it from the surrounding Southern-accented rural terrain. From Mitteleuropa came the founders of St. Louis's great businesses—the Anheuser-Busch brewery, May Company department stores, Joseph Pulitzer's St. Louis Post-Dispatch—and its first great politician, Carl Schurz, the senator and Interior secretary. There is almost a European aura to Forest Park, the site of the 1904 fair, and the mansion-lined private streets nearby.

St. Louis no longer occupies as central a place in the national consciousness and the central city itself has largely emptied out. It has dropped below Denver as the 20th largest metro area in the nation. The German order that made so many people comfortable living in close quarters and commuting by streetcar has yielded to an American desire for suburban spaces and the less restrictive automobile. St. Louis' population peaked at 856,000 in 1950; now it is at its lowest level since the late 19th century —294,890 in 2020, an 8 percent decrease from 2010. In recent years, downtown St. Louis has been spruced up. A new Busch Stadium opened with a panoramic view of the Arch and downtown. The national park surrounding Gateway Arch was refurbished, as a section of Interstate 44 was covered over and the accompanying museum was expanded to provide a more complete portrait of St. Louis' significance. Still, the life of the city continued to struggle. Local icon Anheuser-Busch was taken over by Belgium-based Inbred. The corporate offices and factory operations have remained along the Mississippi just south of the Arch, though the worldwide headquarters are in Belgium and a U.S. commercial strategy office has shifted to New York City. The city suffered a civic blow, though it may have avoided a ruinous financial deal, when the St. Louis Rams of the National Football League returned to Los Angeles in 2016 after the city refused the team owner's demand for a new stadium. In 2018, USA Today ranked St. Louis the third-worst city in which to live, behind Detroit and Flint Michigan.

About 10 miles up Interstate 70 from the Arch is the suburb of Ferguson, which became a center of riots and heated discussion of police practices following the shooting death in August 2014 of Michael Brown, an unarmed 18-year-old, by police officer Darren Wilson. A short time earlier, Brown and a friend had been videotaped in a local convenience store, apparently stealing cigars. The next day, the county police chief said Brown had assaulted Wilson. Ferguson (pop. 20,525), which is 68 percent African-American, the minority white population had managed to keep control of the local government and the police department. As details of Brown's death spread, there were growing protests and then riots in the streets of Ferguson, with police using tear gas and arresting dozens of persons. In July 2020, nearly six years after Brown was killed, a new county prosecutor reviewed the case and decided that there was no basis for charging Wilson, who had left the police department.

News accounts described how several municipalities in St. Louis County, including Ferguson, had profited from poverty and from police and court actions that resulted from often petty offenses, which added to the economic and social dislocation. In 2015, a panel of outside experts working with the Justice Department found persistent racial bias by Ferguson authorities, who had used arrest warrants to raise large sums for the operation of the city. The city agreed to major changes in local laws and police practices. In June 2020, Ella Jones was elected mayor of Ferguson—the first Black and the first woman to hold that position. She pledged to make more changes in local governance. Many residents have told outside reporters that racism remains prevalent in Ferguson, though those earlier protests have been educational in the national debate.

The 1st District takes in all of St. Louis, plus about two-fifths of the people in suburban St. Louis County. It includes all of the predominantly African-American suburbs north of the city, including Ferguson, plus Bellefontaine Neighbors, Spanish Lake and Black Jack. It includes working-class St. Ann, part of Bridgeton and, west of the city, the affluent suburb of University City. African Americans, a 49 percent plurality in the district, account for far more than half the votes in Democratic primaries. Given that the population of St. Louis city is 46 percent Black, the portion of the district that is in St. Louis County has a slight Black majority. Overall, the county is 25 percent Black. The 1st is heavily Democratic, although the party organization has been weakened by the loss of patronage and by state approval of term limits. Joe Biden got 80 percent—the same as President Barack Obama in 2012 and better than Hillary Clinton's 77 percent in 2016.

Ann Wagner (R)

Elected 2012, 5th term, b. Sep 13, 1962; St. Louis, MO; Cor Jesu Academy, 1980; University of MO, B.S., 1984; Roman Catholic; Married (Raymond T. Wagner Jr.); 3 children.

Professional Career: Manager, Hallmark Cards; Manager Ralston Purina; MO Director, George H. W. Bush reelection campaign, 1992; Chair, MO Republican Party, 1999-2005; Co-chair, Republican National Committee, 2001-2005; U.S. ambassador to Luxembourg, 2005-2009; Chairwoman, Roy Blunt for Senate campaign, 2009-2010.

DC Office: 2350 RHOB 20515, 202-225-1621, Fax: 202-225-2563, wagner.house.gov

State Offices: Ballwin, 636-779-5449.

Committees: *Financial Services*: Diversity & Inclusion (RMM); Investor Protection, Entrepreneurship & Capital Markets. *Foreign Affairs*: Asia, the Pacific, Central Asia, Nonproliferation; Europe, Energy, the Environment & Cyber.

Group Ratings

	ADA	ACLU	AFL-CIO	LCV	COC	HAFA	ACU	CFG	FRC
2020	**	20%	**	24%	-	85%	80%	**	-
2019	15%	C	33%	7%	98%	C	82%	67%	91%

Almanac Ratings 2019-2020

	Economy	Social	Foreign	Composite
Liberal	25%	41%	39%	35%
Conservative	75%	59%	61%	65%

Key Votes of the 116th Congress

1. U.S./Mex./Can. trade deal Y	5. Russia sanctions Y	9. Firearms background checks N
2. First Coronavirus response Y	6. Troops in Syria Y	10. Spending at the border Y
3. HEROES Act N	7. Veto arms sales to Saudis N	11. Marijuana liberalized rules N/A
4. CASH Act Y	8. Defense $$$, veto override Y	12. Electoral College objections N

Election Results

Election	Name (Party)	Vote (%)	Cand. Spent	Ind. Exp. Support	Ind. Exp. Oppose
2020 General	Ann Wagner (R)	233,157 (52%)	$6,658,201	$112,679	$5,572,540
	Jill Schupp (D)	204,540 (46%)	$5,039,453	$3,481	$5,470,870
	Martin Schulte (L)	11,647 (3%)			
2020 Primary	Ann Wagner (R)	63,686 (100%)			

Prior winning percentages: 2018 (51%), 2016 (59%), 2014 (64%), 2012 (60%)

A former Republican National Committee co-chair and fundraiser, Ann Wagner was elected in 2012 by overpowering her opponents financially and with her political expertise. But Donald Trump's presidency turned her once-safe seat into a battleground. She spent her first several years in Congress as one of the GOP conference's biggest stars, but has turned to staking out her lane as a moderate and an architect of the party's suburban revival. Following the March 2021 announcement by Sen. Roy Blunt that he would not seek reelection in 2022, Wagner said that she was seriously considering entry into what could be a crowded GOP primary.

Wagner grew up in the St. Louis suburbs, where her father ran a carpet store and her grandfather owned a paint business. At an all-girls Catholic school, she acted in musicals, playing the female roles at all-boys' schools. Her father wanted to see his daughter get a business degree. She graduated with one from the University of Missouri, then went to work for Hallmark Cards and Ralston Purina. Her involvement in politics began in 1989 when her husband, Raymond, took a job with John Ashcroft, then governor of Missouri. She oversaw Missouri's redistricting after the 1990 census, and ran the Missouri campaign for President George H.W. Bush in 1992, which he lost both nationally and in the state. In 1999, Wagner became chair of the Missouri GOP. Both chambers of the General Assembly went Republican in 2002, for the first time in 54 years. President George W. Bush named her ambassador to Luxembourg, and for four years she rotated her family between Missouri and the tiny European nation.

It wasn't until 2012—with two of her children out of the house, the third a high school senior, and a Democratic administration she said was mortgaging her children's future—that she decided to run for office. After GOP Rep. Todd Akin launched his ill-fated bid for the Senate, she announced for his seat, quickly raising money, with substantial contributions from employees of St. Louis-based Enterprise Rent-A-Car, where her husband was an executive. Some Republicans accused Enterprise of essentially buying her the seat, but her campaign said the donations merely reflected the employees' trust in her. Initially, Wagner seemed likely to have a fight on her hands. But Republican Ed Martin, who had unsuccessfully challenged Democratic Rep. Russ Carnahan in 2010, dropped out of the race. And Carnahan, whose district had been dismantled in redistricting, decided to challenge fellow Democrat William Lacy Clay rather than run against Wagner. That left Democrat Glenn Koenen, a former food pantry executive director, who faced insurmountable odds. Wagner won, 60%-37%.

Wagner has had a conservative voting record on economic and foreign policy issues and has ranked a bit more centrist on social issues, according to Almanac ratings. As one of four House members from Missouri to serve on the Financial Services Committee, she has tended to their home state's large financial community. Outside of her committee work, Wagner has worked closely with Democratic Rep. Carolyn Maloney of New York on the issue of human trafficking. She also became a fervent supporter of paid family leave, working with first daughter Ivanka Trump and Florida Sen. Marco Rubio on a plan—which Democrats opposed—that would allow new parents to use Social Security funds to finance a leave. She screamed "yes" with glee when Trump referenced the issue in his 2019 State of the Union address.

Wagner has found roles within the House GOP. She was chosen leader of the freshman class, and became a leading recruiter of candidates by the National Republican Congressional Committee. When Rep. Steve Scalise of Louisiana became whip in June 2014, he selected Wagner as one of five senior deputy whips. She had become politically close to Scalise since her 2012 campaign, when he subbed at a campaign appearance for her on the day after her father died. Wagner spent much of the 2014 cycle dedicated to recruiting female Republican candidates. (That effort yielded mixed success, but a similar effort in 2020 yielded better results.) After she decided not to run in 2016 for chairwoman of the NRCC, she became vice chair for fundraising. She again considered running for the top position after the 2018 midterms, only to back down after it became clear that Minority Leader Kevin McCarthy did not support her, according to The New York Times.

She initially was reelected easily, though her victory in 2016 fell to 59%-38% against lightly financed Democrat Bill Otto. Following the release of the controversial Access Hollywood video in October 2016, she withdrew her endorsement of Donald Trump and said Mike Pence should replace him at the top of the ticket. A few days before the election, she said she would vote for Trump. Following the election, she said she looked forward to working with him. After much speculation, Wagner decided against challenging Sen. Claire McCaskill in 2018 and deferred to Josh Hawley. She finished that cycle with a narrow 51%-47% win over Democrat Cort VanOstran. Wagner outspent the challenger, $4.2 million to $2.3 million.

Her reelection in 2020 was hotly contested. Wagner refocused her efforts on reviving the GOP's Suburban Caucus that had laid dormant for nearly a decade. The group aimed to craft proposals that appeal to that demographic, such as health care and traffic relief. "We cannot be the majority party if we are going to be a party that appeals only to rural America," Wagner told the Washington Post.

After VanOstran passed on another run in 2020, Democrats found a solid recruit in state Sen. Jill Schupp, who in 2014 defeated Jay Ashcroft, son of the former governor and senator, for her state Senate seat by fewer than 2,000 votes. Neither Wagner nor Schupp faced primary competition and both stockpiled cash. Wagner spent $6.7 million to Schupp's $5 million. The national parties and their allies spent more than $10 million on the contest.

As Democrats cast the contest as a referendum on Trump, it became clear to both parties that the president was not polling well in the district. Wagner ran three TV ads that used footage of Joe Biden, warning voters that even the Democratic presidential nominee thought Schupp was too liberal for the district. She accused Schupp of wanting to "Defund the Police" and socialize medicine. Trump barely edged Biden in the district, but didn't fare as poorly as both parties anticipated, and voters didn't take out their anger on Wagner. She won, 52%-46%.

Regardless of whether she decides to run for the Senate, Wagner likely will seek to use her past skills on redistricting to make her district more safely Republican.

MO-2: St. Louis   Cook Partisan Voting Index: R+4

Population		Race and Ethnicity		Income	
Total	751,926	White	88.70%	Median Income	$88,684
Land area (sq. miles)	466	Black	3.70%	District Income Rank	60
Pop/ sq mi	1,614.41	Latino	3.10%	Poverty Rate	5.10%
Born in State	64.90%	Asian	4.60%	With health insurance	96.10%
		Two or more races	2.20%	Cash public assistance	0.70%
Age Groups		Other	0.80%	Food stamp/SNAP	2.70%
Under 18	20.80%				
18-34	18.80%	**Education**		**Work**	
35-64	40.20%	H.S grad or less	23.10%	White Collar	54.10%
Over 64	20.20%	Some college	25.10%	Sales and Service	31.50%
		College Degree, 4 yr	29.60%	Blue Collar	14.40%
Military		Post grad	22.20%	Government	9.40%
Veteran/ Active Duty	6.70%				

2020 Pres. Vote	Trump	222,464	(49%)	Biden	222,349	(49%)		
2016 Pres. Vote	Trump	220,727	(52%)	Clinton	177,731	(42%)	Johnson	16,078	(4%)

St. Louis County, suburbs: Just as the geographic center of U.S. population has moved west from St. Louis to rural Texas County, so has the center of metropolitan St. Louis moved farther west from the Gateway Arch on the Mississippi River. Now the midpoint is suburban St. Louis County, established in 1876 when the city, tired of paying for dusty back roads, separated itself from the sticks. That year, there were 350,000 people in the city and 31,000 in the county. In 2019, there were about 301,000 in the city and 1 million in St. Louis County. The area's office center is fast moving out along the Daniel Boone Expressway (U.S. 40) to Chesterfield. Near the city-county border is Grant's Farm, where Ulysses S. Grant lived in the 1850s and where Anheuser-Busch bred the Budweiser Clydesdales.

The 2nd Congressional District of Missouri consists of central and western St. Louis County, part of St. Charles County across the Missouri River, and a small sliver of Jefferson County to the south. Along the expressway, in the center of St. Louis County, are long-settled suburbs: Kirkwood, LaDue, and high-income Town and Country, where one-acre lots for sale remain common. In Chesterfield, Pfizer broke ground for a new research campus and by spring 2020 its development facilities were preparing to help manufacture a coronavirus vaccine. Meanwhile, Area Development, a facility planning firm, highlighted Chesterfield as a hotspot for company relocations. But Bayer announced it would eliminate 4,200 jobs, a result of its acquisition of the Creve Coeur-based Monsanto biotech company. Chesterfield has the most expensive housing in the area, and upscale shopping. Ballwin is a growing center for immigrants with biotech and health care jobs. For the district, more than four-fifths of the population is in St. Louis County, which has had a big increase in racial minorities. But they are mostly in the 1st District. The 2nd is 87 percent White. St. Louis County has a new district attorney: Wesley Bell, a former councilman from nearby Ferguson, defeated longtime county prosecutor Robert McCulloch in a 2018 primary. McCulloch became a focal point of criticism for his handling in 2014 of a police shooting that led to riots in Ferguson.

These have been historically Republican areas, more so in the newer family-oriented subdivisions than in the leafy precincts of the older enclaves. Fast-growing St. Charles County, where the supply of available land and affordable housing has tightened, has more people and casts more votes than the city of St. Louis, though its Republican vote has become smaller than in the more outlying counties of the St. Louis exurbs. This district voted for Donald Trump in 2016, 52%-42%, a five-point decline from Mitt Romney's performance in 2012. In 2020, that margin dropped to less than one percentage point. Of the six Republican-held districts in Missouri, this is the most suburban, wealthiest and best-educated, and the only one where the Trump vote was below 63 percent in both 2016 and 2020. Suburban St. Louis has become a growing problem for GOP officials, who likely will attempt to make the district a more reliably performing seat for them in the upcoming redistricting.

Blaine Luetkemeyer (R)

Elected 2008, 7th term, b. May 07, 1952; Jefferson City, MO; Lincoln University, B.A., 1974; Catholic; Married (Jackie Luetkemeyer); 3 children; 4 grandchildren.

Elected Office: MO House, 1999-2005.

Professional Career: Bank examiner, State of MO, 1974-1976; Loan officer, Bank of St. Elizabeth, 1978-2008; President, Luetkemeyer Ins. Agency, 1978-2008; Director, MO div. of tourism, 2007-2008.

DC Office: 2230 RHOB 20515, 202-225-2956, Fax: 202-225-5712, luetkemeyer.house.gov

State Offices: Jefferson City, 573-635-7232; Washington, 636-239-2276; Wentzville, 636-327-7055.

Committees: *Financial Services*: Task Force on Financial Technology. *Small Business (RMM)*.

Group Ratings

	ADA	ACLU	AFL-CIO	LCV	COC	HAFA	ACU	CFG	FRC
2020	**	15%	**	5%	-	74%	80%	**	-
2019	10%	C	38%	7%	86%	C	80%	54%	91%

Almanac Ratings 2019-2020

	Economy	Social	Foreign	Composite
Liberal	25%	16%	34%	25%
Conservative	75%	84%	66%	75%

Key Votes of the 116th Congress

1. U.S./Mex./Can. trade deal	Y	5. Russia sanctions	Y	9. Firearms background checks N
2. First Coronavirus response	Y	6. Troops in Syria	N	10. Spending at the border Y
3. HEROES Act	N	7. Veto arms sales to Saudis	N	11. Marijuana liberalized rules N
4. CASH Act	N	8. Defense $$$, veto override	Y	12. Electoral College objections Y

Election Results

Election	Name (Party)	Vote (%)		Cand. Spent	Ind. Exp. Support	Ind. Exp. Oppose
2020 General	Blaine Luetkemeyer (R)	282,866	(69%)	$1,348,365		
	Megan Rezabek (D)	116,095	(29%)			
	Leonard J. Steinman II (L)	8,344	(2%)			
2020 Primary	Blaine Luetkemeyer (R)	80,627	(75%)			
	Brandon Wilkinson (R)	15,901	(15%)			

Prior winning percentages: 2018 (65%), 2016 (68%), 2014 (68%), 2012 (64%), 2010 (77%), 2008 (50%)

Republican Blaine Luetkemeyer, first elected in 2008, once worked in the banking business and has been an assertive conservative advocate of the industry on the Financial Services Committee, where he was a leading player in the GOP rollback of banking regulations in 2017-18. He has moved up the seniority ladder and could be positioned before long to take over the top GOP post on the panel. In 2021, he became the senior Republican on the Small Business Committee.

Luetkemeyer has Missouri roots that stretch back five generations. He grew up in St. Elizabeth, where his father worked as an insurance agent and then owned a bank. Luetkemeyer was a star high school baseball player, but his Major League tryouts were unsuccessful. He graduated from Lincoln University, a historically Black college in Jefferson City, with a degree in political science. He and his wife settled on his great-grandfather's farm in St. Elizabeth. In addition to farming, he joined his family's banking operations and founded the Luetkemeyer Insurance Agency. He was elected in 1999 to the state House, where he was an active legislator. He campaigned for Missouri treasurer in 2004 but lost in the Republican primary. In 2007, Luetkemeyer was appointed director of the Missouri Division of Tourism.

The House seat opened when Republican Rep. Kenny Hulshof ran unsuccessfully for governor. Luetkemeyer was the Republican favorite in a five-way GOP primary. The conservative anti-tax group Club for Growth endorsed GOP state Rep. Bob Onder, but Luetkemeyer gained a critical endorsement from Missouri Right to Life. He led the field with 40 percent to 29 percent for Onder. In the general election, he faced state Rep. Judy Baker, a health care consultant from Columbia. Luetkemeyer emphasized his farming background. He raised $2.8 million, two-thirds of it his own money; Baker raised $1.7 million. Baker carried populous Boone County (Columbia), but Luetkemeyer took the rural counties and those west of St. Louis. In a Democratic year, he won 50%-47.5%.

Luetkemeyer dismissed President Barack Obama's economic stimulus as a "large-scale failure." He successfully amended a House-passed bill in 2011 to bar the United States from contributing to the United Nation's Intergovernmental Panel on Climate Change, which he said engaged in "dubious science." On the Financial Services Committee, Leutkemeyer scorned the Democrats' Dodd-Frank Wall Street reform law as detrimental to small banks. The regulations, he said, had led to "unintended" restrictions of some small and mid-sized banks. In a speech to bankers, he called Massachusetts Democratic Sen. Elizabeth Warren the "Darth Vader of the financial services world." (She replied that she saw herself "more as a Princess Leia type.")

He and Democratic Rep. David Scott of Georgia enacted a bill in 2012 eliminating the physical fee-warning notices on automatic-teller machines in favor of having them displayed on-screen. He organized conservative support for the reauthorization of the Export-Import Bank, which many on the right opposed as corporate welfare. In February 2019, he opposed calls to give the rapidly growing marijuana business access to federally chartered banks. Asserting that Congress must first legalize the weed, he said that the proposal was "putting the cart before the horse."

As Housing Subcommittee chairman in 2015-16, Leutkemeyer worked closely with Democratic Rep. Emanuel Cleaver of Missouri to enact what he called "comprehensive legislation which represents real reforms to our nation's housing programs." He was especially unhappy with what he saw as inadequate funding of the mutual mortgage insurance fund, which he said might require another bailout. In 2016, the House passed his bill to end the Obama administration's Operation Choke Point, which was designed to investigate consumer fraud but allegedly had terminated legitimate banking accounts that had supported industries such as guns and tobacco that the administration disliked.

In 2017, Luetkemeyer became chairman of the Financial Institutions and Consumer Credit Subcommittee, where he said his goal was to "to ensure all Americans have access to the tools they need to reach financial independence." Working with the Trump administration, he used that position to reduce Dodd-Frank coverage and regulations. Because of resistance in the Senate, plus that chamber's 60-vote requirement to force most legislative action, "you can only do rifle shots that are very narrow in focus," he told Politico. He failed to achieve his goal of reining in the Consumer Financial Protection Bureau with management by a multi-member commission rather than by a single administrator, though the Supreme Court later ruled against the CFPB's organization.

He remained mostly positive about President Donald Trump, including his use of tariffs. "The Chinese have been the bullies of trade and dumping poor products here for years," Leutkemeyer told a local newspaper in 2018. "We are trying to push back." Two weeks prior to the mid-term election, he told the St. Louis Post-Dispatch that congressional Republicans needed to defer to Trump. "His popularity as a whole is a lot better than what Congress's is. ... So therefore [he] sets the agenda." Republicans lost 40 House seats.

At a July 2020 Financial Services hearing with Dr. Anthony Fauci, the nation's leading infectious disease doctor, Luetkemeyer urged use of the drug hydroxychloroquine, rejecting Fauci's conclusions about the negative results of a peer review. When he took over in 2021 as the senior GOP member on the Small Business panel, he said his top priority was to assure that federal lending programs assist the recovery "without the weight of needless bureaucracy and harmful mandates."

With his business and legislative backgrounds, Luetkemeyer voiced interest in filling the vacancy for the top Republican at the Financial Services Committee, following the 2018 election. But he deferred to Rep. Patrick McHenry of North Carolina, who had more seniority plus leadership experience. With the prospect that McHenry could return to the leadership track, Leutkemeyer might have other opportunities to lead the panel. He has breezed to reelection every two years.

MO-3: East-central Missouri　　　　　　　　**Cook Partisan Voting Index: R+21**

Population		Race and Ethnicity		Income	
Total	802,919	White	91.70%	Median Income	$69,621
Land area (sq. miles)	6,852	Black	4.00%	District Income Rank	169
Pop/ sq mi	117.19	Latino	2.70%	Poverty Rate	8.20%
Born in State	73.20%	Asian	1.30%	With health insurance	92.10%
		Two or more races	2.10%	Cash public assistance	1.10%
Age Groups		Other	0.90%	Food stamp/SNAP	7.10%
Under 18	23.10%				
18-34	20.40%	**Education**		**Work**	
35-64	39.80%	H.S grad or less	39.10%	White Collar	37.30%
Over 64	16.70%	Some college	32.50%	Sales and Service	37.40%
		College Degree, 4 yr	18.70%	Blue Collar	25.30%
Military		Post grad	9.60%	Government	12.90%
Veteran/ Active Duty	9.40%				

2020 Pres. Vote	Trump	279,638	(67%)	Biden	130,963	(31%)		
2016 Pres. Vote	Trump	254,321	(67%)	Clinton	106,245	(28%)	Johnson	13,524 (4%)

St. Louis area: Missouri was the first state settled west of the Mississippi, and the folks who settled it were a picture of pioneer diversity. Virginians and other Southerners made their way to counties north of the Missouri River, while Germans settled around the small capital, Jefferson City. A taste of that diversity can be found in the capitol, with its mural by Thomas Hart Benton, great-grandnephew of one of Missouri's first senators, who championed hard money and westward expansion for 30 years and lost his seat for opposing the expansion of slavery. The painting depicts dance hall girls, black coal miners and a mother diapering an infant. Fulton is the home of Westminster College, where former British Prime Minister Winston Churchill, accompanied by President Harry Truman, told the world in 1946: "From Stettin in the Baltic to Trieste in the Adriatic, an iron curtain has descended across the continent." In the small town of Washington, Meerschaum Co. remains the largest and oldest manufacturer of corn cob pipes in the world. It has been continually operating in its brick factory since 1869 and a few decades ago, it shipped up to 25 million pipes each year. In recent years, its annual production has been less than a million pipes

The 3rd Congressional District covers east-central Missouri, stretching from Jefferson City to the western St. Louis exurbs of St. Charles and Jefferson counties, and extends like a claw to the Mississippi River both north and south of St. Louis County and city. Its population base is in the western parts of fast-growing St. Charles County, which has about one-third of the voters. In Wentzville, the General Motors plant, which has about 4,000 workers, announced in December 2019 it is building the next-generation midsize pickup truck. The local GM facility has been a boon to parts suppliers, which had been hurt by the closing of Ford and Chrysler plants in the area. With the state agreeing to provide $50 million in tax credits if the company spends at least $750 million to expand its current site, GM won the deal in competition with suitors elsewhere. Up Route 61 in Troy, Toyota said in March 2019 that it was spending $62 million at the plant where it produces more than 3 million cylinder heads each year. In Jefferson City, after years of study, the state legislature in 2020 enacted a bill to give 116 acres to the local port authority to build a Missouri River port. Local leaders contend that cargo vessels would be more efficient than barges—or trucks on local highways—in carrying shipping containers the 100 miles from Columbia to the Mississippi River.

The district is solidly Republican, with Donald Trump winning every county and getting 67 percent of the vote in both 2016 and 2020.

Vicky Hartzler (R)

Elected 2010, 6th term, b. Oct 13, 1960; Harrisonville, MO; University of MO, B.S., 1983; Central MO State University, M.S., 1992; Evangelical; Married (Lowell Hartzler); 3 children.

Elected Office: MO House, 1995-2001.

Professional Career: Teacher, 1983-1994; Spokeswoman, Coalition to Protect Marriage, 2004; Appointee, MO Women's Cncl., 2005-2010; Owner, Hartzler Equipment Co.

DC Office: 2235 RHOB 20515, 202-225-2876, hartzler.house.gov

State Offices: Columbia, 573-442-9311; Harrisonville, 816-884-3411; Lebanon, 417-532-5582.

Committees: *Agriculture*: Livestock & Foreign Agriculture; Subcommittee Nutrition, Oversight & Department Operations. *Armed Services*: Seapower & Projection Forces; Tactical Air & Land Forces (RMM).

Group Ratings

	ADA	ACLU	AFL-CIO	LCV	COC	HAFA	ACU	CFG	FRC
2020	**	17%	**	10%		76%	79%	**	-
2019	5%	C	50%	7%	85%	C	79%	70%	100%

Almanac Ratings 2019-2020

	Economy	Social	Foreign	Composite
Liberal	25%	7%	27%	20%
Conservative	75%	93%	73%	80%

Key Votes of the 116th Congress

1. U.S./Mex./Can. trade deal	Y	5. Russia sanctions	Y	9. Firearms background checks N
2. First Coronavirus response	Y	6. Troops in Syria	Y	10. Spending at the border Y
3. HEROES Act	N	7. Veto arms sales to Saudis	N	11. Marijuana liberalized rules N
4. CASH Act	N	8. Defense $$$, veto override	Y	12. Electoral College objections Y

Election Results

Election	Name (Party)	Vote (%)		Cand. Spent	Ind. Exp. Support	Ind. Exp. Oppose
2020 General	Vicky Hartzler (R)	245,247	(68%)	$1,253,933	$351	
	Lindsey Simmons (D)	107,635	(30%)	$386,148		$1,564
	Steven K. Koonse (L)	9,954	(3%)			
2020 Primary	Vicky Hartzler (R)	80,652	(77%)			
	Neal Gist (R)	24,646	(23%)			

Prior winning percentages: 2018 (65%), 2016 (68%), 2014 (68%), 2012 (60%), 2010 (50%)

Republican Vicky Hartzler, who was elected in 2010 when she defeated the Democratic chairman of the House Armed Services Committee, has created her own niche at the panel. A former activist who led the movement to ban same-sex marriage in Missouri, she retained her focus on social conservative issues, some of which are military-related. As a senior member of the Armed Services panel, Hartzler has advocated the interests of the large military bases in her district. She gave serious thought to running for the Senate in 2018 and said in early 2021 that she was definitely thinking about running for the open Senate seat in 2022.

Hartzler has spent her entire life in rural Cass County, where she grew up on the family farm. After getting her bachelor's degree in education at the University of Missouri, she worked as a high school home economics teacher for 11 years. Later, she got her master's in education at the University of Central Missouri. She and her husband, Lowell, resided on a 1,600-acre farm outside Harrisonville, where they raised corn, soybeans and cattle and ran the Hartzler Equipment Co., which sold farming equipment. Her career changed in 1994 when she got a phone call from a friend while she was grading papers, urging her to run for state representative. "He asked me to think about it and pray about it, and I did," Hartzler said. "After 30 days, I knew I was supposed to run." She served three terms in

Missouri's House, where she overhauled the state's adoption law. With the adoption of her daughter, she had a special interest in the topic.

In 2004, Hartzler headed the Coalition to Protect Marriage in Missouri, a campaign to add an amendment to the state's constitution banning same-sex marriage. Despite being outspent 17-to-1 by pro-gay-marriage groups, the amendment passed with 71 percent of the vote. She wrote the book *Running God's Way: Step by Step to a Successful Political Campaign*, a detailed guide for Christian candidates.

Her bid to unseat Ike Skelton, the 17-term chairman of the Armed Services Committee, drew the interest of tea party groups. In the conservative district, Skelton had relied on crossover GOP voters for reelection. Hartzler assailed his votes with "the liberal leadership" for the $787 billion economic stimulus bill and an energy bill imposing caps on carbon emissions. Hartzler tried to turn Skelton's image as a wise legislative elder into a negative. "So many people in Washington [are] removed from rural America. Ike's lost touch," she said. Skelton raised $3 million and outspent Hartzler 3-to-1. She won, 50%-45%.

Republican leaders made good on their promise to give Hartzler a seat on Armed Services. Using that platform to pursue social issues, she added a provision to the defense bill in 2011 defining marriage as a union between a man and a woman for the purpose of military benefits and policy. The provision was dropped in conference with the Senate. She filed a bill preventing military veterans convicted of sexual abuse of children from being buried in Arlington National Cemetery. She added an amendment to the defense bill that would have banned gender reassignment surgery for members of the military. In July 2017, after the House voted down her provision, President Donald Trump said that transgenders would not be permitted to serve in the military, due chiefly to the medical costs.

As chairwoman of the Oversight and Investigations Subcommittee, the interests of her district remained paramount. The House in 2015 approved her provision for construction at Whiteman Air Force Base of a Consolidated Stealth Operations and Nuclear Alert Facility. She took credit for approval of 12 additional F/A-18F Super Hornet aircraft. After supporting House Republican spending cuts, defense-hawk Hartzler found that the tight-budget demands of fiscal hawks can be objectionable. She opposed the New Year's Day 2013 bipartisan deal aimed at averting the so-called "fiscal cliff." In 2015, she urged Congress to end budget "sequestration" and warned that automatic cuts in Defense Department spending threatened "impending devastation to our military." In August 2020, she and Democratic Rep. John Garamendi wrote to Trump, urging action to increase domestic production of pharmaceuticals, with a goal of "ending China's chokehold."

As the ranking Republican on the Tactical Air and Land Forces Subcommittee, whose jurisdiction over Army and Air Force acquisitions meshes with the interests of her district, Hartzler achieved results in 2019-20. When Congress completed action on the annual defense spending bill in 2020, she cited steps to ensure that members of the military "have the resources they need" and that "our military installations, such as Whiteman Air Force Base, Fort Leonard Wood, and the state of Missouri, continue to play a vital role in our national defense."

Continuing her work on social issues beyond the Pentagon, Hartzler in 2015 joined the special House committee charged with investigating abortion providers, including Planned Parenthood, following the release of undercover videos about the group. Also that year, she filed a resolution to veto a law passed by the District of Columbia that would ban discrimination against LGBT students attending religious schools, which she said "infringed on the fundamental right of religious freedom." With Democratic Rep. Alma Adams, she filed a bill in May 2020 to encourage local schools to take steps to prevent eating disorders.

In 2016, Hartzler said that some comments by Donald Trump were "undefendable," but that she supported him because of the policies he advocated. After his first year as president, she praised Trump for having "really fulfilled his campaign promises," especially on abortion-related issues, including the selection of judges. When Trump suggested cash subsidies for farmers who had lost overseas markets because of his tariffs, Hartzler told reporters in 2018, "farmers want trade, not aid." But she declined to criticize. "He has an unconventional approach."

At home, Hartzler has not been seriously challenged for reelection. Following the 2016 election, she explored a challenge to Democratic Sen. Claire McCaskill. Facing daunting fundraising demands, she said, "this race is for another solid conservative to pursue and win." She was referring to state Attorney General Josh Hawley, who defeated McCaskill. In June 2021, Hartzler joined the wide-open field of GOP candidates seeking the seat of retiring Republican Sen. Roy Blunt.

MO-4: West-central Missouri

Cook Partisan Voting Index: R+20

Population		Race and Ethnicity		Income	
Total	775,664	White	88.70%	Median Income	$53,237
Land area (sq. miles)	14,401	Black	4.70%	District Income Rank	357
Pop/ sq mi	53.86	Latino	3.90%	Poverty Rate	14.80%
Born in State	63.70%	Asian	1.90%	With health insurance	88.80%
		Two or more races	3.50%	Cash public assistance	1.60%
Age Groups		Other	1.20%	Food stamp/SNAP	10.70%
Under 18	22.00%				
18-34	25.10%	Education		Work	
35-64	35.80%	H.S grad or less	44.10%	White Collar	35.10%
Over 64	17.00%	Some college	29.90%	Sales and Service	39.00%
		College Degree, 4 yr	15.10%	Blue Collar	26.00%
Military		Post grad	10.80%	Government	17.60%
Veteran/ Active Duty	11.60%				

2020 Pres. Vote	Trump	243,871	(66%)	Biden	118,042	(32%)			
2016 Pres. Vote	Trump	222,141	(65%)	Clinton	99,858	(29%)	Johnson	13,316	(4%)

Columbia: Roughly equidistant from St. Louis and Kansas City, Columbia in central Missouri has emerged as an economic hub in its own right. Nicknamed the Athens of Missouri, Columbia surpassed Independence in 2015 to become the fourth-largest city in the state, with a population that increased 13 percent from 2010 to 2019. The third-largest is Springfield, though Columbia is the fastest-growing of the 10 largest. The University of Missouri is the biggest employer in Columbia. A number of graduates have remained in the city to work in the health care and insurance industries. In 2015, allegations of racism plus multiple budget cuts led to widespread campus protests, including by its football team, and resulted in the resignation of the university president. That resulted in a decline of applications to the school, especially by African Americans, and a reduction in enrollment from nearly 35,000 in 2015 to 31,000 in 2017. In 2019, following campus reforms, the number of freshmen increased, again pushing the total slightly above 30,000. Improvements at Columbia Regional Airport more than doubled the passenger load from 2014 to 2018. In November 2020, airport authority leaders broke ground for a new terminal—in place of the current hangar for passengers—with completion scheduled for mid-2022.

The 4th Congressional District occupies Columbia and rural west central Missouri. Columbia's Boone County includes about one-fourth of the district's voters. South of Kansas City, the district includes fast-growing Belton and Raymore in ancestrally Democratic Cass County, where President Donald Trump got 65 percent in 2020. Chewy, a company that sells pet food online, announced plans in July 2020 for a fulfillment center in Belton that would employ 1,200 workers. There are two big military bases here: Fort Leonard Wood in Pulaski County, where Marines, sailors and airmen train in joint exercises with Army troops; and Whiteman Air Force Base, near Knob Noster in Johnson County, from which B-2 stealth bombers have flown to drop precision-targeted bombs in Afghanistan. The Air Force has upgraded its B-2 fleet, of which 20 are based at Whiteman. That total fleet is scheduled to be replaced in the late 2020s by the new B-21 Raider bombers. Whiteman will be one of three domestic bases for the plane.

The district overall has become safely Republican, despite its Democratic heritage. Like other non-urban parts of Missouri, Trump scored a big increase in Republican support in the 4th, to 66%-32% in 2020. In each of his campaigns, he lost Boone County by a slender margin. It was one of just three counties he lost statewide.

Emanuel Cleaver (D)

Elected 2004, 9th term, b. Oct 26, 1944; Waxahachie, TX; Murray State College, Att., 1964; Prairie View Agricultural and Mechanical University, B.S., 1972; St. Paul School of Theology, KS City, M.Div., 1974; Methodist; Married (Dianne Cleaver); 4 children (twins); 3 grandchildren.

Elected Office: Kansas City Council, 1979-1991; Mayor, Kansas City, 1991-1999.

Professional Career: Pastor, 1970-present; Radio talk-show host, 2002-2004.

DC Office: 2335 RHOB 20515, 202-225-4535, Fax: 202-225-4403, cleaver.house.gov

State Offices: Higginsville, 660-584-7373; Independence, 816-833-4545; Kansas City, 816-842-4545.

Committees: *Financial Services*: Housing, Community Development & Insurance (RMM); Housing, Community Development & Insurance (Chmn); Investor Protection, Entrepreneurship & Capital Markets; Investor Protection, Entrepreneurship & Capital Markets; Nat'l Security, International Development & Monetary Policy (RMM); Oversight & Investigations (RMM); Oversight & Investigations. *Homeland Security*: Border Security, Facilitation & Operations. *Select Committee on the Modernization of Congress.*

Group Ratings

	ADA	ACLU	AFL-CIO	LCV	COC	HAFA	ACU	CFG	FRC
2020	**	76%	**	86%	-	0%	4%	**	-
2019	90%	C	100%	97%	62%	C	4%	12%	0%

Almanac Ratings 2019-2020

	Economy	Social	Foreign	Composite
Liberal	58%	100%	80%	80%
Conservative	42%	0%	20%	20%

Key Votes of the 116th Congress

1. U.S./Mex./Can. trade deal Y	5. Russia sanctions Y	9. Firearms background checks Y
2. First Coronavirus response Y	6. Troops in Syria Y	10. Spending at the border Y
3. HEROES Act Y	7. Veto arms sales to Saudis Y	11. Marijuana liberalized rules Y
4. CASH Act Y	8. Defense $$$, veto override Y	12. Electoral College objections N

Election Results

Election	Name (Party)	Vote (%)		Cand. Spent	Ind. Exp. Support	Ind. Exp. Oppose
2020 General	Emanuel Cleaver (D)	207,180	(59%)	$946,532	$3,673	
	Ryan Derks (R)	135,934	(39%)	$92,701		$113
	Robin Dominick (L)	9,272	(3%)			
2020 Primary	Emanuel Cleaver (D)	75,040	(85%)			
	Maite Salazar (D)	12,923	(15%)			

Prior winning percentages: 2018 (62%), 2016 (59%), 2014 (52%), 2012 (61%), 2010 (53%), 2008 (64%), 2006 (64%), 2004 (55%)

Democrat Emanuel Cleaver, first elected in 2004, is an ordained minister who is known for his prominent role in the Congressional Black Caucus and his work on housing issues, as well as his efforts to improve civility in Congress. After voicing disappointment when he earlier failed to become chairman of the Financial Services Housing, Community Development, and Insurance Subcommittee, Cleaver in 2021 said he fulfilled his dream when he was selected to lead that panel. His objective, he said, was "ensuring that everyone has somewhere to rest their head at night in a place they call home."

Cleaver grew up in Waxahachie Texas, in a three-room shack with no plumbing or electricity. He graduated from Prairie View A&M University, moved to Kansas City and earned a divinity degree, then became pastor of St. James United Methodist Church. He was elected to the city council in 1979 and as mayor in 1991. In city hall, Cleaver voiced support for the Clinton administration's changes in welfare policy, which he described as "corrective surgery." He backed expansion of downtown's Bartle Hall Convention Center and supported renovation of the deteriorating Liberty Memorial, the country's largest World War I memorial. After leaving office, he hosted a radio talk show.

When the seat became open, Cleaver faced former National Security Council aide Jamie Metzl in the Democratic primary. Metzl hammered him on ethics issues, questioning the propriety of a loan Cleaver took out to purchase a car wash and his failure to pay $36,000 in back taxes on the business. Cleaver won the primary 60%-40%. In the general election, Cleaver faced Republican businesswoman Jeanne Patterson, who spent $3 million of her own money. Like Metzl, she made an issue of Cleaver's ethics, though there was no evidence that he was involved in any crimes. He said Patterson was politically inexperienced and was trying to buy the seat. Cleaver won 55%-42%.

In the House, Cleaver's voting record in the Almanac vote ratings placed him near the center of the Democrats. In his first term, he was one of 22 members, all Democrats, who opposed a Republican House-passed resolution expressing support for Christmas that he dismissed as a sop to social conservatives. He has sponsored bills to promote financial literacy and to make it easier for students to vote. As Speaker, Nancy Pelosi designated Cleaver to act as a liaison with mayors and faith communities.

Cleaver chaired the Black Caucus in 2011-12 at a time when members often expressed dissatisfaction with President Barack Obama for failing to do more to help low-income minorities. Cleaver tried to walk a fine line between joining in the criticism and working to ensure the reelection of the nation's first Black president. "With 14 percent [Black] unemployment, if we had a white president, we'd be marching around the White House. ... The president knows we are going to act in deference to him in a way we wouldn't to someone white," he told The Root in 2012. After the 2014 fatal police shooting of an unarmed Black teenager in Ferguson Missouri touched off riots there, he defended Obama's decision not to visit the city, even as he told MSNBC that it "resembles Fallujah" because of the militarized law-enforcement presence, which he called "un-American."

As ranking member of the Housing and Insurance Subcommittee from 2015 to 2018, Cleaver worked with Republican Rep. Blaine Luetkemeyer of Missouri, who chaired the panel. They enacted in 2016 what they described as the most significant changes in federal housing programs in a quarter-century. The measure included a streamlining of the inspection and income review process for families living in Section 8 housing, improved condo ownership opportunities and increased access to rural housing loans.

With West Virginia Republican Rep. (and now Senator) Shelley Moore Capito in 2011, Cleaver resurrected their call for a "Civility Caucus," and issued regular pronouncements stressing the importance of collegiality. "Bees cannot sting and make honey at the same time; they have to make a choice," he said. During their years in the minority, Cleaver was outspoken among Democrats who believed that they needed to change their leadership team, including Pelosi.

When Democrats took the majority in 2019, Cleaver was disappointed that Rep. Lacy Clay—also from Missouri—asserted his seniority and became chairman of the housing subcommittee. Clay's defeat in the 2020 Democratic primary to Cori Bush opened the door for Cleaver to chair that panel. When that step became official, Cleaver issued a statement, "Since coming to Congress, my only personal dream was to chair the Subcommittee on Housing. ... I know the monumental impact affordable housing can have on American families."

In June 2020, when Pelosi looked to the Black Caucus, where Cleaver has become a senior leader, to craft police reform legislation, Cleaver called it "a CBC moment." He added, "we have been placed on center stage of this American racial and justice moment." He noted, in particular, provisions in the House-passed bill to "hold police accountable in our courts by reforming qualified immunity so that individuals are not entirely barred from recovering damages when police violate their constitutional rights" and to "improve transparency by collecting better and more accurate data of police misconduct."

Cleaver stirred some unhappiness among Democrats in 2018 when he emphasized his close working relationship with Republican Rep. Kevin Yoder, who represented the district across the state line in Kansas. "A lot of Democrats ... did begin to call me and say, 'Hey, what's going on,'" Cleaver told the Kansas City Star. "They were upset." After challenger Sharice Davids defeated Yoder, Cleaver apparently had no problem working with his new Democratic colleague. He became a "mentor" to Davids, whom "he affectionately refers to as his younger sister," according to the metrostl.com website.

In 2020, for the first time in eight elections, Cleaver did not face Republican Jacob Turk. Instead, Ryan Derks, an investment manager, was the Republican nominee. As with Turk, Derks was outspent more than 10-to-1. The outcome was little changed. Cleaver won, 59%-39%. Some Republicans have called for making his district more competitive in redistricting.

MO-5: Kansas City Metro   **Cook Partisan Voting Index: D+7**

Population		Race and Ethnicity		Income	
Total	777,659	White	68.70%	Median Income	$55,239
Land area (sq. miles)	2,425	Black	21.20%	District Income Rank	327
Pop/ sq mi	320.7	Latino	9.40%	Poverty Rate	14.30%
Born in State	59.80%	Asian	1.70%	With health insurance	87.90%
		Two or more races	3.50%	Cash public assistance	2.00%
Age Groups		Other	4.90%	Food stamp/SNAP	10.40%
Under 18	22.70%				
18-34	24.20%	**Education**		**Work**	
35-64	37.40%	H.S grad or less	40.40%	White Collar	35.70%
Over 64	15.80%	Some college	30.00%	Sales and Service	39.60%
		College Degree, 4 yr	19.20%	Blue Collar	24.70%
Military		Post grad	10.50%	Government	11.10%
Veteran/ Active Duty	7.70%				

2020 Pres. Vote	Biden	208,696	(58%)	Trump	141,660	(40%)		
2016 Pres. Vote	Clinton	179,354	(55%)	Trump	130,051	(40%)	Johnson	12,098	(4%)

Jackson County: Kansas City, named after a state it isn't in and a river it doesn't touch, is the center of one of America's largest metro areas, the biggest on the central Great Plains. The first settlers here started little towns on the bluffs above the Missouri River—Independence, Kansas City, Westport—that coalesced a few decades later. Here, traders on the Santa Fe Trail passed through on their way to cross the Sand Hills of Kansas to reach Mexican territory, and pioneers headed for Oregon and California. Kansas City was a rail center and, in the 1920s, had one of the largest stockyards in the country, a major commercial center with lean skyscrapers, and the Country Club Plaza, the first drive-to shopping center in America. Harry Truman grew up on a farm now in the suburb of Grandview and lived in his wife's family's house in Independence, the old county seat just to the east. The Trump administration sought to strengthen the link between the federal bureaucracy and the nation by moving parts of the Agriculture Department to downtown Kansas City. The city is famous for its National Negro Leagues Baseball Museum, its historic jazz district that has been home to musicians like Scott Joplin, Charlie Parker and Count Basie, and for its much-praised barbecue. In 2020, the Kansas City Chiefs franchise in the NFL sought to limit the use of costumes that were most offensive to Native Americans, though the team kept the name of its team and its Arrowhead Stadium. The redevelopment downtown includes the Kauffman Center for the Performing Arts. More than 20,000 people live downtown, most of them millennials. That increase has been accompanied by a small reduction in the Black population in the city from 31 percent in 2000 to 28 percent in 2019. (Kansas City Kansas is about one-third the size of its counterpart.)

A 2.2-mile downtown streetcar, which began service in May 2016, had modest ridership. In September 2020, the local transit authority approved a 3.7 mile extension via Country Club Plaza to the University of Missouri's Kansas City campus, with half of the $350 million cost financed from increases in local sales and property taxes and the other half from a federal grant. That service was projected to start in 2025.

The 5th Congressional District of Missouri includes most of Kansas City, the largest city in Missouri, plus Grandview and the bulk of Independence. On Election Night 1948, when just about everyone thought he would lose, Truman was not far away in the resort town of Excelsior Springs. Most of the Kansas City area's landmarks, including the Truman home, are here, but much of the metropolitan area's growth has been across the state line in Kansas. About 40 percent of the voters live in Kansas City, where about four-fifths of the presidential vote is Democratic. Slightly less than 40 percent live in surrounding Jackson County, which leans a bit Republican. The remainder reside in suburban Clay County and three small counties toward the rural center of Missouri. Twenty-two percent of the district's residents are African-American, the second highest percentage among

Missouri's districts. Joe Biden got 58 percent of the vote, compared to the 55 percent for Hillary Clinton in 2016.

Sam Graves (R)

Elected 2000, 11th term, b. Nov 07, 1963; Tarkio, MO; University of MO, B.S., 1986; Baptist; Married (Lesley Graves); 3 children.

Elected Office: MO House, 1992-1994; MO Senate, 1994-2000.

Professional Career: Farmer.

DC Office: 1135 LHOB 20515, 202-225-7041, Fax: 202-225-8221, graves.house.gov

State Offices: Hannibal, 573-221-3400; Kansas City, 816-792-3976; St. Joseph, 816-749-0800.

Committees: *Armed Services*: Intelligence & Special Operations; Seapower & Projection Forces. *Transportation & Infrastructure (RMM)*: Ex Officio membership on all subcommittees.

Group Ratings

	ADA	ACLU	AFL-CIO	LCV	COC	HAFA	ACU	CFG	FRC
2020	**	18%	**	14%	-	82%	83%	**	-
2019	15%	C	30%	3%	89%	C	83%	83%	95%

Almanac Ratings 2019-2020

	Economy	Social	Foreign	Composite
Liberal	25%	4%	40%	23%
Conservative	75%	96%	60%	77%

Key Votes of the 116th Congress

1. U.S./Mex./Can. trade deal Y	5. Russia sanctions Y	9. Firearms background checks N
2. First Coronavirus response Y	6. Troops in Syria Y	10. Spending at the border Y
3. HEROES Act N	7. Veto arms sales to Saudis N	11. Marijuana liberalized rules N
4. CASH Act N	8. Defense $$$, veto override Y	12. Electoral College objections Y

Election Results

Election	Name (Party)	Vote (%)		Cand. Spent	Ind. Exp. Support	Ind. Exp. Oppose
2020 General	Sam Graves (R)	258,709	(67%)	$1,432,257	$31	
	Gena L. Ross (D)	118,926	(31%)	$6,870		
	Jim Higgins (L)	8,144	(2%)			
2020 Primary	Sam Graves (R)	81,584	(80%)			
	Chris Ryan (R)	20,826	(20%)			

Prior winning percentages: 2018 (65%), 2016 (68%), 2014 (67%), 2012 (65%), 2010 (69%), 2008 (59%), 2006 (62%), 2004 (64%), 2002 (63%), 2000 (51%)

Republican Sam Graves, first elected in 2000, took over in 2019 as ranking member of the Transportation and Infrastructure Committee, where he has joined the widespread desire for far-reaching infrastructure legislation and criticized Democrats in 2020 for advocating a partisan measure, which he described as a "climate" bill. He has promoted aid to the airlines in COVID-relief bills. As chairman of the Highways and Transit Subcommittee, he was instrumental in the enactment in 2015 of the first long-term highway bill in more than a decade.

Graves is a lifelong resident of Tarkio in the northwest corner of the state. An Eagle Scout, he regularly played "Taps" on his bugle at local cemeteries, a practice he has continued in his district each Memorial Day. He graduated from the University of Missouri with a degree in agronomy, farmed with his father and brother, and joined the Farm Bureau. He ran for the state House in 1992 and beat a longtime Democratic incumbent. Two years later, he was elected to the state Senate. He attracted attention with a five-hour filibuster against a school desegregation bill that he said put rural areas at a disadvantage, but the bill eventually passed.

Graves ran for the House when Democratic Rep. Pat Danner dropped her bid for reelection just minutes before the filing deadline. Not by accident, the immediate favorite to succeed her was her son, state Sen. Steve Danner, also a Democrat. Graves entered the race and drew support from national Republicans. Against an opponent who attacked him as the darling of extremist party leaders, Graves won the primary, 68%-17%. In the general, Danner billed himself as a conservative Democrat and switched from pro-abortion rights to opposition. In an editorial endorsing Graves, the Kansas City Star said Danner's switch showed that he "engaged in raw opportunism at the slightest opportunity." Graves won 51%-47%.

Graves has mostly been a rock-solid conservative, though he sometimes has deviated. He opposed barring the use of funds to administer the Davis-Bacon Act, which requires prevailing union wages on federal projects. He has remained a hardliner on immigration. He amended a fiscal 2013 spending bill to stop the Obama administration's family unity waiver system, which allowed illegal immigrants who are married to U.S. citizens to remain with their spouses while their green-card status is reviewed.

As chairman of the Small Business Committee, Graves was a regular critic of the Obama administration. He held hearings on the Environmental Protection Agency's failure to comply with a law requiring agencies to analyze the effects of regulations on small entities and to consider less burdensome alternatives. Graves worked with Democrats to pass a series of bills in 2012 aimed at fixing small business contracting problems. In 2014, he told the Associated Press that he had made the committee "relevant" and forced the administration to analyze the burdens that regulations placed on small business.

With his new focus on transportation programs, Graves said a long-term solution was needed for funding shortfalls in the highway trust funds. On a bipartisan basis, he and Transportation and Infrastructure Committee Chairman Bill Shuster of Pennsylvania secured enactment in 2015 of the five-year Fixing America's Surface Transportation (FAST) Act, which permitted the development of user-funded tools as an alternative to gasoline taxes to finance the highway trust fund; the new law required that each state spend at least 15 percent of its funds to maintain and repair rural bridges. That left the door open for a more sweeping bill, which President Donald Trump advocated, though he failed to offer details. When President Joe Biden, in an early step, called for nearly doubling spending for dredging along the Mississippi River, Graves called that a "huge step forward." In early 2021, he joined bipartisan meetings with Biden on highways and other infrastructure spending, though progress was slow.

An experienced private pilot, Graves has co-chaired the House's General Aviation Caucus and contends that government needs to better understand the impact of its aircraft regulations. At home, Graves has sought to compel the Army Corps of Engineers to emphasize flood control on the Missouri River, telling the St. Joseph News-Press that the agency's focus on environmental recovery over levee operations and maintenance was "out of whack." With his work on highway and aviation issues, plus his district's borders on both the Missouri and Mississippi rivers, Graves jumped over more senior Republicans and replaced Shuster as the senior Republican on the full committee.

Pointing out the need for more funds and the reduced consumption of gasoline, Graves has encouraged public-private partnerships for new highways, though he objects to toll roads. After longstanding opposition to an increase in the gasoline tax as economically regressive, he voiced in 2020 qualified support for indexing the gas tax and has backed a fee on the miles that electric and other alternative-fuel vehicles travel. The federal gas tax, which is 18.4 cents per gallon, was last raised in 1993, though virtually all states impose a gas tax at least that high (though not Missouri, where the state gas tax is 17 cents a gallon).

In 2020, when Democrats unveiled a huge environment-friendly highway bill that had little chance of winning Republican support, Graves criticized them for what he called a partisan approach. Also that year, he worked with Democrats on a bipartisan deal to bail out airlines as part of COVID-relief legislation. And he praised the Trump administration for relaxing rules on safety requirements for the work schedules of truckers.

Graves was the subject of an ethics investigation for arranging testimony before his committee by a family friend. The matter touched off a public squabble in 2009 between the new Office of Congressional Ethics and the House Ethics Committee. OCE recommended further investigation, but the Ethics Committee found deficiencies with OCE and voted unanimously to clear Graves. He and other Republicans in 2017 reportedly cited that experience to seek a House rules change to restrict the powers of the OCE, which Speaker Paul Ryan short-circuited.

In 2008, national Democrats were excited when former Kansas City Mayor and St. Joseph native Kay Barnes announced she would challenge Graves. He attacked Barnes for "San Francisco values" and supporting "a homosexual agenda" because her picture had appeared in a gay magazine; he won, 59%-37%. His recent victory margins have been close to or exceeded 2-to-1.

MO-6: Northern Missouri

Cook Partisan Voting Index: R+18

Population		Race and Ethnicity		Income	
Total	777,104	White	89.20%	Median Income	$62,094
Land area (sq. miles)	18,199	Black	4.50%	District Income Rank	232
Pop/ sq mi	42.7	Latino	4.20%	Poverty Rate	11.20%
Born in State	65.10%	Asian	1.40%	With health insurance	91.40%
		Two or more races	3.30%	Cash public assistance	1.50%
Age Groups		Other	1.50%	Food stamp/SNAP	7.30%
Under 18	23.50%				
18-34	21.10%	**Education**		**Work**	
35-64	38.40%	H.S grad or less	43.10%	White Collar	37.60%
Over 64	16.90%	Some college	28.10%	Sales and Service	35.60%
		College Degree, 4 yr	18.60%	Blue Collar	26.80%
Military		Post grad	10.20%	Government	14.00%
Veteran/ Active Duty	8.20%				

2020 Pres. Vote	Trump	248,231	(63%)	Biden	137,169	(35%)			
2016 Pres. Vote	Trump	226,783	(64%)	Clinton	110,474	(31%)	Johnson	14,252	(4%)

Kansas City suburbs: The rolling fields along the Missouri River in northwest Missouri were settled in a rush in the late 19th century. These lands lost people for most of the 20th century as fewer hands were needed on farms. But increased efficiencies lately have led to resurgent production. In recent years, the meatpacking business has expanded in St. Joseph and has drawn many Hispanics. Barge traffic on the Missouri has successfully reopened, following an increase in water levels and record corn and soybean crops. Although barges move more slowly, many farmers have praised their greater reliability and lower costs than other modes of transportation.

In 2008, Rock Port in the northwest corner was the first town in the country to get all its energy from wind power. Despite earlier interest by neighboring states to use the wind power, the Invenergy utility decided to keep most of the energy from its Grain Belt Express transmission line in northern Missouri, where users welcomed the lower cost. In the northeast corner is Little Dixie, the swath of Missouri along the Mississippi River. This area was settled by southerners from Kentucky and Virginia. Its most famous native son is Mark Twain, born Samuel Langhorne Clemens in Hannibal, then as now a little town on bluffs overlooking the river. Hannibal was the thinly disguised St. Petersburg of Twain's classics, The Adventures of Tom Sawyer and The Adventures of Huckleberry Finn. The overall economy of the area remained sluggish. Twenty counties in northern Missouri lost population from 2000 to 2010.

Hannibal is on the eastern edge of the 6th Congressional District, which takes in all or parts of 36 counties in northern Missouri, stretching more than 200 miles from the Kansas City suburbs and Nebraska to Illinois and the outskirts of St. Louis. On the western edge is the river town of St. Joseph, Missouri's biggest city north of Kansas City, which was the starting point for the Pony Express and its roughly 10-day transport of mail to Sacramento. The 6th also takes in the Kansas City suburbs of Clay and Platte and a slice of eastern Jackson County. That area casts about half the district's vote. The historic political tradition here was mostly Democratic. But the rural vote, as across the nation, has been tempered by dislike for national Democrats and has moved solidly Republican. The Kansas City suburb of Clay County traditionally was a reliable national bellwether, but it has swung the GOP's way too: Democrat Al Gore won in 2000 by one vote. Republican Donald Trump carried Clay by 12 percentage points in 2016, though his lead slipped to five points in 2020, when he won the overall district, 63%-35%. The three counties in the suburbs of Kansas City cast about half of the total vote and they gave 58 percent to Trump.

Billy Long (R)

Elected 2010, 6th term, b. Aug 11, 1955; Springfield, MO; MO Auction School; University of MO, Att., 1976; MO Auction School, 1979; Presbyterian; Married (Barbara Long); 2 children.

Professional Career: Talk show host, 1999-2006; Realtor, 1978-2010; Owner, Billy Long Auctions.

DC Office: 2454 RHOB 20515, 202-225-6536, Fax: 202-225-5604, long.house.gov

State Offices: Joplin, 417-781-1041; Springfield, 417-889-1800.

Committees: *Energy & Commerce*: Communications & Technology; Health; Oversight & Investigations.

Group Ratings

	ADA	ACLU	AFL-CIO	LCV	COC	HAFA	ACU	CFG	FRC
2020	**	20%	**	10%	-	90%	87%	**	-
2019	0%	C	29%	7%	80%	C	86%	81%	90%

Almanac Ratings 2019-2020

	Economy	Social	Foreign	Composite
Liberal	25%	28%	29%	28%
Conservative	75%	72%	71%	72%

Key Votes of the 116th Congress

1. U.S./Mex./Can. trade deal Y	5. Russia sanctions Y	9. Firearms background checks N
2. First Coronavirus response N	6. Troops in Syria N	10. Spending at the border Y
3. HEROES Act N	7. Veto arms sales to Saudis N	11. Marijuana liberalized rules N
4. CASH Act N	8. Defense $$$, veto override N	12. Electoral College objections Y

Election Results

Election	Name (Party)	Vote (%)		Cand. Spent	Ind. Exp. Support	Ind. Exp. Oppose
2020 General	Billy Long (R)	254,318	(69%)	$1,761,073	$537	
	Teresa Montseny (D)	98,111	(27%)			
	Kevin Craig (L)	15,573	(4%)			
2020 Primary	Billy Long (R)	69,407	(66%)			
	Eric Harleman (R)	11,696	(11%)			
	Kevin VanStory (R)	10,486	(10%)			
	Steve Chetnik (R)	7,407	(7%)			
	Camille Lombardi-Olive (R)	5,969	(6%)			

Prior winning percentages: 2018 (66%), 2016 (68%), 2014 (64%), 2012 (64%), 2010 (63%)

Republican Billy Long, elected in 2010, brought a looser style to the House. His orientation has been tea party and rural, and his campaign motto was an anti-Beltway "Fed Up!" He has forged occasional alliances with Democrats. To break the tension, he sometimes resorts to his expertise as an auctioneer. After Speaker Nancy Pelosi tore in half her copy of the State of the Union speech that President Donald Trump delivered in 2020, Long suggested to her that she should have it auctioned for charity. Pelosi responded that she planned to keep it "for posterity." Long tweeted that he would auction his tie that Trump had signed at the event.

Long grew up in Springfield, where he developed an interest in Republican politics at an early age. When he was 9 years old, he told the Springfield News-Leader, he would ride his bike to pass out bumper stickers for a Greene County sheriff candidate. After briefly attending the University of Missouri to study business, he became interested in real estate and attended auction school, eventually starting a company that would conduct as many as 200 auctions a year. He has been inducted into both the national and Missouri auctioneers' halls of fame. He spent six years as a morning-drive talk show host for an AM station covering southwest Missouri.

When Roy Blunt successfully sought a Senate seat, Long ran as a plain-talking conservative who would clamp down on federal spending and set Congress straight. He billed his lack of government service as a plus. "We have enough political experience in Washington D.C. to choke a horse," he told the Associated Press. "That's exactly the problem." In the GOP primary, he defeated seven other candidates, including two veteran state senators, with more than 37 percent of the vote. In the fall, Long advocated a constitutional amendment to limit the federal government's taxation powers and for repeal of the Democrats' health care law. He wore a cowboy hat and inveighed against "elitist politicians." In this Republican bastion, Long won 63%-30%.

Long initially made good on his promise to try to change Washington's ways, though he eventually went along. He voted for a conservative budget alternative with deeper cuts than the version by Budget Committee Chairman Paul Ryan. He adamantly opposed President Barack Obama's 2013 proposals intended to reduce gun violence, including limiting the sale of ammunition clips to those holding 10 rounds or fewer. "If you're lying in bed at 4 in the morning and four people kick your door in, would you like to be restricted to five shots or six shots?" he asked the News-Leader. Long won bipartisan praise for his role in the disaster response to the deadly Joplin tornado in 2011, working closely with the Obama administration to provide funding to the ravaged area. "It was a lot heaped onto a freshman," Missouri Democratic Rep. Lacy Clay told the News-Leader. "But you could see him right before our eyes grow into the job and grow into his responsibility."

On the Energy and Commerce Committee, Long won bipartisan support in 2016 for his amendment to the 21st Century Cures bill to improve information to consumers about new pharmaceuticals. In 2017, when the Republican-controlled House narrowly voted to repeal the Affordable Care Act, Long briefly became the center of attention when he objected that the alternative would not provide sufficient coverage for persons with pre-existing conditions, Republican leaders agreed to add $8 billion to cover such contingencies. That deal was sealed when Long was summoned to the White House—with Republican Rep. Fred Upton, who had similar concerns—to meet with Trump. After the mavericks agreed to support the bill, Long described his role to the News-Leader: "I'm a member of the Show-Me caucus, just one guy."

Not surprisingly, Long showed particular interest in communications issues. In February 2020, he sided with the wireless industry in urging the Federal Communications Commission to reserve a portion of the airwaves it was selling so it could be auctioned for licensed use. Later that year, the House passed the "Media Diversity" bill that he introduced with Democratic Rep. Marc Veasey, which would require the FCC to consider market entry barriers for socially disadvantaged persons applying for a communications license. "Promoting an accurate and diverse communications marketplace is essential," Long said.

Some of Long's votes—such as supporting a raise in the federal debt limit and reauthorizing the Export-Import Bank—annoyed conservatives back home, and he has drawn primary challengers. Long has been held to roughly 60 to 65 percent of the vote, enough to get his attention but not to force big changes.

In October 2016, Long "deplored" 11-year-old comments by Trump about groping women. But he criticized Republicans such as Ryan who distanced themselves from Trump. "If everyone backs away from our nominee for president, that's going to spell disaster down-ticket," Long said. "No one's seen anything like this election before. It's a movement." He became a usually reliable supporter of Trump as president. When Sen. Mitt Romney wrote a harsh op-ed about Trump, Long tweeted that Romney should "get over himself." When the retirement of Sen. Roy Blunt opened a Senate seat in 2022, Long explored running.

MO-7: Western Ozarks

Cook Partisan Voting Index: R+24

Population		Race and Ethnicity		Income	
Total	787,917	White	91.10%	Median Income	$47,679
Land area (sq. miles)	6,273	Black	1.90%	District Income Rank	399
Pop/ sq mi	125.61	Latino	5.40%	Poverty Rate	16.00%
Born in State	60.30%	Asian	1.40%	With health insurance	86.20%
		Two or more races	3.20%	Cash public assistance	1.40%
Age Groups		Other	2.40%	Food stamp/SNAP	12.20%
Under 18	22.70%				
18-34	23.30%	**Education**		**Work**	
35-64	36.20%	H.S grad or less	43.70%	White Collar	33.40%
Over 64	17.80%	Some college	31.40%	Sales and Service	42.30%
		College Degree, 4 yr	16.40%	Blue Collar	24.40%
Military		Post grad	8.50%	Government	10.90%
Veteran/ Active Duty	8.10%				

2020 Pres. Vote	Trump	263,474	(70%)	Biden	105,782	(28%)		
2016 Pres. Vote	Trump	240,700	(70%)	Clinton	84,415	(25%)	Johnson	12,163	(4%)

Springfield, Joplin: One of the biggest tourist destinations in America today is Branson Missouri, something almost no one would have predicted 40 years ago. Branson has only 11,000 year-round residents, but it thrives thanks to the surging popularity of country and western music. It has more than 50 theaters and 57,000 seats—more than Broadway and equaling Las Vegas—and has become a hub for nonstop, low-cost entertainment, attracting 9.1 million visitors a year. As the Kansas City Star put it, each attraction is "more church-loving, more family-friendly, more country than the next." The 150-feet high Ferris wheel that had operated at Chicago's Navy Pier (though not the original wheel) is an entertainment feature. Nearby are fishing, boating and plenty of shopping. These diversions have made southwest Missouri the fastest-growing part of the state, generating new businesses and attracting retirees as well as vacationers. For private and charter flights, Branson even has its own privately financed small airport, a new concept in the United States but more familiar elsewhere. In 2019, prior to the coronavirus, $122 million of local construction was the most robust in more than a decade. Across the lake in Hollister, city officials and resort executives in July 2020 announced plans for a $300 million, 68-acre, family-friendly development—including a water park, convention space and 450 lodging sites.

Springfield is the biggest city in southwest Missouri and the self-styled "buckle of the Bible Belt." It is home to more than 200 churches, including the headquarters of the Assemblies of God, one of the nation's largest Protestant denominations. In 2015, 51 percent of voters agreed in a referendum to repeal the city's prohibitions on LGBT discrimination. Advocates of the anti-discrimination provisions fought back and restored the earlier prohibitions in a 2016 referendum, which also got 51 percent. Southwest Missouri is dairy country and home to a growing poultry industry; the state ranks fourth in the nation for turkey production. Latinos have been moving into McDonald County to work in chicken-processing plants; at least two-thirds of the employees at the Tyson Foods chicken plant in Noel were minorities, including about 500 from Somalia. In June 2020, COVID-19 testing of 1,142 employees revealed that 371 tested positive.

In Jasper County, the city of Joplin rebuilt following a devastating 2011 tornado that killed 158 people and heavily damaged or destroyed 2,000 buildings, including a hospital and schools. With winds exceeding 200 miles per hour, it was the deadliest tornado in the United States since 1950. In October 2020, city officials reported that the city's consumer-based industrial economy had a quicker recovery from the coronavirus than most other locales in the region.

The 7th Congressional District of Missouri includes Springfield and Joplin. This area has been Republican territory since 1861, when it opposed secession. Pro-union Springfield changed hands several times as Missouri staged its own civil war, and now it is solidly Republican. In 2020, President Donald Trump won all the counties here, many by 2-to-1 margins. He took the district, 70%-28%, his second-best in the state, behind the 8th District..

Jason Smith (R)

Elected 2013, 4th full term, b. Jun 16, 1980; St. Louis, MO; Trinity College, Cambridge; MO State University, B.S., 2001; OK City University Law School, J.D., 2004; Assembly of God; Single.

Elected Office: MO House, 2005-2013.

Professional Career: Farmer, practicing Attorney, 2004-2013.

DC Office: 2418 RHOB 20515, 202-225-4404, Fax: 202-226-0326, jasonsmith.house.gov

State Offices: Cape Girardeau, 573-335-0101; Farmington, 573-756-9755; Poplar Bluff, 573-609-2996; Rolla, 573-364-2455; West Plains, 417-255-1515.

Committees: *Budget (RMM)*. *Ways & Means*: Health.

Group Ratings

	ADA	ACLU	AFL-CIO	LCV	COC	HAFA	ACU	CFG	FRC
2020	**	24%	**	5%	-	100%	92%	**	-
2019	0%	C	19%	0%	80%	C	91%	96%	100%

Almanac Ratings 2019-2020

	Economy	Social	Foreign	Composite
Liberal	25%	4%	4%	11%
Conservative	75%	96%	96%	89%

Key Votes of the 116th Congress

1. U.S./Mex./Can. trade deal	Y	5. Russia sanctions	N	9. Firearms background checks	N
2. First Coronavirus response	N	6. Troops in Syria	N	10. Spending at the border	Y
3. HEROES Act	N	7. Veto arms sales to Saudis	N	11. Marijuana liberalized rules	N
4. CASH Act	Y	8. Defense $$$, veto override	N	12. Electoral College objections	Y

Election Results

Election	Name (Party)	Vote (%)	Cand. Spent	Ind. Exp. Support	Ind. Exp. Oppose
2020 General	Jason Smith (R)	253,811 (77%)	$1,575,079	$31	
	Kathy Ellis (D)	70,561 (21%)	$129	$10	
2020 Primary	Jason Smith (R)	114,074 (100%)			

Prior winning percentages: 2018 (73%), 2016 (74%), 2014 (67%), 2013 special (67%)

Republican Jason Smith, who won a special election in 2013, has quietly become a House GOP leader, especially on tax and spending policy. A fervent advocate of limited government, Smith serves on the Ways and Means Committee. He departed the GOP leadership team to become the ranking Republican on the Budget Committee. In 2021, he said that was exploring a bid for the seat of retiring Sen. Roy Blunt.

Smith grew up as the son of a church pastor in Salem Missouri, and he still runs the family farm his great-grandfather started. At the University of Missouri, he received degrees in agricultural economics and business administration. He earned his law degree from Oklahoma City University. After returning to run the family farm and practice law, he became alarmed by "the harm that the overbearing government was inflicting on Missourians and our economy," according to his campaign website. He won a seat in the state House in 2005 and rose to majority whip and speaker pro tempore. He sought to amend the state constitution to protect farmers' rights, which he said was necessary to protect Missouri farmers from out-of-state animal rights groups and "environmental extremists." He joined social conservatives on gun rights and abortion-related legislation.

He ran for the vacant House seat when Republican Rep. Jo Emerson resigned to become president of the National Rural Electric Cooperative Association. Smith campaigned on his opposition to President Barack Obama's health care law and other issues of strong interest to the GOP base. "Voters do not want Obamacare, they are tired of burdensome and costly regulations and they know our $16 trillion national debt is a ticking time bomb," he said.

Democratic nominee Steve Hodges, a state representative with pro-gun rights and anti-abortion views, made an issue of Smith's missed state legislative votes during the special election campaign and criticized his support for an unpopular state sales tax hike. Hodges got little help from national Democrats. Smith raised just over $500,000. The result wasn't close. Smith won 67%-27%, and took all but two counties in the bootheel. He has been reelected with ease.

On the Natural Resources Committees, Smith sought to defend the interests of rural America: opposed to excessive regulations, in search of new markets for farmers and ranchers, and protecting his constituents' way of life. He strongly objected to tentative plans by the Obama administration to restrict recreational use of the Ozarks National Scenic Riverways.

With his seat on Ways and Means, he runs the risk of confusion with a more senior Smith (Adrian) on the committee who is a young GOP policy nerd from neighboring Nebraska. Jason Smith criticized the lack of clarity in the tax code. When Congress approved tax cuts in 2017, he said he was "honored to be part of the team" that cut taxes for working families and repealed the individual mandate in the Affordable Care Act. In 2018, the House unanimously passed a bill he cosponsored with Democratic Rep. Terri Sewell of Alabama that streamlined Internal Revenue Service audit procedures and sought to restore collaboration in disputes with taxpayers. In August 2019, Smith filed with Democratic Rep. Ami Bera a bill that would give Medicare beneficiaries the option to purchase a health savings account.

In 2017, Smith praised the numerous executive orders that President Donald Trump issued during his opening days in office for having "done more to help working-class Americans" than President Barack Obama did in eight years. In February 2018, he was one of 67 House Republicans—and the only GOP elected leader—who voted against the budget deal that included spending agreements for the remainder of the fiscal year. "I hate that I couldn't support it," Smith said. "You don't want to be on an island by yourself. But we also have to get serious about cutting spending." In October 2020, he told The Hill that Speaker Nancy Pelosi "deserved an Emmy" for her pre-election delaying tactics on an pandemic relief bill.

In contrast to some Republicans at Ways and Means, Smith praised Trump's tariffs. He acknowledged that Missouri farmers faced a "bumpy, roller-coaster ride" because of international trade disputes, the Southeast Missourian reported in July 2018. But he added, "I am very supportive of our president. I have trust that he knows what he is doing."

In a partisan exchange in the House during the partial government shutdown in January 2019, Smith shouted across the aisle "Go back to Puerto Rico" in the direction of Democratic Rep. Tony Cardenas of California, who has Mexican ancestry, The Washington Post reported. After nobody responded when Cardenas asked who had said that, Smith apologized to him in a phone call later that day and said he was referring to a group of House Democrats who had recently visited Puerto Rico.

In January 2021, Smith gave up his GOP leadership position—temporarily, at least—to replace Rep. Steve Womack as the ranking Republican on the Budget Committee; Womack took a top subcommittee position at Appropriations. After four years of record-setting federal deficits during the Trump administration, Smith said the working class "feels the pain" of huge deficits. He criticized House Democrats for having gone two years without passing an annual federal budget. "Democrats are afraid to put on paper their budget, which rewards both their progressive base and their wealthy donor class."

MO-8: Southeast Missouri

Cook Partisan Voting Index: R+30

Population		Race and Ethnicity		Income	
Total	736,467	White	92.00%	Median Income	$45,656
Land area (sq. miles)	19,901	Black	4.80%	District Income Rank	415
Pop/ sq mi	37.01	Latino	1.90%	Poverty Rate	18.00%
Born in State	72.10%	Asian	0.90%	With health insurance	87.00%
		Two or more races	1.70%	Cash public assistance	1.90%
Age Groups		Other	0.60%	Food stamp/SNAP	15.40%
Under 18	22.40%				
18-34	20.30%	**Education**		**Work**	
35-64	38.30%	H.S grad or less	54.10%	White Collar	31.30%
Over 64	19.00%	Some college	28.00%	Sales and Service	38.50%
		College Degree, 4 yr	10.80%	Blue Collar	30.20%
Military		Post grad	7.00%	Government	15.90%
Veteran/ Active Duty	9.30%				

2020 Pres. Vote	Trump	261,118	(77%)	Biden	72,104	(21%)		
2016 Pres. Vote	Trump	239,652	(75%)	Clinton	66,884	(21%)	Johnson	7,980	(3%)

Cape Girardeau: The southeast quadrant of Missouri is part river valley, part industrial mining and part agriculture. For years, there has been a population outflow from the Missouri Bootheel, as machines replaced low-wage farm workers and crops shifted from cotton to rice, corn and soybeans. Dairy cattle, pigs, apples and berries, plus some timber, are among the area's other products. The area is also home to Missouri's Lead Belt, a mining region rich in ore minerals such as lead, zinc, copper, silver and cadmium. Reynolds and Iron counties produced about 70 percent of the nation's lead, but many of the local mines have closed because of environmental contamination. Ste. Genevieve County has the nation's largest cement plant, which sparked a mini-economic boom after it opened at a huge limestone quarry.

The area has suffered industrial shutdowns. Doe Run Resources Corp., the largest lead producer in the country, closed its smelter in 2013 after 120 years, following an agreement with Missouri and the Environmental Protection Agency. The Noranda Aluminum smelting plant in New Madrid, which had 850 local jobs, declared bankruptcy in 2016 and closed its operations following a decline in aluminum prices. In 2018, the smelter resumed operations, following President Donald Trump's decision to impose tariffs on imported aluminum. By 2020, amid reports that it might shut down, the facility was losing money and the soot from its smokestacks produced the dirtiest air recorded in the United States, according to a Reuters review of data from the Environmental Protection Agency.

Carrying many industrial goods to market is the Mississippi River, which Mark Twain might not recognize today. The river is hidden behind levees, which ordinarily screen small towns and river roads from rows of barges tethered together, full of coal and corn and soybeans. The Mississippi today is an industrial waterway. But it was never really all that romantic. Twain's steamboats, as he was at pains to point out, were dangerous, noisy contraptions, forever blowing up or getting embedded in roots and branches in the river currents. This is one of the oldest settled parts of the United States. French pioneers founded such Missouri towns as Cape Girardeau in the late 1700s. New Madrid has had some of the most powerful earthquakes in the nation; the most famous was in 1811-12. Recent seismic activity has projected a 90 percent likelihood of at least a 6.0 earthquake along the fault sometime in the next 50 years, according to the U.S. Geological Survey. Meanwhile, the shutdown during the past decade of four nearby hospitals was a factor in the New Madrid area receiving citations as a COVID-19 hot spot in October 2020. In Rolla, the Missouri University of Science and Technology in October 2020 received a $300 million gift from St. Louis businessman Fred Kummer and his wife, June, which will support a new school of innovation, entrepreneurship and economic development.

The 8th District, the largest in Missouri, covers the state's southeast corner, including rural Ste. Genevieve County, the site of Missouri's oldest permanent settlement, and takes in southern Jefferson County in the suburbs of St. Louis. It includes Plato, the tiny Missouri village named the population midpoint of the country based on 2010 census data. The Bootheel was once solidly Democratic, though the mining counties have mostly lost their traces of Democratic sentiment and Republicans have held it since 1980. In 2020, President Donald Trump won here, 77%-21%, placing the district in the top 2 percent of most Republican districts in the Cook-PVI ranking. Trump got at least 65 percent of the vote in the "least Republican" counties in the district—Jefferson, Ste. Genevieve and Phelps.

MONTANA

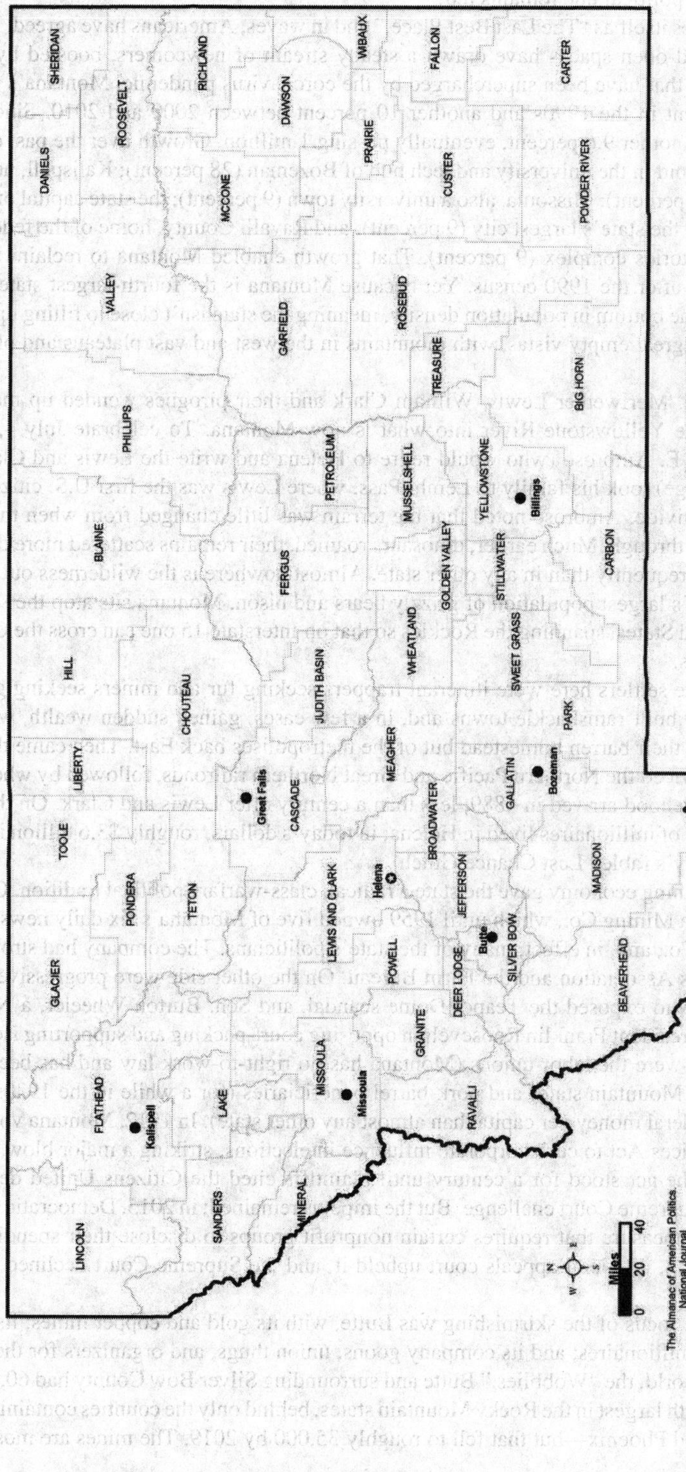

SHERIDAN
DANIELS
ROOSEVELT
RICHLAND
WIBAUX
DAWSON
FALLON
CARTER
PRAIRIE
MCCONE
CUSTER
POWDER RIVER
VALLEY
GARFIELD
ROSEBUD
TREASURE
BIG HORN
PHILLIPS
PETROLEUM
MUSSELSHELL
GOLDEN VALLEY
YELLOWSTONE
CARBON
STILLWATER
SWEET GRASS
BLAINE
FERGUS
WHEATLAND
PARK
HILL
JUDITH BASIN
CHOUTEAU
MEAGHER
GALLATIN
LIBERTY
CASCADE
BROADWATER
MADISON
TOOLE
PONDERA
TETON
LEWIS AND CLARK
JEFFERSON
SILVER BOW
GLACIER
POWELL
DEER LODGE
BEAVERHEAD
GRANITE
FLATHEAD
LAKE
MISSOULA
RAVALLI
SANDERS
MINERAL
LINCOLN

Billings
Great Falls
Bozeman
Helena
Butte
Missoula
Kalispell

U.S. Representative elected at-large.

Miles
0   20   40

N
W   E
S

The Almanac of American Politics,
National Journal

Montana had a cluster of seemingly competitive races in 2020—for a Senate seat, a House seat, the governorship, and several statewide offices. But Republicans ended up winning every one of them by between 10 and 20 points, emphasizing that, despite Montana's rapid population growth, the state's default political hue remains red.

Montana prides itself as "The Last Best Place," and in waves, Americans have agreed. The state's natural beauty and open spaces have drawn a steady stream of newcomers, boosted by advances in telecommuting that have been supercharged by the coronavirus pandemic. Montana's population grew by 13 percent in the 1990s and another 10 percent between 2000 and 2010. Since 2010, it has increased by another 9.6 percent, eventually passing 1 million. Growth over the past decade has been especially rapid in the university and tech hub of Bozeman (28 percent); Kalispell, near Glacier National Park (14 percent); Missoula, also a university town (9 percent); the state capital of Helena (9 percent); Billings, the state's largest city (9 percent); and Ravalli County, home of the federal Rocky Mountain Laboratories complex (9 percent). That growth enabled Montana to reclaim the second House seat it lost after the 1990 census. Yet because Montana is the fourth-largest state in area, it ranks third from the bottom in population density, meaning the state isn't close to filling up. Montana remains a land of great empty vistas, with mountains in the west and vast plateaus and plains in the east.

In April 1805, Meriwether Lewis, William Clark and their pirogues wended up the Missouri River just past the Yellowstone River into what is now Montana. To celebrate July 4, 1976, the historian Stephen E. Ambrose (who would retire to Helena and write the Lewis and Clark history Undaunted Courage) took his family to Lemhi Pass, where Lewis was the first U.S. citizen to cross the Continental Divide. Ambrose noted that the terrain was little changed from when the Corps of Discovery passed through. Much earlier, dinosaurs roamed, their remains scattered more densely and uncovered more frequently than in any other state. Almost nowhere is the wilderness out of sight. It has the Lower 48's largest population of grizzly bears and bison. Montana sits atop the spine of the continental United States, spanning the Rockies so that on Interstate 15 one can cross the Continental Divide three times.

The first white settlers here were itinerant trappers seeking fur and miners seeking gold, silver and copper. They built ramshackle towns and, in a few cases, gained sudden wealth, which made them kings not of their barren homestead but of the metropolises back East. Then came the workers who built and serviced the Northern Pacific and Great Northern railroads, followed by wheat farmers and ranchers. Statehood arrived in 1889, less than a century after Lewis and Clark. On the verge of statehood, dozens of millionaires lived in Helena; in today's dollars, roughly $3.6 billion in gold was taken from the city's fabled Last Chance Gulch.

Montana's mining economy gave the state a radical, class-warfare political tradition. On one side was the Anaconda Mining Co., which until 1959 owned five of Montana's six daily newspapers, the Montana Power Co., and, in effect, many of the state's politicians. The company had strong allies in the Stock growers Association and the Farm Bureau. On the other side were progressives like Sen. Thomas Walsh, who exposed the Teapot Dome scandal, and Sen. Burton Wheeler, a New Dealer who broke with President Franklin Roosevelt in opposing court-packing and supporting isolationism. Allied with them were the labor unions (Montana has no right-to-work law and has been the most pro-union Rocky Mountain state) and pork-barrel beneficiaries (for a while in the 1930s, Montana received more federal money per capita than almost any other state). In 1912, Montana voters passed the Corrupt Practices Act to curb corporate influence in elections, striking a major blow against the Copper Kings. The act stood for a century until plaintiffs cited the Citizens United decision in a successful U.S. Supreme Court challenge. But the impetus remained; in 2015, Democratic Gov. Steve Bullock signed a measure that requires certain nonprofit groups to disclose their spending in state races. In May 2018, a federal appeals court upheld it, and the Supreme Court declined to take the appeal.

For years, the focus of the skirmishing was Butte, with its gold and copper mines; its gamblers, bootleggers and millionaires; and its company goons, union thugs, and organizers for the Industrial Workers of the World, the "Wobblies." Butte and surrounding Silver Bow County had 60,000 people in 1920—the fourth largest in the Rocky Mountain states, behind only the counties containing Denver, Salt Lake City and Phoenix—but that fell to roughly 35,000 by 2019. The mines are mostly closed;

most spectacular is Butte's Berkeley Pit, a disused open copper mine more than a mile in diameter that's now filled with a toxic brew of water contaminated with heavy metals and sulfuric acid. A project that could become Montana's first new copper mine in four decades—the Black Butte Copper Project in White Sulphur Springs, roughly equidistant from Helena and Bozeman—seeks to avoid this fate by drilling diagonally, mining entirely underground, and processing its ore on site. So far, environmentalists remain skeptical. As Montana's mines gradually closed, agriculture—especially wheat growing and cattle grazing—became an economic mainstay. Class warfare died down, but the state's muscular personality remained. Hunting and fishing opportunities abound; development in the small cities and resort areas has not been enough to drive the game away. Montana's libertarian streak persists: For a stretch in the 1990s, the state had no speed limit, and after one was reimposed by the courts, lawmakers raised it to 80 miles per hour on interstate highways in 2015, becoming only the fifth state with a limit that high. In 2020, voters also backed two initiatives to legalize recreational marijuana by comfortable margins.

Over the past quarter-century, Big Sky country attracted at first a trickle and then a flood of affluent Americans who purchased second homes—high-visibility movie stars and billionaires such as CNN founder Ted Turner, but also ordinary people buying small spreads near Big Sky, McLeod or Bozeman, or around Flathead Lake, Big Timber and Whitefish. Now, less than half of residents 25 or older are native to the state, according to a Montana Free Press analysis. Some newcomers, from California and other urban states, are putting down roots amid the coffee houses and gambling parlors one finds along many of Montana's highways; some now dub Bozeman, with a rapidly expanding airport and upscale boutiques, "Boz Angeles." The new Montanans have added a spark of energy and inventiveness to a population that had consisted of people left behind when others moved elsewhere, or who were aging in place; Montana is the oldest state west of the Mississippi, and the median age is especially high in rural areas, where retirements of small business owners can be especially damaging if no one is willing or able to take over. In the cities, by contrast, newcomers have pushed up housing prices beyond the reach of many. It has been "a stampede of transplants descending in Porsche Cayennes and Teslas with cash offers," as The Washington Post put it. "It's multimillionaires grabbing up luxury ranches to serve as second or third homes. It's buyers with more modest resources looking for a way out. It's city dwellers seeking bare land in Montana's wilderness to serve as insurance policies for America's uncertain future." In such hot real estate markets, rising costs have exacerbated the class divide, though perhaps not to its level in the days of the Wobblies.

Montana remains predominantly White—86 percent, ranking fifth in the nation—and only about 2 percent of residents are foreign born. The state is less than 1 percent Black; the biggest minority group is Native Americans, at 6.1 percent. The Hispanic population has climbed fairly quickly, though starting from a small base, to 3.7 percent in 2019; many work in agriculture or in construction in the booming cities. Montana now generates an estimated $2 billion in revenue annually from its rapidly growing high-tech sector. Even bigger (until the coronavirus) was the state's tourism industry, driven by pilgrimages to Yellowstone and Glacier national parks.

The boom in the Bakken shale oil field near the North Dakota border helped the state's economy for a while, but it was followed by a bust. The Keystone XL pipeline that was supposed to run south from Alberta through Montana to Oklahoma was approved under President Donald Trump following long delays under his predecessor, Barack Obama. But Joe Biden, who faced cross-cutting pressures from his allies in the labor and environmental movements, revoked the permit on his first day in office. Meanwhile, Montana's sizable coal reserves face increasing difficulties. The Colstrip Steam Electric Station in Colstrip, one of the largest coal-fired plants in the West, shuttered its oldest units in 2019 amid declining purchases of fossil-fuel generated electricity by its climate-conscious customers in the Pacific Northwest, and the facility's newer units may be next on the chopping block. In recent years, the state has tentatively begun to harness its abundant renewable energy resources; a large wind farm with battery storage is under development at a location near Rapleje, northwest of Billings.

In 2014, Obama signed a measure to increase wilderness areas by 250,000 acres, the first such additions in the state in more than three decades. Meanwhile, the American Prairie Reserve, funded by Manhattan and Silicon Valley millionaires, is buying up land in the northern plains in hopes of creating a 3.2 million-acre preserve where thousands of buffalo (and tourists) would be able to roam, though it's facing opposition from local ranchers. There are lively political arguments over grizzly bears, whose numbers fell from as many as 100,000 in the Lewis and Clark era to 136 in 1975, and over the gray wolves that were reintroduced to Montana in the 1990s. As of 2018, the grizzly bear population in Montana and neighboring states had rebounded to more than 1,800, the Great Falls Tribune reported in December 2020. Some wildlife experts say the grizzlies have gotten used to human beings and vice versa, which might be bad for both.

Montana has often elected Democratic governors, most recently the feisty populist rancher Brian Schweitzer in 2004 and 2008 and Bullock in 2012 and 2016. Under Bullock, the state expanded Medicaid under the Affordable Care Act. During the coronavirus pandemic, Bullock issued a statewide stay-at-home order and closed most schools earlier than other red states did; for much of 2020, Montana's per capita case rate ranked among the bottom half of states. As the infection rate rose in November, Bullock expanded restrictions on restaurants, bars, casinos and breweries. Bullock ran for president in 2019 but dropped out after failing to gain traction with the message that he was a Democrat who could win in red states. More often, Montana has favored conservatives' fierce opposition to higher taxes and federal government dictates. Montana has not elected a Democrat to the House since 1996, and since 1993, Democrats have won the outright majority in the state House or Senate only once. The GOP, meanwhile, has endured a split between establishment and hardline Republicans. When the Medicaid expansion was reauthorized in 2019, moderate Republicans joined with Bullock to make it possible, over the strenuous objections of conservatives. Intra-party tensions were high; the morning of the vote, someone put jars of Vaseline on the desks of some of the bill's supporters, a not-so-veiled, sexualized threat.

In the 2020 presidential contest, Trump defeated Biden in the state by 16 points. That was narrower than Trump's 20-point win in 2016; Biden improved over Hillary Clinton's performance by seven points in Missoula County (Missoula) and six points in Gallatin County (Bozeman), increasing the number of Democratic votes in Gallatin by 53 percent over 2016. Still, even Trump's reduced margin represented a wider victory than Mitt Romney achieved in 2012 (13 points) and John McCain notched in 2008 (three points). And weak performances further down the ballot showed how far the political landscape had tilted against Democrats. Bullock, running against Sen. Steve Daines, managed to outrun Biden but still lost by 10 points. In the race to succeed Bullock as governor, Democratic Lt. Gov. Mike Cooney also outpolled Biden, yet still lost by 13. In the initially competitive attorney general and secretary of state races, the Republican candidates won by even larger margins—18 and 20 points, respectively. Ironically, Republicans had gone to court to stop the state's widespread all-mail balloting; conventional wisdom suggested it would help Democrats. The legal efforts failed and turnout soared. The results turned the conventional wisdom on its head, suggesting that, at least in Montana, easier access to voting tends to draw more Republicans to cast ballots. The takeaway from the 2020 election was that a once reasonably competitive state was turning ever more securely Republican.

Cook Partisan Voting Index: R+11

Population		Race and Ethnicity		Income	
Total	1,068,778	White	88.00%	Median Income	57,153
Land area (sq. miles)	145,546	Black	0.70%	State Income Rank	40 out of 50
Pop/ sq mi	7.34	Latino	3.80%	Poverty Rate	12.60%
Born in state	53.40%	Asian	1.60%	With health insurance	91.70%
		Two or more races	3.40%	Cash public assistance	2.60%
Age Groups		Other	7.00%	Food stamp/SNAP	10.2%
Under 18	21.20%				
18-34	21.90%	**Education**		**Work**	
35-64	37.60%	H.S grad or less	34.10%	White Collar	39.10%
Over 64	19.50%	Some college	32.30%	Sales and Service	38.30%
		College Degree, 4 yr	23.10%	Blue Collar	22.70%
Military		Post grad	10.50%	Government	16.80%
Veteran/ Active Duty	10.70%				

Presidential Politics

2020 Primary (D)	Biden (D)	111,706(74%)	Sanders (D)	22,033(15%)	Warren (D)	11,984 (8%)
2020 Pres. Vote	Trump (R)	343,602(57%)	Biden (D)	244,786(41%)		
2016 Pres. Vote	Trump (R)	279,240(56%)	Clinton (D)	177,709(36%)	Johnson (L)	28,037 (6%)

With its three electoral votes and remote location, Montana doesn't see much of presidential candidates. But it was a close state in 1992, when Democrat Bill Clinton carried it by three percentage points, and in 1996, when he lost by the same margin. The state voted 59%-39% for President George W. Bush in 2004, but went only 50%-47% for John McCain. In 2016, the state swung further in the GOP direction and Donald Trump defeated Hillary Clinton 56%-36%; in 2020 he defeated Joe Biden by 57%-41%, enough coattails to send a trio of strong Democratic statewide candidates to defeat. Trump won 49 of the state's 56 counties. Biden carried only Glacier, home to a huge Blackfeet Indian reservation; Blaine, which includes the Fort Belknap Indian Reservation; Missoula, with the University of Montana; Silver Bow, where Butte was once known as "the Gibraltar of unionism;" Deer Lodge, home to what was once the largest copper smelter in the world; Big Horn, home to a substantial Crow Indian Reservation; and Gallatin, home to Montana State University in Bozeman. Trump carried Flathead County, with its affluent new migrants, and Lewis and Clark County, with its government employees who work in the state capital of Helena, and everything else.

Montana holds its presidential primaries in June when nominations have usually long since been decided. Bernie Sanders won a hard-fought primary in 2016, but in 2020, he suspended his campaign months before the contest; Biden won 75%-15%.

Congressional Districts

117th Congress Lineup	1R	**116th Congress Lineup**	1R

Greg Gianforte (R)

Elected 2020. term expires 2025, 1st term; b. April 17, 1961; San Diego CA; Stevens Institute of Technology, B.S. , 1983; Stevens Institute of Technology, M.S., 1983; Christian - Non-Denominational; Married (Susan Gianforte); 4 children

Elected Office: U.S. House, 2017-2021

Professional Career: Bell Labs; Brightwork Development Inc.; head of North American sales, McAfee Associates; founder and owner, RightNow Technologies.

Office: PO Box 200801 Helena, 59620-0801; 406-444-3111; Fax: 406-444-5529
Lt. Gov.: Kristen Juras (R) **Atty. Gen:** Austin Knudsen (R) **Sec. of State:** Christi Jacobsen (R)
State Legislature: Senate: 19D, 31R **House:** 33D, 67R

Election Results

Election	Name (Party)	Vote (%)
2020 General	Greg Gianforte (R)...	328,548 (54%)
	Mike Cooney (D)...	250,860 (42%)
	Lyman Bishop (L)...	21,479 (4%)
2020 Primary	Greg Gianforte (R)..	119,247 (53%)
	Tim Fox (R)..	60,823 (27%)
	Al Olszewski (R)...	43,080 (20%)

Prior winning percentage: 2012 (49%)

Republican Greg Gianforte traded Montana's at-large House seat for the governor's mansion in 2020, ending 16 years of Democratic control of Montana's governorship and providing the GOP unified control of state government for the first time since 2004.

Gianforte grew up in a Philadelphia suburb and attended Stevens Institute of Technology in Hoboken; he lived and worked in New Jersey before moving to Montana in the mid-1990s. He started the technology firm RightNow Technologies, which he sold to Oracle for $1.8 billion. As the GOP nominee against Democratic Gov. Steve Bullock in 2016, he spent more than $6 million from his own pocket but lost to Bullock by just shy of 19,000 votes. In May 2017, Gianforte ran in the special election to succeed GOP Rep. Ryan Zinke, who had been tapped as Interior secretary by President Donald Trump. Gianforte faced Democrat Rob Quist, a musician who spent 11 years on the Montana Arts Council and served as an ambassador for Montana to its sister state in Japan. Quist, who rarely was seen without a cowboy hat, highlighted his support during the 2016 presidential campaign for Sen. Bernie Sanders of Vermont. This led the Democratic Congressional Campaign Committee to conclude that his prospects were dim; this lack of support dismayed many party activists, who saw an opportunity to take a Republican-held seat, especially in the contentious political climate.

Gianforte ran into problems during the campaign on health care policy. When asked whether he would support the recent House-passed Republican plan, he initially said he would not respond until the Congressional Budget Office had issued its analysis. The CBO issued its report on the day before the Montana election. That led Ben Jacobs, a Washington-based reporter for the Guardian newspaper, to cite the CBO in seeking Gianforte's reaction. Gianforte proceeded to throw Jacobs to the floor, breaking his glasses and leading him to get X-rays at a local hospital. Prominent state newspapers quickly withdrew their endorsements of Gianforte, and he was charged with a misdemeanor. The impact on voters, however, appeared to be negligible; Gianforte won, 50%-44%. (Because Montana allows no-excuse absentee voting, some 75 percent of voters had already cast their ballot by Election Day.) He apologized to the reporter as he delivered his victory speech; he eventually pleaded guilty to misdemeanor assault and received a six-month deferred sentence that included community service and anger-management classes. Gianforte's attack on Jacobs impressed Trump. "Any guy that can do a body slam, he's my kind of — he's my guy," the president said at a campaign rally in Montana in October 2018.

In seeking a full term in 2018, Gianforte faced another competitive and expensive contest, this time against Kathleen Williams, a former state legislator who had worked as a resource economist with the Forest Service and nonprofit conservation groups. In its editorial endorsing Williams, the Missoulian argued that Gianforte had failed to seek consensus and was "the kind of leader who prefers to give orders, rather than follow them." But his victory margin ended up similar to what he'd had in the special election: 51%-46%. Gianforte gained a seat on the Energy and Commerce Committee. But with Bullock term-limited in 2020, Gianforte cast his eye toward the governor's race. Bullock had won two terms in his generally red state, including a reelection victory that came on the same day as Donald Trump's rout of Hillary Clinton. During his two terms, Bullock demonstrated an ability to work with establishment Republicans, achieving victories on expanding Medicaid and tightening campaign finance laws, while using his veto pen to oppose legislation sought by conservatives.

Gianforte promised a different approach from Bullock's. In the GOP primary, Gianforte faced term-limited Attorney General Tim Fox and state Sen. Al Olszewski. (The field initially included Secretary of State Corey Stapleton, but when Gianforte joined the field, Stapleton decided to run for the open House seat instead.) Fox was the establishment candidate, touting his experience in government. Olszewski, a surgeon, came from the GOP's more conservative wing; unlike his two rivals, he urged rescinding Bullock's expansion of Medicaid. Gianforte also courted the party's conservative wing by touting his support from Trump; Donald Trump Jr. was featured at a fundraiser. Gianforte also emphasized his business record, saying it would enable him to jump-start the state's economy. Bolstered by an edge in fundraising, Gianforte took 53 percent, with Fox at 27 percent and Olszewski at 19 percent. Meanwhile, in the Democratic primary, Mike Cooney, who had been appointed to the vacant lieutenant governorship by Bullock, faced Whitney Williams, daughter of former Rep. Pat Williams and former Montana Senate majority leader Carol Williams. Cooney, the grandson of a Montana governor from the 1930s, had a long record in politics, including service as Senate president and secretary of state; he won the primary by a 10-point margin.

National handicappers saw the general election as the only genuinely competitive gubernatorial race in the country. On the one hand, Republicans knew that with Trump at the top of the ticket, they would have the wind at their backs; Trump tweeted his support and Vice President Mike Pence headlined a rally for Gianforte. On the other hand, Democrats felt they had a strong ticket: Bullock was challenging Sen. Steve Daines, and credible Democratic candidates were running for the open House seat and several other statewide offices. Democrats also saw an opening in Gianforte's rough edges. Cooney criticized Gianforte's lax approach to mask-wearing during the coronavirus pandemic, and argued for maintaining public-lands access and increasing school spending. Gianforte attacked Cooney as a political insider. Gianforte held a fundraising edge, spending about three times as much as Cooney. When the results came in, the GOP had swept every statewide race by double digits. Cooney slightly outran Joe Biden in the state, and he notched a win in Lewis and Clark County (Helena) that had eluded Biden. But Gianforte still won by a comfortable 13 points. "You've sent a loud message to Helena, a message to the state capitol from every corner of this great state, that after 16 long years of single-party rule in the governor's office, it's time for Helena to change the way they do business," Gianforte said.

With the last Democratic obstacle to Republican legislation gone—and with some moderate Republican legislators having been defeated in primaries by conservatives—Republicans prepared to pursue a strongly conservative agenda. In his first press conference in office, Gianforte promised to undo Bullock's coronavirus mask mandate. (He would eventually test positive in April 2021.) Gianforte eventually signed legislation erecting liability shields for coronavirus-related lawsuits for businesses, churches and other groups, as well as a measure to keep the state and its localities from enforcing federal bans on firearms, ammunition and magazines. But the state House rejected a "right-to-work" bill before it got to the governor's desk. In the meantime, Gianforte was found to have violated Montana regulations when he trapped and shot a collared wolf near Yellowstone National Park in February 2021. He was given a written warning and promised to take a three-hour online course.

Jon Tester (D)

Elected 2006, term expires 2024, 3rd term, b. Aug 21, 1956; Havre, MT; University of Great Falls, B.S., 1978; Christian; Married (Sharla Tester); 2 children; 2 grandchildren.

Elected Office: Big Sandy School Board, 1983-1992, Chairman, 1986-1991; MT Senate, 1998-2006, Minority Leader, 2003-2005, pres., 2005-2006.

Professional Career: Operations Management, Procter & Gamble, 1984-1997; VP, Clair Daines Construction, 1997-2000; General Manager/VP, Right-Now Technologies, 2000-2012.

DC Office: 311 HSOB 20510, 202-224-2644, Fax: 202-224-8594, tester.senate.gov

State Offices: Billings, 406-252-0550; Bozeman, 406-586-4450; Butte, 406-723-3277; Great Falls, 406-452-9585; Helena, 406-449-5401; Kalispell, 406-257-3360; Missoula, 406-728-3003.

Committees: *Appropriations*: Agriculture, Rural Development, FDA & Related Agencies; Department of Defense (Chmn); Department of Homeland Security; Department of the Interior, Environment & Related Agencies; Energy & Water Development; Military Construction & Veteran Affairs & Related Agencies. *Banking, Housing & Urban Affairs*: Financial Institutions & Consumer Protection; Housing, Transportation & Community Development; National Security & International

Trade & Finance. *Commerce, Science & Transportation*: Aviation Safety, Operations & Innovations; Communications, Media & Broadband; Surface Transportation, Maritime Freight & Ports; Tourism, Trade & Export Promotion. *Indian Affairs. Veterans' Affairs (Chmn).*

Group Ratings

	ADA	ACLU	AFL-CIO	LCV	COC	HAFA	ACU	CFG	FRC
2020	-	77%	-	92%	-	9%	11%	-	-
2019	95%	C	95%	100%	57%	C	11%	17%	0%

Almanac Ratings 2019-2020

	Economy	Social	Foreign	Composite
Liberal	79%	79%	89%	82%
Conservative	21%	21%	11%	18%

Key Votes of the 116th Congress

1. EPA clean energy rules	Y	5. Russia sanctions	Y	9. Barr as Atty. General	N
2. U.S./Mex./Can. trade deal	Y	6. Troops in SYR, AFG	Y	10. Spending at the border	Y
3. Cut unemployment benefits	N	7. Veto arms sales to Saudis	Y	11. Coney Barrett to Sup. Ct.	N
4. Shelton to Fed Reserve	N	8. Defense $$$, veto override	Y	12. Electoral College objections	N

Election Results

Election	Name (Party)	Vote (%)		Cand. Spent	Ind. Exp. Support	Ind. Exp. Oppose
2018 General	Jon Tester (D)	253,876	(50%)	$22,410,746	$3,892,048	$18,519,787
	Matt Rosendale (R)	235,963	(47%)	$5,522,453	$5,182,081	$15,651,214
	Rick Breckenridge (Lib)	14,545	(3%)			
2018 Primary	Jon Tester (D)	114,948	(100%)			

Prior winning percentages: 2018 (50%), 2012 (49%), 2006 (49%)

Democrat Jon Tester won his third close Senate contest in 2018, taking more than 50 percent of the vote for the first time. With his signature flattop haircut and his plain-spoken Western manner inveighing against "D.C. politicians," he doesn't come across like a typical Democrat. But he has compiled a more liberal voting record than other red-state Democratic colleagues and will be a top target in 2024 if he seeks a fourth term. He is Montana's sole remaining statewide elected Democrat.

Tester grew up in a farming family, on the same prairie land his grandparents homesteaded almost a century ago near the tiny town of Big Sandy. His family ran a butcher shop behind their barn; at 9, Tester lost three fingers from his left hand in a meat grinder. The accident, he has said, changed him from a saxophone player to a trumpeter. He earned a music degree from the University of Great Falls and taught music at an elementary school before devoting himself to farming. He has raised wheat, hay, alfalfa, barley, buckwheat, lentils, millet, and peas and served on the local Soil Conservation Service Committee. He then switched to organic farming. "In the '80s, we realized we had to do something to add value to our product. ... That's when we made the conversion to organic," He told Esquire magazine. "It's been a blessing for us. Before we converted, when we sprayed weeds, I just planned on being sick for about a week."

Tester's political career began on the Big Sandy School Board, on which he served a decade. In 1998, when his neighbor, a Republican state senator, decided not to seek reelection, Tester ran for and won the seat. In 2002, he became minority leader, then Senate president in 2005 after Democrats won a majority. In that role, he helped pass a budget that cut taxes for small businesses and middle-class families while increasing funding for public education. When the 2005 legislative session adjourned, Tester challenged three-term Republican Sen. Conrad Burns.

In the primary, Tester faced two-term state Auditor John Morrison, a former president of the Montana Trial Lawyers Association and the son of a state Supreme Court justice. Running as an unabashed populist, Tester gained support from Daily Kos and other progressive internet groups, and in Montana he assembled a formidable grassroots operation with hundreds of volunteers. He beat Morrison 61%-35%.

Tester was taking on the only Republican senator Montana voters had ever reelected. But by 2006, the 71-year-old conservative incumbent had two serious problems. The first was his connection to disgraced lobbyist Jack Abramoff. Burns was the largest congressional recipient of campaign donations from Abramoff's clients, and he faced campaign accusations that he "sold his vote" and betrayed Montana's American Indian population by earmarking funds for Abramoff's Indian clients in other states. Burns' second handicap was a gaffe-prone style; in 2006, while discussing the wars in Afghanistan and Iraq, he spoke of enemies who "drive taxicabs in the daytime and kill at night."

Burns spent $9 million, $3.5 million more than Tester, and argued that the Democrat was too liberal for Montana because of his opposition to the Patriot Act and links to "radical environmentalists" and left-wing bloggers. But Montana voters have a strong libertarian streak, putting Tester's privacy and foreign policy views in the state's mainstream, and Tester was not so easily caricatured as a liberal. His haircut, highlighted in a television ad filmed at the Riverview Barber Shop in Great Falls, and stocky farmer's build, combined with his 3,000 acre farm and down-to-earth style tempered the criticism. The race was decided by 3,562 votes.

In Washington, Tester stressed the importance of transparency and accountability in government, distancing himself from the questionable practices that hurt his predecessor. He co-sponsored a Republican bill to ban former members of Congress from ever lobbying and joined a group of senators seeking to ban secret holds on legislation and nominations, a longtime Senate practice. Tester drew notice for posting his daily schedules on the internet, a Senate first. In 2015, his bill to streamline the federal hiring process for its civil servants was signed into law by President Barack Obama. He was distinctive in other ways, too. He has brought to Washington beef he'd butchered himself.

Tester has supported abortion rights and same-sex marriage and taken a nuanced view of gun rights. He co-sponsored with Republican Sen. John McCain of Arizona an amendment to repeal Washington D.C.'s gun control laws. And early in Obama's presidency, Tester and fellow Montana Democratic Sen. Max Baucus made it clear they would oppose any attempt to reinstate the ban on military-style weapons. But after the 2012 massacre at an elementary school in Newtown Connecticut, Tester was one of the few red-state Democrats to back the legislation from Democratic Sen. Joe Manchin of West Virginia and Republican Sen. Pat Toomey of Pennsylvania to tighten background checks for gun purchases. He voted against a 2016 proposal to close the "gun show loophole" in background checks because it didn't have an exemption for sales and gifts between family members.

Tester has a libertarian view on surveillance issues. He was one of eight senators led by GOP Sen. Rand Paul of Kentucky to filibuster the Patriot Act's reauthorization in 2015, though he backed the eventual compromise legislation. He voted against President Donald Trump's first nominee for CIA director, former GOP Rep. Mike Pompeo of Kansas, saying he was concerned about Pompeo's views on surveillance and "enhanced interrogation"; he also opposed Pompeo's nomination as secretary of State.

Baucus' departure to become ambassador to China in early 2014 gave Tester the chairmanship of the Indian Affairs Committee. In his first few months, he impressed tribal observers with his energy, getting more than a dozen bills through the panel dealing with housing, education, water rights. He also passed a legislative remedy for a 2009 Supreme Court decision that limited the Interior Department's ability to take lands into trusts for tribes. Indian Country Today praised Tester's "shoe leather diplomacy," including visits to Native American communities to gauge education, health, and environmental programs. He called for protecting the Badger-Two Medicine area near Glacier National Park in Montana, a place sacred to the Blackfeet Tribe but long a bone of contention with oil and gas companies. Tester and Montana's junior senator, Republican Steve Daines, have repeatedly won committee-level approval of federal recognition for the Little Shell Tribe of Chippewa Indians. A companion bill passed the House in 2018 but failed in the Senate. In 2020, his bills to address the growing number of missing and murdered indigenous women, Savanna's Act and Not Invisible Act, were signed into law.

Tester has tested the boundaries of party loyalty. He was one of only two Democrats in 2011 to join Republicans in a filibuster of Obama's jobs bill; he said it contained "tax gimmicks" that did not address deficit reduction. He aroused the ire of left-wing bloggers in December 2010 when he voted against the DREAM Act, which would have provided a path to citizenship for immigrants brought to the U.S. illegally as children. Tester has since reversed his position on the issue and was critical of Trump when the president moved to end his predecessor's Deferred Action for Childhood Arrivals program, which gives those same immigrants legal protections. Tester has long supported construction of the Keystone XL pipeline, which would have run through Montana, despite the concerns of environmentalists and most Democrats. "When I fill my tractor up if I'm going to farm, you know what I'm going to fill it full of? It ain't electricity—that's fired by coal, by the way—it's fuel," he told a town hall in 2019. On his first day in office, President Joe Biden canceled the permit for the pipeline, which Trump had signed. Tester and Daines tried to attach an amendment to a

COVID-19 relief bill to override Biden's decision, but the measure failed. "When I disagree with my party, I tell them the truth, and the truth is that the jobs and tax revenue Keystone will create would provide a critical boost to the folks that live and work in rural Montana," Tester said.

Tester has cut a moderate profile on the Banking, Housing, and Urban Affairs Committee, helping community banks and often siding with Republicans to push deregulation. That's made him a top recipient of banking industry donations. He worked in 2009 on the law that banned certain credit card fees and deadlines and provided an extra week for paying bills. A year later, he sponsored a successful amendment requiring large banks to pay higher Federal Deposit Insurance Corp. fees. He sought to block limits on the "swipe fees" that banks and credit card companies charge stores for debit card transactions, arguing fee limits would hurt small rural banks, but the effort fell short.

In early 2018, Tester was a key player in helping Republicans roll back the sweeping Dodd-Frank financial reforms that were enacted after the 2008 financial crisis. The bill, pushed hard by regional banks and credit unions, exempted about two dozen financial companies with assets between $50 billion and $250 billion from the same level of Federal Reserve scrutiny reserved for the largest banks. "The Main Street banks, community banks and credit unions didn't create the crisis in 2008, and they were getting heavily regulated," Tester told the New York Times, adding, "There's not one thing in this bill that gives Wall Street a break." Liberals, including Massachusetts Sen. Elizabeth Warren, disagreed. But the bill passed with moderate Democrats' support. Tester also backed Trump's rewrite of the North American Free Trade Agreement—the United States-Mexico-Canada Agreement—citing a change to how Canada will classify U.S. wheat varieties, which he said will lead to a higher valuation.

None of Tester's statewide races has been easy. In 2012, he faced a tough race in a presidential election year when Obama was deeply unpopular in his home state. His opponent was Republican Denny Rehberg, Montana's sole House member. In 2011, the nonpartisan Center for Responsive Politics found that Tester, despite running as an outsider, had accepted more campaign contributions from lobbyists than any other member of Congress. Republicans pointed to Tester's financial support from large banks as evidence of hypocrisy.

Rehberg relied on the standard Republican strategy of attacking his opponent as a liberal Obama ally, citing Tester's vote in favor of the president's health care law, though that strategy took a hit when it was revealed that the National Republican Senatorial Committee had photoshopped Tester's face onto the body of a man who was embracing Obama for one of its ads. The man was obviously not Tester: He had had all his fingers. Tester defended his Obamacare vote, saying it let people purchase "health care without breaking the bank." He took a page from the national Democratic playbook in sowing doubt about Rehberg's support for Social Security and Medicare. Tester won 49%-45%; Obama lost the state by 14 points.

Tester's campaign trail acumen helped him to take over as chairman of the Democratic Senatorial Campaign Committee for the 2016 cycle; he had to defend just 10 seats, while the GOP had 24 up for reelection. Despite Tester's misgivings about the job's intense fundraising demands, he helped the committee outraise the NRSC by more than $40 million for the cycle. But Democrats failed to recapture the Senate, picking up just two seats in a disappointing election cycle and losing races in which they appeared to have the edge in Wisconsin and Pennsylvania.

Tester headed into 2018 with a target on his back: Trump had won his state by 20 points, a big swing from Obama's 2-point loss there in 2008. Republicans were hopeful they could find a top-tier candidate to challenge Tester, but Trump removed the potential challenger who many believed to be Tester's biggest threat when he chose Republican Rep. Ryan Zinke to become Interior secretary. Tester gleefully introduced Zinke at his committee confirmation hearing and voted for his confirmation.

Republicans were left with second-tier candidates, and state Auditor Matt Rosendale emerged from the primary to face Tester. Rosendale, like Tester, sported a flattop haircut. But he also had a thick Maryland accent—he didn't move to Montana until the early 2000s, after making his millions in real estate. Rosendale branded himself a rancher, but documents showed that he'd never worked on his family ranch and instead had kept working as a developer. Out-of-state developers are despised by many native Montanans who are dismayed by development and the influx of outsiders.

Despite Rosendale's flaws as a candidate, he still had one huge asset: Trump. Tester became the ranking Democrat on the Senate Veterans' Affairs Committee in 2017, and infuriated Trump when he blocked the president's second nominee to head the Department of Veterans Affairs, Ronny Jackson. Jackson had been accused of sexually harassing subordinates and using drugs and alcohol on the job as the White House physician. Tester regularly voted against Trump's nominees in 2017, and in early 2018 he was the only red-state Democrat to stand with his party against reopening the government after Democrats engineered a short-term shutdown over Trump's refusal to help Dreamers after moving to end the DACA program protecting them. (There was also a dispute over funding for Trump's wall along the southern border.) Tester's rationale wasn't about immigration; he didn't like that the short-term funding bill didn't fund Montana hospitals. Trump spent at least as much time and energy trying to take out Tester as any other Democrat in the country after swearing Tester would have a "big price to pay" for blocking Jackson. The former White House physician won a congressional seat from Texas in 2020.

Tester touted his Montana roots and work on the Veterans Affairs' Committee. And like many Democrats, he touted his defense of the Affordable Care Act. That included an ad in which he talked about how he'd lost his fingers and how his parents had to pay for the hospital visit out of pocket because of "junk insurance" plans he said Rosendale wanted to allow back in. Tester led the entire race, but like other red-state Democrats, saw polls head in the wrong direction in the final month as the polarizing hearings over Supreme Court nominee Brett Kavanaugh returned Republicans to their party. Tester prevailed with 50.3 percent of the vote; Rosendale got 46.8 percent. That was the first time that Tester took a majority of the vote.

When Democrats won the Senate majority in 2021, Tester became chairman of the Veterans Affairs' Committee. As a more centrist senator, he has been hesitant to abolish the 60-vote threshold to limit debate on legislation but instead joined a group of 20 bipartisan senators seeking a way to reform the legislative filibuster. He signaled support for Biden's idea of requiring senators wanting to block a bill to speak the entire time on the Senate floor. He told The Washington Post that change is "entirely appropriate." Tester opposed liberal calls to expand the Supreme Court after Justice Amy Coney Barrett's confirmation just ahead of the 2020 elections. Tester has also been critical of his party's failure to reach out to rural voters, which he detailed in his book Grounded: A Senator's Lessons on Winning Back Rural America, suggesting Democrats talk more about infrastructure and broadband access. After Trump strengthened his performance in rural areas in the 2020 election, Tester told The New York Times, "I can go into the list of things that might be insane about this president, but the truth is that rural people connect more with a millionaire from New York City than they do with the Democrats that are in national positions. So that tells me our message is really, really flawed, because I certainly don't see it that way."

Steve Daines (R)

Elected 2014, term expires 2026, 2nd term, b. Aug 20, 1962; Van Nuys, CA; Montana State University, Bozeman, B.S., 1984; Presbyterian; Married (Cindy Daines); 4 children.

Elected Office: U.S. House, 2013-2015.

Professional Career: Employee, Operations and Business Management, Procter & Gamble, 1984-1997; Montana Chair, Governor Mike Huckabee for President, 2007-2008; VP, RightNow Technologies, 2000-2012.

DC Office: 320 HSOB 20510, 202-224-2651, Fax: 202-228-1236, daines.senate.gov

State Offices: Billings, 406-245-6822; Bozeman, 406-587-3446; Great Falls, 406-453-0148; Helena, 406-443-3189; Kalispell, 406-257-3765; Missoula, 406-549-8198; Sidney, 406-482-9010.

Committees: *Banking, Housing & Urban Affairs*: Economic Policy; Housing, Transportation & Community Development; National Security & International Trade & Finance. *Energy & Natural Resources*: National Parks (RMM); Public Lands, Forests & Mining. *Finance*: Energy, Natural Resources & Infrastructure; Health Care (RMM); International Trade, Customs & Global Competitiveness. *Indian Affairs*.

Group Ratings

	ADA	ACLU	AFL-CIO	LCV	COC	HAFA	ACU	CFG	FRC
2020	-	23%	-	15%	-	85%	85%	-	-
2019	5%	C	11%	29%	75%	C	84%	84%	100%

Almanac Ratings 2019-2020

	Economy	Social	Foreign	Composite
Liberal	6%	6%	17%	10%
Conservative	94%	94%	83%	90%

Key Votes of the 116th Congress

1. EPA clean energy rules	N	5. Russia sanctions	Y	9. Barr as Atty. General	Y
2. U.S./Mex./Can. trade deal	Y	6. Troops in SYR, AFG	Y	10. Spending at the border	Y
3. Cut unemployment benefits	Y	7. Veto arms sales to Saudis	N	11. Coney Barrett to Sup. Ct.	Y
4. Shelton to Fed Reserve	Y	8. Defense $$$, veto override	Y	12. Electoral College objections	N

Election Results

Election	Name (Party)	Vote (%)	Cand. Spent	Ind. Exp. Support	Ind. Exp. Oppose
2020 General	Steve Daines (R)	333,174 (55%)	$29,976,534	$8,507,045	$47,138,826
	Steve Bullock (D)	272,463 (45%)	$46,554,801	$12,951,637	$41,879,351
2020 Primary	Steve Daines (R)	192,942 (88%)			
	John Driscoll (R)	13,944 (6%)			
	Daniel Larson (R)	12,319 (6%)			

Prior winning percentages: 2014 (58%), House: 2012 (53%)

Republican Steve Daines of Montana coasted to the Senate in 2014 as the Democrats' chosen candidate imploded. But in 2020, it was a different story. Popular Gov. Steve Bullock entered the race, thrusting the contest into the national spotlight as one that could decide which party controlled the Senate. While the state has voted reliably red at the presidential level for nearly three decades, voters showed a more libertarian, independent streak in choosing governors and senators. After all, Daines, the state's junior senator, had become only the second GOP senator from Montana since 1913. But Daines's convincing 10-point win over Bullock, who had won four successive statewide contests, highlighted that even Montana is bowing to national, partisan trends. If that holds true, Daines could comfortably hold his seat for decades.

Daines grew up in Bozeman, where his father started a home-construction business. He studied chemical engineering at Montana State University. During his senior year, he became one of the youngest delegates at the 1984 Republican National Convention. Daines spent 13 years with consumer goods giant Procter & Gamble, managing operations in the United States before moving his young family for a six-year stint with the company in Hong Kong and China. In 1997, Daines left P&G to join the family construction business in Bozeman. Three years later, he got a call from entrepreneur Greg Gianforte, founder of RightNow Technologies, asking him to come on board as vice president of customer service. Daines has since returned the favor, supporting Gianforte in his failed 2016 gubernatorial run and backing his controversial but successful run for Congress a few months later; Gianforte won the governorship in 2020.

Daines dipped into local politics in 2007 when he and his wife, Cindy, founded GiveitBack.com, a now-defunct nonprofit that pushed for the return of the state's $1 billion budget surplus to taxpayers. Not long after that, former Arkansas Gov. Mike Huckabee asked Daines to serve as Montana state chairman for his presidential campaign. Daines also chaired Montana's delegation to the 2008 Republican National Convention. That same year, he ran for lieutenant governor on a ticket with former state Sen. Roy Brown, but they failed to oust Democratic Gov. Brian Schweitzer.

Two years later, Daines announced his intention to challenge Democrat Jon Tester for his Senate seat. But when Rep. Denny Rehberg said that he would run against Tester, Daines dropped out of the Senate race to seek Rehberg's vacated House seat. He won with 53 percent of the vote; he compiled a conservative record and focused on Montana's energy production.

Daines's rise to the Senate included some good fortune. Rehberg left politics after losing the 2012 race to Tester. The state's other Democratic senator, Max Baucus, resigned when President Barack Obama named him ambassador to China in 2014. Daines jumped into the race, just 14 months after his election to the House. When Schweitzer declined to run, Democrats turned to Lt. Gov. John Walsh, a retired Army general who had been tapped by Bullock to succeed Baucus. But in June, the New York Times published a bombshell story, reporting that Walsh had plagiarized large portions of his master's thesis at the Army War College. Walsh's muddled response made matters worse. In

August, shortly before the ballot deadline, he exited the race. The party chose state Rep. Amanda Curtis to take his place, but a race that had already favored the well-funded Daines in a strong year for Republicans turned into a rout. Daines defeated Curtis 58%-40%.

Daines took seats on two panels of special interest to Montana—the Energy and Natural Resources as well as the Indian Affairs committees—plus Appropriations. The first Senate bill he introduced was the Balanced Budget Accountability Act, which would have forced lawmakers to balance the budget or give up their salaries. He urged approval of the Keystone XL pipeline and decried federal regulations that curbed timber harvests.

Daines has chaired the Western Caucus, a coalition of western Republicans focused on land use and energy issues. In 2017, he introduced a bill that would open a half-million acres of Montana land for development by removing them from a federal Wilderness Study Areas list. He and other western GOP senators proposed a wildfire management bill in 2017.

He has worked across the aisle on several measures, including legislation to reauthorize the Federal Land and Water Conservation Fund, which protects and conserves public lands. The 50-year-old program's funding lapsed in late 2018, but Congress restored the coverage in February 2019. Daines sponsored a bill to bar energy development on the North and Middle forks of the Flathead River, and worked with Tester to push for federal recognition of the Little Shell Tribe of Chippewa Indians. The former tech executive led successful efforts to expand broadband and cellular coverage, with the Federal Communications Commission approving expanded wireless broadband access for 1 million people in Montana and Wyoming in response to his efforts.

In 2019, Daines secured a spot on the Senate Finance Committee. He and Republican Sen. James Lankford of Oklahoma were the first senators in 75 years to serve simultaneously on Finance and Appropriations. He chaired the Energy panel's National Parks subcommittee. In 2021, Daines left Appropriations and was reassigned to the Banking, Housing and Urban Affairs Committee; he became the ranking member on the National Parks panel.

Daines was a steady ally of President Donald Trump, even as he split with the now-former president on some foreign policy and trade issues. Daines, a free-trade advocate, helped engineer a $300 million deal that allowed Montana ranchers to sell beef to China, but he defended Trump's decision to start a trade war with that country. He said he believed U.S. intelligence officials' assessment that Russia meddled in the 2016 presidential election, and he pressed Russian officials not to interfere in future elections during a visit to the country, though he steadily defended Trump when the president rejected the intelligence agencies' assessment. In late 2018, he visited Afghanistan and said it would be a mistake to withdraw troops, disagreeing with Trump.

Daines threatened to vote against Republicans' sweeping tax cuts in late 2017 because he was concerned the package helped big companies more than small businesses. He got what he wanted—a bigger tax cut for pass-through businesses. The change cut his own taxes significantly, according to an analysis from the Billings Gazette.

He opposed his state continuing its Medicaid expansion program unless it defunded Planned Parenthood. In late 2018, he called on Senate leaders to eliminate the filibuster and authorize funding for Trump's long-demanded wall along the U.S.-Mexico border.

In 2020, it looked like Daines would avoid a tough reelection fight after Bullock, the term-limited but popular Democratic governor who had made a brief run for president, repeatedly demurred on a Senate campaign, telling the Montana Standard that he wasn't sure he'd "find being a senator that compelling." But, hoping to expand the Senate battlefield and win back the majority, Democrats set out to woo Bullock. As the March filing deadline approached, both former President Barack Obama and Senate Democratic Leader Chuck Schumer met with Bullock—and it worked. Bullock announced he would run on the last day possible, and all other major Democratic candidates withdrew.

Despite Bullock's repeated denials, Republicans and Daines had anticipated this "Battle of the Steves." The GOP immediately capitalized on positions the governor had taken during his short-lived White House bid, including coming out in favor of a ban on semiautomatic weapons and limits on ammunition magazines—reversals of positions Bullock had taken in his four elections to statewide office in pro-gun Montana. But Bullock wanted to focus more on his tenure as governor, saying in his announcement he'd "make Washington work more like Montana" and emphasizing his support for Medicaid expansion and for public lands. Daines, however, framed the contest in partisan terms. "If I lose this seat here in Montana, we lose the majority," he told Fox Radio. Daines didn't shy away from Trump, who had won the state by 20 percentage points in 2016. Just months before the election, he worked with Colorado Sen. Cory Gardner, another highly endangered Republican, to enact the Great American Outdoors Act, which provided $9.5 billion for a maintenance backlog for national parks and public lands, along with mandatory annual funding for the Land and Water Conservation Fund.

The race was neck and neck. Democrats hoped that Joe Biden would perform better in the state than Hillary Clinton did four years earlier to boost Bullock. As Trump and Republicans sought to blame China for the COVID-19 outbreak, Bullock—boosted in polls by his handling of the pandemic as governor—highlighted Daines' work in China. However, the death of Justice Ruth Bader Ginsburg in September 2020 and the quick confirmation of conservative jurist Amy Coney Barrett to replace her likely boosted Daines. The contest became increasingly nationalized: Daines tied Bullock to Schumer and House Speaker Nancy Pelosi, saying they'd institute "liberal tyranny"; Bullock retorted: "Montanans want a leader, not a lapdog," and he criticized the incumbent for voting to repeal the Affordable Care Act. Ultimately, the vote wasn't even close. Daines beat Bullock 55%-45%, as Trump carried the state by 16 points. The loss made Bullock just the latest Democrat in a red state to fail to translate success as a governor into a Senate victory.

Matt Rosendale (R)

Elected 2020, 1st term, b. Jul 07, 1960; Baltimore, MD; Chesapeake College; Catholic; Married (Jean Rosendale); 3 children.

Elected Office: MT House, 2010-2012; MT Senate, 2013-2017; Majority Leader, MT Senate, 2015-2017; Auditor, State of MT, 2017-2021.

Professional Career: Owner, consulting group; Owner, ranch.

DC Office: 1037 LHOB 20515, 202-225-3211, rosendale.house.gov

State Offices: Billings, 406-413-6720; Great Falls, 406-770-6260; Helena, 406-502-1435.

Committees: *Natural Resources*: Indigenous Peoples of the United States; National Parks, Forests & Public Lands. *Veterans' Affairs*: Health; Technology Modernization (RMM).

Election Results

Election	Name (Party)	Vote (%)		Cand. Spent	Ind. Exp. Support	Ind. Exp. Oppose
2020 General	Matt Rosendale (R)	339,169	(56%)	$3,568,605	$1,150,599	$4,045,840
2020 Primary	Matt Rosendale (R)	104,575	(48%)			
	Corey Stapleton (R)	71,902	(33%)			
	Debra Lamm (R)	14,462	(7%)			
	Joe Dooling (R)	13,726	(6%)			

Matt Rosendale won the House seat as part of Republicans' shuffle of statewide offices in Montana in 2020. He defeated Democrat Kathleen Williams by 13 percentage points. His victory fell within the narrow range of 54.4 to 56.9 percent of the vote by which GOP nominees in Montana won the vote for president, governor, senator and the House.

In his second bid for the House, he succeeded Greg Gianforte, who was elected governor. Rosendale, then the state auditor, challenged Democratic Sen. Jon Tester in 2018 and lost, 50%-47%. His improved showing in the presidential-election year suggested that Rosendale might have his eye on Tester's seat in 2024.

As a Maryland native (which led Democrats to refer to him as "Maryland Matt"), he had been successful in real estate. He moved to Montana in 2002 and expanded his interest in property development, a booming business with more than 60 agents in four offices. He owned a 9,000-acre ranch with cattle and crops in Glendive, which he said he visited a few times each year; that site was close to the state's border with North Dakota and more than 400 miles from his day job in Helena. Rosendale was elected to the state House in 2010. Two years later, he was elected to the state Senate, where he became majority leader.

That led to a series of four contests for three statewide office at two-year intervals, with two victories and two defeats. In 2014, Rosendale ran for the open House seat and finished third in the Republican primary with 29 percent of the vote; Ryan Zinke won with 33 percent. Rosendale was elected in 2016 to the state office with the formal title of Commissioner of Securities and Insurance, Auditor, which he won, 54%-46%, against Democrat Jesse Laslovich; he won that GOP nomination without opposition. As auditor, he clashed with then-Gov. Steve Bullock on health care issues.

Oddly, both Rosendale and Williams were defeated when each ran for Congress in 2018. Williams challenged Gianforte and lost, 51%-46%; that was the best performance by a Democrat running for that House seat since 1994. In Rosendale's Senate bid, he narrowly won the GOP primary with 34 percent of the vote. The high-profile contest put Rosendale on the national political map with four campaign visits from President Donald Trump, who had clashed with Tester. That gave Rosendale an opportunity to mend fences with Trump, after having supported Sen. Ted Cruz in the presidential primary in 2016.

In 2020, Rosendale faced another wide-open primary when he ran for the House. His chief opponent in the six-candidate field was Corey Stapleton, the secretary of state who highlighted that he was a Montana native who graduated from the U.S. Naval Academy and served 11 years in the Navy. As the state's chief election officer, Stapleton gained added responsibilities during the pandemic that spring. Rosendale outspent Stapleton more than 4-to-1 and won the primary, 48%-33%.

Williams, who served six years in the state House, was an expert on water rights during her career in natural resource planning. She criticized Rosendale's work as a developer. "I spent more than 30 years fighting for our outdoor heritage, while Matt Rosendale has advocated for the transfer and sale of our public lands," an unpopular position among some Montana voters, she told the Flathead Beacon newspaper in Kalispell. Rosendale dismissed her as "far left" and ran closely with the GOP ticket led by Trump. "I've got the president's ear, he's got my back, and that's what people are looking for," he said during a campaign debate.

Like many Democrats running for Congress in 2020, Williams outspent Rosendale by about $2 million. But he won the contest, 56.4%-43.6%. In the House, he got seats on the Natural Resources and Veterans' Affairs committees. With Montana gaining a House district following the 2021 reapportionment, Williams might have the opportunity to run again for an open seat in 2022.

NEBRASKA

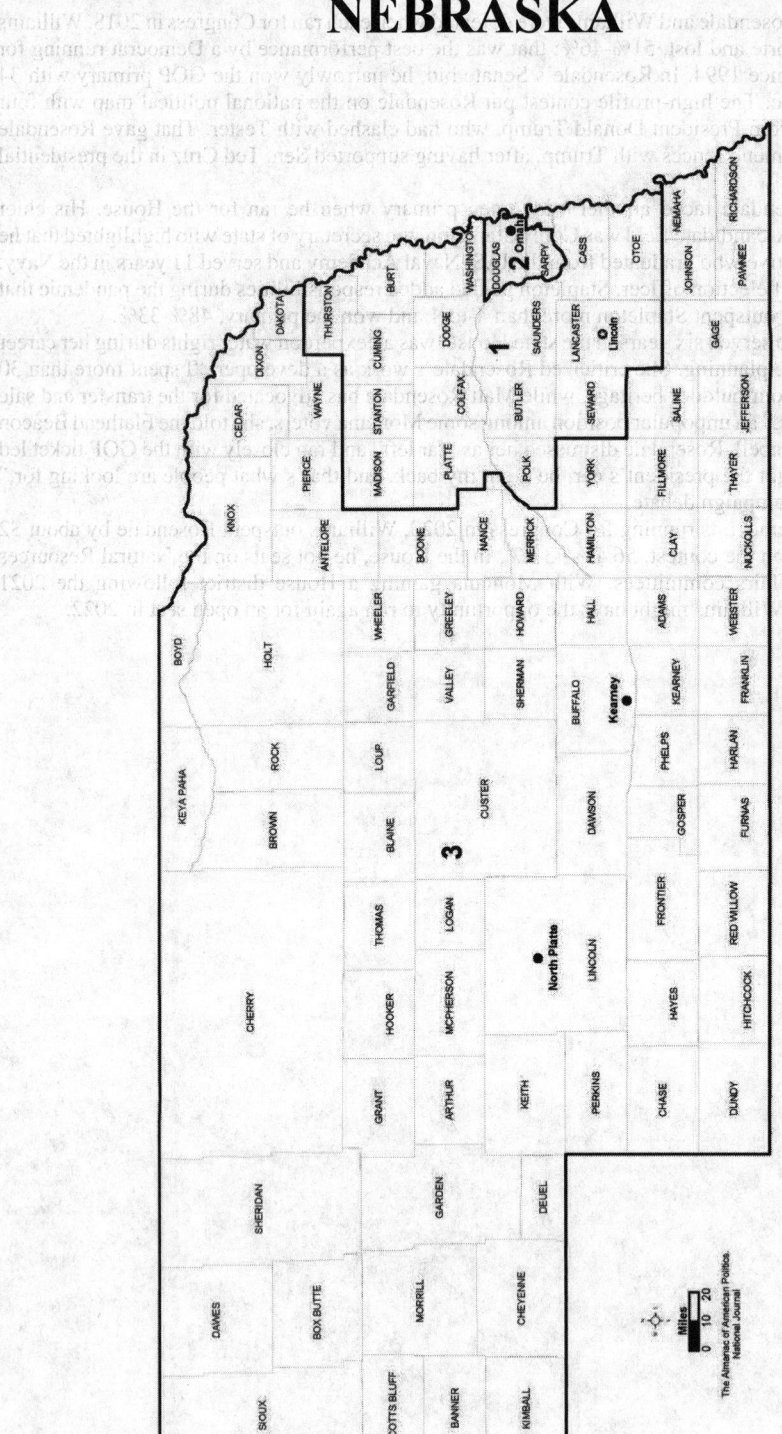

The Almanac of American Politics,
National Journal

Nebraska has long been, and remains, one of the most Republican states in the nation. But its largest and fastest-growing metropolitan area, Omaha, is politically marginal. Thanks to the state's eccentric Electoral College rules, the Omaha-based 2nd District gave one of Nebraska's five electoral votes to Joe Biden in 2020, even as the District's congressman, Republican Don Bacon, was winning reelection. In general, though, Republicans, barring a scandal, are likely to win most of the state's races in the foreseeable future.

The first travelers on the Oregon Trail in the 1840s called what they saw when they crossed the Missouri River and moved west along the Platte River "the sea of Nebraska." The state's ruggedly beautiful sandhills, a blanket of grass tucked roughly over submerged sand dunes, bloom atop the 174,000-square-mile Ogalalla Aquifer and cover about a quarter of the state. In Nebraska, you can see nothing but rolling fields for miles on end, sectioned off here and there by barbed wire fences and perhaps, in the distance, a grain elevator towering over a tiny town and its railroad depot. The Platte is not actually a single river, but a braid of streams that weaves a silver chain around sandbars and islands, flooding the level floor of the Nebraska plain—a mile wide, the saying goes, and six inches deep. (The state's name means "flat water" in the Omaha and Oto languages.) Settlers in Nebraska sliced the top level of earth to prepare for planting, using the layers of sod to construct rustic but practical homes.

Nebraska became a territory with the 1854 Kansas-Nebraska Act. At the time, Nebraska "stretched west from the Missouri River to the Continental Divide in the Rocky Mountains and north to Canada," covering more than 351,000 square miles of the Great Plains and the Rockies, David Hendee wrote in the Omaha World-Herald on the sesquicentennial of statehood in 2017. Within a decade, the Nebraska Territory was chopped up—to help create the Colorado Territory in 1861, the Dakota Territory the same year, and the Idaho Territory two years later. The Homestead Act of 1862 promoted White settlement; 45 percent of all land in Nebraska was taken up by homesteaders, a higher percentage than any other state. "People came to Nebraska because they saw opportunities to get rich," Nebraska Wesleyan University historian Ronald Naugle told Hendee. Statehood was tied up in post-Civil War conflict between President Andrew Johnson and radical Republicans over civil rights. Initially the state intended to restrict voting to free White males, but the radical Republicans insisted on removing the restriction. Twice, Johnson vetoed the measure before the state agreed to remove the restriction, and statehood arrived in 1867.

The state was largely settled in a single rush in the 1880s, when its population increased from 452,000 to 1 million. Omaha became a major railroad center and farming and food products reigned as the main businesses. Czechs, Germans and Danes came to work the factories in Omaha and farms on the Plains—Willa Cather tells the story beautifully in her novels. Nebraska was a major destination for Volga Germans, ethnic Germans who had settled in Russia; they bequeathed runza, a meat-in-bread delicacy kept alive in the state by a popular chain of casual restaurants by that name. For about a century, Nebraska remained pretty much the same. From 1890 to 2010, its population rose from 1 million to just 1.8 million. This is not what its founders envisioned. They hoped that Nebraska would develop a diversified farming, industrial and commercial economy like the ones that emerged in Illinois, Missouri and Ohio. But climate is hard to predict. Rains were plentiful in the 1880s, but the 1890s were years of drought, and Nebraska abruptly stopped growing. Many rural counties, and even Omaha, exported people for much of a century.

For a long time, the creative energies in the American economy seemed to have skipped over the Great Plains and moved west. In the popular imagination, Nebraska has made even less of an impression than the neighboring farm states of Iowa and Kansas, which helps explain why the state tourism office in 2018 settled on a tongue-in-cheek advertising tagline: "Honestly, it's not for everyone." State tourism director John Ricks explained to the World-Herald that Nebraska has typically ranked as the least likely state that tourists plan to visit, so to make them listen, "we had to shake people up."

Since 1990, though, Nebraska has been growing relatively robustly for the first time in decades. Its population expanded 16 percent between 1990 and 2010—more than the increase in the previous 60 years combined—and since 2010, it has grown an additional 7.4 percent. Growth has been concentrated around Omaha: Douglas County (Omaha) has seen population increase 10 percent since 2010; its suburban neighbor, Sarpy County, rose by 17 percent in the same period. The only other big growth spot was Lancaster County (Lincoln), which increased 11.5 percent. These three counties accounted for the entirety of the state's population growth during the past decade, and then some; the rest of the state lost population. Emblematic of rural Nebraska's difficulties was the demise of onetime outdoor-retail giant Cabela's, headquartered in Sidney, a small town in western Nebraska. Amid pressure from an activist investor (and major Republican donor), Cabela's allowed itself to be bought out by Bass Pro Shops, a major rival, in 2017. At its peak, Cabela's had supported 2,000 jobs in Sidney, equal to about a quarter of the town's population.

The Hispanic share of Nebraska's population has risen from 2 percent in 1990 to 11.3 percent today, a higher percentage than such diverse states as Maryland, Virginia, Georgia, Pennsylvania, and Michigan. Many Hispanics came from Texas and Mexico to work in meatpacking factories in such places as Colfax County (Schuyler), which is 46 percent Hispanic, and Dawson County (Lexington), which is 34 percent Hispanic. An estimated two-thirds of meatpacking workers in Nebraska are immigrants. Meanwhile, the state's Asian population is one of the nation's fastest-growing (though starting from a small base) due to an influx of South Asians from such places as Bhutan, Myanmar (Burma), Nepal and Thailand. Nebraska has ranked at or near the top of the list of states for refugees settled per capita. Partly due to these trends, Nebraska's population is no longer quite so elderly. In 2019, Nebraska ranked fourth among states for children as a percentage of its population, behind Utah, Texas and Idaho; the state is tied for 36th in the share of those 65 and older.

Omaha has been thriving economically, and not just because America's second-richest man, Warren Buffett, lives there. Omaha is home to four Fortune 500 companies: Buffett's Berkshire Hathaway, Union Pacific, the $9 billion construction, engineering and mining giant Kiewit, and Mutual of Omaha. The area also harbors such large employers as Green Plains Renewable Energy, TD Ameritrade and Valmont Industries, which manufactures linear irrigation equipment and windmill support structures. The city's robust corporate sector and its sprinkling of early investors in Berkshire Hathaway have spent millions on civic amenities locally, from parks and arts facilities to homeless shelters and investments in education and health. (Nebraska has been consistently near the bottom of state rankings for opioid deaths.) Lincoln, with its skyscraper state capitol and University of Nebraska, has a solid economic base as well. On Saturdays during the fall, when the 'Huskers play in Lincoln, nearly all the 92,000 seats at Memorial Stadium are filled, which equates to roughly one of every 20 people in the state. President Donald Trump's decision to greenlight the 882-mile Keystone XL pipeline from Canada to Nebraska gave the state's energy industry reason for optimism. But grassroots opposition in the state has been surprisingly broad. Amid continued legal wrangling, President Joe Biden scuttled the project on his first day in office.

Nebraska escaped the worst of the Great Recession, and it was protected during the coronavirus recession due to its mix of essential work (agriculture and meatpacking), jobs that can be done remotely (insurance and financial services), and a relatively small footprint for hard-hit sectors like tourism. By October and November 2020, the pandemic was still raging, but Nebraska's unemployment rate had fallen back to its pre-coronavirus rate of about 3 percent. The downside was that Nebraska's slaughterhouses, with their close confines and messy work, became hotspots from the very beginning of the pandemic. The state's median income is a bit below the national average, but those dollars can go further with the state's low cost of living. Measured by cash receipts, Nebraska ranks first by a wide margin for cattle, third in corn and feed crops, and eighth in pork. Nebraskans cheered when Japan opened its market to U.S. beef in 2013 and when China said it would do so in 2016, but they braced for impacts when Trump began implementing an aggressive trade posture.

The sudden boom of the 1880s and the bust of the 1890s produced the most colorful—and atypical —politics of Nebraska's history: the populist movement and William Jennings Bryan, the "silver-tongued orator of the Platte." Bryan was only 36 when he delivered his "Cross of Gold" speech at the 1896 Democratic National Convention and was swept to the nomination. But Bryan was so radical that he lost all three of his campaigns for the presidency. Since Bryan's time, Nebraska's most notable politician has been George Norris. In 1934, Norris spurred adoption of the state's unicameral, nonpartisan legislature, in which every bill gets a public hearing where anyone can speak. In Washington, Norris sponsored the Norris-LaGuardia Anti-Injunction Act, the first federal pro-union legislation, and the Tennessee Valley Authority Act. Today, Nebraska is the only state with entirely public electric utilities. But most Nebraskans were repelled by the New Deal, which they believed threatened their way of life.

A spark of this progressivism has sometimes re-emerged in the state, such as the 2015 bipartisan effort to ban the death penalty (later overturned through a ballot measure pushed by Gov. Pete Ricketts); legislation to permit driver's licenses for undocumented immigrants brought to the U.S. as children; and passage of a 2018 ballot measure to expand Medicaid under the Affordable Care Act. Meanwhile, voters in 2020 approved by a whopping 4-to-1 margin a ballot measure to cap interest rates on payday loans. Even so, Democratic candidates have faced increasing difficulty following the paths of James Exon, Bob Kerrey and Ben Nelson, each of whom served as governor and senator as Democrats.

In the 2020 presidential race, both Trump and Biden lavished attention on the 2nd District, which had popped up in several scenarios as a possible deciding vote in the Electoral College. Trump flew into Omaha during the home stretch, while Biden and his allies spent heavily in the district and sent high-profile surrogates. The reason was clear: The district offered the nation's purest test case of whether an electoral vote could be decided by Trump-era suburban voters shifting from red to blue. "Very simply, Trump offends a deeply ingrained culture of politeness and compromise that, until recently, earned Cornhuskers the very vanilla tourism slogan 'Nebraska Nice,'" wrote Nebraska native Anna Gronewold in Politico. "They are generally not on the news screaming at protesters, waving Confederate flags or brandishing firearms wildly. At its core, Nebraska Nice isn't so much a syrupy sweetness but rather a shared aversion to petty and therefore unproductive conflict."

In the end, Biden won the 2nd District by a comfortable seven points, after Trump had won it by two in 2016. In Douglas County, Biden won by 11 points, up from two for Hillary Clinton in 2016. In Sarpy County, Biden cut Trump's winning margin from 21 points to 11. In the 1st District, Trump's winning margin fell from 20 points to 15, driven by a seven-point Democratic improvement in Lancaster County. Statewide, this enabled Biden to shave Trump's margin from 25 points to 19. But in a sign that Nebraskans were reluctant to go too far in the Democrats' direction, Bacon won reelection by five points, suggesting that lots of Omaha-area voters were happy to split their tickets. And in the heavily rural 3rd District, Trump's margins barely budged, as the Republican won by a gaping 53-point margin.

Population			Race and Ethnicity			Income		
Total		1,934,408	White		86.20%	Median Income		63,229
Land area (sq. miles)		76,824	Black		4.90%	State Income Rank		25 out of 50
Pop/ sq mi		25.18	Latino		11.30%	Poverty Rate		9.90%
Born in state		64.70%	Asian		3.20%	With health insurance		91.70%
			Two or more races		2.80%	Cash public assistance		1.60%
Age Groups			Other		3.70%	Food stamp/SNAP		8.8%
Under 18		24.60%						
18-34		23.00%	Education			Work		
35-64		36.30%	H.S grad or less		33.60%	White Collar		40.00%
Over 64		16.10%	Some college		33.10%	Sales and Service		35.50%
			College Degree, 4 yr		21.80%	Blue Collar		24.50%
Military			Post grad		11.40%	Government		14.40%
Veteran/ Active Duty		8.10%						

Presidential Politics

2020 Primary (D)	Biden (D)	126,444 (77%)	Sanders (D)	23,214 (14%)	Warren (D)	10,401 (6%)
2020 Pres. Vote	Trump (R)	556,846 (58%)	Biden (D)	374,583 (39%)		
2016 Pres. Vote	Trump (R)	495,961 (59%)	Clinton (D)	284,494 (34%)	Johnson (L)	38,946 (5%)

Over the past 50 years, Nebraska has voted an average of 60 percent Republican in presidential elections, more than any other state except Utah, Idaho and Wyoming. In 2016 and 2020, Donald Trump came close to hitting that mark, defeating Hillary Clinton 59%-34% and besting Joe Biden 58%-39%. But Nebraska is one of two states (Maine is the other) that allocate two of its Electoral College votes to the statewide winner and the others to the winners in each of the congressional districts, and that's given Democrats some recent opportunities. In 2008, Barack Obama carried the 2nd District, Omaha and its suburbs, 50%-49%, by 3,370 votes out of 277,809 cast, and won one Nebraska electoral vote, the first for a Democrat since 1964. Hillary Clinton campaigned there in 2016 but fell short. In 2020, Joe Biden's campaign aired ads in Omaha, and he won the district 52%-46%. Like many other cities and towns with larger numbers of college-educated voters, Omaha and its suburbs moved left, as did Lincoln.

Nebraska held its 2020 primary on May 12, after Joe Biden had already clinched the nomination; he won 77%-12% over Bernie Sanders, who'd suspended his campaign more than a month earlier.

Congressional Districts

117th Congress Lineup	3R	116th Congress Lineup	3R

Nebraska has had three congressional districts since it lost one following the 1960 census. Boundaries can generate strong local feelings in Nebraska if only because it has been one of just two states where Electoral College votes are cast by congressional district. The unicameral legislature is technically nonpartisan, but in reality Republicans have long controlled the process. With Joe Biden's comfortable win in the 2nd District in 2020 and the tight vote in 2016, plus its competitive congressional battleground, Republicans have added incentive to eliminate the Electoral College anomaly. But the redistricting change might be easier said than done. Because Omaha and surrounding Douglas County have grown faster than the state as a whole, there are fewer options to add more Republicans to that district—other than a contentious move to split, at least, the county. Still, from a GOP congressional perspective, there will be heavy pressure to protect their three incumbents in a state where Republican statewide candidates typically receive close to 60 percent of the vote.

As the sparse western two-thirds of the state has shed residents, the western 3rd District has needed to expand, and the Lincoln-based 1st District and Omaha-based 2nd District have needed to shrink. In 2011, Republicans passed a map removing from the 2nd politically mixed Bellevue and Offutt Air Force Base south of Omaha in exchange for the deeply Republican western half of Sarpy County, making the 2nd about a percentage point safer overall. To offset the move, the "Big Third" now stretches 460 miles from Wyoming to Missouri and Iowa and includes all or part of 75 counties, more than any other district in the country. That helped Republicans in 2012. But the 2nd then resumed its highly competitive status, with House incumbents ousted the next two cycles. Unless Republican redistricters want to divide Omaha, their options are limited.

Pete Ricketts (R)

Elected 2014, term expires 2023, 2nd term; b. Aug. 19, 1964, Nebraska City; U. of Chicago, B.A., M.A.; Catholic; Married (Susanne); 3 children.

Professional Career: Customer Services, Senior VP Strategy & Business Devel., Senior Vice President of Product Development, Senior Vice President of Marketing, COO at Ameritrade, 1993-2005; Founder, Drakon, LLC.

Office: PO Box 94848 Lincoln, 68509-4848; 402-471-2244; Fax: 402-471-6031
Lt. Gov.: Mike Foley (R) **Atty. Gen:** Doug Peterson (R) **Sec. of State:** John Gale (R)
State Legislature: Unicameral, bipartisan

Election Results

Election	Name (Party)	Vote (%)
2018 General	Pete Ricketts (R)	411,812 (59%)
	Bob Krist (D)	286,169 (41%)
2018 Primary	Pete Ricketts (R)	138,292 (81%)
	Krystal Gabel (R)	31,568 (19%)

Prior winning percentage: 2014 (57%)

Republican Pete Ricketts' last name was well known in Nebraska before he ever tried for public office. His father, Joe, had founded the company that became TD Ameritrade, based near Omaha, and the family owns Major League Baseball's storied franchise, the Chicago Cubs. He won the governorship in 2014 and was reelected with ease in 2018.

Ricketts is one of four children, and the eldest son. On the campaign trail, he told voters that growing up in Omaha, he and his siblings were latchkey kids in a middle-class home where both parents worked and his father built a financial empire. He graduated from Westside High School in Omaha and attended the University of Chicago, earning a bachelor's degree in biology and an MBA. After college, Ricketts joined the family business, rising to president and chief operating officer.

He left TD Ameritrade in 2005 to run against incumbent Democratic Sen. Ben Nelson in 2006. Republicans were not looking for a wealthy scion to be their standard-bearer against Nelson, who was a former two-term governor born in the small plains town of McCook, which had also produced Nebraska icon George Norris. But a number of other notable Republicans, including Gov. Dave Heineman, former Gov. Mike Johanns, and Reps. Lee Terry and Tom Osborne all passed on the race, so Republicans rallied around Ricketts, who could self-fund his campaign. Running on a platform of tax cuts and smaller government, Ricketts won the primary, but in the general election he backed a guest-worker program for immigrants, enabling Nelson to run to his right and call for securing the border. Ricketts, with his investment background, also came out in favor of private Social Security accounts, something Nelson opposed. Ricketts plowed almost $12 million of his own money into the race and outspent Nelson almost 2-to-1. But on Election Day, he lost by a nearly 2-to-1 margin.

For the next five years, Ricketts served on the Republican National Committee, building his connections to the party establishment, grassroots activists in Nebraska and GOP political players around the country. He also invested in startups, served on various boards, and developed philanthropic interests. He founded Drakon LLC, based in Omaha, a management firm that supports local entrepreneurs and new growth companies, and the Platte Institute for Economic Research, a conservative think tank based in Omaha.

When he ran for governor in 2014, Ricketts got endorsements from Wisconsin Gov. Scott Walker, Indiana Gov. Mike Pence, House Budget Committee Chairman Paul Ryan of Wisconsin and Sen. Ted Cruz of Texas, among others—potential White House hopefuls who may have been looking to woo Ricketts' father and his super PAC, as well as his brothers Todd and Tom. (Pete Ricketts' sister Laura was the exception; she was one of 27 high-profile gay and lesbian "bundlers" for President Barack Obama in 2012. Ricketts frequently had to explain how he disagreed with Laura over same-sex marriage, though he always added, "I love her.") Ricketts' main rival for the GOP nod was Attorney General Jon Bruning, who had lost a 2012 Senate primary to long shot Deb Fischer, thanks in part to a last-minute TV ad blitz for Fischer that was funded by Joe Ricketts. Bruning repeatedly accused the Ricketts family of using its wealth to buy another victory, but in a field of six candidates, Ricketts was able to edge Bruning, 27%-26%. Ricketts' Democratic opponent, Center for Rural Affairs Executive Director Chuck Hassebrook, took a few stabs at making Ricketts' family fortune an issue, but it went nowhere; Ricketts overwhelmed Hassebrook, 57%-39%, as he carried 89 of the state's 93 counties. Ricketts' campaign spent roughly $7 million, including almost $1 million from his personal checkbook and more than $1 million from his family members—more than twice what Hassebrook spent.

Entering office, Ricketts enjoyed a state budget surplus and a favorable economy, but that did not help him prevail in a number of tests with the legislature in 2015. First, Nebraska lawmakers overrode Ricketts's veto of a gas-tax hike. Ricketts said the increase would hurt "hardworking Nebraskans," but the legislature wanted the estimated $75 million generated annually by the tax increase for state road repair and maintenance and didn't want to have to cut any other spending to get it. The legislature voted to override Ricketts' veto of a bill that would allow immigrants who were brought into the country illegally as children to get a driver's license; the governor called the measure "an inappropriate benefit to non-citizens." Most spectacularly, the legislature overrode his veto of a bill to end the state's death penalty, becoming the first conservative state in more than four decades to do so. On this issue, the governor was ultimately successful. With his support, voters qualified a ballot measure to reinstate the death penalty and in 2016 it passed easily.

The veto overrides continued in April 2016 with a bill that would allow children who were brought to the country illegally by their parents to acquire occupational licenses. The bill had been supported by business leaders, another indication that Ricketts and the business community were not always on the same page. (Opposing a business-supported effort to protect LGBT workers was another example.) A happier outcome came from a $450 million transportation bill Ricketts signed; the bill was designed to complete the state's 600-mile expressway system by 2033. Ricketts also courted business in Japan, China, Hong Kong and Macau, potential consumers of Nebraska beef.

In January 2016, Ricketts initially declined to meet President Barack Obama during his first presidential visit to the state, then reversed course after an outcry and greeted him at the airport. In that fall's campaign, Ricketts took the unusual step of financially supporting several challengers to members of the legislature who had voted to override one or more of his vetoes. Even though the unicameral legislature is officially nonpartisan, the targeted lawmakers were unofficially Republicans, and Ricketts' offensive did not play well in some GOP circles. Of the 17 members who eventually joined the freshman class, Ricketts had supported eight financially; three of them had ousted Republican antagonists. Strategically, the gambit worked well for the governor. In 2017, he avoided being overridden on vetoes of a felon voting rights bill and on $56.5 million in spending cuts. Meanwhile, the 2018 budget process turned out to be much smoother, attracting no veto fights. One of the budget bills also included a provision to eliminate Title X federal funding for Planned Parenthood, a priority for the state's anti-abortion caucus.

Ricketts, meanwhile, solidified his ties to Trump, joining a White House energy roundtable and a post-World Series visit for the Cubs in 2017 and building relationships to Cabinet members. Despite Trump's protectionist agenda, which put Nebraska farmers at risk, Ricketts downplayed China's retaliatory tariffs on pork products as "part of the overall trade negotiations the Trump administration has," and touted the U.S.-Mexico-Canada Agreement that the administration negotiated to replace the North American Free Trade Agreement. In December 2018, Trump tapped Ricketts to serve on a trade policy advisory committee.

Ricketts had no trouble winning a second term, defeating state Sen. Bob Krist, the Democratic nominee 59%-41%, a slightly larger margin than he'd had in 2014, even though Ricketts lost Douglas County (Omaha), which he had won four years earlier. The bigger surprise was that a ballot initiative to expand Medicaid under the Affordable Care Act also passed, 54%-46%. Ricketts had consistently fought Medicaid expansion; almost two years after passage, the expanded program went into effect in 2020.

In 2019, Ricketts signed a measure allowing the cultivation of hemp, approved the continued acceptance of refugees in the state, and signed a bill to ban a method of abortion known as dilation and evacuation. He also signed a measure adding $51 million to a property tax relief fund—a 23 percent increase but short of the statewide sales tax hike sought by some legislators. Ricketts drew criticism for vetoing a bill that would have outlawed discrimination against Black employees due to their hairstyles; he argued that other races also wore locks, braids, or twists, and that the law would have made it harder for employers to implement safety standards related to grooming. Difficult relations with Nebraska's Black community—5 percent of the population statewide, and 12 percent in Omaha—continued into 2020, as Ricketts had to apologize for addressing a group of Black pastors as "you people." On trade, Ricketts continued to walk a tightrope, saying in 2019 that Trump should "wrap up" his dispute with China after Nebraska farmers had lost more than $1 billion due to tariffs, but softening his perspective in an interview a few days later.

In 2020, Ricketts continued his work on property tax relief, signing into law a new income tax credit aimed at cutting property taxes by 3 percent. After the coronavirus pandemic hit, Ricketts took criticism for a lack of transparency about the virus' spread at meatpacking plants, and like other Republican governors, he pursued only narrow behavioral limits. In June, Ricketts went so far as to tell local officials they would not receive federal coronavirus relief funds if they required people to wear masks in government buildings. He also intervened in August when Douglas County sought to implement a mask mandate. Citing the relatively low economic impact of the pandemic on his state, Ricketts became the only governor to discontinue emergency food aid from the coronavirus relief package, despite urging from state legislators and advocates for low-income residents to keep the aid flowing. In November, voters delivered a blow to Ricketts' efforts to block an expansion of gambling. Ricketts had opposed a group of three ballot measures that collectively allowed casinos to operate at several racetracks around the state. Voters approved the measures on the November 2020 ballot by 2-to-1 margins.

With Ricketts facing a term limit in 2022, and with both of Nebraska's Senate seats filled by fellow Republicans, some have speculated that Ricketts could run for president. Not only does Ricketts have deep pockets, but he strengthened his national connections during his second gubernatorial term by chairing the Republican Governors Association. Meanwhile, former Gov. Dave Heineman has expressed interest in running for his old office. If he doesn't run, there is a potentially large field of possible successors as governor, including Republican state Sens. Brett Lindstrom. Lou Ann Linehan. and Mike Flood; businessman Chuck Herbster; University of Nebraska Board of Regents members Jim Pillen and Tim Clare; Lt. Gov. and former state auditor Mike Foley; Nebraska Chamber of Commerce President Bryan Slone; and Omaha Mayor Jean Stothert. Potential Democratic candidates include Krist and state Sen. Steve Lathrop. Any of the Republicans would be considered a clear favorite.

Deb Fischer (R)

Elected 2012, term expires 2024, 2nd term, b. Mar 01, 1951; Lincoln, NE; University of Nebraska, Lincoln, B.S., 1988; Presbyterian; Married (Bruce G. Fischer); 3 children; 3 grandchildren.

Elected Office: Valentine Rural High School Board of Education, 1990-2004; NE Senate, 2005-2012.

Professional Career: Rancher, 1972-2012.

DC Office: 454 RSOB 20510, 202-224-6551, Fax: 202-228-1325, fischer.senate.gov

State Offices: Kearney, 308-234-2361; Lincoln, 402-441-4600; Norfolk, 402-200-8816; Omaha, 402-391-3411; Scottsbluff, 308-630-2329.

Committees: *Agriculture, Nutrition & Forestry*: Food & Nutrition, Specialty Crops, Organics & Research; Livestock, Dairy, Poultry, Local Food Sys & Food Safety & Sec; Rural Development & Energy. *Armed Services*: Emerging Threats & Capabilities; Readiness & Management Support; Strategic Forces (RMM). *Commerce, Science & Transportation*: Communications, Media & Broadband; Oceans, Fisheries, Climate Change & Manufacturing; Space & Science; Surface Transportation, Maritime Freight & Ports (RMM). *Ethics. Rules & Administration.*

Group Ratings

	ADA	ACLU	AFL-CIO	LCV	COC	HAFA	ACU	CFG	FRC
2020	-	0%	-	0%	-	74%	81%	-	-
2019	0%	C	16%	7%	91%	C	81%	62%	100%

Almanac Ratings 2019-2020

	Economy	Social	Foreign	Composite
Liberal	0%	0%	0%	0%
Conservative	100%	100%	100%	100%

Key Votes of the 116th Congress

1. EPA clean energy rules	N	5. Russia sanctions	N
2. U.S./Mex./Can. trade deal	Y	6. Troops in SYR, AFG	Y
3. Cut unemployment benefits	Y	7. Veto arms sales to Saudis	N
4. Shelton to Fed Reserve	Y	8. Defense $$$, veto override	Y

9. Barr as Atty. General	Y
10. Spending at the border	Y
11. Coney Barrett to Sup. Ct.	Y
12. Electoral College objections	N

Election Results

Election	Name (Party)	Vote (%)	Cand. Spent	Ind. Exp. Support	Ind. Exp. Oppose
2018 General	Deb Fischer (R)....................	403,151 (58%)	$4,983,235		
	Jane Raybould (D)................	269,917 (39%)	$2,078,587	$36,068	
	Jim Schultz (Lib)..................	25,349 (4%)			
2018 Primary	Deb Fischer (R)....................	128,157 (76%)			
	Todd Watson (R)..................	19,661 (12%)			
	Jack Heidel (R).....................	9,413 (6%)			

Prior winning percentages: 2018 (58%), 2012 (58%)

Nebraska's senior senator, Deb Fischer, was the only Republican in the country to flip a Senate seat in 2012, when President Barack Obama cruised to reelection. Since then, she has become a reliable Republican vote while eschewing the spotlight—a stark contrast to the state's junior senator, Ben Sasse, who was a vocal critic of President Donald Trump. Fischer is a close ally of Senate Minority Leader Mitch McConnell, which has helped her push through many of her legislative priorities. She has sought to reach out to Democrats on some issues while maintaining a low profile as a nuts-and-bolts legislator. Fischer is one of the few top GOP women in the chamber, but she has said she'll serve only two terms. Fischer also could jump into Nebraska's open race for governor in 2022.

Fischer much prefers policy over politics. "I like to be able to work with people, figure out what we need to do and then try and get it done," she told the Scottsbluff Star-Herald in 2019. "I love the legislative process. To be able to work on a bill or to be able to offer amendments to change a bill, I like committee work. You get into the details so that we can have some good changes. I was really, really fortunate to have great support now in two elections for U.S. Senate. It is a good job. It is a worthwhile job when you're working with the people of your state to try and make life better."

Her upbringing and career seem to have greatly influenced that outlook. Fischer grew up in Lincoln, the state capital, where her mother, Florence Strobel, was an elementary school teacher and her father, Jerry Strobel, spent many years as an engineer at, and eventually head of, the Nebraska Department of Roads. Transportation funding would later be a legislative focus for Fischer at the state and federal levels. She attended the University of Nebraska, where she met her husband, Bruce Fischer. She left school to marry him, and the couple settled on the Fischer family ranch in Valentine, in northern Nebraska. Despite growing up in what she described as the "big small town" of Lincoln, Fischer said she had little trouble adjusting to ranching life. She honed one talent often associated with farm wives: "She's infamous for her pie-making," her husband told the World-Herald shortly after Fischer was nominated for the Senate. "She doesn't do it very often, but it's a darn-sure treat when she does." As her three sons grew, Fischer returned to the University of Nebraska in Lincoln and earned a degree in education in 1988.

Her first run for elected office came two years later, when she won a seat on the Valentine Rural High School Board of Education. She went on to become president of the Nebraska Association of School Boards and serve on the Nebraska Coordinating Commission for Postsecondary Education, the state's oversight agency for higher education institutions. In 2004, Fischer won a seat in Nebraska's unicameral Legislature, representing a district that sprawled across a dozen counties —an area the size of New Jersey. She was unopposed for a second term in 2008. During her first term, an upheaval in the Legislature gave Fischer the chairmanship of the Transportation and Telecommunications Committee. Among her biggest achievements was passing legislation to shift about $70 million of the state's sales tax revenues to road construction on an annual basis.

Barred by law from seeking a third term in the state Legislature in 2012, Fischer entered the race to succeed retiring Democratic Sen. Ben Nelson. Nelson, like Bob Kerrey, had served as governor before winning a Senate seat. While Nelson had accumulated one of the most conservative voting records among members of his party, he took intense political heat for his crucial 2009 vote in favor of Obamacare.

Fischer began her Senate bid as the underdog in a primary against state Attorney General Jon Bruning and state Treasurer Don Stenberg. Bruning enjoyed the support of the GOP establishment, while tea party leaders rallied behind Stenberg. Fischer, however, steadily gained traction as Stenberg and Bruning turned their fire on each other. She also benefited from the endorsement of one tea party favorite, 2008 vice presidential nominee Sarah Palin, along with a last-minute television ad blitz funded by wealthy businessman Joe Ricketts, founder of Omaha-based TD Ameritrade stock brokerage firm. Fischer won the primary with 41 percent of the vote; Bruning got 36 percent and Stenberg took 19 percent.

In the general election, Kerrey was considered Democrats' best hope in a state where nearly half of all voters identify as Republicans and only about one-third as Democrats. Although Kerrey was a household name, many voters were turned off by the fact that he had been living out of state since leaving the Senate in 2000; he served as president of the New York's New School University from 2001 to 2010.

Fischer vowed not to serve more than two terms in the Senate and backed a constitutional amendment for congressional term limits. She stressed her family's ranching background and her work in the state Legislature on issues important to rural Nebraska. Kerrey made an issue of her family's use of grazing rights on 11,000 acres of federal land, calling her a "welfare rancher." He dubbed her a "bad neighbor" for suing an elderly couple in the 1990s in a dispute over ownership of more than 100 acres along the Snake River and suggested Fischer had used her influence in the Legislature to bar the couple from later selling the land in question to the state. Fischer's campaign called such attacks a "transparent act of desperation." In the end, Fischer won all but a handful of counties and won 58%-42%. Kerrey's loss ended almost four decades of Nebraska splitting its Senate delegation.

One of Fischer's first votes in the Senate, in early 2013, was against Obama's nomination of a former Nebraska senator, Republican Chuck Hagel, as secretary of Defense. She called Hagel's testimony before the Armed Services Committee, which she had just joined, "confusing and contradictory." In opposing Hagel, Fischer parted company with Republican Mike Johanns, then Nebraska's senior senator, whom Fischer had called a role model. Few were particularly surprised by her vote since Hagel, who was viewed as a moderate and had been critical of President George W. Bush's strategy in the Iraq War, had backed Kerrey in the fall election.

Fischer's philosophy has put her in the Republican mainstream on issues ranging from taxes to abortion. She has used her seat on the Environment and Public Works Committee to excoriate the Environmental Protection Agency for what she has called "extreme overreach." But she has shown a pragmatic streak, declining to go as far as other conservatives who have called for abolishing the EPA and the Education Department. When there was conservative blowback against a Supreme Court opinion—authored by Trump-appointed Justice Neil Gorsuch—that extended civil rights protections to LGBTQ workers, Fischer told Politico, "It's important that we recognize that all Americans have equal rights under our Constitution. I'm fine with it."

Fischer joined Republican leadership in 2015—as counsel to the majority leader—and has been called upon to promote GOP alternatives on issues such as pay equity and family leave. In 2017, Fischer reintroduced a proposal to provide tax incentives to businesses that offer employees two weeks of paid family leave each year. But advocacy groups for paid leave criticized Fischer's legislation because it was optional—and not as generous as the leading Democratic bill, which proposed guaranteeing workers two-thirds of their pay for up to 12 weeks. Working alongside Ivanka Trump, Fischer got a two-year trial program in the Republican tax rewrite of 2017. Despite the criticism of its limited scope, this was the first-ever national family leave policy. She has worked with independent Sen. Angus King of Maine to extend the leave program. At the end of 2018, Fischer and Iowa Sen. Joni Ernst battled each other for conference vice chairmanship. Despite being more senior and less critical of Trump, Fischer lost.

On the Commerce Committee, Fischer joined a bipartisan group seeking to promote the economic potential of the internet of things, an expanding market of consumer products in which information can be transmitted without a computer. She stuck to her philosophy of limited government regulation, claiming that legislation she proposed had prompted the Food and Drug Administration to back off from regulating Fitbit and other wearable devices. She also partnered with Minnesota Democrat Amy Klobuchar to expand rural broadband access. She co-sponsored a bill with Virginia Democrat Mark Warner to ban deceptive practices used by Facebook to acquire user data, including phone and email contacts. Fischer also introduced legislation to repeal the 1920 Death on the High Seas Act, which allowed cruise ships to avoid financial liability for wrongful deaths on their ships.

The Nebraska Republican later chaired both the Armed Service subcommittee on strategic forces and the Agriculture panel on research and specialty crops. She helped secure funding for new Veterans Affairs facilities in Omaha and Lincoln and money for a new runway at Offutt Air Force Base in Bellevue, home to U.S. Strategic Command, which oversees the nation's nuclear and missile arsenals. The late Sen. John McCain, who chaired the Armed Services Committee, sometimes called her "the hammer." On the Agriculture Committee in 2019, she introduced the Real MEAT Act, which would require plant-based meat substitutes, such as those made by Impossible Foods and Beyond Meat, to prominently include "imitation" on their labels. "Beef is derived from cattle—period," Fischer said. In an op-ed in the Wall Street Journal, Fischer accused "fake-meat companies" of "running smear campaigns against actual beef" and "using deceptive labeling and marketing practices." She added: "Americans deserve to know what they are eating, particularly when they want to be sure that the meat on their plates is the kind of real, irreplaceable beef for which Nebraska is famous."

For the most part, Fischer has had a good working relationship with the more outspoken Sasse, who succeeded Johanns in early 2015. But Sasse's adamant opposition to Trump as the party's presidential nominee in 2016—he went so far as to advocate a conservative third-party alternative —created some awkward moments. At the Nebraska Republican State Convention in May 2016, delegates overwhelmingly approved a resolution—aimed at Sasse—that condemned a possible third-party candidacy. The force behind the resolution was Sam Fischer, a state political operative—and Deb Fischer's nephew. Sam Fischer and an aide to the senator denied she had any involvement in the resolution. But Politico reported that the view in state political circles was that the nephew would not have acted without his aunt's tacit approval. The senators continued to differ over Trump even after he entered the White House, with Fischer giving him a "B" halfway through his term, adding that only international trade kept him from an "A," while Sasse issued scorching statements and mused about leaving the Republican Party. She later told the Scottsbluff Star-Herald that Sasse had "other avenues he's going down."

Fischer declined an invitation to speak at the 2016 Republican National Convention—not because of concerns about the nominee-in-waiting, Trump, but rather because convention organizers were looking for a "more political speech" than she wanted to give. "I do realize it's a political convention —but I'm kind of known as a policy person, so I wanted to focus on that," Fischer told the Omaha World-Herald. But it was politics that gave her a rare moment in the national spotlight a couple of months later: After a decade-old recording of Trump bragging about sexually assaulting women surfaced, Fischer called on Trump to drop off the ticket. But she took some criticism when she became the first of that group to reverse herself and say she would support him after all. Even on issues like trade, on which Fischer follows the traditional party line of favoring free trade and not Trump's tariff heavy approach, Fischer avoided public confrontations with the president. She has said she gained more ground by staying out of the news. During Trump's first impeachment trial, Fischer said she didn't believe the transcript of his call with the Ukrainian president—during which he threatened to withhold congressionally approved aide to extract political favors—was a "smoking gun."

But as 2020 wore on, Fischer did level some cautious pushback on Trump and his administration. After the president's first debate with Democratic presidential nominee Joe Biden, in which Trump declined to denounce a white nationalist and mysogynist group, Fischer said "he needs to be clear about his stand against white supremacy. It's abhorrent. I've said that over and over again. And I think he needs to clarify that." And as Trump bashed absentee voting, falsely claiming that mail-in ballots would lead to widespread fraud, Fischer pushed back. "It's worked well in Nebraska," she told CNN. "We had tremendous turnout in the primary in May. No issues that I've heard from our secretary of state." During Trump's second impeachment trial in the wake of the Jan. 6, 2021, insurrection at the Capitol, Fischer split with Sasse and voted to acquit the former president, saying, "Congress simply does not have the constitutional authority to impeach a former president" and that the House "had a rushed impeachment process that denied President Trump due process."

In her 2018 reelection, Fischer faced off against Lincoln City Councilwoman Jane Raybould. Raybould had sought to make Fischer's closeness to Trump an issue but struggled to raise money and was swamped by Fischer in rural Nebraska. The senator rarely addressed Raybould even after Raybould called Fischer "corrupt" during their only debate. Fischer won 58%-39%. There's speculation she could be eyeing a run for governor in 2022, when Republican Pete Ricketts will be barred from running for reelection by term limits.

Ben Sasse (R)

Elected 2014, term expires 2026, 2nd term, b. Feb 22, 1972; Plainview, NE; Yale University, M.A.; Yale University, M.Phil; Oxford University, 1992; Harvard University, A.B., 1994; Saint John's College, M.A., 1998; Yale University, Ph.D., 2004; Lutheran; Married (Melissa Sasse); 3 children.

Professional Career: Chief of Staff, U.S Department of Justice Office of Legal Policy, 2004-2005; Chief of Staff, U.S Rep. Jeff Fortenberry, 2005; Assistant Professor, University of TX-Austin 2005-2006; Counselor to secretary, Health & Human Services; Assistant Secretary, Health & Human Services, 2007-2009; President, Professor University of TX-Austin, 2009; Midland University 2010-2014.

DC Office: 107 RSOB 20510, 202-224-4224, sasse.senate.gov
State Offices: Kearney, 308-233-3677; Lincoln, 402-476-1400; Omaha, 402-550-8040; Scottsbluff, 308-632-6032.

Committees: *Budget. Finance*: International Trade, Customs & Global Competitiveness; Social Security, Pensions & Family Policy; Taxation & IRS Oversight. *Intelligence. Judiciary*: Constitution; Federal Courts, Oversight, Agency Action & Federal Rights; Human Rights & the Law; Privacy, Technology & the Law (RMM).

Group Ratings

	ADA	ACLU	AFL-CIO	LCV	COC	HAFA	ACU	CFG	FRC
2020	-	0%	-	0%	-	85%	94%	-	-
2019	5%	C	11%	0%	67%	C	95%	90%	100%

Almanac Ratings 2019-2020

	Economy	Social	Foreign	Composite
Liberal	6%	6%	4%	5%
Conservative	94%	94%	97%	95%

Key Votes of the 116th Congress

1. EPA clean energy rules	N	5. Russia sanctions	Y	9. Barr as Atty. General	Y
2. U.S./Mex./Can. trade deal	Y	6. Troops in SYR, AFG	Y	10. Spending at the border	Y
3. Cut unemployment benefits	Y	7. Veto arms sales to Saudis	N	11. Coney Barrett to Sup. Ct.	Y
4. Shelton to Fed Reserve	Y	8. Defense $$$, veto override	N/A	12. Electoral College objections	N

Election Results

Election	Name (Party)	Vote (%)		Cand. Spent	Ind. Exp. Support	Ind. Exp. Oppose
2020 General	Ben Sasse (R)	583,507	(63%)	$4,264,806	$17,583	
	Chris Janicek (D)	227,191	(24%)	$123,224		
	Gene Siadek (L)	55,115	(6%)			
2020 Primary	Ben Sasse (R)	215,207	(75%)			
	Matt Innis (R)	70,921	(25%)			

Prior winning percentages: 2014 (65%)

Ben Sasse, Nebraska's junior senator, was never really afraid to challenge President Donald Trump's policy and rhetoric—although that criticism diminished as the Republican was running for reelection in 2020, even garnering an endorsement from the commander in chief he often seemed to disdain. But once Sasse avoided a serious primary, he found his voice against Trump again—especially after Trump refused to accept his loss in the 2020 presidential race and incited a deadly insurrection at the U.S. Capitol in an eleventh-hour attempt to overturn the election. Sasse was one of just seven Republicans to vote to convict Trump during his resulting—and second—impeachment trial in February 2021. Now the senator appears poised to push the party away from the former president even as it feels his weighty pull. Sasse was even being mentioned as a possible 2024 candidate.

Sasse is a fifth-generation Nebraskan who spent his childhood summers working in soybean and corn fields; he bears a scar on his forehead from a fall from a hayloft. He was born in the tiny town of Plainview in northeastern Nebraska and went to high school in nearby Fremont. He was recruited by Harvard University, thanks to his prowess as a high school wrestler. ("@BenSasse looks more like a gym rat than a U.S. Senator. How the hell did he ever get elected?" Trump once tweeted in response to Sasse's criticisms.) Sasse earned his undergraduate degree while spending a junior year abroad at the University of Oxford; he then worked for a year at the Boston Consulting Group—the financial firm where Mitt Romney had gotten his start—before returning to school. He collected a master's degree from St. John's College in Annapolis Maryland while tutoring House pages on Capitol Hill, and then he earned two more master's degrees from Yale University before getting a doctorate in American history from Yale. That led to a teaching post at the University of Texas' Lyndon B. Johnson School of Public Affairs. Examples of his erudition: The book worm devoted a chapter of his book "The Vanishing American Adult" to building a "5-foot bookshelf" for his "family canon" of books, and with his wife, he home schools their three children.

But Sasse spent most of the five years after earning his doctorate working in Washington, first for the Justice Department and then briefly as chief of staff to Nebraska Republican Rep. Jeff Fortenberry and then consulting for the Homeland Security Department. He was at the Department of Health and Human Services the last two years of George W. Bush's presidency, first as a counselor to the secretary and later, following Senate confirmation, as assistant secretary for planning and evaluation. At the end of the Bush administration, Sasse returned to Fremont after nearly two decades away from the state to become president of Midland University, a 130-year-old Lutheran school that had financial difficulties. At 37, he was among the youngest college presidents in the country; during the 2014 campaign, he boasted of executing a "turnaround job" that has made Midland University what he termed "one of the fastest growing [schools] in the Midwest." He ended lifetime tenure for professors, persuaded some to take buyouts and brought about a takeover of a rival school.

In early 2013, Republican Mike Johanns, a former Nebraska governor and onetime U.S. secretary of Agriculture, announced he would retire from the Senate after just one term. Sasse said he would run for the seat about a month after former state Treasurer Shane Osborn had announced he would run. As a Navy pilot, Osborn briefly had been detained by the Chinese in 2001 after a midair collision with a Chinese fighter jet forced him to make an emergency landing.

In the primary, Osborn sought to cast Sasse not only as too close to Washington but also insufficiently conservative: Sasse had penned a column in 2009 for U.S. News and World Report calling Medicare Part D, the prescription-drug benefit passed by a GOP-controlled Congress during the Bush administration, "enormously successful" and a "viable model for reform." But conservative groups rallied around Sasse as he headed to the top of the polls, and the Club for Growth and the Senate Conservatives Fund spent heavily on his behalf. Campaign visits by Sen. Ted Cruz of Texas and former Alaska Gov. Sarah Palin cemented Sasse as the conservative choice in the primary. In January 2014, Sasse was featured on the cover of National Review as a "rising conservative star." Sasse prevailed in a three-way primary, winning with 49 percent of the vote; Osborn got 21 percent. National Democrats made no serious attempt to contest the seat in November and Sasse easily won the general election.

In his first floor speech in November 2015—attended by about three dozen of his colleagues— Sasse bemoaned "a real institutional decline in the Senate in recent decades"; he blamed both parties. Underlying this process-oriented critique was an apparent conviction that the long-term priorities the Senate ought to debate involve the basic role of the federal government—which Sasse thought needed to be sharply curtailed. His votes against proposals that he felt exceeded the scope of the federal government—including those broadly embraced by both parties—have exasperated even some fellow Republicans. In March 2016, Sasse was on the losing end of a 94-1 vote on a bill aimed at combating opioid abuse that later became law. When asked for comment by the New York Times on Sasse's vote, then-Sen. Kelly Ayotte of New Hampshire, a fellow Republican and sponsor of the measure, rolled her eyes: "Whatever, dude." Sasse has authored two books since his election, "The Vanishing American Adult" and "Them: Why We Hate Each Other — and How to Heal." Both have been New York Times bestsellers, but they are very different from the usual political tomes.

Several months after taking office, Sasse introduced the Winding Down Obama Care Act, which was seen as a potential Republican fallback position if the Supreme Court failed to uphold a key provision of the Affordable Care Act—subsidies to the federal health insurance exchange—in June 2015. Sasse's bill proposed to do away with the ACA subsidies, replacing them with general tax credits that would disappear within 18 months. He argued this would give the Republican-controlled Congress time to come up with an alternative to Obamacare. But, as the debate over repeal of the law picked up steam in early 2017, Sasse—once hailed as "Obamacare's Nebraska Nemesis" by the National Review—was playing a secondary role. "I'm trying to figure out how to add value, wherever I can, in that fight," Sasse told the Omaha World-Herald.

Sasse's committee assignments changed significantly in 2017: He moved to the Armed Services Committee, where Fischer was already serving, and the Judiciary Committee. He gave up his seat on the Agriculture Committee—marking the first time in nearly a half-century that no Nebraskan served on that panel. That caused consternation among some state farm groups. "I will engage in no less activity in listening to Nebraska farmers and producers about their priorities and concerns," Sasse told the Lincoln Journal Star. Fischer joined the Ag panel in 2018. In 2019, he gave up his seat on Armed Services to join the Intelligence Committee and also became the Republican Senate appointee on the Cyberspace Solarium Commission. The 13-member commission was Sasse's creation and was enacted in the 2018 National Defense Authorization Act. The panel was mandated to deliver a report on cybersecurity policy by September 2019. Sasse also joined the Budget Committee in 2019.

Sasse has been outspoken about Trump since the former reality TV star emerged on the political scene. In 2016, when Trump was the frontrunner for the party's presidential nomination, the Nebraska Republican blistered Trump on social media and questioned both his conservatism and his behavior. "You brag abt many affairs w/ married women. Have you repented?" Sasse tweeted at Trump in late January 2016—before the Iowa caucuses. He later said Trump didn't have "any more core principles than a Kardashian marriage." Sasse's vow not to support Trump as the party's nominee made him a leading member of the "Never Trump" movement—and earned him a rebuke from the Nebraska GOP.

At the end of February 2016, Sasse posted a lengthy "Open Letter to Trump Supporters" in which he compared Trump's and President Barack Obama's views on executive power. "Much like President Obama, [Trump] displays essentially no understanding of the fact that, in the American system, we have a constitutional system of checks and balances, with three separate but co-equal branches of government." Sasse wrote. "The law is king, and the people are boss. But have you noticed how Mr. Trump uses the word 'Reign'—like he thinks he's running for King? It's creepy, actually." Sasse's push for a conservative third-party alternative to Trump prompted speculation about whether he would run, but he disavowed interest—citing his family and Senate duties. When those efforts failed, he announced he would write in Trump's running mate, Mike Pence, for president in November.

Throughout the first years of the Trump administration, Sasse waylaid the president on everything from trade and foreign policy to separating migrant families at the southern border, from bailing out farmers hurt by trade wars and, yes, to the content of Trump's tweets. Even on topics on which his colleagues were critical of Trump, Sasse stood out for his short, stinging jabs. Sasse has been blunt in his unhappiness at times too, saying he thinks "every morning" about leaving the Republican Party and views himself as an "independent conservative who caucuses with the GOP."

That's why it came as a surprise when Trump tweeted in September 2019 that "Senator Ben Sasse has done a wonderful job representing the people of Nebraska. He is great with our Vets, the Military, and your very important Second Amendment. Strong on Crime and the Border, Ben has my Complete and Total Endorsement." A Sasse spokesman said the senator was "grateful for the President's kind words" and that while the two "don't always see eye to eye … they've built a relationship where they work together when they agree and they wrestle hard when they don't."

Former Lancaster County GOP Chairman Matt Innis challenged Sasse in the primary, claiming the incumbent was insufficiently supportive of Trump, but with the president's endorsement that argument held little weight; Sasse defeated Innis 75%-25%. One ad from Sasse touted his independence, admitting that the senator had "ticked off a lot of folks these past six years, from the radical left to, every now and then, even the president from his own party. Here's the deal: Ben's got guts." In November, Sasse easily defeated baker Chris Janicek 67%-26%; the Democrat had all party support withdrawn from him amid allegations he had sexual harassed a campaign staffer.

Sasse's early primary victory freed him once again to criticize Trump as he saw fit. In June 2020, amid demonstrations against police violence and racism outside the White House, Sasse slammed the president for using tear gas and riot control tactics to clear a peaceful crowd so he cross Lafayette Square to pose for a photo outside St. John's Episcopal Church, which had been partially burned amid earlier riots and looting. "There is a fundamental—a constitutional—right to protest, and I'm against clearing out a peaceful protest for a photo op that treats the Word of God as a political prop," Sasse told Politico. In August of that year, Sasse argued against executive orders Trump issued to boost the economy—instead of working with Congress to reach a relief deal—amid the coronavirus pandemic and before the looming election. "The pen-and-phone theory of executive lawmaking is unconstitutional slop," Sasse said. "President Obama did not have the power to unilaterally rewrite immigration law with DACA, and President Trump does not have the power to unilaterally rewrite the payroll tax law." Trump blasted him on Twitter: "RINO Ben Sasse, who needed my support and endorsement in order to get the Republican nomination for Senate from the GREAT State of Nebraska, has, now that he's got it (Thank you President T), gone rogue, again." On an October teletown hall with constituents, Sasse warned Trump could cause a "Republican blood bath" in the Senate. "The debate is not going to be, 'Ben Sasse, why were you so mean to Donald Trump?' It's going to be, 'What the heck were any of us thinking—that selling a TV-obsessed, narcissistic individual to the American people was a good idea?'" the Washington Examiner reported. And as the November elections got closer, and Trump began to suggest he wouldn't accept the results if he were to lose, Sasse told the Omaha World-Herald: "He says crazy stuff. We've always had a peaceful transition of power. It's not going to change."

Trump lost the election to Biden, and in the weeks after, his lawyers alleged widespread voter fraud without evidence and repeatedly failed in court to overturn the election. Sasse blasted the strategy. "Wild press conferences erode public trust. So, no, obviously Rudy [Giuliani] and his buddies should not pressure (Electoral College) electors to ignore their certification obligations under the statute. We are a nation of laws, not tweets," Sasse said. Trump never relented though, and as Congress was tallying the Electoral College votes in favor of Biden on Jan. 6, he incited a crowd of supporters to insurrection and to attack the Capitol. "Lies have consequences. This violence was the inevitable and ugly outcome of the President's addiction to constantly stoking division," Sasse said in a statement. In the ensuing impeachment trial, Sasse voted to convict Trump of inciting the insurrection. Bemoaning the partisan nature of the vote that acquitted Trump, Sasse said, "Here's the sad reality: If we were talking about a Democratic president, most Republicans and most Democrats would simply swap sides. Tribalism is a hell of a drug, but our oath to the Constitution means we're constrained to the facts. ... In my first speech here in the Senate in November 2015, I promised to speak out when a president—even of my own party—exceeds his or her powers. I cannot go back on my word, and Congress cannot lower our standards on such a grave matter, simply because it is politically convenient. I must vote to convict."

Predictably, Sasse faced backlash at home again: The Nebraska Republican Party nearly censured him in a measure expressing "deep disappointment and sadness" about Sasse's tenure; it fell just short of passage. In a video before the vote, Sasse seemed unbothered. "I'm one of the most conservative voters in the Senate—the anger's always been simply about me not bending the knee to … one guy," said Sasse. "Personality cults aren't conservative, conspiracy theories aren't conservative, lying that an election has been stolen isn't conservative, acting like politics is a religion isn't conservative."

Jeff Fortenberry (R)

Elected 2004, 9th term, b. Dec 27, 1960; Baton Rouge, LA; Franciscan University, M.Th.; LA State University, B.A., 1982; Georgetown University, M.P.P., 1986; Franciscan University, M.A., 1996; Roman Catholic; Married (Celeste Gregory Fortenberry); 5 children.

Elected Office: Lincoln City Council, 1997-2001.

Professional Career: Staffer, U.S. House Comm. on Ag., 1986; Research Association, Gulf South Research Inst., 1987-1989; Assistant Director, Baton Rouge Downtown Dev. District, 1989-1992; Sales rep., Sandhills Publishing, 1995-2004.

DC Office: 1514 LHOB 20515, 202-225-4806, Fax: 202-225-5686, fortenberry.house.gov

State Offices: Fremont, 402-727-0888; Lincoln, 402-438-1598; Norfolk, 402-379-2064.

Committees: *Appropriations*: Agriculture, Rural Development, FDA & Related Agencies (RMM); State, Foreign Operations & Related Programs.

Group Ratings

	ADA	ACLU	AFL-CIO	LCV	COC	HAFA	ACU	CFG	FRC
2020	**	22%	**	43%	-	77%	73%	**	-
2019	5%	C	45%	34%	92%	C	73%	60%	100%

Almanac Ratings 2019-2020

	Economy	Social	Foreign	Composite
Liberal	38%	36%	14%	30%
Conservative	62%	64%	86%	70%

Key Votes of the 116th Congress

1. U.S./Mex./Can. trade deal	Y	5. Russia sanctions	N	9. Firearms background checks N
2. First Coronavirus response	Y	6. Troops in Syria	Y	10. Spending at the border	Y
3. HEROES Act	N	7. Veto arms sales to Saudis	N	11. Marijuana liberalized rules	N
4. CASH Act	N/A	8. Defense $$$, veto override	N/A	12. Electoral College objections N

Election Results

Election	Name (Party)	Vote (%)		Cand. Spent	Ind. Exp. Support	Ind. Exp. Oppose
2020 General	Jeff Fortenberry (R)	189,006	(60%)	$2,714,229		
	Kate Bolz (D)	119,622	(38%)	$1,356,958	$10	
	Dennis Grace (L)	8,938	(3%)			
2020 Primary	Jeff Fortenberry (R)	84,017	(100%)			

Prior winning percentages: 2018 (60%), 2016 (70%), 2014 (69%), 2012 (68%), 2010 (71%), 2008 (70%), 2006 (58%), 2004 (54%)

Republican Jeff Fortenberry, elected in 2004, has taken a prime slot on agriculture issues at the Appropriations Committee—a useful assignment for a Nebraskan. He has a reputation as a brainy policy expert and something of a centrist. In the tradition of many Nebraskans in Congress, Fortenberry takes a strong interest in foreign policy.

Fortenberry grew up in Baton Rouge Louisiana, where his father was a life insurance salesman and his mother worked as a 4-H Club extension agent. When Fortenberry was 12, his father was killed in a car accident. "It taught me a hard lesson that you wouldn't want to wish on any other child—you have to figure out a lot of things on your own," he told Esquire magazine. Fortenberry got the political bug early as a page to a Democratic state senator, but switched to the Republican Party after he graduated from Louisiana State University. He earned a master's degree in theology from Franciscan University of Steubenville Ohio, and another in public policy from Georgetown University. For a time, he studied for the priesthood. He moved to Nebraska to take a public relations position with Sandhills Publishing, a publisher of trade magazines for the trucking, aircraft and computer industries, and later got into the sales end of the business. In 1997, he won a seat on the Lincoln City Council. He served for four years, focusing on neighborhood concerns and growing the police force.

When the House seat opened in 2004, three candidates mounted competitive campaigns for the Republican nomination: Fortenberry; Curt Bromm, the speaker of the state's unicameral legislature; and Greg Ruehle, a former executive vice president of the Nebraska Cattlemen Association. The moderate Bromm lost momentum after a barrage of negative television ads financed by the Club for Growth, a national anti-tax group that supported Ruehle. Fortenberry, a social conservative, drew criticism from his opponents as a single-issue candidate, but he had superior grassroots operation and fundraising. Fortenberry won with 39 percent of the vote, to 33 percent for Bromm and 21 percent for Ruehle. In November, Fortenberry faced state Sen. Matt Connealy, a farmer from Decatur who sought to exploit GOP divisions. Fortenberry focused on socially conservative themes: opposition to abortion rights, support of capital punishment and a ban on same-sex marriage. He won 54%-43%, losing only two American Indian reservation counties.

In the House, Fortenberry has moved over time to the ideological center. His Almanac vote ratings have ranked him among moderate Republicans on foreign policy issues. He backed the 2011 compromise to raise the federal debt limit as well as the New Year's Day 2013 budget deal aimed at averting the so-called fiscal cliff. He has won House approval of an increase in visas for Iraqi translators, and enacted a bill barring U.S. assistance for governments using children as soldiers.

His legislative work has been chiefly on the Appropriations Committee. He supported extension of the Export-Import Bank of the United States on the basis that "we don't have a perfect world." He has co-chaired the Caucus on Religious Minorities in the Middle East, the Congressional Study Group on Europe and the Nuclear Security Working Group. In 2016, the House unanimously passed a resolution he authored with Democratic Rep. Anna Eshoo of California that labeled Islamic State atrocities against Christian groups in Syria and Iraq as "genocide." In the summer of 2018, the Obama White House selected Fortenberry to help lead a delegation to northern Iraq to investigate the difficulties minority Christians targeted by ISIS were facing. As a result, he proposed an American-sponsored but Iraqi-led training mission to integrate Christians, Yazidis, Shia Muslims and others into a security force to help stabilize and secure the region.

Fortenberry started off skeptical of Donald Trump during the 2016 campaign. After initially urging him to withdraw as the presidential nominee following the early October release of the Access Hollywood video with his lewd comments on women, Fortenberry said a few days later that he would vote for Trump. When his 17-year-old daughter in tears told Fortenberry, "Daddy, you've got to do something—Trump hates women," he relayed the story to vice presidential nominee Mike Pence during a meeting with other House Republicans and urged the Trump campaign to reach out to women. After the meeting, Pence privately thanked him for his comment, said Fortenberry, who has five daughters. Fortenberry came around on Trump, to some degree. "Many people love him; many do not. But I think it's best to look at outcomes," Fortenberry told the Lincoln Star Journal. "And I've never had better interaction with an administration. I find them willing to help."

Since 2019, he has been ranking member of the agriculture subcommittee at Appropriations. He defended the Trump administration's farm bailout program and said Republicans would not accept any limits on the available credit. In August 2020, when he was invited to a presidential signing ceremony for conservation legislation, the White House background sheet listed him as a congressman from Louisiana.

In 2006, Fortenberry's first reelection campaign was against former Democratic Lt. Gov. Maxine Moul, who made the Iraq war an issue. Fortenberry won 58%-42%. In his past two reelections, he was held below 68 percent for the first time since 2006. In 2018, Democrat Jessica McClure challenged the incumbent's "complacency" with the Trump administration and his vote to repeal the Affordable Care Act; he won 60%-40%. In 2020, he ran against state Sen. Kate Bolz, who criticized Fortenberry as slow to respond to flood damage and for his support of repeal of the Affordable Care Act. Fortenberry said he backed "repair" of the health care law, and he criticized Bolz for missing votes in the legislature. Fortenberry outspent Bolz, $2.7 million to $1.4 million, and won 60%-38%. Bolz led by 746 votes in Lancaster County, which cast nearly half the total vote.

NE-1: Eastern Nebraska

Cook Partisan Voting Index: R+11

Population		Race and Ethnicity		Income	
Total	651,958	White	88.10%	Median Income	$63,921
Land area (sq. miles)	8,879	Black	2.80%	District Income Rank	216
Pop/ sq mi	73.43	Latino	10.00%	Poverty Rate	9.60%
Born in State	67.20%	Asian	2.70%	With health insurance	92.20%
		Two or more races	2.80%	Cash public assistance	2.10%
Age Groups		Other	3.60%	Food stamp/SNAP	7.30%
Under 18	23.70%				
18-34	24.90%	**Education**		**Work**	
35-64	35.70%	H.S grad or less	32.30%	White Collar	38.90%
Over 64	15.50%	Some college	34.60%	Sales and Service	36.50%
		College Degree, 4 yr	21.50%	Blue Collar	24.60%
Military		Post grad	11.50%	Government	17.10%
Veteran/ Active Duty	9.10%				

2020 Pres. Vote	Trump	180,290	(56%)	Biden	132,261	(41%)	Jorgensen	7,495	(2%)
2016 Pres. Vote	Trump	158,576	(56%)	Clinton	100,106	(36%)	Johnson	14,025	(5%)

Lincoln: The eastern half of Nebraska, between the Missouri River and the 98th meridian, was laid out in relentless Midwestern mile-square grids and became some of America's prime farmland during the 1880s. Here the Plains have completed most of their gentle decline from the Rockies to sea level, and the land has contours just regular enough, and weather just favorable enough, to make farming economically viable. The area was settled by Yankee-descended farmers from the Midwest and immigrants from Germany and other countries. Traces of the immigrant heritage can still be found. Many people from Luxembourg, for example, settled along the Platte River in Butler County, where St. Mary's Presentation Parish still has a statue of Our Lady of Luxembourg. Not far away are villages with names that recall other immigrant groups—Prague (Czechs), Malmo (Swedes), Aloys (Germans).

Today, a new wave of immigrants is coming to eastern Nebraska, including Latinos from Mexico and the southwest United States, to work in the region's meatpacking factories, and Vietnamese refugees coming to Lincoln. Some tensions remain. Fremont, a town of 26,000 northwest of Omaha that is about 15 percent Hispanic, made national news when voters overwhelmingly approved an ordinance mandating immigration background checks for anyone seeking to rent an apartment or house; in 2014, the Supreme Court declined to rule on its legality, leaving a lower court ruling in place upholding the policy. Voters in Scribner overwhelmingly approved in 2018 a similar ordinance.

The 1st Congressional District of Nebraska includes 16 counties and parts of two others in the eastern slice of the state. It surrounds but does not take in Omaha-based Douglas County, which is in the 2nd District. Taking up almost half the district is Lancaster County, home to Lincoln and the main campus of the University of Nebraska, which has many scientific units that receive large research grants. The city is home to more than 100 companies and government agencies with 250 or more workers, including a strong manufacturing sector. In the smaller towns, there are many farm equipment and meatpacking factories. Plans were underway to build a 230 megawatt solar farm in Lincoln; despite its plentiful potential for solar energy, the state has been among the slowest to move in that direction. Costco opened in 2019 a chicken processing plant in Fremont, though some local residents were unhappy about it, citing traffic and environmental concerns. The plant employs about 800 workers who process 2 million chickens each week—one-third of Costco's total sales of roasted and fried chickens. A few miles from Omaha, the district includes the eastern part of fast-growing Sarpy County and the city of Bellevue, home of Offutt Air Force Base, headquarters of the Strategic Air Command. In December 2020, the Pentagon began work to repair Offutt's 80-year-old runway. The project, including the closing of the airfield, was scheduled for completion in late 2022.

Politically, Lincoln is fond of moderate Democrats but is still, on balance, Republican in national contests. In 2020, Lancaster was one of two counties—along with Douglas—that voted for Joe Biden, by more than 12,000 votes. The remaining counties were secure for President Donald Trump, who took 56 percent of the district vote, the same as he received in 2016. The district has not elected a Democrat to Congress since 1964.

Don Bacon (R)

Elected 2016, 3rd term, b. Aug 16, 1963; Momence, IL; Northern IL University, B.A., 1984; Officer Intelligence School, 1986; Squadron Officer School, 1989; Navigator/Electronic Warfare School, 1992; University of Phoenix, M.A., 1995; Air Command and Staff College, 1998; National War College, M.A., 2004; MA Institute of Technology, 2006; Eckerd College Leadership Development Institute, 2009; University of VA Darden School of Business, M.A., 2009; Christian - Non-Denominational; Married (Angie Bacon); 4 children.

Military Career: U.S. Air Force 1985-2014

Professional Career: Military Advisor, Rep. Jeff Fortenberry, 2014-2015; Assistant Professor, University of Bellvue , 2014-2017.

DC Office: 1024 LHOB 20515, 202-225-4155, bacon.house.gov
State Offices: Omaha, 402-938-0300.

Committees: *Agriculture*: Biotechnology, Horticulture & Research; Livestock & Foreign Agriculture; Subcommittee Nutrition, Oversight & Department Operations (RMM). *Armed Services*: Intelligence & Special Operations; Tactical Air & Land Forces.

Group Ratings

	ADA	ACLU	AFL-CIO	LCV	COC	HAFA	ACU	CFG	FRC
2020	**	21%	**	24%	-	72%	71%	**	-
2019	0%	C	57%	34%	99%	C	75%	67%	91%

Almanac Ratings 2019-2020

	Economy	Social	Foreign	Composite
Liberal	25%	42%	27%	32%
Conservative	75%	58%	73%	68%

Key Votes of the 116th Congress

1. U.S./Mex./Can. trade deal Y	5. Russia sanctions Y	9. Firearms background checks N
2. First Coronavirus response Y	6. Troops in Syria Y	10. Spending at the border Y
3. HEROES Act N	7. Veto arms sales to Saudis N	11. Marijuana liberalized rules N
4. CASH Act N	8. Defense $$$, veto override Y	12. Electoral College objections N

Election Results

Election	Name (Party)	Vote (%)		Cand. Spent	Ind. Exp. Support	Ind. Exp. Oppose
2020 General	Don Bacon (R)	171,071	(51%)	$3,662,016	$1,989,161	$4,976,918
	Kara Eastman (D)	155,706	(46%)	$4,514,348	$891,211	$5,446,040
	Tyler Schaeffer (L)	10,185	(3%)			
2020 Primary	Don Bacon (R)	68,531	(91%)			
	Paul Anderson (R)	7,106	(9%)			

Prior winning percentages: 2018 (51%), 2016 (49%)

Republican Don Bacon, elected in 2016 in this traditionally reliable Republican district, has proven himself adept at overcoming challenging political environments. In 2016, he was the only GOP candidate nationwide to defeat a House Democratic incumbent. Two years later, Bacon narrowly beat a liberal Democrat, amid a 40-seat loss for the GOP. Facing that same candidate again in 2020, he got reelected even as Joe Biden carried the district, 52.2%-45.7%. His high-level military career was apt for this district, and prepared him for his seat on the Armed Services Committee.

Bacon grew up on a farm in Illinois, earning his bachelor's degree in political science at Northern Illinois University in 1984. The following year, he joined the Air Force, where he served for nearly 30 years and retired as a brigadier general. He specialized in electronic warfare, intelligence, reconnaissance and public affairs. He deployed four times to the Middle East, and commanded an electronic warfare squadron during the invasion of Iraq. In 2009, he was selected as Europe's top Air Force wing commander and later commanded Offutt Air Force Base outside Omaha. After leaving the Air Force, Bacon worked for Republican Rep. Jeff Fortenberry of Nebraska as his military adviser and focused on Offutt. He received two master's degrees, from the University of Phoenix and the National War College in Washington D.C. As an assistant professor at Bellevue University, he taught courses on leadership and American values.

In 2016, he challenged Rep. Brad Ashford, who was one of two Democrats in 2014 to oust a House Republican incumbent. With this district's slight Republican lean, Ashford immediately became a top GOP target. Bacon, with his superior fundraising, became the frontrunner for the Republican nomination against Chip Maxwell, a more outspoken conservative who had been an editorial writer for the Omaha World-Herald. Maxwell accused the National Republican Congressional Committee of siding with Bacon. During the primary, the Democratic Congressional Campaign Committee spent more than $400,000 in ads that extolled Maxwell's conservative credentials, which revealed their concern about Bacon. That may have backfired. Bacon won the primary, 66%-34%.

In the general, Ashford and Bacon discussed foreign policy at length and criticized each other's ads. In a debate, Ashford separated himself from President Barack Obama's nuclear deal with Iran. Bacon parted company with the criticism of NATO by Republican presidential nominee Donald Trump. Ashford led by nearly 9,000 votes in Douglas County, but Bacon won on the basis of his 60 percent of the vote in Sarpy, even though that county cast less than 20 percent of the total vote. He won overall, 48.9%-47.7%, a margin of 3,464 votes.

Bacon got special attention from Republican leaders, including seats on the Armed Services and Agriculture committees. He passed a bill to give Gold Star families better access to benefits at military bases. He passed another bill, named in honor of a fallen Omaha police officer, to allow immediate relatives of immigrant first responders killed in the line of duty to process their immigration applications more quickly. Bacon carved out a moderate profile on immigration, pushing for a pathway to citizenship for young immigrants brought to the country illegally by their parents. In December 2020, he was one of just seven House Republicans to vote with Democrats to continue the DACA program that protects those young immigrants. He was critical of Trump's decision to withdraw from the Paris climate accord. But Bacon was a stalwart supporter of other GOP policies, including the tax overhaul and gun rights.

Running again in 2018 in a primary that largely flew under the radar, the moderate Ashford faced an unexpected challenge from progressive nonprofit CEO Kara Eastman. She criticized Ashford for his GOP past, supported "Medicaid for All" and had the backing of progressive groups. EMILY's List, which supports pro-abortion rights women candidates, stayed neutral in the primary, while the Democratic Congressional Campaign Committee was already helping Ashford. Surprisingly to many national Democrats, Eastman narrowly prevailed, 51.4%-48.6%.

Republicans were enthusiastic about what they saw as an easier race. Eastman's strategy wasn't to win over Republican moderates as the Blue Dog Ashford had done, but to excite the progressive base. She backed a $15 minimum wage, "free" college tuition and no restrictions on abortion—issues that play better in coastal cities than in Omaha. Her positions helped rake in plenty of cash from activists, though the national party was slow to embrace her. National GOP groups carpet-bombed the district with ads painting Eastman as out of touch and pointing to her wilder days in college contrasted with Bacon's military bona fides. Bacon ultimately withstood the blue tide, prevailing 51%-49%. Bacon again lost Douglas County, this time by 6,500 votes; but he led by more than 11,000 votes in Sarpy.

Eastman immediately decided to make another go in 2020. Democrats, meanwhile, tried to recruit around her. Ashford's wife, Ann, decided to run. Ann Ashford, an attorney, said Eastman was "too far to the left" for the district. Eastman outraised Ashford by a 2-to-1 margin and won the May primary, 62%-31%. Republicans were elated. "I have been blessed to have a far-left opponent two times in a row," Bacon told Roll Call, a Capitol Hill newspaper. The incumbent and his allies reprised his 2018 attacks, calling Eastman a "radical socialist" and accused her of supporting violent rioters in Omaha who were protesting for racial justice. Bacon tried to create some distance from Trump. He objected to the president's tweet attacking four minority congresswomen—though didn't back House Democrats' resolution to condemn that tweet—and disavowed Trump's combative demeanor during a presidential debate.

Eastman outspent Bacon $4.5 million to $3.7 million and, unlike in 2018, received consistent help from national Democratic groups and the Justice Democrats, a progressive group. Fourteen different outside groups spent over $10 million in the race. In the end, Bacon prevailed, 51%-46%, a win made all the more impressive because Trump lost the district by an even wider margin.

Bacon will again be a top target in 2022, though Republicans may be able to shore up the seat in redistricting.

NE-2: Greater Omaha   Cook Partisan Voting Index: R+1

Population		Race and Ethnicity		Income	
Total	684,882	White	80.80%	Median Income	$71,277
Land area (sq. miles)	510	Black	9.90%	District Income Rank	152
Pop/ sq mi	1,343.59	Latino	11.90%	Poverty Rate	9.50%
Born in State	59.40%	Asian	3.70%	With health insurance	91.50%
		Two or more races	3.30%	Cash public assistance	1.40%
Age Groups		Other	2.30%	Food stamp/SNAP	7.80%
Under 18	26.20%				
18-34	23.80%	**Education**		**Work**	
35-64	37.00%	H.S grad or less	29.20%	White Collar	45.40%
Over 64	13.20%	Some college	28.70%	Sales and Service	35.40%
		College Degree, 4 yr	27.10%	Blue Collar	19.20%
Military		Post grad	15.00%	Government	11.10%
Veteran/ Active Duty	7.60%				

2020 Pres. Vote	Biden	176,468	(52%)	Trump	154,377	(45%)	Jorgensen	6,909	(2%)
2016 Pres. Vote	Trump	137,564	(47%)	Clinton	131,030	(45%)	Johnson	13,245	(5%)

Omaha: Omaha is the commercial heart of Nebraska and the largest city on the Great Plains north of Kansas City and west of Minneapolis. It got its start from the government, when President Abraham Lincoln picked it as the eastern terminus of the Union Pacific railroad, from which emerged the stockyards and livestock exchange that made it a thriving town. Over the years, Omaha filled up with cattle hands and European immigrants, especially Germans and Czechs. It developed fine civic institutions, from the Joslyn Art Museum to Boys Town, an orphanage founded by the Rev. Edward Flanagan in 1917 and the subject of a 1938 movie. Today, the facility is a gender-neutral home for troubled youth.

Though a major city by the 1880s, Omaha has remained small enough to be intimate. One doesn't feel distant, physically or psychologically, from the other side of town. The older, less affluent part of Omaha is on the Missouri River across from Council Bluffs Iowa. Downtown and the riverfront have experienced substantial growth and development, and a $290 million effort to revitalize the Omaha waterfront is also planned. The 45-story First National Bank Tower is the tallest structure between Minneapolis and Denver. To the west, the city has flourished with the rise of upscale neighborhoods and shopping malls. Omaha has entered the Wall Street vernacular as the place where investor Warren Buffett—ranked by Forbes in 2016 as the world's second-richest person, though he dropped to sixth in 2020—lives and works. His annual Berkshire Hathaway shareholder meeting draws around 40,000 investors to Omaha.

Omaha has experienced a construction boomlet, including a $370 million cancer center with more than 4,600 employees at the University of Nebraska Medical Center. In 2020, an Australian group-travel company acquired the Omaha-based Travel and Transport for $200 million, a sale that will likely boost the city's status as a tech hub. While Omaha's economy remains dependent on overseas sales of food, it has also become the headquarters of more than 30 insurance companies and the nation's telecommunications hub, employing more than 20,000 people at more than two dozen telemarketing centers. Millennials have been 38 percent of this expanding workforce. However, the elderly population has grown over the past decade too, with a 37 percent spike in residents over 65 as baby boomers age. The city has become more ethnically diverse: As of 2019, it was about 12 percent African American and 14 percent Hispanic.

The 2nd Congressional District, the least conservative in the state, includes Omaha and all of Douglas County. Omaha has long had competitive politics, with Democrats strong on the south side around the stockyards and the northeast and Republicans strong on the west side. The district includes nearly two-thirds of more-conservative Sarpy County, but not Offutt Air Force Base, which is in the 1st District. In 2016, Hillary Clinton won Douglas County, 48%-46%. But, with his big lead in Sarpy, Donald Trump prevailed in the district, 47%-45%. But as with other traditionally conservative affluent suburban areas, the district turned against Trump over time. In 2020, he lost this district and its electoral vote, 52%-45%, despite opening a campaign office there. It was only the second time since the 1960s that a Democratic presidential nominee has won the Omaha-based district.

Adrian Smith (R)

Elected 2006, 8th term, b. Dec 19, 1970; Scottsbluff, NE; Liberty University, Att., 1990; University of NE, Lincoln, B.S., 1993; Evangelical; Married (Andrea Smith); 1 child.

Elected Office: Gering City Council, 1994-1998; NE Legislature, 1998- 2006.

Professional Career: Realtor, Buyer Realty, 1997-2006; Owner, My Other Garage, 2003-2006.

DC Office: 502 CHOB 20515, 202-225-6435, Fax: 202-225-0207, adriansmith.house.gov

State Offices: Grand Island, 308-384-3900; Scottsbluff, 308-633-6333.

Committees: *Ways & Means*: Health; Select Revenue Measures (RMM).

Group Ratings

	ADA	ACLU	AFL-CIO	LCV	COC	HAFA	ACU	CFG	FRC
2020	**	19%	**	5%	-	84%	89%	**	-
2019	0%	C	29%	3%	89%	C	89%	85%	100%

Almanac Ratings 2019-2020

	Economy	Social	Foreign	Composite
Liberal	25%	4%	27%	19%
Conservative	75%	96%	73%	81%

Key Votes of the 116th Congress

1. U.S./Mex./Can. trade deal Y	5. Russia sanctions Y	9. Firearms background checks N
2. First Coronavirus response Y	6. Troops in Syria Y	10. Spending at the border Y
3. HEROES Act N	7. Veto arms sales to Saudis N	11. Marijuana liberalized rules N
4. CASH Act N	8. Defense $$$, veto override N	12. Electoral College objections Y

Election Results

Election	Name (Party)	Vote (%)		Cand. Spent	Ind. Exp. Support	Ind. Exp. Oppose
2020 General	Adrian Smith (R)	225,157	(79%)	$758,459		
	Mark Elworth (D)	50,690	(18%)			
	Dustin Hobbs (L)	10,923	(4%)			
2020 Primary	Adrian Smith (R)	96,260	(83%)			
	Arron Kowalski (R)	6,424	(6%)			
	Justin Moran (R)	6,374	(6%)			

Prior winning percentages: 2018 (77%), 2016 (100%), 2014 (75%), 2012 (74%), 2010 (70%), 2008 (77%), 2006 (55%)

Republican Adrian Smith, elected in 2006, is an unwavering conservative who uses his seat on the Ways and Means Committee and his low-key style to focus intently on the rural issues important in his district. In 2017, he became chairman of its Human Resources Subcommittee. After Republicans lost their majority in 2019, he became ranking member on the Select Revenue Measures Subcommittee, which handles tax legislation. He has taken an interest in expanding the use of technology to promote health care, an important issue in rural western Nebraska.

Smith hails from a politically active family; his father is a former county Republican chairman, and his mother has been the state GOP secretary. But the most significant political influence in Smith's life was President Ronald Reagan. When he was in fourth grade, Smith recalls, adults around him were weighing Reagan's attributes against those of Democrat Jimmy Carter, and it sunk into the boy's head that Reagan favored a strong defense. "It just made sense to me that we needed a strong military," said Smith, whose congressional office is filled with portraits of the former president.

At 23, shortly after graduating from the University of Nebraska, he won election to the City Council in his hometown of Gering. Four years later, he knocked off a Democratic incumbent to win the first of two terms in the state legislature. There, Smith devoted his efforts to opposing abortion rights, protecting Nebraskans' right to bear arms, fighting tax increases and blocking efforts to expand casino gambling. He also worked as a real estate agent and owned a storage business.

In 2005, Smith joined the race for an open House seat. Leading the crowded Republican primary field were Grand Island Mayor Jay Vavricek and John Hanson, who had been the incumbent's district director. Smith championed tax incentives to attract new residents and encourage local investment. Touting his support from the Nebraska Farm Bureau, Smith won the nomination with 39 percent of the vote. In the general election, Democrats fielded an unusually strong nominee. Yale-educated cattle rancher Scott Kleeb called for changes in farm policy to emphasize niche markets. Smith portrayed Kleeb as a political carpetbagger who grew up overseas on military bases and attended schools in Colorado and Connecticut before settling in Nebraska on a family-owned ranch. Kleeb was competitive financially. Still, Smith won 55%-45%. In his strongly Republican district, he has easily won reelection since.

In Washington, Smith has pushed for strict fiscal discipline, and in 2018 voted against a bipartisan budget agreement, saying the deal "does not take the necessary steps to rein in our national debt." As founder and co-chairman in 2015 of the Modern Agriculture Caucus, Smith promoted scientifically based policies to move agriculture forward and to educate other lawmakers about the issues farmers face. On the annual defense spending bill in 2016, Smith won approval of his amendment to prevent the exclusion of meat from the Defense Department's food service program manual. To promote ethanol as an alternative fuel, he praised the Environmental Protection Agency for its decision in September 2020 to reject exemptions for small refineries from the Renewable Fuel Standard. Nebraska ranks second nationally in ethanol production.

On Ways and Means, Smith has focused on agriculture and trade issues. He sought to ensure that agriculture was part of the talks held by a U.S.-European Union working group that met to consider a trade agreement. He has advocated lower corporate tax rates to keep the United States more competitive in the world economy, and he contends that free-trade agreements are good for the nation's overall economy, especially agriculture. When President Donald Trump formally abandoned U.S. participation in the Trans-Pacific Partnership three days after he was inaugurated, Smith responded, "Our country should be a leader in writing the rules of the global economy, rather than allowing other world powers to take our place." When the tariffs prompted retaliatory ones that worried many in the agriculture community, Smith argued that farmers in his district still backed the president.

In October 2020, a COVID-19 relief bill was enacted with Smith's provision "promoting policies that incentivize innovation" in health care—specifically, by permitting Medicare reimbursement for greater use of health-care technologies to treat certain nursing-home patients, rather than transferring them to a hospital.

Politically, when many congressional Republicans in July 2020 quickly rejected a trial balloon from Trump about a potential delay in the November election, Smith lent more encouragement to the suggestion. "President Trump is right about the fraud opportunities presented by universal vote-by-mail," he said. "We must do everything we can to ensure a safe, secure election is held on Election Day."

With his safe seat and his relative youth, his seniority at Ways and Means has positioned Smith to take the top Republican slot on the tax-writing committee within a decade.

NE-3: Central and Western Nebraska — Cook Partisan Voting Index: R+30

Population		Race and Ethnicity		Income	
Total	597,568	White	90.20%	Median Income	$55,729
Land area (sq. miles)	67,435	Black	1.50%	District Income Rank	321
Pop/ sq mi	8.86	Latino	12.20%	Poverty Rate	10.70%
Born in State	68.10%	Asian	0.70%	With health insurance	91.30%
		Two or more races	2.10%	Cash public assistance	1.20%
Age Groups		Other	5.40%	Food stamp/SNAP	7.80%
Under 18	23.60%				
18-34	20.10%	**Education**		**Work**	
35-64	36.10%	H.S grad or less	39.70%	White Collar	35.00%
Over 64	20.30%	Some college	36.60%	Sales and Service	34.40%
		College Degree, 4 yr	16.20%	Blue Collar	30.50%
Military		Post grad	7.50%	Government	15.00%
Veteran/ Active Duty	7.70%				

2020 Pres. Vote	Trump	222,179	(75%)	Biden	65,854	(22%)		
2016 Pres. Vote	Trump	199,821	(74%)	Clinton	53,358	(20%)	Johnson 11,676	(4%)

North Platte: West of Grand Island, Nebraska is wheat and livestock country. For miles on end there are rolling brown fields, only occasionally interrupted by barbed wire fences. The wind, rain and tornadoes that come suddenly remind you that the original immigrants likened this part of the country to an ocean and thought themselves in their wooden wagons almost as helpless as passengers at sea in a rowboat. Settlers passed through here on the Oregon, California and Mormon trails in the 1840s and 1850s, then set down roots in the 1880s. But the rain they hoped for fell too unreliably, and wheat lands gave way to pasture and open range. It is a beautiful but hard land, exacting much from its people, as the novels of western Nebraska's Willa Cather make poignantly clear. Chimney Rock—a clay and sandstone spire that marked a good camping spot and offered reliable spring water for travelers and their animals—was the landmark that travelers on the way west most frequently mentioned in their journals.

Dozens of small counties in the region today have fewer people than they did in 1900. Severe droughts in recent years have seemed a kind of endpoint for some, as reservoirs and aquifers began to run dry and ranchers sold off their thinning herds. Still, many farmers have found ways to adapt. The 55,834 farm producers in this district was the most for any congressional district in the nation, according to the Census of Agriculture in 2017. Economic life also sets records in other industries. In North Platte, according to Union Pacific, Bailey Yard is the world's largest railroad classification yard, covering 2,850 acres and handling 14,000 rail cars every 24 hours. The 103-mile Union Pacific line from North Platte east to Gibbon is the busiest freight rail corridor in the world, with 139 trains a day passing through. The railroads employ about 8,000 people in Nebraska.

In 2016, Missouri-based Bass Pro Shops took control of Cabela's in a $5.5 billion merger. Despite initial reassurances by Bass Pro, the move raised warranted fears about the future of Sidney, the small town near the Colorado line where 2,000 were employed by Cabela's. In March 2018, about 700 workers took buyout packages from Bass Pro. By November 2019, only 200 jobs remained with Bass Pro in Sydney, the Sandhills Express reported. "This is extremely sickening," Sand Hills Mayor Roger Gallaway said. "We're very disappointed to see this happen." When the Keystone XL oil pipeline was proposed to go through the environmentally sensitive Sandhills area in north central Nebraska, many Cornhusker politicians pushed to have it rerouted. President Barack Obama rejected the company's application in 2012 in part, he said, because of concerns about this region. That set off a new round of review. When he took office, President Joe Biden pulled the plug on further cooperation with the Keystone project.

The 3rd Congressional District is geographically massive, reaching roughly 460 miles from the Wyoming border to the Iowa border and larger than the state of New York. The district takes in all or part of 75 counties, more than any other district in the nation. Following the 2020 election, this district ranked 8th in the Cook PVI listing of the most Republican districts. President Donald Trump won the district, 75%-22%.

NEVADA

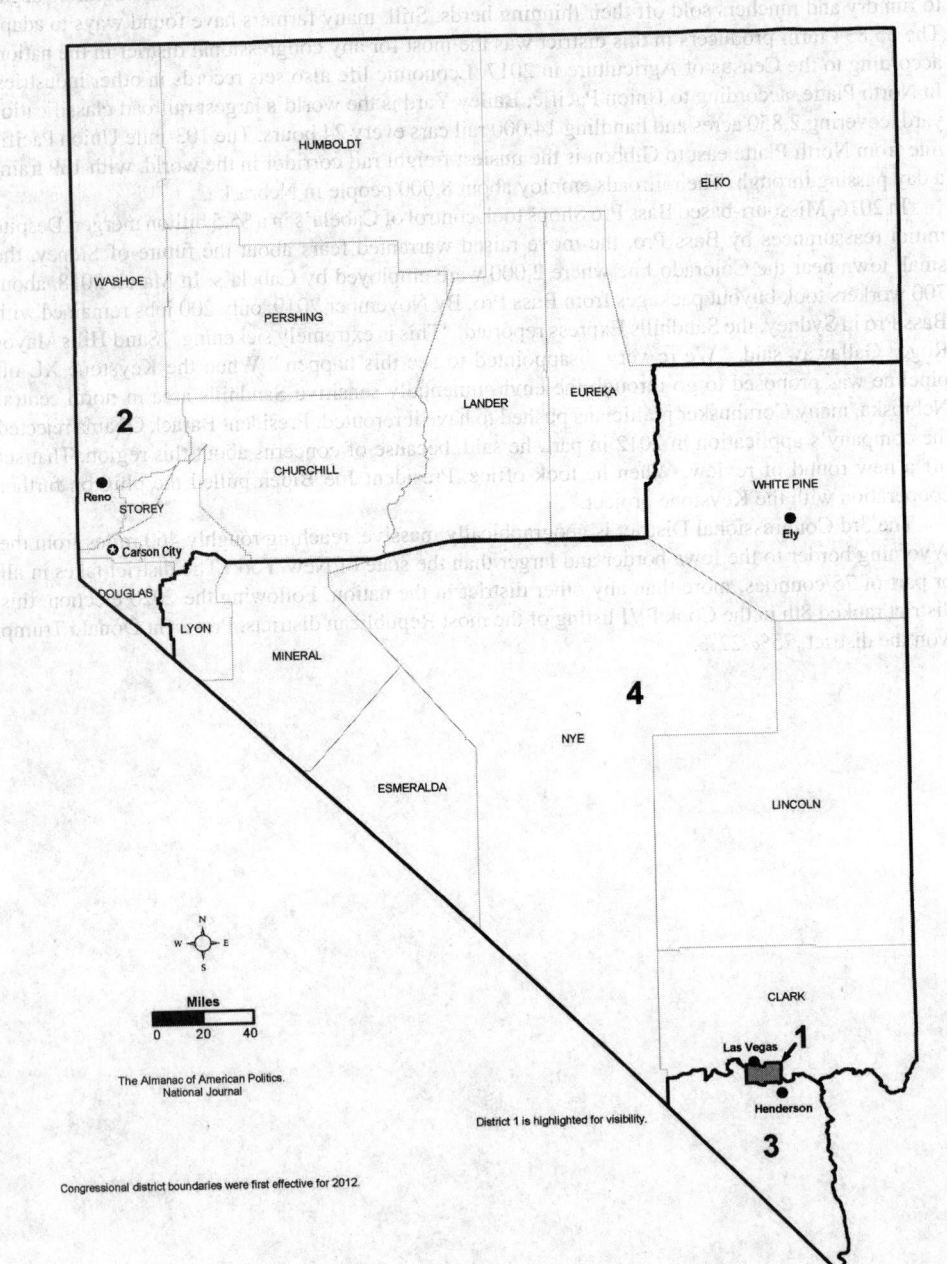

HUMBOLDT

ELKO

WASHOE

PERSHING

LANDER

EUREKA

2

Reno

STOREY

CHURCHILL

WHITE PINE

Carson City

Ely

DOUGLAS

LYON

MINERAL

4

NYE

ESMERALDA

LINCOLN

N
W　E
S

Miles

0　20　40

CLARK

Las Vegas **1**

The Almanac of American Politics.
National Journal

Henderson

3

District 1 is highlighted for visibility.

Congressional district boundaries were first effective for 2012.

Nevada fuses two important, and divergent, demographic groups in today's political scene, minorities and blue-collar whites. The state is more than 29 percent Hispanic (the fifth highest of any state), 9 percent Black and 9 percent Asian (the sixth highest)—all prime voting groups for Democratic candidates. Nevada's white population, meanwhile, accounts for less than 48 percent of the total—the fifth smallest of any state—but it includes many with prickly views about the federal government, which owns about 80 percent of the state's land. These voters are receptive to Republicans, especially those aligned with Donald Trump. Mix in economic upheaval, first during the Great Recession and later during the coronavirus pandemic that flattened the state's crucial tourism industry, and you have the recipe for volatile politics. After a Republican sweep in 2014, Nevada Democrats showed notable strength in two subsequent election cycles. In the 2020 presidential race, Nevada showed less movement from the 2016 results than any other state, handing a narrow victory to Joe Biden.

Nevada has been a land of boom and bust from its very beginnings as a territory. The evidence of the latest boom is apparent as your plane descends at Las Vegas' Harry Reid International Airport (renamed for the former Senate Majority Leader from McCarran International Airport in 2021). You see a pyramid rising from the desert; just across the street from a Sphinx-like lion are New York City-style skyscrapers. Nearby are a fair-sized Eiffel Tower, the gondolas of Venice, and a flaming pirate ship. But there have been signs of bust — giant hotels and condominiums with no lights on at night, retail space up for rent, subdivisions where many houses are unoccupied, and a seamy side of town expertly mined by CSI, the flagship of the long-running TV crime procedural. All this is set in one of North America's most forbidding landscapes, a bowl-shaped desert valley rimmed by barren peaks.

The natural parts would have looked familiar to the prospectors who first came to mine silver and gold in Virginia City, on a mountain 6,700 feet above sea level, or to Mark Twain and Bret Harte, who documented the heyday of the Comstock Lode, which beginning in 1859 produced $500 million worth of silver within two decades. President Abraham Lincoln's Republicans made Nevada a state in 1864, even though it did not meet the population requirement, to win three more electoral votes. But the silver boom went bust, and by 1900, Nevada had only 42,000 residents, down 68 percent from its 1880 peak. For a time, it seemed questionable whether Nevada would be a viable state. In the early 1930s, when there were still only 91,000 Nevadans, the state government was about to go bankrupt. So Nevada decided to roll the dice. It reduced its residency requirement for divorce to six weeks and legalized gambling. The state catered to what most Americans considered sin—casinos, pawnshops, divorce mills, quick-wedding chapels, and legal brothels. (Nevadans remain below average in church attendance.) It turned out to be good business. The 6.75 percent gambling receipts tax generated enough revenue to make it unnecessary for Nevada to impose income, corporate or inheritance taxes.

From mining boom to gambling boom, Nevada has been a second-chance state, a place for outcasts to succeed and misfits to rebound. Only about a quarter of the state's residents were born in Nevada, a rate well below even second-place Florida's, and that percentage has been steady for a half-century. Today, more adult residents of the state were born in California than in Nevada, according to Robert Lang of the University of Nevada-Las Vegas. Nevada has been an avenue of success for ethnic groups who faced roadblocks elsewhere. The four owners of the Comstock Lode—MacKay, Fair, Flood and O'Brien—were Irishmen. The first big hotel on the Las Vegas strip, the Flamingo, was built in 1946 by the Jewish gangster Bugsy Siegel. Most of the big casinos were owned by mobsters until industrialist Howard Hughes—a different kind of outcast—bought them up in the late 1960s. The job market has consistently attracted minorities. But Nevada's median income is 4 percent below the national average, and the state is not highly educated: Less than a quarter of residents had a college degree in 2018, ranking Nevada fifth to last among the states. As for K-12 schools, the Annie E. Casey Foundation's 2020 Kids Count report ranked Nevada 46th in the nation.

Gaming (the state's preferred term for gambling) has generated enormous growth: The 91,000 people in the state who decided to legalize gambling has grown into a population of 3.1 million today. Las Vegas was a dot on the map when gambling became legal, a one-traffic-light crossroads with 8,532 people in all of Clark County. Now, Clark County has almost 2.4 million. Las Vegas' 23,000 hotel rooms in 1973 mushroomed into roughly 150,000 today. Henderson, a Las Vegas suburb, is now the state's third-largest city with 320,000 residents, having grown by about one-quarter during the decade. Reno, known as "the biggest little city in the world," now has about 475,000 people in its metro area. Nevada was America's fastest-growing state in the 1960s, 1970s, 1980s, 1990s and 2000s, and has been ranked fourth between 2010 and 2020. For a long historical moment, gaming was a good economic bet. But in 2007, those revenues declined even before the national economy fell into recession. Nevada suddenly went bust, with the decline in gaming revenues cascading into a housing and construction crash. Nevada recorded the nation's steepest fall in homeownership rates between 2004 and 2012, and foreclosure rates peaked at nearly 10 percent of households.

As the nation began to recover, so did Nevada. Housing prices rebounded, as migrants from other states flocked to a place with a much lower cost of living. Clark County's population grew 16 percent between 2010 and 2019, operating with a revised business model. With some form of gambling available in all of the lower 48 states and with neighboring California dotted with Indian casinos, Las Vegas promoted itself as a family destination, not just a gambling den. While gaming accounted for 57 percent of Nevada casino revenues in 1996, it fell to 43 percent by 2019, and on the Strip specifically, the share declined to 35 percent. The Strip became a luxury shopping center with world-class restaurants. The expansion of sports betting, which was legalized outside Nevada by the Supreme Court in 2018, poses a threat, as does overseas competition; Macau's gaming revenues exceed those in Las Vegas. Las Vegas became a major player in the convention business, and its first major-league sports team, the National Hockey League's Golden Knights, began playing in 2017. The city's second pro sports team, the National Football League's Raiders, began playing in 2020, four years after the legislature approved a financing plan for the $1.9 billion Allegiant Stadium.

The coronavirus pandemic, however, hobbled Nevada's economy to a greater extent than almost any other state. (The pandemic also shuttered its brothels.) Prior to the pandemic, the state's tourism and hospitality sector had an estimated economic impact of $67.6 billion, but that was decimated by the virus and accompanying lockdowns. Statewide unemployment peaked at 30 percent in April 2020 (the highest monthly rate for any state since records have been kept) and fell to a still-high 9.2 percent by November; in Las Vegas, unemployment peaked at 34 percent and fell to 11.5 percent, almost as high as it was during the worst of the Great Recession. Even after partial reopenings, the number of visitors in the fall had shrunk by at least half compared to a year earlier. "If you were to imagine a horror movie when all the people disappear, that's what it looks like," food bank official Larry Scott told The New York Times. (The powerful Culinary Workers Union helped members keep their health insurance and cope with the state's overburdened unemployment system.) Complicating the pandemic response was the state's health care system, which placed third from the bottom in the Commonwealth Fund's 2020 state rankings. By January 2021, Nevada ranked around the national median for per capita coronavirus cases but in the top one-fifth for coronavirus deaths.

Even prior to the pandemic, the state had sought to diversify its economic base. Las Vegas is now a hub for such businesses as Amazon, shoe retailer Zappos, and data firm Switch Inc., as well as a developing medical sector that's piggybacking on the University of Nevada's medical school. In Henderson, Google is building a $600 million data center and Haas Automation, which makes computerized machining tools, is planning a 2.34 million square-foot factory. Meanwhile, solar energy firms, including Tesla, Sunrun and Vivint Solar, have flocked to the state. In 2020, the Trump administration approved the nation's largest solar project, north of Las Vegas. (Conservationists have expressed concern about its impact on habitat for the Mojave desert tortoise.) Reno, for its part, has sunk in the gaming rankings without Las Vegas' luxury attractions, but the surrounding county, Washoe, has ridden its low cost of living and its pleasant combination of sun and ski slopes to a population increase of almost 12 percent since 2010. Economic diversification is also proceeding in Washoe County, with a big push from the state: Apple received $89 million in tax breaks to build a data center, while electric automaker Tesla and Panasonic accepted $1.3 billion in state incentives to build the biggest battery factory in the world. The factory expanded to produce parts for Tesla's Model 3 sports car. The resulting influx of workers has begun pushing up housing prices.

For all its distinctiveness, Nevada has been similar to the nation politically. A silver-producing state, it voted three times for the free-silver populism of William Jennings Bryan, but since his final candidacy in 1908, Nevada has voted only twice for the loser of a presidential election—Gerald Ford in 1976 and Hillary Clinton in 2016. For years, Nevada sent politically shrewd Democrats to Washington and kept them there to protect the interests of a state heavily dependent on the federal government. The most enduring was Harry Reid. In 1982, he won election to the House and in 1986 ran for the Senate and won; he became majority leader in 2007. Keeping him in this position was of immense importance to the gaming industry and the Culinary Workers Union, which is majority Latino and has a crackerjack political organization. When the federal government planned to build a national nuclear waste repository at Yucca Mountain, 90 miles from Las Vegas, Reid fought it mightily— and successfully. (Trump toyed with resurrecting the facility before backing off.) Even in retirement, Reid remains a godfather of Nevada politics—and an influential national Democrat. Meanwhile, Las Vegas-based casino magnate Sheldon Adelson, who died in 2021, was a Republican mega-donor and owner of the Las Vegas Review-Journal.

Between 2000 and 2018, Nevada elected one Democratic and one Republican senator and produced divided House delegations. In 2014, the GOP flipped control of the state legislature and won every statewide office, but two years later the Democrats won back both chambers, as Hillary Clinton, bolstered by nonwhite voters, was taking the state's electoral votes. In 2018, Democrats consolidated their gains, with Democrats Jacky Rosen and Steve Sisolak winning a Senate seat and the governorship, respectively; the party also defended two open House seats and flipped the offices of lieutenant governor, attorney general, treasurer and controller. The GOP was able to hold only the secretary of state's office, eking out a 6,000-vote victory. In the legislature, Democrats extended their control and became the first state to have a female-majority legislature. By 2021, 60 percent of legislators were women.

In 2020, both Biden and Trump courted Nevada voters, but in the end, the Democrats' winning margin remained almost identical to what it was four years earlier. Biden won by 33,596 votes, up only modestly from Clinton's 27,202-vote margin, and Biden's 2.5-point victory was about half as wide as his margin nationally. The race was close enough that Nevada was one of the states where Trump sought to overturn the results. In electorally dominant Clark County, both Clinton and Biden won by 10 points, but in Washoe, Biden increased the winning Democratic margin from one point to five points, consolidating the votes taken in 2016 by third parties and "none of these candidates" (an eccentric option exclusive to Nevada voters). The close presidential margins in 2020, the state's diverse and fluctuating population, and its importance as an early state in the primary and caucus calendar suggest that Nevada will continue to play an outsized role in national politics.

Population		Race and Ethnicity		Income	
Total	3,080,156	White	64.60%	Median Income	63,276
Land area (sq. miles)	109,781	Black	9.60%	State Income Rank	24 out of 50
Pop/ sq mi	28.06	Latino	29.20%	Poverty Rate	12.50%
Born in state	27.20%	Asian	10.50%	With health insurance	88.60%
		Two or more races	4.70%	Cash public assistance	2.60%
Age Groups		Other	12.60%	Food stamp/SNAP	12.3%
Under 18	22.40%				
18-34	22.80%	Education		Work	
35-64	38.60%	H.S grad or less	40.90%	White Collar	30.40%
Over 64	16.20%	Some college	33.40%	Sales and Service	47.30%
		College Degree, 4 yr	16.70%	Blue Collar	22.30%
Military		Post grad	9.00%	Government	11.40%
Veteran/ Active Duty	9.30%				

Presidential Politics

2020 Caucus (D)	Sanders (D)	41,075(40%)	Biden (D)	19,179(19%)	Buttigieg (D)	17,598(17%)
	Warren (D)	11,703(12%)	Klobuchar (D)	7,376 (7%)		
2016 Caucus (D)	Clinton (D)	6,440(53%)	Sanders (D)	5,785(47%)		
2016 Caucus (R)	Trump (R)	34,531(46%)	Rubio (R)	17,940(24%)	Cruz (R)	16,079(21%)
2020 Pres. Vote	Biden (D)	703,486(50%)	Trump (R)	669,890(48%)		
2016 Pres. Vote	Clinton (D)	539,260(48%)	Trump (R)	512,058(46%)	Carson (R)	(5%)
	Johnson (L)	37,384 (3%)				

Nevada has been a battleground in every presidential election since Bill Clinton narrowly carried it in 1992. In 2020, Joe Biden defeated President Donald Trump 50.1%-47.8%, a 2.3-percent margin that was slightly closer than Hillary Clinton's 47.9%-45.5% victory in 2016. That's the fourth presidential election in a row where Democrats' margin has narrowed—though they've carried the state every time.

Democrats win Nevada when they run up the margin in Clark County, home to Las Vegas and its suburbs and about two-thirds of the state's total vote, while winning Washoe County (Reno). Republicans win when they carry Washoe, hold down the margins in Las Vegas' suburbs, and get strong turnout from the state's 15 rural counties, known as the "cow counties." The growing number of Hispanic voters in Nevada—many of whom live in Clark—is another asset for Democratic presidential candidates, though Trump did better with Hispanic voters in 2020 than 2016.

Both campaigns spent heavily to contest the state in 2020, and overall turnout jumped by almost 300,000 votes from 2016, a nearly 25 percent increase. Biden narrowly led Trump in Nevada on election night, but as more mail ballots were tallied his lead grew to more than 34,000. Trump and his lawyers howled about voter fraud, but multiple courts ruled against them as they failed to produce any persuasive evidence. Biden won Washoe County by a wider margin than Clinton, making up for Trump's slightly stronger performance in Clark. Las Vegas Review-Journal owner Sheldon Adelson and his wife, Miriam, were the largest donors to Trump and the GOP in 2020, spending almost $220 million in the last election cycle. Adelson died in early 2021 at age 87.

Since Nevada became an early-caucus state in 2008 after intense lobbying by then-Senate Majority Leader Harry Reid, it has played a key role in both parties' nominating processes. Clinton won the 2008 caucuses, helping her bounce back and leading to a long, drawn-out contest with Barack Obama. Trump scored a huge victory in the 2016 GOP caucuses, defeating Florida Sen. Marco Rubio, 46%-24%. On the Democratic side, Clinton held off Vermont Sen. Bernie Sanders, 53%-47%.

Sanders invested heavily in the state in 2020. "Tío Bernie" campaigned hard in the state's Hispanic community, and his team had by far the largest and best-organized field operation. The powerful Culinary Union, which had attacked Sanders' universal health care plan, ended up staying on the sidelines as it became clear he'd likely win the state. Sanders scored a 34%-18% win over Biden, with Pete Buttigieg at 15% and Elizabeth Warren at 13%. Sanders' win made him the early frontrunner for the nomination and helped convince many in the Democratic establishment to rally hard around Biden as the only viable alternative, setting up his comeback after a South Carolina victory a week later. But Biden's primary weakness in the state hinted at his coming general election problems with some Hispanic voters.

Nevada's 2020 caucuses went smoother than Iowa's, but only because Iowa melted down first— the Nevada Democratic Party had to scrap the app it was planning to use and scramble to put together an alternate. Reid and some other Democrats called afterwards for Democrats to scrap all caucuses and pushed for Nevada to become the first-voting primary state, a move that could set off a primary calendar scramble ahead of 2024.

Congressional Districts

117th Congress Lineup	3D 1R	116th Congress Lineup	3D 1R

Nevada's population gain in the past decade, while in the double digits, will not lead the nation —as it did in the 1990s and 2000s. The boom, in which the state rocketed from one district in 1980 to four in 2012, may finally be subsiding. But redistricting tensions have not disappeared.

In the 2011 redistricting, partisan control was split and tensions ran high. Democrats in charge of the legislature passed maps creating one safely Republican seat in northern Nevada and three Democratic-leaning seats in Clark County. Republican Gov. Brian Sandoval vetoed the maps on the grounds that Latinos deserved a majority Latino seat based in the northeast quadrant of metro Las Vegas. Democrats decried Sandoval's position as a veiled attempt to pack Democratic voters and create three Republican-leaning seats in the process. The debate fractured Latino advocacy groups, and the legislature adjourned in a stalemate. Carson City District Judge James Todd Russell appointed three independent special masters to draw a map. The trio submitted a diplomatic plan that created a safely Democratic, 43 percent Latino 1st District and preserved a Republican-leaning 2nd District in the north. They created a slightly more Republican 3rd District including Henderson to the south, and a new Democratic-leaning 4th District linking substantially Latino North Las Vegas with several rural counties to the north. The result in 2012 was an even 2-2 split.

Since then, multiple developments have shaped the contours for the next round of redistricting. In 2016, Democrats gained two seats to take 3-1 control of the delegation, which they have retained. They also regained control of the legislature. In 2018, they secured their redistricting lock when they won the election for governor. Still, as they seek to reinforce their swing seats, Democrats will face renewed pressure from Latinos eager to win a House seat in a state that has grown to 29 percent Hispanic. With the 1st District in need of additional residents, that could increase the pressure to add Latinos. Latinos might find it difficult to force Democratic Rep. Dina Titus to exit before she is ready. On the other hand, each of the three Democrats holding Las Vegas-area districts has suffered at least one defeat earlier in their career. So, as is the way in Nevada, the incumbents might be forced to take the cards they have been dealt.

Steve Sisolak (D)

Elected 2018, term expires 2023, 1st term; b. Dec. 26, 1953, Milwaukee, WI; University of Wisconsin, Milwaukee, B.S., 1974; University of Nevada, Las Vegas, M.B.A, 1978; Married (Kathy Ong); 2 children (2 from previous marriage)

Elected Office: Member, NV Board of Regents, 1999-2008; Member, Clark County Commission, 2009-2019, Vice chair, 2011-2013, Chair, 2013-2019.

Office: 101 N. Carson St. Carson City, 89701; 775-684-5670; Fax: 775-684-5683; Website: nv.gov
Lt. Gov.: Kate Marshall (D) **Atty. Gen:** Aaron Ford (D) **Sec. of State:** Barbara Cegavske (R)
State Legislature: Senate: 13D, 8R **House:** 28D, 13R, 1V

Election Results

Election	Name (Party)	Vote (%)
2018 General	Steve Sisolak (D)	480,007 (49%)
	Adam Laxalt (R)	440,320 (45%)
2018 Primary	Steve Sisolak (D)	72,749 (52%)
	Chris Giunchigliani (D)	56,511 (40%)

Steve Sisolak—a longtime commissioner in Clark County, which includes Las Vegas—became the first Democrat to win the Nevada governorship in two decades in 2018. Entering office with expanded Democratic majorities in the legislature, Sisolak proceeded to enact a broadly progressive agenda.

Sisolak grew up in Wauwatosa Wisconsin, near Milwaukee. His father worked as a General Motors design engineer; his mother worked in a convenience store. When Sisolak was 10, his father found himself laid off for three years. Sisolak worked his way through college at the University of Wisconsin-Milwaukee. He came to Las Vegas in 1976 to pursue an MBA at the University of Nevada-Las Vegas. After earning his degree, Sisolak built a direct-marketing business and raised two daughters as a single father. In 1979, during a snowstorm, the power went out as Sisolak's appendix was being operated on, and he nearly died. That brought him back to Catholicism; he's said that he attends mass daily.

From 1999 to 2008, Sisolak served on the Nevada Board of Regents, then served on the Clark County Commission from 2009 to 2019, the final six years as chair. On the commission, "he comes across like a gadfly in politician's clothes, demanding accountability for every dollar spent and questioning policies he thinks make no sense," the Las Vegas Review-Journal wrote in 2010. At times he was accused of being too close to unions, but he also "alienated the firefighters' union so much that he received email telling him not to expect red trucks if his house goes up in flames," the newspaper reported. Critics accused him of playing close to the ethical edge. In 2005, he won a $16 million settlement in an eminent domain case, in which he argued that county height limits near McCarran International Airport hurt the value of land he owned nearby. Then, after he was on the county commission, it awarded a six-figure contract to the attorney who had won him the settlement. But Sisolak championed the Vegas Golden Knights expansion NHL team and a stadium deal that enabled the Oakland Raiders to move to Las Vegas.

Sisolak considered running for governor in 2014 against popular Republican incumbent Brian Sandoval but decided against it. Sandoval had been elected Nevada's first Latino governor in 2010 and was reelected with token opposition in 2014. Handsome and telegenic, Sandoval was initially heralded as a trailblazer in Republican circles, but his un-Republican stances on abortion, immigration and tort reform, exacerbated by his support for a tax hike to boost spending on education in 2015, led Sandoval to become increasingly isolated within the GOP. Notably, Sandoval broke with Republican Attorney General Adam Laxalt on several occasions, including Laxalt's desire to join a multistate lawsuit against President Barack Obama's executive actions on immigration.

Laxalt easily won the 2018 gubernatorial primary over state Treasurer Dan Schwartz. On the Democratic side, both main contenders were Clark County commissioners, Sisolak and Chris Giunchigliani. Bolstered by a late robocall from Hillary Clinton, Giunchigliani ran to Sisolak's left. Sisolak countered that his current-day views fit comfortably within the Democratic mainstream. As a top county official, Sisolak played a high-profile role in the 2017 mass shooting in Las Vegas that left 58 dead; he later called bump stocks, which enabled that massacre, "killing machines" that should be banned immediately. While Giunchigliani won the backing of the Nevada State Education Association and the Sierra Club, Sisolak had the crucial support of former Senate Majority Leader Harry Reid, who, even in retirement, controlled a legendary Democratic political machine. Sisolak won the primary, 52%-40%.

Sisolak's general election opponent had a golden name in the state: Paul Laxalt, the candidate's grandfather, had served as a Republican governor and senator from Nevada. To win his 2014 race for attorney general, Laxalt pulled off the unprecedented achievement of losing the state's two big urban counties (Washoe, which includes Reno, and Clark) yet winning the more rural counties by large enough margins to cancel out the urban losses. However, Laxalt's lack of experience, a thin history of living in the state (he grew up in Washington D.C.), and a contentious four years as attorney general hampered his candidacy. Embarrassingly for the candidate, a dozen Laxalt family members penned a Reno Gazette-Journal op-ed opposing their relative, saying they wanted to "protect" the family name "from being leveraged and exploited." They highlighted Laxalt's policies on illegal immigration, which they said disrespected the family's history in the United States, although that began with a legal Basque immigrant in 1900. Laxalt's aunt even appeared in a Sisolak campaign ad.

Sandoval pointedly did not endorse his fellow Republican, and while the outgoing governor never officially endorsed Sisolak, the Democrat aligned himself with some of Sandoval's most popular policies, especially his efforts to boost spending on schools. The pro-Democratic political environment of 2018 gave Sisolak some wind at his back, and President Donald Trump's endorsement of Laxalt probably did not help him with persuadable voters. Sisolak won, 49%-45%, sweeping into office with a bigger Democratic majority in the legislature and Democratic takeovers of the offices of lieutenant governor, attorney general, treasurer and controller.

In his first year in office, Sisolak signed a flurry of bills that pleased progressives. He approved bills that mandated background checks on private gun sales and transfers, authorized temporary "red flag" gun confiscation, sped up the process for ex-felons to resume voting, made it easier to seal old marijuana convictions, approved a doubling of Nevada's renewable fuels standard to 50 percent by 2030, removed a decades-old (and unenforceable) criminal penalty for abortion, instituted collective bargaining for state employees, required paid sick leave for employers with at least 50 workers, tightened laws against workplace discrimination, phased out private prisons, and outlawed the "gay panic" defense in criminal trials. Sisolak also signed a phased-in minimum wage hike to $12. One disappointment for liberals was Sisolak's veto of a measure that would have had Nevada join an interstate compact to allocate its presidential electoral votes to the popular-vote winner; the governor said that joining the compact would "diminish the role of smaller states like Nevada in national electoral contests." Still, the left-wing New Republic applauded the tide of legislation, headlining an article, "The State That Liberal Dreams Are Made Of."

In 2020, Sisolak inflamed critics during the coronavirus pandemic by issuing a statewide mask mandate and restrictions on attendance at religious services; the latter policy was upheld narrowly at the U.S. Supreme Court. (In November, Sisolak himself tested positive for the virus.) Even more challenging was the pandemic's massive economic impact, which wrecked the state's pivotal travel and hospitality industry. Sisolak also took heat for problems with the state's unemployment system; he blamed previous gubernatorial administrations for letting the system's shortcomings fester. Still, Sisolak entered 2021 in reasonably good shape; three efforts to recall him in 2020 failed to make it to the ballot. He said he planned to run for a second term in 2022, a race for which he was expected to start as the favorite.

Catherine Cortez Masto (D)

Elected 2016, term expires 2022, 1st term, b. Mar 29, 1964; Las Vegas, NV; University of Nevada, Reno, B.S., 1986; Gonzaga University School of Law, J.D., 1990; Catholic; Married (Paul Masto).

Elected Office: NV Attorney General, 2007-2015.

Professional Career: Southern District Director, Governor Bob Miller, 1995-1998; Federal Criminal Prosecutor, United States Attorney's Office, 1999-2001; Assistant, United States Attorney, 2000-2002; Chief of Staff, Governor Bob Miller, 1998-2002; Executive Vice Chancellor, NV System of Higher Education, 2003; Assistant County Manager, Clark County, 2002-2007.

DC Office: 516 HSOB 20510, 202-224-3542

State Offices: Las Vegas, 702-388-5020; Reno, 775-686-5750.

Committees: Senate Democratic Outreach Vice Chair. *Banking, Housing & Urban Affairs*: Financial Institutions & Consumer Protection; Housing, Transportation & Community Development; Securities, Insurance & Investment. *Energy & Natural Resources*: Energy; Public Lands, Forests & Mining (Chmn); Water & Power. *Finance*: Health Care; International Trade, Customs & Global Competitiveness; Taxation & IRS Oversight. *Indian Affairs*.

Group Ratings

	ADA	ACLU	AFL-CIO	LCV	COC	HAFA	ACU	CFG	FRC
2020	-	77%	-	92%	-	0%	4%	-	-
2019	95%	C	100%	100%	64%	C	3%	0%	0%

Almanac Ratings 2019-2020

	Economy	Social	Foreign	Composite
Liberal	90%	90%	60%	80%
Conservative	10%	10%	40%	20%

Key Votes of the 116th Congress

1. EPA clean energy rules	Y	5. Russia sanctions	Y	9. Barr as Atty. General	N
2. U.S./Mex./Can. trade deal	Y	6. Troops in SYR, AFG	Y	10. Spending at the border	Y
3. Cut unemployment benefits	N	7. Veto arms sales to Saudis	Y	11. Coney Barrett to Sup. Ct.	N
4. Shelton to Fed Reserve	N	8. Defense $$$, veto override	Y	12. Electoral College objections	N

Election Results

Election	Name (Party)	Vote (%)	Cand. Spent	Ind. Exp. Support	Ind. Exp. Oppose
2016 General	Catherine Cortez Masto (D) 521,994	(47%)	$17,148,576	$6,552,180	$42,462,146
	Joe Heck (R) 495,079	(45%)	$11,707,759	$12,978,487	$38,915,182
2016 Primary	Catherine Cortez Masto (D) 81,971	(81%)			
	Allen Rheinhart (D) 5,650	(6%)			

Prior winning percentages: 2016 (47%)

Democrat Catherine Cortez Masto is the first Hispanic-American woman to serve in the Senate and the state's first female senator, succeeding powerful Nevada politician and former Senate Democratic Leader Harry Reid in 2016. Four years later, she led her party back to a narrow majority as chair of the Democratic Senatorial Campaign Committee. In 2022, she could be the one with a target on her back. Republicans were hoping to unseat her in the battleground state that's been trending blue, but they needed a viable nominee and the GOP doesn't have a deep bench.

Cortez Masto is a lifelong Nevadan whose paternal grandfather immigrated to the state from Mexico; the other side of her family is Italian. Her father, Manny Cortez, an attorney and ally of Reid, was a major player in Nevada politics for three decades—as a member of the Clark County Commission and later as president of the powerful Las Vegas Convention and Visitors Authority. Cortez oversaw a major expansion of the city's airport and the inception of the iconic "what happens here, stays here" marketing campaign: Both moves were credited with reviving the popularity of the nation's longtime gambling mecca.

Cortez Masto earned a degree from the University of Nevada, Reno before getting her law degree from Gonzaga University. After practicing law in Las Vegas, she served as Democratic Gov. Bob Miller's chief of staff. She spent a couple of years in Washington D.C., as a prosecutor in the U.S. attorney's office before returning to Nevada as an assistant Clark County manager on issues relating to juvenile detention alternatives and child services. In 2006, she was elected state attorney general, going after methamphetamine labs and prosecuting sex trafficking and domestic abuse cases. During her second term, Cortez Masto befriended the attorney general in California, Kamala Harris, who would also be elected to the Senate in 2016 and then as vice president in 2020. The women went after several large banks for their foreclosure and lending practices after the 2008 financial crisis. The settlement of a suit against the Bank of America yielded nearly $2 billion for Nevada homeowners —a point widely advertised during Cortez Masto's Senate bid.

Cortez Masto faced controversy in 2008 when she charged Republican Lt. Gov. Brian Krolicki with mismanaging a state-run college savings program in his previous role as state treasurer. At the time, Krolicki was considering a 2010 run against Reid. Krolicki and his defenders decried the felony prosecution as political—and suggested Reid was behind it. Reid denied any involvement. Just days before Krolicki was scheduled to stand trial, the Las Vegas Review-Journal reported that Cortez Masto's husband, retired Secret Service agent Paul Masto, was hosting a fundraiser for a Democrat seeking Krolicki's lieutenant gubernatorial post; Cortez Masto said she had been unaware of the event until contacted by the newspaper. Shortly after that, the indictment against Krolicki was dismissed. Cortez Masto was easily reelected the next year but she had acquired some dents.

Term-limited as attorney general, Cortez Masto declined to take on popular Republican Gov. Brian Sandoval. She was named second in command of the Nevada System of Higher Education —a post she resigned in March 2015 after just three months when Reid opted not to seek a sixth Senate term after injuring himself while exercising. He threw his support behind Cortez Masto within hours of announcing his decision, telling Nevada Public Radio: "She has a background that really is significantly powerful. I hope she runs, and if she does I will help her." Reid had an interest in seeing his seat filled by the Senate's first Latina: It would cement his decades long effort to bring Hispanics and immigrants into the Nevada Democratic Party. Cortez Masto announced a week and a half later, and Reid told the Review-Journal, "We got our wish." His strong support helped Cortez Masto clear the primary field.

Sandoval, also Hispanic-American, was the strongest potential Republican candidate, but he declined to leave the governorship in the middle of his second term. Cortez Masto faced three-term GOP Rep. Joe Heck, an Iraq War veteran from a highly competitive district encompassing much of suburban Las Vegas. Cortez Masto's ads highlighted her family's immigrant roots and featured endorsements from President Barack Obama, who had twice carried the state. Heck touted his experience as a military physician and ran as a law-and-order candidate, attacking Cortez Masto for the state's rising violent crime rate. Cortez Masto outspent him $18.6 million to $11.7 million. That was dwarfed by $90 million in independent expenditures that poured into state. About $50 million of that was intended to benefit Heck in a race that national Republicans saw as their best chance to pick up a Senate seat in 2016.

Republican presidential candidate Donald Trump's harsh rhetoric about immigration proved to be a major headache for Heck in a rapidly diversifying state. Heck held a narrow lead in the polls for much of the election cycle and tried to keep Trump at arm's length; he endorsed Trump only after the latter had secured the presidential nomination. After the "Access Hollywood" video of Trump bragging about sexually assaulting women surfaced in the fall of 2016, Heck retracted his endorsement. "I cannot in good conscience continue to support Donald Trump," Heck told a rally; some Republicans in the crowd booed him. But as Trump recovered politically in the campaign's closing weeks, Heck backed off, calling Trump "qualified" to be president and refusing to say how he would vote. Meanwhile, Cortez Masto ran ads tying Heck to Trump and showing his earlier endorsement of the GOP presidential candidate.

Trump lost Nevada—and likely pulled Heck down with him. Hillary Clinton carried the state 47.9%-45.5%, while Cortez Masto edged Heck 47.1%-44.7%. Heck carried every county in the state but one: Cortez Masto's base of Clark County, where more than 70 percent of the state's residents live. Cortez Masto won Clark by 82,000 votes—three times the statewide margin of 27,000.

Consistent with her status as a vocal critic of Trump's immigration moves, Cortez Masto introduced as her first bill a measure to undo a Trump executive order that both made almost all undocumented immigrants priorities for deportation and sought to block funding for "sanctuary cities" that didn't fully cooperate with immigration authorities. "When he's talking about 'bad hombres,' he's talking about my family," Cortez Masto told MSNBC during a fight between Trump and Mexico's president shortly after she took office. "Really, the only bad hombre in this scenario is the one who's sitting in the White House." In late 2018, when Trump vowed to end birthright citizenship via executive order, Cortez Masto said, "Our president continues to promote hate in America, undermine our country's values and attack our Constitution." Birthright citizenship is enshrined in the Constitution.

Falling more in the middle of her caucus, Cortez Masto has carefully dealt with several initiatives from its progressive wing. In mid-2018, amid controversy over Trump's later-reversed policy of separating migrant families at the southern border, Cortez Masto said the United States needs to "be doing everything it can" to reunify families—including repatriating more than 460 adults deported without their children. But she sidestepped questions about calls from the party's left to abolish Immigration and Customs Enforcement. While accusing the Trump administration of empowering "rogue agents" and creating an "inhumane deportation force," Cortez Masto was quoted by the Nevada Independent as saying: "Do I think we should abolish Homeland Security Investigations as part of ICE? Absolutely not. They're going after international criminals, they're going after human trafficking and child pornography." She has pushed for hiring more immigration judges and offering more legal aid and attorneys to immigrants to speed up the processing—and shorted the detention—of families and unaccompanied minors at the border.

Cortez Masto confronted another hot-button issue in October 2017 after a gunman killed 60 and wounded more than 800 during a concert along the Las Vegas Strip—the worst mass shooting in modern U.S. history. She signed on to a bill, authored by California Democrat Dianne Feinstein, to ban "bump stocks," which modify semi-automatic weapons to fire as quickly as automatic weapons. While Trump promised to ban bump stocks via executive order—which he did at the end of 2018— Cortez Masto earlier that year joined Arizona Republican Jeff Flake, a now-retired Trump critic, to argue that legislation was needed to as a permanent solution.

Cortez Masto aggressively carried on Reid's efforts to block a nuclear waste repository at Yucca Mountain, 90 miles northwest of Las Vegas. Congress voted in 1987 to designate that location for a repository, but Reid bottled up funding until the Obama administration halted the site licensing process in 2010. After taking office, Trump proposed funding to restart that process. The House voted for a bill to do so in mid-2018, but Cortez Masto and Republican Sen. Dean Heller of Nevada blocked action in the Senate. During the 2018 elections, with Heller battling to save his seat, Trump told a Reno-based TV station that he would be "very inclined" to oppose the project if it did not have local support. Trump's proposed 2021 budget did not include funding for the project. In March 2021, Cortez Masto and the rest of Nevada's Democratic congressional delegation re-introduced legislation to block the federal government from moving nuclear waste to a state without approval from the governor and local officials. President Joe Biden has opposed the Yucca site. Cortez Masto also proposed an amendment to the annual defense policy bill to require that the president get approval from Congress for any nuclear test. In 2019, she successfully negotiated a deal with the Department of Energy to remove half a metric ton of weapons-grade plutonium from the Nevada Nuclear Site by 2021 and got the department to agree not to send any more plutonium to Nevada. At the urging of environmental groups, hunters and tribes, Cortez Masto has introduced legislation to bar oil and gas exploration in the Ruby Mountains near Elko.

Cortez Masto was chosen by Democratic Leader Chuck Schumer to lead the DSCC for the 2020 cycle after she raised $10 million for Democratic candidates and organizations in eight states during 2018. Cortez Masto had a much friendlier map than in the previous cycle, with 23 GOP-held seats up for reelection—the 2014 class that had won back the Senate for the GOP—compared to just 12 for Democrats. That meant Democrats needed to flip four seats outright or three if Biden won the presidency, and they started out with obvious targets in Colorado Sen. Cory Gardner and Maine Sen. Susan Collins—the only two GOP incumbents in states Trump lost in 2016—and senators from other swing states like Arizona and North Carolina. Democrats were able to put several other longer-shot races in play with strong recruits, such as Montana, Kansas and South Carolina. The committee endorsed many more moderate candidates in key races early on to try to boost their strongest nominee; that tactic drew ire from progressive groups.

While nonpartisan handicappers and polls estimated Democrats could pick up as many as seven seats, on election night they fell well short of that mark. As expected, Democrats lost a seat in Alabama they had won in a one-of-a-kind 2017 special election. The only contests that flipped were in Arizona and Colorado, as highly touted recruits fell short elsewhere—most notably in Maine, where Biden had won by 9 percentage points but Collins hung on by the same margin, and North Carolina, where Cal Cunningham, one of the committee's earliest endorsements, was embroiled in a sex scandal. Still, dual Georgia contests that required a January 2021 runoff left Democrats with a shot of getting control of a 50-50 Senate with incoming Vice President Harris' tie-breaking vote. Sen. David Perdue had edged out Democrat Jon Ossoff in the regular election but fell short of the 50 percent threshold needed to win outright, while appointed Sen. Kelly Loeffler faced the Rev. Raphael Warnock in a special election for the remaining two years of former Sen. Johnny Isakson's term. Republicans were initially optimistic, given that GOP candidates had the most total votes in the first round. But when Trump began baselessly claiming that widespread fraud had cost him the state's 16 electoral votes, Republican Gov. Brian Kemp and Georgia Secretary of State Brad Raffensperger refused to acquiesce. Both Loeffler and Perdue, however, leaned into the criticism and called for Raffensperger to resign. Trump allies, suggesting the election had not been secure, ended up depleting turnout in GOP-base areas while heavily Black areas saw record turnout. In the end, Ossoff and Warnock both won. By just 128,081 votes, Democrats captured the Senate by the narrowest of margins. What looked like a failure by Cortez Masto and the DSCC in November 2020 had been redeemed.

Cortez Masto was only the second woman to hold the DSCC's top post—often a stepping stone to leadership—and after helping win the Democratic Caucus the majority, she became its vice chair of outreach and also was named chair of the Energy and Natural Resources subcommittee on public lands, forests and mining. Though Cortez Masto had withdrawn from consideration to be Biden's running mate in 2020, her ambitions are likely to continue to draw speculation. After her first year in the Senate, Cortez Masto was asked by the Las Vegas Sun whether she could fill Reid's shoes. "When I was on the campaign trail, people would ask me that all the time," she replied, "and I would say, 'Yeah, not only am I going to fill those shoes, I'm going to do it in heels.'" First, Cortez Masto must win another term in 2022. Republicans were buoyed by the closer-than-expected 2-point presidential margin in the state in 2020. If the GOP persuaded a top-tier candidate like Sandoval to reenter the political fray, it could become a top contest.

Jacky Rosen (D)

Elected 2018, term expires 2024, 1st term, b. Aug 02, 1957; Chicago, IL; University of Minnesota, B.A., 1979; Jewish; Married (Larry Rosen); 1 child.

Elected Office: US House, 2017-2019

Professional Career: Former Computer Programmer/ Designer/ Software Developer, Southwest Gas Company, 1990-1993, Summa Corporation, Citibank.

DC Office: 144 RSOB 20510, 202-224-6244, rosen.senate.gov

State Offices: Las Vegas, 702-388-0205; Reno, 775-337-0110.

Committees: *Aging. Armed Services*: Airland; Cybersecurity; Strategic Forces. *Commerce, Science & Transportation*: Aviation Safety, Operations & Innovations; Communications, Media & Broadband; Tourism, Trade & Export Promotion (Chmn). *Health, Education, Labor & Pensions*: Employment & Workplace Safety; Primary Health & Retirement Security. *Homeland Security & Government Affairs*: Emerging Threats & Spending Oversight. *Small Business & Entrepreneurship*.

Group Ratings (House)

	ADA	ACLU	AFL-CIO	LCV	COC	HAFA	ACU	CFG	FRC
2020	-	75%	-	92%	-	0%	5%	-	-
2019	95%	C	100%	100%	66%	C	4%	0%	0%

Almanac Ratings 2019-2020

	Economy	Social	Foreign	Composite
Liberal	71%	84%	56%	70%
Conservative	29%	16%	44%	30%

Key Votes of the 116th Congress (House)

1. EPA clean energy rules	Y	5. Russia sanctions	Y
2. U.S./Mex./Can. trade deal	Y	6. Troops in SYR, AFG	Y
3. Cut unemployment benefits	N	7. Veto arms sales to Saudis	Y
4. Shelton to Fed Reserve	N	8. Defense $$$, veto override	Y

9. Barr as Atty. General   N
10. Spending at the border   Y
11. Coney Barrett to Sup. Ct.   N
12. Electoral College objections N

Election Results

Election	Name (Party)	Vote (%)		Cand. Spent	Ind. Exp. Support	Ind. Exp. Oppose
2018 General	Jacky Rosen (D)	490,071	(50%)	$26,196,746	$5,613,546	$20,883,471
	Dean Heller (R)	441,202	(45%)	$13,764,061	$4,149,738	$36,310,801
2018 Primary	Jacky Rosen (D)	110,567	(83%)			

Prior winning percentages: 2018 (50%), House: 2016 (47%)

Few sent to Congress can match the rapid—and unlikely—ascent of Democrat Jacky Rosen, Nevada's junior senator. Three years before her election to the Senate, Rosen was president of a synagogue in suburban Las Vegas—and unknown to most Nevadans. A mere eight months after narrowly winning a seat in the House in 2016, she launched a Senate bid in a state that while trending blue remains among the nation's most politically competitive. Rosen ousted Republican Dean Heller, who had never lost an election in three decades in public office.

Rosen launched her political career at the end of 2015, when she was recruited to run for an open House seat by Harry Reid, then the Senate minority leader. Rosen agreed to run after more than a dozen better-known prospects reportedly turned down Reid. Jacklyn Spektor was born the daughter of a housemaker and auto-dealer whose parents were Jewish emigrants from Russia and Austria. Raised in the Chicago suburbs, she graduated from the University of Minnesota in 1979 with a degree in psychology but had an interest in computer science. Rosen's parents moved to Las Vegas while she was in college. She worked as a cocktail waitress at Caesars Palace on the Las Vegas Strip one summer and then moved to the city after graduation—when she was hired as a computer programmer at Summa Corp., the holding company for the business interests of reclusive billionaire Howard Hughes.

Rosen worked in computer programming and management positions for two other large corporations, Citibank and Southwest Gas, before starting an independent consulting business. The scope and nature of that business later would become an issue in her race against Heller. Among her clients was the radiology practice where her husband, Larry Rosen, was a partner. But for much of the quarter of a century before she entered politics, Jacky Rosen found herself in a situation that many other female baby boomers faced: preoccupied with raising a child and caring for her husband's aging parents. She got involved in Congregation Ner Tamid, a synagogue in Henderson—16 miles south of Las Vegas—the state's largest Jewish temple. Putting her computer skills to use, Rosen worked to ensure the synagogue's computers were ready for the year 2000 and became the temple's president in 2013.

When three-term Republican Rep. Joe Heck decided to run for the Senate in 2016, Reid sought to recruit a candidate who could win Heck's politically marginal district, which, since its creation 14 years earlier, had only once been captured by a Democrat. After Reid struck out with numerous potential candidates possessing extensive political and business backgrounds, Rosen was recommended to him by state Judge Elissa Cadish, a member of Ner Tamid. During her Senate bid, Rosen was asked by the Nevada Independent if she would have considered running for Congress if she had not been approached by Reid. She laughed: "That's a good question. I got approached, so here I am. I guess I never had a chance to think about that."

With Reid's support, Rosen had little trouble winning the Democratic primary. In the general election, she faced businessman Danny Tarkanian, son of legendary University of Nevada, Las Vegas basketball coach Jerry Tarkanian. It was one of the closest and most expensive House campaigns of 2016. Tarkanian, an outspoken conservative, had previously lost four elections; he won the Republican nomination with just 32 percent of the vote in a seven-way primary. Rosen and Tarkanian each raised $2 million, but Democratic groups and their allies spent more than $6 million to boost Rosen's profile—while also running extensive advertising that described Tarkanian's business practices as shady. Tarkanian largely failed to respond to the charges, but Republican groups spent more than $9 million on his behalf. Unlike other Republican candidates in Nevada, Tarkanian remained loyal to presidential nominee Donald Trump, who won the district by a single percentage point. Rosen proved successful with what the Las Vegas Sun described as her "under the radar" strategy, winning 47.2%-46.0% and by fewer than 4,000 votes.

Rosen's Almanac vote rating placed her among moderate House Democrats representing swing districts. She joined the House Problem Solvers Caucus, a group equally split between Democrats and Republicans. But she was soon off and running again: Rosen launched her Senate bid in July 2017. Democratic Rep. Lois Frankel of Florida, who helped recruit Rosen for the 2016 House run, told Politico, "The minute I found out she was a synagogue president, I knew she could do anything. There's nothing like the politics of a synagogue." Rosen won the Democratic primary with 83 percent of the vote.

Heller had been appointed to the Senate seat in 2011 after scandal-plagued Republican John Ensign resigned. Heller served three terms as Nevada secretary of state before being elected to the House in 2006. Carving out a reputation as a centrist, Heller showed a willingness to buck his party early in his Senate tenure. He was elected to a full term by a 1-point margin in 2012, a year President Barack Obama carried Nevada. Heller entered the 2018 cycle as the most vulnerable Senate Republican and the only one seeking reelection in a state that Hillary Clinton had won in 2016. Heller soon found himself squeezed between a Republican governor and a Republican president on the hot-button issue of whether to repeal the Affordable Care Act—to say nothing of trying to straddle a conservative Republican base and a rapidly diversifying and increasingly Democratic electorate.

Heller was critical of Trump throughout the 2016 campaign, later refusing to say whether he had voted for the president. Early in the Trump administration, Heller was among several GOP senators who criticized early Republican legislation to repeal Obamacare. Initially, Heller lined up Gov. Brian Sandoval, also a Republican, who had appointed him to the Senate: Sandoval was critical of the repeal efforts, blasting the effect they'd have on federal Medicaid funds coming into the state to insure low-income residents. In July 2017, Heller voted against two Republican-sponsored proposals to repeal the ACA—but split from Sandoval to back a third option that, while not touching Medicaid, was estimated to leave millions of Americans without insurance. After that measure narrowly failed, Heller co-sponsored another proposal that would have led to cuts in Medicaid, although that plan was never brought to a vote. Heller's shift was an effort to mend fences with President Trump, who had made a veiled threat to Heller at a White House event. "This was the one we were worried about," Trump said, gesturing toward Heller, while adding, "Look, he wants to remain a senator, doesn't he?"

The Heller-Trump relationship began to defrost , and, in public and private appearances, the senator increasingly praised the president and his policies. But Heller's shift on Obamacare repeal left him the object of suspicion among many Republicans, while providing no shortage of fodder for Democrats. Rosen ran ads featuring footage of Heller's awkward White House appearance with Trump; one ad featured an inflatable tube man blowing back and forth, while a narrator derided Heller as "Sen. Spineless." Trump—appearing before the Nevada Republican State Convention in mid-2018—called Rosen "Wacky Jacky." Trump said: "Now, that name didn't come from me. That's a name that people have known because people that know her, that's what they call her." In fact, it was not a name that had gained currency even among critics of the restrained, often scripted Rosen. But Trump's comments highlighted Republican efforts to define a candidate who remained largely unknown statewide.

Rosen's limited political background was a two-edged sword: It gave critics little at which to take aim but also opened her to attacks for lack of accomplishment. The Heller campaign launched ads taking issue with Rosen's claims that she had "built a business"—noting there was no evidence that she ever held a business license with the state or the city of Henderson. But state officials told the Reno Gazette-Journal that, before 2003, Rosen would not have been required to obtain a license if she didn't hire anyone; her campaign said she operated a one-woman unnamed consultancy between

1993 and 2002. Rosen suggested the attacks were sexist. "They wouldn't say the same thing to a man: No one ever asks a man if he feels qualified," she told the Nevada Independent. Heller attacked Rosen's legislative record, with one ad saying: "Zero. That's the number of bills Jacky Rosen passed in Congress before announcing she was running for the Senate." The Rosen campaign responded by pointing to eight bills she had co-sponsored that passed the House before she had launched her Senate bid.

Rosen advocated a mainstream Democratic agenda but treaded cautiously in a swing state. She criticized Trump's tax cut plan but stopped short of calling for its repeal. She supported adding a public insurance option to Obamacare but did not favor the "Medicare for All" proposal pushed by progressives. Nor did she endorse progressives' calls for abolishing the Immigration and Customs Enforcement as she pushed for immigration reform. Obama appeared at a rally on her behalf, while Trump flew into the state twice to bolster Heller. Heller praised Trump at a Las Vegas rally in September for the state of the economy. Trump responded: "We started off slow—but I've had no better friend in Congress than Dean Heller."

Heller's strategy of tying himself to Trump was risky in a state where the president's approval rating was hovering below 40 percent: Rosen repeatedly mentioned figures showing Heller voting with Trump's position 96 percent of the time. But the race remained close. Rosen had a clear money advantage. She raised and spent more than $25.5 million; Heller had just over $15 million. Of the $66 million in independent expenditures that poured into the state, $40 million was spent on Rosen's behalf. Heller's strategy rested on energizing the Republican rural base in northern Nevada, while hoping the statewide vote would follow traditional patterns—in a state where Democratic turnout has tended to ebb significantly in off years. Rosen defeated Heller 50%-45%, a difference of nearly 59,000 votes—more than twice the statewide margin by which Rosen's Senate colleague, Catherine Cortez Masto, won in 2016. While Heller carried 15 of the state's 17 counties, Rosen won the two biggest: Clark County, home to Las Vegas, and Washoe County, which contains Reno. Her win made her the first woman to move from the House to the Senate after just one term. According to Smart Politics, only 19 male House freshmen have accomplished this feat since direct election of senators was initiated in 1913.

In her first two years in the Senate, Rosen built a bipartisan reputation. "You just find those places to work together," Rosen told the Nevada Independent. "And then when you do have policy disagreements, that's OK too. That's how we move things forward." She formed a close friendship with Wyoming's John Barrasso, chairman of the Senate Republican Conference, and the two launched the Senate Comprehensive Care Caucus to draw attention to the need for palliative care; they also worked on a bill to give new military recruits a longer time frame to pick their GI Benefits. She called fellow freshman Sen. Mitt Romney of Utah a like-minded legislator who was also "looking for common ground," and the duo partnered on a bill to create congressional committees to preserve and financially strengthen Medicare and Social Security. Rosen and Oklahoma Sen. James Lankford, a conservative Christian, created the Senate Bipartisan Task Force for Combating Anti-Semitism. "As members of Congress, our responsibility to our neighbors, to our friends, to our community, and to our children is to work together in a bipartisan way to prevent anti-Semitism before it starts—to educate, to explain, and to empower," they wrote in a CNN op-ed. The "Never Again Education Act"— which she sponsored with Republicans Kevin Cramer of North Dakota, Marco Rubio of Florida and Democrat Richard Blumenthal of Connecticut—will provide $10 billion for Holocaust education in middle and high schools became law in May 2020.

Rosen and Masto are the first two women to serve as Nevada's senators, and while the state lost its seniority clout with Reid's retirement, the two have picked up the mantle on one of his most important issues: blocking a nuclear waste site at Yucca Mountain. Rosen has been more cautious on other environmental issues though, expressing skepticism of some of the sweeping proposals in the "Green New Deal" pushed by progressives. "I do believe that climate change is real. I do believe we have to have a plan and we have to think carefully about this," she said after a speech to the Nevada Legislature in March 2019. "We have to do it in a measured way so that as we go forward, whatever we're changing ... we'll make sure that we take care of people who might lose jobs or what unintended consequences there are."

Rosen's first bill signed into law by Trump was one close to her heart: It provided additional National Science Foundation grants to encourage more women and people of color to pursue education and careers in STEM fields. "As a former computer programmer, I introduced this bipartisan bill to help break down the gender barriers that I faced as a woman in STEM for current and future generations," Rosen said. She has also proposed legislation to require schools that receive federal funds for computer science to report demographic breakdowns of their number of students to the Department of Education. She also launched a "Tech Time With Jacky Rosen" web series to break down technology and science.

Dina Titus (D)

Elected 2012, 6th term, b. May 23, 1950; Thomasville, GA; College of William and Mary, A.B., 1970; University of GA, M.A., 1973; FL State University, Ph.D., 1976; Greek Orthodox; Married (Thomas Clayton Wright).

Elected Office: U.S. House, 2008-2010; NV Senate, 1988-2008.

Professional Career: Professor, University of NV, Las Vegas, 1977-2011; Professor, N. TX St. University, 1975-1976.

DC Office: 2464 RHOB 20515, 202-225-5965, Fax: 202-225-3119, titus.house.gov

State Offices: Las Vegas, 702-220-9823.

Committees: *Foreign Affairs*: Asia, the Pacific, Central Asia, Nonproliferation; Europe, Energy, the Environment & Cyber. *Homeland Security*: Oversight, Management & Accountability; Transportation & Maritime Security. *Transportation & Infrastructure*: Aviation; Economic Dev't, Public Buildings & Emergency Management (Chmn).

Group Ratings

	ADA	ACLU	AFL-CIO	LCV	COC	HAFA	ACU	CFG	FRC
2020	**	83%	**	100%	-	0%	4%	**	-
2019	95%	C	95%	96%	54%	C	4%	19%	0%

Almanac Ratings 2019-2020

	Economy	Social	Foreign	Composite
Liberal	100%	100%	58%	86%
Conservative	0%	0%	42%	14%

Key Votes of the 116th Congress

1. U.S./Mex./Can. trade deal Y	5. Russia sanctions Y	9. Firearms background checks Y
2. First Coronavirus response Y	6. Troops in Syria Y	10. Spending at the border N
3. HEROES Act Y	7. Veto arms sales to Saudis Y	11. Marijuana liberalized rules Y
4. CASH Act Y	8. Defense $$$, veto override Y	12. Electoral College objections N

Election Results

Election	Name (Party)	Vote (%)		Cand. Spent	Ind. Exp. Support	Ind. Exp. Oppose
2020 General	Dina Titus (D)	137,868	(62%)	$516,022	$2,562	
	Joyce Bentley (R)	74,490	(33%)			$59
	Kamau Bakari (Ind.)	6,190	(3%)	$6,076		
	Robert Van Strawder (L)	4,665	(2%)			
2020 Primary	Dina Titus (D)	31,916	(83%)			
	Anthony Thomas Jr. (D)	4,324	(11%)			
	Allen Rheinhart (D)	2,382	(6%)			

Prior winning percentages: 2018 (66%), 2016 (62%), 2014 (57%), 2012 (64%), 2008 (47%)

Democrat Dina Titus was elected to Nevada's 1st District House seat in 2012 after losing reelection two years earlier in a more competitive district. With an open seat, the former political science professor moved to a Las Vegas-based district that was safe for a Democrat. With nearly half of the district population listed as Hispanic, redistricting could pose a risk for Titus in a state where that community has pressed for its own district.

Raised in Tifton Georgia, Titus retained her thick Southern drawl. "I get teased a lot because I haven't lost the accent, but that's kind of become part of how people know me," she told National Journal. Her upbringing gave her a strong interest in politics. She recalls listening to local politicians talk shop at her grandfather's Greek restaurant across from the courthouse. Her father ran for city council, and her Republican "black sheep" uncle, as she puts it, served in the Georgia legislature.

Titus attended the College of William and Mary, where she majored in political science; she later obtained a master's degree from the University of Georgia and a doctorate from Florida State University. After teaching at the University of North Texas, she joined the faculty at the University of Nevada-Las Vegas. She taught there for 34 years, retiring in 2011. Titus has authored two works on Nevada history, Bombs in the Backyard: Atomic Testing and American Politics, and Battle Born: Federal-State Relations in Nevada During the Twentieth Century. In 1988, Titus put her political knowledge to use and was elected to the state Senate, where she was minority leader for 16 years. She became an advocate for people with disabilities. In 2006, she lost a run for governor to Republican Jim Gibbons.

In 2008, Titus ran for the House, defeating Republican incumbent Jon Porter. That tenure was short-lived. She was swept out of office by the Republican wave in 2010, losing a bruising battle to Joe Heck by 1,748 votes out of more than 314,000 cast. When Democratic Rep. Shelley Berkley retired, Titus ran in 2012 in the 1st District, with its 2-1 Democratic edge in voter registration. In November, she largely avoided engaging Republican Chris Edwards, a Navy officer making his first foray into politics. She won, 64%-32% and has been easily reelected since.

Following her return to the House, Titus was ranking Democrat on the Veterans' Affairs Subcommittee on Disability Assistance and Memorial Affairs. She filed bills that would overturn the VA's prohibition on doctors signing off on marijuana for patients and to permit same-sex couples to be eligible for veterans' benefits. On the Transportation and Infrastructure Committee, Titus has been an enthusiastic advocate of reopening rail service from Las Vegas to Los Angeles. Amtrak shut down the line in 1997, but efforts to revive it with high-speed rail have moved ahead.

Titus has strongly opposed creating a nuclear waste dump at Yucca Mountain and slammed the Trump administration after it sent a half metric ton of plutonium to the Nevada National Security Site at Yucca Mountain, complaining that officials "treat Nevada as the dumping ground for the nation's nuclear waste." When President Donald Trump tweeted in February 2020 that he "respected" the views of Nevadans on Yucca, Titus told a local TV interviewer that he was "pandering" for their votes in November. She has been a staunch ally of the gaming industry, and slammed the Department of Justice for efforts to block online gambling expansion. She has championed liberal causes as well, introducing the Greater Leadership Overseas for the Benefit of Equality (GLOBE) Act to promote LGBTQ equality worldwide. Following the Las Vegas massacre in 2017, she pushed to revive a federal ban on some types of semi-automatic weapons.

In the majority in 2019, Titus chaired the Economic Development, Public Buildings, and Emergency Management Subcommittee, and investigated Trump's real estate holdings, including the government lease for the Trump International Hotel in Washington D.C., which prompted constitutional litigation, and his alleged efforts to influence the FBI headquarters across from his hotel. "Donald Trump is violating the Constitution by accepting money from foreign governments," Titus said, though she took no action while he was president. In 2021, she said that a priority was to permit the Economic Development Administration to promote travel and tourism.

Titus voiced interest in a 2016 run to succeed retiring Senate Majority Leader Harry Reid. But Reid, with whom Titus had a chilly relationship, was firmly behind former state Attorney General Catherine Cortez Masto. Titus decided, "I just love representing Nevada's 1st District." Having lost two elections in the past decade, she was circumspect about giving up her safe seat. She pondered a challenge to Republican Sen. Dean Heller in 2018, even releasing an early poll showing her competitive. But Titus again ran up against Reid, who made clear he thought that more moderate freshman Rep. Jacky Rosen would be the best challenger. As Rosen quickly locked up the support of state and national Democrats, Titus again decided that she preferred to remain in the House.

NV-1: Las Vegas   **Cook Partisan Voting Index: D+12**

Population		Race and Ethnicity		Income	
Total	712,411	White	51.40%	Median Income	$44,078
Land area (sq. miles)	105	Black	12.10%	District Income Rank	421
Pop/ sq mi	6,817.33	Latino	47.00%	Poverty Rate	20.50%
Born in State	24.30%	Asian	9.30%	With health insurance	81.00%
		Two or more races	4.20%	Cash public assistance	4.10%
Age Groups		Other	23.10%	Food stamp/SNAP	16.90%
Under 18	22.80%				
18-34	24.90%	**Education**		**Work**	
35-64	38.20%	H.S grad or less	54.00%	White Collar	19.00%
Over 64	14.20%	Some college	28.50%	Sales and Service	55.20%
		College Degree, 4 yr	11.90%	Blue Collar	25.80%
Military		Post grad	5.60%	Government	6.70%
Veteran/ Active Duty	6.40%				

2020 Pres. Vote	Biden	143,427	(61%)	Trump	84,973	(36%)		
2016 Pres. Vote	Clinton	121,321	(62%)	Trump	64,233	(33%)	Johnson	5,406 (3%)

Las Vegas: Las Vegas, that garish and improbable city, had a fittingly colorful beginning. It began as a Paiute Indian settlement that in the late 1700s served as a watering stop for Spanish priests making the 1,200-mile trek between New Mexico and California. By the 1800s, the Old Spanish Trail, as it came to be known, was used by horse and mule smugglers, by explorers like John C. Fremont, and by Mormon emigrants heading west. Las Vegas was still a small crossroads when Nevada, its mining industry a shambles, legalized gambling in the 1930s. The WPA Guide to Nevada, published in 1940 when the city had 10,000 people, describes a prim Las Vegas: "Relatively little emphasis is placed on the gambling clubs and divorce facilities—though they are attractions to many visitors— and much effort is being made to build up cultural attractions."

All that changed after World War II, when gangster Bugsy Siegel built the Flamingo hotel and casino on what became the Strip, south of the city limits. Pseudo-romantic architectural themes became the order of the day (flamingos are found in the waters of Florida, not in the deserts of Nevada), and one casino followed another. Organized crime provided much of the money and muscle for Las Vegas, and investment capital came from Teamsters pension funds. In the late 1960s, eccentric billionaire Howard Hughes moved into the Desert Inn, bought most of the casinos, and hired Mormons to run them. After Hughes abruptly left town, most of his hotels eventually were torn down, and other operators built huge casinos. Lately, the city has claimed six of the 10 largest hotels in the world.

By the 1990s, diversification became the buzzword. Las Vegas began to produce more family-oriented entertainment, shopping, and even high art, with the Bellagio's museum-quality collection on view. Las Vegas built the largest convention center in the nation. But the city has not neglected its core clientele: people who fly in from elsewhere to be entertained and to be, for a weekend, maybe even a little naughty. "What happens in Vegas stays in Vegas," remained the unofficial motto. The flashy Oscar Goodman, a former mob lawyer, was elected mayor and actively promoted the city. When he was term-limited in 2011, his wife, Carolyn, succeeded him. She continued his habit of taking scantily clad showgirls to events promoting the city; at age 80, she won a third term in 2019.

Because of the city's dependence on leisure-time spending, the recession hit hard here and persisted long after other areas recovered. The more affordable cost of living has attracted many middle-class Californians to Las Vegas, where they find lower taxes and cheaper rents or can buy good-sized homes for less than $300,000. The new visitors were more interested in shopping, concerts and nightlife. The newest big business in Vegas has become professional sports. The former Oakland Raiders moved their NFL franchise to the desert and played in 2020 in the $2 billion Allegiant Stadium, though with no fans because of the pandemic. The stadium was financed largely by an increase in hotel taxes to support bonds for Clark County.

The coronavirus had a devastating impact on the local economy, with more than one-third of workers losing their jobs in this service economy and an initial unemployment rate of 25 percent. Among the victims was the Monorail, which shut down service and declared bankruptcy. But all was not lost. In December 2020, the Las Vegas Convention and Visitors Authority purchased the elevated system for $24 million—largely to cover its debt—and explored cooperation with Elon Musk's Boring Company, which has been planning a series of tunnels under the Strip and to the airport and Allegiant Stadium.

In October 2017, Las Vegas was the site of the deadliest mass shooting in U.S. history after a 64 year-old gunman opened fire on a concert by country singer Jason Aldean at the Route 91 Harvest Music Festival, which attracted more than 30,000 people. The shooter executed the attack from his 32nd floor Mandalay Bay hotel room, killing 58 people and leaving more than 800 injured from the shooting and the panic that ensued. The gunman committed suicide. MGM, which owned the hotel, agreed in September 2020 to an $800 million settlement, without acknowledging liability.

The 1st Congressional District of Nevada consists of the inner core of Las Vegas that visitors are most likely to see. They cross into it as soon as they exit the re-named Harry Reid International Airport. On the three-mile Strip are the nation's 11 largest hotels, each with thousands of rooms that extend far back on their properties. The district is 46 percent Hispanic, the highest proportion in the state, and is the only solidly Democratic district in Nevada. The 61 percent vote for Joe Biden in 2020 fell from 65 percent for President Barack Obama in 2012. The large number of local Latinos with growing doubts about Democrats was a factor in the shift.

Mark Amodei (R)

Elected 2011, 5th full term, b. Jun 12, 1958; Carson City, NV; University of NV, Reno, B.A., 1980; University of the Pacific McGeorge School of Law, J.D., 1983; Presbyterian; Divorced; 2 children.

Military Career: U.S. Army, Judge Advocate General's Corps 1984-1987

Professional Career: NV Assembly, 1997-1998; NV Senate, 1999-2010.

DC Office: 104 CHOB 20515, 202-225-6155, Fax: 202-225-5679, amodei.house.gov

State Offices: Elko, 775-777-7705; Reno, 775-686-5760.

Committees: *Appropriations*: Financial Services & General Government; Interior, Environment & Related Agencies; Legislative Branch.

Group Ratings

	ADA	ACLU	AFL-CIO	LCV	COC	HAFA	ACU	CFG	FRC
2020	**	15%	**	24%	-	76%	73%	**	-
2019	5%	C	33%	10%	93%	C	73%	74%	95%

Almanac Ratings 2019-2020

	Economy	Social	Foreign	Composite
Liberal	25%	37%	13%	25%
Conservative	75%	63%	87%	75%

Key Votes of the 116th Congress

1. U.S./Mex./Can. trade deal	Y	5. Russia sanctions	N	9. Firearms background checks N
2. First Coronavirus response	Y	6. Troops in Syria	Y	10. Spending at the border	Y
3. HEROES Act	N	7. Veto arms sales to Saudis	N	11. Marijuana liberalized rules N
4. CASH Act	N	8. Defense $$$, veto override	Y	12. Electoral College objections N

Election Results

Election	Name (Party)	Vote (%)		Cand. Spent	Ind. Exp. Support	Ind. Exp. Oppose
						$1,657
2020 General	Mark Amodei (R)	216,078	(56%)	$953,524		
	Patricia Ackerman (D)	155,780	(41%)	$444,418	$32,924	
	Janine Hansen (Ind.)	10,815	(3%)			
2020 Primary	Mark Amodei (R)	61,462	(81%)			
	Joel Beck (R)	11,308	(15%)			

Prior winning percentages: 2018 (58%), 2016 (58%), 2014 (66%), 2012 (58%), 2011 special (62%)

Republican Mark Amodei won a 2011 special election to fill the seat of GOP Sen. Dean Heller. A former state Senate president pro tempore and state party chairman, Amodei is a small-government conservative whose governing experience has allied him with the party establishment in pushing for legislation on multiple fronts, though he remained a voice for compromise on immigration reform. With Heller's loss in 2018 and Democrats' success in other districts, Amodei became the lone Republican in the Nevada delegation. He showed occasional independence of President Donald Trump, as with his votes in January 2021 opposing review of the Electoral College results in Arizona and Pennsylvania. He has paid no apparent price for going his own way.

Amodei grew up in Carson City, Nevada's capital, the son of an Italian immigrant father who worked for the state Forestry Division and a mother who was a physician. He attended the University of Nevada, Reno, where he joined ROTC, and earned a law degree from the University of the Pacific's McGeorge School of Law. He joined the Army and became a prosecutor for the Judge Advocate General Corps, handling criminal matters. After opening a law practice in his hometown, Amodei was elected to the state Assembly and then to the state Senate, where he chaired the Judiciary Committee and took his leadership post. In 2007, Amodei became president of the Nevada Mining Association. He said that he saw no conflict of interest, but a year and a half later stepped down from the organization because, he said, he didn't want to have a "distracting" dual role during the legislative session.

In 2009, Amodei announced a challenge to Senate Majority Leader Harry Reid, portraying himself as a common-sense conservative who could appeal to independent voters. He dropped out of the contest six months later, explaining that he was able to raise only about $80,000, a pittance compared to Reid's multimillion-dollar war chest. When Heller was appointed to the Senate in May 2011 to replace Republican John Ensign, who resigned amid a sex scandal with the wife of one of his former aides, Amodei won the nomination with ease. In the special election, Democratic state Treasurer Kate Marshall boasted of support from the National Rifle Association and said she would have voted against increasing the federal debt ceiling, which Amodei also opposed. Amodei played up his more conservative credentials, calling for tax cuts, a balanced budget amendment to the Constitution and opening more public lands to oil and gas production. He used an ad with his mother to deflect Medicare attacks. The National Republican Congressional Committee pumped in more than $600,000 to pummel Marshall, and the Democratic Congressional Campaign Committee never came to her rescue. Amodei won, 58%-36%.

Amodei has been an often pragmatic conservative in the House who emphasizes spending discipline. He has brought a homespun approach to his job and says lawmakers need to talk more with each other. Democratic Rep. John Garamendi of California told the Reno Gazette-Journal that Amodei "knows the legislative process." They worked together in 2016 to enact the Lake Tahoe Restoration Act to "keep Tahoe blue."

On the Appropriations Committee, he won approval of his provision to protect the water rights of private landholders. In the Western Caucus, Amodei has concentrated on natural resource issues. In contrast to the hard-line opposition of many in Nevada, he said the Yucca Mountain proposed burial site for high-level nuclear waste storage should be examined instead as a potential home for nuclear reprocessing and research. Nevada could become "the worldwide leader in reprocessing the fuel so it becomes a commodity instead of trash," he told the Nevada Appeal in 2016.

He clashed with Trump's first Interior Secretary, Ryan Zinke, getting caught on tape addressing a GOP dinner in a profanity-laden tirade after Zinke hadn't alerted him to a shakeup at the Nevada branch of the Bureau of Land Management, according to the Reno Gazette Journal. Citing concerns about Medicaid cuts and changes, Amodei initially wavered in 2017 on whether he would support the American Health Care Act, the GOP's effort to repeal Obamacare. In a 2015 interview with the Sparks Tribune, Amodei said the problems of immigration are "eminently solvable," except that "everybody's got a political angle." In his view, "I'd rather be criticized for trying to do something because I'm tired of defending nothing." After Trump tried to halt the Deferred Action for Childhood Arrivals (DACA) program, Amodei joined a group of Republicans critical of GOP leaders for stalling on a solution. Amodei's district is nearly one-fourth Hispanic.

Amodei has flirted with higher office but hasn't pulled the trigger, and has easily won reelection in his congressional district. During the final weeks of the 2016 contest, while he was the Nevada campaign chairman for Trump, he said that some of the criticism and outrage over Trump's comments about women were "appropriate and deserved." But he stood by Trump. "I am genuinely concerned about the future of our country, and who will set the tone," Amodei said.

In 2018 Amodei faced a primary challenge from tea party activist Sharron Angle, who had unsuccessfully challenged Reid in 2010. Angle slammed Amodei's openness to immigration reform as "amnesty," but she had paltry fundraising and her bid never gained traction. Amodei won 72%-18%. In September 2019, he stirred Republican hostility when he called for increased "oversight" of Trump's actions, though he emphasized that he did not favor an impeachment inquiry. That had no apparent impact of his approval at home in 2020, when he won 81 percent of the primary vote against two challengers and was reelected in November, 56%-41%.

NV-2: Northern Nevada
Cook Partisan Voting Index: R+8

Population		Race and Ethnicity		Income	
Total	736,907	White	78.50%	Median Income	$69,972
Land area (sq. miles)	55,830	Black	2.00%	District Income Rank	164
Pop/ sq mi	13.2	Latino	23.50%	Poverty Rate	11.00%
Born in State	31.90%	Asian	4.50%	With health insurance	90.50%
Age Groups		Two or more races	3.60%	Cash public assistance	2.30%
Under 18	21.20%	Other	11.50%	Food stamp/SNAP	8.90%
18-34	22.90%	**Education**		**Work**	
35-64	38.00%	H.S grad or less	36.70%	White Collar	31.80%
Over 64	17.90%	Some college	36.00%	Sales and Service	40.20%
Military		College Degree, 4 yr	17.00%	Blue Collar	28.00%
Veteran/ Active Duty	10.00%	Post grad	10.30%	Government	14.60%

2020 Pres. Vote	Trump	210,255	(54%)	Biden	171,024	(44%)			
2016 Pres. Vote	Trump	169,631	(52%)	Clinton	129,317	(40%)	Johnson	13,966	(4%)

Reno: Outside of metro Las Vegas, huge, empty and mountainous Nevada has only one sizable population center, a cluster of small cities and towns near the border with California: the casino cities of Reno and Sparks, the mall capital of Carson City, the restored Comstock Lode boomtown of Virginia City, and the resort areas that surround (and endanger) the deep, impossibly blue waters of Lake Tahoe. Reno is so remote from Las Vegas that the only quick way to get there is by air; it takes more than nine hours to drive, although the spectacularly stark scenery makes it time well spent. Ghost towns that once bustled with miners dot the parched, sand-swept deserts, and in some places the land remains distinctly rutted from the wagon trains that crossed here more than 150 years ago. Today, Nevada's small towns survive on mining, ranching and, in some cases, servicing the human sins of greed and lust: Nevada's legal brothels are generally found in the small, desert counties. Another distinction is the Basque influence. Immigrant Basque shepherds once tended their flocks in remote portions of northern Nevada; Basque festivals, social clubs and restaurants can still be found in Winnemucca and Elko.

The military has holdings in the Nevada interior, including Fallon Naval Air Station, home to the Navy Fighter Weapons "Top Gun" School. Many places in Nevada depend on other federal government programs: The Newlands Irrigation Project near Fallon was among the first of its kind. Nevada's gold-mining operations, booming since 2000, do not have to pay royalties to the government, thanks to the Mining Act of 1872. The spread of legalized gambling throughout the country has hurt Reno. In 2019, prior to the pandemic, Washoe County had only 7 percent of the casino revenues in Nevada. Las Vegas-based Clark County had 86 percent of the revenues, with the remainder scattered in places like Carson City, Tahoe and Elko County.

The area has become a tech hub, with solar and wind-energy enterprises and high-precision technologies. Reno has sold itself as close to Silicon Valley but with a lower cost of living and extensive space, though it has struggled to meet demands for new housing and infrastructure. In 2020, northern Nevada had more than 27,000 manufacturing jobs, many of them tech-related, surpassing Clark County. Electric-car manufacturer Tesla Motors opened in 2015 its huge factory near Sparks, with lower-cost cell production for its batteries, and extensive robotics. In 2019, its workforce exceeded 7,000. They work in a facility that is a half-mile long, and as much as one-quarter mile wide. Apple opened a massive solar plant in the Reno area to power its huge data centers; it runs on 100 percent green energy and powered 200,000 servers.

The 2nd Congressional District of Nevada takes in Reno and Carson City in territory that covers nearly the northern half of Nevada. It includes Churchill, Pershing, Humboldt and Elko counties. Washoe County, which includes Reno and Sparks, has nearly two-thirds of the district's population. In Washoe, an important swing county, Joe Biden won, 51%-46%. President Donald Trump won each of the outlying counties with more than 60% of the vote and took the 2nd comfortably, 54%-44%. This was the only Nevada district where he won a majority of the vote.

Susie Lee (D)

Elected 2018, 2nd term, b. Nov 07, 1966; Canton, OH; Carnegie Mellon University, B.S., 1989; Carnegie Mellon University, M.P.A., 1990; Catholic; Married (Dan Lee); 2 children.

Professional Career: Non-Profit Executive; Board President, Communities in School.

DC Office: 522 CHOB 20515, 202-225-3252, susielee.house.gov
State Offices: Las Vegas, 702-963-9336.

Committees: *Appropriations*: Energy & Water Development & Related Agencies; Interior, Environment & Related Agencies; Military Construction, Veterans Affairs & Related Agencies.

Almanac Ratings 2019-2020

	Economy	Social	Foreign	Composite
Liberal	56%	51%	80%	63%
Conservative	44%	49%	20%	37%

Key Votes of the 116th Congress

1. U.S./Mex./Can. trade deal	Y	5. Russia sanctions	Y	9. Firearms background checks Y
2. First Coronavirus response	Y	6. Troops in Syria	Y	10. Spending at the border	Y
3. HEROES Act	Y	7. Veto arms sales to Saudis	Y	11. Marijuana liberalized rules	Y
4. CASH Act	Y	8. Defense $$$, veto override	Y	12. Electoral College objections N

Election Results

Election	Name (Party)	Vote (%)		Cand. Spent	Ind. Exp. Support	Ind. Exp. Oppose
2020 General	Susie Lee (D)	203,421	(49%)	$4,736,224	$162,386	$2,691,167
	Dan Rodimer (R)	190,975	(46%)	$2,894,141	$531,806	$3,478,605
	Steve Brown (L)	12,315	(3%)			
	Edward Bridges (Ind.)	10,541	(3%)			
2020 Primary	Susie Lee (D)	49,223	(83%)			
	Dennis Sullivan (D)	5,830	(10%)			
	Tiffany Watson (D)	4,411	(7%)			

Prior winning percentages: 2018 (52%)

Democrat Susie Lee, after comfortably winning her swing seat in 2018, sought to establish her centrist credentials. She faced a competitive reelection, with a closer result, to win a second term. Her husband, Dan Lee, has been a prominent casino executive—a topic of continuing controversy in Susie Lee's actions.

Lee, a native of Canton Ohio, grew up in a working-class family. "We didn't have much, but we had enough," she told the Las Vegas Review-Journal, which profiled her "humble beginnings." Lee got her bachelor's degree and a master's in public administration from Carnegie Mellon University. She settled in Las Vegas, where her activities included the founding of a homeless shelter, creation of an after-school program and a stint as board president of the Communities in School program.

When Lee ran in the 4th District in 2016, news reports focused on her husband's hefty earnings from casino businesses, which financed nearly one-half of the $1.6 million she spent. PolitiFact confirmed that the Lees owned 17 homes—14 of which they rented—and a private plane. She got 21 percent in the Democratic primary, which was won by Ruben Kihuen, the son of Mexican-born immigrants. He stepped down after one term, following charges of sexual misconduct.

In contrast to other recent Democratic primaries for open seats in Nevada, which have been highly competitive, Lee quickly emerged as the party favorite in 2018. Some unhappy Democratic activists, plus her opponents, criticized the Democratic Congressional Campaign Committee for favoring high-income candidates. "The Washington D.C. and Nevada Democratic establishment anointed Susie Lee for her ease of access to large amounts of money," complained Jack Love, one of her opponents. "Political candidates should be chosen based on a contest of ideas, not the size of their bank accounts." Lee raised more than $1.4 million for the primary against six other candidates, none of whom raised more than $22,000. She got 67 percent of the vote.

Danny Tarkanian, Lee's Republican opponent, was well-known in Nevada as the son of a former prominent college basketball coach—and as a perennial candidate who had lost at least six campaigns in Nevada, including a 47%-46% defeat for this House seat in 2016. Running against eight other candidates, Tarkanian won the primary with 44 percent. In the general election, Tarkanian attacked Lee as "part of the wealthy elite" and "out of touch" with voters. Tarkanian had his own problems in business, including the ownership of a failed bank in California, which resulted in his filing for bankruptcy. Lee emerged with several advantages, including the surge in Democratic fundraising that led her to more than double Tarkanian's spending, and the overall political climate. She had an easy 52%-43% win.

In the House, Lee sought to separate herself from other freshmen who gained attention with their liberal agendas. "There are people that are going to actually try to figure out how we get to common ground and get something done. And that's the type of leadership that I bring to the table," she told local reporters in April 2018, the Nevada Independent reported. She cited an amendment that she added to an education bill that called for a study of the impact of class sizes.

After Lee voted for the $3 trillion COVID-relief bill in March 2020, she reportedly joined the Nevada delegation in urging federal administrators to make sure that gaming companies were covered by the Paycheck Protection Program, which reimbursed some of those costs. According to the Daily Beast, her husband's companies benefited from that action and received $5.6 million in federal loans. A spokesperson for Lee said his firm applied for the loans after the regulatory change had been made.

In her reelection, Lee faced Dan Rodimer, a lawyer and former professional wrestler who criticized her for financial conflicts of interest in her stock transactions. "Big Dan" (with a height of six feet, seven inches) was endorsed by the union representing Las Vegas police officers, which had endorsed Lee in 2018. Aides to Lee said she had no control over the stock sales and criticized Rodimer for a girlfriend's accusation of domestic violence more than a decade earlier while he was living in Florida; no charges were filed in that case. Lee outspent Rodimer, $4.7 million to $2.9 million, and she benefited from $3.5 million in national party aid. Lee won, 48.8%-45.8%.

Following the election, Lee won a seat on the House Appropriations Committee and said her top priority was getting "our economy back on track" in Nevada. The recent history of this district, where two Democrats and two Republicans split the six elections from 2006 to 2016, suggests that redistricting might have a significant impact and that Lee cannot take it for granted.

NV-3: Southern Las Vegas area

Cook Partisan Voting Index: R+2

Population		Race and Ethnicity		Income	
Total	857,197	White	64.50%	Median Income	$79,169
Land area (sq. miles)	2,849	Black	8.80%	District Income Rank	98
Pop/ sq mi	300.88	Latino	17.00%	Poverty Rate	8.20%
Born in State	23.80%	Asian	13.90%	With health insurance	92.30%
		Two or more races	5.60%	Cash public assistance	1.90%
Age Groups		Other	7.20%	Food stamp/SNAP	5.60%
Under 18	21.00%				
18-34	21.70%	**Education**		**Work**	
35-64	40.90%	H.S grad or less	31.00%	White Collar	39.00%
Over 64	16.50%	Some college	34.30%	Sales and Service	46.60%
		College Degree, 4 yr	22.40%	Blue Collar	14.30%
Military		Post grad	12.30%	Government	11.10%
Veteran/ Active Duty	9.10%				

2020 Pres. Vote	Trump	213,299	(49%)	Biden	214,184	(49%)		
2016 Pres. Vote	Trump	154,814	(48%)	Clinton	151,552	(47%)	Johnson	9,971 (3%)

Henderson: Las Vegas, "The Meadows" in Spanish, began as a stop along the Old Spanish Trail trading route between Santa Fe and California in the 1830s. Water from artesian wells had created vast grasslands in the area and let traders replenish their supplies. In the early 20th century, Las Vegas was a terminus of the Las Vegas & Tonopah Railroad, a link to Nevada's silver mines. Even at the end of the 1930s, soon after gambling was legalized in Nevada, it was still a town of fewer than 10,000. Then came decades of amazing growth, as Las Vegas became America's destination for gambling and entertainment. It spread across the desert in every direction from the few blocks around Fremont Street that it occupied in the 1930s, and today it is an exuberant, undisciplined and chaotic city. Following the fast pace of building, Las Vegas was particularly hard hit by the crisis in the credit markets, and the red-hot real estate market tanked. The metro area had the highest foreclosure rate in the nation in 2010.

The 3rd Congressional District covers the southern part of Clark County and several Las Vegas suburbs. It includes retiree communities, small blue-collar towns such as Blue Diamond, and a variety of planned, and often gated, areas like Summerlin South, where young families have sought job opportunities and retired baby boomers have purchased vacation homes. Southeast of Las Vegas, the district takes in the population hub of Henderson and Boulder City, originally built for federal workers at Hoover Dam. (Under an old agreement with the federal government, Boulder City is the only place in Nevada where gambling and prostitution were prohibited.) After the dam was completed, many of the workers unexpectedly decided to stay in the desert. The sale of liquor was legalized in 1969. In 2018, the first 15-mile section of Interstate 11 opened with a bypass around Boulder City, through the Eldorado Mountains overlooking Lake Mead. Officials explored extensions to reduce congestion on the state highway to Phoenix. In the desert outside Boulder City, a solar plant operates with 288,000 panels that can yield 100 megawatts of power.

Henderson resumed its rapid growth following the recession. Since 2010, its population has increased 25 percent to 320,000. To accompany their move to Las Vegas in 2020, the Oakland Raiders located their corporate headquarters and practice facility in Henderson. Also in 2020, Google spent another $600 million to double its investment in a local data center. Fun fact: Henderson provides tours of its "Artisan Booze" district. In Boulder City, where tourists going to and from the Grand Canyon and Hoover Dam have provided half of the revenue, local officials looked for alternative sources.

The 3rd includes the Nevada half of Lake Mohave on the Arizona border, plus the state's southernmost tip, including Searchlight, the hometown of former Senate Majority Leader Harry Reid. The 3rd, with a 17 percent and growing Latino population, is politically competitive. The 2020 presidential election was the third consecutive in which the major party candidates were separated by one percentage point; this time, Joe Biden won by fewer than 1,000 votes.

Steven Horsford (D)

Elected 2018, 3rd term, b. Apr 29, 1973; Las Vegas, NV; University of NV, Reno, B.A., 2014; Baptist; Married (Dr. Sonya Horsford); 3 children.

Elected Office: NV Senate, 2004-2012, Majority Floor Leader 2009-2012; U.S. House, 2013-2015.

Professional Career: NV Legislature Education Committee, Legislative Aide 1995; R&R Advertising, Account Representative 1996; Culinary Training Academy, Chief Executive Officer 2001-2012; R&R Partners, Inc., Senior Vice President, Strategic Integration and Partnerships; Managing Director, Washington, DC Office 2015-2018; Nevada Partners (Employment Training), President of the Board, Chief Executive Officer.

DC Office: 1330 LHOB 20515, 202-225-9894, horsford.house.gov

State Offices: North Las Vegas, 702-963-9360.

Committees: *Armed Services*: Strategic Forces; Tactical Air & Land Forces. *Budget.* *Ways & Means*: Health; Oversight; Social Security.

Almanac Ratings 2019-2020

	Economy	Social	Foreign	Composite
Liberal	100%	100%	92%	98%
Conservative	0%	0%	8%	2%

Key Votes of the 116th Congress

1. U.S./Mex./Can. trade deal	Y	5. Russia sanctions	Y	9. Firearms background checks Y
2. First Coronavirus response	Y	6. Troops in Syria	Y	10. Spending at the border	N
3. HEROES Act	Y	7. Veto arms sales to Saudis	Y	11. Marijuana liberalized rules	Y
4. CASH Act	Y	8. Defense $$$, veto override	Y	12. Electoral College objections N

Election Results

Election	Name (Party)	Vote (%)		Cand. Spent	Ind. Exp. Support	Ind. Exp. Oppose
2020 General	Steven Horsford (D)	168,457	(51%)	$2,967,720	$701,881	$83,500
	Jim Marchant (R)	152,284	(46%)	$1,396,779	$213,704	$627,382
	Jonathan Esteban (L)	7,978	(2%)	$1,603		
2020 Primary	Steven Horsford (D)	39,656	(75%)			
	Jennifer Eason (D)	4,968	(9%)			
	Gabrielle D'Ayr (D)	3,847	(7%)			

Prior winning percentages: 2018 (52%), 2012 (50%)

Democrat Steven Horsford won reelection to his seat in 2020, the first time a candidate has won back-to-back victories in this seat since it was created in 2012, when Nevada gained a fourth district. In May 2020, he acknowledged a longstanding affair with a woman whom he met a decade earlier when she was a political intern. Horsford replaced Democrat Ruben Kihuen, who decided against seeking reelection in 2016 under pressure from national and state Democrats following allegations of improper sexual behavior with a female staffer. Horsford has received high-profile assignments to the Budget and Ways and Means committees.

Horsford grew up in a rough-and-tumble neighborhood in West Las Vegas. The oldest of four, he had responsibility forced on him early in life. His mother struggled with drug and alcohol problems. He attended the University of Nevada, Reno, but had to drop out to support his family when his father was shot and killed during a robbery at a store where he worked. Well-connected to the state's hospitality industry, Horsford was CEO of the Culinary Training Academy of Las Vegas, which trained workers for jobs on the Strip. He served eight years in the state Senate, including a stint as majority leader.

When he ran for the new House district in 2012, Horsford dodged primary opposition. In the general, he defeated Danny Tarkanian, who has become a perennial Republican contender, 50%-42%. During his first term in the House, he was viewed as a rising star. Horsford lost reelection in 2014 to

Republican Cresent Hardy, a state legislator who was significantly outspent. Hardy benefited from the popularity of Gov. Brian Sandoval, a small Democratic turnout, and $1.1 million in late spending by a Republican Super PAC. Hardy won, 49%-46%.

In 2016, the district's Democratic lean reasserted itself as the presidential election and an open Senate seat nearly doubled voter turnout. Kihuen, who was born in Mexico and moved to the United States as a child with his working-class parents, served 10 years in the legislature, including two years as Senate majority whip. He defeated Hardy, 49%-45%. Kihuen's House career imploded after BuzzFeed reported in December 2017 that he had made repeated advances toward a staffer during the 2016 campaign. Kihuen rejected calls that he resign, but announced two weeks after the revelations that he would not seek reelection.

Horsford, who had settled in Washington and opened a public relations firm, announced his candidacy in January 2018. "There are some things that I learned [in 2014] and that I will do differently about this campaign," he told the Nevada Independent. "First is, I will run a very grassroots, community-oriented campaign, listening to voters." Horsford had numerous advantages, including the endorsement of the Democratic Congressional Campaign Committee and a large fundraising lead. In the six-candidate Democratic primary, he got 62 percent of the vote. Hardy was well-financed for his rematch with Horsford. "The people of Nevada fired him four years ago," he told the voters. But state and national politics had changed since 2014. This time, proving that his frontrunner status was warranted, Horsford won, 52%-44%.

On his return to the House, Horsford was named a Democratic whip in addition to his prime committee slots. In October 2019, he filed with Sen. Cory Booker legislation to permit local communities to create violence intervention programs to reduce gun incidents. The proposal was designed "to get ahead of this senseless violence; to allow folks to come together and stem this cruelty in their communities," Horsford said.

His public discussion of his decade-long affair followed the decision of the woman, Gabriela Linder, to describe her affair in a public podcast that did not explicitly name Horsford. She said he had been elected "under false pretenses" and that he should step back from politics. In a statement, Horsford responded that he was "deeply sorry" for "the relationship outside of my marriage over the course of several years."

In his reelection campaign in 2020, Horsford faced Jim Marchant, who served one term in the state Assembly before losing in 2018 and was the chief executive of multiple tech companies. Horsford doubled Marchant's spending and defeated him, 51%-46%; in Clark County, which cast nearly 90 percent of the vote, Horsford led, 54%-43%. Following the election, Horsford, who had endorsed Joe Biden before the state caucuses in February, served as a liaison between the Congressional Black Caucus and Biden's transition team.

NV-4: Central Nevada

Cook Partisan Voting Index: D+1

Population		Race and Ethnicity		Income	
Total	773,641	White	63.60%	Median Income	$62,241
Land area (sq. miles)	50,998	Black	15.60%	District Income Rank	230
Pop/ sq mi	15.17	Latino	32.00%	Poverty Rate	11.40%
Born in State	29.20%	Asian	5.60%	With health insurance	89.60%
		Two or more races	5.10%	Cash public assistance	2.30%
Age Groups		Other	10.20%	Food stamp/SNAP	12.10%
Under 18	24.80%				
18-34	22.10%	**Education**		**Work**	
35-64	37.10%	H.S grad or less	44.60%	White Collar	28.70%
Over 64	16.00%	Some college	34.30%	Sales and Service	48.00%
		College Degree, 4 yr	13.90%	Blue Collar	23.30%
Military		Post grad	7.20%	Government	13.00%
Veteran/ Active Duty	11.60%				

2020 Pres. Vote	Biden	174,851	(51%)	Trump	161,363	(47%)		
2016 Pres. Vote	Clinton	137,070	(50%)	Trump	123,380	(45%)	Johnson	8,041	(3%)

Northern Las Vegas area: A vast majority of the land in Nevada is owned by the federal government—a constant source of tension with local officials, ranchers, loggers and miners. Their pursuits, frequently solitary and often ornery, shaped Nevada's culture from its earliest days. On the desolate frontier, speculation runs wild: Art Bell used to broadcast his popular radio show about the paranormal, aliens and other unexplained phenomena from tiny Pahrump. The federal government's top-secret aviation experiments at places like Area 51 on the Nellis Air Force Gunnery Range have stoked UFO lore to the point that adjoining Route 375 was rededicated as the Extraterrestrial Highway in 1996.

Anti-establishment views also flourish here in more mainstream ways. Nevada residents and most of its politicians have long opposed a nuclear waste repository 1,000 feet beneath Yucca Mountain, 90 miles northwest of Las Vegas. Congress finally approved the project in 2002. President Barack Obama shelved it and a commission recommended alternative storage options. With the arrival of President Donald Trump, Republicans—including some in Nevada—considered new options, though most Nevadans remained steadfast opponents. In 2020, none of the Democratic presidential candidates supported storage at Yucca. Even Trump, whose budgets consistently supported licensing at Yucca, had a change of heart—politically, at least.

The vast interior away from Las Vegas includes the 3-million-acre Nellis Air Force range. Also found here is the Energy Department's Nevada National Security Site, which was created by President Harry Truman. More than 800 underground tests of nuclear weapons were conducted here, as well as 100 above-ground tests, before they ended in 1962. The explosions left the Rhode Island-sized facility pockmarked with unstable "subsidence craters" as far as the eye can see. In a potentially significant twist, Nye County officials in 2015 approved the shipment of uranium waste from Oak Ridge National Laboratory in Tennessee to a landfill at the nuclear site. In December 2018, the Nevada attorney general sued the Trump administration after discovering it had secretly shipped plutonium to the site from South Carolina. Yucca Mountain also is located in Nye County.

The 4th District is a rural and suburban mix that sprawls across most of southern Nevada. It contains much of North Las Vegas and stretches north into the state's interior. The northern part of Clark County, as well as Esmeralda, Mineral, White Pine (and the city of Ely), Nye and Lincoln counties are in the district. Clark County, which dropped from 61 percent non-Hispanic White in 2000 to 42 percent in 2019, has become one of the largest majority-minority counties in the nation, with 32 percent Hispanic, 16 percent Black and 6 percent Asian. Nearly 90 percent of the district vote is cast in Clark. The outlying counties vote heavily Republican. Joe Biden took the 4th in 2020 by four percentage points. The district, which is 29 percent Hispanic and 14 percent Black, has become competitive.

NEW HAMPSHIRE

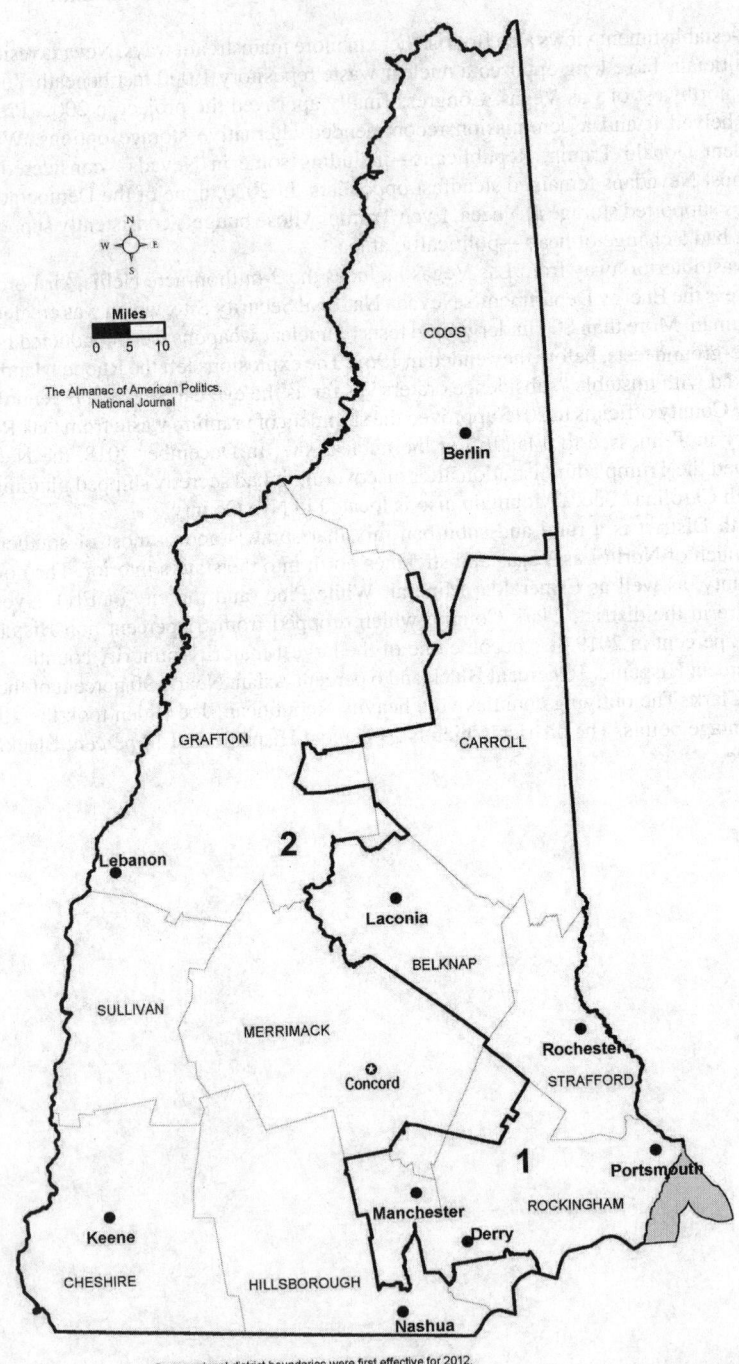

COOS

● Berlin

GRAFTON

CARROLL

2

● Lebanon

● Laconia

BELKNAP

SULLIVAN

MERRIMACK

⊕ Concord

● Rochester

STRAFFORD

1

● Portsmouth

ROCKINGHAM

● Manchester

● Derry

● Keene

CHESHIRE

HILLSBOROUGH

● Nashua

The Almanac of American Politics.
National Journal

N
W ◆ E
S

Miles
0   5   10

Congressional district boundaries were first effective for 2012.

Though it is home to just .41 percent of the nation's population, New Hampshire has historically become the center of the political universe every four years—the place where the contest for the American presidency is temporarily focused, and waged handshake by handshake. The state, once solidly Republican, has become more of a competitive hotbed, though for federal races it increasingly leans Democratic.

In June 1788, New Hampshire voted to ratify the Constitution and, as the ninth state to do so, put the document into effect. New Hampshire has been quirky from its beginnings. In a country that prides itself on its feistiness and freedom from outside direction, the state has always been even feistier and less fettered by authority. Before the Revolutionary War, New Hampshire was almost an outlaw colony, its great fortunes made by poachers in the king's forests and smugglers avoiding taxes. Boxed-in by bossy, Puritan Massachusetts on two sides (Maine was part of that colony and state until 1820), New Hampshire embodied the spirit of Revolutionary War General John Stark's words, " Live free or die." New Hampshire was the first colony with an independent government and was fighting the British even before the Minutemen stood at Lexington and Concord.

In the early republic, New England merchants turned inland and built textile mills along fast-flowing rivers. The Amoskeag Mills in Manchester, lining the Merrimack River for a mile, were once the largest cotton mills in the world, employing 17,000 people and producing enough cloth every two months to extend around the world. Around the mills grew Manchester, a city of red-brick dormitories and three-family frame houses filled with immigrants from Quebec, Ireland, Poland and Greece, set down amid villages of dirt roads and flinty Yankee farmers and mechanics. New Hampshire held to its traditions of local government and little external control, and for years refused to join most other states in enacting an income or sales tax, or to provide statewide guidance of schools and social services.

Instead, low taxes proved to be New Hampshire's fortune. From 1960 to 1990, the state's population grew 83 percent, more than double the national rate of 39 percent. During that time and through the 1990s, it had the fastest growth in the Northeast, attracting businesses from Massachusetts and other high-tax states. It became a location of choice for entrepreneurs and technology innovators. The bedraggled New Hampshire of 60 years ago, of poor Yankee farmers and French-Canadian mill hands, has been overtaken by one of the nation's most prosperous economic communities. The low taxes that spurred New Hampshire's growth would probably have been raised in the late 1960s or early 1970s, as they were in so many states at the time, but for the leadership of Manchester's Union Leader newspaper and its proprietor, William Loeb. The paper (now the New Hampshire Union Leader) insisted that governors and legislators "take the pledge" to vote for no sales or income tax. Almost all did.

The result was that education and social welfare remained local responsibilities. At the same time, New Hampshire boasted the highest average SAT scores in the country and had the brainpower to participate fully in New England's technology boom. The tech sector accounts for almost 14 percent of the state's gross domestic product and 10 percent of its jobs, easily putting it in the top 10 nationally, according to the Computing Technology Industry Association. The old Amoskeag Mills were converted to offices, and once-grimy Manchester became a high-tech center; another cluster of tech companies grew up near Dartmouth College in Hanover. Today, Fidelity Investments, BAE Systems, Fisher Scientific, Liberty Mutual and Timberland are major employers in the state.

New Hampshire's median income ranks eighth in the nation. During the Great Recession, the unemployment rate peaked at only 6.6 percent and, after that, the rate often ranked among the lowest of any state. The population grew 4.6 percent over the past decade, thanks in large part to in-migration from states such as Massachusetts and New York. In fact, only about 35 percent of voting-age residents were born in the state, putting New Hampshire more on par with high-turnover states like Nevada, Florida, and Arizona than its neighbors in the Northeast. But New Hampshire faces a "silver tsunami" —18.6 percent of residents are 65 or older, which ranks as the 10th highest of any state, and that number is on track to reach 30 percent by 2030. In 2019, New Hampshire recorded more deaths than births for the third straight year, an unprecedented stretch in state history. The state is just shy of 90 percent White, ranking fourth-highest nationally. The non-white population remains small: New Hampshire is 1.3 percent Black (one of only seven states with such a small percentage),

3.9 percent Hispanic and 2.6 percent Asian. But the minority population has been growing from this small base, especially the working-age population of 18 to 64.

Opioid use has been a major concern in recent years. In 2018, New Hampshire ranked sixth nationally in per capita overdose deaths. Despite New Hampshire's affluence, a combination of factors, including historically low spending for addiction treatment and the libertarian attitude embodied in the state's motto, has contributed to the problem. An estimated 280 million pills were supplied to the state between 2006 and 2012, or 36 pills per person annually; Interstate 93 north between the Massachusetts border and Manchester became littered with used needles.

New Hampshire's political architecture is quirky. The state House has 400 members, one representative for every 3,416 residents, with each lawmaker paid $100 a year. (California, by comparison, has one Assembly member for every 492,101 residents, and they are paid almost $115,000 annually.) Meanwhile, there's a five-member, elected "executive council" that is essentially a fourth branch of government—one that's able to stymie the governor, who as a result is structurally one of the nation's weakest. There's little impetus among voters to change the way the government works. "We've never had a major scandal, there's no widespread corruption and it's pretty transparent," Tom Rath, a former state attorney general and former Republican National Committee member, told Governing.

The lever with which this small state has sometimes moved the political world is its first-in-the-nation presidential primary. Residents are well-schooled in politics, willing to show up in the snow for town halls, and take the process seriously. The state fiercely defends its first-in-the-nation prerogative, led for decades by Secretary of State Bill Gardner. New Hampshire gave a huge boost to Dwight Eisenhower's candidacy in 1952 and prompted the retirement of Lyndon Johnson in 1968. It helped launch Jimmy Carter in 1976, Ronald Reagan in 1980, George H.W. Bush in 1988, and Bill Clinton in 1992, who had his "Comeback Kid" moment in the Granite State. But this primacy is under unprecedented assault, with some Democrats arguing that New Hampshire's predominantly White electorate (something it shares with the first caucus state, Iowa) offers skewed demographics for sorting out the presidential nomination of a demographically diverse party. Indeed, viewed through the traditional lens, Joe Biden's fifth-place finish in New Hampshire was considered "devastating" to his chances of winning the nomination, as The New York Times phrased it. Yet the former vice president bounced back two and a half weeks later in South Carolina, which has a more heavily Black primary electorate better suited to Biden's coalition. He ended up winning the nomination with ease.

From 1856 to World War II and beyond, New Hampshire voted mostly Republican, with Yankee Protestant farmers outvoting Irish and French-Canadian Catholic mill workers. Manchester and Nashua, formerly Democratic, trended toward Republicans. In the presidential elections from 1972 to 1988, the state voted on average 8 percent more Republican than the nation. But over the past three-plus decades, New Hampshire has become much more Democratic and has become important in presidential elections not just as a primary state but as a target in the general election, albeit one with a small number of electoral votes. Much of New Hampshire is part of the Boston metro area, and like most non-Southern metro areas, it trended Democratic in response to the Republicans' conservative stands on cultural issues. And if New Hampshire voters don't like broad-based taxes, many don't much like politicized religion either. In the 2016 general-election exit poll, 15 percent of New Hampshire respondents identified as born-again or evangelical Christians, below the national percentage of 26 percent. That said, the state's partisan transition has been somewhat unusual. Anti-tax migrants from Massachusetts have made the border towns of Windham, Pelham, Salem, Derry, and Londonderry some of the most Republican towns in the state. By contrast, some of the state's more outlying areas have turned blue due to an influx of affluent migrants seeking open space.

In 2016, Donald Trump came extraordinarily close to winning New Hampshire, losing to Hillary Clinton by less than half a percentage point, the second-closest state in the nation, percentage-wise. This narrow margin suggested that New Hampshire would once again be in play in 2020, and Trump visited the state for a few rallies. But the state's affluence and high education levels made it much more difficult for the president to win than the more heavily blue-collar states of the Midwest. Even New Hampshire's Republicans were not exactly enamored of Trump and his style of politics: The Union Leader endorsed Biden, saying Trump was "100 percent wrong for America" and that Biden would be a "thoughtful and pragmatic public servant." In the end, Biden increased the Democrats' statewide margin of victory to seven points, up from 2,736 votes in 2016 to 59,267 in 2020. Biden flipped four counties from Trump's column by shifting their margins toward the Democrats by between six and eight points: the populous Rockingham County (Portsmouth) and Hillsborough County (Manchester and Nashua), and the less-populated Carroll and Sullivan counties. Biden also expanded the Democrats' winning 2016 margins in Merrimack County (Concord) and Cheshire County (Keene). Republicans could take comfort in 2020's state level races: Not only did Republican Gov. Chris Sununu win reelection by a 2-to-1 margin, he helped flip both chambers of the legislature to GOP control, despite the Biden's victory.

Population		Race and Ethnicity		Income	
Total	1,359,711	White	92.60%	Median Income	77,933
Land area (sq. miles)	8,953	Black	1.60%	State Income Rank	8 out of 50
Pop/ sq mi	151.88	Latino	4.00%	Poverty Rate	7.30%
Born in state	40.60%	Asian	3.50%	With health insurance	93.70%
Age Groups		Two or more races	2.20%	Cash public assistance	2.20%
Under 18	18.80%	Other	1.00%	Food stamp/SNAP	7.6%
18-34	21.60%	**Education**		**Work**	
35-64	40.80%	H.S grad or less	34.80%	White Collar	42.50%
Over 64	18.60%	Some college	27.70%	Sales and Service	35.50%
Military		College Degree, 4 yr	22.90%	Blue Collar	21.90%
Veteran/ Active Duty	8.70%	Post grad	14.70%	Government	12.80%

Presidential Politics

2020 Primary (D)	Sanders (D)	76,384(26%)	Buttigieg (D)	72,454(24%)	Klobuchar (D)	58,714(20%)
	Warren (D)	27,429 (9%)	Biden (D)	24,944 (8%)		
2020 Pres. Vote	Biden (D)	424,937(53%)	Trump (R)	365,660(45%)		
2016 Pres. Vote	Clinton (D)	348,526(47%)	Trump (R)	345,790(46%)	Johnson (L)	30,777 (4%)

New Hampshire's official motto is "Live Free or Die," but it might as well be "Vote First or Die." The state has held its presidential primary first in the nation for a century, though its primaries have as often acted as a brake as a coronation for the eventual nominee. The state's voters haven't backed the Democratic nominee in a contested primary since John Kerry in 2004, though the last three GOP nominees (Donald Trump, Mitt Romney and John McCain) all won its primary. Trump is the only president this century who won a contested primary in the state.

New Hampshire began conducting the first-in-the-nation primary in 1920. Since 1952, when candidates' names were first put on the ballot, it has exerted inordinate influence on the presidential selection process. New Hampshire Secretary of State William Gardner has been in his job since 1976 and has the unilateral authority to select a primary date, a power he has wielded effectively to thwart any state that might attempt to crowd New Hampshire on the primary starting line. Like Iowa, New Hampshire's retail politics offers little-known candidates the ability to propel themselves into the national spotlight. Unlike Iowa, New Hampshire hasn't struggled to run its elections competently, but both states lack racial diversity, and a new challenge to their first-in-the-nation status looms in 2024.

Democratic registered voters surpassed Republicans for the first time in a decade in early 2020 because of a surge in new voter registrations ahead of the primaries. But "undeclared" registrants are the largest bloc of voters in the state, and made up 39 percent of registered voters during the last presidential election. They can vote in either party's presidential primary and on occasion have provided the margin of victory for both Democratic and Republican winners. The two largest cities, Manchester and Nashua, lean Democratic but sometimes vote Republican. Democratic strength is more pronounced in the state capital of Concord, the Seacoast towns of Portsmouth and Dover, and in clusters of towns around universities, like Durham (University of New Hampshire), Keene (Keene State College) and Hanover (Dartmouth College). The New Hampshire counties across the Connecticut River from Vermont are Democratic—a sort of East Vermont. Republican support can be found in the small towns and suburbs around Nashua and Manchester, where lower taxes have attracted Boston commuters, as well as the rural North Country, where towns have been decimated by the declining paper mill industry.

Hillary Clinton's narrow 2008 victory over Barack Obama set up a long, drawn-out primary battle; John McCain edged Mitt Romney that same year, reviving McCain's candidacy and helping him to the eventual nomination. Romney's 2012 win helped him recover from a virtual tie in Iowa to reassert his frontrunner status.

The 2016 primary was memorable for the state's voters, who turned to iconoclasts in both parties. Donald Trump campaigned vigorously in the state after his defeat in the Iowa caucuses, holding massive rallies. He also had a public spat with the Union Leader, the venerable voice of conservatism in New Hampshire, calling its publisher a "low-life" as the paper blasted him in front-page editorials. But the celebrity billionaire's brashness and anti-immigrant sentiment appealed to Republican primary-goers, especially in the old mill towns, and Trump defeated John Kasich, 35%-16%. In the top 25 wealthiest towns in New Hampshire, Trump's average vote was 31 percent. In the bottom 25 downscale towns, Trump's average vote was 40 percent. On the Democratic side, Clinton started out with a substantial lead, but Bernie Sanders' army of grassroots supporters, bolstered by home-state fans from next-door Vermont, fueled his dominant 60%-38% victory. Sanders scored heavily in university towns, but he also won working-class communities like Berlin and Somersworth.

Sanders returned in 2020 looking to repeat his 2016 showing. But he faced a much more crowded field. Elizabeth Warren, like him, represented a state that bordered New Hampshire and pulled support from the progressive wing of the party, and South Bend Mayor Pete Buttigieg's strong Iowa showing (he and Sanders virtually tied) gave him momentum heading into the primary. Buttigieg surged in the polls, but took a beating during the final debate before the primary, with Amy Klobuchar, Elizabeth Warren and Joe Biden attacking his lack of experience and record on race and policing. The pile-on benefited Sanders, who squeaked past Buttigieg 26%-24%, a win of less than 4,000 votes out of roughly 300,000 cast. Klobuchar finished third with 20 percent, siphoning suburban and moderate support from Buttigieg, while Warren and Biden finished a distant fourth and fifth at 9 percent and 8 percent. Buttigieg did best in more upscale Rockingham County on the Seacoast, which he carried, but Sanders won 12 of the state's 15 counties.

New Hampshire was a reliably Republican state for much of the 20th century, but since 1992, Republicans have carried the state in just one of eight presidential elections. It has often been close: Bill Clinton in 1992, George W. Bush in 2000, and John Kerry in 2004 won the state by just one point. Hillary Clinton defeated Trump by fewer than 3,000 votes, or three-tenths of 1 percent. In 2020, Trump's team promised to invest heavily in the state, listing it along with Minnesota as his best pick-up opportunities. But Trump's campaign never followed through, and the Union Leader took the unusual step of endorsing a Democrat. Biden won by a relatively comfortable 53%-45%. Biden improved on Clinton's margins across the state, with his biggest gains in the more upscale, higher-educated southern New Hampshire. He won 13 of the state's 15 counties, flipping upscale Rockingham and Hillsborough counties along the Massachusetts border as well as more rural Sullivan and Carroll counties further north.

Congressional Districts

117th Congress Lineup	2D	116th Congress Lineup	2D

New Hampshire's two congressional districts have had roughly the same boundaries since 1881, neatly separating the Merrimack River mill towns of Manchester and Nashua, the state's largest cities, along a mostly north-south line. That was originally done to split the Catholic Democratic vote, and for years the arrangement helped Republicans hold both districts. But lately, New Hampshire's movement away from its Yankee Republican roots and its high share of independent voters have led to wild gyrations: Both seats swung to Democrats in the wave of 2006, then to Republicans in 2010, and back to Democrats in 2012 and again in 2016. The flinty 2nd District along Vermont's border has crept more Democratic than the eastern 1st District, with its tax-averse Massachusetts exiles, but each remains competitive.

In the 1st District, four consecutive contests between Republican Frank Guinta and Democrat Carol Shea-Porter that resulted in four consecutive defeats of the incumbent were followed in 2018 by the victory of Democrat Chris Pappas, who has won two competitive contests. With their control of the legislature and the governor's office, Republicans signaled their plan to shift redistricting lines in ways that would make the Pappas district more Republican—for example, by adding towns along the Massachusetts border and reducing the vote in Manchester. That might encourage Pappas to accelerate his plans to run statewide.

Chris Sununu (R)

Elected 2016, term expires 2023, 2nd term; b. Nov. 5, 1974, Salem; Massachusetts Institute of Technology, BS 1998; Catholic; Married (Valerie); 3 children.

Elected Office: NH Executive Councilor, 2011-2017.

Professional Career: Engineer 1998-2006; Owner and Director, Sununu Enterprises 2006-2010

Office: 107 N. Main St. Concord, 03301; 603-271-2121; Fax: 603-271-7640
State Legislature: Senate: 10D, 14R **House:** 187D, 213R

Election Results

Election	Name (Party)	Vote (%)
2018 General	Chris Sununu (R)	302,764 (53%)
	Molly Kelly (D)	262,359 (46%)
2020 General	Chris Sununu (R)	516,609 (65%)
	Dan Feltes (D)	264,639 (33%)
2018 Primary	Chris Sununu (R)	91,025 (100%)

Prior winning percentage: 2018 (53%), 2016 (49%)

Chris Sununu, a member of one of New Hampshire's most durable political families, won a Democratic-held open seat in 2016 and then won reelection by increasing margins in 2018 and 2020. Sununu's victories mirrored the success of moderate Republican governors in the blue states of Massachusetts, Vermont and Maryland, and his win in 2020, by a 2-to-1 margin, not only came despite a victory by Joe Biden in the state's presidential race but also helped the GOP flip both legislative chambers.

Sununu, who entered office as the nation's youngest governor, is a son of John H. Sununu, the former three-term governor of New Hampshire and chief of staff to President George H.W. Bush, and Nancy Sununu, a former chairwoman of the New Hampshire Republican Party. He is the brother of former Sen. and Rep. John E. Sununu. His father was legendary for his prickly nature. "Unlike the reserved Yankee reputation of many New England pols, the Sununu family brings a different brand to elected politics: combat," James Pindell wrote in the Boston Globe. Though Chris Sununu was a native of Salem New Hampshire, he graduated from a suburban Virginia high school because his father was working in Washington at the time. As a youngster, Sununu attended National Governors Association meetings and hung out with Chelsea Clinton, whose father, future president Bill Clinton, was then governor of Arkansas. At the Massachusetts Institute of Technology, Sununu earned a degree in civil and environmental engineering, and for a decade he worked as an environmental engineer. He also served as CEO of Waterville Valley Ski Resort. His father didn't think that Chris, among his eight children, would end up going into politics, the Concord Monitor reported. But in 2010, Sununu won a seat on the state's executive council, an unusual "fourth branch of government" whose five members must approve most state contracts and confirm gubernatorial appointees. Sununu was reelected in 2012.

He set his sights higher when Maggie Hassan, the state's two-term Democratic governor, decided to challenge Republican Sen. Kelly Ayotte. Sununu joined a GOP primary field that included state Rep. Frank Edelblut, state Sen. Jeanie Forrester, and Manchester Mayor Ted Gatsas. The September primary ended up as mainly a race between Sununu and Edelblut, who ran an insurgent campaign to Sununu's right. Sununu edged Edelblut by fewer than 1,000 votes. Meanwhile, on the Democratic side, the easy winner was Colin Van Ostern, who like Sununu was an incumbent member of the executive council.

The two nominees shared an opposition to a state sales or income tax—a third-rail of New Hampshire politics—but Sununu proposed shrinking the size of government and instituting a right-to-work law, while Van Ostern supported making the state's Medicaid expansion permanent. Sununu irritated people on both sides of the abortion divide by voting as an executive councilor against renewing a state contract with Planned Parenthood in 2015, then later voting to restore the funding. In the end, Sununu won by two percentage points, or a little over 12,000 votes. That would ordinarily be considered a close race, but in the context of the other statewide contests that year it was a veritable landslide. In the presidential contest, Hillary Clinton won by fewer than 3,000 votes, while in the Senate race, Hassan won by about 1,000 votes.

In office, Sununu worked with a Republican-controlled legislature to enact a bill that got rid of licensing requirements for carrying a concealed pistol or revolver. Sununu achieved a significant victory when he signed a bill to partially fund all-day kindergarten, which conservative Republicans had opposed but which the public favored. Sununu also signed a bill to decriminalize marijuana. But he saw right-to-work legislation hit a roadblock in the state House, thanks to more than two dozen Republicans siding with Democrats and labor unions.

Sununu had another busy legislative year in 2018, with an ideologically mixed set of initiatives. He signed bills to bolster mental health services and child protection; to set water- and air-quality standards; to overhaul permitting for wetlands affected by development; to ban discrimination over gender identity; and to prohibit "gay conversion" therapy. Sununu pleased Democrats by signing a Medicaid expansion bill, which he had previously opposed, though he insisted on including work requirements. But the biggest controversy came when Sununu signed a GOP-backed bill to tighten voting requirements starting in 2019. The measure mandated that voters register their vehicles in the state and either have a valid New Hampshire driver's license or pledge to secure one within 60 days of casting a ballot. Sununu had originally opposed a similar bill, but relented when the state Supreme Court, in a 3-2 decision, cleared it as constitutional.

It's unusual for New Hampshire governors to be ousted after just one two-year term, and Sununu was no exception. State Sen. Molly Kelly won the 2018 Democratic primary against former Portsmouth mayor and 2016 gubernatorial candidate Steve Marchand. One of the strongest contrasts between Sununu and Kelly came in a debate, when the candidates were asked for an occasion when they bucked their party. Sununu cited the bills on kindergarten and Medicaid, but Kelly seemed stumped. Sununu won, 53%-46%, and managed to flip Merrimack County (Concord), which he'd lost in his 2016 run.

The bad news for Sununu was that the GOP lost control of both legislative chambers in the same election, forcing the governor to wield his veto stamp aggressively. In 2019, Sununu vetoed 57 bills; only two were overridden. The sustained vetoes included bills to enhance campaign-finance disclosure, to prohibit employers from using an applicant's credit history in hiring decisions, to enact paid family leave, and to ease the tenure process for public school teachers. He also vetoed a state budget that would have raised business taxes; he later reached a compromise with legislators that allowed the lower rates to continue as long as revenue targets were met. The legislature managed to override Sununu's vetoes of a bill to repeal the state's death penalty, which has not been used since 1939, and a bill to broaden prescribing standards for medical marijuana. Sununu also allowed a bill to become law without his signature that created an "other" category for gender on state driver's licenses. He had a split record on environmental initiatives, signing a bill to ban oil and gas drilling off the New Hampshire coast, but rejecting an invitation to join a regional climate compact that would enact a gasoline tax hike.

Sununu continued his vetoes into 2020, rejecting a minimum wage hike to $12, a more aggressive renewable-energy standard, and a paid family and medical leave measure. Amid national racial justice protests, Sununu signed a criminal justice bill that included a ban on police use of chokeholds. Sununu received broad public approval for his attempts to handle the coronavirus; through early 2021, New Hampshire had among the nation's lowest peak per-capita infection rates.

Sununu was aided in his 2020 reelection bid by his record on the coronavirus and his relative distance from President Donald Trump, at least for a Republican elected official; he easily defeated a primary challenge from the right. The Democrats, meanwhile, had a primary between state Senate Majority Leader Dan Feltes and executive councilor Andru Volinsky. Feltes, the more establishment candidate, prevailed, 52%-47%. He emerged from the state's September primary largely unknown and underfunded, and Sununu ended up winning by a massive 32-point margin, sweeping every county in the state after having lost three of them in 2018. Equally important, Sununu tied the battle for control of the legislature to his own electoral fate, something he hadn't done in 2018. The gamble paid off: The GOP took control of both chambers, suggesting Sununu can spend more time driving the agenda and less time vetoing bills during his third term. Some national Republicans hoped to see Sununu run against Hassan for the Senate in 2022. If that happens, it would be an epic face-off.

Jeanne Shaheen (D)

Elected 2008, term expires 2026, 3rd term, b. Jan 28, 1947; St. Charles, MO; Shippensburg University, B.A., 1969; University of MS, M.S., 1973; Protestant; Married (William Shaheen); 3 children; 7 grandchildren.

Elected Office: NH Senate, 1990-1996; NH Governor, 1997-2003.

Professional Career: Teacher, 1969-1971; A.A., University of NH, 1973-1974; Parents' Association Program Coordinator, 1982-1986; Manager, seasonal retail business, 1973-1976; Campaign Manager, Carter/Mondale NH presidential campaign, 1979- 80; Hart, NH pres. campaign, 1983-1984; McEachern, NH Governor campaign, 1986-1988.

DC Office: 506 HSOB 20510, 202-224-2841, Fax: 202-228-3194, shaheen.senate.gov
State Offices: Berlin, 603-752-6300; Claremont, 603-542-4872; Dover, 603-750-3004; Keene, 603-358-6604; Manchester, 603-647-7500; Nashua, 603-883-0196.

Committees: *Appropriations*: Commerce, Justice, Science & Related Agencies (Chmn); Department of Defense; Department of Homeland Security; DOL, HHS & Education & Related Agencies; Energy & Water Development; State, Foreign Operations & Related Programs. *Armed Services*: Emerging Threats & Capabilities; Readiness & Management Support; Seapower. *Ethics*. *Foreign Relations*: Europe & Regional Security Cooperation (Chmn); Internat'l Dev Instit & Internat'l Econ, Energy & Environ Policy; Near East, South Asia, Central Asia & Counterterrorism; West Hem Crime Civ Sec Dem Rights & Women's Issues. *Small Business & Entrepreneurship*.

Group Ratings

	ADA	ACLU	AFL-CIO	LCV	COC	HAFA	ACU	CFG	FRC
2020	-	85%	-	92%	-	0%	4%	-	-
2019	100%	C	100%	100%	67%	C	4%	0%	0%

Almanac Ratings 2019-2020

	Economy	Social	Foreign	Composite
Liberal	97%	97%	49%	81%
Conservative	3%	3%	51%	19%

Key Votes of the 116th Congress

1. EPA clean energy rules	Y	5. Russia sanctions	Y	9. Barr as Atty. General	N
2. U.S./Mex./Can. trade deal	Y	6. Troops in SYR, AFG	Y	10. Spending at the border	Y
3. Cut unemployment benefits	N	7. Veto arms sales to Saudis	Y	11. Coney Barrett to Sup. Ct.	N
4. Shelton to Fed Reserve	N	8. Defense $$$, veto override	Y	12. Electoral College objections	N

Election Results

Election	Name (Party)	Vote (%)		Cand. Spent	Ind. Exp. Support	Ind. Exp. Oppose
2020 General	Jeanne Shaheen (D)............................	450,778	(57%)	$16,760,410	$285,628	$402,105
	Corky Messner (R)............................	326,229	(41%)	$3,893,089	$88,676	$21,373
	Justin O'Donnell (L).........................	18,421	(2%)	$4,449		
2020 Primary	Jeanne Shaheen (D)............................	142,012	(94%)			

Prior winning percentages: 2014 (52%), 2008 (52%); Governor: 2000 (49%), 1998 (66%), 1996 (57%)

Democrat Jeanne Shaheen, New Hampshire's senior senator, is the first woman in U.S. history to be elected both governor and senator, as well as the first elected to either of those offices in New Hampshire. She has been a political fixture in the Granite State for nearly half a century—first coming to notice not as a candidate but as a behind-the-scenes political operative, engineering victories for Jimmy Carter and Gary Hart in the state's first-in-the-nation presidential primary. Shaheen, 74, was handily elected in 2020 to a third Senate term in a contest that national Republicans had initially eyed as a pickup opportunity. Earlier in the election cycle, she was publicly touted by now-President Joe Biden as a potential vice presidential running mate. But she asked to be taken out of contention once Biden had secured the Democratic nomination and had begun vetting running mates, telling the Biden team privately—and later reiterating publicly—that she wanted to remain on Capitol Hill.

Shaheen has been a reliable Democratic vote, adept at balancing partisan loyalties with the reality that she represents a state that has become a hypersensitive political bellwether. She once taught a university course on how elected officials can overcome partisanship, and she has sought to put her lessons into practice by frequently reaching across the aisle in her legislative efforts. She has acquired a reputation as a disciplined politician who stays on message and refrains from headline-grabbing sound bites. Her low-key style has obscured her increasing influence, enhanced further in early 2021 when Democrats captured the Senate majority and Shaheen became chair of the Appropriations Subcommittee on Commerce, Justice, Science and Related Agencies. Earlier, as a member of the Foreign Relations Committee, Shaheen in the fall of 2016 was the first senator to call for hearings into allegations of Russian interference in that year's presidential race, and she strongly supported legislation the following year to tighten sanctions against Russia. The Russians took notice: They placed Shaheen on a "blacklist" and refused to grant her a visa to travel to their country as part of a congressional delegation.

Born Cynthia Jeanne Bowers, she grew up in the suburbs of St. Louis Missouri, where her father was in the shoe manufacturing business and her mother was a church secretary. Shaheen can trace her Native American lineage to Pocahontas. "I actually have the family tree to show that," she told CNN in 2017. Shaheen graduated from Shippensburg College in Pennsylvania with a degree in education; after teaching for a couple of years, she earned a master's degree in political science from the University of Mississippi. She was raised in a Republican family and cast her first presidential vote for Richard Nixon in 1968. But she registered as a Democrat while at Shippensburg, where her activities reflected the campus activism of the era: She successfully challenged a curfew that applied to women but not men.

While in Mississippi, Shaheen came to admire Carter, then Georgia's governor, for his efforts to foster racial integration. In 1973, she moved to New Hampshire, where she worked as a teacher and ran a seasonal silver and leather business with her husband, attorney Bill Shaheen, a New Hampshire native who has long been a behind-the-scenes political power in the state. The Shaheens were among Carter's earliest New Hampshire supporters when, in 1975, the former Georgia governor began laying the groundwork for his long-shot presidential bid. Carter won the 1976 New Hampshire primary, and, after winning the White House, appointed Bill Shaheen as U.S. attorney for New Hampshire. In 1980, Jeanne Shaheen was Carter's state campaign director and guided him to a win of 10 percentage points in the primary over the insurgent candidacy of Massachusetts Sen. Ted Kennedy. Four years later, another long shot, Colorado Sen. Hart, recruited Shaheen to manage his New Hampshire presidential primary effort. Hart defeated the Democratic frontrunner, Walter Mondale, by 9 points.

At the time, Democrats had limited success in winning statewide office in then-solidly Republican New Hampshire. Shaheen oversaw two unsuccessful efforts to elect Democrat Paul McEachern as governor in the mid-to-late 1980s. In 1990, I decided all the men I'd been working for hadn't gotten it done, so I needed to run myself," she told CNN years later. She won election to the state Senate, where she supported expanded health care coverage and term limits on federal and state legislators. In 1996, Shaheen ran for governor and faced State Board of Education Chairman Ovide Lamontagne, a strong conservative. Shaheen took what is referred to in New Hampshire as "the pledge"—a promise to oppose an income or sales tax. Such a vow had long been politically sacrosanct in a state that has prided itself as the only one in the nation not to impose a broad-based tax. Shaheen won 57%-39%, becoming just the fifth Democrat in more than 100 years to serve as governor.

In 1997, a state Supreme Court ruling outlawed New Hampshire's system of local school financing. Shaheen proposed increasing revenues through slot machine gambling and a hike in the tobacco tax, but the court invalidated her plan in 1998. That year, when her two-year term was up, Shaheen was reelected with 66 percent of the vote. She abandoned her pledge to oppose an income or sales tax but was still reelected in 2000—but with only a 5-point margin. The controversy over school funding continued, and the GOP-controlled Legislature refused to pass either an income or sales tax.

Shaheen ran for the Senate in 2002, as Republicans faced a divisive primary in which Rep. John Sununu, son and namesake of a former governor and White House chief of staff, defeated the incumbent, Robert Smith, 53%-45%. Smith had angered GOP leaders when, after a failed bid for the 2000 Republican presidential nomination, he temporarily left the party. Shaheen backed President George W. Bush's tax cuts and the invasion of Iraq. But her abandoning of the tax pledge came back to haunt her, and Sununu won 51%-46%. In the 2004, Shaheen served as national chair of Democrat John Kerry's presidential campaign and was credited with reviving his campaign in the early primaries—including helping orchestrate a victory in New Hampshire.

After Kerry's general election loss, Shaheen became director of the Kennedy School of Government's Institute of Politics at Harvard University—insisting that she had no interest in running for office again. But after the 2006 election, New Hampshire Democrats pressed her to seek a rematch with Sununu. Nearly a year later, Shaheen quit her job at Harvard and announced she was running. While the 2008 Senate campaign had the same candidates as six years earlier, it took place in a very different political environment. In 2002, Shaheen had emphasized areas in which she agreed with Bush and congressional Republicans; in 2008, she emphasized her disagreements with them. Shaheen led in polls throughout the campaign, but Sununu rebounded after gas prices reached $4 a gallon, and he criticized Shaheen's opposition to offshore oil drilling. But he lost ground in October 2008 after voting for a $700 billion bailout of the financial industry, which Shaheen, like many no incumbent candidates in both parties, opposed. This time, Shaheen won—52%-45%—for the first Democratic Senate victory in New Hampshire since 1974.

Although Shaheen has stuck with her party's leadership on most major votes, Almanac rankings have placed her in the less liberal half of the Senate Democratic Caucus. Her commitment to reaching across the aisle was underscored by a decade long collaboration with Ohio Republican Sen. Rob Portman on energy efficiency legislation. The original bill, introduced in 2011, sought to increase energy efficiency in buildings by offering mortgage incentives and getting the federal government more involved in working with manufacturers. Finally, in spring 2015, a stripped-down version of the bill was signed into law by President Barack Obama. Shaheen and Portman didn't give up there, introducing another energy efficiency bill in 2019; elements of that initiative were incorporated into comprehensive energy legislation that cleared Congress at the end of 2020.

But a provision in the Shaheen-Portman bill for stricter building codes—which, according to an independent analysis, would have reduced carbon dioxide emissions in an amount equivalent to taking 3.1 million cars off the road annually—was stripped from the broader energy package earlier in 2020 as it moved through Senate committee. The two senators made subsequent efforts to revive the provision during Senate floor debate, but came up short. The building codes provision would not have become mandatory unless adopted by states and municipalities; it was praised by environmental groups as well as the U.S. Chamber of Commerce. But the National Association of Home Builders was strongly opposed, and Shaheen blamed that organization for scuttling it. "This special interest group should not be allowed to derail meaningful bipartisan action on energy efficiency in Congress," she told the Washington Post.

Shaheen got several provisions into the Affordable Care Act during her first year on Capitol Hill, including one to close a loophole that had allowed drug companies to avoid competition from generic drugs. On another health issue, Shaheen's interest has been personal: Her granddaughter has Type 1 diabetes and participated in a medical trial for an artificial pancreas. Shaheen has been involved in numerous efforts to highlight the problems associated with juvenile diabetes and worked to persuade the Food and Drug Administration to issue "clear and reasonable guidance" on artificial pancreas devices. She has refrained from embracing the "Medicare for All" plan pushed by her Vermont neighbor, Sen. Bernie Sanders, and other leading progressives. But she backed an unsuccessful effort to add a "public option" when the Affordable Care Act was passed, and, in early 2019, introduced legislation to give those between ages 50 and 64 the option of buying into Medicare.

Throughout her second term, Shaheen focused on a problem that had become an epidemic in her state: opioid addiction. New Hampshire ranked third nationally in per capita deaths from drug overdoses, according to the Centers for Disease Control and Prevention. While the Comprehensive Addiction and Recovery Act sponsored by Shaheen was signed into law in July 2016, it contained no immediate funding. However, most of that bill's initiatives were funded six months later when Obama, as one of his last major acts in office, signed the 21st Century Cures Act, with $1 billion to combat opioid addiction over a two-year period.

In early 2018, Shaheen and other members of her state's congressional delegation successfully pushed to boost funding to combat opioid addiction to $6 billion nationally as part of a bipartisan budget deal. She has since pressed for increased funding as well as greater flexibility for how states can use the money, including in a letter she sent Biden in early 2021 soon after he moved into the White House. As the COVID-19 pandemic took hold a year earlier, Shaheen, as a member of the Small Business Committee, was part of a small bipartisan group that quickly came to agreement on the Paycheck Protection Program. Enacted as part of an economic stimulus package in late March 2020, the PPP disbursed $525 billion in forgivable loans over the next four months in an effort to preserve small businesses and keep their employees paid amid lockdowns and social distancing.

Shaheen has not shied away from the culture wars. As a member of the Armed Services Committee, she got provisions into the 2013 defense authorization bill to repeal a policy denying military women abortion coverage in cases of rape or incest. She got wording into the fiscal 2016 defense authorization bill to increase access to birth control for women covered by military health programs. "Almost 15 percent of our military are now women, but the military has not developed a comprehensive program to make sure they have access to family planning, contraception and counseling," Shaheen said. Another bill that became law in 2016—co-authored by Shaheen and Democratic Sens. Richard Blumenthal of Connecticut and Patrick Leahy of Vermont—required that rape kits be preserved for the entire relevant statute of limitations and that victims be notified in writing 60 days before the kits are destroyed. While the requirement applied only to federal cases, the legislation included incentives for states to give survivors more information at the time they report sexual crimes.

In late 2017, President Donald Trump signed a Shaheen-authored bill titled the "Women, Peace and Security Act," requiring the president to submit a strategy to Congress "to improve the participation of women in peace and security processes, conflict prevention, peace building, and decision-making institutions." It reflected concerns by Shaheen—the only woman on the 22-member Foreign Relations panel—about male dominance in executive branch positions dealing with foreign policy. When Trump nominated Gina Haspel to lead the CIA in early 2018, Shaheen in was among just six Senate Democrats who voted to confirm her—allowing Haspel to squeak through on a 54-45 vote to become the CIA's first female director. Most Democrats refused to support Haspel because of her involvement in the agency's torture program after 9/11. While calling torture inconsistent with the nation's values, Shaheen said she had "been impressed by the strong support for [Haspel's] nomination within the agency and the respect she has earned from her many years of service."

Shaheen's concerns about cybersecurity led her to sponsor legislation, which became law in 2017, to bar federal government use of software from Russia's Kaspersky Lab—an enterprise she described as having "extensive ties to Russian intelligence." Barely two weeks after the bill was signed into law, Russia denied Shaheen a visa to travel there. The congressional delegation was cancelled after two Republicans on the Foreign Relations panel also scheduled to go called it off in solidarity with Shaheen.

With a WMUR/University of New Hampshire poll in February 2013 giving her a 59 percent approval rating, Shaheen was an early favorite to win a second term the next year. But the dynamics of the race changed when former Massachusetts Sen. Scott Brown announced he would run for the Republican nomination. Four years earlier, he had capitalized on public unease over passage of the Affordable Care Act to win a special election to fill the Senate seat left vacant by Sen. Ted Kennedy's death, but he was ousted in 2012 by Democrat Elizabeth Warren. Brown and his wife then sold their Massachusetts home and moved to New Hampshire, where they long had owned a vacation home. His Senate bid gained traction by seeking to tie Shaheen, a co-chair of the 2012 Obama campaign and a leading Obama surrogate that year, to the president. Brown repeatedly charged she had voted with Obama's position 99 percent of the time; Obama, despite having twice won New Hampshire, had seen his popularity there nosedive. Shaheen hung on to win 52%-48%, blocking Brown's bid to become the first person in 135 years to represent two different states in the Senate.

As Shaheen prepared to seek reelection in 2020, her biggest potential threat appeared to come from popular two-term Republican Gov. Chris Sununu—brother of the man whom Shaheen had ousted 12 years earlier. With two polls showing Shaheen and Sununu neck and neck in a hypothetical matchup, Sununu in March 2019 pointedly refused to rule out a run and called Shaheen"very vulnerable." But Sununu announced a couple of months later that he would seek a third two-year term as governor. Trump then all but endorsed his former 2016 campaign manager, Corey Lewandowski, for the Senate nomination. That development hardly thrilled many Republicans in New Hampshire, where Trump's approval rating had dropped precipitously since he came within half a percentage point of winning the state in 2016. Lewandowski—a Trump acolyte and far-right firebrand—toyed with running for months. But at the end of 2019, Lewandowski said he had decided against a Senate bid.

That left multimillionaire attorney Bryant "Corky" Messner and retired Army Gen. Don Bolduc as the leading contenders in what turned into a bitter GOP primary. Messner—a long-time Colorado resident who did not register to vote in New Hampshire until 2018—had to fend off charges of carpetbagging; he said he had bought a second home in the state a dozen years earlier. After an endorsement by Trump, Messner won the nod, 50.5%-42.5%. The Washington Post's "FactChecker" called out Messner for boasting about a Denver foundation he had started to award scholarships to underprivileged students. In fact, only one scholarship had been awarded in 10 years; the largest chunk of largesse from the foundation had gone to an elite school Messner's sons had attended.

For his part, Messner charged that Shaheen had grown wealthy while in office—a reprise of charges leveled at her during the 2014 campaign that another fact-checking entity, PolitiFact, had found "mostly false." He also contended that Shaheen had grown out of touch while in Washington, declaring, "She comes back to New Hampshire and tries to pretend she's a moderate; she's not a moderate." But he made little headway. She trounced Messner in November by 17 points—twice as much as Biden's victory margin in the battleground state.

Maggie Hassan (D)

Elected 2016, term expires 2022, 1st term, b. Feb 27, 1958; Boston, MA; Brown University, A.B., 1980; Northeastern University Law School, J.D., 1985; United Church of Christ; Married (Thomas Hassan); 2 children.

Elected Office: NH Senate, 2004-2010; Majority Leader, NH Senate, 2008-2010; NH Governor, 2013-2016.

Professional Career: Information officer, MA Department of Social Services, 1980-1982; Practicing attorney, 1985-1992, 1996-2009; Assistant General Counsel, Brigham and Women's Hospital/Partners Healthcare, 1993-1996.

DC Office: 324 HSOB 20510, 202-224-3324, Fax: 202-228-0581, hassan.senate.gov

State Offices: Berlin, 603-752-6190; Concord, 603-622-2204; Manchester, 603-622-2204; Nashua, 603-880-3314; Portsmouth, 603-433-4445.

Committees: *Finance*: Energy, Natural Resources & Infrastructure; Health Care; Social Security, Pensions & Family Policy. *Health, Education, Labor & Pensions*: Children & Families; Primary Health & Retirement Security. *Homeland Security & Government Affairs*: Emerging Threats & Spending Oversight (Chmn); Investigations. *Joint Economic. Veterans' Affairs*.

Group Ratings

	ADA	ACLU	AFL-CIO	LCV	COC	HAFA	ACU	CFG	FRC
2020	-	69%	-	92%	-	0%	4%	-	-
2019	95%	C	100%	100%	68%	C	5%	0%	0%

Almanac Ratings 2019-2020

	Economy	Social	Foreign	Composite
Liberal	97%	97%	67%	87%
Conservative	3%	3%	34%	13%

Key Votes of the 116th Congress

1. EPA clean energy rules Y	5. Russia sanctions Y	9. Barr as Atty. General N
2. U.S./Mex./Can. trade deal Y	6. Troops in SYR, AFG Y	10. Spending at the border Y
3. Cut unemployment benefits N	7. Veto arms sales to Saudis Y	11. Coney Barrett to Sup. Ct. N
4. Shelton to Fed Reserve N	8. Defense $$$, veto override Y	12. Electoral College objections N

Election Results

Election	Name (Party)	Vote (%)		Cand. Spent	Ind. Exp. Support	Ind. Exp. Oppose
2016 General	Maggie Hassan (D)	354,649	(48%)	$18,399,896		
	Kelly Ayotte (R)	353,632	(48%)	$17,281,997	$5,671,191	$52,308,296
	Aaron Day (I)	17,742	(2%)			
2016 Primary	Maggie Hassan (D)	Unopposed				

Prior winning percentages: 2016 (48%), Governor: 2014 (53%), 2012 (55%)

When national Democrats persuaded Gov. Maggie Hassan to forgo a bid for a third term to run against Republican Sen. Kelly Ayotte, it marked one of their biggest recruiting coups of the 2016 election cycle. Ayotte and Hassan were among New Hampshire's most popular politicians, and the months-long recruitment of Hassan was key to Democrats' plans to retake the Senate. While they fell short that year, recruiting Hassan still paid off, as she was one of just two Democrats to win a Senate race against an incumbent Republican in 2016—victories that proved crucial when the party took control of the chamber in 2020 by the narrowest possible margin.

With Democrats now seeking to retain and expand that 50-50 Senate majority, Hassan's expected bid for a second term is again shaping up as a marquee contest. As the 2022 election cycle got underway, Republican Gov. Chris Sununu—whom polls have shown to be New Hampshire's most popular politician—declared himself "definitely open" to running for Senate in lieu of reelection. The possibility of a Hassan-Ayotte rematch also loomed.

Hassan's narrow 2016 victory made her only the second woman in U.S. history to have served both as a governor and a senator. The first was Hassan's senior colleague, Democratic Sen. Jeanne Shaheen, whom Hassan considers a mentor. In a chamber where relationships between senators from the same state are sometimes marred by past rivalries and future ambitions, the two women representing the Granite State are notable for their closeness. They have remarkably similar voting records and operating styles: Both are disciplined politicians who choose their words carefully. During her race against Ayotte, Hassan at times was so disciplined that she was dinged for repeating talking points and came off as stiff in media interviews, according to the Concord Monitor.

Born Margaret Wood, Hassan grew up in politics. Raised in the upscale Boston suburb of Lincoln, she was the daughter of Robert C. Wood, a MIT political science professor who was an adviser to John F. Kennedy during the 1960 presidential campaign. Wood later played a leading role in creating the Department of Housing and Urban Development under President Lyndon B. Johnson before serving as president of the University of Massachusetts and superintendent of the Boston school system. A stream of influential guests coursed through the Wood household, and dinner conversations often focused on current events. "My father used to actually go around the table person by person and ask them what they thought, so everybody from family members to our guests were expected to either think out loud or have an opinion, and we did," Hassan recalled to the New Hampshire Union Leader. Hassan earned her undergraduate degree at Brown University and her law degree at Northeastern University. She practiced law in Boston, including a stint as a corporate attorney for Brigham and Women's Hospital.

She met her husband, Tom Hassan, at Brown. The Hassans' connection to New Hampshire dates to the late 1980s when Tom Hassan was appointed to the faculty of the Phillips Exeter Academy, an elite prep school that he later headed. The couple have two children, one of whom, an adult son, has cerebral palsy. Maggie Hassan credits him with inspiring her career in public service, which began in 1999 when then-Gov. Shaheen appointed Hassan as a citizen adviser to the state's Adequacy in Education and Finance Commission. Hassan had become involved in disability rights activism while working to ensure the elementary school attended by her son, Ben, could accommodate his needs. She often has recalled her feelings while watching her son, then 3, get picked up by the bus for his first day of pre-school. "That really got me focused on the work that other families and advocates and elected leaders had done so that, on that day, my son wasn't in an institution," she told Roll Call. Ben Hassan was featured in the first TV ad of his mother's 2016 Senate campaign.

In 2002, Hassan lost a state Senate contest to incumbent Republican Russell Prescott but came back two years later and beat him—serving six years until he reclaimed the seat in 2010. During her three terms, Hassan held several leadership positions, culminating with majority leader. One of her initial accomplishments was helping to pass a bill offering universal kindergarten: At the time, New Hampshire was the only state in the nation without such a law. As majority leader, she proposed a bill in 2010 to set up a commission to regulate health care costs. As the Affordable Care Act was being debated in Washington, state Republicans jabbed at the idea as "Maggie Care." The bill that passed established the commission, but without authority to limit rates. A year earlier, Hassan was more successful on the issue of same-sex marriage. Several of her Democratic colleagues were reluctant to tackle the subject, but Hassan persuaded them to move ahead—and she played an integral role in New Hampshire becoming one of the first states to legalize same-sex marriage, six years before the Supreme Court ruling that recognized such unions nationwide.

After Democratic Gov. John Lynch announced in September 2011 that he would not seek a fifth two-year term, Hassan entered the gubernatorial race. She backed a proposed casino on the Massachusetts border to raise revenue in a state that stands alone in its lack of a broad-based tax. Hassan easily won a three-way Democratic primary; her Republican opponent in November was attorney Ovide Lamontagne, a hard-line conservative who had run unsuccessfully for governor in 1996 against Shaheen and then lost to Ayotte in the 2010 Senate primary. President Barack Obama's strong New Hampshire showing in his 2012 reelection bid helped Hassan to a 55%-43% victory. A historic milestone accompanied Hassan's victory: For the next two years, New Hampshire was the first and only state to have a female governor and an all-female congressional delegation.

Taking office with a state House that had been returned to Democratic control but a Senate that remained in Republican hands, Hassan stressed the need for bipartisanship: It paid off when the two-year budget that she signed her first year passed the Senate unanimously and cleared the 400-member House with fewer than 20 dissenting votes. She made good on one campaign vow when her first budget restored the cuts made to the university system during the Republicans' 2011-2012 control of the Legislature. In her second year in office, Hassan secured bipartisan support to expand Medicaid under the Affordable Care Act. The expansion allowed 50,000 low-income New Hampshire residents to receive subsidized health care and covered substance abuse treatment in a state besieged by heroin and opioid addiction.

In 2014, Hassan faced Republican Walt Havenstein, the former CEO of defense contractor BAE Systems—an international firm with a significant presence in New Hampshire. He pumped $2 million of his own money into his bid. But Hassan prevailed 53%-47% during an election cycle inhospitable to Democrats nationally. Hassan had a bumpy second term, as she faced an all-Republican Legislature. She vetoed bills that would have curbed the Common Core education standards and allowed the concealed carrying of firearms without a license. She also had to deal with a protracted budget impasse in her second year. On the issue that had brought her into politics, she signed the nation's first law banning sub-minimum wages for people with disabilities.

In spring 2015, a string of favorable poll results fueled continuing speculation that she would challenge Ayotte; she announced her Senate bid that fall. First elected in the Republican wave year of 2010, Ayotte was facing the voters again in a purple state that has tended to skew blue in presidential years. During Ayotte's first term, her voting record was moderate, and she sought to play up her differences with her party's leadership on issues ranging from immigration to air pollution. Alluding to Hassan, Ayotte told Boston magazine: "I'm not hesitant to take on my party or the other side. I don't see that same level of independence from her." Hassan, in turn, pointed to her dealings with legislatures partly or totally under Republican control. "I have a real record of working with members of the opposite party, having disagreements with them, to be sure, but then getting results," Hassan told USA Today.

As polls gave Democratic presidential nominee Hillary Clinton a significant lead over GOP nominee Donald Trump, Hassan relentlessly sought to tie Ayotte to Trump. Ayotte, meanwhile, struggled to appeal to both Trump's base and the independents who make up 40 percent of the state's electorate. Ayotte said she would "support" Trump but not "endorse" him—a semantical somersault that elicited reactions ranging from puzzlement to ridicule. In early October, the "Access Hollywood" tape—on which can be heard Trump bragging about sexual assault—emerged, prompting Ayotte to disavow him and write in the name of GOP vice presidential nominee Mike Pence for president. On Election Day, Hassan won by just over 1,000 votes out of more than 708,000 cast, with Clinton's victory margin in the state far narrower than polling had indicated. Total spending by the Senate candidates and outside groups exceeded $131 million, an astounding sum for New Hampshire.

During Hassan's first year in the Senate, Almanac vote ratings scored her as slightly more liberal than Shaheen, although both have placed well within the centrist wing of the Democratic Caucus. In voting on 22 nominees for Cabinet-level and other top positions in the Trump administration, the two had identical records: Each opposed confirmation of half of Trump's nominees. Early on, Hassan gained notice during the confirmation hearing of Betsy DeVos, Trump's choice for Education secretary. As a member of the Health, Education, Labor and Pensions Committee, Hassan pressed DeVos on disability rights. When DeVos said enforcement was best left to the states, Hassan pounced. She asked DeVos if she were aware that such matters were governed by a federal law, the Individuals with Disabilities Education Act. "I may have confused it," DeVos said. Hassan shot back, "I have to say, I'm concerned that you seem so unfamiliar with it."

Hassan worked within the HELP Committee to address the controversy over "surprise medical bills"—invoices that that far exceed patients' expectations after a constituent alerted her to the problem. In one of a number of her bipartisan collaborations, Hassan teamed with a fellow committee member, Republican Bill Cassidy of Louisiana, to introduce legislation in late 2018 on the issue.

The bill sought to require health plans and providers to charge lower "in-network" fees for emergency services and certain nonemergency care provided by "out-of-network" facilities or personnel. House and Senate negotiators in late 2020 reached agreement on a similar measure. Hassan and Cassidy hailed the development, declaring in a joint statement: "For far too long, our constituents have done everything right at the doctor's office or hospital yet still found themselves stuck with surprise medical bills, sometimes to the tune of tens of thousands of dollars. … We are proud that our efforts have now led to the inclusion of legislation to end surprise medical billing in this year's government funding agreement."

In April 2017, after a video showing a passenger being dragged off an overbooked United Airlines flight went viral, Hassan—then a member of the Commerce, Science and Transportation Committee —introduced legislation to strengthen passenger rights. It became law as part of a Federal Aviation Administration authorization bill signed by Trump in late 2018. Hassan also succeeded in adding provisions to the FAA measure to ensure air travel accommodations consider the needs of all people with disabilities. She left the Commerce panel in 2019 to join the Finance Committee.

After 2020 Democratic presidential nominee Joe Biden announced he would select a woman as his running mate, he considered and vetted Hassan before ultimately choosing another senator, Kamala Harris of California.

On the Senate Homeland Security and Governmental Affairs Committee, Hassan has focused on cybersecurity: In early 2021, she became chair of the Subcommittee on Emerging Threats and Spending Oversight. The previous year in the minority, Hassan—working with Republican John Cornyn of Texas—placed a provision in the annual defense authorization bill deploying cybersecurity coordinators in every state. These coordinators, employed by the federal Department of Homeland Security, are responsible for facilitating communication between federal officials and state and local authorities. In late 2020, Hassan and Cornyn introduced a measure to enable states to utilize the National Guard to improve cybersecurity after what Hassan termed "unprecedented cyberattacks" amid the COVID-19 pandemic. "Cyberattacks can jeopardize our national security, shut down electrical grids, and threaten the operations of our hospitals and schools—we must ensure that the National Guard can help with these types of threats just like any other threat that states face," Hassan said.

One cybersecurity breach occurred uncomfortably close to home. In mid-2019, a former systems administrator in Hassan's Washington office was sentenced to four years in prison for hacking into Senate computers and releasing personal information about five Republican senators. His action was apparently spurred by anger over their roles in the confirmation hearings for Supreme Court Justice Brett Kavanaugh the previous year. The former aide—after being fired from Hassan's staff in 2018 —repeatedly used an ex-colleague's key to enter the office and install equipment that enabled him to download a large volume of data from the Senate computer system, Politico reported. Through a spokesman, Hassan praised law enforcement officers and prosecutors for pursuing the matter.

Hassan faced an issue that had emerged as a crisis when she was governor: opioid abuse. With New Hampshire ranking third nationally in per capita deaths from drug overdoses, she sought to turn up the heat on the White House. In an op-ed in Time magazine published in February 2018 —three months after the release of a report by a Trump-appointed commission on the issue—Hassan wrote, "We have seen almost no action from the administration on the commission's recommendations, and the Trump administration has not been willing to lead in pushing for additional federal resources."

Shortly afterward, as part of a two-year bipartisan spending deal on Capitol Hill, Hassan and Shaheen boosted funding to combat the opioid epidemic to $6 billion nationally, up from $1 billion the previous two years. Hassan and other New Hampshire legislators changed the formula for allocating funds to translate into a more than seven-fold increase in money directed to their state to fight opioid addiction.

Just prior to the 2020 elections, Hassan participated in a New Hampshire media call on behalf of the Democratic candidate for governor, state Senate Majority Leader Dan Feltes—during which she tore into Sununu. "We need a governor who is always going to fight to protect and strengthen access to quality, affordable care," she said, referring to the Affordable Care Act. "Not a governor who supports Donald Trump's legislative efforts to undermine the law." Immediately after trouncing Feltes on Election Day, Sununu appeared to fire a warning shot—via a Twitter message by one of his key advisers, Paul Collins: "Hey @SenatorHassan @Maggie_Hassan, what is it like serving in the united states senate these days? asking for a friend."

Sununu—son of former Gov. John H. Sununu and a brother of former Sen. John E. Sununu— also toyed with a run against Shaheen in 2020 but opted to seek reelection. Chris Sununu—who one poll in early 2021 showed with approval ratings 20 points higher than Hassan's—said during a radio appearance that it would be "well into 2021" before he decides whether to run for Senate, seek a fourth two-year term as governor, or pursue other options. If Sununu stays put, a second Hassan-Ayotte race would seem to be in the offing, as Ayotte was renewing her political profile after four years away from elected office.

Chris Pappas (D)

Elected 2018, 2nd term, b. Jun 04, 1980; Manchester, NH; Harvard College, B.A., 2002; Greek Orthodox; Single.

Elected Office: NH House, 2002-2006; Hillsborough County Treasurer, 2007-2011; NH Executive Council, 2013-18.

Professional Career: Co-Owner & Operator, Puritan Restaurant.

DC Office: 323 CHOB 20515, 202-225-5456, pappas.house.gov

State Offices: Dover, 603-285-4300.

Committees: *Transportation & Infrastructure*: Economic Dev't, Public Buildings & Emergency Management; Highways & Transit; Water Resources & Environment. *Veterans' Affairs*: Economic Opportunity; Oversight & Investigations (Chmn); Women Veterans Task Force.

Almanac Ratings 2019-2020

	Economy	Social	Foreign	Composite
Liberal	100%	51%	80%	77%
Conservative	0%	49%	20%	23%

Key Votes of the 116th Congress

1. U.S./Mex./Can. trade deal	Y	5. Russia sanctions	Y	9. Firearms background checks	Y
2. First Coronavirus response	Y	6. Troops in Syria	Y	10. Spending at the border	Y
3. HEROES Act	Y	7. Veto arms sales to Saudis	Y	11. Marijuana liberalized rules	N
4. CASH Act	Y	8. Defense $$$, veto override	Y	12. Electoral College objections	N

Election Results

Election	Name (Party)	Vote (%)		Cand. Spent	Ind. Exp. Support	Ind. Exp. Oppose
2020 General	Chris Pappas (D)	205,606	(51%)	$2,992,126	$21,988	$69,747
	Matt Mowers (R)	185,159	(46%)	$1,687,223	$344,274	$14,162
	Zachary Dumont (L)	9,747	(2%)			
2020 Primary	Chris Pappas (D)	70,643	(100%)			

Prior winning percentages: 2018 (54%)

Democrat Chris Pappas has built on his strong local roots and political experience to defeat vigorous opponents in his two elections to the House. At age 40, he has served in elected office since 2002—most recently, on the influential state Executive Council. Pappas was well-known locally as the hands-on co-owner of Puritan Backroom, a popular Manchester restaurant that his family has operated for more than a century. As far back as 2015, in a profile in the New Hampshire Union Leader, leading state Democrats speculated that he was a prime prospect to run for the Senate.

Pappas, whose paternal great-grandfather emigrated from Greece as a young man, got his bachelor's degree from Harvard University in 2002 and was elected later that year to the state House. After four years in that position, he served four years as treasurer of Hillsborough County. In the Republican year of 2010, he lost reelection by 17 votes, the only loss of his career. He returned in 2012 to win a seat on the five-member Executive Council, defeating the Republican to whom he had lost two years earlier. Pappas had been widely expected for some time to run for Congress or a statewide office.

With the retirement of Democratic Rep. Carol Shea-Porter, who served four terms but lost two reelection campaigns, Pappas was the early frontrunner to succeed her. He was supported by many of his state's Democratic leaders, including its two senators. His road to the Democratic nomination grew more complicated when Maura Sullivan, who had two degrees from Harvard and was an Iraq war veteran, entered the contest. Sullivan held senior jobs at the Veterans Affairs and Defense departments in the Obama administration and was well-financed, though largely from out-of-state.

The chief controversy surrounding her campaign was that she was a native of the Chicago area and had explored a campaign in 2018 for a House seat in Illinois until deciding to settle in New Hampshire. Sullivan responded that she had enjoyed vacations with her family in New Hampshire and that she campaigned for Shea-Porter when she was at Harvard. Pappas largely avoided direct attacks on Sullivan's residency, though he urged all candidates to sign a "Homegrown Candidate Pledge" that they would raise at least half of their campaign funds from the district.

In the 11-candidate field, Pappas and Sullivan raised far more money than the others. Sullivan reported $2 million in spending, while Pappas spent nearly $1 million prior to the primary. Some of his opponents criticized Pappas for not supporting more specific policies, especially on health care. Sullivan sought to link herself to the demand for more women to serve in Congress, though that argument was more difficult in New Hampshire, where all four members of the congressional delegation were Democratic women. Pappas won the nomination with 42 percent of the vote to 30 percent for Sullivan. Among the other candidates was Levi Sanders, son of the Vermont senator, who finished seventh with 2 percent of the vote.

The Republican nominee, Eddie Edwards, ran a small business and had been a local police chief. He embraced President Donald Trump and conservative views and was well-financed, though less than Pappas. A notable feature of the November contest in grassroots New Hampshire was their bios: Edwards is African American and Pappas is openly gay. Those personal details did not appear to be major factors for most voters. Pappas won, 54%-45%.

In the House, he focused his committee work on Transportation and Infrastructure, where he promoted a transportation-funding bill. In July 2020, when the House passed a $1.5 trillion bill, it included $1.3 billion for New Hampshire, including more than $100 million for commuter rail service from Nashua to Boston. With Democratic control of the Senate in 2021, prospects for a version of that measure improved significantly. Pappas said the House-passed measure promotes "bipartisan, common-sense solutions that will help meet our state's urgent transportation needs and help expedite critical projects."

In the 2020 campaign, Matt Mowers, the Republican challenger, talked up his support from Trump plus police unions that had backed Pappas in 2018. Mowers was an aide to Trump's campaign in 2016 and was tapped by the White House to serve as an aide at the State Department. During a campaign debate in October, Mowers said Pappas had given improper support to his boyfriend, who had been a lobbyist for Amazon. Pappas responded that the attack was "baseless" and showed that gay candidates are held to a different standard than other politicians.

Pappas outspent Mowers, $3 million to $1.7 million, and won, 51%-46%, a margin of 20,000 votes. Pappas won all of the southeast corner of the state and took the district's portion of Manchester-based Hillsborough County by nearly 9,000 votes; that county had nearly triple the vote of the next largest county. Mowers won towns that were more inland and mostly rural. Following the election, David Wasserman of the Cook Political Report speculated that Republican-controlled redistricting could jeopardize Pappas if it removed Manchester from the district and substituted Republican-leaning towns.

NH-1: Eastern New Hampshire

Cook Partisan Voting Index: R+1

Population		Race and Ethnicity		Income	
Total	686,735	White	92.80%	Median Income	$79,996
Land area (sq. miles)	2,464	Black	1.60%	District Income Rank	93
Pop/ sq mi	278.75	Latino	4.10%	Poverty Rate	7.70%
Born in State	39.40%	Asian	2.70%	With health insurance	93.10%
		Two or more races	1.80%	Cash public assistance	1.80%
Age Groups		Other	1.10%	Food stamp/SNAP	5.90%
Under 18	18.70%				
18-34	21.80%	**Education**		**Work**	
35-64	41.30%	H.S grad or less	34.20%	White Collar	41.60%
Over 64	18.20%	Some college	27.50%	Sales and Service	36.50%
		College Degree, 4 yr	23.70%	Blue Collar	21.90%
Military		Post grad	14.50%	Government	13.00%
Veteran/ Active Duty	8.70%				

2020 Pres. Vote	Biden	213,662	(52%)	Trump	188,999	(46%)			
2016 Pres. Vote	Trump	179,259	(48%)	Clinton	173,344	(46%)	Johnson	15,994	(4%)

Manchester: The greatest growth in New Hampshire over the past two decades has been in the southeast and south-central parts of the state—the Seacoast and the Manchester area. Manchester was once famous for the Amoskeag Mills, the world's largest textile mill complex. In the first half of the 20th century, it was the quintessential mill town, with a few mansions for mill owners and managers and closely packed neighborhoods of frame houses for mill workers, many of them immigrants from Quebec, Ireland and Greece. A quarter of New Hampshire residents claim French or French-Canadian ties, and racial minorities are sparse here. By the beginning of the 21st century, Manchester was something quite different: a high-tech city, with big shopping malls at freeway interchanges, a spiffy new airport and downtown arena, a more prominent university presence, spruced-up neighborhoods, and growth extending to the wooded suburbs all around. The "Queen City is becoming hip," New Hampshire magazine wrote in 2018. "Manufacturing, in a way, still exists here"—but rather than textiles, it's in the form of engineered human tissues at the Advanced Regenerative Manufacturing Institute. In September 2020, the New Hampshire Tech Alliance said that it hoped to have 100,000 users by early 2021.

The Seacoast, within easy commuting distance of Massachusetts, is a collection of towns of ancient pedigree and high-tech growth along the 18-mile coastline. The biggest city on the coast is Portsmouth, the colonial capital of New Hampshire, with its busy naval shipyard and old seaport with well-preserved homes and a solid local economy that includes many art galleries and bars. In 2019, the shipyard had a total of 7,300 civilian employees, of whom 4,000 lived in New Hampshire and 2,800 in Maine. Pease International Trade port, which had been the site of an Air Force base until 1991, now houses more than 250 businesses and 10,500 jobs on the Seacoast.

The 1st Congressional District of New Hampshire includes the Manchester area and the Seacoast from Manchester and next-door Bedford, its affluent suburb, east to Portsmouth. It extends north to include Laconia and gentrifying Lake Winnipesaukee, studded with summer resorts and new mansions, including the $10 million vacation home in Wolfeboro of freshman Republican Sen. Mitt Romney of Utah. Politically, this is the slightly more Republican of New Hampshire's two congressional districts. It has been the destination of many people fleeing high taxes in Massachusetts.

Portsmouth, with its trendy coffee shops, is Democratic, as are Durham, home of the University of New Hampshire, and nearby Dover, once a mill town and now the second fastest-growing city in the state. Most of the smaller towns on the Seacoast and to the north have been solidly Republican, though that is changing. Joe Biden won this swing district in 2020, 52%-46%. His lead of 24,000 votes was significantly larger than the past two elections, when the winner led by less than 6,000 votes—President Barack Obama in 2012 and Donald Trump in 2016.

Ann Kuster (D)

Elected 2012, 5th term, b. Sep 05, 1956; Concord, NH; Dartmouth College, A.B., 1978; Georgetown University Law Center, J.D., 1984; Christian Church; Married (Brad Kuster); 2 children.

Professional Career: Owner, Newfound Strategies, 2011-2013; Practicing lawyer, 1984-2010; Legislative aide, U.S. Rep. Pete McCloskey, 1978-1981.

DC Office: 320 CHOB 20515, 202-225-5206, Fax: 202-225-2946, kuster.house.gov

State Offices: Concord, 603-226-1002; Littleton, 603-444-7700; Nashua, 603-595-2006.

Committees: *Agriculture*: Commodity Exchanges, Energy & Credit; Conservation & Forestry; Subcommittee Nutrition, Oversight & Department Operations. *Energy & Commerce*: Energy; Health; Oversight & Investigations.

Group Ratings

	ADA	ACLU	AFL-CIO	LCV	COC	HAFA	ACU	CFG	FRC
2020	**	74%	**	100%	-	0%	4%	**	-
2019	95%	C	100%	97%	71%	C	4%	16%	0%

Almanac Ratings 2019-2020

	Economy	Social	Foreign	Composite
Liberal	100%	56%	54%	70%
Conservative	0%	44%	46%	30%

Key Votes of the 116th Congress

1. U.S./Mex./Can. trade deal	Y	5. Russia sanctions	Y	9. Firearms background checks	Y
2. First Coronavirus response	Y	6. Troops in Syria	Y	10. Spending at the border	Y
3. HEROES Act	Y	7. Veto arms sales to Saudis	Y	11. Marijuana liberalized rules	Y
4. CASH Act	Y	8. Defense $$$, veto override	N/A	12. Electoral College objections	N

Election Results

Election	Name (Party)	Vote (%)		Cand. Spent	Ind. Exp. Support	Ind. Exp. Oppose
2020 General	Ann Kuster (D)	208,289	(54%)	$2,332,800	$7,908	
	Steve Negron (R)	168,886	(44%)	$358,587	$6,356	$113
	Andrew Olding (L)	9,119	(2%)			
2020 Primary	Ann McLane Kuster (D)	71,358	(93%)			
	Joseph Mirzoeff (D)	5,500	(7%)			

Prior winning percentages: 2018 (56%), 2016 (50%), 2014 (55%), 2012 (50%)

Democrat Ann McLane Kuster, elected in 2012, has emphasized bipartisanship in both her legislative work and her campaigns. She has achieved some success in Congress dealing with opioid addiction and veterans' health issues. On the Energy and Commerce Committee, she has focused on clean energy, lower prescription drug costs and extended coverage of the Affordable Care Act.

Kuster was born in Concord and is part of a prominent political family in the Granite State. Her great-grandfather John McLane served as governor from 1905 to 1907, while her father, Malcolm McLane, was mayor of Concord and an unsuccessful gubernatorial candidate in 1972. Her mother, Susan McLane, was a Republican state legislator for 25 years. "Politics was sort of a way of life in our family," Kuster said.

Kuster worked on the 1972 presidential campaign of Republican Rep. Pete McCloskey of California, an anti-Vietnam War candidate who launched a quixotic challenge against President Richard Nixon. Kuster later graduated from Dartmouth College and worked in McCloskey's Washington office for three years. Kuster earned her law degree from Georgetown University and returned to Manchester to practice law. She spent many years in Concord as a lobbyist and adoption lawyer. "I represented women with unplanned pregnancies from age 14 to 40, and they ranged from living in their car to living in the nicest neighborhoods in town," she said. "Unplanned pregnancy is an equal-opportunity affliction." Kuster also became immersed in politics, and toured New Hampshire with Barack Obama during his 2008 presidential campaign.

In 2010, Kuster faced off against veteran Republican Rep. Charlie Bass, and was the underdog in a strong year for Republicans. She criticized his role in securing tax rebates for wood-pellet stove buyers before investing in a wood-pellet stove company himself. Bass denied any wrongdoing, but the issue gave her momentum. The incumbent Bass was outspent 2-to-1, but he eked out the victory 48%-47%. Their rematch two years later came in a political climate more favorable to Kuster. She supported the Democrats' 2010 health care overhaul, and Bass called the law a "bureaucratic boondoggle." Kuster again outspent Bass by more than a million dollars and had a comparable advantage in outside money. This time she won, 50%-45%.

In the House, Kuster has had several accomplishments on veterans' issues. During her first term, the House passed her bill to improve health care options for veterans. In 2016, she won support for her bill to create opportunities for veterans to become physicians after their military service. Her interest in opioid addiction extended to the broader community. New Hampshire has been among the states with the highest rates of opioid overdoses. That year, she enacted two proposals that sought additional treatment for addiction that related to mental health or substance abuse. She enacted another bill that assured federal jurisdiction over offenses committed by U.S. personnel stationed in Canada for border-security initiatives.

In 2018, Kuster organized a bipartisan heroin and opioid task force to seek a comprehensive response, both at home and in Washington. That led to passage of multiple bills dealing with treatment, recovery, prevention and law enforcement—including the creation of opioid recovery centers in states that were hardest hit by the epidemic, and loan repayment programs for students who become professionals in treatment of substance abuse. "At a time of heightened partisanship, it's rare in Washington to have such a large group of members put their differences aside," she said. During the coronavirus pandemic, she filed a package of measures in her "roadmap to recovery," which included forgiveness of $25,000 of student loan debt for "front-line heroes" and other essential workers.

In the New Hampshire swing-seat tradition, Kuster has continued to have competitive campaigns. In 2014, she faced a challenge from state Rep. Marilinda Garcia, a conservative Latina activist. Kuster called her opponent "naïve," and won 55%-45%. Against underfunded Republican challenger Jim Lawrence in 2016, Kuster was held to a 50%-45% win. In 2018, she faced state Rep. Steve Negron, a businessman who emphasized his support for President Donald Trump. Kuster criticized Republican tax cuts but cast herself in bipartisan terms, including her work on opioids. Speaking in a campaign ad, she said, "the truth is, both parties, need to stop playing games and work together on the problems we face," which she called "the New Hampshire way." Kuster outspent Negron, $3.4 million to $455,000 and won, 56%-42%.

In 2020, she and Negron had a rematch. Their spending was similar but presidential-year turnout was higher. Kuster's margin slipped to 54%-44%. In the presidential primary, she endorsed Pete Buttigieg, citing his "courage to break from the past to lead us to a better future."

Kuster gained positive notice when she led Democratic women in "raise the roof" dance moves after Trump unexpectedly noted the increased number of women in the House—mostly Democrats and mostly wearing white for that evening—during his State of the Union message in February 2019. "Raise the roof" means "raising expectations, and fulfilling our goals and our dreams," she told a reporter, after she was positively depicted in a sketch on Saturday Night Live that week.

NH-2: Western New Hampshire

Cook Partisan Voting Index: D+1

Population		Race and Ethnicity		Income	
Total	672,976	White	92.30%	Median Income	$76,368
Land area (sq. miles)	6,489	Black	1.60%	District Income Rank	117
Pop/ sq mi	103.71	Latino	3.80%	Poverty Rate	6.80%
Born in State	41.90%	Asian	2.60%	With health insurance	94.40%
		Two or more races	2.60%	Cash public assistance	2.50%
Age Groups		Other	0.90%	Food stamp/SNAP	6.20%
Under 18	19.00%				
18-34	21.50%	Education		Work	
35-64	40.50%	H.S grad or less	35.20%	White Collar	43.60%
Over 64	19.00%	Some college	27.70%	Sales and Service	34.50%
		College Degree, 4 yr	22.10%	Blue Collar	21.90%
Military		Post grad	14.80%	Government	12.60%
Veteran/ Active Duty	8.70%				

2020 Pres. Vote	Biden	211,275	(53%)	Trump	176,661	(45%)		
2016 Pres. Vote	Clinton	175,182	(48%)	Trump	166,531	(45%)	Johnson	14,783	(4%)

Nashua, Concord: Political reporters covering New Hampshire's first-in-the-nation primary usually stay in Manchester, the state's largest city and within an hour's drive of the rest of the state except for the North Country. Yet there are other noteworthy cities and towns in New Hampshire. Concord, north of Manchester, is the state capital. On one side of Main Street is the handsome, small, granite capitol, and on the other you can usually find the headquarters of the two political parties and many candidates: an entire state's politics within 100 yards. A negative sign of everyday life in Concord: In June 2019, National Public Radio reported that the city was among the highest in the nation for opioid death rates. Nashua, south of Manchester and on the Massachusetts line, is twice the size of Concord and the state's second-largest city, a technology and financial services center that has been mostly booming for three decades. Local officials have made progress in seeking to add 10 miles to the commuter rail service from Nashua to Boston. In December 2020, the New Hampshire executive council approved a $5.4 million contract for engineering and public outreach. To the east is prosperous and growing Salem, first chartered in 1750 and the largest of the border suburbs.

To the west near the Vermont border, past the pleasant country around Mount Monadnock, is Keene (pop., 22,949), the hub of southwest New Hampshire, and the largest city in the state north or west of Concord. The town has built a "creative economy" that attracts artists and cultural events. To the north are towns along the Connecticut River; some are mill towns, and some are vacation enclaves. Hanover, home of Dartmouth College, is a tiny, picturesque town set in the mountains. Farther north is Littleton, where the local tax base more than tripled between 1995 and 2018. Every political reporter's itinerary has to include a trip, usually by plane, to the little lumber mill city of Berlin in the middle of the North Country, where the last paper mill has closed; biomass and other forms of renewable energy have been growing, with subsidies from the state. At Dixville Notch in the White Mountains, the town's handful of voters cast their ballots at a minute past midnight and provide the first reported returns in every presidential election.

The 2nd Congressional District of New Hampshire includes Concord, Nashua, Salem, Keene, the Connecticut River counties, Hanover, Berlin and Dixville Notch. It includes Mount Washington, with its spectacularly violent weather and winds that have been measured up to 231 miles per hour; entrepreneurs have considered wind power plants, but the manager of its state park said the location was too windy and icy to be practical. The district takes in the Bretton Woods resort, where the world monetary system was established at a conference in 1944.

Politically, this region is mixed, though it has become the more Democratic of New Hampshire's two congressional districts. The area between Mount Monadnock and Keene and the territory running north along the Connecticut River to Hanover and Dartmouth had become very Democratic, much like Vermont across the river. In 2020 Joe Biden led Donald Trump 53%-45%, a significant increase from Hillary Clinton's 48%-45% lead in 2016 and close to the double-digit leads that Barack Obama had in his two campaigns.

NEW JERSEY

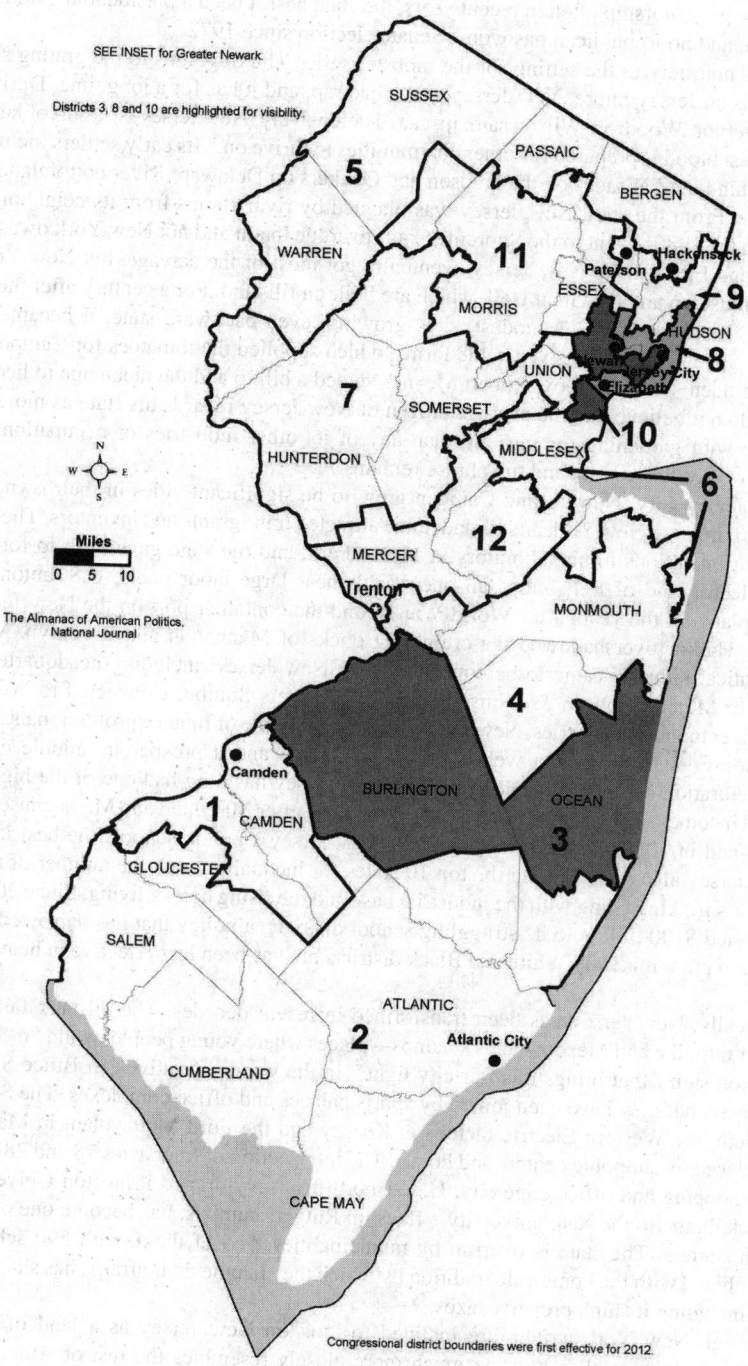

SEE INSET for Greater Newark.

Districts 3, 8 and 10 are highlighted for visibility.

SUSSEX

PASSAIC

BERGEN

WARREN

5

11

Hackensack

Paterson

9

MORRIS

ESSEX

HUDSON

8

UNION

Newark

Jersey City

Elizabeth

7

SOMERSET

10

MIDDLESEX

HUNTERDON

6

N
W   E
S

Miles
0   5   10

The Almanac of American Politics.
National Journal

MERCER

12

MONMOUTH

Trenton

4

Camden

BURLINGTON

OCEAN

1

CAMDEN

3

GLOUCESTER

SALEM

ATLANTIC

2

Atlantic City

CUMBERLAND

CAPE MAY

Congressional district boundaries were first effective for 2012.

New Jersey leaned Republican from the 1940s through the 1980s, but over the past two decades it has become a Democratic bastion due to a growing immigrant population and the presence of many affluent suburbanites who reject the GOP's conservative stands on cultural issues. While Republicans have won the governorship often in recent years, the state hasn't been a presidential battleground for a generation, and no Republican has won a Senate election since 1972.

From its notoriety as the setting for the mobster series The Sopranos to the grating stereotypes of its citizens on Jersey Shore, New Jersey gets a bad rap, and it has for a long time. During his two years as governor, Woodrow Wilson said, just a tad defensively, New Jersey is "a sort of laboratory in which the best blood is prepared for other communities to thrive on." Its early settlers included Dutch in towns behind the Palisades on the Hudson and Quakers on Delaware River bottomlands opposite Philadelphia. From the start, New Jersey was plagued by rival claims from its neighbors and, still defensive in the 1980s, went to the Supreme Court to argue that it and not New York owns the Statue of Liberty and Ellis Island. New Jersey eventually got most of the acreage, but New York got the immigrant museum and the Great Hall, which are built on fill land. For a century after the American Revolution, New Jersey was a modest, slow-growing, even backward state. It became known as the Garden State because of its vegetable farms, which supplied the tomatoes for Campbell's Soup, based in Camden. (In 1954, Gov. Robert Meyner vetoed a bill to add the nickname to license plates, saying, "I do not believe that the average citizen of New Jersey regards his state as more peculiarly identifiable with gardening for farming than any of its other industries or occupations." But the legislature overrode the veto, and the phrase remains.)

While Jersey City, Newark and Camden grew to be significant cities in their own right, New Jersey's proximity to New York and Philadelphia attracted immigrants and inventors. Thomas Edison churned out inventions in his laboratory at Menlo Park, and the state gave birth to forerunners of General Electric and of Bell Labs. On open fields near large labor pools, U.S. automakers built assembly plants in the years after World War II, and the container port on the New Jersey side of New York Harbor overshadowed the crumbling docks of Manhattan and Brooklyn. Much of the pharmaceutical industry came to be concentrated in New Jersey, including headquarters or major facilities for Merck, Johnson & Johnson and Bristol-Myers Squibb. Connected to Wall Street by Hudson River tunnels and ferries, New Jersey became the home of finance professionals and lawyers. This economy gave the state a well-educated workforce and a prosperous middle class, with a high concentration of scientists and engineers. New Jersey has long had one of the highest median household incomes of any state—currently ranking third after Maryland and Massachusetts, at nearly $86,000—and in 2020, Education Week rated New Jersey's public schools the best in the nation. Yet New Jersey also ranks among the top 10 states for inequality, with the number of middle-class households shrinking along with the industrial base and the rising cost of living. Since 2008, the state has redirected $100 billion to its struggling school districts, a policy that has narrowed the funding gap between predominantly White and Black districts but has been less effective in heavily Hispanic districts.

Physically, New Jersey has been transformed in recent decades. The oil tank farms, concrete ribbons of turnpike and Meadowlands swamps—places where young people would "meet 'neath that giant Exxon sign / that brings this fair city light," in the words of native son Bruce Springsteen—are still there, but they have been joined by sports palaces and office complexes. The Singer factory in Elizabeth, the Western Electric factory in Kearny and the Ford Motor plant in Mahwah are all gone, replaced by shopping centers and hotels. The intersection of Interstates 78 and 287 has become a major shopping and office edge city. U.S. 1 north from ivy-draped Princeton University to New Brunswick, home to the state university's flagship Rutgers campus, has become one of the nation's high-tech centers. The state is overrun by municipalities, 565 of them, with 590 school districts. This, combined with the home-rule tradition by which they handle their affairs, has shaped the state's politics, including its high property taxes.

Although New York writers are inclined to look on New Jersey as a land of 1940s diners and 1970s shopping malls, the state much more closely resembles the rest of America than does Manhattan, although drivers will find some peculiarities, such as jug-handle intersections (to make a left turn, you exit to the right and then cross over after the light has changed) and the nation's only remaining state-imposed ban on self-service gas stations. The row houses one used to encounter upon emerging from the Holland Tunnel are now joined by office and apartment towers and, a few miles farther out, by the skyscrapers of Newark and its performing arts center. Farther out still are comfortably packed middle-income suburbs and the horse country around Far Hills, old industrial cities such as Paterson and Trenton (also the state capital), and dozens of suburban towns and small factory cities. In South Jersey is the desolate (and ecologically unique) expanse known as the Pine Barrens, where Christopher Moltisanti and Paulie ("Walnuts") Gualtieri of The Sopranos spent an uncomfortable winter's night trying to dispose of a Russian mobster.

Map for Newark and Jersey City

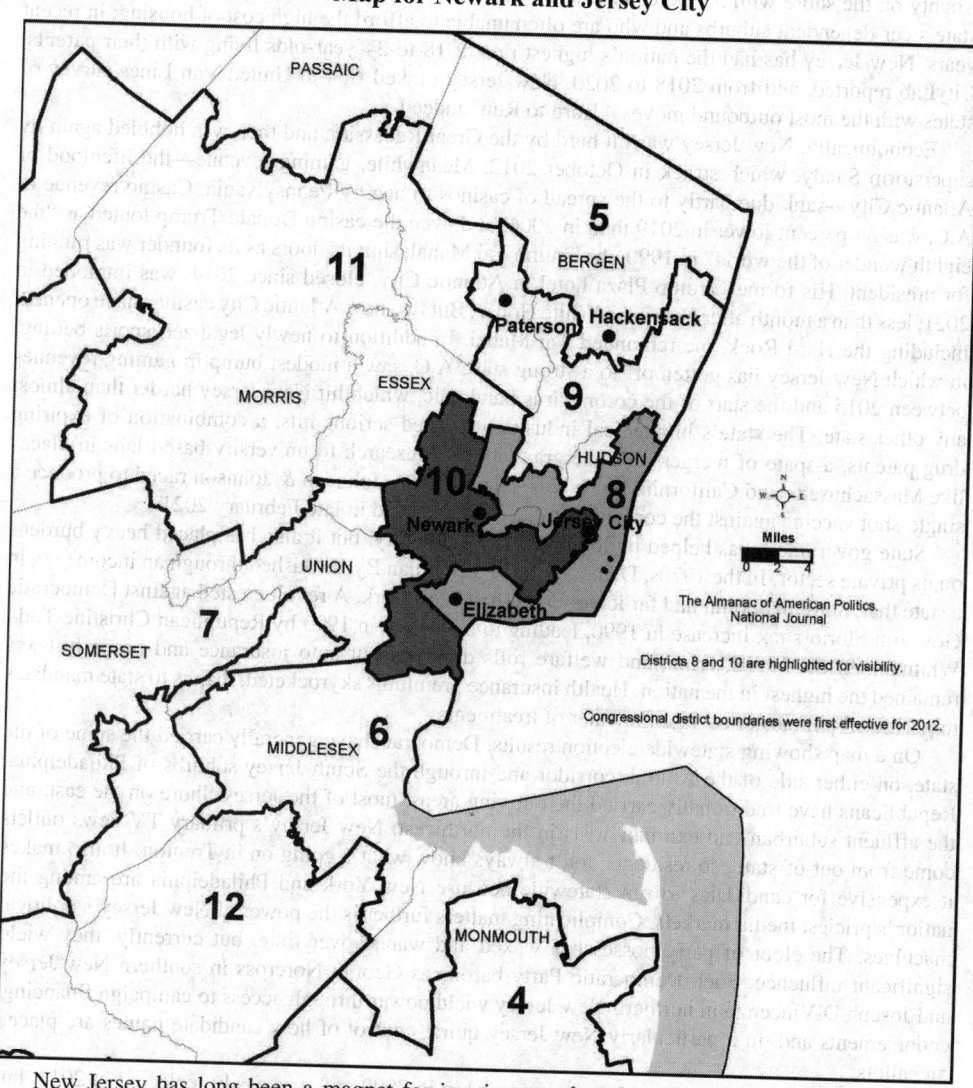

The Almanac of American Politics
National Journal

Districts 8 and 10 are highlighted for visibility.

Congressional district boundaries were first effective for 2012.

New Jersey has long been a magnet for immigrants, though more so in the vicinity of New York City than adjacent to Philadelphia. Today, more than 22 percent of the population is foreign-born, a higher percentage than almost any state. New Jersey's population is 12 percent Black, 21 percent Hispanic (ranking eighth nationally), 10 percent Asian (third behind Hawaii and California), and 56 percent White (ranking among the bottom 10 states). Immigrants are also plentiful in the small, middle-American towns of Bergen County: Filipinos in Bergenfield, Guatemalans in Fairview, Koreans in Leonia, Indians in Lodi, and Chinese in Palisades Park. The old industrial cities of Elizabeth and Paterson are more than 60 percent Hispanic, and Newark is majority Black. In 2020, the state eliminated its unusual term for county commissioner—"freeholder"—due to its origins in the

18th century, when only white, moneyed landowners could hold the office. Also in 2020, Princeton removed the name of former governor, president, and alumnus Woodrow Wilson from its school of public and international affairs due to his "racist thinking and policies," and Gov. Phil Murphy stopped using one of Wilson's desks.

Overall, the state's population has grown by less than 5.7 percent since the 2010 census, slower than the nation as a whole. Of the state's 21 counties, only eight gained any population at all over the past decade, led by Hudson County across from Manhattan with 5.8 percent growth and Ocean County on the shore with 5.1 percent. One weak spot has been millennials, who aren't fond of the state's car-dependent suburbs and who are often unable to afford the high cost of housing; in recent years, New Jersey has had the nation's highest rate of 18-to-34-year-olds living with their parents, CityLab reported, and from 2018 to 2020, New Jersey ranked first in United Van Lines' survey of states with the most outbound moves. "Born to Run" indeed.

Economically, New Jersey was hit hard by the Great Recession and then was hobbled again by superstorm Sandy, which struck in October 2012. Meanwhile, gaming revenue—the lifeblood of Atlantic City—sank due partly to the spread of casinos to nearby Pennsylvania. Casino revenue in A.C. was 34 percent lower in 2019 than in 2006, and even the casino Donald Trump touted as "the eighth wonder of the world" in 1990, the Trump Taj Mahal, shut its doors as its founder was running for president. His former Trump Plaza hotel in Atlantic City, closed since 2014, was imploded in 2021, less than a month after he left the White House. But two new Atlantic City casinos have opened, including the Hard Rock, the rebranded Taj Mahal. In addition to newly legalized sports betting, in which New Jersey has gotten off to a strong start, A.C. saw a modest bump in gaming revenues between 2015 and the start of the coronavirus pandemic, which hit New Jersey harder than almost any other state. The state's biomedical industry sustained serious hits, a combination of expiring drug patents, a spate of mergers and the gravitation of research to university-based labs in places like Massachusetts and California. But home-state company Johnson & Johnson raced to produce a single-shot vaccine against the coronavirus that was approved in late February 2021.

State government has helped build New Jersey's identity, but it also has placed heavy burdens on its private sector. In the 1970s, Democratic Gov. Brendan Byrne pushed through an income tax in a state that, until that point, had far lower taxes than New York. A revolt crested against Democratic Gov. Jim Florio's tax increase in 1990, leading to his defeat in 1993 by Republican Christine Todd Whitman. In the 1990s, crime and welfare rolls dropped, but auto insurance and property taxes remained the highest in the nation. Health insurance premiums skyrocketed, thanks to state mandates requiring all policies to cover all manner of treatments.

On a map showing statewide election results, Democrats have generally carried the spine of the state, on either side of the Amtrak corridor and through the South Jersey suburbs of Philadelphia. Republicans have traditionally carried the outlying areas, most of the Jersey Shore on the east, and the affluent suburban and exurban areas in the northwest. New Jersey's primary TV news outlets come from out-of-state, so residents don't always know what's going on in Trenton. It also makes it expensive for candidates to run statewide because New York and Philadelphia are among the nation's priciest media markets. Complicating matters further is the power of New Jersey's political machines. The clout of party bosses has waxed and waned over time, but currently, they wield significant influence. Such Democratic Party barons as George Norcross in southern New Jersey and Joseph DiVincenzo in northern New Jersey wield power through access to campaign financing, endorsements and, in a particularly New Jersey quirk, control of how candidate names are placed on ballots.

Republican Chris Christie won the governorship in 2009 and was easily reelected in 2013, but shortly after his second victory, he faced investigations into the closing of a lane on the George Washington Bridge to punish a Democratic mayor who spurned Christie's reelection effort. (In 2020, the U.S. Supreme Court threw out two convictions tied to the scandal.) Other stumbles piled up. Christie's presidential bid cratered, voters back home got restless about the time he spent away from the state, and eyebrows were raised when he became the first establishment Republican to back Trump, only to be purged from the transition team after Trump won. Christie's growing unpopularity helped New Jersey turn even bluer. In 2017, Democrat Murphy easily won the governorship, 56%-42%, and, working with a lopsidedly Democratic legislature, he set about enacting such progressive priorities as paid sick leave and gun control. Not even Democratic Sen. Bob Menendez, who had faced corruption charges that ended in a mistrial, was knocked off track in his 2018 reelection bid, defeating a credible Republican opponent by double digits. Democrats also ousted two House incumbents in 2018 and flipped two GOP-held open seats, leaving the delegation with 11 Democrats and one Republican. The GOP gained back some marginal ground in 2019, as Rep. Jeff Van Drew, one of the Democratic winners from 2018, switched parties, and as Republicans narrowed the (still large) Democratic edge in the legislature in the state's off-year elections.

In 2020, as usual, the presidential campaigns all but ignored New Jersey as too blue to flip, although Trump did tap a veteran New Jersey politico, Bill Stepien, to revive his struggling campaign less than four months before Election Day. Moderate former Gov. Christine Todd Whitman, a lifelong Republican, endorsed Biden and spoke at the Democratic National Convention. Biden ended up winning the state by 16 points, up from 14 for Hillary Clinton in 2016, and he flipped Morris County, with its $115,527 median income, as well as Gloucester County in the Philadelphia suburbs. Biden also nibbled away at Trump's margins in Monmouth and Ocean counties along the Jersey shore, though the president still won both easily. (By contrast, Trump's golf club in Bedminster is located in Somerset County, which backed Biden by 21 points.) In the most populous Democratic counties, Latinos proved to be a notable demographic. In the five heavily populated counties where the percentage of Latinos was around the statewide average of 21 percent—Bergen (Hackensack), Middlesex (Edison and New Brunswick), Essex (Newark), Union (Elizabeth), and Camden (Camden and Cherry Hill)—the winning Democratic margin remained roughly the same between 2016 and 2020. But in the two populous counties that are 43 percent Hispanic—Hudson (Jersey City) and Passaic (Paterson)—Trump clawed back the Democratic margins by six and five points, respectively. Despite those shifts, both counties backed Biden by yawning margins, further evidence that the Democrats can feel confident about their chances in New Jersey for the foreseeable future.

Population		Race and Ethnicity		Income	
Total	8,882,190	White	67.10%	Median Income	85,751
Land area (sq. miles)	7,354	Black	13.60%	State Income Rank	3 out of 50
Pop/ sq mi	1,207.77	Latino	20.90%	Poverty Rate	9.20%
Born in state	51.50%	Asian	10.70%	With health insurance	92.10%
		Two or more races	3.00%	Cash public assistance	1.60%
Age Groups		Other	6.60%	Food stamp/SNAP	9.2%
Under 18	21.80%				
18-34	21.40%	**Education**		**Work**	
35-64	40.20%	H.S grad or less	36.60%	White Collar	44.90%
Over 64	16.60%	Some college	22.10%	Sales and Service	36.30%
		College Degree, 4 yr	25.10%	Blue Collar	18.80%
Military		Post grad	16.10%	Government	13.60%
Veteran/ Active Duty	4.60%				

Presidential Politics

2020 Primary (D)	Biden (D)	814,680(84%)	Sanders (D)	140,579(15%)	
2020 Pres. Vote	Biden (D)	2,608,400(57%)	Trump (R)	1,883,313(41%)	
2016 Pres. Vote	Clinton (D)	2,148,278(55%)	Trump (R)	1,601,933(41%)	

New Jersey used to be a close state in close presidential races. In the 1980s, the vast suburban expanses leaned toward Republicans. But Democrats have won the past seven elections. Lately, GOP nominees have barely cleared the 40 percent mark. The suburbs, with many secular voters, reject GOP positions on cultural issues, and rising immigrant communities have generally voted Democratic. As a result, New Jersey, which had voted 56%-43% for George H.W. Bush in 1988, voted 56%-40% for Al Gore over George W. Bush in 2000. In 2012, it was one of five states where President Barack Obama increased his percentage over his 2008 numbers. In 2020, Joe Biden beat President Donald Trump 57%-41%. Trump won the northwestern section of New Jersey that includes the state's two fastest growing counties, Hunterdon and Somerset, home to Trump National Golf Club in Bedminster. Those counties and Morris are among the wealthiest in the country, and like other wealthy, highly educated areas, Biden did better than recent Democratic nominees. Trump ran close to Biden in South Jersey, with its working-class suburbs of Philadelphia, farms around Vineland and Millville, and beach communities in Atlantic, Cape May and Ocean counties. Biden rolled up his biggest margins in Jersey City, Newark and Union City, as well as around the capitol of Trenton and Camden County, Philadelphia's diverse suburbs.

New Jersey has generally held its presidential primary in early June, except for Super Tuesday appearances in 2008 and 2012. In 2016, Trump was the de facto GOP nominee and rolled up 80 percent of the vote in the June 7 primary. The night before the primary, the Associated Press and CNN reported that Hillary Clinton had acquired enough delegates to claim the Democratic nomination. The next day, she defeated Bernie Sanders, 63%-37%. In 2020, New Jersey's primary was scheduled for early June but postponed until July and became all-mail voting because of the coronavirus pandemic. Biden won 85 percent of the vote in the uncontested race.

Congressional Districts

117th Congress Lineup	10D 2R	116th Congress Lineup	11D 1R

For the past three redistricting cycles, New Jersey employed a bipartisan redistricting commission, made up of 12 members—six Democrats and six Republicans—appointed by party leaders in the legislature. The members picked a theoretically dispassionate tie-breaking arbiter. In 1991 and 2011, the outcome was the Republicans' plan. In 2001, the 13 congressional incumbents agreed on a bipartisan, if contorted, map and submitted it to the commission. The arbiter liked the incumbent-protection plan. The consistent result was a House delegation that remained closely balanced: a 7-5 split for the Democrats, prior to the 2018 election.

But politics and election outcomes in New Jersey have changed. The state's quaint traditions of bipartisan redistricting and a divided delegation have become relics, and it's unlikely they will be revived for the foreseeable future. Democrats picked up four suburban seats in 2018—defeating two Republican incumbents, pushing a third into early retirement and taking the fourth seat when a safe Republican retired and the GOP could not find a credible candidate. They relinquished the latter seat when Jeff Van Drew switched to the Republican Party at the end of 2019 and survived a competitive Democratic challenge the following November.

In addition, Democrats have taken control of the governor's office and hold large majorities in the legislature. In December 2018, Trenton Democratic leaders unexpectedly revealed their intentions to reinforce their control of the delegation with a nakedly partisan constitutional amendment to overhaul redistricting procedures, which raised alarms among reformers—as well as the surviving Republicans. Ultimately, that plan was so egregious that it caused some blushing Democratic loyalists to rebel and shelve the proposal. But unless Republicans find a way to become more competitive in New Jersey campaigns, they likely will need to be satisfied with a seat or two in the southern part of the state and a struggle for a seat in north Jersey, where they had three House seats as recently as 2016.

Still, some Republicans have generated hope that they can target Democratic Rep. Tom Malinowski, who has suffered recent ethics problems. With Senate Minority Leader Tom Kean Jr. hoping for a rematch with Malinowski, he also is in position to lead redistricting strategy for Republicans and potential bargaining for a bipartisan deal. A potential deal in north Jersey might boost the prospects for Kean in exchange for securing the seats of Democrats Josh Gottheimer and Mikie Sherrill.

Phil Murphy (D)

Elected 2018, term expires 2022, 1st term; b. Aug. 16, 1957, Needham, MA; Harvard University, B.A.; University of Pennsylvania, M.B.A.; Unknown; Married (Tammy); 4 children.

Professional Career: Partner, Goldman Sachs, 1983-2006; DNC National Finance Chair, 2006-2009; U.S. Ambassador to Germany, 2009-2013.

Office: PO Box 001 Trenton, 08625; 609-292-6000; Fax: 609-292-3454

Lt. Gov.: Sheila Oliver (D)

State Legislature: Senate: 26D, 14R **House:** 54D, 26R

Election Results

Election	Name (Party)	Vote (%)
2017 General	Phil Murphy (D)	1,203,110 (56%)
	Kim Guadagno (R)	899,583 (42%)
2017 Primary	Phil Murphy (D)	243,643 (56%)
	Jim Johnson (D)	110,250 (22%)
	John S. Wisniewski (D)	108,532 (22%)

Phil Murphy, a former Goldman Sachs executive and U.S. ambassador to Germany, won New Jersey's governorship in 2017 in his first run for public office, succeeding two-term Republican Gov. Chris Christie. Murphy pursued a liberal policy agenda, although feuds with state Democratic Party bosses stymied some of his efforts. In 2020, his state had the worst mortality rate from COVID-19.

Murphy grew up in Newton Massachusetts in what he has described as a working-class home (or "middle class on a good day," as he often put it). Murphy worked his way through Harvard University and later earned a degree from the University of Pennsylvania's Wharton School of Business. He spent more than two decades with Goldman Sachs, eventually spending four years posted in Germany and three in Hong Kong. Shortly before leaving Goldman Sachs, Murphy was tapped by acting New Jersey Gov. Richard Codey to chair a panel studying the state's pension system. He stepped further into politics in 2006, when he was named national finance chair of the Democratic National Committee under chairman Howard Dean, the former Vermont governor and 2004 presidential candidate. After Barack Obama won the presidency, he tapped Murphy as ambassador to Germany, a post he held from 2009 to 2013.

In the run-up to the 2017 gubernatorial contest, Democrats were salivating at the chance to succeed Christie, whose approval rating was in the dumps due to the "Bridgegate" scandal and his support for President Donald Trump. Several Democrats were interested in the race, including state Senate President Steve Sweeney, but Murphy moved aggressively and, with seemingly unlimited financial resources, he easily won the nomination. On the Republican side, the outgoing lieutenant governor, Kim Guadagno, won her primary with similar ease. In the general election, Guadagno attacked Murphy as someone whose wealth made it hard to identify with ordinary New Jersey residents, and whose years with Goldman Sachs echoed the resume of Jon Corzine, the Democrat who lost reelection to Christie in 2009. Murphy, for his part, worked to lash Guadagno to Christie's administration, as well as to Trump. The candidates also differed sharply on policy. Guadagno warned voters that Murphy would raise their taxes; Murphy staked out more aggressive stances on gun control and marijuana than his Republican opponent. Notably, Murphy energized progressives with his support for such policies as sanctuary status for undocumented immigrants and a $15 minimum wage. National handicappers never considered the race to be especially competitive; Murphy prevailed, 56%-42%. Exit polls found that eight of every 10 voters disapproved of Christie, making his tenure a bigger driver of the vote than Trump's.

With solid Democratic majorities in the legislature, Murphy signed laws on equal pay, paid family leave, gun control, a ban on drilling for oil and gas in state waters, renewable energy, automatic voter registration, and a restoration of funding for Planned Parenthood. The budget he signed in June 2018 included a surtax on incomes higher than $5 million and a tax hike on some corporations, and directed money toward schools and the NJ Transit commuter rail system. A Murphy appointee, Attorney General Gurbir Grewal, acted to limit local police forces' ability to ask about immigration status and made it harder to hand over undocumented immigrants for deportation. But differences with Sweeney, the powerful Senate leader, prevented progress on other priorities, including a $15 minimum wage and marijuana legalization. Murphy experienced other areas of turbulence. Katie Brennan, who served in Murphy's administration, accused former Murphy campaign aide Albert J. Alvarez of sexual assault, and she criticized Murphy for hiring him even though transition officials were aware of her allegation. Alvarez was not charged with a crime, but he resigned from his senior post. A 2019 report by the legislature offered harsh criticism of several Murphy aides, saying they "failed her at every step of the way." The following year, Brennan agreed to a settlement in which the state and Murphy's campaign paid $1 million, with $600,000 earmarked for a Hudson County nonprofit that helps sexual-assault survivors.

In 2019, relations between Murphy and other key Democrats reached a low ebb—not just Sweeney, but also one of Sweeney's allies, southern New Jersey powerbroker George Norcross. A Murphy-initiated task force found lax oversight of an $11 billion tax incentive program championed by the Democratic bosses. In May, an investigation by WNYC and ProPublica elevated Norcross's role by reporting that some $1.1 billion of $1.6 billion in tax incentives that had been given to companies in the Camden area were directed to entities closely tied to Norcross or his brother Philip, a lawyer-lobbyist. While a state appeals court would eventually uphold the right of Murphy's task force to investigate the program, internal Democratic tempers flared. During a budget stalemate, Sweeney said Murphy "is starting to resemble Donald Trump in bombast, inconsistency and unreliability." Murphy, for his part, told The New York Times, "I didn't come from anyone's machine. So the machine stuff has always been less relevant for me than somebody who grew up in the system."

The factions did manage to work together in 2019 to pass a $15 minimum wage, a bill to let terminally ill residents request life-ending prescriptions, and a restoration of the vote to more than 80,000 parolees. They also avoided a government shutdown over the budget. Then, in 2020, Sweeney softened his opposition to one of Murphy's central agenda items, raising the tax rate on incomes above $1 million from 8.97% to 10.75%, as long as Murphy would increase payments into the state's strained pension fund. By September, Murphy signed a budget that included his long-sought millionaire's tax, as well as rebates for many residents of more modest means. He also signed a bill aimed at preventing the building of new polluting facilities in already polluted neighborhoods, and he set in motion plans for a new port for shipping and assembling huge offshore wind turbines.

But 2020 was mostly the year of the coronavirus, which hit New Jersey early and hard. Murphy didn't become as much of a magnet for attention as Gov. Andrew Cuomo from neighboring New York, but Murphy's profile and public approval rose substantially during the early months of the crisis. (The virus hit as Murphy was recovering from surgery to remove a cancerous growth from his kidney.) Through May, more than 40 percent of deaths were tied to long-term care facilities, or about one of every 13 residents living in long-term care homes when the pandemic started, NJ.com calculated. Under Murphy, New Jersey was the first state to issue temporary medical licenses for doctors with foreign licenses, and he developed a better working relationship with President Donald Trump than other Democratic governors. Republicans, and even Sweeney, eventually urged Murphy to pick up the pace of reopening. But after the state successfully reduced its caseload in the summer, infections rose during the fall and winter, and by February 2021, New Jersey was back again near the top of the state rankings for cases and deaths per capita.

In 2021, amid the pandemic's economic fallout, Murphy enacted an updated, $14 billion tax incentive program with greater oversight provisions than the one that had drawn scrutiny. Putting an end to a years-long standoff, Murphy signed enabling legislation for the legalization of recreational marijuana, following overwhelming voter approval of the change in the November 2020 election. He also proposed an aggressive funding plan for state pensions, as Sweeney had urged.

During the depths of the intra-party feud in 2019, Norcross had suggested that Murphy could get a primary challenger in 2021. But with thawing tensions on the Democratic side, Murphy's reelection was looking more secure, and he bolstered his national credentials as chairman of the Democratic Governors Association. In August 2020, Murphy said he would not join a potential cabinet in a Biden administration, clearing the way for another gubernatorial bid. Jack Ciattarelli, who lost the 2017

GOP primary, and Doug Steinhardt, the state Republican chair, both announced candidacies. But given the state's growing Democratic lean, Murphy is favored to become the first Democrat to win a second gubernatorial term since Brendan Byrne in 1977.

Bob Menendez (D)

Appointed 2006, term expires 2024, 3rd term, b. Jan 01, 1954; New York, NY; St. Peter's College, B.A., 1976; Rutgers University Law School, J.D., 1979; Roman Catholic; Married (Nadine Arslanian); 2 children.

Elected Office: Union City Board of Education, 1974-1982, CFO, 1978-1982; Union City Mayor, 1986-1992; NJ Assembly, 1987-1991; NJ Senate, 1991-1992; U.S. House, 1993-2006.

Professional Career: Practicing attorney, 1980-1992.

DC Office: 528 HSOB 20510, 202-224-4744, Fax: 202-228-2197, menendez.senate.gov

State Offices: Barrington, 856-757-5353; Newark, 973-645-3030.

Committees: *Banking, Housing & Urban Affairs*: Financial Institutions & Consumer Protection; Housing, Transportation & Community Development; Securities, Insurance & Investment (Chmn). *Finance*: Health Care; International Trade, Customs & Global Competitiveness; Taxation & IRS Oversight. *Foreign Relations (Chmn)*.

Group Ratings

	ADA	ACLU	AFL-CIO	LCV	COC	HAFA	ACU	CFG	FRC
2020	-	69%	-	92%	-	0%	7%	-	-
2019	95%	C	100%	100%	54%	C	7%	0%	0%

Almanac Ratings 2019-2020

	Economy	Social	Foreign	Composite
Liberal	97%	97%	84%	93%
Conservative	3%	3%	16%	7%

Key Votes of the 116th Congress

1. EPA clean energy rules	Y	5. Russia sanctions	Y
2. U.S./Mex./Can. trade deal	Y	6. Troops in SYR, AFG	Y
3. Cut unemployment benefits	N	7. Veto arms sales to Saudis	Y
4. Shelton to Fed Reserve	N	8. Defense $$$, veto override	Y

9. Barr as Atty. General — N
10. Spending at the border — N
11. Coney Barrett to Sup. Ct. — N
12. Electoral College objections — N

Election Results

Election	Name (Party)	Vote (%)	Cand. Spent	Ind. Exp. Support	Ind. Exp. Oppose
2018 General	Bob Menendez (D)	1,711,654 (54%)	$10,858,720	$1,000,136	$8,852,569
	Bob Hugin (R)	1,357,355 (43%)	$42,683,739	$431,307	$15,649,323
2018 Primary	Bob Menendez (D)	262,477 (62%)			
	Lisa McCormick (D)	158,998 (38%)			

Prior winning percentages: 2018 (54%), 2012 (59%), 2006 (57%), House: 2004 (76%), 2002 (78%), 2000 (79%), 1998 (80%), 1996 (79%), 1994 (71%), 1992 (64%)

For much of the past decade, Bob Menendez, New Jersey's senior senator, has been the top Democrat on the Foreign Relations Committee—chairing the panel from 2013 to 2015 and again in 2021 after his party recaptured the Senate. Regardless of which party controlled the White House, Menendez has been an equal opportunity critic of the executive branch. He complained of President Barack Obama, a fellow Democrat, failing to consult with Congress before making key foreign policy decisions, and he frequently traded insults with GOP President Donald Trump's second secretary of State, Mike Pompeo. After President Joe Biden—himself a former Foreign Relations chairman—took office in January 2021 facing numerous challenges overseas, he mounted a charm offensive to ensure smoother relations with Menendez. Biden's national security adviser, Jake Sullivan, told Politico he was "making it a personal priority to reach out and regularly engage" with Menendez. Biden's secretary of State, Antony Blinken—a former staff director of the Foreign Relations panel—made similar vows, saying Menendez "has proven himself to be both principled and effective."

Given the traditional tensions between the executive and legislative branches over foreign policy, no one anticipated a conflict-free relationship, and Menendez vowed to conduct vigorous oversight of the new administration's moves abroad. But the overtures were clearly an acknowledgment of the clout of Menendez, who has forged a close working relationship with Senate Republicans on foreign policy matters. For his part, Menendez—in an interview with Politico shortly in early 2021—expressed optimism that Biden would operate differently than the Obama White House and seek to coordinate and consult more closely with Congress. "That makes all the difference in the world," Menendez said. "It doesn't mean that we're going to agree 100 percent of the time. But it does mean that we will understand each other, where we're coming from—and more likely than not, we will agree."

Whatever the future course of the relationship, the Biden administration's overtures capped what amounted to a remarkable political comeback for Menendez—who had spent nearly three years of his second Senate term on leave from his post as the ranking member on the Foreign Relations panel, seeking to exonerate himself of federal corruption charges. An 11-week trial of Menendez and his co-defendant—Salomon Melgen, a wealthy Florida eye surgeon whom the senator characterized as a longtime friend and supporter—ended in a hung jury in November 2017. The Justice Department decided against retrying the case. But the Senate Ethics Committee admonished Menendez for bringing "discredit" upon that chamber, and he was in serious political jeopardy before he hung on to win a third full term in 2018—a victory that required the national Democratic Party to funnel millions in campaign funds into a solidly blue state.

When appointed in January 2006 to fill a vacant seat, Menendez became only the second Cuban-American to serve in the Senate. He grew up in Union City, the son of a carpenter and a seamstress—both Cuban emigrants who arrived in the United States before he was born. His North Jersey political base is home to the largest concentration of Cuban-Americans in the United States outside Miami; Menendez's hard-line stance on Cuba reflects the widespread animosity toward the Castro regime among many of his Cuban-American constituents. When Obama moved in late 2014 to restore diplomatic relations with Cuba, Menendez told reporters, "I think it stinks." In 2017, he offered a rare bit of praise for Trump when the latter ordered a rollback of several aspects of Obama's initiative. Menendez praised the move as a "step in the right direction," declaring, "Allowing the Castro regime, as the previous administration did, to steadily and unilaterally reintegrate into the global economy without firm commitments to improve conditions for the Cuban people only emboldened an oppressive dictatorship to tighten its stranglehold over its citizens."

By the time Menendez graduated from Jersey City-based St. Peter's College—now St. Peter's University—he was a member of the Union City School Board, elected when he was just 20. During this period, Menendez served as an aide to Union City Mayor William Musto, a political mentor. But when Musto was brought up on corruption charges in the early 1980s, Menendez—then in his late 20s—testified against him, wearing a bulletproof vest after receiving death threats. That chapter of his life was widely retold, with some measure of irony, more than three decades later when Menendez himself was hit with corruption charges—becoming only the 12th sitting senator to be indicted.

Shortly after his testimony helped convict Musto, Menendez lost a bid to oust his former boss at the polls. But in 1986, with Musto imprisoned, a 32-year-old Menendez was elected mayor of Union City. Menendez was elected to the New Jersey General Assembly in 1987 and to the state Senate in 1991; he served simultaneously as mayor and state legislator, then a common practice in New Jersey. In 1992, Menendez was easily elected to an open seat in the House, where he was admired—if not always warmly regarded—for his prodigious fundraising and strategic savvy. In 2002, Menendez raised $4 million for Democrats as they sought to recapture the House. The party fell short, but Menendez accumulated chits. After California's Nancy Pelosi defeated Maryland's Steny Hoyer for party whip, the job of caucus chair—then No. 3 in the party hierarchy—opened. Menendez, with Hoyer's support, defeated Pelosi-backed Rosa DeLauro of Connecticut, 104-103.

When Democratic Sen. Frank Lautenberg announced his retirement in 1999, Menendez was expected to run for the seat. But New Jersey Sen. Robert Torricelli, then the chairman of the Democratic Senatorial Campaign Committee, preferred Jon Corzine, a wealthy former investment banker who could self-finance his campaign. Corzine was elected.

Menendez's Senate aspirations were fulfilled when Corzine was elected governor in 2005; he appointed Menendez to serve the remaining year of his Senate term. Running for his first full term in 2006, Menendez faced state Sen. Tom Kean Jr., son and namesake of a popular former governor. Like many races in New Jersey, theirs devolved into a bare-knuckled brawl. Kean called attention to Menendez's activities and influence in Hudson County—a Democratic bastion with a history of machine politics and corruption. Two months before the election, U.S. Attorney Chris Christie subpoenaed records from a lease arrangement between Menendez and an anti-poverty group for which Menendez had sought federal funding and that had paid him $300,000 in rent on a building he owned in Union City. It was then revealed the Kean campaign's opposition researchers had contacted a former Hudson County executive in federal prison on corruption charges. Menendez struck back with a TV spot: "Federal prisoner 25038-050. He's Tom Kean Jr.'s newest adviser." Menendez won 53%-44%.

Menendez chaired the DSCC during the 2010 election cycle. The economic downturn and initial public discontent with the newly passed Affordable Care Act worked against him. But, under his leadership, the DSCC outraised its GOP counterpart. Even though Democrats lost six seats, it marked the first time in 100 years that the party in power held on to the Senate while losing control of the House. At the same time, Menendez acquired a coveted slot on the Finance Committee. In that role, he backed unsuccessful moves to add a "public option" to the Affordable Care Act. That incensed New Jersey tea party activists, who launched a recall attempt in early 2010. Menendez called it an unconstitutional "political stunt," and the state Supreme Court sided with him, halting the effort. In 2012, Republicans struggled to find a top-tier challenger. The task fell to state Sen. Joe Kyrillos, who took in $4.6 million. Menendez again demonstrated his fundraising prowess, raising more than $17 million and winning, 59%-39%.

Menendez has been a major player on immigration reform. A bill he introduced in 2010 failed to become law, but one of its components—the DREAM Act, which would have offered a path to citizenship to immigrants brought to the country illegally as children—was put into policy by Obama, who established the Deferred Action for Childhood Arrivals program by executive order. In 2013, Menendez was among a bipartisan group of eight senators that crafted a reform proposal; it passed the Senate but was never taken up by the GOP-controlled House. In early 2018, he was again part of a bipartisan group that came up with a compromise to retain by law protections for those covered by DACA while providing funds to satisfy Trump's insistence on a wall along the U.S.-Mexico border. The deal fell apart when Trump declined to endorse it. In early 2019, when Trump's demand for funding for a southern border wall led to a protracted government shutdown, Menendez rejected an invitation to appear at a White House signing ceremony for a human trafficking bill he had sponsored. "I did not want to be a potted plant for the president's despicable policies as it relates to immigrants and the whole question of the southern border," he told NJ Advance Media.

During both the Obama and Trump administrations, Menendez was sharply critical of the handling of relations with a longtime Middle Eastern adversary: Iran. He irritated the Obama White House with his outspoken opposition to the Iran nuclear agreement it had negotiated; he was one of only four Senate Democrats to vote against the pact in late 2015. But, when Trump announced in May 2018 he was withdrawing from the pact, Menendez charged, "Trump is risking U.S. national security, recklessly upending foundational partnerships with key U.S. allies in Europe and gambling with Israel's security." Biden vowed to revive the Iran agreement during the campaign, but his early hard line in diplomatic maneuvering won measured praise from Menendez. "I applaud President Biden for saying…his administration will not offer significant [economic] sanctions relief to the Iranians to get them back to the negotiating table," Menendez said in February 2021, adding, "I support the administration's efforts to reach a diplomatic solution with Iran to address its nuclear program that is both longer and stronger than previous commitments and address[es] other pressing challenges."

If there were a common thread between Menendez's criticism of Obama's efforts to engage Cuba and Iran and his skewering of Trump's chumminess toward nations ranging from Russia to Saudi Arabia to Turkey, it is a wariness toward dealings with oppressive regimes. Releasing a report on what he regarded as the Trump administration's foreign policy failures just weeks before the 2020 elections, Menendez recounted a call he received from Trump in May 2019—after the president had met with Viktor Orban, the autocratic leader of Hungary. According to Menendez, Trump sought to convince him that Orban was a "good guy" who had agreed to buy a significant amount of U.S. military equipment. It did little to sway Menendez, who declared in the report: "While the U.S. will need to move forward and set a strong example, it cannot ignore the damage done by the Trump administration to democratic institutions and values. Our country must engage in some accounting of the damage done and take steps to protect our democracy from future abuses."

The call from Trump to Menendez arguably represented a high point in their relationship. Just months earlier, in October 2018, Pompeo had accused Menendez of "putting our nation at risk" by holding up Senate votes on 60 State Department nominees. Menendez responded on the Senate floor: "When the White House, either through negligence or incompetence, sends us unvetted, unqualified nominees incapable and often times offensive, my staff and I must exercise due diligence on behalf of the American people." A month earlier, Menendez introduced a bill to pressure Russia as he assailed "Trump's willful paralysis in the face of Kremlin aggression." In a floor speech, Menendez went so far as to raise "the entirely legitimate question of whether Donald Trump could be compromised by the Russian government." Citing a series of revelations, Menendez said, "The American people deserve to know … if Trump is an agent of the Russian Federation."

The verbal sniping escalated in late 2019, when the Trump administration pulled troops out of northern Syria. Appearing on ABC's "This Week," Menendez belittled Pompeo's claim that the region had been stabilized by the troop withdrawal, gibing, "I think the secretary lives in a parallel, alternate universe." The rhetoric became even more adversarial—and personal—after Trump in May 2020 fired State Department Inspector General Steve Linick. Linick was investigating whether Pompeo had improperly used a political appointee for personal tasks and whether the administration had illegally circumvented Congress to make billions of dollars in arms sales to Saudi Arabia. Pressed during a news conference about Linick's firing, Pompeo accused Menendez of leaking stories, pointedly adding: "I don't get my ethics guidance from a man who was criminally prosecuted—case number 15-155 in New Jersey federal district court—a man for whom his Senate colleagues, bipartisan, said basically that he was taking bribes." Menendez called Pompeo's blast as predictable as it is shameful," adding, "The Secretary should focus on…getting his story straight as to why he wanted to target IG Linick."

Shortly after Menendez first took the gavel of the Foreign Relations Committee in early 2013, he was engulfed in personal controversy—as news outlets reported he had possibly violated Senate rules by accepting and not reporting two round-trip flights to the Dominican Republic in 2010 from Melgen, whose medical offices had been raided by the FBI. Menendez paid the estimated cost of the flights and related expenses—$58,500—saying the matter "unfortunately fell through the cracks." Menendez ultimately repaid Melgen more than $112,400 to comply with the Ethics Committee's decision in his case, according to disclosure reports filed in early 2019. Four months before his joint trial with Menendez began, Melgen was convicted in a separate case in Florida on 67 counts of Medicare fraud, which the judge said involved theft of at least $73 million. He was sentenced to 17 years in prison.

When criminal charges were brought against Menendez in April 2015, a Justice Department spokesman described it as "a bribery scheme in which Menendez allegedly accepted gifts from Melgen in exchange for using the power of his Senate office to benefit Melgen's financial and personal interests." The gifts that Menendez allegedly received included luxury vacations, pricey golf outings and more than $750,000 in campaign contributions. In turn, Menendez was accused of intervening with federal officials after a finding that Melgen had overbilled Medicare by nearly $9 million, working to protect Melgen's $500 million port security contract with the Dominican Republic, and obtaining U.S. visas for several of Melgen's foreign girlfriends. Menendez's legal team argued the gifts from Melgen were simply generosity from one close friend to another—and not tied to any quid pro quo.

Menendez denied any wrongdoing when indicted on charges that included bribery, conspiracy and making false statements; he later blamed the allegations on a smear campaign by the Castro regime. He ignored calls to resign; the trial was delayed multiple times as he fought to dismiss the case. The Supreme Court denied his request to dismiss many of the counts, setting up a September 2017 trial in Newark. In November, after four days of jury deliberations, District Judge William Walls declared a mistrial. One juror told reporters that, by a 10-2 margin, the jury had supported finding Menendez not guilty. In January 2018, the Justice Department announced it would retry the case. But, less than a week later, Walls threw out seven of the 18 counts. In his ruling, he wrote that the prosecution wanted the court "to fashion speculative inferences under the conclusory generalizations of context, chronology, escalation, concealment, and a pattern of corrupt activity—each of which is empty of relevant evidential fact. Quoting Gertrude Stein, the judge concluded, "There is no there there." Citing the impact of Walls' decision, the Justice Department reversed itself and said it would not retry Menendez and Melgen.

Restored to his post as ranking Democrat on the Foreign Relations Committee—which he had temporarily relinquished when indicted nearly three years earlier—Menendez moved to line up endorsements for reelection from virtually every major state Democratic official. But the court case had taken its toll politically; a poll taken as the trial got underway showed 50 percent of likely voters felt he did not deserve to be reelected.

After the mistrial, Senate Republican Leader Mitch McConnell called on the Ethics Committee "to immediately investigate Sen. Menendez's actions, which led to his indictment." In an April 2018 letter of admonishment approved unanimously, the six-member panel found Menendez had "knowingly and repeatedly" violated Senate rules. "You demonstrated disregard for these standards by placing your Senate office in Dr. Melgen's service at the same time you repeatedly accepted gifts of significant value from him," the panel wrote. "Your assistance to Dr. Melgen under these circumstances demonstrated poor judgment, and it risked undermining the public's confidence in the Senate." Two months later, Menendez's political vulnerability was apparent as Lisa McCormick, a newspaper publisher devoid of campaign funds and unknown statewide, received nearly 40 percent of the Democratic primary vote.

By that time, Republican Bob Hugin had spent $2 million on attack ads aimed at Menendez. Hugin, like Menendez, had grown up in Union City in modest circumstances. He went on to make a fortune in the biopharmaceutical industry and ended up spending $36 million from his own pocket in seeking to become the first New Jersey Republican elected to the Senate since 1972. Hugin spent heavily on TV ads reminding voters of the charges on which Menendez had been tried. Menendez responded with spots targeting the firm that Hugin headed before resigning to run for Senate—for sharply increasing the price of a key cancer drug and paying $280 million to settle a Justice Department lawsuit over the marketing of two cancer drugs for unapproved treatments. Two Hugin ads sought to revive unsubstantiated allegations—carried by conservative news sites when Menendez's relationship with Melgen first came under scrutiny—that Menendez had hired underage prostitutes in the Dominican Republic. Dominican police later said an attorney there had paid three women to make up the stories.

National Democratic strategists became alarmed when, in mid-October, private tracking polls had Menendez ahead by only 2 percentage points, according to the New York Times. A super PAC with ties to Senate Democratic Leader Chuck Schumer spent $7.6 million to prop up Menendez in a state where Hillary Clinton beat Trump by 14 points in 2016. Menendez's personal campaign committee spent $13.5 million, barely one-third of the $39 million spent by Hugin.

Menendez could largely thank Trump for winning: The president's approval ratings in New Jersey were stuck in the mid-30s. A Quinnipiac University polling analyst told Roll Call that, while squeamish about pulling the lever for a candidate recently tried for bribery, many voters "may hold their nose to cast a ballot" for Menendez because they wanted "to keep [the] seat in the 'D' column in a blue state where …Trump consistently remains unpopular." Menendez was reelected,54%-43%. In his election night speech, Menendez—defiant throughout his legal ordeal—appeared to acknowledge he faced work to repair the damage to his 45-year political career: "I pledge to spend every day fighting for you and your families and to earn back your respect."

Cory Booker (D)

Elected 2013, term expires 2026, 2nd full term, b. Apr 27, 1969; Washington, DC; Stanford University, B.A., 1991; Stanford University, M.A., 1992; The Queens College, University of Oxford, 1994; Yale Law School, J.D., 1997; Baptist; Single.

Elected Office: Newark City Council, 1998-2002; Newark Mayor 2006-2013.

Professional Career: Attorney; Partner, law firm, 1992.

DC Office: 717 HSOB 20510, 202-224-3224, Fax: 202-224-8378, booker.senate.gov

State Offices: Camden, 856-338-8922; Newark, 973-639-8700.

Committees: *Agriculture, Nutrition & Forestry*: Conservation, Climate, Forestry & Natural Resources; Food & Nutrition, Specialty Crops, Organics & Research (Chmn); Livestock, Dairy, Poultry, Local Food Sys & Food Safety & Sec. *Foreign Relations*: Africa & Global Health Policy; Internat'l Dev Instit & Internat'l Econ, Energy & Environ Policy; Near East, South Asia, Central Asia & Counterterrorism. *Judiciary*: Competition Policy, Antitrust & Consumer Rights; Criminal

Justice & Counterterrorism (Chmn); Federal Courts, Oversight, Agency Action & Federal Rights; Immigration, Citizenship & Border Security. *Small Business & Entrepreneurship.*

Group Ratings

	ADA	ACLU	AFL-CIO	LCV	COC	HAFA	ACU	CFG	FRC
2020	-	90%	100%	-	0%	-	4%	-	-
2019	60%	C	100%	50%	30%	C	4%	-	0%

Almanac Ratings 2019-2020

	Economy	Social	Foreign	Composite
Liberal	100%	100%	97%	99%
Conservative	0%	0%	4%	1%

Key Votes of the 116th Congress

1. EPA clean energy rules	N/A	5. Russia sanctions	Y	9. Barr as Atty. General	N
2. U.S./Mex./Can. trade deal	N	6. Troops in SYR, AFG	N	10. Spending at the border	N/A
3. Cut unemployment benefits	N	7. Veto arms sales to Saudis	Y	11. Coney Barrett to Sup. Ct.	N
4. Shelton to Fed Reserve	N	8. Defense $$$, veto override	N	12. Electoral College objections	N

Election Results

Election	Name (Party)	Vote (%)	Cand. Spent	Ind. Exp. Support	Ind. Exp. Oppose
2020 General	Cory Booker (D)............................	2,541,238 (57%)	$3,269,544	$1,147	
	Rik Mehta (R)................................	1,817,090 (41%)	$571,657	$1,325	$113
2020 Primary	Cory Booker (D)............................	838,110 (88%)			
	Lawrence Hamm (D).........................	118,802 (12%)			

Prior winning percentages: 2014 (56%), 2013 special (55%)

Ever since Democrat Cory Booker, New Jersey's junior senator, arrived on Capitol Hill, the question had been when—not if—the telegenic former Rhodes scholar would run for president. In fact, Booker was a force in national Democratic politics even before winning an October 2013 special election to the Senate. For seven years prior to that, he attracted bountiful media coverage as mayor of Newark—New Jersey's largest municipality—where he became the poster child for the problems and challenges confronting urban America. In addition to charisma and a compelling biography, Booker brought with him an arsenal of advantages when he launched his bid for the 2020 Democratic presidential nomination: A knack for engaging folks on social media and an ability to mesmerize audiences in person and bring crowds to their feet. And, before formally entering the contest in February 2019, Booker had lined up numerous endorsements and assembled a talented campaign staff in the early primary and caucus states.

But Booker exited the race by early 2020, even before voters began choosing delegates for the Democratic National Convention. His failure to gain traction puzzled journalists, and a multitude of explanations were offered. The most prevalent theory: Booker's message of love and unity didn't match the divisive era. Booker "has fallen well short of expectations as his message, grounded in sweetness and light, collides with the sentiments of Democrats who want to see President [Donald] Trump not just beaten in 2020 but battered," the Los Angeles Times observed weeks before he dropped out of the contest. Former South Carolina Gov. Jim Hodges suggested to the newspaper that Booker had fallen between the cracks in a crowded field. "He's not angry enough; the angry vote is divided between [Sens. Elizabeth] Warren and [Bernie] Sanders," Hodges said." He's not new enough; [former South Bend Indiana] Mayor Pete [Buttigieg] has the 'new' vote. [Joe] Biden has the establishment. He's sort of been elbowed out of the race."

Like another rival contender for the 2020 nomination, now-Vice President Kamala Harris, Booker was often compared to Barack Obama: He and the former president both started as community organizers and were involved in local politics before reaching the Senate in their mid-40s. As he sought the nomination, Booker repeatedly portrayed himself as capable of reassembling the coalition that made Obama the first Black president. But race may have hindered Booker's candidacy, despite Obama's having broken that barrier. In a year when many Democratic voters' imperative was ousting Trump, there appeared to be doubt about whether a Black nominee could do so— a political conundrum that similarly bedeviled the numerous female candidates.

Booker is one of only seven Black members elected to the Senate since Reconstruction, a group that also includes Obama and Harris. Booker was born in Washington D.C.—his parents were IBM business executives—but was raised in the affluent, predominantly white New York suburb of Harrington Park New Jersey. Barely five years after the passage of the Civil Rights Act of 1964, the family had a hard time buying a home there because of racism. "My parents tried to move us into a neighborhood with great public schools, but Realtors wouldn't sell us a home because of the color of our skin," Booker said in a video announcing his presidential bid. "A group of white lawyers, who had watched the courage of civil rights activists, were inspired to help Black families in their own community, including mine. And they changed the course of my entire life." Booker was named to the All-USA high school football team and played tight end at Stanford University—where he earned a bachelor's degree and a master's in sociology.

As a Rhodes scholar, he studied at Oxford University before graduating from Yale Law School. In a 2019 interview with the Washington Post, Booker credited his time in the Rhodes program as nurturing the politics of "love" and "common ground" that he espoused on the campaign trail. "My spiritual life really took off at Oxford," he said. Booker, a Baptist, became co-president of the L'Chaim Society—an Orthodox Jewish student group started by an American rabbi with whom he became close friends; years later, it was not unusual for Booker to sprinkle campaign speeches with passages from the Torah. His political ambitions were also apparent at Oxford: Classmates often referred to him as "Sen. Booker." One classmate, future Los Angeles Mayor Eric Garcetti, told the Post, "I didn't know back then if I would run for office, but we knew that Cory was definitely going to run."

In 1998, Booker did run—successfully—for City Council in Newark, 25 miles south of where he had grown up. In his last year of law school, he had begun working there as a tenants' rights advocate, soon moving into one of the city's poorest and most violent housing projects. He lived there until the city housing authority razed it in 2006, the year he was elected mayor. Booker then bought a home nearby in Newark's predominantly African American Central Ward, where he still lives. (As a presidential aspirant, he frequently noted that he was the "only candidate who lives in a low-income, Black and brown community.")In2002, he challenged longtime Mayor Sharpe James, a fellow Democrat and African American. The bitter race prompted the federal government to send in observers on Election Day; the campaign became the subject of a documentary film titled "Street Fight," which was nominated for an Oscar and helped raise Booker's political star. But he lost that election 53%-47%.

Booker practiced law as he geared up for a rematch in 2006. But, after five terms, James declined to run again. Booker won 72 percent of the vote against a former James deputy, and a slate of Booker's allies rode his coattails onto the City Council. As mayor, Booker built an impressive network of celebrity friends and acquaintances in the technology, finance and entertainment sectors, as his contacts yielded $400 million in philanthropic efforts for the city. But his star power was a double-edged sword: He faced criticism for traveling the country to tend to his influential network and build his national profile at the expense of dealing with the day-to-day problems of his constituents. A proclivity toward rhetorical excess—notwithstanding his considerable oratorical abilities—also surfaced (and would continue to plague him in the Senate). In his first term, he frequently referred to a drug dealer who appears to have been a composite character, if not entirely made up.

Booker was elected promising a renaissance of one of the nation's most troubled cities. Newark balanced its budget for the first time in a decade, opened new parks and spent more on mass transit. But Booker was unable to make a lasting dent in the city's notorious crime rate. A Newark Star-Ledger story noted the city had 83 homicides and 2,850 other violent crimes in 2003 under James compared with 95 homicides and 3,220 violent crimes in 2012, the last full year of Booker's mayoralty. His push to improve schools received mixed grades. A member of Booker's celebrity network, Facebook co-founder Mark Zuckerberg, contributed $100 million. Booker and GOP Gov. Chris Christie joined Zuckerberg to announce the donation on "The Oprah Winfrey Show"—whose host had dubbed Booker the "rock star mayor." The initiative doubled the number of students attending public charter schools, which significantly outperform public schools in Newark. But the overall changes didn't show the widespread success many had hoped for; Zuckerberg largely abandoned his plan to use Newark as a national model for education reform, amid criticism of Booker and Christie's top-down approach.

Still, Booker was easily reelected in 2010. His persona as the city's savior gained near-mythical status after he shoveled an elderly resident's walk when a city plow failed to show up and after he rescued a neighbor from a burning house. Booker formed a friendship with Obama and was a featured speaker at the 2012 Democratic National Convention. But Booker created a particularly uncomfortable moment for Obama when, on NBC's "Meet the Press," he criticized Democratic attacks on Republican presidential nominee Mitt Romney's work at Bain Capital—a leading private equity firm—as "crap" and "nauseating." He also contended painting Wall Street "with broad brushes" was unfair to "the good people who work there."

Booker was less defending Romney than sticking up for the private equity industry, which has a significant presence in New Jersey. But his comments continued to haunt him among members of his party's left wing up to and including his presidential run, despite his co-sponsorship of such progressive initiatives as "Medicare for All" and the "Green New Deal"in recent years. To a significant extent, it complicated Booker's candidacy by leaving him dangling between the centrist and progressive lanes that defined the race for the 2020 nomination.

In January 2013, Booker announced plans to seek the Senate seat held by Democrat Frank Lautenberg when it opened in 2014. The 89-year-old Lautenberg had health problems and was all but certain to retire. But he publicly bristled at what he regarded as a lack of deference by Booker; it led to some fallout when Lautenberg's death from viral pneumonia in June 2013 triggered a special election that October. Members of the Lautenberg family endorsed Rep. Frank Pallone, who attracted the backing of organized labor. But Booker won a four-way Democratic primary with 59 percent of the vote to just 20 percent for runner-up Pallone. Booker did collect a few political dents along the way. The New York Times reported that, while full-time mayor of a struggling city, he had founded an internet startup on the side designed to make it easier to collect and share videos; financial backing had come from friends such as Winfrey and Google executive Eric Schmidt. To stem the controversy, Booker stepped down from the company's board and donated his ownership interest to charity.

Booker's general election opponent was Steve Lonegan, a former small-town mayor and hard-line conservative—a decided underdog in a state that had not elected a Republican senator since 1972. Lonegan managed to make the race closer than expected, in part because of a national political climate that was turning difficult for Democrats. Some of Booker's problems were self-inflicted, such as flirtatious tweets he sent to a dancer at an Oregon strip club disclosed in media reports. There was also renewed scrutiny about his earlier claims to a relationship with the drug dealer he called "T-Bone." In his early days as mayor, Booker often spoke of how T-Bone had once threatened him but later came to him to recount a difficult childhood and seek help staying out of prison. The Star-Ledger had been unable to find evidence that T-Bone existed, and—during the 2013 race—a Rutgers University historian who was a Booker supporter told National Review that Booker had admitted to him T-Bone was a composite character. Booker dodged the issue in a Washington Post interview at that time. Several years earlier, he had said T-Bone "is an archetype of so many people that are out there. He is 1,000 percent a real person."

While such controversies enabled Lonegan to cut into Booker's lead, Booker pulled off a solid victory, 55%-44%. He similarly won his first full term in 2014 with 56 percent of the vote—defeating conservative activist Jeff Bell, who had run for the same seat in 1978 and lost to Democrat Bill Bradley. Booker won a second full term in 2020 after dropping out of the presidential race, besting political novice Rik Mehta, a pharmacist and attorney, 57%-41%.

When he launched his presidential candidacy nearly two years earlier, Booker did so with the backing of all Democrats in the state's congressional delegation, including his senior colleague, Sen. Bob Menendez. Menendez's strong endorsement spoke to the close friendship that he and Booker have forged during their tenure together. It stands in notable contrast to two decades earlier, when the toxic nature of the relationship between the state's Democratic senators at the time—Lautenberg and Robert Torricelli—was an open secret on Capitol Hill. As Menendez stood trial in 2017 on federal corruption charges, Booker testified on his behalf as a character witness. After the trial ended in a hung jury and the Justice Department opted not to retry the case, Menendez faced a difficult reelection race in 2018: Booker was a loyal surrogate for Menendez during that campaign, declaring at one point, "I'm the Robin to his Batman."

Like other high-wattage figures elected to the Senate, Booker initially sought to keep a low profile and focus on state-specific issues. Just 44 when sworn in, he told reporters that he "absolutely… unequivocally" was not interested in running for president or vice president in 2016. Nonetheless, he was reported by New York magazine to have been among Democratic presidential nominee Hillary Clinton's top three choices for a running mate. Immediately after the 2016 election, Booker joined Menendez on the Foreign Relations Committee, shoring up his foreign policy credentials. In late 2018, he took a seat on the Judiciary Committee.

Striving to show bipartisanship soon after his election to the Senate, Booker sought to make friends with conservative Sen. Ted Cruz, meeting with the Texan for a three-hour dinner that Booker later described as "one of the best constitutional law discussions since I got out of law school."

He joined with another tea party standard-bearer, Kentucky Sen. Rand Paul, on a bill in early 2015 to prevent federal prosecutions of medical marijuana patients in states where it is legal. In 2017, Booker went a step further by introducing legislation to legalize recreational marijuana, which he had declined to support a couple of years earlier. Booker reintroduced the marijuana bill in early 2019, while also seeking to burnish his progressive credentials on another front: He appeared with a rival presidential contender, Vermont Sen. Bernie Sanders, to promote legislation aimed at lowering what Booker termed "the outrageous and unjustifiably high cost of prescription drugs."

The bill was, in part, an effort by Booker to recover politically from an episode two years earlier, when he attracted scorn from progressives by being one of just 13 Senate Democrats to vote against a largely symbolic amendment to import prescription drugs from Canada. (New Jersey is home to several major pharmaceutical companies.) The financial and pharmaceutical industries have been major donors to Booker, who in 2017 sought to defuse the issue by placing a "pause" on contributions from drug companies "because it arouses so much criticism." In introducing the legislation with Sanders, Booker defended his vote a couple years earlier, which he said had come in conjunction with a "late night messaging amendment." He added that he had gone to work soon afterward to draft an importation bill with adequate safety standards.

Booker's most notable effort in working across the aisle bore fruit in late 2018, when a major criminal justice reform bill—which increased federal judges' discretion over drug-related sentences —was signed into law. Initially, Booker worked closely with South Carolina Sen. Tim Scott— the Senate's only Black Republican—to craft a reform package. He later collaborated with more conservatives, Utah's Mike Lee and Iowa's Chuck Grassley, as well as Democratic Whip Dick Durbin, on a similar proposal that won broad bipartisan backing. But, amid opposition from several hard-line conservatives, the bill died in 2016 when then-Majority Leader Mitch McConnell declined to bring it to the floor. Booker vowed to redouble his efforts to pass the legislation: And he later did—with an assist from President Donald Trump, whose adviser and son-in-law Jared Kushner negotiated with McConnell.

Early in the Trump administration, Booker led the charge against Trump's nomination of then-Alabama Sen. Jeff Sessions as attorney general because of what he described as Sessions' long record of "hostility" toward people of color—apparently becoming the first senator to testify against a fellow senator's Cabinet confirmation. He voted against many of Trump's Cabinet nominees, including Betsy DeVos for Education secretary, despite her role in pushing the Newark school reform experiment he oversaw a decade earlier. And, during a Judiciary Committee hearing in January 2018, Booker yelled at Homeland Security Secretary Kirstjen Nielsen while questioning her about a White House meeting at which Trump reportedly had referred to several African nations as "shithole countries." When Nielsen said she couldn't recall if Trump had used that language, Booker responded, "Your silence and amnesia is complicity."

Eight months later, at a Judiciary Committee hearing on Brett Kavanaugh's Supreme Court nomination, Booker—charging that Republicans were hiding behind arguments of privacy and national security in refusing to publicly release relevant documents—announced that, as an act of "civil disobedience," he would release 12 pages of emails relating to a discussion of racial profiling during Kavanaugh's time as a White House counsel. When a Republican committee member, Texas Sen. John Cornyn, suggested he could be ousted for releasing such material, Booker dared Cornyn to try to do so, as Booker's Democratic colleagues came to his defense. "This is about the closest I'll probably ever have in my life to an 'I am Spartacus' moment," Booker said, alluding to the 1960 film about a slave uprising against the Roman Empire. A problem: The documents at issue had been cleared for public release the morning of the hearing, making Booker's statements appear little more than theatrics. Booker later told CNN he did not know at the time the emails had been cleared for release and, amid widespread guffaws, sought to walk back his comments a bit—saying he did not intend to compare himself to Spartacus.

It was not the only time during the Kavanaugh hearings that Booker's choice of words caused blowback: He retreated from an assertion that those who supported putting Kavanaugh on the Supreme Court were "complicit in evil" after those comments sparked criticism. "I've been exuberant in my beliefs, and I've learned a lot through this process, Booker told committee colleagues, adding, "I know that I have not been as precise and allowed my comments to be mischaracterized."

With the 2020 election looming, Trump appeared to notice Booker as a potential opponent: At an October 2018 news conference, the president derided Booker's tenure in Newark, calling him a "horrible mayor." Booker responded: "I will never let him pull me so low as to hate him. I'm going to continue to be a voice in this country for the love, for bringing the nation together, not driving the nation apart." At the 2016 Democratic National Convention, he delivered a soaring speech that slammed Trump while touting a more hopeful America: It earned comparisons to the stirring speech Obama delivered at the 2004 convention, both for the passion of its delivery and the sweep of its narrative. As with Obama 12 years earlier, it intensified speculation about Booker's future ambitions.

An irony of Booker's bid to become president is that he struggled throughout it to raise money, despite his longtime connections to both Wall Street and Silicon Valley. The latter ties had long caused the party's left wing to view him with skepticism, and, in an effort to take the issue off the table, he initially rejected the support of super PACs, which could have helped him gain traction. Without the type of digital, small-donor apparatus on which his rivals relied, he was left with the worst of both worlds. In September 2019, he warned supporters that he would have to drop out unless he raised $1.7 million in 10 days. The gambit worked, but his fundraising woes made it impossible to overcome the political headwinds he faced in terms of both messaging and the overall dynamics of the race. In the last quarter of 2019, just prior to leaving the contest, Booker raised $6.6 million —about a fifth of what Sanders raised the same quarter.

Booker qualified for the first five primary debates, but low poll numbers kept him out of a sixth debate in Los Angeles in December. He dropped out just before the seventh debate in Des Moines in January, saying he no longer saw a path forward. Polls showed him with the support of barely 3 percent of Iowa caucusgoers. Several weeks later, Booker endorsed Biden over Sanders. He insisted he was enthusiastic about his decision, even though he had sharply criticized the former vice president in mid-2019 when Biden reminisced at a fundraiser about an ability to "bring people together"—and even work with a couple of segregationist Senate colleagues. At the time, Booker also told CNN, "There's a lot of people who are concerned about Joe Biden's ability to carry the ball all the way across the end line without fumbling."

Back on Capitol Hill, Booker joined Sen. Harris in sponsoring police reform legislation after George Floyd, an unarmed Black man, died in Minneapolis after a white police officer knelt on his neck for several minutes. Included in the measure was a ban on federal police officers using chokeholds and a loosening of the legal standards for pursuing criminal and civil penalties for police misconduct. Senate Republicans, then holding a majority, put forth an alternative. Democrats blocked that measure, which they argued was insufficient.

Days earlier, Booker bitterly battled with Paul on the Senate floor over a federal anti-lynching statute, which had passed the House by a bipartisan majority and was being debated in the Senate on the same day as Floyd's funeral. Paul was blocking the measure, arguing that it was overly broad; he wanted to amend it. Booker objected:"Of all days, we're doing this right now when, God, if this bill passed today, what that would mean for America? …It would speak volumes for the racial pain and the hurt of generations. Pointing to Paul, Booker declared, "He is my friend ... but I am so raw today." The measure failed to clear the Senate, but was reintroduced in early 2021.

Donald Norcross (D)

Elected 2014, 4th full term, b. Dec 13, 1958; Camden, NJ; Camden County College, A.S., 1979; Lutheran; Married (Andrea Doran); 3 children; 2 grandchildren.

Elected Office: NJ Assembly, 2010; NJ Senate, 2010-2014.

Professional Career: Electrician; Assistant business Manager, Local 351, Int'l Brotherhood of Electrical Workers; President, Southern NJ AFL-CIO.

DC Office: 2437 RHOB 20515, 202-225-6501, Fax: 202-225-6583, norcross.house.gov

State Offices: Cherry Hill, 856-427-7000.

Committees: *Armed Services*: Seapower & Projection Forces; Tactical Air & Land Forces (Chmn). *Education & Labor*: Health, Employment, Labor & Pensions; Workforce Protections. *Science, Space & Technology*: Energy; Space & Aeronautics.

Group Ratings

	ADA	ACLU	AFL-CIO	LCV	COC	HAFA	ACU	CFG	FRC
2020	**	79%	**	100%	-	0%	3%	**	-
2019	95%	C	90%	97%	53%	C	3%	12%	0%

Almanac Ratings 2019-2020

	Economy	Social	Foreign	Composite
Liberal	100%	100%	96%	99%
Conservative	0%	0%	4%	1%

Key Votes of the 116th Congress

1. U.S./Mex./Can. trade deal	N	5. Russia sanctions	Y	9. Firearms background checks Y
2. First Coronavirus response	Y	6. Troops in Syria	Y	10. Spending at the border	N
3. HEROES Act	Y	7. Veto arms sales to Saudis	Y	11. Marijuana liberalized rules	Y
4. CASH Act	Y	8. Defense $$$, veto override	Y	12. Electoral College objections N

Election Results

Election	Name (Party)	Vote (%)		Cand. Spent	Ind. Exp. Support	Ind. Exp. Oppose
2020 General	Donald Norcross (D)	240,567	(62%)	$1,079,140	$5,823	
	Claire Gustafson (R)	144,463	(37%)	$1,500		$113
2020 Primary	Donald Norcross (D)	94,084	(100%)			

Prior winning percentages: 2018 (64%), 2016 (60%), 2014 (57%), 2014 special (57%)

Democrat Donald Norcross is a usually reliable ally of Democratic leaders and organized labor. He has gained influence on the Armed Services Committee, where he keeps a close eye on New Jersey interests, and now chairs his own subcommittee. He has not been seriously challenged for reelection since first coming to office in 2014. His brother, George Norcross III, is a powerful South Jersey political boss who has recently come into conflict with Governor Phil Murphy.

Norcross graduated from Camden County College. He started his career as an electrician, installing power lines in refineries and on the top of bridges. Later, he became a business manager for the International Brotherhood of Electrical Workers, and president of the Southern New Jersey AFL-CIO. Norcross jumped into politics in 2009, when he won election to the state Assembly. A year later, he was appointed to fill a state Senate seat. He was a leading backer of the state's constitutional amendment to raise the minimum wage. On some issues—notably charter schools—Norcross staked out more centrist positions.

Norcross ran for Congress when longtime Democratic Rep. Robert Andrews resigned to take a job at a Philadelphia law firm. With Andrews' backing, he lined up endorsements from key Democrats across South Jersey. Norcross' two primary opponents, Frank Minor and Frank Broomell, tried to play up his entrenched political ties as a liability. He defeated them with 72 percent of the primary vote. In the general election, he faced Republican Garry Cobb, a local talk-radio personality and former Philadelphia Eagles linebacker. Cobb criticized the "Norcross machine" and said he wanted to clean up politics in South Jersey. Norcross outspent Cobb $2.1 million to $108,000 and won by a comfortable though less than overwhelming 57%-39%.

Norcross is a relatively moderate Democrat, especially on foreign policy, and he occasionally goes his own way. He supported approval of the Keystone XL pipeline, which has been strongly backed by many labor unions but opposed by most Democrats. He opposed President Barack Obama's nuclear deal with Iran, saying that "a better deal can be achieved," though he said that the October 2017 decision by President Donald Trump to decertify the agreement was "reckless" and "could harm our alliances." In January 2018, he was one of 65 House Democrats who voted for the FISA bill to expand government surveillance authority. Since 2014, Norcross has served on the leadership-controlled House Democratic Steering and Policy Committee, where he has the largely honorary title of parliamentarian. He also holds a leadership position in the Congressional Progressive Caucus, serving as vice chair since 2019.

Norcross sits on the Education and Labor panel and has been a leader on issues dealing with organized labor. Norcross worked with others to counter the setback to unions in the Supreme Court's 2018 ruling in the Janus case, which dealt with compulsory membership. "Our goal is to make sure the next generation of workers has a fair playing field to earn enough to take care of a family and retire with dignity," he said. In 2020, Norcross introduced a proposal to spend $3.5 billion over five years in apprenticeship programs. The bill built on his efforts to expand training for energy jobs and opportunities for minority applicants.

Norcross chairs the Armed Services Subcommittee on Tactical Air and Land Forces, which handles the largest share of the Pentagon's procurement spending. He has consistently pledged support for the military installations based in New Jersey, especially nearby Joint Base McGuire-Dix-Lakehurst. In 2019 and 2020, he served on the House-Senate conference committees that hammered out the final versions of the annual National Defense Authorization Act. At the behest of labor allies, he pushed a "Buy American" provision in the 2020 bill that would have required U.S.-based companies to produce an increasing share of the components used in major defense programs, rising to 100 percent by fiscal 2026. Norcross successfully attached the provision to the House bill, but it was not included in the final version.

In 2016, he faced a primary challenge from Alex Law, a 25-year-old political newcomer and supporter of Sen. Bernie Sanders in the presidential campaign. Law ran against the "Norcross machine," which he said had been "marked by corruption and political cronyism." Norcross outspent him more than 20-to-1 and got 70 percent of the vote. He has breezed to reelection against Republicans, winning at least 60 percent of the vote since 2016.

NJ-1: Philadelphia suburbs

Cook Partisan Voting Index: D+11

Population		Race and Ethnicity		Income	
Total	726,825	White	68.00%	Median Income	$75,244
Land area (sq. miles)	350	Black	17.00%	District Income Rank	128
Pop/ sq mi	2,076.52	Latino	14.10%	Poverty Rate	10.00%
Born in State	55.80%	Asian	5.00%	With health insurance	94.10%
		Two or more races	3.10%	Cash public assistance	2.70%
Age Groups		Other	6.80%	Food stamp/SNAP	10.00%
Under 18	22.30%				
18-34	21.80%	**Education**		**Work**	
35-64	39.70%	H.S grad or less	39.90%	White Collar	41.90%
Over 64	16.20%	Some college	26.80%	Sales and Service	37.80%
		College Degree, 4 yr	21.60%	Blue Collar	20.40%
Military		Post grad	11.70%	Government	14.70%
Veteran/ Active Duty	6.20%				

2020 Pres. Vote	Biden	242,213	(62%)	Trump	142,822	(36%)		
2016 Pres. Vote	Clinton	199,386	(60%)	Trump	118,880	(36%)	Johnson	6,512	(2%)

Camden: The closely built streets of Camden, across the Delaware River from Philadelphia, have seen a fair amount of history. This was where poet Walt Whitman lived when he wrote some of the versions of his Leaves of Grass. It was an immigrant-jammed industrial city then, with tinkerers and inventors. In 1894, a Camden machinist named Eldridge Johnson produced the Victor Talking Machine, the birth of the recorded music industry and a company that became RCA Victor in 1929. A few years later, the new Campbell Soup Co. began producing condensed soups. Camden remained for years a major industrial locus on the New Jersey side of the Delaware River, not the broadest and certainly not the most picturesque of Atlantic estuaries, but probably the East Coast's premier industrial waterway, with a concentration of steel mills, chemical plants, and oil tank farms equal to any in the country. The flatlands all around, mostly ignored in the 19th century, had easy access to cheap water transportation and plenty of skilled labor from the Philadelphia area. For a quarter-century starting in the 1940s, this was one of the country's fastest-growing industrial areas.

In the 1980s and 1990s, Camden emptied out as white residents headed to the surrounding suburbs. Many of its factories had closed. Its neighborhoods were beset by crime, its mostly minority residents were heavily dependent on public assistance and its mayor was convicted of doing favors for Philadelphia's organized crime leaders. From 2002 to 2010, the state controlled its finances and government. Camden continues to struggle. Census figures released in 2012 showed Camden with a poverty rate of 42 percent, the highest in the nation. Since then, an influx of jobs modestly lowered the rate to 37 percent, though the population dropped 4 percent between 2010 and 2019. In 2019, its median household income of $27,000 was among the lowest in the state, where the average was $83,000.

Camden has had some bright spots: a redeveloped riverfront park, the New Jersey aquarium and a state-of-the-art amphitheater. Rowan University in 2012 opened a $139 million medical school in the city, the first new medical college in New Jersey in 35 years. As part of the "eds and meds" strategy, it was joined by a health sciences center in 2017. The port of Camden rebounded, spurred by Del

Monte's large fruit-processing plant and increased steel imports. A number of companies, including Subaru, have moved to Camden in recent years to take advantage of state tax incentives.

Violent crime has also plummeted since its peak in the early 2010s, when Camden was known as the most dangerous city in the country. The drop in crime occurred after the city police force was disbanded in 2013 due to financial pressures; policing services were moved to the county level. The restructuring was praised and credited with improving community-police relations. Camden policing received another round of media coverage in the summer of 2020 when racial justice activists called for defunding police departments and cited Camden as a success story. The reality is more complicated though, as the restructured police agency has struggled with high costs, officer retention, and diversity.

The 1st Congressional District is greater Camden, the Delaware riverfront from Palmyra south to a point across the river from the Delaware state line. The district includes two-thirds of adjacent Gloucester County, an area that is nearly one-third of the district, plus a small slice of Burlington County. The 1st is traversed by Black Horse Pike and White Horse Pike, which connect Philadelphia to its South Jersey suburbs. Many of the nearby boroughs and townships developed over the past half-century as a result of white flight from Camden. The district is 17 percent Black and 14 percent Hispanic; the minority population is concentrated in Camden. Joe Biden led President Donald Trump in the safely Democratic district, 62%-36%.

Jeff Van Drew (R)

Elected 2018, 2nd term, b. Feb 23, 1953; New York, NY; Rutgers University, B.S., 1975; Fairleigh Dickinson University, D.D.S., 1979; Veterans Administration NJ Healthcare; Lyons and East Orange Veterans Hospitals, D.D.S., 1979; Catholic; Married (Ricarda Drew); 2 children.

Elected Office: Dennis Township Fire Commissioner, 1983-1986; Cape May County Board of Chosen Freeholders, 1994-1997; Dennis Township Mayor, 1997-2003; NJ General Assembly, 2002-2007; NJ Senate, 2008-2018.

Professional Career: Dentist; Volunteer Fire Fighter

DC Office: 331 CHOB 20515, 202-225-6572, vandrew.house.gov

State Offices: Mays Landing, 609-625-5008.

Committees: *Homeland Security*: Intelligence & Counterterrorism; Transportation & Maritime Security. *Transportation & Infrastructure*: Aviation.

Almanac Ratings 2019-2020

	Economy	Social	Foreign	Composite
Liberal	54%	46%	46%	49%
Conservative	46%	54%	54%	51%

Key Votes of the 116th Congress

1. U.S./Mex./Can. trade deal Y	5. Russia sanctions	Y	9. Firearms background checks Y
2. First Coronavirus response Y	6. Troops in Syria	Y	10. Spending at the border Y
3. HEROES Act N	7. Veto arms sales to Saudis Y		11. Marijuana liberalized rules N
4. CASH Act Y	8. Defense $$$, veto override N		12. Electoral College objections Y

Election Results

Election	Name (Party)	Vote (%)		Cand. Spent	Ind. Exp. Support	Ind. Exp. Oppose
2020 General	Jeff Van Drew (D)	195,526	(52%)	$4,058,109	$428,064	$6,764,933
	Amy Kennedy (D)	173,849	(46%)	$5,020,881	$290,706	$4,922,402
2020 Primary	Jeff Van Drew (R)	45,226	(82%)			
	Bob Patterson (R)	9,691	(18%)			

Prior winning percentages: 2018 (53%)

One year after his initial election, Jeff Van Drew left the Democratic Party and became a Republican. He switched parties over opposition to President Donald Trump's first impeachment. The first party switcher in over a decade, Van Drew mainly shifted his rhetoric and continued to be a moderate on policy issues. After securing Trump's support, he won a tough reelection battle in 2020 against a member of the Kennedy family.

Van Drew graduated from Rutgers University and received a doctorate in dental science from Fairleigh Dickinson University. As a family dentist for more than 35 years, he was president of the New Jersey Dental Society. After serving in several local offices in Cape May County and for six years in the state General Assembly, he was elected in 2007 to the state Senate, where he chaired the Community and Urban Affairs Committee.

Following longtime Republican incumbent Frank LoBiondo's retirement announcement, Van Drew became the frontrunner to replace him in 2018. In the Democratic primary, his opponents and liberal interest groups criticized Van Drew's relatively moderate viewpoints and bipartisan approach, especially on social issues. "We're just too divided," Van Drew told voters in response. "Our country most needs consensus builders." Democratic leaders in all eight counties across the district endorsed Van Drew, whom they largely viewed as the strongest candidate. He also won early backing from the House's Blue Dog Coalition of centrist Democrats. Van Drew benefited from superior fundraising: The $1 million he raised prior to the June primary more than tripled the total of the three more liberal candidates, all political newcomers. Van Drew won the primary with 57 percent. In the general election, Van Drew's Republican opponent, Seth Grossman, self-destructed. Grossman, a former talk-show host, reportedly had connections to white supremacist groups and made several racist remarks, causing the National Republican Congressional Committee to withdraw its endorsement. Still, Van Drew's victory was surprisingly narrow, 53%-45%.

Once in Congress, Van Drew opposed Nancy Pelosi in a vote for Speaker in January 2019 (he said "no" rather than a candidate's name, which the parliamentarian counted as a "present" vote). Although he generally supported the party line on policy issues, including raising the minimum wage to $15, Van Drew found himself increasingly out-of-step with Democrats' approach to Trump. He was an early opponent of impeaching Trump and voted against a motion to open an inquiry in October 2019.

As the impeachment proceeded, Republican leaders, including Trump and Minority Leader Kevin McCarthy, pressured Van Drew to switch parties. Based on polling numbers, Van Drew feared he would either lose to a pro-impeachment challenger in the Democratic primary or to a Republican in the general election. In mid-December, Van Drew told his staff that he would switch parties. Most of his D.C.-based staff subsequently quit And Van Drew became a pariah in the Democratic Caucus and among the mostly Democratic New Jersey delegation. On December 18, Van Drew, still officially a member of the Democratic Party, voted against the articles of impeachment. The next day, he visited Trump at the White House to pledge his "undying support" to the president and officially become a Republican. Shortly afterward, Trump appeared with Van Drew at a rally in Wildwood New Jersey.

The first party-switcher in Congress since Alabama Democrat Parker Griffith joined the GOP in 2009, Van Drew did not change his voting behavior after becoming a Republican. He continued to be one of the most moderate members in the House and to vote for Democrat-backed legislation, including a repeal of the cap on state and local tax deductions that was popular in high-tax New Jersey. But he also became an enthusiastic Trump supporter, appearing on Fox News and speaking at the 2020 Republican convention. Following the 2020 election, he joined other House Republicans in efforts to challenge Joe Biden's victory. His switch to the GOP has yielded him appointments to the Homeland Security Committee and Transportation and Infrastructure Committee, better fits for his district than the Agriculture and Natural Resources assignments he received from Democratic leaders.

Van Drew's party change gamble paid off in his 2020 reelection bid. The month after he switched, the top Republican running for the 2nd District, David Richter, left to run in the 3rd District race. In the primary, Van Drew easily defeated Bob Patterson, a former Trump aide who drew attention to Van Drew's less-than-conservative voting record. In the general election, Van Drew faced Amy Kennedy, a teacher married to former Democratic Rep. Patrick Kennedy, the late Sen. Ted Kennedy's son. Kennedy won a five-candidate primary where her top opponent, Brigid Harrison, was backed by George Norcross' South Jersey political machine. Kennedy scored an endorsement from Governor Phil Murphy. Kennedy won 62%-22%. The general election was closely contested and many observers viewed Kennedy as a slight favorite. She underperformed in her base of Atlantic County and Van Drew prevailed, 52%-46%--with big leads in the rural counties.

NJ-2: South Jersey   **Cook Partisan Voting Index: R+4**

Population		Race and Ethnicity		Income	
Total	707,255	White	74.00%	Median Income	$68,127
Land area (sq. miles)	2,092	Black	12.90%	District Income Rank	182
Pop/ sq mi	338.01	Latino	17.20%	Poverty Rate	10.40%
Born in State	60.70%	Asian	3.70%	With health insurance	92.70%
		Two or more races	3.30%	Cash public assistance	1.90%
Age Groups		Other	6.10%	Food stamp/SNAP	9.80%
Under 18	20.60%				
18-34	20.10%	Education		Work	
35-64	39.50%	H.S grad or less	46.80%	White Collar	34.60%
Over 64	19.80%	Some college	26.10%	Sales and Service	43.20%
		College Degree, 4 yr	17.30%	Blue Collar	22.30%
Military		Post grad	9.90%	Government	16.00%
Veteran/ Active Duty	6.90%				

2020 Pres. Vote	Trump	194,366	(51%)	Biden	183,250	(48%)			
2016 Pres. Vote	Trump	162,486	(50%)	Clinton	147,656	(46%)	Johnson	6,596	(2%)

Atlantic City, Philadelphia exurbs: The builders of the Camden & Atlantic Railroad in 1852 may not have known it, but when they extended their line to the little inlet town of Absecon, they were launching one of America's first beach resorts, Atlantic City. Like all resorts, it was a product of developments elsewhere—of industrialization and spreading affluence. In the years after the Civil War, Atlantic City and the Jersey Shore, from Brigantine to Cape May, became a seaside resort, and Atlantic City developed its characteristic features: the boardwalk in 1870; the amusement pier in 1882; the rolling chair in 1884; salt water taffy in the 1890s; and the Miss America pageant in 1921. In the book Boardwalk Empire, author Nelson Johnson argues that to attract tourists, a powerful alliance of local politicians and racketeers allowed gambling, prostitution and Sunday liquor laws to be flouted. "Nothing could interfere with the visitors' fun or they might stop coming," he writes. But a long period of decline came after World War II, and by the early 1970s Atlantic City was grim, featuring a bedraggled convention hall (site of the 1964 Democratic National Convention), empty hotels and bleak streets.

Then in 1977, New Jersey voters legalized casino gambling in Atlantic City. Gleaming new hotels sprang up, big-name entertainers came, and the resort became more stylish than it had been in 90 years. But it hasn't been that way for everyone. Casino and hotel jobs tend to be low-wage, and decrepit neighborhoods begin just feet from the casinos' massive parking lots. For years, its dozen casinos had net annual revenues nearly as high as Las Vegas' casinos. Then, the recession hit the entertainment sector hard. From 2005 until 2016, casino revenues dropped more than 50 percent, to a bit more than $2 billion. After five of the casinos closed, and others sought tax relief as gambling revenues continued to drop, a turnaround arrived in 2018, with the state's legalization of sports gambling. Two new casinos opened (bringing the total back to nine) and gambling revenue increased 20 percent by the end of the year.Still, Atlantic City came under state control in 2016 due to its dire financial situation and had the highest foreclosure rate of any metropolitan area in the nation for several years, although the situation had improved by 2019.

In 2020, the casino industry was hit hard again by the COVID-19 pandemic. Atlantic City casinos were shuttered from March through July, putting 27,000 people out of work. The Brookings Institution listed Atlantic City as the third most vulnerable economy in the country during the pandemic due to its heavy reliance on tourism and entertainment. Although visitors were slow to return to in-person casino games, sports gambling continued to thrive. New Jersey set a national record for sports bets in August 2020 with $668 million.

Other beach resorts lie south of Atlantic City. There is Wildwood, with its refurbished 1950s motels, and Cape May, with its lovingly preserved Victorian houses. West of the Jersey Shore are swamps and flatlands, the Pine Barrens and abundant vegetable fields that gave New Jersey its "Garden State" nickname. The number of farms decreased 10 percent between 1997 and 2012, though agriculture remained the third largest sector of the state's economy, behind pharmaceuticals and tourism.

The 2nd Congressional District covers the southern end of New Jersey. Atlantic is the largest county, with more than 35 percent of the population. Politically, it has Democratic leanings in the chemical industry towns along the Delaware River and in Vineland and a Republican presence in Cape May County. President Donald Trump--whose casinos in A.C. resulted in three corporate bankruptcies, the final one in 2010--won the district, 51%-48%. The 2nd was one of three New Jersey districts that he won, all of them south of the New York City suburbs.

Andrew Kim (D)

Elected 2018, 2nd term, b. Jul 12, 1982; Boston, MA; Deep Springs College; University of Chicago, B.A., 2004; University of Oxford, B.A., 2004; Oxford University, M.Phil, 2007; Presbyterian; Married (Kammy Kim); 2 children.

Professional Career: Foreign Affairs Officer, U.S. Department of State, 2009-2013; Director for Iraq, National Security Council, 2013-2015.

DC Office: 1516 LHOB 20515, 202-225-4765, Fax: 202-225-0778, kim.house.gov

State Offices: Marlton, 856-703-2700; Toms River, 732-504-0490.

Committees: *Armed Services*: Cyber, Innovative Technologies & Information Systems; Military Personnel. *Foreign Affairs*: Asia, the Pacific, Central Asia, Nonproliferation; Intern'l Dev't, Intern'l Orgs & Global Corporate Social Impact. *Small Business*: Contracting & Infrastructure; Economic Growth, Tax & Capital Access.

Almanac Ratings 2019-2020

	Economy	Social	Foreign	Composite
Liberal	100%	58%	80%	80%
Conservative	0%	42%	20%	20%

Key Votes of the 116th Congress

1. U.S./Mex./Can. trade deal	Y	5. Russia sanctions	Y	9. Firearms background checks	Y
2. First Coronavirus response	Y	6. Troops in Syria	Y	10. Spending at the border	Y
3. HEROES Act	Y	7. Veto arms sales to Saudis	Y	11. Marijuana liberalized rules	Y
4. CASH Act	Y	8. Defense $$$, veto override	Y	12. Electoral College objections	N

Election Results

Election	Name (Party)	Vote (%)		Cand. Spent	Ind. Exp. Support	Ind. Exp. Oppose
2020 General	Andrew Kim (D)	229,840	(53%)	$6,772,405	$186,300	$546,045
	David Richter (R)	196,327	(45%)	$1,508,252	$63,431	$3,350,302
2020 Primary	Andy Kim (D)	79,417	(100%)			

Prior winning percentages: 2018 (50%)

Andy Kim, the first Korean American Democrat to serve in Congress, comfortably won reelection in 2020 after narrowly defeating a Republican incumbent in 2018. He has been active on national security issues from his position on the Armed Services Committee. He stuck with Democratic leaders on tough votes, despite hailing from a swing district.

Kim went to high school in Cherry Hill and graduated from the University of Chicago with a degree in political science. He was a Rhodes Scholar and studied U.S. policy in Iraq while at Oxford University. He attended Oxford with Pete Buttigieg, who Kim endorsed in the 2020 Democratic presidential primary. Kim worked at the State Department and was a civilian adviser to Gen. David Petraeus in Afghanistan. He was Iraq director of the National Security Council under President Barack Obama, helping set policy for dealing with the ISIS terrorist network.

Kim returned to New Jersey to run against incumbent Tom MacArthur in 2018. MacArthur was mostly a party loyalist in a Republican-leaning district. In 2017, MacArthur had played a leading role in cutting a deal on the House Republican bill to repeal the Affordable Care Act. Later that year, he was the only one of the five House Republicans from New Jersey to vote for President Trump's tax cut legislation. That measure stirred heated objections in his home state because of its cap on deductions for state and local taxes.

Kim won the Democratic nomination without opposition. During the general election, Kim out-spent MacArthur, $6.4 million to $4.8 million (MacArthur self-financed $1.4 million). In addition, the national parties and their allies spent more than $6 million. Kim won 50%-49%. The candidates split the two large counties in the district. Kim led by about 33,000 votes in Burlington, which was nearly 60 percent of the district. MacArthur took the smaller Ocean County by 30,000 votes.

Despite coming from a swing district, Kim proved to be a loyal Democrat, supporting Nancy Pelosi for Speaker in January 2019 and voting for President Donald Trump's impeachment later that year. He received a seat on the Armed Services Committee, where he supported Joint Base McGuire-Dix-Lakehurst, located in his district. He also received a spot on the Small Business Committee and was appointed to the House Select Committee on the Coronavirus Crisis in 2020. In line with his background, Kim mainly focused on national security issues. After the United States killed Iranian General Qasem Soleimani in early 2020, Kim wrote an op-ed saying that the assassination would accelerate conflict with Iran. He also cast doubt on the Trump administration's strategy for peace talks with the Taliban. In 2021, he gained a seat on the Foreign Affairs Committee.

Although Kim's 2018 election was the closest race in New Jersey, he had a relatively easy victory in 2020. His opponent, businessman David Richter, switched from the 2nd District race after its incumbent, Jeff Van Drew, changed parties and became a Republican. Richter defeated former Burlington County Freeholder Katie Gibbs in the Republican primary, 61%-39%. Kim did not face a Democratic opponent and focused on fundraising ahead of the general election. He brought in nearly $7 million to Richter's $1.5 million and won, 53%-45%. Richter increased the GOP edge in Ocean County to 26,000 votes, but Kim won Burlington by more than 61,000—slightly better than Joe Biden, who took Burlington by 51,000 votes.

NJ-3: South Central New Jersey   Cook Partisan Voting Index: R+3

Population		Race and Ethnicity		Income	
Total	735,981	White	79.10%	Median Income	$85,746
Land area (sq. miles)	900	Black	11.50%	District Income Rank	70
Pop/ sq mi	818.03	Latino	9.10%	Poverty Rate	5.90%
Born in State	61.30%	Asian	3.80%	With health insurance	95.70%
		Two or more races	3.60%	Cash public assistance	1.20%
Age Groups		Other	2.10%	Food stamp/SNAP	4.80%
Under 18	20.20%				
18-34	19.50%	**Education**		**Work**	
35-64	40.00%	H.S grad or less	37.40%	White Collar	43.40%
Over 64	20.30%	Some college	26.60%	Sales and Service	38.60%
		College Degree, 4 yr	23.40%	Blue Collar	17.90%
Military		Post grad	12.60%	Government	17.90%
Veteran/ Active Duty	8.60%				

2020 Pres. Vote	Trump	218,016	(49%)	Biden	217,223	(49%)		
2016 Pres. Vote	Trump	187,703	(51%)	Clinton	165,090	(45%)	Johnson	7,639	(2%)

Burlington and Ocean Counties: The Pine Barrens of New Jersey are one of the last vacant spots on the eastern seaboard—not quite terra incognita, but still not thickly populated. Encroached on by the Philadelphia suburbs of South Jersey and the Delaware River on the west and burgeoning retirement developments of the Jersey Shore on the east, the 1 million acres of heavy forest and white sand, with their unusual plant life, are crossed mostly by narrow two-lane roads. For years, the Pine Barrens were seen as a barrier to development. Only recently have environment-minded Jerseyites come to see the relatively unspoiled area as a natural treasure. There are a few small towns here, plus Joint Base McGuire-Dix-Lakehurst, the giant amalgamation of an Air Force base, Army military reservation and training site, and Navy air station, which is the second-largest employer in New Jersey, behind the state government. In a major long-term victory for the facility, the Joint Base has become the home of Boeing's KC-46A air-refueling tankers. The new planes are replacing the base's older-model KC-10 refueling planes. The first of the KC-10s was retired in 2020; the KC-46As will not be operational until 2022 or 2023.

East of the Pine Barrens is Ocean County, including the barrier islands from Mantoloking south to Stafford, with older communities on the beachfront and larger clusters of new subdivisions and condominiums inland. Here you can find the house in Seaside Heights where several seasons of MTV's Jersey Shore were set. Ocean County has been the fastest-growing part of New Jersey, a kind of Frost Belt Florida, with many retirees from New York and North Jersey eager to leave urban crime and high taxes. But it hasn't been all paradise lately; Hurricane Sandy in 2012 damaged more than 40,000 buildings in the county, its 20-foot waves smashing boardwalks and flooding dunes. Elected officials in Toms River, the county seat, have drawn criticism for their reaction to an influx of Orthodox Jews from the neighboring township of Lakewood. As of December 2020, the Justice Department was threatening to sue Toms River unless it changed its zoning regulations, which members of the Orthodox community argue infringe on their religious practices. In Lacey Township, the Oyster Creed Generating Station—the oldest nuclear-power plant in the nation—shut down service in September 2018. The decommissioning was expected to take eight years and cost $980 million. In addition to the expected spike in property taxes once the station is gone, locals fear the environmental impact of the remaining radioactive waste.

The 3rd Congressional District of New Jersey spans the Pine Barrens and thousands of acres of farmland, plus the Joint Base. It includes large parts of Burlington and Ocean counties, including several suburban Philadelphia townships. Nearly 60 percent of the population resides in Burlington, which voted for Joe Biden in 2020, 59%-40%. Ocean County is more Republican-leaning and gave President Donald Trump about 64 percent. Overall, Trump narrowly won the district, 49.2%-49.0%-- tighter than his 51%-45% win in 2016.

Chris Smith (R)

Elected 1980, 21st term, b. Mar 04, 1953; Rahway, NJ; Worcester College, 1974; Trenton State College, B.A., 1975; Roman Catholic; Married (Marie Hahn Smith); 4 children.

Professional Career: Sales Executive, family-owned sporting goods business, 1975-1980; Executive Director, NJ Right to Life, 1976-1978.

DC Office: 2373 RHOB 20515, 202-225-3765, Fax: 202-225-7768, chrissmith.house.gov

State Offices: Freehold, 732-780-3035; Hamilton, 609-585-7878; Plumsted, 609-585-7878.

Committees: *Foreign Affairs*: Africa, Global Health & Global Human Rights (RMM).

Group Ratings

	ADA	ACLU	AFL-CIO	LCV	COC	HAFA	ACU	CFG	FRC
2020	**	19%	**	81%	-	56%	57%	**	-
2019	40%	C	76%	72%	87%	C	57%	38%	100%

Almanac Ratings 2019-2020

	Economy	Social	Foreign	Composite
Liberal	46%	45%	27%	40%
Conservative	54%	55%	73%	60%

Key Votes of the 116th Congress

1. U.S./Mex./Can. trade deal Y	5. Russia sanctions Y	9. Firearms background checks Y
2. First Coronavirus response Y	6. Troops in Syria Y	10. Spending at the border Y
3. HEROES Act N	7. Veto arms sales to Saudis N	11. Marijuana liberalized rules N
4. CASH Act Y	8. Defense $$$, veto override Y	12. Electoral College objections N

Election Results

Election	Name (Party)	Vote (%)		Cand. Spent	Ind. Exp. Support	Ind. Exp. Oppose
2020 General	Chris Smith (R)...........................	254,103	(60%)	$1,367,080	$58,325	$113
	Stephanie Schmid (D)...................	162,420	(38%)	$852,294	$6,744	
2020 Primary	Chris Smith (R).................................	51,636	(95%)			
	Alter Richter (R)............................	2,853	(5%)			

Prior winning percentages: 2018 (55%), 2016 (64%), 2014 (68%), 2012 (64%), 2010 (69%), 2008 (66%), 2006 (66%), 2004 (67%), 2002 (66%), 2000 (63%), 1998 (62%), 1996 (64%), 1994 (68%), 1992 (62%), 1990 (63%), 1988 (66%), 1986 (61%), 1984 (61%), 1982 (53%), 1980 (57%)

Republican Chris Smith, first elected in 1980, combines outspoken opposition to abortion with a passionate commitment to human rights and a moderate record on economic policy. Such independence does not always sit well with Republican leaders, though Smith's tenacity has made him one of the most successful legislators at guiding bills into law. Even though he is tied for the second-senior Republican in the House, his independence has kept him from chairing a major committee in recent years.

Smith grew up in the Trenton area, worked in his family's sporting goods business and, after graduating from the College of New Jersey with a degree in business administration, became executive director of the New Jersey Right to Life Committee in 1976. Four years later, he ran for the House in the Trenton-centered district and defeated 26-year Rep. Frank Thompson, a Democrat convicted in the Abscam bribery scandal. Although political observers described his initial election as a fluke, Smith has been reelected 20 times since. After the 2020 election, he became the longest-serving congressman in New Jersey history, surpassing Democrat Peter Rodino, who chaired the House Judiciary Committee during the impeachment of President Richard Nixon.

Smith is a prolific legislator and has won enactment of dozens of bills since he took office. Smith "has a gift for embracing issues that touch nerves and generate publicity," Bob Braun, a columnist for the Star-Ledger of Newark, once wrote. In the 2019-2020 term, Smith worked on legislation related to autism and Lyme disease and largely stayed within his party's mainstream and out of the spotlight. He voted against President Donald Trump's impeachment in 2019 and largely steered clear of the spotlight on Trump-related controversies.

A devout Roman Catholic, Smith is best known for his unwavering fight against legalized abortion. He has worked to stop abortions in military hospitals, and he helped persuade the George W. Bush administration to reinstate Reagan-era restrictions denying federal funds to family-planning organizations that promote abortions abroad. Smith has also been an advocate of legislation to ban "partial birth" abortions and to require doctors to inform pregnant women that some experts say a fetus can feel pain after 20 weeks of gestation. He has a bill to revoke the Food and Drug Administration's approval of the abortifacient RU-486, which Smith calls "baby pesticide." He has opposed federal funding for embryonic stem cell research, which uses excess embryos from in vitro fertilization, but he has been a champion of other stem cell research. In 2005, Congress enacted his Stem Cell Therapeutic and Research Act, which funds research and therapy using umbilical cord stem cells plus cells from bone marrow transplants.

Smith has brought his strong moral views to his work against human rights abuses abroad. He has sharply criticized China for its forced sterilizations and abortions and for its persecution of religious minorities. In 2020, he pushed legislation that would require the Trump administration to impose sanctions on Chinese officials involved in the repression of Uighur Muslims, a minority group in China's Xinjiang region. "We cannot be silent," he said on the House floor, "[Chinese leader] Xi Jinping is smashing and obliterating an entire people."In response, China imposed largely symbolic sanctions on Smith and other Republican lawmakers involved in the effort. Smith has also condemned Russia for barring entry of foreign Catholic priests, criticized the Saudis for treating foreign servants as slaves and worked on legislation aimed at combating anti-Semitism. He is a supporter of Hungarian President Viktor Orbán, a social conservative who is often criticized by some on the left for his supposed authoritarian tendencies and rhetoric they term anti-Semitic.

Overall, Smith has been one of the most moderate members of the House GOP, particularly on economic issues. In 2009, he was one of eight Republicans to support the House-passed energy bill imposing a cap-and-trade system to limit greenhouse gas emissions. In 2017, he voted against Republican tax cut legislation and the effort to repeal the Affordable Care Act. In 2020, he was one of

44 House Republicans to support increasing pandemic-related stimulus checks from $600 to $2,000. He has been supportive of some pro-union and pro-gun control legislation, earning him the backing of the AFL-CIO and former Rep. Gabby Giffords's gun-control group in his 2018 reelection bid.

Earlier in his career, Smith dramatized his willingness to buck his party for the sake of his beliefs and to accept the consequences. As chairman of the Veterans' Affairs Committee, Smith angered budget conservatives by pushing expanded benefits for veterans. In a major breach of party protocol, he voted for the Democratic spending plan because it contained more money for the Veterans Affairs Department. In 2005, the Republican Steering Committee booted Smith from his chairmanship. Since then, Smith's bids to chair the Foreign Affairs Committee have been thwarted when GOP leaders chose more reliable conservatives. Instead, Smith has been the senior Republican on the tailor-made Subcommittee on Africa, Global Health, Global Human Rights and International Organizations.

Smith's devotion to principle and his reputation for tending to constituent problems have made him popular in the 4th District, which has become safely Republican. He faced a relatively serious challenge in 2018 from Democrat Joshua Welle, who outspent Smith $1.9 million to $1.6 million. Smith prevailed, 55%-43%, in his closest election since 1982 (it was also the first time Smith won less than 60% of the vote since 1982). Smith returned to form in 2020, winning 60%-38% against Stephanie Schmid, a former Foreign Service Officer who failed to match Welle's fundraising.

NJ-4: Central New Jersey

Cook Partisan Voting Index: R+8

Population		Race and Ethnicity		Income	
Total	748,199	White	86.00%	Median Income	$91,212
Land area (sq. miles)	692	Black	6.20%	District Income Rank	52
Pop/ sq mi	1,081.4	Latino	11.20%	Poverty Rate	7.90%
Born in State	59.40%	Asian	4.20%	With health insurance	94.60%
		Two or more races	1.30%	Cash public assistance	0.80%
Age Groups		Other	2.30%	Food stamp/SNAP	4.70%
Under 18	24.40%				
18-34	18.20%	**Education**		**Work**	
35-64	38.10%	H.S grad or less	31.60%	White Collar	48.40%
Over 64	19.20%	Some college	24.00%	Sales and Service	36.20%
		College Degree, 4 yr	27.00%	Blue Collar	15.30%
Military		Post grad	17.30%	Government	14.80%
Veteran/ Active Duty	5.60%				

2020 Pres. Vote	Trump	236,896	(55%)	Biden	191,273	(44%)		
2016 Pres. Vote	Trump	198,859	(55%)	Clinton	146,191	(41%)	Johnson	7,184	(2%)

Monmouth and Ocean Counties: An invisible and not-well-defined line divides North Jersey and South Jersey. North of the line, people watch New York television stations, eat hero sandwiches and root for the Yankees. South of the line, they watch Philadelphia television, eat hoagies and root for the Phillies. The state capital of Trenton lies south of the line, which passes east somewhere around Six Flags Great Adventure in the Pine Barrens and heads southeast past Lakewood and Brick to the Jersey Shore. On both sides of the line, a stronger New Jersey identity has developed. The big cities are not all that close, particularly when traffic is heavy. No less a true New Jersey persona than Bruce Springsteen was raised in Freehold Borough, the subject of his bleak portrayal in "My Hometown."The economy of central New Jersey has its own character, with big pharmaceutical companies and the consolidated Joint Base McGuire-Dix-Lakehurst.

Most of the area's growth is occurring in Lakewood, home to the nation's largest population of Orthodox Jews outside of Brooklyn. The Lakewood Orthodox community has existed since 1943, when a Belarusian rabbi fleeing Nazi persecution established a yeshiva, a Jewish educational institution focused on religious learning. As of 1980, Lakewood was a relatively sleepy town of about 38,000. However, high housing costs in Brooklyn and the draw of Beth Medrash Govoha, now the largest yeshiva in the U.S. and the second-largest in the world, brought many Orthodox families into Lakewood. The population rose to 60,000 in 2000 and then to 93,000 in 2010. As of 2019, Lakewood had 106,000 residents and was one of the largest municipalities in New Jersey. Tensions exist within Lakewood as local school enrollments have plummeted (most Orthodox children attend private religious schools but use public school busing, straining the education budget) and the area has been rapidly developed to meet housing needs. An anti-development movement has sprung up in Lakewood's non-Orthodox communities and in neighboring townships, which have passed ordinances aimed at keeping the Orthodox out. Some anti-development activists have used anti-Semitic messaging; local elected officials have also been accused of religious discrimination. The most recent controversy arose during the COVID-19 pandemic as some members of the Orthodox community continued to hold large weddings in defiance of state and local officials.

The Fourth Congressional District of New Jersey is based in Republican-leaning Monmouth County, which has about 60 percent of its population, with parts of Mercer County and the fast-growing exurban Ocean County making up the rest. The district has become relatively safe for Republicans, in part due to the strongly conservative Lakewood Orthodox community. Donald Trump got 55 percent of the vote in both 2016 and 2020, the same as Mitt Romney got in 2012. In each case, the 4th was the best GOP district in New Jersey.

Josh Gottheimer (D)

Elected 2016, 3rd term, b. Mar 08, 1975; Livingston, NJ; University of PA, B.A., 1997; Harvard Law School, J.D., 2004; Jewish; Married (Marla Brooke Tusk Gottheimer); 2 children.

Professional Career: Special Assistant and Speechwriter, President Bill Clinton, 1998-2001; Senior Counselor, Federal Communications Commission, 2010-2012.

DC Office: 213 CHOB 20515, 202-225-4465, Fax: 202-225-9048, gottheimer.house.gov

State Offices: Glen Rock, 201-389-1100; Hackensack, 973-814-4076; Newton, 973-940-1117; Ringwood, 973-814-4076; Vernon Township, 973-814-4076; Washington, 973-814-4076.

Committees: *Financial Services*: Investor Protection, Entrepreneurship & Capital Markets; Nat'l Security, International Development & Monetary Policy; Task Force on Financial Technology. *Homeland Security*: Intelligence & Counterterrorism; Transportation & Maritime Security.

Group Ratings

	ADA	ACLU	AFL-CIO	LCV	COC	HAFA	ACU	CFG	FRC
2020	**	69%	**	100%	-	0%	9%	**	-
2019	80%	C	100%	97%	73%	C	11%	12%	5%

Almanac Ratings 2019-2020

	Economy	Social	Foreign	Composite
Liberal	100%	51%	49%	67%
Conservative	0%	49%	51%	33%

Key Votes of the 116th Congress

1. U.S./Mex./Can. trade deal Y	5. Russia sanctions Y	9. Firearms background checks Y
2. First Coronavirus response Y	6. Troops in Syria Y	10. Spending at the border Y
3. HEROES Act Y	7. Veto arms sales to Saudis Y	11. Marijuana liberalized rules Y
4. CASH Act Y	8. Defense $$$, veto override Y	12. Electoral College objections N

Election Results

Election	Name (Party)	Vote (%)		Cand. Spent	Ind. Exp. Support	Ind. Exp. Oppose
2020 General	Josh Gottheimer (D)	225,175	(53%)	$3,530,908	$197,766	
	Frank Pallotta (R)	193,333	(46%)	$1,937,959	$10,225	$328,511
2020 Primary	Josh Gottheimer (D)	52,406	(67%)			
	Arati Kreibich (D)	26,418	(34%)			

Prior winning percentages: 2018 (56%), 2016 (51%)

Democrat Josh Gottheimer has been one of Capitol Hill's most vocal and successful advocates for bipartisan compromise since he was first elected in 2016. As co-chair of the bipartisan Problem Solvers Caucus, he looks to play a more prominent policymaking role during the Biden administration. A relatively moderate Democrat, he has occasionally butted heads with progressives, among both House colleagues and activists in his district.

Born and raised in New Jersey, Gottheimer was introduced to politics as a high school student when he served as a page for Democratic Sen. Frank Lautenberg. He received his bachelor's from the University of Pennsylvania and attended Oxford University. After working on the rapid response team for President Bill Clinton during his 1996 reelection campaign, he joined the administration as a speechwriter from 1998 until 2001. Gottheimer attended law school at Harvard while working for the 2004 presidential campaigns of Wesley Clark and then John Kerry. Following that election, Gottheimer worked for Ford Motor Co., Burson-Marsteller, and Microsoft. He also served on the staff of the Federal Communications Commission.

In 2016, he challenged seven-term Republican Scott Garrett, the most conservative member of New Jersey's congressional delegation and a founder of the House Freedom Caucus. Garrett attracted largely negative attention when he said he would not support the National Republican Congressional Committee because it was financing LGBT candidates. Gottheimer talked about governing from the center with a broad coalition of support. He supported tax cuts and fewer regulations and opposed President Barack Obama's nuclear deal with Iran. And he benefited from record spending for a New Jersey House candidate—$4.7 million that he raised, plus another $6 million in support from Democratic groups and allies. Garrett spent $4.4 million and had less than $1 million in outside support. Gottheimer won, 51%-47%.

Gottheimer is one of the most moderate and pro-business Democrats in the House. From his seat on the Financial Services Committee, he has worked to reduce regulations on banks. In his 2018 and 2020 reelection bids he was endorsed by the U.S. Chamber of Commerce, which usually supports Republicans. In 2019, the progressive publication The Intercept wrote several critical articles about Gottheimer, focusing on his support for corporate and banking interests and his behind-the-scenes attempt to maintain U.S. support for the Saudi Arabia-led war against Yemen. Although he eventually voted to impeach President Donald Trump in 2019, Gottheimer and other centrist Democrats advocated pushing for censuring Trump rather than removing him from office. In the 2020 Democratic presidential primary, he initially supported former New York City Mayor Michael Bloomberg.

In 2017, Gottheimer and Republican Tom Reed founded and became co-chairs of the bipartisan Problem Solvers Caucus, which has equal numbers of Democrats and Republicans and can act only with three-fourths in agreement. "I've got to do whatever I can to be at the table," he told the Wall Street Journal in July 2017. Following the 2018 election, the caucus—including some of its Republicans—persuaded Nancy Pelosi to agree to rules changes designed to "break the gridlock" in the House by encouraging action on legislation with bipartisan support. In June 2019, the Problem Solvers supported a bipartisan border aid bill passed by the Senate rather than a House proposal with stronger protections for migrant children. After the Senate bill passed the House with mostly Republican votes, Democrat Mark Pocan, co-chair of the Congressional Progressive Caucus tweeted, "Since when did the Problem Solvers Caucus become the Child Abuse Caucus?" In response, Gottheimer said, "You have to understand, you're not going to get everything you want. We just wanted to make sure that none of us went home without getting something done for children and families at the border." In late 2020, the 50-member Problem Solvers Caucus helped forge a compromise on pandemic relief. Although congressional leaders sealed the final deal, the Gottheimer-led Problem Solvers provided a framework for bipartisan compromise by introducing a $1.5 trillion plan in September and then putting forward a smaller $900 billion proposal in December that was similar to the final package. Afterwards Gottheimer said, "This in many ways could be the model for how we govern in the next Congress."

In addition to his work on bipartisan policymaking, Gottheimer has been one of the leading voices opposing "the Squad," a small group of progressive Democrats who have become increasingly influential. He confronted Reps. Rashida Tlaib and Ilhan Omar for remarks about Israel that many considered anti-Semitic. He also called out Rep. Alexandria Ocasio-Cortez for her support of primary challenges against Democratic incumbents. "We need to have a big tent in our party or we won't keep the House or win the White House," he said.

Gottheimer coasted to reelection in 2018; he was unchallenged in the primary and defeated Republican John McCann, 56%-42%, in the general election. In 2020, his pro-business efforts in Congress drew the ire of local Democratic activists. He faced a primary challenge from Glen Rock Councilwoman Arati Kreibich, who said Gottheimer was more loyal to corporations than the district's voters. A prodigious fundraiser, Gottheimer spent $3.6 million to Kreibich's $617,000. Still, she received one-third of the vote. His general election victory was also close relative to 2018; he defeated Republican Frank Pallotta, a former investment banker, 53%-46%.

NJ-5: Northern New Jersey

Cook Partisan Voting Index: R+1

Population		Race and Ethnicity		Income	
Total	734,764	White	79.10%	Median Income	$110,329
Land area (sq. miles)	991	Black	5.50%	District Income Rank	16
Pop/ sq mi	741.21	Latino	14.60%	Poverty Rate	5.00%
Born in State	51.30%	Asian	10.50%	With health insurance	95.50%
		Two or more races	2.90%	Cash public assistance	0.90%
Age Groups		Other	2.10%	Food stamp/SNAP	3.30%
Under 18	21.60%				
18-34	18.00%	**Education**		**Work**	
35-64	41.50%	H.S grad or less	27.40%	White Collar	52.50%
Over 64	18.90%	Some college	22.00%	Sales and Service	34.00%
Military		College Degree, 4 yr	31.10%	Blue Collar	13.60%
Veteran/ Active Duty	4.80%	Post grad	19.50%	Government	13.40%

2020 Pres. Vote	Biden	224,937	(52%)	Trump	202,421	(47%)			
2016 Pres. Vote	Trump	178,058	(48%)	Clinton	173,969	(47%)	Johnson	8,014	(2%)

Bergen County: The northern edge of New Jersey was settled three centuries ago by the Dutch, for whom this plateau of land behind the Hudson River Palisades seemed a natural part of Nieuw Amsterdam. The Dutch influence is seen in old, steep-roofed farmhouses and in many of the place names—Bergen County, Cresskill, Closter. But overall, northernmost New Jersey has the well-settled look of so many northeastern suburbs, with touches of both affluence and small-town hominess, crisscrossed at its edges with limited-access highways and shopping centers. Since the late 1950s, Paramus has been transformed from celery farms to the site of three shopping malls and numerous shopping centers that do more than $5 billion a year in retail sales. One of its main attractions is the Westfield Garden State Plaza mall, right off the New Jersey turnpike. Toys R Us opened a location at the mall in 2019, two years after shuttering all its U.S. stores and declaring bankruptcy. Paramus was also the site of tragedy during the COVID-19 pandemic as dozens of veterans died from the disease at a state-run nursing home. Bergen County was the first part of the state hit by the pandemic and had suffered more than 2,000 deaths by the end of 2020.

North of Paramus are Saddle River and Franklin Lakes, with multimillion-dollar houses on multi-acre lots, and Park Ridge, with office buildings and condominiums. To the east is Bergenfield, which has many people of Filipino descent and is known locally as "Little Manila." In the northeast corner of Bergen County, and within view of Manhattan on a clear day, is tiny Alpine, the wealthiest neighborhood in the state. In Bergen County overall, the population is approaching 1 million and is 21 percent Hispanic and 17 percent Asian. Bergen is the last urban county in the nation that widely complies with "Blue Law" limitations on Sunday retailing, a relic of Puritanism dating back to 1600s. Bergen is the only county in New Jersey that has not opted out—the rest did so from the 1950s through the 1980s. Opponents have been unable to overturn the law in Bergen as many small business owners, particularly those in Paramus, prefer not having to worry about the malls for one day during the week.

The 5th Congressional District of New Jersey comprises most of northern Bergen County, plus a swath of North Jersey stretching west to the upper reaches of the Delaware River. This is the only district in New Jersey that stretches from the Delaware to the Hudson. Nearly three-fourths of its population is in Bergen County, which leans Democratic as a whole. Farther west are exurban and comfortably Republican Sussex and Warren counties, both of which have seen an aging tax base and population losses since 2010. The ongoing local shifts culminated when Joe Biden comfortably took the district, 52%-47%.

Frank Pallone (D)

Elected 1988, 17th term, b. Oct 30, 1951; Long Branch, NJ; Middlebury College, B.A., 1973; Tufts University Fletcher School of Law and Diplomacy, M.A., 1974; Rutgers University Law School, J.D., 1978; Roman Catholic; Married (Sarah Hospodor Pallone); 3 children.

Elected Office: Long Branch City Council, 1982-1988; NJ Senate, 1983-1988.

Professional Career: Assistant Professional, Rutgers University, 1979-1980; Practicing attorney, 1981-1983; Instructor, Monmouth College, 1984-1986.

DC Office: 2107 RHOB 20515, 202-225-4671, Fax: 202-225-9665, pallone.house.gov

State Offices: Long Branch, 732-571-1140; New Brunswick, 732-249-8892.

Committees: *Energy & Commerce (Chmn)*: Ex Officio membership on all subcommittees.

Group Ratings

	ADA	ACLU	AFL-CIO	LCV	COC	HAFA	ACU	CFG	FRC
2020	**	83%	**	100%	-	5%	10%	**	-
2019	100%	C	86%	100%	40%	C	10%	17%	0%

Almanac Ratings 2019-2020

	Economy	Social	Foreign	Composite
Liberal	100%	100%	96%	99%
Conservative	0%	0%	4%	1%

Key Votes of the 116th Congress

1. U.S./Mex./Can. trade deal	N	5. Russia sanctions	Y	9. Firearms background checks Y
2. First Coronavirus response	Y	6. Troops in Syria	Y	10. Spending at the border　　N
3. HEROES Act	Y	7. Veto arms sales to Saudis	Y	11. Marijuana liberalized rules　Y
4. CASH Act	Y	8. Defense $$$, veto override	Y	12. Electoral College objections N

Election Results

Election	Name (Party)	Vote (%)		Cand. Spent	Ind. Exp. Support	Ind. Exp. Oppose
2020 General	Frank Pallone (D)	199,648	(61%)	$1,808,531	$141	
	Christian Onuoha (R)	126,760	(39%)			$59
2020 Primary	Frank Pallone Jr. (D)	56,660	(79%)			
	Russ Cirincione (D)	12,139	(17%)			

Prior winning percentages: 2018 (64%), 2016 (64%), 2014 (60%), 2012 (63%), 2010 (55%), 2008 (67%), 2006 (69%), 2004 (67%), 2002 (66%), 2000 (68%), 1998 (57%), 1996 (61%), 1994 (60%), 1992 (52%), 1990 (49%), 1988 (52%), 1988 special (52%)

Democrat Frank Pallone, elected in 1988, steadily rose to become the powerful Energy and Commerce Committee chairman. In that position, he has been at the center of Democratic Party disputes over healthcare and environmental policy and has also worked with Republicans to address a range of issues with broader consensus. Although Speaker Nancy Pelosi once opposed Pallone's ascension on the committee, they have become close allies.

Pallone is the son of a disabled Long Branch policeman. He became an environmentalist in 1969, when as a Middlebury College freshman in Vermont he worked for that state's first-in-the-nation bottle deposit law. After getting a master's degree in international relations from Tufts University and a law degree from Rutgers, he was elected to the Long Branch City Council at age 31 and to the New Jersey Senate a year later.

Pallone ran in a 1988 special election for a coastal New Jersey House seat that Democrat James Howard held for more than 20 years before his death in office. The district was conservative leaning, but residents were angry about untreated sludge, plastic containers and medical waste washing up on the beach. Pallone's bumper sticker, which didn't mention party affiliation, said, "Stop Ocean

Dumping." That, combined with his moderate views on taxes and crime, helped him win 52 percent of the vote. After redistricting in the early 1990s, Pallone represented a more Democratic-leaning seat that included urban areas in Middlesex County as well as parts of the Jersey Shore.

Given his coastal district, Pallone has had a continuing interest in protecting the New Jersey shoreline. After the BP oil spill in the Gulf of Mexico in 2010, he and other Democrats implored President Barack Obama to oppose oil and gas drilling off the East Coast. After criticizing as "unthinkable" an initial plan for partial approval of drilling, Pallone welcomed the administration's later reversal, including a five-year moratorium, though he continued to urge a permanent ban. He also criticized the Obama administration's response to Superstorm Sandy, which devastated many of his district's coastal communities in 2012. He repeatedly demanded that the Federal Emergency Management Agency provide mobile homes for thousands of stranded residents, then criticized its delivery of 50 trailers. To improve local communications during emergencies, Pallone crafted the Securing Access to Networks in Disasters (SANDY) Act, which the House passed in 2017.

He has also channeled the interests of his district's large Asian populations. In support of the district's Armenians, Pallone helped push congressional approval of normalizing trade relations with Armenia and sponsored the resolution that labeled the 1915 killing of Armenians by Ottoman Turks as genocide. The House and Senate passed separate resolutions recognizing the killings as genocide in 2019.After the Trump administration failed to follow suit, President Joe Biden issued a statement condemning the genocide. He has been active on issues involving India and has introduced a resolution condemning violence against the Hindus known as Kashmiri Pandits.

Before becoming its chairman in 2019, Pallone was an active member of Energy and Commerce and was involved with several major policy initiatives during the Obama administration. As chairman of the Subcommittee on Health, Pallone helped steer the Democrats' expansion of the Children's Health Insurance Program in 2009. On the Democrats' economic stimulus bill, he backed an increase in the federal matching rate for Medicaid as a step to reduce the program's financial burden on states. During the health care overhaul debate that year, he shuttled among various factions of Blue Dogs and progressives to urge flexibility.

When Rep. Henry Waxman retired in 2014 as ranking Democrat on Energy and Commerce, Rep. Anna Eshoo was supported by her longtime friend, then-Minority Leader Nancy Pelosi, as his successor. The Pelosi-controlled Democratic Steering and Policy Committee endorsed Eshoo, 30-19. But Eshoo was edged out by Pallone, 100-90, in secret balloting by the full Democratic Caucus. Pallone highlighted that he had four years more seniority than Eshoo, which appealed to members of the Congressional Black Caucus, who often benefit from seniority. He also received support from Minority Whip Steny Hoyer, who was often at odds with Pelosi.

After moving into his new position, Pallone sought to reduce the fractiousness on the panel. In 2016, the committee was instrumental in enacting the bipartisan Twenty First Century Cures Act, which advanced a series of medical-research innovations. Also that year, the committee completed the long-delayed update of chemical safety laws. The new law resolved numerous manufacturing and public-health issues related to New Jersey and gave new authority to the Environmental Protection Agency to evaluate existing and new chemicals.

With the Democratic takeover of the House in 2019, Pallone stepped in as chairman and confronted many of his party's most contentious policy disputes, particularly the progressive-moderate splits on climate change and healthcare. He made common cause with Pelosi to rein in the progressives while also giving voice to their concerns. At the beginning of 2019, Pelosi created a select committee to address climate change, a key progressive demand. However, at Pallone's insistence, the select committee did not gain legislative authority. In July 2019, Pallone announced that his committee's climate plan would aim for net-zero greenhouse gas emissions by 2050, 20 years later than the progressive-favored Green New Deal.

In December 2019, he held a hearing on "Medicare for all" legislation to push his preference for strengthening the Affordable Care Act rather than moving to fully government-run insurance. In a nod to moderates in the caucus, Pallone has opposed a ban on donations from contributors in the fossil-fuel industry for committee members. He feuded with Rep. Alexandria Ocasio-Cortez, who was denied a spot on the committee following the 2020 elections.

Pallone worked across the aisle, often on less contentious issues before the committee. In late 2020, Pallone helped forge a bipartisan compromise to end most surprise medical billing. Pallone called the provision "the biggest victory for consumers since the Affordable Care Act." He also collaborated with Republicans on a bill to reduce illegal robocalls that was signed into law in late 2019. However, he was unable to find common ground on lowering prescription drug costs. House Democrats passed their own drug bill on a party-line vote; it received no action in the Senate.

Since 1994, Pallone has been reelected with at least 60 percent of the vote, with two exceptions. In 1998, he faced a tough challenge from 28-year-old Republican Mike Ferguson, an ally of former GOP Gov. Thomas Kean, who later won his own seat. An insurance group unhappy with Pallone's support of President Bill Clinton's plan to regulate health maintenance organizations spent nearly $2 million on Ferguson's campaign. Pallone won 57%-40%. In 2010, he drew another formidable opponent in Republican Anna Little, the mayor of Highlands. With strong tea party backing, Little blasted Pallone's efforts to pass the Affordable Care Act. Pallone kept his seat, 55%-44%.

He has had a continuing interest in the Senate, without risking his House seat. When Democratic Sen. Jon Corzine ran for governor in 2005, Pallone endorsed him. Corzine was elected, but he disappointed Pallone by appointing Rep. Robert Menendez to his Senate seat. After Democratic Sen. Frank Lautenberg died in 2013, Pallone ran in the special election and appealed to party regulars. Newark Mayor Cory Booker easily won the Democratic primary with 59 percent to 20 percent for Pallone, the runner-up.

NJ-6: East-Central New Jersey

Cook Partisan Voting Index: D+6

Population		Race and Ethnicity		Income	
Total	739,726	White	61.00%	Median Income	$91,654
Land area (sq. miles)	216	Black	10.80%	District Income Rank	49
Pop/ sq mi	3,431.81	Latino	22.40%	Poverty Rate	9.40%
Born in State	47.80%	Asian	18.50%	With health insurance	91.70%
		Two or more races	3.80%	Cash public assistance	1.80%
Age Groups		Other	5.90%	Food stamp/SNAP	6.40%
Under 18	22.20%				
18-34	24.10%	**Education**		**Work**	
35-64	39.70%	H.S grad or less	36.50%	White Collar	45.60%
Over 64	13.90%	Some college	22.40%	Sales and Service	33.40%
		College Degree, 4 yr	24.80%	Blue Collar	21.00%
Military		Post grad	16.30%	Government	13.00%
Veteran/ Active Duty	3.30%				

2020 Pres. Vote	Biden	191,464	(57%)	Trump	138,919	(41%)
2016 Pres. Vote	Clinton	162,858	(56%)	Trump	117,679	(40%)

Middlesex and Northern Monmouth Counties: For generations, great transportation arteries have brought people out of the huge central cities of New York and Philadelphia and into the flatlands and hills of New Jersey—to vacation, to raise families, to work toward affluence and to build communities. The railroads of the late 19th century created the towns of the Jersey shore. After 1874, when the first train from New York City reached Long Branch, the shore became the summer home of seven presidents from Grant to Wilson (James Garfield, convalescing after he was shot, died there in 1881), and of New York racehorse owners and socialites. Over time, the ambiance degraded, and the fishing pier and much of the boardwalk went up in flames in 1987. A shopping and dining complex took its place.

Middlesex County accounts for about two-thirds of the district's population. Here, the freight rail lines in the New York-Philadelphia corridor sparked electrical and chemical industries—many of them building on the inventions of Thomas Edison, produced in his Menlo Park laboratory just off the rail lines. During the COVID-19 pandemic, a veterans' nursing home in Menlo Park had the highest rate of deaths in the country. South of Menlo Park, the New Jersey Turnpike roars past oil tank farms and petrochemical plants, major rail lines and the oily waters of Raritan Bay. In 2020, the U.S. Department of Transportation gave the city of South Amboy a $5 million grant to build a ferry station at the mouth of the Raritan River that will serve Manhattan commuters. Further up the Raritan River is Sayreville, the site of a $2.5 billion riverfront project – the largest redevelopment in state history. Past Sayreville is New Brunswick, home to Rutgers University. The district's two largest localities are in Middlesex—Woodbridge and Edison Township. "Little India" communities in once-abandoned areas of these cities have attracted Asian business interests from elsewhere in the Northeast. Emirates airline serves this community with a daily flight from Newark to Dubai and beyond; the Indian community provides about one-third of its U.S. passengers.

The district is shaped like a backward capital F, with a string of towns running from Piscataway in Middlesex down the Atlantic coast to Long Branch and Asbury Park in Monmouth County. Asbury Park, which began as a Christian resort and was immortalized in the music of Bruce Springsteen, fell on hard times in the 1970s and 1980s but is now home to expensive condos, luxury hotels, and trendy restaurants. It still maintains a lively music scene. Asbury Park made headlines during the pandemic when its city council openly defied Governor Phil Murphy by voting to reopen indoor dining while a statewide ban was in place. Murphy sued the city in response and a state judge sided with governor. North of Asbury Park is Long Branch, where redevelopment efforts are overseen by Jared Kushner's family company.

The district has become majority-minority: 22 percent Latino, 19 percent Asian and 11 percent Black. It has the third-largest share of Asians of any district on the East Coast, behind two in New York City. This is a safe Democratic district. The presidential elections tightened a bit during Donald Trump's two campaigns. Joe Biden led Trump, 57-41%, compared to Barack Obama's 62%-38% lead over Mitt Romney in 2012.

Tom Malinowski (D)

Elected 2018, 2nd term, b. Sep 15, 1965; Slupsk, Poland; Oxford University; Oxford University; Divorced; 1 child.

Professional Career: Special Assistant, U.S. Sen. Danial Patrick Moynihan, 1988; Research Assistant, Institute for Human Sciences, 1992; Research Assistant, Ford Foundation, 1993; Policy Planning Staff and Speechwriter, U.S. Department of State, 1994-1998; Senior Director, National Security Council, 1998-2001; Washington Director, Human Rights Watch, 2001-2013; Assistant Secretary of State for Democracy, Human Rights, and Labor, U.S. Department of State, 2014-2017.

DC Office: 426 CHOB 20515, 202-225-5361, malinowski.house.gov

State Offices: Somerville, 908-547-3307.

Committees: *Foreign Affairs (VChmn)*: Africa, Global Health & Global Human Rights; Middle East, North Africa & Global Counterterrorism. *Homeland Security*: Intelligence & Counterterrorism. *Transportation & Infrastructure*: Railroads, Pipelines & Hazardous Materials; Water Resources & Environment.

Almanac Ratings 2019-2020

	Economy	Social	Foreign	Composite
Liberal	100%	100%	80%	94%
Conservative	0%	0%	20%	6%

Key Votes of the 116th Congress

1. U.S./Mex./Can. trade deal	Y	5. Russia sanctions	Y	9. Firearms background checks	Y
2. First Coronavirus response	Y	6. Troops in Syria	Y	10. Spending at the border	Y
3. HEROES Act	Y	7. Veto arms sales to Saudis	Y	11. Marijuana liberalized rules	Y
4. CASH Act	Y	8. Defense $$$, veto override	Y	12. Electoral College objections	N

Election Results

Election	Name (Party)	Vote (%)		Cand. Spent	Ind. Exp. Support	Ind. Exp. Oppose
2020 General	Tom Malinowski (D)	219,688	(51%)	$7,716,274	$11,634	$4,223,629
	Thomas Kean Jr. (R)	214,359	(49%)	$3,879,612	$216,383	$4,165,198
2020 Primary	Tom Malinowski (D)	80,334	(100%)			

Prior winning percentages: 2018 (52%)

Democrat Tom Malinowski won his traditionally Republican district in his first bid for elected office. With his national security experience in the Clinton and Obama administrations, most prominently on human rights issues, he was among the most seasoned Washington players in the freshman class. In his first term he proved more confrontational toward President Donald Trump than some of his swing-seat colleagues. And he won reelection by a narrow margin, running far behind Joe Biden's 10-point win in the district. He remains a top GOP target in 2022.

Born in Poland, Malinowski settled with his mother in Princeton when he was age six. He graduated from the University of California, Berkeley, and, as a Rhodes scholar, earned his master's degree in political science at Oxford University. Following brief stints with Democratic Sen. Daniel Patrick Moynihan and the Ford Foundation, he spent four years on the policy planning staff at the State Department. In 1998, he joined the Clinton White House as a speechwriter at the National Security Council.

During the presidency of George W. Bush, Malinowski was Washington director for Human Rights Watch, where he was an outspoken critic of U.S. military and intelligence tactics. He continued in that position during the first term of the Obama presidency. Republican Sen. John McCain said that he was "forever grateful" to Malinowski for his role in the fight in Congress to end the use of "enhanced interrogation techniques" that McCain and others likened to torture. With Secretary of State John Kerry, Malinowski returned to government as assistant secretary for democracy, human rights and labor. In that position, his portfolio included protection of religious minorities targeted by ISIS and sanctions against North Korea.

Malinowski launched his first campaign against Rep. Leonard Lance, a wonky five-term Republican who had survived close primary challenges from more conservative opponents but had seemed secure in general elections. He criticized the incumbent for backing legislation harmful to the district and President Donald Trump for having challenged "everything that I've worked for on behalf of our country."In the Democratic primary, he faced Peter Jacob, a social worker who supported the "Medicare for all" proposal and was backed by groups associated with Sen. Bernie Sanders. Jacob had lost to Lance in 2016, 54%-43%. With the crucial endorsement of county Democratic committees in the district, which were impressed by his superior fundraising, Malinowski won the primary with 67 percent of the vote.

Lance struggled to balance party loyalty with growing antagonism by his constituents toward Trump, including frequent protests at Lance's district office. During a debate, Lance—who voted against House Republican healthcare and tax bills in 2017—said he maintained his support for moderate Republican positions and called Malinowski a "carpetbagger" who had spent most of his career in Washington. In return, Malinowski criticized Lance for failing to be more outspoken in opposing Trump and promised checks on one-party government. As with other leading Democratic challengers in 2018, Malinowski's surge of fundraising prior to the election resulted in spending for his campaign that more than doubled Lance's. In his 51%-48% victory, he easily took Union and Somerset counties, which cast more than half the total vote. Lance won the outlying counties.

In Congress, Malinowski charted a slightly less centrist course than some of his New Jersey colleagues. In spring 2019, he became the first swing-seat Democrat to come out in favor of impeaching Trump and was one of the most outspoken members who condemned Trump for his tweet urging four minority congresswomen to "go back" to their countries.

Republicans recruited an exceptionally strong challenger to take on Malinowski: Tom Kean Jr., the state Senate minority leader and son of a beloved former governor. Kean launched early in 2019, deflecting questions about Trump and suggesting he would govern in the style of his father: "I am a Tom Kean Republican," he told the Newark Star Ledger. And in an acknowledgement that the district is trending more socially liberal, he said he regretted his 2010 vote against legalizing gay marriage. When he became the clear primary frontrunner, his chief opponent, Rosemary Becchi, a tax attorney and former Senate aide, switched districts to run against Democratic Rep. Mikie Sherrill. Kean won a three-way primary with 79 percent of the vote.

The Malinowski-Kean match up was an acrimonious affair. Malinowski ran ads tying Kean to Trump and claiming he would take away access to abortions. When the National Republican Congressional Committee ran an ad claiming Malinowski "worked as the top lobbyist for a radical group that strongly opposed the national sex offender registry," the congressman said he received an onslaught of death threats from believers of the QAnon conspiracy theory. In October 2020, Malinowski joined forces with Republican Rep. Denver Riggleman of Virginia to spearhead a bipartisan resolution condemning the movement. Kean tried to stay above the fray. His father cut a campaign ad for him, stressing his son's commitment to funding common ground.

The incumbent spent $7.7 million to Kean's $3.9 million, and Malinowski won 50.5%-49.3%, a margin of about 5,300 votes. Kean carried Hunterdon and Morris, but couldn't overcome Malinowski's lead in Somerset and Union.

The NRCC quickly named Malinowski a top 2022target, noting that he ran well behind Biden, who carried the district54%-44%. Kean announced in February 2021 that he would not seek reelection to the state Senate, and was widely expected to focus on another congressional run instead. Malinowski subsequently faced charges of insider stock trading. He denied the insider trading, but conceded that he had failed to file requisite reports.

NJ-7: North-Central New Jersey

Cook Partisan Voting Index: D+1

Population		Race and Ethnicity		Income	
Total	734,239	White	74.90%	Median Income	$115,585
Land area (sq. miles)	970	Black	5.00%	District Income Rank	12
Pop/ sq mi	756.8	Latino	14.30%	Poverty Rate	5.40%
Born in State	54.00%	Asian	11.80%	With health insurance	94.40%
		Two or more races	2.40%	Cash public assistance	1.30%
Age Groups		Other	5.80%	Food stamp/SNAP	2.90%
Under 18	21.60%				
18-34	18.30%	Education		Work	
35-64	43.30%	H.S grad or less	26.20%	White Collar	53.70%
Over 64	16.90%	Some college	19.00%	Sales and Service	32.30%
		College Degree, 4 yr	31.60%	Blue Collar	14.00%
Military		Post grad	23.20%	Government	11.90%
Veteran/ Active Duty	4.30%				

2020 Pres. Vote	Biden	239,170	(54%)	Trump	195,284	(44%)			
2016 Pres. Vote	Clinton	180,525	(48%)	Trump	176,386	(47%)	Johnson	9,794	(3%)

Somerset, Union and Hunterdon Counties: The transportation arteries beneath First Watchung Mountain played a large role in New Jersey's development. The rail lines of the late 19th century opened up commuter suburbs. In the 1940s, the four lanes of U.S. 22 made those communities readily accessible by car. Next, Interstate 78, completed in the mid-1980s, put Newark only an hour's distance from the Pennsylvania line. An enormous shopping mall and office development, which included the headquarters of AT&T, rose up in the horse country around Far Hills and Bernardsville, where the likes of Malcolm Forbes and Charles Engelhard owned huge estates. (New Jersey claims more horses per square mile than any other state.) Nearby is the town of Bedminster, more than 40 miles from Manhattan and the site of Trump National Golf Club, which former President Donald Trump turned into an informal "summer White House." These towns are in Somerset County, with a median household income in 2019 of nearly $114,000, the 15thhighest among U.S. counties. Somerset has become an active tourist destination, including for beer and wine enthusiasts. In 2020, Amazon opened a massive 616,000-foot distribution center in the county, creating over 1,000 new jobs.

Nearby, fast-growing Hunterdon County has the nation's 13thhighest median household income, at $115,000.Hunterdon lost about 2 percent of its population between 2010 and 2019, chiefly because some of its kids have grown up and moved away. But the community has resisted some efforts to expand. In 2020, Hunterdon residents opposed a new 333-unit housing development, arguing that the increased sewage would hurt the environment. To the east, Diamond Nation in Flemington is a 35-acre baseball and softball complex and the site of many tournaments. Flemington was also the setting of the "trial of the century," in the kidnapping and murder of the 20-month-old son of aviator Charles Lindbergh.

The 7th Congressional District of New Jersey covers several generations of suburban development. It crosses the breadth of the state, from the edge of Pennsylvania's Lehigh Valley in the west to parts of Union County in the east. It is an agglomeration of places, and includes parts of five counties and all of Hunterdon. The largest slice of population is the 32 percent in Somerset County, with 25 percent in Union County and about 18 percent in Hunterdon County. The district until recently favored Republicans, but not overwhelmingly. Trump in 2016 had less appeal in these upscale precincts. He trailed Hillary Clinton, 48%-47%. This was the only one of the five districts in New Jersey that House Republicans held at the time, where Clinton led, albeit narrowly. But Trump in 2020 only carried three of the state's 12 districts, all in south Jersey, and he lost the 7th overwhelmingly to Joe Biden, 54%-44%.

Albio Sires (D)

Elected 2006, 9th term, b. Jan 26, 1951; Bejucal, Cuba; Middlebury College, M.A., 1985; Saint Peter's College, M.A., 1985; Roman Catholic; Married (Adrienne Sires); 1 stepchild.

Elected Office: West New York Mayor, 1995-2006; NJ Assembly, 2000-2006, speaker, 2002-2006.

Professional Career: H.S. Spanish & ESL teacher, 1975-1985; Special Assistant, NJ Department of Comm. Affairs, 1985; Part-owner, A.M. Title Agency, 1986-2006.

DC Office: 2268 RHOB 20515, 202-225-7919, Fax: 202-226-0792, sires.house.gov

State Offices: Elizabeth, 908-820-0692; Jersey City, 201-309-0301; West New York, 201-558-0800.

Committees: *Budget. Foreign Affairs*: Europe, Energy, the Environment & Cyber; West Hem, Civ Sec, Migration, & Intern'l Econ Policy (Chmn). *Transportation & Infrastructure*: Highways & Transit; Railroads, Pipelines & Hazardous Materials.

Group Ratings

	ADA	ACLU	AFL-CIO	LCV	COC	HAFA	ACU	CFG	FRC
2020	**	81%	**	100%	-	0%	3%	**	-
2019	90%	C	100%	93%	66%	C	3%	12%	0%

Almanac Ratings 2019-2020

	Economy	Social	Foreign	Composite
Liberal	100%	65%	80%	82%
Conservative	0%	35%	20%	18%

Key Votes of the 116th Congress

1. U.S./Mex./Can. trade deal	Y	5. Russia sanctions Y	9. Firearms background checks Y
2. First Coronavirus response	Y	6. Troops in Syria Y	10. Spending at the border Y
3. HEROES Act	Y	7. Veto arms sales to Saudis Y	11. Marijuana liberalized rules Y
4. CASH Act	Y	8. Defense $$$, veto override Y	12. Electoral College objections N

Election Results

Election	Name (Party)	Vote (%)		Cand. Spent	Ind. Exp. Support	Ind. Exp. Oppose
2020 General	Albio Sires (D)	176,758	(74%)	$480,509	$44,263	
	Jason Mushnick (R)	58,686	(25%)			$59
2020 Primary	Albio Sires (D)	47,814	(70%)			
	Hector Oseguera (D)	18,557	(27%)			

Prior winning percentages: 2018 (78%), 2016 (77%), 2014 (77%), 2012 (78%), 2010 (74%), 2008 (75%), 2006 (78%)

Democrat Albio Sires, who won a special election in 2006, is the only Cuban-American Democrat in the House. He is an old-style political boss who remains influential in Hudson County. Sires concentrates on local issues, and on foreign policies that affect his district, including his tough stance against leftist regimes south of the border and his outright opposition to U.S. recognition of Cuba. Despite his willingness to go his separate way from other Democrats, he has chaired the Western Hemisphere Subcommittee, where he has said that he supports the Biden administration's steps to strengthen democratic institutions and protect human rights—especially in dealing with Venezuela.

Sires, who was born in Cuba, remembers the book-burning following the communist revolution there. His family fled Fidel Castro's regime in 1962 when he was 10. He attended St. Peter's College on a four-year basketball scholarship—he is 6-feet-4-inches tall—then earned a master's degree from Middlebury College. He became a high school Spanish teacher.

On his fourth try, he was elected mayor of West New York as a Republican in 1995 and held that post until 2006. He focused on creation of more affordable housing in the small but densely populated town and won praise for merging the fire department with three neighboring departments. He switched parties in 1999 and, with the support of his new party's leaders, defeated a veteran Democratic incumbent to win a state House seat. With strong support from Democratic Gov. Jim McGreevey in 2002, he became speaker of the Assembly.

After Democratic Gov. Jon Corzine appointed Rep. Robert Menendez as his replacement in the Senate, Sires became the frontrunner for the House seat. In the primary, he faced a fierce challenge from Joe Vas of Perth Amboy, who likewise was a state House member and a mayor. Vas assailed Sires as a puppet of the Hudson County Democratic machine. Sires responded by depicting Vas as soft on crime and won the support of most leading Democrats, except for his longtime rival Menendez, who remained neutral. Sires crushed Vas 80%-20% in Hudson County, which cast 74 percent of the total vote. Overall, he won 72%-28%. Sires won the general, 78%-19%, and has been reelected easily since. With his lieutenants, he has gained growing control of the Democratic organization in Hudson County.

In the House, Sires established a voting record that has placed him toward the middle of the House, especially on foreign policy, according to the Almanac vote ratings. He allied himself with South Florida members who have wanted to keep U.S. sanctions on Cuba in place. In 2014, as ranking Democrat on the Foreign Affairs Committee's Western Hemisphere panel, he opposed President Barack Obama's opening to Cuba as "naïve and disrespectful," and said the effort to "encourage a form of Cuban glasnost is a dangerous miscalculation." Sires also opposed Obama's 2015 Iran nuclear deal, pointing out that Iran would be "allowed to enhance its nuclear and weapons capabilities" under the deal.

In December 2019, the House passed his resolution opposing the call by President Donald Trump to invite Russia to attend the annual meeting of the G-7 world leaders unless it ends its occupation of Ukraine. "Time and time again, Russia has shown it has no respect for the territorial or democratic integrity of other nations," he told the House. With the gavel of the Western Hemisphere Subcommittee and a new Democratic president in 2021, Sires pledged to "help tackle the root causes of migration from Central America[and] reinvigorate our bilateral cooperation with Mexico."

On the Transportation and Infrastructure Committee, Sires welcomed completion of the Army Corps of Engineers project to raise the Bayonne Bridge's height to accommodate larger ships. He introduced legislation to revitalize urban parks, and to help commuters find alternative ways to get to work. In 2015, he was one of 28 House Democrats who opposed Obama and sided with some unions in support of the Keystone XL pipeline. In 2018, he criticized Trump for not supporting the Gateway tunnel project under the Hudson River.

In 2020, Sires faced what some local Democrats described as his first real primary challenge since he was elected. Hector Oseguera, who described himself as "an anti-money laundering attorney" from Hudson County, said his chief priority was rooting out political corruption in the district. He embraced "name and shame" tactics to expose corruption, according to HudsonReporter.com.

Each of the candidates criticized the other for having been a Republican earlier in his political career. Sires spent $550,000 during the entire campaign, which was low for an incumbent but far more than the $85,000 Oseguera spent, and won, 70%-27%; he led the challenger by at least 2-to-1 in each of the four counties.

In the 2010 election, Sires was a vice chair of the Democratic Congressional Campaign Committee, in charge of member participation and outreach. After Democrats lost their majority, he called for Speaker Nancy Pelosi to step down. Following the 2018 election, he was among the cadre of Democrats who sought an alternative to Pelosi as Speaker, though he eventually supported her.

NJ-8: Jersey City/Newark Area

Population		Race and Ethnicity		Income	
Total	766,357	White	57.80%	Median Income	$65,658
Land area (sq. miles)	55	Black	10.70%	District Income Rank	204
Pop/ sq mi	14,012.74	Latino	55.40%	Poverty Rate	14.70%
Born in State	35.20%	Asian	9.80%	With health insurance	83.50%
		Two or more races	3.70%	Cash public assistance	1.70%
Age Groups		Other	17.90%	Food stamp/SNAP	13.00%
Under 18	22.10%				
18-34	27.70%	Education		Work	
35-64	39.20%	H.S grad or less	47.20%	White Collar	36.40%
Over 64	11.00%	Some college	17.40%	Sales and Service	36.60%
		College Degree, 4 yr	21.10%	Blue Collar	27.10%
Military		Post grad	14.20%	Government	8.80%
Veteran/ Active Duty	1.50%				

2020 Pres. Vote	Biden	182,965	(72%)	Trump	69,205	(27%)
2016 Pres. Vote	Clinton	173,834	(75%)	Trump	49,336	(21%)

Hudson County: Standing in New York Harbor since 1886, the Statue of Liberty has been the symbol of America's receptiveness to immigrants. The statue is on the New Jersey side of the harbor and so is, as the U.S. Supreme Court ruled in 1998, most of Ellis Island, where immigrants once were processed, though the museum is on the New York side of the island. So it's natural that the towns atop the granite and gneiss ridge of Hudson County, overlooking the harbor, became immigrant territory. Many children and grandchildren of Irish and Italian immigrants stayed in Hudson County, living in the same neighborhoods, working on the same docks or in the factories, and voting the dictates of the same political machine. Hudson County was the setting of one of America's classic political machines, undisciplined by any metropolitan elite. From 1917 to 1949, the boss of Hudson County was Frank ("I am the law") Hague. His machine chose governors and U.S. senators, prosecutors and judges, and had influence in the White House of Franklin D. Roosevelt. Hague collected high taxes from industries clustered here, and then passed them on to consumers. In return, he gave them an orderly city, free of most crime and vice, and a workforce insulated against racketeers and militant unions.

Hudson County has changed. New immigrants arrived—refugees from Fidel Castro's Cuba, and other Latinos and Asians. Starting in the 1980s, huge new condominium and office developments went up in Jersey City, housing big banks, securities firms and, later, internet businesses. The waterfront in Jersey City has been fully built-out, with a high and growing skyline, and many parts have gentrified with young families settling in. In the most expensive municipal referendum campaign in New Jersey history, about 70 percent of Jersey City voters in 2019 approved restrictions on rental housing—a victory for city officials and a major setback for Airbnb.

Upscale young singles moved into Hoboken's five-story Victorians; they were a quick commute through the PATH tubes to Wall Street or Greenwich Village. In Hoboken, the home of Frank Sinatra and the Oreo cookie, shopping and apartment complexes have taken up the waterfront sites where factories were common (and where the classic movie On the Waterfront was filmed). Hoboken attracts urban professionals plus a growing number of families seeking affordable housing; the city, which grew by 38 percent from 2000 to 2019, has been called the "Millennial Capital" of New Jersey. In 2017, Hoboken elected as mayor Ravinder Bhalia—a civil rights lawyer and a Sikh who was unfairly accused in campaign flyers of being a "terrorist." In January 2020, public reaction was pleased with changes in the development plan in and around the ferry terminal in Hoboken, the Jersey Journal reported. Since 2010, the 6 percent population increase in Hudson made it the fastest-growing county in the state. Bayonne has become a cruise ship port. Its 5,780-foot-long bridge, built in 1931, has been raised from 151 feet to 215 feet high so it is tall enough for super-sized container ships. The project was completed in 2017.

The 8th Congressional District includes much of Hudson County, plus most of the immigrant entry ports along the water and the bustling docks along the Hudson River and New York Bay. It takes in Hoboken, now 65 percent Hispanic; nearly half of Newark; West New York and Weehawken;

parts of Jersey City and Bayonne; working-class Harrison, an aging factory town where European immigrants have been replaced by Hispanic immigrants; and part of industrial Kearny. The district is 55 percent Hispanic, by far the largest percentage in the state; 44 percent of the population is foreign-born. In Jersey City, many are from India. About 70 percent of the district is in Hudson, plus sections of Essex and Union and a thin slice of Bergen County. The district lines in Hudson and Essex counties were drawn like pieces of a jig-saw puzzle to assure that the 8th District is heavily Hispanic and the 10th District is heavily Black. Hudson County's vote for the Democratic presidential nominee dropped from 75 percent in 2016 to 72 percent in 2020—another locale where Latino support faded.

Bill Pascrell (D)

Elected 1996, 13th term, b. Jan 25, 1937; Paterson, NJ; Fordham University, B.S., 1959; Fordham University, M.A., 1961; Roman Catholic; Married (Elsie Marie Botto Pascrell); 3 children; 3 grandchildren.

Military Career: U.S. Army 1961-1962; U.S. Army Reserve 1962-1967

Elected Office: President, Paterson Board of Education, 1979-1982; NJ Assembly, 1988-1997, Minority Leader pro temp; Paterson Mayor, 1990-1996.

Professional Career: H.S. teacher, 1960-1974; Director, Paterson Department of Public Works, 1974-1977; Director, Paterson Department of Policy, 1977-1987.

DC Office: 2409 RHOB 20515, 202-225-5751, Fax: 202-225-5782, pascrell.house.gov
State Offices: Englewood, 201-935-2248; Lyndhurst, 201-935-2248; Passaic, 973-472-4510; Paterson, 973-523-5152.

Committees: *Ways & Means*: Oversight (Chmn); Social Security.

Group Ratings

	ADA	ACLU	AFL-CIO	LCV	COC	HAFA	ACU	CFG	FRC
2020	**	79%	**	100%	-	0%	9%	**	-
2019	95%	C	90%	100%	49%	C	9%	12%	0%

Almanac Ratings 2019-2020

	Economy	Social	Foreign	Composite
Liberal	100%	100%	96%	99%
Conservative	0%	0%	4%	1%

Key Votes of the 116th Congress

1. U.S./Mex./Can. trade deal	N	5. Russia sanctions	Y	9. Firearms background checks	Y
2. First Coronavirus response	Y	6. Troops in Syria	Y	10. Spending at the border	N
3. HEROES Act	Y	7. Veto arms sales to Saudis	Y	11. Marijuana liberalized rules	Y
4. CASH Act	Y	8. Defense $$$, veto override	Y	12. Electoral College objections	N

Election Results

Election	Name (Party)	Vote (%)		Cand. Spent	Ind. Exp. Support	Ind. Exp. Oppose
2020 General	Bill Pascrell (D)	203,674	(66%)	$1,397,518	$873	
	Billy Prempeh (R)	98,629	(32%)	$33,342	$825	$113
	Chris Auriemma (I)	7,239	(2%)			
2020 Primary	Bill Pascrell Jr. (D)	52,422	(81%)			
	Zinovia Spezakis (D)	10,998	(17%)			

Prior winning percentages: 2018 (70%), 2016 (70%), 2014 (69%), 2012 (74%), 2010 (63%), 2008 (71%), 2006 (71%), 2004 (70%), 2002 (67%), 2000 (67%), 1998 (62%), 1996 (51%)

Bill Pascrell, elected in 1996, has thrived as an old-style, favor-trading pol with a feisty Jersey-guy demeanor On the House Ways and Means Committee, he suffered a setback in 2019 when his fellow

Democrats replaced him as the top Democrat on the Trade Subcommittee, with a more internationalist Democrat. Instead, he became chairman of the Oversight Subcommittee, where he focused on tax assistance. With coronary bypass surgery in July 2020 and the state designation of a local highway in his name, Pascrell—at age 85 for the 2022 election—seemed ready to complete his apparent plan to deliver his seat to his son.

He grew up in Paterson, the grandson of Italian immigrants. His father worked for the railroad, and Pascrell was the first one in his family to graduate from college. He worked his way through Fordham University, served in the Army, then taught high school for 14 years. From there Pascrell went into politics, first as director of Paterson's public works department, then as school board president. In 1987, he was elected to the New Jersey Assembly. In 1990, Pascrell was elected mayor of Paterson but continued to serve in the Assembly—a common practice in New Jersey until the legislature voted in 2007 to end it.

In 1996, Pascrell challenged first-term Republican Rep. Bill Martini, whom Pascrell portrayed as the tool of an "extremist" House leadership; his ads showed Martini's face on a puppet being manipulated by House Speaker Newt Gingrich. Despite Martini's support from the Sierra Club and labor unions, Pascrell won 51%-48%.

Pascrell has compiled a conventional liberal voting record, especially on economic issues. He has voted for some restrictions on abortion, including a parental notification requirement. In 2002, he voted to authorize the use of force in Iraq and, on the Homeland Security Committee, he was a voice for improved communications among first responders. "How is it we can talk to people on the moon, but we can't talk one block away?" Pascrell asked. He authored the Firefighter Investment and Response Enhancement (FIRE) Act in 2001 and has fought regularly to increase grants to local fire and police departments.

Pascrell has been successful with some pet projects. A bill to designate Paterson's Great Falls as a 120-acre national historical park was enacted in 2009. The following year, the House passed his bill calling for development of a new set of concussion-management guidelines for student athletes. That bill was part of his focus on research for traumatic brain injuries.

As his party's political fortunes declined, Pascrell was among the Democrats who were open in venting frustrations. When President Barack Obama's spokesman Robert Gibbs speculated that the Democrats' House majority was in doubt in the 2010 election, Pascrell told The Washington Post, "What the hell do they think we've been doing the last 12 months? We're the ones who have been taking the tough votes."

As a member of Ways and Means, Pascrell has worked with labor and consumer groups to promote "fair trade," and to expand the Trade Adjustment Assistance program for workers who have lost their jobs. He has become an increasingly harsh critic of international trade agreements. Despite pleas from Obama administration officials, Pascrell strongly opposed giving authority to the president to negotiate the Trans-Pacific Partnership and later praised President Donald Trump for withdrawing the proposal. In January 2017, he became the ranking Democrat on the Trade Subcommittee.

Two years later, he appeared to have been surprised when Ways and Means Democrats, back in the majority, chose Rep. Earl Blumenauer of trade-friendly Oregon to chair the subcommittee. Under party rules, the more-senior Blumenauer was approved in an up-or-down vote, without Pascrell getting his own vote. There were things about the selection process "that I absolutely did not like," he told reporters. The Democrats' action may have resulted from multiple factors—including internal rivalries and Pascrell's failure to protect his interests with committee chairman Richard Neal of Massachusetts. He didn't help himself when he joined Democrats who urged a delay in election of party leaders as they sought an alternative to Nancy Pelosi as Speaker.

After Rep. John Lewis of Georgia died in July 2020, Pascrell succeeded him as chairman of the Oversight Subcommittee. Earlier that year, he attacked Treasury Secretary Steve Mnuchin for refusing to respond to the committee's request to turn over President Donald Trump's tax records. "I think you're breaking the law," Pascrell told Mnuchin at a committee hearing in March. A Supreme Court ruling that June was less definitive on the committee's access. His focus changed with the arrival of a new president. In 2021, the subcommittee's first hearing sought to promote the Internal Revenue Service's program to provide tax-preparation services to low- and moderate-income taxpayers.

Pascrell showed survivor skills at home when the 2011 redistricting placed his seat in jeopardy. The new 9th District included his home base of Paterson, but it contained a large share of Democratic colleague Steve Rothman's former Bergen County-based district. In a battle of turnout, Pascrell's Passaic County machine outmatched Rothman's Bergen County team and he won, 61%-39%.

Since then, Pascrell's campaigns have been uneventful. In 2020, he had a primary challenge from Zina Spezakis, an environmental activist, who called it "unacceptable and horrific" that—at a time when police practices were being questioned—Pascrell had received more campaign contributions during his career from police unions and law enforcement political action committees than any other member of Congress. Pascrell co-chairs the Congressional Law Enforcement Caucus. Voters didn't seem concerned. Spezakis spent $700,000 to Pascrell's $1.8 million. But she was hardly competitive. Pascrell won, 81%-17%.

William Pascrell III, the legal counsel to Passaic County and an ally of Paterson Mayor Andre Sayegh, reportedly has been groomed for when his father decides to step down.

NJ-9: Northeast New Jersey   Cook Partisan Voting Index: D+13

Population		Race and Ethnicity		Income	
Total	762,322	White	62.70%	Median Income	$81,431
Land area (sq. miles)	95	Black	8.90%	District Income Rank	82
Pop/ sq mi	7,995.83	Latino	40.10%	Poverty Rate	11.50%
Born in State	42.20%	Asian	13.70%	With health insurance	86.80%
		Two or more races	2.90%	Cash public assistance	1.50%
Age Groups		Other	11.70%	Food stamp/SNAP	10.80%
Under 18	22.10%				
18-34	22.80%	**Education**		**Work**	
35-64	39.80%	H.S grad or less	44.10%	White Collar	38.70%
Over 64	15.20%	Some college	20.40%	Sales and Service	36.80%
		College Degree, 4 yr	22.70%	Blue Collar	24.50%
Military		Post grad	12.90%	Government	10.70%
Veteran/ Active Duty	2.70%				

2020 Pres. Vote	Biden	200,019	(62%)	Trump	118,376	(37%)
2016 Pres. Vote	Clinton	177,953	(64%)	Trump	91,696	(33%)

Southern Bergen County, Paterson: Paterson is one of the few American cities that has turned out pretty much as planned. It was the brainchild of Alexander Hamilton, who in the 1790s journeyed 20 miles from Manhattan to the Great Falls of the Passaic River in New Jersey. Watching the water surge down 72 feet—the highest falls along the East Coast—he predicted an industrial city would rise on the site. Hamilton formed the Society for Establishing Useful Manufactures, which opened a calico factory in 1794, and got Pierre L'Enfant, the designer of Washington D.C., to design Paterson (named after then-Gov. William Paterson). In 1836, Samuel Colt began manufacturing revolvers there. One of the first American locomotives, the Sandusky, was built in Paterson in 1837. Paterson ultimately became America's "Silk City," employing 25,000 silk mill workers before the great strike of 1913 led by the radical Industrial Workers of the World. Throughout, Paterson attracted immigrants from England, Ireland and, after 1890, Italy and Poland.

The city continues to attract immigrants today, even if its economy produces more service jobs than manufacturing jobs. It has a lively artists' community in its postindustrial setting, and downtown's "Little Ramallah," 10 blocks filled with Middle East shops, reflects the city's sizable Arab community—Palestinians, Lebanese, Jordanians; Syrian refugees settled here after their civil war in 2011. Paterson has suffered from deep-seated poverty and corruption of its politicians and police. In 2018, newly elected mayor Andre Sayegh—his parents were Syrian and Lebanese—sought to encourage optimism with a "One Paterson" promotional campaign.

The 9th Congressional District is based chiefly in the urban parts of Bergen and Passaic counties. It also takes in the leafy suburbs of Englewood, Palisades Park and fast-growing Edgewater. The high-rise towers of Fort Lee became famous in 2013 when top aides to Gov. Chris Christie decided to slow traffic to the George Washington Bridge, an incident that led to felony convictions and an erosion of Christie's cachet; in 2020, the Supreme Court unanimously reversed the convictions because the actions failed to meet the federal definition for fraud. The district also takes in East Rutherford and the Meadowlands Sports Complex, which is along Interstate 95. Once 8,400 acres of wetlands and home to thousands of species of animals and plants, the Meadowlands was developed in the 1970s. A generation later, the state built the $1.6 billion MetLife Stadium at that site for the National Football League's Giants and Jets. In 2018, the EPA announced a $330 million clean-up of mercury waste in a nearby creek—one of the largest such projects in state history. In October 2019, the American Dream Mall—the largest in the nation, by some measures—opened, with features such as ice skating, a ski slope and water park. Because of the Blue Laws in Bergen County, it was closed on Sundays.

A bit more than half the voters reside in Bergen County, with about 40 percent in Passaic and the remainder in a small slice of Hudson. This was a growth area in the 1950s and 1960s, as New Yorkers moved out of the city. It lost population in the next two decades, as young people moved farther out. Now, the population is rising with the influx of new immigrants, many of them low-income. From 2000 to 2019, the number of Hispanics in Bergen County doubled to 195,000 (now, 21 percent of 932,000), and in Passaic County, the Latino population grew to 43 percent of the 502,000 residents. With 40 percent Hispanic and 14 percent Asian, the 9th has become a minority enclave, though Democrats' share of the presidential vote has remained roughly 65 percent.

Donald Payne (D)

Elected 2012, 5th full term, b. Dec 17, 1958; Newark, NJ; Kean College, Att., 1978; Baptist; Married (Bea Payne); 3 children (triplets).

Elected Office: Freeholder-at-large, Essex County, 2005-2012; At-large rep., Newark City Council, 2006-2012, President 2010-2012..

Professional Career: NJ highway authority, 1990-1996; District leader, Newark's South Ward, 1992-2013.

DC Office: 103 CHOB 20515, 202-225-3436, Fax: 202-225-4160, payne.house.gov

State Offices: Hillside, 862-229-2994; Jersey City, 201-369-0392; Newark, 973-645-3213.

Committees: *Homeland Security*: Emergency Preparedness, Response & Recovery; Oversight, Management & Accountability; Transportation & Maritime Security. *Transportation & Infrastructure*: Aviation.

Group Ratings

	ADA	ACLU	AFL-CIO	LCV	COC	HAFA	ACU	CFG	FRC
2020	**	80%	**	86%	-	0%	4%	**	-
2019	95%	C	100%	90%	63%	C	5%	13%	0%

Almanac Ratings 2019-2020

	Economy	Social	Foreign	Composite
Liberal	55%	63%	57%	59%
Conservative	45%	37%	43%	41%

Key Votes of the 116th Congress

1. U.S./Mex./Can. trade deal	Y	5. Russia sanctions	N/A
2. First Coronavirus response	Y	6. Troops in Syria	Y
3. HEROES Act	Y	7. Veto arms sales to Saudis	Y
4. CASH Act	Y	8. Defense $$$, veto override	Y

9. Firearms background checks	Y
10. Spending at the border	Y
11. Marijuana liberalized rules	Y
12. Electoral College objections	N

Election Results

Election	Name (Party)	Vote (%)		Cand. Spent	Ind. Exp. Support	Ind. Exp. Oppose
2020 General	Donald Payne (D)	241,522	(83%)	$447,890	$873	
	Jennifer Zinone (R)	40,298	(14%)		$825	$113
2020 Primary	Mikie Sherrill (D)	79,961	(100%)			
	Donald Payne Jr. (D)	83,436	(89%)			
	Eugene Mazo (D)	6,653	(7%)			

Prior winning percentages: 2018 (88%), 2016 (86%), 2014 (85%), 2012 (88%), 2012 special (97%)

Donald Payne Jr., elected in 2012 to succeed his father, has been a reliable Democratic vote and has made few waves. In 2021, he became chairman of the subcommittee handling railroad issues, which are vital to his metropolitan region.

A Newark native, Payne became involved in politics as a teenager when he founded and became president of the Newark South Ward Junior Democrats. He attended Kean College (now Kean University) and studied graphic arts, but did not graduate. At 21, he began working in the tolls division of the New Jersey Highway Authority; a back injury prompted him to give up the job a few years later. In 1986, at age 27, he became a school bus monitor with the Essex County Educational Services Commission, and went on to become director of student transportation for the county. In 1992, Payne was elected by local Democrats to the party position of South Ward leader in Newark. In 2006, Payne was elected to the Newark Municipal Council and was its president from 2010 to 2012. He co-founded Embracing Arms, a nonprofit youth-advancement organization that sponsors public service projects for young people.

Following the death of his father, Rep. Donald Payne Sr., who served 23 years and died of cancer, Payne entered the Democratic primary. His family pedigree made him a heavy favorite. Not only was his father the first African-American member of Congress to represent New Jersey, but his uncle, William Payne, served in the New Jersey General Assembly for 10 years. Payne Jr. had the backing of the powerful Democratic Party machines in Essex, Hudson and Union counties.

Political opponents and journalists raised questions about his readiness for Congress. In an editorial board meeting with the Star-Ledger before the election, Payne named creating jobs as his chief priority, but declined to provide specific details. He was vague about how he would deal with several other issues. "The dispiriting truth is that his claim to the seat is based entirely on his last name," the newspaper editorialized. "He has only the vaguest grip on key federal issues. He is simply not ready for the job, and hasn't done his homework." Payne won the primary election with 60 percent of the vote, beating fellow Newark Councilman Ron Rice and state Sen. Nia Gill. He got 88 percent in the general election and appears to have become entrenched.

On the Homeland Security Committee, after having served as the ranking Democrat, he chaired for two years the Emergency Preparedness, Response and Recovery Subcommittee. He has noted that the area surrounding Exit 13A of the New Jersey Turnpike, which provides access to Elizabeth and the Newark Airport, has been described by homeland security officials as the "most dangerous two miles in America" because of its cluster of industrial and transportation infrastructure.

Payne won House passage of the bipartisan SMART Grid Study Act of 2014, which sought ways to upgrade and strengthen the nation's electric grid to protect critical infrastructure from natural disasters and cyber-attacks. The annual defense spending bill enacted in 2016 included Payne's provision that required decision-makers in disaster-response planning to gain a complete understanding of a community's vulnerabilities so homeland security grants can have appropriate priority.

Payne has a seat on the Transportation and Infrastructure Committee, an apt assignment, given the extensive air, rail, port and highway services in his district. In 2018, the House passed his bill to create a public area security working group to work with airports and other transportation facilities. The provision was enacted as part of a broader aviation bill. He called for an increase in the gasoline tax to pay for infrastructure repairs. In 2021, when he became chairman of the Railroad, Pipelines and Hazardous Materials Subcommittee, Payne referred to the global pandemic and said, "I want to make sure our nation's rail system has the resources necessary to protect commuters and staff as well as maintain facilities during and after this public health crisis."

With Republican Rep. Markwayne Mullin of Oklahoma, Payne created and co-chairs the Congressional Men's Health Caucus. He has called attention to his father's death from colo-rectal cancer and the need for cancer screenings. In December 2020, Congress included in its year-end spending bill Payne's Colorectal Screening Act, which covers screenings and polyp removal for Medicare beneficiaries.

NJ-10: Newark/Jersey City area

Cook Partisan Voting Index: D+34

Population		Race and Ethnicity		Income	
Total	761,783	White	31.10%	Median Income	$61,975
Land area (sq. miles)	76	Black	51.00%	District Income Rank	234
Pop/ sq mi	10,034.02	Latino	20.00%	Poverty Rate	14.70%
Born in State	47.60%	Asian	6.40%	With health insurance	88.90%
		Two or more races	3.90%	Cash public assistance	2.60%
Age Groups		Other	7.60%	Food stamp/SNAP	14.40%
Under 18	22.40%				
18-34	25.30%	**Education**		**Work**	
35-64	38.90%	H.S grad or less	43.70%	White Collar	36.60%
Over 64	13.40%	Some college	23.90%	Sales and Service	43.00%
		College Degree, 4 yr	21.00%	Blue Collar	20.40%
Military		Post grad	11.30%	Government	16.30%
Veteran/ Active Duty	3.20%				

2020 Pres. Vote	Biden	254,723	(84%)	Trump	45,313	(15%)
2016 Pres. Vote	Clinton	233,822	(85%)	Trump	35,111	(13%)

Essex County: Newark was once the heart of New Jersey. All the main transportation arteries led there, and its corporate headquarters buildings were the tallest in the state. In 1930, 442,000 people lived in Newark, one of every nine in New Jersey. The city fell on hard times in the latter half of the 20th century. Whole sections of the city were dominated by criminals and deserted by most law-abiding residents. By the year 2000, there were just 273,000 people left in Newark, representing one in every 30.

In recent years, Newark has been attempting a turnaround. Population was up to 282,000 in 2019. New office buildings have joined the Prudential and Public Service Enterprise Group headquarters; and the New Jersey Performing Arts Center has been popular with city-dwellers seeking a less expensive experience than Manhattan. There are new restaurants and trendy bars, plus a downtown arena. Facebook founder Mark Zuckerberg in 2010 gave $100 million to Newark public schools. But his program ran into bureaucratic problems and it fell short of expectations. Crime remained intolerably high and downtown office buildings had plenty of empty spaces. After reaching out to gang members to try to reduce crime, Mayor Ras Baraka worked with business groups on expansive plans for a new commercial center and public park downtown. In July 2020, Newark completed a two-year transition and finally regained complete control from the state of its public schools—after a quarter-century. Test scores and graduation rates have increased, with charter schools educating more than one-third of students.

All this activity led some to describe Newark as "the new Brooklyn." Intending that as a compliment, they view Newark as "the place to be," with real estate still inexpensive, busy arts and education scenes, plenty of transportation options, plus an enthusiasm. The fear, in some quarters, is the kind of gentrification that has overtaken Jersey City and Hoboken. "We do not want to wait for the market to dictate to us how to develop and move in our city," Baraka said, with a reference to the "saturation" that has hit those other locales.

The nearby infrastructure continued to expand. At Newark Liberty International Airport, a glass and aluminum facility has been greatly expanded for international carriers. Construction of a new Terminal 1 was underway, which will increase capacity by more than 50 percent and replace the airport's rail system; completion was scheduled for 2022. Port Newark-Elizabeth Marine Terminal is part of the larger Port of New York and New Jersey and the third busiest port in the nation, behind Los Angeles and Long Beach. Plans call for the port to more than double its container traffic by 2050. In 2018, one-third of the imports were from China. The New Jersey Turnpike separates Port Newark from the airport. In December 2020, state officials announced plans to spend $190 million over five years to upgrade the train station. Also underway is a $1.8 billion replacement of the Portal North bridge—a 110-year-old swing bridge, in disrepair—between the Newark station and Penn Station in Manhattan, which carries more than 450 Amtrak and commuter trains daily.

The 10th Congressional District of New Jersey is centered in Essex County, with about 60 percent of its total population, including the majority of Newark. Other parts of Essex extend to Republican suburbs. Smaller parts of the 10th take in Hudson and Union counties. The district includes the predominantly African-American city of East Orange, plus parts of Bloomfield, West Orange, Jersey City and Bayonne. Drawn to maximize the African-American vote, it is a 51 percent Black-majority district and one of the most heavily Democratic in the nation. Joe Biden took 84 percent of the vote in 2020. With a Cook PVI of D+34, the district is in the top three percent for Democrats nationwide.

Mikie Sherrill (D)

Elected 2018, 2nd term, b. Jan 19, 1972; Alexandria, VA; U.S. Naval Academy, B.S., 1994; London School of Economics and Political Science, M.A., 2003; Georgetown University, J.D., 2007; Catholic; Married (Jason Hedberg); 4 children.

Military Career: U.S. Navy 1994-2003

Professional Career: Federal Prosecutor.

DC Office: 1208 LHOB 20515, 202-225-5034, sherrill.house.gov

State Offices: Parsippany, 973-526-5668.

Committees: *Armed Services*: Intelligence & Special Operations; Tactical Air & Land Forces. *Education & Labor*: Higher Education & Workforce Investment. *Science, Space & Technology*: Environment (Chmn).

Almanac Ratings 2019-2020

	Economy	Social	Foreign	Composite
Liberal	100%	58%	80%	80%
Conservative	0%	42%	20%	20%

Key Votes of the 116th Congress

1. U.S./Mex./Can. trade deal	Y	5. Russia sanctions	Y	9. Firearms background checks Y
2. First Coronavirus response	Y	6. Troops in Syria	Y	10. Spending at the border	Y
3. HEROES Act	Y	7. Veto arms sales to Saudis	Y	11. Marijuana liberalized rules	Y
4. CASH Act	Y	8. Defense $$$, veto override	Y	12. Electoral College objections N

Election Results

Election	Name (Party)	Vote (%)	Cand. Spent	Ind. Exp. Support	Ind. Exp. Oppose
2020 General	Mikie Sherrill (D)	235,163 (53%)	$3,760,434	$152,138	$16,818
	Rosemary Becchi (R)	206,013 (47%)	$1,660,735	$21,822	

Prior winning percentages: 2018 (57%)

Freshman Democrat Mikie Sherrill switched party control of one of the most wealthy and old-line Republican districts in the nation. A first-time candidate, she brought to her campaign an impressive profile of military and civilian service, plus experience as a lawyer. She replaced veteran Republican Rep. Rodney Frelinghuysen, the then-chairman of the House Appropriations Committee, when he decided to retire in the face of shifting politics within both his district and Congress. A high-profile freshman who distinguished herself on national security issues, Sherrill was reelected with relative ease in 2020.

Sherrill was born in Alexandria Virginia and graduated from high school in nearby Reston. Following graduation from the U.S. Naval Academy, she was part of the first class of women who were eligible for combat following flight training. As a helicopter pilot, she was deployed to Italy, where her squadron supported the Sixth Fleet during the invasion of Iraq. While in the Navy, she served as a Russian policy officer.

Sherrill retired as a lieutenant commander, and got a master's from the London School of Economics and her law degree from Georgetown University. She practiced with a large law firm in New York City and spent a year in the office of the U.S. Attorney for New Jersey. She declared her candidacy in May 2017, eight months before Frelinghuysen announced his retirement after 24 years; his father earlier had served 22 years in the House. Constituent groups had criticized his limited responses to local queries, while he also voted against the tax and healthcare policies of President Donald Trump and the Republican-controlled Congress. "This whole atmosphere has worn him down," a long-time friend of Frelinghuysen told the New Jersey Daily Record. Other local sources said that he saw "the handwriting on the wall," with a tough reelection campaign.

As the early frontrunner in the Democratic primary, Sherrill gained support from House Democratic leaders and other party allies. She spent about as much as the total of the other four Democrats in that contest and won with 77 percent of the vote. Tamara Harris, a local social worker with backing from the Congressional Black Caucus, was the runner-up with 14 percent in the primary; she had criticized Sherrill's support from "corporate special interests."

Republican nominee Jay Webber initially appeared to pose a challenge to Sherrill. A state Assemblyman for a decade and former chairman of the New Jersey Republican Party, he had long been viewed as a potential successor to Frelinghuysen, though Webber's views were more conservative. The candidates clashed on an array of policy issues, including immigration, guns and Israel. Sherrill attacked Webber's support for Republican-enacted tax cuts, which had been criticized locally because they eliminated tax breaks for high-income earners.

The Newark Star-Ledger endorsed Sherrill in an editorial that described her as a "centrist" with a "sterling background," while criticizing Webber for his "bear hug of President Trump" and calling him "a strict ideologue in the state legislature."In a sign of how local and national politics had shifted from Frelinghuysen's dominance of the district, where he never faced a serious reelection challenge, Sherrill raised more than five times as much in campaign funds as did Webber. In Sherrill's 57%-42% win, she took three of the four counties, losing only more-rural Sussex.

In Congress, Sherrill kept her campaign pledge to vote against Nancy Pelosi for Speaker and was one of several freshmen with military or intelligence background to become outspoken on issues of national intelligence. On the Armed Services Committee, she has been vice-chair of the subcommittee on Tactical Air & Land Forces. In the summer of 2020, amid growing concern that Trump might use the military to hold onto his office, Sherrill and fellow Democratic Rep. Elissa Slotkin of Michigan pressed top Defense officials to assure a peaceful transition of power.

Sherrill moved cautiously in the first impeachment proceedings against Trump, refusing to yield to pressure from progressive groups in her district. But in September 2019, she signed a letter with six other members of her class with a national-security background, signaling their support to begin an investigation into whether Trump committed impeachment offenses when he pressured a foreign country to uncover dirt on his political opponent. In an interview with Politico Magazine, Sherrill said the current crisis felt existential, like a "1776 kind of fight."

Republicans vowed to make her pay at the ballot box for her vote for impeachment. But their plan was foiled by their initial inability to entice a credible candidate into the race. By the end of 2019, Sherrill banked over $2.2 million and had no legitimate opponent. In January 2020, Rosemary Becchi, a tax attorney and former Senate aide, ended her run in a neighboring district against Democratic Rep. Tom Malinowski to challenge Sherrill.

Becchi tried to link Sherrill to Pelosi and the "radical" Defund the Police movement, but she struggled to match Sherrill's financing. Becchi's spent $1.7 million, compared with Sherrill's $3.8 million, and received no help on television from Republican outside groups. With Biden defeating Trump in the district by nearly the same result, Sherrill's 53%-47% victory was much smaller than her 15-point win in 2018.As in that run, she won all the counties except Sussex.

Redistricting will determine the ease of her next reelection, though her political future is bright. Many consider her a strong contender for the Senate someday.

NJ-11: North-Central New Jersey

Cook Partisan Voting Index: EVEN

Population		Race and Ethnicity		Income	
Total	717,657	White	81.70%	Median Income	$120,847
Land area (sq. miles)	505	Black	4.60%	District Income Rank	9
Pop/ sq mi	1,421.19	Latino	11.50%	Poverty Rate	3.80%
Born in State	58.10%	Asian	10.50%	With health insurance	96.30%
		Two or more races	1.90%	Cash public assistance	0.80%
Age Groups		Other	1.20%	Food stamp/SNAP	2.10%
Under 18	21.00%				
18-34	18.50%	**Education**		**Work**	
35-64	42.10%	H.S grad or less	24.30%	White Collar	56.00%
Over 64	18.30%	Some college	18.60%	Sales and Service	32.60%
		College Degree, 4 yr	34.00%	Blue Collar	11.40%
Military		Post grad	23.10%	Government	13.50%
Veteran/ Active Duty	3.70%				

2020 Pres. Vote	Biden	237,986	(52%)	Trump	208,018	(46%)		
2016 Pres. Vote	Trump	185,696	(48%)	Clinton	182,334	(47%)	Johnson	7,911 (2%)

Morris and Essex Counties: Morris County, west of the Watchung Mountains, was one of the first inland parts of the United States to be settled. It has long been a place of comparative wealth, the home of skilled craftsmen working in the water mills and iron forges in the 19th century. But only in the late 20th century did it come into its own, as one of the most affluent parts of the United States. With its over $115,000 median household income, Morris County was the 12th wealthiest county in the nation in 2019.

The very rich have lived here for many decades, connected to Manhattan by commuter rail. But starting in the 1970s, new residents rushed out through the newly completed interstates. Prompted by court-required zoning changes, old farms and woods were cleared to make way for new subdivisions. This is not just a bedroom community. New Jersey's economic energy, entrepreneurial creativity and research expertise are found in office complexes and corporate headquarters. Large forested areas of state parkland remain, and preservation of the state's Highlands region, a 1,000-square-mile forest- and lake-filled oasis, has been a priority. The Highlands Council, tasked with protecting the area from development, fueled controversy as the state legislature overturned a development plan by a pro-business ally of lame-duck Republican Gov. Chris Christie. Local environmentalists had battled constantly with Christie. Subsequently, the conservation-minded appointee of Democratic Gov. Phil Murphy pledged to appreciate "how unique and special the Highlands region is."It provides drinking water to 6.2 million people, or more than 70 percent of the state. But two years after Murphy's swearing-in, the state Sierra Club released a report chiding the governor for "little or no follow through" on environmental initiatives to address climate crises. In March 2019, the U.S. Supreme Court declined a request from Morris County to review a state Supreme Court decision that it could not spend historic preservation funds on religious properties. The justices said the "factual details of the …program are not entirely clear."

The 11th Congressional District of New Jersey takes in about three-fourths of Morris County, including the county seat of Morristown, Randolph and Rockaway. Half the district is in Morris, one-fourth is in western Essex, and there are small parts in Passaic and Sussex. This area is family territory, with relatively few singles. It is predominantly white, though the minority population has grown to 11.5 percent Hispanic and 10.5 percent Asian. The 11th still leans Republican, with a moneyed caste. In 2016, Donald Trump won 48%-47%, a drop from the 52 percent the GOP presidential candidates took in the two previous elections. In 2020, Joe Biden won 52%-46%, a clear repudiation of Trump by upper-crust Republicans.

Bonnie Watson Coleman (D)

Elected 2014, 4th term, b. Feb 06, 1945; Camden, NJ; Rutgers University, Att.; Thomas Edison State College, B.A., 1985; Baptist; Married (William E. Coleman Jr.); 1 child; 2 stepchildren; 3 grandchildren.

Elected Office: NJ Assembly, 1998-2014, Majority Leader, 2006-2009.

Professional Career: Office of Civil Rights, NJ Dept. of Transportation, 1974-1980; NJ Dept. of Community Affairs.

DC Office: 2442 RHOB 20515, 202-225-5801, Fax: 202-225-6025, watsoncoleman.house.gov

State Offices: Ewing, 609-883-0026.

Committees: *Appropriations*: Energy & Water Development & Related Agencies; Labor, Health & Human Services, Education & Related Agencies; Transportation, HUD & Related Agencies. *Homeland Security*: Emergency Preparedness, Response & Recovery; Transportation & Maritime Security (Chmn).

Group Ratings

	ADA	ACLU	AFL-CIO	LCV	COC	HAFA	ACU	CFG	FRC
2020	**	84%	**	100%	-	0%	3%	**	-
2019	100%	C	90%	100%	47%	C	4%	12%	0%

Almanac Ratings 2019-2020

	Economy	Social	Foreign	Composite
Liberal	100%	100%	83%	95%
Conservative	0%	0%	17%	5%

Key Votes of the 116th Congress

1. U.S./Mex./Can. trade deal	N	5. Russia sanctions	Y	9. Firearms background checks Y
2. First Coronavirus response	Y	6. Troops in Syria	Y	10. Spending at the border	Y
3. HEROES Act	Y	7. Veto arms sales to Saudis	Y	11. Marijuana liberalized rules	Y
4. CASH Act	Y	8. Defense $$$, veto override	Y	12. Electoral College objections N

Election Results

Election	Name (Party)	Vote (%)		Cand. Spent	Ind. Exp. Support	Ind. Exp. Oppose
2020 General	Bonnie Watson Coleman (D)	230,883	(66%)	$814,021	$123	
	Mark Razzoli (R)	114,591	(33%)	$1,000		$113
2020 Primary	Bonnie Watson Coleman (D)	81,936	(89%)			
	Lisa McCormick (D)	9,928	(11%)			

Prior winning percentages: 2018 (69%), 2016 (63%), 2014 (61%)

Democrat Bonnie Watson Coleman, easily elected in 2014 to an open seat, was a well-regarded state legislator and has been an activist for liberal causes, She gained recognition for her legislative skills when she won a seat on the Appropriations Committee. where she tends to local concerns and broader social needs.

Watson Coleman grew up in a political family, with her father, a state assemblyman, often guiding debates at the dinner table. She graduated from Thomas Edison State College. Her public service began in 1966, when she went to work for the state public safety department's civil rights division. She later headed the civil rights office of the state's Department of Transportation before taking on senior roles at the Department of Community Affairs. In 1997, she was elected to the General Assembly, where she rose through the ranks to become majority leader. She was the first African-American woman to chair the State Democratic Committee. Watson Coleman promoted staunchly liberal positions on issues such as gun control, the minimum wage and women's health care funding, and worked to reduce recidivism among state prisoners. She took an active role in legislation on identity-theft protection and expansion of urban enterprise zones.

When Democratic Rep. Rush Holt, a leading progressive in Congress, said that he would step down, Watson Coleman announced her bid. She got a boost from the Progressive Change Campaign Committee, major unions and liberal women's groups such as EMILY's List. In the June primary, only state Sen. Linda Greenstein posed any real competition. Watson Coleman topped the field with 43 percent to 28 percent for Greenstein, who ran relatively close only in her Middlesex County base. Watson Coleman breezed in November with 61 percent against Republican Alieta Eck, a physician, who was outspent 6-to-1.

Watson Coleman initially focused her committee work on Homeland Security. In 2015, the House-passed Cybersecurity Protection Advancement Act included her amendment to encourage public awareness and education on personal cybersecurity issues. The House passed her Homeland Security Drone Assessment and Analysis Act, the goal of which was "clarifying the framework for drone manufacturers and enthusiasts alike," she said.

As the senior Democrat on the Oversight Subcommittee, Watson Coleman criticized the Transportation Security Administration for its Quiet Skies programs that tracked domestic air travelers and asked for the legal justification for collecting intelligence on U.S. citizens. In combative Republican-led hearings on the FBI's investigation during the 2016 election, she took her shots at GOP inquisitors and said that they were "out of control." In 2021, she took over as chair of the panel's Transportation and Maritime Security Subcommittee.

With Democratic Reps. Robin Kelly of Illinois and Yvette Clark of New York, Watson Coleman founded the Congressional Caucus on Black Women and Girls. Its objective was to create public policy that "eliminates significant barriers and disparities experienced by black women." Following the election of Donald Trump as president, she was outspoken in leading protest marches and political mobilization. She sought to censure him following his reaction to the violence in Charlottesville, tweeted that he was a "racist" while he was delivering his State of the Union message in 2018, and accused him of "treason" following his meeting in Helsinki with Russian President Vladimir Putin. She continued to file gun-control bills, including limits on the online sale of ammunition and federal licensing and registration for handgun ownership.

In 2019, Watson Coleman got a seat on the House Appropriations Committee, similar to the niche that she held while serving in Trenton. The spending decisions made at that committee, she said, "are a direct representation of our national values." She pursued her interest in funding regional infrastructure, including the long-discussed Gateway Project with New York City, and sought to write off federal loans for the victims of Hurricane Sandy.

Watson Coleman had a cancerous tumor removed from her lung and said in October 2018 that she was cancer-free following chemotherapy treatment. That episode, she told a Democratic meeting in New Jersey, "fortified my resolve to make sure that all Americans have access to world-class health care." Less than a week after the January 2021 riot at the Capitol, she was diagnosed with COVID-19. In an op-ed for The Washington Post, she described her reaction: "I am angry that the attack on the Capitol and my subsequent illness have the same cause: my Republican colleagues' inability to accept facts." She added, "Refusing to wear a mask is not, in fact, an act of self-expression. It's an act of public endangerment."

NJ-12: Central New Jersey

Cook Partisan Voting Index: D+16

Population		Race and Ethnicity		Income	
Total	747,082	White	52.90%	Median Income	$87,559
Land area (sq. miles)	412	Black	17.30%	District Income Rank	65
Pop/ sq mi	1,812.29	Latino	18.40%	Poverty Rate	10.90%
Born in State	45.70%	Asian	17.50%	With health insurance	92.10%
		Two or more races	2.80%	Cash public assistance	1.50%
Age Groups		Other	9.60%	Food stamp/SNAP	6.30%
Under 18	21.30%				
18-34	21.60%	**Education**		**Work**	
35-64	40.50%	H.S grad or less	33.80%	White Collar	50.10%
Over 64	16.70%	Some college	19.10%	Sales and Service	32.90%
		College Degree, 4 yr	26.00%	Blue Collar	16.90%
Military		Post grad	21.10%	Government	13.00%
Veteran/ Active Duty	4.20%				

2020 Pres. Vote	Biden	243,177	(67%)	Trump	113,677	(31%)
2016 Pres. Vote	Clinton	204,660	(65%)	Trump	100,043	(32%)

Middlesex County, Trenton: New Jersey politics is centered in Trenton. The city has been a manufacturing mecca since the 19th century, when it was the setting for the Lenox and Boehm china factories and the old Roebling ironworks, which produced parts for many of the great American bridges. It is a city "that can often feel like two urban areas rolled into one," The New York Times wrote in June 2018. One is the State House and its accompanying buildings for lobbyists and state employees. The other is the "bleak landscape" that they leave behind each day of dilapidated warehouses and a famous but no longer apt sign, "Trenton Makes, the World Takes." The lifeline for Trenton is U.S. 1, on any day crowded with cars taking high-salaried workers and clerical help to one of the East Coast's thickest concentrations of office buildings. The highway also is now a locus of telecommunications and pharmaceutical research, and a vital artery to the brain centers of Princeton and Rutgers.

The 12th Congressional District includes Trenton, which is 50 percent African American and 38 percent Hispanic. It stretches east to East Brunswick, with a significant Asian population, and South River, a city that has attracted Polish, Russian and Portuguese immigrants. In February 2018, East Brunswick announced a plan to create a "city-like vibe" and to redevelop its downtown area, which was filled with vacant buildings and empty strip malls; they will be replaced by "mixed-used transit oriented development," including a bus terminal with service to Manhattan. In Trenton, the weak economy has forced continuing cutbacks in operations. In 2018, Gov. Phil Murphy signed an executive order intended to revitalize Trenton, in which the state committed to identifying funds and resources to implement local initiatives. Two years later, the state sued the city for its failure to upgrade its water system.

Princeton University, which provides $1.6 billion in economic output for New Jersey and supports more than 13,450 jobs, said it would spend $1 billion on campus facilities from 2017 to 2022. The most significant recent development from Old Nassau was its announcement in June 2020 that Woodrow Wilson's name and legacy would be stripped from campus buildings and institutions— given his "racist thinking and policies" as university president, and later as governor and president of the United States. Princeton trustees said, "The question has been made more urgent" by recent urban killings across the nation that have been "tragic reminders of the ongoing need for all of us to stand against racism and for equality and justice."

In the north, the district takes in Plainfield, Scotch Plains and modest-income suburbs such as Franklin. Much of the district's population is in Middlesex County and the more heavily Democratic and Princeton-based Mercer County. Somerset and Union counties have small slices of the district. As recently as two decades ago, with different boundaries, this was a highly competitive district that House Republicans frequently won. Now, its population features a growing 17 percent each for African Americans, Hispanics and Asians. The district has become safe for Democrats. Joe Biden got 67 percent of the vote in 2020, similar to the Democratic vote in the previous two elections.

NEW MEXICO

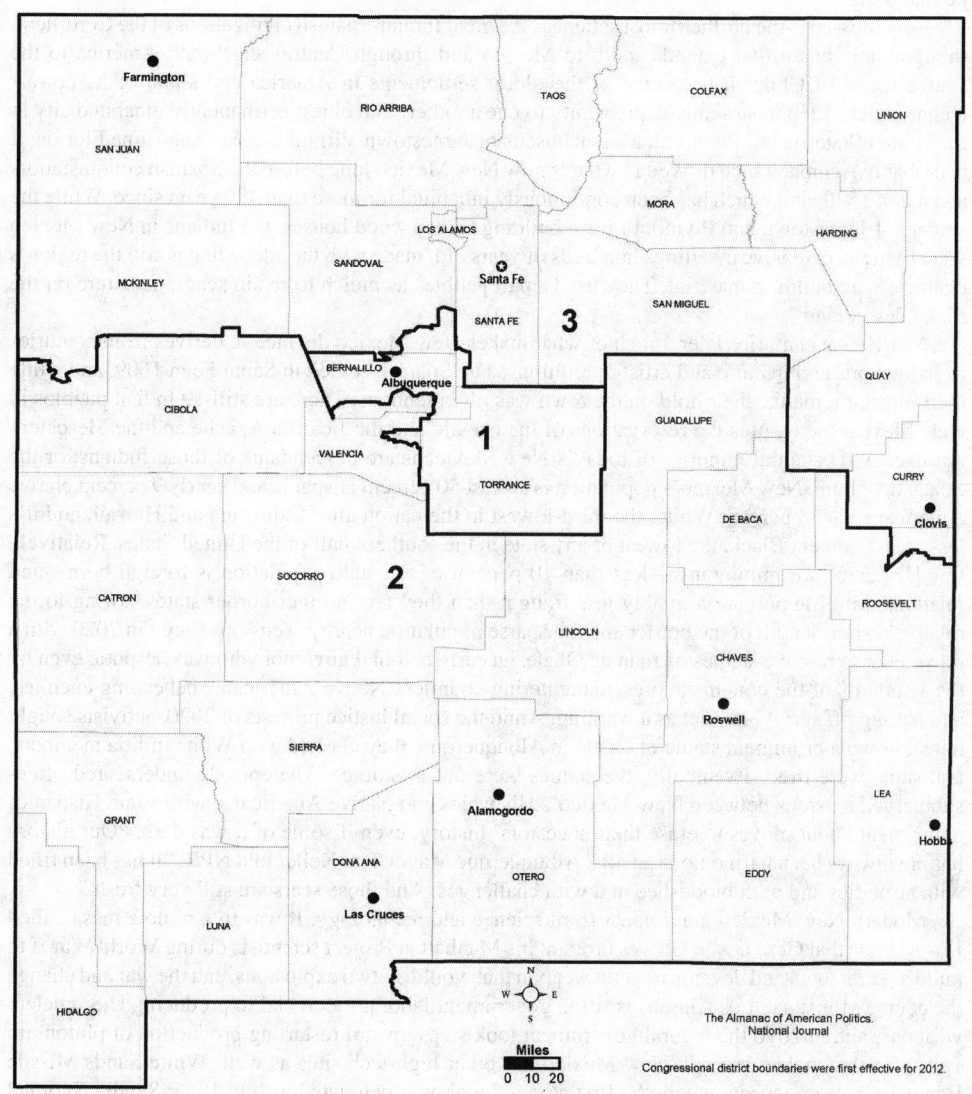

The Almanac of American Politics.
National Journal

Miles
0 10 20

Congressional district boundaries were first effective for 2012.

New Mexico has a higher percentage of Latino residents than any other state, and that has shaped its political transition in recent decades. Republican presidential candidates won the state in every election from 1968 to 1988, but Democrats have won it every four years since, except for 2004. While the state was decided by 366 votes in 2000 and fewer than 6,000 votes in 2004, it has barely been a battleground in ensuing elections. In 2018, non-white candidates, all Democrats, won all three of the state's House seats, the first time that happened in any state with at least a three-member delegation. In the 2020 presidential election, Joe Biden increased the Democrats' winning margin from eight points to 11.

New Mexico is the northernmost salient of the great Indian-Spanish civilizations of the Cordillera, the mountain chain that extends south to Mexico and through Central and South America to the southern end of Chile. It has some of the oldest settlements in America and some of its newest technologies, often in surrealistic proximity to one another. The oldest permanently inhabited city in the United States is not Plymouth Massachusetts or Jamestown Virginia, or St. Augustine Florida; it is probably Acoma, which thrived in what is now New Mexico long before the Spanish conquistadors arrived in 1540, and which has been continuously inhabited for more than 480 years since. While the settlers of Jamestown and Plymouth were building flimsy wood houses, the Indians in New Mexico were living in extensive dwellings hundreds of years old, made with the adobe that is still the region's characteristic building material. They used small pebbles as mulch to retain scarce moisture on the rocky desert land.

Nearly five centuries later, much of what makes New Mexico distinctive derives from centuries of indigenous architecture and artistic traditions. The Spanish settled in Santa Fe in 1609, and while their imprint remains, their hold on the town was often tenuous. There are still 19 Indian pueblos in New Mexico today, plus the reservations of the Navajo and the Jicarilla Apache and the Mescalero Apache. A substantial minority of today's New Mexicans are descendants of those Indians, or the Spanish, or both. New Mexico's population is almost 50 percent Hispanic and nearly 9 percent Native American. It's 38 percent White, the third-lowest in the nation after California and Hawaii, and it's less than 2 percent Black, the lowest of any state in the southern half of the United States. Relatively few Hispanics are immigrants—less than 10 percent of the state population is foreign born—and relations with Mexico are arguably less fraught than they are in other border states, owing to the relatively short length of the border and the sparse population nearby. Tensions flared in 2020 with a movement to remove statues of Juan de Oñate, an early colonial governor who was despotic even by the standards of the conquistadores, slaughtering countless Native Americans, beheading enemies, and cutting off survivors' feet as a warning. Amid the social justice protests of 2020, activists sought to tear down a prominent statue of Oñate in Albuquerque; they clashed with White militia members, and shots were fired. Eventually, the statues were put in storage. The episode underscored often-submerged tensions between New Mexico's Hispanics and Native Americans, with some Hispanics ambivalent about moves to erase their ancestors' history, even if some of it was dark. "Our history has not always been harmonious, at all," Albuquerque Mayor Tim Keller told NPR. "It has been filled with atrocities and with bloodshed and with challenges. And those scars are still very fresh."

Modern New Mexico got a boost from science and technology. It was to a remote mesa called Los Alamos that Gen. Leslie Groves brought his Manhattan Project scientists during World War II to build a secret town and develop a secret weapon that would, in two explosions, end the war and change the course of history. Los Alamos is still a government laboratory crucial to producing U.S. nuclear weapons, and in 2016 the federal government took steps toward restarting production of plutonium "pits" for the nuclear arsenal. New Mexico has other high-tech sites as well: White Sands Missile Range near Alamogordo, where the first atomic bomb was detonated in July 1945; Sandia National Laboratories near Albuquerque, a non-nuclear weapons research facility with one of the fastest computers in the world, used to simulate nuclear explosions; and the Very Large Array National Radio Astronomy Observatory on the Plains of San Agustin, 50 miles west of Socorro. Facebook is constructing a data facility south of Albuquerque that will be powered exclusively by solar power, while Xcel Energy has completed a huge wind-farm complex along the border with Texas. Meanwhile, at the western edge of White Sands in Sierra County is Spaceport America, an 18,000-acre facility with more than $215 million in state and local tax dollars to support space tourism (an investment that has periodically fueled allegations of financial mismanagement). Billionaire Richard

Branson predicted that his Virgin Galactic would be ferrying passengers on space tours by 2014 for up to $250,000 a ticket, but those hopes were dashed in October 2014, when Virgin Galactic's SpaceShipTwo rocket plane broke up on a test flight and crashed. In 2019, after successfully testing a retooled version of the vehicle, Virgin Galactic doubled down on the desert site, moving 100 employees from California in preparation of accelerating efforts.

New and old New Mexico intermingle in varying proportions in this land of majestic vistas. Historic Acoma shares its nickname, "Sky City," with a nearby casino. North and west of Albuquerque are picturesque old towns and active pueblos, low-income Indian reservations, and lavish gambling resorts. A prized variety of chile peppers is cultivated in the Hatch Valley just as it was centuries ago. In the middle of the state is Albuquerque, which grew from a small desert community of 35,000 in 1940 into a Sun Belt metropolitan area of almost 918,000 today. The city's economy is based on technology and, as with many places in New Mexico, government. The high-tech New Mexico, however, coexists with hardship, a dichotomy expertly mined by the acclaimed TV series Breaking Bad and Better Call Saul, which were set in the office parks, strip malls and neighborhoods of Albuquerque.

New Mexico's median income ranks sixth from the bottom in the U.S., a full 21 percent lower than the national average, and its 17.5 percent poverty rate ranked the third-highest of any state, behind only Mississippi and Louisiana. The child poverty rate was 30 percent for Hispanics and 41 percent for Native Americans. Homelessness and crime have been stubborn problems in Albuquerque, with the city setting a homicide record in 2019. By one measure, New Mexico had a higher suicide rate in 2018 than any other state. One bright spot—before the corona virus pandemic, at least—has been tourism. In 2019, White Sands National Monument—the world's largest gypsum dune field and home to specially evolved white lizards, crickets, and spiders— officially became a national park, a change that is expected to increase the number of visitors. Another successful sector, also before the pandemic, has been the arts, especially in Santa Fe and Taos. Over the years, the state's stunning scenery and unique culture have attracted writers such as D.H. Lawrence and painters such as Georgia O'Keeffe. More recently, Netflix has produced increasing amounts of television content in the state, including Longmire, in which the state stands in for Wyoming. NBCUniversal is planning a major television and film studio in Albuquerque.

But in recent years, the biggest economic driver in New Mexico has been the petroleum industry, centered in the Permian Basin in the south eastern part of the state. There, two subterranean structures, the Wolf camp Shale and the Bone Spring Formation, contain the biggest oil and gas reserves the U.S. Geological Survey has ever confirmed; the state is now the nation's third-largest oil producer. Carlsbad, a major hub of the basin, saw its population grow by 14 percent over the decade, overrun by "man camps" and other quickly constructed housing. A flood of truck traffic turned U.S. 285, a two-lane road, into the "Death Highway," and methane emissions, a by product of oil extraction, soared. But the oil boom provided a gusher for state finances—at one point enabling a $1.2 billion budget surplus, allocated in part to early childhood education and higher teacher salaries. But the bust arrived with the pandemic in 2020, as automobile and airplane traffic around the world plummeted, reducing the demand for oil. In the meantime, the state is looking ahead to a post-fossil fuel future. In 2019, the Democratic legislature and Democratic Gov. Michelle Lujan Grisham enacted legislation to require that publicly regulated utilities use only carbon-free energy by 2045, becoming only the third state to mandate a 100 percent phase-out. Cleverly, the legislation might not have much of an impact on the in-state oil industry, since most of that production is exported.

New Mexico's population is up 2.8 percent since 2010, but there has been a divergence between major metro areas and rural regions. The four biggest counties— Bernalillo (Albuquerque), Doña Ana (Las Cruces), Santa Fe (Santa Fe), and Sandoval (the northern suburbs of Albuquerque, including Rio Rancho)—collectively grew almost 4 percent between 2010 and 2019, while the rest of the state was down 1 percent. The residents who are moving away pose a challenge for economic growth. "We are losing young people, and we are losing people who are educated," Jeff Mitchell, an economist with the Bureau of Business and Economic Research, told the Las Cruces Sun News. Another worry is water: Snow packs are down, leaving the state as water-starved as the United Arab Emirates, according to an analysis by the World Resources Institute. Elephant Butte reservoir, the state's largest, hit its lowest level since the early 1970s.Further complicating the issue is the oil and gas industry's heavy reliance on water, and the potential risk of contamination.

For many years, New Mexico politics was a somnolent business. Local bosses— first Republican, later Democratic—controlled the large Hispanic vote. Elections in many counties featured irregularities that would have made a Chicago ward committeeman blush. Politics was a family business in New Mexico that could rival the House of Windsor, most strikingly the extended Luján family, which includes the current governor. Today, as with most states, New Mexico is polarized between a Republican Party and its predominantly White, rural base centered on the oil patch, and a Democratic Party bolstered by urban, suburban, and minority voters. It came as little surprise that Valencia County ended its 68-year streak of voting for the winning presidential candidate in 2020 by backing President Donald Trump. In the county, just 18.5 percent of residents have a college degree, a crucial demographic predictor of voting behaviour these days; that compares to 27.3 percent state wide and 32.1 percent nationally. The Trump campaign spoke periodically of targeting New Mexico in 2020, but that was always a long shot. Biden ended up winning the state by double digits, as the third-party vote, which had ballooned in 2016 due to former New Mexico Gov. Gary Johnson's run on the Libertarian ballot line, shrank from 11 percent to 2 percent. Biden improved the Democrats' winning margins by the low- to mid-single digits in San Juan County (Farmington) as well as Bernalillo, Sandoval, and Santa Fe counties. However, in an echo of Democratic underperformances among Latinos elsewhere, the most heavily Hispanic of the state's five biggest counties, Doña Ana, did not see similar Democratic gains. Republicans can compete in New Mexico with the right candidate; Lujan Grisham succeeded Susana Martinez, a Republican who served two terms as governor, and in 2020, the GOP won back a House seat that represents the oil patch. But the solid Democratic majorities in both chambers of the legislature have enabled Lujan Grisham to govern with a progressive tilt. Democrats, it seems, should be able to maintain the upper hand in New Mexico for the near future.

Population		Race and Ethnicity		Income	
Total	2,096,829	White	73.90%	Median Income	51,945
Land area (sq. miles)	121,298	Black	2.30%	State Income Rank	45 out of 50
Pop/ sq mi	17.29	Latino	49.30%	Poverty Rate	18.20%
Born in state	53.80%	Asian	2.50%	With health insurance	90.00%
		Two or more races	3.50%	Cash public assistance	3.60%
Age Groups		Other	18.50%	Food stamp/SNAP	17.0%
Under 18	22.60%				
18-34	22.70%	Education		Work	
35-64	36.70%	H.S grad or less	40.50%	White Collar	37.60%
Over 64	18.00%	Some college	31.80%	Sales and Service	41.00%
		College Degree, 4 yr	15.50%	Blue Collar	21.30%
Military		Post grad	12.20%	Government	22.50%
Veteran/ Active Duty	9.10%				

Presidential Politics

2020 Primary (D)	Biden (D)	181,700(73%)	Sanders (D)	37,435(15%)	Warren (D)	14,552	(6%)
2020 Pres. Vote	Biden (D)	501,614(54%)	Trump (R)	401,894(44%)			
2016 Pres. Vote	Clinton (D)	385,234(48%)	Trump (R)	319,667(40%)	Johnson (L)	74,541	(9%)

New Mexico was a battleground state in the first two presidential elections in this century but subsequently fell off the list. In 2000, after some ragged vote-counting, the state gave a 366-vote margin to Vice President Al Gore. In 2004, it reported a 5,988-vote margin for President George W. Bush. The 2008 contest was another story, with Sen. Barack Obama deploying a superior campaign organization in the state and beating Sen. John McCain 57%-42%. In 2012, former Republican Gov. Gary Johnson ran as a Libertarian and won 4 percent in his home state, while Obama posted a 53%-43% victory over Mitt Romney. Johnson more than doubled his Libertarian vote to 9 percent when he ran again in 2016, and Hillary Clinton defeated Donald Trump, 48%-40%. In 2020, Trump's team publicly floated competing in the state, but never invested; Biden won, 54%-44%. He handily won the four largest vote-producing counties in the state: Bernalillo (Albuquerque), Santa Fe, Doña Ana (Las Cruces, home to New Mexico State University), and Sandoval (suburban and exurban Albuquerque), which contains several Native American reservations. Trump carried the eastern part of the state, including conservative, oil-producing "Little Texas." Like the rest of the country, Biden did better than previous Democrats in the state's more suburban-heavy areas, while Trump increased his margins in New Mexico's more rural areas.

New Mexico has long held its presidential primary in June. For 2008, the race between Barack Obama and Hillary Clinton was close, and it took nine days to count all the votes, including 17,000 provisional ballots. Clinton won 49%-48%. In 2016, Clinton pulled out another close race, beating Sen. Bernie Sanders 52%-48%. The recent Republican primaries have come after the nomination has been resolved and they have been largely ignored; the same was true in 2020 for the Democratic primary, where Biden took 73 percent of the vote long after he secured the nomination.

Congressional Districts

117th Congress Lineup	2D 1R	116th Congress Lineup	3D

New Mexico's three congressional districts have remained substantially the same since the state gained a third seat in 1982: the heavily Hispanic and Democratic 3rd district in Santa Fe and the north, the more rural and Republican 2nd district in the south, and the competitive Albuquerque 1st in the middle. Both parties have held all three seats at various points. As the 1st District moved away from Republicans, the prevailing balance shifted from a 2-to-1 Republican edge to a 2-to-1 Democratic advantage. But those dynamics have been changing again.

For the next redistricting, Democrats have a strong hand. After winning two open House seats in 2018, including the 2nd for the first time in a decade, they controlled the entire delegation. Plus, they added the governor's office to their majorities in the legislature. But in 2020, Republican Yvette Herrell reclaimed the 2nd by seven percentage points and President Donald Trump won it by 12 points. Democrats likely will seek to increase the Democratic vote share in the 2nd, though they likely would raise objections from Albuquerque leaders if they force extensive changes in the relatively compact 1st in the current map. And Republican strength in the 2nd might be too large for Democrats to make it better than competitive, while they potentially cause problems—and potential gerrymandering—for themselves in one, or both, of the other two districts. National Democrats likely will urge their New Mexico colleagues to make the effort.

Michelle Lujan Grisham (D)

Elected 2018, term expires 2023, 1st term; b. Oct 24, 1959, Los Alamos; University of New Mexico; b.E., 1981; University of New Mexico, J.D., 1987; Roman Catholic; Widow; 2 children.

Elected Office: Secretary, NM Department of Health, 2004-2007; Commissioner, Bernalillo County, 2010-2012; US House, 2013-2018.

Professional Career: Director, NM State Agency on Aging, 1991-2002; Secretary, NM Aging & Long-Term Services Department, 2002-2004; Co-owner, Delta Consulting Group, 2008-present.

Office: 490 Old Sante Fe Trail Room 400, Santa Fe, 87501; 505-476-2200; Fax: 505-476-2226

Lt. Gov.: Howie Morales (D) **Atty. Gen:** Hector Balderas (D) **Sec. of State:** Maggie Toulouse Oliver (D)

State Legislature: Senate: 25D, 16R, 1V **House:** 46D, 24R

Election Results

Election	Name (Party)	Vote (%)
2018 General	Michelle Lujan Grisham (D)	398,368 (57%)
	Steve Pearce (R)	298,091 (43%)
2018 Primary	Michelle Lujan Grisham (D)	116,754 (66%)
	Jeff Apodaca (D)	38,975 (22%)
	Joseph Cervantes (D)	20,169 (12%)

Prior winning percentage: House: 2016 (65%), 2014 (59%), 2012 (59%)

Michelle Lujan Grisham, a member of a family dynasty in her state, took back New Mexico's governorship for the Democrats in 2018, following three terms in the House. Her grandfather, Eugene Lujan, was the state Supreme Court's first Latino chief justice; her uncle, Manuel Lujan Jr., was a GOP congressman and Interior secretary who died in 2019; her apparently distant cousin, Rep. Ben Ray Luján, was elected senator in 2020 after serving in the House. After succeeding another Latina governor, Republican Susana Martinez, in the heavily Hispanic state, Lujan Grisham joined with the Democratic legislature to pursue a progressive agenda.

The daughter of a dentist, Lujan Grisham was born in Los Alamos and attended high school in Santa Fe. Her sister Kimberly was diagnosed with a brain tumor at 2 and died at 21; affordable health care would become a major policy focus in Lujan Grisham's political career. After earning bachelor's and law degrees from the University of New Mexico, she was named director of the State Bar of New Mexico's Lawyer Referral for the Elderly Program, which provides basic legal services to seniors. In 1991, then-Gov. Bruce King appointed Lujan Grisham director of the New Mexico State Agency on Aging. In 1997, she went undercover as a stroke victim in an Albuquerque nursing home; she said her two-day stay was the "longest weekend in her life." Lujan Grisham remained in the post for 13 years, serving under a Republican governor as well as two Democrats, a point she later emphasized as evidence of her bipartisan efforts. Ex-Gov. Gary Johnson, one of her former Republican bosses, told the Albuquerque Journal that Lujan Grisham was "a great communicator" who "really cared. I thought she was the genuine article." She stands 4-foot-11 and sometimes drinks 30 or more cups of coffee per day, according to the Santa Fe New Mexican.

In 2004, Lujan Grisham's college sweetheart and husband of 22 years, Gregory Alan Grisham, collapsed while jogging and died the next day from a ruptured cerebral aneurysm. Three years later, Lujan Grisham filed a wrongful death lawsuit, seeking damages from an Albuquerque physician who had misdiagnosed him with migraines, but the suit was dismissed. After her husband's death, Lujan Grisham was named secretary of the New Mexico Department of Health, which had 3,800 employees and a $440 million budget. In 2007, the Justice Department filed a lawsuit against New Mexico in response to substandard conditions and practices at the state-run Fort Bayard Medical Center. A settlement was reached in four days. Lujan Grisham resigned a month later, telling the Journal that overseeing the Department of Health was the "hardest job on the planet."

In 2008, Lujan Grisham made an unsuccessful run for New Mexico's 1st District seat, placing third in the Democratic primary. Two years later, she won a race for commissioner of Bernalillo County (Albuquerque). When Rep. Martin Heinrich ran for the Senate in 2012, Lujan Grisham started as a long shot candidate to succeed him in the House. She said her real-life hardships gave her insight into voters' problems. "As a widow and a caregiver and a single mother, I'm living the experience that New Mexicans are," she told the Journal. Her primary opponents, state Sen. Eric Griego and former Albuquerque Mayor Marty Chavez, attacked each other and did not take her seriously until it was too late. Lujan Grisham won the primary with 40 percent, defeating Griego with 35 percent and Chavez with 25 percent. In the general election, she easily defeated former state Rep. Janice Arnold-Jones, 59%-41%, and later won reelection easily.

Lujan Grisham served as ranking Democrat on the Agriculture Subcommittee on Conservation and Forestry, an important post for New Mexico, which has more than 9 million acres of Forest Service land. Following the 2016 election, Lujan Grisham took on new partisan dimensions. She chaired the Congressional Hispanic Caucus, which has been open only to Democrats and which took a leading role opposing Trump policies. In December 2016, Lujan Grisham announced her candidacy to succeed Martinez, who had become the first Hispanic woman governor of any state when she was elected in 2010. While Martinez was a rising GOP star who easily won reelection in 2014, her pragmatic instincts left her out of step in a GOP with Trumpian impulses.

Lujan Grisham faced a competitive, and messy, Democratic primary against state Sen. Joseph Cervantes and Jeff Apodaca, a media executive and the son of former Gov. Jerry Apodaca. Her opponents raised questions about Lujan Grisham's past connections to a health care firm that had a state contract to run a high-risk insurance pool. But with the help of a large war chest, she won two-thirds of the votes in the state party convention and then prevailed in the primary with a similar percentage, easily outpacing Apodaca with 22 percent and Cervantes with 12 percent. On the Republican side, Rep. Steve Pearce won the nomination unopposed, enabling him to start the general election campaign with a big edge in campaign funding. Pearce, a former Air Force and commercial pilot and businessman, had initially been elected to the House in 2002, ran unsuccessfully for Senate in 2008, then won back his old seat in 2010. As a House member, Pearce moved further rightward, often aligning with Republicans critical of the party's house leadership. Policy-wise, the race between Lujan Grisham and Pearce offered a fairly conventional liberal-vs.-conservative faceoff. Pearce attacked his opponent's business ties that had come up in the primary, saying that a Lujan Grisham victory would bring New Mexico back to the "cronyism" days of former Democratic Gov. Bill Richardson. Pearce, though, faced questions of his own about his business interests, including how his firms involved in leasing oilfield equipment could shape his views on energy policy. It didn't matter in the end: Lujan Grisham won, 57%-43%. She even exceeded the number of votes won by Hillary Clinton in the presidential year of 2016.

Once in office, Lujan Grisham removed most of the National Guard members assigned to the state's border with Mexico, a clear rebuke to President Donald Trump and his push to build a wall. Lujan Grisham took steps on the environment and gun policy. She signed a bill to require all electricity to be carbon-free by 2045, and an expansion of background checks for gun sales and a "red flag" bill to take guns from people threatening domestic violence. The red flag bill was expanded the following year, despite the opposition of most sheriffs in the state. Lujan repaid her allies in organized labor by signing legislation to bar counties from passing right-to-work labor laws and an education overhaul that ended Martinez-era policies such as grading school performance and the practices for teacher evaluations. Despite her clean-energy legislation, Lujan Grisham was eager to spend the gusher of oil revenues from the state's Permian Basin on raises for teachers, though her proposal to eliminate tuition at state colleges and universities died in 2019 before being passed in a significantly scaled-down version in 2020.

Lujan Grisham signed a constellation of criminal justice bills, including measures to help ex-convicts secure jobs and treatment, and she signed significantly more pardons and commutations than her predecessor had. She approved same-day voter registration and signed New Mexico up for an interstate compact that would sidestep the Electoral College once enough states had joined. She approved a phased-in $12 minimum wage and signed limits on public smoking of e-cigarettes. A bill to legalize recreational marijuana failed, though a more limited decriminalization bill was enacted. Lujan Grisham also approved replacing Columbus Day with Indigenous People's Day, signed an executive order giving state employees paid parental leave, and signed a bill creating a new early childhood education agency. However, she was unable to enact medically assisted suicide and failed to eliminate long-mooted language in the state code that would ban abortion. During the national protests for racial justice in the summer of 2020, Lujan Grisham signed legislation to require most state and local police officers to wear body cameras.

Lujan Grisham generally won plaudits for her efforts to combat the coronavirus, although the state's numbers were no better than middling and deaths outpaced national averages. She declared a health emergency early in the pandemic and worked with tribal officials to limit travel to Navajo areas that had been especially hard hit. She also ordered fines for residents who ignored mask requirements. "I made quick and very broad, decisive actions, telling people to stay at home, closing schools, and narrowing essential businesses," she told Rolling Stone. "We quarantined people coming across borders for 14 days. We were working on taking the temperatures of truckers coming in and out of the state and doing questionnaires about whether they were symptomatic. We really were aggressive on the front end, and I believe, unequivocally, it has paid off in where the state is today." The numbers, however, were more mixed. By February 2021, New Mexico ranked in the bottom half of states for cases per capita, but in the top third for mortality rate.

As a woman and a Hispanic, Lujan Grisham was considered a possible ticket-mate for Joe Biden, and she secured a speaking slot at the Democratic National Convention. When she didn't get the VP nod, she was talked up for a Cabinet job, especially as secretary of Health and Human Services, a position that fit with her policy expertise. Lujan Grisham didn't end up with the HHS job either; she reportedly resisted feelers for Interior secretary, a slot that ultimately went to a fellow New Mexico Democrat, Rep. Deb Haaland. Moving to Washington would have taken Lujan Grisham away from her ailing mother, Sonja Lujan, for whom she is a caretaker.

In 2021, Lujan Grisham signed a measure to bar qualified immunity in lawsuits filed against law enforcement officers. She also signed a bill to require businesses to give their workers paid sick leave. Meanwhile, she reached a reported $62,500 settlement with a former campaign aide who had accused her of sexual harassment. In advance of the 2022 election, Republicans are expected to go after her for allegedly spending lavishly from her discretionary fund on food and beverages. Still, the Republican field is unsettled, and Lujan Grisham starts as a favorite for reelection.

Martin Heinrich (D)

Elected 2012, term expires 2024, 2nd term, b. Oct 17, 1971; Fallon, NV; University of Missouri, B.S., 1995; University of New Mexico; Lutheran; Married (Julie Heinrich); 2 children.

Elected Office: Albuquerque City Council, 2003-2007, President 2005-2006; U.S. House, 2009-2013.

Professional Career: Executive Director, Cottonwood Gulch Foundation, 1997-2002; Principal, public affairs firm, 2002-2005; NM Natural Resources Trustee, 2006-2008.

DC Office: 303 HSOB 20510, 202-224-5521, Fax: 202-228-2841, heinrich.senate.gov

State Offices: Albuquerque, 505-346-6601; Farmington, 505-325-5030; Las Cruces, 575-523-6561; Roswell, 575-622-7113; Santa Fe, 505-988-6647.

Committees: *Appropriations*: Agriculture, Rural Development, FDA & Related Agencies; Department of the Interior, Environment & Related Agencies; Energy & Water Development; Legislative Branch; Military Construction & Veteran Affairs & Related Agencies (Chmn). *Energy & Natural Resources*: Energy; National Parks; Public Lands, Forests & Mining. *Intelligence. Joint Economic.*

Group Ratings

	ADA	ACLU	AFL-CIO	LCV	COC	HAFA	ACU	CFG	FRC
2020	-	92%	-	85%	-	0%	6%	-	-
2019	95%	C	100%	93%	65%	C	6%	0%	0%

Almanac Ratings 2019-2020

	Economy	Social	Foreign	Composite
Liberal	94%	94%	82%	90%
Conservative	6%	6%	18%	10%

Key Votes of the 116th Congress

1. EPA clean energy rules	Y	5. Russia sanctions	Y	9. Barr as Atty. General	N
2. U.S./Mex./Can. trade deal	Y	6. Troops in SYR, AFG	N	10. Spending at the border	Y
3. Cut unemployment benefits	N	7. Veto arms sales to Saudis	Y	11. Coney Barrett to Sup. Ct.	N
4. Shelton to Fed Reserve	N	8. Defense $$$, veto override	Y	12. Electoral College objections	N

Election Results

Election	Name (Party)	Vote (%)		Cand. Spent	Ind. Exp. Support	Ind. Exp. Oppose
2018 General	Martin Heinrich (D)	376,998	(54%)	$6,304,882	$7,431	
	Mick Rich (R)	212,813	(31%)	$995,732		
	Gary Johnson (Lib)	107,201	(15%)	$388,636	$1,012,259	
2018 Primary	Martin Heinrich (D)	152,145	(100%)			

Prior winning percentages: 2018 (54%), 2012 (51%); House: 2010 (52%), 2008 (56%)

Democrat Martin Heinrich, New Mexico's senior senator, has cut a somewhat centrist profile during his more than a decade in Congress, first in the House and then the Senate. It's a model built by the man he succeeded, long time Democratic Sen. Jeff Bingaman, while the Land of Enchantment went from red to purple to blue. As one of the few engineers in Congress, he has frequently focused on issues relating to energy, the environment and technology—areas of interest to New Mexico, home to several large federal government laboratories. And he was a loud voice against President Donald Trump's push to build a wall along the U.S.-Mexico border, nearly 180 miles of which are in New Mexico. "The irony of the wall is it works best the further you are from the border," Heinrich told The New York Times.

Heinrich was born in Fallon Nevada, son of a utility company lineman and a factory worker. He grew up not far from Columbia Missouri, where he attended the University of Missouri and earned a degree in mechanical engineering—while building and racing solar-powered cars. Heinrich took a job doing mechanical drawings at an Albuquerque laboratory. However, he soon went to work for AmeriCorps, President Bill Clinton's public service initiative for recent college graduates. He was later executive director of the Cottonwood Gulch Foundation, which runs adventure programs in the Southwest, and started a political consulting business. Heinrich enjoyed a swift political ascent, beginning with election to the Albuquerque City Council in 2003, when he was 32. His signature issue was increasing New Mexico's minimum wage. In 2006, as council president, he worked with city business leaders and community activists to produce a gradual increase.

Encouraged by then-Democratic Gov. Bill Richardson, Heinrich announced he would challenge six-term GOP Rep. Heather Wilson for the 1st District seat in 2008. National Democrats backed Heinrich's candidacy, and he won 44 percent of the primary vote to defeat three other hopefuls —including Michelle Lujan Grisham, who would later succeed him in the House and is now New Mexico's governor. After Wilson decided to run for the Senate—she lost in the primary— Republicans fielded a strong replacement in Bernalillo County Sheriff Darren White. Heinrich tied White to the unpopular incumbent president by reminding voters that White had served as George W. Bush's county reelection chairman in 2004. Thanks in part to that year's national Democratic wave, Heinrich easily won, 56%-44%. In 2010, he withstood a Republican wave to win reelection by 4 percentage points.

While supporting many of President Barack Obama's major initiatives, including the 2010 Affordable Care Act, Heinrich sought to avoid being a down-the-line Democrat during his House tenure. He endorsed spending cuts in some appropriations bills and, like many Western lawmakers, backed gun owners' rights. The National Rifle Association endorsed Heinrich for reelection in 2010 —citing his vote for an amendment to allow guns in national parks. During the Affordable Care Act debate, Heinrich won inclusion of long-sought measure to improve Native Americans' health care, and he later counted this among his major achievements in the House. "That was something that had been out there for 12-14 years in Congress," he told the Albuquerque Journal. "The negotiations to get that passed … was a real coup for New Mexico." Eleven percent of New Mexico's population identify as American Indian.

As a member of the Natural Resources Committee, Heinrich introduced a bill in 2009 aimed at creating clean-energy jobs by providing a dedicated funding stream for the Bureau of Land Management to process a backlog of clean-energy project applications. Although he initially refrained from signing on to the " Green New Deal"—a nonbinding resolution pushed by the progressives that calls for achieving "net zero greenhouse gas emissions"—Heinrich advocated working toward total reliance on renewable energy. "We can have a future reliable, cheap, resilient grid that is 100 percent powered by clean energy," he told Green tech Media. "I think in my lifetime that is completely doable." But in 2019, he reversed course, telling the Albuquerque Journal that public lands in and beyond New Mexico were changing in the face of a warming planet. "I've spent decades working to build a renewable energy economy. But the progress that we've made simply hasn't kept pace with the speed and the scale of the warming that threatens our very existence." In 2020, amid the corona virus pandemic, Heinrich introduced a bill to provide $1 billion in funding for better ventilation and air quality monitoring in schools. He also helped lead a push in the Senate to make clean energy a focus of COVID-19 recovery bills.

New Mexico's Democratic establishment was eager for Heinrich to run for the Senate as soon as Bingaman announced his retirement. He faced Wilson in the general election. In taking on Heinrich, the former congresswoman stressed her independence, running a biographical ad that played up her military record without mentioning she was a Republican. She got financial help from outside conservative groups. Heinrich benefited from the Obama reelection campaign's heavy presence in the state and won 51%-45%; Wilson went on to serve as Air Force secretary under President Donald Trump.

One of the bigger splashes of Heinrich's first term came when he was cast alongside his then-colleague Republican Jeff Flake of Arizona in a Discovery Channel reality show: "Rival Survival." The duo, who had collaborated a couple times, spent six days with minimal supplies on the isolated island of Eru in the Marshall Islands. "We wanted to show that Republicans and Democrats can get along and survive together," Flake, who retired in 2019, told The Washington Post.

On the Senate Intelligence Committee, Heinrich rebuked federal surveillance of ordinary Americans. After the National Security Agency's bulk collection of phone records was revealed in 2013, he charged that it was "a major invasion of Americans' privacy and has done little if anything to further the fight against terrorism." The program was curtailed in the 2015 Patriot Act reauthorization. Later, when the committee investigated possible assistance by Russia to Trump's 2016 presidential campaign, Heinrich gained attention for his pointed questioning of a tight-lipped Attorney General Jeff Sessions. As Sessions repeatedly said it would be "inappropriate" to answer questions about conversations with the president, Heinrich later told CNN: "He seemed to invent a brand-new legal standard of 'appropriateness.' This is not a backyard barbecue. You either answer the question under oath or you invoke executive privilege." Via Twitter, a Princeton University professor dubbed the performance "the Heinrich maneuver."

Vote ratings have put Heinrich in the center of the Senate Democratic Caucus. A one-time NRA member, his views have evolved in at least one area: gun control. Heinrich appeared on the Senate floor in June 2016 to support Connecticut Democrat Chris Murphy on a proposal denying the sale of firearms to those on the government's terrorist-watch list. Heinrich joined most Democrats in voting for the plan, which failed on a largely party-line vote. He also supported a bipartisan proposal to block gun sales to those on the no-fly list, which is less expansive than the terrorist-watch list. The latter measure also failed to advance, but Heinrich reintroduced it in 2018—while co-sponsoring legislation to ban "bump stocks," devices that allow semi-automatic firearms to fire like automatic weapons. The onetime NRA member told Roll Call in March 2018: "My frustration with them as a group is they just aren't part of any solutions. They're ideologically pure, and they're not interested in doing anything. … I just don't think that's in any way responsible." When former Texas Rep. Beto O'Rourke called for a mandatory gun buyback during his 2020 presidential campaign, Heinrich said such an extraordinary proposal was "a bit of a gift to the NRA."

Heinrich has zeroed in on land issues on the Energy and Natural Resources Committee. He has worked to ensure hunting and fishing access to lands owned by the federal government, while criticizing calls to transfer federal land to state-government control. He and his former colleague, Democrat Tom Udall, pushed for years to create wilderness areas in much of the Organ Mountains-Desert Peaks region of southern New Mexico—which had been declared a national monument by Obama in 2014. A 2019 law written by the two Senators to designate more than 240,000 acres of the national monument as wilderness barred construction of roads and use of mechanized vehicles, while allowing hiking and horseback riding. All told, the bill designated nearly 275,000 acres of new wilderness areas throughout New Mexico. In 2019, Heinrich helped make the state's White Sands—a 275-square mile dune field that had been a national monument—the state's second national park. Heinrich has also proposed legislation to make the 33,000-acre Bandelier National Monument into a national park and worked with Udall to help protect the Gila River from future development. Udall retired in 2021, when Democrat Ben Ray Luján became the state's junior senator.

Heinrich represents a state in which 49 percent of the population—the highest state wide percentage in the nation—is Hispanic. In January 2019, he led 19 other Senate Democrats in introducing a bill to protect Dreamers—children brought to the country illegally as children—from deportation. The bill would have barred the Homeland Security Department—which oversees the Obama-era Deferred Action for Childhood Arrivals program—from sharing information collected on DACA participants with immigration and law enforcement agencies. When the Senate Democratic leadership got behind a legislative compromise in early 2018 that included preserving DACA, Heinrich was one of just three Senate Democrats to vote against it. He and Udall objected to another provision of the compromise that would have provided $25 billion for border security to underwrite Trump's proposed southern border wall. "New Mexicans support smart border security measures, but President Trump's border wall is a symbol of everything that's wrong with this administration," they said in a joint statement. The two also proposed a bill to better equip Border Patrol agents with medical training and interpretation services, invest in technology and equipment, and expand the operating hours of the busiest ports of entry. "Instead of wasting billions of dollars on a border wall that New Mexicans don't want or need, we should make smart, responsible investments," Heinrich said in a statement. Heinrich consistently opposed Trump's push for a border wall, introducing a bill that would have barred the president from using disaster relief money and military construction funds on the barrier. He spearheaded a letter from Senate Democrats urging Trump to stop border wall construction.

After term-limited Republican Gov. Susana Martinez ruled out a challenge to Heinrich in 2018, he faced Mick Rich, an Albuquerque contractor and state Labor and Industrial Commission member making his first run for office. Libertarians nominated former Gov. Gary Johnson—the their nominee for president in 2016.

Johnson's presence enlivened debates during the fall campaign, as he and Heinrich argued over whether Johnson's call to sharply downsize federal spending would harm the state's military installations, which are economically important. Johnson's long time support for marijuana legalization was eliminated as an issue after Heinrich, who supported only medical use in his first campaign, said in the spring of 2018 that it was time to legalize marijuana. Rich, while emphasizing his support for Trump, criticized Heinrich for moving his family to Washington D.C.'s Maryland suburbs. " He has become a Washington politician," Rich said. "He has abandoned New Mexico." It had little effect: Heinrich defeated Rich 54%-31%, as Johnson trailed with 15 percent.

Heinrich's Senate career could last as long as he wants it to. He did show interest in being President Joe Biden's Interior secretary, along with Udall, but that job went to his New Mexico House colleague, Rep. Deb Haaland, who became the first Native American to head the department. Heinrich, who introduced Haaland during her confirmation hearing, said she "will be a true partner for Western states like New Mexico as we diversify our economy, invest in our communities, and remain a global leader in producing and exporting energy."

Ben Ray Lujan (D)

Elected 2020, term expires 2026, 1st term, b. Jun 07, 1972; Santa Fe, NM; University of New Mexico, 1995; New Mexico Highlands University, B.A., 2007; Roman Catholic; Single

Elected Office: Chairman, NM Public Regulation Commission, 2005-2008; U.S. House, 2009-2021; Chief Deputy Whip, U.S. House, 2013-2015; Chair, Democratic Congressional Campaign Committee, 2015-2019; Assistant Speaker, U.S. House, 2019-2021.

Professional Career: NM Deputy Treasurer, Chief Financial Officer, NM Department of Cultural Affairs; Director, Administrative Services, NM Department of Cultural Affairs

DC Office: 498 RSOB 20510, 202-224-6621, Fax: 202-228-3261

State Offices: Las Cruces, 575-526-5475; Portales, 575-252-6188.

Committees: *Agriculture, Nutrition & Forestry*: Commodities, Risk Management & Trade; Conservation, Climate, Forestry & Natural Resources; Rural Development & Energy. *Budget*. *Commerce, Science & Transportation*: Communications, Media & Broadband (Chmn); Consumer Protection, Product Safety & Data Security; Oceans, Fisheries, Climate Change & Manufacturing; Space & Science. *Health, Education, Labor & Pensions*: Employment & Workplace Safety; Primary Health & Retirement Security. *Indian Affairs*.

Election Results

Election	Name (Party)	Vote (%)		Cand. Spent	Ind. Exp. Support	Ind. Exp. Oppose
2020 General	Ben Ray Lujan (D)	474,483	(52%)	$9,863,180	$1,524,296	$404,478
	Mark Ronchetti (R)	418,483	(46%)	$4,002,177	$14,424	$264,345
	Bob Walsh (L)	24,271	(3%)	$5,940		
2020 Primary	Ben Ray Luján (D)	225,082	(100%)			

Two years after orchestrating Democrats' takeover of the House following eight years in the minority, Ben Ray Luján conducted a Senate victory for himself. With a dozen years in the House, chairmanship of the Democratic Congressional Campaign Committee, and two years as assistant speaker as solid credentials, Luján scared off prospective Democratic challengers and won the primary unopposed. In his Democratic-leaning state, Luján defeated his Republican opponent, Mark Ronchetti, but it was closer than expected.

A seventh-generation New Mexican, Luján is the son of Ben Luján, a former state House speaker and legendary figure in state politics. The younger Luján has established his own niche by focusing on complex topics important to the state, especially energy and technology. He was born in Santa Fe and grew up on his family's farm where he and his three siblings helped raise cattle, sheep, and chickens. Luján worked as a card dealer in a casino while attending classes at New Mexico Highlands University. After graduating, he had several state jobs, including chief financial officer and director of administrative services at the Department of Cultural Affairs.

In 2004, Luján was elected to the New Mexico Public Regulation Commission. His most pressing issue as chairman was Qwest Communications' failure to invest a promised $788 million in its New Mexico communications network. Under his leadership, the PRC ordered Qwest to invest in infrastructure or refund the money to customers. When Qwest refused, Luján and the PRC took the company to the New Mexico Supreme Court. In 2006, the court sided with the commission; Qwest agreed to spend $270 million in the state. He worked with commissioners from other states in the West on regional solutions to climate change.

Luján ran for the House in 2008, as then-Rep. Tom Udall ran for—and won—a Senate seat. At the Democratic convention, Luján got 40 percent of the vote to 30 percent for Donald Wiviott, a developer. Both were included on the primary ballot, along with Benny Shendo, former head of the New Mexico Indian Affairs Department. Wiviott ran ads claiming Luján's father had helped him secure his job as deputy state treasurer. Luján claimed that Wiviott's Texas trailer parts company had been charged by the Federal Trade Commission with price-fixing.

Shendo caused the race's biggest controversy when he implied at a candidate forum that Luján was gay, which drew criticism from local gay rights groups. Luján picked up endorsements from Gov. Bill Richardson, local labor unions and the Sierra Club. Wiviott spent almost $1.6 million of his own money. Luján, who spent half that amount, won with 42 percent to Wiviott's 26 percent and Shendo's 16 percent. The general election was a foregone conclusion, as were Luján's subsequent campaigns.

On the Energy and Commerce Committee, he worked on two of his pet causes: alternative energy and the Los Alamos National Laboratory's non-nuclear weapons scientific research. In a 2015 speech to the New Mexico Legislature, Luján urged creation of a public-private consortium for the state's two national labs to bid on federal contracts. Earlier, he organized the bipartisan Technology Transfer Caucus to funnel research from the labs to the private sector. His committee work included legislation to treat and prevent opioid abuse, which was a crisis in New Mexico.

After the 2014 elections, then-Minority Leader Nancy Pelosi chose Luján to lead the DCCC over higher-profile House Democrats. Pelosi described Luján as "a dynamic and forward-looking leader with fresh energy and ideas." But the 2016 campaign revealed little change in DCCC strategy and resulted in widespread disappointment. Democrats grumbled that Pelosi and her close team of operatives remained in control, that they failed to put enough House seats in play in a competitive cycle and that they ran cookie-cutter campaigns that failed to connect with voters, especially in swing states. Like 2016 Democratic presidential nominee Hillary Clinton, House Democrats fell short in reaching out to disaffected voters to whom GOP nominee Donald Trump appealed. Starting the cycle with their smallest number of seats since 1928, they regained only six seats.

Luján acknowledged those shortcomings and other second-guessing in a December 2016 letter to House Democrats, in which he promised "a more inclusive messaging strategy, the need for more member-driven recruitment, and an interest in setting up a regional structure to better tap the expertise of our members." He gained another term at DCCC, without opposition.

Abetted by grassroots anger toward Trump, Luján was boosted by several factors in 2018: the organized "resistance" of Democratic women, especially in the suburbs; more systematic recruitment of candidates; huge fundraising; and more than three dozen open Republican seats, in part a symptom of GOP disillusionment with Trump. After disappointing setbacks in special elections for four GOP-held seats in early 2017, Luján was disciplined in how he used resources and was even willing to take sides in primaries. "We need to do a better job in understanding that we're talking about real people," he told the Los Angeles Times in July 2017. He rejected the use of litmus tests, including on abortion rights.

The resulting 40-seat gain was beyond what most Democrats—and other observers— had forecast. After other aspirants stepped aside, Luján was unopposed for the new position of assistant speaker, with upgraded responsibilities defined by Pelosi. As he described his position, Luján said, "I will welcome ideas from all corners of our caucus to build our agenda, protect our majority, hold the

Trump administration and congressional Republicans accountable, and make a positive difference in peoples' lives."

Economic diversification in New Mexico's economy was one of Luján's priorities in the House, especially amid the havoc wreaked by the novel corona virus in 2020. He backed initiatives to increase spending on renewable energy, encourage commercialization of the various technologies by New Mexico's two national labs, bolster the state's agricultural sector, and expand solar grants and clean energy production.

When Udall announced in March 2019 that he would not seek a third term in the Senate, Luján jumped off the House leadership ladder and ran for that opening, again becoming the frontrunner to succeed Udall. Secretary of State Maggie Toulouse Oliver declared her candidacy in April and spent nearly $500,000 but withdrew six months later with deference to Luján. "When I entered the race for U.S. Senate, I was the only candidate supporting 'Medicare for All'" and impeaching President Trump, she said. "Over the course of this campaign, that has changed." Other prospects with little experience or financing declared but withdrew prior to the June 2020 primary.

Luján raised more than $6 million in the primary and also benefited as a Latino in a state where Hispanics are nearly a majority of the population. New Mexico had not had a Latino senator since 1976, when Democrat Joseph Montoya lost reelection to Republican Harrison Schmitt.

Republicans nominated Ronchetti, a former meteorologist for an Albuquerque television station who was making his first political campaign. Some GOP strategists believed that Ronchetti's background as a TV weatherman—a local news celebrity who had high approval ratings, especially with women—could make the race more challenging. But facing a daunting national map to just defend their own incumbents, Republicans couldn't afford to focus resources on what looked to be a long-shot bid. That left Luján—and Senate Democrats—to retain the New Mexico seat. Amid an otherwise high-stakes and competitive campaign year for Senate Democrats, he was the only incoming freshman with that good fortune. Surprisingly, his 52 percent of the vote fell 2 percentage points short of the state's vote for Joe Biden in the presidential contest, and the contest's 6-point margin was far closer than scant polling had predicted. The Democratic Senate Majority PAC had placed a small $100,000 TV buy to boost Luján in the last leg of the race, which may have portended the tighter margin. Luján ended up running 4 points behind Biden in, the state's most populous county, Bernalillo County, home to Albuquerque.

Nonetheless, in a state where no senator has faced a difficult reelection challenge since Schmitt lost his bid for a second term in 1982, Luján and the state's senior Democratic Sen. Martin Heinrich —both in their late 40s at the start of 2021—appeared well-positioned for lengthy Senate careers. On the Commerce, Science and Transportation Committee, he became chairman of the influential Communication, Media and Broadband Subcommittee, where he can address issues that he handled prior to the Senate.

Melanie Stansbury (D)

Elected 2018, 2nd term; b. Jan. 31, 1979, Farmington, NM; Saint Mary's College of California, B.A., 2002; Cornell University, M.S., 2007; Unknown.

Elected Office: U.S. House, 2018-2020.

Professional Career: Field Ecology Instructor, New Mexico Museum of Natural History and Science, 2002-2004; Researcher, Cornell University, 2004-2010; Policy Fellow, White House Council on Environmental Quality, Energy and Natural Resources Committee, U.S. Senate, 2010-2011; Consultant, Sandia National Laboratories, Utton Transboundary Resources Center; Program Examiner, White House Office of Management and Budget, 2011-2015; Professional Staff, Energy and Natural Resources Committee, U.S. Senate, 2015-2017; Consultant/Senior Adviser, Policy and Community Programs, Utton Center, University of NM.

DC Office: 1421 LHOB 20515, 202-225-6316, stansbury.house.gov

State Offices: Albuquerque, 505-346-6781.

Election Results

Election	Name (Party)	Vote (%)		Cand. Spent	Ind. Exp. Support	Ind. Exp. Oppose
2021 General	Melanie Stansbury (D).................	79,625	(60%)	$867,341		
	Mark Moores (R)................................	47,071	(36%)	$469,618		

Prior winning percentages: 2018 (54%)

Democrat Melanie Stansbury won a special election on June 1, 2021, to fill the vacancy caused by the resignation of Rep. Deb Haaland, who resigned in March after she was confirmed as secretary of Interior. Stansbury defeated Republican Mark Moores, 60% to 36%, in a metro-area district that elected Republican Heather Wilson as recently as 2006. Stansbury had a big advantage in campaign spending and the two national parties largely stayed out of the contest, given what has become the strongly Democratic lean of the district. Both candidates had experience as state legislators.

Haaland, who was elected to the House in 2018 and became one of the first two Native American women elected to Congress, is the first Native American to run the Interior Department, whose Bureau of Indian Affairs has wide influence over tribal lives. That gave her nomination by President Joe Biden added significance among Native Americans and others in the civil rights community. A former Pueblo administrator, Haaland directed business operations of tribal gambling activities in New Mexico. She had lengthy experience as a Democratic candidate and campaign operative in the state.

Stansbury, a native of Albuquerque, earned her bachelor's degree in human ecology and natural science from Saint Mary's College of California and a Master of Science in sociology from Cornell University. She taught science classes in New Mexico schools and later worked in Washington, as an aide in the Obama White House and for Sen. Maria Cantwell at the Senate Energy and Natural Resources Committee. Stansbury was elected to the state House in 2018 in an east Albuquerque district by defeating a seven-term Republican incumbent. She was vice-chair of the Energy, Environment and Natural Resources Committee.

After Haaland resigned, both parties quickly scheduled conventions to select their nominees for the special election. Moores, who ran a pathology laboratory, easily won the Republican nomination. In the two-day vote in which 204 delegates—meeting electronically--selected among a Democratic field that initially included eight candidates, Sen. Antoinette Sedillo Lopez led Stansbury on the first ballot, 74 to 43. A longtime law professor who was supported by some national progressive groups, including Justice Democrats, Sedillo Lopez ran third in the Democratic primary in 2018 when Haaland was first elected.

Some Democrats had urged the nomination of Sedillo Lopez, a Latino, in a district where a slim majority of the population is Hispanic. The Albuquerque Journal called the outcome an "upset" victory for Stansbury, who is Anglo. After her intensive three-month campaign among the small electorate, she won on the second ballot, 103 to 97, the Santa Fe New Mexican reported.

In the general-election campaign, Moores focused heavily on increased crime, which had been an effective issue for Republicans among Latino voters in the November 2020 election. He cited her endorsement of the Breathe Act, a proposal from the Movement for Black Lives that would redirect federal law enforcement grants to social services, the Washington Post reported. A Moores campaign ad called the proposal, "the most dangerous legislation in America." In response, Stansbury ran ads in which police officers and prosecutors vouched for her support for law enforcement. Although Democrats did not spend money on her behalf, White House spouses—Jill Biden and Doug Emhoff, husband of Vice President Kamala Harris—made campaign appearances with Stansbury.

In this district, that was enough for Stansbury's nearly 2-to-1 victory. The outcome virtually assured that the seven special elections created by House vacancies in 2021 would not result in any party switches. It also could encourage Democrats in New Mexico to use redistricting to switch Democratic voters to the neighboring 2nd District, which Republicans captured in November 2020.

NM-1: Central New Mexico

Cook Partisan Voting Index:

Population		Race and Ethnicity		Income	
Total	691,229	White	74.40%	Median Income	$55,318
Land area (sq. miles)	4,600	Black	2.70%	District Income Rank	324
Pop/ sq mi	150.26	Latino	51.00%	Poverty Rate	16.30%
Born in State	54.10%	Asian	2.70%	With health insurance	91.30%
		Two or more races	4.40%	Cash public assistance	3.60%
Age Groups		Other	15.80%	Food stamp/SNAP	15.40%
Under 18	21.00%				
18-34	23.10%	**Education**		**Work**	
35-64	38.10%	H.S grad or less	35.60%	White Collar	42.50%
Over 64	17.70%	Some college	30.00%	Sales and Service	39.90%
		College Degree, 4 yr	18.80%	Blue Collar	17.60%
Military		Post grad	15.70%	Government	21.80%
Veteran/ Active Duty	8.90%				

2020 Pres. Vote	Biden	197,294	(60%)	Trump	122,685	(37%)		
2016 Pres. Vote	Clinton	147,250	(52%)	Trump	100,132	(35%)	Johnson	30,767 (11%)

Albuquerque: New Mexico's past and future come together in its single metropolis, Albuquerque. The city's Spanish and Indian past is memorialized in its name (for a 17th-century Spanish nobleman), its age (founded in 1706) and its quaint Old Town. But Albuquerque's future is decidedly high-tech. For decades, Sandia National Laboratories, Kirtland Air Force Base and the University of New Mexico have attracted scientists and engineers to Albuquerque and promoted private-sector technology growth. The city's minor-league baseball team is the Isotopes, named in part to honor the area's association with the Atomic Age. When rocket scientist Robert Goddard moved here in 1930 and nuclear scientist J. Robert Oppenheimer reconnoitered the site in 1940, Albuquerque was still a town of 35,000 at the junction of the Rio Grande River and old U.S. 66, which paralleled the Santa Fe Railroad. "A dirty, red sod-hut tortilla desert highway city," novelist Tom Wolfe wrote.

Now, metro Albuquerque, spreading out from Bernalillo County into Sandoval and Valencia counties, has more people—546,000 in 2019—than all of New Mexico did when the scientists first arrived. The University of New Mexico has become a magnet for biotechnology, with more than a dozen local start ups working to commercialize UNM's biomedical discoveries. At the Sandia Labs, which have more than 12,000 employees in Albuquerque, officials in 2020 fast-tracked production of ventilators to cope with international demands resulting from the corona virus. The city's prosperous neighborhoods have climbed the gently rising heights to the east; poorer residents have spread north and south along the Rio Grande. Hemmed in by the Sandia Mountains and by federal installations, growth is moving west and north. In 2018, the county approved the first phase of Santolina, a planned 22-square-mile development west of Albuquerque that within a few decades might house 90,000 residents and create 75,000 jobs. Critics continued to voice multiple concerns, including scant water resources and conflicts of interest by county officials.

In the Old Town centered on the plaza, some of the adobe buildings date to the 18th century. Every October, Albuquerque hosts the International Balloon Fiesta, which features more than 500 hot-air balloons and many resident balloonists. Canceled in 2020 because of the corona virus, producers planned to live-stream in 2021 all of the 14 events during their 10-day gathering. The annual Gathering of Nations typically attracts more than 700 tribes, along with 100,000 participants and spectators. Spurred by tax incentives, California-based Netflix took over a large production studio and created 1,600 jobs in 2019—its first year at its Albuquerque site. The company began a training program with NBC Universal to find workers for production jobs.

The 1st Congressional District includes almost all of Albuquerque and some of its suburbs. It is 49 percent Hispanic and takes in most of Bernalillo County, all of sparsely populated Torrance County in the desert, and small corners of Sandoval, Santa Fe and Valencia counties. More than 90 percent of the vote is in Bernalillo. After Hillary Clinton took the county by 17 percentage points, Joe Biden increased the Democratic margin to 23 points. Small slices of Bernalillo are in both the 2nd and 3rd Districts. Until 2008, the 1st District elected only Republicans to Congress. With additional Latino voters, it has become solidly Democratic.

Yvette Herrell (R)

Elected 2020, 1st term, b. Mar 16, 1964; Ruidoso, NM; ITT Technical Institute School of Business, Boise, ID; Christian; Single.

Elected Office: NM House, 2011-2019.

Professional Career: Realtor; Real estate broker.

DC Office: 1305 LHOB 20515, 202-225-2365, Fax: 202-225-9599, herrell.house.gov

State Offices: Las Cruces, 575-323-6390; Roswell, 575-578-6290.

Committees: *Natural Resources*: Energy & Mineral Resources; National Parks, Forests & Public Lands. *Oversight & Reform*: Government Operations; Subcommittee on Environment.

Election Results

Election	Name (Party)	Vote (%)		Cand. Spent	Ind. Exp. Support	Ind. Exp. Oppose
2020 General	Yvette Herrell (R)........................	142,283	(54%)	$3,000,867	$1,405,084	$10,598,255
	Xochitl Torres Small (D)...................	122,546	(46%)	$8,561,438	$1,087,343	$11,284,398
2020 Primary	Yvette Herrell (R).............................	26,968	(45%)			
	Claire Chase (R).................................	19,017	(32%)			
	Chris Mathys (R).................................	14,378	(24%)			

Republican Yvette Herrell won a rematch against first-term Democratic Rep. Xochiti Torres Small. In the traditionally Republican district, where she tied herself closely to President Donald Trump, Herrell prevailed by a larger margin than Torres Small won in 2018. A member of the Cherokee tribe, Herrell was the first Native American woman elected to Congress as a Republican. Former Democratic Rep. (now secretary of Interior) Debra Haaland was elected in 2018 as the first Native American woman from New Mexico.

A native of Ruidoso New Mexico, Herrell received a legal secretary diploma from the ITT Technical Institute School of Business in Boise Idaho and she attended classes at New Mexico State University. For many years, she was a real estate broker in Alamogordo. Her father was a county commissioner in Alamogordo-based Otero County. In 2010, Herrell was elected to the state House, where she served eight years and chaired the Consumer and Public Affairs Committee. During that time, she was a member of the national board of the American Legislative Exchange Council.

Running for the open House seat in 2018, Herrell won the Republican primary, 49%-32%, against Monty Newman, a former chairman of the state Republican Party. Newman was backed by moderate Gov. Susana Martinez, who told the Albuquerque Journal that Herrell's support of oil and gas interests raised questions about her ability to represent New Mexico " in a fair and reasonable way."

Against Torres Small, who outspent her 3-to-1, Herrell in 2018 avoided debates and appeared confident of victory. Vice President Mike Pence spoke at a rally for Herrell in the final days of the campaign. The Journal endorsed her, citing her legislative experience and support for limited government. Torres Small won that contest by fewer than 4,000 votes, 51%-49%, with an 18,000-vote lead in Dona Ana, her home county and the largest in the district.

When Herrell ran again in 2020, House Republican campaign leaders viewed Torres Small as one of the most vulnerable Democratic incumbents. Herrell faced a primary challenge from Claire Chase, an oil and gas executive who had posted negative comments in Facebook about Trump. Herrell, who cited her support from leaders of the House Freedom Caucus, again had a relatively narrow primary victory, 45%-32%.

In the rematch, Torres Small emphasized her bipartisan pragmatism. Herrell criticized the incumbent, citing her vote for the impeachment of Trump as part of the " political circus in Washington." She pitched herself to voters as an ally of Trump, "someone who would defend the conservative values" of the oil-rich district.

"Having President Trump at the top of the ticket has just really energized the base in New Mexico," Herrell said. The campaign featured harsh negative ads on both sides. Herrell and her supporters accused Torres Small of "lies" in her 2018 campaign promises.

As in 2018, Torres Small tripled her opponent's campaign spending. But the increased turnout of the presidential election was a boost for Herrell. In the Republican's 54%-46% victory, Torres Small again had a big lead in her base of Dona Ana County. But Herrell doubled and tripled the vote of Torres Small in several counties in the state's oil-producing southeast corner, which more than made up the difference.

Looking ahead to Democratic-controlled redistricting, Herrell likely will face a more demanding political map in 2022. With their comfortable majorities in New Mexico's two other districts, Democrats could adjust the current relatively straight district lines in an attempt to regain complete control of the state delegation. Still, the 2nd District has moved so far to the GOP that Democrats in the other two districts might be reluctant to relinquish the votes that would be required to make the district at least a toss-up.

In the House, she joined the Natural Resources, and Oversight and Reform committees.

NM-2: Southern New Mexico

Cook Partisan Voting Index: R+8

Population		Race and Ethnicity		Income	
Total	705,615	White	81.90%	Median Income	$46,817
Land area (sq. miles)	71,739	Black	2.40%	District Income Rank	408
Pop/ sq mi	9.84	Latino	55.90%	Poverty Rate	20.70%
Born in State	50.10%	Asian	1.20%	With health insurance	90.00%
		Two or more races	2.00%	Cash public assistance	4.40%
Age Groups		Other	12.40%	Food stamp/SNAP	17.90%
Under 18	23.90%				
18-34	23.00%	**Education**		**Work**	
35-64	35.10%	H.S grad or less	47.40%	White Collar	32.00%
Over 64	17.70%	Some college	32.00%	Sales and Service	41.20%
		College Degree, 4 yr	11.90%	Blue Collar	26.70%
Military		Post grad	8.60%	Government	22.40%
Veteran/ Active Duty	9.70%				

2020 Pres. Vote	Trump	148,608	(55%)	Biden	116,534	(43%)		
2016 Pres. Vote	Trump	117,212	(50%)	Clinton	93,362	(40%)	Johnson	18,903 (8%)

Las Cruces: South eastern New Mexico is a disparate landscape: endless sagebrush-strewn acreage and then, suddenly, 9,000-foot mountain peaks rising along the Continental Divide. (The Robledo Mountains, says the Smithsonian Institution, are the world's greatest repository of pre-dinosaur-era fossil tracks.) The eastern part of this region—places like Lovington and Hobbs—speaks with a Texas twang rather than a northern New Mexico lilt. In Little Texas, as south eastern New Mexico is known, oil has been the economic mainstay. Cattle ranching is common, and cotton is grown on irrigated land. Roswell, the site of a supposed flying saucer landing in 1947, is now home of the International UFO Museum and Research Center. Farther west is White Sands National Park, with its immaculate gypsum dunes and specially evolved animals with white coloration that allows them to elude predators in the harsh environment.

Virgin Galactic, a company started by billionaire Richard Branson, leased land near White Sands to build the nation's first commercial spaceport (called Spaceport America). Despite initial setbacks, including the crash in 2014 of Virgin Galactic's SpaceShipTwo Enterprise, the $218 million facility has grown more active, with several dozen rocket launches. NASA has tested several new technologies, as have the Italian Space Agency and several American aerospace companies. In May 2020, Virgin Galactic completed its first glide flight from the Spaceport. Close by is Alamogordo, not far from where the first atomic bomb was exploded in the empty land at 5:29:45 a.m. Mountain War Time on July 16, 1945.

Las Cruces, New Mexico's second-largest city, has grown at rates well above the state wide average, thanks to migrants from Mexico coming up the Rio Grande. For decades, Anglo and Mexican ranchers across the border spoke " the common language of cattle," and communities frequently shared public services with their cross-border neighbours, not hindered by a wall or other major barrier. This largely empty 150-mile section of the U.S.-Mexico border remains sleepier than elsewhere. In 2019, a private group spent $6 million to build a mile of wall in Sunland Park, though its legality was doubtful, The New York Times reported. In Eunice, along the Texas line, a $4 billion commercial uranium enrichment plant has been built, the first such facility licensed by the Nuclear Regulatory Commission. It takes fuel from nuclear power plants around the world. Surrounding Lea County, where the population grew 10 percent from 2010 to 2019, accounts for more than half the oil production of New Mexico, the third-largest state producer in the nation. In January 2019, Lea was the second-largest oil producing county in the nation, trailing McKenzie County in North Dakota. Lea County had twice as many operating rigs. Oil-field managers complained that immigration crackdowns at the border were depriving them of needed workers.

The 2nd Congressional District of New Mexico covers the southern part of the state, reaching to Albuquerque's southern suburbs. It includes most of Little Texas—majority Anglo and solidly conservative—but also politically marginal Las Cruces and the Indian country around the pueblos, which is strongly Democratic. The district is 54 percent Hispanic and 5 percent Indian. Many of the Latinos are migrant workers. Las Cruces-based Dona Ana County, the population center, has about one-third of the voters. The district—very much of an outlier in New Mexico politics—in 2020 voted for President Donald Trump, 55%-43%, a wider margin than the GOP wins in the two previous presidential elections.

Teresa Leger Fernandez (D)

Elected 2020, 1st term, b. Jul 01, 1959; Las Vegas, NV; Yale University, B.A., 1982; University of TX, Att., 1984; Stanford University Law School, J.D., 1987; Catholic; Divorced; 3 children.

Professional Career: Judicial Law Clerk, U.S. District Court, Northern District of CA, 1987-1989; Fellow, White House Fellows, 1994-1995; Partner/Managing Partner, law firm, 1989-2013; Council Vice Chair, Advisory Council on Historic Preservation, 2013-2016; Counsel/Strategist, law firm.

DC Office: 1432 LHOB 20515, 202-225-6190, Fax: 202-225-1528, fernandez.house.gov

State Offices: Santa Fe, 505-428-4680.

Committees: *Administration*: Elections. *Education & Labor*: Civil Rights & Human Services; Higher Education & Workforce Investment. *Joint Printing*. *Natural Resources*: Indigenous Peoples of the United States (Chmn); National Parks, Forests & Public Lands.

Election Results

Election	Name (Party)	Vote (%)		Cand. Spent	Ind. Exp. Support	Ind. Exp. Oppose
2020 General	Teresa Leger Fernandez (D)	186,282	(59%)	$2,058,302	$826,623	
	Alexis Johnson (R)	131,166	(41%)	$142,378		$113
2020 Primary	Teresa Leger Fernandez (D)	44,480	(43%)			
	Valerie Plame (D)	25,775	(25%)			
	Joseph L. Sanchez (D)	12,292	(12%)			
	Marco Serna (D)	8,292	(8%)			
	Laura M. Montoya (D)	6,380	(6%)			

Teresa Leger Fernandez won the Democratic primary to lock up victory in the open seat in northern New Mexico. She combined a long record of service on both local and national levels, with a well-organized campaign and support from key interest groups. Her victory created the largest state all-women delegation in the House. Prior to the resignation of Debra Haaland to become secretary of Interior, the two others—including a Republican who also was first elected in 2020—are Native American. She replaced Ben Ray Lujan, who was a close ally of House Speaker Nancy Pelosi and won the Senate seat of retiring Democratic Sen. Tom Udall.

Born and raised in Las Vegas New Mexico, Leger Fernandez got her bachelor's degree from Yale University and a law degree from Stanford. She returned to her home state to work on affordable housing and community development, plus advocacy for local tribes. With her "social impact" law firm in Santa Fe, she also represented minority businesses, including with litigation. She was a White House fellow for President Bill Clinton and vice chair of the Advisory Council on Historic Preservation during the Obama administration.

In her first political campaign, she invoked the theme, "Protect What You Love." Contending that families, communities, democracy and the planet were under attack, she added, "when you care deeply about something, you need to act on it." She supported the Green New Deal, including the phase-out of coal-fired power plants in part of her district. In its editorial endorsement of Leger Fernandez, the Santa Fe New Mexican wrote that she "excels at fighting and winning battles" and "brought high achievement at every level of her life."

The other leading Democratic contenders were first-term state Rep. Joseph Sanchez and Valerie Plame, who was a former CIA operations officer and book author. Plame, who cited her familiarity with the Los Alamos National Laboratory when she moved to the district after leaving the CIA, had been well-known in Washington. Amid extensive controversy, her covert status was revealed after she and her husband, a U.S. diplomat, publicly criticized the George W. Bush administration for its handling of the war in Iraq. "I want to take that searing life experience and put it to good use for my community," Plame told the Huffington Post.

With her national fundraising base, Plame's $2.2 million made her the biggest spender in the primary. Leger Fernandez spent $1.4 million in the primary. She was endorsed by the Congressional Hispanic Caucus and EMILY's List, which supports Democratic women who support abortion rights. The political action committees of those two groups spent another $800,000 on her behalf.

Rep. Tony Cardenas of California said the Hispanic Caucus backed Leger Fernandez because minority candidates from low-income areas often struggle financially against candidates with national support whom he called "opportunists."

Leger Fernandez won the primary with 43 percent of the vote to 25 percent for Plame and 12 percent for Sanchez. She took 13 of the 16 counties in the sprawling district, including each of the eight largest except for rural Rio Arriba County, which was the base for Sanchez. In November, she had no problem with her 59%-41% victory over Republican Alexis Johnson, an environmental engineer for oil companies. In the House, she got seats on the Education and Labor plus Natural Resources committees, plus the leadership-centered House Administration Committee.

NM-3: Northern New Mexico

Cook Partisan Voting Index: D+7

Population		Race and Ethnicity		Income	
Total	699,985	White	65.30%	Median Income	$53,357
Land area (sq. miles)	44,959	Black	1.90%	District Income Rank	356
Pop/ sq mi	15.57	Latino	40.80%	Poverty Rate	17.50%
Born in State	57.20%	Asian	1.40%	With health insurance	88.80%
		Two or more races	3.90%	Cash public assistance	2.70%
Age Groups		Other	27.50%	Food stamp/SNAP	16.00%
Under 18	22.80%				
18-34	21.80%	**Education**		**Work**	
35-64	36.80%	H.S grad or less	38.90%	White Collar	37.60%
Over 64	18.60%	Some college	33.50%	Sales and Service	42.00%
		College Degree, 4 yr	15.70%	Blue Collar	20.30%
Military		Post grad	12.00%	Government	23.40%
Veteran/ Active Duty	8.90%				

2020 Pres. Vote	Biden	187,786	(58%)	Trump	130,601	(40%)		
2016 Pres. Vote	Clinton	144,622	(52%)	Trump	102,323	(37%)	Johnson	24,871 (9%)

Santa Fe: "The dancing ground of the sun" is what the Pueblo Indians called the land of northern New Mexico, where the long vistas, dotted with low-lying scrub, are painted in pastel hues in the cold light and clear air. For 100 years, artists have been coming here, attracted by the scenery and by a unique civilization that is part Indian, part Anglo, part Spanish, and a little Mexican. (Northern New Mexico was under Mexican control from 1821 to 1846.) The Indians were here first and built adobe pueblos, including some of the world's earliest apartment buildings. The Spanish conquistadors and priests brought the Catholic religion, the baroque architectural accents, and the Spanish language. The Palace of the Governors, built in Santa Fe in 1610, is now a museum on Santa Fe's Plaza and is the nation's oldest extant public building. Zoning laws vigorously enforce the height and adobe-like appearance of buildings in the historic district.

Along the back roads in Rio Arriba and Taos counties, one can find a religion that mixes Catholicism with adaptations of Indian festivals, buildings not that much different from the old pueblos, and a standard of living reminiscent of the Indian past. Concentrated in and around the Navajo reservation in the west (and outside of Santa Fe), many of the district's Indians live in abject poverty. The corona virus had a devastating impact, with both an economic shutdown resulting from closure of casinos and disproportionate COVID-19 cases because of the poor health care. It's quite a contrast with the ski lodges in the Taos Valley, the high-security research facilities of Los Alamos, which has the second-highest median income of any city in the nation (behind Washington D.C.) and has among the most Ph.D.s per capita, thanks to the National Laboratory, and the affluent lifestyles of modern-day Santa Fe. In September 2020, U.S. News rated Los Alamos the healthiest county in the nation.

The 3rd Congressional District of New Mexico contains most of the state's historic Spanish-speaking and Indian regions. This district, similar in size to Pennsylvania, runs from the High Plains along the Texas border, past the haunting Sangre de Cristo Mountains, through the vast ridges and isolated buttes in the center, to the windy and dusty desert-like plateau in the west. The artsy state capital of Santa Fe, which has the most museums of any city in the nation except New York, remains the lively and dominant center. The local economy has remained strong, with a "gray" growth as the number of residents 65 and older has come close to surpassing those 18 and younger. With 99,000 residents, a 13 percent increase from 2010 to 2019, Rio Rancho began as a retirement community in the 1960s and has become the district's most populous city. Rio Rancho is home to a large Intel plant, which suffered several years of job losses—from 3,300 jobs in 2013 to 1,100—due to the decline of its advanced chip-making. In 2019, the company started to bounce back with the introduction of silicon photonics, a new micro-processing technology that permits faster process, analysis, storage and transfer of data over longer distances. Officials projected 300 new hires. In Farmington-based San Juan County, a lower-income area that suffered a 5 percent population decline from 2010 to 2019, the utility company's plan to close its coal-fired power plant by 2022 caused protests over increased costs. In response, city and utility company officials explored the possibility of installing carbon-capture technology.

The district's Hispanic population is 41 percent, the lowest of the state's three districts. Another 19 percent of the population is Indian, the highest in the state. The politics of northern New Mexico have been unique. For years, votes were bartered in Spanish by Republicans and Democrats, often cynically, sometimes corruptly. Loyalties ran to families and communities more than to principles or parties. Those traditions evolved. Hispanics and Indians are solidly Democratic. In Santa Fe and Taos, the upscale and many elderly migrants have produced a strong liberal tilt. In 2020, Joe Biden took the district, 58%-40%.

NEW YORK

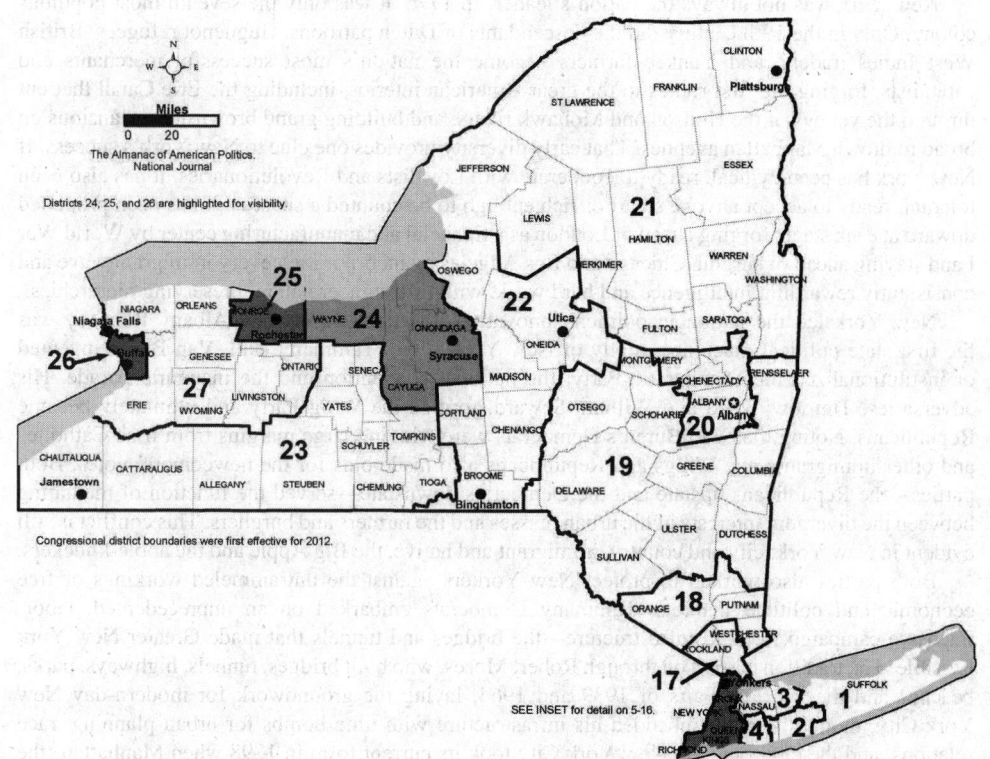

The Almanac of American Politics.
National Journal

Miles
0   20

Districts 24, 25, and 26 are highlighted for visibility.

CLINTON

FRANKLIN   Plattsburg

ST LAWRENCE

ESSEX

JEFFERSON

LEWIS

21

HAMILTON

WARREN

WASHINGTON

OSWEGO

HERKIMER

22

Utica   SARATOGA

FULTON

NIAGARA   ORLEANS

Niagara Falls   Buffalo

26   Buffalo

25   Monroe

Rochester   WAYNE   24

ONONDAGA

Syracuse   ONEIDA

MONTGOMERY

SCHENECTADY   RENSSELAER

ALBANY   Albany

20

GENESEE   ONTARIO   SENECA   CAYUGA   MADISON

27   LIVINGSTON   YATES   CORTLAND   OTSEGO   SCHOHARIE

ERIE   WYOMING   TOMPKINS   CHENANGO   GREENE   COLUMBIA

SCHUYLER

CHAUTAUQUA   CATTARAUGUS   23   STEUBEN   CHEMUNG   TIOGA   BROOME   19   DELAWARE

Jamestown   ALLEGANY   Binghamton

ULSTER   DUTCHESS

Congressional district boundaries were first effective for 2012.

SULLIVAN

18   PUTNAM

ORANGE   WESTCHESTER

ROCKLAND

17   Yonkers

SEE INSET for detail on 5-16.   NEW YORK   3   1   SUFFOLK

NASSAU

4   2

RICHMOND

New York may no longer be the giant among states it once was, but it still packs plenty of heft: Based on gross domestic product, New York City alone would rank as the 13th-largest economy in the world, and it remains a global center. But the state has experienced its share of heartache this century, first with the 9/11 attacks, and then, in 2020, the coronavirus pandemic, which killed more than 50,000 New York residents in just over a year. But it has been resilient, over and over again, fed by a stream of ambitious newcomers.

Today, New York seems far removed from its origins as tiny, rough-hewn Nieuw Amsterdam; fewer than 2 percent of today's New Yorkers are descended from the Dutch. But the character of the place, including its tolerance, endures in daily life and in its great institutions and helps explain its miraculous growth. Combine Amsterdam and America, Dutch character with British-born political freedoms and American military strength, and you have a city-state that can lead the world. In some fields—culture, finance, media—New York City remains, in the words of "Hamilton," the greatest city in the world.

New York was not always the nation's leader. In 1776, it was only the seventh most populous colony. Only in the 19th century did the descendants of Dutch patroons, Huguenot refugees, British West Indies traders, and Yankee farmers become the nation's most successful merchants and capitalists, forging the first routes to the great American interior, including the Erie Canal that cut through the valleys of the Hudson and Mohawk rivers, and building grand brownstone mansions on broad midtown Manhattan avenues. That early diversity provides one clue to New York's success. If New York has been cynical, ready to cooperate with Loyalists and Revolutionaries, it has also been tolerant, ready to accept anyone smart or rich enough to be counted a success. It has been propelled upward at each stage, forging ahead of London as a financial and manufacturing center by World War I and staying ahead of surging Chicago and Los Angeles by incorporating every immigrant wave and consistently rewarding intelligence and hard work, with little concern about preserving hierarchies.

New York led the nation in political innovation. Martin Van Buren's Albany Regency was the first state political machine, an ally of New York City's Tammany Hall. Van Buren invented or institutionalized the Democratic Party, the national convention and the inaugural parade. His adversaries, Thurlow Weed and William Seward, formed the Whig Party and ultimately became Republicans. Noting that Van Buren's Democrats were winning large margins from Irish Catholics and other immigrants, the Whigs and Republicans also made bids for the newcomers' votes. Both parties—the Republicans upstate and the Democrats downstate—served the function of mediating between the divergent interests of the urban masses and the farmers and burghers. This conflict is still evident in New York: city and country, immigrant and native, the Big Apple and the apple-knockers.

Both parties also worked to protect New Yorkers against the untrammeled workings of free economic and political markets. Tammany Democrats embarked on an unprecedented, labor-intensive campaign to build infrastructure—the bridges and tunnels that made Greater New York possible. The tradition carried on through Robert Moses, who built bridges, tunnels, highways, parks, beaches and the World's Fairs of 1939 and 1964, laying the groundwork for modern-day New York City, though he also embedded his infrastructure with time bombs for urban planning, race relations, and the environment. New York City took its current form in 1898 when Manhattan (the nation's largest city) and Brooklyn (the fourth-largest) banded together with the Bronx, Queens and Staten Island to form a megalopolis. Progressive Republicans worked to create civil service laws and bureaucratized purchasing and spending to protect taxpayers from corrupt party machines. The Democratic Tammany machine led by Charles F. Murphy and the talented young men he advanced, Al Smith and Robert Wagner, responded to the 1911 Triangle Shirtwaist fire, in which hundreds of women jumped 11 floors to their death because fire escapes were blocked, by passing labor and safety laws. In the 1920s, the New York metro area produced the nation's first regional plan. New York pioneered public housing and fair housing laws, industry-wide unions (in the garment trades), rent control and dairy price controls to help both New York City tenants and Upstate farmers.

Statewide elections were exceedingly close, with Democrats carrying the New York City Catholic vote and Republicans winning Upstate Protestants. Swing votes were cast by more than 1 million Jewish immigrants, who supported a generous welfare state but mistrusted the Tammany machine and valued civil rights. (For most of its history, New York has used a "fusion voting" system under which candidates can run on multiple ballot lines.) The politician who combined these appeals most cannily was Fiorello LaGuardia, a nominal Republican but almost a socialist, an Episcopalian who was half Jewish as well as Italian, and the man who, as mayor of New York City from 1933 to 1945, built much of the public housing and many of the civic monuments that still stand. Incensed that New York had no airport, he built what is now LaGuardia within a year. Both parties produced politicians whose positions appealed to these swing voters. At a time when the national media was much more heavily concentrated in Manhattan than in Washington, many became nationally prominent and ran for president.

In the immediate pre- and post-War era, the economy was roaring and the country was becoming accustomed to working in big units—being employed by big corporations, represented by big unions, regulated by big government. In this, New York was a natural leader. The financial dominance of Wall Street and the big banks was protected by federal regulation. The high-technology thrust of America in the mid-20th century was directed by big companies headquartered in New York's suburbs or Upstate: Corning, General Electric, IBM, Eastman Kodak, and Xerox.

But in the last quarter of the 20th century, New York's public strengths became weaknesses. The state that was clearly the national leader of a big-unit America—"Mad Men" America— lost the leadership role once growth had shifted to small economic units where flexibility and adaptability had become more important than centralized planning. Competition emerged overseas and elsewhere in the United States, and New York's institutions, practices and infrastructure became ossified. Welfare state benefits became too expensive; measures meant to protect against corruption stifled innovation. Rent control kept housing scarce, school bureaucracies and teacher unions threatened inspired teaching, and public hospitals rationed care. The government that intended to aid growth was cutting it off— not completely, but enough to explain why New York state, which grew 45 percent in population from 1930 to 1970, grew only 6 percent from 1970 to 2010, while California grew 87 percent and Texas 125 percent.

People and businesses started voting with their feet, especially during the terms of Mayor John Lindsay, a liberal Republican turned Democrat who caved to municipal unions' demands and borrowed against next year's revenues to pay this year's bills. Two years after he left office, that approach brought the city to the brink of bankruptcy in 1975. In the 1970s, the population of New York, city and state, dropped by nearly 700,000, an unprecedented hemorrhage of talent and productivity. Retrenchment followed under Gov. Hugh Carey, and private financiers and the state government took control of city government, cut spending, and negotiated cutbacks in jobs and salaries with public employees' unions. In the 1980s, Wall Street boomed, and Manhattan once again brimmed with confidence. Taxes were cut further under Democratic Mayor Edward Koch (1978-89) and Democratic Gov. Mario Cuomo (1983-94) and public-employee unions were for a time reined in. But institutional problems remained. New York's legislature remained tightly controlled by the two chambers' leaders—the Democratic Assembly speaker from New York City and the Republican state Senate president from Upstate or the suburbs, solidified after the mid-1970s through self-reinforcing gerrymanders. They engaged in classic political logrolling, lavishing taxpayers' dollars on each other's pet projects. Public-employee unions reestablished their stranglehold. The mild recession of the early 1990s struck New York with force. Big Upstate companies—Xerox, Kodak, IBM— suffered serious reversals, which only worsened with the advent of new technologies. A private sector that had grown little if at all beyond Wall Street could no longer finance the growing demands of the state.

By the end of the 1990s, New York seemed to have gotten back on track. Building on improvements under Democratic Mayor David Dinkins, Republican Mayor Rudy Giuliani, first elected in 1993, cut crime and welfare rolls in half and cut hard deals with the unions. Republican Gov. George Pataki, first elected in 1994, delivered huge tax and spending cuts. Wall Street and the financial services industry boomed in the late 1990s. Then came September 11, 2001, the beautiful late-summer morning when two planes hit the World Trade Center in the span of 17 minutes. The terrorists had chosen to attack the seat of government in Washington—the Pentagon and a second target saved by the heroes of United Flight 93—and the seat of commerce in New York to inflict the maximum possible damage. Fire fighters, police officers, and rescue workers risked death to help others. Strangers helped strangers, and in less than a week, the New York Stock Exchange reopened. As New York faced an economic downturn, media billionaire Michael Bloomberg, a Democrat-turned-Republican, won the first of three mayoral terms. In time, the financial industry boomed as never before, at least until mortgage-backed securities imploded in September 2008, with repercussions internationally, nationally and locally.

Map for New York City

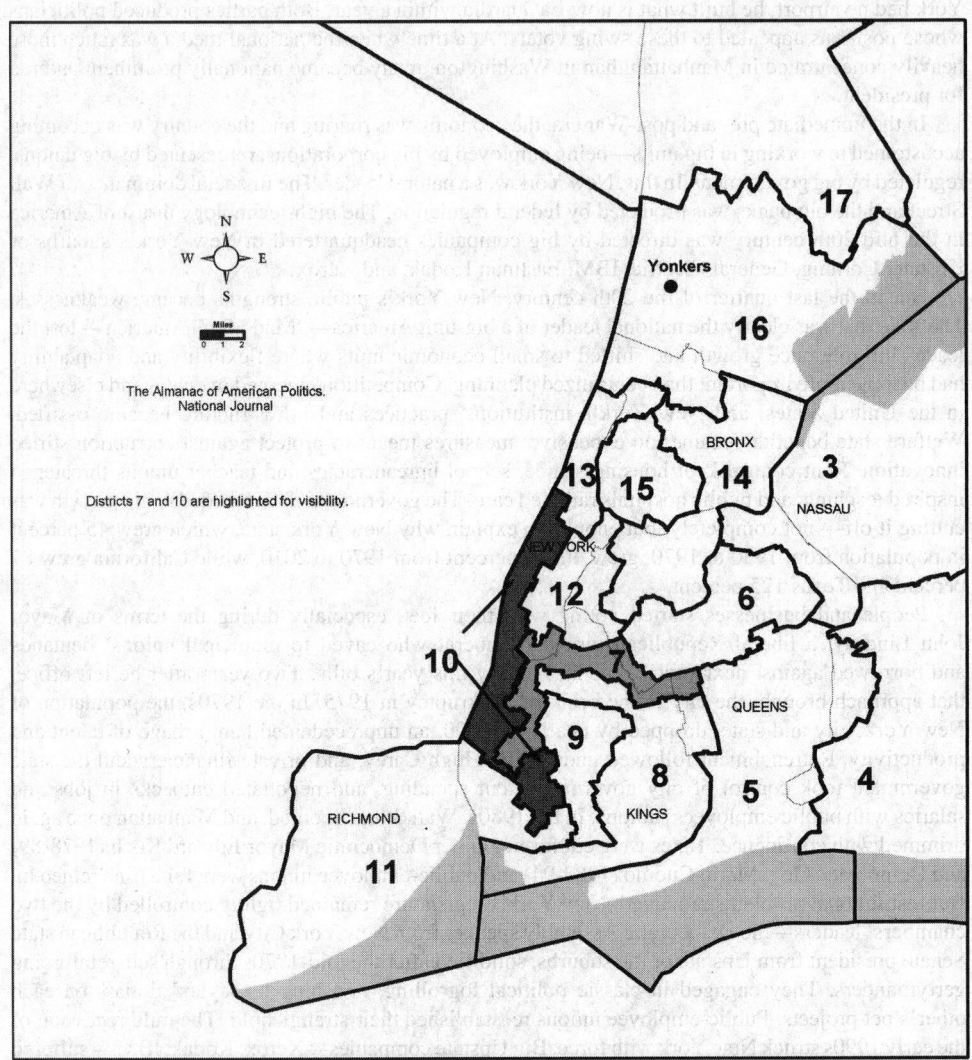

N
W — E
S

Miles
0   2

The Almanac of American Politics.
National Journal

Districts 7 and 10 are highlighted for visibility.

Yonkers

17

16

BRONX

13 15 14   3

NEW YORK   NASSAU

12

6

10   7

9   QUEENS

8   5   4

RICHMOND   KINGS

11

Congressional district boundaries were first effective for 2012.

After another economic recovery driven by the finance sector during the 2010s, New York—and especially New York City—was hit early and hard by the coronavirus pandemic. In March 2020, callers jammed 911 phone lines amid the wail of ambulance sirens; when evening came, stuck-inside New Yorkers opened their windows and clapped for doctors and first responders. At Elmhurst Hospital in Queens, administrators had to call in refrigerated trucks to serve as ad-hoc morgues. The amenities that made New York such a desirable place to live—its restaurants, museums, nightclubs, and Broadway theaters—were shut down, often for a year, and the city's unemployment rate surged to almost 20 percent. For months, Andrew Cuomo, the more-feared-than-loved governor, provided a master class in crisis communications during his televised daily briefings (though it later became clear that he and his administration had badly mishandled the public health policies for nursing home residents and then tried to cover it up). The wealthy who were able to escape to second homes did so, frequently for months at a time. On-again, off-again closures of the public schools drove homebound families crazy. Aggressive public health measures helped bring down the case rate dramatically in the summer of 2020, although the fall and winter brought spikes, and by the spring of 2021, the caseload remained relatively high by national standards.

New York City's population grew 2 percent from 2010 to 2019, to more than 8.3 million. Of the close-in suburban counties, Rockland grew by 4.2 percent during the decade, while Westchester and Nassau grew more slowly than the city, at 1.8 and 1.1 percent, respectively, and Suffolk actually saw its population decrease by 1.1 percent. These modest changes masked much greater movements. The elderly moved out, heading to Florida and other warmer climes, and middle-income workers and young blue-collar workers headed to lower-cost and lower-tax states like the Carolinas, Georgia and Florida. Moving in, meanwhile, were immigrants who streamed into outer-borough neighbourhoods and created new businesses, churches and neighbourhood institutions—Afro-Caribbeans in Flatbush; Chinese in Flushing, Borough Park, and on Staten Island; Colombians and Mexicans in Corona; Pakistanis and Bangladeshis in Jackson Heights; Greeks in Astoria; Russians in Brighton Beach; and Dominicans in Washington Heights and much of the Bronx. At the same time, the city's Black population declined; Hispanics now outnumber Blacks in every borough except Brooklyn. Almost 27 percent of the residents of Queens are Asians; nationally, New York state ranks fifth for its percentage of Asian residents. But the immigrant influx, the main driver of New York's population growth, slowed during the immigration-skeptical presidency of Donald Trump.

New York has long since lost most of its manufacturing jobs, and many corporate headquarters have moved elsewhere. The bright spots are the city's tech sector, which employs an estimated 372,000 people, and the financial-services industry, which pays enormous salaries and bonuses to those at the very top and generates service jobs for those who tend to the needs of the rich. The outer boroughs, particularly Brooklyn, experienced a revival starting in the Bloomberg years, as artisanal-minded, latte-swilling hipsters helped gentrify older neighbourhoods. Hillary Clinton ran her 2016 presidential campaign from Brooklyn. The leftward drift was made clear by the 2013 mayoral victory of Bill de Blasio to succeed Bloomberg as mayor. But growing pains created quality-of-life concerns. Despite de Blasio's efforts, homelessness has risen, due largely to skyrocketing housing costs; in recent years, one of every 100 New York City babies was born to a homeless family, according to the Coalition for the Homeless. New York City's subway system, meanwhile, grappled with broad public frustration, caused by a combination of high ridership, aging infrastructure and inefficient investment —and that was before ridership and revenue plummeted during the pandemic. The open-seat mayor's race in 2021 will help determine the city's future course.

Meanwhile, the suburbs' problems have stemmed from having much higher property taxes than in the city. The high property taxes are in effect tuition to good suburban school districts. New York spends more per pupil than any other state, roughly double the national average. The suburbs have aged, as well. Meanwhile, new businesses have not exactly flocked to New York's suburbs—the hedge-fund sector blossomed across the state line in Connecticut. In 2021, the right-of-center Tax Foundation ranked New York 48th in the nation for its business climate, ahead of only California and New Jersey, and it calculated that the state has the nation's highest overall tax burden. The anti-business sentiment reached new heights when politicians, including Democratic Rep. Alexandria Ocasio-Cortez, helped torpedo a plan by Amazon.com to establish a second headquarters in Long Island City, a project that cities across the country had begged for. (Amazon has since expanded its workforce in New York City, but not at the scale envisioned for the new headquarters.)

Upstate New York has even deeper problems. Large, formerly paternalistic companies have been shedding jobs for decades. Medicaid mandates have forced Upstate counties to drastically raise property taxes, which now rank as the nation's highest relative to values. During the past decade, more than one out of every three counties in New York recorded not a single year of population growth, and several counties in the southern tier and the far north lost between 6 percent and 9 percent of their population during the decade. According to a Moody's Analytics study in 2020, Rochester had the weakest job market of the 53 U.S. metro areas with at least 1 million in population, with Buffalo the second-weakest; among smaller metro areas, Albany and Syracuse also ranked poorly. Per capita income Upstate sits well below the level in the New York City metro area, and the region has experienced high rates of opioid abuse. Unlike similar areas of neighboring Pennsylvania, New York has sworn off one possible economic pursuit: natural gas extraction. Buffalo, once one of the nation's great steel producers, has turned into a center for the debt-collection industry. Cultural differences have emerged as well; in 2019, when the state legalized issuing driver's licenses to undocumented immigrants, some Upstate county clerks threatened not to issue them. Some Upstate legislators have even floated a plan to secede and form a state separate from metropolitan New York City, though the plan would almost certainly be economically and politically unworkable.

In races for statewide office, New York has been voting heavily Democratic. No Republican has won statewide office since Pataki won his final term in 2002, though the GOP maintained control of the state Senate until 2018. Albany's long-festering problems with ethics and corruption have come to a head in recent years. Eliot Spitzer, elected governor in 2006, visited high-end prostitutes, got caught and resigned; his successor, David Paterson, had such low job approval ratings that he decided not to seek a full term. Long time power players in the legislature—Assembly Speaker Sheldon Silver, a Democrat, and Senate Majority Leader Dean Skelos, a Republican—were indicted on separate federal corruption charges and convicted. Then, in late 2020, Cuomo was hit by a barrage of sexual harassment claims; an independent investigation was opened, and the legislature considered impeachment. Meanwhile, prosecutors in both New York state and New York City have been pursuing Trump over a variety of legal matters, even though the former president decamped permanently to Florida.

Joe Biden won the 2020 presidential race in New York by 23 points, a similar margin to the one in 2016 when Hillary Clinton (of Westchester) defeated Trump (of Queens). Biden flipped Broome County (Binghamton), Saratoga County (Saratoga Springs), Rensselaer County (Troy), and Essex County in the Adirondacks, shifting the margin in each by between five and eight points in the Democratic direction. Biden expanded the Democrats' winning margins in most of the populous counties Upstate and in the New York City suburbs, sometimes significantly; he widened the Democratic margins by roughly 10 points each in Albany County (Albany), Dutchess County (Poughkeepsie), Ulster County (Kingston), and Erie County (Buffalo). Biden also narrowed Trump's margin of victory by seven points in each of Suffolk County (outer Long Island), Orange County (Newburgh), and Niagara County (Niagara Falls). Trump did improve on 2016 in a few places, notably suburban Rockland County and four of the five New York City boroughs, thanks to gains in heavily Orthodox Jewish, Latino and Russian-immigrant precincts. (The one borough where Trump didn't improve was the only one he won in the city, Staten Island, by 15 points.) Still, Trump's gains need to be put into perspective: In the Bronx, Trump may have netted a 28,000-vote gain, but he still lost by a yawning margin of more than 67 points. Despite such curiosities, there is little sign that New York is verging toward a Republican comeback.

Population		Race and Ethnicity		Income	
Total	19,453,561	White	63.20%	Median Income	72,108
Land area (sq. miles)	47,126	Black	15.90%	State Income Rank	14 out of 50
Pop/ sq mi	412.80	Latino	19.30%	Poverty Rate	13.00%
Born in state	63.10%	Asian	9.70%	With health insurance	94.80%
		Two or more races	3.30%	Cash public assistance	3.50%
Age Groups		Other	9.00%	Food stamp/SNAP	15.2%
Under 18	20.70%				
18-34	23.80%	Education		Work	
35-64	38.60%	H.S grad or less	38.20%	White Collar	43.10%
Over 64	16.90%	Some college	24.00%	Sales and Service	40.00%
		College Degree, 4 yr	21.20%	Blue Collar	17.00%
Military		Post grad	16.60%	Government	15.70%
Veteran/ Active Duty	4.50%				

Presidential Politics

2020 Primary (D)	Biden (D)	1,136,679(70%)	Sanders (D)	285,908(18%)	Warren (D)	82,917 (5%)
2020 Pres. Vote	Biden (D)	5,244,886(61%)	Trump (R)	3,251,997(38%)		
2016 Pres. Vote	Clinton (D)	4,556,142(59%)	Trump (R)	2,819,557(37%)	Johnson (L)	176,600 (2%)

When Hillary Clinton faced Donald Trump in 2016 — the first time that two New Yorkers were the major party nominees since 1944 when Franklin Roosevelt faced Thomas Dewey — the turnout in the Empire State rose some 10 percent. But the state was an afterthought in the general election. In the first half of the 20th century, New York was the dominant state in presidential politics. It had the most electoral votes (peaking at 47 from 1932 to 1948) and it was usually the most evenly divided between the two parties. Dewey, then the GOP governor, came within five percentage points of FDR in 1944. In 1948, he beat Harry Truman there. But in the 21st century, New York has seen its Electoral College clout drop from 33 in 2000 to 29 in 2016 — tied with Florida (and likely to lose one or two more after the 2020 reapportionment) — while becoming heavily Democratic. In 1988, Republican George H.W. Bush was beaten only 52%-48%.

How did this Democratic dominance come to pass? One reason is that Jewish voters, who did not identify strongly with either major party in the first half of the 20th century, became strong Democrats in the second. Increases in the percentages of black, Hispanic and Asian voters also raised the Democratic percentage. White Catholic voters took conservative positions on cultural issues like crime and abortion in the 1970s and 1980s, but today, these voters and their descendants are more likely to take liberal stands on cultural issues like gun control and gay rights. Republican allegiance in the New York City suburbs — on Long Island and in the upscale commuter towns of Rockland and Westchester counties — faded away starting in 1992. In 2012, the only county in the New York City metropolitan area that was still casting its ballots for GOP presidential hopefuls was tiny Putnam. And urban millennials of all races align Democratic.

Clinton defeated Trump, 59%-37%, but he captured Suffolk County, the first time a Republican carried that suburban enclave since President Bush in 1992. In the Hudson River Valley, Trump won back exurban Orange County, as well as Rensselaer and Saratoga. Upstate, he won blue-collar Oswego, Niagara -- which includes suburbs of Buffalo -- and several other rural central New York counties. In New York City, Trump won only the Borough of Staten Island.

Typically, the New York Republican presidential primary draws little attention. In 2016, Texas Sen. Ted Cruz wooed Orthodox Jewish voters in Brooklyn, but Trump reminded his home state that the Texan had once disparaged "New York values." Ohio Gov. John Kasich repeatedly indulged in deli cuisine in the Big Apple. But Trump easily won the April 19 GOP primary, swamping Kasich 60%-25%, winning 61 of the state's 62 counties. Kasich won Manhattan where Trump resides, but only by about 1,000 votes. From this convincing victory, Trump's march to the GOP nomination was virtually unimpeded.

The Democratic race was an equally important moment for Clinton. In the run up to New York, she had lost one primary (Wisconsin) and four caucuses to Vermont Sen. Bernie Sanders. Clinton had easily captured the 2008 Democratic presidential primary over Barack Obama, 57%-40%, carrying 26 of the 29 congressional districts. Still, Sanders was a native of Brooklyn, many of the state's Democratic primary voters are die-hard liberals, and the rough-and-tumble tabloid media culture of New York City can throw even experienced candidates off stride. But it was Sanders who ran into a political buzz saw. A New York Daily News editorial board interview went poorly and Sanders offered few details on how he planned to break up the big banks on Wall Street, one of his signature issues. Then Sanders blasted Clinton on whether she was qualified to serve as president, a charge that seemed implausible to many New Yorkers who had elected her to the Senate twice. With the support of the entire New York Democratic establishment, Clinton handily defeated Sanders 58%-42%, even though the Vermonter outspent her on television advertising. Turnout was just shy of 2 million, eclipsing the previous record of 1.9 million in 2008. Clinton won 21 of the state's 27 congressional districts, losing six relatively rural ones upstate. Whether the state moves its primary to March, it will remain a major Democratic battleground.

Congressional Districts

117th Congress Lineup	19D 8R	116th Congress Lineup	21D 6R

The next round of redistricting is shaping up as a nightmare for New York, especially its Republicans. Based on the Census Bureau's population totals for 2020, it will lose at least one seat for the eighth consecutive decade. The one-seat loss likely will be taken from the 10 districts Upstate (north of Westchester County), five of which are held by Republicans. Democrats' over whelming control of the legislature plus the governor's office poses risks for all eight Republican seats state wide—three of which are among the 17 districts between Westchester and the eastern end of Long Island. Even in New York City, which has had a notable increase in population in the past few years while most suburban counties have been stagnant or losing, the total of 12 seats could be realigned significantly due to factors such as personal ambitions or minority-group demands. The fact that four insurgent Democrats—all of them young racial minorities, with three replacing veteran white Democrats with influential House posts—won metro-area seats in 2018 and 2020 has increased the sense of change in what had been a stable delegation, especially among Democrats.

With Republicans having regained in 2020 two of the three seats they lost in 2018, Democrats likely will use redistricting to reinforce areas where they have made recent gains, even if they proved to be short-term. Currently, the eight GOP seats include two on the eastern end of Long Island, one on Staten Island, four in central and western New York (from Albany to Buffalo) and the other in the North Country. Some of those districts could be paired, including the two on Long Island, two in central New York and two in the west—making available new seats that would be Democratic opportunities..

The rigors of musical chairs have become familiar in this state. When John F. Kennedy was elected president in 1960, New York elected 43 House members, California 30 and Florida eight. In 2012, New York and Florida each elected 27 members and California 53. Reapportionment has been carnage time for New York: The state lost five districts in the 1980 census, three in 1990, and two each in 2000 and 2010. In recent cycles, those decisions have been made largely by three power brokers: the state Senate president (who until 2018 was Republican), Assembly speaker (a Democrat), and a veto-wielding governor. The partisan dynamics in Albany have shifted to Democratic control. But that doesn't mean that all Democrats will be guaranteed a similar seat—or an easy ride—in 2022.

In 2012, a deadlock in the legislature kicked the conflict to a three-judge federal panel, which appointed a special master in case the legislature failed. As it turned out, the court map was met with reluctant acceptance. The plan even-handedly eliminated retiring Democrat Maurice Hinchey's Upstate seat and the Queens seat of Republican special-election winner Bob Turner, who hadn't expected to win reelection anyway. That election downsized the delegation from 22 Democrats and 7 Republicans to 21-6. The GOP pick-ups in 2020 returned the delegation to 19-8. No doubt, many in the delegation have begun to calculate how they can avoid getting a short straw in 2022.

Andrew Cuomo (D)

Elected 2010, term expires 2023, 3rd term; b. Dec. 6, 1957, Queens; Fordham U., B.A. 1979; Albany Law Schl., J.D. 1982; Catholic; Divorced; 3 children.

Elected Office: NY Attorney General, 2006-2010.

Professional Career: Assistant District Attorney, Manhattan, 1984-1985; Practicing attorney, Blutrich Falcone & Miller, 1985-1988; Founder, Housing Enterprise for the Less Privileged, 1988-1993; Assistant Secretary, Department of Housing & Urban Development, 1993-1997; U.S Secretary, Department of Housing & Urban Development 1997-2001.

Office: Executive Chambers Albany, 12224; 518-474-8390; Fax: 518-474-1513
Lt. Gov.: Kathy Hochul (D) **Atty. Gen:** Letitia James (D) **Sec. of State:** Rossana Rosado (D)
State Legislature: Senate: 40D, 22R, 1V **House:** 106D, 43R, 1I

Election Results

Election	Name (Party)	Vote (%)
2018 General	Andrew Cuomo (D)	3,635,340 (60%)
	Marcus Molinaro (R)	2,207,602 (36%)
2018 Primary	Andrew Cuomo (D)	1,021,169 (65%)
	Cynthia Nixon (D)	537,192 (35%)

Prior winning percentage: 2014 (54%), 2010 (63%)

Few politicians have gone from the heights of adulation to the depths of scandal faster than Andrew Cuomo during his third term as governor of New York. In the first six months of 2020, Cuomo led the state through the misery of the coronavirus pandemic, becoming an unexpectedly reassuring figure during some of his state's darkest days. But 2021 brought a reassessment of his handling of the crisis, including investigations into whether he had released misleading information about the number of coronavirus deaths in nursing homes. In turn, the nursing home controversy helped bring to the surface years of bottled-up resentments against the Democratic governor, including multiple allegations of inappropriate behavior toward women. While Cuomo had planned to run for a fourth term in 2022, that was looking decreasingly likely amid an ongoing impeachment inquiry by the legislature.

"Cuomo can be irritating, confounding, and egotistical. He can also be engaging, intense, and charismatic," Edward-Isaac Dovere wrote in The Atlantic in 2019, before Cuomo's highs and lows of 2020 and 2021. "He deliberately stands apart from the leftward tilt of his party, but his record of bills signed into law on many core progressive issues is unmatched by any other Democrat, in D.C. or the states, with the possible exception of Jerry Brown. He wins in landslides, but most politicians in New York and beyond can't stand him."

Cuomo was born in Queens and grew up in the middle-class neighbourhood of Hollis, the second of five siblings. He showed an early aptitude for repairing and building automobiles. He graduated from Fordham University in 1979, one year after his father was elected lieutenant governor, and from Albany Law School in 1982.He began working for his father's campaign for governor that year and received credit for masterminding his come-from-behind primary victory against New York City Mayor Ed Koch. However, some critics said the younger Cuomo was too willing to engage in dirty politics. He spent several years as an aide to his father as the governor's national profile skyrocketed in the wake of his keynote speech at the 1984 Democratic National Convention.

After a short stint in the Manhattan district attorney's office, Cuomo in 1986 founded the Housing Enterprise for the Less Privileged (HELP USA), a non profit organization dedicated to helping the homeless. He left his private law practice in 1989 to run the group, which became a national model for its formula of offering shelter but also job training, education, drug treatment and other assistance. Two years later, he married Kerry Kennedy, the daughter of Robert F. Kennedy, in a widely publicized union that was described as a merger of two Democratic political dynasties.

Cuomo's work at HELP caught the attention of Arkansas Gov. Bill Clinton, who asked Cuomo to serve on his presidential transition team in 1992 and then as assistant secretary of community planning and development at HUD. After Clinton's reelection in 1996, Cuomo took over as secretary of the department. He won praise for his energetic efforts to make housing more affordable, but he also adopted policies to broaden home ownership for low-income Americans that contributed to the housing crisis a decade later. One of those policies was a dramatic rise in the number of loans that government-sponsored mortgage giants, Fannie Mae and Freddie Mac, were required to buy. HUD also produced rules that explicitly forbade imposing new reporting requirements on the two enterprises.

Cuomo returned to New York in 2001 with the intention of running for governor the following year. But he did himself in with some brash and ill-advised remarks. He said that Republican Gov. George Pataki had done little after 9/11 other than hold New York Mayor Rudy Giuliani's coat. He also angered African Americans who had been looking to State Comptroller Carl McCall as their party's "next in line" candidate. Cuomo dropped out of the race before the primary, and McCall lost to Pataki. Around the same time, Cuomo became engaged in a bitter public divorce and child-custody battle with his wife.

Cuomo largely disappeared from the public eye for several years. In 2006, he came back to run for state attorney general when the incumbent, Eliot Spitzer, ran for governor. He patched up his differences with Democrats and won the primary with ease, then easily beat the Republican nominee, former Westchester District Attorney Jeanine Pirro, 58%-40%. Signaling his ambition for higher office, Cuomo conducted investigations on a wide range of topics, including alleged misdeeds within the financial industry—an issue that had propelled Spitzer to the governorship. He also ended up investigating Spitzer for using the state police to gather information about then-state Senate Majority Leader Joseph Bruno.

When Spitzer resigned in disgrace in 2008 over revelations that he had been the client of a prostitution ring, Lt. Gov. David Paterson took over. Paterson, the state's first African-American governor, took some bold budget stands and inspired many with his ability to overcome his legal blindness, but his job ratings were the lowest in state history. He eventually acceded pressure from the Obama White House and decided not to run for a full term. In May 2010, Cuomo announced his candidacy, declaring the state had slipped from being a "national model" under his father to a "national disgrace." In the general election, Cuomo faced Carl Paladino, a real estate executive who self-funded his campaign. The New York tabloids dubbed Paladino "Crazy Carl" for his sometimes outrageous statements (he also became close to Donald Trump). Cuomo had little trouble rolling to a landslide 63%-33% victory.

In office, Cuomo was fiscally cautious -- in his first year, he struck a budget deal that reduced year-to-year spending by about 2 percent without raising taxes -- but he was liberal on social issues. He carefully organized a broad coalition to support legalizing same-sex marriage, which the state Senate had defeated two years earlier. In the end, six senators who had voted against a legalization bill in 2009 voted for one in June 2011, including three Republicans, and New York became the largest state yet to permit such unions. Political commentators of all stripes said the governor's maneuvering was masterful, and national gay activists as well as prominent liberals began opening their wallets to him. Cuomo also worked more smoothly with the legislature than any of his recent predecessors. He entered 2012 with his highest job-approval rating as governor --- 62 percent in the Siena poll. His name began popping up on the early lists of 2016 presidential prospects; even his father stoked speculation at his 80th birthday party.

In 2013, Cuomo called for action on gun control in the wake of the Sandy Hook school massacre in Connecticut. He quickly signed legislation on military-style weapons and ammunition clips, though this caused his job-approval rating to dip below 60 percent; while downstate Democrats remained in his corner, his support among Republicans, and voters Upstate generally, suffered. His standing eroded further in 2014 after his administration reportedly sought to thwart the progress of an independent panel he had established to investigate corruption, after it had begun delving into issues that involved him and his political supporters. This episode helped Cuomo draw a Democratic primary challenger in Zephyr Teachout, a Fordham University law professor. The New York Times refused to endorse either candidate in the primary. Cuomo prevailed, 63%-34%, but Teachout's showing was stronger than expected, suggesting an increasingly restive left of the Democratic Party. In the general election against Westchester County Executive Rob Astorino, Cuomo used his 9-to-1 fundraising advantage to pull out a victory, but with just 54 percent, well below the 65 percent with which his father had won a second term.

Feeling pressure from his party's progressive wing, Cuomo went around the legislature to set in motion a minimum wage boost for fast-food workers, and he traveled to Havana to promote engagement and trade with Cuba. But he also experienced a string of personal and professional challenges. Mario Cuomo died at 82, and the governor's girlfriend, Food Network cooking show host Sandra Lee, was diagnosed with breast cancer. (She was later declared cancer free; the couple eventually split in 2019.) Meanwhile, Cuomo was mired in a loud feud with New York City Mayor Bill de Blasio. A string of polls in 2015 showed Cuomo's approval ratings falling into the low-to-mid 40s.

Cuomo put significant political capital into building efforts, including a new Tappan Zee bridge named for his father and a rebuild of LaGuardia Airport. But ethics reemerged as an issue in November 2016 when Joe Percoco, a close aide to Cuomo, and Alain Kaloyeros, the former president of SUNY Polytechnic Institute, were indicted in an alleged bribery scheme. In time, concern about Cuomo's inability to clean up Albany helped create room for a new primary challenger in 2018— actress Cynthia Nixon, best known for playing lawyer Miranda Hobbes on "Sex and the City." Nixon criticized the incumbent for being insufficiently liberal, as well as for the ethical problems in his circle, a line of attack that became especially timely when Percoco was convicted in March 2018 and Kaloyeros was found guilty four months later. Nixon attracted significant public attention -- in addition to her celebrity status, she had called Immigration and Customs Enforcement a "terrorist organization" and handed out bongs to promote marijuana legalization. But on primary day, Cuomo won, 65%-35%.

In the legislature, however, a tectonic shift was underway. For seven years, renegade Democrats had joined forces with Republicans to control the Senate -- a longstanding irritant to progressive Democrats, and arguably a relief to Cuomo, who was able to use the GOP's control to excuse his moderate stances to the restive left of his party. But in April 2018, Cuomo negotiated a deal for members of the maverick Independent Democratic Conference to rejoin their fellow Democrats. That still left Democrats one seat short of the number necessary to flip control, but it showed the way the winds were blowing. On primary day, liberal challengers defeated six of the eight breakaway Democrats; Democrats picked up control of the chamber in November. Cuomo's general election race against Dutchess County executive Marcus J. Molinaro was never close, despite Molinaro's argument that Cuomo led "the most corrupted state government in America." Cuomo won, 60%-36%.

During Cuomo's third term, both chambers were newly led by Black progressives: Senate Majority Leader Andrea Stewart-Cousins and House Speaker Carl Heastie. They presented several long-blocked bills to Cuomo, including an electoral reform package and a measure to protect abortion rights in the event the Supreme Court overturned Roe v. Wade; the governor signed both. Cuomo also enacted legislation to implement the nation's most aggressive climate targets, including 100 percent carbon-free electricity by 2040 and net-zero carbon emissions for the whole economy by 2050. He also signed legislation to strengthen tenant rights in New York City, to enable undocumented immigrants to obtain driver's licenses, to allow farm workers to bargain collectively, and—in what would later take on an ironic cast—tougher laws against sexual harassment. Meanwhile, Cuomo and deBlasio promoted New York in the high-stakes quest to become Amazon.com's second headquarters. But after the giant online retailer chose Queens' Long Island City as one of two sites, along with Arlington, Virginia, some local politicians, including Rep. Alexandria Ocasio-Cortez, raised concerns about the billions of dollars of tax breaks the two had promised Amazon, and they criticized the company's working conditions. Irked by the less-than-unified political support, the retailer pulled its offer.

In early 2020, the coronavirus pummeled New York City harder than any other locale. Cuomo's daily press briefings in the Red Room of the state Capitol won wide praise and even an Emmy. "Suddenly the very characteristics that had been criticisms of the governor—his micromanaging, his meddling in local affairs and his sometimes paternalistic preaching—became evidence to some television viewers, particularly those unaccustomed to Mr. Cuomo, of calm, control and compassion," wrote New York Times Albany correspondent Jesse McKinley. Cuomo's approval rating skyrocketed, especially after the state reached -- in one of the governor's favorite metaphors -- the "other side of the mountain" in coronavirus cases. He even published a high-profile book, "American Crisis: Leadership Lessons from the COVID-19 Pandemic." But in the second half of 2020, Cuomo's record increasingly came in for reassessment. Analyses noted a pattern of damaging squabbles between Cuomo and de Blasio; the distribution of substandard ventilators from state stockpiles; low morale among public health officials, some of which led to high-level resignations; and an early order by Cuomo that nursing homes take in coronavirus patients who were considered "medically stable." The nursing home policy was later blamed for unnecessary deaths among a particularly vulnerable group, and its cover-up was alleged to have been linked to fears that it could undercut his book. Meanwhile, Cuomo addressed the other major crisis of 2020 -- race and policing -- by signing a measure to ban police chokeholds and lift a longstanding law that kept police disciplinary records from public view. Meanwhile, in legislative primaries, multiple progressive challengers upset more moderate Democratic incumbents, foretelling an even more left-tilting legislature beginning in 2021.

In early 2021 Cuomo experienced a cascading series of problems, starting with investigations into his handling of the nursing home issue. Attorney General Letitia James -- a fellow Democrat --issued a report that concluded that the state had underreported the coronavirus death toll at nursing homes by perhaps 50 percent. In short order, the U.S. attorney in Brooklyn and the FBI both launched their own investigations. Cuomo didn't apologize, but he acknowledged that "my administration created the void, and that I feel bad about. Not illegal, not unethical, but just failed people in that moment." His position deteriorated further when Assemblyman Ron Kim, a Democrat who had publicly criticized Cuomo's nursing home record, went public with details of a furious call he'd received from Cuomo that, according to Kim, included threats against his career. Soon after that, several women, including former staffers, came forward with accounts of inappropriate behavior by Cuomo. The governor "has created a culture within his administration where sexual harassment and bullying is so pervasive that it is not only condoned but expected," wrote Lindsey Boylan, a former Cuomo aide who went public as an accuser. Cuomo, for his part, denied touching women "inappropriately," but he apologized if his interactions had caused offense or pain; he urged caution until an investigation by the attorney general's office concluded. This didn't stop the legislature from initiating an impeachment inquiry, which, if it led to a successful impeachment vote, would require Cuomo to step back so that the lieutenant governor, Kathy Hochul, could become acting governor. A big reason why Cuomo's political peril was so serious, veteran political consultant George Arzt told the Times, was that "he's a very tough guy and there are many people who don't like him. He doesn't have that reservoir of friends and good feeling to sort of pushback." And despite Cuomo's record of signing progressive bills, the ascendant wing of legislative Democrats had long viewed Cuomo as more of an obstacle than an ally, making them open to ousting him.

Despite the swirling investigations, Cuomo refused to step down through the spring of 2021. In fact, he flexed his legislative muscles by agreeing to several policies he'd opposed previously —recreational marijuana and a "millionaire tax" for New York City. If Cuomo resigns or is impeached, Hochul would become governor. If he stays in office but declines to run for a fourth term, possible successors include Hochul, James, New York City Public Advocate Jumaane Williams, state Comptroller Tom DiNapoli, Suffolk County Executive Steve Bellone, Nassau County Executive Laura Curran, and any number of members of Congress (including Ocasio-Cortez and Antonio Delgado) or the legislature. The GOP's limited hopes could rest on a three-way contest.

Chuck Schumer (D)

Elected 1998, term expires 2022, 4th term, b. Nov 23, 1950; Brooklyn, NY; Harvard University, B.A., 1971; Harvard University, J.D., 1974; Jewish; Married (Iris Weinshall); 2 children; 1 grandchild.

Elected Office: NY Assembly, 1975-1980; U.S. House, 1981-1999.

Professional Career: Attorney

DC Office: 322 HSOB 20510, 202-224-6542, Fax: 202-228-3027, schumer.senate.gov

State Offices: Albany, 518-431-4070; Binghamton, 607-772-6792; Buffalo, 716-846-4111; Melville, 631-753-0978; New York, 212-486-4430; Peekskill, 914-734-1532; Rochester, 585-263-5866; Syracuse, 315-423-5471.

Committees: Senate Majority Leader. *Intelligence. Rules & Administration.*

Group Ratings

	ADA	ACLU	AFL-CIO	LCV	COC	HAFA	ACU	CFG	FRC
2020	-	77%	-	100%	-	0%	5%	-	-
2019	95%	C	95%	100%	31%	C	5%	5%	0%

Almanac Ratings 2019-2020

	Economy	Social	Foreign	Composite
Liberal	97%	97%	75%	90%
Conservative	3%	3%	25%	10%

Key Votes of the 116th Congress

1. EPA clean energy rules	Y	5. Russia sanctions	Y	9. Barr as Atty. General	N
2. U.S./Mex./Can. trade deal	N	6. Troops in SYR, AFG	N	10. Spending at the border	Y
3. Cut unemployment benefits	N	7. Veto arms sales to Saudis	Y	11. Coney Barrett to Sup. Ct.	N
4. Shelton to Fed Reserve	N	8. Defense $$$, veto override	Y	12. Electoral College objections	N

Election Results

Election	Name (Party)	Vote (%)		Cand. Spent	Ind. Exp. Support	Ind. Exp. Oppose
2016 General	Chuck Schumer (D)............................ 5,182,006	(71%)	$13,854,876	$100,000	$39,600
	Wendy Long (R)............................ 1,988,261	(27%)	$685,926	$3,003	
2016 Primary	Chuck Schumer (D)........................ Unopposed				

Prior winning percentages: 2016 (71%), 2010 (66%), 2004 (71%), 1998 (55%); House: 1996 (75%), 1994 (73%), 1992 (89%), 1990 (80%), 1988 (78%), 1986 (93%), 1984 (72%), 1982 (79%), 1980 (77%)

Just out of Harvard Law School, Democrat Chuck Schumer, New York's senior senator, ran for a New York Assembly seat—over the objections of his mother. "Don't run, you'll never win," she is said to have advised her son. She wanted him instead to accept a job from a leading New York law firm. Not only did Schumer win, he has not lost an election in nearly five decades since. And, months before her 93rd birthday in early 2021, Selma Schumer saw her son become the first New Yorker (and first member of the Jewish faith) to assume the post of majority leader since party leadership roles in the Senate were formalized a century ago.

For Chuck Schumer, the majority leader's title came four years later than hoped. Poised to become the Democratic leader with the retirement of Harry Reid of Nevada, Schumer celebrated his overwhelming reelection to a fourth Senate term in 2016. He then rushed to Washington for what he anticipated would be a second celebration—of Senate Democrats regaining the majority lost just two years earlier. However, the event was cancelled after it became clear Democrats had come up three seats short, as Donald Trump unexpectedly captured the White House. Four years later, as Trump's lagging reelection bid renewed prospects for a Democratic Senate majority, Election Day 2020 again yielded disappointment. It was not until after narrow victories in two Georgia runoffs that Democrats clinched control of the chamber, and Schumer's status as majority leader was confirmed while he was hunkered down in a safe room, as a pro-Trump mob rampaged through the Capitol on January 6, 2021.

Schumer immediately faced the challenge of enacting the agenda of Democratic President Joe Biden—a Senate colleague of Schumer's for a decade—in a chamber split 50-50, with Vice President Kamala Harris offering a tie breaking vote, if needed. But, in four years as minority leader, Schumer had kept his ideologically diverse caucus united to a remarkable degree—while winning high marks from centrists and progressives. Schumer's challenge had been that his GOP counterpart, then-Majority Leader Mitch McConnell, was able to achieve a similar degree of unity within his party. The Schumer-McConnell relationship grew increasingly tense through three bitter battles over Trump's Supreme Court nominees. When the COVID-19 pandemic called for consideration of economic relief measures, the two men often negotiated through intermediaries. Ultimately, Schumer's ability to keep his caucus together helped force McConnell to accept significant expansions in the size and scope of that aid—notably a doubling of the size of the first big relief bill, the CARES Act, to $2.2 trillion in March 2020.

Schumer's success in managing the disparate wings of his caucus may be attributable to his having had a foot in both at one time or another. He first became politically active as a Harvard undergraduate in the late 1960s, working with the Young Democrats to promote the anti-Vietnam War candidacy of Minnesota Sen. Eugene McCarthy—whose success in the 1968 primaries prodded President Lyndon B. Johnson to decide not to pursue another term. Thirty years later, seeking a Senate seat for the first time, Schumer branded himself an "angry centrist." He was long the object of suspicion among progressives for exercising legislative clout on behalf of the financial services industry—a major economic force in his home state—with some in the progressive wing unhappy when he became the Senate Democratic leader in 2016. Soon afterward, grassroots activists—in no mood to offer anything but massive resistance to newly elected Trump— rallied outside Schumer's apartment in Brooklyn, waving signs reading, "Grow a spine, Chuck" and chanting, "Filibuster everything!"

More recently, though, Schumer sounded very much like a progressive. Going into the 2020 election, his priorities for the next Congress included many issues key to the party's left wing: "income and wealth inequality, climate [change], racial justice, health care, and improving our democracy." The latter was a reference to protecting voting rights, which took center stage amid efforts by Republican-controlled state legislatures nationwide to reduce voter access after Trump baselessly claimed widespread fraud caused his election loss. He also joined a leading progressive, Massachusetts Sen. Elizabeth Warren, in publicly pressing Biden to issue an executive order forgiving up to $50,000 in federal student loan debt. "I'm not busting my chops to become majority leader to do very little or nothing," Schumer told MSNBC prior to Election Day. There may be some fear behind his leftward lurch: There has been widespread speculation that Rep. Alexandria Ocasio-Cortez, a progressive icon, could challenge Schumer in the 2022 primary.

Notwithstanding his political beginnings in the movement that drove Johnson from the presidency, Schumer was once dubbed a "Jewish LBJ" by a colleague—an allusion to Johnson's hard-charging, arm-twisting days as majority leader in the 1950s. Indeed, the image that accompanied Schumer throughout the early part of his career—part brash partisan, part publicity hound—persists in some quarters. Former Senate Majority Leader Bob Dole once wisecracked that the most dangerous place in Washington was between Schumer and a TV camera. Fellow New York lawmakers upstaged by Schumer came up with a word to describe the experience: "Schumed."

But those who know him say that Schumer has mellowed. "People would say, 'Watch out: If there's a microphone, Sen. Schumer is going to be there,'" Michigan Sen. Debbie Stabenow, a member of Schumer's leadership team, told Politico, adding, "That's what used to be said, and I think he understands that [in] his role as leader, it's his job to make sure that others can get to the microphone." These days, Schumer often appears to have his cellphone attached to his head as he traverses the Capitol corridors, reaching out to as many 20 colleagues per day to counsel and cajole. If there is a rap on the onetime political enfant terrible, it is that he wants to be loved rather than feared: Another Democratic senator told Politico that Schumer is "not as iron-fisted, not as old-school, not as personally intimidating" as Reid was.

When LBJ became majority leader, he had spent a mere 18 years in the House and Senate. By comparison, Schumer comes to the job with 40 years' experience in those chambers—the most congressional experience of anyone ever to hold the position. First elected to the Senate in 1998 after nearly two decades in the House, Schumer began his rise in leadership as chair of the Democratic Senatorial Campaign Committee in the 2006 election cycle—helping his party take the majority, which it held for eight years. He ascended to the vice chairmanship of the caucus, its No. 3 post, and later assumed responsibility for policy and political messaging. When Reid announced his retirement as leader in early 2015, he anointed Schumer over another would-be successor: Whip Dick Durbin of Illinois. Reid's move ended a long behind-the-scenes rivalry between Schumer and Durbin, who for a dozen years were roommates in a Capitol Hill townhouse—an arrangement that inspired the sitcom "Alpha House."

Schumer grew up in and around Brooklyn's Flatbush neighborhood, where his father had a small exterminating business. He graduated first in his class at James Madison High School, also the alma mater of Vermont Sen. Bernie Sanders. Schumer graduated from Harvard College and Harvard Law School, but never practiced law. Months after his 1974 law school graduation, he won election as the youngest member of the New York Assembly since Theodore Roosevelt in the early 1880s.

In 1980, weeks before his 30th birthday, Schumer was elected to an open House seat. His congressional career was threatened almost as soon as it started. Because of the 1980 reapportionment, New York lost five House seats and, under the Voting Rights Act, the state was under pressure to create a second majority-minority district in Brooklyn. Consequently, Schumer's district was widely regarded as on the chopping block. Exhibiting the fundraising prowess that would later help him climb the leadership ladder, Schumer quickly accumulated a large treasury. It saved him: The neighboring district of a House member with more seniority but a smaller campaign bank account was eliminated instead.

Schumer obtained a seat on the now-renamed House Banking Committee, recognizing its importance to Wall Street—just across the East River from his home borough. He served on the Judiciary Committee and chaired its Crime Subcommittee, sponsoring the much-criticized 1994 crime bill that ramped up mass incarceration. That law has become a major target of progressives, with Biden during the 2020 campaign taking heat for his role as a senator in enacting it. At the time, both Biden and Schumer—who during that era labeled himself as a "tough on crime" Democrat—reflected a widely held sentiment among lawmakers. The 1994 law included a 10-year ban on assault weapons sales; efforts by gun control advocates to revive that provision have gone nowhere. Schumer was also House sponsor of the Brady Bill, which created waiting periods for handgun purchases. It became law over the strong opposition of the National Rifle Association.

In early 1997, Schumer considered seeking the governorship. But Republican Gov. George Pataki's strong job approval ratings instead persuaded him to run against GOP Sen. Alfonse D'Amato. D'Amato's initial win in 1980 had been considered something of a fluke, but he had won reelection twice despite the state's Democratic tilt—thanks in large measure to assiduous constituent service. Schumer faced primary opposition from a field that included Geraldine Ferraro, the 1984 vice presidential nominee. Having little difference with his rivals on social issues, Schumer focused on pocketbook concerns. He was much better financed and won the four-way primary with 51 percent of the vote; Ferraro got 26 percent. Late in the general election campaign, D'Amato suffered self-inflicted damage after it leaked out that, in a closed meeting before a Jewish group, he had called Schumer a "putzhead," Yiddish slang for "jerk." Despite being outspent by D'Amato, Schumer won 55%-44%.

The victory helped make him a "historical footnote," he told the New York Times, as he became the only member of Congress to vote against Clinton's impeachment three times: both on the House floor and in committee and then, after he was sworn in to the Senate, in the impeachment trial itself. In 2020, as Schumer unsuccessfully pressed McConnell and Senate Republicans to allow witnesses during Trump's first impeachment trial, they responded by noting that Schumer had opposed witnesses at Clinton's trial. Schumer countered that the witnesses contemplated in the Clinton trial had previously testified, unlike several he sought to summon in the Trump proceeding.

When outgoing first lady Hillary Clinton was elected in 2000 to succeed retiring New York Democrat Daniel Patrick Moynihan, many wondered how the ambitious Schumer would take to being overshadowed by a junior colleague regarded as a potential presidential candidate. "It took a while for us; we're both Type-A personalities," Schumer acknowledged in a Washington Post interview during Clinton's 2016 White House campaign. "We had to learn … that working together was a lot better than working separately." Schumer endorsed Clinton's unsuccessful 2008 bid for the presidential nomination. Her appointment as Barack Obama's secretary of State made Schumer indisputably New York's lead senator. When Democratic Gov. David Paterson dithered over appointing a successor to Clinton in 2009, Schumer weighed in on behalf of little-known upstate Rep. Kirsten Gillibrand. Schumer took his new colleague under his wing, helping lay the political foundation for Gillibrand to acquire national visibility.

In his first reelection bid, in 2004, Schumer raised more than $27 million and won 71%-24%, posting a record margin for a New York Senate race—until Gillibrand received 72 percent of the vote in 2012. With the Senate under Democratic control for only an 18-month period during his first term, Schumer again eyed a run for governor in 2006—with Pataki retiring. But the issue was settled when Reid named Schumer as DSCC chairman, with a seat on the influential Finance Committee added as an enticement to remain on Capitol Hill.

The task facing Schumer in 2006 was formidable: The lineup of Senate seats up for grabs left Republicans with more targets than Democrats. He demonstrated his pragmatic side as he worked on finding strong challengers. In Pennsylvania, Schumer—a strong supporter of abortion rights—recruited state Treasurer Bob Casey Jr., son of the late governor known for his vocal opposition to abortion; the younger Casey ousted Republican Sen. Rick Santorum. In Virginia, Schumer backed Jim Webb, a decorated Vietnam veteran who served as the Reagan administration's Navy secretary, over liberal lobbyist Harris Miller in the primary; Webb went on to defeat heavily favored GOP Sen. George Allen. Schumer's success in helping win a Democratic majority prompted Reid to ask him to stay on as head of the DSCC for the 2008 election season. On top of the six seats picked up in 2006, the Democrats saw a net gain of eight in 2008: A 45-seat minority had become a 59-seat majority in the span of just over two years. Seldom had one senator made such a difference in the partisan composition of the body.

Schumer remains heavily involved in overseeing the DSCC, and the 2020 recruitment of candidates that produced the renewed Democratic majority reflected his strategy of earlier years. Even as former Colorado Gov. John Hickenlooper was pursuing a long-shot bid for the presidential nomination, Schumer spoke with him repeatedly and urged him to run for Senate. Hickenlooper, a centrist, ultimately made the switch, and the DSCC endorsed him—to the unhappiness of others in the primary. Former state House Speaker Andrew Romanoff, challenging Hickenlooper from the left, complained publicly of the DSCC putting pressure on consultants not to work with him. Hickenlooper won the primary and ousted Republican incumbent Cory Gardner. Schumer also spent four months persuading Raphael Warnock, pastor of Atlanta's Ebenezer Baptist Church, to run for a Georgia Senate seat. Warnock's victory in early 2021 was a key to the Democrats' new narrow majority.

After the Democrats' success in 2006 elevated Reid to majority leader, he created the position of vice chair of the Democratic Caucus for Schumer—effectively making the New Yorker a confidant. After the 2010 elections, in which Democrats lost a half-dozen seats, Reid named Schumer chair the Democratic Policy and Communications Center, tasked with sharpening the party's appeal to the middle class. The pragmatism he displayed in these roles won Schumer strong support among party moderates. After Democrats lost the Senate majority in 2014, several moderates urged Schumer to challenge Reid, according to Politico. But Schumer rebuffed their pleas. "Reid made me," Schumer is reported to have told them. Four months later, Reid announced his retirement and anointed Schumer as his successor.

Several months into his leadership, Schumer won praise for holding his caucus together during the July 2017 debate over repealing the Affordable Care Act: Combined with splits in the GOP ranks, Democratic unity stymied efforts by Trump and McConnell to kill Obamacare. Less than three years earlier, after the Democrats' drubbing at the polls in 2014, Schumer created controversy when he gave a speech chastising his party for pushing the Affordable Care Act at the beginning of the Obama administration—rather than focusing on jobs and income growth. "Unfortunately, Democrats blew the opportunity the American people gave them," Schumer said, while making clear he still backed Obama's signature legislative achievement. "We took their mandate and put all of our focus on the wrong problem: health care reform."

Schumer was a key congressional ally for Obama, but they had some highly visible differences. In late 2016, as Obama was leaving office, Schumer led the effort to override his veto of a bill allowing families of 9/11 victims to sue Saudi Arabia for possible involvement in the World Trade Center attacks: It was the only time Congress overrode an Obama veto. A year earlier, when Obama sought "fast track" negotiating authority to expedite a 12-nation Pacific trade deal, Schumer opposed it. "I don't believe in these agreements anymore," he told the Wall Street Journal. "I've changed." In fact, Schumer has been a skeptic of trade deals since at least 1993, when he voted against the North American Free Trade Agreement in the House. Schumer was also among just nine Senate Democrats in early 2020 to vote against the revised version of NAFTA negotiated by Trump—the U.S.-Mexico-Canada Agreement. Schumer said he was voting against the new pact because "it does not address climate change, the greatest threat facing the planet." It was widely seen as part of his effort to head off a possible primary challenge from Ocasio-Cortez, an author of the "Green New Deal."

Trump abandoned pursuit of the Pacific trade deal after taking office; in 2018, in a rare policy accord with Trump, Schumer told a New York radio station, "I'm closer to him on trade than I was to either Obama, a Democrat, or [George W.] Bush, a Republican, because we've got to get tougher on China." Trump sent Schumer a private note thanking him and suggesting they work together on the issue. But, just weeks later, Trump was calling Schumer names on Twitter after the senator criticized the president for withdrawing from the Iran nuclear agreement negotiated by the Obama administration. "Senator Cryin' Chuck Schumer fought hard against the Bad Iran Deal, even going at it with President Obama, & then Voted AGAINST it! Now he says I should not have terminated the deal," Trump wrote.

Trump labeled him "Cryin' Chuck" in the first weeks of his administration, after Schumer teared up at a news conference while criticizing the president's effort to ban citizens from some Muslim-majority nations from entering the U.S. Trump sneered: "I'm going to ask him who is his acting coach." In 2015, Schumer voted against the Iran deal, saying decreased sanctions would enable Iran to eventually obtain a nuclear weapon. But he did not actively lobby against it, and his vote was viewed as a bow to the politics of New York, whose Jewish population is the nation's largest. In criticizing Trump's decision to withdraw from the pact, Schumer argued that "pulling out precipitously without our allies involved does not achieve any of the goals we need to achieve and hurts Americans in different ways."

Such was the roller-coaster relationship between the two tough-talking New York natives. Their paths had been intertwined since Trump, as a real estate developer, was a frequent Democratic donor. He contributed to Schumer's campaigns and held a fundraiser at his Florida estate when Schumer chaired the DSCC in 2008. That relationship had clearly turned toxic before the end of Trump's term. "I've known you for many years, but I never knew how bad a Senator you were for the state of New York until I became President," Trump wrote in an April 2020 letter to Schumer, weeks after Democrats' first effort to convict the president on articles of impeachment. Nine months later, hours after the storming of the Capitol, Schumer declared in a floor speech, "This will be a stain on our country not so easily washed away—the final, terrible, indelible legacy of the 45th President of the United States and undoubtedly our worst." A day later, Schumer called for Trump's removal—via the 25th Amendment or impeachment—less than two weeks before the president was due to leave office.

Just months into his presidency, Trump—to the visible discomfiture of GOP congressional leaders—sided with Schumer by backing a three-month extension of the federal debt ceiling. For the White House, it facilitated a $15 billion aid package for hurricane victims. For Schumer, it pushed further action on the debt ceiling to the end of 2017—when it would converge with a government funding deadline and give Schumer and his House counterpart, Rep. Nancy Pelosi, increased leverage negotiating key issues.

This era of good feeling did not last. When Schumer and Pelosi emerged from a dinner with Trump saying there was a deal to protect Dreamers—immigrants brought to the U.S. illegally as children—from deportation, White House officials put out the word that the two Democrats had gone beyond what Trump had accepted. Several weeks later, Trump sniped via Twitter: "'Chuck and Nancy' … want illegal immigrants flooding into our Country unchecked, are weak on Crime and want to substantially RAISE Taxes. I don't see a deal!"

In January 2018, Schumer led Senate Democrats into a government shutdown, insisting a spending bill include protections for 1.8 million Dreamers. The shutdown ended after just three days, as Democratic moderates seeking reelection in red states feared the wrath of voters. Schumer's handling of the matter spurred grumbling among his caucus' progressive wing, as activists again demonstrated in front of his Brooklyn apartment. But nearly a year later, Schumer and Pelosi—newly restored as House speaker—were the political winners in a record 35-day government shutdown, triggered by Trump's refusal to sign a bill without funding for his wall on the southern border. Schumer and Pelosi's united front helped keep Democratic moderates from bolting; Trump relented after polls showed the White House taking the brunt of voters' blame for the protracted shutdown.

Schumer has been involved with immigration policy since his time on the House Judiciary Committee, when he contributed key provisions to immigration laws passed in 1986 and 1990. In 2013, he was a member of the bipartisan "Gang of Eight" that crafted a comprehensive immigration compromise. It passed the Senate in July 2013, with 14 Republicans joining the entire Democratic Caucus in backing it, but the Republican-controlled House refused to take it up. In January 2018, Schumer—as part of the deal to end the three-day government shutdown—won a commitment from McConnell to hold a floor debate on immigration. Schumer held his caucus together: 46 of 49 Senate Democrats voted for a compromise that contained a path to citizenship for Dreamers and gave Trump $25 billion for border security. But just eight Republicans backed it; the legislation fell a half-dozen votes short of the 60 votes needed to advance.

When Schumer took over the Senate Democrats' top post, the relationship between the chamber's two party leaders had little place to go but up: By most accounts, it had reached a nadir during the eight years in which McConnell and Reid overlapped. But McConnell and Schumer got off to a rocky start in January 2017, when the new Democratic leader cast one of only six Democratic votes against Trump's choice for Transportation secretary, Elaine Chao—McConnell's wife. "She would not commit to spending money on transportation," Schumer later told the New York Times.

Schumer faced his first major test as leader when Trump, days after taking office, nominated federal Judge Neil Gorsuch to the Supreme Court. Schumer worked to restrain hard-line members of his caucus still fuming over McConnell's refusal to hold hearings or a vote on Obama's high court nominee for the seat, Judge Merrick Garland, during the final year of Obama's presidency. He privately urged his caucus to hold off on full-scale opposition until Gorsuch's record had been vetted via hearings. Once that process was complete, Schumer called for a filibuster.

In response, McConnell invoked the "nuclear option," changing Senate rules so that no presidential nominations would be subject to filibuster. It allowed Gorsuch to be confirmed in a Senate that the Republicans controlled by a four-seat margin while diminishing the leverage of the Democratic minority over future Supreme Court openings that followed under Trump. McConnell and other Republicans pointed a finger at Reid, who, in 2013, had executed a similar rules change in response to GOP resistance to Obama administration nominees. In that instance, the change covered presidential nominations except for the Supreme Court.

The Gorsuch showdown aside, there were signs of rapport between McConnell and Schumer early the following year. In February 2018, they negotiated a deal to raise the debt ceiling while providing an additional $300 billion over two years for defense and domestic programs. But the relationship faced intensified strain during the battle over the nomination of federal Judge Brett Kavanaugh to succeed retired Supreme Court Justice Anthony Kennedy later that year. "I will oppose Judge Kavanaugh's nomination with everything I have," Schumer tweeted after the nomination was unveiled. Schumer plotted procedural guerilla tactics with the Judiciary Committee's Democrats to obtain more Kavanaugh-related records. By the White House's count, Democrats interrupted Judiciary Chairman Chuck Grassley 44 times during the first hour of confirmation hearings. Later, amid negotiations with attorneys for Christine Blasey Ford—who had come forward with allegations that Kavanaugh had sexually assaulted her decades earlier—Grassley complained on Twitter: "I feel like I'm playing 2nd trombone in the judiciary orchestra, and Schumer is the conductor."

When the highly charged debate reached the Senate floor in October 2018, McConnell and Schumer all but called each other liars. Referring to McConnell, Schumer spoke of "the blatant falsehoods he tells day after day on this floor," shouting, "Give me a break." McConnell accused Schumer of "a mudslide of wild, uncorroborated accusations … each more outlandish than the last." It didn't stop there: In spring 2019, McConnell's aim of expediting installation of a new generation of conservative judges collided with Schumer's use of the same type of delaying tactics that McConnell had employed on judicial nominations during the Obama administration. Republicans again changed the rules—this time to slash debate on nominees below the Cabinet and Supreme Court levels from 30 hours to just two hours once cloture was invoked. Schumer accused McConnell of seeking to turn the Senate into a "conveyor belt" for judicial nominees and chided Senate Republicans for allowing McConnell's "debasement of the Senate."

In turn, McConnell charged Schumer had set the precedent for filibustering judges when, in 2001, he persuaded fellow Democrats to block a Bush appeals court nominee. "He started this whole thing," McConnell, said, glaring at Schumer. McConnell repeatedly raised the same issue against Schumer in late 2020, when—after having refused to consider the nomination of Garland eight months before the 2016 election—the majority leader pushed through Trump's nomination of federal Judge Amy Coney Barrett to succeed the late Supreme Court Justice Ruth Bader Ginsburg just two weeks before Election Day. "I hope our colleague from New York is happy with what he has built. I hope he is happy with where his ingenuity has gotten the Senate," McConnell declared with his back turned to Schumer and other Democrats in the chamber.

Schumer—with polls showing Senate Democrats likely to win back the majority—vowed retribution prior to the vote on Coney Barrett. "I want to be very clear with my Republican colleagues. You may win this vote … but you will never, never get your credibility back," he said, facing Republicans on the Senate floor. "And the next time the American people give Democrats a majority in this chamber, you will have forfeited the right to tell us how to run that majority."

Weeks before McConnell invoked his version of the nuclear option in 2017, Schumer expressed regret that Reid had opened the door to it four years earlier. "I will say it was a mistake," he told the New Yorker. He also expressed "the hope that the Republican leader and I can find a way to build a firewall around the legislative filibuster. … Let's find a way to further protect the 60-vote rule for legislation." However, Schumer subsequently dropped hints that he might join other Senate Democrats—including many in the caucus' progressive wing—who wanted to end or limit the filibuster if their party won Senate control. "Nothing is off the table," Schumer said repeatedly when asked about the issue prior to the 2020 election.

With the Republicans back in the minority after six years, McConnell sought to use his leverage to preserve the legislative filibuster—threatening in January 2021 to block agreement on rules of procedure needed for the 50-50 Senate to operate. Schumer dismissed what he called McConnell's "extraneous demand" as "unacceptable," noting the Republican leader had engineered two changes in the filibuster rule as majority leader. "What's fair is fair," Schumer asserted. McConnell gave in on the rules of operation—allowing the new Senate to formally organize—when it became clear there would be no immediate change in the filibuster rule; at least two members of the Democrats' centrist wing, Joe Manchin of West Virginia and Kyrsten Sinema of Arizona, expressed strong opposition to any change.

At home, Schumer easily won a third term in 2010, defeating Republican Jay Townsend, owner of a market research firm, 66%-32%. Running for a fourth term in 2016, Schumer overwhelmed Wendy Long, a Manhattan attorney active in conservative circles, 71-27%. After that reelection, Schumer headed off an intraparty battle in the Senate as he prepared to take over as leader. Not eager for a family squabble after the disappointing results of the 2016 elections, Schumer split the proverbial baby: Durbin stayed as whip, while Washington Sen. Patty Murray, who had been eyeing a run for whip, was elevated to the new post of assistant Democratic leader, No. 3 in the hierarchy. Asked about Schumer 18 months later, Durbin told Politico, "We've had good, honest conversations about our relationship, and it's never been better."

The Sept. 11, 2001 attacks hit home for Schumer: Growing up in Brooklyn in the 1960s, he watched the World Trade Center towers being constructed in the distance. When the hijacked planes struck the twin towers, Schumer immediately requested $20 billion in aid for New York, which President George W. Bush approved. In turn, the Bush administration got Schumer's help in rallying support for its centerpiece anti-domestic terrorism law, the Patriot Act. Later, working with Gillibrand, Schumer obtained federal funding to pay more than 22,000 claims filed by first responders sickened by toxins while working at ground zero. In 2019, the compensation fund covering these claims was extended for 75 years, with $10.2 billion allocated for the next decade.

Schumer's newly acquired clout as majority leader was on display in early 2021 when Congress enacted Biden's $1.9 trillion COVID-19 relief package. Tucked away in the measure was $2.75 billion to help private schools recover from the pandemic, which Schumer obtained after lobbying by leaders of New York City's Orthodox Jewish community—notwithstanding unhappiness on the part of the National Education Association and the chairs of congressional committees with jurisdiction over education. Conscious of New York's upstate/downstate divide, Schumer vowed when first elected to visit every one of the state's 62 counties each year—and a spokesman said he planned to continue doing so as majority leader. Such attention to constituents, along with an enhanced ability to deliver federal largesse, will buttress Schumer as he faces the potential of a competitive election race for the first time in nearly a quarter of a century. "He will be in a position to bring significant sums of money at a time when the state and the city need it," Hank Sheinkopf, a veteran Democratic political consultant, told The New York Times. "Money is what's going to talk in the next couple years in New York."

Kirsten Gillibrand (D)

Elected 2009, term expires 2024, 2nd full term, b. Dec 09, 1966; Albany, NY; Dartmouth College, B.A., 1988; University of California, Los Angeles, J.D., 1991; Catholic; Married (Jonathan Gillibrand); 2 children.

Elected Office: U.S. House, 2007-2009.

Professional Career: Practicing attorney, 1991-2006; Law Clerk, Judge Roger Miner, 1992; Special Counsel, Office of the Secretary, United States Department of Housing and Urban Development, 2000; Staff, Hillary Clinton Campaign for Senate.

DC Office: 478 RSOB 20510, 202-224-4451, Fax: 202-228-0282, gillibrand.senate.gov

State Offices: Albany, 518-431-0120; Buffalo, 716-854-9725; Lowville, 315-376-6118; Melville, 631-249-2825; New York, 212-688-6262; Rochester, 585-263-6250; Syracuse, 315-448-0470; Yonkers, 845-875-4585.

Committees: *Aging. Agriculture, Nutrition & Forestry*: Commodities, Risk Management & Trade; Food & Nutrition, Specialty Crops, Organics & Research; Livestock, Dairy, Poultry, Local Food Sys & Food Safety & Sec (Chmn). *Armed Services*: Cybersecurity; Emerging Threats & Capabilities; Personnel (Chmn). *Intelligence*.

Group Ratings

	ADA	ACLU	AFL-CIO	LCV	COC	HAFA	ACU	CFG	FRC
2020	-	92%	-	100%	-	9%	4%	-	-
2019	95%	C	88%	93%	13%	C	4%	26%	0%

Almanac Ratings 2019-2020

	Economy	Social	Foreign	Composite
Liberal	100%	100%	100%	100%
Conservative	0%	0%	0%	0%

Key Votes of the 116th Congress

1. EPA clean energy rules	Y	5. Russia sanctions	Y	9. Barr as Atty. General	N
2. U.S./Mex./Can. trade deal	N	6. Troops in SYR, AFG	N	10. Spending at the border	N/A
3. Cut unemployment benefits	N	7. Veto arms sales to Saudis	N/A	11. Coney Barrett to Sup. Ct.	N
4. Shelton to Fed Reserve	N	8. Defense $$$, veto override	Y	12. Electoral College objections	N

Election Results

Election	Name (Party)	Vote (%)		Cand. Spent	Ind. Exp. Support	Ind. Exp. Oppose
2018 General	Kirsten Gillibrand (D)	4,056,931	(67%)	$10,492,703	$47,032	$609,250
	Chele Farley (R)	1,998,220	(33%)	$1,370,237	$15,000	
2018 Primary	Kirsten Gillibrand (D)		(100%)			

Prior winning percentages: 2018 (67%), 2012 (72%), 2010 special (63%); House: 2008 (62%), 2006 (53%)

Before Democrat Kirsten Gillibrand, New York's junior senator, took her seat, it was held for half a century by political giants: Robert F. Kennedy, Daniel Patrick Moynihan, and, most recently, Hillary Rodham Clinton. That history, combined with the bandwidth of the New York media market, shoved Gillibrand into the national spotlight in 2009, when she was appointed to the seat after Clinton left to become secretary of State. After little more than a term as a moderate-to-conservative Democrat from a red House district from upstate, Gillibrand took a sharp turn to the left in the Senate—becoming an outspoken advocate for greater rights and protections for women and families, notably on the issue of sexual assault. That landed her in Time magazine's "100 Most Influential People in the World" issue in 2014. CBS' "60 Minutes" profiled Gillibrand in February 2018, dubbing her "the political face of the #MeToo movement."

So, it was little surprise when, in January 2019, Gillibrand announced she was joining the crowded contest for the 2020 Democratic presidential nomination—despite having just won a campaign for a second full Senate term during which she promised to serve the full six years. On CBS' "The Late Show with Stephen Colbert," she said, "I'm going to run for president of the United States because, as a young mom, I'm going to fight for other people's kid as hard as I would fight for my own."

Seven months later, her campaign was over. Despite Gillibrand's high profile on Capitol Hill, her presidential bid never really left the launching pad. She remained mired at barely 1 percent in national polls after struggling to raise money, despite a reputation as a prodigious fundraiser.

Unlike many of her Senate colleagues seeking the nomination, Gillibrand didn't receive much support from her home-state colleagues: Just one of the 21 Democrats in New York's House delegation endorsed her. During the first quarter of 2019, she raised only $3 million, the least among the half-dozen Senate Democrats in the race. To reach the donors threshold to qualify for the first debate in June, she was reduced to all but begging. "So please go to KirstenGillibrand.com and just send a dollar," she told a gathering in New Hampshire. "It will help me get to the debate stage." But once she got onto the stage, she failed to breakthrough.

Gillibrand's bid died in the same way as that of New Jersey Sen. Cory Booker, her neighbour just across the Hudson River: Both fell between the cracks in a contest defined by candidates running in the centrist and progressive lanes. While few could outflank Gillibrand on the left—the 2017 Almanac ratings pegged her as one of only two senators with a 100 percent liberal voting score—she nonetheless was viewed skeptically by many in the party's progressive wing. As a House member a decade earlier, Gillibrand was known for anti-immigration and pro-gun positions: She could never escape suspicions that her shift to the left had been fueled by opportunism, despite seeking to put the matter behind her with a combination of candor and contrition. In her "60 Minutes" appearance, Gillibrand said she was "ashamed" of some of her past positions, adding: "As I've gotten older, I've learned more about life. And sometimes you're wrong, and you've got to fix it. And if you're wrong, just admit it and move on."

Ironically, serving as "the political face of the #MeToo Movement" also impeded Gillibrand's presidential prospects. In late 2017, she became the first senator to call on a fellow Democrat, Al Franken of Minnesota, to step down amid allegations of inappropriate sexual behaviour. It set off a veritable stampede of similar calls from other Senate Democrats, prompting Franken to resign. But numerous Democrats, both inside and outside the Senate, later questioned whether Franken—who had built a reservoir of support among progressives for his pointed criticisms of President Donald Trump—had been given a fair chance to defend himself. And several prominent party donors accused Gillibrand of rushing to judgment and suggested she would have trouble raising money if she ran for president. Gillibrand offered no apologies. "We know there were donors who were angry about it," she told The New York Times after withdrawing from the race. But, referring to Franken's accusers, she added, "I wouldn't change what I did, because I would stand with those eight women again today."

Born Kirsten Rutnik in Albany, she comes from a politically wired family. Her father, Douglas Rutnik, is an attorney and lobbyist with close ties to several leading New York Republicans, including former Sen. Alfonse D'Amato—for whom Gillibrand interned in college. Her grandmother, Polly Noonan, was a prominent Democratic activist and long time companion of Albany Mayor Erastus Corning, who held that office for more than 40 years in the political machine run by Daniel O'Connell. Gillibrand attended the exclusive all-girls Emma Willard School in Troy, just across the Hudson River. She graduated from Dartmouth College, where she majored in Asian studies and attained fluency in Mandarin; she was among the first Dartmouth students to visit China after it was opened to students from the United States.

Gillibrand earned her law degree at the University of California, Los Angeles and spent most of the 1990s working for Davis, Polk & Wardwell, a prominent New York City-based firm. Her clients included tobacco giant Philip Morris, then the subject of criminal probes and civil lawsuits: Gillibrand helped defend the company against allegations that it lied about the existence of internal research on the health effects of smoking. Toward the end of the Clinton administration, she was a special counsel to Housing and Urban Development Secretary Andrew Cuomo, later governor of New York, and then joined another major New York law firm, Boies, Schiller & Flexner. (In early 2021, when Gov. Cuomo was accused of sexual harassment, Gillibrand reacted more cautiously than she had regarding Franken three years earlier: She ultimately called for Cuomo's resignation—but only in coordination with her senior in-state colleague, Majority Leader Chuck Schumer, and after a majority of the state's Democratic House delegation had already done so.)

Gillibrand raised money for Clinton's first Senate campaign in 2000, and five years later, she launched what appeared to be a quixotic campaign against four-term GOP Rep. John Sweeney in the upstate region where she had grown up. For the previous century, the district had elected Democrats only rarely; as late as August 2006, polls showed Sweeney with a solid lead. However, Gillibrand was aided by a national wave that swept Democrats into the majority and triumphed in one of that year's nastier races. Sweeney attacked her as a carpetbagger who actually lived in a New York City high-rise and contrasted his working-class background with her prep school pedigree. Gillibrand demanded that Sweeney release police reports from arrests in 1977 and 1978 and an automobile wreck in 2001. A week before the election, the Albany Times Union reported Sweeney's wife had called the police in late 2005 to complain the legislator was "knocking her around." Sweeney denied the report at first, but he later conceded the police had been called to his home. Gillibrand won 53%-47%.

Reflecting her district, she joined the Blue Dog Coalition, a group of conservative Democrats, and her voting record received a 100percent score from the National Rifle Association. Gillibrand boasted she kept two rifles under her bed and that, growing up in a family of hunters, she "always believed in protecting hunters' rights." (A decade later, she told "60 Minutes" she had been "wrong," adding: "What it's about is the power of the NRA and the greed of that industry. ...It is not about hunters' rights, it's about money.")She co-sponsored legislation denying amnesty and benefits to undocumented immigrants; in a 2007 interview, Gillibrand said you have to close the borders as a first step to right size immigration, according to CNN. Gillibrand's fundraising prowess, combined with her issue stances, paid off in 2008 as she defended her seat against former state GOP Chairman Sandy Treadwell—who spent nearly $6 million of his own money in the nation's most expensive House race that year. She won 62%-38%.

After that election, when Clinton became President-elect Barack Obama's choice for secretary of State, Gov. David Paterson seriously thought about appointing Caroline Kennedy, daughter of President John F. Kennedy, to succeed her. But after performing poorly in a New York Times interview and during an upstate "listening tour," Kennedy withdrew. Two days later, in January 2009, Paterson appointed Gillibrand—who, at 42, became the Senate's youngest member at the time.

The reaction from El Diario, New York City's dominant Spanish-language newspaper, was an unflattering photo of Gillibrand with the headline: "Anti-immigrante."Gillibrand quickly changed her stances that were out of step with the statewide Democratic electorate. The day after her appointment, at a rally in Harlem, she won applause by vowing flexibility on gun control. Gillibrand subsequently opposed legislation that would have allowed licensed gun owners to carry concealed firearms across state lines and repealed Washington D.C.'s tough gun laws; while in the House, she had supported a bill lifting gun restrictions in the nation's capital. Within two years, her NRA score grade went from "A" to "F."

At least three Democratic members of the New York House delegation—concerned over Gillibrand's past stances and piqued at being passed over for the appointment in favor of a colleague with less seniority—mulled challenging her in 2010. But, one by one, they dropped out. Gillibrand benefited from the help of two powerful patrons: Obama and Schumer, by then a member of the Senate Democratic leadership. The White House, fearing an expensive primary could cost Democrats a seat in 2010, mounted a full-court press, with the president lobbying would-be challengers to stay out. And Schumer—known for being less than thrilled during the years he had to share the spotlight with Clinton—seemed to delight in taking his new colleague under his wing. He pressed Senate leaders to give her the committee assignments she desired and introduced her to deep-pocketed donors.

Early in her tenure, Gillibrand and Schumer worked closely to enact the James Zadroga 9/11 Health and Compensation Act of 2010. It provided health care and compensation to first responders who became seriously ill after the 2001 terrorist attacks that destroyed Manhattan's World Trade Center. An initial allocation of $4.2 billion in 2011, followed by $7.4 billion in 2015, funded more than 22,000 claims to those sickened by toxins while working at ground zero. Gillibrand and Schumer pushed legislation, enacted in July 2019, to guarantee the law would be funded for the next seven decades, with $10.2 billion set aside over the next 10 years.

Gillibrand didn't face serious GOP competition for the final two years of Clinton's term, and she won63%-35%—despite 2010 being a rough year for Democrats nationally. In 2012, she was up for a full six-year term. Attorney Wendy Long got the GOP nod. Gillibrand outspent Long by nearly 20-1 and won, 72%-26%—a record margin in a New York Senate race. In 2018, Gillibrand largely ignored her opponent, private equity executive Chele Farley, on her way to a 67%-33% victory. She finished the campaign with$10 million left in her treasury,later transferred to help start her presidential bid.

Gillibrand began burnishing her national image early on. In 2012, she founded a political action committee, Off the Sidelines, to mobilize female candidates. She gained a reputation as a fundraising powerhouse: In the three succeeding election cycles, Off the Sidelines distributed more to federal candidates than any other Senate leadership PAC: more than $1.7 million, according to the nonpartisan Center for Responsive Politics.

Playing off the PAC's name, Gillibrand in 2014 published a memoir: "Off the Sidelines: Speak up, Be Fearless, and Change Your World," about her efforts to recruit women into politics. The New York Times bestseller deviated from the usual tomes on the subject by offering self-help and diet advice; it drew attention when Gillibrand wrote about unnamed male colleagues commenting on her weight. In the book, she also confronted the lurking doubts about her intellectual heft that accompanied her arrival in the Senate, acknowledging she was seen by some as a "parakeet" without original thoughts. She said she sought to learn from such critics rather than exact revenge. "I was new at my job, and I needed to address my inexperience and weaknesses head-on," she wrote.

The first issue to bring Gillibrand widespread attention was her call for repeal of the "don't ask, don't tell" policy barring openly gay military service members. It was another about-face from her House tenure. She introduced legislation in July 2009, when interest in repeal of "don't ask, don'tell" was lagging: Its leading champion, Massachusetts Sen. Ted Kennedy, was dying of cancer. Gillibrand lobbied colleagues, pushed for hearings, and set up a website with videos of LBGTQ veterans telling their stories. "If you care about national security, if you care about our military readiness, then you will repeal this corrosive policy," she said in an emotional floor speech. It became law at the end of 2010, earning her widespread praise from progressive and gay rights groups.

In 2012, Gillibrand introduced the Family and Medical Leave Act to guarantee workers at least two-thirds pay for up to 12 weeks annually for health-related leave. The bill made little legislative progress, but served to tout the national Democratic Party's stance on the issue. During the 2020 campaign, she expanded it into a "Family Bill of Rights," including paid family leave as well as other proposals to reduce financial strains on parents of young children.

As the party's progressive wing emerged as a force, Gillibrand not only co-sponsored its legislative touchstones, "Medicare for All" and the "Green New Deal," she also advocated doing away with Immigration and Customs Enforcement, which she told CNN had become a "deportation force." A decade earlier, she voted in the House to increase funding for ICE to work with local law enforcement to increase deportations. Described by Politico early in her Senate career as the "go-to advocate for the financial services industry," Gillibrand by 2018 was describing herself as a "populist," as she co-sponsored Vermont Sen. Bernie Sanders' legislation for a tax on stock market transactions.

Gillibrand's involvement with the issue with which she is most identified began in 2013, when she introduced a bill to remove the military chain of command from handling sexual assault cases. It pitted her against Missouri Democrat Claire McCaskill. As Armed Services Committee members, both aggressively lobbied colleagues on behalf of rival approaches. Gillibrand's proposal fell five votes short of overcoming a Republican filibuster in March 2014; McCaskill's more incremental alternative, to reform the process while keeping responsibility within the chain of command, passed the Senate unanimously. Gillibrand stood firm, but her approach fell 10 votes short when it came up again in 2015.

Her long-term persistence on this front ultimately yielded results: In early 2021, amid a continuing increase in military rapes, a bipartisan majority of more than 60 senators— including most members of the Armed Services Committee— lined up behind legislation for Gillibrand's plan to move responsibility for the matter to independent prosecutors. President Joe Biden— in a switch from both the Obama and Trump administrations— also supported the change. "Since I first started working to reform military justice in 2013, we have twice been blocked by the filibuster standard of 60 votes, despite having a majority of the Senate in support," Gillibrand told Roll Call, adding "This is a defining moment."

Lee Zeldin (R)

Elected 2014, 4th term, b. Jan 30, 1980; East Meadow, NY; State University of NY - Albany, B.A., 2001; Albany Law School, J.D., 2003; Jewish; Married (Diana Zeldin); 2 children (twins).

Military Career: U.S. Army 23-27; U.S. Army Reserves 2007-pres. (Iraq)

Elected Office: NY Senate, 2011-2014.

Professional Career: Practicing attorney.

DC Office: 2441 RHOB 20515, 202-225-3826, zeldin.house.gov

State Offices: Patchogue, 631-289-1097.

Committees: *Financial Services*: Housing, Community Development & Insurance; Nat'l Security, International Development & Monetary Policy. *Foreign Affairs*: Intern'l Dev't, Intern'l Orgs & Global Corporate Social Impact; Middle East, North Africa & Global Counterterrorism.

Group Ratings

	ADA	ACLU	AFL-CIO	LCV	COC	HAFA	ACU	CFG	FRC
2020	**	23%	**	24%	-	93%	67%	**	-
2019	15%	C	38%	28%	82%	C	68%	83%	91%

Almanac Ratings 2019-2020

	Economy	Social	Foreign	Composite
Liberal	38%	33%	11%	28%
Conservative	62%	67%	89%	72%

Key Votes of the 116th Congress

1. U.S./Mex./Can. trade deal	Y	5. Russia sanctions	Y	9. Firearms background checks	N
2. First Coronavirus response	Y	6. Troops in Syria	Y	10. Spending at the border	Y
3. HEROES Act	N	7. Veto arms sales to Saudis	N	11. Marijuana liberalized rules	N
4. CASH Act	Y	8. Defense $$$, veto override	N	12. Electoral College objections	Y

Election Results

Election	Name (Party)	Vote (%)	Cand. Spent	Ind. Exp. Support	Ind. Exp. Oppose
2020 General	Lee Zeldin (R)	205,715 (55%)	$7,901,270	$213,323	$4,220,904
	Nancy Goroff (D)	169,294 (45%)	$8,130,849	$1,380,579	$4,145,991

Prior winning percentages: 2018 (52%), 2016 (58%), 2014 (53%)

Republican Lee Zeldin, elected in 2014 against a Democratic incumbent, brought a burst of energy and occasional independence to the House. In a district that remained competitive and facing a well-financed challenger in 2018, he was responsive to local sentiments, including his opposition to Republican tax cuts that capped the deduction for state and local taxes employed by his affluent and highly taxed constituents, which adversely affected New York. In April 2021, he announced his candidacy for governor, with attacks on Gov. Andrew Cuomo and "one-party Democrat rule."

Zeldin was raised in Shirley New York and received his bachelor's degree from the State University at Albany before earning his law degree at Albany Law School. He received an Army commission as a second lieutenant, spent four years on active duty, and deployed to Iraq in 2006 with an infantry battalion of paratroopers from the 82nd Airborne Division; he remained in the Army Reserve as a major. Zeldin opened a law practice, and in 2010 won election to the state Senate, where he led an effort to fund a pilot program for soldiers suffering from post-traumatic stress disorder. He also led a bid to scale back a transportation-authority payroll tax and sought to end fees for saltwater fishing.

Democratic Rep. Tim Bishop, who had served since 2003, defeated Zeldin in 2008, 58%-42%, but the party gap subsequently narrowed. In his second challenge to Bishop, Zeldin said he would no longer be dragged down by voter fatigue with George W. Bush's presidency and the Iraq War. The American Action Network and the National Republican Congressional Committee spent nearly

$4 million accusing Bishop of being a corrupt Washington insider. Bishop aired two ads to tell voters he was not under FBI investigation for helping a donor secure a fireworks permit for a bar mitzvah. Bishop attacked Zeldin for accepting contributions from industries that he said were polluting New York. Zeldin scored a key endorsement from Newsday, which said Bishop "does not have a significant voice in Congress" and that "Long Island needs this seat at the Republican table." Zeldin got 53 percent of the vote and won with surprising ease.

Zeldin kept a busy pace. In 2015, the House gave voice-vote approval to his amendment to permit states to refuse to comply with Common Core education standards; it subsequently became law. He worked with Democratic Rep. Sean Patrick Mahoney of New York to gain approval of their Safe Bridges Act as part of the highway bill in 2015. Their proposal restored funding to the highway trust fund specifically for bridges and overpasses. On the Financial Services Committee in 2018, Zeldin won unanimous House passage of his bill to clarify rules for banks to create "living wills" for large financial institutions that might be facing jeopardy.

As co-chairman of the House Republican Israel Caucus—with David Kustoff of Tennessee, he is one of two Jewish Republicans in the House—Zeldin said President Barack Obama's conflicts with Israeli Prime Minister Benjamin Netanyahu were an opportunity for House Republicans to increase their Jewish ranks. "President Obama is operating as if he doesn't grasp who truly are America's friends and enemies in that region of the world," he told Bloomberg News. Zeldin defended as "completely true" the comments by President Donald Trump in August 2017 that blamed "both sides" for the violent protests in Charlottesville Virginia. As ranking Republican on the Foreign Affairs Subcommittee on Oversight and Investigation, Zeldin said his goal was to "treat our adversaries as our adversaries, and our friends as our friends."

National Democrats have designated Zeldin as a top target. In 2016, the strategy of their challenger, Anna Throne-Holst, was to link Zeldin to Trump. That might not have been wise, given Trump's double-digit victory in the district. Both candidates were lavishly funded, with more than $5 million available for each side. Zeldin won, 59%-41%.

In 2018, Zeldin faced Perry Gershon, a real estate financier and political newcomer, who attacked Zeldin for his vote to repeal the Affordable Care Act and fought for what he called traditional "values." Zeldin continued his embrace of Trump and the president's allies, including a fundraising event that featured Steve Bannon, a former top Trump aide. After Zeldin in November 2017 voted against the Republican tax cuts, claiming they would have an adverse impact on New York, Speaker Paul Ryan canceled his appearance at a fundraising event. Gershon spent $5.1 million—including nearly $2 million of self-funding—to $4.8 million for the incumbent. Zeldin had his closest win, 52%-47%.

Zeldin faced another high-dollar challenger running as an outsider in 2020. Democrat Nancy Goroff, a physical organic chemist who chaired the chemistry department at Stony Brook University, said that she brought her scientific credentials to seek legislative steps to address the corona virus pandemic. She had been an active contributor to Democratic candidates and liberal causes. Goroff won the nomination, 36%-35%, against Gershon. Goroff out-spent Zeldin, $8.1 million to $7.9 million; the two national parties and their allies spent another $10 million on the contest. Slow vote-counting required a month to declare a winner, though Zeldin won relatively comfortably, 55%-45%.

Regardless of the outcome of sexual-harassment charges against Cuomo, recent state wide contests have shown that Republicans will face an uphill contest against virtually any nominee. Zeldin will have some advantages if he faces a GOP primary, including his experience in Albany and his fundraising ability. Given potential obstacles in redistricting, making an "up or out" move on the political ladder might be good timing for him.

NY-1: Eastern Long Island

Cook Partisan Voting Index: R+6

Population		Race and Ethnicity		Income	
Total	713,168	White	85.50%	Median Income	$101,701
Land area (sq. miles)	650	Black	5.20%	District Income Rank	28
Pop/ sq mi	1,097.15	Latino	17.90%	Poverty Rate	7.00%
Born in State	77.70%	Asian	4.10%	With health insurance	95.20%
		Two or more races	2.10%	Cash public assistance	2.00%
Age Groups		Other	3.10%	Food stamp/SNAP	5.60%
Under 18	21.00%				
18-34	20.70%	**Education**		**Work**	
35-64	40.20%	H.S grad or less	35.50%	White Collar	43.60%
Over 64	18.00%	Some college	26.20%	Sales and Service	38.20%
		College Degree, 4 yr	20.40%	Blue Collar	18.20%
Military		Post grad	17.90%	Government	20.80%
Veteran/ Active Duty	5.30%				

2020 Pres. Vote	Trump	198,826	(51%)	Biden	182,793	(47%)	
2016 Pres. Vote	Trump	183,233	(54%)	Clinton	141,900	(42%)	Johnson 7,217 (2%)

Brookhaven: Long Island—"the Island" to most New Yorkers—is the largest and most populous island in the mainland United States. It stretches 118 miles, from the two-century-old Montauk Point lighthouse on a crumbling bluff to Fort Hamilton at the foot of the Verrazano-Narrows Bridge. Ranging from 12 to 20 miles wide, Long Island is ringed by gentle hills and cliffs above Long Island Sound and sand-spit beaches that front the Atlantic Ocean. Including the populations of Brooklyn and Queens, some 7.7 million people live there, more than in all but 12 states. Brooklyn, at the island's western end, is urban and thickly settled, while the Hamptons in the east are manicured countryside, preserved as a playground for the New York elite. For trend-watchers: In July 2020, the Wall Street Journal reported that real estate prices in the Hamptons that summer reached an all-time high—including a 25 percent increase from a year earlier, as "wealthy New Yorkers flooded the market during the pandemic lockdown."

More important economically—and politically—are the areas immediately west of the Hamptons: the suburbs created in the post-World War II migration out of the city. Developers looking for cheaper land for aircraft factories, shopping centers, subdivisions and office parks found them first in Nassau County, just east of Queens, and then farther out in Suffolk County. Suffolk attracted young families of Irish and Italian descent looking for more space and less crime. More recently the county has been attracting Latinos, who have grown to 20 percent of the population, compared with 9 percent Black in Suffolk. The island's economy soured as defense plants were decimated by the end of the Cold War, and young people fled older suburbs for jobs elsewhere. The waters surrounding Long Island have become filled with wind-power facilities. The South Fork project is scheduled to deliver power to the Long Island Power Authority by the end of 2022, which would be the first that is operational, Offshore Magazine reported in July 2019. Revolutionary Wind, a 15-turbine wind farm that will run from Rhode Island to Montauk, has a 2023 target date for completion.

The 1st Congressional District of New York consists of the eastern end of Long Island and Suffolk, with about half of the county's population. It runs as far west as Smithtown on the North Shore and Patchogue on the South Shore. It includes Shelter Island, between the north and south forks of Long Island's "fishtail," and Plum Island. It takes in Brookhaven National Laboratory, a physics research lab. Also in the 1st are the Hamptons and most of Fire Island National Seashore, the only federal wilderness area in New York state and a magnet for gay vacationers for decades. Suffolk County was long one of the most conservative parts of New York—Richard Nixon won 70 percent of the vote here in 1972—though that changed when the district voted solidly for Democrat Al Gore in 2000. In 2016, Donald Trump was popular here, with a 52%-45% win, a spread of 41,000 votes in Suffolk. It was the only county, other than Staten Island, that Trump won in New York City or its tri-state suburbs. His tough talk on crime and immigration had local appeal. But the tide shifted again in 2020, when Trump won Suffolk by only 232 votes of 770,000 that were cast.

Andrew Garbarino (R)

Elected 2020, 1st term, b. Sep 27, 1984; West Islip, NY; George WA University, B.A.; Hofstra University School of Law, J.D.; Roman Catholic; Single.

Elected Office: Assembly Member, NY State Assembly, District 7, 2013-2021; Minority Joint Conference Vice Chair, NY State Assembly.

DC Office: 1516 LHOB 20515, 202-225-7896, Fax: 202-226-2279, garbarino.house.gov

State Offices: Massapequa Park, 516-541-4225.

Committees: *Homeland Security*: Cybersecurity, Infrastructure Protection & Innovation (RMM); Emergency Preparedness, Response & Recovery. *Small Business*: Economic Growth, Tax & Capital Access; Innovation, Entrepreneurship & Workforce Development.

Election Results

Election	Name (Party)	Vote (%)		Cand. Spent	Ind. Exp. Support	Ind. Exp. Oppose
2020 General	Andrew Garbarino (R)	177,379	(53%)	$1,606,010	$135,951	$5,888,917
	Jackie Gordon (D)	154,246	(46%)	$4,232,476	$2,669,067	$4,984,840
2020 Primary	Andrew Garbarino (R)	17,462	(64%)			
	Mike LiPetri (R)	9,867	(36%)			

Republican Andrew Garbarino won the open seat of retiring Republican Rep. Pete King. Garbarino brought experience on financial issues from serving in the state Assembly. He defeated Jackie Gordon, a member of the Babylon Town Council and former high school guidance counselor. King, who served 28 years in the House, had chaired the Homeland Security Committee and also was influential on financial issues.

A native of Long Island, Garbarino received a bachelor's degree from George Washington University, where he majored in history and classical humanities. He got his law degree from Hofstra University, with an expertise in tax law. He worked at his family's law firm in Sayville, in Suffolk County, and owned some small businesses.

At age 27, Garbarino was elected to the state Assembly in 2012 and served eight years. He was the ranking minority member of the Insurance Committee and served on the executive committee of the National Council of Insurance Legislators, where he worked on legislation to preserve state control of insurance policy.

After King announced his retirement in November 2019, Garbarino expected to defer to more senior Republicans in the Assembly who would seek the seat. "They deserved it," he told City & State New York. But those prospective candidates failed to step forward. With "some convincing" by Rep. Lee Zeldin from the neighboring district in Suffolk County, Garbarino added, he saw that he "could accomplish just as much in Washington as he did in Albany, but on a bigger scale."

In the Republican primary, Michael LiPetri, a first-term member of the state Assembly, referred to William Garbarino, his opponent's father, as the "Islip party boss." Andrew Garbarino said that the 29-year-old LiPetri had originally registered as a Democrat. Garbarino won the primary with 64 percent of the vote.

Democrat Gordon, a native of Jamaica, styled herself as "somebody different" and "challenging the old boy's network." A retired lieutenant colonel in the Army Reserve and a battle captain during the U.S. invasion of Iraq, she told City & State that she sought to identify herself to voters as somebody who "will understand the challenges that they have to go through." In an editorial endorsing Gordon, the Long Island Herald slammed Garbarino and his campaign for his "focus on the fear factor, raising the specter of non-existent bogeymen." It added that he would reinforce the "partisan divisiveness" of President Donald Trump.

In the general election, Gordon outspent Garbarino by nearly 3-to-1. His modest fundraising "alarmed" House Republican campaign officials, according to the Cook Political Report. The two national parties and related groups spent more than $13 million on the campaign, with a slight spending edge on behalf of Gordon.

A Democratic ad attacked Garbarino for "serving the special interests" in Albany. Republicans responded with an ad claiming that Gordon voted herself "perks and pay hikes" on the Babylon council. Garbarino won, 53%-46%. He nearly doubled the total for Gordon in Nassau County, which cast nearly one-third of the vote. In Suffolk County, Gordon led by 3,000 votes—not nearly enough to close the gap.

In the House, Garbarino took the ranking Republican position on the Homeland Security Subcommittee on Cyber security, Infrastructure Protection and Innovation.

NY-2: South-Central Long Island   Cook Partisan Voting Index: R+5

Population		Race and Ethnicity		Income	
Total	698,974	White	73.90%	Median Income	$108,725
Land area (sq. miles)	182	Black	10.00%	District Income Rank	18
Pop/ sq mi	3,840.31	Latino	23.60%	Poverty Rate	5.90%
Born in State	75.60%	Asian	4.10%	With health insurance	96.20%
		Two or more races	2.60%	Cash public assistance	2.00%
Age Groups		Other	9.50%	Food stamp/SNAP	6.30%
Under 18	21.10%				
18-34	21.90%	**Education**		**Work**	
35-64	40.80%	H.S grad or less	38.50%	White Collar	38.90%
Over 64	16.20%	Some college	28.90%	Sales and Service	41.50%
Military		College Degree, 4 yr	19.10%	Blue Collar	19.70%
Veteran/ Active Duty	4.80%	Post grad	13.60%	Government	17.10%

2020 Pres. Vote	Trump	183,204	(51%)	Biden	168,779	(47%)
2016 Pres. Vote	Trump	165,908	(53%)	Clinton	137,680	(44%)

Islip: At the end of World War II, Suffolk County was largely given over to potato fields. It was also directly in the path of one of the major suburban migrations of our day. On the highways that Robert Moses built to connect his parks to the middle-class parts of New York City came tens of thousands of young veterans and their families, forsaking the row-house neighborhoods where they had grown up for comparatively spacious lots and single-family houses. The first wave of post war migration moved into Nassau County, starting in 1947, when 300 families moved into 750-square-foot houses that sold for $6,990, with no money down for veterans. The location was Levittown—America's first mass-produced suburb, where delivery trucks dropped off piles of prefabricated materials 60 feet apart, to be picked up by roving teams of specialized workers with power tools. By the time the final house was sold for $9,500 in 1951, Levittown, a former potato field, had become synonymous with instant suburbanization. This wave represented a cross-section of all but the poorest New Yorkers: almost half Catholic, about one-quarter Jewish, and one-quarter Protestant. As Long Island developed its own employment base, the next wave of migration was more Catholic and less Jewish, more blue-collar (aircraft manufacturers were big Suffolk employers) and less white-collar, more Democratic in ancestral politics.

The 2nd Congressional District of New York takes in Massapequa and Levittown, where the median sale price of a home increased in 2020 to $515,000. These areas in the eastern part of Nassau County are generally Republican, but only about one-third of the district's population resides in Nassau. Most of its residents live in more Democratic areas in the southwest corner of Suffolk County, where the district stretches from Amityville and Babylon east through Bay Shore and Islip to Sayville and Bayport—one community after another strung out along Sunrise Highway. The district takes in Brentwood, which is two-thirds Hispanic and has a per capita income a bit more than half the average in Suffolk, though total household income is 80 percent of the Suffolk average. In July 2020, police arrested the alleged leader of the MS-13 gang, following an earlier indictment describing a vast criminal enterprise that left what Pro Public a earlier described as "killing fields" of immigrant teenagers, especially in Brentwood. Near Islip, plans to expand MacArthur Airport to include international service were abandoned, though the airport has increased its domestic service. Between the Ronkonkoma rail station and the airport, a $1 billion development is underway, including a hotel and retail shops, though plans for a large sports arena were downsized.

In 2020, President Donald Trump won the district, 51%-47%, a dip from his 53%-44% win in 2016.

Thomas Suozzi (D)

Elected 2016, 3rd term, b. Aug 31, 1962; Glen Cove, NY; Boston College, B.S., 1984; Fordham University School of Law, J.D., 1989; Roman Catholic; Married (Helene Suozzi); 3 children.

Elected Office: Glen Cove Mayor, 1994-2001; Nassau County Executive, 2002-2009.

Professional Career: CPA; Practicing Attorney.

DC Office: 214 CHOB 20515, 202-225-3335, Fax: 202-225-4669, suozzi.house.gov

State Offices: Huntington, 631-923-4100; Little Neck, 718-631-0400.

Committees: *Ways & Means*: Oversight; Select Revenue Measures.

Group Ratings

	ADA	ACLU	AFL-CIO	LCV	COC	HAFA	ACU	CFG	FRC
2020	**	79%	**	100%	-	0%	7%	**	-
2019	90%	C	95%	97%	67%	C	8%	18%	5%

Almanac Ratings 2019-2020

	Economy	Social	Foreign	Composite
Liberal	100%	100%	80%	94%
Conservative	0%	0%	20%	6%

Key Votes of the 116th Congress

1. U.S./Mex./Can. trade deal Y	5. Russia sanctions Y	9. Firearms background checks Y
2. First Coronavirus response Y	6. Troops in Syria Y	10. Spending at the border Y
3. HEROES Act Y	7. Veto arms sales to Saudis Y	11. Marijuana liberalized rules Y
4. CASH Act Y	8. Defense $$$, veto override Y	12. Electoral College objections N

Election Results

Election	Name (Party)	Vote (%)		Cand. Spent	Ind. Exp. Support	Ind. Exp. Oppose
2020 General	Thomas Suozzi (D)	208,555	(56%)	$2,156,235	$40,010	$42,919
	George Santos (R)	161,931	(43%)	$332,625	$10,154	
2020 Primary	Thomas Suozzi (D)	36,812	(67%)			
	Melanie D'Arrigo (D)	14,269	(26%)			
	Michael Weinstock (D)	4,284	(8%)			

Prior winning percentages: 2018 (59%), 2016 (53%)

Tom Suozzi, elected to the House in 2016 in a political comeback for a one-time boy wonder on Long Island, showed interest in consensus-building in the House. With his seat on the Ways and Means Committee, he has pursued the tax interests of his upscale district.

A native of Glen Cove, Suozzi graduated from Boston College and got his law degree from Fordham University. He was the mayor of Glen Cove, a position that his father—and two other Suozzis—have held, then served eight years in the more powerful office of Nassau County executive, the first Democrat to hold that position in three decades. In 2004, he spearheaded FixAlbany.com, an initiative that targeted corruption in New York state politics and sought to enact a limit on local Medicaid expenses. Not surprisingly, the initiative ruffled some Democratic chieftains, as well as Republicans, in Albany. From 2006 until 2013, he lost three campaigns: an uphill Democratic primary for governor against Eliot Spitzer, followed by two unexpected defeats for county executive. In private life, he led a state commission that proposed the first state wide cap on property taxes, which subsequently was enacted. He worked as a senior adviser at the investment bank Lazard Freres and as a litigator at the Shearman & Sterling law firm.

When Rep. Steve Israel, a House Democratic leader, announced his decision to step down at the end of 2016, Suozzi quickly voiced interest. The contenders included three other officeholders: North Hempstead councilwoman Anna Kaplan, who had the support of EMILY's List, which supports Democratic women who back abortion rights; Steve Stern, a Suffolk County legislator; and former North Hempstead Supervisor Joe Kaiman. The late June primary had a low turnout of about 20,000 voters. Suozzi won with 35 percent to 22 percent for Stern (who got more than half the vote in Suffolk), 22 percent for Kaiman and 16 percent for Kaplan.

In the peculiar general election, Suozzi faced Jack Martins, a construction businessman who served six years in the state Senate and earlier was mayor of Mineola. When a federal judge ruled in August that another Republican candidate had been improperly excluded from the primary ballot and scheduled a new GOP primary for Oct. 6, Martins sought to delay the general election until Dec. 6. There was speculation that Martins believed that it would be an advantage for him not to appear on the ballot with Donald Trump and Hillary Clinton. Shortly before Labor Day, the judge denied Martins' motion. Then, on Sept. 14, a federal appeals court canceled the rescheduled primary. Suozzi doubled the fundraising of Martins and won, 53%-47%. Martins got 51 percent of the vote in Suffolk, but lost narrowly in Nassau and by nearly 2-to-1 in Queens.

During his first term, Suozzi was a lead sponsor of a bill to hold China responsible for its mistreatment of Uighur Muslims. But he voiced frustration with the limits of the minority party. "I want to get things done. So, I need to build new relationships," he told Newsday. As co-chair of the bipartisan Problem Solvers Caucus, he helped prepare House rules changes to encourage more open debate; that became one of many deals to which Nancy Pelosi agreed to gain support for her return as Speaker.

With an opening for a New York Democrat on Ways and Means in 2019, Suozzi called for a revival of the unlimited federal deduction for state and local taxes, a popular notion in his high-tax state. Also competing for the position was first-termer Alexandria Ocasio-Cortez, who was backed by progressive groups. Suozzi called himself a "fiscal conservative," but said that he had progressive views on issues such as poverty and immigration. In winning the seat, he benefited from his background as a certified public accountant, plus the tradition that freshmen rarely are assigned to the tax-writing committee.

On Ways and Means, he joined Senate Democratic Leader Chuck Schumer on behalf of New York interests in restoring full deductibility of state and local taxes, which they said should be a priority in corona virus-relief legislation. With members of the Problem Solvers Caucus, he held a press conference in December 2020 to urge party leaders to adopt their consensus position for economic stimulus. Their plan, which did not include any income-tax changes, featured Suozzi's strong advocacy of extension of the pay check protection program—especially for restaurants and entertainment venues. His continued demand for restoring the state and local tax break ran the risk of clashing with President Joe Biden's call for increased taxes on wealthy individuals.

In 2020, Republican George Santos, a finance professional and political novice who was the gay first-generation son of Brazilian immigrants, described himself as "a walking living, breathing contradiction" for a Republican candidate. Santos spent $333,000 to $2.2 million for Suozzi in a contest that was not resolved until late November because of New York's arcane vote-counting procedures. Although the initial results described Suozzi's reelection in jeopardy, he won with a relatively comfortable 56%-43%, leading in each of the three counties.

NY-3: Northern Long Island, Eastern Queens

Cook Partisan Voting Index: D+3

Population		Race and Ethnicity		Income	
Total	725,746	White	73.30%	Median Income	$126,191
Land area (sq. miles)	255	Black	2.90%	District Income Rank	5
Pop/ sq mi	2,846.96	Latino	11.10%	Poverty Rate	5.20%
Born in State	68.80%	Asian	16.70%	With health insurance	96.50%
		Two or more races	2.30%	Cash public assistance	1.00%
Age Groups		Other	4.80%	Food stamp/SNAP	3.00%
Under 18	19.70%				
18-34	18.20%	Education		Work	
35-64	40.60%	H.S grad or less	23.50%	White Collar	53.80%
Over 64	21.50%	Some college	20.20%	Sales and Service	35.00%
		College Degree, 4 yr	29.40%	Blue Collar	11.20%
Military		Post grad	26.80%	Government	15.90%
Veteran/ Active Duty	4.00%				

2020 Pres. Vote	Biden	216,247	(55%)	Trump	175,089	(44%)
2016 Pres. Vote	Clinton	178,288	(51%)	Trump	156,942	(45%)

Huntington: The North Shore of Long Island is "Gatsby country," where peninsulas jutting out into the Sound are covered with vast green lawns leading to the mansions of America's great capitalists. Nineteenth-century millionaires commuted by steam yacht from Manhattan to their estates in what is now Queens or Nassau County. In the early 20th century, the richest people in business and show business spent their leisure time here, playing croquet while their servants unloaded bootleggers' boats at their private docks. Inland, behind the expansive lawns, Long Island was still farm country, with little villages clustered at railroad stations, occasional colonial-era houses, and acres of billboard-strewn wasteland on the highways to New York City. But as the city grew outward, affluent neighborhoods developed in Douglaston on the water, just beyond the middle-class Flushing area of Queens inland, and the Great Neck peninsula became a very affluent, mostly Jewish suburb. Farther out, on Sands Point and Oyster Bay, old estates alternated with more modest homes originally built for servants and newer subdivisions. The Sagamore Hill home of President Theodore Roosevelt at Oyster Bay has been restored at a cost of $10 million.

In Glen Cove, the long-delayed Garvies Point development—a Superfund clean-up site—featured $1.3 billion in building along 56 acres of the waterfront, with parks, marinas and an amphitheater, plus 1,100 residences. Growth in Glen Cove, just west of Oyster Bay, resulted in a commuter ferry terminal with planned service to Manhattan, though the launch date of June 2020 was postponed because of the corona virus pandemic. For the longer term, local environmentalists voiced concern that a potential plan for new sea gates to limit flooding in New York City could adversely affect areas along Long Island Sound. "We love New York City but we don't want to be sacrificed to protect it," a local activist told Newsday in October 2018.

The 3rd Congressional District of New York ties together a disparate collection of New York City neighborhoods and suburbs. About one-third of its votes are cast in Suffolk County, where the political leanings are more conservative than elsewhere in the district. Close to 15 percent live at the western end of the district, in upscale neighborhoods of Queens near the Throgs Neck and Bronx-Whitestone bridges to the Bronx and points north: Douglaston, Bellaire and Beechhurst. This area, more affluent than other portions of Queens, is heavily Democratic. In the middle—politically as well as geographically—is northern Nassau County. Roughly half the district's population lives here, many in the posh neighborhoods abutting or near Long Island Sound. This affluence largely continues inland; the median household incomes in Jericho, where nearly one-third of the population is Asian, exceeded $173,000 per year. The district has been politically competitive. Joe Biden's 55%-44% win in 2020 nearly doubled Hillary Clinton's lead four years earlier.

Kathleen Rice (D)

Elected 2014, 4th term, b. Feb 15, 1965; New York, NY; Catholic University of America, B.A., 1987; Touro Law Center, J.D., 1991; Roman Catholic; Single.

Elected Office: Nassau County District Attorney, 2006-2015.

Professional Career: Assistant District Attorney, Brooklyn; Assistant U.S. Attorney, 1999-2005.

DC Office: 2435 RHOB 20515, 202-225-5516, Fax: 202-225-5758, kathleenrice.house.gov

State Offices: Garden City, 516-739-3008.

Committees: *Energy & Commerce*: Communications & Technology; Consumer Protection & Commerce; Oversight & Investigations. *Homeland Security*: Cybersecurity, Infrastructure Protection & Innovation.

Group Ratings

	ADA	ACLU	AFL-CIO	LCV	COC	HAFA	ACU	CFG	FRC
2020	**	71%	**	90%	-	5%	6%	**	-
2019	80%	C	95%	93%	75%	C	6%	21%	0%

Almanac Ratings 2019-2020

	Economy	Social	Foreign	Composite
Liberal	56%	100%	52%	70%
Conservative	44%	0%	48%	30%

Key Votes of the 116th Congress

1. U.S./Mex./Can. trade deal Y	5. Russia sanctions Y	9. Firearms background checks Y
2. First Coronavirus response Y	6. Troops in Syria Y	10. Spending at the border Y
3. HEROES Act Y	7. Veto arms sales to Saudis Y	11. Marijuana liberalized rules Y
4. CASH Act Y	8. Defense $$$, veto override Y	12. Electoral College objections N

Election Results

Election	Name (Party)	Vote (%)		Cand. Spent	Ind. Exp. Support	Ind. Exp. Oppose
2020 General	Kathleen Rice (D)........................	199,762	(56%)	$1,291,184	$123	
	Douglas Tuman (R)..........................	153,007	(43%)	$125,253		$113

Prior winning percentages: 2018 (61%), 2016 (60%), 2014 (53%)

Democrat Kathleen Rice, a veteran Nassau County prosecutor who built a reputation for being tough on drunken drivers, won an open seat in 2014. For a junior lawmaker, she has shown an unusual willingness to challenge authority—namely, that of Speaker Nancy Pelosi. In 2021, Rice finally moved beyond her second-tier committee assignments and joined the Energy and Commerce Committee.

Born in Manhattan and raised in Garden City, Rice was one of 10 children borne by an only-child mother. She graduated from Catholic University in Washington and got her law degree from Touro Law Center in Central Islip, Long Island. Rice registered as a Republican in 1984 and did not vote until 2002, News day reported in 2010. She responded that her lack of voting was a "mistake."

She began her legal career as an assistant district attorney in Kings County, prosecuting burglaries, robberies and sexual assaults. For six years, she was an assistant U.S. attorney in Philadelphia, where she handled white-collar crimes, corporate fraud, gun and drug cases, and public corruption. Rice was elected Nassau County's district attorney in 2005, defeating a Republican who had held the job for three decades. She quickly developed a reputation for prosecution of drunken drivers. She worked to pass legislation imposing harsher penalties on those who had children in the car or who injured other motorists. Rice went after cheating on college admission tests, working to improve test security. She was co-chair of the Moreland Commission to Investigate Public Corruption in New York State, and was president of the state's District Attorneys Association.

As her political ambition increased, Rice ran in the five-candidate Democratic primary for state attorney general in 2010. She trailed eventual winner Eric Schneiderman, 34%-32%, though she led in counties outside of New York City. In Nassau, she was the only countywide Democrat to win reelection in 2013.

In her first campaign for Congress, Rice defeated Republican nominee Bruce Blakeman by a 53%-47% margin. She steadily increased her margin in her next three elections, and Democratic House leaders removed her district from their worry-list.

Rice spent her early House years as one of the foremost internal critics of Pelosi. She blamed the party leader when Democrats underperformed House pickup expectations in 2016, and she kept up the criticism throughout 2017 and 2018. According to Politico, Rice said Pelosi "set women back —and quite frankly, our party back decades" after Pelosi did not more forcefully try to push Rep. John Conyers of Michigan out of Congress amid sexual harassment allegations; Conyers resigned in December 2017.

After the 2018 election, Rice publicly opposed Pelosi's return as Speaker. Pelosi won the gavel anyway, and Rice paid a price. In January 2019, her Democratic colleagues from New York made a push for her to serve on the Judiciary Committee, only to see the re-empowered Pelosi block that effort. During her fourth term, though, Rice appeared to have made peace with Pelosi. To the surprise of many Capitol Hill observers, she landed a choice committee assignment in 2021 on Energy and Commerce. She emerged the winner in a clash with fellow New Yorker Alexandria Ocasio-Cortez —a more junior member, whose outspoken campaign oppositions to several House incumbents had burned bridges with some Democrats.

Rice briefly considered running for state attorney general amid turmoil surrounding the resignation of Schneiderman in 2018. Rice cited the timing of his resignation and a state law that prohibited candidates from seeking two offices simultaneously as her reasons for passing on the race —though those factors didn't stop Rep. Sean Patrick Maloney from his unsuccessful primary bid for the office. Allies have continued to speculate that she might make another state wide run in the not-too-distant future.

NY-4: Southern Nassau County   Cook Partisan Voting Index: D+4

Population		Race and Ethnicity		Income	
Total	730,314	White	64.50%	Median Income	$110,677
Land area (sq. miles)	111	Black	15.20%	District Income Rank	15
Pop/ sq mi	6,588.31	Latino	22.40%	Poverty Rate	5.70%
Born in State	68.60%	Asian	7.30%	With health insurance	94.90%
		Two or more races	4.10%	Cash public assistance	1.50%
Age Groups		Other	8.90%	Food stamp/SNAP	4.90%
Under 18	22.10%				
18-34	21.00%	**Education**		**Work**	
35-64	40.10%	H.S grad or less	33.60%	White Collar	44.00%
Over 64	16.80%	Some college	22.80%	Sales and Service	39.20%
		College Degree, 4 yr	24.60%	Blue Collar	16.80%
Military		Post grad	18.90%	Government	17.40%
Veteran/ Active Duty	3.60%				

2020 Pres. Vote	Biden	211,700	(55%)	Trump	165,073	(43%)	
2016 Pres. Vote	Clinton	179,845	(53%)	Trump	147,469	(44%)	

Hempstead: Nassau County has long been on the cutting edge of American suburban life. It is the home of one of the earliest suburbs: Garden City, founded in 1869 with wide avenues and single-family homes. After World War II, it pioneered large-scale suburban development, as freeways replaced highways, and shopping centers sprang up at intersections. Many of the middle- and upper-income residents continue to depend on the Long Island Railroad to speed them to jobs in New York City. Prominent sites include the county seat of Mineola; Hofstra University in Hempstead, which held a presidential debate during three recent elections; and Roosevelt Field, where Charles Lindbergh took off for Paris in 1927. The fate of this historic airstrip perhaps typifies the extent of suburbanization in Nassau County: It's now the site of an upscale shopping mall, with a longstanding conflict over the exact spot of Lindbergh's departure, either at an escalator in the shopping center or just behind a parking garage near a Best Buy.

The 4th Congressional District of New York comprises Garden City and the towns around it. It is one of six districts in the state that is wholly included within a single county. The 4th takes in several suburbs along the Jericho Turnpike—New Hyde Park, Mineola, Westbury—as well as a large swath of southern Nassau County. This territory includes Hempstead, Uniondale, Rockville Centre and part of ethnically diverse Valley Stream, as well as most of the predominantly Jewish "Five Towns"—the railway suburbs of Lawrence, Cedarhurst, Hewlett and Woodmere; In wood is in the neighboring 5th District. Jones Beach, an early conception of New York master builder Robert Moses, has more than six miles of an expansive ocean beachfront, 2,400 acres for maritime entertainment and hosts about 6 million annual visitors. In 2015, the New York Islanders professional hockey team abandoned the 43-year-old Nassau Coliseum and had a reverse migration to the full-service Barclays Center in rejuvenated Brooklyn. Their move into the city didn't work out. In 2019, the Islanders returned to the Coliseum, while a new arena was under construction on the border with the 5th District that was expected to open for the 2021 season.

Nassau County was traditionally Republican, and once served as the political base of Sen. Alfonse D'Amato, and Garden City remains that way. But the county has become more diverse and more Democratic. Even so, there remain strong pockets of conservatism, both of the Hassidic Jewish strain and another supporting former President Donald Trump. Nearby Roosevelt is only 2 percent non-Hispanic White. The district includes the old resort areas around Lido Beach and Long Beach and suburban Merrick, Bellmore and Wantagh. Joe Biden increased the Democratic margin in the district to 55%-43%. Overall, he got 54 percent of the vote in Nassau.

Gregory Meeks (D)

Elected 1998, 12th term, b. Sep 25, 1953; Harlem, NY; Adelphi University, B.A., 1975; Howard University Law School, J.D., 1978; African Methodist Episcopal; Married (Simone-Marie Meeks); 3 children.

Elected Office: NY Assembly, 1992-1998.

Professional Career: Assistant District Attorney, Queens County, 1978-1983; NY St. Commission of Investigations, 1984-1985; Judge, NY St. Workers' Compensation Board, 1985-1992.

DC Office: 2310 RHOB 20515, 202-225-3461, Fax: 202-226-4169, meeks.house.gov

State Offices: Arverne, 347-230-4032; Jamaica, 718-725-6000.

Committees: *Financial Services*: Investor Protection, Entrepreneurship & Capital Markets. *Foreign Affairs (Chmn)*.

Group Ratings

	ADA	ACLU	AFL-CIO	LCV	COC	HAFA	ACU	CFG	FRC
2020	**	80%	**	100%	-	0%	4%	**	-
2019	95%	C	100%	93%	59%	C	4%	13%	0%

Almanac Ratings 2019-2020

	Economy	Social	Foreign	Composite
Liberal	55%	100%	60%	72%
Conservative	45%	0%	40%	28%

Key Votes of the 116th Congress

1. U.S./Mex./Can. trade deal Y	5. Russia sanctions Y	9. Firearms background checks Y
2. First Coronavirus response Y	6. Troops in Syria Y	10. Spending at the border N
3. HEROES Act Y	7. Veto arms sales to Saudis Y	11. Marijuana liberalized rules Y
4. CASH Act Y	8. Defense $$$, veto override Y	12. Electoral College objections N

Election Results

Election	Name (Party)	Vote (%)		Cand. Spent	Ind. Exp. Support	Ind. Exp. Oppose
2020 General	Gregory Meeks (D)......................	229,125	(99%)	$1,470,549	$113	
2020 Primary	Gregory Meeks (D).........................	50,044	(76%)			
	Shaniyat Chowdhury (D).......................	15,951	(24%)			

Prior winning percentages: 2016 (85%), 2014 (80%), 2012 (75%), 2010 (76%), 2008 (67%), 2006 (70%), 2004 (70%), 2002 (65%), 2000 (69%), 1998 (100%), 1998 special (57%)

Democrat Gregory Meeks, first elected in 1998, is a liberal who is more sympathetic to business than are other New York City Democrats—sometimes to the unhappiness of organized labor. In part, that reflects the commercial interests of his international district. As the senior African American in the delegation, Meeks became an outspoken leader of the Congressional Black Caucus during intra-party clashes in 2020. Also that year, he successfully waged an intensive campaign to chair the House Foreign Affairs Committee.

Meeks grew up in public housing projects in Harlem. He was inspired by his mother, who went back to school when her four children were older and who encouraged volunteerism. After graduating from Adelphi College and Howard University law school, Meeks moved to Far Rockaway. He became an assistant district attorney and a workers' compensation judge. He was elected to the state Assembly in 1992 and became an ally of Democratic Rep. Floyd Flake, a minister whose Allen African Methodist Episcopal Church congregation grew from 1,400 members in 1976 to more than 20,000 members.

When Flake resigned, Meeks won a majority of Democratic committee members at an endorsement meeting and thus became the party's nominee in a 1998 special election. Democratic state Sen. Alton Waldon and Assemblywoman Barbara Clark ran as independents. With the support of Flake and civil rights leaders, Meeks won 57 percent of the vote, to Waldon's 21 percent and Clark's 13 percent. Since then, he has not faced a serious challenge.

Meeks has a voting record toward the center of House Democrats and has been active in the business-oriented New Democrat Coalition. He has backed numerous free-trade agreements. In 2015, he was one of the few outspoken Democratic supporters of President Barack Obama's Trans-Pacific Partnership. These agreements promised new opportunities for JFK airport and its many auxiliary businesses. He joined African-American members in seeking to ensure that legislation addresses minorities' issues.

On the Financial Services Committee, he has been an occasional ally of Wall Street interests. When the House in 2018 took final action on the rollback of the Dodd-Frank financial-regulatory law, he said that he could not "in good conscience" vote for it, chiefly because it exempted many banks from some mortgage disclosure requirements. But he praised provisions in the bill that he sponsored, including benefits for minority-owned banks and credit unions, and encouragement of the use of alternative data in underwriting mortgages.

In 2019, as chairman of the Financial Services Subcommittee on Financial Institutions and Consumer Protection, he encouraged the notion that "the relationship between Wall Street and Main Street should not be as antagonistic."He called for more racial and ethnic diversity among board members of publicly traded companies. Meeks was among a group of moderate Democrats on the committee who pushed back against the more progressive views of committee Chairwoman Rep. Maxine Waters of California and others—including the first-term Democrat from Queens, Rep. Alexandria Ocasio-Cortez, whom Meeks recommended for the panel.

Following the unexpected defeats of 13 House Democrats—and no House Republicans--in the November 2020 election, Meeks said Democrats needed to affirm their opposition to calls to "defund the police." "We've got to be clear about that we're not for defunding the police and allow that lie to continue to be out there," Meeks told Politico. "We're not for defunding the police and we're not socialists. The language has to be clear."

His financial ethics have become fodder for New York's major dailies in recent years. The Federal Election Commission in 2006 reprimanded Meeks for using more than $6,000 in 2004 campaign funds for a personal trainer and other expenses. In 2010, The New York Times wrote that despite acknowledging that he has no more than a few thousand dollars in his savings account, he "lives a life worthy of a jet-setter," staying in luxury hotels, driving a taxpayer-leased $1,000-a-month Lexus and buying a $1 million house built by a developer who was a campaign contributor. He told the newspaper that he observed all campaign finance laws. Meeks blamed the negative attention on conservative groups out to undermine Democrats.

The support by Meeks for the Trans-Pacific trade deal led some national unions to threaten a primary challenge in 2016. Democratic state Sen. James Sanders, an ally of organized labor, filed to challenge him but dropped out of the primary shortly before the deadline. He changed his mind, he said, so he could work with other Democrats to secure a majority in the state Senate. In primaries every two years since 2016, Meeks won the Democratic primary with at least 76 percent of the vote in low-turnout contests—despite mounting opposition to him from progressive activists. Meeks was selected without opposition in March 2019 to chair the Queens Democratic Party, replacing former Rep. Joe Crowley. The post gives Meeks an influential role in selecting local candidates, including judges, and is a throw-back to the Tammany Hall era when county bosses also wielded power as senior members of Congress.

In 2020, as chairman of the CBC's campaign committee, Meeks stirred controversy when he defended its decision to support Rep. Eliot Engel, a 16-term white incumbent who was challenged by Jamaal Bowman, an insurgent African American in his Bronx-based district. Meeks cited the support that Engel had provided to the African-American community. He criticized the anti-incumbent approach of Justice Democrats, which backed Bowman and, earlier, Ocasio-Cortez in her successful challenge to Crowley in 2018. In 2020, Justice Democrats backed Cori Bush in her successful challenge of veteran Democratic Rep. Lacy Clay of Missouri. "We will have to, at some point, sit down and see: Is this something that is directed at members of the Congressional Black Caucus?" Meeks told The Hill in July 2019.

Ironically, the Democratic primary defeat of Engel in late June opened the door for Meeks to succeed him as Foreign Affairs chairman. Despite the fact that Rep. Brad Sherman of California outranked him in seniority—a principle that CBC members traditionally have supported in internal House clashes—"nationwide protests on racial injustice have prompted many House Democrats to push for further diversity in leadership," including the Foreign Affairs Committee, Foreign Policy magazine reported in June 2020. After other House members considered entering the contest, Rep. Joaquin Castro of Texas, a Latino with low seniority and greater advocacy of reshaping foreign policy, announced his candidacy in mid-July.Meeks dismissed criticism that he had been less active on the committee. "I would put up my competency next to anybody's," he told The Washington Post.

Subsequently, in a secret ballot inside the Democratic Caucus, Meeks defeated Castro, 148-78. Sherman dropped out after he trailed during a vote of the leadership-controlled Steering and Policy Committee. In a statement, Meeks said that the committee would make "a leap towards a new way of doing business."

Meeks could be among the several incumbents in New York facing potential jeopardy in redistricting. But he enters that struggle with several political factors, local and national, in his favor.

NY-5: Southeast Queens, Western Nassau　　　　　　Cook Partisan Voting Index: D+34

Population		Race and Ethnicity		Income	
Total	759,001	White	17.30%	Median Income	$76,150
Land area (sq. miles)	52	Black	49.20%	District Income Rank	119
Pop/ sq mi	14,629.93	Latino	20.00%	Poverty Rate	9.90%
Born in State	48.20%	Asian	15.10%	With health insurance	91.70%
		Two or more races	3.70%	Cash public assistance	4.70%
Age Groups		Other	14.70%	Food stamp/SNAP	14.40%
Under 18	21.60%				
18-34	22.80%	Education		Work	
35-64	39.40%	H.S grad or less	47.00%	White Collar	30.80%
Over 64	16.00%	Some college	27.20%	Sales and Service	48.30%
		College Degree, 4 yr	16.70%	Blue Collar	20.80%
Military		Post grad	9.20%	Government	17.90%
Veteran/ Active Duty	2.80%				

2020 Pres. Vote	Biden	229,459	(83%)	Trump	44,495	(16%)
2016 Pres. Vote	Clinton	211,667	(85%)	Trump	31,322	(13%)

JFK Airport: A half-century ago, there was a small black community in southern Queens, near Jamaica Bay. Since then, many African-American families have bought houses and raised their families in neighborhoods that fan east from there. They fought to maintain the relatively spacious streets, relishing the plenitude of natural light, safe schools and good neighbourhood stores. There is block upon block of low-rise, frame and brick houses, built mostly from the 1920s to the 1950s, in the neighborhoods of Springfield Gardens and Laurelton, St. Albans and Rosedale, Cambria Heights and Queens Village. This part of Queens today is home to New York City's largest concentration of middle-class Black homeowners, with a median income higher than other households in Queens. Showing the community's economic strength, multiple developers have launched plans for new residential towers and retail space.

The 5th Congressional District of New York contains all these southeast Queens neighborhoods, plus other less affluent sections of southern Queens. It is bounded on the north, more or less, by Grand Central Parkway. To the east, the Nassau County line has melted away as the unofficial boundary between Black and white Long Island. The district now takes in some precincts in south western Nassau, with about 15 percent of the voters: In wood, Valley Stream and Elmont. Belmont Park is the site of a planned new arena to house the New York Islanders hockey team. To the south, it includes Rockaway Peninsula, with never-completed vast swaths of government-financed housing that were planned by Robert Moses in the 1950s and 1960s. In October 2020, construction began on a six-mile, $336 million storm surge protection plan, which features the equivalent of 24 rock jetties in the ocean. Nearby is the Jamaica Bay Wildlife Refuge, which covers about 20 square miles and is the only wildlife refuge in the nation located entirely within a city; the site includes the open bay, saltmarsh, mudflats and two man-made ponds.

With the start of ferry service to Manhattan, Rockaway has become a more attractive commute. In the middle of all this is John F. Kennedy International Airport, the largest international gateway for air travelers entering the United States. The airport has generated 230,000 jobs in the area. In 2018, New York Gov. Andrew Cuomo announced a $13 billion plan for the airport to improve its transportation systems and create two large international terminals, including more gates, but no additional runway; airlines are providing much of the funding. In February 2020, prior to the pandemic, authorities said the operator of Terminal 4—the busiest at JFK, which accommodated a bit more than one-third of its 60 million annual passengers—planned to spend $3.8 billion on an expanded facility, which houses Delta and several overseas carriers. As of 2019, Uber was competing with Blade Urban Mobility for on-demand helicopter service from Manhattan to JFK. The price, according to CNBC, was $195 per flight.

The 5th Congressional District is 49 percent African American, 20 percent Hispanic and 15 percent Asian. Richmond Hill and Ozone Park, just northwest of JFK, were previously white ethnic neighborhoods, but now have sizable numbers of Latinos and Asians. It has the highest median income of the Queens-based districts. Politically, the vote in 2020 for Joe Biden was 83 percent, his best district in Queens.

Grace Meng (D)

Elected 2012, 5th term, b. Oct 01, 1975; Queens, NY; University of MI, B.A., 1997; Yeshiva University Benjamin N. Cardozo School of Law, J.D., 2002; Christian Church; Married (Wayne Kye); 2 children.

Elected Office: NY Assembly, 2009-2012.

Professional Career: Practicing attorney, 2003-2013.

DC Office: 2209 RHOB 20515, 202-225-2601, Fax: 202-225-1589, meng.house.gov

State Offices: Flushing, 718-358-6364; Forest Hills, 718-358-6364.

Committees: *Appropriations*: Agriculture, Rural Development, FDA & Related Agencies; Commerce, Justice, Science & Related Agencies; State, Foreign Operations & Related Programs.

Group Ratings

	ADA	ACLU	AFL-CIO	LCV	COC	HAFA	ACU	CFG	FRC
2020	**	86%	**	100%	-	0%	4%	**	-
2019	100%	C	90%	100%	40%	C	5%	16%	0%

Almanac Ratings 2019-2020

	Economy	Social	Foreign	Composite
Liberal	100%	100%	97%	99%
Conservative	0%	0%	3%	1%

Key Votes of the 116th Congress

1. U.S./Mex./Can. trade deal	N	5. Russia sanctions	N/A
2. First Coronavirus response	Y	6. Troops in Syria	Y
3. HEROES Act	Y	7. Veto arms sales to Saudis	Y
4. CASH Act	Y	8. Defense $$$, veto override	N

9. Firearms background checks Y
10. Spending at the border N
11. Marijuana liberalized rules Y
12. Electoral College objections N

Election Results

Election	Name (Party)	Vote (%)		Cand. Spent	Ind. Exp. Support	Ind. Exp. Oppose
2020 General	Grace Meng (D)............................ 158,862	(68%)		$1,489,537	$4,123	
	Tom Zmich (R)............................ 74,829	(32%)		$125,352		$113
2020 Primary	Grace Meng (D)............................ 30,759	(66%)				
	Mel Gagarin (D)................................. 9,447	(20%)				
	Sandra Choi (D)............................ 6,757	(14%)				

Prior winning percentages: 2018 (91%), 2016 (72%), 2014 (72%), 2012 (60%)

Democrat Grace Meng, elected to the House in 2012 as the first Asian American from New York, has made her mark in the Democratic Party and as a member of the House Appropriations Committee, where she has pursued her personal interests.

Meng was born and raised in Queens. Her parents had left Taiwan in the early 1970s. After studying history at the University of Michigan, she got her law degree from Yeshiva University's Cardozo School of Law. She did pro bono work for Sanctuary for Families, and joined a law firm. She worked as a volunteer on several New York political campaigns, including Hillary Clinton's reelection to the Senate in 2006. Her father, Jimmy Meng, served one term in the state Assembly and did not seek reelection following reports of legal problems in his campaign. After residency issues disqualified her in 2006, she then defeated his successor. During four years in Albany, Meng enacted a measure to eliminate the word "Oriental" from state documents referring to people of Asian descent.

When she ran for the open congressional seat, Meng received the backing of the Queens Democratic Party, several Asian-American advocacy groups and the powerful New York Hotel and Motel Trades Council. She won the Democratic primary against three other contenders, with 53 percent of the vote to 25 percent for runner-up Assemblyman Rory Lancman. She had little trouble in the general election against Republican Daniel J. Halloran, a member of the New York City Council. The contest became raucous after Halloran accused Meng of running a campaign of "ethnocentrism" based on her roots, referred to her as a "Chinese national" and falsely accused her of having dual citizenship. She won, 68%-31%, and has not been seriously challenged since.

Meng handled an embarrassing episode when her father was arrested in 2014 and accused of soliciting $80,000 from a friend facing criminal charges, claiming he could bribe prosecutors. Jimmy Meng pleaded guilty to wire fraud and was sentenced to one month in prison.

Much of her work has reflected the international interests of her district. She filed a bill with Republican Rep. Tom Emmer of Minnesota to direct the State Department to speed up visa approvals for international physicians who are slated to work at U.S. hospitals. In 2015, Meng was the first House Democrat to oppose the Obama administration's nuclear agreement with Iran, which she described as "simply too dangerous for the American people." In 2016, she enacted a law modeled on her New York statute to remove from U.S. law "Oriental," a word she called "insulting and outdated," and replace it with "Asian American." In February 2021, she filed with Republican Rep. Van Taylor of Texas a bill that seeks to help Korean-American families reunite with their loved ones in North Korea.

On domestic issues, the House twice passed Meng's bill to prohibit a practice known as "spoofing," which has been described as deliberately changing one's cell phone ID when texting another person—a practice used to steal money and personal information. She was a founder and co-chair of the Kids' Safety Caucus. She filed a bill to expand access to free or reduced-price feminine hygiene products as part of healthcare legislation.

She pursued those interests with her seat on Appropriations. She gained prominence during a hearing when she questioned Commerce Secretary Wilbur Ross about the use of citizenship questions in the 2020 census. Following his denial of such a plan, subsequent disclosures led Meng to accuse him of not responding truthfully. 'Hate being lied to!" she tweeted in October 2018. She followed up by demanding a Justice Department review of Ross' response, and filing a bill to prevent use of such questions."There have been so many times where I'm sitting around the table and I realize that I might be the only Asian American, I might be the only woman of color at that table," she told City and State New York in May 2017.

After a temporary appointment in 2016 as a vice chair of the Democratic National Committee, Meng won a full term in that position in 2017.Amid the anti-Asian sentiment that became common following the outbreak of the corona virus, Meng chaired ASPIRE PAC—the political arm of the Congressional Asian-Pacific American Caucus—and ran Facebook ads in the districts of several Republican lawmakers who in September 2020 voted against a House resolution to denounce attacks on Asian Americans. "Some of these Republican members took our Asian American constituents, or their constituents, for granted," she told NBC News the following month.

Meng also used ASPIRE to encourage turnout by Asian-American voters in the 2020 election, especially in California. "AAPI's are the fastest-growing electorate and yet we've been largely passed off," she told Roll Call in October 2020. The following month, two Asian-American Republican women defeated first-term Democratic men in Orange County California.

NY-6: Central Queens

Cook Partisan Voting Index: D+13

Population		Race and Ethnicity		Income	
Total	714,299	White	41.30%	Median Income	$70,529
Land area (sq. miles)	30	Black	5.40%	District Income Rank	161
Pop/ sq mi	23,985.86	Latino	19.90%	Poverty Rate	10.80%
Born in State	43.60%	Asian	40.40%	With health insurance	91.50%
		Two or more races	3.30%	Cash public assistance	2.60%
Age Groups		Other	9.60%	Food stamp/SNAP	11.20%
Under 18	19.80%				
18-34	20.60%	**Education**		**Work**	
35-64	42.10%	H.S grad or less	40.10%	White Collar	40.40%
Over 64	17.40%	Some college	21.70%	Sales and Service	42.70%
		College Degree, 4 yr	22.80%	Blue Collar	17.00%
Military		Post grad	15.40%	Government	13.00%
Veteran/ Active Duty	2.40%				

2020 Pres. Vote	Biden	152,725	(62%)	Trump	92,371	(37%)
2016 Pres. Vote	Clinton	134,970	(65%)	Trump	66,487	(32%)

Forest Hills, Flushing: More than a half-century ago, most of the neighborhoods in New York's outer boroughs were virtually all-white. Most of these areas had filled with descendants of the great mass of immigrants who came from eastern and southern Europe between 1890 and 1924 and from northern Europe earlier—Irish and Italians, Jews and Hungarians, Poles and Czechs and Greeks. A few parts of Queens were WASPy and high-income. Forest Hills in Queens, with its famous tennis stadium and large Tudor houses, was a notable example.

But the only thing permanent in New York is change. The 1960s saw pitched battles in city politics between John Lindsay, a liberal Manhattan Republican, and his mostly outer-borough opponents. During Lindsay's reign as mayor, middle-class New Yorkers fled the city's high taxes and crime-addled neighborhoods, while Forest Hills was the site of sometimes violent protests when Lindsay attempted to place low-income housing projects in the neighbourhood. At the time, Queens had four congressional districts and large portions of two others; today, it is barely entitled to three.

In recent years, the overall picture in Queens has brightened. It has become the borough with the most residential growth in New York City. With the surge of new jobs across the city, Queens was set to pass Brooklyn in 2020 in the number of new housing projects, the Wall Street Journal reported in 2018.Even with the increased supply, the growing demand has forced up rents and the cost of new housing. Much of the growth was in areas with large numbers of recent immigrants. Queens has no real defining quality, The Economist wrote in a December 2018 profile. "But it has the vibrancy of a whole world. Around 160 languages are spoken across the borough; residents hail from almost 200 countries. Nearly half its residents are foreign-born; most speak a language other than English at home." From its start, the corona virus proved "devastating" to many businesses in local Chinese communities. "Chinese business owners say many people fear visiting Chinatown [in Queens] because the disease started in China," CNN reported in March 2020.

The 6th Congressional District is the only district that is entirely in Queens. It begins near the border of Nassau County, at Fresh Meadows, and runs west through Pomonok and the old rail suburbs of Kew Gardens and Forest Hills. It continues west to Rego Park, which has many 1950s high-rise apartments; Middle Village; Glendale; and part of Maspeth. Across Flushing Bay from LaGuardia Airport (which is in the 14th District), it takes in Flushing, long a modest-income white ethnic neighbourhood and now about 70 percent Asian, with several Chinese dialects. West of 138th Street, Queens is dominated by Taiwanese and ethnic Chinese from Malaysia, Vietnam and Thailand. Shops have an urban "Chinatown" feel and feature a wide variety of delicacies. (New York City has three Chinatowns—one each in Manhattan and Brooklyn, with the largest in Queens.) The area east of 138th Street is predominantly Korean.

The district has grown to 40 percent Asian American (the largest share for any district not in a Pacific Coast state), with 19 percent Latino and 4 percent Black. While there are pockets of Republican voting, especially around Middle Village and Kew Gardens Hills, it is solidly Democratic. Joe Bidenled Donald Trump, 62%-37%,his lowest vote in the 10 Democratic-held districts in New York City.

Nydia Velázquez (D)

Elected 1992, 15th term, b. Mar 28, 1953; Yabucoa, PR; University of PR, B.A., 1974; NY University, M.A., 1976; Roman Catholic; Married (Paul Bader).

Elected Office: NY City Council, 1984-1986.

Professional Career: Faculty, University of PR, 1976-1981; Adjunct Professional, Hunter College, 1981-1983; Special Assistant, U.S. Rep. Edolphus Towns, 1983; Migration Director, PR Department of Labor & Human Resources, 1986-1989; Director, PR Department of Community Affairs in the U.S., 1989-1992.

DC Office: 2302 RHOB 20515, 202-225-2361, Fax: 202-226-0327, velazquez.house.gov

State Offices: Brooklyn, 718-599-3658; Brooklyn, 718-222-5819; New York, 212-619-2606.

Committees: *Financial Services*: Consumer Protection & Financial Institutions; Housing, Community Development & Insurance. *Natural Resources*: Oversight & Investigations; Water, Oceans & Wildlife. *Small Business (Chmn)*: Ex Officio membership on all subcommittees.

Group Ratings

	ADA	ACLU	AFL-CIO	LCV	COC	HAFA	ACU	CFG	FRC
2020	**	83%	**	100%	-	0%	3%	**	-
2019	100%	C	90%	100%	45%	C	4%	18%	0%

Almanac Ratings 2019-2020

	Economy	Social	Foreign	Composite
Liberal	100%	100%	100%	100%
Conservative	0%	0%	0%	0%

Key Votes of the 116th Congress

1. U.S./Mex./Can. trade deal	N	5. Russia sanctions	Y	9. Firearms background checks Y
2. First Coronavirus response	Y	6. Troops in Syria	Y	10. Spending at the border N
3. HEROES Act	Y	7. Veto arms sales to Saudis	Y	11. Marijuana liberalized rules Y
4. CASH Act	Y	8. Defense $$$, veto override	Y	12. Electoral College objections N

Election Results

Election	Name (Party)	Vote (%)		Cand. Spent	Ind. Exp. Support	Ind. Exp. Oppose
2020 General	Nydia Velázquez (D)............................	191,073	(85%)	$681,406	$335	
	Brian Kelly (R).......................................	32,520	(14%)			$59
2020 Primary	Nydia Velázquez (D)............................	56,698	(80%)			
	Paperboy Love Prince (D).....................	14,120	(20%)			

Prior winning percentages: 2018 (93%), 2016 (91%), 2014 (83%), 2012 (79%), 2010 (79%), 2008 (67%), 2006 (73%), 2004 (10%), 2002 (55%), 2000 (63%), 1998 (64%), 1996 (83%), 1994 (58%), 1992 (55%)

Nydia Velázquez, first elected in 1992 and the only Puerto Rican woman elected to Congress, again chairs the Small Business Committee. Sometimes called La Luchadora—"The Fighter"—she also is a senior member of the Financial Services Committee, which oversees companies with many employees who are her constituents. With the changes in her district, her constituents increasingly include entrepreneurs and managers, in addition to blue-collar workers.

She grew up in Puerto Rico as one of nine children of sugar-cane field workers. Although her father never finished elementary school, he was a political leader in her hometown of Yabucoa and inspired her to pursue politics as a career. She studied political science at the University of Puerto Rico and taught there in the 1970s. After graduate school in New York City, she went to work for local Democratic Rep. Edolphus Towns. In 1983, she became the first Hispanic woman elected to the New York City Council. She and fellow councilmember Carolyn Maloney, who would become a House colleague and long time political ally, were arrested a year later at the South African Consulate for protesting apartheid in South Africa.

When the new district was created in 1992, Velázquez was a major contender in the Democratic primary. She had to overcome nine-term Rep. Stephen Solarz. Velázquez was endorsed by Mayor David Dinkins and civil rights leader Jesse Jackson. In a light turnout, she beat Solarz 34%-28%. She easily won in November.

Velázquez has a solidly liberal voting record, with occasional pro-business votes on economic issues. Velázquez has been a leading voice on issues related to Puerto Rico and the debate over changing the commonwealth's status. She favors a process that would allow the people of Puerto Rico to determine the status of the island, and has filed legislation authorizing a constitutional convention that would produce a recommendation that would then be subject to a referendum. The results would be submitted to Congress for approval. During the House debate in 2016 on debt relief for Puerto Rico, she was unhappy about the anti-union measures in the bill. "The reality is that Republicans are in control and we have no choice but to compromise," she said in a statement.

Following the devastation left by Hurricane Maria after it tore through Puerto Rico in September 2017, Velazquez took the lead in demanding enhanced disaster assistance, including additional Medicaid funds—beyond what the Republican-controlled Congress would approve. When President Donald Trump low-balled the death-toll on the island, she sought an independent commission to determine the facts. Earlier, she called his tweets that federal aid would be limited "unpresidential" and "shameful."

As chairwoman of the Hispanic Caucus in 2009, Velázquez repeatedly pressed President Barack Obama to move comprehensive immigration reform higher on his agenda. When vehement Republican opposition made clear that such a battle was unwinnable, she worked to separate the DREAM Act, a bill providing a path to legal status for the children of illegal immigrants who attend college or serve in the military. The House approved that bill in late 2010, but Senate supporters could not reach the 60-vote threshold to overcome a filibuster. Later, the Senate passed comparable measures that went nowhere in the Republican-controlled House.

Much of her legislative work has focused on the Small Business Committee. As the panel's chairwoman in 2009, Velázquez praised the Obama administration for requiring the nation's largest banks to report monthly on how much they lend to small businesses. She criticized an administration proposal to give $30 billion of the Troubled Asset Relief Program to community banks for small business, but without any requirement that the money be used for small business loans. "Taking $30 billion and simply handing it to banks—in the hopes that they will make loans—is not sound policy," she said. The administration dropped the idea of using TARP money. While in the House minority, she enacted a bill to improve the disaster-assistance programs of the SBA.

Back in control in 2019, Velázquez sought to expand SBA lending and contract-assistance programs plus oversight of Trump's immigration, trade and tax policies that she said "are harming small firms." She sought assurances that improvements in housing and schools would be part of legislation to expand public infrastructure.

A long time combatant in New York City's political wars, Velázquez has rarely faced serious major-party opposition. In the 2016 primary, she faced a credible challenger: Yungman Lee, a banker in Chinatown, who raised $417,000, which was about half of Velázquez's total. Lee got half of the vote in Manhattan, though that borough cast only one-fourth of the total vote. Velázquez got 69 percent in vote-heavy Brooklyn and defeated Lee overall, 62%-27%. Following the 2018 election, she became an early mentor to Rep. Alexandria Ocasio-Cortez, the first-termer from Queens who created anxiety in the New York delegation with talk of supporting challenges to other incumbents. The two had a "long, long conversation" about congressional dynamics, Velázquez told Politico in January 2019. A year later, news reports emerged about an incident with two Republican congressman in which Ocasio-Cortez said they insulted her. Velázquez sat behind her on the mostly empty House floor as her younger colleague delivered an impassioned speech about respect in politics.

NY-7: Northern Brooklyn, Lower East Side of Manhattan

Cook Partisan Voting Index: D+34

Population		Race and Ethnicity		Income	
Total	698,794	White	48.50%	Median Income	$66,891
Land area (sq. miles)	16	Black	11.70%	District Income Rank	193
Pop/ sq mi	43,242.2	Latino	39.10%	Poverty Rate	19.00%
Born in State	45.60%	Asian	18.30%	With health insurance	92.60%
		Two or more races	4.40%	Cash public assistance	7.00%
Age Groups		Other	17.30%	Food stamp/SNAP	22.30%
Under 18	21.80%				
18-34	28.40%	**Education**		**Work**	
35-64	37.20%	H.S grad or less	46.70%	White Collar	43.80%
Over 64	12.50%	Some college	16.50%	Sales and Service	40.90%
		College Degree, 4 yr	23.40%	Blue Collar	15.30%
Military		Post grad	13.40%	Government	9.70%
Veteran/ Active Duty	1.40%				

2020 Pres. Vote	Biden	190,811	(82%)	Trump	40,366	(17%)
2016 Pres. Vote	Clinton	177,664	(86%)	Trump	21,198	(10%)

Downtown Brooklyn: Over the Fourth of July in 1857, the worst slum in America—the Five Points—exploded into a riot involving a clash between the Irish Dead Rabbits street gang and the nativist Bowery Boys. It is here, in lower Manhattan where wave after wave of immigrants began their lives as Americans and the area still has traces of those cultures. A walk across the East River on the Brooklyn, Manhattan or Williamsburg Bridges delivers a view of the stunning expanse of New York Harbor and delivers the pedestrian to the western-most edges of Long Island and into equally iconic areas of the Brooklyn and Queens Boroughs.

The story of the 7th Congressional District is the story of New York City: a rich immigrant and slum history, gentrification and, as always, looking to the future. About 75 percent of the district's population is in Brooklyn, with the remainder split between Queens and Manhattan. Each borough runs along the East River. Overall, the district is 41 percent Hispanic and 19 percent Asian (mostly Chinese). Of the Hispanics, one-third are Puerto Rican. Chinese, predominantly in Brooklyn, have joined Dominicans as the largest foreign-born groups in the city. But this is New York, so it takes in many other ethnicities as well.

In Brooklyn, the district hugs the upscale and well-preserved Brooklyn Heights waterfront, with its stunning views of the now-rebuilt World Trade Center. Nearby is Carroll Gardens, with young professionals intermingled with Italian immigrants. Inland is Downtown Brooklyn, which has attracted a critical mass of business and residential development to become a "city that never sleeps" in its own right. To the south is Sunset Park, once the home of Irish, Polish and Norwegian immigrants, and now filled with Chinese, Puerto Ricans, Colombians and Ecuadorans; also here are comfortable neighborhoods with brownstones plus new workplaces for the formerly Manhattan-based garment industry.

North of Brooklyn Heights is DUMBO (Down Under the Manhattan Bridge Overpass), with artists in old industrial lofts that have become the most expensive real estate in Brooklyn. The old Brooklyn Navy Yard, which built ships more than two centuries ago and employed 70,000 during World War II but shut down in 1966, now houses a vibrant and rapidly growing industrial park, including new centers for tech companies and the largest movie and television production complex outside Hollywood. Williamsburg has recent Latino arrivals as well as serving as the epicenter of the hipster subculture in recent decades; many of its Orthodox Jews have moved to the exurbs of New York and New Jersey. Inland, the district takes in Bushwick, a former slum that became a beachhead in Brooklyn's urban renewal, and multi-ethnic Cypress Hills. In the Red Hook area in the southwest corner of Brooklyn, planners have envisioned a 246-acre waterfront development with relocation of a longstanding container terminal and perhaps 45,000 residential units.

In Manhattan, the 7th District includes parts of the Lower East Side, East Village and Chinatown. The neighbourhood known as Little Italy has become a few blocks of restaurants surrounded by the expanded Chinatown and gentrified neighborhoods. Like Little Italy, the Lower East Side still carries traces of its immigrant past, with a number of synagogues that served the Jewish community for well over a century. The 82 percent of the vote for Joe Biden in 2020dipped below the 86 percent for Hillary Clinton and the 89 percent for President Barack Obama in 2012.

Hakeem Jeffries (D)

Elected 2012, 5th term, b. Aug 04, 1970; Brooklyn, NY; State University of NY, Binghamton, B.A., 1992; Georgetown University, M.P.P., 1994; NY University Law School, J.D., 1997; Baptist; Married (Kennisandra Jeffries); 2 children.

Elected Office: NY Assembly, 2007-2012.

Professional Career: Clerk, Judge Harold Baer, 1997-1998; Practicing attorney, 1999-2003; Counsel, Viacom, 2004-2005; Assistant General counsel, CBS Broadcasting, 2006.

DC Office: 2433 RHOB 20515, 202-225-5936, Fax: 202-225-1018, jeffries.house.gov

State Offices: Brooklyn, 718-373-0033; Brooklyn, 718-237-2211.

Committees: House Democratic Caucus Chairman. *Budget*. *Judiciary*: Antitrust, Commercial & Administrative Law; Courts, Intellectual Property & Internet.

Group Ratings

	ADA	ACLU	AFL-CIO	LCV	COC	HAFA	ACU	CFG	FRC
2020	**	85%	**	100%	-	0%	4%	**	-
2019	95%	C	100%	97%	53%	C	5%	12%	0%

Almanac Ratings 2019-2020

	Economy	Social	Foreign	Composite
Liberal	100%	100%	92%	98%
Conservative	0%	0%	8%	2%

Key Votes of the 116th Congress

1. U.S./Mex./Can. trade deal Y	5. Russia sanctions Y	9. Firearms background checks Y
2. First Coronavirus response Y	6. Troops in Syria Y	10. Spending at the border N
3. HEROES Act Y	7. Veto arms sales to Saudis Y	11. Marijuana liberalized rules Y
4. CASH Act Y	8. Defense $$$, veto override Y	12. Electoral College objections N

Election Results

Election	Name (Party)	Vote (%)	Cand. Spent	Ind. Exp. Support	Ind. Exp. Oppose
2020 General	Hakeem Jeffries (D)...................... 234,933	(85%)	$2,076,726	$6,523	
	Garfield Wallace (R)...................... 42,007	(15%)			$59

Prior winning percentages: 2018 (94%), 2016 (93%), 2014 (81%), 2012 (78%)

Democrat Hakeem Jeffries, elected in 2012, has brought energy and a spirit of consensus-building to his office. On the House Judiciary Committee in 2019-20, he was among the leading advocates of police reform and won plaudits as a House manager during the Senate trial of the first impeachment charges against President Donald Trump. In 2018, he was narrowly elected chairman of the House Democratic Caucus, a major move up the leadership ladder, which positioned him for increased influence.

Many have viewed him as heir apparent to Speaker Nancy Pelosi. But that assessment may be premature. The House Democrats' disappointing losses in the 2020 election raised questions about how long they will retain the majority—and whether the Democratic successor to Pelosi will be House Minority Leader. Jeffries has clashed with more-progressive activists, including within the Congressional Black Caucus. At home, his establishment profile has spurred rumblings of a possible primary challenge from the left.

Jeffries was born and raised in the Crown Heights neighbourhood of Brooklyn and graduated from the State University at Binghamton. He pledged Kappa Alpha Psi, the predominantly African-American fraternity, where he received the nickname "Kool Ha," for his measured speech. He went to Georgetown University for a master's degree in public policy and later earned a law degree from New York University. He clerked for a federal judge, and worked for large corporate clients at Paul, Weiss, Rifkind, Wharton & Garrison, a law firm known for launching the careers of prominent New York Democrats.

After two unsuccessful campaigns against an entrenched incumbent in the state Assembly, Jeffries won an open seat in 2006. He worked on affordable housing issues and got a bill signed into law forcing the elimination of the New York City Police Department's "stop-and-frisk" database. When the House seat opened, Jeffries faced City Councilman Charles Barron in the Democratic primary. A former Black Panther, Barron had a history of making inflammatory statements critical of Israel and of Jews; local Democrats called him "a hate-monger" and "a bigot." Jeffries raised $1.4 million and won the primary in a rout, defeating Barron 72%-28%. That was tantamount to victory in the heavily Democratic district.

On the Judiciary Committee, Jeffries has focused much of his time on law-enforcement issues. In 2015, he helped enact the Slain Officer Family Support Act. The bill extended the tax deadline for charitable contributions to the families of two Brooklyn police officers who were killed in Bedford-Stuyvesant. Following protests against alleged police excesses in several cities, including Brooklyn, he filed a bill that year to bar the use of chokeholds, which he called a deprivation of civil rights. "It's not sufficient simply to ban a policy through departmental practice. We've got to elevate it, embed it in law, if we really and truly want to end it," he told CNN.

In 2017, Jeffries and Republican Rep. Doug Collins of Georgia took the lead in the House in enactment of the First Step Act, a bipartisan measure advocated by Trump that overhauled criminal justice procedures, including sentencing guidelines. The duo, who had collaborated on earlier issues, worked closely together at the Judiciary Committee and in public forums. "Our friendship is based on a respect that is deeper than legislation," Collins told Politico in 2018.

Jeffries has staked his future as a House leader. In December 2016, he was selected as one of three co-chairs of the House Democratic Policy and Communications Committee. "Jeffries has quickly become a national voice for our party and our caucus," Democratic Leader Nancy Pelosi wrote. In February 2017, he said he was not running for mayor. "The stakes are so high in Washington D.C. right now, and I want to be part of the effort to turn the situation around. It would be a dereliction of duty to abandon ship at the moment when times are tough," he said. At a Martin Luther King Day celebration in January 2019, Jeffries referred to Trump as "a hater in the White House...the grand wizard," though he qualified that the president is not racist.

His selection as Democratic Caucus chairman resulted from a generational and demographic showdown with Rep. Barbara Lee of California, a more senior member of the Congressional Black Caucus and an ally of Pelosi. Jeffries benefited as a younger voice joining a leadership team in which the top three Democrats now are all in their 80s, though plenty of other rising Democratic stars have tired of waiting for the current team to step down. In his bid for the leadership post, he offered a three-part appeal: a commitment that Democrats are "strongest when everyone is on the playing field;" a plan to act aggressively on a bold legislative agenda that includes adequate communication to avoid "the type of mischaracterizations that took place when Barack Obama was president;" and "the best defense is a good offense" against what he termed "the right-wing onslaught in this country."

His 123-113 victory left some intra-party bruises, with Lee—who was supported by several former CBC leaders and was age 72 to 48 for Jeffries—claiming that she was the victim of ageism. A spokesman for Rep. Alexandria Ocasio-Cortez, from a nearby district in New York, said she was "disappointed" with the outcome; her allies reportedly considered a primary challenge to Jeffries. Ironically, the predecessor to Jeffries as Caucus chairman was Joe Crowley, who lost his seat in New York following his stunning primary defeat by Ocasio-Cortez a few months earlier.

When House Democrats argued their case for Trump's impeachment during the Senate trial in January 2020, Jeffries displayed his expertise in legal advocacy. He also showed his cultural connection when he cited The Notorious B.I.G. a well-known rapper who grew up in Brooklyn but died in a Los Angeles shooting at age 24. Responding to Trump's lawyer who asked the Senate, "Why are we here?" Jeffries ended one of his trial arguments by citing the rapper, "And if you don't know, now you know."

In June 2020, when the House took up police reform, Jeffries used his posts as Caucus chairman and a Judiciary Committee member to work with the CBC, which prepared the bill. When the need for consensus among Democrats forced some caution, Jeffries filed a separate bill with Rep. Joe Kennedy that sought to make it easier to charge police with a civil rights violation by setting a standard of "reckless" behaviour, rather than the "willful" standard in the bill. They called their bill the Bend Toward Justice Act. "We're tired of police violence in a country where the Constitution promises equal protection under the law," he told the House.

Jeffries has been reelected four times without a Democratic primary opponent. In 2020, he defeated his first GOP challenger, 85%-15%. But an August 2020 report in The Intercept, the progressive journalistic website, cited political problems for Jeffries at home. In the June primary that year, two of his allies in the Assembly—including his successor—lost renomination to more outspoken challengers in what the publication described as "a bloodbath for Jeffries." He is viewed by the Democratic Socialists of America, which has been a key ally of Ocasio-Cortez, as an "integral member of the Pelosi team that doesn't support single-payer [medical care] or the Green New Deal," The Intercept reported, adding that redistricting in 2022 posed added uncertainties for Jeffries. His continuing tensions with Ocasio-Cortez also could be perilous for Jeffries, both locally and in the House.

NY-8: Brooklyn   **Cook Partisan Voting Index: D+33**

Population		Race and Ethnicity		Income	
Total	776,825	White	31.60%	Median Income	$59,806
Land area (sq. miles)	30	Black	51.90%	District Income Rank	267
Pop/ sq mi	26,191.	Latino	17.10%	Poverty Rate	19.80%
Born in State	53.80%	Asian	6.10%	With health insurance	95.10%
		Two or more races	3.10%	Cash public assistance	5.70%
Age Groups		Other	7.20%	Food stamp/SNAP	23.80%
Under 18	20.70%				
18-34	27.00%	**Education**		**Work**	
35-64	36.60%	H.S grad or less	44.30%	White Collar	42.60%
Over 64	15.50%	Some college	20.40%	Sales and Service	41.80%
		College Degree, 4 yr	21.60%	Blue Collar	15.60%
Military		Post grad	13.60%	Government	17.00%
Veteran/ Active Duty	2.10%				

2020 Pres. Vote	Biden	234,960	(83%)	Trump	46,711	(16%)
2016 Pres. Vote	Clinton	215,689	(84%)	Trump	34,356	(13%)

Bedford-Stuyvesant: African Americans began settling in Brooklyn's Bedford-Stuyvesant neighbourhood in the 1930s, with the opening of the subway line that was celebrated in Duke Ellington and Billy Strayhorn's "Take the 'A' Train." After World War II, the pace accelerated, as crime and crowding in Harlem—as well as a large influx of African Americans from the South —drove Black New Yorkers to the aging but solid brownstones of "Bed-Stuy." When job growth slowed, Bed-Stuy faced more than its share of poverty and crime. After a 1966 visit by New York's two senators, Democrat Robert F. Kennedy and Republican Jacob Javits, Bed-Stuy won a Model Cities designation, which brought the establishment of the Bedford-Stuyvesant Restoration Corporation, the first such community development organization in the United States.

Even as the Black community expanded across Brooklyn, Bed-Stuy became almost as powerful a symbol of Black New York as Harlem, thanks in part to the films of Spike Lee, a Brooklyn native, who hosts an annual block party. With smart planning, the Bed-Stuy neighbourhood's stately, Hopperesque architecture largely avoided the wrecking ball, and community vigilance kept the streets maintained. The revitalized residential area developed a Caribbean flavor that, combined with handsome brownstones and new shops and galleries, led to a wave of gentrification, with a population exceeding 150,000 and more than 1,900 businesses. Owners of the nearby Barclays Center began a $50 million renovation to convert the large Paramount Theater, a surviving Jazz Age movie house on Flatbush Avenue, into an entertainment and educational center. But those plans might have been permanently delayed by its Russian owner, the Bklyner reported in June 2020. New York University has moved into its $500 million science and engineering center in downtown Brooklyn, with several schools and research centers. In July 2020, Gov. Andrew Cuomo unveiled building plans for the state's $1.4 billion "Vital Brooklyn" plan, including 4,000 units of affordable housing.

The 8th Congressional District of New York takes the shape of a sideways "U" as it rambles across Brooklyn. It begins in Fort Greene, a gentrifying arts area, and from there runs east and south through Clinton Hill, Bed-Stuy and East New York. About 7percent of the district is in Queens, taking in Linden wood and Howard Beach, an Italian neighbourhood that was the home of Mob boss John Gotti. The district runs along the Belt Parkway and the edge of Jamaica Bay through Spring Creek and Canarsie, which have become substantially Black neighborhoods mainly due to Caribbean immigrants who prized the backyards and single-family homes. The bay is causing increased flooding of neighborhoods, even on otherwise dry days, as climate change has increased sea levels.

The district continues through parts of heavily African-American Flatlands and the equally heavily white neighborhoods of Bergen Beach, Marine Park and Mill Basin. It includes the Coney Island peninsula, which was an island before the city filled in Coney Island Creek. Today, it is a diverse collection of neighborhoods and home to the famous theme park, site of the annual hot-dog eating contest and including an amphitheater for year-round entertainment. In 2020, the corona virus created a "lost summer" as the amusement park was largely shut down. Brighton Beach, part of Coney Island, has more Russian Jewish immigrants than any other district in the nation. . These factors have slightly reduced the minorities here to 52 percent Black and 17 percent Hispanic. Joe Biden, with 83 percent of the vote in 2020, showed that this remains one of the most Democratic districts in the nation.

Yvette Clarke (D)

Elected 2006, 8th term, b. Nov 21, 1964; Brooklyn, NY; State University of NY - Medgar Evers College; Oberlin College, 1986; African Methodist Episcopal; Single.

Elected Office: NY City Council, 2002-2007.

Professional Career: Childcare specialist, Erasmus Neighborhood Fed., 1987-1989; Legislative aide, Sen. Velmanette Montgomery, 1989-1991; Executive Assistant, NY Workers' Compensation Board, 1992-1993; Youth program Director, Hospital League/Local S.E.I. University 1199 Training & Upgrading Fund, 1993-1997; Business Development Director, Bronx Overall Development Corporation, 1997-2001.

DC Office: 2058 RHOB 20515, 202-225-6231, Fax: 202-226-0112, clarke.house.gov
State Offices: Brooklyn, 718-287-1142.

Committees: *Energy & Commerce*: Communications & Technology; Consumer Protection & Commerce; Environment & Climate Change. *Homeland Security*: Border Security, Facilitation & Operations; Cybersecurity, Infrastructure Protection & Innovation (Chmn).

Group Ratings

	ADA	ACLU	AFL-CIO	LCV	COC	HAFA	ACU	CFG	FRC
2020	**	86%	**	100%	-	0%	3%	**	-
2019	100%	C	90%	100%	40%	C	3%	21%	0%

Almanac Ratings 2019-2020

	Economy	Social	Foreign	Composite
Liberal	100%	59%	100%	87%
Conservative	0%	41%	0%	13%

Key Votes of the 116th Congress

1. U.S./Mex./Can. trade deal	N	5. Russia sanctions	Y	9. Firearms background checks	Y
2. First Coronavirus response	Y	6. Troops in Syria	Y	10. Spending at the border	N
3. HEROES Act	Y	7. Veto arms sales to Saudis	Y	11. Marijuana liberalized rules	Y
4. CASH Act	Y	8. Defense $$$, veto override	N	12. Electoral College objections	N

Election Results

Election	Name (Party)	Vote (%)		Cand. Spent	Ind. Exp. Support	Ind. Exp. Oppose
2020 General	Yvette Clarke (D)	230,221	(83%)	$1,166,184	$123	
	Constantin Jean-Pierre (R)	43,950	(16%)			$59
2020 Primary	Yvette Clarke (D)	52,293	(54%)			
	Adem Bunkeddeko (D)	23,819	(25%)			
	Isiah James (D)	10,010	(10%)			
	Chaim Deutsch (D)	9,383	(10%)			

Prior winning percentages: 2018 (89%), 2016 (92%), 2014 (81%), 2012 (78%), 2010 (85%), 2008 (69%), 2006 (75%)

Democrat Yvette Clarke, elected in 2006, is a liberal who concentrates on immigration and other issues important to her diverse constituency. As vice chair of the influential Energy and Commerce Committee, she has taken an interest in the unusual topic of fake technology that has been used to alter the images and video of candidates seeking office. After surviving a close contest in the 2018 Democratic primary, she more than doubled the challenger's vote in a rematch two years later.

She was born in the Flatbush section of Brooklyn to immigrant parents from Jamaica. As a young girl, she tagged along to political meetings and events with her mother, Una Clarke, who in 1991 became the first Jamaican elected to the New York City Council. Yvette Clarke attended Oberlin College in Ohio but fell short of graduating by six credit hours. She returned to New York, helped train child care workers, worked as a state legislative aide and served as business development director for the Bronx Overall Economic Development Corporation. In 2001, when term limits forced her mother off the City Council, Clarke defeated four other candidates to succeed her in the predominantly Caribbean area of Flatbush and East Flatbush.

From its creation in 1968 until 2006, the congressional district had been represented by just two people, both Democrats—trailblazer Shirley Chisholm, the first black woman elected to Congress and a 1972 presidential candidate, and Major Owens, who succeeded her in 1982. Clarke's mother had run unsuccessfully against Owens, an African American, in the 2000 Democratic primary, a bitter contest that exposed divisions between the local Caribbean-American community and the African-American community.

In the 2006 primary for the open seat, Clarke navigated a competitive primary field. New York City Councilman David Yassky was called a "colonizer" as a white candidate running in a majority-Black district by Chris Owens, a health industry administrator and son of the retiring lawmaker. Yassky raised more than $1.3 million, exceeding the other three candidates' combined fundraising. Clarke's status as the only woman in the contest and her support among Caribbean Americans were helpful. With the endorsement of the Service Employees International Union's powerful Local 1199, which turned out votes, Clarke defeated Yassky 31%-27%; Owens got 19 percent.

Clarke has had a staunchly liberal voting record. She joined some Black Caucus members who expressed frustration with what they considered President Barack Obama's lack of focus on helping minorities. "What we are asking for is that the president use his bully pulpit to look at a more far-reaching, deeper-penetrating jobs initiative. ... The level of unemployment in our communities is unacceptable," she told National Public Radio in 2010. With Reps. Bonnie Coleman Watson of New Jersey and Robin Kelly of Illinois, Clarke organized a Caucus on Black Women and Girls to bring "a balance in the dialogue about Black Americans." She reportedly sought the CBC chairmanship again in 2018, when Karen Bass of California won. Clarke has chaired the CBC's immigration task force.

One of Clarke's priorities has been the DREAM Act, providing in-state college tuition breaks and other benefits to children of illegal immigrants. In 2008, the House passed her bill to create an appeals process for individuals alleging denial of rights in homeland security investigations. In February 2017, she filed a bill to block President Donald Trump's executive actions that targeted sanctuary cities.

On Energy and Commerce, Clarke worked on legislation to urge the Federal Communications Commission to encourage small businesses to participate in spectrum auctions. As vice chair of the committee after Democrats regained House control, Clarke increased her interest in what she called "deep fakes" electronic interference in elections. She filed a bill that would require disclosure of such actions. In 2021, she planned to pursue the issue as chairwoman of the Homeland Security Subcommittee on Cyber security, Infrastructure Protection and Innovation. "The spread of false, deceptive, or misleading statements, information, acts, or practices, amplified by the use of technology and social media, threatens the integrity of democratic institutions, and the rule of law which form the foundation of our democracy," she said.

In 2018, Clarke faced her first serious reelection challenge, when Adam Bunkeddeko—a 30-year-old native of Uganda and a Harvard Business School graduate with experience in community organizing—said that the district had reached "a new inflection point" and that Clarke had failed to enact a bill during her 11 years in Congress. Clarke responded that Bunkeddeko "recently moved to the community and has nothing to show for it." The challenger gained support in the white, gentrified parts of the district, according to news reports. A New York Times editorial endorsed Bunkeddeko for his "refreshing" big thinking and wrote that Clarke's major accomplishments were "regrettably far between." Clarke outspent the challenger, $1.1 million to $309,000, and won, 53%-47%—a clear signal of future vulnerability. Two years later, Bunkeddeko spent nearly twice as much money and again got the Times' endorsement. But, in the five-candidate contest, Clarke led Bunkeddeko, 54%-25%.

NY-9: Brooklyn

Cook Partisan Voting Index: D+32

Population		Race and Ethnicity		Income	
Total	720,316	White	36.20%	Median Income	$69,754
Land area (sq. miles)	16	Black	46.70%	District Income Rank	167
Pop/ sq mi	46,352.38	Latino	12.10%	Poverty Rate	14.00%
Born in State	47.80%	Asian	7.30%	With health insurance	93.50%
		Two or more races	3.70%	Cash public assistance	4.20%
Age Groups		Other	6.10%	Food stamp/SNAP	19.30%
Under 18	21.60%				
18-34	25.10%	**Education**		**Work**	
35-64	37.70%	H.S grad or less	38.60%	White Collar	46.60%
Over 64	15.70%	Some college	20.80%	Sales and Service	40.20%
		College Degree, 4 yr	23.30%	Blue Collar	13.10%
Military		Post grad	17.30%	Government	16.60%
Veteran/ Active Duty	1.80%				

2020 Pres. Vote	Biden	232,347	(81%)	Trump	50,873	(18%)
2016 Pres. Vote	Clinton	211,812	(83%)	Trump	36,600	(14%)

Flatbush, Crown Heights: Brooklyn. Just saying the word in a comedian's monologue used to elicit laughter. It evoked an accent of twisted English, a raucous, in-your-face style, a sense of humor with an edge, and the chip-on-the-shoulder assertiveness of those sure they will always be in second place. As its name testifies, Brooklyn was a separate community from the 17th century on, and in the 19th century, it was one of the largest cities in the country, with its own celebrities—Henry Ward Beecher, Walt Whitman, John Roebling. By 1898, when the five boroughs were welded into Greater New York, 1 million people lived in Brooklyn. In 1913, a transit agreement was struck to link the city's then-independent lines and triple the track to 619 miles. The agreement helped Brooklyn expand well beyond its established neighborhoods near the Brooklyn Bridge.

Suddenly, Manhattan factory workers no longer had to live in the crowded Lower East Side tenements that social reformer Jacob Riis had exposed in the 1890s. They moved in droves into neighborhoods of three- to five-story apartments and four-family houses. Brooklyn grew from 1.1 million in 1900 to 2.6 million in 1930. The old Brooklynites were mostly Protestant—Dutch, Yankee and German, plus some Catholic Irish. The new Brooklynites were heavily Italian and Jewish, and they populated the sports and entertainment businesses for a long generation, making their hometown nationally famous. Around the time Jackie Robinson suited up for the Brooklyn Dodgers in 1947 as the first Black player in Major League Baseball, Brooklyn was experiencing an influx of African Americans into Brownsville and Crown Heights near Ebbets Field. Just as rapid was the flight of ethnic whites, driven away by "blockbusting," in which unscrupulous real estate brokers stoked white fears, then bought homes cheaply and resold them for higher prices. In a different sort of white flight, "Dem Bums" left for Los Angeles in 1958 and Ebbets Field was knocked down and replaced by an apartment complex.

Today, Kings County, which is coterminous with Brooklyn, is New York's largest county, the nation's ninth largest—ranked behind Miami-Dade and Dallas. With a growing population that was back to 2.6 million in 2017, there has been great vitality among upwardly mobile Hispanic, Asian, Caribbean and Russian immigrants, among middle-class Blacks, and among new generations of Italians and Jews. In 2016, Brooklyn had the least affordable housing of any county in the nation. Lower-income groups found themselves priced out. One reason the population hasn't changed much is because there is scant vacant land. Of the 10 largest counties in the nation, Brooklyn has less than one-tenth as many square miles as Orange County California, which is the second-smallest.

The 9th District of New York, the only district that is entirely in Kings County, begins southeast of downtown Brooklyn. At the far north western tip is the Barclays Center, a large arena that is home to basketball's Brooklyn Nets. The New York Islanders hockey franchise, after moving from Nassau County to Barclays, plans to open a new arena at Belmont Park in late 2021. Deeper into the district are some of Brooklyn's jewels: the Grand Army Plaza, the Parisian-style Eastern Parkway (the world's first six-lane parkway), the Brooklyn Public Library, the Brooklyn Museum and the Brooklyn Botanic Garden, with its Japanese landscaping and placid duck ponds.

Park Slope, on Prospect Park's west side, has become affluent, filling up with young professionals who welcome the easy commute to Manhattan. Mayor Bill de Blasio put the local YMCA on the political map by spending an inordinate amount of time exercising at its gym, even though the site is more than 10 miles from his home at Gracie Mansion. On the east side of Prospect Park is Crown Heights, with its mix of modest apartment buildings and nicely restored row houses. Prospect Park South is an upscale neighborhood whose stately late Victorian-era mansions contrast sharply with the vibrant street life nearby in Flatbush's Little Haiti. At the southern end of the district are Midwood, Homecrest and Sheepshead Bay, mostly white communities with substantial Jewish populations. The district's gentrifying population has dipped to 47 percent Black, with 12 percent Hispanic. Politically, the 9th is overwhelmingly Democratic, though it ranked barely behind six other New York districts in support for Joe Biden in 2020.

Jerrold Nadler (D)

Elected 1992, 15th term, b. Jun 13, 1947; Brooklyn, NY; Columbia University, B.A., 1969; Fordham University School of Law, J.D., 1978; Jewish; Married (Joyce L. Miller); 1 child.

Elected Office: NY Assembly, 1977-1992.

Professional Career: Legislative Assistant, NY Assembly, 1972; Law clerk, 1976.

DC Office: 2132 RHOB 20515, 202-225-5635, Fax: 202-225-6923, nadler.house.gov

State Offices: Brooklyn, 718-373-3198; New York, 212-367-7350.

Committees: *Judiciary (Chmn).*

Group Ratings

	ADA	ACLU	AFL-CIO	LCV	COC	HAFA	ACU	CFG	FRC
2020	**	85%	**	100%	-	0%	3%	**	-
2019	95%	C	100%	100%	47%	C	3%	8%	0%

Almanac Ratings 2019-2020

	Economy	Social	Foreign	Composite
Liberal	100%	63%	97%	87%
Conservative	0%	37%	3%	13%

Key Votes of the 116th Congress

1. U.S./Mex./Can. trade deal	N/A	5. Russia sanctions	Y
2. First Coronavirus response	Y	6. Troops in Syria	Y
3. HEROES Act	Y	7. Veto arms sales to Saudis	Y
4. CASH Act	Y	8. Defense $$$, veto override	Y

9. Firearms background checks	Y
10. Spending at the border	N
11. Marijuana liberalized rules	Y
12. Electoral College objections	N

Election Results

Election	Name (Party)	Vote (%)		Cand. Spent	Ind. Exp. Support	Ind. Exp. Oppose
2020 General	Jerrold Nadler (D)	206,310	(74%)	$2,067,085	$6,073	
	Cathy Bernstein (R)	66,889	(24%)	$28,961		
2020 Primary	Jerry Nadler (D)	51,054	(68%)			
	Lindsey Boylan (D)	16,511	(22%)			
	Jonathan Herzog (D)	7,829	(10%)			

Prior winning percentages: 2018 (82%), 2016 (78%), 2014 (79%), 2012 (70%), 2010 (76%), 2008 (63%), 2006 (74%), 2004 (64%), 2002 (55%), 2000 (64%), 1998 (71%), 1996 (66%), 1994 (67%), 1992 (60%)

Democrat Jerrold Nadler, first elected in 1992, is chairman of the House Judiciary Committee, a crucial position during the presidency of Donald Trump. An adversary of Trump since the 1980s in conflicts over real estate development on the West Side of Manhattan and a strong civil libertarian, Nadler initially took a deliberate approach to review of legal issues surrounding the president and a possible congressional response. Once the Democrats launched their initial charges against Trump, Nadler shared the spotlight—sometimes awkwardly—with Rep. Adam Schiff, the more commanding chairman of the Intelligence Committee and a closer ally of Speaker Nancy Pelosi. In the second impeachment case against Trump, Nadler was largely invisible.

With Joe Biden as president, Nadler became a focal point for Democrats' call for broad constitutional change that might strengthen their hand in setting policy. The committee had a more hands-on role with changes in voting rights and police tactics. But Nadler's more immediate interest —his potential legacy--was outside the scope of the Judiciary Committee: his long time advocacy of the Gateway project to add a rail tunnel under the Hudson River to modernize freight service between New York City and much of the nation.

Nadler was born in Brooklyn and moved around with his family as a child. His parents bought a chicken farm in New Jersey, but the business failed, and they moved back to the city. His father ran a gas station on Long Island and owned an auto parts store. Interested in politics from a young age, Nadler campaigned for Democrat Eugene McCarthy for president in 1968 while at Columbia University, where he roomed with Dick Morris, who would later become a top adviser to President Bill Clinton.

After getting his law degree from Fordham University, Nadler ran for the New York Assembly in 1976, at age 29. In the primary, he beat Ruth Messinger, the Democratic nominee for mayor in 1997, by 73 votes. In 1992, he suddenly had the opportunity to run for Congress. Representative Ted Weiss, long an Upper West Side icon, died the day before the September primary, which he won posthumously. The nomination was decided by a convention of almost 1,000 county Democratic committee members. Nadler won 62 percent of the votes to secure the nomination and thus the election.

Nadler's leftward leanings are evident in his fondness for the New Deal. He told a New York audience in 2012 that President Franklin Roosevelt's economic program "put into practice regulations on corporations and banks to prevent economic catastrophes—regulations that worked until they were dismantled, starting in the 1980s." He said Republicans have been misguided in cutting social programs and in letting large corporations pay little or no taxes. After Super storm Sandy ravaged New York and other states in October 2012, he said New York City needed higher seawalls and waterproofed electric power facilities.

With Ground Zero from the 9/11 attacks as part of his district, Nadler has had a continuing focus on the consequences and the cleanup. In late 2010, he helped steer into law a long-delayed post-September 11 measure providing more than $4 billion in compensation to first responders suffering health problems—a development he called "without a doubt the proudest moment of my 34-year career in government." In 2015, he was the original sponsor of the bill that Congress enacted to assure lifetime health benefits for 9/11 survivors. "I am proud of my country today for fulfilling our commitment to never leaving the wounded on the battlefield," he said. That legislation was named for James Zadroga, a city police officer who died in 2006 from toxins at the site.

As the long time liberal pillar on the Judiciary Committee, Nadler has been a counterweight to lawmakers of both parties seeking expanded national security authority to crack down on terrorism. Nadler insists that he is not unsympathetic to their cause. But he has worked to protect detainees' habeas corpus rights. When the House voted in 2012 to extend a warrantless wiretapping program, he bemoaned how much power it gave to presidents. A vigorous opponent of the USA Patriot Act, the Bush administration's center piece anti-terrorism law, he was a leader of the bipartisan coalition that narrowed the law's scope and limited the collection of bulk data by federal intelligence operatives. The renamed USA Freedom Act in 2015 was "the first significant reform of government surveillance carried out by the federal government since 1978," he said.

On domestic issues, he led the fight in the House against proposals to ban same-sex marriage and has blasted the National Rifle Association's resistance to gun control legislation. He called suggestions for putting armed guards in schools "ludicrous and insulting." He worked with Republicans to protect creative performers—many of whom are his constituents—with a proposal to require that radio stations pay royalties to the record companies that own copyrights to records that are played over the airwaves.

On foreign policy, Nadler opposed the Iraq war resolution in 2002. Regarding Afghanistan, he said in 2010, "an intelligent policy is not to try to remake a country that nobody since Genghis Khan has managed to conquer." In 2015, he supported Obama's nuclear agreement with Iran, a difficult vote for many of his Jewish constituents. "My conclusion is that this deal—of the available alternatives to us, not what might or should have been—is the best," he told The New York Times.

Nadler has been an activist on district-related issues at the Transportation and Infrastructure Committee, though he dropped his membership when he became Judiciary chairman. He has fought to add rail service east of the Hudson and to subsidize Amtrak. His biggest idea has been a rail-freight tunnel under the Hudson. Lack of such a line has meant that New York gets only a tiny share of its freight by rail; a new tunnel—at a cost likely exceeding $10 billion—could mean cheaper freight and therefore lower prices. In the 1990s, Nadler successfully fought developer Donald Trump's attempts to alter the West Side Highway to accommodate his proposed luxury housing project in rail yards. Trump in turn called Nadler a "hack." Subsequently, their mutual hostility deepened.

Nadler took over the top Democratic post on Judiciary in December 2017 when Rep. John Conyers of Michigan resigned under pressure following reports of sexual harassment of congressional aides. Nadler, who was next senior on the committee, was challenged by Zoe Lofgren of California, a long time ally of Pelosi, who cited her expertise on immigration and the need for more women to lead House committees. Nadler contended that his expertise in constitutional law made him "the best person to sit in that chair." He won, 118-72.

While in the minority at Judiciary, Nadler said that a Democratic-run committee would review charges that were raised against Supreme Court Justice Brett Kavanaugh during his Senate confirmation hearings in September 2018. "It is not something we are eager to do," he told the Times. "But the Senate having failed to do its proper constitutionally mandated job of advise and consent, we are going to have to do something to provide a check and balance." But that review was set aside in a case of comity between the two chambers and apparent desire to move beyond an incident that was problematic for both parties.

As he prepared to chair the Judiciary Committee, Nadler made clear that the panel would vigorously pursue various allegations against Trump. (Early in 2017, he had filed a "resolution of inquiry," which would have required the Justice Department to provide to the House documents related to Trump's finances; the committee rejected his resolution in a series of party-line votes.) But he initially deferred when Pelosi said—mindful of the political risk of impeachment for Democrats in swing districts—the case was not yet strong enough.

Eventually, Democrats coalesced behind the impeachment charge that Trump sought political assistance from the president of Ukraine and Schiff took the lead in preparing the policy case, while Nadler laid out the narrower constitutional argument for impeachment. By comparison, Schiff had a stronger presence. "If Schiff is a cool television presence, a slim 59-year-old triathlete who speaks in modulated, extemporaneous sound bites," Todd Purdum wrote for The Atlantic in November 2019, "Nadler, 72, is a hotter, blunter personality. His default mode is a wised-up Big Apple belligerence." When Pelosi named the seven trial managers to make the case to the Senate, Schiff—a former federal prosecutor in Los Angeles—took the lead; Nadler, a career legislator, was a team member.

On the second impeachment case against Trump, which followed the January 2021 riot at the Capitol, Nadler barely had a presence. The Judiciary Committee held no hearing or discussion of the charges. News reports widely cited junior members of the committee as drafters of the charges while they were huddled during the insurrection. And Rep. Jamie Raskin, one of those members, led the House managers during the Senate trial—with extensive plaudits from friendly observers.

Another measure of the limits of Nadler's influence under Pelosi's domain came in June 2020, when House Democrats prepared a police reform bill. Many Democrats shared his reservations about police authority as they crafted legislation to respond to incidents across the nation that resulted from abuses by police officers. But, although that bill dealt mostly with issues under the Judiciary Committee's command, Pelosi gave control of the bill to members of the Congressional Black Caucus, with no formal role for Nadler. Some of the CBC leaders on the issue—including Karen Bass of California and Hakeem Jeffries of New York—serve on Judiciary.

Nadler faced unusual competition for reelection in 2016, which he easily survived. In the primary, Oliver Rosenberg, a 30-year-old former investment banker, called Nadler's vote for the Iran nuclear deal "disastrous." Rosenberg, who self-financed $367,000, said Nadler was out of touch with younger voters. The outcome suggested otherwise. Nadler won the primary with 89 percent. The general election was a reprise of sorts. Republican Philip Rosenthal said Nadler's Iran vote was "an existential threat" to both Israel and to New York City. A lawyer with a business in data analytics, Rosenthal raised only $74,000. Nadler, who raised $1.6 million for the campaign, won 78%-22%, including 57 percent in Brooklyn.

Two years later, Nadler got 82 percent against Republican Naomi Levin, a pro-Trump political newcomer, who spent $79,000. In 2020, Nadler took 68 percent in the three-candidate Democratic primary. Runner up Lindsey Boylan, who spent $900,000 and got 22 percent, went public in February 2021 with charges that Gov. Andrew Cuomo sexually harassed her while she was working in his office in Manhattan. Later in 2021, Boylan ran for Manhattan borough president.

NY-10: Lower Manhattan, Southern Brooklyn

Cook Partisan Voting Index: D+27

Population		Race and Ethnicity		Income	
Total	732,732	White	68.70%	Median Income	$103,331
Land area (sq. miles)	14	Black	3.70%	District Income Rank	27
Pop/ sq mi	51,419.79	Latino	13.40%	Poverty Rate	13.60%
Born in State	44.90%	Asian	18.70%	With health insurance	95.80%
		Two or more races	3.10%	Cash public assistance	2.50%
Age Groups		Other	5.80%	Food stamp/SNAP	10.80%
Under 18	19.40%				
18-34	27.10%	**Education**		**Work**	
35-64	37.40%	H.S grad or less	25.70%	White Collar	61.90%
Over 64	16.20%	Some college	10.90%	Sales and Service	30.40%
Military		College Degree, 4 yr	32.60%	Blue Collar	7.70%
Veteran/ Active Duty	1.70%	Post grad	30.70%	Government	7.40%

2020 Pres. Vote	Biden	218,141	(76%)	Trump	65,611	(23%)
2016 Pres. Vote	Clinton	205,114	(78%)	Trump	49,179	(19%)

West Side, Borough Park: Over the course of the 20th century, New York City spread so far beyond its original boundaries in Lower Manhattan that, for a while, it became easy to forget how pivotal the southern end of the island had been in making the city what it is today. That changed in an instant on the morning of Sept.11, 2001, when al-Qaida terrorists flew two hijacked jets into the twin towers of the World Trade Center, killing nearly 3,000 people and laying waste to 13 city blocks. The terrorists struck the tallest buildings in the nation's biggest city, toppling a complex whose name embodied American capitalism. The city, nation and world were forever altered.

Lower Manhattan has long been home to Wall Street and the Financial District. Over the years, it has represented America's striving spirit in other ways as well. The Brooklyn Bridge, begun in 1869 just a few blocks east of the Twin Towers site and completed in 1883, was half again as long as any bridge then standing and seven times higher than any building in the adjoining boroughs. The Holland Tunnel, built in 1927, was the first underwater vehicular tunnel built anywhere in the world. Just offshore are Ellis Island, now split between New York and New Jersey, where members of the great immigration wave first set foot on American soil, and the Statue of Liberty, the symbol of freedom they saw as they sailed in.

Infrastructure remains a local preoccupation. Repairs of the Brooklyn Bridge's deteriorating towers began in 2019, additional repairs required as the result of damage caused by Super storm Sandy in 2012 plus the need to reinforce its foundations; completion was planned for 2023. The Port Authority Bus Terminal on the West Side, originally opened in 1950 and generously described as decrepit, has generated plans for billions of dollars of renovation and expansion to accommodate greatly increased demand. The Hudson Yards, formerly a web of rail tracks that covers more than 14 acres surrounding 34th Street on the Far West Side, has become the platform for a massive real-estate transformation to a growing new neighborhood of residential, commercial and office skyscrapers that has been described as the largest private mixed-use development in U.S. history. At the World Trade Center site, three new skyscrapers, plus a transportation hub and a memorial museum have opened, starting in 2014; one more tower was expected, plus a new performing arts center. The corona virus caused new uncertainties about the demand for downtown office space. In the Chelsea Market area, Google has opened a building that fills one city block and planned to expand to another campus in West Village As of 2019, the tech giant planned a local workforce of more than 14,000.

From the Battery, at the southern tip of Manhattan, the 10th Congressional District of New York runs north up the island's west side, covering the Financial District and many neighborhoods. Battery Park City has attractive, modern apartments and parks—with what reportedly are the most expensive rents in the nation. Sophisticated TriBeCa has artists' lofts and an annual film festival that has spurred economic and cultural revitalization. Art galleries have thrived in Chelsea, and SoHo has become an international shoppers' paradise. Greenwich Village, home of New York University, has long had a taste for the radical, though some of its ideas have become mainstream: Led by Jane Jacobs, its successful fight against the proposed Lower Manhattan Expressway popularized historic preservation and urbanism. A leading antagonist at the time was the local builder, Donald Trump. At 57th Street, the district cuts east to Fifth Avenue and includes most of Central Park, then continues north along Amsterdam Avenue as it excludes Harlem. The Upper West Side is home to Lincoln Center, while the northern end of the district at 122nd Street takes in Morningside Heights, site of Columbia University.

The venerable apartment buildings along Central Park West, West End Avenue and Riverside Drive, and the brownstones on the cross streets, house some of the country's most dedicated liberals. These professional people were satirized on Seinfeld, the long-running sitcom that resonated far beyond Manhattan. In the 1950s, West Siders took up the reform banner and finally killed off the ancient and ailing Tammany Hall Democratic machine. This strip of Manhattan has gained renown among transportation planners for the Gateway Project with New Jersey—proposed rail tunnels under the Hudson River that are needed to expedite commerce in the Northeast and to replace antiquated portals, at a cost exceeding $10 billion. Expectations that Trump would preside over his ultimate deal in his former neighborhood proved futile. But numerous interests pressed the Biden administration to sponsor this epic infrastructure project.

The slice of the 10th District in Brooklyn, which includes 25 percent of the voters, includes a very different set of neighborhoods. Borough Park has one of the nation's largest Orthodox Jewish communities, with Yiddish-language ATMs and Russian bathhouses. Jews have a long history in the city. After World War I, as many as 400,000 disembarked each year at Ellis Island until a 1924 law virtually shut down immigration. Today, New York has the largest Jewish population of any city other than Tel Aviv. The Russians, many of whom live close to poverty, are anti-socialist. The Hasidic

Jews of Borough Park are conservative and hostile to racial preferences, and they favor tough police treatment of crime. After getting about two-thirds of their vote in 2016, Trump won 79 percent in the Assembly district that includes Borough Park. Even with these conservative enclaves, the district remains at the cultural and financial heart of national liberalism. Joe Biden got 76 percent of its vote in 2020.

Nicole Malliotakis (R)

Elected 2020, 1st term, b. Nov 11, 1980; New York, NY; Seton Hall University, B.A., 2001; Wagner College, M.B.A., 2010; Greek Orthodox; Single.

Elected Office: Member, NY State Assembly, 2011-2020; Minority Whip, New York State Assembly, 2019-2021.

Professional Career: Community Liason, New York State Senator John J. Marchi, 2002-2004; Assistant to the Governor, Community Affairs, New York State, 2004-2006; Public and Government Affairs Manager, Consolidated Edison, 2006-2010.

DC Office: 417 CHOB 20515, 202-225-3371, malliotakis.house.gov

State Offices: Brooklyn, 718-306-1620; Staten Island, 718-568-2870.

Committees: *Foreign Affairs*: Europe, Energy, the Environment & Cyber; Intern'l Dev't, Intern'l Orgs & Global Corporate Social Impact (RMM). *Transportation & Infrastructure*: Highways & Transit.

Election Results

Election	Name (Party)	Vote (%)		Cand. Spent	Ind. Exp. Support	Ind. Exp. Oppose
2020 General	Nicole Malliotakis (R)........................ 155,608	(53%)		$3,558,100	$223,053	$7,802,831
	Max Rose (D)..................................... 137,198	(47%)		$9,455,111	$3,808,722	$6,655,403
2020 Primary	Nicole Malliotakis (R)......................... 15,697	(69%)				
	Joe Caldarera (R).................................. 7,046	(31%)				

Nicole Malliotakis returned the Staten Island-based district to its traditional Republican control. She defeated Democrat Max Rose, an outspoken advocate during his one House term, who delighted in confronting powerful forces in New York and Washington. Malliotakis, who served 10 years in the state Assembly, had experience as a political aide before she was elected. In 2017, she unsuccessfully challenged the reelection of New York City Mayor Bill de Blasio, though she ran strongly in the area defined by the 11th Congressional District.

A native of Staten Island, Malliotakis was the daughter of immigrants who ran small businesses; her father was from Greece and her mother was an exile from Cuba. She got her bachelor's degree in communications from Seton Hall University and a master's in business administration from Wagner College. For two years, she was an aide to Gov. George Pataki. In the private sector, she was a public affairs manager for Con Edison, the city utility.

At age 29, Malliotakis was elected to the state Assembly in 2010. She eventually served as minority whip and ranking minority member of the Governmental Employees Committee.

She was not shy about moving up the ladder. When the 11th District opened in 2015 following the resignation of Republican Rep. Mike Grimm, who pleaded guilty to tax evasion, Malliotakis told party leaders that she wanted their support to succeed him. After they backed Daniel Donovan, the local district attorney who was elected to the position, she complained about a "rigged system" and "old boy's network."

In 2017, after other potential GOP contenders stepped aside, Malliotakis got a more daunting opportunity as the GOP challenger to de Blasio. In an interview with The New York Times during that campaign, she said she was tired of defending resident Donald Trump, "instead of all these issues that we should be focusing on as mayor." She got 70 percent of the vote on Staten Island, though De Blasio won citywide, 66%-28%.

After political newcomer Rose defeated Donovan in 2018, Malliotakis launched her challenge in January 2019. "I feel it's important that New York City has at least one Republican voice in

Washington," she told the Brooklyn Reporter. "We have a two-party system to make sure that we have representatives who will stand up and speak out when the majority is not doing the right thing."

Grimm responded by calling her "unprincipled, unaccomplished and underwhelming." But Malliotakis did not face serious opposition in the GOP primary, which she won with 69 percent of the vote. She welcomed Trump's endorsement for the nomination and said she would be "a vocal advocate" for his policies. She attacked Rose for having "turned his back" on his 2018 campaign pledge of independence and instead had become "just another liberal Democrat."

Rose responded with at least as many attacks within his own party—including on the mayor. "Bill de Blasio is the worst mayor in the history of New York City. That's the whole ad," he said in a campaign ad, a recognition that the mayor was highly unpopular with Rose's constituents. He also took issue with what he described as "the limousine liberal trope" of Democratic Rep. Alexandria Ocasio-Cortez of New York, who was elected to the House with Rose in 2018.

Rose spent $9.5 million in the campaign, which nearly tripled his challenger. The two parties spent almost $20 million on the contest. Malliotakis won comfortably, 53%-47%. She ran stronger in the Staten Island portion of the district, where she took 59 percent of the vote. Surprisingly, she also led in its Brooklyn precincts, which cast one-fourth of the total vote and were Rose's political base. As she prepared for the House, she bonded with other newly elected Republican women whose families had escaped persecution overseas. She became ranking Republican on the Foreign Affairs Subcommittee on International Development, International Organizations and Global Corporate Social Impact.

NY-11: New York City

Cook Partisan Voting Index: R+7

Population		Race and Ethnicity		Income	
Total	737,390	White	69.40%	Median Income	$81,253
Land area (sq. miles)	66	Black	7.70%	District Income Rank	84
Pop/ sq mi	11,201.43	Latino	17.30%	Poverty Rate	10.10%
Born in State	62.30%	Asian	15.40%	With health insurance	94.90%
		Two or more races	2.40%	Cash public assistance	3.40%
Age Groups		Other	5.10%	Food stamp/SNAP	14.70%
Under 18	22.40%				
18-34	21.30%	**Education**		**Work**	
35-64	39.30%	H.S grad or less	40.90%	White Collar	42.20%
Over 64	17.10%	Some college	21.10%	Sales and Service	40.60%
		College Degree, 4 yr	22.90%	Blue Collar	17.20%
Military		Post grad	15.20%	Government	18.80%
Veteran/ Active Duty	3.00%				

2020 Pres. Vote	Trump	163,857	(55%)	Biden	132,366	(44%)
2016 Pres. Vote	Trump	133,232	(53%)	Clinton	108,807	(44%)

Staten Island, South Brooklyn: Staten Island is part of New York City, yet is a land apart, closer geographically and culturally to New Jersey than to the city's other boroughs. Its inclusion in Greater New York as part of the great 1898 consolidation was something of an afterthought. It was connected to the rest of the city only by ferry or through Bayonne New Jersey, until the Verrazano-Narrows Bridge—one of Robert Moses' last and most impressive infrastructure achievements—opened to traffic in 1964. Hilly Staten Island (or Richmond County) is the state's southernmost county, one-tenth as densely populated as Manhattan. After doubling in population from 1960 to 2000, it increased by less than 10 percent in the next 20 years. Its rate of home ownership, 69 percent, more than doubles that of the rest of New York City. The $505,000 median value of owner-occupied housing on Staten Island in 2019 was 25 percent higher than in the Bronx and almost as much as Queens.

Ethnically, Staten Island has the highest percentage of residents of Italian ancestry in the nation. The signs on coffee shops read Caffe and on delicatessens, Salumeria. The Staten Island Ferry docks at St. George. The north and south shores that spread out from there are notable for their pleasant Victorian homes. The island's west shore is industrial marshland, where the 2,200-acre Freshkills park—nearly three times as large as Central Park and on top of the former landfill that collected more than 50 years and 150 million tons of the city's trash, which until 2001 received as much as 28,000 tons daily—has taken shape, with varieties of plant and animal life. Staten Island's interior consists of scrubland that has become blocks of suburbia for New Yorkers who like a small-town ambience.

In St. George, Empire Outlets, a $350 million shopping and entertainment complex with extensive waterfront and the first outlet mall in New York City, opened in May 2019. Construction of a $613 million seawall and 20-foot levy on the eastern shore of the island that were planned to extend five miles and designed to limit or delay a repeat of the devastating floods in 2012 from Super storm Sandy has been redesigned, with completion delayed until 2025.

Culturally, Staten Islanders are more conservative than people from the other boroughs, particularly those from Manhattan, which is an18-minute ferry ride away. Fed up with the city's high taxes and costly government, Staten Island residents voted in 1993 for secession, but the legislature never carried out their wish. That year, Staten Islanders provided the margin of victory for Republican Mayor Rudy Giuliani. The Giuliani years contributed a new ferry terminal, additional shops, and hundreds of new houses near cleaned-up beaches. Recent years have featured demographic shifts. The northern shore of Staten Island has gained African-Americans and Asians(12 percent and 11 percent of the total population in 2019, respectively) on the corners of the island, with a large Hispanic community (19 percent) in between the traditional Italian neighborhoods on the southern side.

The 11th Congressional District of New York is made up of Staten Island plus neighborhoods in the southwest corner of Brooklyn. The latter portions, a bit more than 25 percent of the district, include heavily Catholic and Italian Bay Ridge, Dyker Heights and part of Bensonhurst, middle-class enclaves with large single-family brownstones that are nowhere near a subway stop and largely impervious to the economic and social gentrification spreading across Brooklyn, though they are the less conservative part of the district. In 2020, President Donald Trump won this district, 55%-44%. In the county, Trump won 57 percent of the 216,000 votes. Republicans have controlled the congressional seat for all but four years since 1980.

Carolyn Maloney (D)

Elected 1992, 15th term, b. Feb 19, 1946; Greensboro, NC; University Dijon, Paris (France); New School for Social Research; Greensboro College, B.A., 1968; Presbyterian; Widow (Clifton Maloney); 2 children.

Elected Office: NY City Council, 1982-1992.

Professional Career: Community affairs Coordinator, Board of Ed. Welfare ed. program, 1972-1975; Staff, Board of Ed. cntr. for career & occupational ed., 1975-1976; Sr. program analyst, NY Assembly committee, 1977-1979; Legislative aide, NY Assembly & NY Senate, 1979-1982.

DC Office: 2308 RHOB 20515, 202-225-7944, Fax: 202-225-4709, maloney.house.gov

State Offices: Astoria, 718-932-1804; Brooklyn, 718-349-5972; New York, 212-860-0606.

Committees: *Financial Services:* Housing, Community Development & Insurance; Investor Protection, Entrepreneurship & Capital Markets. *Oversight & Reform (Chmn):* Ex Officio membership on all subcommittees.

Group Ratings

	ADA	ACLU	AFL-CIO	LCV	COC	HAFA	ACU	CFG	FRC
2020	**	83%	**	100%	-	0%	4%	**	-
2019	100%	C	90%	100%	45%	C	4%	12%	0%

Key Votes of the 116th Congress

1. U.S./Mex./Can. trade deal N	5. Russia sanctions Y	9. Firearms background checks Y
2. First Coronavirus response Y	6. Troops in Syria Y	10. Spending at the border N
3. HEROES Act Y	7. Veto arms sales to Saudis Y	11. Marijuana liberalized rules Y
4. CASH Act Y	8. Defense $$$, veto override Y	12. Electoral College objections N

Election Results

Election	Name (Party)	Vote (%)		Cand. Spent	Ind. Exp. Support	Ind. Exp. Oppose
2020 General	Carolyn Maloney (D)............................	265,172	(82%)	$3,244,097	$1,656	
	Carlos Santiago-Cano (R).....................	53,061	(16%)			$113
2020 Primary	Carolyn Maloney (D)............................	40,362	(43%)			
	Suraj Patel (D).....................................	37,106	(39%)			
	Lauren Ashcraft (D)..............................	12,810	(14%)			

Prior winning percentages: 2018 (86%), 2016 (83%), 2014 (77%), 2012 (72%), 2010 (71%), 2008 (66%), 2006 (76%), 2004 (81%), 2002 (61%), 2000 (60%), 1998 (66%), 1996 (61%), 1994 (59%), 1992 (42%)

Democrat Carolyn Maloney, first elected in 1992, is known for her forceful efforts on behalf of women and consumers and has been a prolific legislator on Capitol Hill. Following the death in October 2019 of Rep. Elijah Cummings of Maryland, Maloney became chairwoman of the Oversight and Reform Committee, amid the House's impeachment investigation of President Donald Trump. During the following year, she confronted the Trump administration's handling of two prime political issues: the decennial census and the Postal Service, especially its handling of the surge in mailed ballots for the presidential election, amid the corona virus pandemic. With President Joe Biden, she pushed for postal reform and for statehood for the District of Columbia. At home, she recently survived two close challenges in the Democratic primary.

Born and educated in North Carolina, she visited New York at the age of 22, loved it, and "just stayed." She taught adult-education classes in East Harlem and, from 1977 to 1982, was an influential legislative staffer in Albany. She was elected to the New York City Council in 1982. Redistricting in 1992 made the Silk Stocking district more Democratic, and Maloney ran against incumbent Bill Green, an independent Republican who shared the cultural liberalism of Manhattan's East Side. But he was poorly positioned to appeal to voters in the working-class outer-borough neighborhoods that had been added to the district. Maloney lost the Manhattan part of the district 50%-44% but carried Queens heavily, winning 50%-48% overall.

Maloney has a mostly liberal voting record. On the Financial Services Committee—where she has been more willing than many other Democratic lawmakers to listen to bankers, many of whom are her constituents, but not necessarily to support their interests—she had a hand in crafting the Dodd-Frank Wall Street overhaul in 2010. She worked with Democratic Sen. Dick Durbin to achieve a compromise on interchange fees charged on consumers' debit cards. In 2009, she enacted her bill to promote more transparent practices by credit card companies and to restrict lending practices. Maloney had tough rhetoric for bankers who took millions of dollars in bonuses after their firms received federal bailout money in 2008. But she opposed in early 2010 a proposed .25 percent tax on stock transactions above $100,000.

She opposed subsequent Republican-led efforts to weaken the law and she criticized as lax the Trump administration's enforcement of Dodd-Frank. "We have essentially taken the cop off the beat," she said during an April 2018 hearing. In 2019, Maloney was selected to chair the restructured Investor Protection, Entrepreneurship and Capital Markets Subcommittee at Financial Services, where she is the next-senior Democrat behind Chairwoman Maxine Waters of California.

A leader of the Women's Caucus, Maloney drew national attention in 2012 for walking out of an Oversight and Government Reform Committee hearing on contraception and religious liberty after pointing out its all-male witness list. "What I want to know is, where are the women?" she asked. She blasted GOP efforts to bar funding for Planned Parenthood. When conservatives that year removed expanded protections for lesbians and Native Americans in a reauthorization of the Violence Against Women Act, Maloney called it "as chilling and callous as anything I have seen come before this Congress in modern times." The House passed her 2008 bill to give eight weeks of paid leave to federal employees for the birth or adoption of a child. In 2017, she reached out to first daughter Ivanka Trump to seek common ground on paid-leave legislation; they failed to reach agreement.

With part of her district in Lower Manhattan and close to Ground Zero, Maloney has been heavily involved in the government response to the September 11 attacks. She urged President George W. Bush to quickly send New York the $20 billion that Congress approved for cleanup and recovery. In 2010, she and several other New York members steered into law a long-delayed measure to compensate September 11 first responders with health problems. In 2015, she took the lead in extending those benefits to cover the entire life of survivors.

Maloney made a bid for the top Democratic slot on Oversight and Reform after Democrats lost the House majority in 2010. She lost to the less senior Cummings, 119-61, in the Democratic Caucus. Cummings reportedly had the pivotal backing of Minority Leader Nancy Pelosi. A month after the death of Cummings in 2019, the Caucus chose Maloney to chair the committee in a contest with Rep. Gerald Connolly, 133-86.

Initial Democratic plans gave equal billing in the Trump impeachment to the Oversight panel, plus the Judiciary and Intelligence Committees. But Oversight took a diminished role as its internal transition overlapped the impeachment review by the other two committees. Coincidentally, the Judiciary Committee was chaired by Jerrold Nadler, who entered the House the same day as Maloney and worked with her on many issues from his district on the West Side of Manhattan.

Following the first Trump impeachment trial in February 2020, Maloney eagerly confronted the administration. When the Justice and Commerce Departments failed to provide documents subpoenaed by the Oversight committee that related to their controversial efforts to include a question in the census about citizenship, Maloney led efforts to file suit against the top officials of those agencies, who she said "cannot be allowed to disregard and degrade the authority of Congress to fulfill our core constitutional legislative and oversight responsibilities." Although the Supreme Court earlier rejected attempts to ask about citizenship, it separately refused to intervene in the request for documents.

When her panel later investigated news reports that Trump appointee Postmaster General Louis DeJoy urged postal employees to contribute to Trump's reelection campaign, Maloney warned that he could face criminal liability for possibly having lied to the committee. The committee also filed a lawsuit contending that the Postal Service was deliberately delaying the collection of mail-in voting —which DeJoy denied. In that case, a federal judge in the District of Columbia ruled a week before the election that the Postal Service should take steps to increase its on-time delivery of ballots. After Biden took office, Maloney was among the sponsors of bipartisan legislation to adjust USPS finances to eliminate billions of dollars it allegedly owed in Medicare payments for postal employees. "I am laser-focused on fixing the Postal Service's financial problems," she said in February 2021. In May, Maloney took what seemed a significant step when she filed a postal reform proposal with senior Republicans on her committee.Three months later, her committee approved the Postal Service Reform Act, with strong bipartisan support.

At home, Maloney was bitterly disappointed when Democratic Gov. David Paterson appointed the less-seasoned Rep. Kirsten Gillibrand to the Senate seat vacated by Hillary Clinton in 2009. Maloney publicly questioned Gillibrand's stances on issues such as gun control and curbing illegal immigration, and she began raising money for a primary challenge in 2010. Gillibrand quickly moved left in the Senate, and in August 2009 Maloney reluctantly heeded the calls of President Barack Obama and senior New York Democrats to give her a clear path to the nomination.

In 2018 and again in 2020, Maloney faced unusually competitive primary challenges from Suraj Patel, a hotel executive and former Obama campaign aide who appealed to millennials seeking change and said that Maloney had been ineffective. With sizable fundraising from contributors of Indian descent, Patel spent more than $1 million in his initial contest. Maloney won, 60%-40%, chiefly by taking nearly two-thirds of the vote in the Manhattan portion of the district; the candidates were nearly even in Queens and Patel led in Brooklyn. In their four-candidate contest two years later, Maloney led Patel by an unimpressive43%-39%. She got 50 percent of the vote in Manhattan, but ran second in Queens and third in Brooklyn. Her close contests could make Maloney an inviting target post-redistricting, depending on how the lines are drawn. At age 76 in 2022, she is a potential retiree.

NY-12: New York City　　　　　　　　**Cook Partisan Voting Index: D+34**

Population		Race and Ethnicity		Income	
Total	725,760	White	71.00%	Median Income	$124,502
Land area (sq. miles)	15	Black	5.40%	District Income Rank	8
Pop/ sq mi	49,070.99	Latino	14.40%	Poverty Rate	10.00%
Born in State	41.10%	Asian	15.50%	With health insurance	96.40%
		Two or more races	3.40%	Cash public assistance	1.60%
Age Groups		Other	4.80%	Food stamp/SNAP	6.20%
Under 18	12.00%				
18-34	35.10%	**Education**		**Work**	
35-64	36.50%	H.S grad or less	16.40%	White Collar	68.00%
Over 64	16.50%	Some college	11.10%	Sales and Service	27.00%
		College Degree, 4 yr	38.10%	Blue Collar	5.00%
Military		Post grad	34.50%	Government	7.60%
Veteran/ Active Duty	2.30%				

2020 Pres. Vote	Biden	280,012	(84%)	Trump	49,337	(15%)
2016 Pres. Vote	Clinton	255,601	(82%)	Trump	41,384	(13%)

Manhattan's East Side, Queens Astoria: The Upper East Side of Manhattan is home to people with more accumulated wealth than anywhere else in the world. Its western border was established at Fifth Avenue in 1857, when work began on Central Park; originally a swampy, rocky slum, it was completed in 1873. During the 1880s, the avenues—Fifth, Madison, Park, Lexington, Third, Second, First—were paved, and rich New Yorkers as well as many who had made their money elsewhere, built mansions on Fifth Avenue. With its elevated train line, Third Avenue was lined with walk-ups for working-class commuters. The side streets off Fifth Avenue were filled with massive brownstones shielded from the industrial haze along the East River.

The Upper East Side began taking on its present character in 1913, when Grand Central Terminal opened and the New York Central rail line was buried under Park Avenue. What had been a filthy railroad cut became a broad boulevard lined with grand apartment buildings. Although New York has been transformed by gleaming postmodern skyscrapers, its most enduring landmarks are products of the first half of the 20th century: the Flatiron Building, built in 1902; Grand Central, in 1913; the Chrysler Building, in the 1920s; and the Empire State Building and Rockefeller Center, in the 1930s. The United Nations headquarters, the world's first glass-fronted skyscraper, went up after World War II. The Upper East Side remains a world apart from ordinary folks. The neighborhood is overwhelmingly white and expensive.

The 12th Congressional District of New York includes the Upper East Side. It begins at East 96th Street, the historic dividing line between Manhattan's wealthiest and poorest neighborhoods, and runs south through Murray Hill and Gramercy Park all the way to Houston Street, with a few salients protruding further south. It takes in Alphabet City, with its unique lettered avenue names, almost all of the East Village, with its pricey lofts and busy nightlife, and much of the Lower East Side. The district's cultural landmarks are among the world's finest: the Museum of Modern Art, the Guggenheim, the Whitney Museum of American Art, and the Frick Collection. Roosevelt Island, once dubbed Welfare Island and home to massive hospital and prison complexes, was renamed and transformed in the 1970s into an ethnically diverse residential neighborhood. Cornell University has opened on that island a 12-acre "tech campus," in affiliation with the Technion-Israel Institute of Technology and with a $100 million gift from former Mayor Michael Bloomberg's philanthropies. Midtown Manhattan's skyscrapers are also here, along with Times Square and the Theatre District. Starting in March 2020, many of these sites were hollowed out by the corona virus, including hotels that were shut down and office buildings that were virtually empty.Nearly 75 percent of the district resides in Manhattan.

Across the East River in Queens, the 12th encompasses Long Island City and vibrant, historically Greek Astoria, now with many Asians, Latinos and Arabs. Some politicians and neighbors in and close to Long Island City caused a furor when they objected to the November 2018 announcement by Amazon to establish one of its two new office centers in their locale, despite the approval of Gov. Andrew Cuomo and Mayor Bill deBlasio. Their continuing objections to government incentives for Amazon and the impact on local lifestyle led Amazon to reverse its decision, which had been expected to directly create 25,000 jobs. Even without Amazon, nearby areas have been booming—with new housing (both luxury and low-income) plus gentrification. In March 2020, the city unveiled a master plan for a project that would deck over most of the 180-acre Sunnyside Yard—a huge rail hub in Queens—with 12,000 units of affordable housing plus an office complex, which would dwarf the massive Hudson Yards project on the Far West Side of Manhattan. In the northwest corner of Brooklyn, another 10 percent of the district takes in parts of trendy Williamsburg, gritty East Williamsburg, and working-class yet gentrifying Greenpoint—the site of a large new community. As for Amazon, it was part of a tech boom that was offering commercial hope to property owners across the city. As part of its corporate campus in Manhattan, it purchased in March 2020 the former Lord and Taylor department store to house thousands of tech staff.

The district historically has been dominated by its affluent and highly educated voters, leaders in securities, publishing, advertising, entertainment, broadcasting and communications. Historically, they mistrusted the city's usually Democratic immigrant masses. But as the Republican Party increasingly took on cultural conservatism and its Southern accents, the attitude of the Manhattan elite shifted from "silk stocking" liberal Republican to leftish Democratic. In recent years, a new local address consumed the business and political worlds: Trump Tower, on Fifth Avenue, two blocks south of Central Park. But President Donald Trump rarely visited his former hometown. His decision to switch his residence to Palm Beach Florida raised questions about the future of his eponymous super-luxury property in Manhattan. This district, among the top 2 percent wealthiest in the nation, gave 84 percent of its vote to Joe Biden in 2020.

Adriano Espaillat (D)

Elected 2016, 3rd term, b. Sep 27, 1954; Santiago, Dominican Republic; NY University and Rutgers University Leadership for Urban Executives Institute; University of NY Queens College, B.S., 1978; Roman Catholic; Married (Marthera Madera Espaillat); 2 children.

Elected Office: NY Assembly, 1996-2010; NY Senate, 2010-2016.

Professional Career: Coordinator, New York City Criminal Justice Agency, 1980-1988; Director, Washington Heights Victim Services Community Office, 1992-1994; Director, Project Right Start, 1994-1996.

DC Office: 1630 LHOB 20515, 202-225-4365, Fax: 202-226-9731, espaillat.house.gov

State Offices: Bronx, 718-450-8241; New York, 212-663-3900.

Committees: *Appropriations*: Legislative Branch; State, Foreign Operations & Related Programs; Transportation, HUD & Related Agencies. *Education & Labor*: Higher Education & Workforce Investment.

Group Ratings

	ADA	ACLU	AFL-CIO	LCV	COC	HAFA	ACU	CFG	FRC
2020	**	81%	**	100%	-	0%	2%	**	-
2019	100%	C	90%	100%	41%	C	3%	18%	5%

Almanac Ratings 2019-2020

	Economy	Social	Foreign	Composite
Liberal	100%	100%	100%	100%
Conservative	0%	0%	0%	0%

Key Votes of the 116th Congress

1. U.S./Mex./Can. trade deal N	5. Russia sanctions Y	9. Firearms background checks Y
2. First Coronavirus response Y	6. Troops in Syria Y	10. Spending at the border N
3. HEROES Act Y	7. Veto arms sales to Saudis Y	11. Marijuana liberalized rules Y
4. CASH Act Y	8. Defense $$$, veto override N	12. Electoral College objections N

Election Results

Election	Name (Party)	Vote (%)		Cand. Spent	Ind. Exp. Support	Ind. Exp. Oppose
2020 General	Adriano Espaillat (D)....................... 231,841	(91%)	$807,123	$7,325	
	Lovelynn Gwinn (R)....................... 19,829	(8%)	$43,283		$113
2020 Primary	Adriano Espaillat (D)....................... 46,066	(59%)			
	James Felton Keith (D).................. 19,799	(26%)			
	Ramon Rodriguez (D)....................... 11,859	(15%)			

Prior winning percentages: 2018 (95%), 2016 (89%)

Adriano Espaillat, after narrowly losing two primary challenges to the incumbent, took the open seat in 2016. Espaillat's Dominican background marked the gentrification of Harlem and the shift of what had been a legendary African-American district to a Hispanic majority. After serving as an outspoken critic of President Donald Trump, he took a more constructive policymaking role as a member of the Appropriations Committee.

Espaillat was born in Santiago in the Dominican Republic. He arrived in the United States with his mother and sister at the age of nine and overstayed his visa. He described himself as the first undocumented immigrant elected to Congress, though he had become a citizen in his late 20s. He graduated from Bishop Dubois High School, a Roman Catholic school in Harlem, and got his bachelor's from Queens College. He took graduate courses in public administration at New York University and Rutgers University. He got involved in legal services, as a courts coordinator for the New York City Criminal Justice Agency and later as a certified resolution mediator for the Washington Heights In wood Conflict Resolutions and Medication Center. In Washington Heights, he was the director of Project Right Start, a national initiative designed to combat substance abuse by educating parents.

In 1996, Espaillat successfully challenged a 16-year Assemblyman in the Democratic primary and became the first Dominican American elected to a state legislature. He chaired the New York State Black, Puerto Rican, Hispanic and Asian Legislative Caucus. After 14 years, he was elected to an open seat in the state Senate. In 2012, and again in 2014, he challenged Democratic Rep. Charlie Rangel in bitter affairs, reflecting the changes in the minority community and the ethical problems Rangel had experienced in his later years, which resulted in his censure by the House and forced him to step aside in 2010 as chairman of the tax-writing Ways and Means Committee. Espaillat argued that Rangel had overstayed his welcome in Congress after more than 40 years, but Rangel's surrogates maintained that his seniority and experience were valuable to the district.

In 2012, Rangel outspent Espaillat 5-to-1 and won by 1,086 votes, 44.5%-42%. In 2014, Espaillat had become more familiar to voters and was more competitive financially, spending $716,000 for the campaign to $1.5 million for Rangel. But the outcome was little changed. In the four-candidate primary, Rangel won 48%-43%. When Rangel retired in 2016 at age 86, he endorsed influential state Assemblyman Keith Wright, his long time protégé. The large number of serious African-American contenders in the June primary benefited Espaillat. With nine Democratic candidates, Espaillat won 36 percent of the vote to 34 percent for Wright. Wright led by 159 votes in Manhattan, but Espaillat got nearly half the vote in the Bronx. His victory in November was a formality. In 2018 and 2020, he was reelected without a Democratic primary.

Espaillat became an assertive advocate on immigration and a harsh critic of Trump. In September 2017, he was arrested outside of Trump Tower in New York with two other House Democrats urging action on behalf of undocumented immigrants. In June 2018, Espaillat joined another small group of members who shouted at Trump as he walked past them while he was at the Capitol for a meeting.

During the corona virus pandemic in 2020, Espaillat cited his efforts to assist local businesses to take advantage of the Pay check Protection Program. In November, the House passed legislation he sponsored to modernize housing assistance programs for Puerto Rico, including a simplification of applications for relief from hurricane damage. Also that month, he won House approval of his Caribbean Basin Security Initiative bill that he pushed through the Foreign Affairs Committee; that bill improved security cooperation, including in fighting illegal drugs.

Gaining his seat on Appropriations in 2021, his assignments included the Transportation and Housing Subcommittee. With the Hispanic Caucus, he chairs its task force for transportation, infrastructure and housing. On Appropriations, he also joined the Legislative Branch, and State and Foreign Operations subcommittees.

NY-13: Manhattan's Upper West Side

Cook Partisan Voting Index: D+40

Population		Race and Ethnicity		Income	
Total	751,661	White	30.00%	Median Income	$46,298
Land area (sq. miles)	10	Black	29.50%	District Income Rank	410
Pop/ sq mi	73,332.78	Latino	54.50%	Poverty Rate	22.20%
Born in State	48.10%	Asian	4.30%	With health insurance	92.00%
		Two or more races	5.50%	Cash public assistance	7.70%
Age Groups		Other	30.80%	Food stamp/SNAP	27.30%
Under 18	20.10%				
18-34	29.50%	Education		Work	
35-64	37.00%	H.S grad or less	47.50%	White Collar	39.80%
Over 64	13.30%	Some college	19.60%	Sales and Service	46.30%
		College Degree, 4 yr	19.20%	Blue Collar	13.80%
Military		Post grad	13.70%	Government	11.80%
Veteran/ Active Duty	1.50%				

2020 Pres. Vote	Biden	233,234	(88%)	Trump	29,526	(11%)	
2016 Pres. Vote	Clinton	232,925	(92%)	Trump	13,727	(5%)	

Harlem, Washington Heights: Harlem, for many years America's most famous Black ghetto, has turned from grim times to major social evolution. In the late 19th century, Harlem was a commuter neighborhood, first for Germans and then for Jews and Italians. After the turn of the century, real estate speculators began constructing blocks of impressive brownstones, hoping to capitalize on the impending arrival of the subway. Overbuilding led to high vacancy rates. Some landlords agreed to rent to African Americans, as long as they were willing to pay a premium. After generations of being shunted from one neighborhood to the next as the city developed, Black residents were willing, and the neighborhood soon turned into the locus of New York City's African-American community. Many great Americans—W.E.B. DuBois, Thurgood Marshall, Ralph Ellison, Joe Louis—lived in Harlem's Sugar Hill.

The rosters of the Apollo Theater on 125th Street in the 1920s and 1930s were filled with the names of great artists. Then, the WPA Guide described Harlem as "the spiritual capital of Black America." Starting with a riot in the summer of 1964, Harlem endured deterioration. Hundreds of brownstones were abandoned or pulled down. As successful Black families moved out, Harlem's population shifted increasingly toward welfare dependency and criminal gangs. Its population declined by a third between 1970 and 1990.In the 1990s, Harlem began to recover. The federal government provided $300 million in investment capital, and a huge drop in crime restored Harlem real estate. Brownstones were renovated, vacant city buildings sold off, neighborhood schools upgraded and arts spaces opened. Harlem became an enterprise zone, with favorable federal and state tax treatment. Younger African Americans returned. The façade of the Apollo Theater was restored, a new Harlem pier constructed, supermarkets and chain stores opened. In 2001, former President Bill Clinton opened his post-presidential office at 55 West 125th Street in Harlem.

Politically, Harlem has been heavily Democratic since the 1930s, when Blacks switched from the Republican Party of Abraham Lincoln to the Democratic Party of Franklin Roosevelt. Harlem got its own congressional district in 1944 and elected Adam Clayton Powell Jr., minister at the Abyssinian Baptist Church and a brilliant orator. He was instrumental as chairman of the Education and Labor Committee when it crafted many of the Great Society programs, but lost his power when the House in 1967 refused to seat him because of ethical issues.

Today, the 13th Congressional District of New York includes not just Harlem but all of Upper Manhattan, south to 122nd Street on the far west side and lower into Manhattan along both sides of the northern part of Central Park. On the east side, it's East Harlem, once known as Spanish Harlem. This area had been Italian and was Fiorello LaGuardia's political base before it became Puerto Rican. Today, it is dominated by Mexicans and Dominicans and gentrifying whites, some of whom like the close-in location but have had conflicts with local preservationists and residents who want to keep their low rents and worry about "whitewashing." "125th Street, the commercial heart of Harlem, is now a hub for national retailers," New York One reported in February 2019. The result is an "existential" threat to Harlem, The Guardian wrote four months later. "In the home of so much

African American history, churches and other landmarks are disappearing." At the northern tip of Manhattan, the district takes in Washington Heights and In wood, both heavily Latino, with lower incomes and more affordable housing; nearly half their population of about 214,000 are foreign-born, most of them Dominican. Across the Harlem River in the Bronx, the district includes Marble Hill and heavily Hispanic Kingsbridge. Those neighborhoods in the Bronx are about 20 percent of the district.

Overall, the district is 55 percent Hispanic and 25 percent African American, figures that testify to ongoing decades of Black flight from Harlem and the continuing inflow of immigrants from the Western Hemisphere. These changes have altered the identity of Harlem and the 13th. Through all the changes, this remains overwhelmingly Democratic territory. Joe Biden had his third-best showing in the nation in the district in 2020 when he got 88 percent of the vote. It trailed only the 13th District of California and the 3rd District of Pennsylvania.

Alexandria Ocasio-Cortez (D)

Elected 2018, 2nd term, b. Oct 13, 1989; Bronx, NY; Boston University, B.A., 2011; Catholic; Single.

Professional Career: Educational Director, National Hispanic Institute; Founder, Brook Avenue Press.

DC Office: 229 CHOB 20515, 202-225-3965, ocasio-cortez.house.gov

State Offices: Jackson Heights, 718-662-5970.

Committees: *Financial Services*: Nat'l Security, International Development & Monetary Policy. *Oversight & Reform*: Subcommittee on Civil Rights & Civil Liberties; Subcommittee on Environment.

Almanac Ratings 2019-2020

	Economy	Social	Foreign	Composite
Liberal	100%	56%	57%	71%
Conservative	0%	44%	43%	29%

Key Votes of the 116th Congress

1. U.S./Mex./Can. trade deal N	5. Russia sanctions Y	9. Firearms background checks Y
2. First Coronavirus response Y	6. Troops in Syria Y	10. Spending at the border N
3. HEROES Act Y	7. Veto arms sales to Saudis Y	11. Marijuana liberalized rules Y
4. CASH Act Y	8. Defense $$$, veto override N	12. Electoral College objections N

Election Results

Election	Name (Party)	Vote (%)	Cand. Spent	Ind. Exp. Support	Ind. Exp. Oppose
2020 General	Alexandria Ocasio-Cortez (D)............. 152,661	(72%)	$25,158,553	$335	$145,754
	John Cummings (R)........................ 58,440	(27%)	$10,945,305		$113
2020 Primary	Alexandria Ocasio-Cortez (D).............. 46,582	(75%)			
	Michelle Caruso-Cabrera (D)............... 11,339	(18%)			
	Badrun Khan (D).................................... 3,119	(5%)			

Prior winning percentages: 2018 (78%)

Freshman Alexandria Ocasio-Cortez became a sensation for national Democrats after she unexpectedly defeated 10-term Rep. Joseph Crowley in the June 2018 primary. The virtually unknown 28-year-old challenger first drew attention as the giant-killer who defeated the long time party boss in New York City and ambitious chairman of the House Democratic Caucus. With her often bombastic response to Democratic leaders in the House, and elsewhere, Ocasio-Cortez often seemed more focused on serving as an icon for her emerging youthful cadre and less interested in the work of the House, where she made clear that her plans were short-term. Whether and when she would run for the Senate was the topic of Democratic intrigue.

Her media spotlight, which can glow brightly in New York, intensified as Ocasio-Cortez described her humble background and her bold ambitions for the Democrats' future. Although that agenda had its limitations in parts of Middle America, Ocasio-Cortez enhanced her cachet by forming alliances with other relatively young Democratic women—especially racial minorities—who emerged during the 2018 campaign. Four of them—minority women from urban districts who were first elected in 2018—relished their designation as The Squad.

Born in the Bronx—her mother was born in Puerto Rico and her father was a Bronx native—Ocasio-Cortez grew up in in Westchester County. While attending Boston University, where she got a bachelor's degree, she pursued her interest in income inequality and worked on immigration issues for Sen. Edward Kennedy. Returning to the Bronx, she worked in Manhattan as a bartender and as a waitress in a taco stand. She created a small publishing firm, with books for children about urban life, and taught Hispanic students. In 2016, she was a local organizer for the presidential campaign of Sen. Bernie Sanders.

Running against Crowley, who had not faced a Democratic challenge since 2004, Ocasio-Cortez gained attention in her first campaign with a two-minute video that began, "women like me aren't supposed to run for office." A member of the Democratic Socialists of America, she gained support from Sanders alumni and national progressive groups. In her diverse district, she launched her campaign "with the mission of bringing together a broad coalition of groups and communities to listen to their needs and give everyone an open and transparent seat at the table."

Crowley, long time chairman of the Queens Democratic Party, initially relied on his party organization and did not take the challenger seriously until days before the primary. He sent a surrogate to their only scheduled debate. His campaign routinely gained the endorsement of prominent state and local Democratic officials, and spent $3.6 million (much of it for direct mail) to a bit more than $500,000 for Ocasio-Cortez. Even with his belated moves, The New York Times headlined after the outcome, "Crowley never saw defeat coming." (Nor did the Times.)

In a district that Ocasio-Cortez said had been marred by "generations of backroom dealing,"voter turnout typically had been low, to the benefit of the insiders. But in this primary, the novice outsider had the momentum against the party establishment, with the scant turnout of just short of 30,000. In Crowley's base of Queens, which cast more than two-thirds of the vote, Ocasio-Cortez took 59 percent. With her 53 percent of the vote in the Bronx, her overall victory was, 57%-43%. Post-election vote analysis showed that she ran well in gentrifying neighborhoods. Crowley became a Washington-based lobbyist.

As the youngest woman ever elected to Congress, Ocasio-Cortez embraced the national attention, including social media. She generated support for her far-reaching "Green New Deal," which was more aspirational than a legislative proposal. Her policies included "Medicare for all," abolition of the Immigration and Customs Enforcement agency and the shutdown of private prisons. Her maverick style and occasional struggle with details created tensions with other Democrats—including Speaker Nancy Pelosi, who downplayed the impact of the newcomer but often responded by reminding others who was in charge.

That defensiveness was apparent, for example, in Pelosi's decision to create a Select Committee on the Climate Crisis, even though the panel lacked legislative jurisdiction, and in denying Ocasio-Cortez's requests for prime committee assignments in the House. But Ocasio-Cortez limited her influence by stating what had become obvious—that she wasn't "going to be staying in the House forever."

That comment came in an interview that accompanied a lengthy and flattering cover story about Ocasio-Cortez in the December 2020 issue of Vanity Fair, including an elaborate photo shoot. Needless to say, that was unusual attention for a House freshman and it reinforced that she remained a cultural phenomenon. She generated some of that attention when she endorsed Bernie Sanders for president and made appearances on his behalf prior to the Iowa presidential caucuses—though Huff Post reported in March 2020 that the Sanders campaign had grown unhappy that she "refused to campaign more" for the Vermont senator, especially after it became clear that his prospects to gain the Democratic presidential nomination were dwindling.

Her success rate in making congressional endorsements was mixed at best—and at least one incumbent whom she opposed, Henry Cuellar of Texas, subsequently said that he would oppose attempts by Ocasio-Cortez to gain influence in the House, especially with committee assignments. That helped to explain her post-election setback in her clash with Rep. Kathleen Rice of New York for a seat on the Energy and Commerce Committee. Perhaps oddly, her most successful endorsement was on behalf of an aging Senator, Edward Markey of Massachusetts, who was challenged by Joe Kennedy, her youthful House colleague.

Her continuing clashes with Democratic leaders raised the prospect that she might challenge Senate Majority Leader Chuck Schumer in the Democratic primary for his reelection campaign in 2022. For a December 2020 interview with Ocasio-Cortez, in which she called for a sweeping change of Democratic congressional leaders, The Intercept ran the headline: "AOC: Nancy Pelosi Needs to Go, But There's Nobody to Replace Her Yet."

In a separate interview with the Times a few days after the November election, she said the mostly centrist House Democratic incumbents who lost their seats had only themselves to blame. None "were firing on all cylinders," she said, given their limited spending on Facebook ads. "Our party isn't even online, not in a real way that exhibits competence," she said. Referring to the Democratic Caucus generally, she added, "internally, it's been extremely hostile to anything that even smells progressive." Rep. Conor Lamb of Pennsylvania, whom she criticized by name, responded in a follow-up interview.: "She doesn't have any idea how we ran our campaign, or what we spent."

Regardless of whether she takes on Schumer (or perhaps Sen. Kirsten Gillibrand in 2024), Ocasio-Cortez has made her mark and set a model for other insurgent Democrats challenging party fixtures.

NY-14: New York City   **Cook Partisan Voting Index: D+25**

Population		Race and Ethnicity		Income	
Total	696,664	White	41.40%	Median Income	$66,749
Land area (sq. miles)	28	Black	10.50%	District Income Rank	194
Pop/ sq mi	24,625.8	Latino	49.90%	Poverty Rate	12.90%
Born in State	43.20%	Asian	17.80%	With health insurance	88.70%
		Two or more races	4.40%	Cash public assistance	3.30%
Age Groups		Other	25.80%	Food stamp/SNAP	15.00%
Under 18	20.30%				
18-34	25.60%	**Education**		**Work**	
35-64	39.10%	H.S grad or less	50.50%	White Collar	29.50%
Over 64	15.20%	Some college	21.30%	Sales and Service	48.40%
		College Degree, 4 yr	17.70%	Blue Collar	22.10%
Military		Post grad	10.40%	Government	11.00%
Veteran/ Active Duty	2.00%				

2020 Pres. Vote	Biden	161,973	(73%)	Trump	57,174	(26%)
2016 Pres. Vote	Clinton	151,407	(77%)	Trump	38,560	(20%)

Eastern Bronx, Northern Queens: Along the East River, LaGuardia Airport has struggled with short runways and poor commuter access. Gov. Andrew Cuomo has begun to deliver on his promise to upgrade it into a "21st century airport"—an $8 billion project, with two new terminals. The first section of the concourse plus seven new gates opened in August 2020. The remainder of the concourse and 10 additional gates are scheduled for 2022. Also underway, with a 2025completion date, was planning for an above-ground,2.5-mile Air Train link from LaGuardia to subway and Long Island Railroad lines at Willets Point, near Citi Field. This rail link to the airport, despite some neighborhood opposition, will provide access to both Grand Central and Penn Station in midtown Manhattan, plus service to Long Island.

Nearby in Queens is College Point, a middle-class neighborhood. Further south and west are Jackson Heights, home to Little India and a sizable Latino community; East Elmhurst; and Woodside, a long-settled enclave with recent immigrants. Corona was once predominantly Italian and African American (Louis Armstrong, Duke Ellington, and Malcolm X lived here), but it then became home to Dominican and Ecuadoran immigrants and many Asians. More recently, Corona has become the most popular housing site in Queens for millennials. Also in northern Queens are Ditmars, increasingly popular with professionals, as well as Steinway, where the plant that makes pianos for North and South American distribution is still located. Close to LaGuardia is Rikers Island, the site since 1932 of the city prison—now severely out-moded. Mayor Bill de Blasio has made plans for its closing by 2026, with smaller detention centers in all the boroughs except Staten Island. Still under discussion are options for the 415 acres of newly available space at Rikers, with possible new housing, renewable energy or an extended runway for LaGuardia.

Across three bridges over the East River, the Bronx derives its name from its original European settlements. Jonas Bronck, a Swede who emigrated to the New World, started a farm, and once wrote that his new homeland was "a veritable paradise and needs but the industrious hand of man to make it the finest and most beautiful region in the world." His name was given to a nearby river, then to a borough, and it became a county in 1914.Real growth began in 1910, when the subways started connecting these neighborhoods with job sites in Manhattan. The Bronx was rapidly transformed by hundreds of thousands of immigrants flooding to the open spaces northeast of the Harlem River. Today, these neighborhoods are filling with Latinos, with more Mexicans than Puerto Ricans, and many from the Dominican Republic and elsewhere in the Caribbean and Latin America. Out past Eastchester Bay is City Island, a Cape Cod-like resort area with boat makers and plenty of seafood restaurants.

These Bronx and Queens neighborhoods make up the 14th Congressional District of New York.

Other prominent locales include the Bronx Zoo and New York Botanical Garden in the Bronx. The district is a polyglot; it is 49 percent Hispanic, 17 percent Asian and 9 percent Black. More than two-thirds of the voters reside in Queens. Not long ago, Republicans were competitive here. Redistricting and demographic changes reversed GOP expansion. Joe Biden won the district with 73 percent, a slight drop from the 77 percent for Hillary Clinton.

Ritchie Torres (D)

Elected 2020, 1st term, b. Mar 12, 1988; Bronx, NY; NY University, Att.; Christian; Single.

Elected Office: Member, NY City Council, 2014-2020.

Professional Career: Housing Director, council member James Vacca.

DC Office: 317 CHOB 20515, 202-225-4361, Fax: 202-225-6001, ritchietorres.house.gov

State Offices: Bronx, 718-503-9610.

Committees: *Financial Services*: Consumer Protection & Financial Institutions; Housing, Community Development & Insurance; Nat'l Security, International Development & Monetary Policy; Task Force on Financial Technology. *Homeland Security (VChmn)*: Cybersecurity, Infrastructure Protection & Innovation; Oversight, Management & Accountability.

Election Results

Election	Name (Party)	Vote (%)		Cand. Spent	Ind. Exp. Support	Ind. Exp. Oppose
2020 General	Ritchie Torres (D)...............	169,533	(89%)	$1,803,716	$485,502	
	Patrick Delices (R)...............	21,221	(11%)			
2020 Primary	Ritchie Torres (D)...............	19,090	(32%)			
	Michael Blake (D)...............	10,725	(18%)			
	Rubén Díaz Sr. (D)...............	8,559	(14%)			
	Samelys López (D)...............	8,272	(14%)			
	Ydanis Rodríguez (D)...............	6,291	(11%)			

Democrat Ritchie Torres, a New York City Council member, was elected to the House in 2020. As a young, gay, Afro-Latino who grew up in public housing and had limited education, Torres faced many challenges of urban poverty. With his impressive political skills and superior fundraising, Torres was the frontrunner in a competitive primary for one of the most Democratic districts in the nation. He won that contest with a wider margin than many had expected. He replaced Democratic Rep. Jose Serrano, who retired with Parkinson's disease after 15 terms.

Growing up in the East Bronx in Throgs Neck Houses, a housing project with 36 buildings that overlooks Donald Trump's Ferry Point golf course along the East River, Torres and his two siblings were supported by their African-American mother and her modest income; his Puerto Rican father never lived with them. After graduating from Lehman High School in the Bronx, where he was captain of the school's law team, Torres enrolled at New York University. But he struggled with his studies and suffered from severe depression, which was partly due to his difficulty in coping as a gay man. He eventually controlled his illness with medication, according to a profile in The New Yorker.

Meanwhile, Torres began to work with a community organizer in the Bronx who had become a city council member. At age 24, with his boss's support, he ran successfully for the council seat in a neighboring district—the first openly gay person elected to office in the Bronx. At his request, Torres chaired the Public Housing Committee, which had scant legislative authority. He used the position for oversight that sought to hold city officials accountable for deep-seated problems.

Eventually, Torres concluded that the problems could be addressed only in Washington. "I've come to recognize that the policies in housing and health care are largely set at the federal level," he told Gay City News in New York. "That's why I'm running for Congress." With Serrano's retirement opening that door, Torres was the best-organized candidate from the start. In launching his campaign, he tweeted, "My story is the story of the Bronx, a story of overcoming. 12 years ago: I stood on the verge of suicide. 6 years ago: I overcame the odds to become the youngest elected in NYC."

The Democratic field included several other prominent local politicians—most notably, Rubin Diaz Sr., a veteran city and state lawmaker. His son, Rubin Diaz Jr., had been Bronx borough president for a decade, though he was publicly neutral in the congressional contest. The elder Diaz, a Pentecostal minister who often wore a cowboy hat, was colorful and outspoken—with deeply conservative views on social issues, such as gay rights and abortion, that were popular in parts of the district.

Torres gained key organizational and financial support from labor unions, plus Hispanic and gay-rights groups. He spent $1.5 million in the primary, considerably more than any of his opponents; Diaz spent barely one-eighth that amount. Still, the field of 12 Democratic candidates raised concern that Diaz could prevail with a relatively small share of the vote. "There's a real risk that the most Democratic Congressional district in America could be represented by a de facto Trump Republican," Torres told Politico in late 2019.

As it turned out, Torres comfortably won the primary with 32 percent of the vote. Michael Blake, a state assemblyman, got 18 percent. Diaz finished third with 14 percent. With Mondaire Jones, who won another open-seat primary that day in a nearby Westchester County-based district, they were heralded as the first openly gay Black men to be elected to the House. For Torres, that created a new complication: He insisted that he was eligible for both the Congressional Black Caucus and the Hispanic Caucus and was the first House Member to seek membership in each. Eventually, he was accepted in each caucus.

He was assigned to the Financial Services and Homeland Security committees; on the latter, he became vice-chair.

NY-15: Bronx   Cook Partisan Voting Index: D+39

Population		Race and Ethnicity		Income	
Total	739,390	White	16.30%	Median Income	$31,061
Land area (sq. miles)	15	Black	42.00%	District Income Rank	436
Pop/ sq mi	50,852.13	Latino	64.00%	Poverty Rate	34.40%
Born in State	53.80%	Asian	1.80%	With health insurance	90.90%
		Two or more races	4.10%	Cash public assistance	9.30%
Age Groups		Other	35.70%	Food stamp/SNAP	44.40%
Under 18	27.40%				
18-34	26.60%	**Education**		**Work**	
35-64	35.80%	H.S grad or less	60.20%	White Collar	19.60%
Over 64	10.20%	Some college	25.20%	Sales and Service	59.00%
		College Degree, 4 yr	10.20%	Blue Collar	21.40%
Military		Post grad	4.40%	Government	12.20%
Veteran/ Active Duty	2.10%				

2020 Pres. Vote	Biden	171,328	(86%)	Trump	25,855	(13%)
2016 Pres. Vote	Clinton	179,454	(94%)	Trump	9,371	(5%)

South Bronx: It may not quite be "the beautiful Bronx," as borough historian Lloyd Ultan calls it, but the Bronx has rebounded from rock bottom. The borough began its modern development in 1905 with the arrival of the first subway, which allowed the children of immigrants to move from grim Lower East Side tenements to spacious walk-up apartments flooded with light. The population grew from 200,000 in 1900 to 1.2 million in 1930. Its population hit nearly 1.5 million in 1950. Four years later, Supreme Court Justice Sonia Sotomayor was born in a South Bronx tenement before her family moved into the nearby Bronxdale Houses public housing project. The years prior to mid-century were the peak days for the Bronx, when Babe Ruth, Lou Gehrig and Joe DiMaggio knocked home runs out of Yankee Stadium, art deco apartment buildings were built along the Grand Concourse, and shoppers thronged Tremont Avenue stores.

In the mid-1960s, several factors led to the destruction of Bronx neighborhoods. Rent control guaranteed that many owners of low-rent property wouldn't maintain it. Once empty, buildings were torched for the insurance money, sometimes as many as four blocks a week. A decline in low-skill jobs in Manhattan and the Bronx led to a rise in welfare dependency and crime, and empty building shells became the perfect venue for drug dealing. A vicious cycle emerged: Crime drove away jobs, producing more crime. The 13-year, $250 million effort to build the Cross-Bronx Expressway—a brainchild of Robert Moses that crossed 113 streets and avenues, hundreds of utility mains and 10 mass-transit lines—made things worse.

The borough's eventual saviors were churches and creative community groups that built single-family bungalows and small-scale apartment projects for the elderly, single-parent families and the homeless. As immigrants from the Dominican Republic, Jamaica, Ecuador and Central America settled in, the population began to rise. Today, nearly 1.4 million people live in the Bronx, as new immigrants revive neighborhoods that had been given up for dead. Businesses—warehouses, distribution centers and small industrial parks—have begun to move back in. Still, the economic contrast is striking. In 2019, per capita income in the Bronx was $21,800; city-wide, it was $39,800. A promising development has been the city's plans to improve 30 blocks of the waterfront in Mott Haven along the Bronx side of the Harlem River, including the city's first soccer stadium. In South Bronx, drug overdose rates have been among the highest in the nation, second only to West Virginia. Opioids have replaced heroin as the leading cause, and can be far more lethal. Adding to the misery, Bronx residents were twice as likely as others in New York City to die of COVID-19 during the early weeks of the virus.

The 15th Congressional District of New York, which is the only district entirely in the Bronx, includes most of the South Bronx. It is bounded by the Harlem River on the west; the East River on the south; Westchester Creek, the Cross Bronx Expressway, and Bronx Park (home of the Bronx Zoo) on the east; and it goes just past Fordham Road on the north. It includes the gentrifying Belmont to the north, the industrial flatlands of Bruckner Boulevard, and Hunts Point, where meat and produce markets supply the city's tony restaurants, with some new housing. The district is 28 percent Black, and it has the highest share of Hispanics—66 percent—of any New York district; in 2019, it remained at 2 percent white. It has long had New York's largest concentration of Puerto Ricans, but about 69 percent of Hispanics are now from other parts of Latin America. Poverty here remains endemic. The 15th District has the lowest median income in the nation. As longstanding Democratic territory, it is extreme in other ways. The 15th was the most Democratic district in the nation in 2016, giving Hillary Clinton 94 percent of the vote. But the 86 percent for Joe Biden in 2020 was not even his best in the state. That designation went to the 13th District.

Jamaal Bowman (D)

Elected 2020, 1st term, b. Apr 01, 1976; New York, NY; Potomac State Junior College, Att.; Manhattanville College, Ed.D.; University of New Haven, B.A., 1999; Mercy College of NY, M.A., 2007; Married (Melissa Oppenheimer); 3 children.

Professional Career: School Principal, Cornerstone Academy for Social Action Middle School; Education Entrepreneur, NY City Department of Education.

DC Office: 1605 LHOB 20515, 202-225-2464, Fax: 202-225-5513, bowman.house.gov

State Offices: Bronx, 718-530-7710; Mount Vernon, 914-371-9220.

Committees: *Education & Labor (VChmn)*: Civil Rights & Human Services; Early Childhood, Elementary & Secondary Education; Higher Education & Workforce Investment. *Science, Space & Technology*: Energy (Chmn).

Election Results

Election	Name (Party)	Vote (%)		Cand. Spent	Ind. Exp. Support	Ind. Exp. Oppose
2020 General	Jamaal Bowman (D)............................	218,514	(84%)	$2,804,586	$888,645	$806,665
	Patrick McManus (C)...........................	41,094	(16%)			
2020 Primary	Jamaal Bowman (D)............................	49,367	(55%)			
	Eliot Engel (D)...................................	36,149	(41%)			

Democrat Jamaal Bowman, a political newcomer, won a stunning victory in the Democratic primary against veteran Rep. Eliot Engel, who served 16 terms and chaired the House Foreign Affairs Committee. Bowman, a middle-school principal and first-time candidate, combined the support of national progressive groups with his "time for a change" campaign. Engel, who had long emphasized his constituent services, made crucial errors in the final weeks of the campaign, revealing that he had lost touch at home. Bowman won, 55%-41%.

Bowman, born in Manhattan, initially resided with his grandmother in public housing because his working mother was unable to care for him. When his grandmother died, he moved in with his mother and sisters—eventually settling in New Jersey. After receiving his undergraduate degree in sports management from the University of New Haven, Bowman decided that he wanted to be a school teacher. He started by offering crisis intervention to fourth graders in the South Bronx. He switched to a high school in Manhattan, where he was a counselor, teacher and coach.

With a master's degree in school counseling from Mercy College and a doctorate in educational leadership from Manhattanville College, Bowman submitted a proposal to start his own middle school, which New York City education officials accepted. In 2009, his Cornerstone Academy for Social Action Middle School opened in the Bronx. He opposed the emphasis on standardized testing for students and he hired teachers who "believe in innovation and creativity so it's not just learning in an abstract sense," Bowman told New York Amsterdam News.

Bowman was encouraged to seek office by leaders of Justice Democrats and the liberal Working Families Party. He said he was inspired by first-term Rep. Alexandria Ocasio-Cortez, who represented a neighboring district in the Bronx; she endorsed him prior to the primary. With his support for reform of the criminal justice system, the Green New Deal and Medicare for All, his message resonated in the spring of 2020, at a time when national protests were calling for broad social change.

As he sought to continue his responsibilities as a House committee chairman, Engel hurt his own cause. Early during the COVID-19 pandemic, when a reporter for The Atlantic went to his home in Potomac Maryland and asked how he kept in contact with his district, Engel replied, "I'm in both places." At a news conference in early June in the Bronx, he was overheard telling other Democratic officials when he asked to speak about the Black Lives Matter movement, "If I didn't have a primary, I wouldn't care." When Engel cited his support from influential New York Democrats, that fueled Bowman's narrative that it was time to end old-time politics.

Although Engel's campaign slightly outspent his, Bowman's more than $2 million plus another $1 million that outside groups spent on his behalf were enough to deliver the challenger's message. Bowman won easily, taking a slightly larger share of the vote in the Bronx portion of the district. He was assigned to the Education and Labor Committee, where he serves as vice-chair of the panel; on Science, Space and Technology, he chairs the Energy Subcommittee.

With the retirement in the adjacent Westchester County-based district of Democratic Rep. Nita Lowey, who chaired the Appropriations Committee, the area's veteran lawmakers were replaced by two political novices, but with stronger community links. In another Bronx-based district, Ocasio-Cortez in 2018 ousted Rep. Joseph Crowley, who had chaired the House Democratic Caucus.

NY-16: Southern Westchester County, North Bronx

Cook Partisan Voting Index: D+25

Population		Race and Ethnicity		Income	
Total	739,893	White	44.40%	Median Income	$74,799
Land area (sq. miles)	78	Black	32.00%	District Income Rank	132
Pop/ sq mi	9,441.02	Latino	28.10%	Poverty Rate	11.70%
Born in State	55.90%	Asian	5.10%	With health insurance	94.50%
		Two or more races	4.00%	Cash public assistance	3.50%
Age Groups		Other	14.40%	Food stamp/SNAP	15.40%
Under 18	21.60%				
18-34	21.60%	**Education**		**Work**	
35-64	38.30%	H.S grad or less	37.30%	White Collar	44.80%
Over 64	18.60%	Some college	22.10%	Sales and Service	40.10%
		College Degree, 4 yr	20.70%	Blue Collar	15.10%
Military		Post grad	19.90%	Government	16.00%
Veteran/ Active Duty	3.40%				

2020 Pres. Vote	Biden	232,782	(75%)	Trump	73,665	(24%)
2016 Pres. Vote	Clinton	212,644	(75%)	Trump	63,590	(22%)

Yonkers, New Rochelle: The north eastern Bronx wasn't settled until the early 20th century, when it became a collection of middle-class neighborhoods clustered around subway stops, places where the children of immigrants left behind Manhattan's gloomy tenements and walk-ups and basked in the sunlight, wide avenues and hilly vistas. Different ethnic groups collected here: Irish in Kingsbridge; well-to-do WASPs and Jews in Riverdale; and middle-class Blacks in Williams bridge. When neighboring areas in the South Bronx began to deteriorate, many residents fled to Westchester County.

The 16th Congressional District of New York includes the bulk of these Bronx neighborhoods, and a broad swath of Westchester County. It is divided into three parts of similar size. South of the Westchester County line and west of the Bronx River Parkway, the area is about 70 percent white and heavily Democratic. This portion has the century-old Van Cortlandt Park, at 1,146 acres, New York City's fourth-largest park. On opposite sides of the park are Riverdale and leafy Woodlawn, still a magnet for Irish immigrants. The second section of the district is the southern edge of Westchester. It extends from Yonkers, which is the most populous city in the county and 38 percent Hispanic and growing, across the Bronx River Parkway into Mount Vernon, which is 66 percent African American. The sprawling Co-op City is here, consisting of 35 buildings that house more than 35,000 residents in 15,000 apartments that were built by a consortium of labor unions in the late 1960s—the largest affordable-housing development in the nation. Nearby, Metro-North plans to launch by 2023 transit service from Co-op City to the markets in Hunts Point and continuing service in 2024 to Penn Station in Manhattan. After an environmental clean-up along the Hudson River waterfront, more than $2.5 billion of new housing was underway in Yonkers; the city has promoted itself to millennials and others as relatively inexpensive, with the median value of housing virtually the same as in the Bronx and a 30-minute rail commute to Grand Central Station.

The district's third section, to the north in Westchester, stretches from Hastings-on-Hudson eastward to Mamaroneck on Long Island Sound. This section pushes well into Westchester County suburbs, all the way to a touch short of the Connecticut border. It includes a number of affluent suburbs, many within easy reach of Grand Central via the Metro North rail lines—Bronxville, Tuckahoe, Eastchester, New Rochelle, Scarsdale, Larchmont, Mamaroneck and Rye. In New Rochelle, work was underway on a planned $4 billion in downtown redevelopment. In March 2020, that city became a hot spot that The New York Times described as the early "face of the New York epidemic." But city officials successfully took control with a combination of social distancing and aggressive testing to contain the spread of the corona virus.

Historically, Westchester was a Republican county, with a successful GOP machine and an electorate of white-collar professionals who naturally preferred the political party that opposed the big city political bosses and labor union leaders. Today, party registration in Westchester is majority-Democratic, after an influx of racial and ethnic minorities and of Jews who broke down many barriers to residence after World War II. The richly diverse 16th is 32 percent African American and 28 percent Hispanic—and solidly Democratic, though the 69 percent for Joe Biden in 2020 fell from the 75 percent for Hillary Clinton.

Mondaire Jones (D)

Elected 2020, 1st term, b. May 18, 1987; Nyack, NY; Stanford University, B.A., 2009; Harvard University, J.D., 2013; Baptist; Single.

Professional Career: John Gardner Public Service Fellow, U.S. Department of Justice Office of Legal Policy, 2009-2010; Legal Intern, Criminal Division, U.S. Attorney's Office for the Southern District of NY, 2011; Associate, law firm; Attorney.

DC Office: 1017 LHOB 20515, 202-225-6506, Fax: 202-225-0546, jones.house.gov

State Offices: White Plains, 914-323-5550.

Committees: *Communications Standards Commission. Education & Labor*: Higher Education & Workforce Investment; Workforce Protections. *Ethics*.

Election Results

Election	Name (Party)	Vote (%)		Cand. Spent	Ind. Exp. Support	Ind. Exp. Oppose
2020 General	Mondaire Jones (D)	197,354	(59%)	$2,171,677	$590,392	
	Maureen McArdle-Schulman (R)	117,309	(35%)	$56,492		$113
	Yehudis Gottesfeld (C)	8,887	(3%)	$34,542		
2020 Primary	Mondaire Jones (D)	32,796	(42%)			
	Adam Schleifer (D)	12,732	(16%)			
	Evelyn Farkas (D)	12,210	(16%)			
	David Carlucci (D)	8,649	(11%)			
	David Buchwald (D)	6,673	(9%)			

Democrat Mondaire Jones, who was elected in 2020, was raised in poverty in his wealthy House district and scored impressive credentials in the elite meritocracy. Although he was a first-time candidate, Jones had the only Washington-based experience of the three racial-minority men who won Democratic primaries in adjacent New York districts that June. He won his primary with the largest margin of those three newcomers and was the only one elected in a district with a Caucasian majority. Jones succeeded Democratic Rep. Nita Lowey, who chaired the House Appropriations Committee and retired after 32 years, though Jones launched his candidacy before she announced her exit at age 82.

Jones was born to a single mother in the working-class town of Spring Valley in Rockland County. While working multiple jobs, she was diagnosed with a serious mental illness. Starting at age two, her son was raised with the assistance of her parents—who worked locally as a janitor and house cleaner. In high school, Jones became active in a local NAACP youth council; at age 19, he chaired a committee of the NAACP's national board of directors. He got his bachelor's degree at Stanford University, where he was a student leader and active in political and racial issues on campus.

As a college graduate in 2009 at the start of the Obama administration, Jones took a job in the Justice Department's office of legal policy. He worked on judicial nominations, including the selection of Elena Kagan for a Supreme Court vacancy. A year later, he enrolled at Harvard Law School, where Kagan had been the dean. As a law student, he represented impoverished defendants in criminal cases. Following graduation, he joined the New York City law firm of Davis, Polk& Wardwell and later was an attorney for the law department of Westchester County.

In mid-2019, Jones quit his county job and announced his challenge to Lowey, who had not faced a serious Democratic primary challenge since she was first elected. "We're not getting anything at the moment appreciable from her chairing [the Appropriations] Committee," he told City & State, a New York-based publication. "I would bring an energy to the position of a fighter." In October 2019, three days after the release of that interview, Lowey announced her retirement.

The open seat led seven other Democrats to join Jones in the primary. They had a mix of political experiences, ideologies and finances. The top contenders included: Adam Schleifer, a former federal prosecutor who spent more than $5 million, mostly his own money; David Carlucci, a state senator who antagonized many Democrats by joining Republicans in an earlier coalition to run the Senate in Albany; and Evelyn Farkas, a Pentagon official during the Obama administration. (One district resident who did not run was Chelsea Clinton, the daughter of Bill and Hillary Clinton, who had sparked speculation for years that she would run for the seat once Lowey retired.)

In a lengthy preview of the contest, The New Yorker in early June reported the "widely held assumption" that "Carlucci is in as good a position as anyone to win" the primary. The two other "dark horses" were Schliefer and David Buchwald, a state assemblyman, according to the story, which gave scant attention to the prospect for Jones.

Jones blew out the field with 42 percent. Schleifer and Farkas were the runners-up with 16 percent; Carlucci got 11 percent. Jonesran nearly as strongly in Westchester, with 41 percent, as in his home Rockland County, where he got 43 percent.

He got seats on three committees: Education and Labor, Judiciary and Ethics.

NY-17: Northern Westchester, Rockland Counties

Cook Partisan Voting Index: D+9

Population		Race and Ethnicity		Income	
Total	737,355	White	69.10%	Median Income	$108,449
Land area (sq. miles)	383	Black	11.30%	District Income Rank	19
Pop/ sq mi	1,927.07	Latino	22.70%	Poverty Rate	9.10%
Born in State	61.30%	Asian	6.10%	With health insurance	95.90%
		Two or more races	2.80%	Cash public assistance	1.60%
Age Groups		Other	10.70%	Food stamp/SNAP	7.20%
Under 18	24.20%				
18-34	20.60%	**Education**		**Work**	
35-64	38.80%	H.S grad or less	29.10%	White Collar	50.00%
Over 64	16.40%	Some college	21.30%	Sales and Service	36.40%
Military		College Degree, 4 yr	25.30%	Blue Collar	13.60%
Veteran/ Active Duty	3.50%	Post grad	24.30%	Government	16.10%

2020 Pres. Vote	Biden	212,254	(60%)	Trump	140,322	(39%)
2016 Pres. Vote	Clinton	186,437	(58%)	Trump	122,339	(38%)

White Plains: Blessed with some of America's loveliest scenery and easily accessible from Manhattan by train, Westchester County has some of America's earliest suburbs, where grand estates were built by millionaires—Jay Gould's Gothic revival Lyndhurst and John D. Rockefeller's spectacular Kykuit. Today, Westchester still looks suburban, but with the patina of age. It has little commuter railroad stations across from faux Tudor drugstores, soda fountains and cobblestone post offices. But it also has shopping malls and plenty of corporate headquarters. In recent years, Westchester has drawn biotech companies. In February 2020, J.P. Morgan announced that it partnered with the Westchester Biotech Project, which will include a $1.2 billion mixed-use community in Valhalla, that is expected to feature 8,000 jobs, chiefly in life sciences.

Development slows north of White Plains, where Westchester is crossed by the first of several mountain ridges—the closest the Appalachians come to the ocean. In Ossining, on the Hudson River, looms the famed Sing Sing maximum security prison.

The 17th Congressional District of New York contains the largest share of Westchester County, including its northern and western sections: Port Chester, White Plains, Tarrytown, Armonk and Chappaqua, where former President Bill Clinton and Hillary Clinton have a home. Facebook Chairman and CEO Mark Zuckerberg was born in White Plains and grew up in Dobbs Ferry, now the southernmost town in the district on the east bank of the Hudson. Westchester magazine in 2014 described White Plains as the heart of the county that "combines a suburban environment with urban sophistication for a great living and working experience." The twin Indian Point nuclear reactors were scheduled to shut down in April 2021, largely because of fears about the safety risk to New

York City. The decision made the region more dependent on fossil fuels, until renewables become more widely available.

Across the Tappan Zee—a stretch in the Hudson River so wide that Henry Hudson believed he had finally discovered the Northwest Passage to the Pacific Ocean upon entering it—the district takes in all of Rockland County, which comprises about 40 percent of the residents of the 17th and is the second fastest-growing county in the state. First settled by Dutchmen, Rockland featured little towns that grew up as if they were 1,000 miles from Gotham, but which eventually thrived on their proximity to the city once the Palisades Interstate Parkway and Tappan Zee Bridge opened in the 1950s. Today, Rockland is a triangular stretch of suburbia. Its demographics have changed; Haverstraw, on the banks of the Hudson, has a large share of Dominicans; Kaser, a village in the inland town of Rampao, has a large community of Romanians. Orange town is the site of several large high-tech data centers. The second span of the eight-lane, 3.1 mile Mario Cuomo Bridge replaced the deteriorating Tappan Zee in September 2018. The $4 billion cost is being paid from toll revenue of the New York Thruway. On the Sunday before the election in 2020, a large caravan of celebratory supporters of President Donald Trump stopped traffic in the middle of the bridge. Westchester and Rockland counties had the highest property-tax revenues in the nation in 2016.

The 17th District is 22 percent Hispanic and 10 percent Black. In Hillary Clinton's home district, Joe Biden's 60%-39% virtually matched her margin four years earlier.

Sean Maloney (D)

Elected 2012, 5th term, b. Jul 30, 1966; Sherbrooke, Canada; Georgetown University, Att., 1986; University of VA, B.A., 1988; University of VA School of Law, J.D., 1992; Roman Catholic; Married (Randy Florke); 3 children.

Professional Career: Practicing attorney, 1993-1997, 2004-2006, 2009-present; Staff Secretary, President Bill Clinton, 1997-2000; Founder & COO, Kiodex, 2000-2003; First deputy Secretary, Gov. Eliot Spitzer, 2007-2008.

DC Office: 2331 RHOB 20515, 202-225-5441, Fax: 202-225-3289, seanmaloney.house.gov

State Offices: Newburgh, 845-561-1259.

Committees: Democratic Congressional Campaign Committee chairman. *Agriculture*: Biotechnology, Horticulture & Research; Subcommittee Nutrition, Oversight & Department Operations. *Permanent Select on Intelligence*: Counterterrorism, Counterintelligence & Counterproliferation; Defense Intelligence & Warfighter Support. *Transportation & Infrastructure*: Aviation; Coast Guard & Maritime Transportation; Highways & Transit.

Group Ratings

	ADA	ACLU	AFL-CIO	LCV	COC	HAFA	ACU	CFG	FRC
2020	**	79%	**	100%	-	0%	9%	**	-
2019	85%	C	100%	97%	64%	C	10%	12%	0%

Almanac Ratings 2019-2020

	Economy	Social	Foreign	Composite
Liberal	100%	100%	80%	94%
Liberal	100%	100%	96%	99%
Conservative	0%	0%	20%	6%
Conservative	0%	0%	4%	1%

Key Votes of the 116th Congress

1. U.S./Mex./Can. trade deal	Y	5. Russia sanctions	Y	9. Firearms background checks Y
2. First Coronavirus response	Y	6. Troops in Syria	Y	10. Spending at the border	Y
3. HEROES Act	Y	7. Veto arms sales to Saudis	Y	11. Marijuana liberalized rules	Y
4. CASH Act	Y	8. Defense $$$, veto override	Y	12. Electoral College objections N

Election Results

Election	Name (Party)	Vote (%)	Cand. Spent	Ind. Exp. Support	Ind. Exp. Oppose
2020 General	Sean Maloney (D)......................	187,444 (56%)	$1,740,009	$8,248	
	Chele Farley (R)......................	145,145 (43%)	$1,025,449	$168	$113

Prior winning percentages: 2018 (56%), 2016 (56%), 2014 (50%), 2012 (52%)

Elected in 2012, Sean Patrick Maloney of New York was a staffer on Bill Clinton's presidential campaigns and a West Wing aide. With the former president's brand of centrism and a notable ambition, he maneuvered his way to the chairmanship of the House Democrats' campaign arm eight years later. He has long sought a higher-profile position, but fell short in 2018 in his bids for state wide office and a House leadership post, which he won two years later. As chairman of the Democratic Congressional Campaign Committee, his challenge in 2022 will be to protect a five-seat Democratic majority in President Joe Biden's first midterm and in a redistricting cycle.

Maloney was born in Quebec Canada, where his father worked in the lumber industry. He grew up in Hanover New Hampshire, attended Georgetown University for two years and then transferred to the University of Virginia, where he got a bachelor's in international relations and stayed on to earn a law degree. Maloney worked on Clinton's 1992 campaign as a deputy to Susan Thomases, then the chief scheduler. In the 1996 reelection campaign, he was director of surrogate travel. After that, he snagged a job in the White House as the No. 3 official under Chief of Staff John Podesta. Maloney later became staff secretary, responsible for coordinating the flow of information to the president.

After Clinton left office, Maloney worked as the chief operating officer at Kiodex, a firm that developed risk management tools. He made his first bid for office in 2006, when he lost badly to Andrew Cuomo in the Democratic primary for attorney general. Maloney became first deputy secretary to Gov. Eliot Spitzer and, after Spitzer resigned, to Gov. David Paterson. Maloney came under a cloud for possible obstruction of justice following a scheme to release damaging information about then-Senate Majority Leader Joseph Bruno's travel. Bruno, a Republican, was convicted on federal corruption charges, but he was later acquitted in a retrial.

When Maloney ran for the House seat in 2012, his role in Albany became an issue in the five-way Democratic primary. The New York Times editorial board said that during law-enforcement review of the charges, Maloney "appeared to be most interested in holding back the staff's personal emails from investigators." Still, he won the primary handily. He led his closest competitor, Cortlandt Town Council Member Richard Becker, 48%-32%. Against first-term Rep. Nan Hayworth, Maloney painted Hayworth as a tea party extremist, citing her votes for Rep. Paul Ryan's budget and for cutting funding for Planned Parenthood. Hayworth outraised him $3.3 million to $2.3 million and had a comparable edge in outside assistance. Maloney eked out a win, 52%-48%.

Maloney, who is gay, married in 2014 his long time partner, Randy Florke, a prominent real estate agent and interior designer. He has co-chaired the Congressional LGBT Equality Caucus. He has been an active legislator, though with occasional embellishment. In summarizing his work during his first term, Maloney claimed credit for introducing 10 bills that were signed into law. In most of those cases, he appeared to have been a cosponsor of legislation, which often was changed prior to enactment.

Maloney sparked a furor in the House in May 2016 when he offered an amendment to prevent federal contractors from engaging in job discrimination on the basis of sexual orientation. The proposal lost, 213-212, after Republican leaders used strong-arm tactics to urge some of their members to switch their votes. Maloney again offered his amendment the following week and it easily passed, though his provision died in the Senate.

In 2019, as chairman of the Coast Guard and Maritime Transportation Subcommittee, Maloney said his top priority was protecting the Hudson River, which he called "a national treasure" and a key to local commerce. After the outbreak of the corona virus pandemic, he helped lead an inquiry into an outbreak on ships owned by Carnival, the world's largest cruise company. He also gained a coveted assignment to the Intelligence Committee, which gave him a prominent perch during the first impeachment investigation against Trump in 2019.

In 2014, Maloney won a rematch with Hayworth. This time, Maloney outraised his opponent, $4.3 million to $3.5 million, and assistance from super PACs resulted in another $2 million. In a Republican year, he won 49.7%-47.9%, and led in three of the four counties, losing only Putnam His 2016 opponent, Phil Oliva, an aide to the Westchester County executive, accused Maloney of exaggerating or lying about his legislative successes. Oliva raised $224,000 to Maloney's $3.6 million and was limited in getting his message out. Maloney won, 56%-44%.

Following that election, Maloney raised questions about the operations of the DCCC during the 2016 campaign, including its strategy and financing of candidates and was tasked with conducting an autopsy of the disappointing cycle. Summing up his findings in February 2017, Maloney told the Washington Post, "we can win [in districts] where we used to struggle, and we're struggling a bit where we used to win." The DCCC got much-improved results in 2018 with its 40-seat gain, including three in New York.

Maloney had an unusual campaign season in 2018. He ran again for attorney general in a wide-open Democratic primary, citing his experience in the private sector and opposing the Trump administration in Washington. With approval of a state judge, he ran for both the state wide post and for reelection to his House seat; under New York's election law, those primaries were held in separate months. If he had won the September primary for attorney general, he said that he would have given up his House seat, for which he had won the June primary. Instead, though spending more than the combined total of his opponents, he finished third with 25 percent of the vote in the four-candidate primary, which was won by Letitia James. In his House campaign, Republican challenger James O'Donnell criticized Maloney for placing his attention elsewhere. Maloney won, 55%-45%.

Following that election, he ran for DCCC chairman. When he was hospitalized for a bacterial infection, he dropped out of the contest, which Rep. Cheri Bustos of Illinois won. It was not clear that Maloney had strong support against the three other candidates. Bustos fell victim to her own high expectation-setting in 2020; Democrats lost a dozen seats despite her predicting large gains. When she announced that she would not seek a second term at the committee, Maloney quickly declared another bid. He stressed his commitment to updating of polls and eliminating a blanket ban on consultants who worked with candidates who challenged Democratic incumbents. He beat Democratic Rep. Tony Cardenas of California, a leader of the Congressional Hispanic Caucus, 119 to 107.

In his first weeks on the job, Maloney had some early stumbles. Black, Latino and Asian lawmakers urged him to make his senior staff more diverse after he hired a white man as his executive director. And his strategy to yoke GOP members to the QAnon conspiracy theory drew some criticism from vulnerable Democrats. He was widely panned as using elitist language when he told Politico in February 2021 that Republicans "can do QAnon or they can do college-educated voters. They cannot do both."

Maloney faced a tall task. Democrats approached a redistricting cycle that may hand him a more favorable district but will likely have a net nationwide benefit for the GOP.

NY-18: Lower Hudson Valley   Cook Partisan Voting Index: R+1

Population		Race and Ethnicity		Income	
Total	718,624	White	77.20%	Median Income	$91,723
Land area (sq. miles)	1,353	Black	10.60%	District Income Rank	48
Pop/ sq mi	530.97	Latino	18.30%	Poverty Rate	9.70%
Born in State	70.60%	Asian	3.10%	With health insurance	96.30%
		Two or more races	3.30%	Cash public assistance	1.70%
Age Groups		Other	5.80%	Food stamp/SNAP	8.20%
Under 18	22.60%				
18-34	21.40%	**Education**		**Work**	
35-64	40.00%	H.S grad or less	35.00%	White Collar	42.50%
Over 64	15.90%	Some college	28.90%	Sales and Service	39.50%
		College Degree, 4 yr	19.60%	Blue Collar	17.90%
Military		Post grad	16.50%	Government	17.80%
Veteran/ Active Duty	6.00%				

2020 Pres. Vote	Biden	184,181	(52%)	Trump	166,448	(47%)		
2016 Pres. Vote	Trump	152,142	(49%)	Clinton	146,188	(47%)	Johnson	7,930	(3%)

Newburgh, Poughkeepsie: The great interior of America can be said to begin where the Hudson River squeezes through a series of Appalachian ridges at the Hudson Highlands. This chokepoint became a barrier to British military power during the Revolutionary War, when American forces put a chain across the river to keep the British from sailing north. Benedict Arnold betrayed his country over control of this part of the Hudson, and the new nation built its military academy high on the cliffs at West Point. The Hudson was the impetus for the builders of the Erie Canal and the water-level New York Central Railroad, two great projects that made New York City the port of the American interior.

The 18th Congressional District of New York covers much of the southern Hudson Valley, sprawling across four counties. West of the Hudson, the district includes all of Orange County, which takes in about half the voters in the district; it has trailed only Rockland as the state's fastest-growing county outside New York City, with a 13 percent increase between 2000 and 2019. There, old farming villages like Warwick adjoin mountains, farms and new middle-income subdivisions on the nation's biggest deposit of muck soil outside the Everglades. Orange County includes Kiryas Joel, a Hasidic Jewish settlement with more than 26,000 residents, many of whom moved from Brooklyn to find room for their large families. In January 2019, Kiryas Joel separated from Monroe and renamed itself Palm Tree—the first new town in New York in 35 years. With county approval, construction began on the $500 million Lego land theme park—the largest such theme park in the world and the third in the United States, in addition to California and Florida. Also in Orange, the heirs to railroad baron E.H. Harriman successfully resisted plans by Caesars Entertainment to locate a large casino and resort complex next to their parkland; instead, the site was approved for residential development. Environmentalist groups in the area have mobilized to shutter dams that impede fish migration. Stewart International Airport expanded its terminal and nearly doubled its passenger load, including service to Europe with low-cost carrier Norwegian Air. The airport renamed itself "New York International," though it is 60 miles north of New York City.

East of the river, the 18th takes in all of Putnam County and more than half of Dutchess County, including Poughkeepsie, home of Vassar College, and Wappingers Falls. In Poughkeepsie, which has suffered many years of economic hard times, robust development attracted young professionals after officials approved a booming waterfront plan along the Hudson. Local officials believe IBM's new planned center for quantum computing could benefit the Hudson Valley; the company's Poughkeepsie facility is heavily involved in producing mainframes required for computing. The district takes in the lightly populated north eastern reaches of Westchester County, around Somers, North Salem and Lewisboro.

The region has proved attractive to white-collar workers seeking reasonably priced housing in low-crime areas. This has led to population growth at a time when many other areas of the state have been losing residents. Politically, Putnam County is reliably Republican; the rest of the district is swing territory or leans slightly Democratic, resulting in a district that tends to end up near the national average. Donald Trump won the district, 49%-47% in 2016.But it flipped to Joe Biden four years later, by a 52%-47% margin.

Antonio Delgado (D)

Elected 2018, 2nd term, b. Jan 28, 1977; Schenectady, NY; Colgate University, B.A., 1999; Oxford University, M.A., 2001; Harvard University Law School, J.D., 2005; Married (Lacey Delgado); 2 children.

Professional Career: Attorney, Akin, Gump, Strauss, Hauer & Feld; Music Label Owner.

DC Office: 1007 LHOB 20515, 202-225-5614, delgado.house.gov

State Offices: Kingston, 845-443-2930.

Committees: *Agriculture*: Biotechnology, Horticulture & Research; Commodity Exchanges, Energy & Credit (Chmn). *Small Business*: Underserved, Agricultural & Rural Business Development. *Transportation & Infrastructure*: Highways & Transit; Water Resources & Environment.

Almanac Ratings 2019-2020

	Economy	Social	Foreign	Composite
Liberal	100%	58%	80%	80%
Conservative	0%	42%	20%	20%

Key Votes of the 116th Congress

1. U.S./Mex./Can. trade deal Y	5. Russia sanctions Y	9. Firearms background checks Y
2. First Coronavirus response Y	6. Troops in Syria Y	10. Spending at the border Y
3. HEROES Act Y	7. Veto arms sales to Saudis Y	11. Marijuana liberalized rules Y
4. CASH Act Y	8. Defense $$$, veto override Y	12. Electoral College objections N

Election Results

Election	Name (Party)	Vote (%)		Cand. Spent	Ind. Exp. Support	Ind. Exp. Oppose
2020 General	Antonio Delgado (D)............................	192,100	(54%)	$3,011,337	$4,996	$4,375
	Kyle Van De Water (R)........................	151,475	(43%)	$95,334		$113

Prior winning percentages: 2018 (51%)

Democrat Antonio Delgado, first elected in 2018, won a contentious campaign that gained national attention, as Republicans sought to demonize aspects of his diverse career. One of the most robust fundraisers in House campaigns, he was among the African-American newcomers who won districts that leaned Republican and had small minority populations. Despite the competitiveness of his district, he coasted to reelection two years later when Republicans failed to recruit a formidable challenger .

A native of Schenectady, which is in the adjacent 20th District, Delgado graduated from Colgate University, where he was a leading player on the school's basketball team. He studied at Oxford University as a Rhodes Scholar, and got his law degree from Harvard University. In Los Angeles, he was a music-company executive and produced his own rap album, which he said was designed to empower young people with its focus on social justice. He returned to New York, where he represented large businesses and was a litigator with the large Washington-based law firm of Akin, Gump, Strauss, Hauer & Feld.

"I've lived a narrative that's hard to come by," Delgado told the Albany Times-Union. He described his life story as "one of upward mobility," but lamented that the American dream had become out of reach for many Americans, especially in upstate New York.

Days after Donald Trump was inaugurated, Delgado decided to run for Congress against Republican Rep. John Faso—his first bid for political office—and called Trump's election "a moment of awakening."With Faso seen as vulnerable, he faced six other candidates in the Democratic primary. They included businessmen Brian Flynn and Pat Ryan, who each spent more than $1 million, and Gareth Rhodes, a former aide to New York Gov. Andrew Cuomo. Delgado raised the most money for the primary and highlighted his local roots; his parents had both worked at a now-shuttered General Electric plant. He won the primary with 22 percent of the vote, to 18 percent for Ryan and Rhodes, and 14 percent for Flynn. Delgado was the frontrunner in Ulster County.

Faso, who voted for repeal of the Affordable Care Act but opposed the tax cuts passed by House Republicans, sought to depict himself as a bipartisan problem-solver opposed to wasteful spending. His campaign highlighted Trump-style themes that critics said were laced with racial messages and stoked fear of crime. He ran an ad that attacked Delgado as an outsider who moved to the district for the campaign, and as a "big-city rapper," with lyrics that were profane and politically radical.

Delgado responded that he was addressing issues such as income inequality and climate change. His campaign messages included the need for improved healthcare services and his pledge to be a "true independent actor" in Congress. Delgado's spending of $8 million roughly doubled Faso's account, though the incumbent received more than $3 million in national-party support.

Delgado, with his 51%-46% victory, won the three largest counties, which are the closest to New York City: Ulster, where he had his biggest edge, Dutchess and Columbia. Faso took seven of the remaining eight counties in the more rural parts of the district. As a Democrat in a district represented by three Republicans during 20 of the previous 24 years, Delgado became a top 2020 target.

A year into his first term, Delgado voted to impeach Trump, a decision the National Republican Congressional Committee called a "political death sentence." But he doubled down on his efforts at home, holding dozens of town halls and logging thousands of miles to meet with constituents. In October 2019, he aired the first TV ad from a House Democrat that cycle, highlighting his bill to ease the financial burden on farmers by increasing infrastructure and rural broadband. In Congress, he has spoken out about combating racism, including in politics.

Delgado raised over $2.1 million through September 2019 and benefitted immensely from Republicans' failure to recruit a challenger. The NRCC eagerly courted Dutchess County Supervisor

Marc Molinaro, who carried the district by 11 points when he ran for governor in 2018. But he declined. The GOP primary pit fashion designer Ola Hawatmeh against Army veteran and attorney Kyle Van De Water. Van De Water won 57%-42% in a low-turnout race.

Van De Water failed to mount a serious challenge. He spent $95,000 and never aired any broadcast ads. Republican outside groups gave up on the race entirely, even though it was one of just a dozen Democratic-held seats where Trump got over 50 percent in 2016. Delgado won, 54%-43%, and ended the cycle with over $3 million in the bank.

In 2021, Delgado chaired the Agriculture Subcommittee on Commodity Exchanges, Energy, and Credit, where he looked after the interests of his district's dairy farmers. With Democratic control of redistricting in New York, he Delgado may secure more favorable turf.

NY-19: Central Hudson Valley, the Catskills   Cook Partisan Voting Index: R+3

Population		Race and Ethnicity		Income	
Total	701,011	White	87.10%	Median Income	$67,004
Land area (sq. miles)	7,937	Black	4.90%	District Income Rank	192
Pop/ sq mi	88.32	Latino	8.40%	Poverty Rate	11.20%
Born in State	74.60%	Asian	1.60%	With health insurance	95.50%
		Two or more races	3.10%	Cash public assistance	2.00%
Age Groups		Other	3.30%	Food stamp/SNAP	9.10%
Under 18	18.20%				
18-34	20.20%	**Education**		**Work**	
35-64	40.40%	H.S grad or less	40.30%	White Collar	39.20%
Over 64	21.10%	Some college	28.40%	Sales and Service	39.30%
		College Degree, 4 yr	16.60%	Blue Collar	21.50%
Military		Post grad	14.60%	Government	18.60%
Veteran/ Active Duty	7.20%				

2020 Pres. Vote	Biden	182,965	(50%)	Trump	177,569	(48%)			
2016 Pres. Vote	Trump	162,266	(50%)	Clinton	140,517	(44%)	Johnson	10,235	(3%)
	Stein	6,434	(2%)						

Dutchess and Ulster Counties: The Hudson River, an avenue of commerce in colonial days and an inspiration to artists in the early republic, is still one of America's great sights, although it is no longer central to the nation's consciousness and politics. The classic mansions overlooking the river, like Clermont, built by Robert Livingston, who financed the first steamboat, are reminders of the daring nature of the 18th century spirit. The Hudson gave birth to America's passionate party politics. On a visit to this area in the 1790s, James Madison and Aaron Burr welded the Virginia-New York alliance that changed the course of American political history. Nearby is Kinderhook, the home of Martin Van Buren, the innkeeper's son who, in concert with Andrew Jackson, invented the torchlight parade, the national party convention, and, many argue, the Democratic Party. Later in the 19th century, the Hudson was lined with the palaces of the nation's first great millionaires and the comfortable country homes of New York's gentry. One of the latter, Springwood in Hyde Park, was the birthplace and home of Franklin Roosevelt, who, even as president, was most comfortable looking out over his sloping lawn to the river, where he liked to go iceboating in the winter.

On the other side of the Hudson loom the Catskills, where Rip Van Winkle was said to have fallen asleep for 20 years after drinking with nine pipe-playing dwarfs. Eventually, the area became part of a great pathway west, along the Erie Lackawanna and Delaware & Hudson railroad lines, with engines steaming over giant viaducts and along narrow river valleys through the mountains. Later in the 19th century, huge kosher hotels were built in Sullivan County in the Catskills, the resort area popularly known as the Borscht Belt. These thrived when Jews were excluded from other resorts but fell on hard times in the late 20th century. Today, there is little passenger train service, and the Catskills are bypassed by major airlines. A new generation of inns and boutique hotels has sought to create a niche in recent years.

The sprawling 19th Congressional District of New York connects these two regions into a single district. It extends from north of Albany to the exurbs of New York City. It includes seven full counties and parts of four others. It is a collection of small towns and villages. The largest locale is Kingston (pop. 22,793) and only one other place, Hyde Park, has more than 20,000 residents. Like most of

Upstate, all of these counties lost population between 2010 and 2019. The 19th bends around the Albany metropolitan area in the north, taking in a bit of the Mohawk Valley, and the Baseball Hall of Fame in Cooperstown. In Ulster is Bethel, where the 1969 Woodstock music festival took place. Roosevelt lore has contributed to robust tourism in Dutchess County. Its county seat of Poughkeepsie, in particular, is experiencing a revival. Developers have started to build a $300 million community that will include a new hotel, restaurants and office space. Other new additions: craft breweries and refurbished Victorian homes.

Ulster, the largest county, is solidly Democratic at the national level. Like most of Upstate, Republicans fare better at the local level and even control the county legislature. The district was once solidly Republican, part of a tradition that dated to the Civil War (FDR never carried his home territory except when he ran for the state Senate in 1910.) Today, it is swing territory: Donald Trump won here, 50%-44% in 2016. But Joe Biden won it narrowly in 2020.

Paul Tonko (D)

Elected 2008, 7th term, b. Jun 18, 1949; Amsterdam, NY; Clarkson University, B.S., 1971; Roman Catholic; Single.

Elected Office: Montgomery County Board of Supervisors, 1976-1983, Chairman, 1981; NY Assembly, 1983-2007.

Professional Career: NY Department of Transportation, 1972-1974; NY Department of Public Service, 1974-1983; President & CEO, NY St. Energy Research & Development Authority, 2007-2008.

DC Office: 2369 RHOB 20515, 202-225-5076, Fax: 202-225-5077, tonko.house.gov

State Offices: Albany, 518-465-0700; Amsterdam, 518-843-3400; Schenectady, 518-374-4547.

Committees: *Energy & Commerce*: Energy; Environment & Climate Change (Chmn); Oversight & Investigations. *Natural Resources*: National Parks, Forests & Public Lands. *Science, Space & Technology*: Research & Technology.

Group Ratings

	ADA	ACLU	AFL-CIO	LCV	COC	HAFA	ACU	CFG	FRC
2020	**	86%	**	100%	-	0%	3%	**	-
2019	95%	C	90%	100%	43%	C	4%	12%	0%

Almanac Ratings 2019-2020

	Economy	Social	Foreign	Composite
Liberal	100%	100%	100%	100%
Conservative	0%	0%	0%	0%

Key Votes of the 116th Congress

1. U.S./Mex./Can. trade deal	N	5. Russia sanctions	Y	9. Firearms background checks	Y
2. First Coronavirus response	Y	6. Troops in Syria	Y	10. Spending at the border	N
3. HEROES Act	Y	7. Veto arms sales to Saudis	Y	11. Marijuana liberalized rules	Y
4. CASH Act	Y	8. Defense $$$, veto override	Y	12. Electoral College objections	N

Election Results

Election	Name (Party)	Vote (%)		Cand. Spent	Ind. Exp. Support	Ind. Exp. Oppose
2020 General	Paul Tonko (D)	219,705	(61%)	$924,331	$873	
	Elizabeth Joy (R)	139,446	(39%)	$357,688		$113

Prior winning percentages: 2018 (67%), 2016 (68%), 2014 (59%), 2012 (64%), 2010 (57%), 2008 (62%)

Democrat Paul Tonko, elected in 2008, came to Congress with an extensive background in energy issues and parlayed his expertise into a seat on the powerful Energy and Commerce Committee, where he has dealt with similar types of industrial problems that are common to his district. In 2019, as a subcommittee chairman, his domain expanded to include climate change. He has had some bipartisan accomplishments. With the takeover by the Biden administration in 2021, the stars were aligned for Tonko's opportunity to take significant action on the climate issue.

The grandson of Polish immigrants, Tonko was born in the old mill town of Amsterdam New York, where he still lives. He graduated from Clarkson University with a degree in engineering. Attracted from a young age to public service, he built his career in state government, first at the New York Department of Transportation and then as an engineer at the Department of Public Service, the state's utilities regulator. His says his working-class background gave him an appreciation for the "underdog" that remains the underpinning of his political beliefs.

In 1974, at age 26, he became the youngest person elected to the Montgomery County Board of Supervisors, and later became board chairman. Tonko won a seat in the state Assembly in 1983 and served for nearly a quarter century. He won passage of a law requiring health insurers to cover most mental illnesses and another requiring social workers to report all cases of suspected child abuse to the state. He exercised his greatest influence over state energy policy, serving as chairman of the Assembly's energy committee for 15 years, until he resigned to head the state's Energy Research and Development Authority.

When the House seat opened, most of the local Democratic establishment lined up behind Tonko. He won important union endorsements, plus the backing of the Working Families Party. With few differences between the candidates on major issues, the local support likely made the difference. Outraised and outspent by both opponents, Tonko sailed to victory with 40 percent of the vote to 30 percent for Tracey Brooks, a former staffer for Democratic Sen. Hillary Clinton. In the general, Tonko faced Republican Jim Buhrmaster, a Schenectady County legislator; he won. 62%-35%.

Tonko has focused on the issue he knows best, energy policy. Even as a freshman, while Democrats controlled the House, Tonko was quick to exploit his policy expertise. He got a bill through the House in 2009 creating an $800 million research program in wind energy technologies, which would benefit GE in his district. Another of his bills, which passed the same year, created a research program to improve the efficiency of gas turbines used in power generation systems that convert heat into energy.

While Democrats were in the minority, much of Tonko's work was defensive. On Energy and Commerce, he was at the vanguard of defending the Environmental Protection Agency against GOP attacks. He co-chaired the Sustainable Energy and Environment Coalition. On spending bills, he sought to protect EPA's authority to regulate carbon emissions. On the Science, Space and Technology Committee, he worked in 2015 to protect federal research funds that had been directed at Upstate manufacturing facilities.

Tonko pushed ahead with his own proposals. In 2016, the House passed his bill to encourage citizen activities in the federal government to accelerate scientific research. It was enacted as part of a broader package of innovation measures. In 2018, Tonko won enactment of his bill to require increased testing of local drinking water systems.

In the majority, Tonko became chairman of the renamed Environment and Climate Change Subcommittee, which has jurisdiction over the Clean Air Act. "We don't have the time or resources to let this president and his allies in Congress sit on their hands for another two years," he declared, referring to President Donald Trump. Climate-change activists complained that Tonko was not moving fast enough. Protestors rallied on the steps of his office in Albany and demanded that he support the "Green New Deal" proposal backed by many progressive Democrats and their environmental allies. But Tonko was skeptical about the vague guidelines of that proposal, which did not define specific policy action. He also clashed with activists by voicing reservations about Speaker Nancy Pelosi's creation of a select committee on climate change—though she did not give it legislative authority—and responding that House committees "should be allowed to do their work."In 2020, as Congress passed sweeping legislation for corona virus relief, he worked with other Energy and Commerce Democrats to urge inclusion of steps to address climate change unrelated to the pandemic. A lack of interest by the Trump administration made such action a non-starter.

In early March 2021, Tonko joined Energy and Commerce Chairman Frank Pallone and Energy Subcommittee Chairman Bobby Rush in filing legislation to require that the nation produce 80 percent of electricity from clean energy sources by 2030 and 100 percent by 2035, with net zero greenhouse gas pollution by 2050. Their legislation, he said, "invests in the industry and ingenuity of our people and will launch America's next great chapter of sustainable prosperity and real economic and environmental justice." He co-chaired the House's Sustainable Energy and Environment Coalition.

Tonko has had little trouble winning reelection. Albany Times Union columnist Marv Cermak described him in 2011 as "a super-duper campaigner who shows up all over the place," and said "if there is a chink in his armor, colleagues and media types agree it's his penchant for long-winded speeches." Tonko resists hyper-partisanship, Cermak added. "He is frustrated that partisan politics are overshadowing science, math and reason," the Albany Business Review reported in 2018. After a dozen years in Congress, the support of the Biden administration positioned Tonko in 2021 to enact major legislation.

NY-20: Capital Region

Cook Partisan Voting Index: D+7

Population		Race and Ethnicity		Income	
Total	725,669	White	78.30%	Median Income	$71,156
Land area (sq. miles)	1,231	Black	9.30%	District Income Rank	155
Pop/ sq mi	589.36	Latino	6.70%	Poverty Rate	11.60%
Born in State	74.20%	Asian	5.30%	With health insurance	96.90%
		Two or more races	4.80%	Cash public assistance	2.70%
Age Groups		Other	2.40%	Food stamp/SNAP	10.40%
Under 18	19.10%				
18-34	25.70%	**Education**		**Work**	
35-64	37.60%	H.S grad or less	32.10%	White Collar	47.50%
Over 64	17.80%	Some college	27.60%	Sales and Service	37.00%
		College Degree, 4 yr	22.30%	Blue Collar	15.40%
Military		Post grad	18.00%	Government	21.80%
Veteran/ Active Duty	6.30%				

2020 Pres. Vote	Biden	217,340	(59%)	Trump	141,619	(39%)			
2016 Pres. Vote	Clinton	175,384	(53%)	Trump	131,557	(40%)	Johnson	12,538	(4%)

Albany, Schenectady: As readers of novelist laureate William Kennedy know, Albany is an antique city. Its solid row houses recall its 19thcentury prosperity. Its once-teeming lumberyards, railroad car shops, restaurants and hotels have the patina of age and the accumulated grime of decades of coal smoke burned during six-month-long winters. Its history dates to 1609, when Dutch traders from Henry Hudson's ship Half Moon set up a fur trading post. Hudson, his son, and seven crew members were set adrift amidst a mutiny in Canada's James Bay two years later and never seen again, but the trading post endured. The Dutch built Fort Orange on the banks of the Hudson in 1624 so seagoing ships could dock at the edge of the great, gloomy forests near the confluence of the Hudson and the Mohawk. Albany became one of America's biggest lumber towns.

A few miles upriver, Troy was a steel town rivaling Pittsburgh in the 1840s, greatly advantaged by its proximity to the mouth of the Erie Canal. That is where meatpacker Samuel Wilson supplied beef rations to soldiers during the War of 1812; we know Wilson today as "Uncle Sam." Lately, a gentrified Troy has been bustling with antique shops and thousands of shoppers at the farmers' market every Saturday, though many former industrial properties remain vacant. But Bloomberg City Lab reported in November 2020, "the pandemic has exposed just how many people were living on the economic margins: The Albany region has lost more than 19,000 jobs in 2020."

In addition to state government, Albany had one of the nation's most famed Democratic political machines, dating to 1921, when Daniel O'Connell, his brothers, and local aristocrat Edwin Corning took control of City Hall. The machine was sustained by legions of city and county employees, by a certain creativity when it came to counting votes, and by the raffish atmosphere of the speakeasies during Prohibition. In the 1960s, Mayor Corning and Republican Gov. Nelson Rockefeller collaborated on a smorgasbord of civic improvement projects: Empire State Plaza with 11,000 employees in 10 government buildings on 98 acres; the distinctive, ovoid performing arts center known as the Egg; and a renovated Union Station.

The economy in the Capital Region has been stronger than elsewhere in Upstate, with a population gain of 10,000 between 2010 and 2019. The area has remained vibrant with renewable energy jobs and high-tech manufacturing. GE has new plants producing digital X-ray equipment and advanced batteries, though its 4,500-plus area employees are a shadow of the 40,000 in heavy manufacturing at Schenectady Works during World War II. The port of Albany has spent $50 million on an expansion to move additional cargo—partly as an inducement for GE to remain in the area.

The 20th Congressional District of New York includes most of the Albany metropolitan area: all of Albany and Schenectady counties, which take in nearly two-thirds of the district population; most of Montgomery County, including Amsterdam; parts of Rensselaer County, including Troy; and much of Saratoga County. The horse-race track at Saratoga Springs, operating since 1863 and reportedly the oldest sports venue in the nation, has completed a major upgrade, including the grandstand. Politically, Democratic voters in Albany and Troy outweigh the Republican tilt of the outer counties and make this a comfortably Democratic district. After the Democratic presidential vote fell in 2016 to 53 percent, Joe Biden restored the 59 percent that President Barack Obama drew in 2012.

Elise Stefanik (R)

Elected 2014, 4th term, b. Jul 02, 1984; Albany, NY; Harvard University, B.A.; Roman Catholic; Engaged (Matthew Manda).

Professional Career: Staff, President George W. Bush, 2006-2009; Staff, Vice President. candidate Paul Ryan, 2012; Director Communications, Foreign Policy Initiative; Sales, marketing & mgmt operations, Premium Plywood Products.

DC Office: 318 CHOB 20515, 202-225-4611, Fax: 202-226-0621, stefanik.house.gov

State Offices: Glens Falls, 518-743-0964; Plattsburgh, 518-561-2324; Watertown, 315-782-3150.

Committees: House Republican Conference Chairman. *Armed Services*: Cyber, Innovative Technologies & Information Systems; Strategic Forces. *Education & Labor*: Higher Education & Workforce Investment; Workforce Protections. *Permanent Select on Intelligence*: Counterterrorism, Counterintelligence & Counterproliferation; Strategic Technologies & Advanced Research.

Group Ratings

	ADA	ACLU	AFL-CIO	LCV	COC	HAFA	ACU	CFG	FRC
2020	**	31%	**	48%	-	56%	44%	**	-
2019	20%	C	62%	55%	97%	C	41%	40%	68%

Almanac Ratings 2019-2020

	Economy	Social	Foreign	Composite
Liberal	45%	42%	45%	44%
Conservative	55%	58%	55%	56%

Key Votes of the 116th Congress

1. U.S./Mex./Can. trade deal	Y	5. Russia sanctions	Y
2. First Coronavirus response	Y	6. Troops in Syria	Y
3. HEROES Act	N	7. Veto arms sales to Saudis	N
4. CASH Act	Y	8. Defense $$$, veto override	Y

9. Firearms background checks N
10. Spending at the border Y
11. Marijuana liberalized rules N
12. Electoral College objections Y

Election Results

Election	Name (Party)	Vote (%)	Cand. Spent	Ind. Exp. Support	Ind. Exp. Oppose
2020 General	Elise Stefanik (R)............................ 188,655	(59%)	$11,314,760	$86,390	$5,430
	Tedra Cobb (D)................................ 131,995	(41%)	$5,455,681	$1,079	$8,200

Prior winning percentages: 2018 (56%), 2016 (65%), 2014 (55%)

Republican Elise Stefanik, elected to an open seat in 2014 that had been Democratic-held, has taken advantage of her opportunities. When she took office, she was the youngest woman ever elected to Congress. Once a Republican who kept her distance from former President Donald Trump, Stefanik became one of his most prominent congressional supporters and happily engaged with Democrats on his behalf. In May 2021, with support from Trump who called her "a gifted communicator," she won overwhelming support to replace Rep. Liz Cheney as chair of the House Republican Conference.

Born and raised in Albany, Stefanik grew up among entrepreneurs, with both parents running a wholesale plywood business. She became politically engaged during her college years at Harvard, and upon graduation landed a job with the Bush administration's Domestic Policy Council. She worked in the White House chief of staff's office, and later joined Tim Pawlenty's presidential campaign as policy director. After Pawlenty withdrew, she worked for Rep. Paul Ryan of Wisconsin when he became the running mate for Mitt Romney, advising him on vice presidential debate preparation.

After Blue Dog Democratic Rep. Bill Owens announced his retirement, Stefanik unveiled her House bid and earned the backing of the National Republican Congressional Committee's "Young Guns" program, which supports new talent. With nearly $800,000 in help from Karl Rove's American Crossroads—making a rare intervention in a GOP primary—Stefanik dispatched Republican Matt Doheny in the June primary, 61%-39%.

Democrats faced problems in recruiting, and their nominee, Aaron Wolff, was a filmmaker who was a resident of Brooklyn. His only claim to the North Country was that his family owned some land. In the general, Stefanik moderated from the customary GOP line on some issues. Stefanik benefited from nearly $2 million in party-related assistance, far more than Democrats spent for Wolff, who also suffered from an active campaign by Green Party candidate Matt Funicello. Stefanik pulled away to a surprisingly comfortable win, with 55 percent of the vote to 34 percent for Wolff and 11 percent for Funicello. She won nine of the 12 counties, losing three in the northeast corner of the state.

In her first three terms, Stefanik drew considerable publicity, nearly all of it favorable. She cultivated an image of a Republican in the mold of her mentor, Ryan, and burnished a bipartisan reputation. CBS News featured her with an online story headlined, "Is Elise Stefanik the future of the GOP?"

Stefanik's committee assignments put her at the forefront of national security policy. On the Armed Services Committee, she switched in 2021 from the ranking member of the Emerging Threats and Capabilities Subcommittee, which oversees counterterrorism programs, to the Cyber, Innovative Technologies and Information Systems Subcommittee. As a member of the Education and Labor Committee, she worked with Democratic Rep. Cheri Bustos of Illinois to provide more flexible access to Pell Grants.

Stefanik has had multiple party assignments. At the National Republican Congressional Committee, she spent the 2018 cycle as the vice chair for recruitment, the first woman to hold that position. The party's female ranks dwindled to 13 House members. Stefanik announced in December 2018 that she would step back from NRCC duties and instead focus on taking a more active role in supporting women candidates in primaries. NRCC Chairman Tom Emmers called the move "a mistake." Stefanik tweeted that she wasn't asking permission.

In a gracious moment after the 2018 midterms, Stefanik took to Twitter to congratulate Democratic Rep. Alexandria Ocasio-Cortez, who surpassed her as the youngest woman ever elected to Congress. "I proudly hand off that mantle to you," Stefanik wrote. "Work hard to encourage the next generation of women who follow!"

Stefanik initially kept her distance from Trump, emphasizing that she would be "an independent voice for the district." After he became president, she criticized Trump for his handling of the immigration and refugee bans, which she said was "rushed and overly broad."Then came the 2019 impeachment. During Intelligence Committee hearings questioning the appropriateness of Trump threatening to withhold funds from Ukraine in exchange for political support in his reelection, Stefanik turned sharply. Once the darling of the GOP old guard and a Republican some Democrats expressed grudging admiration for, her defence of the president shifted perceptions of her.

Democrats might have now viewed her as a polarizing figure, but they have backed away from seriously competing for Stefanik's district. In both 2016 and 2018, her challengers received virtually no party assistance. In 2020, she coasted to victory, 59%-41%, over Tedra Cobb, a business consultant and former member of the St. Lawrence County legislature, who spent $5.5 million, though she had little national party support.

After House Republicans ousted Cheney as the head of their Conference, Stefanik moved quickly to wrap up support from most wings of the party and took the number-three leadership post, 134--46, in a last-minute challenge from Rep. Chip Roy of Texas, who criticized her lack of conservative credentials. In a potentially deft move, Stefanik said that she would keep the post only until the 2022 election, when she hoped to succeed term-limited Rep. Virginia Foxx as the top Republican at the House Education and Labor Committee.

NY-21: Northern New York   **Cook Partisan Voting Index: R+8**

Population		Race and Ethnicity		Income	
Total	694,835	White	92.50%	Median Income	$57,320
Land area (sq. miles)	15,115	Black	2.80%	District Income Rank	296
Pop/ sq mi	45.97	Latino	3.40%	Poverty Rate	14.40%
Born in State	77.10%	Asian	1.20%	With health insurance	95.70%
		Two or more races	2.20%	Cash public assistance	3.60%
Age Groups		Other	1.20%	Food stamp/SNAP	13.80%
Under 18	20.00%				
18-34	22.40%	**Education**		**Work**	
35-64	38.90%	H.S grad or less	45.70%	White Collar	35.80%
Over 64	18.70%	Some college	29.60%	Sales and Service	40.70%
		College Degree, 4 yr	14.20%	Blue Collar	23.50%
Military		Post grad	10.60%	Government	21.50%
Veteran/ Active Duty	11.40%				

2020 Pres. Vote	Trump	175,347	(54%)	Biden	141,681	(44%)		
2016 Pres. Vote	Trump	150,481	(53%)	Clinton	111,760	(39%)	Johnson	11,620	(4%)
	Stein	5,577	(2%)					

Glens Falls, Watertown: Some early 19th century visionaries believed that the North Country of Upstate New York—a battleground in both the Revolutionary War and the War of 1812—was the land of the future. Politician Gouverneur Morris, French slave trader James LeRay, and Dutch silver speculator David Parish bought up thousands of acres between the Adirondacks and the St. Lawrence River and tried to unload them on farmers unaware of the shortness of the growing season and the unnavigability of the river. These developers left behind grand mansions, but their hopes for huge profits were frustrated when the Erie Canal turned the stream of settlement westward, and Canadians built their new capital of Ottawa far north of the river. But northern New York was not without its business successes: It was in Watertown in 1878 that 26-year-old Frank Woolworth put a sign over a table of odds and ends that read "Any Article 5 Cents," starting America's first retail chain and inventing the concept of discount stores.

More recently, the North Country has looked to government for help. The St. Lawrence Seaway proved too small for most oceangoing freighters and remains frozen three months of the year. A bi national agreement with Canada to return the St. Lawrence River to more natural flowing patterns took effect in 2016. Fort Drum, despite the Army's preference for warm-weather training sites, has been the home since 1985 of the 10th Mountain Division, a 10,000-person light infantry division near Watertown. The unit performed valiantly in difficult environs in Afghanistan and Iraq. In Massena and Plattsburg—places with abandoned aluminum plants—companies use the cheap electricity derived from St. Lawrence River dams to fuel computer servers that produce Bitcoins, a digital currency. Private developers have built big malls in Watertown and Massena, with the cheap dollar attracting Canadian tourism and shopping. In March 2019, The Atlantic found in a national survey that Watertown and the surrounding area were among the most "politically tolerant" places in the United States.

The 21st Congressional District of New York covers most of the North Country, starting at Lake Champlain, running westward along the St. Lawrence Seaway and over the Adirondacks Forest Preserve to Lake Ontario. Lake Placid is here, site of the 1980 Olympic Games and the famous "Miracle on Ice," when a heavily favored Soviet hockey team was upset by an upstart American squad. It stretches to the edges of Saratoga Springs to the southeast, and near Oswego and Syracuse to the southwest. The district has only a few population centers, including Plattsburgh on Lake Champlain, Watertown near Lake Ontario, and Gloversville and Glens Falls in the south. Each is home to fewer than 25,000 residents, with population declining multiple percentage points from 2010 to 2019.

Geographically it is the largest district in New York and one of the largest in the East. It is ancestrally Republican but was more inclined toward moderates than conservatives and increasingly divided in its partisan loyalties. Until recently, Clinton, Franklin and St. Lawrence counties in the northeast corner along the Vermont border were solidly Democratic. The south western counties are more heavily Republican. With each cycle, the GOP has re-established its hold on this region. Donald Trump twice ran well ahead of his national performance, including 54 percent in 2020.

Claudia Tenney (R)

Elected 2020, 2nd term, b. Feb 04, 1961; New Hartford, NY; Colgate University, B.A., 1983; University of Cincinnati, J.D., 1987; Presbyterian; Divorced; 1 child.

Elected Office: Member, NY State Assembly, 2011-2012, 2013-2016.

Professional Career: Attorney; Founder/Publisher, Tenney Media Group, 1997-2004; Chief of Staff/Legal Counsel, Office of Assembly Member David Townsend, 2003-2009; Co-owner, commercial printing company; Radio and television host.

DC Office: 1410 LHOB 20515, 202-225-3665, tenney.house.gov

State Offices: Binghamton, 607-242-0200; Utica, 315-732-0713.

Committees: *Foreign Affairs*: Europe, Energy, the Environment & Cyber; Intern'l Dev't, Intern'l Orgs & Global Corporate Social Impact. *Small Business*: Innovation, Entrepreneurship & Workforce Development; Underserved, Agricultural & Rural Business Development.

Election Results

Election	Name (Party)	Vote (%)		Cand. Spent	Ind. Exp. Support	Ind. Exp. Oppose
2020 General	Claudia Tenney (R)	156,098	(49%)	$2,300,461	$558,171	$7,325,220
	Anthony Brindisi (D)	155,989	(49%)	$6,266,471	$633,421	$10,321,381
	Keith Price (L)	6,780	(2%)			
2020 Primary	Claudia Tenney (R)	23,784	(60%)			
	George Phillips (R)	16,151	(40%)			

Republican Claudia Tenney, who reclaimed her seat in 2020 from first-term Democratic Rep. Anthony Brindisi, has emphasized her conservative pedigree. Disputes over election-count procedures, including inconsistent practices from one county to the next, placed much of the election count under the control of a local judge and delayed Tenney's seating until nearly six weeks after Congress convened in January 2021.

Tenney, the daughter of a New York State Supreme Court justice, was born in New Hartford. She got her bachelor's from Colgate University and a law degree from the University of Cincinnati. Working for the Consulate General of Yugoslavia, she served as an intermediary between ABC Sports and the Yugoslavian government prior to the 1984 Winter Olympics in Sarajevo. The co-owner of a commercial printing company, where she served as publisher and corporate counsel, she also practiced law and was the moderator of a local broadcast called "Common Cents."

Tenney was elected to the state Assembly in 2010 in a district that covered parts of Oswego and Oneida counties and served two terms. In 2014, she challenged moderate Republican Rep. Richard Hanna, who advocated bipartisan compromise and had a voting record that ranked him among the most moderate Republicans in the House. Tenney criticized Hanna's support for gay marriage, and his votes to increase the debt ceiling and oppose delay of implementation of the Affordable Care Act. She raised only $187,000, of which $112,000 came from loans she made to her campaign. Tenney had backing from the tea party and conservative talk-show hosts Laura Ingraham and Sean Hannity.

In the primary, Hanna took five of the eight counties and won 53.5%-46.5%. Hanna, who ran without Democratic opposition that year, spent $862,000 during the cycle, and he had $665,000 support from a Super PAC backed by billionaire investor Paul Singer.

Facing another tough primary challenge from Tenney in 2016, Hanna retired and Democrats had high hopes for recapturing what had become a swing district. Both parties spent heavily on this contest, which was complicated by a big-spending independent candidate. Tenney had competitive primary challenges from businessman Steve Wells and Broome County legislator George Phillips. Unexpectedly, the American Conservative Union ran ads that questioned Tenney's voting record in Albany, and supported Phillips. Hanna endorsed Wells and warned that Tenney could not win in November. In the primary, Tenney won with 41 percent to 34 percent for Wells and 25 percent for Phillips. Tenney got a majority of the votes in Oneida; Phillips did likewise in Broome.

That seemed to give a big opportunity to Democrats. But they encountered recruiting setbacks. After more experienced officials decided not to run, Democrats turned to Broome County legislator Kim Myers, the daughter of the founder of Dick's Sporting Goods. Also running in November was Martin Babinec, a deep-pocket venture capitalist who ran as the "Upstate Jobs" Party candidate. Tenney raised the least money of the three candidates: $1 million to $1.7 million for Wells and $3 million that Babinec self-financed. The National Republican Congressional Committee spent $3 million on behalf of Tenney, while Wells benefited from $3.7 million from national Democrats. Tenney won with unexpected ease, aided in part by Donald Trump's strong local performance. She got 47 percent of the vote to 41 percent for Wells and 12 percent for Babinec.

Tenney got a seat on the Financial Services Committee, where she set a priority of rolling back banking regulations. She became an early Democratic target for 2018.With Trump supporting Tenney, including his participation at a fundraising event in Utica three months before the election, she appeared to have unified GOP voters following her two contentious primaries. "I'm here for Claudia," Trump told the local crowd, in what reportedly was the first presidential visit to the area in 70 years. "She has helped us so much."

Brindisi styled himself as an advocate of "principled bipartisanship" and claimed success with that approach during four terms in the state's Democratic-dominated Assembly. He attacked Tenney for "marching in lockstep with the hard right on critical issues" in Congress. He kept his distance from House Democratic leaders and was more circumspect about taking on Trump. "People see Claudia Tenney as part of the same rigged system that President Trump campaigned against," he told a campaign rally in Binghamton. He told a local reporter that he and Tenney "really didn't work together too much on issues" when they served together in Albany.

His $4.6 million in spending gave him an advantage over Tenney. The two national parties and their allies spent another $15 million on the campaign. In his 51%-49% victory, a margin of 1,473 votes, Brindisi won the two largest counties in the district—Broome, which was the core of his victory margin, and Oneida. Tenney took the smaller, rural counties. One of three Democrats who defeated GOP incumbents in New York in 2018, Brindisi's margin was the tightest.

Tenney in October 2019 announced her campaign to return to Congress. She gained the support of GOP Leader Kevin McCarthy of California and the National Republican Congress Committee, but failed to clear the Republican field. Phillips, a history teacher and former congressional aide, said his local base gave him a better position to defeat Brindisi. Tenney mostly ignored him and focused her attention on Brindisi. She won the primary, 59%-41%, though Phillips got 58 percent of the vote in Broome County.

In their rematch, the candidates pursued national themes. In an October debate, Tenney criticized Brindisi for "holding up" with Speaker Nancy Pelosi a legislative deal for economic "relief to our struggling businesses." Brindisi said that Senate Republican Leader Mitch McConnell was "holding it up." In voting to impeach Trump, Tenney said, Brindisi sided with socialism rather than seeking "to preserve American greatness." Brindisi responded that Trump had signed into law six bills that he had cosponsored.

Brindisi out-spent his opponent, $6.3 million to $2.3 million, though Tenney received more than $10 million in support from the national GOP—about double the Democratic support for Brindisi. The result was another tight contest. Although Tenney had a lead of more than 30,000 from Election Day voting, her final margin was 109 votes as the counties slowly reported their mail-in votes. Tenney did not immediately regain her seat on Financial Services and was assigned to the Foreign Affairs and Small Business Committees. The future of this slow-growing district, with its rapid turnover of incumbents, might be significantly affected by redistricting.

NY-22: Central New York

Cook Partisan Voting Index: R+9

Population		Race and Ethnicity		Income	
Total	688,391	White	88.70%	Median Income	$56,615
Land area (sq. miles)	5,077	Black	3.90%	District Income Rank	304
Pop/ sq mi	135.58	Latino	4.00%	Poverty Rate	15.00%
Born in State	80.80%	Asian	3.00%	With health insurance	95.80%
		Two or more races	3.30%	Cash public assistance	3.20%
Age Groups		Other	1.20%	Food stamp/SNAP	14.70%
Under 18	20.30%				
18-34	23.20%	**Education**		**Work**	
35-64	37.40%	H.S grad or less	42.80%	White Collar	37.00%
Over 64	19.10%	Some college	31.10%	Sales and Service	41.50%
		College Degree, 4 yr	14.60%	Blue Collar	21.50%
Military		Post grad	11.50%	Government	20.00%
Veteran/ Active Duty	7.30%				

2020 Pres. Vote	Trump	177,137	(55%)	Biden	139,990	(43%)		
2016 Pres. Vote	Trump	158,913	(54%)	Clinton	114,016	(39%)	Johnson 12,349	(4%)

Utica, Binghamton: One of the first American frontiers was the Mohawk River Valley of Upstate New York. But from the establishment of Fort Orange in 1624 in what is now Albany until the Revolutionary War, white settlers did not dare move west along the Mohawk. The British used their Iroquois allies as a buffer against the French and in turn kept New England Yankees from venturing very far westward. Only after the French were driven from North America in 1759 did the pressures for westward settlement prevail. Once the Revolutionary War started, Iroquois dominion ended. The later digging of the Erie Canal was an engineering feat that hastened the westward push. In 1811, it cost more to ship goods 30 miles inland from New York City than to send them to England. But after eight years of work by 9,000 men, the canal opened in 1825, ahead of schedule and on budget, effectively tying together the nation and guaranteeing the preeminence of New York City in America's economy.

When the New York Central built its water-line rail route to the west, the Mohawk Valley became one of the nation's early industrial centers. The little Oneida County hamlets of Utica and Rome, where the canal builders had to dig through the route's highest ground, became sizable factory towns. First settled by New England Yankees, these towns attracted a new wave of immigration from the Atlantic coast in the early 20th century, including many Italian and Polish Americans.

The 22nd Congressional District of New York drops from Lake Ontario to the Pennsylvania border in a strip east of Syracuse, as it sprawls through all or parts of eight counties in central New York, most of them lightly populated. The biggest cities are Utica and Rome in Oneida County and Binghamton in Broome County. Each county takes in about 30 percent of the district. This part of Upstate New York has been bypassed by economic growth for decades. Oneida County's population has dropped 15 percent since it peaked in the 1970 census. A similar pattern applied in Broome, which has lost about 13 percent during that time—and 15,000 jobs since 2007. With these losses, it's no surprise that more than 16,000 refugees have settled in Utica in the past 40 years.

In a once economically dynamic area, the largest employer in central New York has become Oneida Nation's Turning Stone Resort Casino, which operates a huge retail outlet and entertainment complex with 4,500 employees; in 2019, the resort began to partner with Caesars Entertainment to offer sports betting. State government has completed dredging for Utica Harbor, which is the successor to the Erie Canal in Utica. In 2019, local officials said they were planning for recreational, retail and residential uses of the Harbor Point area, with the hope of making the city more of a destination point. Cree Inc., a North Carolina semiconductor manufacturer, is constructing a $1 billion silicon-carbide wafer fabrication factory near Utica, which the company said will be the largest such facility in the world.

Politically this area had been Republican since the party came into existence in the 1850s, and the GOP maintains a registration advantage in every county except Broome. After Barack Obama got 49 percent in each of his elections, Donald Trump won the district in 2020 with 55 percent of the vote. Joe Biden took Broome County with 51 percent.

Tom Reed (R)

Elected 2010, 6th full term, b. Nov 18, 1971; Joliet, IL; Alfred University, B.A., 1993; OH Northern University College of Law, J.D., 1996; Roman Catholic; Married (Jean Reed); 2 children.

Elected Office: Corning Mayor, 2008-2010.

Professional Career: Clerk, private firm, 1995; Association Attorney, private firm, 1996-1999; Owner, Law Office of Thomas W. Reed II.

DC Office: 2263 RHOB 20515, 202-225-3161, Fax: 202-226-6599, reed.house.gov

State Offices: Corning, 607-654-7566; Geneva, 315-759-5229; Jamestown, 716-708-6369; Olean, 716-379-8434.

Committees: *Ways & Means*: Health; Social Security (RMM).

Group Ratings

	ADA	ACLU	AFL-CIO	LCV	COC	HAFA	ACU	CFG	FRC
2020	**	40%	**	48%	-	63%	59%	**	-
2019	20%	C	55%	31%	99%	C	60%	64%	52%

Almanac Ratings 2019-2020

	Economy	Social	Foreign	Composite
Liberal	44%	46%	42%	44%
Conservative	56%	54%	58%	56%

Key Votes of the 116th Congress

1. U.S./Mex./Can. trade deal	Y	5. Russia sanctions	Y
2. First Coronavirus response	Y	6. Troops in Syria	N
3. HEROES Act	N	7. Veto arms sales to Saudis	N
4. CASH Act	Y	8. Defense $$$, veto override	N

9. Firearms background checks N
10. Spending at the border Y
11. Marijuana liberalized rules N
12. Electoral College objections N

Election Results

Election	Name (Party)	Vote (%)		Cand. Spent	Ind. Exp. Support	Ind. Exp. Oppose
2020 General	Tom Reed (R)	181,021	(58%)	$3,390,207	$178,022	$412
	Tracy Mitrano (D)	128,976	(41%)	$1,479,711	$421	

Prior winning percentages: 2018 (54%), 2016 (58%), 2014 (62%), 2012 (52%), 2010 (57%)

Republican Tom Reed, who took office in 2010, is a pragmatic and low-key centrist who has sought bipartisan solutions as co-chairman of the Problem Solvers Caucus. On the Ways and Means Committee, he has worked on tax and trade issues and serves as the top Republican on the Social Security Subcommittee. He failed in a House leadership bid, but voiced interest in early 2021 in running for governor of New York. That search ended suddenly in March, when he acknowledged groping a young woman while they were with a political group in Minnesota in 2017. He said that he would not seek reelection.

Reed was born in Joliet Illinois, the youngest of 12 children. His father was an Army veteran and Silver Star recipient who fought in World War II and Korea, but he accidentally died of carbon monoxide poisoning while working on his car when Reed was two years old. Reed's surviving family soon moved to Corning New York, where his mother had grown up. She stayed home to take care of the children, relying on her late husband's military death benefits and Social Security checks for financial support. Reed got his bachelor's at Alfred University in western New York. He went to law school at Ohio Northern University College, then worked at a law firm in Rochester before he returned to Corning to start his own firm. He was elected mayor in 2007.

He ran for a vacant seat in the House after the Democratic incumbent resigned following inappropriate behavior with staff aides. Reed was unchallenged for the Republican nomination. Against Democratic nominee Matthew Zeller, an Afghanistan combat veteran, Reed focused on reducing the deficit and shrinking government. Zeller raised $457,000, compared with Reed's $1 million. Capitalizing on the Republican wave, Reed won, 57%-43%.

Reed has mostly stuck with his party on major legislation, though his Almanac vote ratings have ranked him near the center of the House. He impressed leadership by getting the support of colleagues for free trade agreements with Colombia, Panama and South Korea. In 2011, he won a prized seat on Ways and Means, rare for a freshman. In 2015, he enacted his Trade Facilitation and Trade Enforcement Act, which was largely a law-enforcement measure that overhauled the Customs and Border Protection agency.

After the 2014 election, Reed ran against two other candidates for chairman of the House Republican Policy Committee, which has been viewed as a stepping-stone to higher leadership positions. On the showdown second ballot, he lost to Luke Messer of Indiana, 137-90.

In 2017, Reed shifted much of his focus to the Problem Solvers Caucus, whose objective was "fighting for common-sense principles that impact all Americans—Democrat, Republican, independent—everyone," he said. With the partisan line-drawing that year on the major healthcare and tax policies, the caucus initially had little influence.

But he joined members of both parties who worked prior to the 2018 election to propose in the new Congress rules changes that were designed to open the House floor to additional debate, including amendments. After extended negotiations with Nancy Pelosi resulted in their agreement, Reed praised her for having "opened up the door to giving power back to members." He was one of three Republicans who took the unusual step of voting for the new majority party's rules package— including those changes—when Democrats took control of the House in January. In February 2020, he was one of five Republicans who voted for the bill to extend the time for states to ratify the Equal Rights Amendment to the Constitution.

As ranking Republican on the Social Security Subcommittee, he has been open to working with House Democrats who were eager to address long-term financing demands facing the retirement and disability trust funds. "We will work together with Democrats for the American people to protect this program and ensure Social Security is around for future generations," said Reed, who has cited his personal familiarity with its benefits.

During the extended discussions of providing economic relief during the corona virus pandemic, Reid joined Democratic Rep. Josh Gottheimer of New Jersey, co-chairman of the Problems Solvers Caucus, in working with their group to offer alternatives to break continuing deadlocks. He opposed as "partisan" a $1.9 trillion plan proposed by Biden, with Democratic support, but endorsed its financial relief for state and local governments.

In January 2021, Reed said that he wanted Trump to "face justice" following the riot at the Capitol, though he opposed impeachment with the "inadequate time" at the end of Trump's presidency to complete a trial. Reed suggested options such as a congressional censure, criminal action and steps to prevent Trump from holding federal office in the future. None of those proposals generated serious support.

Reed has faced competitive Democratic challengers from the Ithaca-based eastern edge of his district. In 2012, Nate Shinagawa, the 28-year-old vice chairman of the Tompkins County Legislature, attacked Reed for his support of hydraulic fracturing for natural gas. Reed said he supported an exemption for drilling in the Finger Lakes. He eked out a win, 52%-48%. In 2014, Martha Robinson, chairwoman of the Tompkins Legislature, strongly opposed fossil-fuel production in New York and changes in the Social Security cost-of-living adjustment. Reed outspent her, $3.4 million to $2.3 million and won, 62%-38%, an indication that he had become entrenched in his seat.

In 2018 and 2020, Reed faced Tracy Mitrano, a cyber security expert who had overseen digital information policy at Cornell University. Reed called her "an extreme Ithaca liberal." In each contest, Reed doubled her spending. Reed won 54%-46% in the Democratic year of 2018 and 58%-41% in 2020. He continued to win every county except for Tompkins, where Mitrano got about three-fourths of the vote.

The charges of Reed's sexual harassment came as Democratic Gov. Andrew Cuomo was facing fierce criticism following charges against him by multiple women. In contrast to Cuomo, Reed said, "I was wrong, I am sorry and I take full responsibility." He said that he was suffering alcohol addiction at the time. With his decision not to seek reelection, redistricting in 2022 could divide his district into multiple pieces and attach them to at least three neighboring districts.

NY-23: Southern Tier   **Cook Partisan Voting Index: R+9**

Population		Race and Ethnicity		Income	
Total	687,583	White	90.40%	Median Income	$53,769
Land area (sq. miles)	7,372	Black	2.90%	District Income Rank	348
Pop/ sq mi	93.27	Latino	4.20%	Poverty Rate	15.40%
Born in State	74.10%	Asian	2.40%	With health insurance	94.40%
		Two or more races	2.40%	Cash public assistance	3.60%
Age Groups		Other	1.90%	Food stamp/SNAP	14.70%
Under 18	19.60%				
18-34	23.90%	**Education**		**Work**	
35-64	37.10%	H.S grad or less	41.90%	White Collar	38.90%
Over 64	19.60%	Some college	30.00%	Sales and Service	37.10%
		College Degree, 4 yr	14.30%	Blue Collar	24.00%
Military		Post grad	13.70%	Government	18.10%
Veteran/ Active Duty	8.00%				

2020 Pres. Vote	Trump	175,243	(54%)	Biden	139,037	(43%)		
2016 Pres. Vote	Trump	158,158	(54%)	Clinton	115,014	(39%)	Johnson	11,749	(4%)

Jamestown, Ithaca: The Southern Tier of New York is one of the nation's forgotten stretches of territory, yet it has an interesting and distinctive history. Elmira was the hometown of Mark Twain's beloved wife, Olivia, and it is where Twain is buried. On Lake Chautauqua, not far from Lake Erie, a training camp for Methodist Sunday school teachers was founded in 1874. In summers, on wide green lawns and in Victorian-style gazebos, some 25,000 people heard educational talks and inspirational lectures from the likes of William Jennings Bryan. The area has an Indian presence, with small reservations as wells as the Seneca-Iroquois National Museum in Salamanca, plus miles and miles of dairy farms. Sheltered by hills, the lands at the edge of Upstate New York's deep lakes constitute the nation's largest grape-growing area outside California.

Corning is the headquarters of Corning Glass Works, a company successful over the years not only in manufacturing but also in its artistic distinction, which is showcased at its glass museum. The Fortune 500 company makes key components of the liquid crystal display (LCD) glass used in flat-screen televisions and computers. But the company produces and sells much of that display glass overseas, including in Beijing. At its Big Flats plant in Corning, the company manufactures Valor glass, which is used by the pharmaceutical industry to reduce breakage. In Jamestown, where it employs 1,700 workers, the Cummins Co. Manufactures more efficient engines for industry and heavy-duty trucks. Gov. Andrew Cuomo's ban on fracking in New York caused complaints by landowners along the Southern Tier, who contend that nearby towns in Pennsylvania have benefitted from drilling the oil shale.

The 23rd Congressional District of New York is centered on the state's Southern Tier, extending from Chautauqua near Erie across the Pennsylvania line almost to Binghamton, more than halfway to the Massachusetts line. To the north, it includes the central Finger Lakes: giant gorges torn into the Earth's crust by expanding glaciers, and then naturally dammed up by the debris deposited when the glaciers retreated. Nearby Seneca Falls was the birthplace of the women's rights movement in 1848, when Boston transplants Elizabeth Cady Stanton and Lucretia Mott produced a Declaration of Sentiments that initiated the push for suffrage. The town is believed to be the inspiration for Bedford Falls in the classic film, It's a Wonderful Life. In nearby Jamestown, the $50 million National Comedy Center has more than 50 interactive exhibits. In 2020, the planning commission in Jamestown discussed converting the historic downtown arcade into an apartment complex. Ithaca has become the economic bright spot of the district. The city, which has grown3 percent since 2010,expanded its airport terminal in 2019.

The addition of the heavily Democratic university town of Ithaca made the district more competitive at the federal level, though it is the only Democratic locale; Republicans still perform well elsewhere. President Barack Obama lost this district by two percentage points in 2012, after winning it by one point in 2008. In 2020, President Donald Trump won the district by 11 points and took every county by a double-digit margin except for Ithaca-based Tompkins, where he lost 3-to-1.

John Katko (R)

Elected 2014, 4th term, b. Nov 09, 1962; Syracuse, NY; Niagara University, B.A., 1984; Syracuse University - College of Law, J.D., 1988; Roman Catholic; Married (Robin Katko); 3 children.

Professional Career: Sr. trial Attorney, U.S. Securities & Exchange Comm., 1991-1995; Prosecutor, NY Northern District U.S. Attorney office; Assistant U.S. Attorney, U.S. Justice Department, 1995-2013.

DC Office: 2457 RHOB 20515, 202-225-3701, Fax: 202-225-4042, katko.house.gov

State Offices: Auburn, 315-253-4068; Lyons, 315-253-4068; Oswego, 315-423-5657; Syracuse, 315-423-5657.

Committees: *Homeland Security (RMM)*: Ex Officio membership on all subcommittees. *Transportation & Infrastructure*: Aviation; Highways & Transit; Water Resources & Environment.

Group Ratings

	ADA	ACLU	AFL-CIO	LCV	COC	HAFA	ACU	CFG	FRC
2020	**	35%	**	62%	-	46%	41%	**	
2019	20%	C	67%	48%	98%	C	41%	41%	55%

Almanac Ratings 2019-2020

	Economy	Social	Foreign	Composite
Liberal	45%	46%	44%	45%
Conservative	55%	54%	56%	55%

Key Votes of the 116th Congress

1. U.S./Mex./Can. trade deal	Y	5. Russia sanctions	Y	9. Firearms background checks N/A
2. First Coronavirus response	Y	6. Troops in Syria	Y	10. Spending at the border Y
3. HEROES Act	N	7. Veto arms sales to Saudis	N	11. Marijuana liberalized rules N
4. CASH Act	Y	8. Defense $$$, veto override	Y	12. Electoral College objections N

Election Results

Election	Name (Party)	Vote (%)		Cand. Spent	Ind. Exp. Support	Ind. Exp. Oppose
2020 General	John Katko (R)...............................	182,809	(53%)	$3,780,229	$765,970	$5,374,216
	Dana Balter (D)................................	147,877	(43%)	$3,380,463	$245,244	$5,056,105
	Steven Williams (Work Fam)................	13,264	(4%)			

Prior winning percentages: 2018 (53%), 2016 (61%), 2014 (60%)

John Katko, first elected in 2014, has shown impressive skill as an influential House Republican despite his outspoken opposition to former President Donald Trump. He has become a relatively secure incumbent in what had been a political swing district. Katko has focused his legislative attention on homeland security and the transportation needs of upstate New York. Despite an earlier setback, Katko won the top GOP slot on the Homeland Security Committee following the 2020 election. Weeks later, he was the first House Republican—and, ultimately, one of 10—to support the second impeachment charge against Trump.

Katko grew up in Onondaga County, then attended Niagara University and Syracuse University's law school. He worked for a D.C. law firm before taking a position at the Securities and Exchange Commission. In two decades at the Justice Department, he was a federal prosecutor in Virginia's Eastern District and worked for the narcotics and dangerous drugs section of the criminal division. During that time, he joined multiple organized crime and drug enforcement-related prosecutions with the U.S. Attorney's Office in Syracuse. He contends that his successful prosecution of a major gang case led to a significant drop in the violent crime rate in Syracuse.

Katko retired from the Justice Department to challenge Democratic Rep. Dan Maffei, who was elected in 2012 with just 49 percent of the vote, as President Barack Obama won 57 percent in the district. Maffei had an unusual streak of participating in five consecutive elections with alternating party control of the seat. Depicting Maffei as an out-of-touch Beltway insider, Katko pointed to his purchase of a $700,000 house in the Washington area. Maffei emphasized his moderate stripes and nonideological pragmatism and tried to poke holes in Katko's record as a prosecutor. Katko complained that such campaign attacks "destroyed my character." Katko won with surprising ease, 60%-40%, winning all four counties. Onondaga was the tightest, with 53 percent for Katko.

In the House, Katko chaired the Transportation Subcommittee on the Homeland Security Committee. He passed several bills, which later were enacted as part of the reauthorization of the Federal Aviation Administration. Those measures called for a review of the Transportation Security Administration's security and staffing procedures, enhanced the security of overseas flights and revised TSA's expedited security program. He also took the leadership of a bipartisan Task Force on Combating Terrorist and Foreign Fighter Travel. In 2017-18, his legislative work included enactment of bills to encourage recruitment and retention at the Secret Service, stiffen requirements for biometric transportation security cards and promote more innovative transportation security.

Katko showed occasional independence from the House GOP leadership, as when he voted in 2015 to oppose both the final version of the annual congressional budget and a plan to overturn a District of Columbia law that banned workplace discrimination over employees' reproductive decisions but provided no faith-based exemptions. Katko's Almanac vote ratings have placed him in the center of the House, though he has been a bit more conservative on foreign policy. In 2017, he voted against repeal of the Affordable Care Act, though he voted for the GOP tax cuts.

In November 2018, Katko sought to fill the vacancy of ranking Republican at the Homeland Security Committee. In the backroom vote of a GOP leadership panel, he lost to Rep. Mike Rogers of Alabama, who had more seniority. He became the senior Republican on the Cyber security, Infrastructure Protection and Innovation Subcommittee. With Democratic Rep. Abigail Spanberger of Virginia, he filed a bill to reduce foreign disinformation on social media. Following the 2020 election, when Rogers switched to the top GOP post at Armed Services, Katko ran again for Homeland Security. This time, he defeated outspoken conservative Rep. Scott Perry of Pennsylvania, who had less seniority.

Following the riot at the Capitol, when Democrat filed their second impeachment case against Trump, Katko said prior to the vote, "Trump encouraged this insurrection, both on social media ahead of January 6, and in his speech that day. …To allow the president of the United States to incite this attack without consequence is a direct threat to the future of our democracy." In a subsequent piece he wrote for The Hill, he concluded: "Our nation simply cannot function without the peaceful transfer of power and the recognition of carefully reviewed election results."

At home, Katko has remained a prime Democratic target. After Syracuse Mayor Stephanie Miner decided not to challenge him in 2016, Democrats rallied around Colleen Deacon, who had been the Syracuse district director for Sen. Kirsten Gillibrand. During a debate, she suggested that Katko had misled voters into believing that he was independent. "When the chips are down, he stands with his do-nothing Republican colleagues on the issues that matter," Deacon said. Katko responded that she was a tool of Democratic leaders. "She is 100 percent in the tank with not only her party, but Hillary Clinton," he said. Katko won 61%-39%, with a narrow lead in Onondaga.

In 2018, Democrats suffered from internal divisions. All four Democratic county organizations endorsed Dana Balter, a professor of public administration at Syracuse University. The Democratic Congressional Campaign Committee favored Juanita Perez Williams, who ran unsuccessfully for mayor of Syracuse in 2017 and was a former city official. Balter won the primary, 62%-38%. In the general election, Democrats targeted Katko's vote for the tax bill, which they said favored the wealthy. Katko spent $3 million to $2.7 million for Balter. As one of the few House Republicans from a metro area to survive the Democratic onslaught, Katko won, 53%-47%. In 2020, Balter ran again and had support from the DCCC, though she won her primary with only 61 percent of the vote. This time, Katko outspent Balter, $3.8 million to $3.4 million and the two candidates roughly split more than $10 million from national parties and groups. Katko won, 53%-43%, virtually the reverse of the presidential outcome in the district. He took Onondaga by 3,500 votes.

NY-24: North-Central New York   **Cook Partisan Voting Index: D+2**

Population		Race and Ethnicity		Income	
Total	701,841	White	83.30%	Median Income	$60,899
Land area (sq. miles)	2,389	Black	8.50%	District Income Rank	249
Pop/ sq mi	293.83	Latino	4.70%	Poverty Rate	14.20%
Born in State	80.00%	Asian	2.80%	With health insurance	96.40%
		Two or more races	3.80%	Cash public assistance	3.30%
Age Groups		Other	1.70%	Food stamp/SNAP	13.10%
Under 18	20.80%				
18-34	22.70%	**Education**		**Work**	
35-64	38.90%	H.S grad or less	38.30%	White Collar	38.50%
Over 64	17.70%	Some college	29.70%	Sales and Service	41.60%
		College Degree, 4 yr	17.90%	Blue Collar	19.80%
Military		Post grad	14.00%	Government	17.70%
Veteran/ Active Duty	7.30%				

2020 Pres. Vote	Biden	186,983	(53%)	Trump	155,222	(44%)		
2016 Pres. Vote	Clinton	151,021	(49%)	Trump	139,763	(45%)	Johnson	13,090 (4%)

Syracuse Metro: Syracuse is a Middle American city in the middle of Upstate New York, halfway between Albany and Buffalo on the Erie Canal and the old New York Central Railroad, which were for years the nation's major east-west transportation routes. Built on a swamp that was a salt spring, Syracuse is the home of many practical-minded inventions—the dental chair, Stickley mission furniture, the drive-in bank teller, and the serrated knife. It is the site of the New York State Fair, which attracts more than 1 million visitors annually; of Syracuse University, which plays basketball and football inside the Carrier Dome, the largest domed stadium on a college campus; and of the Museum of Automobile History, home to the largest private collection of automobiles and automobile-related objects in the world.

Nearby, the agricultural hinterland is rich with specialty crops like wine grapes, and its industrial jobs are mostly high-skill. Still, there were 20,000 fewer manufacturing jobs here in 2018 than there were in 2000. An example is Carrier, which once manufactured air-conditioning equipment in Syracuse and employed 7,000 workers; now, it is owned by Connecticut-based United Technologies and has 1,300 workers in Syracuse. The New York State Department of Labor reported that the number of private-sector jobs in the metro area fell nearly 12 percent in 2020.The good news is that housing in Syracuse is among the most affordable in the nation, with a median home value of $94,000 in 2020. The growing communities of immigrants and refugees have been driving the limited economic growth.

The 24th Congressional District of New York centers on Syracuse and surrounding Onondaga County, which takes in two-thirds of the voters; the surrounding counties are comfortably Republican. From 2010 to 2019, both the city and the county lost nearly2percent of their population; the median household income of the county was $61,000, compared to $38,000 for the city, which has one-third of the population. West of Syracuse is territory that dips south from Lake Ontario, with all of Cayuga County, home of abolitionist Harriet Tubman. Near Rochester, in Wayne County, is the village of Palmyra, where Joseph Smith had his vision of the angel Moroni and received the golden tablets that led him to found the Church of Jesus Christ of Latter-day Saints. To the north, the district includes the city of Oswego, whose port facilities on Lake Ontario have made it an attractive tourist destination.

Like much of Upstate, this has become a politically competitive area. Following Barack Obama's double-digit victory margins in his two elections and a 49%-45%win for Hillary Clinton in her home state, Joe Biden restored the Democratic victory to 53%-44%. He grew the Democratic majority in Onondaga from 54 percent to 59 percent.

Joseph Morelle (D)

Elected 2018, 2nd full term, b. Apr 29, 1957; Utica, NY; State University of NY at Geneseo, B.A., 1986; Roman Catholic; Married (Mary Beth Morelle); 3 children (1 deceased).

Elected Office: Monroe County NY Legislature, 1987-1990; NY Assembly, 1991-2018.

Professional Career: Chief executive, MMI Technologies.

DC Office: 1317 LHOB 20515, 202-225-3615, Fax: 202-225-7822, morelle.house.gov

State Offices: Rochester, 585-232-4850.

Committees: *Armed Services*: Cyber, Innovative Technologies & Information Systems; Strategic Forces. *Budget*. *Education & Labor*: Early Childhood, Elementary & Secondary Education; Health, Employment, Labor & Pensions. *Rules*: Legislative & Budget Process; Rules & Organization of the House.

Almanac Ratings 2019-2020

	Economy	Social	Foreign	Composite
Liberal	58%	100%	80%	80%
Conservative	42%	0%	20%	20%

Key Votes of the 116th Congress

1. U.S./Mex./Can. trade deal Y	5. Russia sanctions Y	9. Firearms background checks Y
2. First Coronavirus response Y	6. Troops in Syria Y	10. Spending at the border Y
3. HEROES Act Y	7. Veto arms sales to Saudis Y	11. Marijuana liberalized rules Y
4. CASH Act Y	8. Defense $$$, veto override Y	12. Electoral College objections N

Election Results

Election	Name (Party)	Vote (%)		Cand. Spent	Ind. Exp. Support	Ind. Exp. Oppose
2020 General	Joseph Morelle (D)	206,396	(59%)	$1,172,704	$863	
	George Mitris (R)	136,198	(39%)	$231,890		$113
2020 Primary	Joseph Morelle (D)	42,955	(68%)			
	Robin Wilt (D)	20,070	(32%)			

Prior winning percentages: 2018 special (58%)

Joe Morelle stood out in the House Democrats' freshman class elected in 2018. He was an older white male with an extensive political background in a year when that profile had become the exception for newly elected lawmakers. With his strong base of local support, he easily surmounted the potential stigma of a long career in the tarnished New York state Assembly, where he served six years as majority leader. He replaced another political veteran: 16-term Rep. Louise Slaughter, who died in March 2018 and chaired the Rules Committee when Democrats controlled the House.

Morelle, a native of the Rochester area, graduated from the State University of New York at Geneseo. He served two terms in the Monroe County Legislature before he was elected to the Assembly in 1990. His assignments included the chairmanship of both the Insurance and Tourism committees. As majority leader, he was instrumental in enacting gun-control legislation in 2013. When powerful Assembly Speaker Sheldon Silver was indicted on federal corruption charges in January 2015 and was forced to step down, Morelle spent a week as interim Speaker; he had little chance to win the top post, given the dominance of New York City Democrats in the Assembly.

While serving in Albany, Morelle was the founder and chief executive of MMI Technologies, a small software firm that worked with local healthcare and manufacturing companies. That business background, the Rochester Business Journal reported, made him "a point man for business in the Democratic-controlled and mostly liberal Assembly." Morelle also served nearly a decade as Democratic chairman in Monroe County.

Slaughter's death shortly before the campaign-filing deadline created local interest in what was expected to be an uneventful contest. In the Democratic primary, Morelle faced three opponents, who split support from progressive groups. With his support from the Monroe County Democratic Committee in the abbreviated campaign, Morelle was criticized by his opponents as a political insider."We need different experiences," Rachel Barnhart, a citizen activist who had been a local television reporter, said during a candidate debate. Also running were Rochester City Council member Adam McFadden and Brighton Town Board member Robin Wilt.

In its endorsement of Morelle for the Democratic nomination, the Rochester City Newspaper cited "his long experience in local and state politics and his political connections and influence," which would make him "an effective member of Congress." Morelle also benefited from raising more than $800,000 for the primary, which was eight times more than the combined total reported by his three opponents. In the June primary, Morelle got 46 percent of the vote to 20 percent for Barnhart; the other two Democrats, with limited appeal beyond their local political bases, each got 17 percent.

Republican nominee Jim Maxwell, a long time neurosurgeon and political newcomer, gained some attention by self-funding half of his $1 million campaign. Maxwell attacked Morelle as "a career politician steeped in the ways of corruption and gridlock," and he focused heavily on healthcare issues, including proposals to reduce costs. But House Republicans directed their attention and resources to endangered GOP incumbents elsewhere in upstate New York, and Maxwell gained little traction in the House Democratic tide during the 2018 election. Morelle won, 59%-41%.

In the House, Morelle was one of three freshmen assigned to the Rules Committee. His haul of assignments also included the Budget, and Education and Labor committees. On the Education panel, he worked with Rep. Lori Trahan of Massachusetts to increase access to apprenticeship programs, permit worker training of mentors or supervisors working with apprentices, and financing for the program. The House passed the bill in November 2020. In 2021, Morelle added a seat on the Armed Services Committee.

Seeking reelection in 2020, he faced Robin Wilt, one of his three opponents in the 2018 Democratic primary. A member of the Brighton Town Board, Wilt owned a real estate brokerage firm. She self-financed about 80 percent of the $160,000 that she spent. Morelle spent $1.3 million in the campaign cycle and won the primary 68%-32%. George Metris, his Republican opponent and a Rochester lawyer, voiced sympathy with the Black Lives Matter movement and distanced himself from President Donald Trump. He self-financed most of the $232,000 he spent. Morelle won that contest, 59%-39%.

NY-25: Monroe County   Cook Partisan Voting Index: D+8

Population		Race and Ethnicity		Income	
Total	714,657	White	75.00%	Median Income	$61,336
Land area (sq. miles)	510	Black	15.80%	District Income Rank	243
Pop/ sq mi	1,400.77	Latino	9.40%	Poverty Rate	13.00%
Born in State	72.60%	Asian	3.70%	With health insurance	97.20%
		Two or more races	3.10%	Cash public assistance	4.00%
Age Groups		Other	2.40%	Food stamp/SNAP	15.00%
Under 18	20.60%				
18-34	24.20%	Education		Work	
35-64	37.20%	H.S grad or less	31.80%	White Collar	46.30%
Over 64	17.90%	Some college	27.90%	Sales and Service	37.50%
		College Degree, 4 yr	22.80%	Blue Collar	16.20%
Military		Post grad	17.60%	Government	13.70%
Veteran/ Active Duty	5.40%				

2020 Pres. Vote	Biden	218,504	(60%)	Trump	137,342	(38%)		
2016 Pres. Vote	Clinton	182,896	(55%)	Trump	128,955	(39%)	Johnson	12,514 (4%)

Rochester Metro: Rochester, with a metropolitan area of just over 1 million, is a major city of Upstate New York and was one of America's first boomtowns. Here, the Genesee River descends in a 100-foot drop known as High Falls, which powered the city's early industries. Rochester became known as Flour City for the mills that served western New York farmers. Rochester was also the home base of women's suffrage leader Susan B. Anthony and abolitionist Frederick Douglass, and a popular center of 19th century tent revivals.

It became one of the early high-tech cities, after a bank clerk named George Eastman marketed the first still camera and film for Thomas Edison's motion picture camera. Later, Bausch & Lomb developed its lens business in Rochester. The optics and imaging industry continues to be a significant regional employer. The industries it has produced—Bausch & Lomb, Eastman Kodak and Xerox, which started here as Haloid before moving its headquarters to Connecticut in 1969—thrived on technical innovation, precision workmanship, high reliability and customer service. They gave Rochester an affluent and well-educated population as well as fine civic institutions, including the George Eastman House, one of the world's leading repositories of photographic and motion picture history.

In recent decades, Rochester's big employers have fallen on tough times, and young professionals have been leaving the area. Kodak was hard hit by competition from digital cameras, and although it locally employed 5,000 people (of more than 10,000 worldwide) in 2020, the workforce was down from 60,000 people in 1981. In 2012, it filed for bankruptcy and reemerged a year later as what it called "a technology company focused on imaging for business." In 2020, the company announced plans to add several hundred workers to its new division for pharmaceutical production. Xerox has continued to decline in size but maintained a significant presence in the area, with a payroll of about 3,400. In July 2018, it moved its remaining employees to suburban Webster. The city's population was 332,000 in 1950; it has dropped in each census since, to 206,000 in 2019; the overall metropolitan area has grown by less than 10 percent in the past 40 years. In October 2020, the new owner of Xerox's former 30-story tower announced plans for an Innovation Square in downtown. The University of Rochester is the largest employer, with 30,000 on its payroll.

In September 2020, the city was the site of extended protests by Black Lives Matter after it was disclosed that Daniel Prude died in March of suffocation following the action of police officers who put a hood over his head. Within the following month, the police chief resigned and Mayor Lovely Warren was indicted by the county district attorney on unrelated campaign-finance violations. Tensions in the city already were on edge because more than 50,000 workers had lost their job since March because of the corona virus.

The 25th Congressional District of New York is a compact district that is entirely within Rochester's Monroe County. All but a small northwest corner of the county is in the 25th. Heavily Democratic areas in Rochester mix with more marginal suburbs in a district that is comfortably but not overwhelmingly Democratic. With 60 percent of the vote, Joe Biden improved on Hillary Clinton's performance and virtually matched President Barack Obama's victory margin in 2012.

Brian Higgins (D)

Elected 2004, 9th term, b. Oct 06, 1959; Buffalo, NY; Buffalo State College, B.S., 1984; Buffalo State College, M.A., 1985; Harvard University John F. Kennedy School of Government, M.A., 1996; Catholic; Married (Mary Jane Hannon); 2 children.

Elected Office: Buffalo City Council, 1988-1994; NY Assembly, 1999-2004.

Professional Career: Chief of Staff, Erie County Leg., 1994-1998; Lecturer, Buffalo St. College, 2000-2003.

DC Office: 2459 RHOB 20515, 202-225-3306, Fax: 202-226-0347, higgins.house.gov

State Offices: Buffalo, 716-852-3501; Niagara Falls, 716-282-1274.

Committees: *Budget. Ways & Means*: Health; Social Security; Trade.

Group Ratings

	ADA	ACLU	AFL-CIO	LCV	COC	HAFA	ACU	CFG	FRC
2020	**	79%	**	100%	-	0%	5%	**	-
2019	90%	C	100%	97%	61%	C	5%	12%	0%

Almanac Ratings 2019-2020

	Economy	Social	Foreign	Composite
Liberal	100%	100%	92%	98%
Conservative	0%	0%	8%	2%

Key Votes of the 116th Congress

1. U.S./Mex./Can. trade deal	Y	5. Russia sanctions	Y	9. Firearms background checks	Y
2. First Coronavirus response	Y	6. Troops in Syria	Y	10. Spending at the border	N
3. HEROES Act	Y	7. Veto arms sales to Saudis	Y	11. Marijuana liberalized rules	Y
4. CASH Act	Y	8. Defense $$$, veto override	Y	12. Electoral College objections	N

Election Results

Election	Name (Party)	Vote (%)	Cand. Spent	Ind. Exp. Support	Ind. Exp. Oppose
2020 General	Brian Higgins (D)............................ 223,366	(70%)	$775,577	$6,123	
	Ricky Donovan (R)........................ 91,706	(29%)			$113

Prior winning percentages: 2018 (73%), 2016 (75%), 2014 (68%), 2012 (75%), 2010 (61%), 2008 (74%), 2006 (79%), 2004 (51%)

Democrat Brian Higgins, who was elected in 2004 and devotes his energies to reviving the Buffalo area's economy and focusing on major domestic priorities, is well-placed on the House Ways and Means Committee, with its work on tax and trade issues. He has advocated a trillion-dollar plan to upgrade the nation's infrastructure. After keeping his distance from Nancy Pelosi, he was one of the first renegades to reach an agreement to support her for Speaker following the 2018 election.

Higgins grew up in Buffalo, the son of a skilled tradesman who was prominent in local politics. His mother was a schoolteacher. Higgins graduated from Buffalo State College, where he later became an instructor, and got a master's degree in public administration from Harvard. A political junkie, he launched his career with staff jobs in the Erie County sheriff's office, the state Assembly, and the county legislature. In 1993, after six years on the Buffalo City Council, he ran for county comptroller and lost. In 1998, he was elected to the Assembly and served three terms. In a district crowded with unionized workers, Higgins reminded voters that his father and uncle were bricklayers and stressed his Irish heritage.

When the House seat opened after Republican Rep. Jack Quinn retired, five Democrats sought the nomination. Higgins was the favorite of party leaders, organized labor and The Buffalo News, which called him "an unusually productive member of a largely dysfunctional legislative body" in Albany. He won the primary with 44 percent of the vote. In the contentious general election, Higgins reminded voters that Republican nominee Nancy Naples, a former Merrill Lynch executive in Manhattan, supported many of President George W. Bush's policies, which he claimed shifted the tax burden from the rich to the middle class. He ran on a platform of making health care more widely available. Naples criticized Higgins for supporting tax increases in Albany. Higgins won 51%-49%, about a 3,800-vote victory, in what was then a far more competitive district.

On Ways and Means, he initially opposed the 2010 deal to extend the expiring Bush-era tax cuts because it would not extend the Renewal Communities program, which had brought $150 million in development to his district. But he eventually went along with the deal, saying "the cost of inaction would be far worse for western New York families and seniors." After the Republican takeover of the House in 2011 removed junior Democrats from seats on Ways and Means, Higgins served on the Homeland Security and Foreign Affairs panels.

With increased seniority, he regained his Ways and Means seat in 2017. His priorities included the New Markets Tax Credit program, the solar investment tax credit and tax simplification for middle-class families. He cosponsored the Social Security 2100 proposal to expand benefits and pay for them with increased taxes on higher-income earners. He has been the chief proponent of legislation to expand Medicare to permit early buy-in by those who are age 50.

Hoping to kick off a debate about the importance of infrastructure, he has repeatedly filed a bill calling for $1.25 trillion to be spent over five years to rebuild roads, bridges, railroads, ports and airports. "The time is now for nation-building here at home," he said, while noting that 81 bridges in Erie County have been deemed structurally deficient. He helped create, and co-chaired, a Revitalizing Older Cities Task Force and has sought tax credits to transform older neighborhoods.

In the debate over gun control, Higgins once sided with gun owners, voting in favor of a 2011 amendment to block federal efforts to demand reports from gun dealers on sales of multiple semi-automatic rifles. After the Newtown Connecticut school massacre in 2012, he called for "meaningful reforms" to gun laws.

As Democrats prepared to take House control following the 2018 election, Higgins had signed a letter with 15 other House Democrats stating their opposition to Pelosi as Speaker and the need for new and more assertive leadership. After several discussions, the two of them made a deal in which Higgins supported Pelosi for Speaker in exchange for her agreement to schedule action in 2019 on both his Medicare and infrastructure bills and that he would be given a leading role in those debates. "I have renewed confidence that more voices will be heard, that members will each have greater opportunities to advance policies," he said in a statement, adding that his earlier "principled stand" required a "pragmatic outlook" to succeed. But those two years did not include debate on his two prime concerns.

Since developing skin cancer, Higgins has become a leader of the Cancer Caucus and worked on cancer research, introducing bills to establish a national cancer trust fund and pushing for money for Buffalo's Roswell Park Cancer Institute. He helped to broker an agreement with the New York Power Authority for local financial aid, including improvements of the Buffalo harbor areas, in exchange for its long-term right to operate the Niagara Power Project. When the corona virus pandemic caused unusual hardships for citizens on both sides of the northern border with Canada, he joined Republican Rep. Elise Stefanik of upstate New York in urging expanded definition of essential travelers on both sides of the border.

Higgins has been reelected easily in what has become a safe district. The declining population of Buffalo could prove perilous in pushing him farther into the suburbs during the 2022 redistricting.

NY-26: Western New York

Cook Partisan Voting Index: D+10

Population		Race and Ethnicity		Income	
Total	703,114	White	70.40%	Median Income	$52,122
Land area (sq. miles)	219	Black	18.30%	District Income Rank	366
Pop/ sq mi	3,208.66	Latino	7.00%	Poverty Rate	17.00%
Born in State	79.00%	Asian	4.70%	With health insurance	97.10%
		Two or more races	3.10%	Cash public assistance	3.90%
Age Groups		Other	3.60%	Food stamp/SNAP	18.80%
Under 18	20.20%				
18-34	25.80%	**Education**		**Work**	
35-64	36.70%	H.S grad or less	36.20%	White Collar	39.80%
Over 64	17.40%	Some college	32.30%	Sales and Service	41.40%
Military		College Degree, 4 yr	18.50%	Blue Collar	18.80%
Veteran/ Active Duty	6.30%	Post grad	13.10%	Government	15.30%

2020 Pres. Vote	Biden	209,957	(63%)	Trump	119,410	(36%)			
2016 Pres. Vote	Clinton	175,336	(58%)	Trump	115,558	(38%)	Johnson	8,632	(3%)

Buffalo Metro: With its massive 1920s City Hall overlooking the Niagara River and Lake Erie, Buffalo declares itself to be a city of substance. The butt of jokes about the snow from Lake Erie that supposedly keeps it immobilized half the year, Buffalo also can claim credit for building a heavy industrial base in the late 19th and early 20th centuries, as America's No. 1 grain milling center and as a major steel producer. By 1910, it had installed the first electric streetlight, produced the world's largest office building (Ellicott Square), and erected one of the earliest skyscrapers. It also played a part in producing two presidents: Grover Cleveland was mayor of Buffalo, and Millard Fillmore worked in nearby East Aurora. Today, the area still benefits from cheap hydroelectric power, but the Lackawanna steel mills are shuttered and grain milling waned after the St. Lawrence Seaway opened in the 1950s. Buffalo was eclipsed by the larger Great Lakes industrial cities of Chicago, Detroit and Cleveland.

Buffalo was the nation's 15th-largest city in 1950, when it had a population of 580,000. By 2019, it was 86th-largest—between Reno Nevada and Gilbert Arizona—with a population reduced by more than half to about 255,000. As a further insult, right across Buffalo's Peace Bridge is the richest part of Canada, the "Golden Horseshoe," from Niagara Falls through Hamilton to Toronto. Still, Buffalo retains considerable assets: a high-skill labor force, inexpensive real estate, including a gentrified and handsome waterfront on a now-cleaner Lake Erie, and some impressive cultural institutions. The area has had some encouraging economic developments. General Motors spent $296 million on equipment for engine production at its Tonawanda plant. Both the Tonawanda and Lockport plants, which have nearly 3,000 employees, survived GM's extensive job cutbacks that were announced in 2018. Panasonic teamed with the electric-car company Tesla to make solar cells and modules at Tesla's Solar City factory in south Buffalo. The companies had pledged to create 1,400 jobs by 2020, in exchange for the state building the Solar City factory as part of Gov. Andrew Cuomo's Buffalo Billion plan, an economic development initiative during his first term. In August 2020, the Wall Street Journal reported, Black workers—especially those with manufacturing jobs—suffered disproportionate loss of employment in the Buffalo area because of the pandemic and lockdowns.

In June 2020, the city became part of the nationwide discussion of police tactics following a widely distributed video in which two of its officers aggressively shoved and forced to the ground a 75-year-old man who was peacefully participating in a downtown protest. The officers were charged with felony assault and suspended without pay. In February 2021, a grand jury decided not to indict the officers.

The 26th Congressional District of New York includes all of Buffalo and the cities and townships abutting it, and nearly two-thirds of Erie County. To the north, it takes in a small slice of Niagara County with Niagara Falls and North Tonawanda. About 90 percent of the district is in Erie County. The large number of Eastern European settlers, many of whom hailed from Poland, gave Buffalo a Democratic tilt early on. Unlike much of Upstate, it began electing Democrats with some regularity in the 1860s, and almost exclusively after the 1930s. Today, the district is solidly Democratic. Joe Biden got 63 percent of the vote.

Chris Jacobs (R)

Elected 2020, 1st full term, b. Nov 28, 1966; Buffalo, NY; State University of NY, Buffalo, J.D.; Boston College, B.A.; American University, M.B.A.; Not Known; Not Stated.

Elected Office: NY Secretary of State, 2006-2007; County Clerk, Erie County, 2012-2017; NY Senate, 2017-2020.

Professional Career: Deputy Commissioner, Erie County Office of Planning and Economic Development, 2000-2002; Cabinet Secretary, Department of Housing and Urban Development; Owner, property development company.

DC Office: 214 CHOB 20515, 202-225-5265, Fax: 202-225-5910, jacobs.house.gov

State Offices: Geneseo, 585-519-4002; Williamsville, 716-634-2324.

Committees: *Agriculture*: Biotechnology, Horticulture & Research; Commodity Exchanges, Energy & Credit; Subcommittee Nutrition, Oversight & Department Operations. *Budget*.

Election Results

Election	Name (Party)	Vote (%)		Cand. Spent	Ind. Exp. Support	Ind. Exp. Oppose
2020 General	Chris Jacobs (R)	228,885	(60%)	$2,047,699	$2,544	$65,793
	Nate McMurray (D)	149,449	(39%)	$1,154,414	$57,096	
2020 Primary	Chris Jacobs (R)	40,459	(60%)			
	Beth Parlato (R)	14,805	(22%)			
	Stefan Mychajliw (R)	12,650	(19%)			

Republican Chris Jacobs, a veteran elected official and heir to a prominent local business family, won the special election in June 2020 to fill a House vacancy. Although Jacobs had been a self-styled moderate earlier in his career, he linked himself closely to President Donald Trump in his congressional bid. His 52%-47% victory was unexpectedly close in a district that has been the most strongly Republican in New York state. Jacobs succeeded Republican Rep. Chris Collins, who resigned in October 2019 as he pleaded guilty to federal insider-trading charges.

A Buffalo native, Jacobs was the grandson of Louis Jacobs—the founder of Delaware North, a large hospitality and food-service company based in Buffalo. He graduated from Boston College and got a master's degree in business administration from American University and a law degree from State University of New York at Buffalo. His first job after college was with the late Buffalo-area Republican Rep. Jack Kemp. At home, Jacobs organized a scholarship fund that has supported more than 20,000 students in western New York. In 2002, he started a real estate company that redeveloped many vacant and historic buildings in that area.

Jacobs was first elected to office in 2004 as a member of the Buffalo Board of Education. In 2006, Republican Gov. George Pataki appointed him to fill a vacancy as New York's secretary of state. After Pataki decided not to seek reelection that year, Jacobs planned to run for lieutenant governor on a ticket with William Weld, the former Republican governor of Massachusetts; Weld dropped out of the contest before the Republican primary.

After he was elected county clerk of Erie County in 2011, Jacobs described himself as a "moderate Republican," though he earlier had identified as a Democrat. In the 2016 campaign, he contributed to several Republicans running for president—though not Trump. Later that year, when he ran successfully for the state Senate, Jacobs "dodged the question" of whether he was supporting Trump in the election, the Buffalo News reported.

Collins, an enthusiastic early supporter of Trump's presidential campaign, was indicted in August 2018. After running a largely invisible campaign, he was reelected to his fourth term by a scant 1,087 votes against Democratic challenger Nate McMurray, the town supervisor of Grand Island. Stripped of his committee assignments in the House, Collins focused on preparing for his corruption trial, which was scheduled for early 2020.

In May 2019, Jacobs announced his candidacy for Collins' congressional seat. "Unfortunately, due to the legal problems he is dealing with now and will be dealing with through next year, he's not able to serve in committees right now,"Jacobs said, referring to Collins. Collins responded that Jacobs was "a never-Trump Republican." After Collins stepped down, Jacobs became the frontrunner for the GOP nomination in the special election to succeed him. In that closed-door competition among party leaders in the district's eight counties, Jacobs defeated three more-conservative candidates.

Running against McMurray in the special election, Jacobs styled himself as "an always-Trumper" and he pledged to focus on local issues, the News reported. In return, Trump tweeted his support. With more than $500,000 in self-financing, Jacobs spent twice as much money as McMurray on the campaign. The June contest turned unexpectedly close, especially as the largely Democratic mail-in ballots were counted. With his 8,087-vote lead and a 51%-46% margin, Jacobs led by about 1,400 votes in Erie County, which cast nearly half of the total, and had larger leads in the rural counties; McMurray won the small share of the district in Rochester-based Monroe County and adjacent Ontario County.

On the same day as the special election, Jacobs won the GOP primary for a two-year term, with 60 percent of the vote against two conservatives who earlier sought the party nomination for the special election. In another contest with McMurray, Jacobs had an easier run in November, when he got 60 percent. He increased his vote in Erie to 58 percent. But that smooth result faced the peril of redistricting upheaval, as Democrats in Albany likely planned to eliminate at least one House Republican-held district from Upstate. The retirement of Republican Rep. Tom Reed in an adjacent district could rescue Jacobs from a painful redistricting, though his district almost certainly will expand well beyond the Buffalo suburbs. His seat on the Agriculture Committee could be a good fit.

In January 2021, he joined a majority of Republicans in calling for a review of certification of Electoral College votes, saying that several states had made "unprecedented changes to their electoral systems without the authorization of their respective state legislatures as the Constitution dictates" and that many Americans had "valid concerns about the integrity" of the election results.

NY-27: Northwestern New York Cook Partisan Voting Index: R+12

Population		Race and Ethnicity		Income	
Total	719,554	White	92.70%	Median Income	$69,186
Land area (sq. miles)	3,973	Black	2.60%	District Income Rank	173
Pop/ sq mi	181.11	Latino	2.90%	Poverty Rate	8.10%
Born in State	85.20%	Asian	1.00%	With health insurance	97.10%
		Two or more races	1.90%	Cash public assistance	2.00%
Age Groups		Other	1.80%	Food stamp/SNAP	8.50%
Under 18	19.80%				
18-34	19.40%	**Education**		**Work**	
35-64	40.80%	H.S grad or less	37.00%	White Collar	41.10%
Over 64	19.90%	Some college	29.90%	Sales and Service	36.20%
		College Degree, 4 yr	18.70%	Blue Collar	22.70%
Military		Post grad	14.40%	Government	17.80%
Veteran/ Active Duty	7.80%				

2020 Pres. Vote	Trump	224,305	(57%)	Biden	162,337	(41%)		
2016 Pres. Vote	Trump	206,867	(59%)	Clinton	122,106	(35%)	Johnson	13,162	(4%)

Buffalo and Rochester Suburbs: The destination of the Erie Canal, the great engineering project that made New York the Empire State, was Lake Erie. The final 100 miles of the canal passed through the rolling countryside of western New York when it was scarcely occupied, except by American Indians. The appropriately named Lockport was founded as a site for locks on the canal. Later, the land was settled mostly by New England Yankees, with cultural folkways quite different from those of New York City. By the end of the 19th century, much of the farmland found here had become dominated by heavy industry, especially in Buffalo, where the Yankees were joined by Irish, Italian and Polish immigrants who came to work in the factories. For most of its history, western New York had an economy more prosperous than that of the rest of the country, as is visible in the solid houses and schools, stores and factories built to weather Upstate winters. In some ways, the region has a Midwest flavor, culturally as well as economically. People speak not in the pungent accents of New York City, but in flat Midwestern tones.

In recent decades, economic growth has lagged behind the rest of the nation. Many of Buffalo's factories have closed. The slow growth and population decline have frequently spilled over to the suburbs that sprang up around the city in outer Erie County. From 2010 to 2019, the county had virtually no change in population. Verizon Media Group, which was reorganized in 2018 following its purchase of Yahoo, said it was spending $32 million on its third data center in Lockport. In November 2020, the Common Council approved construction of a solar-power farm in Lockport.

The 27th Congressional District of New York covers much of western New York. It extends from the suburbs that surround Buffalo to suburbs southeast of Rochester, plus the northwest corner of Monroe County. In between are rural areas and small towns, including Attica, scene of a terrible prison uprising in 1970. The district has elected influential national Republicans such as Jack Kemp and Bill Paxon. With population changes, the size of the district has expanded more than 90 miles east of Buffalo. Erie and Niagara counties have been reduced to 60 percent of the district, though Erie remains its heart. Politically, these suburbs are ancestrally Republican country, based on Upstaters' general distrust of New York City. It is the most Republican district in the state by most measures. President Donald Trump's 57%-41% win in 2020 was his best performance in his home state, though the result was eight percentage points tighter than his local lead in 2016.

NORTH CAROLINA

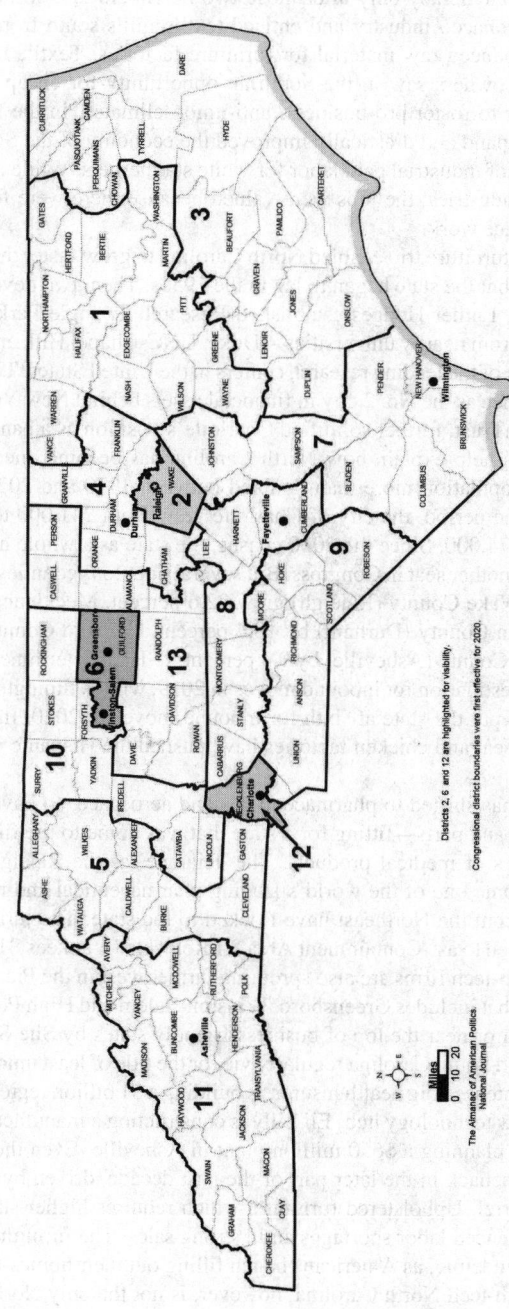

Districts 2, 6 and 12 are highlighted for visibility.

Congressional district boundaries were first effective for 2020.

The Almanac of American Politics
National Journal

In few states today is the political climate more polarized between rural and populated areas as it is in North Carolina—and in few states are the margins between the two parties so consistently narrow.

In the early republic, when Virginia and South Carolina produced statesmen and had grand plantation cultures, North Carolina was often called a valley of humility between two mountains of conceit. It joined the Confederacy only after those two neighbors did. After the Civil War, North Carolina developed its tobacco industry and enticed textile mills south from New England, while its hardwood forests produced raw material for furniture factories. Textile mills were prevalent in the Piedmont region as owners saw in the South an opportunity for cheap land, cheap labor and state governments eager to foster pro-business, anti-union climates. In the following decades, the industry continued to expand and drastically improved the economy of the South. The mill industry became the main source of industrial paid labor for white southerners. While it was one of the lowest paying manufacturing industries, the jobs were valued because there were few other options other than agricultural or service work.

The tobacco-textile-furniture trio enabled North Carolina to grow faster than the national average in the 1920s and 1930s, but the state began to lag in the 1950s. Then, two developments transformed the state. In 1959, Gov. Luther Hodges established Research Triangle Park between Raleigh and Durham. With synergy from nearby universities—Duke, UNC-Chapel Hill, and North Carolina State —the region became one of the leading research centers in the United States. The second development was Charlotte's emergence as the No. 2 city in financial assets behind New York. (In 2019, a merger between BB&T and SunTrust, further solidified Charlotte's position as a banking hub.)

These developments help explain how North Carolina has become one of the fastest-growing and largest states. Its population more than doubled between 1970 and 2020, from 5.1 million to 10.6 million. In the same period, the city of Charlotte grew from 241,000 to 886,000 and Raleigh grew from 123,000 to 474,000. Since the 2010 census, the state as a whole has grown a healthy 9.5 percent, enough to add another seat in Congress. But several populous counties have expanded at rates even higher than that: Wake County (Raleigh) grew 22.6 percent, Mecklenburg County (Charlotte) by 20.3 percent, Durham County (Durham) by 18.4 percent, Guilford County (Greensboro) by 9.7 percent, and Buncombe County (Asheville) by 9.4 percent. U-Haul determined that Raleigh-Durham was the nation's No. 1 destination for inbound moves in 2019, with Wilmington ranking 24th; United Van Lines' calculations put the state at sixth for inbound moves in 2020. Immigrants seeking jobs in construction and in meat and chicken factories have pushed the Hispanic population to nearly 10 percent.

As North Carolina has shifted to pharmaceuticals and aerospace, so have its exports, including civilian aircraft engines and parts—fitting for a state that was home to the first flight at Kitty Hawk —and various categories of medical products. The Triangle, as the Raleigh-Durham-Chapel Hill area is known, has become one of the world's leading pharmaceutical and medical device centers. Highly skilled people from the Northeast have flocked to the state: The jurisdiction of Cary in the Triangle, jokingly referred to as "Containment Area for Relocated Yankees," has grown more than 25 percent since 2010. High-tech firms are also sprouting farther west in the Piedmont Triad, the state's ancestral furniture hub that includes Greensboro, Winston-Salem and High Point. North Carolina has regularly been ranked at or near the top of business-friendly states by Site Selection magazine; not coincidentally, North and South Carolina regularly vie for the title of least unionized labor force in the nation. In Charlotte, Centene, a big health insurer, is building a $1 billion regional headquarters, while Lowe's is building a new technology hub; Eli Lilly is constructing a manufacturing plant in Durham, and Pratt & Whitney is planning a $650 million plant in Asheville. Even the furniture industry has had something of a comeback in the later part of the past decade, driven by the demand from such retailers as Crate & Barrel. Upholstered furniture, which requires higher-skilled labor and custom production lines, experienced labor shortages amid strong sales. The furniture sector even benefited from the coronavirus pandemic, as Americans began filling out their homes-turned-workspaces.

Urban, affluent, high-tech North Carolina, however, is not the only North Carolina. The state's predominantly rural counties saw taxable wages decline 3 percent in the past decade, compared with a 6 percent increase in suburban counties and a 15 percent increase in urban counties, the NC Rural Center calculated. Projections suggest that in 21 counties of 100, population will fall between 2020 and 2038. "Many rural counties in the eastern part of the state are 40 miles from a natural gas line, a non-starter for some corporations," the Wall Street Journal noted. For a time, a $5 billion, 600-mile Atlantic Coast Pipeline running from West Virginia to Pembroke North Carolina promised an economic jolt. But in 2020, amid legal challenges, its sponsors pulled the plug.

North Carolina's agriculture sector is significant: The state is the nation's third-ranking producer of broilers; the biggest producer of sweet potatoes; and the second-biggest for Christmas trees. Notably, it ranks third in hog production, with big feedlots in the southeastern portion of the state. Hurricane Florence, which dropped a record 30-odd inches of rain in 2018 and ranked among the top 10 most expensive storms in U.S. history, spotlighted the problems of hog-waste lagoons, dozens of which overflowed amid the flooding. The psychic draw of rural North Carolina runs deep: If Charlotte is proud of its downtown bank towers and modern art museum, it is also proud of its Billy Graham Library and the NASCAR Hall of Fame. But the federal government's 2004 buyout of tobacco quotas greatly diminished that sector, and retaliatory tariffs by China caused the state's tobacco exports to drop precipitously. Median income has remained in the bottom quarter of states.

Big-government liberalism provided an impetus toward spending on education, but in 2020 Education Week ranked North Carolina's public schools below average. The state has historically spent lavishly on highways and amenities, including the nation's first state-funded symphony and state high schools for science, mathematics and the arts. A different philosophical strand, religious conservatism, has provided a communitarian spirit and charitable impulses, as well as a moral undertone that anchors those who might go astray. With a few notable exceptions, the state's racial conflicts were never as intense as they were in Alabama or Mississippi, though the Greensboro sit-ins in 1960 were a pivotal moment in the civil rights movement. Yet in a state with an African-American population of 21 percent—the eighth-highest of any state—the legacy of segregation persists, including how the state's congressional and legislative district lines have been drawn. The "Silent Sam" confederate statue on the University of North Carolina campus was toppled by protesters, then moved to storage. In 2020, the board of commissioners in Orange County, which includes Chapel Hill, voted to apologize for slavery and discrimination, following similar statements in Asheville, Durham, and Carrboro.

During the latter part of the 20th century, Republicans tended to win federal elections in North Carolina, and Democrats tended to do well in state elections. But in the first two decades of the new millennium, a polarized, increasingly party-line politics evolved, waged partly on economic issues but even more on cultural attitudes. Barack Obama narrowly won the state in 2008, bolstered by high turnout by minorities and affluent Whites. But Republicans achieved big legislative majorities two years later—the first period of GOP legislative control since Reconstruction—and in 2012, Republican Pat McCrory was elected governor and GOP presidential candidate Mitt Romney won the state by 92,000 votes. McCrory ran as a centrist, pro-business mayor of Charlotte, but the legislature produced a virtual assembly line of conservative legislation and dared McCrory to use his veto. Despite some tensions and a series of protests known as "Moral Mondays" led by Rev. William Barber III of the state NAACP, McCrory mostly acceded to their wishes.

A backlash mushroomed in March 2016 when Republicans passed a bill known as H.B. 2. The measure had been spurred by Charlotte's enactment of a non-discrimination ordinance on sexual orientation. The state bill preempted local ordinances and required people to use bathrooms that coincided with one's birth gender. This time, allies of the LGBTQ community peeled off sizable portions of the business community, who predicted, correctly, that national groups would boycott the state. The law became an albatross for McCrory and contributed to his narrow loss in 2016 to longtime Attorney General Roy Cooper. After the election, the two sides agreed to repeal the law in March 2017. In the 2018 midterm elections, voters elected enough Democrats to break the GOP's legislative supermajorities, bolstering Cooper's leverage. Statewide elections also gave Democrats a 6-1 majority on the state Supreme Court.

In both 2016 and 2020, North Carolina was considered a major prize by both presidential candidates, who courted the state accordingly. The GOP planned its convention for Charlotte, before largely abandoning it for a virtual affair during the pandemic. (The pullout was popular in increasingly Democratic Charlotte.) Donald Trump won the state twice, but by narrow margins—by 173,000 votes in 2016 and 74,000 votes in 2020. The Democrats' gains in the big urban-suburban counties of Mecklenburg and Wake, about 120,000 votes net, more than accounted for the Democrats' statewide improvement of almost 99,000 votes. Joe Biden also improved on Hillary Clinton's 2016 showing in the Triad, netting an additional 18,000 votes out of Guilford and Forsyth counties. He flipped New Hanover County (Wilmington) and chipped away at Trump's (still-large) margins in the suburban-exurban Charlotte counties of Union, Gaston, and Cabarrus, and also gained in Johnston County, in the Raleigh exurbs. But Trump strengthened his hold on rural North Carolina—places like Robeson County, notable for its Lumbee Indian population, which shifted its margin 15 points in Trump's direction in 2020.

The presidential race wasn't the only sign of political stability in 2020. North Carolina, arguably the state with the most genuinely bipartisan lineup of statewide elected officials in the nation, voted to keep the incumbent party in power in every office—Cooper as governor, plus the attorney general, secretary of state, and state auditor for the Democrats, while voters backed Republican for six other offices; that included the reelection of Thom Tillis to the Senate. Reinforcing the state's penchant for close races, only one of these contests was decided by more than 5 points. (The race for chief justice of the Supreme Court, which the GOP managed to flip, was decided by just 401 votes.) The GOP also maintained its control of the legislature. Some observers were surprised to see Georgia leapfrog North Carolina as the southern state that went blue in 2020, but Georgia's shift has been amplified by the scale of metropolitan Atlanta, which has a population 29 percent bigger than the combination of Charlotte and Raleigh-Durham. Ultimately, look for continued polarization and tight races. "North Carolina's complex electoral history shows that for the Old North State, the future is really anyone's guess," wrote North Carolina political scholars Michael Bitzer and Virginia Summey just days after the 2020 election.

Population		Race and Ethnicity		Income	
Total	10,488,084	White	68.10%	Median Income	57,341
Land area (sq. miles)	48,618	Black	21.50%	State Income Rank	39 out of 50
Pop/ sq mi	215.72	Latino	9.80%	Poverty Rate	13.60%
Born in state	56.00%	Asian	3.60%	With health insurance	88.70%
		Two or more races	2.80%	Cash public assistance	1.50%
Age Groups		Other	4.70%	Food stamp/SNAP	13.7%
Under 18	21.90%				
18-34	23.00%	**Education**		**Work**	
35-64	38.50%	H.S grad or less	37.00%	White Collar	39.30%
Over 64	16.70%	Some college	30.70%	Sales and Service	37.00%
		College Degree, 4 yr	20.50%	Blue Collar	23.70%
Military		Post grad	11.80%	Government	13.20%
Veteran/ Active Duty	9.10%				

Presidential Politics

2020 Primary (D)	Biden (D)	572,271(43%)	Sanders (D)		322,645(24%)	Bloomberg (D)	172,558(13%)
	Warren (D)	139,912(11%)					
2020 Pres. Vote	Trump (R)	2,758,775(50%)	Biden (D)	2,684,292(49%)			
2016 Pres. Vote	Trump (R)	2,362,631(50%)	Clinton (D)	2,189,316(46%)	Johnson (L)	130,126 (3%)	

Republicans have carried North Carolina in 11 of the last 13 presidential elections, though it's been a battleground state in the past few cycles. The only Democratic victories came in 1976, when southerner Jimmy Carter won the state and 2008, when Barack Obama's campaign built an organization that was able to take advantage of a 2007 state law permitting same-day voter registration and the growing appeal of early voting to mobilize large numbers of college students and African Americans.

The recent arrivals of many Hispanics and affluent professionals in the state's Research Triangle provided opportunities for Democrats to compete in the GOP-leaning state, and it has attracted heavy campaign spending from both sides, though Democrats have failed to repeat Obama's 2008 success. Mitt Romney beat Obama by 50%-48% in 2012, and Donald Trump defeated Hillary Clinton, 50%-46% in 2016. North Carolina was once again vigorously contested in 2020, as one of the six core battleground states that saw heavy ad spending from both campaigns. Polls consistently showed a tight race, though Joe Biden led in more of them. Trump beat Biden 50%-49%, the closest of any of his wins. His 74,000-vote margin was almost 100,000 votes fewer than his 2016 edge, as turnout surged from 4.7 million to 5.4 million votes cast.

Biden made the biggest inroads around Charlotte and in the fast-growing, heavily Democratic Research Triangle; his margins of victory in Mecklenburg County (Charlotte) and Wake County (Raleigh) were both almost six points higher than Clinton's had been, and he ran 10 points ahead of Clinton in Cabarrus County (exurban Charlotte). But Trump made marginal gains in much of North Carolina's more rural areas, including in the Black Belt in the northeast, as well as in Robeson County, a rural county south of Fayetteville with a large number of Lumbee Indians, which swung 14 points his direction. Black turnout was up for Biden compared to Clinton, but not enough to overcome a rural White turnout surge for Trump. The election was close enough that it took 10 days for the Associated Press to officially call the race, as late-arriving mail ballots trickled in.

North Carolina's primary has occasionally played a role in presidential politics. In 1976, after five straight losses, Ronald Reagan won his first major victory over Gerald Ford in the Republican primary, reenergizing his campaign that went all the way to the convention. After Obama trounced Clinton in the 2008 primary, he was the defacto Democratic nominee. In 2016, the state moved its primary up to March 15. In the GOP contest, Trump narrowly defeated Texas Sen. Ted Cruz, 40%-37%. Clinton beat Sanders 55%-41%, and carried 83 of 100 counties. In 2020, North Carolina was one of the Super Tuesday states Michael Bloomberg made a big play for, dropping more than $12 million on TV ads. But Biden's big primary win in neighboring South Carolina just a few days earlier helped him gain momentum, and he won North Carolina's primary, 43%-24%, over Bernie Sanders, with Bloomberg a distant third at 12 percent. It was one of several big wins for Biden that day that helped make him the prohibitive favorite for the nomination.

Congressional Districts

117th Congress Lineup	5D 8R	116th Congress Lineup	3D 8R 2V

North Carolina will gain the 14th House seat that it fell barely short of after the 2010 census. As of early 2021, numerous variables made it difficult to envision the outcome, short of a virtual guarantee that the state faced another partisan and legal brawl.

Republicans retain control of the legislature. Although the governor has no veto power or other formal authority on redistricting, the Democratic governor and attorney general likely will pursue other options—chiefly, court litigation—to protect their party's interests. State Democrats were successful in securing state court action in December 2019 that found the previous redistricting an unconstitutional partisan gerrymander and forced the legislature to radically redraw much of the state's map—for one election cycle. That gave Democrats a two-seat gain in the delegation, which Republicans now control 8-to-5. Their pick-ups were in Wake County (Raleigh) and the Triad (Greensboro and Winston-Salem), which previously were divided into multiple districts. Republican incumbents who held largely exurban seats in those two areas retired, conceding that they had no chance to survive with the new map. Although Democrats welcomed that change, they contend the state's roughly even partisan balance should give them at least one more certain seat, or perhaps a couple of opportunities, especially in the Charlotte metropolitan area. One result of the new map is that the remaining Republican-held seats mostly had stronger GOP majorities.

Since the 1990s, North Carolina has been the epicenter of race-based redistricting litigation. The initial focus was a long, skinny new black-majority12th District that went to the U.S. Supreme Court four times. Throughout these battles, Democrats managed to retain partisan control of the delegation. That ended in 2011, when North Carolina was the site of Democrats' worst redistricting devastation, the seeds of which were sown 15 years prior. In 1996, Democrats in charge of the General Assembly exempted redistricting matters from the governor's veto powers, reasoning they would always hold the legislature but voters might occasionally elect a Republican governor. In the ultimate tale of unintended consequences, Republicans shocked even themselves by taking over the legislature by large margins in 2010, rendering Democratic Gov. Bev Perdue helpless to foil their map makeover. Republicans passed a new plan that unraveled and reversed the Democrats' 2002 map, and then some.

They packed Democratic voters into three of the state's 13 seats: an African-American majority 1st District covering parts of rural northeastern counties and heavily black neighborhoods in Durham; an almost comically gerrymandered and liberal 4th District connecting the academic haven of Chapel Hill, black neighborhoods in Raleigh and faraway Fayetteville; and an even more tightly packed African-American majority 12th District knifing along the I-85 corridor in a strip from Charlotte to Winston-Salem and Greensboro. By 2014, their handiwork eviscerated four of the state's seven Democrats and created 10 safe Republican seats.

The redistricting battles continued. In 2015 and again in 2019, litigation resulted in new maps. The GOP-controlled legislature was given the opportunity to redraw the districts, but with increasingly strict supervision by the state courts. The outcomes largely eliminated gross geographic gerrymanders, though the new districts gained predictable partisan leanings. Although the U.S. Supreme Court, on a 5-4 ruling in 2020, said the federal courts lacked authority to overturn partisan gerrymanders, state courts retained that option under their state's constitution.

In drawing a new 14th district, Republicans likely will return to variations of the map they drew for 2016, in which they retained their 10-3 control of the delegation. They might, for example, seek to break up one or both of the new districts for Wake County and the Triad, perhaps turning them into contests that are closer to "fair fights." The maneuvering could result in clashes between federal and state judges.

Roy Cooper (D)

Elected 2016, term expires 2025, 2nd term; b. Jun. 13, 1957, Nashville; Univ. of North Carolina Chapel Hill, BA 1979; Univ. of North Carolina, JD 1982; Presbyterian; Married (Kristin); 3 children.

Elected Office: NC House 1987-1991; NC Senate 1991-2000; NC Attorney General 2001-2017

Professional Career: Partner, Field and Cooper, Rocky Mount NC, 1982-2000.

Office: Office of the Governor 20301 Mail Service Center, Raleigh, 27699-0301; 919-814-2000; Fax: 919-733-2120

Lt. Gov.: Dan Forest (R) **Atty. Gen:** Josh Stein (D) **Sec. of State:** Elaine Marshall (D)

State Legislature: Senate: 21D, 29R **House:** 55D, 65R

Election Results

Election	Name (Party)	Vote (%)
2016 General	Roy Cooper (D)	2,309,190 (49%)
	Pat McCrory (R)	2,298,927 (49%)
	Lon Cecil (L)	102,986 (2%)
2020 General	Roy Cooper (D)	2,834,790 (52%)
	Dan Forest (R)	2,586,605 (47%)
2016 Primary	Roy Cooper (D)	710,658 (69%)
	Ken Spaulding (D)	323,774 (31%)

Roy Cooper, a Democrat who had served four terms as North Carolina's attorney general, narrowly ousted Republican Gov. Pat McCrory in 2016 and proceeded to do battle with a GOP legislature over the next four years. In 2020, bolstered by public support for his handling of the coronavirus pandemic, Cooper won a second term by a significantly wider margin.

Cooper was born and raised in a rural portion of east-central North Carolina. He earned a bachelor's degree in psychology and political science and a law degree at UNC-Chapel Hill. While Cooper was still in law school, then-Gov. Jim Hunt, a Democrat, named him to a state goals and policy board. Upon graduation, Cooper joined the family law firm, handling civil suits and personal injury and insurance cases; he also served as a Sunday school teacher and deacon at his Presbyterian church. Cooper served in the state House from 1987 to 1991, and in the state Senate from 1991 to 2001, part of that time as majority leader. In 2000, Cooper ran for attorney general against Republican Dan Boyce. It was a hard-fought race, with Cooper airing ads accusing Boyce of overbilling in a class-action lawsuit against the state. (The overbilling allegation prompted a 14-year legal battle that ended with Cooper apologizing.) After outspending Boyce four-to-one, Cooper won the race by five points. He later won reelection three times, serving 16 years. As attorney general, Cooper oversaw the increased use of DNA testing and sought tougher sentences for child predators and pornographers. He took over the bogus Duke lacrosse rape case after Durham District Attorney Mike Nifong recused himself; Cooper re-investigated the allegations and cleared the players of all charges.

In 2013, Cooper actively opposed a voter-ID and election overhaul law driven by the Republican legislature. This and other stances made it increasingly clear that Cooper was aiming for a gubernatorial run against McCrory in 2016. McCrory, a seven-term mayor of Charlotte, had run for governor in 2012 touting a pragmatic, "middle way" philosophy based on pro-business policies and little emphasis on social issues – an approach that had worked for him as a Republican serving on the city level, and that embodied the kind of centrism that had historically carried both Republicans and Democrats to North Carolina's governor's mansion. Once in office, however, McCrory had to work with a Republican-dominated legislature that had little interest in pragmatic centrism and a strong desire to control the agenda, which often included socially conservative issues. McCrory sometimes clashed with GOP legislators and vetoed their bills, but more often he signed them, including the election overhaul bill (later overturned in the courts), a tax overhaul that flattened brackets, and an abortion waiting period.

The biggest threat to McCrory's hopes for reelection came from H.B. 2, a bill that preempted local non-discrimination ordinances on sexual orientation, requiring, among other things, that people use bathrooms corresponding with their birth gender. The types of business interests who had historically aligned with McCrory were unhappy; they feared boycotts would emerge, and they were right. During the campaign, Cooper made opposition to H.B. 2—and particularly its effect on the state's economy—a cornerstone of his message. He also advocated increased funding for K-12 education. Cooper's approach resonated enough to defeat McCrory by a little over 10,000 votes. Donald Trump carried the state, but McCrory underperformed the top of the ticket in some of the industrial areas of the Piedmont and western North Carolina. The McCrory camp raised the specter of election fraud, but election boards headed by Republicans disagreed. In December, the incumbent conceded.

That hardly ended the conflict, however. In an echo of the then-Democratic legislature's actions to remove the governor from the redistricting process in the 1990s, Republican legislators passed laws to strip some of Cooper's powers. In December 2016, the two parties failed to come to agreement on how to repeal H.B. 2. Finally, in March 2017—after Cooper had become governor and after the Associated Press had estimated that the state would suffer $3.76 billion over 12 years in lost business—the two sides agreed to a repeal. However, the repeal measure contained a provision sought by Republicans that continued for three years a restriction on the types of local ordinances that had precipitated H.B. 2 in the first place. The three-year moratorium was a bitter pill for LGBT advocates, and Cooper signed it unhappily, saying it wasn't his "preferred solution."

Cooper came out in favor of removing Confederate monuments after the White nationalist march in Charlottesville. "Some people cling to the belief that the Civil War was fought over states' rights," he wrote. "But history is not on their side. We cannot continue to glorify a war against the United States of America fought in the defense of slavery. These monuments should come down." A year later, Cooper pulled back North Carolina National Guard members from serving at the U.S.-Mexico border in protest of the Trump administration policy of family separations.

On a few issues, Cooper was able to act without being blocked by the legislature. He pledged to oppose a Trump administration proposal to drill for oil and gas offshore, reversing McCrory's position. He also signed an executive order setting a state goal of cutting greenhouse gas emissions by 40 percent by 2025, effectively keeping North Carolina within the terms of the Paris climate accord, which Trump had pulled the U.S. out of. In September 2018, Cooper led the recovery from Hurricane Florence, which left some three dozen North Carolinians dead and caused widespread damage. Meanwhile, the legislature was unable to override two of Cooper's vetoes—one of a bill that would have let nonprofits hold gambling fundraisers, and another of a bill that critics said would have permitted the spraying of "garbage juice" at landfills.

More often, Cooper's efforts were stymied. His campaign pledge to expand Medicaid under the Affordable Care Act stalled, and his vetoes of budget bills were overridden in 2017 and 2018. By January 2019, Cooper had vetoed more than two dozen bills, including several that sought to limit the governor's powers. Many of the bills about gubernatorial authority went through various stages of vetoes, overrides, lower court decisions and judicial appeals. One that became law after an override was a bill to make judicial elections partisan. On Election Day 2018, voters rejected, by 3-to-2 margins, a pair of legislature-backed ballot measures to weaken the governor's powers after all five living former governors, including McCrory, joined with Cooper in opposition.

In an even more important Election Day development, Democrats won enough seats in the state House and Senate to break the GOP's veto-proof supermajority. As a result, the legislature failed to override any of Cooper's vetoes in 2019, including a bill that would have criminalized the failure to treat "any infant born alive after an abortion." Meanwhile, Cooper and the legislature battled for months over the state budget. In June, Cooper vetoed a two-year budget measure, demanding additional teacher pay and an expansion of Medicaid. On Sept. 11, Republican legislators took advantage of Democrats' absence at a commemoration of the 2001 terrorist attacks to hold an unannounced vote with mostly Republicans present. Similar tactics have been employed by both parties in other states at times, but Cooper called it legislating by" trickery, deception, and lies." This gambit failed, as did another override attempt in January 2020. Instead, the state muddled through with temporary spending extensions that did not include any controversial changes. By the time the coronavirus pandemic arrived in 2020, Republican leaders shelved additional efforts to override Cooper's budget veto. Meanwhile, amid racial justice protests across the country, Cooper vetoed a measure that would have tightened confidentiality on investigations of deaths in the custody of police or in prison.

Cooper took an aggressive stance against the coronavirus, especially for a southern governor. He issued a stay-at-home order in March and a mask mandate in May, though his curb on indoor worship was overturned in the courts. Republicans, including Cooper's reelection opponent, Lt. Gov. Dan Forest, tried to make an issue of the governor's restrictions. Forest went to court to curb Cooper's public health powers (he lost) and the legislature passed a bill to open some businesses (but Cooper vetoed it). In the run-up to the Republican National Convention in Charlotte, Cooper insisted on strict guidelines. This clashed with Trump's vision for a traditional confab; blaming Cooper's intransigence, Trump largely pulled the convention out of Charlotte, though the party used the city as a base for some back-office operations.

Polls generally showed North Carolinians approving of Cooper's actions, and the intense media focus gave the relatively low-key governor an unprecedented public platform. Ultimately, Cooper's coronavirus efforts probably sealed his victory in November, though he ended up defeating Forest by well below the double-digit margins that some polls in the summer had indicated. On an Election Day with numerous close races in the state, Cooper defeated Forest relatively comfortably, by 248,000 votes, or about 24 times bigger than his razor-thin edge in 2016. Cooper outran Joe Biden in the state by 150,498 votes, and improved his margins in the two most populous counties, Wake (Raleigh) and Mecklenburg (Charlotte), by 10 and nine points, respectively. After the election, Biden nominated Michael Regan, a key Cooper appointee, to be Environmental Protection Agency administrator. In early 2021, even as the state had one of the lower coronavirus infection rates in the country, Cooper vetoed a measure that would have mandated in-person learning for K-12 public schools.

Richard Burr (R)

Elected 2004, term expires 2022, 3rd term, b. Nov 30, 1955; Charlottesville, VA; Wake Forest University, B.A., 1978; Methodist; Married (Brooke Fauth Burr); 2 children.

Elected Office: U.S. House, 1995-2005; Republican Assistant Whip, U.S. House.

Professional Career: National Sales Manager, wholesale distribution company, 1978-1994.

DC Office: 217 RSOB 20510, 202-224-3154, Fax: 202-228-2981, burr.senate.gov

State Offices: Asheville, 828-350-2437; Rocky Mount, 252-977-9522; Wilmington, 910-251-1058; Winston-Salem, 336-631-5125.

Committees: *Aging. Finance*: Fiscal Responsibility & Economic Growth; Health Care; Taxation & IRS Oversight. *Health, Education, Labor & Pensions (RMM)*: Ex Officio membership on all subcommittees. *Intelligence*.

Group Ratings

	ADA	ACLU	AFL-CIO	LCV	COC	HAFA	ACU	CFG	FRC
2020	-	0%	-	15%	-	58%	86%	-	-
2019	0%	C	17%	29%	93%	C	86%	33%	100%

Almanac Ratings 2019-2020

	Economy	Social	Foreign	Composite
Liberal	0%	0%	0%	0%
Conservative	100%	100%	100%	100%

Key Votes of the 116th Congress

1. EPA clean energy rules N	5. Russia sanctions N	9. Barr as Atty. General N/A
2. U.S./Mex./Can. trade deal Y	6. Troops in SYR, AFG Y	10. Spending at the border Y
3. Cut unemployment benefits Y	7. Veto arms sales to Saudis N	11. Coney Barrett to Sup. Ct. Y
4. Shelton to Fed Reserve Y	8. Defense $$$, veto override Y	12. Electoral College objections N

Election Results

Election	Name (Party)	Vote (%)		Cand. Spent	Ind. Exp. Support	Ind. Exp. Oppose
2016 General	Richard Burr (R)	2,395,376	(51%)	$12,398,612	$2,293,659	$26,170,688
	Deborah Ross (D)	2,128,165	(45%)	$20,299,019	$3,001,651	$28,311,467
	Sean Haugh (L)	167,592	(4%)	$4,298		
2016 Primary	Richard Burr (R)	627,354	(61%)			
	Greg Brannon (R)	257,331	(25%)			
	Paul Wright (R)	86,940	(9%)			

Prior winning percentages: 2016 (51%), 2010 (55%), 2004 (52%); House: 2002 (70%), 2000 (93%), 1998 (68%), 1996 (62%), 1994 (57%)

More Republicans were expected to vote to convict Donald Trump during his second impeachment trial in early 2021 than did in his first a year earlier. One of the most shocking GOP defections came from Sen. Richard Burr, who agreed the former president had incited his supporters to violently storm the Capitol in an eleventh-hour attempt to overturn his election loss. North Carolina's senior senator had already made clear that he wasn't running for reelection in 2022, so there would be no electoral consequences for his vote. By siding with six other Republicans and all Democrats—even though Trump was ultimately acquitted—Burr added to his legacy as a lawmaker often willing to work with the opposite party—as he had during the Senate Intelligence Committee's investigation into Russian interference in the 2016 elections—and call out his party when he felt it was in the wrong

Burr's explanation for his vote was terse: The "evidence is compelling that President Trump is guilty of inciting an insurrection against a coequal branch of government and that the charge rises to the level of high Crimes and Misdemeanors." Backlash at home was swift. Just two days after the trial, the North Carolina Republican Party voted unanimously to censure Burr. "My party's leadership has chosen loyalty to one man over the core principles of the Republican Party and the founders of our great nation," the senator responded.

A distant relative of former Vice President Aaron Burr, Richard Burr grew up a minister's son in Winston-Salem and was a high school and Wake Forest University football star. He then spent nearly two decades in sales for Winston-Salem-based Carswell Distributing, a wholesaler of lawn and garden equipment and home heating appliances. His first run for office was in 1992, against nine-term Democratic Rep. Steve Neal. Although outspent 3-1, he lost by a relatively narrow 53%-46%. Neal retired in 1994 and Burr ran again, this time winning 57 percent of the vote in a Republican wave year. Burr did not have a serious challenge in four reelection bids.

On the House Energy and Commerce Committee, Burr worked to streamline the Food and Drug Administration's drug and medical device approval process, which he argued would speed lifesaving products to the market. With broad bipartisan support, his FDA Modernization Act became law in 1997. He also helped set up the National Institute for Biomedical Imaging and Bioengineering at the National Institutes of Health.

In 2004, his last year in the House, Burr fought to end the tobacco quota system that had been in place since 1938. Burr favored the buyout without FDA regulation, arguing that the toxicity of cigarettes should be regulated by the Centers for Disease Control and Prevention, which he eventually secured, and the bill was enacted to reflect his preferences.

Burr had promised to serve only five terms in the House, and he made clear his interest in running for the Senate. In 2002, when GOP Sen. Jesse Helms announced he would retire, Burr deferred to Elizabeth Dole, who had the backing of the Bush White House. Two years later, Democratic Sen. John Edwards opted to run for president instead of seeking reelection, and Burr had the shot he was waiting for. He had serious opposition from Erskine Bowles, President Bill Clinton's onetime chief of staff, who had lost the 2002 Senate race 54%-45% to Dole. Bowles had deep roots in North Carolina: His father, Skipper Bowles, had been the Democratic nominee for governor in 1972. As Clinton's top aide, Bowles negotiated the 1997 legislation that produced a balanced federal budget for the first time in decades.

Each candidate spent about $13 million. Bowles started running ads in May, while Burr held back until September and, having conserved resources, had a money advantage in the final two months. Bowles touted his ability to work with both parties while depicting Burr as a captive of special interests, especially pharmaceutical and tobacco companies. Burr linked Bowles to Clinton's policies on tax increases, welfare for immigrants and trade with China. Bush carried North Carolina 56%-44% in his re-election bid, and Burr beat Bowles 52%-47%. Later, when Bowles co-chaired President Barack Obama's fiscal commission, he had kind words for Burr: "I think by the grace of God we both ended up in the exact right jobs for North Carolina. ... I can tell you from firsthand experience nobody works harder or is smarter than this guy in Washington."

In the Senate, Burr has shown little interest in calling attention to himself and often reaches across the political aisle. He told the Charlotte Observer in 2009: "I tend to be more of a policy guy than I am a guy who shows up on the 24-hour talk shows or a guy who goes to the floor and speaks." He has leaned conservative on cultural issues and initially toward the center on foreign policy, although he moved further to the right after Obama became president.

One of his most significant legislative achievements came in his first year in the Senate, when he won enactment of a law to create the Biomedical Advanced Research and Development Authority to develop vaccines and other countermeasures to bioterrorism and pandemics. He also wrote the 2019 Pandemic and All-Hazards Preparedness and Advancing Innovation Act, which was particularly relevant amid the 2020 COVID-19 pandemic as it encouraged the FDA to work with companies to produce vaccines for emergency use and helped hospitals set up regional collaborations.

In 2010, Burr surprised his conservative supporters when he voted to end the "don't ask, don't tell" law banning openly gay service members. In 2015, he voted to give married same-sex couples Social Security and veterans' benefits they had earned. Burr occasionally has shown a willingness to take on more-conservative colleagues; he said in 2013 that talk of shutting down the federal government over opposition to the Affordable Care Act was "the dumbest idea I've ever heard." A year later, he worked on a comprehensive alternative to the ACA that retained many of the Obama-era law's most popular elements but guaranteed coverage to those with preexisting medical conditions only if they maintained "continuous coverage."

One area where Burr has taken a strong conservative line is immigration. In 2006, he voted against an immigration overhaul because he said it would lead to "blanket amnesty" for undocumented immigrants. During negotiations on a compromise bill the following year, Burr supported the "touchback" amendment that would have forced undocumented immigrants to return to their native countries before applying for visas. When the amendment was voted down, he voted against the compromise measure. He vowed to keep an open mind as a bipartisan group of his colleagues drafted a comprehensive immigration reform proposal in 2013, but he voted against the bill, saying it didn't do enough to secure the border.

Taking over as Intelligence Committee chairman in 2015, Burr had an at times bumpy relationship with the panel's ranking member, Dianne Feinstein of California—who had chaired the panel for six years. Feinstein had commissioned a staff investigation of the CIA's use of torture after 9/11. It produced a critical report longer than 6,700 pages; a 500-page summary was declassified and released publicly. Burr lambasted the report's conclusions that the CIA's torture program had proved ineffective, calling the report "fiction" and fought its declassification. He wrote to Obama asking that copies of the full classified report sent to the White House and other parts of the executive branch be returned—apparently fearing the report could become available under the Freedom of Information Act. Feinstein opposed Burr's request, later telling the New Yorker, "I was surprised and somewhat suspicious about who put him up to it." The White House declined to return or destroy copies of the report.

Burr resisted reining in the power of intelligence agencies in the face of domestic snooping revelations and fought to turn back attempts at greater openness when sections of the Patriot Act came up for reauthorization. "If I had my way, with the exception of nominees, there would never be a public intelligence hearing," he told reporters in 2014. A year later, Burr helped lead the charge to reauthorize the law, fighting against bipartisan efforts to curtail the program's bulk collection of Americans' phone records. He and Sen. Mitch McConnell, then majority leader, did all they could to renew the act unaltered, even after the House passed a bill with changes by overwhelming bipartisan margins. After an attempt to force a short-term extension of the law failed and the Patriot Act expired, McConnell relented and allowed a vote on the House-passed measure. Burr was among 32 senators to vote against the changes. "I am disappointed in the final bill and, quite frankly, am very concerned about the new system's ability to keep up with the threats we face," he said.

In 2016, Burr got behind Trump when it was clear that he would be the party's presidential nominee. At one point, the usually low-key senator compared himself to the bombastic billionaire. "He's a very nontraditional candidate, and he's run a very nontraditional campaign," Burr told reporters at the Republican National Convention. "Most in Washington would probably say that describes me to a 'T,' and so I can associate with Donald Trump very well." He later signed on as a national security adviser to the Trump campaign, while downplaying the possibility of Russia interfering in the election to help Trump. "I have yet to see anything that would lead me to believe that's the case," Burr told Foreign Policy magazine in early October. He called his congressional colleagues' warnings "probably incorrect," adding, "They give the impression there's one cyber-problem in the world: Russia and the elections, and that's a huge understatement."

Burr vowed impartiality as his panel's investigation of Russian interference—and possible collusion between Moscow and the Trump campaign—got underway in early 2017. "I'll admit that I voted for [Trump]. … But I've got a job in the United States Senate, and I take that job extremely seriously," Butt said. "It overrides any personal beliefs that I have or loyalties that I might have." He quickly developed a cordial relationship with Sen. Mark Warner of Virginia, who had replaced Feinstein as the committee's top Democrat and had a history of working well with Republican senators. With Burr emphasizing the need to determine what had happened during the election, they worked together on much of the investigation and often held joint news conferences. "Contrary to maybe popular belief," Burr told reporters in March 2017, he and Warner are partners.

The committee leaders had little to say in 2017 about their closed-door inquiry, with Burr stressing the extended commitment of his personal time and obligation to protect classified information. By March 2018, he told reporters, "It is clear the Russian government was looking for vulnerabilities in our election system" during 2016. But he said the Russian interference was not responsible for Trump's victory and rejected suggestions that Trump had "colluded" with Russia. As the committee inquiry continued, Burr made a point of avoiding meetings at the White House and didn't heed Trump's pleas to stop investigating, as Republicans had done in the House. Burr again ruffled feathers in 2019 when he subpoenaed Donald Trump Jr. to testify before the committee even though McConnell had declared the Russia investigation "case closed." The committee also told the Department of Justice that Trump's eldest son, his son-in-law Jared Kushner and former Trump strategist Steve Bannon may have misled the committee, though the agency didn't act.

The committee's final 966-page report was released in April 2020, with a unanimous recognition of the intelligence community's verdict that Russia attempted to interfere in the 2016 elections, making it the first bipartisan endorsement of the findings of the CIA, FBI and NSA—conclusions Trump continued to reject. "The committee found no reason to dispute the intelligence community's conclusions," Burr said. The report, though, didn't address the issue of collusion. Senators on both sides of the aisle praised Burr and Warner for the bipartisan way in which they had run the probe, which stood in stark contrast to House Republicans' efforts.

Warner and Burr also worked in concert on other matters, including pressing the Trump administration to declassify information about the murder of Washington Post columnist Jamal Khashoggiat the Saudi consulate in Istanbul; the White House had refused to acknowledge that the grisly killing had come at the direction of Saudi Crown Prince Mohammed bin Salman despite the CIA determining he had ordered it.

Burr was forced to step down as the Intelligence panel's chairman in February 2020 amid controversy: After a briefing on the threat of the looming novel coronavirus, he had dumped shares in businesses that would soon see their value nosedive when COVID-19 hit the U.S. The companies included hotels, restaurants, and drug manufacturers, and the shares were worth between $628,000 and $1.7 million. The transactions, which amounted to his largest total sold in one day since 2016, came as he was receiving daily briefings on the virus' threat and a week before stock markets plummeted. Less than a week before he dumped the stocks, Burr had downplayed the impact the coronavirus would have on the U.S., writing in a column that the country was "better prepared than ever before to face emerging public health threats, like the coronavirus, in large part due to the work of the Senate Health Committee, Congress, and the Trump Administration." But NPR obtained audio of Burr addressing a private group of North Carolina business leaders sounding a different one. "There's one thing I can tell you about this: It is much more aggressive in its transmission than anything we have seen in recent history," Burr said. "It's probably more akin to the 1918 pandemic."

Burr denied any wrongdoing and said he had made the decision after listening to news from Asia. Still, Burr asked the Senate Ethics Committee to investigate the matter, hoping that it would clear him. But in May 2020, the FBI seized his cell phone as part of its investigation with the Securities and Exchange Commission into to whether Burr had violated the Stock Act, which prohibits members of Congress from using any nonpublic information to inform their investments. It was then that Burr said he would temporarily step aside as Intelligence chairman, telling reporters," This is a distraction to the hard work of the committee, and the members and I think that the security of the country is too important to have a distraction," Burr said. Several other senators also found their stock trades under scrutiny, including Feinstein and Georgia GOP Sen. Kelly Loeffler. While other senators were cleared of any wrongdoing months earlier, it was only announced on the final full day of the Trump administration that the Justice Department had concluded its review and would not pursue any charges against Burr.

When he faced reelection in 2010, there was speculation Burr could encounter serious opposition, considering Obama's victory in North Carolina in 2008 and Dole's defeat for reelection that year. Moreover, polls showed Burr had a low profile in the state. But the strongest possible Democratic challenger, state Attorney General Roy Cooper, declined to run. (Cooper is now the state's governor.) Secretary of State Elaine Marshall emerged from the Democratic primary with little money. Burr raised $11 million, nearly four times as much as his opponent. He won 55%-43%.

Democrats also had recruiting difficulties in 2016, when Burr again faced reelection. Former Sen. Kay Hagan, narrowly ousted by Republican Thom Tillis in 2014, declined to take on Burr—as did Obama Secretary of Transportation Anthony Foxx, a former Charlotte mayor. Former state Rep. Deborah Ross, a Raleigh attorney, eventually was embraced by the state Democratic establishment. Initially, the faceoff was not high on the list of competitive Senate races. But Burr was weighed down by a couple of other factors beyond his control: the unpopularity of GOP Gov. Pat McCrory, who ended up losing to Cooper, and the "bathroom bill" passed by the North Carolina General Assembly —which required transgender people to use bathrooms in government buildings consistent with the sex on their birth certificates. Burr sought to distance himself from the law, telling HuffPost, "The Legislature botched what they were trying to do. It was far too expansive."

Burr created some problems for himself. To the frustration of GOP officials, he did not campaign in earnest until late September. Ross sought to paint Burr as a Washington insider and accused him of voting to privatize Medicare and cut Social Security benefits—charges Burr disputed. Meanwhile, Burr and his GOP allies sought to tie Ross to several unpopular stances taken by the state chapter of the

American Civil Liberties Union, of which Ross was a former director. Burr pulled out a 51%-45% win —nearly mirroring Trump's 50%-46% victory in the state. Although short of the $111 million spent in the Hagan-Tillis contest, spending in the Burr-Ross race approached $84 million. The candidates themselves spent about $24 million, with Ross outspending the incumbent by $4 million. That was dwarfed by nearly $60 million from outside spending groups. (After redistricting in 2020, Ross won a new Raleigh-based House district.)

Months before the votes were counted, Burr said that, if he won, it would be his last term."It's real simple: I'm beginning to get old," Burr, who will be 67 in 2022, told reporters at the Republican National Convention. "I still look forward to getting back into the private sector before retirement even comes into the picture. I never envisioned retiring out of the Congress."

In early 2021, the race to replace Burr looked crowded, and the seat was critical for Republicans to protect if they wanted to win back the majority they lost in 2020. Rep. Ted Budd, plus former Gov. McCrory and former Rep. Mark Walker were running on the GOP side. After his daughter-in-law Tara Trump decided not to run, Trump endorsed Budd. That spurred second-guessing about the endorsement, including the role of Mark Meadows—Trump's final White House chief of staff who previously was a House member from North Carolina. Democratic candidates included. Democratic candidates included state Sen. Jeff Jackson, but party leaders were angling for an African-American woman to top the ticket to drive up base turnout, with former state Supreme Court Chief Justice Cheri Beasley and former astronaut Joan Higginbotham both expressing interest.

Thom Tillis (R)

Elected 2014, term expires 2026, 2nd term, b. Aug 30, 1960; Jacksonville, FL; University of MD University College, B.S., 1996; Catholic; Married (Susan Tillis); 2 children.

Elected Office: Board of Commissioners, Cornelius, NC, 2003-2005; NC House, 2007-2014.

Professional Career: Life insurance company consultant, 1981-1982; Executive and Manager, PricewaterhouseCoopers, IBM, 1983-2009.

DC Office: 113 DSOB 20510, 202-224-6342, Fax: 202-228-2563, tillis.senate.gov

State Offices: Charlotte, 704-509-9087; Greenville, 252-329-0371; Hendersonville, 828-693-8750; High Point, 336-885-0685; Raleigh, 919-856-4630.

Committees: *Armed Services*: Airland; Personnel (RMM); Seapower. *Banking, Housing & Urban Affairs*: Economic Policy; Financial Institutions & Consumer Protection (RMM); Securities, Insurance & Investment. *Judiciary*: Competition Policy, Antitrust & Consumer Rights; Federal Courts, Oversight, Agency Action & Federal Rights; Immigration, Citizenship & Border Security; Subcommittee on Intellectual Property (RMM). *Veterans' Affairs*.

Group Ratings

	ADA	ACLU	AFL-CIO	LCV	COC	HAFA	ACU	CFG	FRC
2020	-	8%	-	15%	-	76%	78%	-	-
2019	0%	C	17%	21%	97%	C	79%	60%	100%

Almanac Ratings 2019-2020

	Economy	Social	Foreign	Composite
Liberal	6%	6%	5%	6%
Conservative	94%	94%	95%	94%

Key Votes of the 116th Congress

1. EPA clean energy rules	N	5. Russia sanctions	N	9. Barr as Atty. General	Y
2. U.S./Mex./Can. trade deal	Y	6. Troops in SYR, AFG	Y	10. Spending at the border	Y
3. Cut unemployment benefits	Y	7. Veto arms sales to Saudis	N	11. Coney Barrett to Sup. Ct.	Y
4. Shelton to Fed Reserve	Y	8. Defense $$$, veto override	Y	12. Electoral College objections	N

Election Results

Election	Name (Party)	Vote (%)		Cand. Spent	Ind. Exp. Support	Ind. Exp. Oppose
2020 General	Thom Tillis (R)	2,665,598	(49%)	$23,284,485	$18,051,939	$84,202,719
	Cal Cunningham (D)	2,569,965	(47%)	$52,659,824	$32,304,863	$90,807,771
	Shannon Bray (L)	171,571	(3%)			
2020 Primary	Thom Tillis (R)	608,943	(78%)			
	Paul Wright (R)	58,908	(8%)			
	Larry Holmquist (R)	57,356	(7%)			
	Sharon Y. Hudson (R)	54,651	(7%)			

Prior winning percentages: 2014 (49%)

Republican Thom Tillis, North Carolina's junior senator, won reelection in 2020 despite being Democrats' top target in a fiercely contested year; spending on the campaign totaled $300 million, making it the most expensive Senate race in history until two months later, when it was eclipsed by the Georgia runoffs. Tillis was vulnerable: He began the race with low approval ratings, having irked the state's conservative base in a demographically changing swing state. Polls for much of the race showed him trailing his Democratic challenger, Cal Cunningham, but he was able to ride President Donald Trump's coattails and hang on as Cunningham imploded amid a sex scandal; Tillis won by 95,633 votes out of nearly 5.5 million cast.

Tillis was born in Jacksonville Florida, one of five siblings. By the time he was 17, his family had moved 20 times, at one point living in a trailer park, as his parents sought work. While Tillis graduated near the top of his high school class, he and his siblings "weren't wired to go to college," he told an interviewer shortly after becoming state House speaker. He took a job as a warehouse records clerk—later earning a bachelor's degree in technology management, at 36, through University of Maryland-University College, a largely online institution. By that time, he was a partner at the international accounting and consulting firm PriceWaterhouseCoopers. He previously worked for now-defunct Wang Laboratories. He remained at PWC after it was taken over by IBM and advised banks and other corporations. It was his work for Charlotte-based NationsBank—which later became Bank of America after a merger—that brought him to North Carolina in 1998.

After he settled in Cornelius, a Charlotte suburb, his political rise was little short of meteoric. After getting his start as the president of the PTA at his daughter's high school, he served as a town commissioner before winning election to the state House in 2006. Four years later, Republicans flipped the state House and Tillis was chosen as the fifth GOP speaker in state history. He touted his business background in winning election to the House and later managing it. "A democratic institution is by definition not a business. But there is the business of running the Legislature, which I think we're doing pretty well," he told Business North Carolina magazine in 2012. Critics on the left, however, suggested a contradiction between Tillis' initial pragmatic political image and his later partisan persona.

A business-oriented conservative, Tillis helped enact laws that included restructuring North Carolina's tax code to reduce personal and business income taxes, eliminating the estate tax, and capping the gasoline tax. On his watch, state House Republicans also took on social issues. They passed bills to allow guns in bars and on college campuses and to require women to watch a narrated ultrasound before abortions. The abortion measure was later struck down by a federal judge. In 2013, the Tillis-led House created outrage among civil rights groups when it repealed a law allowing citizens to register to vote and cast a ballot on the same day while adopting a requirement that voters had to present one of six state-approved ID cards at the polls. Democrats attacked Tillis for those moves and for cutting funds from the University of North Carolina system and dragging his feet on teacher pay increases. Nonetheless, some conservatives griped that Tillis wasn't going far enough in pushing changes through the General Assembly.

Indeed, Tillis faced resistance from his right in taking on incumbent Sen. Kay Hagan, a Democrat, in 2014. While a programmatic social and fiscal conservative, he was not a fire-breather—and had no trouble picking up the support of the state's GOP establishment. That helped him prevail in an eight-way primary with 46 percent of the vote, more than the 40 percent needed to avoid a runoff. But for two months after the May primary, pressure from conservatives in the state House kept Tillis focused on his day job more than was helpful for a candidate in a nationally targeted race.

Hagan's seat was high on national Republican lists of pickup opportunities: The incumbent had ousted Republican Sen. Elizabeth Dole in 2008, a good year for Democrats when Barack Obama became only the second Democratic presidential nominee in more than four decades to carry North Carolina. Hagan had backed Obama on his chief legislative priorities. Tillis' main campaign objective was to tie Hagan to Obama, highlighting her support for the Affordable Care Act. He accused his rival of skipping an Armed Services Committee hearing on the threat of the Islamic State to raise campaign money, a particularly potent attack in a state with two large military bases and 800,000 veterans. If tea party activists in the state remained lukewarm at best toward his candidacy, Tillis had the support of major outside groups like Americans for Prosperity, American Crossroads and the U.S. Chamber of Commerce. These organizations spent months and millions of dollars attacking Hagan via television ads.

Hagan responded by campaigning against what she characterized as Tillis' extreme agenda on issues ranging from abortion to education to taxes. "At every opportunity he has fought for policies that are taking our state backwards," Hagan said during an October debate. "Speaker Tillis feels that those who have the most should get the most help." Hagan also emphasized her opposition to a statewide ban on same-sex marriage, which Tillis said he would continue to defend. The North Carolina Constitution's ban on same-sex marriage was overturned in 2014 by a federal judge, prompting Tillis to say during the October debate, "We're in a dangerous time in this country where the president has appointed liberal activist judges—and Sen. Hagan has endorsed them or confirmed them—that are literally trying to legislate from the bench."

As Hagan sought to turn out her base—focusing on equal pay for women, Tillis' opposition to a minimum wage increase and North Carolina Republicans' push to constrain ballot access— Tillis tightened his message: He hammered Hagan on national security issues like ISIS and the Ebola outbreak as well as problems at the Department of Veterans Affairs. Tillis edged Hagan 48.8%-47.2%, the Republicans' closest win of the election cycle; the margin was 45,000 votes out of more than 2.9 million cast. Polls showed neither candidate was well-liked on Election Day—but Obama's low popularity in the state likely was the crucial blow for Hagan. The contest stood as the most expensive Senate race in history at that time. Total spending in the Hagan-Tillis faceoff came to $111 million, with more than two-thirds of that, $77 million, from outside groups. Hagan outspent Tillis by more than 2-1.

In some of his early actions in the Senate, Tillis appeared much the same lawmaker who had steered the North Carolina House sharply to the right. He backed a state push to add anti-abortion "choose life" license plates and called the Department of Justice's investigation into the restrictive voting laws and gerrymandered congressional map he had helped pass in the state House a "waste of resources." He voted against Obama's nomination of Loretta Lynch, a North Carolina native, to be attorney general. But he did vote for a bill to give married same-sex couples Social Security and veterans' benefits they had earned, despite his opposition to same-sex marriage.

He actively reached out to Democrats, seeking to hit the reset button and shed the image he had brought to Capitol Hill. Just weeks after taking office, he became the only Republican to join 13 Democratic senators on a bill to create a mechanism for monitoring conflicts worldwide and detecting early warning signs that might enable the United States to prevent genocides. He also co-authored legislation with Democratic Sen. Tom Carper of Delaware to ensure payments made to eugenics victims did not affect their eligibility for federal benefits like Medicaid and food stamps. The measure, signed by Obama in late 2016, was aimed at protecting the victims of compulsory sterilization programs that operated in 33 states as recently as the 1970s.

Tillis, who first backed Florida Sen. Marco Rubio in the GOP's 2016 presidential primary but went on to become a steadfast Trump supporter, was circumspect after the New York businessman's and congressional Republicans' victories in 2016. "Since the election, I've heard some of my fellow Republicans claim that the party received a decisive mandate from voters," Tillis noted in an opinion column published in the Charlotte Observer. "Let's be clear: the American people didn't give the GOP a stamp of approval or a mandate to ram through an ideologically-driven, far-right agenda. If the election was a mandate for anything, it was for elected officials in both parties to break through the gridlock to finally start producing results."

When, early in his presidency, Trump issued an executive order imposing a temporary ban on immigration from seven predominantly Muslim countries, Tillis, Democrat Claire McCaskill of Missouri and New Hampshire Democrat Jeanne Shaheen sent a letter to the Defense Department protesting the treatment of two Iraqis who had aided U.S. forces but were detained at New York's John F. Kennedy International Airport. Tillis said he supported tighter screening of refugees but that "there is a lot of confusion surrounding the order" and that it needed to be "refined."

Tillis suggested he might not seek reelection unless a bipartisan criminal justice reform measure —within the jurisdiction of the Judiciary Committee, of which Tillis is a member—became law. The bill, intended to reduce mandatory minimum sentences for those with drug convictions and increase rehabilitation programs for prisoners, had cleared the Judiciary panel by a wide margin but was stalled in late 2016 by a handful of hard-line conservatives. It returned to the committee's agenda in 2017. Tillis made the issue one of his top priorities. "I don't run again until 2020, and if we're not able to get things like this done, I don't have any intention of coming back," he said to applause at a juvenile justice forum. "It is time to tell the far-left and the far-right to get productive or get out of the way because we need to solve this problem." With support from Trump's son-in-law, Jared Kushner, the First Step Act was enacted in the lame-duck session after the 2018 elections. Along with Democrat Maggie Hassan of New Hampshire and Republicans Joni Ernst of Iowa and Josh Hawley of Missouri, Tillis in December 2020 introduced legislation to make it easier for rape victims to sue companies that profit from videos of their assaults, like Pornhub.

Tillis downplayed his partisanship. In April 2018, he filed a bill limiting Trump's ability to interfere with special counsel Robert Mueller's probe into whether the 2016 Trump campaign had colluded with Russia. The measure would have allowed Mueller to appeal a possible removal— arguing for such protections regardless of which party controls the White House. Democrats praised the proposal, while many conservatives criticized Tillis and warned that Trump voters would react adversely. Separately, in response to threats from Russia, he created a bipartisan Senate group with Shaheen to demonstrate the chamber's commitment to NATO.

Tillis sided with Trump on other issues. He reportedly told a closed-door meeting of GOP activists that Supreme Court nominee Brett Kavanaugh "will be one of the greatest Supreme Court justices." In November 2018, he said that the president was right to send troops to the border with Mexico to stop illegal immigration. In what seemed a dramatic break, he wrote an op-ed published in the Washington Post in February 2019 saying he opposed Trump's plan to declare a national emergency at the southern border to use funds from other programs to finance a border wall. He cited his responsibility as a member of Congress to "preserve the separation of powers and to curb the kind of executive overreach that Congress has allowed to fester for the better part of the past century." But when the Senate voted in March on a resolution to reject the emergency plan, Tillis sided with Trump. That flip-flop soon drew an early primary challenge from wealthy businessman Garland Tucker, who spent $1 million on TV ads attacking Tillis over his initial opposition to the border wall funding. Garland, however, dropped out just before the December 2019 filing deadline.

Democrats targeted Tillis' seat as critical in their plans to take back the Senate. The Democratic Senatorial Campaign Committee lined up early behind former state Sen. Cunningham. He was a moderate veteran of Iraq and Afghanistan who had run for the Senate in 2010, also with the DSCC's backing, but had lost in the primary.

One of Cunningham's major attacks against Tillis was over heath care. Tillis had voted to repeal the Affordable Care Act, a move that could have harmed those with preexisting conditions —an argument that boosted Democrats in the 2018 midterms; and, when Tillis was state House speaker, the Legislature passed a bill preventing the governor from expanding Medicaid. Amid the COVID-19 pandemic, that criticism took on extra resonance. Cunningham also used Tillis' change of heart to allow military funds to be diverted to border wall funding, pointing out it could harm many of the state's military installments. (Trump siphoned money primarily from the Department of Defense.) Tillis hit back, trying to paint Cunningham as a party-line Democrat despite his opponent's efforts to straddle the middle, and he pointed out that Cunningham had voted to raise taxes in 2001 in the Legislature. The Republican's camp seized on a statement Cunningham made during a September debate that he would be "hesitant" to take a coronavirus vaccine developed under the Trump administration until more details were provided by health officials. "In the middle of a crisis, you don't undermine an effective process of the FDA," Tillis said, arguing that Cunningham's "statement puts lives at risk and it makes it more difficult to manage a crisis."

After Supreme Court Justice Ruth Bader Ginsburg's death in mid-September, Tillis backed the push by Trump and Sen. Mitch McConnell, then the majority leader, to confirm a conservative jurist to replace the liberal icon before the November election, using it to draw a contrast with Cunningham. "There is a clear choice on the future of the Supreme Court between the well-qualified and conservative jurist President Trump will nominate and I will support, and the liberal activist Joe Biden will nominate and Cal Cunningham will support, who will legislate radical, left-wing policies from the bench," Tillis said in a statement the day after Ginsburg's passing. Cunningham pointed out Tillis' seeming hypocrisy: The incumbent had blocked Obama's nomination of Merrick Garland to succeed Justice Antonin Scalia, died in February 2016-the previous presidential election year. "It should be the next president and the next Senate that takes this up, including if Trump is successful," Cunningham said in their final debate. "We should not do this in the midst of an election that is very, very divisive. We need to build up the legitimacy of this court and not continue to tear at it." Cunningham, like many Democratic Senate challengers, pulled in $6 million in online donations from ActBlue in the weekend after Ginsburg's death. But Tillis' support of the confirmation of Amy Coney Barrett to the vacancy may have boosted his standing with conservatives in the state.

Ultimately, October 2, 2020, may have been the most determinative day in the race. On the same day Trump was taken to Walter Reed National Military Medical Center to be treated for COVID-19, Tillis announced he'd also tested positive; he was likely infected at a Rose Garden event for Barrett, which ended up being a called a "super spreader event." That evening, there was an even bigger bombshell—suggestive text messages surfaced showing Cunningham had had an affair over the summer. The married father of two had made his values and integrity a central part of his appeal and the texts were a huge gift to Republicans. "If Cal Cunningham cheats and lies while he asks for your vote, he will continue to cheat and lie as your U.S. senator," Tillis retorted. Cunningham acknowledged his indiscretion: "I have hurt my family, disappointed my friends, and am deeply sorry. The first step in repairing those relationships is taking complete responsibility, which I do." A military investigation was also opened into the Army reservist for violating the code of conduct with his affair. But for the remainder of the race, Cunningham evaded the media and rarely appeared on the campaign trail. As Republican outside groups hammered Cunningham in broadcast ads over the revelations, polling in the race tightened.

Tills narrowly came out ahead, 48.7%-47%, running behind Trump by about 1.2 percentage points, while Cunningham trailed Biden's total by nearly 2 points. By winning a second term, Tillis broke the seat's record of flipping parties every six years since Elizabeth Dole succeeded Jesse Helms in 2002.

G.K. Butterfield (D)

Elected 2004, 9th full term, b. Apr 27, 1947; Wilson, NC; NC Central University, B.A., 1971; NC Central University School of Law, J.D., 1974; Baptist; Divorced; 3 children; 3 grandchildren.

Military Career: U.S. Army 1968-1997

Elected Office: NC Superior Court, 1988-2001, 2002-2004; NC Supreme Court, 2001-2002.

Professional Career: Practicing attorney, 1974-1988.

DC Office: 2080 RHOB 20515, 202-225-3101, Fax: 202-225-3354, butterfield.house.gov

State Offices: Durham, 919-908-0164; Wilson, 252-237-9816.

Committees: *Administration*: Elections (Chmn). *Energy & Commerce*: Communications & Technology; Energy; Health. *Joint Library*.

Group Ratings

	ADA	ACLU	AFL-CIO	LCV	COC	HAFA	ACU	CFG	FRC
2020	**	80%	**	100%	-	0%	5%	**	-
2019	95%	C	100%	93%	56%	C	5%	13%	0%

Almanac Ratings 2019-2020

	Economy	Social	Foreign	Composite
Liberal	100%	53%	92%	82%
Conservative	0%	47%	8%	18%

Key Votes of the 116th Congress

1. U.S./Mex./Can. trade deal Y	5. Russia sanctions Y	9. Firearms background checks Y
2. First Coronavirus response Y	6. Troops in Syria Y	10. Spending at the border N
3. HEROES Act Y	7. Veto arms sales to Saudis Y	11. Marijuana liberalized rules Y
4. CASH Act Y	8. Defense $$$, veto override Y	12. Electoral College objections N

Election Results

Election	Name (Party)	Vote (%)		Cand. Spent	Ind. Exp. Support	Ind. Exp. Oppose
2020 General	G.K. Butterfield (D)......................	188,870	(54%)	$494,183	$190	
	Sandy Smith (R)...............................	159,748	(46%)	$1,432,553	$100	$54

Prior winning percentages: 2018 (70%), 2016 (69%), 2014 (73%), 2012 (75%), 2010 (59%), 2008 (70%), 2006 (100%), 2004 Special (71%), 2004 (64%)

Democrat G.K. (George Kenneth) Butterfield, who won a special election in 2004, rarely makes headlines but has been a key behind-the-scenes strategist for Democratic leaders and a go-to force in the Congressional Black Caucus. He has been a close ally of Majority Whip James Clyburn of South Carolina, and has been a consistent voice for economic revival among low-income African Americans, especially in rural areas. In 2021, he took on two new leadership assignments.

Butterfield grew up in Wilson County, where his father was a dentist and the first Black elected official in Wilson in the 20th century; he lost his seat in 1957 when the White majority switched voting procedures to at-large elections. His mother was a schoolteacher for 48 years. In 1963, at age 16, Butterfield joined his father in Washington when Martin Luther King Jr. delivered his "I Have a Dream" speech. He got his bachelor's and law degrees from North Carolina Central University and participated in many registration drives after enactment of the Voting Rights Act. As a civil rights lawyer, Butterfield took on voting rights cases. He joined hospital employees at Duke University in their drive to organize a union. As a Superior Court judge for 12 years, he handled thousands of civil and criminal cases in 46 counties until 2001, when Democratic Gov. Michael Easley appointed him to the state Supreme Court. After Butterfield lost election in 2002 to a full-term, Easley appointed him as a special Superior Court judge.

He won the vacant House seat in a special election after first-term Rep. Frank Ballance resigned and soon pleaded guilty to personal benefit from his improper use of a charitable fund. Butterfield said his priorities would be strengthening the rural economy and halting job losses. He won 71%-27% and has not been seriously challenged since.

Butterfield has a solidly liberal voting record. He handled an array of racial-discrimination issues. He helped settle claims of up to 74,000 African-American farmers who were discriminated against when applying for Agriculture Department loans and programs between 1983 and 2010. He lobbied to include exhibits in the Capitol Visitor Center on the slave labor that was employed in building the Capitol and on the careers of the 22 African Americans who served in Congress during and after Reconstruction. He pressed Obama administration officials for the appointment of an African American to fill a vacancy for a federal judgeship in North Carolina's Eastern District.

A longtime friend of Clyburn, Butterfield managed his successful campaign for majority whip in 2006, then became a chief deputy whip under Clyburn. A longtime leader of the Black Caucus, he was less confrontational toward President Barack Obama than were other CBC members. Along with Clyburn, he was among the few who supported funding of the wars in Iraq and Afghanistan.

As CBC chairman, Butterfield led a delegation to Ferguson Missouri in 2015 to call for "transformative changes" nationwide in police practices. During a meeting of CBC members with Obama, he told the president that "Black America continues to be in a state of emergency." He met frequently with leaders of Silicon Valley to demand more diversity in the tech industry. At those meetings, and in an April 2018 hearing with Facebook CEO Mark Zuckerberg, he criticized the limited progress. An increase from 2 to 3 percent in the share of the workforce that is Black "does not meet the definition of building a racially diverse community," Butterfield said, urging a strategy to increase diversity in the tech industry.

In June 2020, following the killing of George Floyd while he was in police custody in Minneapolis, Butterfield played a leading role in assembling—with other members of the Congressional Black Caucus—the Justice in Policing Act and in convincing House Democrats to support the measure. "There is a need for bold, transformative legislation that will help change the culture of systemic racism in policing, and this legislation will do just that," he said, following its House passage. The Senate took no action on the measure.

With his connections to Democratic leaders, Butterfield has a seat on the influential Energy and Commerce Committee, where he has worked to prohibit states from passing on their Medicaid costs to counties. In his low-income district—with significant boundary changes from one redistricting to the next—many counties spend more of their property-tax revenues on Medicaid than on public schools. He has taken multiple steps to improve broadband access, especially in rural areas. "While broadband is widely available, the cost of access is often prohibitive, and some residents lack the skills to use the technology effectively," he wrote in The Hill in May 2019. He cited his own district as an example of the "troubling pattern" of racial discrimination, even among groups of similar income. In December 2020, he enacted in the yearend spending bill a provision cosponsored by Republican Rep. Adam Kinzinger to safeguard American telecommunications equipment against cyber threats from untrusted foreign equipment suppliers. On Energy and Commerce, he is next in line for a subcommittee chairmanship.

When Democrats had backroom discussions about changes in their leadership after they regained the majority in the 2018 election, Butterfield made the case for Clyburn to move up a notch or two. When Nancy Pelosi and Steny Hoyer clinched their bids to retain their top-two positions, Butterfield said Democrats needed to retain an African-American among their top leaders. With the growing prospect that some, or all, of those three will move on, Butterfield seems likely to join discussions on the transition. He positioned himself well in filling leadership vacancies in 2021—replacing Rep. Marcia Fudge as chairman of the Elections Subcommittee when she joined President Joe Biden's cabinet, and as senior chief deputy whip, where he succeeded the late Rep. John Lewis of Georgia.

NC-1: Northeastern North Carolina   Cook Partisan Voting Index: D+3

Population		Race and Ethnicity		Income	
Total	763,500	White	47.10%	Median Income	$47,469
Land area (sq. miles)	5,494	Black	44.50%	District Income Rank	403
Pop/ sq mi	138.96	Latino	9.00%	Poverty Rate	19.40%
Born in State	64.00%	Asian	1.80%	With health insurance	87.20%
		Two or more races	2.60%	Cash public assistance	1.40%
Age Groups		Other	3.90%	Food stamp/SNAP	16.60%
Under 18	20.40%				
18-34	25.30%	**Education**		**Work**	
35-64	37.20%	H.S grad or less	43.00%	White Collar	39.10%
Over 64	17.10%	Some college	28.20%	Sales and Service	38.00%
		College Degree, 4 yr	16.00%	Blue Collar	22.90%
Military		Post grad	12.90%	Government	14.70%
Veteran/ Active Duty	6.90%				

2020 Pres. Vote	Biden	190,041	(54%)	Trump	159,605	(45%)		
2016 Pres. Vote	Clinton	240,217	(67%)	Trump	108,565	(30%)	Johnson	7,041 (2%)

Rocky Mount, Goldsboro: In colonial days, the eastern portion of North Carolina was a smaller version of the Chesapeake Bay colonies of Virginia and Maryland. A fertile land laced by rivers and inlets, it had tobacco plantations and farms with docks on waterways accessible to the ocean and so to London. In 1890, James B. Duke founded the American Tobacco Co. in Durham and began mass production of cigarettes. Today, East Carolina survives with remnants of Tobacco Road and is still largely inhabited by descendants of the original white settlers and Black slaves of 250 years ago. They live in small towns and cities.

North Carolina's tobacco production, which peaked at 1 billion pounds in 1951, dropped to 250 million pounds in 2018 and the industry's political influence has diminished, though its production was 47 percent of the total nationwide. Tobacco sales to China were hit hard by President Donald Trump's trade war. More of the local business in this area has turned to hog farming, where its $2 billion in sales make North Carolina the third-largest state for production, behind Iowa and Minnesota. Food-processing plants have replaced textile mills. Reser's Fine Foods began operations locally in 1950 with a potato-salad recipe, and now has 3,000 employees who produce deli foods and salads in the United States and Mexico, with its headquarters in the tiny town of Halifax. CSX rail company has built the $214 million "Carolina Connector" intermodal terminal in Edgecombe County near Rocky Mount; it was scheduled to open in 2021, with the hope of more than 1,000 new local jobs. Rocky Mount also has gained prominence as a distribution center for the pharmaceutical and biotech industries.

The 1st Congressional District of North Carolina covers much of the old tobacco country of East Carolina. The new redistricting map in 2020 sliced the now-academic citadel of Durham from the western end of the district and moved south to add more rural areas, with small cities that have been losing jobs and population: Rocky Mount-based Nash County, Greenville-based Pitt County, Goldsboro-based Wayne County, plus adjacent Wilson and Greene counties; together, this new core constitutes 60 percent of the district. Goldsboro had a 22 percent drop in median income between 2000 and 2017, among the worst in the nation. These areas had been often-forgotten parts of the old 2nd, 3rd and 7th Districts.

The rest of the district is a swath of mostly rural, heavily African-American counties in the northeastern portion of the state. These are Democratic towns along North Carolina's coastal plain, including Roanoke Rapids, Tarboro, Williamston and parts of Albemarle Sound, but none of the Outer Banks. With the switch of Durham to the 4th District, the 1st is among the lowest in the nation in its median income. In rural Warren County, the Raleigh News & Observer reported in December 2018, a relic of Tobacco Road that was prosperous in the mid-20th century faces many of the problems common in rural America: "the loss of manufacturing, a decline in small farming and youth leaving for better opportunities."

Despite its African-American majority, the 2020 election showed that the district was politically divided. Joe Biden's 54%-45% win was his weakest performance in the state's five new Democratic districts and a drop of 13 percentage points from the vote for Hillary Clinton in the previous version of the 1sts.

Deborah Ross (D)

Elected 2020, 1st term, b. Jun 20, 1963; Philadelphia, PA; Brown University, B.A., 1985; University of NC Law School, J.D., 1990; Unitarian; Married (Stephen (Steve) J. Wrinn).

Elected Office: Majority Whip, NC House, 2006-2010; Minority Whip, NC House, 2011-2012; NC House, 2003-2013;

Professional Career: General Counsel, transportation service company, 2013-2015; Counsel, law firm, 2017-2018; Senior Lecturing Fellow, Duke Law School; Adviser, Business Ethics, Duke Kenan Institute for Ethics.

DC Office: 1208 LHOB 20515, 202-225-3032, Fax: 202-225-0181, ross.house.gov

State Offices: Raleigh, 919-334-0840.

Committees: *Judiciary*: Constitution, Civil Rights & Civil Liberties; Courts, Intellectual Property & Internet. *Rules*: Expedited Procedures; Legislative & Budget Process. *Science, Space & Technology*: Energy; Research & Technology.

Election Results

Election	Name (Party)	Vote (%)		Cand. Spent	Ind. Exp. Support	Ind. Exp. Oppose
2020 General	Deborah Ross (D)	311,887	(63%)	$1,681,050	$667	
	Alan Swain (R)	172,544	(35%)	$131,273		$113
	Jeff Matemu (L)	10,914	(2%)			
2020 Primary	Deborah K. Ross (D)	103,574	(70%)			
	Monika Johnson-Hostler (D)	33,369	(23%)			
	Andy Terrell (D)	8,666	(6%)			

Democrat Deborah Ross, a former state legislator and a longtime lawyer in Raleigh, was easily elected to the House in 2020. She was in the right place at the right time, after the Republican incumbent concluded that a court-approved redistricting map left him no realistic chance to win reelection and Democrats had little time to recruit a candidate for the seat. Having run a credible challenge to GOP Sen. Richard Burr in 2016, Ross had the name ID and experience to win the Democratic primary without serious opposition. In November, Ross flipped the district after Republicans failed to wage a serious challenge.

Ross, who was born in Philadelphia and grew up in Connecticut, got her bachelor's degree from Brown University and a law degree from the University of North Carolina. After a brief time in private practice, Ross in 1994 became North Carolina executive director of the American Civil Liberties Union, where she worked on an array of public-policy issues. She stepped down from that position in 2002, when she ran successfully for the state House. During 10 years of service, she chaired the Judiciary, Ethics and Election Laws Committees and held Democratic leadership positions in both the majority and minority.

In 2013, she resigned from the legislature and became legal counsel for Triangle Transit, the metro area's regional transit agency. Following her unsuccessful Senate campaign, Ross became a counselor in the Raleigh law firm of Smith, Moore Leatherwood, which later became part of Fox Rothschild, a national law firm. She taught for more than 10 years at Duke University law school.

In 2016, after Democrats failed in their attempts to recruit better-known candidates, Ross decided to challenge Burr, who was seeking his third Senate term. After winning the primary with 62 percent of the vote against three other candidates, Ross initially was not among the Senate Democrats' leading challengers. But she spent $20 million—to Burr's $12 million. Outside groups spent another $60 million on the contest.

Ross sought to paint Burr as a Washington insider, while accusing him of voting to privatize Medicare and cut Social Security benefits. Republicans said Ross' work with the ACLU showed that she was too liberal. She was boosted by two statewide factors: the unpopularity of Republican Gov. Pat McCrory, who lost in November to Roy Cooper, and her criticism of Burr for failing to speak out more forcefully against the so-called "bathroom bill"—which required transgender individuals to use bathrooms in government buildings consistent with the gender on their birth certificates.

By early August, a Wall Street Journal/Marist poll showed Ross leading Burr, 46%-44%. That poll also showed that Democratic presidential nominee Hillary Clinton led Republican Donald Trump by 9 points in North Carolina. As was the case throughout the nation in 2016, the Senate contest largely tracked the presidential campaign in North Carolina. Ultimately, the Republican Party's intensive focus on the state led Trump to a 50%-46% victory; Ross kept the Senate contest nearly as close, as Burr won 51%-45%.

Ross's political prospects were unexpectedly revived in 2019 when a three-judge state court panel ordered a new round of redistricting. A chief priority for the new map was to create a single House district that would consist of only Wake County. Once the new map was approved in December, Ross quickly announced her candidacy. Republican Rep. George Holding, who had served four terms, decided to retire and said the new district lines were a factor. Three other Democrats who had been running in the earlier version of the district withdrew from the contest.

Ross spent more than $700,000 in the primary, which was five times the total of the runner-up, Monika Johnson-Hosler, a member of the Wake County school board. Ross defeated Johnson-Hosler, 70%-22%. In November, she won 63%-35% against Republican Alan Swain, a retired Army colonel and first-time candidate.

In the House, her assignments to the Judiciary, Rules, and Science, Space and Technology committees likely would keep her busy and signaled that Democratic were confident that they could rely on her..

NC-2: Wake County

Cook Partisan Voting Index: D+12

Population		Race and Ethnicity		Income	
Total	888,547	White	71.80%	Median Income	$75,366
Land area (sq. miles)	3,247	Black	19.20%	District Income Rank	127
Pop/ sq mi	273.68	Latino	9.70%	Poverty Rate	9.60%
Born in State	54.80%	Asian	2.50%	With health insurance	90.40%
		Two or more races	2.70%	Cash public assistance	0.90%
Age Groups		Other	3.70%	Food stamp/SNAP	8.40%
Under 18	24.80%				
18-34	19.70%	**Education**		**Work**	
35-64	41.50%	H.S grad or less	31.30%	White Collar	45.30%
Over 64	14.10%	Some college	30.30%	Sales and Service	34.50%
		College Degree, 4 yr	25.60%	Blue Collar	20.20%
Military		Post grad	12.70%	Government	14.20%
Veteran/ Active Duty	9.00%				

2020 Pres. Vote	Biden	323,249	(64%)	Trump	171,017	(34%)		
2016 Pres. Vote	Trump	210,842	(53%)	Clinton	172,612	(43%)	Johnson	12,564	(3%)

Raleigh, Cary: A half-century ago, Raleigh was a sleepy state capital, moderately prosperous but not very big or showy, while the small cities to the east, such as Rocky Mount, had economies built around tobacco and textile factories. Now, Raleigh has become the center of Wake County—which, with Charlotte-based Mecklenburg—is one of two fast-growing counties that have become the large hubs of North Carolina. Wake County nearly doubled between 2000 and 2020, to a population of more than 1.1 million; Raleigh is nearly 45 percent of the total. In 2019, Wake surpassed Mecklenburg as the largest county in the state. Meanwhile, Rocky Mount and nearby small cities have seen a loss of their jobs and population. Once-rural roads to Raleigh are clogged in the morning with commuters headed for jobs in new office parks, and income levels have risen far above what they once were. Raleigh is 29 percent African American, compared with 21 percent for the county.

The 2020 redistricting map radically revamped the 2nd Congressional District from a mostly exurban area, where outlying parts of Wake County were about one-third of the area, to a new district entirely based in Wake, including nearly all of Raleigh. The new arrivals are changing the politics of Wake in multiple ways. The Democratic presidential vote in Wake grew from 49 percent of 349,000 total votes cast in 2004 to 62 percent of 794,000 votes in 2020. To accommodate the rapid growth, Raleigh officials shifted their transit plans from light-rail to diesel, and added bus service in dedicated lanes. They envision four "bus rapid transit" lines from downtown Raleigh by 2027. In July 2019, officials with the state's Regional Transportation Alliance announced they were studying the option of a "hyperloop" that would connect the three chief cities of the Triangle and the airport with an electric propulsion system that would operate at high speed in vacuum-like tunnels.

From 1990 to 2014, the Raleigh-Durham-Cary "combined statistical area" (in Census Bureau jargon) more than doubled in population, from 855,000 to 2.1 million. Locals joke that the fast-growing city of Cary is an acronym for "Containment Area for Retired Yankees." Just as Northern immigrants helped bring Republicanism to the South in the 1950s and 1960s, today they have made this the most heavily Democratic region in the state. Raleigh has long had an active Lebanese community, which celebrates an annual cultural festival. Zebulon is a growing business area, including the pharmaceutical firm GlaxoSmithKline, which employs nearly 2,000 and produces respiratory drugs and inhalers. In November 2019, UPS collaborated with CVS Pharmacy to make the first commercial distribution of medication by a drone.

Gregory Murphy (R)

Elected 2019, 2nd term, b. Mar 05, 1963; Raleigh, NC; Davidson College, B.S., 1985; University of NC School of Medicine, Chapel Hill, M.D., 1989; university of KY medical center, 1990; University of KY Hospital, 1994; Not Known; Married (Wendy Murphy); 3 children.

DC Office: 313 CHOB 20515, 202-225-3415, Fax: 202-225-3286, gregmurphy.house.gov

State Offices: Edenton, 252-368-8866; Greenville, 252-931-1003; Jacksonville, 910-937-6929; New Bern, 252-636-6612.

Committees: *Education & Labor*: Higher Education & Workforce Investment (RMM). *Veterans' Affairs*: Health.

Almanac Ratings 2019-2020

	Economy	Social	Foreign	Composite
Liberal	43%	42%	41%	42%
Conservative	57%	58%	59%	58%

Key Votes of the 116th Congress

1. U.S./Mex./Can. trade deal	Y	5. Russia sanctions	N/A	9. Firearms background checks	N/A
2. First Coronavirus response	Y	6. Troops in Syria	N	10. Spending at the border	N/A
3. HEROES Act	N	7. Veto arms sales to Saudis	N/A	11. Marijuana liberalized rules	N
4. CASH Act	N	8. Defense $$$, veto override	Y	12. Electoral College objections	Y

Election Results

Election	Name (Party)	Vote (%)	Cand. Spent	Ind. Exp. Support	Ind. Exp. Oppose
2020 General	Gregory Murphy (R)...................... 229,800	(63%)	$1,320,622	$67,695	$725,836
	Daryl Farrow (D)................................ 132,752	(37%)			

Republican Greg Murphy won a September 2019 special election that became an early test of the national party's attempt to boost its scant number of women in the House. A urologist and state representative, Murphy ran first among 17candidates in the GOP primary and then faced a runoff with Joan Perry, a pediatrician running with the endorsement of 13 Republican women in the House.

Despite heavy outside spending for Perry, Murphy easily won what some House Republicans billed as a "battle of the sexes" and sailed to victory in the solidly Republican district. He replaced 13-term Republican Rep. Walter Jones, who died in February 2019.

A native of Raleigh, Murphy graduated from Davidson College and got his medical degree at the University of North Carolina. After a brief residency in Kentucky, he began his practice as a urologist in Greenville. He served on several medical boards and practiced surgery at a 1,000-bed trauma center that served 29 counties in eastern North Carolina. He held multiple leadership positions throughout his career. Murphy was affiliate professor and chief of urology at East Carolina University School of Medicine. He traveled extensively to third-world countries including India, several parts of Africa, Nicaragua and Haiti as a medical missionary.

Murphy was elected in 2015 to the state House, where he chaired two health-related committees and focused on steps to combat the opioid crisis and reduce fraud and waste in the state's Medicaid program.

Following the death of Jones, who had been ill for several months, the special election drew a massive Republican field, including a county commissioner and the former president of a prominent conservative think tank. Murphy spent more than twice as much as any of the 16 other contenders and led with 23 percent to 15 per cent for Perry, who advanced to the runoff.

Murphy was endorsed by Rep. Mark Meadows of North Carolina, plus the Freedom Caucus, which he chaired. Murphy called attention to advertising by Perry in 2012 in a neighboring district on behalf of Democratic Rep. Mike McIntyre, who narrowly defeated a challenge from Republican David Rouzer; McIntyre retired two years later and Rouzer won the seat. Perry had financial support from the Winning for Women political action committee and the Susan B. Anthony List. The 13 Republican women in the House were eager to grow their ranks after bruising setbacks to other GOP women candidates in the 2018 election.

Perry insisted that she was not basing her campaign on gender. "I've never made a statement that I'm running based on the fact that I'm a woman. I'm running on my qualifications," she told Politico. Murphy won the runoff, 60%-40%. He defeated Democrat Allen Thomas, the former mayor of Greenville, 61%-37%.

In the House, Murphy has been active on the Education and Labor Committee. A fervent supporter of President Donald Trump, he tweeted in July during the presidential campaign, "I truly feel sorry for Joe Biden. He has dementia and is being set up by his own party."In October, he tweeted that the vice presidential nominee, Kamala Harris, "is a walking disaster. ... She was only picked for her color and her race." After North Carolina Democrats responded that Murphy was "racist and xenophobic," he deleted the tweet.

The outcome of the Murphy-Perry runoff spurred additional steps for diversity in the House GOP. In 2020, Republican women-centered groups made significant improvements with victories in competitive Republican primaries, which led to the election of women in strongly conservative districts in many states across the nation.

NC-3: Coastal North Carolina

Cook Partisan Voting Index: R+14

Population		Race and Ethnicity		Income	
Total	761,753	White	73.20%	Median Income	$53,545
Land area (sq. miles)	7,810	Black	19.80%	District Income Rank	354
Pop/ sq mi	97.53	Latino	8.40%	Poverty Rate	12.70%
Born in State	52.20%	Asian	1.40%	With health insurance	89.50%
		Two or more races	3.60%	Cash public assistance	2.60%
Age Groups		Other	2.00%	Food stamp/SNAP	12.90%
Under 18	21.50%				
18-34	25.00%	**Education**		**Work**	
35-64	35.70%	H.S grad or less	39.80%	White Collar	35.20%
Over 64	17.80%	Some college	34.90%	Sales and Service	39.70%
		College Degree, 4 yr	16.60%	Blue Collar	25.00%
Military		Post grad	8.70%	Government	19.20%
Veteran/ Active Duty	20.20%				

2020 Pres. Vote	Trump	227,009	(61%)	Biden	140,572	(38%)			
2016 Pres. Vote	Trump	198,972	(60%)	Clinton	120,964	(37%)	Johnson	8,490	(3%)

Jacksonville, Outer Banks: Nearly 500 years ago, Giovanni da Verrazano, a Florentine explorer under the flag of France, sailed past the Gulf Stream and landed on a sand spit island he thought was the outer edge of China. It was the Outer Banks of North Carolina. These are probably America's most unstable barrier islands, constantly changing shape and cut by new inlets as they are battered by ocean currents and storm winds. The islands were settled early by Europeans. Sir Walter Raleigh's Roanoke colony was founded here in 1587, near present-day Manteo, then vanished shortly thereafter when supply ships diverted themselves to loot Spanish galleons rather than deliver their badly needed cargo. Edward Teach, better known as Blackbeard, and other pirates lurked in Pamlico and Albemarle sounds behind the islets.

History is very much alive on the Outer Banks. An antique form of English is spoken by some on Ocracoke Island, reachable only by ferry and largely insulated from the commercialization of the upper islands. A pack of about 100 feral horses — believed to be the last remaining descendants of late-16th century Spanish mustangs — roams free in a 12,000-acre sanctuary in Corolla; fears of their extinction led the Fish and Wildlife Service to approve the introduction of other horses. The 208-foot lighthouse on Cape Hatteras, America's tallest, looks out on some of the most treacherous currents in the Atlantic. The sands along Kitty Hawk, with their winds, brought the Wright brothers to the Outer Banks to undertake mankind's first heavier-than-air flight in December 1903. The Outer Banks are prime vacation and retirement country, with affluent beachfront communities on both the coastal and sound side. Kill Devil Hills has the most millionaires per capita in the state. Those visitors benefit from a new 2.8 mile bridge from the mainland that opened in February 2019. Rising sea levels on the Outer Banks have raised concerns by residents and activists worried about climate change, though few seem worried enough to leave. In March 2020, at the start of the coronavirus pandemic, Dare and Currituck counties banned non-residents from getting access to their vacation properties.

Inland, vestiges of the area's 18th-century past can be seen in New Bern with its reconstructed Tryon Palace, the governor's house when this was the capital, and in the tiny, well-preserved town of Edenton on Albemarle Sound, where 51 women in 1774 protested the taxing of tea and cloth. It is considered the first women's political protest on American shores. Further south in Onslow County, amid swamps outside Jacksonville, is the Marine Corps' Camp Lejeune. With its 14 miles of beachfront and 80 live-fire ranges, it is home base for about 40,000 enlisted Marines and officers, and the Corps' largest installation; including families, veterans and civilian employees, the wider community is about 175,000 persons. On the other side of the Croatan National Forest is Cherry Point, the world's largest Marine Corps air station. That base planned to complete construction in 2023 of an aircraft hangar that would be the home for the first squadron of what were expected to be dozens of F-35 fighter jets.

The 3rd Congressional District of North Carolina covers the Outer Banks and the coastal plain of North Carolina from the Virginia border nearly to Wilmington. Redistricting in 2020 yielded minimal change: the loss of parts of Pitt County in exchange for Duplin County, which has been a center for hog production, plus chickens and turkeys. The three largest counties are in the southern end of the district: Onslow, Craven and Carteret.

David Price (D)

Elected 1996, 17th term, b. Aug 17, 1940; Erwin, TN; Mars Hill College, Att., 1959; The University of NC System, B.A., 1961; Yale University, B.D., 1964; Yale University, Ph.D., 1969; Baptist; Married (Lisa Kanwit Price); 2 children; 2 grandchildren.

Elected Office: U.S. House, 1986-1994.

Professional Career: Legislative aide, U.S. Sen. Bartlett, 1963-1967; Professor, Yale University, 1969-1973, Duke University, 1973-1986, 1995-1996; Executive Director, NC Dem. Party, 1979-1980, Chairman, 1983-1984; Staff Director, DNC Comm. on President Nominations, 1981-1982.

DC Office: 2108 RHOB 20515, 202-225-1784, Fax: 202-225-2014, price.house.gov

State Offices: Chapel Hill, 919-967-7924; Raleigh, 919-859-5999.

Committees: *Appropriations*: Homeland Security; State, Foreign Operations & Related Programs; Transportation, HUD & Related Agencies (Chmn). *Budget*.

Group Ratings

	ADA	ACLU	AFL-CIO	LCV	COC	HAFA	ACU	CFG	FRC
2020	**	83%	**	100%	-	0%	6%	**	-
2019	95%	C	100%	97%	58%	C	7%	12%	0%

Almanac Ratings 2019-2020

	Economy	Social	Foreign	Composite
Liberal	100%	100%	92%	98%
Conservative	0%	0%	8%	2%

Key Votes of the 116th Congress

1. U.S./Mex./Can. trade deal Y	5. Russia sanctions Y	9. Firearms background checks Y
2. First Coronavirus response Y	6. Troops in Syria Y	10. Spending at the border N
3. HEROES Act Y	7. Veto arms sales to Saudis Y	11. Marijuana liberalized rules Y
4. CASH Act Y	8. Defense $$$, veto override Y	12. Electoral College objections N

Election Results

Election	Name (Party)	Vote (%)		Cand. Spent	Ind. Exp. Support	Ind. Exp. Oppose
2020 General	David Price (D)	332,421	(67%)	$781,560	$920	
	Robert Thomas (R)	161,298	(33%)			$59
2020 Primary	David Price (D)	153,322	(87%)			
	Daniel Ulysses Lockwood (D)	23,564	(13%)			

Prior winning percentages: 2018 (72%), 2016 (68%), 2014 (75%), 2012 (75%), 2010 (57%), 2008 (63%), 2006 (65%), 2004 (64%), 2002 (61%), 2000 (62%), 1998 (57%), 1996 (54%%),1992 (65%), 1990 (58%), 1988 (58%), 1986 (56%)

Democrat David Price was first elected in 1986, lost the seat in 1994, and regained it in 1996. Since his return, he has distinguished himself as an influential Appropriations subcommittee "cardinal" and a thoughtful voice on education, security and urban issues. A longtime political science professor, Price has remained a working scholar who has shared his insights on Congress. His lengthy tenure places him among four House Democrats whose service began in January 1987, though he had a two-year break. Although he failed in a bid following the 2020 election to chair Appropriations, he remains an activist on multiple fronts.

Price grew up in East Tennessee, the son of a school principal and an English teacher. He is an interesting blend of political scientist, practical politician and lay Baptist preacher. He attended the University of North Carolina at Chapel Hill, worked as a young aide on Capitol Hill, earned a degree in divinity and a doctorate in political science at Yale University, and taught there for four years. In 1973, he became a political science professor at Duke. He was executive director of the North Carolina Democratic Party in the 1980 election season and chairman in 1983-84. With Democratic Gov. Jim Hunt, Price helped develop North Carolina's robust straight-ticket politics.

In 1986, he ran for the House and beat Republican freshman Rep. Bill Cobey. In 1994, Price lost the seat, 50.4%-49.6%, to Fred Heineman, a former New York City police officer and Raleigh police chief in the 1970s. Two years later, Price outspent Heineman in a rematch, winning 54%-44%.

Price has written four books about Congress, including The Congressional Experience, which focuses on his life as a lawmaker. The polarization of the two chambers has made him pessimistic about finding agreement to solve the nation's fiscal problems. "Our capacity to take them on in the bipartisan fashion that history teaches us is almost always necessary is far weaker" than it was in the 1990s, he said in 2010. Circumstances subsequently proved him correct, and they have worsened.

In the fourth edition of the book, which was published in April 2021, Price focused on changes in Congress during the Obama and Trump presidencies. "I spent a fair amount of time talking about the march toward centralization and the degree to which polarization is responsible for centralization," he told Dan Balz of The Washington Post. "This is certainly not the same institution in terms of where a member like myself gets a foothold or the kind of projects we undertake. That has really changed a great deal in my time there, and I'm trying to make that understandable."

His Education Affordability Act, which he considers his proudest achievement, was folded into the 1997 Balanced Budget Act. It made interest on student loans tax-deductible and allowed penalty-free withdrawals from individual retirement accounts for education expenses. Price founded and now chairs the House Democracy Partnership, a bipartisan, 20-member commission that seeks to strengthen democracy by mentoring more than a dozen legislatures across the world. In February 2020, he voiced concern about democracy at home when he scolded a Trump administration official that it "has no authority" to fail to spend appropriated block-grant funds in Puerto Rico.

From 2007 through 2010, Price chaired the Homeland Security Appropriations Subcommittee. He sought higher levels of spending for homeland security measures, like support for first responders, than were requested by the Bush administration. In 2007, the House passed Price's bill establishing a code of conduct for private security contractors in Iraq and Afghanistan. A target of the bill was North Carolina-based Black water, whose controversial activities in Iraq included the shooting of 17 people in a Baghdad square. After President Barack Obama took office, Price crafted spending bills that rejected the administration's proposal to hold criminal trials for terror suspects in New York City and restored budget cuts the administration had proposed for the Coast Guard. In 2010, he called increased drug trafficking and violence on the U.S. border "an emergency" that merited as much attention as the wars in Afghanistan and Iraq.

In 2015, Price switched to ranking Democrat on the Transportation, HUD Appropriations Subcommittee. He joined a bipartisan group of senior appropriators who strongly opposed a proposal from the Transportation and Infrastructure Committee to create a separate air traffic organization outside the Federal Aviation Administration and removed from the annual appropriations process. The oversight and funding role of Congress, they wrote, was critical "in the operation of our nation's air traffic system." As subcommittee chairman in 2019, he promised increased oversight of housing programs. In July 2020, he told North Carolina-based Spectrum News that the Trump administration was failing to enforce fair-housing rules. He added that both parties had fallen short in assuring sufficient affordable housing. Later that year, he voiced interest in chairing the full Appropriations panel, but he deferred to the more senior Rep. Rosa DeLauro.

Price has been active on campaign finance law. He sponsored the "stand by your ad" requirement for candidates to appear in the full frame of television ads reading their disclaimers on the air, so they would more likely be held responsible for negative ads. His proposal was enacted in the 2002 campaign reform law. He has sought a similar requirement for internet ads and said the Supreme Court's Citizens United decision allowing unlimited spending by corporations, labor unions and wealthy individuals contributed to the flow of misleading ads. "The least we can do is inform viewers who has bought the ads they are seeing," he said.

In 2019, the Democrats' House-passed "good government" legislation included Price's longstanding proposal to give a tax break for small campaign contributions. As vicechair of the House Democrats' democracy reform task force, he sought continued steps to restrain super PACs and to increase transparency by "dark money" groups. "Campaign disclosure requirements are outdated and fail to reflect the rapidly evolving digital world," he said in February 2021.

Price has nurtured local projects for appropriations support, including an Environmental Protection Agency complex in Research Triangle Park, plus defense- and technology-related programs for local universities. He helped to get the Obama administration's support to finance the Raleigh-to-Charlotte high-speed rail corridor.

Since his return to the House in 1996, Price has been reelected by wide margins. Democratic Rep. Brad Miller decided to retire rather than face Price in a primary following the 2012 redistricting. Although he faced another redistricting in 2022, at age 82, Price's handling of frequent redistricting changes—with various pieces of the Research Triangle—suggested that he might handle another round.

NC-4: Research Triangle   Cook Partisan Voting Index: D+16

Population		Race and Ethnicity		Income	
Total	873,270	White	60.00%	Median Income	$75,687
Land area (sq. miles)	1,045	Black	22.60%	District Income Rank	121
Pop/ sq mi	835.39	Latino	11.40%	Poverty Rate	10.30%
Born in State	42.60%	Asian	9.40%	With health insurance	90.70%
		Two or more races	2.60%	Cash public assistance	1.00%
Age Groups		Other	5.40%	Food stamp/SNAP	6.90%
Under 18	21.70%				
18-34	27.90%	**Education**		**Work**	
35-64	38.40%	H.S grad or less	22.10%	White Collar	54.50%
Over 64	11.90%	Some college	22.10%	Sales and Service	31.60%
Military		College Degree, 4 yr	31.20%	Blue Collar	13.80%
Veteran/ Active Duty	5.30%	Post grad	24.70%	Government	15.70%

2020 Pres. Vote	Biden	332,604	(66%)	Trump	160,812	(32%)			
2016 Pres. Vote	Clinton	281,535	(67%)	Trump	116,368	(28%)	Johnson	14,632	(4%)

Durham, Chapel Hill: Back in the 1950s, few people would have predicted that the countryside around Raleigh and Durham would become one of America's high-tech boom areas. But Democratic Gov. Luther Hodges did, and he started the 6,900-acre Research Triangle Park as a research and development industrial park between the musty state capital of Raleigh and the Lucky Strike-manufacturing city of Durham. With the drawing power of three universities—North Carolina State in Raleigh, Duke in Durham, and the University of North Carolina in Chapel Hill—Research Triangle Park slowly began attracting top R&D organizations, which in turn spawned a dynamic entrepreneurial sector. Today, this is among the top tech centers in the nation, with big-name employers that include IBM, Cisco Systems, GlaxoSmithKline and RTI International. Fidelity and Credit Suisse have brought the financial sector to the RTP. Slightly more than half of the 275 employers are in biotech and life sciences or information technology.

A sleepy metro area that once trailed the nation in income is now a vibrant, affluent metropolis and the prime engine of North Carolina's growth. The Triangle has one of the highest concentrations of Ph.D.'s in the nation. The chief population center is Durham, where the district takes in Duke University. Duke is an anchor for the Research Triangle area, whose facilities attract scholars from across the globe in a wide variety of fields and were ranked fourth in the nation in 2015 for tech jobs. The average salary for new researchers hired at the Triangle exceeds $100,000, Gov. Roy Cooper said in August 2020. The population of the county grew by 44 percent between 2000 and 2019, when it reached 322,000. Durham is overwhelmingly Democratic. Joe Biden took 80 percent of the county's presidential vote in 2020.

Even with all those Yankees, the region prides itself on its homier touches. Barbecue is a serious business here. College basketball is the other major preoccupation. UNC attracted different attention in August 2018 when student protestors took down the "Silent Sam" statue, a tribute to the Confederacy.

The 4th Congressional District of North Carolina is the core of the Research Triangle, with all of Durham County, all of Orange County—which includes Chapel Hill—and about one-fifth of Wake County. Together, these three counties are 78 percent of the district. The remainder of the district includes once-rural areas of Granville, Franklin and Chatham counties to the north and south, which have become more exurban as the RTP has grown. Chatham Park, which had been home to 4,000, was projected to grow to 60,000. Following completion in 2018 of a brewery, hotel and senior housing, new development was planned for a hotel and shops; the site had been a trailer park. In 2020, redistricting shifted the core of Raleigh to the new 2nd District in exchange for Durham from the old 1st District. The 2020 election results, with 66 percent for Joe Biden, virtually the same as 2012 and 2016, showed that its partisan mix did not change.

Rolesville is one of several fast-growing boom towns in Wake County, where farmlands have been converted into subdivisions and commercial development, Its population has increased from less than 1,000 in 2000 to 8,500 in 2019, with median household income about 50 percent higher than in the county as a whole.

Virginia Foxx (R)

Elected 2004, 9th term, b. Jun 29, 1943; Bronx, NY; Lees McRae College, 1961; Appalachian State Teachers College, Att., 1963; University of NC Chapel Hill, B.A., 1968; University of NC Chapel Hill, M.A., 1972; University of NC, Greensboro, Ed.D., 1985; Roman Catholic; Married (Thomas A. Foxx); 1 child; 2 grandchildren.

Elected Office: Watauga Board of Education, 1976-1988; NC Senate, 1994-2004.

Professional Career: Owner, Grandfather Mountain Nursery, 1976-2004; Professor, Assistant Dean of General College, Appalachian St. University, 1976-1985; President, May-land CC, 1987-1994.

DC Office: 2462 RHOB 20515, 202-225-2071, Fax: 202-225-2995, foxx.house.gov
State Offices: Boone, 828-265-0240; Clemmons, 336-778-0211.

Committees: *Education & Labor (RMM)*. *Oversight & Reform*: National Security; Select Investigative on the Coronavirus Crisis; Select Investigative on the Coronavirus Crisis; Select Investigative on the Coronavirus Crisis (RMM); Select Investigative on the Coronavirus Crisis (RMM); Select Investigative on the Coronavirus Crisis (RMM); Select Investigative on the Coronavirus Crisis (RMM); Select Investigative on the Coronavirus Crisis; Select Investigative on the Coronavirus Crisis (Chmn).

Group Ratings

	ADA	ACLU	AFL-CIO	LCV	COC	HAFA	ACU	CFG	FRC
2020	**	12%	**	10%	-	87%	93%	**	-
2019	5%	C	24%	10%	74%	C	94%	88%	100%

Almanac Ratings 2019-2020

	Economy	Social	Foreign	Composite
Liberal	25%	31%	27%	28%
Conservative	75%	69%	73%	72%

Key Votes of the 116th Congress

1. U.S./Mex./Can. trade deal Y	5. Russia sanctions Y	9. Firearms background checks N
2. First Coronavirus response Y	6. Troops in Syria Y	10. Spending at the border Y
3. HEROES Act N	7. Veto arms sales to Saudis N	11. Marijuana liberalized rules N/A
4. CASH Act N	8. Defense $$$, veto override Y	12. Electoral College objections Y

Election Results

Election	Name (Party)	Vote (%)		Cand. Spent	Ind. Exp. Support	Ind. Exp. Oppose
2020 General	Virginia Foxx (R)	257,843	(67%)	$1,419,400	$9,559	
	David Wilson Brown (D)	119,846	(31%)	$57,071		
	Jeff Gregory (C)	7,555	(2%)			

Prior winning percentages: 2018 (57%), 2016 (58%), 2014 (61%), 2012 (58%), 2010 (66%), 2008 (58%), 2006 (57%), 2004 (59%)

Republican Virginia Foxx, first elected in 2004, is a vocal conservative who has been savvy in gaining influence. She held a Republican leadership position for four years, and then chaired the House Education and the Workforce Committee for two years. A former teacher and university administrator, she pledged to cut back on federal rules and return education policy to a more traditional state-federal relationship. Her sweeping proposal to overhaul federal higher-education programs stalled in 2018. Term-limited in her top GOP position at the Education Committee in 2022, at age 79, she faced redistricting uncertainty and the prospect of a serious primary challenge.

Foxx grew up in the hardscrabble hollows of western North Carolina; she lived in a home that didn't have running water or electricity until she was 14. She got her bachelor's in English from the University of North Carolina in Chapel Hill and her doctorate in education from UNC-Greensboro, and had a diverse background before she was elected to Congress. She owned with her husband a nursery and landscape company, and she taught sociology and was assistant dean of the General College at Appalachian State University. Later, she was president of Mayland Community College. She served 12 years on the Board of Education of Watauga County. In 1994, Foxx was elected to the state Senate, where she sponsored a constitutional amendment to ban same-sex marriage and a bill to deny Social Security benefits to undocumented immigrants. She actively supported gun rights and home schooling, and she opposed abortion rights.

In 2004, Foxx was one of five candidates in a hotly contested Republican primary for an open seat. Winston-Salem Councilman Vernon Robinson, a retired Air Force officer who campaigned as "the Black Jesse Helms," finished first with 24 percent of the vote. Foxx was second, with 22 percent, just 511 votes ahead of Ed Broyhill, the son of former Republican Sen. James Broyhill. In a hard-fought, four-week runoff campaign, Robinson aired several ads highlighting his tough stance on illegal immigration. Foxx warned voters that Robinson's aggressive style would make him a weak general election candidate who would lose the district for the GOP. She won 55%-45%. In the general election, Foxx won relatively easily, 59%-41%.

Foxx has been close to House GOP leaders and has had a nearly perfect conservative record in the Almanac vote ratings. She was elected Republican Conference secretary in 2012 when she was one of three women to take leadership roles that year.

Foxx has not been afraid to speak her mind in her homespun style. She was one of only 11 House members who voted against a $52 billion relief bill following Hurricane Katrina in 2005 because, she said, there was too little accountability in how the money would be spent. During the health care debate in 2009, she remarked that the public had more to fear from the legislation than from terrorists. During debate on a hate crimes bill named for Matthew Shepard, a Wyoming man tortured and murdered allegedly because of his sexual orientation, she said naming the bill for Shepard was "a hoax" because, she argued, he wasn't gay. She later apologized. Republican leaders saw her as a useful attack dog.

On the Education Committee, Foxx has said the Education Department imposes burdensome regulations on colleges. She is an advocate of for-profit colleges and community colleges. On talk radio in 2012, she expressed her disdain for students complaining about overly burdensome loans. "I have very little tolerance for people who tell me that they graduate with $200,000 of debt or even $80,000 of debt, because there's no reason for that." President Barack Obama later repeated her remarks at a campaign stop at the University of North Carolina. "Can you imagine saying something like that?" he asked. Still, Foxx found common ground with Obama in 2013 during renewal of the student loan program. They tied the rate to the 10-year Treasury bond in what Foxx termed a "market-based approach."

When the chairmanship of the committee opened in 2016, Foxx was eager to take the post. She had curried favor with GOP leaders and Republicans were about to lose their only woman chair. Foxx won the position without opposition. At the committee, her targets have included overtime rules at the Department of Labor, plus restrictions imposed by the National Labor Relations Board. In March 2017, Foxx was one of three House chairs who brought the leadership-drafted American Health Care Act to the House floor, where it was pulled because Republicans were divided on how to replace Obamacare. After additional tinkering, the bill passed in early May but subsequently died in the Senate.

Her chief initiative was her PROSPER (Promoting Real Opportunity, Success and Prosperity through Education Reform)Act to add performance standards for most universities and roll back many regulations on academia, especially on the for-profit and online education sectors. "A hard truth that students, families and institutions must face is that the promise of a postsecondary education is broken," Foxx said, in releasing the proposal in December 2017. The proposal was opposed by committee Democrats and received scant support from most of the traditional education groups in Washington, who had grown comfortable with status quo. Education Secretary Betsy DeVos supported the measure. By June 2018, Inside Higher Education reported "vocal opposition" to the legislation and doubts among many Republicans. Sen. Lamar Alexander of Tennessee, who chaired the counterpart Senate committee, had decided to defer the issue for the year. On the defensive, when Democrats took House control following the 2018 election, Foxx failed on a House vote in July 2020 to remove a Democratic provision in the defense spending bill to restrict the options for military service members and veterans to attend for-profit schools.

In her safely Republican district, Foxx typically was reelected by modest margins against low-profile opponents. In 2012, the Winston-Salem Journal, the largest newspaper in her district, endorsed her Democratic challenger, Elisabeth Motsinger. The newspaper said Foxx "has accomplished little" for the district and "represents the calcification of the political process and is therefore an impediment to reasoned political compromise." She was reelected, 58%-42%, and remained popular with her political base. In 2016, she was challenged in the Republican primary by Pattie Curran, who said that Foxx had moderated her views. "She's establishment and I'm not," Curran told a local reporter. Foxx won 68 percent of the vote and easily took every county.

In 2020, the court-ordered redistricting plan radically changed Foxx's district—removing Winston Salem-based Forsyth County and making Gaston County its new population center. Tracy Philbeck, the veteran chairman of the Gaston County Board of Commissioners, said he had been encouraged to run a primary challenge to Foxx in the two weeks after the plan was approved and before the filing deadline. But he decided not to run after Foxx "asked me to partner with her to be a strong unified voice for the needs and conservative values [of] Gaston County," he said in a statement. She was reelected without Republican opposition and defeated David Brown, 67%-31%. Other than traditionally Democratic Watauga County, where Brown led with 52 percent, Foxx's 63 percent in Gaston was her weakest county. The delay in drawing a new redistricting map for 2022 seems likely to create added uncertainty for Foxx, Philbeck and others.

NC-5: West-central North Carolina

Cook Partisan Voting Index: R+20

Population		Race and Ethnicity		Income	
Total	765,013	White	79.30%	Median Income	$49,376
Land area (sq. miles)	3,572	Black	14.70%	District Income Rank	391
Pop/ sq mi	214.18	Latino	10.00%	Poverty Rate	15.70%
Born in State	64.00%	Asian	1.50%	With health insurance	87.90%
		Two or more races	2.10%	Cash public assistance	1.30%
Age Groups		Other	2.40%	Food stamp/SNAP	11.20%
Under 18	20.40%				
18-34	22.70%	**Education**		**Work**	
35-64	38.30%	H.S grad or less	42.00%	White Collar	36.40%
Over 64	18.50%	Some college	31.30%	Sales and Service	38.10%
		College Degree, 4 yr	16.90%	Blue Collar	25.40%
Military		Post grad	9.90%	Government	12.10%
Veteran/ Active Duty	6.40%				

2020 Pres. Vote	Trump	265,677	(67%)	Biden	124,652	(32%)		
2016 Pres. Vote	Trump	205,332	(57%)	Clinton	142,369	(39%)	Johnson	10,302 (3%)

Gastonia, Boone: From the Atlantic Ocean, the terrain of North Carolina rises slowly through the Piedmont, a transitional land of modest hills that lies between the coastal plain and the Blue Ridge Mountains. The Blue Ridge, named for the mysterious blue haze that blankets it, provides the headwaters of the New River—ironically named given that it is the oldest river in North America —which cuts majestic crevasses in a state park as it flows north near the border with Virginia and Tennessee.

After the Civil War, the surfeit of cheap labor and fast-flowing streams on the Piedmont made it a perfect locus for manufacturing. This hardscrabble country around the county seats of Lenoir and Morganton became a manufacturing area. Textile mill owners moved their operations from New England to western North Carolina for its low-wage workforce. By the end of the 19th century, North Carolina had more textile plants than Connecticut, Maine or Vermont. These companies relied on the "Rhode Island model" of development, where towns were put up around the mills and whole families were placed in small, company-owned homes. Ground zero for the industry was Gaston County and nearby towns. By the 1930s, there were 570 mills within a 100-mile radius of Gastonia. The relationship between workers and management was often uneasy. Gastonia was the site of a massive strike at Loray Mills in the late 1920s, led by the communist-dominated United Textile Workers, which erupted in violence and resulted in the deaths of the local police chief and Ella May Wiggins, the unofficial balladeer of the union who penned tunes such as "A Mill Mother's Song" and "The Big Fat Boss and the Workers." Today, the textile industry is in decline and Gastonia has slower growth than most of the area surrounding Charlotte. Gaston County has explored options to extend light-rail service from Charlotte, which could also serve the Charlotte airport.

The western parts of the state have remained largely rural. Places of interest include chicken-raising Wilkes County and Appalachian State University in Boone (named for Daniel), which has become a center for resurgent pride in the culture of Appalachia. Pre-pandemic, the student population of about 19,000 exceeded the population of the town. The only local area of Democratic strength is in Watauga County, with the university. In 2018, NBC News profiled economically struggling Wilkes County, where half the residents are evangelical Christians, as an example of the changing Republican Party. Residents referred to President Donald Trump, who got 78 percent of the vote in 2016, as "the last hope for an America in decline."

All these places are in the 5th Congressional District of North Carolina. Although the district remained heavily Republican, redistricting radically reshaped what was an east-west configuration in the state's northwest corner to a north-south link to Gaston that connects the Virginia and South Carolina borders. Winston-Salem, which was the center of the old 5th, shifted to the now-urban 6th District. About 70 percent of the population is in the southern end of the district, including Gaston, which is the largest county, plus Caldwell, Burke, Cleveland and part of Rutherford County.

Kathy Manning (D)

Elected 2020, 1st term, b. Dec 03, 1956; Detroit, MI; Harvard University, B.A., 1978; University of MI Law School, J.D., 1978; Jewish; Married (Randall Kaplan); 3 children.

Professional Career: Partner, law firm, 1987-2021.

DC Office: 415 CHOB 20515, 202-225-3065, Fax: 202-225-8611, manning.house.gov

State Offices: Greensboro, 336-333-5005.

Committees: *Education & Labor*: Early Childhood, Elementary & Secondary Education; Higher Education & Workforce Investment. *Foreign Affairs*: Asia, the Pacific, Central Asia, Nonproliferation; Middle East, North Africa & Global Counterterrorism.

Election Results

Election	Name (Party)	Vote (%)		Cand. Spent	Ind. Exp. Support	Ind. Exp. Oppose
2020 General	Kathy Manning (D)	253,531	(62%)	$1,529,188	$2,298	
	Lee Haywood (R)	153,598	(38%)	$54,447		$113
2020 Primary	Kathy Manning (D)	56,986	(48%)			
	Rhonda Foxx (D)	23,506	(20%)			
	Bruce Davis (D)	17,731	(15%)			
	Derwin Montgomery (D)	14,705	(13%)			

Democrat Kathy Manning, an immigration lawyer and longtime Democratic fundraiser, was elected to the House in 2020. After running a competitive challenge to a House Republican two years earlier, she was the beneficiary of court-ordered redistricting that created a solidly Democratic seat ideally suited for her. Republican Rep. Mark Walker, who had represented much of the area, decided not to seek another term.

Manning was born and raised in Detroit. Her father worked for Ford Motor Company for 40years and her mother was a school teacher. She got her bachelor's degree from Harvard University and a law degree from the University of Michigan. After graduating, she moved to Greensboro, which was the hometown of her husband, Randall Kaplan, and where his family owned a large chemical company. Manning was a partner in an immigration law firm and later started her own legal practice dealing with immigration issues..

Manning held leadership positions with several local charitable organizations, including United Way, the Community Foundation of Greater Greensboro, a performing arts center and the University of North Carolina at Greensboro. Nationally, she was the first woman to chair the Jewish Federations of North America. She and her husband were large contributors to the Democratic Party on state and national levels.

In 2018, Manning challenged Republican Rep. Ted Budd in her first political campaign. Citing her own experience with her daughter, Manning focused on the high costs of medical care and prescription drugs—especially for patients with pre-existing conditions. Manning outspent Budd, $4.1 million to $2 million. In a local appearance on the eve of the election, House Speaker Paul Ryan warned of a "green wave of [campaign] money coming at us." In the Republican-leaning district, Manning lost, 52%-46%; she got 62 percent of the vote in Greensboro-based Guilford County, which cast about one-third of the total vote.

In December 2019, a three-judge state court panel approved a new redistricting map that created a Democratic-leaning district based in Greensboro. With encouragement from the Democratic Congressional Campaign Committee, Manning announced her candidacy for the new district. "This is a natural district. It's the Triad district," Manning told the Greensboro News & Record in describing the new district that also included much of High Point and Winston-Salem. "For so many years, we have been trying to build up an economy as the Triad's. This district fits that."

Four other candidates, all African Americans, entered the Democratic primary. Combined, they spent less than one-fourth of the $1.1 million Manning spent in the primary. Some of her opponents complained that national Democrats favored Manning. "We are told to come to the polls, but we are not supported on the ballot," Rhonda Foxx, a lawyer and former chief of staff to Rep. Alma Adams of North Carolina, said in a pre-primary interview with Roll Call, a publication that covers Congress. "I am very concerned about the state and condition of Black women in American politics."

Manning won the primary with 48 percent of the voter; Foxx was the runner-up with 20 percent. In November, Manning won 62%-38% against Lee Haywood, a small businessman and first-time candidate. She matched her 62 percent in Guilford County from two years earlier and got 63 percent in Winston Salem-based Forsyth.

In the House, she got seats on the Education and Labor, and Foreign Affairs committees.

NC-6: Greensboro, Winston-Salem, High Point   **Cook Partisan Voting Index: D+10**

Population		Race and Ethnicity		Income	
Total	791,470	White	70.90%	Median Income	$54,132
Land area (sq. miles)	3,675	Black	19.90%	District Income Rank	344
Pop/ sq mi	215.39	Latino	10.50%	Poverty Rate	15.60%
Born in State	63.20%	Asian	1.70%	With health insurance	88.50%
		Two or more races	3.00%	Cash public assistance	1.50%
Age Groups		Other	4.50%	Food stamp/SNAP	13.80%
Under 18	22.20%				
18-34	19.90%	**Education**		**Work**	
35-64	39.70%	H.S grad or less	45.10%	White Collar	33.50%
Over 64	18.00%	Some college	29.60%	Sales and Service	38.60%
		College Degree, 4 yr	16.40%	Blue Collar	28.00%
Military		Post grad	8.90%	Government	13.40%
Veteran/ Active Duty	7.00%				

2020 Pres. Vote	Biden	257,257	(61%)	Trump	155,401	(37%)		
2016 Pres. Vote	Trump	201,385	(56%)	Clinton	148,693	(41%)	Johnson	8,741	(2%)

Greensboro: The lower Piedmont lands of North Carolina were first settled by independent-minded Scots-Irish farmers and by followers of British and German sects like the Moravians. This was hardscrabble farm country before the Civil War, with few slaves. By the late 19th century it was becoming industrialized, with textile mills alongside streams, furniture factories not far from hardwood forests, and R.J. Reynolds' cigarette factories in the growing city of Winston-Salem.

Today, the Winston-Salem area's pharmaceutical companies, banking institutions and high-skill Piedmont factories have largely supplanted the tobacco and textile industries. At a former R.J. Reynolds Tobacco plant, the booming Wake Forest Innovation Quarter focuses on medical education and biotech research. A smaller and more urban version of the Research Triangle less than 100 miles to the east, it is a broad partnership among the city, state, university and a private developer, with 3,700 workers in more than 170 companies, five colleges with 1,800 degree-seeking students and 8,000 workforce trainees. The biennial National Black Theater Festival, which drew more than 60,000 attendees in 2017, has become a prominent weeklong event.

For more than half a century, furniture store managers and owners from all over the country twice a year have converged on the huge Furniture Mart in High Point, the center of the U.S. furniture business. The giant trade show put on by manufacturers has attracted about 75,000 visitors and 2,000 exhibitors from 100 nations. The furniture business grew here early in the 20th century because of the hardwoods in the mountains not far to the west and the abundance of low-wage labor in the flatlands not far to the east. For many years, the furniture business has proven more resilient than textiles and tobacco. Recently, it has faced serious competition from China, though it continues to call itself the "Furniture Capital of the World." The North Carolina Commerce Department estimated that more than 35,000 workers were employed statewide in furniture manufacturing. The industry has become increasingly tech-oriented to cut costs and increase efficiency. The High Point Market Authority canceled its spring market in 2020 due to the coronavirus—the first cancellation of its semi-annual market since World War II. The markets have been described as the largest economic events in North Carolina each year.

The Triad area—Greensboro, High Point and Winston-Salem—has scrambled for new sources of economic growth to keep pace with booming Raleigh-Durham and Charlotte. In 2018, Site Selection magazine ranked the area second in the nation for its appeal to new and expanded businesses. FedEx has a hub at Piedmont Triad International Airport, between Winston-Salem and Greensboro. That has led other firms to plan distribution centers to utilize the "aerotropolis," otherwise known as a city built around an airport.

The 6th Congressional District of North Carolina was radically reshaped by redistricting in 2020. What had been mostly rural parts of the Piedmont plus the eastern parts of greater Greensboro, became almost entirely urban—including all of the Triad, except for a small corner of Winston-Salem that became part of the 10th District. The remainder of Greensboro shifted from the 13th District; Winston-Salem had been in the 5th. The new district includes 70 percent of Winston-Salem-based Forsyth plus all of Guilford County, which is two-thirds of the district. The changes recast a solidly Republican district to one of the state's two new Democratic districts, along with the Raleigh-based 2nd District. Joe Biden took 62 percent in the new district.

David Rouzer (R)

Elected 2014, 4th term, b. Feb 16, 1972; Landstuhl, Germany; Fund for American Studies; NC State University, B.A., 1994; NC State University, B.S., 1994; Southern Baptist; Single.

Elected Office: NC Senate 2009-2012.

Professional Career: PAC coordinator, 1996; Congressional aide, 1996-2000, 2001-2005; University official, 2000-2001; Administrator, U.S. Department of Agriculture, 2005-2006; Owner, consulting company, 2006-present; Owner, cleaning products business, 2009-present.

DC Office: 2439 RHOB 20515, 202-225-2731, Fax: 202-225-5773, rouzer.house.gov

State Offices: Bolivia, 910-253-6111; Four Oaks, 919-938-3040; Wilmington, 910-395-0202.

Committees: *Agriculture*: General Farm Commodities & Risk Management; Livestock & Foreign Agriculture. *Transportation & Infrastructure*: Highways & Transit; Water Resources & Environment (RMM).

Group Ratings

	ADA	ACLU	AFL-CIO	LCV	COC	HAFA	ACU	CFG	FRC
2020	**	12%	**	14%	-	93%	87%	**	-
2019	0%	C	24%	7%	73%	C	88%	86%	100%

Almanac Ratings 2019-2020

	Economy	Social	Foreign	Composite
Liberal	25%	4%	27%	19%
Conservative	75%	96%	73%	81%

Key Votes of the 116th Congress

1. U.S./Mex./Can. trade deal	Y	5. Russia sanctions	Y	9. Firearms background checks N
2. First Coronavirus response	Y	6. Troops in Syria	Y	10. Spending at the border Y
3. HEROES Act	N	7. Veto arms sales to Saudis	N	11. Marijuana liberalized rules N
4. CASH Act	N	8. Defense $$$, veto override	Y	12. Electoral College objections Y

Election Results

Election	Name (Party)	Vote (%)	Cand. Spent	Ind. Exp. Support	Ind. Exp. Oppose
2020 General	David Rouzer (R)............................	272,443 (60%)	$566,371	$8,062	
	Christopher M. Ward (D)................	179,045 (40%)			$19

Prior winning percentages: 2018 (56%), 2016 (61%), 2014 (59%)

Republican David Rouzer was elected in 2014 as the first Republican to represent southeastern North Carolina since the late 19th century. He settled in at the Agriculture Committee and was influential in the enactment of the farm bill in 2018. In 2021, he switched his chief committee interest to water resources and other public-works projects. Rouzer has styled himself as an expert in public relations and legislative strategy.

Rouzer was born in Landstuhl Germany and was raised in Durham North Carolina. He attended North Carolina State University's College of Agriculture, where he received his bachelor's degree in three majors: agricultural business management, agricultural economics and chemistry. In Washington, he was an aide to home-state Republican senators Jesse Helms and Elizabeth Dole; a Bush administration appointee in the Agriculture Department; and a lobbyist for tobacco companies.

During four years in the state Senate, Rouzer co-chaired the Agriculture and Environment Committee. He became known for his vocal support of a North Carolina law banning the state's use of scientific predictions of how much sea level will rise in developing coastal policy. The law, passed in 2012, drew criticism from environmental groups, which said it amounted to denial of scientific evidence of climate change.

In 2012, Rouzer challenged centrist Democratic Rep. Mike McIntyre, an independent and once-untouchable incumbent. Rouzer had more than $4 million in support from party groups; McIntyre had $1.9million in party assistance and spent $2.3 million of his campaign funds. McIntyre squeaked out a 50.1%-49.9% win, a lead of 654 votes. When McIntyre announced his retirement after nine terms, the seat became an easy pickup for Republicans in 2014.

The real contest was in the primary, where Rouzer's chief opponent was attorney Woody White. The campaign got nasty: White accused Rouzer of being a Beltway lobbyist, and Rouzer derided White's work as a trial lawyer. With more money, more establishment support and more name recognition, Rouzer won, 53%-40%. Democratic nominee Jonathan Barfield, a commissioner in New Hanover County, said he did not want to see U.S. boots on the ground in Syria. National Democrats and their allies had no presence in their longtime bastion. Rouzer spent nearly $1.5 million for the entire campaign, compared with $60,000 for Barfield, and won 59%-37%.

Rouzer got a rare chairmanship for a freshman at the Agriculture Subcommittee on Livestock and Foreign Agriculture, which was well-suited to his background. He talked up export promotion and "the overarching benefits that market development funding brings the U.S. agricultural industry as a whole." He noted growing concerns about devastating animal diseases, especially for livestock, and "the linkages between agriculture and national security." On the House-Senate conference committee that crafted the final version of the 2018 farm bill, Rouzer took credit for two provisions: $300 million in mandatory funding for research and coordination for animal disease preparedness, and $150 million for deployment of a U.S. vaccine bank for foot and mouth disease.

Rouzer was a rare House Member from a coastal district who supported offshore drilling in the Atlantic Ocean. He looked after other coastal needs, as he secured in the 2020 yearend spending bill additional funding for Wrightsville Beach, which needed beach nourishment [i.e., more sand] following storm damage. That was a preview of the work that Rouzer would pursue, starting in January 2021, as the ranking Republican on the Transportation and Infrastructure Subcommittee on Water Resources and Environment—an apt assignment for a House member in a district with long ocean-front. He promised more "attention to mitigation efforts that will better protect property, enhance conservation efforts, and save precious taxpayer dollars when natural disasters hit."

Rouzer breezed to a routine reelection in 2016 against Wesley Canteen, a CPA and attorney in Wilmington. Casteen had run in the 7th as an independent in 2014 and got 4 percent of the vote. This time, he rallied the Democratic base vote, but little more. Rouzer outraised him nearly 100-to-1 and won, 61%-39%.His 2018 contest was a more competitive challenge from Kyle Horton, an internal-medicine physician. Horton, who opposed off-shore seismic testing and drilling for oil and gas, took issue with Rouzer and said their district was "definitely at the epicenter of so many climate challenges." Rouzer outspent Horton, $1.4 million to about $900,000. In a Democratic year, he won more narrowly, 56%-43%; Horton took Wilmington-based New Hanover by nearly 5,000 votes. Following another redistricting in 2020, his opponent spent $5,000 and Rouzer took 60 percent of the vote and won all of the counties, including New Hanover by 4,000 votes.

During the 2020 presidential campaign, Rouzer was an outspoken defender of President Donald Trump and predicted that he would win reelection "in a landslide." When Congress met the following January to count Electoral College votes, he issued a statement with 36 other House Republicans that it was their "solemn duty" to sustain objections to slates of electors from four battleground states that "we believe clearly violated the Constitution," with changes in election procedures that were made by officials other than state legislatures. A week later, he said that he second impeachment charge against Trump was "a knee-jerk reaction grounded in anger and disgust, which are genuine emotions that we all feel. But those are not legitimate or appropriate reasons to impeach."

NC-7: Southeast North Carolina

Cook Partisan Voting Index: R+11

Population		Race and Ethnicity		Income	
Total	816,402	White	74.60%	Median Income	$53,066
Land area (sq. miles)	6,162	Black	17.90%	District Income Rank	359
Pop/ sq mi	132.49	Latino	9.70%	Poverty Rate	14.40%
Born in State	58.60%	Asian	0.90%	With health insurance	88.70%
		Two or more races	2.90%	Cash public assistance	1.30%
Age Groups		Other	3.80%	Food stamp/SNAP	13.70%
Under 18	20.40%				
18-34	21.30%	**Education**		**Work**	
35-64	37.70%	H.S grad or less	38.60%	White Collar	35.10%
Over 64	20.70%	Some college	33.30%	Sales and Service	39.30%
		College Degree, 4 yr	18.50%	Blue Collar	25.60%
Military		Post grad	9.70%	Government	14.10%
Veteran/ Active Duty	10.30%				

2020 Pres. Vote	Trump	267,881	(58%)	Biden	187,839	(41%)		
2016 Pres. Vote	Trump	206,192	(57%)	Clinton	142,782	(40%)	Johnson 8,950	(3%)

Wilmington, Dunn: At the end of the 19th century, North Carolina's lengthy attachment to the Democratic Party and White supremacy seemed to be weakening. A fusion ticket of Populists and Republicans had taken over the state legislature in 1894, and the state elected a rotund, racially egalitarian Republican named Daniel Russell as governor two years later. At the epicenter of this not-so-quiet revolution was Wilmington, a bustling majority-Black city then. It was truly revolutionary, but the changes fell short. The run-up to the 1898 elections was marked by increasing violence and assertion of racial supremacy by many whites. In the ensuing vote, Democrats recaptured the statehouse, though a biracial governing coalition was elected in Wilmington. That, too, was short-lived. A white mob instigated a violent protest, and hundreds of African Americans fled to the nearby woods and swamps. The biracial government was forced to resign at gunpoint in the only successful coup d'état in American history. Wilmington became a majority-white city, which it remains to this day. In June 2020, three white Wilmington police officers were fired after they were heard in a police car exchanging racist and threatening remarks, including discussion of a "civil war," National Public Radio reported.

The coastal counties of southern North Carolina recently have grown smartly. The military has kept things afloat, as have tourism and growing retirement communities. From 1990 to 2019, the population of Wilmington-based New Hanover County increased about 95 percent, and Brunswick County to the south nearly tripled. This metropolitan area was the second-fastest-growing in the nation from 2015 to 2016. The region has some of the busiest movie and television production facilities outside Los Angeles, with more than a dozen credits. South of Wilmington, the Army runs the 16,000-acre Military Ocean Terminal at Sunny Point, the Army's main deep-water port on the East Coast. It is the largest military ammunition port in the world, and often is referred to as "the FedEx of the sea" because it is almost always open.

In Johnston County, Smithfield Foods in Tar Heel runs the largest pork production plant in the world. The smell of hog manure, some of it stored in open-air pits, is a big problem. The northern part of the rapidly growing county borders on Wake County and has become an extension of the Raleigh suburbs.

The 7th Congressional District of North Carolina covers much of this territory. It is ancestrally Democratic, and it was the final white-majority district in the state that hadn't elected a Republican since Reconstruction. That anomaly was resolved in 2014, after redistricting in 2012 made the 7th the second-most Republican district in the state. The 2016 redistricting restored the minority communities of the Wilmington area to the new 7th. The new map for 2020 had relatively modest changes—adding the remaining parts of Johnston County (in the exurbs of Raleigh) and rural Bladen County, and giving up Wilson to the 1st District and Duplin to the 3rd. The area has remained comfortably Republican. President Donald Trump won it in 2020, 58%-41%.

Richard Hudson (R)

Elected 2012, 5th term, b. Nov 04, 1971; Franklin, VA; University of NC, Charlotte, B.A., 1996; Methodist; Married (Ms. Renee Hudson); 1 child.

Professional Career: Deputy chief of Staff, Rep. Robin Hayes, 2000- 05; Chief of Staff, Rep. Virginia Foxx, 2005-2006; Chief of Staff, Rep. John Carter, 2006-2008; Chief of Staff, Rep. Mike Conaway, 2008-2011; President, Cabarrus Marketing Group, 2011-present.

DC Office: 2112 RHOB 20515, 202-225-3715, Fax: 202-225-4036, hudson.house.gov

State Offices: Concord, 704-786-1612; Fayetteville, 910-997-2070; Pinehurst, 910-246-5374.

Committees: House Republican Conference Secretary. *Energy & Commerce*: Communications & Technology; Environment & Climate Change; Health.

Group Ratings

	ADA	ACLU	AFL-CIO	LCV	COC	HAFA	ACU	CFG	FRC
2020	**	17%	**	5%	-	95%	90%	**	-
2019	0%	C	20%	10%	86%	C	91%	90%	100%

Almanac Ratings 2019-2020

	Economy	Social	Foreign	Composite
Liberal	34%	19%	11%	22%
Conservative	66%	81%	89%	78%

Key Votes of the 116th Congress

1. U.S./Mex./Can. trade deal	Y	5. Russia sanctions	Y	9. Firearms background checks	N
2. First Coronavirus response	Y	6. Troops in Syria	Y	10. Spending at the border	Y
3. HEROES Act	N	7. Veto arms sales to Saudis	N/A	11. Marijuana liberalized rules	N
4. CASH Act	N	8. Defense $$$, veto override	Y	12. Electoral College objections	Y

Election Results

Election	Name (Party)	Vote (%)		Cand. Spent	Ind. Exp. Support	Ind. Exp. Oppose
2020 General	Richard Hudson (R)........................ 202,774	(53%)		$4,386,333	$226,952	$2,139,755
	Patricia Timmons-Goodson (D)... 177,781	(47%)		$3,846,683	$427,439	$3,692,645

Prior winning percentages: 2018 (55%), 2016 (59%), 2014 (65%), 2012 (53%)

Republican Richard Hudson, elected in 2012, used a boost from redistricting to take control of a formerly Democratic-held seat, but had to adjust to changes from subsequent re drawings of his district lines. A former senior congressional staffer and usually a party regular, he has worked on health and energy issues from his seat on the Energy and Commerce Committee. In 2020, he won a leadership slot and earlier survived a high-profile challenge for reelection.

Hudson grew up in the Charlotte area, and has a good political bloodline. He helped his grandfather run for the Roanoke Rapids City Council, where he served for 30 years. He put up yard signs for Republican Sen. Jesse Helms. Hudson was student-body president at the University of North Carolina at Charlotte, where he got a bachelor's degree. After college, he worked in Washington, as chief of staff to GOP Reps. Mike Conaway and John Carter of Texas and Virginia Foxx of North Carolina. He was deputy chief of staff for local Rep. Robin Hayes, who lost this seat to Democrat Larry Kissell in 2008. In November 2011, two months after moving back to the district, Hudson said he had a sense that God had a higher purpose for his life and was calling him to run for Congress.

Republicans made two–term Democratic Rep. Larry Kissell's seat a top 2012 takeover target. Hudson led the first round in the five-candidate primary with 32 percent, setting up a runoff with former Iredell County Commissioner Scott Keadle. When Keadle tried to portray Hudson as a Washington insider out of touch with the district, Hudson maintained that his experience on Capitol Hill created connections that would allow him to be more effective than most freshmen. He cruised to a runoff win, 64%-36%.

In the general, Hudson turned the tables by painting Kissell as the Beltway insider. He blamed the incumbent for moving the country toward "skyrocketing debt" and for "out-of-control spending." He accused Kissell of flip-flopping to try to save his seat. "I don't know where my opponent stands on many issues, it depends which day of the week it is," he told the Fayetteville Observer. Kissell stressed his vote against the Affordable Care Act. But styling himself as a conservative Blue Dog who was distant from President Barack Obama alienated Black voters. Hudson took the seat, 53%-45%.

On Energy and Commerce, he has sought to unleash the energy resources of North Carolina and to replace the Affordable Care Act with "a health care system that puts patients first." He helped to form the Atlantic Offshore Energy Caucus, which was designed to promote policies that explore and expand energy production on the Outer Continental Shelf. In 2017, the House unanimously passed his bill to allow emergency medical technicians to dispense medications, subject to general approval of local medical directors. He chaired the agriculture policy group of the House Republican Policy Committee.

Showing his GOP establishment brand during debate in 2017 on repeal of the Affordable Care Act, Hudson criticized Freedom Caucus members who objected to leadership proposals to deliver on the party's promise. "It defies me to understand where they're coming from," he told Politico.

In 2016, a mid-decade redistricting created robust challenges for Hudson, with opponents who had credible financial support. In the Republican primary, he faced Tim D'Annunzio, a former Army paratrooper who went into the military-equipment business. D'Annunzio self-financed most of his $239,000 campaign. He won narrowly in Cumberland, Hoke and Moore counties. Hudson had big margins in the western counties, including 82 percent of the vote in Cabarrus, and won 65%-35%.

In the general, Hudson faced Tom Mills, a veteran Democratic consultant in the area who founded the website, politicsnc.com. The candidates shared doubts about new international trade agreements and agreed on the need to protect U.S. citizens from the Islamic State. They disagreed on gun control and immigration. Hudson raised $2 million overall to $400,000 for Mills. The national parties and their allies spent little money here. In the two biggest counties, Hudson got 62 percent in Cabarrus and Mills got 60 percent in Cumberland. Hudson won overall, 59%-41%. After the election, Mills wrote a scathing piece for Politico in which he ripped the Democratic Congressional Campaign Committee for its failure to give attention to him or his campaign.

After a low-decibel contest in 2018, which Hudson won, 55%-45%, Democrats used another redistricting to make Hudson one of their top targets. Their challenger, Pat Timmons-Goodson, the first African-American woman to win election as a justice on the North Carolina Supreme Court. She resigned from the court in 2012, two years before the end of her eight-year term. In 2016, President Barack Obama nominated her as a federal district court judge, but the Republican-controlled Senate did not act on her nomination.

In her campaign, Timmons-Goodson called for more affordable health-care coverage. In the Cook Political Report, David Wasserman cited her limitations as a candidate: "Adapting her staid courtroom demeanor to the rough-and-tumble of a congressional race could prove a challenge," he wrote in his June 2020 analysis. Aside from health care, she "seemed otherwise unprepared or unwilling to prosecute her case aggressively." Both sides were well financed: Hudson spent $4.4 million to $3.9 million for Timmons-Goodson, with the two parties splitting more than $6 million in outside spending. Timmons-Goodson got 59 percent of the vote in her base in Cumberland County. But Hudson won all of the other counties, including 56 percent in Cabarrus, in his 53%-47 win. The result was the same victory margin that President Donald Trump had in the district.

Following the election, Hudson won election as Republican Conference secretary, the first rung on the GOP leadership ladder. Citing his campaign success, he said, "by running in a targeted district myself, I know what it takes to win."

NC-8: South-Central North Carolina   Cook Partisan Voting Index: R+6

Population		Race and Ethnicity		Income	
Total	815,055	White	64.60%	Median Income	$54,507
Land area (sq. miles)	4,513	Black	23.00%	District Income Rank	339
Pop/ sq mi	180.61	Latino	11.00%	Poverty Rate	12.80%
Born in State	53.70%	Asian	2.90%	With health insurance	88.90%
		Two or more races	4.50%	Cash public assistance	1.70%
Age Groups		Other	5.10%	Food stamp/SNAP	11.60%
Under 18	23.90%				
18-34	24.90%	**Education**		**Work**	
35-64	36.10%	H.S grad or less	37.50%	White Collar	34.50%
Over 64	15.10%	Some college	34.90%	Sales and Service	39.20%
		College Degree, 4 yr	18.00%	Blue Collar	26.30%
Military		Post grad	9.70%	Government	15.10%
Veteran/ Active Duty	16.70%				

2020 Pres. Vote	Trump	202,785	(52%)	Biden	177,876	(46%)		
2016 Pres. Vote	Trump	185,920	(56%)	Clinton	136,191	(41%)	Johnson	9,128 (3%)

Eastern Charlotte Suburbs, Fayetteville: In the Carolina Piedmont, from Atlanta to Durham along Interstate 85, lie the remnants of America's once-mighty textile industry. These sites included Concord and Kannapolis, the latter named for its founding company, Cannon Mills. While eastern Carolina was settled by Englishmen, the Piedmont was settled mainly by Scots and diverse groups like Quakers and Moravian sects, coming down the Blue Ridge from Pennsylvania through Virginia. These migratory patterns were reflected in Civil War divisions and continue to some degree in current voting habits. The textile mill towns along the interstate were anti-secession and have long been Republican.

To the east is military-focused Fayetteville, which is centered on Fort Bragg—operating since 1918 and accounting for half of the area's economic activity. Racial integration on the post took place long before it did in the city. The Army base styles itself as the largest military post in the world, which has had more than 54,000 active-duty military personnel. This is the home of the famed 82nd Airborne Division, which specializes in forcible-entry operations. In 2014, the 82nd lost its "airborne" status because of the high cost of maintenance, plus injuries to the paratroopers and others. The area is home to 100,000 Army retirees and family members. The base was named for Braxton Bragg, an owner of a plantation with slaves and a cantankerous general in the Confederate army. That placed the base on the list of military facilities for which advocates of racial justice sought a name change. The annual defense-spending bill that was enacted in December 2020over the veto of President Donald Trump created a three-year process to remove the names of Confederate leaders from 10 military bases, including Bragg.

These separate areas are the end points of the 8th Congressional District, which stretches across the southern part of the state with four mostly rural and heavily Republican counties between them.

The two areas recently have moved in very different directions. Cabarrus County, which includes the southern end of the textile corridor around Kannapolis and Concord, has been fed by migration from Charlotte and has moved beyond its small-town roots to become a booming exurban county. The county grew 64 percent from 2000 to 2019. In 2018, proposals were unveiled for $300 million of downtown economic revitalization in Concord. In January 2020, General Motors announced it would open a new technical facility in Concord, which would expand GM's performance and racing capabilities. By contrast, Fayetteville-based Cumberland County is less robust economically, with growth of 11 percent since 2000. It casts 40 percent of the district vote and leans Democratic. Lee County, in the outskirts of Raleigh and the Research Triangle, has become a new location for less-expensive bedroom communities.

The 2020 redistricting changes were favorable for Democrats. The new map moved Rowan County—which is north of Cabarrus—to the 13th District and added nearly 150,000 residents on the eastern end, including the remainder of Cumberland plus most of Harnett County to its north. What had become a more Republican district returned to a political swing area. Donald Trump won 55 percent of the old district in 2016; four years later, he got 52 percent of the new district, the lowest of the eight Republican-majority districts.

Dan Bishop (R)

Elected 2019, 2nd term, Charlotte, NC; University of NC, B.S., 1986; University of NC School of Law, J.D., 1990; Not Known; Married (Jo bishop); 1 child.

Elected Office: Commissioner, Mecklenburg County, 2004-2008; NC House, 2014-2017; NC Senate, 2017-2019.

Professional Career: Practicing attorney.

DC Office: 1207 LHOB 20515, 202-225-1976, Fax: 202-225-3389, danbishop.house.gov

State Offices: Lumberton, 910-671-3000; Monroe, 704-218-5300.

Committees: *Homeland Security*: Border Security, Facilitation & Operations; Oversight, Management & Accountability. *Judiciary*: Antitrust, Commercial & Administrative Law; Courts, Intellectual Property & Internet.

Almanac Ratings 2019-2020

	Economy	Social	Foreign	Composite
Liberal	43%	37%	41%	41%
Conservative	57%	63%	59%	59%

Key Votes of the 116th Congress

1. U.S./Mex./Can. trade deal Y	5. Russia sanctions N/A	9. Firearms background checks N/A	
2. First Coronavirus response N	6. Troops in Syria N/A	10. Spending at the border N/A	
3. HEROES Act N	7. Veto arms sales to Saudis N/A	11. Marijuana liberalized rules N	
4. CASH Act N	8. Defense $$$, veto override N	12. Electoral College objections Y	

Election Results

Election	Name (Party)	Vote (%)		Cand. Spent	Ind. Exp. Support	Ind. Exp. Oppose
2020 General	Dan Bishop (R)	224,661	(56%)	$3,974,034	$1,464,866	$1,473,315
	Cynthia Wallace (D)	179,463	(44%)	$779,860	$117,094	$312,091

Republican Dan Bishop in September 2019 won the first repeat congressional election in more than 40 years, defeating a lavishly funded Democrat in a special election that gained national attention. Bishop, a state senator who had crafted North Carolina's "bathroom bill," replaced the 2018 GOP nominee after the state invalidated that election following widespread allegations of absentee-voter fraud. Bishop's win in his historically Republican district was a boost for House Republicans following their devastating losses in 2018,though the contest reinforced some of those problems.

Born and raised in Mecklenburg County, Bishop got his bachelor's and law degrees from the University of North Carolina at Chapel Hill. He practiced law, chiefly on behalf of business clients, for 29 years. In 2004, he began a four-year stint on the Mecklenburg County Commission. After one term in the state House, Bishop was elected to the state Senate in 2016.

In the Legislature, Bishop was a social conservative who adopted a combative stance toward the local news media, denouncing reporters as "jihad media" over their coverage of the state's budget bill. His House Bill 2, which required transgender individuals to use public restrooms that corresponded with their gender at birth, prompted widespread boycotts from businesses and entertainers after GOP Gov. Pat McCrory signed the measure into law in 2016. A year later, it was partially repealed.

The ballot-fraud scandal during the 2018 election in this district gave Bishop his opening to run for Congress. Republican Mark Harris, an evangelical preacher, ousted three-term GOP Rep. Robert Pittenger in a primary rematch by 828 votes. In November, he faced off against Democrat Dan McCready, a Marine veteran-turned-solar-energy entrepreneur.

In the initial outcome, Harris was the apparent winner by 905 votes. But the North Carolina Board of Elections declined to certify the result after it discovered irregularities in voting patterns and learned of suspicious practices with absentee ballots by a Harris campaign operative in rural counties. After a dramatic weeklong hearing in which Harris's son shared his doubts about the campaign operative, the board ordered a new election. Citing his medical problems, Harris bowed out.

Against 10 candidates, Bishop significantly outspent the field and won the Republican primary with 48 percent of the vote. Union County Commissioner Stony Rushing was runner-up, with 20 percent.

Both national parties spent millions on the September election. Bishop described himself as a "pro-life, pro-gun, pro-wall" conservative, embraced President Donald Trump and tried to link McCready to leading liberal Democrats. McCready sought to distance himself from national Democrats by opposing a ban on some semi-automatic weapons, Medicare for All, and the impeachment of Trump.

Trump and Vice President Mike Pence campaigned on behalf of Bishop in the closing days of the campaign. Bishop won 50.7%-48.7%, a margin of 3,800 votes. McCready ran strongly in the *Charlotte suburbs, but Bishop led by large margins in rural and exurban parts of the district.

Barely a month later, a North Carolina court ruled that the state's congressional map, which had reliably elected 10 Republicans and 3 Democrats, was an illegal partisan gerrymander. The new map made minimal change to Bishop's district slightly more favorable for Republicans.

After McCready declined to run a third time, Bishop was challenged in 2020 by Cynthia Wallace, a financial services specialist who chaired the district's Democratic Party. The contest tightened in the closing weeks, as reduced support for Trump in suburbs threatened GOP candidates. Bishop defeated Wallace with 56 percent of the vote—two percentage points more than Trump received. In the two largest counties, which each cast about 30 percent of the vote, Bishop led by 35,400 votes in Union and Wallace led by 5,600 in Mecklenburg.

In the House, Bishop joined the Homeland Security and Judiciary committees.

NC-9: Southern North Carolina   **Cook Partisan Voting Index: R+6**

Population		Race and Ethnicity		Income	
Total	796,413	White	64.40%	Median Income	$66,208
Land area (sq. miles)	857	Black	19.60%	District Income Rank	202
Pop/ sq mi	929.38	Latino	7.60%	Poverty Rate	14.60%
Born in State	56.70%	Asian	2.90%	With health insurance	91.50%
		Two or more races	2.50%	Cash public assistance	1.50%
Age Groups		Other	10.60%	Food stamp/SNAP	13.70%
Under 18	24.40%				
18-34	19.50%	**Education**		**Work**	
35-64	40.80%	H.S grad or less	33.90%	White Collar	43.50%
Over 64	15.30%	Some college	30.10%	Sales and Service	34.60%
		College Degree, 4 yr	23.40%	Blue Collar	21.90%
Military		Post grad	12.60%	Government	11.90%
Veteran/ Active Duty	8.20%				

2020 Pres. Vote	Trump	219,265	(53%)	Biden	187,012	(45%)		
2016 Pres. Vote	Trump	186,926	(54%)	Clinton	147,162	(42%)	Johnson 9,841	(3%)

Southern Charlotte suburbs, Lumberton: "An agreeable village but in a damn rebellious country," recorded British Revolutionary War Gen. Charles Cornwallis when, before the unpleasantness at Yorktown, he visited Charlotte. Settled by Scots-Irish and German colonists who came down from Pennsylvania along the Blue Ridge Mountains, Charlotte has been a rapidly growing metropolitan area and the largest in North Carolina. Before the California gold rush, Charlotte was the gold-mining capital of the country; in 1837, the U.S. Mint established a branch here. And the city continues its preoccupation with the financial sector today. It is headquarters to one of the nation's biggest banks, Bank of America.

In booming Union County east of Charlotte, more than two dozen aerospace manufacturers—with more than 4,000 employees—produce high-precision metal and plastic parts for airplanes around the world. Local high schools and community colleges train these workers. Matthews, whose population more than doubled to 33,000 from 1990 to 2019, has been among the hot real-estate markets south of Charlotte. Union has occasionally struggled with its neighbors. In 2018, its economic development board decided to withhold its $67,000 dues to the Charlotte Regional Partnership. Board members contended that they needed to promote Union County's interests.

The 9th Congressional District has been a microcosm of the changes that have taken place in the South in the past century. In 1928, it elected Republican Charles A. Jonas to Congress. The result was considered a fluke—he lost two years later—but in truth it was a precursor of trends in urban areas across the region. In 1952, the congressman's son, Charles R. Jonas, won the Charlotte district, and this time held it for another nine elections; Republicans subsequently retained control. The remainder of the 9th sprawls east to include four mostly rural counties that extend east along the South Carolina border. Robeson County—the largest county by area in the state and the home of the Lumbee Tribe—gave 56 percent to Barack Obama in 2008 but shifted in 2020 to give 59 percent to President Donald Trump. For decades, the Lumbees have sought to gain full congressional recognition. With 60,000 members, they are the largest tribe east of the Mississippi River that does not have federal recognition. In December 2019, the tribe's leaders testified at a hearing of the House Natural Resources Committee. Trump announced his support for recognition in October 2020, which helps explain the county's increased Republican vote.

Redistricting in 2020made subtle changes in the 9th.In Mecklenburg County, what had been a strip along the southeast edge of the county shifted to one of those corners—though the county population remained similar. On the other end, the pieces of Cumberland and Bladen counties were removed; they were replaced by Hoke and part of Moore County. Likewise, the population totals remained similar. There was no partisan change. Trump won 53 percent of the vote of the new district.

Patrick McHenry (R)

Elected 2004, 9th term, b. Oct 22, 1975; Charlotte, NC; NC State University, Att., 1997; Belmont Abbey College, B.A., 2000; Roman Catholic; Married (Giulia Cangiano McHenry); 2 children.

Elected Office: NC House, 2002-2004.

Professional Career: Real estate broker, 2000-2002; Special Assistant to the U.S. Secretary of Labor, 2001.

DC Office: 2004 RHOB 20515, 202-225-2576, Fax: 202-225-0316, mchenry.house.gov

State Offices: Black Mountain, 828-669-0600; Gastonia, 704-833-0096; Hickory, 828-327-6100.

Committees: *Financial Services (RMM).*

Group Ratings

	ADA	ACLU	AFL-CIO	LCV	COC	HAFA	ACU	CFG	FRC
2020	**	14%	**	14%	-	77%	91%	**	-
2019	5%	C	33%	24%	93%	C	92%	67%	100%

Almanac Ratings 2019-2020

	Economy	Social	Foreign	Composite
Liberal	25%	33%	33%	31%
Conservative	75%	67%	67%	69%

Key Votes of the 116th Congress

1. U.S./Mex./Can. trade deal	Y	5. Russia sanctions	Y	9. Firearms background checks N
2. First Coronavirus response	Y	6. Troops in Syria	Y	10. Spending at the border	Y
3. HEROES Act	N	7. Veto arms sales to Saudis	N	11. Marijuana liberalized rules	N/A
4. CASH Act	N	8. Defense $$$, veto override	Y	12. Electoral College objections N

Election Results

Election	Name (Party)	Vote (%)		Cand. Spent	Ind. Exp. Support	Ind. Exp. Oppose
2020 General	Patrick McHenry (R)	284,095	(69%)	$1,819,865	$9,744	
	David Parker (D)	128,189	(31%)	$28,147		
2020 Primary	Patrick McHenry (R)	62,661	(72%)			
	Lynda Bennett (R)	20,606	(23%)			
	David L. Johnson (R)	14,286	(16%)			
	Ralf Walters (R)	10,484	(12%)			

Prior winning percentages: 2018 (59%), 2016 (63%), 2014 (61%), 2012 (57%), 2010 (71%), 2008 (58%), 2006 (62%), 2004 (64%)

Patrick McHenry, a Republican first elected in 2004, has evolved from a highly partisan GOP guerilla fighter in his early years in the House into a talented insider with both leadership and committee experience seeking to move the party's agenda. Taking over in 2019 as ranking Republican on the Financial Services Committee, he gained opportunities to assist the large financial sector in Charlotte. He occasionally collaborated with the committee chairwoman, Rep. Maxine Waters. As the former chief deputy to GOP Whip Steve Scalise, McHenry is prominent in the next generation of Republicans seeking future influence.

McHenry grew up in Cherryville as the youngest of five children and graduated from Belmont Abbey College, where he was president of the state College Republicans. After school he worked as a real estate broker. As a young conservative, he cut his political teeth on his strenuous opposition to the Clintons. He once dressed up in an Abraham Lincoln costume at a North Carolina appearance by Bill Clinton after Clinton was accused by Republicans of rewarding big contributors with overnight stays in the Lincoln Bedroom in the White House. McHenry worked on several Republican campaigns in North Carolina and was appointed to a job in the Labor Department. In 2002, he was elected to the state House.

When McHenry ran for an open seat, his chief competition in the Republican primary was Catawba County Sheriff David Huffman. Both made conservative Christian values their main issue. After Huffman finished first with 35 percent and McHenry second with 26 percent, the four-week runoff campaign took a negative turn. McHenry accused Huffman of campaign finance irregularities. He ran an energetic, door-to-door grassroots campaign, billing himself as a "pro-life, pro-gun, anti-gay-marriage" Christian conservative. He won the runoff by 85 votes after a recount, rolling up huge majorities in the counties close to his Gaston County home. He easily won the general election and has not faced a serious challenge since.

At age 29, McHenry arrived as the youngest member of the House. Instead of quietly learning the ropes, he made repeat appearances on talk shows to serve up red meat and sound bites. On the House floor, he took on Democrats no matter how powerful or senior. In 2007, he accused Speaker Nancy Pelosi of California of abusing her office by using military jets to fly home to San Francisco during congressional recesses. In 2009, he sidled up to the "birther" movement by saying at a town hall forum that "I haven't seen evidence one way or the other" of President Barack Obama's U.S. citizenship. He backed away from the comment the next day. Looking back at his rambunctious early years in the House, McHenry said in a February 2019 interview with Yahoo News, "I wasn't picking my battles well, nor did I have expertise in a specific area that I could be a leader in that area, nor did I have deep and meaningful relationships." After a few years, he told Yahoo, he abandoned self-promotion and tried to build relationships.

When Republicans took control of the House in 2011, he became more substantive as chairman of a subcommittee specializing in government bailouts. He told the Charlotte Observer that the Troubled Asset Relief Program for the financial industry was "a very uneven response from the federal government," with some banks bailed out and others, notably Charlotte-based Wachovia, forced to merge. He got into a hostile exchange at a 2011 hearing with Elizabeth Warren, then a Harvard professor who helped create the Consumer Financial Protection Bureau.

McHenry won enactment in 2011 of his bill allowing financial institutions involved in multiple transactions to combine them into one contract, something helpful to the banking industry in Charlotte. McHenry passed a provision in the jobs bill enacted in 2012 that allowed companies to more easily raise equity through social media and online platforms. In 2016, he filed a bill to expedite regulatory approval of new products for financial technology companies.

Behind the scenes, he helped his friend Scalise win election as chairman of the Republican Study Committee, the caucus of the House's mainstream conservative members. When Scalise became majority whip in the fallout from Eric Cantor's surprise primary defeat in 2014, he repaid the favor, appointing McHenry as his chief deputy. Like Scalise, McHenry spent much of his time courting his longtime conservative allies, not always successfully. For his new job, McHenry abandoned his earlier presence on the media circuit and went underground.

Given the economic plight of the textile industry, McHenry often voted against trade deals, as he did in 2005 on a pact proposed with Central America and in 2010 on a Haiti trade relief bill. His leadership post created a new twist in 2015 as he engaged in countless discussions to rally support from GOP members for the trade promotion authority request from Obama.

The nearly fatal shooting of Scalise at a congressional baseball practice in June 2017 placed him in charge of the whip team for several months. McHenry largely succeeded in continuing with business-as-usual during often stressful circumstances. "You've got to put in the understanding with people, not simply drive them on some issue, but very much get a sense of where they are and why they are where they are and that gives you a sense of where they can be," he said in described his responsibilities in a September 2017 interview with the Raleigh News & Observer.

The North Carolina delegation has included troublemakers for GOP leaders, including former Rep. Mark Meadows, who chaired the rebellious Freedom Caucus. McHenry's responsibilities to help win enactment of the agenda of Trump and congressional Republicans created additional challenges as he tried to manage the conservative renegades.

When Republicans lost House control in the 2018 election, McHenry took advantage of the opening for the ranking minority member on the Financial Services Committee. In an initial showing of cooperation, Waters and McHenry cosponsored a bill to direct the Securities and Exchange Commission to review corporate executive investment plans. After extended negotiation, the two of them agreed on a bill to reauthorize the Export-Import Bank, but could not win committee support prior to the 2020 election.

On other committee issues, McHenry called for a review of how technology was reshaping banking. In a September 2020 interview with Politico, he said Federal Reserve Board chairman Jerome Powell had done "a fantastic, very smart job" and should be reappointed.

McHenry has had little trouble at election time. He faced several GOP primary challengers who accused him of being insufficiently conservative, but won each contest easily. The 2020 redistricting radically redrew districts in western North Carolina, including McHenry's old 10th District. He selected his new district, which had none of his initial base in Gaston County. The unveiling of the new district lines in December 2019 shortly before the filing deadline left McHenry with weak opponents who spent scant campaign funds. He won the primary with 72 percent of the vote and the general election with 69 percent.

NC-10: West-central North Carolina

Cook Partisan Voting Index: R+21

Population		Race and Ethnicity		Income	
Total	771,791	White	81.20%	Median Income	$53,189
Land area (sq. miles)	2,575	Black	12.60%	District Income Rank	358
Pop/ sq mi	299.71	Latino	7.10%	Poverty Rate	14.00%
Born in State	62.70%	Asian	1.80%	With health insurance	87.90%
		Two or more races	1.90%	Cash public assistance	1.60%
Age Groups		Other	2.60%	Food stamp/SNAP	12.50%
Under 18	20.90%				
18-34	20.20%	**Education**		**Work**	
35-64	39.30%	H.S grad or less	41.80%	White Collar	34.90%
Over 64	19.50%	Some college	32.00%	Sales and Service	36.10%
		College Degree, 4 yr	17.30%	Blue Collar	29.00%
Military		Post grad	8.90%	Government	9.80%
Veteran/ Active Duty	8.10%				

2020 Pres. Vote	Trump	284,458	(68%)	Biden	131,230	(31%)		
2016 Pres. Vote	Trump	216,943	(60%)	Clinton	129,104	(36%)	Johnson	9,088	(3%)

Hickory, Forsyth County: In 1790, one of the most important decisions in North Carolina's history was made—in Pennsylvania. That was when 19-year-old Michael Schenck decided to leave his family farm in Lancaster and settle in western North Carolina. In 1813, on a small creek west of Lincolnton, Schenck built the first cotton mill south of the Potomac River. In 1816, he brought in investors and erected the Lincoln Cotton Mills on the South Fork of the Catawba River, which operated until the Civil War. The North Carolina textile industry was born and soon dominated in an area that had specialized in corn, cotton and whiskey production.

Economic prosperity has become a dim memory in some of these parts, especially in the strip along the border with Virginia. In Rockingham County, the Miller Coors brewery—a 1,365-acre site —and the affiliated Ball Cannery closed and were purchased by a demolition company in 2018. The closure followed a lengthy dispute between Miller and Pabst Brewing, which had an agreement to handle most of the beer production. In Surry County are the remnants of the socks-manufacturing plant of Hanes-Brand in Mount Airy. Iredell County, by contrast, has had rapid growth as the Charlotte metro area has expanded deeper into the suburbs. The purchases of former farmland have jeopardized the county's status as the leading dairy-producer in the state. In January 2019, Catawba County announced that Design Foundry, a new furniture company, would hire 200 workers and start operations in Hickory, in collaboration with Crate &Barrel. The county has lost thousands of furniture-industry jobs since the peak in the 1960s. In January 2020, Duke Energy agreed with environmental activists to remove 80 million tons of coal ash from unlined ponds at six sites in western and central North Carolina; the largest is in Stokes County.

The 10th Congressional District of North Carolina was radically changed by redistricting. Hickory-based Catawba and Lincoln—which are the closest to Charlotte—are the only counties in the " before" and "after" maps of the district. Small slices of each county are in adjacent districts. Previously, the remainder of the district included Gaston County, three other counties to the west along the border with South Carolina and a share of Asheville-based Buncombe County. Instead, the new district heads north from Catawba to the border with Virginia and then turns east to include 30 percent of Forsyth County, with a small piece of Winston-Salem. Granted, the district remained securely Republican. But roughly 70 percent of its constituency had changed. The 10th exchanged many of its counties with the 5th District. Donald Trump won 68 and 67 percent, respectively, in those two districts. In the Republican-drawn map in 2016, which enhanced the number of GOP districts, Trump took 60 and 57 percent.

Madison Cawthorn (R)

Elected 2020, 1st term, b. Aug 01, 1995; Asheville, NC; Patrick Henry College; Christian; Married (Cristina Bayardelle).

Professional Career: Owner, real estate investment firm.

DC Office: 102 CHOB 20515, 202-225-6401, cawthorn.house.gov

State Offices: Burnsville, 828-808-2148; Franklin, 828-452-6022; Hendersonville, 828-435-7310; Waynesville, 828-452-6022.

Committees: *Education & Labor*: Early Childhood, Elementary & Secondary Education; Workforce Protections. *Veterans' Affairs*: Economic Opportunity.

Election Results

Election	Name (Party)	Vote (%)		Cand. Spent	Ind. Exp. Support	Ind. Exp. Oppose
2020 General	Madison Cawthorn (R)	245,351	(55%)	$4,371,795	$724,921	$486,603
	Morris Davis (D)	190,609	(42%)	$2,172,342	$209	$1,881,505
2020 Primary	Madison Cawthorn (R)	18,481	(20%)			
	Jim Davis (R)	17,465	(19%)			
	Chuck Archerd (R)	8,272	(9%)			
	Wayne King (R)	7,876	(9%)			
	Dan Driscoll (R)	7,803	(9%)			
	Joey Osborne (R)	6,470	(7%)			
2020 Primary	Madison Cawthorn (R)	30,636	(66%)			
Runoff	Lynda Bennett (R)	15,905	(34%)			

Prior winning percentages: 2018 (59%)

Republican Madison Cawthorn shocked the Republican political establishment when he won a primary runoff, at age 24, by defeating a candidate handpicked by his predecessor, then-Rep. Mark Meadows. A businessman and motivational speaker, Cawthorn became the youngest member elected to Congress and he sought to position himself to help usher a younger generation of voters into the Republican Party.

Cawthorn, who turned 25 in August 2020, is an eighth-generation resident of western North Carolina, raised in Hendersonville. He said Meadows nominated him to attend the U.S. Naval Academy after graduating from high school. But his life was upended in 2014 during a near-fatal car crash in Florida that left him paralyzed from the waist down and limited to mobility in a wheelchair.

The accident was featured in Cawthorn's campaign. He credited the experience with giving him a unique ability to connect with others facing adversity and to understand the perils of the U.S. healthcare system. After months of recovery, he became the owner of a real estate investment company and offered himself as a motivational speaker

His path to Congress was all the more remarkable given the circumstances of Meadows' retirement. The four-term lawmaker, who had been a key ally of President Donald Trump, revealed his plan to depart only 30 hours before the state's filing deadline. Local Republicans suspected that he timed the announcement to benefit family friend Lynda Bennett, a real estate agent and local GOP activist who launched her campaign that day and appeared to have had advance notice of the retirement.

The field notably lacked state legislators. Meadows made his announcement after the North Carolina deadline for candidates to switch the office for which they are running, boxing out any incumbents who filed for reelection, except for state Sen. Jim Davis, who had planned to retire. Meadows endorsed Bennett after an audio tape of her criticizing Trump began to circulate around the district. (Bennett said she was role-playing and the recording was taken out of context.) In the primary, Bennett won the first runoff spot and Cawthorn edged out Davis for the second slot by barely 1,000 votes.

Cawthorn outraised and outspent Bennett ahead of the runoff. Despite Bennett's Twitter endorsement from Trump, Cawthorn trounced her 66%-34%. Cawthorn capitalized on local resentment of Meadows to win dozens of endorsements from sheriffs, county commissioners and former rivals.Her loss embarrassed Trump, who recorded an automated call for her, and Meadows, who facilitated that endorsement as the president's new chief of staff. The upset made Cawthorn a star and he spoke at the Republican National Convention in August.

Cawthorn said that he hoped to help the GOP gain traction among millennials and Generation Z voters. In an interview with Politico following his primary victory, Cawthorn said Republicans needed to improve their communication of policy proposals. On healthcare, he called the GOP "the party of no, with no real answers." On border security, he said the party's rhetoric came across as "xenophobic."

Democrats nominated Moe Davis, a retired Air Force colonel who had been a chief prosecutor in the trials of terrorists at Guantanamo Bay. Cawthorn was placed on the defensive when reporters dug up an old social-media post that he made during a trip to Adolf Hitler's vacation home in Germany. His caption referred to Hitler as "the Fuhrer" and noted the spot had been on his "bucket list for a while" and "did not disappoint." Cawthorn deleted the photo and forcefully disavowed white nationalism and Nazism.

He caused another controversy when his campaign website accused Sen. Cory Booker of New Jersey of aiming "to ruin white males." Cawthorn later called the mistake a syntax error. Following a lengthy investigation, The Washington Post wrote in a profile in February 2021 that Cawthorn had contrived many details of his biography, including the auto accident and his limited education. Among other things, the Post reported, he had not been accepted at the Naval Academy. Cawthorn and his spokesman did not respond to requests for an interview.

After a court-ordered redistricting in 2019 made the district slightly more favorable to Democrats, House Republicans were sufficiently worried about the contest that the House GOP-aligned Congressional Leadership Fund spent more than $700,000 on broadcast ads to support Cawthorn. He won with 55 percent of the vote.

NC-11: Western North Carolina   Cook Partisan Voting Index: R+9

Population		Race and Ethnicity		Income	
Total	772,612	White	89.50%	Median Income	$51,884
Land area (sq. miles)	6,838	Black	3.30%	District Income Rank	369
Pop/ sq mi	112.98	Latino	6.70%	Poverty Rate	13.20%
Born in State	58.60%	Asian	1.10%	With health insurance	86.80%
		Two or more races	1.80%	Cash public assistance	1.50%
Age Groups		Other	4.50%	Food stamp/SNAP	9.70%
Under 18	18.30%				
18-34	19.60%	**Education**		**Work**	
35-64	38.90%	H.S grad or less	40.70%	White Collar	33.60%
Over 64	23.30%	Some college	33.00%	Sales and Service	39.80%
		College Degree, 4 yr	16.70%	Blue Collar	26.70%
Military		Post grad	9.60%	Government	14.70%
Veteran/ Active Duty	8.80%				

2020 Pres. Vote	Trump	251,903	(55%)	Biden	196,934	(43%)		
2016 Pres. Vote	Trump	230,018	(62%)	Clinton	123,790	(34%)	Johnson	10,246	(3%)

Asheville: Steeped in the hues that gave them the name Blue Ridge, the heavily wooded mountains of North Carolina seem placid and ancient. Geologically, they are some of the oldest ranges in the world; they began forming 400 million years ago, when plant life was just beginning to spread across the continents. After the collapse of the residential furniture industry in Grand Rapids Michigan during the Great Depression, furniture manufacturing took hold in the region because of the abundance of hardwood forests.

Economic interests have continued to evolve. Furniture has faced competition from Asia. So the region has increasingly turned to technology. Asheville, a popular artistic and retirement mecca with its well-preserved and gentrified historic structures in styles ranging from Gothic Revival to Art Deco, has had a spurt of technology-related manufacturing plus craft breweries. Google became the first customer of a Duke Energy program to bring renewable power from a nearby solar farm.

The politics of Asheville are unique in western North Carolina. In July 2020, the city council unanimously agreed to issue an apology for its participation in slavery and to pay reparations by increasing homeownership plus business and career opportunities for Black residents. Weeks later, Buncombe County—which has 10 times the population of the city but only a 6 percent Black population—took a similar action. In September, the Asheville City Council agreed to cut its police budget by 3 percent, though that step fell far short of the 50 percent cut demanded by "defund the police" demonstrators. In January, the council issued a "declaration" that it would eliminate greenhouse gas emissions by 2030. It didn't say how.

With a $2 billion boost, tourism has become a major local business. The Blue Ridge Parkway is the main route that feeds into the Great Smoky Mountains, which cross into Tennessee. In 2019, the Smokies hosted 12.5 million visitors and were rated the most popular park in the National Park Service, with more than double the number of visitors of the Grand Canyon. The scenery along the parkway attracted 15 million visitors—the largest total of any park unit.

The 11th District of North Carolina consists of small, mountainous counties in far western North Carolina. The local politics once were volatile. From 1978 through 2012, the western North Carolina district switched between the parties seven times and threw out six incumbents. That changed when redistricting in 2012 split Asheville, with two-thirds becoming an arm of the old 10th District. But the redistricting of 2020 again unified Asheville-based Buncombe County in the new 11th. Other changes to the district included the addition of Avery and Polk counties and parts of Rutherford, and the shift of Caldwell and Burke counties to the new 5th District.

About a third of the district's residents live in the stretch of counties along the Tennessee border. These include some of the most reliably Republican locales in the nation. Another third is Asheville-based Buncombe, a blue island in a deep red sea and an economic oasis amid extensive poverty. In the remaining area to the south and east of Buncombe, the population center is Henderson County, a retiree-friendly area that is heavily Republican. In 2016, Donald Trump got 62 percent in the old 11th, which was the best GOP-performing district in North Carolina. That changed in 2020, when he got 55 percent in the new 11th.

Alma Adams (D)

Elected 2014, 4th term, b. May 27, 1946; High Point, NC; NC Agricultural and Technical State University, 1968; NC Agricultural and Technical State University, M.S., 1972; OH State University, Ph.D., 1981; Baptist; Divorced; 2 children; 4 grandchildren.

Elected Office: Guilford Cty., School Board, 1984-1986; Greensboro City Council, 1987-1994; NC House, 1994-2014.

Professional Career: Professor, Bennett College, 1972-2012.

DC Office: 2436 RHOB 20515, 202-225-1510, Fax: 202-225-1512, adams.house.gov

State Offices: Charlotte, 704-344-9950.

Committees: *Agriculture (VChmn)*: Subcommittee Nutrition, Oversight & Department Operations. *Education & Labor*: Civil Rights & Human Services; Workforce Protections (Chmn). *Financial Services*: Oversight & Investigations; Task Force on Artificial Intelligence.

Group Ratings

	ADA	ACLU	AFL-CIO	LCV	COC	HAFA	ACU	CFG	FRC
2020	**	80%	**	100%	-	0%	2%	**	-
2019	95%	C	100%	96%	53%	C	2%	12%	0%

Almanac Ratings 2019-2020

	Economy	Social	Foreign	Composite
Liberal	100%	63%	58%	74%
Conservative	0%	37%	42%	26%

Key Votes of the 116th Congress

1. U.S./Mex./Can. trade deal Y	5. Russia sanctions Y	9. Firearms background checks Y
2. First Coronavirus response Y	6. Troops in Syria Y	10. Spending at the border N
3. HEROES Act Y	7. Veto arms sales to Saudis Y	11. Marijuana liberalized rules Y
4. CASH Act Y	8. Defense $$$, veto override Y	12. Electoral College objections N

Election Results

Election	Name (Party)	Vote (%)	Cand. Spent	Ind. Exp. Support	Ind. Exp. Oppose
2020 General	Alma Adams (D)..............................	341,457 (100%)	$324,729	$2,295	
2020 Primary	Alma Adams (D)..............................	109,009 (88%)			
	Keith Cradle (D)....................................	14,713 (12%)			

Prior winning percentages: 2018 (73%), 2016 (67%), 2014 (75%), 2014 special (75%)

Democrat Alma Adams, elected in 2014, has pursued occasional bipartisanship on causes of personal interest. When redistricting in 2016 removed her longtime base, she showed political dexterity in moving 90 miles to her new home, despite some local objections. As chairwoman of the Workforce Protections Subcommittee, she accused federal regulators during the Trump administration of failing to protect workers during the coronavirus pandemic

Adams arrived in Washington as a rarity: a lawmaker with a fine-arts background. She grew up in New Jersey, with her single mother who did domestic work. She got her bachelor's degree from North Carolina A&T State University, a master's and her doctorate in art education and multicultural education from Ohio State University. Until 2012, she taught art history at Bennett College, a historically Black women's college. She got her first taste of politics in the 1980s, with election to the Guilford County School Board and the Greensboro City Council; she was the first African-American woman elected to the school board. A single mother from a working-class African-American community, she focused on educational and housing disparities. She helped organize Greensboro for the 1988 presidential campaign of Jesse Jackson.

In 1994, Adams was appointed to the state Assembly, where she served for 20 years. She chaired the Legislative Black Caucus and became known as "the minimum-wage lady" because of her advocacy. Adams is known for her hats. "It's a part of my wardrobe," she told National Public Radio in 2015. "I started wearing hats because I was sick a lot. And I remember my grandmother telling me, 'Cover your noggin; you'll stay healthy.'" Serving in Congress has expanded her collection from 903 when she started to more than 1,100, as of 2018.

When the House seat opened in 2014, seven Democrats jumped into the race. Adams was backed by progressive and abortion-rights organizations that funneled at least $186,000 to super PACs that took aim at her top Democratic rival, Malcolm Graham, a former Charlotte City Council member and state senator. Adams also won support from organized labor.

In a heavily Democratic district, the candidates largely agreed on the core issues: supporting the Affordable Care Act, opposing the decision of Republican Gov. Pat McCrory to block Medicaid expansion, and taking aim at Republican efforts to curtail early voting. Adams emphasized her participation in the Democratic pushback in a state where partisan politics had become fractious. She easily topped the field in the primary with 44 percent to 24 percent for Graham. Adams won huge majorities in Guilford and Forsyth counties; she ran third in Mecklenburg, where the turnout was lighter. She got 75 percent in her general election victory. She also won a special election to fill the remaining two months of the vacant seat.

Adams displayed her activism on numerous issues. With Republican Rep. Bradley Byrne of Alabama, she founded the Historically Black Colleges and Universities Caucus. In 2016, the House passed their bill with improvements in capital financing of HBCUs. Adams introduced with Democratic Rep. Rosa DeLauro the Paycheck Fairness Act for gender equality on wages, and she filed a measure to raise the federal minimum wage to $12 hourly by 2020. She said that voting must be made easier for all Americans, and claimed that mandatory voter ID laws did the opposite.

In 2016, Adams filed the Small and Disadvantaged Businesses Act, which called for a review of government purchasing procedures. That measure was enacted as part of that year's defense spending bill. Earlier, the House approved her amendment calling on the Pentagon to assure that service members have enough resources and treatment for post-traumatic stress disorder.

With Democrats in the majority, Adams has chaired the Education and Labor Subcommittee on Workforce Protections. Her top priorities included an increase in the minimum wage and a requirement of equal pay for equal work. She filed a paycheck fairness bill to update the 2009 Lily Ledbetter Fair Paycheck Act, which was designed to make it easier to sue for gender discrimination. In June 2020, she chaired a subcommittee hearing that focused on what she said was the failure of the Occupational Safety and Health Administration to "fully use the tools it has" to protect workers during the pandemic.

With Rep. Lauren Underwood and then-Sen. Kamala Harris in March 2020, Adams filed a bill to improve maternity care for Black mothers. Adams and Underwood created the Black Maternal Health Caucus in the House.

When redistricting in 2016 reduced her district to only Mecklenburg County, Adams picked up roots from her home in Greensboro to run in the Democratic primary. The Charlotte Observer, saying that it preferred "someone with a better grounding in Charlotte's history, culture and neighborhoods," endorsed Graham, who ran again, and cited his "deep varied local experience." Graham ran an ad with the slogan, "A house is not a home." State Rep. Tricia Cotham, another candidate, said Adams was "intentionally deceiving" voters by claiming that she had changed her residence. Outspending the combined spending of her two opponents by nearly four-to-one, Adams got 43 percent to 29 percent for Graham and 21 percent for Cotham.

By 2020, Adams appeared to have entrenched herself. In the Democratic primary, she initially was challenged by Keith Cradle, director of youth and juvenile programs for the Mecklenburg sheriff's office. He withdrew from the contest, citing his "inability to raise the needed funds for a competitive race. But Cradle's name remained on the ballot for the primary, which Adams won with 88 percent of the vote.

NC-12: Mecklenburg County

Cook Partisan Voting Index: D+19

Population		Race and Ethnicity		Income	
Total	891,792	White	44.90%	Median Income	$61,658
Land area (sq. miles)	441	Black	37.50%	District Income Rank	237
Pop/ sq mi	2,022.2	Latino	15.90%	Poverty Rate	11.50%
Born in State	41.70%	Asian	5.80%	With health insurance	86.00%
		Two or more races	3.30%	Cash public assistance	1.20%
Age Groups		Other	8.40%	Food stamp/SNAP	8.30%
Under 18	23.10%				
18-34	28.30%	Education		Work	
35-64	38.10%	H.S grad or less	28.90%	White Collar	41.90%
Over 64	10.50%	Some college	29.70%	Sales and Service	38.50%
		College Degree, 4 yr	27.50%	Blue Collar	19.60%
Military		Post grad	13.90%	Government	8.00%
Veteran/ Active Duty	5.20%				

2020 Pres. Vote	Biden	308,165	(70%)	Trump	125,324	(28%)			
2016 Pres. Vote	Clinton	243,693	(67%)	Trump	101,178	(28%)	Johnson	11,425	(3%)

Charlotte: "This is perhaps the Negro's temporary farewell to Congress," began the peroration of the last speech given by George White, an African-American lawyer from Tarboro North Carolina, and a Republican, in his last days in the House in 1901. Segregation was being imposed by law, and Blacks were informally but effectively driven from the voting rolls in the rural South. The conclusion of White's speech proved prophetic: "Phoenix-like, he will rise up some day and come again. These parting words are in behalf of an outraged, heart-broken, bruised, and bleeding, but God-fearing people, faithful, industrious, loyal people—rising people, full of potential force." When White said his farewell, most North Carolina Blacks lived on farms or in tiny towns. Through the 20th century, few moved to the textile towns, where most mills hired only Whites, but some moved to its larger cities. After the Voting Rights Act of 1965, their "potential force" began to be felt. Some Blacks won in White-majority constituencies, notably Charlotte Mayor Harvey Gantt. Voters elected their next African Americans to Congress from North Carolina after the Democratic legislature, following the 1990 census, drew two irregularly shaped Black-majority districts—in the mostly rural and small-town 1st District and in the mostly urban 12th District.

Charlotte-based Mecklenburg County and Raleigh-based Wake are the two largest counties and they include about one-fifth of the population in North Carolina, with half of the population gain from 2010 to 2019. Charlotte, which is about 80 percent of Mecklenburg, has a boosterish pride in its capacity for accommodation. The downside of its rapid growth is that the city has had the worst sprawl of 15 fast-growing metro areas nationwide. Charlotte has promoted cultural development and entertainment. It boasts the NASCAR Hall of Fame and a $50 million performing arts center across from the 60-story Bank of America tower. In July 2020, Centene, a national healthcare provider, announced it would locate its East Coast headquarters in Charlotte, with more than 3,200 employees. The city has long been the financial center for North Carolina and much of the South. Republican plans to hold their national convention in Charlotte in August 2020 were disrupted by the coronavirus and the insistence of Democratic local officials on safe distancing, over the strong objections of President Donald Trump. In a virtually last-minute scheduling switch, he delivered his acceptance speech on the White House lawn.

The 12th Congressional District of North Carolina has been the most litigated district in the country since the 1990s and has been the focus of no fewer than five cases that went to the Supreme Court. It originally comprised a series of Black precincts connected in some places by nothing wider than the lanes of Interstate 85, and stretched 160 miles from Gastonia to Durham. Over the years, it grew a bit shorter. Finally, in the 2016 redistricting, the 12th took on regular lines and was entirely in Mecklenburg. It remained a Democratic island.

With the 2020 redistricting, the new 12th remained entirely in Mecklenburg, with 80 percent of the county. The four surrounding districts changed more than did the 12th. The changes reduced the vote in 2012 for President Barack Obama from 79 percent, among the highest in the nation in 2008, to 68 percent. In 2020, Joe Biden won 70 percent here—still the strongest Democratic district in the state.

Ted Budd (R)

Elected 2016, 3rd term, b. Oct 21, 1971; Winston-Salem, NC; Appalachian State University, B.S., 1994; Dallas Theological Seminary, M.Th., 1998; Wake Forest University, M.B.A., 2007; Christian - Non-Denominational; Married (Amy Kate); 3 children.

Professional Career: Investment analyst; Business owner.

DC Office: 118 CHOB 20515, 202-225-4531, budd.house.gov

State Offices: Advance, 336-998-1313; High Point, 336-858-5013.

Committees: *Financial Services*: Consumer Protection & Financial Institutions; Diversity & Inclusion; Task Force on Artificial Intelligence.

Group Ratings

	ADA	ACLU	AFL-CIO	LCV	COC	HAFA	ACU	CFG	FRC
2020	**	20%	**	10%	-	100%	97%	**	-
2019	0%	C	19%	7%	79%	C	99%	100%	100%

Almanac Ratings 2019-2020

	Economy	Social	Foreign	Composite
Liberal	25%	14%	7%	16%
Conservative	75%	86%	93%	84%

Key Votes of the 116th Congress

1. U.S./Mex./Can. trade deal	Y	5. Russia sanctions	Y	9. Firearms background checks	N
2. First Coronavirus response	N	6. Troops in Syria	N/A	10. Spending at the border	Y
3. HEROES Act	N	7. Veto arms sales to Saudis	N	11. Marijuana liberalized rules	N/A
4. CASH Act	N	8. Defense $$$, veto override	N	12. Electoral College objections	Y

Election Results

Election	Name (Party)	Vote (%)	Cand. Spent	Ind. Exp. Support	Ind. Exp. Oppose
2020 General	Ted Budd (R)......................................	267,181 (68%)	$1,103,254	$236,580	
	Scott Huffman (D)................................	124,684 (32%)	$184,988		

Prior winning percentages: 2018 (52%), 2016 (56%)

Ted Budd, elected in 2016 as a political newcomer, became an active member of the Financial Services Committee, where he worked with banking groups to roll back the Dodd-Frank financial regulatory law. He survived a more competitive challenge in his first reelection campaign than in his initial contest. The court-ordered redistricting for the 2020 election gave him a much safer district. In April 2021, he entered the growing field of candidates for the seat of retiring Sen. Richard Burr. Budd immediately picked up the support of the business-oriented Club for Growth, which often spends generously on behalf of its candidates. Then, in June, Budd won the endorsement of former President Donald Trump, which likely will provide an additional boost.

Budd grew up on a 300-acre cattle and commercial chicken farm and he continues to reside there in the town of Advance, which had a population of 1,171 in 2018. His father built a janitorial supply house into a facility-services company that employed 3,400 people in 10 states, the Charlotte Observer reported. He graduated from Appalachian State University, where he worked on phone banks for Republican Sen. Jesse Helms. He got graduate degrees in theology from Dallas Theological Seminary and in business administration from Wake Forest University. Budd met his wife, Amy Kate, while they were on a mission trip to the former Soviet Union. He worked for his father's company and owned his own gun store and shooting range, which he called ProShots. He opposes gun control, and he views terrorism and mental health problems as the chief causes of gun-related violence.

The Republican primary included 17 candidates, none of whom spent sizable amounts of money. Budd raised about $150,000 for the primary, which was more than any of the next three candidates in the contest. He got a big boost from the Club for Growth, which viewed him as a true outsider and spent $500,000 on his behalf, with ads that highlighted his conservative values and firm resolve. In a remarkably low-turnout contest for a new seat, Budd got 6,340 votes and won the primary with 20 percent. Budd won Davie and Davidson counties, finished second in Iredell and third in Guilford, which cast about one-third of the vote.

In the general election, Budd faced Democrat Bruce Davis, a Marine Corps veteran who served 12 years as a Guilford County commissioner. The two candidates had similar views on several issues, including support of gun ownership, opposition to the Trans-Pacific Partnership, and the need to address Islamic extremism. Davis disagreed with Budd's support for a wall on the southern border to keep out illegal immigrants. Davis raised only $91,000, while Budd raised nearly $600,000 overall. Budd won, 56%-44%. Davis won 60 percent in Guilford, which cast slightly more than half the vote. Budd won Davie, Davidson and Iredell by margins of more than two-to-one.

With a seat on the Financial Services Committee, Budd has sought to use "my real-world experience to roll back the restrictive regulations that strangle job creation in this country." With a Republican-controlled Congress and White House in his first term, his timing was right. He took a special interest in repealing the Durbin amendment to the Dodd-Frank banking law. Sponsored by Democratic Sen. Richard Durbin of Illinois, that provision placed limits on the rates that credit-card companies could charge retailers for their swipe fees. "Command and control government policies benefit powerful interests as much as they do the disadvantaged," Budd said.

With strong support for the Durbin proviso from small business groups, Budd's initiative proved a step too far. Still, the American Bankers Association supported Budd and Democratic Sen. Jon Tester of Montana in its first broadcast ads of the midterms. "Rep. Budd understands the important role North Carolina banks play in the economy," said the president of the North Carolina Bankers Association.

Budd faced a more organized and better financed challenge for reelection in 2018. Democrat Kathy Manning, a Greensboro attorney and civic activist, said her top issue was the need for more affordable and accessible health care. She criticized Budd for the failure of Republican-passed legislation to protect patients with pre-existing conditions with a federal mandate. In an election-eve appearance, House Speaker Paul Ryan praised Budd as an "impact player." Manning spent an impressive $4.1 million to $2 million for Budd; outside groups spent more than $4 million on the contest. Budd won, 52%-46%. Manning led in Guilford, 62%-37%, a margin of 34,000 votes. Budd survived with more than 70 percent of the vote in Davidson and Davie counties. (The 2020 redistricting created a Guilford County-based district, which was ideally suited for Manning, who was easily elected.)

In the Democratic-controlled House in 2019, Budd worked with Democratic Rep. Stephen Lynch on a House-passed bill that would create an inter-agency task force to research how new financial technology(fintech) is being used in financial crimes and terrorism, and prepare federal responses. "As we move into an increasing digital and virtual world, criminals and terrorists will start to use new technologies that are available to them," Budd said. He said he was the first member of Congress to call for a travel ban from China at the outbreak of the coronavirus. In February 2021, he filed a bill that would permanently ban the use of earmarks.

In 2020, Budd breezed to reelection in his new district that leaned far more Republican— chiefly with the removal of Guilford County. Against first-time candidate Steve Huffman, Budd won, 68%-32%. He won all 10 counties. Alamance was the most competitive, with Budd getting 55 percent of the vote. The redistricting wars in North Carolina have shown that prospective successors to his House seat cannot take anything for granted for 2022.

NC-13: Piedmont   Cook Partisan Voting Index: R+20

Population		Race and Ethnicity		Income	
Total	780,466	White	68.00%	Median Income	$56,718
Land area (sq. miles)	2,281	Black	22.80%	District Income Rank	301
Pop/ sq mi	342.22	Latino	8.50%	Poverty Rate	14.40%
Born in State	58.60%	Asian	3.70%	With health insurance	89.40%
		Two or more races	3.00%	Cash public assistance	1.80%
Age Groups		Other	2.50%	Food stamp/SNAP	12.50%
Under 18	21.40%				
18-34	23.70%	**Education**		**Work**	
35-64	37.80%	H.S grad or less	38.80%	White Collar	36.00%
Over 64	17.10%	Some college	30.80%	Sales and Service	35.60%
		College Degree, 4 yr	20.10%	Blue Collar	28.30%
Military		Post grad	10.40%	Government	10.50%
Veteran/ Active Duty	7.40%				

2020 Pres. Vote	Trump	267,638	(67%)	Biden	126,861	(32%)		
2016 Pres. Vote	Trump	193,990	(53%)	Clinton	160,204	(44%)	Johnson	9,678 (3%)

Lexington, Burlington: The rolling hills of the Piedmont, which are really the foothills of the long ridges of the Appalachian Mountains, are a geographic feature that helped define North Carolina politically. The Piedmont was settled not by the aristocratic planters who typified the Southern lowlands, but by the more hardscrabble Scots-Irish who colonized the Appalachian regions. These settlers clustered in small towns, usually around a mill or a factory. Even today, there isn't a large population center between High Point and the ancient sand dunes in the Sandhills region toward Fayetteville. Instead, the landscape is a collection of small towns, places like Siler City, burial place of Francis Bavier, best known as Aunt Bee on The Andy Griffith Show in the 1960s. Davidson County, in the heart of the Piedmont, styles itself as the Barbecue Capital of the World and features many renowned golf courses.

In Alamance County, a voting-rights controversy gained national attention in 2018 when the local prosecutor filed felony charges against 12 individuals who had voted in violation of a state law that prohibits voting by convicted felons—including while they remain on probation or post-release supervision. Many of the "Alamance 12," nine of whom were African-Americans, said they were not aware of the restrictions and their names had not previously been removed from the voting rolls. The local district attorney said he was committed to strict prosecution of the law. At least nine of the group pleaded guilty to subsequent misdemeanor charges, without additional prison time, and the judge waived court costs, the Burlington Times-News reported. In January 2020, the Davidson County Commission showed another facet of the Old South: It unanimously agreed to make the county a "Second Amendment sanctuary" that implored the state and the nation to "to preserve, uphold, and protect the rights of all citizens to keep and bear arms" and opposed any effort to restrict those rights.

The 13th Congressional District is shaped like a backward capital "L," which wraps around the eastern and southern edges of Greensboro-based Guilford County. The four largest counties, which comprise 80 percent of the district's population, are relatively equal size and adjacent to each other. Starting with the largest, they are Lexington-based Davidson County, Burlington-based Alamance, Salisbury-based Rowan and Siler City-based Randolph. The 13th has had a disruptive decade. Following the 2016 redistricting, it was based in parts of Guilford County and extended west; that version had no overlap with the previous 13th, which was east of Raleigh. The 13th in the 2020 redistricting took from the 2016 map: Davidson and Davie counties, plus part of Rowan—35 percent of the old district. The remainder of the previous 13th extended east and then north to the outskirts of Durham and Chapel Hill.

The latest changes removed the Democratic parts in Guilford, which had nearly half of the previous population, and turned a district that had been the most politically competitive of the 10 Republican-held districts into a solidly GOP domain. In the map for 2016, Donald Trump led, 53%-44%. In the new version, he defeated Joe Biden with 67 percent of the vote.

NORTH DAKOTA

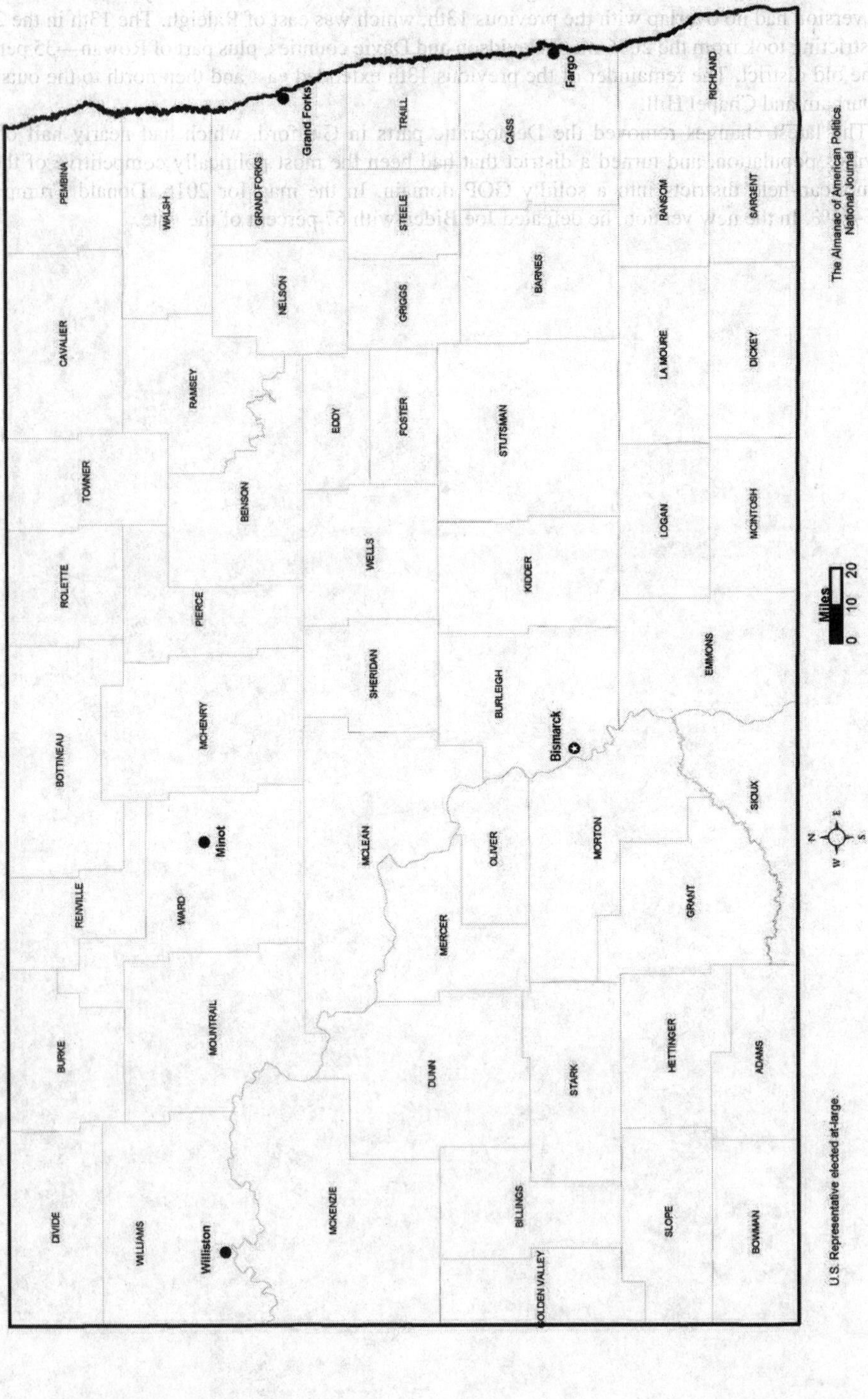

The Almanac of American Politics,
National Journal

U.S. Representative elected at-large.

Miles
0   10   20

Grand Forks

Fargo

Bismarck

Minot

Williston

PEMBINA
CAVALIER
TOWNER
ROLETTE
BOTTINEAU
RENVILLE
BURKE
DIVIDE
WILLIAMS
MOUNTRAIL
WARD
MCHENRY
PIERCE
BENSON
RAMSEY
WALSH
NELSON
GRAND FORKS
STEELE
TRAILL
CASS
GRIGGS
FOSTER
EDDY
WELLS
SHERIDAN
MCLEAN
MCKENZIE
DUNN
MERCER
OLIVER
BURLEIGH
KIDDER
STUTSMAN
BARNES
TRAILL
LOGAN
LA MOURE
DICKEY
RICHLAND
SARGENT
RANSOM
MONTOSH
EMMONS
MORTON
GRANT
SIOUX
STARK
BILLINGS
GOLDEN VALLEY
SLOPE
BOWMAN
ADAMS
HETTINGER

North Dakota, one of the most remote states in the Lower 48; has been transformed by a shale-oil boom in the western part of the state in recent years. But the coronavirus pandemic left the oil and gas industry—and the state as a whole—grappling with a severe bust. Through it all, the state has remained strongly Republican.

In late 1804, members of the Lewis and Clark Expedition paddled up the Missouri River and reached what is now North Dakota. The explorers bivouacked for the winter across the river from where the state capital of Bismarck now stands, and they spent 146 nights in North Dakota. On the Lewis and Clark Trail, you can still see traces of the pristine landscape the expedition encountered — a vast unfenced land where the Indians built a civilization based on the buffalo and the horse, a Spanish import. Less than a hundred years later, railroads crisscrossed the prairie and the Sioux were herded onto reservations; it was from Fort Abraham Lincoln, built on the site of an old Mandan Indian village in central North Dakota, that the post's commander, Lt. Col. George Armstrong Custer, rode out to his death at the Battle of the Little Bighorn in what was then the Montana Territory in 1876. Theodore Roosevelt owned a ranch in the rugged Badlands of the Dakota Territory in the late 19th century. By the time he visited the state as president in 1903, so many buffalo had been killed he needed perseverance to find one to shoot. Roosevelt's ranching days are credited with inspiring his vision for a national conservation program that established national parks and wildlife refuges during his presidency. North Dakota's lush, green farmland is pockmarked in places by placid blue "prairie pothole" lakes carved by glaciers. But its flatness encourages flooding, as in the massive Grand Forks flood in April 1997. North America's geographic center is near the town of Rugby, about 40 miles south of the Canadian border.

North Dakota was admitted to the Union in 1889, on the same day as South Dakota—no one knows which is the 39th state and which is the 40th, thanks to some quick paper shuffling by President Benjamin Harrison's secretary of State—and settlers poured in. Its prairies turned out to be some of the best wheat-growing acreage in the world, and while wheat—mostly spring wheat but also durum, used in pasta—remains the biggest crop, it is not the only one. North Dakota ranks first, second, or third in the production of dry edible beans, oats, dry peas, sunflowers, barley, sugar beets, rye, flaxseed, and canola. There is also plenty of cattle ranching on the arid plains in the western half of the state; all told, about 90 percent of the state's land is devoted to farming or ranching. While North Dakota's cold climate discouraged many Americans from settling this far north, it was no deterrent to emigrants from Germany, Norway, Bohemia (now the Czech Republic), Iceland and Russia. North Dakota's population shot up from 191,000 in 1890 to 319,000 in 1900 and to 647,000 in 1920. For the next nine decades, its population oscillated in the 600,000s, until it began to rise dramatically after 2007, reaching 765,309 in the census estimate for 2020. Just a decade after worries about an emptying-out of the northern plains, North Dakota was at times the fastest-growing state in the nation. In all, the population has risen 15.8 percent since the 2010 census.

Behind those numbers are two stories. The contraction owed to the state's dependence on an agriculture sector growing ever more productive and efficient, and thus requiring less labor. The subsequent rise came from a different economic engine: oil and natural gas from the Bakken shale formation in the western part of the state. North Dakota had seen energy booms before, but they paled in comparison to the Bakken. Discovered in 1951 and named after a Williston-area farmer, it remained untapped for many years. Then, in 2006, oil producers began using extended-reach horizontal drilling to reach more deposits, along with hydraulic fracturing to break up the shale in which the oil is embedded. North Dakota climbed to No. 2 in the nation in petroleum production; natural gas output rose as well. During the Great Recession, unemployment maxed out at a ridiculously low 4.3 percent in early 2009 and never rose above 3.3 percent between 2012 and the onset of the coronavirus pandemic. Fueling this boom was a surge of men (and fewer women) to western North Dakota, lured by annual earnings of $100,000 and more. Initially, many lived in RVs or modular living pods lined up on farm fields, because Williston, improbably, had the highest average rent in the nation for an entry-level apartment. Trucks carrying water in for fracking and oil out for refining jammed the two-lane roads and buckled the pavement; there were long lines at stores and fast-food takeout lanes, and schools were strained. The milieu spawned human and drug trafficking, organized crime and homicides—a situation worrisome enough that the FBI opened an office there. Worker deaths spiked, and the lack of government regulation attracted questions.

The energy sector is volatile, and production began to decline in 2015, with lower prices on the global market. The global shift away from fossil fuels also hampered the industry, as did controversies over pipelines. For 10 months starting in 2016, the Standing Rock Sioux, joined by the Cheyenne River Sioux and a small group of celebrities and other supporters, camped out to oppose the $3.7 billion Dakota Access Pipeline, which would run for 1,170 miles from North Dakota to Illinois. Living in teepees and rallying behind the cry "Mni wiconi!"—"water is life"—they said the pipeline would threaten drinking water supplies and harm ancestral lands. Work was temporarily halted by the Obama administration. But President Donald Trump reversed that decision as one of his first actions. The remaining demonstrators were cleared in February 2017 after burning some of their teepees as a final act of protest (and leaving tons of trash behind); tensions between the protest camp and nearby ranchers had become so heated that one state lawmaker proposed a bill to legalize running over protesters in the road as long as it was done accidentally. (The bill was defeated in the state House.) In 2019, a portion of a different pipeline, the Keystone 1, was shut down following a leak of more than 9,000 barrels of oil. For Native Americans, the state's largest minority group, choosing between economic growth and cultural and environmental protection was often wrenching.

But during its first three years of operation, the Dakota Access Pipeline significantly cut transportation costs, and in 2019, an optimistic Williston inaugurated a new, $273 million airport. Within months, however, came the most serious bust to date, prompted by the global economic slowdown from the pandemic, which caused a dramatic decline in air and automobile travel. Further hampering the oil sector was an OPEC price war and the Bakken's relatively high cost of production, transportation, and storage, which put producers in the state at a disadvantage compared to other oil-producing regions in the U.S. and overseas. In April 2020, Whiting Petroleum Corp., once the largest oil producer in the state, filed for Chapter 11 bankruptcy. Continental Resources, another large oil producer, stopped drilling and "shut in" many of its wells. With oil and gas production levies accounting for 53 percent of all taxes collected, North Dakota officials worried about the impact on the state budget. In the meantime, a federal judge in 2020 ordered a temporary shutdown of the Dakota Access Pipeline while an environmental review was being completed; a few months later, the pipeline was reopened after an appeals court overturned the decision.

By the fall of 2020, the coronavirus was becoming a serious problem for the health of its residents as well. By autumn, North Dakota was vying with South Dakota for the unwanted title of worst coronavirus hot spot in the nation. While North Dakota's per-capita caseload had declined dramatically by early 2021, the cumulative impact was significant: Almost one of every 500 North Dakota residents alive at the beginning of the pandemic had died of the virus by February 2021.

In what is the eighth-whitest state in the country, the share of African Americans and Hispanics has more than doubled, from a small base, driven by oil industry work available for qualified out-of-staters. The state's second-largest group after Whites is Native Americans; only five states have a higher percentage. The low-income Native American population fought a restrictive state voter identification law that required an ID with a residential address, even though many residents of reservations use post office box numbers. In 2020, the state settled the case in a way that significantly eased the law's impact. Meanwhile, the state saw a sizable increase in foreign-born residents, including refugees settled from Congo, Iraq and Somalia. After Trump signed an executive order allowing states and localities to opt out of refugee resettlement, Gov. Doug Burgum agreed to continue the state's participation in resettlement; after a vociferous debate, commissioners in Burleigh County (Bismarck) narrowly reaffirmed their resettlement efforts.

Until recently, North Dakota politics was shaped by agriculture, not oil. The boosterish optimism of the first settlers was soon followed by cries, reverberating with varying intensity, for government protection against market forces. Since commodity prices tend to fall during periods of economic growth, there was often a countercyclical force at work in North Dakota politics—a tendency to vote against the national trends, and a radical strain going back to the 1910s. That strain also owes much to the Scandinavian and German origins of many of the state's early settlers, who produced orderly small towns and grain cooperatives and supported the Nonpartisan League, which operated as a faction within the Republican Party from its founding in 1915 until its alliance with the Democratic Party in 1956. The NPL's program was socialist—government ownership of railroads and grain elevators —and it often determined the outcome of the usually decisive Republican primary, but sometimes swung its support to the otherwise heavily outnumbered Democrats, instituting reforms and creating the state-owned Bank of North Dakota and a state grain elevator. (In 2020, efforts by the Bank of North Dakota enabled the state to distribute federal Paycheck Protection Program funds to employers more effectively than any other state, according to The Washington Post.)

With rare exceptions, such as Democrat Heidi Heitkamp's narrow Senate victory in 2012, North Dakota has become solidly Republican. When Heitkamp ran for a second term in 2018, she fared significantly better than Hillary Clinton had two years earlier, yet still lost to GOP Rep. Kevin Cramer, 55%-44%. Her loss meant that for the first time since 1960, the state's federal delegation became all-Republican; in addition, no Democrat held any statewide elected office, and the GOP held large majorities in both legislative chambers.

In the 2016 presidential race, North Dakota's urban and suburban areas—contrary to almost every other state—moved toward Trump and away from the Democrats. Then, in 2020, with Joe Biden the Democratic nominee, these areas backed off Trump slightly. In Cass County (Fargo), Biden cut Trump's winning margin from 10 points to 3, and he cut Trump's margins by four and five points, respectively, in Grand Forks and Burleigh counties. But the gains for Biden came only on the margins; statewide, he was barely able to pare Trump's margin of victory, from 36 points to 33 points. More telling, Biden was largely unable to reach the percentages won by Barack Obama in the state just a few years earlier. Indeed, Biden won only two counties that collectively cast fewer than 5,000 votes. Expect North Dakota to remain strongly Republican for the foreseeable future.

Cook Partisan Voting Index: R+20

Population		Race and Ethnicity		Income	
Total	762,062	White	85.80%	Median Income	64,577
Land area (sq. miles)	69,001	Black	2.90%	State Income Rank	20 out of 50
Pop/ sq mi	11.04	Latino	4.00%	Poverty Rate	10.60%
Born in state	61.80%	Asian	2.10%	With health insurance	93.10%
		Two or more races	3.30%	Cash public assistance	1.70%
Age Groups		Other	6.60%	Food stamp/SNAP	7.2%
Under 18	23.20%				
18-34	26.00%	**Education**		**Work**	
35-64	34.90%	H.S grad or less	33.20%	White Collar	38.30%
Over 64	15.80%	Some college	36.40%	Sales and Service	36.10%
		College Degree, 4 yr	21.50%	Blue Collar	25.60%
Military		Post grad	8.90%	Government	16.50%
Veteran/ Active Duty	9.30%				

Presidential Politics

2020 Caucus (D)	Sanders (D)	7,682(53%)	Biden (D)	5,742(40%)			
2016 Caucus (D)	Sanders (D)	253(64%)	Clinton (D)	101(26%)			
2020 Pres. Vote	Trump (R)	235,595(65%)	Biden (D)	114,902(32%)			
2016 Pres. Vote	Trump (R)	216,794(63%)	Clinton (D)	93,758(27%)	Johnson (L)	21,434 (6%)	

In the past 21 presidential elections, North Dakota has voted only once for a Democratic nominee: Lyndon Johnson in 1964. So it came as no surprise that President Donald Trump defeated Joe Biden here, 65%-32%. Biden carried just two of the state's 53 counties, Rolette and Sioux, where the Native American population exceeds 75 percent, though he held Trump to a three-point win in Cass County, the state's most populous and the home to Fargo. North Dakota was the state that turned most Republican in the 2016 election: Trump's margin over Hillary Clinton was 36 percentage points, a whopping 16-point increase from Mitt Romney's margin over President Barack Obama in 2012. Republicans now have a near-lock on the state, whose population has boomed this past decade because of fracking; oil and natural gas production from the Bakken shale formation in the state's west has had a significant impact on its politics and economy.

North Dakota Democrats and Republicans use caucuses to help select their national convention delegates. In 2016, the state GOP declined to include a presidential preference poll at the first stage of its caucuses, opting to elect individuals who would then select a delegation to the national Republican confab in Cleveland that was technically unbound to any candidate. After Texas Sen. Ted Cruz suspended his campaign, many of the Cruz delegates switched their allegiance to Trump. In the Democratic caucuses in June, Vermont Sen. Bernie Sanders campaigned in Bismarck and won 64 percent of the county delegates selected to the state convention to Clinton's 26 percent, with 10 percent uncommitted. The state's 2020 Democratic caucuses were held on March 10, a week after Super Tuesday; Sanders prevailed over Biden 53%-40%, making it the only state he won after Super Tuesday.

Congressional Districts

117th Congress Lineup	1R	116th Congress Lineup	1R

Doug Burgum (R)

Elected 2016, term expires 2024, 2nd term; b. Aug. 1, 1956, Arthur, ND; North Dakota State University, B.A., 1978; Stanford University, M.B.A., 1980; Married (Kathryn); 3 children.

Professional Career: CEO, Great Plains Software 1983-2001; Senior Vice President, Microsoft Business Solutions Group,2001-2007; Founder, Arthur Ventures.

Office: 600 E. Boulevard Ave. Bismarck, 58505-0001; 701-328-2200; Fax: 701-328-2205
Lt. Gov.: Brent Sanford (R) **Atty. Gen:** Wayne Stenehjem (R) **Sec. of State:** Al Jaeger (R)
State Legislature: Senate: 10D, 37R **House:** 15D, 79R

Election Results

Election	Name (Party)	Vote (%)
2016 General	Doug Burgum (R)	259,863 (77%)
	Marvin Nelson (D)	65,855 (19%)
	Marty Riske (L)	13,230 (4%)
2020 General	Doug Burgum (R)	235,479 (66%)
	Shelley Lenz (D)	90,789 (25%)
	Write-In (W-I)	17,538 (5%)
	DuWayne Hendrickson (L)	13,853 (4%)
2016 Primary	Doug Burgum (R)	68,042 (59%)
	Wayne Stenehjem (R)	44,158 (39%)

Doug Burgum, a successful software entrepreneur, was easily reelected governor of North Dakota in 2020. When he first won the office, North Dakota had a booming oil and gas sector. By the end of Burgum's first term, his state was grappling with the economic and health effects of the coronavirus pandemic.

Burgum grew up near tiny Arthur, northwest of Fargo, and attended North Dakota State University, where he was a cheerleader. He earned an MBA at Stanford before returning to North Dakota. In 1983, he mortgaged the family farm to get into the computer business. He became CEO of Fargo-based Great Plains Software, expanded the company, took it public in 1997, then sold it to Microsoft for $1.1 billion in 2001, when it had 1,200 local employees. Burgum then led

Microsoft Business Solutions for six years before founding a group to revitalize downtown Fargo and establishing a venture-capital firm.

After Gov. Jack Dalrymple said he would not seek another term in 2016, Burgum announced his intention to run for the seat. With a deep Republican bench in the state, others were ahead of him in the establishment queue, notably long-serving state Attorney General Wayne Stenehjem. Burgum seized the outsider's mantle, touting his business experience ("when I think about the governor's job, I like it because it's a CEO position," Burgum told Fortune) and announcing that he would forgo his gubernatorial salary if elected. At the state Republican convention in April, he finished a distant third behind Stenehjem and state Rep. Rick Becker. In the June primary, Stenehjem had the endorsements of Dalrymple, Sen. John Hoeven and most Republican state lawmakers. But amid a $1.6 billion state budget shortfall and the Republican surge for Donald Trump, Burgum's outsider approach proved to be more effective with rank-and-file primary voters. Burgum endorsed Trump in May and spoke more favorably about him than Stenehjem did. Burgum defeated Stenehjem, 59%-39%, carrying 49 of North Dakota's 53 counties.

The general election was anticlimactic, as the Democrats put up underfunded state Rep. Marvin Nelson. Burgum won, 77%-19%. That 58-point margin was double Dalrymple's already substantial 29-point victory in 2012. Nelson won only two counties, down from the six won by the Democratic nominee in 2012. Strikingly, Burgum increased the GOP's winning margins from 2012 by roughly double digits in each of the state's four most populous counties—Cass (Fargo), Burleigh (Bismarck), Ward (Minot) and Grand Forks.

Upon taking office, Burgum kept most of Dalrymple's cabinet and sought more extensive spending cuts to balance the state budget with declining tax revenues from oil and gas. Drawing from his own background, Burgum touted the role of technology in economic growth and the diversification of the state's economy. In his first state of the state address, he choked up while telling the story of a young man he had met in Fargo who was homeless, suffering from addiction to methamphetamine, and facing a parole violation. "Jail time without rehab is not a cure for addiction," Burgum said. "We need to start treating addiction like the chronic disease it is, and by moving these services upstream we will save lives and we will save taxpayer money." His wife, Kathryn Helgaas Burgum, overcame alcohol addiction and now spearheads a statewide "Recovery Reinvented" initiative.

Burgum supported the Dakota Access Pipeline, which had drawn intense protests on environmental and cultural grounds from the Standing Rock Sioux tribe and a band of celebrity allies. Burgum said he offered a "fresh start" to critics of the pipeline, which was eventually greenlighted by Trump. Weeks after taking office, Burgum signed a bill to allow the carrying of concealed firearms without a permit. The state's fiscal picture had a roller-coaster couple of years, due in part to fluctuating conditions in the oil and gas industry. Burgum urged spending a portion of the state's Legacy Fund—a voter-created account funded by oil and gas revenue—on such projects as a proposed Theodore Roosevelt Presidential Library and infrastructure for developing and deploying drones. (During Burgum's 2020 state of the state speech, a small drone emerged to deliver him the remote control for his slide show.)Burgum and the legislature skirmished over the limits of the governor's line-item veto powers, and the governor established a task force to reconsider how the state's 11 public colleges and universities were governed. In 2019, Burgum signed a bill that eliminated mandatory minimum sentences for certain drug crimes, and another that eased strict prohibitions on Sunday shopping.

Burgum faced his biggest challenge in 2020, when the coronavirus pandemic hit. The initial impact was economic, as the state's oil and gas industry faced plummeting demand nationally and globally. This, in turn, threatened the state's fiscal health; in June, Burgum ordered state agencies to start cutting their budgets 5-15 percent. The health impacts took later to develop, as the state's isolation helped keep the infection rate low. Burgum ordered some business closures and made an emotional call for residents to wear masks that drew national attention, but he resisted a statewide stay-at-home order. In the fall, as North Dakota was becoming one of the hardest-hit states in the nation, Burgum issued a mask requirement. (Fargo, Grand Forks, Minot, and Bismarck had already put mandates into place by then.)

In the run-up to the 2020 election, Burgum ruffled feathers within his own party by working to defeat Jeff Delzer, the long-serving chairman of the state House Appropriations Committee, in the GOP primary.David Andahl, Burgum's favored candidate, did defeat Delzer in the primary but died a month before the election due to the coronavirus. Following a ruling by the North Dakota Supreme Court that Burgum did not have the authority as governor to fill legislative vacancies, Delzer was appointed by the local district GOP to fill the seat, and he returned to his chairmanship. As for Burgum, his own reelection was easy. After easily winning the GOP primary, Burgum faced Democrat Shelley Lenz, a veterinarian and founder of an overseas economic development nonprofit. Burgum won, 66%-25%, a wide margin but smaller than his victory four years earlier. Lenz secured 38 percent more votes than the 2016 Democratic nominee had, and she narrowed Burgum's winning margins by double digits in each of the state's four largest counties—Cass, Burleigh, Grand Forks and Ward. Still, it was hardly enough to give North Dakota Democrats hope of becoming a genuinely competitive party any time soon.

John Hoeven (R)

Elected 2010, term expires 2022, 2nd term, b. Mar 13, 1957; Bismarck; Dartmouth College, Hanover, B.A., 1979; Northwestern University Kellogg School Management, M.B.A., 1981; Roman Catholic; Married (Mikey Hoeven); 2 children; 3 grandchildren.

Elected Office: ND Governor, 2000-2010.

Professional Career: Executive VP, First Western Bank, 1986-1993; President & CEO, Bank of ND, 1993-2000.

DC Office: 338 RSOB 20510, 202-224-2551, Fax: 202-224-7999, hoeven.senate.gov

State Offices: Bismarck, 701-250-4618; Fargo, 701-239-5389; Grand Forks, 701-746-8972; Minot, 701-838-1361.

Committees: *Agriculture, Nutrition & Forestry*: Commodities, Risk Management & Trade (RMM); Conservation, Climate, Forestry & Natural Resources; Food & Nutrition, Specialty Crops, Organics & Research. *Appropriations*: Agriculture, Rural Development, FDA & Related Agencies (RMM); Department of Defense; Department of Homeland Security; Energy & Water Development; Military Construction & Veteran Affairs & Related Agencies; Transportation, HUD & Related Agencies. *Energy & Natural Resources*: Energy (RMM); National Parks; Water & Power. *Indian Affairs*.

Group Ratings

	ADA	ACLU	AFL-CIO	LCV	COC	HAFA	ACU	CFG	FRC
2020	-	17%	-	15%	-	64%	70%	-	-
2019	0%	C	21%	14%	94%	C	69%	29%	100%

Almanac Ratings 2019-2020

	Economy	Social	Foreign	Composite
Liberal	0%	0%	0%	0%
Conservative	100%	100%	100%	100%

Key Votes of the 116th Congress

1. EPA clean energy rules	N	5. Russia sanctions	N	9. Barr as Atty. General	Y
2. U.S./Mex./Can. trade deal	Y	6. Troops in SYR, AFG	Y	10. Spending at the border	Y
3. Cut unemployment benefits	Y	7. Veto arms sales to Saudis	N	11. Coney Barrett to Sup. Ct.	Y
4. Shelton to Fed Reserve	Y	8. Defense $$$, veto override	Y	12. Electoral College objections	N

Election Results

Election	Name (Party)	Vote (%)		Cand. Spent	Ind. Exp. Support	Ind. Exp. Oppose
2016 General	John Hoeven (R)	268,788	(79%)	$2,055,899		
	Eliot Glassheim (D)	58,116	(17%)	$32,799		
	Robert Marquette (L)	10,556	(3%)			
2016 Primary	John Hoeven (R)	Unopposed				

Prior winning percentages: 2016 (79%), 2010 (76%), Governor: 2008 (74%), 2004 (71%), 2000 (55%)

John Hoeven became the first Republican senator from North Dakota in 24 years in 2011—and two years later he became that state's senior senator. After presiding over the state's new prosperity

—from an oil and gas boom—he has been a reliable member of the GOP team. He has protected home state interests, with his growing seniority on the Appropriations and Agriculture committees. His continued popularity at home suggested another landslide reelection in 2022.

Hoeven was born in Bismarck and grew up in Minot. His father was a banker who in 1969 took over the First Western Bank & Trust of Minot, which became a family business. Hoeven started working there as a bookkeeper at 15. He graduated from Dartmouth College and went on to earn his master's degree in business administration from Northwestern University. He later returned home to become First Western Bank's executive vice president. In 1993, he was chosen to head the Bank of North Dakota, the only state-owned bank in the country, by a board that included his predecessor as governor, Republican Ed Schafer, and then-Attorney General Heidi Heitkamp, a Democrat. Under Hoeven's stewardship, the bank's worth rose from $990 million to $1.6 billion, and its loan portfolio increased from $200 million to $1 billion. Hoeven's banking career and successful investments have placed him among the 25 wealthiest members of Congress, according to Roll Call's survey of congressional assets. Financial disclosure forms show him with a net worth of at least $17 million.

Though he's credited with putting North Dakota in the red column, Hoeven had declared himself a Democrat as recently as four years before his 2000 election as governor. In a 1996 letter to a local newspaper, Hoeven wrote: "I have always been moderate in my political views, but now that I am considering elective office, I realize I must join a political party and stick to it. I have decided to join the Democratic-NPL Party because I believe that is the best fit for my views." The Bank of North Dakota was created in 1919 at the initiative of the Nonpartisan League, a coalition of reformers and radicals that was a major force in North Dakota for decades before it merged with the state Democratic Party in 1960.

When the letter surfaced during Hoeven's 2010 Senate bid, his campaign manager, Don Larson, told Talking Points Memo that, shortly after writing the letter, Hoeven "realized his views were more in line with the Republicans than the Democrats. So, he got involved with the Republican Party, became a Republican district chairman, helped Republican candidates around North Dakota and then ran for and won the governorship. Before that, he had not been involved in politics at all, either as a Republican or a Democrat." Throughout his tenure as governor and a senator, Hoeven has been in the conservative Republican mainstream on most social issues, ranging from abortion to gun control. Unlike those in the party's tea party wing, Hoeven has been open to increasing funds for education and infrastructure; while he was governor, the state budget grew dramatically, especially in those categories.

Hoeven ran for governor against Heitkamp in 2000 when Republican Gov. Ed Schafer retired. He cited his work attracting and retaining jobs and organizing the effort to keep Minot Air Force Base off the government's base closure list. He called for economic development in the state with an emphasis on the technology industry and on improving education, and he pledged more money for teacher training and salaries. He won 55%-45%, as Heitkamp was compelled to all but end her campaign after she was diagnosed with breast cancer.

As governor, Hoeven used North Dakota's burgeoning revenues to fund programs to stimulate economic development. In 2002, he announced an ambitious research and development program, borrowing $50 million for university projects to commercialize new technology. From 2005 to 2007, more than $40 million in state funds and double that amount in private funds were invested in several research centers. Much of this was aimed at exploiting North Dakota's abundant energy resources, including oil, coal, ethanol, wind, and hydrogen. In 2002, he announced his EmPower North Dakota energy plan, aimed at building three biodiesel plants by 2015 and having wind supply 10 percent of the state's electricity by 2015. By 2014, wind energy supplied 17.5 percent of electricity generated in North Dakota.

During his second term, Hoeven submitted budgets with reductions in property taxes and big increases in education spending, especially for raising teachers' salaries. Despite the pleas of national Republicans, he opted not to challenge Democratic Sen. Kent Conrad in 2006. In 2008, he won a third term against state Sen. Tim Mathern, capturing nearly 75 percent of the vote.

By all indications, Democratic Sen. Byron Dorgan was planning to run for a fourth term—he had been raising money for the campaign—until he stunned Senate colleagues in January 2010 by saying he would retire. Shortly thereafter, Hoeven announced he was running for the open Senate seat, criticizing President Barack Obama's economic agenda and what he called the overly bureaucratic overhaul of the health care system. He didn't have to campaign very hard. Democratic nominee state Sen. Tracy Potter struggled for attention and momentum. Hoeven spent $4 million; Potter spent $28,000. Hoeven won 76%-22%.

In the Senate, Hoeven worked on the 2014 farm bill that renewed federal agriculture and nutrition programs. On the Agriculture Committee, he supported an earlier version of the bill that cleared the Senate in 2012, which ended direct payments to farmers but included a new form of crop insurance favored by farm-state senators outside the South. Both features were included in the final 2014 legislation. Hoeven also worked to ensure that the legislation contained an extension of the sugar program—important to North Dakota, one of the nation's leading producers of sugar beets, but decried by critics who say it has raised the cost of sugar for consumers.

On the next farm bill, in 2018, Hoeven called crop insurance "the primary risk management tool for many producers" and cited a countercyclical safety net that he added to the coverage that was designed to reduce disparity in protection between counties. He worked on another provision in the final agreement to ensure producers have access to enough capital. "This increased credit is especially helpful to young producers," he said.

In February 2020, he and Rep. Collin Peterson of Minnesota, chairman of the House Agriculture Committee, announced their agreement with the Agriculture Department to provide $285 million in disaster assistance for sugar co-ops, a move designed to help growers facing bad weather—ranging from flooding to drought. The deal was designed to assist producers, "as many are struggling with cash flow issues as they head into spring 2020 planting," Hoeven said. The agreement was part of a larger disaster-aid package that Congress enacted two months earlier. Peterson, who was defeated for reelection in November 2020, resided in northwest Minnesota, close to the North Dakota border —an area with similar farm interests.

On the Energy and Natural Resources Committee, Hoeven advocated a national energy plan similar to EmPower North Dakota— an approach that encompassed renewable and traditional energy resources. He was an outspoken critic of Obama's decision to block construction of the Keystone XL pipeline, which was designed to carry 100,000 barrels of oil a day from Canada to the Gulf Coast, partly through North Dakota. In 2014, he led the effort to allow the pipeline to move ahead; it cleared the House and Senate. Pipeline advocates fell five votes short of the two-thirds majority needed to override Obama's veto. Finally, with the election of President Donald Trump, Hoeven won legislative approval of the pipeline in early 2017. But the project later was abandoned by its corporate overseers.

Hoeven played a leading role in another pipeline controversy. In 2016, members of the Standing Rock Sioux Tribe protested that the Dakota Access pipeline—built to transport 470,000 barrels of oil daily from North Dakota to Illinois —grazed its reservation. Tribal opponents of the project said it violated a 170-year-old treaty with the U.S. government and that a leak in the pipeline —routed under a reservoir adjacent to the reservation— could have disastrous consequences for drinking-water supplies. As the Sioux were joined by thousands of Native American allies, the protests attracted international attention as a symbol of the continuing fight for Native American rights. Hoeven rebuked the protests as often violent and disruptive of the economic livelihood of farmers and ranchers in the area.

In a Senate speech, he dismissed the arguments against the pipeline as specious, noting the pipeline had been "twice challenged and twice upheld—including by the Obama administration's own appointees" and saying,"the federal courts found that the Army Corps had followed the appropriate process, the Standing Rock Sioux Tribe was properly consulted and the project could lawfully proceed." While Obama was still in office, the Army Corps of Engineers denied an easement to allow pipeline builders to burrow under the reservoir. As it had with the Keystone pipeline, the Trump administration quickly reversed that decision and granted the easement, although tribal leaders vowed to continue fighting.

Given this history, Hoeven's ascension in early 2017 to the normally low-profile chairmanship of the Senate Indian Affairs Committee drew pushback from progressive activists.With bipartisan support in December 2018, he enacted his bill to give Native American tribes greater flexibility to manage their energy resources by streamlining their agreement with the Interior Department. The measure was supported by tribes in North Dakota, where about a fifth of state's oil production is on the Fort Berthold Indian Reservation.

As committee chairman, Hoeven spent the next two years working to enact what proved to be an uncontroversial bill designed to give greater control and flexibility to American Indian tribes in the administration of federal programs. The bill had a lengthy title: the Practical Reforms and Other Goals To Reinforce the Effectiveness of Self-Governance and Self-Determination for Indian Tribes Act of 2019. Trump signed the measure, known as the PROGRESS for Indian Tribes Act, in October 2020. The bill "reduces unnecessary red tape and streamlines the Department of the Interior's Self-Governance program," Hoeven said.

Hoeven has been open to federal regulation in other areas. He was 1 of 15 Republicans to vote to reauthorize the Violence Against Women Act in 2012.The next year, he supported the bipartisan immigration overhaul pushed by Republican Sens. Marco Rubio of Florida and John McCain of Arizona. Later that year, he was one of only nine Senate Republicans to back a bipartisan budget deal crafted by the chairmen of the Senate and House budget committees; conservative groups said the measure would spend too much.

Continuing as senator his gubernatorial efforts to spur economic development through technology, Hoeven joined Democratic Sen. Cory Booker of New Jersey in 2015 on legislation to set guidelines for drones—an effort to increase commercial use of unmanned aircraft. At the end of 2016, he helped gain approval from the Federal Aviation Administration for a drone test site in Grand Forks. That site became the first in the nation to operated drones beyond line of sight.

In the 2016 campaign, Hoeven spent more than $2 million while running against state Rep. Eliot Glassheim. Glassheim, owner of a Grand Forks used-bookstore called Dr. Eliot's Twice Sold Tales, spent a mere $33,000. Hoeven won in a 78%-17% blowout, running 15 points ahead of Trump in the state.He took 52 of 53 counties: Glassheim won Sioux, the only county entirely within the boundaries of the Standing Rock Reservation.

Hoeven was rated as the GOP senator who most consistently supported his party in 2017 and 2018, according to Pro Publica. In the Almanac vote ratings for that period, his scores were solidly conservative. Still, he voiced concern that while Trump's tariffs might benefit steel and other industries, "we want to be very careful to make sure that it doesn't hurt our [farmers'] ability to export in other areas."He criticized early drafts of the Senate bill to repeal and replace the Affordable Care Act, which he said would have adversely affected healthcare providers in North Dakota; he voted for the final version, which failed to win Senate approval.

In the spring of 2020, amid the international economic collapse amid the coronavirus pandemic, Hoeven sought to protect his state's economy. He played a central role in crafting a provision for$50 billion of aid to farmers, which was a small portion of the huge economic-relief measure enacted in late March of that year.

Hoeven also led six Republican senators from energy-producing states who criticized decisions by Saudi Arabia and Russia to drop restrictions on their petroleum refining as "economic warfare against the United States." In April, as energy prices plummeted, he claimed credit for a measure buying $3 billion of U.S. crude oil for the Strategic Petroleum Reserve. He called the action a step "to support our domestic energy producers and provide stability to global energy markets."

Kevin Cramer (R)

Elected 2018, term expires 2024, 1st term, b. Jan 21, 1961; Rolette; Concordia College, B.A., 1983; University of Mary, M.A., 2003; Evangelical; Married (Kris Neumann); 5 children (1 deceased); 5 grandchildren.

Elected Office: ND Public Service Commission, 2003-2012; U.S. House 2013-2019.

Professional Career: Director, Harold Schafer Leadership Foundation, 2001-2003; Director, ND tourism, 1993-1997; Chairman, ND Republican Party, 1991-1993.

DC Office: 400 RSOB 20510, 202-224-2043, cramer.senate.gov

State Offices: Fargo, 701-232-5094; Minot, 701-837-6141.

Committees: *Armed Services*: Emerging Threats & Capabilities; Seapower (RMM); Strategic Forces. *Banking, Housing & Urban Affairs*: Economic Policy; Financial Institutions & Consumer Protection; Housing, Transportation & Community Development. *Budget*. *Environment & Public Works*: Clean Air & Nuclear Safety; Fisheries, Water, and Wildlife; Transportation & Infrastructure (RMM). *Veterans' Affairs*.

Group Ratings (House)

	ADA	ACLU	AFL-CIO	LCV	COC	HAFA	ACU	CFG	FRC
2020	-	18%	-	15%	-	63%	73%	-	-
2019	0%	C	21%	14%	96%	C	72%	29%	100%

Almanac Ratings 2019-2020

	Economy	Social	Foreign	Composite
Liberal	8%	6%	0%	5%
Conservative	92%	94%	100%	95%

Key Votes of the 116th Congress (House)

1. EPA clean energy rules	N	5. Russia sanctions	N	9. Barr as Atty. General	Y
2. U.S./Mex./Can. trade deal	Y	6. Troops in SYR, AFG	Y	10. Spending at the border	Y
3. Cut unemployment benefits	Y	7. Veto arms sales to Saudis	N	11. Coney Barrett to Sup. Ct.	Y
4. Shelton to Fed Reserve	Y	8. Defense $$$, veto override	Y	12. Electoral College objections	N

Election Results

Election	Name (Party)	Vote (%)		Cand. Spent	Ind. Exp. Support	Ind. Exp. Oppose
2018 General	Kevin Cramer (R)............................... 179,720	(55%)		$6,121,645	$807,062	$7,244,464
	Heidi Heitkamp (D)............................ 144,376	(44%)		$18,948,236	$1,896,604	$8,518,167
2018 Primary	Kevin Cramer (R)................................. 61,529	(88%)				
	Thomas O'Neill (R)............................. 8,509	(12%)				

Prior winning percentages: 2018 (55%), House: 2016 (69%), 2014 (56%), 2012 (55%)

Republican Kevin Cramer, after struggling for decades to gain a seat and influence in Congress, showed insider skills after he was elected to the Senate in 2018—the culmination of a long career in North Dakota politics that has had its ups and downs. After President Donald Trump was slow to embrace his challenge to Democratic Sen. Heidi Heitkamp during a tough campaign, Cramer followed up his victory with occasional displays of independence and moves to become a Senate insider.

In 2020, he urged compromise on economic stimulus legislation in response to the COVID-19-related economic collapse, and he was willing to publicly voice concerns that led to the scuttling of a Trump nominee to the Pentagon—independence that many GOP senators were reluctant to display. Cramer, who was candid in conceding the importance of retaining the Republican majority in the Senate, also was eager to exploit opportunities resulting from that control.

His relatively smooth transition to the Senate followed his 55%-44% victory over Heitkamp— by far the widest margin of the four GOP challengers who ousted Democratic senators in 2018 and a signal that he might have a lengthy Senate career. Although his campaign had bumps, Cramer benefited from the overwhelming rightward shift in his home state, especially once he gained the support of Trump.

Cramer grew up in Kindred, southwest of Fargo. Throughout high school, he worked for the same electric cooperative as his father. He earned his bachelor's degree from the Evangelical Lutheran Church-affiliated Concordia College in Minnesota, where he was a pre-seminary student majoring in social work. Cramer was inspired to get involved in politics by Ronald Reagan, whom he described as a "joyful conservative." He was a campaign aide to Sen. Mark Andrews in his failed 1986 reelection bid and worked for the state Republican Party, where he rose to executive director. At 30, he was the youngest-ever state party chairman. A self-described leader of a GOP "youth movement," he was courted by national party bigwigs. Looking back, Cramer said, he was naïve enough to be "quite bold —you might say reckless, even."

After serving as state tourism director, he ran for the House in 1996. Cramer lost to veteran Democratic Rep. Earl Pomeroy 55%-43%. After the loss, Cramer became the state's economic development director. He ran for the House seat a second time in 1998, but again lost to Pomeroy, this time with 41 percent of the vote. He later called that run a political mistake that cost him the state party's endorsement when he ran for the seat in 2010. That year, he dropped out before the GOP primary. From 2003 to 2012, he served on North Dakota's public service commission, helping oversee an energy-driven boom in the state economy. He worked for a foundation offering faith-based training for students at the University of Mary in Bismarck, where he earned a master's degree in management.

When Republican Rick Berg defeated Pomeroy in 2010 and then ran for the Senate in 2012, Cramer tried again, spurning the state party's endorsement and taking his campaign directly to the primary. He beat party-backed Brian Kalk, a fellow public service commissioner, 55%-45%. Against

Democrat Pam Gulleson, a former state representative, Cramer ran as a strong social conservative, saying on his campaign website, "I hope you know that my public service is an extension of my service to Christ." He called himself "a strong advocate for the free market system." Gulleson was competitive financially, but the state's Republican tilt gave the win to Cramer by 13 percentage points.

In the House, Cramer advocated for a host of North Dakota interests. He often told President Barack Obama "you're welcome" for the huge economic boost to the nation from oil and gas drilling in North Dakota and urged Obama to open more federal lands to production. He was one of the few congressional Republicans to support Obama's bid to normalize relations with Cuba. In addition to the opportunity for agriculture sales, he said that the move was "an opportunity to influence an oppressed country." In 2016, Cramer won enactment of a measure to set procedures for criminal background checks of adults working in foster care or tribal social service agencies. His Almanac vote ratings put him toward the center of House Republicans.

In 2014, Cramer faced a competitive contest with Democratic state Sen. George Sinner, the son of former Gov. George Sinner. The challenger complained that Cramer's campaign ads were dishonest and proposed "truth in politics" legislation. Cramer responded that his ads were true and that Sinner's proposal would violate the free speech guarantee of the First Amendment. Cramer won 56%-39%.

As one of seven House members who served single-district states, Cramer was well-positioned to run for the Senate when the opportunity knocked. He became the early front-runner among possible challengers to Heitkamp. Before their faceoff became official, both took steps to show their ambition and their reluctance to face each other in the election.

Soon after Heitkamp met with Trump in New York after the 2016 election and voiced interest in joining his Cabinet, reports surfaced that she was under consideration for Agriculture secretary. Cramer, in turn, had a well-publicized meeting with then-Senate Majority Leader Mitch McConnell to discuss the possibility that he would run in a special election for a vacant seat. He also had his own meeting with Trump in New York to discuss the possibility of becoming secretary of Energy. During the presidential campaign, he had written a white paper for Trump about energy policy and his skepticism about climate change. Neither Heitkamp nor Cramer was selected for the Cabinet, though their political dances with Trump had begun.

While GOP leaders thought Cramer was the strongest challenger to Heitkamp, some Republicans were concerned about his penchant for making controversial comments. They were worried about a repeat of the 2012 campaign, in which Heitkamp narrowly defeated Berg. Despite facing an uphill reelection fight, which was laid bare by Trump's 63%-27% win in North Dakota in 2016, Heitkamp maximized her opportunities. Her strong support for the rollback of the Dodd-Frank financial reforms was instrumental in the bipartisan approval of the Senate-passed bill. She was the only Democrat to attend the bill-signing ceremony at the White House, where she stood in front of other supporters—including Cramer—and directly at Trump's side. Americans for Prosperity—the political network of the conservative Koch brothers—took the unusual step of backing the Democrat in a priority contest, including digital ads.

In June 2018, the Washington Post headlined a story about Cramer: "GOP candidate seethes as Trump embraces Democratic senator." Trump's positive remarks about Heitkamp made other large conservative campaign donors reluctant to offend the president. As a result, Heitkamp outspent Cramer, $25 million to $6 million; party committees from both sides spent more than $15 million on the contest—huge sums for a sparsely populated state. Reflecting the views of his home state's businesses, Cramer voiced disagreement with Trump's crackdown on immigration. The adverse effects of Trump's tariffs on North Dakota farmers—who included the three largest soybean producers in the nation—became another concern for Cramer.

As Cramer tended to his campaign, his victory gained a sense of inevitability. He was bolstered by Trump's appearances at three rallies. Probably the final strike against Heitkamp's campaign prospects was her election-eve opposition to Supreme Court nominee Brett Kavanaugh. Heitkamp, one of three Democratic senators who voted to confirm Neil Gorsuch to the high court in 2017, concluded that Kavanaugh was "tearing our country apart"; she tried to shift the discussion to other issues, which proved difficult during the dramatic Senate hearings. Cramer's double-digit victory marked the first time since 1960 that Republicans controlled both Senate seats from North Dakota.

In the Senate, Cramer did not walk away from conflict or the opportunity to show influence. On the Armed Services Committee, he voiced concern over Trump's nominee for Pentagon undersecretary of policy, Anthony Tata, a retired Army general and an occasional inflammatory Fox News commentator. Prior to Tata's scheduled confirmation hearing in July 2020, which was expected to focus on Tata's harsh criticism of former President Barack Obama, Cramer was noncommittal to reporters who sought his view on the nomination. The committee cancelled the hearing amid signs that opposition by Cramer, and perhaps other Republicans, would sink the nomination. Later that year, when Trump fueled concerns that he might fail to acknowledge his reelection defeat, Cramer dismissed the controversy as an example of the President's "very extreme manners."

Cramer criticized bipartisan congressional leaders for their failure to reach agreement on an economic stimulus bill in the final weeks before the 2020 election. He told a reporter that a more expensive legislation likely would result in less Republican support, though he added, "the substance also matters." When a Democratic challenger for Senate in North Carolina acknowledged sending romantic text messages to a woman who was not his wife, Politico cited Cramer's reaction: "The entire majority of the United States Senate could rest not just on this one race, but this one issue." Asked before the 2020 elections about the potential effect of a partisan deadlock in the Senate, he said, "A 50-50 Senate makes it really difficult for the party of the president to do everything that they may want to do."

Regardless of internal Senate politics, there's no reason to believe the Republican brand of its North Dakotans will end any time soon.

Kelly Armstrong (R)

Elected 2018, 2nd term, b. Oct 08, 1976; Dickinson, ND; University of ND, B.A., 2000; University of ND, B.A., 2000; University of ND School of Law, J.D., 2003; Lutheran; Married (Kjersti Armstrong); 2 children.

Elected Office: ND Senate, 2012-2018.

Professional Career: Attorney; Vice President, Armstrong Corp.

DC Office: 1004 LHOB 20515, 202-225-2611, armstrong.house.gov

State Offices: Bismarck, 701-354-6700; Fargo, 701-353-6665.

Committees: *Energy & Commerce*: Consumer Protection & Commerce; Energy. *Ethics. Select Committee on the Climate Crisis.*

Almanac Ratings 2019-2020

	Economy	Social	Foreign	Composite
Liberal	34%	16%	27%	26%
Conservative	66%	84%	73%	74%

Key Votes of the 116th Congress

1. U.S./Mex./Can. trade deal	Y	5. Russia sanctions	Y	9. Firearms background checks	N
2. First Coronavirus response	Y	6. Troops in Syria	Y	10. Spending at the border	Y
3. HEROES Act	N	7. Veto arms sales to Saudis	N	11. Marijuana liberalized rules	N
4. CASH Act	N	8. Defense $$$, veto override	Y	12. Electoral College objections	N

Election Results

Election	Name (Party)	Vote (%)		Cand. Spent	Ind. Exp. Support	Ind. Exp. Oppose
2020 General	Kelly Armstrong (R)	245,229	(69%)	$637,861	$858	$750
	Zach Raknerud (D)	97,970	(28%)	$22,541		
	Steven Peterson (L)	12,024	(3%)			
2020 Primary	Kelly Armstrong (R)	99,582	(100%)			

Prior winning percentages: 2018 (60%)

With his diverse background, Republican Kelly Armstrong showed as a House freshman that he was comfortable in dealing with national issues. In the minority, he found that his views were not always accepted. But, with a seat on the Energy and Commerce Committee, he was well-positioned for the long term. At home, he was a lawyer and a leader of his family business in energy and farming. As an ally of North Dakota's governor, Doug Burgum, and chairman of the state Republican Party, he easily won the GOP nomination for the open House seat in 2018and showed independence from President Donald Trump by criticizing the trade war with China as harmful to his home state's soybean exports.

Armstrong got his bachelor's and law degrees from the University of North Dakota. He served as vice president of Armstrong Corp., his family's oil and gas business, which has been active in farming and other commercial activities in the booming energy-production region in the western part of the state. Harold Hamm of Oklahoma, a billionaire oil investor and a pioneer of North Dakota drilling, has been a partner of the Armstrong projects. Hamm also has been a prominent financier of Republican politics, both nationally and in North Dakota.

Elected to the state senate in 2012, Armstrong chaired the Judiciary Committee. He helped enact measures on issues ranging from criminal sentences to disputes over private mineral ownership. He took special interest in a bill that established guidelines for the use of confidential informants, which followed a controversial local incident. Armstrong also practiced law in his hometown of Dickinson.

Rep. Kevin Cramer announced his ultimately successful campaign for the Senate in February 2018, leaving Republicans a brief period to select a House candidate to succeed him. Armstrong, who called himself "a conservative guy with a conservative record," stepped down as chairman of the state party. That experience proved helpful as he won the endorsement of the Republican convention in April. State Sen. Tom Campbell, a potato farmer who had been seeking the GOP nomination to oppose Heitkamp before Cramer entered that contest, was the distant runner-up at the convention.

Campbell subsequently reversed his decision to run in the House primary, though he was too late to remove his name from the ballot. Campbell spent $1.2 million overall, including $745,000 in personal loans; Armstrong spent $1 million to get the GOP nomination, including $300,000 in personal loans.

Armstrong, who described himself as a "Trump Republican," occasionally went his own way from the president during his first congressional campaign. In an interview with the Grand Forks Herald following the GOP convention, he warned that Chinese retaliation for the president's tariffs would harm North Dakota's soybean exports and other parts of the state's agriculture industry. "This cannot happen," he said. In November, Armstrong defeated Democrat Mac Schneider, a former state Senate minority leader, 60%-36%.

In the House, Armstrong weighed in on issues as a member of the Judiciary Committee, though he acknowledged that the partisan lines often were sharply drawn on that panel. In June 2020, after he had privately discussed with committee Democrats a plan to require federal law enforcement agencies to record all interviews in criminal inquiries, they refused to go along after he made clear that he was partly motivated by a desire to vindicate Michael Flynn, Trump's initial national security adviser; Flynn resigned after he became the target of an FBI investigation and later pleaded guilty to lying to the FBI, though Trump gave him a pardon in December 2020.

When the House passed by voice vote in September a bill to make the hacking of voting systems a federal crime, Armstrong said the measure could assist states in taking actions against "bad actors" who "must be punished for their actions." He also agreed with Democrats that Facebook and other social-media sites should be investigated for their influence on federal elections.

He was routinely reelected with 69 percent of the vote, which was the biggest vote for the seven Republicans running statewide in 2020 with a Democratic opponent. Each got at least 59 percent.

Armstrong started his second term by gaining a seat on Energy and Commerce. He cited the panel's impact on a "wide range of topics that have a major impact on our way of life" in North Dakota, including energy development and agriculture. He seems secure in his House seat. Recent North Dakota politics suggest that Armstrong has an eye on his state's two Republican-held Senate seats. Both senators are in their early 60s. So, Armstrong—who is nearly two decades younger than each—might have a long wait.

OHIO

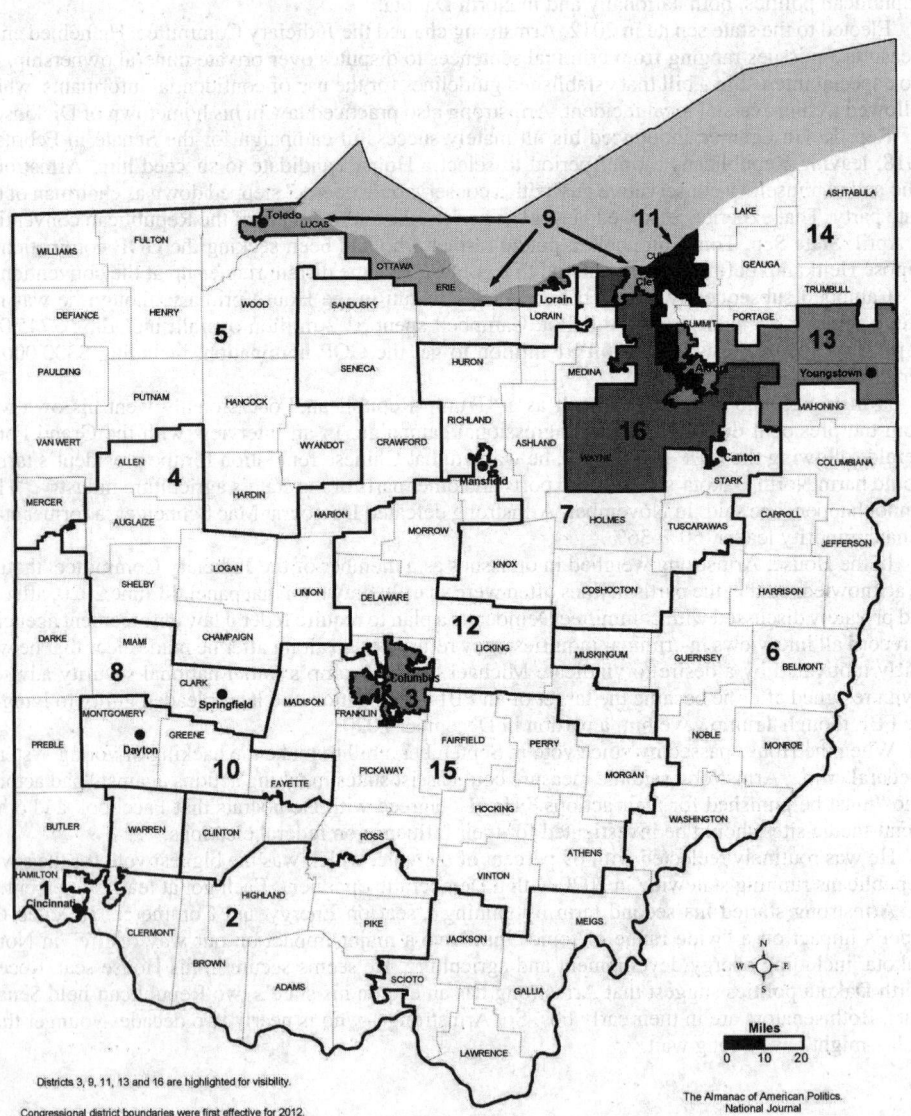

Districts 3, 9, 11, 13 and 16 are highlighted for visibility.

Congressional district boundaries were first effective for 2012.

The Almanac of American Politics.
National Journal

Ohio, a crossroads of the Midwest, was for a long time a bellwether state politically – it did not vote for a presidential loser between 1960 and 2016. But Donald Trump's solid, eight-point wins in both 2016 and 2020 have put an end to Ohio's bellwether status, largely because its disproportionately aging, White, working-class population makes the Buckeye State a notch or two more Republican than the nation.

Ohio was the first entirely American state. The original 13 started as British colonies, and the next three—Vermont, Kentucky and Tennessee—were spun off from them. But Ohio sprang, Athena-like, from the head of Congress, as the first state formed from the Northwest Territory. The Northwest Ordinance of 1787 established 6-mile-square townships, which imposed geometric order on diverse new American landscapes to the west. It set aside one square mile per township for public schools, and the land was soon peppered with schoolhouses and small colleges, the foundation stones of a literate republic. The ordinance prohibited slavery at a time when most northern states still had it, opening the way for free labor to clear fields, raise crops, and build mills and factories. In less than half a century, the former wilderness wrested from British-aided Indian control only in 1796 was one of the most productive parts of the young republic. In the years after the Civil War, Ohio became one of the great industrial states, the original headquarters of John D. Rockefeller's Standard Oil, the site of major steel mills along the narrow Cuyahoga and Mahoning rivers, and the location of the biggest soap companies, machine tool makers and tire manufacturers. Dayton was the home of the Wright brothers, who developed the airplane; Akron was the home of Harvey Firestone, B.F. Goodrich and F.A. Seiberling, the great tire manufacturers. Cincinnati was and is the headquarters of Procter & Gamble.

Ohio was settled by New Englanders in the northeast (in the Western Reserve) and by Virginians in the southwest, creating a split between the Southern-accented counties south of the National Road and U.S. 40 and the Yankee-accented cities and towns to the north. In the middle were the Amish, who moved west from Pennsylvania. (Ohio is home to 62 Amish settlements with 75,830 people, slightly behind Pennsylvania.) Ohio's split heritage was an early reason why it became a closely divided state politically—and a nationally pivotal one. Ohio produced the winning candidate for president in 1896 and 1900, William McKinley, who inaugurated a 34-year period of mostly Republican national majorities. McKinley's Republicans backed high tariffs and hard money and were friendly to some unions, but not large ones. They preached a nationalist Americanism tempered by wariness about making major commitments abroad. Republicans were the majority in this increasingly industrial Ohio, losing rural Butternut counties but carrying the big industrial cities of the north.

Then came the Great Depression of the 1930s, and Ohio became the scene of class warfare, with sit-down strikes and victories for industrial unions in autos, steel and tires. The industrial union cities of the CIO—Cleveland, Akron, Youngstown and Toledo—moved sharply toward the Democrats, while places with fewer union members, such as Cincinnati and Columbus, remained Republican. The political fighting was fierce and the stakes were high. CIO leaders hoped to organize the entire workforce, but Republican leaders like Ohio Sen. Robert Taft, fearing that union control of business would throttle the economy, acted to curb union power with the Taft-Hartley Act of 1947. Ohio thrived in the industrial economy after World War II, thanks to new auto and auto-parts plants and a growing population. In those years it was often said that Ohio was a great test market—close to the national average in income levels, urban-rural balance, ethnic mix and partisan proclivities.

But Ohio is not so typical today. It remains industrial in an increasingly post-industrial country. In Ohio, manufacturing accounted for 16 percent of state GDP in 2019, compared with 11 percent for the U.S. as a whole. The ArcelorMittal steel mill in Cleveland, once again operating after being closed in 2002, makes specialized, advanced-technology steel that allows it to compete against cheaper foreign competitors. But like other industrial operations in an era of automation, the mill employs far fewer employees than it once did. Indeed, Ohio's manufacturing economy has been shrinking relative to other sectors of the economy. Manufacturing accounted for 18.2 percent of Ohio's jobs in 2000 but just 12.3 percent on the cusp of the coronavirus pandemic in 2020; the number of manufacturing workers in the state declined by 340,000 during that period. Ohio's median income has remained mired in the bottom third of states, and its opioid overdose death rate ranked in the top five states nationally. In 2018, General Motors shuttered its massive Lordstown plant near Youngstown, which had produced the Chevy Cruze.

Still, Ohio is slowly adapting to new economic realities. The Lordstown facility has since been sold to a startup, the Lordstown Motors Corporation, that aims to build electric trucks, and GM announced a joint venture with the Korean company LG Chem to build a $2.3 billion electric vehicle battery plant nearby. In 2016, a Chinese glass manufacturer, Fuyao, reopened a GM plant in Dayton that had been closed eight years earlier. Akron, once hailed as the tire and rubber capital of the world, has attracted new jobs in polymers, information technology and biomedical engineering. Perhaps most notable is the growth in health services, led by the world-renowned Cleveland Clinic, now the state's largest employer (at a time when General Motors, once No. 1 in the state, has sunk to 72nd). The clinic has midwifed an array of biomedical firms, including Invacare, Philips Healthcare and Steris; overall, Cleveland's Cuyahoga County ranks 31st among all U.S. counties in gross domestic product and has a bigger GDP than 13 states. Culturally, Cleveland has moved past its days as the "mistake by the lake" in the 1960s and '70s. The city still faces challenges, including tensions over the use of force by the city's police department. But downtown Cleveland around the Rock and Roll Hall of Fame has blossomed, a clear lesson that visitors and media took away from the 2016 Republican National Convention. Indeed, 2016 was a banner year for the city. The city opened the renovated Public Square, transforming the asphalt-heavy, traffic-snarled plaza into a lush urban park. In the spring, the Cleveland Cavaliers, led by local hero LeBron James, won the NBA championship and prompted a massive victory parade. Then in the fall, the Cleveland Indians made it to the World Series, losing in extra innings in the seventh game to the Chicago Cubs.

In Ohio's Appalachian region, horizontal drilling and hydraulic fracturing—fracking—enabled drillers to tap into huge reservoirs of oil and natural gas in the Marcellus and Utica shale formations. By 2019, Ohio ranked fifth nationally in the production of dry natural gas (a methane leak from a well in Belmont County exceeded, over 20 days in 2018, the annual methane emissions of some oil-producing nations). Agriculture remains a significant industry, although foreign owners, led by Germany, control some half a million acres in the state. Ohio ranks third nationally in egg production and sixth in soybeans.

Ohio's population has stagnated in recent decades. Between 1970 and 2010, the state's population grew only 8 percent, a lower rate than all but New York, West Virginia, Pennsylvania and Iowa. Since the 2010 census, Ohio's population has grown just 2.3 percent, meaning it will lose one of its 16 House seats after the 2020 census. The exception is metro Columbus, which has experienced some of the fastest growth of any area outside the southern and western United States: Franklin County (Columbus) grew 12.9 percent, while suburban Delaware County grew 19.5 percent. The city of Columbus recently passed San Francisco in population. The Cincinnati suburbs of Butler, Clermont, and Warren counties have grown at more modest rates. However, several large counties saw their populations decline during the past decade, including Cuyahoga (Cleveland), Mahoning (Youngstown), Montgomery (Dayton), Stark (Canton), and Trumbull (Warren). African Americans make up 12 percent of Ohio's population—exactly on par with the nation. But part of the reason for Ohio's slow population growth has been a relative lack of Hispanics: The state ranks in the bottom 10 states for the percentage of residents who are Hispanic. Moreover, the percentage of foreign-born residents in Ohio is 4.6 percent, well below the national average of 13 percent.

Traditionally, northeast Ohio—centered on Cleveland and extending west to Toledo and south and east to the factory towns of Akron and Canton, Youngstown and Warren—has been the state's Democratic heartland, with the highest percentages of union members and African Americans. The other part of Ohio—south and west of the industrial belt and including Columbus, Cincinnati and Dayton—was never as heavily unionized and in national elections tended to vote Republican, like most of neighboring Indiana, although not always by wide margins. But these patterns have shifted significantly in recent years. Metro Columbus has trended Democratic, while the hill country along the Ohio River—where fossil fuel extraction is now king—has trended sharply Republican.

It became clear that Ohio's demographic makeup made it ripe for Trump to win in 2016, and on Election Day, he did, in a romp. Whereas President Barack Obama won the state by three points in 2012, Trump won it by eight in 2016. Hillary Clinton won eight counties, half as many as Obama. In 2018, a good year for Democrats nationally, Ohio proved to be a disappointment for the party. While populist, labor-friendly Democratic Sen. Sherrod Brown was reelected, a credible Democratic gubernatorial candidate, Richard Cordray, lost to Republican Mike DeWine, and the GOP won the other four statewide executive offices on the ballot.

In 2020, a string of favorable poll numbers for Democrats, plus the expectation that Joe Biden would be a stronger candidate than Clinton was four years earlier, pushed Democrats to give Ohio some investment and attention in the campaign's closing months. Still, it was never as high a priority for the Biden campaign as Michigan, Pennsylvania, and Wisconsin—a wise decision, it turned out, as Trump won Ohio a second time and by a barely diminished margin. Biden managed to flip Montgomery County, but Trump neutralized that by flipping Mahoning County and Lorain County (west of Cleveland). Biden improved on the Democrats' winning margins by about six points in Franklin County, Hamilton County, and Summit County (Akron), and narrowed Trump's margins of victory in the suburban counties surrounding both Cincinnati and Columbus. In a sign of the times, former Republican Gov. John Kasich, who had represented portions of the Columbus area in Congress and who had run for president as a Republican in 2016, endorsed Biden in 2020. Not all news out of Ohio was good for Republicans in 2020; for the second time in two years, a Republican state House speaker left under a cloud, as Larry Householder was indicted in an alleged bribery scheme involving electric utilities. In 2022, the GOP will face a test when they have to defend the Senate seat being vacated by Rob Portman, an establishment figure out of step with the Trump-era GOP. But on the whole, Republicans are in a good spot in Ohio, a state that's now less competitive between the parties than it has been in decades.

Population		Race and Ethnicity		Income	
Total	11,689,100	White	80.90%	Median Income	58,642
Land area (sq. miles)	40,861	Black	12.60%	State Income Rank	36 out of 50
Pop/ sq mi	286.07	Latino	4.00%	Poverty Rate	13.10%
Born in state	74.70%	Asian	3.00%	With health insurance	93.40%
		Two or more races	2.90%	Cash public assistance	2.40%
Age Groups		Other	1.20%	Food stamp/SNAP	14.2%
Under 18	22.00%				
18-34	22.40%	**Education**		**Work**	
35-64	38.20%	H.S grad or less	41.80%	White Collar	38.10%
Over 64	17.50%	Some college	28.80%	Sales and Service	37.40%
Military		College Degree, 4 yr	18.20%	Blue Collar	24.50%
Veteran/ Active Duty	7.40%	Post grad	11.10%	Government	12.40%

Presidential Politics

2020 Primary (D)	Biden (D)	647,285(72%)	Sanders (D)	149,686(17%)		
2020 Pres. Vote	Trump (R)	3,154,834(53%)	Biden (D)	2,679,165(45%)		
2016 Pres. Vote	Trump (R)	2,841,006(51%)	Clinton (D)	2,394,169(43%)	Johnson (L)	174,498 (3%)

Since 1892, Ohio has sided with the winner in all but three presidential elections: 1944, when it cast its votes for Thomas Dewey over President Franklin D. Roosevelt; 1960, when it favored Richard Nixon over John F. Kennedy; and 2020, when President Donald Trump carried it over Joe Biden. That last result suggests that the Buckeye State's preeminence as a crucial bellwether state might be a thing of the past.

The shift from must-win to "would be nice" in Democrats' calculations has been abrupt and dramatic. As recently as 2016, Ohio was second behind only Florida in total ad spending. Hillary Clinton pulled out all the stops in her quest to corral the state's 18 electoral votes, with Beyonce and Jay Z headlining a concert in Cleveland and LeBron James appearing at events. Trump campaigned vigorously too, and his criticism of trade deals like NAFTA, anti-elites rhetoric, and vow to restore manufacturing jobs played well throughout the Rust Belt. He faced some resistance from within: Ohio Gov. John Kasich, Trump's former primary rival, never endorsed, and other Ohio Republicans, including Sen. Rob Portman and State Auditor Dave Yost, repudiated their support after a video of Trump bragging about groping women surfaced in October. Yet amid all that strife, Trump handily defeated Clinton, 52%-44%.

Clinton won just eight of the state's 88 counties: Athens (Ohio University), Cuyahoga (Cleveland), Franklin (Columbus), Hamilton (Cincinnati), Lorain (working-class Cleveland suburbs), Lucas (Toledo), Mahoning (Youngstown), and Summit (Akron). Trump made dramatic gains across the state, flipping blue-collar counties like Ashtabula, Ottawa, Sandusky and Trumbull, all carried by Obama in 2012, and turned agricultural counties like Marion and Tuscarawas that Obama had kept close into 30-point routs.

The 2020 election was the first time Democrats didn't prioritize Ohio in a generation. The state wasn't included in early ad buys, and didn't start seeing serious ad spending until October, when a cash-flush Biden campaign moved to expand the map. Polls showed a tight race, and Biden made a few October campaign appearances in the state. But Trump over-performed public and private polls in the state and across the Midwest, just as he had in 2016, and won Ohio, 53%-45%. That margin was almost identical to his 2016 win in the state. Biden ran ahead of Clinton in some of the state's higher-educated areas, flipping Montgomery County (Dayton) and running ahead of Clinton in Hamilton County (Cincinnati) and around greater Columbus. But Trump flipped Mahoning County, the home of Youngstown and heart of the Rust Belt, making him the first Republican to win it since 1972, and carried blue-collar Lorain County outside Cleveland.

It's clear that Ohio won't be at the center of the presidential map unless there's a shift in the parties' coalitions in the coming years. Democrats came closer to carrying Texas than Ohio in the past two presidential elections, and Trump's eight-point Ohio win was only slightly smaller than his 10-point win in Alaska. Trump's 8-point margin in Ohio was closer to his 16-point victory in Mississippi than his four-point loss in the national vote.

Ohio has scheduled its primary for March since 1996, and has occasionally played a significant role in the nomination process. Hillary Clinton extended her 2008 campaign by beating Obama 53%-45% in 2008, and in 2016 she used a 56%-43% victory to halt Bernie Sanders' momentum a week after he'd won Michigan. In 2012, Mitt Romney scored a pivotal victory when he squeaked past Rick Santorum, 38%-37%. The 2016 GOP primary was heated: Trump blasted Kasich for voting for NAFTA, while Kasich alleged a "toxic atmosphere" at Trump rallies. Kasich won his home state, 47%-36%, but Trump scored big wins in other states that day on his inexorable march to the nomination.

The 2020 primary was historic, but for a different reason: After initially insisting that they'd hold the March 17 election even as the coronavirus surged, Ohio Republican Gov. Mike DeWine and Republican Secretary of State Frank LaRose reversed themselves at the last minute and delayed it until late April while making it an all-mail election. Their decision made Ohio the first of many states to postpone their primary because of COVID-19, and one of the first where officials changed voting rules to make it easier to vote during the pandemic, foreshadowing a major shift in the voting process for the fall election. Biden won three other states on the day Ohio was initially set to vote, all but guaranteeing his nomination. Sanders dropped out two weeks later; Biden then won the rescheduled April 28 primary 72%-17% over Sanders.

Congressional Districts

117th Congress Lineup	3D 11R 2V	116th Congress Lineup	4D 12R

Ohio is losing one seat in the 2022 reapportionment. As was the case following the most recent redistricting when they also were in control, Republicans may find that they are victims of their own success.

Following the 2010 census, the state lost two House seats. That reduced the delegation to 16 members, the fewest since Ohio was frontier country in the 1820s. During the previous decade, the map had been somewhat competitive: Democrats won a 10-8 majority in 2008 and Republicans a 13-5 majority in 2010. Even with their complete control of redistricting, GOP strategists conceded that they had too many Democrats to allocate to preserve all 13 of their seats. To resolve the dilemma, they forced one pair of Democrats to run against each other in the Cleveland-Toledo area. Furthermore, for decades Republicans had cracked Columbus into multiple districts to shortchange Democrats. But the state capital was growing and attracting progressive-minded voters at such a rate that neither the Republican-held 12th nor 15th might hold until 2020. So, Republican legislative aides hatched an innovative scheme to pack Democrats into a new Columbus 3rd District. The creation of that Democratic vote sink produced a beneficial ripple effect, allowing Republicans to shore up their freshmen and keep a 12-4 advantage. To attract the two-thirds support in the legislature required to avoid a veto referendum in the next election, Republicans plotted minor changes designed to appease enough Democrats. Chiefly, those were allies of Toledo-based Marcy Kaptur, who got the better draw of the new district with Cleveland-based (and former presidential candidate) Dennis Kucinich. Republican Mike Austria, a low-key sophomore, retired. Republicans got the 12-4 delegation they envisioned in a state that Barack Obama twice won. Not one of those seats changed party hands in the next decade.

Reforms of Ohio's redistricting procedures gained support after the 2014 election. Spurred by Republican Secretary of State Jon Husted, a bipartisan coalition voted for a compromise plan that transferred redistricting authority for legislative districts from a handful of statewide elected officials to a broader group that would require support from both parties. The plan was approved by 71 percent of voters in a 2015 referendum. In 2018, voters approved a separate referendum for congressional districts. The new rules require support for a redistricting plan by at least half the members of each party in the legislature and limit the splitting of counties. If the legislature deadlocked, then a commission of elected officials would draw the map; without sufficient bipartisan support, the map would be subject to revision after four years.

Republicans' best option might be to squeeze the four House Democrats and their voters into three districts, most likely by carving into several pieces the 13th District in northeast Ohio, where Democratic control has weakened and Democratic Rep. Tim Ryan is running for the open Senate seat. Alternatively, Republicans facing the greatest jeopardy would be those in eastern Ohio—the 6th, 7th, 14th and 16th districts. Many of the remaining Republicans in the Ohio delegation would find that their districts shift a bit to the east. Back in Columbus, the resignation in May 2021 of Rep. Steve Stivers in the 15th District—and the scheduled special election in November—could add new uncertainty; a special election in 2018 to fill a vacancy in the 12th was tight, though the GOP prevailed.

Mike DeWine (R)

Elected 2018, term expires 2023, 1st term; b. Jan. 05, 1947, Springfield; Miami University of Ohio, B.S., 1969; Ohio Northern University, J.D., 1972; Roman Catholic; Married (Frances); 8 children.

Elected Office: Greene County Prosecutor, 1977-1981; OH Senate, 1981-1982; US House, 1983-1991; OH Lt. Gov., 1991-1995; US Senate, 1995-2007; OH Attorney General, 2011-2018.

Professional Career: Attorney.

Office: 77 S. High St. 30th Floor, Columbus, 43215; 614-466-3555; Fax: 614-466-9354
Lt. Gov.: Jon Husted (R) **Atty. Gen:** Dave Yost (R) **Sec. of State:** Frank LaRose (R)
State Legislature: Senate: 9D, 24R **House:** 38D, 61R

Election Results

Election	Name (Party)	Vote (%)
2018 General	Mike DeWine (R)	2,231,917 (50%)
	Richard Cordray (D)	2,067,847 (47%)
2018 Primary	Mike DeWine (R)	499,639 (60%)
	Mary Taylor (R)	335,328 (40%)

Prior winning percentage: Senate: 2000 (60%), 1994 (53%), House: 1988 (74%); 1986 (100%); 1984 (74%); 1982 (56%)

Mike DeWine, a fixture in Ohio politics for four decades, was elected governor in 2018. In 2020, he received praise for his early handling of the coronavirus pandemic, though members of his own party objected to some of his policies.

DeWine grew up in Yellow Springs, the home of liberal Antioch College, where his family owned a successful seed business. DeWine's great-great-great-grandfather came from Ireland during the potato famine and settled in Yellow Springs. His mother, Jean, wrote a conservative column for the local Yellow Springs News in the 1960s. DeWine met his future wife, Frances Struewing, when they were first graders. They began dating during high school and married while both were attending Miami University. DeWine earned a law degree from Northern Ohio University and settled in Cedarsville, where he and his wife for years hosted an annual ice cream social. There, DeWine was elected Greene County prosecutor in 1976 at age 29. He resisted plea bargaining; once, to nail a drug dealer, he put up the collateral to get $50,000 in cash to stage a buy.

In 1980, at 33, DeWine was elected to the state Senate. In 1982, when incumbent Clarence Brown ran for governor, DeWine won a six-way Republican primary for a seat in Congress with 69 percent of the vote. In 1990, he was elected lieutenant governor. Two years later, DeWine sought to unseat legendary astronaut and Democratic Sen. John Glenn. It was a hard-hitting campaign and while Glenn won, 51%-42%, it was his closest general election margin ever. In 1994, DeWine ran for the Senate again, this time to fill the seat of retiring Democrat Howard Metzenbaum, and won, 53%-39%. In 2000, Democrats initially thought DeWine might be vulnerable, but no top-tier candidate surfaced; after vastly outspending his challenger Ted Celeste, brother of former Democratic Gov. Dick Celeste —DeWine prevailed, 60%-36%, winning 83 of 88 counties.

A common motif of DeWine's time in Congress was a concern for children and families, shaped by the loss of his 22-year-old daughter Becky in a car accident in 1993. As chairman of the Appropriations Subcommittee on the District of Columbia, regarded on Capitol Hill as a thankless post, DeWine worked to reform the city's child welfare system. He was also chief sponsor of a bill to make it a crime to injure or kill a fetus in the course of a federal crime; it passed, 61-38. A bipartisan bill he sponsored to provide $82 million for teen suicide prevention became law in 2004. But DeWine lost his Senate seat in 2006 to Democrat Sherrod Brown. Four years later, DeWine defeated incumbent Democrat Richard Cordray to become attorney general. He served two terms.

DeWine announced he was running for governor at his family ice cream social. He was running to succeed term-limited Republican Gov. John Kasich, whose career in Ohio politics was almost as long as his own, including 18 years in the House and two terms as governor. In 2016, Kasich ran for president and outlasted 15 rivals before conceding the nomination to Donald Trump. Kasich became a critic of Trump and eventually grew more popular among Ohio Democrats than Republicans. The initial Republican primary for governor included DeWine, Lt. Gov. Mary Taylor, Secretary of State Jon Husted, and Rep. Jim Renacci. But early on, Husted joined forces with DeWine as his running mate, while Renacci chose to challenge Brown in the Senate contest instead. That left DeWine facing Taylor in a bare-knuckled fight for the nomination. The party establishment strongly favored DeWine, and he won the primary, 60%-40%.

The Democratic primary included Cordray, former Congresswoman Betty Sutton, Dayton Mayor Nan Whaley, onetime Cleveland mayor and former Rep. Dennis Kucinich, former state Senate Minority Leader Joe Schiavoni, and former Ohio Supreme Court Justice Bill O'Neill. The primary eventually narrowed to a two-man contest—the progressive Cordray, who had served as state treasurer, attorney general, and as the first director of the federal Consumer Financial Protection Bureau, facing off against the even more progressive Kucinich. For a time, it seemed like the left-leaning Democratic electorate might flock to the eclectic, eccentric Kucinich. But Cordray boasted support from President Barack Obama, Sen. Elizabeth Warren and the state AFL-CIO, and his sober style seemed the safer choice for voters concerned about electability in November. Cordray won 62 percent, with Kucinich far behind at 23 percent.

The general election between DeWine and Cordray was dubbed a contest of nerds. Cordray was a multiple winner of Jeopardy! who "tweets Ohio trivia and strange observations regularly," the Cleveland Plain Dealer noted. DeWine, for his part, had an old-school approach, "handing out thousands of his wife's cookbooks a year" and arguably out walking anyone in a small-town parade, the paper wrote. The two divided over social issues, including abortion and marijuana legalization. For months, Kasich stayed out of the campaign, but despite efforts by Cordray to woo the outgoing governor and his supporters, he eventually campaigned for his fellow Republican. DeWine prevailed, 50%-47%, even as other midwestern GOP gubernatorial candidates were losing. He became Ohio's oldest-ever governor at 72.

In office, DeWine extended gender-identity protections for state employees and took some detours from conservative orthodoxy by proposing a gas tax hike to fund infrastructure, additional spending for public health and early-childhood programs, and a fund to protect Lake Erie and other bodies of water. But the most notable bill of his first term in office was legislation to bail out nuclear and coal plants in the state while undercutting previous policies to encourage renewable energy. The measure, contentious as it was being passed, became fully toxic in 2020 when Republican House Speaker Larry Householder, the bill's champion, was indicted in an alleged $61 million bribery case that involved the bill's biggest beneficiary, the utility FirstEnergy. After Householder's indictment in July 2020, DeWine called for the law to be repealed, saying that "the process by which it was created stinks. It's terrible. It's not acceptable." (By early 2021, the law remained in place.)

When the coronavirus pandemic hit in 2020, DeWine took earlier steps to combat the virus than many of his fellow governors, regardless of party. Even before a single case was reported in Ohio, DeWine acted to shut down major gatherings and ordered school and business closures before most other governors did. "The lifelong Republican public servant has been calm, sober and data-driven," wrote Politico in April 2020 as it named DeWine the most successful governor to date in fighting the virus. "He has not only been uninterested in emulating Donald Trump's style—he has been willing to defy Trump's edicts." DeWine's early moves bolstered his approval ratings, but a vocal group of opponents emerged. Anti-lockdown protesters tried to break into the state capitol in April and May and converged on the home of Amy Acton, DeWine's health director and a fixture of televised coronavirus briefings. ("The buck stops with me," DeWine said in urging protesters to focus on him instead; Acton eventually stepped down from her role in June.) During the late spring and summer, DeWine focused on reopening the state, but amid a surge of cases in November 2020, he reimposed a statewide mask order. The following month, several GOP legislators filed articles of impeachment, though legislative leaders tamped down the rebellion. By March 2021, Ohio ranked in the bottom one-third of states for per capita cases. Meanwhile, on criminal justice, DeWine broke with his past skepticism of reform measures by signing bills that benefited incarcerated pregnant women, low-income residents faced with suspended driver's licenses, convicts seeking professional licenses, and teenaged and mentally ill defendants. DeWine also bolstered the use of substance abuse treatment in the criminal-justice system and implemented an easier process for sealing conviction records.

DeWine is expected to run for another term in 2022, even though he would be 76 by the time of his next inauguration. But Trump, perceiving DeWine as insufficiently loyal, sent a tweet after the 2020 election that was widely perceived as a call for a GOP primary challenge. While Democrats have been in an increasingly weakened position in Ohio, a few Democrats could become credible challengers if they run, including Dayton Mayor Nan Whaley, who's already announced a bid, Cincinnati Mayor John Cranley, or Columbus City Attorney Zach Klein. Still, DeWine has history on his side: No incumbent Republican governor of Ohio has been kept from a second term since 1958.

Sherrod Brown (D)

Elected 2006, term expires 2024, 3rd term, b. Nov 09, 1952; Mansfield, OH; Yale University, B.A., 1974; Ohio State University, M.A., 1979; Ohio State University, M.P.A., 1981; Lutheran; Married (Connie Schultz); 2 children; 2 stepchildren; 6 grandchildren.

Elected Office: OH House, 1974-1982; OH Secretary of State, 1982-1990; U.S. House, 1993-2007.

Professional Career: Professor, Ohio State University, 1979-1981.

DC Office: 503 HSOB 20510, 202-224-2315, Fax: 202-228-6321, brown.senate.gov

State Offices: Cincinnati, 513-684-1021; Cleveland, 216-522-7272; Columbus, 614-469-2083; Lorain, 440-242-4100.

Committees: *Agriculture, Nutrition & Forestry*: Commodities, Risk Management & Trade; Conservation, Climate, Forestry & Natural Resources; Rural Development & Energy. *Banking, Housing & Urban Affairs (Chmn).* *Finance*: International Trade, Customs & Global

Competitiveness; Social Security, Pensions & Family Policy (Chmn); Taxation & IRS Oversight. *Veterans' Affairs*.

Group Ratings

	ADA	ACLU	AFL-CIO	LCV	COC	HAFA	ACU	CFG	FRC
2020	-	92%	-	92%	-	0%	6%	-	-
2019	100%	C	100%	100%	59%	C	6%	0%	0%

Almanac Ratings 2019-2020

	Economy	Social	Foreign	Composite
Liberal	97%	97%	88%	94%
Conservative	3%	3%	12%	6%

Key Votes of the 116th Congress

1. EPA clean energy rules	Y	5. Russia sanctions	Y
2. U.S./Mex./Can. trade deal	Y	6. Troops in SYR, AFG	N
3. Cut unemployment benefits	N	7. Veto arms sales to Saudis	Y
4. Shelton to Fed Reserve	N	8. Defense $$$, veto override	Y

9. Barr as Atty. General	N
10. Spending at the border	Y
11. Coney Barrett to Sup. Ct.	N
12. Electoral College objections	N

Election Results

Election	Name (Party)	Vote (%)		Cand. Spent	Ind. Exp. Support	Ind. Exp. Oppose
2018 General	Sherrod Brown (D)............................	2,355,923	(53%)	$23,969,911	$4,855,471	$674,215
	Jim Renacci (R)................................	2,053,963	(47%)	$5,036,235	$491,708	$57,006

Prior winning percentages: 2018 (53%), 2012 (51%), 2006 (56%); House: 2004 (67%), 2002 (69%), 2000 (65%), 1998 (62%), 1996 (60%), 1994 (49%), 1992 (53%)

Heading into the 2020 election, some Democrats felt that Sherrod Brown, Ohio's senior senator, would make an ideal presidential candidate: He's a blunt-talking populist with the potential to bridge the party's progressive and centrist wings and has demonstrated an ability to win consistently in what has long been a bellwether state. But despite being on 2016 presidential nominee Hillary Clinton's shortlist for a running mate, Brown for years had insisted he has little interest in a White House bid of his own. His view, however, appeared to shift after he comfortably won a third term in November 2018 in a state that had voted for President Donald Trump by an 8-point margin two years earlier. "It never occurred to me to actually do it until … the response to election night," Brown told New York magazine. He said he had been overwhelmed by the number of people urging he consider a presidential run after a victory speech in which he characterized his campaign as a "blueprint for America in 2020"—particularly in Ohio and other Midwestern states that had swung to from Democrat Barack Obama to Republican Trump.

In early 2019, Brown announced he had decided to stay put—"The pull on me was always [to] do my work here," he told reporters outside the Senate chamber—but only after a "Dignity of Work" tour of early presidential primary states, during which he highlighted working-class economic issues. "For too long, Democrats, have not focused on these issues," he declared. If he took a pass on an opportunity to advance these concerns from the bully pulpit of the presidency, the results of the 2020 elections provided him another high-profile platform: Democrats' new Senate majority handed him the gavel of the Banking, Housing and Urban Affairs Committee—to the discomfiture of many in the nation's financial services industry. "Wall Street doesn't get to run this entire economy," Brown told reporters. After six years of Republican control in which the committee had focused on loosening financial regulations, Brown vowed to investigate the relationship among stock prices, executive compensation and workers' wages, the New York Times reported, as part of taking on a corporate business model he charged "treats workers as expendable."

With Democrats regaining Senate control by only the narrowest possible margin, it remained uncertain to what extent Brown would be able to translate his expansive policy agenda into legislation. Nonetheless, "the chairman of the Senate Banking Committee has a gigantic megaphone and spotlight that he can use, and I expect will use, to identify problems, shape public opinion and change banking regulation and behavior, Better Markets President and CEO Dennis Kelleher, an advocate for Wall Street oversight, told Politico. Brown served notice that he would be calling the chief executive officers of the nation's largest financial institutions before the committee on a routine basis. "I'm not suggesting that CEOs of U.S. banks, of Wall Street banks—I'm not suggesting they're Deutsche Bank," Brown said, referring to the numerous probes the German bank has faced from U.S. and British regulators. "But I am suggesting that they have a lot of power, and we need to know more about how they do their business. The more we hear from them, the better."

And, in a symbolic move, Brown quickly set out to modify the panel's shorthand name—"Senate Banking"—used around Capitol Hill. He told his hometown newspaper, the Cleveland Plain Dealer, "You will always hear me call it 'Banking Housing.' Housing was a word left out of this committee's title for far too many years and it won't be left out anymore." Brown often notes that his home zip code, 44105, topped the national list of housing foreclosures in early 2007 at the outset of the Great Recession. "I want to devote the rest of my career to helping people have affordable, decent, clean, safe housing," Brown said upon becoming committee chair.

The Senate seat Brown now holds was occupied for nearly two decades by the late Howard Metzenbaum, with whom Brown is sometimes compared. Metzenbaum, a self-made multimillionaire, was dubbed "the last angry liberal." As with Brown, Metzenbaum positioned himself as a populist whose acerbic attacks on big business and other powerful interests gave him an appeal that transcended ideological lines. Brown's rhetoric, too, can be biting—but behind the sharp tongue is a personal style often cheerful and informal. Besides for wearing sneakers—always American-made —and off-the-rack suits sold not far from his Cleveland home, Brown is known for a gravelly voice and tousled hair. He is so often described as "rumpled" that it appears to be part of his given name. Brown loves to talk about baseball: "Damn Yankees" is the beginning of his personal email address. "I really didn't grow up with this dream of running for president," he told the Washington Post while exploring a White House bid. "My dream was to play center field for the Cleveland Indians."

Brown has held elected office virtually his entire adult life. He grew up in Mansfield in northeast Ohio, the son of a physician. After graduating from Yale University in 1974, he went directly to the campaign trail, winning a seat in the Ohio House that year as he was turning 22. Brown earned master's degrees in education and public administration from Ohio State University while serving in the Legislature. In 1982, he was elected secretary of state and worked to increase voter registration and turnout. After two terms, he lost in 1990 to Republican Bob Taft, a scion of Ohio's most famous political family and later the state's governor. It didn't take long for a political comeback: In 1992, Brown won an open House seat that stretched from the western suburbs of Cleveland south to Akron, 53%-35%. He had a close call in the Republican wave year of 1994, but, after that, was regularly reelected with more than 60 percent of the vote.

On most issues, Brown's House record was unerringly liberal: He voted against the Iraq War in 2002 and was a supporter of same-sex marriage a decade and a half before a 2015 Supreme Court ruling made it legal nationwide. But he gained the greatest attention for being among the most voluble "fair trade" members from the manufacturing-reliant Great Lakes region. He campaigned hard against the North American Free Trade Agreement in his initial House campaign—Congress approved it a year later, in 1993—while attacking a string of trade agreements and free-trade policies that followed NAFTA. In 2005, Brown helped lead the effort to defeat the U.S.-Central American free trade agreement, which cleared the House by just two votes. One of two books he published during his House years was titled "Myths of Free Trade: Why American Trade Policy Has Failed."

As Brown observed years later to Bloomberg News while seeking a third Senate term, "I will get a number of Trump voters because I fought for the things that Trump campaigned on long before he did." Notwithstanding Brown's disdain for much of what Trump stood for—"I mean, why does anyone even describe Trump as a populist? Because he says he's 'for people' and he has big rallies? So did Mussolini," Brown rhetorically asked Yahoo News in 2019—the two shared the same skepticism of trade agreements. Brown split from many Democratic colleagues fearful of a trade war when he praised Trump's April 2018 imposition of tariffs on steel and aluminum from China and several U.S. allies. The "action finally sends a clear message to our trading partners that we aren't going to allow them to cheat Americans out of their jobs and infect global markets," Brown asserted.

Shortly after Trump's 2016 victory, Brown wrote him urging a renegotiation of NAFTA and received a note back from the president reading: "Great letter. I will never let our workers down. Best wishes!" Brown worked with administration officials—notably Trade Representative Robert Lighthizer, a native of Ashtabula Ohio—as a deal was reached to replace NAFTA. But, after initially offering tentative praise for the new U.S.- Mexico-Canada Agreement, he later strongly objected to what he considered insufficient worker protections. "We can go back to the table with the Mexicans and the Canadians and do stronger labor standards," Brown asserted.

After modifications were made, Brown in January 2020 sided with a majority of Senate Democrats in voting for the pact—a political first for him. "I have never … voted for a trade agreement because every trade agreement presented to Congress is all about corporate interest and investor protections and corporate special interest protections and never about workers," Brown told CNN a month prior to the vote, charging, "When President Trump put out his NAFTA revision ... it was a pro-corporate deal that helped Washington special interests." However, Brown said that he—and Democratic Sen. Ron Wyden of Oregon, House Speaker Nancy Pelosi and organized labor—had come up with language that "simply says these agreements should be about workers." He added, "This will mean that workers in the United States and with our trading partners will see their standard of living increase."

During nearly a decade and a half in the House, Brown eyed a return to statewide office. But, in 2005, he initially said he would not challenge two-term Republican Sen. Mike DeWine. Brown later reconsidered at the urging of state Democratic leaders, who had concerns about the viability of the remaining field of candidates; he breezed to the Democratic nomination. DeWine—elected governor in 2018—suffered at the time from association with the Bush administration and from various scandals associated with the Republican-controlled state government. Brown won 56%-44% in a year in which Democrats regained control of both houses of Congress. He carried the state's major population centers and the area east of Interstate 77, where his hard-line trade views resonated in coal- and steel-dependent counties.

Brown's voting record has been as reliably liberal as it was in the House, even though he represents a state that has long been politically marginal and, in recent years, trended red. In 2015, Almanac vote rankings put him in a three-way tie for the Senate's most liberal score. However, he has refrained from co-sponsoring recent high-profile initiatives touted by progressives: "Medicare For All" and the "Green New Deal." On health care, he said in 2019: "I want to get something done: I see too many 58-year-olds and 62-year-olds whose plants have closed going without insurance." After that, "we move towards Medicare for All. But I just don't know how it happens in this political climate." Brown has authored legislation to lower the Medicare eligibility age to 55 and worked to include a similar proposal during debate over the Affordable Care Act. But it was dropped after then-Connecticut Sen. Joe Lieberman threatened to torpedo the bill if it was included. Brown remains angry about the episode, telling Vox in 2019: "Lieberman killed it, saying it was a matter of conscience when it was clearly a matter of insurance industry interests in Hartford. And I'm speaking on the record."

Representing a coal-producing state, Brown has tread carefully on environmental issues. In 2010, the last time the Senate seriously endeavored to pass a climate change bill, he was point man for a bloc of Democrats that dubbed itself the "Brown Dogs;" its members refused to support the bill without more protections for U.S. firms on carbon emissions. The measure was never brought to the Senate floor after passing the House. More recently, Brown has worked to make Ohio a leader in wind energy production. In early 2021, noting that he now chaired a committee whose jurisdiction also included mass transit as well as banking and housing, Brown said he planned legislation to replace approximately 60,000 city buses around the country with zero-emission substitutes. He described the move as a "a jobs bill" that would lead to manufacturing of buses "in states like mine that know how to make vehicles."

In 2015, Brown became ranking member on the Banking panel. Before the 2014 election, with Senate control in the balance, one bank executive anonymously told the Washington Post that the prospect of Brown becoming committee chairman was "frightening." When Brown finally achieved his goal of chairing the panel six years later, some on-the-record assessments were similar—if put a bit more delicately. "We're under no illusion, Consumer Bankers Association President Richard Hunt, whose organization represents such large lenders as JPMorgan Chase and Bank of America, told Politico. "We have our work cut out for us. Other banking interests, however, expressed a more nuanced view. "Sen. Brown has strong views on the regulatory regime, which often places him in diametric opposition to the banking industry during key policy debates," acknowledged Isaac Boltansky, director of policy research for Compass Point, an investment bank. "But he has an appreciation for the industry's role in Ohio and the national economy". The finance industry is a major employer in Brown's home state.

In the wake of the 2008 financial crisis, as Congress debated what became the Dodd-Frank financial reform law, Brown led a bipartisan effort to preempt future bank bailouts by breaking up the "too-big-to-fail" banks through limits on size. He failed to garner sufficient support, but among his allies was Democrat Ted Kaufman of Delaware—appointed in 2009 to fill the seat vacated by Joe Biden when the latter became vice president. By the same token, Brown later advocated for a business-friendly provision that was one of the first changes to Dodd-Frank. The result was a 2014 revision that worked to the benefit of insurers facing stiff capital requirements.

A year later, the new GOP majority on the Banking panel sought a broader loosening of Dodd-Frank. Brown and the committee chair, Alabama Republican Richard Shelby, had a bumpy relationship. They produced competing bills to revise the 2010 law; Shelby's bill cleared the panel but went no further amid the prospect of a Democratic filibuster. Brown was happy to see Idaho Republican Mike Crapo replace Shelby as chairman at the end of 2016. "We have a working relationship. He's way more conservative than I am, but he's straightforward and honorable," Brown said of Crapo, according to The Hill.

In early 2017, it appeared Crapo and Brown were poised to pursue a bipartisan approach to change Dodd-Frank. But, at the end of October, Brown announced he and Crapo had been unable to reach a compromise. Crapo then began negotiations with several moderate Democrats, some up for reelection in states that had voted overwhelmingly for Trump in 2016. The upshot was a bill signed by Trump after passing the Senate 67-31 in spring 2018—with 17 members of the Senate Democratic Caucus backing it. The debate opened an acrimonious rift among Senate Democrats: While supporters of the measure pointed to relief for community banks and local credit unions, Brown and Massachusetts' Elizabeth Warren blasted a provision that loosened regulations on banks with assets greater than $50 billion but less than $250 billion. Brown and Warren, among other Democrats, pushed a counterproposal aimed at relief for the smallest banks. Bemoaning what he called "collective amnesia" about the banking crisis a decade earlier, Brown warned on the Senate floor: "This legislation threatens to undo important rules protecting us from risk. [It] again puts taxpayers on the hook for bailouts.

Brown, who also serves on the Finance Committee, scored a victory early in the Biden administration when a major expansion of the child tax credit—which he had co-sponsored with Colorado Democrat Michael Bennet two years earlier—was included in the new president's $1.9 trillion stimulus package. Brown, Bennet and a leading House advocate of the plan—Connecticut Democrat Rosa DeLauro— spent months lobbying Biden's inner circle to include it in the stimulus package; Brown told the Washington Post he had been "working" his former colleague Kaufman, the head of Biden's transition team. According to the Center on Budget and Policy Priorities, expanding the credit—to $3,600 annually for children younger than 6 and $3,000 for those 6 to 17—and making it refundable would cut the U.S. child poverty rate in half. The expanded credit contained in the stimulus package expires in a year, but Brown and Bennet vowed to make it permanent.

The benefits from the expanded child tax credit would be distributed throughout the year, which could help make the case for a top Brown priority at the Banking Committee—bank accounts set up through the Federal Reserve for members of the public who don't have accounts at commercial banks. Brown has long argued that citizens unable to afford the latter need a "public option" to cash paychecks and receive government benefits.

In 2012, Brown faced 35-year-old Ohio Treasurer Josh Mandel, who raised $19 million and was aided by $23.5 million in spending by outside conservative groups. Mandel labeled Brown's support for the auto industry bailout "un-American." Brown spent more than $24.5 million, and liberal outside groups funneled in another $15 million. Boosted by Obama's substantial political investment in Ohio, Brown turned what was a neck-and-neck race in August into a 51%-45% win. Obama carried the state 50%-48% over Republican Mitt Romney.

With the endorsement of Trump and the state GOP establishment, Rep. James Renacci—a multimillionaire recruited in part because of his ability to self-finance—challenged Brown in 2018. Despite loaning his campaign $8 million, he used less than $300,000 and repaid himself the rest. Brown raised $28.7 million and outspent Renacci by more than 5-1. Notwithstanding Trump's backing, Renacci was largely written off by national Republicans: After an initial ad buy in June, his campaign did not go back on the air until October's second week. Still, the contest developed into one of the nastiest of the 2018 cycle. Taking little for granted in a state increasingly Republican, Brown ran ads attacking Renacci for his wealth and lengthy fight to avoid paying nearly $360,000 on his 2000 taxes. When Renacci's campaign finally went on TV in the closing weeks, it focused on an issue generally avoided by Republicans in previous campaigns: Brown's contentious 1986 divorce from his first wife.

The ads aired just after Brown's vote against confirming Brett Kavanaugh, who was accused of sexual assault, to the Supreme Court. Citing filings from Brown's divorce proceeding, Renacci's ads highlighted that the incumbent's former wife, Larke Recchie, had gotten a restraining order against him after alleging Brown had been rough with her. Brown repeated past statements denying any violence toward Recchie, who is remarried—and now a political supporter of her ex-husband. She recorded a campaign ad decrying Renacci's effort to bring the matter into the political arena, contending the divorce proceedings had led "only to angry words." Renacci continued to hammer

Brown during three debates over what he called "substantiated claims of abuse"; Brown called Renacci and his allegations "despicable."

Brown won 53.4%-46.6%, as Republicans swept Ohio's statewide executive offices. Brown took only 16 of the 88 counties, but again captured the state population centers and most of traditionally Democratic northeast Ohio. While it was unclear whether Renacci's attacks had an effect, there was later speculation about the role they played in Brown's decision to forgo a national campaign. Brown told the Plain Dealer shortly after his reelection that, if he decided to run for president, he expected Trump, "who has made a career of attacking people personally, would recycle the allegations that Renacci had used.

Brown married Pulitzer Prize-winning columnist Connie Schultz in 2004. His 2012 reelection bid created professional complications: She resigned after 18 years with the Plain Dealer, telling colleagues "it has become painfully clear that my independence, professionally and personally, is possible only if I'm no longer writing for the newspaper that covers my husband's Senate race on a daily basis." Schultz, who currently writes a nationally syndicated column, authored a 2007 book of her experiences on the campaign trail, titled "… and His Lovely Wife: A Memoir from the Woman Beside the Man."

Rob Portman (R)

Elected 2010, term expires 2022, 2nd term, b. Dec 19, 1955; Cincinnati, OH; Cincinnati Country Day School, 1974; Dartmouth College, B.A., 1979; University of MI Law School, J.D., 1984; Methodist; Married (Jane Portman); 3 children.

Elected Office: U.S. House, 1993-2005.

Professional Career: White House Legislative Affairs Director, 1989-1991; U.S Trade Rep., 2005-2006; Director, Office of Management & Budget, 2006-2007; Practicing attorney, 1984-1988, 2007-2010.

DC Office: 448 RSOB 20510, 202-224-3353, Fax: 202-224-9075, portman.senate.gov

State Offices: Cincinnati, 513-684-3265; Cleveland, 216-522-7095; Columbus, 614-469-6774; Toledo, 419-259-3895.

Committees: *Finance*: International Trade, Customs & Global Competitiveness; Social Security, Pensions & Family Policy; Taxation & IRS Oversight. *Foreign Relations*: Europe & Regional Security Cooperation; Internat'l Dev Instit & Internat'l Econ, Energy & Environ Policy (RMM); West Hem Crime Civ Sec Dem Rights & Women's Issues. *Homeland Security & Government Affairs (RMM)*: Ex Officio membership on all subcommittees. *Joint Economic*.

Group Ratings

	ADA	ACLU	AFL-CIO	LCV	COC	HAFA	ACU	CFG	FRC
2020	-	31%	-	15%	-	66%	79%	-	-
2019	10%	C	26%	29%	99%	C	79%	29%	100%

Almanac Ratings 2019-2020

	Economy	Social	Foreign	Composite
Liberal	0%	0%	3%	1%
Conservative	100%	100%	97%	99%

Key Votes of the 116th Congress

1. EPA clean energy rules	N	5. Russia sanctions	N	9. Barr as Atty. General	Y
2. U.S./Mex./Can. trade deal	Y	6. Troops in SYR, AFG	Y	10. Spending at the border	Y
3. Cut unemployment benefits	Y	7. Veto arms sales to Saudis	N	11. Coney Barrett to Sup. Ct.	Y
4. Shelton to Fed Reserve	Y	8. Defense $$$, veto override	Y	12. Electoral College objections	N

Election Results

Election	Name (Party)	Vote (%)		Cand. Spent	Ind. Exp. Support	Ind. Exp. Oppose
2016 General	Rob Portman (R)............................ 3,118,567	(58%)		$33,851,658	$3,264,568	$15,540,944
	Ted Strickland (D)........................... 1,996,908	(37%)		$10,231,752	$4,827,629	$34,525,870
2016 Primary	Rob Portman (R)............................ 1,336,686	(82%)				
	Don Elijah Eckhart (R)...................... 290,268	(18%)				

Prior winning percentages: 2016 (58%), 2010 (57%), 2004 (72%), 2002 (74%), 2000 (74), 1998 (76%), 1996 (72%), 1994 (77%), 1993 special (70%)

The election of Republican Rob Portman as Ohio's junior senator in 2010 was just another stop for a consummate insider whose career has alternated between Capitol Hill and the White House. After serving in the administration of President George H.W. Bush—to whom Portman at times was compared, both in his center-right views and even-keeled modesty—Portman won a Cincinnati-based House seat in a 1993 special election, only to head back up Pennsylvania Avenue a dozen years later when he was appointed U.S. trade representative and later director of the Office of Management and Budget by President George W. Bush. After his arrival in the Senate, it appeared that another White House stint might be in his future. Portman was on 2012 GOP presidential nominee Mitt Romney's short list of running mates, and, early in the 2016 election cycle, he made the requisite visits to Iowa and New Hampshire as he mulled a presidential bid himself. But at the end of 2014, Portman cited the GOP's newly restored Senate majority as a key factor in not seeking the presidency—and went on to handily win reelection less than two years later.

So, it was a major surprise to Washington when, in January 2021, Portman announced he would not seek a third term the next year—barely two months after he indicated that he planned to run again. The decision came after his brand of pragmatic, bipartisan politics began to fade amid intensifying polarization, fueled in part by Donald Trump and his takeover of the Republican Party. It has gotten harder and harder to break through the partisan gridlock and make progress on substantive policy, and that has contributed to my decision, Portman said. But some viewed him not merely as a victim but also as part of the problem. "To some people, including some Republicans, Portman proved a major disappointment for not showing more backbone and speaking out forcefully against a president who trampled norms and threatened institutions," wrote Dan Balz, the Washington Post's chief national politics correspondent.

Appearing on the same ballot as Trump in 2016, Portman ran well ahead of his party's presidential candidate—while keeping his political distance. He endorsed Trump only in the most perfunctory terms after the New York businessman secured the party's nomination, and he didn't even vote for Trump—announcing he would instead write in the name of the GOP vice presidential nominee, Mike Pence, after the October 2016 disclosure of the "Access Hollywood" tapes in which Trump can be heard bragging about sexually assaulting women. However, once Trump was in the White House, Portman became a reliable vote for the president, notwithstanding occasional differences in areas such as immigration and international trade. According to FiveThirtyEight, Portman voted in accord with Trump's positions 88.3 percent of the time—significantly more than fellow GOP centrists such as Maine's Susan Collins (65.1%), Alaska's Lisa Murkowski (72.6%) and Utah Sen. Romney (75%).

"I think there's 50 instances where I disagreed with the president and I said so, but I tried to say so respectfully," Portman told the Post's Balz. "If you look at my Twitter account ... there's not a single partisan attack in there. I tried to stay away from, you know, following suit with the president's approach." He defended his strategy in dealing with the often-vengeful Trump, saying: "I was pleased that [Trump] signed 82 of my bills into law and it was important to have a relationship with the administration in order to do that. ... But yeah, I was put on the spot more than I would have liked."

Emblematic of Portman's balancing act was his vote, days after his retirement announcement, in Trump's second impeachment trial. Unlike several fellow GOP centrists, Portman voted to acquit Trump of charges of inciting the mob that had stormed the Capitol a month earlier; like many other Republicans, he said it was unconstitutional to impeach a former president even though constitutional scholars said it was OK. But Portman also said Trump's conduct "was inexcusable, because in his speech he encouraged the mob, and that he bears some responsibility for the tragic violence that occurred." Four protesters died in the violence and so did a police officer (another killed himself days later), and at least 138 police officers were wounded, 15 of whom were hospitalized. Financially, the toll passed $30 million.In May 2021, Portman did join five other Republican senators to support legislation to create a bipartisan commission to investigate the Jan. 6 violence— but the bill failed in the face of a filibuster engineered by Senate Republican Leader Mitch McConnell.

Portman grew up in Cincinnati, where his father in 1960 started a small forklift distribution company. The five-employee firm grew into a 350-person operation before being sold to a Dutch conglomerate in 2004. Portman's grandfather in 1926 purchased the Golden Lamb Inn in the Cincinnati suburb of Lebanon, which had opened in 1803 and says it is Ohio's oldest continuously operated business. A dozen presidents have stayed at the hotel, now owned by Portman and his siblings. As an undergraduate at Dartmouth College, Portman took a semester off to work for Republican Rep. Bill Gradison, whom he would later succeed, and, after graduation, worked on the advance team for George H.W. Bush's 1980 presidential campaign. It was the beginning of a long association with the Bush family.

After earning a law degree at the University of Michigan, Portman was hired by a leading Washington lawyer/lobbying firm, Patton, Boggs and Blow. He returned to Cincinnati to practice law before coming back to Washington in 1989 as an associate White House counsel and then head of the Office of Legislative Affairs. Portman was back practicing law in Cincinnati when, in January 1993, Gradison resigned his House seat to head a D.C.-based trade association. Portman ran in a special election to fill the vacancy, with former first lady Barbara Bush recording a radio ad for him. He won a seven-candidate primary in the GOP-dominated district, and was easily re-elected six times.

Portman got on the House Ways and Means and Budget committees and became known for his fiscal conservatism and ability to work across the aisle. He co-chaired the National Commission on Restructuring the Internal Revenue Service, and worked with his then-House and current Senate colleague, Maryland Democrat Ben Cardin, on issues ranging from land conservation to pensions. Portman and Cardin co-sponsored the 1998 Internal Revenue Service reform law, and in 2001, when Congress enacted the Bush administration's tax cut, it included their provision to increase the limits for IRA and 401(k) contributions.

In 2005, President George W. Bush appointed Portman as U.S. trade representative. A year later, Bush appointed him OMB director; the president nicknamed him "The Mule" in tribute to Portman's persistence in trying to push the federal budget toward balance. During the Bush administration, Portman befriended Brett Kavanaugh, who was associate White House counsel and later staff secretary. In September 2018, Portman introduced Kavanaugh before the Senate Judiciary Committee after the latter had been nominated by Trump to the Supreme Court. During the highly charged floor debate on Kavanaugh's confirmation, Portman defended him against sexual assault allegations: "If the new normal is eleventh-hour accusations, toxic rhetoric like calling a candidate 'evil' and those of us who support him 'complicit in evil' and guilt without any corroborating evidence, who would choose to go through that? Portman asked. How many good public servants have we possibly already turned away by this display?

Portman left OMB in 2007 and returned to Cincinnati. When Republican Sen. George Voinovich announced that he would not run for a third term, Portman entered the contest to replace him. Despite his long record, Portman had virtually no name recognition beyond the Cincinnati area. Unfazed, Portman campaigned around the state while raising serious money: $16.5 million. In the fall campaign, Lt. Gov. Lee Fisher derided Portman's association with the Bush family; George W. Bush had left the presidency two years earlier with his popularity at a low point. But Fisher was strapped for cash—much of the $6.4 million he had raised was spent in during a fractious Democratic primary. Portman fended off criticism of his work as trade representative by saying he would make enforcement of trade laws a high priority. Portman won 57%-39% in a difficult year for Democrats nationally.

Portman attracted widespread attention during his first term when he reversed his opposition to same-sex marriage after he disclosed that his 21-year-old son, Will, had come out as gay. It made him the first Republican senator to openly support same-sex marriage. Some conservatives vowed to oppose him for renomination in 2016, but a serious primary challenge never materialized. In 2014—a year before the Supreme Court legalized same-sex marriage nationwide—Portman told the Associated Press, "I feel very comfortable in taking a position of respecting people for who they are, which is what I think ultimately same-sex marriage is about."

Portman was among the first senators to call attention to the opioid epidemic. With statistics for Ohio showing a death every three hours from an opioid overdose, Portman joined four other Republicans to back a March 2016 effort led by New Hampshire Democrat Jeanne Shaheen to add $600 million for treatment and prevention programs to a bill funding continued government operations. The move failed because of opposition from Senate GOP leaders. But President Barack Obama later that year signed the 21st Century Cures Act, which included $1 billion to combat opioid abuse. When an $8.4 billion bipartisan bill aimed at the problem was signed by Trump in October 2018, it included several Portman-authored provisions—most notably one requiring the U.S. Postal Service to screen packages shipped from overseas for fentanyl.

Republican efforts to get rid of Obamacare during Trump's tenure would have translated into a significant loss of Medicaid funds to Ohio, prompting Portman to decline to tip his hand until shortly before the legislation was brought to the floor in July 2017. Portman joined a half-dozen other Republicans in opposing the "partial repeal" bill favored by hard-line conservatives, but he voted for the option that came the closest to passing—the"skinny repeal," a bare-bones measure that was an attempt to attract enough votes to move to conference committee with the House, where a comprehensive bill could be written. It failed narrowly, as three Republicans joined all Democrats in opposition.

Portman has had to navigate between his past as a negotiator of trade agreements and the widespread skepticism toward such deals in his home state—where free trade has been widely blamed for a shrinking manufacturing base. In 2015, he was at odds with many in his own party as he pushed an amendment to Obama's request for "fast track" negotiating authority to expedite a 12-nation trade deal known as the Trans-Pacific Partnership. Teaming with Michigan Democrat Debbie Stabenow, Portman unsuccessfully sought an amendment to require establishing "enforceable rules" to combat currency manipulation. The effort was backed by the nation's automakers, but the Wall Street Journal's editorial board suggested Portman was "abandoning his policy chops in favor of reelection politics." Portman early the next year came out against the draft TPP agreement; the Ohio Teamsters cited his opposition in endorsing his 2016 reelection campaign. The TPP did not come before Congress for a vote before the end of the Obama administration, and Trump withdrew the United States from the agreement days after entering the White House.

Nearly two years into the Trump administration, Portman in a speech praised the president's hard line on trade relations with China. "China has been violating and circumventing our trade laws for decades," he said. "I think the Trump administration now has China's attention, and I applaud the president for taking a tough stand." But he disagreed with Trump's use of a 1962 law—known as Section 232—to impose tariffs ostensibly on national security grounds. Alluding to an investigation launched by the Commerce Department into whether imports of autos and auto parts were damaging national security, Portman—representing an auto manufacturing state—was quoted by the Columbus Dispatch: "Autos help run our economy. They don't run a national security risk."

Portman also split with Trump in early 2019 when he was among 12 Senate Republicans to support a resolution blasting the president's declaration of a national emergency at the southern border —an attempt to bypass Congress and siphon military money for a border wall. While he backed the border wall, Portman expressed concern about the usurpation of Congress' power of the purse. He complained it "opens the door for future presidents to implement just about any policy they want and to take funding from other areas Congress has already decided upon without Congress' approval."

The previous year, Portman took issue with Trump's immigration policies, as he joined in criticism of the administration's policy of separating immigrant children from their families at the U.S.-Mexico border. Portman complained the policy, later reversed under pressure, was aggravating a problem uncovered by the Homeland Security and Governmental Affairs Subcommittee on Investigations, which he chaired. It involved the failure of the Department of Health and Human Services to adequately track unaccompanied immigrant children placed with sponsors in the U.S. Portman convened a hearing after it was revealed human traffickers had forced teenagers from Guatemala to work on farms in central Ohio.

At a time when Trump was widely excoriated for his coziness with Russian President Vladimir Putin, Portman utilized the investigations panel to target a couple of Russian oligarchs, Arkady and Boris Rotenberg—longtime friends of Putin. Barred from doing business in the U.S. because of their role in Russia's 2014 invasion of Ukraine's Crimea region, the Rotenbergs circumvented sanctions by buying $18 million in art work through intermediaries and shell companies, according to a 2020 report released by Portman. The subcommittee had launched the probe to determine why sanctions had not encouraged Russia to withdraw from Crimea. "It is shocking that U.S. banking regulations don't currently apply to multimillion-dollar art transactions," Portman said. He and Delaware Democrat Tom Carper said they would introduce legislation to close such loopholes. (Portman became ranking Republican of the full Homeland Security panel in early 2021.)

Trump faced his first Senate impeachment trial in early 2020, accused of withholding congressionally approved aid unless the president of Ukraine announced an investigation into a prospective election opponent, Democrat Joe Biden. Portman told reporters: "The president should not have raised the Biden issue on that call, period. It's not appropriate for a president to engage a foreign government in an investigation of a political opponent." At the same time, he said "these actions do not rise to the level of removing President Trump from office and taking him off the ballot in a presidential election season that's already well underway." Two decades earlier, as a House member, Portman had not only voted to impeach President Bill Clinton but he also asked Clinton to resign "to spare the country from going through a long, divisive and distracting impeachment process." In an interview with the Dayton Daily News, Portman contended Clinton had broken the law by lying to a grand jury while Trump's behavior, though "wrong," was not illegal.

As chair of the Senate Ukraine Caucus, Portman was credited by Trump himself with persuading the president to release $400 million in aid to Ukraine that the president had withheld to force an investigation of Biden. Initially, Trump contended he had blocked the money because European nations had failed to come up with sufficient aid for Ukraine's security; Portman, a Foreign Relations Committee member, echoed similar arguments during the fall of 2019. "The president was very clear with me. He only raised one issue, and that issue only, and that was about Europeans not doing enough. I don't disagree with him on that," Portman told Fox News. But it later turned out that Europe had, in fact, provided more than two-thirds of the security aid to Ukraine since the Russian annexation of Crimea. A senior Portman aide acknowledged to NBC News that the claim about Europe falling short in its financial obligations to Ukraine was incorrect and said that Portman's staff had later reminded the senator of this. The aide added Portman was referring specifically to $250 million in military aid and felt NATO should be contributing more to Ukraine's security.

In 2012, Portman put his Ohio organization behind Romney before the state's crucial presidential primary, which the former Massachusetts governor won by just over 10,000 votes. He and Romney—now a Senator from Utah—got along well, and Portman later assumed the role of Obama in Romney's debate preparation sessions. (Portman also served as a debate prep partner for George W. Bush and Dick Cheney in 2000 and 2004.) But Portman's association with the still-unpopular Bush was probably a mark against him in the 2012 vice presidential sweepstakes, along with the perception that his personality was, well, dry. Comedy Central's Colbert Report parodied a Romney-Portman ticket as the bland leading the bland." Those who know Portman say such characterizations are off the mark—that, in fact, he has a reputation as a prankster. His outdoor exploits include smuggling a kayak into China in the 1980s to paddle the Yangtze River.

Portman's reelection appeared at risk early in the 2016 cycle, as some polls showed him trailing the likely Democratic nominee, former Gov. Ted Strickland, by nearly double digits. But Strickland ran a problem-plagued campaign: By July 2016, Portman had raised more than $15 million, twice as much as Strickland. It allowed Portman to go on air during the summer with negative ads, to which the Strickland campaign was slow to respond.

While viewed with suspicion by the GOP's tea party wing, Portman got a big assist from the billionaire Koch brothers, the tea party's financial angels—who were determined to see the Senate remain in Republican control. Groups aligned with the Kochs poured in nearly $12 million for advertising, most of it before Labor Day. By that time, the ad blitz had sliced Strickland's favorability ratings in half. Portman scored a 58%-37% victory, running well ahead of Trump (51%-43%) in Ohio.

Portman was a times criticized for not steering a course more independent of Trump, but the first two Republicans who announced plans to run to replace him—former state Treasurer Josh Mandel and former Ohio Republican Chair Jane Timken— sought to outdo each other in declaring fealty to the former president. Mandel, who unsuccessfully challenged Democratic Sen. Sherrod Brown in 2012, blasted Ohio Rep. Anthony Gonzalez—one of 10 House Republicans to vote to impeach Trump after the January 2021 Capitol insurrection—as a "traitor." Rep. Tim Ryan announced his candidacy and appeared to be the frontrunner on the Democratic side. Ryan has represented the blue-collar Youngstown area, a onetime Democratic stronghold that veered toward Trump—a shift that has helped put Ohio, a onetime bellwether state, increasingly in the Republican column.

Steve Chabot (R)

Elected 2010, 13th term, b. Jan 22, 1953; Cincinnati, OH; College of William and Mary, B.A.; Northern KY University Salmon P. Chase College of Law, J.D.; Roman Catholic; Married (Donna Chabot); 2 children; 1 grandchild.

Elected Office: Cincinnati City Council, 1985-1990; Hamilton County Commission, 1990-1994; U.S. House, 1995-2009.

Professional Career: Teacher, St. Joseph School, 1975-1976; Practicing attorney, 1978-1994.

DC Office: 2408 RHOB 20515, 202-225-2216, Fax: 202-225-3012, chabot.house.gov

State Offices: Cincinnati, 513-684-2723; Lebanon, 513-421-8704.

Committees: *Foreign Affairs*: Asia, the Pacific, Central Asia, Nonproliferation (RMM). *Judiciary*: Courts, Intellectual Property & Internet; Crime, Terrorism & Homeland Security.

Group Ratings

	ADA	ACLU	AFL-CIO	LCV	COC	HAFA	ACU	CFG	FRC
2020	**	19%	**	14%	-	91%	95%	**	-
2019	5%	C	24%	10%	84%	C	96%	94%	100%

Almanac Ratings 2019-2020

	Economy	Social	Foreign	Composite
Liberal	25%	20%	27%	24%
Conservative	75%	80%	73%	76%

Key Votes of the 116th Congress

1. U.S./Mex./Can. trade deal	Y	5. Russia sanctions	Y	9. Firearms background checks	N
2. First Coronavirus response	Y	6. Troops in Syria	Y	10. Spending at the border	Y
3. HEROES Act	N	7. Veto arms sales to Saudis	N	11. Marijuana liberalized rules	N
4. CASH Act	N	8. Defense $$$, veto override	Y	12. Electoral College objections	Y

Election Results

Election	Name (Party)	Vote (%)		Cand. Spent	Ind. Exp. Support	Ind. Exp. Oppose
2020 General	Steve Chabot (R)	199,560	(52%)	$2,878,369	$696,788	$6,019,358
	Kate Schroder (D)	172,022	(45%)	$4,049,474	$14,272	$4,329,455
	Kevin David Kahn (L)	13,692	(4%)	$7,381		
2020 Primary	Steve Chabot (R)	44,746	(100%)			

Prior winning percentages: 2018 (51%), 2016 (59%), 2014 (63%), 2012 (58%), 2010 (52%), 2006 (52%), 2004 (60%), 2002 (65%), 2000 (53%), 1998 (53%), 1996 (54%), 1994 (56%)

Republican Steve Chabot first came to the House in the historic GOP Class of 1994. After losing reelection in 2008, he returned two years later as the most senior member of another huge freshman class. As Small Business Committee chairman, he wielded his power to help entrepreneurs weather the coronavirus pandemic. After two relatively close reelections in 2018 and 2020, redistricting will determine Chabot's fate in 2022. He might not get a district as favorable as the one he now enjoys.

Chabot grew up in the Cincinnati area and graduated from La Salle High School. He earned a degree in history and physical education from the College of William & Mary. He took night classes at Northern Kentucky University to get his law degree while teaching at an elementary school during the day. Chabot won a seat on the Cincinnati City Council, where he served for four years. He followed that with a four-year stint on the Hamilton County Commission. During that time, Chabot tried to find innovative ways to reduce the cost of government, such as using jail inmates for some public services.

In 1994, Chabot was among the successful conservative Republicans who ended 40 years of Democratic control of the House. For 14 years, he sometimes took politically risky stands opposing federal spending on projects in his district and was a leader on social issues, particularly opposition to abortion rights. In 2003, on the Judiciary Committee, he helped enact a ban on "partial-birth" abortions, and he pushed a bill to prevent minors from crossing state lines to get abortions. Chabot was a House manager during the 1998 impeachment of President Bill Clinton.

Chabot lost his seat in 2008 when Democrat Steve Driehaus defeated him by five percentage points. In a rematch, Chabot in 2010 criticized the incumbent for voting for the Affordable Care Act and the $787 billion economic-stimulus package. Driehaus defended the actions of Democrats, including the health care overhaul, which he called "the right thing" to do. Each candidate raised about $2 million. Chabot won, 52%-46%.

When he returned to the House, Chabot used his seniority to become chairman of the Foreign Affairs Subcommittee on the Middle East and South Asia. He criticized the Obama administration's policies in the region and called its explanation of events before and after the deadly 2012 attack at the U.S. consulate in Benghazi Libya, "ham-handed at best and a cover-up at worst." During the next two years, he chaired the Asia and the Pacific Subcommittee. He filed the Burma Human Rights and Democracy Act, which restricted military aid to that country and signaled the Obama administration to move more cautiously to normalize relations. In December 2018, he won House passage of a resolution that condemned the military in the renamed Myanmar for its genocide of Rohingya Muslims. In 2020, Chabot added an amendment to a defense bill that expressed support for India in its border skirmishes with China.

On domestic issues, he filed a bill to revamp the Section 8 housing initiative for low-income residents, calling it "a broken program that rewards dependency on government with our tax dollars." He crusaded against federal funding of Cincinnati's streetcar project on economic grounds. In 2014, Chabot enacted a bipartisan bill to strengthen the law school clinic certification program of the Patent and Trademark Office, which he said would encourage innovation.

For four years, he chaired the Small Business Committee. "If there's one thing government can do for small business, it's to get the heck off their backs," Chabot told the Associated Press. In June 2018, he enacted his bill that reorganized the Small Business Administration's loan program and increased its lending authority. Later, during the coronavirus pandemic, he helped secure flexible relief loan programs and bailouts for small businesses.

Following the 2018 election, Chabot made a bid for the vacancy as the ranking Republican on the Judiciary Committee, citing his lengthy experience. But he lost to Doug Collins of Georgia, who had closer ties to GOP leaders. Chabot's bid might have been handicapped by the bid of Jim Jordan, another Ohioan, for the top post. Chabot resumed his position as the ranking Republican on Small Business. A year later, Jordan replaced Collins.

After redistricting in 2012 made the 1st District substantially more Republican by adding solidly GOP Warren County, Chabot won reelection easily. "Unless Steve Chabot commits a felony, he will be there for as long as he wants to be," Hamilton County Democratic Party Chairman Tim Burke lamented to the Cincinnati Enquirer.

Not all Democrats accepted that caution. In 2018, Chabot was challenged by Aftab Pureval, the clerk of courts for Hamilton County, who styled himself as a moderate and claimed that the incumbent had lost touch with his district. Pureval was criticized when a supporter secretly did work for the Chabot campaign. Chabot won 51%-47%. Pureval had a 20,000 vote lead in Hamilton County. Chabot prevailed with two-thirds of the vote in Warren. This was a case where artful redistricting likely was a savior for the GOP.

In 2020, the Democratic primary featured Air Force reservist Nikki Foster and Kate Schroder, a Lymphoma survivor and public health expert who worked for the Clinton Health Access Initiative in Africa. Schroder outspent Foster and touted her unique skill set to address to pandemic; she won 68%-32%.

The matchup was among the most hotly contested nationwide. It drew over $11 million in TV ads from the candidates and their allies and the attacks turned personal. Chabot's sister blasted him in a Facebook post for being too "intertwined with Trump." Schroeder was forced to correct an ad that accused Chabot of facing a grand jury investigation over $123,000 in missing campaign funds. A former Chabot aide was accused of stealing those funds, but Chabot says he was a victim of the heist. In turn, Chabot accused Schroder of mismanagement while serving on the Cincinnati Board of Health. Schroder outspent Chabot by more than $1 million, but she lost 52%-45%. She led by nearly 18,000 votes in Hamilton, but Chabot more than doubled her in Warren.

Following the election, Chabot announced he would run again in 2022 "whatever happens with redistricting this time around." With Ohio's loss of a seat, the state's redistricting reform might make it harder to splice Hamilton County in a way that advantages a Republican.

OH-1: Southwest Ohio   **Cook Partisan Voting Index: R+4**

Population		Race and Ethnicity		Income	
Total	749,773	White	70.70%	Median Income	$63,648
Land area (sq. miles)	687	Black	21.40%	District Income Rank	218
Pop/ sq mi	1,091.44	Latino	3.40%	Poverty Rate	12.40%
Born in State	70.30%	Asian	4.00%	With health insurance	94.10%
		Two or more races	3.00%	Cash public assistance	1.60%
Age Groups		Other	0.80%	Food stamp/SNAP	9.40%
Under 18	23.50%				
18-34	23.90%	Education		Work	
35-64	38.00%	H.S grad or less	36.20%	White Collar	44.90%
Over 64	14.60%	Some college	25.90%	Sales and Service	36.00%
		College Degree, 4 yr	22.80%	Blue Collar	19.00%
Military		Post grad	15.10%	Government	11.30%
Veteran/ Active Duty	6.40%				

2020 Pres. Vote	Trump	198,433	(51%)	Biden	185,947	(48%)			
2016 Pres. Vote	Trump	185,025	(51%)	Clinton	160,988	(44%)	Johnson	11,250	(3%)

Western/Northern Cincinnati Metro: Cincinnati, with its long-settled good looks, was Ohio's first major metropolis, a heavily German beehive of riverboats and sausage factories, nicknamed in the 1850s "Porkopolis." In the 19th century, it was the nation's fourth-largest city, and at the outbreak of the Civil War, it was a chief destination for slaves on the Underground Railroad. The National Underground Railroad Freedom Center is now located downtown. In the middle of the city is Mill Creek, named by the advocacy group American Rivers the most endangered urban river in North America in 1997. Two decades later, fish and wildlife had returned to the Mill Creek, with a reduction of sewage, and the cleanup of nearby contaminated sites.

The Cincinnati area was the site of great innovations: the first municipal fire department; the first professional baseball team, the Red Stockings, who began playing in 1869; and the nation's first concrete skyscraper, the 15-story Ingalls building built in 1902. Cincinnati spawned not flashy but solid industries, including America's biggest concentration of machine tool makers and the Procter & Gamble soap business. General Electric has its Global Operations Center downtown, with more than 1,300 employees. In suburban Evendale, the company maintains a huge jet-engine manufacturing facility. With more than 9,000 employees in southwest Ohio, GE is the largest manufacturer statewide. P&G opened in 2017 its new Beauty Innovation Center, a $400 million expansion of its campus in Mason that is thriving. And in May 2019 Jeff Bezos broke ground on a $1.5 billion Amazon hub at the airport outside Cincinnati.

Downtown, Fountain Square shows off well-maintained skyscrapers plus a revival of museums, arts institutions and retail shops. Old ethnic neighborhoods on the west side, crowded with brick row houses on steep hills, maintain their thick local accents and special foods, from German sauerbraten to Cincinnati chili. With fewer recent immigrants than comparable northern cities, Cincinnati's population declined in every decade from 1940 until 2010. From 2010 until 2019, the population remained roughly the same size in the city—Hamilton County, however, added 15,100 new residents.

The 1st Congressional District of Ohio includes almost all of Cincinnati, except for parts of its affluent eastern side. It contains most of Cincinnati's distinctive neighborhoods, like Over-the-Rhine, named for its heavily German-American early population. This was a premier entertainment district until the late 1910s, when Prohibition shut down the breweries. With increased African-American population, it was the epicenter of race riots in 2001, though it has been gentrifying since. The district takes in Avondale, now more than 90 percent African American. After Hillary Clinton won Hamilton County, 53%-43%, Joe Biden's margin there grew to 57%-41%. The district also takes in overwhelmingly Republican Warren County.

Historically, Cincinnati was an island of Republicanism in a sea of Democratic sentiment. Today, the reverse is true. It has an overwhelmingly Democratic urban core, but beyond that, the rest of the district is largely Republican. The 1st includes most of the heavily Republican middle-class suburbs and exurbs to the west of the city and some Democratic-leaning inner suburbs to the north. The district is divided into three roughly equal parts: the city, the Hamilton suburbs and Warren County. This was one of only two Republican-held districts in Ohio where the GOP presidential vote declined in 2020. Trump took 51 percent to Biden's 48 percent.

Brad Wenstrup (R)

Elected 2012, 5th term, b. Jun 17, 1958; Cincinnati, OH; University of Cincinnati, B.A., 1980; Rosalind Franklin University, B.S., 1985; William M. Scholl College of Podiatric Medicine, Rosalind Franklin University, 1985; Roman Catholic; Married (Monica Klein); 1 child.

Military Career: U.S. Army Reserve Medical Service Corps 1998-pres. (Iraq)

Professional Career: Physician, Wellington Orthopedic & Sports Medicine, 1999-2013; Private practice, 1986-1999.

DC Office: 2419 RHOB 20515, 202-225-3164, Fax: 202-225-1992, wenstrup.house.gov

State Offices: Cincinnati, 513-474-7777; Peebles, 513-605-1380.

Committees: *Permanent Select on Intelligence*: Counterterrorism, Counterintelligence & Counterproliferation; Defense Intelligence & Warfighter Support (RMM). *Ways & Means*: Health; Oversight; Worker & Family Support.

Group Ratings

	ADA	ACLU	AFL-CIO	LCV	COC	HAFA	ACU	CFG	FRC
2020	**	17%	**	5%	-	93%	91%	**	-
2019	0%	C	24%	3%	86%	C	92%	88%	100%

Almanac Ratings 2019-2020

	Economy	Social	Foreign	Composite
Liberal	25%	4%	27%	19%
Conservative	75%	96%	73%	81%

Key Votes of the 116th Congress

1. U.S./Mex./Can. trade deal	Y	5. Russia sanctions	Y	9. Firearms background checks	N
2. First Coronavirus response	Y	6. Troops in Syria	Y	10. Spending at the border	Y
3. HEROES Act	N	7. Veto arms sales to Saudis	N	11. Marijuana liberalized rules	N
4. CASH Act	N	8. Defense $$$, veto override	Y	12. Electoral College objections	N

Election Results

Election	Name (Party)	Vote (%)		Cand. Spent	Ind. Exp. Support	Ind. Exp. Oppose
2020 General	Brad Wenstrup (R)	230,430	(61%)	$1,684,441		
	Jaime Castle (D)	146,781	(39%)	$268,841		
2020 Primary	Brad Wenstrup (R)	53,674	(94%)			
	H. Robert Harris (R)	3,326	(6%)			

Prior winning percentages: 2018 (58%), 2016 (65%), 2014 (66%), 2012 (59%)

Republican Brad Wenstrup, elected in 2012 when he defeated the Republican incumbent in the primary, is a foot surgeon and Iraq War veteran. He used those experiences to become an influential player on national security issues. As the only physician serving on the Ways and Means Committee, he took a seat on the Health Subcommittee in 2021 and said he would seek patient-centered solutions. He earned the gratitude of many in the House when his medical skills—and quick response—probably helped save the life of Rep. Steve Scalise following the shooting at a baseball practice in 2017.

Wenstrup was born and raised in Cincinnati. His father was an optician, and his mother worked at a Stein Mart department store. As a kid, Wenstrup thought about a career in medicine as well as serving in the military. He got his bachelor's degree from the University of Cincinnati and a medical degree from the Scholl College of Podiatric Medicine in Chicago. His medical practice was incorporated into Wellington Orthopedic & Sports Medicine. He joined the Army Reserve in 1998 and served as a combat surgeon in Iraq in 2005 and 2006. "I tell people, it's the worst thing I ever had to do, but the best thing I ever got to do," he said. Not long after the prisoner-abuse scandal at the Abu Ghraib prison erupted, he was stationed at a combat support hospital within the prison walls. He treated U.S. troops, civilians and some enemy combatants.

Politics grew more intriguing to Wenstrup when he returned from Iraq. "I started to see people in Washington making military decisions that have never served, making health care plans that have never seen a patient or dealt with insurance companies or Medicaid and Medicare," he said. Running for mayor of Cincinnati in 2009 against incumbent Democrat Mark Mallory, Wenstrup lost but took a respectable 46 percent of the vote in the Democratic-leaning city.

In 2011, he launched a primary challenge to Rep. Jean Schmidt, who had sometimes offended colleagues in Washington and Ohio and was dubbed "Mean Jean" in the blogosphere. Wenstrup was endorsed by the Ohio Liberty Council, a coalition of tea party groups. Wenstrup ran an ad attacking Schmidt's votes to raise the debt limit and to support the Wall Street bailout, while mentioning that she planted a kiss on President Barack Obama at the State of the Union address. He won the nomination, 49%-43%. In his comfortably Republican district, he has not faced a serious primary challenge since then.

Veterans issues have drawn Wenstrup's attention. In 2015, he passed bills in the House that improved the electronic processing by the Veterans Benefits Administration of claims for educational assistance, and established the Veterans Economic Opportunity and Transition Administration to assist veterans with health, education assistance and vocational rehabilitation. Those measures became part of a broader veterans bill that was enacted in 2016. In 2017, as chairman of the Health Subcommittee at Veterans Affairs, Wenstrup won committee approval of his bill to ban smoking inside VA facilities—striking a 25-year mandate to require smoking areas. The House did not act on the bill. In the Army Reserves, where Wenstrup is a colonel, he serves as medical policy adviser for the chief of the Army Reserve at Fort Belvoir in Washington.

In 2018, as a member of the Armed Services Committee, Wenstrup worked on the defense spending bill to increase military readiness of troops with gear designed to reduce the risk of injury and to require an intelligence report on the interference by Russia and China in U.S. elections. He has used his national security experience as a member of the Intelligence Committee, where he has been ranking Republicans on the Subcommittee on Defense Intelligence and War fighter Support. In February 2020, he criticized committee Chairman Adam Schiff for holding a public hearing as a "publicity stunt" on what Wenstrup said was a classified issue related to intelligence surveillance. Republicans boycotted the hearing.

Joining Ways and Means in 2018, Wenstrup has focused on steps to reduce opioid abuse, including cutbacks in what he said was the excessive writing of prescriptions by physicians. As co-chairman of the Republican Doctors Caucus, he said that he "fought hard" in working with Ways and Means Chairman Richard Neal to assure final action in December 2020 on the bill to restrict "surprise" medical billing. He cited two provisions he had advocated: creating accurate directories of providers so patients can be certain which doctors are in their insurance network and promoting access to every type of doctor patients might need.

Wenstrup's medical experience in stressful circumstances proved invaluable when he happened to be with a group of House Republicans at an early-morning baseball practice in June 2017. When a gunman shot and seriously wounded then-Majority Whip Steve Scalise of Louisiana, Wenstrup applied a tourniquet to care for Scalise until a rescue squad arrived. Nearly four months later, when Scalise made a dramatic return to the House, he said that Wenstrup "saved my life." Wenstrup, who remained a colonel in the Army Reserve, received a Pentagon award for valor.

At home, Wenstrup in 2018 had his closest election. Democrat Jill Schiller, who was a White House aide during the Obama administration, said her top issue was expanded health coverage. Schiller—who spent about $600,000 compared with $1.6 million for Wenstrup—took 55 percent in Hamilton County, which cast nearly half the total vote. Wenstrup rolled up huge majorities in the remaining seven counties and won, 58-41%. In 2020, political newcomer Jaime Castle decided to challenge Wenstrup after she was offended by what she called his "grandstanding" at Intelligence Committee hearings in the Trump impeachment inquiry. Wenstrup won, 61%-39%; Castle, who spent $269,000, got 54 percent in Hamilton County, which cast nearly half of the vote.

OH-2: Southern Ohio

Cook Partisan Voting Index: R+9

Population		Race and Ethnicity		Income	
Total	730,151	White	86.20%	Median Income	$61,220
Land area (sq. miles)	3,222	Black	9.20%	District Income Rank	244
Pop/ sq mi	226.64	Latino	2.40%	Poverty Rate	12.80%
Born in State	74.40%	Asian	1.40%	With health insurance	94.00%
		Two or more races	2.60%	Cash public assistance	2.10%
Age Groups		Other	0.60%	Food stamp/SNAP	11.20%
Under 18	22.70%				
18-34	20.80%	**Education**		**Work**	
35-64	38.50%	H.S grad or less	40.40%	White Collar	42.70%
Over 64	17.90%	Some college	26.50%	Sales and Service	35.90%
		College Degree, 4 yr	20.20%	Blue Collar	21.50%
Military		Post grad	12.90%	Government	10.40%
Veteran/ Active Duty	7.60%				

2020 Pres. Vote	Trump	214,585	(56%)	Biden	165,605	(43%)		
2016 Pres. Vote	Trump	197,856	(55%)	Clinton	140,786	(39%)	Johnson	12,111 (3%)

Eastern Cincinnati Metro: Back in the 1850s, Cincinnati, with its large German population, was heavily Republican and anti-slavery. The city's ethnic character and political preference, like its physical appearance, remained pretty well fixed for a long time. Cincinnati attracted fewer European immigrants than did Great Lakes industrial cities such as Cleveland, Detroit and Chicago, so the New Deal had less impact on the local political dynamic. Appalachian immigrants who settled here in the 1940s to work in the factories were typically Republicans. Economically, it was never a strong union town, and culturally it is conservative.

The city of Ripley was a hub for the Underground Railroad, a natural point of egress from the South because the Ohio River narrows near the city. In 1838, escaped slave Eliza Harris leapt from one ice floe to the next, while carrying her 2-year-old son, to cross the river and make it to the city. A young abolitionist and Underground Railroad participant named Harriet Beecher Stowe lived in Cincinnati at the time and likely borrowed from Harris' experiences to create one of the most riveting scenes in Uncle Tom's Cabin.

The area to the east on the Ohio River includes distinctly different places—"the richest to the poorest, and everything in between," as one area mayor put it. Chillicothe, on the Scioto River and the first capital of Ohio, has suffered from the opioid epidemic, with a rising death rate. Heroin overdoses have become an almost daily occurrence, a local police captain wrote in Vox in 2017. "People are silent about their addiction or an addiction in their family—until it's too late." In an October 2019 profile, the Boston Globe described Portsmouth as "so ravaged by opioid abuse that it earned the notorious moniker of America's Pill Mill. ... one more washed-up Rust Belt city with a sad story, known for its abandoned factories." Work on the Energy Department's uranium cleanup project to decontaminate and decommission the Portsmouth Gaseous Diffusion Plant, which enriched uranium for the nation's nuclear arsenal from 1954 to 2001, reached a major milestone in 2018: turnover of the first 80 acres of formerly toxic property for possible development by a community group. The original site was 3,700 acres. The bad news: Radioactive uranium contamination in adjacent Pike County led to a cancer incidence rate that is 10 times the national average, the Ohio Department of Health reported in 2019.

Ohio's 2nd Congressional District includes the eastern edge of Cincinnati, taking in Hyde Park Square, with its farmer's market and many shops and boutiques; most of the largely affluent suburbs of eastern Hamilton County; and fast-growing Clermont County. In once-rural Clermont, Miami Township has become a bedroom community and a center of commercial development along the Interstate 275 loop. . In 2019, the median household income in Clermont was $67,000; in Portsmouth, it was $29,000. Reflecting national trends, suburban Hamilton has shifted to Democrats, while more exurban Clermont remains strongly Republican. The counties farther east have become pockets of high unemployment and poverty. In rural Pike County, which once had a Democratic tradition, President Donald Trump in 2020 got 74 percent of the vote. The low-income county is 96 percent white; only 13 percent of residents have a college degree. The district still leans substantially Republican, and Democrats have rarely competed here. In 2020, Trump took the district, 56%-43%.

Joyce Beatty (D)

Elected 2012, 5th term, b. Mar 12, 1950; Dayton, OH; Central State University, B.A., 1972; Wright State University, M.S., 1974; University of Cincinnati, Att., 1979; Baptist; Married (Justice Otto Beatty Jr.); 2 stepchildren; 2 grandchildren.

Elected Office: OH House, 1999-2008.

Professional Career: Sr.Vice President., OH St. University, 2008-2013; President, Joyce Beatty & Associates, 1992-2013; Director, Montgomery County Department of Comm. Human Services, 1983-1992; Director, Adult & Elderly services, Montgomery County Mental Health Board, 1983; Professor, Capital University, 1979-1992; Professor, Sinclair Community College, 1975-1983; Caseworker, City of Dayton, 1971-1975.

DC Office: 2303 RHOB 20515, 202-225-4324, Fax: 202-225-1984, beatty.house.gov
State Offices: Columbus, 614-220-0003.

Committees: *Financial Services*: Diversity & Inclusion (Chmn); Housing, Community Development & Insurance. *Joint Economic*.

Group Ratings

	ADA	ACLU	AFL-CIO	LCV	COC	HAFA	ACU	CFG	FRC
2020	**	81%	**	95%	-	0%	3%	**	-
2019	95%	C	100%	96%	67%	C	4%	13%	0%

Almanac Ratings 2019-2020

	Economy	Social	Foreign	Composite
Liberal	58%	100%	54%	71%
Conservative	42%	0%	46%	29%

Key Votes of the 116th Congress

1. U.S./Mex./Can. trade deal Y	5. Russia sanctions Y	9. Firearms background checks Y
2. First Coronavirus response Y	6. Troops in Syria Y	10. Spending at the border Y
3. HEROES Act Y	7. Veto arms sales to Saudis Y	11. Marijuana liberalized rules Y
4. CASH Act Y	8. Defense $$$, veto override Y	12. Electoral College objections N

Election Results

Election	Name (Party)	Vote (%)		Cand. Spent	Ind. Exp. Support	Ind. Exp. Oppose
2020 General	Joyce Beatty (D)	227,420	(71%)	$2,222,465	$18,898	
	Mark Richardson (R)	93,569	(29%)			$113
2020 Primary	Joyce Beatty (D)	44,995	(68%)			
	Morgan Harper (D)	21,057	(32%)			

Prior winning percentages: 2018 (74%), 2016 (69%), 2014 (64%), 2012 (68%)

Democrat Joyce Beatty's election to the House in 2012 gave Ohio its first African-American member outside of Cleveland. Consistent with the spirit of Columbus, Beatty often takes a consensus-building approach and has worked with Republicans. She looks after the large academic and financial interests of her constituents. As chairwoman of a new Financial Services subcommittee, she has pressed for increased diversity, including racial, in the nation's banks. In 2021, she became chairwoman of the Congressional Black Caucus at a time of growing demands for racial justice and increased legislative opportunity with Democratic control.

Beatty is the daughter of a brick mason and a stay-at-home mom. Her parents moved from the inner city to a predominantly White neighborhood in Dayton with better schools when Beatty was young. She did her undergraduate work in speech and psychology at Central State University and later earned a master's degree in counseling from Wright State University, both in Ohio. Beatty's interest in politics was fueled by hearing Jesse Jackson speak at the 1984 Democratic National Convention. She owned a management consulting business and had several jobs in local government and academia, eventually becoming senior vice president for engagement and outreach at Ohio State University. She served in the Ohio House for nearly a decade, including a stint as minority leader. She was instrumental in passing measures that helped women without health insurance get cancer screenings, reined in home foreclosures and encouraged financial literacy education. Her husband, Otto Beatty Jr., an attorney, was a member of the state House for nearly two decades until he resigned and was succeeded by his wife.

When she entered the race in the new Columbus-based district, Beatty cited her knowledge of how to "make a payroll" and her ability to work with businesses and labor unions to bring jobs to central Ohio. She drew on her background to make education a central focus of her campaign, with her calls for making college more affordable and encouraging public-private partnerships to work on job-training initiatives with community colleges and training centers. With the endorsement of Columbus Mayor Michael Coleman and strong financial support from labor unions, her toughest opponent in the primary was former Rep. Mary Jo Kilroy, who had served one term in the 15th District and was defeated in 2010. Beatty took the primary, 38%-35%. She easily won in November.

On the Financial Services Committee, Beatty has a useful platform for the robust financial sector in Columbus. In 2015, she filed the Housing Financial Literacy Act to improve first-time homebuyers' financial knowledge. She has been a leading advocate for placing a woman on the $20 bill, and praised the Obama administration plan in 2016 for Civil War-era abolitionist Harriett Tubman to replace President Andrew Jackson on the currency. She urged that the Treasury Department act more speedily than its original timetable, which could extend until 2030.

As chairwoman of the new Diversity and Inclusion Subcommittee, which she urged committee Chairwoman Maxine Waters of California to create, she filed a bill with her "Beatty" rule. That required an interview of at least one racial minority when there was an opening for the head of one of the regional Federal Reserve banks. "It's hard to believe that in 2018, in the Federal Reserve's 105-year history, only one African American has ever served as a Reserve Bank president," she said. With that partly symbolic step, Beatty added, she planned to encourage the entire financial-services industry to look more like America. "It's about changing the culture, the quality of service and the benefits to constituents or customers."

In February 2020, Beatty released a report on behalf of committee Democrats that documented the lack of racial and gender diversity in the top ranks of the nation's largest banks. She urged more transparency as an initial step. At a committee hearing the previous October that dealt chiefly with cryptocurrency, Beatty harshly criticized Facebook chief executive Mark Zuckerberg, who was testifying, for his company's "appalling and disgusting" lack of diversity in management positions. She had earlier pursued the topic in private meetings with Facebook executives.

With Rep. Ann Wagner of Missouri, who is the ranking Republican on her subcommittee, Beatty won House passage of legislation to combat sex trafficking in the United States by making it easier for people to report incidents. In 2018, she and Wagner enacted a bill to penalize website operators that facilitate online sex trafficking. Beatty took her pursuit of bipartisanship an additional step by creating the Civility Caucus.

As vice chair of the Black Caucus in 2020, she participated in community events on behalf the Black Lives Matter movement. At a May protest in Columbus with other local African-American officials following the death of George Floyd in Minneapolis, Beatty was pepper-sprayed by police officers who were seeking to control the demonstration. After describing the "burning sensation" in her eyes, the 70-year-old Beatty the next day told The Atlantic "it was unnecessary force." In December when she became CBC chairwoman, she said the nation faced "three pandemics that have disproportionately impacted the lives of Black Americans: COVID-19, economic turmoil and social injustice."

Also in 2020, Beatty faced her most serious campaign challenge since she was elected to the House: a Democratic primary contest with Morgan Harper, a Columbus native and consumer-rights attorney who had recently returned to the district from her work in New York City. Harper was supported by Justice Democrats, an organization that had earlier assisted young minority candidates against entrenched incumbents. In a campaign ad, she said Beatty was "profiting off of gentrification and taking money from corporations." Beatty outspent Harper, $2.5 million to $858,000 and won 68%-32%.

The insurgent challenge caused anger among other CBC members, who defended Beatty as an effective House member. "We worked hard," Rep. Gregory Meeks told Politico. "For people who seem to come out of nowhere, who have done nothing. ... Does that make sense?"

OH-3: Franklin County

Population		Race and Ethnicity		Income	
Total	813,890	White	52.80%	Median Income	$51,435
Land area (sq. miles)	228	Black	34.60%	District Income Rank	376
Pop/ sq mi	3,569.69	Latino	7.20%	Poverty Rate	17.80%
Born in State	64.80%	Asian	4.40%	With health insurance	90.00%
		Two or more races	4.70%	Cash public assistance	2.00%
Age Groups		Other	3.50%	Food stamp/SNAP	14.30%
Under 18	24.50%				
18-34	29.40%	**Education**		**Work**	
35-64	35.00%	H.S grad or less	40.70%	White Collar	36.60%
Over 64	11.00%	Some college	29.40%	Sales and Service	41.70%
Military		College Degree, 4 yr	19.70%	Blue Collar	21.80%
Veteran/ Active Duty	6.20%	Post grad	10.10%	Government	12.70%

2020 Pres. Vote	Biden	231,858	(70%)	Trump	93,437	(28%)			
2016 Pres. Vote	Clinton	210,489	(66%)	Trump	89,634	(28%)	Johnson	9,210	(3%)

Columbus Metro: In 1972, the first Almanac of American Politics noted that Columbus had just surpassed Cincinnati to become Ohio's second-largest city. Today, Columbus is by far the largest city in the state, with a gain of 110,000 from 2010 to 2019. Franklin County (which is about 50 percent larger than the city) grew 9 percent during the 2000s and another brisk 13 percent in the nine subsequent years. In 2019, the population of the metro area was nearly 2.1 million, now surpassing the Cleveland metro area and expecting to replace metro Cincinnati by 2024, and it is booming while much of the state has stagnated or declined. The reasons are simple: location, location, location—and government. Not only the geographical center of Ohio, the city lies just a one-day truck drive from more than half of the nation's population, making it the perfect location for a Midwestern hub. It is also the capital of the nation's seventh-most-populous state and home to the Ohio State University system's flagship campus. Columbus, NBC News reported in September 2018, "is riding a knowledge economy into prosperity."

In a region known for its blue-collar accents, Columbus has retained a distinctly white-collar flavor and attracted the type of upscale, enterprising people who have produced much of America's growth in recent years. It is home to four Fortune 500 companies. The area is the home of the Battelle Memorial Institute, the think tank that helped invent photocopying, compact discs and the Universal Product Code. Columbus has been rated one of the best cities for a start-up business. Its leaders point to an inviting civic culture.

The city's rapidly growing foreign-born population—Latinos, Koreans, Ethiopians, Chinese, Russian Jews and Somalis—exceeds 13 percent. This population growth has brought political change. Columbus had been Democratic during the Civil War years but became reliably Republican in the late 1800s. As the metropolitan area grew, more people headed for the suburbs and one of the largest Republican cities in the country slowly became Democratic again.

The 3rd Congressional District represents a bow by Republicans to political and demographic realities. Columbus had traditionally been split between the 12th and 15th districts, enabling suburban areas to trump Democratic-leaning portions of the city even in landslide Democratic years. Republicans chose to protect the 12th and 15th and create a Democratic "vote sink" in Franklin County, the only district in the state entirely contained in a single county. The 3rd takes in the skyscrapers of downtown Columbus; heavily Jewish Bexley, the site of the governor's mansion; the capitol, with the statue of President William McKinley out front; most of the university (except for the Ag Lab, which is in the 15th) plus its neighborhoods; the capital further south at the curve of the Scioto River; city slums; and the Democratic portions of upscale New Albany and Westerville. The district includes working-class, mixed-race communities west of the city like Greater Hilltop and Franklinton, which has begun to revitalize. These sometimes-disparate areas have Democratic voting patterns in common. The 3rd is the second-most Democratic district in Ohio. Joe Biden won here, 70%-28%, virtually the same as President Barack Obama in 2012 and four percentage points higher than Hillary Clinton. As Republican redistricters have planned for 2022, they have looked elsewhere in Ohio to slice up a district.

Jim Jordan (R)

Elected 2006, 8th term, b. Feb 17, 1964; Urbana, OH; University of WI, B.S., 1986; OH State University, M.A., 1991; Capital University, J.D., 2001; Evangelical; Married (Polly Jordan); 4 children; 2 grandchildren.

Elected Office: OH House, 1994-2000; OH Senate, 2000-2006.

Professional Career: Assistant wrestling coach, OH St. University, 1987-1995; Wrestling camp coach, clinician, 1987-2006.

DC Office: 2056 RHOB 20515, 202-225-2676, Fax: 202-226-0577, jordan.house.gov

State Offices: Bucyrus, 419-663-1426; Lima, 419-999-6455; Norwalk, 419-663-1426.

Committees: *Judiciary (RMM). Oversight & Reform*: Select Investigative on the Coronavirus Crisis; Subcommittee on Civil Rights & Civil Liberties.

Group Ratings

	ADA	ACLU	AFL-CIO	LCV	COC	HAFA	ACU	CFG	FRC
2020	**	16%	**	5%	-	94%	100%	**	-
2019	0%	C	19%	0%	65%	C	100%	100%	100%

Almanac Ratings 2019-2020

	Economy	Social	Foreign	Composite
Liberal	25%	4%	37%	22%
Conservative	75%	96%	63%	78%

Key Votes of the 116th Congress

1. U.S./Mex./Can. trade deal Y	5. Russia sanctions Y	9. Firearms background checks N
2. First Coronavirus response N	6. Troops in Syria N	10. Spending at the border Y
3. HEROES Act N	7. Veto arms sales to Saudis N	11. Marijuana liberalized rules N
4. CASH Act N	8. Defense $$$, veto override N	12. Electoral College objections Y

Election Results

Election	Name (Party)	Vote (%)		Cand. Spent	Ind. Exp. Support	Ind. Exp. Oppose
2020 General	Jim Jordan (R)...............................	235,875	(68%)	$12,418,992	$95,091	$24,224
	Shannon Freshour (D).....................	101,897	(29%)		$113	
	Steve Perkins (L)...........................	9,854	(3%)			
2020 Primary	Jim Jordan (R)................................	64,695	(100%)			

Prior winning percentages: 2018 (65%), 2016 (68%), 2014 (68%), 2012 (58%), 2010 (72%), 2008 (65%), 2006 (60%)

Republican Jim Jordan, elected in 2006, has endeared himself to conservatives while annoying his party's leaders with his confrontational approach. In 2019-20, he took the top Republican post on the Oversight and Reform Committee and later took the same position on the Judiciary Committee, where he served as a relentless ally of President Donald Trump. Jordan's first platform was as chairman of the Republican Study Committee. Later, he was a founder and the first chairman of the House Freedom Caucus, which conservative members on economic and social policy organized as a forum for their resistance to President Barack Obama's agenda and then became cheerleaders for Trump. But he has fallen short in leadership bids.

Jordan grew up in Champaign County and graduated from Graham High School, where he was a champion wrestler. At the University of Wisconsin, he won two NCAA wrestling championships in the 134-pound weight class and was inducted into the Badger Hall of Fame. With his bachelor's in economics, Jordan worked as an assistant wrestling coach at Ohio State University, where he earned a master's degree in education before getting a law degree at Capital University. (Years later, in 2018, charges were raised, especially by former Ohio State wrestlers, that he was aware of sexual-harassment allegations in the wrestling program.)

Soon, he began thinking about elected office. "You get married and have kids, and you get sick of having the government take your money and tell you what to do," he told columnist George Will in 2011. He won a state House seat in 1994 and served six years before he won a tough primary for the state Senate. His solidly conservative record included legislation creating Ohio's "Choose Life" license plates, a ban on same-sex marriage and government vouchers for private-school tuition.

Jordan ran for the House when Republican Rep. Michael Oxley retired as chairman of the Financial Services Committee. In the six-way Republican primary, he had the most name recognition plus support from Ohio Right to Life, the National Rifle Association and the national anti-tax group Club for Growth. With the benefits of geography and connections, Jordan won 51 percent, carrying eight of 11 counties. Findlay real estate developer Frank Guglielmi self-financed $1.6 million and carried his home county and one other to get 30 percent. In the solidly Republican district, Democrats barely mounted a competitive campaign.

In the House, Jordan established an unfailingly conservative voting record, with consistent perfect scores and a 100 percent lifetime rating from the American Conservative Union. "With the exception of the military, the federal government doesn't do anything very well," he told the Mansfield News Journal. He said he weighs all issues based on whether they benefit families. He is a father of four whose desk calendar is crowded with his children's athletic schedules.

With his right-wing bona fides well established, Jordan became head of the 170-member Republican Study Committee in 2011, when the GOP reclaimed control of the House. Jordan vowed to be independent of the leadership. Under Jordan's guidance, the RSC unveiled a congressional budget plan that called for cuts of $2.5 trillion in planned spending over 10 years. When the House approved a measure in March to keep the government running temporarily as Speaker John Boehner and Obama tried to hammer out an agreement on spending cuts, Jordan was openly scornful. "We must do more than cut spending in bite-sized pieces," he said. That summer, Jordan dug in his heels during the showdown over whether to raise the federal debt limit. He denied speculation that he and allies were eager to shut down the government.

As the founding chairman in 2015 of the House Freedom Caucus, whose chief purpose was to move the Republican agenda to the right, he created a new base for friction with Boehner. Those divisions became apparent in the next few months, notably opposition by Jordan and his allies to giving trade promotion authority to Obama, and their demand that new limits on national security data collection go even further. Despite his high regard among the rebels and his continued poor-mouthing of GOP leaders, Jordan pointedly was not directly involved with the internal pressure campaign that ultimately led Boehner to step down as Speaker in September 2015.

With Republicans in control of the White House and Congress after the 2016 election, some Republicans speculated that Jordan would lose his leverage as Trump and Speaker Paul Ryan took command. Jordan disagreed. "I actually think our influence is as strong as ever," he told the New York Times a week after the election.

Initially at least, Jordan proved to be correct. In March 2017, he and his Freedom Caucus allies stood firm against party leaders, whom they criticized for failing to keep their promise to repeal the Affordable Care Act. Singling out Jordan and two others, an unhappy Trump tweeted in response, "The Freedom Caucus will hurt the entire Republican agenda if they don't get on the team, & fast. We must fight them, & Dems, in 2018!"

In May 2018, a similar scenario of Republican infighting played out when Jordan and other Freedom Caucus members voted against House passage of a bill to extend farm programs. Conservatives objected that the bill did not impose stricter work requirements on recipients of food stamps. The following month, Jordan led a group of eight conservatives who switched their previous opposition to the farm bill when Republican leaders agreed to oppose separate immigration legislation.

Jordan became a vocal defender of Trump and persistent critic of special counsel Robert Mueller and his investigation of the 2016 presidential campaign. The president viewed Jordan and Rep. Mark Meadows of North Carolina, his successor as Freedom Caucus chairman, as his "tough-talking, unapologetic allies," Politico reported in July 2018.

The limits of the support for Jordan among House Republicans became apparent when he challenged Rep. Kevin McCarthy for minority leader a week after the party's setbacks in the 2018 election. On Fox News, Jordan complained that House GOP leaders failed to demonstrate the "same intensity" toward party goals that conservatives had shown on behalf of Trump. The outcome was not close. McCarthy won, 159-43.

In December, Jordan had another setback in his bid to become the senior Republican on the Judiciary Committee. Instead, the McCarthy-controlled panel gave the position to Rep. Doug Collins of Georgia. In what seemed a consolation prize, Jordan got the vacant top GOP slot on the Oversight committee—defending Trump in Democratic investigations. But, with Republicans unified behind Trump during the initial impeachment inquiry, Jordan got a temporary assignment on the Intelligence Committee to become Trump's stalwart defender. And, Jordan reversed his earlier setback, when he easily won GOP approval to replace Collins at the Judiciary Committee when he stepped down for his Senate campaign in Georgia.

Jordan has survived intraparty conflicts at home. During preparation for the 2012 redistricting in Ohio, The Columbus Dispatch reported that Boehner's allies were considering a plan that would make Jordan's seat substantially more competitive. Boehner denied any such effort, and Jordan's new district became securely Republican, though it moved east, well beyond his thinly populated base in western Ohio. That ruffled some feathers in Cleveland.

"There was no good reason to punish Greater Cleveland by making the person who's now the second most contemptible human being in the entire U.S. government part of the region's delegation to Congress," Brent Larkin, the former editorial director for the Cleveland Plain Dealer, wrote in that newspaper in November 2019. But the next round of redistricting could push the district of Jordan (and other Republicans in western Ohio) even farther east, as a result of the state's loss of a House seat.

OH-4: Central Ohio   Cook Partisan Voting Index: R+20

Population		Race and Ethnicity		Income	
Total	712,261	White	89.30%	Median Income	$60,212
Land area (sq. miles)	4,665	Black	5.20%	District Income Rank	257
Pop/ sq mi	152.69	Latino	3.90%	Poverty Rate	11.50%
Born in State	82.70%	Asian	1.20%	With health insurance	95.00%
		Two or more races	3.10%	Cash public assistance	3.40%
Age Groups		Other	1.20%	Food stamp/SNAP	10.70%
Under 18	21.80%				
18-34	20.60%	**Education**		**Work**	
35-64	39.20%	H.S grad or less	49.00%	White Collar	30.70%
Over 64	18.40%	Some college	31.00%	Sales and Service	34.90%
		College Degree, 4 yr	12.90%	Blue Collar	34.40%
Military		Post grad	7.10%	Government	11.20%
Veteran/ Active Duty	8.10%				

2020 Pres. Vote	Trump	237,156	(67%)	Biden	110,327	(31%)			
2016 Pres. Vote	Trump	208,736	(64%)	Clinton	99,626	(30%)	Johnson	11,741	(4%)

Lima, Sandusky: Central and western Ohio look mostly like farmland to the traveler. Yet this is manufacturing country, indeed one of America's premier manufacturing areas, where the economy is based on factories in small towns and on rural highways. These places seem far from anywhere "important," yet the region has been quietly prosperous most of the years since World War II. While there have been some manufacturing job losses, most of this area emerged from the recession in better shape than other parts of the state.

Each population center has its own pet industry: In Lima, the Joint Systems Manufacturing Center has been building versions of the Abrams tank since 1980 and is the only factory in the United States that produces tanks, with sizable overseas sales. In 2019, it got a $700 million contract to upgrade 174 of the battle tanks, with a workforce of about 1,000. A month earlier, the JSMC got a contract to build a new prototype—good news for a facility that came close to shutting down a few years earlier. Also in Lima, Ford spent $500 million to develop "EcoBoost" technology for its F-150 pick-up truck. Dannon in Minster in 2019 expanded what it described as the world's largest yogurt plant, with adaptations for the transition to Greek yogurt; it relies on 4,500 cows that operate on an assembly-line basis in what the company describes as "free-stall" barns. In Jackson Center, Airstream completed in 2019 the expanded production of its iconic trailers, with a workforce of about 1,000. Honda has invested more than $6 billion at four sites in Marysville and East Liberty since it opened its first plant in Union County, for motorcycles, in 1979. Today, it employs about 13,000 Ohioans and is the largest automobile employer in the state. Production of the hybrid Honda Accord returned to Marysville from Japan in 2018. That plant can assemble about 440,000 vehicles each year. Many other local companies provide parts and supplies.

These small towns have historical significance. Marion was the home of President Warren G. Harding and socialist Norman Thomas; the latter, as a young boy, delivered the newspaper edited by the former. Fremont, settled by abstemious Yankees and named after explorer (and first Republican presidential candidate) John C. Fremont, was the home of President Rutherford B. Hayes, whose wife, Lucy, served only lemonade in the White House. Although it has been home to an aromatic Heinz ketchup plant that produced daily the equivalent of 4.1 million 14-ounce bottles, the most in the world, the company said it was moving most of those operations to Ontario in 2021. Wapakoneta, a typically Ohioan-Indian name, is the hometown of Neil Armstrong, the first man to walk on the moon, and the site of the Neil Armstrong Air and Space Museum.

This terrain in central Ohio makes up the 4th Congressional District. The district extends north and east into Seneca, Sandusky, Erie and Lorain counties, and the outer Cleveland suburbs. But it has been carefully wedged into the countryside to avoid metro areas, including Dayton and Toledo. The GOP lean of the small towns mitigates the impact of places like Oberlin College, one of the most liberal colleges in the country and the first to admit African Americans (1835) and women (1841). President Donald Trump in 2020 got 67 percent of the vote here, second in Ohio only to the 6th District.

Bob Latta (R)

Elected 2007, 7th full term, b. Apr 18, 1956; Bluffton, OH; OH Northern University, Att., 1975; Bowling Green State University, B.A., 1978; University of Toledo College of Law, J.D., 1981; Roman Catholic; Married (Marcia Sloan Latta); 2 children.

Elected Office: Wood County commissioner, 1991-1996; OH Senate, 1997- 2001; OH General Assembly, 2001-2007.

Professional Career: Attorney, 1981-1991.

DC Office: 2467 RHOB 20515, 202-225-6405, Fax: 202-225-1985, latta.house.gov

State Offices: Bowling Green, 419-354-8700; Defiance, 419-782-1996; Findlay, 419-422-7791.

Committees: *Energy & Commerce*: Communications & Technology (RMM); Consumer Protection & Commerce; Energy. *Select Committee on the Modernization of Congress*.

Group Ratings

	ADA	ACLU	AFL-CIO	LCV	COC	HAFA	ACU	CFG	FRC
2020	**	19%	**	10%	-	91%	90%	**	-
2019	5%	C	19%	7%	77%	C	90%	96%	100%

Almanac Ratings 2019-2020

	Economy	Social	Foreign	Composite
Liberal	25%	20%	27%	24%
Conservative	75%	80%	73%	76%

Key Votes of the 116th Congress

1. U.S./Mex./Can. trade deal	Y	5. Russia sanctions	Y	9. Firearms background checks N
2. First Coronavirus response	Y	6. Troops in Syria	Y	10. Spending at the border	Y
3. HEROES Act	N	7. Veto arms sales to Saudis	N	11. Marijuana liberalized rules	N
4. CASH Act	N	8. Defense $$$, veto override	Y	12. Electoral College objections N

Election Results

Election	Name (Party)	Vote (%)	Cand. Spent	Ind. Exp. Support	Ind. Exp. Oppose
2020 General	Bob Latta (R)...................................	257,019 (68%)	$1,058,457	$506	$863
	Nick Rubando (D)............................	120,962 (32%)	$233,778	$123	
2020 Primary	Bob Latta (R)...................................	57,537 (100%)			

Prior winning percentages: 2018 (62%), 2016 (71%), 2014 (67%), 2012 (57%), 2010 (68%), 2008 (64%), 2007 special (57%)

Republican Bob Latta, who was elected in 2007 to the seat that his father, Delbert Latta, earlier held for 30 years, has a conservative voting record like his father. He has been a practical legislator on the Energy and Commerce Committee, where he has become a GOP leader on communications policy—including his promotion of self-driving automobiles and steps to reduce annoying telephone robocalls.

Bob Latta was born in Ohio but split his early years between his native Bluffton and Washington D.C. Helping his father's campaigns, Latta says he learned the business of catering to constituents. Young Latta frequently interrupted his homework to answer their phone calls and remembers his father following up with federal agencies to get results from the bureaucracy. While attending Bowling Green State University, he volunteered in his father's office, where he met his wife, Marcia, who worked for his father. When he graduated from law school at the University of Toledo, his father had one bit of career advice for him: Don't get into politics.

He followed that guidance and practiced law for several years. When his father retired in 1988, the 31-year-old sought to follow in his footsteps. Paul Gillmor, a Republican state senator, had been waiting to succeed Del Latta. After a spirited race, Gillmor beat Latta by just 27 votes out of 57,361 cast. Latta retreated to local politics, on the Wood County Commission and then to the Ohio legislature. One of his major efforts was to repeal the estate tax for most Ohioans. An avid hunter, Latta championed longer hunting seasons and expanded wildlife reserves.

After Gillmor died in September 2007, Latta ran for the open seat. His chief primary opponent was state Sen. Steve Buehrer, who was backed by the Club for Growth, which ran several ads attacking Latta as an advocate of higher taxes. Latta defeated Buehrer by 2,542 votes out of 74,191 cast. Democrat Robin Weirauch had backing from labor unions and the abortion-rights group EMILY's List. She attacked Latta on economic issues and his support for the Iraq war. Latta won 57%-43%.

Latta's Almanac voting record has been nearly perfect conservative. On Energy and Commerce, he initially made energy independence his central issue. He successfully amended a House-passed air-quality bill in 2011 to require the Environmental Protection Agency to take costs into account in setting standards under the Clean Air Act. Latta's Protect Our Great Lakes Act, which was designed to reduce algal blooms by prohibiting discharge of dredged material into the lakes, evolved and was enacted in 2015 as his Drinking Water Protection Act.

Latta has taken an interest in technology. In 2010, he was the first House member to release an iPhone app. He filed in 2011 a resolution declaring that to continue aggressive growth in telecommunications and technology industries, the federal government "should get out of the way and stay out of the way." He co-chaired the Republican New Media Caucus and the Rural Broadband Caucus. With Democratic Rep. Jerry McNerney of California, another member of Energy and Commerce, Latta started the Wi-Fi Caucus. They addressed aspects of the digital divide between communities with and without internet access.

As chairman of the Digital Commerce and Consumer Protection Subcommittee, Latta in September 2017 got voice-vote passage in the House of his bill to set a policy framework for autonomous, self-driving vehicles. "U.S. companies are investing major resources in the research and development of this tech and should not be held up by regulatory barriers," he said. The Senate did not act on the bill. In September 2020, he filed a bill to set standards for the safety and security of those vehicles, with upgraded enforcement by federal transportation regulators. In the global race, he said, "Congress must act to create a national framework that provides developers certainty and a clear path to deployment."

In the minority, Latta has been ranking Republican on the Communications and Technology Subcommittee. In January 2019, he told an industry audience that government should not stand in the way of innovators. But he has raised concern with industry practices. With Federal Communications Commission Chairman Ajit Pai, Latta co-authored in August 2019 an op-ed for the Cleveland Plain

Dealer in which they described how the FCC—in response to Latta's legislation—had voted to allow phone companies to block unwanted robocalls and also closed a loophole that had "benefited international fraudsters" in taking advantage of caller ID spoofing. Separately, he pushed in 2019 for nationwide standards for data privacy.

Following the 2020 election, Latta sought to fill the opening for ranking Republican on Energy and Commerce. But he finished a distant third in the contest that was won by Rep. Cathy McMorris Rodgers of Washington.

At home, Latta has won reelection by wide margins. His closest race was in 2012. The Toledo Blade endorsed his Democratic opponent, Angela Zimmann, a college professor, and said Latta "has not been pragmatic or constructive." Latta outspent her nearly 3-to-1 and won convincingly, 57%-39%.

OH-5: Northwest Ohio

Cook Partisan Voting Index: R+15

Population		Race and Ethnicity		Income		
Total	721,212	White	91.20%	Median Income	$63,702	
Land area (sq. miles)	5,626	Black	3.00%	District Income Rank	217	
Pop/ sq mi	128.18	Latino	6.00%	Poverty Rate	9.00%	
Born in State	79.50%	Asian	1.40%	With health insurance	95.50%	
		Two or more races	2.60%	Cash public assistance	1.20%	
Age Groups		Other	1.80%	Food stamp/SNAP	7.80%	
Under 18	22.20%					
18-34	22.40%	**Education**		**Work**		
35-64	37.50%	H.S grad or less	40.90%	White Collar	35.50%	
Over 64	18.00%	Some college	31.20%	Sales and Service	34.70%	
Military		College Degree, 4 yr	17.30%	Blue Collar	29.80%	
Veteran/ Active Duty	7.10%	Post grad	10.70%	Government	12.50%	

2020 Pres. Vote	Trump	237,760	(62%)	Biden	141,528	(37%)		
2016 Pres. Vote	Trump	214,661	(59%)	Clinton	124,407	(34%)	Johnson	15,370	(4%)

Toledo Area, Bowling Green: Undergirded by limestone, as flat and fertile as any place in America, northwest Ohio was economically productive from the time it was settled. That settlement came relatively late. Conflicts with Native Americans played a large role in the delay. In 1791, near Fort Recovery in Mercer County, the U.S Army was routed by a confederation of Indian tribes: Only 48 of the 1,000 soldiers led into battle escaped unharmed, and a quarter of them died. Three years later, the Battle of Fallen Timbers near present-day Maumee put a temporary end to outright conflict between Indians and Americans, and the ensuing Treaty of Greenville set aside northwestern Ohio for Native American use; the area wasn't made formally available for white settlement until the end of Tecumseh's War some 20 years later. What we know today as fecund farmland was part of a giant swamp in the early 1800s.

Today, this is prime industrial country. Its limestone, rail connections, and location between Lake Michigan and Lake Erie have spurred a factory economy that financially is far more important than agriculture. After the first settlements, northwest Ohio grew steadily for many decades, with Germany supplying many of the immigrants. Its small factories supplied the big auto plants in Detroit and northeast Ohio. Growth lagged in the 1980s when the domestic industry collapsed, but rebounded somewhat as small firms sold not only to the Big Three but to foreign customers. Honda has dozens of suppliers in the area. In February 2019, leaders of the Regional Growth Partnership—a private planning group that covers 17 counties in northwest Ohio—listed $3.2 billion in new investments, with 5,700 jobs, during the previous year, with the potential of $6.7 billion in additional projects.

The 5th Congressional District sweeps across northwest Ohio, including the suburbs of Toledo, the university town of Bowling Green, the Marathon Petroleum home in Findlay, and the towns of Napoleon and Defiance en route to Ohio's borders with Michigan and Indiana. Its factories are numerous and widespread. Bowling Green is the site of the state's first wind turbines. Napoleon has the world's largest Campbell soup plant. Upper Sandusky (more than 60 miles inland from Sandusky on Lake Erie) is home to about 30 industrial firms; it promotes its "small town living with big business appeal."

This had been a solidly Republican district. About three-tenths of the district is in suburban Lucas County, though its Toledo neighborhoods are mostly in the solidly Democratic 9th District. With adjacent Wood County, the area surrounding Toledo accounts for nearly one-half of the district. From 2010 to 2019, Lucas lost 3 percent of its population and Wood gained 4 percent. The outlying areas are strongly Republican. As with several other mostly rural Ohio districts, Donald Trump boosted the Republican presidential performance here in each of his campaigns—with 62 percent in 2020.

Bill Johnson (R)

Elected 2010, 6th term, b. Nov 10, 1954; Roseboro, NC; Air Command and Staff College; Troy University, B.S., 1979; GA Institute of Technology, M.S., 1984; Protestant - Unspecified Christian; Married (LeeAnn Johnson); 4 children; 6 grandchildren.

Military Career: U.S. Air Force 1973-1999

Professional Career: President, Johnson-Schley Mgmt. Group, 1999-2003; Owner, J2 Business Solutions, 2003-2006; Director, Lockheed Martin, 2005; CIO, Stoneridge Inc., 2006-2010.

DC Office: 2336 RHOB 20515, 202-225-5705, Fax: 202-225-5907, billjohnson.house.gov

State Offices: Cambridge, 740-432-2366; Ironton, 740-534-9431; Marietta, 740-376-0868; Salem, 330-337-6951.

Committees: *Energy & Commerce*: Communications & Technology; Energy; Environment & Climate Change.

Group Ratings

	ADA	ACLU	AFL-CIO	LCV	COC	HAFA	ACU	CFG	FRC
2020	**	18%	**	14%	-	76%	75%	**	-
2019	0%	C	40%	7%	88%	C	76%	69%	95%

Almanac Ratings 2019-2020

	Economy	Social	Foreign	Composite
Liberal	25%	24%	33%	28%
Conservative	75%	76%	67%	72%

Key Votes of the 116th Congress

1. U.S./Mex./Can. trade deal Y	5. Russia sanctions Y	9. Firearms background checks N
2. First Coronavirus response Y	6. Troops in Syria Y	10. Spending at the border Y
3. HEROES Act N	7. Veto arms sales to Saudis N	11. Marijuana liberalized rules N
4. CASH Act Y	8. Defense $$$, veto override Y	12. Electoral College objections Y

Election Results

Election	Name (Party)	Vote (%)		Cand. Spent	Ind. Exp. Support	Ind. Exp. Oppose
2020 General	Bill Johnson (R)	249,130	(74%)	$1,628,303	$9,000	$750
	Shawna Roberts (D)	85,661	(26%)	$500		
2020 Primary	Bill Johnson (R)	57,790	(87%)			
	Kenneth Morgan (R)	8,721	(13%)			

Prior winning percentages: 2018 (69%), 2016 (71%), 2014 (58%), 2012 (53%), 2010 (50%)

Republican Bill Johnson, elected in 2010 in what was a Democratic bastion not long ago, had been a business consultant and founded an anti-tax group. After learning the ropes, he has become an active member of the Energy and Commerce Committee, where he has been a zealous opponent of environmental regulation and an advocate of more business-friendly government, especially for energy companies. He has lost two bids to be the top Republican on the House Budget Committee. Wisely in this district, Johnson has been an enthusiastic advocate for former President Donald Trump.

Johnson was born in Roseboro North Carolina and raised on his family's cotton and tobacco farm. He joined the Air Force when he was 17. While serving, he graduated with a degree in computer science from Alabama's Troy University. Later, he earned his master's degree in computer science from Georgia Tech. In the military, he was stationed at many bases. As a director at U.S. Special Operations Command, he briefed congressional and intelligence officials. He retired from the military in 1999 as a lieutenant colonel, having managed communications and computer systems. He worked for multiple tech companies and became an information-technology consultant, especially for the military. He moved to Ohio in 2006, when he began working for Stone ridge, which makes electronic components for automobiles. Upset that shoppers were pouring across the border into Pennsylvania to buy certain goods free of sales taxes, Johnson in 2009 founded an organization called the Ohio Sales Tax Reform Incentive with the goal of creating tax holidays for shoppers.

Johnson challenged two-term Democratic Rep. Charlie Wilson. In the GOP primary, he defeated Donald Allen, a veterinarian, 43%-37%. Wilson cast fiscally conservative votes and backed gun rights, but he voted for the Democrats' $787 billion economic stimulus bill and the Affordable Care Act. Johnson characterized Wilson as a puppet of liberal House Speaker Nancy Pelosi and out of touch with his constituents. Wilson accused Johnson's company of exporting jobs. Johnson replied that the company created jobs in Ohio and called Wilson's attacks "the desperate act of a career politician who cannot defend his record for his tax-and-spend policies." The U.S. Chamber of Commerce ran ads that attacked Wilson as "Party-Line Charlie." Johnson won, 50%-45%, even as Wilson outspent him almost 2-to-1.

Johnson was an adamant critic of the Obama administration. He won House passage in 2012 of his "Stop the War on Coal Act," which barred the Environmental Protection Agency from restricting greenhouse gas emissions, quashed stricter fuel efficiency standards for cars and gave states control over disposal of coal byproducts.

On the Energy and Commerce Committee, Johnson promoted energy independence. In 2015, the House passed his bill to expedite exports of liquefied natural gas by setting a deadline for federal approval. After a trip to four European nations, he said they were "begging" for U.S. energy exports so they could reduce their dependence on Russia. At a 2016 committee hearing, he called the EPA "un-American" and said the agency was "draining the lifeblood out of our businesses." Democrats criticized him as "extreme." In 2018, he won committee approval of a bill to streamline approval of small-scale LNG facilities. On the House Budget Committee, Johnson ran unsuccessfully in January 2018 to fill the vacancy for chairman. Rep. Steve Womack of Arkansas was the easy winner of that contest. Johnson ran again for the committee's top GOP slot following the 2020 election, but lost to Rep. Jason Smith of Missouri.

In February 2017, Trump used one of his first bill-signings to enact a Johnson measure to overturn a regulation on mining waste that President Barack Obama had approved shortly before he left office. Johnson said the sole purpose of the rule was "to put a death knell into the coffin of the coal industry." Co-chairman of the House Natural Gas Caucus, he said EPA's decision in June 2019 to replace the Obama-era Clean Power Plan showed that its leaders understood that "we can have smart environmental regulations and protect coal jobs and our economy at the same time."

Johnson became a reliable advocate for Trump. "You don't have to like what he says," Johnson told a Lincoln Day dinner in Athens in April 2018. "But you can't argue with the idea of returning America to that age of innovation and ingenuity." As Trump faced growing difficulties, Johnson became a more outspoken booster. When the House in December 2019 debated the first impeachment charges against Trump, Johnson called on the House to "observe a moment of silent reflection" for the 63 million voters who had supported Trump in 2016 and "Democrats today are wanting to silence." In June 2020, after police used tear gas to clear protestors for Trump to walk to St. Matthews Church across Pennsylvania Avenue, Johnson tweeted that it was "a powerful reminder that Americans will not be intimidated by lawlessness and violence."

Wilson sought a comeback in 2012 against Johnson, who tried to preserve his outsider status with ads referring to his rival as "Congressman Charlie Wilson." Wilson got about $2 million in help from the DCCC, but the anti-tax lobbying group Americans for Tax Reform spent more than $3 million on Johnson's behalf. Johnson won again, 53%-47%. In 2014, Johnson faced Democrat Jennifer Garrison, a lawyer who served six years in the state Assembly and described herself as "pro-life, pro-gun and pro-coal." She called Johnson "the face of Washington dysfunction." Johnson outspent her $1.9 million to $900,000. He won 58%-39% and took 17 of the 18 counties. Since then, Democrats have turned their attention elsewhere. In redistricting, his district might gain additional parts of Mahoning County.

OH-6: Ohio River Valley   **Cook Partisan Voting Index: R+24**

Population		Race and Ethnicity		Income	
Total	698,284	White	95.20%	Median Income	$52,442
Land area (sq. miles)	7,215	Black	2.10%	District Income Rank	364
Pop/ sq mi	96.78	Latino	1.20%	Poverty Rate	13.40%
Born in State	69.70%	Asian	0.50%	With health insurance	93.60%
		Two or more races	1.60%	Cash public assistance	1.60%
Age Groups		Other	0.50%	Food stamp/SNAP	13.60%
Under 18	21.00%				
18-34	19.20%	**Education**		**Work**	
35-64	39.40%	H.S grad or less	53.40%	White Collar	32.20%
Over 64	20.40%	Some college	28.90%	Sales and Service	38.20%
		College Degree, 4 yr	11.10%	Blue Collar	29.70%
Military		Post grad	6.70%	Government	13.10%
Veteran/ Active Duty	8.60%				

2020 Pres. Vote	Trump	248,573	(72%)	Biden	91,279	(26%)		
2016 Pres. Vote	Trump	221,872	(69%)	Clinton	85,501	(27%)	Johnson	8,833	(3%)

Steubenville: In the years after the American Revolution, shipping goods downriver by raft was cheaper than sending them over the Appalachian Mountains, and so the Ohio River became a great highway of commerce. From Pittsburgh, where the Allegheny and Monongahela Rivers meet to form the Ohio, the river led south and west toward the Mississippi and the great port of New Orleans. For hundreds of miles, it twisted this way and that through mountains and rolling hills, land that marked the boundary between post-Revolutionary Virginia and the Northwest Territory. Across this boundary, settlers made their way in those years to Ohio—Yankees and, in larger numbers, Virginians.

By the late 19th century, the Ohio was an industrial river. Coal was nearby, barge transportation was available, and railroads were built in the narrow valleys between the hills. Steel mills went up on the riverfront. This produced prosperity for a while, but it also produced pollution—Steubenville on the Ohio River once had the nation's dirtiest air—and after the old-line steel industry fell on hard times, the Ohio River was lined with some of the most impoverished parts of America. So many people left what became known as Appalachia to find jobs in Detroit and the big industrial cities that the road to the north was called the Hillbilly Highway. Decades later, many landowners reaped a windfall after rising prices made feasible the extraction of vast reserves of oil and natural gas from the Marcellus and Utica shale beds miles under their land. The petroleum industry, abetted by local developers, has ambitious plans for those reserves. In Guernsey County, work was underway on a $1.4 billion natural gas power plant, with commissioning expected in 2022. A $250 million underground salt cavern ethane storage facility was planned for Monroe County, with storage capacity of a million barrels, WTRF-TV in Wheeling West Virginia reported in July 2020. In January 2019, local economic progress ranked Steubenville and Jefferson County first in the nation for its percentage gain in construction jobs. From 2011 to 2018, $74 billion was invested in Ohio's shale energy sector, according to a Cleveland State University study in April 2019.

The 6th Congressional District of Ohio is a string of counties running 325 miles along the Ohio River, plus part of the Mahoning Valley. It includes Canfield and a few small suburbs of Youngstown in Mahoning County. The district curves along the lightly populated stretch of the river south from Marietta, past the old industrial town of Ironton, and extends to Wheelersburg, which is not quite in the Cincinnati metro area.

This mix of communities has become a Republican enclave with a cultural conservatism much like that of West Virginia and eastern Kentucky across the river. The population is 95 percent white, the third highest in the nation, but with the lowest median income of any Republican-held district in Ohio. (Strikingly, all four of the Democratic-held districts—largely in urban areas—have a lower median income than the 6th.) In 2020, President Donald Trump won this district, 72%-26%. That margin, the largest in Ohio, was all the more extraordinary given that Mitt Romney in 2012 won, 55%-43%. In Columbiana, the Republican chairman called the area, "the very epicentre of the Trump groundswell." For now, that's hard to challenge.

Bob Gibbs (R)

Elected 2010, 6th term, b. Jun 14, 1954; Peru, IN; OH State University Agricultural Technical Institute, A.A.S., 1974; Methodist; Married (Jody Gibbs); 3 children.

Elected Office: OH House, 2003-2008; OH Senate, 2008-2010.

Professional Career: Technician, OH Ag. Research & Devel. Center, 1974-1978; Owner, Hidden Hollow Farms, 1978-2004; Owner, Gibbs Enterprises.

DC Office: 2446 RHOB 20515, 202-225-6265, Fax: 202-225-3394, gibbs.house.gov

State Offices: Ashland, 419-207-0650; Canton, 330-737-1631.

Committees: *Oversight & Reform*: National Security; Subcommittee on Environment. *Transportation & Infrastructure*: Coast Guard & Maritime Transportation (RMM); Highways & Transit.

Group Ratings

	ADA	ACLU	AFL-CIO	LCV	COC	HAFA	ACU	CFG	FRC
2020	**	13%	**	19%	-	83%	81%	**	-
2019	0%	C	40%	7%	81%	C	81%	69%	91%

Almanac Ratings 2019-2020

	Economy	Social	Foreign	Composite
Liberal	25%	26%	7%	20%
Conservative	75%	74%	93%	80%

Key Votes of the 116th Congress

1. U.S./Mex./Can. trade deal	Y	5. Russia sanctions	Y	9. Firearms background checks	N
2. First Coronavirus response	Y	6. Troops in Syria	N/A	10. Spending at the border	Y
3. HEROES Act	N	7. Veto arms sales to Saudis	N	11. Marijuana liberalized rules	N
4. CASH Act	N	8. Defense $$$, veto override	Y	12. Electoral College objections	Y

Election Results

Election	Name (Party)	Vote (%)		Cand. Spent	Ind. Exp. Support	Ind. Exp. Oppose
2020 General	Bob Gibbs (R)	236,607	(68%)	$370,585		$750
	Quentin Potter (D)	102,271	(29%)	$12,042		
	Brandon Lape (L)	11,671	(3%)	$1,478		
2020 Primary	Bob Gibbs (R)	55,009	(100%)			

Prior winning percentages: 2018 (59%), 2016 (64%), 2014 (100%), 2012 (56%), 2010 (54%)

Republican Bob Gibbs, elected in 2010, is a hog farmer and ex-state farm bureau president who takes seriously agriculture and public works projects. As chairman of the Water Resources and Environment Subcommittee, he was a prime dispenser of congressional pork—or, as his website described his domain, "cost effective water infrastructure improvements that provide jobs." He has avidly sought to cut back excessive regulations. In the minority, as ranking Republican on the Coast Guard and Maritime Transportation Subcommittee, Gibbs has had a close watch on the interests of the Great Lakes.

Gibbs grew up on the west side of Cleveland, "as far away from agriculture as you can get," he said. After working in the garden center of his high school, he enrolled in Ohio State University's Agricultural Institute. Gibbs went into business in Holmes County with his Hidden Hollow Farms, where he mostly raised market hogs. His two terms as president of the Ohio Farm Bureau Federation sparked his interest in politics. In 2002, Gibbs won a seat in the Ohio House. He was elected six years later to the Senate, where he chaired the Ways and Means Committee. He focused on agriculture, small business and private property issues. He co-authored a 21 percent cut in Ohio's personal income tax rates.

Gibbs challenged two-term Democratic Rep. Zack Space, a self-described moderate and a prolific fundraiser. They attacked each other on climate change, health care reform and the "don't ask, don't tell" policy prohibiting gay men and women from serving openly in the military. Republicans blasted Space for his vote for the 2009 House-passed bill to create a cap-and-trade system to reduce greenhouse-gas emissions. Space ran ads with footage of Gibbs telling an audience, "I'm a free-trader," and tying him to trade deals that, Space said, sent Ohio jobs overseas. Space outspent Gibbs, $2.9 million to $1.1 million; each had more than $1 million in national party help. In the 2010 Republican tidal wave, Gibbs won easily, 54%-40%.

With a boost from Speaker John Boehner, Gibbs got the Water Resources subcommittee chairmanship, a prime plum for a freshman. He enacted in 2014 the Water Resources Reform and Development Act, the first such reauthorization since 2007. The law reformed the review process of the Army Corps of Engineers for the nation's ports and flood control projects, "deauthorized" $18 billion in inactive projects and included no specific earmarks.

Gibbs worked to provide clear guidance to the Army Corps for new projects. "Typically, it would take 10 to 15 years to complete the studies necessary prior to beginning construction. WRRDA will reduce that time to three years so that projects are able to begin as they are needed and create jobs," he summarized. Subsequently, Gibbs said he was "disappointed" with the slow pace and the priorities of the Army Corps in its implementation of the new law.

The election of President Donald Trump provided a policy breakthrough for Gibbs. In February 2017, he joined a White House ceremony where Trump signed an executive order that overturned Obama's proposed Waters of the United States (WOTUS) rules. Trump called those rules one of the worst examples of government "run amok." Gibbs praised Trump for keeping his campaign promise.

On the farm bill enacted in 2018, Gibbs took the lead in the House on a provision that encouraged farmers to make more use of clean-water sources. In 2019, as the senior Republican on the Coast Guard Subcommittee, he pursued his interest in water navigation, especially on the Great Lakes. In April 2020, he called EPA's attention to the extra $20 million that Congress allotted to controlling invasive species in the Great Lakes and remediating other environmental problems, the Cleveland Plain-Dealer reported.

Gibbs has not been shy about sending a partisan dagger. When the Ohio Democratic Party took a loan under the Paycheck Protection Program, he objected and filed a bill to require that any political organization return such a loan to the federal government. He called his bill, the Stop Pilfering Everyone's Paycheck Protection for Election Results (PEPPER) Act. The chairman of the Ohio Democrats was David Pepper. The following day, Pepper agreed to pay back the loan under conventional financing terms.

In 2012, redistricting gave Gibbs a district in which six of the 10 counties were completely new to him, but the new district leaned more Republican. Democrats nominated Joyce Healy-Abrams, who ran a corporate record-keeping business and whose brother, William Healy, was mayor of Canton. She spent $905,000 to $1.3 million for Gibbs. Healy-Abrams won 55 percent of the vote in Stark, but Gibbs rolled up big majorities in the other counties and won 56%-44%.

In 2018, Democratic challenger Ken Harbaugh, a Navy veteran with support from veterans groups, spent $3 million to $1.8 million for Gibbs. His campaign theme was "country over party" and he styled himself as a political centrist. The Plain Dealer endorsed Harbaugh, though it said his campaign views were "noticeably thin;" it criticized Gibbs for his "blind partisanship" in support of Trump. Gibbs won, 59%-41%; he took all 10 counties, with 51 percent in Stark.

In the next few years, the seniority Gibbs has on the Transportation and Infrastructure Committee, plus House Republican term-limit rules, could position him to seek the top GOP position on that panel.

OH-7: North-Central Ohio **Cook Partisan Voting Index: R+18**

Population		Race and Ethnicity		Income	
Total	727,011	White	92.10%	Median Income	$57,897
Land area (sq. miles)	3,865	Black	4.20%	District Income Rank	289
Pop/ sq mi	188.11	Latino	2.90%	Poverty Rate	10.90%
Born in State	83.80%	Asian	0.70%	With health insurance	90.20%
		Two or more races	2.40%	Cash public assistance	3.40%
Age Groups		Other	0.60%	Food stamp/SNAP	10.80%
Under 18	23.30%				
18-34	19.50%	**Education**		**Work**	
35-64	38.30%	H.S grad or less	51.90%	White Collar	32.50%
Over 64	19.00%	Some college	27.10%	Sales and Service	36.70%
		College Degree, 4 yr	14.00%	Blue Collar	30.80%
Military		Post grad	7.10%	Government	11.10%
Veteran/ Active Duty	7.50%				

2020 Pres. Vote	Trump	237,285	(65%)	Biden	120,713	(33%)			
2016 Pres. Vote	Trump	205,572	(62%)	Clinton	107,942	(33%)	Johnson	10,856	(3%)

Canton, Cleveland Suburbs: A little more than a century ago, Canton was at the center of American politics. It was already an industrial city, though without the huge steel mills of Youngstown or Cleveland. Its high-skill workers were fashioning new kinds of plows and reapers, making watches and, beginning in 1899, roller bearings. It did not attract masses of immigrants, its factories did not run on harsh stopwatch discipline, and the class-warfare politics of other northern Ohio industrial cities did not take root here. Canton's most famous citizen was Republican President William McKinley, who rose to the rank of major at age 22 in the Civil War and was later elected to Congress. In 1896, he campaigned for president from his front porch in Canton, meeting with delegations brought in by train from around the country. This spectacle, displaying both technological virtuosity and personal modesty, sounded a reverberating note in American politics, as did the McKinley platform—the "full dinner pail," the gold standard and the enforcement of law and order in labor relations—a platform that mostly severed the Democrats' ties to northern blue-collar whites until the 1930s.

Today, Canton remains based on manufacturing and has had some recovery from job losses In 2017, community leaders issued a report warning that surrounding Stark County was growing "smaller, older and poorer," unless there was major economic development. Canton has become best known as the home of the Professional Football Hall of Fame, with a roof shaped like a football. The Canton Bulldogs were one of the first teams in the Ohio League, the predecessor to the modern National Football League. The NFL has pursued lavish plans for a $700 million Hall of Fame village in Canton, which has been described as sports and entertainment "Disney for football fans." A scaled-back version of Phase One opened in September 2020, the centennial of the league. Those features included stadium improvements, five new fields, plus expansion of the Hall of Fame and its museum. At the same time, the village owners broke ground on Phase Two—scheduled for completion by the end of 2023—with a new office building ("Center for Excellence"), Performance Center, water theme park, and a hotel and retail shops. But the village lost $57 million in 2020, much of that due to the coronavirus pandemic, which could cause additional refinements.

The area includes Holmes County, which has moved toward becoming the first Amish-majority county in the nation. The Amish village in Holmes and surrounding counties includes about 36,000 residents. Ashland is a rural county where Johnny Appleseed lived on land that is now Ashland University. The campus includes the Ashbrook Center, which has become a hub for conservative academicians and politicians.

The 7th Congressional District of Ohio is a hodgepodge of counties forming a crescent across northeastern Ohio and avoiding Democratic areas of Cleveland, Akron and Lorain. It includes all of Canton, the old Ohio and Erie Canal town of Massillon, and most of Stark County, which has about a third of the district's population. Much of the area west and southwest of Canton is part of the Appalachian Plateau. The remaining swath of lightly populated counties arches west to Knox County on the outskirts of Columbus and north to North Ridgeville and Avon nearly to Lake Erie in Lorain County. The district extends through Medina County in the outer reaches of the Cleveland metropolitan area. The Stark County portions of the district, formerly Democratic, were described as a political bellwether by the Trump campaign in 2020, when President Donald Trump added two percentage points to the 56 percent he scored in 2016. The remainder of the district is mostly Republican. The result has been a dramatic increase in Republican presidential performance, from 54 percent in 2012 to 65 percent in 2020.

Warren Davidson (R)

Elected 2016, 3rd full term, b. Mar 01, 1970; Troy, OH; University of Notre Dame, M.B.A.; U.S. Military Academy - West Point, B.A., 1995; Married (Lisa Davidson); 2 children.

Military Career: U.S. Army 1995-2000

DC Office: 1107 LHOB 20515, 202-225-6205, Fax: 202-225-0704, davidson.house.gov

State Offices: Springfield, 937-322-1120; Troy, 937-339-1524; West Chester, 513-779-5400.

Committees: *Financial Services*: Investor Protection, Entrepreneurship & Capital Markets; Nat'l Security, International Development & Monetary Policy; Task Force on Financial Technology (RMM).

Group Ratings

	ADA	ACLU	AFL-CIO	LCV	COC	HAFA	ACU	CFG	FRC
2020	**	28%	**	10%	-	92%	97%	**	-
2019	0%	C	14%	7%	65%	C	99%	100%	95%

Almanac Ratings 2019-2020

	Economy	Social	Foreign	Composite
Liberal	33%	20%	40%	31%
Conservative	67%	80%	60%	69%

Key Votes of the 116th Congress

1. U.S./Mex./Can. trade deal	Y	5. Russia sanctions	N	9. Firearms background checks N
2. First Coronavirus response	N	6. Troops in Syria	N	10. Spending at the border Y
3. HEROES Act	N	7. Veto arms sales to Saudis	N	11. Marijuana liberalized rules N
4. CASH Act	N	8. Defense $$$, veto override	N	12. Electoral College objections Y

Election Results

Election	Name (Party)	Vote (%)		Cand. Spent	Ind. Exp. Support	Ind. Exp. Oppose
2020 General	Warren Davidson (R)	246,277	(69%)	$629,393	$1,279	$750
	Vanessa Enoch (D)	110,766	(31%)	$28,092		
2020 Primary	Warren Davidson (R)	53,542	(91%)			
	Edward Meer (R)	5,125	(9%)			

Prior winning percentages: 2018 (67%), 2016 (69%), 2016 special (77%)

Warren Davidson won a special election in June 2016 to replace Speaker John Boehner, who had resigned from the House. With his business background, he has centered his work at the Financial Services Committee. He has been an active member of the Freedom Caucus, though—unlike some of the group's members—he did not automatically support the views of President Donald Trump. He has worked across the aisle to set limits on federal monitoring of internet use.

Davidson grew up in Sydney, which is between Dayton and Lima. In high school, he was not a motivated student. As Davidson recounted to the Cincinnati Enquirer, he told a guidance counselor during his senior year that he wanted to attend West Point. She told him, "Baby, that's not going to happen." Instead, he enlisted in the Army. He gained a series of promotions and became an elite Army Ranger. He witnessed the fall of the Berlin Wall while he was serving in Germany. With this background, he eventually won an appointment to West Point, where he graduated with a degree in American history.

When he left the military, he returned home and planned to join his father's tool making manufacturing business. But, the Enquirer reported, the business was "floundering" and his father was "leery of change." Davidson started his own tool making business. He was successful and bought out his father. The company grew from 20 employees to more than 200. During that time, he got an MBA from the University of Notre Dame and settled in Concord Township, where he served two years as a trustee. He was appointed to the position after having lost an election for the seat.

After Boehner resigned, Davidson voiced interest in running. Republican Rep. Jim Jordan of the neighboring district arranged an appointment for him with the Washington-based Club for Growth. Davidson won the endorsement. "It was a pretty easy call for us," said Andrew Roth, the group's vice president of government affairs told the Enquirer. "It was clear that what he was telling us was based on principle." That support proved vital when the Club spent $1.1 million on behalf of Davidson during the primary. His two chief opponents, Bill Beagle and Tim Derickson, raised $500,000 and $300,000, respectively. Each was a member of the state legislature. For the entire campaign, Davidson spent nearly $1 million.

In the 15-candidate March primary for the special election, Davidson won with 32 percent of the vote to 24 percent for Derickson and 20 percent for Beagle. Davidson defeated Democrat Corey Foister, 77%-12%, with a thin turnout. Foister was described as a 25-year-old whose biggest political achievement was serving in student government at Northern Kentucky University.

Davidson joined the Freedom Caucus, the group that spurred Boehner's downfall and where Jordan has been a leader. By 2018, he expressed interest in becoming the group's leader after Rep. Mark Meadows of North Carolina stepped down. Instead, he took the new position of policy chair of the caucus. At the end of the year, Davidson was among the House members who took a hard line during the government shutdown in demanding that Congress approve funds for a border wall with Mexico.

On the Financial Services Committee, he filed in 2017 with Rep. Ted Budd of North Carolina the "Drain the Swamp" bill, which required that each federal agency relocate its employees across the nation and retain no more than 10 percent of its staff in the Washington area. With Democratic Rep. Darren Soto of Florida, Davidson proposed a bill to permit the regulation of so-called crypto-currencies separately from securities law. Their goal, Davidson said, was to promote "American leadership in this innovative space." Bitcoin has had few consumer protections, as its value has gyrated widely. In June 2019, he took the additional step of filing a bill that defined the currencies and offered more specific regulation. "We have all the innovations," Davidson complained. "We have these phenomenal capital markets, and we're driving that capital out of our country."

Davidson voiced occasional disagreements with Trump. At a local farm forum in 2018, he opposed the president's trade war with China and said he was "very concerned" about the adverse impact on farm commodities. Later, he said he was frustrated by "the amount of spending" that Trump approved, including farm legislation and hurricane relief. "The oath of office says to support and defend the Constitution, not support the president," Davidson told the Enquirer in 2018.

His libertarian views occasionally led Davidson to seek bipartisan action. During debate on intelligence legislation in May 2020, he and Democratic Rep. Zoe Lofgren proposed an amendment to restrict surveillance of Internet browsing; they voiced concern about excessive government access to personal information. Democratic leaders blocked consideration of their proposal.

OH-8: West-Central Ohio   **Cook Partisan Voting Index: R+19**

Population		Race and Ethnicity		Income	
Total	733,811	White	87.50%	Median Income	$62,845
Land area (sq. miles)	2,450	Black	6.80%	District Income Rank	227
Pop/ sq mi	299.45	Latino	3.70%	Poverty Rate	11.90%
Born in State	73.90%	Asian	2.40%	With health insurance	93.70%
		Two or more races	2.30%	Cash public assistance	2.10%
Age Groups		Other	0.90%	Food stamp/SNAP	10.40%
Under 18	23.00%				
18-34	22.00%	**Education**		**Work**	
35-64	37.90%	H.S grad or less	46.00%	White Collar	33.90%
Over 64	17.10%	Some college	28.80%	Sales and Service	37.40%
		College Degree, 4 yr	15.90%	Blue Collar	28.60%
Military		Post grad	9.40%	Government	11.80%
Veteran/ Active Duty	8.10%				

2020 Pres. Vote	Trump	243,072	(66%)	Biden	119,844	(33%)		
2016 Pres. Vote	Trump	223,215	(65%)	Clinton	104,929	(30%)	Johnson	10,948	(3%)

Cincinnati and Dayton Suburbs, Springfield: Since the early 20th century, the far west edge of Ohio—where U.S. 40, the old National Road, heads into Indiana—was some of the nation's prime industrial country. The Great and Little Miami rivers drain south into the Ohio, and the Miami and Erie Canal system continues its northward march to Toledo. The small cities and towns around and between Dayton and Cincinnati were rising industrial country a century ago. In the years since, they have weathered economic downturns and sought to adapt to changing markets and circumstances. Butler County, in between the two cities, was dominated by the large factory towns of Hamilton and Middletown, which style themselves as "reinvention cities." Butler is reliably Republican and has had an economic boom since the recession, including a new $600 million natural-gas power plant in Middletown and an Amazon fulfillment center that employs more than 1,000 in Monroe.

Butler's population has grown with the outflow of people from Cincinnati and Dayton, an increase of 15 percent from 2000 to 2019. The county has five universities, including Miami in Oxford. The center of growth has been West Chester Township, situated on Interstate 75 south of Wright-Patterson Air Force Base and rated by Money magazine in 2019 as the only Ohio community listed among the best places to live in the nation. It has attracted an Amylin Pharmaceuticals facility, which produces diabetes medication and is owned by AstraZeneca. CFM manufactures jet engines in a partnership between GE and French-owned Safran. The town remains the home of former House Speaker John Boehner.

The 8th Congressional District of Ohio includes all of Butler County. It extends north along the Indiana border to take in Preble County and Darke County, the birthplace of Phoebe Ann Moses, later known as sharpshooter Annie Oakley. The district includes Clark County, with economically depressed Springfield, where manufacturing has collapsed, the poverty rate is 23 percent and residents are disproportionately aging. Its declining population is at a 90-year low, with a 10 percent drop from 2000 to 2019. In 2016, the Pew Research Center listed Springfield as tied with Goldsboro North Carolina as the cities with the largest decline in economic status since 2000. But city officials in 2019 projected a turnaround in Springfield, citing the $400 million invested in its downtown during the previous decade. Springfield votes Democratic, but its presence does not alter the partisan balance of the district, which has been comfortably Republican. About half the voters are in Butler County and 17 percent are in Clark. President Donald Trump got 66 percent of the vote in 2020. He surpassed that in Ohio only in the 4th and 6th Districts.

Marcy Kaptur (D)

Elected 1982, 20th term, b. Jun 17, 1946; Toledo, OH; St. Ursula Academy, Att.; University of WI, B.A., 1968; University of Manchester, Att., 1974; University of MI, M.A., 1974; MA Institute of Technology, Att., 1981; Catholic; Single.

Professional Career: Urban planner, Lucas County Planning Comm., 1969-1975; Urban planning consultant, 1975-1977; White House Assistant Director for Urban Affairs, 1977-1980; Deputy Secretary, National Consumer Coop. Bank, 1980-1981.

DC Office: 2186 RHOB 20515, 202-225-4146, Fax: 202-225-7711, kaptur.house.gov

State Offices: Cleveland, 216-767-5933; Lorain, 440-288-1500; Toledo, 419-259-7500.

Committees: *Appropriations*: Defense; Energy & Water Development & Related Agencies (Chmn); Interior, Environment & Related Agencies. *Veterans' Affairs*: Disability Assistance & Memorial Affairs.

Group Ratings

	ADA	ACLU	AFL-CIO	LCV	COC	HAFA	ACU	CFG	FRC
2020	**	68%	**	90%	-	0%	12%	**	-
2019	85%	C	95%	100%	62%	C	12%	6%	0%

Almanac Ratings 2019-2020

	Economy	Social	Foreign	Composite
Liberal	100%	100%	84%	95%
Conservative	0%	0%	16%	5%

Key Votes of the 116th Congress

1. U.S./Mex./Can. trade deal	N	5. Russia sanctions — Y	9. Firearms background checks Y
2. First Coronavirus response	Y	6. Troops in Syria — Y	10. Spending at the border — N/A
3. HEROES Act	Y	7. Veto arms sales to Saudis Y	11. Marijuana liberalized rules Y
4. CASH Act	Y	8. Defense $$$, veto override Y	12. Electoral College objections N

Election Results

Election	Name (Party)	Vote (%)		Cand. Spent	Ind. Exp. Support	Ind. Exp. Oppose
2020 General	Marcy Kaptur (D)	190,328	(63%)	$510,864	$10	
	Rob Weber (R)	111,385	(37%)	$121,050		
2020 Primary	Marcy Kaptur (D)	52,433	(91%)			
	Peter Rosewicz (D)	5,370	(9%)			

Prior winning percentages: 2018 (68%), 2016 (69%), 2014 (68%), 2012 (73%), 2010 (59%), 2008 (74%), 2006 (74%), 2004 (68%), 2002 (74%), 2000(75%), 1998 (81%), 1996 (77%), 1994 (75%), 1992 (74%), 1990 (78%), 1988 (81%), 1986 (78%), 1984 (56%), 1982 (58%)

Democrat Marcy Kaptur, first elected in 1982, has set the record for the longest-serving woman in the House. Kaptur is a plainspoken Democrat and a dedicated opponent of free trade who does not always toe the party line, but whose old-fashioned ways have proven popular at home. In 2019-20, she enacted what she called the two "most significant climate change bills" during that Congress—referring to the annual spending bills that she crafted as chair of the Appropriations Subcommittee on Energy and Water Development. In marking her longevity record, the Washington Post ran a lengthy and favorable profile headlined, "The Quiet Endurance of Marcy Kaptur."

Kaptur grew up in a blue-collar neighborhood in Toledo, the daughter of Polish-American parents who worked at local auto plants. The family also operated a small grocery store, but her father sold it to get a job with health benefits. "It broke his heart," she said. She has spent almost her entire career in public service. She graduated from the University of Wisconsin, the first in her family to attend college, got a master's degree from the University of Michigan, then spent eight years as an urban planner in Toledo. She worked on urban revitalization in the Jimmy Carter White House.

She interrupted her studies for a doctorate at M.I.T. to return home and run for office. In 1982, she challenged first-term Republican Rep. Ed Weber and won 58%-39%, despite being outspent 3-to-1.

Kaptur has long been convinced that Toledo and places like it have lost jobs and industry because of unfair trade practices and low-wage competition from countries like Mexico and China. She was featured prominently in left-wing filmmaker Michael Moore's 2009 movie Capitalism: A Love Story. "I have always said there's a great injustice being done here, because the power rests with a handful of megabanks and millions of Americans are being affected," she told the Toledo Blade when the film opened.

She criticized President Bill Clinton for ignoring Democrats opposed to the 1993 North American Free Trade Agreement. In 1995, she made a rousing speech on trade before Texas businessman Ross Perot's United We Stand Party. Perot, running as a third-party candidate for president in 1996, offered her the vice presidential nomination, but she turned it down. She was a vocal opponent of normal trade relations with China and the Central American Free Trade Agreement.

Reflecting on those trade wars years later, Kaptur criticized Nancy Pelosi's support of NAFTA. "That's where the real knife was put in the flesh," she said. When Pelosi announced in 2007 an agreement with Treasury Secretary Hank Paulson on principles for international trade policy, an uninvited Kaptur glared from the back of the room. When the House narrowly voted in 2015 to give trade promotion authority to President Barack Obama, Kaptur slammed proponents who she said sold out "working families and American industries that have been the backbone of the U.S. economy for decades."

Kaptur has departed from party orthodoxy on abortion, though she hasn't completely shut the door. She opposes federal funding for the procedure, but she has also voted against proposals to deny federal money to Planned Parenthood. She contended that federal funds were not used for abortions, and that Planned Parenthood provided valuable medical care for women.

On the Appropriations Committee, Kaptur in 2012 hoped to fill the vacancy as the ranking Democrat. But the post instead went to Nita Lowey of New York, who was a more predictable liberal and a favorite of Pelosi. Kaptur became ranking Democrat on the Energy and Water Development Subcommittee. She is a strong advocate of Ohio-produced alternative energy such as ethanol and bio fuels. Kaptur has also promoted solar energy, a growing industry in Toledo.

In 2019, as subcommittee chairwoman, she invoked Ohio's long history in energy innovation and suggested that she could help to promote those interests. "Many, many of the firms in Ohio, or the inventors who are patenting, don't necessarily see the institutions here in Washington as being a helpful partner to them," Kaptur told an interviewer with Spectrum News. "And I think we need a little more shoulder-to-the-wheel in that arena." In summarizing the funding she secured for northern Ohio in the yearend bill for 2020, she listed several Army Corps of Engineers projects in the Great Lakes, research on harmful algae blooms, and solar energy technologies developed at the University of Toledo.

Prior to the temporary House ban on earmarks, Kaptur in 2010 ranked 24th for her district among the top earmark recipients, according to the group Taxpayers for Common Sense. She once challenged Republicans on Appropriations to limit farm payments, but when they threatened her favorite spending projects, she backed off. "I may be blockheaded sometimes, but I'm not stupid," Kaptur said.

After Lowey announced she would not seek reelection in 2020, Kaptur was one of three women-and, again, the most senior committee member--who campaigned to succeed her as Appropriations chairwoman. This time, it was Rep. Rosa DeLauro of Connecticut who benefited as a longtime ally of Pelosi. After Kaptur finished third in voting at the Democratic leadership panel, she dropped out and backed DeLauro.

Kaptur keeps close tabs on her district. A constituent gave her the idea to sponsor the legislation that created the World War II Memorial on the National Mall. She is exceedingly popular in the Toledo area and rarely has faced a credible challenge. In 2012, Republicans drawing the new redistricting map put her in a district with Cleveland-based Democratic Rep. Dennis Kucinich, a result that she described as "appalling." Kucinich's bids for president had given him a reputation at home for hobnobbing with celebrities and not accomplishing much for the district. Kaptur won the Democratic primary, 56%-40%. In Lucas County, she led 94%-4%. Since then, she has breezed to reelection.

Kaptur's dealings with Pelosi and other Democratic leaders have evolved. In 2002, she ran a quixotic, one-day campaign for minority leader against Pelosi but, predictably, got nowhere. In 2008, she challenged Xavier Becerra of California for Democratic Caucus vice chair and lost badly, 175-67. She backed Pelosi for minority leader in 2011 when Pelosi faced internal dissension. The two appeared to have reached an entente following the 2018 election when Kaptur gave early and enthusiastic support to her return as Speaker, even as other Ohio Democrats explored possible leadership challenges.

Kaptur earlier secured the record for the longest House tenure for a woman. When she reaches the end of 2022, she will tie Barbara Mikulski of Maryland, who had 40 years of combined House and Senate service. She is the second most-senior House Democrat, trailing Steny Hoyer of Maryland by 19 months.

In the Washington Post profile in August 2019, which described her as "an economic populist from America's heartland with progressive values and a conservative disposition," Kaptur described the keys to her success and was dismissive of junior House members who generate lots of attention. "It's exciting to get elected and it's exciting to get all this notoriety," she said. "But for people of ordinary means, the answer is to persevere and to immerse yourself in the subject matter of your district and how that relates to others in the country."

OH-9: Lakefront   Cook Partisan Voting Index: D+9

Population		Race and Ethnicity		Income	
Total	697,570	White	74.50%	Median Income	$45,076
Land area (sq. miles)	465	Black	15.90%	District Income Rank	417
Pop/ sq mi	1,501.28	Latino	10.90%	Poverty Rate	20.00%
Born in State	74.60%	Asian	2.10%	With health insurance	92.60%
		Two or more races	4.40%	Cash public assistance	3.50%
Age Groups		Other	3.10%	Food stamp/SNAP	19.40%
Under 18	23.00%				
18-34	23.70%	**Education**		**Work**	
35-64	36.60%	H.S grad or less	45.20%	White Collar	31.80%
Over 64	16.70%	Some college	30.90%	Sales and Service	42.20%
		College Degree, 4 yr	15.50%	Blue Collar	26.00%
Military		Post grad	8.30%	Government	10.80%
Veteran/ Active Duty	6.40%				

2020 Pres. Vote	Biden	184,332	(59%)	Trump	124,576	(40%)	
2016 Pres. Vote	Clinton	177,147	(58%)	Trump	110,178	(36%)	Johnson 9,495 (3%)

Toledo, Cleveland Suburbs: Lake Erie, the southernmost and shallowest of the Great Lakes, played a critical role in the history of America's interior. For decades, its shoreline was the locus of a four-way battle among French, Indian, British and American claimants. Additional conflicts over various claims to the area made by the various American colonies bubbled underneath. Once the federal government finally assumed full control of the Lake Erie shoreline in 1800, development proceeded quickly. Cleveland, at the mouth of the Cuyahoga River, had a population of 1,000 in 1830. Toledo and Cleveland became the biggest cities once the Ohio & Erie and Miami & Erie canals were completed. All the towns benefited from the trade that flowed from the Atlantic seaboard, up the Erie Canal to Buffalo, across the lake and into the burgeoning American interior. Canal traffic declined in the late 1800s, but Lake Erie retained an important role in the economy. Erie contains only 2 percent of the water of the Great Lakes, but 50 percent of its fish. It houses one of the largest commercial freshwater fisheries in the world, including a large yellow perch yield.

Fiat Chrysler in 2017 shut down its Toledo assembly line for Jeep Cherokees and moved their production to Belvidere Illinois. In its place, the company upgraded its plant to produce Jeep Wranglers and then pick-up trucks. Its local workforce grew to about 6,500. Gritty Lorain has survived decades of job losses and shutdowns as a steel town. That changed briefly as the result of President Donald Trump's trade war, which placed domestic steel production as a high priority. But the U.S. Steel plant, where 250 workers had been producing seamless pipe for less than two years, shut down again in June 2020. Pollution poses a continued threat to the native fisheries. The canals brought in invasive species—notably, Asian carp—while runoff from farms still promotes algae blooms. In July 2020, the National Oceanic and Atmospheric Administration said the United States and Canada had failed to reach their goal of a 20 percent reduction in algae from 2019 to 2020. Months earlier, scientists said the algae level was the worst that they had seen in Lake Erie.

The 9th Congressional District sprawls across the Lake Erie shoreline, rarely venturing more than 10 miles inland and sometimes less than a mile or two. From Toledo-based Lucas County, with about 30 percent of its voters, it goes east through Port Clinton and Sandusky, home to the giant Cedar Point amusement park, with some of the country's fastest roller coasters, and on to Lorain and Avon Lake. About 40 percent are in Cuyahoga County, where the district takes in western Cleveland, including Hopkins International Airport. This portion includes some inner suburbs, such as revived Lakewood, with its many Victorian-era houses. (Three other districts include parts of Cuyahoga.) The two ends of the district, which are 120 miles apart, have shared other features: generally blue-collar economies and Democratic voting patterns. That has changed since 2012. With a minority population of about 30 percent and a large white blue-collar cadre, the 59 percent for Joe Biden dropped from the 68 percent that President Barack Obama got in 2012. The Toledo end of the district, which has a large share of its African-American population, has become more reliable for Democrats than its white ethnics in the Cleveland area.

Michael Turner (R)

Elected 2002, 10th term, b. Jan 11, 1960; Dayton, OH; OH Northern University, B.A., 1982; Case Western Reserve University School of Law, J.D., 1985; University of Dayton, M.B.A., 1992; Presbyterian; Divorced; 2 children.

Elected Office: Dayton Mayor, 1993-2001.

Professional Career: Practicing attorney.

DC Office: 2082 RHOB 20515, 202-225-6465, Fax: 202-225-6754, turner.house.gov

State Offices: Dayton, 937-225-2843.

Committees: *Armed Services*: Strategic Forces (RMM); Tactical Air & Land Forces. *Permanent Select on Intelligence*: Intelligence Modernization & Readiness (RMM); Strategic Technologies & Advanced Research.

Group Ratings

	ADA	ACLU	AFL-CIO	LCV	COC	HAFA	ACU	CFG	FRC
2020	**	23%	**	33%	-	76%	66%	**	-
2019	10%	C	42%	14%	97%	C	67%	58%	95%

Almanac Ratings 2019-2020

	Economy	Social	Foreign	Composite
Liberal	38%	39%	33%	37%
Conservative	62%	61%	67%	63%

Key Votes of the 116th Congress

1. U.S./Mex./Can. trade deal	Y	5. Russia sanctions	Y	9. Firearms background checks	Y
2. First Coronavirus response	Y	6. Troops in Syria	Y	10. Spending at the border	Y
3. HEROES Act	N	7. Veto arms sales to Saudis	N	11. Marijuana liberalized rules	N
4. CASH Act	N	8. Defense $$$, veto override	Y	12. Electoral College objections	N

Election Results

Election	Name (Party)	Vote (%)		Cand. Spent	Ind. Exp. Support	Ind. Exp. Oppose
2020 General	Michael Turner (R)	212,972	(58%)	$1,889,035	$3,911	$113
	Desiree Tims (D)	151,976	(42%)	$2,030,551	$26,450	
2020 Primary	Mike Turner (R)	44,704	(86%)			
	John Anderson (R)	4,110	(8%)			
	Kathi Flanders (R)	2,944	(6%)			

Prior winning percentages: 2018 (56%), 2016 (64%), 2014 (65%), 2012 (60%), 2010 (68%), 2008 (63%), 2006 (59%), 2004 (62%), 2002 (59%)

Republican Mike Turner, first elected in 2002, is a former Dayton mayor who has retained his strong interest in urban issues. He has gained significant influence and an assertive role on national security policy, which he has used on behalf of his district's military presence. Following the 2020 election, he lost his bid to become the ranking Republican on the House Armed Services Committee.

Turner grew up in Dayton, where his father spent his career with General Motors. He graduated from Ohio Northern University, Case Western law school and the University of Dayton business school, and became a corporate lawyer. At age 33, he narrowly defeated a scandal-tainted Democratic incumbent to win the first of two terms as Dayton mayor. He created Rehabarama, an acclaimed private-public partnership to rehabilitate neglected housing in Dayton's historic neighborhoods. He narrowly lost reelection in 2001.

Republican leaders recruited him to challenge Democratic Rep. Tony Hall, who had served 12 terms but was vulnerable following redistricting changes. A week after Turner announced he was running for Congress, President George W. Bush nominated Hall as ambassador to the U.N. Food and Agriculture Organization in Rome. In the Republican primary, Turner faced fierce opposition from newspaper publisher Roy Brown, grandson and son of former Reps. Clarence Brown and Clarence Brown Jr. Brown spent $1.3 million of his own money, largely on ads attacking Turner's record on taxes and lambasting him for being insufficiently conservative. Turner defeated Brown, 80%-14%. Rick Carne, Hall's chief of staff, had little national party support as the Democratic nominee, though he raised nearly $600,000 and benefited from a local appearance by actor—and Dayton native—Martin Sheen. Turner won, 59%-41%.

Turner has supported his party on most major issues, though he has shown occasional independence. In a stark contrast to Freedom Caucus leader Jim Jordan, who holds a nearby district, Turner's Almanac vote ratings have ranked him toward the center of the House, especially on economic issues. He has voted against conservative efforts to cut science funding and has helped to save the Community Development Block Grant program. In 2019, he was one of 20 House Republicans who voted against the GOP plan to repeal and replace the Affordable Care Act, which he said "will leave our most vulnerable citizens with inadequate health coverage."

Turner has remained focused on urban issues and formed a caucus of former mayors serving in Congress. He worked on House-passed legislation to accelerate the cleanup of polluted brown fields by making it easier for communities to apply for federal grants. He has promoted the kind of public-private partnerships that he used for economic development in Dayton.

On the Armed Services Committee, Turner has offered protection from Defense Department cuts for Wright-Patterson Air Force Base. He said the base added more than 10,000 jobs since he was first elected. He has worked to make Dayton into a center for unmanned aerial vehicle research and testing. In 2016, he opposed President Barack Obama's proposed budget cuts for the military, which Turner said "could break the Army." With his seat on the Intelligence Committee, Turner was successful in locating at Wright-Patt the new National Space Intelligence Center, where it joined the National Air and Space Intelligence Center headquarters, which is scheduled to be housed in a new $156 million complex.

Turner has co-chaired the bipartisan Military Sexual Assault Prevention Caucus. In 2018, he criticized the Veterans' Affairs Department for improper handling of assault claims. Turner has tried for years to get Congress to pass a bill aimed at protecting service members from losing custody of their children because of military deployments; the measure passed the House and stalled in the Senate.

As ranking Republican on the Strategic Forces Subcommittee, Turner raised extensive questions about creation of the proposed Space Force, including its impact on Wright-Patterson. He said it was important that the new unit remain under the control of the Air Force. But he lost that fight when Wright-Patt did not make the list of six finalists; President Donald Trump located its headquarters in Huntsville Alabama during his final week as president.

Turner has sought to lead Republicans on the Armed Services Committee. In 2014, he deferred to Rep. Mac Thornberry of Texas, but made clear his interest in the next such vacancy. When Thornberry was term-limited in 2020, Turner competed with Rep. Mike Rogers of Alabama for the top spot. House Republicans selected Rogers, who had been a more active party fundraiser with a more easy-going reputation than the policy-oriented Turner.

Turner frequently clashed with Trump. In July 2015, he endorsed Ohio Gov. John Kasich for the Republican presidential nomination. During a December interview with CNN, he said Trump was "not qualified to … hold any elective office." He harshly criticized some of Trump's actions as president. He said that the president's comments following his July 2018 meeting with Russian President Vladimir Putin were "deeply damaging" for U.S. relations in Europe. In a December 2018 letter to Trump, Turner wrote that suggested cuts in Pentagon spending would be "disastrous." Following the 2020 election, he was in the minority of House Republican who opposed Trump's efforts to challenge the results.

In the past two cycles, Turner faced serious reelection challenge. In 2018, Democrat Theresa Gasper, a political newcomer, attacked Trump's immigration policies, including family separation at the Mexican border. She added that Turner has supported Trump's policies and that he had not sufficiently addressed the problems of Dayton. Turner outspent Gasper, $1.5 million to $1.2 million. He was reelected, 56%-42%, his lowest-ever vote.

Two years later, Desiree Tims, a former Senate aide who became a Washington lobbyist with environmental and child-care organizations, was the Democratic nominee. She called Turner a "career politician" and cited her working-class background in Dayton. Tims outspent the incumbent, $2.1 million to $1.7 million, though neither national party showed much interest in the contest. "Absent her lobbyist connections and outside money, she doesn't have enough money to run for office," Turner said in a campaign ad. He increased his victory margin to 58%-42%, taking 55 percent in Montgomery County.

OH-10: Montgomery County   Cook Partisan Voting Index: R+5

Population		Race and Ethnicity		Income	
Total	723,716	White	75.50%	Median Income	$56,595
Land area (sq. miles)	1,130	Black	16.20%	District Income Rank	306
Pop/ sq mi	640.59	Latino	3.10%	Poverty Rate	14.40%
Born in State	70.10%	Asian	2.10%	With health insurance	93.00%
		Two or more races	4.40%	Cash public assistance	2.90%
Age Groups		Other	1.70%	Food stamp/SNAP	12.10%
Under 18	21.60%				
18-34	23.60%	**Education**		**Work**	
35-64	36.60%	H.S grad or less	35.50%	White Collar	39.90%
Over 64	18.20%	Some college	33.50%	Sales and Service	38.50%
		College Degree, 4 yr	18.50%	Blue Collar	21.50%
Military		Post grad	12.50%	Government	14.50%
Veteran/ Active Duty	9.60%				

2020 Pres. Vote	Trump	188,657	(51%)	Biden	172,479	(47%)			
2016 Pres. Vote	Trump	178,674	(51%)	Clinton	153,346	(44%)	Johnson	11,898	(3%)

Dayton Area: For decades, underestimated Dayton has held its own against bigger cities for fostering creative American genius in commerce. It has strong traditions of tinkering and innovation, practical organization and mechanical dreaming, as well as small-town neighborliness. Just south of the old National Road that spans the Midwest was the home of James Ritty, who in 1879 invented the cash register, that indispensable instrument of retail trade that led to the establishment in 1884 of the National Cash Register Co. Tom Watson Sr., an employee of NCR, feuded with owner John Henry Patterson and went off in a huff to found International Business Machines, better known by its initials, IBM. In 1887, George Huffman moved the Davis Sewing Machine Co. to Dayton, and in 1892 began producing Huffy bicycles. Around the same time, Wilbur and Orville Wright experimented with kites and gliders and constructed the first wind tunnel in the world and the first heavier-than-air flying machine, which they took to windy Kitty Hawk North Carolina for a test flight in 1903. A few years later, Dayton's Charles Kettering invented the automatic starter for cars and became one of the leaders of the budding automobile industry. Not long ago, Montgomery County was home to the most patents per capita of any county in the United States. Boston's Suffolk County has claimed that title.

Dayton's economy in recent years suffered serious setbacks, though there have been signs that it has been bouncing back. During the financial recession, DHL closed an air cargo hub at the Wilmington Air Park in Clinton County, costing the region 10,000 jobs. NCR departed to suburban Atlanta in 2009, taking away Dayton's last Fortune 500 company and the 1,300 jobs it provided. An encouraging feature has been General Electric, which has a huge presence in southwest Ohio and employs 1,200 in the Dayton area. It builds jet engines here, and has a center that develops advanced electric power systems for aircraft, ships and hybrid automobiles. A former General Motors assembly plant has been converted to a highly automated automotive glass factory, which is a Chinese subsidiary; the pay scales for employees have been cut roughly in half. Dayton remains "a manufacturing town," with those plants covering 13 percent of its workforce, NBC News reported in 2018. In May 2020, Site Selection magazine ranked the Dayton area first for economic development projects among metro areas of its size.

Dayton-area universities and Wright-Patterson Air Force Base have made the area a magnet for technology companies. The world's most advanced centrifuge, which is used for aerospace medical research, became operational in 2018 and was expected to train thousands of military pilots. Wright-Patt in 2019 had more than 30,000 military and civilian employees, the largest single-site employer in Ohio. In February 2020, Boeing won a contract to modernize the Global Decision Support System, which supports military missions. Many of the system's operations are based at Wright-Patt.

The 10th Congressional District of Ohio includes all of Dayton and surrounding Montgomery County, which is about three-fourths of the district. To the east, it includes Greene County, with upscale Beaver Creek and middle-class Fairborn, and most of rural Fayette County. This has been a Republican-leaning district, although not overwhelmingly so. Donald Trump won 51 percent in both of his campaigns, a smaller increase for the GOP than in other districts in Ohio.

OH-11 - VACANT (V)

DC Office: 2344 RHOB 20515, 202-225-7032, Fax: 202-225-1339, fudge.house.gov
State Offices: Akron, 330-835-4758; Warrensville Heights, 216-522-4900.

Democrat Marcia Fudge, after being elected to seven terms, resigned from the House on March 10, 2021, after the Senate confirmed her as secretary of Housing and Urban Development. Party primaries for the special election were scheduled for August 3, with the general election on November 2. In this heavily Democratic district, the winner of the primary was virtually certain to take the seat. A wide-open primary was expected, with the initial skirmishing underway even before Fudge vacated the seat.

Initial attention for the special election focused on Nina Turner, a former state senator and a vocal supporter of Sen. Bernie Sanders in his presidential campaigns, and Shontel Brown, who chaired the Cuyahoga County Democratic Party and has styled herself as a protégé of Fudge. Each had a long list of endorsements, though Turner had more support from national Democrats and progressive groups and Brown had more local supporters, including labor unions. Turner, who had a quicker start to her campaign, raised nearly $1.6 million in the first quarter of 2021, compared to $643,000 for Brown.

During her 12 years in the House, Fudge had parlayed her organizational and networking skills into leadership of the Congressional Black Caucus and an active role in the Democratic Caucus. She was an outspoken advocate of change among House Democrats.

Like many African Americans of her generation, Fudge was greatly influenced by the civil rights movement and got active politically when she was young. She practiced mainly criminal defense law in the Cleveland area until she went to work for her mentor and friend, Rep. Stephanie Tubbs Jones. hen Tubbs Jones was elected to Congress in 1998, Fudge followed her to Washington as chief of staff. After a few years, Fudge pursued her own elected office. After the Warrensville Heights mayor resigned, she was the first African-American woman to be elected mayor of the city.

Tubbs Jones died unexpectedly from a cerebral aneurysm after having won the Democratic primary in 2008 for another term. Fudge called each member of the district's Democratic Executive Committee, which selected a replacement on the ballot. The committee nominated Fudge with 175 votes. She won the general election with 85 percent of the vote.

Representing an urban area, Fudge was outspoken on the Agriculture Committee in defending food stamps. She used the committee niche during debate on the 2018 farm bill to oppose House Republicans' proposals for work requirements. With bipartisan Senate support in the House-Senate conference committee, she largely prevailed. In 2019, Fudge gained direct influence over the program as chairwoman of the Nutrition, Oversight and Department Operations Subcommittee.

After the House Democrats' election success in 2018, Fudge continued to press for internal changes. With foes of Democratic Leader Nancy Pelosi foes struggling to find a challenger to her return as Speaker, Fudge said that an African-American woman should be part of the leadership team and that Pelosi had not wrapped up the requisite 218 votes. For a short time, Fudge said that she was considering a bid for Speaker. But her interest ran into numerous obstacles, including the support of many Black Caucus members for Majority Whip James Clyburn and the support of many women for Pelosi — including two other House Democrats from Ohio.

Seeing the opportunity to neutralize a prospective opponent, Pelosi reached out to Fudge. Within a few days, Fudge agreed to take the gavel of the House Administration Elections Subcommittee, where she prepared legislation to reinstate and overhaul a provision of the Voting Rights Act that the Supreme Court had ruled against in 2013. In exchange, Fudge undermined the rebels by agreeing to support Pelosi. With her Nutrition Subcommittee post, that gave Fudge the unusual cachet of two chairmanships.

When President-elect Joe Biden in December 2020 initially considered Fudge for his Cabinet, some supporters urged Fudge's selection as Agriculture Secretary. After some farm groups objected to her inexperience with farm programs, Biden announced that Fudge was his nominee to head the Housing Department, The Senate confirmed her, 66-34; the 16 Republican votes was relatively large support for Biden's domestic officials.

OH-11: Cuyahoga County   **Cook Partisan Voting Index:**

Population		Race and Ethnicity		Income	
Total	684,617	White	39.80%	Median Income	$42,207
Land area (sq. miles)	244	Black	52.90%	District Income Rank	427
Pop/ sq mi	2,800.53	Latino	4.80%	Poverty Rate	22.70%
Born in State	74.20%	Asian	2.40%	With health insurance	94.40%
		Two or more races	3.00%	Cash public assistance	3.70%
Age Groups		Other	1.90%	Food stamp/SNAP	23.20%
Under 18	20.90%				
18-34	24.60%	**Education**		**Work**	
35-64	37.00%	H.S grad or less	39.70%	White Collar	38.20%
Over 64	17.60%	Some college	32.20%	Sales and Service	42.30%
		College Degree, 4 yr	15.00%	Blue Collar	19.40%
Military		Post grad	13.00%	Government	12.90%
Veteran/ Active Duty	6.50%				

2020 Pres. Vote	Biden	252,778	(80%)	Trump	60,861	(19%)
2016 Pres. Vote	Clinton	260,311	(80%)	Trump	55,013	(17%)

Cleveland, Downtown Akron: Like most great American cities, Cleveland grew in great bursts of migration, during periods when the economy expanded and attracted low-wage workers from around the country and the world. After the Ohio and Erie Canal connected Lake Erie with the Ohio River in the 1830s, Cleveland became a critical destination for goods traveling from the north to the interior and vice versa. Its greatest surge of growth started in the 1890s and lasted through the 1920s, when the city was transformed from a bustling city of 250,000 to a burgeoning metropolis of over 900,000. Tens of thousands of immigrants from central and southern Europe arrived, looking for jobs in the steel and automobile factories. Bohemians came to the tightly packed neighborhoods along Broadway, Hungarians settled in the northeast, Jews lived north of University Circle along East 105th Street, and Italians ran produce markets along Mayfield Road. As heavy industries geared up for World War II and enjoyed years of prosperous growth afterward, another surge of immigrants came, this time from the South.

These bursts of migration led to political changes. A string of ethnic mayors—Frank Lausche, Anthony Celebrezze, Ralph Locher—was followed by the election in 1967 of Carl Stokes, the nation's first Black big-city mayor. Cleveland had racially polarized politics for much of the 1970s. Even so, the west side stayed mostly white, and Cleveland did not have a Black majority until the 2000 census; its 2019 population declined to 381,000, only 42 percent of what it was in 1950. In a hopeful sign, the loss of 81,000 people from 2000 to 2010 was followed by a reduction of only 15,000 in the next nine years. Nearly all Clevelanders exalted in the NBA title that their Cavaliers, led by Akron-native LeBron James, won in 2016. Two years later, he escaped to Los Angeles. More significantly for Cleveland, the economy recently has grown. And the downtown improvements, which James helped create, have spurred new development.

For decades, Akron was the rubber capital of the world. The four largest tire companies had their headquarters and factories here, with close to 60,000 workers in the rubber industry in the 1930s. By the 1980s, those plants had largely shut down, except for the production of a few specialty tires. Goodrich, Firestone and General left town to manufacture tires with cheaper labor in the South, and then outside the country. Goodyear remained, with an impressive new office building plus its innovation center. One positive result was that the air was cleaner, and the smell of rubber was gone. The population dropped from 290,000 in 1960 to 198,000 in 2019. Like Cleveland, where the influx of new residents from around the world has enriched the city, Akron has benefited from immigration. Many refugees have moved into North Hill—from Myanmar and Bhutan, and more recently from Iraq and Syria. But the revitalization of downtown Akron remained a distant goal.

The 11th Congressional District of Ohio includes most of the east side of Cleveland, plus the suburbs just to the east. Some of these areas—deteriorating East Cleveland, more robust Warrensville Heights—are mostly Black. Shaker Heights has increased to 35 percent Black, though median family income for whites is nearly three times higher than for Blacks, The Washington Post reported in October 2019. Still others, like the old Slavic enclave of Garfield Heights, are populated by the heirs of the ethnic whites who settled Cleveland in the early 20th century. The district includes exurbs of Cleveland, minority segments of downtown, plus Fairlawn and a few other suburbs of Akron. Nearly one-third of Summit County is in the district, which accounts for about 15 percent of its population. The 11th exists for two reasons: To provide a minority-majority district in compliance with the Voting Rights Act, and to satisfy the desire of Republicans in control of redistricting to place as many Democrats as possible in a single district and protect Republicans in nearby districts. The 11th is 53 percent Black, and is in the top five percent of Democratic districts, according to the Cook PVI scale. . Joe Biden took 80 percent, the same as Hillary Clinton in 2016.

Troy Balderson (R)

Elected 2018, 2nd full term, b. Jan 16, 1962; Zanesville, OH; Muskingum College; OH State University; Christian Church; Married (Angie Albright); 1 child.

Elected Office: OH House, 2009-2011; OH Senate, 2011-2018.

Professional Career: General Manager, Balderson Motor Sales, 1987-2008.

DC Office: 1221 LHOB 20515, 202-225-5355, Fax: 202-226-4523, balderson.house.gov

State Offices: Worthington, 614-523-2555.

Committees: *Agriculture*: Biotechnology, Horticulture & Research; Commodity Exchanges, Energy & Credit. *Transportation & Infrastructure*: Aviation; Highways & Transit; Railroads, Pipelines & Hazardous Materials.

Group Ratings

	ADA	ACLU	AFL-CIO	LCV	COC	HAFA	ACU	CFG	FRC
2020	**	19%	**	24%	-	82%	70%	**	-
2019	1000%	C	33%	3%	85%	C	79%	75%	86%

Almanac Ratings 2019-2020

	Economy	Social	Foreign	Composite
Liberal	25%	41%	27%	31%
Conservative	75%	59%	73%	69%

Key Votes of the 116th Congress

1. U.S./Mex./Can. trade deal Y	5. Russia sanctions Y	9. Firearms background checks N
2. First Coronavirus response Y	6. Troops in Syria Y	10. Spending at the border Y
3. HEROES Act N	7. Veto arms sales to Saudis N	11. Marijuana liberalized rules N
4. CASH Act N	8. Defense $$$, veto override Y	12. Electoral College objections N

Election Results

Election	Name (Party)	Vote (%)	Cand. Spent	Ind. Exp. Support	Ind. Exp. Oppose
2020 General	Troy Balderson (R)........................ 241,790	(55%)	$1,851,400	$5,215	
	Alaina Shearer (D)......................... 182,847	(42%)	$1,039,404	$4,988	
	John S. Stewart (L)............................... 13,035	(3%)	$62,649		
2020 Primary	Troy Balderson (R)..................... 51,412	(84%)			
	Tim Day (R)........................ 9,877	(16%)			

Prior winning percentages: 2018 special (50%)

Republican Troy Balderson in 2018 won two elections in three months to secure a vacant seat the GOP had long controlled. Each outcome was close and produced high anxiety among Republicans, with Democrats outspending Balderson and his allies and placing him on the political defensive in a prelude to the Democrats' recent gains in suburban districts similar to this one—though they have failed to make a breakthrough in Ohio. Balderson, a veteran state legislator from the rural part of the district, has adapted to his largely suburban district. And he has taken committee assignments that focus on what he can deliver back home.

A native of Zanesville, Balderson took business administration classes at Muskingum College and Ohio State University but did not graduate. He owned and operated a family farm and was general manager of the family's auto dealership in Zanesville. He won election to the state House in 2008 and was appointed in 2011 to a seat in the state Senate, where he chaired the Energy and Natural Resources Committee. He calls himself a "principled conservative" who opposes abortion, supports gun rights and believes that government should create an environment for economic growth.

In the special election following the resignation of Republican Rep. Pat Tiberi, who left Congress to become president of the Ohio Business Roundtable, Balderson was endorsed by Tiberi. He had close ties to retiring GOP Gov. John Kasich, who held this House seat for 18 years prior to Tiberi, and was an early supporter of Kasich's 2016 presidential campaign. Balderson narrowly won the competitive Republican primary in May 2018 against nine other candidates. Of the 68,000 votes cast, he led by 775 votes—29%-28%— against runner-up Melanie Leneghan, the trustee for Liberty Township who ran as a supporter of President Donald Trump and was backed by Rep. Jim Jordan, also of Ohio, a leader of conservative Republicans. Democratic nominee Danny O'Connor, who handily defeated six other candidates in his primary, had been elected as recorder of Franklin County.

In their initial faceoff, Balderson's campaign ads attacked national Democratic leaders, including then-Minority Leader Nancy Pelosi, and their liberal agenda. O'Connor attacked the pending Republican tax bill as "a corporate tax giveaway." Balderson emphasized his background and seemed more comfortable in the rural part of the district, which had a smaller share of the vote. In the high turnout for an August special election, Balderson won 50.1%-49.3%, a margin of 1,680 votes of the 208,000 cast. In Franklin County, the most populous part of the district, O'Connor got 65 percent and led by more than 22,000 votes. Balderson led in the other six counties.

With barely a chance to catch their breath, Balderson and O'Connor plunged into the general election. O'Connor maintained his large financial advantage. In the two campaigns combined, he outspent Balderson $8.5 million to $2.5 million. National Republican groups spent more than $6 million on behalf of O'Connor. The Democratic momentum from the growing political expectation that they would win the House majority failed to boost O'Connor. Balderson won 51%-47%, a margin of more than 14,000 votes, a sign of the district returning to its roots. He narrowed O'Connor's lead in Franklin to 62 percent. Balderson took 55 percent in Delaware County and got at least 60 percent of the vote in each of the other five counties.

Balderson got seats on the Transportation and Infrastructure Committee and the Agriculture panel. In October 2020, he filed what he called the SMART Transportation bill, which he said would "spur innovation, improve efficiency and promote advanced technology" for transportation—which could benefit auto research firms in central Ohio. He voiced concern that national cuts of more than $7 billion from highway funding would cut $337 million for projects in Ohio. Also that year, the

Motorcycle Riders Foundation named him its Legislative Champion of the Year for work on their behalf.

With Democratic Rep. Lizzie Fletcher, with whom he served on Transportation, Balderson filed a proposal that would allow pipeline operators to use new safety technologies and practices on portions of their existing pipelines. Current regulations have placed workers in harm's way, Balderson said, because they "haven't kept pace with technological advancements."

Balderson's work on agriculture included the Rural Equal Aid Act, which he filed with Democratic Rep. Cindy Axne of Iowa, which would give loan borrowers from the Agriculture Department during the coronavirus pandemic the same loan terms that were available to loan borrowers from the Small Business Administration. During the pandemic, he also pushed for enhanced broadband internet access and for the purchase of $3 billion of meat and produce for nationwide distribution.

In the 2020 election, Balderson faced Democrat Alaina Shearer, a political newcomer; she had a background in marketing and started a network for women in tech. Balderson outspent Shearer, $2 million to $1 million. The national parties showed no interest in the contest this time. Balderson won, 55%-42%, a significant increase in his victory margin. He grew his vote to 39 percent in Franklin County and 57 percent in Delaware. That improvement likely will serve Balderson well in redistricting, where Ohio is losing a seat and his district might gain rural areas to the east.

Following the 2020 election, Balderson bucked President Donald Trump and a majority of House Republicans by objecting to review of the Electoral College outcome. "It is my strong belief, and reading of the Constitution, that Congress does not have the authority to overturn elections, nor to overrule decisions made in state or federal courts," he said. None of the legal challenges, he added, "pointed to widespread fraud that would change the outcome of this election."

OH-12: Central Ohio   **Cook Partisan Voting Index: R+6**

Population		Race and Ethnicity		Income	
Total	788,335	White	86.50%	Median Income	$76,631
Land area (sq. miles)	2,272	Black	5.00%	District Income Rank	113
Pop/ sq mi	346.99	Latino	2.60%	Poverty Rate	9.20%
Born in State	71.10%	Asian	4.90%	With health insurance	94.50%
		Two or more races	2.80%	Cash public assistance	1.60%
Age Groups		Other	0.80%	Food stamp/SNAP	8.30%
Under 18	22.80%				
18-34	21.00%	**Education**		**Work**	
35-64	40.20%	H.S grad or less	31.80%	White Collar	48.10%
Over 64	16.00%	Some college	26.00%	Sales and Service	33.60%
Military		College Degree, 4 yr	26.00%	Blue Collar	18.30%
Veteran/ Active Duty	7.10%	Post grad	16.20%	Government	13.90%

2020 Pres. Vote	Trump	232,995	(52%)	Biden	206,168	(46%)		
2016 Pres. Vote	Trump	205,978	(52%)	Clinton	162,218	(41%)	Johnson	14,308	(4%)

Northern Columbus Metro: Columbus was overshadowed by its much larger cousins for most of its existence—Cincinnati to the south and Cleveland to the north. It remained a surprisingly small town for the capital of such an important state. Today, Columbus is a major metropolis and, with 899,000 people in 2019, has breezed past the total of Cleveland and Cincinnati. Columbus' Franklin County has grown close to 1.3 million, surpassing Cleveland's Cuyahoga in 2016. Columbus and Franklin increased their populations 14 and 13 percent, respectively, from 2010 to 2019; during the same time, Cuyahoga and Cincinnati's Hamilton were nearly flat. With this explosive growth has come sprawl in all directions. Most American cities grew up around a coastline or river, which tended to direct their growth. The plains to the north and west of Columbus have done little to inhibit growth, while the rolling hills that mark the end of the Appalachian Plateau to the south and east provide no meaningful barrier to expansion.

The 12th Congressional District contains a northern slice of the city and Franklin County, with portions of the University District filled with pre-World War II Craftsman-style bungalows, as well as the more spacious homes of Clintonville, one of the original "streetcar" communities. It takes in suburbs to the north and east: Worthington, increasingly indistinguishable from the encroaching city;

newly fashionable Dublin, with its lush Muirfield Village Golf Club; Gahanna; and upscale New Albany. Dublin is the headquarters of Cardinal Health, a health-services company and wholesaler of prescription drugs with 50,000 employees worldwide, which ranked 16th in the Fortune 500 in 2019.

To the north is fast-growing Delaware County, home to the highly rated Columbus Zoo and traditionally Republican. It last voted for a Democratic presidential candidate in 1916. Its upscale suburbs help give Delaware the highest median income of any county in Ohio. Growth here has spread to the northern townships. In May 2018, the Columbus Dispatch reported that Evans Farm is a "new urbanist" project of business, with more than 2,000 homes in Orange Township mostly within walking distance. Delaware County grew 20 percent from 2010 to 2019. In October 2020, Otterbein University in Westerville proposed the purchase of 58 acres of farmland that it would turn into residential and commercial uses to combine with the Innovation Hub the university opened in 2018. Outside of Columbus' orbit, Licking County is home to picturesque Granville and Denison, its small liberal arts college. Industrial parks across the county have attracted new manufacturing companies. Newark, an old manufacturing town that was in decay, has begun to revive its downtown area, including a historic district. Corn fields have turned into business parks. In Muskingum County, rural Zanesville, with its famous "Y"-shaped bridge, is known as the Y-city.

Franklin is the population center in the 12th District, with about one-third of the vote, but Delaware and Licking are not far behind. Donald Trump twice won the district with 52 percent. Despite his poor performance statewide and in the rural parts of the 12th, Joe Biden's loss of Delaware County by seven percentage points was a significant improvement from Hillary Clinton's 16-point loss. His 46 percent of the vote was the best Democratic performance in the county since 1964. By contrast, Biden's 28-point loss in Licking County was virtually the same as four years earlier.

Tim Ryan (D)

Elected 2002, 10th term, b. Jul 16, 1973; Niles, OH; Dickinson School of Law's International Law Program (Italy), Att.; Youngstown State University, Att., 1992; Bowling Green State University, B.A., 1995; Franklin Pierce College Law Center, J.D., 2000; Catholic; Married (Andrea Zetts); 1 child; 2 stepchildren.

Elected Office: OH Senate, 2000-2002.

Professional Career: Aide, U.S. Rep. Jim Traficant, 1995-1997.

DC Office: 1126 LHOB 20515, 202-225-5261, Fax: 202-225-3719, timryan.house.gov

State Offices: Akron, 330-630-7311; Warren, 800-856-4152; Youngstown, 330-740-0193.

Committees: *Appropriations*: Defense; Energy & Water Development & Related Agencies; Legislative Branch (Chmn). *Joint Library*.

Group Ratings

	ADA	ACLU	AFL-CIO	LCV	COC	HAFA	ACU	CFG	FRC
2020	**	75%	**	100%	-	0%	10%	**	-
2019	85%	C	100%	66%	65%	C	11%	13%	0%

Almanac Ratings 2019-2020

	Economy	Social	Foreign	Composite
Liberal	56%	53%	55%	55%
Conservative	44%	47%	45%	45%

Key Votes of the 116th Congress

1. U.S./Mex./Can. trade deal Y	5. Russia sanctions Y	9. Firearms background checks Y
2. First Coronavirus response Y	6. Troops in Syria N/A	10. Spending at the border N/A
3. HEROES Act Y	7. Veto arms sales to Saudis Y	11. Marijuana liberalized rules Y
4. CASH Act Y	8. Defense $$$, veto override Y	12. Electoral College objections N

Election Results

Election	Name (Party)	Vote (%)		Cand. Spent	Ind. Exp. Support	Ind. Exp. Oppose
2020 General	Tim Ryan (D).................................	173,631	(52%)	$2,171,378	$25,054	
	Christina Hagan (R).....................	148,648	(45%)	$697,984	$343,331	$75,113
	Michael Fricke (L)........................	8,522	(3%)			
2020 Primary	Tim Ryan (D).................................	61,813	(100%)			

Prior winning percentages: 2018 (61%), 2016 (68%), 2014 (69%), 2012 (73%), 2010 (54%), 2008 (78%), 2006 (80%), 2004 (77%), 2002 (51%)

Tim Ryan, a Democrat elected in 2002 at age 29, has been a pro-union centrist who is usually a party regular and tries to encourage occasional hope for his economically battered constituency. His views on guns and abortion have moved to the left. He sought the 2020 Democratic presidential nomination with an appeal to his working-class Midwest base. But he struggled to make an impact and withdrew in October 2019.

After Sen. Rob Portman of Ohio announced in February 2021 that he would not seek reelection, Ryan stepped forward in April and became the early frontrunner for the 2022 Democratic nomination. Although Democrats have struggled in Ohio in recent years, Ryan's approach likely will echo the populist-tinged progressive approach of Sherrod Brown, the state's third-term Senator. Ryan earlier had turned down multiple opportunities to run statewide.

In the House, he criticized Minority Leader Nancy Pelosi's handling of the 2016 campaign and challenged her bid for another term. He lost the Democratic Caucus vote, 134-63. When Democrats regained House control in 2018 and Pelosi was the beneficiary, Ryan quietly stepped aside. He kept busy at the Appropriations Committee, as chairman of the Legislative Branch Subcommittee.

Ryan grew up in Niles, was a star quarterback before a knee injury ended his career, and graduated from Bowling Green State University. His first job was with Rep. James Traficant, a blue-collar and often maverick Democrat. In 2000, after graduating from Franklin Pierce Law Center, Ryan was elected to the state Senate. His opening to run for Congress came when the increasingly flaky Traficant was forced to resign in disgrace after his conviction in 2002 for racketeering and bribery.

Akron-based Rep. Tom Sawyer, a Democrat who had been thrown into the district by redistricting, was the early favorite to succeed Traficant. He outspent Ryan nearly 6-to-1 and had the perks of incumbency. But Sawyer had voted for the 1993 North American Free Trade Agreement, and he was one of the few Rust Belt Democrats to vote for normalizing trade relations with China. Ryan hammered on these votes in the Mahoning Valley. He was endorsed by the National Rifle Association in a district with many hunters. With greater voter intensity in Youngstown than in Akron, Ryan defeated Sawyer 41%-27%. In the general, Ryan slammed state Rep. Ann Womer Benjamin and the GOP legislature for votes that he said led to higher tuition at state universities. Republicans fired back with ads highlighting several disorderly conduct charges lodged against Ryan while he was in college. The district's Democratic leanings and Ryan's labor support proved decisive. He won 51 percent of the vote to 34 percent for Womer Benjamin and 15 percent for Traficant, who ran from jail as an independent.

Ryan has leaned to the left on economic policy. His splits with Democrats on abortion rights and gun control initially placed him closer to the center on social issues, but he has shifted and worked with others to seek common ground. After the deadly school massacre in Newtown Connecticut, he held meetings with gun enthusiasts and law enforcement officials to try to "thread the needle" on a solution to gun violence. With Democratic abortion-rights advocate Rosa DeLauro of Connecticut, he sponsored the Reducing the Need for Abortion and Supporting Parents Act, with federal dollars to fight teen pregnancy and increased aid for women who become pregnant. In 2015, he said his position had "evolved" further. "I have come to believe that we must trust women and families — not politicians — to make the best decisions for their lives," he wrote in the Akron Beacon-Journal.

In 2006, Ryan endeared himself to Pelosi when he was a vocal backer of her close ally John Murtha of Pennsylvania in his unsuccessful bid for majority leader against Steny Hoyer of Maryland. That earned Ryan a seat on Appropriations. He used that niche to secure earmarked projects for his hard-pressed district.

Reflecting his district, Ryan has remained a harsh critic of international trade deals. For several years, he sponsored the Chinese Currency Act, a proposal to counter China's alleged manipulation and undervaluation of its currency. He has co-chaired the Congressional Manufacturing Caucus, which seeks to revive the nation's industrial base and to revise its trade policy. When General Motors shut down its Lordstown plant in his district, Ryan criticized the failure of President Donald Trump to contribute to the revival of manufacturing in the Mahoning Valley. "What we've gotten instead are broken promises and petty tweets."

Ryan has drawn attention for his meditation. "My mind and body were in the same place at the same time, synchronized in a way I had rarely experienced," he told the Beacon Journal. In 2015, he expanded his spiritual revival to include healthier eating, with a book, The Real Food Revolution: Healthy Eating, Green Groceries, and the Return of the American Family Farm. He became a devotee of hot yoga.

When House Democrats convened after their traumatic 2016 election setbacks, Ryan joined those calling for political introspection. Some Democrats, mostly junior, were looking for an alternative to Pelosi, who had been Democratic leader for 14 years, all but four of them in the minority. They urged Ryan to run. In a letter to House Democrats, he agreed. "Keeping our leadership team completely unchanged will simply lead to more disappointment in future elections," he wrote.

Although his voting record was more centrist and consensus-driven than that of Pelosi, his two-week campaign was more generational and geographic. His 63 votes were potentially a path to additional Democratic influence. Oddly, he became chairman of the Appropriations Subcommittee on the Legislative Branch, which traditionally is a position that requires cooperation with party leaders. Following the January 2021 riots at the Capitol, he took early steps to investigate the law-enforcement breakdown and explore alternative approaches.

His interest in House leadership became a springboard for his presidential campaign, which he launched in April 2019. "At the end of the day, the progressive agenda is what's best for working families," he said in an interview on The View. But the nearly two dozen Democratic candidates made it difficult for Ryan to create a niche. And Sen. Amy Klobuchar of Minnesota and Mayor Pete Buttigieg of South Bend Indiana already had staked out the appeal to white Midwest voters. As the months passed, Ryan found that he was consumed with meeting party eligibility requirements for joining debates of the presidential candidates. When he dropped out of the contest in October 2019, Geoffrey Skelley wrote on the 538 website that Ryan also suffered from inadequate fundraising. "Ryan's poor fundraising was probably the nail in his campaign's coffin."

At home, Ryan's political dilemma at home has been a repeated refusal to step up the ladder for other offices, despite his ambition. He considered a run for the Senate in 2006 but decided against challenging the more senior Brown. Democratic Gov. Ted Strickland discussed a shared ticket with Ryan in 2010, but he decided to remain in the House, largely because of his new influence at Appropriations. He took another serious look at running for governor in 2014 after Strickland said he wouldn't run, but announced that it still wasn't worth the risk to give up his committee seat. He turned down the opportunity to run for the Senate in 2016, with the explanation that he wanted to be close to his "new and growing family."

Portman's retirement changed his calculation. He regained national political prominence, perhaps with the benefit of his national campaign experience and his limits for advancement in the House, plus the risk that Ohio Republicans in redistricting would make it hard for him to win reelection in a district increasingly supportive of Trump, where Ryan survived a narrow reelection in 2020. The day after Portman's announcement, Ryan told CNN, "the U.S. Senate needs another working-class voice and I'm very serious about the opportunity to continue representing the people of Ohio." Though Democrats in Ohio have faced uphill battles in running statewide, his prospects could be enhanced by the outcome of the expected messy Republican primary.

With the huge cost of competitive Senate campaigns, Ryan will face the early challenge of showing that he has learned lessons from his presidential bid. If he becomes the Democratic nominee, he likely will rely on the huge national fundraising support that several Senate Democratic candidates received in 2020—though many of them lost.

OH-13: Northeast Ohio

Cook Partisan Voting Index: D+1

Population		Race and Ethnicity		Income	
Total	704,191	White	81.20%	Median Income	$46,582
Land area (sq. miles)	894	Black	12.60%	District Income Rank	409
Pop/ sq mi	787.42	Latino	3.50%	Poverty Rate	17.60%
Born in State	76.60%	Asian	2.40%	With health insurance	92.70%
		Two or more races	3.20%	Cash public assistance	3.70%
Age Groups		Other	0.60%	Food stamp/SNAP	15.90%
Under 18	18.60%				
18-34	24.10%	**Education**		**Work**	
35-64	37.80%	H.S grad or less	47.70%	White Collar	30.60%
Over 64	19.50%	Some college	28.60%	Sales and Service	42.10%
		College Degree, 4 yr	15.60%	Blue Collar	27.40%
Military		Post grad	8.10%	Government	11.80%
Veteran/ Active Duty	7.50%				

2020 Pres. Vote	Biden	171,221	(51%)	Trump	159,955	(48%)			
2016 Pres. Vote	Clinton	163,600	(51%)	Trump	142,738	(44%)	Johnson	8,810	(3%)

Youngstown, Akron Area: For nearly a century, the Mahoning Valley—between the Lake Erie docks that unload iron ore from Great Lakes freighters and the coalfields of western Pennsylvania and West Virginia—was a steel capital of the United States. The first blast furnace opened in 1803, and the first coal mine opened in 1826. Canals followed, and in 1892 the first steel mill was built. The valley soon filled up with mills, converters and furnaces. But in the 1950s and 1960s, worldwide overcapacity in steel grew as almost every developing country decided it needed its own mills. After a 119-day strike in 1959, an agreement between the United Steelworkers and management boosted wages and fringe benefits to levels that helped price domestic steel out of the market. When the oil shock of the 1970s collapsed the U.S. auto and steel markets, every plant in the Mahoning Valley closed, with a loss of 40,000 jobs.

Steel has since revived, although not at its previous peak and not in Youngstown. The high-wage living standard of the area vanished. Organized crime infiltrated local government, and a federal investigation in the late 1990s led to more than 70 convictions, including a prosecutor, a sheriff and a congressman. In 2019, Youngstown's population was 65,500, little more than a third its size in the 1950s, when the area stopped growing. Since 2000, two-thirds of the manufacturing jobs in the area have disappeared. Still, there is some benefit to the weak economy. In 2018, the Youngstown area had the second-lowest home prices in the nation, higher than only Cumberland Maryland. The median price for a single-family home was $90,200.

The 13th Congressional District of Ohio encompasses most of the Mahoning Valley industrial area: Youngstown, Warren and most of Trumbull County. It includes nearly all of Portage County and the less-minority parts of Summit County and Akron. Mahoning, Trumbull and Summit, with similar shares of the population, comprise most of the district. It contains two loci of 1970s protest —Kent State University, where four students were killed by National Guardsmen, and Lordstown, site of the General Motors plant where workers purposely built shoddy cars to protest the tedium of the assembly line. Lordstown's auto-based facility grew obsolescent as market demand shifted to SUVs and trucks—plus, increasingly, hybrid and autonomous vehicles. In March 2019, GM shut down Lordstown; two years earlier, its workforce was about 4,500. After union protests and political posturing, two businesses agreed to build factories on the former Chevrolet site: GM announced a joint venture with a South Korean chemical company to manufacture electric batteries, with about 1,100 jobs; and Lordstown Motors, a start-up company, made plans to manufacture electric pick-up trucks at the site, with about 400 workers. Both plants would have a United Auto Workers workforce, though a large share of the earlier GM crew had moved to jobs at other GM sites.

Of the four Democratic-held districts in Ohio, this Rustbelt patchwork is the least Democratic and least urban. In a district President Barack Obama won with 63 percent in 2012, Hillary Clinton and Joe Biden each got 51 percent. In Mahoning County, Donald Trump was the first Republican to win since 1972. Republican redistricters have viewed the 13th as a prime target for slicing and dicing in 2022.

Dave Joyce (R)

Elected 2012, 5th term, b. Mar 17, 1957; Cleveland, OH; University of Dayton, B.S., 1979; University of Dayton, J.D., 1982; Roman Catholic; Married (Kelly Joyce); 3 children.

Elected Office: Prosecutor, Geauga County, 1988-2013.

Professional Career: Public defender, Geauga County, 1985-1988; Public defender, Cuyahoga County, 1983-1984.

DC Office: 1124 LHOB 20515, 202-225-5731, Fax: 202-225-3307, joyce.house.gov

State Offices: Mentor, 440-352-3939; Twinsburg, 330-357-4139.

Committees: *Appropriations*: Financial Services & General Government; Interior, Environment & Related Agencies (RMM). *Ethics. Select Committee on the Modernization of Congress.*

Group Ratings

	ADA	ACLU	AFL-CIO	LCV	COC	HAFA	ACU	CFG	FRC
2020	**	21%	**	33%	-	70%	54%	**	-
2019	10%	C	52%	21%	98%	C	54%	57%	86%

Almanac Ratings 2019-2020

	Economy	Social	Foreign	Composite
Liberal	38%	43%	27%	36%
Conservative	62%	57%	73%	64%

Key Votes of the 116th Congress

1. U.S./Mex./Can. trade deal Y	5. Russia sanctions Y	9. Firearms background checks N
2. First Coronavirus response Y	6. Troops in Syria Y	10. Spending at the border Y
3. HEROES Act N	7. Veto arms sales to Saudis N	11. Marijuana liberalized rules N
4. CASH Act Y	8. Defense $$$, veto override Y	12. Electoral College objections N

Election Results

Election	Name (Party)	Vote (%)		Cand. Spent	Ind. Exp. Support	Ind. Exp. Oppose
2020 General	Dave Joyce (R)	238,864	(60%)	$2,472,971	$171,856	$113
	Hillary O'Connor Mueri (D)	158,586	(40%)	$573,959	$5,039	
2020 Primary	David Joyce (R)	43,970	(83%)			
	Mark Pitrone (R)	8,932	(17%)			

Prior winning percentages: 2018 (55%), 2016 (63%), 2014 (63%), 2012 (54%)

Republican David Joyce, a former prosecutor who was elected in 2012 against a weak opponent after the GOP incumbent unexpectedly retired, quickly showed his political skills when he got a seat on the Appropriations Committee. As the ranking Republican on its subcommittee that deals with environmental issues, he has secured funds for his interest in protecting the water quality of the Great Lakes. Although he occasionally goes his own way, including as co-chair of the Cannabis Caucus, Joyce usually is a reliable member of the GOP establishment and politically secure at home.

Joyce, born in Cleveland, is the son of a coal salesman. He went to the University of Dayton, where he got his bachelor's in accounting and earned a law degree. He said that he expected to get a job at a national accounting firm, but he was told during interviews that he would have little opportunity for trial work. Instead, he took a job as a public defender in Cuyahoga County, eventually moving to nearby Geauga County. Rising through the ranks quickly, Joyce was elected as the youngest prosecutor in Geauga County's history. He worked in political campaigns, starting on phone banks for then-Cleveland Mayor George Voinovich. In 1999, he organized "Prosecutors for Bush," with George W. Bush's presidential campaign.

In July 2012, nine-term GOP Rep. Steven LaTourette announced that he would not seek reelection, despite having won the GOP primary. He soon suffered serious health problems and died of cancer in 2016. Needing a new candidate, a group of 14 Republican leaders selected Joyce, a friend of LaTourette with a credible background and no political record to attack. Democratic nominee Dale Blanchard, an obscure accountant and a 10-time candidate for Congress, continued to run despite pressure to step aside for a stronger challenger. Joyce ran a mostly positive campaign and generally did not engage Blanchard. He won, 54%-39%.

Although Joyce has been more of a party regular than his predecessor, his Almanac vote ratings have ranked him near the center of the House and as the most moderate member of the Ohio delegation. In 2017, he was one of 20 Republicans who voted against House passage of a bill to repeal and replace the Affordable Care Act. He said it was "unacceptable" that premiums for people with pre-existing conditions "could potentially skyrocket."

On Appropriations, Joyce has pursued bipartisan efforts to restore the environmental health of the Great Lakes, with $300 million in annual funding. In 2016, Joyce claimed a victory when enactment of water resources legislation included a provision for the Great Lakes states to create an action plan to determine future funding projects. That bill continued regular dredging of the Cuyahoga River, with removal of dangerous sediments. In both 2017 and 2018, Joyce worked with the Ohio delegation and got the full $300 million; President Donald Trump had proposed eliminating the funds. With Joyce taking over in 2019 as ranking Republican on the Appropriations Subcommittee on Interior and the Environment, long-term funding appeared secure for the Great Lakes, which Joyce termed "the greatest natural resources and economic powerhouses we have in the United States." In the 2020 yearend spending bill, he got $330 million for the Great Lakes, including $25 million to combat Asian carp infestation. In December 2020, he also was part of a bipartisan group that enacted a five-year extension of the authorization for the Great Lakes program.

With the bipartisan Cannabis Caucus, Joyce has filed legislation to permit each state to go its own way in deciding whether to legalize marijuana. Current federal policy, he said, "has stifled important medical research, hurt legitimate businesses and diverted critical law enforcement resources needed elsewhere." But he held his ground in December 2020 when a separate group sought federal legalization. The decision by Democratic leaders to push that proposal to its virtually party-line House passage showed that Congress was "failing to enact sensible and meaningful cannabis reform."

After handing Joyce his seat on a silver platter, Democrats failed to make a more serious effort in 2014. In the Republican primary, Joyce won 55%-45% over pro-life state Rep. Matt Lynch, who was helped by tea party groups. Joyce had more than $600,000 in help from the U.S. Chamber of Commerce, American Hospital Association and a Super PAC run by LaTourette, whose daughter won Lynch's seat in the state House. Michael Wager, a Democratic fundraiser and former chairman of the Cleveland-Cuyahoga County Port Authority. Joyce won, 63%-33%. In 2016, Joyce breezed past two rematches. Against Lynch, who repeated his tea party themes, Joyce increased his margin to 64%-36%. Wager tried again, with rhetorical boosts from national Democrats but not much else. He spent $240,000 to $2 million for Joyce and lost 63%-37%.

In 2018, Joyce faced a well-funded and credible challenger. Democrat Betsy Rader, an attorney who handled employment discrimination cases, said she was "horrified" by Trump's proposed budget cuts. She told the Cleveland Plain Dealer that "she has nothing against Joyce personally," but that he had "gone missing" in failing to attend a town-hall meeting organized by supporters of Obamacare. Joyce, who outspent Rader $2.7 million to $2.2 million, ran an ad that cited his willingness to challenge Trump on behalf of the Great Lakes. "I'll do what's right for northeast Ohio, even if it means standing up to my own party," he said. He won, 55%-45%. Rader led narrowly in Cuyahoga and Summit counties. In 2020, Joyce was challenged by Hillary Mueri, an attorney and former Navy flight officer who served in Iraq. He outspent her $2.5 million to $575,000 and won 60%-40%, taking all seven counties.

OH-14: Northeast Ohio   **Cook Partisan Voting Index: R+7**

Population		Race and Ethnicity		Income	
Total	714,870	White	90.20%	Median Income	$67,698
Land area (sq. miles)	1,953	Black	4.90%	District Income Rank	184
Pop/ sq mi	366.01	Latino	3.30%	Poverty Rate	8.90%
Born in State	76.80%	Asian	1.90%	With health insurance	93.40%
		Two or more races	2.30%	Cash public assistance	1.40%
Age Groups		Other	0.60%	Food stamp/SNAP	8.10%
Under 18	21.20%				
18-34	18.20%	**Education**		**Work**	
35-64	39.70%	H.S grad or less	37.20%	White Collar	41.50%
Over 64	20.70%	Some college	28.90%	Sales and Service	36.40%
		College Degree, 4 yr	21.00%	Blue Collar	22.20%
Military		Post grad	12.90%	Government	10.80%
Veteran/ Active Duty	7.50%				

2020 Pres. Vote	Trump	222,995	(54%)	Biden	185,672	(45%)		
2016 Pres. Vote	Trump	197,943	(53%)	Clinton	155,561	(42%)	Johnson	11,325	(3%)

Cleveland and Akron Suburbs, Ashtabula: The imprint of the westward track of New England Yankee migration is still apparent today on the shores of Lake Erie in northern Ohio. The British crown had granted the Colony of Connecticut all the land due west of its borders in 1662. Connecticut ceded most of this land in 1786 in exchange for the newly created federal government taking over its Revolutionary War debts, but it retained a 3 million-acre claim in Ohio for its excess population, which became known as the Western Reserve. As European claims to North America subsided and Native Americans were placed on reservations or relocated, these Yankees, cooped up in New England for 200 years, moved west, through Upstate New York, across Ohio and Michigan to Chicago, and on to Kansas, Oregon and California.

During the Civil War, the Western Reserve, ceded by Connecticut to the federal government in 1800, produced some of the nation's strongest opposition to slavery and hardiest support of the Union armies and the Republican Party; Lake Erie ports were prime transit points for the Underground Railroad to Canada. Its thrifty, hardworking, well-educated citizens built communities with fine schools and, with their accumulated savings, invested in what became some of the nation's leading industries. Now, like Connecticut and Massachusetts, northeastern Ohio has moved toward a post-industrial economy. Small, adaptive business units with highly skilled workers are the growth sectors.

In 2018, a private economic development report found that northeast Ohio remained globally competitive in manufacturing and that the number-one challenge for businesses was finding skilled workers to meet the expected demand and to replace retiring workers. In late 2020, a South African company began construction in the harbor of Ashtabula on a $474 million pig-iron production facility, which will produce a commodity that is vital in the metal casting industry; scheduled for completion at the end of 2022, the facility will be the first such plant in the United States. FirstEnergy stirred controversy when it filed a notice in 2018 that it would shut down by 2021 its nuclear power plant in Lake County, plus others near Toledo and Pittsburgh. The company later filed for bankruptcy; it was losing money because of the low price of natural gas and other fuels. The state legislature responded in 2019 with energy legislation that included numerous subsidies, including support for retention of the plant in Perry. In February 20211, the new owner of the plant indicated that it was not interested in the subsidies, the Associated Press reported.

The 14th Congressional District of Ohio takes in parts or all of seven counties of northeast Ohio and the old Western Reserve. It includes the suburbs of eastern and southern Cleveland-based Cuyahoga County; northern Summit; some of Portage to the east; and Geauga. Lake County has nearly one-third of the population. The more diverse areas are rural Ashtabula, home to a historic port district, 18 covered bridges and several wineries, and the northern part of Trumbull County, which is industrial and close to Youngstown. Historically, the area was Republican. Since the 1930s, it has remained politically competitive. Even with the Democratic-leaning portions in Cuyahoga and Summit, which are more than one-third of the district, the 14th has enough Republican territory to give it a GOP lean. Donald Trump got 53 percent and then 54 percent in his campaigns. In Ashtabula, he got 61 percent in 2020 and was the first Republican presidential candidate to win the county since Ronald Reagan.

OH-15 - VACANT (V)

DC Office: 2234 RHOB 20515, 202-225-2015, stivers.house.gov
State Offices: Hilliard, 614-771-4968; Lancaster, 740-654-2654; Wilmington, 937-283-7049.

Republican Steve Stivers, who was serving his sixth term, resigned from the House on May 15, 2021, and became chief executive officer of the Ohio Chamber of Commerce. His exit opened the door to a special election, with the primary on August 3 and the general election on November 2. Republicans were the initial favorites to hold the seat. Stivers was not seriously challenged after he defeated a Democratic incumbent in 2010, which was followed by a redistricting that increased the Republican lean of his seat. The winner likely will be determined in the GOP primary.

The unexpected move by Stivers came as he was exploring the possibility of seeking the seat of retiring Sen. Rob Portman. Several GOP candidates already had entered that contest. Following the resignation of the previous head of the Ohio Chamber in late 2020, the business lobby reportedly had been pursuing Stivers, according to the Cleveland Plain-Dealer. Stivers was well-known in state government following his years as a state legislator sand as a banking lobbyist in Columbus.

In the House, Stivers focused his legislative work on the Financial Services Committee. In 2017-18, he had the challenging assignment of chairing the National Republican Congressional Committee. After the House GOP lost 40 seats, he suffered the inevitable second-guessing and offered some hindsight judgments about other Republicans. He gained an early entry into Republican leadership circles as an ally of Speaker John Boehner of Ohio, who held that position from 2011 to 2015. Former Rep. Pat Tiberi, another Republican ally of Boehner, resigned in 2018 to become president of the Ohio Business Roundtable. Tiberi and Stivers represented the two House districts based in the suburbs of Columbus.

Stivers grew up in the Cincinnati suburbs, moved to Columbus to attend Ohio State University, and never left, except for deployments with the Ohio Army National Guard. For most of his career, he was associated with the Ohio legislature. He was a staffer in the state Senate, and in 1995 began working as a lobbyist for BankOne, which was based in Columbus (and later absorbed into Bank of America). He was appointed in 2003 to fill the seat of a retiring state senator and became vice chairman of the Finance Committee. Soon afterward, he served tours in Kuwait and Iraq, for which he received a Bronze Star.

When Republican Rep. Deborah Pryce retired in 2008, Democrats nominated Franklin County Commissioner Mary Jo Kilroy. After initially declining amid speculation that he wanted to be Ohio Senate president, Stivers entered the contest. He campaigned as a moderate, with a blend of support for abortion rights and fiscal discipline plus his military experience. Kilroy emphasized her background as a former Columbus school board president and slammed Stivers for his stint as a bank lobbyist. Stivers portrayed Kilroy as "way outside the mainstream." In a strongly Democratic year, Kilroy won 46%-45%, a margin of 2,312 votes.

In her one term, Kilroy was a faithful supporter of the majority Democrats' programs, including the cap-and-trade bill to reduce carbon emissions and the Affordable Care Act. Stivers said the health law's mandate to buy insurance would be a heavy burden on small business. Kilroy portrayed him as a flip-flopper, arguing that he had supported an individual mandate and a carbon emissions bill in the past. They raised roughly $2.7 million each, but the Democratic Congressional Campaign Committee abandoned the race in October as unwinnable. Stivers prevailed 54%-41%.

In the House, Stivers was "the type of sensible moderate that most Ohioans want to see," the Columbus Dispatch wrote in endorsing him for reelection. Retaining his interest in veterans, he enacted in 2020, as part of a broader bill, his provision that required the Veterans Affairs Department to report on its steps to implement a suicide-prevention program.

On the Financial Services Committee, Stivers worked with other Republicans to rein in what they viewed as the excesses of the Dodd-Frank banking law. In the minority, he became ranking member of the Housing, Community Development and Insurance Subcommittee. Ironically, he said that he would work closely with Fudge, his former House colleague from Ohio who became the new secretary of Housing and Urban Development.

After he gave up his leadership responsibilities, Stivers was outspoken about what he viewed as excesses in each party. When President Donald Trump raised doubts about whether he would comply with the outcome of the 2020 election, Stivers cited the need for a peaceful transfer of power. Although he said that Trump's actions related to the riot at the Capitol in January 2021 were "unacceptable and contributed to what will be remembered as one of the darkest days in our nation's history," he opposed what he called the "snap impeachment" without evidence or committee action.

OH-15: Central Ohio   **Cook Partisan Voting Index: R+9**

Population		Race and Ethnicity		Income	
Total	769,664	White	89.30%	Median Income	$69,844
Land area (sq. miles)	4,739	Black	4.70%	District Income Rank	166
Pop/ sq mi	162.41	Latino	2.40%	Poverty Rate	10.60%
Born in State	77.10%	Asian	2.80%	With health insurance	94.80%
		Two or more races	2.40%	Cash public assistance	1.90%
Age Groups		Other	0.70%	Food stamp/SNAP	10.20%
Under 18	21.00%				
18-34	23.90%	**Education**		**Work**	
35-64	39.70%	H.S grad or less	39.50%	White Collar	44.50%
Over 64	15.40%	Some college	25.70%	Sales and Service	33.10%
		College Degree, 4 yr	21.20%	Blue Collar	22.30%
Military		Post grad	13.50%	Government	17.30%
Veteran/ Active Duty	7.20%				

2020 Pres. Vote	Trump	222,259	(56%)	Biden	165,740	(42%)			
2016 Pres. Vote	Trump	196,762	(55%)	Clinton	141,648	(39%)	Johnson	12,381	(3%)

Southern Columbus Metro, Athens: Not long ago, when Columbus was a smaller and more provincial city, a Republican could compete there. But as that city and its metro area have become the largest— and continually growing—part of Ohio, the new arrivals have been younger and they leaned Democratic. Coincidentally for Republicans, that growth in the heart of the state left the metro area with nearly enough people to control three congressional districts, rather than the two of the past. For Republican redistricters in 2011, the solution became obvious: Create a heavily Democratic district based in the city, and carefully draw the two outlying districts to make them safely Republican.

That partisan shift resulted in radical changes in the 15th Congressional District. A slim majority of the district's residents live in Columbus and its suburbs, mostly in the southern parts of the metro area. In a vast swath of mostly Republican counties stretching from the exurbs of Cincinnati nearly to West Virginia, disparate areas were stitched together to help prevent a non-Columbus Republican from amassing a power base in a primary election. About 40 percent of the population is in Franklin County, with 20 percent in adjacent Fairfield. The district also features disparate economic levels. In 2019, quarterback Joe Burrow highlighted the disparity. When he won the Heisman Trophy as the top college football player in 2019, after having transferred from Ohio State to Louisiana State University, he cited his experience growing up in Athens, where "all those kids … go home to not a lot of food on the table, hungry after school."

The parts of Columbus were mostly south and west of the capital and the campus: half of the Short North neighborhood just north of downtown, an up-and-coming area with a large gay population and many of the fashionable new clubs and restaurants of Columbus, though high real estate costs have forced some businesses to move elsewhere; a few other downtown communities; the old money suburb of Upper Arlington; and the up-and-coming suburbs of Hilliard and Grove City, which grew 29 percent and 17 percent, respectively, from 2010 to 2019. These upscale suburbs have been shifting to the Democrats. In Upper Arlington, where President George H.W. Bush led by 34 percentage points in 1992, Hillary Clinton led by 16 points in 2016, the Chicago Tribune reported. In

Fairfield, downtown Lancaster has combined its historic roots and downtown revitalization to create an attractive community.

The only Democratic county is Athens, the poorest county in the state (31 percent of its residents met poverty standards in 2019) and home of Ohio University, the oldest college west of the Appalachians. Athens has been one of 31 counties in the Appalachian region listed as "distressed," and it was one of only seven counties in Ohio to vote for Joe Biden in 2020—and, by far, the smallest in population. Nearby is Hocking Hills, the most visited state park in Ohio, with features that include a cave, a gorge, nature preserves, log cabins and access to the 1,444-mile Buckeye Trail that circles most of the state. The district has a distinct Republican lean. Donald Trump took 55 and then 56 percent of the vote, compared to 52 percent for Mitt Romney.

Anthony Gonzalez (R)

Elected 2018, 2nd term, b. Sep 18, 1984; Avon Lake, OH; OH State University, B.A., 2007; Stanford University, M.B.A., 2014; Catholic; Married (Elizabeth Gonzalez); 1 child.

Professional Career: Indianapolis Colts, Wide Receiver 2007-2011; New England Patriots, Wide Receiver 2012-2012; Manager, InformedK12.

DC Office: 1023 LHOB 20515, 202-225-3876, anthonygonzalez.house.gov

State Offices: Canton, 330-599-7037; Strongsville, 440-783-3696.

Committees: *Financial Services*: Diversity & Inclusion; Investor Protection, Entrepreneurship & Capital Markets; Nat'l Security, International Development & Monetary Policy; Task Force on Artificial Intelligence (RMM). *Science, Space & Technology*: Environment; Research & Technology. *Select Committee on the Climate Crisis*.

Almanac Ratings 2019-2020

	Economy	Social	Foreign	Composite
Liberal	41%	40%	35%	39%
Conservative	59%	60%	65%	61%

Key Votes of the 116th Congress

1. U.S./Mex./Can. trade deal	Y	5. Russia sanctions	Y	9. Firearms background checks	N
2. First Coronavirus response	Y	6. Troops in Syria	Y	10. Spending at the border	Y
3. HEROES Act	N	7. Veto arms sales to Saudis	N	11. Marijuana liberalized rules	N
4. CASH Act	N	8. Defense $$$, veto override	Y	12. Electoral College objections	N

Election Results

Election	Name (Party)	Vote (%)		Cand. Spent	Ind. Exp. Support	Ind. Exp. Oppose
2020 General	Anthony Gonzalez (R)	247,335	(63%)	$1,747,873		$750
	Aaron Paul Godfrey (D)	144,071	(37%)	$58,386		
2020 Primary	Anthony Gonzalez (R)	43,026	(100%)			

Prior winning percentages: 2018 (57%)

Republican Anthony Gonzalez was elected in 2018 in his first campaign. Before entering politics, he had extensive experience in the public spotlight as a star football player at Ohio State University and then for five years as a wide receiver with the Indianapolis Colts in the National Football League. Gonzalez brought to the campaign a compelling life story as the grandson of refugees from Cuba, the son of a successful businessman and the manager of his own enterprises. He is the first Hispanic Republican in the House from outside the South or West. After a quiet first term, he set off political bombshells when he was one of 10 House Republicans who voted for the second impeachment charge against President Donald Trump.

Gonzalez proudly embraced his grandfather, who was a successful lawyer in Cuba before he fled with his family to Miami in 1960, when their lives were in jeopardy following the takeover by Fidel Castro. They settled in Ohio, where his father started up a steel plant on the west side of Cleveland. At Ohio State, where Gonzalez got an athletic scholarship, the team won two Big Ten championships during his career.

Following his career with the NFL's Colts, which was cut short by injuries after he was a first-round draft choice, Gonzalez got a master's in business administration from Stanford University. That led to his work as chief operating officer for Chalk Schools, a San Francisco-based tech company that sought to reduce excessive paperwork in public schools.

Returning to Ohio to run for Congress, Gonzalez won the GOP primary against state Rep. Christina Hagan, who had served eight years in the state House. Hagan more closely identified with Trump. Her ardent pro-gun and anti-abortion views drew support from conservative leaders. She criticized Gonzalez for his lack of political experience. "Legislating isn't quite as easy as catching a football," she said in an interview with Fox News.

Gonzalez, while mostly avoiding discussion of Trump, emphasized his own policy and campaign themes. He more than doubled Hagan's campaign financing and benefited from $300,000 in expenditures by the U.S. Chamber of Commerce. House Republican Leader Kevin McCarthy of California contributed to his campaign during the primary. Gonzalez won the primary, 53%-41%. In Cuyahoga County, which had a bit more than one-third of the vote, Gonzalez took 59 percent. Hagan led narrowly in her base of Stark County, plus nearby Portage, and Gonzalez took the other three counties.

In November, Gonzalez handily defeated Democrat Susan Palmer, a health product sales executive and another political newcomer. She had limited campaign funds and received scant national-party assistance. Gonzalez won, 57%-43%. Two years later, Gonzalez was reelected with 63 percent of the vote against a challenger whom he outspent by more than 30-to-1.

In the House, Gonzalez got a seat on the Financial Services Committee and pursued some eclectic issues. As a former successful college athlete, he sought to expand the discussion of commercial endorsements of current student athletes, which is prohibited by intercollegiate rules. With a bipartisan House group—including Democratic Rep. Colin Allred, who also played in the NFL—he filed a bill that would prevent universities from banning endorsements except for a limited number of commercial products. "The college athlete, as it sits today, is the only person in America who cannot capitalize on their name, image or likeness," he said.

As a co-chair of the House China task force, he enacted in December 2020 a bipartisan bill that sought to end the practice of companies based in China—and often financed by their government— that have escaped coverage by U.S. securities law, often by an unintended loophole. China represents one of the biggest existential threats facing our nation today," he said. "It is time that we significantly recalibrate the relationship between the United States and China and hold the Chinese Communist Party accountable for their actions."

On the impeachment charge following the January 2021 riot at the Capitol, Gonzalez said that Trump "helped organize and incite a mob that attacked the United States Congress in an attempt to prevent us from completing our solemn duties as prescribed by the Constitution." He added that Trump "abandoned his post while many members asked for help, thus further endangering all present." Calling those actions "fundamental threats … to the very foundation of our republic," Gonzalez said that he was "compelled" to vote for impeachment. A month later, Trump endorsed Max Miller, one of his former White House aides, who had announced his challenge to Gonzalez. Trump said that Gonzalez did not represent his constituents' "interest or their heart."

OH-16: Northern Ohio   **Cook Partisan Voting Index: R+10**

Population		Race and Ethnicity		Income	
Total	719,744	White	92.70%	Median Income	$68,534
Land area (sq. miles)	1,205	Black	1.90%	District Income Rank	181
Pop/ sq mi	597.13	Latino	2.60%	Poverty Rate	6.80%
Born in State	77.70%	Asian	2.50%	With health insurance	93.80%
		Two or more races	1.90%	Cash public assistance	1.60%
Age Groups		Other	0.90%	Food stamp/SNAP	6.20%
Under 18	20.80%				
18-34	19.50%	**Education**		**Work**	
35-64	39.10%	H.S grad or less	36.00%	White Collar	42.00%
Over 64	20.70%	Some college	28.40%	Sales and Service	36.10%
		College Degree, 4 yr	22.70%	Blue Collar	21.90%
Military		Post grad	12.80%	Government	11.40%
Veteran/ Active Duty	7.00%				

2020 Pres. Vote	Trump	232,235	(56%)	Biden	173,675	(42%)		
2016 Pres. Vote	Trump	207,149	(56%)	Clinton	145,670	(39%)	Johnson 11,451	(3%)

Cleveland/Akron/Canton Suburbs: The rapidly growing Cleveland of the early 1900s—it went from 93,000 residents in 1870 to more than 900,000 in 1930—was crammed into a compact area. The eclectic mix of newcomers that populated the city sorted itself into Cleveland's so-called "cosmo wards:" Italians in Big Italy to the southeast of Public Square; Croats, Serbs and Slovenians in the St. Clair area on the northeast side of town; Irish in Whiskey Island to the west of downtown; Russians, Germans, Poles and Slovaks in the Ohio City and Tremont areas near present-day Newburgh Heights; and Czechs and Poles in Praha and Slavic Village to the north of present-day Garfield Heights. The cosmo wards began to empty out in the 1950s as the original immigrants died off and their children fled to the suburbs. For a half-century, Cleveland's population has been in decline. With the population of Greater Cleveland barely over 2 million, only 19 percent now live in the city itself.

The now-graying great-grandchildren of those immigrants live in places like those found in the 16th Congressional District of Ohio, a political creation whose precincts are bound more by Republican voting habits than by any coherent geographic locale. A bit more than one-third of the district's votes are cast in Cuyahoga County, mostly in Cleveland's western outer suburbs: comfortable places like Westlake, a stone's throw from Lake Erie, plus Strongsville and North Royalton. Many residents here tend to be descended from the Hungarians and Bohemians who settled southwest of Public Square, near present-day Brooklyn. Parma—the second-largest city in Cuyahoga and the seventh-largest in Ohio—has had a population decline from 100,000 in 1960 to 78,000 in 2019. It is 87 percent non-Hispanic white. Its share of the population with a college degree is two-thirds of that in Cuyahoga overall.

The district also takes in exurban Medina County, Portage and Stark (but not including Canton) counties, and Wayne County, home to the College of Wooster. Both Medina and Stark include about one-sixth of the 16th. Wayne is the headquarters of Smuckers, whose familiar consumer brands have included Smucker jellies and Folgers coffee; in recent years, it has added Big Heart pet foods and Ainsworth Pet Nutrition. The southern part of Wayne County is Amish country, where people drive horse-drawn tractors, eschew automobiles and electricity (except from their own generators), and quit school after the eighth grade. Tourism has been a growth industry in the Amish region, with a profusion of restaurants, bed-and-breakfasts, and gift shops. The 16th leans Republican just enough to avoid serious Democratic challenges. The vote for Donald Trump was consistent with that pattern; he won 56 percent in each of his campaigns.

OKLAHOMA

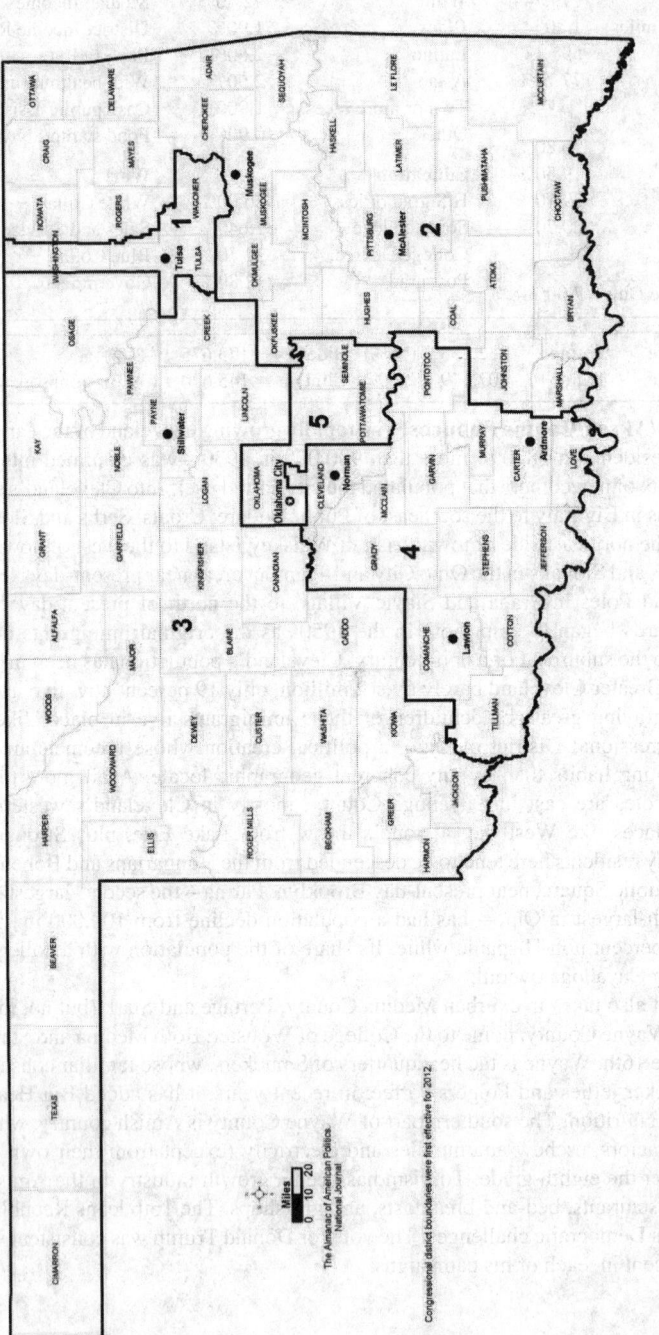

It wasn't that long ago that Democrats held sway in Oklahoma. They controlled the state House until 2004, the state Senate until 2008, and the governorship until 2010. Since then, though, the GOP has had a virtual lock on the state. Not a single county in Oklahoma has voted Democratic in a presidential election since 2000—a 385-for-385 record for the GOP. Oklahoma Democrats have begun notching modest gains in urban and suburban areas, notably Oklahoma City, where President Donald Trump beat Joe Biden by just a percentage point in 2020. But such gains have been counterbalanced by Democrats' continued erosion in rural counties.

Oklahoma, the subject of the classic Broadway musical, is one of the newest states, the 46th to be admitted to the Union, in 1907. Its capitol, located atop a large oil field, opened in 1917, though the dome was not finished until 2002. As that chronology suggests, Oklahoma's history has been a story of sudden stops and starts. It was settled in a rush, first by the "Five Civilized Tribes"— Chickasaw, Choctaw, Creek, Cherokee and Seminole—driven west by Andrew Jackson on the Trail of Tears in the 1830s. Then came white settlers. One morning in April 1889, in the great land rush memorialized by novelist Edna Ferber and Hollywood movies, thousands of homesteaders drove their wagons across the territorial line at the sound of a gunshot, the most adventurous or unscrupulous of them literally jumping the gun—the Sooners.

In 1905, a convention of the Five Tribes sought to have eastern Oklahoma admitted as a separate state of Sequoyah. The federal government turned a deaf ear and ended the tribal government, parceled out reservation land to tribe members, and combined the Indian and Oklahoma Territories into a single state. Oklahomans of Indian ancestry—almost 8 percent of the population, fourth-highest of any state—have made their way forward in the larger society while still cherishing their heritage. There has been much intermarriage over the years, and many Oklahomans—and not a few of its politicians—proudly claim Indian blood. Such murky ancestral ties caused problems for Massachusetts Sen. Elizabeth Warren, an Oklahoma native whose claims of Native American family history came under scrutiny; her attempts to use DNA testing to prove her lineage outraged the Cherokee leadership, and Warren eventually apologized. Despite assimilation, there's an ongoing struggle to keep the Cherokee, Choctaw, Chickasaw and Seminole languages from dying out—you can see street signs in the Cherokee alphabet in Tahlequah, the Cherokee Nation's capital. In 2019, the Cherokee Nation for the first time nominated a delegate to the U.S. House, acting on a provision of a treaty signed in 1835. Then, in 2020, the Supreme Court delivered a landmark decision in favor of the Muscogee (Creek) Nation, ruling, 5-4, that broad swaths of eastern Oklahoma, including Tulsa, were territory of the 86,100-member Muscogee nation, based on an 1866 treaty. The most immediate consequence was that Native Americans could no longer be tried by state or local courts for major crimes within the reservation and instead must be tried by federal or tribal courts. Left uncertain were additional effects, such as those on taxation and regulation of the area's substantial oil and gas deposits.

The Rodgers and Hammerstein musical was set in a mythical Oklahoma on the brink of statehood in 1906. Soon thereafter, the territory rapidly filled up with farmers, rising from 1.5 million people in 1907 to 2.4 million in 1930. Oil helped. The first well was drilled here in 1897, and by 1920 Tulsa was an oil boom town complete with art deco skyscrapers. Then in the 1930s came a decade of bust —and dust—as soil loosened by erosion was whipped into giant swirling clouds: the Dust Bowl. "People sat in Oklahoma City, with the sky invisible for three days in a row, holding dust masks over their faces and wet towels to protect their mouths at night, while the farms blew by," wrote author John Gunther. Okies headed in droves west on U.S. 66 to greener California, and Oklahoma's population steadily declined, falling to 2.2 million in 1950. It did not reach its 1930 level again until 1970.

Then came another oil boom. As the oil shocks of 1973 and 1979 sent prices up, Oklahoma's population rose from 2.5 million in 1970 to 3 million in 1980. The collapse of oil prices in the 1980s produced another bust. In the 1990s, Oklahoma began building a more diversified economy that included high-tech employers. The population rose 10 percent in the 1990s, 9 percent from 2000 to 2010, and 5.5 percent since 2010. Oklahoma became a leader in hydraulic fracturing, or fracking, and horizontal drilling to extract natural gas embedded in shale rock. The state now ranks fourth in dry natural gas production and sixth in shale-gas production; it also produces coalbed methane, and much of the nation's helium supply comes from natural gas extracted from Oklahoma's Hugoton field. Oil remains big as well. Oklahoma ranks fourth among the states in petroleum production, and the pipeline terminus and storage hub of Cushing, in the central part of the state, is the pricing point for benchmark U.S.-produced crude oil, known as West Texas Intermediate. But the market has whipsawed, and in 2020, during a pandemic-driven bust, a leading shale driller based in Oklahoma City, Chesapeake Energy, filed for bankruptcy.

Energy extraction may also have come at an environmental cost, namely earthquakes. As recently as 1990, the Soviet Union sent scientists to Oklahoma to verify that the United States was not testing nuclear weapons underground, choosing Oklahoma because of its unusually low levels of seismic activity. That all changed around 2011, when Oklahoma began experiencing hundreds of quakes a year. The culprit wasn't fracking per se, the Oklahoma Geological Survey has concluded, but the reinjection back into "disposal wells" of the water produced in drilling. Tighter regulation instituted by the Oklahoma Corporation Commission in 2015 has helped reduce the number of quakes, from 903 in 2015 to below 200 in 2018, but the level remains far higher than it was a decade earlier. Concerns continue because building codes in the state were never intended to handle quakes. Meanwhile, Oklahoma has joined Texas in signing legislation to prevent Oklahoma cities and counties from banning fracking on their own.

The growth of the energy business has juiced the state's capital. The area around its stockyards, the nation's largest, has become a tourist attraction, and civic leaders have channeled the North Canadian River (and renamed a portion of it the Oklahoma River) to create North America's premier rowing center, even if the arid landscape does not match verdant Henley-on-Thames. At the same time, Oklahoma has been investing in renewable energy. Oklahoma now ranks second to Texas in electricity generation from wind. In Oklahoma, wind can also be a serious problem. Between 1890 and 2013, metropolitan Oklahoma City saw at least 156 tornadoes—about one each year, including the 2013 EF5 that killed 24 in and around Moore. The state also has 10 hydropower plants; Oklahoma has more man-made lakes than any other state.

Despite its oil riches, Oklahoma has its share of problems. It has the second-highest percentage of divorced residents in the nation, its median income ranks in the bottom 10 states, and its health system ranks only above Mississippi, according to annual rankings by the Commonwealth Fund. In July 2020, voters narrowly backed a ballot measure to expand Medicaid under the Affordable Care Act, a step that politicians in the red state had been reluctant to take. Oklahoma has the fourth-highest rate of teenage pregnancy, ranks 12th in violent crime, and is eighth from the bottom in bachelor's degrees. After protests by teachers in 2018, Oklahoma has raised K-12 teacher pay enough to move up from 49th in the nation to 34th, according to National Education Association rankings. Oklahoma has been neck-and-neck with Louisiana for highest rate of incarceration of any state. It has taken some steps toward criminal justice reform, and voters easily approved a medical marijuana ballot measure, which produced both a bustling retail sector and the nation's highest percentage of residents with medical marijuana cards, at about 10 percent. (Wags call it "Tokelahoma.") The state aggressively pursued opioid makers Purdue Pharma, Teva Pharmaceuticals, and Johnson & Johnson and received hundreds of millions of dollars in settlements and court judgments. But criminal justice reforms stalled in 2020, when a ballot measure that would have kept courts from enhancing sentences for any defendant without a history of a violent felony was rejected by 61 percent of voters. Also in 2020, the state said it would resume executions, five years after several botched lethal injections drove the state to declare a moratorium.

Racial tension has cast a shadow over Oklahoma for decades. The state is 7 percent Black, well under the national average; most live in Oklahoma City and Tulsa. The latter city was the site of racial slaughter of 1921, "a firestorm of hatred and violence that is perhaps unequaled in the peacetime history of the United States," as historian John Hope Franklin called it. The violence by White mobs destroyed nearly 40 square blocks of African-American homes and businesses and likely killed up to 300 people, many of them the descendants of freed slaves of the Creek Indians. The carnage was largely forgotten for decades, though the history became more widely known after the Emmy-winning HBO superhero series Watchmen was set in Tulsa. (On April 19, 1995, the state's other major city, Oklahoma City, was the site of another mass slaughter, when a truck bomb placed by anti-government domestic terrorists blew apart the Alfred P. Murrah Federal Building, killing 168.) Two studies found that Oklahoma police in 2015 killed people more often than those in any other state; in 2019, a handcuffed Black man, Derrick Scott, died in Oklahoma City police custody after saying, "I can't breathe," to which an officer replied, "I don't care." Oklahoma has other minorities as well: Hispanics, who account for 11 percent of the state's population, are concentrated in the two big cities and in meatpacking counties in the west. White students are now a minority in the state's public schools.

Oklahoma ranks fifth in the nation in number of farms, first in rye production, fifth in canola, and sixth in cattle and wheat. But the population gains in the past decade have come in urban and suburban areas: Canadian County (the western suburbs of Oklahoma City, with 27.5 percent growth), Oklahoma County (Oklahoma City, 10.6 percent), Cleveland County (the southern Oklahoma City suburbs and Norman, 10.5 percent) and Tulsa County (7.7 percent).

Historically, Oklahoma saw big Democratic margins in eastern counties and in Little Dixie in the southeast, while northwestern Oklahoma, settled by Kansans, has always been Republican. Starting in the 1950s, Tulsa and Oklahoma City leaned Republican too. Then, in the last decade or two, parts of the state outside the metro regions moved sharply away from their Democratic heritage. This evolution has made Oklahoma one of America's most Republican states. It has not voted Democratic for president since 1964. Since 1966, Oklahoma has elected only one Democratic senator, David Boren. The state GOP is fractured between tea partiers, Chamber of Commerce types, movement conservatives, evangelicals and others, but Democrats are usually too weak to take advantage.

The partisan tide turned slightly during the Trump era. In 2017, Democrats won a flurry of legislative special elections, and the following year, Democrat Kendra Horn surprised even some in her own party by defeating Rep. Steve Russell in an Oklahoma City-based district that hadn't voted for a Democrat in more than four decades. Democratic gubernatorial nominee Drew Edmondson lost the 2018 gubernatorial race to Republican Kevin Stitt by 12 points, but he posted marked improvement in and around Oklahoma City. Still, Republicans gained legislative seats overall by flipping Democratic-held seats in rural areas, and Republican candidates for lieutenant governor, attorney general and state treasurer won their races by larger margins than Stitt did.

While Democrats were disappointed in 2020 when Horn lost her House seat after just one term, Biden managed to increase the number of Democratic presidential votes in the state by 20 percent compared to 2016, largely because the GOP continued to bleed support in urban and suburban areas. In Tulsa County, where Trump had held a June rally that had disappointing turnout and was blamed for becoming a coronavirus super-spreader, Biden narrowed Trump's winning margin by almost six points in November. The shifts to the Democrats were even bigger in Cleveland County (seven points), Canadian County (eight points) and Oklahoma County (nine and a half points). Still, Trump won the state by 33 points, well above the GOP's 22-point winning margin 20 years earlier, a sign that Democrats will have a long, difficult path to becoming genuinely relevant in Oklahoma again.

Population		Race and Ethnicity		Income	
Total	3,956,971	White	72.40%	Median Income	54,449
Land area (sq. miles)	68,595	Black	7.30%	State Income Rank	43 out of 50
Pop/ sq mi	57.69	Latino	11.10%	Poverty Rate	15.20%
Born in state	60.60%	Asian	2.90%	With health insurance	85.70%
Age Groups		Two or more races	7.60%	Cash public assistance	2.90%
		Other	10.40%	Food stamp/SNAP	13.4%
Under 18	24.10%				
18-34	23.20%	**Education**		**Work**	
35-64	36.50%	H.S grad or less	43.10%	White Collar	36.20%
Over 64	16.10%	Some college	30.70%	Sales and Service	38.40%
		College Degree, 4 yr	17.10%	Blue Collar	25.40%
Military		Post grad	9.10%	Government	17.10%
Veteran/ Active Duty	9.50%				

Presidential Politics

2020 Primary (D)	Biden (D)	117,633(39%)	Sanders (D)	77,425(25%)	Bloomberg (D)	42,270(14%)	
	Warren (D)	40,732(13%)					
2020 Pres. Vote	Trump (R)	1,020,280(65%)	Biden (D)	503,890(32%)			
2016 Pres. Vote	Trump (R)	949,136(65%)	Clinton (D)	420,375(29%)	Johnson (L)	83,481 (6%)	

Since the FDR era, Oklahoma has voted only twice for a Democratic presidential candidate: Harry Truman in 1948 and Lyndon Johnson in 1964. The last Democratic nominee to carry a county in Oklahoma was Al Gore in 2000 (he won nine out of 77). Traditionally, Tulsa and Oklahoma City were Republican strongholds, but starting in 2004 that's reversed—those areas have become more competitive, while the counties outside the two big metro areas have become overwhelmingly Republican. In 1996, Bob Dole defeated President Bill Clinton 48%-40%, but Clinton won nearly half the counties. Most of those were in the region's old Indian Territory, where in-migration from Texas, Arkansas and especially Mississippi brought with it Democratic traditions—the region became known as "Little Dixie." But in 2020, President Donald Trump crushed Joe Biden, 65%-32%, carrying 70 percent or more of the vote in 68 of the state's 77 counties. Biden's best county was Oklahoma (Oklahoma City), where he took 48 percent of the vote—the only county in the state with a single-digit margin. Oklahoma's biggest role in the 2020 race was a Tulsa Trump rally as COVID-19 cases were spiking in late June that drew significantly fewer people than anticipated, and cost Trump campaign manager Brad Parscale his job.

In the 2008 Democratic primary, Hillary Clinton handily defeated Barack Obama 55%-31%. In 2016, Vermont Sen. Bernie Sanders beat Clinton 52%-42%. Sanders visited the state in 2019 as he mulled a comeback, but Biden defeated him in the state's Super Tuesday primary, 39%-25%, one of a string of disappointing results that night that torpedoed Sanders' hopes for the nomination.

Republican presidential primaries have been closer. John McCain defeated Mike Huckabee 37%-33% in 2008 and Rick Santorum beat Mitt Romney 34%-28% in 2012. In 2016, Texas Sen. Ted Cruz defeated Trump 34%-28%.

Congressional Districts

117th Congress Lineup	5R	116th Congress Lineup	1D 4R

Oklahoma redistricting following the 2010 census was a breeze. Republicans controlled the process for the first time and they had little incentive to rock the boat. Dan Boren, whose family name is revered in state politics, was the sole Democrat in the delegation, but he voted with Republicans more often than any other Democrat in the House. All five incumbents, including Boren, agreed to minimal changes in their districts, and legislators passed them with a yawn. Then, Boren surprised observers and made the GOP job even easier by announcing his retirement at age 37, from what had long been known as the Little Dixie (2nd) district—a former Democratic stronghold in the southeast. Fiercely conservative Republican Markwayne Mullin easily picked up the seat the following November. From 2012 through 2016, Republicans won each of the five districts with at least 57 percent of the vote.

Then, the unexpected happened. In 2018, Democrat Kendra Horn took the Oklahoma City-based 5th District from Republican Rep. Steve Russell, with some help from GOP over-confidence and shifting demographics. Two years later, Republican Stephanie Bice regained the seat in another close contest. So, the Republican vulnerability in Oklahoma has shifted from Little Dixie to Oklahoma City. With Republicans retaining complete control of the redistricting process, the apparent solution is to switch some Republican precincts into the 5th District and remove some of its most Democratic areas. Since most of the remainder of the state is solidly Republican, the options are nearly endless. There might be practical limitations, including the Tulsa and Norman communities likely will want to remain whole. But the 5th could easily reach north to Stillwater, south to Ardmore, or to rural areas east and west. The fact that some Democratic-leaning precincts in Oklahoma County already are in the 4th District might be a starting point.

Kevin Stitt (R)

Elected 2018, term expires 2023, 1st term; b. Dec. 28, 1972, Milton, FL; Oklahoma State University, B.S., 1996; Unknown; Married (Sarah); 6 children;

Professional Career: CEO, Gateway Mortgage Group, 2000-2018; Loan Officer, First City Financial, 1998-2000.

Office: 2300 N. Lincoln Blvd. Room 212, Oklahoma City, 73105; 405-521-2342; Fax: 405-521-3353; Website: ok.gov

Lt. Gov.: Matt Pinnell (R) **Atty. Gen:** Mike Hunter (R)

State Legislature: Senate: 9D, 39R **House:** 24D, 77R

Election Results

Election	Name (Party)	Vote (%)
2018 General	Kevin Stitt (R)	644,579 (54%)
	Drew Edmondson (D)	500,973 (42%)
	Chris Powell (Lib)	40,833 (3%)
2018 Primary runoff	Kevin Stitt (R)	164,892 (55%)
	Mick Cornett (R)	137,316 (45%)
2018 Primary	Mick Cornett (R)	132,806 (29%)
	Kevin Stitt (R)	110,479 (24%)
	Todd Lamb (R)	107,985 (24%)
	Dan Fisher (R)	35,818 (8%)
	Gary Jones (R)	25,243 (6%)

Republican Kevin Stitt, founder of a mortgage company, was elected governor of Oklahoma in 2018, running as an outsider who defeated experienced politicians in both the primary and the general election. In office, he grappled with the coronavirus pandemic and intra-party friction in the solidly Republican state.

Stitt, a fourth-generation Oklahoman, grew up in Norman, where his father was a pastor, and spent summers in Skiatook, where his grandfather owned a dairy farm. He is a member of the Cherokee Nation, making him the first Native American to be elected governor in the United States, though when tensions rose with officials in Indian Country over his stance on gaming compacts, some of his adversaries raised questions about how solid Stitt's ancestral ties actually were. Stitt earned his bachelor's degree at Oklahoma State University, working his way through college as a door-to-door book salesman. In his late twenties—with just $1,000 and a computer, he has often said—Stitt founded Gateway Mortgage, turning it into a company with $16 billion in loans, 1,200 employees and 164 field offices in 41 states by 2018. He stepped down as CEO shortly before securing the GOP nomination. The company's record drew questions from opponents, who cited a Business Insider article after the 2008 financial crisis that called Gateway one of the "15 shadiest mortgage lenders." Stephen Curry, Stitt's successor as CEO, acknowledged to the Associated Press that the firm's default rate was high, but that it stemmed from the challenging times in the lending industry; he said it improved substantially in later years.

Stitt was one of the contenders to succeed Gov. Mary Fallin, a Republican who had been elected in 2010 as the state's first female chief executive and who was easily reelected in 2014. Her record of cutting taxes, curbing abortion rights and relaxing handgun restrictions pleased conservatives, but an oil and gas downturn hit the state—and the state budget—hard, lowering Fallin's approval ratings during her second term. Her final year in office was dominated by a teacher walkout, driven by spending cuts that had left one-fifth of schools operating only four days a week and that left teacher salaries second-to-last in the nation.

The 2018 GOP primary featured 10 candidates, though only three of them were considered to be in the top tier: Mick Cornett, the outgoing four-term Oklahoma City mayor; two-term Lt. Gov. Todd Lamb; and Stitt. Lamb had long since distanced himself from Fallin, but his establishment ties and career-politician label were an albatross. The little-known Stitt spent more than $2 million from his own pocket prior to primary day to raise his profile. Cornett finished first with 29 percent, while Stitt took the other runoff slot. In the runoff, Stitt continued spending from his own pocket, positioning himself as a newcomer to politics and emphasizing his loyalty to President Donald Trump and his immigration policies (although Trump didn't publicly endorse Stitt until after he won the nomination). In ads, Cornett rejected the notion that he was disloyal to Trump, calling the charge "Bull Stitt." Stitt won, 55%-45%. In the Democratic primary, former 16-year attorney general Drew Edmondson easily defeated state Sen. Connie Johnson, 61%-39%.

Stitt framed Edmondson as part of the Oklahoma political establishment, but Edmondson questioned whether a political outsider like Stitt could be successful as governor. (When the Tulsa World looked at voting records, it found that Stitt had not voted in a gubernatorial race since at least 1999.) In a state where Trump's approval rating was above water, Stitt made use of the president's endorsement as well as a visit from Vice President Mike Pence during a rally at Oral Roberts University. The National Rifle Association also took out ads against Edmondson. Bolstered by nearly $5 million of his own funds, Stitt won all but four of the state's counties, though he notably lost Oklahoma County (Oklahoma City) and Cleveland County (Oklahoma City suburbs and Norman), both of which had voted for Fallin in 2014. Edmondson won his home base of Muskogee County by one vote.

In office, Stitt signed a series of executive orders that restructured the cabinet, increased transparency requirements on the use of contract lobbyists by state agencies, and gave agency managers more flexibility in hiring. He signed a bill allowing Oklahomans to carry firearms without a permit. And he signed legislation that strengthened the governor's authority over hiring and firing the heads of the state's five largest agencies. Benefiting from a $600 million budget surplus that stemmed from the rebounding economy, Stitt had a relatively easy time working with the legislature on the budget in 2019, enacting an additional teacher pay raise, shoring up the state's rainy-day fund, and offering more money for attracting businesses to the state. Stitt also signed legislation to apply the terms of a 2016 criminal justice ballot reform measure retroactively, a change that led to more than 400 inmates being released from prison a few months later, something the governor described as the largest one-day mass commutation in U.S. history. Stitt also signed a measure designating the second Monday in October Oklahoma Native American Day, and he recommitted to continuing to accept refugees in the state. Meanwhile, after the university town of Norman imposed a 5 cent tax on plastic bags, Stitt signed a measure to prevent all local jurisdictions from banning or taxing plastic bags.

Stitt's second year in office proved to be more difficult, on several fronts. One effort by Stitt that ruffled feathers was his push for new compacts for the 130 tribal casinos operating in the state. The original 15-year compacts, signed in 2004, obligated the tribes to pay 4%-6% of their revenues to the state, much of which went to fund public schools. Stitt argued that subsequent agreements in other states were in the 20%-25% range. Most Indian officials saw this as the latest in a long line of broken agreements and opposed any such move; they took the issue to federal court. Stitt found little support among Republicans; the state attorney general withdrew from the case, and several other prominent GOP officials sided with the tribes. The Supreme Court's decision in a case giving greater authority to Indian tribes in the state also proved to be an irritant. The antagonism on Indian policy spilled over into other areas of governance, as well, including the budget, which was written without significant input from Stitt. He vetoed it, and the legislature overrode his veto. Stitt also suffered a setback when voters in July 2020 narrowly approved an expansion of Medicaid under the Affordable Care Act, a policy he had opposed.

But Stitt's biggest challenge came with the emergence of the coronavirus. Early in the pandemic, as health officials were urging Americans to stay home whenever possible, Stitt drew criticism for tweeting a photo of himself and his family in a crowded restaurant, with the comment, "Eating with my kids and all my fellow Oklahomans at the @CollectiveOKC. It's packed tonight!" When Stitt did issue a stay-at-home order in April, he broke with most other governors and limited it to senior citizens and those with immune-system concerns, those most at risk from the virus. He told a Tulsa World virtual forum that it was "not reasonable" to ask everyone to "just bunker in place." Some bigger cities such as Oklahoma City and Tulsa went further and issued broader orders. Then, when Stitt began to lift closure orders for nonessential businesses, he did so without adhering to the

White House coronavirus task force guidelines for doing so. In July, he became the first governor to become infected with the coronavirus; after a two-week recovery, he ignored CDC recommendations by conducting his first news briefing without a mask. (Stitt also donated plasma to aid the recovery effort.) All told, Oklahoma saw a relatively high case rate in the summer, as other states were beating back their own caseloads; the number of cases peaked in the fall and winter, before falling to the middle of the national pack by March 2021. Meanwhile, in April 2021, Stitt signed a bill to shield drivers who unintentionally injure or kill protesters during riot.

Stitt has drawn one announced Republican challenger for 2022, Ervin Yen, a physician and former state senator. But with such a deep Republican bench, potentially stronger GOP primary challengers may emerge.

Jim Inhofe (R)

Elected 1994, term expires 2026, 5th full term, b. Nov 17, 1934; Des Moines, IA; University of Tulsa, B.A., 1973; Presbyterian; Married (Kay Kirkpatrick Inhofe); 4 children (1 deceased); 16 grandchildren.

Military Career: U.S. Army 1957-1958

Elected Office: OK House, 1967-1969; OK Senate, 1969-1977, Republican leader, 1975-1977; Tulsa Mayor, 1978-1984; U.S. House, 1987-1995.

Professional Career: Businessman, land developer, 1962-1986.

DC Office: 205 RSOB 20510, 202-224-4721, Fax: 202-228-0380, inhofe.senate.gov

State Offices: Enid, 580-234-5105; McAlester, 918-426-0933; Oklahoma City, 405-208-8841; Tulsa, 918-748-5111.

Committees: *Armed Services (RMM)*: Ex Officio membership on all subcommittees. *Environment & Public Works*: Clean Air & Nuclear Safety (RMM); Fisheries, Water, and Wildlife; Transportation & Infrastructure. *Intelligence*. *Small Business & Entrepreneurship*.

Group Ratings

	ADA	ACLU	AFL-CIO	LCV	COC	HAFA	ACU	CFG	FRC
2020	-	0%	-	0%	-	74%	95%	-	-
2019	0%	C	16%	0%	69%	C	95%	69%	100%

Almanac Ratings 2019-2020

	Economy	Social	Foreign	Composite
Liberal	6%	6%	0%	4%
Conservative	94%	94%	100%	96%

Key Votes of the 116th Congress

1. EPA clean energy rules	N	5. Russia sanctions	N	9. Barr as Atty. General	Y
2. U.S./Mex./Can. trade deal	N/A	6. Troops in SYR, AFG	Y	10. Spending at the border	Y
3. Cut unemployment benefits	Y	7. Veto arms sales to Saudis	N	11. Coney Barrett to Sup. Ct.	Y
4. Shelton to Fed Reserve	Y	8. Defense $$$, veto override	Y	12. Electoral College objections	N

Election Results

Election	Name (Party)	Vote (%)		Cand. Spent	Ind. Exp. Support	Ind. Exp. Oppose
2020 General	Jim Inhofe (R)	979,140	(63%)	$4,925,015	$9,337	$28,587
	Abby Broyles (D)	509,763	(33%)	$2,034,492	$597	
	Robert Murphy (L)	34,435	(2%)			
2020 Primary	Jim Inhofe (R)	277,868	(74%)			
	J.J. Stitt (R)	57,433	(15%)			
	John Tompkins (R)	23,563	(6%)			

Prior winning percentages: 2014 (68%), 2008 (57%), 2002 (57%), 1996 (57%), 1994 special (55%), House: 1992 (53%), 1990 (56%), 1988 (53%), 1986 (55%)

Republican Jim Inhofe became one of the most influential senators when he became Armed Services Committee chairman in September 2018, after the death of Sen. John McCain. Inhofe, the seventh longest-serving senator, was a strong supporter of President Donald Trump, and he used his committee position to the benefit of military installations in his home state of Oklahoma. Earlier in his career, he served more than a decade as chairman or ranking member of the Environment and Public Works Committee, on which he was a strong voice—in the Capitol and later with the Trump administration—in denying the hazards of climate change, of which there is scientific consensus. After political setbacks early in his career, Inhofe has been comfortably reelected in his strongly Republican home state. At 85 at the start of the Biden presidency, Inhofe remained a leader of Senate conservatives.

Inhofe's political career dates back more than a half-century. He grew up in Tulsa, served in the Army, and worked in real estate and insurance. He was elected to the state House in 1966 and to the state Senate in 1969. During his time in the state Senate, he earned a bachelor's degree from the University of Tulsa. As a state legislator, he promoted a balanced budget constitutional amendment. His career then hit a couple of bumps at a time when now-solidly Republican Oklahoma still tilted Democratic. In 1974, Inhofe ran for governor and lost to Democrat David Boren—whom he later succeeded in the Senate—64%-36%. Two years later, he ran for the House against Democratic Rep. Jim Jones and lost. Inhofe made a political comeback by winning election as mayor of Tulsa in 1978, an office he held until 1984.

When Jones left to run for Senate in 1986, Inhofe was elected to his House seat. He was reelected three times, albeit with uninspiring margins: He was held to 53 percent of the vote on two occasions. Negative publicity from a family business lawsuit and charges of campaign finance irregularities impaired his support in his strongly Republican district. Inhofe's most notable accomplishment while serving eight years in the minority was reforming the arcane rules for discharge petitions, used chiefly by the minority party to force a floor vote on legislation bottled up in committee. For years, House rules kept secret the names of signers of discharge petitions. That was changed in 1993, and one of the first bills to benefit from the new rules was an aviation liability reform bill co-sponsored by Inhofe, an avid flyer of small airplanes. The legislation limited the liability of small-airplane manufacturers in lawsuits resulting from crashes.

In 1994, when conservative Democrat Boren resigned from the Senate to become president of the University of Oklahoma, Rep. Dave McCurdy, a moderate Democrat, was the initial front-runner in the special election to fill the final two years of Boren's term. But the Clinton administration's unpopularity among conservatives was too much for McCurdy, who had voted for 1993 budget increases and tax hikes and for the 1994 crime bill with its ban on assault weapons. Inhofe won 55%-40%. In the Senate, Inhofe was elected president of the large GOP freshman class of 11.

In the Almanac's vote ratings, Inhofe consistently has been among the most conservative senators. For many years, he has been an outspoken leader of the GOP faction that disputes the mainstream scientific view of climate change—which holds that carbon dioxide emissions will cause catastrophic damage absent action by the United States and other major nations. In 2003, Inhofe termed the contention that man-made emissions have caused global warming "the greatest hoax ever perpetrated on the American people." In 2012, he published a book: The Greatest Hoax: How the Global Warming Conspiracy Threatens Your Future. In a Senate floor speech in 2015, Inhofe suggested climate change was due to forces beyond the control of modern civilization. "Climate is changing, and climate has always changed. There's archeological evidence of that. There's biblical evidence of that. There's historic evidence of that," he said. Inhofe's position on the Environment and Public Works Committee gave him a prominent platform for those views.

Representing a major petroleum-producing state, Inhofe has been an avid proponent of oil drilling in the Arctic National Wildlife Refuge, as well as more oil and gas exploration throughout the nation at large. After the April 2010 BP oil spill in the Gulf of Mexico, he opposed a Democratic initiative to remove the $75 million cap on damages for offshore drilling accidents. Environmental activist Robert F. Kennedy Jr. in 2012 called Inhofe "Big Oil's top call girl."

Inhofe's first stint as chairman of the Environment panel was from 2003 to 2007, ending when Democrats regained the majority. He devoted much of his attention to the reauthorization of the federal surface transportation bill funding highways and transit systems. By early 2004, Inhofe had hammered out an agreement in the Senate for a six-year, $318 billion transportation bill. His goal was to guarantee that every state got 95 percent of its gas tax money back. Following a two-year deadlock, GOP leaders in 2005 were eager to cut a final deal with President George W. Bush. Inhofe agreed to a scaled-down bill of $286 billion over six years.

It took another decade for Congress to agree on the next long-term surface transportation measure, after a period of short-term extensions of two years or less. In 2015, when Inhofe had returned for his third and final term as chairman of the Environment Committee, President Barack Obama signed a five-year, $305 billion extension of the highway bill into law. Left unresolved was a long-term solution to funding the nation's transportation infrastructure: Gas tax revenues continued to decline because of more fuel-efficient vehicles, and lawmakers resisted increasing the per gallon amount of the tax. Trump promised—but failed—to address that challenge.

Initial prospects for cooperation between Inhofe and Sen. Barbara Boxer of California, the senior Democrat on the committee for many years, had appeared dim. He spoke out strongly against her bill to impose a mandatory cap on carbon dioxide emissions, which died in the Senate in 2010. But Inhofe insisted their working relations were nonetheless good. After the two worked together in 2012 to pass a two-year transportation bill, Boxer told reporters that Inhofe "has been just the best partner for me as chairman ... in the best traditions of how the highway bill has been done until now."

Besides transportation, perhaps the most notable accomplishment of Inhofe's final term as Environment chairman was a revision to the federal Toxic Substances Control Act. Facing growing pressure to improve the much-criticized law, which had remained largely unchanged since its enactment in 1976, Inhofe's panel in 2015 cleared a sweeping bill on a bipartisan vote. The measure had backing from some environmental groups—which felt it gave the Environmental Protection Agency significantly increased powers—and from industry, which liked the fact that it provided a single federal regulatory regimen rather than a patchwork of state laws.

Inhofe initially served as the top Republican on the Armed Services Committee from 2013 to 2014 after Republicans' internal term limits forced McCain to step aside as that panel's ranking minority member. Inhofe began that tenure by crusading against his former Senate colleague Nebraska Republican Chuck Hagel's bid to become Obama's secretary of Defense. While other senators said that Hagel's inadequate support for Israel was a cause for concern, Inhofe went even further: He suggested that Hagel was "cozy" with countries promoting terrorism because Iran had expressed support for his nomination.

When Republicans regained Senate control in 2015, the same term-limits rule restored McCain as chairman and returned Inhofe to chairing the Environment Committee for two final years. But McCain was diagnosed with brain cancer in July 2017. He received intensive treatment that severely diminished his work time at the Capitol, and he died 13 months later. Inhofe served as acting chairman during much of that time.

When Inhofe formally regained the chairmanship in September 2018, his experience made the transition relatively smooth, despite the different styles of the two veteran senators. With his quick temper and experience as a Naval Academy graduate and pilot who was a prisoner of war for six years during the Vietnam War, McCain wasn't shy about voicing his views and demanding accountability from the Pentagon brass. Inhofe, by contrast, usually refrained from public criticism of military officials and was less familiar with the operational side.

Inhofe's more conservative record than the famously independent McCain gave him a more positive relationship with Trump. He acknowledged that tension when Trump initially refused to lower the flag over the White House after McCain's death. "John McCain is partially to blame for that because he is very outspoken," Inhofe told reporters. "He disagreed with the president in certain areas and wasn't too courteous about it." When Inhofe disagreed with Trump, the chairman usually was low-key in seeking to convince the president of legislative or political realities.

The annual defense spending bill that Congress approved in 2018, which became law two weeks before McCain died and was named in his honor, had much of Inhofe's imprint. Most significantly, it increased military spending by $160 billion over two years. As chairman, Inhofe took credit for added funding of military facilities in his home state, including the new KC-46 tanker stationed at Altus Air Force Base and upgrades of the B-52 bomber, some of which have been stationed at Tinker Air Force Base.

Even with the gush of military spending that Congress had recently approved, Inhofe warned about threats that the nation continued to face, especially because the Pentagon budget had been downsized in earlier years. "China and Russia have increased all during the years that we have decreased," he told the Senate in January 2019. "It would take over 40 years to modernize a fleet that's already too old and too small."

The handling of the military spending bill in 2020 became one of Trump's final showdowns with Congress and led to the only time during his presidency that Congress overrode his veto. Inhofe and Sen. Jack Reed of Rhode Island, the senior Democrat on the Armed Services Committee, hammered out a bill with broad bipartisan support in the Senate. The pair, who have a mostly harmonious relationship, also collaborated in conducting an on-site investigation in September 2020 of serious charges of sexual harassment and assault at Fort Hood in Texas.

Democrats recapture of the House in 2018 ended the free-spending practices at the Pentagon. And it pushed some social issues front and center on the annual defense bill, notably the growing public demand to remove Confederate symbols and names from military bases, especially in the South. The pressure for action was fueled by nationwide protests against police brutality and systemic racism during in the summer of 2020. When the Senate and House completed final negotiations on the defense bill, Inhofe joined the broad agreement to gradually remove symbols of the Confederacy —despite having earlier assured Trump that he would eliminate provisions that the president strongly opposed. Inhofe also was committed to the bill because it gave significant additional support to Oklahoma-based military facilities.

The lame-duck Trump was further miffed because he saw the military spending bill as his final opportunity to repeal "Section 230," a part of the 1996 Communications Decency Act that gives immunity to big online platforms for user-generated content that might otherwise create legal liability. Despite repeated warnings from Inhofe and other congressional Republicans that the internet proposal would not be considered as part of the defense bill, Trump exercised his veto, based on the two issues that had little to do with national military policy. "You can't do it in this bill," Inhofe told reporters. Both the House and Senate comfortably overrode his veto, with Inhofe joining other senior Republicans defying Trump.

Inhofe has for years regularly flown airplanes and is one of the few certified commercial pilots in Congress. He flew around the world following the historic route of Wiley Post, the first pilot to fly solo around the globe. But he has had several close calls, most recently a 2016 forced landing in northeastern Oklahoma amid severe weather; he was 81. A decade earlier, Inhofe encountered problems when the experimental plane he was flying spun out of control and suffered significant damage on landing in Tulsa, though he and an aide escaped injury.

In 2010, his apparent flouting of air safety rules became a serious issue. Inhofe narrowly missed hitting a group of construction workers during an aborted landing attempt and set his six-seat Cessna down on a clearly closed runway at a South Texas airport. The Federal Aviation Administration ordered him to take remedial flying lessons but did not take away his pilot's license. An unrepentant Inhofe contended he had been cleared to land. He responded legislatively with what he called a bill of rights that gave pilots accused of wrongdoing more authority to review the evidence against them. It was signed into law in 2012. Inhofe didn't stop there: In 2015, he introduced "Pilots Bill of Rights 2," which was enacted the following year. In 2013, his son Perry Inhofe died when the small single-engine plane he was flying crashed in Oklahoma. Discussing how the loss affected him, the senator told NBC News: "You don't change in terms of your positions, in terms of what you believe in, but you change in terms of your understanding of individuals."

Jim Inhofe was reelected by almost identical margins in 2002 and 2008, both somewhat smaller than recent Republican presidential margins in Oklahoma. In 2002, he defeated former Gov. David Walters, who had years earlier pleaded guilty to a misdemeanor count of violating campaign finance laws, 57%-36%. In 2008, he beat state Sen. Andrew Rice 57%-39%. In 2014, he won a fourth full term with a more convincing 68 percent of the vote against little-known Democratic challenger Matt Silverstein. The previous year, Inhofe had quadruple bypass surgery to repair extreme blockages in his arteries.

In 2016, Inhofe's first choice for the Republican presidential nomination was Florida Sen. Marco Rubio. When it became clear that Trump would be the nominee, Inhofe reportedly forged ties through Alabama Sen. Jeff Sessions—later, Trump's first attorney general—and was named an adviser to the Trump campaign on national security and regulatory issues. That stirred the animosity of environmental groups. "Inhofe was like the original climate denier in chief. He was one of the first people spouting this gibberish—fact-free but dangerous gibberish," Gene Karpinski, president of the League of Conservation Voters, told the Washington Post. "Now he and his cronies have far more reach and are far more dangerous than they've ever been."

Trump's selection of Scott Pruitt to run the EPA initially was a big boost for Inhofe and his home state. Pruitt had twice been elected as Oklahoma attorney general, and he had made his mark fighting environmental and energy regulations of the Obama administration. He vigorously pursued that approach as one of Trump's favorite officials. But Pruitt got into trouble with questionable ethical and financial practices in how he ran EPA and lived in the nation's capital. He became the target of numerous investigations in Congress and even within the Trump administration for his handling of official funds.

When Pruitt resigned in July 2018, that was hardly the end of Inhofe's influence. Andrew Wheeler, who succeeded Pruitt at EPA, had been staff director at the Environment and Public Works Committee when Inhofe was chairman. Other former Inhofe aides became part of Wheeler's inner circle. "With these Inhofe staff, you get all of the Pruitt policy and none of the Pruitt baggage," an energy lobbyist told E&E News.

Inhofe remained a strong ally of Trump on most policy issues. He typically defended the president —either with denial of criticisms or blame-shifting to other officials. But he was less enamored of Trump's style. "I have to admit—confession's good for the soul—every time I hear that a tweet is coming out, I cringe a little," he told defense officials in December 2018, according to The Hill. "But how else can he circumvent a media that hates him?"

In May 2020, Inhofe escaped potential legal and political problems when the Justice Department cleared him and two other senators of insider-trading allegations after they old stocks after being briefed on the coronavirus threat but before the pandemic caused markets to crash.

As Inhofe sought reelection that year at 85, his Democratic challenger, Abby Broyles, a 30-year-old Oklahoma native who was a lawyer and former television reporter in Oklahoma City, said that she wanted to hold Inhofe "accountable" and "give Oklahomans back their voice in Washington." In a TV ad, her campaign noted that Inhofe had been in office since 1967 and that he "misses so many votes, so many meetings."

Inhofe, though refusing to debate Broyles, vigorously responded to her criticisms in an October interview with the Claremore Daily Progress. "My opponent says that I don't do anything for Oklahoma," Inhofe said. "But last year the National Farm Bureau gave me their biggest award ... because I saved [Oklahoma] farmers from Obama's water rules." At a time that military bases across the nation have closed, he added, "Oklahoma's military installations have grown."

Broyles spent $2 million, though her campaign attracted little national attention or financial support. Inhofe, who spent $4.9 million, won handily, 63%-33%. He fell barely short of Trump's victory in Oklahoma, 65%-32%. With another six years, his platform and voice assured his continuing influence.

James Lankford (R)

Elected 2014, term expires 2022, 1st full term, b. Mar 04, 1968; Dallas, TX; University of Texas, B.S., 1990; Southwestern Theological Baptist Seminary, M.Div., 1994; Baptist; Married (Cindy Lankford); 2 children.

Elected Office: U.S. House 2011-2014; Chair, Majority Policy Committee, U.S. House, 2013-2014.

Professional Career: Director, Falls Creek Youth Camp, 1996-2009; Director of Student Ministry, Baptist Convention of OK.

DC Office: 316 HSOB 20510, 202-224-5754, lankford.senate.gov

State Offices: Oklahoma City, 405-231-4941; Tulsa, 918-581-7651.

Committees: *Energy & Natural Resources*: Energy; National Parks; Public Lands, Forests & Mining. *Ethics. Finance*: Energy, Natural Resources & Infrastructure (RMM); Health Care; Social Security, Pensions & Family Policy. *Homeland Security & Government Affairs*: Government Operations & Border Management (RMM); Investigations. *Indian Affairs*.

Group Ratings

	ADA	ACLU	AFL-CIO	LCV	COC	HAFA	ACU	CFG	FRC
2020	-	8%	0%	-	85%	89%	-	-	-
2019	0%	C	11%	0%	68%	C	89%	76%	100%

Almanac Ratings 2019-2020

	Economy	Social	Foreign	Composite
Liberal	15%	1%	1%	6%
Conservative	85%	99%	99%	94%

Key Votes of the 116th Congress

1. EPA clean energy rules	N	5. Russia sanctions	N	9. Barr as Atty. General	Y
2. U.S./Mex./Can. trade deal	Y	6. Troops in SYR, AFG	Y	10. Spending at the border	Y
3. Cut unemployment benefits	Y	7. Veto arms sales to Saudis	N	11. Coney Barrett to Sup. Ct.	Y
4. Shelton to Fed Reserve	Y	8. Defense $$$, veto override	Y	12. Electoral College objections	N

Election Results

Election	Name (Party)	Vote (%)		Cand. Spent	Ind. Exp. Support	Ind. Exp. Oppose
2016 General	James Lankford (R)	980,892	(68%)	$3,079,878	$2,000	
	Mike Workman (D)	355,911	(25%)			
	Robert Murphy (L)	43,421	(3%)			
	Sean Braddy (I)	40,405	(3%)	$4,518		
2016 Primary	James Lankford (R)	Unopposed				

Prior winning percentages: 2016 (68%), 2014 special (68%), House: 2012 (59%), 2010 (63%)

Republican James Lankford, during his decade in Congress, has impressed party leaders with his ability to toe the line in delicate situations. In exchange, he has received a growing number of coveted assignments that should guarantee his growing influence. With his low-key style, he has managed the unusual feat of serving simultaneously on the Senate's two most powerful committees: Appropriations and Finance. If Oklahoma's junior senator keeps his hands clean and remains connected to his solidly Republican state, the wonders of seniority could make him a very influential senator within a couple of decades. Lankford in 2020 served as chairman of the Senate Ethics Committee.

Part of the internal respect for Lankford, a former church youth camp director who entered politics at 41, is that he can be trusted to take the politically sound approach for congressional Republicans. When President Donald Trump was firing inspectors general at federal agencies because he didn't like their work, Lankford emphasized the need for "reasonable oversight." Responding to concerns prior to the 2020 election that the new postmaster general would not prioritize the delivery of mailed ballots, he told an interviewer that voters "need to have every option," while urging voters to plan for delayed delivery. As President Donald Trump stymied the transition to the Biden administration, Lankford said that the president-elect ought to receive intelligence briefings—though he sidestepped the question of whether Biden had won the election.

Lankford grew up impoverished in Dallas. His parents divorced when he was 4, and, with his mother and older brother, he moved into the garage behind his grandparents' house. Lankford has said he became a Christian when he was 8 and that his faith has helped him endure tough times. He graduated from the University of Texas with a degree in secondary education and then earned a master's degree in divinity from the Southwestern Baptist Theological Seminary. In 1995, Lankford began working for the Baptist General Convention of Oklahoma. A year later, he was made director of the Falls Creek Christian youth summer camp, which touts itself as the largest religious camp in the world. He was in charge of organizing activities for more than 50,000 campers each summer.

In 2009, Lankford resigned to run for the Oklahoma City-based House seat of GOP Rep. Mary Fallin after she decided to run for governor. With grassroots support among conservative Christians —Southern Baptists constitute a significant portion of Oklahoma's population—Lankford led in the initial round of voting and then won 65 percent of the vote in the primary runoff against state Rep. Kevin Calvey, who had the backing of national Republicans. Lankford also benefited from tea party support. In the general election, Lankford easily defeated a Democratic attorney.

In the House, Lankford got a seat on the Oversight and Government Reform panel and won committee passage of several bills, including a measure setting standards to promote transparency in the awarding of federal grants. On the Budget Committee, he became a firm supporter of Republican Chairman Paul Ryan's push to cut spending. Politico named him and California Democrat Karen Bass as the freshmen "most likely to succeed."

When there was an opening for chairman of the House Republican Policy Committee after the 2012 elections, Lankford quietly lined up support. Making the case that he provided fresh blood, he was elected without opposition to the party's No. 5 post, a sign of respect from ambitious colleagues. In his leadership post, he tried to define agenda items beyond the typical week-ahead congressional perspective, and he described his role as serving as the "eyes and ears" of then-Speaker John Boehner in the Republican Conference. As it turned out, he had little time to make an impact: He left the House sooner than Boehner.

GOP Sen. Tom Coburn, a physician first elected to the Senate in 2004, was diagnosed with prostate cancer and announced in January 2014 that he would resign at the end of that year rather than serve out the final two years of his term. Lankford jumped into the Senate race. Despite his earlier backing from tea party interests, he rankled some in the movement by joining the GOP leadership and with some of his House votes. "We won't support Congressman Lankford's bid for the Senate because of his past votes to increase the debt limit, raise taxes and fund Obamacare," an official of the tea party-aligned Senate Conservatives Fund said at the time.

Several of the tea party's most visible figures—including former vice presidential nominee Sarah Palin, Texas Sen. Ted Cruz and Utah Sen. Mike Lee—coalesced around T.W. Shannon, the former speaker of the Oklahoma House, in the Republican Senate primary. The candidacy of Shannon, an African-American and a member of the Chickasaw Nation, was seen by some of his high-profile supporters as an opportunity to rebut criticisms of the Republican Party as overly white. "The Democrats accuse us of not embracing diversity? Oh, my goodness. He is it," Palin said at an April event also attended by Cruz and Lee.

Meanwhile, Coburn, who had emerged as one of the Senate's most outspoken conservatives, said he would remain out of the contest. But, two weeks before the primary, he released a statement calling Lankford "a man of absolute integrity." Lankford ran an ad featuring Coburn's words and drew on his long-standing support from the Southern Baptist community, including former Arkansas Gov. Mike Huckabee. Lankford defeated Shannon 57%-34%; the remaining 9 percent was spread among five other candidates. The outcome was a surprise—particularly for conservative groups that were planning a big push for Shannon in an August runoff that would have resulted if no candidate got more than 50 percent of the vote.

In the solidly conservative state, Lankford received 68 percent of the vote against Democratic state Rep. Connie Johnson, the first woman and the first African-American to be nominated for the Senate from Oklahoma. Seeking a full term in 2016, Lankford faced no primary challenger; against Democratic political operative Mike Workman, he again won with 68 percent of the vote.

In the Senate, Lankford got a plum assignment to the Appropriations Committee, on which he became chairman of the Legislative Branch Subcommittee in 2017. He pulled off a coup in 2019 when he and Republican Steve Daines of Montana gained seats on the Finance Committee, while each remained a member of Appropriations; they reportedly were the first senators to have such dual assignments in several decades. The caveat for Lankford was that he lost, at least temporarily, his seniority and subcommittee chairmanship at Appropriations. He has used a seat on the Intelligence Committee to gain increased visibility, making the rounds of cable news shows while the panel investigated allegations of Russian interference in the 2016 president election.

Lankford has taken a particular interest in freedom of religion. When the Senate granted President Barack Obama expedited authority to negotiate the proposed Trans-Pacific Partnership in 2015, Lankford won inclusion of an amendment into the measure that U.S. trading partners should encourage religious freedom. After President Donald Trump had taken office, Lankford sponsored a resolution with Florida Republican Marco Rubio and Delaware Democrat Chris Coons "reaffirming the commitment of the United States to promoting religious freedom" and pointing to a recent Pew Center finding that nearly 80 percent of the world's population lives in countries where freedom of religion is highly restricted.

Some of Lankford's efforts in the name of religious freedom have been controversial. In 2017, he filed a bill to overturn a 1954 provision in the tax code—included at the behest of influential Sen. Lyndon B. Johnson—that prohibited ministers and leaders of nonprofits from advocating for or against political candidates if they wanted to keep their organizations' tax-exempt statuses. "The federal government and the IRS should never have the ability to inhibit free speech," Lankford said. Three months after Lankford introduced his legislation, Trump issued an executive order "promoting free speech and religious liberty" that also took aim at the Johnson amendment. But Lankford and other social conservatives failed to make legislative progress when Congress completed its sweeping revision of the tax code in 2017.

Lankford has worked with other libertarian-minded Republicans to reduce mandatory questionnaires from the Census Bureau that they viewed as overly intrusive. On the Homeland Security and Governmental Affairs Committee, he worked across the aisle on several bills. Citing an increase in embezzlement of government benefits by representatives of retirees, the Senate in 2015 passed his bill to give U.S. attorneys the power to prosecute retiree representatives who misuse funds. Lankford collaborated with Democratic Sens. Cory Booker of New Jersey and Mark Warner of Virginia to make permanent the Presidential Innovation Fellows program, which paired outside technology experts and entrepreneurs with high-ranking civil servants to solve challenges facing the public sector.

Lankford has been eager to take assignments on behalf of McConnell. He was a leader among Republicans seeking to reduce from 30 hours to two hours the time available for discussion in the Senate after a majority has voted to close debate on a presidential nomination. After reducing the time for Supreme Court nominees in 2017, the Senate moved in April 2019 to impose those rules for all judicial nominees; two Republicans opposed the otherwise party-line vote.

When Sen. Johnny Isakson of Georgia resigned at the end of 2019 because of poor health, Lankford succeeded him as chairman of the Ethics Committee. That signaled McConnell's trust that Lankford would protect the interests of both Republicans and the Senate and that he would work with others on the bipartisan panel to assure the integrity of senators, when necessary.

Lankford continued to distance himself from Trump's leadership. When the president spoke positively about his meeting with Russian President Vladimir Putin in Helsinki in 2018, Lankford tweeted, "I trust the assessments of Dan Coats, Gina Haspel & their [intelligence] teams more than I trust a former KGB agent." Two months earlier, he said in an interview on MSNBC, "I don't consider the president a role model for my kids. ... I don't speak that way. I don't tweet that way. I don't interact with people that way. I don't treat my staff the way that he treats his staff."

In June 2020, when Trump scheduled his first political rally since large gatherings were halted because of the novel coronavirus, Lankford said that he was among those who gave "encouragement to the president" to change the date of the event: It was set to take place in Tulsa, the site a racial massacre, on Juneteenth, the June 19 holiday that celebrates the end of slavery and is important to many African-Americans.

Facing reelection in 2022 in a state where Democrats have not had a competitive candidate in a Senate race since 1994, Lankford's only potential cause for concern would be a Republican primary.

Kevin Hern (R)

Elected 2018, 2nd full term, b. Dec 04, 1961; Belton, MO; University of AR-Little Rock, B.S., 1986; University of AR-Little Rock, M.B.A., 1999; Evangelical; Married (Tammy Hern); 3 children.

Professional Career: McDonald's national leadership team; chairman, finance committee, OK Turnpike Authority, 2011-2015.

DC Office: 1019 LHOB 20515, 202-225-2211, Fax: 202-225-9187, hern.house.gov

State Offices: Tulsa, 918-935-3222.

Committees: *Ways & Means*: Select Revenue Measures; Social Security; Worker & Family Support.

Almanac Ratings 2019-2020

	Economy	Social	Foreign	Composite
Liberal	25%	14%	6%	15%
Conservative	75%	86%	94%	85%

Key Votes of the 116th Congress

1. U.S./Mex./Can. trade deal	Y	5. Russia sanctions	N	9. Firearms background checks	N
2. First Coronavirus response	N	6. Troops in Syria	Y	10. Spending at the border	Y
3. HEROES Act	N	7. Veto arms sales to Saudis	N	11. Marijuana liberalized rules	N
4. CASH Act	N	8. Defense $$$, veto override	N	12. Electoral College objections	Y

Election Results

Election	Name (Party)	Vote (%)		Cand. Spent	Ind. Exp. Support	Ind. Exp. Oppose
2020 General	Kevin Hern (R).................................	213,700	(64%)	$799,754		$750
	Kojo Asamoa-Caesar (D)................	109,641	(33%)	$171,092		
	Evelyn Rogers (I)...........................	12,130	(4%)			

Prior winning percentages: 2018 (59%)

Republican Kevin Hern of Oklahoma won his first bid for elected office in 2018 after a successful career in business. He positioned himself in that contest as a relative centrist in the competitive primary, and some Republicans criticized him as not sufficiently conservative. But his House votes during his first two years often positioned Hern as the most conservative member of the state's House delegation. He sufficiently impressed House GOP leaders that they rewarded him with a coveted seat on the Ways and Means Committee in 2021.

Hern described his life as a child living in poverty and on government assistance, including food stamps. He got his bachelor's degree from Arkansas Tech University, where he majored in engineering, and an MBA from the University of Arkansas. Early in his professional career, he worked for several companies—including the Rockwell aerospace firm, where he wrote computer programs. His turning point in business came in 1999, when he bought two McDonald's franchises in Muskogee. At the time, he later said, he came home "to a house with no furniture and a sleeping bag as a bed."

Eventually, Hern owned 10 McDonald's restaurants and took a national leadership position with the company, chairing the systems economic team for more than 3,000 franchisees. With his profits, he expanded into other businesses. He took on additional projects, including chairman for four years of the finance committee of the Oklahoma Turnpike Authority and finance committee chairman of the Oklahoma Republican Party.

In the campaign to succeed Republican Rep. Jim Bridenstine, who resigned to become administrator of the National Aeronautics and Space Administration, the crucial contest was the wide-open GOP primary, which featured five candidates. Hern was endorsed by the business-friendly and relatively centrist Republican Main Street Partnership. His chief opponents were Tim Harris, who served 16 years as district attorney for Tulsa County and taught constitutional law, and Andy Coleman, a retired military intelligence officer who was backed by the Club for Growth and other national conservative groups. Harris led the first round of voting with 27 percent of the vote, to 23 percent for Hern and 22 percent for Coleman. Hern qualified for the runoff, with his 858-vote lead over Coleman.

In the runoff, Harris emphasized law-enforcement issues and his experience in government. Hern embraced President Donald Trump, attacked Harris as a "career politician" and called for term limits. Harris voiced reservations about Trump's policies on international trade and said the president "has to temper some of his verbiage," the Tulsa World reported. The Club for Growth ran ads that attacked Hern's past political contributions to Democratic candidates. Hern spent more than $2 million in the primary, including $1.5 million in self-financing; Harris spent about $480,000. Hern won the runoff, 55%-45%. In Tulsa County, where Harris was well-known, Hern took 53 percent. Hern increased his vote by about 17,000 over the primary; Harris's total grew by fewer than 5,000 votes.

Democratic nominee Tim Gilpin, a Tulsa attorney and former state education official, described himself as the "serious candidate." He criticized Trump and Republican handling of issues such as tax cuts and changes to the Affordable Care Act. His campaign struggled financially. Hern won, 59%-41%; in Tulsa County, which cast 80 percent of the vote, Hern was held to 56 percent. The district has not elected a Democrat since 1984.

In the House, Hern showed that he was willing to go his own way. In July 2020, he voted against the Great American Outdoors Act, a bipartisan bill that increased funding for national parks. "Increasing the federal real estate holdings should not be on anyone's to-do list," he said. In September, he was the only Oklahoman in the House to vote against a bill that was intended to prevent employers from discriminating against pregnant workers. The House passed the bill, 329-73.

In July 2020, in an opinion column with the headline "McCongressman Gets a Large Order of PPP," Bloomberg News reported that federal records showed Hern's burger franchises received between $1 million and $2 million from the Paycheck Protection Program, which was created to provide relief to small businesses, including franchises, during the coronavirus pandemic. Earlier, Bloomberg reported that Hern had been one of four members of Congress who wrote to congressional leaders with a request that PPP benefits should be made available to franchises. Hern provided no comment to the columnist.

Hern was reelected without Republican opposition and faced Democratic challenger Kojo Asamoa-Caesar, who founded a leadership academy and whose parents were immigrants from Ghana. He won, 64%-33%.

As the first Oklahoman to serve on the Ways and Means Committee in 20 years, Hern cited his business experience. "I know what it feels like to be on the receiving end of federal regulations and restrictive tax codes, so I believe I can be a unique voice to provide the business owner perspective on Ways and Means," he said.

OK-1: Tulsa Area   **Cook Partisan Voting Index: R+15**

Population		Race and Ethnicity		Income	
Total	809,500	White	71.10%	Median Income	$59,660
Land area (sq. miles)	1,632	Black	8.60%	District Income Rank	269
Pop/ sq mi	496.12	Latino	11.90%	Poverty Rate	13.30%
Born in State	57.70%	Asian	3.30%	With health insurance	86.10%
		Two or more races	8.00%	Cash public assistance	3.00%
Age Groups		Other	8.90%	Food stamp/SNAP	10.60%
Under 18	24.90%				
18-34	22.90%	**Education**		**Work**	
35-64	36.90%	H.S grad or less	36.60%	White Collar	39.40%
Over 64	15.20%	Some college	31.30%	Sales and Service	37.80%
		College Degree, 4 yr	21.20%	Blue Collar	22.80%
Military		Post grad	10.80%	Government	11.20%
Veteran/ Active Duty	7.50%				

2020 Pres. Vote	Trump	202,879	(60%)	Biden	125,905	(37%)			
2016 Pres. Vote	Trump	191,343	(61%)	Clinton	101,757	(33%)	Johnson	18,406	(6%)

Tulsa: The gushers of the 1905 Glenn Pool discovery made Tulsa one of America's oil boomtowns, settled not just by people from the immediate hinterland but also by Midwesterners and New Englanders of Yankee stock. In the 1920s, as its art deco skyscrapers rose on the heights above the Arkansas River, it was still a raw town, but one bent on becoming more cultured. It was optimistic and ready to seek economic change, yet culturally and politically conservative, with a Yankee elite and an American Indian heritage recalled today in one of the nation's best collections of Western art at the Gilcrease Museum—left by oil millionaire Thomas Gilcrease, who was one-eighth Creek Indian. Tulsa, also the home of Oral Roberts University, has remained cosmopolitan and conservative. After forensic archeologists used radar that found that mass graves likely were dug following the Black Wall Street 1921 massacre in which a White mob burned Black neighborhoods and killed more than 300 people in Tulsa, excavation began in April 2020 in an attempt to resolve multiple historical questions about the event.

In recent decades, Tulsa has boomed and occasionally busted. The "Vision 2025" tax of six-tenths of a cent has helped pay for everything from Arkansas River protection work to new university buildings to upgrades at city parks and golf courses. Gathering Place—a 66-acre, $465 million park—is a feature of the downtown area. The American Airlines maintenance center in Tulsa is the largest such facility in the world, with 5,500 employees at the maintenance base, which has added engine service to the workload. The facility services more than 900 aircraft annually at its plant, with 22 buildings over 330 acres. American's presence spurred other aerospace-related development in Tulsa, which has become the base of the Oklahoma Aerospace Alliance. More than 400 aerospace firms in the state have an annual output of about $12 billion, including more than 20,000 workers in Tulsa.

In June 2020, Tulsa became the center of unwanted attention when President Donald Trump scheduled his first campaign rally since the outbreak of the coronavirus. The arena featured large sections of empty seats; plus, an outdoor event was canceled. Several Trump campaign aides tested positive hours before the rally.

The 1st Congressional District of Oklahoma includes Tulsa, Wagoner and Washington counties, and small slices of Rogers and Creek counties—with about 80 percent in Tulsa. The political tradition here is heavily Republican, strengthened in recent decades by opposition to national Democrats' cultural liberalism. Trump got 60 percent of the vote here in 2020, but the 1st ranked only fourth among the five Oklahoma districts in its vote for Trump. In Tulsa County, Trump got 56 percent. It's not likely that Republican presidential candidates will need to worry about Oklahoma any time soon.

Markwayne Mullin (R)

Elected 2012, 5th term, b. Jul 26, 1977; Tulsa, OK; MO Valley College, Att., 1996; OK State University Institute of Technology, Assc. Deg., 2010; Pentecostal; Married (Christie Mullin); 5 children (twins).

Professional Career: Owner, Mullin Plumbing, 1996-present.

DC Office: 2421 RHOB 20515, 202-225-2701, Fax: 202-225-3038, mullin.house.gov

State Offices: Claremore, 918-283-6262; McAlester, 918-423-5951; Muskogee, 918-687-2533.

Committees: *Energy & Commerce*: Communications & Technology; Environment & Climate Change; Health. *Permanent Select on Intelligence*: Defense Intelligence & Warfighter Support; Strategic Technologies & Advanced Research.

Group Ratings

	ADA	ACLU	AFL-CIO	LCV	COC	HAFA	ACU	CFG	FRC
2020	**	24%	**	5%	-	92%	84%	**	-
2019	0%	C	25%	0%	75%	C	84%	92%	100%

Almanac Ratings 2019-2020

	Economy	Social	Foreign	Composite
Liberal	25%	35%	12%	24%
Conservative	75%	65%	88%	76%

Key Votes of the 116th Congress

1. U.S./Mex./Can. trade deal Y	5. Russia sanctions N	9. Firearms background checks N
2. First Coronavirus response N/A	6. Troops in Syria N	10. Spending at the border N/A
3. HEROES Act N	7. Veto arms sales to Saudis N	11. Marijuana liberalized rules N/A
4. CASH Act N/A	8. Defense $$$, veto override N/A	12. Electoral College objections Y

Election Results

Election	Name (Party)	Vote (%)		Cand. Spent	Ind. Exp. Support	Ind. Exp. Oppose
2020 General	Markwayne Mullin (R)	216,511	(75%)	$1,280,719		
	Danyell Lanier (D)	63,472	(22%)	$35,677		
	Richie Castaldo (L)	8,544	(3%)	$900		
2020 Primary	Markwayne Mullin (R)	53,149	(80%)			
	Joseph Silk (R)	8,445	(13%)			
	Rhonda Hopkins (R)	4,917	(7%)			

Prior winning percentages: 2018 (65%), 2016 (71%), 2014 (70%), 2012 (57%)

Republican plumber Markwayne Mullin, elected in 2012, has been an outspoken conservative, but a usually reliable vote for the GOP leadership. As a member of the Energy and Commerce Committee, he has pursued rural issues and various topics of interest to Native Americans. A fitness buff, he has led early morning workout sessions for a devoted bipartisan following of House members.

Mullin was born in Tulsa and grew up in Westville, a small town on the Arkansas line, as the youngest of seven children. His father ran a small plumbing business, which Mullin took over at age 19 after briefly attending Missouri Valley College. He expanded the company from six employees to more than 100. He hosted a local talk show advising callers on home repair. Mullin, a Cherokee, has operated the Oklahoma Fight Club in Broken Arrow, a training center for jujitsu and mixed martial arts. He earned an associate's degree in business from the Oklahoma State University Institute of Technology in Okmulgee.

Mullin was one of six Republican candidates for the open seat of retiring Rep. Dan Boren, who was one of the House's most conservative Democrats. Arguing that it was "time to fire Barack Obama," he became the frontrunner. His fundraising outpaced that of his GOP rivals, although a good portion was self-financed. In the primary, he coasted to a first-place finish with 42 percent of the vote. In the runoff, state Rep. George Faught accused Mullin of carpet bagging when property records showed he had claimed homestead tax exemptions in Wagoner County, outside the district. Mullin labeled Faught a career politician and won the runoff handily, 57%-43%.

In September, news broke that Mullin Plumbing had received about $370,000 in federal economic stimulus money for housing projects with the Cherokee and Muscogee nations. Mullin had campaigned heavily against Obama's stimulus program, and Democratic nominee Rob Wallace accused him of acting like an "out-of-touch, typical Washington politician." Mullin claimed not to know that the projects got stimulus money, but documents from the Cherokee Nation contradicted that assertion. Attacks on Mullin's business practices mostly fell flat. He outspent Wallace, $1.7 million to $1.2 million, and won, 57%-38%.

On Energy and Commerce, Mullin has provided an "Oklahoma business owner perspective" on its broad agenda of regulatory and health care issues. He took on an unusual adversary, when he filed a bill in 2016 to require the rapidly growing Ultimate Fighting Championship to disclose more information about its finances, including how it handles its martial-arts competitors. He also sponsored a bill to extend safety protections to those fighters. In 2017, the House passed his bill to transfer authority over pipelines and power transmission lines that cross international borders from the State Department to the Federal Energy Regulatory Commission; the Senate did not act on the measure. Mullin enacted a bill the following year to extend health coverage in sparsely served rural areas.

Mullin has helped enact several bills related to Indian tribes. In September 2020, Congress sent to President Donald Trump legislation that ordered the Justice Department to develop guidelines to prepare cases involving missing or murdered Native Americans, especially women. In December, the House passed a bill that Mullin cosponsored with Democratic Rep. Tom O'Halleran of Arizona to assure that tribal governments have access to federal assistance to advance their energy development initiatives.

Mullin has taken a personal approach to his work. He used his fitness expertise to bond with members from both parties, including interval training exercises at the House gym and the formation with Democratic Rep. Donald Payne of New Jersey of the Men's Health Caucus.

Mullin's initial pledge to serve only three terms in the House caused political complications. In 2016, he had a competitive primary against Jarrin Jackson, a West Point graduate who served two tours of duty in Afghanistan. Jackson criticized Mullin for having "only voted to grow government" and for perhaps backing away from his earlier campaign pledge to serve only three terms in the House. Three months before the primary, Mullin had issued a brief statement to The Oklahoman that he and his wife "will continue to seek the Lord's guidance and do what is best for our family and the 2nd District of Oklahoma" on his term-limits pledge. Sens. Jim Inhofe and James Lankford endorsed Mullin. He won the primary, 63%-37%.

In 2018, Mullin said he had found that his term-limits pledge was a "mistake" and "I'm going to learn from" it. With the support of Trump, Mullin added, he can "make a difference" in Washington. Jackson ran again; not surprisingly, he attacked Mullin for abandoning his pledge. Mullin spent $1.7 million, nearly 10 times as much as Jackson, and won 54%-25%. In the general election, Democrat Jason Nichols, the mayor of Tahlequah, ran an active campaign, but did not raise the term-limits issue. Mullin won easily, 65%-30%.

Two years later, against low-profile challengers, Mullin won the primary with 80 percent and the general election with 75 percent. He has entrenched himself in a formerly Democratic stronghold.

OK-2: East Oklahoma

Cook Partisan Voting Index: R+29

Population		Race and Ethnicity		Income	
Total	747,337	White	65.90%	Median Income	$45,207
Land area (sq. miles)	20,995	Black	3.20%	District Income Rank	416
Pop/ sq mi	35.6	Latino	5.70%	Poverty Rate	19.80%
Born in State	61.70%	Asian	0.70%	With health insurance	81.70%
		Two or more races	11.00%	Cash public assistance	3.30%
Age Groups		Other	19.30%	Food stamp/SNAP	15.60%
Under 18	23.10%				
18-34	20.80%	**Education**		**Work**	
35-64	36.80%	H.S grad or less	50.80%	White Collar	30.10%
Over 64	19.30%	Some college	31.80%	Sales and Service	39.70%
		College Degree, 4 yr	12.10%	Blue Collar	30.20%
Military		Post grad	5.40%	Government	20.20%
Veteran/ Active Duty	9.20%				

2020 Pres. Vote	Trump	221,123	(76%)	Biden	64,353	(22%)		
2016 Pres. Vote	Trump	198,155	(73%)	Clinton	62,022	(23%)	Johnson	11,667	(4%)

Tulsa Suburbs, Muskogee: The land that is now northeast Oklahoma used to be Indian territory, the place where in the 1830s the Five Civilized Tribes were driven from Georgia and Alabama over the Trail of Tears. A sizable minority here report their race as American Indian. The Native American identity is highest in the hilly counties west of the Ozarks of Arkansas, where county names —Cherokee, Osage, Sequoyah—recall the Civilized Tribes. The street signs in scenic Tahlequah, the Cherokee capital since 1839, are written in both English and Cherokee. The Creek Nation chose its tribal site in Okmulgee in the belief that tornadoes would not strike the area; history has proven the choice correct so far. Tornadoes have done minimal damage here. Bicyclists from the Cherokee Nation have an annual three-week trip for 950 miles across seven states to retrace the Trail of Tears. South of Indian country is Oklahoma's Little Dixie, settled between 1889 and 1907 by White Southerners, most of them poor. In July 2020, the Supreme Court issued a historic decision that much of eastern Oklahoma remains on tribal land. The 5-4 opinion, which might take years to fully decipher and implement, could mean—among other things—that criminal justice authority in the area, including much of Tulsa, is subject to Native American rulings. As a result of the opinion, written by Justice Neil Gorsuch, "the boundaries of Muscogee (Creek) Nation still exist—meaning the tribe, not the state of Oklahoma, holds some key jurisdictional powers," the Tulsa World wrote.

This pleasant land of gentle hills and man-made lakes recently has grown at a healthy pace with population spread from Tulsa. Interstate highways and turnpikes connect people to jobs in more-vibrant metropolitan areas, while the lakes have spurred resort and retirement communities. The largest city here is Muskogee, an old railroad community with a manufacturing economy that had slowed in recent years; despite efforts at local revival, the population of both Muskogee city and county dipped 5 percent and 4 percent, respectively, from 2010 to 2019. The largest local employer is a Georgia-Pacific paper mill, with 800 workers. Natural-gas production has increased in this area, which is part of the Anadarko Basin. In 2017, a local field was the third most active in the nation, behind two in Texas. In November 2020, the Muscogee Nation broke ground on a $10 million meat-processing facility in Glenpool, with assistance from federal coronavirus relief.

The 2nd Congressional District includes eastern Oklahoma, except for the Tulsa area. It borders four states and takes in Muskogee; Claremore, Will Rogers' hometown; and McAlester, hometown of former House Speaker Carl Albert. The median income here is the lowest of the five districts in Oklahoma and in the bottom 10 percent nationwide. McAlester is the site of a massive Army ammunition plant that manufactures non-nuclear bombs and is the largest local employer. The plant has worked to upgrade and extend the life of 1,400 Stinger missiles, which can be shoulder-launched or mounted on a vehicle or helicopter. The area was ancestrally Democratic. Since the retirement in 1976 of Albert, a New Deal Democrat who presided over the House during the Watergate scandal, the area has become as solidly Republican as most of Oklahoma. In 2020, Donald Trump won the presidential vote, 76%-22%, his best district in the state and among his top two percent nationwide.

Frank Lucas (R)

Elected 1994, 14th term, b. Jan 06, 1960; Cheyenne, OK; OK State University, B.S., 1982; Baptist; Married (Lynda Bradshaw Lucas); 3 children; 2 grandchildren.

Elected Office: OK House, 1988-1994.

Professional Career: Farmer & rancher.

DC Office: 2405 RHOB 20515, 202-225-5565, Fax: 202-225-8696, lucas.house.gov

State Offices: Yukon, 405-373-1958.

Committees: *Financial Services*: Consumer Protection & Financial Institutions; Diversity & Inclusion. *Science, Space & Technology (RMM)*.

Group Ratings

	ADA	ACLU	AFL-CIO	LCV	COC	HAFA	ACU	CFG	FRC
2020	**	15%	**	10%	-	81%	85%	**	-
2019	5%	C	32%	7%	92%	C	86%	70%	100%

Almanac Ratings 2019-2020

	Economy	Social	Foreign	Composite
Liberal	28%	20%	30%	26%
Conservative	72%	80%	70%	74%

Key Votes of the 116th Congress

1. U.S./Mex./Can. trade deal	Y	5. Russia sanctions	Y	9. Firearms background checks	N
2. First Coronavirus response	Y	6. Troops in Syria	Y	10. Spending at the border	N/A
3. HEROES Act	N/A	7. Veto arms sales to Saudis	N	11. Marijuana liberalized rules	N
4. CASH Act	Y	8. Defense $$$, veto override	Y	12. Electoral College objections	Y

Election Results

Election	Name (Party)	Vote (%)		Cand. Spent	Ind. Exp. Support	Ind. Exp. Oppose
2020 General	Frank Lucas (R).....................................	242,677	(78%)	$622,460		
	Zoe Midyett (D)............................	66,501	(22%)			

Prior winning percentages: 2018 (74%), 2016 (78%), 2014 (79%), 2012 (75%), 2010 (78%), 2008 (70%), 2006 (68%), 2004 (82%), 2002 (76%), 2000 (59%), 1998 (65%), 1996 (64%), 1994 special (54%), 1994 (70%)

Republican Frank Lucas, who won a 1994 special election, is a soft-spoken, unflashy farmer and rancher who has become a savvy lawmaker in a party where such traits are diminishing. As chairman of the Agriculture Committee until 2015, he eventually found a way to bridge deal-oriented lawmakers from farm states and budget-conscious conservatives. After being term-limited as chairman, he moved to new niches at other committees. In the minority, as the senior Republican on the Science, Space and Technology Committee, he has made some bipartisan moves.

Lucas' family roots in western Oklahoma extend more than 100 years; he owns a farm and cattle ranch in Roger Mills County that features about 100 cattle, mostly adult females. He studied agricultural economics at Oklahoma State University, where he was active in the College Republicans and student government. He was elected to the Oklahoma House at age 28 after losing two races. He shared an office there with Jim Reese, who became the state's secretary and commissioner of agriculture. "He's not a showboat," Reese told The New York Times in 2012. "He just goes about doing his work and tries to work with everybody and is not about getting credit for himself."

He ran for Congress in a special election after veteran conservative Democratic Rep. Glenn English resigned to head the National Rural Electric Cooperative Association. In the primary, he trailed state Sen. Brooks Douglass, who campaigned from his Oklahoma City base, 36%-34%. In the runoff, Lucas ridiculed "some Johnny-come-lately dressed up like a drugstore cowboy" and carried the rural areas to win 56%-44%.Then, he faced Dan Webber, the 27-year-old press secretary for Democratic Sen. David Boren. Lucas ran an ad depicting the Capitol and saying, "This is where Dan Webber has worked his entire adult life." The ad displayed a picture of Oklahoma farmland and said, "This is where Frank Lucas has worked his entire adult life." Lucas won 54%-46%. At age 34, he settled in for a lengthy tenure.

Lucas' voting record is mostly conservative. As shown by his Almanac vote ratings, he has occasionally broken from conservative orthodoxy on economic matters, chiefly to support parochial interests. He has voted against GOP amendments to abolish or cut funding for federal programs such as rural airport subsidies and the Economic Development Administration.

For many years, his chief base was the Agriculture Committee. On the 2002 farm bill, Lucas helped to unravel the 1996 Freedom to Farm Act and its rollback of government subsidies, although he had once embraced the law and its conservative philosophical underpinnings. Lucas helped write provisions to control erosion, aid farmers hit by drought, and protect air and water quality. In the minority during work on the 2008 farm bill, Lucas strongly opposed an overhaul of farm programs as "a threat to the nutrition of the whole, entire world," and he mostly succeeded in preserving subsidies for his district, which ranked 14th in subsidies between 1995 and 2009. He has been a proponent of government support for alternative fuels, particularly switch grass.

As Ag chairman in 2011, he found himself leading a committee full of freshmen and new members who did not share his bipartisan leanings. He worked closely with Agriculture's ranking Democrat Collin Peterson of Minnesota to report a five-year farm bill from the committee in 2012. But the measure never came to a vote that year in the full House. Some conservatives wanted deeper cuts to the food stamp program, which Democrats resisted. The delays frustrated Lucas, who labored for months to strike a deal acceptable to House GOP leaders, whom he referred to as "the management."

In 2013, the legislation he managed to get to the floor looked to be a conservatives' dream: It cut spending, including $20 billion from the food stamp program, and it had bipartisan support from farm-state Democrats. Discontented conservatives passed an amendment to give states the option of imposing work requirements on food stamp recipients, a move that shattered the delicate political coalition behind the bill. Despite a desperate last-minute plea by Lucas on the House floor, the farm bill failed, 195-234. Sixty-two Republicans voted against it while only 24 Democrats voted for it. "It shouldn't be this hard to pass a farm bill," he lamented

When he finally passed the bill in 2014, which Lucas called his "single biggest accomplishment" as chairman, he said its "fundamental guise" was that it became an insurance measure in place of the direct payment program for farm commodities. The House passed the bill, 251-166, with bipartisan support. After term limits forced him to step down as Agriculture chairman in 2015, he remained active on the committee. When a final deal was reached in 2018, he praised it for "protecting the safety net for producers" and "maintaining critical conservation programs." Then, he quit the committee. But he still knew the issues and he occasionally intervened on farm issues, as when he added to the yearend spending bill in December 2020 a provision to protect farm interests, including cattle producers, who suffered in the pandemic.

Lucas found himself, like other term-limited House GOP chairmen, looking for opportunities to remain relevant. As vice chairman of the Science, Space and Technology Committee. Lucas shaped a bipartisan bill to improve weather forecasting and research capabilities (useful tools for farmers), which was enacted in 2017. With his Democratically Peterson, Lucas in 2015 passed a bill to create a science advisory board at the Environmental Protection Agency.

As senior Republican on the Science Committee in 2019, he said he wanted more data collected from satellites to chart short-term and long-term weather. That information would be useful to energy entrepreneurs as well as farmers. With what he called "a solid relationship" with Democratic Rep. Eddie Bernice Johnson of Texas, who chaired the committee, Lucas filed bills to combat sexual harassment in science and engineering, and to improve water conservation and resources for clean water. The House passed each bill, with some revisions.

In his efforts to encourage cutting-edge research for scientific and technological development, Lucas grew especially interested in the use of carbon-capture technology to produce natural gas that was environmentally cleaner. In July 2019, he filed a bipartisan bill to achieve that objective. "This bill will expand early-stage research and development of carbon-capture technologies to make natural gas an even cleaner energy source," he said.

Meanwhile, Lucas has become the number-two Republican on the Financial Services Committee behind Rep. Patrick McHenry and could move to the top slot on that panel within a few years.

Lucas has been reelected by wide margins—winning at least 67 percent since 2000. Despite the unhappiness of national conservative groups, he has not faced serious competition in GOP primaries.

The Club for Growth threatened but failed to recruit a primary opponent in 2014 after he scored in the bottom-third among Republicans in the anti-tax group's legislative ratings. He said the criticism didn't bother him. "Any time I have to choose between the influences of D.C. political groups and my fellow Oklahomans, I will always side with my fellow Oklahomans," he told the Tulsa World.

OK-3: Western and Central Oklahoma   Cook Partisan Voting Index: R+29

Population		Race and Ethnicity		Income	
Total	782,091	White	79.80%	Median Income	$54,629
Land area (sq. miles)	34,117	Black	3.60%	District Income Rank	336
Pop/ sq mi	22.92	Latino	10.60%	Poverty Rate	15.10%
Born in State	63.90%	Asian	1.40%	With health insurance	86.90%
		Two or more races	6.00%	Cash public assistance	2.50%
Age Groups		Other	9.20%	Food stamp/SNAP	11.40%
Under 18	24.10%				
18-34	23.00%	Education		Work	
35-64	36.40%	H.S grad or less	47.00%	White Collar	33.20%
Over 64	16.40%	Some college	29.30%	Sales and Service	38.00%
		College Degree, 4 yr	15.80%	Blue Collar	28.80%
Military		Post grad	7.90%	Government	18.00%
Veteran/ Active Duty	8.60%				

2020 Pres. Vote	Trump	232,416	(75%)	Biden	72,141	(23%)		
2016 Pres. Vote	Trump	216,078	(74%)	Clinton	61,179	(21%)	Johnson 16,160	(6%)

Suburbs of Oklahoma City and Tulsa: Settled at the turn of the 20th century, western Oklahoma is a fertile land forever at the mercy of the elements. The western plains are scorching hot under the summer sun and blown frozen by bitter winter winds. Visitors to the Tall grass Prairie Preserve, maintained by the Nature Conservancy near Pawhuska, can experience what settlers found when they arrived here: a swaying ocean of 10-foot-high grasses filled with insects emitting a dull, incessant roar. Many rural counties here are not much more populated than they were 100 years ago.

Today, local entrepreneurs see the possibility of economic revival in another abundant natural resource: the wind. Kansas company TradeWind has purchased multiple wind farm properties in western Oklahoma. As of 2018, 11 of those projects had begun operations. Two of those wind farms have long-term contracts with large corporations: Anheuser-Busch, T-Mobile and Google. Developers proposed a transmission line that could transform the prairie into a national wind energy hub. In 2019, Oklahoma ranked second in the nation after Texas for electricity generated from wind and was third behind Iowa and Kansas in wind's share of power in each state, the Energy Information Administration reported. Wind supplied more than 35 percent of Oklahoma's net generation, more than any other source. Solar power has increased in the Panhandle, with a subsidiary of Arkansas Electric Cooperatives owning a 1-megawatt solar project in Hooker. The region is home to the world's largest plot of switch grass, and there are hopes that it too can become a profitable source of alternative energy.

The 3rd Congressional District includes Oklahoma's western plains and nearly half of the state's land. It includes the university town of Stillwater, and Osage County, site of the state's lone Indian reservation. A few of the southern counties, settled by farmers crossing the Red River from Texas, are ancestrally Democratic. Farmers coming south from Kansas settled most of these plains, and they were heavily Republican. In February 2019, Altus Air Force Base became the home of a squadron of KC-46 refueling tankers. To the west in the Panhandle is Beaver County, which claims to be the cow-chip-throwing capital of the world. The Hispanic population has grown to 26 percent, with many moving here to work on hog farms and in meatpacking plants. One of the largest operations is Seaboard Corp.'s plant in Guymon, which has more than 3,300 employees. In February 2020, Seaboard announced plans to spend $100 million to upgrade its facility in the city of Guymon, which is 58 percent Hispanic. Texas County, a wheat-growing area in the Panhandle, is 47 percent Hispanic, the highest percentage in the state. For many elections, this was the most Republican district in the state. But it has been overtaken by the 2nd District. Still, President Donald Trump got 75 percent of the vote here in 2020. In several counties in the thinly populated Panhandle, his vote exceeded 90 percent.

Tom Cole (R)

Elected 2002, 10th term, b. Apr 28, 1949; Shreveport, LA; Grinnell College, B.A., 1971; Institute for Historical Research - London, B.A., 1972; Yale University, M.A., 1974; University of London - Queens College, 1978; University of OK, Ph.D., 1984; Methodist; Married (Ellen Elizabeth Decker Cole); 1 child.

Elected Office: OK Senate, 1988-1991.

Professional Career: Staff, U.S. Rep. Mickey Edwards, 1982-1984; OK GOP Chairman, 1985-1989; Executive Director, NRCC, 1991-1995; OK Secretary of st., 1995-1999; Chief of Staff, RNC, 1999-2000; Political consultant, 2000-2002.

DC Office: 2207 RHOB 20515, 202-225-6165, Fax: 202-225-3512, cole.house.gov
State Offices: Ada, 580-436-5375; Lawton, 580-357-2131; Norman, 405-329-6500.

Committees: *Appropriations*: Defense; Labor, Health & Human Services, Education & Related Agencies (RMM). *Rules (RMM)*: Ex Officio membership on all subcommittees.

Group Ratings

	ADA	ACLU	AFL-CIO	LCV	COC	HAFA	ACU	CFG	FRC
2020	**	19%	**	10%	-	76%	77%	**	-
2019	10%	C	38%	17%	99%	C	78%	58%	91%

Almanac Ratings 2019-2020

	Economy	Social	Foreign	Composite
Liberal	38%	38%	34%	37%
Conservative	62%	62%	66%	63%

Key Votes of the 116th Congress

1. U.S./Mex./Can. trade deal	Y	5. Russia sanctions	N	9. Firearms background checks N
2. First Coronavirus response	Y	6. Troops in Syria	Y	10. Spending at the border	Y
3. HEROES Act	N	7. Veto arms sales to Saudis	N	11. Marijuana liberalized rules	N
4. CASH Act	Y	8. Defense $$$, veto override	Y	12. Electoral College objections Y

Election Results

Election	Name (Party)	Vote (%)		Cand. Spent	Ind. Exp. Support	Ind. Exp. Oppose
2020 General	Tom Cole (R)	213,096	(68%)	$2,444,414		
	Mary Brannon (D)	90,459	(29%)	$3		
	Bob White (L)	10,803	(3%)			
2020 Primary	Tom Cole (R)	55,699	(76%)			
	Terry Neese (R)	24,828	(37%)			
	James Taylor (R)	11,081	(37%)			
	Trevor Sipes (R)	4,357	(6%)			

Prior winning percentages: 2018 (63%), 2016 (70%), 2014 (71%), 2012 (68%), 2010 (unopposed), 2008 (66%), 2006 (65%), 2004 (78%), 2002 (54%)

Tom Cole, first elected in 2002, is a politically savvy and experienced Republican who has become a key ally of House GOP leaders. On the Appropriations subcommittee that handles discretionary spending for health and education programs, he has been an active policy leader for the GOP. Following the 2018 election, he failed in his bid to become the senior Republican on Appropriations, but got an impressive consolation prize: the top GOP slot on the traffic-cop Rules Committee, while retaining his prime spending post. Cole shows little restraint in offering his candid assessments—with zingers directed at both parties, as warranted.

Cole grew up in Moore, south of Oklahoma City. He is a fifth-generation Oklahoman, and his mother was a state representative and senator. He is a member of the Chickasaw Nation tribe; more than half of the nation's Chickasaw Indians live in his district. Until they were joined by two Democratic women in 2019, Oklahoma GOP colleague Markwayne Mullin and Cole were the only

Native Americans in Congress. Cole's father served in the Air Force and later worked at Tinker Air Force Base. Cole graduated from Grinnell College, got a master's degree at Yale University, and a Ph.D. in British history at the University of Oklahoma, studying for a year at the University of London. From 1985 to 1989, he was the Oklahoma Republican Party chairman. In 1988, he was elected to the state Senate.

He moved to Washington in 1991 to become executive director of the National Republican Congressional Committee, and over the next decade held jobs as the appointed Oklahoma secretary of state, president of a polling and political consulting firm in Oklahoma City, and chief of staff for the Republican National Committee during the 2000 election. When the House seat opened, Cole was the early frontrunner, though he faced formidable opposition from attorney Marc Nuttle. The two shared positions on most issues and extensive party connections. Nuttle had been Cole's predecessor at the NRCC. In the showdown between the strategists, Cole won 60%-33%.

In the general election, he faced former state Senate Majority Leader Darryl Roberts, who appealed to the "yellow dog" Democratic tradition in the Red River counties. Cole countered by linking Roberts to past Democratic presidential nominees he had supported, and described him as "pro-tax, pro-abortion, and pro-lawsuit." Cole won 54%-46% and has been reelected with ease.

Cole has a voting record that usually fits with mainstream conservatives. From his plum seat on the Appropriations Committee, he tends to the needs of his district's military installations and supports federal programs that help his constituents. In the wake of the influence-peddling scandal involving Republican lobbyist Jack Abramoff, who represented several tribes, Cole strongly opposed the proposed limits on the right of tribes to contribute to political campaigns. In 2018, he continued his efforts to protect Native American rights by enacting a bill that expanded the definition of eligibility for tribal membership.

In late 2013, Cole was one of four House Republicans appointed by Speaker John Boehner to a conference committee seeking to end the partisan brinkmanship that had led to a 16-day government shutdown in October. Working with then-Budget Committee Chairman Paul Ryan, Cole was a skillful conciliator trusted by mainstream Republicans and conservative enough to maintain credibility with the restive tea party faction. Earlier, during the late 2012 negotiations over tax and spending to avoid the so-called "fiscal cliff," he urged his party to accept a tax-cut extension for all but the highest-earning Americans. A profile in Politico that October likened him to "the friendly uncle sent out to smoke a cigar and explain to the neighbors what all the noise is about in the basement."

For four years, Cole was an Appropriations "cardinal" as chairman of the Subcommittee on Labor, Health and Human Services, Education and Related Agencies. In recent years, that spending bill typically made little progress toward agreement with the Senate and instead became part of a status quo "continuing resolution" in the new fiscal year. With Republican Sen. Roy Blunt of Missouri, a Cole ally when he served in the House, serving as chairman of the counterpart Senate panel, they were successful in reaching House-Senate consensus on those major spending categories. Their agreement in 2018 was the first time since 1996 that their bill was enacted—with bipartisan support—before the start of the fiscal year. Cole called it "a monumental moment," though Republicans lost House control five weeks later.

In a sign of his increasing value to Ryan and GOP leaders, Cole was named in 2017 as vice chairman of the leadership-driven Rules Committee. Along with his seat on the Budget Committee, where he also applied his political and parliamentary skills, he became the eyes and ears—and occasionally a gentle enforcer—for Republican strategists. Following the 2018 election, Kevin McCarthy, House GOP leader, selected Cole to fill the vacancy as top Rules Committee Republican, though in the minority. Earlier, he was unsuccessful in his bid to take the top post at Appropriations. He lost to Kay Granger of Texas, who had more seniority, plus the support of the influential Texas delegation. Granger named Cole as the vice ranking member of the committee and he remained as the senior Republican on the Labor-HHS panel.

Campaign politics have been a longstanding part of Cole's portfolio in the House. Following the dismal 2006 election for Republicans, he became chairman of the NRCC, where he had cut his teeth as a political strategist years earlier. He expanded the playing field of competitive seats, but his tenure was a difficult time for the GOP. The party suffered a rough transition to the minority with many retirements, and the committee was $19 million in debt. The party lost 24 seats during the cycle.

Cole found his way back into Boehner's good graces through aggressive fundraising, plus his combination of legislative skills and political instincts. He called Republicans who voted against Boehner for Speaker in 2015 "pretty unprofessional and very disappointing." Later, both Ryan and McCarthy tapped him as a skillful legislative tactician.

With the House GOP's return to the minority, he offered plenty of second guessing of the Democrats' legislative actions. When Speaker Nancy Pelosi negotiated details of the $3 trillion coronavirus-relief bill with Treasury Secretary Steven Mnuchin and then struggled to win House passage in May 2020, Cole said the deal was "crafted behind closed doors and without any Republican input at all." In September, he called the failure to include farm assistance in another spending bill "an unfortunate and unnecessary outcome." In July, he said placing public-health agencies on emergency spending was a bad precedent.

He occasionally clashed with Trump. In March 2020, when the coronavirus struck the United States with many casualties, Cole said the administration failed to heed his advice in 2017 not to pursue their plan to reduce funds for public-health agencies to monitor pandemics and other disease outbreaks. Asked in August whether he shared Trump's concern about the prospect of election fraud, Cole said election administrators are "a very able and honorable group of public servants."

But Cole stuck with Trump on one controversial topic. In January 2021, he voiced an apparent lack of enthusiasm as he joined other congressional Republicans who sought to challenge the Electoral College results, saying that he voted against certification "on behalf of my constituents." He added: "They have asked me to express their concerns with my vote on the floor today, and as their representative, I intend to do so."

OK-4: South-Central Oklahoma　　　　　　　　　　**Cook Partisan Voting Index: R+20**

Population		Race and Ethnicity		Income	
Total	792,928	White	75.10%	Median Income	$59,463
Land area (sq. miles)	9,777	Black	7.10%	District Income Rank	273
Pop/ sq mi	81.1	Latino	8.80%	Poverty Rate	12.50%
Born in State	60.10%	Asian	2.40%	With health insurance	88.60%
		Two or more races	7.50%	Cash public assistance	2.50%
Age Groups		Other	7.80%	Food stamp/SNAP	9.50%
Under 18	23.10%				
18-34	25.20%	**Education**		**Work**	
35-64	36.40%	H.S grad or less	42.10%	White Collar	39.10%
Over 64	15.40%	Some college	32.10%	Sales and Service	37.00%
		College Degree, 4 yr	16.50%	Blue Collar	24.00%
Military		Post grad	9.10%	Government	21.30%
Veteran/ Active Duty	13.80%				

2020 Pres. Vote	Trump	207,217	(66%)	Biden	101,121	(32%)		
2016 Pres. Vote	Trump	194,160	(66%)	Clinton	83,648	(28%)	Johnson	17,617 (6%)

Parts of Oklahoma City, Norman: In the years after 1900, the brown hills west of Oklahoma City and north of the Red River suddenly filled up with farmers riding north from Texas, past the quenched green lands of the east toward the bare pasturelands of the west. The first settlers here arrived just as the buffalo were dying out, down from an estimated 60 million animals to no more than 1,000. So in 1901, Republican President William McKinley established the nation's first wildlife preserve in the Wichita Mountains, 25 miles northwest of Lawton. Fifteen bison were donated by the New York Zoological Society and arrived at the preserve via rail in 1907—a major factor in the survival of the species. Today, this habitat supports grazing for Rocky Mountain elk, white-tailed deer and Texas longhorn cattle.

Government has played a role in the survival of the people, too. Norman, which housed the world's first school of petroleum geology, is now home to the National Weather Center. Tinker Air Force Base in southern Oklahoma City and the Army Field Artillery School at Fort Sill in Lawton are major facilities. Tinker will provide maintenance for the new fleet of B-21 Raider stealth bombers (replacing the B-1 and B-2), when they become operational in the mid-2020s. In 2020, the base had a total of 26,000 military and civilian employees, the largest employer in the state. With 125,000 people, a growth of 13 percent from 2010 to 2019, Norman is the third-largest city in Oklahoma and the home of the University of Oklahoma, with booming commercial and residential development underway. In 2015, 72 percent of voters approved the Norman Forward initiative, with $148 million of capital improvements financed by bonds and a half-cent increase in the sales tax for 15 years. In 2018, the Norman city council agreed on a transition to 100 percent renewable energy by 2035. In the summer of 2020, the debate over police reform reached Norman, with *intense divisions over a city council proposal to reduce spending for the police department. At football-crazed OU, the cancellation of each home game because of the coronavirus pandemic cost an estimated $3.6 million in direct business sales.

The 4th Congressional District of Oklahoma begins smack dab in the middle of the state not far from the capitol in Oklahoma City, and spreads south and west to cover half of Oklahoma's Red River Valley. Demographically, this district is becoming more suburban, but the cultural tone remains countrified. Norman-based Cleveland County is about 40 percent of the population; a snip of Oklahoma County is less than 10 percent. Lawton-based Comanche County is another 10 percent. The area is at the heart of Tornado Alley. Moore, outside Oklahoma City, has been the site of several deadly strikes, including one in 1999 that remains the strongest ever recorded. In 2013, an EF-5 tornado struck Moore, killing 24 people, damaging at least 12,000 buildings, and leveling entire neighborhoods; its estimated $2 billion in damage placed it among the costliest tornados in the nation's history. Ancestrally, this is Democratic country. Norman, Lawton and the Oklahoma City outskirts have voted solidly Republican since the 1990s, though some of the suburban and campus enclaves limit the GOP vote. In the three presidential elections from 2012 to 2020, the Republican vote ranged from 65 percent to 67 percent.

Stephanie Bice (R)

Elected 2020, 1st term, b. Nov 11, 1973; Oklahoma City, OK; OK State University, B.S., 1995; Catholic; Married (Geoffrey Bice); 2 children.

Elected Office: OK Senate, 2014-2020.

Professional Career: Marketing Manager, IT services company, 2004-2013; Director of Business Development, digital marketing company, 2013-2015; Assistant Majority Floor Leader, OK State Senate, 2017-2020.

DC Office: 1223 LHOB 20515, 202-225-2132, bice.house.gov

State Offices: Oklahoma City, 405-300-6890.

Committees: *Armed Services*: Cyber, Innovative Technologies & Information Systems; Military Personnel. *Science, Space & Technology*: Environment (RMM).

Election Results

Election	Name (Party)	Vote (%)		Cand. Spent	Ind. Exp. Support	Ind. Exp. Oppose
2020 General	Stephanie Bice (R)	158,191	(52%)	$3,429,098	$1,439,322	$7,067,435
	Kendra Horn (D)	145,658	(48%)	$6,211,197	$747,980	$7,282,440
2020 Primary	Stephanie Bice (R)	17,292	(25%)			
	David Hill (R)	12,922	(19%)			
	Janet Barresi (R)	6,799	(10%)			
2020 Primary Runoff	Stephanie Bice (R)	27,402	(53%)			
	Terry Neese (R)	24,369	(47%)			

Republican Stephanie Bice in 2020 returned Oklahoma to its normalcy of GOP dominance, as she won back the seat that Kendra Horn had taken for one term. Bice, the first Iranian-American elected to Congress, brought legislative experience and an insider perspective.

A native of Oklahoma City, Bice got her bachelor's degree in marketing from Oklahoma State University. She worked eight years for her family's technology company and later was vice president of business development for Smirk New Media, a marketing agency in Oklahoma City that helped clients to manage their online presence.

Elected to the state Senate in 2014, Bice chaired its Finance Committee and was assistant floor leader for Republicans. She led efforts to impose spending controls in state government by requiring legislative approval of line-item budgets for the largest state agencies. She claimed credit for overhauling the state's liquor laws to permit on-site sales by local breweries and distilleries, plus sales in grocery stores. Those laws had not been updated since Oklahoma repealed statewide prohibition in 1959. "This was never about alcohol," she told The Oklahoman after enactment of her bill. "This was always about the economy and jobs," with an estimated 5,000 new workers.

In the nine-candidate Republican primary for the House seat in 2020, the frontrunners with 25 and 36 percent of the vote, respectively, were Bice and Terry Neese, a businesswoman who had been the Republican nominee for lieutenant governor in 1990. Each spent more than $1 million in competing for the nomination. The Club for Growth spent an additional $1 million on behalf of Neese. Bice won the runoff, 53%-47%. Neese led in the two outlying counties, but Bice took 55 percent of the vote in Oklahoma County, which cast nearly 90 percent of the total.

Horn, the first Democrat to hold a House district in the state since Dan Boren retired in 2012, was one of the most unexpected Democrats elected in 2018. Her challenge to Republican Rep. Steve Russell was largely ignored by national Democratic groups and political pundits. She ran an energetic campaign that took advantage of voter unhappiness with state Republicans. Russell, who left more than $300,000 in his campaign account on Election Day, apparently was surprised by his defeat.

Running against Horn, Bice in a debate attacked her party-line votes. "You vote with Nancy Pelosi 90 percent of the time," she charged. Horn responded that she "stood up to the Speaker," was a member of the bipartisan Problem Solvers Caucus and opposed the Green New Deal proposed by progressive Democrats. Horn cited the endorsement she received from the Chamber of Commerce of the United States as proof of her bipartisanship. Officials of the state Chamber of Commerce objected to that support, contending that Horn "voted four times to limit energy exploration."

Bice won, 52%-48%. Horn led by roughly 2,000 votes in Oklahoma County, which again cast nearly 90 percent of the total vote. But Bice got more than 70 percent of the vote in more rural Pottawatomie and Seminole counties, where Horn failed to win a single precinct. Horn's campaign spending nearly doubled that of Bice. The two national parties split a total of $15 million of additional spending on the general election.

With Republicans' control of redistricting in Oklahoma, it's a good bet they will attempt to reinforce Bice and her district. One option could be swapping Democratic parts of Oklahoma City for more of the heavily Republican suburbs, perhaps in an exchange with the adjacent and firmly Republican 4th Congressional District. With her Oklahoma City base, Bice likely will need to introduce herself to rural voters.

OK-5: Oklahoma City Area   Cook Partisan Voting Index: R+7

Population		Race and Ethnicity		Income	
Total	825,115	White	70.10%	Median Income	$54,928
Land area (sq. miles)	2,074	Black	13.20%	District Income Rank	331
Pop/ sq mi	397.86	Latino	17.60%	Poverty Rate	15.50%
Born in State	59.70%	Asian	3.40%	With health insurance	85.20%
		Two or more races	5.50%	Cash public assistance	3.30%
Age Groups		Other	7.80%	Food stamp/SNAP	12.90%
Under 18	25.10%				
18-34	24.40%	**Education**		**Work**	
35-64	36.10%	H.S grad or less	39.60%	White Collar	37.70%
Over 64	14.30%	Some college	28.80%	Sales and Service	39.60%
		College Degree, 4 yr	19.50%	Blue Collar	22.70%
Military		Post grad	12.00%	Government	16.10%
Veteran/ Active Duty	8.50%				

2020 Pres. Vote	Trump	156,645	(51%)	Biden	140,370	(46%)	
2016 Pres. Vote	Trump	149,400	(53%)	Clinton	111,769	(40%)	Johnson 19,631 (7%)

Oklahoma City: Oklahoma City, like many state capitals, was not the spontaneous creation of commerce but the deliberate creation of government, sited in the geographic center of the state on what turned out to be oil land. Rigs were pumping crude on the grounds of the capitol until 1989. The land here is browner and more eroded by creeks than the rolling Oklahoma farmland to the east. Oklahoma City's population grew briskly from 506,000 in 2000 to 655,000 in 2019, a 29 percent increase. A survey of housing affordability in 2019 ranked Oklahoma City as the third most affordable city in the United States; the top two were Pittsburgh and Rochester, New York.

Oklahoma City was scarred by a profound tragedy: the day in April 1995 when a bomb destroyed the Alfred P. Murrah Federal Building, killing 168 people and injuring more than 680. Five years later, the Oklahoma City National Memorial opened on the site of the blast. Timothy McVeigh, who was convicted for the attack, was executed three months before the September 2001 terror attacks —a coincidence that might be apt, given that the Oklahoma City killing was the deadliest attack on U.S. soil in the 60 years from Pearl Harbor to 9/11. Local pride spiked in 2008 when the Seattle SuperSonics of the National Basketball Association relocated to the city and became the Oklahoma City Thunder, the state's first major professional sports franchise. The team's run to the NBA finals in 2012 energized the city's fan base. But, alas, the team's star players escaped for more cosmopolitan venues and its title prospects waned. A local builder planned to complete by late 2021 redevelopment of the historic 31-story First National Center—with its Art Deco exterior—into a hotel, with retail stores and apartments. A new $288 million, downtown convention center, completed in 2020, is across the street from a new 70-acre park along the Oklahoma River. Streetcar service connects these sites along six miles of track. All this activity, financed with a 1 percent sales tax, was bolstered by the growing number of young professionals moving into the city, plus an increase in the minority population (20 percent Hispanic and 14 percent Black).

The 5th Congressional District is centered in Oklahoma City and includes most of Oklahoma County. It takes in Pottawatomie and Seminole counties to the east. Oklahoma County, which is the least-red in the state, casts nearly 90 percent of the vote. In 2020, President Donald Trump took the district, 51%-46%—a drop from the 59 percent the Republican presidential nominees took in 2008 and 2012 and a notable contrast to the 75-plus percent for Trump in the adjacent 2nd and 3rd districts. The local influx of new voters has been trending Democratic. "Minorities and millennials turn Oklahoma City blue," The Oklahoman—with some over-statement--sheadlined the election results in 2018.

OREGON

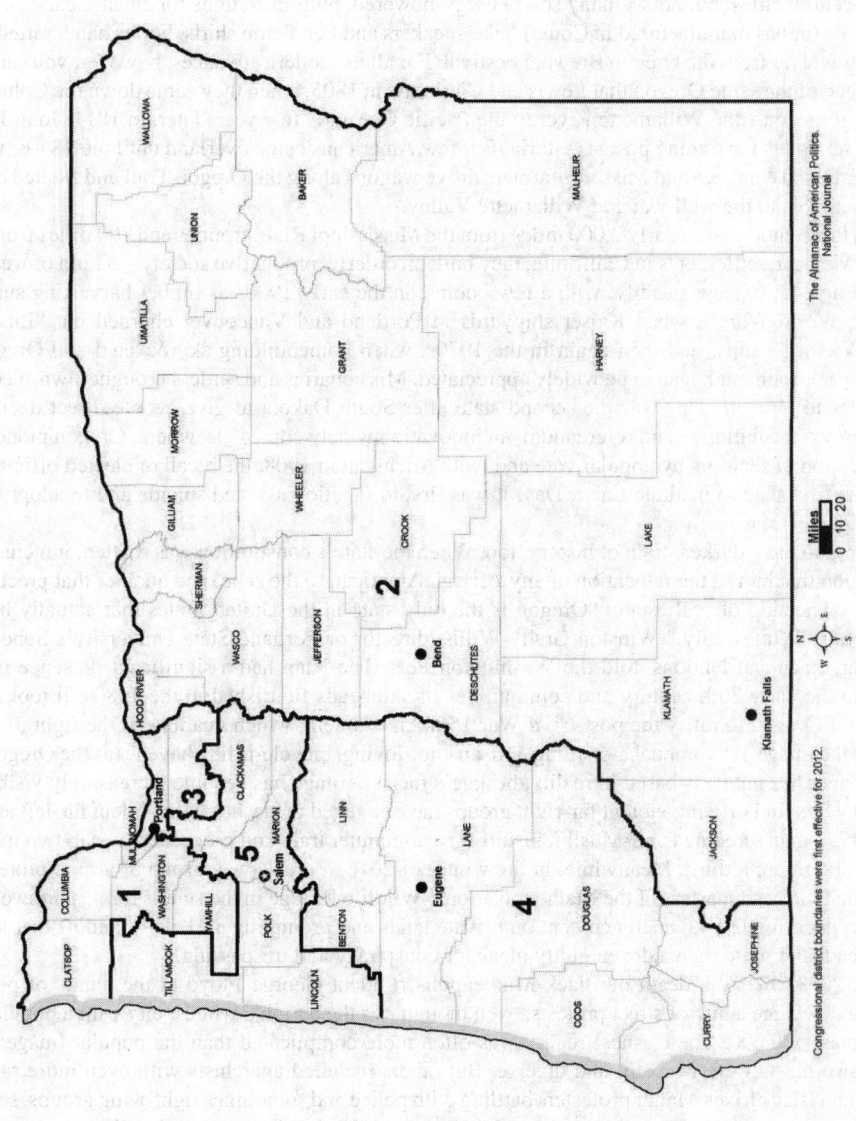

Congressional district boundaries were first effective for 2012

Miles
0 10 20

Oregon is a blue state, even though its rural areas are as Republican as other portions of the American West. That's because almost half of the state's population lives in the counties in and around Portland, the city whose hippie-liberal sensitivities were lovingly satirized by Fred Armisen and Carrie Brownstein in the television comedy series Portlandia, though more recently the city has been known as the location of violent face-offs driven by anarchists.

Oregon is an experimental commonwealth, a laboratory of reform, a maker of national trends—with varying results. Bike trails now exist throughout the country. You can find light-rail trams in many central cities, but not as many solar energy-powered, plug-in stations for electric cars. Oregon produces (or has manufactured in China) Nike sneakers and Pendleton shirts, but its handcrafted ales don't travel far from the Oregon Brewers Festival. For all its modern advances, however, you can still see much of the same Oregon that Lewis and Clark saw in 1805, when they came down the Columbia River gorge, past the Willamette River to the Pacific Ocean. A few years later, in 1811, John Jacob Astor set up his fur trading post at Astoria. But few Americans came overland until the 1840s, when New England Yankees and Missouri farmers drove wagons along the Oregon Trail and floated down the Columbia to the well-watered Willamette Valley.

In this remote spot, nearly 2,000 miles from the Mississippi River frontier and 700 miles from the small Mexican settlements in California, they built an orderly, productive society—a kind of western New England. It grew steadily, with a few booms: in the early 1900s as timber harvesting surged; during World War II, when Kaiser shipyards in Portland and Vancouver churned out "Liberty" and "Victory" ships; and then again in the 1970s, when homebuilding skyrocketed and Oregon's natural environment began to be widely appreciated. Missionaries and settlers brought town-meeting attitudes to Oregon. This was the second state after South Dakota to give people direct decision-making via the initiative and referendum, an innovation widely copied elsewhere. Oregon pioneered the election of senators by popular vote and, with Michigan in 1908, the recall of elected officials. It was the first state to institute Labor Day. It was first to sanction assisted suicide and to adopt mail-in ballot elections.

Oregon has a darker strain of history, too. When the state's constitution was written, it included a provision that barred the relocation of any African American to the state, and another that precluded Black ownership of real estate. "Oregon is the only state in the United States that actually began as literally Whites-only," Winston Grady-Willis, director of Portland State University's School of Gender, Race and Nations, told the Washington Post. The Klan had a significant presence in the state in the early 20th century and communities of skinheads flourished in the 1980s. It took until 1959 for Oregon to ratify the post-Civil War 15th Amendment, which guaranteed the right to vote. While the image of "kombucha-swilling, artisan knot-loving, bicycle-riding haven" (as the Oregonian newspaper has put it) is based in reality,thestate's racist heritage has become increasingly visible in recent years. In Portland, violent far-right groups have engaged in clashes with violent far-left antifa. In 2017, a man screamed anti-Muslim insults on a commuter train and proceeded to stab two men to death and injure a third. Meanwhile, in the winter of 2016, a breakaway group of armed protesters occupied the headquarters of the Malheur National Wildlife Refuge in the state's rural, southwestern corner, decrying federal encroachment on private lands and prompting a 41-day standoff that led to one death and more than a dozen guilty pleas for conspiracy and trespassing.

In 2020, after the death of Black Minneapolis resident George Floyd at the hands of police, Portland became a hub of street protests, even though it is the nation's whitest city with a population of at least 500,000. The clashes' reality was often more complicated than the popular image: The biggest protests were peaceful and diverse. But others included anarchists with even more radical aims than Black Lives Matter protesters battling with police and sometimes right-wing groups, setting fires in certain areas of the city, and vandalizing the federal courthouse and police headquarters. President Donald Trump seized on the conflict as he was running for reelection, blaming Democrats for tolerating, if not fomenting, and violence. The clashes lingered for weeks, but eased somewhat in June, when the Portland City Council redirected $15 million from police to other city programs, and the state enacted police reform measures, including a ban on most chokeholds, tougher discipline for police misconduct, and a higher threshold for using tear gas. In July, Trump sent federal personnel into Portland to protect federal property, but without the support of local officials. Gov. Kate Brown, who had tolerated the "occupation" of large swaths of the city, called it "political theater" and a "blatant abuse of power."The administration was put on the defensive when reports emerged of more than 100 unidentified federal personnel snatching protesters off the streets without normal judicial processes. Eventually, negotiations between Brown and Vice President Mike Pence brokered an agreement for the federal forces to leave; while some clashes continued, the unrest ratcheted down, although the "occupied zone" in Portland remained occupied.

Oregon grew much faster than the national average in the 1940s, when war industries brought thousands of people to the West Coast, and again in the 1970s, when the pleasant environment attracted so many young people that the state's population shot up 26 percent. Containing growth became the hot local issue. "Come and visit us again and again," Republican Gov. Tom McCall told outsiders. "But for heaven's sake don't come here to live." At his prodding, the legislature in 1973 passed a law that limited development, and in the 1990s, the Portland metropolitan area sharply restricted growth and sprawl. These measures were also popular in the university towns of Eugene and Corvallis and to a lesser extent in the suburbs. Oregon is still attempting to find the right mix for development. In 2019, Brown signed the nation's first statewide rent control law as well as a separate measure requiring cities of at least 10,000 residents to permit duplexes in areas of single family-homes, and even quadriplexes in the Portland area. Meanwhile, employment in the lumber industry has been shrinking amid tighter federal and state regulation and greater automation. The state has also grappled with one of the downsides of its verdant surroundings: In 2020, Oregon faced its worst fire season in memory, with more than 1,400 square miles burned in just three days, double the usual amount for a whole year. Urban and rural Oregon have often been at odds over environmental policy, but in 2020, timber interests, green groups, and political leaders were able to hammer out a roadmap for negotiating a new framework for logging practices, rather than fighting it out via ballot measures.

In Portland and the university towns, newcomers helped build the state's new economy. The growth of high-tech companies around Portland was such that the area became known as Silicon Forest, where Intel, the largest tech employer in the state, is expanding its already considerable footprint in the Portland suburbs. The chipmaker shares the stage with homegrown firms like Mentor Graphics, FEI Co., Rentrack Corp., Open Sesame, and Twist lock. Oregon is also a top exporter; semiconductors and electronic components are the biggest, totaling $9.1 billion, thanks largely to Intel. The port of Portland also ships more than a billion dollars of motor vehicles and agricultural crops every year. Befitting Oregon's location on the Pacific Rim, the state's top trading partners save Canada are all in Asia: China, Vietnam, South Korea, Japan, Malaysia, Taiwan, and Singapore.

While Oregon's population growth rate has fallen from its earlier peaks, the state is still expanding at a healthy clip, up 10.6 percent since 2010, enough for an additional seat in the House. Its three biggest counties—Multnomah, Washington and Clackamas, each in the Portland metro area —have each grown between 10 and 13 percent since 2010. Deschutes County, for its part, has grown a stunning 25 percent in the last decade, driven by a boom in Bend, a onetime blue-collar locale that has recently become a destination for scenic tourism and families looking to relocate in pleasant surroundings. (Bend is home to the planet's only remaining Blockbuster Video store.) Oregon's rural population is a rapidly diminishing proportion of the state, contributing to its resentment of metro Portland. Oregon's population is less than 2 percent Black, 13 percent Hispanic and 5 percent Asian. Washington County in suburban Portland is increasingly diverse ethnically—12 percent Asian and 17 percent Hispanic. The state capital of Salem and farming counties east of the Cascades also have relatively high Hispanic percentages.

Though it was largely founded by missionaries, Oregon has America's highest percentage of self-described agnostics (8 percent) according to the Pew Research Center's most recent U.S. Religious Landscape Study. The religiously unaffiliated form the core constituency for some of the state's policy innovations over the last two generations, when Oregon legalized most abortions prior to the Supreme Court'sRoe v. Wade decision, decriminalized medical marijuana, and legalized assisted suicide in referendums in 1994 and 1997, to the point that doctors can prescribe but not administer lethal drugs. In 2007, the Democratic-controlled legislature banned discrimination on the basis of sexual orientation and mandated recycling of discarded electronics. Running counter to the anything-goes atmosphere, it also imposed limits on smoking. Oregon eagerly expanded Medicaid under the Affordable Care Act, adding 438,000 mostly able-bodied adults to the rolls. When costs skyrocketed, voters in 2018 approved tax increases on health care providers to pay for it. (The providers weren't opposed; they just passed the cost along to patients.) Meanwhile, the state has some of the oldest sanctuary policies for undocumented immigrants, and in 2018, voters rejected a ballot measure that would have overturned the sanctuary law. Oregon was also among the most active states in filing lawsuits opposing the Trump administration's immigration policies. Legalized recreational marijuana, approved by voters in 2014, is flourishing. (Unlike most products for sale in the state, marijuana is taxed at 17 percent.) Then, in 2020, voters approved a move to the next frontier—the regulated medical use of psilocybin, a hallucinogen sometimes called "magic mushrooms." It passed by double-digit margins.

Voting in Oregon has featured huge margins for progressive candidates and positions in Portland and the university towns of Eugene and Corvallis and huge conservative margins in counties east of the Cascades and in much of southwestern Oregon, where discontent over the policies that decimated the logging industry has lingered. (Some rural Oregonians have been pushing an effort to join a conservative "greater Idaho.") There are no polls open on Election Day—there really is no Election Day—and voters have until that night to get their ballots to an election clerk. Oregon has recently had more women in senior legislative leadership roles than any other state, and by 2020, women accounted for half of the members of the state House. But the state has had to grapple with explosive sexual harassment allegations in the legislature; a $1.3 million legal settlement with nine women who had been harassed was signed in 2019.

Oregon has not been a presidential battleground in recent elections; it voted for Hillary Clinton by 11 points in 2016 and Joe Biden by 16 points in 2020. (In the 2016 presidential race, 11 percent of voters chose a third-party nominee or write-in candidate; that share plummeted to 3 percent in 2020.) Biden flipped two counties that Trump had won four years earlier: Marion, home of the state capital of Salem, and Deschutes. Biden also improved on Clinton's margins by between five and nine points in the other five most populous counties: Multnomah, Clackamas, and Washington in metro Portland, Lane County (Eugene), and Jackson County (Medford). In early 2019, the only Republican to win statewide in years, Secretary of State Dennis Richardson, died of brain cancer; in 2020, a Democrat won the office. In Oregon, the GOP's options for the gubernatorial race, and other statewide contests, are limited. While moderate Republicans dominated the party through the 1990s, the remnants of the party have shifted too far to the right to be competitive in a solidly blue state.

Population		Race and Ethnicity		Income	
Total	4,217,737	White	83.50%	Median Income	67,058
Land area (sq. miles)	95,988	Black	1.80%	State Income Rank	18 out of 50
Pop/ sq mi	43.94	Latino	13.40%	Poverty Rate	11.40%
Born in state	45.60%	Asian	6.20%	With health insurance	92.80%
		Two or more races	4.90%	Cash public assistance	3.10%
Age Groups		Other	5.10%	Food stamp/SNAP	17.8%
Under 18	20.50%				
18-34	22.70%	**Education**		**Work**	
35-64	38.60%	H.S grad or less	31.70%	White Collar	40.40%
Over 64	18.20%	Some college	33.80%	Sales and Service	38.10%
		College Degree, 4 yr	21.00%	Blue Collar	21.40%
Military		Post grad	13.50%	Government	14.50%
Veteran/ Active Duty	8.10%				

Presidential Politics

2020 Primary (D)	Biden (D)	408,315(66%)	Sanders (D)	127,345(21%)	Warren (D)	59,355(10%)
2020 Pres. Vote	Biden (D)	1,340,383(56%)	Trump (R)	958,448(40%)		
2016 Pres. Vote	Clinton (D)	1,002,106(50%)	Trump (R)	782,403(39%)	Johnson (L)	94,231 (5%)
	Stein (G)	50,002 (3%)				

Oregon has the distinction of being the site of the first presidential broadcast debate. During the 1948 GOP primary, Portland radio station KEX hosted Thomas Dewey and Harold Stassen, who debated whether the Communist Party should be outlawed. The debate was carried on national radio networks and some 40 million Americans tuned in to listen for an hour without commercial interruption. Oregon once tilted Republican in close presidential contests, voting for other losing GOP nominees in 1960 and 1976, in addition to Dewey, but it's gone Democratic every year since 1988, and by double-digit margins every presidential election since 2008, as Portland and its growing suburbs moved increasingly left. In 2020, Joe Biden defeated President Donald Trump, 57%-40%. Biden won Multnomah County (Portland), the state's largest vote producer, by a whopping 79%-18%, carried three neighboring counties as well as the counties that include the state capitol of Salem and the college town of Eugene. He also flipped fast-growing Deschutes County, where California transplants have remade Bend. Trump won every county in eastern Oregon, which is more similar to Idaho than Portland politically, with at least 60 percent of the vote.

Oregon holds its presidential primary in late May. In 2008, when the race between Clinton and Barack Obama was still raging, Obama carried Oregon 59%-41%. Eight years later, Vermont Sen. Bernie Sanders beat Clinton, 56%-42%, winning all but one small rural county. Biden was the presumptive nominee by late May 2020, and won the primary 66%-21% over Sanders, who'd suspended his campaign more than a month earlier.

Congressional Districts

117th Congress Lineup	4D 1R	116th Congress Lineup	4D 1R

Oregon will gain the sixth seat it narrowly missed following the 2010 census. The good news for Democrats is that they control the governorship and the legislature. The challenge they face is whether they can create a safe seat for their party in a delegation that has had four Democrats and one Republican for more than two decades. The 4th and 5th districts have been competitive in both presidential and congressional elections, and each seat might be at risk. Democrats likely will seek to reinforce those two districts, though that might pose the risk of providing Republican voters for the new district. The Portland-based 1st and 3rd Districts have plenty of Democrats to sacrifice, though the map-drawers probably would need to divide the city or suburban Washington County to create a new Democratic-leaning district; either option likely would meet wide resistance. Alternatively, Democrats could draw the new district to give their candidate a reasonable opportunity in a competitive district. Each of the Portland-area districts has had population surges in the past decade. The Republican-controlled 2nd District east of the Cascade Mountains likely will sacrifice its increasingly Democratic-leaning Bend-based Deschutes County.

In 2011, the legislature accomplished something that it hadn't been able to do in more than 100 years: It passed its own congressional redistricting plan. The prospects had seemed unlikely because the parties were tied at 30 seats apiece in the state House. But there was a compromise to be had: Democrats wanted to shift Corvallis, home of Oregon State University, to the Eugene-based 4th District. In the deal, Democrats let the 3rd pick up some of Democrat Kurt Schrader's already tiny share of Portland, keeping his 5th District competitive. That kind of deal might be more difficult to pull off with the complexities created by an additional seat. Traditionally progressive Oregon is the last West Coast state without an independent redistricting commission of some kind.

Kate Brown (D)

Assumed office in 2015, term expires 2023, 1st full term; b. Jun. 21, 1960, Torrejón de Ardoz, Spain; U. of CO Boulder, B.A. 1981; Northwestern Schl. of Law, J.D. 1985; Married (Dan); 2 children.

Elected Office: OR House, 1991-1996; OR Senate, 1997-2008, Majority Leader, 2004; OR Secretary of State, 2008-2015.

Professional Career: Practicing attorney; Instructor, Portland State University.

Office: 900 Court St. NE Rm. 160, Salem, 97301-4047; 503-378-4582; Fax: 503-378-8970; Website: oregon.gov

Atty. Gen: Ellen Rosenblum (D) **Sec. of State:** Leslie Cummings (R)

State Legislature: Senate: 18D, 11R, 1V **House:** 38D, 22R

Election Results

Election	Name (Party)	Vote (%)
2018 General	Kate Brown (D)	934,498 (50%)
	Knute Buehler (R)	814,988 (44%)
	Patrick Starnes (I)	53,392 (3%)
2018 Primary	Kate Brown (D)	324,451 (84%)
	Ed Jones (D)	33,464 (9%)
	Candace Meville (D)	29,110 (8%)

Prior winning percentage: 2016 (51%)

Kate Brown was elevated to the governorship of Oregon in 2015, succeeding scandal-plagued Gov. John Kitzhaber, a fellow Democrat. She won an election for the remainder of Kitzhaber's term in 2016, then secured a full term of her own in 2018. Brown, the nation's first openly bisexual governor, has worked with the Democratic legislature to enact a largely liberal agenda; she grappled with a series of crises in 2020, including anarchist protests in Portland, the coronavirus pandemic, and widespread fires.

Brown was born in Spain, where her father served in the Air Force, but she grew up in Minnesota. She received a bachelor's degree in environmental conservation, with a certificate in women's studies, from the University of Colorado at Boulder, then obtained her law degree from Lewis & Clark College in Portland. She practiced family law in Portland and worked for a nonprofit legal services group. Brown got her start in politics in 1991 when, while working as an advocate for the Women's Rights Coalition, she was appointed by the Multnomah County Board of Commissioners to fill a vacancy in the Oregon House. A year later, the state representative Brown replaced, Judy Bauman, wanted her seat back and challenged Brown in the Democratic primary. Bauman had stronger political connections, but Brown went door-to-door and waged a vigorous grassroots campaign, winning the primary by seven votes. In 1996, Brown won a seat in the Oregon Senate and quickly was named its Democratic caucus leader. Brown married in 1997; she publicly acknowledged her bisexuality after The Oregonian reported on it when she was a state lawmaker. Brown rose to majority leader in 2004, becoming the first woman to occupy that post.

Brown ran for secretary of state in 2008 and won, 51%-46%. In that post, Brown attracted attention for helping Oregon implement an online voter-registration system and for using iPad technology to make voting more accessible to people with disabilities. But in 2012, she came under fire when her office notified two candidates for labor commissioner that their election would be held in November instead of the following May, a move that critics said appeared to be aimed at helping the Democratic candidate. In her reelection bid, The Oregonian endorsed Republican Knute Buehler—who would run against her for governor in 2018—saying her decision had "eroded public confidence in Brown, if not the office itself." But Brown won reelection anyway.

Prior to his resignation, Kitzhaber was a giant figure in Oregon politics. During the summer before his reelection, he became engaged to Cylvia Hayes, who ran an environmental consulting business. But investigative reporting by Willamette Week in 2014 raised questions about whether Hayes had benefited financially from her relationship with the governor and whether she had properly disclosed the consulting fees she had been paid. Although Kitzhaber won his race, the controversy didn't die down. It reached a crescendo in February 2015, and Kitzhaber stepped down. Brown, the next in line as secretary of state, became governor.

On the whole, lawmakers seemed to welcome Brown and her more collegial approach; Kitzhaber was seen by some as aloof and arrogant. Brown emphasized the need to restore trust in government and within months she signed an ethics package. Separately, she signed a bill that would automatically register voters who obtained or renewed their driver's license, becoming the first state to make voter registration automatic. Brown also signed other progressive measures approved by the state legislature, including mandatory paid sick leave for most Oregon workers; more permissive rules for acquiring a medical-marijuana card; a bill making it illegal for employers to ask about an applicant's criminal background on job applications; a new system for collecting data about racial profiling by law enforcement officers; an employee-funded workplace-based retirement savings program; a bill to end "conversion therapy" for homosexuality; and protections for transgender students. The most controversial measure, however, was a bill Brown signed in 2015 to require a background check for most private sales of guns. Reaction to the measure highlighted the divide between the Portland region and the state's rural areas.

Brown's second year in office began with a crisis, as an armed group protesting federal land policies occupied the headquarters of the Malheur National Wildlife Refuge, in rural southeast Oregon. Brown vented frustration with federal officials' take-it-slow approach. The incident ended after 41 days, with one protester dead; more than a dozen people eventually pled guilty to conspiracy and trespassing charges. (In 2018, President Donald Trump pardoned the cattle ranchers whose legal case had initially inspired the armed occupation.) The Malheur refuge takeover, combined with lingering anger at Brown's gun control policies, raised concerns about the governor's safety. In July 2016, The Oregonian reported that Brown's security procedures had been tightened and coordination with the FBI had increased. Two months later, Brown was burned in effigy on the front steps of the state capitol by gun-rights demonstrators.

Despite such tensions, Brown had legislative successes in 2016. She signed a phased-in minimum wage increase scaled to three different territories—the Portland metro area, rural areas, and everywhere else. She signed new protections for tenants, and she allowed jurisdictions to require builders to include housing priced below market rates. Lawmakers also approved new renewable energy mandates; a lodging-tax increase; a boost for the backlogged testing of rape kits; the lifting of the statute of limitations on rape; and permission for banks to take on marijuana businesses as clients.

Brown ran in a 2016 special election for the final two years of Kitzhaber's term; Republicans hadn't won an Oregon gubernatorial race since 1982. She faced William "Bud" Pierce, a moderate former president of the Oregon Medical Association. During a debate, Pierce said well-educated and accomplished women are less susceptible to sexual harassment; after an outcry, he apologized. Brown courted opposition from pro-gun Republicans by accepting a $250,000 campaign donation from former New York City mayor and gun control advocate Michael Bloomberg. In the end, she won by seven points, less than the polls had indicated.

As Brown prepared for another election in just two years, she had a productive time with the legislature. In 2017, she signed a measure to keep private any changes transgender people make on their birth certificates; Oregon was the second state with such a measure, following California. She also signed one of the most pro-abortion laws in the nation, requiring abortion coverage and birth control without any co-pay, and allotting state funds to pay for abortions for non-citizens who aren't permitted to sign up for Medicaid. The following year, Brown signed a bill to require internet providers who do business with the state to maintain so-called net neutrality, while signing another measure to close the "boyfriend loophole" that had permitted gun access for those convicted of domestic violence against non-married intimate partners. Brown signed an executive order to ban offshore drilling. She also persuaded her fellow Democrats to support a narrowly tailored tax cut for an estimated 6,000 sole proprietors. Meanwhile, Brown and Attorney General Ellen Rosenblum protected the state's longstanding sanctuary-state law, a stance that would receive the voters' support in November when a ballot measure for its repeal failed by nearly a 2-to-1 margin.

In the 2018 GOP primary, Buehler, an orthopedic surgeon and state legislator, prevailed against a split conservative field, winning 46 percent against Trump-aligned businessman Sam Carpenter, with 29 percent, and former Navy pilot Greg Wooldridge, with 20 percent. Buehler ran a center-right campaign, backing abortion rights and saying climate change needed to be tackled; he was bolstered by millions of dollars donated by Nike co-founder Phil Knight. Buehler criticized Brown's record on educational achievement, mental health, foster care, and the state's pension challenges. Buehler sought to distance himself from Trump, who was unpopular in the state. But Brown got a boost in October when independent candidate Patrick Starnes dropped out and endorsed the incumbent, saying she would be best positioned to enact campaign finance reform, Starnes' highest-profile issue. Brown won, 50%-44%.

In 2019, Brown signed a pension overhaul bill that narrowly passed the legislature. The measure, which refinanced the system's ballooning debt and trimmed employees' secondary retirement accounts, later drew a lawsuit from aggrieved employees and retirees, but the state Supreme Court upheld it. She also enacted a tax on large businesses designed to increase funding for K-12 schools by $1 billion a year. The bill received a vote after Republicans ended a quorum-denying walkout in exchange for Democrats' promise to pull other measures from consideration, including a gun control bill. Brown also expanded the state's family and medical leave law by guaranteeing full wage-replacement for minimum-wage workers, and joined a national compact designed to be a workaround to the Electoral College. In good news for taxpayers, the state was able to return a record "kicker," or tax rebate, worth $1.6 billion. The biggest legislative battle, however, revolved around a bill to attack climate change by instituting a cap-and-trade system for emissions. Republican lawmakers representing resource-rich areas of the state fled the capital for points unknown and evaded state troopers in order to keep the legislature from proceeding with consideration of the climate bill. Eventually, the Democrats' own support for the bill waned, and GOP lawmakers returned to work on other legislative business. The cycle repeated itself in early 2020 when Democrats tried to pass a modified version of the climate bill. When that failed, Brown issued an executive order that sought to cobble together some of the proposal's main goals, though it was unclear how effective that approach would be.

In 2020, Oregon survived the coronavirus pandemic better than almost any other state. But Brown and officials in Portland struggled to contain anarchist-driven clashes, provocations by right-wing groups, extensive vandalism, and a deployment of federal forces sent by Trump. In addition, broad swaths of the state were set ablaze by a freak lightning storm. Republicans blamed Brown for not engaging in more aggressive forest management to forestall the fires. Brown acknowledged the point, but she said forest management was not the only factor: "It's decades of mismanagement of our forests in this country, and it is the failure to tackle climate change. We need to do both." Brown faced three recall attempts driven by her conservative critics, but each of them fizzled.

Heading into the open-seat election in 2022, Democrats will likely have a large primary field, possibly including Attorney General Ellen Rosenblum, Secretary of State Shemia Fagan, House Speaker Tina Kotek, state Treasurer Tobias Read, state Labor Commissioner Val Hoyle, former Oregon House minority leader and current chair of the Multnomah County Commission Deborah Kafoury, and investment executive and attorney Rukaiyah Adams. Buehler left the GOP in 2021 to become an independent and has ruled out a run for governor; the GOP bench is thin.

Ron Wyden (D)

Elected 1996, term expires 2022, 4th full term, b. May 03, 1949; Wichita, KS; University of California, B.A., 1969; Stanford University, B.A., 1971; University of OR Law School, J.D., 1974; Jewish; Married (Nancy Bass Wyden); 5 children (2 from previous marriage).

Elected Office: U.S. House, 1981-1996.

Professional Career: Co-Director & co-founder, OR Gray Panthers, 1974-1980; Director, OR Legal Svcs. for the Elderly, 1977-1979; Instructor, University of OR, 1976, Portland St. University, 1979, University of Portland, 1980.

DC Office: 221 DSOB 20510, 202-224-5244, Fax: 202-228-2717, wyden.senate.gov

State Offices: Bend, 541-330-9142; Eugene, 541-431-0229; La Grande, 541-962-7691; Medford, 541-858-5122; Portland, 503-326-7525; Salem, 503-589-4555.

Committees: *Budget. Energy & Natural Resources*: Energy; Public Lands, Forests & Mining; Water & Power (Chmn). *Finance (Chmn)*: Ex Officio membership on all subcommittees. *Intelligence. Joint Taxation.*

Group Ratings

	ADA	ACLU	AFL-CIO	LCV	COC	HAFA	ACU	CFG	FRC
2020	-	77%	-	92%	-	0%	8%	-	-
2019	95%	C	95%	100%	49%	C	8%	5%	0%

Almanac Ratings 2019-2020

	Economy	Social	Foreign	Composite
Liberal	100%	100%	92%	97%
Conservative	0%	0%	8%	3%

Key Votes of the 116th Congress

1. EPA clean energy rules	Y	5. Russia sanctions	Y	9. Barr as Atty. General	N
2. U.S./Mex./Can. trade deal	Y	6. Troops in SYR, AFG	N	10. Spending at the border	N
3. Cut unemployment benefits	N	7. Veto arms sales to Saudis	Y	11. Coney Barrett to Sup. Ct.	N
4. Shelton to Fed Reserve	N	8. Defense $$$, veto override	N	12. Electoral College objections	N

Election Results

Election	Name (Party)	Vote (%)		Cand. Spent	Ind. Exp. Support	Ind. Exp. Oppose
2016 General	Ron Wyden (D)	1,105,119	(57%)	$6,565,807		
	Mark Callahan (R)	651,106	(33%)		$37,221	
	Eric Navickas (G)	48,823	(3%)			
2016 Primary	Ron Wyden (D)	501,903	(84%)			
	Kevin Stine (D)	78,287	(13%)			

Prior winning percentages: 2016 (57%), 2010 (57%), 2004 (63%), 1998 (61%), 1996 special (48%), House: 1994 (73%), 1992 (77%), 1990 (81%), 1988 (99%), 1986 (86%), 1984 (59%), 1982 (78%), 1980 (72%)

Democrat Ron Wyden, Oregon's senior senator, is tied with Senate Majority Leader Chuck Schumer as the second longest-serving Democrat on Capitol Hill, behind only Sen. Patrick Leahy of Vermont. He arrived in the Senate via a special election in January 1996, after a decade and a half in the House. After 40 years in Congress, including a quarter-century in the Senate, he chairs the tax-writing Finance Committee—one of the most powerful seats on Capitol Hill and potentially a challenging slot for an often independent lawmaker. Wyden has pursued an array of often eclectic interests. As a member of the Intelligence Committee, Wyden has emerged as perhaps the Senate's most implacable critic of government efforts to expand electronic surveillance of citizens for the sake of national security.

Like President Joe Biden, Wyden has relentlessly worked to bridge the partisan divide on high-wattage issues—often to the consternation of his Democratic colleagues. In 2013, he became chairman of the Senate Energy and Natural Resources Committee. Just over a year later, when Montana Sen. Max Baucus resigned to become ambassador to China, Wyden briefly took the Finance gavel—bringing along his reputation for trying to craft bipartisan deals on highly polarizing issues. "Sometimes folks tease him, [saying]'If Ron Wyden hasn't used the word 'bipartisan' in a sentence today, it's not our Ron,'" Republican Sen. Lisa Murkowski of Alaska, who worked closely with him on the Energy panel, told the Oregonian. "But then he's genuine about it, and it's important to him."In the Senate minority during the Trump administration, he found such opportunities were scant. With Biden, Wyden would help determine the limits of Democratic patience with the GOP on issues such as taxes and health care.

Wyden was born in Wichita Kansas, while his father, Peter, a journalist, was working for the Wichita Eagle. Peter shortened the family surname from Weidenreich three years before his son was born; both Wyden's father and his mother, Edith, were Jews who had fled Nazi Germany. Presaging Wyden's involvement in overseeing U.S. intelligence policy years later, Peter Wyden was trained as a U.S. spy during World War IIand returned to Europe to help run an Allied propaganda campaign aimed at Nazi-held territory. Ron Wyden grew up in California, graduated from Stanford University and moved to Oregon to attend the University of Oregon Law School. After graduating in 1974, he founded the Oregon chapter of the Gray Panthers, an advocacy group for the elderly. Under Wyden, the group ventured into electoral politics by sponsoring a successful referendum reducing the price of dentures.

As a 19-year-old undergraduate, Wyden worked as a campaign driver for Sen. Wayne Morse, who became a mentor— and whose Senate seat Wyden now occupies. In 1968, the famously independent-minded Morse, an early opponent of the Vietnam War, got a challenge in the Democratic primary from former Rep. Robert Duncan, a supporter of the war. Morse won the primary, but lost the general election to a young Republican state legislator, Bob Packwood. Twelve years later, at 31, Wyden launched a primary challenge to Duncan, who had returned to the House representing the Portland-based 3rd District. Wyden won the primary 60%-40% and easily captured the heavily Democratic seat in 1980. As a member of the Energy and Commerce Committee, his interests included health care, energy and telecommunications.

Wyden's path to the Senate was opened by the Senate Ethics Committee's decision in September 1995 to expel Packwood for sexually harassing aides and lobbyists. Wyden, who had long eyed the seat, ran in the special election to replace Packwood, who resigned before the scheduled expulsion vote. With his base in Portland, Wyden had greater name recognition than his rivals. He had spirited opposition in the primary, but he won 50%-44%. Senate President Gordon Smith, a moderate, won the Republican nomination. Smith, a frozen-vegetable tycoon from Eastern Oregon, spent $2 million of his own money. Most polls suggested a dead heat, and negative ads flooded the airwaves. Wyden won 48%-47%.Ten months later, Smith won the state's other Senate seat after Republican Mark Hatfield retired.

Wyden and Smith became friends and collaborators, holding dozens of joint town meetings across Oregon and having lunch every Thursday with their chiefs of staff. Facing a tough reelection campaign in 2008 against Democrat Jeff Merkley, Smith boasted of bipartisanship in ads that included images of Wyden. Merkley narrowly won.

Wyden has sought other opportunities to pursue counterintuitive political alliances and creative ideas. In early 2009, he and Republican Sen. Olympia Snowe of Maine predicted that high-dollar bonuses and "golden parachutes" for executives of financial companies being bailed out by U.S. taxpayers would be unpopular with the public, and they won passage of a provision in that year's economic stimulus bill to prevent such payments. But the stipulation was dropped from the final bill at the insistence of aides to President Barack Obama, who argued that employees might sue to keep their bonuses. Public anger boiled over in March 2009 after lucrative bonuses were paid to employees of troubled insurance giant AIG.

One of the more memorable moments of Wyden's career came during a 2013 Intelligence Committee meeting. He asked then-Director of National Intelligence James Clapper, "Does the [National Security Agency] collect any type of data at all on millions or hundreds of millions of Americans?"

Clapper replied, "No, sir."

"It does not?"Wyden pressed.

"Not wittingly," Clapper answered.

Three months later, whistleblower Edward Snowden created a national firestorm by leaking thousands of NSA documents that proved Clapper had not been straight with Wyden. Snowden later said that Clapper's answer to Wyden had been a "major motivating factor" in his decision to leak information illustrating the extent to which intelligence agencies were electronically collecting information on U.S. citizens. Clapper later acknowledged he had answered Wyden in the "least most untruthful manner."

After Snowden's revelations, Wyden achieved success in 2015, when the revised USA Freedom Act reined in the government's ability to collect phone data. It put Wyden in yet another bipartisan alliance, this time with libertarian-minded Sen. Rand Paul of Kentucky. Two years earlier, Wyden was the only Democrat to stand on the floor while Paul filibustered John Brennan's nomination to be director of the CIA—a protest of the Obama administration's use of drone strikes overseas. Wyden voted to confirm Brennan, but he called on the administration to produce more documents about its drone policy.

In January 2017, Wyden battled President Donald Trump's first nominee for CIA director, then-Rep. Mike Pompeo, forcing a six-hour debate on the Senate floor before Pompeo was confirmed. Wyden took aim at an op-ed piece that Pompeo had written a year earlier that called for establishing programs collecting Americans' metadata, which Congress had restricted in 2015. Pompeo said such metadata should be combined with publicly available financial and lifestyle information into a "comprehensive searchable database." Wyden said on the Senate floor: "I have never heard an idea so extreme, so overarching and so intrusive of Americans' privacy. We are headed into dangerous times."

Wyden's interest in the internet goes back to the mid-1990s. He was an early champion of internet freedom, often siding with the tech sector against Hollywood and other content producers who sought strict anti-piracy laws. He and then-California Republican Rep. Christopher Cox sponsored a three-year ban on taxation of access to the internet that passed in 1998. The ban on such taxes was extended several times until Congress made the prohibition permanent in 2016.

Wyden's efforts to cross the aisle on health care date to the George W. Bush's presidency. He was one of 11 Senate Democrats to vote for the Republican-authored Medicare prescription drug law in 2003. "It wasn't a bill I would have written. But I thought it was the right thing to do to get started," he said. Later, with Snowe, he sponsored a bill to allow the federal government to negotiate drug prices with pharmaceutical companies.

As Obama's health care overhaul was debated in 2009, Wyden joined Republican BobBennett of Utah on a bill to replace the tax exclusion for employer-provided health insurance with a tax deduction for individuals to buy insurance from private insurers. The Obama administration and key Senate committee chairmen disagreed that changes in tax incentives alone would achieve the goal of insuring millions of Americans without health insurance. "Ron Wyden's brand is as a guy who wants to get things done," Bennett, who lost reelection in 2010, later said. "Anything he does with a Republican who is reasonable builds that brand, even if it doesn't come to fruition. ...He's built this brand and he loves it."

Wyden did not get a lot of love from his own party when he joined forces with Rep. Paul Ryan of Wisconsin—then chairman of the House Budget Committee and later House speaker— in December 2011to offer a plan to partially privatize and radically transform Medicare. The Democratic Party had already campaigned against—and condemned—Ryan's budget blueprint to change Medicare, and Wyden's move undermined the party's message. The Obama White House said the plan would "end Medicare as we know it." The Wyden-Ryan plan would have allowed insurers to compete with traditional Medicare and give patients subsidies they could use for either fee-for-service Medicare or private insurance.

The next summer, Ryan was chosen as Republican Mitt Romney's running mate in the presidential race. In arguing that Ryan'sMedicare plan had bipartisan support, the Romney campaign cited Wyden. By then, Wyden had disavowed the plan. He denounced Romney's claims and sought to downplay his involvement with the plan by noting he had not drafted actual legislation with Ryan. But critics on the left complained that Wyden "gave cover" to Ryan while the Republicans were on the political defensive.

Wyden has long promoted a broad restructuring of the tax code, including reductions in tax rates and an expansion of the tax base by eliminating tax preferences and deductions. In 2010, he and Republican Judd Gregg of New Hampshire sponsored a measure with three income tax brackets—15 percent, 25 percent and 35 percent—a lower corporate tax rate and immediate expensing of inventory and equipment for businesses with receipts under $1 million.

During his short-lived Finance chairmanship, which ended with the Republican takeover of the Senate in 2015, Wyden ran the committee with a lighter touch than his predecessors had—he even granted subcommittee chiefs more freedom to hold their own hearings. He didn't achieve much of what he wanted, in part because the leaders of his own party were leery of his independent ways. As the Washington Post put it, Wyden was "shoved aside by his majority leader, snubbed by his House counterpart and handcuffed by his president." The newspaper published a quote from a former aide to then-Senate Democratic Leader Harry Reid, Jim Manley, that was dismissive of Wyden's leadership style. "He's prone to quixotic causes and never really got into the nitty-gritty of the legislative process," Manley said.

The debate over the Trans-Pacific Partnership trade deal in 2015 allied Wyden with the Obama White House—albeit on the opposite side from most Democratic senators. Representing a Pacific Rim state heavily dependent on exports, Wyden was one of his party's most notable free-trade voices. Oregon is "the face of the opportunity to grow more good-paying jobs" from trade, he told the Post. Wyden and 11other Democrats joined most Republicans in voting to give Obama expedited negotiating authority for the 12-nation trade deal. His critics expressed their dismay: Activists back home chased him with a blimp and an RV and AFL-CIO President Richard Trumk a visited Portland just to scold Wyden and other free-trade backers in the state's delegation. Trump withdrew from the deal after taking office.

Wyden's attention to state issues, and his visibility at home—he holds forums in all 36 counties every year—have arguably made him the state's most enduring politician. Wyden has been a staunch defender of Oregon's landmark assisted-suicide law. He irritated allies in the environmental movement by backing a proposed liquefied natural gas terminal at Coos Bay in southern Oregon; opponents said it would lead to significant greenhouse-gas emissions. When a company in 2016 withdrew its application for a liquefied natural gas site at the mouth of the Columbia River in northwest Oregon amid strong local opposition, Wyden said he was relieved, adding, "I shared the concerns that the…project would have had negative environmental and economic impacts."

After Trump's selection, Wyden voiced worry about other nations, especially Russia, hacking U.S. government computers—including in Congress. In September 2018, he wrote to Senate leaders, saying their security office had claimed it lacked the authority to defend senators and their aides. Months later, he and Republican Sen. Tom Cotton of Arkansas requested that Senate authorities immediately inform senators if their computer networks get hacked.

Attacking the Federal Communications Commission in October 2020 when it sought to clarify the tech companies' immunity from lawsuits related to third-party content on their sites, Wyden—who helped to write the so-called Section 230 of the Communications Decency Act—tweeted, the "FCC does not have the authority to rewrite the law, and [the FCC chairman] can't appoint himself commissioner of the speech police." Three months later, after the elections, the FCC chairman resigned and support for his party-line proposal disappeared.

With Merkley, Wyden opposed the 2018 nomination of Ryan Bounds, a federal prosecutor in Oregon, to a judgeship on the 9th U.S. Circuit Court of Appeals. On the Senate floor, they read extensive excerpts from earlier writings by Bounds that Wyden described as "appalling stuff" in its "disdain for multicultural values." In an unusual concession by Senate Republicans, Bounds' nomination was withdrawn after it became clear that he lacked support for confirmation. Wyden voiced relief, hoping the move meant "the Senate [was] coming to its senses on judges."

In early 2019, Wyden backed House Ways and Means Committee Chairman Richard Neal's attempts to obtain Trump's tax returns. He filed a bill that affirmed the authority of Congress to require the delivery of such records, though the Supreme Court largely sided with Trump's continued resistance to those requests. In 2020, Wyden was an early proponent of expanding unemployment compensation so that workers who lost a job during the coronavirus pandemic could receive what had been the full amount of their income. Officials of the Trump administration contended that his proposal was not workable because of the complexity of such calculations. Congress approved other options for expansive jobless aid.

Wyden's call for congressional activism was an early indicator of how the two tax committees would deal with the tax code when both chambers were under Democratic control, and Wyden took back the Finance Committee gavel—as happened in January 2021. As chairman, one of his prime interests was expansion of retirement programs for workers, including 401(k) plans. He promoted a proposal that would tax capital gains as they appreciate (and permit deduction of losses as they mount), especially as a tool to assure that the wealthiest taxpayers are accountable for benefits that have been realized. Wyden said that another top priority would be enforcement crackdowns by the Internal Revenue Service against wealthy taxpayers who have abused tax breaks.

On health care, Wyden told Vox in 2019 that he had abandoned the prospect of reaching bipartisan agreements. Democrats, he said, were "united around the proposition that Americans need and want Medicare-type choices," including a revival of the "public option" that many Democrats supported during debate on the Affordable Care Act. Adding that it was vital to cut costs for individuals who already were insured, he said, "Congress should have gone much further when it had the chance [in 2009] and had a laser like focus on holding health care costs down." With Republican Sen. Chuck Grassley of Iowa, who was the Finance Committee chairman until January 2021, Wyden filed a bill to cap drug-price increases at the rate of inflation for Medicare beneficiaries.

In 2016, Wyden won a fourth full term 57%-33%, defeating Republican Mark Callahan, a perennial candidate who surprised even himself by winning a four-way primary for the GOP nomination. Although the Democratic vote in statewide contests in Oregon has been decreasing in recent years, Wyden faced no threat of a serious challenge in 2022. Assuming he is reelected, at 73, he could have an extended tenure as the top Democrat at Senate Finance and in his other Senate assignments.

Jeff Merkley (D)

Elected 2008, term expires 2026, 3rd term, b. Oct 24, 1956; Myrtle Creek; Stanford University, B.A., 1979; Princeton University, M.P.P., 1982; Lutheran; Married (Mary Sorteberg); 2 children.

Elected Office: OR House, 1999-2008, Speaker, 2007-2008.

Professional Career: President Fellow, Office of the Secretary of Defense, 1982-1985; National Security Analyst, CBO, 1985-1989; Executive Director, Portland Habitat for Humanity, 1991-1994; Director of Housing Development, Human Solutions, 1995-1996; President, World Affairs Council of OR, 1996-2003.

DC Office: 313 HSOB 20510, 202-224-3753, Fax: 202-228-3997, merkley.senate.gov

State Offices: Bend, 541-318-1298; Eugene, 541-465-6750; Medford, 541-608-9102; Pendleton, 541-278-1129; Portland, 503-326-3386; Salem, 503-362-8102.

Committees: *Appropriations*: Agriculture, Rural Development, FDA & Related Agencies; Commerce, Justice, Science & Related Agencies; Department of the Interior, Environment & Related Agencies (Chmn); DOL, HHS & Education & Related Agencies; Energy & Water Development; State, Foreign Operations & Related Programs. *Budget*. *Environment & Public Works*: Chem Safety, Waste Mngmnt, Enviro Justice & Reg Oversight (Chmn); Clean Air & Nuclear Safety; Transportation & Infrastructure. *Foreign Relations*: Africa & Global Health Policy; East Asia, the Pacific & International Cybersecurity Policy; West Hem Crime Civ Sec Dem Rights & Women's Issues. *Rules & Administration*.

Group Ratings

	ADA	ACLU	AFL-CIO	LCV	COC	HAFA	ACU	CFG	FRC
2020	-	92%	-	92%	-	0%	4%	-	-
2019	100%	C	95%	100%	32%	C	3%	8%	0%

Almanac Ratings 2019-2020

	Economy	Social	Foreign	Composite
Liberal	100%	100%	92%	97%
Conservative	0%	0%	8%	3%

Key Votes of the 116th Congress

1. EPA clean energy rules	Y	5. Russia sanctions	Y
2. U.S./Mex./Can. trade deal	Y	6. Troops in SYR, AFG	N
3. Cut unemployment benefits	N	7. Veto arms sales to Saudis	Y
4. Shelton to Fed Reserve	N	8. Defense $$$, veto override	N

9. Barr as Atty. General	N
10. Spending at the border	N
11. Coney Barrett to Sup. Ct.	N
12. Electoral College objections	N

Election Results

Election	Name (Party)	Vote (%)		Cand. Spent	Ind. Exp. Support	Ind. Exp. Oppose
2020 General	Jeff Merkley (D)	1,321,047	(57%)	$4,464,611	$1,130	
	Jo Rae Perkins (R)	912,814	(39%)	$109,383	$12	$113
2020 Primary	Jeff Merkley (D)	564,878	(99%)			

Prior winning percentages: 2014 (56%), 2008 (49%)

Democrat Jeff Merkley, Oregon's junior senator, has attracted a following among activists beyond his home state for his aggressive pursuit of his agenda. "I'm absolutely a risk-taker," Merkley said, " and it kind of catches people off guard." In 2016, he became the only senator to endorse his colleague Bernie Sanders of Vermont for the Democratic presidential nomination. His hard-charging tactics have caused him to at times run afoul of the chamber's Democratic leader, Chuck Schumer of New York.

In March 2019, after several months of exploration, Merkley decided not to run for president the following year. Instead, he said in a video announcing that he would seek a third term, "I'm going to work to fix our broken and dysfunctional Senate so it isn't just a graveyard for good ideas. To fix America, we must fix the Senate." At the time, he acknowledged that Oregon lawmakers were unwilling to change a state law that would have prohibited him from running for president while also seeking reelection to the Senate. Unlike 2016, he did not make an early endorsement in the Democratic presidential primary.

Merkley was born in Myrtle Creek in Oregon's Douglas County, where his parents worked at a sawmill. The saw mill closed when Merkley was 2, and his father went to work as a logger and a homebuilder in the neighboring town of Roseburg. When those jobs disappeared, the family moved to Portland, where his father took a job as a mechanic. He still resides in the East Portland neighborhood in which he grew up, and his kids went to the same schools that he attended. "My parents lived with an ethic of making sure they saved and spent very little money on frills," he recalled.

In high school, Merkley spent a summer in Ghana as part of the American Field Service Exchange Program. At Stanford University, he earned a bachelor's degree in international affairs. As an intern with the Carnegie Endowment for International Peace in 1980, he and a fellow intern traveled through Central America by bus. He earned a master's degree in public policy from Princeton University, landed a presidential fellowship at the Pentagon in 1982 and worked as an analyst in the Congressional Budget Office.

Merkley returned to Portland in the early 1990s and accepted a job as director of the city's Habitat for Humanity chapter, where he concentrated on affordable housing and skills training for at-risk youth and low-income families. He worked for the World Affairs Council in Oregon. Merkley was elected to the state House in 1998, having campaigned on a platform to improve the state's school system. In 2003, state House Democrats cited his consensus-building ability as they chose him for minority leader. Once he became party leader, Merkley exhibited his no-holds-barred side as he campaigned on behalf of Democratic candidates in 2006, including running a television ad that accused the Republican House speaker of covering up suspected sexual misconduct by her brother-in-law. State Republicans condemned the ad as over the line. Democrats won control of the Oregon House for the first time in 16 years, and Merkley was elected speaker.

He had a busy two years as speaker. The Legislature passed an expanded indoor smoking ban and extended more rights to same-sex couples. Merkley pushed through an ethics bill aimed at curbing gifts from lobbyists to lawmakers. He took on Oregon's payday loan industry with a bill that imposed an interest rate cap of 36 percent annually on consumer loans of less than $50,000, and he negotiated establishment of a rainy-day fund to protect schools and other state services from recessions; an increase in the state's corporate minimum tax paid for the fund. The Oregonian called the session " one of the most successful…of recent years."

In 2008, after two House Democrats passed on the opportunity to challenge GOP Sen. Gordon Smith, Schumer— then chairman of the Democratic Senatorial Campaign Committee— recruited Merkley."The fact that I ended up in that campaign was a real shock to me," Merkley reminisced years later.Despite the endorsements and financial backing of the national party, Merkley faced stiff primary competition from liberal activist and political consultant Steve Novick, who had opposed Merkley's elevation to House minority leader five years earlier. Merkley initially ignored Novick and focused his campaign on Smith. But Novick labeled Merkley as pro-war for a vote cast in favor of a 2003 resolution that praised both President George W. Bush and U.S. troops for courage in the war in Iraq. Merkley narrowly won the primary, 45%-42%.

The general election was among the most expensive and closely watched contests of 2008. Smith had broken with his party by voting for higher automobile mileage standards and against oil drilling in the Arctic National Wildlife Refuge. Merkley allied himself with Democratic presidential nominee Barack Obama and his campaign theme of change. The message resonated in a state where Bush's approval ratings were particularly weak. Smith touted his reputation for bipartisanship, particularly his good relationship with fellow Oregon Sen. Ron Wyden, a Democrat. He attempted to distance himself from Bush, running ads that featured shots of Wyden, Sen. Ted Kennedy of Massachusetts and even Obama. Merkley won 49%-46%. Smith out raised Merkley $13 million to $7 million, but the Democratic Senatorial Campaign Committee and outside groups poured in $11 million to help Merkley. The election gave Oregon two Democrats in the Senate for the first time in 40 years.

"When he was running, people didn't expect him to be quite as progressive as he turned out to be," Tim Carpenter of the Progressive Democrats of America said. Arriving on Capitol Hill just months after the financial crisis of 2008 began, Merkley hammered Wall Street. During debate over the 2010 Dodd-Frank law on financial regulation, he joined Democrat Carl Levin of Michigan to craft a tough version of the "Volcker Rule" banning banks from engaging in risky investment practices that may have contributed to the crisis. Their provision remained in the final bill, albeit in a weakened version.

Merkley was one of 11 Democrats to oppose President Obama's nomination of Ben Bernanke in 2010 for a second term as Federal Reserve chairman. He contended Bernanke was partly at fault for the recession and was the wrong person to trust with an economic recovery. Four years later, Merkley was among the progressives whose opposition stymied Obama's plan to nominate former Treasury Secretary Larry Summers to succeed Bernanke; the party's left wing saw Summers as too accommodating to Wall Street. Merkley also joined progressive Democrats in the debate over the Affordable Care Act, as they unsuccessfully pushed for a Senate vote on a government-run "public option" to compete with private insurers.

As a follow-on to his advocacy while speaker of the Oregon House for extending rights to same-sex couples, Merkley played a leading role in drafting and moving the Employment Non-Discrimination Act, which would protect members of the LGBTQ community from job discrimination. The legislation passed 64-32in November 2013 with bipartisan backing. The bill didn't make it out of the House. Prominent on Merkley's office wall is a letter from Kennedy— for years the Senate's leading liberal voice—turning over leadership on the issue to Merkley.

Merkley has courted progressive activists outside the Beltway. "He gets the value of an inside-outside partnership— of really using pressure from around the country to get Washington D.C., to pay attention," said Adam Green, co-founder of the Progressive Change Campaign Committee. He was upfront in standing alone among his Senate colleagues in endorsing Sanders. "It doesn't feel lonely, it just feels right," Merkley told the Atlantic, adding, "I think we need to fundamentally change the system that has been so deeply moving towards consolidation of power by the very few." In turn, once the Sanders campaign had fallen short, some progressive activists floated his name as a running mate for Hillary Clinton before the Democratic National Convention in July 2016. Notwithstanding his limited name recognition outside his home state and a reputation as a less-than-fiery stump speaker, Merkley, they argued, would bring progressive enthusiasm to the ticket.

Merkley was aligned with Sanders, Warren and other leading progressives—and against most Oregon legislators, as well as Obama—in opposing the Trans-Pacific Partnership trade deal in 2015. While free trade receives notable support in export-friendly Oregon, Merkley opposed the pact. "Here we are repeating the same basic structure of the other agreements with no changes for America and therefore no improvement for the workers," he said in a floor speech.

Representing a state where the sale of both medical and recreational marijuana is legal, Merkley has regularly filed legislation to allow Veterans Affairs physicians to discuss with patients marijuana as a treatment option for pain and symptoms related to post-traumatic stress disorder. With Republican Sen. Steve Daines of Montana—another state where medical marijuana is legal—he sponsored a bill to make medicinal cannabis easier to access for veterans. In both 2015 and 2016, the Senate and House approved amendments to appropriations bills for which Merkley had advocated. But the marijuana language was quietly stripped in House-Senate conference committees. Merkley blasted the removal as "outrageous" but failed to get the provision reinserted.

In 2018, he made progress on steps to legalize hemp and make it readily available. This time, he had the vital assistance of Sen. Mitch McConnell of Kentucky, then the Senate majority leader and an advocate for hemp—a productive home-state crop; hemp is derived from a cannabis plant but does not provide a high like marijuana and is typically used as a fiber. With Wyden and Rand Paul, the other two senators from their states, Merkley and McConnell won approval of the Hemp Farming Act as part of the sweeping farm bill that was enacted in December 2018. That legislation defined hemp as an agricultural commodity and removed it from the list of controlled substances. Merkley welcomed that result and teamed with Democratic Sen. Cory Booker of New Jersey on a bill that would legalize marijuana nationwide.

Merkley received extensive news coverage in June 2018 when he traveled to a site along the southern border in McAllen Texas, where hundreds of migrant children were housed after having been separated from their families. He sought entry into the facility as a senator, but the police denied him access. He said that the Trump administration had acted to "deliberately inflict trauma on [asylum-seekers'] children." He returned to the border six months later, this time with several other congressional Democrats, and visited an encampment where 2,700 migrant children were being held near El Paso. "This is a child prison strategy that inflicts trauma on children," he said. "It's part of the broader strategy of the Trump administration. ...It's completely unacceptable." He was again denied access to the facility. Republicans accused him of grandstanding.

Merkley has been outspoken on both sides of the Senate filibuster. Earlier, when Senate Democrats were in the majority, he lobbied outside groups to support efforts to restrict Republicans' ability to block progressive-backed legislation via a filibuster. In 2010, he told the New Yorker he winces when he hears the Senate described as the world's greatest deliberative body. "The amount of real deliberation, in terms of exchange of ideas, is so limited," he said. Arguing that the Senate was broken, he joined then-Democratic Sen. Tom Udall of New Mexico on a proposal to ban the filibustering of motions to proceed to legislation. After initially resisting their efforts, then-Majority Leader Harry Reid in 2013 pushed through a no-filibuster rule for most judicial and executive appointments. To Democrats' dismay, McConnell—as majority leader in in 2017, after Republicans had taken the majority—extended the Democrats' rules change to cover Supreme Court nominees, in the face of a filibuster of President Donald Trump's nomination of Neil Gorsuch to the high court.

By that time, Merkley's perspective on filibustering had shifted. In January 2017, he vowed to filibuster Gorsuch to exact revenge for McConnell's refusal to allow hearings or a vote on Obama's nominee for the same seat, Merrick Garland, a year earlier. According to Politico, an irritated Schumer —having succeeded Reid as Democratic leader—warned Merkley about making the battle about retribution for Garland instead of the nominee's merits. That warning was futile. Shortly before McConnell's move to change the filibuster rules on nominations, Merkley delivered the eighth-longest floor speech in Senate history; it was nearly 15 hours and 30 minutes long. He charged the Republicans had "stolen" a Supreme Court seat and detailed Democratic concerns about Gorsuch. McConnell already had set the vote on the Senate rules change, and Merkley's move did not delay Senate business.

When Democrats in 2021 reclaimed Senate control, albeit with a razor-thin majority, Merkley resumed his role as a leading foe of the filibuster. Gaining a seat on the Senate Rules and Administration Committee, he joined with Chairwoman Amy Klobuchar of Minnesota in taking the lead on behalf of the House-passed For the People Act, which would make a litany of changes to election and congressional rules. When he was wrestling with whether to seek reelection in 2020, he told The Hill in March 2021, "I thought, well, if I run for reelection it's going to be because I make an all-out push to restore the Senate as a functioning body." In a separate interview a month earlier with Northwest Labor Press, he said that Democrats would give Republicans an opportunity to show whether they would cooperate in debating major legislation. "That process, I think, will help solidify the sense that we have to move quickly for reform if there isn't cooperation from the Republican side on letting the Senate function."

After a handful of senators were accused of using secret information about the looming coronavirus pandemic to benefit themselves on the stock market, Merkley in June 2020filed a bill that would prohibit members of Congress from trading any individual stocks, though they would be allowed to trade mutual funds. The Stock Act, which was enacted in 2012 and imposed additional limits on insider trading, "was not strong enough medicine for the problem," he told the New York Times.

In the majority, Merkley gained home-state influence when he became chairman of the Appropriations Subcommittee on Interior, Environment and Related Agencies. As the first Oregonian from the Senate or House to serve on Appropriations since 1996, when Republican Mark Hatfield retired as chairman of the Senate panel, he told E&E News that "addressing climate change and creating more healthy forests [were] steps toward combating wildfires that have devastated Oregon in recent years." A supporter of the "Green New Deal,"Merkley said that climate change should be declared a national emergency.

In his two reelection campaigns, Merkley faced GOP outsiders. In 2014, Republicans sought to portray him as out of touch with most Oregon voters. His opponent, Monica Wehby, a pediatric neurosurgeon with moderate positions, faced media reports alleging she had stalked her ex-husband and a former boyfriend. No charges were filed and Wehby blamed Democrats for trying to "shred" her family. But she never recovered politically from the allegations. Merkley won, 56%-37%.

Six years, later, Merkley faced Republican Jo Rae Perkins, a perennial candidate and outspoken conservative who embraced the QAnon conspiracy theories. In a message to supporters, the Washington Post reported after her primary victory, she said, "I stand with President Trump; I stand with Q and the team." Perkins spent a paltry $109,000. Merkley, who spent $4.5 million on the campaign, largely ignored her. The day after she won the GOP primary, he told a Portland television station, "I have no comment on my potential Republican opponent." He won, 57%-39%. Perkins, who had lost GOP primaries in previous years, said that she planned to challenge Sen. Ron Wyden in 2022.

During the 2020 campaign, the George Floyd and Black Lives Matter protests in Portland dominated local news coverage for weeks— and they occasionally became violent. When Trump sent federal law enforcement to the city, over the objections of state and local officials, Merkley attacked the presence of what he called "paramilitary" forces and called for an investigation by federal inspectors general.

Suzanne Bonamici (D)

Elected 2012, 5th term, b. Oct 14, 1954; Detroit, MI; Lane Community College, A.A.; University of OR Law School, J.D.; University of OR, B.A., 1980; Episcopalian; Married (Michael H. Simon); 2 children.

Elected Office: OR House, 2007-2008; OR Senate, 2008-2011.

Professional Career: Attorney, Federal Trade Commission, 1983-1986; Practicing attorney, 1986-1989; Legislative aide, 2001-2006.

DC Office: 2231 RHOB 20515, 202-225-0855, Fax: 202-225-9497, bonamici.house.gov

State Offices: Beaverton, 503-469-6010.

Committees: *Education & Labor*: Civil Rights & Human Services (Chmn); Higher Education & Workforce Investment. *Science, Space & Technology*: Energy; Environment. *Select Committee on the Climate Crisis*.

Group Ratings

	ADA	ACLU	AFL-CIO	LCV	COC	HAFA	ACU	CFG	FRC
2020	**	83%	**	100%	-	0%	4%	**	-
2019	95%	C	95%	97%	48%	C	4%	18%	0%

Almanac Ratings 2019-2020

	Economy	Social	Foreign	Composite
Liberal	100%	100%	92%	98%
Conservative	0%	0%	8%	2%

Key Votes of the 116th Congress

1. U.S./Mex./Can. trade deal	Y	5. Russia sanctions	Y
2. First Coronavirus response	Y	6. Troops in Syria	Y
3. HEROES Act	Y	7. Veto arms sales to Saudis	Y
4. CASH Act	Y	8. Defense $$$, veto override	N

9. Firearms background checks	Y
10. Spending at the border	N
11. Marijuana liberalized rules	Y
12. Electoral College objections	N

Election Results

Election	Name (Party)	Vote (%)		Cand. Spent	Ind. Exp. Support	Ind. Exp. Oppose
2020 General	Suzanne Bonamici (D)	297,071	(65%)	$683,546	$8,123	
	Christopher Christensen (R)	161,928	(35%)	$648		$113
2020 Primary	Suzanne Bonamici (D)	100,733	(84%)			
	Heidi Briones (D)	8,260	(7%)			
	Amanda Siebe (D)	8,055	(7%)			

Prior winning percentages: 2018 (64%), 2016 (60%), 2014 (57%), 2012 (60%), 2012 special (54%)

Democrat Suzanne Bonamici, who won a special election in 2012, usually has been a reliable liberal. The chief exception has been that she is responsive to the needs and overseas interests of local businesses, often to the dismay of unions on international trade issues. She improved those relationships with her leadership in the House on education and child-care issues. Her coastal district has increased her advocacy on climate change.

Bonamici was born in Detroit and grew up in the small town of Northville Michigan. Her father worked at a local bank, and her mother was a piano teacher. After high school, Bonamici traveled with friends in a van to Oregon, fell in love with the state and moved to Eugene. "It was a very '70s thing to do," Bonamici told The Oregonian. She attended Lane Community College and worked at a legal-aid center in Eugene. Bonamici got her bachelor's and law degrees from the University of Oregon. She moved to Washington D.C. to take a job as a consumer protection lawyer at the Federal Trade Commission. There, she met her husband and they went back to Oregon, where Bonamici was a lawyer in private practice. After working in the Oregon House of Representatives, she won a state

House seat and focused on consumer protection. She was appointed to fill a vacancy in the state Senate and then was elected.

When Democratic Rep. David Wu resigned amid charges of improper sexual advances, Bonamici jumped into the special election. In the Democratic primary, she faced off against state Labor Commissioner Brad Avakian and state Rep. Brad Witt; both opposed U.S. trade pacts with Colombia, Panama and South Korea that were being debated in Congress. After she initially declined to take a position and drew criticism for indecisiveness, Bonamici supported the South Korea pact. She raised the most money of the three candidates and won with 66 percent of the vote.

In the general, Bonamici faced Rob Cornilles, a sports business consultant. Cornilles played up his business experience and kept his distance from the national GOP. Bonamici ran an ad attacking him for an old federal tax lien against his business over failure to pay payroll taxes. The Democratic Congressional Campaign Committee, EMILY's List and other liberal interest groups poured millions into the race, while national Republican groups mostly stayed away. Bonamici won, 54%-40%.

On the Education and the Workforce Committee, she focused on making college more affordable and reforming the No Child Left Behind Act. On the renewal of student-loan legislation in 2014, she worked with others to add increased financial counseling for recipients. As chairwoman of the Subcommittee on Civil Rights and Human Services, Bonamici in February 2021 outlined plans for "making our system of public education more equitable so all students have the opportunity to succeed" and addressing the problem that "too many women, people of color, older workers, workers with disabilities and LGBTQ workers still experience harassment and discrimination in the workplace."With Democratic Rep. Katherine Clark, she was a leading advocate of party plans to expand child-care services, especially during the disruption of the pandemic. Bonamici was a founder and remained co-chair of the bipartisan Congressional STEAM Caucus, which encourages innovation in science, technology, engineering, art and design, and math education.

On the Science, Space and Technology Committee, Bonamici focused on global climate change, including ocean policy. In 2017, she enacted her bill to improve warnings and education in coastal communities about the threat of tsunamis. With Republican Rep. Don Young of Alaska; she wrote an op-ed in 2018 about the economic stakes in protecting the health of the oceans, including marine life. In 2019, she co-chaired the Oceans Caucus and was a member of the Select Committee on the Climate Crisis, where she advocated comprehensive policies to "protect our planet." In 2019, she was part of a House Democratic working group that reached agreement with the Trump administration on what she described as "meaningful improvements" in environmental standards and access to prescription drugs, as part of the renegotiation of the North American Free Trade Agreement.

In 2015, Bonamici was one of 28 House Democrats who voted to give trade promotion authority to President Barack Obama, whose prospective Trans-Pacific Partnership was touted as an economic boon for West Coast companies and ports. She cited the benefits for local wheat and potato farmers. She accompanied Obama on a visit to Nike headquarters, where he said the deal would benefit Oregon companies. A few days later, AFL-CIO President Richard Trumka spoke in Portland and warned that he was "blowing the whistle, quite frankly" on Bonamici and other Portland-area Democrats in Congress for being on "the wrong side" of TPP, which he said most Oregonians opposed.

Bonamici has been reelected easily. Despite the threat of a challenge backed by organized labor or a loss of enthusiasm among her base, she suffered neither. In the Democratic primary in 2016, her opponent was Shabba Woodley, a 25-year-old videographer who had no money or political experience and read poetry to a reporter. Bonamici won the primary with 90 percent of the vote.Her Republican opponent, Brian Heinrich, was a sales representative who was running his first campaign. He did not file a campaign-finance report. Bonamici won, 60%-37%, and retained support from a broad array of interest groups. She was reelected in 2018 with no Democratic primary and with comparable ease. In 2020, she won the Democratic primary with 84 percent of the vote against three challengers.

During the months-long protests in Portland in 2020, Bonamici joined other Oregon Democrats in demanding that federal inspectors general investigate the unrequested presence of federal law enforcement officials on downtown streets, plus the resulting violence.

OR-1: Northwest Oregon

Cook Partisan Voting Index: D+12

Population		Race and Ethnicity		Income	
Total	858,875	White	78.50%	Median Income	$81,473
Land area (sq. miles)	3,007	Black	1.80%	District Income Rank	81
Pop/ sq mi	285.63	Latino	15.00%	Poverty Rate	8.90%
Born in State	43.70%	Asian	9.00%	With health insurance	94.20%
		Two or more races	4.90%	Cash public assistance	2.60%
Age Groups		Other	5.90%	Food stamp/SNAP	8.90%
Under 18	21.60%				
18-34	23.50%	**Education**		**Work**	
35-64	39.50%	H.S grad or less	27.20%	White Collar	45.00%
Over 64	15.40%	Some college	32.10%	Sales and Service	35.20%
		College Degree, 4 yr	24.40%	Blue Collar	19.80%
Military		Post grad	16.40%	Government	11.50%
Veteran/ Active Duty	7.00%				

2020 Pres. Vote	Biden	298,701	(63%)	Trump	160,855	(34%)	Jorgensen	9,562	(2%)
2016 Pres. Vote	Clinton	219,369	(55%)	Trump	132,195	(33%)	Johnson	22,061	(6%)
	Stein	9,036	(2%)						

Western Portland Area: Just over the hills from downtown Portland are the valleys and interstices between green mountains of suburban Washington County. This was once farm country, with 39,000 people in 1940; now it has almost 602,000 and is an integral part of metro Portland. Its population zoomed up 70 percent between 1990 and 2010, with an increase of another 72,000 in the next nine years. Its towns enjoy a high-tech, healthy-lifestyle affluence, cushioned by protected forests and anchored by major employers that include Intel, Tektronix, IBM and Columbia Sportswear. Like Silicon Valley, the Silicon Forest has an environment that appeals to a highly skilled workforce. Nestled at the foot of mountains, it is woodsy and even rustic, but is outfitted with all the comforts of modern life. The Asian population of the county is 12 percent.

Intel is the largest private employer in Oregon, many of them at its 530-acre campus in Hillsboro, with the start of construction in early 2019 of a huge expansion to house the next generation of computer chips. The new facility at Ronler Acres, its most advanced production site, was expected to add 1,750 employees—a total of 21,000 for Intel in Oregon. The tech industry's move away from standard chips has led Intel to new markets, such as data and memory. In August 2019, a Japanese company that specializes in chip-industry supply and helps other chip companies with the growing complexity of their manufacturing announced its plan for a $100 million factory in rapidly growing Hillsboro. Intel reportedly was years behind schedule in development of its latest-generation micro-processor, The Oregonian reported at the time. In November 2020, Intel was contemplating moving to Asia much of its advanced production, according to the paper.

Near Beaverton is the world headquarters of Nike, housed in 75 buildings spread over 300 acres, with more than 11,000 local employees. Many of them work on breakthrough products that are designed and developed for the world's athletes and those who emulate them. In November 2020, Nike announced layoffs of 700 employees—an unusual move that appeared to be pandemic-related.

The 1st Congressional District of Oregon includes the western slice of Portland and all of suburban Washington County, which includes two-thirds of the voters. It extends nearly 100 miles northwest from Portland along the Columbia River to the rain-swept port of Astoria on the Pacific Coast, where Lewis and Clark spent the winter of 1805-06. (The event is memorialized at the Lewis and Clark National Historical Park.) Yamhill County and Beaverton are known for wineries. Coastal Astoria, at the mouth of the Columbia River, retains many century-old buildings and has been a popular site to shoot movies. Its booming tourism businesses were hit hard by the pandemic. Like Oregon overall, the 1st was historically New England Republican, electing only Republicans to Congress from 1892 to 1972. It trended left on cultural issues, and since 1974 has elected only Democrats. In a big increase in the Democratic vote that grew the parallel to Silicon Valley, Joe Biden won 63 percent of the presidential vote in 2020.

Cliff Bentz (R)

Elected 2020, 1st term, b. Jan 12, 1952; Salem, OR; Eastern OR State College; Northwestern School of Law, Lewis and Clark College; Roman Catholic; Married (Dr. Lindsay Norman); 2 children.

Elected Office: OR House, 2008-2018; OR Senate, 2018-2020.

Professional Career: Associate, law firm, 1977-1980; Partner, law firm; Assistant Republican Leader, OR House, 2017-2018; Deputy Republican Leader, OR Senate.

DC Office: 1239 LHOB 20515, 202-225-6730, Fax: 202-225-5774, bentz.house.gov

State Offices: Medford, 541-776-4646; Ontario, 541-709-2040.

Committees: *Judiciary*: Antitrust, Commercial & Administrative Law; Courts, Intellectual Property & Internet. *Natural Resources*: Indigenous Peoples of the United States; Water, Oceans & Wildlife (RMM).

Election Results

Election	Name (Party)	Vote (%)		Cand. Spent	Ind. Exp. Support	Ind. Exp. Oppose
2020 General	Cliff Bentz (R)	273,835	(60%)	$1,376,747	$226,184	$54,141
	Alex Spenser (D)	168,881	(37%)	$5,000		
	Robert Werch (L)	14,094	(3%)			
2020 Primary	Cliff Bentz (R)	37,488	(31%)			
	Knute Buehler (R)	26,405	(22%)			
	Jason Atkinson (R)	23,274	(20%)			
	Jimmy Crumpacker (R)	21,507	(18%)			

Republican Cliff Bentz won a competitive primary and rolled to victory in the only GOP-held seat in the Oregon congressional delegation. As a resident of the eastern edge of the vast district, he had a distinctive base from the two other leading contenders, both of whom resided near its western border. All three had been active in state politics, though their professional experience varied. Bentz succeeded Greg Walden, who held the seat for 22 years and was the influential chairman of the House Energy and Commerce Committee and, earlier, a partisan strategist as head of the National Republican Congressional Committee.

Bentz, who was raised on his family's cattle ranches in eastern Oregon, graduated from Eastern Oregon State College and got his law degree from Lewis and Clark Law School in Portland. He joined a law firm in Ontario, where he specialized in ranch organizations and water law. He chaired a local school board and served eight years as a member of the state's Water Resources Commission, which he also chaired. He owns an alfalfa farm.

In 2008, Bentz was appointed to a seat in the state House, where he served 10 years, until he was appointed to fill a Senate vacancy. His rural Senate district was roughly the size of Indiana. In the legislature, he was a leader on energy and infrastructure issues.

In June 2019, he joined a Republican boycott that prevented action on a Democratic climate-change bill. "When the Democratic majority decided to trade Oregon's economic free-market system for one of government control—while ignoring our constitution and making a shambles of Oregon's rural and low-income economies—we walked," he wrote at the time.

As the Republican challenger to Gov. Kate Brown in 2018, Knute Buehler, a physician, was the best-known candidate and the early frontrunner in the field. The other leading contenders were business consultant Jason Atkinson and Jimmy Crumpacker, who operated an investment fund. Both Buehler and Crumpacker more than doubled the spending by Bentz during the primary. Bentz got significant backing from the Republican Main Street Partnership, a centrist party group. Conservatives opposed Buehler's pro-abortion rights views.

On his campaign website, Bentz wrote that what separated him from the other candidates in the primary was, "I have been a resident of, and I have stood up for [the district] and eastern Oregon my entire life."

Bentz won the GOP primary with 31 percent of the vote to 22 percent for Buehler, 20 percent for Atkinson and 18 percent for Crumpacker. Bentz took 16 of the 20 counties in the district, but led in only one of the four largest counties. Buehler led in Bend-based Deschutes, which was his home county. Atkinson took the adjacent counties of Jackson and Josephine, where he resided. Those three counties are on the western edge of the district and about 300 miles from the Idaho border, where Bentz resided near Ontario.

In an editorial endorsement, The Oregonian—the state's largest newspaper—said Bentz was "deeply attuned to the natural resources and economic development issues" that concern farmers and ranchers, and cited his expertise in environmental law and water rights. The Bend-based Bulletin wrote that, as a state legislator, Bentz "was known as somewhat of a wonk on transportation issues."

Bentz took the general election with 60 percent of the vote against Democrat Alex Spenser, a writer and performance coach, who had been an aide to Democratic candidates. Bentz won each county except for Hood River, which is the part of the district that is closest to Portland.

In the House he got seats on the Judiciary and Natural Resources committees and became ranking Republican on the Water, Oceans and Wildlife Subcommittee.

OR-2: Eastern Oregon   Cook Partisan Voting Index: R+11

Population		Race and Ethnicity		Income	
Total	841,022	White	89.70%	Median Income	$57,870
Land area (sq. miles)	69,443	Black	0.80%	District Income Rank	290
Pop/ sq mi	12.11	Latino	14.20%	Poverty Rate	13.00%
Born in State	43.10%	Asian	1.10%	With health insurance	91.70%
		Two or more races	3.70%	Cash public assistance	2.60%
Age Groups		Other	4.60%	Food stamp/SNAP	16.00%
Under 18	21.10%				
18-34	19.50%	Education		Work	
35-64	37.70%	H.S grad or less	37.80%	White Collar	35.90%
Over 64	21.60%	Some college	35.30%	Sales and Service	40.50%
		College Degree, 4 yr	16.40%	Blue Collar	23.50%
Military		Post grad	10.50%	Government	15.70%
Veteran/ Active Duty	10.60%				

2020 Pres. Vote	Trump	261,602	(55%)	Biden	197,922	(42%)		
2016 Pres. Vote	Trump	215,711	(55%)	Clinton	139,059	(35%)	Johnson	18,600	(5%)
	Stein	8,191	(2%)					

Medford, Bend: The Cascade Mountains that wall off eastern Oregon from the rest of the state are a magnificent chain of once active volcanic mountains that drain almost every drop of moisture out of the air blowing in from the Pacific Ocean. They separate green, wet western Oregon from brown, parched eastern Oregon. The eastern part has 70 percent of the state's land, but only around half a million of its 4 million people, many of whom still make their living off the land: beef and dairy cattle, timber and lumber, fish from the Columbia River, and wheat and sugar beets from the irrigated plains. The effect of the Cascades can be felt in the one place they are breached—the Columbia River Gorge. Here, funneled winds pound in steadily from the west, making the confluence of the Columbia and Hood rivers the best windsurfing site in the United States.

The 2nd Congressional District of Oregon covers nearly three-fourths of the state: everything east of the Cascades and the southernmost valley between the Cascades and the Coast Range. Much of this land is forested and unpopulated. In Bend and the surrounding area, the wilderness and high desert plateau have attracted software developers, outdoor activity, upscale tourists and telecommuters. With its 31 percent growth between 2010 and 2019, Bend has been one of the fastest-growing cities in the nation. CNBC reported in March 2018 that the city is so appealing—and relatively cheap— that some workers commute to their Silicon Valley jobs, in California. Prior to the pandemic, about 20 percent of the professionals in Bend worked from home. The influx of techies has shifted politics in surrounding Deschutes County, the largest in the district. In 2020, Joe Biden won the county with 53 percent of the vote—the only blue county east of the Cascades. Also in that election, progressives gained control of the city council in Bend.

In the town of The Dalles, Google was a pioneer in 2006 when it opened a data center on 30 acres of land on the Columbia River. Since then, Google has expanded its campus with a total investment of close to $2 billion. Oregon is an appealing site for these power-intensive facilities because it has no sales tax. To the south, other tech giants—including Apple and Facebook—have taken advantage of property tax breaks and opened huge data centers in once-tiny Prineville. With expanded solar energy, the area has quickly boosted its electrical power. In August 2020, the regional jail in The Dalles said it would no longer house prisoners for the Immigration and Customs Enforcement agency.

The 2nd District has been solidly Republican. In 2009, rural Jackson County saw its last remaining large sawmill dismantled; it had 91 in its heyday. In 2014, according to The Oregonian, "the pendulum had swung so far that Oregon's high-tech industry accounted for the same number of workers and share of wages as the forest sector did in the 1970s." This has been the only district in Oregon where Republican presidential candidates are competitive. Donald Trump got 55 percent of the vote, virtually the same as the GOP vote in the previous two presidential elections.

Earl Blumenauer (D)

Elected 1996, 13th full term, b. Aug 16, 1948; Portland, OR; Lewis & Clark College, B.A., 1970; Northwestern Law School, Lewis and Clark College, J.D., 1976; Married (Margaret Kirkpatrick Blumenauer); 2 children.

Elected Office: OR House, 1973-1978; Multnomah County Commissioner, 1978- 86; Portland City Council, 1986-1996.

Professional Career: Assistant to President, Portland St. University, 1970-1977; Portland Community College Board of Director, 1975-1981.

DC Office: 1111 LHOB 20515, 202-225-4811, Fax: 202-225-8941, blumenauer.house.gov

State Offices: Portland, 503-231-2300.

Committees: *Ways & Means*: Health; Social Security; Trade.

Group Ratings

	ADA	ACLU	AFL-CIO	LCV	COC	HAFA	ACU	CFG	FRC
2020	**	83%	**	100%	-	5%	5%	**	-
2019	95%	C	90%	93%	45%	C	5%	29%	5%

Almanac Ratings 2019-2020

	Economy	Social	Foreign	Composite
Liberal	100%	100%	92%	98%
Conservative	0%	0%	8%	2%

Key Votes of the 116th Congress

1. U.S./Mex./Can. trade deal	Y	5. Russia sanctions	N/A
2. First Coronavirus response	Y	6. Troops in Syria	Y
3. HEROES Act	Y	7. Veto arms sales to Saudis	Y
4. CASH Act	Y	8. Defense $$$, veto override	N

9. Firearms background checks	Y
10. Spending at the border	N
11. Marijuana liberalized rules	Y
12. Electoral College objections	N

Election Results

Election	Name (Party)	Vote (%)		Cand. Spent	Ind. Exp. Support	Ind. Exp. Oppose
2020 General	Earl Blumenauer (D)	343,574	(73%)	$1,605,423	$9,323	
	Joanna Harbour (R)	110,570	(24%)	$13,832	$12	$113
2020 Primary	Earl Blumenauer (D)	140,812	(81%)			
	Albert Lee (D)	29,311	(17%)			

Prior winning percentages: 2018 (73%), 2016 (72%), 2014 (72%), 2012 (75%), 2010 (70%), 2008 (75%), 2006 (74%), 2004 (71%), 2002 (67%), 2000 (67%), 1998 (84%), 1996 special (68%), 1996 (67%)

Democrat Earl Blumenauer, who won a special election in 1996, has pursued an idiosyncratic approach that is socially liberal with a "smart growth" economic approach that has sought to combat urban sprawl. On the Ways and Means Committee, where he chairs the International Trade subcommittee, he was part of Speaker Nancy Pelosi's working group in 2019 that negotiated final details of the updated North American Free Trade Agreement. In the majority, Blumenauer has been active on other committee issues, including his leadership role in securing COVID-19 relief for the restaurant industry. He is known for his distinctive bow ties and bike rides.

Blumenauer grew up in Portland and graduated from Lewis and Clark College and its Northwestern Law School. In his teens, he was inspired by the civil rights and anti-war movements of the 1960s. In college, he headed a statewide campaign to lower Oregon's voting age. He has held public office for almost all his adult life—nearly a half-century. In 1972, at age 23, he was elected to the Oregon House. He subsequently was elected as a Multnomah County commissioner and as a Portland city councilor; in the latter job, he also served as commissioner of public works.

He championed many of the policies that have made Portland distinctive—regional light-rail transit, curbside recycling and aggressive land-use planning. He encouraged bicycle riding and "regional rail summits," which bring neighborhood residents into the planning for higher densities at transit nodes. Blumenauer has had some setbacks, notably when he lost the 1992 mayoral race. He was the obvious successor when Ron Wyden was elected to the Senate, and he won the special election 67%-25%. His campaign slogan was "Vote Earl, Vote Often." In his Democratic bastion, he has never drawn less than 67 percent of the vote since and has not faced a serious primary challenge.

Blumenauer has had a consistently liberal voting record, as shown by his Almanac vote ratings. He has been a lead sponsor of a bill allowing states to legalize medical marijuana and to regulate it in a manner similar to alcohol. "We're still arresting two-thirds of a million people for use of a substance that a majority feel should be legal," Blumenauer told the Associated Press. In 2015, the House narrowly defeated a proposal that he cosponsored to give states the authority to legalize marijuana. In April 2016, Rolling Stone profiled him as the "top legal pot advocate" in Congress.

Blumenauer, who has ridden his bicycle everywhere he travels around Washington, formed a Congressional Bike Caucus. Blumenauer was astonished to find that the House subsidized parking for employees, but not mass transit; now employees can get subsidized transit fares. He is interested in what seem like quixotic projects now, but may seem less so in time: an interstate highway system for bicycle paths and reduced dependence on driving as a tool to improve public health. "The rise of bicycles is a metaphor for change in this country," Blumenauer says. To rescue the depleted highway trust fund, he has called for a 15-cent hike per gallon in the federal gas tax over a three-year period, plus eventual movement toward a mileage-based tax.

On economic issues, he has actively promoted trade across the Pacific, a key element of Portland's economy. He was an outspoken supporter of approving Trade Promotion Authority for President Barack Obama, noting in 2015 that "Oregon will not only be able to export more of its products, but also its values," including human rights, worker rights and environmental protections. He was caustic in criticizing other House Democrats, including party leaders, for their votes against extending trade adjustment assistance for workers adversely affected by overseas trade deals. "Political gamesmanship within our party won out over substance," he said.

Despite Blumenauer's support of some trade deals that in recent years has placed him among a minority of Democrats, Ways and Means Democrats selected him to become Trade Subcommittee chairman when they organized the committee in January 2019. In the seniority-based selection, Blumenauer was selected over Rep. Bill Pascrell of New Jersey, who had been ranking Democrat on the trade panel and complained that he was replaced without a vote on his own credentials.

The outcome made Blumenauer a leading participant in congressional handling of President Donald Trump's proposed revision of the U.S. trade deal with Canada and Mexico, though Pelosi's coordination of the House response weakened the customary authority of Ways and Means. When they reached agreement with the Trump administration's trade officials in December 2019, Blumenauer called it "a huge victory for Democrats, who insisted that radical change over old NAFTA be made and demanded that we set a new template for all future trade agreements."

In 2020, Blumenauer became a leading congressional advocate of financial support for the restaurant industry during the coronavirus pandemic. In October 2020, when House Democrats passed their own $2.2 trillion relief measure, it included his call for $120 billion for restaurants and bars. It was the first targeted relief for 500,000 independent restaurants that was passed by either the House or Senate. "What started as a local Portland effort to save our beloved food establishments has turned into a national movement," he said. Although Congress did not complete action on that measure in 2020, the $1.9 trillion COVID relief bill that President Joe Biden signed in March 2021 included $25 billion for local restaurants and their workers.

During the often destructive protests against racism that wracked Portland for weeks in 2020, he led legislative protests of what he called "federal paramilitary occupations" in Portland and elsewhere.

In October, he filed a proposal to prevent federal agents from deputizing local law-enforcement officers. With the election of Biden, his proposal had less salience, although the local violence continued.

OR-3: Multnomah County   Cook Partisan Voting Index: D+24

Population		Race and Ethnicity		Income	
Total	853,116	White	78.20%	Median Income	$73,091
Land area (sq. miles)	1,074	Black	4.80%	District Income Rank	142
Pop/ sq mi	794.	Latino	11.60%	Poverty Rate	11.60%
Born in State	43.10%	Asian	7.40%	With health insurance	92.80%
		Two or more races	5.60%	Cash public assistance	4.40%
Age Groups		Other	4.00%	Food stamp/SNAP	11.80%
Under 18	19.00%				
18-34	26.10%	**Education**		**Work**	
35-64	40.70%	H.S grad or less	26.90%	White Collar	45.30%
Over 64	14.30%	Some college	28.80%	Sales and Service	37.10%
		College Degree, 4 yr	26.80%	Blue Collar	17.60%
Military		Post grad	17.50%	Government	12.20%
Veteran/ Active Duty	5.50%				

2020 Pres. Vote	Biden	356,714	(74%)	Trump	112,509	(23%)		
2016 Pres. Vote	Clinton	282,402	(68%)	Trump	89,631	(22%)	Johnson	14,294	(4%)
	Stein	12,886	(3%)					

Greater Portland: Postmodern skyscrapers rising above the riverfront and below a range of hills: This is downtown Portland. The city—which would have been named Boston if a coin toss had gone the other way—started here, along the Willamette River just before it flows into the Columbia. Downtown Portland was once a dowdy place, proper in a New England kind of way, with a few formal buildings above the warehouses and factories. But the past four decades here have witnessed an explosion of affluence and creativity, symbolized by handsome high-rises, restored Victorian storefronts, a downtown transit trolley, and a light-rail line known as MAX (for Metropolitan Area Express). The population of the city increased 12 percent from 2010 to 2019.

On the Pacific Rim, Portland makes much of its living on trade with Asia. It has become a home to high-tech industries, particularly in the Silicon Forest suburbs. Local government also has produced change. Metro, the regional agency established just as growth was accelerating, is a counterweight against the endless population sprawl outward. The city encouraged development of high-density commercial space and housing around transit stops, and bicycle paths wind throughout the metropolitan area. Local leaders have sought to make Portland the nation's leader for biodiesel and other renewable fuels. In 2018, the local transit authority started using electric buses, with a goal to eliminate diesel buses by 2034.

The city's hipster sensibility was satirized on the IFC television show Portlandia, which featured Carrie Brownstein and Fred Armisen and had its final episode in 2018. That year, a survey ranked the Portland metro area second behind San Francisco in the share of its population that is gay, lesbian, bisexual or transgender. In other ways, the city is notably less diverse: Its population is 6 percent African American and 10 percent Hispanic. In 2016, The Atlantic headlined a story about the city, "The Racist History of Portland, the Whitest City in America."

In 2020, the weeks of nationwide protest that followed the death of George Floyd at the hands of police in Minneapolis were a troubling time for Portland residents—in their image to outsiders as well as their self-image. They voiced resentment of outsiders—ranging from radical agitators to President Donald Trump—who exploited local tensions and sporadic violence for their own benefit. What seemed new was that, without a local request, Trump sent federal law-enforcement officials who had little experience or training in quelling domestic protests, but conveyed a sense of military force. In The Atlantic, Anne Applebaum described the federal presence as "performative authoritarianism, a form of politics that reached new heights of sophistication in Russia in the past decade." The purpose of the troops, she added, was not to bring peace to Portland. "Instead of working with local leaders, they have antagonized them. Instead of coaxing people to go home, their behavior has caused more people to come out onto the streets. Instead of calming the situation, they are infuriating people."Still, the violence had pre-dated the arrival of the feds and persisted long after their departure.

Video tapes of the street clashes became campaign ads—not in Portland, but in political swing states. Among the troubling implications was that federal forces should assume the traditional local responsibility of enforcing law and order. As The Washington Post headlined the operation, "Trump showcased federal power in Portland, making a culture war campaign pitch."

The 3rd Congressional District of Oregon includes most of Portland, including downtown. It also takes in Multnomah County east of the city and a small part of suburban Clackamas County to the south, which includes a bit more than 10 percent of its voters. Small slices of Multnomah are in the 1st and 5th Districts. Politically, the 3rd is dominated by progressives. In 2020, Joe Biden increased the Democratic vote to 79 percent in Multnomah County and 74percent in the district. The Clackamas part of the district tilts Republican.

Peter DeFazio (D)

Elected 1986, 18th term, b. May 27, 1947; Needham, MA; Tufts University, B.A., 1969; University of OR, Att., 1971; University of OR, M.S., 1977; Roman Catholic; Married (Myrnie Daut).

Military Career: U.S. Air Force 1967-1971

Elected Office: Lane County Board of Commissioners, 1983-1986, chmn, 1985-1986.

Professional Career: District Director, U.S. Rep. James Weaver, 1977-1982.

DC Office: 2134 RHOB 20515, 202-225-6416, Fax: 202-226-3493, defazio.house.gov

State Offices: Coos Bay, 541-269-2609; Eugene, 541-465-6732; Roseburg, 541-440-3523.

Committees: *Transportation & Infrastructure*: Aviation; Coast Guard & Maritime Transportation; Economic Dev't, Public Buildings & Emergency Management; Highways & Transit; Water Resources & Environment.

Group Ratings

	ADA	ACLU	AFL-CIO	LCV	COC	HAFA	ACU	CFG	FRC
2020	**	82%	**	100%	-	0%	11%	**	-
2019	100%	C	90%	97%	44%	C	11%	15%	0%

Almanac Ratings 2019-2020

	Economy	Social	Foreign	Composite
Liberal	100%	54%	83%	79%
Conservative	0%	46%	17%	21%

Key Votes of the 116th Congress

1. U.S./Mex./Can. trade deal N	5. Russia sanctions Y	9. Firearms background checks Y
2. First Coronavirus response Y	6. Troops in Syria Y	10. Spending at the border N
3. HEROES Act Y	7. Veto arms sales to Saudis Y	11. Marijuana liberalized rules Y
4. CASH Act Y	8. Defense $$$, veto override Y	12. Electoral College objections N

Election Results

Election	Name (Party)	Vote (%)		Cand. Spent	Ind. Exp. Support	Ind. Exp. Oppose
2020 General	Peter DeFazio (D).......................... 240,950	(52%)		$5,838,408	$244,929	$308,792
	Alek Skarlatos (R)............................. 216,081	(46%)		$5,220,646	$100,931	$2,383,465
	Daniel Hoffay (G)........................ 10,118	(2%)				
2020 Primary	Peter DeFazio (D)......................... 96,077	(84%)				
	Doyle Elizabeth Canning (D)....... 17,701	(15%)				

Prior winning percentages: 2018 (56%), 2016 (56%), 2014 (59%), 2012 (59%), 2010 (55%), 2008 (82%), 2006 (62%), 2004 (61%), 2002 (64%), 2000 (68%), 1998 (70%), 1996 (66%), 1994 (67%), 1992 (71%), 1990 (86%), 1988 (72%), 1986 (54%)

Peter DeFazio, a Democrat first elected in 1986, is a persistent—and sometimes outspoken—populist who doesn't mind showing his independence from his party or loudly criticizing the conservative ideas he disdains. With his lengthy tenure, he has been eager to use his influential post as chairman of the Transportation and Infrastructure Committee to press for sweeping legislation to expand the nation's infrastructure.

DeFazio grew up in Massachusetts, moved to Oregon for graduate school, was a bike mechanic and went to work for Democratic Rep. Jim Weaver. In 1982, DeFazio moved to Springfield and won a seat on the county commission. When Weaver retired in 1986, DeFazio won his House seat in close contests. He beat Bill Bradbury 34%-33% in the primary and took the general election 54%-46%.

DeFazio has compiled a record that seems to satisfy both liberal Eugene and the more conservative parts of the district: The Almanac vote ratings have shown that he's liberal on most issues, and moderate on social issues. An original founder of the Progressive Caucus, he channeled the anger from millions of working Americans.

DeFazio often takes maverick views. He introduced a bill in 2011 allowing people to opt out of the health care law's individual mandate reviled by Republicans—but only if they waived the right to any government-backed medical help for at least three years. He voted against climate legislation in 2009 putting caps on carbon emissions, he said, because there were better ways to reduce greenhouse gas emissions, such as a carbon tax. Sometimes, his views are enacted: He took the lead in 2007 in the House effort to permit airline pilots to carry guns in the cockpit. Although the Bush administration initially opposed it, DeFazio won by an astonishing 250-175. The Senate followed suit.

DeFazio was the only member of Congress to oppose the final economic stimulus bill in 2009 after backing the original House version, saying it did not sufficiently boost transportation spending. In 2012, he made sure that a surface transportation bill contained a temporary extension of federal payments for Oregon counties. DeFazio has called for replacing the federal gasoline tax with a per-barrel tax on oil. "What if we got rid of the tax that people don't like and move it upstream to something that most people don't like—the oil industry?" he asked The Oregonian.

When he took the top Democratic post on Transportation and Infrastructure after the 2014 election, DeFazio urged Congress to get serious about fixing what he called the nation's decaying transportation facilities and stop "relying on short-term patches for longstanding problems." He called for financing the highway trust fund with a one-time 14 percent transition tax on foreign earnings by U.S. companies, followed by a 19 percent minimum tax on their global profits. He pledged bipartisan cooperation and said his goals were "job creation, increased efficiency and strategic growth."

Long before most other congressional Democrats, he was a critic of international trade deals. He opposed the Clinton-era North American Free Trade Agreement and was a leader in the fight against normal trade relations with China. In 2015, he was an outspoken foe of granting authority to President Barack Obama to expedite his prospective Trans-Pacific Partnership. The agreement, he said, was "informed and manipulated by corporate interests" and would have "relegated Congress to be used as a doormat… [for an agreement that] has been negotiated in secret and will export jobs, drive down U.S. wages, and undermine U.S. sovereignty." The House approved the presidential authority the following week, with support from the other three Democrats from Oregon.

After Donald Trump was elected and called for extensive new building of infrastructure, DeFazio said he would be willing to work with him. But he added, "I will not hesitate to fight short-sighted proposals that seek to privatize our transportation systems, jeopardize American jobs and manufacturing, or gut critical regulations that protect our workers and communities." He filed a new financing plan, with an annual increase of one cent in the gasoline tax, plus authorization for the Treasury Department to issue 30-year bonds to finance highway construction.

Taking over as committee chairman in January 2019, DeFazio said he would push for a bipartisan deal that would require Trump to be "fully on-board" with any increase in the gas tax or other new funding. Trump never submitted a financing proposal and congressional Republicans hesitated to take the lead. Instead, in July 2020, the House passed in a nearly party-line vote a $1.5 trillion bill crafted by DeFazio that was a sweeping overhaul and expansion of federal highway and mass-transit programs. The measure included steps to address climate change and broad incentives for electric vehicles. Although the Republican-controlled Senate took no action, that bill offered useful background to the incoming Biden administration and its eventual transportation plan.

DeFazio pursued a detailed investigation of the Federal Aviation Administration's review of Boeing's two 737-MAX airplanes that crashed in October 2018 and March 2019, which resulted in the grounding of its entire fleet for more than a year. He harshly criticized Boeing officials for ignoring multiple warnings of flaws with the model, especially the failure of a sensor. In an investigative report the committee released in September 2020, the panel found "a disturbing pattern of technical miscalculations and troubling management misjudgments" by Boeing and "numerous oversight lapses and accountability gaps by the FAA." In November, the House passed, on a voice vote, DeFazio's bill to overhaul the FAA's airline certification process. "Our intent is to ensure a U.S.-manufactured airplane never again crashes due to design issues or regulatory failures," he said.

At his committee, which has jurisdiction over the General Services Administration, DeFazio demanded information about GSA's lease agreement with the Trump International Hotel on Pennsylvania Avenue. In October 2019, when the agency failed to respond, he issued a subpoena to GSA for the details. GSA offered limited access, which DeFazio rejected. After Trump left office, DeFazio said that his investigation was continuing.

After Republican Sen. Bob Packwood resigned in 1995, DeFazio ran in the special election. His opposition to gun control and NAFTA provided clear contrasts with Portland liberal Democratic Rep. Ron Wyden. The better-funded Wyden won the primary 50%-44% and prevailed in the general.

Until 2010, DeFazio routinely won reelection with more than 60 percent in his marginal district. That year, Republican Art Robinson held him to 55 percent of the vote after getting a boost from outside groups' ads tying DeFazio to House Speaker Nancy Pelosi. Robinson, a biochemist who owned a sheep ranch, received hundreds of thousands of dollars of support from Robert Mercer, a hedge-fund manager and prominent supporter of Trump in the 2016 campaign. DeFazio faced Robinson in the next four elections. In each contest, he got between 56 and 59 percent.

In 2020, a new opponent, Alex Skarlatos, brought a more serious challenge. Skarlatos, a political newcomer who gained fame in 2015 when he foiled a terrorist attack on a French train, stressed that DeFazio had held the seat since before Skarlatos was born. He took strongly conservative views on issues ranging from health care to guns and said DeFazio's cosponsorship of the Green New Deal showed he was out of touch with the district. His $5.2 million in spending nearly matched DeFazio's $5.8 million. National Democrats spent more than $2 million on the contest, several times more than Republican spending. DeFazio won, 52%-46%, his closest victory ever. He took 62 percent of the vote in Eugene-based Lane County, which cast nearly half the vote. In the other six counties, Skarlatos led by 30,000 votes—a signal that redistricting will be vital to DeFazio's future.

OR-4: Southwest Oregon   Cook Partisan Voting Index: R+1

Population		Race and Ethnicity		Income	
Total	820,504	White	87.90%	Median Income	$55,886
Land area (sq. miles)	17,274	Black	0.90%	District Income Rank	320
Pop/ sq mi	47.5	Latino	8.50%	Poverty Rate	13.80%
Born in State	45.90%	Asian	2.30%	With health insurance	93.40%
		Two or more races	5.00%	Cash public assistance	2.90%
Age Groups		Other	3.80%	Food stamp/SNAP	16.80%
Under 18	18.30%				
18-34	23.60%	**Education**		**Work**	
35-64	36.40%	H.S grad or less	34.00%	White Collar	35.50%
Over 64	21.70%	Some college	38.00%	Sales and Service	40.00%
		College Degree, 4 yr	16.50%	Blue Collar	24.40%
Military		Post grad	11.60%	Government	18.10%
Veteran/ Active Duty	9.90%				

2020 Pres. Vote	Biden	238,619	(50%)	Trump	219,851	(46%)		
2016 Pres. Vote	Clinton	180,872	(45%)	Trump	180,318	(44%)	Johnson	19,141	(5%)
	Stein	11,675	(3%)					

Eugene, Albany: Eugene is nestled in the southernmost bit of lowland in Oregon's Willamette Valley, and is surrounded by mountains on three sides. It is a farming center, a lumber provider and, most notably, a university town. In 1876, the University of Oregon was established, a symbol of the state's strong Yankee cultural ethic. Eugene and next-door Springfield, which has become a center for the manufacture of computer chips, have grown into comfortable midsized towns. Eugene has bicycle paths along the riverbanks and its main streets. It likes to bill itself as the "Running Capital of the Universe"—Phil Knight and his former University of Oregon track coach, Bill Bowerman, started Nike here, the first soles formed on a waffle iron. Now the third-largest city in Oregon, Eugene has small-town ambience and urban sensibilities, and its progressive voters have been vital to Democrats statewide. A longtime contributor, Knight in 2016 donated $500 million to the University of Oregon for its new science campus. Critics—s including journalist Joshua Hunt, who in 2018 wrote a book, University of Nike—have contended that the university has provided commercial benefits to Nike.

Beyond Eugene and Springfield are southwest Oregon's green-clad mountains. For years, the region cut more timber than anywhere else in the country. But Timber Country, including forest-product businesses, has struggled. Recent economic development has been diverse, with gains in health care, tourism and retiree migration from California. Springfield is the putative home of the popular television show The Simpsons, according to its creator, Oregon native Matt Groening. Local groups have protested the proposed Jordan Cove liquefied natural gas terminal and a 229-mile pipeline in coastal Coos County. In March 2020, the Federal Energy Regulatory Commission granted a temporary license to revive the site for overseas exports. But in January 2021, on the final day of the Trump administration, FERC upheld the state's decision to deny a water-quality certification for the terminal—which likely was a lethal blow.

The 4th Congressional District of Oregon includes Eugene, Springfield and surrounding Lane County. It includes the state's other main college town, Corvallis, home to Oregon State University. Also in the 4th is Douglas County and the southern half of Oregon's stunning Pacific coastline, a roughly 200-mile drive to the California border. About half the voters are in Eugene-based Lane County. Eugene is heavily Democratic, while Douglas County votes Republican; the travails of the logging industry hurt the Democrats here. The 4th has leaned Democratic but is far more blue-collar and less liberal than the Portland area's districts. Joe Biden won the district, 50%-46%, a boost for Democrats from 2016 when Hillary Clinton won by a few hundred votes.

Kurt Schrader (D)

Elected 2008, 7th term, b. Oct 19, 1951; Bridgeport, CT; Cornell University, B.A., 1973; University of IL, B.A., 1975; University of IL College of Veterinary Medicine, D.V.M., 1977; Episcopalian; Married (Susan Mora); 5 children.

Elected Office: OR House, 1997-2003; OR Senate, 2003-2008.

Professional Career: Former aide, AK gov.; Veterinarian, 1978-2008.

DC Office: 2431 RHOB 20515, 202-225-5711, Fax: 202-225-5699, schrader.house.gov

State Offices: Oregon City, 503-557-1324; Salem, 503-588-9100.

Committees: *Energy & Commerce*: Communications & Technology; Energy; Health.

Group Ratings

	ADA	ACLU	AFL-CIO	LCV	COC	HAFA	ACU	CFG	FRC
2020	**	76%	**	86%	-	10%	12%	**	-
2019	85%	C	90%	93%	72%	C	12%	23%	0%

Almanac Ratings 2019-2020

	Economy	Social	Foreign	Composite
Liberal	48%	58%	83%	63%
Conservative	52%	42%	17%	37%

Key Votes of the 116th Congress

1. U.S./Mex./Can. trade deal	Y	5. Russia sanctions	Y	9. Firearms background checks Y
2. First Coronavirus response	Y	6. Troops in Syria	Y	10. Spending at the border	N/A
3. HEROES Act	N	7. Veto arms sales to Saudis	Y	11. Marijuana liberalized rules	Y
4. CASH Act	N	8. Defense $$$, veto override	Y	12. Electoral College objections N

Election Results

Election	Name (Party)	Vote (%)		Cand. Spent	Ind. Exp. Support	Ind. Exp. Oppose
2020 General	Kurt Schrader (D)................................ 234,863	(52%)	$1,676,173	$104,461	
	Amy Ryan Courser (R)................ 204,372	(45%)	$212,762	$24	$113
	Matthew James Rix (L)....................... 12,640	(3%)			
2020 Primary	Kurt Schrader (D)................................ 73,060	(69%)			
	Mark F. Gamba (D)............................. 24,327	(23%)			
	Blair G. Reynolds (D)..................... 7,910	(8%)			

Prior winning percentages: 2018 (55%), 2016 (54%), 2014 (54%), 2012 (54%), 2010 (51%), 2008 (54%)

Kurt Schrader, elected in 2008, has been a business-oriented Democrat in a district that is divided between urban and rural. A veterinarian and organic farmer, he has dealt with health care and energy issues on the Energy and Commerce Committee. Schrader has urged change in the Democratic leadership and has been an outspoken critic of Nancy Pelosi; he was one of 15 House Democrats who did not support her in the 2019 vote for Speaker, though he backed her in 2021. He sought alternatives to the first impeachment charges against President Donald Trump.

Schrader was born in Bridgeport Connecticut, where his father was a chemical engineer. He studied government and got a degree at Cornell University, then received his doctorate in veterinary medicine at the University of Illinois. He settled in Oregon and ran two veterinary clinics in Canby. From his farm, he sold organic fruits and vegetables. Schrader entered politics on the Canby planning commission, assisting in development of the city's land-use plan. He was elected to the state House, where he served six years, followed by another six in the state Senate. He was co-chairman of the Joint Ways and Means Committee, where he developed a reputation as a conservative Democrat and opposed his party on increasing the minimum wage.

When the House seat opened, Schrader lent his campaign $130,000 during the primary and won more than 54 percent of the vote against three opponents. In the general, he faced Republican shipping entrepreneur Mike Erickson, who was the GOP nominee two years earlier. The general election was initially considered wide open. This was George W. Bush territory in 2000 and 2004, but a surge in new voters gave Democrats their first registration advantage in 12 years. Erickson was unable to shake allegations about an earlier relationship with a woman for whose abortion he had paid. Schrader received endorsements from the Oregon Farm Bureau and several newspapers. Erickson outspent Schrader by more than $1 million, but Schrader prevailed 54%-38%. He has not exceeded 55 percent of the vote in his six reelections.

Schrader has been willing to go his own way from his party. He has been co-chair of the fiscally conservative Blue Dog Coalition and was one of 22 House Democrats in 2012 to support fellow Blue Dog Jim Cooper's unsuccessful budget proposal based on the bipartisan Simpson-Bowles commission's recommendations. He has voted for Republican alternatives to weaken the 2010 health care law by allowing consumers to purchase insurance plans that don't meet the terms of that law. He originally cosponsored the DREAM Act for children of illegal immigrants but later voted against it, saying he wanted a more comprehensive reform. In 2015, he was among only 28 House Democrats voting for trade promotion authority, though three of them were from Oregon.

Schrader joined the nonpartisan No Labels group, which has urged a bipartisan congressional agenda. And he has participated in the bipartisan Problems Solvers Caucus. On social issues, Schrader has frequently crossed the party line. In 2017, he was one of six Democrats who voted for a Republican-sponsored bill to permit gun-owners licensed for concealed carry to carry their weapons in all 50 states. In 2018, he cosponsored a bill to override a federal court decision that instructed operators of dams to spill more water to assist endangered salmon; all but eight House Democrats voted against it.

On Energy and Commerce, Schrader advocated more spending on renewable energy and access to health coverage without increased government regulations. In September 2020, he filed with Republican Rep. David McKinley a proposal to require utility companies to reduce their carbon emissions by 80 percent by 2050—a less aggressive approach than many other Democrats advocated. "We need a new approach to develop realistic solutions that will enjoy support from both parties in Congress," they wrote in USA Today.

In 2019, Schrader was among a small group of House Democrats who explored options short of impeachment—such as censure—prior to the House's first charges against Trump; he favored an approach that "might be a little more bipartisan." In February 2021, he was one of two Democrats to oppose House approval of the $1.9 trillion pandemic-relief bill. But when the final version returned to the House two weeks later with limited changes, he voted for the measure.

National Republicans went after Schrader in 2010 and recruited state Rep. Scott Bruun, who accused him of not being the fiscal hawk he claimed and of going "on a world-class spending spree with your money." Schrader parried that Bruun wanted to privatize Social Security. Schrader won 51%-46%. After redistricting changes made the district slightly more favorable for Republicans, they nominated in 2014 Clackamas Commissioner Tootie Smith, a conservative who once raffled off a Glock pistol to raise campaign funds. Schrader won 54%-39%. Two years later, he again got 54 percent, this time against Colm Willis, the top lobbyist for Oregon Right to Life. In the 2016 primary, Schrader was challenged by a former state representative who decided to run after Schrader announced his support for the Trans-Pacific trade deal.

Following the 2018 election, Schrader was among 16 Democrats who signed a letter vowing to oppose Pelosi for Speaker. Some Democratic activists in Oregon cited that vote in supporting a 2020 primary challenge by Mark Gamba, the mayor of Milwaukie and a supporter of Sen. Bernie Sanders for president. "Kurt Schrader falls soundly into representing the corporations," Gamba said. They disagreed on Medicare for All and the Green New Deal. In a three-candidate contest, Schrader got 69 percent of the vote. In November, he defeated Amy Ryan Courser, a former member of the Ketzer City Council, 52%-45%. Schrader will be seeking a safer seat in redistricting.

OR-5: West-Central Oregon   Cook Partisan Voting Index: D+2

Population		Race and Ethnicity		Income	
Total	844,220	White	83.80%	Median Income	$68,757
Land area (sq. miles)	5,190	Black	0.90%	District Income Rank	177
Pop/ sq mi	162.67	Latino	17.70%	Poverty Rate	9.70%
Born in State	52.20%	Asian	2.90%	With health insurance	92.00%
		Two or more races	5.40%	Cash public assistance	3.00%
Age Groups		Other	6.90%	Food stamp/SNAP	13.40%
Under 18	22.20%				
18-34	21.20%	Education		Work	
35-64	38.30%	H.S grad or less	32.80%	White Collar	38.40%
Over 64	18.20%	Some college	35.30%	Sales and Service	38.70%
		College Degree, 4 yr	20.60%	Blue Collar	22.90%
Military		Post grad	11.40%	Government	16.00%
Veteran/ Active Duty	7.20%				

2020 Pres. Vote	Biden	248,427	(53%)	Trump	203,631	(44%)	
2016 Pres. Vote	Clinton	180,404	(46%)	Trump	164,548	(42%)	Johnson 20,135 (5%)
	Stein	8,214	(2%)				

Salem, Clackamas County: The Willamette River Valley was the great Promised Land at the end of the Oregon Trail, shielded from the cold storms of the Pacific by mountains but squeezing most of the moisture out of the clouds in the form of rain, fog and persistent mist. New England Yankees planted small towns they called Salem and Oregon City, founded schools and colleges, built tall-spired churches and eventually Salem's distinctive Art Deco state capitol, a few blocks east of the river. This was one of the few valleys in the West that settlers found readily suitable for agriculture. The soil is fertile, and the plain created by the waters of the Willamette sweeping down from the mountains is broad. Ironically in this environmentally friendly state, agricultural and polluted stormwater runoff have continued to make the river among the dirtiest in the nation. The Willamette Valley is home to a burgeoning wine industry with more than 750 wineries, as of 2018, many of which are known for their pinot noir. By some measures, Oregon is the third-largest wine producing state, behind California and Washington.

Salem and Eugene have battled for the distinction of Oregon's second-largest city, after Portland. Salem, the state capital, has pulled slightly ahead; its 23 percent Hispanic population is more than twice the share in Eugene. Planners expect Salem to gain nearly 100,000 more residents between 2019 and 2035. In Wilsonville, German-based Siemens owns Mentor Graphics, a sophisticated electronic-design company with 1,000 employees at its 53-acre headquarters campus. In 2015, Microsoft began to manufacture giant touch screens in Wilsonville, with a retail price up to $22,000, depending on size. But the company shut the facility two years later and switched the product to its larger operations in China.

The 5th Congressional District of Oregon includes much of the northern Willamette Valley. The district has about 40 percent of its voters in Clackamas County on the outskirts of Portland; more than three-fourths of Clackamas is in the 5th. It spreads south to Salem-based Marion County, which has one-third of the voters and is home of Willamette University, the oldest university in the West. It crosses the Coast Range to take in Lincoln and Tillamook counties, which are fishing, logging and cheese-making communities. In the thinly populated coastal areas, Newport has a busy port and a state beach. Historically, the valley was Republican, but it has trended Democratic. Overall, the 5th has remained competitive. In 2020, Joe Biden took the district, 53%-44%. He took 54 percent in Clackamas, which helped to balance the Republican-leaning rural counties.

PENNSYLVANIA

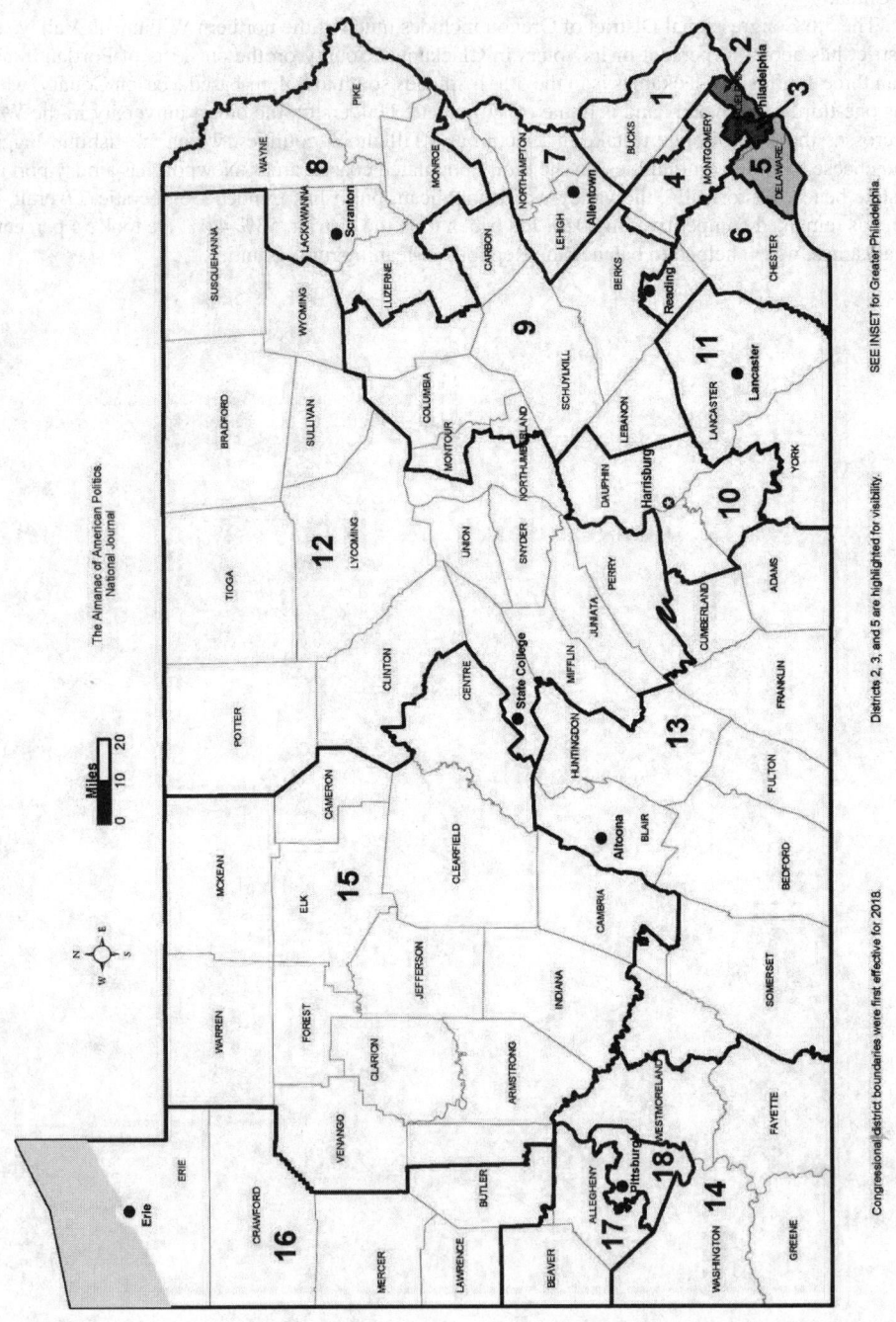

The Almanac of American Politics.
National Journal

SEE INSET for Greater Philadelphia.

Districts 2, 3, and 5 are highlighted for visibility.

Congressional district boundaries were first effective for 2018.

Pennsylvania has long been a state targeted by Democrats and Republicans alike, with competitive contests at almost every level of government. In the 2020 presidential race—four years after it helped send Donald Trump to the White House by giving him a 44,000-vote victory—both parties lavished attention on the Keystone State. Ultimately, Joe Biden won the state of his birth by about 82,000 votes, sealing his national victory.

Pennsylvania "sprawls from the Northeast corridor to Appalachia to the Midwest," the Philadelphia Inquirer's Jonathan Tamari has written. "It's a place of big, crowded cities, affluent suburbs, and vast farmland. Cascading mountains, forested lakefronts, fracking wells, cul-de-sacs, corner stores, and gleaming skyscrapers. Sheetz and Wawa. World-class colleges and shuttered factories. Diverse, dynamic cities and huge rural stretches where the population is almost entirely white. Each piece is big enough that no one aspect dominates the rest. "Indeed, the combination of votes from Philadelphia, its collar suburbs, and Pittsburgh's Allegheny County do not provide the Democrats with enough of a cushion to win the state comfortably; they also need to do well in other, far-flung parts of the state that have been consistently moving in the Republicans' direction.

The state where the Founders declared American independence and wrote the Constitution started out as a Quaker haven, founded in 1682 by the pacifist William Penn, son of an admiral to whom King Charles II owed political debts. Pennsylvania's policy of tolerance attracted Englishmen of many religious sects and thousands of pietist Germans—ancestors of the Pennsylvania Dutch. Soon, Pennsylvania became the major settlement in the Middle Colonies and Philadelphia the largest colonial port. In the 18th century, border men from Scotland, the north of England and Northern Ireland landed in Philadelphia and crossed the corduroy ridges of the Appalachians and settled the mountainous interior. The geometric lines William Penn had obtained from the king included two major river systems—the wide Delaware estuary with its thriving commerce and rich hinterland, and the golden triangle where the Allegheny and Monongahela Rivers joined to form the Ohio. They remain today important geographical features defining the eastern and western parts of the state. Philadelphia was the natural host for the Continental Congresses that began meeting in 1774, and in the early republic it seemed destined to become the London of America, the metropolis of government, commerce and culture. Pittsburgh, founded in 1758, was the young republic's key frontier metropolis, the fulcrum of American expansion.

But Philadelphia—and Pennsylvania—failed to maintain the central position the Founders expected. As part of a political deal, the young republic's capital was located some 80 miles south of the Mason-Dixon line, at a site along the Potomac River. And the Erie Canal from the Hudson River to Lake Erie, completed in 1825, channeled trade away from Philadelphia to New York. Pennsylvania evolved into America's early capital of energy and heavy industry. Northeast Pennsylvania was the nation's primary source of anthracite, the hard coal used for home heating, and western Pennsylvania was laced with bituminous coal, the soft coal used in steel production. Connected to Philadelphia by the Pennsylvania Railroad, Pittsburgh was the center of the nation's steel industry by 1890; it became synonymous with industrial prosperity and, led by its adopted son, steel mogul Andrew Carnegie, for philanthropy as well. Immigrants poured in from Europe and from the surrounding hills to work in the hardscrabble environment of western Pennsylvania's mines and factories.

Pennsylvania was the nation's second-largest state from the first census in 1790 through 1940. It stopped growing rapidly during the Great Depression, and in some parts of the state growth has never returned. After World War II, both home heating and industry shifted away from coal. Only the embers remain, or the fires: The Red Ash colliery fire, ignited in 1915, burns on beneath the hills above Wilkes-Barre, as do a few dozen other fires in abandoned coal mines. Similarly, Pennsylvania steel began a sharp decline in the 1960s. The result has been the slowest population growth of any major state. Pennsylvania cast 36 electoral votes for Franklin Roosevelt in 1940 but only 20 for Biden in 2020. In 1960, it had 30 House members, as many as California and more than Texas. In 2023, it will have 17 to California's 52.

Since 2010, the state has grown by just 2.4 percent. (A consolation prize was that Pennsylvania in 2017 regained fifth place among most populous states, surpassing Illinois.) Some pockets have expanded more than others: Since the last census, Cumberland County (Harrisburg suburbs and Carlisle) grew 7.4 percent, Lebanon County (east of Harrisburg) grew 6.1 percent, Lehigh County (Allentown-Bethlehem) grew 5.5 percent, and Lancaster County (Lancaster) grew 4.9 percent, while

Philadelphia, along with two of its collar counties, Montgomery and Chester, grew in the 4-5 percent range. But other corners of the state have shrunk slightly, including Lackawanna County (Scranton) and Luzerne County (Wilkes-Barre) in the northeast, and Erie County (Erie) in the northwest. Some smaller counties have contracted by even more. With relatively few outsiders moving in, Pennsylvania has become increasingly old—it ranks eighth in the percentage of residents age 65 and over. It also remains one of the Whitest big states—10 percent Black, 8percent Hispanic, and 3.5 percent Asian. Pockets of the state, however, have seen rapid Hispanic increases, notably Hazleton in Luzerne County, a shift that has prompted bitter battles over immigration. Hispanics from New York and North Jersey have also moved out Interstate 78 to Reading (67 percent Hispanic), Allentown (53 percent Hispanic) and Bethlehem (30 percent Hispanic).

Map for Greater Philadelphia

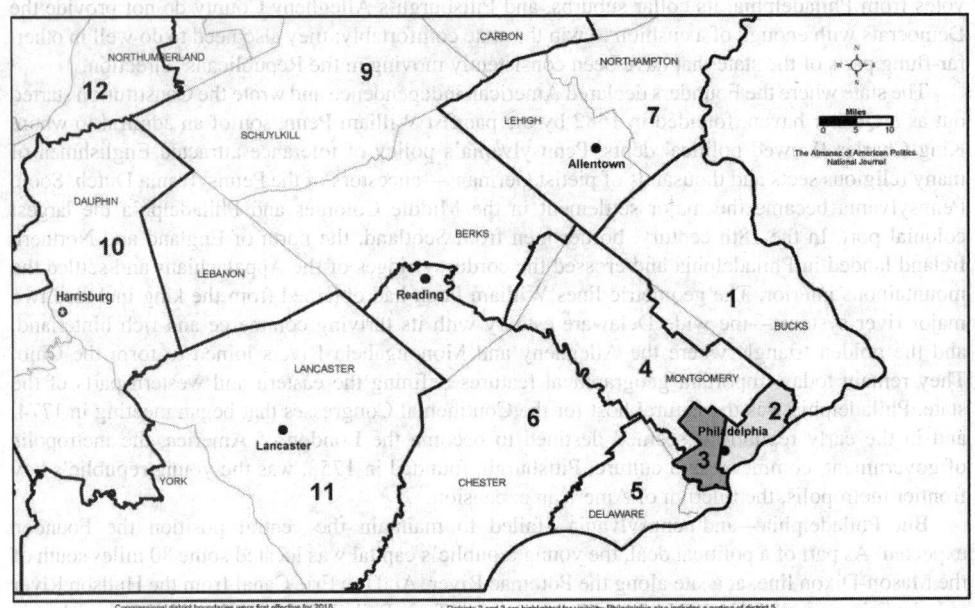

Economically, Pennsylvania has begun to perk up a bit over the past two decades. Big hospitals have replaced big steel mills as employers in metro Pittsburgh, although in 2019, U.S. Steel said it would pursue a $1 billion upgrade for its Pittsburgh-area plants, collectively known as the Mon Valley Works, and a major "ethane cracker" plant is being built in Monaca. Metro Philadelphia and the surrounding countryside have experienced diversified economic growth, while the Lehigh Valley has capitalized on its convenient access to transportation routes to lure warehouse jobs for Amazon, Walmart, FedEx and UPS. Manufacturing remains important outside the big cities, but manufacturing employment in Pennsylvania declined 34 percent between 2000 and the start of the coronavirus pandemic, a significantly faster rate than the national decline of 26 percent. Pennsylvania has held state taxes down more than many of its Northeastern neighbors, which has been a factor in luring New Yorkers to retire near the Delaware Water Gap and the Poconos. Meanwhile, both Philadelphia and Pittsburgh have become hip destinations with impressive cultural and nightlife amenities. While the number of farms has fallen, agriculture remains a significant industry in Pennsylvania—it ranks among the top seven states for production of eggs, milk, pumpkins, apples, and peaches, and ranks first nationally in mushroom production, centered on Kennett Square in Chester County, "The Mushroom Capital of the World." The state's median income ranks slightly below the national average.

James Carville once famously described the state as Pittsburgh and Philadelphia with Alabama in between. Those parts in the "T" of rural Pennsylvania were once the site of the world's first oil well and first commercial nuclear power plant. More recently, they have benefited from the Marcellus Shale that lies beneath 60 percent of Pennsylvania and much of upstate New York. The Marcellus Shale contains the nation's largest reserves of natural gas embedded in hard rock; these reserves can be brought to the surface by hydraulic fracturing, or fracking. Pennsylvania has become the second-largest producer of natural gas after Texas, economically transforming portions of the southwestern part of the state. But in addition to longstanding worries about pollution, the industry has had to grapple with both an energy glut and the global economic slowdown from the pandemic. The industry has also spooked investors with its record of heavy indebtedness.

For generations after the Civil War—whose turning point is often pegged to quiet Gettysburg—Pennsylvania was the most Republican of the large states, due in part to the legacy of Abraham Lincoln and the Union, and due in part to the steel industry and high tariffs. Its Republican machines built parties that were representative not of one ethnic segment, but had a place for just about everyone. In 1932, Pennsylvania was the only big state that stuck with Republican Herbert Hoover over Democrat Franklin Roosevelt. Then the political landscape changed. The New Deal, John L. Lewis' United Mine Workers, the CIO industrial union movement, and a series of bloody strikes made industrial Pennsylvania almost as Democratic in the late 1930s and 1940s as it had been Republican from the 1860s to the 1920s. Even then, parts of Pennsylvania not heavy with big steel factories and coal mines—the northern tier of counties along the New York border, the central part of the state around Altoona, and the Pennsylvania Dutch country around Lancaster—remained among the strongest Republican voting blocs in the East. Philadelphia became a heavily Democratic city after the last Republican mayor left office in 1952, but in the suburban counties the old Republican machines stayed in control.

By the 1980s, prosperous eastern Pennsylvania was trending Republican while ailing western Pennsylvania was trending Democratic. By the 1990s, though, the pattern began to reverse. Fiscally conservative but socially moderate suburban Republicans in the east increasingly voted for Democrats, while economically liberal but socially conservative Democrats in the west flocked to the GOP. Pennsylvania voted Republican for president three times in the 1980s but Democratic for president in 1992 and the subsequent five elections. But western Pennsylvania, other than Pittsburgh's increasingly blue Allegheny County, has been moving in the other direction, with voters strongly supporting socially conservative policies, gun rights and energy extraction. In four heavily working-class counties surrounding Allegheny—Beaver, Fayette, Greene and Washington—Al Gore won better than 53 percent of the two-party vote in 2000. By 2016, those four counties gave Hillary Clinton only 29 percent to 40 percent of the two-party vote. Biden, with a more favorable profile than Clinton for the region's voters, fared only marginally better. In southwestern Pennsylvania, "Trump has laid the foundation for a Republican Party realignment that will outlast him and set the party on a sustainable path for the future," Mike Ward, a GOP strategist, told Politics PA. Such shifts were echoed in demographically similar areas of the state: In 2016, Trump flipped three counties Obama won: Luzerne (by shifting the margin 24 points in the GOP's direction), Erie (by shifting it 19 points), and Northampton (Easton, by shifting it nine points).

The silver lining for Democrats was Clinton's ability to improve on Obama's performance in more affluent and educated cities and suburbs. She flipped Philadelphia-area Chester County from red to blue, as well as Centre County, the home of Penn State University. The areas that saw Democratic gains in 2016 helped drive a successful 2018 for the party. That year, a newly Democratic-controlled state Supreme Court threw out the congressional district lines that had given the GOP a consistent 13-5 House delegation edge for most of the decade. On Election Day, Democrats pulled into a 9-9 tie in the delegation, which became a crucial building block of the party's new majority in the House.

In 2020, both the Trump and Biden camps focused aggressively on Pennsylvania, with Scranton-native Biden framing the race as "Scranton vs. Park Avenue" and Trump touting fracking and other issues tailored to rural audiences. (Biden also traveled to Allegheny County and articulated more support for fracking than many in his party's base would have liked.) In the end, Biden did well enough to reverse Trump's 2016 margin—and a bit more. Biden flipped Erie and Northampton counties back to the Democratic column, but more importantly he was able to chalk up gains almost everywhere, in counties won by both parties. Biden increased the Democratic margin of victory between two and eight points in the four Philadelphia collar counties (Bucks, Chester, Delaware, and Montgomery) as well as in Allegheny County; Lehigh County; Dauphin County (Harrisburg); and most sweetly for the nominee, Scranton's Lackawanna County. Perhaps equally notable, Biden cut Trump's winning margins between two and eight points each in York County (York), Berks County

(Reading), Westmoreland County (Pittsburgh suburbs), and Luzerne, Lancaster, and Cumberland counties. Even though Democrats had already notched gains in the Philadelphia suburbs for several election cycles running, Biden was still able to squeeze out more: He won 171,000 more votes from the four collar counties than Clinton had in 2016, and that was enough, by itself, to flip the state his way. The only major jurisdiction where Biden lost ground was in the city of Philadelphia, thanks to Trump gains among Latino and Black voters. Still, the winning Democratic margin in the city remained huge, 81%-18%. Down ballot races were less favorable to the Democrats, however, as several of the House seats they targeted remained in GOP hands, as did both chambers of the legislature.

The presidential race was close enough that Trump and his allies tried to overturn Biden's victory, including lawsuits, entreaties to state legislative leaders (which were rebuffed), and a mystifying press conference by Rudy Giuliani at Four Seasons Total Landscaping in Philadelphia. Burned by the loss and upset by the high court's late intervention to expand mail-in balloting beyond what state law allowed, Republicans began pushing to change the way judges are selected by introducing a regional system to replace the current method of statewide elections; the change would be expected to advantage the GOP. Meanwhile, the 2022 election promised to be a big one, with open-seat gubernatorial and Senate races. All told, Pennsylvania looks likely to continue as a battle ground state for the near future.

Population		Race and Ethnicity		Income	
Total	12,801,989	White	79.60%	Median Income	63,463
Land area (sq. miles)	44,743	Black	11.40%	State Income Rank	23 out of 50
Pop/ sq mi	286.12	Latino	7.80%	Poverty Rate	12.00%
Born in state	71.40%	Asian	4.20%	With health insurance	94.20%
		Two or more races	2.60%	Cash public assistance	3.20%
Age Groups		Other	2.80%	Food stamp/SNAP	13.0%
Under 18	20.60%				
18-34	22.20%	Education		Work	
35-64	38.50%	H.S grad or less	43.40%	White Collar	40.30%
Over 64	18.70%	Some college	24.30%	Sales and Service	37.20%
		College Degree, 4 yr	19.50%	Blue Collar	22.40%
Military		Post grad	12.80%	Government	11.00%
Veteran/ Active Duty	7.10%				

Presidential Politics

2020 Primary (D)	Biden (D)	1,264,625(77%)	Sanders (D)	287,834(18%)			
2020 Pres. Vote	Biden (D)	3,461,221(50%)	Trump (R)	3,379,055(49%)			
2016 Pres. Vote	Trump (R)	2,970,733(48%)	Clinton (D)	2,926,441(47%)	Johnson (L)	146,715 (2%)	

Pennsylvania has been a presidential battleground state for close to a half-century, and in the past two elections has seen more attention and spending than just about any other state. It's not as demographically diverse as emerging battlegrounds like Arizona or Georgia, but it is a state where the shifting politics of wealthier suburbs and blue-collar communities have been apparent for several elections—and these crosscurrents have kept the state near the center of the country politically, as well as at the heart of its presidential battles.

Pennsylvania has been seriously contested in just about every presidential election since 1976, and only once in that time, in 2008, has any candidate received more than 52 percent of the vote. But the state's political coalitions have changed dramatically in that stretch. Democrats used to rely heavily on White working-class and union voters in western Pennsylvania and the Lehigh Valley, but those voters have moved to the GOP in the past two decades. Democrats have made up for those losses by gaining college-educated voters in more upscale Philadelphia suburbs, keeping the state closely divided. In 2016, Trump ran up the score in the rural, more culturally conservative areas outside of metro Pittsburgh and Philadelphia, known as "Pennsyltucky" or "The T" because of its geographic layout. Trump eked out a 48.2%-47.5% victory statewide, with a margin of 44,000 votes, to become the first Republican since George H.W. Bush in 1988 to carry the state.

Pennsylvania was clearly at the top of both parties' target lists during 2020. Joe Biden, a Scranton native who made sure everyone knew it, picked Philadelphia for his campaign headquarters. And he spent 13 days in the state after he returned to in-person campaigning for the race's final two months —thrice the time he spent in any other battleground state. Trump wasn't far behind, with 10 days campaigning in Pennsylvania in September and October.

Biden's final margin of victory was 49.9%-48.7%, a win of more than 82,000 votes, almost double Trump's 2016 margin in the state. He won back the state for Democrats by running just a bit ahead of Hillary Clinton across much of the map—and running up the score in suburban Philadelphia.

He won Bucks, Chester, Delaware and Montgomery counties by a combined 59%-40%, a wider margin than any Democrat in modern history. His 290,000-vote margin in those counties accounted for more than three times his total statewide victory. Barack Obama won the Philadelphia suburbs 57%-42% as he won statewide by 10 points in 2008; in 2012, he won them 54%-45% as he carried the state by five points. Clinton won those four counties by a combined 55%-42%. Chester County swung the hardest of any county toward the Democrat: Biden won it by 17 points, up from Clinton's 10-point win four years earlier.

Biden also flipped blue-collar Erie County in the state's northwest corner, and made marginal but important improvements over Clinton's numbers throughout much of his childhood home region of Northeast Pennsylvania, including flipping back Northampton County. Overall turnout jumped 13 percent, a huge spike considering the state also was hotly contested in 2016, and rose by double digits in 64 of the state's 67 counties.

Biden won despite Trump's gains in Philadelphia itself, driven by a voting surge from a handful of conservative white ethnic neighborhoods in South and Northeast Philadelphia, plus some Trump gains among Blacks and Latinos. Biden netted 471,305 votes from Philadelphia County—about 4,000 fewer votes than Clinton's net of 475,277. Biden increased Clinton's vote in Philadelphia by more than 20,000 votes, but Trump had an even larger jump of 24,000 votes.

The state's court-imposed voting law changes made it a post-election lightning rod, as well. State Republicans and Democrats came together to legalize widespread mail voting in the state ahead of the 2020 election, though Trump's campaign objected to many of those changes—especially following his defeat. But as Trump began claiming the process was rife with fraud, local Republicans followed suit. They refused to permit localities to begin counting mail ballots until Election Day, meaning they were counted later than in-person ballots, creating a "red mirage." Trump led on election night and prematurely declared victory. But hundreds of thousands of ballots remained uncounted—many of them in Democratic-heavy Philadelphia and its suburbs. Biden eventually pulled ahead on Friday morning; on Saturday, once most of the ballots were counted, the Associated Press and a number of television networks called the state and the election for Biden.

But Trump and his Republicans allies continued to claim voter fraud, even as numerous judges rejected their claims. The U.S. Supreme Court dismissed appeals that the state courts had exceeded their authority. Pennsylvania was one of the two states that congressional Republicans targeted to try to throw out their Electoral College votes on Jan. 6, the day that pro-Trump rioters overran the Capitol.

Since 1924, Pennsylvania has held its presidential primary in April. It was a battleground in the 2008 Democratic primary, when Clinton had a 55%-45% victory over Obama, who got in trouble for saying Pennsylvanians in small towns "cling to guns or religion" because they were "bitter" about their economic circumstances. Eight years later, Clinton defeated Vermont Sen. Bernie Sanders by a similar 56%-44%. On the Republican side, Trump defeated Texas Sen. Ted Cruz, 57%-22%. In 2020, the Democratic contest was already decided before Pennsylvania's scheduled primary, and the state postponed it to June because of the coronavirus. Biden defeated Sanders, 77%-18%.

Congressional Districts

117th Congress Lineup	9D 9R	116th Congress Lineup	9D 9R

In February 2018, Pennsylvania Democrats convinced the state's Democratic-dominated Supreme Court to issue a mid-decade redistricting. The 4-3 ruling eviscerated the previous Republican-drawn map and replaced it with a new map largely along the lines Democrats had proposed. The resulting upheaval left a 9-9 delegation the GOP had previously controlled 12-6. Republicans, who have succeeded with their share of partisan redistricting gambits in other states, were outraged—not surprisingly. The results were a reminder of the power of redistricting, whatever the timing or whoever the map-drawer. The district revisions in swing areas—chiefly, in the suburbs outside Philadelphia—were so dramatic that three GOP incumbents threw in the towel and their party made little, if any, effort to contest the new seats. The redistricting resulted in the defeat of a fourth House Republican (Rep. Keith Rothfus lost to Democratic Rep. Scott Lamb) in the Pittsburgh suburbs, though the GOP managed to retain its 4-2 control of districts in western Pennsylvania.

Among the notable results of the election changes in 2018, a total of six incumbents (including one Democrat) decided not to seek reelection. All four newly elected Democrats in the Philadelphia area were women. The other three freshmen were Republican men from central and western parts of the state. Four of those seven had not previously held elected office. In 2020, each party was unsuccessful in targeting additional seats.

With Pennsylvania losing another seat in reapportionment and with political power divided in Harrisburg between a Democratic governor and Republican-controlled legislature, the likely prospect is that another court-drawn map will cause new upheaval and unpredictable partisan consequences in 2022. It's anybody's guess which districts and which party will be at greatest risk. With the state's loss of one House seat, virtually every district will need to gain some population; that could be precarious for a few incumbents. Rural and small-town areas likely will be at greatest risk of losing a district, which is bad news for Republicans.

History offers useful insights into the complexities of Pennsylvania redistricting. Republicans held the governorship and legislative majorities in both 2001 and 2011, and were in firm control of redistricting. In 2001, under heavy pressure from White House strategist Karl Rove, they overreached. With Republicans having overplayed their hand and two of their incumbents damaged by scandals, Democrats in Pennsylvania gained by 2008 six seats the GOP had intended as its own. Then, in their party's national wave of 2010, Republicans' regained five of those seats and reversed Democrats' 12-7 edge.

By 2011, Republicans had learned their lesson. Needing to cut a seat while protecting 12 of their own, including five in districts President Barack Obama had carried in 2008, Republicans retained all their seats and picked up one more when they merged two junior House Democrats in the west; both ran, and lost, in the same district in 2012. The new Republican plan ruthlessly sewed the state, particular the Philadelphia suburbs, into a crazy quilt. Montgomery County, about the population of one district, was split five ways to boost three suburban Republicans. In the three elections from 2012 to 2016, Republicans emerged with what appeared to be a lock-tight 13-5 delegation in what has been an essentially 50-50 state.

Democrats finally turned the tables, in a June 2017 lawsuit filed by the League of Women Voters of Pennsylvania that challenged the congressional map as an unconstitutional partisan gerrymander. Democratic Gov. Tom Wolf played an instrumental role, in working with state Democrats to offer legal arguments and an alternative. The Republican-controlled legislature objected to the proceedings and defended the existing boundaries. The state Supreme Court ruled that the map violated the state constitution and ordered the legislature to submit a new plan. When Republican lawmakers refused, Stanford University law professor Nathaniel Persily prepared the new map, following guidance by the court—with alternatives submitted by Democrats and others.

Moving quickly, Persily presented his alternative, which the court—on a 4-3 vote—imposed. It met the redistricting dictates of relatively straight boundaries and a minimum number of divided counties. The result was the first case in which any congressional redistricting plan has been overturned as a partisan gerrymander, though the violation was based on the Pennsylvania constitution.

The Republican response was aptly summarized by GOP Rep. Ryan Costello, whose gerrymandered district in the Philadelphia suburbs was a target of the redistricting critics. He decided not to seek reelection." I was surprised and am still absolutely shocked that the Supreme Court got away with what it did," he told a local reporter. "Their objective was to take me out politically, and that's what they did." Costello was not the first politician across the country to voice such outrage. And he likely won't be the last.

Tom Wolf (D)

Elected 2014, term expires 2023, 2nd term; b. Nov. 17, 1948, York; Dartmouth Col., B.A. 1972; U. of London, M.A. 1978; MA Inst. of Technology, PhD 1981; Episcopalian; Married (Frances); 2 children.

Professional Career: Peace Corps, India; CEO & President, Wolf Organization, 1986-2006, Chairman & CEO, 2009-present; Secretary of Revenue, Governor Ed Rendell, 2007-2009.

Office: Main Capitol Building Rm. 225, Harrisburg, 17120; 717-787-2500; Fax: 717-772-8284

Lt. Gov.: John Fetterman (D) **Atty. Gen:** Josh Shapiro (D)

State Legislature: Senate: 22D, 26R, 2V **House:** 93D, 108R, 2V

Election Results

Election	Name (Party)	Vote (%)
2018 General	Thomas Wolf (D)...	2,895,652 (58%)
	Scott Wagner (R)...	2,039,882 (41%)
2018 Primary	Thomas Wolf (D)...	749,812 (100%)

Prior winning percentage: 2014 (55%)

Pennsylvanians have twice elected Democrat Tom Wolf, a latecomer to politics, as their governor.

Born in York and raised in Mount Wolf—named for his great-great-grandfather—Wolf earned degrees from Dartmouth College, the University of London and the Massachusetts Institute of Technology. During that time, he interrupted his studies to join the Peace Corps, serving two years in a village in India. After graduation, Wolf went to work for the family business, initially employed as a forklift operator at the Wolf Organization, a cabinet and building-materials company. In 1985, Wolf and two cousins bought the company and more than doubled its size. After selling the company to a private-equity firm in 2006, Wolf was tapped by Democratic Gov. Ed Rendell to be state revenue secretary in 2007 and 2008. Wolf intended to mount a campaign for governor to succeed Rendell, who was term-limited, but when the family business was on the brink of bankruptcy and collapse, Wolf abandoned the campaign, repurchased the company and restored it to solvency. He stepped down as CEO in 2013 to focus on his 2014 bid for governor, targeting first-term Republican Gov. Tom Corbett, who was saddled with low approval ratings.

Democratic Rep. Allyson Schwartz was anointed the early frontrunner in the primary, and state Treasurer Rob McCord and former state Environmental Protection Secretary Kathleen McGinty ran as well. But Wolf poured $10 million of his own money into the race, allowing him to blanket the airwaves from January 2014 until the May primary, which Wolf won easily with 58 percent of the vote. (Wolf later tapped McGinty as his chief of staff.) In the general, Wolf had the air and campaign strategy of an incumbent, bolstered by double-digit leads in the polls. Wolf said that, unlike Corbett, he would raise taxes on the fast-growing natural gas industry, though he was generally supportive of the industry's right to expand. Scrutiny of Corbett's role as attorney general in the investigation of former Penn State assistant football coach Jerry Sandusky on accusations of child molestation became another albatross for the incumbent. Wolf won the high-spending race with 55 percent of the vote, shattering Pennsylvania's rigid, post-World War II pattern of the two parties trading off the governorship every eight years.

Wolf moved to broaden the state's Medicaid expansion under the Affordable Care Act, and he ordered a moratorium on the death penalty. But budget issues proved the most intractable. Wolf came into office facing a $2 billion budget gap—and two Republican-controlled legislative chambers. In June 2015, Wolf vetoed the first GOP budget. That instigated a battle that lasted until March 2016 and included skirmishes not only over revenues and spending but also vetoes of GOP-backed changes to the state pension system and to tightly regulated liquor sales. The standoff also led to a credit downgrade for the state and fears of layoffs and closed public schools. Ultimately, Wolf allowed a budget to become law without signing it.

The relationship between Wolf and lawmakers grew lower-key and generally more productive. In 2016, he signed a medical-marijuana law, and he issued an executive order protecting persons from discrimination based on sexual orientation and gender identity. Wolf signed bipartisan legislation to overhaul the state liquor system, including permission for grocery stores to sell wine and for wine to be shipped directly to customers, as well as an extension of hours at state liquor stores. He signed new regulations governing horizontal oil and gas drilling, and he signed several measures aimed at curbing opioid addiction. The 2016 election was a downer for Pennsylvania Democrats, as presidential nominee Hillary Clinton lost the state and Republicans expanded their majorities by three seats in the state Senate and two seats in the state House. That gave Senate Republicans their widest edge in the Senate in seven decades, enough to override vetoes if Republicans managed to stick together.

In 2017, Wolf and the legislature faced the biggest budgetary shortfall since the Great Recession; the independent legislative fiscal office projected a deficit of about $3 billion for the two-year fiscal period ending in June 2018. Wolf once again allowed the budget to be enacted without his signature, and it took another three months before the two sides could come up with enough funding to close the budget gap. It took until June 2018 for the two sides to finally notch a harmonious budget session, as Wolf signed a $32.7 billion spending package, bolstered by projections of strong revenue gains. Wolf signed an executive order to raise state employees' and contractors' minimum wages to $12 initially and to $15 an hour in 2024. Wolf signed a bipartisan criminal justice reform bill that sealed nonviolent criminal records after an individual had been free of convictions for 10 years. Wolf also wielded his veto pen: He nixed one bill that would have banned abortions at 20 weeks, as well as a business-backed, union-opposed measure that would have limited the prescriptions permitted for injured workers. For the fourth consecutive year, Republicans blocked Wolf's proposal to institute a severance tax on the volume of natural gas extracted. Wolf also played a key role in the state's redistricting battle: After the state Supreme Court struck down the congressional district map as a Republican gerrymander, Wolf rejected the alternative proposed by legislative Republicans, which effectively left the Democratic-dominated state Supreme Court to draw the new maps, which not surprisingly proved to be significantly more favorable to the Democrats.

Wolf faced no primary opposition in 2018, although voters did knock out the lieutenant governor, Mike Stack, in favor of John Fetterman, with Wolf's tacit support. Stack had a controversial term in office that included scrutiny of his family's treatment of state employees. Fetterman, the burly, 6-foot-8 mayor of Braddock in Allegheny County, had attracted attention for his black T-shirt, jeans and tattoos, as well as his grassroots brand of progressivism. The GOP, meanwhile, held a raucous primary between state Sen. Scott Wagner, businessman and former McKinsey consultant Paul Mango, and attorney Laura Ellsworth. Wagner's outspoken, Trumpian style carried him to victory with the GOP primary electorate; he took 44 percent, followed by Mango with 37 percent and Ellsworth with 19 percent. In the general election, Wolf outspent the Republican and was aided by the Democratic lean of the 2018 cycle. Wagner attracted national criticism for remarks he made in a video posted on his campaign's Facebook page in which he told Wolf, "Between now and Nov. 6, you better put a catcher's mask on your face, because I'm going to stomp all over your face with golf spikes." In the end, Wolf won easily, 58%-41%; he collected nearly 1 million more votes than in his 2014 victory. Meanwhile, Democrats made gains in both legislative chambers but not enough to flip partisan control.

After the budget battles of his first term, Wolf set more modest goals for his second term, telling Penn Live in January 2019 that he wanted to improve competence in government. "I'll look back and I'm hoping that of the eight years I've been in office people will say: 'Yeah, I think what goes on in Harrisburg, those folks are actually trying to do the right thing.'" The budget he signed in 2019 was opposed by many legislators from his own party. Some objected to Wolf's approval of language to end a longstanding cash assistance program for residents temporarily unable to work. Republicans once again blocked Wolf's push for a severance tax on natural gas drilling. Wolf signed a sweeping electoral overhaul that would come to loom large during the 2020 election and its aftermath; among other things, the measure allowed absentee voting without an excuse and provided funding for jurisdictions to upgrade their balloting machines to ones with a voter-verified paper trail. Wolf vetoed a bill that would have banned abortions for women contending that their fetus had Down syndrome, as well as a bill that would have expanded tax credits for businesses that donate to K-12 scholarship funds. (The latter veto drew a rebuke from Trump in his 2020 State of the Union address.) On the minimum wage, Wolf did a workaround after being stymied by the legislature in seeking an increase from $7.25—the federal floor—to $9.50. Instead, Wolf left the issue to a regulatory board that moved to extend the eligibility for overtime pay to some 80,000additional workers in the state. Meanwhile, despite active support from Fetterman, Wolf was unable to make significant progress in legalizing recreational marijuana. On the business front, a multifaceted, cross-state pipeline project called Mariner East became a recurring headache. The FBI was among those investigating whether members of Wolf's administration had been too cozy with the companies backing it. The project was supported by energy interests and labor unions but opposed by environmentalists and neighborhood groups near its path.

When the coronavirus pandemic hit in 2020, Wolf worked with other governors in the region on a coordinated response. He began with jurisdiction-by-jurisdiction stay-at-home orders, only issuing a statewide stay-at-home order (and a statewide mask order) after other nearby states had already done so. Wolf earned strong marks for communications, but he took criticism for inconsistent rules on what types of businesses were allowed to stay open. He sparred with Republicans seeking to open the economy more aggressively, and by December some businesses were flouting state restrictions. That month, Wolf reported that he had tested positive for the virus. In all, Pennsylvania was spared the early surges of neighboring New York and New Jersey, but its caseload peaked in the fall and winter and, after declining, rose again in the spring of 2021. Meanwhile, in another high-profile issue of 2020—the nation's reckoning over race and policing—a Black man, Walter Wallace Jr., armed with a knife and acting erratically, was shot dead by Philadelphia police in October, triggering protests and looting.

Wolf is term-limited, leaving an open-seat election in 2022. The presumed Democratic frontrunner is Attorney General Josh Shapiro, whose stature would make him an initial favorite. With a U.S. Senate seat also open in 2022, both parties' primary fields were in flux as of early 2021.

Bob Casey (D)

Elected 2006, term expires 2024, 3rd term, b. Apr 13, 1960; Scranton, PA; College of The Holy Cross, B.A., 1982; Catholic University of America, J.D., 1988; Roman Catholic; Married (Terese Foppiano Casey); 4 children.

Elected Office: PA Auditor General, 1997-2005; PA Treasurer, 2005-2007.

Professional Career: Practicing attorney, 1991-1996.

DC Office: 393 RSOB 20510, 202-224-6324, Fax: 202-228-0604, casey.senate.gov

State Offices: Allentown, 610-782-9470; Bellefonte, 814-357-0314; Erie, 814-874-5080; Harrisburg, 717-231-7540; Philadelphia, 215-405-9660; Pittsburgh, 412-803-7370; Scranton, 570-941-0930.

Committees: *Aging (Chmn)*. *Finance*: Health Care; International Trade, Customs & Global Competitiveness; Social Security, Pensions & Family Policy. *Health, Education, Labor & Pensions*: Children & Families (Chmn); Primary Health & Retirement Security. *Intelligence*.

Group Ratings

	ADA	ACLU	AFL-CIO	LCV	COC	HAFA	ACU	CFG	FRC
2020	-	54%	-	92%	-	28%	7%	-	-
2019	90%	C	100%	100%	65%	C	6%	0%	67%

Almanac Ratings 2019-2020

	Economy	Social	Foreign	Composite
Liberal	93%	93%	60%	82%
Conservative	7%	7%	40%	18%

Key Votes of the 116th Congress

1. EPA clean energy rules	Y	5. Russia sanctions	Y	9. Barr as Atty. General	N
2. U.S./Mex./Can. trade deal	Y	6. Troops in SYR, AFG	Y	10. Spending at the border	Y
3. Cut unemployment benefits	N	7. Veto arms sales to Saudis	Y	11. Coney Barrett to Sup. Ct.	N
4. Shelton to Fed Reserve	N	8. Defense $$$, veto override	Y	12. Electoral College objections	N

Election Results

Election	Name (Party)	Vote (%)		Cand. Spent	Ind. Exp. Support	Ind. Exp. Oppose
2018 General	Bob Casey (D).....................................	2,792,437	(56%)	$19,869,640	$769,690	$36,085
	Lou Barletta (R)............................	2,134,848	(43%)	$7,423,020	$89,756	$2,321,087
2018 Primary	Bob Casey (D)...		(100%)			

Prior winning percentages: 2018 (56%), 2012 (54%), 2006 (59%)

Bob Casey, Pennsylvania's senior senator, is an old-style, working-class populist who's find success while opposing abortion and supporting international trade tariffs. Casey has locked down his seat—in a swing state—and he has been a reliable Democratic vote in the chamber. He endorsed Joe Biden for president in April 2019, the day that the former vice president announced his candidacy. They share roots in Scranton.

During his own reelection in 2018, Casey needed to motivate swing voters to vote against President Donald Trump's agenda—and for him. Casey's brand of economic populism had some overlap with Trump's—and with some blue-collar Democrats, but not with the party's suburban voters. He supported the president's international trade war. On those economic issues, he was closer to Trump than was Pennsylvania's Republican senator, Pat Toomey, who was an outspoken opponent of the president on trade. Casey was easily reelected, as his Republican challenger failed to reignite the Trump coalition. His victory was the latest example of the appeal Casey, like his father before him, has had with his state's voters.

Born the oldest son in a large Irish-Catholic family in the former coal town of Scranton in northeast Pennsylvania, Casey grew up in the Green Ridge neighborhood—also the boyhood home of Biden. His father, Bob Casey Sr., served as a state senator and Pennsylvania's auditor general; he lost three Democratic primaries for governor before winning that office in 1986 and serving two terms. He was a feisty, tradition-minded practitioner of New Deal-style politics but was best known nationally for his steadfast opposition to abortion and his frequent clashes with national party leaders over that issue. In 1992, he was prevented from speaking at the Democratic National Convention, a decision related to his abortion stance but also brought on by his skepticism of Bill Clinton.

The younger Casey graduated from the College of the Holy Cross in Massachusetts. He taught in an inner city Philadelphia school for the Jesuit Volunteer Corps and earned his law degree from The Catholic University of America in Washington D.C. He practiced law in Scranton and then began his political career in 1996 by winning election as state auditor general. He was reelected in 2000, and, two years later, he ran as a cultural conservative with strong labor support in a nasty and expensive primary for governor against former Philadelphia Mayor Ed Rendell. Casey voiced similar views on abortion as his late father had as he sought to follow his footsteps into the governor's mansion. Casey's negative ads tarnished his image and he lost, but he showed resilience by returning in 2004 to win the state Treasurer's Office.

A year later, national Democrats were looking for a strong challenger to two-term Republican Sen. Rick Santorum, a high-profile social conservative with a red-state following and blue-state constituency. First in the House and then in the Senate, Santorum showed a knack for winning elections against tough odds—but the state's political landscape had shifted considerably since his first election to the Senate in 1994. Casey was waiting to make another run for governor in 2005 when New York Sen. ChuckSchumer—then head of the Democratic Senatorial Campaign Committee—wanted him to run for the Senate and quickly cleared the field to avoid a cash-draining primary.

While Casey's opposition to abortion rights made him anathema to many cultural liberals in the Philadelphia area, Schumer believed Casey could make inroads into Santorum's culturally conservative base—particularly in the western part of the state, where Santorum lived. Meanwhile, as the Democratic alternative to Santorum, Casey would be acceptable to voters in suburban Philadelphia, Schumer reasoned. The national party's heavy-handed involvement in recruiting Casey rankled many Democrats in the state. But resistance to Casey's candidacy faded in the run-up to the election, as he maintained a sizable lead over Santorum in the polls.

Though Santorum was being mentioned as a potential presidential candidate, his standing at home was tenuous. In the summer of 2005, he released a book titled, "It Takes a Family: Conservatism and the Common Good. "The book didn't have the best timing for a frank discourse on some of the most divisive cultural issues of the day. Santorum's support of the unpopular Bush administration in 2006 didn't help him either. Casey's socially conservative positions—at the time, he opposed gun control and same-sex marriage—helped cut into Santorum's advantage outside the state's metropolitan areas. Santorum outspent Casey by more than $8 million, but it wasn't enough. Casey won in a landslide, 59%-41%, becoming the first Pennsylvania Democrat elected to a full Senate term since 1962.

In the Senate, Casey has been a reliable supporter of his party's agenda and has moved leftward on several social issues. He angered some anti-abortion groups in 2011 when he voted against denying federal funds to Planned Parenthood; they noted the group provides many family planning services beyond abortion. He used a similar line of argument in 2014 when he supported a bill to overturn the Supreme Court's Hobby Lobby decision, another move that irked some abortion foes. The legislation was an effort to put congressional Democrats on record in favor of forcing most businesses to offer employees a full range of contraceptive coverage, even if the businesses' owners raised religious objections. "The healthcare service that's at issue here is contraception, which means prior to conception," Casey told the Philadelphia Inquirer, even as he added, "I'm a pro-life Democrat, always have been, always will be." Christopher Borick, a political scientist at Muhlenberg College, told the newspaper, "He has remained a pro-life Democrat, but one who has stretched the bounds of that definition."

Casey held to his traditional anti-abortion stand in spring 2015, voting with three other Democrats and most Republicans to advance a bill related to human trafficking. Most Democrats joined a filibuster of the measure over a provision they believed would expand the scope of the so-called Hyde amendment, which bars federal dollars from being spent on abortions. He signed on to the anti-abortion view in 2015 and again in 2018 when he joined two Democratic senators—Joe Donnelly of Indiana and Joe Manchin of West Virginia—to vote to start debate on a bill to prohibit abortions after 20 weeks of pregnancy. A Pennsylvania official of Planned Parenthood, who seemed reconciled to Casey's views, told the Pittsburgh Post-Gazette in early 2017 that he had "become more comfortable in distinguishing the women's health work we do" from abortion. In a July 2018 interview with Politico, Casey said that he remained a "pro-life Democrat," which meant, "I try to support policies that help women and children both before and after birth."

Casey reversed himself on two other social issues of perennial controversy: gun control and same-sex marriage. In 2013, he supported a measure—co-authored by his in-state colleague Toomey—to expand background checks for gun purchasers. The bill, which came after the 2012 school massacre in Newtown Connecticut in which more than two dozen were killed, failed to overcome a filibuster. Two years before the Supreme Court legalized same-sex marriage nationwide; Casey dropped his opposition to such unions. In 2016, after a massacre at a gay club in Orlando, he reinforced his shift on guns with a proposal ban those convicted of hate crimes from buying or owning guns.

On the Senate Finance Committee, Casey has been a party regular on economic issues. He has shared the skepticism of other Democrats from Rust Belt states toward international trade deals. "Our workers are losing over and over again when you have these trade agreements," Casey told the Allentown-based Morning Call. He voted against South Korea, Panama and Colombia trade agreements that became law in 2011, and, in 2015, was among the large majority of Democrats to oppose giving President Barack Obama "fast track" negotiating authority to expedite a 12-nation Pacific trade agreement.

Casey serves on the Health, Education, Labor and Pensions Committee and chairs its subcommittee dealing with children and families. He has consistently promoted legislation to award grants to states that provide full-day prekindergarten programs, while complaining that Congress has ignored the business community's support for investment in early childhood education. He has been an avid booster of funding for the Children's Health Insurance Program, which is similar to a program his father instituted in Pennsylvania. In February 2020, he unveiled his bill to expand child-welfare coverage, including guaranteed healthcare and childcare coverage, enhanced nutrition programs in schools, plus a guaranteed savings account for children born into families earning less than $100,000 annually. He told the Pittsburgh Tribune-Review that "it will take a long time" to enact the measure.

Like other coal-state senators, Casey had his differences with the Obama administration on environmental and energy policies. Responding in late 2014 to the administration's proposed climate change rules, Casey emphasized his commitment to environmental protection, saying a plan by the Environmental Protection Agency was necessary but asking for revisions and saying the plan set the carbon emissions target for Pennsylvania too high. In 2015, he was one of only eight Democrats to support an unsuccessful effort to override Obama's veto of the Keystone XL pipeline, a project opposed by environmentalists.

Republicans hoped to unseat Casey in 2012, but they had a hard time recruiting a top-tier candidate to take on the well-funded incumbent. Former coal executive Tom Smith, who spent almost $5 million of his own money, won the nomination with almost 40 percent of the vote. Initially, Smith was given little chance to beat Casey. But Smith went on the attack, calling Casey "Sen. Zero" and claiming he had accomplished little in the Senate. As a precaution, Casey kept his distance from Obama. His supporters worried he was underestimating Smith. "They've run a noncampaign up until now," Rendell told the Scranton Times-Tribune just weeks before the general election. Around that time, Smith invested another $10 million into his campaign, flooding the airwaves with attack ads. Casey won endorsements from most of the state's major newspapers. Smith outspent him, $21 million to $14 million, but Casey won 54%-45%; the margin was half of big as it was in his victory over better-known Santorum. He ran slightly ahead of Obama, who took the state with 52 percent of the vote.

Heading into the 2018 campaign, Casey saw that the political tide again was shifting. In early 2017, he spoke out against several of Trump's Cabinet nominees and went to the Philadelphia airport to join a protest of Trump's executive order banning entry of citizens of seven majority-Muslim nations. Although he had been moving in recent years to the left on social issues, the cautious Casey was mindful of the 2016 results in Pennsylvania: Democrats had narrowly lost high-stakes presidential and Senate contests. Republican Rep. Lou Barletta received encouragement from Trump. Barletta, an early and outspoken supporter of Trump, shared Casey's home ground in northeastern Pennsylvania.

In his customary way, Casey played to both sides as he responded to Trump's actions as president. He supported Trump's increased tariffs, especially on steel and aluminum. "I commend the president for announcing his intent to take action to protect our steelworkers from countries like China that cheat on trade," he said in March 2018. In July, Casey said Trump "shamed the office of the presidency" during his "dangerous and reckless" news conference with Russian President Vladimir Putin after their meeting in Helsinki.

Barletta followed Trump's 2016 small-town strategy instead of Toomey's more-suburban emphasis in his close reelection that year. But Barletta was no Trump. And politics in Pennsylvania shifted between 2016 and 2018. Midterm turnout dropped by about 1 million voters, with anti-Trump voters in the suburbs more motivated than many of Trump's core voters. Casey outspent him, $21.4 million to $7.8 million, and won 56%-43%.

In April 2019, less than an hour after Biden announced his candidacy on Twitter, Casey endorsed him, citing "a lifetime fighting battles on behalf of hardworking Americans while ensuring America's values and interests are represented abroad."

In the Senate, Casey's seniority lifted him to the chairmanship of the Senate Aging Committee, a useful platform though the panel lacks legislative jurisdiction. He might be close to becoming the top Democrat on the HELP Committee. Despite his earlier interest in following his father as governor of Pennsylvania, he told the Washington Post after the 2020 elections that he would not seek the open seat in 2022. "I'm very happy with the work I'm doing in the Senate," he said.

Pat Toomey (R)

Elected 2010, term expires 2022, 2nd term, b. Nov 17, 1961; Providence, RI; La Salle Academy ; Harvard University, B.A., 1984; Roman Catholic; Married (Kris Toomey); 3 children.

Elected Office: Allentown Government Study Commissioner, 1994-1996; U.S. House, 1999-2005.

Professional Career: Investment banker, Chemical Bank, 1984-1986; Investment banker, Morgan Grenfell, 1986-1990; Financial consultant, Springfield Ltd., 1990-1991; Restaurateur, 1990-2001; President, Club for Growth, 2005-2009.

DC Office: 248 RSOB 20510, 202-224-4254, Fax: 202-228-0284, toomey.senate.gov

State Offices: Allentown, 610-434-1444; Erie, 814-453-3010; Harrisburg, 717-782-3951; Johnstown, 814-266-5970; Philadelphia, 215-241-1090; Pittsburgh, 412-803-3501; Wilkes-Barre, 570-820-4088.

Committees: *Banking, Housing & Urban Affairs (RMM). Budget. Finance*: Health Care; International Trade, Customs & Global Competitiveness; Taxation & IRS Oversight.

Group Ratings

	ADA	ACLU	AFL-CIO	LCV	COC	HAFA	ACU	CFG	FRC
2020	-	23%	-	8%	-	85%	93%	-	-
2019	5%	C	11%	0%	63%	C	93%	95%	100%

Almanac Ratings 2019-2020

	Economy	Social	Foreign	Composite
Liberal	0%	0%	0%	0%
Conservative	100%	100%	100%	100%

Key Votes of the 116th Congress

1. EPA clean energy rules	N	5. Russia sanctions	N	9. Barr as Atty. General	Y
2. U.S./Mex./Can. trade deal	N	6. Troops in SYR, AFG	Y	10. Spending at the border	Y
3. Cut unemployment benefits	Y	7. Veto arms sales to Saudis	N	11. Coney Barrett to Sup. Ct.	Y
4. Shelton to Fed Reserve	Y	8. Defense $$$, veto override	Y	12. Electoral College objections	N

Election Results

Election	Name (Party)	Vote (%)	Cand. Spent	Ind. Exp. Support	Ind. Exp. Oppose
2016 General	Pat Toomey (R)...............................2,951,702	(49%)	$27,373,876	$15,146,525	$59,455,201
	Kathleen McGinty (D)................ ...2,865,012	(47%)	$14,968,292	$14,558,232	$47,543,382
	Edward Clifford (L)...................... 235,142	(4%)			
2016 Primary	Pat Toomey (R)............................Unopposed				

Prior winning percentages: 2016 (49%), 2010 (51%), House: 2002 (57%), 2000 (53%), 1998 (55%)

Pat Toomey, Pennsylvania's junior senator, has repeatedly evolved with his state's complex politics. In his improbable reelection in 2016, he took a different path to victory than did Donald Trump, who won even more narrowly in the Pennsylvania presidential contest that year. With an emphasis on the suburban battlegrounds outside Philadelphia, Toomey succeeded by coalition-building. Toomey mostly retained his Main Street Republican views and his role as a busy Senate insider, including a willingness to challenge Trump.

He asserted his independence when he bucked most Pennsylvania Republicans and voted to convict Trump in his second impeachment trial, which came after he goaded his supporters into storming the Capitol in an eleventh-hour attempt to overturn his election loss. At that time, Toomey became the top Republican on the Senate Banking, Housing and Urban Affairs Committee, a perch from which he envisioned some opportunity to cooperate with the chairman, Democratic Sen. Sherrod Brown of Ohio. Toomey's decision to retire in 2022 initially left Republicans struggling to retain his seat.

Toomey's success in the 2016 election was notable because of the stark differences from that campaign and the way he ran in 2010, though both wins were narrow. He spent several years as the president of the Club for Growth, a national organization that has spent generously to support candidates who share its conservative economic views. As head of the group, Toomey frequently backed candidates opposed by the local party establishment in Republican primary contests. But, facing reelection in a state that had become reliably blue in presidential elections, he moved perceptibly to the center on some social issues. The most noteworthy example came in 2013, when Toomey—a gun-rights supporter with an "A" rating from the National Rifle Association—broke with his party to sponsor expanded background checks on would-be gun purchasers.

A New Englander by birth, Toomey grew up in Providence Rhode Island, the third of six children of a union worker and a part-time church secretary. He graduated from Harvard University, paid for by scholarships and earnings from part-time jobs. After college, he worked in investment banking —founding a successful international financial services consulting firm and amassing considerable wealth. After six years on Wall Street, Toomey moved to Allentown, where he joined his brothers to start Rookies Restaurant and Sports Bar, which grew into a statewide chain. In 1994, he was elected to the Allentown Government Study Commission, where he pushed to lower taxes and require the City Council to have a supermajority to raise taxes.

As one of six candidates in the 1998 Republican primary for an open House seat in the Allentown area, Toomey advocated individual Social Security investment accounts, a flat tax to replace the income tax system and term limits for members of Congress; he promised to serve only six years. He won the close primary with 27 percent of the vote. In the general election, he won 55%-45%. He was twice reelected with a similar margin in a district that had consistently voted for Democrats in presidential elections since 1992.

In the House, Toomey focused primarily on economic issues, pushing to limit spending and force Congress to set aside money for debt reduction. Toomey ran in 2004 for the Senate seat held by then-Republican Arlen Specter. Specter was supported by President George W. Bush and conservative Pennsylvania colleague, Sen. Rick Santorum. Specter raised far more money than Toomey, while spotlighting the projects he had obtained for the state over his 24 years in the Senate. Toomey criticized Specter's voting record as too liberal and emphasized the latter's support from trial lawyers. Specter won 51%-49%, by a margin of 17,000 votes out of more than 1 million casts. Specter carried metro Philadelphia, his home, with 57 percent of the vote, but Toomey carried metro Pittsburgh with 58 percent.

In 2005, Toomey signed on as the head of the Club for Growth, a post he held until 2009 and which enabled him to make contacts around the country with conservative activists and major fundraisers. He defended the group's strategy in 2008 after Oklahoma Rep. Tom Cole, then chairman of the National Republican Congressional Committee, excoriated the Club for Growth's involvement in a contentious Ohio congressional primary. "The problem I have with the club is, I think they're stupid," Cole told The New York Times. "They spend more money beating Republicans than Democrats." In a Wall Street Journal op-ed piece titled, "In Defense of RINO Hunting,"—which used a derisive term meaning "Republican in Name Only"—Toomey shot back: "This is the argument of politicians who care more about maintaining power than using that power to implement conservative policies."

Toomey challenged Specter again in 2010 after the incumbent cast one of three Republican votes for Democrats' $787 billion economic stimulus bill amid the Great Recession. In April 2009, Specter announced he was switching parties to become a Democrat, saying he did not want to put his service at the mercy of Republican primary voters. Specter had a rocky path to the Democratic nomination, despite his backing from party heavyweights. Two-term Democratic Rep. Joe Sestak, a retired Navy admiral, entered the race. Sestak won the primary 54%-46%, carrying all but three counties: Philadelphia and those containing Harrisburg and Scranton.

The general election presented a clear contrast on issues: Sestak had voted not only for the stimulus bill but for the Democrats' health care overhaul and their cap-and-trade bill to limit carbon emissions. Toomey called for extending the Bush-era tax cuts for everyone, including those in the wealthiest bracket, and for lower corporate and capital gains tax rates. He spent $17 million, while Sestak spent $12 million, much of it in the primary. In a year in which Republicans rode a political wave, Toomey beat Sestak 51%-49%. Sestak's independence left intraparty scars that affected his candidacy in 2016, when he sought a rematch against Toomey.

In the Senate, Toomey has shown a preference for serious policy over sound bites. He has won praise for articulating conservative ideals in a manner that has not offended those who disagree. He introduced legislation making permanent an earmark ban on pet projects in spending bills; it did not pass, but continuing opposition by then-House Speaker John Boehner to earmarks resulted in a prohibition of the practice for the next decade.

Toomey gained attention while floating a couple of far-reaching plans to reduce the deficit. When a standoff developed in 2011 between President Barack Obama and Republican congressional leaders over raising the federal debt ceiling, Toomey disputed warnings from the Treasury Department and business leaders that a failure to raise the debt ceiling risked a financial default; he argued the United States could prioritize its payments to avoid a true default. He was one of three Republican senators appointed to the Joint Committee on Deficit Reduction—the "Supercommittee"—that was created by the legislation. The committee, evenly divided between Democrats and Republicans and the House and Senate, was charged with coming up with at least $1.2 trillion in budget savings over a decade.

The committee's efforts ended in partisan stalemate. Toomey, with the support of several other Republicans, floated a proposal to raise $400 billion in revenue—the majority coming from a reduction in tax breaks—coupled with $800 million in spending cuts. But Democrats reportedly rejected Toomey's plan because it did not phase out the Bush-era tax cuts for the wealthiest Americans. Toomey's proposal aimed to balance the budget in nine years with defense cuts already proposed by then-Defense Secretary Robert Gates, along with an overhaul of Medicaid into a block grant program. His plan did not touch the two largest entitlement programs: Medicare and Social Security.

In 2013, with a coveted seat on the Finance Committee, Toomey supported the compromise on taxes and spending to avoid the "fiscal cliff." But he blunted criticism from conservatives who didn't like the deal by saying Republicans needed to be ready to shut down the government in future debates over raising the deficit. "We absolutely have to have this fight over the debt limit," he said. In October of that year, Toomey was one of just 18 senators to vote against the spending deal to end a 16-day federal government shutdown, saying he opposed the new borrowing it allowed.

Toomey's first-term record on social issues was mixed. In late 2010, he favored repealing the military's ban on openly gay service members. Although he reiterated shortly before the Supreme Court's 2015 ruling on same-sex marriage that he believes marriage should be between a man and a woman, he voted for several measures that acknowledged gay rights. They included domestic violence protections for LGBTQ people, a ban on workplace discrimination and a requirement that groups receiving federal money do not discriminate based on sexual orientation.

Toomey's teaming with Democratic Sen. Joe Manchin of West Virginia in April 2013 on a compromise on gun control rippled across Capitol Hill. Their proposal called for expanding background checks to gun shows and online sales while maintaining record-keeping provisions that law enforcement officials said were essential in tracking criminal gun use. Toomey said that, while the volatile issue wasn't something he had sought, he considered it important to take action. The measure came after the December 2012 school massacre in Newtown Connecticut, in which 28 people, including the shooter and his mother, were killed; most of the victims were elementary-school children. The Manchin-Toomey proposal fell five votes short of the 60-vote supermajority needed to overcome a filibuster; only three Republicans joined Toomey in supporting the measure, which was strongly opposed by the NRA. Later, Toomey said he regretted his bill hadn't passed and "that it took me so long before I raised my voice on this very important issue."

In 2015, national Democratic leaders spent months searching for an alternative candidate to Sestak to take on Toomey. Finally, in August, Katie McGinty entered the contest, hoping to rally the support of feminists, organized labor and environmentalists. Republicans pointed out that the former Al Gore aideran a distant fourth in the 2014 primary for governor. In a view that became more prevalent in postelection second guessing, some Democrats argued that Sestak, given his outsider appeal and narrow loss to Toomey in a year unkind to Democrats, would have been a formidable challenger in a rematch, notwithstanding his scratchy relations with Democratic leaders. McGinty won 43%-33%.

Toomey presented himself as more well-rounded than a politician who cared only about cutting taxes and regulations, his campaign strategist Jon Lerner told Roll Call after the election. Emphasizing that Toomey had not backed away from his conservatism, Lerner said, "It was an attempt to put something else on top of it, it was a tonal aspect. It was a guy who's thoughtful, a guy who's serious." He sought to demonstrate this approach on several issues, including opposition to the Iranian nuclear agreement and the response to sanctuary cities, in addition to his actions on the federal debt and gay rights.

The approach was designed to appeal, in particular, to voters in the Philadelphia suburbs. The results there showed his success. He narrowly won in Bucks and Chester counties, and lost narrowly in Montgomery and Delaware counties. In the four counties combined, Toomey got about 48 percent of the vote; Trump got only43 percent. Trump outperformed Toomey in blue-collar strongholds outside Pittsburgh, which responded to more socially conservative appeals. Toomey won every other county west of the Philadelphia suburbs, including Centre and Dauphin, which Trump narrowly lost. During the campaign, Toomey would not endorse Trump, though he said on Election Day that he voted for Trump. The Senate contest was one of the most expensive in congressional history. In addition to nearly $50 million in spending by the candidates, outside groups spent more than $130 million, which was split about evenly between the two parties.

After the election, Toomey worked on significant Republican policies. On the Finance Committee, he worked with party leaders to seek common ground on major healthcare and tax bills in 2017. As Senate Republicans failed to repeal the Affordable Care Act in July 2017, Toomey said he could not reach common ground on alternatives that might draw support from Democrats. "I'm not interested in perpetuating a failed system and just throwing more dollars at it," he told the Pittsburgh Post-Gazette. "I've expended an awful lot of political time and energy and political capital. It's really important to me, and it'll be extremely disappointing if we don't get this done."

After the GOP meltdown on healthcare legislation, Toomey had a more rewarding experience with the party's measure to cut taxes. In reviewing Toomey's "intimate role" on the tax bill, the Allentown Morning Call gave him credit for crafting the key deal that set the amount of the cuts, for serving as a public "cheerleader" for the bill, and for making a closing pitch to the final undecided

Republican senators. "Let's face it, he was central," GOP Sen. Bob Corker of Tennessee, who was part of the deal-making, told The Washington Post in December 2017. For that story, Toomey described his experience as "gratifying and fulfilling."

As chairman of the Banking panel's Subcommittee on Financial Institutions and Consumer Protection, he helped prepare the Senate bill to reduce the scope of the 2010 Dodd-Frank banking regulation law. Trump signed the measure in May 2018.

Toomey faced his limits as a team player on steps that Trump took overseas. In March 2018, he called the president's tariff hikes "very, very counter-productive." He told a telephone town hall in July that Trump's meeting with Russian President Vladimir Putin was "very troubling" and showed "inexplicable blindness." In March 2019, he was one of 12 senators who voted to reject Trump's declaration of an emergency at the southern border to secure funds for a border wall without Congress. When the Senate overwhelmingly approved the revised U.S. trade deal with Mexico and Canada in January 2020, Toomey was the only Republican to vote against it. The fact that Democrats and organized labor were enthusiastic about the agreement, he told reporters, showed that it had "clearly moved way to the left."

Toomey also grew unhappy with Trump's political actions. In July 2020, he said that the president's decision to commute the prison sentence of political ally Roger Stone was a "mistake," given the severity of his offenses of lying to Congress and obstructing an investigation. After the 2020 election, he said that it was "completely unacceptable" for the president to pressure state legislators in Pennsylvania to overturn the results in that state. "It's all very, very unhelpful to people's confidence in our government," he told the Philadelphia Inquirer in December 2020.

When other Republican senators in January objected to certifying the state's Electoral College results, Toomey said their effort directly undermines "the right of the people to elect their own leader." As one of seven Republican senators who voted to convict Trump after his second impeachment trial, Toomey said, "For the first time in American history, the transfer of presidential power was not peaceful. ... [Trump's] betrayal of the Constitution and his oath of office required conviction."

A month before the election, Toomey announced that he would not seek reelection in 2022 nor run for the open seat for governor in Pennsylvania. "The reasons I have reached this decision are not political, they're personal," he said. Wide-open primaries were expected in each party. The early frontrunner to replace Toomey was Democratic Lt. Gov. John Fetterman, who finished third in the 2016 Democratic Senate primary to oppose Toomey. The dimension of the challenge facing Republicans is that Toomey is one of only two surviving Republican senators from the New England and Mid-Atlantic regions—areas that were the heart of the Republican establishment a few decades ago.

For his final two years in the Senate, Toomey moved up to ranking Republican on the Banking Committee. When Democrats took control of the Senate in early 2021, Toomey said he and Brown "have had a constructive working relationship" and that he looked forward to "continuing to work" with him.

Brian Fitzpatrick (R)

Elected 2016, 3rd term, b. Dec 17, 1973; Levittown, PA; LaSalle University, B.A., 1996; PA State University, M.B.A., 2001; PA State University School of Law, J.D., 2001; Roman Catholic; Single.

Professional Career: Judicial Clerk, Eastern District of PA, 2001-2002; Special Agent, FBI.

DC Office: 1722 LHOB 20515, 202-225-4276, Fax: 202-225-9511, brianfitzpatrick.house.gov

Committees: *Foreign Affairs*: Europe, Energy, the Environment & Cyber (RMM). *Joint Security & Cooperation in Europe. Permanent Select on Intelligence*: Defense Intelligence & Warfighter Support; Intelligence Modernization & Readiness. *Transportation & Infrastructure*: Aviation; Highways & Transit; Railroads, Pipelines & Hazardous Materials.

Group Ratings

	ADA	ACLU	AFL-CIO	LCV	COC	HAFA	ACU	CFG	FRC
2020	**	48%	**	84%	-	26%	33%	**	-
2019	60%	C	86%	86%	91%	C	37%	27%	50%

Almanac Ratings 2019-2020

	Economy	Social	Foreign	Composite
Liberal	47%	49%	47%	48%
Conservative	53%	51%	53%	52%

Key Votes of the 116th Congress

1. U.S./Mex./Can. trade deal Y	5. Russia sanctions Y	9. Firearms background checks Y
2. First Coronavirus response Y	6. Troops in Syria Y	10. Spending at the border Y
3. HEROES Act N	7. Veto arms sales to Saudis N	11. Marijuana liberalized rules N
4. CASH Act Y	8. Defense $$$, veto override Y	12. Electoral College objections N

Election Results

Election	Name (Party)	Vote (%)	Cand. Spent	Ind. Exp. Support	Ind. Exp. Oppose
2020 General	Brian Fitzpatrick (R)............ 249,804	(56%)	$4,557,659	$2,149,217	$2,855,983
	Christina Finello (D)............ 191,875	(43%)	$2,437,475	$208,739	$4,149,409
2020 Primary	Brian Fitzpatrick (R)............ 48,017	(63%)			
	Andy Meehan (R)............................ 27,895	(37%)			

Prior winning percentages: 2018 (51%), 2016 (54%)

Republican Brian Fitzpatrick, elected in 2016, had deep experience with law enforcement at the FBI, where he pursued political corruption and global terrorism. His independence from GOP leaders on high-stakes votes likely served Fitzpatrick well, as he twice withstood well-financed reelection challenges and survived as the only remaining House Republican in the Philadelphia suburbs. In 2021, he became a leader of the House's chief forum for bipartisanship, though he voted against both impeachments of former President Donald Trump.

Fitzpatrick was raised in Bucks County. He got his bachelor's degree from LaSalle University and his MBA and law degrees from Penn State University. He has been a licensed certified public accountant and an attorney. Fitzpatrick served as a special assistant U.S. attorney focused on drug crimes. He graduated first in his class at Quantico, the FBI academy, and served for 15 years as an FBI supervisory special agent. During the war in Iraq, Fitzpatrick was embedded with U.S. Special Forces. In his portfolio with the FBI, he was the national director for its Campaign Finance and Election Crimes Enforcement Program and was a national supervisor for its political corruption unit.

Fitzpatrick's brother Mike retired after having served eight years in the House between 2005 and 2017 (he lost reelection in 2006 and regained his seat four years later) and died of cancer in January 2020. Although Brian Fitzpatrick was a newcomer as a political candidate and had not resided in his district for many years, his last name and bio were obvious assets when he sought to succeed his brother. The Republican primary became a low-key contest in which the candidates had few major differences and Fitzpatrick's two opponents spent less than $50,000 between them. He won that contest with 78 percent of the vote.

His Democratic challenger, state Rep. Steven Santarsiero, said Fitzpatrick had spent little time in the district, and that "it's clear that if his last name were not Fitzpatrick, he wouldn't be running." Local reporters said Fitzpatrick was rarely available for interviews. His ads described him as "Levittown's own," and he emphasized his professional credentials and national security expertise. He said he could not vote for Donald Trump. Santarsiero spent $2.8 million for the cycle to $2 million for Fitzpatrick. Each candidate benefited from more than $7 million in national party support. In a district where the presidential election was virtually even, Fitzpatrick won 54%-46%.

In the House, Fitzpatrick quickly showed his independence. In January 2017, he was one of nine Republicans who voted against his party's plan to permit expedited House votes on health care reform. He opposed the House GOP plan to replace the Affordable Care Act. Following Trump's meeting in Helsinki with Russian President Vladimir Putin in 2018, Fitzpatrick said Trump was "manipulated" and that he was "frankly sickened by the exchange" between the two presidents in describing their meeting.

In 2019, Fitzpatrick was one of seven House Republicans who voted to end the partial government shutdown and was among 13 Republicans who opposed Trump's declaration of a national emergency to justify funding construction of a wall along the border with Mexico. He was the only Republican who joined 50 Democrats in sponsoring a bill that affirmed support for the Paris climate agreement that Trump had rejected.

On the first impeachment of Trump, Fitzpatrick—who had investigated corruption in Ukraine while he was an FBI agent—opposed the charges and said the Democrats' inquiry of Trump's disputed telephone call with the president of Ukraine had been "partisan." When the House impeached Trump following the riot at the Capitol, Fitzpatrick slammed Trump's "outrageous conduct." But he again opposed impeachment and said that the only way to "unify our nation with a bipartisan voice" would be a vote for censure. He was the only one of the nine House Republicans from Pennsylvania who voted to certify the Electoral College result that Joe Biden had won their home state.

In January 2021, Fitzpatrick became the ranking Republican on the Foreign Affairs Subcommittee on Europe, Energy, the Environment and Cyber. Two months later, he got a seat on the Intelligence Committee and said, "It is imperative that we have reliable intelligence and accountable agencies that the American people can trust." In April, after Rep. Tom Reed acknowledged improper behavior with a woman at a congressional event and stepped down as Republican co-chairman of the bipartisan Problem Solvers Caucus, Fitzpatrick was tapped as his successor.

In 2018, Fitzpatrick was challenged by Scott Wallace, who self-financed about 90 percent of the $13.5 million his campaign spent. Wallace, whose Grandfather Henry Wallace was vice president under Franklin Roosevelt, ran a foundation that contributed to many strongly left-wing causes; some of those recipients, including the Black Panthers and anti-Israel groups, became the focus of Republican campaign attacks. Wallace sought to link Fitzpatrick to Trump and to Republican attempts to cut back government health spending. Fitzpatrick highlighted his attempts to rebuild the political center. He was endorsed by the AFL-CIO and by the Philadelphia Inquirer, which wrote that "Fitzpatrick's emphasis on bipartisanship is a breath of fresh air." Fitzpatrick spent $3.5 million and was aided by more than $9 million in national GOP assistance. He won, 51.3%-48.7%, a margin of 8,300 votes.

In the 2020 Republican primary, Fitzpatrick was challenged by Andy Meehan, a financial adviser who called him a "fake Republican" and criticized the incumbent's insufficient support of Trump. Meehan spent only $59,000, but he held Fitzpatrick to a 63%-37% win. In the general election, Christina Finello, who served a decade as deputy director for housing and human services in Bucks County, voiced the familiar Democratic refrain that Fitzpatrick had not stood up to Trump. Noting the irony of the opposite primary and general election criticisms related to Trump, he responded to a news site in Levittown, "the far-left and far-right want to oppose me because I'm not an ideological purist." He outspent Finello $4.6 million to $2.4 million and had a relatively comfortable win, 56%-43%.

PA-1: Northern Philadelphia Suburbs   Cook Partisan Voting Index: EVEN

Population		Race and Ethnicity		Income	
Total	713,411	White	85.40%	Median Income	$93,474
Land area (sq. miles)	638	Black	4.70%	District Income Rank	46
Pop/ sq mi	1,117.52	Latino	5.50%	Poverty Rate	5.30%
Born in State	64.90%	Asian	6.20%	With health insurance	96.10%
		Two or more races	2.10%	Cash public assistance	1.80%
Age Groups		Other	1.70%	Food stamp/SNAP	6.60%
Under 18	20.40%				
18-34	18.90%	**Education**		**Work**	
35-64	41.80%	H.S grad or less	32.60%	White Collar	47.20%
Over 64	18.90%	Some College	24.70%	Sales and Service	34.30%
		College Degree, 4 yr	25.30%	Blue Collar	18.50%
Military		Post grad	17.30%	Government	9.30%
Veteran/ Active Duty	6.40%				

2020 Pres. Vote	Biden	233,462	(52%)	Trump	207,442	(46%)	
2016 Pres. Vote	Clinton	189,327	(49%)	Trump	181,716	(47%)	Johnson 9,729 (3%)

Bucks County: Bucks County was one of Pennsylvania founding father William Penn's three original settlements and the launching point for George Washington's crossing of the frigid Delaware River to surprise English and Hessian forces on Christmas Day 1776. But it has had a split personality from the start. Upper Bucks County was at once a bucolic paradise of rolling hills and creeks. In the 1920s, Bucks County's well-settled farmland, old fieldstone houses and covered bridges captured the imagination of writers and artists, attracting the New York theatrical crowd—Oscar Hammerstein, Moss Hart, Dorothy Parker and S.J. Perelman. Doylestown, the county seat, has beautiful old homes and several impressive museums. New Hope remains a popular weekend spot, with its hip boutiques and restaurants. Tourism and conventions are big business in Bucks.

After World War II, its location between Philadelphia and Trenton New Jersey brought industrial Lower Bucks County to the forefront. The ocean-navigable Delaware River and several rail lines resulted in huge new developments: U.S. Steel's Fairless Works, one of the few big postwar steel plants, and the Levitt organization's second Levittown in what had been a swamp between U.S. 13 and U.S. 1. The steel mill closed in 1991. A wind turbine plant moved onto part of the site Development in Bucks came later than in other suburban Philadelphia counties, where most blue-collar immigration settled decades earlier. Fairless Works and Levittown, with their tightly packed homes filled with blue-collar workers, became Democratic decades ago. Upper Bucks was a Republican bastion for many decades. As the area began to attract trendy New Yorkers, it has increasingly favored Democratic policies such as green space programs to keep developers away, while working-class Lower Bucks has become less strongly Democratic. Overall, Bucks County has remained politically marginal.

The 1st Congressional District of Pennsylvania includes all of Bucks County. Its small part of northeast Montgomery County is slightly more than 10 percent of the district. The redistricting in 2018 had less impact here than in any other district in the state. The modest change from the old 8th District, which already had relatively compact boundaries, moved its Montgomery County townships to the south along the Northeast Extension of the Pennsylvania Turnpike—from the area surrounding Upper Hanover to Franconia and Hatfield townships, including the borough of Lansdale. Bucks has a notably small minority population of 5 percent for both Blacks and Asians, plus 6 percent for Hispanics—smaller than other Philadelphia suburbs—and the third-highest median household income of any county in the state (behind Chester and Montgomery). The district has hosted some of the most hotly contested House races in the country, and it remained competitive. The latest redistricting changes increased the Democratic vote by about one percentage point. Plus, Joe Biden increased the Democratic presidential performance in Bucks from a lead of 2,700 votes in 2016 to more than 17,000 votes. That gave Democrats 52 percent in the district in 2020 and a more comfortable advantage of 6 percentage points.

Brendan Boyle (D)

Elected 2014, 4th term, b. Feb 06, 1977; Philadelphia, PA; University of Notre Dame, B.A., 1999; Harvard University John F. Kennedy School of Government, M.P.P., 2005; Roman Catholic; Married (Jennifer Morgan); 1 child.

Elected Office: PA House, 2009-2014.

Professional Career: Radio broadcaster; Management Consultant; Adjunct Professional, Drexel University.

DC Office: 1133 LHOB 20515, 202-225-6111, Fax: 202-226-0611, boyle.house.gov

State Offices: Philadelphia, 215-426-4616.

Committees: *Budget. Ways & Means*: Select Revenue Measures; Trade.

Group Ratings

	ADA	ACLU	AFL-CIO	LCV	COC	HAFA	ACU	CFG	FRC
2020	**	83%	**	100%	-	0%	4%	**	-
2019	90%	C	95%	97%	59%	C	5%	18%	0%

Almanac Ratings 2019-2020

	Economy	Social	Foreign	Composite
Liberal	100%	100%	92%	98%
Conservative	0%	0%	8%	2%

Key Votes of the 116th Congress

1. U.S./Mex./Can. trade deal	Y	5. Russia sanctions	Y
2. First Coronavirus response	Y	6. Troops in Syria	Y
3. HEROES Act	Y	7. Veto arms sales to Saudis	Y
4. CASH Act	Y	8. Defense $$$, veto override	Y

9. Firearms background checks Y
10. Spending at the border   N
11. Marijuana liberalized rules Y
12. Electoral College objections N

Election Results

Election	Name (Party)	Vote (%)		Cand. Spent	Ind. Exp. Support	Ind. Exp. Oppose
2020 General	Brendan Boyle (D)	198,268	(72%)	$768,754	$13,276	$158
	David Torres (R)	75,083	(27%)			$113
2020 Primary	Brendan Boyle (D)	73,980	(100%)			

Prior winning percentages: 2018 (79%), 2016 (100%), 2014 (67%)

Democrat Brendan Boyle, whose political base is in northeast Philadelphia, got a boost when court-ordered redistricting in 2018 removed Montgomery County from his district and located it entirely in Philadelphia. On the tax-writing House Ways and Means Committee, with his working-class views, he has emphasized the need to strengthen Social Security. The youthful Boyle has shown his willingness to challenge Democratic dogma.

Raised by working-class parents in northeast Philadelphia, Boyle was the first in his family to go to college. After his bachelor's in government at Notre Dame, he got a master's degree in public policy at Harvard's John F. Kennedy School of Government. In 2008, he was elected to the state House. His brother Kevin was elected two years later, making them the first pair of siblings to serve together in the state House.

When Democratic Rep. Allyson Schwartz ran unsuccessfully in the Democratic primary for governor in 2014, Boyle was one of four Democrats seeking to replace her. Boyle was financially outgunned by the three other contenders. Each spent at least $1.5 million in the primary, while Boyle spent only $900,000 for his entire campaign. Boyle hit the pavement with old-school populism and held 225 voter events that played up his grassroots candidacy, noting that his father was a public-transit maintenance worker and his mother a school crossing guard. He got a boost from union support, with a labor-backed PAC spending $350,000 on Boyle's behalf, plus a crucial endorsement by then-Rep. Robert Brady, boss of the Philadelphia Democratic organization. NARAL, a leading abortion-rights group, accused him of "tap dancing around votes he took that would throw roadblocks in front of women seeking reproductive health care."

Boyle's targeted route to victory went decidedly through Philadelphia, where he got 70 percent of the vote, with Brady's help. He called himself "a Northeast guy." He finished a distant fourth with only 16 percent in Montgomery, which cast 54 percent of the primary vote. But that was enough to give him the victory with 41 percent, to 27 percent for former Rep. Marjorie Margolies, who is Chelsea Clinton's mother-in-law. In the general election, the contest was never in doubt. Boyle won 67%-33%, and took 75 percent of the vote in Philadelphia.

At the St. Patrick's Day reception at the White House in 2015, President Barack Obama gave a shout-out to Boyle, plus his brother and father. He told the immigrant story of their father, who was born in Donegal. His Almanac vote ratings have ranked Boyle toward the center of the House, especially on foreign policy.

In 2017, on the Budget Committee, Boyle joined other Democrats in attacking Republican plans to repeal and replace the Affordable Care Act. He said the GOP alternative broke the promises made by Donald Trump during his presidential campaign. With Democratic Rep. Marc Veasey of Texas, he organized the Blue Collar Caucus for Democrats to reach out to Trump voters. In 2019, he gained additional influence with his seat on Ways and Means. That made him, he said, "one of the youngest members of Congress' oldest committee" at what he termed a "relatively early" point in his career.

In October 2019, Boyle joined four other Ways and Means Democrats in writing a piece for The Hill in which they pitched their Social Security 2100 bill, which is designed to fix the growing deficit in the system's financing. With their 1 percentage point increase in the payroll tax, which would be phased in over more than 20 years, plus a more beneficial cost-of-living adjustment, they wrote, "This is the time to fulfill the promise and guarantee of Social Security."

During his speech at the Democratic convention in 2020, Boyle said a Biden administration would bring stability and predictability. "You deserve health care that you can afford, a job that pays you fairly," he said, speaking symbolically from his kitchen table.

His foreign policy interests have included advocacy on behalf of Ireland and the need to address the genocide in Syria. With Republican Rep. Adam Kinzinger, Boyle has created the Friends of a Free, Stable and Democratic Syria Caucus in the House.

In 2017, Philadelphia magazine ran a lengthy profile of the Boyle brothers that described their skill in reaching out to working-class voters, a constituency with which national Democrats had been falling short, they said. "Now that I've been inside the room of the Democratic Congressional Campaign Committee, one of the first questions that's asked when we're looking to recruit a Democratic candidate for Congress is: Can that person self-fund?" Brendan Boyle said critically. He added that Democrats need to "widen the tent" to include voters with different views on abortion and guns, for example.

Following the redistricting in 2018, the Philadelphia Inquirer reported, former City Councilman Bill Green—whose father and grandfather were influential members of the House—filed papers for his candidacy. But he changed his mind just before the filing deadline because of legal uncertainty whether he could retain his membership on a local school board. Green told the Inquirer that he might have had enough support to win the party endorsement. A Boyle spokesman responded, "it would have been awfully difficult to beat" the incumbent. He has been easily reelected in his new district.

PA-2: North Philadelphia   Cook Partisan Voting Index: D+21

Population		Race and Ethnicity		Income	
Total	722,722	White	45.00%	Median Income	$46,248
Land area (sq. miles)	63	Black	25.20%	District Income Rank	411
Pop/ sq mi	11,537.71	Latino	27.90%	Poverty Rate	25.40%
Born in State	62.60%	Asian	8.80%	With health insurance	90.00%
		Two or more races	4.00%	Cash public assistance	6.80%
Age Groups		Other	17.00%	Food stamp/SNAP	32.70%
Under 18	24.90%				
18-34	24.00%	**Education**		**Work**	
35-64	37.50%	H.S grad or less	55.30%	White Collar	30.60%
Over 64	13.50%	Some College	22.10%	Sales and Service	46.20%
		College Degree, 4 yr	14.90%	Blue Collar	23.20%
Military		Post grad	7.70%	Government	11.70%
Veteran/ Active Duty	4.50%				

2020 Pres. Vote	Biden	207,491	(70%)	Trump	86,128	(29%)
2016 Pres. Vote	Clinton	207,154	(73%)	Trump	70,663	(25%)

Delaware River areas: Everywhere in Philadelphia, American history is close at hand. Independence Hall is where Americans in the 1780s drew up the Constitution, and not far away are the restored townhouses of Society Hill. Nearby sits the Liberty Bell and its signature crack. City founder William Penn was a Quaker, a member of one of the 17th-century sects that prized reason, and he imposed order on his new environment: no cow-path street patterns here, but a grid of numbered and named streets. Penn's "City of Brotherly Love" grew to be a commercial and industrial metropolis that spread out over the countryside until it was the young nation's largest city. Since 2005, the metro area has dropped from the fourth-largest in the nation to seventh.

Northeast Philadelphia is relatively new urban territory, with more than half its houses built after 1950. Many of Philadelphia's Hispanics, who are mostly from Puerto Rico, live in the industrial wards along the Delaware River. Other wards in the Northeast have remained mostly white and blue-collar. Trip advisor recommends Fish town, which is centered on Frankford Avenue, for "some of the coolest hipster neighborhood bars in the city." Housing prices in Fish town climbed 70 percent in the past decade, WPVI reported in February 2020. Nearby is Northern Liberties, another gentrifying neighborhood that has received national recognition and is not far from Center City. Along Broad Street and close to downtown, with a boost from real-estate developers, Temple University has spent hundreds of millions of dollars to create a campus experience in a more residential and gentrified university; the African-American population in this area had declined nearly 20 percent from 2000 to 2014.Kensington, a more troubled area to the north, has suffered from a wave of opioid-related deaths. Expansion of container cargo facilities plus additional dredging at the port, which are part of a $300 million capital improvement plan to accommodate ultra-large container vessels and to double overall capacity, have resulted in the fastest-growing port on the Atlantic coast.

The 2nd Congressional District of Pennsylvania contains North Philadelphia and eastern sections of Philadelphia along the Delaware River. It extends south to Franklin Square. The new 2nd District, now entirely in Philadelphia, does not include areas that were based in Center City and South Philadelphia or Delaware and Montgomery counties. As a whole, Philadelphia grew 4 percent from 2010 to 2019 to a population of 1.6 million. Minority groups are 44 percent Black, 15 percent Hispanic and 8 percent Asian-American. To keep the neighboring 3rd District an African-American majority, the 2018 redistricting decreased the Black population and the Democratic vote of the 2nd. But this is a two-thirds majority-minority and solidly Democratic district. In 2020, Joe Biden won 70 percent in the district.

Dwight Evans (D)

Elected 2016, 3rd full term, b. May 16, 1954; Philadelphia, PA; Community College of Philadelphia, A.A., 1973; La Salle College, B.A., 1975; Baptist; Single.

Elected Office: PA House, 1980-2016.

Professional Career: Teacher, Philadelphia Public Schools.

DC Office: 1105 LHOB 20515, 202-225-4001, Fax: 202-225-5392, evans.house.gov

Committees: *Small Business*: Economic Growth, Tax & Capital Access; Oversight, Investigations & Regulations. *Ways & Means*: Health; Oversight; Worker & Family Support.

Group Ratings

	ADA	ACLU	AFL-CIO	LCV	COC	HAFA	ACU	CFG	FRC
2020	**	80%	**	100%	-	0%	2%	**	-
2019	95%	C	100%	97%	60%	C	3%	12%	0%

Almanac Ratings 2019-2020

	Economy	Social	Foreign	Composite
Liberal	100%	100%	92%	98%
Conservative	0%	0%	8%	2%

Key Votes of the 116th Congress

1. U.S./Mex./Can. trade deal	Y	5. Russia sanctions	Y	9. Firearms background checks Y
2. First Coronavirus response	Y	6. Troops in Syria	Y	10. Spending at the border N
3. HEROES Act	Y	7. Veto arms sales to Saudis	Y	11. Marijuana liberalized rules Y
4. CASH Act	Y	8. Defense $$$, veto override	Y	12. Electoral College objections N

Election Results

Election	Name (Party)	Vote (%)		Cand. Spent	Ind. Exp. Support	Ind. Exp. Oppose
2020 General	Dwight Evans (D)............................	341,922	(91%)	$882,259	$3,775	$158
	Michael Harvey (R)......................	33,728	(9%)			$59
2020 Primary	Dwight Evans (D)........................	164,871	(100%)			

Prior winning percentages: 2018 (93%), 2016 (90%)

Dwight Evans, who was influential and well-known locally during his 36 years in the state House, had the support of Democratic state and city leaders when he won the Democratic primary in 2016 against 11-term Rep. Chaka Fattah, who was convicted on corruption charges two months later. In the House, he got a seat on the Ways and Means Committee, where he has addressed the consequences of income inequality, including protection of pensions.

Evans was born in Philadelphia and got his bachelor's degree from La Salle University. He went to work as a teacher in Philly and for the Urban League as a community activist. In 1980, he was elected as a state representative, where he began a busy legislative career. He helped create the Public Transportation Assistance Fund, which was a dedicated funding source for mass transit. He was an author of the state's charter school program, which increased the school choices for parents and their children.

For 20 years, Evans was the chairman or senior Democrat on the House Appropriations Committee, where he directed funds to communities across the state. As chairman of the Budget Committee of the Southeast Pennsylvania Transportation Authority, Evans participated in labor negotiations, including the weeklong transit strike in 2016 that was settled on the eve of Election Day. Evans had several unsuccessful runs for higher office, including governor and lieutenant governor and two bids for mayor.

Evans got his big opening when Fattah was indicted in July 2015 on federal corruption charges —including bribery, money laundering and mail fraud—for his mixing of personal and campaign finances when he ran for mayor in 2007. Evans was endorsed by, among others, Pennsylvania Gov. Tom Wolf and Philadelphia Mayor Jim Kenney, each of whom Evans had endorsed when they sought their current office. Many of the ward leaders in the Democratic organization stayed with Fattah.

Fattah, who was beleaguered by legal bills, raised only $220,000 to $1.5 million for Evans. In the four-candidate April primary, Evans won 42%-35%. Subsequently, Fattah resigned from the House three days after his conviction. He was sentenced to 10 years in prison, one of the longest-ever criminal sentences for a current or former member of Congress. In addition to the general election, which Evans won with 90 percent of the vote, he won a simultaneous special election for the remainder of Fattah's term, and took office a week after the election.

Evans joined the Agriculture Committee, where he worked on hunger and nutrition programs during debate on the farm bill in 2018. A week after President Donald Trump took office, Evans joined local Democrats in criticizing the new administration's decision to deny admission to Syrian refugees who reportedly were seeking to enter the nation legally at the Philadelphia airport. He called the prohibition "cruel and unusual … [and] a very sad day in the city of Brotherly Love." Evans called for the removal of cannabis and hemp from federal drug-sentencing schedules, which he said have targeted African-American males. He won enactment of his bill to reduce costs for small business owners who apply for a loan with the Small Business Administration.

In 2019, Evans got his seat on Ways and Means on the same day Rep. Brendan Boyle also was assigned to the committee. They hold adjacent districts in Philadelphia, which gives the city additional clout on tax and social-welfare legislation. Evans took a special interest in a bill the House passed in July 2019 that sought to protect pensions of businesses that had failed to provide adequate financing. Evans called the bill, which allowed private investors to purchase bonds guaranteed by the federal government, "a vital preventive tool" to lift workers and retirees out of poverty.

In 2019, Evans filed a bill to repeal provisions of a law enacted in 2005 that makes it difficult for victims of gun violence to sue manufacturers of firearms. With Senator Bob Casey of Pennsylvania, he filed a separate bill that would provide information about programs and benefits that are available to gun-violence victims.

PA-3: West Philadelphia, Center City   **Cook Partisan Voting Index: D+41**

Population		Race and Ethnicity		Income	
Total	741,654	White	33.30%	Median Income	$49,897
Land area (sq. miles)	53	Black	56.40%	District Income Rank	388
Pop/ sq mi	14,051.80	Latino	4.30%	Poverty Rate	21.80%
Born in State	65.60%	Asian	5.60%	With health insurance	93.60%
		Two or more races	3.00%	Cash public assistance	5.10%
Age Groups		Other	1.80%	Food stamp/SNAP	22.90%
Under 18	18.10%				
18-34	34.40%	**Education**		**Work**	
35-64	32.90%	H.S grad or less	37.20%	White Collar	48.80%
Over 64	14.50%	Some College	22.30%	Sales and Service	40.00%
		College Degree, 4 yr	21.30%	Blue Collar	11.10%
Military		Post grad	19.30%	Government	10.80%
Veteran/ Active Duty	4.60%				

2020 Pres. Vote	Biden	357,956	(91%)	Trump	31,769	(8%)
2016 Pres. Vote	Clinton	339,564	(91%)	Trump	26,216	(7%)

City Hall: Looking out over the Schuylkill River north of Center City Philadelphia, you can still see the landscape painted 100 years ago by Philadelphia artist Thomas Eakins: the tightly packed but formidable row houses, the old fieldstone houses of Germantown and the boat houses below the small Greek temples of the Water Works. West Philadelphia's long-established Black neighborhoods run across the Schuylkill on either side of Market Street. Pennsylvania was the first state to abolish slavery, thanks to William Penn and his Quaker legacy, and Philadelphia has been home to a large African-American community since before the Civil War. Northwest Philadelphia includes distinguished old neighborhoods such as Chestnut Hill, with its cobblestone streets and classic architecture. East Falls was the childhood home of Grace Kelly, who grew up to be a Hollywood starlet and princess of Monaco. Some neighborhoods here continue to suffer from poverty and blight. But in recent years, city officials have made a concerted effort to bring young, affluent people back to the city.

For all its historical grandeur, Philadelphia seldom has had a city government to be proud of. It has had crime-ravaged neighborhoods, with the highest crime rates of the nation's 10 largest cities, including 351 homicides in 2018.The adult poverty rate of 26 percent was the highest in the nation for big cities. There are signs of renewal. Center City remains attractive to young professionals—a growing number with families. The changes may be creating a political "power vacuum" in the city as the Democratic Party machine suffers from corruption charges and decay and the insurgents are "just not scared anymore," the Philadelphia Inquirer reported in December 2019.

The 3rd Congressional District takes in the African-American neighborhoods in West Philadelphia, and north Philadelphia west of 15th Street. It includes City Hall, an ornate building where a statue of city founder William Penn stands 37 feet high, well-heeled Rittenhouse Square, the Philadelphia Zoo (America's first), and the University of Pennsylvania and Drexel University across the Schuylkill. It also includes most of Fairmount Park, the largest landscaped urban park in the world, which climaxes at the Philadelphia Museum of Art, where a Rocky-like run up the steps has become de rigueur for tourists. For many, including visitors, the 30th Street train station is the heart of the district. A $10 billion master plan envisioned a new concourse, connections to local rail and bus lines, and long-term development of the area over the tracks—which occupies88 acres of prime urban real estate. In June 2020, Amtrak launched a $400 million renovation of the station, including new offices and expansion of retail and dining services.

Also here is much of 18th century Philadelphia: Independence Hall; the U.S. Mint; and historic Christ Church, where George Washington and Benjamin Franklin worshipped. The district takes in Chinatown, Society Hill, the Northern Liberties village, two miles of prime real estate along the Delaware River, and Old City, with its flourishing night life. The National Constitution Center is on Independence Mall. The Gallery Mall shopping area, part of wider-scale development between City Hall and Independence Mall, was transformed in 2019 into the Fashion District across three city blocks. In September 2020, the Delaware River Waterfront Corp. selected a developer for the Penn's

Landing area that will create a four-acre park over Interstate 95 south of Chestnut Street, which will include 12 residential and office towers by 2030.

The court-ordered redistricting in 2018 had little impact on the politics of the district, which has been among the five most Democratic districts in the nation. Joe Biden got 91 percent in the 3rd—his best district in the nation. The chief geographic shifts were the addition of Center City and the historic areas of the city and the removal of a few wealthy suburbs on the Main Line of Montgomery County. As a result, the new 3rd—like the new 2nd—is entirely in Philadelphia. Together, they cover nearly 95 percent of the city; the remainder is in the Delaware County-based 5th District.

Madeleine Dean (D)

Elected 2018, 2nd term, b. Jun 06, 1959; Glenside, PA; La Salle University; Montgomery County Community College; University of PA, Att.; Widener University School of Law - DE, J.D., 1984; Christian Church; Married (Patrick J. Cunnane); 3 children; 1 grandchild.

Elected Office: PA House, 2012-2018.

Professional Career: Counsel, Cunnane Bicycle Company, Inc.; General Law Practice Attorney; Philadelphia Daily News, Contributor

DC Office: 129 CHOB 20515, 202-225-4731, dean.house.gov

State Offices: Glenside, 215-884-4300; Norristown, 610-382-1250.

Committees: *Financial Services*: Diversity & Inclusion; Nat'l Security, International Development & Monetary Policy. *Judiciary (VChmn)*: Antitrust, Commercial & Administrative Law; Crime, Terrorism & Homeland Security.

Almanac Ratings 2019-2020

	Economy	Social	Foreign	Composite
Liberal	100%	100%	80%	94%
Conservative	0%	0%	20%	6%

Key Votes of the 116th Congress

1. U.S./Mex./Can. trade deal Y	5. Russia sanctions Y	9. Firearms background checks Y
2. First Coronavirus response Y	6. Troops in Syria Y	10. Spending at the border Y
3. HEROES Act Y	7. Veto arms sales to Saudis Y	11. Marijuana liberalized rules Y
4. CASH Act Y	8. Defense $$$, veto override Y	12. Electoral College objections N

Election Results

Election	Name (Party)	Vote (%)		Cand. Spent	Ind. Exp. Support	Ind. Exp. Oppose
2020 General	Madeleine Dean (D)	264,645	(59%)	$834,936	$4,008	$158
	Kathy Barnette (R)	179,934	(40%)	$908,938	$81,010	$113
2020 Primary	Madeleine Dean (D)	122,657	(100%)			

Prior winning percentages: 2018 (64%)

In 2018, Madeleine Dean had the easiest path to the House of the four Philadelphia-area Democratic newcomers—all women—to the Pennsylvania delegation. She also had the most political experience of that group. Probably her biggest challenge was navigating the complex redistricting changes in her Montgomery County-based seat. In the once-competitive battleground, which has become solidly Democratic, Dean's victory in the primary virtually assured her election in November. Pending the outcome of redistricting, she appears to have a lock on the seat.

Dean offered a diverse background. A graduate of LaSalle University and Widener University Law School, she had been a lawyer, writer and teacher. She practiced law with the Philadelphia Trial Lawyers, where she became executive director, and she later opened a three-woman firm that practiced general law. As a writer, she contributed to local newspapers and taught writing as an English professor at LaSalle.

Dean launched her political career in 2012, when she was elected to the first of three terms in the state House. In Harrisburg, she was vice chair of the Finance Committee and co-chaired the PA Safe Caucus, a coalition that sought to curb gun violence through action and awareness; she filed legislation to ban the use of bump stocks with firearms. As a member of the Governor's Commission for Women, she advised on policies that promoted equality issues ranging from sexual assault to business initiatives. That advocacy led to her focus on the need for more women in politics.

In 2017, Dean announced her campaign for lieutenant governor. But she switched her plan when the state Supreme Court in February 2018 approved a new congressional redistricting map. State Sen. Daylin Leach, who finished fourth in the 2014 Democratic primary for an open seat in the previous version of the district, dropped his bid to run because of sexual-harassment claims. Rep. Brendan Boyle, who won that contest, switched to run in a redrawn Philadelphia seat.

After no strong contender showed interest during the brief filing period, Dean launched what she called a "once in a lifetime opportunity to serve." Her campaign was endorsed by labor unions and EMILY's List, the Democratic abortion-rights group. She emphasized the lack of women in the Pennsylvania delegation, though two women had been elected to earlier versions of this district during the previous quarter-century: Marjorie Margolies and Allyson Schwartz, each of whom turned down the opportunity to return to Congress. The Philadelphia Inquirer endorsed Dean as "the person who seems better prepared to not only represent Pennsylvanians but counter" President Donald Trump.

In what became a surprisingly easy contest, her chief opponent appeared to be former Rep. Joe Hoeffel, who served three terms in the Montgomery County-based district (prior to Schwartz) before he ran unsuccessfully against Republican Sen. Arlen Specter in 2004. Hoeffel was under-financed in his bid to return to Congress and had lost support from party regulars. Also competing in the primary was Shira Goodman, a gun-control advocate who was new to electoral politics. Dean won 73 percent of the vote, with runner-up Goodman getting 16 percent. In November, Dean got 64 percent of the vote against Republican Dan David, a political newcomer who started up an equities research firm.

In the House, Dean got prime committee assignments on Financial Services and Judiciary. Following an October 2019 Financial Services hearing with Facebook chief executive Mark Zuckerberg, Dean said she was un persuaded by his claim that antitrust issues were not discussed when he had an earlier meeting at the White House with Trump and that he had no notes from that meeting. "Of course, people took notes. You don't go into that high-powered a meeting and not document what was said," Dean told CNN. In response to her question whether Facebook had booked blocks of rooms at the Trump International Hotel in Washington, which often were not used, Zuckerberg said, "I would be very surprised to hear if that were the case." Dean—the former writer and lawyer—said later, "he didn't have a response."

In August 2020, Dean discussed with People magazine her forthcoming joint memoir, Under Our Roof, with her 30-year-old son Harry about his 10-year recovery from drug addiction. "Writing a book like this—told from our dueling perspectives—was difficult and yet ultimately rewarding," she and Harry said in a joint statement. "We can't combat the stigma around addiction and recovery unless we talk about it, so we figured we'd start at home by writing about our own story." Harry later served as a resource director for the same treatment center where he sought help for his addiction.

Asked by a reporter for The Washington Post in December 2019 whether her freshman class had changed Washington or if Washington had changed them, Dean paused and responded, "That's a great question. ...I think we're changing things. I really do."

Dean was reelected, 59%-40%, against Republican Kathy Barnette, each spent nearly $1 million. Barnette, who served 10 years in the Army Reserve, worked in corporate finance and was a conservative commentator.

PA-4: Northwestern Philadelphia Suburbs   **Cook Partisan Voting Index: D+9**

Population		Race and Ethnicity		Income	
Total	730,701	White	79.60%	Median Income	$91,030
Land area (sq. miles)	477	Black	9.70%	District Income Rank	53
Pop/ sq mi	1,531.80	Latino	5.70%	Poverty Rate	6.40%
Born in State	72.50%	Asian	6.70%	With health insurance	96.30%
		Two or more races	2.70%	Cash public assistance	1.70%
Age Groups		Other	1.30%	Food stamp/SNAP	5.80%
Under 18	21.20%				
18-34	20.50%	**Education**		**Work**	
35-64	39.90%	H.S grad or less	29.10%	White Collar	51.70%
Over 64	18.40%	Some College	22.50%	Sales and Service	33.30%
		College Degree, 4 yr	28.00%	Blue Collar	15.00%
Military		Post grad	20.50%	Government	8.30%
Veteran/ Active Duty	6.00%				

2020 Pres. Vote	Biden	276,499	(61%)	Trump	168,178	(37%)			
2016 Pres. Vote	Clinton	221,308	(57%)	Trump	147,219	(38%)	Johnson	9,663	(3%)

Montgomery County: Montgomery County is the proximate hinterland of Philadelphia: rolling hills cut on one side by the Schuylkill River and at intervals by the Pennsylvania and Reading Railroad lines radiating outward from Center City. Older suburbs, both rich and modest, grew up around rail stations, with comfortable houses within walking distance for commuters. Farther out are 18th and 19th century villages, once surrounded by farm fields, now encroached upon by subdivisions where people depend on cars, not rail lines, to get to work. Historically, the moderate Republican style of politics in Montgomery was set by Ivy League graduates. In the 1990s, the county swung toward Democrats in national politics, with abortion rights and other cultural issues usually trumping economic concerns. Now, as in much of the nation's suburbia, Republican influence has become scarcer. Montgomery County from 2010 to 2019 had the fastest growth in the region in the first ring of counties outside Philadelphia and it has been the second most affluent county, behind Chester, in the state. It is a distant third as the most populous county, behind Philadelphia and Allegheny.

In Horsham, downsizing of the Willow Grove Naval Air Station resulted in plans for a large housing development following an environmental clean-up of the area. Instead, local officials approved the land for open-space preservation. Also in the Horsham area, the Navy has spent more than $63 million to investigate and start the clean-up of groundwater contamination that was caused by the chemicals (known as "forever chemicals") in a firefighting foam that was used by the Naval Air Warfare Center, which was based in Warminster; the center manufactured military aircraft, starting in World War II, and shut down in 1996. Just to the east of Valley Forge, where Gen. George Washington and his men spent the terrible winter and spring of 1777-78, is the King of Prussia mall. With three expansions in recent years and more than 450 stores, it has gained the distinction of the largest amount of leased space of any mall in the nation. The Mall of America in Minnesota retained the record for the most stores. SEPTA has approved a $2 billion plan to extend high-speed rail service to the mall, with a four-mile extension on the Norristown Line, which is scheduled for completion by 2027. The mall is 16 miles from Center City.

The 4th Congressional District of Pennsylvania is 97 percent in Montgomery County and largely unified the county in one district for the first time since 2002; the remaining 3 percent is in Berks County. Two small salients, which border Bucks and Delaware counties in the 1st and 5th Districts, include an additional 15 percent of the county. The new 4th is one of four solidly Democratic districts in the Philadelphia metro area—two of them in the city and two others based in Montgomery and Delaware counties. The loss of Northeast Philadelphia from the old 13th District reduced the Democratic base vote here by a few percent. Joe Biden won the district, 61%-37%, a marked increase from President Barack Obama's 56%-43% win in 2012. The return to Republican control of this area, which predominated as recently as 1998, seems a distant prospect.

Mary Gay Scanlon (D)

Elected 2018, 2nd full term, b. Aug 30, 1959; Syracuse, NY; Colgate University, B.A., 1980; University of PA Law School, J.D., 1984; Catholic; Married (Mark Scanlon); 3 children.

DC Office: 1535 LHOB 20515, 202-225-2011, Fax: 202-226-0280, scanlon.house.gov

State Offices: East Lansdowne, 610-626-1913.

Committees: *Communications Standards Commission (Chmn). Judiciary:* Antitrust, Commercial & Administrative Law; Crime, Terrorism & Homeland Security; Immigration & Citizenship. *Rules:* Legislative & Budget Process.

Almanac Ratings 2019-2020

	Economy	Social	Foreign	Composite
Liberal	100%	100%	92%	98%
Conservative	0%	0%	8%	2%

Key Votes of the 116th Congress

1. U.S./Mex./Can. trade deal	Y	5. Russia sanctions	Y	9. Firearms background checks	Y
2. First Coronavirus response	Y	6. Troops in Syria	Y	10. Spending at the border	N
3. HEROES Act	Y	7. Veto arms sales to Saudis	Y	11. Marijuana liberalized rules	Y
4. CASH Act	Y	8. Defense $$$, veto override	Y	12. Electoral College objections	N

Election Results

Election	Name (Party)	Vote (%)		Cand. Spent	Ind. Exp. Support	Ind. Exp. Oppose
2020 General	Mary Gay Scanlon (D)	256,021	(65%)	$1,150,085	$6,385	$158
	Dasha Pruett (R)	139,686	(35%)	$71,988	$158	$113
2020 Primary	Mary Gay Scanlon (D)	103,194	(100%)			

Prior winning percentages: 2018 (65%)

Democrat Mary Gay Scanlon, who won her seat with a big boost from redistricting in the revamped Delaware County-based district, quickly gained influential assignments in the House. A longtime legal activist, Scanlon had scant experience in elected office beyond her tenure on the Wallingford-Swarthmore School Board. She campaigned on her extensive resume on education issues and her background in the area's legal community. Republican Rep. Pat Meehan, who had been elected to four terms, resigned from the seat in April 2018 following disclosure of his settlement of a sexual-harassment claim with a female staffer. The new district lines made it virtually impossible for Meehan—or any other Republican—to win the seat.

Scanlon was born in upstate New York, where her father and grandfather were local judges. A graduate of Colgate University and the University of Pennsylvania Law School, Scanlon served 14 years as the national pro bono counsel at Ballard Spahr, a large Philadelphia-based law firm where she supervised the public-oriented legal services. (Her husband, Mark Stewart, was chairman of the firm, where he has been a prominent litigator.)

Working with the Education Law Center of Pennsylvania, Scanlon's expertise included federal laws on special education; at home, she worked with statewide councils implementing those laws. She co-chaired the Philadelphia Bar Association's Commission on Children at Risk and served as president of her school board, where she was a member for eight years. "With the rise of the corporate social responsibility movement, pro bono work has become an important indicator [of] a law firm's values," she wrote for a legal journal in 2009.

In her extensive portfolio, Scanlon helped to win two class-action lawsuits on behalf of children with disabilities. She worked on voting-rights issues, including allegations of voter suppression and gerrymandering. Her efforts on behalf of women included successful pursuit of fair pay and equitable treatment of the U.S. national women's hockey and soccer teams. When President Donald Trump sought a travel ban targeting several majority-Muslim nations shortly after he took office, Scanlon led a team of lawyers defending international passengers arriving at U.S. airports. "I am running to continue doing that work, just in a new forum," she told the Philadelphia Inquirer in an interview prior to the primary.

The Democratic primary was a wide-open contest, with 10 candidates—including six women. None had been widely known in the population center of Delaware County. Scanlon benefited from the endorsement of the Inquirer, which praised her "deep understanding of pressing national, state, and local issues." Former Philadelphia Mayor and Gov. Ed Rendell appeared prominently in her advertising, which described Scanlon as a "progressive Democrat...[who] will fight for us."

Richard Lazer, a former deputy mayor for labor of Philadelphia who was endorsed by organized labor and Sen. Bernie Sanders, drew early attention. But he failed to grow beyond his local electoral base. The other leading contender was Ashley Lunkenheimer, a former federal prosecutor who then worked with a group to expand Medicare and Medicaid services. Scanlon and Lunkenheimer, the leading fundraisers among the Democrats, each loaned at least $300,000 to their campaigns.

Scanlon won the primary with 28 percent of the vote; Lunkenheimer got 15.3 percent and Lazer had 15 percent. In Delaware County, which cast 70 percent of the vote, Scanlon got 33 percent—double the vote for Lunkenheimer. She took a similar share in the Montgomery County sliver of the district, which cast nearly10 percent of the vote. Lazer got 41 percent in the Philadelphia portion, where Scanlon got 8 percent; but Lazer ran poorly in the suburban counties. In November, Scanlon defeated Pearl Kim, the daughter of immigrants who became a prosecutor and law-enforcement official.

In the House, Scanlon showed skill in drawing multiple leadership assignments. In her first term, she was vice chair of the Judiciary Committee and a member of the Rules Committee. In an example of her ability to handle insider assignments, Roll Call reported in September 2019 that Scanlon was instrumental in revising the text of a House resolution calling on the inspector general of the intelligence community to forward the complaint of the whistleblower who cited improper behavior by Trump in dealing with the president of Ukraine. Her actions led to a unanimous House vote for the nonbinding measure, rather than the customary party-line splits.

In her second term, Scanlon gained a seat on the House Administration Committee. Party leaders generally award seats on Rules and House Administration to members who have shown they are capable, reliable and loyal. When she gained the additional post of vice chair on House Administration, Scanlon referred to the issues handled by the panel and said, "election law and civics education have been the focus of my legal and volunteer work for almost 30 years, and that experience will guide my approach to this new role as we work to make our elections more accessible, safeguard our democracy and deliver accountability to the American people." (At the start of 2021, the Rules Committee had two other Democrats who entered the House two years earlier with Scanlon, and House Administration had one.)

Scanlon showed her public-relations savvy when she and Rep. Madeleine Dean, a Democrat from a neighboring district, arrived without advance notice at a family detention center for immigrants in Reading Pennsylvania to make eyewitness observations about the treatment of the detainees. They noted, for example, the lack of on-site medical care. Given the availability of assignments for House members who are willing and able to handle such tasks, Scanlon has shown the ability to perform as an insider.

PA-5: Southern and Western Philadelphia Suburbs   Cook Partisan Voting Index: D+13

Population		Race and Ethnicity		Income	
Total	719,973	White	63.30%	Median Income	$71,880
Land area (sq. miles)	212	Black	25.80%	District Income Rank	150
Pop/ sq mi	3,400.27	Latino	4.50%	Poverty Rate	11.40%
Born in State	69.20%	Asian	7.00%	With health insurance	94.70%
		Two or more races	2.30%	Cash public assistance	3.30%
Age Groups		Other	1.60%	Food stamp/SNAP	14.30%
Under 18	22.30%				
18-34	22.90%	Education		Work	
35-64	38.60%	H.S grad or less	38.00%	White Collar	45.40%
Over 64	16.30%	Some College	22.80%	Sales and Service	38.30%
		College Degree, 4 yr	22.60%	Blue Collar	16.30%
Military		Post grad	16.60%	Government	10.70%
Veteran/ Active Duty	5.10%				

2020 Pres. Vote	Biden	263,626	(65%)	Trump	137,694	(34%)		
2016 Pres. Vote	Clinton	230,060	(62%)	Trump	126,361	(34%)	Johnson	6,828	(2%)

Delaware County: A century ago, Delaware County, southwest of Philadelphia, was already filling up, with industrial towns strung out along the rail lines paralleling the Delaware River and residential suburbs along the inland commuter lines. Politics in Delaware County in those days was run by a Republican machine headed by state Sen. John McClure. Such was his power that, in 1960, presidential candidate Richard Nixon stopped by the ailing McClure's home to pay homage. McClure exercised his influence through the War Board, a 15-member panel that decided on all nominations for public office. The board technically went out of business in 1975, but one of its products, Tom Judge, remained county Republican chairman until 2010.

In recent decades, Blacks have moved out of Philadelphia into adjacent Delaware County in large numbers, and cultural liberalism has led many affluent suburbs to vote Democratic. In the 1988 presidential race, Delaware County voted 60%-39% for Republican George H.W. Bush. Joe Biden in 2020 got 63 percent in the county, which was 23 percent Black. In 2017, Democrats for the first time won countywide offices; two years later, they won control of the county council for the first time since the Civil War. The bad news for the Democrats: In taking control, they lacked sufficient time to organize a health department prior to the outbreak of the coronavirus; that initially left them "scrambling to protect" their residents, NBC News reported.

The area is filled with colonial history. At the Brandywine Battlefield, Gens. George Washington and Henry Knox unsuccessfully tried to prevent British forces from taking Philadelphia during the Revolutionary War. Villanova University, the oldest Catholic university in Pennsylvania and the home of the NCAA basketball champions in 2016 and 2018, is in Radnor. A driving economic force here is Boeing's plant in Ridley Park, with 4,600 employees, where the V-22 Osprey and helicopters have been assembled for decades. In 2018, the Air Force announced a new $2.4 billion deal with Boeing to build MH-139 helicopters, to protect the nation's intercontinental ballistic missile bases. In August 2019, Boeing opened a new $115 million plant for production of the Osprey, which takes off and lands like a helicopter, flies like a turboprop plane and carries up to 24 Marines.

The 5th Congressional District of Pennsylvania covers all of Delaware County. The remaining 20 percent of the district is chiefly in once heavily Italian South Philadelphia, where the Delaware River turns its southerly direction to the west as it heads toward Delaware Bay. That area takes in the city's stadium and arena complex, the CSX rail yards, as well as Pat's and Geno's, well-established haunts for late-night cheesesteaks. A small section extends northwest from the city line into the upscale Ardmore and Bryn Mawr sections of Montgomery County. The new 5th replaced the unconventional shape of the old 7th, which had been one of the most discredited gerrymanders in post-2010 redistricting, as it meandered to parts of Chester and Berks counties and a few conservative precincts in Lancaster County. The Philadelphia Daily News complained that it was "a new poster child for why we must find a better way to do redistricting." Making the lines more regular and adding parts of the city switched the district from marginal territory to solidly Democratic. Biden won, 65%-34%.

Chrissy Houlahan (D)

Elected 2018, 2nd term, b. Jun 05, 1967; Patuxent River, MD; Stanford University, B.S., 1989; MA Institute of Technology, M.S., 1994; Married (Bart Houlahan); 2 children.

Military Career: U.S. Air Force 1989-1992; U.S. Air Force Reserves 1992-2006

Professional Career: Chief Operating Officer, AND1 Basketball; Founding Chief Operating Officer, B-Lab, ; Chemistry Teacher, Teach for America Corps; President, Chief Operating Officer and Chief Financial Officer, Springboard Collaborative.

DC Office: 1218 LHOB 20515, 202-225-4315, houlahan.house.gov

State Offices: Reading, 610-295-0815; West Chester, 610-883-5050.

Committees: *Armed Services:* Cyber, Innovative Technologies & Information Systems; Military Personnel. *Foreign Affairs:* Asia, the Pacific, Central Asia, Nonproliferation; Intern'l Dev't, Intern'l Orgs & Global Corporate Social Impact. *Small Business:* Innovation, Entrepreneurship & Workforce Development; Underserved, Agricultural & Rural Business Development.

Almanac Ratings 2019-2020

	Economy	Social	Foreign	Composite
Liberal	100%	100%	80%	94%
Conservative	0%	0%	20%	6%

Key Votes of the 116th Congress

1. U.S./Mex./Can. trade deal Y	5. Russia sanctions	Y	9. Firearms background checks Y
2. First Coronavirus response Y	6. Troops in Syria	Y	10. Spending at the border Y
3. HEROES Act Y	7. Veto arms sales to Saudis Y		11. Marijuana liberalized rules Y
4. CASH Act Y	8. Defense $$$, veto override Y		12. Electoral College objections N

Election Results

Election	Name (Party)	Vote (%)	Cand. Spent	Ind. Exp. Support	Ind. Exp. Oppose
2020 General	Chrissy Houlahan (D)	226,545 (56%)	$1,192,591	$56,312	$158
	John Emmons (R)	177,598 (44%)	$611,811	$4,843	$113
2020 Primary	Chrissy Houlahan (D)	89,411 (100%)			

Prior winning percentages: 2018 (59%)

Democrat Chrissy Houlahan, a political newcomer who had an unusually easy ride to Congress, has continued to show impressive political skills. With her military background, business experience and recent political activism, she was one of the prime recruits for House Democrats in the 2018 cycle and prevailed in what became an unexpectedly easy contest. In the House, she joined the Armed Services Committee and focused initially on military issues. With the retirement of Republican Sen. Pat Toomey in 2022, Houlahan said she was considering a run for his seat. She would bring a lot to the table, including in a contested Democratic primary.

Houlahan got her bachelor's degree in engineering from Stanford and a master's in technology and policy from the Massachusetts Institute of Technology. As a captain in the Air Force Reserve, she worked on missile-defense systems. Following her military service, she helped to start up and became chief operating officer of And1 Basketball, a successful t-shirt company. Later, she became president of a Philadelphia-based nonprofit that sought to improve literacy in inner-city schools.

Her political activism was launched in January 2017 when she organized a busload of women traveling to the Washington Women's March to protest the inauguration of President Donald Trump. Following that experience, Houlahan decided to run for Congress. By summer, she decided to challenge two-term Republican Rep. Ryan Costello; she won the support of the Democratic

Congressional Campaign Committee and EMILY's List, which supports Democratic women who favor abortion rights.

That positioned her for what seemed an uphill challenge to Costello, who won his two campaigns with 56 and 57 percent of the vote in a district that Hillary Clinton won by 2,299 votes in 2016.Costello had prepared for the contest, but he was knocked off-balance by the state Supreme Court redrawing of district lines in February 2018, with new lines in his Chester County-based district measurably jeopardized his reelection.

With only a few days from the release of the new map until the filing deadline for candidates, Costello—unexpectedly facing a radical change in his political prospects—decided not to seek reelection. "I was…absolutely shocked that the Supreme Court got away with what it did," he told a local reporter. "Their objective was to take me out politically, and that's what they did. "In his announcement on the eve of the filing deadline for candidates, he also cited the political tumult created by Trump. "It's very difficult to move forward in a constructive way today," said Costello, who was an emerging leader of House Republican centrists.

Costello's late decision angered House GOP leaders and made it nearly impossible for other candidates from either party to enter the campaign. Houlahan added to the steep challenge facing potential opponents with her prolific financing: $2.8 million raised and $2.2 million cash on hand by mid-year. Her Republican opponent, Greg McCauley, a tax lawyer with little political experience, had less than 10 percent of those totals. He became a token opponent who was largely written off by the GOP.

Perhaps the biggest stumbling block Houlahan faced during the campaign were reports of sweatshop labor at the Chinese firms that manufactured her company's sportswear, plus allegations of large pay raises at the nonprofit she led, which were uncovered by Republican researchers. Her campaign dismissed the charges as "grossly misleading," and McCauley had little success in stirring the pot. Her 59%-41% November victory included 59 percent in the once-Republican leaning Chester County core of the district.

In the House, Houlahan was named freshman leader of the New Democrat Coalition of business-oriented party moderates. With other first-term House Democrats who had experience in the military or in other national security position, she signed a statement in September 2019 calling for Trump's impeachment, which led Speaker Nancy Pelosi to direct committee action in the subsequent days. "It's my job to say, 'no, there's something here that we should really be looking into,'" Houlahan told the New Yorker at that time.

On the Armed Services Committee, Houlahan claimed several successes in the annual military spending bill that Congress enacted over Trump's veto in December 2020. They included the availability of higher quality mammography tests in the healthcare plans of military veterans, plus additional research on the clean-up of chemicals that had created groundwater contamination on or near military sites, including in the Philadelphia area.

Her highest-profile provision in the defense bill was a requirement that law enforcement or military personnel called by federal authorities during a civil disturbance must display identifiable credentials. As she described, the requirement was a response to Trump's use of "unidentified, uniformed personnel on our streets during protests this summer." Her proposal received bipartisan legislative support.

Houlahan took other actions that displayed her sharp political antennae. In early January 2020, when Joe Biden was struggling to remain in the pack of Democratic presidential candidates, she endorsed him, citing his potential strength in the battleground state of Pennsylvania and his more favorable standing than other contenders. Later that month, she wrote a letter to Iowa and New Hampshire Democratic voters—that CNN posted on its website—in which she requested "one important thing: Send us someone who can win a state like mine in the general election this November."

Her political skills became all the more important in early 2021 as she considered seeking the Democratic nomination for Toomey's Senate seat. Although Lt. Gov. John Fetterman already had entered the contest, with experience as a statewide candidate and official, Houlahan would bring numerous assets to the table—including her fundraising skill and her political success as a woman in the battleground Philadelphia metro area.

PA-6: Southeast Pennsylvania   **Cook Partisan Voting Index: D+5**

Population		Race and Ethnicity		Income	
Total	735,283	White	78.00%	Median Income	$85,665
Land area (sq. miles)	913	Black	7.00%	District Income Rank	71
Pop/ sq mi	805.49	Latino	16.10%	Poverty Rate	8.50%
Born in State	61.80%	Asian	4.70%	With health insurance	95.20%
		Two or more races	3.10%	Cash public assistance	1.90%
Age Groups		Other	7.20%	Food stamp/SNAP	9.20%
Under 18	23.20%				
18-34	21.20%	**Education**		**Work**	
35-64	39.00%	H.S grad or less	33.00%	White Collar	48.60%
Over 64	16.40%	Some College	20.40%	Sales and Service	34.20%
		College Degree, 4 yr	27.70%	Blue Collar	17.20%
Military		Post grad	18.90%	Government	9.00%
Veteran/ Active Duty	6.20%				

2020 Pres. Vote	Biden	232,017	(57%)	Trump	170,600	(42%)		
2016 Pres. Vote	Clinton	185,866	(52%)	Trump	153,034	(43%)	Johnson	10,169	(3%)

Chester County, Reading: The gentle hills of southeastern Pennsylvania, settled in the 18th century by Quaker townsmen, Welsh farmers, German peasants and members of pietistic sects who became known as the Pennsylvania Dutch, were America's first polyglot interior. Before and after independence, a diverse lot looking for tolerance in the area above Philadelphia and the Delaware River found a land that yielded riches, first in crops, then in ironworking. In Revolutionary times, the area was countryside, a long day's ride from the markets and docks of Philadelphia. Then, rail lines were built from Philadelphia: The Main Line of the Pennsylvania Railroad headed west to industrial Pittsburgh and the Midwest, and the Reading Railroad headed northwest through Berks County and the anthracite coalfields beyond. Factories were built in some of the towns, and many farms continued to thrive; but by the late 19th century, some of the land had become commuter territory. Parts of Chester County, such as the refined farm country of Chadds Ford, have been home to generations of Wyeth artists.

Much of this area offers idyllic, rustic living. Chester has a disproportionate share of well-educated voters. Its $100,000 median household income in 2019was the highest in Pennsylvania, though it has dipped in the national rankings. Its 5 percent population growth from 2010 to 2019 was the highest in the metro area. With the rich soil, fruits and vegetables are a pillar of the local economy. Kennett Square is the Mushroom Capital of the World. It grows two-thirds of domestic consumption at more than 50 family-owned commercial farms; annual revenues exceed $400 million. The industry employs about 8,600 workers; most of them are permanent residents because many of the mushroom farmers have six crops each year, most of them indoors. In September, the annual mushroom festival —a mile-long street fair—attracts about 100,000 attendees.

The 6th Congressional District of Pennsylvania, the only district in the state that retained its number in the 2018 redistricting, was redrawn to include all of Chester County plus about half of Berks County, including heavily urban—and Democratic—Reading. An old industrial town that inspired John Updike's Rabbit novels and many of his short stories, Reading has become 67 percent Hispanic and ranked recently among the poorest cities in the nation; its median household income of $32,000 in 2019 was half that of Berks County. The old6th snaked through nearly two-thirds of Chester County, clipped the northwest corner of Montgomery County and the southeast corner of heavily Republican Lebanon County and stretched through the center of Berks County but did not include Reading.

Those changes turned an artfully drawn Republican-held seat into a district where Republicans in 2018 threw in their cards. Chester has more than three-fourths of the population. The northern, and more Republican, portion of Berks was shifted to the 9th District. In 2017, Democrats won the four countywide offices in Chester that were on the ballot—the first-ever victory by the party; all four were women. Chester has been a presidential battleground. Joe Biden won the county, 58%-41%, a margin of more than 53,000 votes, after Mitt Romney took it by about 1,000 votes in 2012.Biden took the new 6th by 15 percentage points after Hillary Clinton won the old version by less than one point in 2016.

Susan Wild (D)

Elected 2018, 2nd full term, b. Jun 07, 1957; Wiesbaden, Germany; American University, B.A., 1978; George WA University, J.D., 1982; Jewish; Divorced; 2 children.

Professional Career: Attorney, Gross McKinley firm, 1995-2017; City Solicitor, Allentown PA, 2015-2017.

DC Office: 1607 LHOB 20515, 202-225-6411, wild.house.gov

State Offices: Allentown, 484-781-6000; Easton, 610-333-1170.

Committees: *Education & Labor*: Health, Employment, Labor & Pensions. *Ethics. Foreign Affairs*: Africa, Global Health & Global Human Rights; Europe, Energy, the Environment & Cyber. *Science, Space & Technology*: Research & Technology.

Almanac Ratings 2019-2020

	Economy	Social	Foreign	Composite
Liberal	54%	100%	80%	78%
Conservative	46%	0%	20%	22%

Key Votes of the 116th Congress

1. U.S./Mex./Can. trade deal	Y	5. Russia sanctions	Y
2. First Coronavirus response	Y	6. Troops in Syria	Y
3. HEROES Act	N	7. Veto arms sales to Saudis	Y
4. CASH Act	Y	8. Defense $$$, veto override	Y

9. Firearms background checks Y
10. Spending at the border Y
11. Marijuana liberalized rules Y
12. Electoral College objections N

Election Results

Election	Name (Party)	Vote (%)		Cand. Spent	Ind. Exp. Support	Ind. Exp. Oppose
2020 General	Susan Wild (D)	195,669	(52%)	$4,726,664	$44,951	$127,592
	Lisa Scheller (R)	181,582	(48%)	$3,780,801	$602,639	$1,219
2020 Primary	Susan Wild (D)	76,878	(100%)			

Prior winning percentages: 2018 (53%)

Democrat Susan Wild, a newcomer to elected office, won hard-fought contests. One of four House Democratic women from southeast Pennsylvania who won their seats in 2018, she was the only one who ran in a swing district. Wild, an experienced trial lawyer had been the part-time solicitor of Allentown for more than two years while the mayor was tried and convicted for corruption. She won a competitive reelection in 2020.

Wild lived for more than a decade in the Washington D.C. area, where she got her bachelor's degree at American University and law degree from George Washington University, and worked for a local law firm for five years. In 1988, she settled in the Allentown area and practiced law for three decades. As a partner and the head of the litigation group in the prominent Allentown-based Gross McGinley firm, Wild handled hundreds of cases and described herself as an expert in the use of legal technologies for a courtroom practice. Her clients included healthcare practitioners, insurance companies and local governments.

In 2015, following her selection by Allentown Mayor Ed Pawlowski, Wild was approved by the city council to serve as the city's part-time solicitor. Her tenure was a chaotic time, as Pawlowski was charged in a federal indictment for pay-to-play crimes that occurred before Wild became a city official. She resigned to run for Congress shortly before Pawlowski was convicted in March 2018. "No evidence was presented during the trial signaling Wild participated in Pawlowski's criminal scheme," the Allentown Morning Call reported. Prosecutors said Wild cooperated with the investigation, though her role was an issue during the campaign.

In running for the open House seat that had been held by Republican Charlie Dent, a leader of GOP moderates, Wild embraced local concerns. "It's working-class families that deserve a break in this economy—not big city billionaires and wealthy corporations," she said. Wild was well-positioned among the Democrats in the primary. She was the only woman running against two men, and she was a relatively mainstream Democrat. The alternatives were Greg Edwards, an African-American pastor who was supported by Sen. Bernie Sanders and progressive groups, and John Morganelli, the more-conservative Northampton County district attorney for 25 years, who occasionally spoke positively about President Donald Trump. Both criticized House Democratic campaign strategists for their lack of support.

Wild had been largely unknown to voters when the campaign began, the Morning Call reported. EMILY's List, which supports Democratic women candidates who back abortion rights, was a leading ally. She ran well in the suburbs, while Edwards was strong with urban voters and Morganelli relied on his local base. She won the primary with 33 percent of the vote, to 30 percent for Morganelli and 25 percent for Edwards. In the two counties that dominated the redrawn district, Wild led by nearly 4,000 votes in Lehigh and Morganelli led by nearly 3,000 in Northampton; Wild won overall by 1,508 votes.

Republicans initially were hopeful about their nominee, Marty Nothstein, a Lehigh County commissioner. He was well-known among many voters after having won an Olympic gold medal for cycling in 2000. But "GOP operatives and insiders have been sharply critical of his campaign, marked by sluggish fund-raising," the Philadelphia Inquirer reported in September. Wild won, 53%-43%, and led in each of the three counties. She benefited from the opposition to Trump in many suburbs.

Four months after Wild took office, she unexpectedly gained a cause when her "life partner"— Kerry Acker, a local attorney—committed suicide. In addition to mourning his death, Wild told the House, "mental health issues know no boundaries." She supported legislative steps to expand insurance coverage for mental health. On the Foreign Affairs Committee, she took an interest in human-rights abuses—notably, with letters to State Department officials about problems in Brazil and Chile.

In 2020, Wild was challenged by Republican Lisa Scheller, a former chair of the Lehigh County Board of Commissioners. Scheller, who was president of the successful aluminum pigment producer that her family had built in the area, told her story of having overcome alcohol and heroin addictions. She praised Trump, though she had been a donor to Marco Rubio and John Kasich in the 2016 GOP presidential contest. Both Wild and Scheller are Jewish and supported actions taken by Israel. Wild outspent Scheller, $4.7 million to $3.9 million; Scheller self-financed $2.5 million of her campaign. The outcome was closer than Wild's initial victory. She won, 52%-48%, losing Northampton County by 548 votes, but taking Lehigh with 53 percent and Monroe with 55 percent,.

The district is sufficiently competitive that Wild cannot take reelection for granted, especially with the uncertainties of redistricting.

PA-7: Lehigh Valley

Cook Partisan Voting Index: EVEN

Population		Race and Ethnicity		Income	
Total	731,467	White	82.00%	Median Income	$69,105
Land area (sq. miles)	857	Black	7.50%	District Income Rank	174
Pop/ sq mi	853.88	Latino	20.50%	Poverty Rate	10.00%
Born in State	56.90%	Asian	3.00%	With health insurance	94.70%
		Two or more races	3.10%	Cash public assistance	3.60%
Age Groups		Other	4.30%	Food stamp/SNAP	12.40%
Under 18	21.10%				
18-34	22.00%	**Education**		**Work**	
35-64	38.60%	H.S grad or less	44.20%	White Collar	37.20%
Over 64	18.10%	Some College	25.80%	Sales and Service	38.50%
		College Degree, 4 yr	18.90%	Blue Collar	24.30%
Military		Post grad	11.20%	Government	10.00%
Veteran/ Active Duty	6.40%				

2020 Pres. Vote	Biden	199,520	(52%)	Trump	180,936	(47%)			
2016 Pres. Vote	Clinton	160,346	(48%)	Trump	156,771	(47%)	Johnson	8,272	(2%)

Allentown, Bethlehem: Billy Joel's song "Allentown" was a source of both controversy and praise upon its release in 1982. Its grim picture of closed factories, joblessness and human despair sonated with some area residents, while others found the song derisive and inaccurate. Joel was actually singing about the neighboring town of Bethlehem and the struggles of Bethlehem Steel, which was dissolved in 2003. Fences were mended when a petition drive helped bring Joel to play a concert at Lehigh University's Stabler Arena. The empathy Joel showed toward the region's economic plight has generated mostly pleasant memories.

Today's Lehigh Valley has a much more diverse economy, with a mix of regional health care networks, telephone call centers for insurance companies and banks, and long-surviving manufacturing industries. The valley's population increased almost 12 percent from 2000 to 2010. Growth slowed to 4 percent in the next nine years, though that was still better than most of Pennsylvania. Commuters seeking to avoid big-city housing costs are connected by Interstate 78 to New York City and by the Northeast Extension to Philadelphia. The region has a cluster of colleges —Lehigh, Muhlenberg and Moravian—and a strong newspaper in the Morning Call. Still, the area has been shedding manufacturing jobs, and even its health care sector was struggling. In Allentown, the 2014 opening of a new $200 million hockey arena was described as "the biggest happening in 30 years."Planned development in Allentown of a $425 million, 12-building commercial and residential complex along the Lehigh River was delayed after it broke ground in 2015.Not much happened until February 2021, when a development company from New Jersey offered what seemed an ambitious plan to take over the project. In Easton, old industrial buildings have become a magnet for artists seeking inexpensive loft and warehouse space.

The 7th Congressional District of Pennsylvania includes the Lehigh Valley, covering all of Allentown-based Lehigh County and Bethlehem-based Northampton County. Half the population is in Lehigh, about 42 percent is in Northampton and the remainder is in a southern slice of Monroe County, which is more rural. These lines are far more compact than the old 15th District, which extended west almost to Harrisburg. The loss of those exurban areas marginally shifted the district from its previous Republican lean to a slight Democratic lean—though Lehigh and Northampton have been politically competitive and the 7th is more competitive than suburban districts closer to Philadelphia. In 2016, Hillary Clinton took Lehigh County by nearly 8,000 votes and lost Northampton by 5,500. Joe Biden had a small improvement in each: winning by 14,000 and 1,200 votes, respectively. He took the district, 52%-47%.

Matthew Cartwright (D)

Elected 2012, 5th term, b. May 01, 1961; Erie, PA; Hamilton College, A.B., 1983; Temple University School of Law, Att., 1984; University of PA, J.D., 1986; Roman Catholic; Married (Marion Munley); 2 children.

Professional Career: Practicing attorney, Munley, Munley & Cartwright, 1986-2012.

DC Office: 1034 LHOB 20515, 202-225-5546, Fax: 202-226-0996, cartwright.house.gov

State Offices: Hawley, 570-576-8005; Hazleton, 570-751-0050; Tannersville, 570-355-1818.

Committees: *Appropriations*: Commerce, Justice, Science & Related Agencies (Chmn); Financial Services & General Government; Interior, Environment & Related Agencies.

Group Ratings

	ADA	ACLU	AFL-CIO	LCV	COC	HAFA	ACU	CFG	FRC
2020	**	76%	**	100%	-	6%	6%	**	-
2019	90%	C	100%	96%	62%	C	6%	13%	0%

Almanac Ratings 2019-2020

	Economy	Social	Foreign	Composite
Liberal	100%	63%	80%	81%
Conservative	0%	37%	20%	19%

Key Votes of the 116th Congress

1. U.S./Mex./Can. trade deal Y	5. Russia sanctions Y	9. Firearms background checks Y
2. First Coronavirus response Y	6. Troops in Syria Y	10. Spending at the border Y
3. HEROES Act Y	7. Veto arms sales to Saudis Y	11. Marijuana liberalized rules Y
4. CASH Act Y	8. Defense $$$, veto override Y	12. Electoral College objections N

Election Results

Election	Name (Party)	Vote (%)		Cand. Spent	Ind. Exp. Support	Ind. Exp. Oppose
2020 General	Matthew Cartwright (D)..................... 178,039	(52%)		$3,943,640	$203,468	$134,446
	Jim Bognet (R)................................. 165,809	(48%)		$1,328,752	$249,863	$1,300,144
2020 Primary	Matt Cartwright (D)..................... 75,101	(100%)				

Prior winning percentages: 2018 (55%), 2016 (54%), 2014 (57%), 2012 (60%)

Scranton lawyer Matt Cartwright, elected in 2012, has faced competitive challenges in this district where blue-collar support for Democrats has been declining. With a seat on the Appropriations Committee, he promised to deliver in the Pennsylvania tradition of servicing local constituents. In 2021, he took over as chairman of an Appropriations subcommittee

Cartwright was born in Erie. His mother earned a law degree but didn't practice. After his father served in the Army during World War II, that wartime experience with radar technology led to a job with General Electric and relocation to Toronto, where Cartwright got his bachelor's degree from Hamilton College. He studied at the London School of Economics and Political Science. He earned his law degree from the University of Pennsylvania and practiced law in Philadelphia for several years. He and his wife moved to Scranton to join the law firm of his father-in-law, Robert Munley. Cartwright represented consumers tangling with large corporations on a variety of civil claims. He served on the board of governors of the American Association for Justice, a trial lawyers' group.

Cartwright decided to take on 10-term Democratic Rep. Tim Holden, who had been severely damaged by the Republican-orchestrated redistricting. "I had always thought about running for high political office, and I was kind of waiting for the stars to line up," Cartwright said. "And, you know, they don't hold the door open for you. You kind of have to muscle your way in. "For the Democratic primary, Cartwright raised around $600,000, much of it from fellow trial lawyers; he ran as a progressive, pushing for environmental protections and criticizing corporate tax breaks. He supported the 2010 Affordable Care Act. Holden had voted against it while serving his more conservative district. The challenger won the primary, 57%-43%, with more than 70 percent of the vote in both Lackawanna and Luzerne. In the general election, Cartwright defeated Scranton Tea Party founder Laureen Cummings, 60%-40%.

With Rep. Joaquin Castro of Texas, Cartwright was elected one of two presidents of the Democratic freshman class. During his first two years, he took credit for having developed and introduced 60-plus bills, more than any other House Democrat. True to his campaign promise, Cartwright mostly voted the party line.

In the Almanac vote ratings, he has been more liberal on economic issues and conservative on foreign policy. He was part of a bipartisan group that enacted in 2016 the Megabyte Act, which reduced government costs for software licenses. Also that year, Cartwright filled a vacancy on the Appropriations Committee. Explaining his selection to the Wilkes-Barre Times Leader, Cartwright said, "as soon as I got to Washington, I set about the business of making friends. And the best way to make friends is to be a friend."

In January 2021, Cartwright moved up to chairman of the Commerce, Justice and Science Subcommittee at Appropriations. Citing the benefit for northeast Pennsylvania, he said, "I look forward to directing money to help our small businesses recover from the pandemic, bring home new jobs and expand opportunities for local companies to do business with the federal government." During the two previous years, he said, he helped to deliver more than $270 million in federal funds to his district, including funds for stormwater projects and for abandoned coal mine land reclamation.

Following the 2018 election, Cartwright won election in the Democratic Caucus as one of three co-chairs of the Democratic Policy and Communications Committee, working to develop the party's agenda and message. In November 2020, Democrats gave him a second term in that post.

Cartwright has needed to work to secure his seat. In 2016, little-known Republican challenger Matt Connolly, a real estate investor, said Cartwright's views were "not aligned with this district." Connolly spent a mere $31,000 to nearly $1 million for Cartwright. The outcome was unexpectedly close, 54%-46%.In 2018, in the redrawn district, he faced a well-funded challenger. John Chirin, an investment banker who had been a managing director at JP Morgan Chase and then joined his wife's investment advisory firm, offered his "practical business experience." He ran ads attacking Cartwright for voting for sanctuary cities. Former Vice President—and Scranton native—Joe Biden made an election-eve campaign stop. Chirin outspent Cartwright $3million to $2.6 million. The incumbent won, 55%-45%,with 64 percent in Lackawanna and 53 percent in Luzerne.

In 2020, Cartwright had his closest contest. Jim Bognet, a native of Hazleton who was senior vice president of the Export-Import Bank of the United States during the Trump administration, told Breitbart News that Cartwright was "toast" for having voted for the impeachment of President Donald Trump in a district that supported him by 10 percentage points in 2016. Cartwright tripled the spending of Bognet and benefited from a large share of the more than $2 million the political parties spent on the contest. He won, 52%-48%, and again won Lackawanna, Luzerne and Monroe counties, though by narrower margins.

PA-8: Northeast Pennsylvania   Cook Partisan Voting Index: R+5

Population		Race and Ethnicity		Income	
Total	698,973	White	84.30%	Median Income	$56,149
Land area (sq. miles)	2,668	Black	7.90%	District Income Rank	314
Pop/ sq mi	262.00	Latino	12.70%	Poverty Rate	14.60%
Born in State	60.40%	Asian	1.90%	With health insurance	93.70%
		Two or more races	2.20%	Cash public assistance	3.10%
Age Groups		Other	3.70%	Food stamp/SNAP	16.20%
Under 18	19.70%				
18-34	20.90%	**Education**		**Work**	
35-64	39.50%	H.S grad or less	47.40%	White Collar	32.80%
Over 64	19.90%	Some College	28.30%	Sales and Service	40.90%
		College Degree, 4 yr	15.00%	Blue Collar	26.30%
Military		Post grad	9.30%	Government	11.80%
Veteran/ Active Duty	8.60%				

2020 Pres. Vote	Trump	184,892	(52%)	Biden	169,148	(47%)		
2016 Pres. Vote	Trump	165,168	(53%)	Clinton	135,590	(43%)	Johnson	5,742 (2%)

Scranton, Wilkes-Barre: "Coal is the theme song of this city in the hills," the WPA Guide said of Scranton in 1940, but even as those words were written, the anthracite kingdom around Scranton and Wilkes-Barre was crumbling. In the 19th century, anthracite had become America's main home heating fuel, and the valley along the East Branch of the Susquehanna River was the No. 1 source. Thousands of immigrants flocked to the valley, settling in a chain of little cities north and south of Wilkes-Barre and Scranton. They took jobs with long hours, modest pay, poor working conditions and high death rates—facts of life that made the violently pro-union Molly Maguires popular here and that spawned periodic clashes between workers and the Pinkerton security forces hired by the industrial moguls.

While the supply of coal seemed endless, demand proved fleeting. Anthracite production peaked in 1917, with long strikes in 1922 and 1925 quickening the conversion to oil and gas. Demand for anthracite began to fall in the 1920s and plummeted in the 1940s. The counties containing Wilkes-Barre and Scranton, Luzerne and Lackawanna, had 755,000 people in 1930 and 527,000 in 2019. Scranton is the birthplace of President Joe Biden, and Hillary Clinton's paternal grandparents were natives. Scranton's $16 million budget shortfall in 2012 threatened to push the city into bankruptcy. Crisis was averted, though plans for the city to end its "distressed" status in 2020 were extended for at least two more years.

Hazleton is a small city that gained national notoriety for its crackdowns on illegal immigrants, which were repeatedly contested in the courts and not implemented. Those problems have subsided with a combination of new warehouse jobs, "white flight" to nearby towns and a population that was nearly 60 percent Hispanic in 2019. In a lengthy report, the Boston Globe in October 2019 described how the network of interstate highways near Hazleton helped to create "a booming sector of distribution warehouses." The Pocono Mountains are a destination for weekend skiers and, for a few days each November, for bear hunters. In April 2018, developers unveiled plans for Pocono Springs, a $350 million entertainment center, with completion of the first phase scheduled for 2021. As of September 2020, those construction plans were still being finalized, the Pocono Record reported.

The 8th Congressional District takes in the Democratic strongholds Scranton and Wilkes-Barre, and nearly all of surrounding Lackawanna and Luzerne counties. The remaining 30 percent of the population is in the more rural Pike and Wayne counties and most of Monroe; the eastern boundaries of these counties drop from New York to New Jersey. Democratic performance in these blue-collar areas took a sharp and unexpected downward turn in the 2016 election. The old district shifted from a double-digit victory in 2012 for President Barack Obama—with Biden on the ticket—to a double-digit loss in 2016 for Clinton against Donald Trump. Biden improved Democratic performance in the district by a few percentage points in 2020. But with the exception of Lackawanna County, where Biden increased the Democratic victory from 3,600 votes to nearly 10,000, northeast Pennsylvania remained mostly Republican. In 2020, Trump took the district, 52%-47%.

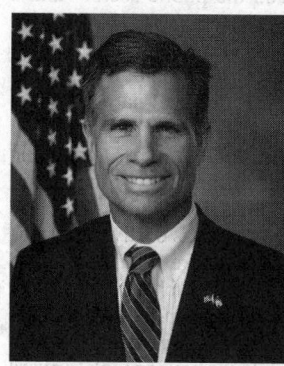

Daniel Meuser (R)

Elected 2018, 2nd term, b. Feb 10, 1954; Babylon, NY; Cornell University, B.A., 1986; Cornell University, B.A., 1986; Catholic; Married (Shelley Van Acker); 3 children.

Elected Office: Secretary, PA Department of Revenue, 2011-2015

Professional Career: Executive, Pride Mobility Products, 1988-2008.

DC Office: 326 CHOB 20515, 202-225-6511, meuser.house.gov

State Offices: Pottsville, 570-871-6370.

Committees: *Foreign Affairs*: Africa, Global Health & Global Human Rights; Europe, Energy, the Environment & Cyber. *Small Business*: Contracting & Infrastructure; Economic Growth, Tax & Capital Access (RMM); Oversight, Investigations & Regulations.

Almanac Ratings 2019-2020

	Economy	Social	Foreign	Composite
Liberal	27%	22%	5%	18%
Conservative	73%	78%	95%	82%

Key Votes of the 116th Congress

1. U.S./Mex./Can. trade deal	Y	5. Russia sanctions	Y	9. Firearms background checks	N
2. First Coronavirus response	Y	6. Troops in Syria	N	10. Spending at the border	Y
3. HEROES Act	N	7. Veto arms sales to Saudis	N	11. Marijuana liberalized rules	N
4. CASH Act	N	8. Defense $$$, veto override	Y	12. Electoral College objections	Y

Election Results

Election	Name (Party)	Vote (%)		Cand. Spent	Ind. Exp. Support	Ind. Exp. Oppose
2020 General	Daniel Meuser (R)............................	233,124	(66%)	$601,616	$8,579	$750
	Gary Wegman (D)............................	118,372	(34%)	$180,738	$2,500	$158
2020 Primary	Dan Meuser (R)..................................	77,350	(100%)			

Prior winning percentages: 2018 (60%)

Republican Dan Meuser easily won the redrawn seat that was the successor to the district represented by Republican Rep. Lou Barletta. Meuser, who embraced President Donald Trump, had been a fixture in the local business community and earlier held a prominent position in state government. As the leading Republican to announce for the seat, he stuck with his plans, even with the significant local disruptions from the redistricting the state Supreme Court approved in February 2018. After winning the GOP primary, he breezed to victory in November.

Meuser spent most of his professional life in business. After graduating from Cornell University, he settled in Luzerne County and joined Pride Mobility Products, which he built with his father and brother and managed for more than two decades. He became president of the company—an industry leader in the manufacturing of power wheelchairs, scooters and other personal mobility products.

Meuser made an earlier bid for Congress. In 2008, he lost a contentious primary for the Republican nomination in the district in the northeast corner of Pennsylvania, which was held at the time by Democratic Rep. Christopher Carney; two years later, Republican Tom Marino won that seat. From 2011 to 2015, he held the powerful state office of secretary of revenue under Gov. Tom Corbett, a Republican for whom Meuser had been a major contributor in the 2010 campaign. During his four years in government, Meuser said, the Council on State Taxation raised the rating of his department from D to A-minus.

Making another run in 2018, Meuser had a huge fundraising advantage in the GOP primary for the open seat. He raised nearly $1 million against his two opponents: Schuylkill County Commissioner George Halcovage and former CIA station chief and Fox News analyst Scott Uehlinger. With his endorsement by the Trump-supporting Making America Great PAC, he described himself as "a problem-solving conservative" with "a record of success in business and the public sector" and a commitment to helping Trump implement his agenda.

In the primary, Meuser took 53 percent of the vote to 24 percent for Halcovage and 23 percent for Uehlinger. He ran strongly in the five northern counties in the district, where he got between 61 and 85 percent of the vote. Uehlinger took his base in Berks County and Halcovage narrowly won Schuylkill; in those two counties, Meuser was second.

Democrat Denny Wolff, a dairy farmer who was secretary of agriculture under former Democratic Gov. Ed Rendell, ran a credible campaign in the general election. But in the face of the strong Republican tilt of the district and national Democrats' focus on several nearby districts, he was outmatched by the fundraising dominance of Meuser, who won 60%-40%. He was easily reelected.

Following the 2020 election, Meuser objected to changes in election procedures that were made by judges and election officials in his home state of Pennsylvania. Listing such action as late acceptance of ballots and inconsistent standards for verifying signatures on mail-in ballots, Meuser joined all but one of the nine House Republicans from Pennsylvania in voting not to certify the state's Electoral Collee results. "If such unlawful actions are to be accepted, what do we have to look forward to next year? The Pennsylvania secretary of state allowing online voting because it may be raining in Pennsylvania? It was a free for all," he told the House.

In 2021, Meuser became ranking Republican on the Small Business Subcommittee on Economic Growth, Tax and Capital Access. "I look forward to fighting for small businesses across the country, many of which have suffered from unfair treatment over the past year due to arbitrary lockdowns," Meuser said.

Meuser faced the uncertain impact of redistricting in 2022 on a district that sprawls across a wide area of eastern Pennsylvania, with no central urban core.

PA-9: East-Central Pennsylvania   **Cook Partisan Voting Index: R+18**

Population		Race and Ethnicity		Income	
Total	699,832	White	92.20%	Median Income	$62,078
Land area (sq. miles)	3,295	Black	2.60%	District Income Rank	233
Pop/ sq mi	212.37	Latino	7.10%	Poverty Rate	9.80%
Born in State	80.10%	Asian	1.20%	With health insurance	94.50%
		Two or more races	1.40%	Cash public assistance	2.30%
Age Groups		Other	2.40%	Food stamp/SNAP	10.60%
Under 18	19.50%				
18-34	20.40%	**Education**		**Work**	
35-64	40.10%	H.S grad or less	54.10%	White Collar	32.60%
Over 64	20.20%	Some College	24.70%	Sales and Service	36.40%
		College Degree, 4 yr	13.60%	Blue Collar	31.00%
Military		Post grad	7.70%	Government	12.20%
Veteran/ Active Duty	8.10%				

2020 Pres. Vote	Trump	232,000	(64%)	Biden	122,474	(34%)	
2016 Pres. Vote	Trump	205,191	(65%)	Clinton	97,810	(31%)	Johnson 8,369 (3%)

Exurbs of Lancaster and Wilkes-Barre: In the late 19th and early 20th centuries, towns existed in Berks and Schuykill counties solely to mine rich veins of anthracite coal, which long served as the nation's chief energy supply. These mountain towns were less orderly, filled with tough-talking miners and factory workers—the Pennsylvania that novelist John O'Hara knew growing up and wrote about in the 1930s and 1940s. Although the big companies abandoned the mines long ago, some local entrepreneurs still go deep underground to blast their way into the anthracite. With incentives from the Trump administration's trade policies, several abandoned coal mines in Schuykill have reopened, though the surrounding towns have been hollowed out by economic distress. In 2020, the vote for President Donald Trump in Schuykill was virtually unchanged, at 69 percent. As Reuters astutely forecast in its September 2020 report from this area, the miners stuck with Trump not because he delivered more jobs or coal production. He didn't. But "they fear Biden's clean-energy plan would hasten coal's decline, and that the new green jobs wouldn't come quickly enough to keep their families financially secure," Reuters reported.

Pottsville is the home of Yuengling lager (known locally as "Vitamin Y") and produced the Maroons, the team that may have won the 1925 National Football League championship. The league disputed the claim, to the eternal chagrin of Pottsville. The city's ties to coal country are emblematic of the hardscrabble roots of the NFL in the old Rust Belt.

The 9th Congressional District is centered in the small cities of east-central Pennsylvania, west of Philadelphia. Two-thirds of the population is in the three largest and adjacent, counties: Berks, Schuykill and Lebanon. The portion of Berks does not include economically distressed Reading, which is in the 6th District. The remainder of the new 9th is in the more rural area to the north, including the small part of Luzerne County that is not in the 8th District.

For decades, this area leaned Democratic. When Republican redistricting in 2011 removed Wilkes Barre, Scranton and other Democratic urban centers, the old 11th district became solidly Republican. It increased from 52 percent for John McCain in the 2008 presidential election to 65 percent for Trump with the new lines in 2016.The latest round of redistricting further entrenched GOP control in the 9th, which has become a "vote sink" that protects adjacent Democratic districts—chiefly, the 7th and 8th. In 2020, Trump won the district with 64 percent. The fact that Democrats have abandoned these blue-collar areas but have become entrenched not far away in upscale Montgomery County illustrates how the politics of the state—and nation—have been upended in the past half-century.

Scott Perry (R)

Elected 2012, 5th term, b. May 27, 1962; San Diego, CA; U.S. Army War College, M.S.; PA State University, B.S., 1991; Church of the United Brethren in Christ; Married (Christy Perry); 2 children.

Military Career: PA Army National Guard 1980-pres. (Iraq)

Elected Office: PA House, 2007-2012.

Professional Career: Dock worker, Dauphin Distribution, 1981-1982; Insurance sales agent, 1984-1985; Co-owner, Hydrotech Mechanical Services, 1993-present.

DC Office: 1207 LHOB 20515, 202-225-5836, Fax: 202-226-1000, perry.house.gov

State Offices: Harrisburg, 717-603-4980.

Committees: *Foreign Affairs*: Asia, the Pacific, Central Asia, Nonproliferation; Middle East, North Africa & Global Counterterrorism. *Transportation & Infrastructure*: Aviation; Highways & Transit; Railroads, Pipelines & Hazardous Materials.

Group Ratings

	ADA	ACLU	AFL-CIO	LCV	COC	HAFA	ACU	CFG	FRC
2020	**	21%	**	5%	-	98%	96%	**	-
2019	5%	C	20%	3%	70%	C	96%	100%	95%

Almanac Ratings 2019-2020

	Economy	Social	Foreign	Composite
Liberal	27%	16%	11%	18%
Conservative	73%	84%	89%	82%

Key Votes of the 116th Congress

1. U.S./Mex./Can. trade deal	Y	5. Russia sanctions	Y	9. Firearms background checks N
2. First Coronavirus response	Y	6. Troops in Syria	Y	10. Spending at the border	Y
3. HEROES Act	N	7. Veto arms sales to Saudis	N	11. Marijuana liberalized rules	N
4. CASH Act	N	8. Defense $$$, veto override	N	12. Electoral College objections Y

Election Results

Election	Name (Party)	Vote (%)	Cand. Spent	Ind. Exp. Support	Ind. Exp. Oppose
2020 General	Scott Perry (R)............................	208,896 (53%)	$3,731,242	$1,513,216	$5,421,138
	Eugene DePasquale (D)...............	182,938 (47%)	$4,528,909	$381,072	$4,793,458
2020 Primary	Scott Perry (R)............................	79,365 (100%)			

Prior winning percentages: 2018 (51%), 2016 (66%), 2014 (75%), 2012 (60%)

Republican Scott Perry was elected in 2012 after easily prevailing in a crowded primary. With an agenda that emphasized a leaner federal government, gun rights, traditional marriage and his lengthy military career, Perry became an active member of the House Freedom Caucus. Democrats contended that his views had grown out of sync with his district. Since 2018, when redistricting made his district more competitive, he has won two close campaigns.

Perry was born in San Diego but moved at age 7 to central Pennsylvania, where he lived in a home without electricity or plumbing. He grew up in what he described to National Journal as a "little dysfunctional and a little disjointed family." After graduating from high school, Perry worked as an auto mechanic before enlisting in the Pennsylvania Army National Guard. He became an instructor pilot and distinguished himself as a helicopter pilot, rising to the rank of brigadier general. While a state representative, he served for a year in Iraq, flying 44 missions. He has commanded the Fort Indiantown Gap National Training Site and remained active as an assistant adjutant general at headquarters.

With his bachelor's in business administration from Penn State University, Perry and a partner built a contracting firm specializing in meter calibration and line work for municipalities. In 2002, the Pennsylvania attorney general's office accused Perry of falsifying reports to the state Environmental Protection Department. The matter ended with a $5,000 fine and his record being expunged. Perry maintained his innocence.

As a past president of the Pennsylvania Young Republicans, Perry was elected to the state House in 2006. He expanded the law allowing residents to use deadly force in self-defense. He bucked Republican Gov. Tom Corbett by proposing legislation that would have declined federal money to fund insurance exchanges under the Affordable Care Act.

When he ran for the House, Perry's past legal troubles were raised in the seven-person Republican primary, but they never gained traction. He got endorsements from Corbett and GOP Sen. Pat Toomey. He benefited from his military background. Perry was outspent 2-to-1, but won 54 percent of the primary vote. In November, he had no trouble in what was a heavily Republican district.

In the House, Perry was a co-founder of the post-9/11 veterans' caucus. As a member of the Foreign Affairs Committee, he has taken a hard line on overseas issues. In 2014, when the Iraqi military lost control of major parts of their country, he voiced bitterness as he recalled his own service. "Right now, I wonder what that was all about. What was the point of all of that?" In 2015, he criticized President Barack Obama's "lack of leadership" in dealing with terror threats overseas and worried publicly about the potential threat to the homeland from domestic jihadists.

After President Donald Trump met with Russian President Vladimir Putin in Helsinki in July 2018, Perry told a town-hall meeting that news coverage of the two standing next to each other "makes you feel uncomfortable." On Foreign Affairs in 2019, Perry deferred to less-senior Republicans who took ranking positions on subcommittees.

In 2017, the House, on a 185-234 vote, defeated Perry's move to strip from the defense spending bill a provision that would have blocked a Pentagon study of the impact of climate change on national security. The proposed review "detracts from the central mission of securing our nation against enemies," he told the House. On the Homeland Security Committee, the House passed his bill to improve management of the vehicle fleet at the Department of Homeland Security.

As an active member of the Freedom Caucus, Perry supported the partial government shutdown that Trump hoped would result in funding of a wall along the border with Mexico. In 2019, he was one of three members seeking to succeed Rep. Mark Meadows of North Carolina as the group's chairman. Rep. Andy Biggs of Arizona won the position.

In 2018, Perry faced his first well-financed challenger—George Scott, a retired Army lieutenant colonel and Lutheran pastor who ran "common sense" ads to contrast himself to Perry. He cited, for example, the need for gun safety and more "compassionate" treatment of immigrants at the border. In endorsing Scott, the York Daily Record criticized Perry's participation in the Freedom Caucus, with its "their way or the highway" approach. Scott outspent Perry, $2.2 million to $1.6 million. In the district that had become less Republican following the court-drawn redistricting, Perry won, 51%-49%, a margin of 7,700 votes.

Democrats were enthusiastic about Eugene DePasquale, the state auditor general and a native of York County, who challenged Perry in 2020. In a contest in which each candidate ran closely to his party's presidential candidate, DePasquale sought to position himself as a centrist. One of his ads featured his father, who was imprisoned for eight years for selling drugs. Democrats cited Perry as one of 18 House Republicans who voted against a resolution that condemned the QAnon conspiracy group. Perry ran ads that sought to connect DePasquale to the Democrats' "radical socialist agenda." DePasquale outspent Perry, $4.5 million to $3.7 million, and the two national parties spent more than $10 million in the contest.

Perry won surprisingly easily, 53%-47%, taking 58 percent in York and 55 percent in Cumberland; DePasquale took 52 percent in Dauphin. According to the Harrisburg Patriot-News, Perry benefited from Trump's narrow lead in the district, his own incumbency and ads that targeted an indicted union boss in Philadelphia who had backed DePasquale.

PA-10: South-Central Pennsylvania   Cook Partisan Voting Index: R+5

Population		Race and Ethnicity		Income	
Total	744,681	White	78.10%	Median Income	$67,155
Land area (sq. miles)	1,080	Black	11.40%	District Income Rank	191
Pop/ sq mi	689.35	Latino	9.10%	Poverty Rate	9.90%
Born in State	68.60%	Asian	4.10%	With health insurance	94.70%
		Two or more races	3.70%	Cash public assistance	2.90%
Age Groups		Other	2.50%	Food stamp/SNAP	10.00%
Under 18	21.70%				
18-34	21.70%	**Education**		**Work**	
35-64	38.90%	H.S grad or less	42.80%	White Collar	40.40%
Over 64	17.70%	Some College	25.10%	Sales and Service	36.10%
Military		College Degree, 4 yr	20.40%	Blue Collar	23.50%
Veteran/ Active Duty	8.40%	Post grad	11.90%	Government	14.30%

2020 Pres. Vote	Trump	201,367	(51%)	Biden	189,804	(48%)			
2016 Pres. Vote	Trump	180,979	(52%)	Clinton	150,076	(43%)	Johnson	10,542	(3%)

Harrisburg, York: Harrisburg, the capital of Pennsylvania, features a string of mansions-turned-lobbying headquarters lining the banks of the Susquehanna and boasts Pennsylvania's marvelously restored capitol. Beyond that building, the city has suffered financially. In 2012, its $1.5 billion debt was the largest per capita in the nation. The legislature in 2016 tightened municipal debt procedures in an attempt to prevent a repeat of apparent abuses. During a campaign visit that summer, Donald Trump said Harrisburg "looked like a war zone" because of its closed factories. Local business leaders and journalists disagreed. In 2019, the state took control of the city's school system.

Nearby in Dauphin County are centers of American heritage. Hershey was erected by chocolate magnate Milton S. Hershey as a planned utopian village for his factory workers and their families. The surrounding area is fed by a steady flow of tourists to the Hershey park amusement site. With automation and the smell of chocolate still in the air, the facility produced more than 70 million Kisses each day. Middletown has leafy, gridded streets and handsome homes that give no hint that it is the location of the Three Mile Island nuclear plant, which in 1979 was the site of the worst nuclear accident in U.S. history. In September 2019, Exelon shut down TMI because it was no longer profitable, plus natural gas and renewable fuels had become cheaper, with plentiful supply.

The area was home to the westernmost capital of the United States during the Revolutionary War: the city of York, where the Continental Congress passed the Articles of Confederation and received word from Benjamin Franklin in Paris that the French would help the colonies with money and ships. More than two centuries later, a different kind of European intervention proved more troublesome. A large Harley-Davidson manufacturing plant has been based in York, though automation and fewer sales downsized its payroll from 2,000 workers in 2009 to about 950 in 2018. With the closing of a Harley plant in Kansas City Missouri that year, the York facility gained450 additional workers. Harley's decision to shift some of its motorcycle operations across the Atlantic to avoid much higher tariffs prompted harsh criticism from President Donald Trump and added new uncertainty.

The 10th Congressional District of Pennsylvania is in the south-central part of the state and includes all of Dauphin County, which is the largest share of the district, plus large portions of York and Cumberland counties. Like York, Cumberland—whose 6 percent population increase from 2010 to 2017 was the fastest in the state—has remained conventionally Republican. With portions of Democratic-leaning Dauphin added to the old 4th District, plus its loss of some rural areas, redistricting in 2018 made the 10th more politically competitive. Trump took the district, 51%-48%.

Lloyd Smucker (R)

Elected 2016, 3rd term, b. Jan 23, 1964; Lancaster, PA; Lebanon Valley College, Att.; Franklin & Marshall College, Att., 1991; Lutheran; Married (Cynthia Smucker); 3 children.

Elected Office: Western Lampeter Board of Supervisors, 2001-2005.

Professional Career: Business Owner; West Lampeter Planning Commission.

DC Office: 127 CHOB 20515, 202-225-2411, Fax: 202-225-2013, smucker.house.gov

State Offices: Hanover, 717-969-6132; Red Lion, 717-969-6133.

Committees: *Budget*. *Ways & Means*: Oversight; Worker & Family Support.

Group Ratings

	ADA	ACLU	AFL-CIO	LCV	COC	HAFA	ACU	CFG	FRC
2020	**	15%	**	14%	-	83%	82%	**	-
2019	5%	C	20%	7%	76%	C	84%	93%	95%

Almanac Ratings 2019-2020

	Economy	Social	Foreign	Composite
Liberal	27%	39%	27%	31%
Conservative	73%	61%	73%	69%

Key Votes of the 116th Congress

1. U.S./Mex./Can. trade deal Y	5. Russia sanctions Y	9. Firearms background checks N
2. First Coronavirus response Y	6. Troops in Syria Y	10. Spending at the border Y
3. HEROES Act N	7. Veto arms sales to Saudis N	11. Marijuana liberalized rules N
4. CASH Act N	8. Defense $$$, veto override N	12. Electoral College objections Y

Election Results

Election	Name (Party)	Vote (%)		Cand. Spent	Ind. Exp. Support	Ind. Exp. Oppose
2020 General	Lloyd Smucker (R)	241,915	(63%)	$670,490	$9,217	$750
	Sarah Hammond (D)	141,325	(37%)	$20,771	$2,500	$158
2020 Primary	Lloyd Smucker (R)	78,842	(100%)			

Prior winning percentages: 2018 (59%), 2016 (54%)

Lloyd Smucker, elected in 2016, fit comfortably with the mostly establishment Republicans in his state delegation. He won competitive contests in both the primary and general election and styled himself as a problem-solver. Two years later, following court-ordered redistricting, Smucker survived in a district that had become more safely Republican, as three other GOP members from southeast

Pennsylvania walked away and were replaced by Democrats. In 2021, he joined the Ways and Means Committee.

Smucker grew up locally and attended but did not graduate from local colleges. He founded Smucker Co., a commercial construction firm that specialized in dry wall, and ran the business for a quarter-century. He served on the West Lampeter Township Planning Commission for four years and was elected to the state Senate for eight years. In Harrisburg, Smucker chaired the Senate Education Committee and mostly advocated local control over educational standards. He supported steps to encourage legalization of undocumented immigrants but was unable to enact such a measure.

When the House seat opened, Smucker became the frontrunner. In the primary, he faced businessman Chet Beiler, whose family-owned Amish Country Gazebos was the nation's leading retailer of custom-built gazebos. The two candidates were second cousins who graduated in the same class at Lancaster Mennonite High School. In the primary, each spent more than $600,000, with a large share self-financed. Smucker was endorsed by the Chamber of Commerce and the National Rifle Association. He won, 54%-46%, with 56 percent in Lancaster County, which cast more than 80 percent of the total vote.

The general election was competitive against Democrat Christina Hartman, who was a consultant to nonprofit groups after having spent 15 years in international development. She described herself as "moderate to progressive" and said the district was moving to the left. Her campaign ran negative ads that sought to link Smucker to GOP presidential nominee Donald Trump. David Wasserman of the Cook Political Report wrote that Hartman ran a "surprisingly energetic campaign," and was competitive financially, even though national Democrats did not become active until late in the campaign. Smucker outraised Hartman, $1.5 million to $1.2 million, and received more than $800,000 in additional party support. He won, 54%-43%. Lancaster cast about three-fourths of the total vote, of which Smucker took 59 percent.

In the House, Smucker was usually a party loyalist. His Almanac vote ratings showed a consistently conservative pattern. He advocated steps to reduce health care costs and said he was "very disappointed" by the initial failure of House Republicans to reform the Affordable Care Act. Smucker showed some independence when he joined the bipartisan Problem Solvers Caucus, where he said he would "focus on navigating—not obstructing—our path forward," while maintaining his "conservative principles." After the 2018 election, he was part of the group that persuaded Nancy Pelosi to agree to its plan for more open House debates, especially on bills with bipartisan support.

As ranking Republican on the Education and Labor Subcommittee on Higher Education and Workforce Investment, Smucker said he would draw on his experience as chairman of the Senate Education Committee in Harrisburg. During a committee debate on higher education, he said Democrats' proposed revisions to the Pell student-loan "layer on so many requirements and bureaucratic mandates that those programs will be unworkable."

In March 2019, a broad public lands bill was enacted that included Smucker's legislation to create the Susquehanna National Heritage Area, which would prepare a plan for historic preservation, natural-resource conservation and local tourism. In August, following a visit to the southern border with a bipartisan group, he called for changes in asylum laws, "allowing individuals claiming persecution to apply in either their home country or the first country they pass through."

With his seat on Ways and Means, Smucker said that with his background as a business owner, "I will work to advocate for a tax code that allows small businesses to thrive."

In his redrawn district, Smucker in 2018 had another competitive primary with Beiler, who accused Smucker of being insufficiently conservative and of sending campaign mailers that had "no basis in reality." Smucker won the primary 59%-41%. Smucker's general-election contest with Jessica King, a Mennonite with a career of anti-poverty work, ended with the same spread. She was supported by Bernie Sanders, which helped her raise and spend $1.9 million—more than the $1.5 million for Smucker. But that endorsement carried less weight with voters in this district. In 2020, Smucker had an easier road, as he faced no opponent in the Republican primary and a lightly funded Democrat.

PA-11: Philadelphia exurbs

Cook Partisan Voting Index: R+14

Population		Race and Ethnicity		Income	
Total	734,038	White	89.10%	Median Income	$68,811
Land area (sq. miles)	1,503	Black	3.70%	District Income Rank	176
Pop/ sq mi	488.39	Latino	8.90%	Poverty Rate	10.10%
Born in State	70.50%	Asian	1.80%	With health insurance	90.70%
		Two or more races	3.20%	Cash public assistance	2.70%
Age Groups		Other	2.20%	Food stamp/SNAP	7.50%
Under 18	22.90%				
18-34	21.30%	**Education**		**Work**	
35-64	37.10%	H.S grad or less	48.70%	White Collar	37.10%
Over 64	18.70%	Some College	23.10%	Sales and Service	35.60%
		College Degree, 4 yr	18.40%	Blue Collar	27.30%
Military		Post grad	9.70%	Government	8.30%
Veteran/ Active Duty	7.00%				

2020 Pres. Vote	Trump	233,091	(60%)	Biden	148,531	(38%)		
2016 Pres. Vote	Trump	201,586	(60%)	Clinton	115,388	(34%)	Johnson	11,343	(3%)

Lancaster, part of York County: The Pennsylvania Dutch Country, settled by Germans in the 18th century when it was Pennsylvania's frontier, remains a distinctive part of America. These Germans were Amish and Mennonite, pietistic sects seeking religious liberty and determined to farm rich lands in the same intensive way they had in Germany. Today, many of their descendants—the Eisenhower family is the most famous example—have blended into mainstream America. But in the Dutch area around Lancaster, many "Plain People" still live in the old way, though today they are willing to use some modern devices, such as battery-powered electricity. Tourists can still see families of Plain People clad in black, clattering over the back roads in horse-drawn carriages, with scrupulously tended farms set amid rolling hills and barns decorated with hex signs. Beneath the surface, Amish communities have faced the strains of modernity and economic dislocation. In 2017, the York Daily Record reported that some Amish were leaving Lancaster to start settlements in more rural areas. According to a book author who has written about the Amish, one factor might be that Lancaster had become too "crowded, fast paced." Still, the Associated Press reported in April 2019 that the Amish accounted for nearly half the population gain in the county.

With an easy drive from Philadelphia, Baltimore and Washington, the area is home to many outlet malls; the first Woolworth's store opened in Lancaster in 1879. Pennsylvania Dutch Country draws more than 8 million tourists annually. Lancaster has gained national attention for its livability. In October 2018, U.S. News & World Report rated it as the best place to retire in the United States. New York Times columnist Tom Friedman in July 2018 praised Lancaster as a model for local development. Citing "the societal innovation the town's leader's had employed to rebuild their once-struggling city," Friedman described its "adaptive coalition in which business leaders, educators, philanthropists, social innovators and the local government would work together to unleash entrepreneurship." The wide variety of tastes in the central market in a century-old downtown building attests to the many nationalities in the area.

The Mason-Dixon Line, the historic boundary between Maryland and Pennsylvania, runs through pleasant rolling farmlands from the Susquehanna River through the Appalachian Mountains. Hanover, in York County, is the self-styled "Snack Food Capital of the World," home to Snyder's of Hanover and potato chip giant Utz, including many varieties of pretzels.

The 11th Congressional District of Pennsylvania includes all of Lancaster County, plus nearly half of York County, which is along the Maryland border. Until the 1980s, Lancaster County was one of the most Republican counties in the state. Suburbanization and demographic change have reduced that share. But it remains firmly Republican, with 57 percent for Donald Trump in both 2016 and 2020, and is the second-fastest growing county in the state. The county includes nearly 75 percent of the population in the 11th. (Amish rarely vote, but their social views seem consistent with the overall local attitudes.) Overall, the 2018 redistricting increased the GOP base in the new 11th.With a boost from the vote in York, Trump took 60 percent of the vote in each of his campaigns.

Fred Keller (R)

Elected 2019, 2nd term, b. Oct 23, 1965; Page, AZ; Don Paul Shearer Real Estate School, 1995; Christian Church; Married (Kay Keller); 2 children; 1 grandchild.

DC Office: 1717 LHOB 20515, 202-225-3731, Fax: 202-225-9594, keller.house.gov

State Offices: Selinsgrove, 570-374-9469; Tunkhannock, 570-996-6550; Williamsport, 570-322-3961.

Committees: *Education & Labor*: Early Childhood, Elementary & Secondary Education; Workforce Protections (RMM). *Oversight & Reform*: Government Operations; Subcommittee on Economic & Consumer Policy.

Almanac Ratings 2019-2020

	Economy	Social	Foreign	Composite
Liberal	43%	39%	40%	41%
Conservative	57%	61%	60%	59%

Key Votes of the 116th Congress

1. U.S./Mex./Can. trade deal	Y	5. Russia sanctions	N/A	9. Firearms background checks N/A
2. First Coronavirus response	Y	6. Troops in Syria	Y	10. Spending at the border	Y
3. HEROES Act	N	7. Veto arms sales to Saudis	N	11. Marijuana liberalized rules	N
4. CASH Act	N	8. Defense $$$, veto override	Y	12. Electoral College objections	Y

Election Results

Election	Name (Party)	Vote (%)	Cand. Spent	Ind. Exp. Support	Ind. Exp. Oppose
2020 General	Fred Keller (R)	241,052 (71%)	$1,026,205	$80,530	$750
	Lee Griffin (D)	99,216 (29%)	$41,293	$2,500	$158
2020 Primary	Fred Keller (R)	87,886 (100%)			

Prior winning percentages: 2019 special (68%)

Republican Fred Keller, who won in May 2019 the first special election since Democrats took control of the House in January, styled himself as a conservative Republican with mainstream credentials. Keller replaced Republican Tom Marino, who had served four terms before resigning for health reasons three weeks after the new Congress convened. In this solidly Republican district, the contest was perfunctory, aside from the election-eve campaign rally with President Donald Trump..

Marino's resignation announcement in January was surprising and gave little explanation. He became counsel and vice president of Williamsport-based Miele Manufacturing, which provides technology and software for gambling devices.

At the Republican convention in March to select their nominee for the special election, the 202 delegates selected among 14 candidates. Keller won a majority on the fourth ballot. The Associated Press described him as "largely a back-bencher and one of the most conservative state House members."

Keller graduated from Shikellamy High School in Northumberland County and attended the Don Paul Shrear Real Estate School, which is a state-certified appraiser. He spent 25 years with the Conestoga Wood Specialties Corp. in Lancaster County, which manufactures cabinet doors and wood products for kitchens and bathrooms; he eventually became plant manager. He served as the auditor for Middle creek Township in Somerset County. In 2010, he was elected to the state House from a district serving parts of Snyder and Union counties; he served on the Appropriations and Finance committees.

The special election attracted little attention, locally or nationally. Keller spent $464,000 to $220,000 for the Democratic nominee, Marc Friedenberg, a Penn State University professor who taught cyber law and the global economy. Keller said he would be "a champion for the agriculture industry" and he backed "pragmatic, conservative principles." Trump appeared at an election-eve rally at the Williamsport airport, during which he briefly introduced Keller and he focused chiefly on prospects for the 2020 presidential contest. "I'll be here a lot," Trump told the crowd, Roll Call reported. Keller won, 68%-32%. He took at least 63 percent in every county, except for Friedenberg's home of Penn State-based Centre County, where Friedenberg took 66 percent.

In the House, Keller created in August 2020 the bipartisan Bureau of Prisons Reform Caucus, which called for greater oversight of the federal prison system. In previous months, more than 40 cases of the coronavirus were confirmed at the federal prison in Lewisburg. The leader of the local prison counsel said that inmates with the illness had been isolated and treated multiple times each day. After the Pennsylvania Department of Health announced that it was planning in-person instruction for prison officers, Keller said that step was "unacceptable and we must bring greater accountability to the federal unelected bureaucrats in Washington D.C." He said coronavirus surges in prisons often resulted from transfers of inmates from one facility to another.

In February 2021, Keller became ranking Republican on the Education and Labor Subcommittee on Workforce Protections. He cited his 25 years of experience in private industry where "I learned the importance of ensuring our employees have the necessary tools to do their jobs safely and efficiently." He also got on a seat on the Oversight and Reform Committee.

PA-12: North-central Pennsylvania   **Cook Partisan Voting Index: R+20**

Population		Race and Ethnicity		Income	
Total	701,387	White	93.80%	Median Income	$55,203
Land area (sq. miles)	9,893	Black	2.20%	District Income Rank	328
Pop/ sq mi	70.89	Latino	2.60%	Poverty Rate	12.70%
Born in State	76.90%	Asian	1.70%	With health insurance	92.00%
		Two or more races	1.70%	Cash public assistance	2.90%
Age Groups		Other	0.70%	Food stamp/SNAP	11.60%
Under 18	19.60%				
18-34	23.80%	**Education**		**Work**	
35-64	36.70%	H.S grad or less	52.90%	White Collar	34.40%
Over 64	19.90%	Some College	23.30%	Sales and Service	36.10%
		College Degree, 4 yr	14.10%	Blue Collar	29.50%
Military		Post grad	9.70%	Government	13.60%
Veteran/ Active Duty	8.60%				

2020 Pres. Vote	Trump	232,414	(67%)	Biden	107,807	(31%)			
2016 Pres. Vote	Trump	202,538	(65%)	Clinton	91,175	(29%)	Johnson	8,843	(3%)

Williamsport: The sprawling northern tier of Pennsylvania is a land of crevassed valleys and rugged mountains, crisscrossed by giant viaducts built for the railroads linking the East Coast with the Great Lakes and the mines that produced the region's anthracite coal. This area still has a throwback look to it. The region has numerous long-established small towns, with solidly built courthouses and banks and elderly citizens. It's a part of the Northeast that seems worlds away from the region's huge central cities and growing suburbs. Notable towns include Williamsport, home of the Little League World Series, and Lewisburg, home of Bucknell University. The area's most consequential member of Congress was probably David Wilmot of Bradford County, a founding member of the Republican Party. In the 1840s, he introduced the Wilmot Proviso barring slavery from the New Mexico and California territories acquired in the Mexican War, raising the issue that led proximately to the Civil War. Most people in this part of Pennsylvania have been Republicans ever since.

The rural area recently has benefited from major building and energy development. Work on the 12-mile, $865 million Central Susquehanna Valley Thruway project was scheduled for completion in 2027, with a new bridge across the Susquehanna River between rural Snyder and Northumberland counties set to open in 2022. Two new Marcellus Shale-gas power plants in Lycoming and Bradford counties will convert the natural gas from nearby wells to generate electricity to power up to 2 million homes.

The 12th Congressional District includes the less-populated areas of north-central Pennsylvania. Williamsport-based Lycoming County is the population center of the 15 counties. None of them have a substantial Democratic presence. The district dips deep into central Pennsylvania west of Harrisburg in the rural counties of Juniata and Mifflin. In its southwest corner, the new 12th includes about half of Centre County, including the cutting-edge facilities of Penn State University that have spawned a high-skills job market. Centre, along with Harrisburg-based Dauphin, are the only counties between Pittsburgh and the suburbs of Philadelphia that have voted Democratic in presidential elections. The 12th and 15th District share the largest in the state; combined, they extend from nearly Ohio to the Catskills in New York. Along with the adjacent 13th to the south, they also are the most Republican. In 2020, Trump took the 12th, 67%-31%.

John Joyce (R)

Elected 2018, 2nd term, b. Feb 08, 1957; Altoona, PA; PA State University, Att., 1977; PA State University, B.S., 1979; Temple University, M.D., 1983; Catholic; Married (Alice Joyce); 3 children.

Military Career: U.S. Navy, Portsmouth Naval Hospital

Professional Career: Dermatologist.

DC Office: 1337 LHOB 20515, 202-225-2431, johnjoyce.house.gov

State Offices: Altoona, 814-656-6081; Chambersburg, 717-753-6344.

Committees: *Energy & Commerce*: Health; Oversight & Investigations.

Almanac Ratings 2019-2020

	Economy	Social	Foreign	Composite
Liberal	27%	9%	4%	14%
Conservative	73%	91%	96%	86%

Key Votes of the 116th Congress

1. U.S./Mex./Can. trade deal Y	5. Russia sanctions N	9. Firearms background checks N
2. First Coronavirus response Y	6. Troops in Syria N	10. Spending at the border Y
3. HEROES Act N	7. Veto arms sales to Saudis N	11. Marijuana liberalized rules N
4. CASH Act N	8. Defense $$$, veto override N	12. Electoral College objections Y

Election Results

Election	Name (Party)	Vote (%)		Cand. Spent	Ind. Exp. Support	Ind. Exp. Oppose
2020 General	John Joyce (R)..................................... 267,841	(73%)		$400,077	$10,693	$750
	Todd Rowley (D)........................ 96,664	(27%)		$63,593	$2,500	$158
2020 Primary	John Joyce (R)............................. 94,171	(100%)				

Prior winning percentages: 2018 (71%)

Republican John Joyce, elected in 2018, is the first representative of this west-central Pennsylvania district since 1972 who has not been named Shuster. But Joyce, a physician who styled himself as a political outsider, attracted a late endorsement and other encouragement from retiring Rep. Bill Shuster. In the decisive GOP primary, he defeated other candidates who had challenged or criticized Shuster in recent campaigns.

An Altoona native, Joyce graduated from Pennsylvania State University, got his medical degree from Temple University and was a resident in dermatology at Johns Hopkins. Following a tour of duty with the Navy during the 1991 war in Iraq, he established his practice as a dermatologist in Altoona. He was active in community activities and became a quiet supporter of the Shusters.

Bill Shuster in 2001 had succeeded his father, Bud Shuster, who served 28 years. The two Shusters had the unusual cachet that each chaired the powerful House Transportation and Infrastructure Committee, which controls the largesse for many public works programs. Each also faced ethical challenges and criticisms that they were too close to lobbyists.

Facing a six-year term limit as committee chairman, Bill Shuster's retirement had been widely expected. Joyce launched his campaign by styling himself as a political outsider and problem-solver. He received early support from the centrist Republican Main Street Partnership, which included Shuster among its members. With $1.5 million spent on his campaign, more than half of which was from personal loans, Joyce nearly doubled the total spent in the primary by the other seven GOP candidates combined. With themes that he was a caring physician and "a pro-life, common-sense conservative," his ads sought to reach across the party.

The conservative Club for Growth ran ads that opposed Joyce as an occasional supporter of Democrats. In the closing days of the campaign, Shuster announced support for Joyce—who was a longtime financial supporter of the incumbent, despite Joyce's campaign criticism of "career politicians." Joyce's son Sean, a Washington lobbyist, had served as Shuster's campaign chairman, the Chambersburg Public Opinion reported.

Joyce, with 22 percent of the vote in the primary, benefited from the other candidates splitting what remained of the anti-Shuster sentiment from their geographic bases across the district. Like the Shusters, Joyce's core support was in Blair County, which cast the most votes in the primary. His chief opponents— who each received between 15 and 20 percent of the total vote—were state Sen. John Eichelberger, who took Huntingdon County; state Rep. Stephen Bloom, who ran strongest in Cumberland County; Douglas Mastriano from Franklin County; and Art Halvorson, whose base was Bedford County.

Halvorson, who had held Shuster to a 51%-49% win in the 2016 GOP primary, said following the latest outcome, "the swamp won."Democrat Brent Ottaway, a communications professor at St. Francis University, had no chance in this Republican bastion. Joyce won, 70%-30%. In 2020, Joyce won the GOP primary without opposition.

Older than both Shusters when they took office, Joyce took a different route to influence in the House than climbing the seniority ladder at the Transportation committee. In 2021, he got a seat on the influential Energy and Commerce Committee. "It is critical that we advance conservative and free-market solutions for the vital health care, energy and telecom issues under the Energy and Commerce Committee's jurisdiction," he said following his selection. He noted his interest in expanding access to broadband in rural areas and increasing the number of doctors in rural communities.

PA-13: Southwest Pennsylvania   **Cook Partisan Voting Index: R+25**

Population		Race and Ethnicity		Income	
Total	697,051	White	93.40%	Median Income	$56,618
Land area (sq. miles)	6,018	Black	3.20%	District Income Rank	303
Pop/ sq mi	115.83	Latino	3.50%	Poverty Rate	11.00%
Born in State	75.90%	Asian	0.50%	With health insurance	92.90%
		Two or more races	1.70%	Cash public assistance	2.70%
Age Groups		Other	1.20%	Food stamp/SNAP	13.40%
Under 18	20.20%				
18-34	19.30%	**Education**		**Work**	
35-64	39.10%	H.S grad or less	56.00%	White Collar	31.10%
Over 64	21.30%	Some College	23.40%	Sales and Service	36.70%
		College Degree, 4 yr	12.60%	Blue Collar	32.20%
Military		Post grad	8.00%	Government	12.70%
Veteran/ Active Duty	9.10%				

2020 Pres. Vote	Trump	263,933	(71%)	Biden	100,422	(27%)		
2016 Pres. Vote	Trump	227,448	(71%)	Clinton	81,407	(25%)	Johnson	7,228 (2%)

Pittsburgh Exurbs, Altoona: The old towns of the southern tier of Pennsylvania look much as they did a century ago: farmhouses and red barns set amid rolling hills in the shadow of mountain ridges, seemingly isolated from the pulsing rhythms of modern America. During the 18th century, the Appalachian Mountains provided Quaker Pennsylvania with a rampart against Indian attacks, and allowed the commonwealth to become the richest and most populous of the colonies. In July 1863, Robert E. Lee's Confederate troops crossed the invisible Mason-Dixon line and were repelled at the Battle of Gettysburg. Not much today suggests that these hills were a frontier or the object of bloody struggle. President Dwight Eisenhower, of Pennsylvania Dutch stock, quietly spent his retirement years in Gettysburg. The mountains became a barrier to commerce for later pioneers, and it took the aggressive capitalists who built the Pennsylvania Railroad to get trains over the ridges. Though Pennsylvania's rail links remained important, a war-bound nation in1940 opened the road of the future here: the Pennsylvania Turnpike, the first highway in America that was able to move vehicles dependably at high speeds over long distances.

The region recorded a tragic mark in transportation history: On Sept. 11, 2001, United Airlines Flight 93 crashed into an empty former coalfield near Shanksville in Somerset County, killing all 40 passengers and crew on board. To Americans, the crash site became a symbol of both sadness and pride at the passengers' effort to wrest back control of the plane and possibly thwart a greater disaster, initiated by the now-famous cry of "Let's roll!" The National Park Service opened a memorial to Flight 93.

The 13th Congressional District takes in a wide swath of southern Pennsylvania, extending from east of Gettysburg almost to the northern panhandle of West Virginia and the eastern fringes of the Pittsburgh metro region, with seven full counties and parts of three others. Parts of the district are slow-growth and low-income. Blair County includes the city of Altoona, which continues to wither, from 82,000 people in 1930 to 43,400 in 2019.In Cambria County is Johnstown, the site of the cataclysmic flood in 1889. Johnstown, whose population fell from 67,000 in 1920 to a bit above 19,000 in 2019, has been ranked as the poorest city in Pennsylvania, with 38 percent living in poverty. Other areas have prospered. The largest county in the 13th is Franklin, where several international manufacturers have built local plants; its population jumped 20percent from 2000 to 2019. In December 2019, the Chambersburg Public Opinion headlined, "Franklin County's biggest story of the 2010's: Commercial development skyrockets."

The court-ordered redistricting moved the boundary of the district east to include all of Adams County and dropped Fayette County in the west. Politically, this part of Pennsylvania has been solidly Republican since 1860and has remained the strongest GOP district in the state, with little partisan shift from redistricting. President Donald Trump in 2020 increased the Republican presidential vote to an impressive 71 percent. The top Republican county in the district and in the state was Fulton, where he got 86 percent— though the county also was among the smallest in Pennsylvania.

Guy Reschenthaler (R)

Elected 2018, 2nd term, b. Apr 07, 1983; Pittsburgh, PA; PA State University, B.A., 2004; Duquesne University, J.D., 2007; Protestant; Single.

Military Career: U.S. Navy 2007-2012 (Iraq)

Elected Office: PA Magisterial District Judge, 2013-2015; PA Senate, 2015-2018.

Professional Career: Attorney.

DC Office: 531 CHOB 20515, 202-225-2065, reschenthaler.house.gov

State Offices: Greensburg, 724-219-4200; Washington, 724-206-4800.

Committees: *Appropriations*: Energy & Water Development & Related Agencies; State, Foreign Operations & Related Programs. *Rules*: Rules & Organization of the House (RMM). *Select Committee on the Modernization of Congress.*

Almanac Ratings 2019-2020

	Economy	Social	Foreign	Composite
Liberal	25%	30%	27%	28%
Conservative	75%	70%	73%	72%

Key Votes of the 116th Congress

1. U.S./Mex./Can. trade deal	Y	5. Russia sanctions	Y	9. Firearms background checks	N
2. First Coronavirus response	Y	6. Troops in Syria	Y	10. Spending at the border	Y
3. HEROES Act	N	7. Veto arms sales to Saudis	N	11. Marijuana liberalized rules	N/A
4. CASH Act	N	8. Defense $$$, veto override	N	12. Electoral College objections	Y

Election Results

Election	Name (Party)	Vote (%)	Cand. Spent	Ind. Exp. Support	Ind. Exp. Oppose
2020 General	Guy Reschenthaler (R)................... 241,768	(65%)	$1,581,630	$11,384	$750
	Bill Marx (D)................................ 131,943	(35%)	$44,908	$2,500	$158
2020 Primary	Guy Reschenthaler (R)................... 66,671	(100%)			

Prior winning percentages: 2018 (58%)

Republican Guy Reschenthaler restored order to a firmly Republican seat that moved into the national spotlight during a special election earlier in 2018. As the youngest Republican to join the House delegation from Pennsylvania after retirements, redistricting and election losses depleted the once-influential group, he showed influence when he got seats on the Appropriations and Rules committees.

A graduate of Pennsylvania State University and Duquesne Law School, Reschenthaler joined the U.S. Navy Judge Advocate General Corps. He served in Iraq, where he prosecuted terrorists from al-Qaida. Back home, he was nominated by both parties and elected as a district judge in Allegheny County. In 2015, as a Republican, he won a special election to the state Senate for what had been a Democratic-held seat. In the Senate, he claimed credit for passing a bill to outlaw sanctuary cities in Pennsylvania.

The political chaos in what had become a reliably partisan district ensued after veteran GOP Rep. Tim Murphy resigned in October 2017, amid reports that the married lawmaker asked his mistress to get an abortion after she told him she thought she was pregnant. At the closed-door GOP contest that attracted about 200 Republican insiders to nominate a candidate for the special election to replace Murphy, Reschenthaler led by one vote following the first ballot. But the third candidate in that contest, state Sen. Kim Ward, threw her support to Rick Saccone, a veteran state legislator, who she called "a very fiery guy." She dismissed Reschenthaler, her Senate colleague, as a "very nice young man," the Pittsburgh Post-Gazette reported.

Saccone proved a poor candidate with a weak organization that failed to take advantage of Trump's personal support. In March 2018, Democrat Conor Lamb, a political newcomer, rallied working-class voters as an alternative to Trump and defeated Saccone by 755 votes out of more than 217,000 cast. When the court-ordered redistricting made this district even more Republican, Lamb in November ran—and won—in a more favorable adjacent district against GOP Rep. Keith Rothfus.

In the May primary for a full term in the new district, Reschenthaler conveyed a youthful and patriotic appeal as "a new voice" who was "born to lead and called to serve." He drew the contrast to 60-year-old Saccone, who he called "an embarrassment" and "a career politician," and criticized Saccone's failure in the special election, the Post-Gazette reported. "The president said that Rick was a weak candidate. The national Republicans said his campaign was a joke." With scant public attention compared to the special election, Saccone appealed to the "grassroots." This time, Ward backed Reschenthaler.

For the second time in two months, Saccone was defeated. In the redrawn district, 43,000 voters participated in the May 2018 primary. Reschenthaler won the primary, 55%-45%. He took 58 percent in Westmoreland County and 56 percent in Washington County, the population centers of the district. Saccone took rural Fayette and Greene Counties, but they cast less than 20 percent of the total vote. Reschenthaler spent nearly twice as much money as his opponent and benefited from more than $100,000 spent by a group organized by former Rep. Murphy. With national Democratic attention having moved elsewhere, he won in November, 58%-42%,against Democrat Bibiano Boerio, a businesswoman and former congressional aide.

Unlike many of the large class of freshman Republicans, in Pennsylvania and elsewhere, Reschenthaler reached across the aisle to find Democratic cosponsors on his legislation. With Rep. Lisa Blunt Rochester of Delaware, he filed the Clean Slate Act, which would automatically seal an offender's federal criminal record if that individual had been convicted of certain nonviolent drug crimes. "Working on the front lines of our judicial system [as a local judge] showed me we can reduce crime by giving these individuals the tools they need to live productive and fulfilling lives," Reschenthaler said Their bill was supported by the conservative Freedom Works and the liberal Center for American Progress.

In January 2021, Reschenthaler scored the impressive feat of winning seats on two of the House's most powerful committees: Appropriations and Rules. Rep. Tom Cole of Oklahoma, the senior

Republican on Rules, called Reschenthaler "one of the most able and hardworking members of the House, with a brilliant future ahead of him."

PA-14: Southwest Pennsylvania   Cook Partisan Voting Index: R+16

Population		Race and Ethnicity		Income	
Total	678,915	White	93.40%	Median Income	$59,165
Land area (sq. miles)	2,848	Black	3.00%	District Income Rank	278
Pop/ sq mi	238.41	Latino	1.50%	Poverty Rate	12.00%
Born in State	83.50%	Asian	0.90%	With health insurance	95.40%
		Two or more races	2.20%	Cash public assistance	3.40%
Age Groups		Other	0.40%	Food stamp/SNAP	15.70%
Under 18	18.80%				
18-34	19.10%	**Education**		**Work**	
35-64	39.90%	H.S grad or less	45.40%	White Collar	36.80%
Over 64	22.00%	Some College	27.00%	Sales and Service	38.30%
		College Degree, 4 yr	18.00%	Blue Collar	24.90%
Military		Post grad	9.60%	Government	9.50%
Veteran/ Active Duty	7.90%				

2020 Pres. Vote	Trump	240,521	(63%)	Biden	135,934	(36%)			
2016 Pres. Vote	Trump	209,536	(62%)	Clinton	112,882	(34%)	Johnson	7,665	(2%)

Southern and eastern Pittsburgh Suburbs: The mountains and valleys within a 100-mile radius of Pittsburgh comprise one of America's most beautiful—and economically troubled—regions. This has been tough, hardworking country ever since Scots-Irish farmers settled here in the 1790s. Their first big product was whiskey—this was the site of the Whiskey Rebellion of 1794—but historically the most important product was bituminous coal. Discovered in the 19th century, it was the basic energy source for the production of iron and steel.

The cities and towns of Greater Pittsburgh are discontinuous, separated from each other not just by miles but by altitude. So, the region's high-income suburbs and its gritty factory towns are not concentrated in one area, but are scattered all around. This is long-settled country, with many more old towns than sparkling new suburbs. Unlike the economically diverse Pittsburgh-based Allegheny County, Westmoreland and Washington counties here are more dependent on manufacturing and more susceptible to industry-wide cuts. That, in turn, has led young people to leave to find work elsewhere. In Westmoreland, the Pittsburgh Post-Gazette in 2017 described "a slipping population and evaporating jobs. "The population of the county—the second-largest in the metro area but less than one-third the size of Allegheny—fell 4 percent from 2010 to 2019. Westmoreland is 94 percent White, compared to 78 percent for more robust Allegheny.

Fayette County is a blue-collar area, where the loss of jobs accompanied a 5 percent drop in population from 2010 to 2019; since 1940, the population has declined 35 percent. There has been a spiraling effect as prospective employers have "struggled with hiring" because the workforce has dried up, the Post-Gazette reported in 2018. "The truth is not a lot of people want to live in Fayette County," said an executive with a new company in the area. The jobs problems have been "aggravated by rising substance abuse," the Post-Gazette reported. Youth poverty in Fayette has made teens vulnerable to human trafficking. One positive factor: Washington County has benefited from the growth in energy production and led the state in new permits for natural-gas drilling from the Marcellus Shale.

The 14th Congressional District of Pennsylvania covers the southern part of the Pittsburgh metropolitan area and the southwest corner of Pennsylvania. It includes nearly 90 percent of Westmoreland County, which is nearly half of the district population; the eastern edge of Westmoreland is part of the rural 13th District. During the 2020 presidential campaign, both parties talked about increasing their vote in Westmoreland from 2016. President Donald Trump took 63 percent—his best showing among the 10 largest counties in Pennsylvania. The three other counties along both sides of the West Virginia border—Washington, Fayette and Greene—are entirely in the 14th; Washington is the largest. The court-ordered redistricting in 2018 turned an area that already had been a struggle for Democratic candidates into a safe Republican bastion.

Glenn Thompson (R)

Elected 2008, 7th term, b. Jul 27, 1959; Bellefonte, PA; PA State University, B.S., 1981; Temple University, M.Ed., 1998; Marywood College, 2006; Protestant; Married (Penny Thompson); 3 children.

Elected Office: Bald Eagle Area School Board, 1990-1995.

Professional Career: Therapist, Williamsport Hosp., 1982-1995; Adjunct faculty, Cambria County Comm. College, 1997-1999; Manager, Susquehanna Health Rehabilitation Services, 1995-2008; Centre County GOP Chairman, 2002-2008; Firefighter & EMT.

DC Office: 400 CHOB 20515, 202-225-5121, Fax: 202-225-5796, thompson.house.gov

State Offices: Ebensburg, 814-419-8583.

Committees: *Agriculture (RMM)*: Ex Officio membership on all subcommittees. *Education & Labor*: Civil Rights & Human Services.

Group Ratings

	ADA	ACLU	AFL-CIO	LCV	COC	HAFA	ACU	CFG	FRC
2020	**	15%	**	10%	-	72%	72%	**	-
2019	5%	C	38%	7%	91%	C	71%	65%	95%

Almanac Ratings 2019-2020

	Economy	Social	Foreign	Composite
Liberal	27%	33%	13%	25%
Conservative	73%	67%	87%	75%

Key Votes of the 116th Congress

1. U.S./Mex./Can. trade deal	Y	5. Russia sanctions	N	9. Firearms background checks N
2. First Coronavirus response	Y	6. Troops in Syria	Y	10. Spending at the border	Y
3. HEROES Act	N	7. Veto arms sales to Saudis	N	11. Marijuana liberalized rules	N
4. CASH Act	N	8. Defense $$$, veto override	Y	12. Electoral College objections Y

Election Results

Election	Name (Party)	Vote (%)		Cand. Spent	Ind. Exp. Support	Ind. Exp. Oppose
2020 General	Glenn Thompson (R)	255,059	(73%)	$1,393,110	$9,440	$750
	Robert Williams (D)	92,157	(27%)		$2,500	$158
2020 Primary	Glenn Thompson (R)	88,364	(100%)			

Prior winning percentages: 2018 (68%), 2016 (67%), 2014 (64%), 2012 (63%), 2010 (69%), 2008 (57%)

Glenn Thompson, who won the seat in 2008, is an amiable centrist with practical experience on many issues. In 2021, he became the top Republican on the House Agriculture Committee, where he was comfortable with the traditional bipartisanship on farm issues. "GT" played a prominent role in helping to enact the 2018 farm bill, though the final deal dropped most of the new restrictions on food stamp recipients that Thompson had moved through the House. He also is a senior member of the Education and Labor Committee.

A lifelong resident of Centre County, Thompson graduated from nearby Penn State. He launched his career in health care at Williamsport Hospital, where he worked as a rehabilitation services manager. He later worked as a licensed nursing home administrator. Thompson served as a member of the board of the Bald Eagle Area School District. He ran twice for state representative, both times unsuccessfully, but was elected to three terms as chairman of the Centre County Republican Party.

When the House seat opened, Thompson jumped into the nine-candidate primary. His hopes appeared dim against big-spending rivals. Thompson instead crisscrossed the district in a low-key and low-cost campaign that emphasized his Republican positions and focused on rural issues. He called for expanding rural Medicare initiatives and spoke of the Iraq war in personal terms; his son, Logan, was injured by a landmine in 2007 while serving.

Less than two weeks before the primary, retiring GOP Rep. John Peterson endorsed Thompson as the candidate who best understood rural issues. A week later, the Clearfield County district attorney filed charges against Derek Walker, one of his leading rivals, for allegedly breaking into his ex-girlfriend's apartment. Vastly outspent, Thompson won 19 percent of the vote to beat Walker by 835 votes. In the general election, Thompson won 57%-41%. He has not been seriously challenged for reelection.

Thompson has shown some independence. His Almanac vote ratings have ranked him toward the center of the House. He dissed tea party advocates by voting to raise the federal debt limit in 2011 and to support the tax and spending legislation that averted the so-called fiscal cliff in 2013. He called the latter "not perfect, but a pretty good deal." In 2014, he included in the yearend spending bill $155 million for the Essential Air Service program, which promotes rural airports and is opposed by many conservatives. C-SPAN has frequently ranked Thompson first among members in the yearly number of speeches on the House floor.

Rural causes have been a priority for Thompson. On the Agriculture panel, he chaired the Subcommittee on Conservation and Forestry for six years. He worked to strengthen voluntary conservation programs as part of the farm bill enacted in 2014. With many dairy farmers in his district, he filed a bill in 2019 to allow participants in the school-lunch program to serve whole milk as an option. He has sought to amend a law enacted in 2010 that limited public schools to offering skim or 1 percent milk. Those restrictions have reduced overall consumption of milk by school kids, according to Thompson and dairy industry allies.

In 2017-18, Thompson chaired the Nutrition Subcommittee, where Republicans have placed a high priority on adding work requirements for most beneficiaries of food stamps. When the House passed its version of the farm bill, its restrictions included 20 hours of weekly work or participation in a state-run training program for most recipients. Democrats have traditionally opposed such requirements, often with the support of Senate Republicans. So, when the farm bill was included on the "to do" list for the lame-duck session after Democrats had won House control, Thompson and his allies had lost much of their leverage. "If we could get this one done with some bad modifications, it will be so much better than what will be negotiated under the Democrat majority" in 2019, Thompson said at the start of the final negotiations. Most House Republicans accepted those changes that Thompson had forecast.

When Rep. Mike Conaway of Texas retired in 2020 after being term-limited as the top Republican on the ag committee, Thompson was next in line to succeed him. Reps. Austin Scott of Georgia and Rick Crawford of Arkansas also competed for the position. When a GOP leadership panel gave the position to Thompson, he said he expected to work with Rep. David Scott of Georgia, who took over at the same time as committee chairman.

"I reach across the aisle. That's my style with committee work, as well," Thompson told American Agriculturist. For a new farm program he hoped to enact in 2022, Thompson called for "full and complete connectivity" for broadband in rural America and for expanded access to commodity purchases at no cost for low-income Americans.

Thompson has retained his interest in education issues as a member of the Education and Labor Committee. With Democratic Rep. Jim Langevin of Rhode Island, Thompson filed a bill in November 2019 to promote career counseling in secondary schools. They have been leaders of the Career and Technical Education Caucus.

PA-15: West-central Pennsylvania

Cook Partisan Voting Index: R+24

Population		Race and Ethnicity		Income	
Total	672,749	White	95.20%	Median Income	$53,741
Land area (sq. miles)	9,729	Black	2.40%	District Income Rank	349
Pop/ sq mi	69.15	Latino	1.30%	Poverty Rate	12.30%
Born in State	84.90%	Asian	0.70%	With health insurance	94.40%
		Two or more races	1.30%	Cash public assistance	3.10%
Age Groups		Other	0.40%	Food stamp/SNAP	14.10%
Under 18	18.50%				
18-34	20.80%	**Education**		**Work**	
35-64	39.50%	H.S grad or less	55.20%	White Collar	30.50%
Over 64	21.30%	Some College	24.10%	Sales and Service	37.60%
		College Degree, 4 yr	13.10%	Blue Collar	31.80%
Military		Post grad	7.50%	Government	14.60%
Veteran/ Active Duty	8.80%				

2020 Pres. Vote	Trump	250,610	(71%)	Biden	96,907	(27%)		
2016 Pres. Vote	Trump	215,591	(69%)	Clinton	81,962	(26%)	Johnson	7,771	(2%)

Cambria and Indiana Counties: West-central Pennsylvania, isolated from the rest of the country by mountains and off the main east-west rail and highway lines until the 1970s, is one of those empty spaces that make even the Northeastern states seem lightly populated compared to the densely packed terrain of Western Europe or East Asia. This is a prime area for hunting, fishing and snowmobiling. The Allegheny National Forest sprawls across four counties and is a popular recreational area. In 2018, it was the second most popular camping destination in the nation, trailing only Cape Cod in Massachusetts. Neatly preserved Ridgway holds the largest chainsaw carving event in the world.

For several years recently, production of natural gas deep underground in the Marcellus Shale formation generated extensive local spending and considerable optimism. In 2017, with 802 new wells developed—nearly 300 more than a year earlier—the area has become the second-largest producer of natural gas in the nation, closely behind Texas. The number of new wells drilled in 2019 declined, but there was an increase in the amount of gas produced. About 80 percent of the drilling permits were for fracking—horizontal shale gas wells. In Centre County, there has been "a quiet renaissance of manufacturing," led by small businesses, the Centre Daily Times reported in 2018.Punxsutawney in Jefferson County is home of the legendary groundhog Phil, who predicts the arrival of spring every February 2 by looking for his shadow on Gobbler's Knob. Phil doesn't see many Democrats. In 2020, President Donald Trump got 79 percent of the vote in Jefferson.

The 15th Congressional District of Pennsylvania, rural and sprawling, reaches more than 150 miles across the western half of the state—from the New York state border south nearly to the Mason-Dixon line and from Butler east to Bellefonte. Court-ordered redistricting removed its portion of Erie County and cut back parts of Centre County, including Pennsylvania State University. Those had been the two most populous and least Republican areas of the old 5th District. In their place, the new map extended toward the exurbs of Pittsburgh. Indiana County and two-thirds of Cambria County, new to the district, have become its two largest counties, though Johnstown is in the 13th. Those shifts increased the already ample Republican vote in the district, which rivals the adjacent 13th as the most Republican in the state. In 2020, Trump won each district by an identical 71%-27%.

Mike Kelly (R)

Elected 2010, 6th term, b. May 10, 1948; Pittsburgh, PA; University of Notre Dame, B.A., 1970; Roman Catholic; Married (Victoria Kelly); 4 children; 10 grandchildren.

Elected Office: Butler City Council, 2006-2009.

Professional Career: Butler Area School Board, 1992-1996; Owner, Manager, Kelly Chevrolet-Cadillac Inc.

DC Office: 1707 LHOB 20515, 202-225-5406, Fax: 202-225-3103, kelly.house.gov

Committees: *Ways & Means*: Health; Oversight (RMM).

Group Ratings

	ADA	ACLU	AFL-CIO	LCV	COC	HAFA	ACU	CFG	FRC
2020	**	15%	**	19%	-	89%	73%	**	-
2019	5%	C	24%	7%	78%	C	71%	86%	95%

Almanac Ratings 2019-2020

	Economy	Social	Foreign	Composite
Liberal	27%	32%	27%	29%
Conservative	73%	68%	73%	71%

Key Votes of the 116th Congress

1. U.S./Mex./Can. trade deal Y	5. Russia sanctions Y	9. Firearms background checks N
2. First Coronavirus response Y	6. Troops in Syria Y	10. Spending at the border Y
3. HEROES Act N	7. Veto arms sales to Saudis N	11. Marijuana liberalized rules N
4. CASH Act N	8. Defense $$$, veto override Y	12. Electoral College objections Y

Election Results

Election	Name (Party)	Vote (%)	Cand. Spent	Ind. Exp. Support	Ind. Exp. Oppose
2020 General	Mike Kelly (R)	210,088 (59%)	$1,201,415	$135,032	$750
	Kristy Gnibus (D)	143,962 (41%)	$583,599	$3,794	$2,072
2020 Primary	Mike Kelly (R)	68,199 (100%)			

Prior winning percentages: 2018 (52%), 2016 (100%), 2014 (61%), 2012 (55%), 2010 (56%)

Republican Mike Kelly is an ex-college football player and auto dealer who has been known for his fiery pep talks to colleagues behind closed doors. He has been mostly loyal to his party and its leaders. On the Ways and Means Committee, he has advocated core issues for House Republicans. In 2019, as part of the minority for the first time, he defended President Donald Trump against what Kelly viewed as excessive investigations by the panel's Democrats, especially his taxes.

Kelly was born in Pittsburgh and four years later his family moved to Butler, where his father started a small automobile business, working seven days a week. "He took the cars off the trains himself, and he serviced them himself. And he built a business, based around a strong work ethic, which was similar to his parents. It's pretty much the story of western Pennsylvania," Kelly said. In high school, Kelly was an all-state football player and was recruited to play for the University of Notre Dame. But he tore up a knee during his freshman year and dislocated it again in his sophomore season, ending his football career. After college, he worked as a salesman in the family business, Kelly Chevrolet-Cadillac, eventually becoming general manager. He bought the dealership from his father, and expanded it to include Hyundai and Kia autos. In 2005, Kelly was elected to the Butler City Council.

Running for Congress in 2010, Kelly's toughest opponent in the primary was business executive Paul Huber. He eked out a victory by 954 votes out of 54,000 cast. His general election foe was Rep. Kathy Dahlkemper, a Democrat who in 2008 had narrowly defeated the Republican incumbent. Dahlkemper opposed abortion rights, but she took heat from conservatives for voting for the Affordable Care Act. She outspent Kelly by about 3-to-2. He stressed his football background, which was an asset in the football mecca of western Pennsylvania, and he promised to cut government spending and curtail interference with small business. With the strong Republican wave at his back, Kelly won 56%-44%.

During the 2011 fight over raising the debt limit, he gave what Rep. Peter King of New York called a well-delivered "Knute Rockne-type speech" to rally conservatives. "Mike Kelly's the one that steps up to the microphone and says, 'Hey, we're all in this together. ... Nobody in this room is going to get everything they want. Let's go do this,'" Republican Rep. Austin Scott of Georgia told the Pittsburgh Tribune-Review.

On Ways and Means, Kelly won approval in 2015 of his bill to remove protections for Internal Revenue Service employees who improperly review or reveal taxpayer information. The committee approved his bill to improve the transparency of Medicare Advantage programs for individuals who have enrolled. He co-founded the bipartisan Retirement Security Caucus to encourage more savings. Kelly has been a vocal advocate of expanded international trade, which he said is a boost for workers and assures that the nation "is leading, shaping, and dominating the global economy." He strongly backed trade promotion authority for President Barack Obama, a step that he said would be "a crucial victory to the principles of American dominance, domestic prosperity, and government accountability that we hold so dear." In 2017, he was an avid proponent of the Republican-passed tax cuts, which he later said had "successfully revived our economy."

During the 2016 presidential campaign, Kelly was an enthusiastic supporter of Trump. "Only a Trump presidency can undo the current damage caused by explosive government growth and chart a new direction," he wrote for CNN in October 2016. In 2019, Kelly took over as ranking Republican on the Oversight Subcommittee at Ways and Means, where he said he would serve "as a guardian of America's precious taxpayer dollars. "He warned that Democratic efforts to get the president's tax returns would be "an abuse of power [and] open a Pandora's box" and "set a very dangerous precedent." In a mixed result in July 2020, the Supreme Court largely deferred on the clash between Congress and the president, but gave broad access to the prosecutor in Manhattan. Following the November election, Kelly was a prominent advocate in the unsuccessful efforts by Republicans to challenge the results in Pennsylvania, based largely on their claim that state officials had made unconstitutional changes in election procedures.

At home, Kelly easily won reelection in his first three contests. Encouraged by the redistricting changes, Democrats in 2018 gave Kelly his first serious contest. Democratic challenger Ron DiNicola, a criminal defense lawyer who narrowly lost a bid for the seat in 1996, attacked Kelly for his vote to repeal the Affordable Care Act and called Congress "corrupt. "During an October campaign rally in Erie, Trump said "Mike is strong on crime…and he is really great on jobs." Kelly outspent DiNicola, $3.3 million to $1.8 million, and won, 52%-47%. DiNicola took 59 percent of the vote in Erie County, but Kelly swept the four outlying counties. Two years later, Kelly was challenged by Kristy Gnibus, a schoolteacher and cancer survivor. She spent $584,000. Kelly won, 59%-41%, nearly the same result for Trump in the district.

PA-16: Northwest Pennsylvania

Cook Partisan Voting Index: R+12

Population		Race and Ethnicity		Income	
Total	678,333	White	90.60%	Median Income	$54,627
Land area (sq. miles)	3,312	Black	4.50%	District Income Rank	337
Pop/ sq mi	204.83	Latino	2.70%	Poverty Rate	13.50%
Born in State	80.30%	Asian	1.10%	With health insurance	94.80%
		Two or more races	3.00%	Cash public assistance	3.80%
Age Groups		Other	0.90%	Food stamp/SNAP	16.90%
Under 18	20.00%				
18-34	21.40%	**Education**		**Work**	
35-64	38.70%	H.S grad or less	47.10%	White Collar	36.60%
Over 64	20.10%	Some College	24.60%	Sales and Service	38.40%
		College Degree, 4 yr	18.00%	Blue Collar	25.10%
Military		Post grad	10.30%	Government	11.70%
Veteran/ Active Duty	8.50%				

2020 Pres. Vote	Trump	212,969	(59%)	Biden	145,211	(40%)		
2016 Pres. Vote	Trump	187,203	(57%)	Clinton	122,582	(38%)	Johnson	9,392 (3%)

Erie, Pittsburgh Exurbs: The best natural harbor on Lake Erie is in Erie Pennsylvania, protected by the Presque Isle ("almost an island") peninsula—a cowlick-shaped, seven-mile-long sand spit blanketed by mature forest, with a lighthouse dating to 1872. Erie is in Pennsylvania's far northwest corner, closer to Cleveland (about 100 miles) than to Pittsburgh (125 miles). There are farmlands here, and even some woods, but the land between the Great Lakes and the basin of the Ohio River has been prime heavy industry territory for more than a century. The jeep, which Gen. George Marshall called America's greatest contribution to World War II, was invented in Butler County. In the 1990s, under Republican Gov. Tom Ridge, who grew up in Erie, the state spent$100 million on the city's waterfront to develop a cruise ship terminal, hotel and convention center, a ballpark for the double-A Erie SeaWolves baseball team, and a renovated Warner Theatre.

These efforts "haven't worked," the Wall Street Journal reported in October 2019. They failed to buffer Erie from a new downturn during which International Paper, American Meter, Gunite/EMI and American Sterilizer laid off employees and closed plants. General Electric Transportation, which had remained the area's largest industrial employer, in 2017 ended locomotive production in Erie, citing the decline in freight rail traffic. That resulted in a loss of 575 jobs. In 2018, what remained of the GE division was sold to Wabtec, a Pittsburgh-based rail-equipment company known as the Westinghouse Air Brake Company. At that time, 2,000 workers remained of the more than 15,000 who once worked locally for GE, which had been a force in Erie for more than a century. "The GE of the past has been gone for a long time," said Erie County Executive Kathy Dahlkemper. A new project was underway to draw more people to live and work downtown. Erie officials have created a downtown innovation district that invites 10 start-ups to visit the county each year and consider it as a hub for cyber security and data science.

The 16th Congressional District of Pennsylvania occupies the northwest corner of the state. It takes in all of Erie County and two-thirds of Butler County outside Pittsburgh. The court-ordered redistricting in 2018 resulted chiefly in population switches with the new 15th District to the east: The 16th added the portion of Erie County that had been in the old 5th District in exchange for Armstrong. About two-fifths of the population is in Erie, and one-fifth in Butler. From 2010 to 2019, Erie County lost 4 percent of its population, while Butler gained 2 percent. The population of the city of Erie declined more than 30 percent from 1960 to its 2018 total of 95,500. The growing number of refugees coming to the city was slowed by restrictions imposed by the Trump administration. The redistricting changes increased the Democratic vote in the district by a few percentage points, though it remained comfortably Republican. In 2020, President Donald Trump took the district, 59%-40%. Erie County, which Trump won by almost 2,000 votes in 2016, swung to Biden by 1,400. Erie was the only one of 67 counties statewide that voted for the winner in all seven statewide elections in 2016 and 2018.

Conor Lamb (D)

Elected 2018, 2nd full term, b. Jun 27, 1984; Washington, DC; University of PA, B.A., 2006; University of PA Law School, J.D., 2009; Catholic; Married.

Professional Career: Asst. U.S. Attorney, U.S. Attorney office, Pittsburgh. 2014-2017.

DC Office: 1224 LHOB 20515, 202-225-2301, Fax: 202-225-1844, lamb.house.gov

State Offices: Monaca, 724-206-4860.

Committees: *Science, Space & Technology*: Energy; Research & Technology. *Transportation & Infrastructure*: Aviation; Highways & Transit. *Veterans' Affairs*: Health; Oversight & Investigations; Women Veterans Task Force.

Almanac Ratings 2019-2020

	Economy	Social	Foreign	Composite
Liberal	54%	49%	50%	51%
Conservative	46%	51%	50%	49%

Key Votes of the 116th Congress

1. U.S./Mex./Can. trade deal Y	5. Russia sanctions Y	9. Firearms background checks Y
2. First Coronavirus response Y	6. Troops in Syria Y	10. Spending at the border Y
3. HEROES Act N	7. Veto arms sales to Saudis Y	11. Marijuana liberalized rules N
4. CASH Act Y	8. Defense $$$, veto override Y	12. Electoral College objections N

Election Results

Election	Name (Party)	Vote (%)		Cand. Spent	Ind. Exp. Support	Ind. Exp. Oppose
2020 General	Conor Lamb (D)	222,253	(51%)	$3,915,005	$274,986	$151,493
	Sean Parnell (R)	212,284	(49%)	$3,397,137	$172,129	$525,430
2020 Primary	Conor Lamb (D)	111,828	(100%)			

Prior winning percentages: 2018 special (50%)

Democrat Conor Lamb achieved the unusual distinction of winning two House elections in less than eight months in 2018 in two notably different districts in the Pittsburgh metro area. One was a special election, in which he defeated a relatively weak Republican opponent by fewer than 800 votes. In the second, in a new district changed significantly by court-ordered redistricting, Lamb defeated a veteran GOP incumbent by more than 40,000 votes. Lamb, a political newcomer, kept his distance from Democratic Leader Nancy Pelosi. His dual successes were a harbinger of the national election changes and offered useful tips to other centrist Democrats running in red districts. In 2020, he became an important surrogate for Joe Biden and together they offered a blueprint for how Democrats can win in the Rust Belt. In early 2021, he explored running for the seat of retiring Sen. Pat Toomey.

Lamb, a native of Mount Lebanon, went to Central Catholic High School in Pittsburgh. He got his bachelor's and law degrees from the University of Pennsylvania. He served four years on active duty in the Marine Corps and remained in the Marine Corps Reserve, with the rank of captain. That was followed by work as a prosecutor in the U.S. attorney's office in Pittsburgh, where he handled narcotics cases and worked to build partnerships between law enforcement and hard-hit communities.

Lamb's political opportunity opened when veteran Republican Rep. Tim Murphy—a physician who became a leader in Congress on mental health issues—resigned in October 2017. His decision followed news reports in Pittsburgh that Murphy had urged his mistress to have an abortion, despite his own pro-life views; it turned out that she was not pregnant. The reports also described his allegedly abusive treatment of his congressional aides. Under pressure at home and from House GOP leaders, Murphy quit what he had turned into a safely Republican seat.

Lamb brought a profile that was old-style, blue-collar Democrat, in some ways. He embraced organized labor and was an advocate of gun ownership. As a devout Catholic, he said, he opposed abortion but he did not favor new anti-abortion laws. In the Republican-leaning district during the special election, he styled himself as a bipartisan problem-solver. He was widely viewed as the underdog in a district that President Donald Trump had won by 20 points.

But Lamb got a boost when Republicans at their closed-door party convention narrowly selected state Rep. Rick Saccone as their nominee. He proved to a be a weak fundraiser and communicator who struggled with the national attention the special election received. Saccone sought to turn the contest into a referendum on Trump, who made a campaign appearance on his behalf. Lamb sought to remain neutral on the president, whose increased tariffs were popular in parts of the steel-producing region. He notably shunned most national Democratic figures, save for Biden, who held a rally in the district for him.

Lamb won by 755 votes in the March 2018 special election, which had a turnout of nearly 230,000 voters. He led, 57%-42%, in Allegheny County, which cast more than 40 percent of the vote. Saccone won handily in the more exurban and rural parts of the district. The outcome was the first House district that changed parties since the 2016 election.

Meanwhile, the legal victory by Democrats in their court challenge to the Republican-drawn redistricting plan in 2012, caused major changes of district lines across Pennsylvania. Among other things, the old 18th District that Lamb had won became even more Republican. Lamb decided that he had a better chance in a neighboring district that had a large share of Allegheny County, including some precincts in the district that Lamb had won. That placed Lamb in the new 17th District with three-term Republican Rep. Keith Rothfus. (In the new 14th District, Saccone ran again. But he lost the GOP primary to Guy Reschenthaler, who easily won the district in November.)

The fiscally conservative Rothfus was a mainstream Republican. When he was first elected in 2012, after having narrowly lost his first congressional campaign in 2010, he was the beneficiary of redistricting that drew a Republican-leaning seat, plus a bitter primary between two Democratic incumbents who were forced into the new district.

The Rothfus-Lamb contest initially seemed a toss-up in the new district where Trump had led by about two points in 2016. But Lamb benefited from favorable publicity from his special-election victory and the national surge in Democratic support in 2018, especially in suburban areas. Lamb continued his campaign strategy of not discussing Trump. Citing the need for new leadership, he said he would not support Pelosi for House Speaker.

With polls showing a double-digit lead for Lamb, the National Republican Congressional Committee in mid-September canceled its planned ads on behalf of Rothfus, a sure sign of its pessimism. Lamb won, 56%-44%, with a nearly 43,000-vote lead in Allegheny.

Lamb stayed true to his pledge of independence. He was one of 15 House Democrats who did not vote for Pelosi for Speaker in 2019 and one of five who did so again in 2021. Still, he got two plums: vice chairman of the Veterans' Affairs Committee and chairman of the Science, Space and Technology Subcommittee on Energy, which he later surrendered.

In the 2020 Democratic presidential primary, Lamb endorsed Biden early, calling him the best candidate for western Pennsylvania, and he campaigned with Biden. "We need the person who's best able to beat President Trump," he told The Washington Post. Biden and Lamb hit similar themes in their campaign, vowing to protect Social Security and Medicare and keeping a laser-focus on protecting working-class jobs.

Lamb continued to stake out moderate positions on climate and energy. Eschewing the Green New Deal, he pledged to protect his district's manufacturing and natural gas sectors while lambasting the Trump era rollback of environmental protections. He served on the Biden campaign's climate task force.

In his reelection, Lamb faced Sean Parnell, an Army veteran-turned author who had a strong fundraising network, thanks to his frequent Fox News appearances and Trump connections, and he spent nearly as much as Lamb. He criticized Lamb for voting to impeach Trump and cast him as a Pelosi crony.

National Republicans declined to spend significantly for Parnell, but the results suggest they missed an opportunity. Lamb won 51%-49%, thanks to hiseight-point edge in Allegheny County, which comprised more than 75 percent of the total vote. Parnell handily carried Beaver County.

Redistricting in 2022 could make Lamb's seat more challenging, though he seriously explored a run for the open Senate seat. In either chamber, he would be well poised for a promising future in national politics.

PA-17: Allegheny County

Cook Partisan Voting Index: R+2

Population		Race and Ethnicity		Income	
Total	706,961	White	88.10%	Median Income	$70,857
Land area (sq. miles)	883	Black	6.00%	District Income Rank	158
Pop/ sq mi	800.74	Latino	1.70%	Poverty Rate	7.70%
Born in State	77.20%	Asian	2.70%	With health insurance	96.80%
		Two or more races	2.60%	Cash public assistance	1.90%
Age Groups		Other	0.60%	Food stamp/SNAP	9.10%
Under 18	19.80%				
18-34	19.20%	**Education**		**Work**	
35-64	40.60%	H.S grad or less	30.80%	White Collar	47.90%
Over 64	20.50%	Some College	26.70%	Sales and Service	35.20%
		College Degree, 4 yr	25.70%	Blue Collar	17.00%
Military		Post grad	16.90%	Government	9.40%
Veteran/ Active Duty	7.50%				

2020 Pres. Vote	Biden	221,555	(51%)	Trump	209,683	(48%)			
2016 Pres. Vote	Trump	188,250	(49%)	Clinton	178,625	(46%)	Johnson	10,569	(3%)

Northern and western Pittsburgh suburbs: Pittsburgh was built on the unlikeliest terrain of any major U.S. city. Just about the only level places in the city or its suburbs are the bottomlands along the rivers. Everything else is built on hills that approach the magnitude of mountains. Only a propitious location, where the Allegheny and Monongahela rivers join to form the Ohio, and the confluence of economically valuable natural resources—coal from the mountains and iron ore from the Great Lakes—can explain why a large metropolitan area sprang up there.

This is long-settled country, with many more old towns than new suburbs. The population in the area has been declining, but with some increase in high-wage jobs to counter an ongoing loss of blue-collar jobs. With government aid, companies in the area have developed improved batteries and energy storage. The massive $6 billion ethane cracker plant along the Ohio River in Beaver County—powered by natural-gas reserves from the Marcellus Shale—brought in 8,000 construction jobs. The pandemic delayed construction but it was more than 70 percent completed by the spring of 2021. When the petrochemical facility is finished, it expects a permanent payroll of 600 workers. The project is the most significant economic development in the region in 40 years, local officials report. Perhaps optimistically, they view the facility—and others that might follow—as successors to the steel industry, though some in the community are already raising questions about potential environmental risk.

The Allegheny County suburbs north of Pittsburgh include old-money Fox Chapel and Sewickley, which have attracted the region's high-tech wealth. In the North Hills are affluent McCandless and more middle-class Ross. In contrast to adjacent Beaver and Butler counties, which have gained many young families and are comfortably Republican, the Allegheny suburbs—which include many senior citizens—have remained politically marginal. Several small towns in Allegheny County have had above-average growth since 2010, especially those that are close to the Pittsburgh airport. One of them, Findlay Township, received a $30 million Amazon fulfillment center and 800 new jobs in 2020.

The 17th Congressional District stretches from the Ohio border to the suburbs surrounding Pittsburgh on all but its eastern side. It varies economically from the shrinking rust belt cities of Aliquippa and Beaver Falls to comfortable Pittsburgh suburbs. Nearly three-fourths of the population is in Allegheny County. The remainder is all of Beaver County and the southwest corner of Butler in Cranberry Township. In the court-ordered redistricting in 2018, Republican-leaning areas in northern Westmoreland County plus Johnstown-based Cambria that were in the old 12th District were removed. The 17th added large parts of the western and southern Allegheny suburbs. Those changes made the new district virtually a political toss-up. President Donald Trump lost to Joe Biden, 51%-48%.

The 2018 redistricting changes were part of a long-running evolution in the region. It reversed recent gains by Republicans in the old 12th District and elsewhere in southwest Pennsylvania, which were abetted by the GOP-controlled redistricting in 2012 that had been a disaster for Democrats. The four seats that Democrats held in the southwest corner in 2002 were reduced to one a decade later. The southwest corner likely faces a few more twists as the state loses a seat in the 2022 redistricting.

Mike Doyle (D)

Elected 1994, 14th term, b. Aug 05, 1953; Swissvale, PA; PA State University, B.S., 1975; Roman Catholic; Married (Susan Erlandson Doyle); 4 children.

Elected Office: Swissvale Borough Council, 1977-1981.

Professional Career: Ins. agent, 1975-1977; Executive Director, Turtle Creek Valley Citizens Union, 1977-1979; Chief of Staff, PA Sen. Frank Pecora, 1979-1994; Co-founder/owner, Eastgate Ins. Agency, 1983-present.

DC Office: 306 CHOB 20515, 202-225-2135, Fax: 202-225-3084, doyle.house.gov

Committees: *Energy & Commerce*: Communications & Technology (Chmn); Energy.

Group Ratings

	ADA	ACLU	AFL-CIO	LCV	COC	HAFA	ACU	CFG	FRC
2020	**	86%	**	95%	-	0%	13%	**	-
2019	95%	C	95%	97%	52%	C	13%	19%	0%

Almanac Ratings 2019-2020

	Economy	Social	Foreign	Composite
Liberal	100%	100%	80%	94%
Conservative	0%	0%	20%	6%

Key Votes of the 116th Congress

1. U.S./Mex./Can. trade deal Y	5. Russia sanctions N/A	9. Firearms background checks Y
2. First Coronavirus response Y	6. Troops in Syria Y	10. Spending at the border Y
3. HEROES Act Y	7. Veto arms sales to Saudis Y	11. Marijuana liberalized rules Y
4. CASH Act Y	8. Defense $$$, veto override Y	12. Electoral College objections N

Election Results

Election	Name (Party)	Vote (%)		Cand. Spent	Ind. Exp. Support	Ind. Exp. Oppose
2020 General	Mike Doyle (D)	266,084	(69%)	$831,483	$3,260	$158
	Luke Negron (R)	118,163	(31%)	$49,485	$158	
2020 Primary	Mike Doyle (D)	90,353	(67%)			
	Jerry Dickinson (D)	44,170	(33%)			

Prior winning percentages: 2016 (74%), 2014 (100%), 2012 (76.9%), 2010 (69%), 2008 (91%), 2006 (90%), 2004 (100%), 2002 (100%), 2000 (69%), 1998 (68%), 1996 (56%), 1994 (55%)

Mike Doyle, an ardently pro-labor Democrat first elected in 1994, has become a senior member of the Energy and Commerce Committee, where he has shown deal-making skills. As chairman of the subcommittee handling communications and technology issues, a priority has been a bill to restore "net neutrality" regulations designed to impose restrictions on use of the spectrum, which Republicans had repealed. His work on these issues plays well with his district's growing tech interests.

Of Irish and Italian descent, Doyle grew up in the Monongahela Valley town of Swissvale and worked in steel mills during summers off from Penn State. He became an insurance agent and was elected to the Swissvale Borough Council at age 24. In 1978, he became chief of staff to state Sen. Frank Pecora, a Republican. In 1994, Doyle, who followed his boss in switching to the Democratic Party, ran for the House seat vacated by Republican Rep. Rick Santorum, who was elected to the Senate. With endorsements from labor unions and community leaders, he won the seven-candidate primary. In November, he faced John McCarty, an aide to the late Republican Sen. John Heinz. McCarty was pro-abortion rights and Doyle opposed abortion rights—a sign of the change since he was first elected. In a Republican year, Doyle won 55%-45%.

Doyle initially had a mixed voting record, often on the right on cultural issues. Over the years, he became more of a progressive populist. His Almanac vote ratings have been almost uniformly liberal. As a pro-life Catholic, he helped broker the deal on abortion during the final days of the 2010 health care debate that brought on board other anti-abortion members of his party. When Republicans regained control, he complained that GOP budgets would "eviscerate" social services.

On Energy and Commerce, his focus has been on high-tech initiatives, including the need for broadband services in underserved areas. On the Communications and Technology Subcommittee, he has supported policies such as modernized 911 services, greater competition for devices and services, and what he sees as protection of the open internet. In 2017, Doyle joined other senior Democrats calling for the Federal Communications Commission to investigate Russian media interference in the 2016 election. In 2018, he called for a federal agency to assure that social-media companies make proper use of data. Recent abuses, he said, have shown that "self-regulation hasn't worked."

Seeking to restore "net neutrality" rules that Democrats had approved at the FCC during the Obama administration but that Republicans repealed when they took control in 2017, he called his bill the "Save the Internet Act." It would prohibit internet service providers from creating tiered services with different pricing and service options. His legislation "puts consumers first by once again putting a cop on the beat at the FCC," Doyle said. Most Republicans opposed the proposal. "This commonsense legislation would recodify an ethical practice that protects consumers from corporate malfeasance and ensures that all information is equally accessible online," the Pittsburgh Post-Gazette wrote in an April 2019 editorial.

During the 2009 debate over cap-and-trade legislation, which would have capped carbon emissions while allowing companies to trade emissions credits, he vigorously advocated the interests of steel and other job-creating Rust Belt industries, even as he worked out a compromise with environmentalists. The House-passed bill died in the Senate, largely because of opposition from Rust Belt Democrats. With other Democrats on Energy and Commerce, Doyle filed in January 2020 the CLEAN Future Act, which would require a 100 percent clean-energy economy by 2050. Although progressive Democrats contend that their "Green New Deal" would reach that goal years earlier, Doyle and his allies highlight that their plan includes more detailed steps.

Doyle has worked to reduce foreign imports. During debate over the Keystone XL pipeline, he unsuccessfully offered an amendment that would have required at least three-quarters of the iron and steel in the pipeline to be made in North America. In 2016, Republicans defeated his effort to add a "buy America" provision to a water infrastructure bill. Doyle founded and co-chaired the House Distributed Generation Caucus, which promotes decentralized power generation technology that is fuel efficient and environmentally friendly.

He has voiced unhappiness with the lack of generational change among House Democratic leaders. Following the 2018 election, Doyle said in an interview with a public radio station in Pittsburgh that he wished Democrats had "choices" in the selection of party leaders. "A new generation of Democrats [is] ready to assume the mantle and they've been blocked from doing that," he said.

Doyle has been politically untouchable at home. In 2018, he was challenged in the Democratic primary by Janis Brooks, a community activist and former pastor. Doyle got 76 percent in that contest. Two years later, Doyle had a primary challenge from Jerry Dickinson, a University of Pittsburgh law professor who advocated more immediate solutions for climate change and said it was "time for change." In contrast to Brooks, who spent less than $5,000, Dickinson spent $259,000. Doyle, who spent $1 million, won 67%-33%. In November, he won with 69 percent.

PA-18: Allegheny County   **Cook Partisan Voting Index: D+13**

Population		Race and Ethnicity		Income	
Total	693,858	White	73.50%	Median Income	$58,743
Land area (sq. miles)	293	Black	18.10%	District Income Rank	282
Pop/ sq mi	2,371.84	Latino	2.70%	Poverty Rate	14.10%
Born in State	75.80%	Asian	4.30%	With health insurance	95.60%
		Two or more races	3.30%	Cash public assistance	3.90%
Age Groups		Other	0.80%	Food stamp/SNAP	15.20%
Under 18	17.60%				
18-34	27.90%	**Education**		**Work**	
35-64	35.80%	H.S grad or less	33.10%	White Collar	48.30%
Over 64	18.80%	Some College	26.90%	Sales and Service	36.70%
		College Degree, 4 yr	22.60%	Blue Collar	14.90%
Military		Post grad	17.30%	Government	11.20%
Veteran/ Active Duty	6.60%				

2020 Pres. Vote	Biden	252,857	(64%)	Trump	134,830	(34%)		
2016 Pres. Vote	Clinton	225,321	(62%)	Trump	125,266	(34%)	Johnson	7,903	(2%)

Pittsburgh metro: The Golden Triangle is the inevitable focus of Pittsburgh, the tip of land where the Allegheny and Monongahela rivers come together to form the Ohio. It has been a strategic site for more than 250 years. During the French and Indian War, British Gen. Edward Braddock's army was heading to Fort Duquesne, with George Washington helping lead the way, when it was ambushed and famously defeated in 1754. A few years later, the first American city west of the Appalachian chain was carved out of the wilderness and named after the English statesman William Pitt. Pittsburgh did nicely when railroads became ascendant because rail lines tend to run along the riverside. Then Andrew Carnegie, a Scottish immigrant, foresaw that steel would replace iron for railroad bridges. He built a steel factory in Pittsburgh, one blessed with ready deposits of coal and access to iron ore via the Great Lakes. Carnegie built his capacity to the point that when he sold out in 1901, the resulting U.S. Steel Corp. held a near-monopoly.

As the steel industry and other blue-collar industries contracted over the years, so did Pittsburgh. In 1940, it was the nation's 10th largest city, with 672,000 people. In 2019, it was the 66th largest, with 300,000. The population loss has been easing, with an increase in young people. Economic diversity helped Pittsburgh survive the recession better than other Rust Belt cities. The University of Pittsburgh Medical Center is the largest employer in the region. Carnegie Mellon University has been a pioneer in machine-learning technologies, including for self-driving cars. The city has a rich cultural heritage. The predominantly African-American Hill District inspired playwright August Wilson's chronicles. The Brookings Institution in 2017 ranked Pittsburgh third among 100 metro areas in a combination of productivity, wage increases and standard of living.

In February 2018, a columnist for Bloomberg described the city as a "growing mecca for millennials" who enjoy "an art scene, fashionable neighborhoods and a lively downtown."Still, grim events intrude. In October 2018, a gunman killed 11 Jewish worshippers at a Sabbath service inside the sanctuary of a synagogue in upscale Squirrel Hill. The economic slowdown caused by the pandemic led U.S. Steel to idle its blast furnace in Braddock, laying off 2,700 workers at least temporarily.

The 18th Congressional District of Pennsylvania includes Pittsburgh and the mostly working-class suburbs to the east, south and west. All of it is in Allegheny County. The district remains safely Democratic, but the 2018 redistricting reduced by a few percentage points the Democratic vote in the old 14th District. The Pittsburgh neighborhoods it lost—chiefly in areas to the west (such as Green Tree and Carnegie) and north (Penn Hills and Verona) of downtown—shifted to the new 17th to boost Democrats and make that district more competitive. In return, the district smoothed out some missing pieces from the southeastern part of Allegheny County. For Joe Biden, the city took on added prominence. It hosted his first campaign rally in April 2019 and his final election-eve rally in

November 2020. He returned in March 2021 to unveil his infrastructure plan. He won the district, 64%-34%.

RHODE ISLAND

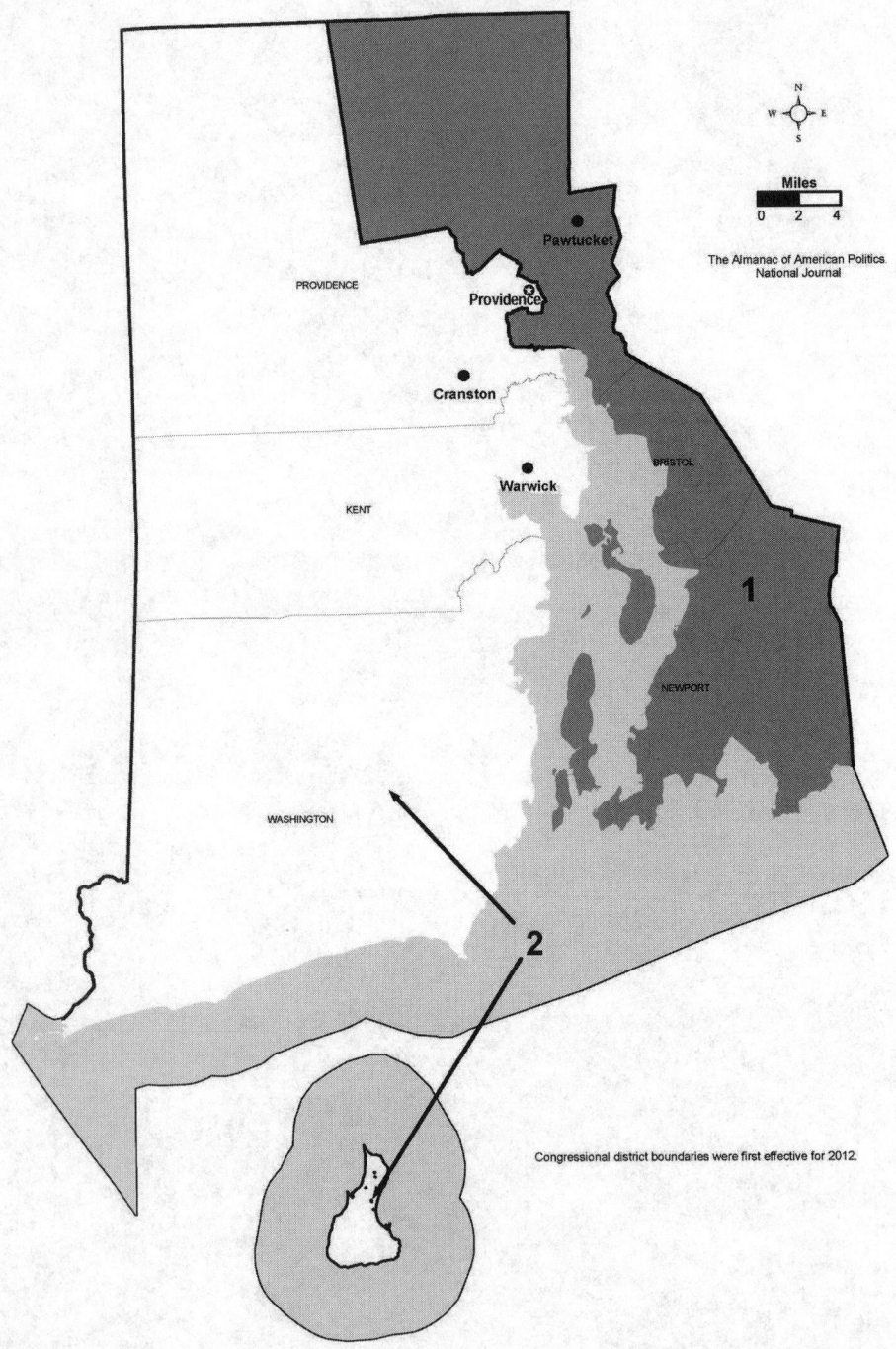

PROVIDENCE

Pawtucket

Providence

Cranston

BRISTOL

Warwick

KENT

NEWPORT

WASHINGTON

2

1

The Almanac of American Politics
National Journal

Miles
0   2   4

Congressional district boundaries were first effective for 2012.

Rhode Island has a lopsidedly Democratic legislature and a Democratic governor, and it supported Joe Biden for president by more than 20 points. But more so than in almost any other blue state, Rhode Island's Democratic party is so dominant that it has been riven by a bitter dispute between ideological factions.

"Little Rhody," the nation's smallest state in size, has often been set apart, with a turbulent history. It was founded by Roger Williams as a refuge for religious dissenters—"the sewer of New England," as the Puritan Cotton Mather put it. It has been a successful trading community since the late 17th century and a leader in manufacturing since Samuel Slater replicated from memory an English water-powered cotton textile mill in Pawtucket in 1791. Rhode Island profited from slavery (two-thirds of America's slaves arrived from Africa on ships owned by Rhode Islanders) and war (the state boomed during the Civil War), and it carried its tradition of tolerating just about anything into its politics. Rhode Island refused to pay its share for the Revolutionary War and declined to send delegates to the 1787 Constitutional Convention. It delayed joining the union until the other 12 states already had.

In the 1930s, Rhode Island had something resembling a political revolution. Thousands of immigrants from Ireland, Italy, Portugal and French Canada came to the state to work in textile mills, and the colony founded by dissident Protestants became the most heavily Catholic state in the nation –more than 40percent in the recent estimates, three quarters of whom are non-Hispanic whites. Yankee Republicans tried to appeal to Catholics by running French Canadians for office. But national events—including Catholic Democrat Al Smith's presidential candidacy in 1928 and Franklin Roosevelt's New Deal—moved Catholic voters toward the Democrats. Then came a revolution. In 1935, although they had won only 20 of the 42 state Senate seats, Democrats under Gov. Theodore Green refused to seat two Republicans. With the lieutenant governor breaking the tie, they voted Democrats into the seats and proceeded in 14 minutes to declare the state Supreme Court vacant, to abolish state boards that controlled Democratic cities, to increase the power of the governor, and to reorganize state government to purge Republicans. The uprising of the 1930s ended the political control of Rhode Island's "Five Families"—the Browns, Metcalfs, Goddards, Lippitts and Chafees—who owned or ran many of the textile mills, the Rhode Island Hospital Trust (long the largest bank), the Providence Journal-Bulletin, Brown University, the Rhode Island School of Design and the state Republican Party. Democrats have won most elections since. (Speaking of influential Rhode Island families, Ray Patriarca ran much of New England's organized crime from the 1950s to the 1980s from Coin-o-Matic Distributors on Atwells Avenue in Providence.)

Rhode Island today has a diverse ethnic and racial mix: 6 percent Black, 17 percent Hispanic and 3 percent Asian. The white population includes substantial numbers of Irish, Italian, French, and French Canadian residents, as well those of Portuguese ancestry, many from the Azores. But if the population is diverse, it has been extremely slow-growing in recent years, increasing by 4.3 percent since 2010; the only one of Rhode Island's five counties to gain population during the decade was Providence, which includes the state capital. This slow growth created local fears that Rhode Island would drop to one House seat for the coming decade—the first time in more than two centuries that the state's representation would have been so small. But the Census Bureau's April 2021 announcement of statewide population totals showed that the state narrowly retained its second House seat. Rhode Island is also disproportionately old. Only three other states—New England neighbors Maine, Vermont, and New Hampshire—have a smaller percentage of children than Rhode Island.

Rhode Island has experienced a long and often painful economic transformation, from blue collar to white collar, and from textiles toward technology. In the early 1990s, the state suffered job losses when the naval air base at Quonset Point and the state's costume jewelry manufacturers shed jobs; neighboring Massachusetts, with a more educated population and a much bigger high-tech sector, surged ahead. All told, Rhode Island has lost 60 percent of its manufacturing jobs in the past 30 years. Toy giant Hasbro floated the idea of leaving its headquarters in Pawtucket, though the company eventually decided to stay. Rhode Island has consistently ranked last or near last in CNBC's annual rankings of best states for business, based on its troubled finances and pension system, its aging infrastructure, and its relatively high cost of living.(The pension system's health has been improving thanks to 2011 reforms pushed by then-Treasurer, and later Governor, Gina Raimondo.) Today, one of every seven children live in poverty, slightly behind Maine for the highest rate in New England. On a per capita basis, Rhode Island has about twice the rate of child

United States as a whole. The state has taken over the Providence School System; in 2019, the Johns Hopkins Institute for Education Policy issued a searing indictment of the system, citing evidence of vermin, lead paint, asbestos, bureaucratic dysfunction, and low academic achievement. The state also struggled with the coronavirus, due in part to its density; the per capita case rate soared during the fall and winter of 2020, and while it fell in early 2021, the case and mortality rates remained among the highest in the country by March 2021.

On the upside, Rhode Island's median income ranks in the top one-third of states, and it has attracted investment in the biosciences, such as an Amgen manufacturing plant in the Providence suburbs and a Rubius Therapeutics facility in Smithfield, though neighboring Massachusetts remains a bigger tech hub. After Pawtucket lost the Boston Red Sox AAA farm team to Worcester Massachusetts, officials announced a $400 million project anchored by a professional soccer stadium, a sports center and hotel, partly funded by state dollars. Rhode Island became home to the nation's first operational offshore wind farm, a 30-megawatt project off Block Island. One economic bright spot is the state's calamari industry, which received national attention with a cameo during a roll call vote during the 2020 Democratic National Convention. Calamari's path to becoming the official "state appetizer" in 2014 attracted a surprising amount of controversy from partisans of the quahog, a clam, but the state's squid catch has reached 22 million pounds and $28 million a year in value.

The anti-corruption group Coalition for Integrity rates Rhode Island's ethics laws among the strongest in the country, yet Rhode Island is sometimes called "Rogues Island" for its history of public corruption. No political figure embodied Rhode Island's spotty ethical history better than Buddy Cianci, the Providence mayor who spent time in a "federally funded gated community" for assaulting with a fire log a man whom he accused of having an affair with his wife. Later, after becoming a radio talk show host, Cianci was reelected mayor in 1990, before resigning again amid federal racketeering charges that ultimately led to another conviction. Cianci died in 2016.

Rhode Island has backed the Democrat in every presidential election following Ronald Reagan's 49-state landslide in 1984. Democrats currently hold all of Rhode Island's four seats in Congress, with Sens. Jack Reed and Sheldon Whitehouse well-positioned to hold on as long as their Democratic predecessors Green, John Pastore and Claiborne Pell (24,24 and 36 years, respectively). Republicans have done better with the governor's office. Starting in 1994, Republicans Lincoln Almond and Donald Carcieri were elected governor two times each; in 2010, Lincoln Chafee, former Republican Sen. John Chafee's son, was elected as an independent. It wasn't until 2014 that Democrats returned to the governor's chair, as Raimondo, the state's first female governor, won the office. Despite never attaining high popularity, Raimondo easily secured a second term in 2018before being tapped by President Joe Biden as Commerce secretary.

Explaining the Democrats' dominance in Rhode Island requires some important caveats. The party has become so strong in the state that its big tent has experienced some rips and tears. Tensions have flared between a restive progressive wing and the more moderate Democratic establishment that, with the support of the influential Catholic Church, has opposed legislation expanding abortion rights and assisted suicide. Rhode Island is the rare Democratic state where many legislative Democrats are pro-life; many have also been aligned with the National Rifle Association. The party, led for years by influential House Speaker Nicholas Mattiello, took heat for backing moderate candidates in the Democratic primary, including one who had supported Donald Trump for president in 2016; after some federal and statewide Democrats officeholders expressed their displeasure, the party backed down from some of the endorsements. Progressive candidates ended up making incremental gains in the 2018 elections, and Mattiello declared himself after the election to be "the firewall" against "ultra left-wing groups." Mattiello opposed legislative efforts to preserve abortion rights if Roe v. Wade were overturned, but the measure passed anyway. In 2019, the state Democratic Party sought to stop its women's caucus from endorsing candidates and making statements as a group without approval from the state party chairman; the women responded by forming an independent group, the Rhode Island Democratic Women's Caucus. In the 2020 Democratic primaries, the progressive wing made even bigger gains in the legislature, and in the general election, Mattiello lost his legislative seat to a Republican. Although Mattiello's defeat created opportunities, a Trumpified GOP could end up seeing its meager number of legislators decline further; the Democrats' big tent will be ready to accept the disaffected, but an even bigger tent could become even messier.

In the 2020 presidential election, Biden won Rhode Island by almost 21 points, an improvement on Hillary Clinton's 15.5-point victory in 2016 but a decline from President Barack Obama's 28-point win in 2012. Biden won all five counties, flipping Kent County (Warwick), which had narrowly backed Trump in 2016. In the same election, voters, by a 53%-47% margin, approved a ballot measure to eliminate "Providence Plantations" from the state's official name, a decade after a similar effort had failed by a large margin. While the term "plantation" generically meant "colony" in early Rhode Island, the word's later connection to slavery caused unease among some and drove the effort to remove it—and in some ways amounted to a delayed symbolic reckoning with the state's role in the slave trade centuries before.

Population		Race and Ethnicity		Income	
Total	1,059,361	White	78.70%	Median Income	71,169
Land area (sq. miles)	1,034	Black	7.40%	State Income Rank	15 out of 50
Pop/ sq mi	1,024.72	Latino	16.30%	Poverty Rate	10.80%
Born in state	56.60%	Asian	4.50%	With health insurance	95.90%
Age Groups		Two or more races	4.20%	Cash public assistance	3.90%
Under 18	19.20%	Other	6.20%	Food stamp/SNAP	16.1%
18-34	24.30%	**Education**		**Work**	
35-64	38.80%	H.S grad or less	39.10%	White Collar	42.20%
Over 64	17.70%	Some college	26.00%	Sales and Service	38.80%
Military		College Degree, 4 yr	20.90%	Blue Collar	18.90%
Veteran/ Active Duty	6.20%	Post grad	13.90%	Government	13.40%

Presidential Politics

2020 Primary (D)	Biden (D)	79,728(77%)	Sanders (D)	15,525(15%)			
2020 Pres. Vote	Biden (D)	307,486(59%)	Trump (R)	199,922(39%)			
2016 Pres. Vote	Clinton (D)	252,525(54%)	Trump (R)	180,543(39%)	Johnson (L)	14,746 (3%)

Rhode Island has been one of the most Democratic states in presidential elections. Joe Biden easily beat President Donald Trump 59%-39%, a five-point net improvement over Hillary Clinton's performance, though it lagged behind Barack Obama's 63%-35% victories in both 2008 and 2012. No Republican candidate has cracked 40 percent of the presidential vote since George H.W. Bush did it in 1988. Voter registration split 43 percent Democratic, 43 percent independent and 14 percent Republican as of early 2021. Rhode Island is also the most Catholic state in the country. White ethnic voters dominate the political culture of the state and places like Johnston, North Providence, West Warwick and Woonsocket can tilt more Republican for a candidate who is conservative on social issues and crime, but is not opposed to forced union membership and growing the social safety net.

Biden bested Clinton's numbers in all five of the state's counties—and carried all five of them after Trump had narrowly won Kent County (Warwick) in 2016. The biggest swing toward Biden came in Newport County, which he carried 64%-34%, an 11-point improvement over Clinton's performance. He defeated Trump in the capital city of Providence 80%-18%. Trump carried a handful of inland townships, but Biden won every coastal township in the state.

Rhode Island used to hold a presidential primary in early-to-mid March, but in 2011 the state legislature moved the date back in hopes of increasing its relevance in a regional Eastern states primary. The state succeeded somewhat in 2016: In the final days before the April 26 primary, all four of the top contenders campaigned in Rhode Island. Trump defeated Ohio Gov. John Kasich 64%-24%, while Vermont Sen. Bernie Sanders defeated Clinton 55%-43%. In 2020, the state postponed its primary because of the coronavirus, and it was uncontested in June, with Biden winning 77%-15% over Sanders.

Congressional Districts

117th Congress Lineup	2D	116th Congress Lineup	2D

To local surprise and relief, Rhode Island got good news when the Census Bureau statewide population reports showed that it barely retained its second seat when the Commerce Department delivered the decennial reapportionment results in April 2021. That avoided the prospect of a bitter showdown between the two veteran House Democrats—David Cicilline and Jim Langevin—and created the welcome opportunity for each to continue his growing influence in the House. Langevin, in particular, had been considering new opportunities for his political career—though he lost one option with the March 2021 succession of Dan McKee to replace two-term Gov. Gina Raimondo after she was confirmed as Commerce Secretary for President Joe Biden. Ironically, with the Census Bureau in her department, Raimondo was the first to share the good news with her home state.

Although Langevin has served in the House a decade longer, Cicilline is three years older. In the event of a matchup, Cicilline—the former mayor of Providence—appeared to have the stronger local base. Now, the two have at least another decade in which they can assert growing clout in the House before they face the possibility of musical chairs in which one of them loses his seat.

Dan McKee (D)

Appointed 2021, term expires 2023, 1st term; b. Jun. 16, 1951, Cumberland, RI; Assumption College, B.A., 1973; Harvard University, M.P.A., 2005; Catholic; Married (Susan); 2 children.

Elected Office: Mayor, Town of Cumberland, 2007-2015; Lt. Governor, State of RI, 2015-2021.

Professional Career: VP, McKee Brothers Oil Corporation.

Office: 82 Smith St. Providence, 02903; 401-222-2371; Fax: 401-222-2012; Website: ri.gov

Lt. Gov.: Sabina Matos (D) **Atty. Gen:** Peter Neronha (D) **Sec. of State:** Nellie Gorbea (D)

State Legislature: Senate: 33D, 5R **House:** 66D, 9R

Election Results

Election	Name (Party)	Vote (%)
2018 General	Gina Raimondo (D)	198,122 (53%)
	Allan Fung (R)	139,932 (37%)
	Joseph Trillo (I)	16,532 (4%)
	Bill Gilbert (Mod)	10,155 (3%)
2018 Primary	Gina Raimondo (D)	67,370 (57%)
	Matt Brown (D)	39,518 (34%)
	Spencer Dickinson (D)	10,987 (9%)

Prior winning percentage: Lt. Governor: 2018 (62%), 2014 (54%)

Dan McKee was elevated to governor of Rhode Island in March 2021 after two-term Gov. Gina Raimondo, a fellow Democrat, was tapped by President Joe Biden as Commerce secretary and confirmed by the Senate. McKee was little known in the state before becoming governor, partly because Rhode Island's lieutenant governorship is relatively powerless; he is expected to run for a full term in 2022, likely as a moderate facing off against more progressive rivals in the Democratic-dominated state.

McKee graduated from Cumberland High School, then earned a bachelor's degree in political science from Assumption College in Worcester Massachusetts and a master's in public administration from Harvard University's Kennedy School of Government. He went into business, owning and operating a heating oil firm, a real estate brokerage, and a fitness center. He also coached youth basketball, which he had played in high school. McKee served two terms on the Cumberland Town

Council, and then defeated the incumbent mayor in a primary. He was later ousted as mayor before regaining the office; in all, he served six terms as Cumberland's mayor. McKee was a champion of mayoral academies, which are like charter schools, and he served as a board member of Blackstone Valley Prep.

In 2014, McKee ran for lieutenant governor, an office that was coming open as Republican Elizabeth Roberts was term-limited out. (In Rhode Island, lieutenant governors run on their own, rather than as part of a ticket.) McKee won 43 percent of the Democratic primary vote, outpacing the outgoing secretary of state, Ralph Mollis, who won 36 percent, and state Rep. Frank Ferri, who won 21 percent. Mollis was better known than McKee, but he was hampered by fallout from the controversy over 38 Studios, an ill-fated, state-backed video game enterprise headed by former Boston Red Sox pitcher Curt Schilling. While McKee's advocacy for charter schools made him an enemy of the state's influential teachers' unions, Mollis and Ferri ended up dividing the pro-union vote. In the general election, McKee faced Republican Catherine Terry Taylor, a former aide to moderate former Sens. John Chafee and Lincoln Chafee. Taylor made a cross-party play for labor support, but McKee won, 54%-34%, with candidates from the Moderate and Libertarian parties taking the rest of the vote.

McKee's first term was largely quiet, focusing on such issues as the opioid crisis, workforce training for small businesses, assistance for people with Alzheimer's, and electricity costs. When he ran for reelection in 2018, McKee nearly lost the Democratic primary; in an increasingly common pattern in Rhode Island, the primary involved a face-off between a moderate (McKee) and a progressive (state Rep. J. Aaron Regunberg). Regunberg, a 28-year-old who had cut his teeth as an activist while attending Brown University, won the endorsement of Sen. Bernie Sanders of Vermont, while McKee won the backing of Sen. Jack Reed, a pillar of Rhode Island's Democratic establishment. In the end, McKee held on by fewer than 2,500 votes, largely on the strength of his support from minority and working-class voters. During his second term, McKee paid a $250 fine after the Ethics Commission cited his failure to disclose a trip to Taiwan that had been paid for by an affiliate of the Taiwanese government.

In the run-up to his elevation to governor, McKee had little contact with Raimondo. The two reportedly didn't see each other in person for more than a year, and McKee was reduced to asking capitol police officers to deliver letters to her office. During the coronavirus pandemic, Raimondo won some plaudits for her early efforts to control the virus, but she took more flak as the pandemic wore on and Rhode Island had the highest infection rate in the nation outside the Dakotas. McKee had almost no official role in fighting the virus, and before taking office he took a shot at her handling of the crisis. "Like most Rhode Islanders, I am not satisfied with the current administration's progress on vaccine distribution, especially as we see our neighbors in Connecticut ranked among the top in the nation," he said in a statement. "Rhode Island has much more work to do to get shots in arms quickly and efficiently." At a press briefing, Raimondo was asked whether she'd had any substantive discussions with McKee. "Not often," she acknowledged. McKee, for his part, framed himself as a "backup quarterback ... that's not part of a team. I don't even have a uniform." McKee did win appreciation from his old adversaries, the teachers' unions, when he urged that educators receive priority for coronavirus vaccinations.

After taking office, McKee urged a phase-out of the auto tax and legalization of recreational marijuana. He also prepared to negotiate a new contract with teachers in the Providence school system, which was in the midst of a state takeover. Meanwhile, McKee faced a legislature he had never served in, and which was to his left ideologically.

McKee's best hope for winning the governorship in 2022 would be to occupy the Democratic Party's moderate lane and watch as more progressive challengers split up the remainder of the vote. But the Democratic primary field could include some strong rivals—Secretary of State Nellie M. Gorbea, Treasurer Seth Magaziner, and Providence Mayor Jorge O. Elorza, among them. To McKee's relief, reapportionment preserved its second congressional seat for Rhode Island, which meant that Rep. James Langevin no longer had an interest in running for governor instead of being forced into a member-vs.-member contest against Rep. David Cicilline. Possible Republican contenders include Cranston Mayor Allan Fung, House Minority Leader Blake Filippi, and Moderate Party founder-turned-Republican Ken Block. But whoever wins the Democratic nomination will start as the favorite in the general election.

Jack Reed (D)

Elected 1996, term expires 2026, 5th term, b. Nov 12, 1949; Cranston, RI; La Salle Academy, 1967; U.S. Military Academy, B.S., 1971; Harvard University John F. Kennedy School of Government, M.P.P., 1973; Harvard University School of Law, J.D., 1982; Roman Catholic; Married (Julia Hart Reed); 1 child.

Military Career: U.S. Army 1967-1979; U.S. Army Reserve 1979-1991

Elected Office: RI Senate, 1985-1991; U.S. House, 1991-1997.

Professional Career: Associate Professor, U.S Military Academy at West Point, 1977-1979; Practicing attorney, Southerland, Asbill & Brennan, Edwards & Angell, 1982-1990.

DC Office: 728 HSOB 20510, 202-224-4642, Fax: 202-224-4680, reed.senate.gov
State Offices: Cranston, 401-943-3100; Providence, 401-528-5200.

Committees: *Appropriations*: Commerce, Justice, Science & Related Agencies; Department of Defense; Department of the Interior, Environment & Related Agencies; DOL, HHS & Education & Related Agencies; Legislative Branch (Chmn); Military Construction & Veteran Affairs & Related Agencies; Transportation, HUD & Related Agencies. *Armed Services (Chmn)*: Ex Officio membership on all subcommittees. *Banking, Housing & Urban Affairs*: Economic Policy; Housing, Transportation & Community Development; Securities, Insurance & Investment. *Intelligence*.

Group Ratings

	ADA	ACLU	AFL-CIO	LCV	COC	HAFA	ACU	CFG	FRC
2020	-	92%	-	100%	-	0%	4%	-	-
2019	100%	C	100%	100%	32%	C	3%	0%	0%

Almanac Ratings 2019-2020

	Economy	Social	Foreign	Composite
Liberal	90%	90%	67%	82%
Conservative	10%	10%	33%	18%

Key Votes of the 116th Congress

1. EPA clean energy rules	Y	5. Russia sanctions	Y	9. Barr as Atty. General	N
2. U.S./Mex./Can. trade deal	N	6. Troops in SYR, AFG	Y	10. Spending at the border	Y
3. Cut unemployment benefits	N	7. Veto arms sales to Saudis	Y	11. Coney Barrett to Sup. Ct.	N
4. Shelton to Fed Reserve	N	8. Defense $$$, veto override	Y	12. Electoral College objections	N

Election Results

Election	Name (Party)	Vote (%)		Cand. Spent	Ind. Exp. Support	Ind. Exp. Oppose
2020 General	Jack Reed (D)	328,574	(66%)	$2,228,072	$113	
	Allen Waters (R)	164,855	(33%)	$19,661		$113
2020 Primary	Jack Reed (D)	65,859	(100%)			

Prior winning percentages: 2014 (71%), 2008 (73%), 2002 (78%), 1996 (63%), House: 1994 (68%), 1992 (71%), 1990 (59%)

During nearly a quarter of a century in the Senate, Democrat Jack Reed, Rhode Island's senior senator, has been among that chamber's most respected policy wonks, making his influence felt on banking issues and, most prominently, national security matters. In early 2021, Reed became chairman of the Armed Services Committee after his party gained a narrow Senate majority; it put him in charge of a panel with jurisdiction over half of the federal government's annual discretionary budget. Reed is a graduate of the United States Military Academy—among only eight senators in history with a degree from West Point—and one of the few senators of his generation with military experience. He has largely operated within the Senate's longstanding tradition of bipartisanship on defense matters, although he found his ability to do so strained during the tenure of President Donald Trump.

Reed has accumulated a reliably liberal voting record while representing one of the nation's bluest states—including opposing the 2002 resolution that authorized the war in Iraq. But, with Joe Biden as president, Reed was expected to temper demands from his party's left wing for large reductions in the Defense Department. "I think there are issues where Jack Reed might be a little bit of a foil to some of the progressive orthodoxy that's going on in the Democratic Party right now, because if he's not a centrist, he holds mainstream national security views that aren't necessarily aligned with folks who want to cut the defense budget by 10 percent across the board," one Senate Armed Services Committee staffer told Defense News. In fact, when Vermont Sen. Bernie Sanders unsuccessfully proposed such an amendment in the summer of 2020, Reed parted ways with Senate Democratic leaders to oppose it. "This across-the-board approach, it's good for a headline, it's good to make a point, but we're here to make policy," Reed said in a floor speech.

As the top Democrat on Armed Services since 2015, Reed collaborated closely with Republican John McCain of Arizona—who chaired the panel until his death in August 2018. McCain and Reed enjoyed a highly respectful partnership, based partly on common experience as military academy graduates with lengthy service in uniform. "We work together, never surprise each other," McCain said of Reed in a 2016 interview with Rhode Island-based WPRI. "We also happen to be good friends, which is very helpful. That's not always the case with a Republican and Democrat." Days before McCain died of cancer, Reed told NPR, "His whole demeanor was one of encouraging bipartisan participation in the committee." McCain was succeeded as chair by Oklahoma Republican James Inhofe, a more orthodox Republican than McCain; Reed told the Boston Globe he nonetheless had a "good working relationship" with Inhofe. But Reed's efforts to operate in a bipartisan manner were challenged by differences with Trump over issues ranging from the president's Middle East policies to his antagonism toward NATO allies.

Rhode Island has tended to send scions of the state's blue-blooded families to the Senate; Theodore Francis Green, Reed's predecessor once removed, traced his ancestry to colonists who arrived with Roger Williams, Rhode Island's founder, in 1636. Reed is an exception to that political pedigree: He grew up in working-class Cranston, just outside Providence, the second of three children of a school custodian and a housewife. Disappointed she never attended college, Mary Reed prepared her children for educational success. She insisted on music and art classes for Jack beginning when he was5. Her son, fascinated by history and World War II as a child, decided he wanted to attend West Point. First, he played football at LaSalle Academy, a Catholic prep school in Providence (also the alma mater of Republican Sen. Pat Toomey of Pennsylvania).

After graduating from West Point in 1971, Reed served in the 82nd Airborne Division and received a master's degree from Harvard's Kennedy School of Government. After eight years of active duty, Reed enrolled in Harvard Law School. He spent another 12 years in the Army Reserve, retiring with the rank of major in 1991. Throughout his life, he has maintained connections to West Point, teaching there briefly in the late 1970s, serving on the academy's governing board and choosing its chapel as the site of his wedding in 2005. (Reed, whom friends long joked was married to his work, married for the first time in his mid-50s. His wife, Julia Hart, was working in the Senate's Interparliamentary Services Office when she met Reed—on a congressional trip to Afghanistan.)

After graduation from law school, Reed was an associate at a Washington D.C. firm before returning to Rhode Island in 1983 to work for Providence-based Edwards & Angell, then one of the state's oldest and most prominent law firms. A year later, Reed won public office for the first time, beating an incumbent in the primary for state Senate. During his six-year tenure, he headed a commission that investigated a corruption scandal involving a state agency created to make affordable housing loans to low-income Rhode Islanders. When Republican Claudine Schneider gave up her House seat in 1990 to run against Sen. Claiborne Pell, Reed ran for Congress. He captured 49 percent of the vote in a four-way Democratic primary. In the general election, he won 59%-41%.

In 1995, when Pell announced his retirement, Reed had no serious competition for the Democratic nomination to succeed him. State Treasurer Nancy Mayer was his general election opponent. National Republicans spent nearly $1 million on ads attacking Reed as a liberal for opposing bills requiring welfare recipients to work and supporting labor unions—not especially harmful charges in largely liberal, heavily unionized Rhode Island. Reed outspent Mayer by well over 3-1. His biography was his message: He launched his campaign in a public school conference room named for his late father, stressed his rise from a working-class background, and called for education spending to help others achieve the same success. He won 63%-35% and has not had serious competition since, winning with more than 70 percent of the vote in his first three reelection bids. In November 2020, Reed won a fifth term by defeating Allen Waters—a Black Republican who had returned to Rhode Island from neighboring Massachusetts less than a year earlier to run. Reed won 66%-33%, running ahead of the party's presidential nominee, Biden, who beat Trump 59%-39%.

His influence in the national security arena has been such that former Defense Secretary Robert Gates said Reed was instrumental in persuading him to remain in the post under President Barack Obama after initially being appointed by President George W. Bush. "In terms of reaching out to me, and whether I would stay on, Obama couldn't have picked a person I was more willing to listen to or respected more than Jack," Gates later told Rhode Island Monthly. Reed—on at least two occasions when Obama was president—rejected opportunities to become Defense secretary. One occurred just after the 2014 election, when Defense Secretary Chuck Hagel was eased out. A Reed spokesman told the Providence Journal at that time that Reed "has made it very clear that he does not wish to be considered for secretary of Defense or any other Cabinet position. "Avoidance of such a high-profile perch is consistent with Reed's low-key persona. He rarely appears on national television and —unlike many of his Senate colleagues—tends to avoid stopping to talk with reporters at the Capitol; when he does, they often have to strain to hear what he is saying.

Obama—who developed a close relationship with Reed while serving with him in the Senate —in his 2020 memoir described the Rhode Islander as "slightly built, studious and understated." After Obama won the 2008 Democratic presidential nomination, Reed accompanied him on a trip to Iraq and Afghanistan, and Obama later considered him as a potential running mate until Reed ruled himself out. As Obama mulled strategy in Afghanistan during his first year as president, Reed expressed doubts about sending more troops and said the burden of proof was on commanders to justify a troop increase. In the final months of Obama's presidency, Reed said the president's decision to maintain U.S. troops in Afghanistan and provide support to the country's armed forces had" laid the foundation for a sustainable U.S. and international security presence in Afghanistan," and urged the incoming Trump administration to continue a "conditions-based approach" in that country. "It is critical that we not cede space or territory to Iranian influence," Reed said.

Reed has visited Afghanistan 18 times and Iraq 20 times over the past two decades, often straying from the safe zones—thanks to his military background and his close relationship with many military commanders. In a February 2019 hearing, he issued a warning amid reports that Trump was planning large cutbacks in U.S. troop levels in Afghanistan. "In considering the prospect of conflict termination, we must also weigh the cost of getting it wrong," he said. Two years later, with Biden in office, Reed spoke out against what he had earlier characterized as a "precipitous withdrawal" of troops negotiated by the Trump administration and the Taliban. He told reporters the deadline should be extended to allow more time to negotiate an agreement between the Taliban and the Afghan government. Alluding to reports of increased activity by terrorists allied to the Islamic State, Reed said, "We've got to be able to assure the world and the American public that Afghanistan will not be a source of planning, plotting to project terrorist attacks around the globe," adding: "That's the minimum. I'm not sure we can do that without some presence there."

Biden announced in early 2021 that he would withdraw all troops from Afghanistan by September11, 2021—the 20th anniversary of the terror attacks that sparked the invasion.Trump's deal with the Taliban had called for a withdrawal three months earlier, on June 1.

In March 2018, Reed was among only 10 Democratic senators who voted against a resolution that would have ended U.S. support for a Saudi-led coalition intervening in Yemen's civil war. But he reversed his position later in the year, spurred in part by the grisly killing of Saudi journalist and U.S. resident Jamal Khashoggi at the Saudi consulate in Istanbul. Echoing CIA findings, Reed called it "inconceivable" that the killing had taken place "without the direction or blessing" of Saudi Crown Prince Mohammed bin Salman and criticized Trump for having too cozy a relationship with Saudi leaders. "This outrageous [killing of Khashoggi] can't be followed by a business-as-usual arms deal," he added. In mid-2019, Reed joined a bipartisan group of senators in an effort to block the White House from utilizing emergency authority to sell$8.1 billion in arms to Saudi Arabia and the United Arab Emirates. Measures to prevent the sale cleared the Senate as well as the House, but were vetoed by Trump.

Perhaps Reed's sharpest criticism of Trump was in response to the president's moves to cut back the U.S. military presence in Europe. In July 2018, the Senate approved Reed's motion to reaffirm support for NATO 97-2; it came amid concern about Trump's ambivalence. "Our allies are starting to wonder whether they can rely on the United States to come to their defense in a crisis," Reed said. In June 2020, Trump moved to withdraw a third of the 36,000 U.S. troops stationed in Germany after complaining repeatedly that the latter nation was not contributing sufficient funding to the NATO alliance. Reed blasted the move: "It's another favor to [Russian President Vladimir] Putin and another leadership failure by this administration that further strains relations with our allies." When Trump's plan was outlined in detail a month later, Reed described it as a "self-inflicted wound," adding, "This is the type of move Secretary [James] Mattis was able to stand up to in the past, but this administration seems to be unraveling under the strain of the pandemic." It was a reference to Trump's first Pentagon chief, who had resisted moves to weaken traditional defense alliances. In April 2021, Biden not only stopped the withdrawal but increased the number of troops in Germany by 500.

At the outset of the Trump administration, Reed—to enable Mattis to serve as Defense secretary —voted for a waiver of the seven-year "cooling off" period required by law between military service and the top civilian Defense job; Mattis had retired from the military only four years earlier. Reed had vowed not to vote for such a waiver again, saying, "Waiving the law should happen no more than once in a generation." However, he changed his mind four years later when Biden nominated another retired general, Lloyd Austin, as his Defense secretary. In a statement, Reed cited "historic circumstances"—including the COVID-19 pandemic, Trump's "irresponsible efforts to hollow out the Pentagon and politicize the military," and the "unprecedented storming of the U.S. Capitol by pro-Trump extremists seeking to overturn the outcome of the presidential election." Reed said: "I backed the waiver for Gen. Mattis in large part because of Donald Trump's inexperience and temperament and had no intention of supporting another waiver so soon. That rationale seems almost quaint now, considering the seismic forces we are currently facing."

Reed has long backed efforts to permanently increase the size of the Army. While in 2012 he defended Obama's plans to shrink the size of the Army and Marines, he later expressed concern about the 2011 Budget Control Act's effect on the armed forces. That bipartisan deal created automatic spending cuts—so-called sequestration—while putting both defense and domestic spending limits in place. When Trump became president, Reed did welcome increased Pentagon spending, which has boosted jobs at General Dynamics' Electric Boat Division—a major employer in Rhode Island. While annual defense spending levels grew to $740 billion under Trump, Reed in late 2020 cautioned a group representing communities with defense facilities: "I think President Biden will send a budget up that recognizes essentially the same reality that President Trump would have to recognize, which is that the increases of the last several years are not going to be carried forward, that we're in more of a steady-state, sort of flat-line budget, and within that budget we're going to have to make savings."

After taking Armed Services gavel, Reed spoke of the need to examine potential cuts in "legacy" weapons programs and facilities. "It's going to be a very challenging period of time in which there are now significant strategic rivals," he told the Boston Globe. "Also, we as an institution have to demand more value in terms of what we are buying for equipment and other aspects of the military." Reed pointed to the increasing size of China's military, saying, "It requires looking at the equipment systems of the last two decades, which have been essentially focused on counter-terrorism and counter-insurgency in Iraq and Afghanistan. It requires a different mindset and equipment." In comments to Bloomberg News, Reed pointed to "the invulnerability—or the less vulnerability, I should say—of a submarine, adding, "As we operate in the Pacific, given the precision missiles the Chinese have, I think, [the] submarine looks more and more important every day. Electric Boat employs 4,000 people in his home state—mostly in submarine production at Quonset Point—and has plans announced in early 2021 to add 1,300 more jobs.

In 2009, a National Journal examination of roll call votes dating to the 1980s found Reed to be the most liberal senator, slightly ahead of Barbara Boxer of California and Ted Kennedy of Massachusetts. In recent years, he has remained among the more liberal senators in the Almanac vote ratings, particularly on economic matters. Sometimes overlooked in Reed's high-profile status as a defense expert is his grounding in financial issues. As a member of the Banking, Housing and Urban Affairs Committee, he played a key role in the crafting of the 2010 Dodd-Frank financial regulation law. The committee's chair, Connecticut Democrat Chris Dodd, asked Reed to work with New Hampshire Republican Judd Gregg. According to "Act of Congress," a book by Washington Post editor Robert Kaiser on Dodd-Frank, Reed spent months working with Gregg to craft a regulatory framework in the complex area of derivatives—financial contracts based on the value of other assets, from interest rates to corn and soybeans. "Reed was an atypical senator," Kaiser wrote. "A small, compact man with a formidable intellect, he did mountains of homework. He mastered complicated issues."

In 2008, Rhode Island was among the 10 states with the most subprime mortgage foreclosures amid the Great Recession; Reed played a quiet, but major role in securing an agreement on a foreclosure rescue bill. It included an affordable housing fund that he had been seeking for six years. More recently, as a member of the powerful Appropriations Committee, he used his position as ranking Democrat on the Subcommittee on Transportation, Housing and Urban renovation of the Amtrak station in downtown Providence. When the COVID-19 pandemic hit in early 2020, Reed helped lead efforts to include a $150 billion relief fund for states in the CARES Act. He succeeded in inserting a $1.25 billion small-state minimum—directing more aid to Rhode Island than a per capita formula would have.

Rhode Island Senate seats tend to turn over infrequently; Reed is only the third person to occupy his seat since 1937. Such seniority has translated into a number of committee chairmanships for the pocket-sized state. Green served 24 years and retired at 93; Pell served for 36, retiring at 77. Each chaired the Foreign Relations Committee. When Reed arrived in the Senate, his senior colleague, Republican John Chafee, was chairing the Environment and Public Works Committee. At 71, Reed has joined them as he wields the gavel at Armed Services—the first Rhode Islander in history to chair that panel.

Sheldon Whitehouse (D)

Elected 2006, term expires 2024, 3rd term, b. Oct 20, 1955; New York City, NY; Yale University, B.A., 1978; University of Virginia Law School, J.D., 1982; Episcopalian; Married (Sandra Thornton Whitehouse); 2 children.

Elected Office: RI Attorney General, 1999-2003.

Professional Career: RI special Assistant Attorney General, 1984-1990; Legal counsel, Governor Bruce Sundlun, 1991; Policy Director, Governor Bruce Sundlun, 1992; Director, RI Department of Business Regulation, 1992-1994; U.S Attorney for RI, 1994-1998; Practicing attorney, 2003-2006.

DC Office: 530 HSOB 20510, 202-224-2921, Fax: 202-228-6362, whitehouse.senate.gov

State Offices: Providence, 401-453-5294.

Committees: *Budget. Environment & Public Works*: Clean Air & Nuclear Safety; Fisheries, Water, and Wildlife; Transportation & Infrastructure. *Finance*: Energy, Natural Resources & Infrastructure; Health Care; Taxation & IRS Oversight (Chmn). *Judiciary*: Constitution; Criminal Justice & Counterterrorism; Federal Courts, Oversight, Agency Action & Federal Rights (Chmn); Privacy, Technology & the Law.

Group Ratings

	ADA	ACLU	AFL-CIO	LCV	COC	HAFA	ACU	CFG	FRC
2020	-	69%	-	100%	-	0%	2%	-	-
2019	95%	C	100%	86%	35%	C	2%	0%	0%

Almanac Ratings 2019-2020

	Economy	Social	Foreign	Composite
Liberal	97%	97%	67%	87%
Conservative	3%	3%	33%	13%

Key Votes of the 116th Congress

1. EPA clean energy rules	Y	5. Russia sanctions	Y	9. Barr as Atty. General	N
2. U.S./Mex./Can. trade deal	N	6. Troops in SYR, AFG	Y	10. Spending at the border	Y
3. Cut unemployment benefits	N	7. Veto arms sales to Saudis	Y	11. Coney Barrett to Sup. Ct.	N
4. Shelton to Fed Reserve	N	8. Defense $$$, veto override	Y	12. Electoral College objections	N

Election Results

Election	Name (Party)	Vote (%)		Cand. Spent	Ind. Exp. Support	Ind. Exp. Oppose
2018 General	Sheldon Whitehouse (D)	231,477	(61%)	$4,732,417	$49,716	
	Robert Flanders Jr. (R)	144,421	(38%)	$1,191,815	$155,000	
2018 Primary	Sheldon Whitehouse (D)	89,140	(77%)			
	Patricia Fontes (D)	26,947	(23%)			

Prior winning percentages: 2018 (61%), 2012 (65%), 2006 (54%)

Democrat Sheldon Whitehouse, Rhode Island's junior senator, often has relished the role of partisan attack dog. During the Trump administration, he was cheered by progressives for taking aim —in legal briefs and rhetoric— at the U.S. Supreme Court, which slid to the right with President Donald Trump's nominees . Central to Whitehouse's criticism was the role of "dark money"—cash raised by political groups not required to disclose the identity of their donors—and what Whitehouse has viewed as its compromising influence on the judicial process. His sharp critiques have drawn searing responses—including in a letter signed by all Republican senators and in a speech by one of the high court's justices.

By the same token, Whitehouse frequently has worked to reach across the political aisle on a variety of issues, foreign and domestic. He drew criticism from his left when, in 2019, he and a handful of other Democrats joined a largely Republican effort to overhaul the much-criticized congressional budget process. On the issue with which Whitehouse has been most identified during his Senate tenure —alleviating climate change—he has continually sought avenues for attracting Republican support.

The ambitions of Whitehouse, who's spent a decade and a half on Capitol Hill, were evident when Democrats regained the Senate majority in 2021.He told Roll Call that Vermont Sen. Bernie Sanders —ranking Democrat on the Budget Committee for the previous six years—"just may very well have a better offer from other committees." That would have put Whitehouse in line to chair the Budget panel—but the post went to Sanders, after other scenarios didn't play out. Then, when California Sen. Dianne Feinstein stepped down as top Democrat on the Judiciary Committee, Whitehouse—who elevated his profile during the late 2020 hearings on the Supreme Court nomination of Amy Coney Barrett—made a play for that gavel. He had the support of some progressive groups, which said he would aggressively take on committee Republicans. But he fell short again: The Judiciary post went to the more senior Illinois Sen. Dick Durbin despite Whitehouse's push for an internal caucus ruling barring Durbin from serving as both committee chair and Democratic whip.

Whitehouse is the latest in a series of senators from wealthy, blue-blooded families elected to represent predominantly working-class Rhode Island in recent decades. He is a descendant of Charles Crocker, one of California's"Big Four" who built the Central Pacific Railroad. His father, diplomat Charles Whitehouse, served as U.S. ambassador to Laos and Thailand in the 1970s. Sheldon Whitehouse was born in New York City and grew up overseas; as a teenager, he taught English to Vietnamese children in Saigon. He graduated from St. Paul's preparatory school, Yale University and the University of Virginia Law School.

Whitehouse moved to Rhode Island in 1984 to take a job as an assistant state attorney general. He was named a top staffer to Democratic Gov. Bruce Sundlun in 1991 and served two years as head of the state Department of Business Regulation under Sundlun. In 1994, on the recommendation of Democratic Sen. Claiborne Pell, a family friend, Whitehouse was appointed U.S. attorney for Rhode Island during the Clinton administration. He launched an undercover probe that culminated in the conviction of Providence Mayor Buddy Cianci on corruption charges. He also led an investigation that resulted in the largest fine in state history for an oil spill in Narragansett Bay.

In 1998, Whitehouse ran for state attorney general. In the Democratic primary, his two opponents portrayed him as an inexperienced fox-hunting patrician trying to buy his way into public office. But Whitehouse was better-known and captured the nomination with about half of the total vote. In the general election, the Republican nominee, state Treasurer Nancy Mayer, forced Whitehouse to concede he had tried drugs as a student and questioned whether he was tough enough for the job. Whitehouse later told the Providence Journal, "The book on me was, 'Smart kid, works hard, but, you know, has no common touch, can't relate to people, will be a disaster.'" But highly negative ads by Mayer on the drug issue backfired in the absence of evidence that the incident was more than a brief chapter from Whitehouse's distant past. He won 67%-33%.In 2002, despite being seen as a strong contender for governor, Whitehouse lost the primary by 926 votes after being outspent 2-1.

Not long after his election as attorney general, Whitehouse considered running for the Senate in 2000.Republican Sen. John Chafee had announced he would not seek a fifth term. But Chafee —a roommate of Whitehouse's father while they were Yale undergraduates—died in November 1999. Republican Gov. Lincoln Almond appointed the senator's son, Lincoln Chafee, then mayor of Warwick, to fill the vacancy; Whitehouse deferred his bid, and Chafee was elected to a full term.

In 2006, Whitehouse easily won the Democratic Senate primary, while Chafee faced an intraparty challenge from his right—winning 54%-46%,but with little cash remaining. The general election pitted candidates of fairly similar views who shared an upper-crust background: Chafee was heir to one of Rhode Island's most prominent families, whose members had held high office in the state going back to the 1870s. Both candidates backed abortion rights, gun control and federal funding of stem cell research. Whitehouse campaigned against the unpopular Bush administration, running ads with the tagline, "Finally, a Whitehouse in Washington you can trust." He won 54%-46%—it was the first time in 70 years a sitting Rhode Island senator had been ousted. He was among eight new Democratic senators whose election pushed the party into the majority.

In the final year of his first term, Whitehouse began delivering weekly Senate floor speeches on the dangers posed by climate change. He started the practice in April 2012 and kept it up until early 2021.In the process, he became perhaps Congress' most persistent voice on the issue. Whitehouse credited his wife, Sandra, a marine scientist, with helping him recognize the importance of oceans in everyone's lives. Speaking each week when the Senate was in session, Whitehouse—standing in front of a picture of Earth taken from space, emblazoned with words "time to wake up"—claimed never to have given the same speech twice due to breadth of the topic.

A year into the Trump administration, Whitehouse began his 200th speech by pointedly noting: "The fact that stands out for me, here at No. 200, is the persistent failure of Congress to even take up the issue of climate change. One party will not even talk about it. One party in the executive branch is even gagging America's scientists and civil servants and striking the term 'climate change' off of government websites." Three years later, in a Washington Post webcast, Whitehouse said he had advised the new administration of President Joe Biden that "the most important thing they can do now is to try to convene the American business community, which has completely sucked on climate in Congress." Of business, he added: "At best, they've been doing zero; at worst, they've been supporting really horrible trade associations that have been the worst climate obstructers in America." In a March 2019 op-ed for NBC News, Whitehouse pointed a finger at the U.S. Chamber of Commerce for what he called its "obstructive stance on climate."

Whitehouse, however, declined to sign on to the "Green New Deal" pushed by leading progressives in early 2019, telling Bloomberg Law: "I fear that those forces that vehemently oppose climate action and are constantly up to no good around here will take every opportunity to try and use something like this to divide us. We're more likely to…be effective if we stay united and work with each other rather than get into the usual Democratic circular firing squad."He sought to make a carbon dioxide emissions tax on industry more politically palatable by crafting it as revenue neutral —proposing legislation under which more than $2 trillion raised over 10 years went to corporate tax cuts and worker tax credits. Whitehouse initially introduced his plan in mid-2017 with Hawaii Democrat Brian Schatz, unveiling it before the conservative American Enterprise Institute. "Sen. Schatz and I extend an open hand—an olive limb," Whitehouse was quoted as saying by The Hill. "Find [us] a Republican to negotiate with."

In 2019, Whitehouse joined with Indiana Republican Mike Braun and West Virginia Republican Shelley Moore Capito on a bill creating a federal advisory board to propose ways to make heavy industry less carbon intensive. And, in 2020, he combined with Braun and South Carolina Republican Lindsey Graham on legislation to make it easier for farmers and forest managers to earn income through sale of credits for reducing greenhouse gas emissions from their land. It was not Whitehouse's only recent collaboration with Graham, a close ally of Trump. In early 2020, the two led the congressional delegation to the Munich Security Conference, amid a shared concern that the Trump administration was seeking to withdraw too quickly from Afghanistan. A year earlier, at the same conference, Whitehouse drafted a letter of concern over Trump's planned withdrawal of troops from northeast Syria—which Graham delivered to the White House. "That bipartisan message seemed to slow Trump's rush for the exit," Washington Post foreign affairs columnist David Ignatius later wrote.

In early 2017, Whitehouse wrote a book, Captured: The Corporate Infiltration of American Democracy. In its introduction, he wrote: "In the Senate, I see every day how power works in the political sphere. …Never in my life have I seen such a complex web of front groups sowing deliberate deceit to create public confusion about issues that should be clear. The corporate propaganda machinery is of unprecedented size and sophistication." While the book was targeted in part at the institution in which Whitehouse serves, he has increasingly taken aim at the role of "dark money" across the street from the Capitol: at the Supreme Court. "A decades long effort by big corporations and partisan donors to rig the courts using dark money is working; they've won over 80 partisan, 5-4 [Supreme Court] decisions," Whitehouse said in July 2020. He later told the Washington Post, "Right now, probably the most consequential influence-seeking in America is not done by lobbyists, it's done by people showing up in the Supreme Court and asking the Supreme Court to make decisions in their favor."

During the first round of questioning during confirmation hearings for Barrett in October 2020, Whitehouse spent the time allotted to him for a lengthy presentation of his views on this subject, telling the nominee that she needed to understand the "forces outside of this room who are pulling strings and pushing sticks and causing the puppet theater to react." In an op-ed the same month for NBC News, Whitehouse called out the "corporate-funded Federalist Society," which, he said, "is 'in-sourced' to the Trump White House";he added: "Trump admitted it picks his [judicial] nominees." He also cited a group with links to the Federalist Society, the Judicial Crisis Network, which "takes anonymous donations —some as much as $17 million—to fund political ad campaigns for those nominees' confirmations."

Whitehouse's op-ed continued, "Meanwhile, dark-money-funded private organizations hunt for plaintiffs of convenience to bring cases before the Supreme Court that advance the big donors' agenda, while other dark money-funded organizations appear at the court by the orchestrated dozen as "friends of the Court" to instruct the corporate-selected judges how to rule." The conservative targets of such criticism have responded in kind—pointing out that Whitehouse has given speeches to liberal groups benefiting from dark money and told reporters that he would accept such money himself. In early 2021, Americans for Public Trust, a conservative nonprofit, launched a six-figure ad buy, the Boston Globe reported. "Sheldon Whitehouse has a dirty little secret, the ad declared. He relentlessly attacks dark money, harping on its supposed evils. But at the same time, he's backed by liberal dark money. A lot of it."

The most furious reaction came in the summer of 2019, when five Democratic senators led by Whitehouse filed a friend of the court brief in a case brought by a New York gun owners group. The senators were seeking to preempt the Supreme Court from using the case to loosen laws on the carrying of firearms; in the brief, Whitehouse argued that because New York had changed the law in question, there was no longer a live controversy to be decided. He suggested that for the court to hear the case anyway would be to reveal a bias, writing: "The Supreme Court is not well. And the people know it. … Perhaps the Court can heal itself before the public demands it be 'restructured in order to reduce the influence of politics.'" The latter phrase was taken from an opinion poll question on which a majority of Americans agreed, the Washington Post noted.

In response, all Republicans senators signed a letter—drafted by Senate GOP Leader Mitch McConnell—to the Supreme Court's clerk, charging that Whitehouse and the other Democrats had "openly threatened this court with political retribution if it failed to dismiss the petition as moot." The justices "must not be cowed by the threats of opportunistic politicians," the letter added. In a statement, Whitehouse was defiant: "The response to our brief from Republicans and the partisan donor interests driving the court's polarization shows exactly why it's time to speak out. They want us to shut up about their capture of the court; we will not."(Borrowing from his strategy for highlighting the hazards of climate change, Whitehouse in May 2021 launched another series of floor speeches to take aim at dark money.)

In April 2020,the Supreme Court ruled the case moot by 6-3. Seven months later, one of the dissenters in that ruling, Justice Samuel Alito, slammed Whitehouse's brief in a speech to the Federalist Society. Alito called the statements in the brief "an affront to the Constitution and the rule of law," the Boston Globe reported, and compared the episode to an incident from an authoritarian country—in which a military tank pointed its gun toward a courthouse to intimidate a judge. "The Supreme Court was created by the Constitution, not by Congress," Alito said. "Under the Constitution, we exercise the judicial power of the United States. Congress has no right to interfere with that work, any more than we have the right to legislate."

The furious Republican reaction to the brief came at around the same time that Whitehouse and four other Democratic senators allied themselves with 19 Republicans in an unsuccessful push to overhaul the congressional budget process. Whitehouse went so far as to co-author a November 2019 op-ed in Roll Call with Republican Mike Enzi of Wyoming, then chairman of the Budget panel. "Our current budget process is broken, as evidenced by mounting debt and deficits, a patchwork of temporary spending bills, government shutdowns, and budgets that, if passed at all, are quickly ignored," Whitehouse and Enzi wrote. Their plan proposed a two-year budget cycle, "providing more predictability in the spending process."

But in an op-ed in The Hill, David Super—a former counsel for the Center on Budget and Policy Priorities, a liberal think tank—complained the legislation would force a vote on deficit reduction whenever the Congressional Budget Office's deficit estimate worsened from that of the prior year's budget resolution. Whitehouse's support of the bill appeared to reflect his past frustrations with the Budget Committee. In late 2020, as he eyed the panel's gavel, Roll Call noted that Whitehouse five years earlier had called the committee "preposterous and meaningless" during a hearing. He later termed the panel a "nullity" when it comes to fiscal policy, griping during a January 2018 hearing, "We don't do anything in this committee."

Whitehouse has been reelected easily in a solidly blue state. If Democrats maintain Senate control, Whitehouse, 65, in the near future could find himself chairing one of three committees on which he is high on the seniority leader: Budget, Environment and Public Works, or Judiciary. In addition, in 2018, Whitehouse won a long-sought seat on the influential Finance Committee.

Six years earlier, his Republican opponent in his first reelection race, software executive Barry Hinckley, campaigned as a moderate on social issues while calling for the repeal of Obama care and supporting offshore oil drilling. Whitehouse won 65%-35%. In April 2018, Chafee announced plans to challenge Whitehouse in the Democratic primary. After losing to Whitehouse in 2006, Chafee had been elected governor as an independent and then had run an eccentric 2016 campaign for the Democratic presidential nomination. He told the Providence Journal that supporters of Sanders, unhappy that Whitehouse had supported Hillary Clinton in 2016, had encouraged Chafee to seek his former Senate seat. A month later, Chafee abandoned his plan. Whitehouse won 77 percent against a little-noticed primary challenger and went on to defeat Republican Robert Flanders 61%-38%. Borrowing a page from Whitehouse's first run for office, Flanders, a former state Supreme Court justice, referred to the incumbent as "Silver Spoon Sheldon"—while also criticizing his focus on climate change.

David Cicilline (D)

Elected 2010, 6th term, b. Jul 15, 1961; Providence, RI; Brown University, B.A., 1983; Georgetown University Law Center, J.D., 1986; Jewish; Single.

Elected Office: RI House, 1995-2003; Providence Mayor, 2003-2011.

Professional Career: Public defender, 1986-1987; Practicing attorney; Faculty, Roger Williams Law School.

DC Office: 2233 RHOB 20515, 202-225-4911, Fax: 202-225-3290, cicilline.house.gov

State Offices: Pawtucket, 401-729-5600.

Committees: *Foreign Affairs*: Africa, Global Health & Global Human Rights; Europe, Energy, the Environment & Cyber; Middle East, North Africa & Global Counterterrorism. *Judiciary*: Antitrust, Commercial & Administrative Law (Chmn); Crime, Terrorism & Homeland Security.

Group Ratings

	ADA	ACLU	AFL-CIO	LCV	COC	HAFA	ACU	CFG	FRC
2020	**	82%	**	100%	-	0%	5%	**	-
2019	95%	C	100%	97%	57%	C	5%	12%	0%

Almanac Ratings 2019-2020

	Economy	Social	Foreign	Composite
Liberal	100%	100%	92%	98%
Conservative	0%	0%	8%	2%

Key Votes of the 116th Congress

1. U.S./Mex./Can. trade deal	Y	5. Russia sanctions	Y
2. First Coronavirus response	Y	6. Troops in Syria	Y
3. HEROES Act	Y	7. Veto arms sales to Saudis	Y
4. CASH Act	Y	8. Defense $$$, veto override	Y

9. Firearms background checks Y
10. Spending at the border   N
11. Marijuana liberalized rules Y
12. Electoral College objections N

Election Results

Election	Name (Party)	Vote (%)		Cand. Spent	Ind. Exp. Support	Ind. Exp. Oppose
2020 General	David Cicilline (D)	158,550	(71%)	$1,023,581	$9,013	
	Jeffrey Lemire (I)	35,457	(16%)			
	Frederick Wysocki (I)	28,300	(13%)	$10,680		
2020 Primary	David Cicilline (D)	25,224	(100%)			

Prior winning percentages: 2018 (67%), 2016 (65%), 2014 (60%), 2012 (53%), 2010 (51%)

Democrat David Cicilline, elected in 2010 with a niche as a gay and often outspoken liberal lawmaker, gained two plum assignments when Democrats took House control. He used those busy platforms in the party leadership and at the Judiciary Committee to assert influence on issues ranging from antitrust and gay rights to the second impeachment of former President Donald Trump. At home, he recovered politically from his rocky start in the House, when his popularity plummeted with news of his messy stewardship of the city's finances while he was mayor of Providence.

Cicilline was born in Providence, the middle of five children. His parents eloped when his Jewish mother was 16 and his Catholic father 17. He grew up celebrating the traditions of both religions, and now identifies as Jewish. His father was a criminal-defense attorney who has been described in news accounts as a "Mafia lawyer." Cicilline attended Brown University, where he majored in political science and founded, along with classmate John F. Kennedy Jr., a chapter of the College Democrats. He was active in student government and worked two jobs waiting tables. Cicilline came out as gay in college and says he was fortunate to have a supportive family. After getting a law degree from Georgetown University, he worked in Washington as a public defender for juveniles.

He returned to Rhode Island to campaign for the state Senate. He lost that bid, but ran for the state House two years later and won. In the legislature, he pushed to raise the legal age to buy a gun from 13 to 18, introduced a bill creating a needle exchange program for drug users, and fought attempts to restrict abortion rights. In 2002, he was elected to the first of two terms as mayor of Providence, becoming the first openly gay mayor of a state capital city. He campaigned as a reformer, promising to clean up the city after the two-decade reign of Buddy Cianci, who was convicted of corruption. As the city's revenue shriveled in the recession, he laid off nearly 500 employees and raised property taxes. Cicilline was president of the National Conference of Democratic Mayors.

When Democratic Rep. Patrick Kennedy decided not to seek reelection, Cicilline won the primary with 37 percent of the vote against three opponents. In the general election, he campaigned as a pragmatist seeking to create jobs. Republican state Rep. John Loughlin focused on the state's poor economy and said he would balance the federal budget. Cicilline spent $2 million to $800,000 for Loughlin and won 51%-45%. The unexpectedly close outcome in a heavily Democratic district raised residual problems for Cicilline.

Cicilline spent his first term under a cloud from his actions as mayor. The Providence Journal reported in early 2011 that the city had a $180 million deficit for the next two fiscal years and that its reserve fund was almost depleted. A nonpartisan bond rating agency, Fitch Ratings, criticized Cicilline's administration for "imprudent budgeting decisions." Cicilline said he had to use reserve money to prevent sharp cuts to city programs. He went on an apology tour to acknowledge he should have been more forthcoming about Providence's fiscal problems.

Cicilline established a solidly liberal voting record. He spoke out forcefully against proposed GOP budget cuts to programs for low-income citizens. On the Judiciary Committee, he criticized Facebook and its chairman, Mark Zuckerberg, for lying to Congress about its data-sharing practices and for turning "a blind eye to the spread of hate speech and Russian propaganda on its platform."

That led to his selection in 2019 to chair the Antitrust, Commercial and Administrative Law Subcommittee, where his agenda included the goal to "hold big tech companies accountable." He gained notice when he launched extended hearings on anti-competitive practices in Big Tech, particularly Facebook and Google, the first major antitrust review by Congress in decades. His review, Cicilline said, "really underscored for me how broken this market is, how broken the internet is, and that we are in a very serious monopoly moment."

What was distinctive about the hearings, Franklin Foer wrote in The Atlantic in July 2020, was "the broad agreement they evinced." They represented a return to century-old "worries about corporate behemoths, about how they use their size to hurt small businesses, how concentrated economic power can so easily distort the functioning of democracy."

While in the House minority, Cicilline filed legislative proposals that had no prospects in a Republican-controlled Congress, but they gave Democrats and progressives talking points. Then, once they gained the majority, Democrats secured House passage of some of his measures. In 2015, following the shooting deaths of nine people in a Charleston South Carolina church, he filed legislation to prohibit gun purchases by children, people with a criminal record and those with a mental illness. He has pushed another bill to reinstate a ban on certain classes of semi-automatic weapons. He has sponsored legislation for automatic voter registration in the 50 states, which shifts the burden for registering from the individual to the state. As chair of the LGBT Equality Caucus, he led the preparation and passage of the Equality Act, which affirmed, he said, "that LGBTQ people should enjoy the same rights and responsibilities as all other Americans."

Following the 2018 election, Speaker Nancy Pelosi created a new leadership position that was intended for Cicilline: chairman of the Democratic Policy and Communications Committee, with responsibility to develop a policy agenda and communications strategy to unify Democrats in Congress and beyond. Two years later, he sought the open position of assistant Speaker, but was defeated by Rep. Katherine Clark of Massachusetts.

At the start of 2021, a new opportunity arose with the January riot at the Capitol. During the hours-long chaos, while House members were sheltered in a secure place, Cicilline discussed options with Reps. Ted Lieu of California and Jamie Raskin of Maryland, two other members of the Judiciary Committee. That led to their preparation of the second impeachment charge against Trump. "We had never witnessed an American president incite a violent mob on the citadel of our democracy in a desperate attempt to cling to power," he wrote in an op-ed piece for The New York Times, which explained their rationale.

After serving as a House manager during the subsequent Senate trial, Cicilline said he had no regrets. The fact that seven Republican senators voted to convict Trump was vital, he subsequently told the Boston Globe. "What we wanted to avoid at all costs was a vote of 50-50 where it would look completely partisan."

At home, he turned back a Democratic challenge in 2012 from businessman Anthony Gemma, who was the runner-up in the 2010 primary. Gemma accused Cicilline of voter fraud. The incumbent called the allegation "absolutely absurd" and won 62%-38%. His general election rival was Republican Brendan Doherty, a former state police superintendent. Cicilline outspent Doherty, $2.4 million to $1.5 million, and again won modestly, 53%-41%. Since then, Cicilline has won more comfortably against lightly funded opponents.

RI-1: Eastern Rhode Island   **Cook Partisan Voting Index: D+12**

Population		Race and Ethnicity		Income	
Total	530,066	White	75.90%	Median Income	$66,652
Land area (sq. miles)	268	Black	8.60%	District Income Rank	197
Pop/ sq mi	1,974.25	Latino	19.10%	Poverty Rate	12.20%
Born in State	51.70%	Asian	3.20%	With health insurance	95.30%
		Two or more races	4.70%	Cash public assistance	4.50%
Age Groups		Other	7.70%	Food stamp/SNAP	15.80%
Under 18	20.10%				
18-34	24.50%	**Education**		**Work**	
35-64	38.30%	H.S grad or less	41.50%	White Collar	39.60%
Over 64	17.10%	Some college	24.30%	Sales and Service	40.60%
		College Degree, 4 yr	20.30%	Blue Collar	19.80%
Military		Post grad	13.90%	Government	12.10%
Veteran/ Active Duty	6.50%				

2020 Pres. Vote	Biden	154,430	(64%)	Trump	83,607	(34%)	
2016 Pres. Vote	Clinton	130,682	(59%)	Trump	75,510	(34%)	Johnson 6,767 (3%)

Parts of Providence, Newport: Economic woes have hit hard in some Rhode Island cities, and have not been easy to shake. Central Falls declared bankruptcy in 2011, becoming the second city in the nation to exhaust its pension fund; it significantly cut benefits for retirees under court direction. In 2012, Providence, on the brink of bankruptcy, averted fiscal disaster by cutting back pensions and education spending, and raising property taxes. Since then, each city has continued to struggle with its finances. In Pawtucket, the AAA baseball franchise affiliated with the Boston Red Sox announced in August 2018 that it will relocate 40 miles away in Worcester Massachusetts, where it will have a taxpayer-financed new stadium and a growing metropolis. In December 2018, the chief executive of Hasbro, the Fortune 500 toy company that has been headquartered in Pawtucket for more than a half-century and employs 1,600 locally, announced the company was exploring all options for its new headquarters location and planned a decision in the next six months. Two years later, nothing was new. These dispiriting conditions contrast sharply with the comfortable—in some cases, aristocratic—lifestyle only a few miles away, in parts of Providence and in tony towns along Narragansett Bay. In October 2018, a study by economists at Brown University found that Providence, known for its progressive political base, "is among the most unequal cities in the country," with pockets of prosperity alongside areas of deep poverty.

The 1st Congressional District is the eastern half of Rhode Island, divided from the state's other congressional district by a boundary line that extends about 40 miles from Woonsocket to Newport and Little Compton. The district takes in much of Providence, including the elite East Side and College Hill around Brown University. In recent years, the once down-on-its-luck city has revived physically, with an accessible waterfront adjacent to downtown and restoration of neighborhoods around the state capitol. The district captures all of next-door Pawtucket, whose Slater Mill is known as the birthplace of the American Industrial Revolution; the city has rehabbed many of its abandoned mills into lofts for artists and commercial space for entrepreneurs. In Central Falls, the coronavirus added to local woes when the crowded city became a hot spot in May 2020, with one of the highest rates in the nation.

The onetime textile mill towns of the Blackstone Valley, Woonsocket and Central Falls (with an area of one square mile) are in the 1st, along with high-income Barrington and Bristol along the eastern coast of Narragansett Bay. To the south, on the ocean, is the old city of Newport, with its restored 18th-century houses and summer "cottages" that are more like mansions, plus the smaller island of Jamestown. Newport has been home to the America's Cup races and has hosted a popular jazz festival every summer since 1954. It is also the site of the oldest synagogue in North America, where George Washington once told a congregation that the United States gives "to bigotry no sanction, to persecution no assistance." Ethnically, the 1st District is the more French-Canadian and the less Italian of Rhode Island's two congressional districts. Politically, it has become nearly 2-to-1 Democratic in presidential elections.

Jim Langevin (D)

Elected 2000, 11th term, b. Apr 22, 1964; Providence, RI; RI College, B.A., 1990; Harvard University John F. Kennedy School of Government, M.P.A., 1994; Roman Catholic; Single.

Elected Office: RI House, 1989-1995; RI Secretary of St., 1995-2001.

Professional Career: RI Secretary of State; State Representative

DC Office: 2077 RHOB 20515, 202-225-2735, Fax: 202-225-5976, langevin.house.gov

State Offices: Warwick, 401-732-9400.

Committees: *Armed Services*: Cyber, Innovative Technologies & Information Systems (Chmn); Seapower & Projection Forces; Strategic Forces. *Homeland Security*: Cybersecurity, Infrastructure Protection & Innovation; Intelligence & Counterterrorism.

Group Ratings

	ADA	ACLU	AFL-CIO	LCV	COC	HAFA	ACU	CFG	FRC
2020	**	76%	**	100%	-	0%	9%	**	-
2019	90%	C	100%	97%	61%	C	9%	12%	0%

Almanac Ratings 2019-2020

	Economy	Social	Foreign	Composite
Liberal	100%	100%	80%	94%
Conservative	0%	0%	20%	6%

Key Votes of the 116th Congress

1. U.S./Mex./Can. trade deal	Y	5. Russia sanctions	Y	9. Firearms background checks	Y
2. First Coronavirus response	Y	6. Troops in Syria	Y	10. Spending at the border	Y
3. HEROES Act	Y	7. Veto arms sales to Saudis	Y	11. Marijuana liberalized rules	Y
4. CASH Act	Y	8. Defense $$$, veto override	Y	12. Electoral College objections	N

Election Results

Election	Name (Party)	Vote (%)		Cand. Spent	Ind. Exp. Support	Ind. Exp. Oppose
2020 General	Jim Langevin (D).................... 154,086	(58%)	$1,535,806		
	Robert Lancia (R)............................ 109,894	(42%)	$46,755	$183	
2020 Primary	James Langevin (D)................. 31,599	(70%)			
	Dylan Conley (D)............................. 13,482	(30%)			

Prior winning percentages: 2018 (64%), 2016 (58%), 2014 (62%), 2012 (56%), 2010 (60%), 2008 (70%), 2006 (73%), 2004 (75%), 2002 (76%), 2000 (62%)

Democrat Jim Langevin, elected in 2000, is the first quadriplegic to serve in Congress and has worked on behalf of others with similar physical challenges. He has been a leader in promoting action on cyber security and other national security issues on the Armed Services and Homeland Security committees. In 2020, Langevin was instrumental in the enactment of landmark legislation setting cyber security policies at the Pentagon and throughout the federal government, including a new national cyber director within the White House. In 2021, he became chairman of a new Armed Services Subcommittee handling cyber issues.

Langevin grew up in Warwick and as a boy hoped to become an FBI agent. in 1980, at age 16, when he was a police cadet in the Boy Scout Explorer program, he was shot by a police officer when a gun accidentally discharged. The bullet went through his upper back and throat and damaged the upper part of his spinal column, leaving him a quadriplegic. He received a $2.2 million settlement from the city of Warwick. Although he disliked the attention it brought him, he says he became determined to do something meaningful with his life. He worked as an intern at the state House and for Sen. Claiborne Pell. While a student at Rhode Island College, where he got his bachelor's, he was elected to the state House, where he styled himself as a reformer. He got a master's degree in public administration from the John F. Kennedy School of Government at Harvard. In 1994, Langevin was elected Rhode Island's secretary of state.

When the House seat opened, Langevin's chief opponent was Kate Coyne-McCoy, executive director of the Rhode Island Association of Social Workers, who criticized his opposition to abortion rights. Langevin had support from many Democratic leaders and some unions, and won the party's convention endorsement. Coyne-McCoy waged an aggressive campaign financed by unions, health care workers and EMILY's List. Langevin called her positions "unrealistic and extreme." She said, "there's no such thing as being too liberal." He spoke often about the accident that paralyzed him. "Certainly, being disabled is part of who I am, but it doesn't define me," he said. Langevin defeated Coyne-McCoy, 47%-29%. In the general, Rodney Driver, nominee of the Conscience for Congress Party and a retired mathematics professor, spent $300,000 of his retirement savings. Langevin won easily, 62%-21%.

The House chamber in the Capitol was made wheelchair-accessible for Langevin, with two seats in the front removed to give him space to maneuver and to talk to colleagues. In July 2010, he became the first person in a wheelchair to preside over the House. In February 2018, Langevin opposed a Republican-passed bill he said would weaken compliance with the Americans with Disabilities Act. "I am saddened that Congress sent a message to people with disabilities that we are not equal or worthy of the same civil rights protections as others," he said.

Langevin has been a member of the Democratic whip team. In 2005, he sided with conservatives in the case of Terri Schiavo, a severely brain-damaged Florida woman in a court battle over removing her life-sustaining feeding tube. He returned to the liberal fold on embryonic stem cell research, which anti-abortion groups opposed. Langevin took the view that the research might alleviate suffering from certain diseases and injuries, which drew heat from the Roman Catholic bishop of Providence. He has been among the scant Democrats in the Pro-Life Caucus.

Langevin has sponsored several gun-control bills, including increased inspections of firearms dealers' sales records and stiffened penalties for dealers who have been untruthful. In 2006, Langevin won passage of a bipartisan bill that established a respite program for caregivers of individuals with special needs. He was a staunch supporter of the Democrats' health care initiative in 2009 and 2010.

On the Armed Services Committee, Langevin worked successfully to thwart the Obama administration's proposed cut in production of Virginia-class submarines in Rhode Island and Connecticut. As ranking Democrat, and then chairman, of the Intelligence, Emerging Threats and Capabilities Subcommittee, he has been an expert and leading policymaker on cyber security programs and what he has termed "the increasingly competitive security environment," including "new forms of hybrid warfare and cyber intrusions."

In December 2020, final action on the annual defensespending bill featured extensive organizational changes and policy direction for the nation's cybersecurity, much of which Langevin had sought to enact for the past decade. Included was his long-sought goal of a national cyber director, with "centralization of cybersecurity efforts for the industrial base" and "specialized cyber teams with blended authorities." This new office in the Executive Office of the President would overhaul the estimated 87 cyber provisions in the defense bill enacted a year earlier. In a statement, Langevin and House Armed Services Committee Chairman Adam Smith of Washington said they will push the Pentagon "not only to account for utilizing the tools Congress has afforded, but toward the novel application of these authorities to different problem sets."

Smith reorganized his panel to create a new Subcommittee on Cyber, Innovative Technologies, and Information Systems, chaired by Langevin. "As technology continues to advance at an incredibly rapid rate—from artificial intelligence to biotechnology and everything in between—it is critical that the Armed Services Committee redoubles our efforts to bridge the gap between current capabilities and future requirements," they said in a February 2021 statement.

State and national Democrats urged Langevin to challenge Republican Sen. Lincoln Chafee in 2006, but abortion rights groups objected to his candidacy. In 2020, Langevin faced challengers in both the primary and general election. He won with 70 percent and 58 percent, respectively; his $1.5 million was about 20 times the total spent by his two opponents. Langevin's future has been a topic of speculation for years. In 2017, he said in an interview that he might run for governor "at some point in the future," but not in 2018. Making such a move in 2022 would have avoided a potential House showdown when reapportionment was expected to eliminate one of Rhode Island's two House seats. As it turned out, Rhode Island retained both of its seats. Langevin doesn't have to worry about a face-offwith Rep. David Cicilline for the state's surviving seat. And he will continue his work on national security issues from his senior slot on two House committees.

RI-2: Western Rhode Island

Cook Partisan Voting Index: D+4

Population		Race and Ethnicity		Income	
Total	529,295	White	81.50%	Median Income	$74,180
Land area (sq. miles)	765	Black	6.20%	District Income Rank	135
Pop/ sq mi	691.6	Latino	13.50%	Poverty Rate	9.50%
Born in State	61.60%	Asian	3.80%	With health insurance	96.50%
		Two or more races	3.70%	Cash public assistance	3.20%
Age Groups		Other	4.70%	Food stamp/SNAP	13.20%
Under 18	18.30%				
18-34	24.10%	**Education**		**Work**	
35-64	39.60%	H.S grad or less	37.00%	White Collar	44.70%
Over 64	18.20%	Some college	27.70%	Sales and Service	37.20%
		College Degree, 4 yr	21.50%	Blue Collar	18.00%
Military		Post grad	14.00%	Government	14.60%
Veteran/ Active Duty	5.90%				

2020 Pres. Vote	Biden	153,056	(56%)	Trump	116,315	(42%)		
2016 Pres. Vote	Clinton	121,843	(50%)	Trump	105,033	(43%)	Johnson	7,979 (3%)

Parts of Providence, Warwick, Cranston: For a small state, Rhode Island plays a major role in the construction of the nation's submarine fleet. The combined workforce at the Quonset Point Shipyard exceeds 15,000 and was expected to grow another 13,000 by 2027, with the official announcement in December 2019 that the yard will manufacture a new class of nine ballistic missile submarines, with delivery starting in 2025. These subs will be able to remain up to 800 feet underwater for months. The shipyard already has been producing a class of attack submarines. Much of the work for the new subs will be performed at a new $800 million facility a short distance down Narragansett Bay in North Kingston.

The 2nd Congressional District is the western half of Rhode Island. The largest cities are working-class Cranston and more upscale Warwick, which was the second-largest in the state. But Cranston in 2019surpassed Warwick by 452 in 2019in the number-two slot behind Providence. One reason why Cranston has had more growth has been because it had more undeveloped land, while Warwick had little space for growth. Cranston was reportedly the inspiration for FOX's animated comedy Family Guy, with a cultural edge; the show, which has run for several seasons and has been one of the most popular on the network, was set in the fictitious town of Quahog, which happens to be a Rhode Island species of clam. The 2nd includes the fastest-growing part of the state, South County, which is not an official place but the common name for Rhode Island south of East Greenwich. The Electric Boat company, a division of General Dynamics, has sprawling plants in Quonset Point—a few miles from Warwick—and across the Connecticut line in Groton and New London. This area takes in the affluent suburbs and beachfront communities along Narragansett Bay, the Kingston home of the University of Rhode Island, and the area around Westerly, where many residents work at the Electric Boat shipyards.

Another important segment of the economy is sailing and tourism. In addition to its rolling farmland (this is Rhode Island, so there is not much acreage), the district includes communities along the bay and the ocean, where many people still make their living building boats and catching fish. The Block Island Revolution Wind Farm began to produce energy in 2017 from the nation's first offshore wind farm. The five-turbine, 30-megawatt facility, which is three miles off the coast, uses a submarine cable to connect to the mainland and is expected to power 17,000 homes. In October 2020, the contractor reached agreement with Rhode Island to add another 400 megawatts of capacity. Wind farms on land are cheaper to build, but those in the ocean have stronger winds.

This has been a comfortably Democratic district. In 2012, Mitt Romney took only 38 percent of the vote. Donald Trump ran strongly in the small towns and increased the Republican vote to 43 and then back to 42 percent.

SOUTH CAROLINA

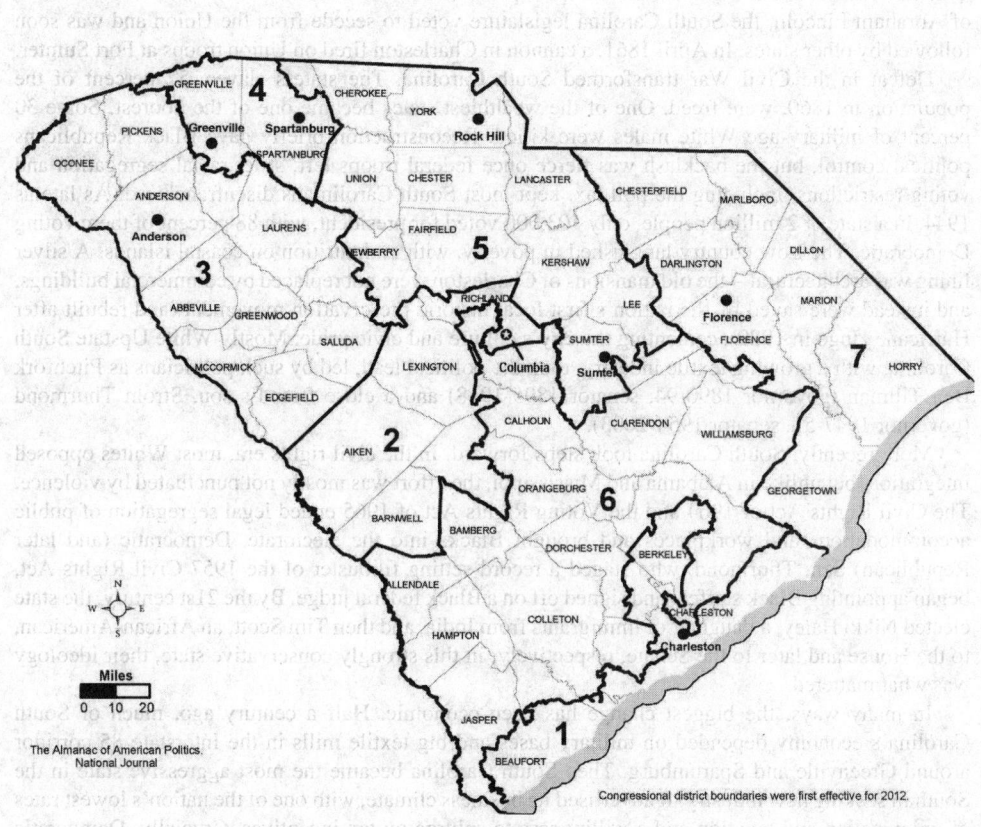

The Almanac of American Politics.
National Journal

Miles
0   10   20

Congressional district boundaries were first effective for 2012.

In recent years, South Carolina has been vaulted into the headlines for tragic incidents and efforts at reconciliation. In 2020, it helped elect a president.

Tragedy and coexistence have been dueling parts of South Carolina's history from the beginning. The state's early influence was the slave-majority, sugar-producing island of Barbados, which produced its original settlers; until 1855, South Carolina was the only colony or state with a Black majority. On the one hand, Carolina plantation owners were tolerant of some groups, opening their colony to French Huguenots and Sephardic Jews. At the same time, they were also slave masters of giant plantations that produced rice and indigo. South Carolinian Charles Pinckney led the effort to enshrine the principle of no religious tests for political office in the Constitution; he was also a slaveholder. Low country planters maintained effective control of the legislature, and therefore the state's two Senate seats and presidential electors, up through 1860. In that year and the next, South Carolina did more than any other state to precipitate the Civil War. In December, after the election of Abraham Lincoln, the South Carolina legislature voted to secede from the Union and was soon followed by other states. In April 1861, a cannon in Charleston fired on Union troops at Fort Sumter.

Defeat in the Civil War transformed South Carolina. The state's slaves, 57 percent of the population in 1860, were freed. One of the wealthiest states became one of the poorest. Some 30 percent of military-age White males were killed. Reconstruction briefly gave Black Republicans political control, but the backlash was fierce once federal troops left; strict racial segregation and voting restrictions, including the poll tax, kept most South Carolinians disenfranchised. As late as 1944, in a state of 2 million people, only 103,000 voted for president, with 88 percent of them voting Democratic. The Low country languished in poverty, with malnutrition on coastal islands. A silver lining was architectural—the old mansions of Charleston were not replaced by commercial buildings, and instead were saved by the nation's first local historic preservation movement (and rebuilt after Hurricane Hugo in 1989), cementing the city's culture and civic pride. Mostly White Upstate South Carolina, with a growing textile industry, took the political lead, led by such politicians as Pitchfork Ben Tillman (governor 1890-94, senator 1895-1918) and a close friend's son, Strom Thurmond (governor 1947-51, senator 1954-2003).

More recently, South Carolina took steps forward. In the civil rights era, most Whites opposed integration, but unlike in Alabama and Mississippi, the effort was mostly not punctuated by violence. The Civil Rights Act of 1964 and the Voting Rights Act of 1965 ended legal segregation of public accommodations and workplaces and brought Blacks into the electorate. Democratic (and later Republican) Sen. Thurmond, who staged a record-setting filibuster of the 1957 Civil Rights Act, began appointing Black staffers and signed off on a Black federal judge. By the 21st century, the state elected Nikki Haley, a daughter of immigrants from India, and then Tim Scott, an African-American, to the House and later to the Senate, respectively; in this strongly conservative state, their ideology was what mattered.

In many ways, the biggest change has been economic. Half a century ago, much of South Carolina's economy depended on military bases and big textile mills in the Interstate 85 corridor around Greenville and Spartanburg. Then South Carolina became the most aggressive state in the South in seeking new industry. It advertised its business climate, with one of the nation's lowest rates of unionization and taxation and a willingness to splurge on tax incentives. Crucially, Democratic Gov. (later Sen.) Ernest Hollings spearheaded the creation of the state's technical colleges, which today educate and train hundreds of thousands of residents a year. (Hollings died in 2019.) Michelin opened the first of several South Carolina plants in 1975, and the first BMW vehicles rolled off the Spartanburg assembly line in 1992. Volvo chose a South Carolina site 30 miles northwest of Charleston as the location of its first North American assembly plant, while companies such as Bosch, Fujifilm and Adidasbuilt factories throughout central and Upstate South Carolina. In recent years, South Carolina has been neck-and-neck with North Carolina for the nation's lowest rate of unionization, just above 2 percent of all workers.

Navy bases were the mainstay of Charleston's economy in the 1970s, but they were closed in the early 1990s and subsequently became a center of aircraft production, particularly after Boeing in 2009 chose North Charleston as the location of a plant to assemble its 787 Dreamliner. The aircraft giant now employs 6,800 people in the Charleston area, though the company has been enmeshed in a long-running battle over unionization. Charleston has become a major port, which is especially helpful for the state's international exporters; the state wants to dredge Charleston Harbor so container ships can traverse it regardless of tidal conditions. Charleston's downtown has not only survived but thrived, thanks in large part to the creative energy of longtime Mayor Joseph P. Riley Jr., who was first elected in 1975 and who served for 40 years. With a keen aesthetic eye, he made the city's historic center a magnet for tourists; statewide, tourism has grown consistently, passing the military's statewide economic impact in 2016.

Despite economic gains, South Carolina has only three Fortune 500 companies headquartered locally, compared to 14 each in neighboring North Carolina and Georgia. But the state dodged a bullet with the trade war waged by President Donald Trump. Exports hit a record $41.5 billion in 2019, up almost 20 percent, and exports shipped through the Port of Charleston rose more than 5 percent. Despite bilateral trade tensions, the flow of goods with China remained steady. BMW maintained its lead as the top U.S. vehicle exporter; collectively, jets from Boeing and vehicles from BMW and Volvo accounted for more than half of South Carolina's exports in 2019. One of every six vehicles exported from the U.S. now comes from South Carolina, as well as one-third of tire exports. However, the coronavirus pandemic caused economic distress in 2020, particularly in tourism-heavy regions such as Myrtle Beach and Charleston.

In the meantime, poverty remains in many areas of the state. South Carolina's median income ranks in the bottom 10 states nationally, a full 14 percent below the national average; the poverty rate is a few percentage points higher than the nation as a whole. South Carolina ranks in the bottom quarter of states for the percentage of residents with a college degree, and teacher pay has not kept up with inflation since 2003, when the GOP gained full control of state government, according to a Charleston Post and Courier analysis.

Race has continued to be a defining issue for South Carolina. In 2015, Dylann Roof, a man with a history of White supremacist beliefs, entered a historic African-American church in Charleston, sat down for Bible study, then systematically gunned down nine Black worshippers—including the pastor, state Sen. ClementaPinckney–as he squeezed the trigger more than 75 times. The attack took place in the successor to the very same church that was the epicenter of the 1822 slave rebellion led by Denmark Vesey, which ended with the execution of Vesey and numerous lieutenants, as well as the destruction of the church. (Before his death, Pastor Pinckney had been active in erecting a memorial to Vesey.)Amid the mourning, a debate about old subjects—race and Confederate heritage —reemerged. Critics said the state should finally do what it had previously balked at:Remove the Confederate battle flag from the state capitol grounds in Columbia, where it had flown, in one way or another, since 1962. Haley, who prior to the killings had shown little interest in following her predecessors' failed efforts to pull down the flag, offered her support for removal, and the tide began to turn. On July 10, 2015, the flag was lowered from the statehouse grounds for good. Roof was sentenced to death in 2017, the nation's first federal hate-crime defendant to face the death penalty. Meanwhile, another high-profile case—a videotaped police shooting in North Charleston in which a Black man, Walter Scott, was shot in the back by a white police officer—produced first a deadlocked jury and then a plea agreement that resulted in a 20-year prison sentence.

Through the 1960s, few people except military personnel moved to South Carolina. That has changed in a big way. Since 2010, the population has grown 10.7 percent, driven by migration from other states. The growth has been fastest on and near the coast—31 percent during the past decade in Horry County (Myrtle Beach), 27 percent in Berkeley County (northern suburbs of Charleston), 19 percent in Dorchester County (the northwestern suburbs of Charleston), 18 percent in Beaufort County (Hilton Head), and 17 percent in Charleston County (Charleston). The York County suburbs of booming Charlotte North Carolina, meanwhile, have grown 24 percent. These booming areas attract predominantly White tourists and affluent retirees who are eager to spend days with pleasant weather on the golf course and in time-shares. The percentages of White residents (63 percent) and Black residents (26 percent) have remained stable for a decade, with relatively small populations of Hispanics (5.7 percent) and Asians (1.7 percent). The fastest-growing portion of South Carolina's population consists of senior citizens, a group that has increased from 12 percent in 2000 to 14 percent in 2010 to 18 percent today. By 2030, the state is expected to have more residents 65 and older than children in school.

The influx of White retirees has moved South Carolina politically toward Republicans. Politics cleaves the electorate along racial lines, and the hard math of the population figures makes it difficult for Democrats to win statewide. South Carolina has voted Republican for president in every election but one since 1960—in 1976, when son of the South Jimmy Carter was running. But it's South Carolina's early primary that often plays a pivotal role for one party or the other, and few were more consequential than the 2020 Democratic primary. Coming off poor finishes in Iowa, New Hampshire, and Nevada, Joe Biden bet everything on a win in South Carolina. And after Rep. James Clyburn, the state's most influential Black Democrat, endorsed Biden three days before the primary, he ended up winning the state so convincingly that most of the remaining Democratic candidates fell in line. "You brought me back," Biden told Clyburn—all the way to the presidency.

Trump—who had forged ties with such leading South Carolina Republicans as Sen. Lindsey Graham, Gov. Henry McMaster, Haley, and White House Chief of Staff Mick Mulvaney—won the state easily in both 2016 and 2020, with Trump's winning margin narrowing by only two points statewide. The seven most populous counties all shifted in the Democrats' direction by between three and seven points, but less-populated areas shifted toward Trump, including two counties, Clarendon and Dillon, that flipped from Hillary Clinton in 2016 to Trump in 2020. Graham managed to win reelection by double digits, despite a strong Democratic opponent in Jaime Harrison, a massive fundraising deficit, and lots of baggage accumulated during the Trump years. Indeed, Trump's and Graham's showings were almost in lockstep, underscoring how inflexible South Carolina's racially driven voting patterns are. And they are likely to persist.

Population			Race and Ethnicity		Income	
Total	5,148,714		White	66.70%	Median Income	56,227
Land area (sq. miles)	30,061		Black	26.50%	State Income Rank	41 out of 50
Pop/ sq mi	171.28		Latino	5.80%	Poverty Rate	13.80%
Born in state	55.00%		Asian	2.20%	With health insurance	89.20%
			Two or more races	2.40%	Cash public assistance	1.10%
Age Groups			Other	2.70%	Food stamp/SNAP	14.0%
Under 18	21.60%					
18-34	22.10%		Education		Work	
35-64	38.00%		H.S grad or less	40.10%	White Collar	36.90%
Over 64	18.20%		Some college	30.30%	Sales and Service	38.10%
			College Degree, 4 yr	18.40%	Blue Collar	25.10%
Military			Post grad	11.20%	Government	14.90%
Veteran/ Active Duty	9.80%					

Presidential Politics

2020 Primary (D)	Biden (D)	262,336(49%)	Sanders (D)	106,605(20%)	Steyer (D)	61,140(11%)
	Buttigieg (D)	44,217 (8%)	Warren (D)	38,120 (7%)		
2020 Pres. Vote	Trump (R)	1,385,103(55%)	Biden (D)	1,091,541(43%)		
2016 Pres. Vote	Trump (R)	1,155,389(55%)	Clinton (D)	855,373(41%)	Johnson (L)	49,204 (2%)

South Carolina has been reliably Republican in presidential elections since 1980. But that's also the year it became a major player in the presidential primary process, helping boost Ronald Reagan to the GOP nomination. Since then, it's played a key, if sometimes ugly, role in both parties' nomination processes.

The primary's significance for Republicans started when Ronald Reagan defeated John Connolly in 1980. Connolly had the backing of the state's legendary segregationist Sen. Strom Thurmond. Reagan's 55%-30% victory confirmed his widespread popularity among Southern Republicans and helped propel him to the GOP nomination. In 1988, Republicans moved the primary to right before Super Tuesday; Texas' George H.W. Bush won a 49%-21%-19% victory over GOP Senate leader Bob Dole and evangelical champion Pat Robertson that foreshadowed a sweep of the Southern primaries that clinched the nomination for him three days later. In 1992, Bush beat Pat Buchanan 67%-26%, squashing Buchanan's claims to conservative Southern support. Four years later, Dole, after his disappointing showings elsewhere, won an impressive 45%-29% victory over Buchanan. In

2000, George W. Bush beat John McCain 53%-42% in a particularly bruising and bitter contest that included a whisper campaign that McCain's adopted daughter was actually illegitimate; the contest left relations between McCain and Bush strained throughout the latter's presidency. In 2008, McCain defeated former Arkansas Gov. Mike Huckabee 33%-30%. The Arizonan's victory established him as the frontrunner for the nomination and gave him momentum that he carried into the Florida primary 10 days later and then the subsequent Super Tuesday contests. The 2012 Republican primary was held just 10 days after New Hampshire, and got nasty as well; Mitt Romney faced attacks on his Mormon religion, while Newt Gingrich turned a bombshell report about his marital infidelities to his advantage by attacking a debate moderator and the media, and defeated Romney, 40%-28%.

The 2016 edition of the South Carolina GOP primary was another Republican slugfest. Donald Trump questioned Texas Sen. Ted Cruz's citizenship and accused former President George W. Bush of lying about the presence of weapons of mass destruction in Iraq in the run-up to the 2003 Iraq War. After that debate the former president made his only appearance at a campaign rally for his brother, Jeb, who also got an endorsement from South Carolina Sen. Lindsey Graham. Florida Sen. Marco Rubio won endorsements from Gov. Nikki Haley and Sen. Tim Scott. But it was Trump's fiery rhetoric and disdain for the GOP establishment and the media that excited South Carolina Republicans and enabled him to defeat Rubio, 33%-23%. Cruz finished third with 22 percent and Bush's 8 percent prompted him to withdraw from the race.

In 2008, the Democratic National Committee chose South Carolina as the only state other than New Hampshire to hold an early primary. Since then, the Democrat who won South Carolina also won the nomination. It's not just a momentum-builder: South Carolina is the first primary state with a large Black population, and African Americans make up a significant share of the overall Democratic primary electorate. The most coveted endorsement for Democrats is from House Majority Whip James Clyburn, an African American and a force in a presidential primary in which the electorate is more than 50 percent Black. Candidates and surrogates flock to his annual spring fish fry in Columbia, where the crowd consumes more than 1,000 pounds of whiting. Clyburn didn't endorse in 2008; Barack Obama won a crushing victory, defeating Hillary Clinton 55%-26%. Years later in his memoir, Clyburn, who said he voted for Obama, wrote that he received a 2 a.m. phone call the day after the primary from Bill Clinton blaming him for his wife's defeat and vowing, "If you bastards want a fight, you damn well will get one." The 2016 Democratic primary was much less contentious and saw a reversal of fortune for Clinton, who consolidated African-American support and was endorsed by Clyburn one week before the primary. Clinton won more than 80 percent of Black voters.

Republicans canceled their 2020 primary to protect Trump (both parties have done this before for incumbent presidents—Democrats in 1996 and 2012, Republicans in 1984 and 2004).

South Carolina (and Clyburn) played an even bigger role in the 2020 nomination process. Joe Biden limped into the state; he'd lost the first three nominating contests of Iowa, New Hampshire and Nevada, hadn't finished with more than 18 percent of the vote in any of them, and was almost out of money. But Obama's former vice president was also the only candidate left who had a deep connection to the African American community—and arguably the only candidate left with the potential coalition to stop Bernie Sanders from the nomination. Clyburn endorsed Biden three days ahead of the primary, arguing that he was the only candidate left who could beat Trump and warning of "down-ballot carnage" if Sanders won the nomination.

Sanders had invested heavily in a field operation to try to make inroads with the state's Black voters, while billionaire philanthropist Tom Steyer poured millions into the state. But Biden's longstanding connection with African-American voters and Clyburn's last-minute boost made a big difference. He won, 49%-20% over Sanders, with Steyer at 11 percent. According to exit polls, Biden won more than three-fifths of the Black vote, which accounted for almost 60 percent of the total electorate; more than half of primary voters said Clyburn's endorsement was an important factor in who they voted for. Biden knew it: "My buddy Jim Clyburn, you brought me back!" he declared in his primary victory speech that Saturday night.

The results drove Minnesota Sen. Amy Klobuchar and South Bend Mayor Pete Buttigieg from the race; both endorsed Biden almost immediately afterward, along with former Texas Rep. Beto O'Rourke. The win showed Black voters stood with Biden, while the subsequent endorsements helped him unify white voters That combination propelled him to a huge Super Tuesday victory three days later that turned Biden from a foundering candidate into the eventual nominee—and president.

The state's general elections have been much less suspenseful. Its racially polarized vote means Democrats have a relatively high floor and low ceiling for their overall state vote, and have won between 40 and 45 percent in every presidential election since 1996. In 2020, Trump defeated Biden 55%-43%. Trump won 33 of the state's 46 counties. Biden carried Charleston and Richland counties (Columbia) and did well in the counties with larger African-American populations. Four years earlier, Trump won, 55%-43%.

Congressional Districts

117th Congress Lineup	1D 6R	116th Congress Lineup	2D 5R

As was the case a decade ago, Republicans likely will split the seven districts of South Carolina so that so that the 6th District continues to reach into several urban and rural areas to create an African-American majority. Republicans might also seek to strengthen their vote in the 1st and 2nd Districts, where the urban precincts have made those districts more competitive. With the state's population 27 percent African American, the key question will be where, and how, Democrats push for a second district that has at least a sizable African-American influence and perhaps a majority. That likely would require reduction of the number of Black voters in the 6th, and carving up the 5th or the 7th. In 2011, the Obama Justice Department tersely granted preclearance of the Republican plan. And a three-judge panel upheld the map. Subsequently, Republicans controlled all six of their districts until an internal GOP split in 2018 unexpectedly gave Democrats control of the Charleston-based 1st District. Republicans narrowly regained that seat two years later.

The 2011 redistricting had another twist that might remain relevant. In that case, the state House passed a proposal adding its new 7th District in the Pee Dee region anchored by Myrtle Beach and surrounding Horry County, a rapidly growing Republican bastion. But the state Senate surprised the House with its own scheme, placing the new 7th District in the Charleston suburbs and Beaufort to the south. Republicans in the two chambers reached a compromise, greased by support from Upstate legislators, to place the 7th District in the Pee Dee, which has the most Blacks of any district in the state other than the 6th. Since then, Tom Rice has easily held the7th District for the GOP.

Henry McMaster (R)

Assumed office in 2017, term expires 2023, 1st full term; b. May. 27, 1947, Columbia; Univ. of South Carolina, BA 1969; Univ. of South Carolina, J.D 1973; Presbyterian; Married (Peggy); 2 children.

Military Career: U.S Army JAG, 1969-1975.

Elected Office: Chairman, SC Republican Party, 1993-2002; SC Attorney General 2003-2011; SC Lt. Governor, 2015-2017.

Professional Career: Legislative Assistant to U.S Sen. Strom Thurmond, 1973-1974; SC Law Enforcement Coordinating Committee head, 1981-1985;

Office: 1205 Pendleton St. Columbia, 29201; 803-734-2100; Fax: 803-734-5167; Website: sc.gov
Lt. Gov.: Pamela Evette (R) **Atty. Gen:** Alan Wilson (R) **Sec. of State:** Mark Hammond (R)
State Legislature: Senate: 19D, 27R **House:** 44D, 78R, 2V

Election Results

Election	Name (Party)	Vote (%)
2018 General	Henry McMaster (R)	921,342 (54%)
	James E. Smith, Jr. (D)	784,182 (46%)
2018 Primary runoff	Henry McMaster (R)	184,286 (54%)
	John Warren (R)	159,349 (46%)
2018 Primary	Henry McMaster (R)	155,723 (42%)
	John Warren (R)	102,390 (28%)
	Catherine Templeton (R)	78,705 (21%)
	Kevin Bryant (R)	24,790 (7%)

Henry McMaster, a longtime Republican officeholder in South Carolina, was elevated to the governorship in 2017 after Nikki Haley was confirmed as President Donald Trump's ambassador to the United Nations. He won a full term in 2018 and is expected to run again in 2022, when he'll be 75 on Election Day.

McMaster, a native of Columbia, received his bachelor's degree from the University of South Carolina in 1969 and his law degree from the same university four years later. He served a year as a legislative assistant to Sen. Strom Thurmond, after which he built a private practice in South Carolina. In 1981, President Ronald Reagan appointed McMaster to serve as U.S. attorney. During his four years in the post, his office helped convict more than 100 people for importing nearly $1 billion in illegal drugs. In 1986, McMaster ran against longtime Democrat Sen. Ernest Hollings, but lost. Four years later, he ran for lieutenant governor and lost again. In 1991, then-Gov. Carroll Campbell appointed McMaster to the state Commission on Higher Education, and for most of the 1990s he headed the state Republican Party.

McMaster finally won elected statewide office—attorney general—2002. After securing the GOP nomination in a contested primary, McMaster defeated Democrat Steve Benjamin, 56%-44%, and easily won a second term four years later. As attorney general, McMaster took a leading role in opposing the Affordable Care Act. He threw his hat into the ring for the open-seat gubernatorial race in 2010. The large Republican primary field also included Lt. Gov. André Bauer, Rep. Gresham Barrett, state Sen. Larry Grooms, and state Rep. Nikki Haley; Haley won the primary and then the general election. In 2014, McMaster ran for lieutenant governor, winning the Republican primary and defeating Democrat Bakari Sellers in the general election, 59%-41%.

After being elevated to governor, McMaster's early tenure featured plenty of legislative drama. McMaster vetoed a bill that would have raised the state's gasoline tax for the first time since 1987, but the measure—which received support from the party's business wing—became law after the legislature voted by a wide margin to override. He also drew fierce legislative opposition to a spending-bill veto that would have allotted $20.5 million to replace aging and fire-prone school buses; McMaster said it was unwise to earmark lottery funds for that purpose rather than for scholarships. The legislature overwhelmingly overrode that veto, too.

Both vetoes were widely believed to be fodder for the GOP's anti-tax, small-government base as McMaster headed into what promised to be a tough primary season. McMaster made other moves that pleased the GOP base, however. He asked the federal government to stop the resettlement in South Carolina of refugees from the countries targeted by Trump's travel ban; he signed an executive order protecting a foster care agency that limited its services to Christian families; and he vetoed almost $16 million in women's health services to end state funding for Planned Parenthood. McMaster also worked, unsuccessfully, to block a proposed tariff that could have hit Samsung washing machines being built in a newly opened plant in the state, and he sought to derail a Trump administration plan to allow drilling off the Atlantic coast. McMaster, joined by the state's congressional delegation, fought the Trump administration's plan to shut down a partially built facility at the Savannah River Site that would reprocess plutonium from weapons into nuclear fuel. He also urged a sale of Santee Cooper, a state-owned electric utility saddled with $4 billion in nuclear-related debts, though some in the legislature pushed back on the idea. (In 2020, the utility would settle with ratepayers for $520 million over the nuclear plant debacle.)

In the 2018 primary, McMaster faced former state agency head Catherine Templeton, Lt. Gov. Kevin Bryant, former Lt. Gov. Yancey McGill, and businessman John Warren. McMaster received endorsements from South Carolina Citizens for Life and the National Rifle Association, and he touted a strong economy. But his opponents attacked him as an apostle of a tired and corrupt political establishment. Late in the campaign, Warren gained ground by leveraging his outsider profile. A 39-year-old Marine veteran from Upstate, he owned a mortgage lending firm; a relatively late entrant in the race, Warren spent $3 million from his own pocket, including a heavy run of television ads. McMaster finished first with 42 percent, followed by Warren with 28 percent, Templeton with 21 percent, Bryant with 7 percent, and McGill with 2 percent. That made McMaster the first modern South Carolina governor in either party to be forced into a primary runoff. On the eve of the runoff, Trump visited South Carolina to promote McMaster, who had been the first statewide official anywhere to back Trump before the state's 2016 primary. Trump had the magic touch: McMaster prevailed, 54%-46%, ceding only a few counties in Warren's Upstate home base. South Carolina Republicans "picked the candidate Trump liked over the Trump-like candidate," The State newspaper wrote.

In the general election—running for the first time on a ticket with a lieutenant governor candidate, following a change in state law—McMaster faced state Rep. James Smith, who Democrats considered a strong candidate. Smith was an Afghanistan combat veteran and an experienced legislative hand who had easily won a three-way primary with the support of national Democratic leaders. But McMaster benefited from a fundraising edge and strong marks for handling the economy, and he won, 54%-46%. Despite some modest gains over their 2014 performance, including areas in and around Charleston and Columbia, Democrats found that the final few percentage points needed to score a statewide victory remained elusive.

In 2019, McMaster shepherded a $115 million incentive plan to support a state-of-the-art facility for the NFL's Charlotte Panthers to be constructed in Rock Hill, just across the border from the team's North Carolina base. The facility was designed to be a hub for further economic development along I-77, which would be upgraded with a new interchange. He also approved a $159 million teacher pay raise and additional funding for school counselors. In general, legislators' hopes of a more collaborative governorship than Haley's or that of her predecessor, Mark Sanford, came true, though McMaster did have a rough time with several personnel matters. The Senate rejected the nominations of two figures close to McMaster: Stephen Morris to lead the Office on Aging and Charlie Condon as head of Santee Cooper. And McMaster's efforts to name Robert Caslen, a retired three-star Army general, to the presidency of the University of South Carolina were met with student and faculty opposition, citing Caslen's lack of experience in academia. Caslen was ultimately approved, but the university's accreditor later concluded that McMaster had used undue influence in the hiring process. In 2021, Caslen resigned after portions of his commencement speech were found to have been given without attribution.

During the coronavirus pandemic in 2020, McMaster's approach mirrored that of other Republican governors. He issued a stay-at-home order relatively late—he was the last of the 42 governors who did so—and then, within weeks, loosened restrictions on a wide swath of businesses and public amenities. And despite a summer spike in cases, McMaster declined to issue a statewide mask order. "We cannot live in fear of the virus and shut down every institution in sight," he said. "It will not work, and it certainly won't work here." As in most other states, outcomes were generally independent of policy. South Carolina was in the middle of the pack in terms of COVID-19 death rates among the states.

In September, as Trump was facing a tight reelection contest, the president backed off his plans to allow oil and gas drilling off the coast of South Carolina, as well as the coasts of Florida and Georgia, a victory for McMaster. And in early 2021, McMaster signed a "fetal heartbeat" bill that would ban all abortions if a heartbeat is detected, unless the pregnancy was caused by rape, incest, or threatened the life of the mother. The measure would also put the abortion provider at risk of a felony, with a possible prison sentence of two years.

Despite having already become South Carolina's oldest governor, McMaster is widely expected to run again in 2022. (His father, an attorney, was handling cases at 93 and died at 99.) In a development that should raise his profile and enhance his fundraising, McMaster joined the executive board of the Republican Governors Association in 2020. But he won't have the field to himself. In a move that could portend a primary challenge, Warren formed a political action committee, and Templeton could mount another primary bid. On the Democratic side, the frontrunner is Steve Benjamin, who after his 2002 loss to McMaster for attorney general became the first African-American mayor of Columbia and served as president of the U.S. Conference of Mayors in 2018 and 2019.

Lindsey Graham (R)

Elected 2002, term expires 2026, 4th term, b. Jul 09, 1955; Seneca, SC; University of South Carolina, B.A., 1977; University of South Carolina School of Law, J.D., 1981; Baptist; Single.

Military Career: U.S. Air Force 1982-1988; SC Air National Guard 1989-1995; Colonel/Senior Instructor, Air Force Judge Advocate Generals (JAG) School, United States Air Force Reserves, 1995-2015; U.S. Air Force Reserve 1995-2015 (Afghanistan & Iraq)

Elected Office: SC House, 1992-1994; U.S. House, 1995-2003.

Professional Career: U.S Air Forces Europe Circuit Trial Counsel, 1984-1988; Assistant Oconee County Attorney, 1988-1992; Practicing attorney, 1988-1994; Judge advocate, McEntire Air National Guard Base, 1989-1994; Central, SC, city Attorney, 1990-1994.

DC Office: 290 RSOB 20510, 202-224-5972, Fax: 202-224-3808, lgraham.senate.gov

State Offices: Columbia, 803-933-0112; Florence, 843-669-1505; Greenville, 864-250-1417; Mt. Pleasant, 843-849-3887; Pendleton, 864-646-4090; Rock Hill, 803-366-2828.

Committees: *Appropriations*: Commerce, Justice, Science & Related Agencies; Department of Defense; DOL, HHS & Education & Related Agencies; Energy & Water Development; State, Foreign Operations & Related Programs (RMM); Transportation, HUD & Related Agencies. *Budget (RMM)*. *Environment & Public Works*: Chem Safety, Waste Mngmnt, Enviro Justice & Reg Oversight; Clean Air & Nuclear Safety; Transportation & Infrastructure. *Judiciary*: Criminal Justice & Counterterrorism; Federal Courts, Oversight, Agency Action & Federal Rights; Immigration, Citizenship & Border Security; Privacy, Technology & the Law.

Group Ratings

	ADA	ACLU	AFL-CIO	LCV	COC	HAFA	ACU	CFG	FRC
2020	-	0%	-	15%	-	61%	82%	-	-
2019	5%	C	21%	29%	91%	C	83%	29%	100%

Almanac Ratings 2019-2020

	Economy	Social	Foreign	Composite
Liberal	9%	9%	8%	9%
Conservative	91%	91%	92%	91%

Key Votes of the 116th Congress

1. EPA clean energy rules	N	5. Russia sanctions	N	9. Barr as Atty. General	Y
2. U.S./Mex./Can. trade deal	Y	6. Troops in SYR, AFG	Y	10. Spending at the border	Y
3. Cut unemployment benefits	Y	7. Veto arms sales to Saudis	Y	11. Coney Barrett to Sup. Ct.	Y
4. Shelton to Fed Reserve	Y	8. Defense $$$, veto override	N/A	12. Electoral College objections	N

Election Results

Election	Name (Party)	Vote (%)		Cand. Spent	Ind. Exp. Support	Ind. Exp. Oppose
2020 General	Lindsey Graham (R)	1,369,137	(54%)	$89,824,110	$6,140,126	$13,586,701
	Jaime Harrison (D)	1,110,828	(44%)	$115,088,830	$3,344,517	$26,319,510
2020 Primary	Lindsey Graham (R)	317,512	(68%)			
	Michael LaPierre (R)	79,932	(17%)			
	Joe Reynolds (R)	43,029	(9%)			
	Dwayne "Duke" Buckner (R)	28,570	(6%)			

Prior winning percentages: 2014 (55%), 2008 (58%), 2002 (54%), House: 2000 (69%), 1998 (100%), 1996 (60%), 1994 (60%)

Republican Lindsey Graham, South Carolina's senior senator, may have undergone the biggest —and most confounding—political transformation of any lawmaker over the past four years. He was once seen as a maverick alongside his late friend Republican Sen. John McCain of Arizona, who was unafraid to challenge his party and collaborate with Democrats. But after McCain's death, Graham morphed into one of President Donald Trump's most loyal allies—after having called him a "kook" and "unfit for office" during his own short-lived 2016 presidential campaign. After that unusual metamorphosis, Democrats saw an opportunity to defeat him in 2020. But in the most expensive race in South Carolina's history, Graham prevailed by 10 percentage points over highly touted Democrat Jaime Harrison, who raised over $130 million. With Republicans now in the minority in the Senate —and Trump out of office—the question is which version of Graham will appear on Capitol Hill.

Graham grew up in Pickens County, where his parents owned a tavern in the textile mill town of Central. Both his parents died young, while Graham was attending the University of South Carolina, and he became his younger sister's legal guardian so that she could receive his military benefits. He was first in his family to graduate from college; he received a law degree from the University of South Carolina. He was an Air Force prosecutor who worked on assignments overseas, including one case that led to major changes in the service's drug testing program for troops. In 1988, he returned home and practiced law in Seneca. In 1992, he was elected to the state House. Graham was called to active duty and served stateside during the Gulf War. In 1995, he joined the Air Force Reserve and served as a senior instructor in the Judge Advocate General's school and as a reserve judge on the Air Force Court of Criminal Appeals. He was awarded the Bronze Star in 2014 for meritorious service for his role as a senior legal adviser to the Air Force during combat operations in Afghanistan. Graham retired from the reserves in June 2015.

In 1994, with the retirement of 20-year Democratic Rep. Butler Derrick, Graham ran for the House. Graham won the Republican primary with 52 percent of the vote. In the general election, he faced state Sen. Jim Bryan. Graham called for term limits, supported more defense spending and the "don't ask, don't tell" ban on LGBTQ people serving openly in the military. His attitude toward the Clinton administration and Democratic leadership was unequivocal. "I'm one less vote for an agenda that makes you want to throw up," he said. Graham won 60%-40%, a smashing victory in a district that had been represented only by Democrats since Reconstruction.

As a member of the House Judiciary Committee, Graham played a major role in the 1998 impeachment of President Bill Clinton. In the Senate trial, Graham's folksy manner and clear description of Clinton's offenses—"Where I come from, a man who calls someone up at 2:30 in the morning is up to no good"—made him one of the most effective GOP impeachment managers. In 2000, Graham was one of McCain's staunchest supporters in his first bid for the presidency.

In 2002, Graham ran for the seat of Republican Sen. Strom Thurmond, who was 99 and did not seek a ninth term. Even though there had not been an open South Carolina Senate seat since 1941, Graham had no opposition in the Republican primary. His work on impeachment and the McCain campaign made him well-known and popular statewide, and he had the endorsements of three former governors and Thurmond. Democrats portrayed him as lacking in substance and recruited Alex Sanders, president of the College of Charleston, who in 1985 was appointed to the state Court of Appeals.

Sanders was a gifted raconteur, charming and well-connected around the state. He was a solid fundraiser as well, raising $4.2 million—less than Graham's $6.2 million, but a considerable achievement for a candidate consistently behind in the polls. Sanders supported the Bush tax cuts and Iraq War, but he opposed the death penalty—on religious grounds—and a constitutional amendment to allow criminalization of flag burning. Graham hammered him on the death penalty and the flag amendment, but most of all, labeled him as a liberal, saying Sanders would advance the agenda of Sens. Hillary Clinton of New York and Ted Kennedy of Massachusetts. Graham won 54%-44%.

Graham has long combined a foreign policy hawkishness with sometimes surprising breaks with his party on domestic issues. After the Supreme Court legalized same-sex marriage nationwide, he said the party should accept the ruling and drop language calling for a constitutional amendment barring same-sex marriage nationwide from its platform. Graham was the only Judiciary Committee Republican to support President Barack Obama's choice of Sonia Sotomayor for the Supreme Court in 2009, saying the president deserved the prerogative to nominate a qualified person of his choice even if the GOP disagreed with her ideology. He took the same position a year later when Obama nominated Solicitor General Elena Kagan for the court. He praised her intellect and, he said, "She's funny, and that goes a long way in my book."

But his limits of understanding the other side were tested amid Trump's nomination of Brett Kavanaugh to the Supreme Court in 2018. After the initial confirmation hearing, allegations surfaced from psychology professor Christine Blasey Ford, who said Kavanaugh had sexually assaulted her while he was drunk at a high school party decades earlier. Kavanaugh denied the allegations, and a subsequent public hearing with both the nominee and accuser was held. Republicans on the committee —all white men—had hired a female prosecutor to question Blasey Ford, cognizant of the optics. At first, most also ceded their time to the prosecutor when it was Kavanaugh's turn, but Graham was the first not to do so. He erupted in anger, accusing Senate Democrats of "the most unethical sham since I've been in politics. … Boy, you guys want power. God, I hope you never get it." Seething, Graham pointed out he had been willing to cross the aisle and vote for Obama's nominees, but Democrats wouldn't consider doing so. "This is not a job interview. This is hell," the senator said. His indignation shocked many Democrats as he was attacking a woman who said she had been sexually assaulted, but Graham was undeterred. "I know I'm a single white man from South Carolina and I've been told to shut up, but I will not shut up," he said. His impassioned defense of Kavanaugh, who was eventually confirmed, won praise from the White House and Trump allies.

But Graham's confrontational stance was nothing new. He took similar tacks in several high-profile issues involving national security. He and McCain led a successful push to derail the chances of Susan Rice, then the ambassador to the U.N., to become secretary of State after they sharply questioned her role in responding to the deadly September 2012 terrorist attack on the U.S. consulate in Benghazi Libya. Graham told Fox News that Secretary of State Hillary Clinton "got away with murder" for not foreseeing the threat in Benghazi. The two senators were at the forefront of opposing the nomination of their former colleague Republican Chuck Hagel of Nebraska to become Obama's secretary of Defense because of what they considered his insufficient support for Israel and hawkishness on Iran, although Hagel was confirmed. And he warned in June 2014 that the "seeds of 9/11 are being planted all over Iraq and Syria" in calling for a more aggressive U.S. response in both nations.

Graham has taken a hard line against new gun control measures, including an assault-weapons ban. Graham stuck by his view that tighter gun control wasn't necessary even after the murders of nine Black churchgoers by a white man in Charleston in June 2015, though he suggested he would support more enforcement of background check laws already on the books. Graham said there's "no doubt" the murders were racially motivated but initially demurred when asked if he thought the Confederate flag should be removed from official use in the state, calling it "part of who we are." Later, he backed South Carolina Gov. Nikki Haley when she called for the removal of the Confederate flag from Statehouse grounds after the Charleston shooting.

Graham had worked in a bipartisan fashion on immigration, an issue with which he has long grappled. In 2006 and 2007, Graham supported the McCain-Kennedy and Kennedy-Kyl immigration bills, positions that got him in considerable trouble with conservatives who opposed giving undocumented immigrants a path toward citizenship. Radio talk show host Rush Limbaugh belittled him as "Lindsey Grahamnesty," and the Greenville County Republican Party voted to censure him. Graham's public comments suggesting that immigration bill opponents were "bigots" did not help his cause. Undeterred, Graham joined a group of senators, four Democrats and four Republicans, that hammered out a plan in early 2013 to tighten border security, visa tracking and workplace verification in exchange for providing a path toward citizenship for the country's estimated 11 million undocumented workers. The bill passed by a wide margin in the Senate, but House GOP leaders refused to take it up in the face of withering criticism from conservative talk radio. During the 2016 campaign, he criticized Trump for his hostility toward immigrants. "My party is in a hole with Hispanics. The first rule of politics when you're in a hole is stop digging. And somebody needs to take a shovel out of Donald Trump's hand."

But, as on other issues, once Graham allied with Trump, his rhetoric and policy positions on immigration began to change. He supported Trump's call to end birthright citizenship and took a much harder line on Muslim immigration and purported, but unproven, links to possible terrorism. Using words that seemed straight out of Trump's mouth, Graham said in November 2017 that the president "is right to make sure when somebody comes into the country from a place where radical Islam [flourishes] ... we're going to ask extra hard questions." And he added that Trump was "right to slow down who comes into this country" and applauded him for recognizing "that we're in a religious war"—a stark shift from the Graham who in 2011 convened a hearing on "Protecting the Civil Rights of American Muslims" and said that "if I don't stand up for" religious freedom for Muslims, "you won't stand up for mine." Amid the 35-day government shutdown in late 2018 and early 2019 over funding for a southern border wall, the senator tried to broker a comprehensive reform push despite initially saying he was "glad [Trump] picked this fight" because capitulating would "probably [be] the end of his presidency." During negotiations, Graham said he'd "never been more depressed about moving forward."

Before his transformation, Graham had varied experiences in national politics. Comparing his political style to McCain's, Graham told the New York Times: "I've never been a Luke Skywalker; I'm a much more calculating guy than that. I understand that you just don't charge into these things based on some moral belief that you're right and the other guy's wrong." Without much of a threat to his own reelection bid, Graham in 2008 traveled the country with McCain, then the Republican presidential nominee. McCain, Graham, and Democratic Sen. Joe Lieberman of Connecticut formed a bipartisan triumvirate on the campaign trail, dubbed the Three Amigos. Graham's support helped McCain in the pivotal January 2008 South Carolina primary, in which McCain redeemed his 2000 loss by winning with 33 percent of the vote.

Graham lost one of his best friends when McCain died from brain cancer in August 2018. "The void to be filled by John's passing is more than I can fill. Don't look to me to replace this man," Graham said in a tearful speech from the Senate floor, next to McCain's desk, which was draped in black. "There is a little John McCain in all of us, and the little John McCain practiced by a lot of people can make this a really great nation." But to others, McCain's death only magnified the evolution Graham had undergone, especially as remembrances of the late senator's patriotism and war career rolled in—which stood in stark contrast to Trump, who had belittled the former prisoner of war and said he wasn't a hero. He told the Washington Post in October 2018, "I'm not living my life going forward around John McCain."

Graham had long mused about running for president. He launched his campaign in June 2015, saying, "I want to be president to protect our nation that we all love so much from all threats foreign and domestic." Graham began the campaign as a long-shot candidate and never caught fire. With Trump taking an "America First" approach, Graham argued for a more aggressive national security strategy. Early in the campaign, he got under Trump's skin so much that the billionaire businessman called him a "light-weight" and urged supporters at his rallies to call Graham's cellphone, while Graham called Trump a "jackass" after he belittled McCain. Graham ended his campaign in December 2015 after failing to break out of the second tier of presidential candidates.

However, his relationship with Trump began to evolve around the time that McCain was diagnosed with cancer. The two played golf together often and Trump frequently called Graham for advice. "I'm going to try to stay in a position where I can have input to the president," Graham told the New York Times in October 2017. "I can help him where I can, and he will call me up and pick my brain. Now, if you're a United States senator, that's a good place to find yourself." And, in the same interview, he admitted there was also an ulterior electoral motive: "He's very popular in my state. When I help him, it helps me back home." Earlier, in an April 2017 interview with Fox News, Graham said, "I am like the happiest dude in America right now. ... We have got a president and a national security team that I've been dreaming of for eight years." In February 2019, Graham reminded the New York Times Magazine that McCain, too, had to reinvent himself as more conservative when he faced primary challenges in 2010. "If you don't want to get reelected, you're in the wrong business. ... I have never been called this much by a president in my life." He lashed out at other Republicans who dared to criticize Trump, including his onetime immigration reform collaborator, Arizona Sen. Jeff Flake, who retired in 2018 rather than face a Trump-inspired primary challenge. Democrats bemoaned the disappearance of the Graham they once knew. "People have black armbands on around the Democratic Caucus because it feels like we've lost Lindsey Graham," Missouri Sen. Claire McCaskill told NPR in November 2018 after she lost her reelection bid. "He is someone who was willing to step outside that bubble from time to time and really do the hard work on issues like immigration. " Notably, in 2018, Graham campaigned against Senate Democrats for the first time, targeting those who had opposed Kavanaugh's nomination, reneging on his past practice to never campaign against colleagues.

Another notable shift was on his approach to the Russia investigation. Far from an initial partnership with Ben Cardin of Maryland, the top Democrat on the Foreign Relations Committee, in voicing concerns over that country's interference in the 2016 elections, Graham downplayed the need for a bill he had once co-authored to protect the man leading it, special counsel Robert Mueller, because no one in their "right mind" would fire him. (Trump tried several times). Graham had also once defended Jeff Sessions as attorney general, saying in 2017 there would be "holy hell to pay" if Trump fired him. But after Trump did just that November 2018, Graham defended Trump, saying, "Every president deserves an attorney general they have confidence in and they can work with."

There have remained flashes of Graham's formerly "maverick" self, and some accounts have posited that Graham simply sidled up to Trump to try to wield the most influence on defense issues, especially on a president with an often incoherent foreign policy and strong isolationist beliefs. In late 2018, he criticized Trump's decision to withdraw troops fighting ISIS from Syria, saying on the

Senate floor that such a move would be "dishonorable" to allies in the region and "a stain on the honor of the United States." He renewed his opposition in 2019 when Trump decided to abandon Kurdish allies in the country. He also broke with Trump after Washington Post columnist Jamal Khashoggi, a Saudi citizen living in the U.S., was murdered inside the Saudi consulate in Istanbul, arguing that Saudi Crown Prince Mohammed bin Salman must be held accountable—even as Trump wanted to give him a pass because of their alliance—and saying that the prince had said he didn't know about the murder. On Fox News, Graham said, "Nothing happens in Saudi Arabia without MBS knowing it."

Graham took the gavel of the Senate Judiciary Committee in 2019. He promised to "push for the appointment and Senate confirmation of highly qualified conservative judges to the federal bench and aggressive oversight of the Department of Justice and FBI." And he said he would reopen probes into Hillary Clinton, again one of Trump's top talking points. "We need a special counsel to look at all this," he told Fox News host Sean Hannity about Clinton's use of a private email server while secretary of State, "but I intend to look at it." Graham also planned a "deep dive" into FBI and Justice Department surveillance of Trump campaign advisers during the 2016 race. One of his earliest actions was to get William Barr confirmed as Trump's second attorney general. After initially opposing a Republican push to use Senate resources to investigate the Ukrainian ties of Hunter Biden, the Democratic nominee's son, saying he didn't want to "turn the Senate into a circus" in 2020, Graham backed the inquiry into unproven conspiracy theories Trump had latched onto.

Graham's conversion during the Trump era led to his most serious reelection challenge in 2020. While he didn't have a major primary challenge as once seemed possible, instead Democrats were bullish on their chances to send a Democrat to the Senate from South Carolina for the first time since 1998. Their candidate, Harrison, was a former chairman of the South Carolina Democratic Party who later became a chair of the national party. He tried to exploit the incumbent's flip flops while hoping that as a Black candidate he could register and mobilize more of the state's African-American voting bloc and create a coalition of disaffected independents and moderate GOP voters. Like Graham, Harrison had a hardscrabble upbringing, growing up in impoverished Orangeburg with his teenage mother and grandparents before going to Yale University and Georgetown Law. A former floor director for and political acolyte of powerful South Carolina Rep. James Clyburn, now the House majority whip, Harrison said he was spurred to enter the race after seeing Graham's treatment of Blasey Ford during the Kavanaugh hearings. "It was all fake. It was all him performing for President Trump," Harrison told Esquire.

One of Harrison's main arguments was that Graham had fundamentally changed and was too worried about Trump's approval instead of the best interests of his state. "It used to be, in the past, you always thought Lindsey was doing stuff for us. But since this last term, he's been too much on his own theatrics and political relevance," Harrison told The Washington Post. "Getting in front of every TV camera he can. He doesn't understand that when you lose your job, it also means you lose your health benefits." Harrison zeroed in on GOP efforts to repeal the Affordable Care Act, which would have endangered coverage for those with preexisting conditions. Harrison supported expanding Medicaid in the state and broadband in its rural areas, but he worked to distance himself from his party's progressive wing: He opposed "Medicare for All" and the "Green New Deal." To Graham and Republicans, though, that distinction didn't matter, and just painting a Democratic candidate with that same brush is often enough in the Palmetto State. "The more liberal he becomes in the eyes of the voters, the better I will do," Graham told voters. He also seized on Harrison's past work as a lobbyist for the Podesta Group, which had ties to Clinton. But Graham had become a bogeyman of the left for his vocal support of Trump and frequent media appearances; millions of dollars began flowing to Harrison as a result. Throughout 2020, the Democrat outraised Graham, and polling showed the race was tightening. But the COVID-19 pandemic upended many of Harrison's plans to barnstorm the state, and as a pre diabetic, he conducted a nearly all-virtual campaign, while Graham still held physical events.

If it was Kavanaugh's confirmation hearing that spurred Harrison to run, it may have been the next Supreme Court vacancy that sealed the Democrat's fate. In mid-September, liberal icon Justice Ruth Bader Ginsburg died after being diagnosed with pancreatic cancer at 87. Even though Republicans refused to hold a hearing on Obama's nominee to replace conservative Justice Antonin Scalia who died in February 2016, saying the election cycle had already started, they rushed to confirm Trump's nominee, Amy Coney Barrett. As Judiciary chairman, Graham was front and center, reminding wavering Republicans at home that his race was about the importance of conservative judges that could be threatened if Democrats won back the majority. "A president serves for four years—not three," Graham said, arguing the situation was different than in 2016 because now the same party controlled the Senate and the White House. "I hope it's OK that you can be pro-life and adhere to your faith and still be considered by your fellow citizens worthy of this job," he told Barrett during her hearing—another subtle reminder to conservative religious voters at home.

But Ginsburg's death and the rush to confirm her replacement had another unintended consequence: Small-dollar online donors flooded Senate Democratic candidates with cash. Harrison, who had long had impressive fundraising totals outpacing Graham, saw his bank account explode, raising $57 million alone in the third quarter, blowing past the record set by Texan Beto O'Rourke's in 2018. By the end, Harrison has spent more than $130 million to Graham's $96 million; GOP outside spending added $33.7 million while Democratic groups put in $17.5 million. Despite Harrison's financial advantage, when Election Day came, Graham won by 10 points, a margin nearly identical to that of Trump, who won 55%-43% over Democratic nominee Joe Biden in the state. Democrats had hoped for more ticket splitting and that a third-party candidate would draw voters away from Graham, but the Constitution Party candidate—who had withdrawn just weeks before and endorsed Graham but remained on the ballot—only got 1.4%.

Graham didn't challenge Trump's false claims of widespread voter fraud after the elections. With the president focused on his narrow loss in Georgia and irate at that state's Republican secretary of State, Brad Raffensperger, for not helping him overturn the results, the GOP election official said Graham had called him and suggested he find a way to throw out legal ballots. Graham denied the "ridiculous" allegation, saying he was simply trying to discover "how do you verify signatures for mail in ballots in these states." But after the perpetuation of that election lie led to the violent January 6 insurrection at the Capitol, Graham was blunt in saying Biden had won and that he had "never been so humiliated and embarrassed for the country" when Trump incited a mob of his supporters. who stormed the Capitol in an eleventh-hour attempt to overturn Trump's loss. "Trump and I, we've had a hell of a journey. I hate it to end this way. Oh, my God; I hate it. From my point of view, he's been a consequential president," Graham said on the Senate floor. "But today, first thing you'll see. All I can say is count me out. Enough is enough." But Graham's rare break with Trump wouldn't last, and their golf games resumed in Mar-a-Lago. "I'm trying to keep a relationship with him after the riot," Graham told Axios. "I still consider him a friend. What happened was a dark day in American history. And we're going to move forward." In the same interview, Graham admitted Trump "could make the Republican Party something that nobody else I know could make it. He could make it bigger. He could make it stronger. He could make it more diverse. And he also could destroy it."

Tim Scott (R)

Appointed 2013, term expires 2022, 1st full term, b. Sep 19, 1965; North Charleston, SC; Presbyterian College, Att., 1984; Charleston Southern University, B.S., 1988; Evangelical; Single.

Elected Office: Charleston County Council, 1995-2008, Chairman, 2007-2008; SC House, 2009-2010; U.S. House, 2011-2013.

Professional Career: Partner, real estate firm; Owner, Tim Scott Allstate.

DC Office: 104 HSOB 20510, 202-224-6121, Fax: 202-228-5143, scott.senate.gov

State Offices: Columbia, 803-771-6112; Greenville, 864-233-5366; North Charleston, 843-727-4525.

Committees: *Aging (RMM)*. *Banking, Housing & Urban Affairs*: Economic Policy; Financial Institutions & Consumer Protection; Securities, Insurance & Investment (RMM). *Finance*: Energy, Natural Resources & Infrastructure; Health Care; International Trade, Customs & Global Competitiveness. *Health, Education, Labor & Pensions*: Employment & Workplace Safety; Primary Health & Retirement Security. *Small Business & Entrepreneurship*.

Group Ratings

	ADA	ACLU	AFL-CIO	LCV	COC	HAFA	ACU	CFG	FRC
2020	-	17%	-	8%	-	87%	91%	-	-
2019	0%	C	11%	14%	77%	C	92%	80%	100%

Almanac Ratings 2019-2020

	Economy	Social	Foreign	Composite
Liberal	0%	0%	0%	0%
Conservative	100%	100%	100%	100%

Key Votes of the 116th Congress

1. EPA clean energy rules	N	5. Russia sanctions	N	9. Barr as Atty. General	Y
2. U.S./Mex./Can. trade deal	Y	6. Troops in SYR, AFG	Y	10. Spending at the border	Y
3. Cut unemployment benefits	Y	7. Veto arms sales to Saudis	N	11. Coney Barrett to Sup. Ct.	Y
4. Shelton to Fed Reserve	Y	8. Defense $$$, veto override	Y	12. Electoral College objections	N

Election Results

Election	Name (Party)	Vote (%)		Cand. Spent	Ind. Exp. Support	Ind. Exp. Oppose
2016 General	Tim Scott (R)................................	... 1,241,609	(61%)	$4,751,790	$161,399	
	Thomas Dixon (D)........................	 757,022	(37%)	$35,176		
2016 Primary	Tim Scott (R)...............................	. Unopposed				

Prior winning percentages: 2016 (61%), 2014 special (61%); House: 2012 (62%), 2010 (65%)

Tim Scott, South Carolina's junior senator, is the first Black senator elected from the Deep South since Reconstruction and the first Republican nationwide since 1979 as well as the first African-American to serve in both chambers of Congress. That unique, and sometimes fraught, position has led him to be a major voice against racist policing practices and efforts to reform them. During the Trump administration, he frequently pushed back against the president's sometimes racist language and policies, even torpedoing several judicial nominees with problematic backgrounds. The Republican Party has sought to elevate him during these debates, especially amid a push for tighter voting restrictions that could disenfranchise Black voters. That's led some Democrats to imply Scott is Republicans' Black "token" senator. He was selected to give the GOP response to President Joe Biden's first speech to Congress in April 2021, and the rising star has been frequently mentioned as a possible presidential contender in 2024.

He has had a remarkable ascent in local and state politics and has become a prominent national spokesman on topics from conservatism to racist policing practices. Scott and his siblings were raised by a single mother who worked 16-hour days as a nurse's assistant. Scott got his first job at 13. He was on the verge of flunking out of high school when he met the man who he has said changed his life: John Moniz, the owner of a Chick-fil-A next to the movie theater where Scott worked and where he would regularly buy french fries, the only food he could afford. Moniz, a Christian, became a father figure for Scott, teaching him the value of personal discipline and hard work. In a speech at the 2012 Republican National Convention, Scott said Moniz taught him that "having a job is a good thing, but creating jobs was even better." Scott finished high school and went on to earn a partial football scholarship to Presbyterian College in Clinton South Carolina. He transferred to Charleston Southern University, where he earned a bachelor's degree in political science.

Scott went on to run an insurance company, own part of a real estate agency and win a seat on the Charleston County Council. Just after his first election, in 1995, he received a handwritten note of congratulations from Republican Sen. Strom Thurmond of South Carolina, who had run for president on a pro-segregation platform in 1948. Thurmond's past didn't stop Scott from accepting the job as statewide co-chairman of Thurmond's final senatorial campaign in 1996. Asked how an African-American could help Thurmond, Scott told The New York Times, "The Strom Thurmond I knew had nothing to do with that" and noted that Thurmond's views on race had evolved. He later served as chairman of the county council and was elected to one term in the state House.

In 2010, Scott ran for an open House seat in the 1st District, which includes Charleston. In the GOP primary, he faced opposition from candidates with better name recognition, including Carroll Campbell III, son of former South Carolina Gov. Carroll Campbell Jr., and Paul Thurmond, the late senator's son. Scott got help from national Republican organizations and was the front-runner in the primary. He took 47 percent of the vote, which was just short of avoiding a runoff; Thurmond took second. There were few policy differences between the two, although Thurmond did not share Scott's willingness to abide by term limits and swear off earmarked spending. Scott claimed that in his 15 years in elected office, he never voted for a tax increase. His conservative credentials won him praise from prominent Republicans like former Alaska Gov. Sarah Palin and former House Speaker Newt Gingrich. In the runoff, Scott defeated Thurmond 68%-32%. In the general election, he easily beat Democrat Ben Frasier, a retired federal worker, 66%-29%. His race appeared to be a nonissue for the district's voters, about 70 percent of whom were white.

As a House member, Scott's voting record was marginally more moderate than those of the rest of South Carolina's deeply conservative delegation. He was less outspoken than the state's other members. He joined conservatives in refusing to support a 2011 bill to raise the federal debt limit, a 2012 tax and spending compromise to avert a "fiscal cliff" and several leadership-backed spending bills to keep the government running. Republican leaders didn't mind; they realized his value to their party and heaped praise on him. Scott served as a deputy whip and a freshman-class liaison to the leadership, and he was given a seat on the influential Rules Committee.

After the 2012 elections, Sen. Jim DeMint quit the Senate to lead the conservative Heritage Foundation think tank after he suffering setbacks with the defeat of some tea party candidates whom he had supported, which contributed to Republicans' failure to win Senate control. Attention then turned to whom Gov. Nikki Haley would appoint. Haley, who is Indian-American, chose Scott over four other finalists, a decision she said was based on his devotion to the state and his ability to advocate for it. "It is very important to me, as a minority female, that Congressman Scott earned this seat," she said. His selection proved popular with Republicans.

At first, Scott shunned the spotlight, turning down several opportunities to raise his national profile and refusing to highlight his race, even declining to join the Congressional Black Caucus (which is comprised mostly of Democrats). He'd introduce himself: "I am a Christian, who is a conservative, and you may have noticed that I'm Black." He concentrated on getting to know the state, holding numerous town halls and meeting constituents in creative circumstances, such as volunteering incognito at a local Goodwill store to talk about their problems without tipping them off that he was a politician. In 2014, he flew under the national radar without serious primary or general election opposition, winning 61 percent of the vote.

But when major race-related events shook South Carolina, Scott took advantage of his unique position. After a white policeman killed Walter Scott [no relation], an unarmed Black man in Scott's hometown of North Charleston in April 2015, the senator was one of the first to support issuing body cameras to police officers, and he introduced a bill to provide millions of dollars for police departments to acquire them. Similar legislation became law in South Carolina in early June. Weeks later, when nine Black churchgoers were murdered by a white supremacist in Charleston, Scott joined Haley and other South Carolina leaders to back removal of the Confederate flag from Statehouse grounds. During an emotional speech on the Senate floor, Scott choked up when repeating comments from a relative of a victim that "this evil attack would lead to reconciliation, restoration and unity in the nation." He later told the Senate that he had been subject to racial discrimination at the Capitol. "I have felt the anger, frustration, sadness and humiliation that comes with feeling like you're being targeted for nothing more than being yourself," Scott said in a floor speech detailing how he'd been racially profiled throughout his life.

Once President Donald Trump was elected, Scott began separating himself from his party by opposing many of Trump's judicial and administration nominees, often raising past statements or actions on race. In 2017, Senate Majority Leader Mitch McConnell was forced to withdraw Trump's nomination of Ryan Bounds to the 9th U.S. Circuit Court of Appeals after Scott announced he would oppose Bounds—and persuaded Florida Sen. Marco Rubio to do so, too—over past racist writings. In late 2018, Scott also helped derail Thomas Farr's nomination to the District Court for the Eastern District of North Carolina after he was scrutinized for defending a controversial voter ID law and other possible suppression of Black voters in North Carolina. Scott wrote in the Wall Street Journal about those votes, telling his party that "the solution isn't simply to decry 'racial attacks.' Instead, we should stop bringing candidates with questionable track records on race before the full Senate for a vote." However, Scott has not been complimentary of Democratic efforts to address race and has criticized Sen. Chuck Schumer of New York, now the majority leader, for opposing a South Carolina judicial nominee because he was white and would be replacing two Black men that President Barack Obama had nominated. "Perhaps Senate Democrats should be more worried about the lack of diversity on their own staffs than attacking an extremely well-qualified judicial nominee from the great state of South Carolina," Scott tweeted.

Scott was deeply critical of Trump's response to violent protests by neo-Nazi groups in Charlottesville Virginia in August 2017. The president claimed there were "some very fine people on both sides" of clashes between white supremacists and counter protesters. "What we want to see from our president is clarity and moral authority," Scott told Vice News. "And that moral authority is compromised. ... There's no question about that." Trump later reached out to Scott and the two met. Scott told CBS afterward that the president "was very clear that the perception that he received on his comments was not exactly what he intended with those comments." However, Trump repeated his those comments the next day.

There were areas where Scott worked with the Trump administration. As a member of the Senate Finance Committee, Scott successfully pushed in 2017 for his "Investing in Opportunity Act," which encouraged private investment in distressed communities via tax advantages. He also worked with Ivanka Trump, the president's daughter and adviser, to expand the child tax credit in the GOP's tax overhaul and praised her as someone who has "a strong, powerful backbone." Scott also successfully inserted a provision in the 2018 farm bill to allow the heirs of property owners to qualify for federal farm programs—something especially important to Black farmers in the South.

Scott was influential in passing the 2018 First Step Act, a bipartisan criminal justice reform bill that overhauled sentencing guidelines. He called Trump "the MVP" for helping get the bill across the finish line, but it was Scott and other lawmakers like Utah Sen. Mike Lee who persuaded undecided senators to support it. However, he was unsuccessful at getting his Walter Scott Act, named after an unarmed Black man who was fatally shot by a white North Charleston policeman in 2015, included in the criminal justice reform overhaul. The measure would have forced states receiving federal law enforcement funding to keep track of certain data points for each officer-involved shooting.

In 2016, Scott told the Senate that there was no single solution to law enforcement problems affecting minorities. "Believe it or not, the government is not the answer to what ails us," he said. He called for improved police training, increased personal interaction between law enforcement officers and community groups, and federal legislation to provide broader assistance—including expanded police use of body cameras. His critics pointed out that he received "F" ratings from the NAACP on its annual scorecards, supported voter ID laws many civil rights groups view as racist, and refused to endorse a congressional fix to the Voting Rights Act after the Supreme Court struck down a key enforcement provision of the law. He also has been a loud advocate for school choice, a more controversial issue. Scott believes it can improve education for poor and minority children. "There is a trend that can be broken at its foundation if we focus first on education and second on work skills," he said on ABC's "This Week" in 2015.

As racial justice protests swept the country during the spring and summer of 2020 after white police officers killed Breonna Taylor and George Floyd, both unarmed African-Americans, Scott was thrust into the spotlight as he began pushing again for policing reform. As polling increasingly showed a shift in public opinion toward changes in policing procedures and accountability, McConnell tapped Scott to lead a working group to produce new legislation, noting the senator had experience "dealing with this discrimination that persists some 50 years." With the Senate majority on the line, the issue took on outsize importance for the GOP. Of Scott's selection, McConnell told The Washington Post, "The best way is to listen to one of our own who has had these experiences." After he was chosen, Scott tweeted about some of the blowback he'd gotten from liberals on social media: "Not surprising the last 24 hours have seen a lot of 'token' 'boy' or 'you're being used' in my mentions. Let me get this straight ... you DON'T want the person who has faced racial profiling by police, been pulled over dozens of times, or been speaking out for YEARS drafting this?" In an interview with the Associated Press, Scott said he'd been pulled over by police repeatedly without cause over the years. "I'm thinking to myself how blessed and lucky I am to have 18 different encounters and to have walked away from each encounter," he said.

Scott's proposal was much more conservative than the more widespread reforms Democrats wanted. His "Justice Act" included his previous suggestion of federal data collection of the use of force and no-knock warrants. It also would discourage the use of chokeholds but wouldn't ban them. The measure also included grant programs to encourage the use of body cameras and would create a database of police disciplinary records and add criminal penalties for falsifying reports on civil rights violations. Additionally, it would direct the Justice Department to provide training on de-escalation techniques and require an officer to intervene if another officer was using unjustified deadly force. Democrats, however, wanted to revoke "qualified immunity"—which protects police from most civil suits—to allow victims' families to sue police officers as well as ban chokeholds and no-knock warrants.

After the Democratic-controlled House passed its more stringent bill, Democrats in the Senate, then in the minority but backed by the NAACP, blocked debate on Scott's bill, demanding bipartisan talks. Scott bristled at the development, asking on the Senate floor, "If we're all watching the same pictures that we have all found disgusting and unbelievable, why can't we agree to tackle the issues in a substantive way here on the floor of the world's greatest deliberative body? Because that's what we're supposed to do here: We debate the issues. I want the nation to see. I want the public to see. I want the world to see. I want all of America to see us debating this issue." Sen. Dick Durbin, then the minority whip, had to apologize after saying the GOP bill was "a token, half-hearted approach"; the white Illinois Democrat said he wasn't talking about Scott but about the bill, which he saw as doing way too little. Scott told the Wall Street Journal, "I'm just really ticked off about how casual and cavalier he gets to be, as a Democrat leader, to race-bait in an intentional, and unnecessary, and unfortunate way." A few months later, House Majority Whip Jim Clyburn, who is also Black and is the only Democrat in South Carolina's delegation, also suggested that Scott was a Republican token.

Scott never seemed fully comfortable with having to be the GOP's face on the issue, especially as he kept having to defend things Trump did or said. After the president re tweeted a video of supporters in Florida shouting "white power," Scott went on CNN and said Trump should take it down; three hours later, he did. "Of all the issues that are going on, I know the racial ones are the most provocative," Scott told the Post in June 2020. "But I'm not the only person that people can talk to about it. I don't want to be racially profiled into a position where I only get to talk about what the president does." After attending a 2017 event for South Carolina GOP women that came, shortly after he had criticized Trump for his comments on Charlottesville, he told his best friend, former Rep. Trey Gowdy, that the attendees didn't think he supported the president enough. "There are days, I am sure, he feels like a man without a home," Gowdy—who wrote a 2017 book titled, "Unified: How Our Unlikely Friendship Gives Us Hope for a Divided Country," with Scott—told the Dispatch in 2020. Scott also spoke out in 2020 after Biden told a radio host, "If you have a problem figuring out whether you're for me or Trump, then you ain't Black." Scott accused the former vice president and then-Democratic presidential nominee of "negative race baiting." He added: "I'd say I'm surprised, but it's sadly par for the course for Democrats to take the Black community for granted and brow beat those that don't agree."

That uncomfortable dichotomy, though, was again on display when Scott was tapped to deliver the official GOP response to the president's first speech to a joint session of Congress—often a thankless, and sometimes awkward, job. Even as he talked about being racially profiled, Scott declared, "America is not a racist country," and, "It's wrong to try to use our painful past to try to dishonestly shut down debates in the present." Alluding to Democrats' voting rights bill, Scott said he was offended by attempts to frame it in a racial context. "This is not about civil rights or our racial past. It's about rigging elections in the future," Scott said, claiming Democrats were trying to fight "discrimination with different discrimination" in their approach to race. "President Biden promised you a specific kind of leadership. He promised to unite a nation, to lower the temperature, to govern for all Americans, no matter how we voted," Scott said. "But three months in, the actions of the president and his party are pulling us further apart."

Scott had an easy reelection in 2016. Perhaps the most notable aspect was that he won 61 percent of the vote—6 percentage points more than Trump in the state. The chief difference in their performances was that Scott took 56 percent in his home county of Charleston, where Trump took 43 percent. He's up for reelection again in 2022 but isn't expected to face serious Democratic opposition for what he's said will be his final term in the Senate. However, Scott's political career may not be over after that, as he's continued to be mentioned as a possible 2024 presidential candidate. But even that prospect could put Scott in yet another precarious position, as the racist elements of the Republican Party that embraced Trump battle those who want to see the party become less homogenous.

Nancy Mace (R)

Elected 2020, 1st term, b. Dec 04, 1977; Fayetteville, NC; The Citadel University, B.A., 1999; University of GA, M.S., 2004; Christian - Non-Denominational; Divorced; 2 children.

Elected Office: SC House, 2018-2021.

Professional Career: Author; Real Estate Agent; Management Consultant, Accenture, 1999-2001; Public Relations and Marketing Employee, 2004-2014; Coalitions Director/Field Director, Donald J. Trump for President, Inc., 2015-2016.

DC Office: 212 CHOB 20515, 202-225-3176, mace.house.gov

State Offices: Beaufort, 843-521-2530.

Committees: *Oversight & Reform*: Government Operations; Subcommittee on Civil Rights & Civil Liberties. *Transportation & Infrastructure*: Aviation; Highways & Transit; Water Resources & Environment. *Veterans' Affairs*: Economic Opportunity.

Election Results

Election	Name (Party)	Vote (%)		Cand. Spent	Ind. Exp. Support	Ind. Exp. Oppose
2020 General	Nancy Mace (R)...............................	216,042	(51%)	$5,823,046	$1,332,140	$5,882,742
	Joe Cunningham (D)......................	210,627	(49%)	$7,286,529	$706,403	$7,099,689
2020 Primary	Nancy Mace (R)................................	48,411	(58%)			
	Kathy Landing (R)...........................	21,835	(26%)			
	Chris Cox (R).....................................	8,179	(10%)			
	Brad Mole (R).................................	5,800	(7%)			

Republican Nancy Mace, who was the first woman to graduate from The Citadel military college, became the first Republican woman elected to Congress from South Carolina. Although Mace enthusiastically supported President Donald Trump, she showed her independence as a member of the state House when she spoke out against his support for offshore drilling along her state's coastline. Mace narrowly defeated first-term Democratic Rep. Joe Cunningham, who unexpectedly won the district in 2018.

Mace was born at Fort Bragg North Carolina to military parents. Her father, an Army brigadier general, served as commander of cadets at The Citadel. In getting her bachelor's degree at that school, she majored in business administration. Mace wrote a book about her undergraduate experience, In the Company of Men: A Woman at the Citadel. Later, she earned a master's degree in journalism and mass communication at the University of Georgia.

In business, Mace ran what she described as a multi-service business consulting group in Charleston. Her clients included local Republican candidates, such as Sen. Tim Scott. In 2014, Mace joined several candidates who challenged Sen. Lindsey Graham in the Republican primary. "Unfortunately, our senator has a track record of trusting this government and working to grow this government." Graham won the seven-candidate primary with 56 percent. Mace placed fifth, with 6 percent of the vote.

As a member of the state House, where she won a special election in 2017 and a full term the following year, Mace had a productive record. Citing her own experience as a rape victim when she was a teenager, she successfully advocated an exception for rape and incest to a bill that otherwise banned an abortion where there was a fetal heartbeat. Her break with Trump on offshore drilling helped to earn her a perfect record of support from the League of Conservation Voters. Mace enacted a bill that ended the shackling of pregnant mothers in state prisons.

In 2020, Mace won the Republican primary with 57 percent of the vote against three opponents. Cunningham was the first Democrat to represent the district since 1980. Mark Sanford, who held the seat for a total of 12 years before and after his 8 years as governor of South Carolina, lost the Republican primary in 2018 to Katie Arrington. She then lost the general election to Cunningham, 51%-49%.

Mace's challenge to Cunningham had some lively moments. In a debate, he criticized her for missing dozens of votes in the state House. In response, she said she was a single mother who was home-schooling her two children. "You should be ashamed of yourself and disqualified because of this personal attack," Mace told Cunningham. When Cunningham described Mace's politics as "more partisan, more toxic and more divisive," she responded, "You can't be independent when you vote with Nancy Pelosi 90 percent of the time."Mace's motto was, "Send a new Nancy to Congress." Cunningham described the contest as a choice between "people who want to change politics and the people who relish in chaos."

The Columbia-based State newspaper, in its editorial, endorsed Cunningham as "clearly deserving" a second term, describing him as "a hard-working, pragmatic and results-driven member of Congress." But the editorial added that the decision was "a close call" and that Mace was a "highly impressive candidate" who had shown that she was "unafraid to stand up to powerful leaders in her own party."

Mace won, 50.6%-49.4%, a margin of 5,400 votes. In Charleston County, which cast 40 percent of the vote, Cunningham led by 17,000 votes. Mace took the other four counties, with leads of about 10,000 votes in both Beaufort and Berkeley counties, which each cast 20 percent.

SC-1: Lowcountry

Population		Race and Ethnicity		Income	
Total	821,107	White	72.00%	Median Income	$77,185
Land area (sq. miles)	1,548	Black	19.00%	District Income Rank	108
Pop/ sq mi	530.48	Latino	6.10%	Poverty Rate	8.80%
Born in State	40.80%	Asian	2.10%	With health insurance	89.90%
		Two or more races	3.00%	Cash public assistance	0.80%
Age Groups		Other	3.80%	Food stamp/SNAP	5.30%
Under 18	21.70%				
18-34	21.80%	**Education**		**Work**	
35-64	37.70%	H.S grad or less	29.20%	White Collar	43.10%
Over 64	18.80%	Some college	30.00%	Sales and Service	37.60%
		College Degree, 4 yr	25.20%	Blue Collar	19.40%
Military		Post grad	15.70%	Government	16.60%
Veteran/ Active Duty	12.50%				

2020 Pres. Vote	Trump	222,867	(52%)	Biden	197,130	(46%)		
2016 Pres. Vote	Trump	178,181	(54%)	Clinton	134,541	(40%)	Johnson	12,450 (4%)

Charleston, Hilton Head: Looking out across the harbor to Fort Sumter are the glorious mansions of the Battery, gazing on the same view that the hot-blooded young swells of Charleston did in April 1861, when they fired the shots that began the Civil War. Today, there are few more beautiful urban scenes in America than the pastel single houses of Charleston, built flush with the sidewalk, turning their shoulders to the streets, with open piazzas inside their iron gateways facing south to catch the breeze. Founded in 1670, Charleston was blessed with one of the finest harbors on the Atlantic, at the point where, Charlestonians like to say, the Ashley and Cooper rivers meet to form the Atlantic Ocean. Cargoes of rice, indigo, cotton and slaves crossed its docks, enriching the White planters and merchants who dominated the state's economic and political life. After the war, Charleston became an economic backwater, enabling the old buildings to survive. The loving restorations of recent years have attracted a considerable tourist trade. Charleston remains one of the top tourist destinations in the world—ranked for five years straight by Travel + Leisure magazine as the best city in the U.S. to visit.

Charleston's old society—descended from planters from Barbados, French Huguenots, Sephardic Jews and the second sons of English gentry—was once a leading force in American political life. The hotheads in the gallery disrupted the 1860 Democratic National Convention here so boisterously that it adjourned and reconvened in Baltimore, while Southern Democrats split off and nominated their own candidate, enabling Abraham Lincoln to win with 38 percent of the popular vote. The history of black South Carolinians, memorialized in George Gershwin's Porgy and Bess, is noteworthy, but the tale of slavery, once hidden under a blanket of politeness, was slow to emerge. Many plantations near Charleston have added programs on the history of slavery to tours once dominated by romantic tales of the old South.

The decision by Gov. Nikki Haley in 2015 to remove the Confederate flag from the state capitol grounds accelerated that rethinking. In 2018, the Charleston City Council formally apologized for its role in slavery, the slave trade and Jim Crow. The Old Slave Mart Museum, the onetime site of slave auctions, details the history along with displaying African-American arts and crafts. The city plans to open in 2022 a $100 million, 40,000-square-foot International African American Museum where slave ships once docked; historians estimate that 90 percent of African Americans can trace at least one ancestor to that spot. Still, inequality persists. An analysis from the College of Charleston found that around 60 percent of downtown Charleston's restaurant and hotel workers live outside the peninsula. Black Lives Matter showdowns in 2020 damaged more than 100 buildings in Charleston. Another longer-term problem is growing: In 2020, Charleston Harbor suffered 68 "flooding events," second only to 2019. The seven "major" tidal floods in 2020, with water levels of more than eight feet, were a record—all the more of a concern because there was no hurricane.

The 1st Congressional District of South Carolina stretches along the coast from Charleston down to Hilton Head. It includes the coastal parts of Beaufort County, taking in the old county seat of Beaufort and the carefully manicured developments of Hilton Head Island, plus parts of burgeoning inland suburbs in Berkeley and Dorchester counties. It includes the heavily white Battery and the area west of the Ashley River. About 40 percent of the population of the 1st is in Charleston, another 40 percent in the inland counties, and 20 percent in Beaufort. The posh condominium developments and golfing resorts around Hilton Head helped drive up Beaufort County's population, which increased 18 percent between 2010 and 2019. On nearby St. Helena Island, slave owners escaping the heat and the mosquitoes ran largely absentee operations, thus allowing Gullah culture, a fusion of English and African elements, to thrive, and it lingers in the Low country today. The district takes in the Marine Corps' Parris Island training base and the nearby air station at Beaufort.

This has been comfortable Republican country, but the conservatism of the Low country—the term for South Carolina's coastal counties, including Charleston—is more economic and less cultural than the conservatism of the Upstate region. Many voters here oppose offshore drilling, favor environmental restrictions—the city banned plastic bags, straws and foam containers—and efforts to curb sprawl. The area has moderated as more northern retirees settle here. In 2020, President Donald Trump won the 1st, 52%-46%, his lowest performance in the state's six Republican districts and notably closer than Mitt Romney's 58%-40% win over President Barack Obama in 2012.

Joe Wilson (R)

Elected 2001, 10th full term, b. Jul 31, 1947; Charleston, SC; WA and Lee University, B.A., 1969; University of SC, J.D., 1972; Presbyterian; Married (Roxanne Dusenbury McCrory Wilson); 4 children; 7 grandchildren.

Military Career: U.S. Army Reserve 1972-1975; South Carolina Army National Guard 1975-2003

Elected Office: SC Senate, 1985-2001.

Professional Career: Practicing attorney, 1972-2001.

DC Office: 1436 LHOB 20515, 202-225-2452, Fax: 202-225-2455, joewilson.house.gov

State Offices: Aiken, 803-642-6416; West Columbia, 803-939-0041.

Committees: *Armed Services*: Readiness; Strategic Forces. *Education & Labor*: Health, Employment, Labor & Pensions. *Foreign Affairs*: Middle East, North Africa & Global Counterterrorism (RMM).

Group Ratings

	ADA	ACLU	AFL-CIO	LCV	COC	HAFA	ACU	CFG	FRC
2020	**	25%	**	10%	-	82%	90%	**	-
2019	5%	C	42%	7%	85%	C	90%	66%	100%

Almanac Ratings 2019-2020

	Economy	Social	Foreign	Composite
Liberal	25%	36%	33%	32%
Conservative	75%	64%	67%	68%

Key Votes of the 116th Congress

1. U.S./Mex./Can. trade deal Y	5. Russia sanctions Y	9. Firearms background checks N
2. First Coronavirus response N	6. Troops in Syria Y	10. Spending at the border Y
3. HEROES Act N	7. Veto arms sales to Saudis N	11. Marijuana liberalized rules N
4. CASH Act N	8. Defense $$$, veto override Y	12. Electoral College objections Y

Election Results

Election	Name (Party)	Vote (%)	Cand. Spent	Ind. Exp. Support	Ind. Exp. Oppose
2020 General	Joe Wilson (R)............................ 202,715	(56%)	$2,026,248	$5,386	$750
	Adair Boroughs (D)............................ 155,118	(43%)	$2,670,152	$10,594	
2020 Primary	Joe Wilson (R)............................ 55,557	(74%)			
	Michael Bishop (R)........................ 19,397	(26%)			

Prior winning percentages: 2018 (56%), 2016 (60%), 2014 (62%), 2012 (96%), 2010 (54%), 2008 (54%), 2006 (63%), 2004 (65%), 2002 (84%), 2001 special (73%)

Republican Joe Wilson, elected in 2001, has a reputation in his committee roles as a hardworking fiscal and defense hawk. With his seniority, he has been a mentor to many junior Republicans. Following the 2020 election, he was passed over when had sought the top GOP slot on the Armed Services Committee—one of a series of such setbacks, despite having the most seniority.

Wilson grew up in Charleston and graduated from Washington & Lee University and the University of South Carolina law school. He got his Republican stripes as an aide to Rep. Floyd Spence and then for Sen. Strom Thurmond. Wilson was deputy general counsel at the Energy Department during the Reagan administration. He practiced law in West Columbia for 25 years while working on several political campaigns. In 1984, he was elected to the state Senate, where he chaired the Transportation Committee. Throughout this period, he served as a staff judge advocate in the South Carolina Army National Guard. All four of Wilson's sons have been Eagle Scouts and served in the military, two of them in Iraq. His son, Alan, was reelected state attorney general in 2018.

In 2001, when Spence died after more than 30 years in the House, Wilson became the frontrunner to replace his longtime friend and mentor. In the special election, he won the Republican primary with 76 percent of the vote and defeated his Democratic opponent easily.

Wilson has advocated a closer military relationship with India, and he traveled frequently to Iraq and Afghanistan to review those conflicts when U.S. forces were engaged. He urged President Donald Trump to loosen restrictions on the U.S. military fighting the Taliban in Afghanistan. In 2017-18, Wilson chaired the Readiness Subcommittee, to provide the resources for the military to respond to what he described as an "unprecedented readiness crisis."

Wilson was largely unknown outside his district, and barely known in Washington, before his outburst during Obama's September 2009 speech at the Capitol. As Obama was answering what he called critics' "bogus claims" about his health care legislation, Wilson called out, "You lie!" His behavior provoked stinging criticism on editorial pages and talk shows around the country. He apologized to Obama in a phone call but rebuffed Democratic demands for a more public apology from the well of the House. His South Carolina Democratic colleague, Majority Whip James Clyburn, alleged there was a taint of racism in Wilson's reaction, noting that no other president to that point had been the target of a similar breach in protocol during a joint session. The House passed a "resolution of disapproval" on a mostly party-line vote.

On the Education and the Workforce Committee, Wilson worked with Democrats to make permanent the child adoption tax credit. He failed to get the top Republican slot on the committee when it came open in 2009. Although he had more seniority, he lost out to John Kline of Minnesota. After Kline stepped down in 2016, Wilson supported Rep. Virginia Foxx of North Carolina as the next chair. In 2019, he vied for the ranking Republican slot on the House Foreign Affairs Committee after working vigorously to help vulnerable Republicans in the 2018 cycle to boost his chances, doling out $1.8 million to more than 100 candidates and incumbents. Even though Wilson had more seniority and had made a case that his working relationship with the new chairman, Eliot Engel of New York, would be an asset, he lost out to Rep. Michael McCaul of Texas.

Wilson has typically been reelected by wide margins. In 2018, he had his closest challenge since 2010, besting Army veteran Sean Carrigan 56%-43%. Carrigan attacked him for his support for Trump and for not taking Russian interference in U.S. elections seriously enough. In 2020, Wilson was an enthusiastic supporter of Trump's reelection, citing his support for "a very strong national defense," even though Wilson sometimes disagreed with the details. During that year, for example, he joined other senior Republicans on a letter to Trump in which they objected to his plans to cut troop levels in Germany. And he unsuccessfully urged granting refugee status to persecuted Uighur Muslims in China. In his own reelection, Wilson had the same 56%-43% victory as two years earlier—the closest margin of any of the six successful incumbents in South Carolina.

SC-2: West-Central South Carolina   **Cook Partisan Voting Index: R+9**

Population		Race and Ethnicity		Income	
Total	722,542	White	69.40%	Median Income	$60,781
Land area (sq. miles)	3,022	Black	24.60%	District Income Rank	250
Pop/ sq mi	239.08	Latino	5.90%	Poverty Rate	11.60%
Born in State	52.80%	Asian	1.90%	With health insurance	90.50%
		Two or more races	2.40%	Cash public assistance	1.10%
Age Groups		Other	1.70%	Food stamp/SNAP	9.60%
Under 18	22.50%				
18-34	22.40%	**Education**		**Work**	
35-64	38.30%	H.S grad or less	35.40%	White Collar	41.90%
Over 64	16.80%	Some college	29.60%	Sales and Service	36.70%
		College Degree, 4 yr	21.40%	Blue Collar	21.50%
Military		Post grad	13.70%	Government	19.50%
Veteran/ Active Duty	11.40%				

2020 Pres. Vote	Trump	200,712	(55%)	Biden	158,360	(43%)			
2016 Pres. Vote	Trump	176,615	(57%)	Clinton	119,812	(38%)	Johnson	8,289	(3%)

Parts of Columbia Metro, Aiken: In 1786, soon after the Revolutionary War, the South Carolina legislature decided to move the state capital away from the Charleston aristocracy and into the interior, away from a city named after a king to a new city named after a discoverer of America. So began Columbia. The State House was built on high ground above the Congaree River in a town of one-and-a-half story houses with first-floor porticos, dormers and raised brick basements—"Columbia cottages." In 1865, Gen. William Tecumseh Sherman's army burned almost everything here but the State House. Columbia recovered but grew slowly, with the state government, the state university, the Army's Fort Jackson, and local insurance companies providing steady employment.

Columbia's politics were personified by Jimmy Byrnes, the Democrat who was elected to Congress in 1910 and returned from top posts in the administrations of Franklin D. Roosevelt and Harry Truman to serve as governor. Byrnes adamantly opposed the Brown v. Board of Education decision in 1954. Since then, upwardly mobile White South Carolinians have turned Republican. Metro Columbia is competitive: Richland County, which is 49 percent African-American, votes Democratic and gave 68 percent of the vote to Joe Biden in 2020. Across the river, Lexington County is 16 percent Black and heavily Republican and gave 64 percent to President Donald Trump.

The 2nd Congressional District of South Carolina includes parts of metro Columbia, excluding Black neighborhoods in central and north Columbia that are in the Black-majority 6th District. It contains the city's affluent white neighborhoods and the spread-out towns and countryside beyond. It includes all of Lexington and Aiken counties. Aiken, with its horsey trappings for polo and steeplechase, has long attracted affluent transplants. About 40 percent of the vote is in Lexington, and 30 percent is in Richland. The Midlands area overall has been rapidly growing, and in 2017 the financial website Smart Asset found that Columbia gained the second most millennia's in the country, behind only Seattle. The Columbia metro area's population is projected to double by 2050. Aiken County, which runs along the Georgia border, has grown in recent years thanks to employers such as Bridgestone Tires, Kimberly-Clark Corp., Shaw Industries carpet and flooring and UPS. At a plant in Lexington, Michelin manufactures radial and earthmover tires.

The district takes in Barnwell County and the Savannah River Site near Aiken, which from 1954 to 1991 was one of the nation's nuclear weapons manufacturing complexes. Since then, the 310 square miles have been undergoing a multibillion-dollar cleanup, an important economic driver regionally. The state has pursued extensive litigation with the federal government over the project. In 2017, a federal judge dismissed part of the lawsuit seeking compensation for the delay, but continued to review the pace of the cleanup. The Department of Energy in 2019 shuttered the Mixed Oxide (MOX) Fuel Fabrication Facility at the site, moving nuclear material to New Mexico. The site transitioned to plutonium pit production. Still, important work continues at the Savannah River Site. Its employees "have been at the forefront of national security, environmental stewardship and world-class innovation" Energy Secretary Dan Brouilette said in October 2020.

The district is comfortably Republican, though mirroring the area's suburban culture the vote for President Donald Trump in 2020 dropped to 55 percent from the 62 percent Mitt Romney received in 2012.

Jeff Duncan (R)

Elected 2010, 6th term, b. Jan 07, 1966; Greenville, SC; Clemson University, B.A., 1988; Baptist; Married (Melody Duncan); 3 children.

Elected Office: SC House, 2002-2010.

Professional Career: Assistant Vice President., M.S. Bailey & Son, 1989-1993; Assistant Vice President., Palmetto Bank, 1993-1995; President, J. Duncan & Assocs., 1995-2010.

DC Office: 2229 RHOB 20515, 202-225-5301, Fax: 202-225-3216, jeffduncan.house.gov

State Offices: Anderson, 864-224-7401; Clinton, 864-681-1028.

Committees: *Energy & Commerce*: Communications & Technology; Energy; Environment & Climate Change.

Group Ratings

	ADA	ACLU	AFL-CIO	LCV	COC	HAFA	ACU	CFG	FRC
2020	**	24%	**	5%	-	98%	97%	**	-
2019	0%	C	19%	7%	69%	C	97%	100%	100%

Almanac Ratings 2019-2020

	Economy	Social	Foreign	Composite
Liberal	25%	15%	4%	15%
Conservative	75%	85%	96%	85%

Key Votes of the 116th Congress

1. U.S./Mex./Can. trade deal Y	5. Russia sanctions	N	9. Firearms background checks N
2. First Coronavirus response N	6. Troops in Syria	N	10. Spending at the border Y
3. HEROES Act	N	7. Veto arms sales to Saudis N	11. Marijuana liberalized rules N
4. CASH Act	N	8. Defense $$$, veto override N	12. Electoral College objections Y

Election Results

Election	Name (Party)	Vote (%)	Cand. Spent	Ind. Exp. Support	Ind. Exp. Oppose
2020 General	Jeff Duncan (R)................................ 237,544	(71%)	$1,085,193	$10,762	$750
	Hosea Cleveland (D)......................... 95,712	(29%)			

Prior winning percentages: 2018 (68%), 2016 (73%), 2014 (71%), 2012 (67%), 2010 (66%)

Republican Jeff Duncan, elected in 2010 to an open seat, has often gone his own way from GOP leadership. His deeply held conservative beliefs can prompt fierce rhetoric, which angers Democrats but plays well among his like-minded colleagues and at home.

Duncan was born in Greenville. His family moved frequently, mostly in the Carolinas, as they followed his father's job as a textile industry manager tasked with turning around underperforming plants. He got his bachelor's at Clemson University, where he was a wide receiver on the football team and majored in political science. After college, he worked as a community banker and then for a real estate auction company, which inspired him to start his own real estate marketing firm that specialized in auctions. In the state House, he worked on updating the funding formula for education and on lowering taxes. In 2009, Duncan sponsored a bill creating an alternative state budget that did not use federal stimulus money, as a way of protesting President Barack Obama's $787 billion measure.

In the six-candidate GOP primary for the House seat, Duncan was endorsed by the anti-tax group Club for Growth, built a 2-to-1 fundraising advantage and prevailed in a runoff with 51 percent of the vote against businessman Richard Cash. In the general, he faced token Democratic opposition in the solidly Republican district. He widened his victory margin in each of his first three reelections.

Duncan believes in the "Jeffersonian principles of limited governments, free markets and individual liberties," and says the federal government has gone beyond its constitutional authority. In 2011, he became the first member of Congress to receive a perfect score from the conservative activist group Heritage Action. A member of the Tea Party Caucus, Duncan has been part of the cadre of conservatives who have voted against GOP leadership priorities. In January 2015, he voted against giving John Boehner another term as Speaker. Soon after that, he quit as a member of the Republican whip team and was among the GOP rebels who helped create the Freedom Caucus. Duncan is a steadfast supporter of gun rights, and in 2017 sponsored the Hearing Protection Act to legalize silencers; he suffered damage in his left ear during his youth as a result of not using proper noise suppressors when he was hunting with his dad.

On the Foreign Affairs Committee, he enacted a bill in 2012 that called for a strategy to address the Iranian threat in the Western Hemisphere. At a hearing in 2013 on the terrorist attack in Benghazi Libya, he rebuked outgoing Secretary of State Hillary Clinton for "gross negligence" in allowing the consulate there to "become a death trap." As chairman of the Subcommittee on the Western Hemisphere, Duncan was outspoken in his opposition to President Barack Obama's opening of diplomacy to Cuba.

After joining the Energy and Commerce Committee in 2017, Duncan supported the Mixed Oxide Fuel Fabrication Facility (MOX) at the Savannah River Site, which was shut down by President Donald Trump's Energy Department. Calling it "part of God's "intelligent design," Duncan supported offshore drilling, telling a group at Lander University that "God gave us the ability to discover there are resources known as fossil fuels inside the Earth that we can extract." Duncan grilled Facebook CEO Mark Zuckerberg during his April 2018 appearance before the committee, arguing that the social media site has censored conservative and Christian content unfairly. Duncan gave Zuckerberg a pocket copy of the U.S. Constitution, asking him, "Why not have a community standard for free speech and freedom of religion that is simply a mirror of the First Amendment?"

During the 2016 presidential campaign, Duncan criticized as "horrendous and indefensible" comments about women by Donald Trump. Then, he added, "I continue to be more concerned with Hillary Clinton's actions than I am with Donald Trump's words." He became a steadfast supporter of Trump's policies as president, though he said in a speech in South Carolina that "I'm proud of this president. Now, I'm not proud about what he says or how he says it, and maybe not proud of what he's done in the past. But from the time he was sworn into office until now, he has kept his eye on the Americans."

In October 2020, Duncan was among 18 House Members who voted against a resolution to condemn QAnon conspiracy theories. "I wasn't sent to Congress to play along with Democrats' messaging bills that try to ignore what's actually going on in this country right now—violence in the streets by left-wing mobs, supported by Democrat politicians," he told the House. Four months earlier, he opposed a House-passed resolution to remove Confederate statues from the Capitol. "Every leader in history, including ourselves, has flaws and imperfections," he wrote in a letter to Speaker Nancy Pelosi that sought to preserve the statue of a former House Speaker from South Carolina. Removing the memorabilia was a "slippery slope," he added.

Duncan had been interested in running for governor in 2018, when there was the prospect of an open seat. That option faded in January 2017 when Henry McMaster succeeded Nikki Haley after she became ambassador to the United Nations. He might look to move up if there is an open Senate seat or for the next gubernatorial vacancy.

SC-3: Northwestern South Carolina   **Cook Partisan Voting Index: R+21**

Population		Race and Ethnicity		Income	
Total	706,961	White	75.10%	Median Income	$50,815
Land area (sq. miles)	5,268	Black	19.20%	District Income Rank	378
Pop/ sq mi	134.19	Latino	4.70%	Poverty Rate	15.10%
Born in State	65.40%	Asian	1.00%	With health insurance	89.80%
		Two or more races	2.60%	Cash public assistance	1.30%
Age Groups		Other	2.00%	Food stamp/SNAP	11.20%
Under 18	21.60%				
18-34	21.90%	**Education**		**Work**	
35-64	37.60%	H.S grad or less	45.60%	White Collar	33.90%
Over 64	18.90%	Some college	30.50%	Sales and Service	35.00%
		College Degree, 4 yr	14.40%	Blue Collar	31.10%
Military		Post grad	9.50%	Government	14.10%
Veteran/ Active Duty	7.70%				

2020 Pres. Vote	Trump	228,038	(68%)	Biden	102,363	(31%)			
2016 Pres. Vote	Trump	190,605	(67%)	Clinton	82,618	(29%)	Johnson	5,616	(2%)

Anderson, Greenville Suburbs: The Upstate in South Carolina was once many days' travel by wagon from the Low country plantations along the coast. It was first settled by Scots-Irish farmers, including the family of future Vice President John C. Calhoun, around the time of the Revolutionary War. The pioneers wanted to make big plantations of these forests, but the land was too hilly for the labor-intensive rice crops grown in the Low country and sometimes too cold for cotton. So, relatively few slaves were brought here and the land became mostly small farms. Today, the racial and cultural tone of the Upstate shows traces of these roots. Clemson University was founded here by Calhoun's son-in-law and is one of the state's two land-grant institutions. (South Carolina State, a historically Black university in Orangeburg, is the other.) This is a mostly white part of the South, with a hell-of-a-fella tone to daily life and a tradition-minded slice of Middle America.

Yet it is not untouched by change. The textile factories and mills have been shutting down, and a way of life in many of these rural areas has vanished with them. The few surviving textile plants have limited payrolls. On the positive side, high-tech and automobile manufacturers have expanded, with growth throughout the Upstate. In 2018, Michelin, which has its North American headquarters in nearby Greenville, reopened a dormant jumbo tire plant in Anderson County. The county is now home to manufacturing centers such as Electrolux appliances, First Quality tissue products and Glen Raven fabrics. Bosch, the second-largest plant in Anderson, announced a $45 million expansion in 2018, and there's a growing presence and influence of German companies in the Upstate.

Clemson—both the university and the city—have helped lead the growth. In 2016, the university became part of a $300 million program, including support from the Defense Department, to expand textile manufacturing and technology. In October 2020, a start-up biotech company run by two Clemson professors announced progress in developing screws used in orthopedic surgery that employ easy-to-use sensors to determine the status of fracture healing. Also that month: The Clemson city council looked for ways to manage the city's rapid growth, the Greenville News reported. The bad news: In November 2020, Clemson reported more than 4,300 cases of COVID, the most for any university in the nation.

The 3rd Congressional District of South Carolina follows the Georgia border from Augusta through the tree-harvesting country around McCormick County to Appalachian foothills along the North Carolina border. The 18 percent Black populations is the smallest of any district in the state. The southern part of the 3rd has a few heavily African-American areas, including Edgefield County, where Sen. Strom Thurmond first won public office in the 1930s. Anderson is the largest county in the district, with nearly 30 percent of the voters. This part of South Carolina, ancestrally Democratic, began trending Republican in the 1950s as cultural issues became more important in this fervently religious region. President Donald Trump won 68 percent of the vote here in 2020, nine percentage points better than his showing in other South Carolina districts.

William Timmons (R)

Elected 2018, 2nd term, b. Apr 30, 1984; Greenville, SC; Christ Church Episcopal School; George WA University, B.A., 2006; University of SC, M.A., 2009; University of SC, J.D., 2010; Church of Christ; Married.

Elected Office: SC Senate, 2016-2018.

Professional Career: Staff Assistant, Sen. Bill Frist, 2006-2007; Prosecutor, SC 13th Circuit Solicitor's Office.

DC Office: 313 CHOB 20515, 202-225-6030, timmons.house.gov

State Offices: Greenville, 864-241-0175; Spartanburg, 864-583-3264.

Committees: *Financial Services*: Consumer Protection & Financial Institutions; Diversity & Inclusion; Oversight & Investigations. *Select Committee on the Modernization of Congress (VChmn)*.

Almanac Ratings 2019-2020

	Economy	Social	Foreign	Composite
Liberal	25%	29%	27%	27%
Conservative	75%	71%	73%	73%

Key Votes of the 116th Congress

1. U.S./Mex./Can. trade deal	Y	5. Russia sanctions	Y	9. Firearms background checks	N
2. First Coronavirus response	N	6. Troops in Syria	Y	10. Spending at the border	Y
3. HEROES Act	N	7. Veto arms sales to Saudis	N	11. Marijuana liberalized rules	N
4. CASH Act	N	8. Defense $$$, veto override	Y	12. Electoral College objections	Y

Election Results

Election	Name (Party)	Vote (%)		Cand. Spent	Ind. Exp. Support	Ind. Exp. Oppose
2020 General	William Timmons (R)......................	222,126	(62%)	$785,930	$6,409	$750
	Kim Nelson (D).................................	133,023	(37%)	$174,289		

Prior winning percentages: 2018 (60%)

Republican William Timmons was elected as the more mainstream candidate in a hard-fought primary in 2018. He narrowly won the GOP runoff against Lee Bright, an outspoken conservative who generated controversy as a state legislator and in his 2014 primary challenge to Sen. Lindsey Graham. The general election became an afterthought in the solidly Republican district. In the House, Timmons took steps that showed his interest in bipartisan actions.

Timmons, part of a prominent family in the Greenville business community, graduated from George Washington University and got his master's and law degrees from the University of South Carolina. He worked in the state prosecutor's office and later started his own small businesses in the Greenville area. In 2016, he defeated a veteran Republican incumbent to win election to the state Senate.

Bright had been a controversial figure in the Legislature for his conservative views on social issues, such as defense of flying the Confederate flag on State House grounds and a limitation on the rights of transgender people. In his 2014 challenge to Graham, Bright attacked the senator's collaboration with "gun grabbers" in attempts at gun-control legislation; he was criticized during that campaign for his plan to give away an AR-15 rifle at a raffle during a political event. He was a distant runner-up in that primary with 15 percent to Graham, who got 56 percent. In 2016, Bright narrowly lost the GOP primary to retain his state Senate seat. Then-Gov. Nikki Haley, among other leading Republicans, backed his opponent.

In their contest for the House seat, Timmons said Bright had a "history of embarrassing stunts" and that he had run a "dirty, name-calling campaign" against him, including references to Timmons' wealthy family background. "He is going to say things that embarrass you, and it is going to cause problems for the Upstate," warned Timmons, who contrasted his own skills as a thorough prosecutor. Bright dismissed Timmons as the "establishment-backed candidate."

With his base in Spartanburg County, where he more than doubled the vote for Timmons, Bright led with 25 percent in the initial round of voting in the 13-candidate Republican field. Bolstered by his narrow lead in Greenville County, Timmons finished second by a scant 391 votes over state Rep. Dan Hamilton.

That forced a runoff two weeks later, which took on larger dimensions within the national party. Timmons was endorsed by Sen. Marco Rubio of Florida; Bright had the support of Sen. Ted Cruz of Texas. The Club for Growth spent more than $400,000 on advertising that attacked Timmons for his inadequate support of President Donald Trump. Overall, he had a big fundraising advantage, with $1.4 million—including $1.1 million in personal loans—to $343,000 for Bright. Timmons prevailed, 54%-46%. This time, Timmons led in both counties, with similar margins. Nearly two-thirds of the vote was cast in Greenville. In November, Timmons easily defeated Brandon Brown, a local businessman.

Timmons was the only freshman among the six House Republicans assigned to the Select Committee on the Modernization of Congress. Discussing the work of that panel, he told Roll Call, a publication that covers Capitol Hill, that during the initial orientation, he was "shocked" that new House Members traveled to meetings on separate busses. He called that separation an early signal that "this kind of partisanship was encouraged from the very start." The 12-member panel made nearly 100 bipartisan recommendations to improve House operations.

Midway through his first term, Timmons filled a Republican vacancy on the Financial Services Committee, another sign that he had won the early trust of Republican leaders. He cosponsored a bipartisan proposal that would require Congress to create a bipartisan "rescue committee" of lawmakers to propose steps to address federal trust funds that were nearing insolvency. In May 2020, when Tesla chief executive Elon Musk threatened to move his company from Fremont California because he was unhappy with local regulations and taxes, Timmons Tweeted him, "May we suggest South Carolina instead? We are a business-friendly state with large-scale automotive manufacturing already taking place." There was no public indication that Musk replied.

In August 2019on a balcony of the Capitol, Timmons married Sarah Anderson, a lawyer in private practice in Greenville. Sen. Tim Scott of South Carolina officiated. At age 36 when he entered Congress, Timmons was positioned for a lengthy career in Congress.

SC-4: Upcountry   Cook Partisan Voting Index: R+14

Population		Race and Ethnicity		Income	
Total	754,148	White	73.50%	Median Income	$60,731
Land area (sq. miles)	1,299	Black	17.60%	District Income Rank	251
Pop/ sq mi	580.43	Latino	9.00%	Poverty Rate	11.00%
Born in State	55.20%	Asian	2.60%	With health insurance	89.70%
		Two or more races	2.50%	Cash public assistance	0.90%
Age Groups		Other	3.80%	Food stamp/SNAP	7.20%
Under 18	22.50%				
18-34	23.00%	**Education**		**Work**	
35-64	38.10%	H.S grad or less	36.60%	White Collar	38.80%
Over 64	16.50%	Some college	30.10%	Sales and Service	35.80%
		College Degree, 4 yr	21.10%	Blue Collar	25.50%
Military		Post grad	12.30%	Government	9.70%
Veteran/ Active Duty	7.20%				

2020 Pres. Vote	Trump	215,250	(59%)	Biden	140,897	(39%)	
2016 Pres. Vote	Trump	181,637	(60%)	Clinton	103,848	(34%)	Johnson 8,171 (3%)

Greenville and Spartanburg: A century ago, Northern investors seeking sites for textile mills looked at the Upstate of South Carolina and found what was described then as "mild climate, abundant water power, proximity to the cotton fields, and plenty of native labor already accustomed to a low standard of living." As mills fled New England, textile factories settled along the Southern Railway and Seaboard Coast Line tracks between Charlotte and Atlanta, especially in the Piedmont of South Carolina. The textile country might look bucolic, but Greenville, Spartanburg and the dozens of mill towns thick in the surrounding countryside became as industrial as Lancashire or the Ruhr. In the days before child labor laws, factory work sometimes began at age 6, condemning workers to a life of illiteracy. Escapes to a brighter future, such as the brilliant but brief baseball career of West Greenville's "Shoeless" Joe Jackson, were rare.

Today, along Interstate 85, which parallels the Southern Railway, little remains of what was once the largest textile-producing area in the United States. In 2016, Greenville Online reported that the 18 textile mills that were operating a century earlier within three miles of downtown had been reduced to three. The old mills have been turned into historic centers and are the topics of documentaries. But the multinational corporations that have sprung up in their place have listed Greenville among the fastest growing cities in the country, with a 37 percent uptick from 2000 to 2019.

Financial sweeteners, tax incentives, the absence of unions, and solid infrastructure—airports, highways and the busy Port of Charleston—attracted an enormous BMW plant in Spartanburg that continues to expand production of 412,000 vehicles and a payroll of 11,000, and an investment to date of more than $10 billion. About 70 percent of the vehicles are exported to more than 125 countries, which exceeds the exports of GM and Ford combined. The Greer plant, BMW's largest in the world and its first outside Germany, manufactures many of its X-series cars, including two plug-in hybrid models. Michelin is another large employer in the Greenville area, with 5,700 workers at six plants that manufacture tires. GE Power produces gas turbines at its first advanced manufacturing center, which employed 3,200. Greenville's revitalized downtown boasts fancy hotels and restaurants, which cater to the new corporate manager class, along with glitzy condos, apartments and other mixed-use developments. In 2020, the city of Spartanburg, which is barely 10 percent of the population of the county and is 48 percent Black, launched a comprehensive plan; "racial equity" is a guiding principle.

The 4th Congressional District of South Carolina includes about 90 percent of Greenville and Spartanburg counties, with nearly two-thirds living in Greenville. Along with nearby Anderson, Greenville and Spartanburg comprise the largest population area in South Carolina, with more than 1 million residents. Culturally, the this strongly influenced by Greenville's many evangelical and fundamentalist churches. Bob Jones University dropped its ban on interracial dating in 2000, finally regaining its tax-exempt status in 2017 three decades after losing it because of that ban. Here, the real political divide is between religious and economic conservatives. As Greenville continues to grow and diversify, many young people stay in the area after graduating from Furman University or nearby Clemson. Hispanics grew from 4 percent of Greenville County's population in 2000 to 10 percent in 2019. The 4th remains comfortably Republican. President Donald Trump got 59 percent of the vote in 2020.

Ralph Norman (R)

Elected 2017, 2nd full term, b. Jun 20, 1953; York County, SC; Presbyterian College, B.S., 1975; Presbyterian; Married (Elaine Rice); 4 children; 16 grandchildren.

Elected Office: SC House: 2005-2006; 2009-2017.

Professional Career: Real estate developer, Warren Norman Co.

DC Office: 319 CHOB 20515, 202-225-5501, Fax: 202-225-0464, norman.house.gov

State Offices: Rock Hill, 803-327-1114.

Committees: *Homeland Security*: Cybersecurity, Infrastructure Protection & Innovation; Transportation & Maritime Security. *Oversight & Reform*: Subcommittee on Environment (RMM).

Group Ratings

	ADA	ACLU	AFL-CIO	LCV	COC	HAFA	ACU	CFG	FRC
2020	**	20%	**	0%	-	98%	95%	**	-
2019	0%	C	10%	7%	69%	C	94%	100%	95%

Almanac Ratings 2019-2020

	Economy	Social	Foreign	Composite
Liberal	25%	22%	8%	19%
Conservative	75%	78%	92%	81%

Key Votes of the 116th Congress

1. U.S./Mex./Can. trade deal	Y	5. Russia sanctions	N	9. Firearms background checks N
2. First Coronavirus response	N	6. Troops in Syria	N	10. Spending at the border Y
3. HEROES Act	N	7. Veto arms sales to Saudis	N	11. Marijuana liberalized rules N/A
4. CASH Act	N	8. Defense $$$, veto override	N	12. Electoral College objections Y

Election Results

Election	Name (Party)	Vote (%)		Cand. Spent	Ind. Exp. Support	Ind. Exp. Oppose
2020 General	Ralph Norman (R)..............................	220,006	(60%)	$763,514	$579	$863
	Moe Brown (D).................................	145,979	(40%)	$480,749	$35,523	

Prior winning percentages: 2018 (57%), 2017 special (51%)

Republican Rep. Ralph Norman was first elected in a June 2017 special election to succeed former Rep. Mick Mulvaney, who resigned to join the Trump administration, first as director of the Office of Management and Budget and later as acting chief of staff. The special election was closer than expected a harbinger of things to come in suburban House districts in the midterm elections as a backlash to President Donald Trump. After damaging information about his Democratic opponent's past surfaced in a rematch, Norman easily won a full term in 2018. He collaborated with conservative House Republicans.

A Rock Hill native, Norman got a degree in business from Presbyterian College in Clinton South Carolina. He joined his family's real estate development company. The business began by building homes and planning subdivisions in and around Rock Hill, and expanded into commercial real estate throughout York and Lancaster counties. The ventures were highly successful.

In 2004, Norman won an open seat in the state House, winning the three-way primary with 52 percent of the vote. Two years later, he challenged longtime Democratic Rep. John Spratt, who was in line to chair the House Budget Committee. National Republicans had long lobbied Norman to take on Spratt. The incumbent spent more than $2.6 million, double Norman's $1.3 million. In a poor year for the GOP that saw Democrats take back the House, Spratt won 57%-43%.

In 2009, Norman won back his old state House seat. When the congressional seat opened again in 2017, he couldn't resist another try. The Republican primary was hard-fought, with Norman and state Rep. Tommy Pope emerging as frontrunners. Norman received more than $700,000 of support from the Club for Growth, while Pope was backed by the Chamber of Commerce. Norman painted himself as the natural successor to Mulvaney, underscoring his support for Trump and opposition to Obamacare, saying at one forum, "If you liked Mick Mulvaney's votes, you'll like my votes." Pope cast himself as a more pragmatic figure. In the first round of voting, each got 30 percent of the vote in the seven-candidate primary; Pope led by 135 votes. The run-off was just as close. Norman prevailed by 221 votes out of the more than 35,000 tallied. Pope took 54 percent of the vote in York County, which cast slightly more than half the vote; Norman won nine of the other 10 counties.

Archie Parnell, the Democratic nominee, was new to local politics, but he had extensive experience in Washington as a tax attorney at the Justice Department and with the House Ways and Means Committee. Later, he was an international tax and trade adviser to large companies. The contest was overshadowed by another special election the same day about 200 miles west in a suburban Atlanta district that had been nearly as solidly Republican. Norman won that far less costly contest by a much closer margin than did Karen Handel, the successful GOP candidate in Georgia, 51%-48%.

Parnell started gunning to challenge Norman for a full term in 2018, and Democrats saw him as a top-tier candidate until divorce records surfaced from the 1970s showing he had physically abused his ex-wife. Parnell admitted to the abuse, saying it occurred when he was in college and he "did something that I have regretted every single day since," but that it had led to a "monumental change in my life," pointing to his second marriage of 40 years and two grown daughters. Parnell's staff quit en masse and the national party largely abandoned him, but he refused to drop out. Norman refused to debate Parnell, saying, "I'm not going to debate a man who beats his wife."

During a Rock Hill event in April 2018, Norman put his loaded gun on a table while talking with women from the gun control group Moms Demand Action. Saying he was trying to make the point that guns aren't dangerous in the right hands, Norman told the Charleston Post & Courier, "I'm not going to be a Gabby Giffords. … I don't mind dying, but whoever shoots me better shoot well, or I'm shooting back," a reference to the former Arizona Democratic congresswoman who was shot and nearly killed during a constituent event in 2011. The Moms group said they felt "unsafe." None of that seemed to hurt Norman, who won, 57%-42%.

Norman joined the House Freedom Caucus, as he had promised. At a meeting of House Republicans in July 2020, when conservatives objected that Rep. Liz Cheney had not been sufficiently supportive of Trump, Norman referred negatively to her father—former Vice President Dick Cheney—as part of the hawkish Bush administration. As reported by Politico, Cheney responded, "I'm not a Bush."

In January 2021, he was selected as the ranking Republican on the Environment Subcommittee of the Oversight panel. Norman said he was honored to have been selected because "so much is at stake when it comes to our nation's environmental policies."

SC-5: North-Central South Carolina   Cook Partisan Voting Index: R+11

Population		Race and Ethnicity		Income	
Total	738,205	White	68.10%	Median Income	$56,282
Land area (sq. miles)	5,506	Black	26.20%	District Income Rank	310
Pop/ sq mi	134.08	Latino	4.40%	Poverty Rate	12.40%
Born in State	53.60%	Asian	1.70%	With health insurance	90.00%
		Two or more races	2.60%	Cash public assistance	1.20%
Age Groups		Other	1.40%	Food stamp/SNAP	9.60%
Under 18	22.70%				
18-34	20.20%	**Education**		**Work**	
35-64	39.70%	H.S grad or less	40.40%	White Collar	36.00%
Over 64	17.40%	Some college	33.20%	Sales and Service	37.70%
		College Degree, 4 yr	17.20%	Blue Collar	26.40%
Military		Post grad	9.20%	Government	13.70%
Veteran/ Active Duty	9.90%				

2020 Pres. Vote	Trump	212,162	(58%)	Biden	150,693	(41%)		
2016 Pres. Vote	Trump	175,488	(57%)	Clinton	118,656	(39%)	Johnson	6,525	(2%)

Charlotte Suburbs, Sumter County: Some of the fiercest battles of the Revolutionary War were fought in South Carolina's Upstate, on hilly lands just being settled by Scots-Irish farmers moving up from the Low country or down the Virginia Piedmont valley. This was a country of violent passions and unclear lines. Carolinians argued for years over which side of the North and South Carolina boundary Andrew Jackson was born on in 1767. Ever since, the fighting spirit and Calvinist faith of Upstate Carolinians have not wavered. This "Olde English District" remains intensely religious and pro-military, but it is no longer impoverished. The area has been moving on from the Civil War in other ways. In 2017, the Confederate flag and photos of local war generals were removed from a room in the courthouse in York.

For many years, the dominant industry here was textiles, traditionally the first factory enterprise of industrializing countries, with low pay and poor working conditions. With unemployment exceeding 20 percent in some small counties during the 2007-09 recession, the number of textile jobs declined markedly, though more sophisticated manufacturing has boomed. In 2018, South Korean company Samsung opened a $380 million plant in Newberry to manufacture home appliances, creating more than 1,200 jobs. The growth of suburbia south of Charlotte in York and Lancaster counties has been rapid. From 2010 to 2019, the counties grew 24 and 28 percent, respectively.

Located 30 miles from downtown Charlotte and with an average home price of about $225,000 in January 2021, an increase from $139,000 in 2015, Rock Hill has become an attractive destination for city workers looking for affordable housing, and some businesses are taking advantage, too. Its population is 39 percent Black. In October 2020, a group of local Black economic leaders issued a statement that hiring of Black residents should be "reflective of the opportunities." In Cherokee County, Gaffney is the heart of peach country. It is home to the famed Peachoid, a four-story water tower tank off Interstate 85 that is shaped like a peach. South Carolina has shipped more peaches than neighboring Georgia since the 1950s, despite the latter's Peach State nickname.

The 5th Congressional District consists of all or part of 11 counties, mostly in the Upstate and some in the Midlands. Over half the population is in Lancaster and York counties and in Cherokee County, along I-85 and in the Charlotte exurbs. Politically, this Jacksonian homeland is ancestrally Democratic but has become increasingly Republican. Much of the population growth in York and Lancaster comes from Charlotte suburban commuters with few ties here but with strong conservative views. In the outskirts of Columbia, the rural counties of Fairfield and Lee are majority-Black. Sumter, which is 48 percent Black, has grown only 2 percent since 2000. The district is 27 percent Black. Overall, this has been a Republican district in presidential elections, and President Donald Trump got 58 percent of the vote in 2020. Demographics have placed a lid on the partisan balance. If York County and its surrounding areas continue to explode with college educated professionals, that balance could shift again.

James Clyburn (D)

Elected 1992, 15th term, b. Jul 21, 1940; Sumter, SC; SC Executive Institute, 1957; Mather Academy, Camden, 1957; SC State University, B.S., 1962; University of SC School of Law, B.S., 1974; African Methodist Episcopal; Widower (Emily England Clyburn); 3 children; 4 grandchildren.

Professional Career: Teacher, 1962-1966; Director, Charleston Neighborhood Youth Corps, 1966-1968; Executive Director, SC Comm. for Farm Workers, 1968-1971; Assistant, Gov. West, 1971-1974; SC Human Affairs Comm., 1974-1992.

DC Office: 200 CHOB 20515, 202-225-3315, Fax: 202-225-2313, clyburn.house.gov

State Offices: Columbia, 803-799-1100; Kingstree, 843-355-1211; Santee, 803-854-4700.

Committees: House Majority Whip.

Group Ratings

	ADA	ACLU	AFL-CIO	LCV	COC	HAFA	ACU	CFG	FRC
2020	**	79%	**	100%	-	0%	7%	**	-
2019	90%	C	100%	92%	63%	C	7%	12%	0%

Almanac Ratings 2019-2020

	Economy	Social	Foreign	Composite
Liberal	51%	52%	54%	53%
Conservative	49%	48%	46%	47%

Key Votes of the 116th Congress

1. U.S./Mex./Can. trade deal	Y	5. Russia sanctions	Y	9. Firearms background checks	Y
2. First Coronavirus response	Y	6. Troops in Syria	Y	10. Spending at the border	Y
3. HEROES Act	Y	7. Veto arms sales to Saudis	Y	11. Marijuana liberalized rules	Y
4. CASH Act	Y	8. Defense $$$, veto override	Y	12. Electoral College objections	N

Election Results

Election	Name (Party)	Vote (%)		Cand. Spent	Ind. Exp. Support	Ind. Exp. Oppose
2020 General	James Clyburn (D)	197,477	(68%)	$1,695,128	$873	
	John McCollum (R)	89,258	(31%)			$113

Prior winning percentages: 2018 (70%), 2016 (70%), 2014 (73%), 2012 (94%), 2010 (63%), 2008 (68%), 2006 (64%), 2004 (68%), 2002 (67%), 2000 (72%), 1998 (73%), 1996 (69%), 1994 (64%), 1992 (65%)

James Clyburn, a Democrat elected in 1992, is the highest ranking African-American in Congress and again serves as the House majority whip. With Democrats back in control, he's a major spokesman for the party, especially on issues of race. His endorsement of Joe Biden three days before the 2020 presidential primary in South Carolina was instrumental in Biden's sweeping win in that contest and in his stunning turnaround that resulted in his capture of the Democratic nomination and the presidency. Biden made clear his deep appreciation.

Clyburn,the son of a minister, grew up in Sumter and was educated at a private, all-Black boarding school. As a young man, he joined the Student Nonviolent Coordinating Committee, which usually took its cues from the Rev. Martin Luther King Jr.'s Southern Christian Leadership Conference. In 1960, he was one of seven people who organized the state's first sit-ins, at a five-and-dime store in the Orangeburg town square. Clyburn worked as a teacher, as an employment counselor and in government antipoverty programs. In 1970, he ran for the South Carolina House and lost narrowly. Democratic Gov. John West appointed Clyburn as state Human Affairs commissioner, and he served 18 years, under two Democratic and two Republican governors. He ran twice for secretary of state, losing narrowly.

Then, the new Black-majority 6th District was created. Clyburn ran for the seat and won 56 percent of the vote in the Democratic primary against four African-American opponents. Clyburn was better known, ran first or second in every part of the district, and piled up 88 percent of the vote in his home county of Sumter. He became the first African American to represent South Carolina in Congress since George Washington Murray (a distant relative of his) left in 1897. He has not faced serious opposition for reelection.

In the House, Clyburn established a moderate-to-liberal voting record. He joined the moderate New Democrat Coalition, the only African-American House member to do so at the time. Like other South Carolina lawmakers, he has been a proponent of expanding the use of nuclear power, which provides more than half of the state's electricity. On the Appropriations Committee, Clyburn focused on securing federal funds to develop the Interstate 95 corridor, which passes through rural counties in the district that historically were dependent on tobacco and cotton. The House enacted in 2006 his bill to create a Gullah/Geechee Cultural Heritage Corridor from south of Jacksonville Florida to north of Wilmington North Carolina.

After the 2002 election, Clyburn ran for vice chairman of the Democratic Caucus, arguing that the leadership needed to better reflect the party's diversity, and he prevailed over New York Rep. Gregory Meeks and California Rep. Zoe Lofgren. In 2006, he was elected Democratic Caucus chairman; later that year, after Democrats won control of the House, he was chosen majority whip, the No. 3 post.

Clyburn sought enhanced influence for his whip organization in crafting policy, a way of getting more points of view into the drafting of major legislation. He held a series of "listening sessions" with Democrats to explore options for an immigration bill. He led the Hurricane Katrina Task Force, which met regularly with local officials to coordinate the House's response to the devastation caused in 2005. "I truly believe that if the demographics of the affected areas had been different, the response of the federal government would have been different," he said in a 2007 speech in Baton Rouge. Clyburn finessed a solution to a longstanding complaint by CBC members that they were prevented from advancing in the Democratic caucus because they couldn't raise large amounts of political donations in their low-income districts. Clyburn persuaded Pelosi to adopt a modified system that rewarded Democrats for non-financial contributions, such as making appearances for candidates and doing press interviews.

In 2009, Clyburn got into a conflict with Republican Gov. Mark Sanford, who said he would not use all the money available to South Carolina from the $787 billion economic stimulus bill. Clyburn called the action a "slap in the face" to the predominantly Black constituents who would benefit. He wrote a clause into the bill that enabled state legislatures to bypass governors who rejected the money. Clyburn took on another South Carolina conservative, Rep. Joe Wilson, after he infamously called out "You lie!" during President Barack Obama's health care address to Congress in 2009. Clyburn —contending that the outburst was racially motivated--pressed a resolution formally reproaching Wilson for a breach of House rules, which passed on a largely party-line vote.

When Democrats lost the House majority in 2010, they lost one spot in their leadership lineup. An intense, behind-the-scenes battle shaped up for the No. 2 position between Clyburn and former Majority Leader Steny Hoyer of Maryland. To avoid a divisive outcome, Pelosi created the new job of assistant leader and made it the No. 3 post in the minority hierarchy. Clyburn took that position.

Clyburn's new job wasn't well-defined, but he became one of his party's main messengers. After the Newtown Connecticut school massacre, he compared the push for gun control to the civil rights movement. When Obama's health care law was a hot topic on the 2012 campaign trail, he told a gathering of South Carolina Democrats, "Do not be afraid to use the term 'Obamacare.' You should be proud of Obamacare." He spoke out forcefully against state voter-identification laws that he said disenfranchised minority voters.

As the most prominent black politician in the state, Clyburn has been a player in South Carolina's often pivotal Democratic presidential primary. In 2004, after his initial candidate, Rep. Dick Gephardt of Missouri, withdrew following the Iowa caucuses, Clyburn endorsed frontrunner John Kerry rather than Sen. John Edwards of North Carolina. Although he did not take sides in the 2008 primary, he clashed with Hillary Clinton when she seemed to suggest that President Lyndon Johnson, in signing the Civil Rights Act of 1964, had a more important role than King and other key civil rights figures at the time. He later wrote in his 2014 memoir, Blessed Experiences: Genuinely Southern, Proudly Black, that an angry Bill Clinton called to blame him for his wife's defeat in the primary.

In February 2016, Clyburn enthusiastically endorsed Hillary Clinton a week before the South Carolina primary. During the closing weeks of the general election, Clyburn publicly urged the Clinton campaign to step up its activity in minority neighborhoods to assist in down-ballot contests. He turned out to be correct about the lack of grassroots enthusiasm. Clyburn has carved out his own space that often was more hostile to President Donald Trump than other Democratic leaders. Just ahead of Trump's first State of the Union address, Clyburn told CNN that "I can only equate one period of time with what we experience now, and that was what was going on in Germany around 1934, right after the 1932 elections when Adolf Hitler was elected chancellor."

After they were victorious in the 2018 elections, Clyburn re-assumed the position of majority whip. He was reelected unanimously after Colorado Rep. Diana DeGette dropped her bid amid pressure from the CBC. Clyburn said he would consider running for Speaker if Pelosi didn't have the necessary votes amid a revolt of some within the caucus. Pelosi eventually quelled any rising rebellion, with her promise that the trio of now-octogenarian leaders—herself, Hoyer and Clyburn —would serve no more than four more years to make way for a new generation of Democratic leadership, though both Clyburn and Hoyer subsequently said Pelosi was not speaking for them.

In 2019-20, Clyburn suffered the death of two close allies, whose partnership dated back to the early years of the civil rights protests: His wife, Emily, whom he met while he was in jail for three days, and Rep. John Lewis, who was another young King ally. Clyburn called for renaming the Edmund Pettis Bridge in Selma Alabama for the iconic Lewis.

During the 2020 presidential primary, Clyburn showed that his influence at home remained supreme. Three days before the vote, he endorsed Biden, whose campaign was lagging. "I know Joe. We know Joe. But most importantly, Joe knows us," he told supporters. As Clyburn aptly wrote at the time, "In South Carolina, we choose presidents." With huge support from African-American voters, Biden swept the South Carolina primary with 49 percent of the vote, while Bernie Sanders was runner-up among the seven candidates with 20 percent. None other than George W.Bush told Clyburn at Biden's inaugural, "You're the savior, because if you had not nominated Joe Biden, we would not be having this transfer of power today."

In one way, Clyburn was disappointed with the outcome of the 2020 election and he was candid in assigning responsibility. The Democrats' unexpected loss of a dozen House seats partly resulted, he said on CNN days after the election, from the "sloganeering" that accompanied the Black Lives Matter protests that summer, specifically citing calls to "defund the police." Referring to his long-time ally Jaime Harrison, who lost his challenge that year to Sen. Lindsey Graham, Clyburn added, "that stuff hurt Jaime." Biden subsequently selected Harrison to chair the Democratic National Committee.

Clyburn has shown no signs of slowing down. "My health is good. I feel fine," Clyburn told The State after former state Rep. Bakari Sellers, a CNN analyst and former Clyburn intern, said he "will be raring and ready" to run for the 6th District seat whenever Clyburn retires. The congressman's three daughters are all politically active, and at least one, Jennifer Clyburn Reed, has expressed interest in following her father in the seat. "That learning curve[for Congress] won't be as much for me as it would be for someone else," Reed told the Post and Courier. Clyburn replied: "I don't know whether she will run for office, but I know if she is planning to run for my seat, she's going to have to wait for a while."

SC-6: Central South Carolina   **Cook Partisan Voting Index: D+17**

Population		Race and Ethnicity		Income	
Total	665,215	White	38.10%	Median Income	$41,128
Land area (sq. miles)	8,063	Black	54.30%	District Income Rank	430
Pop/ sq mi	82.5	Latino	6.00%	Poverty Rate	23.50%
Born in State	66.60%	Asian	1.20%	With health insurance	86.90%
		Two or more races	2.20%	Cash public assistance	1.80%
Age Groups		Other	4.20%	Food stamp/SNAP	16.60%
Under 18	20.20%				
18-34	27.30%	**Education**		**Work**	
35-64	36.40%	H.S grad or less	48.10%	White Collar	30.20%
Over 64	16.20%	Some college	29.00%	Sales and Service	41.40%
		College Degree, 4 yr	14.20%	Blue Collar	28.50%
Military		Post grad	8.60%	Government	18.70%
Veteran/ Active Duty	9.70%				

2020 Pres. Vote	Biden	195,338	(67%)	Trump	91,350	(31%)
2016 Pres. Vote	Clinton	179,272	(67%)	Trump	79,798	(30%)

Parts of Charleston and Columbia: South Carolina's coastal lowlands and islands are laced with sluggish rivers and swamps. Its early settlers, planters from Barbados, brought thousands of slaves from Africa, and colonial South Carolina quickly became one of the richest parts of North America, with dazzling Georgian architecture in Charleston and classic plantation gardens. The planters built great irrigation systems and grew rice, cotton and the dye-plant indigo, all heavily in demand in Britain and elsewhere. All this wealth, of course, was built on the slave labor of countless African Americans. In colonial times, a majority of South Carolinians were slaves, as were a majority of lowland residents. South Carolina's Black heritage has left a lasting imprint on American culture. Gullah, a mixture of English, French and African dialects, is still spoken on the Sea Islands, and Gullah customs survive—oyster roasts and sweet potato feasts at Christmas, handmade dolls and sweet grass baskets. The poverty that was the almost universal lot of lowland blacks after the Civil War has eased only in the last generation, as development came to the coast and cultural isolation dissipated. But many African Americans decided not to wait for progress. They abandoned South Carolina for opportunities in the North or for metro areas in the South.

At the Emanuel African Methodist Episcopal Church in downtown Charleston—which sits within the 1st District by just one block— a 21-year-old white gunman in 2015 opened fire on a Bible study group, killing nine people before he escaped and was captured a few hours later. The victims included the church pastor, Clementa Pinckney, who also was a state senator. "Emanuel A.M.E. Church is the rock upon which the A.M.E. Church throughout the South is built," local Rep. James Clyburn said at a prayer vigil the next day. Dylann Roof was convicted of the nine murders and became the first federal hate-crime defendant sentenced to death.

The 6th Congressional District of South Carolina, created in 1992 as a Black-majority district, takes in the Black central city neighborhoods of Charleston, North Charleston and Columbia, but leaves out their larger affluent white areas. Columbia-based Richland has nearly 30 percent of the population; Charleston and Orangeburg are close to 15 percent each. The remainder of the district is mostly rural. The poorer counties, which run along the I-95 corridor, stretch from southern Florence County to Jasper County along the Georgia border. They were given the distressing moniker "Corridor of Shame" after a 2005 documentary highlighted the lack of attention paid to rural, dilapidated schools that are largely minority and low-income, leaving many students illiterate and unable to meet state standards. Orange burg County dropped 7 percent of its population from 2010 to 2019.

Only a small strip of the 6th, south of Hilton Head, touches the Atlantic Ocean. Inland, Boeing's North Charleston assembly plant, adjacent to the airport, has become the sole factory that produces the 787 Dreamliner. With the decline of orders accelerated by the coronavirus pandemic, Boeing announced in October 2020 that it was shutting down 787 assembly at its Everett Washington plant and consolidating those operations in North Charleston, which employs about 7,000 workers. Deliveries that year of the 787 declined by more than half compared to 2019.In 2018, local officials said that earlier plans by Chinese Wanli Tire Corp. to build a factory in Orangeburg County that would employ 1,200 people had been delayed indefinitely because of growing economic tensions with China.

Republicans packed the 6th District with African-American Democrats, seeking to ensure that the remaining six of the state's seven congressional seats would solidly favor Republicans. Joe Biden in 2020 won the district, 67%-31%.

Tom Rice (R)

Elected 2012, 5th term, b. Aug 04, 1957; Charleston, SC; University of SC, B.S., 1979; University of SC, M.A., 1982; University of SC School of Law, J.D., 1982; Episcopalian; Married (Wrenzie Rice); 3 children.

Elected Office: Horry County Council, 2010-2012.

Professional Career: Staff accountant, Deloitte Haskins & Sells, 1982-1984; Practicing lawyer, 1984-present.

DC Office: 512 CHOB 20515, 202-225-9895, Fax: 202-225-9690, rice.house.gov

State Offices: Florence, 843-679-9781; Myrtle Beach, 843-445-6459.

Committees: *Ways & Means*: Select Revenue Measures; Social Security; Trade.

Group Ratings

	ADA	ACLU	AFL-CIO	LCV	COC	HAFA	ACU	CFG	FRC
2020	**	18%	**	5%	-	95%	87%	**	-
2019	0%	C	15%	10%	66%	C	87%	96%	90%

Almanac Ratings 2019-2020

	Economy	Social	Foreign	Composite
Liberal	25%	31%	35%	31%
Conservative	75%	69%	65%	69%

Key Votes of the 116th Congress

1. U.S./Mex./Can. trade deal Y	5. Russia sanctions Y	9. Firearms background checks N
2. First Coronavirus response Y	6. Troops in Syria N	10. Spending at the border Y
3. HEROES Act N	7. Veto arms sales to Saudis N	11. Marijuana liberalized rules N
4. CASH Act N	8. Defense $$$, veto override N	12. Electoral College objections Y

Election Results

Election	Name (Party)	Vote (%)		Cand. Spent	Ind. Exp. Support	Ind. Exp. Oppose
2020 General	Tom Rice (R)	224,993	(62%)	$1,190,077	$4,794	$750
	Melissa Watson (D)	138,863	(38%)	$142,294	$10,640	

Prior winning percentages: 2018 (60%), 2016 (61%), 2014 (60%), 2012 (56%)

Republican Tom Rice was elected in 2012 with a focus on his business background and conservative politics in the growing region. Compared to the often-raucous members of the state's congressional delegation, Rice has been more focused on his legislative work, with occasional bipartisan interest. That style proved useful when he got a seat on the Ways and Means Committee, where his accounting expertise has been helpful on tax policy. In January 2021, following the riot at the Capitol, Rice was one of 10 House Republicans—and the only Southerner—to vote for the second impeachment charge against President Donald Trump. He acknowledged that his vote would cause some opposition from local Republicans.

Growing up amid the sand dunes of Myrtle Beach, Rice spent most days at the beach. His mother was a schoolteacher; his father, a repairman, died when he was young. Rice worked every summer after he turned 12, busing tables at the local tourist restaurants. At the University of South Carolina, he volunteered with Big Brothers Big Sisters. He stayed at the university to earn his master's in accounting and a law degree.

Rice moved to Charlotte to work for the accounting giant Deloitte. After gaining experience on larger cases, he returned home to practice tax law. Rice served on the board of the Myrtle Beach Haven homeless shelter and, during 10 years as president, helped it build an expanded facility. In 2010, he was elected Horry County Council chairman, where he focused on rebuilding the Myrtle Beach Regional Economic Development Corporation and bringing jobs to the county.

In 2012, Rice came in second in the crowded GOP primary field to former Lt. Gov. André Bauer, who raised almost double the amount of campaign cash as Rice and labeled him a "moderate" in a wave of attack ads. In the runoff, Rice crushed Bauer, 56%-44%, thanks in part to a powerful endorsement from popular GOP Gov. Nikki Haley. In the general, Rice faced former economics professor Gloria Bromell Tinubu, who ran on a platform of union advocacy. Rice got support from the state tea party and National Right to Life Committee. He won 56%-44%, with his entire margin of victory coming from his base in Horry County, where he led 65%-35%.

Rice has been outspoken in his call to raise the gasoline tax by as much as 13 cents per gallon to pay for improvements to highways and bridges. "Infrastructure is the foundation on which competitiveness is based," he said. He said that the increase should be offset by cuts in income taxes. Rice has made a big push to build the local section of Interstate 73. "We need some infrastructure, we need it terribly, we needed it 50 years ago and it's ridiculous we're trying to do it right now (with sandbags)," Rice told the Charleston Post and Courier in the aftermath of Hurricane Florence in 2018.

After Democrats won back Congress, Rice was hopeful that infrastructure looked ripe for bipartisan agreement. The susceptibility of his coastal district to hurricanes made Rice an expert on federal disaster assistance. During his 2020 reelection campaign, he said he would seek ways to aid the Grand Strand, where the economy was "terribly affected" by the coronavirus.

Rice disagreed with GOP conservatives who sought to shut down the Export-Import Bank, which earned him the ire of the anti-tax Club for Growth. "In a perfect world, I wish it wasn't there. And I wish that banks would step up to fill the void. But the problem is it's not a perfect world," Rice said. When he voted in 2015 to extend the Bank, he said that during the previous five years it "has facilitated $4 billion in exports from South Carolina, and has helped over 60 companies in the state." Also in 2015, he filled a vacancy on tax-writing Ways and Means. His initiatives on the panel included legislation to provide tax credits to businesses to assist them in reopening during the pandemic, including precautions to assist employees and patrons—especially at restaurants.

Rice resisted entreaties to join the Freedom Caucus and got some pushback from local tea party activists as a result. But local leaders like the influence he wields on Ways and Means, despite his low-key style. "People don't pay me for smiling," Rice told the Post and Courier. "They pay me to get results." He opposed Trump's push for offshore drilling, saying that "tapping new reserves in the Atlantic has become less and less feasible." Rice added that he's cognizant that his district voted overwhelmingly for the president and that "while I don't necessarily agree with his tactics, I agree with 95 percent of his policies."

Following the 2020 election, Rice joined other members of the Problem Solvers Caucus in pushing for bipartisan action on a COVID-19 relief bill, including coverage of the costs of vaccine distribution plus expanded testing programs. "Each vaccination is a step towards combating the spread of COVID-19 and getting our economy back on track," said Rice, who tested positive for COVID in the summer of 2020.

Rice drew considerable attention with his vote to impeach Trump in January 2021. "Any reasonable person could see the potential for violence" in Trump's speech preceding the riot, Rice said in a statement. Referring to Trump's subsequent failure to urge calm or to comment on the consequences of the riot, he added, "this utter failure is inexcusable." In an interview with the Associated Press the day after the vote, he said he knew that his vote could cost him his seat. "If it does, it does," he said. "It's the honor of my life to do this job. ... I've tried to do my best to do the right thing and represent [my constituents'] interests."

In his four reelections, Rice has received between 60 and 62 percent of the vote. With pressure to create a second Black majority district in South Carolina, he might face a challenge from redistricting in 2022, though his base in booming Horry County likely will serve him well.

Republican Tom Rice was elected in 2012 with a focus on his business background and conservative politics in the growing region. Compared to the often-raucous members of the state's congressional delegation, Rice has been more focused on his legislative work, with occasional bipartisan interest. That style proved useful when he got a seat on the Ways and Means Committee, where his accounting expertise has been helpful on tax policy. In January 2021, following the riot at the Capitol, Rice was one of 10 House Republicans—and the only Southerner—to vote for the second impeachment charge against President Donald Trump. He acknowledged that his vote would cause some opposition from local Republicans.

Growing up amid the sand dunes of Myrtle Beach, Rice spent most days at the beach. His mother was a schoolteacher; his father, a repairman, died when he was young. Rice worked every summer after he turned 12, busing tables at the local tourist restaurants. At the University of South Carolina, he volunteered with Big Brothers Big Sisters. He stayed at the university to earn his master's in accounting and a law degree.

Rice moved to Charlotte to work for the accounting giant Deloitte. After gaining experience on larger cases, he returned home to practice tax law and eventually open his own practice. Rice served on the board of the Myrtle Beach Haven homeless shelter and, during 10 years as president, helped it build an expanded facility. In 2010, he was elected Horry County Council chairman, where he focused on rebuilding the Myrtle Beach Regional Economic Development Corporation and bringing jobs to the county.

In 2012, Rice came in second in the crowded GOP primary field to former Lt. Gov. André Bauer, who raised almost double the amount of campaign cash as Rice and labeled him a "moderate" in a wave of attack ads. In the runoff, Rice crushed Bauer, 56%-44%, thanks in part to a powerful endorsement from popular GOP Gov. Nikki Haley. In the general, Rice faced former economics professor Gloria Bromell Tinubu, who ran on a platform of union advocacy. Rice got support from the state tea party and National Right to Life Committee. He won 56%-44%, with his entire margin of victory coming from his base in Horry County, where he led 65%-35%.

Rice has been outspoken in his call to raise the gasoline tax by as much as 13 cents per gallon to pay for improvements to highways and bridges. "Infrastructure is the foundation on which competitiveness is based," he said. He said that the increase should be offset by cuts in income taxes. Rice has made a big push to build the local section of Interstate 73. "We need some infrastructure, we need it terribly, we needed it 50 years ago and it's ridiculous we're trying to do it right now (with sandbags)," Rice told the Charleston Post and Courier in the aftermath of Hurricane Florence in 2018.

After Democrats won back Congress, Rice was hopeful that infrastructure looked ripe for bipartisan agreement. The susceptibility of his coastal district to hurricanes made Rice an expert on federal disaster assistance. During his 2020 reelection campaign, he said he would seek ways to aid the Grand Strand, where the economy was "terribly affected" by the coronavirus.

Rice disagreed with GOP conservatives who sought to shut down the Export-Import Bank, which earned him the ire of the anti-tax Club for Growth. "In a perfect world, I wish it wasn't there. And I wish that banks would step up to fill the void. But the problem is it's not a perfect world," Rice said. When he voted in 2015 to extend the Bank, he said that during the previous five years it "has facilitated $4 billion in exports from South Carolina, and has helped over 60 companies in the state." Also in 2015, he filled a vacancy on tax-writing Ways and Means. His initiatives on the panel included legislation to provide tax credits to businesses to assist them in reopening during the pandemic, including precautions to assist employees and patrons—especially at restaurants.

Rice resisted entreaties to join the Freedom Caucus and got some pushback from local tea party activists as a result. But local leaders like the influence he wields on Ways and Means, despite his low-key style. "People don't pay me for smiling," Rice told the Post and Courier. "They pay me to get results." He opposed Trump's push for offshore drilling, saying that "tapping new reserves in the Atlantic has become less and less feasible." Rice added that he's cognizant that his district voted overwhelmingly for the president and that "while I don't necessarily agree with his tactics, I agree with 95 percent of his policies."

Following the 2020 election, Rice joined other members of the Problem Solvers Caucus in pushing for bipartisan action on a COVID-19 relief bill, including coverage of the costs of vaccine distribution plus expanded testing programs. "Each vaccination is a step towards combating the spread of COVID-19 and getting our economy back on track," said Rice, who tested positive for COVID in the summer of 2020.

Rice drew considerable attention with his vote to impeach Trump in January 2021. "Any reasonable person could see the potential for violence" in Trump's speech preceding the riot, Rice said in a statement. Referring to Trump's subsequent failure to urge calm or to comment on the consequences of the riot, he added, "this utter failure is inexcusable." In an interview with the Associated Press the day after the vote, he said he knew that his vote could cost him his seat. "If it does, it does," he said. "It's the honor of my life to do this job. … I've tried to do my best to do the right thing and represent [my constituents'] interests."

In his four reelections, Rice has received between 60 and 62 percent of the vote. With pressure to create a second Black majority district in South Carolina, he might face a challenge from redistricting in 2022, though his base in booming Horry County likely will serve him well.

SC-7: Pee Dee/Waccamaw Region

Cook Partisan Voting Index: R+11

Population		Race and Ethnicity		Income	
Total	740,536	White	67.50%	Median Income	$49,494
Land area (sq. miles)	5,355	Black	27.80%	District Income Rank	390
Pop/ sq mi	138.3	Latino	4.20%	Poverty Rate	16.50%
Born in State	53.70%	Asian	1.10%	With health insurance	87.00%
		Two or more races	1.70%	Cash public assistance	0.80%
Age Groups		Other	1.90%	Food stamp/SNAP	11.10%
Under 18	19.90%				
18-34	19.60%	**Education**		**Work**	
35-64	38.20%	H.S grad or less	48.10%	White Collar	31.60%
Over 64	22.30%	Some college	29.40%	Sales and Service	43.00%
Military		College Degree, 4 yr	14.10%	Blue Collar	25.40%
Veteran/ Active Duty	9.50%	Post grad	8.30%	Government	12.80%

2020 Pres. Vote	Trump	214,724	(59%)	Biden	146,760	(40%)
2016 Pres. Vote	Trump	173,065	(58%)	Clinton	116,626	(39%)

Myrtle Beach, Florence, Georgetown: The Pee Dee region of South Carolina was named for the river that lazily winds its way through the northern lowlands of the Palmetto State. It was here that Francis Marion's penchant for conducting lightning-fast raids on larger British forces and then vanishing into the swamps earned him the name "Swamp Fox" during the Revolutionary War. In 2016, researchers raised from the muddy Pee Dee River three cannons, which Confederate forces apparently had pushed overboard from a ship in their futile battle against the oncoming forces of Gen. William Tecumseh Sherman.

The 7th Congressional District takes in almost the entire Pee Dee region. The 7th consists of two distinct areas of roughly equal size. The inland counties remain reminiscent of the Old South. Crossroads communities and farms dot the landscape, and on Labor Day weekend the Cook Out Southern 500 fills the air around Darlington with the roar of stock car engines. Florence, historically the hub of the Pee Dee, is the only city in this portion of the district with a population in excess of 30,000. The county overall had new investments that created more than 1,000 jobs, with companies like Honda, McCall Farms, Otis Elevator and GE Healthcare expanding. In November 2020, voters in Florence, which is 48 percent Black, elected as mayor Teresa Ervin—the first woman and the first African-American to hold the position.

The second half of the district is coastal. A century ago, this was largely uninhabited forestland. Myrtle Beach wasn't incorporated until 1938. Today, the two coastal counties of the Pee Dee—Horry and Georgetown—are home to the 60-mile Grand Strand, comprising miles of beachfront and golf courses and drawing 17 million visitors annually to the year-round vacation spot. There's been a push here for years to build Interstate 73, which would run from Michigan to Myrtle Beach. The hit of Hurricane Florence to the area in 2018 gave local officials another justification, arguing that an interstate was necessary for evacuation. Environmentalists have opposed the plan.

The combined vote of Horry and Georgetown counties has increased to a bit more than half the total for the district. From 2000 to 2019, Horry County (pronounced OR-e) grew 77 percent to 354,000 people, and was the fastest-growing county in the state; it expects to add another 100,000 people over the next 20 years. The Myrtle Beach metro area was the second fastest-growing in the country from 2016 to 2017, much of it migration from out-of-state. The coastal areas of the district are overwhelmingly Republican, while the inland portions of Florence and Darlington are more competitive. Rural Marion and Marlboro counties are majority-Black and vote Democratic.

The district is 28 percent Black, similar to the 5th District and the largest in the state other than the Black-majority 6th District. Despite legal challenges, the Obama administration concluded that the state was not required by the Voting Rights Act to draw an additional minority-majority district. President Donald Trump won 59 percent of the vote here in 2020.

SOUTH DAKOTA

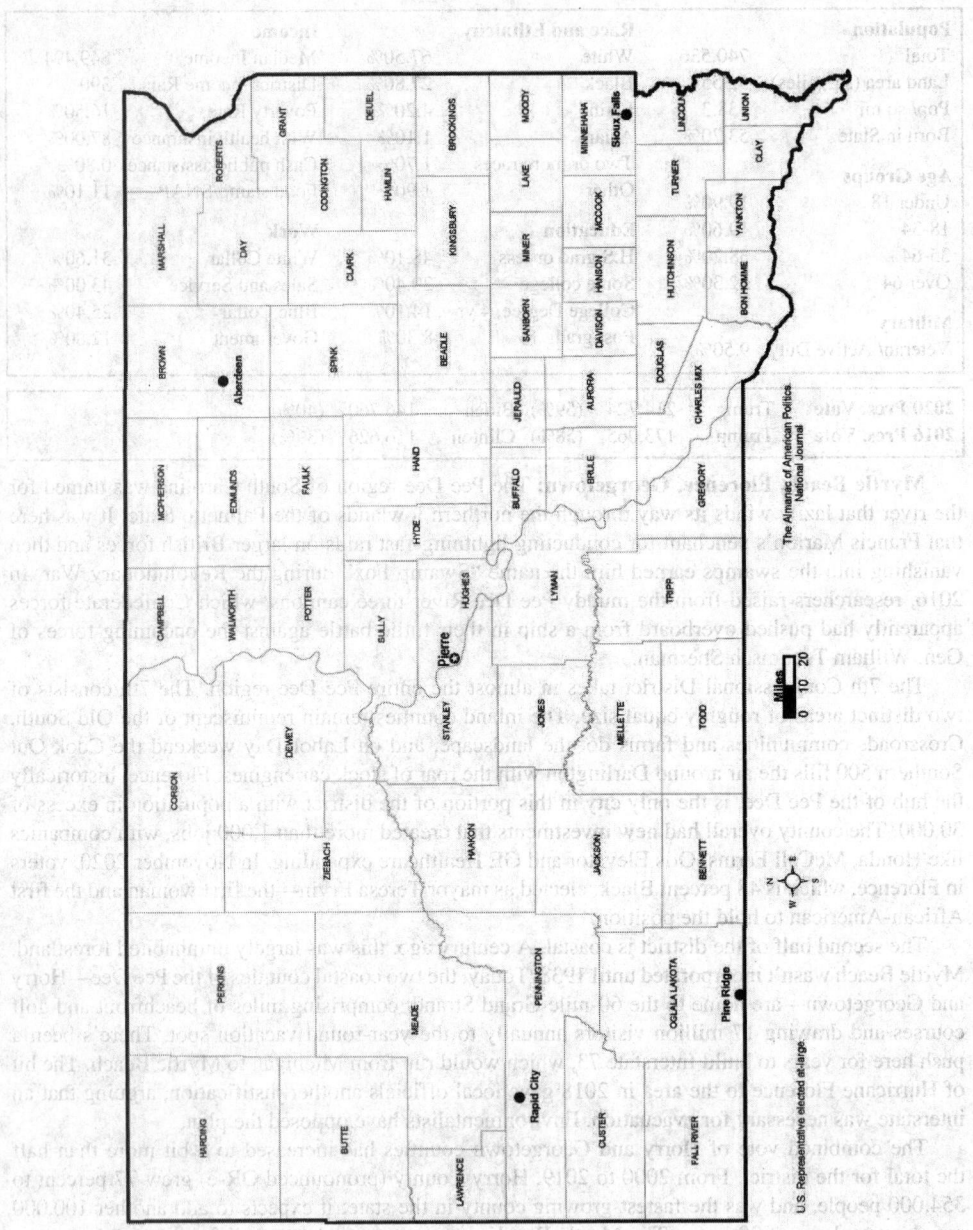

South Dakota is one of the most Republican states in the nation. It last supported a Democratic nominee for president in 1964, and it last elected a Democratic governor in 1974, a Democratic senator in 2006, and a Democratic House member in 2008. In the 2020 presidential election, President Donald Trump won in a 26-point romp.

The Lewis and Clark expedition encountered herds of buffalo as the Corps of Discovery paddled up the Missouri River in the fall of 1804 through land where the Oglala Sioux became masters of the horses the Spaniards had imported to North America 300 years earlier. (Today, you can still see bison, bighorn sheep and elk at Custer State Park near Rapid City, a preserve on par with many of the finest national parks.) Fort Pierre was established as a fur-trading post in 1817 and Congress established the Dakota Territory in 1861, but few White men settled here until the 1880s. The Sioux remained dominant, and their warrior chief Sitting Bull, now buried on a bluff above the Missouri River, destroyed Gen. George Armstrong Custer and his 7th Cavalry at Little Big Horn in 1876 next door in Montana. Fourteen years later, many of the remaining Oglala Sioux Indians in South Dakota were massacred at Wounded Knee. After half a century of disease and a decade of setbacks against the westward advance of White settlement, the Sioux were a traumatized people.

In many ways, they still are. Indians account for 8.4 percent of South Dakota's population, the third-highest behind Alaska and New Mexico. (By contrast, African Americans account for 2.2 percent, ranking the state 12th from the bottom nationally, while Hispanics account for just 3.7 percent.) Most Native Americans live on reservations with proud traditions but terrible poverty. Isolated from the mainstream economic marketplace, they are beset by high rates of alcoholism, diabetes, and suicide. Five South Dakota counties—Ziebach, Todd, Buffalo, Corson, and Oglala Lakota (known as Shannon County prior to 2015)—rank among the most impoverished counties in the country. In 2015, a federal judge ruled that the South Dakota Department of Social Services and other state agencies had "failed to protect Indian parents' fundamental rights" over many years when they removed hundreds of Native American children after cursory hearings and placed them in foster-care homes. In 2018, a federal appeals court sided with the state and sent the case back to a lower court. In 2020, Native American plaintiffs sued the state for failing to provide sufficient voter registration services.

Once the Sioux were forced to surrender their territory, White settlement of South Dakota came quickly. After gold was discovered in the Black Hills in 1874, the mountains swarmed with settlers. Deadwood became a city of 20,000 where Calamity Jane ruled the saloons and Wild Bill Hickok was shot in the back while holding two pair—aces and eights. Because barbed wire could not fence in the buffalo, hired hunters massacred them so thoroughly that when Theodore Roosevelt visited the Dakota Territory in 1884, he had a hard time finding one to shoot. It was not long before the railroad came through, followed by permanent settlers, many of them German and Scandinavian immigrants recruited by the railroads. They built sod houses, broke the land, and set down roots. There were 98,000 South Dakotans in 1880; 401,000 in 1900; and 636,000 in 1920—at which point settlement pretty much stopped. Farmers settled the eastern third of the state, sectioned off Midwestern-style. But moving westward, before a traveler reaches the Missouri River in the middle of the state, green turns to brown, cultivation grows sparse, and then simply stops. The West River plains are open grazing land. Beyond the 100th meridian the land is punctuated not by roads meeting every mile at precise angles, but by buttes, gullies, and grasslands sweeping to the horizon with no sign of human habitation except the occasional missile silo that once pointed weapons toward the Soviet Union. The badlands did not get their name for nothing.

South Dakota is coming to resemble the Rocky Mountain States, with most people concentrated around a few prosperous and growing cities and towns, with vast acreage remaining vacant, punctuated by the occasional farm or ranch house. Statewide, the population has grown 8.9 percent since 2010, mostly driven by increases in the Sioux Falls area, including 13.6 percent in Minnehaha County and 35.3 percent in suburban Lincoln County.

South Dakota's business climate is unapologetically pro-business; the Tax Foundation ranks it second best in the country for its business-tax climate. (Some taxes, though, are readily accepted: It was a South Dakota lawsuit that led the Supreme Court, in a landmark 2018 ruling, to allow states to impose sales taxes on online merchants even if they lack a physical presence in the state.) South Dakota ranks high in credit ratings, low in foreclosures, high in repayment of college loans, and low in commute times. The agriculture sector is something of an exception. It began a downturn around 2014, as prices for livestock, corn, soybeans and wheat fell. Farm income fell 76 percent between 2011 and 2016 before rising again; the number of farms has declined, and the number of farm bankruptcies has risen.

What has really set South Dakota apart is its focus on financial services. In 1979, Sioux Falls banker Thomas Reardon suggested that the state get rid of its usury law limiting interest rates; state officials agreed in 1981, and the laws they passed enticed Citibank to move its credit-card operations to Sioux Falls, where it could charge market interest rates, all in a state with no corporate or personal income taxes, and a community with a literate but lower-wage work force. It didn't take long for other companies such as Wells Fargo and Capital One to move their credit-card operations to the Sioux Falls metro area. Today, South Dakota has $3.3 trillion in bank assets. The finance sector bequeathed Sioux Falls a secondary industry—mail-order pharmaceuticals, which piggybacked on a logistics network that had been built to enable credit-card companies to deliver replacement cards quickly and securely to their customers. Most strikingly, the state has become a hotbed for trusts for wealthy families, aided by laws that ensure secrecy and protect holdings from divorced spouses and creditors. A decade ago, trust companies in South Dakota held $57.3 billion in assets; by the end of 2020, the total had reached $355.2 billion, according to estimates cited by the Guardian. A crucial element has been that South Dakota, unlike most jurisdictions around the world, protects trusts in perpetuity. As a result, South Dakota has become, in the Guardian's words, "the best place in the world to stay rich."

The coronavirus pandemic arguably hit South Dakota harder than almost any other state. First, the Smithfield pork factory in Sioux Falls became the nation's biggest coronavirus hot spot, infecting its heavily immigrant workforce and forcing a temporary closure. But the real damage emerged after the state and Republican Gov. Kristi Noem welcomed bikers to the annual motorcycle rally in Sturgis in early August 2020 while downplaying the need to abide by social distancing and other precautions. One study suggested that the rally might be implicated in hundreds of thousands of cases nationwide, but even if that assessment is high, there was no doubt that the virus spiked in nearby states over the succeeding weeks. By September, South Dakota led the nation in cases per capita, and by October, nearly one half of tests came back positive, a rate eight times the World Health Organization's standard. In the face of withering criticism from political opponents outside the state, Noem focused on letting people make up their own minds, writing in an op-ed, "Those who don't want to wear a mask shouldn't be shamed into wearing one." And, by early 2021, cases and deaths had fallen significantly. Overall, South Dakotan was among the 10 worst states in mortality rate, with the second highest rate of infection, trailing only North Dakota.

South Dakota's political patterns were largely set by the early 1900s. Its early settlers were mostly Midwesterners who brought their Republicanism with them, of New England Yankee and German stock primarily, and also some Norwegians. South Dakota, unlike North Dakota, never had much use for the Non-Partisan League, and unlike in Minnesota, there was never anything comparable to the Farmer-Labor Party. But the nature of the farm economy—its dependence on the great railroads and milling companies and on the vagaries of international markets — meant that South Dakota was subject to periodic farm revolts. South Dakota briefly supported the New Deal, and it rebelled against the Eisenhower administration in the late 1950s by electing to Congress a young Dakota Wesleyan University professor named George McGovern. South Dakota shared the isolationist impulse of much of the Great Plains; McGovern's opposition to the Vietnam War in the late 1960s was not a liability back home.

Like the residents of other small states, South Dakotans expect to meet and chat with their elected officials repeatedly. Pierre (pronounced "peer") is the nation's second smallest state capital city, outranking only Montpelier Vermont, and personal campaigning enabled Democrats such as Sens. Tom Daschle and Tim Johnson to be competitive in congressional elections, particularly when they articulated populist themes. In general, though, South Dakota has leaned strongly Republican. Since 2008, no Democrat has been elected to statewide office, though in 2018, the Democratic gubernatorial nominee—Billie Sutton, a legislator who was paralyzed in a rodeo accident at age 23 —ran a surprisingly strong race before losing narrowly to Noem.

In the 2016 presidential election, the state became even redder: Trump's winning margin was 30 points, well above Mitt Romney's 18-point edge in 2012. In 2020, Joe Biden was able to shave

Trump's winning margin modestly, by four points; he managed to increase Hillary Clinton's 2016 vote total by 28 percent, outpacing Trump's 15 percent increase from his first campaign. The state's most populous counties remained heavily Republican but the margins shifted incrementally toward Biden: a 5.5-point Democratic improvement in Minnehaha County (Sioux Falls), an eight-point improvement in Pennington County (Rapid City), and a six-point improvement in Lincoln County (Sioux Falls suburbs). Biden narrowed Trump's winning margins by more modest amounts in Hughes County (Pierre), Brown County (Aberdeen), and Brookings County (Brookings). But Biden did nowhere near as well as Sutton did in his gubernatorial race two years earlier, and it's hard to see Democrats competing effectively for federal office in South Dakota in the near future.

Cook Partisan Voting Index: R+16

Population		Race and Ethnicity		Income	
Total	884,659	White	84.10%	Median Income	59,533
Land area (sq. miles)	75,811	Black	2.40%	State Income Rank	33 out of 50
Pop/ sq mi	11.67	Latino	3.70%	Poverty Rate	11.90%
Born in state	63.60%	Asian	1.60%	With health insurance	89.80%
		Two or more races	2.80%	Cash public assistance	1.70%
Age Groups		Other	9.50%	Food stamp/SNAP	10.6%
Under 18	24.30%				
18-34	22.20%	**Education**		**Work**	
35-64	36.10%	H.S grad or less	37.90%	White Collar	39.20%
Over 64	17.40%	Some college	32.40%	Sales and Service	36.60%
		College Degree, 4 yr	20.60%	Blue Collar	24.10%
Military		Post grad	9.10%	Government	16.00%
Veteran/ Active Duty	9.00%				

Presidential Politics

2020 Primary (D)	Biden (D)	40,800(77%)	Sanders (D)	11,861(23%)		
2020 Pres. Vote	Trump (R)	261,043(62%)	Biden (D)	150,471(36%)		
2016 Pres. Vote	Trump (R)	227,721(62%)	Clinton (D)	117,458(32%)	Johnson (L)	20,850 (6%)

South Dakota has voted Democratic for president just four times since statehood—in 1896, 1932, 1936 and 1964. But it was fairly close in five of the seven elections between 1972, when South Dakota Sen. George McGovern was the Democratic nominee, and 1996, when Democrat Bill Clinton came within three points of winning. Since then, its closest call for a Republican came in 2008 when John McCain carried the state 53%-45% over Barack Obama. But it's been solidly Republican since: Mitt Romney beat Obama 58%-40% in 2012, Donald Trump beat Hillary Clinton 62%-32% in 2016, and Trump beat Joe Biden by 62%-36% in 2020. Trump won 60 of the state's 66 counties, and took Minnehaha County (Sioux Falls) by 10 points; Biden won Clay County, home of the University of South Dakota. as well as five counties with large Native American reservations (though Trump narrowly carried Corson County, which contains the South Dakota portion of the Standing Rock Indian Reservation, and Bennett County, which contains part of the Pine Ridge Indian Reservation).

South Dakota holds a June presidential primary that seldom sees much action. In 2008 there was a robust race for the Democratic nomination when South Dakota voted. Obama had a long list of endorsements from leading South Dakota Democrats, but Hillary Clinton, Bill Clinton and daughter Chelsea crisscrossed the state in the two weeks before the primary, and Clinton won 55%-45%. In the 2016 primary, South Dakotans stuck with Clinton, giving her a narrow 51%-49% victory over Sen. Bernie Sanders. In 2020, Biden had already locked up the nomination when he beat Sanders, 77%-23%.

Congressional Districts

117th Congress Lineup	1R	116th Congress Lineup	1R

Kristi Noem (R)

Elected 2018, term expires 2023, 1st term; b. Nov 30, 1971, Watertown; Mount Marty College (SD), Att.; Northern State University, Aberdeen (SD), Att., 1992; South Dakota State University, Bach. Deg., 2012; Evangelical; Married (Bryon Noem); 3 children.

Elected Office: SD House, 2007-2011; US House, 2011-2018.

Professional Career: Farmer, rancher.

Office: 500 E. Capitol Ave. Pierre, 57501-5070; 605-773-3212; Fax: 605-773-4711

Lt. Gov.: Larry Rhoden (R) **Atty. Gen:** Jason Ravnsborg (R) **Sec. of State:** Steve Barnett (R)

State Legislature: Senate: 5D, 30R **House:** 11D, 59R

Election Results

Election	Name (Party)	Vote (%)
2018 General	Kristi Noem (R)	172,912 (51%)
	Billie Sutton (D)	161,454 (48%)
2018 Primary	Kristi Noem (R)	57,598 (56%)
	Marty J. Jackley (R)	45,174 (44%)

Prior winning percentage: House: 2016 (64%), 2014 (67%), 2012 (57%), 2010 (48%)

Republican Kristi Noem, a former House member, was elected governor in 2018. She rocketed to national prominence in 2020 by embracing President Donald Trump and echoing his approach to the coronavirus even as the state became a virus hotspot.

Noem was born in Hamlin County South Dakota. She attended college but returned home to help run the family farm after her father died in a fall into a grain bin while trying to unclog a feeder line, an accident she discussed in her first campaign ad. She raised Angus cattle and quarter horses on a ranch with her husband, Bryon. An avid hunter of elk, pheasant and other game, Noem owned a hunting lodge and worked a variety of jobs, including a stint as a restaurant manager. She finished her bachelor's degree at South Dakota State University in 2011, when she was already serving in Congress.

After developing an interest in conservative causes, Noem ran for the South Dakota House and narrowly won in 2006, eventually becoming assistant majority leader. In 2010, Noem challenged Democratic Rep. Stephanie Herseth Sandlin. In the GOP primary, Noem won 42 percent, besting two-term Secretary of State Chris Nelson with 35 percent and state Rep. Blake Curd with 23 percent. With substantial campaign contributions from out-of-state Republicans, Noem outraised Herseth Sandlin. The state Democratic Party sought to make an issue of Noem's 20 speeding tickets and other traffic violations over two decades; she received six notices for failing to appear in court. Noem responded that she was not proud of her driving record and was working to be a better example to young drivers. Noem won 48%-46%.

In Washington, Noem was named one of two freshman class representatives to the GOP leadership and became a favorite with activists on the right. In 2015she joined the powerful Ways and Means Committee, leaving the Agriculture Committee; it was the first time since 1978 that South Dakota did not have a member on the Ag panel, which irked some critics back home. In 2012, Noem faced a challenge by Democrat Matt Varilek, a former aide to Democratic Sen. Tim Johnson. Varilek impressed local observers by raising close to $1 million and hitting Noem on missing Agriculture Committee hearings. But Noem raised $2.8 million and won, 57%-43%. She won easily after that. Noem played significant roles on the Republican tax bill that passed in 2017 and on the farm bill in 2018. She helped to lessen the impact of the estate tax, a longtime concern dating back to the death of Noem's father, which left his family with an estate tax obligation, at a time when the tax's threshold was much lower.

Noem announced that she would run for governor in 2018, seeking to succeed two-term Republican Gov. Dennis Daugaard. She faced a bitter GOP primary against Attorney General Marty Jackley but won, 56%-44%, by portraying her opponent as a Pierre insider. After the primary win, Noem's treasury was drained, and some Jackley supporters were left with raw feelings. Meanwhile, Billie Sutton, 34, was as strong a candidate as Democrats had put forward in South Dakota in years. He had been a champion saddle bronc rider until, at age 23, he was thrown by his horse and paralyzed from the waist down. After a stint in banking, Sutton won a state Senate seat in 2010 and became minority leader in 2015.Sutton painted the state GOP as arrogant and corrupt because of its longstanding control of Pierre, and he articulated views more in tune with the state than with the national Democratic Party: He was anti-abortion, pro-gun and anti-income-tax, although Noem sought to tie him to pro-tax views. Sutton's message resonated, and polls showed a close race. In the home stretch, Trump, Vice President Mike Pence, and other top Republicans visited the state, and the Republican Governors Association invested substantially in the contest. In the end, Noem pulled out a 51%-48% victory. Sutton won 22 counties, up from just four the Democratic nominee against Daugaard had won in 2014. Sutton won populous Minnehaha County (Sioux Falls)by seven points after the Democrats had lost it by 49 points four years earlier. Sutton became the first Democratic gubernatorial nominee since 1972 to win Hughes County (Pierre),by five percentage points, after Democrats had lost it by 66 points in 2014. Sutton also flipped Brookings County (Brookings) and Brown County (Aberdeen) and made dramatic gains in Lincoln County (suburban Sioux Falls) and Pennington County (Rapid City).

In her first year in office, Noem pursued a solidly conservative agenda, signing bills that legalized concealed handguns without a permit, required schools to prominently display the motto "In God We Trust," and barred universities from interfering with unpopular speech. Meanwhile, Native Americans feuded with Noem, decrying her support for laws that cracked down on demonstrations like the ones that tribal members had carried out against the Keystone XL pipeline; the Oglala Sioux Tribal Council banned Noem from the Pine Ridge Reservation. Noem raised eyebrows nationally when a state-supported anti-methamphetamine ad campaign drew derision online for its tagline: "Meth. We're on it." (Noem dismissed the outcry, saying it was an intentional "play on words.")

In 2020, Noem backed off her opposition to legalizing hemp; in 2019, she vetoed a hemp bill, but in 2020, she signed one after saying it provided adequate enforcement, regulation, and funding. In 2021, she said she would delay, but not block, enactment of a ballot measure to legalize medical marijuana that passed with 70% of the vote. She did register a win in court when a more expansive recreational marijuana ballot measure was struck down. Meanwhile, Noem was denied a chance to fulfill her campaign promise of signing an anti-transgender bill when the measure was scuttled by a Senate committee. It would have banned "puberty blocking" medication, hormone replacement therapy, and surgency for transgender minors. However, in March 2021, Norm issued a pair of executive orders that barred transgender girls from taking part in girls' sports, either at the K-12 level or in college.

But Noem's biggest challenge in 2020 was the coronavirus. Noem declined to issue stay-at-home orders or business closures, telling Laura Ingraham of Fox News, "I believe in our freedoms and liberties." Noem initially balked at urging the closure of a Smithfield pork plant near Sioux Falls that had become a virus hotspot, though she eventually relented. Noem also announced a clinical trial of hydroxychloroquine, a drug touted by Trump but which most medical experts looked at skeptically. Tensions flared again with Native Americans after Noem criticized tribal checkpoints that were intended to keep the virus out of reservations. After a series of large public events in the summer and fall, including the South Dakota State Fair and the Sturgis Motorcycle Rally, South Dakota became the hottest of the nation's coronavirus hotspots. Noem bristled at public-health advice from what she called an "elite class of so-called experts," as she called them in her Republican National Convention address. She also took heat for spending $5 million in federal coronavirus relief funds on a state tourism ad she narrated; it premiered on Fox News along with her convention speech.

Noem's response to the pandemic helped her win a loyal following among Trump-aligned Republicans nationally. She received advice from Trump insider Corey Lewandowski and installed a TV studio in the governor's office; both helped increase her airtime on Fox. On July 4, 2020, Noem hosted Trump at Mount Rushmore, where he delivered a speech to a mostly non-socially distanced audience. Noem successfully lobbied federal officials to approve fireworks for the event, breaking a decade-long moratorium prompted by wildfire concerns. No fires ensued. She also presented Trump with a four-foot-tall, $1,000-plus model of Mount Rushmore with his face on it. After the event, Noem and Lewandowski flew to Washington on Air Force One; she later visited with Pence to assure him that she was not looking to replace him on the ticket, The New York Times reported. Trips to political events in Iowa and Ohio fueled speculation that Noem might run for president in 2024 if Trump doesn't. In the 2021 Conservative Political Action Conference straw poll, Noem finished second to Florida Gov. Ron DeSantisin a contest in which Trump didn't compete; her finish outpaced Donald Trump Jr., former Secretary of State Mike Pompeo, and Texas Sen. Ted Cruz, among others.

John Thune (R)

Elected 2004, term expires 2022, 3rd term, b. Jan 07, 1961; Pierre, SD; Biola University, B.B.A., 1983; University of South Dakota, M.B.A., 1984; Evangelical; Married (Kimberley Joe Weems Thune); 2 children; 2 grandchildren.

Elected Office: U.S. House, 1997-2003.

Professional Career: Legislative Assistant, U.S Sen. James Abdnor, 1985-1986; Special Assistant, U.S Small Business Admin., 1987-1989; Executive Director, SD Republican Party, 1989-1991; SD railroad Director, 1991-1993; Executive Director, SD Municipal League 1993-1996.

DC Office: 511 DSOB 20510, 202-224-2321, Fax: 202-228-5429, thune.senate.gov

State Offices: Aberdeen, 605-225-8823; Rapid City, 605-348-7551; Sioux Falls, 605-334-9596.

Committees: Senate Republican Whip & Assistant Republican Leader. *Agriculture, Nutrition & Forestry*: Commodities, Risk Management & Trade; Conservation, Climate, Forestry & Natural Resources; Livestock, Dairy, Poultry, Local Food Sys & Food Safety & Sec. *Commerce, Science & Transportation*: Aviation Safety, Operations & Innovations; Communications, Media & Broadband; Consumer Protection, Product Safety & Data Security; Surface Transportation, Maritime Freight & Ports. *Finance*: Health Care; International Trade, Customs & Global Competitiveness; Taxation & IRS Oversight (RMM).

Group Ratings

	ADA	ACLU	AFL-CIO	LCV	COC	HAFA	ACU	CFG	FRC
2020	-	0%	-	8%	-	66%	84%	-	-
2019	0%	C	21%	14%	85%	C	85%	29%	100%

Almanac Ratings 2019-2020

	Economy	Social	Foreign	Composite
Liberal	6%	6%	0%	4%
Conservative	94%	94%	100%	96%

Key Votes of the 116th Congress

1. EPA clean energy rules N	5. Russia sanctions N	9. Barr as Atty. General Y
2. U.S./Mex./Can. trade deal Y	6. Troops in SYR, AFG Y	10. Spending at the border Y
3. Cut unemployment benefits Y	7. Veto arms sales to Saudis N	11. Coney Barrett to Sup. Ct. Y
4. Shelton to Fed Reserve Y	8. Defense $$$, veto override Y	12. Electoral College objections N

Election Results

Election	Name (Party)	Vote (%)	Cand. Spent	Ind. Exp. Support	Ind. Exp. Oppose
2016 General	John Thune (R)	265,516 (72%)	$2,424,179		
	Jay Williams (D)	104,140 (28%)	$59,126		
2016 Primary	John Thune (R)	Unopposed			

Prior winning percentages: 2016 (72%), 2010 (100%), 2004 (51%), House: 2000 (73%), 1998 (75%), 1996 (58%)

Republican John Thune of South Dakota has held the No. 2 position in Senate GOP leadership since 2019. His ascension to Republican whip was accompanied by his stepping down as chairman of the Commerce, Science and Transportation Committee, where he focused on transportation and communications issues—often with home-state interests. Before and after the 2020 election, South

Dakota's senior senator engaged in frequent spats with President Donald Trump, has who called for Thune's ouster in 2022—when he is expected to seek a fourth Senate term. Trump's intervention is unlikely to have much effect on Thune's prospects. But the former president's broadsides—plus changes among the Senate GOP rank and file—could affect another contest for which Thune has been planning: that to be the next Senate GOP leader, succeeding Mitch McConnell of Kentucky.

Thune has seemed well-positioned to gain additional influence in the years ahead—perhaps more so than any other of the relatively junior GOP senators. Those prospects depend, in part, on the longevity of McConnell of and the plans of Sen. John Cornyn of Texas, the previous GOP whip, who was forced to step down because of internal GOP term limits. Alternatively, the seniority tables could leave Thune as the top Republican on the powerful Senate Finance Committee within the next decade.

He first gained national notice in 2004, when he defeated the Senate Democratic leader, Tom Daschle, in a hard-fought and costly contest. With his relative youth, extensive Capitol Hill experience and impressive fundraising, Thune has had numerous opportunities inside and outside the Senate. In effect, he has become a Republican version of his Democratic predecessor.

Thune grew up in Murdo, on the dusty plains west of the Missouri River, a small town with a cluster of restaurants and motels at the interchange of Interstate 90 and U.S. Route 83. His father, the son of a Norwegian emigrant and a Navy veteran of World War II, was a teacher and the family was Democratic. Thune graduated from Biola University in La Mirada California and then earned an MBA from the University of South Dakota. Thune's political career dates to his freshman year of high school, when he was spotted at a grocery checkout counter by Republican Rep. Jim Abdnor, who recalled the tall boy had missed only one of six free throws in his high school basketball game the previous night. They kept in touch, and Thune joined his staff a year after finishing business school, when Abdnor was in the Senate. He worked there until he was 25 and Abdnor lost his 1986 bid for reelection to Daschle. Thune then worked for the Small Business Administration.

Thune returned to South Dakota in 1989 and became executive director of the state Republican Party. In 1991, he was appointed state railroad director by Gov. George Mickelson and in 1993 he became director of the South Dakota Municipal League. In 1996, Thune ran for the state's at-large House seat. The favorite in the Republican primary was Lt. Gov. Carole Hillard. But Thune attracted the support of religious conservatives and won the primary 59%-41%. In the general election, he faced Democrat Rick Weiland, a former state director for Daschle. Thune opposed all tax increases and promised to serve only three terms. He won 58%-37%. In the House, Thune was chosen as freshman class representative to the Republican leadership.

As he bumped up against his self-imposed three-term limit in the House, Thune considered running for the open governor's seat in 2002, and he was a heavy favorite to win it. But, at a White House dinner in April 2001, President George W. Bush urged Thune to challenge Democratic Sen. Tim Johnson. Thune launched his Senate bid, clearing the way for Republican Mike Rounds —now Thune's junior colleague in the Senate—to run successfully for governor. In taking on Johnson, Thune argued South Dakota would be better off with a bipartisan Senate delegation. Johnson emphasized votes he had cast for Bush administration policies in a state that had not voted for a Democratic presidential nominee since 1964. Johnson and Thune spent about $6 million each, a record amount for South Dakota; the national parties and independent groups spent much more.

The election was the closest Senate races in the nation that year. The last two precincts reporting from Shannon County, which includes most of the Pine Ridge Indian Reservation, voted for Johnson by a mammoth margin, putting him on top by 524 votes. Many Republicans urged Thune to contest the election results. In a decision that won him respect and appreciation from both parties in South Dakota, he declined and went to work as a lobbyist and consultant in Washington.

Encouraged by Republican leaders, he decided to run in 2004 against Daschle, who had beaten lightly funded opponents in 1992 and 1998. Daschle had been majority leader for 18 months beginning in 2001, and he had been Democratic leader since 1995. In South Dakota, Thune's favorability ratings remained high; he enjoyed the full support of the Bush White House.

Thune sought to portray Daschle as the chief obstructionist to the Bush agenda in the Senate. Daschle ran ads arguing that a freshman senator could not hope to match his influence in Washington and emphasizing the federal largesse he had brought to South Dakota. He also cited his support of some Bush initiatives. But Daschle was hobbled politically by a difficult balancing act—serving as a spokesman for national Democratic policies without putting off voters in a Republican-leaning battleground state. "Sen. Daschle at the time was using his leadership position in a way that was contrary to where a majority of South Dakotans were," Thune told CSPAN nearly a decade after that campaign. "Eventually, that caught up with him."

Thune portrayed Daschle as a political insider who lived in a $2 million house in Washington and had lost touch with folks back home. The state Republican Party sent a mailer attacking the work of Daschle's wife, an aviation industry lobbyist. It was the most expensive congressional election of the year, as both national parties and numerous third-party interest groups spent $35 million. Thune won 51%-49%; Daschle was the first Senate party leader to lose reelection since Democrat Ernest McFarland of Arizona lost to Republican Barry Goldwater in 1952. The contours of the vote were similar to 2002, although Thune significantly increased his share of the vote in the Pine Ridge and Rosebud Indian reservations.

Republicans celebrated Thune as a giant killer, and he became a talk show favorite and a fundraising star, quickly rising in the ranks. He served as vice chairman of the Senate Republican Conference before moving up to Republican Policy Committee chairman in 2009. In early 2012, Thune became chairman of the Republican Conference after Tennessee Sen. Lamar Alexander gave up that post. It made Thune the No. 3 Senate Republican, behind McConnell and Cornyn.

Thune has established a mostly conservative voting record, especially on cultural issues. His Almanac vote ratings ranked him near the center of Senate Republicans. "He is conservative, but his message usually is not bombastic, and he doesn't say things that scare off moderates and independents," the largest newspaper in Thune's home state, the Sioux Falls-based Argus Leader, wrote in 2013.

Taking over as Commerce Committee chairman in 2015, Thune attended to railroads, which were a specialty of his lobbying days and remain a prime interest of many farmers and businesses in South Dakota. He has been especially concerned about the availability of rail transportation for agriculture. In 2015, he won enacted of a bill to reform operations of the Surface Transportation Board, which regulates rail freight. Thune said that the changes were designed to make the board "more accountable and effective in addressing rail rate and service disputes," including severe rail backlogs and service delays that had hindered agricultural shipments. On another transportation issue that is vital to South Dakota, Thune has split with fellow conservatives who have sought to kill the Essential Air Service program, which ensures small airports get commercial flights.

Another prime issue for Thune has been net neutrality, which the Democratic majority of the Federal Communications Commission approved on a 3-2 vote in 2015. The rules were designed to ensure all internet content is treated equally by classifying internet providers as public utilities, as telephone companies have long been. Thune called the FCC action the "most radical, polarizing and partisan path possible." He told the FCC majority at a hearing of his committee: "Instead of working with me and my colleagues in the House and Senate on a bipartisan basis to find a consensus, the three of you chose an option that I believe will only increase political, regulatory and legal uncertainty, which will ultimately hurt average internet users."

In February 2017, Thune filed legislation that defined net neutrality principles and codified them into law, including a measure blocking internet service providers from selectively slowing down traffic or creating special "fast lanes" for sites that pay more. After Trump selected new commissioners, the FCC rescinded the earlier rules. In May 2018, Thune said Senate Democrats were grandstanding with a bill aimed at reinstating net neutrality and said that they were unwilling to negotiate on his proposal. On an issue that is vital for rural areas, Thune criticized the FCC for failing to ensure "sufficient and predictable funding" of broadband to rural areas.

On the Agriculture Committee in 2017, Thune proposed a new category of land conservation, which he has called the Soil Health and Income Protection Program. The voluntary program, which compensates farmers during times of excessive crops, was approved as a pilot program in six prairie states as part of the 2018 farm bill. Thune said that his income protection program for farmers did not require a long-term commitment. Earlier, he helped author a section of the 2008 farm bill establishing a permanent disaster-relief program to provide financial aid to farmers whose crops are harmed by natural disasters. He pushed successfully to include those provisions in the 2014 farm bill and made sure they were retroactive to 2012 to cover drought losses in the Upper Midwest.

Thune has used his seat on the Finance Committee to push legislation to repeal the estate tax, which he has said disproportionately affects farmers. The Republican tax bill that was enacted in December 2017 doubled the exemption for all estates to $11.4 million. Thune also emphasized the lower rates that resulted for middle-class taxpayers. For business, he highlighted the steps toward reducing the "double taxation" on American firms operating overseas. Thune has supported proposals for a biennial budget and a presidential line-item veto as steps to encourage fiscal discipline.

After his initial close Senate races, Thune has breezed to reelection. In 2010, Democrats did not field a challenger. He became only the third Republican senator to run unopposed since direct election of senators began in 1913. Thune faced token opposition in 2016 from Jay Williams, a small businessman who spent $67,000—1percent of what Thune spent during the two-year cycle. Thune won 72%-28%. With the lack of serious competition, Thune in 2016 gave $2 million to the National Republican Senatorial Committee to assist other Senate GOP candidates. In early 2021, he retained more than $13 million in his campaign account. His investment of those funds has resulted in yearly interest and dividends of several hundred thousand dollars for his campaign fund.

After the 2018 elections, Senate Republicans tapped Thune as their whip. The fact that he ran without opposition was a tribute to his skill in garnering support from his colleagues. Some of them undoubtedly explored a bid for the position, but they realized that challenging Thune would have been a futile exercise. Given his decade of serving on the GOP leadership team, his selection resulted in little immediate change. On the day that Thune was selected as whip, both he and Cornyn issued statements that lavished praise on the other. As the most likely heirs to McConnell, it's been fair to expect that they will cautiously eye each other as they build their separate teams and seek opportunities to show their strength.

But with Senate Republicans increasingly embattled, Thune revised the role of the whip—especially to highlight contrasts to Trump and to urge the bombastic president to modify his persona. For example, Thune regularly second-guessed the president, including his criticism of the intelligence community. "I prefer the president would stay off Twitter—particularly with regard to these important national security issues where you've got people who are experts and have the background and are professionals," he said in January 2019 after Trump had criticized their testimony before Congress. In October 2020, when Treasury Secretary Steven Mnuchin was seeking a pre-election deal on an economic stimulus bill with House Speaker Nancy Pelosi, Thune splashed cold water on those prospects: Republicans' "natural instinct, depending on how big it is and what's in it, is probably going to be to be against it," he told reporters.

He voiced concern about the adverse effect for Senate Republicans fighting to retain their majority. "Right now, obviously, Trump has a problem with the middle of the electorate, with independents," Thune told reporters in June 2020. "I think he can win those back, but it'll probably require not only a message that deals with substance and policy but, I think, a message that conveys, perhaps, a different tone." When the president tweeted in July that the November election might be delayed, Thune was one of several GOP senators to take issue. "I think that's probably a statement that gets some press attention, but I doubt it gets any serious traction." Two weeks before the election, Thune said that Trump needed to talk more about issues that were important to undecided voters. "That's what our members are trying to do, and hopefully that's a pivot the president can make as well." In an interview with CNN at that time, he advised Trump, "Stay away from personal attacks. Quit attacking the media. Quit attacking Fauci and focus on issues."

When Thune dismissed the president's postelection claims about voter fraud, Trump lashed out—sometimes pairing Trump unfavorably with McConnell. "RINO John Thune, 'Mitch's boy', should just let it play out," Trump tweeted in late December, using a derogatory term that means "Republican in Name Only." South Dakota doesn't like weakness. He will be primaried in 2022, political career over!!!" Trump encouraged Gov. Kristi Noem to challenge Thune. But she was pursuing a possible run for president in 2024 and showed no interest in an intraparty contest in her home state.

Cory Allen Heidelberger, who writes a newsletter about South Dakota politics, at that time dismissed prospects of a primary challenge to Thune. "If you think anyone in the SDGOP establishment is going to run against our three-term senator, you clearly don't understand the lay of our one-party land."

At a time when several Republican senators said that they won't seek reelection in 2022, Thune said that he was deferring his decision. Thune is young by the standards of the Senate—he turned 60 in January 2021—and he could be an influential presence on Capitol Hill for years to come. But he may have been considering his place in a Trump-dominated party. Multiple establishment GOP senators retired or have announced retirements in 2020 and 2022 and have been replaced by Trump sympathizers; that could spell trouble for Thune's ambitions.

Mike Rounds (R)

Elected 2014, term expires 2026, 2nd term, b. Oct 24, 1954; Huron, SD; SD State University, B.S., 1977; Roman Catholic; Married (Jean Vedvei Rounds); 4 children; 6 grandchildren.

Elected Office: SD Senate, 1991-2000, Majority Leader, 1995-2000; SD governor, 2003-2010.

Professional Career: Insurance & Real Estate Executive.

DC Office: 502 HSOB 20510, 202-224-5842, Fax: 202-224-7482, rounds.senate.gov

State Offices: Aberdeen, 605-225-0366; Pierre, 605-224-1450; Rapid City, 605-343-5035; Sioux Falls, 605-336-0486.

Committees: *Armed Services*: Cybersecurity (RMM); Readiness & Management Support; Strategic Forces. *Banking, Housing & Urban Affairs*: Financial Institutions & Consumer Protection; Housing, Transportation & Community Development (RMM); Securities, Insurance & Investment. *Foreign Relations*: Africa & Global Health Policy (RMM); East Asia, the Pacific & International Cybersecurity Policy; Internat'l Dev Instit & Internat'l Econ, Energy & Environ Policy. *Indian Affairs*. *Veterans' Affairs*.

Group Ratings

	ADA	ACLU	AFL-CIO	LCV	COC	HAFA	ACU	CFG	FRC
2020	-	15%	-	0%	-	69%	77%	-	-
2019	0%	C	25%	21%	93%	C	75%	39%	100%

Almanac Ratings 2019-2020

	Economy	Social	Foreign	Composite
Liberal	6%	6%	0%	4%
Conservative	94%	94%	100%	96%

Key Votes of the 116th Congress

1. EPA clean energy rules	N	5. Russia sanctions	N	9. Barr as Atty. General	Y
2. U.S./Mex./Can. trade deal	Y	6. Troops in SYR, AFG	Y	10. Spending at the border	N/A
3. Cut unemployment benefits	Y	7. Veto arms sales to Saudis	N/A	11. Coney Barrett to Sup. Ct.	Y
4. Shelton to Fed Reserve	Y	8. Defense $$$, veto override	Y	12. Electoral College objections	N

Election Results

Election	Name (Party)		Vote (%)	Cand. Spent	Ind. Exp. Support	Ind. Exp. Oppose
2020 General	Mike Rounds (R)	276,232	(66%)	$2,660,613	$1,698	$7,697
	Dan Ahlers (D)	143,987	(34%)	$240,863		
2020 Primary	Mike Rounds (R)	70,365	(75%)			
	Scyller Borglum (R)	23,164	(25%)			

Prior winning percentages: 2014 (50%), Governor: 2006 (62%), 2002 (57%)

Like other former governors in the Senate, Republican Mike Rounds has stayed attuned to the needs of his home state and has pursued bipartisan deals to break through the gridlocked Senate. Arriving in the Senate in 2015, the former two-term governor of South Dakota gravitated toward a range of topics on which he could build consensus. Those interests have included cyber security, banking regulations and immigration enforcement. Rounds has not always been successful, given the deepening polarization in the Senate. But South Dakota's junior senator has shown that opportunities remain for deal-making. In contrast to his bumpy campaign when he first ran for the Senate, his easy reelection in 2020 positioned him to control his destiny.

Rounds had been urged by some Republicans to challenge Democratic Sen. Tim Johnson in 2008, but he declined to do so. At 2006's end, Johnson suffered a cerebral hemorrhage that required brain surgery; he had only partially recovered. When Johnson retired in 2014, Rounds won comfortably, but only after the contest took some unusual twists. His swearing-in gave South Dakota its first all-GOP congressional delegation in more than a half-century. Although the state has voted reliably Republican in presidential races, it had a history of sending Democrats to Congress, where some became highly influential—including 1972 presidential nominee George McGovern and Tom Daschle, who was Senate Democratic leader for a decade. That era seems long gone.

Rounds, named for an uncle who was killed in World War II, was born in Huron. He has lived in Pierre, the state capital, since he was 3. The eldest of 11 siblings, Rounds earned a degree in political science from South Dakota State University. In 1990, he was elected to the South Dakota Senate, where he served six years as majority leader before departing in 2000 because of term limits. In 2002, he ran for governor and won the Republican primary in one of the biggest political upsets in state history. Rounds faced former Lt. Gov. Steve Kirby and state Attorney General Mark Barnett, who waged a highly negative campaign against each other. Their attack ads backfired, benefiting Rounds —who won with 44 percent of the vote. That fall, he took 57 percent of the vote against Democrat Jim Abbott, who had been president of the University of South Dakota.

As governor, Rounds enjoyed high approval ratings. They briefly slumped in spring 2006 after he signed a law banning all abortions except those necessary to save the mother's life. The law was challenged in court and never took effect. The statute—criticized because it did not include exceptions for rape, incest or the mother's health—was repealed by voters in a state referendum—55%-45%— on the same day that Rounds won his second term with 62 percent of the vote.

Rounds started his second term by calling for the creation of a pilot preschool program in Sioux Falls as part of his long-term goal to increase school retention. He won enactment of a bill to cut the tax on biodiesel fuel blends, which consist of diesel fuel and soybean or corn oil, by 2 cents per gallon. In 2009, he signed legislation banning smoking in South Dakota restaurants and bars. At the end of 2010, Rounds returned to his insurance and real estate firm, where he had put his ownership interest in a blind trust after being elected governor.

When Johnson's retirement from the Senate in 2014 seemed to open the door to his easy victory, Rounds ran and won a five-way primary with 56 percent of the vote. After top Democratic prospects declined to run, the national party all but threw in the towel on the seat. Rick Weiland, a former congressional aide and a two-time unsuccessful candidate for the state's at-large House seat, became the Democratic nominee.

Weiland hammered Rounds on his handling, while governor, of the EB-5 visa program, which allows foreigners to obtain U.S. green cards by investing $500,000 in U.S. business projects that create jobs. A beef processing plant, Northern Beef Packers, received almost $100 million from EB-5 funding but went bankrupt in 2013—a year after it opened. The problem for Rounds was that, a month before leaving office as governor, his economic development secretary, Richard Benda, had signed a contract with a private firm, SDRC, to take over the state's EB-5 program. Benda subsequently went to work for that firm. It was later revealed that Benda failed to disclose his plans to work for SDRC while signing contracts that benefitted that firm. Benda killed himself in 2013 after the South Dakota attorney general, in a draft indictment, accused him of diverting a $550,000 state grant to his own enrichment. Rounds, who acknowledged that he had been aware of Benda's conflict of interest, dropped in the polls amid voter anger over the EB-5 scandal.

Rounds campaigned on a conservative platform, favoring gun rights and opposing abortion and same-sex marriage; he wanted to repeal the Affordable Care Act and suggested he wanted to abolish the Department of Education. Still, some Republicans fretted that he was not doing enough to defend himself.

Public polling revealed another problem: An independent candidate—former Republican Sen. Larry Pressler—made it a three-way contest. Pressler had served for 18 years until losing to Johnson in 1996. A Rhodes scholar and Vietnam veteran who was regarded as an oddball by colleagues on Capitol Hill, Pressler had moved back to South Dakota. Eighteen years after his defeat, he ran as a maverick committed to reforming the way things are done in Washington. Weiland charged that the Democratic Senatorial Campaign Committee undercutting him and boosting Pressler. Rounds went along with national GOP strategists and ran ads contrasting his views on the Affordable Care Act and the Keystone XL pipeline with those of Pressler and Weiland. Rounds won comfortably, taking 50 percent of the vote; Weiland took 30 percent for and Pressler nabbed 17 percent.

Rounds took his problem-solving approach to cyber security, especially regarding national security. That topic had attracted growing bipartisan interest after Russia hacked computers as it sought to influence the 2016 presidential election. In 2017, Rounds became chairman of the newly created Armed Services Cyber security Subcommittee. He was especially interested, he said, in "the Defense Department's role in responding to an attack on our nation's civilian critical infrastructure and in deterring bad actors from conducting such an attack in the first place." It was vital, he said, to deter a potential attack on the nation's infrastructure.

With independent Angus King of Maine, another former governor, Rounds went to work on a plan for a national cyber director to address cyber security threats. When they and their House counterparts were unable to pass a stand-alone bill, they decided in 2020 that they would attempt to add their plan to the annual defense-authorization bill. But the proposal received pushback from the Trump White House, which feared restrictions on its national-security actions. Rounds voiced some sympathy for the administration's view that the plan might "add more bureaucracy."

Finally, after nearly four years of efforts, Rounds announced in December 2020 a bipartisan and bicameral agreement, which would "strengthen our nation's cyber security planning and coordination at all levels of government as well as between the public and private sectors." That defense bill included another provision that was vital to Rounds' constituents: making Ellsworth Air Force Base the home of the first two squadrons of the new ultra long-range B-21 stealth Raider bomber.

Rounds also led bipartisan group seeking to increase security of election systems. In September 2018, he praised President Donald Trump for issuing an executive order that imposed sanctions on foreign countries and people who interfere with U.S. elections. "Today's executive order draws a clear line in the sand and puts our adversaries on notice that we will not tolerate any meddling in our election process," Rounds said.

As a member of the Banking, Housing and Urban Affairs Committee, Rounds looked after large banking and credit card interests in South Dakota. He helped assemble a broad Senate coalition, including 17 Democrats, that voted in 2018 to relax the Dodd-Frank financial regulations. Rounds was interested in reducing regulations on small, local banks and credit unions. He cited a provision that he had sponsored and was part of the final bill, which relaxed rules on banks with less than $3 billion in assets. The result, he said, permits financial institutions to "focus on providing services to their customers."

Rounds has pursued other constituent-based concerns. As chairman of the Environment and Public Works Subcommittee on Superfund, Waste Management and Regulatory Oversight while Republics were still in the majority, he welcomed repeal of Obama-era environmental regulations, notably rules that had given the Environmental Protection Agency new authority over water sources. In December 2018, he praised the Trump administration for issuing new regulations on water policy. They replaced Obama-era rules, which Rounds called "one of the largest federal land grabs in U.S. history."

He fell short on a bipartisan proposal with King and other members of the Senate's self-styled Common Sense Coalition, which sought to address immigration conflicts. The group backed steps to provide a pathway to citizenship for "Dreamers"—immigrants who were brought to the United States illegally as children. In late January 2018, Rounds issued a statement that claimed broad bipartisan support for making permanent changes by law for such immigrants enrolled in the Obama-era Deferred Action for Childhood Arrivals program. Two weeks later, Trump tweeted that the proposal by Rounds and others was "a total catastrophe."

Rounds clashed with Trump on other issues. In June 2019, he complained that the president's trade war with China had slashed soybean prices by 20 percent and that South Dakota farmers were losing patience. When Trump announced a trade agreement with China at the White House in January 2020, the president pointedly called out Rounds for his continuing demands to resolve the conflict. "Where is Mike Rounds?" Trump said, as he scanned his audience. "He kept calling me, 'We've gotta get it done.'" Rounds responded that the deal was "great news" for his home state, though the subsequent coronavirus pandemic reduced sales below the limits in the deal.

In this bid for a second term in 2020, Rounds faced a Republican primary contest with Scyller Borglum, a one-term state representative who called for increased attention to rural education and described her bid as a challenge to the South Dakota "Republican establishment." She lost, 75%-25%. Democratic nominee Dan Ahlers, who owned a video rental store in Dell Rapids, said that he was more moderate than other Democrats and criticized Rounds as "part of the swamp," especially for helping confirm Amy Coney Barrett to the Supreme Court just before the election. Rounds outspent him by more than 100to1 and won, 66%-34%, taking all but five counties.

Dusty Johnson (R)

Elected 2018, 2nd term, b. Sep 30, 1976; Pierre, SD; University of SD, B.A., 1999; University of KS, M.P.A., 2002; Christian Church; Married (Jacquelyn Johnson); 3 children.

Elected Office: SD Public Utilities Commission, Chair 2005-2011

Professional Career: Chief of Staff, Gov. Dennis Daugaard; Management Analyst; Adjunct Professor, Dakota Wesleyan, Adjunct Professor; Senior Policy Advisor, Gov. Mike Rounds, Truman Fellow, U.S. Department of Agriculture.

DC Office: 1508 LHOB 20515, 202-225-2801, dustyjohnson.house.gov

State Offices: Aberdeen, 605-622-1060; Rapid City, 605-646-6454; Sioux Falls, 605-275-2868.

Committees: *Agriculture*: Conservation & Forestry; Livestock & Foreign Agriculture (RMM). *Transportation & Infrastructure*: Highways & Transit; Railroads, Pipelines & Hazardous Materials.

Almanac Ratings 2019-2020

	Economy	Social	Foreign	Composite
Liberal	25%	20%	44%	30%
Conservative	75%	80%	56%	70%

Key Votes of the 116th Congress

1. U.S./Mex./Can. trade deal Y	5. Russia sanctions Y	9. Firearms background checks N
2. First Coronavirus response Y	6. Troops in Syria Y	10. Spending at the border Y
3. HEROES Act N	7. Veto arms sales to Saudis N	11. Marijuana liberalized rules N
4. CASH Act N	8. Defense $$$, veto override Y	12. Electoral College objections N

Election Results

Election	Name (Party)	Vote (%)		Cand. Spent	Ind. Exp. Support	Ind. Exp. Oppose
2020 General	Dusty Johnson (R)	321,984	(81%)	$642,874		$750
	Randy Luallin (L)	75,748	(19%)			
2020 Primary	Dusty Johnson (R)	71,496	(77%)			
	Liz Marty May (R)	21,779	(23%)			

Prior winning percentages: 2018 (60%)

Republican Dusty Johnson had extensive experience in government and business in South Dakota. After winning election as a state regulator and later serving as chief of staff to Gov. Dennis Daugaard, Johnson became a corporate consultant. He easily won election in 2018 with a pragmatic approach in a competitive GOP primary. Compared to most other successful Republican congressional candidates, he kept his distance from President Donald Trump. His committee assignments should serve his state well, as he prepares for a potentially lengthy career in Congress.

Johnson, a South Dakota native, graduated from the University of South Dakota and got a master's in public administration from the University of Kansas. After serving as a policy aide to Gov. Mike Rounds, he was elected in 2004 to the state's Public Utilities Commission; two years later, he became its chairman. During his tenure, Johnson took credit for "hundreds of megawatts of new electrical generation, more than 100 new cell towers, and assistance provided to thousands of consumers."

Following the 2010 election, when Johnson won another term on the commission, Daugaard tapped him as his chief of staff. In 2014, he joined the private sector as vice president of Vantage Point Solutions, a local telecommunications engineering and consulting firm.

When Kristi Noem made her long-expected move to run for governor, Johnson was an early contender to succeed her in the House. He embraced what he called the optimistic appeal of President Ronald Reagan. "I am not going to hurl insults," Johnson told the Rapid City Journal. "I really do believe that constructive governance is about building bridges. …I'm not gonna be anybody's foot soldier in Washington D.C." He criticized Trump's personal behavior and said the president was "too easily distracted" and "too thin-skinned."

During his campaign, Johnson voiced concerns about the mounting federal deficit plus the "general dysfunction" in Washington, and supported changes in how Congress handles the budget. He voiced concern that the tax cuts enacted by Republicans in 2017 will increase the federal debt. He cautioned that Trump's international trade policies could cause problems for South Dakota's farmers. His chief primary opponent, Secretary of State Shantel Krebs, kept closer to Trump and was endorsed by several conservative groups and political leaders.

The Sioux Falls Argus-Leader endorsed Johnson as "a mature and moderate Republican voice," with "a consistency in his ideals and demeanor." He generally avoided campaign attacks on his opponents. Johnson had a slight edge over Krebs in fundraising. He benefited from more than $310,000 in independent spending by Citizens for a Strong America, a North Carolina-based super PAC that backed centrist Republicans.

Johnson won the GOP primary with 47 percent of the vote to 29 percent for Krebs and 24 percent for state Sen. Neal Tapio. Johnson led in 62 of the state's 66 counties. In November, he faced Tim Bjorkman, who served 10 years as a state court judge before stepping down to run for the House; Johnson won, 60%-36%.

In the House, he joined the Agriculture Committee, where his expertise led to his selection to the Republican whip team that urged approval of the revised trade agreement with Mexico and Canada. In 2021, he became ranking Republican on the Agriculture Subcommittee on Livestock and Foreign Agriculture, a position where he said he would highlight "the challenges and opportunities facing South Dakota's small feeders and cow-calf operators." He added that ranching and livestock "often gets less attention in D.C. than it deserves."

Johnson said he was "grateful" for his selection in 2021 to the Transportation and Infrastructure Committee, where its handling of a sweeping transportation bill was expected to be "among the most important pieces of legislation" facing Congress that year. He said he would assure that "rural priorities aren't forgotten."

During his first term, he pursued bipartisanship as a member of the Problem Solvers Caucus. In early October 2020, he joined other Republicans in the coalition who said "inaction is not an option" as they criticized Trump's decision to abandon discussion of a new pandemic-relief bill. At that time, he co-authored an op-ed piece for the Sioux Falls Argus Leader with Democratic Rep. Dean Phillips of Minnesota—another member of the coalition—in which they cited their "five weeks and countless hours deliberating, developing and drafting" a framework that the 50 members of their bipartisan group endorsed.

Johnson also took issue with Trump's handling of his reelection campaign. When the president raised doubts prior to the election whether he would comply with the results, he tweeted that "the peaceful transition of power is a hallmark of our American system of government." When the House and Senate convened in January 2021 to ratify the Electoral College vote, Johnson was among the minority of House Republicans who voted against review of election results in Arizona and Pennsylvania. "There is no constitutional basis for Congress to substitute its judgment for that of the states and courts," he said.

Seeking reelection in 2020, Johnson was challenged in the GOP primary by Liz Marty May, a former state lawmaker, who said that Johnson was not conservative enough. He defeated her, 77%-23%. In November, Democrats did not run a challenger. Johnson took 81 percent of the vote against a Libertarian candidate. In Republican-controlled South Dakota, where he already has won multiple statewide elections, the youthful Johnson could have additional electoral opportunities.

TENNESSEE

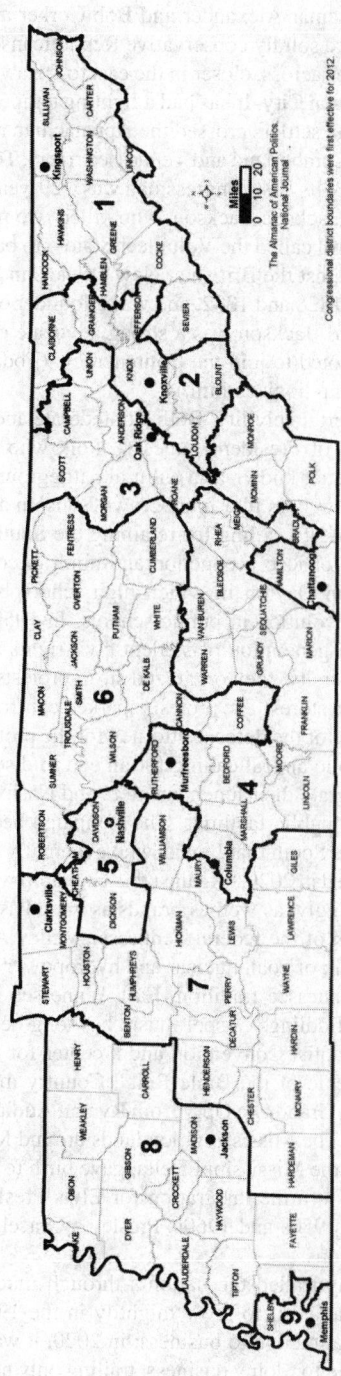

Tennessee, once a political battleground, is no longer. It has become one of the most solidly Republican states in the country, with just a few pockets of blue in its biggest cities. And while Tennessee has long been home to an influential strain of moderate Republicanism, the tradition's most recent exemplars—Sens. Lamar Alexander and Bob Corker and Gov. Bill Haslam—are now out of politics, succeeded by more solidly conservative Republicans.

Tennessee is almost 500 miles across, closer in the east to Delaware than to Memphis, and closer in the west to Dallas than to Johnson City. It has had a fighting temperament since the days before the Revolutionary War, when the first settlers crossed the Appalachian ridges and headed for the rolling country in the watersheds of the Cumberland and Tennessee rivers. Tennessee became a state in 1796, the third state after the original 13. Its first congressman was a 29-year-old lawyer who was the son of Scots-Irish immigrants: Andrew Jackson. Jackson, who killed two men in duels, was a general who led Tennessee volunteers—it's still called the Volunteer State—to battle against the Creek Indians at Horseshoe Bend in 1814 and against the British at New Orleans in 1815. He was the first president from an interior state, elected in 1828 and 1832, and was a founder of the Democratic Party, now the oldest political party in the world. Jackson was a strong advocate of the union, but 16 years to the day after his death, Tennessee voted to join the Confederacy. (Today, Jackson's own party largely disowns him, while Donald Trump lionized him.)

Tennessee is a state with a certain civility: Both Confederate and Union generals paid respectful calls on Sarah Polk, the widow of President James K. Polk who stayed carefully neutral, in her Nashville mansion. Yet it was better known as a cultural battleground for much of the 20th century. On one side were the Fugitives, writers like John Crowe Ransom and Allen Tate, who contributed to "I'll Take My Stand," a manifesto calling for retaining the South's rural economy and heritage. (Today, the state ranks third in tobacco production and ninth in cotton.) Tennessee is also known for the momentous 1925 trial in Dayton in which high school biology teacher John T. Scopes defied a state ban on teaching evolution in public schools. In 1959 and 1960, Vanderbilt divinity student James Lawson trained a generation of student civil rights activists, notably John Lewis, a student at Nashville's Fisk University; they organized sit-in protests at segregated lunch counters at Kress, Woolworth and McClellan stores. The protests sparked confrontations, arrests and ultimately a bombing that destroyed the home of the defense attorney for the protestors. That prompted Nashville Mayor Ben West to make a public appeal calling for an end to discrimination in the city. Within a few weeks, stores began to integrate their lunch counters and Nashville later became the first major city in the South to desegregate public facilities. The campaign became a template for student-run civil rights efforts throughout the South that Lewis, who eventually became a Georgia congressman, would heroically lead. (Lewis died in 2020.) Against this backdrop were business leaders who created the first supermarket, Piggly Wiggly, as well as brands as varied as Holiday Inn, FedEx, and Moon Pies. The New Deal-era creation of the federal Tennessee Valley Authority also provided the state with bountiful energy, from a mix of coal, nuclear and hydropower plants.

Music is another strong Tennessee tradition. East Tennessee is one of the original homes of bluegrass music and mountain fiddling. Gospel music has long been centered in Nashville, which is also home to the Southern Baptist Convention and a center for religious publishing; justifiably, Nashville is known as the "buckle of the Bible Belt." Country music got its commercial start in Nashville, with broadcasts of the Grand Ole Opry from Ryman Auditorium in 1925, and it remains the capital of country music today. The Mississippi lowlands around Memphis, which is economically and culturally the metropolis of the Mississippi Delta, gave birth to the blues in the years from 1890 to 1920, and the blues were in turn the inspiration for Elvis Presley and countless other rock 'n' roll musicians beginning in the 1950s and 1960s. Presley's Graceland mansion remains one of the country's major tourist destinations.

While Tennessee's economy trailed the nation's through much of the 20th century, its open climate for entrepreneurism enabled it to grow mightily in the 1980s and 1990s. The absence of strong unions made Tennessee attractive to business; in 2020, it was chosen by Area Development magazine as the second-best state for doing business, trailing only neighboring Georgia. The relative lack of bitter racial discord was a factor as well, with the obvious exception being the assassination of Martin Luther King Jr. in Memphis in 1968. Alexander, governor through most of the 1980s, was a deft salesman in his efforts to bring foreign auto plants to Middle Tennessee; Nissan opened a plant in Smyrna, south of Nashville, where the land was flat and the bedrock was strong. It has since built another and relocated its U.S. headquarters to Tennessee. Volkswagen built a $1 billion "green" plant for the Passat in Chattanooga that, after a $900 million investment, is now being used to build the Atlas, a midsize crossover SUV, and is now being fitted to produce an electric vehicle. (In both 2014 and 2019, workers at the Volkswagen plant rejected a unionization effort.) Among domestic producers, General Motors built the short-lived Saturn, a cult favorite, at Spring Hill; the plant is now producing the Cadillac XT5 and XT6 and the GMC Acadia. Meanwhile, Nashville has become a tech center since Dell Computer built its second major U.S. facility there in 1999. It's also a health care hub, led by HCA and Vanderbilt University.

Tennessee's population has grown 8.9 percent since 2010, with especially rapid expansion in the Nashville area. Davidson County, which includes Nashville, grew by 10.6 percent, while the suburbs grew even more rapidly—growth of almost 30 percent in Williamson County, 26 percent in Rutherford and Wilson counties, and almost 19 percent in Sumner County. The economic-analysis firm POLICOM rated Nashville fourth among the nation's metro areas in "economic strength" for 2021. Meanwhile, the populations of Knox County (Knoxville) and Hamilton County (Chattanooga) grew 8.6 percent and 9.1 percent, respectively, and Blount County, south of Knoxville, grew 8 percent. Among the state's largest counties, only Shelby County (Memphis) lagged, with growth of less than 1 percent; the poverty rate in the city of Memphis is 25 percent, higher than any of Tennessee's other three big cities.

Tennessee ranks among the bottom 10 states in median income, the attainment of bachelor's degrees, and health status as measured by America's Health Rankings; it has high rates of obesity and smoking. The Nashville area experienced twin disasters in 2020—an outbreak of EF3 and EF4 tornadoes in March that caused at least 20 fatalities and an estimated $1 billion in damage, and a downtown bombing by a troubled man in an RV on Christmas Day, damaging dozens of buildings. The liberal-leaning Institute on Taxation and Economic Policy rated Tennessee's tax system the nation's sixth most regressive, thanks in large part to its heavy reliance on the sales tax, which does not exempt food and clothing. (Tennesseans seem to prefer it; in 2014, voters by an almost a 2-1 margin ratified a constitutional amendment banning the adoption of any state or local personal income or payroll tax.) Tennessee was ahead of the curve in offering free community college or technical school to all high school graduates, in a bill signed by Haslam in 2014. Demand quickly exceeded expectations for the program, which chiefly benefits lower-income and working-class families. "The way they talk about free college in Tennessee is very different than the way they talk about free college on the Democratic side," Kim Dancy of the Institute for Higher Education Policy told Politico. "It wasn't as strongly associated with Democratic politics at that time. I would be very surprised if a Republican governor was able to do this today."

For more than a century, Tennessee's political divisions were rooted in Civil War loyalties. In two referenda on secession (one that failed in February 1861 and one that embraced it in June after the attack on Fort Sumter) most East Tennessee counties voted heavily for the Union and have remained heavily Republican ever since. Pro-secession counties in Middle and West Tennessee long voted heavily Democratic. Reform-minded liberal Democrats Estes Kefauver and Albert Gore Sr. became national figures, with reliable enough backing from Tennessee's yellow-dog Democratic majority to vote for civil rights bills. Gore was defeated in 1970. He died in 1998, but lived to see his son twice elected vice president.

As the Democrats' cultural liberalism strained the ancestral loyalties of rural voters in West and Middle Tennessee, and as the surging growth around Nashville created a new voting bloc that was conservative both economically and culturally, Republicans gained the upper hand. Gore won his Senate seat in 1990 with two-thirds of the vote, but just 10 years later, he couldn't win his home state in the presidential election. By 2012, with President Barack Obama at the top of the Democratic ticket, Republicans won supermajorities in both legislative chambers. In the space of a decade, Democrats went from controlling all three branches of state government to barely being relevant in the capital. By 2018, the American Conservative Union ranked the Tennessee legislature as the nation's most conservative. The rump Democratic Party has become largely urban and more progressive as old-style conservative Democrats have died or become Republicans. The only significant base of power for Democrats is in mayoral offices, which they now hold in Memphis, Nashville, Chattanooga and Knoxville, the state's four largest cities.

The 2018 elections represented a death blow to a long tradition of pragmatic, technocratic Republicanism. On the strength of Republican support in rural and exurban areas, the GOP candidates for senator and governor—Rep. Marsha Blackburn and businessman Bill Lee—won their races for senator and governor, respectively, by 11 and 21 points, respectively. The winning party label might not have changed, but the brand of Republicanism did: The state's political elite articulate a more confrontational message than was typical of politicians in the East Tennessee mold, such as former Senate Republican Leader Howard Baker, former Sens. Bill Brock, Alexander and Corker, and Haslam.

In 2020, Trump won the state by 23 points, a slightly smaller victory than in 2016, when he won by 26 points. In both elections, Trump lost only three counties: urban Shelby and Davidson, and small, majority-Black Haywood. Joe Biden made incremental gains in the other two big urban counties, narrowing Trump's winning margin by six points in Hamilton and nine points in Knox. Biden also made 5-to-10-point gains in the suburban counties of Rutherford, Williamson, Sumner, Wilson, and Blount. But even in those counties where the Democrats made modest gains, Trump still won by margins of 16 to 44 points, enough to secure his wide victory in the state. Perhaps an even more illustrative race in 2020 was the primary to succeed Alexander, in which two Republicans, Bill Hagerty and Manny Sethi, sought to one-up each other in displays of loyalty to Trump. Hagerty won the primary with Trump's endorsement, and in November won by 27 points, outrunning Trump slightly. All in all, there's little sign of significant weakening of the Republican brand in Tennessee.

Population		Race and Ethnicity		Income	
Total	6,829,174	White	77.20%	Median Income	56,071
Land area (sq. miles)	41,235	Black	16.70%	State Income Rank	42 out of 50
Pop/ sq mi	165.62	Latino	5.70%	Poverty Rate	13.90%
Born in state	59.10%	Asian	2.40%	With health insurance	89.90%
		Two or more races	2.30%	Cash public assistance	1.60%
Age Groups		Other	2.00%	Food stamp/SNAP	15.7%
Under 18	22.10%				
18-34	22.90%	Education		Work	
35-64	38.30%	H.S grad or less	43.50%	White Collar	36.20%
Over 64	16.70%	Some college	27.70%	Sales and Service	38.20%
		College Degree, 4 yr	18.00%	Blue Collar	25.60%
Military		Post grad	10.70%	Government	13.00%
Veteran/ Active Duty	8.40%				

Presidential Politics

2020 Primary (D)	Biden (D)	215,390(42%)	Sanders (D)		129,168(25%)	Bloomberg (D)	79,789(15%)
	Warren (D)	53,732(10%)					
2020 Pres. Vote	Trump (R)	1,852,475(61%)	Biden (D)	1,143,711(37%)			
2016 Pres. Vote	Trump (R)	1,522,925(61%)	Clinton (D)	870,695(35%)	Johnson (L)	70,397 (3%)	

Most of Tennessee is part of the Jacksonian belt of America running along the Appalachians, territory that has turned more and more Republican since 2000. That year, Al Gore carried 36 of its 95 counties and came within four points of carrying his home state. By 2008, Barack Obama carried just six: Memphis' Shelby County, which is majority African American; Nashville's Davidson County; and four other small counties. Hillary Clinton and Joe Biden both won only three: Shelby, Davidson and tiny Haywood, the only other county in the state with a majority-Black population. President Donald Trump defeated Biden, 61%-38%.

Tennessee set its primary on Super Tuesday in 2008, and Clinton defeated Obama 54%-40%. In 2016, she defeated Bernie Sanders 66%-33%. In 2020, Tennessee was one of the states where Michael Bloomberg made the most effort, but Biden won 42%-25% over Sanders, with Bloomberg at 15%. Recent GOP primaries have offered mixed results. In 2008, Mike Huckabee defeated John McCain, 34%-32%, with Mitt Romney third at 24 percent. In 2012, Rick Santorum defeated Romney,

37%-28%. In 2016, Trump defeated Texas Sen. Ted Cruz, 39%-25% and carried 94 of the state's 95 counties.

Congressional Districts

117th Congress Lineup	2D 7R	116th Congress Lineup	2D 7R

Republicans swept the governorship and both houses of the Tennessee legislature in 2010, earning unbridled authority to reverse the jig-sawed map Democrats had drawn in 2002. Back then, Democrats had created a fragile arrangement that gave them a 5-4 edge for eight years. Tennessee's cultural shift away from Democrats rendered the map a ticking time bomb even before the next redistricting. In 2010, Republicans defeated one incumbent and had double-digit wins to take two open seats. That gave them 7-2 control of the delegation, which has not been seriously threatened since. In early 2011, there was chatter that Republicans would seek more revenge by splitting Nashville Democrat Jim Cooper's 5th District four ways. But Republicans determined the move too risky and passed a map strengthening Cooper and straightening most district lines across the state. They had enough maneuvering room to tweak two of the districts to remove potential primary foes for two of their GOP incumbents. Democrats comfortably control the Memphis-based 9th plus the 5th. Of the 45 House elections since 2012, the winner has received at least 60 percent of the vote in each, except for the first two contests in the 4th District.

With Republicans again in firm control, the logical scenario for the next redistricting would be to continue the current map for another decade. The 8th and 9th districts in West Tennessee have grown the least, which likely will require each to extend a bit farther to the east. But the fate of the 5th might be an even more tempting target for Republicans, given their huge majorities in the three adjacent districts in the Nashville metro area, plus Cooper's narrow victory in the 2020 Democratic primary. Still, the nationwide changes in suburban politics—including parts of the Nashville area--might pose eventual risks for one or two of the GOP incumbents.

Bill Lee (R)

Elected 2018, term expires 2023, 1st term; b. Oct. 09 1959, Franklin, TN; Auburn University, B.S.; Married (Maria); 4 children.

Professional Career: Rancher; President, Lee Company, 1992-2016, Chair, 2016-2018.

Office: Tennessee State Capitol 1st Floor, Nashville, 37243; 615-741-2001; Fax: 615-532-9711
Lt. Gov.: Rand McNally (R) **Atty. Gen:** Herbert Slatery III (R)
State Legislature: Senate: 5D, 28R **House:** 26D, 73R

Election Results

Election	Name (Party)	Vote (%)
2018 General	Bill Lee (R)...	1,336,106 (60%)
	Karl Dean (D)..	864,863 (39%)
2018 Primary	Bill Lee (R)...	289,699 (37%)
	Randy Boyd (R)...	191,940 (24%)
	Diane Black (R)...	181,719 (23%)
	Beth Harwell (R)...	120,910 (15%)

Businessman Bill Lee easily won the governorship of Tennessee in 2018, becoming the first Tennessee Republican to succeed a Republican governor since 1869. Lee's victory shattered another longstanding pattern in Tennessee: Since the 1960s, partisan control of the governor's office had changed with every new governor. This electoral habit finally came to an end as Tennessee became one of the most Republican states in the union.

Lee, a seventh-generation Tennessean from Williamson County south of Nashville, earned a mechanical engineering degree at Auburn University, then returned home to join the Lee Co., a business founded by his grandfather in 1944 that specializes in HVAC, electrical work, and plumbing. Starting in 1992, Lee served as president and CEO; by the time of his gubernatorial run, the company was employing 1,200 people and earning annual revenue of more than $220 million. The company collected $13.8 million from state contracts between 2012 and 2018, but it stopped signing new state contracts during his campaign, and Lee put his holdings into a blind trust. Separately, Lee helped operate the Triple L Ranch, a 1,000-acre farm founded by his grandparents with 300 head of Hereford cattle. Carol Ann, Lee's wife and the mother of their four children, died in a horse-riding accident in 2000. Lee eventually became close to a third-grade teacher of one of his children, and in 2008, they married. Bill and Maria Lee attend a conservative, charismatic church, and Lee serves as a board member of the Men of Valor prison ministry.

Lee was one of several Republicans to enter the race to succeed two-term Gov. Bill Haslam. A major business figure in the state, Haslam had come to the governorship after serving as mayor of Knoxville. He fit with the East Tennessee tradition of pragmatic Republicanism, producing achievements in education and transportation policy. Haslam often sparred with the more conservative members of his own party in the GOP-controlled state legislature, and declared he would not vote for Donald Trump in 2016, even though Trump was poised to win the state by 26 points.

In addition to Lee, the Republican primary field seeking to succeed Haslam included Rep. Diane Black, state House Speaker Beth Harwell and Knoxville businessman Randy Boyd. Black came into the race as something of a frontrunner, winning endorsements from Vice President Mike Pence and the National Rifle Association. Boyd, who spent $21 million on his candidacy, came the closest to following Haslam's more pragmatic approach, but Republican primary voters seemed to be in a mood for a more conservative choice, and he veered right in response. As Boyd and Black beat up on each other, Lee framed himself as an outsider, campaigning from an RV and a tractor and refraining from negativity. The low-key approach enabled Lee to climb in the polls. He finished first with 37 percent, followed by Boyd at 24 percent, Black at 23 percent, and Harwell at 15 percent. The Tennessean called Lee's victory "arguably the biggest Cinderella story in Tennessee Republican politics in decades." On the Democratic side, former Nashville Mayor Karl Dean easily won the primary with 75 percent of the vote. But Dean was unsuccessful in his efforts to woo Republican moderates. Lee won, 60%-39%.

After taking office, Lee signed executive orders to increase ethics and transparency within state government. He signed a bill to create education savings accounts to provide private-school tuition for qualifying public school students, but in 2020 the law was struck down in the courts. He also signed a bill that would apply criminal penalties to voter registration groups if they submit incomplete forms; this law, too, was enjoined by a federal court in 2019. Over several months, Lee grappled with a running controversy over memorializing the state's Confederate history. Lee attracted national attention when he signed a proclamation declaring July 13 as Nathan Bedford Forrest Day, honoring the Confederate general and Ku Klux Klan figure. Lee said he had no choice but to sign it, given longstanding state law. (Complicating matters, USA Today had earlier discovered a 1980 photograph from Lee's Auburn days in which he had posed in a Confederate uniform.) In 2020, after racial justice protests flared nationally, Lee signed a law that eliminated the requirement that the governor denote the commemoration, though the law disappointed critics who noted that the measure did not eliminate

Nathan Bedford Forrest Day altogether. Meanwhile, the State Capitol Commission approved removal of Forrest's bust from the capitol, reversing the panel's vote in 2017 to keep the bust where it was.

In 2020, Lee proposed a $117 million pay increase for K-12 teachers, but the proposal was shelved after the coronavirus pandemic hit. Lee, like other Republican governors in red states, began opening Tennessee's economy during the pandemic relatively early; in July, he rebuffed a suggestion by Dr. Deborah Birx to close bars and tighten indoor-dining rules, and he resisted calls for a statewide mask mandate. In August, Lee signed legislation to shield businesses, schools, and nursing homes from coronavirus lawsuits. However, Lee did largely allow local officials the option of imposing their own, stricter rules. Cases spiked in the fall and winter, as they did nationally; by March, the case rate had fallen significantly, but Tennessee remained in the top one-third of states for per capita cases. Even beyond the coronavirus, 2020 was a challenging year for the state, with a cluster of large tornadoes hitting Nashville and a Christmas Day bombing in the city's downtown.

Lee took heat from some in his own party for continuing to accept refugees, but he did please conservatives by signing several bills in 2020. One protected adoption and foster care agencies with religious objections to same-sex adoptive parents; another was a bill to bar abortions after a fetal heartbeat is detected, unless the mother's life is in danger. Lee outraged liberals by signing a bill targeting protesters who camp out on state property; the measure upped potential charges to felonies, meaning defendants could be stripped of their voting rights if they were convicted. Lee has announced that he'll run for a second term in 2022. As long as he doesn't get a top-tier GOP primary challenger, he should be in good shape for reelection.

Marsha Blackburn (R)

Elected 2018, term expires 2024, 1st term, b. Jun 06, 1952; Laurel, MS; MS State University, B.S., 1973; Presbyterian; Married (Chuck Blackburn); 2 children; 2 grandchildren.

Elected Office: Chair, Williamson County Republican Party, 1989-1991; TN Senate, 1998-2002; U.S. House, 2003-2019.

Professional Career: Retail marketing consultant, 1973-1998; Executive Director, TN Film, Entertainment, and Music Commission, 1995-1997.

DC Office: 357 DSOB 20510, 202-224-3344, Fax: 202-228-0566, blackburn.senate.gov

State Offices: Chattanooga, 423-541-2939; Jackson, 731-660-3971; Jonesborough, 423-753-4009; Knoxville, 865-540-3781; Memphis, 901-527-9199; Nashville, 629-262-8423.

Committees: *Armed Services*: Cybersecurity; Emerging Threats & Capabilities; Readiness & Management Support. *Commerce, Science & Transportation*: Communications, Media & Broadband; Consumer Protection, Product Safety & Data Security (RMM); Oceans, Fisheries, Climate Change & Manufacturing; Tourism, Trade & Export Promotion. *Judiciary*: Competition Policy, Antitrust & Consumer Rights; Immigration, Citizenship & Border Security; Privacy, Technology & the Law; Subcommittee on Intellectual Property. *Veterans' Affairs*.

Group Ratings (House)

	ADA	ACLU	AFL-CIO	LCV	COC	HAFA	ACU	CFG	FRC
2020		15%	-	0%		98%	95%	-	100%
2019	0%	C	11%	21%	70%	C	95%	89%	100%

Almanac Ratings 2019-2020

	Economy	Social	Foreign	Composite
Liberal	2%	7%	6%	5%
Conservative	98%	93%	94%	95%

Key Votes of the 116th Congress (House)

1. EPA clean energy rules	N	5. Russia sanctions	N	9. Barr as Atty. General	Y
2. U.S./Mex./Can. trade deal	Y	6. Troops in SYR, AFG	Y	10. Spending at the border	Y
3. Cut unemployment benefits	Y	7. Veto arms sales to Saudis	N	11. Coney Barrett to Sup. Ct.	Y
4. Shelton to Fed Reserve	Y	8. Defense $$$, veto override	Y	12. Electoral College objections	N

Election Results

Election	Name (Party)	Vote (%)		Cand. Spent	Ind. Exp. Support	Ind. Exp. Oppose
2018 General	Marsha Blackburn (R)....................... 1,227,483	(55%)		$16,298,206	$9,551,771	$19,797,103
	Phil Bredesen (D)............................... 985,450	(44%)		$19,285,588	$6,461,866	$22,204,717
2018 Primary	Marsha Blackburn (R)......................... 613,513	(85%)				
	Aaron Pettigrew (R)......................... 112,705	(16%)				

Prior winning percentages: 2018 (55%), House: 2016 (72%), 2014 (70%), 2012 (71%), 2010 (72%), 2008 (69%), 2006 (66%), 2004 (100%), 2002 (71%)

Republican Marsha Blackburn won a closely watched race in 2018 to become the first woman elected to the Senate from Tennessee and rose to become the state's senior senator after just two years when Sen. Lamar Alexander retired. A conservative firebrand who was a legislative activist and influential lawmaker in the House for 16 years, Blackburn represented a sharp shift from a pragmatic conservative—like Bob Corker, whom she replaced—to a tea party acolyte who was a fierce supporter of President Donald Trump. In the Senate, she's kept up that tone, seizing on conservative complaints of online censorship by Silicon Valley and attacking the veracity of witnesses who claimed Trump had urged Ukraine to help dig up dirt on his eventual 2020 opponent—a scandal that sparked his first impeachment.

Blackburn grew up in Laurel Mississippi, where her father sold oil-field production equipment. Her interest in gardening and canning won her a 4-H scholarship at Mississippi State University, where she majored in merchandising and clothing. She helped pay her way through college by selling books door to door for Southwestern Co., which sold educational materials that attracted many conservative students. Blackburn, however, was rejected when she first applied because she was a woman and there were concerns about a single woman going out to sell alone. The company finally hired her as one of its first saleswomen, albeit with a catch—she had to live in Mississippi with her parents, while the salesmen were allowed to go between cities. "People have been brainwashed that they think women aren't capable of this type of work," she told her college newspaper. Blackburn worked her way up and eventually became a sales manager and earned enough money to pay for her sophomore year college tuition and buy a blue Ford sedan, which she called the "Can-Do."

After graduation, she married and moved to Tennessee, settling in the tony Nashville suburb of Brentwood. Her hilltop home in Brentwood is known as "Up Yonder," named by its former owner, Grand Ole Opry star Minnie Pearl. Blackburn became director of retail fashion for the Nashville department store Castner Knott Company and later found her own marketing company. She was appointed by Republican Gov. Don Sundquist as executive director of the Tennessee Film, Entertainment and Music Commission, and her interest in politics grew. In 1992, she challenged Democrat Rep. Bart Gordon but lost 57%-41%. She then won a state Senate seat, where she built a grassroots campaign to defeat Sundquist's proposed income tax. In 2014, Tennessee voters approved a constitutional amendment that prohibited a state income tax.

When the 7th District House seat, which then stretched from the Nashville to Memphis suburbs, opened, Blackburn was the only well-known candidate from the Nashville area. Of the six other candidates, three were familiar figures in the Memphis area. She benefited from financial support of the national anti-tax Club for Growth and from attacks by the Shelby County candidates on one another. She ran as an anti-abortion, pro-gun, pro-military conservative and won the primary with 40 percent of the vote and then easily won the general election. She was the first woman elected to Congress from Tennessee without following her husband, though gender wasn't something she emphasized—even asking to be called "congressman" rather than "congresswoman."

Blackburn staked out conservative positions in the House, often seeking leadership roles. She was active on the Republican Study Committee, and in 2012, she co-chaired the Republican National Convention's platform committee. She co-sponsored the "birther" bill, requiring future presidential candidates to prove they were born in the United States, a measure that played off attacks from the right on President Barack Obama's qualifications to hold office, although the measure would not have applied to him. In 2015, she wrote a letter to the IRS challenging the tax-exempt status of the Clinton Foundation. A champion of gun owners' rights, Blackburn has boasted about her perfect marksmanship score with her Smith & Wesson .38. After the Newtown Connecticut elementary school massacre, she said the debate should focus on mental health because disturbed people predisposed toward violence could use "a hammer, a hatchet, a car" instead of a gun. In 2016, she chaired the House's Select Panel on Infant Lives, which was a special committee created to review allegations by anti-abortion activists of an illicit trade of fetal tissue. The panel held hearings and issued recommendations for changes in what Blackburn described as "the abortion and fetal tissue procurement industries." Democrats opposed creation of the panel and its activities.

In the majority, Blackburn played a prominent role on technology policy at Energy and Commerce. A fervent advocate of the Nashville-based music industry and founder of the Congressional Songwriters Caucus, she fought to protect intellectual property rights of artists against illegal music downloads. In 2015, she co-sponsored the bipartisan Fair Play, Fair Pay bill to ensure musicians are compensated for their work. The recording industry has given her a congressional Grammy. Blackburn has often challenged the Federal Communications Commission. In 2014, the House passed on a largely party-line vote her amendment to prevent the FCC from pre-empting state laws that block the ability of cities to create local government-run broadband networks; she cited state sovereignty on behalf of her proposal, which was supported by large cable companies. In 2015, she sought to deny funding for the FCC to implement its net-neutrality rules that were designed to bar tiered pricing for internet services; she contends that such authority is solely the responsibility of Congress. In taking over in 2017 as chairwoman of the revamped Communication and Technology Subcommittee, she encouraged Ajit Pai, Trump's choice to chair the FCC, to cut back its regulations.

Blackburn was an early Trump supporter and served as a vice chairwoman of his presidential transition team, which sparked speculation that she might be named to a Cabinet position. When Corker announced in September 2017 he wouldn't run for a third term, her attention turned to the open seat. After term-limited Tennessee Gov. Bill Haslam announced he wouldn't run, Blackburn became the GOP front-runner. She made clear in her announcement video she would be a very different senator than the collegial Corker. "I'm a hard core, card-carrying Tennessee conservative. I'm politically incorrect and proud of it," Blackburn said. "I know the left calls me a wing-nut, or a knuckle-dragging conservative. And you know what? I say that's all right; bring it on."

Corker, however, soon appeared to have a change of heart. Some in the Tennessee Republican establishment had concerns about Blackburn's statewide viability—especially after popular centrist former Gov. Phil Bredesen got in on the Democratic side—and began encouraging Corker to reconsider his decision to retire. Corker's office confirmed the pressure campaign, saying he was "listening closely." A spokeswoman for Blackburn issued an irate response: "Anyone who thinks Marsha Blackburn can't win a general election is just a plain sexist pig. ... We aren't worried about these ego-driven, tired old men." She made clear Blackburn was staying in the race, whether or not Corker jumped back in. The prospect of such a primary—which many Republicans admitted Corker likely could not win—would bleed their war chests dry, while Bredesen was left a clear path to the general election. Corker stuck with his original decision. Blackburn won the primary with 85 percent of the vote against a little-known challenger.

The rift between Blackburn and the state establishment was cause for pause, initially. And those concerns were magnified by Corker's repeated praise of Bredesen, with whom he had worked closely while mayor of Chattanooga to bring a Volkswagen plant to the area. He gave Blackburn only a tepid endorsement, repeatedly refusing to say her name during one live TV interview. Bredesen was a strong recruit for Democrats—their last candidate to win statewide, first elected in 2002 and reelected in 2006 with 69 percent of the vote, including carrying all of Tennessee's 95 counties. He argued the race was a test of the centrist brand he had built in the state and would show whether a Southern Democrat could still be victorious despite a national party very much disliked in Tennessee. "I'm not going up there to be lockstep in some way with what the national Democratic Party has become," Bredesen told NPR. "You have to join the party to participate in electoral politics but the party for me is an organization I belong to—it's not a religion, and I don't think that I will go to hell if [then-Senate Minority Leader] Chuck Schumer doesn't like what I say about something or other." Instead, the low-key policy wonk tried to localize issues, holding small events with a focus on topics like agriculture and trade—emphasizing his opposition to Trump's tariffs—and health care and even on hyper local issues like Asian Carp, an invasive species that was harming the state's fishing industry. The former businessman and health care executive also pointed out places where he agreed with Trump, such as rolling back regulations. Bredesen made the case he was the centrist choice and would bring that mentality to Washington.

Blackburn worked to nationalize the race as much as possible—a smart strategy in a state that Trump won by 26 percentage points. The Tennessee seat was a key piece to Democrats' path to a majority—another thing Blackburn and other Republicans repeatedly emphasized. She argued that even if you may have liked Bredesen as governor, going to Washington with a "D" beside your name was a far different matter. Trump traveled to Tennessee to campaign for Blackburn several times, telling voters that she would be the best person to uphold his agenda. Her biggest break may have been the retirement of Supreme Court Justice Anthony Kennedy. Blackburn's fervent support for the president's nominee to replace him, Brett Kavanaugh, underscored just how important having a Republican vote in the Senate would be, and she stood by Kavanaugh even after he was accused of sexual assault, a charge he denied. Bredesen said he would have supported Kavanaugh's nomination. Regardless, Blackburn's poll numbers rose.

Outside money poured into the race—with $19.4 million spent hitting Bredesen compared with $17.5 attacking Blackburn. Both had large war chests of their own—Bredesen spent $19.2 million, including $7.5 million of his own money, while Blackburn spent $16.3 million. Republicans had been worried about this seat up until the end, but Blackburn won 55%-44%. Bredesen, who 12 years before had swept every county in the state, only won three counties. Blackburn's victory was a major shift in Tennessee politics—away from the genial, bipartisan lawmakers who have typically won in the state and toward vocal, conservative partisans. That former pragmatic approach was extinguished with Alexander's departure.

Blackburn and Iowa Sen. Joni Ernst got seats on the Judiciary Committee—adding Republican women to the panel just months after their absence was especially stark during the hearings into the sexual assault allegations against Kavanaugh. The first Senate bill Blackburn introduced would have stopped federal funding of organizations that perform abortions, such as Planned Parenthood. In 2019, along with Republican Sen. Josh Hawley of Missouri, she proposed the Helping Infrastructure Restore the Economy Act, which would have moved federal departments out of Washington D.C. and into areas struggling economically throughout the nation; Tennessee would get the Department of Education.

Blackburn maintained her frequent presence on conservative TV and penchant for contentious language. After National Security Council aide Lt. Col. Alexander Vindman testified before the House Intelligence Committee's impeachment inquiry about a phone call he'd been on in which Trump pressured the Ukrainian president to investigate then-presidential candidate Joe Biden or else he'd withhold military aid, she launched a long campaign against the Iraq veteran and Purple Heart-winner. Tweeting at first that he was "Vindictive Vindman," she questioned on Twitter why House Democratic impeachment managers were hailing Vindman as a "hero": "How patriotic is it to badmouth and ridicule our great nation in front of Russia, America's greatest enemy?" Her comments about an unverified conspiracy played into efforts to question Vindman's patriotism, given that his family had emigrated from the Soviet Union to the U.S. when he and his brother were 3. "I work with a lot of military folks, and they all had questions about him as someone in uniform," Blackburn told Politico. "They were offended. That what he would do is go against, try to undermine the commander in chief. And so we have weighed in on that." Blackburn later blocked election security bills proposed by Democrat Mark Warner of Virginia, including two that would require campaigns to alert the FBI if they're offered help by a foreign power.

She also joined the Commerce Science and Transportation Committee, which has jurisdiction over the technology issues she pursued in the House. In 2019, amid growing furor and claims of censorship from conservatives against tech giants, she was tapped to lead a Judiciary Committee tech task force. "You'll see some of all of it: privacy, data security, prioritization, censorship, competition, antitrust. It's all there," she told Politico. Blackburn didn't go as far as Trump, who wanted to abolish Section 230 of the Communications Decency Act, which immunizes tech companies from lawsuits related to content posted on their sites by third parties and allows them to broadly moderate what is posted on their sites. She and Republican Sens. Roger Wicker of Mississippi and Lindsey Graham of South Carolina introduced a bill to modify the law, allowing companies to remove only content that is illegal, promotes terrorism or promotes self-harm. "Big Tech companies have stretched their liability shield past its limits, and the national discourse now suffers because of it," Blackburn said. In October 2020, she and Texas Sen. Ted Cruz threatened to subpoena executives at Twitter and Facebook after they blocked sharing of an unsubstantiated New York Post article about Hunter Biden, the then-Democratic presidential nominee's son.

After Biden won the election, Blackburn called the former vice president the "president-elect" in an ABC interview, a comment her staff later walked back as Trump refused to concede and was pushing unsubstantiated conspiracy theories about widespread voter fraud. As the certification of the Electoral College votes neared, Blackburn said she "cannot in good conscience turn a blind eye to the countless allegations of voter fraud in the 2020 presidential election" and that she would vote to object to the certification of votes from certain states. However, in a rare break from Trump, she and her newly elected in-state colleague, Bill Hagerty, reversed course after Trump supporters stormed the Capitol during the vote, and they both voted to certify Biden's win.

Bill Hagerty (R)

Elected 2020, term expires 2026, 1st term, b. Aug 14, 1959; Gallatin, TN; Vanderbilt University, B.A., 1981; Vanderbilt University Law School, J.D., 1984; Episcopalian; Married (Chrissy Hagerty); 4 children.

Professional Career: International Management Consultant/ Senior Expatriate Japan, Boston Consulting Group, 1984-1991; White House Fellow, Economic Advisor, Bush Administration, 1991-1993; Venture Capital/Private Equity Investor, Trident Capital, LP, 1993-1994; TN Commissioner of Economic and Community Development, 2011-2014; U.S. Ambassador to Japan, 2017-2019; Co-Founder, Hagerty Peterson & Company, LLC.

DC Office: Suite B11 RSOB 20510, 202-224-4944, Fax: 202-228-3398, hagerty.senate.gov

State Offices: Blountville, 423-325-6240; Chattanooga, 423-752-5337; Cookeville, 615-736-5129; Jackson, 901-544-4224; Knoxville, 865-545-4253; Memphis, 901-544-4224; Nashville, 615-736-5129.

Committees: *Appropriations:* Commerce, Justice, Science & Related Agencies; Department of the Interior, Environment & Related Agencies; Energy & Water Development; Military Construction & Veteran Affairs & Related Agencies; State, Foreign Operations & Related Programs. *Banking, Housing & Urban Affairs:* Financial Institutions & Consumer Protection; Housing, Transportation & Community Development; National Security & International Trade & Finance (RMM). *Foreign Relations:* East Asia, the Pacific & International Cybersecurity Policy; Near East, South Asia, Central Asia & Counterterrorism; State Dept & USAID Mngmnt, Internat'l Ops & Internat'l Dev (RMM); West Hem Crime Civ Sec Dem Rights & Women's Issues. *Rules & Administration.*

Election Results

Election	Name (Party)	Vote (%)		Cand. Spent	Ind. Exp. Support	Ind. Exp. Oppose
2020 General	Bill Hagerty (R)	1,840,926	(62%)	$11,663,315	$69,356	$1,006,805
	Marquita Bradshaw (D)	1,040,691	(35%)	$1,376,724	$33,861	
2020 Primary	Bill Hagerty (R)	331,267	(51%)			
	Manny Sethi (R)	257,223	(39%)			

Republican Bill Hagerty, a successful financier and former ambassador to Japan, was elected to the Senate—with important boosts from prominent Tennessee Republicans and President Donald Trump, whom Hagerty assisted during the 2016 presidential campaign. He wrapped up his victory in a bitter primary clash with two largely self-financing political newcomers. Hagerty succeeded Sen. Lamar Alexander, who retired after a lengthy political career. Alexander's bipartisan collegiality has largely faded from the Senate—and from Tennessee politics. Hagerty's election and Marsha Blackburn's win in 2018 to succeed the retiring Bob Corker have pushed the Volunteer State's delegation from the pragmatic Republican—such as Howard Baker, Bill Frist and Fred Thompson —to the hard-line conservative.

Born in Gallatin, Hagerty earned his bachelor and law degrees from Vanderbilt University, where he graduated Phi Beta Kappa and was an editor of the law review. He worked for the Boston Consulting Group, including three years in its Tokyo office. Returning to the United States, he joined

Trident Capital, a private equity firm, before he became the founder and managing director of Hagerty Peterson & Company, a merchant bank and private equity investment firm with offices in Nashville and Chicago. With his wife and young children, he initially lived in the home that his grandfather built in Sumner County.

Hagerty was also active in government and politics with several leaders of the Republican establishment, at both federal and state levels. He served as a member of the domestic policy staff on the President George W. Bush's Council on Competitiveness. As a White House fellow, Hagerty worked for the NASA administrator and in the office of Vice President Dick Cheney. He was national finance chairman of Mitt Romney's 2008 presidential campaign and later was a member of John McCain's transition-planning team. In 2012, he repeated his earlier role with Romney when he was the Republican nominee for president and handled appointments for what was again an aborted presidential transition.

In Tennessee, Hagerty joined Gov. Bill Haslam's Cabinet for four years as Commissioner of Economic Development, where he brought large international business deals to the state. Later, he co-chaired the committee to organize Haslam's second inauguration. After leaving that office, he was co-founder of the committee that brought a Major League Soccer franchise to Nashville.

Hagerty signed up early in the 2016 presidential campaign as a delegate for former Florida Gov. Jeb Bush. After Bush dropped out, Hagerty supported Sen. Marco Rubio, also of Florida. Finally, after Trump had virtually clinched the GOP's 2016 presidential nomination, he became Trump's victory chair in Tennessee. In August 2016, he was named director of appointments for Trump's presidential transition team, which placed him in charge of vetting, interviewing and recommending presidential appointments.

Hagerty's selection as ambassador to Japan was announced in early January 2017, prior to Trump's inauguration. Before that appointment, he had been mentioned as a prospective candidate for Tennessee governor in 2018. Coincidentally, former Tennessee Sen. Baker served as ambassador to Japan under the younger President Bush. In that position, Hagerty later took credit for strengthening Japan's role as the most strategic U.S. partner in the Indo-Pacific region, including an increased military presence and a new bilateral trade deal that reduced tariffs on American farm exports.

After Alexander announced that he would not seek reelection in 2020, ending a political career as governor and senator that extended more than a half-century, Hagerty left his position in Tokyo and announced his Senate candidacy in September 2019. He got a boost when Trump endorsed him. "It was actually President Trump who announced my candidacy for this office, and I don't think that's ever happened—for a president to announce a Senate campaign," Hagerty said prior to the GOP primary. In his campaign materials, though, Hagerty failed to mention his connections with presidential candidates other than Trump.

That support proved vital when Manny Sethi, an orthopedic trauma surgeon and first generation Indian immigrant in Nashville who was mentored by the heart surgeon Frist, opposed Hagerty as a political outsider for the party nomination. In a contest that featured highly negative attacks, Sethi criticized Hagerty for his support of moderate Republicans such as the Bush brothers and Romney and called him a "Washington insider." Sethi won endorsements from prominent conservatives, including Sens. Ted Cruz of Texas and Rand Paul of Kentucky; notably, the doctor held indoor campaign events across Tennessee without masks at a time when the coronavirus pandemic was surging in the state. Hagerty also held indoor events without requiring masks or social distancing.

Hagerty was endorsed by other leading Republicans, including Blackburn; Sen. Mitch McConnell of Kentucky, then the Senate majority leader; and Sen. Tom Cotton of Arkansas—as well as the Chamber of Commerce. To stave off his opponent's criticism of his ties to Romney, he even used one ad to brand both Sethi and Romney, now a Utah senator, as "weak-kneed Republicans." Hagerty branded Sethi as "Massachusetts Manny" for being on the Massachusetts Medical Society Board, which supported the Affordable Care Act, and later for applying for a nonpartisan White House fellowship program while President Barack Obama was in office. His campaign also seized on a $50 donation that his wife had made to former Democratic Rep. Tom Perriello of Virginia, who was a family friend; Maya Sethi appeared in her husband's ad explaining the donation, again hitting Hagerty for his donations to Romney and to former Democratic Vice President Al Gore, a onetime and senator from Tennessee.

Both candidates spent a lot of their personal money. Hagerty spent close to $12 million on the primary, with $7.3 million of self-financing. Sethi financed $2.2 million of the nearly $6 million that he spent. Hagerty won the primary, 51%-39%. Oddly, Sethi led in five of the six counties with the largest vote: Knox, Hamilton, Davidson, Williamson, Rutherford. But his total victory margin in those counties was less than Hagerty's nearly 13,000-vote lead in Memphis-based Shelby County.

With the support of many local GOP leaders across the state, Hagerty took all but a handful of the remaining counties, posting especially strong margins in many rural counties.

The Democratic Senatorial Campaign Committee backed in the primary James Mackler, a Nashville attorney who was a helicopter pilot with the Army's 101st Airborne Division in Iraq. But he ran third to Marquita Bradshaw, a lightly funded environmental activist who was boosted by African-American voters. Tennessee, which had two Democratic senators as recently as 1994, has elected only Republicans to the Senate since then. In 2020, the outcome was never in doubt, as Hagerty was elected with 62 percent of the vote. He won all but three counties, though those they included the two largest in Tennessee: Shelby and Davidson.

Shortly after he was sworn in, Hagerty indicated he would back the president's efforts to block certification of the Electoral College votes on January 6, amid the losing incumbent's false claims that the election had been beset by fraud in swing states he lost. But after the Capitol was overrun by Trump-supporting violent insurrections before the Senate votes could be held, both Hagerty and Blackburn backed away from their opposition and voted to certify the electoral counts in Arizona and Pennsylvania. "Last night we reconvened with our Senate colleagues to fulfill our constitutional duty to certify the 2020 election results and prepare for a peaceful transition of power," the two senators said in a statement. "On January 20th, we will prove to the world that America is still the shining city on the hill." Hagerty's change of heart might indicate that he isn't as much of a partisan as he seemed during his primary; many Tennessee Republican insiders reached that conclusion, given his background with Bush and Romney. He got a seat on both the Appropriations and Foreign Relations committees. No other freshman in either party was assigned to even one of those panels. The coming years will tell which path he takes.

Diana Harshbarger (R)

Elected 2020, 1st term, b. Jan 01, 1960; Kingsport, TN; East TN State University, B.S.; Mercer University, PharmD; Baptist; Married (Robert Harshbarger); 1 child.

Professional Career: Pharmacist; Owner, compounding pharmacy.

DC Office: 167 CHOB 20515, 202-225-6356, Fax: 202-225-5714, harshbarger.house.gov

State Offices: Kingsport, 423-398-5186.

Committees: *Education & Labor:* Health, Employment, Labor & Pensions; Higher Education & Workforce Investment. *Homeland Security:* Cybersecurity, Infrastructure Protection & Innovation; Oversight, Management & Accountability.

Election Results

Election	Name (Party)	Vote (%)		Cand. Spent	Ind. Exp. Support	Ind. Exp. Oppose
2020 General	Diana Harshbarger (R)	228,181	(75%)	$1,873,560		$381,165
	Blair Walsingham (D)	68,617	(22%)	$128,655	$10	
	Steve Holder (I)	8,621	(3%)			
2020 Primary	Diana Harshbarger (R)	18,074	(19%)			
	Timothy Hill (R)	15,731	(17%)			
	Rusty Crowe (R)	15,179	(16%)			
	Josh Gapp (R)	13,379	(14%)			
	Steve Darden (R)	11,647	(12%)			
	John Clark (R)	8,826	(9%)			
	David B. Hawk (R)	4,717	(5%)			

Diana Harshbarger led the 16-candidate Republican primary with 19 percent of the vote to lock up victory in the longtime GOP sanctuary. A pharmacist with her own business, who self-financed most of her campaign in her first bid for public office, she was the most successful of the candidates in reaching beyond their local base in the rural district. Harshbarger replaced Rep. Phil Roe, a physician who worked on health issues in the House and chaired the Veterans' Affairs Committee. He retired after six terms.

Harshbarger was born in Kingsport, where she has resided for most of her life. The first person in her family to attend college, she got her bachelor's degree from East Tennessee State University and a doctor of pharmacy degree from Mercer University. As a licensed pharmacist since 1987, she owned her business since then. She was a board member of the International Academy of Compounding Pharmacists.

In her campaign, Harshbarger described herself as "an unapologetic conservative Trump Republican." Her numerous broadcast ads were largely biographical or they invoked standard Republican themes, including her promise to deliver "the right medicine" to Washington. In ads about the pandemic, she blamed China for a cover-up and said, "China's Government Lied." She called for "bringing medical manufacturing back to America."

Her biggest vulnerability stemmed from a criminal indictment to which her husband and business partner, Robert Harshbarger, pleaded guilty in 2013 and was sentenced to four years in prison plus penalties of more than $1 million: allegations that he committed health care fraud by substituting cheaper drugs from China in place of medication the Food and Drug Administration had approved for kidney dialysis patients. Robert Harshbarger admitted that health insurers paid his business more than $845,000 for the drugs with an inaccurate brand, the Kingsport Times News reported at the time. There reportedly was no information that patients were harmed during the five years in which they received the drugs.

In response to those charges, a campaign spokesman for Diana Harshbarger said her husband "made medications" with the imports as part of a separate company in which she claimed to have no role. Corporate documents listed her as one of the two officers—with her husband—of the import firm and showed that their multiple businesses had the same address in Kingsport.

Campaign opponents attacked Harshbarger for her links to the criminal violations. On behalf of Timothy Hill, a veteran state representative, the political action committee of the conservative Club for Growth paid several hundred thousand dollars for advertising, including the claim that "Harshbarger's company charged taxpayers full price for cut-rate Chinese drugs." Harshbarger said the attacks against her were lies and "a lot of hot air" from "politicians who have over 80 years of combined political experience."

Harshbarger won the primary by fewer than 3,000 votes over both Hill and Rusty Crowe, a state senator for 30 years and chairman of the Senate's Health and Welfare Committee. Harshbarger led in 5 of the 11 counties; Crowe won three counties and Hill took one. Harshbarger led the primary field in spending with $1.6 million, of which about 80 percent was financed with personal loans. Crowe and Hill each spent less than $500,000, and each loaned about 10 percent of their separate funds.

In her historically Republican district, Harshbarger got 75 percent of the vote against Democrat Blair Walsingham, an Air Force veteran and certified dog trainer who spent $135,000. She got at least 65 percent in each of the 12 counties. Harshbarger won seats on the Education and Labor, and Homeland Security committees.

TN-1: Northeast Tennessee   Cook Partisan Voting Index: R+30

Population		Race and Ethnicity		Income	
Total	725,173	White	94.10%	Median Income	$47,478
Land area (sq. miles)	4,142	Black	2.30%	District Income Rank	402
Pop/ sq mi	175.08	Latino	4.10%	Poverty Rate	16.80%
Born in State	61.40%	Asian	0.80%	With health insurance	88.50%
		Two or more races	1.90%	Cash public assistance	2.20%
Age Groups		Other	1.00%	Food stamp/SNAP	11.70%
Under 18	19.60%				
18-34	20.50%	**Education**		**Work**	
35-64	39.10%	H.S grad or less	50.60%	White Collar	31.70%
Over 64	20.80%	Some college	27.50%	Sales and Service	41.30%
		College Degree, 4 yr	13.90%	Blue Collar	27.10%
Military		Post grad	8.00%	Government	13.80%
Veteran/ Active Duty	8.80%				

2020 Pres. Vote	Trump	242,684	(76%)	Biden	70,462	(22%)		
2016 Pres. Vote	Trump	203,651	(77%)	Clinton	52,237	(20%)	Johnson	6,488	(2%)

Kingsport, Bristol, Johnson City: Between the corduroy-like ridges of the Appalachian chains, as they bend west and then south, the Great Valley of Virginia extends far into northeastern Tennessee. These ridges guide travel today (even the interstates follow the valleys here) just as they guided settlement more than 200 years ago. The land rush immediately after the Revolutionary War populated the area, mostly with Scots-Irish immigrants. In tiny Jonesborough, the early settlers attempted to establish the free state of Franklin in 1784. The original town had an ordinance requiring settlers "to within three years build a brick, stone, or well framed house, 20 feet long and 16 feet wide, and at least 10 feet in the pitche, with a brick or stone chimney"—a sort of early restrictive covenant— and many pioneer cabins, Federal-style mansions and Greek Revival churches are lovingly preserved today. In Elizabethton, European settlers established the Watauga Association in 1772, the first majority-rule system of government in America and the first permanent settlement outside the 13 colonies.

The building of the railroads in the 1850s determined the winners and losers for the modern era, and today some of those dormant railroad routes have been converted into biking and hiking trails. The small industrial cities that originally developed—Johnson City, Kingsport and Bristol, now collectively known as the Tri-Cities—were on the main lines of national commerce before the Civil War. Mountainous northeast Tennessee had few slaves and, with its connection to Northern industry, was Union and Republican territory. East Tennesseans twice voted against secession. It remains heavily Republican to this day.

The area developed the sort of industrial economy that produced unions and Democrats in the North. Its skilled labor force, low electric power rates because of the Tennessee Valley Authority, and good transportation routes (rail lines and Interstates 26 and 81) spurred growth. With companies such as Kingsport-based Eastman Chemical Co. and Bell Helicopters taking the lead, the area has been a strong market for exports. Bristol is home to a major NASCAR track, nicknamed "The World's Fastest Half-Mile." Despite a NASCAR ban, a Confederate flag flew over the Speedway in July 2020. Bristol, the birthplace of country music, is a split city—half in Tennessee, half in Virginia, divided literally in the middle of State Street—though the Tennessee side has been more economically successful. In Sevier County near Knoxville, Gatlinburg and Pigeon Forge (home of Dolly Parton's Dollywood theme park) have more than 10,000 hotel rooms near the entrance to Great Smoky Mountains National Park, the nation's busiest. In 2019, the park had more than 12.5 million visitors, twice as many as the runner-up, Grand Canyon. Still, the Tri-Cities region has succumbed, as have many poor and rural regions, to the opioid epidemic.

The 1st Congressional District takes in the far northeastern end of Tennessee. Sullivan and Washington counties, which include the Tri-Cities, include 40 percent of the population. Greeneville was the birthplace of member of Congress and Alamo hero Davy Crockett, and the longtime home of President Andrew Johnson. Over the years, this district's politics haven't budged an inch. It hasn't elected a Democrat to the House since 1878. True to its roots, it gave President Donald Trump 76 per cent of the vote in 2020, his highest in Tennessee and in the top 2 percent of GOP districts nationwide.

Tim Burchett (R)

Elected 2018, 2nd term, b. Aug 25, 1964; Knoxville, TN; University of TN, B.S., 1988; Presbyterian; Married (Kelly Burchett); 1 child.

Elected Office: TN House, Member 1995-1999, TN Senate, 1998-2010; Knox County Mayor, 2010-2018.

Professional Career: Small Businessman.

DC Office: 1122 LHOB 20515, 202-225-5435, burchett.house.gov

State Offices: Knoxville, 865-523-3772; Maryville, 865-984-5464.

Committees: *Foreign Affairs*: Asia, the Pacific, Central Asia, Nonproliferation; Middle East, North Africa & Global Counterterrorism. *Transportation & Infrastructure*: Aviation; Highways & Transit; Railroads, Pipelines & Hazardous Materials.

Almanac Ratings 2019-2020

	Economy	Social	Foreign	Composite
Liberal	34%	27%	33%	32%
Conservative	66%	73%	67%	68%

Key Votes of the 116th Congress

1. U.S./Mex./Can. trade deal	Y	5. Russia sanctions	Y	9. Firearms background checks	N	
2. First Coronavirus response	N	6. Troops in Syria	N	10. Spending at the border	Y	
3. HEROES Act	N	7. Veto arms sales to Saudis	N	11. Marijuana liberalized rules	N	
4. CASH Act	N	8. Defense $$$, veto override	N	12. Electoral College objections	Y	

Election Results

Election	Name (Party)	Vote (%)		Cand. Spent	Ind. Exp. Support	Ind. Exp. Oppose
2020 General	Tim Burchett (R)	238,907	(68%)	$852,147		$2,528
	Renee Hoyos (D)	109,684	(31%)	$833,625	$2,233	
2020 Primary	Tim Burchett (R)	78,990	(100%)			

Prior winning percentages: 2018 (66%)

Republican Tim Burchett was elected in 2018 as the most experienced officeholder among the House GOP freshmen. He has cited his 24 years in state and local elected positions as a model for more efficient federal spending. In his heavily Republican district, Burchett survived a bruising primary contest. His victory marked the first time since 1964 that the seat was not held by one of the Duncans, a father and son team who typically were backbenchers but remained attentive to local politics in their Knoxville-based district.

Burchett, a Knoxville native, graduated from the University of Tennessee. In his first job, he sold mulch; government regulations put him out of business, he later complained. He served four years in the state House and 12 years in the Senate before winning election in 2010 as mayor of Knox County —a separate post from the mayor of the city of Knoxville.

During eight years as county mayor, he took credit for reducing taxes and the county's debt. He called himself a "limited libertarian," who believed that individuals should be responsible for their own actions. "I've never seen where government has come into a situation and made things better," he told City view magazine. In that 2017 interview, he said that both "national parties have continuously failed us." With Burchett's position term-limited in 2018, he planned to seek another office. When Rep. Jimmy Duncan announced his retirement in August 2017, Burchett days later said he would seek to replace him.

His chief opponent was Jimmy Matlock, who owned a chain of local tire and auto-repair shops and served 12 years in the state House. He styled himself as the more-conservative candidate, and was endorsed by leaders of the House Republican Freedom Caucus. Duncan supported Matlock, citing his "real heart for service." Matlock charged that Burchett backed tax increases when he served in the legislature and that he supported a Democrat to lead the Senate. Five other candidates entered the GOP primary, but none of them gained significant support. Sarah Nickloes, the only woman in the field, received national publicity for her experience in the Air Force as commander of an aircraft tanker.

Burchett won the primary with 48 percent of the vote to 36 percent for Matlock and 11 percent for Nickloes. His lead of more than 17,000 votes in Knox County, which cast a bit more than half the total vote, accounted for his overall advantage of about 12,000 votes. Democrat Renee Hoyos, executive director of the Tennessee Clean Water Network, who opposed Burchett in November, styled herself as a problem-solver and said voters wanted a change from "the same old, same old." With his 66%-33% victory, Burchett upheld the district's tradition as a Republican stronghold since the 19th century.

In November 2019, Burchett won passage of a bill he filed with Democratic Rep. Andy Kim that encourages the Small Business Administration to give incentives to companies that hire members of the military reserves. In 2021, as a member of the Transportation and Infrastructure Committee, he said he would keep highway costs under control by reducing federal regulatory hurdles.

Burchett was reelected, 68%-31%, in a rematch with Hoyos. Her spending of $819,000 was n nearly the total spent by Burchett. Burchett took 61 percent in his home county of Knox and more than 70 percent in the remaining counties.

TN-2: East Tennessee

Cook Partisan Voting Index: R+18

Population		Race and Ethnicity		Income	
Total	758,519	White	89.00%	Median Income	$57,777
Land area (sq. miles)	2,321	Black	5.90%	District Income Rank	292
Pop/ sq mi	326.85	Latino	4.40%	Poverty Rate	12.70%
Born in State	58.10%	Asian	1.60%	With health insurance	91.10%
		Two or more races	2.50%	Cash public assistance	2.00%
Age Groups		Other	1.00%	Food stamp/SNAP	10.00%
Under 18	20.20%				
18-34	23.30%	**Education**		**Work**	
35-64	38.10%	H.S grad or less	40.30%	White Collar	36.40%
Over 64	18.30%	Some college	28.60%	Sales and Service	40.40%
		College Degree, 4 yr	18.80%	Blue Collar	23.20%
Military		Post grad	12.40%	Government	13.40%
Veteran/ Active Duty	8.90%				

2020 Pres. Vote	Trump	228,992	(64%)	Biden	124,230	(34%)		
2016 Pres. Vote	Trump	188,973	(65%)	Clinton	86,217	(30%)	Johnson	10,457	(4%)

Knoxville: Knoxville, the largest city in East Tennessee, was the state's first capital. It is nestled between mountain ridges where the Holston and French Broad rivers join to form the Tennessee River. It was established not long after the first wave of pioneers came through the gaps and down the mountains of the Appalachian chain. During the Civil War, it was Union territory, and it has remained Republican in allegiance and progressive on civil rights ever since.

Its Republican heritage has been affected by another tradition, that of the Tennessee Valley Authority. A bold program when created in the 1930s, it is now part of the fabric of life in East Tennessee, sometimes criticized as it has reached capacity to produce hydroelectric power and begun to rely more on nuclear power. In a competitive electricity market, TVA has labored with billions of dollars in debt, mostly incurred in building its nuclear plants. In February 2019, the TVA board ignored President Donald Trump's tweet objecting to its shutdown of two coal-fired power plants. But he removed two of the board members in August 2020 after they hired foreign workers. Heavy ozone pollution in Knoxville led the Environmental Protection Agency to impose growth limits, so TVA spent several billion dollars to reduce pollution at its coal-fired plants. The result has improved local air quality and the EPA has ruled that the Knoxville area met its ozone standard. Even with its more rigorous standards, the American Lung Association in 2016 gave Knoxville an "F" for air quality. By 2019, the city had its lowest pollution level in the 20 years of the ratings, though it still ranked 25th worst of the nation's 201 metro areas.

Knoxville has overcome other setbacks and grown, at times robustly. The University of Tennessee's football complex, Neyland Stadium, on fall Saturdays contains one of the nation's largest crowds, over 100,000, cheering on the Volunteers. Women's basketball has historically been nearly as popular as football here. In 2009, Lady Vols' Coach Pat Summitt became the first Division I basketball coach, men's or women's, to win 1,000 career games. She retired in 2012, after having won 1,098 games and eight national championships, and died in 2016 after suffering Alzheimer's disease.

The 2nd Congressional District of Tennessee includes Knoxville and Knox County, plus all or part of six mountainous counties to the north and south. More than 60 percent live in Knox County, where the landmark Sunsphere tower from the 1982 World's Fair remains visible from Interstate 40. The heavily Republican district has not elected a Democratic congressman since the early 1850s. That record is not in jeopardy, though its 64 percent vote for Donald Trump in 2020 was the lowest of the seven Republican-held districts in Tennessee.

Chuck Fleischmann (R)

Elected 2010, 6th term, b. Oct 11, 1962; New York, NY; University of IL, B.A., 1983; University of TN College of Law, Knoxville, J.D., 1986; Roman Catholic; Married (Brenda Fleischmann); 3 children.

Professional Career: Practicing attorney, 1987-2010.

DC Office: 2410 RHOB 20515, 202-225-3271, Fax: 202-225-3494, fleischmann.house.gov

State Offices: Athens, 423-745-4671; Chattanooga, 423-756-2342; Oak Ridge, 865-576-1976.

Committees: *Appropriations*: Energy & Water Development & Related Agencies; Homeland Security (RMM); Labor, Health & Human Services, Education & Related Agencies.

Group Ratings

	ADA	ACLU	AFL-CIO	LCV	COC	HAFA	ACU	CFG	FRC
2020	**	19%	**	10%	-	77%	83%	**	-
2019	0%	C	33%	7%	89%	C	84%	68%	95%

Almanac Ratings 2019-2020

	Economy	Social	Foreign	Composite
Liberal	25%	18%	4%	16%
Conservative	75%	82%	96%	84%

Key Votes of the 116th Congress

1. U.S./Mex./Can. trade deal	Y	5. Russia sanctions	N
2. First Coronavirus response	Y	6. Troops in Syria	N
3. HEROES Act	N	7. Veto arms sales to Saudis	N
4. CASH Act	N	8. Defense $$$, veto override	Y

9. Firearms background checks N
10. Spending at the border Y
11. Marijuana liberalized rules N
12. Electoral College objections Y

Election Results

Election	Name (Party)	Vote (%)	Cand. Spent	Ind. Exp. Support	Ind. Exp. Oppose
2020 General	Chuck Fleischmann (R)	215,571 (67%)	$376,694		$750
	Meg Gorman (D)	97,687 (31%)	$75,512		
2020 Primary	Chuck Fleischmann (R)	69,890 (100%)			

Prior winning percentages: 2018 (64%), 2016 (66%), 2014 (62%), 2012 (61%), 2010 (60%)

Republican Charles (Chuck) Fleischmann, first elected in 2010, has settled into his seat after surviving tough primary challenges. With his seat on the Appropriations Committee, where he is ranking Republican on the Homeland Security Subcommittee, he pursues funding for the Oak Ridge lab. He has successfully advocated rebuilding of the Chickamauga Lock on the Tennessee River.

When he was a boy, Fleischmann's father, Max, worked in the food services business. Fleischmann lived in Philadelphia and New Jersey before finishing high school in Chicago. He graduated from the University of Illinois in three years with a bachelor's degree in political science. He got his law degree at the University of Tennessee and started his own firm in Knoxville with his wife, Brenda.

When Rep. Zach Wamp ran unsuccessfully for governor, Fleischmann ran, saying he was "very, very upset with the way things were going in Washington D.C." In the primary, health care consultant Robin Smith, a former Republican state party chairwoman, attacked Fleischmann's record as a personal injury lawyer, saying he had sued gun clubs, Walmart stores and churches, all popular institutions in the state. Fleischmann put $544,000 of his own money into the campaign and defended himself by saying, "I make a living standing up for the little guy, people who have traditionally not had a voice and who have been dealt injustices and harm." Fleischmann edged out Smith, 30%-28%. In November, he defeated radio talk-show host John Wolfe, 57%-28%.

Fleischmann has been a conservative mainstay. He is capable of serving up red-meat rhetoric. Asked at a debate for his views on climate change, he responded: "I think we ought to take Al Gore, put him on an iceberg, and put him way out there." He opposed the debt ceiling hike in 2011 and the deal to avoid the so-called fiscal cliff in 2013.In 2018, the Chattanooga Free Press editorial board endorsed Fleischmann and acknowledged he had become more pragmatic as he gained seniority, writing that "while not changing his stripes, we believe he has lost some of the stridency he had in his first few years on the job and has learned the value of working with colleagues across the aisle on issues important to the state and to this district."

His position on Appropriations has given Fleischmann a critical voice on issues of vital interest to the region. He advocated replacing Chickamauga's deteriorating 75-year-old river lock by overhauling the project's funding mechanism, the Inland Waterway Trust Fund, by raising the fuel tax on barges. After the lock shut down in 2016 because of cracked concrete, that work began in 2018, with a new, larger 110-foot-by-600-foot lock. In 2020, Fleischmann restored full funding for the lock after President Donald Trump proposed eliminating support in his budget proposal. The replacement was set to be completed by2024.Fleischmann has become a chief advocate for the Oak Ridge National Laboratory.

In 2019, he was part of the bipartisan group that negotiated a deal following the 35-day government shutdown. The agreement included only $1.375 billion for border barriers—far short of the $5.7 billion Trump wanted—but Fleischmann considered it a victory. "Republicans got more border wall funding," he told NPR after the bill passed. He later supported Trump's decision to declare a national emergency to get the rest of the border wall funds, though he said he had constitutional concerns. After Joe Biden was elected, Fleischmann said they can find agreement by supporting clean energy, especially nuclear power.

Fleischmann has survived two grueling primary fights. In 2012, he drew spirited challenges from 25-year-old Weston Wamp and dairy magnate Scottie Mayfield. He won the primary with 39 percent, as Mayfield took 31 percent and Wamp 29 percent. Democrat Mary Headrick accused him of being in the pocket of special interests and blasted his proposal to cut capital gains tax rates. He coasted to a 61 percent win.

Wamp, the son of Fleischmann's predecessor, returned for another try in 2014 in a one-on-one primary. He called himself an "independent-minded conservative" and courted votes from Democrats, who were eligible to vote in the primary. Fleischmann rebuked him at one debate, saying, "if he wants to run as a Democrat, let him run as a Democrat." He accused Wamp of being a "show horse" and supporting "amnesty" for illegal immigrants. He eked out a win, 51%-49%. The outcome in many of the counties was exceedingly close.

In 2016, Bo Watson, the veteran speaker pro tem in the Tennessee Senate, said publicly that he was giving serious thought to a primary challenge. Instead, Watson decided to stick with his influential state post. That has left Fleischmann with easy campaigns since then. In 2020, he and Wamp staged a surrogate battle with competing endorsements in the GOP primary for the open Senate seat. Fleischmann prevailed by supporting the winner, Bill Hagerty.

If he emerges unscathed in the 2022 redistricting, Fleischmann may have finally settled into this district for as long as he wants.

TN-3: East Tennessee

Cook Partisan Voting Index: R+19

Population		Race and Ethnicity		Income	
Total	743,225	White	84.40%	Median Income	$52,491
Land area (sq. miles)	4,570	Black	10.50%	District Income Rank	362
Pop/ sq mi	162.62	Latino	4.30%	Poverty Rate	15.30%
Born in State	61.20%	Asian	1.40%	With health insurance	89.80%
		Two or more races	2.10%	Cash public assistance	2.20%
Age Groups		Other	1.60%	Food stamp/SNAP	12.40%
Under 18	20.90%				
18-34	21.10%	**Education**		**Work**	
35-64	39.10%	H.S grad or less	44.40%	White Collar	37.30%
Over 64	19.00%	Some college	29.40%	Sales and Service	37.10%
		College Degree, 4 yr	16.70%	Blue Collar	25.60%
Military		Post grad	9.40%	Government	12.80%
Veteran/ Active Duty	8.50%				

2020 Pres. Vote	Trump	219,253	(65%)	Biden	110,461	(33%)		
2016 Pres. Vote	Trump	181,189	(65%)	Clinton	83,297	(30%)	Johnson	8,665	(3%)

Chattanooga, Oak Ridge: Etching its way through the serrated ridges of East Tennessee, with some of the most vivid scenery in the Appalachian Mountain chain, is the river that gave the state its name. From Knoxville, the Tennessee River cuts through a ridge and then plunges down a long valley to the city of Chattanooga at the Georgia line. There it switches course again, winding around the tabletop Lookout Mountain and then moving into northern Alabama before eventually swinging back north to empty into the Ohio River at Paducah Kentucky. Chattanooga was just a village when it became a Civil War battlefield. It grew to be the industrial "Dynamo of Dixie," rising to prominence as a part of the "New South." Four decades ago, it was labeled America's most polluted city. But regional political leaders, prodded by civic-minded scions of its Industrial Age aristocracy, used creative measures, such as locally built electric shuttle buses, to reduce pollution and to spruce up the city's scenic river banks. With big job cuts at the Tennessee Valley Authority, the region has pinned its hopes for economic growth more on the private sector, including tourism and a large food-service industry that includes Moon Pie and Little Debbie confectioners.

Chattanooga, the state's fourth-largest city, is challenging Knoxville for third place. After declining in the 1980s and stagnating in the 1990s, the city has had a double-digit increase since 2000. As old businesses have shut down, more than two dozen companies from 20 countries employing more than 20,000 people have found homes in the region. By 2018, Chattanooga's Hamilton County was growing new businesses at the fastest rate in the state. Volkswagen is building a second production line in Chattanooga, an $800 million investment that will add 1,000 jobs, to build electric vehicles set to roll out in 2022. In 2019, the United Auto Workers failed in its effort to unionize the plant.

The technology industry is transforming more than the local economy, The city features a state-of-the-art, publicly owned, 10-gigabyte citywide fiber network. The city is a growing tourist destination, featuring the popular Tennessee Aquarium and Rock City atop Lookout Mountain, narrowly situated on the Georgia side. Chattanooga has moved closer to the growing orbit of metropolitan Atlanta, which is 110 miles away, and it has been discussed as a site for the latter city's second airport.

The 3rd Congressional District of Tennessee includes Chattanooga, stretches from Georgia to Kentucky, and stops a few miles short of both Alabama and Virginia. A bit more than half its population is in Hamilton County. The district includes Oak Ridge National Laboratory, which was secretly constructed during World War II in virgin Appalachian forest to house the facility that made uranium isotopes for the Hiroshima bomb. In February 2021, TVA said its members could use the reactors at Oak Ridge. The district contains the Museum of Appalachia in Clinton, which maintains dozens of frontier structures, including a cabin owned by Mark Twain's father. Historically, the area was split politically, with Chattanooga voting Democratic and the mountain counties solidly Republican. Today, the city leans Republican. Donald Trump twice won 65 percent of the vote.

Scott DesJarlais (R)

Elected 2010, 6th term, b. Feb 21, 1964; Des Moines, IA, IN; University of SD, B.S., 1987; University of SD School of Medicine, M.D., 1991; Episcopalian; Married (Amy DesJarlais); 4 children (1 from previous marriage).

Professional Career: Practicing physician, 1993-2010.

DC Office: 2301 RHOB 20515, 202-225-6831, Fax: 202-226-5172, desjarlais.house.gov

State Offices: Cleveland, 423-472-7500; Columbia, 931-381-9920; Murfreesboro, 615-896-1986; Winchester, 931-962-3180.

Committees: *Agriculture*: Conservation & Forestry; Livestock & Foreign Agriculture; Subcommittee Nutrition, Oversight & Department Operations. *Armed Services*: Strategic Forces; Tactical Air & Land Forces.

Group Ratings

	ADA	ACLU	AFL-CIO	LCV	COC	HAFA	ACU	CFG	FRC
2020	**	23%	**	10%	-	100%	93%	**	-
2019	0%	C	25%	3%	80%	C	93%	94%	100%

Almanac Ratings 2019-2020

	Economy	Social	Foreign	Composite
Liberal	28%	23%	4%	19%
Conservative	72%	77%	96%	81%

Key Votes of the 116th Congress

1. U.S./Mex./Can. trade deal	Y	5. Russia sanctions	N	9. Firearms background checks N
2. First Coronavirus response	N	6. Troops in Syria	N	10. Spending at the border	Y
3. HEROES Act	N/A	7. Veto arms sales to Saudis	N	11. Marijuana liberalized rules	N
4. CASH Act	N	8. Defense $$$, veto override	N	12. Electoral College objections Y

Election Results

Election	Name (Party)	Vote (%)	Cand. Spent	Ind. Exp. Support	Ind. Exp. Oppose
2020 General	Scott DesJarlais (R)........................... 223,802	(67%)	$255,211	$9,474	$750
	Christopher J. Hale (D)................. 111,908	(33%)	$311,366		
2020 Primary	Scott DesJarlais (R)............................. 55,194	(71%)			
	Doug Meyer (R).............................. 14,184	(18%)			
	Randy Sharp (R).................................... 8,298	(11%)			

Prior winning percentages: 2018 (63%), 2016 (65%), 2014 (58%), 2012 (56%), 2010 (57%)

Republican Scott DesJarlais, elected in 2010, has overcome explosive accusations about his personal life and has survived serious primary challenges. He has continued to show skills as a campaigner and was a strong supporter of President Donald Trump.

DesJarlais grew up in Sturgis South Dakota. He earned a bachelor's degree in chemistry and psychology from the University of South Dakota in 1987. After receiving his medical degree from the school in 1991, DesJarlais moved to Jasper Tennessee, where he practiced medicine.

The 2010 House race was DesJarlais' first bid for elected office. He challenged Rep. Lincoln Davis, a Democrat who had earned the endorsements of the U.S. Chamber of Commerce, the National Rifle Association and National Right to Life. DesJarlais billed himself as a "doctor, not a politician." Davis made headlines with an ad featuring accusations by DesJarlais' first wife, Susan, who claimed that he physically intimidated her during their 2000 divorce and threatened to commit suicide.

DesJarlais called the charges "completely false," and the ad exposed Davis to accusations of mudslinging. Davis pointed out his votes against the Democrats' health care overhaul and cap-and-trade bill to limit greenhouse gas emissions, both unpopular in the district. But he backed the $787 billion economic stimulus. DesJarlais won 57%-39%.

DesJarlais joined fellow Tennessee Rep. Chuck Fleischmann in opposing an Energy Department plan to consolidate management of Oak Ridge's Y-12 weapons plant with the Pantex facility in Texas. He defended as essential outreach his unusually high spending on constituent mailings. On the Armed Services Committee, he tended to the needs of Arnold Air Force Base, an advanced testing facility in Coffee and Franklin counties.

Desjarlais was an early supporter of Donald Trump and served as his liaison to the conservative Freedom Caucus. He was an outspoken supporter of the new trade deal with Mexico and Canada. "Under new confident leadership, the United States is winning again," he said.

Scandal has so overshadowed DesJarlais' legislative work that survival sometimes seemed his most significant accomplishment. According to the transcript of a phone recording made prior to his divorce a few weeks before the 2012 election, DesJarlais reportedly urged his pregnant mistress—who was one of his medical patients—to get an abortion. He issued a statement accusing opponents of "the same gutter politics" as his earlier race, but he later said in a letter to supporters that he encouraged the abortion because he was trying to get her to admit she wasn't pregnant. Conservatives abandoned him in droves, and national Democrats raced to assist challenger Eric Stewart, who had been seen as a longshot. DesJarlais won, 56%-44%.

After the election, the state Democratic Party released court transcripts showing that DesJarlais and his ex-wife mutually agreed that she would have two abortions, and that he admitted having sex with at least two patients, three coworkers, and a drug company representative. DesJarlais later acknowledged having used "very poor judgment" but dismissed suggestions that he resign or not run again. In 2013, the Tennessee Board of Medical Examiners fined him $500 and reprimanded him for having sex with multiple patients.

In 2013, state Sen. Jim Tracy announced a primary challenge and began to peel off DesJarlais' donors. Tracy told supporters, "I'm a conservative in word and deed. I'm 100 percent pro-life." Tracy outraised DesJarlais and won endorsements from many in the state's GOP establishment. He campaigned on bringing "integrity" to the office, but was slow to attack DesJarlais directly. The incumbent countered that his personal life was old news, noting that he had been married for 12 years to his second wife. He emphasized his conservative values and efforts in Washington.

DesJarlais won the high-turnout primary by 38 votes. Tracy had a big lead in Rutherford County, but DesJarlais rolled up the vote in rural areas. After 18 days of recounts, Tracy said that further challenges "would not be the right thing for the Republican Party and the conservative cause in Tennessee." In November, DesJarlais faced Democrat Lenda Sherrell, an accountant, who spent more than $1 million. DesJarlais increased his victory margin to 58%-35%.

In 2016, his chief Republican challenger was Grant Starrett, a lawyer and real estate investor who worked for Mitt Romney in the 2012 presidential campaign. Starrett self-financed nearly $900,000 of the $1.7 million he spent on his campaign. DesJarlais won the four-candidate contest, 52%-43%. Since then, he has easily defeated routine primary challenges. In 2020, Democratic challenger Christopher Hale, running as a pro-life Democrat, said DesJarlais "pressured [his mistresses] into three abortions, he's not pro-life." The two candidates spent less than $400,000 each. DesJarlais won easily, 67%-33%, with 56 percent in Rutherford County.

Redistricting offers an opportunity for disaffected Republicans to wage another challenge to DesJarlais.

TN-4: Middle Tennessee   Cook Partisan Voting Index: R+22

Population		Race and Ethnicity		Income	
Total	812,697	White	83.30%	Median Income	$59,461
Land area (sq. miles)	5,985	Black	9.90%	District Income Rank	274
Pop/ sq mi	135.79	Latino	7.30%	Poverty Rate	12.90%
Born in State	60.40%	Asian	2.00%	With health insurance	89.80%
		Two or more races	3.00%	Cash public assistance	1.50%
Age Groups		Other	1.70%	Food stamp/SNAP	10.50%
Under 18	23.50%				
18-34	23.40%	**Education**		**Work**	
35-64	38.20%	H.S grad or less	46.40%	White Collar	31.20%
Over 64	15.00%	Some college	29.80%	Sales and Service	38.30%
		College Degree, 4 yr	15.70%	Blue Collar	30.50%
Military		Post grad	8.10%	Government	12.90%
Veteran/ Active Duty	7.80%				

2020 Pres. Vote	Trump	239,401	(68%)	Biden	108,740	(31%)	
2016 Pres. Vote	Trump	189,318	(68%)	Clinton	76,133	(27%)	Johnson 7,806 (3%)

Murfreesboro Area: The invisible line between Republican and Democratic territory during the Civil War in Tennessee ran along Walden Ridge, the westernmost swelling of the Appalachians. This invisible line also separates the Tennessee Valley, which had few slaves and whose economic ties were to the North, from the rolling farmlands of Middle Tennessee, first settled by Andrew Jackson in the 1790s and resolutely Democratic from 1829, when Jackson became the first president to call himself a Democrat. This is an America of small towns, where every hamlet seems to have its own annual festival, like the RC Moon Pie Festival in Bell Buckle. Lynchburg is where Jasper Newton Daniel, better known by the nickname "Jack," began brewing his "Old No. 7" whiskey, an operation that continues to this day. Oddly, Moore County, where the distillery is located, is a dry county.

There is an industrial base here as well, particularly in the automobile industry. General Motors launched its Saturn brand in Spring Hill in 1990, igniting growth in the region. When the erstwhile auto giant went bankrupt in 2009, it furloughed most of its 2,700 employees. Since then, it has had an impressive comeback. Assembly-line production resumed in 2012 on the Chevrolet Equinox, and the plant produces engines and other components for GM assembly plants elsewhere. In 2019, GM announced it was making a $300 million investment to start building the Cadillac XT6, as well as another $22 million to shift production toward high-tech, fuel-conserving V-8 engines. By late 2022, GM plans to run its plant—with about 3,000 workers—entirely by solar power from the Tennessee Valley Authority. Nissan has a large engine assembly plant in Decherd in Franklin County and operates a plant in Smyrna with about 7,000 employees, where the assembly line can produce 640,000 vehicles annually; it also manufactures batteries for its Leaf electric cars.

The 4th Congressional District of Tennessee takes in all these places. About 40 percent of its population is in Rutherford County, which has become part of suburban Nashville. Murfreesboro is the sixth-largest city in the state, with a population of 47,000; it grew 35 percent from 2010 to 2019. In May 2020, police responded with tear gas to protestors who demanded removal of a Confederate statue. Rutherford is the most blue-collar of Nashville's major suburban counties and the least-heavily Republican. The rest of the district is a scattering of small towns and rural areas. Dayton is where the famous Scopes Monkey Trial was held in 1925; John T. Scopes was convicted of teaching evolution and fined $100 (although the conviction was later overturned). This was once reliably blue territory, but Democrats have become scarce in most of Tennessee outside Nashville and Memphis. Donald Trump twice won the 4th with 68 percent.

Jim Cooper (D)

Elected 2002, 17th term, b. Jun 19, 1954; Nashville, TN; University of NC, Chapel Hill, B.A., 1975; Oxford University, M.A., 1977; Harvard University Law School, J.D., 1980; Episcopalian; Widower (Martha Hays Cooper); 3 children.

Elected Office: U.S. House, 1983-1995.

Professional Career: Practicing attorney, 1980-1982; Investment banker, 1995-1999; Founder & partner, investment bank, 1999-2002.

DC Office: 1536 LHOB 20515, 202-225-4311, Fax: 202-226-1035, cooper.house.gov

State Offices: Nashville, 615-736-5295.

Committees: *Armed Services*: Intelligence & Special Operations; Seapower & Projection Forces; Strategic Forces (Chmn). *Budget*. *Oversight & Reform*: Subcommittee on Environment. *Permanent Select on Intelligence*: Intelligence Modernization & Readiness; Strategic Technologies & Advanced Research.

Group Ratings

	ADA	ACLU	AFL-CIO	LCV	COC	HAFA	ACU	CFG	FRC
2020	**	76%	**	100%	-	5%	24%	**	-
2019	90%	C	90%	93%	65%	C	25%	20%	0%

Almanac Ratings 2019-2020

	Economy	Social	Foreign	Composite
Liberal	100%	100%	50%	84%
Conservative	0%	0%	50%	16%

Key Votes of the 116th Congress

1. U.S./Mex./Can. trade deal Y	5. Russia sanctions Y	9. Firearms background checks Y
2. First Coronavirus response Y	6. Troops in Syria Y	10. Spending at the border Y
3. HEROES Act Y	7. Veto arms sales to Saudis Y	11. Marijuana liberalized rules Y
4. CASH Act Y	8. Defense $$$, veto override Y	12. Electoral College objections N

Election Results

Election	Name (Party)	Vote (%)	Cand. Spent	Ind. Exp. Support	Ind. Exp. Oppose
2020 General	Jim Cooper (D).....................................	252,155 (100%)	$1,479,706	$873	
2020 Primary	Jim Cooper (D)............................	50,752 (57%)			
	Keeda Haynes (D).............................	35,472 (40%)			

Prior winning percentages: 2018 (68%), 2016 (63%), 2014 (62%), 2012 (65%), 2010 (57%), 2008 (66%), 2006 (69%), 2004 (69%), 2002 (64%), 1992 (66%), 1990 (69%), 1988 (100%), 1986 (100%), 1984 (75%), 1982 (66%)

Jim Cooper, a Democrat elected in 2002 who also served from 1982 to 1994, is a brainy moderate with a tart tongue—especially when it comes to his own party's leadership. Despite the polarized political climate, he persistently seeks bipartisanship on fiscal matters. He has shifted his legislative focus chiefly to defense issues. In 2020, he survived a close primary challenge that pulled him to the left.

His father, Prentice Cooper, was governor for six years; his brother John was elected mayor in 2019 with calls to reduce downtown development. Jim Cooper, educated at the University of North Carolina, Oxford and Harvard Law School, was first elected in 1982 at age 28, by defeating Republican Cissy Baker, daughter of then-Senate Majority Leader Howard Baker. During his first stint in Congress, when his district was mostly rural, he spoke out against tobacco use and opposed the National Rifle Association in a state where both were popular. He participated actively in the "Group of Nine" Democrats on the Energy and Commerce Committee that produced a compromise on the Clean Air Act of 1990. In 1994, Cooper ran against Republican Fred Thompson for the Senate seat that Democrat Al Gore had vacated when he was elected vice president; in a bad year for Democrats, Thompson won, 60%-39%.

Cooper went to work as an investment banker in Nashville and as a teacher at Vanderbilt University's business school. In 2002, when the city-based district opened, Cooper joined a flurry of Democratic candidates. His toughest opponent was Davidson County Sheriff Gayle Ray, the first female sheriff in Tennessee, who had support from the EMILY's List, which supports women candidates who back abortion rights. Ray attacked Cooper's voting record on abortion. An abortion-rights supporter, Cooper said Ray's charges were inaccurate. The AFL-CIO and The Tennessean endorsed Ray. Cooper had support from the Sierra Club and several smaller newspapers and raised twice as much money as Ray, including $700,000 in self-financing. He won the primary, 47%-23%, in a seven-candidate field.

Since his return to Congress, he has served on the Armed Services Committee. When Democrats won back the House in 2018, he became chairman of its Strategic Forces Subcommittee, which oversees the nation's nuclear arsenal and usually acts on a bipartisan basis. In December 2019, following a years-long battle, he played a leading role with Republican Rep. Mike Rogers in the creation of the Space Force. "This is like the birth of a new baby," Cooper said. "Its mother is the Air Force for some time. But this child will grow up to be independent."

Cooper has been a consistent voice for fiscal discipline. He called for a panel to examine entitlement spending—an idea that led to President Barack Obama's creation in 2010 of the Simpson-Bowles commission on the national debt. When the House in 2012 debated Cooper's amendment to have a budget resolution based on the commission's recommendations, it drew just 38 votes. He has introduced numerous measures with GOP support. He said that finding Republicans to support him "is really not hard" but gets overlooked. "The press is only focused on the leaders," he said. "They barely know the names of the backbenchers, and those are the people who can make things happen if they choose to."

Cooper has sought to reform Congress, which he has accused of being "too lazy to prioritize." In 2012, he became the first lawmaker to sign a pledge by the activist group Root strikers not to lobby after leaving office. He was an early advocate of limits on spending earmarks and enforcement of pay-as-you-go rules that require tax cuts or spending increases to be offset elsewhere in the budget. A longtime proponent of increased government oversight, his bill to strengthen the independence of federal inspectors general passed Congress and became law in 2008. In 2020, he filed a bill with Democratic Sen. Chris Murphy that would give inspectors general a seven-year term and set very limited circumstances in which they could be fired.

Cooper has been a leader of the fiscally conservative Blue Dog Coalition, where he has described himself as "the nerd" of the group, and an advocate of consensus-building among Democrats. He once said of his fellow Democrats under California's Nancy Pelosi, "we're just told how to vote. We are treated like mushrooms most of the time." In the January 2017 vote for House Speaker, he voted for Democratic Rep. Tim Ryan of Ohio, who earlier had challenged Pelosi within the Democratic Caucus. In 2019, he simply voted "present," joining more than a dozen Democrats in not casting their votes for Pelosi. He has continued to say that Democrats need new leadership.

Cooper's centrism came under attack in 2020 from the growing influence of the Democrats' progressive wing—his first primary challenge in a decade. Keeda Haynes, a former public defender and a legal adviser for prisoners who herself served four years in federal prison for a marijuana-related crime that she said she did not commit, described her voice as "part of both the American dream and its nightmare." She said that Cooper had not given enough focus to the criminal justice system, including systemic racism. In response to a plea from former Vice President Al Gore, a longtime friend who endorsed him, Cooper switched his previous opposition to the Green New Deal, which he had dismissed as not a legislative proposal. Cooper outspent Haynes nearly 10-to-1 and she failed to win support from Justice Democrats, which has backed several insurgent Democrats. He won the primary, 57%-40%. Cooper faced a continuing risk that Republicans would carve up his district in redistricting.

TN-5: Davidson County

Cook Partisan Voting Index: D+9

Population		Race and Ethnicity		Income	
Total	778,094	White	66.50%	Median Income	$63,295
Land area (sq. miles)	1,249	Black	24.40%	District Income Rank	220
Pop/ sq mi	623.19	Latino	9.70%	Poverty Rate	11.90%
Born in State	49.80%	Asian	3.40%	With health insurance	88.90%
		Two or more races	2.20%	Cash public assistance	0.70%
Age Groups		Other	3.50%	Food stamp/SNAP	7.90%
Under 18	20.80%				
18-34	29.30%	**Education**		**Work**	
35-64	37.10%	H.S grad or less	32.90%	White Collar	44.60%
Over 64	13.00%	Some college	24.20%	Sales and Service	35.30%
		College Degree, 4 yr	26.90%	Blue Collar	20.10%
Military		Post grad	16.00%	Government	10.20%
Veteran/ Active Duty	5.50%				

2020 Pres. Vote	Biden	210,071	(60%)	Trump	127,900	(37%)		
2016 Pres. Vote	Clinton	156,730	(56%)	Trump	105,720	(38%)	Johnson	10,431	(4%)

Nashville Metro: Country music, an art form that emerged from the settlers of the hardscrabble, mountainous counties of East Tennessee, is now a more than $2 billion-a-year business. The heart of country music is located in the city that is increasingly the cultural, political and economic heart of Tennessee: Nashville. Run out of a series of deceptively modest homes-turned-offices on Music Row, the industry congregated in Nashville because local radio station WSM had a clear channel in the 1920s from which to beam its weekly "barn dances" throughout the South. The broadcasts later became known as the Grand Ole Opry, the nation's longest continuously running radio show. Music Row has become a corporate juggernaut that views itself as more influential than the entertainment meccas on the East or West Coasts. The city has about 75 sound recording studios—second in the nation to New York City; annual income from Nashville music exceeds $3 billion—of a combined $10 billion from music and entertainment. Music City has supported 56,000 jobs here, more per capita than either New York or Los Angeles. The music industry is increasingly intertwined with the television industry. The eponymous ABC and then CMT show "Nashville" filmed here for six seasons, closing in 2018; it highlighted some of the smaller performance spaces, including honky tonks that line Lower Broadway, where live music from aspiring singer/songwriters is played at all hours of the day—a big reason why Nashville has become the country's top destination for bachelorette parties.

For years, the city's elite and its religious leaders resented the growing local influence of country music. But all three made their peace in the 1970s, and since then Nashville has become one of the South's boom cities—one of the fastest-growing metropolitan areas behind the much larger Atlanta and Dallas-Fort Worth Metroplex, though with that growth has also come wealth disparities. An agreeable quality of life, plenty of highly skilled labor, a central location and absence of urban strife have all enhanced Nashville as the largest metropolitan area in the state, with suburban growth in all directions, though suburban population has increased far more rapidly in recent decades than has the growth in Nashville. An estimated 100 people move into Nashville every day, sending real estate prices skyrocketing. It is also a center of the for-profit health industry, the area's largest and fastest-growing employer.

The dominant cultural tone in the metropolitan area is conservative—Nashville has more than 700 churches and is the headquarters for the publishing arms of the Southern Baptist Convention, United Methodist Church, and National Baptist Convention. But Nashville and Davidson County remain Democratic islands in an ocean of Republicanism. The metro area has a large immigrant population and one of the fastest-growing foreign-born populations in the country, at 13 percent. Davidson County is 56 percent white (down from 80 percent in the 1960s and 70s), more than a quarter African American, and 11 percent Hispanic, up from just 1 percent Hispanic in the 1990s.

2020 was a cataclysmic year for Nashville. In addition to the immediate and sweeping shutdown of music sites as the result of the coronavirus pandemic, the city was devastated in March 2020 by tornadoes, which hit especially hard in the Black neighborhoods of North Nashville. Then, on Christmas morning, a truck bomb exploded in the center of downtown. Although there were minimal personal casualties, dozens of buildings were damaged or destroyed. One man, who blew himself up when he detonated the explosive device, was believed solely responsible.

The 5th Congressional District of Tennessee includes all of consolidated Nashville-Davidson County. Neighboring Cheatham and Dickson counties, which lean Republican, include about 5 percent of the district's vote. The 5th is reliably Democratic, one of only two districts in Tennessee where a Democrat has a chance, but it is more centrist than the Memphis-based 9th District. Joe Biden got 60 percent of the vote, an increase from the 56 percent for Hillary Clinton and for President Barack Obama in 2012.

John Rose (R)

Elected 2018, 2nd term, b. Feb 23, 1965; Cookeville, TN; TN Tech University, B.S., 1988; Purdue University, M.S., 1990; Vanderbilt University, J.D., 1993; Christian Church; Married (Chelsea Rose); 1 child.

Professional Career: TN Agriculture Commissioner, 2002-2003; Owner & President, Boson Software.

DC Office: 1232 LHOB 20515, 202-225-4231, Fax: 202-225-6887, johnrose.house.gov

State Offices: Cookeville, 931-854-9430; Gallatin, 615-206-8204.

Committees: *Financial Services*: Consumer Protection & Financial Institutions; Diversity & Inclusion; Housing, Community Development & Insurance.

Almanac Ratings 2019-2020

	Economy	Social	Foreign	Composite
Liberal	25%	9%	4%	13%
Conservative	75%	91%	96%	87%

Key Votes of the 116th Congress

1. U.S./Mex./Can. trade deal	Y	5. Russia sanctions	N	9. Firearms background checks N
2. First Coronavirus response	N	6. Troops in Syria	N	10. Spending at the border Y
3. HEROES Act	N	7. Veto arms sales to Saudis	N	11. Marijuana liberalized rules N
4. CASH Act	N	8. Defense $$$, veto override	N	12. Electoral College objections Y

Election Results

Election	Name (Party)	Vote (%)		Cand. Spent	Ind. Exp. Support	Ind. Exp. Oppose
2020 General	John Rose (R)......................................	257,572	(74%)	$530,588	$50	$750
	Christopher Finley (D)..................	83,852	(24%)			
	Christopher Monday (I).........................	8,154	(2%)			
2020 Primary	John Rose (R).......................................	78,340	(100%)			

Prior winning percentages: 2018 (69%)

Republican John Rose, elected in 2018, was a family farmer and a lawyer who became wealthy after starting a technology-training business. His chief experience in government was a few months as Tennessee's commissioner of agriculture. He was initially elected with a larger financial war chest and a broader base of support across the district. In the House, he has worked on financial issues and has shown occasional independence.

Rose, a native of rural Putnam County, graduated from Tennessee Tech University, got a master's degree in agricultural economics from Purdue and a law degree from Vanderbilt. After practicing law for a few years with a Chattanooga firm, he co-founded the Transcender Corp., a fast-growing provider of information technology certification training. In 2000, he and his partners sold that company for $60 million, the Tennessean reported the following year. In 2002, as he was about to leave office, Gov. Don Sundquist appointed Rose to the state's top agricultural position. He later held several public service posts, including with the Tennessee Tech Foundation, a state conservation trust fund and the Tennessee State Fair Association.

After Rep. Diane Black gave up the House seat to run unsuccessfully for the GOP nomination for governor, the chief contenders to replace her were Rose and Bob Corlew, who served 30 years as a Rutherford County judge before retiring in 2014. Each was largely a self-funder, though Rose's $3 million campaign fund roughly doubled Corlew's account. Several weeks before the primary, the Volunteer State Report wrote that Corlew "has come out of the gate flat" and that Rose's "connections with both the political class and the agricultural community" made him the frontrunner. Corlew was disadvantaged because Rutherford County shifted from the 6th District to the 4th District in the 2012 redistricting.

In their campaign ads, Rose and Corlew both emphasized their support of President Donald Trump and the need for tougher enforcement of immigration laws. Rose described himself as a "businessman, farmer and outsider." In a closing ad, Corlew's unusual message that he was not Sen. Bob Corker, who was retiring, revealed that he had problems in building his name-identification. Also running was state Rep. Judd Matheny, who was backed by members of the House Republicans' Freedom Caucus.

Rose won the primary with 41 percent of the vote to 31 percent for Corlew and 16 percent for Matheny. He took 15 of the 19 counties, with his largest margins in Sumner and Putnam. Corlew led Rose by 111 votes in Wilson County, which had the largest turnout. Matheny got 64 percent in Coffee County but finished no higher than third in the other counties. On a 69%-28% vote, Rose defeated Democratic nominee Dawn Barlow, a medical doctor who campaigned mostly on health care reform. Barlow had scant financing and gained little notice in this once-firmly Democratic district.

Rose was assigned to the Financial Services Committee—a logical move, given his success in business. He showed skill in finding Democratic allies, a necessity to pass legislation in the Democratic-controlled House. In April 2019, the House passed a non-binding resolution that he filed with freshman Democratic Rep. Sean Casten, which urged steps to combat the financial exploitation of senior citizens. "It is time to empower community partnerships and law enforcement in their work to safeguard seniors against deception and scams which threaten their stability and security daily," Rose told the House. In July 2019, the House passed his bill—with bipartisan sponsors—that gave small businesses in rural communities the same opportunity to receive capital formation technical assistance that was already available to many other entrepreneurs. Each proposal passed with all but a handful of House members voting in favor.

He voiced support for local law-enforcement agencies when many of them were under attack during civil rights protests in 2020. "I reject the idea that our local police forces or America as a whole are inherently or irredeemably racist. America is not a perfect nation, but no nation is," he wrote in an op-ed to a local newspaper. "We recognize that two things can be true at once: that we have made progress, but that progress can still be made. That discrimination exists, but that our nation is not systemically discriminatory."

Rose showed his free spirit when he joined Republican Rep. Thomas Massie in demanding a roll-call vote on emergency disaster-aid relief that House leaders had hoped to pass by voice vote. His move forced a delay in final action during a week in May 2019 when the House was not conducting legislative business.

Rose faced no Republican primary opposition. Christopher Finley, his Democratic challenger, reported to the Federal Election Commission that he spent no money on his campaign. Rose won, 74%-24%.

TN-6: Middle Tennessee   Cook Partisan Voting Index: R+26

Population		Race and Ethnicity		Income	
Total	799,365	White	89.40%	Median Income	$59,421
Land area (sq. miles)	6,474	Black	5.20%	District Income Rank	276
Pop/ sq mi	123.47	Latino	4.60%	Poverty Rate	12.40%
Born in State	61.10%	Asian	1.10%	With health insurance	91.00%
		Two or more races	1.90%	Cash public assistance	1.30%
Age Groups		Other	2.50%	Food stamp/SNAP	10.70%
Under 18	22.00%				
18-34	20.60%	Education		Work	
35-64	39.40%	H.S grad or less	47.40%	White Collar	34.10%
Over 64	18.00%	Some college	27.60%	Sales and Service	38.00%
		College Degree, 4 yr	16.40%	Blue Collar	27.90%
Military		Post grad	8.60%	Government	13.50%
Veteran/ Active Duty	8.30%				

2020 Pres. Vote	Trump	273,977	(73%)	Biden	96,461	(26%)			
2016 Pres. Vote	Trump	216,516	(72%)	Clinton	70,428	(24%)	Johnson	7,578	(3%)

Eastern Nashville Suburbs: Middle Tennessee is hilly and fertile, cut by deep, curvy rivers. The terrain was never much suited for plantation crops, and there were few big landholdings. This has long been a land of small farmers and small county-seat towns, nestled amid some of the loveliest scenery in the country. As one of the heartlands of the Democratic Party, it was the political base of President Andrew Jackson and supported him nearly unanimously in his 1832 reelection. For 140 years after Jackson, it voted solidly Democratic and elected as its representatives in Congress some of the luminaries of the national party: Cordell Hull (1907-21, 1923-31), later senator and secretary of State; Albert Gore Sr. (1939-53), later senator; and Albert Gore Jr. (1977-85), later senator and vice president.

The 6th Congressional District includes 17 Middle Tennessee counties, plus small parts of two others. These counties largely retain a rural heritage. Dan Evans, founder of the Cracker Barrel Old Country Store chain, grew up in Smithville. The populated areas evoke the small-town charm for which those stores are famous. Just over half of the district's population lives in the three counties that adjoin Nashville. These are generally upscale places with median incomes that are among the highest in the state. Sumner and Wilson, the two largest counties in the district, grew 19 and 27 percent respectively from 2010 to 2019. Sumner, which includes Nashville bedroom communities such as Hendersonville, Gallatin, White House and Portland, has seen a major spike in new homes as working professionals have moved to the suburbs, along with an influx of retirees. In Gallatin, the Tennessee Valley Authority ended a five-year fight with environmental groups and agreed in June 2019 to remove 12 million tons of coal ash that had been stored in unlined pits and to clean up the contamination at its fossil fuel plant. In a sign of the future for Gallatin, Facebook announced in August 2020 that it would build an $800 million data center; all the energy will be supplied by renewable sources. Putnam County and Cookeville are an industry and manufacturing hub in the district. In 2018, Brazilian ceramic tile manufacturer Portobello America Inc. chose Baxter as the location of its first U.S. production facility, investing $150 million in Putnam and adding 220 jobs.

Because this part of Tennessee had few African Americans, the racial politics of the 1960s largely bypassed the region, and Democratic loyalties outlasted those in other parts of the South. With Gore, Bill Clinton swept the area in 1992. Then, as the Democratic Party became an increasingly urban coalition in the 2000s, the party's local fortunes plummeted. Its 73 percent for President Donald Trump in 2020 placed it among his top 5 percent of districts nationwide. It likely will be a long time before Democrats return to competitiveness in Al Gore's former district.

Mark Green (R)

Elected 2018, 2nd term, b. Nov 08, 1964; Jacksonville, FL; U.S. Military Academy - West Point, B.S., 1986; University of Southern CA, M.A., 1987; Wright State University, M.D., 1999; Christian Church; Married (Camilla Joy Guenther); 2 children.

Military Career: U.S. Army 1987-2006 (Afghanistan & Iraq)

Elected Office: TN Senate, 2012-2018.

Professional Career: President and Chief Executive Officer, Align MD, 2006-2015.

DC Office: 533 CHOB 20515, 202-225-2811, markgreen.house.gov

Committees: *Armed Services*: Readiness; Tactical Air & Land Forces. *Foreign Affairs*: Asia, the Pacific, Central Asia, Nonproliferation; West Hem, Civ Sec, Migration, & Intern'l Econ Policy (RMM).

Almanac Ratings 2019-2020

	Economy	Social	Foreign	Composite
Liberal	33%	29%	27%	30%
Conservative	67%	71%	73%	70%

Key Votes of the 116th Congress

1. U.S./Mex./Can. trade deal	Y	5. Russia sanctions	Y	9. Firearms background checks	N
2. First Coronavirus response	N	6. Troops in Syria	Y	10. Spending at the border	Y
3. HEROES Act	N	7. Veto arms sales to Saudis	N	11. Marijuana liberalized rules	N
4. CASH Act	N	8. Defense $$$, veto override	Y	12. Electoral College objections	Y

Election Results

Election	Name (Party)	Vote (%)		Cand. Spent	Ind. Exp. Support	Ind. Exp. Oppose
2020 General	Mark Green (R)	245,188	(70%)	$899,808	$454	$750
	Kiran Sreepada (D)	95,839	(27%)	$209,111		
	Ronald Brown (I)	7,603	(2%)			
2020 Primary	Mark Green (R)	73,540	(100%)			

Prior winning percentages: 2018 (67%)

Republican Mark Green, elected in 2018, brought a diverse background to Congress: West Point graduate, flight surgeon, war veteran, founder of his own medical-services business, state senator, and a failed nomination in 2017 for secretary of the Army. He won nomination to the House without a primary in his heavily Republican district, which opened when Rep. Marsha Blackburn ran successfully for the Senate. Green's general election victory wasn't much more difficult. His Democratic opponent had extensive experience in Hollywood, but he was new to Tennessee and to politics. Despite his earlier expression of interest in the Senate, he quickly ruled out running for the seat of retiring Sen. Lamar Alexander

Green, a native of Mississippi, graduated from the U.S. Military Academy with a degree in business management. During 20 years in the Army, with a final rank of lieutenant colonel, he began as an infantry officer and then served as an airborne battalion supply officer with the renowned 82nd Airborne Division. While in the Army, he attended medical school, where he was a resident in emergency care and became a flight surgeon. That background prepared Green to be in the elite crew that captured Saddam Hussein in 2003; Green wrote a book, A Night with Saddam, about his six hours of interrogation of the former Iraqi president.

Following his military service, Green founded and became chief executive of Align MD, a business that provided hospital and emergency room services. In 2015, he sold that company to a competitor for $24 million. He remained as its president for the following year, then became chief executive of the firm. The Nashville Business Journal cited Green as a Health Care Hero. Green began his political career in 2012, when he defeated a Democratic incumbent to win a seat in the Tennessee Senate. He sponsored legislation to provide a health savings account for Medicaid beneficiaries, and he played a leading role in the phased repeal of taxes on income from savings and investment.

In April 2017, President Donald Trump nominated Green as secretary of the Army. Critics cited Green's controversial remarks on various topics, including the status of transgender persons and the rights of Muslims in the United States. Senate Armed Services Committee Chairman John McCain said that some of Green's comments were "very concerning." Green called the attacks "false and misleading," and subsequently blamed his failure on "obstruction from Senate Democrats and attacks on his Christian faith." When Green requested the withdrawal of his nomination, Secretary of Defense Jim Mattis had no public comment, the Washington Post reported.

In January 2017, Green filed papers to run for governor in 2018. He switched that plan in October when Blackburn announced her campaign for the Senate, and he said he would seek her House seat. Despite speculation about a more moderate GOP candidate, none stepped forward. Green won the primary without opposition—an unusual result for an open seat in which one party has firm control. Democrats nominated Justin Kanew, a film producer and writer who was a former contestant on the reality TV show, The Amazing Race. Kanew moved from Los Angeles to the district in 2017. He called Green an "extremist" and urged a "return to civility." With his ample fundraising and the district's pedigree, Green won, 67%-32%.

Green quickly ran into controversy a month after his election when he raised doubts about the efficacy of vaccines. "There is some concern that the rise in autism is the result of the preservatives that are in our vaccines," Green told a town hall forum, The Tennessean reported. Six months later, in response to a complaint that was filed with the Tennessee Department of Health, a spokesman for Green issued a statement that the complaint was "frivolous" and that Green "supports vaccination and has said so repeatedly."

Green had been mentioned as a potential Senate candidate, especially if Alexander decided to seek reelection in 2020. Once Alexander announced in July 2019 his decision to retire, Green dismissed the option of running for the Senate and said his top priorities were the reelection of Trump and a GOP takeover of the House. News reports at the time speculated that the flap over vaccines might have damaged Green's credibility.

In June 2020, Green had a setback in the House when he was one of three candidates for the opening of ranking Republican at the Oversight and Reform Committee. A GOP leadership panel selected James Comer of Kentucky, who had more seniority. Separately, Minority Leader Kevin McCarthy named Green as one of five Republicans on the House select committee to oversee spending for coronavirus relief.

In his reelection bid, Green again ran without Republican opposition and faced Kiran Sreepada, a newcomer to the district who had lengthy experience as a federal employee and had received a master's degree in public policy. Green outspent the challenger, $900,000 to $209,000. This time, he won, 70%-27%.

Following his reelection, Green got assignments to the Armed Services and Foreign Affairs committees. On the latter panel, he was named ranking Republican on the Western Hemisphere, Civilian Security, Migration and International Economic Policy Subcommittee. In a statement, Green said, "I am deeply committed to protecting the American people from the devastating consequences of illegal immigration and the transnational drug trade." Two weeks after his selection, he was joined by other House Republicans in writing a letter to President Joe Biden urging him to recognize the "threat to democracy" posed by the government of Cuba.

TN-7: Middle Tennessee

Cook Partisan Voting Index: R+21

Population		Race and Ethnicity		Income	
Total	800,536	White	83.40%	Median Income	$62,720
Land area (sq. miles)	9,160	Black	9.70%	District Income Rank	228
Pop/ sq mi	87.39	Latino	5.40%	Poverty Rate	11.00%
Born in State	50.70%	Asian	2.10%	With health insurance	92.00%
		Two or more races	3.50%	Cash public assistance	1.30%
Age Groups		Other	1.30%	Food stamp/SNAP	9.40%
Under 18	24.30%				
18-34	21.30%	**Education**		**Work**	
35-64	39.10%	H.S grad or less	41.60%	White Collar	38.60%
Over 64	15.30%	Some college	26.30%	Sales and Service	37.70%
		College Degree, 4 yr	20.20%	Blue Collar	23.60%
Military		Post grad	11.90%	Government	14.20%
Veteran/ Active Duty	12.30%				

2020 Pres. Vote	Trump	245,875	(67%)	Biden	115,160	(31%)			
2016 Pres. Vote	Trump	196,893	(67%)	Clinton	82,236	(28%)	Johnson	9,071	(3%)

Western Nashville Suburbs, Clarksville: Rural Tennessee north of Mississippi is mostly a sparsely settled area. Along each side of the Tennessee River, as it flows north and widens out into Kentucky Lake, are small rural communities. Many date to pre-Civil War days and have not grown much since. One of these is Waynesboro, where Davy Crockett delivered campaign speeches from the base of a huge natural stone double bridge overlooking the Buffalo River. Farther west is McNairy County, where Sheriff Buford Pusser of Walking Tall fame carried his big stick and fought organized crime until his death in a 1974 car crash. Even some of the roads have changed little; the Natchez Trace Parkway follows the same basic path as the trail carved out by prehistoric bison from Mississippi grazing lands to the salt licks of central Tennessee.

This land is complemented by two urban areas: Greater Nashville to the east and Clarksville to the north. South of Nashville is Williamson County, where the bedroom communities of Franklin and Brentwood are affluent, highly educated, and fast-growing. The county grew by 30 percent from 2010 to 2019. In 2019, Mitsubishi moved its corporate headquarters to Franklin—the county seat of Williamson—joining Nissan North America, which recently moved its headquarters from California to Franklin. In January 2019, the Tennessean profiled Williamson as "an anomaly in Tennessee." Its high median income ($113,000 per household) and education (60 percent of adults with at least a bachelor's degree) plus low poverty rate (four percent in 2019) far outperform other parts of the state. The fact that the county's support for Donald Trump dropped from 65 percent in 2016 to 62 percent in 2020 is one measure of how the county continues to reflect Tennessee more than upscale suburbia nationwide.

Along the Cumberland River is Clarksville, the fifth-largest city in the state, with many restored 19th-century homes and a large industrial park. Straddling the Kentucky border north of Clarksville is the Army's sprawling Fort Campbell, home of the 101st Airborne Division, which has become a rapid deployment unit and is the Army's only air assault division; Campbell is the Army's fifth largest base and a military boomtown. The military community and jobs in Clarksville have helped make it the youngest city in the state. In November 2019, Google opened its $500 million data center. In September 2019, Money magazine rated Clarksville "the best place to live in America right now"—citing its large number of millennials, growing community of military retirees, commuters to Nashville, high-performing school system, relatively inexpensive housing and "charming downtown." The area around Clarksville retains some of its historic attachment to the Democratic Party dating to the Civil War. Trump got 55 percent of the vote in the city in 2020.

The 7th Congressional District covers this territory, which is the largest district in Tennessee. Close to 40 percent live in Tennessee's Central Basin, in Williamson County. Another fifth of its population lives in Clarksville-based Montgomery County, which has seen 21 percent population growth since 2010. The median income in Montgomery is half of Williamson. The remainder live in the lightly populated, rural counties traversing the state from northern border to southern. Trump twice took the district with 67 percent, with a much higher vote in its rural areas.

David Kustoff (R)

Elected 2016, 3rd term, b. Oct 08, 1966; Memphis, TN; University of Memphis, B.B.A., 1989; University of Memphis School of Law, J.D., 1992; Jewish; Married (Roberta Kustoff); 2 children.

Professional Career: Practicing attorney; Chairman, Shelby County GOP, 1995-1999; U.S. Attorney, Western District of Tennessee, 2006-2008.

DC Office: 523 CHOB 20515, 202-225-4714, Fax: 202-225-1765

State Offices: Dyersburg, 731-412-1037; Jackson, 731-423-4848; Memphis, 901-682-4422.

Committees: *Financial Services*: Consumer Protection & Financial Institutions; Oversight & Investigations.

Group Ratings

	ADA	ACLU	AFL-CIO	LCV	COC	HAFA	ACU	CFG	FRC
2020	**	15%	**	10%	-	85%	83%	**	-
2019	10%	C	33%	10%	85%	C	85%	65%	100%

Almanac Ratings 2019-2020

	Economy	Social	Foreign	Composite
Liberal	25%	23%	15%	21%
Conservative	75%	77%	85%	79%

Key Votes of the 116th Congress

1. U.S./Mex./Can. trade deal	Y	5. Russia sanctions	N
2. First Coronavirus response	Y	6. Troops in Syria	Y
3. HEROES Act	N	7. Veto arms sales to Saudis	N
4. CASH Act	N	8. Defense $$$, veto override	Y

9. Firearms background checks N
10. Spending at the border   N/A
11. Marijuana liberalized rules N
12. Electoral College objections Y

Election Results

Election	Name (Party)	Vote (%)		Cand. Spent	Ind. Exp. Support	Ind. Exp. Oppose
2020 General	David Kustoff (R)	227,216	(68%)	$960,618		$750
	Erika Stotts Pearson (D)	97,890	(30%)	$11,552		
2020 Primary	David Kustoff (R)	70,677	(100%)			

Prior winning percentages: 2018 (68%), 2016 (69%)

Republican David Kustoff was elected to an open seat in 2016 after winning a hard-fought primary. With his experience as a U.S. attorney in West Tennessee and his political connections to leading Republicans in the state, Kustoff was the establishment favorite in the contest. He showed his continued establishment credentials when he was the only one of the nine congressional Republicans from Tennessee who voted to accept the Electoral College results from Arizona when they were challenged by allies of President Donald Trump.

Born and raised in Shelby County, Kustoff got his bachelor's and law degrees from the University of Memphis. He opened a law firm with Jim Strickland, a Democrat who was elected mayor of Memphis in 2016. Kustoff served in various positions for the Republican Party, including Shelby County chairman, and state chairman of the George W. Bush presidential campaigns in 2000 and 2004. He ran for Congress in the 7th District in 2002, but finished second with 20 percent, to 40 percent for Marsha Blackburn in the Republican primary, when he split the vote from Shelby County with two other local Republicans.

Kustoff was nominated as U.S. attorney in 2006 and served until 2009. He gained attention for winning the conviction of state Sen. John Ford and others in the "Tennessee Waltz" political corruption trial. Later, Kustoff served on the board of the Bank of Tennessee, a community bank, and was appointed by Gov. Bill Haslam as vice chairman of the Tennessee Higher Education Commission, where he oversaw implementation of state assistance programs.

When three-term GOP Rep. Stephen Fincher retired, there was a wide-open field of 13 Republican candidates, two Democrats and five independents. Kustoff emphasized his law-enforcement background by criticizing President Barack Obama for having "unfairly and severely impugned the reputation of law enforcement" officers in high-profile cases of alleged police misconduct. Former Shelby County Commissioner George Flinn, a radiologist and TV station owner who had two previous unsuccessful runs for Congress, raised by far the most money with $3 million, of which $2.7 million was self-financed. Kustoff raised about $700,000 for the primary, including $100,000 from a personal loan.

Kustoff won the primary with 28 percent of the vote to 23 percent for Flinn, 18 percent for Shelby County Mayor Mark Luttrell and 13 percent for state Sen. Brian Kelsey. Kustoff took nearly half the vote in Shelby County. Democratic nominee Rickey Hobson did not file a financial report with the Federal Election Commission, and Kustoff won the general, 69%-25%.

Flinn challenged Kustoff again in the 2018 Republican primary, and again put more than $3 million of his own money into the race. Flinn argued Kustoff wasn't conservative enough and touted his own "Christian conservative" background, which many saw as a not-so-veiled swipe at Kustoff, who is one of the few Jewish Republicans in Congress. It was Kustoff, however, who got the coveted endorsement from President Donald Trump, who tweeted that "Congressman David Kustoff has been a champion for the Trump Agenda." Despite being outspent more than 3-to-1, he again defeated Flinn, 56%-40%. Otherwise, he has breezed to reelection.

Kustoff got a seat on the Financial Services Committee, where he sought to reduce the restrictions imposed by the 2010 Dodd-Frank banking law, arguing that it hampered small business growth, especially in rural communities. In a 2017 op-ed for CNBC, he wrote that "Dodd-Frank created two Americas, but I see a unified U.S. economy that serves all Americans." In 2018, Kustoff—still a freshman—had an unusual, and confidential, one-on-one meeting with Jay Powell, the chairman of the Federal Reserve Board, CNBC reported in February 2019. Kustoff was "the first stop in the chairman's charm offensive on Capitol Hill" for Powell, who had been confirmed to his position days earlier, according to the report. "I was pleasantly surprised because you don't see that very often," Kustoff later said.

In actions that appeared to reflect his experience as a federal prosecutor, Kustoff collaborated on security issues with Republican Sen. Tom Cotton. They filed in May 2019 a bill to restore a tool for prosecutors to seek enhanced penalties against violent, serial criminals. In May 2020, they filed in the House and Senate legislation that would bar Chinese nationals from receiving student or research visas to the United States for graduate or postgraduate studies in science, technology, engineering or mathematics fields. "Student visas should be only for those who want to contribute to our research institutions and advance our national interests," Kustoff said about their proposal; Blackburn, now a Senator, was the other chief sponsor.

Kustoff has forged a close working relationship with neighboring Memphis Democratic Rep. Steve Cohen; the two attend the same temple and are both alumni of the University of Memphis. Cohen helped to whip votes for Kustoff's first bill in the House, which would protect religious institutions; it passed 402-2. And Kustoff used his leverage with the Trump administration to successfully lobby for Clayborn Temple in Memphis to be named a National Treasure by the National Trust for Historic Preservation; striking sanitation workers in 1968 used that site as their staging ground during the civil rights movement.

When Sen. Lamar Alexander announced in July 2019 that he would not seek reelection, Kustoff —after suggesting that he was considering a run for the Senate—announced days later that he would remain in the House. Following the 2020 election, he was among the small number of House Republicans who voted to certify the Electoral College result for one state (Arizona, in his case), but voted for additional review of another state (Pennsylvania). Although Kustoff offered no immediate explanation, he said a week later after the House voted to impeach Trump a second time that even in "this time of turmoil and uncertainty," an impeachment "during [Trump's] last seven days in office would only further divide us as Americans."

TN-8: West Tennessee

Cook Partisan Voting Index: R+19

Population		Race and Ethnicity		Income	
Total	711,068	White	73.00%	Median Income	$60,152
Land area (sq. miles)	6,851	Black	22.00%	District Income Rank	258
Pop/ sq mi	103.8	Latino	3.10%	Poverty Rate	11.90%
Born in State	65.40%	Asian	1.70%	With health insurance	91.80%
		Two or more races	1.80%	Cash public assistance	1.20%
Age Groups		Other	1.50%	Food stamp/SNAP	10.90%
Under 18	23.00%				
18-34	19.40%	**Education**		**Work**	
35-64	39.70%	H.S grad or less	42.70%	White Collar	40.30%
Over 64	17.80%	Some college	26.60%	Sales and Service	34.50%
		College Degree, 4 yr	17.60%	Blue Collar	25.20%
Military		Post grad	13.00%	Government	14.50%
Veteran/ Active Duty	7.80%				

2020 Pres. Vote	Trump	225,464	(65%)	Biden	114,520	(33%)		
2016 Pres. Vote	Trump	197,432	(66%)	Clinton	90,006	(30%)	Johnson 6,370	(2%)

Memphis Suburbs, Jackson: West of Nashville and north of Memphis, the rivers roll lazily through flat or gently rolling land that has similarities to the northern end of Mississippi. Cotton and soybeans are the main crops—the annual Tennessee Soybean Festival is held in Martin, near the Kentucky border—and they often are abundant. African Americans remain in rural areas here, a reminder of the old plantation economy. Henning is the hometown of Alex Haley, who used to sit on his porch and listen to his aunts tell him stories about slave ships and the Civil War; these became his best-selling book Roots. The plantation economy also bequeathed a fierce loyalty to the Democratic Party; before 2011, much of this district hadn't been represented by a Republican since Reconstruction.

The small towns in this area are sustained by manufacturers such as the NSK automotive plant and light industry such as Dot Foods, the nation's largest food redistributor, both in Dyersburg. In August 2020, Tyson Foods completed the second expansion of its plant in Union City that hired 1,600 workers, producing fresh tray-packed chicken for retail sales. In January 2021, the Jackson Sun reported, county and city officials voiced "frustrations" with the slow progress with The Memphis Regional Mega site, which includes 4,100 acres in Haywood and Fayette counties executives were working to attract a major employer after receiving a $106 million grant from the state. Those redevelopments have helped to soften the blow after other companies once prominent in the area closed—including Brown Shoe Co. and Plastech Corp. in Gibson County, where Tyson has expanded, and a Goodyear Tire & Rubber Co. plant in Obion County.

Crockett County, with a county seat named Alamo, is named after Davy Crockett, who represented the area for three terms in the House before he moved to Texas. The area carries the highest earthquake risk in the United States outside the West Coast. In the early 1800s, four earthquakes rocked the region, permanently altering the topography. Perhaps the most extreme example is Reelfoot Lake, the only large natural lake in Tennessee, which was a dry area before the quakes occurred; the land dropped almost 20 feet in places before the Mississippi River filled in the newly formed depression. Kentucky Lake draws big crowds for its annual BASS fest in Henry County.

The 8th Congressional District of Tennessee includes much of this West Tennessee farmland. Its largest city is Jackson, founded shortly after the area was opened for White settlement in 1818, and the site of one of Crockett's final speeches before heading west to his doom—and immortality —at the Alamo. In Jackson, which is 45 percent Black, a marker was erected to note the site of two lynchings in the late 19th century. Nearby Haywood is a Black-majority county. Overall, the population is 20 percent Black. Suburban Shelby County east of Memphis includes 40 percent of the district population. President Donald Trump got 65 percent of the vote in 2020.

Steve Cohen (D)

Elected 2006, 8th term, b. May 24, 1949; Memphis, TN; Vanderbilt University, B.A., 1971; Memphis State University - Cecil C. Humphreys School of Law, J.D., 1973; Jewish; Single1 child.

Elected Office: Shelby County Commissioner, 1977-1978; TN Senate, 1982-2006.

Professional Career: Practicing attorney, 1974-2006.

DC Office: 2104 RHOB 20515, 202-225-3265, Fax: 202-225-5663, cohen.house.gov

State Offices: Memphis, 901-544-4131.

Committees: *Judiciary*: Constitution, Civil Rights & Civil Liberties; Constitution, Civil Rights & Civil Liberties (Chmn); Courts, Intellectual Property & Internet; Crime, Terrorism & Homeland Security. *Natural Resources*: Oversight & Investigations; Water, Oceans & Wildlife. *Transportation & Infrastructure*: Aviation; Highways & Transit; Railroads, Pipelines & Hazardous Materials; Water Resources & Environment.

Group Ratings

	ADA	ACLU	AFL-CIO	LCV	COC	HAFA	ACU	CFG	FRC
2020	**	80%	**	100%	-	0%	4%	**	-
2019	95%	C	95%	96%	53%	C	4%	18%	0%

Almanac Ratings 2019-2020

	Economy	Social	Foreign	Composite
Liberal	100%	100%	55%	85%
Conservative	0%	0%	45%	15%

Key Votes of the 116th Congress

1. U.S./Mex./Can. trade deal	Y	5. Russia sanctions	Y	9. Firearms background checks Y
2. First Coronavirus response	Y	6. Troops in Syria	Y	10. Spending at the border Y
3. HEROES Act	Y	7. Veto arms sales to Saudis	Y	11. Marijuana liberalized rules Y
4. CASH Act	Y	8. Defense $$$, veto override	Y	12. Electoral College objections N

Election Results

Election	Name (Party)	Vote (%)		Cand. Spent	Ind. Exp. Support	Ind. Exp. Oppose
2020 General	Steve Cohen (D)	187,905	(77%)	$258,515	$873	$15,685
	Charlotte Bergmann (R)	48,818	(20%)	$97,545	$28,298	$113
2020 Primary	Steve Cohen (D)	56,312	(84%)			
	Corey Strong (D)	9,994	(15%)			

Prior winning percentages: 2018 (80%), 2016 (79%), 2014 (75%), 2012 (75%), 2010 (74%), 2008 (88%), 2006 (60%)

Democrat Steve Cohen, elected in 2006, is a rare white member of Congress representing a majority-minority district. He has easily fended off primary challenges from the district's African-American majority by maintaining one of the House's most liberal voting records. He was an outspoken opponent of President Donald Trump at the Judiciary Committee and sometimes grew frustrated that other Democrats were slow to reach his conclusions on impeachment.

Cohen is a fourth-generation Memphian and the son of a psychiatrist. At age 5, he was diagnosed with polio. Cohen got his bachelor's at Vanderbilt University and his law degree from the University of Memphis. He worked as a legal adviser for the Memphis Police Department and then started a law practice. He was elected to the Shelby County Commission and, in 1982, to the state Senate, where he served for 24 years. He became known as the father of the Tennessee State Lottery for his efforts in 2002 to pass a referendum creating a lottery, with revenue to fund college scholarships.

Cohen wanted to run for Congress in 1996 when 22-year African-American Rep. Harold Ford Sr., announced his retirement, but he found his path blocked by the incumbent's 26-year-old son, who secured the seat. He got his chance in 2006 when Harold Ford Jr. ran unsuccessfully for the Senate. As the only serious White contender among the 15 candidates who filed to run, Cohen faced criticism from local Black leaders, who said that an African American should represent the district. Cohen's supporters charged that another primary foe paid for a push poll that asked, "Are you more likely to vote for a born-again Christian or a Jew?" Cohen quipped that his staunchly liberal record would make people mistake him for a black woman.

The district's Black leaders did not sufficiently narrow the field, and the primary results splintered. Cohen won with 31 percent. Nikki Tinker, the former campaign manager for Ford Jr., finished second with 25 percent. The incumbent's cousin, Joe Ford Jr., finished third with 12 percent. Cohen faced a challenge in November from yet another Ford—Jake Ford, the incumbent's younger brother, who ran as an independent. Jake Ford was a high school dropout who had a few scrapes with the law, but he had support from his father and other African-American leaders who opposed Cohen. He won the general election with 60 percent of the vote, ending the Ford family's 32-year hold on the district. Cohen wanted to join the Congressional Black Caucus, but backed off when CBC leaders made it clear they objected.

Cohen quickly secured his hold on the seat. Among his first moves was a resolution apologizing for slavery, which passed the House on a voice vote days before the 2008 primary. Many constituents charged that the measure was a political ploy. In that primary, African-American leaders in the district coalesced around Tinker. "He's not Black, and he can't represent me," one minister told the Memphis Commercial Appeal. Tinker got financial help from the CBC and EMILY's List, the abortion-rights fundraising group that supports women candidates. But prominent Black leaders from outside the district made radio ads for Cohen and donated to his campaign. He outraised Tinker more than 2-to-1 and crushed her, 79%-19%.

On the Judiciary Committee, Cohen worked on bills to force radio broadcasters to pay money to performers and to study racial disparities in the criminal justice system. As the ranking Democrat on the Constitution and Civil Justice Subcommittee, he championed a bipartisan bill that would make marijuana legal for some medical purposes.

After Democrats won back the House in 2018, Cohen became chairman of the renamed Constitution, Civil Rights and Civil Liberties subcommittee. In November 2017, he and several other liberal Democrats had introduced five articles of impeachment against Trump. "The time has come to make clear to the American people and to this president that his train of injuries to our Constitution must be brought to an end through impeachment," Cohen said. Although Democratic leaders had little appetite to proceed with the risky push, he pressed ahead. In May 2019, he told MSNBC, "80 to 90 percent of the committee is on board to go forward" with impeachment. It took another six months before Speaker Nancy Pelosi gave her OK. She did not include him as a House manager in either of the Senate impeachment trials of Trump. Cohen filed constitutional amendments to eliminate the Electoral College and prohibit presidents from pardoning themselves; each made a liberal statement but failed to move, even in a Democratic House.

In the face of repeated primary challenges, Cohen has become entrenched. In 2010, his opponent was Willie Herenton, Memphis' first elected black mayor. Cohen was ready, with an endorsement from President Barack Obama, a popular figure in the district, as well as support from a dozen CBC members. He trounced Herenton, 79%-21%, in the primary and sailed to reelection. Two years later, his challenger was Memphis Urban League CEO and school board member Tomeka Hart. Cohen won the primary, 89%-11%.

Against the less well-known Ricky Wilkins in 2014, Cohen had his closest primary since he was first elected. Wilkins campaigned publicly on how Cohen's race and ethnicity differed from that of most of his constituents. Cohen won, 66%-33%. Since then, he has easily dispatched primary challengers. The threat of a serious primary challenge now seems virtually nil.

TN-9: Shelby County

Cook Partisan Voting Index: D+28

Population		Race and Ethnicity		Income	
Total	700,497	White	27.60%	Median Income	$43,708
Land area (sq. miles)	483	Black	65.10%	District Income Rank	423
Pop/ sq mi	1,449.13	Latino	8.10%	Poverty Rate	20.70%
Born in State	65.60%	Asian	2.40%	With health insurance	85.50%
		Two or more races	1.60%	Cash public assistance	2.10%
Age Groups		Other	3.30%	Food stamp/SNAP	20.20%
Under 18	24.80%				
18-34	26.50%	**Education**		**Work**	
35-64	35.40%	H.S grad or less	45.90%	White Collar	29.70%
Over 64	13.20%	Some college	29.90%	Sales and Service	42.10%
		College Degree, 4 yr	15.10%	Blue Collar	28.20%
Military		Post grad	9.10%	Government	12.30%
Veteran/ Active Duty	7.20%				

2020 Pres. Vote	Biden	193,606	(79%)	Trump	48,929	(20%)
2016 Pres. Vote	Clinton	173,411	(78%)	Trump	43,233	(19%)

Memphis Metro: Memphis had long been the largest city in Tennessee, until it lost that title in 2015 to fast-growing Nashville, which also has a much larger metropolitan area. In the state's southwestern corner, 20 miles from Mississippi's cotton fields and riverboat casinos, Memphis' share of African Americans is among the largest in the country, evidence of the city's economic heritage as a capital of the Cotton Kingdom. Big Mississippi planters used to come north to sell their crops in the courtyard of the Peabody Hotel, then make financial arrangements for the next growing season.

The city's most celebrated tradition is blues music. Unlike Nashville's country music, which emerged from mountainous East Tennessee, the Memphis sound originated from the self-taught musical stylings of poor, rural Blacks in the Mississippi Delta. Throughout the first half of the 20th century, talented Black musicians migrated north to Memphis and congregated downtown on Beale Street. The blues sound was adapted by Elvis Presley, a poor white boy from rural Mississippi, in July 1954 at Sam Phillips' Sun Studio in Memphis—the birth of rock 'n' roll. In the early 1960s, Memphis again became the crucible of a new sound, soul music, which emerged as a counterpoint to rock, its increasingly white-dominated cousin. Graceland, Presley's garishly decorated mansion, attracts hordes of musical pilgrims from all over the world.

Memphis is the home of the first supermarket chain: Piggly Wiggly, founded in 1916. St. Jude's Children's Research Hospital is also in Memphis, opened in 1962 by actor Danny Thomas to provide free treatment for children with cancer and to advance cancer research. The biggest private employer by far is FedEx, where nearly 10,000 employees scan, sort, weigh and route 1.4 million packages on 42 miles of conveyor belts to and from 150 aircraft that arrive and depart within a six-hour period almost every night at the world's busiest cargo airport. As part of its $1 billion investment to enlarge and modernize the Memphis super hub, FedEx said in October 2019 that it was building a new package sorting facility at the Memphis airport. However, there have been economic struggles in the city too. Electrolux, a home appliance manufacturer, planned to close its Memphis plant in 2021, putting 530 people out of work; the company is combining operations with its facility in Springfield Tennessee. And studies have shown that the city lags behind other cities economically, citing high tax rates and rising crime and poverty as deterrents. In the Economic Innovation Group's 2020 Distressed Communities Index, Memphis ranked most distressed among 100 major metro areas.

Racial discord has scarred the political life of Memphis, which has been a major site in the civil rights movement. Rev. Martin Luther King Jr. was assassinated there in 1968, and the site, the Lorraine Motel, has been converted into the National Civil Rights Museum. Resurgent Beale Street is one of the few racially integrated spaces in the city, a division that holds equally true in voting. Blacks vote almost unanimously Democratic, and whites vote Republican by margins almost as great. A Chalk beat analysis in 2018 found that Memphis schools are more segregated than 50 years ago.

The 9th Congressional District of Tennessee remains the strongest Democratic district in the state. African Americans are 66 percent of the population. In 2020, Joe Biden won 79 percent in the district.

TEXAS

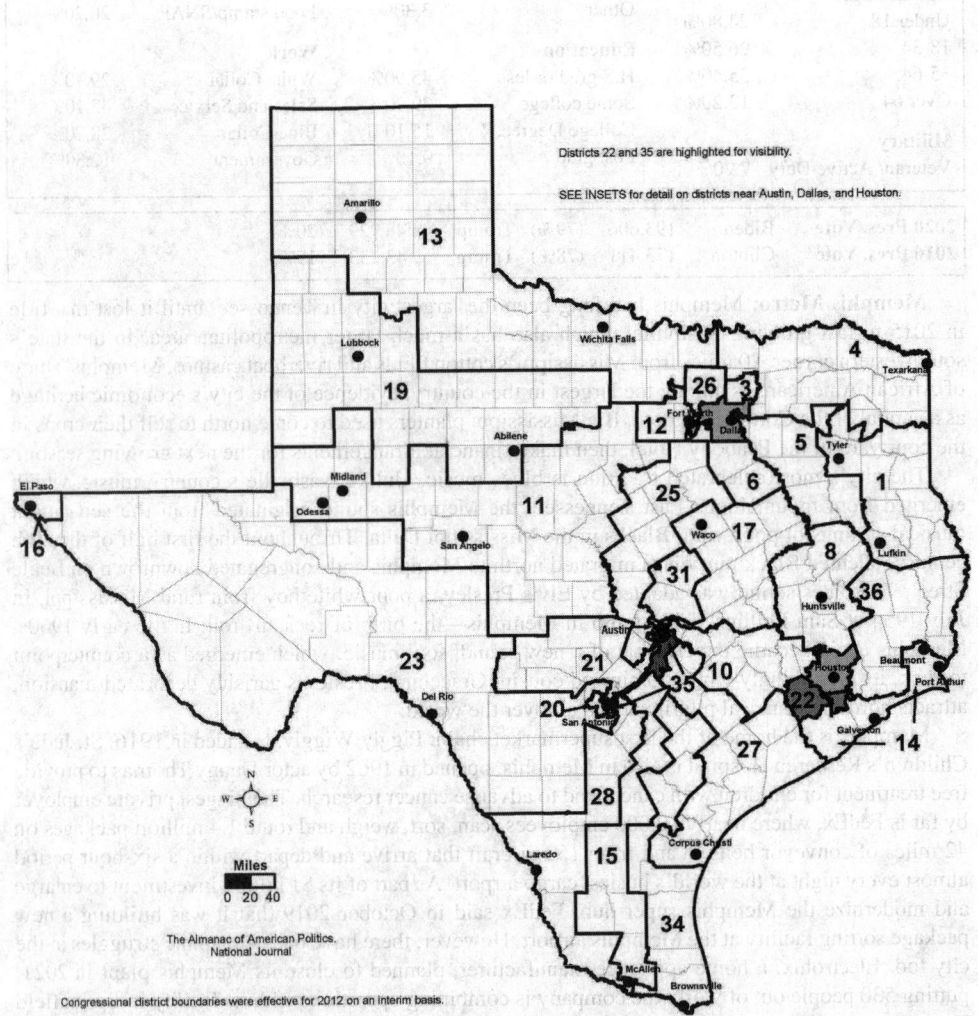

Districts 22 and 35 are highlighted for visibility.

SEE INSETS for detail on districts near Austin, Dallas, and Houston.

Miles
0 20 40

The Almanac of American Politics.
National Journal

Congressional district boundaries were effective for 2012 on an interim basis.

Texas hasn't elected a Democrat to statewide office in more than a quarter century, and it hasn't voted for a Democratic presidential candidate since Jimmy Carter. But after years of watching the state's demographics slowly shift in their direction, the Democrats are finally on an upswing in the Lone Star State. Over the past three presidential elections, the Republican nominee has won the state by diminishing margins—16 points in 2012, then 9 points in 2016, and finally 5.6 points in 2020. Joe Biden won 10 of the state's 13 most populous counties in 2020, up from seven when President Barack Obama won a second term in 2012, and Biden made substantial gains in the remaining three counties that President Donald Trump managed to win. Still, Democrats haven't yet pulled off "Blue Texas," particularly down the ballot.

David Oshinsky, a former University of Texas historian, has written of Texas that "no state can match its swagger or eccentricities; no state generates more loyalty within its borders, or more controversy beyond." At its origin, Texas was an independent republic, freed from Mexico before it agreed to annexation by the United States in 1845. Today it is a nation-state, almost 29 million strong, larger in area than any of the 28 nations of the European Union and more populous than all but five. Texas has been the second-largest state in area since Alaska was admitted to the Union in 1959, and it became the second largest in population in 1994, when it surpassed New York. Texas was founded by Southerners, particularly Tennesseans, who were invited to establish their own enclave within the borders of Mexico, then dreamed of a republic with Anglo-Saxon freedoms and African-American slavery. They defended their dream to the death at the Alamo and to a bloody victory at San Jacinto. They entered the Union willingly in 1845 and left it enthusiastically in 1861.

The Texas that emerged from the Civil War was still young and poor. It began as a marshland on the border of the Third World, with an economy based on commodities, mainly cotton, when cotton prices were in long-term decline. Its farmers felt as if they were part of a colonial economy controlled by bankers and Wall Street financiers. But in 1901, oil was discovered in Beaumont, near the Gulf Coast, at a well that would be named Spindle top. "It was the greatest oil discovery in history," Texas journalist Lawrence Wright has written. "For the next nine days, until the well was capped, the gusher spurted into the air a hundred thousand barrels of oil a day—an output that exceeded the production of all the other wells in America combined." To develop Spindletop, two future oil giants were established, Gulf Oil and Texaco.

Without the underpinnings and burdens of tradition, 20th century Texas produced fabulous wealth, generously rewarding success while being unforgiving of failure. It has respect for learning and style—think of its great universities and Neiman Marcus—and it revels in rough manners and Western wear. Texans are prone to wild swings in fortune—think of Sam Houston and Lyndon B. Johnson, the Yankee wildcatter George H.W. Bush and his son George W. In the 21st century. Texans, despite their history of slavery and segregation, have proved open to immigrants and have generally been friendly with their Mexican neighbors. The North American Free Trade Agreement and the coming together of these two countries that are at such different economic levels and have such different cultures, was a project mainly of Texans of both political parties—of the two Republican presidents named Bush and two top Democrats, Treasury Secretary Lloyd Bentsen and Gov. Ann Richards. At the same time, Texas has become a high-technology powerhouse with some of the nation's most creative businesses. But its success is not just economic. There are elements of heroism —some mythical, some genuine—in the Texas history that every public school student is taught.

Texas became the nation's—and for a time the world's—leading producer of oil. But oil prices were subject to declines, and producers were propped up by politicians. These politicians also secured subsidies for cotton growers and contracts for defense plants and space facilities during World War II and through the Cold War. Most Texas voters supported Democrats up to 1970 because of Confederate memories, New Deal affections, and the clout and competence of Texas Democratic officeholders. By the 1970s, Texas was no longer dependent on raw commodities. The "awl bidness" here became less a matter of extracting oil than it was playing host to the world's greatest concentration of highly skilled specialists in extracting oil and natural gas. Also beginning in the 1960s, Texas became a center for technology with the critical mass of knowledge and finances needed to produce firms like Texas Instruments and Dell Computer and an academic infrastructure in the University of Texas and Texas A&M. There are 50 Fortune 500 companies with Texas headquarters, slightly behind New York and California; Texas A&M educated four of the Fortune 500 CEOs, ranking first for any university.

Map for Austin and San Antonio

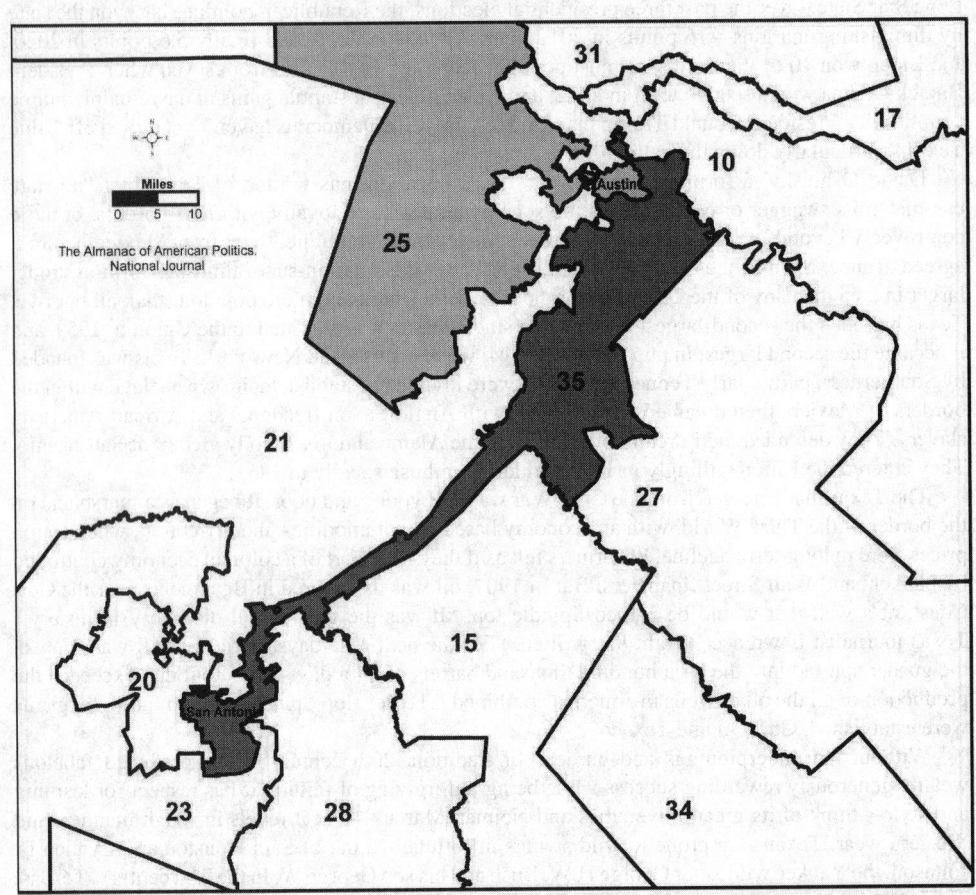

Congressional district boundaries were effective for 2012 on an interim basis.   Districts 25 and 35 are highlighted for visibility.

Today, oil extraction remains important in the state—revered, and still protected by politicians. Texas accounts for 45 percent of the nation's crude oil production, and recent discoveries in the Permian Basin of West Texas—the Alpine High and the Wolf camp shale—have boosted the state's recoverable oil and gas reserves. The state has played host to key developments in horizontal drilling and hydraulic fracturing, or "fracking," and those developments have further boosted the state's footprint in resource extraction. (In the meantime, Texas has assembled the nation's No. 1 capacity in wind power.) The fracking boom has taken a toll on roads—every well requires some 1,200 truck deliveries—and possibly on air quality. While it has produced jobs, mechanization has reduced the number. Meanwhile, Texas ranks sixth per capita among the states in energy consumption, due in part to the needs of oil and gas drillers, combined with heavy air-conditioning loads. In 2020, the fossil fuel industry, already hobbled by an international oil glut, suffered from a pandemic-driven decline in global demand. This stressed Permian Basin operators, whose expansion had been supported by substantial debt.

The recent oil slump has not hurt Texas' economy as severely as the 1980s oil bust, which helped tank the real estate and banking sectors. A big reason is diversification. The Dallas-Fort Worth Metroplex is rich with defense contractors and small firms that grew large through exports to Mexico; the suburb of Plano is now home to a 2-million-square-foot U.S. headquarters for Toyota, and the company is expanding its existing facility near San Antonio where Tacomas and Tundras are built. Austin has become a major tech hub, with attracting the headquarters of Oracle and the venture capital firm of Palantir co-founder Joe Lonsdale. Elon Musk has established a Cybertruck factory and his Boring Company in the Austin area, while his SpaceX also has built out a major presence outside Brownsville, near the border with Mexico. In 2020, Hewlett Packard Enterprise announced it would be moving its headquarters from Silicon Valley to Houston, a city that already had a large HP footprint from the company's 2001 acquisition of Compaq. Houston, the nation's leading city for exports, is home to firms like Schlumberger, the global oil services company, and high-tech spinoffs from the enormous Texas Medical Center and from the space program. Houston also has one of the nation's busiest ports; officials are now trying to widen and deepen the Houston Ship Channel so it can handle two-directional traffic, in an estimated $1 billion effort that would be completed in the 2030s. San Antonio, with the Air Force's prime hospital, has significant medical technology and biotech industries, as well as a growing cybersecurity sector.

Map for Dallas-Fort Worth

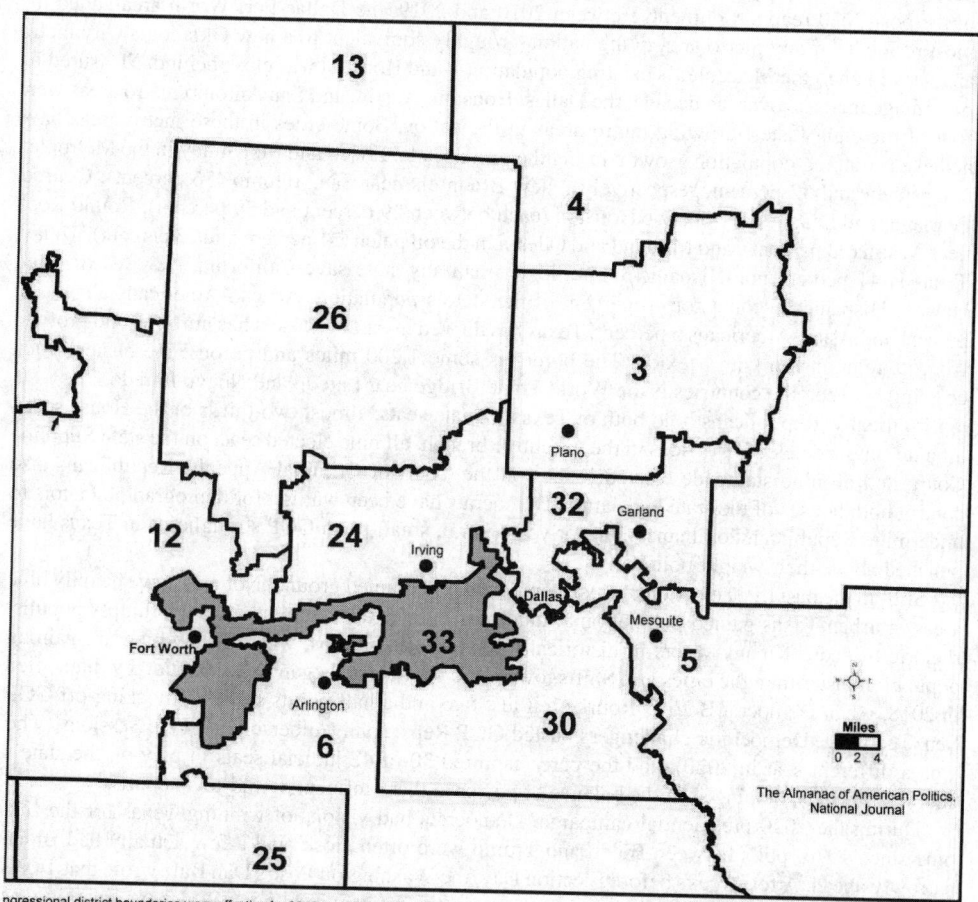

ngressional district boundaries were effective for 2012 on an interim basis.

District 33 is highlighted for visibility.

Texas has developed a civic culture of adaptability and resilience, as it demonstrated by taking in thousands of Hurricane Katrina evacuees in 2005. In 2017, after slow-moving Hurricane Harvey dumped as much as 52 inches of rain on the Houston area, the region and its industries recovered from massive damage more quickly than expected. Yet by some indicators, the state is underperforming. As its leading public colleges prosper, Texas has the nation's second-lowest percentage of residents who graduated from high school. It's in the top quarter of states for child poverty rate, and the state's imprisonment rate ranks fifth in the nation. Texas also faces health care challenges. Its 18.4 percent uninsured rate is easily the highest in the nation, and lawmakers have been resistant to expanding Medicaid under the Affordable Care Act. In all, 159 of the state's 254 counties have no general surgeons, 121 have no medical specialists, and 35 have no doctors at all, according to The Washington

Post. Texas' approach to the coronavirus, like that of many Republican-governed states, prioritized reopening the economy, though more urban (and predominantly Democratic) areas applied tighter public health restrictions. At one point, Lt. Gov. Dan Patrick baffled seniors when he said, in defense of reopenings, that "there are more important things than living, and that's saving this country for my children and my grandchildren and saving this country for all of us." Such ideas "represent the stubborn if expediently applied strain of anti-government independence that is inherent in the Texas character," wrote Mimi Swartz of the Texas Monthly. Despite several surges in infections during the pandemic, Texas' case rate was roughly at the national average by March 2021, besting many states that had kept tight restrictions in place.

Newcomers—think of the Bushes—have done much to put the stamp of Texas on the whole of the United States. The state's population grew from 21 million in 2000 to 25 million in 2010, a 21 percent increase, and by an additional 16 percent since 2010, enough to gain the state additional seats in the post-2020 reapportionment. Between 2010 and 2019, the Dallas-Fort Worth area added the most residents of any metro area in the nation—roughly equivalent to a new Oklahoma City metro area tacked on to the Metroplex's existing population—and Houston was close behind. Measured by percentage increase over the decade, the Dallas, Houston, Austin, and San Antonio metro areas were four of the eight fastest-growing metro areas in the nation. Some cities in these metro areas have achieved stunning population growth during the past decade: Frisco and McKinney in the Metroplex (71 percent and 52 percent, respectively); New Braunfels near San Antonio (56 percent); Conroe, Pearland, and League City outside Houston (each between 29 percent and 39 percent); Round Rock near Austin (33 percent); and Midland and Odessa in the oil patch (31 percent and 23 percent). Today, Texas is 41 percent non-Hispanic White, lower than any state save California, New Mexico and Hawaii. Hispanics account for 40 percent of the state's population, African-Americans almost 12 percent and Asian-Americans 5 percent. Texas has thrived in part because it has nurtured and profited from its relationship with Mexico. The border is some 1,200 miles and porous; the busiest truck crossing between the countries is the World Trade Bridge near Laredo and Nuevo Laredo.

Politically, Republicans hold both of Texas' Senate seats, almost two-thirds of the House seats, all nine statewide elective offices in the executive branch, all nine elected seats on the state Supreme Court, and all nine statewide elected judges on the Court of Criminal Appeals. Republicans also control both houses of the state legislature. Democrats have been waiting for demographic factors to undermine Republican dominance, but for years, rural, small-town GOP strongholds in Texas have punched above their weight politically.

Still, in the past three election cycles, Democrats have gained ground. Not only have heavily blue areas in urban Texas gained population at much faster rates than rural areas, but Trump's populist rhetoric turned off many voters in historically Republican suburbs, which if anything are gaining population faster than the cities are. Shifts toward the Democrats began in 2016, but they intensified in 2018, when Democrat Beto O'Rourke fell just two and a half points short of knocking off GOP Sen. Ted Cruz, Democratic challengers ousted GOP Reps. John Culberson and Pete Sessions (who won a different seat in 2020), and the party captured 30 of 42 judicial seats in play on the state's courts of appeals, helping shift the balance of power in these influential mid-level courts.

During the 2020 presidential campaign, Democrats had visions of winning Texas for the first time since 1976; polls between Biden and Trump were often close, and a few actually had Biden narrowly ahead. A few weeks before Election Day, the Washington Post's Dan Balz wrote that Texas "might just be the most politically intriguing state in the country right now. Whichever way it goes in November, there's no question that President Trump is a problem for Republicans in the Lone Star State." Democrats also worked to put down-ballot races in play. Democrats targeted at least 10 GOP-held House seats, most of which, as the Austin American-Statesman noted, had a higher median income than the state as a whole and a higher percentage of residents with at least a college degree than the statewide average. Democrats also worked to flip the state House in advance of the 2021 round of redistricting; on the eve of the election, the Cook Political Report moved the chamber to toss-up.

Ultimately, Trump won the state again, but his margin shrank from nine points in 2016 to about five and a half points in 2020. In addition to holding Fort Bend County near Houston, which Clinton had flipped in 2016, Biden achieved some flips of his own by making double-digit gains in Tarrant

County (Fort Worth) and Williamson and Hays counties in the Austin suburbs. Biden also narrowed Trump's winning margin to single digits in Denton and Collin counties near Dallas-Fort Worth; only eight years earlier, both counties had handed Republican Mitt Romney winning margins of more than 30 points. Trump posted some gains, notably in the heavily Hispanic Rio Grande Valley, which is not only ancestrally Democratic but which as recently as four years earlier had given Clinton comfortable victories. Trump flipped six counties, shifting the margin in the GOP direction by as much as 38 points. Analysts noted that not only did Latino voters elsewhere respond favorably to Trump, but that voters in the Rio Grande Valley, who consider themselves "Tejanos," are predominantly blue-collar, socially conservative, and have an economy that's dependent on oil and gas, all factors that generally align with support for Trump.

Map for Greater Houston

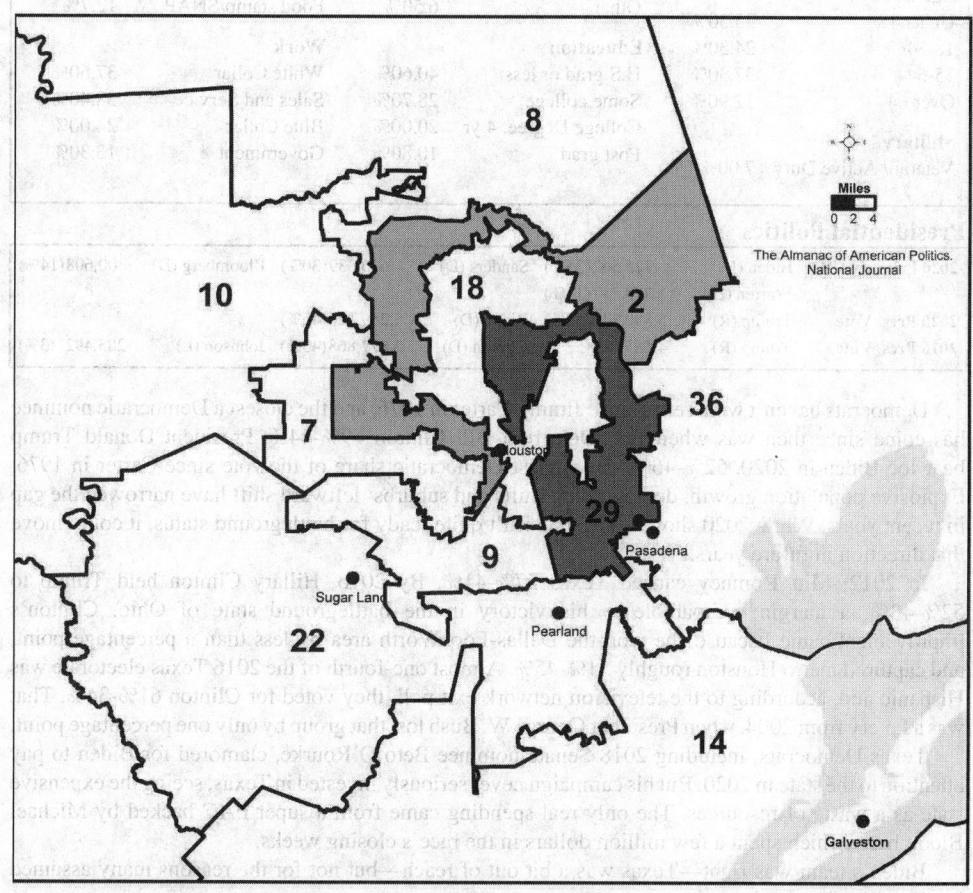

Congressional district boundaries were effective for 2012 on an interim basis.   Districts 2 and 29 are highlighted for visibility.

But if this amounted to a trade of suburban voters for rural voters, the Democrats have reason for optimism. Urban Latino voters did not show the same degree of support for Trump, and the six counties Trump flipped were so small that the president gained only 6,000 votes collectively in them, plus another 80,000 votes in four nearby counties where Biden won with diminished margins: Cameron, Hidalgo, Starr, and Webb. By contrast, in 12 populous counties—Harris (Houston), Dallas, Travis (Austin), Bexar (San Antonio), El Paso, Fort Bend, Tarrant, Williamson, Hays, Denton, Collin, and Montgomery (Houston suburbs) —Biden increased the number of Democratic votes by more than 1 million. This accounted for about 75 percent of his statewide increase, enough to wipe out Trump's gains in the Rio Grande Valley many times over. However, Republicans took solace that Democrats were unable to flip a single GOP-held congressional district in 2020, and that the Republican majority in the state House held firm.

In February 2021, an unusually harsh winter storm cut power and water for millions of Texans for days, killing dozens and causing billions of dollars in damage. Whether these failures will boomerang against the GOP, which has been exclusively in charge of Texas' energy policy for roughly two decades, remains to be seen.

Population		Race and Ethnicity		Income	
Total	28,995,881	White	73.40%	Median Income	64,034
Land area (sq. miles)	261,232	Black	12.30%	State Income Rank	22 out of 50
Pop/ sq mi	111.00	Latino	39.70%	Poverty Rate	13.60%
Born in state	59.50%	Asian	5.80%	With health insurance	81.60%
		Two or more races	2.90%	Cash public assistance	1.40%
Age Groups		Other	6.50%	Food stamp/SNAP	12.7%
Under 18	25.50%				
18-34	24.30%	Education		Work	
35-64	37.30%	H.S grad or less	40.60%	White Collar	37.60%
Over 64	12.90%	Some college	28.70%	Sales and Service	38.40%
		College Degree, 4 yr	20.00%	Blue Collar	24.00%
Military		Post grad	10.80%	Government	13.30%
Veteran/ Active Duty	7.00%				

Presidential Politics

2020 Primary (D)	Biden (D)	725,562(35%)	Sanders (D)	626,339(30%)	Bloomberg (D)	300,608(14%)
	Warren (D)	239,237(11%)				
2020 Pres. Vote	Trump (R)	5,890,347(52%)	Biden (D)	5,259,126(46%)		
2016 Pres. Vote	Trump (R)	4,685,047(52%)	Clinton (D)	3,877,868(43%)	Johnson (L)	283,492 (3%)

Democrats haven't won Texas since Jimmy Carter in 1976, and the closest a Democratic nominee has come since then was when Bob Dole beat Bill Clinton 49%-44%. President Donald Trump beat Joe Biden in 2020, 52%-46%, the highest Democratic share of the vote since Carter in 1976. Explosive population growth, demographic shifts and suburbs' leftward shift have narrowed the gap in recent years. While 2020 showed the state isn't quite ready for battleground status, it could move that direction in future years.

In 2012, Mitt Romney carried Texas 57%-41%. By 2016, Hillary Clinton held Trump to 52%-43%, a margin comparable to his victory in the battleground state of Ohio. Clinton's improvement came because she won the Dallas-Fort Worth area by less than a percentage point, and captured metro Houston roughly 51%-45%. Almost one-fourth of the 2016 Texas electorate was Hispanic and, according to the television network exit poll, they voted for Clinton 61%-34%. That was a far cry from 2004, when President George W. Bush lost that group by only one percentage point.

Texas Democrats, including 2018 Senate nominee Beto O'Rourke, clamored for Biden to pay attention to the state in 2020. But his campaign never seriously invested in Texas, seeing the expensive state as a waste of resources. The only real spending came from a super PAC backed by Michael Bloomberg, which spent a few million dollars in the race's closing weeks.

Biden's team was right—Texas was a bit out of reach—but not for the reasons many assumed heading into the election.

Biden flipped Williamson and Hays counties in suburban Austin and Tarrant County (Fort Worth), and posted double-digit improvements over Clinton in four counties around the Dallas-Fort Worth metroplex in North Texas. In Texas' five most populous counties—Bexar (San Antonio), Harris (Houston), Dallas, Tarrant and Travis (Austin), Biden won 2.8 million votes, up from Clinton's 2.1 million, and he netted a quarter-million more votes. Biden's vote total of almost 5.3 million statewide far outpaced Clinton's 3.9 million votes in 2016—and Trump's 4.7 million votes in 2016. But Trump's 2020 total was 5.9 million votes.

The Rio Grande Valley along the U.S.-Mexico border saved Trump from a closer call. The heavily Tejano, mostly poor, rural and culturally conservative region has long been one of the Democratic Party's best regions in the state. But it showed Trump's biggest improvement of anywhere in the country besides Miami-Dade County in Florida. He flipped six South Texas counties, and improved by 20-point margins in 18 counties, most along the Rio Grande River. That included a 55-point swing in Starr County and a 40-point swing in tiny Kenedy County in the valley, and a 46-point swing in Maverick County further west.

Biden won the Texas Hispanic vote 58%-41%, according to exit polls, weaker than Clinton four years earlier.

Texas has been sporadically important in both parties' primary contests. The 2016 Republican primary came at a critical phase. Texas Sen. Ted Cruz campaigned hard in his home state, knowing that if he lost it he was out. Cruz defeated Trump, 44%-27%, but disappointing results for him in other states put Trump in the driver's seat to the nomination. On the Democratic side, Clinton swamped Vermont Sen. Bernie Sanders, 65%-33%.

Sanders campaigned hard there in 2020, part of his heavy focus on winning Hispanic voters, and was banking on a win on Super Tuesday. But Joe Biden's nationwide momentum helped him to a 35%-30% win, one of the biggest blows to Sanders on a night that anointed Biden the heavy frontrunner.

Congressional Districts

117th Congress Lineup	13D 22R 1V	116th Congress Lineup	13D 23R

Texas redistricting, once the plain prerogative of Anglo Democrats, involves a complex set of partisan, racial and legal dynamics. In the 2000 census, Texas gained two seats, and in 2010, another four. The latest reapportionment again yielded two seats to Texas. In 2001, after a split legislature failed to agree on a map, a federal court drew a plan protecting 17 Democratic incumbents and adding two new Republican seats, for a 17-15 breakdown. In 2012, the four seats—in effect—were split between the two parties. Since then, the Republicans' grip on state politics has coincided with a Hispanic population boom and—more recently—the Democratic resurgence in large suburban areas across the state. The result: Texas has endured what seems like a never-ending legislative and legal rollercoaster ride. There is every reason to believe that will continue with the redistricting scheduled for 2022.

The 2018 election results introduced important new dynamics: Democrats took two Republican-held seats in the Dallas and Houston suburbs, plus Latina Democrats replaced Anglo Democrats in Houston and El Paso, giving Republicans 23-13 control of the delegation. Strong Democratic performances left them with several other opportunities. But, unexpectedly, Republicans managed to hold all their seats in 2020—even with the retirement of seven GOP House incumbents and the tighter presidential election.

The history of this disruption began in 2002, when Republicans took over the legislature and House Majority Leader Tom DeLay pressured his party to replace a court-drawn plan for 2002 with a design to maximize Republican seats in 2004. Months later, 51 Texas House Democrats, who became known as the "Killer D's," fled to Oklahoma to thwart a two-thirds quorum. But Republicans eventually rammed through their map, converting a 15-17 deficit that wildly underrepresented GOP strength into a 21-11 edge in 2004 by defeating five "WD-40s"—white Democrats over age 40—whom DeLay had targeted for extinction. In 2010, Republicans captured 23 of 32 seats, and it was Democrats rather than Republicans who were underrepresented.

In the initial skirmishing for 2012, Gov. Rick Perry and Republican legislators in Austin were horrified by the idea of "giving" Democrats any seats. In June, they passed their own plan to split the Dallas-Fort Worth Metroplex's Hispanic population six ways, stuff Austin Democrat Lloyd Doggett into a heavily Hispanic seat stretching to San Antonio, and create three new safely Republican enclaves: one in Fort Worth's western suburbs, another in Houston's eastern suburbs, and a third running along the I-35 corridor from the fringes of the Metroplex to the outskirts of Austin. The plan created one new Democratic seat in the Rio Grande Valley.

Doggett and the Democrats immediately blasted the "Perry-mander" as a gross overreach. Hispanic advocacy groups denounced it as discriminatory and sued in a San Antonio federal court. The Justice Department declared the map had been drawn with discriminatory intent and assumed the opposition. Attorney General Greg Abbott, in an end-around attempt, sought preclearance from a three-judge panel at the U.S. Court of Appeals in Washington. The San Antonio panel halted the map's implementation and announced its intent to draw its own interim plan if the state map did not obtain federal preclearance before the December 2011 opening of the candidate filing period.

The San Antonio judges delighted Democrats with their own plan: Not only did it preserve Doggett's existing Austin-based 25th District, it essentially drew three of four new seats for Democrats—one minority "coalition" seat in Fort Worth, and one Hispanic majority seat each in the Rio Grande Valley and San Antonio areas. But the Supreme Court ruled that the San Antonio court had "exceeded its mission" to fix only the districts that had violated the Voting Rights Act and faulted the court for failing to use an elected legislature's original plan as a baseline for its own. So in February, the San Antonio court issued a second interim map. This time, it resembled the Republicans' plan, except it created a new 66 percent Hispanic seat linking Dallas and Fort Worth and restored Hispanic voting strength in the San Antonio-based 23rd District. The result was nearly identical to what Republican incumbents had lobbied for in the first place: a 2-2 division of new seats. Democrats picked up the 23rd in November, for 12 of 36 seats overall; Republicans regained that seat two years later.

Following further legal maneuvering, the San Antonio panel ruled in August 2017 that Doggett's 35th District, plus the Republican-held 27th district in Corpus Christi were discriminatory violations of the Constitution and the Voting Rights Act. But the judges failed to offer an alternative. In September 2017, the Supreme Court blocked immediate changes. In June 2018, in a 5-4 ruling that was a legal victory for Republicans, the high court found that alleged discrimination by the state was not intentional. As it turned out, Democrats turned the map to their favor in the November 2018 election, as the broader demographic and political shifts in the suburbs gave them a two-seat gain— their first pick-up of House seats in Texas since 2012.

In the political and legal thickets that are certain to accompany the 2022 redistricting, Republicans might agree to concede the two seats they lost in 2018, while they seek a new seat in the Rio Grande Valley. Democrats likely will make competitive challenges for the several seats where they have narrowly fallen short. Regardless, Republicans will use their initial control in Austin to reinforce control of their newly vulnerable seats and they likely will use the state's two additional seats following reapportionment to gain new ground in 2022—perhaps in the rapidly growing exurban areas.

For Democrats, the total of their prospective gains will be accompanied by the demographic implications. Of their four freshmen following the 2018 election, they included two Latinas (in Democratic seats that previously were held by Anglo men), a white woman and an African-American man. Of the six Republican newcomers to the delegation in 2019, all were white men; of the seven GOP newcomers in 2021, five were White men, one was Latino and one a White woman. Overall, when Congress convened in January 2021, 20 of the 23 Republicans are white men.

Of the 36 seats, Hispanics hold 7 (6 Democrats and 1 Republican) in a state where they are 39 percent of the population. Of the Democrats, four are in districts along the border with Mexico, and one each is in Houston and San Antonio. Freshman Tony Gonzalez, the sole GOP Latino, holds a San Antonio-based seat. Blacks, with 12 percent of the population, hold five House seats—three in the Metroplex and two in Houston. All of the African-Americans are Democrats: four of them have held a seat since at least 2012 that is minority-majority population, and the fifth—Colin Allred—took a - white plurality seat in 2018. The two white Democrats hold seats that are minority-majority.

The return to Democratic control of the House in 2019 left only one Texan—Eddie Bernice Johnson—chairing a committee. Under Republican control of the House in 2018, the Texas delegation included seven committee chairs and three Appropriations subcommittee chairs. Of those 10 Republicans, four retired and two have lost reelection bids since 2018, though Pete Sessions won a different seat in 2020. The prospect of additional turnover among Republicans and the longer-term increase of Hispanic influence, especially among Democrats, promise continuing turmoil in the Texas delegation.

Greg Abbott (R)

Elected 2014, term expires 2023, 2nd term; b. Nov. 13, 1957, Wichita Falls; U. of TX, B.B.A. 1981; Vanderbilt U., J.D. 1984; Catholic; Married (Cecilia); 1 child.

Elected Office: TX State Trial Judge 129th District Court, 1992-1995; TX Supreme Court, 1995-2001; TX Attorney General, 2002-2014.

Professional Career: Practicing attorney, Butler & Binion, 1984-1992.

Office: PO Box 12428 Austin, 78711-2428; 512-463-2000; Fax: 512-463-5571

Lt. Gov.: Dan Patrick (R) **Atty. Gen:** Ken Paxton (R)

State Legislature: Senate: 12D, 19R **House:** 67D, 83R

Election Results

Election	Name (Party)	Vote (%)
2018 General	Greg Abbott (R)	4,656,196 (56%)
	Lupe Valdez (D)	3,546,615 (43%)
2018 Primary	Greg Abbott (R)	1,389,562 (90%)
	Barbara Krueger (R)	127,134 (8%)

Prior winning percentage: 2014 (59%)

Republican Greg Abbott has twice been elected governor of Texas, following 12 years as state attorney general. In both positions he's amassed a solidly conservative record; he once described his job as attorney general as, "I go into the office in the morning, I sue Barack Obama, and then I go home." But after years of economic gains and population growth in Texas, Abbott faced major challenges from the coronavirus pandemic in 2020 and from a winter storm in 2021 that shut down power and water for millions of residents. These ordeals put Abbott's governance in the political crossfire from both parties.

Abbott was born in Wichita Falls and raised in Duncanville in Dallas County. He earned a bachelor's degree in finance from the University of Texas at Austin and got his law degree from Vanderbilt University in Nashville Tennessee. In 1984, the year he finished law school, a falling tree injured Abbott while he was out for a run. The incident left him a paraplegic, and he has used a wheelchair ever since. After a stint in private practice, Abbott became an associate justice on the Texas Supreme Court in 1995, appointed to fill a vacancy by then-Gov. George W. Bush. Abbott won election twice more to the state's highest civil court, and in 2001 he resigned to run for attorney general in 2002. Abbott won reelection twice and became the longest-serving state attorney general in Texas history. He sued the federal government more than two dozen times, on issues ranging from the Affordable Care Act to abortion, voter ID and environmental regulations. In 2005, Abbott argued before the U.S. Supreme Court on the constitutionality of the Ten Commandments monument on the Texas State Capitol grounds. The high court ruled 5-4 in his favor.

Less than a week after Gov. Rick Perry announced he would not seek another term, Abbott declared his candidacy for the job. He faced only token opposition in the GOP primary; in the general, he squared off against state Sen. Wendy Davis, whom supporters hoped would benefit from the national attention she got from her unsuccessful filibuster of a bill to ban most abortions after the 20th week of pregnancy. Davis tapped Hispanic state Sen. Leticia Van de Putte as her running mate. Abbott was joined at the top of the GOP ticket by state Sen. Dan Patrick, the nominee for lieutenant governor, and state Sen. Ken Paxton, the nominee for attorney general; both were tea party favorites who had prevailed over establishment favorites in contentious primaries and runoffs. Davis sought to portray Abbott as an Austin "insider" siding with the interests of his rich and powerful friends at the expense of "hard-working Texans." Abbott saturated the airwaves with spots that reminded voters how, despite using a wheelchair, he had persevered and succeeded in life. His ads portrayed

Davis as closely aligned with Obama, who was not popular in the Lone Star State, and he featured his Hispanic mother-in-law in TV ads and on billboards to appeal to Hispanic voters. Abbott ended up winning, 59%-39%; exit polls showed he won roughly 44 percent of the Hispanic vote.

In 2015, Abbott signed legislation to provide $130 million in funding to school districts whose pre-kindergarten programs met certain standards, including having certified teachers and using a state-approved curriculum. The measure won bipartisan approval in the legislature. He also signed legislation that expedited hiring of law-enforcement officers on the border, increased penalties for human trafficking, and established a center to analyze border-crime data. Abbott got a further boost when a federal judge in Brownsville blocked Obama's executive order on immigration, which he had personally fought in court as attorney general. After Donald Trump won the presidency, Abbott praised his efforts to build a border wall and to expand federal spending on border security, and Abbott signed a measure to cut state funding for sanctuary cities.

Under pressure from GOP majorities in the legislature, Abbott also took up social issues, including a "bathroom bill" that would require transgender individuals to use the bathroom of their birth sex. Abbott ranged from neutral to supportive of a more moderate version, though in the end, the bill failed to pass in a special session. Abbott and the legislature did agree on a measure requiring women who wanted abortion coverage to buy it in a separate insurance policy. The legislature considered a "red-flag law" that would let judges temporarily take firearms from a person deemed to be an imminent threat; Abbott indicated that he was open to the idea, but amid opposition from gun-rights advocates citing due process concerns, the measure floundered.

Abbott was always considered a strong favorite to win a second term. In a runoff for the Democratic nomination, Dallas County Sheriff Lupe Valdez, a child of migrant workers who had previously served as a captain in the Army and as a U.S. Customs and Border Protection agent, defeated businessman Andrew White, son of the late Democratic Gov. Mark White, 53%-47%. In the general election, Abbott far outraised Valdez, and used his money to tout his conservative stances on immigration policy and his efforts to fund pre-kindergarten. Valdez attacked Abbott for not calling a special session to generate recovery funds for Hurricane Harvey. In the end, Abbott won, 56%-43%, about three points below his percentage in 2014, though still not enough to produce a genuinely competitive race. Indeed, Abbott fared about five points better than GOP Sen. Ted Cruz in his Senate race against Democrat Beto O'Rourke.

In 2019, Abbott signed a bill allocating $6.5 billion in additional funding for public schools—including raises for teachers and full-day pre-K for eligible four-year-olds—as well as another bill devoting $5.1 billion for lowering property tax bills. He also responded to a mass shooting at Santa Fe High School that killed 10 and wounded 13 by signing bipartisan legislation to increase mental health services for children and to fund security measures at schools. In 2020, he told the federal government that Texas would no longer accept refugees.

During the coronavirus pandemic, Abbott appeared torn between following the urgings of public health experts and members of his own party's base. Abbott delayed imposition of a stay-at-home order (and when he relented, he insisted that it not be referred to as a stay-at-home order); he lifted the order after only about a month. His early lifting of restrictions was followed by a surge of cases, and Abbott eventually moved to tighten limits on restaurants and outdoor gatherings and to allow local authorities—mostly Democrats with whom he had sparred on public health matters—to go further than his orders. Abbott expressed regret in a radio interview for reopening too quickly, saying, "If I could go back and redo anything, it probably would have been to slow down the opening of bars, now seeing in the aftermath of how quickly the coronavirus spread in the bar setting." However, such moves, plus a statewide mask order, alienated Abbott from his party's base, and various local and county Republican organizations censured him in protest. Then, at the state GOP convention, an insurgent slate led by outspoken former Florida Rep. Allen West easily won control of the party apparatus. Abbott kept the mask order and capacity restrictions in place until March 2021, when he said, "It is now time to open Texas 100 percent. … People and businesses don't need the state telling them how to operate" any longer. In June, West resigned as state GOP chairman and said that he was considering a challenge to Abbott.

The other crisis, the winter storm, struck in February 2021. Amid record-breaking cold and massive utility failures, millions of Texas homes lost power, some for days at a time; water systems were down even longer and affected an even larger share of the population. Public frustration was intense. On Fox News, Abbott blamed the outages on the unreliability of wind power and said it illustrated the dangers of the Green New Deal, the Democrats' climate change plan; Democrats blamed what they called lax regulation that had allowed conventional utilities to skimp on winterization, exacerbated by the state's decision to maintain its own power grid separate from the rest of the nation. Days into the crisis, Abbott acknowledged that "many of you are angry—and you have a right to be. I'm angry, too. At a time when essential services were needed the most, the system broke. You deserve answers. You will get those answers." He said he would push for an overhaul of the state's grid authority, the Electric Reliability Council of Texas, or ERCOT. But it was unclear how much such a wide-scale winterization program would cost, and question of reversing utility price spikes for ratepayers during the crisis turned into another political football.

Abbott is widely expected to run for another term in 2022, but his reelection bid could be more challenging than his earlier campaigns. The winter storm put decades of unitary Republican governance in the spotlight, and even before that Texas Democrats had been making strides due to demographic shifts and a backlash by independents and moderate Republicans against a Trump-aligned GOP. Once bereft of a bench, Democrats now have such potential contenders as O'Rourke, former cabinet member Julián Castro, Reps. Veronica Escobar and Joaquin Castro, Dallas Mayor Eric Johnson, Harris County Judge Lina Hidalgo, and Dallas County Judge Clay Jenkins. Meanwhile, Abbott's stock has fallen within the GOP, making it possible that he could face a primary, though he'd remain the favorite.

John Cornyn (R)

Elected 2002, term expires 2026, 4th term, b. Feb 02, 1952; Houston, TX; Trinity University, B.A., 1973; St. Mary's School of Law, J.D., 1977; University of Virginia, L.L.M., 1995; Church of Christ; Married (Sandra Hansen Cornyn); 2 children.

Elected Office: Judge, TX 37th Judicial District Court, 1985-1991; Associate Justice, TX Supreme Court, 1991-1997; TX Attorney General, 1999-2002; Minority Whip, U.S. Senate, 2012-2015; Majority Whip, U.S. Senate, 2015-2019.

Professional Career: Practicing attorney, 1977-1984.

DC Office: 517 HSOB 20510, 202-224-2934, Fax: 202-228-2856, cornyn.senate.gov

State Offices: Austin, 512-469-6034; Dallas, 972-239-1310; Harlingen, 956-423-0162; Houston, 713-572-3337; Lubbock, 806-472-7533; San Antonio, 210-224-7485; Tyler, 903-593-0902.

Committees: *Finance*: Energy, Natural Resources & Infrastructure; International Trade, Customs & Global Competitiveness (RMM); Taxation & IRS Oversight. *Intelligence*. *Judiciary*: Constitution; Criminal Justice & Counterterrorism; Immigration, Citizenship & Border Security (RMM); Subcommittee on Intellectual Property.

Group Ratings

	ADA	ACLU	AFL-CIO	LCV	COC	HAFA	ACU	CFG	FRC
2020	-	0%	-	8%	-	74%	88%	-	-
2019	0%	C	16%	7%	84%	C	88%	49%	100%

Almanac Ratings 2019-2020

	Economy	Social	Foreign	Composite
Liberal	0%	0%	0%	0%
Conservative	100%	100%	100%	100%

Key Votes of the 116th Congress

1. EPA clean energy rules N	5. Russia sanctions N	9. Barr as Atty. General Y
2. U.S./Mex./Can. trade deal Y	6. Troops in SYR, AFG Y	10. Spending at the border Y
3. Cut unemployment benefits Y	7. Veto arms sales to Saudis N	11. Coney Barrett to Sup. Ct. Y
4. Shelton to Fed Reserve Y	8. Defense $$$, veto override Y	12. Electoral College objections N

Election Results

Election	Name (Party)	Vote (%)	Cand. Spent	Ind. Exp. Support	Ind. Exp. Oppose
2020 General	John Cornyn (R)................................ 5,962,983	(54%)	$33,523,577	$6,111,388	$15,396,338
	MJ Hegar (D).................................. 4,888,764	(44%)	$31,306,197	$11,350,233	$8,044,018
2020 Primary	John Cornyn (R)................................ 1,470,669	(76%)			
	Dwayne Stovall (R)............................ 231,104	(12%)			
	Mark Yancey (R)................................ 124,864	(6%)			

Prior winning percentages: 2014 (62%), 2008 (55%), 2002 (55%)

Long overshadowed by a succession of larger-than-life Texas politicos, John Cornyn, Texas' senior senator, has spent the past two decades quietly accumulating so much influence in Washington that he is the most powerful Texan to serve in the Senate since Lyndon Johnson.

First elected in 2002, the Republican rose quickly through his caucus' leadership ranks. After two terms as chairman of the National Republican Senatorial Committee, his GOP colleagues chose him as their minority whip in 2013. Two years later, after the GOP regained control of the Senate, Cornyn became majority whip. In that role, Cornyn was known for using the carrot over the stick and had close relationships with members of his conference. But he had to cede that post in 2019 to Sen. John Thune of South Dakota because of Senate Republicans' term limits for their party leaders.

Cornyn has made little secret of his desire to succeed Mitch McConnell as Republican Leader. But McConnell, 79, holds the one GOP leadership post not subject to term limits, and he has shown no interest in stepping down. "A lot depends on what his decision is going to be," Cornyn told Politico. Even so, Senate Republicans carved out a counselor role for Cornyn, allowing him to attend leadership meetings and offer guidance.

The workload has been bumpy at times. Since 2013, Cornyn has served alongside erstwhile presidential contender Ted Cruz. The two could not take more wildly divergent approaches to the job. Cornyn is a coalition-builder, the central force of Texas' congressional delegation during a crisis; Cruz is the national firebrand. Cornyn is frequently overshadowed by his junior colleague but is the more effective legislator. In early 2018, a shaken Cornyn responded to a massacre at a Sulphur Springs church by pushing enhanced background checks for some firearm sales; later that year, he quarterbacked a sweeping criminal justice reform bill that had widespread bipartisan support.

Cornyn was born in Houston and spent much of his childhood in San Antonio. His father was an oral pathologist in the Air Force and stationed in Japan, where Cornyn attended high school. After his father retired from the service, the family settled in San Antonio. Cornyn graduated from Trinity University and St. Mary's University School of Law, both in San Antonio. He practiced law for five years with a firm that defended physicians and insurance companies in medical malpractice cases. In 1984, he ran for District Court judge in Bexar County and, at 32, upset a strong favorite in the race. In 1990, Cornyn was elected to the state Supreme Court. Five years later, he wrote a 5-4 decision upholding the state's "Robin Hood" school finance system, in which property-wealthy school districts had to send money to property-poor districts.

In 1997, Cornyn resigned from the court to run for attorney general. Facing two better-known opponents, he placed second in the initial round of the primary but won the runoff. In the general election, he faced a grizzled political knife fighter—former Attorney General Jim Mattox, a populist Democrat. Cornyn won 54%-44%, becoming the first Republican attorney general in Texas since Reconstruction. He argued two cases before the U.S. Supreme Court, including the Santa Fe Independent School District's defense of reading the Lord's Prayer at football games. The high court nixed it.

When GOP Sen. Phil Gramm announced he would not seek reelection in 2002, Cornyn ran and had no serious opposition in the primary. Democrats nominated two-term Dallas Mayor Ron Kirk, who was vying to become Texas' first African-American senator. Cornyn ran as a strong supporter of President George W. Bush, a former Texas governor; he called for making Bush's 2001 tax cuts permanent. He supported government vouchers for private school tuition, individual investment accounts as part of Social Security and "colorblind" standards for college and university admissions. Kirk took opposite stands on most issues, but portrayed himself as a moderate Democrat who would support Bush in many instances. Republicans ran ads linking Kirk to then-New York Sen. Hillary Clinton and liberal out-of-state contributors.

Kirk—who later served as U.S. trade representative under President Barack Obama—campaigned with a sense of humor, making fun of his bald pate, but he made some mistakes. Cornyn came out in favor of a bill in the Texas Legislature that would require district attorneys to seek the death penalty for killers of law enforcement officials after the Austin-based district attorney had not done so for the killer of a Travis County sheriff's deputy. Kirk said Cornyn was acting like he was running for district attorney and then apologized to a convention of law enforcement officials a few days later—as Cornyn met with the deputy's widow. Democrats operated on the assumption that Kirk had to win 85 percent of African Americans, 65 percent of Hispanics and 35 percent of whites to win. He achieved the first and probably the second of those goals but failed on the third. Cornyn won 55%-43%.

Cornyn is known as one of the most mannered members of the Senate. "He's quiet by nature and isn't excitable," his friend Jim Lunz, a retired San Antonio businessman, told the New Republic. "So when he does speak, you are more inclined to listen to what he has to say." As Republicans prepared to assume the majority in 2014, South Carolina Sen. Lindsey Graham told NPR in that Cornyn was "the best guy in the [GOP] Conference to bring us together. ... Nobody doubts his conservatism, but he's a very practical, let's-move-the-ball-forward kind of guy." But he has an edge on Twitter that can infuriate Democrats. "One thing I have to sort of keep in mind is you can't take them back once you unleash them," he told the Texas Tribune in 2019.

Cruz and Cornyn come from different sides of the Texas GOP and, for that matter, different eras. Cornyn represents the George W. Bush-style Republicans while Cruz is of the anti-establishment tea party. The two men did not overtly support each other in Cruz's 2012 Senate bid or in Cornyn's 2014 reelection. Cruz's main GOP foil in the Senate was McConnell, and at times that put the two Texans in adversarial positions. In 2015, Cruz accused McConnell of a "flat out lie," a stunning statement in chamber known for its comity. It was Cornyn who responded on the floor in a remark considered blunt by the chamber's genteel standards: "I have listened to the comments of my colleague, the junior senator from Texas, both last week and this week, and I would have to say that he is mistaken." Cornyn did little later in the 2016 campaign to support Cruz when he was in a one-on-one delegate fight with Donald Trump. Cruz also frustrated Cornyn's vote counting as the party whip, most notably in June 2015, when Cruz abruptly pulled his previously stated support on a leadership-backed trade vote, with just a few hours' notice.

Political necessity, however, brought the two men closer together. Sensing a threat to Cruz from Democratic Rep. Beto O'Rourke, Cornyn endorsed him in his 2018 Senate race. Cruz swiftly returned the favor in early 2019 for Cornyn, signaling that a Democratic wave in the state would leave no room for GOP primary fights in 2020.

Cornyn's legislative passion in recent years has been criminal justice reform, a measure he eventually passed in late 2018. The First Step Act was one of the few bipartisan pieces of legislation during the Trump era. Modeling an approach based on Texas prison reforms, the bill allowed low-risk inmates to move to less restrictive confines, allowed for reduced sentences if inmates engaged in programs that would reduce recidivism, scaled back the use of restraints on pregnant prisoners, sought to reduce prison rap and increased preparation for a prisoner's return to society.

Cornyn first worked on immigration reform in 2007 before abandoning the effort. The late Republican John McCain of Arizona accused Cornyn at the time of raising arcane legal issues to scuttle the bill. Cornyn said of the talks, "I didn't so much walk away as got chased away." His amendment to bar undocumented immigrants convicted of identity theft from a legalization processes was defeated, 51-46. From then on, he opposed the larger immigration bill. As a push for reform heated up in 2013 with the bipartisan "Gang of Eight" negotiations, Cornyn remained a skeptic about a comprehensive approach. He said giving undocumented immigrants a path to citizenship remained premature and insisted on focusing on border enforcement. Frank Sharry, founder of the pro-immigration group America's Voice, complained in HuffPost that Cornyn "is famous for posing as a reformer even as he works to derail reform."

In 2009, Cornyn became chairman of the National Republican Senatorial Committee, the campaign arm of the Senate GOP. The assignment came at a tumultuous moment in Republican politics. The emergence of anti-establishment tea party activism and candidates would dog his two terms at the helm of the committee. Democrats had gained 14 Senate seats between the 2006 and 2008 campaign cycles, when their Senate campaign committee was headed by New York Sen. Chuck Schumer, now the majority leader; Cornyn wanted to reverse those results. Cornyn adopted Schumer's strategy of recruiting candidates who could win in states not naturally inclined to his party. It didn't always work out. Cornyn urged Gov. Charlie Crist to run in Florida and Rep. Mike Castle to run in Delaware. In Florida, former state House Speaker Marco Rubio gained steam against Crist, eventually forcing him from the party and then crushing his independent bid. Castle lost in a stunning primary upset to a tea party challenger, Christine O'Donnell, with the Democrats retaining the seat in the fall.

Despite these setbacks, Cornyn succeeded in the chairman's major duty: raising large sums. He brought in $115 million for the cycle and came close to matching the $130 million raised by rival Democrats. Republicans gained six seats, many more than seemed likely in January 2009 but fewer than later expected.

Cornyn earned another term as NRSC chairman for the 2012 election cycle. Irritated by then-South Carolina Republican Sen. Jim DeMint's endorsements of candidates whose chances Cornyn had thought to be dim in 2010, he urged colleagues to bring concerns they had about candidates to him. Cornyn, in turn, made it plain that he would be more wary of taking sides in primaries. The downside was that a pair of far-right Republicans became nominees: Richard Mourdock in Indiana and Todd Akin in Missouri. Both blew what were nearly seen as sure things after they made politically disastrous comments about rape and abortion; in 2018, Republicans captured each seat. When Republican Whip Jon Kyl of Arizona retired at the end of 2012, Cornyn ran for the position. Lamar Alexander of Tennessee said he would run for whip but later dropped out. Richard Burr of North Carolina also considered running but decided against it, giving Cornyn a clear path to the post.

Democrats failed to attract a well-known challenger to Cornyn in in 2008. Their nominee was Houston state Rep. Rick Noriega, an Afghanistan veteran. Cornyn outraised Noriega by more than 4-1 and won 55%-43%, the same margin by which he won in 2002. He captured 36 percent of the Hispanic vote, an improvement over 2002.

After Cruz's surprise 2012 primary win over an establishment Republican, Cornyn's biggest reelection threat in 2014 appeared to be from the right. But Cornyn assiduously courted conservatives in the state, careful not to split with Cruz's hard-line postures on most high-profile votes. His efforts, and huge early fundraising, helped scare off serious primary challengers. Even though Cruz declined to endorse him, Cornyn drew no serious tea party opposition—just an impulsive last-minute challenge from quirky far-right Rep. Steve Stockman. Cornyn finished way ahead of Stockman, 59%-19%. Cornyn's race against Democratic businessman David Alameel was little more than a formality; he won 62%-34%.

In the Senate, Cornyn was close to former Alabama Sen. Jeff Sessions, who—as Trump's first attorney general—asked Cornyn to consider the FBI job after Trump fired Director James Comey in May 2017. Cornyn was interviewed, but a week after Comey's ouster, he took himself out of the running.

Facing reelection in 2020, Cornyn made clear that he would take the race—and its effects on down-ballot contests—seriously. When Rep. Joaquin Castro decided not to run, the Democratic frontrunner was M.J. Hegar, a military veteran who ran a well-financed and unexpectedly close—though unsuccessful—challenge to GOP Rep. John Carter in 2018. Hegar benefitted from a burst of late-stage fundraising after the death of Supreme Court Justice Ruth Bader Ginsburg. Down-ballot Democrats for the U.S. House and state legislative seats threatened Republican incumbents across the state, particularly in the suburbs. Cornyn dispatched Hegar 54%-44%, and Texas Republicans widely credited him with running a stabilizing Senate campaign that supported their potentially endangered down-ballot candidates.

Now in his fourth term, Cornyn returned to the Senate floor just hours after the Jan. 6 insurrection at the Capitol to vote against objections to certifying President-elect Joe Biden's wins in Arizona and Pennsylvania. A month later, Cornyn voted against convicting former President Trump in his second impeachment trial on charges of inciting that mob to attack the building and its occupants.

In the early days of the Biden administration, Cornyn was the highest-profile Texas Republican willing to engage with the new president—a former Senate colleague.

Ted Cruz (R)

Elected 2012, term expires 2024, 2nd term, b. Dec 22, 1970; Calgary, Alberta, Canada, AB; Princeton University, A.B., 1992; Harvard Law School, J.D., 1995; Southern Baptist; Married (Heidi Nelson); 2 children.

Professional Career: Clerk, Judge J. Michael Luttig, 1995-1996; Clerk, Supreme Court Justice William Rehnquist, 1996-1997; Attorney, law firm, 1997-1999; Domestic policy adviser, Bush-Cheney campaign, 1999-2000; Associate Deputy Attorney General, U.S. Department of Justice, 2001; Director, Office of Policy Planning, Federal Trade Commission, 2001-2003; Texas Solicitor General, 2003-2008; Adjunct Professor of Law, University of TX, 2004-2009; Attorney, law firm, 2008-2012.

DC Office: 404 RSOB 20510, 202-224-5922, Fax: 202-228-0755, cruz.senate.gov

State Offices: Austin, 512-916-5834; Dallas, 214-599-8749; Houston, 713-718-3057; McAllen, 956-686-7339; San Antonio, 210-340-2885; Tyler, 903-593-5130.

Committees: *Commerce, Science & Transportation*: Aviation Safety, Operations & Innovations (RMM); Communications, Media & Broadband; Oceans, Fisheries, Climate Change & Manufacturing; Space & Science. *Foreign Relations*: East Asia, the Pacific & International Cybersecurity Policy; Near East, South Asia, Central Asia & Counterterrorism; State Dept & USAID Mngmnt, Internat'l Ops & Internat'l Dev; West Hem Crime Civ Sec Dem Rights & Women's Issues. *Joint Economic. Judiciary*: Constitution (RMM); Criminal Justice & Counterterrorism; Federal Courts, Oversight, Agency Action & Federal Rights; Immigration, Citizenship & Border Security. *Rules & Administration.*

Group Ratings

	ADA	ACLU	AFL-CIO	LCV	COC	HAFA	ACU	CFG	FRC
2020	-	23%	-	0%	-	96%	97%	-	-
2019	0%	C	6%	0%	59%	C	98%	95%	100%

Almanac Ratings 2019-2020

	Economy	Social	Foreign	Composite
Liberal	6%	6%	8%	7%
Conservative	94%	94%	92%	93%

Key Votes of the 116th Congress

1. EPA clean energy rules	N	5. Russia sanctions	N	9. Barr as Atty. General	Y
2. U.S./Mex./Can. trade deal	Y	6. Troops in SYR, AFG	N	10. Spending at the border	Y
3. Cut unemployment benefits	Y	7. Veto arms sales to Saudis	N	11. Coney Barrett to Sup. Ct.	Y
4. Shelton to Fed Reserve	Y	8. Defense $$$, veto override	N/A	12. Electoral College objections	Y

Election Results

Election	Name (Party)	Vote (%)	Cand. Spent	Ind. Exp. Support	Ind. Exp. Oppose
2018 General	Ted Cruz (R)	4,260,553 (51%)	$40,647,923	$1,205,710	$3,186,483
	Beto O'Rourke (D)	4,045,632 (48%)	$74,424,994	$1,770,046	$9,138,593
2018 Primary	Ted Cruz (R)	1,315,146 (85%)			
	Mary Miller (R)	94,274 (6%)			

Prior winning percentages: 2018 (51%), 2012 (56%)

In the modern political era, there have been few senators as controversial—or disliked—as Ted Cruz. Nor has the Senate seen a member whose fortunes have reversed so quickly. Once a dominant force in conservative politics, Cruz, Texas' junior senator, has been rebuilding his career since nearly being ousted by a Democrat, former Rep. Beto O'Rourke, in 2018 and losing the 2016 GOP presidential nomination to Donald Trump. Now well into his second term, Cruz appears to be gearing up for another presidential run in 2024, even as his popularity in the Senate reached a nadir after the January 2021 Capitol insurrection.

Cruz was born in Calgary Alberta, where his parents worked in the oil business. Thanks to an American-born mother, he is considered a natural-born citizen under the Constitution, notwithstanding Trump's suggestion during the 2016 race that Cruz's place of birth made him ineligible for the White House. The life story of Cruz's father figures prominently into his political narrative. Rafael Cruz fought to overthrow Fulgencio Batista's regime in Cuba in the 1950s before fleeing to Texas at 18 with nothing more than $100 sewn into his underwear. He worked as a dishwasher for 50 cents an hour to put himself through the University of Texas, and he later started a business in Houston. There, he met Cruz's mother, an Irish-American who studied math at Rice University.

As a high school student, Ted Cruz earned a scholarship by entering speech contests organized by the Free Enterprise Institute, in which participants studied the "Ten Pillars of Economic Wisdom," a libertarian manifesto, and delivered 20-minute speeches about it. As part of the program, Cruz memorized the Constitution and traveled around Texas discussing conservative ideas. He was educated at elite East Coast universities not usually associated with political outsiders: After earning his undergraduate degree from Princeton University, where he was a champion debater, Cruz graduated from Harvard Law School and clerked for Supreme Court Chief Justice William Rehnquist.

After a few years with a Washington law firm, Cruz joined George W. Bush's presidential campaign in 2000 as a domestic policy adviser. It was there that he met his wife, Heidi Nelson Cruz, another member of the Bush team. Both were dispatched to Florida in the chaos of the recount between Bush and Democratic nominee Al Gore, which led to jobs in the Bush administration. In his autobiography, Cruz admits he was "far too cocky for my own good" in those years and "burned a fair number of bridges" that hurt his chances at landing a higher-level administration job. He served as associate deputy attorney general at the Justice Department and then as director of the Federal Trade Commission's Office of Policy Planning.

Cruz returned to Texas in 2003 when he was appointed state solicitor general, making him the first Hispanic-American to hold the position. During his five-year tenure, Cruz argued before the Supreme Court nine times and participated in a number of high-profile cases, including one in which Texas fought to execute a Mexican citizen who raped and murdered two teenage girls and another in which he defended the display of the Ten Commandments on the state Capitol grounds. Cruz in July 2012 told The Texas Tribune: "We ended up, year after year, arguing some of the biggest cases in the country. There was a degree of serendipity in that, but there was also a concerted effort to seek out and lead conservative fights." His successor, James Ho, told the New Yorker: "He was and is the best appellate litigator in the state of Texas."

Cruz was in private practice when he decided to run to replace retiring Republican Sen. Kay Bailey Hutchison in 2012. He began the race as an underdog against Lt. Gov. David Dewhurst, an influential figure in the Texas GOP establishment who had the backing of almost every prominent Republican officeholder, including Gov. Rick Perry. Dewhurst was much better-known than Cruz and had millions of dollars to throw into the race. But Cruz got the backing of national conservative heavyweights and outside groups such as the Club for Growth and Freedom Works. Cruz sank $1 million of his own money into the primary in an effort to keep Dewhurst under 50 percent and force a runoff. In the nine-candidate first round, Dewhurst finished with 45 percent of the vote, followed by Cruz with 34 percent.

Dewhurst sought to cast Cruz as a creature of Washington, given his government experience, and suggested Cruz did not have the state's best interests in mind. Cruz portrayed Dewhurst as just another moderate Republican, though one in a position that required a large amount of deal-cutting and horse trading. Cruz trounced Dewhurst 57%-43%, capturing every major county. In the general election, he had little trouble defeating former state Rep. Paul Sadler.

Within a year of his election, Cruz revealed his headstrong, take-no-prisoners legislative tactics that helped shut down the federal government for 16 days—thrilling tea party activists but infuriating Democrats and many of his Republican colleagues. "If you killed Ted Cruz on the floor of the Senate, and the trial was in the Senate, nobody would convict you," Republican Lindsey Graham of South Carolina said in early 2016.

Cruz established himself as a strong voice for the right. Summarizing what he would do to enact a conservative agenda, Cruz told National Review: "What it takes is backbone, the willingness to stand and fight for those principles in the face of opposition and derision. Of those who have firm principles, even fewer have the backbones to stand for those principles when the heat is on." Underpinning such convictions was a political calculation: At least before Trump's surprise 2016 victory, the Republican

Party was divided over whether success lay in seeking to energize the political right or following a more centrist approach in an effort to broaden the party's base. Cruz was firmly in the former camp.

He won ecstatic reviews from conservative activists for his aggressiveness on issues, but his hyper-confident style won him few friends in the Senate of either party. He sought to block a vote on a measure to fund the federal government past the September 30, 2013, budget deadline unless Congress barred any funding to implement the Affordable Care Act. "I believe we can win this fight," he told reporters and conservative activists.

But other Republicans weren't buying it; North Carolina Sen. Richard Burr called it "the dumbest idea I've ever heard." In September, Cruz staged a 21-hour talk marathon on the Senate floor in which he read portions of Dr. Seuss' "Green Eggs and Ham" as a bedtime story to his two young daughters supposedly watching via C-SPAN. The resulting 16-day shutdown damaged the GOP brand, and Cruz took a significant share of the blame. "It wasn't about the shutdown. It wasn't about the Affordable Care Act. It was about launching Ted Cruz," Oklahoma GOP Sen. Tom Coburn told the Washington Post. Cruz's tactics created a continuing series of headaches for his in-state colleague, Sen. John Cornyn, leading to a frosty relationship between the two Texans.

Indeed, the episode caused Cruz's star to shine even brighter in right-wing circles. He won several straw polls at conservative events during and after the shutdown. He traveled across the country giving speeches, accompanied by his father, who introduced him saying, "He will not compromise!" His dad also was in the spotlight later during the presidential campaign after Trump, citing a National Enquirer story, made the unfounded claim that the elder Cruz had been with Lee Harvey Oswald before the assassination of President John F. Kennedy. Ted Cruz's numbers as a potential 2016 presidential contender reached double digits in mid-2014 surveys.

Cruz became the first major Republican in the presidential race when he launched his long-expected bid in March 2015 at Liberty University, a hotbed of social conservatism founded by the late Jerry Falwell. But his star had faded somewhat with the base since his first years in office—he began the race in the low single digits in national polling, stuck in the second tier of a crowded GOP field. Undeterred, Cruz kept up his bomb-throwing rhetorical approach on the campaign trail, seeking to put together a coalition of religious and economic ultraconservatives. His calls to abolish the IRS and Common Core national education standards earned regular cheers on the campaign trail. Cruz leaned hard into religious liberty arguments as well, introducing legislation for a constitutional amendment that would reinstate states' rights to bar same-sex marriage just days before the Supreme Court legalized such unions nationwide.

At first, Cruz went out of his way to maintain a "bromance" with Trump—to the point of defending the New York businessman after Trump described Mexicans coming to the U.S. as "rapists" and criminals while launching his candidacy. In contrast with the insult-laden blasts aimed at other rivals, Trump was kinder to Cruz, calling him a "nice guy." The sentiment did not last. Before the race was over, Trump had posted an unflattering picture of Heidi Cruz—on whom he threatened to "spill the beans"—while Ted Cruz had blasted Trump as a "serial philanderer" and "utterly amoral."

Cruz pulled off a surprise win in the first delegate selection contest: the Iowa caucuses—in which Trump was the favorite. The Cruz campaign raised $93.2 million on its own, a record for a Republican presidential primary candidate. According to a compilation by the Washington Post, this did not include another $89.6 million raised by super PACs and other independent groups supporting Cruz. In addition to Iowa and his home state of Texas, Cruz won primaries and caucuses in nine other states and outlasted two other freshman senators seeking the nomination: Rand Paul of Kentucky, who dropped out after Iowa, and Marco Rubio of Florida, who called it quits after losing his home state to Trump. But, for most of the campaign after the Iowa win, Cruz had a bumpy ride. Trump recovered to win the first-in-the-nation New Hampshire primary and followed with a victory in South Carolina. On Super Tuesday in March, Trump captured seven states; Cruz took three.

Cruz scored a significant 15-point victory over Trump in Wisconsin, but, by that time, there was no mathematical possibility of Cruz winning the nomination outright. In an informal alliance with the other remaining contender besides Trump, Cruz and Ohio Gov. John Kasich pursued a strategy of seeking to deny Trump a first-ballot victory—and thereby force a contested convention. Cruz picked a former contender for the GOP nomination, businesswoman Carly Fiorina, as his running mate, as he sought to present himself as the true conservative in the race.

In the end, the animosity toward Cruz precluded him from emerging as the standard-bearer of the "Never Trump" movement. Former House Speaker John Boehner of Ohio called Cruz "Lucifer in the flesh" and a "miserable son of a bitch." Josh Holmes, McConnell's chief of staff when Cruz arrived in the Senate, told Politico, "The idea that there's ever been a spokesperson less equipped to make an argument for party unity—I don't think there is anybody." In early May, Cruz lost the Indiana primary to Trump 53%-36% and withdrew from the race.

Cruz was slow to rebound from the bitterness of that campaign: He was virtually booed off the stage at the 2016 Republican National Convention after refusing to endorse Trump. The backlash from that episode spurred some intraparty fence-mending on his part. And Trump's unexpected victory in November prompted Cruz—whose path to the White House was blocked for at least eight years—to blunt his hard political edges.

Cruz announced he would seek reelection in Texas in 2018, but the blowback from his prime-time convention speech—including criticism of his refusal to endorse Trump—prompted speculation that his Senate seat could be at risk. "You don't come to the convention after you have lost the nomination and not support the nominee," Cornyn told Fox News Radio. "I think it was a mistake, and I don't know what it means in terms of his future, but I think he miscalculated."

Cruz took steps to repair the damage: He and Cornyn co-sponsored October events in Texas to raise money for endangered Senate Republicans. A month earlier, Cruz endorsed Trump in a Facebook post, declaring: "After many months of careful consideration, of prayer and searching my own conscience, I have decided that on Election Day, I will vote for the Republican nominee, Donald Trump. … If you don't want to see a Hillary Clinton presidency, I encourage you to vote for him."

At that time, Trump was the clear underdog, and Cruz appeared to be contemplating a bid for the 2020 GOP nomination to run against a President Hillary Clinton. After the election, he pivoted again. According to Politico, Cruz visited Trump Tower in mid-November and told the Trump transition team that the incoming president would need a "champion"—and volunteered for the task. "I think everyone recognizes we are in a markedly different environment today," Cruz told the outlet in January 2017. "And that environment is going to change how everyone approaches getting our job done."

Two months later, less than a year after Trump and Cruz had slung insults at each other over their wives and respective moral standards, the two dined at the White House at Trump's invitation —accompanied by their spouses. On Capitol Hill, a kinder, gentler Cruz invited colleagues to weekly basketball games.

While some were skeptical about the authenticity of Cruz's changed modus operandi, McConnell —at a weekly luncheon of Republican senators—labeled his erstwhile tormentor "the new Ted Cruz" and Graham apologized for his much-quoted wisecrack of a year earlier. "Love is everywhere," Graham said as he and Cruz made a joint appearance on MSNBC.

In 2018, Cruz needed all the friends he could find. O'Rourke, a little-known El Paso Democrat, challenged him for the Senate. O'Rourke spent the early stages of the campaign visiting all 254 Texas counties. It was a mixture of internet savvy—most of O'Rourke's events and even car rides were live streamed—and old-style retail politics. The result was astonishing: He came within 3 percentage points of ousting Cruz. It was even more shocking on the financial side. O'Rourke had raised $79 million to Cruz's $45 million. That left O'Rourke running for president in 2020, built on the political capital gained from nearly defeating the conservative firebrand in one of the most conservative states.

By 2021, that measure of goodwill he had built up with colleagues evaporated. Weeks after Trump lost reelection, he reportedly asked Cruz to argue his lawsuit to overturn the election before the U.S. Supreme Court, should the case make its way to the high court. Cruz accepted.

Then, just ahead of the usually ceremonial certification of the Electoral College votes, Cruz led a band of Republican senators in challenging the results. On the day of certification, McConnell delivered a sharp speech with implied criticisms toward Cruz. Cruz took to the floor to make his case. Minutes later, Trump supporters attacked the Capitol, hoping to violently force members of Congress to overturn the results.

A number of Democrats called on Cruz to resign for giving credibility to the specious claims of voter fraud that led to the insurrection. When asked if Cruz and Sen. Josh Hawley of Missouri should resign for those actions, President-elect Joe Biden said, "I think they should just be flat beaten the next time they run. … I think the American public has a real good clear look at who they are. They're part of the big lie, the big lie."

A little over a month later, the Senate held an impeachment trial of Trump for inciting the riot. Cruz served as a juror and actively helped Trump's defense team. Unsurprisingly, he voted to acquit Trump for a second time.

Back in Texas a few days later, a winter storm struck his home state, and millions of his constituents lost electricity. Some even died of hypothermia. Cruz flew to a resort in Cancun Mexico with his family, prompting yet another round of criticism.

Louie Gohmert (R)

Elected 2004, 9th term, b. Aug 18, 1953; Pittsburgh, TX; TX Agricultural and Mechanical University, B.A., 1975; Baylor University School of Law, J.D., 1977; Baptist; Married (Kathy Gohmert); 3 children.

Military Career: U.S. Army 1978-1982

Elected Office: Smith County District Court judge, 1993-2002.

Professional Career: Practicing attorney, 1982-1992; Chief justice, TX 12th Court of Appeals, 2002-2003.

DC Office: 2267 RHOB 20515, 202-225-3035, Fax: 202-226-1230, gohmert.house.gov

State Offices: Longview, 903-236-8597; Lufkin, 936-632-3180; Marshall, 903-938-8386; Nacogdoches, 936-715-9514; Tyler, 903-561-6349.

Committees: *Judiciary*: Courts, Intellectual Property & Internet; Crime, Terrorism & Homeland Security. *Natural Resources*: National Parks, Forests & Public Lands; Oversight & Investigations.

Group Ratings

	ADA	ACLU	AFL-CIO	LCV	COC	HAFA	ACU	CFG	FRC
2020	**	20%	**	5%	-	92%	95%	**	-
2019	0%	C	20%	3%	67%	C	95%	96%	100%

Almanac Ratings 2019-2020

	Economy	Social	Foreign	Composite
Liberal	25%	11%	38%	25%
Conservative	75%	89%	62%	75%

Key Votes of the 116th Congress

1. U.S./Mex./Can. trade deal Y	5. Russia sanctions Y	9. Firearms background checks N
2. First Coronavirus response N	6. Troops in Syria N	10. Spending at the border N
3. HEROES Act N	7. Veto arms sales to Saudis N	11. Marijuana liberalized rules N
4. CASH Act N	8. Defense $$$, veto override N	12. Electoral College objections Y

Election Results

Election	Name (Party)	Vote (%)		Cand. Spent	Ind. Exp. Support	Ind. Exp. Oppose
2020 General	Louie Gohmert (R)	219,726	(73%)	$564,742	$12,776	$1,539
	Hank Gilbert (D)	83,016	(27%)	$728,619		
2020 Primary	Louie Gohmert (R)	83,887	(90%)			
	Johnathan Davidson (R)	9,659	(10%)			

Prior winning percentages: 2018 (72%), 2016 (74%), 2014 (61%), 2012 (71%), 2010 (90%), 2008 (88%), 2006 (68%), 2004 (61%)

Louie Gohmert, a Republican first elected in 2004, has concentrated most of his efforts on provoking Democrats and even some fellow Republicans. He was an unabashed supporter of President Donald Trump.

Gohmert grew up in Mount Pleasant and graduated on an Army scholarship from Texas A&M University, where he was class president. He earned a law degree from Baylor University, then served as a captain in the Army. He practiced law in Tyler and spent a decade as a district court judge. Republican Gov. Rick Perry named him chief justice of the Texas Appellate Court in 2002. He earned a reputation as a tough law-and-order judge with a knack for attracting attention. In 1996, he ordered an HIV-positive convicted car thief, as a condition of probation, to notify future sexual partners of his HIV status and to obtain written consent from them before engaging in sexual activity.

After the 2003 redistricting in Texas, Gohmert was one of six Republicans to challenge four-term Democratic Rep. Max Sandlin, who was a close ally of Minority Leader Nancy Pelosi. Gohmert led in the primary with 42 percent of the vote to 30 percent for lawyer John Graves. In the runoff campaign, few differences separated the two conservatives; Gohmert prevailed 57%-43%. Gohmert won 77 percent of the vote in his home base of Smith County, where half the votes were cast. In the general election, Gohmert linked Sandlin to the national Democratic Party and its 2004 presidential nominee, John Kerry. The result wasn't close. Gohmert beat Sandlin, 61%-38%, winning 79 percent in Smith County.

For his first few years in Congress, Gohmert was one of the more obscure members of the massive Texas Republican delegation. Then in a 2010 CNN appearance, Gohmert screamed at Anderson Cooper with allegations regarding "terror babies," children born in America to terrorists. From then on, his career became a succession of inflammatory remarks and actions. When the bailout for the financial industry came to the House floor in 2008, he made a motion to adjourn the chamber "so we don't do this terrible thing to our nation." It was defeated 394-8. He had little regard for President Barack Obama or Hillary Clinton. During a 2016 speech to the Values Voters Summit of social conservatives, Gohmert said Clinton was "mentally impaired." "We need to be praying for Hillary Clinton," he added. "There's special needs there." Also that year, he said on the House floor that gay people should not be sent into space.

Gohmert serves on the House Natural Resources Committee, but it's his perch from the Judiciary Committee where he has garnered the most attention. At a well-publicized Judiciary hearing in July 2018 with FBI agent Peter Strzok, whose law-enforcement inquiries were challenged by Trump and his allies, Gohmert said the witness was a "disgrace" and asked "how many times did you look so innocent into your wife's eye and lie about" his reported affair with a former FBI attorney. During a 2019 impeachment hearing, Gohmert named an intelligence official Republicans believed to be the whistleblower making allegations about Trump's conversations with a Ukrainian official.

Throughout the 2020 COVID-19 pandemic, Gohmert often refused to wear a mask around the halls of Congress. When he did, it was in the form of a bandana that often did not cover his nose. That summer, when he revealed he tested positive, colleagues reacted with fury. A political watchdog group filed an ethics complaint against him. Gohmert finished out the year by traveling to Philadelphia after the presidential vote-fraud allegations, alleging Democrats were "manufacturing" votes.

Gohmert often has tangled with House Republican leaders. After the 2014 election, he launched his own candidacy as conservative unhappiness with Speaker John Boehner deepened. He received three votes, including his own. Allies referred to Gohmert as "a stalking horse" who encouraged others to enter the contest. After Boehner resigned in October 2015, he was one of nine who voted against Paul Ryan for Speaker. "I simply cannot vote for a candidate who demands more power before he agrees to be Speaker," Gohmert said. Despite his seniority, Republican leaders have bypassed Gohmert for a senior position on his two House committees.

When Democrats regained House control in 2019, they imposed what he proudly referred to as the "Louis Gohmert rule," which limited how often a member could speak in the House on non-legislative topics. In January 2021, he objected to certifying Joe Biden's Electoral College victories in Pennsylvania and Arizona. He joined a group of House Republicans who filed a lawsuit seeking to declare that the law describing the count of the Electoral College was unconstitutional and that "exclusive authority and sole discretion in determining which electoral votes to count" rested with Vice President Mike Pence. "We continue to hold out hope that there is a federal judge who understands that the fraud that stole this election will mean the end of our republic," Gohmert said. They failed to find such a judge.

In part because of the outrage he stirs up nationally, he is beloved in East Texas. Gohmert has never been reelected with less than 68 percent of the vote. His notoriety allowed his 2020 Democratic opponent, Hank Gilbert, to gain national prominence. Gilbert outraised Gohmert-- $729,000 to $565,000--but the money made no difference: Gohmert defeated him, 73%-27%, with at least 66 percent in each county.

TX-1: East Texas   **Cook Partisan Voting Index: R+25**

Population		Race and Ethnicity		Income	
Total	726,094	White	77.50%	Median Income	$54,396
Land area (sq. miles)	7,859	Black	17.20%	District Income Rank	340
Pop/ sq mi	92.39	Latino	18.00%	Poverty Rate	16.70%
Born in State	71.60%	Asian	1.10%	With health insurance	83.20%
		Two or more races	2.50%	Cash public assistance	1.50%
Age Groups		Other	1.60%	Food stamp/SNAP	12.80%
Under 18	24.10%				
18-34	23.00%	**Education**		**Work**	
35-64	35.20%	H.S grad or less	43.20%	White Collar	32.60%
Over 64	17.80%	Some college	34.70%	Sales and Service	38.90%
		College Degree, 4 yr	14.50%	Blue Collar	28.40%
Military		Post grad	7.50%	Government	15.70%
Veteran/ Active Duty	7.20%				

2020 Pres. Vote	Trump	218,700	(72%)	Biden	83,229	(27%)		
2016 Pres. Vote	Trump	189,604	(72%)	Clinton	66,389	(25%)	Johnson	5,501 (2%)

Tyler, Longview: The gently rolling, pine tree-covered land of East Texas was settled by Tennessee farmers in the years before the Civil War. It sits at the western edge of Scots-Irish America, a swath of territory that starts in the Appalachian ridge and is inhabited by a combative, honor-bound and highly religious populace. A hundred years ago, this was one of the poorest parts of America, where farmers scratched a living off the land and hoped for good weather and decent prices in the marketplace. When a peach blight in the early 20th century wiped out much of the local fruit industry, many farmers turned to growing roses, which proved ideally suited to the climate and soil of East Texas. By the 1940s, more than half the nation's rose bushes were grown within 10 miles of Tyler, which has become known for its annual Texas Rose Festival, which draws 120,000 visitors every October. About 75 percent of the garden roses in the country have found their way through Tyler and are distributed throughout the country. As the western edge of the Deep South, East Texas has a complicated racial history. In the summer of 2020, Tyler officials voted to change the name of Robert E. Lee High School to Tyler Legacy.

Longview, which in the 1870s was the western terminus of the Southern Pacific Railroad, became a trading center for wagon trains and local cotton growers and timber cutters. One of the most dramatic moments in East Texas history came in 1930, when oil was discovered outside Henderson. It took a while for oil producers to realize the scale of what was beneath them: a giant underground lake of oil that spanned five counties and would become known as the East Texas Oilfield. In 1943, the Big Inch pipeline began sending millions of barrels of crude oil from the "Black Giant" oil field near Longview —at the time, the largest ever in the state—to the East for refining. This oil supply was pivotal in assisting the Allied cause in World War II. Since then, the area has become an industrial center for earth-moving equipment and chemicals. Eastman Chemical Co., which once produced chemicals for film company Eastman Kodak, has had a booming business because of lower natural gas prices; its Longview site has employed about 1,500. Geologists have identified the shale formations in east Texas as the largest reserves of natural gas in the nation. Agriculture and timber are major industries here, and feral hogs are a local menace.

The 1st Congressional District of Texas, covering the heart of East Texas, is made up of 12 counties, the most populous being Tyler's Smith County and Longview's Gregg County, which total nearly half the population. East Texas is ancestrally Democratic, a region that responded to the populist rhetoric of presidential candidate William Jennings Bryan in the 1890s and President Franklin D. Roosevelt in the 1930s and 1940s. Republicans first made inroads in Tyler and Longview in the 1950s. By the time George W. Bush ran for reelection as Texas governor in 1998, the area was solidly Republican. In the 2003 redistricting, GOP-friendly Smith and Gregg counties were added to the district. In the Cook Political Report's latest PVI listings, this was the 21th most Republican district in the nation. But it is only the 7th most Republican district in Texas.

Daniel Crenshaw (R)

Elected 2018, 2nd term, b. Mar 14, 1984; Aberdeen, Scotland; Tufts University, B.A., 2006; Taubman Center for State & Local Government – Harvard Kennedy School, M.P.A., 2017; Methodist; Married (Tara Crenshaw).

Military Career: U.S. Navy SEAL 2006-2016 (Afghanistan, WIA)

DC Office: 413 CHOB 20515, 202-225-6565, crenshaw.house.gov

State Offices: Kingwood, 713-860-1330.

Committees: *Energy & Commerce*: Environment & Climate Change; Health. *Select Committee on the Climate Crisis.*

Almanac Ratings 2019-2020

	Economy	Social	Foreign	Composite
Liberal	25%	26%	27%	26%
Conservative	75%	74%	73%	74%

Key Votes of the 116th Congress

1. U.S./Mex./Can. trade deal	Y	5. Russia sanctions	Y	9. Firearms background checks	N
2. First Coronavirus response	Y	6. Troops in Syria	Y	10. Spending at the border	Y
3. HEROES Act	N	7. Veto arms sales to Saudis	N	11. Marijuana liberalized rules	N
4. CASH Act	N	8. Defense $$$, veto override	Y	12. Electoral College objections	N

Election Results

Election	Name (Party)	Vote (%)		Cand. Spent	Ind. Exp. Support	Ind. Exp. Oppose
2020 General	Daniel Crenshaw (R)	192,828	(56%)	$17,408,276	$195,934	$262,493
	Sima Ladjevardian (D)	148,374	(43%)	$4,023,254	$50,311	
2020 Primary	Dan Crenshaw (R)	53,938	(100%)			

Prior winning percentages: 2018 (53%)

A political newcomer when he entered the House in 2019, Dan Crenshaw became a genuine national star. The Republican sophomore brought new blood and enthusiasm when he was the unexpected Republican nominee in a Texas open seat in 2018. In the GOP primary, he barely survived into the runoff against a big-spending party contributor. Then he easily defeated a state legislator who was backed by business groups. Crenshaw, a retired Navy lieutenant commander who served as a SEAL for 10 years, wore a distinctive eye patch. He lost his right eye to an explosive blast that nearly killed him while he was deployed in Afghanistan in 2012.

More distinctively, the youthful Crenshaw generated excitement among suburban Houston voters. He ran as an outsider who emphasized the importance of "service before self," and appealed to young voters with his call for long-term steps to preserve Social Security. Following his easier than expected victory in the Republican runoff, the Houston Chronicle wrote that Crenshaw "became a potential star on the national stage because of his war-hero story and a charisma that is drawing younger voters."

A native of Houston, where his father worked in the oil business and traveled around the world, Crenshaw graduated from Tufts University, where he joined the Reserve Officers' Training Corps. Following his military retirement as a lieutenant commander and his recuperation from the war injuries that also badly damaged his other eye, he received a master's in public administration from Harvard's Kennedy School of Government. He returned to Houston just in time to assist as a volunteer in the recovery from the devastation of Hurricane Harvey in September 2017. That experience spurred his decision to run for Congress.

In the first round of voting in the Republican primary, he finished second by a scant 155 votes ahead of Republican donor Kathaleen Wall, who spent $6.2 million of her own funds but lacked basic skills as a campaigner. Crenshaw, by contrast, raised about $200,000 in the initial round of the contest, as he sought to introduce himself as a fresh spirit against the party insider. State Rep. Kevin Roberts led the opening round with 33 percent of the vote, to 27 percent each for Crenshaw and Wall.

Roberts, the chief operating officer of a Houston law firm, began the runoff with support from much of the state's Republican establishment and he outspent Crenshaw nearly 2-to-1. He campaigned on his legislative experience plus support from conservative groups, including the National Rifle Association. Crenshaw, by contrast, styled himself as a policy expert and wrote his campaign's position papers.

His appeal was enhanced by several national appearances on Fox News. He received a late campaign boost from former Texas Lt. Gov. David Dewhurst, who criticized a negative campaign mailing from the Roberts camp for "lying about his opponent."

Crenshaw won the runoff with an impressive 70 percent of the vote. He won, 53%-46%, in November against Democrat Todd Litton, a lawyer and political activist. Although national Democrats had voiced hopes of being competitive in this contest, they instead focused elsewhere in Texas. Crenshaw burnished his cultural appeal when he responded magnanimously to a sarcastic reference to his eye patch by an entertainer on Saturday Night Live prior to the election.

Once in Congress, Crenshaw attracted a massive online following, a conservative foil to the celebrity surrounding first-term Democratic Rep. Alexandria Ocasio-Cortez. In the 2020 cycle, he raised nearly $20 million. He was not just the strongest Texas House member in fundraising, he was the top Republican member who was not in leadership. In 2020, Crenshaw released a book, "Fortitude: American Resilience in the Era of Outrage," that in part recounted his recovery from his war injury. Between that factor and his star power, fellow Texas Republicans are watching him closely for a future statewide run.

In 2020, Democrats continued their push into the district with a widely touted recruit in Sima Ladjevardian. Crenshaw easily won that race as well, 56%-43%. House leaders rewarded him with a seat on the Energy and Commerce Committee, a key assignment for any member representing Houston. With that assignment, Crenshaw said, he would be "fighting for personalized health care, lowering drug costs, commonsense solutions to climate change, and protecting Texas energy jobs and our economy."

Crenshaw walked a fine line in the weeks after the 2020 election, as President Donald Trump sought to discredit and eventually overturn the election results. "If Trump loses, he loses. It was never an impossible outcome and we must accept the final results when it is over," Crenshaw wrote on Twitter. "But the unfortunate reality is that there is very little trust in the process, where irregularities have been flagrant and transparency lacking." When Rep. Marjorie Taylor Greene criticized him for not more fully supporting Trump, Crenshaw retorted: "No one said give up. I literally said investigate every irregularity and use the courts. You're a member of Congress now, Marjorie. Start acting like one."

When Republicans in Congress pushed to overturn Biden's victory over Trump, Crenshaw voted against objecting to the results. He described the proposed congressional failure to certify electoral votes as "deeply unconstitutional." A week later, he voted against impeaching Trump for inciting a riot in which attackers overtook the Capitol.

TX-2: Harris County　　　　　　　　　　Cook Partisan Voting Index: R+4

Population		Race and Ethnicity		Income	
Total	787,271	White	66.40%	Median Income	$80,922
Land area (sq. miles)	309	Black	11.90%	District Income Rank	86
Pop/ sq mi	2,549.87	Latino	31.60%	Poverty Rate	10.10%
Born in State	50.40%	Asian	8.30%	With health insurance	84.40%
		Two or more races	3.20%	Cash public assistance	1.10%
Age Groups		Other	10.20%	Food stamp/SNAP	4.90%
Under 18	23.60%				
18-34	25.10%	**Education**		**Work**	
35-64	38.50%	H.S grad or less	30.00%	White Collar	47.40%
Over 64	12.80%	Some college	25.40%	Sales and Service	33.40%
		College Degree, 4 yr	27.70%	Blue Collar	19.10%
Military		Post grad	16.80%	Government	10.20%
Veteran/ Active Duty	5.40%				

2020 Pres. Vote	Trump	174,980	(50%)	Biden	170,430	(49%)		
2016 Pres. Vote	Trump	145,530	(52%)	Clinton	119,659	(43%)	Johnson	10,323　(4%)

West Houston and Northern Suburbs: Houston, which remains one of the fastest growing metropolitan areas in the country, has become an internationally renowned energy hub that provides the largest share of the nation's jobs in oil and gas extraction. The city's Energy Corridor, a sprawling 4,000-acre business district on both sides of the Katy Freeway west of the city, is a state-established district whose vision is to become the world's premier location for energy-related businesses. It houses more than 300 companies and 94,000 employees, including U.S. headquarters for BP, ConocoPhillips and Shell. In late 2020, Hewlett Packard Enterprise announced its relocation to Spring, which is north of Houston. And northeast of downtown near Lake Houston along the Sam Houston Tollway is Generation Park, a 4,000-acre master-planned enterprise park for corporate and residential development, with office, shopping and industrial sites that could eventually host 150,000 employees.

Growth in the Houston area has been phenomenal. The oil and gas rush in South Texas' Eagle Ford Shale region alone supported 155,000 jobs, according to a 2013 University of Texas-San Antonio study. Many of those field operation and management jobs have been centered in Harris County. Harris' growth to 4.7 million to 2017 was a 37 percent increase from 2000; the metropolitan area's 16 percent growth from 2010 to 2017 was the fifth-fastest in the nation. New office space and condominiums have been concentrated on the west side of Houston.

When Hurricane Harvey devastated the Houston area in August 2017, it didn't spare these upscale sections. After long-term sedimentation had reduced the depth of Lake Houston, the flooding from the San Jacinto River was severe in nearby Kingwood and Atascocita, plus Humble, which is near the entrance to George Bush International Airport. West of the city, the Army Corps of Engineers made a deliberate decision to flood parts of the Energy Corridor to prevent a possible failure of massive reservoirs at the Addicks and Barker dams, which form the Buffalo Bayou through downtown. Residents in these wealthy neighborhoods filed huge lawsuits against the Army Corps. In December 2018, the Federal Claims Court ruled that the government was liable for damages resulting from the floods.

The 2nd Congressional District of Texas is a swirl-shaped district located entirely within Harris County. It comes close to downtown, covering Rice University, the museum district and Memorial Park, which at 1,466 acres is larger than New York City's Central Park. It also takes in the heavily Democratic neighborhood of Montrose, southwest of downtown, which has been the center of Houston's gay and lesbian community and claims President Lyndon Johnson (who lived there after he graduated from Southwest Texas State) and Howard Hughes as former residents. In 2017, Texas Monthly wrote that Montrose had been changed by gentrification but that "enough of its spirit remains intact for it to remain Houston's, and Texas's, coolest neighborhood." It is home to the only LGBT pride crosswalk in Texas. The district, which includes some of the most Republican precincts in Harris County, was the only one of the five that are mostly in Houston that voted for Donald Trump. In 2020, Trump took the district by 4,550 votes, with 49.9 percent of the vote. That was a huge drop from the 63 percent for Mitt Romney in 2012.

Van Taylor (R)

Elected 2018, 2nd term, b. Aug 01, 1972; Dallas, TX; Harvard College, A.B., 1995; Harvard Business School, M.B.A., 2001; Episcopalian; Married (Anne Taylor); 3 children.

Military Career: U.S. Marine Corps 1995-1999; U.S. Marine Corps Reserve 1999-2005 (Iraq)

Elected Office: TX House, 2011-2018.

Professional Career: Director, Churchill Capital Company.

DC Office: 1404 LHOB 20515, 202-225-4201, vantaylor.house.gov

State Offices: Plano, 972-202-4150.

Committees: *Financial Services*: Housing, Community Development & Insurance; Nat'l Security, International Development & Monetary Policy; Task Force on Artificial Intelligence.

Almanac Ratings 2019-2020

	Economy	Social	Foreign	Composite
Liberal	25%	26%	27%	26%
Conservative	75%	74%	73%	74%

Key Votes of the 116th Congress

1. U.S./Mex./Can. trade deal	Y	5. Russia sanctions	Y	9. Firearms background checks	N
2. First Coronavirus response	Y	6. Troops in Syria	Y	10. Spending at the border	Y
3. HEROES Act	N	7. Veto arms sales to Saudis	N	11. Marijuana liberalized rules	N
4. CASH Act	N	8. Defense $$$, veto override	Y	12. Electoral College objections	N

Election Results

Election	Name (Party)	Vote (%)		Cand. Spent	Ind. Exp. Support	Ind. Exp. Oppose
2020 General	Van Taylor (R).......................................	230,512	(55%)	$2,659,122	$570,537	$863
	Lulu Seikaly (D).................................	179,458	(43%)	$1,631,544	$5,886	
	Christopher Claytor (L)..........................	8,621	(2%)			
2020 Primary	Van Taylor (R)....................................	53,938	(100%)			

Prior winning percentages: 2018 (54%)

Republican Van Taylor has brought a more bipartisan approach than most of the other newcomers to the House. And he has been proud to discuss his efforts and his friends across the aisle. That's a sound approach in his district, which has grown more rapidly and shifted more politically in the past decade than virtually any other district in the nation. Facing little competition—in either party—to win the seat, he was the only one of six House GOP freshmen from Texas who was nominated in 2018 without a primary runoff. Taylor largely cleared the field, with support from both economic and social conservatives in the GOP. Two years later, he faced a well-financed challenger who received encouragement from national Democrats.

Taylor is a Dallas native with deep Texas roots. He was a descendant of Robert Lee Blaffer, who helped found Humble Oil Co., and he resided in Plano on land near where another great-grandfather farmed during the Depression. He got his undergraduate and business degrees from Harvard University. As a captain in the Marine Corps and a paratrooper, Taylor won awards for his service as a platoon commander and intelligence officer in Iraq, including a successful mission to rescue wounded Marines during a battle in An Nasiriyah.

In business, Taylor was a director of the Dallas-based Churchill Capital Co., a real estate investment firm that has financed many large projects across the South. He also has experience in cellular infrastructure financing and home building, and has been a board member of Texas Gulf Bank. His wife, Anne, has been an executive at another Dallas-based real estate firm.

He had an unsuccessful start in politics in 2006, when he lost to veteran Rep. Chet Edwards, 58%-40%, the largest victory margin in that decade for the embattled Democrat in his Waco-based district. Edwards attacked Taylor for having recently moved into the district. That setback became largely overlooked as Taylor rebuilt his political career in Collin County, more than 100 miles to the north. After serving four years in the state House, he had tea party support when he was elected to the Texas Senate in 2014. He received awards from conservative groups for his efforts to restrict government spending and taxes, and he was a consistent conservative on social issues.

Taylor won Senate adoption of a Truth in Taxation rule, which required that legislation state clearly in its first line if there is an attempt to raise taxes or fees. Americans for Tax Reform has cited the rule as a blueprint for other states. For his work in the Republican-controlled chamber, the Dallas Morning News in its endorsement described Taylor as "a solid conservative who can point to a series of bills he got passed as a state legislator with bipartisan support."

Although many local Republicans for years had their eyes on the seat held by Republican Rep. Sam Johnson, who was held as a prisoner of war for more than six years during the Vietnam War and retired at age 88 as the oldest member of Congress, Taylor had a virtual free ride. For the GOP primary, he raised $1.8 million—including a $1 million personal loan that he mostly paid back—compared with $54,000 for runner-up David Niederkorn, who had experience as a professor and in the Baptist ministry. Taylor swamped him in the vote, 85%-9%.

In November, he defeated Democrat Lorie Burch, an attorney, in a contest that received little outside attention. His surprisingly narrow 54%-44% win was a flashing signal of change in Taylor's slice of the Dallas suburbs.

In the Democratic-controlled House, Taylor said that he deliberately spends as much time on the Democratic side of the chamber as with Republicans—not a common practice in the mostly polarized House. In a May 2019 story headlined "Taylor of Plano is not like other Congress members as he works to be 'Mr. Bipartisan'," the Morning News wrote that Taylor said when he was deployed in Iraq, "you're not there asking what their political party is or what they believe." Democratic Rep. Jimmy Panetta of California, who was a founding member with Taylor of the House's veterans caucus, Our Country, said Taylor is "willing to talk to anybody, to get to the truth, and that's what he bases his policies on."

Taylor talked up his cooperation with Democratic Rep. Colin Allred, whose adjacent district serves north Dallas and who was a fellow freshman with Taylor. In a post-election story in November 2020, Allred told the News that he and Taylor usually share the same goals. "I never question Van's motivations and we've become friends," Allred said. He said they have worked together on local highway, water and veterans' issues. Oddly, each represents what has become a competitive district, though each was solidly Republican a decade ago.

Democrat Lulu Seikaly, a lawyer in Plano, challenged Taylor for reelection and sought to tie him to President Donald Trump. "He's Trump's puppet," said Seikaly, who was seeking to become the first Arab-American woman elected to Congress. The Democratic Congressional Campaign Committee placed the contest on its target list, though neither party spent much money there. Taylor outspent Seikaly, $2.7 million to $1.6 million, and won, 55%-43%.

Taylor got a seat on the Financial Services Committee, which matches his professional interests and the business sector is a major employer in his district. In January 2021, he was among the minority of House Republicans—especially from Texas—who opposed steps to review the electoral college results in Pennsylvania and Arizona.

TX-3: Northern Dallas Suburbs   Cook Partisan Voting Index: R+6

Population		Race and Ethnicity		Income	
Total	913,161	White	67.20%	Median Income	$95,619
Land area (sq. miles)	481	Black	9.90%	District Income Rank	43
Pop/ sq mi	1,898.94	Latino	14.90%	Poverty Rate	6.20%
Born in State	42.70%	Asian	17.80%	With health insurance	89.70%
		Two or more races	2.90%	Cash public assistance	0.60%
Age Groups		Other	2.20%	Food stamp/SNAP	2.50%
Under 18	25.30%				
18-34	21.00%	**Education**		**Work**	
35-64	42.10%	H.S grad or less	20.80%	White Collar	54.90%
Over 64	11.60%	Some college	24.70%	Sales and Service	33.40%
		College Degree, 4 yr	33.50%	Blue Collar	11.80%
Military		Post grad	21.00%	Government	9.30%
Veteran/ Active Duty	5.10%				

2020 Pres. Vote	Trump	214,359	(50%)	Biden	209,859	(49%)		
2016 Pres. Vote	Trump	174,561	(54%)	Clinton	129,384	(40%)	Johnson	12,304	(4%)

Plano, McKinney: The Dallas and Fort Worth metropolitan area, once a railroad junction and cotton-shipping center, now has 7.6 million people, the fourth largest in the nation and more than all of Texas had during World War II. More than two-thirds of them live beyond the city limits of Dallas and Fort Worth. In Dallas, the city's old elite occupies the mansions of Highland Park north of downtown, but its business and professional classes have moved farther up into Collin County's scrub-covered hills. Collin's population exploded from 67,000 in 1970 to more than 1 million in 2019, with an impressive 32 percent growth since 2010. The county has the sixth-largest population and third-highest median income in Texas.

Its biggest city is Plano, with 288,000 people. The former farming community is the corporate headquarters of Dr. Pepper, J.C. Penney and HP Enterprise Services. Toyota has its seven-building headquarters at a state-of-the-art campus on 100 acres near the Dallas North Tollway in Plano. Relocation costs from Torrance California exceeded $1 billion. Toyota executives said the result, with about 4,200 employees, was "a more nimble, mobility-focused company, rather than just an automaker," the Dallas Morning News reported. Officials reviewed more than 100 other potential sites before they decided to move. JPMorgan Chase moved 6,000 employees to its new campus in Plano in 2017. Plans for their four-building campus on a 50-acre campus envision more than 11,000 employees, the News reported in 2019. Nearby, Boeing located the headquarters of its global services division. Plano is the Spanish word for "flat," referring to the local topography. Settlers looking for fertile land first came west from Kentucky and Tennessee about 1840.

Plano and nearby Richardson have growing Asian-American populations that were 21 percent and 16 percent, respectively, in 2019. Sixty Chinese cultural organizations are based in North Texas, mostly in Collin County, serving more than 30,000 Chinese-American residents. More than 20,000 Indian-American residents moved into Collin County from 2000 to 2010, with many working at high-tech firms and medical centers in the region. Restaurants, grocery stores and boutiques cater to the Indian community. North of Plano is Frisco, which was the fastest-growing city in the nation in 2017. Nearby McKinney ranked ninth. Wallet Hub in 2018 listed them as the top real-estate markets nationwide. The Professional Golfers Association is making plans to move its headquarters from Palm Beach Gardens Florida to a 600-acre hotel and convention-center complex in Frisco, which also will include two championship golf courses, a retail village and a park. The courses are scheduled to open in 2022.

The 3rd Congressional District of Texas, based entirely within Collin County, includes all but two small corners of the county and centers on Plano. Historically, Collin has been heavily Republican. As in other upscale suburban GOP districts in Texas, that has changed in the past decade. The 49.8 percent vote for President Donald Trump in 2020 was a big drop from the 64 percent for Mitt Romney in 2012.

Pat Fallon (R)

Elected 2020, 1st term, b. Dec 19, 1967; Pittsfield, MA; University of Notre Dame, B.A.; University of MA; Roman Catholic; Married (Susan Garner-Sherrill); 2 children.

Military Career: Second Lieutenant, U.S. Air Force.

Elected Office: Member, Frisco City Council, 2009-2011; Mayor Pro Tempore, Frisco City Council, 2011-2012; TX House, 2012-2019; TX Senate, 2019-2021.

Professional Career: President/CEO, clothing company.

DC Office: 1118 LHOB 20515, 202-225-6673, fallon.house.gov

State Offices: Rockwall, 972-771-0100; Sherman, 903-820-5170; Texarkana, 903-716-7500.

Committees: *Armed Services*: Cyber, Innovative Technologies & Information Systems; Military Personnel. *Oversight & Reform*: Subcommittee on Environment.

Election Results

Election	Name (Party)	Vote (%)		Cand. Spent	Ind. Exp. Support	Ind. Exp. Oppose
2020 General	Pat Fallon (R)................................	253,837	(75%)	$93,742	$11,194	
	Russell Foster (D).........................	76,326	(23%)			

Republican Pat Fallon was easily elected after taking an unusual route to the ballot. He was nominated during a meeting of Republican officials in his district that was held in August 2020, after Rep. John Ratcliffe resigned his House seat. Ratcliffe, who earlier won the GOP primary without opposition, stepped down after President Donald Trump selected him as the Director of National Intelligence. With experience as a state legislator and his record as a self-styled "movement conservative," Fallon was an obvious choice to fill the opening. He cruised to victory against his little-known Democratic opponent.

Fallon, who was born in Massachusetts, got his bachelor's degree in government and international relations from the University of Notre Dame, where he was on the reserve squad of the football team that won the national championship in 1988. After joining the Air Force Reserve

Officer Training Corps, he served as a second lieutenant and was stationed at Sheppard Air Force Base in Wichita Falls Texas. He was successful in business, chiefly in starting and operating an apparel company that specialized in military clothing. According to his official bio, he completed in the 2016 World Marathon Challenge, in which participants run seven marathons on seven continents in seven consecutive days; he contends he is the only person ever to complete the challenge with no previous marathon experience.

In 2009, Fallon was elected to the city council in Frisco Texas; later, he was selected as mayor by council members. Running as a "fierce taxpayer advocate," he was elected in 2012 to the state House, where he served three terms. With $1.8 million of his own funds, plus endorsements from prominent statewide GOP officials and grassroots conservative organizations, he then defeated a veteran Republican incumbent to join the state Senate; his 62%-23% victory in that contest was the widest margin of victory against a Senate incumbent in Texas history, Fallon said.

In 2019, he considered a primary challenge to Sen. John Cornyn of Texas, but concluded that "a statewide U.S. Senate race right now is simply not something that fits with the chapter in my life that we're in."

Less than a year later, Fallon's opportunity opened for an easier route to Congress. To replace Ratcliffe, who had been elected to three House terms, 12 candidates were nominated at an afternoon meeting in Sulphur Springs of Republican officials from the 16 counties in the district. Fallon won on the first ballot, with 82 of the 145 votes that were cast. Jason Ross, who had been the district chief of staff for Ratcliffe and was endorsed by Ratcliffe's wife, finished second with 34 votes.

Sen. Ted Cruz attended the meeting and "stumped for Fallon … before two groups of 40 delegates," the Texas Tribune reported. Cruz "needs reinforcements in D.C. and he wants me by his side," Fallon told the GOP delegates. Opponents criticized Fallon because his home in Prosper was a short distance outside the district.

In the general election, the Dallas Morning News endorsed Fallon in an editorial that cited his "legislative experience and a record that mixes commonsense legislation with overt appeals to cultural politics." He was elected with 75 percent of the vote, sweeping every county. Russell Foster, the Democratic nominee, did not file the customary financial reports with the Federal Election Commission. In the 18 counties, Fallon's lowest vote was 69 percent in Morris.

In the House, Fallon was one of two freshmen to get a seat on the Armed Services Committee among the seven Texas Republicans who took office in 2021.

TX-4: Northeast Texas   Cook Partisan Voting Index: R+28

Population		Race and Ethnicity		Income	
Total	782,743	White	80.40%	Median Income	$60,060
Land area (sq. miles)	10,123	Black	10.90%	District Income Rank	261
Pop/ sq mi	77.32	Latino	15.20%	Poverty Rate	13.30%
Born in State	65.30%	Asian	1.60%	With health insurance	84.00%
		Two or more races	3.30%	Cash public assistance	1.10%
Age Groups		Other	3.80%	Food stamp/SNAP	10.70%
Under 18	24.50%				
18-34	20.10%	**Education**		**Work**	
35-64	38.80%	H.S grad or less	42.60%	White Collar	33.50%
Over 64	16.70%	Some college	33.80%	Sales and Service	39.50%
		College Degree, 4 yr	15.00%	Blue Collar	26.90%
Military		Post grad	8.60%	Government	15.50%
Veteran/ Active Duty	9.10%				

2020 Pres. Vote	Trump	258,470	(74%)	Biden	84,680	(24%)	
2016 Pres. Vote	Trump	210,587	(75%)	Clinton	60,841	(22%)	Johnson 6,530 (2%)

Eastern Dallas Area, Denison: The Red River Valley is hardscrabble farm country along an unnavigable river. First settled in the 1830s, in the days of the Texas Republic, many counties here reached their population peak around 1900, when a large extended farm family worked every 160 acres. It includes towns like Denison, due north of Dallas, best-known as the birthplace of Dwight Eisenhower, and Sherman, which was the site of a major race riot in 1930 when a Black farm worker accused of rape was attacked by a White mob. To the east is Texarkana, noteworthy because its neat grid streets cross the Texas-Arkansas state line, which is straddled by the city's downtown post office. The contrast between the laws of the two states has created competition for which side of the border is more attractive. This small city and its hinterland have produced three recent presidential candidates: Ross Perot grew up in Texarkana, while Bill Clinton and Mike Huckabee hail from Hope Arkansas, just 30 miles east.

Northeast Texas in 1912 sent Democrat Sam Rayburn to Congress, where he became the powerful House Speaker from 1940 until his death in 1961 (except for two terms when Republicans had the majority). The region was once a Democratic bastion, with a sentimental regard for Confederate veterans and a seething hatred of Wall Street bankers. That was Rayburn's politics, and he arguably was the most skillful lawmaker of the 20th century. Today, Rayburn's style of politics has almost completely vanished from the area.

The 4th Congressional District of Texas is the lineal descendant of the seat Rayburn held, and still includes his hometown of Bonham in Fannin County, which houses a Rayburn museum. But it is quite a different district today. In Rayburn's time, it was farm country, separate and distinct from citified Dallas. Today, it retains its farm counties, but they are only a short hop on the interstate from the Dallas-Fort Worth Metroplex, and about one-third of the district's residents live in the DFW metropolitan area. Rockwall County's population more than doubled between 2000 and 2019, Its median household income in 2019 was a robust $101,000. In addition to Rockwall, other population centers are Sherman-based Grayson County and Texarkana-based Bowie. In Texarkana, the Red River Army Depot has a robotics mission in partnership with the local campus of Texas A&M University. Less than 10 percent of the district is in suburban Collin County. Bonham is the site of the state's first new reservoir since 1999, which will pump water into northeast Dallas.

In 1940, the year Rayburn became Speaker, his district voted 90 percent for Franklin D. Roosevelt. In 2020, the 4th District voted 74 percent for President Donald Trump, which placed it third most-Republican in the state, behind two rural west Texas districts and among the top three percent of Republican districts nationwide in the Cook PVI.

Lance Gooden (R)

Elected 2018, 2nd term, b. Dec 01, 1982; Terrell, TX; Trinity Valley Community College; University of TX, B.A., 2004; Church of Christ; Married (Alexa Calligas).

Elected Office: TX House, 2011-2018.

Professional Career: Legislative Aide, Rep. Betty Brown; Insurance Broker.

DC Office: 425 CHOB 20515, 202-225-3484, gooden.house.gov

State Offices: Mesquite, 214-765-6789.

Committees: *Financial Services*: Diversity & Inclusion; Housing, Community Development & Insurance.

Almanac Ratings 2019-2020

	Economy	Social	Foreign	Composite
Liberal	27%	9%	5%	14%
Conservative	73%	91%	95%	86%

Key Votes of the 116th Congress

1. U.S./Mex./Can. trade deal	Y	5. Russia sanctions	Y	9. Firearms background checks N
2. First Coronavirus response	N	6. Troops in Syria	N	10. Spending at the border	Y
3. HEROES Act	N	7. Veto arms sales to Saudis	N	11. Marijuana liberalized rules	N
4. CASH Act	N	8. Defense $$$, veto override	N	12. Electoral College objections Y

Election Results

Election	Name (Party)	Vote (%)		Cand. Spent	Ind. Exp. Support	Ind. Exp. Oppose
2020 General	Lance Gooden (R)...............................	173,836	(62%)	$1,588,563	$7,953	$750
	Carolyn Salter (D)..............................	100,743	(36%)	$312,755		
	Kevin Hale (L)...................................	5,834	(2%)	$6,443		
2020 Primary	Lance Gooden (R)..............................	57,253	(83%)			
	Don Hill (R)......................................	11,372	(17%)			

Prior winning percentages: 2018 (62%)

Republican Lance Gooden, who showed impressive campaign skills to win his seat, joined the social conservative wing of House Republicans and was a hardline supporter of President Donald Trump in the allegations of voter fraud following the 2020 election. Gooden took the seat of Rep. Jeb Hensarling, who retired when he was term-limited as chairman of the House Financial Services Committee. Gooden's campaign success has been evidence that "all politics is local" remains an apt adage among some Republicans.

A resident of Terrell in rural Kaufman County, Gooden got bachelor's degrees in government and business administration from the University of Texas. He worked as an insurance broker and consultant for energy companies. In 2010, he was elected to the first of three terms in the state House. After losing reelection in 2014, he regained his seat two years later. His accomplishments included passage of a bill that stopped municipalities from annexing rural land into their city limits without the approval of local voters; the legislation resulted from a property conflict between Dallas and Kaufman counties. In the legislature, he was an ally of Speaker Joe Straus, whose desire for bipartisan coalition-building sparked internal Republican conflicts.

After Hensarling announced his retirement, the frontrunner was Bunni Pounds, a Republican political consultant who earlier had been Hensarling's campaign manager. With support from the Club for Growth and other national conservative groups, she had the initial fundraising lead. Gooden, with his base in the rural part of the district, was endorsed by many local officials from those areas. He emphasized his support for "traditional values" of those rural communities, in contrast to the "establishment" support for his opponent from insiders with "no connection to our district;" they included Vice President Mike Pence, a Hensarling ally. Gooden styled himself as "a new congressman of rural Texas, by rural Texas and for rural Texas."

Gooden led the first round of voting in the March primary, with 30 percent to 22 percent for Pounds; six other candidates divided the remainder. In Dallas County, which cast about one-fifth of the vote, Gooden won only 9 percent to 24 percent for Pounds and 38 percent for Kenneth Sheets, a former state representative. Gooden won an outright majority of the vote in Kaufman and Henderson counties, which were the core of his state House district.

Gooden was endorsed as the "hands-down choice" in the runoff by the Dallas Morning News, which cited his free-market views on economic issues, plus his "strong legislative experience," in contrast to the lack of legislative background by the "doctrinaire" Pounds. The final days of the contest featured a theological conflict between the Texas Catholic Conference of Bishops, which backed Gooden, and the Pounds-supporting Texas Right to Life Political Action Committee. In the runoff, Pounds led in Dallas and three of the outlying rural counties. Gooden again ran strongly in Kaufman and Henderson, which were the two largest county votes in the runoff, and he won, 54%-46%. Pounds outspent him by more than $200,000. Gooden benefited from significant spending by a super PAC, Our Conservative Texas Future, which was largely financed by Monty Bennett, an influential Dallas businessman, the Texas Tribune reported.

In November, Gooden faced Dan Wood, a lawyer and former member of the Terrell City Council. Wood got 59 percent of the vote in Dallas County, which cast 40 percent of the vote. Gooden took at least 70 percent in each of the six outlying counties and won, 62%-38%.

Gooden joined the Financial Services Committee, where he had professional experience in addition to the Hensarling connection. In October 2019, he filed a bill that was intended to reduce the risk for investors in the options markets, which would require federal regulatory agencies to develop a framework that would better calculate and account for the risk of those investments. "Recent options volatility has indicated the immediate need for adjustments to existing regulations," Gooden said.

He took strongly conservative views on illegal immigration across the southern border, despite the large number of Hispanics in his district. In January 2019, during the federal shutdown because of the conflict over Trump's call to increase funding of the border wall, Gooden said he would support declaration of a national emergency so Trump could secure additional funding. He filed a bill that would cut off federal funding to local governments that become so-called "sanctuary cities" that refuse to aid in enforcement of federal immigration law.

In his reelection, Gooden got 83 percent of the vote in the Republican primary and faced Democrat Carolyn Salter, an anesthesiologist and the former mayor of Palestine. "I'm going to represent my constituents," she said, trying to distance herself from national Democrats. Salter self-financed more than half of her $290,000 in spending. The November outcome was similar to two years earlier. Salter took 58 percent in Dallas County, which cast 40 percent of the vote. Gooden won the remaining counties with at least 68 percent and won overall, 62%-36%. Redistricting of Dallas-area districts could significantly influence his political future.

In December 2020, when the presidential election results had been determined, Gooden took the lead in sending a letter to Trump—signed by 27 House Republicans—urging him to direct Attorney General William Barr to appoint a special counsel to investigate alleged election fraud. Americans "deserve a definite resolution" of the election uncertainty, Gooden wrote. The letter came shortly after Barr told a reporter that he saw no evidence of fraud that would have affected the outcome.

TX-5: Dallas County   Cook Partisan Voting Index: R+15

Population		Race and Ethnicity		Income	
Total	759,749	White	75.30%	Median Income	$57,026
Land area (sq. miles)	5,044	Black	15.10%	District Income Rank	299
Pop/ sq mi	150.63	Latino	30.10%	Poverty Rate	13.00%
Born in State	65.10%	Asian	2.80%	With health insurance	78.30%
		Two or more races	2.20%	Cash public assistance	1.30%
Age Groups		Other	4.50%	Food stamp/SNAP	11.30%
Under 18	24.80%				
18-34	23.00%	**Education**		**Work**	
35-64	37.30%	H.S grad or less	49.10%	White Collar	30.30%
Over 64	14.80%	Some college	31.10%	Sales and Service	39.50%
		College Degree, 4 yr	13.10%	Blue Collar	30.20%
Military		Post grad	6.70%	Government	12.80%
Veteran/ Active Duty	6.40%				

2020 Pres. Vote	Trump	172,395	(61%)	Biden	107,494	(38%)		
2016 Pres. Vote	Trump	145,841	(62%)	Clinton	79,759	(34%)	Johnson	5,776 (3%)

Eastern Dallas Suburbs, Mesquite: Not all of Dallas is glitz and postmodern marble. East of downtown is an older Dallas with neighborhoods of old mansions, modest bungalows and shotgun houses. Some of these areas have been renovated and rebuilt, with chic cafes and trendy stores. Other once middle-class neighborhoods are filling up with immigrants from Mexico and are again noisy with children, as they were in the 1950s when people moved here not from Mexico or Central America, but from the almost all-Anglo counties of North and Central Texas.

The 5th Congressional District includes much of east and southeast Dallas County, including neighborhoods in east Dallas and suburban Mesquite, which has become a destination for immigrants moving up the economic ladder. The population of Mesquite was 141,000 in 2019—42 percent Hispanic and 26 percent Black. What started as a train depot in 1873 became the "Rodeo capital of Texas" on an 18-acre site in 1950, the Dallas Morning News reported in March 2020. In 1959, the Big Town mall opened: the first enclosed, air-conditioned mall in Texas. But downtown Mesquite declined in the 1980s, leading the city council to unveil a development plan in 2016. In 2015, the Breitbart.com website ran a story headlined, "Mesquite Texas — The Gun Show Capital of America," which described its several hundred shows annually as a mix of "trade shows, swap meets and raw capitalism," with crowds that are usually male, White and over 40. Since then, Mesquite has grown and become more suburban, with a new health care center and a furniture distribution facility. Per capita income in 2019 was half of that in upscale Plano. In 2018, the city had a 47 percent increase in building permits from a year earlier. The district also covers a more upscale slice of Dallas inside the LBJ freeway, including parts of Lakewood and White Rock Lake.

The minority population in the district has been steadily increasing, to 28 percent Hispanic and 15 percent Black in 2019. About 40 percent of the district's voters are in Dallas County. The 5th takes in six other counties in East Texas, the largest of which are Henderson and Kaufman. Anderson County was the site in 1910 of the little-noted Slocum Massacre in which a White mob attacked and killed as many as 25 Black residents and forced the remainder to flee, according to a report in 2015 on Texas Public Radio. Each of the outlying counties is heavily Republican. As rural areas have swung away from Democrats, the district switched from being a battleground in the early 1990s to safely Republican. In 2020, President Donald Trump won 61 percent of the vote. Aided by rural voters, that gave him the largest share of any Dallas-area district.

TX-6 - VACANT (V)

DC Office: 1725 LHOB 20515, 202-225-2002, wright.house.gov
State Offices: Arlington, 817-775-0370.

The Feb. 7, 2021 death of Republican Rep. Ron Wright triggered a special election, which was scheduled for July 27. In the 23-candidate all-party primary, Republicans got a break when they took the top two slots—blocking a Democrat from the July runoff. In something of a rematch of Wright's initial election in 2018, the final GOP contenders were Susan Wright, the widow of the late incumbent, and Jake Ellzey, who narrowly lost he GOP primary runoff to Ron Wright in 2018.

In the first round of voting for the vacant seat, Susan Wright led Ellzey, 19% to 14%. Trailing in third place by 347 votes was Democrats Jana Sanchez, a public relations consultant with experience as a campaign manager and some national Democratic connections. Even though Joe Biden got 48 percent of the district vote in November 2020, the 10 Democratic candidates running six months later got a total of only 37 percent.

In the July 2021 runoff, Susan Wright had the support of former President Donald Trump and the Wall Street-based Club for Growth. In addition to her work for her late husband, she had been active in local government and politics in Tarrant County and the city of Arlington. This was her first campaign for office.

Ellzey, a former Navy officer and fighter pilot who flew combat missions in Afghanistan and Iraq later became an aide to President George W. Bush and worked as a commercial airplane pilot. Following his unsuccessful contest with Ron Wright, he was elected to the state House in 2020—with easy victories in both the primary and general election in his Ellis County-based district.

In 2018, Ron Wright took the seat of 17-term Rep. Joe Barton, for whom Wright served as a longtime aide and had become his heir apparent. Even with his own extensive experience in city and county politics in the district, plus his conservative credentials, Wright struggled in the GOP primary, when he first sought the seat. Barton, who had been prominent as chairman of the House Energy and Commerce Committee, decided not to seek reelection after a nude photo of him appeared on social media in November 2017. Local unhappiness with Barton, who did not endorse in the GOP primary, had some negative impact on Wright's campaign.

A native of Tarrant County, Wright spent more than a decade as district director and then chief of staff for Barton. During much of that time, he pursued his own career as a member of the Arlington City Council and served as mayor pro tempore. He was appointed as Tarrant County tax assessor-collector and later was elected to two terms in that position.

Although Wright did not disavow Barton following his former boss' embarrassing social-media revelations, he said that he knew nothing about those actions and criticized Barton for "some terrible mistakes and choices." He emphasized his own experience in local office and distanced himself from Barton on some issues, notably by voicing hardline opposition to rights for illegal immigrants, even with his district's population that is more than 40 percent African-American and Hispanic. Wright cited support from the Club for Growth and pledged to join the conservative House Freedom Caucus.

In the March primary against Ellzey, who had a limited public profile in the district, Wright led, 45%-21%; nine other candidates split the remaining vote. In the runoff, the Dallas Morning News recommended Ellzey in an editorial and criticized Wright's plan to join the Freedom Caucus, which it called "one of the farthest right groups on Capitol Hill." Ellzey was endorsed by former Texas Gov. Rick Perry, who had become secretary of Energy in the Trump administration. Despite his commanding lead in the primary, Wright narrowly won the runoff, with 52 percent of the vote. In Tarrant, he took 68 percent, though turnout in that county dipped to less than half of the total vote. Ellzey got 63 percent in Ellis County and 57 percent in Navarro in the runoff.

In the November contest between Ron Wright and Sanchez, Democratic strategists switched their attention to other congressional campaigns in Texas. Wright prevailed, with 53 percent of the vote, with leads of more than 2-to-1 in Ellis and Navarro. Sanchez led 52%-47% in Tarrant.

The outcome of the 2020 election was similar. Wright was challenged by Stephen Daniel, a lawyer and long-time top aide to the Dallas County chief executive. Wright won, 53%-44%. Daniel took the vote in Tarrant County, 51%-46%, though Wright again prevailed with more than 2-to-1 leads in the outlying counties. Both won their party nomination without opposition.

TX-6: Southwest Metroplex — Cook Partisan Voting Index:

Population		Race and Ethnicity		Income	
Total	818,442	White	64.10%	Median Income	$71,161
Land area (sq. miles)	2,148	Black	21.10%	District Income Rank	154
Pop/ sq mi	380.95	Latino	25.40%	Poverty Rate	8.70%
Born in State	58.50%	Asian	4.80%	With health insurance	85.40%
		Two or more races	3.20%	Cash public assistance	1.40%
Age Groups		Other	6.90%	Food stamp/SNAP	8.40%
Under 18	25.90%				
18-34	23.80%	**Education**		**Work**	
35-64	38.00%	H.S grad or less	35.60%	White Collar	37.00%
Over 64	12.30%	Some college	32.00%	Sales and Service	38.30%
		College Degree, 4 yr	21.80%	Blue Collar	24.70%
Military		Post grad	10.60%	Government	13.20%
Veteran/ Active Duty	7.80%				

2020 Pres. Vote	Trump	175,101	(51%)	Biden	164,746	(48%)		
2016 Pres. Vote	Trump	148,945	(54%)	Clinton	115,272	(42%)	Johnson	8,552 (3%)

Arlington, Fort Worth Area: The Dallas-Fort Worth Metroplex—a name even the locals use— has spread outward from its historic nodes in downtown Dallas and downtown Fort Worth. Although Dallas is the larger population center, much of the development has moved west, across the plains and the barely perceptible Balcones Escarpment, the geologist's boundary between green and grassy East Texas and brown and barren West Texas. The plains have been filled in with subdivisions and shopping centers under the enormous Texas sky. Among the larger suburbs is Arlington, right between Dallas and Fort Worth and an easy highway commute to both cities. Named in 1877 after Robert E. Lee's hometown in Virginia (another suburb, but not quite so booming as the Texas locale), its location has been ideal as a site for regional attractions like Six Flags over Texas and Globe Life Park in Arlington, commissioned by the former part-owner of the Texas Rangers, George W. Bush. In 2009, the Dallas Cowboys opened the $1.1 billion domed AT&T Stadium in Arlington, which hosted the 2011 Super Bowl and the 2014 NCAA Final Four basketball tournament. In August 2018, developers opened in Arlington the $250 million Texas Live entertainment center, including hotel and dining facilities; a new feature was the largest e-sports stadium in the United States. The Rangers relocated to a new, air-conditioned stadium, due to declining attendance blamed on global warming. They played their first game there in July 2020, a delayed season start resulting from the coronavirus pandemic. (Redistricting in 2011 placed those complexes in a small area just outside the 6th District, in the 33rd District.)

Arlington's population of nearly 400,000 in 2019 was 30 percent Hispanic, 23 percent African American, and 7 percent Asian. Enrollment at the University of Texas campus in Arlington reached a new high of 42,733 students in 2020, making it the second-largest in the UT system behind Austin. GM's Arlington assembly plant produces the company's popular and highly profitable SUVs and employs about 4,800 workers. In 2018, GM switched the factory entirely to wind power as part of an expansion. As Arlington has filled up, the big growth has been to the south in Mansfield, where the population increased from 28,000 to 72,000 from 2000 to 2019.

The 6th Congressional District of Texas includes most of Arlington and the southern and northeastern fringes of Fort Worth to the west. Nearly three-fourths of the people live in Arlington and Tarrant County, which is the 15th largest in the nation. To the south is Ellis County, which grew 24 percent between 2010 and 2019. Beyond Ellis is small-town Navarro County, home to the Collin Street Bakery, which ships its famed fruitcakes around the world during Christmas season each year. Ellis and Navarro lean heavily Republican and provide the partisan ballast for the 6th. This territory was ancestrally Democratic for many years, then became solidly Republican. With non-Hispanic whites declining to 50 percent of the district, the GOP margin at the presidential level has tightened. In 2020, President Donald Trump took the district, 51%-48%.

Lizzie Fletcher (D)

Elected 2018, 2nd term, b. Feb 13, 1975; Houston, TX; William & Mary Law School, J.D., 2006; Kenyon College, B.A., 1997; Methodist; Married (Scott Fletcher PE); 2 stepchildren.

Professional Career: Attorney, Vinson & Elkins, Ahmad, Zavitsanos, Anaipakos, Alavi & Mensing.

DC Office: 1429 LHOB 20515, 202-225-2571, Fax: 202-226-3805, fletcher.house.gov

State Offices: Houston, 713-353-8680.

Committees: *Energy & Commerce*: Communications & Technology; Consumer Protection & Commerce; Health. *Science, Space & Technology*: Environment.

Almanac Ratings 2019-2020

	Economy	Social	Foreign	Composite
Liberal	51%	59%	80%	64%
Conservative	49%	41%	20%	36%

Key Votes of the 116th Congress

1. U.S./Mex./Can. trade deal	Y	5. Russia sanctions	Y	9. Firearms background checks	Y
2. First Coronavirus response	Y	6. Troops in Syria	Y	10. Spending at the border	Y
3. HEROES Act	Y	7. Veto arms sales to Saudis	Y	11. Marijuana liberalized rules	Y
4. CASH Act	Y	8. Defense $$$, veto override	Y	12. Electoral College objections	N

Election Results

Election	Name (Party)	Vote (%)		Cand. Spent	Ind. Exp. Support	Ind. Exp. Oppose
2020 General	Lizzie Fletcher (D)......................	159,529	(51%)	$6,268,633	$5,951	$3,193,550
	Wesley Hunt (R)...........................	149,054	(47%)	$7,237,428	$1,247,039	$1,434,331
2020 Primary	Lizzie Fletcher (D)........................	55,253	(100%)			

Prior winning percentages: 2018 (53%)

Democrat Lizzie Pannill Fletcher, elected in 2018, is part of a class that at times can seem larger than life, packed with retired military heroes, former NFL players and ex-spooks. At times she flew under the radar, and that seemed to be exactly how she wanted it. Fletcher scored a significant victory in the battle to shift control of suburban seats from Republicans' decades-long dominance that began with an earlier congressman, future President George H.W. Bush. As such, Republicans wanted badly to defeat her, not just for political reasons but symbolic ones as well. Fletcher is a cautious member, who is studious and a strong fundraiser and deeply engaged with her hometown of Houston.

Fletcher, a Houston native, first engaged in national politics in high school as a protestor at the 1992 Republican National Convention at the Astrodome. She linked arms with like-minded demonstrators and prevented abortion opponents from overrunning a nearby Planned Parenthood clinic. She went on to graduate from Kenyon College and earned her law degree from William and Mary. She began her career at the Houston-based and politically connected Vinson & Elkins law firm. As a partner at another firm that specialized in business litigation, she represented a cross-section of Houstonians facing difficult legal issues. She was a co-founder of Planned Parenthood Young Leaders and worked with local charitable groups.

Fletcher decided to run for Congress in early 2018 in reaction to the Trump presidency. The incumbent, Rep. John Culberson, who was an influential "cardinal" on the House Appropriations Committee. Culberson was one of three Republicans—starting with Bush—to hold the suburban Houston seat since it was created in 1966. He had never faced a credible Democratic challenger even as the district grew more diverse, but became an early target of House Democrats after Hillary Clinton in 2016 took it, 48%-47%. "Changing demographics, the #MeToo movement, and [Hurricane] Harvey may give the Democrats their best chance in decades to capture the West Houston seat," headlined Houston Public Media.

Fletcher won a hard-fought primary that spurred national controversy when House Democrats intervened on her behalf against her more progressive opponent. The Democratic primary attracted seven contenders. The frontrunners who advanced to the runoff were Fletcher and Laura Moser, a former journalist who had lived much of her adult life in the Washington D.C. area.

In an extraordinary move, the House Democratic campaign arm unleashed a blast of opposition research against Moser out of fear that she was too liberal for the district. She and her progressive allies gained more attention as she criticized the Democratic campaign committee for taking sides. Fletcher, meanwhile, reaffirmed her Texas roots and appealed to mainstream Democrats and other voters unhappy with President Donald Trump and congressional Republicans. She won the runoff, 67%-33%.

Culberson was slow to respond politically, saying he was busy arranging relief for victims of devastating local hurricane damage in 2017 and with his responsibilities in the House. In their only debate, Culberson praised the House Republican alternative to the Affordable Care Act and defended his low profile. "I don't go looking for the headlines," he said. Fletcher alleged long-term failure on Culberson's part to address hurricane threats to the Houston area and questioned the honesty of his campaign claims.

In endorsing Fletcher, the Houston Chronicle said she was "so well prepared, so knowledgeable about the job, so right for the district" and praised her for having "reclaimed the center." Although the editorial credited Culberson's handling of recent hurricane relief, it added, "his career has been spent promoting his own pet projects rather than serving the local needs of his home district."

Fletcher spent more than $6 million on the campaign, which nearly doubled Culberson's total. Each party and its allies spent more than $5 million for its candidate. Fletcher won, 53%-47%.

She faced a tougher challenge for reelection, this time against veteran Wesley Hunt—an African-American graduate of West Point. He ran a more robust campaign than Culberson—out-spending her $7.3 million to %6.3 million--and was a favorite recruit among national Republicans. While he narrowed the margin, Fletcher defeated him, 51%-47%.

Following her reelection, she got a coveted seat on the Energy and Commerce Committee. She was in the House gallery when rioters breached the Capitol. Terrified, she wore a gas mask and removed her congressional pin for fear of attackers on the hunt for members of Congress. "For me, who's relatively new here, there's really a majesty to this place, and it is … it is the Capitol of the United States of America," she told the Texas Tribune hours later. "To see it attacked? And to be present on this assault for our democracy, and our country was just … it's an assault on everything that we do right."

TX-7: Harris County   **Cook Partisan Voting Index: D+1**

Population		Race and Ethnicity		Income	
Total	762,826	White	60.00%	Median Income	$73,730
Land area (sq. miles)	162	Black	15.50%	District Income Rank	137
Pop/ sq mi	4,710.55	Latino	30.30%	Poverty Rate	10.30%
Born in State	45.00%	Asian	12.10%	With health insurance	82.80%
		Two or more races	3.40%	Cash public assistance	1.00%
Age Groups		Other	9.10%	Food stamp/SNAP	6.40%
Under 18	23.90%				
18-34	25.20%	**Education**		**Work**	
35-64	39.20%	H.S grad or less	24.90%	White Collar	49.60%
Over 64	11.80%	Some college	24.90%	Sales and Service	32.40%
		College Degree, 4 yr	30.40%	Blue Collar	18.00%
Military		Post grad	19.90%	Government	9.20%
Veteran/ Active Duty	4.30%				

2020 Pres. Vote	Biden	170,060	(54%)	Trump	143,176	(45%)			
2016 Pres. Vote	Clinton	124,722	(48%)	Trump	121,204	(47%)	Johnson	9,126	(4%)

West Houston and Suburbs: West Houston, particularly ritzy River Oaks, is the premiere address in all of Texas. It is here where many of the state's oil billionaires go to live, along with retired politicians, medical researchers and partners at some of the most powerful law firms in the country. In the early 1980s, the greatest civic contention in the area was noise from Houstonians flying to work downtown via helicopter. That problem solved itself when locals went broke in the 1980s oil bust and sought to pawn their commuter aircraft. For a while in the mid-2000s, the River Oaks mansions of convicted felons were even stops on an Enron bus tour.

The lavish Galleria, one of the largest malls in the United States with an ice rink and tennis club, draws more than 30 million visitors a year under its impressive glass atriums. Downtown Houston is sprouting apartment buildings. Oil companies have prospered, and many businesses moved here from the New Orleans area following the devastation of Hurricane Katrina in 2005.

When George H.W. Bush moved from Midland in West Texas to Houston in 1960, he bought a house in Briarwood in what were then the western outskirts of the fast-growing city. He returned to Houston in 1993 after losing his reelection bid for the presidency and built a new house one mile from his old one, near lush Memorial Park. The 7th Congressional District of Texas is the lineal descendant of the district that in 1966 elected Bush as the first Republican to represent Houston in the House. That this district is trending toward Democrats is a source of sentimental heartbreak not just for Republican operatives, but for the GOP donors who live there. In successive redistricting rounds, its boundaries have been pared back, as the population of the west side of Houston has skyrocketed. Today, more than 2 million people reside in an area where 350,000 lived when Bush was first elected. The district, based entirely in Harris County, includes most of the territory between the Katy Freeway (Interstate 10) and Westheimer Road from downtown. In Texas style, Katy's 26 lanes when it crosses Beltway 8 may be the widest highway in the world. The district takes in the affluent neighborhoods southwest of downtown Houston and a swath of Houston west of the 610 loop; Bellaire is the fourth-wealthiest town in Texas. During the torrential rains of Hurricane Harvey in August 2017, the Barker reservoir overflowed and caused extensive damage in the western end of the district. In 2018, voters in Harris County approved $250 million in bonds for flood-control projects.

Outside the loop is Gulfton, a rural area in the 1950s that became a haven for young oil workers in the 1970s and is now a predominantly Hispanic town the Houston Chronicle called an "ersatz Ellis Island for economic refugees from Mexico and Central America." Continued surges of immigration from Mexico have strained the public schools in Gulfton, whose sprawling apartment complexes have become the most densely populated neighborhood in Houston. The district is also home to Rev. Joel Osteen's Lakewood evangelical mega church, which describes itself as the largest congregation in the nation and draws more than 45,000 worshipers a week, with many more viewing the service on an internationally televised Sunday program.

The 7th long was a solidly Republican district, but its demographics are changing. After redistricting in 2011, it became a majority-minority district: Whites are about 43 percent of the population, Hispanics 30 percent, Blacks 15 percent and Asian Americans 12 percent. Among the voting-age population, Hispanics skewed younger and turned out to vote at a lower rate. President Donald Trump played poorly among this educated population, a factor that elevated Democrats down-ballot here. The district that Mitt Romney won with 60 percent in 2012 and Joe Biden won, 54%-45% in 2020 is a district in upheaval—with further change likely in redistricting.

Kevin Brady (R)

Elected 1996, 13th term, b. Apr 11, 1955; Vermillion, SD; University of SD, B.S., 1990; Roman Catholic; Married (Cathy Brady); 2 children.

Elected Office: TX House, 1991-1996.

Professional Career: Executive, The Woodlands Chamber of Commerce, 1978-1996.

DC Office: 1011 LHOB 20515, 202-225-4901, Fax: 202-225-5524, kevinbrady.house.gov

State Offices: Conroe, 936-441-5700; Huntsville, 936-439-9532.

Committees: *Joint Taxation. Ways & Means (RMM).*

Group Ratings

	ADA	ACLU	AFL-CIO	LCV	COC	HAFA	ACU	CFG	FRC
2020	**	14%	**	5%	-	78%	92%	**	-
2019	0%	C	32%	7%	75%	C	93%	77%	100%

Almanac Ratings 2019-2020

	Economy	Social	Foreign	Composite
Liberal	25%	11%	30%	22%
Conservative	75%	89%	70%	78%

Key Votes of the 116th Congress

1. U.S./Mex./Can. trade deal Y	5. Russia sanctions N	9. Firearms background checks N
2. First Coronavirus response Y	6. Troops in Syria Y	10. Spending at the border Y
3. HEROES Act N	7. Veto arms sales to Saudis N	11. Marijuana liberalized rules N
4. CASH Act N	8. Defense $$$, veto override Y	12. Electoral College objections N/A

Election Results

Election	Name (Party)	Vote (%)		Cand. Spent	Ind. Exp. Support	Ind. Exp. Oppose
2020 General	Kevin Brady (R)	277,327	(73%)	$3,563,499	$7,468	$750
	Elizabeth Hernandez (D)	97,409	(25%)	$12,270		
	Chris Duncan (L)	7,735	(2%)			
2020 Primary	Kevin Brady (R)	75,044	(81%)			
	Kirk Osborn (R)	15,048	(16%)			

Prior winning percentages: 2018 (73%), 2016 (100%), 2014 (89%), 2012 (77%), 2010 (80%), 2008 (73%), 2006 (67%), 2004 (69%), 2002 (93%), 2000 (92%), 1998 (93%), 1996 (59%)

Republican Kevin Brady, first elected in 1996, served three years as chairman of the House Ways and Means Committee. As one of the most powerful players in Congress, he sat at the starting point for much of President Donald Trump's legislative program—notably, the tax cuts that were enacted in December 2017. After Republicans lost House control in the 2018 election, Brady defended Trump's objections to efforts by House Democrats to get copies of the president's tax returns. He voiced major differences with Trump on his use of tariff increases in international trade. Term-limited in the top Republican slot at Ways and Means in 2022, he announced his retirement.

Brady comes easily to his pro-business viewpoint. He grew up and went to college in South Dakota, moved in 1978 to what was then rural Texas in Montgomery County and headed The

Woodlands Chamber of Commerce for 18 years. In 1990, he was elected to the Texas House. When Brady ran for the open seat in Congress, his chief opponent in the decisive Republican primary was Eugene Fontenot, a physician who said he wanted "to restore America to its Christian heritage." Brady was the choice of party regulars; Fontenot was backed by religious conservatives.

Fontenot attacked Brady for being one of two Republicans to vote against the state's concealed weapons law. Brady had opposed most gun control bills but not the concealed weapons bill. When he was 12 years old, his father, an attorney, was shot and killed while trying a case in a South Dakota courtroom. "I couldn't look Mom in the eye and vote for this," he told the Houston Chronicle after the vote. (In 2013, he said he regretted the vote. "I've been remarkably impressed with how well concealed-carry has worked in Texas," he told National Journal.) The campaign was grueling and convoluted. After Fontenot led Brady in the March primary, Brady won the April runoff 53%-47%. After the Supreme Court in June ordered a redrawing of 13 districts, Brady led Fontenot 41%-39% in an all-party primary in November. Finally, in the December runoff, turnout was sharply down and Brady won their third face-off, 59%-41%.

Brady has compiled a conservative voting record, though he has often been more of a pragmatist than other Texas conservatives. He is known for being easygoing and soft-spoken, but that doesn't mean he never gets mad. His November 2009 showdown with Treasury Secretary Timothy Geithner made national news when Brady savaged Geithner's handling of the Wall Street crisis, saying, "The public has lost all confidence in your ability to do the job." A year earlier, Brady was the only Houston-area member of the House in either party to vote for the financial industry rescue. "As much as I detest this bill, doing nothing is worse," he said.

At Ways and Means, Brady has focused on economic issues. For many weeks in 2015, he worked closely with Ways and Means and House GOP leaders to win the House's narrow approval of trade promotion authority for President Barack Obama to submit his Trans-Pacific Partnership.

Much of his work has been on the tax code. Brady in 2014 got a bipartisan bill through the House to make permanent and expand the research and development tax credit. The Obama administration, however, opposed the measure because it would expand the credit without offsetting the cost. On an important local matter, Brady was a central figure in the successful effort in 2004 to make state and local sales taxes deductible in the seven states, including Texas, that have no personal income tax.

When the Ways and Means chairmanship became open after the 2014 election, Brady made his case for the job. He challenged Rep. Paul Ryan, the 2012 vice presidential nominee, who had chaired the House Budget Committee. "I'm qualified and prepared to lead this committee," Brady told Bloomberg TV. "This is all about the ideas and how we can move tax reform, trade, entitlement reform forward, so it's good to have a healthy competition."

Ryan had less seniority than Brady, but he had the support of Speaker John Boehner and made at least an implicit disavowal of plans for another national campaign. Ryan prevailed, though Brady retained his Health Subcommittee post. He would later benefit from running a respectful campaign. Brady continued as the senior House Republican on the Joint Economic Committee, which studies fiscal policy but has no power to consider legislation.

His next opportunity at Ways and Means came sooner than expected amid the internal House Republican chaos. When Boehner in late September 2015 announced his resignation as Speaker under pressure, House Republicans struggled to find a successor. After other contenders fell short, Ryan became the consensus choice of virtually all Republicans and became Speaker a month later. That created uncertainty and awkwardness at Ways and Means, especially for Brady. Although Brady seemed to be the heir apparent, Rep. Pat Tiberi of Ohio—a Boehner ally—said that he would seek the chairmanship.

Five days after Ryan became Speaker, one of his first official duties was to chair the leadership committee meeting as it selected his Ways and Means successor. Shortly before the secret-ballot vote, Ryan said he was supporting Brady. This time, Brady won.

With 2016 consumed by the presidential election, Brady's start as chairman was relatively quiet. That respite ended with Republicans in control of Congress and, unexpectedly, Donald Trump as president. It took time for Brady and GOP leaders to establish a working relationship with Trump on the handling of major legislation. That resulted in missed deadlines on budget actions and an extended scramble before the House passed in May 2017 its first major legislation during the Trump presidency: the bill to repeal and revise the Affordable Care Act. On that legislation, the final deals were brokered chiefly by Ryan and other GOP leaders.

Later in the year, Brady had primary responsibility for handling the Republican tax cuts which will likely be his legacy. He faced an early setback when Republicans abandoned his plan to impose a "border adjustment" tax on imports, as a tool to assist U.S. manufacturers. That proposal was actively opposed by retail groups, who ran an extended lobbying campaign. Within the House, Brady faced resistance from Republicans and Democrats from high-tax states who were unhappy with his plan to limit deductions for state and local taxes for high earners. On that issue, Brady prevailed.

Democrats complained that the Republican legislation favored the wealthy and that Ways and Means Republicans were acting mostly behind closed doors—with coordination by Ryan, the previous chairman. For Brady and his allies, failure was not an option and their party usually responds favorably to tax cuts. In November 2017, the House passed the bill, 227-205, with no Democratic support and opposition from 12 Republicans—chiefly from the high-tax states of California, New Jersey and New York. After Senate Republicans made limited tweaks, the House sent the final version to Trump a month later. "This is an incredibly exciting day for the American people, who have waited years—even decades—for a simpler, fairer tax code that will grow our economy and allow them to keep more of their hard-earned money," Brady exulted.

That was not the final move on taxes by the House Republican majority. In July 2018, Brady unveiled a "tax cut 2.0" plan, with lower rates, incentives for savings and steps to make permanent the 2017 cuts. The House planned "to look at the tax code every year—not just once a generation— to consider how we do things better," Brady said. The House passed the Brady-crafted tax-relief plan in one of its final votes before adjourning for the election. The Senate during its lame-duck session had no time to consider the bill, which had no hope after Democrats took House control.

Brady clashed with Trump on his use of tariff hikes. Resorting to his customary free-trade view, Brady told CNBC in July 2018 that "tariffs are taxes [that] impede economic growth. ... We do worry about that." Also that month, he urged Trump to resolve the "escalating trade dispute" with China.

In the minority, Brady quarreled with a fellow Texan, Democratic Rep. Lloyd Doggett, who was outspoken in the new majority's attempt to gain access to Trump's tax returns. "Weaponizing the tax code for political purposes sets a dangerous precedent," Brady told reporters in February 2019. In October 2020, when The New York Times published extensive details from Trump's tax returns, Brady said that publication of the information was a "felony crime" that demanded investigation.

Amid his new prominence in Washington, Brady ran into a major problem at home in 2016: his first significant Republican primary contest. He faced three challengers, who spent a total of less than $200,000, compared with the $4 million Brady spent during the campaign cycle. Steven Toth, an ordained minister and a former state representative, was his chief challenger. In a pre-primary story, The Texas Tribune reported, "Brady is in enough trouble that outside groups—including the leadership-aligned Congressional Leadership Fund super PAC—are spending big to protect him." Brady subsequently was routinely nominated and elected. In April 2021, he announced that he will not seek reelection and said that Republican term limits on committee leaders was a "factor into that decision." Although Republicans were nearly certain to retain the district, it could have significant changes in redistricting—with its population center either closer to Houston, or farther away.

TX-8: Northern Houston Suburbs

Cook Partisan Voting Index: R+25

Population		Race and Ethnicity		Income	
Total	895,861	White	83.00%	Median Income	$78,615
Land area (sq. miles)	6,054	Black	8.40%	District Income Rank	100
Pop/ sq mi	147.98	Latino	24.20%	Poverty Rate	10.10%
Born in State	57.60%	Asian	3.00%	With health insurance	86.90%
		Two or more races	2.70%	Cash public assistance	0.90%
Age Groups		Other	2.80%	Food stamp/SNAP	6.70%
Under 18	24.90%				
18-34	21.20%	**Education**		**Work**	
35-64	39.50%	H.S grad or less	38.60%	White Collar	40.60%
Over 64	14.30%	Some college	30.80%	Sales and Service	36.40%
		College Degree, 4 yr	20.70%	Blue Collar	23.00%
Military		Post grad	9.80%	Government	15.50%
Veteran/ Active Duty	7.00%				

2020 Pres. Vote	Trump	274,224	(71%)	Biden	109,291	(28%)			
2016 Pres. Vote	Trump	214,605	(72%)	Clinton	70,532	(24%)	Johnson	8,418	(3%)

Montgomery County: Montgomery County, north of Houston, was once fenceless cattle country, dotted with roadside stands and barbecues. In 1931, wildcatter George Strake struck oil near

Conroe. Thousands of other wildcatters and roughnecks quickly joined in the boom, and this became one of the richest oil-producing areas in the nation. Active production continues today.

The oil boom centered on Conroe was followed by a population and economic boom. In 1974, a planned community called The Woodlands opened 30 miles north of Houston and 15 miles south of Conroe. Development of this new city has barreled along since, with corporate parks, glistening condo towers, pristine golf courses and a man-made waterway. Its real estate, which is among the most expensive in the Houston area, was home to more than 117,000 residents and 2,200 businesses with 68,000 employees, as of January 2019. Anadarko Petroleum, with two office towers, has been the chief corporate presence, with 3,400 employees. In early 2019, Chevron and Occidental were in a bidding war for Anadarko. The Cynthia Woods Mitchell Pavilion in The Woodlands, which opened in 1990, was listed as the third-busiest outdoor concert venue in the nation in 2018. The Woodlands is the home to five large hospitals and has styled itself as a prominent medical center. Entergy expected to complete construction in 2021 of a $1 billion natural gas-fired power plant north of Conroe; officials said it would pay for itself in 10 years because of energy efficiency.

The 8th Congressional District includes all of Montgomery County, which is one of the fastest-growing counties in Texas and contains about two-thirds of the district's people. This area is potent with conservatism and serves as a bulwark against Democratic statewide ambitions. About 10 percent of the district is a small slice of Harris County, a few miles from George Bush International Airport. The district extends north through parts of the thinly populated Brazos Valley and covers Sam Houston National Forest and Davy Crockett National Forest. It encompasses all of seven counties and parts of two. The district takes in Huntsville, with one of Texas' oldest prisons, and "Big Sam," a 67-foot-tall statue of Sam Houston outside the town along Interstate 45. This is in the top five percent of Republican districts in the nation, with a Cook PVI of +25 for Republicans. President Donald Trump won 71%-28% in 2020.

Al Green (D)

Elected 2004, 9th term, b. Sep 01, 1947; New Orleans, LA; Tuskegee University, B.A.; University of FL, Att., 1971; TX Southern University, Thurgood Marshall School of Law, J.D., 1973; Baptist; Marital status unknown.

Elected Office: Harris County justice of the peace, 1977-2004.

Professional Career: Practicing attorney, 1973-1977; President, Houston NAACP, 1986-1995.

DC Office: 2347 RHOB 20515, 202-225-7508, Fax: 202-225-2947, algreen.house.gov

State Offices: Houston, 713-383-9234.

Committees: *Financial Services*: Consumer Protection & Financial Institutions; Housing, Community Development & Insurance; Oversight & Investigations (Chmn). *Homeland Security*: Border Security, Facilitation & Operations; Emergency Preparedness, Response & Recovery.

Group Ratings

	ADA	ACLU	AFL-CIO	LCV	COC	HAFA	ACU	CFG	FRC
2020	**	83%	**	100%	-	0%	6%	**	-
2019	95%	C	95%	97%	58%	C	7%	18%	0%

Almanac Ratings 2019-2020

	Economy	Social	Foreign	Composite
Liberal	100%	100%	80%	94%
Conservative	0%	0%	20%	6%

Key Votes of the 116th Congress

1. U.S./Mex./Can. trade deal	Y	5. Russia sanctions	Y	9. Firearms background checks	Y
2. First Coronavirus response	Y	6. Troops in Syria	Y	10. Spending at the border	Y
3. HEROES Act	Y	7. Veto arms sales to Saudis	Y	11. Marijuana liberalized rules	Y
4. CASH Act	Y	8. Defense $$$, veto override	Y	12. Electoral College objections	N

Election Results

Election	Name (Party)	Vote (%)		Cand. Spent	Ind. Exp. Support	Ind. Exp. Oppose
2020 General	Al Green (D)	172,938	(75%)	$354,425	$995	$361
	Johnny Teague (R)	49,575	(22%)	$81,322	$156	$113
	José Sosa (L)	6,594	(3%)			
2020 Primary	Al Green (D)	48,387	(84%)			
	Melissa Wilson-Williams (D)	9,511	(16%)			

Prior winning percentages: 2018 (89%), 2016 (81%), 2014 (91%), 2012 (78%), 2010 (76%), 2008 (94%), 2006 (100%), 2004 (72%)

Democrat Al Green, first elected in 2004 and a champion of the homeless and poor, became the earliest and most outspoken advocate of the impeachment of President Donald Trump—even when party leaders wanted to downplay that option for fear of stoking conservative counter-action. His legislative work has focused on the Financial Services Committee, where he represents the interests of low-income groups. With his engaging demeanor, he has had some success in building bipartisanship. Like his namesake soul-singer-turned-preacher, Green is deeply religious, usually sporting a "God Is Good" lapel pin.

Green grew up in New Orleans. He attended college at Florida A&M University and graduated from Texas Southern University's law school, where he later taught. He was elected justice of the peace for Harris County in 1977 and served 26 years. For a decade, he also was president of the Houston chapter of the NAACP.

After the congressional redistricting in 2003 that largely benefited Republicans, Green saw an opening to run for Congress. The representative from the old district that covered much of this area was Chris Bell, a white Democrat elected in 2002, when he defeated a more conservative Black candidate. Green said he wanted to fight discrimination in law enforcement and used subtle racial references on the campaign trail, including his promise to bring "a mountain of soul" to the new district. He amassed endorsements from prominent local and national Black leaders. Bell responded by asking voters "not to focus on the color of my skin, but on the size of my heart." He was endorsed by the AFL-CIO, teachers unions, abortion rights groups and Democratic Minority Leader Nancy Pelosi. But he struggled as a white candidate running in a heavily minority district. Green won the primary in a landslide, 66%-31%, and faced no real opposition in the general election.

Green began with a relatively moderate voting record but has become a more liberal Democrat. The Almanac ratings have ranked him among the most liberal House member from Texas. On the Financial Services Committee, he chairs the Oversight and Investigations Subcommittee, where he has worked to eliminate housing practices that discriminate against minorities, at times successfully enlisting Republicans in his efforts. In October 2019, he held a hearing with the LGBTQ community on discrimination in lending and housing. In 2015, the House passed his "Homes for Heroes" bill to increase housing assistance to low-income and homeless veterans, and give the topic a higher priority at the Department of Housing and Urban Development. An estimated 50,000 veterans are homeless.

Like most Texas lawmakers, Green is protective of the oil and gas industry, joining a group of Democrats in 2009 warning that President Barack Obama's proposal to raise taxes and impose new fees on the industry would hamper domestic production. Green broke with House Democrats by voting in 2012 for a bill to double the number of offshore oil and gas drilling leases, probably the smart vote in a Houston-based district that relies on oil profits. In 2015, he was one of 28 House Democrats who voted for the Keystone XL oil pipeline.

Green has focused on a diverse set of social issues. After Democrats were criticized before their 2012 convention for initially leaving the word "God" out of the party platform, Green was added as a speaker to reinforce the party's commitment to religion. As part of the congressional delegation that accompanied Obama to Cuba in 2016, Green voiced concern about the racism experienced by Afro-Cubans, who are more than one-fourth of the population on the island.

Green did not take long to advocate the impeachment of Trump. "I will not be moved. The president must be impeached," he told the House in May 2017. His position initially was based on Green's view that Trump had damaged the social fabric of the nation. The damage to American society could be "irreparable," Green said in September 2018. He filed the initial articles of impeachment, which were tabled in December 2017 on a 364-58 vote. After Democrats won the House and Pelosi said impeachment could not go forward without bipartisan support, Green in February 2019 filed new impeachment charges, which were based on what he called "400 years of bigotry culminating in the Trump presidency." In July, he forced a vote on his revised charges; his proposal was tabled, 332-95. "Dr. King reminds us that there are times that you have to do that which is neither safe nor politic nor popular. You do them because they are right," Green said. Two months later, Democratic leaders and most of the Caucus joined him.

In June 2019, Green was among the first members of Congress to endorse Kamala Harris for president. Ignoring the two Texans who were then running, he said, "Kamala Harris represents the future of our nation." In 2020, Green faced his first primary challenge since he was first elected. "I am not going to be bullied out of challenging him," Melissa Wilson-Williams, a mortgage banker, told the Houston Chronicle. Opposed to abortion and a ban on semi-automatic weapons, she spent $57,000. In its endorsement of Green, the Houston Chronicle wrote, "we do admire his courage to step out boldly for what he believes in" and added, "there is no evidence that Green's more traditional liberal positions are out of step with his district." He won, 84%-16%.

TX-9: Harris County, Eastern Fort Bend County

Cook Partisan Voting Index: D+27

Population		Race and Ethnicity		Income	
Total	769,335	White	34.50%	Median Income	$49,147
Land area (sq. miles)	166	Black	39.00%	District Income Rank	393
Pop/ sq mi	4,644.62	Latino	38.00%	Poverty Rate	20.60%
Born in State	50.00%	Asian	12.10%	With health insurance	73.80%
		Two or more races	2.30%	Cash public assistance	1.70%
Age Groups		Other	12.00%	Food stamp/SNAP	16.90%
Under 18	25.30%				
18-34	25.40%	Education		Work	
35-64	38.10%	H.S grad or less	46.90%	White Collar	28.00%
Over 64	11.20%	Some college	26.70%	Sales and Service	44.90%
		College Degree, 4 yr	17.20%	Blue Collar	27.20%
Military		Post grad	9.30%	Government	10.80%
Veteran/ Active Duty	3.90%				

2020 Pres. Vote	Biden	178,908	(76%)	Trump	54,944	(23%)
2016 Pres. Vote	Clinton	151,559	(79%)	Trump	34,447	(18%)

South Houston: A half-century ago, the steaming flatlands south of Houston running down to the Gulf of Mexico did not seem a likely site for one of the world's most advanced civilizations. But spreading out in all directions from its historic center at Allen's Landing on Buffalo Bayou, Houston has become one of the great metropolises of North America. Most of the scientific work in NASA's early years was done in Houston, and the first word spoken when man landed on the moon was "Houston." It is the undisputed center of expertise in the oil business and has been at the center of innovations in fracking, leading to a resurgence in drilling throughout South Texas. Houston is the fourth-largest city in the nation, with a population that grew 21 percent from 2000 to 2020. Demographers expect it will surpass Chicago as the third-largest in the next decade. It is now the most ethnically diverse major metropolitan area, according to a Rice University report, citing its status as an "immigration gateway."

The famed Astrodome, which was once the "Eighth Wonder of the World," has been closed since 2009 and came close to demolition. After voters in 2013 rejected a referendum to turn it into a giant convention center, the Harris County Commission in 2016 decided to create a parking lot on its lower two levels. Work was scheduled to start in 2019 on a renovation, which would raise its floor by 30 feet to ground level and encourage more open space for festivals and events. The projected $105 million cost was supposed to be paid by revenues and fees, with support from a nonprofit conservancy. But city officials forced a delay because, they said, the air conditioning system was not large enough. By the end of 2020, the Houston Chronicle reported, the plan was "all but dead."

Houston has become a medical mecca. The giant Texas Medical Center—the largest in the world —has more than 50 medical institutions, including 21 hospitals. The Memorial Hermann Health System, the largest in Houston, completed in 2020 a $700 million expansion and renovation at the TMC. The MD Anderson Cancer Center, which U.S. News in 2019 ranked as the top cancer hospital in the nation, has more than 20,000 employees, including 1,700 faculty members. The TMC has not only a swanky new Intercontinental Hotel as a center for medical tourism, but also a residential community with 375 units.

The 9th Congressional District of Texas slices across the southern part of metropolitan Houston in Harris County. It takes in two wedges of Fort Bend County, which form a crescent around the 22nd District and include about 30 percent of the district's voters. The 9th includes many African-American neighborhoods, low-income and middle-income, in both counties. Its population is 39 percent Hispanic and 38 percent Black, although many of the former are not citizens or do not vote. Another 12 percent are Asians, many clustered along Bellaire Boulevard in the Chinese-American community. Entrepreneurial Vietnamese boat people settled in Alieve and have created quality schools, an Asian-oriented shopping mall and businesses that serve one of the largest Vietnamese communities in the nation. Overall, this is a heavily Democratic district, which gave Joe Biden 76 percent of the vote in 2020, his second best in Texas, trailing only the Dallas-based 30th District.

Michael McCaul (R)

Elected 2004, 9th term, b. Jan 14, 1962; Dallas, TX; Trinity University, B.A., 1984; Harvard University John F. Kennedy School of Government, Att., 2002; St. Mary's University School of Law, J.D., 1987; Catholic; Married (Linda McCaul); 5 children (triplets).

Professional Career: Federal prosecutor, 1990-1999; Deputy Attorney General, 1999-2003; Chief, Western Div. of TX. U.S. Attorney's Office, 2003-2004.

DC Office: 2001 RHOB 20515, 202-225-2401, Fax: 202-225-5955, mccaul.house.gov

State Offices: Austin, 512-473-2357; Brenham, 979-830-8497; Katy, 281-398-1247; Tomball, 281-255-8372.

Committees: *Foreign Affairs (RMM). Homeland Security.*

Group Ratings

	ADA	ACLU	AFL-CIO	LCV	COC	HAFA	ACU	CFG	FRC
2020	**	14%	**	33%	-	77%	84%	**	-
2019	15%	C	38%	21%	94%	C	86%	50%	95%

Almanac Ratings 2019-2020

	Economy	Social	Foreign	Composite
Liberal	25%	38%	27%	30%
Conservative	75%	62%	73%	70%

Key Votes of the 116th Congress

1. U.S./Mex./Can. trade deal	Y	5. Russia sanctions	Y	9. Firearms background checks N
2. First Coronavirus response	Y	6. Troops in Syria	Y	10. Spending at the border Y
3. HEROES Act	N	7. Veto arms sales to Saudis	N	11. Marijuana liberalized rules N
4. CASH Act	Y	8. Defense $$$, veto override	Y	12. Electoral College objections N

Election Results

Election	Name (Party)	Vote (%)		Cand. Spent	Ind. Exp. Support	Ind. Exp. Oppose
2020 General	Michael McCaul (R)	217,216	(52%)	$4,109,004	$86,300	$100,913
	Mike Siegel (D)	187,686	(45%)	$3,000,314	$178,793	$276,787
	Roy Eriksen (L)	8,992	(2%)			
2020 Primary	Michael McCaul (R)	60,323	(100%)			

Prior winning percentages: 2018 (51%), 2016 (57%), 2014 (62%), 2012 (61%), 2010 (65%), 2008 (54%), 2006 (55%), 2004 (79%)

Michael McCaul, a Republican first elected in 2004 as a protégé of Texas GOP Sen. John Cornyn, has been an activist legislator. As chairman of the Homeland Security Committee for six years, he pursued an agenda of timely issues, often on a bipartisan basis, and warned of threats facing the nation. Following the 2018 election, he switched to the top Republican post on the Foreign Affairs Committee. McCaul remained interested in a Senate seat, if available.

McCaul grew up in Dallas, studied business and history at Trinity University, earned his law degree at St. Mary's University, both in San Antonio. He worked as a federal prosecutor and then moved to Austin in 1999 to be a deputy to state Attorney General Cornyn. In 2002, he joined the U.S. attorney's office and was chief of the Terrorism and National Security Section for West Texas.

McCaul was one of eight candidates in the 2004 Republican primary for the newly created congressional district. The other top Republican contenders were mortgage company owner Ben Streusand and former Judge John Devine. McCaul focused on his anti-terrorism work, calling himself the only candidate who "won't have a learning curve." Streusand, based in Harris County, called for less government regulation. Devine had the support of Christian conservatives and called for a crackdown on illegal immigration. In the primary, Streusand carried seven of the eight counties to finish with 28 percent of the vote, to 24 percent for McCaul, who ran strongly in his Travis County base, and 21 percent for Devine.

In the runoff campaign, McCaul criticized Streusand's past donations to Democratic candidates, while Streusand questioned McCaul's service in the Clinton administration Justice Department. McCaul used his connections—his father-in-law is Clear Channel Communications founder and Chairman Lowry Mays—to collect major Republican endorsements. McCaul won 63%-37%, carrying both Travis and Harris counties. McCaul is perennially at the top of the wealthiest members of Congress lists. The Center for Responsive Politics estimated his net worth in 2017 at close to $120 million. In the House, McCaul has a mostly conservative voting record. Early in his career, he cast moderate votes that included requiring insurers to treat mental illness the same as other health conditions, and allowing the Food and Drug Administration to regulate tobacco products. He worked with Democratic Rep. G.K. Butterfield of North Carolina in 2012 to enact a bill encouraging companies to develop drugs for rare childhood cancers and other diseases. After Republicans took control of the House in 2011, his voting record grew more conservative, particularly on fiscal matters. McCaul earned the gratitude of House GOP leaders for leading the protracted 2010 ethics investigation of Democratic Rep. Charles Rangel of New York that culminated in Rangel's censure by the full House.

In 2011, as chairman of Homeland Security's Oversight, Investigations and Management Subcommittee, McCaul filed legislation to have six Mexican drug cartels designated as foreign terrorist organizations, a move that could have led to much stiffer penalties for drug traffickers. Later, he pressed Obama administration officials at a hearing over their failure to define "spill-over violence" from the drug wars in Mexico. McCaul cosponsored a cybersecurity bill with bipartisan support that would develop standards for dealing with cyberthreats; it passed the House in 2012 but fell victim to partisan squabbling in the Senate.

After the 2016 election, he was on President-elect Donald Trump's initial short list to lead the Homeland Security Department and publicly voiced interest in the job. Although McCaul had advised the Trump campaign and transition team on immigration enforcement, he said in January 2017 that the new president's executive order on immigration "went too far" in restricting lawful entry.

Later that year, when Homeland Security Secretary John Kelly gave up that job to become White House chief of staff, McCaul again was considered for the job. But it had become clear that he didn't see eye-to-eye with Trump on some issues, including immigration policy and his management style. He had differences—at least in tone—with Trump's proposal for a wall on the border with Mexico.

"I don't think we need a 2,000 mile wall down there," McCaul said in an interview with PBS in 2017. A year later, he criticized Trump's handling of his meeting in Helsinki with Russian President Vladimir Putin as "demoralizing" to U.S. intelligence agencies and said that he was "astounded at the inability" of Trump to criticize Russian meddling in the 2016 presidential election.

Term-limited as chairman of the Homeland Security Committee, McCaul in 2018 earned the opening as the top Republican at the Foreign Affairs Committee. His previous experience was an advantage in winning the position—now in the minority. He had early cooperation with Democratic Chairman Eliot Engel of New York. In February 2019, McCaul said he was "deeply troubled" by the Trump administration's response to Saudi Arabia's murder of dissident Jamal Khashoggi.

At home, McCaul voiced interest in the seat of Sen. Ted Cruz during the latter's presidential campaign in 2016 and later, at the national convention when many of the party faithful were unhappy with Cruz's failure to endorse Trump. Cruz eventually rebuilt his bridges with the Texas GOP. Likewise, McCaul was mentioned as a possible successor when Cornyn was briefly considered in 2017 for the opening of FBI director. With his deep pockets and law-enforcement persona, McCaul could be a credible statewide contender.

McCaul is a cooler force in a delegation that is often full of hotheads He's known for striking up friendships with an occasional Democrat, counting Rep. Henry Cuellar, a Laredo Democrat, as one of his best friends. He publicly described his terror during the Jan. 6, 2021, insurrection, in which he and his staff barricaded their office door shut and he prepared for battle with a baseball bat. He opted against impeaching Trump for allegations of inciting the riot, but did so reluctantly. "I will, with a heavy heart, oppose impeachment at this time," he said. "I did not come to this decision lightly. And I truly fear there may be more facts that come to light in the future that will put me on the wrong side of this debate."

His reelection bid in 2018 proved to be unexpectedly competitive. Democrat Mike Siegel, a civil rights lawyer in Austin, endorsed much of the progressive agenda and said McCaul "refused to act as a check on Trump." McCaul declined to participate in campaign debates and missed a meeting with editors at the Houston Chronicle. Siegel had little national party support and was outspent by McCaul, $1.9 million to $486,000. McCaul won, 51%-47%, his narrowest outcome in eight elections. Siegel took Travis County by 50,000 votes and McCaul led in Harris by nearly 31,000. The incumbent's huge margins in the rural counties pushed him over the top. In a 2020 rematch against Siegel, McCaul was better prepared with a campaign infrastructure and defeated Siegel by a more comfortable 52%-45% margin. This time, McCaul outspent Siegel, $4.1 million to $3 million. He increased his margin in Harris to 43,000 votes, while Travis was little changed.

TX-10: Western Harris County, Northern Travis County

Cook Partisan Voting Index: R+5

Population		Race and Ethnicity		Income	
Total	925,348	White	70.10%	Median Income	$80,528
Land area (sq. miles)	5,071	Black	12.70%	District Income Rank	88
Pop/ sq mi	182.48	Latino	30.70%	Poverty Rate	8.10%
Born in State	54.70%	Asian	5.10%	With health insurance	86.00%
		Two or more races	3.30%	Cash public assistance	0.50%
Age Groups		Other	8.90%	Food stamp/SNAP	6.30%
Under 18	25.70%				
18-34	23.10%	**Education**		**Work**	
35-64	38.80%	H.S grad or less	31.00%	White Collar	46.70%
Over 64	12.30%	Some college	27.60%	Sales and Service	32.80%
		College Degree, 4 yr	26.50%	Blue Collar	20.50%
Military		Post grad	14.80%	Government	15.20%
Veteran/ Active Duty	5.90%				

2020 Pres. Vote	Trump	210,770	(50%)	Biden	203,975	(48%)	
2016 Pres. Vote	Trump	164,912	(52%)	Clinton	135,984	(43%) Johnson	11,251 (4%)

Austin/Houston Corridor: Two of Texas' major cities are named for leaders of the old Texas Republic, Sam Houston and Stephen F. Austin. They were not entirely attractive characters: Houston had episodes of alcoholic depression, and Austin was a slaveholder who argued that Mexico infringed on Texas' liberty when it freed its slaves. But they were also men of courage and determination who built a distinctively American culture in what was then the northeast of Mexico. Today, the two metropolises named for them are quite different in character. Houston is about commerce, the capital of the oil business, an entrepreneurial hub spread out over the swampy, humid plains north of the Gulf of Mexico. Austin is the creature of the state government headquartered in the grand capitol building and of the University of Texas, with a huge endowment of land in West Texas that turned out to be full of oil. Still, Austin has as much oil in its DNA as does Houston.

Politically, these two urban centers have moved in very different directions. The historic Austin is a liberal enclave in the heart of a conservative state. North of the capitol and the university, an entrepreneurial Austin has taken shape, one that embraces technology and the free market, and is a major center for technology startups and the manufacturing of computer and electronic products. It is host to the annual South by Southwest (SXSW) conference, which had more than 417,000 participants in 2019. Started in 1986 by journalists chiefly as a music festival, it has become a 10-day phenomenon of policy, culture, food, entertainment and networking. The area around north Austin and its suburbs has taken on some of Houston's character in recent years. Apple has built a campus in northwest Austin, which handles hardware technologies, customer service and human resources; its payroll of 6,700 at the end of 2020 was scheduled to grow by at least another 5,000 on a new 133-acre campus less than a mile away.

With 160 miles between Austin and Houston, the drive goes through thinly populated counties dotted with plaques recalling the days of the Texas Republic. This area includes seven lightly populated rural counties, including Austin County and its small town of Sealy, where the same-named mattress company was founded. On that route is the town of La Grange, which is famous for the nearby "Chicken Ranch" that while closed in 1973 became the setting of the Broadway musical "The Best Little Whorehouse in Texas." The town of Brenham is home to renowned ice cream manufacturer Blue Bell Creamery. The company suffered a setback with Listeria contamination that caused three deaths and closed the facility for most of 2015; three years later, it had rebounded. Brenham is a popular rest stop for travelers between the two cities.

The 10th Congressional District of Texas is like a barbell (politically, if not visually) that connects the western suburbs of Houston with the northern precincts of Austin through a corridor of rural counties. It is split into three parts. About 40 percent live on the western edge of Houston's Harris County, a fast-growing and overwhelmingly Republican area, with lots of young families, new subdivisions and mega-churches. Another 35 percent of the voters are in Austin and Travis County, where the Democratic arm of the district includes the northern third of Austin, with one tentacle reaching northwest beyond the city limits and another dropping south to Austin State Hospital. In 2020, the congressional vote in the 10th was 62 percent Republican in Harris and 69 percent Democratic in Travis. The small towns between the two ends are heavily Republican. With minority growth on each end, the Hispanic population is 28 percent and Blacks account for 11 percent. The Republican presidential vote dropped from 59 percent in 2012 to 50 percent in 2020, when Joe Biden trailed by fewer than 7,000 votes.

August Pfluger (R)

Elected 2020, 1st term, b. Dec 28, 1977; Harris County, TX; United States Air Force Academy, B.S.; Georgetown University, M.S.; Embry-Riddle Aeronautical University, M.S.; Christian; Married (Camille Coley); 3 children.

Military Career: Lieutenant Colonel, U.S. Air Force, 2000-2020.

Professional Career: National Defense Fellow, The Washington Institute for Near East Policy, 2018-2019; Director, Defense Policy and Strategy, National Security Council, 2019-2020;

DC Office: 1531 LHOB 20515, 202-225-3605, Fax: 202-225-1783, pfluger.house.gov

State Offices: Brownwood, 325-646-1950; Granbury, 682-936-2577; Llano, 325-247-2826; Midland, 432-687-2390; Odessa, 432-331-9667; San Angelo, 325-659-4010.

Committees: *Foreign Affairs*: Europe, Energy, the Environment & Cyber; West Hem, Civ Sec, Migration, & Intern'l Econ Policy. *Homeland Security*: Intelligence & Counterterrorism (RMM).

Election Results

Election	Name (Party)	Vote (%)		Cand. Spent	Ind. Exp. Support	Ind. Exp. Oppose
2020 General	August Pfluger (R)................... 232,568	(80%)		$2,085,100	$480,467	
	Jon Mark Hogg (D)................... 53,394	(18%)		$132,949		
	Wacey Alpha Cody (L)............... 5,811	(2%)				
2020 Primary	August Pfluger (R)................... 56,093	(52%)				
	Brandon Batch (R)................... 16,224	(15%)				
	Wesley W. Virdell (R)............... 7,672	(7%)				
	Jamie Berryhill (R)................... 7,496	(7%)				

Republican August Pfluger, a former Air Force fighter pilot and national security advisor to President Donald Trump, was elected in one of the strongest Republican districts in the nation. As a first-time candidate, he scored the impressive mark of winning a majority of the votes in the 10-candidate Republican primary. Bolstered by his huge advantage in campaign spending, Pfluger was one of only two freshmen from Texas—of the seven Republicans who were elected in 2020—to avoid a runoff following the March primary. He took the seat of retiring Rep. Mike Conaway, who chaired three House committees during his eight terms.

Pfluger, a seventh-generation Texan, grew up on his family's several ranches near San Angelo. He graduated with honors from the Air Force Academy and served for nearly 20 years. Flying T-38 Talon trainers and F-22 Raptor and F-15 Eagle fighters, he had more than 250 hours of direct action against sites in Iraq and Syria that were held by the Islamic State. Later, he commanded hundreds of combat pilots who were based in the United Arab Emirates and served in operational offices at the Pentagon and NATO Command in Italy.

Pfluger received master's degrees in aeronautical sciences and military strategy from Embry-Riddle University and later pursued a master's in international business and policy at Georgetown University. For three months in 2019, prior to announcing his candidacy for Congress, he was an adviser on the White House National Security Council staff. He remained active in his family's ranching business and founded an energy investment company in the Permian Basin of West Texas.

After Conaway announced his retirement, Pfluger launched his campaign with consistently conservative views. He was endorsed in the primary by Trump plus two military veterans in Congress: Sen. Tom Cotton of Arkansas and Rep. Dan Crenshaw of Texas, both Republicans. One endorsement he did not receive was from the conservative House Freedom Caucus; its leaders backed Jamie Berryhill, a local businessman. Pfluger spent $800,000 in the primary, which nearly matched the combined total spent by the nine other Republican candidates.

His results in the primary were impressive. With 52 percent of the vote, he took all 29 counties in the sprawling district. Brandon Batch, a businessman and former congressional aide, finished second with 15 percent. Berryhill, a real estate developer and business consultant, and businessman Wesley Virdell each received 7 percent.

Against Jon Mark Hogg, who won the Democratic primary without opposition, Pfluger won 80%-18% in November.

In the House, he was assigned to two committees: Foreign Affairs and Homeland Security, where he was ranking Republican on the Intelligence and Counterterrorism Subcommittee.

TX-11: West-Central Texas   **Cook Partisan Voting Index: R+32**

Population		Race and Ethnicity		Income	
Total	790,264	White	83.10%	Median Income	$64,070
Land area (sq. miles)	27,832	Black	4.30%	District Income Rank	215
Pop/ sq mi	28.39	Latino	39.90%	Poverty Rate	11.60%
Born in State	68.60%	Asian	1.10%	With health insurance	82.20%
		Two or more races	2.60%	Cash public assistance	1.50%
Age Groups		Other	8.90%	Food stamp/SNAP	7.10%
Under 18	25.60%				
18-34	23.30%	**Education**		**Work**	
35-64	35.50%	H.S grad or less	44.20%	White Collar	33.00%
Over 64	15.60%	Some college	32.60%	Sales and Service	36.30%
		College Degree, 4 yr	15.40%	Blue Collar	30.70%
Military		Post grad	7.70%	Government	12.60%
Veteran/ Active Duty	8.00%				

2020 Pres. Vote	Trump	235,697	(79%)	Biden	58,592	(20%)		
2016 Pres. Vote	Trump	193,620	(78%)	Clinton	47,468	(19%)	Johnson	6,659 (3%)

Midland, Odessa: In the 1540s, the conquistador Francisco Coronado and his men rode their horses over the plains of the land they called the Llano Estacado, or "palisaded plains," which is now West Texas. They found a vast emptiness, gradually and imperceptibly rising in elevation to the west, with only scrub vegetation and small bands of Comanche Indians. What they did not see, lying far beneath the surface, was oil, discovered in the 1940s in large amounts in the Permian Basin. When oil was found, two tiny county seats 25 miles apart suddenly became small cities—Odessa, home of the roughneck oil well workers, and Midland, the more upscale town where oil entrepreneurs lived and started their own Petroleum Club. The Permian Basin boomed in the years just after World War II. In 1940, Ector and Midland counties had a population of 26,000. By 1960, they had grown to 159,000. Midland in the 1950s was an affluent town by West Texas standards, but hardly luxurious. Air conditioning had not yet become standard in homes or schools, and there were no mansions at the edge of town, just barren desert and oil derricks. George and Barbara Bush moved to the Permian Basin in 1948 in search of success in the oil industry and room for a growing family. They rented houses in Odessa before upgrading to a series of larger, but by no means grand, ranch houses in Midland. President George W. Bush's wife, Laura, also is from Midland. Odessa is perhaps best known as the high school football-crazed town depicted in the 1990 book Friday Night Lights, later turned into a movie and hit TV series.

In an area that still yields much of the state's oil, production and land sales have increasingly been driven by new hydraulic fracturing techniques. As recently as early 2014, 536 of the 1,540 onshore oil rigs operating in the United States were in the Permian Basin. As a result, there are few American cities that feel the swing of a boom-and-bust market quite like Midland. Tales of the 1980s oil bust are legion. In recent years, it has been mostly boom. In 2018, Midland had the hottest housing market in the country. Midland's population grew 18 percent from 2000 to 2010 and an even more impressive 31 percent in the next nine years. In November 2019, CNN headlined Midland as "America's ultimate boomtown," with unemployment at 2 percent. A few months later, when the coronavirus pandemic slowed the world's economy, virtually everyone in Midland felt the pain and wondered how long until—and whether—the old normal would return.

The 11th Congressional District of Texas covers much of West Texas. It sweeps through 29 counties and across 300 miles of often barren land from the New Mexico border to the outskirts of both Fort Worth and Austin. More than half the population is in Midland, Ector and Tom Green (San Angelo) counties. The district's Hispanic population has steadily increased to 38 percent. West Texas in the 1940s was, like nearly every other part of Texas, almost totally Democratic. That began to change in the 1950s. The 11th today is overwhelmingly Republican, giving President Donald Trump 79 percent of the vote in 2020. Slightly behind the adjacent 13th District, it remained the second-most Republican district in Texas, though they no longer were the top-two in the nation, as in 2016 and 2012. Instead, they ranked third and fourth in the Cook PVI.

Kay Granger (R)

Elected 1996, 13th term, b. Jan 18, 1943; Greenville, TX; TX Wesleyan University, B.S., 1965; University of TX - Arlington, 1976; Methodist; Divorced; 3 children; 5 grandchildren.

Elected Office: Ft. Worth City Council, 1989-1991; Ft. Worth Mayor, 1991-1996.

Professional Career: Teacher, 1965-1978; Life ins. agent, 1978-1985; Chairman, Ft. Worth Zoning Comm., 1981-1989; Founder & President, Kay Granger Ins. Co. Inc.

DC Office: 1026 LHOB 20515, 202-225-5071, Fax: 202-225-5683, kaygranger.house.gov

State Offices: Fort Worth, 817-338-0909.

Committees: *Appropriations (RMM)*: Ex Officio membership on all subcommittees.

Group Ratings

	ADA	ACLU	AFL-CIO	LCV	COC	HAFA	ACU	CFG	FRC
2020	**	11%	**	14%	-	83%	82%	**	-
2019	15%	C	35%	10%	89%	C	83%	59%	100%

Almanac Ratings 2019-2020

	Economy	Social	Foreign	Composite
Liberal	28%	36%	33%	33%
Conservative	72%	64%	67%	67%

Key Votes of the 116th Congress

1. U.S./Mex./Can. trade deal	Y	5. Russia sanctions	Y	9. Firearms background checks	N
2. First Coronavirus response	Y	6. Troops in Syria	Y	10. Spending at the border	Y
3. HEROES Act	N/A	7. Veto arms sales to Saudis	N	11. Marijuana liberalized rules	N
4. CASH Act	Y	8. Defense $$$, veto override	Y	12. Electoral College objections	N/A

Election Results

Election	Name (Party)	Vote (%)		Cand. Spent	Ind. Exp. Support	Ind. Exp. Oppose
2020 General	Kay Granger (R)	233,853	(64%)	$2,631,579	$971,135	$2,266,419
	Lisa Welch (D)	121,250	(33%)	$89,892		
	Trey Holcomb (L)	11,918	(3%)	$259		
2020 Primary	Kay Granger (R)	43,240	(58%)			
	Chris Putnam (R)	31,420	(39%)			

Prior winning percentages: 2018 (64%), 2016 (69%), 2014 (71%), 2012 (71%), 2010 (72%), 2008 (68%), 2006 (67%), 2004 (72%), 2002 (92%), 2000 (63%), 1998 (62%), 1996 (58%)

Kay Granger, first elected in 1996 and the only Republican woman in the state's delegation, is one of the most powerful Texans in Congress. Less conservative than most other Texas Republicans, she became the ranking member on the Appropriations Committee in 2019. Granger quietly wields her power on behalf of her district, including a massive public works project and production of F-35 fighter planes in Fort Worth.

Granger grew up in Fort Worth, graduated from Texas Wesleyan College and worked as a high school journalism and English teacher in North Richland Hills. She raised three children and started her own insurance agency, which she operated for more than 20 years. In 1989, she was elected to the Fort Worth Council, and two years later was elected as the nonpartisan mayor. When the House seat opened, leaders of both parties recruited Granger.

She decided to run in the Republican primary. In a three-candidate race, she was attacked as a liberal, partly for her support of abortion rights. She won with 69 percent of the vote. Her Democratic opponent was Hugh Parmer, a former Fort Worth mayor and the challenger to GOP Sen. Phil Gramm in 1990. Parmer attacked Republican cuts in Medicare and the stewardship of House Speaker Newt Gingrich. Granger called for a balanced budget and tax cuts for business and ran on her record as mayor. She won 58%-41%, a stunning Republican victory in the district held for 18 terms by Democratic Speaker Jim Wright until 1989.

Granger's voting record has been in the center of House Republicans, as shown by the Almanac vote ratings. In 2007-08, she was vice chair of the Republican Conference, but her leadership ambitions were limited. One of Granger's legislative achievements was enactment of tax-free savings accounts for higher education expenses. In 2014, Speaker John Boehner named her to chair a working group on the border crisis, chiefly in the Rio Grande Valley. Her proposal was far less costly than the plan submitted by President Barack Obama. She takes her work seriously and rarely seeks media attention. "Kay Granger chooses work over recognition," the Fort Worth Star-Telegram headlined a March 2015 news story.

After six years chairing the subcommittee that controls spending for the State Department and foreign aid, she took over in 2017 as chairwoman of the Defense Subcommittee. Her expertise on national security issues and local funding have been instrumental for the major defense plants in her district.

Over the years, she has kept a close eye on local Pentagon spending and worked to maintain production in her district of Lockheed Martin planes, especially the F-35 fighter jet. Her selection to chair the subcommittee was all the more timely because Donald Trump following his election had tweeted, "F-35 program and cost is out of control." After the October 2016 release of Trump's crude comments about women, Granger said that he "should remove himself from consideration as commander in chief." Following the election, she said Trump had a "mandate for change" and "I will work with whoever is the president."

The key constituent project of Granger's career has been a water control project, "Panther Island." She has directed hundreds of millions of dollars to the north side of downtown Fort Worth to reroute the Trinity River. The project's plans also have aimed to create a new entertainment district in the city. With her son, J.D. Granger, as executive director of the Trinity River Vision Authority that has been responsible for the plan and its ballooning costs, Granger faced extended negative publicity. In October 2019, he was forced out of his position at the authority, which reportedly was taken over by the city; he took on new responsibilities with flood control projects for the water district.

As ranking member of the Appropriations Committee, Granger prevailed over other senior Republicans on the committee. As she rose through committee ranks, Granger formed a close and productive working relationship with Democratic Rep. Nita Lowey of New York, who retired in 2021.

Granger has been reelected by wide margins. Her moderate tendencies inspired challenges in the 2010 and 2012 Republican primaries by underfunded challengers from her right, whom she dispatched with ease. She wrote a book, What's Right About America: Celebrating Our Nation's Values, published in 2006. Granger faced her toughest race in early 2020, when Republican Chris Putnam challenged her in the district's Republican primary. While she ran an unsteady campaign and Putnam pummeled her for her criticisms of Trump and for Panther Island, she soundly defeated him 58%-42%.

TX-12: Tarrant County

Cook Partisan Voting Index: R+15

Population		Race and Ethnicity		Income	
Total	844,563	White	78.90%	Median Income	$73,000
Land area (sq. miles)	1,441	Black	9.70%	District Income Rank	145
Pop/ sq mi	586.03	Latino	23.20%	Poverty Rate	8.30%
Born in State	60.20%	Asian	3.80%	With health insurance	84.00%
		Two or more races	3.00%	Cash public assistance	1.20%
Age Groups		Other	4.70%	Food stamp/SNAP	7.20%
Under 18	24.70%				
18-34	23.90%	**Education**		**Work**	
35-64	38.00%	H.S grad or less	37.20%	White Collar	39.90%
Over 64	13.30%	Some college	30.90%	Sales and Service	37.80%
		College Degree, 4 yr	21.10%	Blue Collar	22.30%
Military		Post grad	10.80%	Government	11.60%
Veteran/ Active Duty	7.90%				

2020 Pres. Vote	Trump	224,490	(60%)	Biden	140,683	(38%)		
2016 Pres. Vote	Trump	177,939	(62%)	Clinton	92,549	(33%)	Johnson	10,173 (4%)

Fort Worth and Western Suburbs: Fort Worth has a fair claim to being the quintessential American city. It is "where the West begins," as its 19th century boosters proclaimed, coining the slogan that's still used by the city. Situated halfway across the continent, it is just west of the Balcones Escarpment that divides the dry, treeless grazing lands of West Texas from the humid green croplands of East Texas This was the last stop for cattle drives before they returned to Kansas. In the 20th century, the city became a favorite place for oil wildcatters to do business. It is Southern in heritage and Northern in its advanced post-industrial economy. It has the nation's longest row of Western wear shops and one of the nation's richest families, the Basses, whose steel skyscrapers dominate the skyline. The family developed Sundance Square, a 35-block entertainment, office and retail district that has helped revive the downtown district. The area was named for the running mate of famed outlaw Butch Cassidy, who regularly frequented Fort Worth for its saloons and gambling establishments at the turn of the 20th century.

"Cowtown," "Panther City" or "Funky Town," as the city is sometimes called, surpassed Indianapolis in 2018 to become the 15th most populous city in the nation. It has a high-tech economy and has been an aviation center since the 1940s, though one that was hard hit by defense cuts. The huge Lockheed Martin plant, which employs about 14,000 people, produces numerous bombers and fighter planes, including the F-35 fighter jet. Next door is the Naval Air Station Fort Worth Joint Reserve Base, formerly Carswell Air Force Base, the home of B-52 bombers for years. The New York Times has called the city "an irresistible combination of cowboys and culture," in part because it has some of the nation's premier small museums, including the Amon Carter Museum, the Kimbell Art Museum, the Modern Art Museum of Fort Worth, and the Sid Richardson Museum. The newly opened Dickie Arena is a new source of civic pride that honors the city's cowboy roots and will host sporting events and rodeos.

City leaders have sought to tamp down the city's historic little-brother rivalry with nearby Dallas. While many in Fort Worth commute to Dallas, many of the city's residents resent the Dallas shadow. Newspaper publisher Amon Carter was known to pack a sack lunch for trips to Dallas, to avoid supporting the city's economy.

The 12th Congressional District includes about half of Fort Worth and western suburban Tarrant County, as well as all of Parker County to the west and part of Wise County to the north. About 76 percent of the population is in Tarrant, which has grown an impressive 41 percent since 2000. It has narrowed its population gap with Dallas County to less than 600,000 residents. Parts of Tarrant are in six districts, of which the 12th has the largest share. The district includes northern and western Fort Worth neighborhoods and the affluent southwest quarter beyond Texas Christian University, downtown and the stockyards. Parker County was once windswept open land around the courthouse town of Weatherford, where Rep. Jim Wright, a Democrat, grew up and later served two-plus years as Speaker, before he quit in 1989 in the face of ethics sanctions. Today, Parker is sprouting subdivisions; it has grown 22 percent from 2010 to 2019, to a population of 143,000.

Fort Worth and Tarrant County stayed Democratic in the 1950s when Dallas went Republican. With Dallas recently swinging back to Democrats, Fort Worth and Tarrant County continued to swing Republican. In 2018, Tarrant, the last urban Republican county in the state, fell to the Democrats when Rep. Beto O'Rourke carried the county by 4,400 votes (less than one percentage point margin) in his challenge to Sen. Ted Cruz. Democrats made a ferocious challenge for Tarrant County in 2020, with a slate of state legislative and congressional candidates. While Joe Biden carried the county by fewer than 2,000 votes, the rest of the Democratic challengers fell short. The 12th remained strongly Republican, with President Donald Trump winning, 60%-38%.

Ronny Jackson (R)

Elected 2020, 1st term, b. May 04, 1967; Levelland, TX; South Plains College, A.S., 1988; TX A&M University System, B.S., 1991; University of TX Medical Branch, M.D., 1995; Church of Christ; Married (Jane Ely); 3 children.

Military Career: Rear Admiral, U.S. Navy, 1995-2019 (Iraq); U.S. Marine Corps.

Professional Career: Commander, White House Medical Unit; Physician to the President, 2013-2018; Chief Medical Advisor to the President, 2019.

DC Office: 118 CHOB 20515, 202-225-3706, Fax: 202-225-3486, jackson.house.gov

State Offices: Amarillo, 806-641-5600; Wichita Falls, 940-285-8000.

Committees: *Armed Services*: Military Personnel; Tactical Air & Land Forces. *Foreign Affairs*: Africa, Global Health & Global Human Rights; Middle East, North Africa & Global Counterterrorism.

Election Results

Election	Name (Party)	Vote (%)		Cand. Spent	Ind. Exp. Support	Ind. Exp. Oppose
2020 General	Ronny Jackson (R)	217,124	(79%)	$1,719,547	$994,722	$167,617
	Gus Trujillo (D)	50,477	(18%)	$16,956		
	Jack Westbrook (L)	5,907	(2%)			
2020 Primary	Josh Winegarner (R)	29,327	(44%)			
	Ronny Jackson (R)	20,048	(20%)			
	Chris Ekstrom (R)	15,387	(15%)			
	Elaine Hays (R)	7,701	(8%)			
2020 Primary Runoff	Ronny Jackson (R)	36,684	(56%)			
	Josh Winegarner (R)	29,327	(44%)			

Republican Ronny Jackson, a retired Navy rear admiral and a familiar Washington figure as the White House physician for three presidents, was elected to the House following a bitter Republican primary in one of the strongest GOP districts in the nation. He won the primary run-off against Josh Winegarner, a lobbyist for a Texas farm group, who had a big lead in the first round of voting.

Jackson turned the contest in his favor by citing his close relationship with President Donald Trump, who earlier had nominated Jackson to serve as secretary of Veteran Affairs; Jackson withdrew his name from Senate consideration for that position following allegations of professional misconduct. In the House, he succeeded GOP Rep. Mac Thornberry, a former chairman of the House Armed Services Committee, who strongly backed Winegarner.

Jackson was raised and continued to reside in Levelland, which became a sore point in the primary because it is west of Lubbock in the 11th District. He graduated from Texas A&M University at Galveston and went to medical school at the University of Texas Medical Branch, while he served in the Navy Reserve.

He was assigned as an officer to the Naval Hospital in Portsmouth Virginia. From there, he joined the Navy's undersea medical officer program in Groton Connecticut and qualified as a Navy deep-sea diver trained in hyperbaric and submarine medicine. He served in multiple aquatic operations around the world dealing with explosive ordnance disposal, special warfare and salvage diving,

After he completed his residency in emergency medicine at Portsmouth, Jackson was assigned in 2005 to the Marine Corps. He was deployed to Iraq as the physician in charge of resuscitative medicine for a surgical shock trauma platoon in Taqaddum Iraq. A year later, Jackson was selected as the White House physician to President George W. Bush. The Navy extended his active duty as Jackson retained that position with President Barack Obama and then with Trump. In that position, Jackson directed health care for the Cabinet and senior staff, and he led the White House medical unit as its commanding officer.

In 2018, Trump nominated Jackson to join his Cabinet as head of the Department of Veterans Affairs. But the Republican-controlled Senate's review ran into problems, including allegations that

Jackson was drinking on the job and overprescribing medication. After the nomination stalled, Trump appointed him as an assistant to the president and to the new position of chief medical advisor to the White House and Executive Office of the President.

After Thornberry announced his retirement, Jackson was late in joining the field of 15 candidates in the Republican primary. He centered his campaign on his military experience and his close relationship to Trump. But he needed time to learn about fundraising and other campaign skills and to get acquainted with the sprawling rural district.

With a boost from having served as an aide to several congressional Republicans from Texas, including Thornberry, Winegarner led the first round of voting, with 39 percent; Jackson finished a distant second with 20 percent, which placed him ahead of Chris Ekstrom, a businessman who self-financed his campaign with $1 million and finished third with 15 percent.

In the runoff, support from Trump's political team and the vote delay because of concerns about COVID-19 gave Jackson time to become more familiar with voters. With the two candidates sharing strong conservative views, Jackson emphasized his close connection to Trump plus Winegarner's time in the "Washington swamp." Winegarner's broadcast ads depicted him as "one of our own" and attacked Jackson as an outsider. Each spent more than $1 million in seeking the nomination. Jackson won the July contest, 56%-44%. He led Winegarner in each of the district's nine largest counties. His election in November, by contrast, was a breeze, 79%-18%. He got seats on the Armed Services and Foreign Affairs committees.

TX-13: North Texas/Panhandle   Cook Partisan Voting Index: R+33

Population		Race and Ethnicity		Income	
Total	714,733	White	85.10%	Median Income	$54,004
Land area (sq. miles)	38,349	Black	5.50%	District Income Rank	346
Pop/ sq mi	18.64	Latino	28.40%	Poverty Rate	13.20%
Born in State	66.70%	Asian	2.40%	With health insurance	83.40%
		Two or more races	2.80%	Cash public assistance	1.40%
Age Groups		Other	4.10%	Food stamp/SNAP	10.00%
Under 18	24.90%				
18-34	22.80%	**Education**		**Work**	
35-64	36.40%	H.S grad or less	47.50%	White Collar	30.10%
Over 64	16.00%	Some college	31.10%	Sales and Service	39.40%
		College Degree, 4 yr	14.50%	Blue Collar	30.40%
Military		Post grad	6.80%	Government	16.30%
Veteran/ Active Duty	9.90%				

2020 Pres. Vote	Trump	219,888	(79%)	Biden	54,002	(19%)			
2016 Pres. Vote	Trump	190,838	(80%)	Clinton	40,253	(17%)	Johnson	6,709	(3%)

Amarillo, Wichita Falls: The farther west one travels in Texas, the browner the land gets and the smaller the towns get, until you arrive at counties containing only a few hundred people each —plus quite a few more head of cattle. At that point, the land rises nearly 1,000 feet in elevation, up steep hillsides from the gullies along the rivers that for most of the year are just trickles, to the tilted tableland that makes up the High Plains of West Texas. The winds here sweep down from the Rockies, the land is barren except where irrigated, often with the now dangerously depleted waters of the Ogallala Aquifer. The land alternates between grazing areas and cotton fields. But here and there in this demanding environment—sticky hot in the summer, swept by north winds from Canada in winter, always threatened by tornadoes—comfortable cities have been built to house the people and businesses that bring forth some of the nation's most abundant oil, natural gas, helium and other elements from the earth. The area produces cotton and milo, a variety of sorghum, and is home to one of the nation's oldest cattle auctions. Researchers have discovered dangerous levels of uranium at some sites in the Ogallala Aquifer. Support has grown for greater use of renewable energy in the Panhandle, especially wind.

Around Wichita Falls is the agricultural land of the Red River Valley. Cadillac Ranch, located just off I-40 west of Amarillo, is a famous roadside sculpture featuring "10 tail-finned, brightly painted Cadillacs planted nose down in a pasture," as Texas Monthly described it. Built in 1974, the attraction inspired the 1980 Bruce Springsteen song Cadillac Ranch. Archer City, home of the late novelist Larry McMurtry, was chronicled in The Last Picture Show and Texasville. Female entrepreneur Enid

Justin founded Nocona Boots in its namesake Montague County town in 1925. The boot company eventually relocated, but Nokona baseball mitts are still produced in the town.

The 13th Congressional District spans 39 counties and parts of two others, from the New Mexico border to just north of Denton in the Dallas exurbs. That is a Texas-sized drive of more than 450 miles. The area was long dominated by Texas Anglos, but Latinos lately have been moving here in large numbers to work in the fields or in crop processing. Still, the population in the region has been either in decline or stagnant for three decades. Today, the district is 28 percent Hispanic. In need of workers, the city has become a haven for refugees. Amarillo is the largest city in the heart of cowboy country. It is famously windy—windier than Chicago, in fact. Just outside town is the Pantex plant that secretly assembled and then dismantled thousands of nuclear warheads and was the epicenter of American defense in the Cold War. Much of the facility has decayed, including leaky roofs. Pantex has become the site of a renewable energy project that removes carbon dioxide emissions from the air. In November 2020, high case levels of COVID-19 left local officials responding that they were facing war-like challenges, including the need for mobile morgues. At the same time, the city reported the lowest unemployment rate in Texas. To the east, close to the Red River Valley, the district borders Denton County at the northwest corner of the Metroplex.

Settled by Confederate veterans, the valley was heavily Democratic through the 1970s. The High Plains were for years more Republican. Both are now solidly Republican, and so is the 13th District. In 2020, President Donald Trump got 79 percent of the vote here, which was no longer his strongest performance in the nation. This Texas district slightly trailed the 4th District of Alabama and the 5th District of Kentucky.

Randy Weber (R)

Elected 2012, 5th term, b. Jul 02, 1953; Pearland, TX; Alvin Community College; University of Houston, Clear Lake, B.S., 1977; Baptist; Married (Brenda Weber); 3 children; 7 grandchildren.

Elected Office: Pearland City Council, 1990-1996; TX House, 2008-2013.

Professional Career: Owner, Weber's Air & Heat, 1981-present.

DC Office: 107 CHOB 20515, 202-225-2831, Fax: 202-225-0271, weber.house.gov

State Offices: Beaumont, 409-835-0108; Lake Jackson, 979-285-0231; League City, 281-316-0231.

Committees: *Science, Space & Technology*: Energy (RMM). *Transportation & Infrastructure*: Coast Guard & Maritime Transportation; Railroads, Pipelines & Hazardous Materials; Water Resources & Environment.

Group Ratings

	ADA	ACLU	AFL-CIO	LCV	COC	HAFA	ACU	CFG	FRC
2020	**	20%	**	0%	-	96%	92%	**	-
2019	0%	C	32%	3%	74%	C	90%	86%	100%

Almanac Ratings 2019-2020

	Economy	Social	Foreign	Composite
Liberal	40%	6%	4%	17%
Conservative	60%	94%	96%	83%

Key Votes of the 116th Congress

1. U.S./Mex./Can. trade deal	Y	5. Russia sanctions	N	9. Firearms background checks	N
2. First Coronavirus response	N	6. Troops in Syria	N	10. Spending at the border	Y
3. HEROES Act	N	7. Veto arms sales to Saudis	N	11. Marijuana liberalized rules	N
4. CASH Act	N	8. Defense $$$, veto override	N	12. Electoral College objections	Y

Election Results

Election	Name (Party)	Vote (%)		Cand. Spent	Ind. Exp. Support	Ind. Exp. Oppose
2020 General	Randy Weber (R)........................ 190,541	(62%)		$684,755	$7,445	$750
	Adrienne Bell (D)............................ 118,574	(38%)		$4,980	$500	
2020 Primary	Randy Weber (R)........................ 51,837	(85%)				
	Joshua Foxworth (R)...................... 8,856	(15%)				

Prior winning percentages: 2018 (59%), 2016 (62%), 2014 (62%), 2012 (54%)

Republican Randy Weber has used his business background to craft energy legislation, a prime interest to many of his constituents. Weber joined the Freedom Caucus and posed challenges to House GOP leaders. In 2019, he made an unsuccessful bid for the top GOP slot on the Science, Space and Technology Committee.

Before he was elected to Congress, Weber always resided within a five-mile radius of his hometown of Pearland. His father owned a gas station and later ran an RV business. After getting his bachelor's from the University of Houston, he started Weber's Air and Heat, making all the service calls as an air conditioning contractor and putting flyers on every doorstep in town to drum up business. "Did we struggle? Man, did we," Weber said, recalling the number of times the electric company threatened to turn off his power. "Nobody came to bail out Randy Weber. My company, I made it the old-fashioned way." In the 1980s, President Ronald Reagan's message of limited government inspired Weber to get politically involved. From 1990 to 1996, he served on the Pearland City Council. Twelve years later, he was elected to the Texas House, where he worked on issues ranging from veterans affairs to domestic human trafficking—usually with a strongly conservative view.

Running in 2012 for the House seat of retiring libertarian icon Ron Paul, Weber emerged from a field of nine GOP contenders. He was endorsed by Paul and Texas Gov. Rick Perry. Weber styled himself as a devoted family man and Christian and he ran "to everyone else's right," wrote David Wasserman of the Cook Political Report. After leading the first round with 28 percent to 19 percent for Felicia Harris, an attorney and councilwoman from Pearland, he easily won the runoff with 63 percent of the vote.

Weber faced off in the general election against former Democratic Rep. Nick Lampson, who distanced himself from his national party and retained some of his local popularity from two earlier stints in the House; he had served five terms and represented Jefferson County. The unique makeup of the redrawn district—thick with working-class voters—forced Republicans to work harder than expected, especially when Weber ran short of cash. Lampson took 58 percent in Jefferson. Weber ran strongly in his base, with 68 percent in Brazoria. In the swing county of Galveston, which cast 45 percent of the total vote, Weber got 57 percent. Overall, he won, 54%-45%. He has been easily reelected.

In the House, Weber unabashedly said that nobody would "out-conservative" him—unlike Paul, whose views on some social and foreign policy issues sometimes fit more comfortably with Democrats. In 2014, he filed a resolution condemning President Barack Obama for having routinely refused to enforce the law and said the president was provoking a constitutional crisis. "In my view, the president has not faithfully executed the law," Weber said.

He got an opportunity to deal with local issues as chairman of the Science, Space and Technology Subcommittee on Energy. When the House passed in 2017 an authorization bill for the Energy Department, it included Weber's provisions to encourage spending on advanced nuclear reactor technologies. In 2018, he took the lead in the House on enactment of the Nuclear Energy Innovation Capabilities Act, which updated programs for civilian use of nuclear energy, including advanced reactors. The legislation opened the door, he said, to "the next generation reactor designs, materials and nuclear fuels."

Weber clashed frequently with Republican leaders. In January 2015, he voted for Rep. Louie Gohmert of Texas—and against John Boehner—for House Speaker. He said he hoped his vote sent a signal to GOP leaders that "we need to be more forceful in fighting this president and his liberal agenda." In the October 2015 selection of a successor to Boehner, Weber voted for Rep. Daniel Webster of Florida and expressed hope that Paul Ryan will "have the strength to make tough decisions."

Following the 2018 election, Weber ran for the opening of top Republican on the Science committee. He cited his familiarity with the panel and the connection of his district to its agenda. The slot went to Frank Lucas of Oklahoma, who also had oil and gas interests at home, plus the experience of chairing the Agriculture Committee and usually operating as a leadership ally. Instead, Weber became ranking member on the Energy Subcommittee. In September 2020, the House passed a Science committee bill that Weber filed with Democratic Rep. Ami Bera that enhanced research and development on the security of the power grid.

Following the 2020 election, Weber joined Republicans who challenging the validity of the presidential election results and told a rally in Beaumont, "if [Democrats] secure the presidency, we will no longer recognize this country."

TX-14: Gulf Coast

Cook Partisan Voting Index: R+12

Population		Race and Ethnicity		Income	
Total	760,530	White	73.10%	Median Income	$67,459
Land area (sq. miles)	2,441	Black	19.30%	District Income Rank	188
Pop/ sq mi	311.52	Latino	26.30%	Poverty Rate	12.40%
Born in State	67.30%	Asian	3.20%	With health insurance	82.90%
		Two or more races	2.10%	Cash public assistance	0.80%
Age Groups		Other	2.30%	Food stamp/SNAP	10.50%
Under 18	24.00%				
18-34	23.00%	**Education**		**Work**	
35-64	38.60%	H.S grad or less	41.80%	White Collar	36.50%
Over 64	14.40%	Some college	33.20%	Sales and Service	36.80%
		College Degree, 4 yr	16.60%	Blue Collar	26.80%
Military		Post grad	8.40%	Government	17.30%
Veteran/ Active Duty	7.30%				

2020 Pres. Vote	Trump	185,961	(59%)	Biden	124,630	(40%)		
2016 Pres. Vote	Trump	153,191	(58%)	Clinton	101,228	(38%)	Johnson 7,352	(3%)

Galveston, Beaumont-Port Arthur: The spongy land of the Texas Gulf Coast remained mostly unsettled until well into the 19th century. When oil was found at the Spindle top field near Beaumont in 1901, the area all around it boomed, first with oil exploration, then petroleum refining, then petrochemical production. The rig workers and mechanical engineers they attracted have given a kind of permanent roughneck air to the region, and it's one of the few places in Texas where unions have any strength. The Humble oil field was once the largest in Texas, and the local Humble Oil and Refining Company is now known as ExxonMobil. Galveston, on a barrier island in the Gulf, was an immigrant port until a 1900 hurricane killed thousands. It is now guarded by a 17-foot seawall and connected to the mainland by a hurricane-resistant bridge. Its cruise port, the only one in Texas and ranked fourth in total passengers; a third cruise terminal was scheduled to open in 2021.

Hurricanes Gustav and Ike in 2008 shut down oil pipelines for months and toppled some platforms. To limit a possible recurrence of the "storm surge" in Galveston Bay, the Army Corps of Engineers in 2018 proposed a 70-mile coastal barrier ("Ike Dike"). In October 2020, the revised plan from the Corps envisioned massive sea gates across the Houston ship channel plus 43 miles of sand dunes, at a cost of $26 billion, the Houston Chronicle reported. In addition to dredging a second channel, the navigation gates would be anchored in new man-made islands. The dunes would require unprecedented amounts of sand. Once the study is completed, it could take 12 to 20 years for congressional approval, plus design and construction.

The 14th Congressional District of Texas stretches along the southeast Gulf Coast, from Port Arthur and Beaumont to Freeport at its southernmost point. Nearly half the district is in the solidly Republican confines of Galveston. One-third of the population lives in Jefferson County, around the highly polluted "Golden Triangle" oil refining area of Beaumont and Port Arthur. While refineries are Port Arthur's economic lifeline, the city's downtown has been virtually abandoned, and over a quarter of residents live below the poverty level. The BP oil spill disaster and subsequent offshore drilling moratorium hurt that industry and the local shrimping economy, as well. This industrial area is the planned site of two new huge petrochemical steam cracker plants. In January 2019, ExxonMobil began work on expansion of its refinery complex in Beaumont, which has 2,100 employees. Completion of the $20 billion construction project, which was delayed until 2023 because of the pandemic, was expected to add 250,000 barrels of daily crude oil distribution. That would nearly double the existing amount and become the largest refinery in the nation.

Galveston County is about half of the district and is comfortably Republican. The population in Jefferson County is 34 percent African American and 21 percent Hispanic; the county leans Democratic and is about one-third of the 14th. The remaining 20 percent of the district is inland Brazoria County, home to the first capital of the Republic of Texas; about half of Brazoria is in the 14th; the remainder is in the 22nd. The district, working-class and ancestrally Democratic, since the 1980s has become safely Republican, with help from redistricting changes. Galveston County grew 17 percent from 2010 to 2019. In north Galveston, "if you drive a mile in any direction, there's construction everywhere, largely residential," a local official told the Chronicle in March 2020. That area is well-located between downtown Houston and Galveston Bay. Overall, the 26 percent Latino and 19 percent Black populations have not affected the comfortably Republican tilt of the district. In this area, President Donald Trump took 59 percent of the vote in 2020, the same as Mitt Romney in 2012.

Vicente Gonzalez (D)

Elected 2016, 3rd term, b. Sep 04, 1967; Corpus Christi, TX; Harvard University School of Law; Embry-Riddle Aeronautical University, B.A., 1992; TX A & M University School of Law (formerly TX Wesleyan School of Law), J.D., 1996; Catholic; Married (Lorena Saenz).

Professional Career: Attorney and Owner, V. Gonzalez & Associates.

DC Office: 113 CHOB 20515, 202-225-2531, Fax: 202-225-5688, gonzalez.house.gov

State Offices: Benavides, 888-217-0261; Falfurrias, 361-209-3027; McAllen, 956-682-5545; San Diego, 888-217-0261; Seguin, 830-358-0497.

Committees: *Financial Services*: Housing, Community Development & Insurance; Investor Protection, Entrepreneurship & Capital Markets. *Foreign Affairs*: Europe, Energy, the Environment & Cyber; West Hem, Civ Sec, Migration, & Intern'l Econ Policy.

Group Ratings

	ADA	ACLU	AFL-CIO	LCV	COC	HAFA	ACU	CFG	FRC
2020	**	79%	**	95%	-	0%	13%	**	-
2019	75%	C	95%	86%	68%	C	15%	30%	5%

Almanac Ratings 2019-2020

	Economy	Social	Foreign	Composite
Liberal	52%	100%	80%	78%
Conservative	48%	0%	20%	22%

Key Votes of the 116th Congress

1. U.S./Mex./Can. trade deal	Y	5. Russia sanctions	Y
2. First Coronavirus response	Y	6. Troops in Syria	Y
3. HEROES Act	N/A	7. Veto arms sales to Saudis	Y
4. CASH Act	Y	8. Defense $$$, veto override	Y

9. Firearms background checks	Y
10. Spending at the border	Y
11. Marijuana liberalized rules	Y
12. Electoral College objections	N

Election Results

Election	Name (Party)	Vote (%)		Cand. Spent	Ind. Exp. Support	Ind. Exp. Oppose
2020 General	Vicente Gonzalez (D)	115,605	(51%)	$813,623	$993	$10,000
	Monica de la Cruz-Hernandez (R)	109,017	(48%)	$332,466		$113
2020 Primary	Vicente Gonzalez (D)	44,444	(100%)			

Prior winning percentages: 2018 (60%), 2016 (57%)

Democrat Vicente Gonzalez of Texas was elected in 2016 to an open seat along the border with Mexico. His years growing up had a boot-strap quality in an area that faced demanding imperatives. But his professional success as a trial lawyer allowed him to mostly self-finance his campaign. In the House, he showed some independence but narrowly won reelection in 2020 amid a Trump-fueled GOP surge in South Texas, and he's at risk in the next round of redistricting.

Gonzalez was born to a military family in Corpus Christi. His mother stressed the importance of education, which motivated Gonzalez to go back to high school and get his GED certificate. He attended community college classes at Del Mar College and earned his bachelor's in business aviation at Embry Riddle Aeronautical University at Corpus Christi Naval Air Station. Continuing to heed his mother's advice, he got a law degree at Texas A&M. While in law school, he interned for Democratic Rep. Solomon Ortiz of Texas to learn more about government. He founded his own law firm, which focused on business litigation, catastrophic accidents and property damage. In that work, he successfully handled several major lawsuits against South Texas school districts, which recovered millions of dollars from contractors who misspent bond money.

When Rep. Rubén Hinojosa announced his retirement, Gonzalez faced five other candidates in the Democratic primary. Gonzalez said he self-financed his campaign so he would not have to accept corporate contributions. The $2.3 million he spent more than doubled the total for all of his opponents combined in both parties. With the benefit of some Washington connections, Gonzalez won the endorsement of the Congressional Progressive Caucus and campaign contributions from several House Democrats, including now-Majority Leader Steny Hoyer. In the first round of voting, Gonzalez got 42 percent; the runner-up with 19 percent was Juan "Sonny" Palacios Jr., an attorney who was a member of the Edinburg school board. Gonzalez won the runoff with 66 percent of the vote.

In the general election, Republican nominee Tim Westley was an Army veteran whose campaign slogan was "Putting God Back into Politics." He spent $16,000, which was less than 1 percent of the total for his opponent. Gonzalez won, 57%-38%. That might seem close, but it was roughly the share of the vote Hinojosa typically received during his 10 terms as Gonzalez's predecessor. Two years later, Gonzalez had no Democratic opposition and got 60 percent against Westley.

On the Financial Services Committee, Gonzalez joined the bipartisan coalition that enacted cutbacks in the Dodd-Frank banking regulatory law that had been enacted following the Wall Street meltdown. He joined the fiscally conservative Blue Dog Coalition in Congress and is not a member of Progressive Caucus—despite its initial support of his bid.

A week after President Donald Trump took office, Gonzalez invited him to the Rio Grande Valley to discuss international trade policy. "I would appreciate having the opportunity to visit with you in a bipartisan way to discuss how commerce between the two nations affects border communities and the overall economy," he wrote to Trump. Instead, Trump visited other parts of the border to make other rhetorical points. Following a meeting with Trump at the White House in January 2019, Gonzalez questioned the president's grasp of the border and called his comments "crazy" and "irrational," he said to the Houston Chronicle. "Just crazy stuff." He told the Rio Grande Guardian, an independent news service, that the root cause of the immigrant crisis was the failure of three governments in Central America—El Salvador, Guatemala and Honduras—which need economic and security aid. "Until we deal with that, we will continue to have problems," he said.

Following the 2018 election, he joined the Problem Solvers Caucus meetings with Nancy Pelosi, who needed their support to become Speaker. She agreed to the group's changes in House rules that were designed to produce more open debate. With the others, Gonzalez voted for Pelosi for Speaker. "For too long we have fallen victim to partisan bickering and witnessed congressional inaction," he said. "Legislators must find practical, common-sense solutions to the nation's most pressing issues."

In 2020, Gonzalez led an effort to get the Congressional Hispanic Caucus to coalesce behind Joe Biden, warning any other candidate would lose to Trump. He got his wish, but the presidential race upended Gonzalez's normally sleepy reelection campaign. His challenger, Monica De La Cruz-Hernandez, a small business owner, spent just $333,000—less than half that of Gonzalez—and ran no broadcast TV ads, but still came within 6,600 votes of winning. Yoking herself to Trump, she lost 50.5%-47.6%. Gonzalez carried Hidalgo County but De La Cruz-Hernandez swept Guadalupe--which cast more than one-fourth of the district vote--and the rural counties that stretch up toward San Antonio.

In an election post mortem, Gonzalez attributed his narrow margin to Trump's appeal in the district. Trump lost the district in 2016 by 17 points; in 2020 he lost by just two. Gonzalez said Trump inspired 49,000 new voters to turnout and had strong appeal with the Hispanic district. "He was the rock star—I say in Spanish: lucha libre candidate, if you will—that Latinos love," he told Politico. GOP hits on Democratic policy positions also didn't help: "Defund police, open borders, socialism —it's killing us," he told the New York Times.

The close margin gave Republicans hope of ousting Gonzalez in 2022. De La Cruz-Hernandez launched another run. The Democratic Congressional Campaign Committee named Gonzalez to its Frontline program, which offers support to endangered incumbents. The retirement of Rep. Filemon Vela in the neighboring 34th suggested that Democrats in south Texas were concerned that redistricting could pose problems. A majority-minority seat that leans conservative and has less presence at the border would be a boon to Texas Republicans—and a threat to Gonzalez.

TX-15: South Texas   Cook Partisan Voting Index: D+3

Population		Race and Ethnicity		Income	
Total	804,562	White	83.80%	Median Income	$48,113
Land area (sq. miles)	7,804	Black	1.90%	District Income Rank	398
Pop/ sq mi	103.1	Latino	82.00%	Poverty Rate	22.30%
Born in State	65.70%	Asian	1.20%	With health insurance	72.30%
		Two or more races	2.60%	Cash public assistance	1.40%
Age Groups		Other	10.50%	Food stamp/SNAP	22.80%
Under 18	29.70%				
18-34	24.60%	**Education**		**Work**	
35-64	34.00%	H.S grad or less	53.90%	White Collar	28.90%
Over 64	11.70%	Some college	24.80%	Sales and Service	45.20%
		College Degree, 4 yr	14.60%	Blue Collar	25.80%
Military		Post grad	6.60%	Government	17.00%
Veteran/ Active Duty	5.30%				

2020 Pres. Vote	Biden	119,784	(50%)	Trump	115,315	(49%)		
2016 Pres. Vote	Clinton	104,454	(57%)	Trump	73,689	(40%)	Johnson	4,501	(2%)

McAllen/San Antonio Corridor: A century ago, there was little but desert wilderness in the Lower Rio Grande Valley in South Texas. Only a handful of people lived anywhere near the shallow, sluggish Rio Grande. There was no U.S. Border Patrol because very few people wanted to venture across desert. Then came pioneers like Lloyd Bentsen Sr., father of the former senator and Treasury secretary, who arrived after World War I with $5 in his pocket and became one of the valley's biggest landowners. Bentsen and others cleared the land and dug canals, hired Mexican and Mexican-American workers, and with irrigated water from the Rio Grande planted citrus groves, cornfields and palm windbreaks, ran cattle and drilled for oil and gas. Along U.S. 83, north of the Rio Grande, these pioneers built a string of towns with Anglo names and storefronts. But most of the people were Latino in culture and language.

The 15th Congressional District of Texas is one of three adjacent districts in the Lower Rio Grande Valley that run from the heavily populated areas along the border to just north of San Antonio; the 15th has a much smaller slice of the border than do the districts to the east and west. The days are past when ranchers and oilmen wielded absolute political power here. There is instead a robust, mostly Hispanic politics. The Hispanic population in the district is 82 percent, one of the highest in the state. Although the district includes the rural area between Corpus Christi and San Antonio, three-quarters of its residents live just north of the river in McAllen-based Hidalgo County. Reasonably priced real estate and wages that are higher than across the border contributed to fast-paced growth in the region. Hidalgo's population tripled since 1980 and increased 50 percent from 2000 to 2019, when it passed 868,000. Hidalgo has surpassed El Paso as the largest Texas metro area along the border.

The local infrastructure has barely kept up as subdivisions have replaced citrus groves. In the McAllen area, new suburbanites work just across the border in booming Reynosa as corporate managers in the low-wage "maquiladoras," or factories. Poverty is pervasive. As of 2019, 23 percent of residents lived below the poverty line. The abortion clinic in McAllen, which became a flashpoint in federal litigation over state-imposed restrictions, reopened in 2017. The region is struggling to handle crime from the trade in illegal immigration and drugs. A Gallup survey in 2014 found that McAllen had the highest rate of fear of walking alone at night. "This town built on immigration has become ground zero for the nation's nastiest political battle," The Washington Post reported in July 2018. The chain-link fenced detention the huge customs facility has been called the "dog kennel" that housed many of the child detainees after the Trump administration instituted a family separation policy in 2018. Yet President Donald Trump's determination to erect hundreds of miles of border wall caused consternation among McAllen landowners and environmental advocates who feared land seizures.

The 15th shares Hidalgo with the 28th and 34th Districts, but includes about 70 percent of the county population. The district, where President Barack Obama in 2012 and Hillary Clinton in 2016 each took 57 percent, was a prime example of the shift by Hispanic voters to the GOP in 2020; Trump held Joe Biden. to a 50.4%-48.5% win..

Veronica Escobar (D)

Elected 2018, 2nd term, b. Sep 15, 1969; El Paso, TX; University of TX, El Paso, B.A., 1991; NY University, M.A., 1993; Catholic; Married (Michael Pleters); 2 children.

Elected Office: El Paso County Commissioner, 2007-2010.

Professional Career: El Pasoans Judge 2011-2017; Community Scholars, Executive Director; Communications Director, El Paso Mayor Raymond Caballero.

DC Office: 1505 LHOB 20515, 202-225-4831, escobar.house.gov

State Offices: El Paso, 915-541-1400.

Committees: *Armed Services*: Cyber, Innovative Technologies & Information Systems; Military Personnel. *Ethics. Judiciary*: Crime, Terrorism & Homeland Security; Immigration & Citizenship. *Select Committee on the Climate Crisis.*

Almanac Ratings 2019-2020

	Economy	Social	Foreign	Composite
Liberal	100%	100%	59%	87%
Conservative	0%	0%	41%	13%

Key Votes of the 116th Congress

1. U.S./Mex./Can. trade deal Y	5. Russia sanctions Y	9. Firearms background checks Y
2. First Coronavirus response Y	6. Troops in Syria Y	10. Spending at the border N
3. HEROES Act Y	7. Veto arms sales to Saudis Y	11. Marijuana liberalized rules Y
4. CASH Act Y	8. Defense $$$, veto override Y	12. Electoral College objections N

Election Results

Election	Name (Party)	Vote (%)	Cand. Spent	Ind. Exp. Support	Ind. Exp. Oppose
2020 General	Veronica Escobar (D)............	154,108 (65%)	$1,011,225	$1,730	
	Irene Armendariz-Jackson (R)............	84,006 (35%)	$147,140	$5,246	$113
2020 Primary	Veronica Escobar (D)............	54,910 (100%)			

Prior winning percentages: 2018 (68%)

Democratic Veronica Escobar brought extensive experience in El Paso County politics, plus an independence at home that is similar to that of her predecessor, Beto O'Rourke, who stepped down in 2018 for his unsuccessful challenge to Sen. Ted Cruz. She and Sylvia Garcia, who was elected at the same time to an open seat in the Houston area, are the first Latina women from Texas elected to Congress. Representing a gateway that is on the border with Mexico, she had a strong interest in immigration issues and was an outspoken critic of President Donald Trump's handling of those policies.

A native of the El Paso valley area, Escobar grew up near her family's dairy farm. She graduated from the University of Texas at El Paso, earned her master's degree in English literature from New York University and returned home to teach Chicano literature at UTEP. She served as communications director to the El Paso mayor and was Executive Director for Community Scholars, a local non-profit organization that hired high school students to do public policy research.

When she entered public office as a county commissioner, Escobar kept her distance from the local Democratic Party, which she viewed as resistant to change and to newcomers. "The local Democratic Party has been very fractured and not as inclusive as I think it should have been," she told the El Paso Inc. website in a 2011 interview. In 2010 she was elected El Paso County judge, the chief executive manager, and held that position for seven years until she stepped down to run for Congress.

In the primary for the open seat, her chief opponent was Dori Fenenbock, a former El Paso School Board president. With the endorsement of O'Rourke plus several national Democratic-allied and progressive organizations, Escobar was the early frontrunner. Each contender spent about $1 million. Escobar cited her record in cleaning up and modernizing county government, and in addressing border issues such as immigration and trade. In the spirit of Sen. Bernie Sanders, she supported single-payer health care and no-cost-to-students college tuition. She criticized Trump as "nothing short of dangerous" and said that "injustice is at our doorstep."

Escobar won the March primary with 62 percent of the vote to 22 percent for Fenenbock. Four other candidates split the remainder. In an April interview with the Texas Tribune, Escobar said Trump was not fit to be president because of his "rampant corruption and collusion," and that he should be impeached. She added that Latino voters were a "sleeping giant"—a longstanding political prediction, especially in Texas—and that the "perfect combination" of inspiration and anger had motivated her and many other Democratic women to seek office in 2018. In a district that Hillary Clinton won with 68 percent in 2016, Escobar defeated Republican Rick Seeberger with that same vote share.

There have been high expectations for Escobar's political future. Her class colleagues elected her as a freshman representative to leadership. The most obvious path ahead is her ascendancy within the House. But her name has emerged at times as a possible statewide candidate. She serves on the Armed Services, Judiciary, Ethics Committees and the Select Committee on the Climate Crisis.

Escobar was in the House chamber during the January 2021 insurrection and was one of the first members to post on social media amid the crisis, giving the public an opportunity to grasp in real time the gravity of the circumstances.

"The Capitol building has been breached and both chambers are locked down," she wrote on Twitter. "This is the chaos and lawlessness @realDonaldTrump has created."

TX-16: El Paso area   Cook Partisan Voting Index: D+18

Population		Race and Ethnicity		Income	
Total	747,648	White	79.00%	Median Income	$49,013
Land area (sq. miles)	710	Black	3.80%	District Income Rank	395
Pop/ sq mi	1,052.51	Latino	81.30%	Poverty Rate	18.90%
Born in State	59.20%	Asian	1.30%	With health insurance	77.90%
		Two or more races	2.70%	Cash public assistance	2.30%
Age Groups		Other	13.10%	Food stamp/SNAP	20.20%
Under 18	26.80%				
18-34	26.60%	**Education**		**Work**	
35-64	34.20%	H.S grad or less	43.90%	White Collar	32.50%
Over 64	12.40%	Some college	31.60%	Sales and Service	44.80%
		College Degree, 4 yr	16.90%	Blue Collar	22.60%
Military		Post grad	7.60%	Government	19.30%
Veteran/ Active Duty	11.00%				

2020 Pres. Vote	Biden	160,809	(66%)	Trump	77,473	(32%)		
2016 Pres. Vote	Clinton	130,784	(68%)	Trump	52,334	(27%)	Johnson	6,900	(4%)

El Paso: El Paso Texas and Ciudad Juaréz Mexico face each other across the narrow Rio Grande, their tree-shaded streets spread out below the rough brown face of Comanche Peak. Downtown El Paso is only a few blocks from the bridge to Ciudad Juaréz. The two border cities are surrounded by hundreds of miles of some of North America's most rugged and desolate landscape. El Paso is closer to San Diego than to Houston, and it's in a different time zone from the rest of the state. The region has grown significantly. In the 1950s, El Paso and Ciudad Juaréz each had a population around 130,000. In 2019, there were 840,000 people in El Paso County (including 682,000 in the city of El

Paso), 83 percent of them Hispanic; the Mexican census counted 1.4 million in metro Juaréz. This is a bilingual, bicultural pair of cities.

One of the most dynamic of American cities, it has of late became a place of heartbreak. In August 2019, a 21-year-old white supremacist allegedly drove across the state with the aim to kill Hispanics. Once he arrived in El Paso, he was accused of shooting and killing 21 people in a local Walmart. And in the fall of 2020, El Paso was a hotspot for COVID-19. So much so, local officials pleaded with residents to stay home. By late November, the National Guard was deployed to the region to assist overwhelmed morgues.

El Paso is one of the lowest-wage and lowest-education locales in the United States, though statistically it has been one of the safest, with the lowest crime rate of any large U.S. city. After President Donald Trump in his February 2019 State of the Union message said that El Paso "used to have extremely high rates of violent crime" before the barrier along the border was reinforced, Mayor Dee Margo said that he was "wrong." Ciudad Juaréz, though struggling with drug cartel violence and crime, is one of the highest-wage cities in Mexico. At the border, undocumented immigrants released by the Immigration and Customs Enforcement agency have overwhelmed shelters and other services.

In the wake of the North American Free Trade Agreement, maquiladora factories enhanced the cross-border economy. Much of the local economy is built on cheap, low-skill labor. South of the border, there is a large General Motors technical center. The other important factor sustaining the economy has been Fort Bliss, which had a $5 billion expansion following the 2005 base closing review; in 2018, Bliss had 39,000 military personnel, more than 40,000 family members and nearly 13,000 civilian employees. The base is home to the First Armored Division and covers 1,700 square miles, which is nearly four times the size of Delaware. One in three jobs in El Paso depends directly or indirectly on Fort Bliss. There has been deep concern about the potentially devastating impact of another base-closing review.

The 16th Congressional District of Texas is based entirely in El Paso County—the city itself, the suburban fringe, Fort Bliss to the north, and rural housing settlements known as colonias, most without electricity and running water, spreading out to the east and south. The district is solidly Democratic. The remaining 9 percent of El Paso voters are in the sprawling 23rd District. In 2020, Joe Biden won the 16th with 66 percent of the vote.

Pete Sessions (R)

Elected 2020, 12th term, b. Mar 22, 1955; Waco, TX; Southwest TX State University, Att., 1973; Southwestern University, B.S., 1978; Methodist; Married (Juanita Sessions); 2 children ; 3 stepchildren.

Elected Office: U.S. House, 1997-2019.

Professional Career: Vice President, Public Policy, National Center for Policy Analysis, 1994-1995; District Manager for marketing, telephone company; Principal, Sessions Partners, LLC.

DC Office: 2204 LHOB 20515, 202-225-6105, Fax: 202-225-0350, sessions.house.gov

State Offices: College Station, 979-431-6340; Waco, 254-633-4500.

Committees: *Oversight & Reform*: Subcommittee on Civil Rights & Civil Liberties (RMM). *Science, Space & Technology*: Investigations & Oversight; Research & Technology.

Election Results

Election	Name (Party)	Vote (%)	Cand. Spent	Ind. Exp. Support	Ind. Exp. Oppose
2020 General	Pete Sessions (R)	171,390 (56%)	$1,739,995	$46,166	
	Rick Kennedy (D)	125,565 (41%)	$186,411		
	Ted Brown (L)	9,918 (3%)	$2,505		
2020 Primary	Pete Sessions (R)	21,706 (32%)			
	Renée Swann (R)	13,072 (19%)			
	George W. Hindman (R)	12,405 (18%)			
	Elianor Vessali (R)	6,286 (9%)			
	Scott Bland (R)	4,947 (7%)			
	Trent Sutton (R)	3,662 (5%)			
2020 Primary Runoff	Pete Sessions (R)	18,524 (54%)			
2021 Primary Runoff	Renée Swann (R)	16,096 (46%)			

Pete Sessions, who previously served 22 years in the House and held multiple Republican leadership posts before he was defeated in 2018, returned to the House in a Waco-based district 100 miles from his former Dallas-area district. He earlier was known as a tough partisan in-fighter and a crafter of back-room political deals. As chairman of the House Rules Committee for six years, he was a legislative traffic cop.

His return to Waco—the city where he was born and went to school—was not fully embraced by local leaders. Republican Rep. Bill Flores, who held the seat for 10 years before he retired in 2020, called Sessions "a career politician" and actively backed his opponent in the competitive Republican primary run-off. Sessions also faced criticism of some backroom moves during his earlier service.

Sessions graduated from Southwestern University and worked at Southwestern Bell in Dallas for 16 years. His father was William Sessions, a former federal judge who then served as director of the Federal Bureau of Investigation from 1987 to 1993. In 1993, he resigned from the phone company to run against Democratic Rep. John Bryant in a district that included much of the east side of Dallas and several rural counties to the south. Sessions ran a vigorous campaign, making a two-day, 12-city tour of the district's rural portions with a livestock trailer full of horse manure and a sign saying, "the Clinton health care plan stinks worse than this trailer."

Although he outspent Sessions 2-to-1 in 1994, Bryant won by just 50%-47%. Two years later, Bryant ran, unsuccessfully, for the Senate. Sessions faced Democrat John Pouland, a former regional General Services Administration director. Sessions charged that Pouland was a big-government liberal and would abandon U.S. military bases overseas. He won 53%-47%.

Sessions' voting record routinely placed him in the top 10 percent of conservative Republicans in the Almanac vote ratings. Still, some conservative blogs and websites questioned whether he was too much a part of the Washington establishment that they loathe. Among his conservative actions, Sessions sponsored a constitutional amendment to require a two-thirds vote to raise taxes, was a leading advocate of the Republican proposal to stop the government from spending Social Security and Medicare surpluses, and called for scrapping the income tax code. When President Barack Obama laid out a liberal agenda in his 2013 State of the Union address, Sessions told the New York Times: "We're now managing America's demise, not America's great future."

After the 2008 election, Sessions won a second try to head the NRCC. He had the strong support of Republican Leader John Boehner: Sessions was among the few Texas Republicans who had backed Boehner for party leader against Roy Blunt of Missouri in 2006.

Sessions had a rocky start as chairman. He drew criticism for holding fundraisers at risqué venues that were at odds with the party's family-values image. He was lampooned by Democrats for what they considered odd comments, including his statement that Obama was trying "to inflict damage and hardship on the free enterprise system, if not to kill it." Sessions set a challenging goal of gaining the 40 seats the party needed to recapture the majority in 2010. He was not in complete command of the job, as Boehner reportedly sat in on major strategy meetings. Sessions joined the Tea Party Caucus and channeled its members' anger at big spending, while helping to mesh the GOP message to that theme. The Republicans' huge 63-seat gain in November was the largest party switch since 1948.

With his seat on the Rules Committee, Sessions promoted the Republican message. Boehner chose him as chairman in 2013. When Majority Leader Eric Cantor unexpectedly lost his primary in June 2014, Sessions flirted with seeking a leadership post. Some conservatives reportedly approached Sessions about running for Kevin McCarthy's former whip job, but he declined after brief consideration. A failed leadership bid would have jeopardized his continuation as chairman of Rules.

In 2016, Sessions became part of two internal House conflicts. After Democrats held their overnight sit-in on the House floor to protest Republicans' refusal to consider gun-control legislation, he threatened an investigation of House rules violations. Republicans later changed House rules to penalize lawmakers who use their phones to broadcast videos in the House. He supported a change in House ethics rules to reduce the independence of the Office of Congressional Ethics. Following widespread public objections, including from President-elect Donald Trump, GOP leaders dropped the proposal.

Sessions has had a roller-coaster electoral history. The vagaries of redistricting in Texas have led him to run in several different House districts. In 2001, he unexpectedly decided to run in a newly created and more upscale district based in north Dallas. He said he wanted to spend less time traveling around his district in east Texas and he thought it more compatible with his pro-business philosophy. Sessions had only token primary opposition and won the seat, 68%-30%.

In 2003, Tom DeLay of Texas, the powerful House majority leader, persuaded the Republican-controlled Texas Legislature to draw the lines yet again. Although most GOP members were well-served by the new lines, Sessions wound up in a somewhat less Republican district and with a reelection challenge from 13-term Democratic Rep. Martin Frost, whose district had been shorn of its most Democratic precincts. The contest became the most expensive House campaign of 2004. Sessions spent $4.5 million and Frost $4.8 million, and much more was spent by party committees and independent groups. Sessions won 54%-44%, capturing more than 80 percent of the vote in some Park Cities precincts.

Following the 2016 election, in which Democrats failed to post a challenger, they listed Sessions as a top target in 2018 and contended that Trump's brand of conservatism would cause complications for him. They proved correct, when political newcomer Colin Allred defeated Sessions by nearly 18,000 votes.

Determined to have a political comeback, Sessions ruled out a rematch and saw an opportunity in a comfortably Republican district after Flores announced his retirement. The usually understated Flores voiced vocal opposition. "The conservative leaders and community leaders in the district who are aware of Pete's intentions have told me they would prefer someone who currently lives, works and serves in our communities," he told the Texas Tribune.

With 12 candidates in the Republican primary, Sessions led with 32 percent. Renee Swann, who had been endorsed by Flores, was the runner-up with 19 percent. Swann, who managed her husband's longtime practice as an eye surgeon, ran as a "citizen legislator." Sessions styled himself as "a proven conservative leader."

During their runoff contest, Sessions unexpectedly faced two controversies that resulted from his previous tenure. In an October 2019 federal indictment of two Ukraine allies of former New York City Mayor Rudy Giuliani—who was serving as a lawyer for Trump—Sessions reportedly was the unnamed congressman who had been an intended beneficiary of campaign contributions from those men. A spokesman responded that Sessions had cooperated with investigators. Later, the Associated Press reported that Sessions was part of a potential deal to remove Nicolas Maduro as the president of Venezuela—apparently with the knowledge of the Trump White House. His spokesman said that Sessions was asked to perform a diplomatic mission on behalf of the State Department. Those incidents fed Swann's narrative that she was an outsider. "Frankly, I don't want that kind of experience at all," she told the Tribune.

With each candidate spending a bit more than $1 million through the runoff, Sessions won 54%-46%. He got 59 percent in Waco-based McLennan County, which cast 40 percent of the total vote, and took most of the other counties except for Swann's base of Brazos. In the general election, against Democratic nominee Rick Kennedy, who lost to Flores 57%-41% in 2018, Sessions took 56 percent of the vote, including every county except Travis.

In the House, Sessions became ranking member of the Oversight and Reform Subcommittee on Civil Rights and Civil Liberties.

TX-17: Central Texas

Population		Race and Ethnicity		Income	
Total	786,023	White	76.10%	Median Income	$58,929
Land area (sq. miles)	7,651	Black	13.70%	District Income Rank	281
Pop/ sq mi	102.73	Latino	26.70%	Poverty Rate	16.90%
Born in State	67.30%	Asian	4.50%	With health insurance	87.10%
		Two or more races	3.40%	Cash public assistance	2.30%
Age Groups		Other	2.30%	Food stamp/SNAP	10.40%
Under 18	22.20%				
18-34	30.20%	**Education**		**Work**	
35-64	34.90%	H.S grad or less	38.50%	White Collar	38.80%
Over 64	12.70%	Some college	29.20%	Sales and Service	38.40%
Military		College Degree, 4 yr	19.90%	Blue Collar	22.90%
Veteran/ Active Duty	6.70%	Post grad	12.40%	Government	18.80%

2020 Pres. Vote	Trump	172,342	(55%)	Biden	137,632	(44%)		
2016 Pres. Vote	Trump	139,415	(56%)	Clinton	96,156	(38%)	Johnson	10,055	(4%)

Waco, College Station: Waco, about midway between Dallas and Austin, is deep in the heart of Texas. In the late 19th century, it was one of the largest cotton markets in the world, a rip-roaring town with legalized prostitution. In 1870, Waco opened across the Brazos River what was then the largest single-span suspension bridge in the United States. It became the main depot along the Chisholm Trail, which cattlemen used to drive their longhorns north to Kansas stockyards. The city has embarked on an "Imagine Waco" program to restore a walk able downtown; development along the riverfront also is underway. The city's growing tourism business, with many conventions and attractive vacation sites, in 2017 surpassed that of Austin. It had been the site of "Fixer Upper," the popular HGTV program about home-buying.

The 17th Congressional District of Texas includes all of eight counties and parts of four more, but centers on Waco and all of McLennan County, which has a third of the district's population. The southwestern tip of the district covers a small slice of northern Austin and most of socially diverse suburban Pflugerville, whose population jumped from 4,400 in 1990 to more than 65,000 residents in 2019, an increase of 35 percent since 2010. The other population center is Brazos County, whose largest city, College Station, is home to Texas A&M University, with nearly 70,000 students; Brazos is entirely in the 17th and is one-fourth of the population. The school's agricultural and military traditions have given it a much more conservative ambience than the similarly selective University of Texas at Austin. College Station is the site of the George H.W. Bush Presidential Library, where the former president enjoyed spending time during his final years. Both he and his wife, Barbara, died in 2018. Following funeral services in Houston, each was interred at the site. In December 2019, Smart Asset, a financial technology company, ranked College Station sixteenth among the nation's top boomtowns, as measured by seven statistical variables.

The political tradition in Central Texas for more than a century after the Civil War was heavily Democratic. As recently as 1990, it voted Democratic for governor, supporting Waco native Ann Richards. Since then, the district has followed most of non-urban Texas to the Republican Party. The arm of the district that extends into Travis County is its heavily Democratic enclave on the north side of Austin, which includes the large and rapidly growing campus of Apple, with more than 6,700 employees at the end of 2019—the company's largest hub outside its headquarters in Cupertino California. The 17th is one of five Republican-held districts that slice up small parts of the area surrounding Austin. Donald Trump won 56 percent and then 55 percent of the district-wide vote in his two campaigns, a drop from the 60 percent vote for Mitt Romney in 2012.

Sheila Jackson Lee (D)

Elected 1994, 14th term, b. Jan 12, 1950; Jamaica, NY; NY University; Yale University, B.A., 1972; University of VA Law School, J.D., 1975; Seventh-Day Adventist; Married (Elwyn C. Lee); 2 children; 2 grandchildren.

Elected Office: Houston City Council, 1990-1994.

Professional Career: Practicing attorney, 1975-1977, 1978-1987; Staff counsel, U.S. House Select Assassinations Committee, 1977-1978; Houston Association municipal judge, 1987-1990.

DC Office: 2079 RHOB 20515, 202-225-3816, Fax: 202-225-3317, jacksonlee.house.gov

State Offices: Houston, 713-691-4882; Houston, 713-861-4070; Houston, 713-655-0050; Houston, 713-227-7740.

Committees: *Budget. Homeland Security*: Cybersecurity, Infrastructure Protection & Innovation; Emergency Preparedness, Response & Recovery; Intelligence & Counterterrorism. *Judiciary*: Constitution, Civil Rights & Civil Liberties; Crime, Terrorism & Homeland Security (Chmn); Immigration & Citizenship.

Group Ratings

	ADA	ACLU	AFL-CIO	LCV	COC	HAFA	ACU	CFG	FRC
2020	**	83%	**	100%	-	0%	5%	**	-
2019	95%	C	95%	93%	53%	C	5%	23%	0%

Almanac Ratings 2019-2020

	Economy	Social	Foreign	Composite
Liberal	58%	100%	92%	84%
Conservative	42%	0%	8%	16%

Key Votes of the 116th Congress

1. U.S./Mex./Can. trade deal Y	5. Russia sanctions Y	9. Firearms background checks Y
2. First Coronavirus response Y	6. Troops in Syria Y	10. Spending at the border N
3. HEROES Act Y	7. Veto arms sales to Saudis Y	11. Marijuana liberalized rules Y
4. CASH Act Y	8. Defense $$$, veto override Y	12. Electoral College objections N

Election Results

Election	Name (Party)	Vote (%)		Cand. Spent	Ind. Exp. Support	Ind. Exp. Oppose
2020 General	Sheila Jackson Lee (D)	180,952	(73%)	$808,413	$16,471	
	Wendell Champion (R)	58,033	(24%)	$270,051		$113
2020 Primary	Sheila Jackson Lee (D)	49,729	(77%)			
	Marc Flores (D)	5,353	(8%)			

Prior winning percentages: 2018 (75%), 2016 (74%), 2014 (72%), 2012 (75%), 2010 (70%), 2008 (77%), 2006 (77%), 2004 (89%), 2002 (77%), 2000 (77%), 1998 (90%), 1996 (77%), 1994 (74%)

Sheila Jackson Lee, a Democrat first elected in 1994 and long known for her high staff turnover, is hugely popular at home, always winning at least 70 percent of the vote in elections and rarely facing a primary challenge. In 2021, she regained her chairmanship of the Judiciary Subcommittee on Crime, Terrorism and Homeland Security, which she had been forced to yield for two years because of serious allegations involving her aides.

A native of Queens New York, Jackson Lee graduated from Yale University and the University of Virginia law school. She practiced law in Houston, where she was a local judge and won two terms as an at-large member of the Houston City Council. After a local term-limits law took effect in 1994, she ran against Democratic Rep. Craig Washington, a talented but iconoclastic legislator. He had voted against funding for the space station, a source of many local jobs, and against the 1993 North American Free Trade Agreement, which was a boon to Houston's port traffic. Jackson Lee supported NAFTA and raised a lot of money from business interests that favored it. She won the primary, 63%-37%, and swept the general election.

The Almanac vote ratings have shown that Jackson Lee has shifted toward the center of the House in each of the three issue areas. She has been among the most prolific members of the House in proposing bills and offering amendments on the floor. In 2017-18, she filed 65 bills. Typically, her measures call for studies on one topic or another, add small amounts to spending bills, or are noncontroversial, such as one that called on Afghanistan to prohibit the use of children as soldiers. She told the Houston Chronicle that while she can ruffle feathers, she is unflagging in her desire to serve constituents. "I just want to be called an Energizer bunny that keeps on working for the people of this great district," she said. At times, her prolific amendments irk her colleagues. Even so, Jackson Lee has a deep well of loyalty within the Democratic caucus. She is a much-sought after surrogate in the districts of her colleagues, and Rep. Frank Pallone of New Jersey enlisted her as a top lieutenant during his successful run in 2014 for the top Democratic slot at the Energy and Commerce Committee.

Jackson Lee has been active on the Homeland Security Committee, especially the Border and Maritime Security Subcommittee, an assignment that suits a port city. In 2016, one of her bills was enacted. It required the Transportation Security Administration to make a comprehensive risk analysis of security threat assessment procedures for vessels and maritime facilities. In 2015 and again in 2017, the House passed her bill to require the Homeland Security Department to prepare a report on the effectiveness and availability of first responders in the case of a terrorist threat or attack.

On the Judiciary Committee, she has faced conflicting tensions from Latino constituents, who favor more generous treatment of immigrants, and African-American constituents who see immigrants as competition for jobs. She frequently has taken the pro-immigrant side. She favors an increase in visas and access to permanent resident status. As ranking Democrat on the Subcommittee on Crime, Terrorism, Homeland Security, and Investigations for several years, Jackson Lee introduced the "Build Trust Act," which was intended to decrease the excessive reliance by some local governments on traffic fines and court costs to generate revenue to fund operations. She has called for reparations for African Americans and filed a House resolution to create a commission to study the concept.

In January 2019, news stories reported that a former aide to the Congressional Black Caucus Foundation, which Jackson Lee chaired, had filed a lawsuit against the foundation and Jackson Lee's office, claiming that she had been wrongly fired in March 2018. The ex-staffer alleged that her supervisor at the foundation had sexually assaulted her in 2015, when she was a 19-year-old student.

Jackson Lee denied any wrongdoing on her part, including retribution against the aide, and she said that she would be exonerated. But she stepped down from her position with the foundation. And she relinquished her chairmanship of the Crime Subcommittee; that position went to Rep. Karen Bass of California, who also chaired the Congressional Black Caucus. An advocacy group supporting the victims of domestic violence said Jackson Lee should no longer handle legislation dealing with violence against women. The allegations were sufficiently resolved for her to reclaim the post in January 2021.

Jackson Lee was outspoken in her opposition to Donald Trump. At the Democratic convention in 2016, she delivered a speech in which she called him "a man of fear" and "willfully ignorant to the outcry of young people who want real criminal justice reform." In January 2017, during the joint session of Congress that certifies the Electoral College count, she led several House members who protested the vote count in some states. When she failed to get the required support of at least one senator, then-Vice President Joe Biden overruled her objections.

Jackson Lee has remained popular at home. In 2010, she faced a primary challenge from Houston City Councilman Jarvis Johnson, who cited her reputation as difficult to work with, and local lawyer Sean Roberts. Neither came remotely close to her in fundraising. She released an endorsement from President Barack Obama calling her "a tireless champion for Houston's working families." She drew 67 percent of the vote to Johnson's 28 percent and Roberts' 5 percent. She did not face another primary challenge until 2018, when she took 85 percent against Richard Johnson, an aide to a Houston-area state representative. In 2020, she faced a crowded Democratic primary of six challengers, but again dominated that contest with 77 percent of the vote.

TX-18: Harris County   **Cook Partisan Voting Index: D+26**

Population		Race and Ethnicity		Income	
Total	827,015	White	51.00%	Median Income	$48,625
Land area (sq. miles)	235	Black	33.70%	District Income Rank	396
Pop/ sq mi	3,516.22	Latino	44.80%	Poverty Rate	19.80%
Born in State	58.60%	Asian	4.40%	With health insurance	73.30%
		Two or more races	2.20%	Cash public assistance	1.80%
Age Groups		Other	8.60%	Food stamp/SNAP	16.30%
Under 18	25.90%				
18-34	28.50%	**Education**		**Work**	
35-64	35.60%	H.S grad or less	50.70%	White Collar	30.30%
Over 64	10.00%	Some college	26.20%	Sales and Service	39.50%
		College Degree, 4 yr	14.50%	Blue Collar	30.30%
Military		Post grad	8.50%	Government	9.70%
Veteran/ Active Duty	4.40%				

2020 Pres. Vote	Biden	189,823	(76%)	Trump	57,669	(23%)			
2016 Pres. Vote	Clinton	157,117	(76%)	Trump	41,011	(20%)	Johnson	5,346	(3%)

Central and Northern Houston: Within its sprawling boundaries, Houston contains income and wealth disparities as striking as any city in America, the product of an expanding city with dynamic economic growth, a high rate of immigration and the absence of centralized planning. The contrast is most obvious at the edge of Houston's gleaming downtown. Just blocks from the Heritage Plaza, Pennzoil and Bank of America buildings, and the sports complexes for baseball's Astros and basketball's Rockets are slums where many people live in unpainted frame houses with cracks wide enough to let in Houston's humid, smoggy air.

Until the 1960s, Houston had a Third World economy. It was a low-skill producer of basic commodities, where a few got rich and many lived near subsistence level. Since then, Houston has built a high-tech economy offering myriad opportunities and a wider range of economic outcomes. It has also greatly expanded its international trade. Many of Houston's African Americans and Hispanics have moved to comfortable middle-class neighborhoods. In 2007, Hispanics for the first time outnumbered Anglos in Harris County, which grew 20 percent from 2000 to 2010 and another 15 percent from 2010 to 2019. Houston accounts for about half the county. With its rapid growth, it was expected to surpass Chicago as the third-largest city in the nation by about 2025. By 2050, state demographers project, Houston will be 60 percent Hispanic and 15 percent Black. (In 2019, the 45 percent Hispanic population doubled the 23 percent Black share.)

While oil has remained king, the city has diversified economically. In 2015, Forbes ranked Houston as the fastest-growing city in the nation. In 2018, the metro area led the nation in new construction jobs. The city's long tradition of limited urban planning has drawn growing criticism, especially following the devastation in August 2017 of Hurricane Harvey—the third "500-year flood" to hit the city in three years. The contrasts between rich and poor remain. In a 2014 report, the Brookings Institution ranked Houston 11th among cities with the highest income inequality. The diversity also has applied to local elections. With the retirement of three-term Mayor Annise Parker, one of the first mayors in the nation who was openly gay, voters in 2015 selected African-American state Sen. Sylvester Turner over Republican Bill King, a longtime local businessman, 50.2%-49.8%; Turner won a runoff to take his second term in 2019. In 2018, Republican Ed Emmett, who had been county judge (the chief executive position) since 2007, was defeated by 27-year-old Lina Hidalgo, a Democrat and native of Colombia.

The 18th Congressional District of Texas contains Houston's downtown area and the African-American and Latino neighborhoods immediately south of it. The district has two arms extending beyond Loop 610 and nearly encircling the city—one is northeast, between the Eastex Freeway and Beaumont Freeway, and the larger one is northwest, between the Northwest Freeway and Interstate 45, extending east to take in George Bush Intercontinental Airport. African Americans make up a declining 34 percent of the district's population and Hispanics a rising 45 percent. This is the third most Democratic district in Texas. Joe Biden got 76 percent of the vote here in 2020.

Jodey Arrington (R)

Elected 2016, 3rd term, b. Mar 09, 1972; Kansas City, MO; TX Tech University, B.A., 1994; TX Tech University, M.P.A., 1997; Georgetown University-McDonough School of Business, 2004; Presbyterian; Married (Anne Arrington); 3 children.

Professional Career: Special Assistant, President George W. Bush, 2001; Chief of Staff, FDIC Chairman Don Powell, 2001-2005; Deputy Federal Coordinator, COO, Office of the Federal Coordinator for Gulf Cost Rebuilding, 2005-2006; Administrator, Texas Tech University, 2007-2014.

DC Office: 1029 LHOB 20515, 202-225-4005, Fax: 202-225-9615, arrington.house.gov

State Offices: Abilene, 325-675-9779; Lubbock, 806-763-1611.

Committees: *Joint Economic. Ways & Means:* Select Revenue Measures; Social Security; Trade.

Group Ratings

	ADA	ACLU	AFL-CIO	LCV	COC	HAFA	ACU	CFG	FRC
2020	**	15%	**	0%	-	91%	93%	**	-
2019	0%	C	14%	7%	77%	C	92%	96%	100%

Almanac Ratings 2019-2020

	Economy	Social	Foreign	Composite
Liberal	25%	4%	33%	21%
Conservative	75%	96%	67%	79%

Key Votes of the 116th Congress

1. U.S./Mex./Can. trade deal Y	5. Russia sanctions Y	9. Firearms background checks N
2. First Coronavirus response Y	6. Troops in Syria Y	10. Spending at the border Y
3. HEROES Act N	7. Veto arms sales to Saudis N	11. Marijuana liberalized rules N
4. CASH Act N	8. Defense $$$, veto override N	12. Electoral College objections Y

Election Results

Election	Name (Party)	Vote (%)		Cand. Spent	Ind. Exp. Support	Ind. Exp. Oppose
2020 General	Jodey Arrington (R)	198,198	(75%)	$1,560,306	$7,452	$750
	Tom Watson (D)	60,583	(23%)	$55,717		
	Joe Burnes (L)	6,271	(2%)			
2020 Primary	Jodey Arrington (R)	71,234	(89%)			
	Vance Boyd (R)	8,410	(11%)			

Prior winning percentages: 2018 (75%), 2016 (87%)

Republican Jodey Arrington was elected in 2016 to an open seat. His narrow win in the primary runoff was tantamount to victory in this Republican stronghold. Arrington benefited from strong political connections, which resulted from his extended experience as an aide to President George W. Bush. He gained influence with a seat on the Ways and Means Committee.

Arrington was born in Plainview, where his father was a farm equipment salesman. He earned a bachelor's and a master's degree in public administration from Texas Tech University. A high school tennis player, he was a walk-on player for the Red Raider football team. Soon after that, he joined the staff of then-Gov. Bush as a manager of appointments in state government. After Bush was elected president, Arrington become a White House special assistant to the president and associate director of presidential personnel. He was among the White House staffers who were evacuated from the building on September 11, 2001. He specialized in appointments relating to energy, the environment and natural resources. Late that year, he became chief of staff to the chairman of the Federal Deposit Insurance Corporation, who was a native of Amarillo.

In 2002, Arrington returned to Texas to become chief of staff for the Texas Tech University System, which has more than 40,000 students and a budget of about $1.3 billion. Initially, he worked for Chancellor Kent Hance, who had defeated Bush a quarter-century earlier in a campaign for Congress. Later, he was appointed vice chancellor of research and commercialization, where he helped to spur the university's growth. In 2014, he ran for the state Senate and lost the Republican primary, 53%-30%. In the private sector, he became president of Scott Laboratories, which commercializes health care innovations.

When Rep. Randy Neugebauer retired, nine Republican candidates ran for the open seat. The chief contenders, in addition to Arrington, were Glen Robertson, who was completing four years as mayor of Lubbock, and Michael Bob Starr, who had been commander of Dyess Air Force Base near Abilene. In the first round of the primary, Starr got 48 percent of the vote in Abilene-based Taylor County. Arrington and Robertson each got 30 percent in Lubbock County, which was the base for each. The district-wide vote in the primary gave 27 percent to Arrington, 26 percent to Robertson and 21 percent to Starr, with the top two advancing to the runoff.

Arrington touted his support from Bush and many of his advisers, plus former Gov. Rick Perry, and said he was the candidate who best represented "conservative values." Robertson said he had more political experience as mayor and as a local businessman for 38 years. Robertson had an edge in campaign spending with $1.8 million, of which 90 percent was self-financed. Arrington spent $1.3 million during the cycle. He won, 54%-46%, and led in both Lubbock and Taylor counties. In November, no Democrat had filed and Arrington took 87 percent of the vote. Since then, he has coasted to reelection. He has been reelected twice with 75 percent of the vote. In 2020, he got 89 percent against a challenger in the Republican primary.

In the House, Arrington was assigned to the Agriculture Committee, his first choice. He said that a priority on the farm bill was the resumption of commodity coverage for cotton. That objective was bolstered by committee Chairman Mike Conaway representing the neighboring 11th District, which also is heavily rural. "I want to carry his water, help him any way I can," Arrington said. His cotton provision, with detailed specifications, was included as a rider in a disaster-relief appropriation bill that was enacted in February 2018. It restored the price support, which had been overturned in 2014 in a ruling by the World Trade Organization. The cotton crop in Texas exceeds $2 billion in annual value.

His prized seat on Ways and Means, Arrington said, expands the influence of West Texas and "the decibel of the voice of rural America." He told the Abilene Reporter News that he would "fight for free-market policies" that encourage energy production. Arrington created a bipartisan House caucus that would discuss options to handle the national debt and take steps to address the nation's fiscal crisis. Following the 2020 election, he joined Republicans who objected to certifying the Electoral College result and he dismissed the move to impeach former President Donald Trump. "The president didn't incite a riot. The president didn't lead an insurrection. And there are no 'high crimes or misdemeanors' requisite of impeachment," he told the House. "I'm not saying the president didn't exercise poor judgment, but to criminalize political speech by blaming lawless acts on the president's rhetoric is wrong, Madame Speaker, and a very dangerous precedent."

In March 2019, Arrington welcomed the decision by the Air Force to select Dyess Air Force Base in Abilene as the only base that will house the operational test squadron and the weapons training school for the prospective B-21 bomber. The action, he said, "secures the future of Dyess as a bomber base in the 21st century." He later urged steps to assure "a seamless transition," with "the least disruptions."

TX-19: West Texas   **Cook Partisan Voting Index: R+26**

Population		Race and Ethnicity		Income	
Total	729,664	White	83.60%	Median Income	$55,278
Land area (sq. miles)	25,836	Black	6.20%	District Income Rank	326
Pop/ sq mi	28.24	Latino	37.40%	Poverty Rate	15.60%
Born in State	71.30%	Asian	1.60%	With health insurance	82.30%
		Two or more races	2.80%	Cash public assistance	1.30%
Age Groups		Other	5.80%	Food stamp/SNAP	11.50%
Under 18	24.30%				
18-34	27.00%	**Education**		**Work**	
35-64	34.10%	H.S grad or less	46.10%	White Collar	32.90%
Over 64	14.50%	Some college	30.00%	Sales and Service	40.30%
		College Degree, 4 yr	15.40%	Blue Collar	26.70%
Military		Post grad	8.50%	Government	15.80%
Veteran/ Active Duty	7.80%				

2020 Pres. Vote	Trump	195,515	(72%)	Biden	71,237	(26%)		
2016 Pres. Vote	Trump	165,384	(72%)	Clinton	53,519	(23%)	Johnson	7,849	(3%)

Lubbock, Abilene: Until water was discovered in the giant Ogallala Aquifer that lies under Lubbock and its environs, this was Indian country, a land of Army forts and cattle ranches. When the water was tapped, well into the 20th century, what had been grazing land suddenly became cotton-growing territory, with green crops grown in circles where the sprinklers reached and parched ground beyond. Lubbock became a regional center, the home of Texas Tech University, and grew rapidly at mid-century. Lubbock County's population increased from 101,000 in 1950 to 156,000 in 1960. Since then, the regional economy has grown more slowly, though it had an 11 percent gain from 2010 to 2019, when the county's population reached 311,000. Nearby Gaines County has led the nation in cotton production. Cotton growers have struggled with international competitors and adverse trade rulings, as well as pressure to reduce agricultural subsidies. The region's economy is strong. Lubbock and nearby counties have made an outsized contribution to American popular culture with a disproportionate share of renowned musicians, including Buddy Holly, Tanya Tucker, Jimmy Dean, Waylon Jennings, Mac Davis, Roy Orbison and the Dixie Chicks' Natalie Maines.

Nearly 200 miles southeast of Lubbock, over gully-ridden territory, are Abilene and the surrounding Big Country, with ranches specializing in Angora goats and sheep and exotic animals like ostriches, emus and aoudad sheep. Sweetwater, near Abilene, features an annual "rattlesnake roundup," with a noise from thousands of snakes that apparently can be fearsome. There also are cotton fields, pecan trees, mesquite and many oil wells. Some of the nation's B-1 bombers are stationed at Dyess Air Force Base. Texas officials successfully lobbied for Dyess as the principal training base for the B-21 long-range bomber, which is scheduled for delivery in the mid-2020s. Abilene is a college town, but the culture is conservative as the three most prominent schools —Abilene Christian University, Hardin-Simmons University and McMurry University— are all religiously affiliated. Like other parts of Texas, Abilene has become a haven for resettlement of refugees, mostly from Africa. In 2019, about 1,200 resided in Abilene, a city of 123,000.

The 19th Congressional District of Texas takes in the Lubbock and Abilene areas. The two counties combined account for about 62 percent of the district's population. In 1978, this part of West Texas was Democratic enough that in an open-seat election, voters rejected the candidacy of a young Midland oilman named George W. Bush in favor of Lubbock Democrat Kent Hance. Today, the area is heavily Republican. Bush received 77 percent of the vote in his 2004 reelection, and Republican candidate Mitt Romney won the district with 74 percent in 2012—among their highest scores in the nation. In 2020, the vote for President Donald Trump dipped to 72 percent; that was seven percentage points less than his vote in the 13th District to the north, which can be explained partly by the larger Hispanic population in the 19th.

Joaquin Castro (D)

Elected 2012, 5th term, b. Sep 16, 1974; San Antonio, TX; Stanford University, A.B., 1996; Harvard University Law School, J.D., 2000; Roman Catholic; Married (Anna Flores); 2 children.

Elected Office: TX House, 2003-2013.

Professional Career: Practicing attorney, 2000-2013.

DC Office: 2241 RHOB 20515, 202-225-3236, Fax: 202-225-1915, castro.house.gov

State Offices: San Antonio, 210-348-8216.

Committees: *Education & Labor*: Higher Education & Workforce Investment. *Foreign Affairs*: Intern'l Dev't, Intern'l Orgs & Global Corporate Social Impact (Chmn); West Hem, Civ Sec, Migration, & Intern'l Econ Policy. *Permanent Select on Intelligence*: Counterterrorism, Counterintelligence & Counterproliferation; Strategic Technologies & Advanced Research.

Group Ratings

	ADA	ACLU	AFL-CIO	LCV	COC	HAFA	ACU	CFG	FRC
2020	**	83%	**	100%	-	0%	4%	**	-
2019	85%	C	95%	93%	59%	C	5%	28%	0%

Almanac Ratings 2019-2020

	Economy	Social	Foreign	Composite
Liberal	56%	52%	83%	64%
Conservative	44%	48%	17%	36%

Key Votes of the 116th Congress

1. U.S./Mex./Can. trade deal	Y	5. Russia sanctions	Y	9. Firearms background checks Y
2. First Coronavirus response	Y	6. Troops in Syria	Y	10. Spending at the border	N/A
3. HEROES Act	Y	7. Veto arms sales to Saudis	Y	11. Marijuana liberalized rules	Y
4. CASH Act	Y	8. Defense $$$, veto override	Y	12. Electoral College objections N

Election Results

Election	Name (Party)	Vote (%)		Cand. Spent	Ind. Exp. Support	Ind. Exp. Oppose
2020 General	Joaquin Castro (D)..........................	175,078	(65%)	$595,641	$8,618	
	Mauro Garza (R).............................	89,628	(33%)	$265,463		$113
	Jeffrey Blunt (L).....................................	6,017	(2%)			
2020 Primary	Joaquín Castro (D).........................	61,861	(92%)			

Prior winning percentages: 2018 (81%), 2016 (80%), 2014 (76%), 2012 (64%)

Democrat Joaquin Castro was elected to his San Antonio-based seat in 2012. As a young, telegenic Hispanic, Castro mostly earned attention when he first came to Congress as the identical twin brother of fellow politician, Julián Castro. Now in his fifth term in the House, Castro has made several flirtations with climbing the ladders of politics only to back off. But expectations for his future and potential remain high.

Politics is in Castro's blood. His mother, Rosie Castro, was a noted Latina activist in the 1960s and 1970s, and she instilled a belief in civil rights and equality of opportunity in her sons. Both he and his brother earned their bachelor's in political science at Stanford University. Both continued to Harvard Law School, where they graduated and then returned to San Antonio to join the politically well-connected Akin, Gump, Strauss, Hauer & Feld law firm and launch their local political careers. Joaquin Castro successfully challenged a Democratic incumbent in the Texas House in 2002, running a change-themed campaign. In the legislature, he focused on education and eventually became the Democratic floor leader. "I've always been in deep minorities" in the legislature, Castro said. "The silver lining is that you learn, almost in a Darwinian way, how to be effective without using sheer force of numbers." That included restoring education funding amid budget-cutting after the 2010 elections.

Castro has had an unusually charmed electoral history. He initially announced he would run in 2012 for Texas' new 35th Congressional District, which runs from San Antonio's east side to Austin. That pitted him against veteran Democratic Rep. Lloyd Doggett and foretold an expensive primary battle dividing two cities and two ethnic groups of Democrats. Soon, longtime Democratic Rep. Charles Gonzalez of San Antonio called Castro and said he had decided to retire. "At that point," Castro said, "it became clear I should run for my home district." He has occasionally faced perfunctory opposition from each party.

Castro has pushed on various fronts to urge legislative action on immigration, including a pathway to citizenship for those in the country illegally. In 2016, he unsuccessfully pleaded to the House Rules Committee to abandon Republican efforts to force the Library of Congress to continue using the term "alien" to refer to immigrants, which he described as "a prejudicial term that's particularly offensive to Hispanics. ... These folks may not be U.S. citizens, but they're not from outer space."

On the House Intelligence Committee, Castro spoke out on the "need to determine not only the extent of Russia's attempts to undermine our election and democracy, but also whether any Americans participated in those efforts." He was harshly critical during most of the Trump era, and his Intelligence perch gave him a platform as a frequent broadcast critic.

Following the 2018 election, in the legislative majority for the first in his career, Castro was selected as chairman of the Congressional Hispanic Caucus. A comprehensive immigration bill was a priority, he said, as was "shedding light on [President Donald] Trump's inhumane immigration policies." Castro has remained active among Democrats as a chief deputy whip. In 2020, Castro launched an unsuccessful bid to chair the House Foreign Affairs Committee after the chairman, Rep. Eliot Engel, lost reelection. It was a longshot bid requiring a leapfrog over a number of more senior members. Castro eventually lost the race to Rep. Gregory Meeks, but he beat expectations in his vote count and in placing second. He became chairman of the Subcommittee on International Development, International Organizations, and Global Corporate Social Impact. Also in 2021, Castro put his legal training to use when Speaker Nancy Pelosi named him as a House manager in Trump's second impeachment for allegedly inciting a riot at the Capitol on Jan. 6. Castro earned plaudits for his calm presentations to the Senate.

In 2017, Castro mulled a run for the Democratic nomination to take on Sen. Ted Cruz. But by the time he came around to a decision, Rep. Beto O'Rourke had started to gain traction. His support for his brother's presidential campaign grew potentially more complicated when Joaquin Castro voiced interest in challenging Republican Sen. John Cornyn for reelection in 2020. Those plans grew more active after O'Rourke said he would not challenge Cornyn and instead launched his own presidential campaign.

A statewide bid remained a daunting challenge for any Texas Democrat, though O'Rourke's narrow loss to Sen. Ted Cruz in 2018 encouraged some Democrats. Journalists have written for years about Castro's frequent travels to meet with grassroots Democrats across the state. But party leaders in Washington made plain their preference for military veteran MJ Hegar and Castro opted against a run. Castro has a safe seat in the House. When or if he makes the jump to a statewide run remains one of the biggest open questions in Texas politics.

TX-20: Bexar County   **Cook Partisan Voting Index: D+13**

Population		Race and Ethnicity		Income	
Total	832,518	White	78.50%	Median Income	$54,908
Land area (sq. miles)	200	Black	5.70%	District Income Rank	332
Pop/ sq mi	4,169.26	Latino	68.40%	Poverty Rate	16.30%
Born in State	63.60%	Asian	3.00%	With health insurance	80.70%
		Two or more races	3.80%	Cash public assistance	1.80%
Age Groups		Other	8.90%	Food stamp/SNAP	17.50%
Under 18	25.80%				
18-34	27.80%	**Education**		**Work**	
35-64	34.70%	H.S grad or less	44.20%	White Collar	33.10%
Over 64	11.80%	Some college	31.40%	Sales and Service	45.70%
		College Degree, 4 yr	15.90%	Blue Collar	21.30%
Military		Post grad	8.60%	Government	12.80%
Veteran/ Active Duty	9.50%				

2020 Pres. Vote	Biden	177,058	(64%)	Trump	96,537	(35%)		
2016 Pres. Vote	Clinton	132,363	(61%)	Trump	74,386	(34%)	Johnson	7,373	(3%)

San Antonio: With its antique past and Hispanic heritage, San Antonio is unlike any other city in the United States. It is the home of the Alamo, preserved by the Daughters of the Republic of Texas, where Davy Crockett, Jim Bowie and 184 others were killed in 1836. Its Spanish architecture recalls San Antonio's days as the most important town in Texas, when the state was part of Mexico; it contrasts with the 30-story Tower Life Building and with the armadillo-like Alamodome. Its Paseo del Rio, the Riverwalk along the tiny San Antonio River that was redeveloped in the 1970s, recalls an earlier era.

For most of the 20th century, San Antonio's economy was built on the military. What the locals call "Military City, U.S.A." remains the home of Lackland Air Force Base, Fort Sam Houston and a giant military hospital. San Antonio has many military retirees and is the largest tourist center in Texas. The city's recent strength has resulted from a diversifying economy that has attracted good-paying jobs in its booming medical research industry. Health care and biosciences have grown to a $37 billion business, led by the military units and the University of Texas Health Science Center. More than one of every six San Antonio employees works in these fields, according to the city's

Chamber of Commerce. San Antonio's manufacturing center contributes more than $22 billion to the local economy, more than triple the revenue it generated in 1991. It is home to the world headquarters of Valero Energy, Clear Channel Communications and USAA Insurance. The 30 percent increase in the gross regional product of the metro area from 2011 to 2016 was the third-highest in the nation, behind San Jose and Austin.

From 2000 to 2019, San Antonio's population increased 34 percent, and it has surpassed Dallas as Texas' second-largest city, after Houston. Of its metropolitan area population of 2.6 million, 56 percent are Hispanic and that share is growing. In November 2018, when Texas Attorney General Ken Paxton sued San Antonio for the first alleged violation of a state law barring the practices of a sanctuary city, he cited a decision by the city's police department not to bring charges against a trailer carrying 12 undocumented individuals from Guatemala. The police department responded that its policy is not to refer individuals to immigration agencies unless they have a federal deportation warrant.

Just over half of San Antonio's population—or one-third of Bexar County—is in the 20th Congressional District of Texas, which is centered in its lower-income west side; the downtown area where most of the city's attractions are located is in the 35th District. To dilute the Democratic vote, parts of five districts are in Bexar; only the 20th is wholly contained in the county. With a Hispanic population share of 69 percent, it is one of the state's nine Hispanic-majority districts. Joe Biden took 64 percent of the district vote, a notable increase from the 59 percent for President Barack Obama in 2012—especially with Biden's problems with Latino voters elsewhere in Texas and beyond.

Chip Roy (R)

Elected 2018, 2nd term, b. Aug 07, 1972; Bethesda, MD; University of VA, B.S., 1994; University of VA, M.S., 1995; University of TX, J.D., 2003; Baptist; Married (Carrah Roy); 2 children.

Professional Career: Counsel, U.S. Senate Subcommittee on Constitution, Civil Rights, and Property Rights, 2005; Counsel, U.S. Sen. John Cornyn 2009; Senior Counsel, U.S. Senate Subcommittee on Immigration, Refugees and Border Security, 2009; Director, Office of Texas Governor Rick Perry, Washington DC Office, 2011; Chief of Staff, U.S. Sen. Ted Cruz, 2012-2014; TX First Assistant Attorney General; Vice President of Strategy, Texas Public Policy Foundation; Senior Advisor, Governor Rick Perry; Special Assistant U.S. Attorney in the Eastern District of Texas.

DC Office: 1319 LHOB 20515, 202-225-4236, Fax: 202-225-8628, roy.house.gov

State Offices: Austin, 512-871-5959; San Antonio, 210-821-5024.

Committees: *Judiciary*: Constitution, Civil Rights & Civil Liberties; Immigration & Citizenship. *Veterans' Affairs*: Health.

Almanac Ratings 2019-2020

	Economy	Social	Foreign	Composite
Liberal	27%	5%	44%	26%
Conservative	73%	95%	56%	74%

Key Votes of the 116th Congress

1. U.S./Mex./Can. trade deal	Y	5. Russia sanctions	Y	9. Firearms background checks	N
2. First Coronavirus response	N	6. Troops in Syria	N/A	10. Spending at the border	N
3. HEROES Act	N	7. Veto arms sales to Saudis	N	11. Marijuana liberalized rules	N
4. CASH Act	N	8. Defense $$$, veto override	N	12. Electoral College objections	N

Election Results

Election	Name (Party)	Vote (%)	Cand. Spent	Ind. Exp. Support	Ind. Exp. Oppose
2020 General	Chip Roy (R)....................................	235,740 (52%)	$4,737,275	$1,532,259	$4,557,136
	Wendy Davis (D).........................	205,780 (45%)	$10,513,880	$107,145	$7,773,240
2020 Primary	Chip Roy (R).....................................	75,389 (100%)			

Prior winning percentages: 2018 (50%)

Republican Chip Roy, a veteran congressional aide and partisan insider who narrowly won his first elected office, showed occasional independence from the GOP mainstream and a willingness to go his own way, including criticism of former President Donald Trump. He won reelection more easily against a prominent and well-financed Democratic challenger.

Born in Maryland to Texas natives and raised in northern Virginia, Roy got his bachelor's degree and a master's degree in management information systems from the University of Virginia, plus his law degree from the University of Texas. With his blue-chip credentials, he served as a federal prosecutor with then-U.S. Attorney John Cornyn, became a senior aide when Cornyn was elected to the Senate and later was a top official for the Texas attorney general. He also was a top aide to, among others, Texas Sen. Ted Cruz and former Gov. Rick Perry, including their separate presidential campaigns. In the private sector, Roy was an investment banking analyst and a top officer of the conservative Texas Public Policy Foundation.

"For years, Roy has operated behind the scenes on behalf of top Texas GOP officeholders," the Austin American-Statesman wrote in a campaign profile, which emphasized that he used his experience chiefly to oppose federal actions. "Now he's trying to make a name for himself as a politician in his own right." But that became an unexpectedly challenging effort.

Roy was the most politically experienced and well-connected of the six Texas Republicans in 2018 who won contests for open House seats that had been GOP-held and were largely determined in the March primary. He won a tight victory in the runoff against a local businessman who ran a low-profile campaign and was significantly outspent.

Roy received 27 percent of the vote to 17 percent for Matt McCall; an unwieldy 16 other candidates split the remainder of the vote. In Bexar County, the population center of the district that cast nearly one-third of the vote, Roy barely led with 26 percent. McCall spent less than half as much money as Roy, who also benefited from more than $1 million in spending by the conservative Club for Growth.

Roy struggled in the runoff. McCall, a tea party ally, criticized Roy "as an outsider in the district who is leaning hard on his political connections to get him across the finish line," the Texas Tribune reported prior to the runoff. Roy won the GOP nomination by an unimpressive 53%-47%. He led McCall in Bexar and Travis, the urban anchors of the district, and won the three exurban counties that were closest to those areas. McCall took the other five counties in the rural western part of the district, including the Hill Country.

In November, Roy faced Democrat Joseph Kopser, a businessman who once was affiliated with the Republican Party. Despite Kopser's nearly 2-to-1 lead in spending and Roy's continued learning curve, the Republican history of the district ultimately secured Roy's victory, 50%-48%. The vote was split in three roughly equal parts: Kopser won 76 percent in Travis County; Roy took a slim 51 percent in Bexar County and rolled up huge majorities in the exurban and rural counties.

In the House, Roy was positioned to take advantage of his deep familiarity with Capitol Hill, especially among Texans. But his early independence caused some annoyance, even among Republicans, as he forced numerous votes on procedural tactics and uncontroversial amendments. "I think it's really important that the people in this town not get comfortable that they can just kind of move through business," he told The Washington Post. "I get that it causes some pain; I understand that. I don't take joy in that, but I'm not bothered by it, either."

When several senators were investigated for charges of insider trading, Roy joined Democratic Rep. Abigail Spanberger of Virginia in filing a bill to require all members of Congress to place stocks and commodities in a blind trust. He cited "a lack of public trust" when lawmakers "are gaming financial markets." In the lame-duck session following the 2020 election, he criticized Trump for raising a peripheral issue that would have stymied final action on the defense spending bill.

In his reelection campaign, after winning the GOP primary without opposition, Roy faced Democrat Wendy Davis—who became well known when she filibustered an anti-abortion bill in the state senate and in 2014 ran unsuccessfully for governor. She called Roy's views "extreme," criticized his failure to wear a mask during the coronavirus pandemic and cited "a failure of leadership" by Republicans. Davis outspent Roy, $10.4 million to $4.8 million, with the national parties spending more than $12 million on the contest. Davis got 73 percent in Travis County, which cast a bit more than one-fourth of the total vote, but Roy won, 52%-46%.

Following the election, Roy rejected Republican calls to review the Electoral College votes of Pennsylvania and Arizona and said Trump "deserves universal condemnation for what was clearly impeachable conduct" in seeking to pressure Vice President Mike Pence to side with the objectors. Although he voted against the impeachment charge, he said Republican Conference Chairwoman Liz Cheney "should be commended, not condemned, for standing up in defense of the Constitution" when she voted in favor. And he rejected initial calls by other House Republicans to discipline her.

After Cheney was ousted from her leadership position in May 2021, Roy made a last-minute challenge to Rep. Elise Stefanik, who already had locked up support from most wings of the party as the successor to Cheney. Roy criticized Stefanik's lack of conservative credentials. But his bid was too little and too late, and resulted in Trump's criticism that Roy had "not done a great job" in Congress. He lost, 134-46.

TX-21: Northern Bexar County, Southern Travis County

Cook Partisan Voting Index: R+5

Population		Race and Ethnicity		Income	
Total	829,628	White	84.70%	Median Income	$73,472
Land area (sq. miles)	5,921	Black	4.20%	District Income Rank	140
Pop/ sq mi	140.12	Latino	30.50%	Poverty Rate	9.60%
Born in State	56.00%	Asian	3.80%	With health insurance	87.90%
		Two or more races	3.50%	Cash public assistance	1.30%
Age Groups		Other	3.90%	Food stamp/SNAP	4.70%
Under 18	19.00%				
18-34	25.70%	**Education**		**Work**	
35-64	38.00%	H.S grad or less	24.60%	White Collar	48.20%
Over 64	17.10%	Some college	28.00%	Sales and Service	38.50%
		College Degree, 4 yr	30.00%	Blue Collar	13.30%
Military		Post grad	17.40%	Government	13.70%
Veteran/ Active Duty	9.40%				

2020 Pres. Vote	Trump	232,949	(51%)	Biden	220,572	(48%)			
2016 Pres. Vote	Trump	188,336	(52%)	Clinton	152,528	(42%)	Johnson	14,130	(4%)

San Antonio/Austin Corridor: The Balcones Escarpment is a bulwark of cracked and weathered rock that crosses Texas diagonally from the Dallas-Fort Worth Metroplex southwest to Austin and San Antonio and all the way to the Rio Grande. It separates the flatlands of central Texas from the stony hills to the north and west. It is a boundary between cropland and grazing land, between acres rich with greenery and acres whose rolling brown hills blaze out in color when the wildflowers bloom in early spring. But the Balcones Escarpment is less familiar to Texans today than the highway that runs pretty much along the same line: Interstate 35. This is one of the most heavily traveled and congested interstates in America, thick with truck traffic in the populated stretches between the Metroplex and the Mexican border even as it passes through the lightly populated near-desert between San Antonio and Laredo. I-35 connects Austin and San Antonio, two booming Texan cities with very different beginnings and different characters now.

In the counties between these two cities and in the Hill Country to the west is the Texas German country, originally settled by Germans in the mid-1800s. It consists of economically prosperous communities that were anti-slavery and politically Republican in a state whose enthusiasm for the Democratic Party had roots in Confederate loyalties and populist rebellions. Texas Germans introduced the long-barbecued beef brisket that has become synonymous with Lone Star State cuisine; an antique German dialect is sometimes heard on the streets of New Braunfels, Boerne and Fredericksburg. Parts of this area, chiefly small cities, are among the most rapidly growing in the nation. Hays and Comal, which are between Travis and Bexar counties, ranked second and fourth among the fastest-growing counties in the nation between 2017 and 2019, with gains of 47 and 44 percent, respectively. New Braunfels, the county seat of Comal ranked third among cities nationwide, with 56 percent growth during those years. San Marcos, which is about halfway between the two anchors on I-35, was the fastest-growing city in 2014. But it suffered extensive flooding from Hurricane Harvey in 2017 and sought long-term solutions to its problems in what has been called "Flash Flood Alley."

The 21st Congressional District of Texas includes much of this territory. About one-third of its people are in San Antonio and Bexar County. It includes the northeast corner of the city and county, taking in Fort Sam Houston, and the affluent north side neighborhoods of Terrell Hills, Olmos Park and Alamo Heights just outside San Antonio. In the expansive Hill Country, the district takes in Gillespie County; along the Pedernales River is the LBJ Ranch, where the 36th president was born, vacationed during his presidency and is buried. As a New Deal congressman, Johnson famously brought electricity and other services to this hinterland.

Nearly one-third of the district is in Travis County, with parts of downtown Austin's central business district that border the University of Texas and the state capital. Amid the booming corporate development, downtown Austin has cherished its fame of more bars per capita than any other ZIP code in the nation. While Travis County was always Democratic and the Texas German country was Republican, San Antonio was mixed. As was the case in other suburban parts of Texas, President Donald Trump underperformed the GOP presidential vote here; he got 50.5 percent in 2020, compared with 60 percent for Mitt Romney in 2012.

Troy Nehls (R)

Elected 2020, 1st term, b. Apr 07, 1968; Beaver Dam, WI; Liberty University, B.A.; University of Houston, M.A.; Christian - Non-Denominational; Married (Jill Nehls); 3 children.

Military Career: Major, U.S. Army (Bosnia, Iraq, Afghanistan).

Professional Career: Constable, Fort Bend County Precinct 4 Constable's Office, 2005-2012; Sheriff, Fort Bend County Sheriff's Office, 2013-2021.

DC Office: 1104 LHOB 20515, 202-225-5951, Fax: 202-225-5241, nehls.house.gov

State Offices: Richmond, 346-762-6600.

Committees: *Transportation & Infrastructure*: Aviation; Highways & Transit; Railroads, Pipelines & Hazardous Materials. *Veterans' Affairs*: Disability Assistance & Memorial Affairs (RMM).

Election Results

Election	Name (Party)	Vote (%)		Cand. Spent	Ind. Exp. Support	Ind. Exp. Oppose
2020 General	Troy Nehls (R)............................ 210,259	(52%)		$1,758,541	$1,111,246	$7,900,719
	Sri Preston Kulkarni (D)............ 181,998	(45%)		$6,104,969	$322,098	$5,933,127
	Joseph LeBlanc, Jr. (L).................. 15,791	(4%)				
2020 Primary	Troy Nehls (R)............................ 29,538	(41%)				
	Kathaleen Wall (R)............................. 14,201	(19%)				
	Pierce Bush (R)............................... 11,281	(15%)				
	Greg Hill (R).................................. 10,315	(14%)				

Republican Troy Nehls, a local sheriff, defeated better-financed opponents and won a competitive contest in a district that has been the site of major demographic and political shifts. In a contest that featured extensive discussion of law enforcement, Nehls distanced himself from President Donald Trump. He replaced Republican Rep. Pete Olson, who retired after six terms and a narrow reelection victory in 2018 against a Democrat who ran again two years later.

A native of Beaver Dam Wisconsin, where his father was sheriff, Nehls graduated from Liberty University and got a master's degree in criminal justice from the University of Houston. He enlisted in the Army Reserves and served for 21 years, including tours of duty in Bosnia, Iraq and Afghanistan, where he managed large projects. He earned two Bronze Stars and retired as a major. He served with the police department in Fort Bend County and then as a local constable, which is a law-enforcement position. As the elected sheriff of the county for eight years, Nehls supervised more than 800 employees.

When Olson retired, rather than face an election rematch, 15 Republicans entered the contest. They included Pierce Bush, the chief executive of a large nonprofit group and grandson of President George H.W. Bush and son of Neil Bush. In his first political campaign, Bush spent $1.5 million and was endorsed by the Houston Chronicle, which praised his vision and his support for a "pathway to legal status" for illegal immigrants.

In the first round of the primary, Bush finished third with 15 percent of the vote. Nehls led with 40 percent, including 52 percent in Fort Bend County, which cast about two-thirds of the vote. He ran well behind the field in Brazoria and Harris counties. The runner-up was Kathaleen Wall, with 19 percent.

Wall, who self-financed her campaign with proceeds from the sale of her computer company, took a hardline position on immigration. After spending $6 million of her own money in her 2018 bid for the Houston-area seat that was won by Republican Dan Crenshaw, she spent another $9.4 million running against Nehls. In her ads, she accused Nehls of not taking serious action against sex trafficking as sheriff. Nehls denied her charges and won the primary runoff with 70 percent of the vote.

Democrat Sri Preston Kulkarni, who defeated three opponents to win the primary without a runoff, had challenged Olson in 2018 and called him a "do-nothing congressman." Kulkarni lost, 51%-47%. A former foreign service officer and the son of a native of India, he was a national security aide to Sen. Kirsten Gillibrand of New York.

Running against Nehls, Kulkarni cited the sheriff's history of misconduct and complaints about his department's actions. In 1998, Nehls had been fired by a local police department after he had committed 19 violations in one year. In a statement, Nehls cited "my long record of service to the district" and criticized Kulkarni for taking campaign contributions from groups that support "defunding the police." Nehls refused to debate his opponent.

In an editorial endorsement of Kulkarni, the Chronicle praised his "intelligence and cooperative attitude," and criticized Nehls for his handling of immigration and for a sheriff department's narcotics task force that was accused of "egregious racial profiling." The Chronicle earlier reported that Nehls had removed Trump-friendly features from his campaign website. Its news story cited the "strong headwinds" that Trump had created for local candidates. Nehls defeated Kulkarni, 52%-45%, and led by single digits in each of the three counties. Kulkarni outspent Nehls by more than 3-to-1. The two national parties roughly split another $13 million on the contest.

In April 2021, Nehls gained attention when he unexpectedly talked up President Joe Biden as he was leaving the House chamber following his first speech to Congress. He told Biden, "I want to help with the criminal justice reform. I want to be part of that," but that he didn't know how to reach out to him, the Texas Tribune reported. As Biden promised, a White House aide contacted him the next morning, Nehls said.

TX-22: Southern Houston Suburbs   **Cook Partisan Voting Index: R+4**

Population		Race and Ethnicity		Income	
Total	960,957	White	59.70%	Median Income	$101,658
Land area (sq. miles)	1,033	Black	14.50%	District Income Rank	29
Pop/ sq mi	930.4	Latino	26.80%	Poverty Rate	5.60%
Born in State	51.80%	Asian	18.30%	With health insurance	87.60%
		Two or more races	3.70%	Cash public assistance	1.40%
Age Groups		Other	3.90%	Food stamp/SNAP	5.50%
Under 18	27.40%				
18-34	20.10%	**Education**		**Work**	
35-64	41.30%	H.S grad or less	26.30%	White Collar	52.70%
Over 64	11.30%	Some college	28.30%	Sales and Service	32.10%
		College Degree, 4 yr	27.70%	Blue Collar	15.30%
Military		Post grad	17.70%	Government	11.80%
Veteran/ Active Duty	5.00%				

2020 Pres. Vote	Trump	210,011	(50%)	Biden	206,114	(49%)		
2016 Pres. Vote	Trump	159,717	(52%)	Clinton	135,525	(44%)	Johnson	9,322	(3%)

Sugar Land: The story of the Houston area's booming growth is well captured in a drive out the Southwest Freeway to Sugar Land. Much has changed from the days before the Civil War, when sugar plantations flourished here. In 2018, archeologists at the construction site for a new local school found 95 graves that they concluded were the remains of Black prison laborers who worked in indentured servitude on plantations in the late 19th century. The school board decided to move the new school elsewhere and approve a historical memorial for the "Sugar Land 95." Sugar Land is a privately planned city of more than 118,000 people, with privatized water and other services. (In 1990, its population was 45,000.) The surrounding Fort Bend County has been among the nation leaders in job growth since 2000. In November 2018, a University of Houston study projected that Fort Bend would be the third-fastest growing county in the nation between 2010 and 2050, with an increase to perhaps 2.7 million. Its population of 812,000 in 2019 was a 39 percent increase from 2010. The local baseball team is the Sugar Land Skeeters, a reference to the area's uncomfortable proliferation of the biting insects.

When former House Majority Leader Tom DeLay represented the 22nd Congressional District, whites were a majority. Although much of Fort Bend's Black population resides in the adjacent 9th District, the 22nd has become a minority-majority district. Suburban Sugar Land and Fort Bend County are among the most-diverse areas in the country. A quarter of the county's population is Hispanic, 21 percent each are African American, and Asian. In 2018, voters elected as county judge —the top county executive—KP George, a Democrat and a native of a small village of India who immigrated and became a certified financial planner; he was described as the Indian American with the most prominent position in local government in the United States. With growth and diversification has come wealth: The median income in the district is nearly $94,000, the highest in Texas. In 2020, Joe Biden took the county, 55%-45%, a 17-point swing from 2012 and an encouraging omen for Democrats. About two-thirds of the district is in Fort Bend.

The district includes 80 percent of the voters in Fort Bend County, including Sugar Land, and a bit more than half of Brazoria County, centering on Pearland, just south of Houston. In Pearland, a suburb that was positioning itself as a health care hub for the region, the population exploded from 46,000 in 2000 to 122,000 in 2019; the local economy in 2017 was the third fastest-growing in the nation. In February 2020, the Houston Chronicle reported that Census Bureau data showed that Pearland ranked 15th in the nation among cities with the most new homeowners; 36 percent had lived in the same home for less than a decade. The district, which takes in a small slice of southwestern Houston, has been solidly Republican, with Mitt Romney getting 62 percent in 2012. Eight years later, that had changed notably. President Donald Trump was not so good a fit and took 49.8 percent, a lead of fewer than 4,000 votes over Joe Biden.

Tony Gonzales (R)

Elected 2020, 1st term, b. Oct 10, 1980; Fort McClellan, AL; Georgetown University, B.A.; American Public University System, M.A.; University of Southern MS, Ph.D.; Catholic; Married (Angel Gonzales); 6 children.

Military Career: Master Chief Petty Officer, U.S. Navy, 1999-2019 (Iraq, Afghanistan).

Professional Career: National Security Fellow, Foundation for Defense of Democracies; Legislative Fellow, U.S. Senator Marco Rubio's Office, Department of Defense; Assistant Professor, University of Maryland.

DC Office: 1009 LHOB 20515, 202-225-4511, Fax: 202-225-2237, gonzales.house.gov

State Offices: Del Rio, 830-308-6200; Fort Stockton, 432-299-6200; San Antonio, 210-806-9920; Socorro, 915-490-7551; Uvalde, 830-333-7410.

Committees: *Appropriations*: Military Construction, Veterans Affairs & Related Agencies; Transportation, HUD & Related Agencies.

Election Results

Election	Name (Party)	Vote (%)		Cand. Spent	Ind. Exp. Support	Ind. Exp. Oppose
2020 General	Tony Gonzales (R)	149,395	(51%)	$2,719,511	$308,857	$5,702,065
	Gina Ortiz Jones (D)	137,693	(47%)	$7,167,731	$1,446,067	$4,319,467
	Beto Villela (L)	8,369	(3%)			
2020 Primary	Tony Gonzales (R)	11,522	(28%)			
	Raul Reyes (R)	9,555	(23%)			
	Alma Arredondo-Lynch (R)	5,391	(13%)			
	Ben Van Winkle (R)	4,427	(11%)			
	Jeff McFarlin (R)	4,241	(10%)			
	Sharon Thomas (R)	2,511	(6%)			

Republican Tony Gonzales upended initial political expectations of a Democratic victory and won an open seat in Texas. He got a boost from the unexpectedly strong vote for President Donald Trump in the Rio Grande Valley.

Gonzales, who retired as a Navy cryptologist, defeated Democrat Gina Ortiz Jones, an Air Force veteran who was an intelligence officer in Iraq. This was the second campaign in the district by Jones, who lost by 926 votes to Republican Rep. Will Hurd in 2018. Gonzales succeeded Hurd, who retired after three terms, though he left the door open for another political campaign.

A native of San Antonio, Gonzales received a graduate certificate in legislative studies from Georgetown University and a master's degree in international relations from the online American Public University. He has been a Ph.D. candidate in security studies and international politics at the University of Southern Mississippi.

Gonzales served 20 years in the Navy, retiring as a master chief petty officer. He was stationed at multiple U.S. bases and was deployed to support combat operations in Iraq and Afghanistan and with security operations elsewhere in Asia. He was a Defense Department fellow in the office of Sen. Marco Rubio of Florida and has been an assistant professor at the University of Maryland, where he has taught counterterrorism and political science courses. In San Antonio, he was elected as the community representative for the local Head Start policy council.

Hurd's retirement attracted nine Republican candidates. Gonzales led the first round of the Republican primary, with 28 percent of the vote; Raul Reyes was second with 23 percent. In the runoff, Gonzales was endorsed by Hurd and House Republican leaders, plus Trump. Sen. Ted Cruz of Texas endorsed Reyes, a retired Air Force lieutenant colonel who was a senior officer in the command and control of cyber defense operations.

Their contest featured some angry exchanges. As reported by the San Antonio Current, Reyes accused Gonzales of supporting the liberal agenda of the League of United Latin American Citizens; Gonzales claimed that Reyes had been fired from the administration of a local college, which Reyes denied. Following a lengthy recount, Gonzales won the runoff by 45 votes out of the nearly 25,000 cast. In Bexar County, which cast nearly half the vote, Gonzalez got 60 percent. Reyes took most of the lightly populated rural counties.

Jones, who won the Democratic primary with 66 percent of the vote against four opponents, had five months to prepare before Gonzales was the GOP nominee. She criticized his opposition to the Affordable Care Act and mandated protections for pre-existing conditions. Republican ads attacked Jones, who was openly lesbian, for supporting taxpayer money for gender-reassignment surgery.

Gonzales won 51%-47%. In Bexar County, which cast 54 percent of the vote, he led 50%-48%. Jones took 69 percent in the slice of El Paso County, which casts nearly one-tenth of the vote. Gonzales had big leads in most of the small rural counties.

The outcome was an unpleasant surprise to leading Democrats. During the summer, Rep. Joaquin Castro of Texas introduced Jones at an event and said, "if we win no other races, I'm sure we're gonna win this one," the Texas Tribune reported. Each national party spent more than $4 million in the contest. From her own campaign account, she spent $7 million, which was more than twice what Gonzales spent.

Gonzales likely will face instances of mistaken identity with Rep. Anthony Gonzalez, an Ohio Republican in his second term. Anthony has a shaved head and is a former wide receiver in the National Football League. He also was one of the 10 House Republicans who voted for the second impeachment charge against Trump.

With Republican Rep. Ashley Hinson of Iowa, Tony Gonzalez was one of only two freshmen who got a seat on the Appropriations Committee in 2021. He said that his priorities were "to advocate for our district's veterans, protect Texas bases from the next round of Base Realignment and Closure, and deliver much needed investments to Texas' infrastructure." Gonzalez also will be seeking help from state Republicans during redistricting.

TX-23: Bexar County Exurbs, West Texas   Cook Partisan Voting Index: R+1

Population		Race and Ethnicity		Income	
Total	786,712	White	84.30%	Median Income	$59,074
Land area (sq. miles)	58,059	Black	3.50%	District Income Rank	279
Pop/ sq mi	13.55	Latino	69.60%	Poverty Rate	15.50%
Born in State	64.70%	Asian	2.00%	With health insurance	83.20%
		Two or more races	2.50%	Cash public assistance	2.20%
Age Groups		Other	7.70%	Food stamp/SNAP	15.80%
Under 18	27.50%				
18-34	23.60%	Education		Work	
35-64	35.80%	H.S grad or less	48.80%	White Collar	32.10%
Over 64	13.10%	Some college	27.20%	Sales and Service	41.60%
		College Degree, 4 yr	16.00%	Blue Collar	26.30%
Military		Post grad	7.90%	Government	16.30%
Veteran/ Active Duty	9.10%				

2020 Pres. Vote	Trump	151,964	(50%)	Biden	146,559	(48%)		
2016 Pres. Vote	Clinton	115,157	(50%)	Trump	107,273	(46%)	Johnson	7,077	(3%)

San Antonio: Fifty or so miles west of San Antonio, the hills flatten out and become the parched uplands of West Texas. This is a borderland, just north of Mexico, where people are concentrated in tiny hamlets amid the empty ranchlands. Most are Hispanic. Once, Indians were the threat on this frontier. Now the challenge is a lack of water. The aquifers of West Texas are being drained, and state law still permits landowners to pump out as much water as they want. The Rio Grande, dried out by a dam in New Mexico, gets most of its water from the Rio Conchos in the Mexican state of Chihuahua. Rising above the Rio Grande are the mountains of Big Bend National Park, where in the clean air you can see for 180 miles. Texas' frontier in many ways is thriving; its remote location makes it one of the least-visited national parks. The tiny town of Marfa first became a landmark when director George Stevens and actors Rock Hudson, Elizabeth Taylor and James Dean stayed in the glamorous Hotel El Paisano and shot the movie Giant. Marfa has become known as an eccentric art colony. Near the Mexican border is Dimmit County, where more than a dozen companies have drilled thousands of wells in an oil and gas field known as the Eagle Ford shale formation. In oil-producing Loving County, the population more than doubled from 82 to 169 residents from 2010 to 2019, which made it the fastest-growing—and still the least populous—county in the nation. Discovery of shale oil and improved fracking techniques have opened additional parts of the Permian Basin to production.

The 23rd Congressional District of Texas is geographically the largest in the state, stretching from the outskirts of San Antonio to the edge of El Paso, from Eagle Pass and Maverick County to the New Mexico border. It takes in 23 percent of the state's land area, spanning more than 800 miles of the Texas-Mexico border and covering 29 counties. Many local communities along the border have strong views—often hostile—about national politicians who want to build a large wall here. Local residents also understand the logistical complications, especially in Big Bend.

About half of the district's population is in Bexar County, chiefly in a C-shaped ring in the county's western suburbs that surround downtown San Antonio and is the more heavily Republican part of the district. San Antonio's Mexican-American community has produced many politicians who are liberal on economic issues and civil rights but also are pro-military and at home with traditional cultural values. Only 8 percent of the 23rd is in El Paso County, which is disproportionately Democratic, as are some of the rural counties. The district is 70 percent Hispanic, but this has remained a battleground district. This was among the few seats won by Hillary Clinton that Mitt Romney carried four years earlier—narrowly, in each case. President Donald Trump in 2020 flipped his earlier setback of two percentage points.

Beth Van Duyne (R)

Elected 2020, 1st term, b. Nov 16, 1970; Ithaca, NY; Cornell University, B.A.; Greenhill School, Addison, TX; Episcopalian; Divorced; 2 children.

Elected Office: Member/Deputy Mayor Pro Tem, Irving City Council, 2004-2010; Mayor, City of Irving, 2011-2017.

Professional Career: Vice President of Marketing, information consulting firm, 2008-2009; Senior Director of Corporate Communications, aviation service company, 2010-2011; President, Digital Marketing Agency, 2002-2011; Vice President of Strategic Alliances, information consulting firm, 2013-2015; Regional Administrator, U.S. Department of Housing and Urban Development, 2017-2019.

DC Office: 1337 LHOB 20515, 202-225-6605, Fax: 202-225-0074, vanduyne.house.gov

State Offices: Dallas, 972-966-5500.

Committees: *Select Committee on the Modernization of Congress. Small Business*: Economic Growth, Tax & Capital Access; Oversight, Investigations & Regulations (RMM). *Transportation & Infrastructure*: Aviation; Economic Dev't, Public Buildings & Emergency Management; Highways & Transit.

Election Results

Election	Name (Party)	Vote (%)		Cand. Spent	Ind. Exp. Support	Ind. Exp. Oppose
2020 General	Beth Van Duyne (R)......................	167,910	(49%)	$3,413,036	$453,027	$7,597,905
	Candace Valenzuela (D).....................	163,326	(47%)	$4,869,833	$1,474,936	$7,970,056
2020 Primary	Beth Van Duyne (R).....................	32,067	(64%)			
	David Fegan (R).................................	10,295	(21%)			
	Desi Maes (R).:.............................	2,867	(6%)			
	Sunny Chaparala (R)......................	2,808	(6%)			

Republican Beth Van Duyne narrowly won an open House seat that has shifted dramatically from its once-solidly GOP control. The former mayor of Irving, she was a well-known candidate running against Candace Valenzuela, a political activist who generated enthusiasm among local and national Democrats. Van Duyne succeeded Republican Rep. Kenny Marchant, who retired after eight terms and was a senior member of the House Ways and Means Committee. In 2018, he barely survived reelection, 51%-48%.

Van Duyne, a native of upstate New York, moved with her family to Texas when she was in high school. She got her bachelor's degree from Cornell University, where her studies included city and regional planning, government and law. She worked with several companies in Texas and, with her husband, ran a consulting business that advised executives on strategic business plans.

After serving six years on the Irving city council, Van Duyne was elected mayor in 2011. In that office, she generated controversy when she opposed a local effort to create what was described as "the first sharia tribunal in Texas;" she supported state legislation to bar such a practice, though the bill was not approved. In 2017, President Donald Trump named her a regional administrator of the Department of Housing and Urban Development. Van Duyne won the five-candidate Republican primary with 64 percent of the vote. David Fegan, who worked in commercial real estate, got 21 percent.

In the Democratic primary, Kim Olson and Valenzuela led the seven candidates, with 41 and 30 percent respectively. Olson, a former Air Force colonel, later was director of human resources for the Dallas school district. Valenzuela unexpectedly won the runoff with 60 percent, leading in all three counties: Dallas, Tarrant and Denton.

In seeking to become the first Black Latina elected to Congress, Valenzuela described the homelessness she experienced as a child and the hardships she faced as a political outsider. In 2017, when she was elected to the Carrollton-Farmers Branch school board, she said her victory shattered the conventional political narrative that "everything outside of Dallas is red and there'd be no opportunity to change things."

"As soon as my constituents hear my story, it's incredibly easy for them to relate," she told the Texas Tribune, which profiled her in September as "a new face of Democrats' optimism" for 2020. "I think a lot of people [in the suburbs] were politically disengaged."

In the closing days of their campaign, the candidates clashed over their handling of the coronavirus pandemic. Citing photos of Van Duyne at public events where she was not wearing a mask, Valenzuela's campaign manager accused her of "recklessly opposing Texas' statewide mask mandate and refusing to social distance." Van Duyne criticized her opponent for her failure to campaign in person. Valenzuela responded that she lived with her elderly mother-in-law, who was at greater risk of illness from the virus.

The Dallas Morning News, in its editorial endorsement, said it "cautiously recommended" Van Duyne. It voiced concern over her hardline on immigration and wrote that she was "unnecessarily combative."

In the final election result declared for Texans in the House, Van Duyne wrapped up the unexpected retention of the status quo for the relieved GOP: 23 Republicans, 13 Democrats. Van Duyne won, 48.8%-47.5%. In Tarrant County, she took 58 percent of the vote, a lead of nearly 27,000 votes. Valenzuela won the other two counties, with 55 percent in Dallas, which had a slightly larger turnout than Tarrant, and 50 percent in Denton, which cast one-sixth of the total votes. Valenzuela outspent Van Duyne by $1.5 million. The national parties and interest groups spent more than $15 million on the contest, which was about evenly split..

In the House, Van Duyne gained useful assignments for her district, as a member of the Transportation and Infrastructure Subcommittees on Aviation and Highways. She likely will be seeking redistricting assistance from Republicans in the Texas Legislature.

TX-24: North-Central Metroplex

Cook Partisan Voting Index: R+2

Population		Race and Ethnicity		Income	
Total	832,445	White	62.20%	Median Income	$79,667
Land area (sq. miles)	263	Black	13.10%	District Income Rank	96
Pop/ sq mi	3,168.08	Latino	23.60%	Poverty Rate	7.40%
Born in State	42.50%	Asian	15.50%	With health insurance	86.10%
		Two or more races	3.60%	Cash public assistance	0.90%
Age Groups		Other	5.50%	Food stamp/SNAP	4.10%
Under 18	22.30%				
18-34	26.70%	**Education**		**Work**	
35-64	40.10%	H.S grad or less	26.10%	White Collar	48.00%
Over 64	10.90%	Some college	25.50%	Sales and Service	35.10%
		College Degree, 4 yr	31.60%	Blue Collar	16.90%
Military		Post grad	16.80%	Government	7.20%
Veteran/ Active Duty	5.00%				

2020 Pres. Vote	Biden	180,609	(52%)	Trump	161,671	(46%)		
2016 Pres. Vote	Trump	140,128	(50%)	Clinton	122,872	(44%)	Johnson	10,753	(4%)

Fort Worth Suburbs: The gigantic (larger than Manhattan Island) Dallas-Fort Worth International Airport bisects the Metroplex and its two adjacent counties with its large terminals and the Texas-sized highway network that feeds them. Its total of flight operations makes it the third largest airport in the world, with seven runways, five terminals, 165 gates and 60,000 employees in an area of 27 square miles. DFW, as the locals call it, has been a focal point for development in both Dallas and Tarrant counties. "DFW is no longer solely an airport. DFW is our home," the Fort Worth Star-Telegram wrote. New cities, with as many people as Dallas and Fort Worth had in the 1950s —Grand Prairie and Irving—grew up around the airport during the next two decades in an area that had been an open prairie. In November 2018, the airport authority announced plans to sell about $10 billion in bonds; one possible project was the building of a sixth terminal. "Our airfield is in pretty good shape, but we're out of gates again," an executive said. Two years later, the Austin Business Journal reported that DFW—now "the epicenter of national and global logistics"—was positioned to help lead Texas out of the pandemic.

North and west of DFW are newer and more upscale suburbs in northeast Tarrant County: Southlake, with huge shopping malls and resort centers, and Grapevine, home to the largest consumer-judged wine competition in the country. The Texas 114 corridor (also known as the Northwest

Freeway) has become a booming business zone from Southlake to Roanoke. Across the International Parkway in northwest Dallas County are Coppell, Farmers Branch and Carrollton. To the north are the fast-growing suburbs and exurbs of Denton County. The Dallas-Fort Worth-Arlington Metropolitan Statistical Area has passed Philadelphia as the nation's fourth-largest MSA.

The 24th Congressional District of Texas is based in the suburban territory around DFW Airport. The line between its two principal counties, which goes through the eastern part of the terminal, is roughly the central axis of the district. Dallas and Tarrant each provide slightly more than 40 percent of the population, with the remainder beyond Dallas in Denton County. The area in Dallas takes in part of Irving, including ExxonMobil's corporate headquarters, part of Carrolton and all of Farmers Branch and Coppell. Irving, which business executives describe as "the headquarters of headquarters," has six Fortune 500 corporate offices—the most per capita of any city in the United States. McKesson, the giant pharmaceutical company, relocated from San Francisco in early 2019. The slice in Tarrant is the strongest Republican part of the district. Colleyville—which had no sanitary sewer system in 1956—had become the city in Texas with the highest percentage of college graduates, with an average household income of $200,000, the Dallas Morning News wrote in July 2020. It was also a "mecca for conservatives," the Fort Worth Star Telegram reported in May, as evidenced a month earlier by the proclamation of Mayor Richard Newton to reopen the town's restaurants. The town has shown "a strong sense of conservatism and liberty more common among rural towns, making it an outlier among the Metroplex's rapidly growing and changing suburbs."

In once solidly Republican territory, Joe Biden's 52%-46% win over President Donald Trump was a stunning turnaround from the 60 percent that Mitt Romney got in 2012.

Roger Williams (R)

Elected 2012, 5th term, b. Sep 13, 1949; Evanston, IL; TX Christian University, B.S., 1972; Disciples of Christ; Married (Patty Williams); 2 children.

Professional Career: Owner, Roger Williams Chrysler Dodge Jeep Ram, 1971-present; Atlanta Braves farm team, 1971-1974; Baseball coach, TX Christian University, 1974-1976; TX Secretary of st., 2005-2007.

DC Office: 1708 LHOB 20515, 202-225-9896, Fax: 202-225-9692, williams.house.gov

State Offices: Austin, 512-473-8910; Cleburne, 817-774-2575.

Committees: *Financial Services*: Consumer Protection & Financial Institutions; Nat'l Security, International Development & Monetary Policy. *Small Business*: Innovation, Entrepreneurship & Workforce Development; Underserved, Agricultural & Rural Business Development.

Group Ratings

	ADA	ACLU	AFL-CIO	LCV	COC	HAFA	ACU	CFG	FRC
2020	**	19%	**	10%	-	91%	92%	**	-
2019	10%	C	25%	0%	87%	C	92%	83%	95%

Almanac Ratings 2019-2020

	Economy	Social	Foreign	Composite
Liberal	25%	10%	39%	25%
Conservative	75%	90%	61%	75%

Key Votes of the 116th Congress

1. U.S./Mex./Can. trade deal	Y	5. Russia sanctions	Y	9. Firearms background checks N
2. First Coronavirus response	Y	6. Troops in Syria	N	10. Spending at the border	Y
3. HEROES Act	N	7. Veto arms sales to Saudis	N	11. Marijuana liberalized rules	N
4. CASH Act	N	8. Defense $$$, veto override	Y	12. Electoral College objections Y

Election Results

Election	Name (Party)	Vote (%)		Cand. Spent	Ind. Exp. Support	Ind. Exp. Oppose
2020 General	Roger Williams (R)...............................	220,088	(56%)	$3,365,900	$7,713	$5,196
	Julie Oliver (D).................................	165,697	(42%)	$2,546,998	$4,219	$259,020
	Bill Kelsey (L)..................................	7,738	(2%)			
2020 Primary	Roger Williams (R).............................	63,146	(88%)			
	Keith Neuendorff (R)...........................	8,965	(12%)			

Prior winning percentages: 2018 (54%), 2016 (58%), 2014 (60%), 2012 (58%)

Republican Roger Williams, a former Texas secretary of state and prolific fundraiser, in 2012 took a district that had become reliably Republican in redistricting. He has quietly gone about his work, which includes a seat on the Financial Services Committee. Facing an ethics complaint dealing with his ownership of an auto dealership, he got a wrist slap.

Williams grew up in Fort Worth, where his father was a Chevrolet dealer and his mother ran a needlepoint business. He distinctly remembers that, as a 14-year-old, he was the last person to shake President John F. Kennedy's hand as he left the Texas Hotel in Fort Worth on the morning of Nov. 22, 1963. He attended Texas Christian University on a baseball scholarship. After graduating, he played in the Atlanta Braves minor league system for four years until he injured a shoulder while sliding into first base. He returned home to run the family car dealership and to coach baseball at TCU for three years. He continues to own the dealership, which led to the ethics inquiry.

Their shared love for baseball connected Williams and George W. Bush. A former owner of the Texas Rangers, Bush invited Williams to be a regional finance chairman for his two campaigns for governor, which was Williams' first foray into politics. In 2000, Bush appointed him to run the Republican National Committee's Eagles program. Later, Gov. Rick Perry appointed him as secretary of state. He was also Perry's chief liaison to Mexico. Having voiced interest in running for the open Senate seat that Ted Cruz later won in 2012, Williams announced in 2011 that he would instead run for the 25th District seat.

Williams overwhelmingly outspent the GOP primary field and defeated tea party activist Wes Riddle in a runoff, 58%-42%. Williams ran on what he called a "pretty simple" platform. "It's lower taxes, less government, cut the spending, defend the borders, listen to your generals, and understand the 10th Amendment," he said. He generated controversy when he called President Barack Obama a socialist at a campaign event, but said he saw no reason to apologize. "Here's a man that wants to own the banks, the car manufacturers, the student loan programs," he said. "It's basically socialism versus entrepreneurialism and capitalism. That's what we're fighting." In November, Williams defeated Democrat Elaine Henderson, 58%-37%.

In the House, Williams generated controversy in seeking to award the Medal of Honor to former Navy SEAL Chris Kyle, who inspired the movie American Sniper for having killed more than 160 of the enemy during combat in Iraq, then was the victim of a shooting at a Texas rifle range. Critics from some veterans' groups contended that Kyle did not meet the required standard of a single extraordinary act of valor. Williams disagreed, and filed his bill in 2015. The House took no action on his proposal.

After serving as finance chairman of the National Republican Congressional Committee, he voiced interest in taking over as chairman of the full committee in 2014. When House Republicans made a double-digit gain in that election, then-chairman Greg Walden of Oregon. made clear that he was not giving up the post. Following the 2016 election, Williams and Rep. Steve Stivers of Ohio competed to replace Walden. Stivers, who had more experience within the NRCC, won on a 143-96 vote among House Republicans.

Questions dealing with his legislation related to car dealerships led the Office of Congressional Ethics to recommend that the House Ethics Committee conduct an investigation, given his continued ownership of a large auto dealership in the Fort Worth area. Williams denied any conflict. In August 2017, the committee ended its inquiry and said Williams' conduct "did not create a reasonable inference of improper conduct." Its statement added a general reminder that lawmakers who take legislative actions that could affect their personal financial interests "should contact the committee before doing so." In 2018, the Center for Responsive Politics listed his net assets at close to $70 million.

His personal finances were again questioned following a July 2020 report in the Dallas Morning News that his dealership took a loan between $1 million and $2 million from the Payroll Protection Program, which was created to assist small businesses during the coronavirus pandemic. He said in a subsequent interview that he had no regrets. "Why would I not want to make sure that I preserve jobs for my employees?"

In 2016, Democrat Kathi Thomas, a special events planner, challenged Williams for reelection. She talked about the need for bipartisanship and getting big money out of politics, though she had little money to make her case. Williams won, 58%-38%. In 2018, Democratic challenger Julie Oliver—an attorney and health care finance professional—spent $646,000. The victory for Williams was reduced to 54%-45%, chiefly because Oliver increased the Democratic vote in Travis County to 64 percent. In a rematch in 2020, Oliver spent $2.5 million to $3.4 million for Williams. She supported Medicare For All and the Green New Deal and criticized Williams for taking the PPP loan as "using his position of public trust to vote for something that benefits him." The national parties largely steered clear of the contest. Williams widened his margin to 56%-42%.

TX-25: Northern Travis County; the Hill Country   **Cook Partisan Voting Index: R+8**

Population		Race and Ethnicity		Income	
Total	818,807	White	82.40%	Median Income	$79,975
Land area (sq. miles)	7,621	Black	7.40%	District Income Rank	95
Pop/ sq mi	107.45	Latino	18.70%	Poverty Rate	9.70%
Born in State	57.10%	Asian	3.80%	With health insurance	87.90%
		Two or more races	3.60%	Cash public assistance	0.80%
Age Groups		Other	2.90%	Food stamp/SNAP	6.40%
Under 18	23.20%				
18-34	22.60%	**Education**		**Work**	
35-64	40.10%	H.S grad or less	32.00%	White Collar	47.50%
Over 64	14.10%	Some college	27.40%	Sales and Service	32.30%
Military		College Degree, 4 yr	25.80%	Blue Collar	20.10%
Veteran/ Active Duty	10.40%	Post grad	14.80%	Government	16.40%

2020 Pres. Vote	Trump	216,264	(54%)	Biden	177,852	(44%)			
2016 Pres. Vote	Trump	172,476	(55%)	Clinton	125,949	(40%)	Johnson	11,772	(4%)

Austin: Austin, the capital of the second-largest state in the country and the site of the largest capitol building, had long been styled as laid-back and countrified. After World War II, in Sen. Lyndon Johnson's time, Austin had a metropolitan population of just over 130,000. There had never been much commerce. State government provided much of the local employment. Its skies were untainted by industrial smoke. Its biggest industry was the University of Texas, now with 52,000 students and an endowment of thousands of West Texas acres that turned out to sit on top of oil. The university has long had a distinguished faculty and some of the world's great scholarly collections, including the LBJ Presidential Library and its 45 million pages of documents. The Austin of old was also the central focus of Texas' hardy but almost always outnumbered liberals, based in the university, state government and Texas Observer magazine. They mocked the business lobbyists who they were certain called the shots when the "Leg" (pronounced lej) was in session.

Today's Austin is quite a different place. Greater Austin's population stands at 2.2 million. In 2019, it was the fastest-growing metro area in the nation with at least 1 million people, with an increase of 30 percent since 2010. The city, with a 22 percent increase from 2010 to 2019, has a population of 979,000. Some businesses cater to the old liberal bastions: The upscale organic-food chain Whole Foods Market was based in Austin until its purchase by Amazon in 2017. The tone of the area overall has grown more corporate, especially as its private sector began to make up a larger share of the local economy. The techies who settled in the Silicon Hills tended to vote Republican. Housing prices across much of the city have soared, though they still seem cheap compared with San Francisco and Boston. Travis County in 2017 declared itself a "sanctuary" for immigrants. But when the state passed a law prohibiting such designations, the county sheriff announced a reversal of its sanctuary status.

The 25th Congressional District of Texas, which includes the capitol and the nearby UT campus, has about 30 percent of the residents of Travis County. To dilute the liberal votes cast in Austin, they have been split among five districts, of which the 25th has the largest share and is the only district that runs across the county. That part of the district leans notably Democratic, though not as much as the lower-income neighborhoods of southeast Austin, which are in the 35th District. The huge new Apple plant and the planned Tesla factory are in other districts. To the west of downtown, Mopac Boulevard operates as a dividing line for the more suburban, Republican-leaning areas of the county near Lake Travis. The remaining 55 percent of the district's population resides in a string of Republican-leaning counties that include the Hill Country. This stretch extends 180 miles north to Burleson in the Fort Worth exurbs. Rural Coryell County includes much of Fort Hood, which covers more than 25 percent of the county's land area. The 25th has been a solidly Republican district, though many of its new business class did not respond well to President Donald Trump. He got 54 percent of the vote in 2020.

Michael Burgess (R)

Elected 2002, 10th term, b. Dec 23, 1950; Rochester, MN; The Selwyn School, 1968; North TX State University, Dallas, B.S., 1972; North TX State University, M.S., 1976; University of TX-Houston, M.D., 1977; University of TX at Dallas, M.S., 2000; Anglican; Married (Laura Burgess); 3 children; 2 grandchildren.

Professional Career: Practicing obstetrician, 1981-2003.

DC Office: 2161 RHOB 20515, 202-225-7772, Fax: 202-225-2919, burgess.house.gov

State Offices: Lake Dallas, 940-497-5031.

Committees: *Budget. Energy & Commerce*: Energy; Health; Oversight & Investigations. *Rules*: Legislative & Budget Process (RMM).

Group Ratings

	ADA	ACLU	AFL-CIO	LCV	COC	HAFA	ACU	CFG	FRC
2020	**	22%	**	10%	-	100%	92%	**	-
2019	0%	C	29%	10%	79%	C	92%	84%	100%

Almanac Ratings 2019-2020

	Economy	Social	Foreign	Composite
Liberal	25%	15%	29%	23%
Conservative	75%	85%	71%	77%

Key Votes of the 116th Congress

1. U.S./Mex./Can. trade deal Y	5. Russia sanctions Y	9. Firearms background checks N
2. First Coronavirus response Y	6. Troops in Syria N	10. Spending at the border Y
3. HEROES Act N	7. Veto arms sales to Saudis N	11. Marijuana liberalized rules N/A
4. CASH Act Y	8. Defense $$$, veto override N	12. Electoral College objections Y

Election Results

Election	Name (Party)	Vote (%)		Cand. Spent	Ind. Exp. Support	Ind. Exp. Oppose
2020 General	Michael Burgess (R)	261,963	(61%)	$1,684,206	$19,413	$750
	Carol Iannuzzi (D)	161,009	(37%)	$76,881		
	Mark Boler (L)	9,243	(2%)			
2020 Primary	Michael C. Burgess (R)	51,312	(74%)			
	Jack Wyman (R)	7,816	(11%)			
	Michael Armstrong (R)	5,745	(8%)			
	Jason Mrochek (R)	4,846	(7%)			

Prior winning percentages: 2018 (59%), 2016 (66%), 2014 (83%), 2012 (68%), 2010 (67%), 2008 (60%), 2006 (60%), 2004 (66%), 2002 (75%)

Michael Burgess, a conservative Republican physician first elected in 2002, has become an activist House leader and GOP spokesman on health care. An outspoken member of the Energy and Commerce Committee, he served as chairman of its Health Subcommittee from 2017 to 2018. Republicans failed to achieve their paramount objective during that time, but they had success on some lower-profile issues. Following the 2020 election, he lost a bid to become the committee's ranking Republican to Rep. Cathy McMorris Rodgers.

Burgess was born in Rochester Minnesota and grew up in Denton County, the son of a physician. He graduated from the University of North Texas and the University of Texas Medical School in Houston. He trained at Parkland Hospital in Dallas and set up an obstetrics-gynecology practice in Lewisville. After 21 years in practice, Burgess decided to run for Congress after the Sept. 11 attacks, his first bid for elective office. When Majority Leader Dick Armey announced that he would not run again, there was no doubt that a Republican would succeed him in his overwhelmingly Republican district. The frontrunner was the majority leader's son, Scott Armey, the former Denton County judge.

In the primary, Armey outspent Burgess by more than 6-to-1. With no statewide Republican contests on the ballot, there seemed to be no suspense about the outcome. But Armey took only 45 percent of the vote, failing to gain the required majority. Burgess won 23 percent. In the four-week runoff campaign, Burgess benefited from a series of hard-hitting articles in the Dallas Morning News about Armey's record as a county judge, which suggested he had used his position to steer government jobs and contracts to close friends. Burgess focused on health care and taxes. He had helped draft the Texas Patients' Bill of Rights and vowed to do the same on a national level. With a low-turnout of 19,259 voters, Burgess won the runoff 55%-45%. Armey tellingly lost 60%-40% in Denton County, where he was known best. Burgess breezed to victory in November, 75%-23%. He has been reelected comfortably since.

Burgess has a reliably conservative voting record, especially on social issues, according to the Almanac vote ratings. He joined the Tea Party Caucus when it was formed in 2010. He has pushed legislation to simplify or replace the federal income tax—either with a single flat rate or with a 23 percent sales tax on goods and services. Those proposals received little attention when Republicans approved tax cuts and major changes to the tax code in 2017.

During both the GOP fight against President Barack Obama's 2010 health care law and the more recent COVID-19 pandemic, Burgess served as a top party spokesman. In his bid for the top GOP slot at Energy and Commerce, he had seniority. But McMorris Rodgers, a former member of the GOP leadership, had better connections in the Republican Conference and she prevailed.

Even so, he has been an active member on the committee. He was a persistent opponent of Obama administration policies. His nine-part plan for health care included many ideas that GOP candidates have espoused and that have become mainstream within the party, including allowing patients to shop for insurance across state lines and limiting damages in malpractice lawsuits.

He made a steady rise to influence, with work on a cross-section of health care issues. In 2009, Burgess joined a bipartisan agreement to permit the Food and Drug Administration to approve generic versions of biologic drugs. He was part of a bipartisan group in 2011 that proposed legislation ensuring that seniors who show signs of Alzheimer's receive a formal diagnosis from their doctor. In 2015, he filed with then-Rep. Chris Van Hollen of Maryland the Advancing Research for Neurological Diseases Act of 2015, which would create a national data collection system at the Centers for Disease Control and Prevention for disorders such as Parkinson's disease and multiple sclerosis.

In 2015, Burgess was chief sponsor of a landmark law when Congress resolved the "doc fix" issue that limited reimbursements for patients with Medicare coverage. The bipartisan deal, which he called the most significant entitlement reform in years, included other changes in Medicare, such as performance incentives and new payment procedures for health care providers. Several provisions from Burgess were part of the enactment in 2016 of the Twenty First Century Cures Act, including neurological research and interoperability standards for electronic health records.

When Burgess became chairman of the Health Subcommittee in 2017, he said the position is "what I asked for" when first elected to Congress. "That's going to be my life for the next two years," he told the Texas Tribune. He described his role as "educator" of other members of Congress as well as the public. In a profile, McClatchy News headlined that Burgess was "the GOP's policy wonk behind Obamacare repeal." When House action was delayed, he blamed the Freedom Caucus. "There were people who were not interested in solving the problem," Burgess said in March 2017, according to Politico. House Republicans passed a slightly revised version of their proposal a few weeks later, but it died in the Senate that summer.

He led action on other health care issues. The House passed in 2017 the bipartisan Improving Access to Maternity Care Act, of which Burgess was the lead sponsor. The proposal sought to improve the availability of maternity services, a topic with which he has deep familiarity. In 2018, President Donald Trump signed the "right to try" legislation that he had advocated, which authorized dying patients to use experimental drugs that had not been approved by the Food and Drug Administration. "Why do you not want to allow these patients to exercise their right to fight for the future?" Burgess asked opponents during House debate. He advocated research into the potential medical benefits of marijuana.

At home, Burgess has kept his distance from the Texas GOP establishment. He was an early supporter of Ted Cruz, including his successful Senate primary bid against Lt. Gov. David Dewhurst in 2012. Early in the 2016 campaign, he said that it would be "inappropriate" for vaccination against measles to become an issue. His position took issue with Trump, who occasionally raised questions about vaccines when he was a candidate.

TX-26: Northern Metroplex   Cook Partisan Voting Index: R+12

Population		Race and Ethnicity		Income	
Total	920,865	White	76.00%	Median Income	$96,307
Land area (sq. miles)	907	Black	9.10%	District Income Rank	41
Pop/ sq mi	1,015.12	Latino	19.80%	Poverty Rate	6.10%
Born in State	48.80%	Asian	7.80%	With health insurance	88.70%
		Two or more races	3.80%	Cash public assistance	1.10%
Age Groups		Other	3.30%	Food stamp/SNAP	4.00%
Under 18	25.60%				
18-34	22.40%	**Education**		**Work**	
35-64	41.10%	H.S grad or less	25.30%	White Collar	46.70%
Over 64	10.80%	Some college	29.10%	Sales and Service	36.80%
		College Degree, 4 yr	30.30%	Blue Collar	16.50%
Military		Post grad	15.30%	Government	12.50%
Veteran/ Active Duty	7.20%				

2020 Pres. Vote	Trump	248,196	(56%)	Biden	185,956	(42%)			
2016 Pres. Vote	Trump	194,033	(60%)	Clinton	109,536	(34%)	Johnson	12,577	(4%)

Denton County: Until the Texas Land and Immigration Company settled this portion of north Texas with a land grant from the Texas Congress in 1841, settlers were scarce and Indian raids were common. The area now known as Denton County takes its name from John Bunyan Denton, a Methodist pioneer preacher and lawyer killed in a skirmish with Indians. Today, this area on the northern edge of the Dallas-Fort Worth Metroplex is teeming with new arrivals and filling up with young, well-educated, middle-class families. In 1940, there were 34,000 people in Denton County, and they voted 88 percent Democratic for president. Population for the county grew from 432,000 in 2000 in 887,000 in 2019. The University of North Texas, with more than 40,000 students, is the sixth-largest in the state, while Texas Woman's University is the largest state-supported university for women in the United States (although it does accept men).

The county's chief cities are Denton, Flower Mound and Lewisville, and there is plenty of room for more growth along Interstates 35E and 35W. Two of the most noteworthy landmarks in the district are the Alliance Airport, an industrial transportation hub, and the Texas Motor Speedway racetrack. Truck manufacturer Peterbilt Motors, the largest employer in Denton with 2,300 employees, has expanded to improve its efficiency. Near Justin, in the southwest corner of Denton County, a pipeline allows for the production of up to 1 billion cubic feet of natural gas daily. With sophisticated imaging and drilling technology, other natural gas wells operate within 10 miles of downtown Fort Worth. The sale of GE Transportation, which manufactures rail locomotives in Fort Worth, to the local Westinghouse Air Brakes Technology firm in 2018 restored hope that the business would fare better outside of the chaos that has surrounded GE in recent years; company officials voiced confidence about continued demand for their products. More broadly, Oxford Economics, a forecasting firm, projected that Denton County from 2017 to 2022 would have the strongest economic growth of any county in the nation. Sufficient open space remains so that Denton has more horse ranches than any other county in the United States.

The 26th Congressional District of Texas is at the heart of the northern expansion of the Metroplex. It includes more than 80 percent of Denton County, and a small fragment of urban Tarrant County, including the old railroad town of Keller, now a bustling upscale suburb. There are some Democratic areas here, especially around Denton's universities. The county voted 65 percent for Mitt Romney in 2012, though it fell to 58 percent for Donald Trump in 2016. By 2020, Republicans had legitimate reasons for concern in Denton: Trump carried the county over Biden, but defeated Biden by only 53%-45%.

Michael Cloud (R)

Elected 2018, 2nd full term, b. May 13, 1975; Baton Rouge, LA; Oral Roberts University, B.S.; Protestant; Married (Rosel Cloud); 3 children.

Professional Career: Owner, Bright Ideas Media; chairman; Victoria County TX Republican Party, 2010-2017.

DC Office: 1314 LHOB 20515, 202-225-7742, Fax: 202-226-1134, cloud.house.gov

State Offices: Corpus Christi, 361-884-2222; Victoria, 361-894-6446.

Committees: *Agriculture*: Commodity Exchanges, Energy & Credit; Subcommittee Nutrition, Oversight & Department Operations. *Oversight & Reform*: Subcommittee on Economic & Consumer Policy (RMM).

Group Ratings

	ADA	ACLU	AFL-CIO	LCV	COC	HAFA	ACU	CFG	FRC
2020	**	21%	**	0%	-	94%	100%	**	-
2019	0%	C	19%	0%	73%	C	100%	96%	100%

Almanac Ratings 2019-2020

	Economy	Social	Foreign	Composite
Liberal	25%	4%	43%	24%
Conservative	75%	96%	57%	76%

Key Votes of the 116th Congress

1. U.S./Mex./Can. trade deal Y	5. Russia sanctions Y	9. Firearms background checks N
2. First Coronavirus response N	6. Troops in Syria Y	10. Spending at the border Y
3. HEROES Act N	7. Veto arms sales to Saudis N	11. Marijuana liberalized rules N
4. CASH Act N	8. Defense $$$, veto override N	12. Electoral College objections Y

Election Results

Election	Name (Party)	Vote (%)		Cand. Spent	Ind. Exp. Support	Ind. Exp. Oppose
2020 General	Michael Cloud (R)	172,305	(63%)	$954,078	$7,386	$750
	Ricardo de la Fuente (D)	95,466	(35%)	$312,082		
	Phil Gray (L)	5,482	(2%)			
2020 Primary	Michael Cloud (R)	60,945	(100%)			

Prior winning percentages: 2018 special (61%)

Republican Michael Cloud, a newcomer to public office, in 2018 won a special election to fill the seat of Blake Farenthold. The incumbent had quit following allegations of ethics violations that resulted from sexual harassment claims by a former House employee. Cloud, a veteran party activist, skillfully learned the political ropes and settled into his House seat, facing significant local demands for aid in recovery from Hurricane Harvey in 2017. Following the turmoil that surrounded Farenthold, the low-profile Cloud has emphasized his outsider status.

Cloud, a graduate of Oral Roberts University, owned a small business in which he advised on media relations. He was the communications director of the Faith Family Church in Victoria, served seven years as chairman of the Victoria County Republican Party and was a local leader of the tea party. His core message was that "Congress is broken" and failed to serve the public's interests.

He entered the GOP primary two months prior to Farenthold's decision not to seek reelection, which ensued from additional controversy that he used $84,000 in office funds to settle the discrimination claim from his ex-aide. (Farenthold subsequently became a lobbyist for Port Lavaca, a tourist site north of Corpus Christi. He reneged on his pledge to reimburse the $84,000.) Once Farenthold stepped aside, the frontrunner was Bech Bruun, who held several senior positions in Texas government, including chairman of the Water Development Board. Key Republican officials, including Gov. Greg Abbott, quickly endorsed Bruun, who had a fundraising advantage in the primary.

In the first round of voting for the full term, Bruun got 58 percent of the vote in his base of Nueces County, which had the largest turnout. Cloud got 62 percent in Victoria County, his base, which had the second-largest turnout. With six other candidates splitting the vote in the 11 other mostly rural counties, Bruun led Cloud in the first round, 36%-34%. Cloud's strength grew in the May runoff. He took 85 percent of the vote in Victoria and led in each of the other counties except for Nueces, where he reduced Bruun's vote to 53 percent. Overall, Cloud won, 61%-39%.

Cloud's victory in November over Democrat Eric Holguin, a gay activist and former congressional aide, was largely a formality. Instead, following the resignation of Farenthold, attention turned to the special election on June 30. The filing deadline had been set prior to the runoff for the full term. In the nonpartisan primary in which a majority of all votes was required to avoid a runoff, the initial expectation was that another contest would be required in September.

Bruun reduced the suspense by endorsing Cloud following the May runoff and urging his voters to switch their allegiance. That tactic proved successful. With only 4 percent of the vote going to Bruun, Cloud won 55 percent against eight opponents in the special election. Cloud led narrowly in Nueces County, and comfortably elsewhere. In November, he won a full term with 60 percent; he took all 11 counties, though Cloud led by only 232 votes in Nueces, which cast nearly 45 percent of the total vote.

In the House, Cloud fit comfortably with supporters of President Donald Trump. In October 2019, he joined Republican protestors who interrupted a closed-door meeting of the House Intelligence Committee that was hearing witnesses in its impeachment inquiry. He said they were "demanding a transparent process." Following the election in November 2020, Cloud objected to the presidential vote-counting process in Pennsylvania. Since 2019, he has been the ranking Republican on the Oversight and Reform Subcommittee on Economic and Consumer Policy. In 2021, he joined the Agriculture Committee.

Seeking reelection, Cloud had no opposition in the Republican primary. In November, he won, 63%-35%; he took 53 percent in Nueces County.

Perhaps the most notable feature of that contest was that Democratic challenger Ricardo de la Fuente also ran that year in House contests in California and Florida; in those two other campaigns, the 30-year-old de la Fuente badly trailed the Democratic incumbent in the primary. (His father, Rocky de la Fuente, was a Republican candidate for president in 2020.) A San Diego County resident, he described himself as a graduate of Harvard University and a clean energy entrepreneur. "My life goal is to get more Latinos elected, so I'm going into districts where there's a huge community of Latinos," he told the Dallas Morning News in April 2020. "Eventually, we're going to build enough name ID and get elected."

TX-27: Central Gulf Coast   **Cook Partisan Voting Index: R+14**

Population		Race and Ethnicity		Income	
Total	745,526	White	85.70%	Median Income	$55,987
Land area (sq. miles)	9,128	Black	4.90%	District Income Rank	318
Pop/ sq mi	81.67	Latino	54.30%	Poverty Rate	16.80%
Born in State	75.30%	Asian	1.60%	With health insurance	81.30%
		Two or more races	2.00%	Cash public assistance	1.60%
Age Groups		Other	5.70%	Food stamp/SNAP	13.40%
Under 18	24.60%				
18-34	22.80%	Education		Work	
35-64	35.90%	H.S grad or less	49.00%	White Collar	29.20%
Over 64	16.70%	Some college	30.90%	Sales and Service	40.20%
		College Degree, 4 yr	13.40%	Blue Collar	30.70%
Military		Post grad	6.70%	Government	14.50%
Veteran/ Active Duty	9.20%				

2020 Pres. Vote	Trump	170,800	(61%)	Biden	104,511	(37%)		
2016 Pres. Vote	Trump	140,787	(60%)	Clinton	85,589	(36%)	Johnson	6,491	(3%)

Corpus Christi, Victoria: The Nueces River rises on the Edwards Plateau in Central Texas, almost a half mile above sea level. From there it cascades across the Texas Hill Country and passes through the coastal plain before emptying into the Gulf of Corpus Christi. Early attempts at establishing settlements near the river's terminus were half-hearted and unsuccessful, and the area was uninhabited until Henry Lawrence Kinney and William Aubrey established a trading post on the west shore of the bay in 1839. Growth came slowly here at first; a population of 2,100 in 1870 was barely 11,000 in 1920. Hurricanes, the occasional outbreak of yellow fever and, more importantly, the lack of a deep-water port, frustrated attempts to expand the city.

Then, in 1926, the federal government completed the dredging of a shipping channel and the modern Port of Corpus Christi was born. The city's population almost tripled in the 1920s, then doubled in the 1930s. By 2019, it topped 326,000. The port is the sixth largest in the United States in total tonnage shipped, a center for exporting cotton, sorghum and grains, and importing steel and construction equipment; the port includes numerous factories and industrial plants. Barge traffic of oil has increased greatly along the Gulf Intracoastal Waterway. In 2018, a $15 billion liquefied natural gas facility, the first in Texas, was opened in nearby Gregory; it was the first "greenfield" liquefaction plant built in the lower 48 states. Work on the new Harbor Bridge, which will replace a nearby bridge that is more than 60 years old, was halted in 2020 for six months because of design questions and expected completion was delayed until 2023; it will give larger ships entry to the port. The Naval Air Station at Corpus Christi is another major contributor to the local economy.

The Eagle Ford Shale, which in 2020 suffered a drop in active rigs from 81 to 18, yielded more than 1.1 million barrels of daily oil production. In San Patricio County, a $10 billion petrochemical complex owned by ExxonMobil and its Saudi partner was expected to start operations in late 2021; it has been described as the world's largest steam-cracker. Corpus Christi's population is 63 percent Hispanic. Only 9 percent of residents were foreign-born. According to an earlier Pew Research Center report, the city had the smallest such share of any of the 60 metro areas with sizable Hispanic populations.

The 27th Congressional District of Texas is centered on Corpus Christi, and almost half its residents live in the city and surrounding Nueces County. Corpus Christi is the county seat and 90 percent of Nueces; the city extends into three adjacent smaller counties. The district takes in most of the Gulf Coast north of Corpus Christi, up to Bay City and the outskirts of Houston's suburbs. The only other city of any size in the district is Victoria, an industrial town of 68,000. An arm of the 27th reaches to Bastrop and Caldwell counties, in the Austin area, and takes in Gonzales, where the first shots of the Texas Revolution were fired. The redrawn district, unlike its predecessor, is safe Republican territory. In 2020, President Donald Trump got 61 percent of the district vote.

Henry Cuellar (D)

Elected 2004, 9th term, b. Sep 19, 1955; Laredo, TX; Laredo Community College, A.A., 1976; Georgetown University, B.S., 1978; University of TX School of Law, J.D., 1981; TX A and M International University, M.B.A., 1982; University of TX, Ph.D., 1998; Roman Catholic; Married (Imelda Rios Cuellar); 2 children.

Elected Office: TX House,1987-2001; TX Secretary of st., 2001.

Professional Career: Practicing attorney, 1981-2004; Adjunct Professional, TX A&M University, 1984-1986.

DC Office: 2372 RHOB 20515, 202-225-1640, Fax: 202-225-1641, cuellar.house.gov

State Offices: Laredo, 956-725-0639; Mission, 956-424-3942; Rio Grande City, 956-487-5603; San Antonio, 210-271-2851.

Committees: *Appropriations*: Agriculture, Rural Development, FDA & Related Agencies; Defense; Homeland Security.

Group Ratings

	ADA	ACLU	AFL-CIO	LCV	COC	HAFA	ACU	CFG	FRC
2020	**	67%	**	90%	-	0%	25%	**	-
2019	70%	C	90%	79%	73%	C	26%	24%	14%

Almanac Ratings 2019-2020

	Economy	Social	Foreign	Composite
Liberal	46%	54%	52%	51%
Conservative	54%	46%	48%	49%

Key Votes of the 116th Congress

1. U.S./Mex./Can. trade deal	Y	5. Russia sanctions	Y	9. Firearms background checks	Y
2. First Coronavirus response	Y	6. Troops in Syria	Y	10. Spending at the border	Y
3. HEROES Act	Y	7. Veto arms sales to Saudis	Y	11. Marijuana liberalized rules	N
4. CASH Act	Y	8. Defense $$$, veto override	Y	12. Electoral College objections	N

Election Results

Election	Name (Party)	Vote (%)		Cand. Spent	Ind. Exp. Support	Ind. Exp. Oppose
2020 General	Henry Cuellar (D)	137,494	(58%)	$3,146,124	$356,778	$948,790
	Sandra Whitten (R)	91,925	(39%)	$24,623		
	Bekah Congdon (L)	6,425	(3%)			
2020 Primary	Henry Cuellar (D)	38,834	(52%)			
	Jessica Cisneros (D)	36,144	(48%)			

Prior winning percentages: 2018 (84%), 2016 (66%), 2014 (82%), 2012 (68%), 2010 (56%), 2008 (69%), 2006 (68%), 2004 (59%)

Henry Cuellar, elected in 2004, is one of the most conservative Hispanic Democrats, with a voting record putting him near the center of the House. He barely survived a 2020 primary from a progressive primary challenger, only to see President Donald Trump more competitive in his district in November. Even with his coveted seat on the Appropriations Committee, he has remained a maverick. He has delivered funds to his district for its many needs, including homeland security and agriculture.

Cuellar was the oldest of eight children of migrant workers who had only elementary school educations. He graduated from Georgetown University and the University of Texas law school, and later got a Ph.D. in government from UT. With his five degrees, he claims to be the "most degreed" member of the House. From his base in Laredo, he served in the Texas House from 1986 to 2000, where he helped to author the Texas Grant college aid program. In 2001, Republican Gov. Rick Perry appointed him secretary of state even though he is a Democrat.

Cuellar resigned in 2002 to run against veteran Republican Rep. Henry Bonilla in the sprawling 23rd District. Bonilla claimed he didn't need Laredo to win. In response, the Webb County GOP chairman endorsed Cuellar. The challenger attacked Bonilla for his votes against funding for the Children's Health Insurance Program, the Family and Medical Leave Act, and Pell grants. Cuellar carried Webb County 84%-15%. When the Bexar County votes were counted, Bonilla's confidence turned out to be warranted. He won 52%-47%.

Redistricting in 2003 gave Cuellar an opportunity to run against Democratic Rep. Ciro Rodriguez of San Antonio, who was chairman of the Hispanic Caucus. Rodriguez expressed disbelief that a friend and former legislative colleague for whom he had raised money in 2002 would run against him. The ambitious Cuellar told a local reporter, "nobody died and made him king." Cuellar criticized Rodriguez for voting against the GOP's 2003 Medicare prescription drug bill, while Rodriguez pointed out Cuellar's cooperation with Republicans as secretary of state. Cuellar was the Democratic nominee by 58 votes out of 49,000 cast. He won in November, 59%-39%.

Cuellar's voting has placed him among the most conservative Democrats. The Almanac ratings for 2015 and 2017 gave him the second-highest conservative score for a House Democrat behind Collin Peterson of Minnesota, who lost reelection in 2020. Cuellar has been a leader of the Blue Dog Coalition of his party's fiscal conservatives. He joined most of the Texas delegation in voting against lifting the financial liability cap on oil spills. In response to criticism of his independence, Cuellar often says, "I will die as a Democrat." Cuellar's family is somewhat of an institution in the district. His brother is the Webb County Sheriff; his sister was the tax assessor-collector.

His middle ground positions on immigration have irritated both parties. He was the only House Democrat who voted for a bill that would have made it easier to deport unaccompanied minors from Central America. He criticized President Barack Obama and said that Obama looked "aloof and detached" by not going to the Mexican border when he was in Texas for political fundraisers in 2014. When Trump became president, Cuellar attacked his proposal for a border wall as "a 14th century solution," and said illegal immigration ought to be addressed as a 21st century problem, with steps such as military surveillance and a "virtual border." During the January 2019 partial government shutdown when Trump was seeking additional funds for a wall, Cuellar joined a bipartisan delegation to meet with the president. He continued to advocate multiple steps, such as more personnel and improved technology. As an appropriator who works on border bills, Cuellar slammed Trump for derailing attempts to increase security at legal ports of entry.

Cuellar has had success passing legislation that benefited his district. In 2016, he enacted his bill for alternative financing arrangements to construct and maintain facilities at ports of entry along the border. In a spending bill that was approved in 2017, he claimed credit for $947 million for his 10-20-30 agriculture program: at least 10 percent of funds go to counties where 20 percent or more of the population has lived in poverty for the past 30 years. In 2018 and again in January 2019, Cuellar won House passage of his U.S.-Mexico Economic Partnership Act, which would expand educational and professional exchange programs. Cuellar was a big supporter of Trump's United State-Mexico-Canada trade agreement, but called the president "petty" for leaving key House Democrats off the invite list for the White House signing ceremony.

In Cuellar's first reelection bid in 2006, Rodriguez challenged him in the primary but struggled to match his fundraising. Cuellar won the primary comfortably, 53%-40%. He got national media attention in 2018 when he sponsored a fundraising event for Texas Republican Rep. John Carter, who was facing a difficult reelection challenge. "Judge Carter is a dear friend and trusted colleague with whom I work on Appropriations," Cuellar said in a statement. He added that he raised more money for House Democrats than has any other Democrat from Texas.

With his seniority on Appropriations, Cuellar is close to becoming the top Democrat on a subcommittee—assuming he retains the support of other Democrats when there is a vacancy.

Cuellar, who endorses some abortion restrictions and opposes gun restrictions and Medicare-for-All, has long been ripe for a primary challenge. Justice Democrats—a political committee of progressive activists that has sought to reshape the party through primary challenges—handpicked a challenger: Jessica Cisneros, a 26-year-old immigration attorney and Laredo native who once interned for Cuellar. She nabbed endorsements from EMILY's List, Sen. Elizabeth Warren of Massachusetts and Rep. Alexandria Ocasio-Cortez of New York. Cuellar was backed by Speaker Nancy Pelosi, who fundraised for him in the district.

Cisneros backed the Green New Deal, an odd stance in an area where oil and gas dominate the economy, and stressed her commitment to abortion rights. She said Cuellar was too conservative for the district and knocked him as "Trump's favorite Democrat." Cuellar refused to debate her and insisted he was a good fit in a district where Democrats are more moderate and conservative. An impressive fundraiser, Cisneros spent nearly $2 million—though the incumbent nearly doubled her spending—and received over $1 million in help from progressive groups. On Super Tuesday, she came within 2,700 votes, a near-miss she described as proof "a brown girl from the border ... could take on the machine." In contrast to Cuellar's rout in Webb County against Rodriguez, he got only 55 percent against Cisneros.

Despite a primary electorate that nearly rejected him, Cuellar may have been right ascribing a conservative lean to his district. He beat Republican Sandra Whitten, 58%-39%, as Trump enjoyed an unexpected swell of support in the district and came within five points of carrying it. Cuellar called it a wake-up call but predicted it wouldn't last. "I think it's more of a Trump effect," he told the San Antonio Express-News. "But is there an alarm? Heck yes."

TX-28: South Texas

Cook Partisan Voting Index: D+5

Population		Race and Ethnicity		Income	
Total	772,410	White	87.70%	Median Income	$53,597
Land area (sq. miles)	9,379	Black	3.90%	District Income Rank	352
Pop/ sq mi	82.36	Latino	78.90%	Poverty Rate	21.40%
Born in State	65.70%	Asian	0.70%	With health insurance	73.60%
		Two or more races	2.40%	Cash public assistance	1.20%
Age Groups		Other	5.40%	Food stamp/SNAP	19.40%
Under 18	30.40%				
18-34	24.20%	**Education**		**Work**	
35-64	33.50%	H.S grad or less	53.50%	White Collar	29.40%
Over 64	11.90%	Some college	26.50%	Sales and Service	43.30%
		College Degree, 4 yr	14.20%	Blue Collar	27.40%
Military		Post grad	5.80%	Government	16.60%
Veteran/ Active Duty	6.20%				

2020 Pres. Vote	Biden	125,755	(52%)	Trump	115,160	(47%)			
2016 Pres. Vote	Clinton	110,020	(58%)	Trump	72,520	(38%)	Johnson	4,401	(2%)

Laredo/San Antonio Corridor: The border country along the Rio Grande is in some ways a region all its own, a mixture of the United States and Mexico. As former Laredo Mayor Betty Flores has said, "The river for us is more like some street that we cross. It's really not a border." This is where, in "Streets of Laredo," singer Marty Robbins summoned up images of lonely cowboys on dusty streets outside of saloons in a tiny town. But that is not the Laredo of today. It is the busiest border crossing for U.S.-Mexico trade. About 20,000 trucks and railcars cross its four bridges daily; with about $303 billion in two-way trade crossing the Rio Grande in 2017, the Laredo customs district was the second busiest in the nation behind Los Angeles. Local enthusiasts believe the region stands to benefit from the deal that replaced NAFTA, the United States-Mexico-Canada free trade agreement, through increased infrastructure, jobs and economic growth along the border. Laredo grew at a 34 percent pace in the first decade of the 21st century and another 11 percent from 2010 to 2019. Its old downtown streets are filled with Mexicans who cross the border on foot.

Laredo's Webb County had a population of nearly 277,000 in 2019, of which 95 percent was Hispanic. Nearly three-fourths of all businesses are minority owned, which is the largest share in the nation. The region has its problems, including crime from the trade in illegal immigration and drugs; its positioning at the end of Interstate 35 makes it an important point of entry for both. The county retained a 21 percent poverty rate in 2019. The coronavirus pandemic hit the region hard, causing unprecedented fatalities in Laredo. Four of the five metro areas with the highest death rates in the country in the first half of August 2020 were in South Texas's border region, according to The New York Times. Good news for the local economy: Production in the Eagle Ford Shale increased in 2018, with 175 new permits to drill oil and gas wells.

The 28th Congressional District of Texas is centered in Laredo and Webb County, which has the largest population in the district. South along the Rio Grande, it crosses Starr County, one of the poorest counties in Texas and home of many blatant and wealthy drug smugglers. It also takes in Mission in a narrow strip of Hidalgo County. These border counties make up about two-thirds of the district. To the north, it extends through thinly settled ranch and oil well country, plus about 160,000 residents on the eastern side of Bexar County, including a small portion of San Antonio. It includes the Joint Base San Antonio, formed from the joining of Randolph and Lackland Air Force bases and Fort Sam Houston. About 79 percent of the residents of the 28th are Hispanic.

The district leans Democratic locally, but Republicans sometimes do well. President George W. Bush in 2004 and some state GOP officials have carried the district as currently configured. In 2016, Hillary Clinton got 58 percent and won by 19 points. But a fascinating boomerang pattern occurred in 2020; Joe Biden got just 52 percent in his five-point win. In the rural counties along the border, President Donald Trump saw a surge. He won Zapata County, the first time a Republican presidential candidate has carried it since Reconstruction.

Sylvia Garcia (D)

Elected 2018, 2nd term, b. Sep 06, 1950; San Diego, TX; TX Woman's University, B.A., 1972; TX Southern University, Thurgood Marshall School of Law, J.D., 1978; Catholic; Single.

Elected Office: Presiding Judge, Houston Municipal System; City of Houston Controller, 1998-2002; Harris County Commissioner, 2003-2008; TX Senate, 2013-2018.

Professional Career: Social Worker; Attorney.

DC Office: 1620 LHOB 20515, 202-225-1688, sylviagarcia.house.gov

State Offices: Houston, 832-325-3150.

Committees: *Financial Services*: Diversity & Inclusion; Oversight & Investigations; Task Force on Artificial Intelligence. *Judiciary*: Constitution, Civil Rights & Civil Liberties; Immigration & Citizenship.

Almanac Ratings 2019-2020

	Economy	Social	Foreign	Composite
Liberal	100%	100%	92%	98%
Conservative	0%	0%	8%	2%

Key Votes of the 116th Congress

1. U.S./Mex./Can. trade deal Y	5. Russia sanctions Y	9. Firearms background checks Y
2. First Coronavirus response Y	6. Troops in Syria Y	10. Spending at the border N
3. HEROES Act Y	7. Veto arms sales to Saudis Y	11. Marijuana liberalized rules Y
4. CASH Act Y	8. Defense $$$, veto override Y	12. Electoral College objections N

Election Results

Election	Name (Party)	Vote (%)	Cand. Spent	Ind. Exp. Support	Ind. Exp. Oppose
2020 General	Sylvia Garcia (D)	111,305 (71%)	$13,892	$4,212	
	Jaimy Blanco (R)	42,840 (27%)			$113
2020 Primary	Sylvia Garcia (D)	28,180 (100%)			

Prior winning percentages: 2018 (75%)

It took Sylvia Garcia longer than most to get to Congress: She first ran for the House in 1992 and was not sworn in until 2019. During the interim, she compiled one of the most extensive records in local and state government by any member of the large freshman class. Garcia and Veronica Escobar, who won the El Paso-based 16th District, became the first two Latinas elected to Congress from Texas. "I never really wanted to be the first. I wanted to be the best," Garcia told the Texas Tribune.

Garcia grew up the eighth in a family of 10 children in the South Texas town of Palito Blanco. That farming community was so sparsely populated at the time that her immediate family constituted about one-fifth of the town's population. She graduated from Texas Woman's University in Denton, with a degree in social work and political science. Garcia earned her law degree from Texas Southern University in Houston, where she worked at several jobs to pay her tuition. Early in her career, Garcia was a social worker and a legal-aid attorney.

She served five terms in the appointed position of director and presiding judge of the Houston Municipal System. In her first run for Congress, she was defeated by Gene Green, an Anglo who held the newly created Latino-majority district for the next 26 years. Garcia ran third in the Democratic primary, with 21 percent of the vote. Six years later, she was elected Houston City Controller, the city's chief financial officer. In a further sign of shifting local politics, she was elected in 2002 to the Harris County Commissioner's Court, the first woman and first Latina to hold that position; eight years later, she unexpectedly lost reelection to a Republican. She won a special election for the state Senate in 2013.

After Green, a senior Democrat on the House Energy and Commerce Committee, announced his retirement, Garcia was the early frontrunner to succeed him. In 2018, Green and most of the local political establishment backed her. During the campaign, she said her top national concern was passage of legislation to grant permanent legal status to "dreamers," who entered the U.S. illegally as minors. In an interview with the Houston Chronicle, she said her chief local concern was the need to protect against a repeat of the hurricane devastation that recently had jarred the Houston area.

Garcia contended with an unexpected Democratic primary challenge from Tahir Javed, a health care entrepreneur who raised $1.8 million (including $1.3 million from himself), far more than the other candidates; he had been a prominent fundraiser for Hillary Clinton in the 2016 presidential campaign. With endorsements from Indian-American groups and national Democrats, including Senate Minority Leader Chuck Schumer of New York, Javed hoped to keep Garcia below 50 percent in the primary and force a runoff. Schumer spoke at a Houston fundraising event for him, to the dismay of some Hispanic Democrats.

Garcia, who raised $700,000 for the primary, had a robust campaign organization and was supported by organized labor and EMILY's List. In the March primary, she easily prevailed with 63 percent of the vote to 21 percent for Javed; five other candidates split the remainder. Following the primary, she was more cautious in criticizing President Donald Trump than were many other House Democratic hopefuls. But she has been out front with Democratic activists in leading demonstrations against Trump's policies along the border and seeking to abolish the Immigration and Customs Enforcement agency.

After a 26-year wait to enter Congress, Garcia made a quick impression. She scored with assignments to the Financial Services and Judiciary committees, including the Immigration Subcommittee. Citing her background as a judge, Garcia told the Texas Tribune in April 2018, "the facts are not there yet" to warrant impeachment proceedings. And she was one of the last House Democrats to sign onto impeachment in September 2019 as Trump's Ukrainian scandal began to break open. A few months later, though, she found herself at the center of the process when a close political ally, House Speaker Nancy Pelosi, named her to serve as a House impeachment manager. When Joe Biden's presidential campaign was considering prospects for minority women as his running mate, Los Angeles Mayor Gil Garcetti spoke with Garcia to get her input "It's time to make sure that Latinas are part of the conversation," she told Politico in May 2020.

On Jan. 6, 2021, police rushed Garcia out of a ladies room off the House floor and into the chamber. She said she was startled to see that Pelosi was not presiding. "When I walked in, Nancy wasn't at the podium, and I thought this is … serious," she told the Texas Tribune.

TX-29: Harris County   Cook Partisan Voting Index: D+19

Population		Race and Ethnicity		Income	
Total	783,915	White	72.20%	Median Income	$48,300
Land area (sq. miles)	187	Black	10.50%	District Income Rank	397
Pop/ sq mi	4,190.49	Latino	78.70%	Poverty Rate	22.20%
Born in State	61.00%	Asian	1.80%	With health insurance	67.20%
		Two or more races	1.60%	Cash public assistance	1.10%
Age Groups		Other	13.80%	Food stamp/SNAP	18.50%
Under 18	31.50%				
18-34	25.60%	**Education**		**Work**	
35-64	34.10%	H.S grad or less	65.90%	White Collar	19.20%
Over 64	8.80%	Some college	22.50%	Sales and Service	38.80%
		College Degree, 4 yr	8.30%	Blue Collar	41.90%
Military		Post grad	3.40%	Government	9.70%
Veteran/ Active Duty	2.30%				

2020 Pres. Vote	Biden	106,229	(66%)	Trump	52,937	(33%)	
2016 Pres. Vote	Clinton	95,027	(71%)	Trump	34,011	(25%)	Johnson	3,136	(2%)

East Houston and Pasadena: Many areas of Texas have large Mexican-American communities that can be traced back to statehood. But not Houston. The swampy area in what was originally called Harrisburg County had few inhabitants of any ethnicity until the 20th century. Houston and its Mexican-American community had to be built from the ground up. The city's economy was also built from the ground up, based on a combination of cotton, oil and trade via the 52-mile Houston Ship Channel. Cotton and oil were gifts of nature, though they required much human effort and ingenuity to produce in commercial quantities. The ship channel has been almost totally man's creation and a massive public works project. Along with the unsettled conditions created by the Mexican Revolution of 1910, it provided the impetus for Mexican immigration to the city.

After the sand-spit port of Galveston was destroyed by a hurricane in 1900, Houston's elders decided to dredge out Buffalo Bayou and make their inland city a seaport. When the channel officially opened in November 1914, a sluggish, 6-foot-deep creek had become a 40-foot-deep waterway that would turn Houston into one of the nation's biggest ports. Today, the channel is 45 feet deep and 530 feet wide. In the port, which is the second-largest in the nation in tonnage, more than half the cargo is energy-related. Total exports from the port of Houston exceeded imports in 2018 by about $20 billion—the first-ever surplus.

On its west side, Houston seems entirely a white-collar, office-bound city. But on the east and north, around the port and through the maze of refinery towers and pipelines, it remains blue-collar and a job magnet for Mexican Americans and workers from the rural South. To the south is Hobby Airport, whose art-deco terminal served the city until what is now called the George Bush Intercontinental Airport opened in 1969. Hobby serves about 25 percent of the area's airline passengers. The three devastating hurricanes that struck Houston in three years, capped by Harvey in 2017, temporarily shut down refineries, pipelines and chemical plants. In August 2018, voters in Harris County approved $2.5 billion in new bonds for more than 200 flood-control projects.

The 29th Congressional District of Texas, which is entirely in Harris County, covers much of the ship channel area and working-class Houston. Its unusual shape—some say it resembles a seated dragon—connects heavily Hispanic sections north of Houston with the Hispanic community around the ship channel and Pasadena. The district wraps around the Sam Houston Tollway, taking in blue-collar neighborhoods in northeast Houston as well. In the southeast, Pasadena, once part of the giant Allen Ranch, is now a working-class city of 154,000 centered on the oil and aerospace industries. Construction was nearing completion on an $820 million high-capacity marine terminal along the ship channel in Pasadena. It will chiefly handle refined petroleum products and will be able to dock Panamax-size ships, with room for expansion. Pasadena was also once home to Gilley's, the nightclub setting in Urban Cowboy and a venue that became a top tourist attraction before it closed in 1989. The district is 79 percent Hispanic and firmly Democratic. Joe Biden won the district with 66 percent, the same share that President Barack Obama received in 2012, but five percentage points less than the total for Hillary Clinton.

Eddie Bernice Johnson (D)

Elected 1992, 15th term, b. Dec 03, 1935; Waco, TX; St. Mary's College at the University of Notre Dame, M.P.A., 1955; TX Christian University, B.S., 1967; Southern Methodist University, M.P.A., 1976; Baptist; Divorced; 1 child; 3 grandchildren.

Elected Office: TX House, 1973-1977; TX Senate, 1987-1993.

Professional Career: Registered nurse, 1955-1972; Regional Director, U.S. Department of HEW, 1977-1981; Mgmt. consultant, Sammons Corporation, 1979-1981; Owner, Eddie Bernice Johnson & Association.

DC Office: 2306 RHOB 20515, 202-225-8885, Fax: 202-226-1477, ebjohnson.house.gov

State Offices: Dallas, 214-922-8885.

Committees: *Science, Space & Technology (Chmn). Transportation & Infrastructure*: Aviation; Highways & Transit; Water Resources & Environment.

Group Ratings

	ADA	ACLU	AFL-CIO	LCV	COC	HAFA	ACU	CFG	FRC
2020	**	75%	**	95%	-	0%	6%	**	-
2019	90%	C	100%	97%	63%	C	6%	13%	0%

Almanac Ratings 2019-2020

	Economy	Social	Foreign	Composite
Liberal	59%	100%	80%	80%
Conservative	41%	0%	20%	20%

Key Votes of the 116th Congress

1. U.S./Mex./Can. trade deal	Y	5. Russia sanctions	Y
2. First Coronavirus response	Y	6. Troops in Syria	Y
3. HEROES Act	N/A	7. Veto arms sales to Saudis	Y
4. CASH Act	Y	8. Defense $$$, veto override	Y

9. Firearms background checks Y
10. Spending at the border Y
11. Marijuana liberalized rules Y
12. Electoral College objections N

Election Results

Election	Name (Party)	Vote (%)		Cand. Spent	Ind. Exp. Support	Ind. Exp. Oppose
2020 General	Eddie Bernice Johnson (D)	204,928	(77%)	$280,192	$995	
	Tre Pennie (R)	48,685	(18%)	$239,778	$4,215	$113
	Eric Williams (I)	10,851	(4%)			
2020 Primary	Eddie Bernice Johnson (D)	58,804	(71%)			
	Shenita Cleveland (D)	11,358	(14%)			
	Barbara Mallory Caraway (D)	10,452	(13%)			

Prior winning percentages: 2018 (91%), 2016 (78%), 2014 (88%), 2012 (79%), 2010 (76%), 2008 (82%), 2006 (80%), 2004 (93%), 2002 (74%), 2000 (92%), 1998 (72%), 1996 (55%), 1994 (73%), 1992 (72%)

Eddie Bernice Johnson, a Democrat first elected in 1992, is the dean of the Texas congressional delegation and has been a revered figure in Dallas politics, an advocate for the city for nearly a half-century. Some of her younger rivals and the Dallas Morning News' editorial page have said it's time for her to step aside, even as she acknowledged that she was considering retirement. As chairwoman of the Science, Space and Technology Committee, she promised a more bipartisan approach, especially in contrast to her often-fractious relationship with the previous Republican chairman. Johnson is the second-oldest House member, trailing only Republican Rep. Don Young of Alaska. When Democrats regained House control, she was the only committee chair from Texas.

Johnson grew up in Texas, graduated from Texas Christian University with a nursing degree, and later got a master's degree in public administration at Southern Methodist University. She worked at St. Paul Hospital and was the chief psychiatric nurse at the Veterans Administration Hospital in Dallas. She told the Morning News in 1987 that she first got interested in politics in the early 1960s, when she went to buy a new hat and was shocked to learn that Blacks in the city weren't allowed to try on such headgear. She organized a boycott of the store. In 1972, she was elected to the Texas House, the first Black woman elected to the legislature from Dallas. That year, she came to know two out-of-state young Democratic staffers working to elect George McGovern president: Bill Clinton and Hillary Rodham. She became a regional director of the Health, Education and Welfare Department under President Jimmy Carter. She was elected to the Texas Senate in 1986. As the Senate's Redistricting Committee chair in 1991, she was instrumental in creating the new 30th District, where she went on to win the Democratic primary with 92 percent of the vote. She remains the only person to have held the seat.

In the House, Johnson—known by her initials "EBJ"—has a mostly liberal voting record. A former chairwoman of the Congressional Black Caucus, she was more supportive of President Barack Obama than other CBC members critical of what they saw as limited efforts for low-income and unemployed Blacks. She has been attentive to business interests in Dallas. Johnson once pledged to labor unions to oppose the North American Free Trade Agreement, but she changed her mind and voted for it in 1993. Dallas is a large exporter to Mexico and many jobs depend on that trade. Johnson also sided with business on normalizing trade relations with China and was one of 28 House

Democrats who backed trade promotion authority for Obama in 2015. National unions were unhappy, though she suffered no political damage.

Johnson became ranking Democrat on the Science, Space, and Technology Committee in 2011. What had long been a bipartisan committee has become increasingly polarized. At a 2013 hearing, she accused chairman Lamar Smith, a fellow Texan, of representing the interests of "industry hacks." In 2015, they clashed over his criticism of scientists at the National Oceanic and Atmospheric Administration who had studied global warming. As a health care professional, she takes an interest in minority health issues. She has regularly filed her bipartisan bill to create a federal National Nurse for Public Health to work alongside the surgeon general.

Taking the committee gavel in 2019, Johnson focused on the panel as "the only one that really truly examines the future in a profound way." She said her objectives included ensuring the United States leads the world in science and innovation and has "the right educational and workforce development programs." Her hopes for bipartisanship were improved by the retirement of Smith and the selection of the more collegial Frank Lucas of Oklahoma as the panel's ranking Republican. Following the election, she told a meeting of scientists, "climate change is perhaps the biggest challenge of our time."

As a senior member of the Transportation and Infrastructure Committee, Johnson has worked to secure funds for the Interstate 30 suspension bridge over the Trinity River, and she continues to support Trinity River projects. She has supported the Dallas-Fort Worth area's mass transit projects to alleviate traffic congestion and other area transportation priorities. She has been well-positioned as an ally of Dallas-Fort Worth International Airport.

In the 2020 presidential campaign, she was an early endorser of former Vice President Joe Biden and was a part of the contingent of powerful Black lawmakers who pushed him toward the nomination.

Johnson generally has sailed to reelection, though she has faced some local impatience over when she will step down. In 2012, she faced two young Democratic challengers: attorney Taj Clayton and state Rep. Barbara Mallory Caraway, both of whom avoided criticizing Johnson directly but made clear their view that the district needed fresh representation. The Morning News endorsed Clayton, saying Johnson "once had what it takes, but now it's time for new leadership." Johnson ripped into both of her opponents, calling Clayton a stooge for Republicans and Caraway a disgruntled former aide. She won the primary with 70 percent to Caraway's 18 percent and Clayton's 12 percent. In subsequent rematches with Caraway, whose husband Dwaine Caraway is a city council member in Dallas, Johnson has won the primary by declining—but still safe— margins, winning 70 percent in 2014, 69 percent in 2016 and 64 percent in 2018. As a sign that she remains in control, Johnson won the primary in 2020 with 71 percent.

Following the 2016 election, Johnson broadly hinted that she would not seek reelection. "I want to wind it down and move on to what's out there for me," she told a local television station. By April 2017, the Morning News reported that she had changed her mind and was planning to seek one more term. If nothing else, her uncertainty and the recent futile challenges have opened the door for Johnson's potential successors to make plans. Another possible signal that Johnson has focused on her legacy: In April 2019, she received extended tributes when the century-old train station in Dallas was dedicated in her name. "If my work highlights any one thing in particular, it is that I have made it a point to help others," she said at the event. Whenever it occurs, given Johnson's dominance in Dallas politics it's likely she will retire on her terms.

TX-30: Dallas County   **Cook Partisan Voting Index: D+29**

Population		Race and Ethnicity		Income	
Total	792,445	White	47.90%	Median Income	$51,819
Land area (sq. miles)	356	Black	41.20%	District Income Rank	370
Pop/ sq mi	2,224.28	Latino	40.50%	Poverty Rate	18.70%
Born in State	62.30%	Asian	1.80%	With health insurance	77.30%
		Two or more races	1.90%	Cash public assistance	2.10%
Age Groups		Other	7.30%	Food stamp/SNAP	15.20%
Under 18	26.90%				
18-34	25.90%	Education		Work	
35-64	36.30%	H.S grad or less	50.40%	White Collar	29.40%
Over 64	10.90%	Some college	27.30%	Sales and Service	41.30%
		College Degree, 4 yr	14.30%	Blue Collar	29.30%
Military		Post grad	8.00%	Government	10.60%
Veteran/ Active Duty	4.90%				

2020 Pres. Vote	Biden	212,373	(80%)	Trump	50,270	(19%)			
2016 Pres. Vote	Clinton	174,528	(79%)	Trump	40,333	(18%)	Johnson	4,276	(2%)

Central and Southern Dallas Metro: In 1923, Texas adopted the "white primary," which barred Blacks from participating in statewide Democratic primary elections, although Blacks who could pay a poll tax were permitted to vote in general elections, municipal elections, school board elections, special elections and on ballot propositions. By 1947, Dallas County had a majority-Black electorate, and yet despite this, there was no congressional district in North Texas that was considered likely to elect a Black representative until the creation of the 30th Congressional District in 1991. Its creation was insisted on by the then-chairwoman of the Texas Senate's redistricting committee, and the result was a grotesquely shaped district. Since then, lawsuits and four more rounds of redistricting have smoothed out the lines and left the 30th as one of two heavily minority Democratic districts in the Dallas-Fort Worth Metroplex.

The Dallas-Fort Worth metro area in 2017 surpassed Houston as the fastest growing area in the nation; in the previous year, they grew by 146,000 and 94,000, respectively. With its population of 7.6 million, Dallas in 2019 claimed bragging rights as the largest metro area in Texas, over Houston, with its 7.1 million. Nationally, they trailed only New York, Los Angeles and Chicago. The Dallas metro area has been responding to the growth in multiple ways. Construction was scheduled to start in 2019 on a privately financed high-speed rail line that would take 90 minutes from Dallas to Houston on an elevated 240-mile route. But the project was delayed as cost estimates soared. The Dallas Area Rapid Transit approved a two-mile downtown subway line, which was scheduled for completion in 2024 and will connect to the existing light rail system and bus lines. Love Field, which Congress in 1979 confined to short routes so it would not interfere with the new DFW airport, was the fastest-growing airport in the nation from 2007 to 2017, with a 90 percent increase in passengers; that progress was expedited by repeal in 2014 of the Wright amendment, the 1979 law named for Rep. Jim Wright of Texas.

Today, the 30th District consists of most of the south side of Dallas, with one tentacle running northwest, out Stemmons Freeway to Love Field. In between is the "mix master," where three busy highways—Interstates 30, 35E and 45—come together within a square mile, surrounding many of the prominent sites in Dallas. Further south, it embraces African-American majority towns such as Cedar Hill, Glenn Heights and upscale DeSoto, as well as minority-majority locales like Duncanville and Hutchins. The district also includes Fair Park, home to the Texas State Fair each fall and the Cotton Bowl. The court-drawn map placed much of the district's previous Hispanic population in the newly created 33rd District. But Hispanics have continued to surge in South Dallas. The 30th District's population is now split 41 percent among both African Americans and Hispanics; the latter are mostly young and 90 percent of them are from Mexico. The growing influence of racial minorities in the city has been a major factor in Democrats' virtual takeover of Dallas County offices. In 2018, local Democrats won 12 of the 14 House seats in the Texas legislature; with the Republican redistricting map in 2012, they had six of the 14. This district is overwhelmingly Democratic and the party's strongest in Texas. Joe Biden took 80 percent of the vote.

John Carter (R)

Elected 2002, 10th term, b. Nov 06, 1941; Houston, TX; TX Technical University, B.A., 1964; University of TX School of Law, J.D., 1969; Lutheran; Married (Erika Carter); 4 children; 6 grandchildren.

Elected Office: Williamson County TX District Court judge, 1981-2001.

Professional Career: Practicing attorney, 1969-1981.

DC Office: 2110 RHOB 20515, 202-225-3864, Fax: 202-225-5886, carter.house.gov

State Offices: Round Rock, 512-246-1600; Temple, 254-933-1392.

Committees: *Appropriations*: Defense; Military Construction, Veterans Affairs & Related Agencies (RMM).

Group Ratings

	ADA	ACLU	AFL-CIO	LCV	COC	HAFA	ACU	CFG	FRC
2020	**	26%	**	10%	-	87%	86%	**	-
2019	10%	C	35%	3%	82%	C	86%	67%	95%

Almanac Ratings 2019-2020

	Economy	Social	Foreign	Composite
Liberal	39%	31%	15%	29%
Conservative	61%	69%	85%	71%

Key Votes of the 116th Congress

1. U.S./Mex./Can. trade deal	Y	5. Russia sanctions	Y
2. First Coronavirus response	Y	6. Troops in Syria	N
3. HEROES Act	N/A	7. Veto arms sales to Saudis	N
4. CASH Act	N/A	8. Defense $$$, veto override	N/A

9. Firearms background checks	N
10. Spending at the border	Y
11. Marijuana liberalized rules	N/A
12. Electoral College objections	Y

Election Results

Election	Name (Party)	Vote (%)		Cand. Spent	Ind. Exp. Support	Ind. Exp. Oppose
2020 General	John Carter (R)	212,695	(53%)	$2,261,754	$88,131	$18,743
	Donna Imam (D)	176,293	(44%)	$1,016,121	$10,004	
	Clark Patterson (L)	8,922	(2%)			
2020 Primary	John Carter (R)	53,070	(82%)			
	Mike Williams (R)	5,560	(9%)			

Prior winning percentages: 2018 (51%), 2016 (58%), 2014 (64%), 2012 (61%), 2010 (83%), 2008 (60%), 2006 (59%), 2004 (65%), 2002 (69%)

John Carter, a conservative Republican first elected in 2002, has brought an ex-judge's no-nonsense perspective to his work on homeland security and immigration, and later to military construction and veterans' issues, as the top Republican of the Appropriations subcommittees handling those issues. "Judge Carter" has been respected as an informal leader among House Republicans. In 2018, he sweated his first tough reelection challenge since taking office against a well-funded challenger, a woman who was a former military pilot. Two years later, in a contest that got much less attention and financing, Carter increased his victory margin by six percentage points. At age 80 heading into 2022, he could be on the retirement watch.

Carter grew up in Houston and graduated from Texas Tech University and the University of Texas law school. He practiced law in Williamson County and served as a municipal judge in Round Rock. He was appointed a district judge in 1981 by Republican Gov. Bill Clements and in 1982 stood for election. Judicial elections are partisan in Texas, and Carter was the first GOP judge elected in Williamson County. He became known as the father of the county Republican Party.

In 2001, he ran in a new Republican district stretching from Williamson County to Houston. The real contest was for the Republican nomination. Carter's main rivals were Peter Wareing, the son-in-law of Texas oilman Jack Blanton, and Brad Barton, son of Rep. Joe Barton. In the primary, Wareing led with 37 percent to 26 percent for Carter and 16 percent for Barton.

In the runoff, Carter attacked Wareing as a liberal in disguise, pointing to his campaign contributions to Democrats. He offered what he called a "homestead pledge"—a ploy to highlight his charge that Wareing was a Houston carpetbagger who had rented an apartment in the district to run for the seat. Wareing outspent Carter more than 2-to-1, but Carter won 57%-43%. He got 78 percent of the vote in Williamson County, which cast 33 percent of the vote. Carter won the general election easily.

Carter has been a reliable conservative, but not a hardliner. As an Appropriations Committee member, he opposed some of the bolder GOP proposals to cut spending in 2012, such as an across-the-board cut in energy and water spending. He fought off a Republican attempt in 2011 to sharply cut spending for military bands, arguing that they "are an integral part of the patriotism that keeps our soldiers' hearts beating fast."

Carter retained an interest in law-enforcement issues. In 2016, he enacted his POLICE (Protecting Our Lives through Initiating COPS Expansion) Act, which was designed to increase active-shooter training for officers. In 2017, he joined Rep. Jeff Duncan in filing a bill to relax restrictions on gun silencers, which is a priority of the National Rifle Association. In 2018, he enacted a bill that provided additional resources to assist local prosecutors with DNA analysis.

As chairman of the Homeland Security Appropriations Subcommittee starting in 2011, Carter fought for spending more to secure the U.S.-Mexico border, but also acknowledged the need to "show compassion" to immigrants who are already in the United States. In 2015, he cooperated on the House GOP leadership strategy to use the Homeland Security spending bill to try to force President Barack Obama to back down on his executive actions to protect some illegal immigrants from deportation. Senate Democrats held firm against any compromise.

In 2017, Carter switched to chair the Military Construction and Veterans Affairs Subcommittee. His work on Appropriations brought added benefits to Fort Hood, including funding of a new hospital, $61 million to upgrade the barracks and $50 million to renovate the cavalry headquarters. He has served several terms as co-chairman of the bipartisan House Army Caucus.

On immigration legislation, Carter took part in bipartisan discussions on a broader measure. He quit the group in September 2013 because, he said, Obama was using the immigration issue to "advance his political agenda." In 2018, with President Donald Trump demanding a wall along the border with Mexico, Carter cautioned that the demands of private landowners would complicate the building of a wall.

Carter served three terms in the leadership as House Republican Conference secretary. In 2009, he was the chief antagonist on ethics charges against Democratic Rep. Charles Rangel, who stepped down as chairman of the Ways and Means Committee.

In 2016, Carter had a GOP primary challenge from political newcomer Mike Sweeney, who criticized Carter for his "votes to fund the Obama agenda." Sweeney, who had a successful software business, spent a mere $10,000. Carter spent $1.2 million in the campaign cycle and got 71 percent of the vote, a signal of some conservative unrest. Facing Sweeney again in the 2018 Republican primary, Carter touted his support for Trump plus the $367 million he delivered to Fort Hood; with Sweeney spending $55,000 this time, Carter won with 66 percent.

The real challenge for Carter in 2018 came from Democrat M.J. Hegar, who gained attention with a campaign ad that described her experience serving as a decorated Air Force officer in Afghanistan, where she was shot down while operating as a "search and rescue" helicopter pilot. Later, she complained, Carter refused to provide her sufficient assistance as a constituent in Round Rock. She outspent Carter, $5.1 million to $2 million, and criticized him as a "coward" for his failure to agree to a campaign debate. Carter escaped with a 51%-48% win. Hegar led by 3,500 votes in Williamson, but Carter prevailed with a nearly 12,000-vote edge in Bell County.

In 2020, Donna Imam, a tech entrepreneur and a native of Bangladesh, defeated five Democrats in the primary. Carter outspent her, $2.3 million to $1 million. In contrast to the contest with Hegar, the national parties showed no interest. This time, Carter took Williamson by 14,600 votes. Still, the political newcomer Imam kept it relatively close, 53%-44%. With redistricting uncertainties and the shifting demographics north of Austin, Carter faces more political change and challenges.

TX-31: Central Texas   Cook Partisan Voting Index: R+6

Population		Race and Ethnicity		Income	
Total	916,064	White	74.60%	Median Income	$75,813
Land area (sq. miles)	2,154	Black	12.30%	District Income Rank	120
Pop/ sq mi	425.19	Latino	25.30%	Poverty Rate	8.40%
Born in State	49.50%	Asian	5.90%	With health insurance	88.50%
		Two or more races	4.50%	Cash public assistance	1.30%
Age Groups		Other	2.80%	Food stamp/SNAP	7.50%
Under 18	26.00%				
18-34	24.10%	**Education**		**Work**	
35-64	37.60%	H.S grad or less	30.20%	White Collar	43.70%
Over 64	12.30%	Some college	33.40%	Sales and Service	38.50%
		College Degree, 4 yr	24.20%	Blue Collar	17.80%
Military		Post grad	12.30%	Government	15.90%
Veteran/ Active Duty	14.90%				

2020 Pres. Vote	Trump	204,096	(50%)	Biden	192,599	(48%)		
2016 Pres. Vote	Trump	153,823	(53%)	Clinton	117,181	(40%)	Johnson	13,735	(5%)

Williamson and Bell Counties: In 1932, Williamson County was a rural backwater that cast a little more than 7,000 votes for president; Franklin Roosevelt won all but 431 of them. Today it has become a major population and business center deep in the heart of Texas, casting 200,000 votes in 2016. Its population has nearly doubled in every recent decade. It had 40,000 people in 1970 and 591,000 in 2019. Williamson County is just north of Austin, and much of this growth has been generated by the area's high-technology boom—Austin's city limits actually now spill over into Williamson. The county long ago moved beyond a bedroom suburb. Hugely successful computer producer Dell is headquartered in Round Rock (the rock, which served as an important wagon crossing, is in the middle of Brushy Creek, with wheel ruts still visible). In December 2018, Apple announced its plan for a second campus in northwest Austin, where it expected to hire 5,000 employees.

Texas 130, a 49-mile, 10-lane toll road with a speed limit of 85 miles per hour in parts, has steered more growth. Georgetown, home to Southwestern University, has become a popular retirement destination and is one of the fastest-growing cities in the nation. As one of the fastest-growing cities in the nation, it has seen a population increase from 28,000 in 2000 to 80,000 in 2019. In May 2020, the Torque News reported that Tesla purchased several large parcels of land near Taylor—on the outskirts of Round Rock—that were expected to become a rail-served logistics park to serve its new factory in Austin.

Bell County, just north of Williamson County, is home to part of Fort Hood, the largest U.S. military base in the world in terms of acreage. The base is the only U.S. post capable of supporting two full armored divisions. Its mission—maintaining combat readiness, including training Army reservists in urban combat—explains its size; it covers 218,000 acres, or, 340 square miles, an area larger than New York's five boroughs. Killeen, home of the base, has been growing rapidly. In February 2019, the Austin American-Statesman reported "deplorable" housing conditions at Hood, where the barracks housed 18,000 soldiers. The situation became serious enough that a congressional delegation visited the base in 2020 as part of an investigation. To the east is Temple, a rail center and the birthplace of Miriam "Ma" Ferguson, wife of Gov. James "Pa" Ferguson, who was elected governor in 1925 after her husband was impeached and convicted.

The 31st Congressional District is an unusually compact district by modern Texas standards. It is entirely contained within Bell and Williamson counties, and takes in almost all of each. Williamson has 70 percent of the population. Historically this was solidly Democratic country, devoted to the party of the Confederacy and then the New Deal. It was populated by cotton farmers who distrusted Wall Street and railroads and who trusted politicians like Sam Rayburn and Lyndon Johnson. These people took a shine to Ronald Reagan's and George W. Bush's brand of Republicanism. Now, places like suburban Williamson County have become the central fight as Democrats battle Republicans for control of Texas. This is another Texas district where the partisan gap has narrowed significantly. Mitt Romney won here, 60%-38%. In 2020, President Donald Trump led, 50.4%-47.6%.

Colin Allred (D)

Elected 2018, 2nd term, b. Apr 15, 1983; Dallas, TX; Baylor University, B.A., 2005; University of CA, Berkeley, J.D., 2014; Religion unknown; Married (Alexandra Allred); 1 child.

Professional Career: Linebacker, Tennessee Titans, 2006-2010; Special Assistant, U.S. Department of Housi., Attorney

DC Office: 328 CHOB 20515, 202-225-2231, allred.house.gov

State Offices: Richardson, 972-972-7949.

Committees: *Foreign Affairs*: Middle East, North Africa & Global Counterterrorism. *Transportation & Infrastructure*: Aviation; Highways & Transit. *Veterans' Affairs*: Health; Women Veterans Task Force.

Almanac Ratings 2019-2020

	Economy	Social	Foreign	Composite
Liberal	100%	56%	54%	70%
Conservative	0%	44%	46%	30%

Key Votes of the 116th Congress

1. U.S./Mex./Can. trade deal	Y	5. Russia sanctions	Y	9. Firearms background checks Y
2. First Coronavirus response	Y	6. Troops in Syria	Y	10. Spending at the border	Y
3. HEROES Act	Y	7. Veto arms sales to Saudis	Y	11. Marijuana liberalized rules	Y
4. CASH Act	Y	8. Defense $$$, veto override	Y	12. Electoral College objections N

Election Results

Election	Name (Party)	Vote (%)		Cand. Spent	Ind. Exp. Support	Ind. Exp. Oppose
2020 General	Colin Allred (D)............................ 178,542	(52%)	$5,940,316	$159,311	$703,055
	Genevieve Collins (R)...................... 157,867	(46%)	$5,989,519	$540,786	$113
2020 Primary	Colin Allred (D)............................... 72,761	(100%)			

Prior winning percentages: 2018 (52%)

Democrat Colin Allred won a district north of Dallas that had recently shifted toward Democrats. Although a first-time candidate, he had experience in Democratic politics and with civil rights issues as an attorney. Allred defeated Republican Rep. Pete Sessions, who served 22 years and led the GOP campaign committee when the party regained the House majority in 2010. Hillary Clinton's 48%-46% lead in this district in 2016 signaled an opportunity for Democrats, though they oddly failed to run a candidate against Sessions that year. Sessions relocated to the Waco-based 17th District and was elected again to the House in 2020.

Allred was raised in North Dallas and graduated from Baylor University, where he received an athletic scholarship. He played for five years as a defensive lineman for the Tennessee Titans in the National Football League. After getting his law degree from the University of California, Berkeley, he was a special assistant in the general counsel's office at the Housing and Urban Development Department. In 2014, he entered politics as the Dallas-Fort Worth director of the Texas Democrats' voter protection program. He worked as a voting-rights litigator with the Washington-based law firm of Perkins Coie.

Following the results of the 2016 election, Democrats weren't going to repeat their mistake of not posing a challenge to Sessions. His voting record often was among the most conservative in the House, which posed a potential clash with his district, and he could be a tough partisan—both at home and in the Capitol. House Democrats enthusiastically made Sessions one of their prime targets in 2018; he had not faced a serious reelection challenge since the redistricting wars of 2004.

Of the seven candidates in the Democratic primary, none of the four leading contenders had held elected office, though each had been actively involved in party politics; three of them spent at least $700,000 in the primary. Allred was forced into a runoff, where he won the nomination easily. He led runner-up Lillian Salerno, a senior Agriculture Department official in the Obama administration, by more than 2-to-1 in each round.

Sessions sought to wrap himself in multiple wings of the Republican Party. He embraced the mantra of President Donald Trump to "make America great again." In an interview with a Dallas radio station, he called himself "the business community member of Congress." And he posed the election as a stark partisan choice: "You get somebody that's for Nancy Pelosi or you get a market-based system, which is what I have stood for." Each of those themes seemed politically outdated, given the demographic and political shifts in his district.

In an editorial, the Dallas Morning News endorsed Sessions as more experienced and wrote that he "better represents the principles of limited government that we favor." The endorsement criticized Allred for his lack of "comprehensive solutions" and his support for the Affordable Care Act.

Each candidate spent more than $5 million and outside groups spent another $10 million, mostly in negative ads. Allred won, 52%-46%, with more than 90 percent of the vote cast in Dallas County, where he led by 20,000 votes. The remainder was in outlying Collin County, where Sessions got 55 percent of the vote.

Allred's classmates elected him freshman class co-president in his first term, and he landed assignments on the Transportation and Infrastructure, Foreign Affairs and Veterans' Affairs Committees. He came to Congress with a bit of star power around him, given his NFL background. But for the most part, he kept his head down and did little to draw attention to himself. He pursued bipartisan alliances, which were a good fit with his evolving district. Following the 2020 election, he won a Democratic leadership position representing members who have been elected to no more than five terms.

On the second day of his second term, Allred grew increasingly alarmed from the House floor as he watched House Speaker Nancy Pelosi shuffled off the rostrum. As rioters attempted to break down the doors, he readied himself for the worst. Allred texted his wife that he loved her, removed his tie, rolled his sleeves up and prepared for a fight. A number of members who were on the floor that day later said they moved toward their 6-foot-1-inch former pro football player for protection.

In his first bid for reelection, Allred faced a spirited challenge from Republican Genevieve Collins. Each candidate spent about $6 million, though both national parties gave their attention and resources to other districts in Texas. Allred won, 52%-46%, even as many of his classmates lost in similar districts elsewhere in the country.

TX-32: Dallas County   **Cook Partisan Voting Index: D+1**

Population		Race and Ethnicity		Income	
Total	778,087	White	67.40%	Median Income	$76,464
Land area (sq. miles)	186	Black	14.90%	District Income Rank	115
Pop/ sq mi	4,190.92	Latino	27.00%	Poverty Rate	9.90%
Born in State	50.60%	Asian	8.20%	With health insurance	81.60%
		Two or more races	3.70%	Cash public assistance	0.80%
Age Groups		Other	5.80%	Food stamp/SNAP	5.90%
Under 18	24.50%				
18-34	25.00%	**Education**		**Work**	
35-64	37.70%	H.S grad or less	28.70%	White Collar	46.30%
Over 64	12.70%	Some college	26.10%	Sales and Service	36.10%
		College Degree, 4 yr	27.90%	Blue Collar	17.60%
Military		Post grad	17.40%	Government	9.50%
Veteran/ Active Duty	4.90%				

2020 Pres. Vote	Biden	187,919	(54%)	Trump	151,944	(44%)			
2016 Pres. Vote	Clinton	134,895	(48%)	Trump	129,701	(46%)	Johnson	11,358	(4%)

Northern Dallas Metro: North Dallas has long been the home of the city's elite and, indeed, a slice of the nation's elite. Early in the 20th century, the richest citizens started moving away from old neighborhoods adjacent to downtown and out past Turtle Creek to the area around the suburbs of Highland Park and University Park. Dallas grew lustily from mid-century. Beyond the Park Cities, miles of affluent neighborhoods were built, especially between the Central Expressway and the Dallas North Tollway. Galleries and office complexes followed. An entertainment and singles apartment corridor runs along Greenville Avenue, plus working-class neighborhoods here and there, and pockets of Latino neighborhoods near the freeways. The Texas transportation department is expanding a section of Interstate 635 that is east of the Central Expressway—the LBJ East project.

The Park Cities, Highland Park and University Park, are well-heeled and over 90 percent White in increasingly diverse Dallas. They comprise one of the top school districts in the state. University Park is the larger of the two exclusive cities, which have a combined population of 34,000 and median household income exceeding $200,000. After eight years in the White House, George and Laura Bush returned to their Preston Hollow neighborhood a few miles from his presidential library at Southern Methodist University; they have decided that they will be buried at the library. The much larger and still-growing urban center is Garland, with a population of 240,000, majority-minority residents and household income of $55,000. Its largest private-sector employers are the Baylor Medical Center and Kraft Foods.

North Dallas and the 32nd Congressional District of Texas reflect the political trends driving 21st century politics: As upper-income suburbanites drifted toward the Democrats and the minority population of north Dallas County increased, the district has moved leftward. The Republican-engineered redistricting in 2011 dropped the Hispanic share of the population from 43 percent to 26 percent. The district includes a thin slice of Collin County that takes in some of fast-growing, upscale Wylie; more than 90 percent of the 32nd is in Dallas County. The 32nd has Democratic pockets around racially diverse Richardson and the downtown area. Still, few were prepared for the stunning shift toward the Democratic Party up and down the ballot in this area in recent years. Joe Biden led Donald Trump, 54%-44%.

Marc Veasey (D)

Elected 2012, 5th term, b. Jan 03, 1971; Tarrant County, TX; TX Wesleyan University, B.S., 1995; Christian Church; Married (Tonya Veasey); 1 child.

Elected Office: TX House, 2005-2013.

Professional Career: Staffer, Rep. Martin Frost, 1998-2004; Commercial real-estate broker.

DC Office: 2348 RHOB 20515, 202-225-9897, Fax: 202-225-9702, veasey.house.gov

State Offices: Dallas, 214-741-1387; Fort Worth, 817-920-9086.

Committees: *Armed Services*: Military Personnel; Tactical Air & Land Forces. *Energy & Commerce*: Communications & Technology; Energy. *Joint Security & Cooperation in Europe.*

Group Ratings

	ADA	ACLU	AFL-CIO	LCV	COC	HAFA	ACU	CFG	FRC
2020	**	78%	**	100%	-	0%	5%	**	-
2019	85%	C	100%	97%	63%	C	6%	12%	0%

Almanac Ratings 2019-2020

	Economy	Social	Foreign	Composite
Liberal	100%	61%	92%	85%
Conservative	0%	39%	8%	15%

Key Votes of the 116th Congress

1. U.S./Mex./Can. trade deal Y	5. Russia sanctions Y	9. Firearms background checks Y
2. First Coronavirus response Y	6. Troops in Syria Y	10. Spending at the border N
3. HEROES Act Y	7. Veto arms sales to Saudis Y	11. Marijuana liberalized rules Y
4. CASH Act Y	8. Defense $$$, veto override Y	12. Electoral College objections N

Election Results

Election	Name (Party)	Vote (%)		Cand. Spent	Ind. Exp. Support	Ind. Exp. Oppose
2020 General	Marc Veasey (D)...............................	105,317	(67%)	$1,064,518	$995	
	Fabian Vasquez (R)............................	39,638	(25%)	$22,136	$1,715	$113
	Carlos Quintanilla (I)..................	8,071	(5%)	$6,800		
2020 Primary	Marc Veasey (D).............................	23,869	(64%)			
	Sean Paul Segura (D)...................	13,678	(36%)			

Prior winning percentages: 2018 (76%), 2016 (74%), 2014 (87%), 2012 (73%)

Democrat Marc Veasey, first elected in 2012, has faced competitive primaries as an African American in this heavily Hispanic district. His deep political experience gave him a head start in the House, where he looked after the needs of local defense contractors. His seat on the Energy and Commerce Committee has been useful for home-state interests. A McClatchy News profile in August 2017 described Veasey as "the future of the Democratic Party: Moderate, African-American and focused on helping Democrats reconnect with the working-class voters who abandoned them for Donald Trump."

Veasey, a commercial real estate broker, was born and still lives in Fort Worth. His uncle worked for Rep. Jim Wright, the House Speaker from 1987 to 1989. After watching a White House press briefing on television in his mid-teens, Veasey remembers asking what it would take to get such a job. His uncle advised he get a college degree. After graduating from Texas Wesleyan University, Veasey held a string of jobs. As a staffer to Democratic Rep. Martin Frost, he attracted a grocery store to a poor section of Fort Worth to create jobs and enable residents to buy fresh produce. Veasey ran successfully for the state House in 2004 against an incumbent who refused to join other Texas Democrats in leaving the state to protest GOP-led redistricting. He chaired the Democratic Caucus.

His main competition in the decisive primary for the newly created House seat was Dallas attorney Domingo Garcia. The contest polarized Black voters who supported Veasey and Hispanics who largely supported Garcia; it also developed into a regional spat between Veasey from Fort Worth and Garcia from Dallas. In the initial balloting, Veasey led Garcia, 37%-25%. In the runoff, Veasey targeted Black voters on his home turf. Garcia accused him of "playing the race card." But it was a good strategy. Voters in Tarrant County turned out in higher proportions than those in Dallas County.

Garcia failed to galvanize Hispanics, who outnumbered Blacks 4-to-1, though more narrowly among registered voters. Veasey won the runoff 53%-47%. He got 68 percent in Tarrant County, which cast 59 percent of the total. "This election was about making sure North Texans were represented fairly and honestly," he said. In November, Veasey defeated Republican Chuck Bradley, 73%-26%.

At the Armed Services Committee, he tended to the interests of the many military contractors in or near his district. On the defense spending bill in 2015, he claimed credit for additional weapons procurement plus a bipartisan agreement that required the Pentagon to review how illegal immigrants were serving in the military. He has filed a bill to create a monument to recipients of the Medal of Honor. The monument in Washington D.C. would complement a museum planned for Arlington, in Veasey's district.

With his assignment to Energy and Commerce, Veasey and Democratic Rep. Rick Larsen of Washington filed in January 2019 a bill to remove "discriminatory" restrictions on voting participation, such as ID cards. Their measure was incorporated into the sweeping political reform bill that House Democrats passed in February. In July 2020, the House passed on a party-line vote Veasey's resolution that rejected the Trump administration's plan to give states more authority to shape how they run their Medicaid programs. In 2021, he rejoined the Armed Services panel, while retaining his seat on Energy and Commerce.

Veasey has organized two caucuses to promote Democratic interests. The Congressional Voting Rights Caucus was designed to update the Voting Rights Act, following the 2013 ruling by the Supreme Court that struck down a key enforcement provision. With Rep. Brendan Boyle of Pennsylvania, he launched the Blue Collar Caucus to respond to what Veasey called the "scam" of President Donald Trump's outreach to workers. "Trump's focus on America's workers started and ended with his campaign rhetoric," Veasey and Boyle wrote in an op-ed in the Philadelphia Inquirer in November 2018.

In 2020, Veasey showed the other side of his centrism when he said prior to the Democratic presidential primary in Texas that the nomination of Bernie Sanders would be disastrous for down-ballot Democrats. "It's going to be Bernie and his cause taking the party down with him," said Veasey, who endorsed Joe Biden for the nomination.

Veasey has faced varied primary challenges from Latino opponents. In 2014, Tom Sanchez, a telecommunications lawyer, self-financed nearly all of his $1.5 million campaign. Although outspent, Veasey won easily, 73%-27%. The 2016 primary sent a warning to Veasey. Democratic challenger Carlos Quintanilla, a self-described "activist," did not report spending any money. But his grassroots campaign gave him 52 percent in Dallas County, which cast 43 percent of the total vote. Veasey took 75 percent in Tarrant, which gave him 63 percent overall. Quintanilla ran again in 2018. Veasey increased to 70 percent his share of the smaller midterm turnout, including 57 percent of the Dallas vote. In 2020, Veasey got 64 percent in the Democratic primary against political newcomer Sean-Paul Segura; he took 70 percent in Tarrant.

Local Democrats have talked up the possibility that the next round of redistricting could create separate minority seats for Blacks and Hispanics in the Metroplex, in addition to the longstanding 30th District. For Veasey, those dynamics could be complicated by the potential retirement of veteran Rep. Eddie Bernice Johnson in the 30th and the interests of Rep. Colin Allred in the 32nd District, both of which are Dallas-based. All three are African American Democrats.

TX-33: Central Metroplex — Cook Partisan Voting Index: D+23

Population		Race and Ethnicity		Income	
Total	751,182	White	60.80%	Median Income	$45,997
Land area (sq. miles)	212	Black	16.20%	District Income Rank	414
Pop/ sq mi	3,544.31	Latino	66.80%	Poverty Rate	20.10%
Born in State	56.40%	Asian	2.10%	With health insurance	67.70%
		Two or more races	1.80%	Cash public assistance	3.00%
Age Groups		Other	19.10%	Food stamp/SNAP	18.60%
Under 18	30.30%				
18-34	25.60%	**Education**		**Work**	
35-64	35.50%	H.S grad or less	67.10%	White Collar	17.20%
Over 64	8.50%	Some college	19.80%	Sales and Service	39.80%
		College Degree, 4 yr	9.50%	Blue Collar	43.00%
Military		Post grad	3.60%	Government	7.10%
Veteran/ Active Duty	3.30%				

2020 Pres. Vote	Biden	117,340	(73%)	Trump	41,209	(26%)		
2016 Pres. Vote	Clinton	94,513	(73%)	Trump	30,787	(24%)	Johnson	3,157 (2%)

Parts of Fort Worth and Dallas: In the 1950s, the Dallas-Fort Worth Turnpike was built on empty land to link the two cities' downtowns. Over the next three decades, the land got filled, with as many people as the central cities had. Irving, Grand Prairie and Arlington grew up along the highway in the once impoverished region and became central to one of America's richest and most productive metropolitan areas. Major civic landmarks followed: Rangers Ballpark in Arlington, built by one-time managing partner George W. Bush, and the domed AT&T Stadium, home of the Dallas Cowboys. Arlington and Grand Prairie are in their second generation, taking on the patina of age. The turnover brought newcomers to these fast-growing areas: Arlington is now only 38 percent non-Hispanic White; Irving is 22 percent; Grand Prairie 21 percent.

The 33rd Congressional District of Texas, which covers this suburban zone, is a judicial creation. A court drew the minority-majority district, which is 66 percent Hispanic and 16 percent African American. In its southeast corner, its jagged boundaries mesh with those of the African-American-controlled 30th District in Dallas. The 33rd doesn't take in many of the industrial plants in the area, but its blue-collar workforce provides much of the manpower for Northrop Grumman, General Motors, Hughes Training, Bell Textron Helicopter and Lockheed Martin, all of which have facilities in or near the district. It has neighborhoods in western Dallas, including Oak Cliff, a collection of Victorian era mansions near the Trinity River that became heavily African American and is now heavily Hispanic. Lee Harvey Oswald, who lived in a rooming house in Oak Cliff, took a cab from near Dealey Plaza to his home after killing President John F. Kennedy in November 1963 and then was arrested in the nearby Texas Theater.

The district includes much of Grand Prairie and Irving, as well as tiny, almost-entirely Hispanic Cockrell Hill. The $180 million Toyota Music Factory entertainment and retail venue in Irving features a concert hall and amphitheater. Across a narrow tentacle of lightly populated precincts, the district has about a third of Fort Worth, including the old stockyards, formerly the site of meatpacking plants and where cattle drives are still conducted twice a day by real cattle drovers. The Tarrant County part of the district includes Forest Hill and parts of Arlington, including the sports stadiums. Several major commercial and retail projects have sparked the district, including the $175 million Stockyards real estate and retail development, which features the Texas Cowboy Hall of Fame, and the voter-approved $1 billion baseball stadium in an entertainment complex. Globe Life Field, which opened in 2020 during the pandemic, has been hailed for its design that places many Rangers spectators closer to the field. North of the stockyards, Fort Meachem International Airport, which offers private and charter flights, planned to offer commercial service for the first time since 1998. The extensive redevelopment of the land and buildings, which the city has owned since 1925, was scheduled for completion in 2021. Tarrant and Dallas counties each have about 50 percent of the voters of the 33rd. Overall, Joe Biden got 73 percent in 2020, which fell short of his 80 percent in the adjacent 30th.

Filemon Vela (D)

Elected 2012, 5th term, b. Feb 13, 1963; Harlingen, TX; St. Joseph's Academy, Brownsville, TX; Loyola University, New Orleans, Att., 1982; Georgetown University, B.A., 1985; University of TX, Ausitn, J.D., 1987; Roman Catholic; Married (Rose Vela).

Professional Career: Practicing attorney, 1988-2012.

DC Office: 307 CHOB 20515, 202-225-9901, Fax: 202-225-9770, vela.house.gov

State Offices: Alice, 361-230-9776; Brownsville, 956-544-8352; San Benito, 956-276-4497; Weslaco, 956-520-8273.

Committees: *Agriculture*: Conservation & Forestry; General Farm Commodities & Risk Management. *Armed Services*: Intelligence & Special Operations; Seapower & Projection Forces.

Group Ratings

	ADA	ACLU	AFL-CIO	LCV	COC	HAFA	ACU	CFG	FRC
2020	**	79%	**	100%	-	0%	8%	**	-
2019	85%	C	95%	86%	63%	C	9%	27%	5%

Almanac Ratings 2019-2020

	Economy	Social	Foreign	Composite
Liberal	51%	100%	92%	81%
Conservative	49%	0%	8%	19%

Key Votes of the 116th Congress

1. U.S./Mex./Can. trade deal Y	5. Russia sanctions Y	9. Firearms background checks Y
2. First Coronavirus response Y	6. Troops in Syria Y	10. Spending at the border N
3. HEROES Act Y	7. Veto arms sales to Saudis Y	11. Marijuana liberalized rules Y
4. CASH Act Y	8. Defense $$$, veto override Y	12. Electoral College objections N

Election Results

Election	Name (Party)	Vote (%)	Cand. Spent	Ind. Exp. Support	Ind. Exp. Oppose
2020 General	Filemon Vela (D)............................ 111,439	(55%)	$975,934	$768	
	Rey Gonzalez (R).................................. 84,119	(42%)	$29,602		
2020 Primary	Filemon Vela (D)............................. 39,484	(75%)			
	Diego Zavala (D)................................. 9,707	(18%)			
	Osbert Rodriguez Haro III (D)...... 3,413	(7%)			

Prior winning percentages: 2018 (60%), 2016 (63%), 2014 (59.5%), 2012 (61.9%)

Democrat Filemon Vela won the 34th District House seat in part on the strength of his illustrious political family. Brownsville's federal courthouse bears the name of his late father, a federal district judge who served more than two decades, and his mother was the city's first elected woman mayor. In March 2021, President Joe Biden named his wife, Rose Vela, director of the President's Commission on White House Fellowships. A week later, Vela announced that he was not seeking reelection, which was a signal that Democrats in the Rio Grande Valley—following their poor performance in 2020-- were worried about Republican-controlled redistricting in 2022. During nearly a decade in the House, Vela does not seem to have paid a price for his notable independence from Speaker Nancy Pelosi.

Vela was born in Harlingen and raised in nearby Brownsville. After receiving a bachelor's degree from Georgetown University and a law degree from the University of Texas, he returned to Brownsville to practice law. Vela represented school districts seeking restitution for shoddy construction by contractors. In one case, he won recompense for a malfunctioning air-quality control system.

When Vela launched his campaign in 2012, some political observers were surprised by the "D" next to his name. His wife had been a Republican justice on the Texas Court of Appeals. Vela acknowledged that he sometimes backed GOP office-seekers. He aligned himself with the Democratic agenda, calling for "a realistic and fair way" to deal with illegal immigration, protection of Medicare and Social Security benefits, and tax cuts for small businesses as an incentive to hire workers. Undoubtedly, he was mindful of the district's Democratic tilt.

His main rival for the Democratic nomination, Cameron County District Attorney Armando Villalobos, led the field in fundraising but was indicted on federal fraud charges two weeks before the primary. Vela had a 40%-13% lead in the opening round and got 67 percent in the runoff against Denise Saenz Blanchard, who was chief of staff to former Democratic Rep. Solomon Ortiz, who represented the area for 28 years before he was defeated in 2010. Following the runoff, she told the Associated Press, "we now have a Republican who has converted to being a Democrat, who I believe is taking a seat from the Democrats." Pelosi, the House Democratic leader, dismissed those concerns and headlined a fundraiser for Vela in August. He won in November, 62%-36%.

Vela showed an informed and forceful interest in immigration issues. In 2013, he temporarily resigned from the Hispanic Caucus, saying it was not objecting strongly enough to a provision in the Senate-passed immigration reform bill, which he believed was spending too much money on new barriers and border officials. During the 2016 campaign, he was outspoken in his opposition to Donald Trump, especially his views on immigration. Vela sent him an open letter after Trump said he would not get a fair trial from a judge who was Hispanic in a case dealing with Trump University. "Your ignorant anti-immigrant opinions, your border wall rhetoric, and your recent bigoted attack on an American jurist are just plain despicable," he wrote. "Mr. Trump, you're a racist and you can take your border wall and shove it up your ass."

When Trump took initial steps to build a wall during his first few days as president in January 2017, Vela called it "a ridiculous proposition." Later, he said it was "difficult to believe any Democrat would be willing to give President Trump a nickel to fund his 'big beautiful wall.'" A large border wall, Vela wrote in 2019, "would trample on the property rights of many Texas families." Alternatively, he advocated improved security at the nation's ports of entry.

On the Agriculture Committee, Vela has focused on assuring sufficient water from the Rio Grande for South Texas farmers and he opposed cuts in food stamps. On the bipartisan farm bill that was enacted in December 2018, he took credit for a national animal disease preparedness and response program and for protections for cotton and sugar growers. He has chaired the General Farm Commodities and Risk Management Subcommittee. "It is imperative that we mitigate the risks inherent to farming with robust credit and insurance programs," he said. On the Armed Services

Committee, he has sought to protect an army depot—with more than 3,000 employees—and two naval air stations in and near his district.

Pelosi's willingness to accommodate Vela has been notable, given his repeated calls for new Democratic leaders. "She just doesn't help our candidates in those swing districts with independent voters and Republican voters," he told CNN in June 2017. Following the Democrats' House takeover in November 2018, he remained a vocal dissident who opposed her return as Speaker. "She's been in power 16 years, and the time has just come for us to have a new leader. It's just that simple," he told the Austin American-Statesman. Weeks later, when Vela was part of the final crucial group of House Democrats who agreed to support her, he cited Pelosi's decision to name Rep. Ben Ray Lujan of New Mexico as assistant speaker. Following the riot at the Capitol in January 2021, Vela told a reporter that the Capitol police were outmanned and that congressional leaders "weren't ready for it. They should have seen it coming. They didn't."

In 2014, Vela was reelected 59%-39% over Republican Larry Smith, who spent $120,000 and had a small lead among the one-third of district voters who did not reside in Cameron or Hidalgo counties. In the past three cycles, Vela opposed Rey Gonzalez Jr., a lawyer and former Air Force captain, who spent a total of less than $50,000 in those campaigns. Vela's vote dropped from 63% to 60% to 55% in 2020—a sign of the hazards that Democrats in south Texas face with redistricting.

In announcing that he would not seek reelection in 2022, Vela said he would remain as a vice chair of the Democratic National Committee.

TX-34: Southern Gulf Coast   Cook Partisan Voting Index: D+5

Population		Race and Ethnicity		Income	
Total	712,596	White	91.70%	Median Income	$42,092
Land area (sq. miles)	8,190	Black	1.40%	District Income Rank	428
Pop/ sq mi	87.	Latino	84.50%	Poverty Rate	24.70%
Born in State	71.60%	Asian	0.50%	With health insurance	72.40%
		Two or more races	1.50%	Cash public assistance	1.90%
Age Groups		Other	4.90%	Food stamp/SNAP	24.40%
Under 18	28.60%				
18-34	24.30%	Education		Work	
35-64	32.60%	H.S grad or less	58.30%	White Collar	26.30%
Over 64	14.40%	Some college	26.20%	Sales and Service	48.50%
		College Degree, 4 yr	11.10%	Blue Collar	25.20%
Military		Post grad	4.40%	Government	17.00%
Veteran/ Active Duty	4.70%				

2020 Pres. Vote	Biden	106,771	(52%)	Trump	98,462	(48%)		
2016 Pres. Vote	Clinton	101,796	(59%)	Trump	64,767	(38%)	Johnson 4,042	(2%)

Brownsville, McAllen: At the far southern tip of Texas, just before the waters of the Rio Grande end their 1,900-mile journey from southern Colorado by washing out into the Gulf of Mexico, stands the fast-growing city of Brownsville. Situated across the river from Matamoros Mexico, it is one of the country's major border crossings, and its history has been intertwined with U.S.-Mexican relations. Fort Texas, later renamed Fort Brown, was established in the run-up to the Mexican-American War.

Fort Brown was decommissioned in 1946, but Brownsville still stands at the crossroads of Mexican-American relations. The 1993 North American Free Trade Agreement has lifted the economy in parts of the area, and there has been a boom in commercial construction. In February 2019, the port of Brownsville announced that it will build its second new dock in five years to accommodate the increased shipping. Officials contend that more than 8,000 jobs result directly from the port, with $3 billion in annual economic activity for Texas. More than 90 percent of the cargo in the Brownsville port is to or from Mexico. Brownsville has gained a new niche as the "ship-breaking" capital of the nation. In 2014, it dismantled a former aircraft carrier, the Constellation. The dismantling of other Navy hulks ensued, including the USS Tripoli assault ship. The SpaceX company of Elon Musk has tested its super-heavy booster rocket at its launch site in Boca Chica, near Brownsville. Some of the nearby residents, unwilling to sell their homes, have grown concerned about potential hazards. Although the company cannot force them to leave, Cameron County officials were considering action, The Atlantic reported in February 2020.

National politicians have made visits to Brownsville to assess its migration patterns and security needs. In June 2018, Sen. Jeff Merkley of Oregon was among several congressional Democrats who complained that they were denied access to a converted Walmart supercenter that had become the largest shelter of migrant children in the nation, with nearly 1,500 boys aged 10 to 17. In January 2019, President Donald Trump visited nearby McAllen to make his case for a border wall. Officials in Brownsville have rejected his claim that their city was plagued by crime. In 2019, Brownsville, which is 94 percent Hispanic, had a 29 percent poverty rate, the highest for any city in the nation.

The 34th Congressional District of Texas stretches nearly 300 miles while reaching across 11 counties. More than half its population is at the far southern end in Brownsville-based Cameron County and another 15 percent is in McAllen-based Hidalgo County. The rest of the district is mostly ranching country, with a handful of small towns that lean heavily Republican. Kleberg County is home to the vast grazing and oil lands of the 825,000-acre King Ranch, which is bigger than Rhode Island. South Padre Island, part of the lengthy national seashore, is a popular spring-break beach destination. In rural Willacy County, San Perlita has been ranked among the poorest school districts in the nation. With its 84 percent Hispanic population, the 34th has been a Democratic district. But the 2020 election raised questions about its political future. After Hillary Clinton got 59 percent in 2016 and President Barack Obama took 61 percent in 2012, Joe Biden was held to 52 percent.

Lloyd Doggett (D)

Elected 1994, 14th term, b. Oct 06, 1946; Austin, TX; University of TX, B.B.A., 1967; University of TX Law School, J.D., 1970; Methodist; Married (Libby Belk Doggett); 2 children; 4 grandchildren.

Elected Office: TX Senate, 1973-1985; TX Supreme Court justice, 1989-1994.

Professional Career: Practicing attorney, 1970-1989; Adjunct Professional, University of TX Law School, 1989-1994.

DC Office: 2307 RHOB 20515, 202-225-4865, Fax: 202-225-3073, doggett.house.gov

State Offices: Austin, 512-916-5921; San Antonio, 210-704-1080.

Committees: *Budget. Joint Taxation. Ways & Means*: Health (Chmn); Oversight; Select Revenue Measures.

Group Ratings

	ADA	ACLU	AFL-CIO	LCV	COC	HAFA	ACU	CFG	FRC
2020	**	83%	**	100%	-	5%	7%	**	-
2019	95%	C	90%	97%	45%	C	8%	35%	0%

Almanac Ratings 2019-2020

	Economy	Social	Foreign	Composite
Liberal	100%	56%	92%	83%
Conservative	0%	44%	8%	17%

Key Votes of the 116th Congress

1. U.S./Mex./Can. trade deal Y	5. Russia sanctions Y	9. Firearms background checks Y
2. First Coronavirus response Y	6. Troops in Syria Y	10. Spending at the border N
3. HEROES Act Y	7. Veto arms sales to Saudis Y	11. Marijuana liberalized rules Y
4. CASH Act Y	8. Defense $$$, veto override Y	12. Electoral College objections N

Election Results

Election	Name (Party)	Vote (%)		Cand. Spent	Ind. Exp. Support	Ind. Exp. Oppose
2020 General	Lloyd Doggett (D)..............................	176,373	(65%)	$379,163	$995	
	Jenny Sharon (R)...................................	80,795	(30%)	$11,406		$113
	Mark Loewe (L).....................	7,393	(3%)			
2020 Primary	Lloyd Doggett (D)...............................	51,169	(73%)			
	Rafael Alcoser (D)........................	18,922	(27%)			

Prior winning percentages: 2018 (71%), 2016 (63%), 2014 (63%), 2012 (64%), 2010 (53%), 2008 (66%), 2006 (67%), 2004 (68%), 2002 (84%), 2000 (85%), 1998 (85%), 1996 (56%), 1994 (56%)

Lloyd Doggett, first elected in 1994, is a liberal Democrat and a respected voice in his party on tax and poverty issues. He has been a vocal figure in Texas politics for a half-century. As a senior member of the House Ways and Means Committee, he has pressed for steps to reduce prescription drug prices and chairs the Health Subcommittee. Doggett was outspoken in seeking copies of former President Donald Trump's tax returns and raising questions about possible tax-code violations.

Doggett grew up in west Austin in the 1950s and 1960s, when it was concentrated with the homes of state and national leaders — families like the John Connollys and Lyndon Johnsons and J.J. Pickles. He finished first in his class at the University of Texas business school and was student body president; he then earned his law degree at UT. At age 26, he began his relentless career with election to the state Senate, which had been under the control of conservative Democrats. In the 1970s, as part of a large liberal bloc, he pushed for laws against job discrimination and cop-killer bullets, and for generic drugs. He has long been a close ally of trial lawyers, a strong force supporting liberal Democrats in Texas. He was one of the "Killer Bees" who hid out to prevent a quorum for changing the rules in the Democratic primary.

In 1984, he ran for the Senate, narrowly edging out two House members to win the Democratic nomination. His campaign team included political strategy stars James Carville, Mark McKinnon and Paul Begala. He lost the general election 59%-41% to Rep. Phil Gramm, a former Democrat who had switched parties. Doggett was elected to the Texas Supreme Court in 1988. When Democratic Rep. Jake Pickle retired after 31 years, Doggett ran for his Austin-based seat. He won the Democratic primary with token opposition and took the general 56%-40%.

Doggett is consistently a leader of liberal Democrats and one of the few Anglos to survive Republican redistricting efforts. At times highly partisan, he was a frequent critic of Republican Speaker Newt Gingrich when he first arrived in Congress and worked with Democratic leaders to raise questions about his ethics.

As a longtime member of the Ways and Means Committee, Doggett has used that perch to advocate his policy positions through the tax code. During nearly three decades in the House, he's put emphasis on eliminating tax shelters, lowering prescription drug prices, increasing use of electric cars and cracking down on overseas tax avoidance.

Doggett was persistent in seeking votes on his proposals to force Trump to release his tax returns for closed-door review. Once Democrats won House control and gained added leverage, Doggett pushed for moves by Ways and Means Chairman Richard Neal to get the records. Sunlight is "a weapon against corruption, bias and self-dealing," he told the Houston Chronicle in February 2019.

Republicans have sought and failed with numerous redistricting schemes to end Doggett's congressional career. In 2004, the GOP stretched his district 300 miles south to the Mexican border. But he took up the challenge. As other dislocated Texas Democrats took their fight to the courts, Doggett took his case to the voters of his new district. Doggett won the primary 64%-36%, with 88 percent of the vote in Travis County and holding Leticia Hinojosa, a former district court judge from McAllen, to a standoff in her base in Hidalgo County. He won handily in November. In 2010, he drew a tough challenge from Republican Donna Campbell, a doctor and hospital emergency department director who raised $765,000. But Doggett spent $1.2 million and won 53%-45%.

In 2011, Texas Republicans again carved up Doggett's stronghold, by attaching his liberal Austin base to a predominantly San Antonio district. Doggett easily won a three-way Democratic primary with 73 percent of the vote, then crushed Republican San Marcos Mayor Susan Narvaiz in November with 64 percent. In March 2017, after federal judges ruled that his district had been unconstitutionally gerrymandered, Doggett agreed and said the GOP map "reduces the amount of accessibility and accountability of elected officials, regardless of their party." Part of his success is attributed to maintaining a fundraising war chest that scares off potential Democratic rivals.

Long-standing Republican ambitions to remove Doggett through redistricting plans might take a back seat in 2022 to the practical politics for the GOP of maximizing their own seats. That likely will warrant the return of an Austin-based Democratic district. An alternative Republican hope might be that, at age 76 for the next election, Doggett might end his career. On the other hand, he might conclude that his position as the number-two Democrat at Ways and Means is sufficient reason to await the gavel.

TX-35: Eastern Bexar County, Eastern Travis County

Cook Partisan Voting Index: D+17

Population		Race and Ethnicity		Income	
Total	857,654	White	76.90%	Median Income	$53,898
Land area (sq. miles)	594	Black	9.20%	District Income Rank	347
Pop/ sq mi	1,444.42	Latino	60.60%	Poverty Rate	18.40%
Born in State	62.90%	Asian	1.80%	With health insurance	78.90%
		Two or more races	2.70%	Cash public assistance	1.60%
Age Groups		Other	9.40%	Food stamp/SNAP	15.30%
Under 18	23.80%				
18-34	29.70%	**Education**		**Work**	
35-64	35.90%	H.S grad or less	47.60%	White Collar	32.00%
Over 64	10.50%	Some college	27.10%	Sales and Service	43.40%
		College Degree, 4 yr	17.10%	Blue Collar	24.70%
Military		Post grad	8.10%	Government	14.30%
Veteran/ Active Duty	7.30%				

2020 Pres. Vote	Biden	188,164	(68%)	Trump	84,808	(31%)		
2016 Pres. Vote	Clinton	128,535	(64%)	Trump	61,136	(30%)	Johnson	7,664	(4%)

San Antonio/East Austin Corridor: "There are only four unique cities in America: Boston, New Orleans, San Francisco and San Antonio." This quote may well be apocryphal—it has been attributed to both Mark Twain and Will Rogers—and today one would have to add a few other cities to the list. But San Antonio still stands as a one-of-a-kind American locale. It started out as a collection of five Spanish missions, including the Mission San Antonio de Valero, better known today as the Alamo. From there it grew into a colonial capital, a hub for cattle drives, a railroad base, and eventually the heart of South Texas' increasingly transnational economy. Southerners and Mexicans played a large role in the city's growth, but Germans also settled here in large numbers in the mid-19th century. Frederick Law Olmsted referred to antebellum San Antonio as a "jumble of races, costumes, languages, and buildings," and as late as 1877, German speakers outnumbered Anglos and Mexican Americans. Even the city's politics ran against the grain. In 1920, a district that included Bexar County elected Republican Harry Wurzbach to Congress, the only member of his party the Lone Star State sent to Congress in the first half of the 20th century.

The 35th Congressional District of Texas covers many of the downtown features that helped make San Antonio unique. The Alamo, which had been maintained by the private Daughters of the Republic of Texas for 110 years, switched to management by the state's general land office soon after George P. Bush became land commissioner in 2015. The district takes in the 2.5-mile-long River Walk, lined with restaurants, museums and hotels; the 30-story, octagonal Tower Life Building; the Alamodome, a 65,000-seat basketball/football stadium; and the Henry B. Gonzalez Convention Center. On the east side of downtown, the city council has approved an innovation district as a center for bioscience start-ups and research. About 40 percent of the district's voters live in Bexar County.

There has been rapid growth in the often-thin strip of neighborhoods running along Interstate 35 through the outskirts of Texas Hill Country, in the German settlement of New Braunfels, the old mill town of San Marcos, and Kyle, a booming suburb of Austin. The remaining 30 percent of the district's population lives in southeastern Travis County, in the mostly Hispanic neighborhoods of east Austin. The Austin airport, a former military base, has had a spurt in traffic and expanded its facilities with nine new gates in 2019. That increase was halted by the coronavirus pandemic. A four-mile highway to the airport, including toll lanes, opened in September 2020. In July 2020, Tesla leaders announced

Austin would be the site of its second and larger assembly plant. Gentrification and high housing prices in Austin and San Antonio continue to be pressing civic concerns.

The district owes its unique shape to two goals of Republicans during the 2011 redistricting. They wanted to pack as many Democrats as possible into a single district, and they wanted to make a majority-Hispanic district that would endanger longtime Austin-based Democratic Rep. Lloyd Doggett in a primary. They attained their objective with a district that has become 61 percent Hispanic. In March 2017, a three-judge federal court ruled that the gerrymandered shape of the district was unconstitutional, though the panel did not offer a solution. A year later, the Supreme Court, in a 5-4 ruling, largely overturned that decision, though the majority agreed that the district was a racial gerrymander. Three other districts—the 10th, 21st and 25th—cover larger parts of Austin and Travis County than does the 35th. Each has consistently elected a Republican, even though the Travis County part of each of those districts votes heavily Democratic. The logic of that math, plus the continued growth in this area, suggests that the next round of redistricting will return to Austin its own Democratic district, which it had prior to 2005.

Brian Babin (R)

Elected 2014, 4th term, b. Mar 23, 1948; Port Arthur, TX; University of TX-Houston, Att., 1969; Lamur University, B.S., 1973; University of TX-Houston, D.D.S., 1976; Southern Baptist; Married (Roxanne Babin); 5 children; 13 grandchildren.

Military Career: TX Army National Guard 1969-1975; U.S. Air Force 1975-1979

Elected Office: Woodville City Council, 1981-1982, 1984-1989; Woodville Mayor, 1982-1984; Woodville School Board, 1992-1995.

Professional Career: Dentist, 1979-2014; TX St. Board of Dental Examiners, 1981-1987; TX Historical Comm., 1989-1995; Lower Neches Valley Authority, 1999-2014.

DC Office: 2236 RHOB 20515, 202-225-1555, Fax: 202-226-0396, babin.house.gov
State Offices: Deer Park, 832-780-0966; Orange, 409-883-8075; Woodville, 409-331-8066.

Committees: *Science, Space & Technology*: Space & Aeronautics (RMM). *Transportation & Infrastructure*: Highways & Transit; Water Resources & Environment.

Group Ratings

	ADA	ACLU	AFL-CIO	LCV	COC	HAFA	ACU	CFG	FRC
2020	**	15%	**	0%	-	91%	94%	**	-
2019	0%	C	35%	7%	75%	C	93%	77%	100%

Almanac Ratings 2019-2020

	Economy	Social	Foreign	Composite
Liberal	30%	12%	4%	16%
Conservative	70%	88%	96%	84%

Key Votes of the 116th Congress

1. U.S./Mex./Can. trade deal	Y	5. Russia sanctions	N	9. Firearms background checks	N
2. First Coronavirus response	N	6. Troops in Syria	N	10. Spending at the border	Y
3. HEROES Act	N	7. Veto arms sales to Saudis	N	11. Marijuana liberalized rules	N
4. CASH Act	N	8. Defense $$$, veto override	N	12. Electoral College objections	Y

Election Results

Election	Name (Party)	Vote (%)		Cand. Spent	Ind. Exp. Support	Ind. Exp. Oppose
2020 General	Brian Babin (R)	222,712	(74%)	$1,296,327	$15,676	$750
	Rashad Lewis (D)	73,418	(24%)	$11,528		
2020 Primary	Brian Babin (R)	75,277	(90%)			
	RJ Boatman (R)	8,774	(10%)			

Prior winning percentages: 2016 (89%), 2014 (76%)

Brian Babin, a dentist and local Republican leader who was elected in 2014, has sought to bolster NASA and make his own mark as the top Republican on the Space Subcommittee, an apt assignment for his district. In the majority, he had limited success. Babin was a loyal ally of President Donald Trump. But he clashed with other members of the conservative Freedom Caucus and quit the group in 2017, amid internal divisions among House Republicans over their attempts to repeal the Affordable Care Act.

Babin grew up in Beaumont, attended Lamar University and got his degree in dentistry at the University of Texas at Houston; friends refer to him as "Doc Babin." After dental school, he served overseas in the Air Force, and later was an airborne artilleryman in the Army Reserve. He settled in Woodville in rural Tyler County, where he maintained his dental practice. Babin entered local politics by serving as an alderman and mayor of Woodville. He was a regional chairman for Ronald Reagan's 1980 presidential campaign and claimed some credit for the shift to the Republican Party in these parts of east Texas that had been "yellow dog" conservative Democratic territory. When the colorful Democratic Rep. Charlie Wilson retired in 1996, Babin ran for the seat, only to lose to Democrat Jim Turner 52%-46%. He tried again two years later and lost by a wider margin.

When the more suburban 36th became open in 2014, he ran in the 12-candidate field. In the March primary, Babin ran first with 33 percent of the vote, followed by tea-party favorite Ben Streusand at 23 percent. In the May runoff, Streusand brought up Babin's role in a long-ago Texas campaign finance scandal, noting that he received $37,000 in illegal corporate money from his friend, businessman Peter Cloeren, when he ran for the House in 1996. The FEC gave Babin a light penalty, ordering him to pay $30,000 in civil fines. His years of local political work gave him the edge. Streusand, a Houston banker who lived outside the district, led in Harris County with 65 percent of the vote, but he underperformed on turnout as Harris cast only one-third of the vote. Babin rolled up huge majorities in the rural areas, including 85 percent in his native Tyler County. He won the runoff, 58%-42%. The general election was largely a formality. He has not been seriously challenged.

Babin has served on two committees well-suited to his district: Transportation and Infrastructure; and Science, Space and Technology. In his first year, Babin became chairman of the Space Subcommittee. He wanted to resume manned space flight as NASA's top priority, and to end NASA's reliance on other nations to send astronauts to the International Space Station. He supported expansion of commercial space flight and criticized the agency's lack of focus. "NASA's primary missions are aeronautics and human spaceflight," he told the Houston Chronicle. "We seem to have gotten off of that in many respects."

With other Texans, Babin sought to revitalize the Johnson Space Center, whose share of the NASA budget dropped from about half to less than one-fourth during the Obama administration. The 2017 NASA authorization bill, which he helped to enact, included Babin's provision to care for former astronauts and enhance public understanding of the effects of spaceflight on the human body. With Democratic Rep. Ami Bera of California, Babin wrote that Trump's call in December 2017 for a return to manned space flight was "welcome and encouraging news."

In 2018, Babin pursued more ambitious legislation for NASA. In April, the Science Committee approved a bill, with bipartisan support, that boosted funds for the International Space Station. Babin called it "an important step forward for America's economic competitiveness." But the bill failed to generate enough support for Republican leaders to bring it to the House floor that year. In October 2020, Babin joined a bipartisan group that backed the new Space Force, with his goal of educating other House members about national security objectives in space.

On his other committee, Babin won approval in 2016 of two provisions in the water resources bill, which the Transportation Committee helped enact. They improved the navigation and maintenance of the Houston Ship Channel. In 2018, he took the leadership in creating—and then co-chairing—the I-14 Caucus, which advocated a proposed new east-west interstate in the South that would serve "forts and ports," including Beaumont Texas. On the water resources bill that was enacted in December 2020, he cited provisions that benefited Houston and the region's energy sector, including additional widening and dredging of the ship channel.

In March 2017, Babin voiced disappointment that the Freedom Caucus delayed House approval of the revision of the Affordable Care Act. "I worked very hard to get President Trump elected," Babin said. "So we need to support that agenda." The following month, he quit the caucus and told Fox Business Network, "we have the opportunity of a lifetime … so we must make the best use of our opportunity." In May, the House narrowly passed the bill. It died in the Senate.

Following the 2020 presidential election, Babin organized a post-election "integrity rally" in Lumberton Texas. "This thing is going to continue until we are shown that it was a legitimate election and these questions about all these concerning issues anomalies are answered," Babin said, according to KBMT television in Beaumont.

TX-36: Harris County, Southeast Texas

Cook Partisan Voting Index: R+25

Population		Race and Ethnicity		Income	
Total	758,238	White	82.40%	Median Income	$62,206
Land area (sq. miles)	7,126	Black	9.00%	District Income Rank	231
Pop/ sq mi	106.41	Latino	28.50%	Poverty Rate	13.00%
Born in State	68.80%	Asian	1.80%	With health insurance	80.60%
		Two or more races	2.80%	Cash public assistance	1.50%
Age Groups		Other	4.10%	Food stamp/SNAP	10.60%
Under 18	25.10%				
18-34	22.00%	**Education**		**Work**	
35-64	38.40%	H.S grad or less	48.30%	White Collar	32.70%
Over 64	14.50%	Some college	32.20%	Sales and Service	36.00%
		College Degree, 4 yr	13.80%	Blue Collar	31.30%
Military		Post grad	5.60%	Government	13.90%
Veteran/ Active Duty	8.00%				

2020 Pres. Vote	Trump	221,600	(72%)	Biden	82,881	(27%)			
2016 Pres. Vote	Trump	183,176	(72%)	Clinton	64,225	(25%)	Johnson	5,704	(2%)

Eastern Houston Suburbs : East Texas is thick with landmarks of Lone Star history. There's still an Indian reservation in Polk County, and the swampland Big Thicket National Preserve reminds you of what the area looked like before humans first settled the region some 2,500 years ago. These were some of the first parts of Texas to be settled by Anglos; Anahuac in Chambers County was a port of entry for early colonists. Later, the area became a destination for other colonists during the famed "Runaway Scrape," as they fled eastward, leaving beds unmade and breakfasts sitting on the table, in the face of Santa Anna's approaching army. Today, much of East Texas looks frozen in time —farm towns that the railroads passed by and the interstates overlooked. Of course, some things have changed. Racial segregation has been abolished—this area is home to a large portion of the state's rural Black population—and the isolation of the small towns has been reduced.

Urban development, sprinting outward from Houston's loop freeways, is spreading in between the pine forests and reservoirs. The industrial age is on steroids in Baytown. The growth of Houston's port has been an incentive. Exxon began production in 2018 at its petrochemical plant, with a major expansion of chemical manufacturing. Chevron completed the $6 billion expansion of its "methane cracker," which is instrumental in the production of plastics. JSW, an Indian steelmakers, has expanded its mill in Baytown.

The southeastern corner of Harris County tends to be more upscale, populated by highly educated employees of the Lyndon B. Johnson Space Center and the space and aeronautics industry that grew around it. The location of that iconic center, which opened in 1961, was influenced by its namesake, the Texas senator who was the majority leader when the site was selected and later became the 36th president and a continuing advocate of NASA. After its discouraging recent years, during which the Houston Press in 2014 reported that the JSC "lost its identity and purpose" with the demise of NASA's manned space flights and roughly half its buildings were torn down or consolidated, several factors have contributed to its brighter prospects, including the boom in commercial space flight.

The 36th Congressional District of Texas was a compromise: Both suburban Houston Republicans and East Texas Republicans wanted a new congressional district, and the result is one evenly divided between the two groups. About half of the district's population lives in a collection of eight lightly populated counties, where lumbering, farming, ranching, and oil and gas dominate. The other half of the district's population lives in the suburbs on the eastern edge of Harris County. They include blue-collar Baytown, Deer Park, La Porte and part of Pasadena, near the Houston Ship Channel. Further south are Clear Lake, Taylor Lake Village and part of Webster. The district is among the top 5 percent of the most Republican nationwide, with a Cook PVI of +25 for Republicans. Donald Trump got 72 percent in each of his campaigns; Mitt Romney took 73 percent in 2012.

UTAH

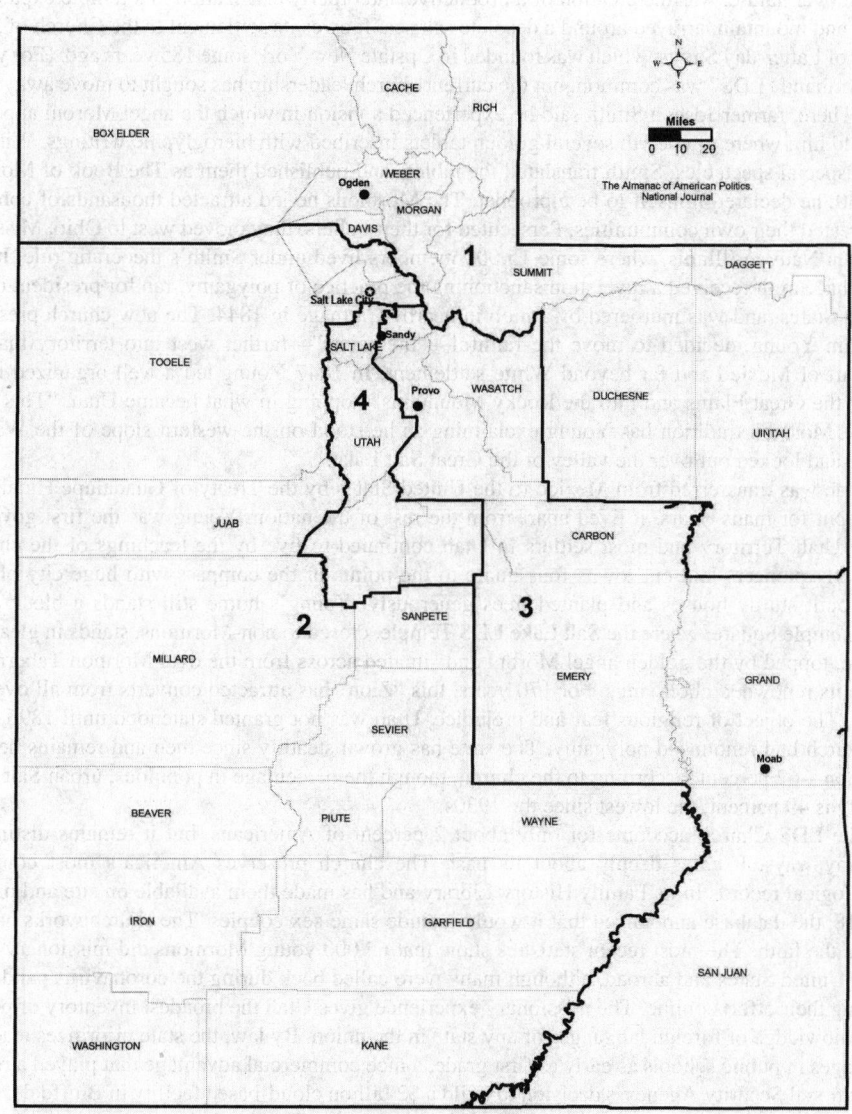

CACHE

RICH

BOX ELDER

WEBER

Ogden

MORGAN

DAVIS

SUMMIT

DAGGETT

Miles

0   10   20

The Almanac of American Politics.
National Journal

1

SALT LAKE CITY

Sandy

SALT LAKE

TOOELE

Provo

WASATCH

DUCHESNE

4

UINTAH

UTAH

JUAB

CARBON

SANPETE

3

MILLARD

EMERY

GRAND

2

SEVIER

Moab

BEAVER

PIUTE

WAYNE

IRON

GARFIELD

SAN JUAN

WASHINGTON

KANE

Congressional district boundaries were first effective for 2012.

Utah has long been one of the most Republican states in the union. The highly religious state had reservations about President Donald Trump, and Utahns seemed to tolerate Sen. Mitt Romney's 2019 vote to convict in Trump's impeachment. But in the 2020 presidential election, Utah decided that Trump was still preferable to Joe Biden, by a margin of 20 points.

Other American states were founded by leaders of religious sects—Massachusetts, Connecticut, Pennsylvania—but only in colonial times and along waters navigable by ocean ships. Utah, a triumph of man over nature, was the creation of a productive and orderly civilization in a remote expanse of desert and mountain, arrayed around a desolate salt sea. It owes its settlement to the Church of Jesus Christ of Latter-day Saints, which was founded in Upstate New York some 185 years ago. (For years, the shorthand "LDS" was common, but the current church leadership has sought to move away from that.) There, farmer Joseph Smith said he experienced a vision in which the angel Moroni appeared and told him where to unearth several golden tablets inscribed with hieroglyphic writings. With the aid of special spectacles, Smith translated the tablets and published them as The Book of Mormon in 1830; he declared himself to be a prophet. The Mormons he led attracted thousands of converts and created their own communities. Persecuted for their beliefs, they moved west to Ohio, Missouri, and then Nauvoo Illinois, where some 15,000 members lived under Smith's theocratic rule. It was there that Smith received a revelation sanctioning the practice of polygamy, ran for president of the United States, and was murdered by a mob in nearby Carthage in 1844. The new church president, Brigham Young, decided to move the faithful—"the saints"—farther west into territory that was still part of Mexico and far beyond White settlement. In 1847 Young led a well-organized march across the Great Plains and into the Rocky Mountains, stopping in what became Utah. "This is the place," Mormon tradition has Young exclaiming as he stood on the western slope of the Wasatch Range and looked out over the valley of the Great Salt Lake.

Utah was transferred from Mexico to the United States by the Treaty of Guadalupe Hidalgo of 1848, but for many years, it lived apart from the rest of the nation. Young was the first governor of the Utah Territory and most settlers in Utah continued to live by the teachings of the church. The early pioneers laid out towns foursquare to the points of the compass with huge city blocks. They built sturdy houses and planted trees generously. Young's home still stands a block away from Temple Square, where the Salt Lake LDS Temple, closed to non-Mormons, stands in gleaming granite, topped by the golden angel Moroni and situated across from the oval Mormon Tabernacle, where its renowned choir sings. For 170 years, this "Zion" has attracted converts from all over the world. The object of religious fear and prejudice, Utah was not granted statehood until 1896, after the church had renounced polygamy. The state has grown steadily since then and remains heavily Mormon—62 percent, according to the church, though the percentage in populous, urban Salt Lake County is 49 percent, the lowest since the 1930s.

The LDS Church accounts for only about 2 percent of Americans, but it remains distinctive in many ways. It cares deeply about its past. The church preserves America's most complete genealogical records in its Family History Library and has made them available on site and online; in 2018, the database announced that it would include same-sex couples. The church works hard to spread the faith: The most recent statistics show that 65,000 young Mormons did missionary work in the United States and abroad, although many were called back during the coronavirus pandemic, pushing their efforts online. The missionary experience gives Utah the broadest inventory of people with knowledge of foreign languages of any state in the union. By law, the state prioritizes teaching languages in public schools as early as first grade, a nice commercial advantage that played a role in the National Security Agency's decision to build a $2 billion cloud-based facility in Bluffdale, south of Salt Lake City. It's now joined by a 1.5-million-square-foot Facebook data center.

Mormon teaching prohibits the consumption of tobacco, alcohol, coffee and tea. Only in 2009, amid concerns about the impact on tourism, could you finally get a drink served at a bar without joining a private club, and even then it had to be poured out of sight, behind what became known as a "Zion curtain." After years of trying, lawmakers finally got rid of the Zion curtain in 2017. The same year, the state lowered the blood alcohol limit from .08 to .05, the nation's lowest threshold. (Possibly related: Utahns buy candy at the highest rate in the United States, about 50 percent higher than the national average.)

The church encourages hard work and large families; Utah ranks first in the nation for the share of its population under 18 (31 percent) and between 19 and 25 (11 percent). On average, Mormons are better educated, work longer hours, and earn more money than Americans at large. The LDS Church has no paid clergy, but members serve in positions for which they are chosen, conducting religious services but also keeping in touch with members and counseling them when they need help. The church also maintains its own social-service organizations. While American mainline denominations have been losing members, the LDS Church is growing. Starting with just 30 members, the church took a century to reach 1 million. There were 2.9 million Mormons in 1970, 5 million in 1982 and about 16.1 million today. The United States has 6.6 million members in 14,255 congregations, but about three-fifths of LDS members today live outside the U.S.

In some ways, Utah resembles the America of the 1950s. In recent years, it has had the highest percentage of households headed by married couples and households with children, the highest fertility rate for non-Hispanic Whites, the youngest median age of first marriages, and the lowest birth rate for unmarried women. Sometimes this makes its economic statistics misleading: Utah has a per capita income 11 percent below the national average—because all those kids aren't earning salaries —yet the median household income is 23 percent above the national average and the poverty rate is more than three full percentage points below the nation's as a whole. It also has the highest rate of volunteerism and charitable giving. Utahns' trusting nature even prompted state Attorney General Sean Reyes to note that Utahns are "sadly known" for falling for scams that take advantage of personal relationships. Utah was the first state where women voted and it elected the first female state senator. But in recent years, the percentage of women in elected office has been below the national average.

Historically, Utah has been a bastion of social conservatism. The LDS Church's opposition to abortion rights is widely shared by its membership, and in 2020, the state enacted a law that would ban most abortions if Roe v. Wade was overturned, including felony charges for the physician and woman involved. The church has always discouraged gambling; Utah is one of just two states (Hawaii is the other) without any legal gambling. The church has made notable overtures to the LGBT community in recent years. In 2019, the church declared that "while we cannot change the Lord's doctrine, we want our members and our policies to be considerate of those struggling with the challenges of mortality." That same year, the church backed a change to state licensing requirements that banned "gay conversion therapy." The state also repealed a 1973 law criminalizing sex outside of marriage. In 2020, Utah passed a law decriminalizing bigamy; doing so removed a barrier to cooperation by abuse victims.

While Utah's Black population—1 percent—is among the nation's lowest, its Hispanic population now exceeds 14 percent. While that's lower than Arizona or Nevada, it still represents a sharp contrast with Utah's past. Utah's Hispanic population has grown by more than a quarter over the past decade, or more than double the roughly 11 percent growth among non-Hispanic Whites. The Hispanic population is also younger than the state's population as a whole, making it a growing demographic force. The Asian population has grown even faster, although from a small base. These shifts have evoked a different response in Utah than in Arizona. Utah businesses have been interested in maintaining an immigrant work force, and LDS leaders, many with experience as overseas missionaries, have expressed compassion. In 2018, the church threw its weight behind protection for "dreamers" who were brought illegally to the United States as children, saying that while "immigration is a complex and sometimes divisive issue … we believe that our first priority is to love and care for one another as Jesus Christ taught." In 2019, Gov. Gary Herbert referenced the state's founding generation in affirming his state's willingness to continue resettling refugees. "We empathize deeply with individuals and groups who have been forced from their homes, and we love giving them a new home and a new life," he said.

Overall, Utah has been on a growth spurt. From 2000 to 2010, the state's population rose 24 percent, and since 2010, it has grown by another 18.4 percent, faster than any state. Two Utah metro areas ranked among the 10 fastest-growing in the nation during the past decade: St. George, which is closer to Las Vegas than Salt Lake City, and Provo-Orem. Meanwhile, Wasatch County (Heber City), Morgan County (suburban Salt Lake City and Ogden), Washington County (St. George), and Utah County (Provo) have all grown by at least 22 percent since 2010, and Davis County (suburban Salt Lake City) and Summit County (Park City) have grown by 15 percent. One reason for this growth has been the scenery, which includes five national parks—Arches, Bryce Canyon, Canyonlands, Capitol Reef and Zion—and countless pleasant vistas that have made Utah a popular destination for shooting films and TV shows. The drilling industry has sometimes faced challenges in expanding its footprint in the state; in 2020, the Trump administration scuttled plans to auction tens of thousands of acres to oil and gas interests, after complaints by officials in Grand County and Moab, which are dependent on tourism.

Before World War II, Utah saw itself as a colonial victim of East Coast bankers and financiers, and Mormons saw themselves as suffering religious discrimination and bigotry—with considerable cause. Utah's income levels were well below the national average, and its cost of living was higher. In political terms, this perspective translated into Democratic allegiance. In 1940, Utah was represented by staunch New Dealers in Congress and voted 62%-38% for Franklin Roosevelt. Since then, Utah has come to see itself as a busy generator of wealth, pushing Mormons and Utahns toward the GOP. Utah has not voted Democratic for president since 1964, it hasn't elected a Democratic governor since Scott Matheson in 1980, and it hasn't sent a Democratic senator to Washington since 1970. In fact, as the Salt Lake Tribune's Robert Gehrke has noted, no Utah Democrat since 1994 has come within 15 points of winning any of those races, and the last time a Democrat won any statewide office was in the 1996 attorney general race.

Salt Lake City has been the state's primary pocket of liberalism, with the resort area of Park City a close second. The neighborhoods close to the church headquarters, with their gracious old houses and a smaller street grid, have attracted academic and professional newcomers and so have become the most heavily "gentile" (the Mormon term for non-Mormons) part of the state. Starting in 2008, Democrats won control of the Salt Lake County government and elected most of its state legislators. But Democrats have won few legislative seats in the rest of the state. The Republican dominance has grown so great that GOP factions have sometimes fought over control of the party. In an activist-dominated convention in 2010, insurgent Mike Lee won enough votes to keep incumbent Sen. Robert Bennett off the primary ballot; after that, establishment Republicans pushed successfully to allow candidates alternate paths to the primary.

The 2016 presidential race in Utah was the most topsy-turvy in memory. The eventual Republican nominee, Donald Trump, got a measly 14 percent of the GOP primary vote, and he was so unpopular that even Democratic nominee Hillary Clinton made the rare move of spending general election money in the state, sending a mailer to Utah voters in late August. About two weeks before the election, the Trump campaign felt pressed to dispatch vice presidential nominee Mike Pence to Salt Lake City, a move unheard of for a Republican nominee. While native son Romney had won the state with 73 percent in 2012, Trump won it with just 46 percent four years later, garnering 225,000 fewer votes statewide than Romney had. Most of the "missing" Republican vote went to Evan McMullin, a third-party Utah resident and LDS member, who took 21.5 percent. In 2018, Democrat Ben McAdams, the Salt Lake County mayor, narrowly ousted GOP Rep. Mia Love, and several ballot initiative results pleased center-left voters in the state: Medical marijuana passed with 53 percent, an expansion of Medicaid under the Affordable Care Act passed with 53 percent, and a redistricting commission passed with just over 50 percent.

In 2020, there was no quirky, multi-candidate presidential field; the third party and write-in vote declined from 26 percent to 5 percent. In the end, Trump's margin over the Democratic nominee expanded from 18 points to 20, making Utah one of only a half-dozen states where Trump improved his margin in 2020, and making the biggest improvement in any state he won. In fact, in a reversal from the pattern in most states, Utah gave Trump stronger margins in several more populated counties in 2020, including Utah, Davis, and Cache (Logan); Trump expanded his margin of victory by between three and 10 points in each. Biden did manage to flip Grand County, and he marginally expanded the winning margins in the two counties Clinton had won, Salt Lake and Summit. All told, Biden won nearly 250,000 more votes than Clinton had, almost half of this increase coming from Salt Lake County. However, McAdams was narrowly ousted from his House seat in 2020, leaving the congressional delegation all-Republican once again. "Change will come, but not in a couple cycles —more like a couple decades," wrote the Tribune'sGehrke.

Population		Race and Ethnicity		Income	
Total	3,205,958	White	87.30%	Median Income	75,780
Land area (sq. miles)	82,170	Black	1.20%	State Income Rank	11 out of 50
Pop/ sq mi	39.02	Latino	14.40%	Poverty Rate	8.90%
Born in state	61.70%	Asian	3.70%	With health insurance	90.30%
		Two or more races	3.20%	Cash public assistance	1.30%
Age Groups		Other	5.90%	Food stamp/SNAP	7.7%
Under 18	29.00%				
18-34	26.00%	Education		Work	
35-64	33.50%	H.S grad or less	30.00%	White Collar	40.40%
Over 64	11.40%	Some college	35.20%	Sales and Service	37.30%
		College Degree, 4 yr	23.40%	Blue Collar	22.30%
Military		Post grad	11.30%	Government	14.80%
Veteran/ Active Duty	5.40%				

Presidential Politics

2020 Primary (D)	Sanders (D)	79,728(36%)	Biden (D)	40,674(18%)	Warren (D)		35,727(16%)
	Bloomberg (D)	33,991(15%)	Buttigieg (D)	18,734 (8%)			
2016 Caucus (D)	Sanders (D)	62,991(79%)	Clinton (D)	16,162(20%)			
2016 Caucus (R)	Cruz (R)	132,904(69%)	Kasich (R)	31,992(17%)	Trump (R)		26,434(14%)
2020 Pres. Vote	Trump (R)	865,140(57%)	Biden (D)	560,282(37%)			
2016 Pres. Vote	Trump (R)	515,231(45%)	Clinton (D)	310,676(27%)	McMullin (I)		243,690(21%)
	Johnson (L)	39,608 (3%)					

Utah has been the most Republican state in seven of the past 11 presidential elections, though it grew slightly less ruby red during the Donald Trump era. Joe Biden's 37.7 percent showing in 2020 may not sound like a lot, but it was the best Democratic performance since President Lyndon Johnson carried the state in 1964.

Biden's relatively strong showing came after years of booming growth in the state, with the blue trend of Salt Lake County and nearby Summit County (Park City) slightly outpacing booming population growth in the state's deeply conservative, heavily Mormon rural areas. Barack Obama's 296-win in Salt Lake County was a breakthrough in 2008, but he still took just 34.4 percent of the vote statewide. In 2012, when Republicans nominated Mitt Romney, a Mormon who was widely known for his work in rescuing the 2002 Salt Lake City Winter Olympics, the state saw the biggest Republican swing in the nation, as Romney won 73%-25% and carried Salt Lake County 58%-38%.

Mormons' skepticism towards Trump made for an odd race in the state in 2016, and an independent bid by Utah native Evan McMullin, a Mormon and former senior GOP congressional aide, further complicated the picture. Trump won the state over Hillary Clinton, 46%-28%, with McMullin taking 21 percent, his best showing by far. Clinton carried Salt Lake and Summit counties.

The state swung back some in 2020, even with Romney a constant thorn in Trump's side. Both Trump and Biden picked up votes in a two-party race. Trump ran ahead of his 2016 numbers in six counties including Utah County (Provo), but Biden improved in Salt Lake and Summit and flipped tiny Grand County (Moab and Arches National Park); Trump prevailed, 58.2%-37.7%.

In their March 2016 caucus, Democrats gave Vermont Sen. Bernie Sanders a 79%-20% landslide over Clinton. In the GOP caucus, Romney cut radio ads for Sen. Ted Cruz in Utah, and the Texan captured 70 percent of the vote, to Ohio Gov. John Kasich's 17 percent and Trump's 14 percent. Utah switched to a primary and voted on Super Tuesday in 2020; Sanders rallied there and won 36%-18% over Biden, a rare bright spot as it was just one of four states he carried that night and seven he won all campaign.

Congressional Districts

117th Congress Lineup	4R	116th Congress Lineup	1D 3R

Democrats twice won a seat in the past decade after Republicans drew Utah's districts in 2012 and expected to sweep the delegation, including a new fourth seat. The two Republicans who won that seat—Mia Love and Burgess Owens—have both been African-Americans. With a Republican governor and legislature, it's likely they will reallocate a few precincts and make it more difficult for Democrats to prevail again in this state that has been comfortably Republican.

The next round could be a reprise of the 2012 redistricting when many Utah Republicans argued, in their party's interest, that all the state's districts should contain both urban and rural areas, splitting Democratic-leaning Salt Lake City like a "pizza pie." After lengthy debate and some Republican internal bickering, the legislature agreed the new 4th District would be a "doughnut hole," with its core in the heavily Republican suburbs south of Salt Lake City and the northern reaches of prohibitively Republican northern Utah County. Each of the remaining three districts included parts of the metropolitan area plus vast open spaces.

In 2012, Democratic Rep. Jim Matheson ran in the 4th. Like Houdini, he cheated the Republicans' plan, prevailing by 768 votes. The feat was all the more impressive, given that Republican presidential nominee Mitt Romney won 68 percent in the 4th. Love prevailed twice—though by unexpectedly narrow margins, before the popularity of Salt Lake County Mayor Ben McAdams and the unpopularity of President Donald Trump worked against her in 2018. This time, she lost by 694 votes. Even with the improved performance of Trump in 2020, the three victories by Love and Owens took no more than 54 percent. Republican map-drawers likely will be more rigorous in advancing their interests the next time.

Spencer J. Cox (R)

Elected 2020. term expires 2025, 1st term; b. July 11, 1975; Fairview, UT; Utah State University, B.A., 1998; Washington and Lee University, J.D., 2001; Mormon; Married (Abby); 4 children.

Elected Office: City councilor and Mayor, Fairview; Commissioner, Sanpete County, 2009-13, State House, 2013; Lt. Gov., 2013-21.

Professional Career: Atty, Fabian and Clendenin; VP and general counsel, CentraCom Interactive.

Office: 350 North State St. Suite 200, Salt Lake City, 84114-2220; 801-538-1000; Fax: 801-538-1133
Lt. Gov.: Deidre Henderson (R); **Atty. Gen:** Sean Reyes (R)
State Legislature: Senate: 6D, 23R   **House:** 17D, 58R

Election Results

Election	Name (Party)	Vote (%)
2020 General	Spencer Cox (R)...	918,754 (63%)
	Chris Peterson (D)...	442,754 (30%)
	Daniel Cottam (L)..	51,393 (4%)
2020 Primary	Spencer Cox (R)...	190,505 (36%)
	Jon Huntsman (R)...	184,246 (35%)
	Greg Hughes (R)...	110,835 (21%)
	Thomas Wright (R)...	41,532 (8%)

Prior winning percentage: 2012 (68%), 2010 (64%)

Spencer Cox was elected governor of Utah in 2020 after surviving a competitive Republican primary. Cox—like Gary Herbert, the governor with whom he served as lieutenant governor—has carved out a pragmatic path in solidly red Utah.

Cox grew up as the oldest of eight children in rural Fairview, where his family had lived for six generations. In addition to operating a 150-acre farm, the family ran CentraCom, a telecommunications company bought by his grandfather in 1919. (The Cox family sold the company in 2001 but continued to manage it.) When he was 10, Cox's parents divorced, and he later told of being bullied at school, once being stuffed in a trash can in sixth grade. Cox considered suicide, he told the Salt Lake Tribune. "I was very fortunate to have loving parents and family—specifically, a stepmom who really came to my rescue and helped to save me," he told the newspaper. "It gave me a little insight into the plight of the underdog." Cox earned an associate's degree at nearby Snow College, then went on a two-year Mormon mission in Mexico. After returning, he married Abby, who had grown up on a nearby ranch, and followed her to Utah State University, where he earned his bachelor's degree. Cox then earned his law degree at Washington & Lee University, clerked for a federal district judge, and worked for a law firm in Salt Lake City. But he moved back to Fairview in 2008 after his father asked him to help run CentraCom. "The Coxes live in a Norman Rockwell painting," the Deseret News wrote in 2014. "Their handsome, two-story brick home sits on seven acres that overlook the valley, backed by a small red barn. On a summer day, the only sounds are meadowlarks, aspen stirring in the breeze and the clack-clack-clack of large Rain Bird sprinklers in the adjacent alfalfa fields."

In Fairview, with a population of about 1,200, Cox began his political rise. He was appointed to a vacant city council seat, then was elected mayor, followed by a stint on the Sanpete County Commission. In 2012, Cox won a state House seat, but he didn't serve long: The following year, at age 38, Cox was tapped by Herbert to succeed departing Lt. Gov. Greg Bell. Cox's appointment was unexpected: The Deseret News' political columnists, LaVarr Webb and Frank Pignanelli, had not included Cox on a list of more than 30 potential candidates for the post. Cox made one demand before taking the job—that he would be able to commute from Fairview to Salt Lake City, a four-hour round trip. As lieutenant governor, Cox attracted national notice when he gave a speech after the mass shooting at a gay nightclub in Orlando in which he offered support for LGBT rights and apologized for his own past mistreatment of fellow students he later learned were gay. "How did you feel when you heard that 49 people had been gunned down by a self-proclaimed terrorist?" Cox asked. "That's the easy question. Here's the hard one: Did that feeling change when you found out the shooting was at a gay bar at 2 a.m.? If that feeling changed, we're doing something wrong." Cox was also tasked with improving the quality of life for the homeless population of Salt Lake City. On occasion, he criticized President Donald Trump.

The governorship, which Herbert had held since 2009, was coming open in 2020, and Cox won Herbert's endorsement to replace him. Both men, while conservative, had generally taken stances in line with the party's more pragmatic wing, including positions supportive of the LGBT community and immigrants. But Cox did not have a free ride to the nomination. Jon Huntsman Jr., Herbert's predecessor as governor, announced a comeback bid, and several other candidates joined the race, including former House Speaker Greg Hughes and former state GOP Chairman Thomas Wright. By then, however, Huntsman had alienated both wings of the party, first by leaving the governorship to become President Barack Obama's ambassador to China, and then by accepting President Donald Trump's offer to become ambassador to Russia. It didn't help that Huntsman was hobbled by the coronavirus during the home stretch of the primary campaign, even as Cox was taking a key, public-facing role in managing the pandemic. Hughes accused Cox of being a "never-Trumper," but Cox, like his primary rivals, reiterated his support for Trump's reelection. In the end, Cox won the primary with 36 percent, edging Huntsman with 35 percent, Hughes with 21 percent, and Wright with 8 percent.

Once Huntsman decided against running in the fall as a write-in candidate, the general election was anti-climactic, as is usually the case in Utah. Cox faced University of Utah law professor Chris Peterson, who had served during the Obama administration in the Consumer Financial Protection Bureau. Cox won, 63%-30%, running six points ahead of Trump in the state. In populous Salt Lake County, Cox managed an impressive five-point victory even as Joe Biden was winning the county by 11 points. In the two other Utah counties Biden won, Summit (Park City) and Grand (Moab), Peterson noticeably underperformed Biden. The most notable artifact from the general election, however, was probably the joint video Cox and Peterson cut calling for political civility, which won praise on social media.

Mike Lee (R)

Elected 2010, term expires 2022, 2nd term, b. Jun 04, 1971; Mesa, AZ; Brigham Young University, B.A., 1994; Brigham Young University, J.D., 1997; Mormon; Married (Sharon Lee); 3 children.

Professional Career: Law Clerk, Judge Samuel Alito, U.S Court of Appeals, 1998-1999; Practicing attorney, 1999-2002; Assistant U.S Attorney, 2002-2005; Gen. Counsel, Gov. Jon Huntsman, 2005-2006; Law Clerk, Supreme Court Justice Samuel Alito, 2006-2007; Practicing attorney, 2007-2010.

DC Office: 361-A RSOB 20510, 202-224-5444, Fax: 202-228-1168, lee.senate.gov

State Offices: Ogden, 801-392-9633; Salt Lake City, 801-524-5933; St. George, 435-628-5514.

Committees: *Aging. Commerce, Science & Transportation*: Aviation Safety, Operations & Innovations; Communications, Media & Broadband; Consumer Protection, Product Safety & Data Security; Space & Science. *Energy & Natural Resources*: National Parks; Public Lands, Forests & Mining (RMM); Water & Power. *Joint Economic (RMM). Judiciary*: Competition Policy, Antitrust & Consumer Rights (RMM); Constitution; Criminal Justice & Counterterrorism; Federal Courts, Oversight, Agency Action & Federal Rights.

Group Ratings

	ADA	ACLU	AFL-CIO	LCV	COC	HAFA	ACU	CFG	FRC
2020	-	46%	-	0%	-	85%	99%	-	-
2019	15%	C	0%	0%	66%	C	99%	100%	100%

Almanac Ratings 2019-2020

	Economy	Social	Foreign	Composite
Liberal	11%	11%	28%	17%
Conservative	89%	89%	72%	83%

Key Votes of the 116th Congress

1. EPA clean energy rules	N	5. Russia sanctions	N	9. Barr as Atty. General	Y
2. U.S./Mex./Can. trade deal	Y	6. Troops in SYR, AFG	N	10. Spending at the border	N
3. Cut unemployment benefits	Y	7. Veto arms sales to Saudis	Y	11. Coney Barrett to Sup. Ct.	Y
4. Shelton to Fed Reserve	Y	8. Defense $$$, veto override	N	12. Electoral College objections	N

Election Results

Election	Name (Party)	Vote (%)		Cand. Spent	Ind. Exp. Support	Ind. Exp. Oppose
2016 General	Mike Lee (R)...................................... 760,220	(68%)	$4,420,800	$316,173
	Misty Snow (D)................................... 301,858	(27%)	$95,199	
	Stoney Fonua (I)................................. 27,339	(3%)		
2016 Primary	Mike Lee (R)................................. Unopposed			

Prior winning percentages: 2016 (68%), 2010 (62%)

Utah's senior senator is Mike Lee, who in 2010 ousted the incumbent at the Republican State Convention. Though low-key and outwardly unassuming, Lee has strong convictions, especially an abiding and wide-ranging interest in reducing the power of the federal government. After refusing to endorse fellow Republican Donald Trump in the 2016 presidential election, Lee became an outspoken foe of his impeachment and strategized with Trump allies during his first Senate trial—as well as Trump's choices for Supreme Court nominees. He also emerged as a leading Big Tech critic and has backed antitrust action. His independence appears to play well in Utah, despite the state's hostility to former President Trump and its booming tech business.

Lee grew up in Provo, where his father, Rex Lee, was the founding dean of Brigham Young University's law school. As a boy, Mike Lee lived part time in McLean Virginia, when his father was an assistant attorney general from 1975 to 1976 and solicitor general from 1981 to 1985. Lee remembers watching his father argue cases before the Supreme Court. "It took me a while before I realized it wasn't entirely an ordinary experience to get to do that frequently," he recalled. Lee returned to Provo at 14 and later graduated from college and law school at Brigham Young. He clerked for two federal judges, including Samuel Alito. He practiced law in Washington D.C. and in Utah, where he served as legal counsel to Republican Gov. Jon Huntsman. In 2006, after Alito was confirmed to the Supreme Court, Lee returned to Washington to clerk for him once again.

Lee said he decided to challenge 18-year Senate veteran Bob Bennett in 2009 after Congress passed the $700 billion bailout of the financial industry and the $787 billion stimulus bill that President Barack Obama sought. "The Republican Party had in so many ways deviated from what it professes," Lee said. Bennett was a solid conservative, but he had voted for the Troubled Asset Relief Program for the financial industry and had been a chief supporter of bipartisan health care legislation with Democratic Sen. Ron Wyden of Oregon.

Bennett was endorsed by soon-to-be presidential nominee Mitt Romney and Utah GOP Sen. Orrin Hatch. But to get on the primary ballot, he needed either 60 percent of the delegate vote or to finish first or second at the 2010 Republican State Convention. In the meantime, Lee had caught the fancy of tea party activists, who were making inroads with their attacks on government spending.

At the May convention, Bennett was hammered as a member of the Appropriations Committee when the government debt kept growing. He was swept out after the second ballot. Business consultant Tim Bridgewater came in first with 37 percent of the vote; Lee got 35 percent of the delegates and Bennett finished third with 27 percent. In the primary election, Lee prevailed 51%-49%. The general election was anticlimactic in this heavily Republican state. Lee easily won 62%-33%.

At 39, Lee was the youngest senator when he took office in 2011. He got early notice when he was one of the few Republicans to vote against extending the Patriot Act after expressing concern that it did not sufficiently protect civil liberties and privacy. Also that year, he penned a book titled, "The Freedom Agenda: Why a Balanced Budget Amendment is Necessary to Restore Constitutional Government." During the standoff over raising the debt limit in summer 2011, he pushed his balanced budget amendment that would have required a two-thirds vote of both houses of Congress to raise the limit on spending. When the Democratic-controlled Senate approved a plan with more modest deficit reduction, Lee voted against it. In December, his balanced budget amendment was narrowly rejected.

Lee jumped into the fray on judicial nominations. Outraged over Obama's recess appointments, he voted, as a member of the Judiciary Committee, against Utah lawyer Robert Shelby for a federal judgeship in 2012. He made it clear that he supported Shelby but voted "no" to protest recess appointments. His persistence was rewarded when the Supreme Court ruled unanimously in 2014 that such recess appointments were unconstitutional if made when the Senate said it is in session.

Lee's tenacity became evident in his battle to dismantle the Affordable Care Act. During the initial legal challenge to Obamacare, Lee was active as the lawsuit wended its way to the Supreme Court. He published three health care-related videos to YouTube. But the high court in 2012 upheld the law's requirement that individuals must carry health insurance or face a penalty as part of the government's tax authority.

That setback did not stop Lee from targeting the law. He emerged as a leader, along with his friend and ally Ted Cruz of Texas, in formulating the strategy to defund Obamacare. That approach led to a government shutdown in October 2013, much to the consternation of party leaders. When the 16-day shutdown ended without having made a dent in Obamacare, he faced widespread unhappiness in the Senate from fellow Republicans. Lee was criticized at home, where the federal government is the largest employer, too. That downturn proved to be temporary as Lee rebounded by explaining his relentless push for smaller and less meddlesome government. He had the strong backing of well-funded conservative groups that were poised to spend lavishly to help him fend off would-be GOP primary challengers. As it turned out, their help was not needed.

Lee has not shied from bucking his party's establishment and has pressed some controversial stances. With other conservative Republicans, he co-sponsored a measure declaring that the 14th Amendment's birthright citizenship is limited to children of citizens, legal residents and members of the military and does not extend to children of undocumented immigrants. Showing his independence, he crossed party lines in an unusual alliance with New York Democratic Sen. Chuck Schumer to advance a visa reform bill that included helping foreigners who have invested at least $500,000 in a house in the United States. At Schumer's behest, Lee took part in bipartisan talks on a comprehensive immigration reform bill in early 2013 but backed out and refused to sign the group's draft giving immigrants a path to citizenship. "Reforms to our complex and dysfunctional immigration system should not in any way favor those who came here illegally over the millions of applicants who seek to come here lawfully," he said.

On foreign policy, Lee has been less hawkish than some other conservatives. In 2011, he opposed a congressional resolution authorizing U.S. military involvement in Libya. He was the first GOP senator to join Kentucky colleague Rand Paul during Paul's 13-hour filibuster in 2013 that protested the Obama administration's potential use of drones to attack U.S. citizens. Lee's Almanac vote ratings mostly have been conservative, except on foreign policy, where his votes have leaned toward the center.

During the high-stakes fight over the Trans-Pacific Partnership trade pact in 2015, Politico reported Lee had blindsided Republican leaders by failing to show up on a critical vote. Though he had stated he backed the effort, he stayed in Utah when the vote was called because, his office said, he had a family commitment. In 2016, he pursued a quixotic bid for a GOP leadership seat, even though there appeared to be no opening.

Lee has worked hard to elect other tea party-backed candidates. In 2012, he formed a political action committee to support like-minded conservative candidates and produced a policy blueprint for them to use on the trail. Lee has traveled across the country to campaign with such candidates in tough primaries. After his enthusiastic support for Cruz during the 2016 presidential primaries, Lee was outspokenly "Never Trump" at the Republican National Convention and during the fall campaign. He complained that Republican officials violated party rules by denying the anti-Trump forces their right to participate in convention activities. At home, he coasted to reelection, 68%-27%, against Democrat Misty Snow, one of the first openly transgender people to win a major-party nomination for a congressional seat.

From a state where Trump won with 45 percent of the vote in 2016, Lee continued to show his independence. He filed a bill to limit Trump from raising tariffs with what Lee called "unilateral trade actions." The purpose of his legislation, Lee said, was "to restore the proper balance of power between the branches of government." In 2018, he opposed a budget deal that congressional leaders reached with Trump as "a betrayal of everything limited government conservatism stands for." A year later, he was one of 12 Republican senators who voted for a bill to oppose Trump's use of a national emergency to shift federal funds to pay for a wall on the border with Mexico.

Lee spoke out against some of Trump's foreign policy actions. Referring in April 2018 to a possible U.S. military response to conflicts in Syria, he said, "The president of the United States should come to Congress and ask for authorization before military force is used." With liberal Sen. Bernie Sanders of Vermont, Lee filed a resolution to end U.S. military support for the Saudi-led coalition intervening in Yemen's civil war. "This legislation is neither liberal nor conservative. It's constitutional," he said at a news conference in February 2019. After it was passed by the Senate and House, Trump in April vetoed the measure as "an unnecessary, dangerous attempt to weaken my constitutional authorities."

Continuing his opposition to the Foreign Intelligence Surveillance Act, Lee worked with a bipartisan group that advocated limits in the law's authority. In March 2020, he complained after the House adjourned—because of the expanding threat posed by the COVID-19 pandemic—and failed to address Senate alternatives, and he demanded "a real, open honest debate". After Trump ordered the killing of Qasem Soleimani, the commander of Iran's Revolutionary Guard, in the January 2020 in Baghdad, Lee complained that Trump had OK'd the strike without consulting Congress. He described a presentation on the operation by administration officials as "probably the worst briefing, at least on a military issue, I've seen in nine years I've been here." In some areas, especially on law-related controversies, Lee grew more comfortable with Trump. In 2018, he was a vocal supporter of the Supreme Court nomination of Brett Kavanaugh and actively lobbied other Republican senators on Kavanaugh's behalf. They had been friends since Lee clerked at the Supreme Court. Perhaps oddly, given Lee's independence, a conservative group included him on a list of 25 potential Supreme Court nominees that it submitted to Trump during the 2016 campaign. Cruz was among those who publicly urged Trump to nominate Lee to the high court.

Immediately after the death of liberal Justice Ruth Bader Ginsburg in September 2020, Lee contacted other Republicans to urge that the Senate confirm a successor in the weeks before the November elections. He praised Trump's nomination of conservative Amy Coney Barrett and her performance before the Judiciary Committee. And he chastised Democrats for leaping to conclusions on how Barrett might eventually rule on cases before the court. It's "simply not the case," Lee said at the committee hearing, that the constitutionality of abortion options is "contingent on anyone's confirmation to the Supreme Court." Also in that preelection season, Lee reportedly urged other Senate Republicans not to yield to Democratic demands for a COVID-relief bill, which might backfire with Republican voters.

Earlier in 2020, as the Senate prepared for Trump's first impeachment trial, Lee worked closely with White House lawyers on their defense strategy. Politico called Lee "the quiet force to get Trump acquitted" and reported that he strategized regularly with Trump and White House counsel Pat Cipollone. According to the story, Lee said Trump "has every reason to be confident about this, every reason to be unapologetic and defiantly confident about his case. Because he has a really good case. ... I don't think what he did was even wrong." Trump was accused of abusing his office by withholding congressionally approved aid to Ukraine in order to extract election help. Even Mitt Romney, his home-state colleague and the only Republican who voted to convict Trump, said that he respected Lee's expertise on impeachment process.

After Trump was impeached a second time in early 2021—after inciting a mob to storm the U.S. Capitol in an eleventh-hour attempt to overturn his election loss—Lee again voted to acquit the now-former president. Romney again voted against Trump.

Also at the Judiciary Committee, Lee used his chairmanship of the Antitrust, Competition Policy and Consumer Rights Subcommittee to grill executives of large tech companies about social media practices that might have a "disparate impact" on political conservatives. At his panel's hearing a week before the 2020 election, he told chief executives from Twitter, Facebook and Google that "there is a good case" that they were engaging in unfair or deceptive practices that violated federal law. He said the platforms targeted conservatives for censoring.

As Lee prepared for reelection in 2022, his Senate activities seemed popular at home. The reelection defeat of freshman Rep. Ben McAdam in 2020 dampened speculation that he might be a Democratic challenger to Lee.

Mitt Romney (R)

Elected 2018, term expires 2024, 1st term, b. Mar 12, 1947; Detroit, MI; Brigham Young University, B.A., 1971; Harvard University School of Business, M.B.A., 1975; Harvard University Law School, J.D., 1975; Mormon; Married (Ann Davies); 5 children; 16 grandchildren.

Elected Office: MA Governor, 2003-2007.

Professional Career: Boston Consulting Group, Management Consultant, 1975-1977; Bain & Company, VP, 1978-1984, CEO, 1991-1993; Bain Capital, Founder, Managing Partner 1984-2001; Salt Lake City Winter Olympics Organizing Committee, President and CEO, 1999-2002.

DC Office: 124 RSOB 20510, 202-224-5251, romney.senate.gov

State Offices: Salt Lake City, 801-524-4380.

Committees: *Budget. Foreign Relations*: East Asia, the Pacific & International Cybersecurity Policy (RMM); Europe & Regional Security Cooperation; Near East, South Asia, Central Asia & Counterterrorism. *Health, Education, Labor & Pensions*: Children & Families; Employment & Workplace Safety. *Homeland Security & Government Affairs*: Emerging Threats & Spending Oversight; Government Operations & Border Management.

Almanac Ratings 2019-2020

	Economy	Social	Foreign	Composite
Liberal	48%	26%	29%	34%
Conservative	52%	74%	71%	66%

Key Votes of the 116th Congress

1. EPA clean energy rules	N	5. Russia sanctions	N	9. Barr as Atty. General	Y
2. U.S./Mex./Can. trade deal	Y	6. Troops in SYR, AFG	Y	10. Spending at the border	Y
3. Cut unemployment benefits	N	7. Veto arms sales to Saudis	N	11. Coney Barrett to Sup. Ct.	Y
4. Shelton to Fed Reserve	N	8. Defense $$$, veto override	Y	12. Electoral College objections	N

Election Results

Election	Name (Party)	Vote (%)		Cand. Spent	Ind. Exp. Support	Ind. Exp. Oppose
2018 General	Mitt Romney (R)...............................	665,215	(63%)	$5,248,693	$58,790	$7,960
	Jenny Wilson (D)..........................	328,541	(31%)	$923,979		
	Tim Aalders (CNP).......................	28,774	(3%)	$74,518		
	Craig Bowden (Lib).......................	27,607	(3%)	$37,321		
2018 Primary	Mitt Romney (R)...............................	240,021	(71%)			
	Mike Kennedy (R)................................	96,771	(29%)			

Prior winning percentages: 2018 (63%), Governor: 2002 (50%)

When he was elected Utah's junior senator in November 2018, Republican Mitt Romney already had earned himself a place in history. But he never planned to rest on his laurels. During his first two years in the Senate, perhaps more than during any other time since he entered politics, Romney felt liberated to speak his mind—regardless of the consequences. And more than any other Senate freshman in recent memory, he created a unique niche that displayed his independence and occasional influence. As a former presidential nominee who had made his mark in business, government and religion, he brought a broad range of experience.

Romney has always been willing to go his own way. He became only the third American to serve as governor of one state and senator for another. The last person to pull off this feat was Sam Houston, governor of Tennessee from 1827 to 1829 and later a senator from the new state of Texas. Romney was governor of Massachusetts from 2003 to 2007 before twice seeking the presidency, securing the Republican nomination in 2012. He declined to make a third presidential bid in 2016, only to emerge as a scathing critic of Donald Trump, whose nomination Romney tried to derail. The two had a tempestuous relationship during Trump's presidency; Romney was the only Republican in either chamber of Congress to vote against Trump in February 2020 during his first impeachment. In other ways, too, he was an anything-but-typical freshman as he sought to become an elder statesman and perhaps a counterforce to a president of his own party. Once Trump was ousted by voters, Romney felt more comfortable to help his party find its way—with occasional bipartisanship.

Willard Mitt Romney was born in Detroit, the youngest of four children of George and Lenore Romney. He grew up in Bloomfield Hills Michigan, as his father, CEO of American Motors, rescued the nearly bankrupt automaker. In 1962, George Romney was elected governor of Michigan, and, after an unsuccessful bid for the 1968 Republican presidential nomination, was secretary of Housing and Urban Development during President Richard Nixon's first term. Lenore Romney, his wife, unsuccessfully ran for a Senate seat from Michigan in 1970.

Mitt Romney initially enrolled in Stanford University, but—as a member of a prominent Mormon family—left after his freshman year to spend 30 months in France as a missionary for the Church of Jesus Christ of Latter-day Saints. He graduated from Mormon-founded Brigham Young University and earned degrees from both Harvard Law School and Harvard Business School, where he overlapped with George W. Bush. Romney stayed in the Boston area and became a vice president of Bain & Co., a management consulting firm.

In 1984, he founded Bain Capital, an investment company that provided crucial capital to such retailers as Staples, Domino's Pizza, and Brookstone. In 1990, he returned to Bain & Co., for a year as interim CEO to rescue it from financial difficulties. During his years with Bain, he accumulated a considerable fortune: Disclosures during his 2012 presidential campaign put it as high as $250 million. He also served from 1986 to 1994 as president of the Mormon Church's Boston Stake, making him the rough equivalent of a bishop in the Roman Catholic Church—although he would downplay his faith throughout much of his political career.

In 1994, as Massachusetts Democrat Ted Kennedy was seeking a sixth full Senate term, Romney made his first run for office. Kennedy's approval ratings had plummeted three years earlier when his nephew William Kennedy Smith was charged with rape after a night of drinking in Palm Beach Florida. The senator had been present that night. Polls in mid-September showed the race even, but Kennedy recovered to win 58%-41% despite it being a strongly Republican year. The Kennedy campaign aired ads on how Bain Capital's purchase of an Indiana paper plant had led to layoffs and a bitter strike. It presaged attacks on Romney's ties to Bain during the 2012 presidential primary and general elections.

Romney relinquished day-to-day management of Bain Capital in early 1999 to head the Salt Lake Olympic Organizing Committee for the Olympics, which was in debt and reeling from scandal. He erased a $379 million deficit, mobilized 23,000 volunteers and ran an effective security operation at the 2002 Games; 87 percent of Utahans rated his performance positively. At the time, however, Romney was eyeing a campaign 2,000 miles to the east. Massachusetts Republican Lt. Gov. Jane Swift, who became acting governor in 2001 when her predecessor resigned to accept an ambassadorship, was engulfed in controversy. Amid low poll ratings, Swift dropped a bid for election in March 2002; hours later, Romney announced. He was embarrassed when it was disclosed he had listed his home in Park City Utah as his principal residence for tax purposes from 1999 to 2001. He said he had intended all along to return to Massachusetts, where he owned a home in the Boston suburb of Belmont.

Romney ran as a professional manager and outsider who wasn't part of the Beacon Hill crowd. The Democratic nominee was Treasurer Shannon O'Brien. O'Brien attacked Romney in debates, arguing he was out of place in Massachusetts and trying to "mask a very conservative set of belief systems." Although she avoided making an issue of his religion, she criticized him for making contributions to Brigham Young University, whose policies bar expressions of homosexuality. She also advocated legalizing same-sex marriage; Romney sidestepped the issue by saying he opposed all extramarital sex. During his 1994 Senate bid, Romney had written a letter promising a gay Republican group he would be a stronger supporter of gay rights than Kennedy. Romney won, 50%-45%.

With his business background, he was less inclined than his Republican predecessors to make deals with the Democratic-dominated Legislature. But his major accomplishment turned out to be a plan for universal health insurance coverage enacted by working closely not only with the legislative leadership but also with his erstwhile opponent, Kennedy. "Romneycare" became a model for the President Barack Obama's Affordable Care Act. (Despite that, Romney campaigned for president in 2012 while advocating repeal of Obamacare.) In signing the legislation in 2006, Romney hailed it as "an achievement that comes around once in a generation."

Romney unveiled his plan in a Boston Globe op-ed just weeks after the 2004 elections. At a time when the state was in danger of losing $600 million in Medicaid funding because federal officials felt the money was being used for ineligible services, Romney persuaded Washington to provide funding for the experiment. It featured an individual mandate requiring all who could afford insurance to purchase it. The final compromise that emerged from the Legislature included an annual fee for companies that didn't offer health insurance. Romney initially did not voice objections but, as conservatives grumbled that it amounted to a new tax, he exercised a line-item veto over the "employer assessment"—which, as expected, was later overridden by the Legislature.

At the end of 2005, Romney announced he would not seek reelection. He became chairman of the Republican Governors Association the next year and traveled the country building a political network. Hours before leaving the governorship in early 2007, he registered a presidential exploratory committee at the Federal Election Commission. His approval ratings at home tumbled to less than 40 percent—amid extensive out-of-state travel and frequent use of liberal Massachusetts as a rhetorical foil, as he curried favor with conservatives in early presidential primary states.

Romney shifted rightward on several hot-button social issues. In 2002, he had called his support for abortion rights "unequivocal" despite personal opposition to abortion. But in May 2005, he told USA Today he was "in a different place" and vetoed a bill promoting emergency contraception that he had supported during his gubernatorial run. He began to criticize Roe v. Wade and, as a presidential candidate, said the Supreme Court decision legalizing abortion nationwide should be overturned. After he had sidestepped the same-sex marriage issue during the governor's race, a 2004 decision by the state's highest court made Massachusetts first in the nation to legalize gay marriage; Romney worked to have a constitutional amendment reversing the ruling put on the ballot. That effort was later thwarted by his Democratic successor, Deval Patrick. After saying during the 1994 Senate race that he didn't "line up with the NRA" and signing an assault-weapons ban as governor, Romney touted himself as a "lifelong hunter" during his 2008 presidential bid, disclosing he had recently joined the National Rifle Association.

Romney presenting himself as a conservative alternative to the frontrunner for the 2008 Republican presidential nomination—Arizona Sen. John McCain, a political maverick who had been runner-up to President Bush in the race for the 2000 nomination. After early stumbles by McCain, Romney finished first in the quadrennial straw poll of Iowa Republican activists in August 2007. But in the Iowa caucuses the next January, Romney came in second despite heavily outspending the winner, former Arkansas Gov. Mike Huckabee. McCain, after righting his campaign, skipped Iowa to focus on New Hampshire—where he defeated Romney 37%-32%, despite Romney's longtime ownership of a vacation home in the state. Romney won Michigan, where he had grown up, but finished a distant fourth to McCain in South Carolina and lost to the Arizonan in Florida. McCain had the nomination sewn up by Super Tuesday in early February, and Romney suspended his campaign several days later.

After McCain was defeated in the 2008 general election by Obama, Romney began laying the groundwork for another run, which he announced in April 2011. While Romney started as the frontrunner, conservatives remained leery, and several contenders emerged to challenge him from the right. Minnesota Rep. Michele Bachmann won the Iowa straw poll this time but dropped out after a poor finish in the Iowa caucuses in January 2012. For a time, Texas Gov. Rick Perry was a leading alternative, but his bid collapsed after a late 2011 debate at which he couldn't recall one of the three federal agencies he had proposed to eliminate. (It was the Energy Department, which Perry went on to head during the Trump administration.) In late 2011, polls showed businessman Herman Cain in a tie with Romney after Cain won a straw vote in Florida. But Cain dropped out after allegations of sexual harassment and an extramarital affair surfaced.

Two other hard-line conservatives fared better: Former Pennsylvania Sen. Rick Santorum battled Romney to a draw in the Iowa caucuses, and, while Romney won the New Hampshire primary, he was badly beaten by former House Speaker Newt Gingrich in South Carolina. Romney recovered after winning a half-dozen states on Super Tuesday; Santorum dropped out in April and Gingrich in early May, guaranteeing Romney the nomination. In November, Obama was vulnerable as the national economy struggled to recover from the 2008 recession. However, Romney's selection of Wisconsin Rep. Paul Ryan—a leading proponent of reforming entitlement programs—as his running mate kicked off a debate that overshadowed the Republicans' desire to make the election a referendum on Obama's handling of the economy. A Romney-Ryan premium support proposal called for new Medicare beneficiaries, beginning in 2023, to have the option of choosing between traditional Medicare and a private health plan. Democrats attacked it as an effort to dismantle the social safety net.

In September 2012, Romney was put on the defensive after footage from a private fundraiser he had held in Florida the previous May leaked. Romney told attendees at the event: "There are 47 percent of the people who will vote for the president [Obama] no matter what ... who believe that they are victims, who believe the government has a responsibility to care for them, who believe that they are entitled to health care, to food, to housing, to you name it. ... These are people who pay no income tax. ... And, so, my job is not to worry about those people. I'll never convince them that they should take personal responsibility and care for their lives."

Obama jumped on the remarks, saying Romney was out of touch with middle class America. On Election Day, exit polls showed Obama ahead of Romney by 4-1 on the question of which candidate "cares about people like me." In a post-election interview, Romney told Fox News: "I didn't express myself as I wished I would have. ... There's no question that hurt and did real damage to my campaign." Obama won the Electoral College 332-206, with Romney carrying two more states than McCain had in 2008. In the popular vote, Romney's biggest margin of victory was in Utah, where he defeated Obama 73%-27%. In Massachusetts, he lost 61%-38%.

In 2014, Romney registered to vote in Utah and built a house next to the home of one of his five son in a Salt Lake City suburb. After contemplating a third presidential bid, he announced in January 2015 he would not run. He returned to the spotlight a year later when Trump established himself as the clear frontrunner for the 2016 GOP nomination. Romney demanded Trump release his income tax returns, suggesting they might contain a "bombshell." While saying he lacked proof, Romney told Fox News: "I think there is something there. Either he is not nearly as wealthy as he says he is or he hasn't been paying the kind of taxes you would expect him to." Trump responded via Twitter, calling Romney a "dope" who "totally blew an election that should have been won."

Romney's volley turned out to be prelude to a speech at the University of Utah a month later, during which he let Trump have it with both barrels. "Donald Trump is a phony, a fraud," Romney said. "He has neither the temperament nor the judgment to be president." It was an unprecedented rebuke in the modern political era—the party's immediate past nominee devoting an entire speech to condemning the current frontrunner for the nomination in withering terms. When Trump was nominated, Romney said he would not vote for him; in mid-2018 he revealed he had written in the name of Ann Romney, to whom he has been married since 1969, for president.

Romney's tone mellowed after Trump's election; he told the Deseret News, "Now the time has come for us to recognize we have a new president and we have hopes he will be successful leading our country." Trump and Romney met twice after the election, reportedly to discuss the possibility of Romney becoming secretary of State. It appeared Trump never seriously entertained appointing

Romney—who differed with the president on issues ranging from Russia to free trade—but was instead toying with his frequent antagonist.

A more consequential discussion of Romney's future took place in March 2017, when Romney met with Orrin Hatch, the longest serving Republican in Senate history. Hatch indicated he planned to retire after 42 years and urged Romney to consider succeeding him. Months later, Trump, during a visit to Utah, publicly said he hoped Hatch would seek reelection. It reportedly capped a series of private efforts by Trump to block Romney's ascension by pushing Hatch to stay, despite Hatch's low approval ratings. Hatch declined to run, and Trump offered Romney "my full support and endorsement" on Twitter. At the Utah Republican State Convention, Romney was forced into a June primary after losing the vote of the delegates by 51%-49% to state Rep. Mike Kennedy. Such gatherings are often not reflective of Utah's GOP electorate, and Romney defeated Kennedy 71%-29%. In November, he defeated the Democratic nominee, Salt Lake County Councilwoman Jenny Wilson, 63%-31%—running 18 percentage points ahead of the 45 percent plurality by which Trump had won Utah in 2016.

In an op-ed in the Salt Lake Tribune two days before the June primary, Romney was conciliatory toward Trump, while also offering a warning. "I will support the president's policies when I believe they are in the best interest of Utah and the nation," he wrote, noting that "the first year of his administration has exceeded my expectations." But in a Washington Post op-ed published just before he was sworn into the Senate in January 2019, Romney issued a critique reminiscent of his biting comments during the 2016 campaign. He wrote that Trump had not "risen to the mantle of the office," adding, "With the nation so divided, resentful and angry, presidential leadership in qualities of character is indispensable. And it is in this province where the incumbent's shortfall has been most glaring."

In his first months in the Senate, Romney picked his shots carefully, adhering to his vow in the Post op-ed to not "comment on every tweet or fault." Although he supported building a wall on the U.S.-Mexico border, Romney joined 11 other Republican senators in voting to overturn Trump's effort to obtain money for such a wall by issuing an emergency declaration. Romney said the action set a bad precedent. In April, Romney broke from many Republicans who argued special counsel Robert Mueller's probe into connections between Russia and Trump's 2016 campaign had exonerated the president. While saying it was "good news" that Mueller didn't find sufficient evidence to prove collusion, Romney added, "I am sickened at the extent and pervasiveness of dishonesty and misdirection by individuals in the highest office of the land, including the president."

Romney was one of the few Republicans voicing concern about Trump's behavior as president even before he was impeached the first time. After revelations in September 2019 that Trump had threatened to withhold congressionally approved aid from Ukraine unless it announced a criminal probe into a political rival—Joe Biden, then the frontrunner for the Democratic presidential nomination—Romney said that he was "deeply troubled" by a president seeking foreign assistance in an election. Unlike most other Republican senators, Romney had little to fear politically, and he was willing to withstand the inevitable attacks from Trump. Some thought he was voicing the private views of other Republican senators. "I do think these are critical times," he told the Atlantic prior to House action on impeachment. "And I hope that what I'm doing will open the way for people to take a different path." Trump responded with harsh tweets about Romney, mocking his failed presidential campaigns and calling him a "pompous ass" and "a fool."

As the Senate prepared for Trump's first impeachment trial, with some Republicans seeking a quick dismissal with little discussion, critics looked to Romney to insist that the Senate conduct credible proceedings that fully examined the charges. But he said he was unwilling to make demands, such as calling White House aides or other key witnesses to testify, until he discussed such options with other senators. Once the trial began in January 2020, he joined the unified Republican Conference in rejecting Democratic efforts to broaden the focus of the trial and request additional documents. Only after much of the lawyers' presentations had been completed did Romney support a move by Senate Democrats to subpoena John Bolton, Trump's former national security adviser. Romney was joined by Republican Sen. Susan Collins of Maine, but their votes were not enough to approve the subpoena. Calling it "the most difficult decision I have ever faced," Romney told the Senate he would vote to convict Trump for abuse of his power as president, describing Trump's dealings with Zelensky: "The president's purpose was personal and political. … Corrupting an election to keep oneself in office is perhaps the most abusive and destructive violation of one's oath of office that I can imagine." He voted against the second impeachment charge—that Trump had obstructed Congress by defying House subpoenas. Romney was one of seven Republican senators in February 2021 to vote to convict Trump during his second impeachment trial—which came after he incited a mob of supporters to violently storm the Capitol in an attempt to overturn his election loss. Trump was acquitted by the GOP-controlled chamber. As he expected, Romney was harshly criticized by Republicans, both nationally and in his home state, for the votes. Although the state Republican Party defeated a move to censure him, some county parties voted a censure.

In the volatile political year of 2020, Romney sought other opportunities to show his independence. During the nationwide protests that followed George Floyd's death in Minneapolis police custody, Romney joined a march of demonstrators near the White House. He echoed their chant, "Black Lives Matter," and described it as a call to "end violence and brutality." He noted that his father, as governor, had joined a civil rights protest event in Detroit.

In the Senate, which had become consumed by the coronavirus, he sought an aggressive national response. In April 2020, he joined Democratic Sen. Kyrsten Sinema of Arizona in urging the Centers for Disease Control and Prevention to move more aggressively to track the spread of the novel coronavirus. That month, Trump deliberately excluded Romney when he invited the 52 other Republican senators to join a task force on reopening the national economy. "I'm not a fan of Mitt Romney," Trump told reporters. "I don't really want his advice."

Romney rejected calls to campaign against Trump. He said that he voted against the president's reelection, though he kept his choice private. After the election 2020, he was the first Republican senator to congratulate Biden on his victory. And he renewed his call for a bipartisan national response to the pandemic.

Blake Moore (R)

Elected 2020, 1st term, b. Jun 22, 1980; Ogden, UT; UT State University, B.A.; Northwestern University, M.P.P.; University of UT, Salt Lake City, B.A.; Mormon; Married (Jane Moore); 3 children.

Professional Career: Sales Representative, medical equipment supplier, 2005-2007; Business Development Consultant, healthcare consulting company, 2007-2011; Foreign Service Officer, U.S. Department of State, 2012-2013; Senior Associate/Engagement Manager/Principal, management consulting firm.

DC Office: 1320 LHOB 20515, 202-225-0453, Fax: 202-225-5857, blakemoore.house.gov

State Offices: Ogden, 801-625-0107.

Committees: *Armed Services*: Cyber, Innovative Technologies & Information Systems; Readiness. *Natural Resources*: National Parks, Forests & Public Lands; Oversight & Investigations.

Election Results

Election	Name (Party)	Vote (%)		Cand. Spent	Ind. Exp. Support	Ind. Exp. Oppose
2020 General	Blake Moore (R)............................	237,988	(70%)	$774,699	$8	$13,380
	Darren Parry (D)...........................	104,194	(30%)	$39,789		
2020 Primary	Blake Moore (R)............................	39,260	(31%)			
	Bob Stevenson (R)........................	36,288	(29%)			
	Kerry Gibson (R)...........................	29,991	(24%)			
	Katie Witt (R).............................	21,317	(17%)			

Republican Blake Moore narrowly won the primary and coasted to victory in his strongly GOP district. A veteran of the U.S. Foreign Service and a management consultant, he won his first political campaign while voicing concern about "the lack of conservative leadership for the next generation of Americans." Moore succeeded Rep. Rob Bishop, who served nine terms and chaired the House Natural Resources Committee. Bishop ran unsuccessfully for lieutenant governor in 2020.

A native of Ogden, Moore won national awards as a football quarterback when he was in high school. He got his bachelor's degree at the University of Utah and a master's in public policy and administration at Northwestern University. He served his Mormon mission in South Korea. As a Foreign Service officer, he was assigned to intelligence and defense communities in Washington. In that work, Moore said, "I gained first-hand knowledge of the threats we face from foreign enemies," especially China. He also learned "what is vital and what is wasteful in our federal government." Later, he was a business consultant in Singapore.

Returning to Utah in the private sector, Moore joined the Cicero Group, a management consulting firm, where he worked with businesses to help them grow and solve complex problems. During that time, he collaborated with the George W. Bush Institute's school leadership team to assist school districts in recruiting and developing administrators. In Utah, he co-chaired Better Boundaries, a group that won narrow approval in 2018 of a voter initiative to create an independent commission to handle redistricting.

In a profile in the Salt Lake Tribune that described how he went from a political unknown to a seat in Congress, Moore said voters were looking for "a new face and a new perspective." He said he struck a political chord with his diverse experiences and when he criticized President Donald Trump for sending military forces to control domestic protests during 2020; Utah Republicans have been notably critical of Trump. "We need that kind of perspective when we have a global crisis and an economic meltdown," Moore said. He called for steps to address racial inequality and social justice.

The other leading contenders were Bob Stevenson, a home builder who served as mayor of Layton and commissioner of Davis County; Kerry Gibson, a dairy farmer and Utah's Commissioner of Agriculture and Food, and Katie Witt; the mayor of Kaysville in Davis County.

In the GOP primary, Moore led Stevenson, 31%-29%, with 24 percent for Gibson and 17 percent for Witt. In the two largest counties, Stevenson got 43 percent of the vote in Davis and Moore took 35 percent in Weber. Moore won three additional counties and Gibson led in five mostly small counties. Moore and Stevenson also led the field in spending, with about $400,000 each. In a district where no Democrat has topped 40 percent of the vote in the past 30 years, Moore won in November with 70 percent against Darren Parry—a tribal leader of the Shoshone Nation.

In the House, he got a seat on the Armed Services Committee and was tapped as vice ranking member on the Natural Resources Subcommittee on Oversight and Investigations, where he called for "more effective management of our lands and resources nationwide."

UT-1: Northern Utah   Cook Partisan Voting Index: R+20

Population		Race and Ethnicity		Income	
Total	787,582	White	91.40%	Median Income	$73,964
Land area (sq. miles)	19,561	Black	0.90%	District Income Rank	136
Pop/ sq mi	40.26	Latino	13.50%	Poverty Rate	7.70%
Born in State	65.50%	Asian	1.70%	With health insurance	91.60%
		Two or more races	2.90%	Cash public assistance	1.30%
Age Groups		Other	3.00%	Food stamp/SNAP	6.70%
Under 18	30.10%				
18-34	25.30%	**Education**		**Work**	
35-64	34.10%	H.S grad or less	33.20%	White Collar	38.10%
Over 64	10.60%	Some college	35.00%	Sales and Service	37.40%
		College Degree, 4 yr	21.60%	Blue Collar	24.50%
Military		Post grad	10.20%	Government	17.40%
Veteran/ Active Duty	7.40%				

2020 Pres. Vote	Trump	230,314	(63%)	Biden	113,343	(31%)	Jorgensen	9,182	(3%)
2016 Pres. Vote	Trump	139,503	(49%)	Clinton	62,733	(22%)	Johnson	10,231	(4%)

Ogden, Logan: In May 1869, a motley crowd of Irish and Chinese laborers, teamsters, engineers, train crews, officials and guests from Salt Lake City gathered at Promontory Summit to watch the opening of the transcontinental railroad. Leland Stanford's blow with a silver sledge, intended to drive the ceremonial "Last Spike" into the railroad ties, missed its mark, but telegraphs nevertheless conveyed the word "done" across the nation. It wasn't just the railroad that was complete. As long as America had been America, there had been a frontier. But as the civilized East and the mostly untamed West were finally united, that frontier began to shrink and then vanish.

Ogden Utah is in many ways a microcosm of the impact the railway could have. At the time the railroad was completed, Ogden was a small farming community of 1,500 inhabitants. Had it not won the right to become the junction of the Union Pacific and Central Pacific railroads—which meant that all the passengers and shipping crossing the nation changed trains in Ogden—it might have suffered the same fate as Corinne, the nearby and forgotten town that lost out to Ogden in the competition for the railroad. The city adopted the motto, "You can't get anywhere without coming to Ogden!" Today, with a population of 88,000, Ogden has developed as a hub for outdoor sports equipment makers. As a manufacturing center for bicycles, it has become known as "biketown." Like other cities in Utah, Ogden has become a center for technology jobs. In 2019, pre-pandemic, the metro area's 5 percent annual increase in jobs was among the highest in the nation.

The 1st Congressional District of Utah takes in Ogden and areas to the north of Salt Lake City. While it sprawls from the Colorado border to Idaho, about two thirds of its residents live in the stretch north of Salt Lake City from Kaysville to Brigham City. Hill Air Force Base, which houses F-35 fighter jets, is in the district, as is Utah State University, farther north in Logan. Northrop Grumman, with more than 5,000 employees in the state, primarily in Clearfield, is upgrading the nation's Minuteman intercontinental ballistic missiles. Much of the district is farm country. Great Salt Lake, which is the largest water mass west of the Mississippi River and much of which is in this district, has been disappearing. Ecologists worry about the threat to the ecosystem of the area, including wildlife. The National Audubon Society has advocated less use of irrigation. In August 2020, the Deseret News reported that failure to act could cause the water level to drop another three to four feet in less than a decade and cost the state billions of dollars. An exception to the Mormon dominance is Park City, in the mountains east of Salt Lake City, which is a fashionable ski resort and home of actor Robert Redford's annual Sundance Film Festival, the largest independent film festival in the nation. The event in January-February 2021 combined virtual and in-person programs and attracted attendees from 120 nations.

When Mitt Romney got 78 percent in 2012, the 1st was among the top 10 most heavily Republican districts in the nation. The antipathy of Mormons for Donald Trump changed that. His 63%-31% win over Joe Biden was his highest in the state but a double-digit increase in Democratic performance.

Chris Stewart (R)

Elected 2012, 5th term, b. Jul 15, 1960; Logan, UT; UT State University, B.S., 1984; Mormon; Married (Evie Stewart); 6 children.

Military Career: U.S. Air Force 1984-1998

Professional Career: Owner, Shipley Group, 2000-present.

DC Office: 2242 RHOB 20515, 202-225-9730, Fax: 202-225-5629, stewart.house.gov

State Offices: Salt Lake City, 801-364-5550; St. George, 435-627-1500.

Committees: *Appropriations*: Financial Services & General Government; Interior, Environment & Related Agencies. *Permanent Select on Intelligence*: Counterterrorism, Counterintelligence & Counterproliferation; Strategic Technologies & Advanced Research (RMM).

Group Ratings

	ADA	ACLU	AFL-CIO	LCV	COC	HAFA	ACU	CFG	FRC
2020	**	17%	**	14%	-	89%	83%	**	-
2019	0%	C	29%	3%	86%	C	83%	77%	100%

Almanac Ratings 2019-2020

	Economy	Social	Foreign	Composite
Liberal	25%	15%	11%	17%
Conservative	75%	85%	89%	83%

Key Votes of the 116th Congress

1. U.S./Mex./Can. trade deal	Y	5. Russia sanctions	Y	9. Firearms background checks N
2. First Coronavirus response	Y	6. Troops in Syria	Y	10. Spending at the border	Y
3. HEROES Act	N	7. Veto arms sales to Saudis	N	11. Marijuana liberalized rules	N/A
4. CASH Act	N	8. Defense $$$, veto override	Y	12. Electoral College objections Y

Election Results

Election	Name (Party)	Vote (%)	Cand. Spent	Ind. Exp. Support	Ind. Exp. Oppose
2020 General	Chris Stewart (R)................................ 208,997	(59%)	$745,189	$8,000	$769
	Kael Weston (D)........................... 129,762	(37%)	$299,118		
	J. Robert Latham (L)......................... 15,465	(4%)			

Prior winning percentages: 2018 (56%), 2016 (62%), 2014 (60%), 2012 (62%)

Republican Chris Stewart, a former Air Force pilot and author, won an open seat in 2012. Following impressive careers in the military and private sector, he established his credentials as a member of the Appropriations and Intelligence committees. Stewart typically takes a hard line on national security issues, which resulted in occasional criticism of former President Donald Trump.

Stewart and his nine siblings grew up on a dairy farm in southern Idaho. His parents, both Mormon, had moved there from nearby Utah. Stewart enrolled in Utah State University, serving as a Mormon missionary in Texas before completing a degree in economics. After graduating from college, he entered the Air Force. He was first in his class in both officer training school and undergraduate pilot training. In 14 years in uniform, he attained the rank of major and in 1995 set the world record for the fastest nonstop flight around the world in a B-1 Lancer. (His crew flew nearly 23,000 miles in just over 36 hours, for an average speed of about 630 mph.) He also flew rescue helicopters. Five of Stewart's six sons have served in the military.

Stewart began writing in the military and took it up full time after his discharge to spend more time with his children. After two years, he bought the Shipley Group, an energy and environment consulting firm that did government and corporate security work. While he ran the business, Stewart's writing career flourished. He has written 18 books. One of his New York Times best sellers was a collaboration in 2013 with Utah native Elizabeth Smart on the story of her kidnapping. He says that he found more meaning in writing a six-part fiction series, The Great and Terrible, a religious epic about the struggle between good and evil.

When Democratic Rep. Jim Matheson decided to run in 2012 in the newly created 4th District, Stewart got into the open-seat contest, emerging on top in an acrimonious GOP primary. Stewart prevailed with more than 60 percent of the vote in the only contest that really mattered in the heavily Republican district.

After the October 2013 government shutdown, which cost local Utah governments and businesses millions of dollars, Stewart filed a bill that would allow states to fund the operations of national parks, monuments and other facilities related to tourism and other commercial activity in the event of a future lapse of federal spending. In 2014, the House passed on a largely party-line vote his bill to revamp the selection of members to the Environmental Protection Agency's Science Advisory Board to require more representatives of state and local governments. In March 2019, enactment of a wide-ranging public lands bill included two provisions from Stewart, which increased disclosure on the settlement of claims against the United States and permitted Utah to purchase federal land along the old Pony Express route.

In October 2020, Trump signed a bill that Stewart filed, with bipartisan cosponsors, to establish a national suicide and mental health crisis hotline number: 988. The bill also provided funding and resources to boost the capacity of local crisis centers to handle the expected increase in calls beyond existing phone numbers.

His seats on the Appropriations and Intelligence committees positioned him to use his Air Force experience to oversee national security activities, notably the Obama administration's nuclear-arms talks with Iran. In March 2015, Stewart wrote in the Wall Street Journal that, as a B-1 pilot, he was a military representative in arms-reduction talks with the former Soviet Union. On that basis, he contended, "the record is bare" of Iran partnering with the United States or an ally "in a productive way. Congress must do everything in its power to stop it," he said. The House and Senate failed to secure the two-thirds to override President Barack Obama's veto in an unusual procedure. Stewart praised the decision by President Donald Trump to withdraw the United States from the "deeply flawed" agreement.

In December 2016, Stewart voiced concern that the "Cold War-esque" relationship with Russia had become difficult and dangerous, especially its cyber-attacks against American interests, including the election that year. "What Russia is doing is aggressive. It's illegal and harmful," he told a Utah reporter. On the Intelligence Committee, he has become ranking Republican on the Defense Intelligence and Overhead Architecture Subcommittee.

During the Republican presidential primaries, Stewart supported Sen. Marco Rubio of Florida. While speaking to University of Utah students in March 2016, he called Donald Trump "our Mussolini," referring negatively to the fascist dictator of Italy. A few days before the election, he said he would vote for Trump as "a better choice than Hillary Clinton." He occasionally disagreed with Trump's actions as president. Many of his tweets, Stewart told CNN, were "just unpresidential" and "not helpful." When Trump said that he accepted the assurances of Russian President Vladimir Putin during their meeting in Helsinki and praised him in July 2018, Stewart said, "Trump is wrong. Russia meddled in the 2016 elections. Russia is led by a former KGB thug who only understands lies and manipulations."

That background seemed to make it odd that Trump considered Stewart in early 2000 to fill the vacancy of Director of National Intelligence. Reportedly, Stewart's earlier reference to Mussolini was a factor in Trump's decision to select Rep. John Ratcliffe for the position.

UT-2: Southwest Utah   Cook Partisan Voting Index: R+10

Population		Race and Ethnicity		Income	
Total	788,484	White	83.40%	Median Income	$69,852
Land area (sq. miles)	39,988	Black	1.50%	District Income Rank	165
Pop/ sq mi	19.72	Latino	15.80%	Poverty Rate	10.10%
Born in State	59.00%	Asian	3.10%	With health insurance	88.70%
		Two or more races	3.00%	Cash public assistance	1.20%
Age Groups		Other	9.10%	Food stamp/SNAP	5.90%
Under 18	26.50%				
18-34	25.50%	Education		Work	
35-64	34.00%	H.S grad or less	31.60%	White Collar	39.40%
Over 64	14.00%	Some college	36.30%	Sales and Service	37.50%
		College Degree, 4 yr	20.50%	Blue Collar	23.10%
Military		Post grad	11.70%	Government	16.00%
Veteran/ Active Duty	6.00%				

2020 Pres. Vote	Trump	207,667	(56%)	Biden	148,890	(40%)	Jorgensen	8,122	(2%)
2016 Pres. Vote	Trump	130,525	(46%)	Clinton	90,686	(32%)	McMullin	47,862	(17%)
	Johnson	8,914	(3%)						

Salt Lake City: At the center of the Mormon Church is Temple Square, illuminated by 300,000 lights during Christmas week and nestled beneath the towering mountains that flank Salt Lake City. The Mormon Tabernacle is here, home to the famous choir, as is the Salt Lake LDS Temple itself, crowned with the golden angel Moroni. The area has been the focal point of Utah since Mormon leader Brigham Young looked down at the valley and said (according to church tradition), "This is the place." Ironically, this part of Salt Lake City has become the least Mormon and most cosmopolitan part of Utah, with the state university and businesses bringing in outsiders who, flouting Mormon strictures, keep purveyors of alcohol and caffeine in business. The state has ended its private club system at bars, though prohibitions remained on bartenders pouring drinks in plain sight. In October 2020, the Salt Lake Tribune and Deseret News announced the end of their 68-year joint publishing agreement. Each newspaper, which had published daily for more than 140 years, moved to a weekly print edition in addition to their online publishing.

The 2nd Congressional District of Utah consists of most of Salt Lake City and the vast and mostly empty southwestern portion of the state. In Salt Lake, which includes about one-third of the district's population, it takes in the historic downtown, its distinctive Avenues District, and the airport. The county has had one Mormon chapel every 1.3 square miles, many of which are relatively small. The already huge construction of a new terminal at the airport has been expanded to add a third concourse, which is scheduled to open by 2024. The first two concourses were completed in 2020. The population of the city, which peaked at 189,000 in 1960 and then fell 15 percent by 1990 as residents moved to the suburbs, has rebounded. In 2019, it surpassed 200,000, though the faster-growing Salt Lake County reached nearly 1.2 million.

The neighboring open land of stark beauty, much of it federally owned, has been used roughly by humans, as a repository for hazardous wastes at civilian and military dumps in Tooele County and as a place for military experimentations at the Dugway Proving Grounds, where scientists test defenses against chemical and biological agents. About 20 percent of the district's residents live in the stretch of the Wasatch Front, between the mountains and Great Salt Lake, just north of Salt Lake City, in suburban and fairly affluent Davis County. Another 25 percent live in the stretch of lightly populated counties in the southwest corner of the state, chiefly Washington County, which is the home of Zion National Park. The park has coped with a surge of visitors. Even after the coronavirus pandemic forced a shutdown during the spring, the September 2020 attendance of 521,000 was a record for that month.

Politically, this is a mostly Republican area, with pockets of Democratic strength in Salt Lake City. Joe Biden carried Salt Lake County by nearly 60,000 votes over President Donald Trump in 2020. The 68%-29% win in 2012 for Mitt Romney in the 2nd District dropped to a 46%-32% lead for Trump four years later and then settled at 56%-40% in 2020.

John Curtis (R)

Elected 2017, 2nd full term, b. May 10, 1960; Salt Lake City, UT; University of UT, Salt Lake City, Att., 1979; Brigham Young University, B.S., 1985; Mormon; Married (Sue Snarr); 6 children; 5 grandchildren.

Elected Office: Mayor, Provo UT, 2010-2017.

Professional Career: CEO, Action Target Company.

DC Office: 125 CHOB 20515, 202-225-7751, Fax: 202-225-5629, curtis.house.gov

State Offices: Provo, 801-922-5400.

Committees: *Energy & Commerce*: Communications & Technology; Environment & Climate Change; Health.

Group Ratings

	ADA	ACLU	AFL-CIO	LCV	COC	HAFA	ACU	CFG	FRC
2020	**	19%	**	5%	-	100%	84%	**	-
2019	0%	C	20%	3%	82%	C	90%	100%	95%

Almanac Ratings 2019-2020

	Economy	Social	Foreign	Composite
Liberal	25%	27%	27%	27%
Conservative	75%	73%	73%	73%

Key Votes of the 116th Congress

1. U.S./Mex./Can. trade deal Y	5. Russia sanctions Y	9. Firearms background checks N
2. First Coronavirus response Y	6. Troops in Syria Y	10. Spending at the border Y
3. HEROES Act N	7. Veto arms sales to Saudis N	11. Marijuana liberalized rules N
4. CASH Act N	8. Defense $$$, veto override Y	12. Electoral College objections N

Election Results

Election	Name (Party)	Vote (%)		Cand. Spent	Ind. Exp. Support	Ind. Exp. Oppose
2020 General	John Curtis (R)................................	246,674	(69%)	$540,959		$750
	Devin Thorpe (D)...............................	96,067	(27%)	$185,534		
	Daniel Cummings (C)..................	8,889	(2%)			
	Thomas McNeill (UU).................	7,040	(2%)	$4,984		

Prior winning percentages: 2018 (68%), 2017 Special (58%)

Republican John Curtis in 2017 won a special election to fill a vacancy, following a party primary in which he highlighted his independence from President Donald Trump, though he has supported much of the GOP agenda. Curtis, who was a Democrat earlier in his career, has emphasized the need for bipartisanship. He became a regular critic of Trump, including actions that led to two impeachments—though Curtis voted against each. He got a seat in 2021 on the influential Energy and Commerce Committee.

Curtis, a native of Salt Lake City, was class president at Skyline High School. After graduating from Brigham Young University, he was a Mormon bishop and served on a mission in Taiwan. With his wife, Sue, whose family was politically active in the area, they settled in Provo; she later became president of the school board. Curtis became a salesman for a watch company and soon won the company's award for "salesman of the year." He worked for local businesses and developed his own firm: Action Target, a shooting range.

Curtis registered as a Democrat, he told the Deseret News, so that he could counter the "one-party dominance" of Utah, though he said that he continued to "sound just like a Republican." He switched to a Republican in 2006, but lost two bids for the state House. In 2009, Curtis narrowly won a nonpartisan election for mayor of Provo, where he built a reputation for economic development and tight-fisted budgets. He is "a self-professed introvert" and often seeks to avoid crowds, the News reported. His chief extrovert trait has been a penchant for colorful socks, of which he owns more than 200 pairs.

Months before Republican Rep. Jason Chaffetz announced his surprise resignation in 2017 (and became a contributor to Fox News), Curtis had decided not to seek a third term as mayor of Provo. He moved quickly to seek the House seat. At a party convention to secure the Republican nomination for the House seat, he was defeated on the fourth ballot by Christopher Herrod. His political experience and familiarity with voters were advantages when Curtis decided to run in the GOP primary. Tanner Ainge outspent his two opponents and ran ads that linked Curtis with "tax and spend liberals" such as Nancy Pelosi. Curtis responded by emphasizing gun rights and defending his record as mayor. He was endorsed by Mitt Romney, who was elected a year later as senator from Utah.

During the campaign, Curtis said he had written in a "good friend's name" in the 2016 presidential election, the Salt Lake Tribune reported. But he added that he wanted Trump to be successful. With surprising ease, Curtis won the August primary with 43 percent of the vote to 33 percent for Herrod and 24 percent for Ainge. He led comfortably in both Utah and Salt Lake counties, the two population centers. In this district, he was a shoo-in against Democrat Kathie Allen. He won, 58%-26%, with four other candidates splitting the remaining votes.

In the House, one of his first votes was for the Republican-crafted tax bill. Curtis said he read the 400-plus pages before deciding to vote for it. After Trump acted to reduce the size of Bears Ears National Monument, Curtis filed a bill to formalize that action in a statute. In seeking his first full term, Curtis easily prevailed, 73%-27%, in a primary rematch with Herrod. And he defeated Democrat James Singer, 68%-27%. In the sweeping public lands bill that was enacted in March 2019, Curtis sponsored provisions that resolved a long-running conflict in Emery County and set rules for fish recovery in the Colorado River Storage Project.

Curtis became increasingly outspoken about the Republican agenda, especially as defined by Trump. On the president's trade war with China, he said, "unfortunately it's having a disproportionate impact on small businesses." He said Trump's cuts in foreign aid "will hurt America more than it helps." He said Republicans should stop calling climate change a "hoax." With Democratic Rep. Jerry McNerney, he won House subcommittee approval in March 2020 of a bill that authorized the National Oceanic and Atmospheric Administration (NOAA) to study potential approaches to atmospheric climate intervention.

When the House in December 2019 took up the first impeachment charge against Trump, Curtis called the president's telephone call with the president of Ukraine "troubling and problematic," but added, "I do not feel that his actions have met that high standard" to warrant removal. Following the January 2021 riot at the Capitol, Curtis said the president's actions were "grossly incompatible with self-governance and the rule of law," but he objected to a "48-hour impeachment process." Instead, he filed a resolution with five other Republicans to "censure and condemn Trump, though Democrats rejected the call by Curtis for a vote. Curtis voted against both attempts by House Republicans to defer certification of the Electoral College results.

When the new Congress convened in January 2021, Curtis was assigned to Energy and Commerce. "No committee in Congress has more impact on Utah, including its oversight of all policy related to health care, technology, commerce, environment, energy, and much more," he said.

UT-3: Central and East Utah   Cook Partisan Voting Index: R+17

Population		Race and Ethnicity		Income	
Total	779,460	White	90.30%	Median Income	$78,931
Land area (sq. miles)	20,071	Black	0.70%	District Income Rank	99
Pop/ sq mi	38.84	Latino	10.90%	Poverty Rate	9.80%
Born in State	59.70%	Asian	1.90%	With health insurance	91.20%
		Two or more races	3.40%	Cash public assistance	1.00%
Age Groups		Other	3.60%	Food stamp/SNAP	5.10%
Under 18	29.20%				
18-34	28.40%	**Education**		**Work**	
35-64	31.10%	H.S grad or less	23.20%	White Collar	44.20%
Over 64	11.10%	Some college	34.90%	Sales and Service	37.80%
		College Degree, 4 yr	28.20%	Blue Collar	18.00%
Military		Post grad	13.70%	Government	12.80%
Veteran/ Active Duty	3.60%				

2020 Pres. Vote	Trump	225,830	(59%)	Biden	131,845	(35%)	Jorgensen	10,945	(3%)
2016 Pres. Vote	Trump	136,782	(47%)	McMullin	70,933	(24%)	Clinton	67,461	(23%)
	Johnson	9,580	(3%)						

Provo Area, Salt Lake City Suburbs: Provo is in a geographically isolated valley between 11,000-foot peaks of the Wasatch Range and the shores of Utah Lake. It is the third-largest city in the state and home of Brigham Young University, the heart of Mormonism and an institution long known for old-fashioned moral standards and the conservative views of its faculty. In 2018, its student population of 33,000 was 98 percent Mormon, and about 25 percent of students were married. It is annually ranked as the most-sober university in the nation. In March 2020, the university reiterated—despite student protests, that "same-sex romantic behavior" was still prohibited. BYU is known for its welcoming of technological innovation. The Mormon commonwealth, after all, started off with a huge shortage of both labor and water, and its inhabitants were motivated to use technology to prosper in the fearsome terrain. Provo is where the vast majority of Mormon missionaries are trained; 36,000 annually have gone through Provo's Missionary Training Center, which has had the effect of producing a disproportionately high number of foreign language speakers in the area.

Today, the city is a technology center, the home of Novell and hundreds of other computer-related firms. Provo produced Philo Farnsworth, the inventor of television, and Harvey Fletcher, inventor of the hearing aid. Nearby Lehi is home to a large office site for the software maker Adobe and to Micron's master planned community for technology leadership. In October 2019, Micron completed the purchase of the share that its partner Intel held in their jointly operated IM Flash plant, where it was developing new computer chips for use in manufacturing, in an effort to reverse the big drop in the U.S. share of the chip market. But Micron announced in March 2021 its plan to sell the chip plant and focus on data centers. In the past decade, Provo has had the fastest-growing tech economy in the nation. Statewide, there were nearly 120,000 tech jobs in 2019, plus 50,000 in aerospace and defense, and 44,000 self-employed tech workers.

The 3rd Congressional District of Utah includes all or part of seven counties in central and eastern Utah. More than 50 percent of the district's residents live in Utah County and 30 percent in Salt Lake. The 3rd takes in affluent suburbs southeast of Salt Lake City, including Holladay and Cottonwood Heights. In Utah County, which grew 23 percent from 2010 to 2019, the district takes in Provo and the string of towns between the mountains and Utah Lake. The area around Moab is a destination for outdoor-loving tourists. The land is mostly owned by one federal agency or another, and there have been bitter fights between locals dependent on mining and environmentalists who want to preserve the scenery, including recently discovered dinosaur tracks. Donald Trump fared poorly throughout Utah, though he improved in 2020. He won the 3rd with 47 percent of the vote in 2016, which then grew to 59 percent. In 2012, Mitt Romney got 79 percent in the district, among his highest in the nation.

Burgess Owens (R)

Elected 2020, 1st term, b. Aug 02, 1951; Columbus, OH; University of Miami-Teacher's Certificate, B.S.; Mormon; Divorced; 6 children.

Professional Career: Player, NFL, 1973-1983; Corporate/National Account Executive, software company, 1989-1994, Sprint/Nextel Inc., 2001-2008, Motorola, 2008-2009; Senior Vice President, Summit Financial Sports Division; Owner, appliance company; Motivational Keynote Speaker, Burgess Owens Talks; Founder/CEO, Utah Mentoring Initiative, Second Chance 4 Youth.

DC Office: 1039 LHOB 20515, 202-225-3011, owens.house.gov

State Offices: West Jordan, 801-999-9801.

Committees: *Education & Labor*: Early Childhood, Elementary & Secondary Education (RMM); Workforce Protections. *Judiciary*: Antitrust, Commercial & Administrative Law; Constitution, Civil Rights & Civil Liberties; Crime, Terrorism & Homeland Security.

Election Results

Election	Name (Party)	Vote (%)		Cand. Spent	Ind. Exp. Support	Ind. Exp. Oppose
2020 General	Burgess Owens (R)...........................	179,688	(48%)	$4,930,684	$1,649,149	$6,434,597
	Ben McAdams (D)...........................	175,923	(47%)	$5,551,611	$778,061	$5,247,874
	John Molnar (L).............................	13,053	(3%)			

Republican Burgess Owens, who was a defensive back for 10 years in the National Football League and later became a mentor to troubled youth, narrowly defeated first-term Rep. Ben McAdams. A veteran local official, McAdams had won the seat two years earlier by 694 votes. By contrast, the Owens victory by almost 3,800 votes seemed nearly a landslide. With Rep. Byron Donalds of Florida, he became one of two African-American Republicans who won House seats in 2020.

Owens was born in Columbus Ohio, where his father was a graduate student. His family moved to Tallahassee Florida, where his father became a professor at Florida A&M University, but the family lived in segregated neighborhoods into the 1960s. He got a bachelor's degree in biology and chemistry from the University of Miami, where he was only the third African-American to receive a scholarship.

His football exploits in college earned him first-team All American status. In 1973, Owens was drafted in the first round by the New York Jets. He spent a total of 10 years with the Jets and Oakland Raiders. With the Raiders, he was credited with six tackles as they won the Super Bowl in 1980. Near the end of his football career, Owens explored conversion to the Mormon Church, with encouragement from teammates.

When his football career ended, Owens started a business with his brother that sold electronic equipment to other businesses. The firm went bankrupt. For a time, he lived with his children in a one-bedroom apartment in Brooklyn New York and worked as a chimney sweep. "That was a very humbling moment," Owens told the Salt Lake Tribune. His professional interest in the computer business resumed with a job at Word Perfect, a software company. Later, he became an account executive with Sprint and Motorola.

Throughout his business career, Owens sought to mentor young people as part of his interest in encouraging conservative values. In 2012, he moved to Utah. With his mentoring, he started up and became chief executive of Second Chance 4 Youth, a nonprofit that assisted those who had been incarcerated.

With political views that he described as "very conservative," Owens was outspoken in opposing demands for reparations by some African-Americans and objected to athletes who kneeled during the national anthem. He became politically active, he told the Tribune, at a time when many Blacks began leaving "the Democrat plantation." He was inspired by President Donald Trump who, Owens said, "was getting the job done." He wrote books about his political views and was an occasional commentator on Fox News.

In his first political campaign, Owens joined several candidates seeking the Republican nomination to oppose McAdams. Launching his campaign, he cited his commitment to four tenets, which he said were first outlined by civil rights pioneer Booker Washington: head, heart, hands and home. In a debate during the Republican primary, the Utah Policy.com website wrote, "Owens was clearly the most partisan of the bunch." He won the nomination with 44 percent against three other candidates. State Rep. Kim Coleman was second, with 24 percent.

In his single debate with McAdams, Owens rejected the suggestion that racism was systemic. "I can tell you with a family that has the color of a rainbow, my personal family, that's not the case," he said. McAdams disagreed, saying that local residents had told him "that doors aren't open to them." Pressed on his views about an alternative health care plan to Obamacare, Owens referred generally to an executive order issued by Trump that assured coverage of individuals with pre-existing conditions.

During their campaign, McAdams slightly outspent Owens. With an extended vote count, their contest was among the last nationwide to be resolved, Owens won, 47.7%-46.7%. In his base of Salt Lake County, which cast four-fifths of the total, McAdams led 52%-43%. Owens swamped him in the outlying areas, with at least two-thirds of the vote in each of the three other counties.

In the House, Owens became ranking Republican on the Education and Labor Subcommittee on Early Childhood, Elementary and Secondary Education. He also served on the Judiciary Committee.

UT-4: Central Utah

Cook Partisan Voting Index: R+6

Population		Race and Ethnicity		Income	
Total	850,432	White	84.50%	Median Income	$80,918
Land area (sq. miles)	2,550	Black	1.50%	District Income Rank	87
Pop/ sq mi	333.46	Latino	17.10%	Poverty Rate	8.10%
Born in State	62.50%	Asian	2.80%	With health insurance	90.00%
		Two or more races	3.60%	Cash public assistance	1.50%
Age Groups		Other	7.80%	Food stamp/SNAP	4.50%
Under 18	30.20%				
18-34	25.30%	**Education**		**Work**	
35-64	34.60%	H.S grad or less	31.80%	White Collar	40.00%
Over 64	9.90%	Some college	34.50%	Sales and Service	36.60%
		College Degree, 4 yr	23.90%	Blue Collar	23.50%
Military		Post grad	10.00%	Government	13.30%
Veteran/ Active Duty	4.30%				

2020 Pres. Vote	Trump	201,329	(52%)	Biden	166,204	(43%)	Jorgensen	10,198	(3%)
2016 Pres. Vote	Trump	108,421	(39%)	Clinton	89,796	(32%)	McMullin	62,348	(22%)

Suburbs of Salt Lake City and Provo: Driving along the Wasatch Front on the 90-mile stretch of Interstate 15 from North Ogden to Provo, one passes within about five miles of two-thirds of the state's population. In Utah, 65 percent of the people occupy about 2 percent of the land area. Salt Lake City accounts for a surprisingly small portion of this: Its population of 200,000 is only slightly larger than the 189,000 it had in 1960. Suburbs and small cities stretch out to the north, south, and west of the city, and even into the foothills of the Wasatch. Salt Lake County, consequently, quadrupled its population from 275,000 in 1950 to nearly 1.2 million in 2019.

The 4th Congressional District of Utah, the smallest district in the state, takes in much of the suburban area to the south of Salt Lake City. About 40 percent of the district's population is in Salt Lake County south of the Interstate 215 Belt Route—West Jordan, South Jordan, Sandy and Riverton—all of which are Republican. Sandy was an old mining town and West Jordan was a farming community, but their populations shot up as suburban growth took off in the 1960s. Today, West Jordan has more than 116,000 people. South Jordan and Lehi, which is farther south, are the new growth centers. Each was among the fastest-growing cities in the nation between 2010 and 2019: 52 percent and 46 percent, respectively. Technology-related employment has expanded strongly in this area since 2010. With recent office openings by Adobe, eBay and Microsoft, some now refer to Lehi as "Silicon Slopes." Bluffdale is the site of the intelligence community's Comprehensive National Cyber security Initiative Data Center.

These are all upscale places, with median incomes well above the national average. More than 80 percent of the 4th is in Salt Lake County, where the Mormon population in 2017 fell below 50 percent for the first time since at least the 1930s. The district also takes in western Utah County, including Eagle Mountain and Saratoga Springs, which were created in the early 1990s and have grown rapidly; in September 2020, the Deseret News reported that Facebook planned to add another

500,000 square feet to its giant data center under construction in Eagle Mountain, at a total cost of $1 billion. Only one area in Salt Lake County has had a population drop since 2010: Draper, the site of the state prison, has moved to make its 700-acre site in the Tech Corridor along Interstate 15 available for development.

This has been a solidly Republican district, which Mitt Romney won in 2012 with 68 percent of the vote, though it is the least Republican district in deep-red Utah. The antipathy toward Donald Trump throughout Utah was especially pronounced here. In 2016, he won the 4th 39%-32%, with much of the remaining vote going to Evan McMullin. In 2020, Trump won, 52%-43%, evidence that Utah includes some Democratic bastions.

VERMONT

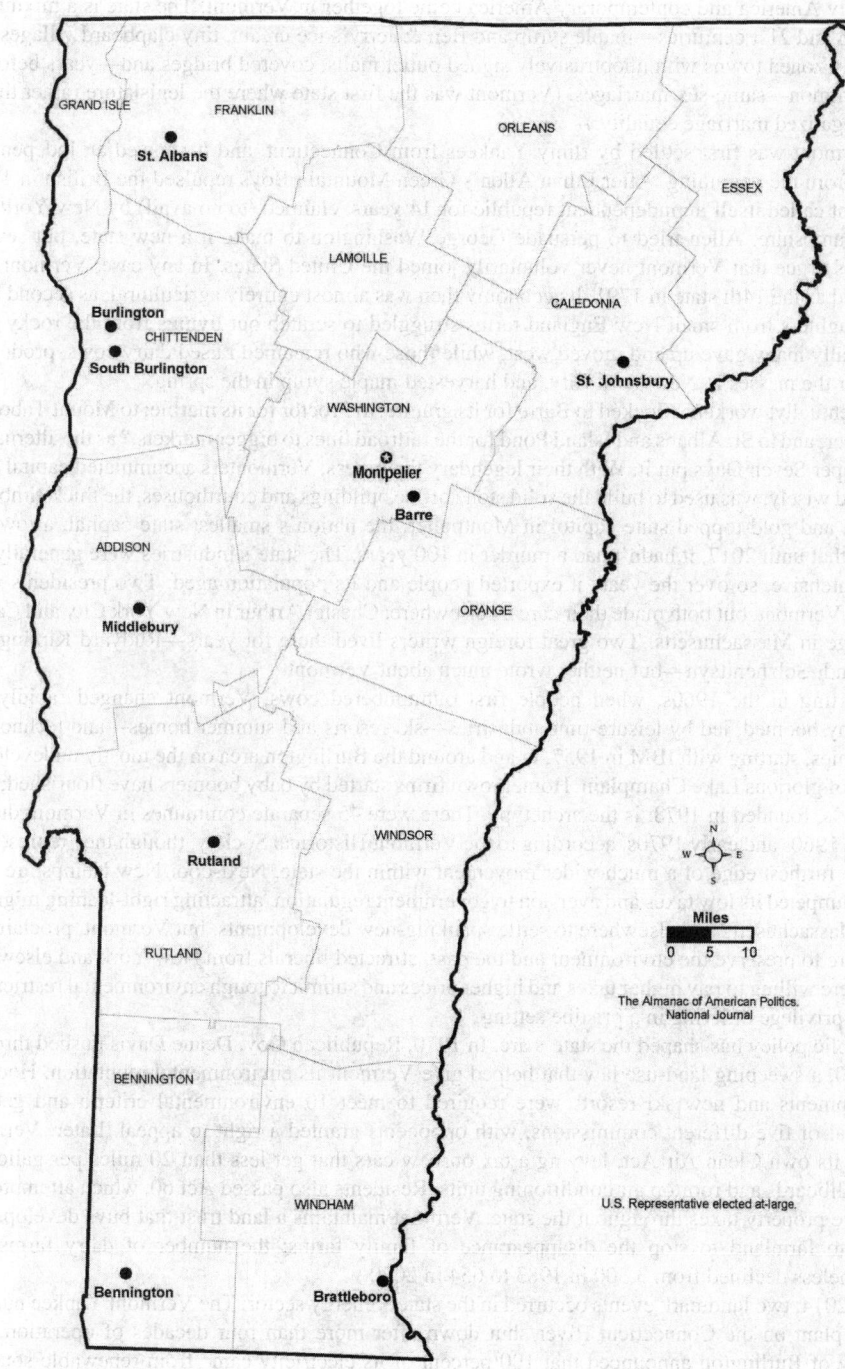

GRAND ISLE

FRANKLIN

ORLEANS

St. Albans

ESSEX

LAMOILLE

CALEDONIA

Burlington

CHITTENDEN

South Burlington

St. Johnsbury

WASHINGTON

✪ **Montpelier**

Barre

ADDISON

ORANGE

Middlebury

WINDSOR

Rutland

RUTLAND

Miles

0   5   10

BENNINGTON

U.S. Representative elected at-large.

WINDHAM

Bennington

Brattleboro

Vermont is one of the bluest states in America. But while the state has overwhelmingly elected socialist Bernie Sanders to Congress, it also elected Republican Phil Scott as its governor in 2016, 2018, and 2020.

Early America and contemporary America come together in Vermont. The state is a mixture of the 19th and 21st centuries—maple syrup and Ben & Jerry's ice cream, tiny clapboard villages and carefully zoned towns with unobtrusively signed outlet malls, covered bridges and—years before it was common—same-sex marriages. (Vermont was the first state where the legislature rather than a court legalized marriage equality.)

Vermont was first settled by flinty Yankees from Connecticut, and it showed an independent streak from the beginning. After Ethan Allen's Green Mountain Boys repulsed the British in 1777, Vermont called itself an independent republic for 14 years, claimed (to no avail) by New York and New Hampshire. Allen tried to persuade George Washington to make it a new state, but several histories argue that Vermont never voluntarily joined the United States. In any case, Vermont was admitted as the 14th state in 1791. Its economy then was almost entirely agricultural, as second sons and daughters from small New England farms struggled to scratch out livings from the rocky soil. Eventually many gave up and moved west, while those who remained raised dairy cows, producing milk for the masses in New York City, and harvested maple syrup in the spring.

Eventually, workers "flocked to Barre for its granite; to Proctor for its marble; to Mount Tabor for its timber; and to St. Albans and Island Pond for the railroad lines to bigger markets," as the alternative newspaper Seven Days put it. With their legendary thriftiness, Vermonters accumulated capital that, invested wisely, was used to build the solid stone office buildings and courthouses, the thick-timbered houses, and gold-topped state capitol in Montpelier, the nation's smallest state capital, a town so sleepy that until 2017, it hadn't had a murder in 100 years. The state's industries were generally not labor-intensive, so over the years it exported people and its population aged. Two presidents were born in Vermont, but both made their careers elsewhere: Chester Arthur in New York City and Calvin Coolidge in Massachusetts. Two great foreign writers lived there for years—Rudyard Kipling and Aleksandr Solzhenitsyn—but neither wrote much about Vermont.

Starting in the 1960s, when people first outnumbered cows, Vermont changed rapidly. Its economy boomed, led by leisure-time industries—ski resorts and summer homes—and technology companies, starting with IBM in 1957, in and around the Burlington area on the mostly undeveloped shores of glorious Lake Champlain. Homegrown firms started by baby boomers have flourished; Ben & Jerry's, founded in 1978, is the archetype. There were 45 separate communes in Vermont during the late 1960s and early 1970s, according to the Vermont Historical Society, though they represented just the furthest edge of a much wider movement within the state. Next-door New Hampshire may have trumpeted its low taxes and aversion to government regulation, attracting right-leaning migrants from Massachusetts and elsewhere to settle spanking-new developments, but Vermont, proclaiming its desire to preserve the environment and the past, attracted liberals from New York and elsewhere who were willing to pay higher taxes and higher prices and submit to tough environmental restrictions for the privilege of living in a pristine setting.

Public policy has shaped the state's arc. In 1970, Republican Gov. Deane Davis pushed through Act 250, a sweeping land-use law that helped give Vermont its environmental reputation. Housing developments and new ski resorts were required to meet 10 environmental criteria and get the approval of five different commissions, with opponents granted a right to appeal. Later, Vermont passed its own Clean Air Act, levying a tax on new cars that get less than 20 miles per gallon. It bans billboards and rooftop air conditioning units. Residents also passed Act 60, which attempted to equalize property taxes throughout the state. Vermont maintains a land trust that buys development rights to farmland to stop the disappearance of family farms; the number of dairy farms has nevertheless declined from 3,300 in 1983 to 654 in 2020.

In 2014, two landmark events occurred in the state's energy sector: The Vermont Yankee nuclear power plant on the Connecticut River shut down after more than four decades of operation, and the city of Burlington announced that 100 percent of its electricity came from renewable sources, including renewably farmed wood chips, hydroelectric power, wind turbines and solar panels. In 2019, Burlington announced a goal of becoming a net-zero energy locality by 2030, meaning it would have a carbon-neutral footprint for heating and transportation. Meanwhile, the state's largest electric utility, Green Mountain Power, has set a goal of securing all-renewable power by 2030, something that two of the state's smaller utilities, Burlington Electric and Washington Electric, had already met. Liberal policies have proven to be compatible with economic success: The unemployment rate was 2.4 percent in February 2020, just before the coronavirus pandemic; it spiked briefly but returned to 3.1 percent by December 2020, less than half the national rate of 6.7 percent. Part of that could be attributable to Vermont's wage growth over the last decade, among the nation's lowest.

The quintessential Vermont commercial strip is the Church Street Marketplace in downtown Burlington, a four-block pedestrian mall known for its tasteful shopping venues and street fairs—the polar opposite of the big-box stores sprouting elsewhere. (No state has a smaller largest city than Burlington, with 42,000 residents.) Target opened its first Vermont location in South Burlington in 2018, making it the last state to get one. Dollar General was required to face its Chester store with clapboard wood rather than vinyl siding and keep its shopping carts off the street. For a long time, Vermont had one exception to its tight regulatory impulse—few restrictions on gun rights, tolerated even by leading Vermont Democrats, to the consternation of others in their party who represent more urbanized areas. But that changed after the 2018 Parkland Florida high school mass shooting, as the Democratic legislature and the Republican governor worked together to enact a gun-control package. The bipartisan leadership also helped it battle the coronavirus, with the state adopting an early mask mandate, cautious reopening measures, and aggressive testing and contract-tracing efforts. Vermont's approach "should be the model for the country," Dr. Anthony Fauci told state leaders during the pandemic.

Population growth in Vermont has been sluggish, due to the quadruple whammy of a low birth rate, an aging population, out-migration of residents to other states, and low international immigration. Only four of the state's 14 counties have grown since the 2010 census, all of them in the northwest around Burlington: Chittenden, Franklin, Lamoille, and Grand Isle. Vermont has a smaller percentage of children under 15 than any other state. When Moody's downgraded Vermont's bond rating slightly in 2018 and Fitch Ratings followed suit in 2019, they did so less for the state's fiscal picture than for the risk that slow population growth and aging pose for its economic base. The state has established the Remote Worker Grant Program, which provides $10,000 to anyone who moves to the state and works remotely in their existing job; it has aided a couple hundred newcomers, though in 2019 the state auditor concluded that it's hard to tell whether these households would have relocated to Vermont anyway. Sparsely populated southern Vermont and the even more sparsely populated Northeast Kingdom have experienced economic stagnation, and their remoteness and lack of reliable broadband is hobbling their ability to take advantage of post-coronavirus opportunities for remote work. Vermont might also be having trouble attracting new residents because of its low diversity: It's the second-whitest state in the nation after Maine, and Blacks, Hispanics and Asian-Americans each account for less than 2 percent of the population. Residents were forced to do a gut check when Kiah Morris, the first African-American woman to be elected to the state legislature, resigned from her seat in 2018 following a series of racist threats, ranging from social media attacks to vandalism at her home. (The state attorney general filed no charges.) Vermont also suffers from an aging populace and low birth rate.

Starting in the 19th century, Yankee Vermont was the most Republican state in the nation, voting Republican in every presidential election from 1856 to 1960. In 1936, Vermont and Maine were the only states to resist Franklin D. Roosevelt's landslide, inspiring Roosevelt's campaign manager, James Farley, to joke, "As Maine goes, so goes Vermont." For three decades thereafter, Vermont's Yankee Protestant Republicans outnumbered its French Canadian and Irish Catholic Democrats. As newcomers kept arriving, Vermont was divided politically along different lines: between liberal, highly educated newcomers and conservative, less educated, old Vermonters. A key figure was Howard Dean, who grew up on Park Avenue in New York City, was educated at Yale and moved to Vermont, where he and his wife practiced medicine. He was elected lieutenant governor in 1986 and became governor when incumbent Republican Richard Snelling died in August 1991, learning of his elevation while treating a patient. He was elected to five terms in his own right (Vermont and New Hampshire are the last states with two-year gubernatorial terms) before running unsuccessfully for president in 2004.

Sanders, a self-styled socialist, has managed to hold office almost continuously in Vermont since 1981, though Democratic Gov. Peter Shumlin faced the limits of Vermont's liberalism when he was forced to pull back from a proposed single-payer health insurance system in 2014, citing its cost. Republicans haven't become extinct in Vermont, but the ones who survived tended to be much more moderate than their peers within the national GOP. When Shumlin opted not to seek another term in 2016, Scott, the moderate Republican lieutenant governor, won the open seat and has easily won reelection twice. Even today, Sen. Patrick Leahy is the only Democrat ever to be elected senator from Vermont. Leahy, Sanders, and Rep. Peter Welch collectively have 90 years of congressional service. The state has never elected a woman to the Senate or the House.

In 2020, Vermont had the nation's second strongest swing to the Democrats in the presidential election, exceeded only by Colorado; Joe Biden won by a 35-point margin, compared to the 27-point edge for Hillary Clinton in 2016. But that increase was largely an artifact of the drastically shrunken third-party vote, which plunged from 13 percent in 2016 to 3 percent in 2020. Write-in votes alone, many of them for Sanders, accounted for 7 percent of presidential ballots cast in 2016, compared to just half a percent in 2020. Trump won just one county in each election—Essex, in the Northeast Kingdom, population 6,163—and each of the four most populous counties saw the winning margin shift toward Democrats by between 6 and 12 points. Except for Scott-style centrists, Vermont should retain its blue tint for the foreseeable future.

Cook Partisan Voting Index: D+15

Population		Race and Ethnicity		Income	
Total	623,989	White	93.80%	Median Income	63,001
Land area (sq. miles)	9,217	Black	1.50%	State Income Rank	26 out of 50
Pop/ sq mi	67.70	Latino	2.00%	Poverty Rate	10.20%
Born in state	48.80%	Asian	2.40%	With health insurance	95.50%
		Two or more races	2.50%	Cash public assistance	2.60%
Age Groups		Other	0.90%	Food stamp/SNAP	12.8%
Under 18	18.20%				
18-34	22.70%	**Education**		**Work**	
35-64	39.00%	H.S grad or less	35.90%	White Collar	42.90%
Over 64	20.10%	Some college	25.40%	Sales and Service	36.10%
Military		College Degree, 4 yr	22.70%	Blue Collar	21.00%
Veteran/ Active Duty	7.00%	Post grad	16.00%	Government	14.70%

Presidential Politics

2020 Primary (D)	Sanders (D)	79,921(51%)	Biden (D)	34,669(22%)	Warren (D)	19,785(13%)	
	Bloomberg (D)	14,828 (9%)					
2020 Pres. Vote	Biden (D)	242,820(66%)	Trump (R)	112,704(31%)			
2016 Pres. Vote	Clinton (D)	178,573(57%)	Trump (R)	95,369(30%)	Johnson (L)	10,078 (3%)	
	Stein (G)	6,758 (2%)					

No state has voted more often for Republican presidential candidates than Vermont: From the birth of the GOP in 1856 until the 1992 election, Lyndon Johnson in 1964 was the only Democrat to carry the state. Times have certainly changed. Since 1992, the state has been reliably Democratic, and in 2020 it was the most Democratic state in the country (it was No. 2 in both of Barack Obama's elections, behind only his home state of Hawaii). Vermont has become solidly liberal on foreign policy, economic and cultural issues (though less so on gun control). In 2016, Hillary Clinton defeated Donald Trump, 57%-30%, with 6 percent of Vermonters writing in home-state Sen. Bernie Sanders' name on the general election ballot. In 2020, with Sanders more committed to campaigning for the Democrat, Joe Biden defeated Trump 66%-31%, winning all but one county.

In the 2008 primary, Obama and Hillary Clinton were locked in a struggle for the nomination. Obama beat Clinton 59%-39%. In 2012, when the Republican race was still raging, Mitt Romney led with 40 percent, to 26 percent for Ron Paul and 24 percent for Rick Santorum. In 2016, John Kasich held several town-hall events, but Trump beat him, 33%-30%; Sanders crushed Clinton in the Democratic race, 86%-14%. The 2020 primary, held on Super Tuesday, was a bit closer: Sanders beat Biden 51%-22%.

Congressional Districts

117th Congress Lineup	1D	116th Congress Lineup	1D

Phil Scott (R)

Elected 2016, term expires 2023, 3rd term; b. Aug. 4, 1958, Barre; Univ. of Vermont, BS 1980; Married (Diana); 2 children.

Elected Office: VT Senate 2001-2010; VT Lt. Governor 2011-2017

Professional Career: Stock Car Racer 1996-2005; Co-owner, DuBois Construction, 1986-2016.

Office: 109 State Street Pavilion Montpelier, 05609-0101; 802-828-3333; Fax: 802-828-3339; Website: vermont.gov

Lt. Gov.: Molly Gray (D) **Atty. Gen:** T. J. Donovan (D) **Sec. of State:** Jim Condos (D)
State Legislature: Senate: 22D, 6R, 2P **House:** 94D, 43R, 5I, 7P, 1V

Election Results

Election	Name (Party)	Vote (%)
2018 General	Phil Scott (R)	151,261 (55%)
	Christine Hallquist (D)	110,335 (40%)
2020 General	Phil Scott (R)	248,412 (68%)
	David Zuckerman (D)	99,214 (27%)
2018 Primary	Phil Scott (R)	24,142 (67%)
	Keith Stern (R)	11,669 (33%)

Prior winning percentage: 2016 (53%)

Vermont may be one of the most liberal states in the union, but voters have elected Phil Scott, a Republican, as their governor three times, and by increasing margins.

Scott was born in Barre, earned a bachelor's degree from the University of Vermont, and co-owned a company, DuBois Construction, that he sold, as he had promised, prior to his inauguration as governor. A stock-car enthusiast, Scott also founded a program called Wheels for Warmth, which enabled Vermont residents to donate tires they no longer need, with some being resold to benefit heating-fuel assistance programs and others recycled. Scott won a state Senate seat in 2000 and served for a decade. In 2010, he ran for lieutenant governor, which in Vermont is elected separately from the governor. In the general election, he defeated Democrat Steven Howard, 49%-42%, as Democrat Peter Shumlin was winning the open-seat gubernatorial race. As lieutenant governor, Scott started the "Vermont Everyday Jobs" initiative, in which he worked a few hours several times a month in different jobs, aiming to promote state businesses and highlight local workers. Scott was fiscally conservative but steered a moderate course overall; by the time he ran for reelection in 2012, he was endorsed by the state affiliate of the National Education Association. Scott won a second term over Democrat Cassandra Gekas, 57%-40%. Two years later, he won a third term without even facing a Democratic candidate.

When Shumlin decided against running for a fourth two-year term as governor in 2016, Scott jumped into the race. First, though, Scott had to win the August GOP primary against former Wall Street executive Bruce Lisman. On the big issues, such as their stances toward business, taxation and the state's health care system, Scott and Lisman were generally on the same page. Instead, the race boiled down to a faceoff between a Montpelier insider (Scott) and a political outsider (Lisman). With the backing of much of the party establishment, Scott won the primary, 60%-39%. In the competitive Democratic primary, state Transportation Secretary Sue Minter prevailed decisively over former state Sens. Matt Dunne and Peter Galbraith. But Scott was able to maintain his image as a moderate pragmatist in the mold of the state's two most recent Republican governors, Richard Snelling and Jim Douglas. Even as Hillary Clinton was defeating Donald Trump by a 57%-30% margin, voters backed Scott over Minter, 53%-44%. (Scott had withheld his support from Trump.) Scott's victory made him the only Republican to hold statewide office in Vermont.

In his first year, Scott vetoed a marijuana legalization bill, though by January of the following year he reversed himself and signed a similar bill, acknowledging "mixed emotions." With the bill's enactment, Vermont became the first state to approve recreational marijuana through legislative action rather than by a popular vote. In 2018, Scott vetoed a range of proposed fee increases as well as a minimum wage hike to $15. Republicans in the legislature sustained Scott's vetoes. His most consequential action, however, addressed a third rail of Vermont politics: gun control. Scott and legislators enacted a package that included a ban on bump stocks and large magazines; a requirement that gun sales be handled through a licensed dealer; and permission for police to temporarily confiscate guns from individuals deemed to pose an immediate threat. In 2016, Scott had campaigned on not changing the state's gun laws, but he said he changed his mind after the mass school shooting in Parkland Florida in February 2018, as well as a case that involved a Columbine-style plan to shoot up a school in Vermont that was stopped in time. Scott's change of heart enraged many Republicans: At the bill signing, he was heckled with calls of "Traitor!" and "BS!"

As the GOP base grew restive, Scott's once-charmed approval ratings sank and Keith Stern, a political novice and owner of Stern's Quality Produce in White River Junction, challenged Scott from the right in 2018. But with help from the Republican Governors Association, Scott prevailed, 67%-33%. The Democrats, meanwhile, had a four-way primary, won by Christine Hallquist, the former CEO of Vermont Electric Cooperative and a transgender woman. Despite national media attention, Hallquist was a heavy underdog, due to Scott's ability to maintain support among moderate-to-liberal voters by openly defying Trump. Scott opposed Trump's immigration policies; he pledged to uphold the Paris climate accord after Trump pulled out; he declined to endorse Brett Kavanaugh's Supreme Court nomination; and he opposed GOP efforts to roll back the Affordable Care Act. Scott won another term, 55%-40%, with Hallquist taking only one county, Windham (Brattleboro). Scott flipped the state's most populous county, Chittenden (Burlington), though Democrats gained ground in both legislative chambers, making it harder for Republicans to sustain Scott's vetoes.

In 2019, Scott signed a bill that enshrined abortion rights and another that officially changed Columbus Day to Indigenous Peoples' Day, making Vermont the third state to make that switch. But he vetoed a measure that would have instituted a waiting period for gun purchases. Scott explained his veto by saying that with the earlier package of gun laws in place, "we must now prioritize strategies that address the underlying causes of violence and suicide" rather than passing new restrictions. Scott went on to veto three major bills in 2020; two of them were overridden by the legislature. Scott's veto of a statewide family leave bill was sustained; he objected to the required $29 million payroll tax. But the legislature overrode Scott's veto of a bill to increase the minimum wage to $12.55 by 2022 and then index it to inflation. And they overrode his veto of a measure that set targets for reducing carbon emissions to 80 percent below 2005 levels by 2050. Scott said he supported efforts to tackle climate change but opposed the bill's provision that allowed lawsuits against the state if it fell short of the targets. Meanwhile, Scott signed a bill to accelerate expungements of past marijuana convictions, and he allowed a second bill, to legalize marijuana sales, to become law without his signature. A law to overhaul the rules for the use of deadly force by police also became law without his signature.

What bolstered Scott's standing among voters the most was his handling of the coronavirus pandemic. He issued an early stay-at-home order and mandated masks statewide in July. Between mid-June and mid-July, Vermont was the only state in the nation to go a full month without a death from the virus. Meanwhile, Scott continued to distance himself from Trump. Scott backed former Massachusetts Gov. Bill Weld over Trump in the GOP primary, and he announced on Election Day that he had crossed party lines to vote for Joe Biden. "I put country over party," he said, adding that Biden could "heal the country." In his own election, Scott faced Democratic Lt. Gov. David Zuckerman, who had won a competitive primary against former state Education Secretary Rebecca

Holcombe and two other candidates. But with Scott's approval consistently high, the race never became competitive; moreover, the last time an incumbent Vermont governor lost a reelection bid was 1962. In the end, Scott almost tripled his margin of victory compared to 2018, from 15 points to 41; he won every county, flipping Windham County and increasing his winning margin in Chittenden County from four points to 37. Scott more than doubled Trump's vote in Vermont. These days, there aren't many Vermont Republicans with bright political futures, but Scott's reputation remains strong.

Patrick Leahy (D)

Elected 1974, term expires 2022, 8th term, b. Mar 31, 1940; Montpelier, VT; St. Michael's College, B.A., 1961; Georgetown University Law Center, J.D., 1964; Roman Catholic; Married (Marcelle Pomerleau Leahy); 3 children; 5 grandchildren.

Elected Office: VT State Attorney, Chittenden County, 1966-1974.

Professional Career: Practicing attorney, 1964-1974.

DC Office: 437 RSOB 20510, 202-224-4242, Fax: 202-224-3479, leahy.senate.gov

State Offices: Burlington, 802-863-2525; Montpelier, 802-229-0569.

Committees: Senate President Pro Tempore. *Agriculture, Nutrition & Forestry*: Conservation, Climate, Forestry & Natural Resources; Food & Nutrition, Specialty Crops, Organics & Research; Livestock, Dairy, Poultry, Local Food Sys & Food Safety & Sec. *Appropriations (Chmn)*: Ex Officio membership on all subcommittees. *Judiciary*: Competition Policy, Antitrust & Consumer Rights; Criminal Justice & Counterterrorism; Federal Courts, Oversight, Agency Action & Federal Rights; Subcommittee on Intellectual Property (Chmn). *Rules & Administration*.

Group Ratings

	ADA	ACLU	AFL-CIO	LCV	COC	HAFA	ACU	CFG	FRC
2020	-	92%	-	92%	-	0%	5%	-	-
2019	100%	C	100%	100%	44%	C	5%	0%	0%

Almanac Ratings 2019-2020

	Economy	Social	Foreign	Composite
Liberal	100%	100%	89%	96%
Conservative	0%	0%	11%	4%

Key Votes of the 116th Congress

1. EPA clean energy rules	Y	5. Russia sanctions	Y	9. Barr as Atty. General	N
2. U.S./Mex./Can. trade deal	Y	6. Troops in SYR, AFG	N	10. Spending at the border	Y
3. Cut unemployment benefits	N	7. Veto arms sales to Saudis	Y	11. Coney Barrett to Sup. Ct.	N
4. Shelton to Fed Reserve	N	8. Defense $$$, veto override	Y	12. Electoral College objections	N

Election Results

Election	Name (Party)	Vote (%)		Cand. Spent	Ind. Exp. Support	Ind. Exp. Oppose
2016 General	Patrick Leahy (D)	192,243	(61%)	$2,558,664		
	Scott Miline (R)	103,637	(33%)	$57,826		
	Cris Ericson (M)	9,156	(3%)			
2016 Primary	Patrick Leahy (D)	62,249	(89%)			
	Cris Ericson (D)	7,596	(11%)			

Prior winning percentages: 2016 (60%), 2010 (64%), 2004 (71%), 1998 (72%), 1992 (54%), 1986 (63%), 1980 (50%), 1974 (50%)

Democrat Patrick Leahy, Vermont's senior senator, was first elected in 1974, and, at the outset of 2021, was the fifth longest serving senator in history. By the time his current term ends at the beginning of 2023, he will have moved up to third on the all-time list. Should he seek reelection, he would become the longest serving senator ever in the middle of his ninth term, surpassing the late Sen. Robert Byrd of West Virginia. In nearly five decades on Capitol Hill, Leahy has wielded influence over a wide range of issues—running the gamut from agricultural subsidies to civil liberties to international humanitarian aid. He has chaired three Senate committees: Agriculture, from 1987 to 1995; Judiciary, from 2001 to 2003 and again from 2007 to 2015; and now, Appropriations, whose gavel he claimed in early 2021 when Democrats retook the Senate.

Leahy is a stalwart liberal known for periodic flashes of temper and can be a sharp-tongued partisan. Republican Vice President Dick Cheney infamously told Leahy, "Go f--- yourself," after a 2004 picture-taking session at the Capitol; Cheney apparently was angered by Leahy's criticism of the activities of Halliburton, a company Cheney once headed, during the Iraq War. More recently, Leahy theatrically ripped up a copy of the Judiciary Committee's rules of procedure during an August 2019 session—after the panel's then-chair, South Carolina Republican Lindsey Graham, had suspended the rules to win approval of bill sought by the Trump administration to change procedures for those seeking asylum in the U.S. "This is supposed to be the Senate Judiciary Committee, not the Donald Trump Committee," Leahy snarled.

But Leahy arrived in the Senate in a more collegial time and has continued to reach across the aisle in a highly polarized era. He has found common ground on civil liberties and criminal justice issues with some of the Senate's most outspoken conservatives, including Kentucky Sen. Rand Paul and Utah Sen. Mike Lee. And he has enjoyed a good working relationship with his longtime Judiciary Committee colleague Iowa Republican Chuck Grassley—even though Leahy did not hesitate to lambaste Republicans' handling of Brett Kavanaugh's 2018 nomination to the Supreme Court, when Grassley chaired the Judiciary panel.

As the chamber's most senior member, Leahy initially served as Senate president pro tempore from late 2012 until early 2015, when the GOP regained the majority; he reassumed that position in early 2021. It soon put him in the spotlight. When both Chief Justice John Roberts and Vice President Kamala Harris declined to preside over the second impeachment trial of former President Trump—on charges of inciting the mob that stormed the Capitol on Jan. 6 with the goal of keeping him in power—the task fell to Leahy. It made him both judge and one of 100 jurors, sparking complaints of conflict-of-interest from Trump's attorneys as well as some Republican colleagues. "This is not something I requested," Mr. Leahy told the New York Times, adding: "I've presided hundreds of hours—I don't know how many rulings I've made. I've never had anyone, Republican or Democrat, say my rulings were not fair." Leahy avoided major controversy in his handling of the four-day trial, which ended as he joined his 49 Democratic colleagues and seven Republicans in voting to convict—a majority but still short of the two-thirds supermajority required.

Leahy grew up in Vermont when the Green Mountain State, now one of the nation's bluest, was rock-ribbed Republican. Born in Montpelier, he graduated from St. Michael's College, just north of Burlington. He earned a law degree at Georgetown University and returned home to join the law firm of Philip Hoff, who, in 1962, had become the first Democrat since before the Civil War to win election as Vermont's governor. In 1966, Hoff appointed Leahy, then just 26, to fill a vacancy as state's attorney for Chittenden County, which includes Burlington. He was elected to full terms in 1966 and 1970.

In 1974, at 34, he ran for the Senate seat vacated by liberal Republican George Aiken, first elected the year Leahy was born. Leahy had made a name for himself in the pocket-sized state as a prosecutor who tried major felony cases; he also had a solid base in Democratic Burlington, the state's largest city, with the thoughtful temperament Vermonters like in their public officials. In a year when Democrats benefited from the Watergate scandal, Leahy defeated Rep. Richard Mallary 50%-46%; today, Leahy is the only Democrat still on Capitol Hill among the wave of "Watergate babies" elected that year to the House and Senate. He was also the first Democrat to win a Vermont Senate seat—and remains the only one. His colleague, Sen. Bernie Sanders, though now a force in the national Democratic Party, has won three Senate terms running as an independent.

In 2012, Leahy had the seniority to claim the chairmanship of the Appropriations Committee upon the death of Hawaii Sen. Daniel Inouye. Instead, he opted to remain at the helm of the Judiciary Committee because the latter panel was confronting two issues that could shape his legislative legacy. One was the first attempt at comprehensive immigration reform in six years; the other was the first major gun control legislation in nearly two decades. Leahy was an unlikely figure on the latter issue: A gun enthusiast, he was a member of his college shooting team and still enjoys the sport. In 1993, Leahy voted against passage of the so-called Brady Bill, which requires background checks for individuals purchasing firearms. Vermont continues to have one of the highest rates of gun ownership in the country—and, until recent years, some of the nation's least restrictive gun laws.

After the December 2012 school massacre in Newtown Connecticut in which 28 people including the shooter were killed, Leahy moved a series of bills through his committee to bar the straw purchase and trafficking of guns. His legislation included reinstatement of a ban on assault weapons, which then-Senate Majority Leader Harry Reid refused to schedule because it lacked the votes for passage. Even so, efforts to pass more modest gun control legislation fell apart when a bipartisan compromise to expand background checks to more gun buyers fell five votes short of the 60-vote threshold needed to end a filibuster.

On immigration, Leahy held hearings to try to build support for reform, while leaving much of the legislative work to a bipartisan group of eight senators. He guided the major overhaul of immigration laws, providing a path to citizenship for undocumented immigrants, through the Senate on a 68-32 vote. The GOP-controlled House never took up the measure.

Leahy's first stint as Judiciary chairman coincided with the attacks of Sept. 11, 2001. He worked with the Bush administration to hammer out the sweeping law that sparked a national debate over government investigative powers at the expense of individual liberties. The Patriot Act, enacted a month after the 9/11 attacks, was essentially the version crafted in Leahy's committee. Leahy fought attempts to expand police powers after the attacks and opposed a proposal to allow the government to detain and deport immigrants suspected of terrorism without presenting evidence in court.

In 2013, when onetime National Security Agency contractor Edward Snowden revealed the agency was collecting Americans' telephone and email data en masse, Leahy and Utah's Lee introduced a bill to require targeted warrants to obtain Americans' data from telecommunications firms. The effort came to fruition in 2015. Chairman Grassley's failure to move a bill through the Judiciary Committee strengthened Leahy's hand. It left the Leahy-Lee measure and a proposal backed by GOP Sen. Mitch McConnell of Kentucky, then the majority leader—to continue the law in its current form—as the major options. McConnell was forced to concede to the approach contained in the Leahy-Lee bill and a similar House-passed measure. "It's historical. It's the first major overhaul of government surveillance in decades," Leahy said after Congress stripped the NSA of authority to collect from U.S. citizens' phone and internet communications in bulk.

Leahy and Lee have since collaborated on several efforts to place restrictions on a related law: the Foreign Intelligence Surveillance Act. Section 702 of the latter permits the government to collect phone and email data of foreigners abroad without a warrant—even when they communicate with U.S. citizens. Leahy and Lee again teamed up in 2018 on an amendment requiring the government to get a warrant to access Americans' phone and email data collected incidentally under Section 702. Their effort failed narrowly. Leahy and Lee were more successful in 2020 in targeting another aspect of FISA: Their amendment expanding the role of outside legal experts in secret FISA court proceedings overwhelmingly cleared the Senate. In a Washington Post op-ed, Leahy and Lee said their move added "a layer of protection for those who will likely never know they have been targeted for secret surveillance."

Leahy was an early supporter of Barack Obama in the 2008 presidential primaries and guided his two Supreme Court nominees, Sonia Sotomayor and Elena Kagan, through the Judiciary Committee to swift Senate confirmation. He accused Republicans of seeking to play the race card against Sotomayor, the court's first Latina justice, and of gender bias toward Kagan. As the GOP blocked numerous Obama nominees to district and appeals courts, Leahy lamented in 2013, "I have repeatedly asked Senate Republicans to abandon their destructive tactics." Soon thereafter, Reid sought to end to such tactics by invoking the "nuclear option"—changing the Senate rules to prevent filibusters for all appointees except Supreme Court justices; in 2017, Republicans under McConnell extended the move to include high court nominees.

Leahy often held up President George W. Bush's judicial nominations. He led filibusters against 10 Bush appeals court nominees, tactics about which Republicans bitterly complained. Leahy countered that the committee had approved most appellate and trial court nominees and argued he had been fairer to Bush's appointees than Republicans had been to those put forth by President Bill Clinton. When Leahy returned as chairman in 2007, he instituted "blue slip" procedures that gave all senators the ability to object to judicial nominees within their home states. "I have steadfastly protected the rights of the minority," Leahy said in 2012. "I have done so despite criticism from Democrats." Under Trump, Senate Republicans abandoned Leahy's blue slip procedures. It prompted some progressives to grumble that judgeships Obama had been unable to fill remained open to conservatives appointed by Trump.

Leahy led the criticism in 2016 when Republicans, spearheaded by McConnell, refused to hold hearings on Obama's nomination of federal Judge Merrick Garland to succeed the late Justice Antonin Scalia, ostensibly because it was an election year. It's sleazy, Leahy told USA Today. "Have the courage to do your job and actually ask the questions." It put Leahy at odds with Grassley, whom Leahy tried to prod into breaking with McConnell to convene hearings on the nomination. Grassley had breakfast with Garland but went no further, and the seat remained vacant until Trump took office and nominated Judge Neil Gorsuch to fill it in early 2017. In late 2020, when McConnell said he would move to confirm federal Judge Amy Coney Barrett to replace the late Justice Ruth Bader Ginsburg just before the election, Leahy accused the Kentucky senator of a "flip flop" that would "stain the Supreme Court." On NPR, Leahy declared: "I've never seen political hypocrisy at this level. I mean, it will actually go down in the journals of political hypocrisy."

Leahy announced he would vote against Kavanaugh before sexual assault allegations against the nominee were aired, saying he didn't believe Kavanaugh had been truthful about several policy questions. Leahy was overshadowed by junior Democratic colleagues during Kavanaugh's confirmation hearings, but his rhetoric was no less pointed. As the hearings opened in September 2018, Leahy said, "This is the most incomplete, most partisan and least transparent vetting for any Supreme Court nominee I have ever seen—and I've seen more than anyone else in the Senate. … I'm just sorry to see the Senate Judiciary Committee descend this way." He slammed the unwillingness of Grassley and other committee Republicans to request records relating to Kavanaugh's tenure as a top aide in the George W. Bush White House. In a New York Times op-ed, Leahy contrasted his cooperation with Republicans during Kagan's 2009 confirmation to obtain records relating to her tenure as an aide in the Clinton White House.

In 2005, Leahy led the Democratic minority's questioning of Bush's Supreme Court nominees, John Roberts and Samuel Alito. He surprised many when he voted to approve the conservative Roberts, but he voted against Alito. "This president is in the midst of a radical realignment of the powers of government and its intrusiveness into the private lives of Americans. This nomination is part of that plan," Leahy said in opposing Alito. In 2017, he voted against Gorsuch, taking aim at not only several of Gorsuch's rulings but at what Leahy termed his "nonresponsive testimony" before the Judiciary panel. "Compared to Chief Justice Roberts, there is a yawning crevasse between the words Judge Gorsuch spoke to us and his actual record," Leahy said. He lodged a similar complaint in 2020 after the Coney Barrett hearings. "Judge Barrett refused to stand up for even the most basic tenets of our democracy," Leahy said. "And she refused to recuse herself from any election dispute." Speaking weeks before Trump refused to accept the results of the 2020 election, Leahy warned, "Make no mistake, President Trump was listening and he sees this as a green light to do whatever he wants."

In 2017, Leahy used his seniority to become the top Democrat on the Appropriations Committee. A year later, when Alabama Republican Richard Shelby became the Appropriations chairman, the two set out to restore "regular order" to an annual funding process plagued by partisan gridlock and brinkmanship—amid increasing reliance on stopgap continuing resolutions to keep the government running. Leahy and Shelby shared concerns that the breakdown of the appropriations process—the last time all 12 annual appropriations measures were passed and individually signed was 2005—had concentrated increasing power with congressional leaders to cut last-minute deals at the expense of rank-and-file lawmakers. "We took a couple of trips together and we talked about it, and just said, 'Unless we get this back, the Senate is really screwed,'" Leahy told the New York Times. "We have to get back to doing it the regular way."

Leahy and Shelby persuaded their respective party leaderships to keep "poison pill" policy riders off appropriations bills. Shelby and Leahy by the end of 2018 had shepherded nine of the 12 annual appropriations measures to Senate passage on bipartisan votes. Those bills did not include the Department of Homeland Security measure that was a focal point in the battle over Trump's proposed southern border wall; the 35-day government shutdown of 2018-2019 complicated the efforts of Shelby and Leahy in restoring the traditional appropriations process. It was complicated further in the 2020 election year, amid the COVID-19 pandemic and the Black Lives Matter movement. According to Roll Call, Shelby planned to mark up a half-dozen annual appropriations bills in early summer but changed his mind after Leahy and other Democrats signaled plans to offer amendments adding pandemic relief and social justice-related provisions. Shelby said he would "not allow the appropriations process to be hijacked and turned into a partisan sideshow." A Senate Democratic appropriations aide countered that previous agreements were meant to avoid poison pill policy— not funding—amendments.

For many years, Leahy was the top Democrat on the Appropriations subcommittee with jurisdiction over the State Department and foreign aid programs; he reluctantly gave that up in 2021 when a new Democratic Caucus rule preempted him from chairing the subcommittee as well as the full committee. In a 2020 interview with the Vermont Digger, Leahy listed efforts to eliminate land mines and to free government contractor Alan Gross from a Cuban prison as among his proudest accomplishments. Since 1989, he has crusaded against land mines—easy and cheap to implant yet difficult and expensive to remove. The Leahy War Victims Fund was created that year within the U.S. Agency for International Development, initially to assist victims of land mine explosions; in 1994, he persuaded the United Nations to unanimously call for the eventual elimination of land mines. As an opponent of the U.S. embargo against Cuba, Leahy was actively involved in successful negotiations to free Gross in 2014—a move that paved the way for Obama's decision to restore diplomatic relations with the island nation. Leahy was among those who flew to Cuba to bring Gross home.

Earlier in his career, Leahy became one of the few senators to chair the Agriculture Committee who did not represent a state with crops like wheat, corn or cotton. As the panel's ranking Democrat, he worked with Indiana Republican Richard Lugar in the mid-1990s to phase out the subsidy system. But after their success in enacting the Freedom to Farm Act of 1996, crop prices fell. Congress took to supporting large annual subsidies as emergency relief to farmers, and in 2002, largely rolled back the 1996 act. Leahy lists the Organic Foods Production Act—included in the 1990 Farm Bill to establish uniform national standards for foods labeled "organic" —as among his leading legislative accomplishments.

In Leahy's first race for Senate in 1974, 4 percent of the vote went to the candidate of the Liberty Union Party: Sanders, Vermont's junior senator since 2006. In 2016, Leahy endorsed Hillary Clinton for the Democratic presidential nomination, saying he had committed to Clinton before Sanders got into the race. When Sanders announced a second presidential run in February 2019, Leahy endorsed him. He also co-sponsored Sanders' "Medicare For All" legislation.

Leahy had a close call in his first reelection bid, surviving a 1980 challenge by a single percentage point amid a national Republican landslide. In 1986, a year more favorable for Democrats, he had little trouble defeating popular Gov. Richard Snelling; he won 63%-35%. In 1992, Leahy was held to 54 percent by Republican Jim Douglas, later elected governor. Leahy has easily won reelection since. In 2016, Leahy faced businessman Scott Milne—who sought to make an issue of Leahy's past advocacy of the EB-5 program, which provides foreigners with a path to permanent residency in exchange for investments in U.S. projects. Milne's charges followed a Securities and Exchange Commission lawsuit alleging two Vermont developers, including one with ties to Leahy, had operated what the SEC called a "Ponzi-like scheme" to defraud foreign investors of $200 million. Leahy snapped: "If he is accusing me of doing something wrong, he should call the U.S. attorney's office." Leahy won 61%-33%.

Following past tradition, Leahy—who turned 81 in early 2021—planned to make a decision on seeking a potentially history-making ninth term later in the year, after he and his wife retreat to their Vermont farm. "I walk around our fields and woods and go hiking and talk about it and make the decisions," he told the Vermont Digger of past such deliberations.

Around the Capitol, Leahy is known for his hobbies. He is an accomplished photographer, despite being legally blind in his left eye since birth; his work has been published in The New York Times, USA Today and several news magazines. Leahy has been a high-profile fan of the Grateful Dead and can recite lyrics from the band's songs. He became a fan of Batman comic books in childhood, and, in recent years, has appeared briefly in five Batman movies. He had a speaking part in "The Dark Knight" in 2008, telling the Joker, "We're not intimidated by thugs."

Bernie Sanders (I)

Elected 2006, term expires 2024, 3rd term, b. Sep 08, 1941; Brooklyn, NY; Brooklyn College, Att., 1960; University of Chicago, B.A., 1964; Jewish; Married (Jane O'Meara Driscoll); 1 child; 3 stepchildren.

Elected Office: Burlington Mayor, 1981-1989; U.S. House, 1991-2007.

Professional Career: Writer; Director, American People's Historical Soc., 1977-1981; Lecturer, Harvard University, 1989; Lecturer, Hamilton College, 1990.

DC Office: 332 DSOB 20510, 202-224-5141, Fax: 202-228-0776, sanders.senate.gov

State Offices: Burlington, 802-862-0697; St. Johnsbury, 800-339-9834.

Committees: Senate Democratic Outreach Committee Chairman. *Budget (Chmn)*. *Energy & Natural Resources*: Energy; National Parks; Water & Power. *Environment & Public Works*: Chem Safety, Waste Mngmnt, Enviro Justice & Reg Oversight; Clean Air & Nuclear Safety; Transportation & Infrastructure. *Health, Education, Labor & Pensions*: Children & Families; Primary Health & Retirement Security (Chmn). *Veterans' Affairs*.

Group Ratings

	ADA	ACLU	AFL-CIO	LCV	COC	HAFA	ACU	CFG	FRC
2020	-	100%	-	62%	-	0%	6%	-	-
2019	60%	C	100%	69%	3%	C	6%	-	0%

Almanac Ratings 2019-2020

	Economy	Social	Foreign	Composite
Liberal	100%	100%	100%	100%
Conservative	0%	0%	0%	0%

Key Votes of the 116th Congress

1. EPA clean energy rules	N/A	5. Russia sanctions	N/A	9. Barr as Atty. General	N
2. U.S./Mex./Can. trade deal	N	6. Troops in SYR, AFG	N	10. Spending at the border	N/A
3. Cut unemployment benefits	N	7. Veto arms sales to Saudis	Y	11. Coney Barrett to Sup. Ct.	N
4. Shelton to Fed Reserve	N	8. Defense $$$, veto override	N	12. Electoral College objections	N

Election Results

Election	Name (Party)	Vote (%)		Cand. Spent	Ind. Exp. Support	Ind. Exp. Oppose
2018 General	Bernie Sanders (I)	183,649	(67%)	$5,222,961		$2,232,449
	Lawrence Zupan (R)	74,815	(27%)			
2018 Primary	Bernie Sanders (D)	63,322	(94%)			
	Folasade Adeluola (D)	3,748	(6%)			

Prior winning percentages: 2018 (67%), 2012 (71%), 2006 (65%), House: 2004 (67%), 2002 (64%), 2000 (69%), 1998 (63%), 1996 (55%), 1994 (50%), 1992 (58%), 1990 (56%)

When independent Bernie Sanders, Vermont's junior senator, unveiled "Medicare for All" in 2013, he did so without a single co-sponsor. When Sanders again re-introduced the bill, which calls for replacing private health insurance with a public single-payer plan, in late 2017, one-third of the Senate Democratic Caucus co-sponsored it. The change was emblematic of the clout the onetime outlier had acquired after the surprising success of his 2016 campaign for the Democratic presidential nomination. Down nearly 50 percentage points in some polls when he started, Sanders battled the front-running candidate, Hillary Clinton, to the end of the primary elections. By the time he arrived at the Democratic National Convention, he had won contests in 22 states, along with 46 percent of the pledged delegates—after attracting massive crowds and energizing millennial voters, as he railed against the "billionaire class" and urged a "political revolution."

While Sanders didn't end up as the nominee, he could still claim a major moral victory: He had pulled the Democratic Party's center of gravity in his direction on major issues, ranging from free college tuition to a $15 hourly minimum wage, as well as Medicare for All. "During our 2016 campaign, when we brought forth our progressive agenda, we were told that our ideas were 'radical' and 'extreme,'" the self-described democratic socialist wrote to supporters in February 2019, as he launched a second presidential bid. "Three years have come and gone. And, as result of millions of Americans standing up and fighting back, all of these policies and more are now supported by a majority of Americans."

Sanders began his second presidential run as a leading contender, with national name recognition and a committed base of backers in all 50 states, to say nothing of an ability to raise large amounts of money from a massive list of small donors. But, competing in a splintered Democratic field of more than 20 candidates, he was no longer the sole alternative on the party's left flank. Notably, the 2020 field included fellow Sen. Elizabeth Warren of Massachusetts, another progressive icon; she had declined to get into the nomination contest four years earlier. Kicking off the campaign with a couple of large enthusiastic rallies, Sanders had a year of ups and downs—including a heart attack that prompted questions about his future as a candidate—on the trail. He recovered, however, to emerge briefly in early 2020 as the frontrunner for the nomination—a development that panicked many in the party establishment who feared he'd be unable to defeat President Donald Trump. It led to a rapid consolidation behind the eventual nominee, Joe Biden; by early April, Sanders was out of the race.

Nonetheless, the denouement of this nomination contest was decidedly different from 2016, when many Democrats complained Sanders was more interested in transforming the party's prevailing orthodoxy than in its near-term success. In a post-campaign memoir, Clinton said Sanders had run to disrupt the Democratic Party rather than to make sure a Democrat won the White House and that his candidacy did lasting damage to her campaign. In turn, the Sanders camp griped of being disrespected by Clinton's team. But a friendlier relationship between Sanders and Biden—combined with Democratic fears of a repeat win for Trump, whose prospects for victory had been widely discounted four years earlier—served to tamp down such sniping in 2020. While Sanders had refused to leave the race well after it became clear Clinton would be the nominee, he appeared on a live cast with Biden in early spring and endorsed his erstwhile rival "to make certain that we defeat somebody who I believe is the most dangerous president in the modern history of this country." Pledged Sanders, "I will do all that I can to see that that happens, Joe."

Sanders afterward told the New Yorker, "I think the difference now is that … I have a better relationship with Joe Biden than I had with Hillary Clinton and that Biden has been much more receptive to sitting down and talking with me and other progressives than we have seen in the past." For his part, Biden said, "Sanders and his supporters have changed the dialogue in America. Indeed, the work of joint policy task forces involving the two camps, followed by the party's 2020 platform, underscored Biden indeed had been nudged to the left by Sanders.

In early 2021, as Biden assumed the presidency, Sanders returned to Capitol Hill in an unfamiliar role: influential insider, as chairman of the Budget Committee. And the same politician who two decades earlier had authored a memoir on his congressional career titled, "Outsider in the House," demonstrated his skill at playing the inside game. Sanders was credited with a key role in guiding Biden's $1.9 trillion pandemic relief package through a Senate in which the Democrats had no votes to spare—working to assuage restive members of the party's progressive wing while parrying demands from moderates who wanted the package trimmed. He did this while coordinating closely with a Biden White House that had seen to it that former Sanders staffers were placed in a number of administration posts.

If some were startled by Sanders' apparent metamorphosis, it was little surprise to those who had long known him. Behind the face of this longtime fomenter of upheaval lies a savvy strategist who has demonstrated a willingness to—yes—compromise during and before his congressional career. "Bernie has been a movement builder for a long time, and the unfair critique of him is that he didn't know how to operate within the Congress itself as effectively," Hawaii Democratic Sen. Brian Schatz told Politico. "He's put to rest this idea that he's only an outside player." During a prior chairmanship —of the Senate Veterans' Affairs Committee—Sanders steered a major overhaul of the Department of Veterans Affairs into law in 2014 despite difficulty negotiating with the House GOP. In closing that deal, Sanders recalled his days as mayor of Burlington in the 1980s. "When I took office, [in terms of] people who supported me on the City Council, we had two out of 13, and I had to make things happen while being in the minority," he told Roll Call. "So, I do know how to negotiate fairly. Negotiation is part of the political process. I certainly have been prepared to do that since Day One."

As his thick Brooklyn accent indicates, Sanders grew up in the Flatbush section of New York's largest borough. His father was a paint salesman who had emigrated from Poland. He graduated from James Madison High School—also alma mater of Majority Leader Charles Schumer—before attending Brooklyn College. Sanders graduated from the University of Chicago, where he became involved in left-wing politics, and moved to Vermont as part of the hippie migration of 1968. Sanders worked as a carpenter upon arriving in the Green Mountain State. In 1971, he ran in a special election for a vacant state Senate seat as the candidate of the Liberty Union Party, winning just 2 percent of the vote. He went on to lose four statewide races. Running against Democrat Patrick Leahy, now his senior Senate colleague, in 1974, Sanders raised his vote on the Liberty Union line to 4 percent. In 1981, Sanders' earnest persona finally won over the Burlington electorate, which made him mayor of the state's largest city by just 10 votes.

"There was anger in the air, plenty of it," the Burlington Free Press wrote years later. "Bernie Sanders, a self-proclaimed socialist of all people, had somehow stolen City Hall from" the Democrats. He served until 1989, winning reelection three times. "I am a socialist. Of course I am a socialist," Sanders said during a 1983 debate, according to the Associated Press. He added, "To hold a vision that society can be fundamentally different, to believe that all people can be equal, that is not a new idea."

Though he has arguably become the dominant figure of the Democratic Party's progressive wing—and always has caucused with the Democrats on Capitol Hill—Sanders has made eight successful runs for the House and three for the Senate without appearing on the Democratic line on the ballot. Asked whether he identified as a Democrat on MSNBC after his first presidential run, Sanders replied, No, I'm an independent. Such assertions help explain why many in the Democratic establishment remain leery of him—and why Sanders had little success increasing his base of support during his second presidential bid.

Further fueling Democratic establishment nervousness were fears Sanders' candidacy would revive Cold War era use of the socialist label as a cudgel. Here in the United States, we are alarmed by the new calls to adopt socialism in our country, Trump said during his 2019 State of the Union address, a line echoed by other Republicans. Sanders later told NPR: I think what we have … to do a better job, maybe, in explaining what we mean by 'socialism'—'democratic socialism.' Obviously, my right-wing colleagues here want to paint that as authoritarianism and communism and Venezuela, and that's nonsense." Sanders stepped on that message during a key juncture in 2020, when an overwhelming win in the Nevada caucuses for a time made him the Democratic frontrunner. While telling CBS' "60 Minutes" he opposed the Cuban regime's "authoritarian nature," he added: "But you know, it's unfair to simply say everything is bad. When Fidel Castro came to office, you know what he did? He had a massive literacy program. Is that a bad thing? Even though Fidel Castro did it?" His comments produced immediate backlash among the large Cuban-American community in the battleground state of Florida.

Sanders' first congressional bid came in 1988, when Vermont's at-large House seat opened. He ran as an independent but lost by 3 points to Republican Peter Smith in a three-way race. Two years later, he defeated Smith 56%-40%, becoming only the third socialist elected to the House—and the first since the late 1920s. Sanders benefited from his opposition to gun control: Smith had voted to ban semi-automatic weapons, and the National Rifle Association had come out against him. Three years later, Sanders voted against the "Brady Bill," which required background checks for those buying firearms. And in 2005, he supported an NRA-backed bill to shield gun manufacturers and dealers from most lawsuits. Sanders' early gun control opposition haunted him as a presidential candidate: Clinton raised it in 2016 candidate forums, and it was used in ads by a super PAC supporting her. More recently, Sanders has sided with gun control advocates—voting in 2013 to expand background checks and in 2016 to bar firearm sales to those on the government's terrorist watch list. He represents a state where gun ownership remains widespread, and where it was loosely restricted until a 2018 law expanding background checks and banning high-capacity ammunition magazines.

In the House, Sanders formed the Congressional Progressive Caucus with an agenda that, in addition to a single-payer health insurance system, included progressive tax reform, a 50 percent cut in military spending, a national energy policy, and—a Vermont touch—support for family farms. Notwithstanding much of what he has advocated is unlikely to be enacted anytime soon—even co-sponsors of Medicare for All see it as largely aspirational in the short term—Sanders has played the long game throughout his career, hoping to influence opinion by speaking out early and often. "Everybody [now] talks about income inequality," he told The New York Times in 2015. "Well, check it out. Find out who was talking about it 20 years ago." Sanders helped make the cost of prescription drugs a national issue: He was the first member of Congress to lead bus trips to Canada to buy pharmaceuticals at lower costs.

All of this played well at home, where Sanders regularly won reelection with more than 60 percent of the vote. After eight House terms, he became the early frontrunner when Independent Sen. Jim Jeffords announced his retirement in 2005. Sanders quickly amassed endorsements from top Vermont Democrats; with his consent, Democrats put his name on their primary ballot, and he won 94 percent of the vote. He declined the nomination and petitioned to be listed on the general election ballot as an independent. Gov. Jim Douglas, considered the only Republican with a real shot at defeating Sanders in 2006, declined to run. The GOP nominee, multimillionaire businessman Richard Tarrant, ran ads portraying Sanders as an ineffective radical soft on sexual predators and drug dealers. The strategy didn't work in a small state where voters were well-acquainted with Sanders and his iconoclastic ways. Sanders won 65%-32%.

Sanders had no trouble winning reelection in 2012 over underfunded Republican John MacGovern, winning 71%-25%. In 2018, he bested Lawrence Zupan, a real estate broker and critic of Medicare for All, 67%-27%—after again winning the Democratic nomination with 94 percent of the vote and declining it to run as an independent. Sanders will be 83 when his current term is up at the end of 2024. State-by-state polling in late 2019 showed him to be the most popular senator in the nation among his constituents, with a 65 percent approval rating.

Sanders initially settled with surprising ease into the Senate's more structured ways. Leahy told a Vermont reporter that other senators—presumably expecting a political bomb-thrower in their midst—had confided "what a pleasant surprise [Sanders] has turned out to be" with his willingness to craft legislative deals. His more familiar side was on display when, as the Occupy Wall Street protests energized the American left in 2011, Sanders endorsed the goals of the upstart movement. His breakout moment on the national stage came with an eight-hour, often apoplectic, Senate speech at the end of 2010: He excoriated the extension of tax cuts for the highest-income Americans—enacted early in the Bush administration—as "Robin Hood in reverse."

At one point, Sanders sarcastically asked: "How can I get by on one house? I need five houses, 10 houses! I need three jet planes to take me all over the world! Sorry, American people. We've got the money, we've got the power, we've got the lobbyists here and on Wall Street. Tough luck." The speech proved so popular it temporarily shut down the Senate video server. (When Sanders released 10 years of his income tax returns early in his 2020 presidential run, it confirmed that the onetime carpenter was now among the nation's wealthiest 1 percent: Thanks largely to proceeds from sales of his books, he and his wife, Jane Sanders, reported $1 million in annual income for both 2016 and 2017.)

As Budget Committee chair, Sanders moved quickly to use the new platform to continue to target income inequality. Jeff "Bezos and [Elon] Musk now own more wealth than the bottom 40 percent. Meanwhile, we're looking at more hunger in America than at any time in decades, Sanders said while opening a March 2021 hearing, taking aim at the country's two richest people. It was not the first time he had targeted Bezos, CEO of Amazon. In September 2018, he introduced legislation titled, "Stop Bad Employers by Zeroing Out Subsidies Act"—"Stop BEZOS"—requiring Amazon and other large employers to cover the cost of food stamps, public housing, Medicaid and other federal assistance received by its employees. Not long afterward, Bezos announced the online retailer would raise its minimum wage to $15 per hour for 350,000 permanent and seasonal U.S. employees.

Sanders took the plunge for the first time in May 2015. His populist rhetoric and outsider appeal appeared to be a key element of his allure to voters younger than 30, as he captured them 5-2 over Clinton; they continued to be the bedrock of his 2020 run. Sanders' fundraising efforts were a notable departure from previous presidential campaigns fueled by super PACs and other outside groups: They relied heavily on small individual donors, lending credibility to his attacks on moneyed interests and their influence on the political system. His 2016 campaign collected nearly $234 million from 8 million donations. He raised almost as much in 2020—$211.2 million, according to data from the Center for Responsive Politics.

Sanders' fundraising success propelled his campaign through the 2016 primary season, even as the mathematical odds against his capturing the nomination mounted. But working against him were 700 "superdelegates" with automatic votes at the convention as elected officeholders or high-ranking party officials—a large majority of whom backed Clinton early on. That extended to Sanders' own state, where four of five superdelegates lined up behind Clinton, despite Vermont giving more than 85 percent of its primary vote to its favorite son. Among the Vermont superdelegates backing Clinton was Leahy, who said he had committed to her well before Sanders decided to run. Sanders' sharpest criticisms were reserved for the Democratic National Committee and what he considered its rigging of the system to bolster Clinton. The DNC's chairwoman, Rep. Debbie Wasserman Schultz, resigned just before the convention in July 2016 after a series of stolen emails confirming Sanders' suspicions were leaked. In an olive branch to Sanders backers, the DNC in 2018 changed the party's nominating rules to reduce the influence of superdelegates.

The start of Sanders' second presidential bid in early 2019 brought a reminder that, as a leading contender this time around, he would face more intense scrutiny than he had as a long-shot prospect four years earlier. They included published reports of allegations by several women who said they were harassed or mistreated while working for his male-dominated campaign in 2016. Although Sanders offered multiple apologies and shook up his campaign staff heading into 2020, some detected signs of tone deafness when he was asked if he had been aware of the complaints during his earlier campaign. "I was a little bit busy running around the country trying to make the case," he told CNN. Sanders triggered another gender-related controversy when—during a private dinner a couple of months prior to announcing his candidacy—he reportedly told Warren that a woman could not win the presidency. When CNN reported that comment in January 2020, Sanders denied having said it during a televised debate a day later—prompting Warren to accuse him of calling her a liar in a post-debate exchange picked up by an open mic.

The Sanders campaign hit its low point in October 2019—just as Warren emerged for a time as the frontrunner in the race. The then-78-year-old Sanders was hospitalized after complaining of chest pains during an event in Las Vegas. After three days of his campaign dodging questions on the issue, Sanders disclosed he had suffered a heart attack. Nearly three months later, three of his physicians acknowledged he had suffered "modest heart muscle damage" but was in good health and capable of continuing the campaign.

New York Rep. Alexandria Ocasio-Cortez—who had achieved near-cult status among young progressives after her upset 2018 win—almost single-handedly rescued the Sanders campaign with her endorsement, as he was forced to spend weeks away from the campaign trail. "The only reason that I had any hope in launching a long-shot campaign for Congress is because Bernie Sanders proved that you can run a grassroots campaign and win in an America where we almost thought it was impossible," she said in endorsing him. Ocasio-Cortez's blessing had been actively sought by both Sanders and Warren; when she heard Sanders was in the hospital, Ocasio-Cortez moved quickly, according to the Washington Post, telling an aide, "Bernie needs us and needs us now."

Sanders came back to win a virtual tie (with Pete Buttigieg, a former mayor of South Bend Indiana) for first place in the Iowa caucuses in early February 2020. He followed that with a victory in the New Hampshire primary a week later. Warren finished third in both contests, with the other early frontrunner, Biden, finishing in fourth and fifth place, respectively. In the Nevada caucuses, Sanders won his most resounding victory—capturing just about every demographic group, including more than half of Hispanic-Americans. Although Biden finished a distant second in Nevada, he recovered to win the South Carolina primary—where Black voters constituted a majority of the electorate—by better than 2-1 over Sanders.

The South Carolina results underscored the continuing struggle encountered by Sanders—who has long represented a state that is 93 percent white—in attracting the national Democratic Party's sizable Black electorate. In 2016, African-American voters favored Clinton by more than 3-1, according to exit poll data compiled by the Wall Street Journal; most of Sanders' primary season wins that year were in less populated states with smaller minority populations. Sanders worked in the run-up to his second presidential bid to build ties to minority communities, and his endorsements helped two African-American candidates, Andrew Gillum and Ben Jealous, win 2018 gubernatorial primaries in Florida and Maryland, respectively—although both lost in November. But the crucial South Carolina primary in 2020 showed he had made limited inroads: Exit polls had Biden winning two-thirds of Black voters, to just 15 percent for Sanders.

The South Carolina results led to a consolidation around Biden, sparked by widespread fear among the party establishment that nominating Sanders could forfeit the presidency as well as control of Congress. Buttigieg bespoke such concerns after the Nevada caucuses. "Before we rush to nominate Sen. Sanders in our one shot to take on this president, let us take a sober look at the consequences," he said, contending Sanders "believes in an inflexible, ideological revolution that leaves out most Democrats, not to mention most Americans." Both Buttigieg and another contender in the centrist lane for the nomination, Minnesota Sen. Amy Klobuchar, dropped out and endorsed Biden immediately after South Carolina—and just hours before the "Super Tuesday" primaries in 14 states.

Biden went on to win 10 of the latter primaries and, over the next three weeks, won eight of the 11 succeeding contests—with Sanders victorious only in North Dakota and the Northern Mariana Islands as well as among Democrats living abroad. Several Biden victories came in states that Sanders had won four years earlier, an indication that "electability" against Trump was foremost on the minds of the 2020 Democratic primary electorate. His campaign was effectively over after a March 10 loss in Michigan, where he had upset Clinton four years earlier. Sanders' failure to hold it in 2020 undermined his argument that he could appeal to white working-class voters in a way that centrists such as Biden could not.

Peter Welch (D)

Elected 2006, 8th term, b. May 02, 1947; Springfield, MA; College of The Holy Cross, B.A., 1969; University of CA, Berkeley, J.D., 1973; Roman Catholic; Married (Margaret Cheney); 5 children; 3 stepchildren.

Elected Office: Elected Office: VT Senate, 1981-1989, 2002-2007, Minority Leader, 1983-1985, President pro tem, 1985-1989, 2003-2007.

Professional Career: Robert F. Kennedy fellow, 1969-1970; Practicing attorney, 1974-2006.

DC Office: 2187 RHOB 20515, 202-225-4115, Fax: 202-225-6790, welch.house.gov

State Offices: Burlington, 888-605-7270.

Committees: *Energy & Commerce*: Communications & Technology; Energy; Health. *Oversight & Reform*: National Security. *Permanent Select on Intelligence*: Counterterrorism, Counterintelligence & Counterproliferation; Defense Intelligence & Warfighter Support (Chmn).

Group Ratings

	ADA	ACLU	AFL-CIO	LCV	COC	HAFA	ACU	CFG	FRC
2020	**	83%	**	100%	-	0%	5%	**	
2019	95%	C	95%	97%	48%	C	6%	19%	0%

Almanac Ratings 2019-2020

	Economy	Social	Foreign	Composite
Liberal	100%	63%	96%	87%
Conservative	0%	37%	4%	13%

Key Votes of the 116th Congress

1. U.S./Mex./Can. trade deal Y	5. Russia sanctions Y	9. Firearms background checks Y
2. First Coronavirus response Y	6. Troops in Syria Y	10. Spending at the border N
3. HEROES Act Y	7. Veto arms sales to Saudis Y	11. Marijuana liberalized rules Y
4. CASH Act Y	8. Defense $$$, veto override Y	12. Electoral College objections N

Election Results

Election	Name (Party)	Vote (%)		Cand. Spent	Ind. Exp. Support	Ind. Exp. Oppose
2020 General	Peter Welch (D)	238,827	(67%)	$787,280	$873	
	Miriam Berry (R)	95,830	(27%)		$175	$113
	Peter Becker (I)	8,065	(2%)			
2020 Primary	Peter Welch (D)	101,566	(95%)			

Prior winning percentages: 2018 (69%), 2016 (90%), 2014 (64%), 2012 (72%), 2010 (65%), 2008 (83%), 2006 (53%)

Vermont's only House member is Peter Welch, a Democrat first elected in 2006. He is highly regarded within his party as a strategist and spokesman. He serves as a chief deputy whip and has been active on energy and health care issues—occasionally on a bipartisan basis. On the Intelligence Committee, he pushed aggressively for the impeachment of President Donald Trump. Welch has been viewed as the heir apparent to a Senate seat if either of Vermont's more elderly senators creates a vacancy. As he turns age 74 in 2021, he might be close to missing his chance.

Welch grew up in Springfield Massachusetts, the son of a dentist, and graduated from the College of the Holy Cross. The summer before his junior year, he worked for a Jesuit group that did community outreach in poor Black neighborhoods in Chicago, where he was inspired by a speech by the Rev. Martin Luther King Jr. After graduating from law school at the University of California, Berkeley, Welch backpacked down the Pan-American Highway to Santiago Chile, then worked on a freighter that sailed to Portugal. After that, he was ready to practice law and chose White River Junction as his home. He worked as a public defender before founding his small firm.

In 1980, Welch became the first Democrat to represent Windsor County in the state Senate since the Civil War. Two years later, he became Senate minority leader. After Democrats in 1984 won a majority in the Senate for the first time ever, he was elected president pro tem. He focused on environment, education and tax issues and helped establish the Housing and Land Conservation Trust, which worked to create affordable housing and conserve farmland and forests. In 1988, Welch aimed for the House but lost the Democratic primary by 266 votes. In 1990, he ran for governor, but lost 52%-46% to Republican Richard Snelling. For some years after that, Welch was out of political life. His wife, Joan, who had been his closest adviser and campaign manager, fought cancer for nine years, and Welch at times was her full-time caregiver. She died in 2004.

In 2001, Democratic Gov. Howard Dean appointed Welch to the state Senate to fill a vacancy. In 2003, he became president pro tem once again and focused on health care issues. When Rep. Bernie Sanders, after 16 years in the House, ran for the Senate, Welch ran again for the House and won the Democratic nomination unopposed. In the general election, Welch ran as an opponent—from the start—of military action in Iraq, and he condemned the "corrupt" Republicans in Washington. He supported universal health care. Republican nominee Martha Rainville, commander of the Vermont National Guard, criticized some decisions of the Bush administration. Both candidates favored abortion rights. Welch spent $1.7 million to Rainville's $1.1 million. Welch won, 53%-45%.

Welch features an understated and collegial style. On the Energy and Commerce Committee, he has helped shape energy and climate-change legislation, including billions of dollars in subsidies to promote energy efficiency. He won committee approval of a measure to provide tax rebates to consumers for installing upgraded insulation, storm windows and other energy-efficiency aids. Practicing what he preached, he made his office the first in the House to install new lights and water fixtures to reduce energy use.

After the GOP takeover of the House, he helped liberals articulate their opposition on various issues, but Welch is not a strict partisan. He joined Republican Rep. David McKinley of West Virginia on a broad proposal that included efficiency standards for utility companies and a requirement that federally backed home mortgages must include efficiency ratings for the property. The House passed the bill in 2015 and it was enacted with Senate revisions. In 2016, he joined a bipartisan group that enacted a bill that directed the Commerce Department to quantify the financial impact of outdoor recreation. Welch has been a member of the bipartisan citizen activist effort, No Labels.

In March 2017, Welch and Democratic Rep. Elijah Cummings of Maryland met with Trump to discuss their proposal for the federal government to negotiate lower prices for prescription-drug coverage under Medicare. Following the nearly hour long meeting, the two Democrats said that Trump agreed to support their plan. There was no apparent follow-up. Welch strongly opposed Trump's tariffs on Canada, which has long enjoyed a lucrative trade relationship and friendly border with Vermont. "The president is abusing his authority," he said.

Back in the majority, Welch said it was vital to revive open debate in the House. "Too much power has landed in the Speaker's office," regardless of which party was in House control, he told Seven Days, a Vermont news site. Welch remained a chief deputy whip and joined the Intelligence Committee, with a pledge to "protect our national security, as well as our privacy and civil liberties."

On the Intelligence panel, Welch worked with other Democrats to narrow the charges against Trump. In an October 2019 interview, he told National Public Radio that two major questions were at stake: "One is, is a president above the rule of law? ... [The second question] is about whether Congress is going to defend what has been our constitutional system of checks and balances. ... [Trump] has repudiated the notion that Congress has any authority whatsoever to even ask the question about what his conduct was."

In his continuing advocacy of energy efficiency, Welch endorsed the "Green New Deal" framework of progressive Democrats. And his proposal with Republican Rep. David McKinley to provide rebates up to $4,000 to homeowners who renovate their homes to reduce energy use was included in the Democrats' infrastructure bill the House approved in July 2020.

At home, Welch has faced no serious reelection threats. In 2009, he married state Rep. Margaret Cheney, who later became a member of the Vermont Utility Commission. After a question arose about a possible conflict, he said he would not accept campaign contributions from political action committees of companies with cases before the board. When Seven Days in 2018 raised new allegations of possible conflicts involving his wife, he responded, "her responsibilities and my responsibilities are completely separate." Welch turned down an opportunity to run for governor in 2016. Even with his age, he remained a distinct possibility to seek to succeed either Sen. Patrick Leahy or Sen. Bernie Sanders if an opening occurs; they are seven and six years older than Welch.

VIRGINIA

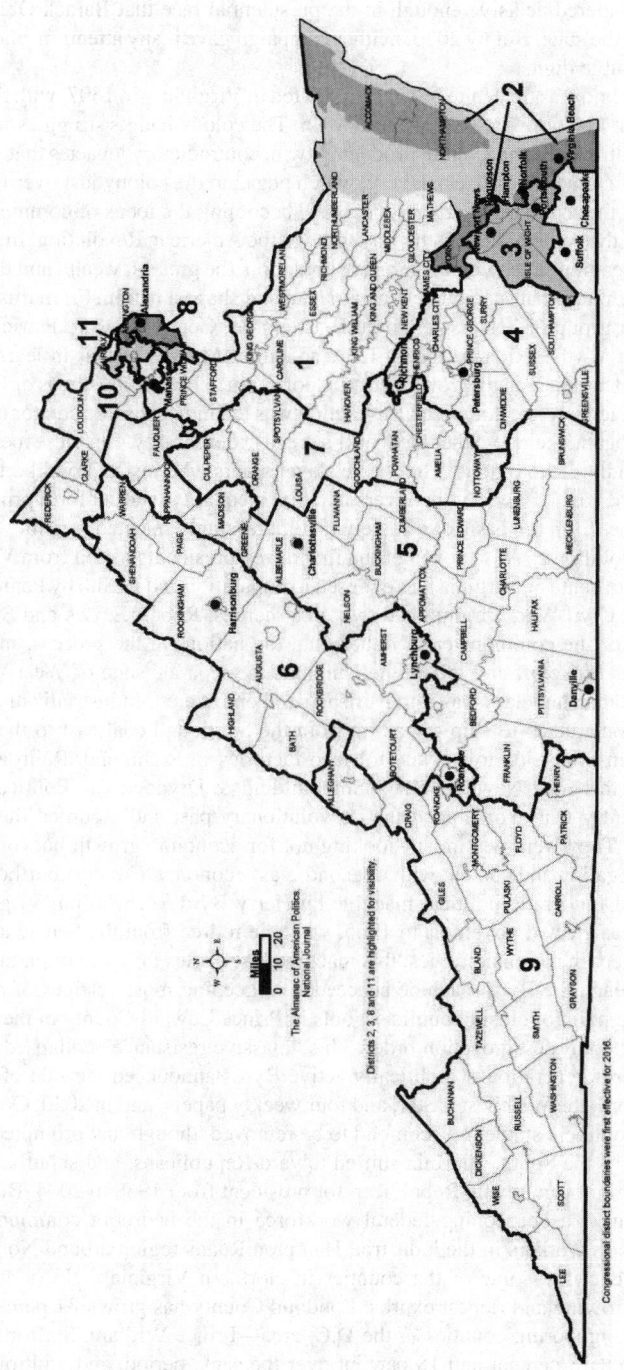

Districts 2, 3, 8 and 11 are highlighted for visibility

The Almanac of American Politics
National Journal

Miles
0 10 20

N
W   E
S

Congressional district boundaries were first effective for 2016.

Virginia may have been home to the capital of the Confederacy a century and a half ago, but in the historical blink of an eye, the state has shifted from Republican to Democratic control, driven by the increasingly diverse and government-focused suburbs of Washington D.C. As recently as 2008, Virginia was considered decisive enough in the presidential race that Barack Obama held his final campaign rally in the state. But by 2020, neither campaign gave it any attention, and Joe Biden ended up winning by double digits.

What we now know as the United States originated in Virginia—in 1607, with the first permanent English settlement in North America at Jamestown. The colony had its struggles with food, weather and Indians, but ultimately persevered, producing twin, contradictory legacies that shaped the nation: representative democracy and Black slavery, which began in the colony just over four centuries ago. Virginia's capital moved to Williamsburg in 1699, becoming the locus of commercial, cultural and intellectual life of the colonial era, all the way through the American Revolution. In the early republic, Virginia was the leading state, with the largest population, the greatest wealth and the most illustrious political figures, a place that seemed destined to lead and shape a nation. From this tobacco-growing region emerged a group of leaders—George Washington, George Mason, Patrick Henry, Thomas Jefferson, George Wythe, Richard Henry Lee and James Madison—that in learning, wisdom and strength of character equaled any group from any polity since Periclean Athens or Republican Rome. The Virginia they led into the American Revolution was the indispensable creator of the republic and the Constitution that has held together the world's greatest democracy. But these men embodied ideals that were profoundly dichotomous. They were slaveholders who insisted on liberty, revolutionaries who insisted on the rule of law, and believers in racial inequality who set forth principles of equality that would, in time, form the basis of a society that increasingly rejected racism.

After the Revolutionary War, seven of the first dozen presidents hailed from Virginia. But in the first half of the 19th century, Virginia was eclipsed in population and wealth by Pennsylvania and New York. During the Civil War, Virginia had two great heroes, Robert E. Lee and Stonewall Jackson, but they fought for the commonwealth rather than the nation. In the process, many of Virginia's mountain counties broke off and joined the Union as the separate state of West Virginia. After the war, Virginia's leadership class was impoverished and embittered. Industrialization was haphazard. Railroads were constructed to ship cotton up from the South and coal east to the seaports. Textile mills were built in Southside towns and tobacco factories in Richmond. Railroad magnate Collis Huntington built the giant Newport News Shipbuilding & Drydock Co. Politically, Virginia was ruled by local gentry who worshipped their revolutionary past and mourned the "Lost Cause" of the Confederacy. They were pessimists, looking not for economic growth but for stability, bent on maintaining segregation and content with a second-class economy. County courthouse organizations were united in a Democratic political machine by Harry Byrd Sr., who ran Virginia politics from 1925, when he was elected governor, to 1965, when he retired from the Senate as chairman of the Finance Committee. In national politics, this machine lost battles far more often than Lee lost on the battlefield. For years, the Byrd machine succeeded in keeping most vestiges of racial equality out of Virginia, to the point of closing public schools in Prince Edward County in the 1950s rather than obeying a federal court desegregation order. This "massive resistance" collapsed in the late 1950s. (In 2018, the fourth generation of politically active Byrds announced the sale of the Harrisonburg Daily News-Record, the Winchester Star, and four weekly papers, and in 2020, Gov. Ralph Northam directed Lee's prominent statue in Richmond to be removed, though that prompted a legal battle.)

Like the rest of the South, Virginia shifted toward Republicans, and suburban growth kept the party strong; Virginia would vote Republican for president from 1968 to 2004. But political change came in the form of a burgeoning federal workforce in the bedroom communities of Northern Virginia, along with workers in the industrial Hampton Roads region around Norfolk and Newport News. Over the decades, some of the counties in Northern Virginia ("NoVa") have become the nation's fastest-growing and richest exurbs. Loudoun County has grown 31 percent since the 2010 census. Several neighboring counties in the D.C. area—Prince William, Stafford and Arlington—each grew between 13 percent and 18 percent over the same period. and multiple D.C.-area cities chalked up impressive growth rates during the decade, including 21 percent in Manassas Park, 19 percent in Fredericksburg, 18 percent in Falls Church, and 13 percent in Alexandria. The region can expect further growth: After a closely watched national search, Amazon chose Crystal City in

Arlington County as the location of its second headquarters, with 25,000 projected new jobs over 12 years. To boost regional infrastructure, Northam negotiated a $3.7 billion deal with rail company CSX to buy 225 miles of track that would extend and expand commuter rail from D.C. to Richmond, including a new bridge over the Potomac River.

Meanwhile, the city of Richmond, undeterred by the marginalization of tobacco, has grown 13 percent since 2010, and its reach has expanded outward, with suburbs like New Kent County growing 25 percent during the decade. Further to the south, Hampton Roads grew out into swampy lands on either side of the James River and swelled due to a large military presence in Norfolk and Virginia Beach. The region's population growth has been led by the city of Chesapeake, which grew 10 percent over the past decade. Counties elsewhere in the state that grew by double digits included Frederick (Winchester) and Albermarle (Charlottesville and the University of Virginia). But "RoVa" (the "rest of Virginia") —places like the Northern Neck, the two Eastern Shore counties, Southside Virginia, and the Shenandoah Valley—saw their population stagnate, along with the economy. The mountains of Southwest Virginia suffered the most: Since 2010, the Appalachian counties of Bath, Buchanan, Dickenson, Tazewell and Wise have seen their populations decline between 10 and 13 percent.

Virginia's population growth was accompanied by significant demographic change. Statewide, the population is 19 percent Black, 10 percent Hispanic and 7 percent Asian; both the Black and Asian percentages ranked Virginia among the top 10 states in the nation. The biggest groups of immigrants have come from El Salvador, India, South Korea, and Mexico. Norther Virginia saw the heaviest diversification: Prince William County is 25 percent Hispanic and 9 percent Asian; Fairfax County is 17 percent Hispanic and 20 percent Asian; and Loudoun County is 14 percent Hispanic and 20 percent Asian. Each of these jurisdictions was not just diverse but also affluent, thanks to the relatively high wages and good benefits enjoyed by federal employees. Loudoun, Fairfax, and Arlington counties and Falls Church and Fairfax cities all rank among the 10 highest-income localities in the country, with medians ranging from $116,000 to $132,000. Virginia also has the sixth-highest percentage of any state for residents with bachelor's degrees.

Growth and change produced unstable politics. In the 1970s, conservatives who left the Democratic Party and ran as independents or Republicans held Democrats at bay. In the 1980s, three moderate Democrats were elected governor—Charles Robb in 1981, Gerald Baliles in 1985 and Douglas Wilder in 1989. (Virginia is the last state that bars its governors from running for reelection, though they can run again after at least one term out of office.) The three Democratic governors did not attempt to impose a liberal agenda on an unwilling Virginia, instead arguing that government could be used effectively to improve education and build the commonwealth's economy. (Virginia has been chosen as the best state for business by CNBC four times since 2006, under governors of both parties.) In the 1990s, Virginia split increasingly along ideological lines. George Allen, elected governor by a wide margin in 1993, was a Republican who believed in lower taxes and traditional cultural values, but he leavened confrontational issue positions with a sunny temperament. Four years later, Republican James Gilmore made his centerpiece issue the phasing-out of the property tax on automobiles and won a 56%-43% victory. Republicans for the first time swept the top three statewide offices, and in the 1999 legislative elections Gilmore led Republicans to majorities in both chambers for the first time ever.

But the 21st century has tilted Virginia toward the Democrats. Mark Warner won the governorship in 2001 after an intensive campaign in rural Virginia in which he paid attention to regions not blessed by 1990s growth. He left office with high ratings and later became a senator; his success represented the first of several Democratic breakthroughs. While George W. Bush carried Northern Virginia in 2000, he lost it four years later, 51%-48%. The trend accelerated as Democrat Tim Kaine was elected governor in 2005 over Republican Jerry Kilgore, whose conservative stands were a tough sell in Northern Virginia. Three years later, Barack Obama became the first Democratic presidential candidate to carry Virginia since 1964. Virginia politics zig-zagged back, at least temporarily, in 2009, amid dissatisfaction with Obama's agenda; Republican Bob McDonnell deemphasized cultural issues and ran instead as a job-creating candidate ready to tackle the recession. He won, but 2009 proved to be the last year any Republican has won statewide. Obama carried the commonwealth again in 2012, and after a money-and-influence scandal hobbled McDonnell, voters elected Democratic Party fixer Terry McAuliffe as governor in 2013 over socially conservative attorney general Ken Cuccinelli. In the 2016 presidential election, Hillary Clinton, with Kaine as her running mate, won Virginia by a slightly wider margin than Obama had in 2012, as such Northern Virginia jurisdictions as Arlington, Fairfax, Loudoun and Prince William counties and the city of Alexandria pushed their winning margins by between five and 20 points in the Democrats' direction. The Richmond suburbs also moved toward the Democrats.

In August 2017, Virginia became a battleground when white nationalists and neo-Nazis converged on Charlottesville to protest the city's decision to remove Lee's statue. A few months later, Virginia voters rebelled against President Donald Trump, with Democrats winning the governorship, lieutenant governorship and the attorney general's office and coming close to seizing the state House, foiled primarily by a Republican-friendly map. (Control hinged on a tied race that was decided by drawing the winner's name from a bowl—a Republican, as it turned out.) The Democrats' gains were focused in suburban districts that had been turning bluer, and one of the newly elected Democratic legislators, Danica Roem, became the first openly transgender candidate to be elected and serve as a state legislator in the country, ousting socially conservative, 13-term Del. Bob Marshall.

The strong Democratic showing at the ballot box paid policy dividends, as Northam, the newly elected governor, persuaded enough Republicans to join him to enact an expansion of Medicaid under the Affordable Care Act. Virginia Democrats had another good election in 2018, as Kaine easily won reelection to the Senate and Democratic challengers ousted three Republican House incumbents. But Northam didn't have long to celebrate. In early 2019, it emerged that Northam's 1984 medical school yearbook page included a photograph of one man in blackface and another in a KKK outfit —one of whom was suspected of being Northam. In short order, two women accused Lt. Gov. Justin Fairfax of sexual assault, and Attorney General Mark Herring volunteered that he had once appeared in blackface. The panoply of scandals had the ironic effect of securing Northam's hold on his office, although the turmoil nudged the governor to take a lower-profile role in the pivotal 2019 legislative elections. Democrats got a boost in those elections when the Supreme Court let stand a new and friendlier legislative map, and gun control—an archetypal issue for widening rural-urban divisions—rose in importance after a mass shooting that summer in Virginia Beach. In November, with opposition to Trump energizing suburban voters, Democrats seized both legislative chambers, teeing up unified party control that, among other things, produced a tightening of gun restrictions in early 2020.

In the 2020 presidential race, Virginia, for the first time in a generation, was never considered a battleground state. Biden won by 10 points—twice Hillary Clinton's margin four years earlier— and he extended the ongoing pro-Democratic shifts in more populated parts of the state. Biden flipped counties in both the D.C. suburbs (Stafford) and the Richmond area (Chesterfield), along with two large cities in the Hampton Roads area (Chesapeake and Virginia Beach). He also flipped the city of Lynchburg (the home of the Jerry Falwell-founded Liberty University) and James City County (Williamsburg). In each of these jurisdictions, Biden improved on Clinton's margins by between seven and 12 points. "As Virginia has moved into the Democratic column, the state Republican Party has become more populist, more nationalist, and more culturally conservative. The dwindling number of Republicans who spoke the language of suburbia could not escape their party's national reputation for hostility to immigrants and opposition to progressive ideals," wrote conservative commentator Matthew Continetti.

Population		Race and Ethnicity		Income	
Total	8,535,519	White	67.00%	Median Income	76,456
Land area (sq. miles)	39,490	Black	19.40%	State Income Rank	10 out of 50
Pop/ sq mi	216.14	Latino	9.70%	Poverty Rate	9.90%
Born in state	49.50%	Asian	8.10%	With health insurance	92.10%
		Two or more races	3.80%	Cash public assistance	1.70%
Age Groups		Other	3.30%	Food stamp/SNAP	9.1%
Under 18	21.80%				
18-34	23.30%	Education		Work	
35-64	39.10%	H.S grad or less	33.60%	White Collar	45.40%
Over 64	15.90%	Some college	26.90%	Sales and Service	36.10%
		College Degree, 4 yr	22.40%	Blue Collar	18.50%
Military		Post grad	17.20%	Government	19.80%
Veteran/ Active Duty	11.90%				

Presidential Politics

2020 Primary (D)	Biden (D)	705,501(53%)	Sanders (D)	306,388(23%)	Warren (D)	142,546(11%)
	Bloomberg (D)	128,030(10%)				
2020 Pres. Vote	Biden (D)	2,413,568(54%)	Trump (R)	1,962,430(44%)		
2016 Pres. Vote	Clinton (D)	1,981,473(50%)	Trump (R)	1,769,443(44%)	Johnson (L)	118,274 (3%)

Once a solidly Republican state, Virginia suddenly became a national bellwether in 2008 and 2012, when its 53%-46% and 51%-47% margins for Barack Obama were the same as those in the nation as a whole. It has since continued to drift left, driven by an increasingly diverse electorate, rapid growth in well-educated and government-employee rich Northern Virginia, and suburbanites' antipathy to the GOP under Trump, and it appears its bellwether status may have just been a blip in its transformation into a Democratic-leaning state.

In the first half of the 20th century, Virginia was part of the solid Democratic South. But from 1952 to 1960 it voted Republican, following the "golden silence" of segregationist Democratic Sen. Harry Byrd Sr., who declined to endorse presidential candidates, but quietly signaled his preference for the more fiscally conservative GOP standard bearers. It voted for Democrat Lyndon Johnson for president in 1964, then backed Republicans in the next 10 elections. But over time, the GOP margins narrowed. In 2008, Obama targeted Virginia from start to finish. His organizing efforts for the February primary gave him a head start when he defeated Hillary Clinton 64%-35%. Obama ran seven percentage points ahead of John Kerry in 2004 on his way to defeating John McCain. In 2012, Obama's margin over Mitt Romney was reduced, but patterns were similar. Close-in Northern Virginia D.C. suburbs voted heavily for Obama, and he narrowly carried the Northern Virginia exurbs. The vote was almost identical to 2008 in the Tidewater and metro Richmond, while Romney increased Republican margins in rural areas.

The growth and diversity of the Northern Virginia suburbs and exurbs will continue to make the region's voters a critical component of the Democratic coalition in the state. In 2016, Hillary Clinton beat Donald Trump by 50%-44%, four points wider than her national popular vote margin.

The state kept moving left in 2020, and after seeing a decrease in campaigning and ad spending from both parties in 2016 it saw almost none in 2020. Joe Biden defeated Trump 54%-44%, the first time a Democrat won Virginia by a double-digit margin since Franklin Delano Roosevelt in 1944. He improved on Clinton's margins across the state, doing even better than her already-impressive performance in Northern Virginia and suburban Richmond and nearly matching Obama's numbers in the African-American heavy Tidewater region. He won Virginia Beach, which Obama never managed to do, and carried Stafford County in exurban D.C., a first for a Democrat in modern history. Trump improved in some Appalachian counties, but Biden ran ahead of both Clinton and Obama almost everywhere else. His 10-point margin was six points better than his national popular vote victory.

In the 2008 Democratic presidential primaries, held early in the calendar in mid-February, Obama captured the state the same day he won in neighboring Maryland and the District of Columbia, making him the clear frontrunner in the race. In the GOP competition, McCain defeated Mike Huckabee

50%-41. Since 2012, Virginia has held its primary on Super Tuesday. That year only two Republicans gathered enough signatures to make it onto the ballot on March 6; Romney beat Ron Paul 60%-40%. This was Paul's highest percentage in any 2012 primary. The 2016 primary was held on March 1, when both parties' nominations were up for grabs. The Republican contest saw Trump narrowly defeat Florida Sen. Marco Rubio, 33%-30%. The Democratic primary was a one-sided affair in which Clinton reversed her 2008 fate and walloped Vermont Sen. Bernie Sanders, 64%-35%. In 2020, Biden did the same thing to Sanders, winning 53%-23%, with Elizabeth Warren at 11 percent and Michael Bloomberg at 10 percent. It was one of Biden's biggest Super Tuesday wins, on a night that made him the dominant frontrunner for the nomination.

Congressional Districts

117th Congress Lineup	7D 4R	116th Congress Lineup	7D 4R

Despite above national average population growth, Virginia has failed to gain a seat in reapportionment since 1991 and the size of its delegation appeared unlikely to change in 2021. At the start of this decade, Virginia was a prime target for Democratic redistricters. Republicans had maximized their opportunities with creative map-drawing in a state that was leaning Democratic. Since then, Democrats have picked up four seats — through a combination of legal and election successes. And they might have additional opportunities.

Federal judges in 2016 ordered a mid-decade redrawing of lines following the relentless push by state Democrats, led by Gov. Terry McAuliffe, to seek court revision of the plan that had been enacted in 2011 by the Republican-controlled legislature and Gov. Bob McDonnell. That map had shored up incumbents in both parties, especially Republicans, and left the 8-3 GOP delegation — in a state whose statewide officials are all Democrats and Republican haven't won a presidential campaign since 2004. At the time, Democrats offered a competing plan converting Republican Rep. Randy Forbes' 4th District into a second minority-majority seat. The Senate Democrats' plan took on new life in October 2014, when a three-judge federal court panel ruled that the state's map was an unconstitutional violation of the 14th Amendment's civil rights protections. The court found that the legislature had improperly packed minorities into the 3rd District of Democratic Rep. Bobby Scott. After the Republican-controlled legislature was unwilling to make the sacrifice, Democrats persisted on court resolution. The judges agreed to a version of the Democrats' map, in which Petersburg and large parts of Richmond were moved to the 4th, and much of Forbes' base of Chesapeake was shifted to the 3rd District. Forbes concluded that he could not win his revised district. With little time to prepare, he ran in the revamped Virginia Beach-based 2nd District, which had none of his previous constituents. In the primary for an open seat, Forbes ran as an outsider against Del. Scott Taylor and fared poorly. In what became a missed opportunity for Democrats, Taylor won easily in November. The court's map made changes in the 1st and 7th Districts, but their Republican incumbents were unscathed. The remaining six districts in Virginia were untouched.

In 2018, the Republican collapse deepened. Three of their incumbents in suburban seats — Tidewater, the Richmond area and the Northern Virginia suburbs — succumbed to their own mistakes plus well-financed challengers who took advantage of divisions among the state's Republicans and hostility toward President Donald Trump. That left Democrats with 7-4 control of the delegation. The prospects for redistricting will be shaped significantly by whether those three Democrats survive in 2020 and whether Democrats in November 2019 finally crack the GOP's narrow majorities in each chamber of the state legislature. Another uncertainty is the role — and disposition — of federal judges, whose continued role seems inevitable. Whatever the dynamics, Democrats likely will retain control of at least three seats in Northern Virginia and one minority district in the Tidewater area; Republicans start with their two seats in the western part of the state. The shape and the outcome of the five remaining districts — from Tidewater to the center of the state -- likely will be up for grabs.

Ralph Northam (D)

Elected 2017, term expires 2022, 1st term; b. Sept. 13, 1959, Nassawadox; Virginia Military Institute, B.S., 1981; Eastern Virginia Medical School, M.D., 1984; Unknown; Married (Pam); 2 children.

Military Career: US Army, 1984-1992.

Elected Office: VA Senate, 2008-2014; VA Lt. Gov., 2014-2018.

Professional Career: Pediatric Neurologist, Children's Hospital of the King's Daughters.

Office: P.O. Box 1475 Richmond, 23218; 804-786-2211; Fax: 804-371-6351

Lt. Gov.: Justin Fairfax (D) **Atty. Gen:** Mark Herring (D)

State Legislature: Senate: 19D, 21R **House:** 49D, 51R

Election Results

Election	Name (Party)	Vote (%)
2017 General	Ralph Northam (D)...	1,409,175 (54%)
	Ed Gillespie (R)..	1,175,731 (45%)
2017 Primary	Ralph Northam (D)...	303,846 (56%)
	Tom Periello (D)...	239,505 (44%)

Ralph Northam, a low-key pediatric neurologist, has had a wild term as governor of Virginia. A Democrat, Northam rode a blue wave into the governorship in 2017. But just over a year later, a 35-year-old medical school yearbook surfaced, showing a photograph on Northam's page that featured a pair of men in blackface and a KKK outfit. Chastened by the controversy, he took a low profile and worked on mending relationships with Black lawmakers and voters. Later that year, the Democrats won both chambers of the legislature. The yearbook scandal faded and Northam signed a raft of bills long sought by Democrats.

Northam was born on Virginia's eastern shore, an isolated, tight-knit peninsula between Chesapeake Bay and the Atlantic Ocean—"a flat strip of farm fields and fishing villages, pine trees and crape myrtles and marsh grass," as the Washington Post described it. "When Northam was born in 1959, the area was connected to the rest of Virginia only by ferryboats; the 20-mile Chesapeake Bay Bridge-Tunnel linked the region to Norfolk in 1964." (The most recent governor from the eastern shore had served just before the Civil War.) Northam's father, Wescott, returned from World War II and earned a law degree, practicing locally and eventually serving as a prosecutor and circuit court judge; his wife, Nancy, was a nurse. While still a teen, Northam worked on ferries and fishing charters. He attended Virginia Military Institute, where he served as president of the honor court. He earned his medical degree at Eastern Virginia Medical School and rose to the rank of major in the Army. His service included treating wounded soldiers from Operation Desert Storm who had been airlifted to Germany. After eight years in the Army, Northam practiced pediatric neurology and taught at his medical alma mater.

Northam was recruited to politics to challenge Nick Rerras, a Republican state senator in a district that spanned the eastern shore and portions of Hampton Roads. He won the 2007 race by eight points. In the Senate, Northam forged ties to Republicans—sometimes too much so for Democratic leaders' tastes—but also had a good relationship with Democratic Gov. Tim Kaine, who asked him to take a lead role on legislation to ban smoking in restaurants. Northam also worked against a transvaginal ultrasound mandate for women seeking abortions. In 2011, he won reelection.

Democratic gubernatorial candidate Terry McAuliffe recruited Northam to run for lieutenant governor in 2013, seeking geographical balance. He easily beat Rev. E.W. Jackson, an outspoken social conservative, in November, and took office alongside McAuliffe and fellow Democrat Mark Herring, who won the race for attorney general. With the Virginia governorship coming open every four years, Northam was considered the frontrunner for the Democratic nomination in 2017, but he faced a challenge from the left by former Rep. Tom Perriello. Northam, who counted most of the in-state Democratic establishment in his corner, moved to the left to compete with Perriello, who touted supportive words from Sens. Bernie Sanders and Elizabeth Warren. In addition to his reputation for bipartisanship, Northam had to explain his votes for George W. Bush in 2000 and 2004. But Northam got to Perriello's left on abortion and both candidates earned F ratings from the National Rifle Association, a badge of honor to primary voters. In an ad, Northam told primary voters that "I'm listening carefully to Donald Trump, and I think he's a narcissistic maniac." Northam, boosted by strong support from African Americans, beat Perriello 56%-44%.

In the general election, Northam faced Ed Gillespie, a Washington insider and lobbyist who had made a surprisingly strong run at Democratic Sen. Mark Warner in 2014. Northam backtracked from the "narcissistic maniac" rhetoric about Trump, but on most issues he took a progressive line. Northam even joined in a protest at the National Rifle Association headquarters in Fairfax two weeks after the 2017 mass shooting in Las Vegas. (The gun group was airing ads for Gillespie and against Northam.) In the end, he won easily, 54%-45%, much wider than McAuliffe's 2.5-percentage-point victory four years earlier. Northam was aided by a surge in voting by White suburbanites angered by Trump. He flipped two locales that Republican Ken Cuccinelli had won four years earlier: Chesterfield, near Richmond; and Virginia Beach. Northam also extended McAuliffe's margins in the Richmond, Hampton Roads and Northern Virginia areas. Meanwhile, Democrats nearly wiped out the GOP's 66-to-34 majority in the House, losing a shot at control only because of a tied outcome that was decided in favor of the GOP by drawing lots.

The Democratic gains in the legislature helped Northam deliver an expansion of Medicaid that had eluded McAuliffe. He also signed legislation to create a dedicated source of funding for the D.C. area's Metro transit system. But Northam would soon suffer a reversal of fortune. First, he drew the ire of anti-abortion advocates when he offered garbled remarks about a pending bill that would have eased the rules governing third-trimester abortions. Critics said he endorsed infanticide. Soon after, a conservative website published the yearbook images. The reaction was immediate and viscerally negative, not least from most elected Democrats in Virginia, and the furor was compounded after Northam equivocated about whether he was one of the men in the picture and after he gave a peculiar press conference in which he acknowledged once wearing blackface to portray Michael Jackson in a dance contest, then seemed to consider an impromptu demonstration of a moonwalk before his wife urged him to move on. Northam's resignation seemed imminent—until the lieutenant governor, Justin Fairfax, was accused of two sexual assaults, and the attorney general, Mark Herring, acknowledged that he, too, had worn blackface at a college party. With the line of succession mired in controversy, Northam remained in office. He pledged to undertake efforts to better understand racial injustice throughout American history and offered to "take a harder line" on Confederate monuments. And, after a brief flurry of coverage, the press largely ignored the incident.

Northam rebuilt trust slowly but steadily over several months, including among Black lawmakers and voters. He established one commission to weed out vestiges of Jim Crow in the state's laws and another to ensure that school textbooks were teaching racial history fairly. He also secured a funding boost for historically Black colleges. In the pivotal 2019 legislative elections, when every seat in the legislature would be on the line, Northam took something of a backseat to McAuliffe on the campaign trail. But Northam played a key role in the wake of a mass shooting at Virginia Beach government building in which 12 died and four were injured. Northam called a special legislative session to consider gun restrictions, but the GOP-controlled chambers adjourned after just 90 minutes. Democrats effectively leveraged the GOP's response to the gun issue, especially in traditionally Republican suburbs that had become increasingly swingy. "The calling of the special session turned out to be brilliant," veteran political analyst Bob Holsworth told the New York Times. "Republicans couldn't bring themselves to go against their rural base to make changes. This put a totally different dynamic on the election."

With state government now in unified Democratic hands, Northam came out of the gate fast, and effectively, in 2020. By the time the coronavirus pandemic began to sideline legislative business, Northam had already signed several new gun restrictions, including universal background checks; a "red flag" law allowing judges to remove firearms from individuals deemed to be a threat; and reinstatement of a one-gun-a-month purchase limit the GOP legislature had nixed. (Other gun measures, including bans on some semi-automatic weapons, silencers, and magazines with a capacity greater than 12 rounds, were defeated.) Northam also signed a minimum-wage increase to $12, an expansion of rights for public-employee unions, a decriminalization of marijuana, a gasoline tax hike to pay for transportation improvements, and an overhaul of voting rules. He also enacted a wide-ranging anti-discrimination law for LGBT individuals and a ban on "gay conversion therapy," as well as loosening abortion regulations that had been enacted by the former Republican majority. Northam also signed a law enabling local governments to remove Confederate monuments, and he embarked on an effort, delayed by the courts, to remove the statue of Robert E. Lee from a prominent location in Richmond. When the pandemic hit, Northam, like other Democratic governors, took an aggressive course, including issuance of a statewide mask mandate and safety rules for workplaces that went beyond what most other states enacted, but the results didn't match the rhetoric. By April 2021, Virginia was in the middle of the pack nationally for per-capita cases. Meanwhile, in October 2020, Northam signed a wide-ranging overhaul of criminal justice and policing laws, and in March 2021, he signed legislation to end the death penalty, making Virginia the first former Confederate state to do so. "Few back-from-the-dead narratives have been as swift and sure-footed as the one Virginia Gov. Ralph Northam has managed this year," wrote the Washington Post editorial board.

With Virginia's unique one-term-and-out restriction on governors, attention soon turned to the 2021 off-year election. The gubernatorial restriction bars consecutive terms, so McAuliffe decided to run and immediately became a top-tier candidate; he received the endorsement of Northam, marking a stunning turnaround from when McAuliffe had called for Northam's resignation after the blackface scandal broke. But McAuliffe would not have a free ride to the nomination. In a sign of the state's increasing diversity, the field included two Black women, former Del. Jennifer Carroll Foy and state Sen. Jennifer McClellan; a Black man, Fairfax; and a white socialist, Del. Lee Carter. Meanwhile, the Republicans chose their nominee using a ranked-choice convention ballot, featuring candidates that were "Trumpy, Trumpier and Trumpiest," in the words of University of Virginia political scientist Larry Sabato. One of the least Trumpy candidates, Glenn Youngkin, a former Carlyle Group executive with the ability to self-fund, won the nomination over state Sen. Amanda Chase, former House speaker Kirk Cox, retired Army Col. Sergio de la Peña, former think tanker Peter Doran, former Roanoke sheriff Octavia Johnson, and businessman Pete Snyder. Given the state's strong blue shift in recent years, Democrats began the contest as favorites to hold the governorship.

Mark Warner (D)

Elected 2008, term expires 2026, 3rd term, b. Dec 15, 1954; Indianapolis, IN; George Washington University, B.A., 1977; Harvard University Law School, J.D., 1980; Presbyterian; Married (Lisa Collis); 3 children.

Elected Office: VA Governor, 2002-2006.

Professional Career: Fundraiser, Democratic National Committee, 1980-1982; Venture capitalist, 1982-1989; Managing Director, Columbia Capital Corporation, 1989-2001; Commonwealth Transportation Board, 1990-1994; Chairman, VA Democratic Party, 1993-1995; Chairman, National Governors Association, 2004-2005.

DC Office: 703 HSOB 20510, 202-224-2023, Fax: 202-224-6920, warner.senate.gov

State Offices: Abingdon, 276-628-8158; Norfolk, 757-441-3079; Richmond, 804-775-2314; Roanoke, 540-857-2676; Vienna, 703-442-0670.

Committees: *Banking, Housing & Urban Affairs*: Financial Institutions & Consumer Protection; National Security & International Trade & Finance (Chmn); Securities, Insurance & Investment. *Budget. Finance*: Energy, Natural Resources & Infrastructure; Health Care; International Trade, Customs & Global Competitiveness. *Intelligence (Chmn). Rules & Administration.*

Group Ratings

	ADA	ACLU	AFL-CIO	LCV	COC	HAFA	ACU	CFG	FRC
2020	-	62%	-	92%	-	0%	7%	-	-
2019	95%	C	100%	100%	64%	C	7%	0%	0%

Almanac Ratings 2019-2020

	Economy	Social	Foreign	Composite
Liberal	90%	90%	20%	67%
Conservative	10%	10%	80%	33%

Key Votes of the 116th Congress

1. EPA clean energy rules Y	5. Russia sanctions Y	9. Barr as Atty. General N
2. U.S./Mex./Can. trade deal Y	6. Troops in SYR, AFG Y	10. Spending at the border Y
3. Cut unemployment benefits N	7. Veto arms sales to Saudis Y	11. Coney Barrett to Sup. Ct. N
4. Shelton to Fed Reserve N	8. Defense $$$, veto override Y	12. Electoral College objections N

Election Results

Election	Name (Party)	Vote (%)	Cand. Spent	Ind. Exp. Support	Ind. Exp. Oppose
2020 General	Mark Warner (D)............................ 2,466,500	(56%)	$15,362,198	$11,383	$105,750
	Daniel Gade (R)............................ 1,934,199	(44%)	$4,526,068	$18,490	$113
2020 Primary	Mark Warner (D)........................... Unopposed	(0%)			

Prior winning percentages: 2014 (49%), 2008 (65%), Governor: 2001 (52%)

Democrat Mark Warner, Virginia's senior senator, is a former governor whose tenure in Richmond was widely seen as a template for fellow Democrats seeking ways to win and effectively govern in the states once a part of the Confederacy. In the Senate, he's emerged as an adept and respected policymaker, particularly on national security and tech issues. Warner has served as the top Democrat on the Senate Intelligence Committee, including during its investigation of Russian efforts to influence the 2016 presidential election. As vice chairman, his close cooperation with the then-Republican chairman, Sen. Richard Burr of North Carolina, was consistent with his approach to much of his Senate career. Once Democrats won the Senate majority in 2021, he became the chairman of the committee and was poised to be a leading voice on election security.

Warner was born in Indianapolis, where his father was a safety evaluator for Aetna Life & Casualty Inc. The family moved to Connecticut when Warner was in the eighth grade. He graduated from The George Washington University, becoming the first college graduate in his family, and from Harvard Law School. Although he has emphasized his business experience in his campaigns, his first love appears to have been politics: Soon after graduating from law school in 1980, he took a job fundraising for the Democratic National Committee. In 1989, he managed Democrat Douglas Wilder's successful campaign to become the first African-American governor elected anywhere in the nation since Reconstruction.

Warner spent most of the 1980s and 1990s as a highly successful venture capitalist and gaining political contacts. While working for the DNC, Warner met Rep. Tom McMillen, a Maryland Democrat, who told him about the potential of cell phone markets just as the Reagan administration was about to award 1,500 free licenses for metropolitan markets. Warner cobbled together investor groups and packaged their applications in exchange for a fee and a 5 percent ownership stake if they received the licenses. The best-known of these ventures was Nextel, and Warner soon became wealthy. According to the nonpartisan Center for Responsive Politics, his estimated net worth in 2020 was estimated at more than $214 million, making him the second wealthiest member of Congress. A political career remained very much on Warner's mind. From 1993 to 1995, he was Virginia Democratic Party chairman. In 1996, he ran against Republican Sen. John Warner (no relation) in what seemed a quixotic race: The incumbent Warner, elected narrowly in 1978, had won reelection in a landslide in 1984 and had no Democratic opponent in 1990. Mark Warner pitched his campaign not to his home turf in Northern Virginia, but to the Shenandoah Valley and southwest Virginia. He carried southwest Virginia but lost the part of the state outside the three big metropolitan areas by only 51%-49%, a considerable achievement for a Democrat. But John Warner's strength among moderates enabled him to carry Northern Virginia 55%-45% and to win Hampton Roads and metropolitan Richmond with smaller majorities. The result was a 52%-47% statewide win for John Warner. But it wasn't the end of upstart Mark Warner's electoral ambitions.

In the late 1990s, Mark Warner put millions of dollars into philanthropic efforts and set up regional business investment funds in Hampton Roads, Richmond, and Southside—the area south of Richmond—as well as southwest Virginia. By 1999, he had an eye on running for governor in 2001 as an entrepreneur who could bring savvy business methods to government. He picked a good year. Republican Gov. Jim Gilmore had helped elect Republican majorities in both houses of the Legislature, but then battled with them over the budget. Republicans had an intraparty fight over the gubernatorial nomination in 2001 between Lt. Gov. John Hager and Attorney General Mark Earley.

After winning the nomination, Earley had little money and no clear strategy. Warner poured $5 million of his own money into his candidacy.

Warner has lived in a mansion in Old Town Alexandria but avoided being typecast as an urban liberal. He characterized himself as a fiscal conservative and pledged not to raise income or sales taxes. Responding to complaints from traffic-choked Northern Virginia and Hampton Roads, he called for regional referendums on local sales tax increases for transportation. He opposed new gun control measures and wooed the National Rifle Association, which remained neutral in the contest. Warner ran ads featuring old pickups and bluegrass music, and he sponsored a local NASCAR team. He traveled to all parts of rural Virginia, much as Wilder had in 1989, to show he was in touch with everyday folks and to remind them of his investment funds and philanthropic initiatives.

Warner defeated Earley 52%-47%. He carried all major regions of the state, albeit by narrow margins. And he attracted notice from national Democrats for winning a Southern state through business-friendly, fiscally responsible policies combined with cultural conservatism—a combination Warner dubbed "radical centrism."

Once in office, Warner persuaded the Legislature to approve transportation tax referendums in Northern Virginia and Hampton Roads, but the House of Delegates rejected his education initiative in 2002. As a budget shortfall grew, Warner cut more than $850 million in spending and laid off 1,800 state employees. In November 2003, after the legislative elections and when Virginia seemed to be in danger of losing its AAA bond rating, Warner presented his new fiscal plan: a $1 billion tax increase, with increases in the income, sales, and cigarette taxes, and tax reductions for those with low incomes and in car and food taxes. In early 2004, his plan was rejected by the heavily Republican House of Delegates, which moved to increase taxes by just $520 million and provide few spending increases. But House Speaker William Howell was unable to hold his Republicans in line, and 17 of them abandoned their anti-tax positions. The Senate agreed to a $1.3 billion tax increase, more than Warner had requested, and the House went along, a major victory for the governor. By December 2004, the fiscal picture had changed: The state government was facing a $1.2 billion surplus, and Warner called for more spending.

When John Warner in August 2007 announced his retirement from the Senate, Mark Warner's next move seemed obvious. He had no serious opposition for the Democratic nomination. On the Republican side, Gilmore, Warner's predecessor as governor, decided to run. At the 2008 Republican State Convention, he barely prevailed after being challenged from the right because of his support for abortion rights in some cases. It turned out not to be a seriously contested campaign. Warner argued Gilmore had left the state in poor fiscal shape and that he had turned things around as Gilmore's successor. Warner won 65%-34%, losing only two counties in the Shenandoah Valley, two exurban Richmond counties and two small independent cities. For the first time since 1970, Virginia had two Democratic senators.

In the Senate, Warner lamented the adjustment former governors face in becoming one of 100 senators. In 2013, he toyed with running again for governor, which he called "the best job I ever had," but opted against it. His driven and frenetic personality became a source of humor among his colleagues. In recounting his close working relationship with the laid-back Republican Saxby Chambliss of Georgia, Warner told reporters in 2013, "The way he starts each day is, 'Well, Mark, did you take your Ritalin today?'"

Warner's voting habits have put him in the political center. He supported President Barack Obama on the health care overhaul in 2009; during that debate, he led 11 freshman Democrats in proposing a series of amendments intended to control costs and boost accountability of the new program. He also backed the Budget Control Act of 2011 and other Obama administration efforts to raise the federal debt ceiling, but he joined Republicans in backing caps on discretionary spending.

Despite his "A" rating from the NRA, Warner said after the December 2012 Newtown Connecticut school massacre in which 27 teachers and young children were killed that "the status quo isn't acceptable" on guns. "There needs to be appropriate restrictions on these tools of mass-killing," he said. In April 2013, Warner joined most Democrats in backing a compromise measure—opposed by the NRA—to expand background checks on gun buyers. But he was among 15 Democrats to vote against an assault weapons ban and one of 10 Democrats to oppose a ban on high-capacity magazines. Warner took blowback from the party's liberal wing, as the president of MoveOn.org called Warner's votes on the latter issues "shameful." After the high school massacre in Parkland Florida, he shifted and said he backed a ban on assault weapons. It might be impossible to reach "a perfect solution," he told the Virginian-Pilot, but "it's time for action."

Warner won a seat on the Finance Committee in 2014, a plum assignment he had pursued for years. It provided him with an influential platform to pursue longtime interests in reforming the tax code and curbing entitlement spending. He worked closely with Republicans on the Senate Banking Committee to craft the bipartisan deal in 2018 that rolled back the Dodd-Frank financial regulatory law. When Sen. Chuck Schumer of New York became Democratic leader in 2017, he named Warner and Sen. Elizabeth Warren of Massachusetts as vice chairs of the Democratic Caucus.

He retained his interest in the tech industry, occasionally raising tough questions. With Sens. Amy Klobuchar of Minnesota and John McCain of Arizona, in 2017 Warner filed legislation that would have forced social media companies to disclose who paid for online ads. "Americans deserve to know whether the ads they're seeing are generated by Americans or generated by foreign interests," he told reporters. In 2018, he circulated a white paper in which he wrote that he was "very annoyed" with Silicon Valley for its "pathetic" response to revelations of massive data breaches. In 2019, he and Republican Sen. Deb Fischer of Nebraska introduced a bill to ban social media companies from using deceptive practices to obtain user information, such as requiring access to phone and email contacts to continue using the application. Another bill with GOP Sen. Josh Hawley of Missouri would require major platforms such as Facebook and Google to disclose the value of personal user data. "This senator's patience is wearing very thin. It's time for these companies to put their money where their mouth is," Warner told Axios.

Warner came within 1 percentage point of losing reelection in 2014. He started the campaign as a prohibitive favorite, and polls as late as September showed him up by 20 points over his challenger, former Republican National Committee Chairman Ed Gillespie. By the end of the campaign, Warner had outspent Gillespie by almost 2-1, $15.7 million to $7.9 million. Warner's ad campaign attacked Gillespie, founder of a prominent Washington lobbying firm, for lobbying on behalf of Enron—the Texas-based energy firm that collapsed amid scandal in 2001. Gillespie in 2010 had helped found American Crossroads, an outside group that pumped millions into Republican campaigns around the country. But he was unable to attract the group's interest to his seemingly long-shot bid, and his own campaign couldn't afford to go on the air until October.

Two major factors conspired to almost defeat Warner. First, Democratic turnout in 2014 was low nationwide—but especially low in Virginia. Warner was later criticized in Democratic circles for not getting his campaign up and running earlier in the cycle and for not doing more to turn out the vote, especially in Democratic areas such as Northern Virginia. Plus, Gillespie relentlessly tied Warner to Obama, pointing to a CQ Roll Call analysis that found Warner had voted with Obama 97 percent of the time. PolitiFact noted the 97 percent figure was based on just 419 of the 1,473 votes Warner had cast in the Senate. Nevertheless, this line of attack proved potent. Obama's approval ratings had sunk to 40 percent after he carried the state in 2008 and 2012. Warner eked out a win by 49%-48%, a statewide margin of fewer than 17,000 votes.

Warner, who focused heavily during the campaign on the centrist, fiscally responsible persona he had developed during his time as governor, brushed aside suggestions that the election results were an indication his moderate stance no longer played well in an increasingly polarized state. "I'm going to continue to be bipartisan," he said. He attributed his close call to voters "grumpy" over congressional inaction and saying that "they want results." The voters, he added, were telling him: "'Warner, show us some more of being that change agent.' I'm taking that message to heart."

His big opportunity arrived in January 2017 when changes on the Intelligence Committee left Warner as the ranking Democrat as the panel became the Senate vehicle to investigate claims of Russian interference in the 2016 presidential election. As Warner told the New York Times, the investigation would be "probably the most important thing I've done in public life." After committee Chairman Burr—backed by Sen. Mitch McConnell, the majority leader—initially rejected demands for an inquiry, Warner organized committee Democrats to reverse his decision. With a combination of public and private pressures, Warner succeeded. As the investigation began, Warner seemed to have succeeded with his practice of bonding with a relatively pragmatic Republican senator. In this case, Warner and Burr were both mid-South white men of similar age and serious purpose. Their congenial approach to the inquiry stood in stark contrast to the partisan fireworks on the House Intelligence Committee.

Warner seemed to have placed himself at the center of a complex international web of 21st-century statecraft and competition. For the most part, he was careful to respect Burr's occasional caution with the challenges in their fact-finding. Still, he pursued some clues on his own, including his private meetings and exchanges with Russian oligarchs and others who had dealt with them. In February 2018, the alt-right conservative website Breitbart charged that Warner was responsible for "Democrat-Russian collusion."

In April 2020, the committee's long-awaited final report was released, backing up the intelligence community's assessment that Russia had worked to undermine and influence the 2016 elections, still over the protests of Trump. Both Burr and Warner championed the bipartisan result, though the two ended up with divergent opinions on whether the Trump campaign had colluded with the Kremlin. They agreed, though, that Russia was likely emboldened by its successes in 2016 and would attempt the another disinformation campaign during the 2020 elections. In August, the committee passed the report on a 14-1 vote. By then, Rubio had taken over as chairman after Burr stepped aside amid investigations into his stock trades. Rubio said the report proved "without any hesitation" that the Trump campaign had not colluded with the Russian government. But Warner differed, saying that it laid out "unprecedented contacts between Russians and folks on the Trump campaign. The Trump campaign officials welcomed that help. And maybe one of the most stunning was the level of detail of the then-campaign manager Paul Manafort sharing very specific campaign information with a Russian agent." Rubio, who also developed a good working relationship with Warner, distanced himself from Trump in other instances, including a push by Homeland Security and Governmental Affairs Chairman Ron Johnson to investigate Biden's son Hunter ahead of the 2020.

Warner proposed several election security bills to try to derail the possibility of a similar scenario repeating itself in 2020, including one that would require campaigns to report offers of assistance from foreign entities to the FBI, but they were repeatedly blocked by Republicans. "In a different time, with a different president, this bill wouldn't be controversial at all," Warner said on the Senate floor. When a foreign power reaches out, "the appropriate response is not to say, 'Thank you.' The appropriate response is, 'Call the FBI.' What a sad statement about partisan politics in our country when we can't even agree on that."

After his near-death experience in 2014, Warner took his reelection bid for a third term in 2020 more seriously. "I can assure you one thing: I still have nightmares about 2014," he told Politico. Warner also had the benefit of being on the ballot during the highest-turnout presidential election in modern history, as Virginia continued its streak of boxing out Republicans statewide since 2009. No major Republican stepped forward to run, and Warner faced off against political newcomer Daniel Gade, a retired Army officer who had lost a leg during a Humvee explosion in Iraq. Warner spent $15 million compared to Gade's $4.5 million, and the Democrat won easily by 12 points, running slightly ahead of Biden's 54%-44% victory in the commonwealth.

Tim Kaine (D)

Elected 2012, term expires 2024, 2nd term, b. Feb 26, 1958; St. Paul, MN; University of Missouri, A.B., 1979; Harvard Law School, J.D., 1983; Roman Catholic; Married (Anne Bright Holton); 3 children.

Elected Office: Richmond City Council, 1994-1998; Richmond Mayor, 1998-2001; VA Lt. Governor, 2002-2006; VA Governor, 2006-2010; Chairman, Democratic National Committee, 2009-2011.

Professional Career: Law Clerk, Judge R. Lanier Anderson, U.S. Court of Appeals, 1983-1984; Attorney; Lecturer, University of Richmond, 1987-1993, 2010-2012.

DC Office: 231 RSOB 20510, 202-224-4024, Fax: 202-228-6363, kaine.senate.gov

State Offices: Abingdon, 276-525-4790; Danville, 434-792-0976; Manassas, 703-361-3192; Richmond, 804-771-2221; Roanoke, 540-682-5693; Virginia Beach, 757-518-1674.

Committees: *Armed Services*: Emerging Threats & Capabilities; Readiness & Management Support (Chmn); Seapower. *Budget. Foreign Relations*: Africa & Global Health Policy; State Dept & USAID Mngmnt, Internat'l Ops & Internat'l Dev; West Hem Crime Civ Sec Dem Rights & Women's Issues (Chmn). *Health, Education, Labor & Pensions*: Children & Families; Primary Health & Retirement Security.

Group Ratings

	ADA	ACLU	AFL-CIO	LCV	COC	HAFA	ACU	CFG	FRC
2020	-	85%	-	92%	-	0%	2%	-	-
2019	100%	C	100%	100%	51%	C	2%	0%	0%

Almanac Ratings 2019-2020

	Economy	Social	Foreign	Composite
Liberal	97%	97%	61%	85%
Conservative	3%	3%	39%	15%

Key Votes of the 116th Congress

1. EPA clean energy rules	Y	5. Russia sanctions	Y	9. Barr as Atty. General	N
2. U.S./Mex./Can. trade deal	Y	6. Troops in SYR, AFG	Y	10. Spending at the border	Y
3. Cut unemployment benefits	N	7. Veto arms sales to Saudis	Y	11. Coney Barrett to Sup. Ct.	N
4. Shelton to Fed Reserve	N	8. Defense $$$, veto override	Y	12. Electoral College objections	N

Election Results

Election	Name (Party)	Vote (%)	Cand. Spent	Ind. Exp. Support	Ind. Exp. Oppose
2018 General	Tim Kaine (D)................................ 1,910,370	(57%)	$16,951,669	$108,120	$270,375
	Corey Stewart (R)......................... 1,374,313	(41%)	$2,769,385	$39,676	$26,613
2018 Primary	Tim Kaine (D)..	(100%)			

Prior winning percentages: 2018 (57%), 2012 (53%), Governor: 2005 (52%)

Democrat Tim Kaine, a former Virginia governor who was elected in 2012 as the state's junior senator, took a star turn in 2016 as his party's vice presidential nominee in a campaign that had seemed likely to cap his diverse career in local and national government and politics. But now he seems content to make his mark in the Senate with a lengthy career like that of 30-year veteran Virginia Republican John Warner, a feat made easier by the Old Dominion's further lurch leftward. "When I walked in here the day after I got back from 2016, my feeling was, I think the Senate is going to be incredibly important to saving this country in the next few years," he told The Atlantic. Kaine has emerged as one of the most prominent voices for a check by Congress on a president's military power—whether they be Democrat or Republican.

Born in St. Paul Minnesota, Kaine grew up outside Kansas City. His father ran his own ironworking and welding shop, with Kaine and his younger brothers frequently helping. Kaine attended the University of Missouri, where he graduated in three years, before going to Harvard Law School. Midway through law school, Kaine left to spend nine months teaching at a Jesuit mission in Honduras. In a Washington Post interview three decades later, Kaine said of his time in Honduras: "It made a public servant out of me. … And the Jesuits themselves kind of became my heroes." It also gave him fluency in Spanish. As the Senate debated a major immigration overhaul bill in 2013, Kaine became the first senator ever to deliver a floor speech entirely in Spanish. "I think people were probably surprised," Kaine told The New York Times afterward. "One of my people got a call by a Latino staffer in the House [who] said, 'I have waited 20 years to see this happen.'"

Kaine returned to Harvard to complete his law degree in 1983. It was there that he met his wife, Anne Holton, a daughter of Linwood Holton, Virginia's first Republican governor since Reconstruction. Anne Holton made national headlines as a child when her father, as governor from 1970-1974, ended the state's resistance to desegregation—and enrolled his children in Richmond's public schools, whose student population was largely African-American. For a time, Kaine worked for a federal judge in Macon Georgia, while Holton was working for a federal judge in Richmond. They decided to marry and settle in Richmond. Kaine worked as a civil rights lawyer, specializing in representing those who had been denied housing because of race or disability. In 1994, he won a seat on the Richmond City Council and four years later was elected mayor. In 2001, he was elected lieutenant governor.

Kaine ran for governor in 2005 against former state Attorney General Jerry Kilgore. Kaine, who held positions well to the left of Kilgore, pitched a quality-of-life agenda designed to appeal to urban and suburban voters. He emphasized tax relief for homeowners, a statewide pre-kindergarten initiative, a balanced approach to growth and new transportation solutions. Kilgore relied on hot-button issues such as the death penalty and illegal immigration, while dismissing Kaine as "too liberal for Virginia." In one Kilgore ad, a man whose son and daughter-in-law were murdered criticized Kaine for opposing the death penalty for "the worst mass murderer in modern times." Kaine said his opposition to capital punishment was based on religious convictions, and the issue gave him an opportunity to talk about his Catholic faith. Kaine emphasized that, despite his personal beliefs, he would allow executions as governor; his opposition didn't stand in the way of four executions of incarcerated people. Kaine won 52%-46%, a victory powered by large margins in suburban Northern Virginia.

In his first year, Kaine had some successes dealing with the Republican-controlled Legislature, including passage of a bill requiring rigorous teacher evaluations. A year later, Kaine reached agreement with the Republican-controlled House and Senate on a $1 billion transportation bill, representing the state's biggest funding increase in two decades. Since Republicans would not agree to a significant statewide tax increase, the scheme called for borrowing up to $3 billion over 10 years and giving taxing powers to regional authorities in the two traffic-choked big metro areas, Northern Virginia and Hampton Roads. That plan was hobbled when the state Supreme Court ruled that the regional authorities couldn't raise taxes. In 2008, Kaine proposed $1.1 billion for transportation, with a penny sales tax increase in Northern Virginia and Hampton Roads. But House Republicans resisted it.

While Kaine was in Japan on a trade mission in April 2007, a Virginia Tech student opened fire on campus during classes, killing 32 people before killing himself. Kaine immediately flew home and won praise for his handling of the tragedy. Kaine in his last year in office reached agreement with House Speaker William Howell, a Republican, to ban smoking in bars and restaurants. Later as a senator in 2019, he and Sen. Mitch McConnell of Kentucky, then the majority leader, successfully raised the age to buy tobacco products from 18 to 21 nationwide. But Kaine failed to get the Legislature to agree to proposals for universal pre-kindergarten and background checks on sales at gun shows. Kaine pleaded with legislators to enact tighter controls in a 2019 special session after a gunman killed 12 people in a Virginia Beach municipal building. The following year, after Democrats won back control of both the state Senate and House of Delegates, a slate of new restrictions was enacted, including universal background checks.

In February 2007, Kaine endorsed Barack Obama for the Democratic presidential nomination, the first governor to do so outside Obama's home state. He campaigned heavily for Obama in Virginia and helped him win one of his biggest primary victories there. On his vice presidential short list, Obama named Kaine chairman of the Democratic National Committee after he won, a post he held until 2011.

When Democratic Sen. Jim Webb decided not to seek re-election in 2012 after serving just one term, Kaine entered the Senate race at the urging of Obama and other leading Democrats eager to find a high-profile challenger to George Allen. The son and namesake of a legendary football coach, Allen was first elected to the Senate in 2000. But he narrowly lost re-election in 2006 to Webb, after Allen sparked widespread controversy when he referred to an Indian-American aide to Webb—who had been assigned to tape Allen's public campaign appearances—with the racist term "macaca."

Flooding the airwaves with ads, Kaine spent nearly $18 million and Allen spent $14.4 million. The outside group Crossroads GPS spent millions attacking Kaine, while Allen ridiculed him for accepting a position to head the DNC while still governor; Kaine criticized Allen for increased spending while in the Statehouse and for past support of partial privatization of Social Security. Kaine won, 53%-47%, making him among roughly 20 people in U.S. history to have served as mayor, governor and senator.

Assigned to the Foreign Relations and Armed Services committees, Kaine, whose son is in the Marines, focused on national security—and, specifically, the process for authorizing the United States to engage in military action. Kaine and Arizona Republican John McCain in 2014 introduced legislation to clarify the then-40-year-old War Powers Act—and the underlying question of the degree to which the president and Congress possess, or share, the power to initiate military action abroad. In 2016, Kaine said that it was hypocritical for the Obama administration to criticize Russia's invasion of Ukraine when it has put troops in Syria without authority. "We are carrying out escalating military operations in Syria without the permission and really even against the will of the sovereign nation," he told a Senate hearing.

In addition, Kaine has pushed repeatedly for a congressional debate and vote on a new authorization for U.S. military action against the Islamic State group. This stance put him at odds with Obama, who had asserted that an Authorization for Use of Military Force passed a week after 9/11 allowed for current U.S. military activities in and around Syria and Iraq. Kaine contended that current military action against ISIS "goes well beyond the intent" of the 2001 AUMF. In June 2014, Kaine engaged Obama at the White House in what the senator later referred to as a "spirited discussion." Kaine is reported to have firmly told Obama that, if he intended to go to war, he would need Congress' permission, while the president—politely, but just as firmly—disagreed. Republican Jeff Flake of Arizona and Kaine advocated for an authorization for action against ISIS, but they failed.

Kaine told The New York Times in 2014 that his adamant position on this issue grew not only out of the large military presence in his home state, but also Virginia's place in the nation's founding. "They know I feel strongly about this because I'm a Virginian," Kaine said of the Obama White House. "Until we have a vote, and we live by that vote, I am going to keep pushing them hard."

In 2016, Hillary Clinton selected Kaine as her running. The choice was well-received, but Kaine did not escape second-guessing. He did not excite liberal activists and his support for international trade deals did little to generate enthusiasm among blue-collar union members. Clinton based the selection, in part, on their compatibility and his preparation to do the job, She told PBS her decision showed that she was "afflicted with the responsibility gene."

Kaine's persistent attack mode in the vice presidential debate was described by commentators as "over-caffeinated." He played the attack dog, especially against Republican presidential nominee Donald Trump. "A dark and twisted journey through the mind of Donald Trump [is] a very scary place to be," was an occasional attack line. But, like the Clinton campaign generally, he failed to convince battleground-state voters that Trump was an unacceptable choice or generate enthusiasm for the Democratic alternative. Kaine's Spanish speaking and experience in Latin America did not have a noticeable effect with Hispanic voters.

Back in the Senate, with even more resolve, Kaine resumed his quest to debate the use of military force, citing the new element of a president whose actions could be unpredictable or not fully explained. With Flake, he filed his resolution again. "We owe it to the American public to define the scope of the U.S. mission against terrorist organizations, including ISIS, and we owe it to our troops to show we're behind them in their mission," Kaine said in May 2017. In 2019, he again tried, and failed, to attach an amendment to a defense bill requiring Trump to seek congressional approval before any military action in Iran. The next year, he and GOP Sen. Mike Lee of Utah persuaded enough Senate Republicans to sign on to the same war powers resolution, which passed 55-45. However, when Trump vetoed it, the Senate was unable to muster the two-thirds vote needed to override. "He's not worried about war. He's worried about himself and his reelection, and so he can only look at this important constitutional matter—and there isn't a more important one than war and peace—through the lens of Donald Trump and my own reelection," Kaine told reporters after the veto. Amid summer 2020 protests for racial justice, Kaine threatened to defund portions of the Defense budget if Trump tried to use troops against protesters.

In a 2018 reelection campaign that turned out to be his easiest statewide contest, Kaine faced Corey Stewart, the Prince William County board chairman, whose right-wing populism, occasional demagoguery and support for Confederate statues bore similarities to Trump's political style. He called himself "Trumpier than Trump." More than Trump, Stewart had problems unifying his party after a narrow primary win. The National Republican Senatorial Committee did not spend money on his behalf. Americans for Prosperity—the political arm of the Koch network—refused to endorse him, in part because of his hard-line opposition to immigration and international trade. Virginia Business, a statewide magazine that had not endorsed a candidate during its more than 30 years of publication, endorsed Kaine as "good for business."

In a campaign debate, Stewart criticized Kaine's record in the Senate. "He's had six years in the Senate, four of which were under a Democratic president, and he's got nothing done," Stewart said. Kaine cited his pragmatic and occasionally bipartisan approach and said that Trump had signed his bills dealing with career education and cyber security.

Stewart's challenge to Kaine never posed a serious threat. He spent only $2.8 million—far less than successful Democratic challengers for House seats in Virginia in 2018—while Kaine spent $19.6 million. In the closing days, the incumbent focused much of his attention on aiding other Democratic candidates. Kaine won 57%-41%. In Stewart's home of Prince William County, Kaine won 65%-33%.

Kaine has cut a centrist profile in the Senate. He endorsed Biden in the Democratic presidential primary just ahead of Super Tuesday 2020, when Virginia would vote. "Joe Biden has exemplary heart, character, and experience," Kaine said. He and other moderates had warned the year prior of their party's leftward lurch, fearing a more progressive nominee couldn't defeat Trump. As part of that pushback, Kaine and Colorado Democrat Michael Bennet—who would make a brief run for president—introduced a "Medicare X" plan, which would create a public option for health insurance but allow people to keep their private insurance plans, as opposed to the progressive "Medicare for All" proposal that would create a single-payer system. One of Kaine's departures from the center came in a summer 2020 warning that Republicans shouldn't fill a Supreme Court vacancy should it occur after they blocked Obama's nominee to fill the late Justice Antonin Scalia's seat 2016. "If they show that they're unwilling to respect precedent, rules and history, then they can't feign surprise when others talk about using a statutory option that we have that's fully constitutional in our availability," Kaine told NBC News, threatening that Democrats could subsequently add seats to the court. "I don't want to do that. But if they act in such a way, they may push it to an inevitability. So they need to be careful about that." Of course, Kaine's fear came true in September 2020 with Justice Ruth Bader Ginsburg's death and Republicans' confirmation of conservative jurist Amy Coney Barret the next month.

Rob Wittman (R)

Elected 2007, 7th full term, b. Feb 03, 1959; Washington, DC; VA Polytechnic Institute, B.S., 1981; University of NC in Chapel Hill, M.PH, 1990; VA Commonwealth University, Ph.D., 2002; Episcopalian; Married (Kathryn Jane Sisson Wittman); 2 children; 4 grandchildren.

Elected Office: Montross Town Council, 1986-1996; Montross Mayor, 1992-1996; Westmoreland County Board of Supervisors, 1996-2005, chmn, 2004-2005; VA House, 2006-2007.

Professional Career: Environmental health specialist, VA health Department; Field Director, VA Health Department Div. of Shellfish Sanitation.

DC Office: 2055 RHOB 20515, 202-225-4261, Fax: 202-225-4382, wittman.house.gov

State Offices: Mechanicsville, 804-730-6595; Stafford, 540-659-2734; Tappahannock, 804-443-0668.

Committees: *Armed Services*: Seapower & Projection Forces (RMM); Tactical Air & Land Forces. *Natural Resources*: Water, Oceans & Wildlife.

Group Ratings

	ADA	ACLU	AFL-CIO	LCV	COC	HAFA	ACU	CFG	FRC
2020	**	24%	**	19%	-	89%	86%	**	-
2019	5%	C	29%	3%	87%	C	87%	79%	100%

Almanac Ratings 2019-2020

	Economy	Social	Foreign	Composite
Liberal	38%	17%	27%	28%
Conservative	62%	83%	73%	72%

Key Votes of the 116th Congress

1. U.S./Mex./Can. trade deal	Y	5. Russia sanctions	Y
2. First Coronavirus response	Y	6. Troops in Syria	Y
3. HEROES Act	N	7. Veto arms sales to Saudis	N
4. CASH Act	N	8. Defense $$$, veto override	Y

9. Firearms background checks N
10. Spending at the border Y
11. Marijuana liberalized rules N
12. Electoral College objections Y

Election Results

Election	Name (Party)	Vote (%)		Cand. Spent	Ind. Exp. Support	Ind. Exp. Oppose
2020 General	Rob Wittman (R)	260,614	(58%)	$1,853,761		$750
	Qasim Rashid (D)	186,923	(42%)	$1,529,312	$104,741	$1,408

Prior winning percentages: 2018 (55%), 2016 (60%), 2014 (63%), 2012 (56%), 2010 (64%), 2008 (57%), 2007 special (61%)

Republican Rob Wittman, who won the seat in a 2007 special election, has engaged on national security, with a focus that includes and goes beyond the parochial concerns of his district. He combines military expertise with a professional interest in environmental protection, a pairing not often found among officials in either party. Wittman has gained growing influence in the House, especially on the Armed Services Committee, where he has worked to expand the Navy's fleet, including two new aircraft carriers, plus a commitment to increased submarine production. Following his closest election ever in 2018, he won more comfortably in 2020 against a well-funded challenger. Redistricting could pose risks.

Wittman was born in Washington D.C. and became a marine scientist. He has a Ph.D. in public policy and administration from Virginia Commonwealth University. Wittman served for many years as an environmental health specialist in the Northern Neck and Peninsula regions, including as field director for the state's shellfish sanitation division. His first public office was a seat on the Montross Town Council, where he served for 10 years, including four as mayor. In 1995, he began a decade on the Westmoreland County Board of Supervisors. In 2005, he was elected to the Virginia House of Delegates.

When the seat was vacant in 2007, after GOP Rep. Jo Ann Davis died of breast cancer, Republicans held a convention to choose their nominee. Wittman's chief opponent was Paul Jost, a businessman and anti-tax activist. Wittman cited his experience in public office and "the basics of good government." With help from several busloads of supporters, Jost led in early balloting, which began with 11 candidates. The key moment came after five ballots, when Davis' widower, Chuck Davis, threw his support to Wittman. Against Democrat Philip Forgit, a school teacher and Navy reservist who won a Bronze Star in Iraq, Wittman emphasized his conservative credentials, including his support for gun rights and opposition to abortion. Democrats paid little attention to the contest, and Wittman won 61%-37%.

Wittman got a seat on the Armed Services and Natural Resources committees. He usually sticks with Republicans on major issues but is not an automatic vote. Coming from a district with a large government presence, he is less enamored of eliminating federal programs and dramatically reducing spending than some other conservatives.

Wittman has worked with lawmakers in both parties on efforts to clean up Chesapeake Bay. In March 2019, he joined Democratic Reps. Elaine Luria and Bobby Scott to call for $455 million for pollution control in the bay and assistance to states in the watershed to manage their runoffs into its tributaries. An advocate of an "all of the above" approach to energy resources, he has supported offshore drilling.

Wittman has had key position on the Armed Services Committee. In 2013, he became chairman of the Readiness Subcommittee. As co-chair of the Congressional Shipbuilding Caucus, he aggressively advocates expanding the fleet and he has maintained that it is more critical than ever for the military to project power around the world.

Republican Rep. Randy Forbes of Virginia lost reelection in an adjacent district following the redistricting changes in 2016, opening for Wittman the chairmanship of the Sea power and Projection Forces Subcommittee. He grabbed that position, which was vital for the extensive shipbuilding interests of Virginia.

He has made the most of the opportunity. That chairmanship was all the more attractive because of the support from President Donald Trump to expand the Navy from its roughly 285 ships to 355 ships. Wittman embraced that ambitious long-term objective, which could require at least 30 years to achieve. Hampton Roads is home to the world's largest naval base and the headquarters of Huntington Ingalls Industries, the largest U.S. military shipbuilder.

As an immediate priority, Wittman worked in the House and with the Trump administration to win approval of two new aircraft carriers, which were part of the defense spending bill enacted in December 2018. When Trump's budget in March 2019 called for an early decommissioning of one of the existing 12 carriers and for a halt in funding of a new attack submarine, Wittman strongly objected, calling the budget "strategically and fiscally irresponsible."

Wittman has worked closely with Democratic Rep. Joe Courtney of Connecticut, the subcommittee chairman, whose district includes the nation's other submarine-building yard. He said the Navy needs to be "much more aggressive" in achieving its objectives. In December 2020, when Congress enacted the annual defense spending bill—with both submarines—over Trump's veto, Wittman said, "our service members and our national security professionals need this legislation."

Wittman has not been seriously threatened for reelection. In a state that has not elected a Republican statewide since 2009, he has explored but then rejected possible runs for governor and the Senate. In 2018, Wittman had his most competitive House contest. Democratic challenger Vangie Williams, who filed for bankruptcy years earlier because of a sick child's medical bills, proposed a "Medicare for all" system. Wittman outspent her, $2.1 million to $317,000, but was held to a 55%-45% win. In a strongly Democratic year in Virginia, Williams led by nearly 10,000 votes in Prince William County. In 2020, he faced a better-financed challenge from Qasim Rashid, a native of Pakistan and human rights attorney, who spent $1.5 million. Wittman won, 58%-42. He narrowed his loss in Prince William to 6,500 votes and also trailed in the far smaller city of Fredericksburg, while winning all the other counties.

Following the election, he voted against certifying the Electoral College result in Pennsylvania. He cited judicial changes in election administration, which he said "bypassed the constitutionally vested power of the state legislature."

With Democrats in control of redistricting plus the continued growth of northern Virginia, Wittman faces the risk that his seat will move further into the Washington exurbs. Still, if he retains his hold on the district, he is young enough that he could be positioned to be the top Republican on the Armed Services Committee, especially now that his statewide plans have been curtailed.

VA-1: Eastern Virginia   Cook Partisan Voting Index: R+6

Population		Race and Ethnicity		Income	
Total	824,492	White	72.40%	Median Income	$90,181
Land area (sq. miles)	3,684	Black	16.40%	District Income Rank	58
Pop/ sq mi	223.78	Latino	11.10%	Poverty Rate	7.90%
Born in State	48.60%	Asian	3.60%	With health insurance	92.30%
		Two or more races	4.20%	Cash public assistance	1.30%
Age Groups		Other	3.40%	Food stamp/SNAP	6.40%
Under 18	23.60%				
18-34	20.50%	**Education**		**Work**	
35-64	40.20%	H.S grad or less	34.30%	White Collar	43.90%
Over 64	15.70%	Some college	27.90%	Sales and Service	36.50%
		College Degree, 4 yr	22.50%	Blue Collar	19.60%
Military		Post grad	15.20%	Government	22.80%
Veteran/ Active Duty	15.30%				

2020 Pres. Vote	Trump	233,398	(51%)	Biden	213,535	(47%)		
2016 Pres. Vote	Trump	210,618	(53%)	Clinton	161,476	(41%)	Johnson 12,298	(3%)

DC and Richmond Exurbs: When the English first sailed up the estuaries that flow into Chesapeake Bay, they were searching for gold. But they couldn't help noticing that the spot where the James River fed into the bay, now Hampton Roads, was a fine natural harbor with calm, deep water and good anchorages. So, some of them stayed and established communities farther up the river that achieved not only the high craftsmanship of Williamsburg, but endured the pitiless hardship of Jamestown and other early settlements. Tidewater Virginia brought slavery to America and tobacco to the world, and slave-raised tobacco was the center of its economy in the colonial era and in the years afterward. Today, more than 1.7 million people live in the area. Because of the heavy military presence, it's a population collected from all over the country. Like most of Northern Virginia, it has less of a southern atmosphere than other regions of the Old Dominion. In response to protestors, Fredericksburg officials in June 2020 agreed to remove a slave auction block from a downtown site to a local museum.

About half the population of the 1st Congressional District of Virginia lives south and east of Fredericksburg, the unofficial southern terminus of Northern Virginia. Most of the major Hampton Roads military installations are in surrounding congressional districts. But the 1st remains steeped in military culture, and the Department of Defense and NASA are significant employers. In Caroline County, Fort A.P. Hill serves as a training site for active and reserve-component units. Not far from there is the Naval Surface Warfare Center in Dahlgren, located on the Potomac River, originally established as the Navy's main proving ground for large-caliber guns.

The other half of the district's population lives in the southern reaches of exurban Washington D.C., effectively making its representative the fourth member of Congress from Northern Virginia. This part has become a political swing area, with Fredericksburg, Stafford County and portions of Prince William and Fauquier counties. Prince William and Stafford remain the two largest counties in the district. They comprise nearly 40 percent of the population. Prince William, other parts of which are in two suburban Washington districts, has grown 65 percent between 2000 and 2017; it surpassed Virginia Beach in population and is the second-largest locality in Virginia, behind Fairfax County. Stafford County, which is more rural and 42 miles from Washington, also is rapidly growing, with a 64 percent increase during that time; projections are that it will more than double between

2015 and 2040. The district has a large military presence here as well, including the Quantico Marine Corps base. With drivers in this area suffering some of the worst commutes in the nation, Virginia transportation officials have taken steps to upgrade the rail line, including additional tracks, between Richmond and Washington to reduce the time along that route by about an hour. The changes might be fully completed by 2030. The estimated $3.7 billion cost includes nearly $2 billion to build a new passenger rail bridge over the Potomac River into Washington. With its military population and growing retirement communities, the 1st has been reliably Republican in most elections and is the most Republican district in Tidewater. In 2020, President Donald Trump took the district, 51%-47%, a Republican dip since 2012, when Mitt Romney won, 55%-43%.

Elaine Luria (D)

Elected 2018, 2nd term, b. Aug 15, 1975; Birmingham, AL; U.S. Naval Academy, B.S., 1997; Old Dominion University, M.E.M., 2004; Jewish; Married (Bob Blondin); 1 child ; 2 stepchildren.

Military Career: U.S. Navy 1997-2017

DC Office: 534 CHOB 20515, 202-225-4215, luria.house.gov

State Offices: Onley, 757-364-7631; Virginia Beach, 757-364-7650.

Committees: *Armed Services (VChmn)*: Readiness; Seapower & Projection Forces. *Homeland Security*: Transportation & Maritime Security. *Veterans' Affairs*: Disability Assistance & Memorial Affairs (Chmn); Oversight & Investigations; Women Veterans Task Force.

Almanac Ratings 2019-2020

	Economy	Social	Foreign	Composite
Liberal	54%	51%	46%	51%
Conservative	46%	49%	54%	49%

Key Votes of the 116th Congress

1. U.S./Mex./Can. trade deal	Y	5. Russia sanctions	Y	9. Firearms background checks	Y
2. First Coronavirus response	Y	6. Troops in Syria	Y	10. Spending at the border	Y
3. HEROES Act	N	7. Veto arms sales to Saudis	Y	11. Marijuana liberalized rules	Y
4. CASH Act	Y	8. Defense $$$, veto override	Y	12. Electoral College objections	N

Election Results

Election	Name (Party)	Vote (%)	Cand. Spent	Ind. Exp. Support	Ind. Exp. Oppose
2020 General	Elaine Luria (D)............................	185,733 (52%)	$6,478,323	$1,129,512	$2,893,311
	Scott Taylor (R)............................	165,031 (46%)	$2,349,905	$546,656	$1,856,810
	David Foster (I).....................................	9,170 (3%)			

Prior winning percentages: 2018 (51%)

Freshman Elaine Luria was among several Democrats elected in 2018 with extensive military experience who have become outspoken on national security issues. She was an officer and nuclear engineer in the U.S. Navy, which has a major presence in her district. Luria won her seat by defeating Rep. Scott Taylor after he became enmeshed during the campaign in an investigation of the filing papers of an independent candidate. That scandal doomed him again when he sought a 2020 comeback.

A native of Birmingham Alabama, Luria graduated from the Naval Academy, where she majored in physics and history. She later received a master's degree in engineering management from Old Dominion University. Luria was trained as an officer in the surface warfare division and in Tomahawk land-attack missile launch.

During her 20-year Navy career, Luria was deployed on numerous vessels, including aircraft carriers. Much of that time was in the Middle East and western Pacific, including for support of operations in Iraq and Afghanistan. As an engineer, she operated nuclear reactors to conduct air operations. In the private sector, she started a business, Mermaid Factory, with two local shops that sold clay souvenirs of aquatic symbols. Her husband, Robert Blondin, is a retired Navy commander.

In the Democratic primary, Luria faced Karen Mallard, a school teacher who was a progressive advocate for organized labor. With early support from the Democratic Congressional Campaign Committee, which drew complaints from Mallard, Luria had a big fundraising advantage and won, 62%-38%.

Taylor, a retired Navy Seal sniper, was severely injured while on a combat mission in Iraq. He was elected in 2016, when he defeated Rep. Randy Forbes—a senior member of the Armed Services Committee—in a redrawn district. He easily defeated Democrat Shaun Brown, a business consultant who had lost several previous local campaigns. Luria said she voted in both contests for Taylor, a fellow Navy officer.

In 2018, Taylor ran into problems when his campaign aides forged signatures on petitions for Shaun Brown to run as an independent against Taylor and Luria. Given her background, Brown's candidacy likely would have drawn votes chiefly from Luria. Following an investigation by a special prosecutor, a local judge ordered Brown's name removed from the ballot because of what he termed "out-and-out fraud."

Taylor fired the aides, saying he was aware of their assistance for Brown but that he knew nothing about their illegal actions. In a separate case days before the election, Brown was convicted of fraud in mishandling funds for a federal nutrition program for needy children. In a campaign debate, Taylor contended that he had delivered on his campaign promises from 2016, when Luria had voted for him. Luria said his vote to repeal the Affordable Care Act ran counter to his promises. She cited the flap over Brown's candidacy to question Taylor's honesty. Each candidate spent more than $4 million and had $2 million in party support. Citing Taylor's handling of the ballot controversy, the Virginian-Pilot endorsed Luria.

Luria won, 51%-49%. She took 51 percent in Virginia Beach, which cast about 60 percent of the vote. Taylor got 55 percent in York County, the next-largest locality in the district. Luria led in most other areas. She was one of three Democratic women who ousted GOP incumbents in Virginia that year.

In her first term, Luria protected the interests of her coastal district; in 2020, the House passed her bill to reauthorize the Chesapeake Bay clean-up. Ideologically she became an outspoken moderate, eager to publicly disavow the progressive wing of her party. She endorsed Joe Biden during the Democratic presidential primaries, suggesting Sen. Bernie Sanders of Vermont would be too divisive. A devout Jew, Luria co-wrote a letter urging colleagues to condemn anti-Semitic language after Democratic Rep. Ilhan Omar of Minnesota wrote tweets using Jewish tropes.

With a keen eye on her swing district, she initially was loath to call for an impeachment inquiry against President Donald Trump. But in September 2019, she signed a letter with six other first-term members with national-security backgrounds signaling their support after allegations surfaced that Trump pressured the president of Ukraine to uncover dirt on a political opponent. "I didn't spend 20 years in uniform defending our country to watch something like this," she told a town hall in her district that October.

That stance convinced Taylor to abandon his challenge to Sen. Mark Warner and seek a rematch with Luria. "The last straw for me was impeachment," he told a local TV station. But Taylor again struggled to overcome the signature-forgery scandal that plagued him in 2018. Democratic outside groups ran TV ads relitigating the investigation. Taylor again defended himself by noting he was not a target of the investigation. Luria outspent Taylor $6.5. million to $2.3 million, though the Congressional Leadership Fund spent more than $3 million on his behalf.

Luria prevailed again, 52%-46%, this time with 52 percent in Virginia Beach and 60 percent in Norfolk. Taylor won York County, but lost most other localities. Biden carried the district in 2020, though more narrowly than Luria.

Virginia Democrats ceded control of redistricting to an independent commission, reducing their ability to make Luria's seat more favorable. She remained a top target for House Republicans, who hoped to recruit a female Navy veteran.

VA-2: Hampton Roads   **Cook Partisan Voting Index: R+1**

Population		Race and Ethnicity		Income	
Total	723,927	White	67.20%	Median Income	$74,704
Land area (sq. miles)	992	Black	19.30%	District Income Rank	133
Pop/ sq mi	730.00	Latino	8.30%	Poverty Rate	8.50%
Born in State	43.00%	Asian	6.20%	With health insurance	93.50%
		Two or more races	4.90%	Cash public assistance	0.90%
Age Groups		Other	2.60%	Food stamp/SNAP	6.20%
Under 18	20.60%				
18-34	26.50%	**Education**		**Work**	
35-64	37.40%	H.S grad or less	28.10%	White Collar	43.90%
Over 64	15.60%	Some college	34.20%	Sales and Service	38.30%
		College Degree, 4 yr	22.20%	Blue Collar	17.80%
Military		Post grad	15.50%	Government	21.40%
Veteran/ Active Duty	26.50%				

2020 Pres. Vote	Biden	186,427	(51%)	Trump	169,365	(47%)			
2016 Pres. Vote	Trump	158,067	(48%)	Clinton	147,217	(45%)	Johnson	12,379	(4%)

Virginia Beach, Colonial Virginia: Virginia Beach, once a sleepy beach resort, is now the state's largest city, with 450,000 people. It began attracting tourists when rail service to Norfolk began in 1883. Since then, it has become the anchor to a metropolitan area of 1.7 million people that is centered on the local Navy community—active duty and civilian personnel, dependents, retirees and workers at the Newport News Shipyard. Virginia Beach also is home to the headquarters of the Christian Broadcasting Network, which produces The 700 Club and features evangelist Pat Robertson, the son of former Democratic Sen. A. Willis Robertson of Virginia. The city has a growing industrial base, including a large power tool plant of the German-based Stihl company. Like Norfolk, Virginia Beach is infused with military culture. The city is the base of East Coast Navy SEAL teams; these elite commandos endure punishing training, and they took on some of the military's most secretive and daring missions in Iraq and Afghanistan, including the Pakistan compound raid that killed Osama bin Laden in 2011. A monument in tribute to the SEALs was dedicated in 2017. The boardwalk helped Virginia Beach attract a record 19 million visitors that year. But tourism was hit hard by the COVID-19 pandemic.

Military history of a different sort is commemorated in Yorktown, site of the decisive battle of the Revolutionary War in 1781, which is adjacent to a naval weapons station on the banks of the York River. Not far away is Williamsburg, where major parts have been restored to look as they did in colonial times; actors play the roles of colonists, which is a major tourist draw. Also in Williamsburg is the College of William & Mary, America's second-oldest college. Jamestown, with the nation's first permanent settlement, is the third leg of what has been called the "Historic Triangle." Another historic site, on a spit of land in Chesapeake Bay, is Fort Monroe, where Jefferson Davis was confined after the Civil War. As the area faced a reckoning with that part of its past, the Virginia Beach City Council in the summer of 2020 removed a 115-year-old Confederate monument.

Virginia Beach plunged into the national debate on gun control in 2019 after an employee massacred a dozen of his coworkers in a municipal building. Mayor Bobby Dyer called it the "most devastating day" in the city's history. In 2020, the City Council adopted a resolution declaring it a "Second Amendment Constitutional City," which has no legal effect but rankled those still reeling from the shooting.

The 2nd Congressional District of Virginia includes all of Virginia Beach, plus several small cities on thin stretches of land that Virginians refer to as necks (peninsulas to outsiders). Across the Chesapeake Bay Bridge-Tunnel, the district transforms into a more placid area, including the two Virginia counties of the Delmarva Peninsula, site of the annual roundup of wild Chincoteague ponies in the national wildlife refuge. Dominion Resources operates in Accomack County what has been promoted as the largest solar power facility on the East Coast. More than 60 percent of the district's population is in Virginia Beach, which has leaned narrowly Republican in recent decades. In 2016, Donald Trump won the district, 48%-45%. Four years later, Joe Biden flipped both the city, 52%-46%, and the district, 51%-47%.

Bobby Scott (D)

Elected 1992, 15th term, b. Apr 30, 1947; Washington, DC; Harvard University, B.A., 1969; Boston College Law School, J.D., 1973; Episcopalian; Divorced.

Military Career: U.S. Army Reserve 1970-1976; MA National Guard 1974-1976

Elected Office: VA House, 1978-1983; VA Senate, 1983-1993.

Professional Career: Practicing attorney, 1973-1991.

DC Office: 1201 LHOB 20515, 202-225-8351, Fax: 202-225-8354, bobbyscott.house.gov

State Offices: Newport News, 757-380-1000.

Committees: *Budget. Education & Labor (Chmn)*: Ex Officio membership on all subcommittees.

Group Ratings

	ADA	ACLU	AFL-CIO	LCV	COC	HAFA	ACU	CFG	FRC
2020	**	79%	**	100%	-	5%	5%	**	-
2019	90%	C	100%	97%	58%	C	6%	12%	0%

Almanac Ratings 2019-2020

	Economy	Social	Foreign	Composite
Liberal	100%	59%	80%	80%
Conservative	0%	41%	20%	20%

Key Votes of the 116th Congress

1. U.S./Mex./Can. trade deal	Y	5. Russia sanctions	Y
2. First Coronavirus response	Y	6. Troops in Syria	Y
3. HEROES Act	Y	7. Veto arms sales to Saudis	Y
4. CASH Act	Y	8. Defense $$$, veto override	Y

9. Firearms background checks Y
10. Spending at the border Y
11. Marijuana liberalized rules Y
12. Electoral College objections N

Election Results

Election	Name (Party)	Vote (%)		Cand. Spent	Ind. Exp. Support	Ind. Exp. Oppose
2020 General	Bobby Scott (D)	233,326	(68%)	$782,365	$863	
	John Collick (R)	107,299	(31%)	$166,859		$113

Prior winning percentages: 2016 (67%), 2014 (94%), 2012 (81%), 2010 (70%), 2008 (97%), 2006 (96%), 2004 (69%), 2002 (96%), 2000 (98%), 1998 (76%), 1996 (82%), 1994 (79%), 1992 (79%)

Democrat Bobby Scott, first elected in 1992, has been an influential civil libertarian, an intellectual force in the Congressional Black Caucus and an important figure in Virginia politics. As chairman of the House Education and Labor Committee since 2019, he has taken significant steps to help Democrats achieve their goals, which he described as "advancing equity in education, expanding access to affordable health care [and] ensuring workers have a safe workplace." Depending on the success of the Biden administration, he had the opportunity in 2021 to help enact numerous landmark bills.

Scott grew up in Newport News, the son of a doctor. He got his bachelor's at Harvard University, where he was a classmate of Al Gore, and his law degree at Boston College. He served in the National Guard and Army Reserve and returned home to practice law. In 1977, he was elected to the House of Delegates, and later to the state Senate, representing a multiracial district in a community that had been shaped by the military tradition of integration.

In 1986, he ran a credible race for Congress and lost to Republican Rep. Herb Bateman, 56%-44%. In 1992, with his base in a new district that had been redrawn to have an African-American majority, Scott won the Democratic primary with 67 percent of the vote against two Richmond-based candidates. He easily won the general election to become the first African-American elected from Virginia since 1891. He has been reelected by overwhelming margins, with occasional changes in his district lines in the Tidewater region.

Scott's Almanac vote ratings have placed him among the most liberal House members, especially on social issues. On the Judiciary Committee, he raised First Amendment objections when bipartisan coalitions in 2012 passed legislation to permit states to display the Ten Commandments in schools or government buildings.

In 2010, Scott enacted the Fair Sentencing Act to narrow the discrepancies between sentences for powder and crack cocaine, an issue he had long contended led to Blacks receiving disproportionately longer sentences. After the Newtown Connecticut elementary school massacre in 2012, Minority Leader Nancy Pelosi named Scott vice chair of the Democrats' gun-violence prevention task force. He worked with Republicans to reduce certain mandatory drug sentences, restore judicial discretion in sentencing for some offenses, and promote alternatives to incarceration. He played a leading role in reducing national security collection of telephone metadata records, as part of a revision of the Patriot Act in 2015.

On the Education and Labor Committee, Scott has combined his longtime interest in K-12 education with a special focus on equity. In 2015, he was among the four lawmakers chiefly responsible for rewriting the No Child Left Behind education law, which Scott had contended was outdated. Despite his initial objections to Republican alternatives, he praised the final version of the Every Student Succeeds Act as "the embodiment of what we can do when we work together in Washington—a workable compromise that does not force either side to desert its core beliefs." In a February 2017 speech at the University of Virginia, he discussed his efforts to bridge the partisan divide during what he called a "difficult" moment in Congress.

When he moved up as chairman after Democrats regained House control in 2019, Scott said his priorities included funds for school construction and renovation, steps to promote school safety, and a revival of the higher education bill the previous Congress had deadlocked on, including increased affordability. In October 2019, he drafted legislation designed to make college more affordable by reducing student loan costs and simplifying the available options, with the option of having the loan balance forgiven after 20 to 25 years.

Scott coordinated House Democratic efforts to increase the minimum wage to $15 per hour, which would be phased in over five years. He also assembled legislation that would make drastic changes in labor-management relations to benefit unions. The so-called PRO (Protecting the Right to Organize) Act, among other things, would permit unions to organize workplaces with a "card check" process rather than a secret ballot and expand the National Labor Relations Board ability to impose penalties on employers that violate labor law.

Scott was largely dismissive of Trump administration policies. The logic behind its proposal to merge the Education and Labor departments was "painfully thin," he said. For the final two years of that administration, Scott had an ongoing battle to pursue oversight, especially with Education Secretary Betsey DeVos. "It's kind of hard to do oversight when they're not answering our questions," he told the Associated Press in January 2019. Scott was especially interested in the Education Department's regulation of for-profit colleges, changes in Title IX sexual-misconduct investigations on campuses and student-debt relief.

Scott has taken a leadership role on issues that go beyond his committee work. In 2007, he joined with then-Sens. Barack Obama of Illinois and Joe Biden of Delaware in pushing for legislation to compensate Black farmers who had been victims of government discrimination; the bill was enacted in 2010. Scott has been the prime sponsor of the CBC's alternative budget plan to raise taxes on upper-income taxpayers to finance more spending on domestic programs. The House has routinely defeated his annual proposal.

Scott has hosted an annual Labor Day picnic that has become a required stop for Democratic candidates in Virginia for state and federal office. He used the 2011 picnic to announce that he wouldn't run for retiring Democrat Jim Webb's Senate seat, clearing the way for former Gov. Tim Kaine to get the nomination. At the 2016 picnic, guests enthusiastically speculated that Scott would be the frontrunner for Gov. Terry McAuliffe's appointment to succeed Kaine, who was the vice presidential nominee that year. He did not object. Privately, some Democrats worried that Scott would have been too liberal and unknown outside his district to win statewide. That became a moot point.

In redistricting fights, Scott operated mostly behind the scenes in encouraging a second district in the Tidewater area with a substantial minority presence. That removed from his district many African-American locales, though he has never been at risk of losing reelection. He has grown stronger politically and reached the top ranks of House seniority as Democrats have gained seats elsewhere in the Old Dominion and he has chaired a House committee with sweeping jurisdiction.

VA-3: Tidewater

Cook Partisan Voting Index: D+16

Population		Race and Ethnicity		Income	
Total	760,127	White	43.30%	Median Income	$56,455
Land area (sq. miles)	947	Black	47.40%	District Income Rank	309
Pop/ sq mi	802.58	Latino	6.80%	Poverty Rate	14.80%
Born in State	56.20%	Asian	2.60%	With health insurance	90.90%
		Two or more races	4.40%	Cash public assistance	2.30%
Age Groups		Other	2.20%	Food stamp/SNAP	13.30%
Under 18	22.50%				
18-34	27.40%	**Education**		**Work**	
35-64	35.90%	H.S grad or less	39.50%	White Collar	33.70%
Over 64	14.20%	Some college	33.90%	Sales and Service	42.30%
		College Degree, 4 yr	16.00%	Blue Collar	24.10%
Military		Post grad	10.50%	Government	19.80%
Veteran/ Active Duty	17.60%				

2020 Pres. Vote	Biden	233,646	(67%)	Trump	108,728	(31%)		
2016 Pres. Vote	Clinton	205,746	(63%)	Trump	103,064	(32%)	Johnson	9,072 (3%)

Newport News, Norfolk: The U.S. Navy Atlantic fleet berthed in its home port of Norfolk is one of the most awe-inspiring sights in America, or anywhere. Norfolk has been a Navy port since 1801 and has long been recognized as having one of the best natural harbors on the East Coast, one that never freezes, has a channel 50 feet deep, and is within 750 miles of three-quarters of U.S. manufacturing capacity. The Norfolk Naval Station is the world's largest naval base, situated on 4,300 acres on Sewell's Point. Almost a quarter of the nation's uniformed military personnel are stationed in the Hampton Roads area, and the aggregation of destructive power in the line of towering gray ships is probably greater than in any other single port.

Once a small city, Norfolk is now part of a metropolitan area of 1.7 million people, anchored by Virginia Beach. The local Navy community—active duty and civilian personnel, dependents, retirees, and workers at the Newport News Shipyard—is estimated at more than 300,000, and military spending pours some $11 billion annually into the local economy. The shipyard, a division of Huntington Ingalls Industries, and Virginia's largest industrial employer, increased from 23,000 workers in 2017 to 26,000 workers in February 2021, in part due to work on two new aircraft carriers. The Newport News yard is the only manufacturer of nuclear-powered aircraft carriers. Work also was underway with Electric Boat in Groton Connecticut on the new Columbia-class nuclear submarines that will replace the Navy's Ohio-class subs—a $22 billion deal to build nine vessels by 2029.

The 3rd Congressional District of Virginia includes all of the majority-Black city of Portsmouth, a Navy port and industrial town with a charming old section. It travels up the James River to the communities of Norfolk and Newport News, which form its population centers. In 2018, Norfolk Southern—a Fortune 500 company—announced it was moving its headquarters to Atlanta. In February 2019, the company announced a further reduction of 3,000 employees from its workforce, which already had shrunk in recent years to below 27,000. The district takes in areas with high concentrations of white liberals, such as Ghent in Norfolk. In Smithfield, where the town museum offers the "World's Oldest Ham," pork products have been iconic. That ended in 2018 when Smithfield Foods closed its final smokehouse, which had prepared the genuine Smithfield cured ham for more than 50 years. The business had been purchased by a large Chinese company, which began shipping a large share of the pork to consumers in its home country.

As the result of the redistricting changes in 2016, the district no longer includes parts of Richmond. Those areas, especially the African-American neighborhoods, have shifted to the new 4th District. The District dropped to 46 percent Black from the 56 percent Black population of the old 3rd, which had been drawn to place the largest possible number of Democrats in a single district. In exchange, a Black plurality—and Democrats—gained control of a second district in Tidewater. In 2020, Joe Biden won, 67%-31%, the same result by which President Barack Obama in 2012 would have won with the new lines.

A. Donald McEachin (D)

Elected 2016, 3rd term, b. Oct 10, 1961; Nuremberg, Germany; St. Christopher School, 1979; American University, B.S., 1982; University of VA Law School, J.D., 1986; VA Union University Samuel DeWitt Proctor School of Theology, M.Div., 2008; Baptist; Married (Colette Wallace McEachin); 3 children.

Elected Office: VA Assembly, 1996-2002, 2006-2008; VA Senate, 2008-2016.

DC Office: 314 CHOB 20515, 202-225-6365, Fax: 202-226-1170, mceachin.house.gov

State Offices: Richmond, 804-486-1840; Suffolk, 757-942-6050.

Committees: *Energy & Commerce*: Communications & Technology; Energy; Environment & Climate Change. *Natural Resources*: Energy & Mineral Resources. *Select Committee on the Climate Crisis*.

Group Ratings

	ADA	ACLU	AFL-CIO	LCV	COC	HAFA	ACU	CFG	FRC
2020	**	84%	**	100%	-	0%	6%	**	-
2019	95%	C	94%	100%	52%	C	5%	7%	0%

Almanac Ratings 2019-2020

	Economy	Social	Foreign	Composite
Liberal	49%	52%	52%	51%
Conservative	51%	48%	48%	49%

Key Votes of the 116th Congress

1. U.S./Mex./Can. trade deal N	5. Russia sanctions N/A
2. First Coronavirus response Y	6. Troops in Syria N/A
3. HEROES Act Y	7. Veto arms sales to Saudis Y
4. CASH Act Y	8. Defense $$$, veto override Y
9. Firearms background checks Y	
10. Spending at the border N	
11. Marijuana liberalized rules Y	
12. Electoral College objections N	

Election Results

Election	Name (Party)	Vote (%)	Cand. Spent	Ind. Exp. Support	Ind. Exp. Oppose
2020 General	A. Donald McEachin (D)	241,142 (62%)	$615,402	$876	
	Leon Benjamin (R)	149,625 (38%)	$505,524	$40,874	$113
2020 Primary	Donald McEachin (D)	45,083 (80%)			
	R. Cazel Levine (D)	11,287 (20%)			

Prior winning percentages: 2018 (63%), 2016 (58%)

Democrat Donald McEachin has been easily elected since 2016 to represent a district that changed significantly in a court-ordered redistricting plan. McEachin, with extensive experience as a legislator, serves on the Energy and Commerce Committee, where his chief interests have been climate change and the pursuit of what he calls environmental justice. He has had extended absences from the House because of health problems.

McEachin was born in Nuremberg Germany to an Army veteran and a public-school teacher. He grew up in Richmond, got his bachelor's from American University and law degree from the University of Virginia. He served six years in the state House of Delegates, then ran unsuccessfully in 2001 for state attorney general. "The defeat stung, and he found himself struggling to find a purpose," the Washington Post reported. McEachin enrolled in the Samuel Proctor Theological Seminary at Virginia Union University, received his masters of divinity degree and became an ordained Baptist minister. Meanwhile, he returned to the state House and later was elected to the state Senate, where he chaired the Democratic Caucus. He co-founded his law firm in Richmond.

When a federal court in 2016 reviewed redistricting in Virginia, it agreed to a version of the map proposed by Democratic Gov. Terry McAuliffe that revamped the Republican-held 4th District. It appeared to be tailor-made politically and geographically for McEachin. He ran and got 75 percent of the vote in the low-turnout Democratic primary. After eight-term Republican Rep. Randy Forbes concluded that he could not win in the new 4th district, he decided to run in the Virginia Beach-based 2nd District, where he lost the Republican primary. Henrico County Sheriff Mike Wade, who spent his career in law enforcement, switched from a campaign in the 7th District and won the GOP nomination for the open seat in the 4th.

With McEachin running a mostly quiet campaign, the lightly funded Wade had little opportunity to engage. He referred to his opponent as "Dodging Don." Wade took offense at McEachin's claim of excessive police profiling of racial minorities. The greater problem, he said, was with individuals who have mental-health or substance-abuse problems. "When I got pulled over … I didn't have a mental health problem and I wasn't on my way to jail," McEachin responded. He won, 58%-42%, rolling up huge majorities in Richmond, Petersburg and Henrico, which cast nearly half of the vote.

During his first term, McEachin had seats on the Armed Services and Natural Resources committees, and promoted "quality of life" issues for the military and veterans. In the Tidewater tradition, he was an enthusiastic proponent of increased shipbuilding. In 2018, he was "disappointed" that the budget plan from President Donald Trump proposed only 10 new ships. He opposed plans for seismic testing for offshore oil drilling. "Unlike the Trump administration, we have not forgotten about the Deepwater Horizon oil spill" in the Gulf of Mexico in 2010, McEachin said in 2018. He moved to Energy and Commerce in 2019, when Democrats took House control. "For me, protecting our environment is a moral obligation and an act of faith," he said, in describing his new assignment.

He found the pace in Congress slower and less stressful than serving in Richmond, he said in an interview midway through his first year. "We have the ability to actually dig down and figure what exactly should the right policy be, as opposed to what we did in the General Assembly," McEachin told the Virginian-Pilot.

Speaker Nancy Pelosi tapped him to serve on the Select Committee on the Climate Crisis. As the panel completed its work in November 2019, McEachin took the lead in filing a bill—with more than 150 Democratic cosponsors--to direct federal agencies to determine how to reduce net U.S. carbon emissions to zero by 2050.

Three months later, he filed with Natural Resources Committee Chairman Raul Grijalva a more targeted bill, the "Environmental Justice for All Act," that would impose new fees on energy producers to assist communities to transition from reliance on fossil fuels. "In far too many American communities, the fundamental rights to clean air, pure water and an environment free of toxic pollution remain unrealized," McEachin said. "We are taking meaningful action toward ameliorating those wrongs and empowering … communities disproportionately affected by environmental injustice."

In the 2018 campaign, Republican Ryan McAdams—a pastor and former social worker in Williamsburg, and a political newcomer—challenged McEachin. "I'm not your normal Republican," McAdams told the Richmond Times-Dispatch, in describing his appeal to urban voters. He was outspent, $931,000 to $239,000, in a contest that received little attention from either national party. McEachin improved his victory margin to 63%-36%.

Two years later, he faced a similar challenger with a similar outcome. His challenger was Leon Benjamin, the senior pastor of a church in Richmond, who also was chairman of the Republican Party in Richmond and a member of a group of evangelical leaders who were informal advisers to Trump. Benjamin spent $505,000—close to what McEachin spent. The incumbent won, 62%-38%.

McEachin lost more than 60 pounds in the several months prior to his reelection in 2018 as the result of a medical condition caused by earlier treatment for cancer. His medical problems continued, including a blood clot in his foot in April 2019 and two surgeries in August that his staff did not describe. In 2018, his doctor told the Times-Dispatch that McEachin had developed a fistula, which is "an abnormal connection between the bladder and colon." New photos each year showed that he had become notably thinner.

VA-4: Southeast Virginia   Cook Partisan Voting Index: D+10

Population		Race and Ethnicity		Income	
Total	768,382	White	51.30%	Median Income	$60,407
Land area (sq. miles)	4,310	Black	41.10%	District Income Rank	254
Pop/ sq mi	178.26	Latino	6.00%	Poverty Rate	12.30%
Born in State	62.70%	Asian	1.70%	With health insurance	92.00%
		Two or more races	3.40%	Cash public assistance	2.30%
Age Groups		Other	2.50%	Food stamp/SNAP	11.90%
Under 18	20.70%				
18-34	24.90%	**Education**		**Work**	
35-64	38.80%	H.S grad or less	40.30%	White Collar	39.10%
Over 64	15.50%	Some college	28.90%	Sales and Service	39.10%
		College Degree, 4 yr	18.70%	Blue Collar	21.90%
Military		Post grad	12.10%	Government	20.60%
Veteran/ Active Duty	11.00%				

2020 Pres. Vote	Biden	246,583	(62%)	Trump	146,900	(37%)		
2016 Pres. Vote	Clinton	212,677	(58%)	Trump	134,676	(37%)	Johnson	9,595 (3%)

Richmond and its Exurbs, parts of Chesapeake: The history of African slavery in America began along the tidal expanse of the James River. Only a dozen years after the founding of Jamestown in 1607, the first slave ship sailed up the James and offloaded its human cargo, giving birth to the slave-based economy of the American South. In the 21st century, some of the big plantation houses of the Tidewater still dot the banks of the James. Charles City County—the site of William Byrd II's Westover, Benjamin Harrison III's Berkeley, and John Carter's Shirley—also was the birthplace of two successive presidents, William Henry Harrison and John Tyler. Virginia famously produced a total of eight U.S. presidents—almost 20 percent of the individuals to serve—but none since Woodrow Wilson, whose racial views have led to an unfavorable reckoning with his legacy.

The 4th Congressional District of Virginia travels back and forth across the James River north of Jamestown to string together Black precincts and communities. Upriver on the south bank of the James, it takes in 77 percent African-American Petersburg, as well as eastern Henrico County and eastern Chesterfield County, though more than two-thirds of each is in the more politically balanced 7th District. All of Richmond is in the district, including the state's capitol, designed by Thomas Jefferson; the historic Jefferson Hotel; and the African-American neighborhoods around Church Hill, where Patrick Henry famously proclaimed "give me liberty or give me death." Monument Avenue was famous for its statues of Confederate luminaries and tennis player Arthur Ashe. Following protests that culminated in the summer of 2020, all the Confederate statuary—except for Robert E. Lee, who was preserved by a court order—were removed. "As protesters have remade this avenue, forcing the removal of memorials to men who betrayed their country," The Washington Post's art and architecture critic wrote in July 2020, "they also have underscored deep connections between urban planning and old ideologies of whiteness, greatness and cultural ambition." Hollywood Cemetery in Richmond is where Presidents James Monroe and John Tyler share a final resting place with 25 Confederate generals and Jefferson Davis.

The district also takes in the flat lands of Southside Virginia. These were tobacco fields after the English first settled here in the 17th century. The tiny town of Wakefield is home to the Shad Planking, the iconic fish-eating event where Virginia politicians have made pilgrimages every spring for more than a half-century to meet and greet each other and voters. The gathering has been renamed as the Barbecue and Shad Homecoming (BASH), where more traditional fare has been added to the oily fish to increase the turnout. Closer to the Atlantic coast and almost an appendage to the 4th is Chesapeake, a site of epic battles in both the Revolutionary War and the Civil War and now the second-largest jurisdiction in the district; its Republican lean is easily outweighed by Richmond, with its larger and more sharply partisan Democratic bent. The redistricting changes in 2016 increased the African-American population in the district from 31 percent to 41 percent. Although some of the outlying areas remain Republican, the overwhelming Democratic vote in Richmond and parts of Henrico, plus Petersburg, controls the outcome of the district. In 2020, Joe Biden took 62 percent of the vote.

Bob Good (R)

Elected 2020, 1st term, b. Sep 11, 1965; Wilkes Barre, PA; Liberty Christian Academy; Liberty University, B.A., 1988; Liberty University, M.B.A., 2010; Christian Church; Married (Tracey Good); 3 children.

Elected Office: Member, Campbell County Board of Supervisors.

Professional Career: District Manager, CitiFinancial, 1988-2005; Senior Associate Athletics Director, Liberty University, 2005-2020.

DC Office: 1213 LHOB 20515, 202-225-4711, Fax: 202-225-5681, good.house.gov

Committees: *Budget. Education & Labor*: Higher Education & Workforce Investment; Workforce Protections.

Election Results

Election	Name (Party)	Vote (%)		Cand. Spent	Ind. Exp. Support	Ind. Exp. Oppose
2020 General	Bob Good (R)	210,988	(52%)	$1,309,786	$117,677	$4,795,520
	Cameron Webb (D)	190,315	(47%)	$5,760,042	$966,122	$3,005,678

Republican Bob Good was elected to the House largely as the result of a controversial drive-in nominating convention. Overcoming the refusal of ousted Republican Rep. Denver Riggleman to close ranks, Good then defeated Cameron Webb, a charismatic young African-American physician, to stifle Democratic hopes. National Republicans worried that Good lacked sufficient campaign funds or the outreach to his diverse constituents. But he benefited from positive national and local Republican trends in 2020.

Riggleman, who served one term, made the politically fatal error in his district of offending social conservatives by officiating at the gay marriage of two campaign volunteers. That triggered the internal GOP challenge, though the iconoclastic Riggleman might have been vulnerable to an intra-party clash in any case. In rapid turnover, Good became the fourth Republican to win this seat in the past four elections, and the sixth person elected in the district since 2006, five of them Republicans.

Good, who was born in Pennsylvania, settled with his family in Lynchburg Virginia, where his father attended a local seminary. He graduated from high school at Liberty Christian Academy, where he was a champion wrestler, and got his bachelor's degree in finance and a master's in business administration at Liberty University. Good joined the lending division of CitiFinancial and was district manager at three sites during 17 years. In 2005, he became executive director of the Flames Club at Liberty University, which supported student-athletes.

He first won elected office in 2015, as a member of the Board of Supervisors of Campbell County; the county borders the city of Lynchburg, which is in the 6th Congressional District. A born-again Christian, he has been an ardent social conservative and a supporter of individual rights of property owners, in the workplace and with firearms, though he opposed gay marriage. Good has styled himself as a "biblical Republican."

Riggleman, the owner of a successful distillery, was elected to the House in 2018, when Rep. Tom Garrett cited problems with alcoholism as he abandoned his bid for reelection after he had been nominated for a second term. In response, a 37-member Republican committee selected a new nominee. Riggleman was the winner by one vote on the fourth ballot. In his first bid for elected office, he called himself a "liberty Republican." He defeated Democrat Leslie Cockburn, 53%-47%, in a competitive contest.

Riggleman's version of liberty included support for gay marriage. After he presided at such a ceremony in July 2019, some Republicans objected that his action clashed with his representation of the district. The Cumberland County Republican Committee passed a motion of "no confidence" in Riggleman. He responded that "government shouldn't be involved in marriage."

Good launched his candidacy and convinced the district's Republican committee to select the GOP nominee in 2020 at a church in Campbell County, his home base. When the coronavirus pandemic prevented an on-site meeting, the organizers decided to count votes in a full-day drive-through; delegates voted from their vehicles in the parking lot of the Tree of Life Ministries. Good won, reportedly with 58 percent of the roughly 2,500 participants—though the precise count was disputed.

Webb, who won a routine Democratic primary with 67 percent against three opponents, was a professor at the University of Virginia, where he was director of health policy and equity at its medical school. He emphasized "a point of commonality" as an American ideal among diverse interests. His nearly $6 million in campaign spending was four times the total spent by Good. National party and ideological groups spent nearly $10 million more.

Good won the contest, 52%-47%. Webb got nearly three-fourths of the vote in Charlottesville and surrounding Albemarle County, which cast about 22 percent of the total. He also won Danville. Good rolled up double-digit leads in most of the other localities.

Following the election, Democratic Rep. Abigail Spanberger—who narrowly won her neighboring district—said Webb was the victim of aggressive ads that incorrectly described his purported support to "defund the police." Webb told The Washington Post that the GOP attacks "did shift the conversation" in the contest, though his own statements gave an opportunity to Good.

VA-5: Southside   Cook Partisan Voting Index: R+7

Population		Race and Ethnicity		Income	
Total	735,766	White	74.90%	Median Income	$57,615
Land area (sq. miles)	10,030	Black	19.40%	District Income Rank	293
Pop/ sq mi	73.36	Latino	3.80%	Poverty Rate	12.90%
Born in State	64.30%	Asian	1.70%	With health insurance	92.20%
		Two or more races	2.80%	Cash public assistance	3.40%
Age Groups		Other	1.10%	Food stamp/SNAP	10.20%
Under 18	19.30%				
18-34	21.60%	Education		Work	
35-64	38.10%	H.S grad or less	41.80%	White Collar	39.00%
Over 64	21.00%	Some college	29.20%	Sales and Service	37.90%
		College Degree, 4 yr	16.80%	Blue Collar	23.10%
Military		Post grad	12.20%	Government	18.30%
Veteran/ Active Duty	8.60%				

2020 Pres. Vote	Trump	217,535	(53%)	Biden	183,175	(45%)		
2016 Pres. Vote	Trump	195,190	(53%)	Clinton	154,665	(42%)	Johnson	9,230	(3%)

Charlottesville, Danville: Southside Virginia is technically defined as the parts of the commonwealth east of the Blue Ridge, west of the Fall Line and south of the James River. But it really is a cultural designation: an outcropping of Deep South culture in the Old Dominion. The eastern counties are flat and humid—frontier in the late-colonial period, plantation country by 1800, and now peanut fields and pine forests. Along U.S. 58, which snakes across southern Virginia from Virginia Beach almost to the Cumberland Gap, are the vestiges of the state's Tobacco Road, including the Tobacco Farm Life Museum of Virginia in South Hill. The largest metropolitan area in Southside is Danville, where the tobacco auction originated in 1858. Two of the most important battles for African-American equality were won northeast of Danville. The first was at Appomattox Court House, the serene little hamlet where Robert E. Lee surrendered to his onetime subordinate Ulysses S. Grant. The second was in Prince Edward County, where one of the five cases consolidated into the landmark Brown v. Board of Education case arose.

Charlottesville was the scene of a controversial "Unite the Right" protest in August 2017, which resulted in the death of a counter-protestor and the December 2018 conviction on murder charges of the automobile driver who caused her death and was later sentenced to life imprisonment, plus a national debate over the deepening political polarization the incident revealed. The initial protest, which had been organized to oppose removal of a statue of Lee, started with an evening torchlight march on the campus of the University of Virginia; it included a few hundred hooded members of the Ku Klux Klan and other White nationalists. The next day, the political right and left clashed in the small several-block area of downtown Charlottesville. The angry exchanges turned lethal when the young driver, a white supremacist, rammed his car into a small group on the street and killed Heather Heyer, a liberal activist. President Donald Trump stoked the tensions a few days later when he said that there were good people—as well as blame—on "both sides," though he also said that "the neo-Nazis and the white nationalists...should be condemned totally." The raw feelings left by the incident also resulted in criticism of local officials. The city council in Charlottesville subsequently voted to remove the birthday of Thomas Jefferson from the list of city holidays. And the statue of a Confederate soldier was removed from outside the county courthouse.

The 5th District of Virginia covers most of Southside Virginia west of metro Richmond, spreading out to the Blue Ridge Mountains. This is the heart of the district; about two-thirds of its population lives south of the James River. The district includes overwhelmingly liberal Charlottesville, with Jefferson's University of Virginia, and surrounding Albemarle County, but their 20 percent of the vote has had little impact in this district. An arm extends north to the western part of Fauquier County in the Washington D.C. exurbs. Southside Virginia was long conservative and Democratic. In recent decades, the district has voted predominantly Republican. Democrats running statewide have energized the Charlottesville area and the African-American precincts, especially in Danville, which is 51 percent Black. Donald Trump twice won 53 percent of the district vote. Joe Biden won 86 percent in Charlottesville, 66 percent in Albemarle, 60 percent in Danville, and not much else.

Benjamin Cline (R)

Elected 2018, 2nd term, b. Feb 29, 1972; Stillwater, OK; Bates College, B.A., 1994; University of Richmond, J.D., 2007; Roman Catholic; Married (Elizabeth Rocovich); 2 children.

Elected Office: VA House, 2002-2018; Roanoke Valley Higher Education Authority Board, 2004-2018.

Professional Career: Policy Advisory & Chief of Staff, U.S. Rep. Bob Goodlatte, 1994-2002; President, New Dominion Solutions, L.L.C., 2002-2007; Assistant Commonwealth Attorney, Rockingham County and City of Harrisonburg, 2007-2013; Private Practice Attorney.

DC Office: 1009 LHOB 20515, 202-225-5431, Fax: 202-225-9681, cline.house.gov

State Offices: Harrisonburg, 540-432-2391; Lynchburg, 434-845-8306; Roanoke, 540-857-2672; Staunton, 540-885-3861.

Committees: *Appropriations*: Commerce, Justice, Science & Related Agencies; Labor, Health & Human Services, Education & Related Agencies. *Budget*.

Almanac Ratings 2019-2020

	Economy	Social	Foreign	Composite
Liberal	25%	7%	35%	23%
Conservative	75%	93%	65%	77%

Key Votes of the 116th Congress

1. U.S./Mex./Can. trade deal Y	5. Russia sanctions Y	9. Firearms background checks N
2. First Coronavirus response N	6. Troops in Syria Y	10. Spending at the border Y
3. HEROES Act N	7. Veto arms sales to Saudis N	11. Marijuana liberalized rules N
4. CASH Act N	8. Defense $$$, veto override N	12. Electoral College objections Y

Election Results

Election	Name (Party)	Vote (%)		Cand. Spent	Ind. Exp. Support	Ind. Exp. Oppose
2020 General	Benjamin Cline (R)........................	246,606	(65%)	$519,148	$847	$750
	Nicholas Betts (D)............................	134,729	(35%)	$41,272		

Prior winning percentages: 2018 (60%)

Republican Ben Cline has established a niche in his heavily Republican district in the Shenandoah Valley region of Virginia. Cline served eight terms in the state House of Delegates and earlier was chief of staff to his predecessor, Rep. Bob Goodlatte, who retired after 13 terms.

A graduate of Bates College and the University of Richmond Law School, Cline was an assistant prosecutor in Rockingham County. He worked for Goodlatte for eight years following college.

He was first elected to the state House in 2002. He chaired the Militia, Police and Public Safety Committee, where he was a strong opponent of gun control, and was vice chair of the Finance Committee. His successful legislation included a limitation on the use of unmanned drone aircraft by state and local law enforcement agencies. Cline was the House chairman of the Conservative Caucus. In addition to practicing law, he served as a business advisor who gave marketing assistance to internet and high-tech companies in rural areas.

For years, he had been viewed as the heir apparent in the district. Following Goodlatte's retirement, Cynthia Dunbar challenged Cline for the GOP nomination. Dunbar, a member of the Republican National Committee, who styled herself as a political outsider, criticized Cline as a "career politician" and a resident of "the swamp."

Under pressure from Dunbar, who voiced strongly conservative views on social issues and viewed the limited turnout at a convention as her best option, district GOP leaders agreed to select the nominee at a convention rather than a primary. At Dunbar's insistence, they took the unusual step of including an additional stipulation that there would be only one ballot and the winner was not required to get the customary majority of convention votes.

When the convention met in May, some Republicans—including Cline—questioned the legality of the planned procedure. Over the objections of Dunbar and her allies, they modified the rules to require a majority vote. The parliamentary conflict became a moot point. With an initial field of eight candidates and more than 2,200 voters, Cline led Dunbar on the first ballot, 52%-39%. In an unusual effort, Dunbar two weeks later unsuccessfully sought the GOP nomination for the open seat in the adjacent 5th District.

In a year marked by competitive House races across Virginia, Cline defeated Democrat Jennifer Lewis, a liberal activist, 60%-40%. Cline got national attention following an unusual incident in his hometown of Lexington when White House press secretary Sarah Huckabee Sanders was asked to leave the local Red Hen restaurant because its employees objected to President Donald Trump. Cline called the restaurant's action "disappointing" and he tweeted an apology to Sanders.

In the House, Cline initially followed in the footsteps of Goodlatte, with a seat on the Judiciary Committee. On that panel, he voiced conventional Republican arguments in opposing legislation to reform police practices and immigration changes to provide citizenship to individuals who came to the United States as children. But he pursued a bipartisan measure with Rep. Dean Phillips of Minnesota to require that the text of legislation is available for at least 48 hours before the House can vote on the measure. The reform "will bring greater accountability regardless of which party is in the majority," Cline said.

He won reelection, 65%-35%, against Nicholas Betts, a clerk in a Roanoke law firm, whom Cline outspent more than 10-to-1.

Following the election, Cline got seats on the Appropriations and Budget committees. With other House Republicans, he opposed certification of the Electoral College results in January 2021. Judicial changes of election rules in some states, he said, were a "usurpation of the legislatures constitutional authority [and] a primary reason why the 2020 election became riddled with an unprecedented number of allegations of irregularities and improprieties."

VA-6: Shenandoah Valley   Cook Partisan Voting Index: R+14

Population		Race and Ethnicity		Income	
Total	755,012	White	82.20%	Median Income	$59,939
Land area (sq. miles)	5,930	Black	11.90%	District Income Rank	265
Pop/ sq mi	127.32	Latino	5.60%	Poverty Rate	12.20%
Born in State	65.00%	Asian	1.50%	With health insurance	92.40%
		Two or more races	2.90%	Cash public assistance	2.40%
Age Groups		Other	1.50%	Food stamp/SNAP	8.80%
Under 18	19.80%				
18-34	24.40%	**Education**		**Work**	
35-64	37.10%	H.S grad or less	44.70%	White Collar	35.40%
Over 64	18.80%	Some college	27.00%	Sales and Service	39.20%
		College Degree, 4 yr	16.90%	Blue Collar	25.40%
Military		Post grad	11.40%	Government	15.80%
Veteran/ Active Duty	8.30%				

2020 Pres. Vote	Trump	231,248	(60%)	Biden	149,254	(38%)		
2016 Pres. Vote	Trump	206,303	(59%)	Clinton	120,596	(35%)	Johnson	10,801 (3%)

Roanoke, Harrisonburg: The sturdy men and women who settled the Shenandoah Valley of Virginia west of the Blue Ridge were quite different from the "second sons" of the European aristocracy who cleared the marshy forests of the Tidewater and built grand plantations. Even before the Revolutionary War, Scots and Scots-Irish, German Protestants, and Mennonites and Moravians—members of religious communities and fiercely independent farmers—poured down the Great Wagon Road from Pennsylvania to the valley, planting farms and founding towns with names like Strasburg, Edinburg, Mount Jackson and Glasgow. They were looking not for the flat, mahogany colored land that Eastern tobacco growers sought, but for land that could support wheat, corn and hay, crops that could be rotated and that an individual farmer and his family could handle. A young George Washington surveyed portions of the land; what are believed to be his carved initials are still visible on Natural Bridge in Rockbridge County.

The same independent spirit nurtured the growth of higher education here. In Lexington are Washington and Lee University, which Robert E. Lee headed after the Civil War, and the Virginia Military Institute, where Stonewall Jackson taught philosophy and artillery tactics before the war. Leaders of both universities have been reviewing—and removing--the names and memorials on campus that might offend some, including symbols of the Confederacy. Harrisonburg is the home of James Madison University. . President Woodrow Wilson's birthplace is in Staunton. Industry flourished here more than in most of Virginia east of the Blue Ridge. In the 19th century, the Norfolk and Western Railway established its chief junction at Roanoke; as the years passed, the city became the headquarters of the railroad and many other companies. In 2015, the renamed Norfolk Southern moved its corporate headquarters to Norfolk—but soon shifted again to Atlanta. More bad news came in February 2020 when the company announced it was closing its distribution center in Roanoke and moving its locomotive shop to Altoona Pennsylvania. The chief factor, according to Norfolk Southern, was a 48 percent decline during the past decade in coal tons shipped through Roanoke and further reductions expected. The population of Roanoke was on the cusp of 100,000 in 2019 for the first time since 1980. The city was thriving, according to CityLab, with its attractiveness to "outdoorsy millennials," including new craft breweries and the revived downtown in a historic district.

The 6th Congressional District of Virginia covers the heart of the Valley of Virginia, from Front Royal to Roanoke. In recent decades, the ancestral conservatism of the region and the feisty politics of the mountain rebels have melded into a single conservative Republicanism, more populist than elitist in tone and prickly about interference from Washington and Richmond. Those roots go deep: Many of these counties have shown Republican tendencies dating back more than 100 years. In 1952, the district's voters did something extremely rare at the time: They voted out an incumbent Southern Democrat in favor of a Republican. The GOP has held the seat ever since, save for an interlude in the 1980s. Donald Trump twice won 59 percent of the vote, though Democrats each time took Roanoke, Harrisonburg and Lexington. In 2020, Joe Biden was the first Democratic presidential candidate to win Lynchburg since 1948.

Abigail Spanberger (D)

Elected 2018, 2nd term, b. Aug 07, 1979; Red Bank, NJ; University of VA, B.A., 2001; Christian Church; Married (Adam Spanberger); 3 children.

Professional Career: Federal Law Enforcement Officer, Narcotics and Money Laundering Cases, U.S. Postal Inspection Service; Operations Officer, Central Intelligence Agency; Page, Office of U.S. Sen. Chuck Robb.

DC Office: 1239 LHOB 20515, 202-225-2815, spanberger.house.gov

State Offices: Glen Allen, 804-401-4110; Spotsylvania, 202-225-2815.

Committees: *Agriculture*: Conservation & Forestry (Chmn); Livestock & Foreign Agriculture. *Foreign Affairs*: Asia, the Pacific, Central Asia, Nonproliferation; Europe, Energy, the Environment & Cyber.

Almanac Ratings 2019-2020

	Economy	Social	Foreign	Composite
Liberal	54%	48%	80%	61%
Conservative	46%	52%	20%	39%

Key Votes of the 116th Congress

1. U.S./Mex./Can. trade deal	Y	5. Russia sanctions	Y
2. First Coronavirus response	Y	6. Troops in Syria	Y
3. HEROES Act	N	7. Veto arms sales to Saudis	Y
4. CASH Act	Y	8. Defense $$$, veto override	Y

9. Firearms background checks	Y
10. Spending at the border	Y
11. Marijuana liberalized rules	Y
12. Electoral College objections	N

Election Results

Election	Name (Party)	Vote (%)		Cand. Spent	Ind. Exp. Support	Ind. Exp. Oppose
2020 General	Abigail Spanberger (D)	230,893	(51%)	$8,074,730	$767,705	$7,661,868
	Nick Freitas (R)	222,623	(49%)	$3,564,566	$2,020,282	$6,093,093

Prior winning percentages: 2018 (50%)

Freshman Democrat Abigail Spanberger was elected in 2018 to a seat that had been a Republican stronghold by defeating Republican Rep. Dave Brat. A former CIA analyst, she brought a deep national security background plus extended familiarity with the Richmond-area district and has become a prominent voice for the moderate wing of the party.

Spanberger, a native of New Jersey, moved with her family to a Richmond suburb and attended high school there. She graduated from the University of Virginia, where her major was French literature, and she got a master's in business administration while living in Germany. She started her career as a law enforcement officer with the U.S. Postal Inspection Service.

At the Central Intelligence Agency, Spanberger was an operations officer who gathered intelligence on terrorism, making use of her knowledge of other languages and her experiences overseas. Agency rules barred her from discussing the details of her work. When she returned to Henrico County, she joined a consulting firm that specialized in higher education.

In declaring her candidacy, Spanberger said she wanted to talk not only about problems, but also solutions. "Beating the drum about how terrible the president [Donald Trump] is, is just beating the drum," she told the Chesterfield Observer. "It's not actually doing something productive." In the Democratic primary, she easily defeated Dan Ward, a former Marine who was a pilot and worked at the State Department. Ward spent nearly $1 million. Spanberger won, 73%-27%.

Brat, who had been an economics professor at Randolph-Macon, compiled a modest legislative record. At home, he had limited reconciliation with allies of former House Majority Leader Eric Cantor, whose stunning defeat in the 2014 primary threw GOP leadership succession into chaos. Brat also suffered from mid-decade redistricting changes that added suburban Democrats. In an interview with the Orange County Review prior to the election, he said that enactment of tax cuts was his proudest accomplishment in Congress, referring especially to subsequently abandoned plans for post-election tax cuts targeted to the middle class.

The Congressional Leadership Fund, a Republican Super PAC, caused a stir in the campaign when it released a confidential security-clearance application that Spanberger had filed for a job, which showed that she had taught for a short time at a Washington-area school that was financed by Saudi Arabia. Although the Postal Service said that it had mistakenly released the document, Republicans ran ads that suggested Spanberger was aiding terrorists. Her campaign responded that the ad was a smear and that she spent her career "on the front line" fighting terrorists.

In their only debate, both candidates mostly avoided talking about Trump, though Brat sought repeatedly to link his opponent to the "Nancy Pelosi liberal agenda." Brat, who noted that his defeat of Cantor had killed plans for House action on immigration legislation, said that Spanberger supported undocumented immigrants. She responded that such a charge was "frankly comical," given her intelligence work to keep communities safe.

Spanberger, with $7.3 million, more than doubled Brat's spending. National party groups spent more than $8 million on the contest. Spanberger won, 50.3%-48.4%. She took the two largest counties, each of which cast about one-third of the total vote: Henrico, with 59 percent; and Chesterfield, with 54 percent. Brat took the other eight, mostly rural, counties.

In her first term, Spanberger fulfilled her campaign promises of promptly holding a town hall in every county in the district and voting for the replacement to the North American Free Trade Agreement. She was one of only five Democrats to vote against Nancy Pelosi as Speaker in 2019 and 2021. She was placed on the House Foreign Affairs Committee and the Agriculture Committee, where she sought to increase rural broadband access.

Spanberger has become a leader among centrist Democrats in the House and often voices concern that leaders of the progressive movement don't realize that maintaining the majority requires that Democrats remain palatable in conservative districts. "There's some people that just think that we're out of touch and that if we just worked hard, more Democrats would come out of the woodwork and so we should just try to say all the things that excite all the Democrats," she told The New York Times. "You can say that until you're blue in the face, but there are just not that many Democrats in my district."

Spanberger angered Republican constituents in September 2019 when she signed onto an op-ed column in the Washington Post with six other members of her freshman class, supporting an impeachment inquiry against Trump after allegations that he pressured Ukraine to uncover dirt on Joe Biden. In December 2019, she joined all but two House Democrats in voting to impeach.

Several Republicans lined up to take on Spanberger, though she benefitted from a primary that was delayed until mid-July because of the coronavirus pandemic. Republicans selected their nominee through a convention; state Del. Nick Freitas, a favorite of the fiscally conservative Club for Growth, won on the third ballot. Republican ads yoked Spanberger to Pelosi; one spot from the National Republican Congressional Committee tried to revive the attack line that she aided terrorists.

Spanberger had a marked financial edge, spending $8.1 million to Freitas' $3.6 million. In addition, party groups and their allies spent more than $10 million. She won 50.8%-49%, a margin of 8,270 votes. She again carried Henrico and Chesterfield counties, with 61 percent and 55 percent; they made up over 60 percent of the vote. Freitas took the other eight counties by double-digit margins. Biden narrowly carried the district, a likely plus for Spanberger.

Following the election, Spanberger again attacked her liberal colleagues for rhetoric that she felt made it harder for moderates to win. "Don't say socialism. Don't say 'defund the police' when that's not what we mean," Spanberger told colleagues, according to CNN.

She remained a top target for House Republicans in 2022. With Virginia Democrats having tentatively ceded control to a redistricting commission, they might be more limited in their ability to secure a safer seat for Spanberger.

VA-7: Central Virginia   Cook Partisan Voting Index: R+3

Population		Race and Ethnicity		Income	
Total	802,921	White	69.00%	Median Income	$81,364
Land area (sq. miles)	2,776	Black	18.00%	District Income Rank	83
Pop/ sq mi	289.20	Latino	8.00%	Poverty Rate	7.90%
Born in State	54.50%	Asian	5.40%	With health insurance	92.10%
		Two or more races	3.30%	Cash public assistance	1.40%
Age Groups		Other	4.30%	Food stamp/SNAP	5.90%
Under 18	22.90%				
18-34	20.70%	**Education**		**Work**	
35-64	39.80%	H.S grad or less	32.40%	White Collar	43.60%
Over 64	16.50%	Some college	27.00%	Sales and Service	38.10%
Military		College Degree, 4 yr	24.90%	Blue Collar	18.30%
Veteran/ Active Duty	8.70%	Post grad	15.70%	Government	16.50%

2020 Pres. Vote	Biden	228,335	(50%)	Trump	223,268	(49%)			
2016 Pres. Vote	Trump	198,032	(50%)	Clinton	172,544	(44%)	Johnson	14,206	(4%)

Richmond Suburbs: The metro area of Richmond, now the third-largest in the commonwealth, has grown far past its city borders, covering most of suburban Henrico and Chesterfield counties and spreading into what was, until recently, countryside. As the area has grown, its tone has shifted. No longer is this the heart of the Old South. Some of these areas are closer in outlook to Washington D.C. Richmond, the centrally located capital of Virginia, still sets the tone for the commonwealth. It is home to many of the state's great institutions—Dominion Resources, Main Street banks, big law firms and the Richmond Times-Dispatch. Likewise, the city has changed, as it has become less insular and more cosmopolitan.

The 7th Congressional District of Virginia sprawls across 120 miles from southwest of Richmond to the outer reaches of the Washington exurbs, though it is centered in Henrico and Chesterfield; each county is about one-third of the population. Surrounding much of Richmond, Henrico was once a linchpin of the state Republican coalition—it gave GOP nominee Barry Goldwater 70 percent of the vote in 1964. But demographic change, especially in the eastern portion of the county and the movement of suburbanites toward Democrats in the past two decades have changed its makeup. In 2008, Barack Obama became the first Democrat to carry Henrico since Franklin Roosevelt. In 2016, Hillary Clinton increased the Democratic vote in Henrico to 58 percent. And in 2020, Joe Biden took 64 percent. In 2019, Henrico was 31 percent Black and 6 percent Hispanic. To the south of Richmond, Chesterfield County has been exurban and largely Republican. With rapid population growth and increases to 25 percent Black and 10 percent Hispanic, Chesterfield has surpassed Henrico in population and become more competitive. Biden beat President Donald Trump here 52%-46% in 2020, a marked switch from Bob Dole's 60%-32% lead over Bill Clinton in 1996. Solidly Democratic Richmond is in the 4th District. Not all these areas are middle-class suburbia. "The growth of suburban poverty continues to outpace that of the city's," especially in Henrico, the Times-Dispatch reported in 2017. Rising drug overdoses in the county led the city to build a $14 million detox and recovery center. Though the pandemic was not kind to Henrico's economy, a T-Mobile customer service center in the county is expanding and hiring up to 500 new employees.

The outlying parts of the district are rural and heavily Republican. For Washingtonians willing to endure a long commute or simply wanting to get away from the metro area, Spotsylvania and Culpeper counties have become popular destinations in the Washington exurbs; each grew about 50 percent from 2000 to 2019. The redistricting in 2016 added areas west of Richmond that had been in the old 4th District, and in exchange moved New Hanover and Kent counties north and east of Richmond to the 1st District. That switch resulted in a slight increase in the Democratic vote. The demographic and redistricting shifts have made this a more competitive area. Trump won, 50%-44% in 2016. The GOP's decades-long control flipped in 2020 when Biden beat him 50%-49%.

Don Beyer (D)

Elected 2014, 4th term, b. Jun 20, 1950; Trieste, Italy; Williams College, B.A., 1972; Episcopalian; Married (Megan Carroll); 4 children; 2 grandchildren.

Elected Office: VA Lt. Governor, 1990-1998.

Professional Career: Automobile dealer; Chairman, Jobs for VA Graduates, 1999-2013; U.S. Ambassador to Switzerland and Liechtenstein, 2009-2013.

DC Office: 1119 LHOB 20515, 202-225-4376, Fax: 202-225-0017, beyer.house.gov

State Offices: Arlington, 703-658-5403.

Committees: *Joint Economic (Chmn). Science, Space & Technology*: Research & Technology; Space & Aeronautics (Chmn). *Ways & Means*: Trade.

Group Ratings

	ADA	ACLU	AFL-CIO	LCV	COC	HAFA	ACU	CFG	FRC
2020	**	83%	**	100%	-	0%	3%	**	-
2019	95%	C	100%	97%	57%	C	2%	13%	0%

Almanac Ratings 2019-2020

	Economy	Social	Foreign	Composite
Liberal	100%	100%	59%	87%
Conservative	0%	0%	41%	13%

Key Votes of the 116th Congress

1. U.S./Mex./Can. trade deal	Y	5. Russia sanctions	Y	9. Firearms background checks	Y
2. First Coronavirus response	N/A	6. Troops in Syria	Y	10. Spending at the border	N
3. HEROES Act	Y	7. Veto arms sales to Saudis	Y	11. Marijuana liberalized rules	Y
4. CASH Act	Y	8. Defense $$$, veto override	Y	12. Electoral College objections	N

Election Results

Election	Name (Party)	Vote (%)		Cand. Spent	Ind. Exp. Support	Ind. Exp. Oppose
2020 General	Don Beyer (D)..................................... 301,454	(76%)	$1,029,847	$123	
	Jeff Jordan (R)..................................... 95,365	(24%)	$97,113		$113

Prior winning percentages: 2018 (76%), 2016 (68%), 2014 (63%)

Democrat Don Beyer has easily won election in this district, which covers the wealthy and heavily Democratic Northern Virginia suburbs. After his long record as a successful businessman and public official, he sought opportunities for bipartisanship. With the Democratic majority, Beyer gained multiple opportunities to show his influence—including a seat on the Ways and Means Committee, where the former car dealer's top priority was action on a carbon tax. He remained active as co-chair of the Safe Climate Caucus.

Beyer was born in Trieste Italy, where his father was serving as an Army officer, grew up in Washington, went to Gonzaga High School in the shadow of the Capitol, and got his bachelor's degree from Williams College. American politics is rich in examples of second and third chances, and Beyer is no exception. He built a reputation as an affable dealmaker who could work with both sides of the aisle when he served two terms as Virginia's lieutenant governor, starting in 1990. But in 1997, when he sought the prize of the governorship, he floundered in his campaign against Republican James Gilmore III, stumbling in particular over the issue of the state's contested car tax. When he lost by 10 percentage points, many Virginians thought it would mark the end of Beyer's political career.

Beyer turned toward building his family's car-dealership business, which features Volvos, but he found he couldn't stay away from politics for good. In 2004, he served as campaign treasurer for Howard Dean's presidential campaign, and in 2008 he helped raise substantial sums for the Obama campaign. He led the new administration's transition planning at the Commerce Department and was rewarded with a plum ambassadorship to Switzerland and Liechtenstein, which he held for four years.

When 12-term Democratic Rep. Jim Moran announced his retirement, Beyer promptly launched his bid and tapped his extensive network of high-level Democratic contacts. His name recognition and connections proved to be advantages in a crowded primary race that drew six other Democrats. Of the $2.7 million he spent, $415,000 was self-financed. He stood out in candidate forums by demonstrating a strong grasp of both foreign and domestic policy. In the June primary, he topped the field with 46 percent of the vote, followed by state Del. Patrick Hope at 18 percent. The general election is a formality in this district.

On the Science, Space and Technology Committee, Beyer worked with Republicans on cyber security issues, including at the Office of Personnel Management and in the banking industry. The House passed his Science Prize Competition Act, which encourages federal agencies to use prize competitions as incentives for innovative scientific research and development. A self-styled "science nerd," Beyer has said he wants to make it easier for experts to clarify the facts on complex topics such as climate change.

Beyer brought his international experience to bear as well. To the dismay of labor unions that had supported him, he was an enthusiastic backer in 2015 of President Barack Obama's request for trade promotion authority and the prospective trans-Pacific trade deal. Union threats to challenge his reelection proved empty in this upscale district. He praised Obama's nuclear agreement with Iran, and took a bit of credit. As ambassador to Switzerland, he recounted, he hosted the initial discussions with Iran that launched the broader negotiations.

In 2017, he unsuccessfully urged the Trump administration to comply with international climate-change agreements. In 2019, as one of four co-chairs of a climate-change task force of the New Democrat Coalition, Beyer said the group planned to propose "common-sense solutions" to build a green economy. With the Safe Climate Caucus, Beyer said its mission was to "stand up to the White House" and "show the world that the United States has leaders who are willing to lead on climate and find bold solutions."

On Ways and Means, Beyer said he advocated a carbon tax to achieve the progressive goals of the "Green New Deal," which he supported. He endorsed "an economic mechanism that would rapidly elevate wind, solar and other clean energy and phase out carbon pollution, while minimizing the negative effects on American families." Also on Ways and Means, he worked actively in 2019 on the U.S.-Mexico-Canada trade agreement. Although the Trump administration's initial deal had "a number of positive elements," it was "also fundamentally flawed," Beyer said. The result "has been fixed by House Democrats."

In 2021, Beyer gained two chairmanships: At the Joint Economic Committee, he said he would "return the committee's focus to core issues facing the country, including economic inequality, climate change, corporate governance, health care and college affordability." As the new head of the Science, Space and Technology Subcommittee on Space and Aeronautics, Beyer said he planned to "advance a climate-driven agenda, working hand-in-hand with NASA's new climate adviser and advancing research into cleaner modes of flight." He added that he was "an unabashed science-fiction enthusiast."

VA-8: Northern Virginia

Cook Partisan Voting Index: D+27

Population		Race and Ethnicity		Income	
Total	813,568	White	62.90%	Median Income	$111,627
Land area (sq. miles)	149	Black	14.10%	District Income Rank	14
Pop/ sq mi	5,451.41	Latino	18.50%	Poverty Rate	8.40%
Born in State	25.10%	Asian	12.20%	With health insurance	91.00%
		Two or more races	4.60%	Cash public assistance	0.60%
Age Groups		Other	6.10%	Food stamp/SNAP	3.60%
Under 18	21.50%				
18-34	26.00%	**Education**		**Work**	
35-64	40.20%	H.S grad or less	19.60%	White Collar	60.20%
Over 64	12.40%	Some college	17.10%	Sales and Service	29.00%
		College Degree, 4 yr	31.20%	Blue Collar	10.90%
Military		Post grad	32.10%	Government	23.70%
Veteran/ Active Duty	10.70%				

2020 Pres. Vote	Biden	311,470	(77%)	Trump	84,711	(21%)			
2016 Pres. Vote	Clinton	270,415	(72%)	Trump	76,854	(21%)	Johnson	10,396	(3%)
	McMullin	7,334	(2%)						

Fairfax, Arlington, Alexandria: When George Washington strolled the brick sidewalks of Alexandria on his way to market or church or Gadsby's Tavern (where he celebrated his final two birthdays), it was the largest city in Northern Virginia, and larger than Georgetown just up the Potomac River. The areas that are now Capitol Hill and downtown Washington D.C. were hills above the river's mud flats. But Washington became the national capital; as it grew, Northern Virginia seemed left behind. In 1846, the District of Columbia retroceded its land south of the Potomac—now Alexandria and Arlington—to Virginia because it seemed then that the federal government would never need it. It would be another 97 years before the first federal building was constructed on the Virginia side—the Pentagon. When that occurred, Alexandria and the rural countryside of Northern Virginia were represented in Congress by Judge Howard W. Smith, for many years the influential chairman of the House Rules Committee, a Democrat who saw as his mission the maintenance of the standards of George Washington, Thomas Jefferson and Robert E. Lee, including on racial segregation. Yet by the 1950s, the area was changing around him. New subdivision dwellers with white-collar jobs wanted schools with good academic programs, not the segregated schoolhouses Judge Smith's friends were willing to finance. Smith lost the Democratic primary in 1966.

Today, the onetime suburbs of Arlington and Alexandria are "edge cities," with far more progressive policies. In 2014, Arlington County led the nation with the greatest share of its people who have college degrees (72 percent) and graduate degrees (37 percent). Cranes dot its cityscape, as giant office and housing developments have sprung up from rail yards in Crystal City and from used car lots upriver in Rosslyn. Amazon announced in 2018 the location of its second headquarters between Crystal City and Alexandria, with at least 25,000 workers and 4 million square feet of office space. The plan, renamed National Landing, was described as a "generationally transformative project." The move was accompanied by $750 million in tax incentives, with up to $295 million in transportation improvements, from the state and county—with relatively little controversy, especially compared to the quick reversal of comparable plans in New York City. For years, local commuters have found roads jammed: Washington suffers from some of the worst traffic congestion in the country, plus nagging slowdowns with its Metrorail system. In 2018, the Army completed its first expansion of Arlington National Cemetery since the 1980s; the 27 acres were removed from woodlands adjacent to nearby Fort Myer.

The 8th Congressional District of Virginia consists of Arlington County and the cities of Alexandria and Falls Church, where slightly more than half its population resides. The district covers all of Virginia that is inside the Capital Beltway except for small pockets in Annandale and McLean. The balance lives in Fairfax County, either in precincts near the perimeter of Arlington/Falls Church/ Alexandria or in areas south of the Beltway. The district takes in George Washington's Mount Vernon estate and the more rural areas around Fort Belvoir. Joe Biden got 77 percent of the vote in 2020, a marked increase from the 68 percent for President Barack Obama in 2012. This is the most Democratic district in Virginia.

Morgan Griffith (R)

Elected 2010, 6th term, b. Mar 15, 1958; Philadelphia, PA; Emory and Henry College, B.A., 1980; WA and Lee University School of Law, J.D., 1983; Episcopalian; Married (Hilary Davis); 3 children.

Elected Office: VA House, 1994-2010, Majority Leader, 2000-2010.

Professional Career: Practicing attorney, 2008-2010.

DC Office: 2202 RHOB 20515, 202-225-3861, Fax: 202-225-0076, morgangriffith.house.gov

State Offices: Abingdon, 276-525-1405; Big Stone Gap, 276-525-1405; Christiansburg, 540-381-5671.

Committees: *Energy & Commerce*: Energy; Health.

Group Ratings

	ADA	ACLU	AFL-CIO	LCV	COC	HAFA	ACU	CFG	FRC
2020	**	25%	**	14%	-	92%	82%	**	-
2019	5%	C	24%	7%	69%	C	81%	96%	91%

Almanac Ratings 2019-2020

	Economy	Social	Foreign	Composite
Liberal	25%	19%	43%	29%
Conservative	75%	81%	57%	71%

Key Votes of the 116th Congress

1. U.S./Mex./Can. trade deal	Y	5. Russia sanctions	Y	9. Firearms background checks	N
2. First Coronavirus response	Y	6. Troops in Syria	Y	10. Spending at the border	Y
3. HEROES Act	N	7. Veto arms sales to Saudis	N	11. Marijuana liberalized rules	N
4. CASH Act	N	8. Defense $$$, veto override	N	12. Electoral College objections	Y

Election Results

Election	Name (Party)	Vote (%)	Cand. Spent	Ind. Exp. Support	Ind. Exp. Oppose
2020 General	Morgan Griffith (R)............................ 271,851	(94%)	$372,344	$799	$750

Prior winning percentages: 2018 (65%), 2016 (69%), 2014 (72%), 2012 (61%), 2010 (51%)

Republican Morgan Griffith, a former Virginia House majority leader, has used his Energy and Commerce Committee seat to protect his region's coal industry, inveigh against the Environmental Protection Agency and restrict the distribution of opioid prescriptions. Following his election in 2010, he has become entrenched in a district that his Democratic predecessor held for 28 years. He has shown insider skills and occasional independence.

Griffith was born in Philadelphia and moved to Salem as a child. He was president of his high school student body and an avid swimmer. He attended Emory & Henry College, in part because it had just installed a new pool. He went on to get a law degree from Washington and Lee University. Griffith opened a private practice in Salem. After winning a seat in the House of Delegates in 1994, Griffith worked to repeal restrictions on gun ownership, limit abortion rights, and block a $1.4 billion tax increase. In 2000, he became the first Republican in Virginia to serve as House majority leader and earned a reputation as a skilled parliamentarian. Griffith bucked his party in 2010 when he helped draft a bill to legalize marijuana for medicinal use.

When he first ran for Congress, Griffith was at a 3-to-1 spending disadvantage to Rep. Rick Boucher. The incumbent, though he sought a middle ground, had been a leader at the Energy and Commerce Committee on his party's cap-and-trade bill aimed at limiting greenhouse gas emissions, which passed the House in 2009. The bill was unpopular in Appalachia's coal country. Griffith made Boucher's work on the bill a centerpiece of his campaign. He argued that the measure would have killed jobs and raised electricity costs. Boucher framed his support for the bill as a way to ensure that Congress and not the EPA had power over regulating carbon emissions. Griffith ran an ad with a video clip of President Barack Obama saying, "I love Rick Boucher." Boucher attacked Griffith as a carpetbagger who lived outside the district, running a television ad that said, "Morgan Griffith: He's not from here … and it shows." Griffith was bolstered by nearly $2 million in spending by national party and conservative groups. As Republicans swept across the country, especially in rural areas, Griffith won 51%-46%.

In the House, Griffith has mostly been a loyal Republican, though less of an ideologue than many of his GOP classmates. He followed Boucher with a plum seat on Energy and Commerce and steered a bill through the House in 2011 that sought to limit the EPA's power to regulate boilers. He and West Virginia Republican Rep. David McKinley complained in a 2013 op-ed about "the destructive consequences of this administration's regulatory assault" on the coal industry. He contended that EPA regulations treated dairy milk spills the same as oil spills, an assertion that the fact-checking site PolitiFact labeled false. Griffith took the lead in seeking to reverse "stream protection" regulations imposed by the Obama administration, which were designed to prevent coal debris from being dumped into nearby waters. In 2017, he praised President Donald Trump for signing a bill to overturn the new rules and "bring relief" to coal miners.

On other issues at Energy and Commerce, Griffith focused on home-style rural issues. He filed with Democratic Rep. Joyce Beatty of Ohio the Furthering Access to Stroke Telemedicine (FAST) Act, to expand Medicare coverage of health technology in rural areas. He urged the inclusion of expanded broadband services in any legislation for additional infrastructure. In 2018, Griffith won enactment of his bill to expedite permits for hydropower plants that potentially use existing infrastructure, including abandoned coal mines, and provide renewable energy. These pumped-storage facilities have been promoted by some miners. He continued to seek other opportunities for the use of coal, especially with the support of Trump.

With the scourge of opioids in many rural areas, including his district, Griffith worked with Democratic Rep. Diana DeGette to press for harsher punishment of pharmaceutical companies. "Anybody who knew ought to be sued criminally," he told the Martinsville Bulletin. In November 2020, the House passed his bill to close legal loopholes that "could enable opioid abuse." In an example of his independence, Griffith was one of six House Republicans in March 2020 who voted for a Democratic-sponsored bill that directed Trump to "terminate the use" of military actions against Iran.

Griffith has easily won reelection. In 2018, Democratic nominee Anthony Flaccavento launched a rematch of his challenge in 2012, which Griffith won, 61%-39%. Flaccavento ran on what he called "rural progressive" themes, including "Medicare for all," taxpayer-funded community college tuition, and protections for organized labor. Flaccavento avoided criticism of Trump and said Democrats had become too liberal. He spent a bit more than $1 million, nearly as much as Griffith. Aside from taking Blacksburg-based Montgomery County, which is the largest in the district, his revival bid fell short. Griffith won, 65%-35%, reinforcing the political transformation of rural America. In 2020, he was reelected without opposition.

VA-9: Southwest Virginia　　　　　　　　　　　　　**Cook Partisan Voting Index: R+23**

Population		Race and Ethnicity		Income	
Total	704,078	White	90.80%	Median Income	$46,909
Land area (sq. miles)	9,114	Black	5.50%	District Income Rank	407
Pop/ sq mi	77.25	Latino	2.80%	Poverty Rate	17.20%
Born in State	64.50%	Asian	1.50%	With health insurance	92.10%
		Two or more races	1.50%	Cash public assistance	2.80%
Age Groups		Other	0.70%	Food stamp/SNAP	12.40%
Under 18	18.10%				
18-34	22.10%	**Education**		**Work**	
35-64	38.60%	H.S grad or less	48.10%	White Collar	35.50%
Over 64	21.10%	Some college	30.00%	Sales and Service	38.70%
		College Degree, 4 yr	12.90%	Blue Collar	25.80%
Military		Post grad	9.00%	Government	19.80%
Veteran/ Active Duty	7.80%				

2020 Pres. Vote	Trump	244,996	(70%)	Biden	98,653	(28%)		
2016 Pres. Vote	Trump	217,837	(68%)	Clinton	86,463	(27%)	Johnson 7,481	(2%)

Blacksburg, Bristol: As early as 1765, settlements were carved out of the great Valley of Virginia, bending westward and south toward Tennessee and the Cumberland Gap. Most of these founders were of Scots-Irish lineage, and they moved to a mountainous area that developed almost apart from the rest of Virginia. The fiercely independent settlers eventually spilled into the heart of the Appalachian Mountains. Here, they followed the same political and economic development patterns as those in West Virginia, which wasn't a separate state until 1863. They were first farmers and later coal miners. Politically, this virtually all-White area opposed slavery and was skeptical, if not hostile, to the Confederacy. It is a long way from here to plantation country—the state's extreme southwest corner is closer to nine other state capitals than to Richmond. Out of the crucible of struggle between secessionists and unionists, Southwest Virginia developed a robust two-party politics after the Civil War, sooner than in the rest of the state.

In recent decades, as development moved down Interstate 81 from Roanoke to Bristol, the region has become more like the rest of Virginia. With encouragement from state officials, businesses have created jobs at high-tech companies and telephone call centers. Agriculture has thrived, especially produce and dairy, while coal mining has diminished. Coal has not entirely disappeared, either economically or socially.

The 9th Congressional District covers all of Southwest Virginia west of Roanoke; the city and most of Roanoke County are in the 6th District. Over the years, it became known as the "Fighting Ninth" because of its taste for raucous politics, which by and large were culturally conservative and economically populist. This is NASCAR country; Martinsville's speedway is here, and Bristol's is just across the Tennessee line. Bristol, a former rail hub, has adjacent cities on opposite sides of the state line that share many services; its Virginia locale has suffered from poor local management. Blacksburg, with a population of 45,000 plus the 37,000 students on campus at Virginia Tech University, is the largest city in the area. Buchanan County, in the far western part of the district, shows how the political winds have shifted. It gave Bill Clinton 63 percent of the vote in both 1992 and 1996, but the Democratic vote then dropped precipitously. In 2020, President Donald Trump took Buchanan by a stunning 84%-16%. As Democratic support collapsed, this has become the most Republican district in the state. Even with Sen. Tim Kaine of Virginia as her running mate, Hillary Clinton fell far short. Trump won 68%-27% in 2016 and 70%-28% four years later. This is the only district in Virginia where the GOP nominee exceeded 60 percent of the vote in the past three presidential elections.

Jennifer Wexton (D)

Elected 2018, 2nd term, b. May 27, 1968; Washington, DC; University of MD, Baltimore (UMB), B.A., 1991; College of William and Mary - Marshall-Wythe Law School, J.D., 1995; Married (Andrew Wexton); 2 children.

Elected Office: VA Senate, 2014-2018.

Professional Career: Assistant Commonwealth Attorney, Loudon County 2001-2005; Attorney; Loudoun County Circuit Court Substitute Judge.

DC Office: 1217 LHOB 20515, 202-225-5136, Fax: 202-225-0437, wexton.house.gov

State Offices: Sterling, 703-234-3800.

Committees: *Appropriations*: Legislative Branch; State, Foreign Operations & Related Programs; Transportation, HUD & Related Agencies. *Budget*.

Almanac Ratings 2019-2020

	Economy	Social	Foreign	Composite
Liberal	100%	100%	80%	94%
Conservative	0%	0%	20%	6%

Key Votes of the 116th Congress

1. U.S./Mex./Can. trade deal	Y	5. Russia sanctions	Y	9. Firearms background checks	Y
2. First Coronavirus response	Y	6. Troops in Syria	Y	10. Spending at the border	Y
3. HEROES Act	Y	7. Veto arms sales to Saudis	Y	11. Marijuana liberalized rules	Y
4. CASH Act	Y	8. Defense $$$, veto override	Y	12. Electoral College objections	N

Election Results

Election	Name (Party)	Vote (%)		Cand. Spent	Ind. Exp. Support	Ind. Exp. Oppose
2020 General	Jennifer Wexton (D)............................	268,734	(57%)	$1,757,198	$1,115	$1,500
	Aliscia Andrews (R)............................	206,253	(43%)	$1,306,147	$8,941	$113

Prior winning percentages: 2018 (56%)

Jennifer Wexton received the largest share of the vote among the more than two dozen Democratic challengers who defeated a House Republican incumbent in the 2018 election. That and her smooth reelection two years later highlighted the gains Democrats have made in wealthy suburbs since the election of President Donald Trump, not only in Virginia but in many metro areas across the nation. In 2018, Wexton defeated Republican Rep. Barbara Comstock, who received hefty financial support from national Republican groups despite her dim prospects. Those groups did not spend at all in 2020.

Wexton, a native of Bethesda Maryland, graduated from the University of Maryland and got her law degree from the College of William & Mary School of Law. She was a prosecutor for the Commonwealth's Attorney of Loudoun County Virginia. As a partner in the Laurel Brigade law group in Leesburg, she had an interest in mental health issues. Wexton was a member of an advisory board to the county's mental health department and handled pro bono work on behalf of abused and neglected children. For a year, she chaired the Loudoun County Bar Association.

Wexton won a special election in 2014 for the state Senate, where she pursued her interest in issues affecting children. She claimed credit for enacting 40 bills, though she had served entirely in the minority party.

In the Democratic primary for the House seat, Wexton faced five other candidates. Three of them spent more than $1 million: Lindsey Davis Stover and Alison Friedman, both of whom held positions in the Obama administration, and Army veteran Dan Helmer. Opponents criticized Weston for not refusing to accept corporate campaign contributions. The political geography of the district allowed Wexton to avoid a lurch to the left that often occurs in swing-seat primaries. Her base in Loudoun County cast nearly half the vote. The other top contenders were dividing up Fairfax County. "I've represented a moderate, centrist district in the state Senate," she told The Associated Press. "For myself, I've got to be me." She won the primary with 42 percent of the vote to 23 percent for Friedman, 16 percent for Stover and 13 percent for Helmer. Wexton got 49 percent in Loudoun.

In the general election, both Wexton and Comstock ran extensive advertising, much of it negative. Comstock cast blame on Wexton for traffic congestion and for tolls that she had supported in the state legislature.

Wexton sought to link "Trumpstock" to President Donald Trump. The ads were replete with exaggerations and falsehoods, according to campaign observers.

In a campaign debate, Wexton described her opponent as "a masterful political chameleon." Comstock responded by defending her record of "getting results." Wexton accused Comstock of a double standard when she refused to say whether she believed allegations of sexual misconduct that had been lodged against Supreme Court nominee Brett Kavanaugh, who was a longtime friend of hers.

In an editorial endorsing Wexton, The Washington Post praised her "clear and convincing competence" and said she would be "a breath of fresh air." The editorial added that Comstock's earlier promise to be independent of Trump had "turned to dust" and that she had been an "often unquestioning foot soldier" among GOP loyalists. The district's proximity to the capital drew some high-profile members to the stump. James Comey, the former FBI director and self-proclaimed lifelong Republican-turned-Trump critic, campaigned for Wexton.

This was one of the costliest House contests in the nation. Each candidate spent more than $6 million. Total spending exceeded $25 million. Some Republicans objected during the campaign that the GOP campaign committee was wasting money here that could have been spent more effectively elsewhere. Their complaints proved to be valid. Wexton won, 56%-44%. In suburban Loudoun and Fairfax counties, which cast nearly three-fourths of the total vote, she got 60 percent and 59 percent of the vote, respectively. Comstock won two small, outlying counties.

Wexton entered the House with more legislative experience than most of her colleagues and seemed politically secure. In Congress, she joined the moderate New Democrat Coalition, but her relatively safe district has afforded her the ability to become more outspoken on progressive causes than others in her cohort. She was an early supporter of statehood for the District of Columbia.

Capitol staff and visitors made a pilgrimage to her office in 2019 to praise her decision to hang a transgender pride flag outside the door, a show of solidarity with her transgender niece. She quipped that she had become "the patron saint of the transgender community" in an interview with the Post after she urged Ben Carson, the then-secretary of Housing and Urban Development, to resign after he declared federally funded homeless shelters would require transgender women to use men's restrooms. In 2020, the House passed her bill aimed at cracking down on imports from China's forced labor camps that target Uyghur Muslims.

Republicans made only a half-hearted attempt to challenge Wexton in 2020. She outspent Republican Aliscia Andrews, a Marine veteran, by about $500,000 and still ended with over $2 million left in the bank. Wexton won, 57%-43%. She took 60 percent in both Loudoun and Fairfax.

Virginia Democrats ceded redistricting power to an independent commission, but the rapid growth and diversification of the Washington suburbs will provide a buffer for Wexton.

VA-10: Northern Virginia | Cook Partisan Voting Index: D+6

Population		Race and Ethnicity		Income	
Total	857,693	White	69.10%	Median Income	$132,226
Land area (sq. miles)	1,372	Black	8.00%	District Income Rank	3
Pop/ sq mi	625.03	Latino	14.40%	Poverty Rate	3.50%
Born in State	35.80%	Asian	15.60%	With health insurance	93.40%
		Two or more races	4.50%	Cash public assistance	0.80%
Age Groups		Other	2.90%	Food stamp/SNAP	3.60%
Under 18	26.30%				
18-34	18.40%	Education		Work	
35-64	42.50%	H.S grad or less	22.00%	White Collar	57.20%
Over 64	12.90%	Some college	21.40%	Sales and Service	30.50%
		College Degree, 4 yr	31.20%	Blue Collar	12.30%
Military		Post grad	25.30%	Government	17.80%
Veteran/ Active Duty	8.70%				

2020 Pres. Vote	Biden	281,817	(59%)	Trump	189,376	(39%)		
2016 Pres. Vote	Clinton	210,692	(52%)	Trump	170,580	(42%)	Johnson	12,563	(3%)

Loudoun and Fairfax Counties: What we think of today as the outer suburbs and exurbs of Washington D.C. was still open country as late as World War II. Gen. George Marshall, driving from his office in the Pentagon to the old house he bought in Leesburg 40 miles away, would pass a few gas stations, crossroads villages and countless acres of farm fields. If Marshall made the trip today, his drive would take a lot longer and he would see something very different. As the federal government grew, Fairfax County's population doubled in the 1940s and very nearly tripled in the 1950s. It has continued to grow, though at a much slower rate, passing 1 million in 2002 and 1.15 million in 2019. Loudoun County, where Dulles International Airport opened in the 1960s as the outer limit to the region, lately has experienced that type of explosive expansion. It grew more than 30 percent over the last decade, one of the fastest growing counties in the nation. Its population increased from 174,000 in 2000 to 414,000 in 2019. This has become the richest area of the country: Loudoun and Fairfax counties ranked first and third in the nation in median household income in 2019, with $142,000 and $125,000, respectively. Nearby Falls Church took second and Arlington is close behind. The Asian and Latino populations have increased rapidly in both Fairfax and Loudoun: a combined 37 percent and 34 percent, respectively.

Growth continues apace, and the Washington metro area now extends past those two counties and over the Blue Ridge into the Shenandoah Valley. No longer simply a collection of bedroom communities, Northern Virginia has become an employment center and focus of innovation in its own right. The Dulles Access Road is lined with high-tech firms and entrepreneurial startups, defense contractors and "Beltway bandit" lobbying firms. Traffic is mightily congested and Loudoun has taken steps to curb sprawl; Metrorail service to and beyond the airport is scheduled to launch in 2022.

The 10th Congressional District covers much of Northern Virginia's western suburbs. It includes most of well-heeled McLean, home of many of Washington's political and lawyer-lobbyist elites, but it skirts the increasingly liberal—and growing—residential enclaves in the booming Tysons commercial area. It includes the conservative Clifton area of southwest Fairfax, northern Prince William County, and the cities of Manassas and Manassas Park. Beyond the Beltway, it takes in woodsy Great Falls and the Dulles Airport corridor. It includes all of Loudoun County, which is heavily built-up in the east with some still-rural areas west of Leesburg. Middleburg, with both old and new money, is horse country with many gated mansions. Beyond the Blue Ridge, it takes in the fast-growing, Republican Winchester-based Frederick County, which not long ago was best known for its apple orchards. Winchester was the home of the Byrd family, who published the local newspaper and spawned a powerful political "machine" of conservative Democrats, led by longtime Sen. Harry Byrd, who firmly resisted racial desegregation. Nearly 50 percent of the district's population is in Loudoun, and 25 percent in Fairfax.

The district was once reliably Republican. It gave George W. Bush 56 percent of the vote in 2000. With an influx of immigrants and federal workers and the election of Donald Trump, Northern Virginia has transformed into Democrats' country. In 2020, Joe Biden completed the rapid turnaround with his 59%-39% win.

Gerald Connolly (D)

Elected 2008, 7th term, b. Mar 30, 1950; Boston, MA; Maryknoll College, B.A., 1971; Harvard University, M.P.A., 1979; Roman Catholic; Married (Cathy Connolly); 1 child.

Elected Office: Fairfax County Board of Supervisors, 1995-2009, Chairman, 2004-2009.

Professional Career: Non-profit Executive; U.S. Senate aide; Defense contractor.

DC Office: 2238 RHOB 20515, 202-225-1492, Fax: 202-225-3071, connolly.house.gov

State Offices: Annandale, 703-256-3071; Woodbridge, 571-408-4407.

Committees: *Foreign Affairs*: Asia, the Pacific, Central Asia, Nonproliferation; Middle East, North Africa & Global Counterterrorism. *Oversight & Reform*: Government Operations (Chmn).

Group Ratings

	ADA	ACLU	AFL-CIO	LCV	COC	HAFA	ACU	CFG	FRC
2020	**	86%	**	100%	-	0%	6%	**	-
2019	90%	C	100%	97%	59%	C	7%	12%	0%

Almanac Ratings 2019-2020

	Economy	Social	Foreign	Composite
Liberal	100%	100%	92%	98%
Conservative	0%	0%	8%	2%

Key Votes of the 116th Congress

1. U.S./Mex./Can. trade deal Y	5. Russia sanctions	Y	9. Firearms background checks Y
2. First Coronavirus response Y	6. Troops in Syria	Y	10. Spending at the border N
3. HEROES Act Y	7. Veto arms sales to Saudis	Y	11. Marijuana liberalized rules Y
4. CASH Act Y	8. Defense $$$, veto override	Y	12. Electoral College objections N

Election Results

Election	Name (Party)	Vote (%)		Cand. Spent	Ind. Exp. Support	Ind. Exp. Oppose
2020 General	Gerald Connolly (D)	280,725	(71%)	$2,395,768	$873	
	Manga Anantatmula (R)	111,380	(28%)	$265,264		$113
2020 Primary	Gerry Connolly (D)	50,626	(78%)			
	Zainab Mohsini (D)	14,610	(22%)			

Prior winning percentages: 2018 (71%), 2016 (88%), 2014 (57%), 2012 (61%), 2010 (49%), 2008 (55%)

Democrat Gerald (Gerry) Connolly, elected in 2008, is a former Capitol Hill staffer and county executive who remains an ardent champion of the federal workers and government contractors who populate his Northern Virginia district. Although he failed in his 2019 bid to chair the Oversight and Reform Committee, his subcommittee chairmanship gave him wide-ranging jurisdiction over federal operations and many aspects of metropolitan Washington. He retains influence on international issues.

Connolly grew up in the Boston area and graduated from Maryknoll College. He considered joining the priesthood and studied for six years at a Catholic seminary. His interest in public policy led him to Washington, where he managed the American Freedom from Hunger Foundation and the U.S. Committee for Refugees. He got a master's degree from Harvard and worked for a decade on the staff of the Senate Foreign Relations Committee, where he specialized in Middle Eastern affairs and foreign aid.

He left Capitol Hill to run the Washington office of Stanford Research Institute International and then became vice president of the San Diego-based defense contractor SAIC. In 1995, Connolly won a seat on the Fairfax County Board of Supervisors, and later was elected board chairman, taking responsibility for a large government at a time of rapid growth. His biggest project was the Metrorail extension to Tysons and Dulles.

When Republican Rep. Tom Davis, who could see that Northern Virginia was moving away from the GOP, retired in 2008, Connolly had a primary clash with former Rep. Leslie Byrne. Connolly outpaced her finances, with support from defense contractors, and won by a solid 58%-33%. Republican nominee Keith Fimian, a businessman and newcomer to Northern Virginia politics, self-financed much of his campaign. Democrats attacked Fimian as too conservative on cultural issues; Fimian got little help from national Republicans. Connolly won 55%-43%.

Connolly has been a leader of the centrist New Democrat Coalition and he has established a moderate voting record. His Almanac vote ratings have placed him toward the center of the House, though he was more liberal on social issues. Connolly was an enthusiastic supporter of trade promotion authority for President Barack Obama and his prospective Trans-Pacific Partnership deal. In turn, he was strongly criticized by labor and liberal groups that opposed the measure. Connolly's close alliance with federal employees' unions gave him some political cover.

On the Oversight and Reform Committee, Connolly often worked well with Republicans. He was instrumental in 2014 in the enactment of the landmark Federal Information Technology Acquisition

Reform Act, which was the first major overhaul of federal IT management since 1996. He enacted a bill in 2010 to encourage teleworking. When Republicans controlled the House, Connolly blasted their budget-cutting efforts that he said unfairly targeted government workers.

As chairman of the Oversight Subcommittee on Government Operations since 2019, Connolly has responsibility for a range of federal issues, including the U.S. Postal Service and the Census Bureau. In July 2019, he cited the transcript of the telephone call that President Donald Trump had with Ukraine president Volodymyr Zelensky and said that Congress had "the smoking gun" to proceed with impeachment.

Following the death of Rep. Elijah Cummings later that year, Connolly sought the chairmanship of the full committee and cited his extensive work on the panel. After other prospective challengers withdrew, he lost, 133-86, to Rep. Carolyn Maloney, who had the most seniority.

Following up on his work as a Senate staffer, Connolly has been an active member of the House Foreign Affairs Committee, where he tends to voice an internationalist view. As chairman of the U.S. delegation to the NATO Parliamentary Assembly, he supported, "with absolute clarity, the longstanding U.S. commitment to NATO and Euro-Atlantic security."

Connolly was a harsh critic of Trump's foreign policy, with often cutting remarks. During the 35-day federal shutdown that began in December 2018, he said in an interview on CNN: "I think the president lives in this delusional world fed by Fox News and a couple of right-wing talking heads and does not connect actions with consequences."

At home, Connolly faced a rematch with Fimian in 2010, a perilous year for Democrats. This time, Fimian raised $2.9 million to Connolly's $2.4 million. Fimian stuck to the national Republican message of "outrageous spending" and rising deficits and attacked Connolly as a "career politician." Five days after the election, Fimian conceded, having won 48.8 percent to his opponent's 49.2 percent —a margin of 981 votes out of 227,000 cast. Connolly has had it easier since then, with assistance from new district lines and the Democrats' domination of Northern Virginia.

VA-11: Northern Virginia

Cook Partisan Voting Index: D+19

Population		Race and Ethnicity		Income	
Total	789,553	White	55.50%	Median Income	$118,099
Land area (sq. miles)	185	Black	13.90%	District Income Rank	10
Pop/ sq mi	4,265.78	Latino	19.10%	Poverty Rate	6.30%
Born in State	29.70%	Asian	18.70%	With health insurance	91.10%
		Two or more races	4.40%	Cash public assistance	1.00%
Age Groups		Other	7.70%	Food stamp/SNAP	3.50%
Under 18	22.90%				
18-34	23.30%	**Education**		**Work**	
35-64	41.10%	H.S grad or less	22.10%	White Collar	56.50%
Over 64	12.60%	Some college	20.70%	Sales and Service	32.00%
		College Degree, 4 yr	29.70%	Blue Collar	11.50%
Military		Post grad	27.40%	Government	20.30%
Veteran/ Active Duty	9.90%				

2020 Pres. Vote	Biden	280,673	(70%)	Trump	112,905	(28%)			
2016 Pres. Vote	Clinton	238,982	(66%)	Trump	98,222	(27%)	Johnson	10,253	(3%)

Fairfax and Prince William Counties: Rising on a hill west of Washington D.C., Tysons Corner was a back-country intersection 50 years ago. By the late 1980s, it was an edge city, with the largest concentration of office space to be found anywhere between Washington and Atlanta, and with a modern skyline and busy multi-lane avenues that served as arteries to the Capital Beltway. Fairfax County, which includes Tysons Corner, had been a typical postwar suburb. It had only 99,000 people in 1950, far fewer than Washington's 802,000. But in the years that followed, the trickle moving into Fairfax became a gusher. In 2019, it had 1.15 million people, nearly twice as many as Washington. Today, it is packed with mostly affluent communities, with dazzlingly high percentages of residents with college degrees and two or more cars.

In the last decade, the once-sedate "Mother Fairfax" has once again changed. Just as Tysons Corner (now referred to as simply Tysons) made it a major corporate and shopping center, developers are transforming that complex to approximate a walkable, downtown urban area. By 2050, planners envision 100,000 residents and 200,000 jobs in Tysons, which will become a 24-hour urban center.

Except for Tysons, population growth in Fairfax has slowed since the 1980s; the 12 percent growth rate of the 2000s, the slowest since the 1910s, was followed by 6 percent from 2010 to 2019. The next Silver Line extension of the Metrorail system from Reston past Dulles Airport, which is scheduled for completion in 2022, is expected to boost the number of passengers who fly from Dulles; it also will expand development at the new subway stations. Meanwhile, Prince William County has been growing at a fast clip, 65 percent between 2000 and 2019, attracting the young families that Fairfax once did. Immigrants—Koreans and Vietnamese, Ethiopians and Afghans, Salvadorans and Mexicans—have put their stamp in Fairfax on what once were mostly white, heavily Protestant neighborhoods.

The 11th Congressional District of Virginia consists of much of Fairfax County and southeastern Prince William County. Stretching across northern Virginia, its southern end borders the Potomac River but its northern edge falls a bit short of the river. Republicans in control of redistricting in 2011 packed as many Democratic voters into the district as possible to shore up neighboring Republican districts. Fairfax County has had a dramatic political shift. President Bill Clinton won 46 percent of the county vote in his 1996 reelection; Joe Biden took 70 percent in 2020. The 11th takes in sprawling Tysons, parts of Annandale that are the only area of the district inside the Capital Beltway, and also Oakton, Vienna, Fairfax City, Lorton, Burke and part of Centreville. An arm extends west to the heavily Democratic planned community of Reston, neighboring Herndon and the entrance to Dulles Airport. In Prince William County, it includes Woodbridge and Dale City, areas with large Latino immigrant populations. The district has the most federal employees of any district that does not have a military base. It is majority-minority. including: 19 percent Asian, 19 percent Hispanic, and 14 percent African American. It is solidly Democratic, as intended. In 2020, Biden got 70 percent of the district.

WASHINGTON

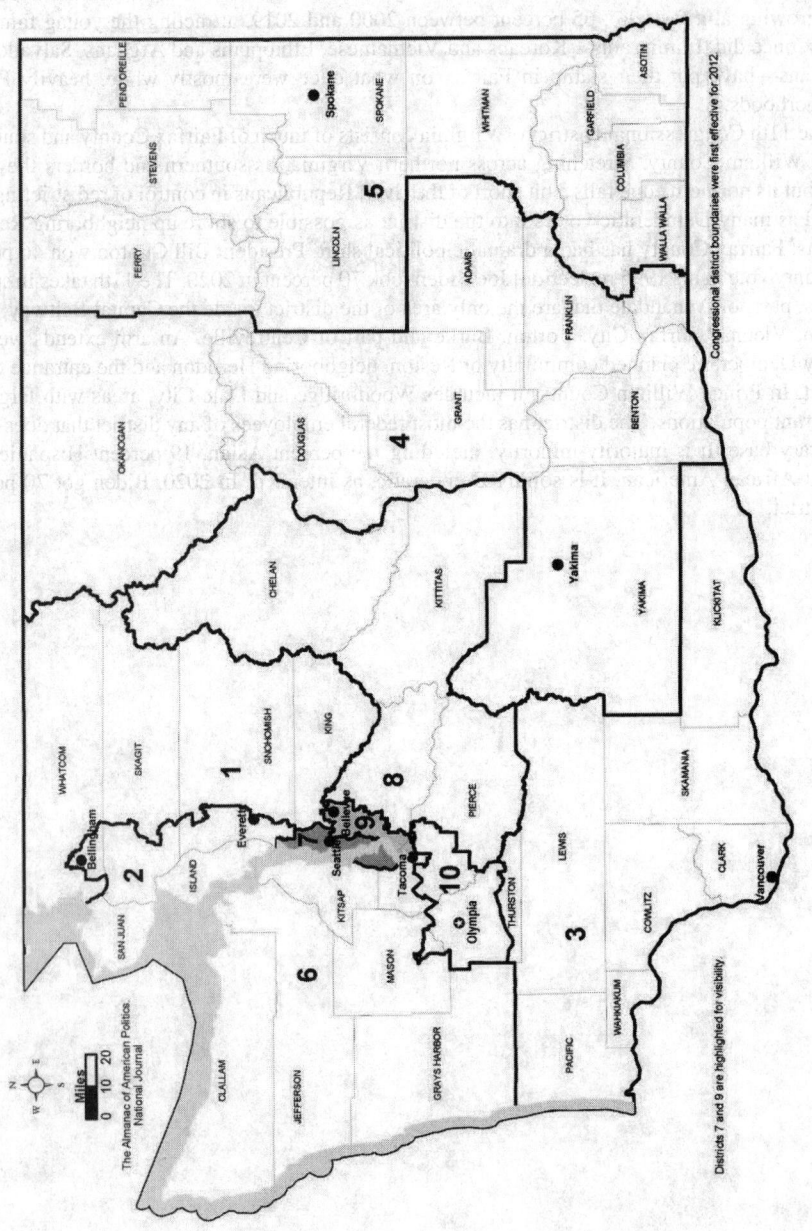

The Almanac of American Politics.
National Journal

Congressional district boundaries were first effective for 2012.

Districts 7 and 9 are highlighted for visibility.

Washington is a hotbed for high-tech and export industries, disproportionately populated by affluent, well-educated, and culturally liberal residents, at least in the Seattle metropolitan area, which accounts for just over half of the state's population. As such, it embodies a key wing of the modern Democratic Party. At the same time, the eastern part of the state is rural and more heavily Republican.

Off in the far northwest corner of the continental United States, Washington was settled by indigenous peoples who cultivated the land and engaged in commerce. Washington likes to think of itself as a national trendsetter and model for the rest of the country: As the headquarters of Microsoft, Starbucks and Amazon, it has been on the cutting edge of innovation. An unusual environment and human creativity combined to produce these achievements. Seattle's cold, misty air and 226 overcast days a year—the cloudiest pattern of any big U.S. city—stimulate the appetite for strong, aromatic coffee. Boeing's airframe business took off during World War II because the Pacific Northwest's abundant hydroelectric power made cheap aluminum possible, and the boom in air travel in the 1980s and 1990s kept Boeing's huge assembly lines humming. Redmond-based Microsoft, founded by the tie-less and tousle-haired Bill Gates and the late Paul Allen, became one of America's great success stories as its software became embedded in computers across the world.

In the two decades after it became a state in 1889, transcontinental railroads reached the great ports of Puget Sound, the wheat-processing city of Spokane, and the region's orchard towns, fishing ports and lumber settlements. Shielded from the storms of the Pacific Ocean by the Olympic Mountains and Puget Sound, Seattle grew quickly as a city, a lusty town full of lumbermen and railroad workers. When gold was struck in the Klondike and in Alaska, Seattle became a metropolis of miners, prospectors, and get-rich-quick operators; it is the site of the original "Skid Road," where logs were rolled downhill to the port. (Today it's in gentrified Pioneer Square.) In the years before World War I, thriving young Seattle was a hotbed of radical politics, as class warfare pitted the radical Industrial Workers of the World (the IWW, or Wobblies) against city business and civic leaders. The city birthed worker cooperatives and a general strike in 1919. Businessmen, after some violence from both sides, prevailed. Adding to the area's distinctiveness was its large number of Scandinavian immigrants, with their favorable views of cooperative enterprises and government ownership.

Over time, Washington was transformed by a series of national decisions that set its course. One was government development of hydroelectric power. The Columbia River and its tributary, the Snake River, fall thousands of feet in a relatively short distance, offering far greater hydroelectric potential than any other American river system. President Franklin D. Roosevelt took an interest in projects there: In 1937, Bonneville Dam was completed on the lower Columbia, followed three years later by Grand Coulee Dam, the largest man-made structure in the world at the time and still the nation's single greatest producer of electricity. When war came, Washington's hydroelectric power—the cheapest electricity in the country—made it the natural site for huge, electricity-sucking aluminum plants. The Seattle area became the home not only of shipbuilders but also of the biggest aircraft manufacturer in the country, Boeing. William Boeing founded the company in 1916 in a converted shipyard on the Duwamish River in south Seattle. The Navy had a large presence locally as well, with depots in Seattle, Bremerton and other locations. Cheap power, aluminum, aircraft, and high unionized wages—these became the starting point for the state's post-World War II economy. Further inland, the Hanford plant on the Columbia was secretly one of the government's main manufacturing sites for the plutonium used in nuclear weapons until 1987; it is currently undergoing a multi-decade cleanup, a troubled effort that has left some parts of the site uninspected for 50 years.

Today, Washington lives less off the brawn of hydroelectric power and rail and ship tonnage, and more off the brains that made Boeing, Microsoft and Amazon global giants. The torn blue jeans and flannel shirts once worn year-round have morphed into hi-tech fleece and hipster beards. Today, Washington ranks 11th in attainment of bachelor's degrees, 3rd in per-capita patents granted, and 7th in median income. Microsoft survived a major antitrust case, a huge fine from the European Union, Gates' retirement, and vigorous competition from California-based Apple and Google; it has grown to 150,000 full-time employees, more than 50,000 of them in metro Seattle. As Microsoft overhauls its Redmond headquarters, it has pledged $500 million for affordable housing in the region. (Gates and his foundation became major players during the coronavirus pandemic, sponsoring public health and vaccination efforts, though the split with his wife Melinda in 2021 cast a cloud over his future philanthropy.) Starbucks cut back during the Great Recession but has been expanding again, abroad and at home. Amazon, meanwhile, was transformed from an internet bookseller that wreaked havoc on big bookstores to a behemoth rewriting the rules of retailing everywhere, especially during the pandemic as bricks-and-mortar retail suffered. The company expanded into streaming video and web hosting services; its founder, Jeff Bezos, purchased the Washington Post (in the other Washington) and proceeded to bolster its fortunes. The company has had a profound impact on Seattle, creating some 75,000 jobs and counting, redeveloping large swaths of the city, and encouraging transit-oriented development. It has promised up to $2 billion for affordable housing.

But Amazon and Seattle's other tech firms have also attracted intense criticism. Tech growth has contributed to Seattle becoming an expensive city to live in, exacerbating income inequality. Amazon has continually battled tax proposals by Seattle's left-wing City Council; in the 2019 local elections, the company spent heavily to seek the defeat of incumbents such as Kshama Sawant, an Indian-born Trotskyist socialist. But the effort failed: In 2020, the council approved a tax on the highest salaries at large companies that could raise an estimated $200 million annually. Meanwhile, Boeing has floundered. In early 2019, two newly introduced (and initially fast-selling) 737 MAX airplanes crashed back to back, forcing a grounding of the fleet. Later in 2019, a Star liner space capsule the company had built for NASA botched its mission. In took until November 2020 for the Federal Aviation Administration to approve the MAX for flights again, by which time the international aviation market had been decimated by the coronavirus pandemic.

In 2020, Seattle was also riven by protests that were sparked by the racial reckoning after the death of George Floyd in police custody in Minneapolis, but which were also shaped by the city's longstanding left-wing undercurrents. Shortly after Floyd's death, the Seattle police were faced with growing standoffs in the Capitol Hill neighborhood and abandoned a police building, leaving several square blocks to protesters as a police-free experiment—"part street festival, part commune," as the New York Times put it, with speeches, poetry, music, a medic station, and a "no-cop co-op." Initially, city officials such as Mayor Jenny Durkan defended the area from criticism by President Donald Trump that it was a den of "domestic terrorists." But within weeks, a series of shootings and growing unhappiness among nearby residents and businesses led the city to retake the police building and arrest anyone who didn't follow dispersal orders. "Our job is to support peaceful demonstrations," said police chief Carmen Best, calling the previous few weeks "lawless," "brutal," and "simply unacceptable." (Best was the first Black woman to serve as chief of the department, which had drawn federal oversight in 2011 for excessive force on minority residents; she later resigned amid efforts to slash the department's budget.) Complicating matters was that Washington remains predominantly white, although the percentage has fallen in recent years; overall, the state is 13 percent Hispanic, 9 percent Asian, and only 4 percent Black. "Theregion's homeowners may vote Democratic and plant racial solidarity signs in their front yards but often resist higher densities that can increase the affordable housing supply," wrote Margaret O'Mara, a University of Washington historian.

Washington's population expanded 14 percent between 2000 and 2010—faster than Oregon or California—and it has risen another 14.6 percent since 2010, initially driven by migration from other states and now increasingly by newcomers from India and China, drawn by the tech sector. The Seattle metro area has grown by more than 15 percent since 2010, and Washington's biggest counties have expanded by healthy rates over that period: King County (Seattle) by 16 percent and neighboring Snohomish County (Everett) and Pierce County (Tacoma) by 15 percent and 14 percent, respectively. Outside metro Seattle, Clark County (Vancouver, across from Portland Oregon) has grown by 14 percent. Even Spokane County, in the slower-growing eastern half of the state, has grown 11 percent. Some of the highest minority proportions are in agricultural areas, such as apple-growing Yakima County, a minority-majority jurisdiction that is 50 percent Hispanic and 7 percent Native American. Rural areas continue to have a healthy agricultural sector—Washington ranks first nationally in the production of apples, cherries, and hops—despite challenges with securing labor, especially during the pandemic.

Four of the nation's 15 most dangerous volcanoes, according to the U.S. Geological Survey, are in Washington: Mount St. Helens, which erupted spectacularly in 1980 and continues to produce periodic earthquakes; 14,000-foot Mount Rainier, situated just 60 miles from Seattle and Tacoma; Mount Baker; and Glacier Peak. Another risk is an earthquake and tsunami stemming from the obscure Cascadia subduction zone. A regional director of the Federal Emergency Management

Agency told the New Yorker in 2015 that, in the worst-case scenario, "our operating assumption is that everything west of Interstate 5 will be toast," meaning 140,000 square miles and 7 million people living in and around Seattle, Tacoma and Olympia in Washington and Portland, Eugene and Salem in Oregon. In 2020, an invasive insect with a terrifying name—the "murder hornet" —was discovered near Blaine, spooking Americans already exhausted by the pandemic.

Situated in a region with abundant natural beauty, Washington has taken environmental concerns seriously. Puget Sound Energy has become a major player in wind energy, bolstering the state's renewable energy capacity. However, green priorities have often been pitted against industries that created the state's original wealth. A key flashpoint has been coal—not extracted from mines in the state (the last one closed in 2006) but rather shipped by rail from places such as Wyoming, destined for terminals and then ships bound for Asia. Activists have fought the construction of a half-dozen new cargo terminals, and they have been successful. But in 2020, Wyoming hit back, filing a lawsuit at the Supreme Court challenging Washington's blockage of a coal export terminal. (Port expansions for containerized cargo have generally prompted less opposition.) The state's environmental leanings do have limits. In 2016, voters overwhelmingly rejected a ballot measure that would have taxed carbon dioxide emissions at $25 per ton, in exchange for sales tax rollbacks. Two years later, voters, by a 57%-43% margin, rejected a measure to enact a carbon emissions fee with revenues funding environmental programs; it won King County by double digits but lost in rural areas and in the suburban counties of Snohomish and Pierce. A hopeful sign of détente is that environmentalists and loggers are increasingly aligned on more aggressive forest management practices in the wake of devastating wildfires.

Politically, Washington was one of the most Democratic northern states in the 1930s. Roosevelt's campaign manager, James Farley, used to refer to "the 47 states and the Soviet of Washington." Its mainstream Democrats believed in an activist federal government that built dams, bought military aircraft and pursued an internationalist, anti-Communist foreign policy abroad. Their political strength came out of a blue-collar base, augmented by the respect big business had for its political clout. Today, the state remains among the top five unionized states, but the fulcrum of the electorate has moved from blue collar to white collar, and from economic class warfare to culture wars. On balance, the Democrats have benefited. In presidential races, Washington has voted exclusively Democratic since 1988 and has elected only Democratic governors since 1984, though some gubernatorial races have been competitive. The GOP today controls one statewide office: secretary of state.

The biggest share of votes comes from the three counties closest to Seattle—King, Snohomish and Pierce. In the 1980s, King County was closely divided, with higher-income suburbs voting Republican and working-class neighborhoods in Seattle voting Democratic. But Seattle has become a relatively childless city, while Hispanics have been moving to southern King County suburbs and Asians have been relocating to suburbs like Bellevue and Redmond east of Lake Washington. All these groups tend to vote heavily Democratic. Pierce County was long a blue-collar Democratic bastion, and that remains true in Tacoma, though it's less so elsewhere in the county. Snohomish County leans blue in many races but can be competitive.

Two other regions account for the remainder of the statewide vote. One is eastern Washington beyond the Cascade Range; this region votes consistently Republican, often sharply at odds with the population-heavy Puget Sound region. Some in the region have urged splitting the state so the eastern half joins with Idaho or rural eastern Oregon, where voters share a cultural conservatism. The third area that casts the remainder of the state's votes is west of the Cascades but outside King, Snohomish and Pierce. A notable portion of this region is Clark County, a fast-growing area adjoining Portland. (Washington has no income tax and Oregon no sales tax, so you can avoid lots of taxes by living in Clark County and shopping across the line.)

Joe Biden expanded the Democrats' already impressive winning margin in Washington from 16 points in 2016 to 19 in 2020, due in part to a shrinkage of the third-party and write-in vote from 11 percent to 3 percent. King, Snohomish, and Pierce counties accounted for about 60 percent of Biden's vote, slightly down from Clinton's 62 percent in 2016 but higher than the 55 percent for President Barack Obama in 2012. Biden held all of Clinton's counties and was able to flip Clallam (Port Angeles). Strikingly, in each of the state's 10 most populous counties, the 2020 margin shifted toward Democrats by a consistent four to seven points, even in the eastern counties won by Trump —Spokane, Yakima, and Benton (Kennewick). While Democrats in Metro Seattle will continue to face friction on their left, the state party as a whole is in no danger of collapsing anytime soon.

Population		Race and Ethnicity		Income	
Total	7,614,893	White	74.20%	Median Income	78,687
Land area (sq. miles)	66,456	Black	4.00%	State Income Rank	7 out of 50
Pop/ sq mi	114.59	Latino	13.00%	Poverty Rate	9.80%
Born in state	46.40%	Asian	11.60%	With health insurance	93.40%
		Two or more races	6.00%	Cash public assistance	2.50%
Age Groups		Other	6.90%	Food stamp/SNAP	13.3%
Under 18	21.80%				
18-34	24.00%	Education		Work	
35-64	38.40%	H.S grad or less	30.40%	White Collar	43.30%
Over 64	15.90%	Some college	32.70%	Sales and Service	35.40%
		College Degree, 4 yr	22.80%	Blue Collar	21.30%
Military		Post grad	14.20%	Government	15.50%
Veteran/ Active Duty	9.90%				

Presidential Politics

2020 Primary (D)	Biden (D)	591,403 (38%)	Sanders (D)	570,039 (37%)	Warren (D)	142,652 (9%)
	Bloomberg (D)	122,530 (8%)				
2016 Caucus (D)	Clinton (D)	420,461 (52%)	Sanders (D)	382,293 (48%)		
2020 Pres. Vote	Biden (D)	2,369,612 (58%)	Trump (R)	1,584,651 (39%)		
2016 Pres. Vote	Clinton (D)	1,742,718 (53%)	Trump (R)	1,221,747 (37%)	Johnson (L)	160,879 (5%)

For three decades, Washington was one of the most contrarian states in presidential politics, voting for Republican losers Richard Nixon in 1960 and Gerald Ford in 1976 and Democratic losers Hubert Humphrey in 1968 and Michael Dukakis in 1988. But no Republican has won it since Ronald Reagan in 1984, and it has become one of the country's most reliably Democratic states: Barack Obama won it by 58%-40% and 56%-41% in 2008 and 2012, Hillary Clinton won it by 53%-37% in 2016 and Joe Biden won it by 58%-39%, the largest margin in the state for any presidential candidate since President Lyndon Johnson in 1964. The traditional partisan dividing line is the Cascades mountain range. West to the Pacific is Democratic territory. East to the Idaho border is Republican turf. Anchoring the Democratic terrain is King County, which accounts for more than a quarter of the state's vote. King once had plenty of Seattle suburbs that backed moderate Republicans. But as the GOP adopted more conservative stands on social issues and Seattle became a high-tech haven that attracted younger voters, the county became a Democratic bastion. It voted for Biden over President Donald Trump, 75%-22%. Biden won 11 of the 12 counties along the Puget Sound, including Pierce and Snohomish counties in suburban Seattle, the state's next-largest counties after King. All the counties east of the Cascades backed Trump except for Whitman, home to Washington State.

Washington's 2016 caucuses were held on March 26, and Vermont Sen. Bernie Sanders walloped Clinton 73%-27%. He carried every county in the state, and the caucuses gave him a larger delegate boost than any other caucus or primary. Republicans held a May primary, after all of Trump's GOP rivals had withdrawn from the race, and he garnered 76 percent of the vote. In March 2020, the state switched to an all-mail presidential primary. It turned out to be a pivotal week both in the Democratic primary and in the country: It marked the turning point when the coronavirus began shutting down the country, and the week Biden locked down the nomination. He beat Sanders in a close race, 40%-37%, one of the five states he won that day to just one for Sanders (though Washington's took six days to call).

Congressional Districts

117th Congress Lineup	7D 3R	116th Congress Lineup	7D 3R

In 1983, voters approved a constitutional amendment that created a bipartisan redistricting commission, made up of two Democrats and two Republicans appointed by legislative leaders. If the commission deadlocks, the issue goes to the Supreme Court; lines also can be changed by a two-thirds vote in both houses of the legislature. The Washington plan originally was lauded for encouraging cooperation and creating more districts that both parties can win. But unlike Iowa or California, where commissions are not supposed to take political considerations into account, the result in Washington has become incumbent protection.

Washington gained a House seat in the reapportionment following the 2010 census. In 2011, Democrats held a 5-4 lead in House seats, and 56 percent of the state's growth between 2000 and 2010 had taken place in the four Republican-held districts. The two Republican commissioners proposed placing a new "fair fight" 10th District in the state's highly competitive northwest and North Puget Sound. The two Democrats countered with proposals putting the new 10th District in the more reliably Democratic South Puget Sound area around Olympia. Three days before their New Year's Eve deadline, the commissioners forged a compromise. The new 10th District went to the South Sound and was a perfect fit for Democrat Denny Heck, who had lost to Republican Rep. Jaime Herrera Beutler in 2010. In exchange, Democrats strengthened two incumbent Republicans, and stretched the suburban Seattle 1st District all the way north to the Canadian border to make it marginally more competitive. Democrats have easily controlled the 1st and the 10th since then. When Republicans lost the incumbency advantage after Rep. Dave Reichert retired in 2018, Democrats took the 8th in the eastern Seattle-Tacoma suburbs.

That left Democrats with all seven districts that surround Seattle and Puget Sound. Republicans continued to hold the three seats in the hinterlands. Based on recent election results and population shifts, Democrats likely will seek to reinforce the 8th in their favor. Absent an improved performance in the suburbs, Republicans will be hard-pressed to take back that seat. Their greater concern might be incumbent protection in their three remaining districts, especially Herrera Beutler's Vancouver-based 3rd District. Switching some counties east of the Cascades from the 8th in exchange for some Democratic precincts in the exurbs might accommodate both parties.

Jay Inslee (D)

Elected 2012, term expires 2025, 3rd term; b. Feb. 9, 1951, Seattle; Stanford U., 1969-70, U. of WA, B.A. 1973; Willamette U., J.D. 1976; Protestant; Married (Trudi); 3 children.

Elected Office: WA House, 1988-1992; U.S. House, 1993-1995, 1999-2012.

Professional Career: City prosecutor, Selah, WA, 1976-1984; Practicing attorney, 1976-1992, 1995-1996; Regional Director, U.S. Department of Health and Human Services, 1997-1998.

Office: PO Box 40002 Olympia, 98404-0002; 360-902-4111; Fax: 360-753-4110
Lt. Gov.: Denny Heck (D) **Atty. Gen:** Bob Ferguson (D) **Sec. of State:** Kim Wyman (R)
State Legislature: Senate: 28D, 20R, 1V **House:** 57D, 41R

Election Results

Election	Name (Party)	Vote (%)
2016 General	Jay Inslee (D)...	1,760,520 (54%)
	Bill Bryant (R)...	1,476,346 (45%)
2020 General	Jay Inslee (D)...	2,294,243 (57%)
	Loren Culp (R)...	1,749,066 (43%)
2016 Primary	Jay Inslee (D)...	687,412 (49%)
	Patrick O Rourke (R)...	40,572　(3%)

Prior winning percentage: 2012 (52%); House: 2010 (58%), 2008 (68%), 2006 (68%), 2004 (62%), 2002 (60%), 2000 (55%), 1998 (50%), 1992 (51%)

Democrat Jay Inslee was easily elected to his third term as governor of Washington in 2020, the year after he ran, unsuccessfully, as the Democratic presidential hopeful most focused on tackling climate change.

Inslee grew up in north Seattle; his mother worked at Sears-Roebuck and his father was a high school coach who later became athletic director for the Seattle Public Schools. Inslee graduated from the University of Washington and Willamette University College of Law. He moved to Selah, in Yakima County east of the Cascades, to practice law. In 1988, at age 37, he was elected to the state House over a former Yakima mayor. In 1992, when 4th District Rep. Sid Morrison ran for governor, Inslee won the election to succeed him, 51%-49%, over Republican Doc Hastings. In the House, Inslee voted for President Bill Clinton's tax increase and for a crime bill that banned some types of semi-automatic weapons; these votes came back to haunt him in the 1994 Republican wave election, as Hastings challenged him and won, 53%-47%. After his defeat, Inslee moved across the state to Bainbridge Island and practiced law in Seattle. In 1996, he ran for governor and finished fifth in the all-party primary, with 10 percent of the vote. He briefly served as regional director of the U.S. Health and Human Services Department.

In 1998, Inslee decided to run for Congress again, this time in the 1st District against Republican Rep. Rick White, an economic conservative with liberal votes on some cultural issues. In the September all-party primary, White led 50%-44%. But by November, two issues changed the balance. Inslee ran ads claiming that White intended to spend 10 years in the House and then become a lobbyist, a charge his ex-wife had made in divorce papers. He also ran ads highlighting White's vote to impeach Clinton. White's vote share was hurt by a third-party Christian conservative, Bruce Craswell. The primary numbers were reversed in November, and Inslee won 50%-44%.

In Congress, Inslee was a moderate-to-liberal Democrat. He joined in protecting the privacy of consumer financial records—an issue important to Microsoft, his largest single source of campaign funds as a congressman. When security experts reported in 2011 that Apple's iPhone could secretly track its users' movements, Inslee called for greater government oversight of data collection. On the Energy and Commerce Committee, Inslee focused on conservation and increasing renewable energy sources. As early as 2005, he introduced bills to address global warming and reduce U.S. dependence on foreign oil. When Republicans regained control of the House, Inslee criticized what he called the GOP's "allergy to science," and toted a stack of more than 20 books to a March 2011 hearing, claiming they contained irrefutable evidence of the problem. He co-wrote a book of his own, "Apollo's Fire," on green energy, though not all the companies he wrote about proved to be successful.

By the time two-term Democratic Gov. Christine Gregoire decided to retire in 2012, Inslee had already laid the groundwork for a bid. Nine months after launching his candidacy, he decided in March 2012 to resign his House seat to campaign full-time. Inslee's stature cleared the Democratic contenders, and he finished first in the state's top-two primary in August with 47 percent of the vote. That set up a general-election matchup against Republican Rob McKenna, the state's attorney general, who had taken 43 percent in the primary. Republicans accused Inslee of notching no significant legislative accomplishments or attaining a leadership position.

Even though a Republican hadn't won a gubernatorial race in the state since 1980, the GOP liked McKenna's chances. McKenna campaigned as a business-friendly moderate, playing up his pro-environment views and saying he would work with unions if elected. He said he personally opposed abortion, but that ultimately it was up to the woman to decide. President Barack Obama's strong reelection showing in the state helped put Inslee over the top, 52%-48%.

During his first term, Inslee proposed a cap-and-trade program aimed at reducing greenhouse gases in stages. He also urged phasing out coal-derived electricity, reducing vehicular emissions, increased spending on alternative energy and curbing emissions by state government. But the cap-and-trade plan faced resistance, including from some Democrats, and even modified versions of the proposal fell by the wayside. Meanwhile, Inslee supported the "Connecting Washington" program, which allocated billions of dollars for expanding and replacing state highways, paid for by gasoline and car taxes. He also worked with the legislature to raise salaries for school employees and cut college tuition.

The 2016 election pitted Inslee against Republican Bill Bryant, a former Port of Seattle commissioner. In the August primary, Inslee took first place with 49 percent and Bryant took second with 38 percent. In the general election, Bryant attacked Inslee's oversight of the state's biggest psychiatric facility and the corrections system. Inslee touted the state's economic health and reductions in tuition at state colleges and universities; he was also a leading supporter of a ballot measure that would raise the minimum wage in steps to $13.50 an hour. Inslee beat Bryant by nine points; Democrats kept their House majority, but the GOP held its majority in the state Senate. Voters approved the minimum-wage ballot measure but rejected one that would have imposed the nation's first carbon tax, abetted by dissatisfied environmentalists who wanted the money to be earmarked for renewable energy subsidies and other pet projects.

The $43.7 billion two-year budget Inslee signed in 2017 raised state property taxes by $1.6 billion to fund education, while also expanding online sales taxes and raising taxes on bottled water and extracted fuels. He also signed a bipartisan measure to guarantee paid family leave. Meanwhile, Inslee became a leading national Democratic voice against the immigration policies of President Donald Trump. In 2017, the state, led by Attorney General Bob Ferguson, became an important litigant against Trump's travel ban. Inslee received rhetorical backing from the state's influential tech sector, which relied on a well-functioning immigration system to hire workers from overseas. Inslee signed an executive order limiting state cooperation on federal immigration enforcement, and he called the administration "morally bankrupt" and the White House "a den of deceit." When Trump made increasingly protectionist moves on trade, Inslee, the governor of an export-dependent state, spoke out.

In 2018, Inslee spearheaded the nation's first effort to pass a law requiring so-called net neutrality. He signed one bill to ban "bump stocks," which make semi-automatic weapons more deadly, and signed another to ban "conversion therapy" for LGBT youth. He also signed a measure to guarantee that health insurers in the state cover abortions and contraception if they also cover maternity care. The same year, the state Supreme Court validated Inslee's earlier death penalty moratorium, abolishing the practice and commuting the sentences of existing death row inmates to life in prison.

In March 2019, Inslee launched a presidential bid, with climate change the centerpiece. He proposed spending $3 trillion on green energy, saying it would create 8 million new jobs; he also said that by 2030, all electric plants should be carbon-neutral and all cars should be electric. "When I thought about what I was going to do with the rest of my life, I wanted to be able on my deathbed to look my three grandchildren in the eye and say that I did everything within my power to give them a healthy life and a no degraded place to live," he said in New Hampshire. The Democratic National Committee rebuffed Inslee's idea for an all-climate candidate debate, however, and his candidacy never gained traction. He exited the race in August 2019, shifting to a campaign for a third term as governor. Inslee was credited, however, with raising the profile of climate change during the primary and helping nudge the eventual nominee, Joe Biden, toward a more aggressive climate agenda.

Back in Olympia, Inslee found more success in 2019. Aided by a Democratic-controlled legislature, he signed a bill to end power generated by fossil fuels by 2045 (and coal by 2025); enshrine energy efficiency standards for buildings and appliances; and phase out hydro fluorocarbons. He also enacted the nation's first "public option" health care law, in which the state offers health insurance as an option while leaving private coverage in place. To get it passed, however, sponsors had to provide more generous reimbursement caps for health care providers, which reduced the amount of projected savings in health care spending. Meanwhile, Inslee signed a measure to repeal the state's 20-year-old ban on affirmative action, and he was able to provide funding bumps for higher education and the mental health system.

As Inslee headed into his reelection year of 2020, the state's challenges swelled. The first known coronavirus case was discovered in suburban Seattle in January, with a patient who had traveled from Wuhan, China. Then in late February came an outbreak at a Washington nursing home. Much of Seattle went into lockdown even before Inslee officially issued a stay-at-home order. In June, Inslee issued a statewide mask order. Compared to most states, Washington saw a significantly lower peak caseload, and by April 2021 it ranked in the bottom third of states for cases per capita. Meanwhile, Inslee had to grapple with violent unrest in Seattle after the death of George Floyd and with wildfires that scorched hundreds of thousands of acres across the state.

In the 2020 gubernatorial election, some three dozen candidates ran in the August primary. The Republican candidates included Tim Eyman, a well-known sponsor of anti-tax ballot initiatives; Joshua Freed, a businessman and ex-mayor of Bothell; and Loren Culp, a pro-gun rights, small-town police chief from eastern Washington. Inslee finished first with 50.1 percent, followed by Culp with 17.4 percent. The general election was never considered competitive, with Culp's conservative positions non-starters in the state's politically dominant Seattle area. (No nominee from eastern Washington has won the governorship since 1932.) In the end, Inslee won by 14 points—five points better than his victory in 2016—and he roughly tracked Biden's performance in and around Seattle. Inslee flipped three counties he'd lost four years earlier: Skagit (north of the Seattle suburbs); Whitman (in the far northeastern part of the state); and Clark (Vancouver, adjoining Portland Oregon). But he failed to capture Clallam County (Port Angeles), which Biden managed to win narrowly on the same ballot.

Patty Murray (D)

Elected 1992, term expires 2022, 5th term, b. Oct 11, 1950; Bothell, WA; WA State University, B.A., 1972; Roman Catholic; Married (Robert Randall Murray); 2 children.

Elected Office: Shoreline School Board, 1985-1989, President, 1985-1986; WA Senate, 1988-1992.

Professional Career: Instructor, Shoreline Community College, 1984-1987.

DC Office: 154 RSOB 20510, 202-224-2621, Fax: 202-224-0238, murray.senate.gov

State Offices: Everett, 425-259-6515; Seattle, 206-553-5545; Spokane, 509-624-9515; Tacoma, 253-572-3636; Vancouver, 360-696-7797; Yakima, 509-453-7462.

Committees: Senate Assistant Majority Leader. *Appropriations*: Department of Defense; Department of Homeland Security; DOL, HHS & Education & Related Agencies (Chmn); Energy & Water Development; Military Construction & Veteran Affairs & Related Agencies; Transportation, HUD & Related Agencies. *Budget*. *Health, Education, Labor & Pensions (Chmn)*: Ex Officio membership on all subcommittees. *Veterans' Affairs*.

Group Ratings

	ADA	ACLU	AFL-CIO	LCV	COC	HAFA	ACU	CFG	FRC
2020	-	73%	-	92%	-	0%	3%	-	-
2019	90%	C	100%	93%	48%	C	3%	0%	0%

Almanac Ratings 2019-2020

	Economy	Social	Foreign	Composite
Liberal	100%	100%	82%	94%
Conservative	0%	0%	18%	6%

Key Votes of the 116th Congress

1. EPA clean energy rules	Y	5. Russia sanctions	Y	9. Barr as Atty. General	N
2. U.S./Mex./Can. trade deal	Y	6. Troops in SYR, AFG	Y	10. Spending at the border	Y
3. Cut unemployment benefits	N	7. Veto arms sales to Saudis	Y	11. Coney Barrett to Sup. Ct.	N
4. Shelton to Fed Reserve	N	8. Defense $$$, veto override	Y	12. Electoral College objections	N

Election Results

Election	Name (Party)	Vote (%)		Cand. Spent	Ind. Exp. Support	Ind. Exp. Oppose
2016 General	Patty Murray (D)................................ 1,913,979	(59%)	$5,676,043	$33,423	
	Chris Vance (R)................................. 1,329,338	(41%)	$441,718		
2016 Primary	Patty Murray (D)................................. 745,421	(54%)			
	Chris Vance (R)................................... 381,004	(28%)			

Prior winning percentages: 2016 (59%), 2010 (52%), 2004 (55%), 1998 (58%), 1992 (54%)

Patty Murray is the senior senator from Washington, first elected in 1992. She has come a long way from her entry into politics as a parent-activist. Even as Murray maintains a low-key, plainspoken style, she has become a powerful, senior backroom player, with a seat at her party's leadership table. She plays a key role in advancing Democrats' positions, especially on health care and education—a lofty status she partly ascribes to her preschool teacher training. "You don't walk into a class with 4-year-olds without a direction of where you're going to go," she told Huff Post. Murray is preparing to seek her sixth term in 2022, with little serious challenge so far. A win would place her in the amongst the longest-serving senators.

Her more daunting challenge has become managing the myriad issues facing the Senate HELP Committee, which she chairs. In addition to Murray's long-standing interests in expanding the Affordable Care Act and making quality education more widely available, especially at the college level, many of the diverse ambitions of President Joe Biden have been sent to her committee. They include expanded childcare, job training and a minimum-wage increase. At the Appropriations Committee, she has kept busy with a similar range of issues and she tends to the diverse needs of her home state.

Murray grew up in the Seattle suburb of Bothell, one of seven children of a disabled World War II veteran. She graduated from Washington State University in 1972, married, and stayed home to raise her children. In 1980, she was in Olympia trying to save a parenting class she was teaching at Shoreline Community College, which was the target of budget cuts. A state legislator told her: "You're just a mom in tennis shoes. You can't make a difference." She later said, "Almost every woman I've ever met in politics got into it because she was mad about something." She won her fight over the parenting class and then ran for the Shoreline School Board. She eventually was chosen board president. In 1988, she challenged a Republican state senator, knocked on 17,000 doors and won the seat. While there, she worked on issues that resonated with voters, from school bus safety to extending a family leave bill for a parent whose child is ill or dying. In late 1991, Murray decided to run against Sen. Brock Adams, a Democrat who was under a cloud following charges of sexual molestation. He decided not to seek reelection.

Amid a crowd of better-known, conventional male politicians, Murray, with her flat, Midwestern-style accent and "mom in tennis shoes" line, attracted most of the campaign attention. In the 1992 all-party primary, her main Democratic opponent was former Rep. Don Bonker, who had narrowly lost a Senate nomination in 1988. Murray won 28 percent of the vote to Bonker's 19 percent. She sprinted to a big lead in polls against Republican Rep. Rod Chandler, who had served for a decade. She won 54% to 46% in November in what came to be called "the year of the woman."

With a largely liberal voting record, Murray is a skillful lawmaker. She is known for being attuned to the needs of Senate conservatives, being adept at ingratiating herself with veteran colleagues and recognizing and exploiting the possibility of a deal even in a partisan environment. "She's a pretty good arbiter and proxy for the caucus as a whole," Rich Tarplin, a lobbyist close to Senate Democrats, told National Journal. Murray generally leaves the spotlight for others but does not shy from asserting senatorial prerogatives. In what she calls her "angry mom" voice, she has rebuked Republican and Democratic secretaries of the Department of Veterans Affairs for proposals that would make veterans pay more for health care.

Murray became chairwoman of the Budget Committee in 2013. To counter the budget proposal offered by her House counterpart, Wisconsin Republican Paul Ryan, she unveiled a spending plan that was the first from her party since 2009. It included about $1 trillion in new revenues over 10 years, mostly from closing tax loopholes and incentives, and had about $1 trillion in spending cuts. Unlike Ryan's budget, which some House GOP moderates found draconian, her plan was geared toward getting broad Democratic support. It included $100 billion for a new "economic recovery protection plan" that would fund infrastructure projects and education programs. But in a surprise, it would have cut more than twice as much from the biggest health entitlement, Medicare, than Ryan's would have. Though Republicans vilified her proposal as unworkable, they said Murray was easy to work with. "You've allowed us to have free ability to speak out; you've been respectful," Republican Jeff Sessions of Alabama, the ranking Republican on the panel, told her at a hearing.

Murray forged a working relationship with Ryan through her combination of affability and a can-do, pragmatic style. Their partnership enabled them in December 2013 to strike a two-year budget deal that called for raising new revenue through fee increases without tax increases or changes to Social Security or Medicare. It replaced steep across-the-board spending cuts under the looming "sequester" in January with targeted spending cuts. Democrats groused about the deal, which didn't add much money for party priorities such as infrastructure spending, and it failed to close any of the tax loopholes they had targeted. But it easily passed both chambers and became law. Each chairman scored a personal achievement.

Being Budget chairwoman was Murray's second time being a leader on the issue. After the protracted standoff over raising the federal debt limit in 2011, she and Texas Republican Rep. Jeb Hensarling were named as co-chiefs of the Joint Select Committee on Deficit Reduction, the "super committee" charged with finding a bipartisan consensus on future spending in just a few months. To nearly no one's surprise, the effort was fruitless. In this case, she had less maneuverability. "The one thing the Republicans wouldn't put on the table was revenue," Murray told The Seattle Times. "I knew what a bad deal would mean for the middle class in this country. Many of us are where we are in our lives because we had a country that was there for us."

As a junior member on the Appropriations Committee, Murray made a point to get along with senior senators. After Alaska's Ted Stevens, the former GOP chairman, lost his bid for reelection in 2008, he gave Murray the desk that once belonged to Washington Democrat Warren Magnuson, who served in the Senate for nearly 40 years. When West Virginia Democrat Robert Byrd was too ill in 2007 and 2008 to manage spending bills on the floor as chairman, he gave Murray the task ahead of more senior senators. Now, only Patrick Leahy of Vermont and Dianne Feinstein of California have more years as Democrats in the Senate than Murray; those two senators also are senior to her on Appropriations. Murray has delivered for her state and then some: The Washington watchdog group Taxpayers for Common Sense dubbed her the "Queen of Pork." Despite a subsequent ban on earmarking, Murray worked to include funding for a variety of Washington projects in spending bills, including money for a Seattle light-rail system, a bridge over the Columbia River and removal of dams along the Snake River to restore salmon runs. The earmark ban was lifted in early 2021.

In 2015, Murray became the ranking Democrat at the HELP Committee. She worked with Tennessee Republican Lamar Alexander, the chairman of the committee, on a measure to overhaul No Child Left Behind, a bipartisan legacy of President George W. Bush. She dissuaded Alexander from writing his own bill and then seeking some moderate Democrats' support and, instead, he agreed to develop a bipartisan proposal from the start. No Child Left Behind had become unpopular because of its heavy reliance on standardized testing.

Though efforts to change the law had failed for several years, Alexander and Murray crafted a proposal that gave states and school districts more control of academic standards and teacher and school performance. In 2015, the Senate passed it 81-17.

That collaboration on the HELP Committee ended with the election of President Donald Trump. The confirmation of Betsy DeVos as Education secretary was a contentious affair. Murray complained that DeVos had not sufficiently disclosed her complex personal finances or answered questions from Democrats, who were unhappy with Alexander's rush to confirm DeVos. Murray made stopping sexual harassment a central part of her agenda during the Trump administration. The two women clashed over a range of issues but tensions boiled over in 2018 when Murray went after DeVos on Twitter over proposed changes to the department's guidelines to universities on how to handle sexual assault and sexual misconduct. DeVos called Murray's action "unbecoming and irresponsible."

With Republicans in complete control of Congress and the White House, Murray had less leverage to push her objectives, like lowering tuition costs and increasing access to education for those with low incomes. Plus, Murray had little interest in House Republicans' proposal, which changed and cut back on student-aid programs. Alexander and Murray also ran into broader partisan problems in 2018 when they again failed to find common ground on incremental changes to the Affordable Care Act. Their discussions included ideas like giving states more flexibility in setting up their own programs in exchange for Democrats' goal of providing billions of dollars more to support the states. They found themselves hamstrung by peripheral issues, especially the Republican insistence to prohibit funding of abortion in the Obama care marketplaces. "I greatly respect the senator from Washington and enjoy working with her, but on this issue, I think we've reached an impasse," Alexander told the Senate in 2018.

Earlier, Murray worked with Republican Sen. John Cornyn of Texas to end a stalemate over a noncontroversial measure to combat human trafficking that became ensnared in the always-combustible abortion debate. Democrats objected to what they saw as an anti-abortion provision in the legislation that would have prevented money from the victims fund from being used for abortions in keeping with the Hyde Amendment's prohibition on taxpayer money being used for abortion services. Murray and Cornyn found a creative compromise: They clarified that money from the fines would go to non-health care concerns, which would not be subject to the Hyde prohibition, and that federal funds, which are subject to the prohibition, would cover health care.

In 2020, Murray grew outspoken about Trump's slow response to the novel coronavirus, which was reported in Seattle before other parts of the nation. In April, the Seattle Times reported, she grew frustrated with the lack of a federal strategy to test and create a public-health response to the crisis. "We need testing to be fast, free and everywhere," she said. Murray called for an investigation of delays and mismanagement by the Trump administration, which she said had undermined the nation's ability to control the spread of COVID-19, the diseased caused by the virus. In July, she called for creation of a $50 billion fund to expand childcare, as an essential step for parents to return to work after months employees being laid off or asked to work from home. She also advocated $345 billion for an education fund, which would be split between K-12 programs and higher education.

Her role flipped in 2021, when Democrats took the White House and, narrowly, the Senate. In April, when Biden sent domestic spending proposals to Congress, Murray hailed the plan as "a framework that shows our country values our students, workers, families and communities most of all and acknowledges the need to not just go back to normal but build back stronger and better from COVID-19." A month earlier, when Biden signed the initial $1.9 trillion economic rescue bill, she said that she was "proud to have partnered" with him in providing badly needed money and services. She also worked with Democratic congressional leaders on legislation to strengthen federal labor laws to protect the rights of workers to organize and collectively bargain for higher pay, enhanced benefits and safer workplaces.

Murray chaired the Appropriations subcommittee overseeing the Labor, HHS and Education departments, which gave her unique influence in Congress over domestic spending programs at both the authorizing and outlay levels. For years, she has worked closely with Democratic Rep. Rosa DeLauro of Connecticut, who chairs the counterpart subcommittee in the House and took over in January 2021 as chair of the full House committee.

Murray first served as the head of the Democratic Senatorial Campaign Committee in 2002. After the Sept. 11 terrorist attacks, it was a tough year for the party, which lost a net two seats. Even so, Murray impressed colleagues with her fundraising. In 2012, Democrats faced a daunting map, and the party was on defense. Several ambitious Democrats passed on the job, but Murray stepped in to lead the committee once again. She picked up two seats. Democrats got some fortunate breaks from Republicans and successful female candidates, such as Massachusetts' Elizabeth Warren, Wisconsin's Tammy Baldwin and North Dakota's Heidi Heitkamp. "Oftentimes, when you're looking at people to run, they rule the women out, saying, 'They can't win,'" Murray told The Oregonian. "I ruled them in."

In her first years on Capitol Hill, Murray was criticized as too staff-reliant. But she has grown into the role of senator. She immersed herself in Washington state issues, becoming one of the Senate's staunchest proponents of normal trade relations with China, a position strongly backed by Boeing, a major employer in Washington state. At the Appropriations Committee, she worked to maximize funding for the ongoing cleanup at the Hanford nuclear reservation. In 2019, she successfully challenged the Trump administration's proposed cuts at the site. "Our government has a moral and legal obligation to clean up Hanford," she said amid a dispute over compensation between the Energy Department and local workers.

Murray's most recent reelection was her easiest: In in 2016, she beat Chris Vance, a former chairman of the Washington Republican Party, which failed to recruit a more formidable challenger, 59%-41. In earlier campaigns, Murray had won reelection three times by steadily diminishing margins. In 1998, she was challenged by Rep. Linda Smith, a strong opponent of abortion and free trade deals. Murray raised far more money than Smith and won 58%-42%. In 2004, she faced Republican George Nethercutt, another House member, who in 1994 earned a reputation as a giant killer for defeating Democratic House Speaker Tom Foley. The mom in tennis shoes had become a hardball fundraiser. An aide put out the word to lobbyists that the senator would regard contributions to Nethercutt as hostile, even if contributors gave to her too. Murray raised $11.5 million, compared with Nethercutt's $7.7 million. Murray won 55%-43%. In 2010, Republicans landed a top-tier recruit in former state Sen. Dino Rossi, a fiscal conservative who had twice run impressive but losing campaigns against Democratic Gov. Christine Gregoire. He criticized Murray's involvement in shaping the Democratic agenda. But Murray did not back down from her record and said Rossi would bankrupt the nation by giving tax breaks to the wealthy. In a strongly Republican year, she won 52%-48%.

When Senate Democratic Leader Harry Reid announced in 2015 that he would not seek reelection, Murray did not rule out a move to climb up the Democratic leadership ladder. Though she endorsed New York Sen. Chuck Schumer to succeed Reid in the top post, she declined to back Sen. Dick Durbin of Illinois to retain his position as Democratic whip. After the Democratic setbacks in the 2016 election, she decided not to challenge Durbin, who said that he had a majority of the votes. Schumer gave her more responsibilities and the title assistant Democratic leader. As the relentless Murray has shown in playing the long game, it's a good bet that she will have additional opportunities.

Maria Cantwell (D)

Elected 2000, term expires 2024, 4th term, b. Oct 13, 1958; Indianapolis, IN; Miami University of Ohio, B.A., 1980; Roman Catholic; Single.

Elected Office: WA House, 1987-1993; U.S. House, 1993-1995.

Professional Career: Owner, public relations firm, 1985-1991; Senior VP, technology company, 1995-2000.

DC Office: 511 HSOB 20510, 202-224-3441, Fax: 202-228-0514, cantwell.senate.gov

State Offices: Everett, 425-303-0114; Richland, 509-946-8106; Seattle, 206-220-6400; Spokane, 509-353-2507; Tacoma, 253-572-2281; Vancouver, 360-696-7838.

Committees: *Commerce, Science & Transportation (Chmn)*: Ex Officio membership on all subcommittees. *Energy & Natural Resources. Finance. Indian Affairs. Joint Taxation. Small Business & Entrepreneurship.*

Group Ratings

	ADA	ACLU	AFL-CIO	LCV	COC	HAFA	ACU	CFG	FRC
2020	-	77%	-	92%	-	0%	8%	-	-
2019	95%	C	100%	100%	64%	C	8%	0%	0%

Almanac Ratings 2019-2020

	Economy	Social	Foreign	Composite
Liberal	100%	100%	77%	92%
Conservative	0%	0%	23%	8%

Key Votes of the 116th Congress

1. EPA clean energy rules	Y	5. Russia sanctions	Y	9. Barr as Atty. General	N
2. U.S./Mex./Can. trade deal	Y	6. Troops in SYR, AFG	N/A	10. Spending at the border	Y
3. Cut unemployment benefits	N	7. Veto arms sales to Saudis	Y	11. Coney Barrett to Sup. Ct.	N
4. Shelton to Fed Reserve	N	8. Defense $$$, veto override	Y	12. Electoral College objections	N

Election Results

Election	Name (Party)	Vote (%)		Cand. Spent	Ind. Exp. Support	Ind. Exp. Oppose
2018 General	Maria Cantwell (D)	1,803,364	(41%)	$10,393,463	$32,056	
	Susan Hutchison (R)	1,282,804	(29%)			
2018 Primary	Maria Cantwell (D)	929,961	(55%)			
	Susan Hutchison (R)	413,317	(24%)			

Prior winning percentages: 2018 (58%), 2012 (60%), 2006 (57%), 2000 (49%), House: 1992 (55%)

Democrat Maria Cantwell, Washington's junior senator, was elected in 2000. She has been active on energy, technology and tax matters and is known for her legislative tenacity. After two decades in the Senate, she has entered the most senior ranks, though she remains relatively young. When Democrats regained Senate control in 2021, Cantwell—at 62—became chairman of the Commerce, Science and Transportation Committee, where she could have extended influence over industries that are vital to her home state, including aviation and technology. Although a home-state booster, she has called out some of those companies—including Boeing and Google—when they have harmed the interests of consumers. She has suggested, for example, steps be taken to compel more rigorous safety standards in the certification of new aircraft and to break up the power of big tech companies.

As the ranking member on the Energy and Natural Resources Committee when Republicans controlled the chamber, she developed a close partnership with Republican Chairwoman Lisa Murkowski of Alaska; the two share a Northwestern perspective and views on many issues. In 2017, they split when Murkowski achieved her long-sought goal of opening part of the Arctic National Wildlife Refuge to oil development. But the two senators later collaborated to enact major revisions in conservation programs and use of the national forests.

Cantwell grew up in Indianapolis, where her father worked as a construction worker and served as county commissioner, a city councilman and a state legislator. As a child, Cantwell observed politics firsthand as he advised union members, laborers and politicians who stopped by to talk politics. During her father's stint as an aide to Democratic Rep. Andy Jacobs of Indiana, she awoke one morning to the distinctive Boston accent of Sen. Ted Kennedy downstairs.

Cantwell graduated from Miami University of Ohio, the first in her family to graduate from college. She worked in Ohio for Cincinnati mayor-turned-television personality Jerry Springer's 1982 campaign for governor. Then she worked for California Democratic Sen. Alan Cranston's presidential campaign in 1984, setting up a regional campaign office in Seattle. The Cranston campaign went nowhere, but Cantwell loved the Pacific Northwest and stayed. She moved to Mountlake Terrace, a suburban city in Snohomish County, where she organized a coalition to build a new library. In 1986, she was elected to the Washington state House.

In 1992, Cantwell ran for an open House seat and won 55%-42%, becoming the first Democrat to represent Washington's 1st District in 40 years. In the House, she showed her independence by not supporting President Bill Clinton's health care plan, but she did back the family and medical leave bill, Clinton's economic plan and NAFTA. Cantwell was a strong supporter of abortion rights and protecting the environment. She sounded early alarms about encroachments on digital privacy and persuaded the Clinton administration to drop its support of the "clipper chip," which would have enabled the government to monitor personal electronic communications. Still, she lost her 1994 bid for reelection to Republican Rick White by 4 percentage points, as Republicans rode a nationwide wave and ousted six Democrats from the nine-member Washington delegation.

In the Seattle area in 1995, Cantwell joined a startup firm called Progressive Networks. Five years later, it had become Real Networks, a leader in internet-based audio and visual software. In late 1999, her stock was worth about $40 million, and Cantwell was ready to resume her political career. She challenged Republican Sen. Slade Gorton. Gorton had an increasingly conservative record on environmental and economic issues. Insurance Commissioner Deborah Senn, who also was running, was widely considered too liberal to defeat the incumbent. Cantwell called herself a New Democrat in the Clinton mode and backed permanent normal trade relations with China—a move that Senn opposed. But the real difference was money. Cantwell spent freely, while Senn was on television only during the two weeks before the September all-party primary. In the first round, Gorton got the most votes, capturing 44 percent. Cantwell got 37 percent, and Senn received 13 percent.

Cantwell said she would spend "whatever it takes" to win. At the same time, she refused to take contributions from political action committees or large donations known as "soft money" from the Democratic Party; the party had already pumped $640,000 into the state before Cantwell won the primary. She charged that Gorton was beholden to special-interest contributors, singling out his late-night Senate amendment that paved the way for a cyanide leach gold mine in rural Okanogan County, which environmentalists were fighting. She talked about her work in tech and compared her experience with his, saying: "I've just spent the last five years in the private sector learning how to do things on the outside. Sen. Gorton's been in office for 41 years. He seems to like government a lot." Gorton described Cantwell as an old-style liberal Democrat who would have government meddling in health care, education and the environment. Overall, she spent $11.5 million—$10.3 million of it her own money—to Gorton's $6.4 million. Gorton was hurt when American Indian tribes, some flush with casino cash, said that he did not respect their sovereignty when he sought to bind them to the same laws as other people. Cantwell won by 2,229 votes out of 2.4 million cast. She carried only five counties: King, Snohomish, Thurston, and two small counties in the west.

Cantwell's voting record has been consistently liberal on social issues but moderate on economic and foreign policy matters. She was one of just nine Senate Democrats to oppose creating the Troubled Asset Relief Program for ailing financial institutions in 2008, saying the government had no business getting so deeply involved with the private sector.

To help her state's hydropower industry, which produces almost three-fourths of Washington's electricity, Cantwell has been active in efforts to remove barriers to licensing new facilities. In 2010, when the Obama administration and Democrats in Congress pushed unsuccessfully for legislation aimed at curbing greenhouse gases, Cantwell and GOP Sen. Susan Collins of Maine stepped up efforts to push their cap-and-dividend bill that skirted the idea of a carbon trading market. Instead, their bill would have capped emissions from sources such as coal mines and oil refineries, and those emitters would have been required to purchase carbon permits. The Senate failed to take action on the bill.

In 2014, after a shuffling of Senate Democratic chairmanships, Cantwell nabbed the gavel on the Small Business Committee. She worked with Jim Risch of Idaho, the panel's ranking Republican, on a measure to renew the State Trade and Export Promotion program, which awards grants to states to help small businesses begin or expand exports of their products. She held separate hearings on helping veterans and women grow small businesses. Working with Murkowski, Cantwell put together a bill on multiple energy topics that won bipartisan approval in committee and overwhelmingly passed the Senate in 2016. "It's a positive test for the Congress being able to legislate across the bitter partisan divide, and frankly Chairman Murkowski and Sen. Cantwell deserve considerable credit," former Democratic Rep. Philip Sharp of Indiana, who worked on energy issues for decades, told The Washington Post. The Senate bill addressed such issues as enhancement of the electrical grid, energy efficiency in buildings and exports of natural gas. Negotiators failed to resolve differences with the House, which had passed a measure that focused more on resource production. "It is really irresponsible for our House colleagues to drop the ball," Cantwell said. She and Murkowski also collaborated on a proposal to increase the fleet of icebreakers for the Coast Guard, which has an active presence in their home states.

In 2017, President Donald Trump's nomination of former Texas Gov. Rick Perry to be Energy secretary halted bipartisanship on the Energy committee. Perry, who had called for abolishing the department as a presidential candidate in 2011, was "not the direction that the Energy Department needs to go," Cantwell said. When the Trump administration teamed with Murkowski to add Arctic oil drilling to the Republicans' sweeping 2017 tax bill, Cantwell sought to block the parliamentary maneuver but was defeated on a nearly party-line vote.

Months later, Cantwell and Murkowski resumed their collaboration, working on a sweeping public lands bill that combined more than 100 measures that had been introduced in the Senate. She called it "the biggest public lands package in more than a decade." It included a prohibition of new mining activities on federal land in Washington's Methow Valley and a multibillion-dollar plan for more efficient water use in the Yakima basin. The package was enacted soon after the Senate passed it—on a 92-8 vote—in February 2019.

In June 2020, the two senators spearheaded a landmark conservation measure, which included steps to address maintenance needs at national parks and to guarantee full funding for the Land and Water Conservation Fund. Some Senate Republicans seeking to score political points changed the name of the bill to the Great American Outdoors Act. Cantwell pointed out that the fund was supported by off-shore oil and gas royalties and that the outcome was "a big win for the American people." She cited "the economic value of land and open space." The Seattle Post-Intelligencer said Cantwell's success on the bill showed she was "a policy wonk for Washington's great outdoors." Separately from Murkowski, Cantwell has taken the lead in the Senate in proposing legislation to prevent logging in national forests. The measure has stirred heated opposition in Alaska, where Tongass National Forest is a prime target for logging.

Cantwell gave up her ranking post on the Energy committee in 2019 to lead Democrats on the Commerce panel. Her priorities have included expanding the Coast Guard's Arctic fleet and improving cyber security for the nation's electrical grid. Cantwell was the point person on the ambitious Next Gen air traffic control modernization effort, which was part of the Federal Aviation Administration reauthorization bill that became law in 2012.

On the committee, she has kept a close eye on Boeing and the rest of her state's aerospace businesses. That grew more complicated after two Boeing 737-Max passenger planes crashed overseas in 2018 and 2019. After the second crash, she criticized the federal certification of new planes as "a system that is in clear need of improvement." Although she had helped to enact legislation years earlier that gave Boeing more autonomy in review of "low and medium risk" operational problems, Cantwell said in January 2020 that there were "shortcomings" that needed to be corrected in the FAA's delegation to industry of parts of the certification process.

In September 2020, she teamed with Sen. Roger Wicker of Mississippi, the senior Republican on the Commerce panel, in filing a proposal that more clearly defined the authority of the FAA. "Congress needs to make sure aviation safety in the United States is the strongest in the world," with the FAA "in the driver's seat," Cantwell said.

Cantwell issued a report in September 2020 that lambasted tech giants—especially Google and Facebook—for "unfair, deceptive and abusive practices" that have severely damaged news organizations across the nation. "There is a clear need for Congress to address the market failures created by the search and social-media platforms," said her report, which called for the tech giants —which have outpaced aerospace in job creation and economic impact in the Seattle area—to make regular payments to local news outlets. But she objected to the "chilling" attempts by Republicans to launch these attacks with subpoenas days before the 2020 elections.

In April 2021, Cantwell chaired a hearing of the Commerce committee to highlight her proposal for the tech giants to make payments to local news organizations. She has cited the legacy of Democratic Sen. Warren Magnuson of Washington, who chaired the committee for 22 years and left a long legacy of consumer-protection legislation.

Cantwell has a coveted seat on the Finance Committee. She secured passage of a 2008 measure to temporarily extend the deductibility of state sales taxes, a popular tax break in Washington because the state doesn't have a personal income tax. She objected when Republicans' eliminated that provision in their 2017 tax overhaul. The result, she said, was to "gouge middle-class taxpayers in King County and make them pay $1,000 more [to] open the Arctic Wildlife Refuge."

In 2015, Cantwell took the lead in seeking to extend the life of the U.S. Export-Import Bank —another priority for Boeing. The bank, which finances U.S. exports abroad, became the center of a fierce political debate. Tea party conservatives argued that it is a prime example of corporate cronyism and welfare to companies that don't need it. Defenders, like Cantwell, saw it as vital to U.S. competitiveness. With her home-state colleague Patty Murray, Cantwell played tough with GOP Sen. Mitch McConnell of Kentucky, then-the majority leader, and won a promise for a floor vote on the bank's renewal; in return, they supported a bill to give President Barack Obama fast-track authority to negotiate new trade deals. That led to a sequence of votes in which Congress agreed to revive the bank, which has aided Boeing's jet sales. The Seattle Times editorial board said Cantwell deserved "credit for helping bring back the Ex-Im Bank." She has continued her advocacy of the Ex-Im Bank.

Although a strong supporter of campaign finance regulation, Cantwell has had some personal problems. To fund her 2000 campaign, she sold $5.6 million of her Real Networks stock and had borrowed $3.8 million from a bank using the company's stock as collateral. That enabled her to run last-minute ads that were essential to her victory. The Federal Election Commission ruled in 2004 that she had violated the law by failing to disclose the terms of the loans, but it took no punitive action. With her earlier net worth of $40 million, paying off the loans should have been easy. But Real Networks saw its stock price plummet from $80 per share in spring 2000 to $6 per share in spring 2001. Suddenly, Cantwell owed far more than the collateral was worth. Over the course of the next several years, she paid off the debt.

Cantwell's narrow victory in 2000 placed her high on Republicans' target list in 2006. National Republicans recruited Mike McGavick, chairman and chief executive officer at Safeco Insurance. McGavick, a moderate who managed Gorton's 1988 campaign and served as his chief of staff, appeared formidable. Cantwell faced lingering discontent from liberals in the party for her 2002 vote in favor of the Iraq War. In a Democratic year in a Democratic-leaning state, she won 57%-40%. In 2012, another good year for Democrats, Cantwell had an easy race against Republican state Sen. Michael Baumgartner. He was from eastern Washington, which hasn't produced a senator since 1934, and was unable to raise the kind of money necessary to compete with Cantwell. She won 60%-40%. In 2018, Cantwell outspent former television news anchor Susan Hutchison, $12 million to $1.9 million, and won 58%-42%.

Suzan DelBene (D)

Elected 2012, 5th term, b. Feb 17, 1962; Selma, AL; Reed College, B.A., 1983; University of WA, M.B.A., 1990; Episcopalian; Married (Kurt Delbene); 2 children.

Professional Career: Director of Marketing, Microsoft, 1989-1998; Vice President., Drugstore.com, 1998-2000; President, CEO, Nimble Tech., 2000-2003; Vice President., Microsoft, 2004-2007; Consultant, Global Partnerships, 2008-2009; Director, WA Department of Revenue, 2010-2012.

DC Office: 2330 RHOB 20515, 202-225-6311, Fax: 202-226-1606, delbene.house.gov

State Offices: Bothell, 425-485-0085; Mount Vernon, 360-416-7879.

Committees: *Ways & Means (VChmn):* Select Revenue Measures; Trade.

Group Ratings

	ADA	ACLU	AFL-CIO	LCV	COC	HAFA	ACU	CFG	FRC
2020	**	83%	**	100%	-	0%	3%	**	-
2019	90%	C	100%	97%	67%	C	4%	12%	0%

Almanac Ratings 2019-2020

	Economy	Social	Foreign	Composite
Liberal	100%	100%	80%	94%
Conservative	0%	0%	20%	6%

Key Votes of the 116th Congress

1. U.S./Mex./Can. trade deal Y	5. Russia sanctions Y	9. Firearms background checks Y
2. First Coronavirus response Y	6. Troops in Syria Y	10. Spending at the border Y
3. HEROES Act Y	7. Veto arms sales to Saudis Y	11. Marijuana liberalized rules Y
4. CASH Act Y	8. Defense $$$, veto override Y	12. Electoral College objections N

Election Results

Election	Name (Party)	Vote (%)	Cand. Spent	Ind. Exp. Support	Ind. Exp. Oppose
2020 General	Suzan DelBene (D)	249,944 (59%)	$1,253,251	$2,484	
	Jeffrey Beeler (R)	176,407 (41%)	$55,015		$113

Prior winning percentages: 2018 (59%), 2016 (55%), 2014 (55%), 2012 (54%)

Democrat Suzan DelBene, a former Microsoft executive who was elected to an open seat in 2012, has become an activist lawmaker who was a leader in the enactment of an expanded child tax credit—an early accomplishment of the Biden administration. She has used her coveted seat on the Ways and Means Committee to work on multiple issues, including economic growth and international trade. With her corporate experience, she became chairwoman in 2021 of the business-oriented New Democrat Coalition. Earlier, she fell short in her bid to chair the Democratic Congressional Campaign Committee, but took on other party assignments.

DelBene was born in Selma Alabama. When she was a toddler, her parents divorced and DelBene lived with her mother, who married an airline pilot. The family moved often. When she was in high school, DelBene's stepfather got a job with Iran Air and her parents relocated overseas. She majored in biology at Reed College, originally hoping to become a veterinarian. Changing her career interests, her first job after college was with a biotechnology firm in Seattle. She got her master's degree in business administration and interned at Microsoft. She landed a full-time job there, where she met and married her husband, Kurt, then-president of Microsoft's Office division. She spent 12 years at Microsoft, rising to the position of corporate vice president of the company's mobile communications business. (Later, Kurt spent about a year with the Obama administration managing the government website for citizen enrollment in the Affordable Care Act. He returned to Microsoft, where he held senior executive positions before announcing his retirement in June 2021.)

DelBene left Microsoft in 1998 and joined two high-tech startups. She later worked on microfinance with an international nonprofit; a job that she said taught her the ways in which policy could create opportunities for families. Inspired to run for Congress, she spent more than $2 million of her own money in a 2010 challenge to Republican Rep. Dave Reichert in the east Seattle suburbs. Her narrow 52%-48% loss in the GOP-leaning district was impressive during a disastrous year for national Democrats. Democratic Gov. Christine Gregoire appointed her director of the state Department of Revenue, where she helped to enact a tax amnesty program that generated $345 million.

That job didn't last long. In 2012, DelBene was one of five Democrats running in the newly drawn 1st District that was vacated by now-Gov. Jay Inslee. With a reported net worth of more than $50 million, her Democratic opponents cast her as just another millionaire running for Congress. Endorsed by Gregoire and Rep. Rick Larsen, her campaign ads focused on the financial struggles of her youth. Republican state legislator John Koster, who had lost two contests a decade apart in the adjacent 2nd District, led the all-party primary with 45 percent . DelBene was the top Democrat with 22 percent to 14 percent for liberal Darcy Burner, also a Microsoft executive. In the runoff, DelBene consolidated support among Democrats and won, 54%-46%.

DelBene spent much of her time during her first year tending to two unexpected local disasters and their follow-up: the collapse of a bridge on Interstate 5 in Skagit Valley and a destructive mudslide in rural Oso that killed 43 people. Later, she introduced the National Landslide Preparedness Act, which would create a national program to identify and reduce losses from landslide hazards.

In 2015, DelBene was one of 28 House Democrats who voted to give trade promotion authority to Obama, noting that "Washington is the most trade-dependent state in the nation and 40 percent of our jobs depend on trade." In 2018, the farm bill was enacted with a section authored by DelBene to encourage additional research and development of wood products by the Forest Service. In the Almanac vote ratings, her scores were centrist on the economy and liberal on social issues.

In 2017, DelBene joined Ways and Means, while Republicans retained House control. Like other committee Democrats for the next two years, she had little opportunity to shape health care or tax legislation. With the GOP measure, she said, "ultra-wealthy and well-connected Americans receive the majority of the tax cuts." When Democrats took House control in 2019, DelBene showed interest in international trade issues, including the revised trade deal with Mexico and Canada and other steps to respond to Trump's "reckless trade and tariff policies." She also pressed her economic views as vice chair for policy coordination of the New Democrats.

Working with Rep. Rosa DeLauro, DelBene played a lead role in pressing for expansion of the child tax credit, which Republicans originally made part of their tax cuts in 2017. At Ways and Means, she took the initiative to coordinate support and details of the measure. Following the Democratic convention, she helped to convince Biden's policy advisers to join the initiative. In September 2020, Vox reported, the Biden campaign "made official the most significant antipoverty proposal of his candidacy: making the child tax credit much bigger, and available to all parents as a monthly check." At the urging of DelBene, DeLauro and others, the expanded child credit became a centerpiece of the $1.9 trillion economic relief bill that was enacted in March 2021. When the credit was approved for only two years because of budget rules, DelBene insisted on its permanent enactment.

Other DelBene initiatives have included leadership among Democrats in repealing the ban on transgender in the military, setting requirements that tech companies take additional steps to protect privacy in their handling of data, and creating a bipartisan Medical Technology Caucus to encourage public support of new tools.

In 2017-18, DelBene was finance co-chair of the DCCC. Following the election, she lost a bid to chair the full committee, but was named a co-chair of the Frontline program to assist Democrats defending competitive districts. DelBene has won easy reelection. In 2018 and 2020, she got 59 percent of the vote, her strongest performances.

WA-1: Interior Northwest Washington

Cook Partisan Voting Index: D+8

Population		Race and Ethnicity		Income	
Total	791,545	White	75.10%	Median Income	$106,190
Land area (sq. miles)	6,186	Black	1.50%	District Income Rank	23
Pop/ sq mi	127.95	Latino	9.70%	Poverty Rate	6.30%
Born in State	47.20%	Asian	13.00%	With health insurance	94.80%
		Two or more races	5.30%	Cash public assistance	2.40%
Age Groups		Other	5.10%	Food stamp/SNAP	6.30%
Under 18	23.20%				
18-34	20.80%	**Education**		**Work**	
35-64	41.60%	H.S grad or less	24.80%	White Collar	51.90%
Over 64	14.30%	Some college	29.90%	Sales and Service	29.40%
		College Degree, 4 yr	26.80%	Blue Collar	18.60%
Military		Post grad	18.50%	Government	11.00%
Veteran/ Active Duty	7.30%				

2020 Pres. Vote	Biden	257,631	(59%)	Trump	166,460	(38%)	Jorgensen	9,347	(2%)
2016 Pres. Vote	Clinton	188,952	(52%)	Trump	132,109	(37%)	Johnson	19,396	(5%)

Seattle and Everett Suburbs: With the high-tech growth since the 1980s, metropolitan Seattle grew to the north and to the east, as a wave of newcomers arrived seeking the area's distinctive blend of natural beauty, robust and creative economic expansion, and freewheeling culture. The heart of the new Seattle is east of Lake Washington, in the edge city of Redmond. That is where you find the turquoise-shaded, low-rise buildings of the 500-acre Microsoft campus—a tranquil environment for a booming and boisterously aggressive company. In 2019, officials announced plans for a huge expansion of the campus, with 18 new and taller buildings replacing 12 buildings scheduled for demolition and expected to add 8,000 workers to the existing 50,000 in the Puget Sound area, when the redevelopment is completed in 2023. Plans call for the new buildings to be clustered in five villages. Microsoft has fueled Redmond's transformation from a sleepy hamlet of 1,426 people in 1960 to a hip center of commerce with a population of more than 72,000, of whom 36 percent are Asian; from 2010 to 2019, Redmond grew 32 percent. Mindful of the limited amount of affordable housing, which Microsoft President Brad Smith termed a "crisis," the company pledged in 2019 low-interest loans for new housing in the Seattle area. Its affordable housing initiative included a $750 million commitment to reduce area rents—an increase from its initial $500 million plan.

The 1st Congressional District of Washington includes most of Redmond and many of the other King County suburbs east of Seattle. Technology is a huge factor in the local economy. Redmond is also home of Nintendo of North America and expanding research facilities for Facebook and Amazon. In neighboring Kirkland, Google maintains its research and development center, which developed Google Maps. The company purchased a 10-acre plot close to its existing campus and planned to expand in the area, Bloomberg News reported in 2020. On the eastern shore of Lake Washington are the homes and estates of the "Microsoft millionaires," many of whom exercised company stock options before the economic bust. The affluent suburbs include Medina, Clyde Hill, Yarrow Point and Hunts Point, as well as Bill Gates' $60 million, 66,000-square-foot home. In January 2020, this area was the site of the first known COVID case in the United States—a local man who had recently returned from Wuhan China.

The 1st crosses the Cascades to take in the eastern extremities of King County. It also takes in the interior portions of Snohomish, Skagit and Whatcom counties, all the way to the Canadian border. Along the way, the economy gradually shifts from software code to raspberries and dairy farming. At the far north end of the district is the fishing and lumber town of Blaine, with America's most attractively landscaped border crossing and the International Peace Arch, just south of British Columbia. About 40 percent of the population is in King, and nearly as many in Snohomish. The King County areas of the district are strongly Democratic, while the inland portions are swing territory. The resulting district leans Democratic, but can be competitive. After Hillary Clinton won 52 percent in 2016, Joe Biden raised the Democratic vote in the district to 59 percent.

Rick Larsen (D)

Elected 2000, 11th term, b. Jun 15, 1965; Arlington, WA; Pacific Lutheran University, B.A., 1987; University of MN, M.P.A., 1990; Methodist; Married (Tiia Karlen Larsen); 2 children.

Elected Office: Snohomish City Council, 1998-2000, President, 1999-2000.

Professional Career: Econ. dev. official, Port of Everett, 1990-1991; Director pub. affairs, WA St. Dental Assn., 1991-1998.

DC Office: 2113 RHOB 20515, 202-225-2605, Fax: 202-225-4420, larsen.house.gov

State Offices: Bellingham, 360-733-4500; Everett, 425-252-3188.

Committees: *Armed Services*: Cyber, Innovative Technologies & Information Systems; Intelligence & Special Operations. *Transportation & Infrastructure*: Aviation (Chmn), Coast Guard and Maritime Transportation

Group Ratings

	ADA	ACLU	AFL-CIO	LCV	COC	HAFA	ACU	CFG	FRC
2020	**	81%	**	100%	-	0%	7%	**	-
2019	95%	C	100%	93%	64%	C	7%	12%	0%

Almanac Ratings 2019-2020

	Economy	Social	Foreign	Composite
Liberal	100%	100%	80%	94%
Conservative	0%	0%	20%	6%

Key Votes of the 116th Congress

1. U.S./Mex./Can. trade deal Y	5. Russia sanctions Y	9. Firearms background checks Y
2. First Coronavirus response Y	6. Troops in Syria Y	10. Spending at the border Y
3. HEROES Act Y	7. Veto arms sales to Saudis Y	11. Marijuana liberalized rules Y
4. CASH Act Y	8. Defense $$$, veto override Y	12. Electoral College objections N

Election Results

Election	Name (Party)	Vote (%)		Cand. Spent	Ind. Exp. Support	Ind. Exp. Oppose
2020 General	Rick Larsen (D)	255,252	(63%)	$1,213,963	$2,257	
	Tim Hazelo (R)	148,384	(37%)	$47,871		$113
2020 Primary	Rick Larsen (D)	120,694	(49%)			
	Jason Call (D)	34,537	(14%)			

Prior winning percentages: 2018 (71%), 2016 (64%), 2014 (61%), 2012 (61%), 2010 (51%), 2008 (62%), 2006 (64%), 2004 (64%), 2002 (50%), 2000 (50%)

Rick Larsen, a moderate Democrat first elected in 2000, has been well-positioned in the House to deal with aviation, maritime and national security issues that are vital at home. As chairman of the Aviation Subcommittee, he has sought to assist Boeing Co., the largest employer in his district. Boeing's epic problems in recent years have created challenges for Larsen in balancing the needs of his constituents with his own responsibilities. Following the crash of two new 737 Max jets, he sought an evenhanded approach to the controversy, though he eventually placed much of the blame on the Federal Aviation Administration.

When Boeing announced in 2020 that it was shutting down its jumbo jet production in his district, Larsen blasted the company's management, though he also noted the economic impact of the pandemic. In the state's tradition, he remains an outspoken proponent of international trade and has taken an avid interest in issues related to China, a country that does substantial business with his state.

Larsen grew up in Arlington, in Snohomish County, graduated from Pacific Lutheran University, and got a master's degree at the University of Minnesota. He spent a year doing research on economic development for the Port of Everett. For six years, he was director of public affairs for the Washington

State Dental Association. In 1998, he won a seat on the Snohomish County Council and later became its president.

In 2000, when Republican Jack Metcalf retired after three terms in Congress, the Democratic field was cleared for Larsen. Republicans nominated state Rep. John Koster, creating one of that year's premier contests. Anti-abortion rights groups and the National Rifle Association backed Koster, and unions and abortion-rights groups supported Larsen. Larsen criticized Koster for referring to "our American holocaust," a familiar term among anti-abortion activists. Larsen won 50%-46%.

Larsen has been a leader of the centrist New Democrat Coalition, although he became more reliably Democratic after President Barack Obama took office and he has taken progressive positions on most social issues. He voted for the Bush-era tax cuts in 2001, but later opposed extending the cuts for upper-income taxpayers. He was one of 22 Democrats in 2012 to support a failed plan for a budget along the lines of the Simpson-Bowles deficit reduction commission. In 2015, he was one of 28 House Democrats who voted to give trade promotion authority to Obama, especially for the prospective Trans-Pacific Partnership.

Larsen has co-chaired the U.S.-China Working Group, which has called for greater U.S. engagement with China on diplomatic and military issues. In 2016, Larsen applauded an agreement by China to reduce its export subsidies. In March 2019, he led a bipartisan House delegation to China, where they held discussions about ongoing trade negotiations.

As anti-China sentiment in the United States grew following the outbreak of the coronavirus, Larsen took a more nuanced approach. "I think that there's still room in this debate for economic policy," Larsen told a panel at the Brookings Institution in October 2020, adding that "we need China to deal with North Korea, international terrorism, despite the security concerns we have with China." He also remained mindful of the economic stakes for his district. "The Boeing company is not going to move manufacturing out of China," he said.

As the "Congressman from Boeing," Larsen has what has been a plum assignment as chairman of the Transportation and Infrastructure Committee's Aviation panel. Boeing and its employees have been among Larsen's major campaign contributors. He has urged innovative technologies to advance air safety. When specific controversies have arisen, he often has deferred to federal regulators. He supported the FAA's decision in 2013 to ground the company's new 787 Dreamliner fleet over concerns about the plane's fire-plagued batteries, saying that safety should be paramount. He has warned against proposals to privatize the air traffic control system.

Following the overseas crashes of two 737 Max jets, plus the subsequent questions about Boeing's rollout of the new planes and federal certification, Larsen in March 2019 joined committee Chairman Peter DeFazio of Oregon in asking the FAA to engage an "independent, third-party review" of Boeing's handling of its aircraft. They also called for the inspector general at the Transportation Department to review the FAA's certifying of the plane. In a November 2019 letter to the FAA, they wrote, the two crashes "raise questions about how the agency weighs the validity of safety issues raised by its own experts compared to objections raised by the aircraft manufacturers the F.A.A. is supposed to oversee." In their own report in September 2020, DeFazio and Larsen placed blame on each sector.

When Boeing announced it was consolidating at its South Carolina plant the assembly lines for its 787 Dreamliner plane, Larsen called the decision "shortsighted and misplaced." Despite the economic devastation caused by the pandemic, Larsen continued to praise "Northwest Washington's aviation and aerospace workforce [as] the best in the world." In economic-relief legislation that Congress enacted in March 2021, he included provisions that sought to save aviation jobs by covering pay and benefits for many workers and including $8 billion in aid for the nation's airports.

On the Armed Services Committee, Larsen works closely with Chairman Adam Smith, his home-state colleague. He has pushed to secure funds for upgraded border security at Bellingham. He co-founded the Congressional Arctic Working Group, with the chief focus of protecting U.S. environmental, economic and strategic interests in the region.

Larsen won reelection easily until 2010, when he was challenged by Koster, his opponent of a decade earlier who gained support from tea party activists. Larsen outspent the challenger $2.1 million to $1.1 million and stressed job creation and expanding credit for small business. He declared victory a week after the election, 51%-49%, a margin of 6,500 votes.

After the 2012 redistricting boosted the Democratic base in the district by five percentage points, Larsen has won more than 60 percent of the vote in each general election. But he has faced a difficult political balance. In 2016, the State Labor Council withheld its endorsement. Democrat Mike LaPointe, a coffee shop owner in Everett, challenged Larsen in the primary from the left, with objections to his international trade votes. In the all-party primary, Larsen got 53 percent and

LaPointe had 10 percent, with the remainder going to Republicans. In the 2020 primary, Larsen led seven challengers in the all-party primary, with 49 percent of the vote. Jason Call, a high school math teacher and liberal Democrat who supported Medicare for All and attacked Larsen's "corporate friendly politics," narrowly missed making the runoff, finishing one percentage point behind Republican Timothy Hazelo. Whether the liberal criticism of Larsen becomes more than a nuisance remains to be seen.

As a relatively youthful and senior member of two committees with sweeping coverage, Larsen might be might be influential for many more years. In a unique local twist, Larsen and Adam Smith—the top Democrat on Armed Services—were born on the same day: June 15, 1965. At the Transportation Committee, DeFazio is 18 years older.

WA-2: Upper Puget Sound   **Cook Partisan Voting Index: D+11**

Population		Race and Ethnicity		Income	
Total	760,064	White	76.10%	Median Income	$75,095
Land area (sq. miles)	1,015	Black	3.30%	District Income Rank	130
Pop/ sq mi	748.82	Latino	11.10%	Poverty Rate	9.00%
Born in State	48.10%	Asian	9.50%	With health insurance	93.60%
		Two or more races	5.40%	Cash public assistance	2.80%
Age Groups		Other	5.60%	Food stamp/SNAP	10.10%
Under 18	19.90%				
18-34	24.70%	**Education**		**Work**	
35-64	38.10%	H.S grad or less	29.60%	White Collar	39.30%
Over 64	17.30%	Some college	36.90%	Sales and Service	37.40%
		College Degree, 4 yr	22.10%	Blue Collar	23.30%
Military		Post grad	11.30%	Government	15.10%
Veteran/ Active Duty	11.30%				

2020 Pres. Vote	Biden	257,291	(62%)	Trump	145,138	(35%)	Jorgensen	8,647	(2%)
2016 Pres. Vote	Clinton	185,821	(55%)	Trump	113,670	(34%)	Johnson	16,880	(5%)
	Stein	7,477	(2%)						

Everett Metro: The Seattle metropolitan area has marched north along the shore of Puget Sound, beyond the old lumber port and railroad terminus of Everett. The huge Boeing assembly plant has produced 747s, 767s, 777s and the long-range 787s. In October 2020, citing the precipitous decline in air travel during the pandemic, the company announced that it would shut down 787 productions in Everett in mid-2021 and consolidate manufacturing of those jumbo airplanes at its newer and lower-cost facility in South Carolina. The company earlier announced that it was ending all production of 747s. Those two planes accounted for nearly a third of the payroll at Everett.

Company officials said that they did not envision shifting production of other aircraft to Everett.

Overall, business had been booming. In 2018, Boeing increased its statewide payroll to 70,000 —its first increase since 2012, when it peaked at 87,000 employees. With Boeing's internal shifts plus automation, that total was expected to drop well below 70,000. At the port, the chief long-term concern aside from former President Donald Trump's trade war has been the widening of the Panama Canal. As expected, that has shifted away from the West Coast some destinations for Asia-based shipping. The 20,000 jobs at the Port of Seattle in 2018 had an average salary of $95,000.

In the waters of Puget Sound are the 176 San Juan Islands, which were the last part of the continental United States to be turned over to this country. The waters were great whaling grounds, and not until 1860 did the British relinquish them. Today, ferryboats connect the islands to mainland Washington and to British Columbia, directly to the west. The publicly operated Washington State Ferries system in 2019 had 23.9 million passengers (the 24.7 million in 2018 were the most since 2002) and 10.5 million vehicles on 22 auto-passenger vessels to 20 terminals, the largest ferry operator in the United States. (Ridership fell about 40 percent in 2020, as a result of the coronavirus.) With planned expansion of service, the system prepared to purchase 16 new vessels by 2040; most of the new vessels were expected to replace the aging existing fleet and to run on low-pollution electric power.

This is some of the most beautiful coastline in North America: the steely blue sound with forested hills rising behind it, shielded from the full force of Pacific rains by the Olympic Mountains, though still seldom dry. The little towns, on bits of level land between the water and the mountains, have the look of pristine New England villages. Further north is Bellingham, which grew up as a supply station for gold miners in the 1850s and was the source of much of the lumber used to rebuild San Francisco after the 1906 earthquake and fire. In late 2020, local officials continued to explore plans to redevelop the waterfront, which was devastated by the shutdown of a Georgia-Pacific plant in 2007.

The 2nd Congressional District of Washington encompasses the San Juan Islands, including 45-mile-long Whidbey Island, and most of the mainland along the east side of the sound. The district has several military installations, including a Navy base at Everett and a naval air station on Whidbey. The political tradition in most of the lumbering and fishing areas here is Democratic, as is the political culture in Everett. In addition to Everett, the district takes in most of the major ports on Puget Sound. Nearly 60 percent of the population resides in Snohomish County, which is closest to Seattle. The 2nd leans strongly Democratic. Joe Biden took 62 percent of the vote in 2020.

Jaime Herrera Beutler (R)

Elected 2010, 6th term, b. Nov 03, 1978; Glendale, CA; Seattle Pacific University, Att., 1998; Bellevue Community College, A.A., 2003; University of WA, B.A., 2004; Christian Church; Married (Daniel Beutler); 3 children.

Elected Office: WA House, 2007-2011.

Professional Career: Legislative aide, Rep. Cathy McMorris Rodgers, 2005-2007.

DC Office: 2352 RHOB 20515, 202-225-3536, Fax: 202-225-3478, herrerabeutler.house.gov

State Offices: Chehalis, 360-695-6292; Vancouver, 360-695-6292.

Committees: *Appropriations*: Energy & Water Development & Related Agencies; Labor, Health & Human Services, Education & Related Agencies; Legislative Branch (RMM). *Joint Economic*.

Group Ratings

	ADA	ACLU	AFL-CIO	LCV	COC	HAFA	ACU	CFG	FRC
2020	**	34%	**	33%	-	63%	65%	**	-
2019	20%	C	59%	24%	91%	C	65%	68%	86%

Almanac Ratings 2019-2020

	Economy	Social	Foreign	Composite
Liberal	46%	44%	45%	45%
Conservative	54%	56%	55%	55%

Key Votes of the 116th Congress

1. U.S./Mex./Can. trade deal Y	5. Russia sanctions Y	9. Firearms background checks N
2. First Coronavirus response Y	6. Troops in Syria Y	10. Spending at the border Y
3. HEROES Act N	7. Veto arms sales to Saudis N	11. Marijuana liberalized rules N
4. CASH Act Y	8. Defense $$$, veto override Y	12. Electoral College objections N

Election Results

Election	Name (Party)	Vote (%)		Cand. Spent	Ind. Exp. Support	Ind. Exp. Oppose
2020 General	Jaime Herrera Beutler (R)	235,579	(56%)	$4,661,929	$325,503	$1,021,237
	Carolyn Long (D)	181,347	(43%)	$4,125,515	$105,230	$2,339,989

Prior winning percentages: 2018 (53%), 2016 (62%), 2014 (62%), 2012 (60%), 2010 (53%)

Republican Jaime Herrera Beutler is a young Latina who assists the GOP in its outreach while compiling a business-friendly centrist voting record. In the 2016 presidential campaign, Herrera Beutler said she was open to supporting Donald Trump. Following the early October release of a 2005 tape in which Trump made lewd comments about women, she said, "that door has now slammed shut." She split with Trump on his immigration enforcement actions and on repeal of the Affordable

Care Act. In 2021, she voted to impeach him. Following the January riot at the Capitol, she used her position on the Appropriations Committee to demand accountability and more effective security. Her independence may have helped her survive narrow reelections.

Herrera Beutler grew up in the region. Her father was a printer. Her parents raised six children and finances were tight. She took a job as a nanny to help pay for college. After concluding that nursing studies weren't the right field for her, Herrera Beutler got a degree in communications from the University of Washington. As a teenager, she knocked on doors for Republicans in 1994. During college, she had a White House internship. After graduating, she was a legislative aide to Rep. Cathy McMorris Rodgers of eastern Washington, who became her mentor. When a seat opened in the state legislature in 2007, she was appointed. She became the assistant floor leader, the only woman and minority on the Republican leadership team.

When six-term Democratic Rep. Brian Baird retired in 2010, Herrera Beutler was 31 and a newlywed. Her husband, Daniel Beutler, who was about to start law school, delayed his plans so she could run. In the all-party primary, Herrera Beutler led a crowded Republican field, with 28 percent of the vote.

In the general, media and technology entrepreneur Denny Heck spent $2 million, including $350,000 of his own money, to her $1.5 million. Heck ran as a moderate Democrat and emphasized his experience creating jobs. She criticized Heck for his support of the health care overhaul championed by Democrats and of President Barack Obama's economic stimulus bill. Riding that year's GOP tidal wave, she won 53%-47%. Heck subsequently served eight years in an adjacent district that was created by redistricting.

Herrera Beutler was among the moderate members of the Class of 2010. Oregon GOP Rep. Greg Walden appointed her vice chair for minority outreach at the National Republican Congressional Committee. "I think we can do a better job of tone," she told The Columbian of Vancouver about her party's relationship with Hispanics. She expressed reservations about legislative proposals to restrict gun rights, citing her own experience in her early 20s when a man repeatedly tried to break into her home. She said owning a gun gave her peace of mind. On immigration, she favored comprehensive reform, but opposed Obama's unilateral efforts to impose changes.

In 2017, she voted against the House Republican proposal to repeal Obama care. When Trump at a White House meeting urged Herrera Beutler to support the bill, she told him that that she was helping him to "keep your promise" to his supporters that he would not back a bill that failed to protect people with pre-existing conditions, she later told The (Longview) Daily News. She also took issue with the policy of separating immigrant families at the border. As a member of the bipartisan Problem Solvers Caucus, she told The Hill in December 2020 that the group's role in encouraging COVID-19 relief showed "we're trying to be more of a governing group."

On Appropriations, Herrera Beutler worked to secure funds for the nuclear waste cleanup at the Hanford plant in her home state. She took the lead on other health care initiatives, including organ-donor assistance and mental health awareness.

Following the Capitol riot in January 2021, Herrera Beutler was one of 10 House Republicans who voted to impeach Trump. "I see that my own party will be best served when those among us choose truth," she said. The Clark County Republican Party censured her. During the subsequent Senate trial, when her comments raised the option that she might be called as a witness, she confirmed that House Minority Leader Kevin McCarthy had told her that Trump had said to him that the rioters were "more upset about the election than you are." As the ranking Republican on the Appropriations Subcommittee on the Legislative Branch, she joined chairman Tim Ryan in urging the Capitol Police Board to be more transparent in its review of the riot.

In 2013, Herrera Beutler took six months away from the Capitol to be with her daughter Abigail, who was born premature and without kidneys; she unexpectedly survived with unprecedented surgical intervention and kidney dialysis. In 2016, her husband provided a donor kidney to their daughter, whose health seemed miraculously robust. As a result of that experience, Herrera Beutler has pushed for several related health care bills, including measures to help create a nationwide network of providers to assist medically complex children and to assure insurance coverage for such children. Those proposals were enacted in 2018.

Herrera Beutler had coasted to reelection with at least 60 percent of the vote and entrenched herself in the previously Democratic district. That changed in 2018, when Democratic challenger Carolyn Long, a political science professor at Washington State University, advocated expansion of the Affordable Care Act and said Herrera Beutler was not accessible to her constituents. Long outspent her, $3.9 million to $3 million, but Herrera Beutler won, 53%-47%. In 2020, they had a rematch. During a debate, the incumbent said that climate change is "real" and she challenged Long on her earlier support for a carbon tax. Herrera Beutler outspent Long, $4.7 million to $4.1 million, and won, 56%-43%. This time, she flipped Clark County, which she took with 52 percent, and won all eight counties.

WA-3: Southwest Washington

Cook Partisan Voting Index: R+5

Population		Race and Ethnicity		Income	
Total	756,675	White	85.90%	Median Income	$70,936
Land area (sq. miles)	9,114	Black	1.60%	District Income Rank	157
Pop/ sq mi	83.02	Latino	10.20%	Poverty Rate	10.10%
Born in State	40.30%	Asian	3.20%	With health insurance	93.90%
		Two or more races	5.80%	Cash public assistance	2.20%
Age Groups		Other	3.40%	Food stamp/SNAP	12.30%
Under 18	22.60%				
18-34	21.00%	**Education**		**Work**	
35-64	38.50%	H.S grad or less	35.50%	White Collar	35.30%
Over 64	18.00%	Some college	37.30%	Sales and Service	38.60%
		College Degree, 4 yr	17.70%	Blue Collar	26.10%
Military		Post grad	9.40%	Government	15.20%
Veteran/ Active Duty	9.90%				

2020 Pres. Vote	Trump	214,391	(50%)	Biden	198,429	(47%)		
2016 Pres. Vote	Trump	157,359	(48%)	Clinton	134,009	(41%)	Johnson	15,707	(5%)

Vancouver: From the Pacific Ocean to the majestic row of active and inactive volcanoes of the Cascades, southwest Washington was long one of America's most productive lumber areas. The moist air and almost constant rain blown in from the Pacific have kept the trees on the coast growing rapidly. Precipitation is heavy in the valleys just past the Coast Range, and the forests there are also fast-growing. Then come the high mountains. The Cascades are a genuine divide, wringing almost all the moisture out of the atmosphere and making an arid climate eastward for a thousand miles. Americans had long been taught that the lower 48 states had no active volcanoes, but Mount St. Helens in Skamania County proved that wrong in 1980 when it erupted after lying dormant for 123 years, killing 57 people (many from asphyxiation), destroying its own peak and paving the land around it with lava. In January 2018, seismologists reported an increased number of quakes, with intensity up to 3.9 on the Richter scale.

For many years, this part of Washington was sparsely settled, with lumber-mill and fishing-boat towns scattered between mountains and water. It was flannel shirt country, Democratic since New Deal days. In the early 1990s, its resource-based economy was threatened by the environmental movement, which restricted fishing practices and produced a court decision shutting down logging in old-growth forests to save spotted owl habitat. This roiled local politics and gave Republicans an opening. The GOP's efforts in the region have been assisted by the growth of Clark County, across the Columbia River from Portland Oregon; Vancouver has filled with new residents eager to avoid Oregon's income tax, one of the highest in the country, but who want to make big purchases in Oregon free of sales tax. Clark County, where one-third of the residents commute to work in Portland, grew by 38 percent from 2000 to 2017; 10 percent of the county population is Hispanic and the fast-growing Asian community accounts for 5 percent.

In January 2018, Gov. Jay Inslee rejected a permit for a proposal to build an oil-by-rail terminal in Vancouver, which would have been the largest in the nation. A year later, local shipbuilder Vigor announced a nearly $1 billion contract to build a new landing craft for the U.S. Army. Corporate planners rejected options to do the work in Seattle or Portland. The port of Vancouver employs about 4,000 workers, the Columbian reported in September 2019.

The 3rd Congressional District of Washington covers the southwestern corner of the state, between the ocean and the Cascades. Economic growth and diversification and the arrival of many new residents with no roots in the old industries have made the area politically marginal. Nearly two-thirds of the district's residents live in Clark County. To the north, the district includes a small slice of Thurston County, but not the state's capital, Olympia. President Donald Trump won in 2020, 50%-47%.

Dan Newhouse (R)

Elected 2014, 4th term, b. Jul 10, 1955; Sunnyside, WA; WA State University, B.S., 1977; Presbyterian; Married (Joan Galvin); 2 children (from previous marriage).

Elected Office: WA House, 2003-2009.

Professional Career: Farmer; WA Director of Agriculture, 2009-2013.

DC Office: 1414 LHOB 20515, 202-225-5816, Fax: 202-225-3251, newhouse.house.gov

State Offices: Richland, 509-713-7374; Twisp, 509-433-7760; Yakima, 509-452-3243.

Committees: *Appropriations*: Agriculture, Rural Development, FDA & Related Agencies; Energy & Water Development & Related Agencies; Legislative Branch.

Group Ratings

	ADA	ACLU	AFL-CIO	LCV	COC	HAFA	ACU	CFG	FRC
2020	**	19%	**	14%	-	66%	74%	**	-
2019	0%	C	52%	14%	89%	C	74%	62%	86%

Almanac Ratings 2019-2020

	Economy	Social	Foreign	Composite
Liberal	25%	38%	36%	33%
Conservative	75%	62%	64%	67%

Key Votes of the 116th Congress

1. U.S./Mex./Can. trade deal Y	5. Russia sanctions Y	9. Firearms background checks N
2. First Coronavirus response Y	6. Troops in Syria Y	10. Spending at the border Y
3. HEROES Act N	7. Veto arms sales to Saudis N	11. Marijuana liberalized rules N/A
4. CASH Act N	8. Defense $$$, veto override Y	12. Electoral College objections N

Election Results

Election	Name (Party)	Vote (%)		Cand. Spent	Ind. Exp. Support	Ind. Exp. Oppose
2020 General	Dan Newhouse (R)............................	202,108	(66%)	$920,008	$506	$8,816
	Douglas McKinley (D)......................	102,667	(34%)	$52,854	$480	
2020 Primary	Dan Newhouse (R)............................	101,539	(57%)			
	Sarena Sloot (R)...............................	11,823	(7%)			
	Tracy Wright (R)..................................	9,088	(5%)			

Prior winning percentages: 2018 (63%), 2016 (58%), 2014 (51%)

Dan Newhouse, who won the seat in 2014 with a promise of greater bipartisanship to address local priorities, has grown comfortable as a leadership ally and House insider. He has been willing to buck conservative Republicans on issues that are vital to business and in his vote to impeach President Donald Trump.

Newhouse grew up in a Yakima Valley family that was active in local politics. His father, Irv, was a state legislator for 34 years; a state Senate office building was named after him. The younger Newhouse operated a 600-acre farm that grows hops, grapes and alfalfa. He got his bachelor's degree in agricultural economics from Washington State University and is a former president of the Hop Growers of America. Newhouse won election to the state House in 2002. Six years later, Democratic Gov. Christine Gregoire named him state agriculture director, calling him "the best person for the job." He served four years in the position. When Gregoire's successor, Democrat Jay Inslee, declined to keep Newhouse in the position, he became a frequent television spokesman for the victorious opponents of a 2013 state ballot initiative that would have required labeling of genetically modified food products.

When the House seat opened, Clint Didier and Newhouse led the field in the all-party primary with 32 percent and 26 percent, respectively. Didier, a former tight end in the National Football

League, was a major figure in the state's tea party movement. He emphasized gun rights, patriotism and religion.

Newhouse won endorsements from former Rep. Doc Hastings, his predecessor, the National Rifle Association and the Yakima Herald-Republic, which noted the importance of the federal government in the district. "Newhouse by far shows a better grasp of the federal government's influence," the newspaper said. Newhouse outspent Didier, $982,000 to $579,000, and won the general election, 51%-49%, a margin of 2,465 votes. Didier led in six of the eight counties. Newhouse took Benton and Yakima counties, which cast 64 percent of the total vote.

When an opening occurred in 2015 on the Rules Committee, which operates as an arm of the leadership, Speaker John Boehner tapped Newhouse as the only freshman on the panel. He supported renewal of the Export-Import Bank, a split with many junior Republicans but a popular move in his home state, where Boeing is a major beneficiary of the agency's subsidies, as are many farmers. He enacted a bill in 2017 that extended the deadline to start construction of the hydroelectric project at the Enloe Dam near Oroville. In 2019, he failed in his bid to become ranking Republican on the Rules Committee and exited the panel.

With his seat on the Appropriations Committee, Newhouse has supported the district's Hanford nuclear cleanup and opposed calls to breach four dams on the Columbia River. In 2021, he joined the Agriculture Subcommittee and pledged support for "funding priorities of our agricultural communities."

Newhouse has urged steps to "improve the nation's broken immigration system." With Democratic Rep. Zoe Lofgren, he filed a bill to revise the guest worker program and provide a path to legalization for farm workers. In December 2019, the House passed their bill, with bipartisan support. "Our farmers and ranchers desperately need relief," he said. Newhouse repeatedly voiced concerns about President Donald Trump's international trade actions, including increased tariffs that are "harmful" for the economy in his district.

He was one of 10 House Republicans who voted to impeach Trump, stating that he "failed to fulfill his oath of office" during the January 2021 riot at the Capitol. In response, six Republican county chairmen in his district condemned Newhouse and demanded that he resign. He responded, "I am still a conservative Republican … and we have a lot of work to do to keep the Biden administration accountable."

In the 2016 campaign, Newhouse had a rematch with Didier. This time, Didier—who had a radio show on a Christian network—was an enthusiastic supporter of Trump. Newhouse, who had a fundraising advantage of 15-to-1, won the general election, 58%-42%. Since then, Newhouse has faced minor Republican opposition. In 2018, against Democrat Christine Brown, a former local television news anchor who criticized his support of Republican efforts to repeal the Affordable Care Act, Newhouse won 63%-37%. He outspent the challenger, $1.1 million to $467,000. In 2020, he defeated Doug McKinley, an attorney who represented workers in a class-action suit on behalf of the pension rights of Hanford workers. Newhouse won, 66%-34%.

WA-4: Central Washington — Cook Partisan Voting Index: R+13

Population		Race and Ethnicity		Income	
Total	735,797	White	75.20%	Median Income	$59,872
Land area (sq. miles)	19,250	Black	1.40%	District Income Rank	266
Pop/ sq mi	38.22	Latino	39.70%	Poverty Rate	15.10%
Born in State	55.90%	Asian	1.40%	With health insurance	87.70%
		Two or more races	3.80%	Cash public assistance	2.60%
Age Groups		Other	18.20%	Food stamp/SNAP	16.70%
Under 18	28.50%				
18-34	22.40%	**Education**		**Work**	
35-64	34.60%	H.S grad or less	46.70%	White Collar	32.30%
Over 64	14.40%	Some college	31.10%	Sales and Service	34.00%
		College Degree, 4 yr	14.50%	Blue Collar	33.80%
Military		Post grad	7.70%	Government	16.20%
Veteran/ Active Duty	7.60%				

2020 Pres. Vote	Trump	179,022	(58%)	Biden	122,691	(39%)	
2016 Pres. Vote	Trump	140,560	(56%)	Clinton	85,083	(34%) Johnson	12,039 (5%)

Richland, Yakima: The rugged peaks of the Cascade Mountains divide the state of Washington into two starkly different climate zones and two almost as starkly different political cultures. West of the Cascades, Washington is moist, green and crammed with watery inlets. To the east, it is barren and brown, except where irrigation ditches channel the water of the Columbia River into thirsty valleys and where the mountaintop waters fall east, as they do above the apple orchards in the Yakima Valley.

As Washington has become mostly Democratic west of the Cascades, it has become mostly Republican on the eastern side. This shift in political inclinations has followed the development of national politics and the local economy. The federal government has been a presence east of the Cascades since the 1930s, when it began to build dams to provide cheap power and boost economic development in this forbidding landscape. A giant bust of Franklin D. Roosevelt gazes out from a bluff on the Columbia over 550-foot-high Grand Coulee Dam, one of Roosevelt's favorite projects. Other dams are strung along the Columbia to Bonneville Dam near Portland, where the river breaks through the Cascades. This was Democratic territory then; Grant County, which includes the dam, gave Roosevelt 86 percent of the vote in 1936. As the region became wealthier—in part because of the federal projects—the area shifted to the Republicans. Rising costs, especially the projected $256 million annual maintenance in 2021, raised questions about the future of the Bonneville Power Administration, when its contracts expire in 2028, the Seattle Times reported in July 2019. Farmers in the Yakima Valley, which produces most of the nation's apples and many other crops, were enraged when environmentalists proposed breaching the Snake River dams upriver to save salmon. The Trump administration decided in July 2020 not to remove the dams, though their plan continued the practice of spilling the water over the dams at crucial times to assist the salmon in their migration.

The 4th Congressional District of Washington covers much of the center of the state east of the Cascades, running from the vast wilderness of Okanogan County, which has long been gold country, past the Grand Coulee and the Columbia River. The biggest population center here is the Tri-Cities area of Richland, Kennewick and Pasco in Benton County. Like Benton, Yakima County has about one-third of the voters in the district, of which 50 percent is Hispanic. In 2017, ConAgra Foods opened its second French fry processing line at its manufacturing campus in Richland; it produces more fries than any other company. Benton is the location of the Hanford Nuclear Reservation. Since 1997, the federal government has spent more than $240 billion to clean up the residue from the nuclear weapons that had been produced here. In January 2021, new 10-year contracts began for the Hanford clean-up, which employs 1,650 workers.

The district's population is 40 percent Hispanic. Many are farm workers or the children of farm workers who have picked fruit for generations. The area was narrowly split between the parties as recently as the 1990s, but the 4th has become the most Republican district in the state; the cultural liberalism of Seattle seems very far away from here. Donald Trump twice got 58 percent here.

Cathy McMorris Rodgers (R)

Elected 2004, 9th term, b. May 22, 1969; Salem, OR; Pensacola Christian College, B.A., 1990; University of WA, M.B.A., 2002; Evangelical; Married (Brian Rodgers); 3 children.

Elected Office: WA House, 1994-2004, Minority Leader, 2002-2004.

Professional Career: Owner-operator, Peachcrest Fruit Basket orchard, 1984-1998; St. Legislative aide, 1990-1994.

DC Office: 1035 LHOB 20515, 202-225-2006, Fax: 202-225-3392, mcmorris.house.gov

State Offices: Colville, 509-684-3481; Spokane, 509-353-2374; Walla Walla, 509-529-9358.

Committees: *Energy & Commerce (RMM)*: Ex Officio membership on all subcommittees.

Group Ratings

	ADA	ACLU	AFL-CIO	LCV	COC	HAFA	ACU	CFG	FRC
2020	**	30%	**	14%	-	81%	85%	**	-
2019	5%	C	29%	10%	86%	C	85%	83%	95%

Almanac Ratings 2019-2020

	Economy	Social	Foreign	Composite
Liberal	25%	37%	44%	36%
Conservative	75%	63%	56%	64%

Key Votes of the 116th Congress

1. U.S./Mex./Can. trade deal	Y	5. Russia sanctions	Y	9. Firearms background checks	N
2. First Coronavirus response	Y	6. Troops in Syria	Y	10. Spending at the border	Y
3. HEROES Act	N	7. Veto arms sales to Saudis	N	11. Marijuana liberalized rules	N
4. CASH Act	N	8. Defense $$$, veto override	Y	12. Electoral College objections	N

Election Results

Election	Name (Party)	Vote (%)		Cand. Spent	Ind. Exp. Support	Ind. Exp. Oppose
2020 General	Cathy McMorris Rodgers (R)..............	247,815	(61%)	$4,000,750	$153,525	$496
	Dave Wilson (D)............................	155,737	(39%)	$107,854	$580	
2020 Primary	Cathy McMorris Rodgers (R).............	122,744	(53%)			
	Stephen T. Major (R).....................	20,000	(9%)			

Prior winning percentages: 2018 (55%), 2016 (60%), 2014 (61%), 2012 (62%), 2010 (68%), 2008 (65%), 2006 (56%), 2004 (60%)

Cathy McMorris Rodgers, after serving several years in Republican leadership as a trusted on-message lieutenant, shifted her focus to her work on the Energy and Commerce Committee. In 2021she became the senior Republican on the committee, the first woman of either party to take a leadership position on that panel. In 2018, she easily prevailed in her first serious reelection challenge at home.

McMorris Rodgers spent much of her childhood in northern British Columbia but moved with her family to Kettle Falls, where her parents bought a fruit orchard. Her father was a county Republican chairman. She graduated from Pensacola Christian College in Florida and got an MBA from the University of Washington. After college, she became a legislative assistant in the legislature and then was appointed to her state House seat at age 24. She served for 10 years and chaired the Commerce and Labor Committee. She rose to minority leader, the first woman to hold such a post in state history.

In 2004, George Nethercutt, who defeated Democratic House Speaker Tom Foley in 1994, ran for the Senate. McMorris Rodgers and two other Republicans competed in the primary. They agreed on most major issues. McMorris Rodgers won 50 percent of the vote in the primary to 27 percent for state Sen. Larry Sheahan. The Democratic nominee, businessman Don Barbieri, had a large financial advantage and no primary opposition. The National Republican Congressional Committee spent heavily for McMorris Rodgers, highlighting her pro-business credentials and agricultural background. She won, 60%-40%, a sign of the change in Foley's old district.

She leaned toward the center of the House on some issues. In 2007, she voted to expand the Children's Health Insurance Plan, a move favored by Democrats but opposed by President George W. Bush. She backed Bush's Iraq war policies, but also criticized the administration on veterans' health care and on a delay in rules for country-of-origin meat labeling.

McMorris Rodgers became an ally of Republican Leader John Boehner. She served as the GOP Conference vice chair and took on several tasks. She helped recruit women to run and served as a liaison to newly elected Republican women, including with fundraising. McMorris Rodgers has broadened her party's use of social media tools. During the 2012 presidential campaign, Mitt Romney tapped her to serve as his House liaison, partly as a reward for her early endorsement. After the 2012 election, McMorris took over as Republican Conference chair. She defeated Tom Price of Georgia, who had the backing of Paul Ryan—Romney's running mate that year.

Along with senior GOP leaders, she considered the party's perceived weaknesses to be less about its policies than about how it conveys its message. "I don't think it's about the Republican Party needing to become more moderate," she told CNN. "I really believe it's the Republican Party becoming more modern." She created video products for other members to use on social media and in their districts. In 2015, McMorris Rodgers was instrumental in crafting a compromise between GOP women and pro-life conservatives on a House-passed abortion bill that would have barred most abortions after 20 weeks.

Her voting record has become more conservative. Although House Republicans praised McMorris Rodgers for her hard work, she passed up several opportunities to try to move up the leadership ladder. When there were leadership shuffles in 2014 and 2015, she quickly said she would not seek to move up—a continuing signal that that she doubted that she could win. She stepped down from leadership following the 2018 election, when she was term-limited as Conference chair.

On Energy and Commerce, McMorris Rodgers has worked across the aisle on several issues. With Democratic Rep. Diana DeGette, she enacted in 2013 the Hydropower Regulatory Efficiency Act, which streamlined the permitting process for small hydropower projects as a tool to expand clean energy. As ranking Republican on the Energy and Commerce Subcommittee on Consumer Protection and Commerce in September 2020, she criticized Twitter for its "inconsistent application" of its content management practices that limited access by Trump because of his purportedly false statements during the campaign.

Following the 2020 election, McMorris Rodgers was selected the ranking GOP member on Energy and Commerce. Showing her leadership experience, she sent a video to other Republicans in which she made a pitch for her bid. "I have a detailed strategy to maximize the Energy and Commerce Committee to counter Pelosi and the squad," she said, referring to the House Speaker and a cadre of junior Democratic members. Unlike the other two Republicans from Washington, McMorris Rodgers voted against the impeachment of Trump. She said that his encouragement to supporters prior to their riot at the Capitol was "constitutionally protected speech" and did not "constitute an incitement of violence." But she voted with the minority of House Republicans to certify the Electoral College results.

In December 2019, the House Ethics Committee concluded a five-year investigation of McMorris Rodgers' office practices and unanimously ruled that her dealings with consultants and use of campaign funds violated House rules. Her violations showed an "indifference [to laws and House rules that] led to myriad instances of resources being used inappropriately," the panel concluded in its 1,365-page report. She reimbursed the government for $7,576 and, according to the committee, "accepted responsibility" for its conclusions.

In 2007, McMorris Rodgers and her husband had their first child, Cole McMorris Rodgers, who was diagnosed with Down syndrome. She subsequently gave birth to two daughters, making her the first member of Congress to deliver multiple babies while in office. She formed the Congressional Down Syndrome Caucus in 2008 to raise awareness about institutional barriers that face individuals with Down syndrome, and she became a leader in the disabilities community. In 2013, she enacted her National Pediatric Research Network Act. In 2014, she helped enact the Achieving a Better Life Experience (ABLE) Act, which was designed to empower individuals with disabilities.

Following the 2016 election, though McMorris Rodgers reportedly was considered for Interior Secretary, the Spokane Spokesman-Review earlier reported that she had a "tepid alliance" with Trump during the presidential campaign. With Trump as president, she occasionally found herself in an awkward position of avoiding criticism when she disagreed with his policies. In a June 2018 profile, The Washington Post reported that she deflected questions about Trump, though she said, "I have stood up to him when I thought that was appropriate."

In 2018, McMorris Rodgers was challenged by Democrat Lisa Brown, who had been majority leader during 20 years in the state Senate and then served as chancellor of the Spokane campus of Washington State University. Brown contrasted their actions on health care issues, saying McMorris Rodgers was out of touch with the district and complained that "Congress just isn't getting the job done." Each candidate spent about $5.5 million. McMorris Rodgers scored an impressive victory, 55%-45%, taking 52 percent of the vote in Spokane County, which cast more than two-thirds of the vote. In 2020, she won, 61%-39%, over Dave Wilson, a retired health care administrator; Wilson, who had run as an independent in earlier campaigns against McMorris Rodgers, spent only $108,000.

With her increasing policy experience, McMorris Rodgers retained options to emulate Foley, who had been a committee chairman before he was a party leader in the House.

WA-5: Eastern Washington   Cook Partisan Voting Index: R+8

Population		Race and Ethnicity		Income	
Total	734,322	White	87.30%	Median Income	$57,837
Land area (sq. miles)	15,473	Black	1.70%	District Income Rank	291
Pop/ sq mi	47.46	Latino	6.80%	Poverty Rate	14.00%
Born in State	52.00%	Asian	2.50%	With health insurance	94.10%
		Two or more races	4.70%	Cash public assistance	3.40%
Age Groups		Other	3.80%	Food stamp/SNAP	14.80%
Under 18	21.10%				
18-34	24.90%	**Education**		**Work**	
35-64	36.60%	H.S grad or less	30.10%	White Collar	40.00%
Over 64	17.40%	Some college	39.50%	Sales and Service	39.90%
		College Degree, 4 yr	18.70%	Blue Collar	20.20%
Military		Post grad	11.70%	Government	18.90%
Veteran/ Active Duty	11.30%				

2020 Pres. Vote	Trump	215,706	(53%)	Biden	178,895	(44%)	Jorgensen	9,608	(2%)
2016 Pres. Vote	Trump	166,765	(50%)	Clinton	125,112	(38%)	Johnson	18,499	(6%)

Spokane: Eastern Washington is a land of great rivers and bare parched land, where the Columbia, Spokane and Snake rivers wind among vast plateaus, bringing water from the Rockies to the desert. Spokane grew up at the falls of the Spokane River when the railroads first came through. It was initially a gold rush town, and later became a major wheat, mining and railroad center. Nearby are some of the most fascinating landscapes in the United States: undulating yellow wheat fields on the rolling ridges of the Palouse, where the wheat-growing topsoil is 200 feet deep; acres of protected forestland in Colville National Forest, home to the last surviving herd of caribou in the lower 48 states; and bare-rock coulees rising above dammed-up lakes and barren desert. Much of this area is remote and inhospitable. The summers can be blazingly hot and the winters bitterly cold. But the water from the Grand Coulee and other dams irrigates some of the richest farmland in the country.

The 5th Congressional District of Washington covers the easternmost part of the state. Nearly three-fourths of the people live in Spokane County, where the voting habits have grown apart from the Washington west of the Cascades, especially on natural resource issues. Spokane, with four local universities, has become a "second-tier" city where companies locate for quality of life and lower housing costs. From 2010 to 2019, the population of Spokane County grew 11 percent and exceeded 500,000.

A prospective round of base closures has had residents concerned about the fate of Fairchild Air Force Base, the area's largest employer. Fairchild lost two bids to be the home for the new KC-46A aerial tankers; in 2017, it gained 12 additional KC-135s, the military's experienced refueling tanker. The area also is a farming center. Near the Oregon border is Walla Walla, long dependent on alfalfa, wheat and sweet onions. Its budding wine industry had 120 wineries in 2018. Travelocity that year named Walla Walla the best small-city destination for a road trip. The city's name is an American Indian term for "many waters."

The district's political inclinations lean Republican. Spokane County voted for Democrat Bill Clinton in 1992 and 1996, but Republicans have won it since. In 2020, President Donald Trump took 53 percent of the vote, virtually the same as Mitt Romney's performance in 2012. Democrat Tom Foley was the local congressman for 30 years and served as Speaker of the House from 1989 until 1994, when he lost his seat and Democrats lost their majority. Since then, Democrats have twice regained the House but they have not been competitive for the seat.

Derek Kilmer (D)

Elected 2012, 5th term, b. Jan 01, 1974; Port Angeles, WA; Princeton University, A.B., 1996; University of Oxford, Ph.D., 2003; Methodist; Married (Jennifer Kilmer); 2 children.

Elected Office: WA House, 2005-2007; WA Senate, 2007-2013.

Professional Career: Mgmt. consultant, McKinsey & Co., 1999-2002; Vice President., Economic Development Board, Tacoma Pierce County, 2002-2012.

DC Office: 1410 LHOB 20515, 202-225-5916, Fax: 202-226-3575, kilmer.house.gov

State Offices: Bremerton, 360-373-9725; Port Angeles, 360-797-3623; Tacoma, 253-272-3515.

Committees: *Appropriations*: Defense; Energy & Water Development & Related Agencies; Interior, Environment & Related Agencies. *Select Committee on the Modernization of Congress (Chmn)*.

Group Ratings

	ADA	ACLU	AFL-CIO	LCV	COC	HAFA	ACU	CFG	FRC
2020	**	79%	**	100%	-	0%	5%	**	-
2019	90%	C	100%	97%	71%	C	6%	12%	0%

Almanac Ratings 2019-2020

	Economy	Social	Foreign	Composite
Liberal	100%	100%	80%	94%
Conservative	0%	0%	20%	6%

Key Votes of the 116th Congress

1. U.S./Mex./Can. trade deal Y	5. Russia sanctions Y	9. Firearms background checks Y
2. First Coronavirus response Y	6. Troops in Syria Y	10. Spending at the border Y
3. HEROES Act Y	7. Veto arms sales to Saudis Y	11. Marijuana liberalized rules Y
4. CASH Act Y	8. Defense $$$, veto override Y	12. Electoral College objections N

Election Results

Election	Name (Party)	Vote (%)		Cand. Spent	Ind. Exp. Support	Ind. Exp. Oppose
2020 General	Derek Kilmer (D)	247,429	(59%)	$2,014,634	$2,572	
	Elizabeth Kreiselmaier (R)	168,783	(40%)	$144,713		$113
2020 Primary	Derek Kilmer (D)	125,019	(47%)			
	Rebecca Parson (D)	35,631	(14%)			

Prior winning percentages: 2018 (64%), 2016 (62%), 2014 (63%), 2012 (59%)

Democrat Derek Kilmer, elected in 2012, has had a steady rise in influence with a seat on the Appropriations Committee and as a leader of the business-friendly New Democrat Coalition. Kilmer has been a centrist whose interest in defense and resource issues mirrors the needs of his district. As chairman of the select committee to consider ways to modernize Congress, he has worked doggedly to build bipartisan support for steps to improve operations in the House, including Members' offices, while avoiding policy battles and turf conflicts.

Kilmer grew up as the son of two public school teachers in Port Angeles. Watching the town's economic struggles in the wake of the timber industry's decline led Kilmer to pursue a career linking public policy and economic development. He got a bachelor's from Princeton University and a doctorate in social policy from the University of Oxford in England, with a focus on economic development. After working as a business consultant for McKinsey and Co., he went to work for the nonprofit Economic Development Board for Tacoma-Pierce County. As a vice president, he talked with 200 businesses a year in an effort to broaden the economies of communities like Port Angeles, long dependent on timber. Kilmer was elected to the state House in 2004 and two years later moved to the state Senate, where he was the chief author of the state's capital budget and promoted legislation to create jobs by borrowing money for public construction.

Rep. Norm Dicks, who was the senior Democrat on Appropriations, announced his retirement in 2012, Kilmer moved quickly and was the only Democratic contender. In the all-party primary, Kilmer got 53 percent of the vote. Republican businessman Bill Driscoll, an ex-Marine who served in Iraq and Afghanistan, led the six Republican candidates with 18 percent. He departed from Republican orthodoxy in supporting abortion rights and same-sex marriage. Kilmer made sure to let voters know that he was running with the backing of Dicks, his former mentor. The Seattle Times endorsed him as "a problem solver who can be bipartisan." Each candidate spent close to $2 million. Kilmer won 59%-41%.

Kilmer has sought consensus-building with the Bipartisan Working Group and the Problem Solvers Caucus, which have tried to forge greater consensus on a variety of issues. With Republican Rep. Doug Collins of Georgia, he filed the "Keeping American Jobs Act," which sought to assure that employers can't require American workers to train cheaper staff who are working with U.S. visas. He helped organize the Puget Sound Recovery Caucus to bring increased focus and attention to cleanup work. His Almanac vote ratings have placed him near the center of House Democrats. With other junior Democrats, Kilmer won Democratic Caucus approval in 2017 of a requirement that Democrats add a "vice ranking member" to each House committee, with the goal of giving more leadership opportunities to junior Democrats. Fortuitously, Kilmer took that new position at Appropriations.

On Appropriations, he has added district-oriented provisions to subcommittee bills. In the Pentagon appropriations bill for fiscal 2019, he secured funding to upgrade facilities at the Puget Sound shipyard and got $2 million to review steps to reduce military jet noise at the Naval Air Station on Whidbey Island. In July 2020, he got a $5 million increase for the Puget Sound Geographic Program, which supports projects to improve water quality and protect shorelines. He joined House Democrats with districts that represent large military shipyards in urging the Biden administration in March 2021 to prioritize steps to strengthen, modernize and maintain the nation's fleet. Kilmer has been active on the New Democrat Coalition. As chairman in 2019-20, he welcomed more than 40 freshman Democrats to the group as they sought—with mixed success—to offer alternatives to Republican critiques that Democrats were advocating "socialist" views.

After Speaker Nancy Pelosi agreed to demands by many House members for a review of and recommendations for reforms to congressional operations, the House in 2019 created a bipartisan select committee to study ways to modernize Congress. Citing Kilmer as an "innovator and pioneer," she named him as chairman. Two years later, Kilmer listed 97 internal changes the panel approved —far greater success than other congressional reform panels in recent decades. The steps include a bipartisan members-only meeting space in the Capitol, a bipartisan retreat at the start of each Congress, and updated technology and communication for the House. "We all need to work together to solve problems. Too often, that's missing in our government today," Kilmer said. The select committee was renewed in January 2021.

In HR 1, the sweeping political reform bill the House passed in March 2021, Kilmer claimed credit for two provisions: requiring disclosure of who paid for online political advertising and reducing the number of members of the Federal Election Commission from six to five to limit partisan gridlock.

On local interests, Kilmer enacted a bill in 2014 that renamed a memorial on Bainbridge Island in honor of Japanese Americans who were forced from their homes during World War II. With the campaign arm of the New Democrat Coalition, he secured its endorsement of Marilyn Strickland in her competitive open-seat contest in Washington against a more liberal candidate, which Strickland won. He has been reelected easily and appears to have settled in for a lengthy and productive career.

WA-6: Lower Puget Sound, Olympic Peninsula

Cook Partisan Voting Index: D+6

Population		Race and Ethnicity		Income	
Total	726,540	White	80.80%	Median Income	$72,169
Land area (sq. miles)	6,903	Black	4.00%	District Income Rank	148
Pop/ sq mi	105.25	Latino	8.00%	Poverty Rate	8.90%
Born in State	47.80%	Asian	3.80%	With health insurance	94.60%
		Two or more races	7.00%	Cash public assistance	2.20%
Age Groups		Other	4.40%	Food stamp/SNAP	10.90%
Under 18	19.30%				
18-34	21.80%	**Education**		**Work**	
35-64	37.80%	H.S grad or less	30.80%	White Collar	40.10%
Over 64	21.30%	Some college	36.20%	Sales and Service	38.40%
		College Degree, 4 yr	20.60%	Blue Collar	21.40%
Military		Post grad	12.50%	Government	23.20%
Veteran/ Active Duty	17.10%				

2020 Pres. Vote	Biden	244,141	(57%)	Trump	168,250	(39%)	Jorgensen	10,001	(2%)
2016 Pres. Vote	Clinton	172,596	(50%)	Trump	131,449	(38%)	Johnson	19,038	(6%)
	Stein	6,950	(2%)						

Tacoma, Bremerton: The rainiest part of the continental United States is its far northwest corner, where the Olympic Mountains of Washington jut into the Pacific Ocean. The waters of the Pacific evaporate, condense, and then mist or rain on the hills and mountains along Puget Sound. The mountains here are always green, the trees that line the inlets towering, and during heavy rainfalls the rivers can rise six feet in a day. This has long been lumbering and fishing country, where people start work at 6 a.m. and where the vagaries of nature and environmental laws—like the ban on old-growth logging to protect the habitat of the spotted owl—have strengthened a traditional surly independence and suspicion of authority. Still, respect for the beauty of nature endures, including at the 3,310-square-mile Olympic Coast National Marine Sanctuary, a vast underwater reserve.

The many inlets of Puget Sound, winding sinuously through mountains, are among America's most picturesque waterways and strategically among its most important. During World War II, shipyards were built to shelter much of the Navy's Pacific fleet. During the Cold War, some of the nuclear submarine fleet was anchored at the giant Kitsap Navy base. The Puget Sound Naval Shipyard now has five installations. It employed more than 14,000 in 2018. Navy officials have been making plans for an additional dry dock at the shipyard, which already has six. The new one likely would accommodate the Navy's new aircraft carriers, the Kitsap Sun reported in October 2019. The Tacoma Narrows Bridge replaced the original bridge which, in a scene preserved on newsreel and still viewed by civil engineering students, started vibrating on the wrong harmonic in high winds and collapsed in 1940. On the other side is Tacoma, long the second city on Puget Sound, with its massive docks, former pulp mills, pleasant hilly residential neighborhoods and recently revived waterfront. On the northern coast, Port Angeles has been ranked among the nation's best small towns. A retooled paper mill reopened in early 2020 at the site of a 98-year-old factory that had been idle for three years. The Olympic Peninsula extends from the Pacific Ocean to Puget Sound, and from the Canadian border to Oregon.

The 6th Congressional District of Washington includes the Olympic Peninsula, Bremerton and about 40 percent of Tacoma, but not the port; Tacoma also is part of the 9th and 10th Districts. Kitsap County is the largest population center, including Bainbridge Island; "fast ferry" service now offers a 30-minute trip from Bremerton to downtown Seattle. (No bridges cross the sound.) Kitsap has become a popular residential area for residents who can't afford the housing costs in Seattle. About two-thirds of the 6th's residents live in Kitsap or in Tacoma's Pierce County. Politically, the Olympic Peninsula and Tacoma are working-class Democrat, though the remainder of the district is more balanced. Joe Biden in 2020 got 57 percent of the vote—a seven-point increase in Democratic performance from 2016, which was similar to other Seattle-area districts. Port Angeles-based Clallam County might be the only county in the nation that has voted for the winning presidential candidate in every election since 1980. Prior to 2020, there had been 19 such counties, the Wall Street Journal reported. But only Clallam remained perfect.

Pramila Jayapal (D)

Elected 2016, 3rd term, b. Sep 21, 1965; Chennai, India; Georgetown University, A.B., 1986; Northwestern University, M.B.A., 1990; Hinduism; Married (Steve Williamson); 1 child ; 1 stepchild.

Elected Office: WA Senate, 2015-2016.

Professional Career: Financial Analyst; Non Profit Executive.

DC Office: 1510 LHOB 20515, 202-225-3106, Fax: 202-225-6197

State Offices: Seattle, 206-674-0040.

Committees: *Budget. Education & Labor*: Higher Education & Workforce Investment; Workforce Protections. *Judiciary*: Antitrust, Commercial & Administrative Law; Immigration & Citizenship.

Group Ratings

	ADA	ACLU	AFL-CIO	LCV	COC	HAFA	ACU	CFG	FRC
2020	**	87%	**	95%	-	0%	5%	**	-
2019	100%	C	90%	100%	39%	C	4%	18%	0%

Almanac Ratings 2019-2020

	Economy	Social	Foreign	Composite
Liberal	54%	100%	100%	85%
Conservative	46%	0%	0%	15%

Key Votes of the 116th Congress

1. U.S./Mex./Can. trade deal N	5. Russia sanctions Y	9. Firearms background checks Y
2. First Coronavirus response Y	6. Troops in Syria Y	10. Spending at the border N
3. HEROES Act N	7. Veto arms sales to Saudis Y	11. Marijuana liberalized rules Y
4. CASH Act Y	8. Defense $$$, veto override N	12. Electoral College objections N

Election Results

Election	Name (Party)	Vote (%)		Cand. Spent	Ind. Exp. Support	Ind. Exp. Oppose
2020 General	Pramila Jayapal (D)	387,109	(83%)	$1,508,567	$2,311	
	Craig Keller (R)	78,240	(17%)	$511		$113

Prior winning percentages: 2018 (84%), 2016 (56%)

Pramila Jayapal of Washington, who won her seat in 2016 in a runoff against another Democratic state legislator, has become an outspoken leader of House progressives. She has been out front on topics such as government-run health care and taxpayer-funded college tuition for many. Following the 2018 election, Jayapal fell short in her bid for a seat on the Ways and Means Committee. But she has gained prominence as co-chair of the Progressive Caucus. In sparking debate on Medicare for All and leading a liberal rebellion to Democratic leaders' spending plans, she was "steering the progressive legislative agenda" and was "becoming a force party leaders must reckon with," the Wall Street Journal reported in April 2019.

Jayapal, the first Indian-American woman elected to Congress, was born in Chennai India, where her family has continued to reside. Her father was in the oil business, and the family traveled in Asia when she was a child. At 16, she moved to the United States to attend Georgetown University. She worked on Wall Street for PaineWebber as a financial analyst in leveraged buyouts and got an MBA from Northwestern University. After briefly selling cardiac defibrillators in the medical equipment industry, she pursued a career in the nonprofit world, starting with a Seattle-based group working on international public health. She wrote a book about living two years in small towns in India: Pilgrimage to India: A Woman Revisits Her Homeland.

Following the 9/11 terrorist attacks, Jayapal started and was executive director of Hate Free Zone, an advocacy group for South Asians, Arabs and Muslims. She led a national coalition, We Belong Together, which addressed gender-related issues in the Senate-passed immigration reform bill in 2013. She was recognized by President Barack Obama as a White House "Champion of Change." In 2014, Jayapal was elected as the first woman of color to the state Senate, where she worked on tuition-free community college, a state voting rights act, automatic voter registration and measures to help survivors of sexual assault. Her husband, Steve Williamson, has held senior positions with labor unions.

When Democratic Rep. Jim McDermott retired, five Democrats entered the contest to succeed him. In the first round of voting, Jayapal was the frontrunner with 42 percent. The runner-up with 21 percent was Brady Walkinshaw, an openly gay Democratic state representative who styled himself as a bipartisan bridge-builder. In the general election, Jayapal was endorsed by EMILY's List, several labor unions and Sanders. She raised $3 million to $1.9 million for Walkinshaw, who won endorsements from many local Democrats and support from a Latino advocacy group. Jayapal won the runoff, 56%-44%.

Jayapal didn't wait long to get attention. Three days after taking office, during the typically ceremonial count of the Electoral College vote, she raised objections to the 2016 presidential vote count in Georgia, which Donald Trump had easily won. Vice President Joe Biden, who was presiding over the joint session of Congress, gaveled her to silence and advised her, to some laughter, "it's over." Jayapal was one of seven House Democrats who voted against certifying the Trump victory.

In April 2017, she filed in coordination with Sen. Bernie Sanders a bill to make public colleges and universities tuition-free for families with less than $125,000 in income and to significantly reduce student debt. "The College for All Act renews our compact with our young people," Jayapal said. Her centerpiece proposal became the "Medicare for All" plan, on which she took the lead with Rep. Debbie Dingell of Michigan. "One of the best ways to ensure health care for all is to use the system that already exists for millions of seniors over the last half century: Medicare," Jayapal said.

Following the 2018 election, Jayapal was elected with Wisconsin Rep. Mark Pocan as co-chair of the Progressive Caucus. She described her commitment to "ensuring our caucus is as bold and strategic as possible." A January 2019 profile in The Nation headlined that Jayapal's "inside-outside strategy is changing the future of progressive politics."

In March 2019, Politico profiled her as "a mentor with a maternal touch, helping to shepherd a raucous faction that includes a pack of freshman superstars under immense scrutiny on the national stage and even within their own caucus." Noting that she too has faced attacks, Jayapal said, "I know the fear of it, and I also know what it takes to steel yourself and get yourself through that."

As an early endorser of Sanders and the national health policy chair of his campaign, she told the Washington Post in January 2020, "he has a clarity on policy prescriptions that goes right to the heart of what working people need." Her support was all the more important for Sanders as a White man. She sought to draw the contrast between Sanders and Elizabeth Warren, on the one hand, and Joe Biden, whom Jayapal initially referred to as part of the "entrenched interests."

As the campaign evolved, the Seattle Times reported, she came "full circle" with Biden. After he wrapped up his victory, Jayapal said that his success and leftward shifts on some issues "prove that our democracy still works and that the power always belongs to the people through the power of the vote."

At home, Jayapal has clashed with local business leaders—especially Amazon executives. When its chief executive, Jeff Bezos, testified in July 2020 with other large tech leaders before the House Judiciary Committee, Jayapal asked him about Amazon's access to data that gives the company unfair advantages. "So, you can set the rules of the game for your competitors, but not actually follow those same rules for yourself," she said. Bezos defended the company's actions.

WA-7: Seattle Metro   **Cook Partisan Voting Index: D+36**

Population		Race and Ethnicity		Income	
Total	817,787	White	69.70%	Median Income	$100,991
Land area (sq. miles)	144	Black	5.00%	District Income Rank	32
Pop/ sq mi	5,673.95	Latino	8.10%	Poverty Rate	8.60%
Born in State	38.00%	Asian	14.70%	With health insurance	94.90%
		Two or more races	6.80%	Cash public assistance	2.00%
Age Groups		Other	3.80%	Food stamp/SNAP	7.10%
Under 18	15.80%				
18-34	32.40%	Education		Work	
35-64	38.50%	H.S grad or less	15.80%	White Collar	60.10%
Over 64	13.20%	Some college	21.90%	Sales and Service	30.20%
		College Degree, 4 yr	36.10%	Blue Collar	9.70%
Military		Post grad	26.10%	Government	12.60%
Veteran/ Active Duty	4.60%				

2020 Pres. Vote	Biden	410,067	(85%)	Trump	58,832	(12%)			
2016 Pres. Vote	Clinton	341,412	(80%)	Trump	50,615	(12%)	Johnson	13,495	(3%)
	Stein	8,374	(2%)						

Seattle: Seattle rises from the Puget Sound harbor of Elliott Bay on steep hills once covered with 300-foot-high Douglas firs. Behind the hills and buildings, on a clear day you can see the nimbus of Mount Rainier. On the picturesque waterfront, below gleaming high-rises, is Pike Place Market, where you can get fresh salmon and Dungeness crabs. Nearby, where the ferries from Bainbridge and Vashon islands and Bremerton dock in the nation's busiest ferry system, is Pioneer Square, where stores and warehouses from the turn of the 20th century have been restored.

Seattle has some old ethnic neighborhoods, like the once heavily Scandinavian Ballard, which now features boutiques and nightspots, and Capitol Hill, where shoppers jam busy stores, galleries and clubs. Highly educated, affluent single professionals have made the Victorian houses overlooking the harbor and the 1940s houses in Capitol Hill among the nation's highest-priced residential real estate. The counter-culture in that area grabbed the attention of the nation during the summer of 2020 when residents created an "autonomous zone," with no conventional policing; the four blocks were cordoned off from the city for nearly a month, initially to protest the killing of George Floyd in Minneapolis while he was in police custody.

The city's economic foundation is sound, and parts are bustling. Its population increased 24 percent from 2010 to 2019, with more construction of new skyscrapers than any other city in the nation. It has been home to three of the nation's iconic companies—each of which didn't exist 50 years ago and has become an international brand. Rejecting Microsoft's local model of a suburban campus, robust Amazon has a huge downtown campus with office towers in the South Lake Union area. In 2018, the company had more than 40,000 local workers who occupy more than 20 percent of the city's prime office space. Amazon founder Jeff Bezos, the wealthiest person in the world, announced in February 2021 his plan to step down as CEO, perhaps removing himself as a regular local presence. His company grew stronger than ever during the pandemic, though "the lockdown that boosted the company's dominance also threw into higher relief its consequences for other businesses," Time reported in July 2020.

Microsoft founder Bill Gates' decision to turn his attention to global health philanthropy has made Seattle the Davos of health care, drawing experts in malaria, tuberculosis, AIDS and other global scourges. Seattle is the headquarters, in an old industrial district, of Starbucks. In 2020, Starbucks had 32,600 stores worldwide, with a bit more than half of them overseas; the total number doubled since 2010, when two-thirds of the shops were in the United States.

In 2014, the city council spurred a nationwide movement when it increased Seattle's minimum wage to $15 per hour, on a phased timetable to 2021. A further financial twist was the city's move in May 2018 to impose a corporate tax that would raise an estimated $50 million annually to finance steps to aid the homeless; one month later, large businesses—led by Amazon—successfully pressured the city to repeal the fee. In November 2019, Amazon failed in its attempt to defeat City Council member Kshama Sawant, a leading foe of Amazon. Subsequently, the council passed a new payroll tax that was aimed at large companies.

Seattle ranks as one of the nation's most desirable cities. It is a growing haven for young singles, as married couples with children make up only 13 percent of Seattle households. As many as 40 percent of Seattle households have a single occupant. It has a new ethnic mix, with thousands of recent Asian immigrants boosting the total to 15 percent. Still, stark contrasts remain. Yesler Way was America's original Skid Road—literally a path for skidding newly cut logs to transportation terminals. Many worry that it is remains a haven for the homeless and a frequent locale for open-air drug dealing. In March 2019, local KOMO TV aired a documentary that centered on Skid Row and had the title, "Seattle is Dying." The Justice Department investigated the city's police and concluded that the department had engaged in a pattern of excessive force that violated the Constitution and federal law.

The 7th Congressional District of Washington includes nearly all of Seattle, some industrial suburban fringes to the south, a white-collar suburban fringe to the north, and artsy, bucolic Vashon Island in Puget Sound. Less than 10 percent of the population is in the southwest corner of Snohomish County, in Lynnwood. Joe Biden got 85 percent of the vote—an increase of five percentage points from Hillary Clinton's support in 2016. Its Cook PVI of D+36 placed it in the top two percent of most Democratic districts nationwide.

Kim Schrier (D)

Elected 2018, 2nd term, b. Aug 23, 1968; Los Angeles, CA; Universidad Complutense de Madrid (Spain); University of CA, Berkeley, B.A., 1991; University of CA, M.D., 1997; Jewish; Married (David Gowing); 1 child.

Professional Career: Pediatrician, Virginia Mason Medical Center (Issaquah, WA).

DC Office: 1123 LHOB 20515, 202-225-7761, schrier.house.gov

State Offices: Issaquah, 425-657-1001.

Committees: *Agriculture*: Biotechnology, Horticulture & Research; Conservation & Forestry. *Energy & Commerce*: Energy; Health; Oversight & Investigations.

Almanac Ratings 2019-2020

	Economy	Social	Foreign	Composite
Liberal	100%	100%	80%	94%
Conservative	0%	0%	20%	6%

Key Votes of the 116th Congress

1. U.S./Mex./Can. trade deal Y	5. Russia sanctions	Y	9. Firearms background checks Y
2. First Coronavirus response Y	6. Troops in Syria	Y	10. Spending at the border Y
3. HEROES Act Y	7. Veto arms sales to Saudis Y		11. Marijuana liberalized rules Y
4. CASH Act Y	8. Defense $$$, veto override Y		12. Electoral College objections N

Election Results

Election	Name (Party)	Vote (%)	Cand. Spent	Ind. Exp. Support	Ind. Exp. Oppose
2020 General	Kim Schrier (D)................................. 213,123	(52%)	$3,424,540	$62,951	
	Jesse Jensen (R)................................. 198,423	(48%)	$838,748	$50,500	$5,670

Prior winning percentages: 2018 (52%)

Democrat Kim Schrier in 2018 won a district that Republicans had held since 1982. A pediatrician, she said that Republican attempts to repeal the Affordable Care Act spurred her to launch her first political campaign. She became the first woman doctor to serve in Congress. Schrier defeated Dino Rossi, a well-known Republican who had run three competitive statewide campaigns. In her second term, she took her health care experience to a seat on the powerful Energy and Commerce Committee.

Schrier, a native of Los Angeles, graduated from the University of California, Berkeley, with a degree in astrophysics and got her medical degree from the university's Davis campus. She practiced at a medical center in Issaquah Washington for 16 years. As Congress prepared to overhaul the Affordable Care Act in early 2017, Schrier met with an aide to Republican Rep. Dave Reichert to describe the adverse impact of the GOP legislation on her patients. Reichert's decision to support the bill led her to run for his seat. Reichert, who worked on health care issues as a member of the Ways and Means Committee, retired after seven terms.

"The [2016] election and the utter failure of this Congress to provide checks and balances, or to work together on just about anything has compelled me to step up," Schrier said. She made health care the centerpiece of her campaign and said "she'd work to cut drug costs and stabilize Obamacare while moving gradually toward a 'Medicare for all' system," the Seattle Times reported.

In Washington's "top two" primary, Rossi was the frontrunner with 43 percent of the vote. Schrier got 19 percent to edge out Democratic attorney Jason Rittereiser by 1,129 votes for second place. Rittereiser and other Democrats criticized Schrier for failing to take a more activist approach on health care changes. The total vote in the primary split 50%-47% for the Democrats over the Republican candidates.

Rossi, a former state legislator and a commercial real estate investor, lost a bid for governor in 2004 by 139 votes, plus subsequent bids for governor and the Senate. He said Schrier was too liberal for the district and did not share his interest in bipartisanship. Schrier described Rossi as a "career politician" and cited his opposition to abortion as out of step with local voters. In their only debate, Rossi cited his legislative experience and said Schrier's approach to health care "will destroy Medicare as we know it." Schrier said Rossi would place the interests of President Donald Trump above those of constituents.

In its editorial endorsing Rossi, the Seattle Times praised "his demonstrated record of working across the aisle with Democrats" and said he could do that in the "hopelessly dysfunctional Congress." Schrier, according to the editorial, would require more time to show her influence and "falls short in explaining how to manage the cost" of her health care proposals.

Schrier was an impressive fundraiser, with more than $8 million in spending, and she benefited from more than $10 million in spending by national Democrats and progressive interest groups. That nearly doubled Rossi's campaign funds. The combined spending of more than $25 million made the contest "the costliest House race in the nation," the Times reported. In a prime example of suburban hostility to Trump across the nation, Schrier won, 52%-48%. Rossi won four of the five counties and ran best in areas more distant from the Seattle metro area. In King County, which cast about three-fifths of the vote, Schrier took 58 percent.

During the coronavirus pandemic, Schrier sought to secure funds for local public health agencies and to expedite the availability of vaccines. The economic-relief bill Congress enacted in December 2020 included her VACCINES Act, which increased public awareness of immunizations and their benefits. In January 2021, she took a seat on Energy and Commerce, which handles most health care issues. "As the only woman doctor and first pediatrician to serve in Congress, I look forward to being a voice for America's 74 million children and to continue my work to lower health costs for families, expand health care access for children and to improve vaccine confidence and coverage," she said.

During a hearing in February, she cited data showing pregnant mothers are not at greater risk of contracting COVID, but that they are 70 percent more likely to die than the general population if they contract the virus. She filed a bipartisan bill that month that would change the reimbursement rates for Medicaid to expand access for children. "As a pediatrician, I know that now, more than ever, it's critical that children and families can receive the care they need in a timely fashion," she said.

In her reelection, Schrier won, 52%-48%, against Jesse Jensen, a former Army captain and Amazon manager. She outspent him $3.4 million to $839,000. In contrast to 2018, national parties largely passed on this contest. The geographic split in the vote was very similar to 2018. In King County, Schrier got 59 percent. She likely will seek to shift more of her district into King in redistricting.

WA-8: Outer Seattle-Tacoma Suburbs   **Cook Partisan Voting Index: D+1**

Population		Race and Ethnicity		Income	
Total	770,177	White	72.40%	Median Income	$95,968
Land area (sq. miles)	7,360	Black	3.10%	District Income Rank	42
Pop/ sq mi	104.65	Latino	12.00%	Poverty Rate	7.90%
Born in State	50.70%	Asian	9.60%	With health insurance	94.00%
		Two or more races	5.80%	Cash public assistance	2.20%
Age Groups		Other	9.10%	Food stamp/SNAP	7.30%
Under 18	25.10%				
18-34	19.80%	**Education**		**Work**	
35-64	40.90%	H.S grad or less	31.80%	White Collar	42.10%
Over 64	14.40%	Some college	31.40%	Sales and Service	36.00%
		College Degree, 4 yr	23.90%	Blue Collar	21.80%
Military		Post grad	12.90%	Government	13.70%
Veteran/ Active Duty	8.50%				

2020 Pres. Vote	Biden	218,274	(52%)	Trump	190,801	(45%)	Jorgensen	8,573	(2%)
2016 Pres. Vote	Clinton	153,167	(46%)	Trump	143,403	(43%)	Johnson	17,644	(5%)

Auburn, Wenatchee: In the shadow of the majestic 14,410-foot Mount Rainier, Seattle in the last 50 years has spread out to all four points of the compass. In 1960, surrounding King County had 935,000 residents, 557,000 of whom lived in Seattle. Since then, the city has added about 200,000 people, but the county has more than doubled to 2.3 million. At first these newcomers moved into places like Bellevue, Redmond and Renton, on the flat lands to the north and west of Cougar Mountain. As those places have filled in, the metropolitan area expanded out past Lake Sammamish and into the foothills of the Cascades, the valleys between the peaks of the Issaquah Alps and the southern flatlands of the Puget Trough. Auburn, an old center for hop farming that became a factory town for Boeing in the 1960s, doubled its population from 1999 to 2019, as a new super mall attracted businesses, jobs and new residents.

The 8th Congressional District of Washington takes in much of this new frontier in greater Seattle's development, as well as some of its last remaining areas of undeveloped land. It encompasses all of Mount Rainier, as well as one of the nation's last inland old-growth rain forests. Other areas include the southern edge of King County, including Auburn and smaller towns like Algona, Milton and Lakeland North. In Issaquah, which grew 30 percent from 2010 to 2019, Costco has expanded its corporate headquarters. In 2019, Costco ranked 14th in revenues among the Fortune 500. The district extends into Pierce County, where it includes some of the suburbs east of Tacoma. The risk of mud slides and volcanic debris at Rainier have led Pierce County officials to prepare improved detections and warnings. The district also takes in three agricultural counties that extend east of the Cascades. Kittitas County is a major producer of hay, most of which is shipped overseas. Wenatchee, the county seat of Chelan, has been discovered as the "go-to place for everything from wine tourism and real-estate speculation to cannabis farming and bitcoin mining," the Seattle Times wrote in August 2018. Close to 60 percent of the district is in King, nearly 25 percent in Pierce, and the remainder is in or beyond the Cascades.

Of the three districts that are based chiefly in King County, the 8th has the preponderance of Republican precincts. Even with redistricting changes in 2012 that increased the GOP vote by several percentage points, the district has moved to the Democrats. Barack Obama won the district by two points in 2012; Joe Biden led, 52%-45%. The district "all but oozes red and blue," the Times wrote perceptively in October 2020. "It illustrates the stark divide between Eastern and Western Washington voters, especially so in the last four years." In the congressional vote in November 2020, the King County portion of the district went Democratic, 59%-41%. In the remaining four counties, the GOP candidate won 58 percent.

Adam Smith (D)

Elected 1996, 13th term, b. Jun 15, 1965; Washington, DC; Western WA University, Att.; Fordham University, B.A., 1987; University of WA, J.D., 1990; Christian Church; Married (Sara Bickle-Eldridge Smith); 2 children.

Elected Office: WA Senate, 1990-1996.

Professional Career: Practicing attorney, 1991-1992; City prosecutor, 1993-1995.

DC Office: 2264 RHOB 20515, 202-225-8901, adamsmith.house.gov

State Offices: Renton, 425-793-5180.

Committees: *Armed Services (Chmn).*

Group Ratings

	ADA	ACLU	AFL-CIO	LCV	COC	HAFA	ACU	CFG	FRC
2020	**	83%	**	100%	-	0%	10%	**	-
2019	85%	C	95%	97%	52%	C	10%	18%	0%

Almanac Ratings 2019-2020

	Economy	Social	Foreign	Composite
Liberal	100%	66%	92%	86%
Conservative	0%	34%	8%	14%

Key Votes of the 116th Congress

1. U.S./Mex./Can. trade deal Y	5. Russia sanctions Y	9. Firearms background checks Y
2. First Coronavirus response Y	6. Troops in Syria Y	10. Spending at the border N
3. HEROES Act Y	7. Veto arms sales to Saudis Y	11. Marijuana liberalized rules Y
4. CASH Act Y	8. Defense $$$, veto override Y	12. Electoral College objections N

Election Results

Election	Name (Party)	Vote (%)	Cand. Spent	Ind. Exp. Support	Ind. Exp. Oppose
2020 General	Adam Smith (D)............................ 258,771	(74%)	$523,505	$2,095	
	Doug Basler (R)............................ 89,697	(26%)	$18,026		$113

Prior winning percentages: 2018 (68%), 2016 (73%), 2014 (71%), 2012 (72%), 2010 (55%), 2008 (65%), 2006 (66%), 2004 (63%), 2002 (59%), 2000 (62%), 1998 (65%), 1996 (50%)

Adam Smith of Washington, a Democrat first elected in 1996, has become an expert on military policy and logistics and often a blunt critic as the chairman of the House Armed Services Committee. Although he has joined the panel's tradition of bipartisanship, the polarization of Congress occasionally has led Smith to go his own way. His takeover as committee chairman could give him a lengthy tenure and enhance the clout of home-state defense facilities and industries.

Smith grew up in the Sea-Tac area. His father, a baggage handler for United Airlines who was active in the Machinists Union, died when Smith was 17. The family went on welfare. Smith worked his way through Fordham University driving trucks for UPS, and got his law degree at the University of Washington. He worked as a Seattle prosecutor, handling drunk-driving and domestic-abuse cases. In 1990, at age 25, he was elected to the state Senate, beating an incumbent Republican by canvassing the district door-to-door.

In 1996, he ran against first-term Republican Rep. Randy Tate. The two had similar backgrounds. They had been born in the same year to families of modest means, were elected to office at a young age and were firm believers in grassroots campaigning. Tate was a religious conservative and a strong supporter of House Speaker Newt Gingrich, while Smith campaigned as a pro-business moderate Democrat, supporting the death penalty and tougher penalties for criminals. Tate attacked Smith for his opposition to assigning youthful offenders to adult courts and prisons and for voting for a tax increase in 1993. This was one of the closest races in the country. In the September all-party primary, Smith led 49%-48%. In November, he won 50%-47%.

Smith joined the New Democrat Coalition, established a moderate voting record and showed a willingness to take on established views and interests in his party. He voted to authorize military action in Iraq and sought to improve compensation and other quality-of-life benefits for military personnel. He supported the House-passed health care overhaul in 2009, but refused to commit publicly on the final version until the very end in March 2010, finally agreeing to back it after pleas from President Barack Obama and others. In 2012, he lamented "the hyper-partisanship that is making Congress so dysfunctional." In opposing the New Year's Day 2013 tax and spending deal to avoid the so-called fiscal cliff, he accused Obama of "bad math" and of being unrealistic. In 2015, in a switch of his customary free-trade views, Smith cited problems for workers and the environment when he voted against giving trade promotion authority to Obama.

On the Armed Services Committee, Smith earned praise for his work as chairman of two of its subcommittees. When Armed Services Chairman Ike Skelton of Missouri lost his reelection bid in 2010, Smith made a bid for ranking Democrat on the panel. Intelligence Committee Chairman Silvestre Reyes of Texas and California Rep. Loretta Sanchez—two Latinos—also got into the race. In the Democratic Caucus, Sanchez and Smith tied at 64 votes apiece, while Reyes got 53. In the runoff, Smith won by 11 votes.

Smith joined efforts to help the military adapt to automatic spending cuts that took effect in 2013. As Armed Services chairman, Republican Rep. Mac Thornberry of Texas said Smith has helped make the committee less partisan. Ironically, Smith for the first time voted in May 2015 against passage of the defense spending bill, and called it "extremely damaging" to national security because it did not remove the budgetary spending caps and shifted some funding off-budget. In November, after a budget deal was reached, he rejoined the bipartisan majority on the defense bill. In 2016, he again switched his earlier opposition after hot-button social issues were removed and the bill made "positive improvements" to defense policy.

In 2014, Smith was appointed to the select committee investigating the terrorist attacks at U.S. facilities in Benghazi Libya. "This is a committee that should not have been formed," he said when it was unveiled. "But since the Republicans chose to form it, I think we have to participate to do our best to bring out the correct arguments." Earlier, he said Obama "could have done a better job" in working with Congress before taking military action against Libya in 2011, but he backed the president's strategy.

In the debate over the Islamic State, he dismissed hawks' calls for swift military action and emphasized the need to build coalitions. "We need reliable partners to work with in the region," Smith told CBS News. "We can't simply bomb first and ask questions later." He said a formal request for authorization for use of military force should be sharply limited in how much power it gave to the president. "I don't think we should give the executive a blank check," he said. On the defense spending bill that was enacted in August 2018, Smith took credit for more public disclosure of civilian casualties in U.S. military operations, limits on military support of Saudi Arabia and restrictions on the military use of public lands.

After Donald Trump was elected, Smith voiced serious doubts about his national security views. "I don't think it's intellectually possible to digest what he's talking about, and I'm not just being a wise-ass here," he told McClatchy News in November 2016. As time passed, his fears about Trump deepened. "There is no sugar coating," he said following Trump's meeting with Russian President Vladimir Putin in Helsinki in July 2018. "It is hard to see … as anything other than treason" Trump's taking sides against the views of the U.S. intelligence community. Congress needed to "begin an impeachment investigation," he added. Smith said Trump's demand for a wall along the border with Mexico was rooted in "xenophobia and racism."

Taking over as Armed Services Committee chairman in January 2019, at age 53, Smith said he would hold the administration accountable for military operations overseas and for wasteful military spending. He called the past approach by the Pentagon, "scare the crap out of you and convince you to spend more money." He showed leadership in modernizing military operations, including creation of the Space Force and improved organization of cyber actions.

Smith harshly criticized Trump's use of the military during domestic protests in 2020 and the administration's refusal to explain their actions to Congress. When Trump fired Defense Secretary Mark Esper following the 2020 election, Smith called the action "not just childish, it's also reckless" for national security.

As Joe Biden prepared to take over as president, Smith said he would support him in expected clashes with liberal Democrats over cuts in Pentagon spending. He became a consistent advocate of reducing forces in Afghanistan, agreeing with actions by both Trump and Biden to reduce the U.S. military presence. "There are other means to monitor that threat and manage risk and, at this point, the cost and risk of a continued troop presence—both U.S. troops and those of our allies—outweigh the benefits," he said in April 2021.

Smith's independence has worked well for him at home and he usually has won reelection easily. His closest contest was a 55%-45% win over Pierce County Council member Dick Muri during the Republican wave in 2010. Redistricting changes in 2012 removed most of his base in Pierce County and gave him a King County-based district that was ethnically diverse and largely new to him, but more safely Democratic.

In 2016, Democrat Jesse Wineberry, an African American and former state representative, challenged Smith for not being a local advocate. Smith responded that 160 languages were spoken in the district and said, "I consistently reach out to these communities." In the all-party primary, Smith got 56 percent to 23 percent for Republican Doug Basler and 15 percent for Wineberry. He defeated Basler in November, 73%-27%. Smith eagerly supported Pramila Jayapal in the neighboring 7th District. She was a resident of the 9th and might have been a serious threat if she had instead challenged Smith. In 2018, styling himself as "progressive," he won the runoff with 68 percent against Democrat Sarah Smith, a political newcomer and member of the Democratic Socialists of America.

Redistricting could affect Smith's exposure to criticism by local activists and the potential tensions with his responsibilities as Armed Services chairman.

WA-9: Southern and Eastern Seattle Metro   Cook Partisan Voting Index: D+23

Population		Race and Ethnicity		Income	
Total	751,595	White	49.20%	Median Income	$90,353
Land area (sq. miles)	183	Black	12.00%	District Income Rank	57
Pop/ sq mi	4,097.45	Latino	12.90%	Poverty Rate	8.70%
Born in State	37.10%	Asian	23.90%	With health insurance	92.90%
		Two or more races	6.70%	Cash public assistance	2.20%
Age Groups		Other	8.30%	Food stamp/SNAP	10.10%
Under 18	20.80%				
18-34	26.80%	Education		Work	
35-64	38.40%	H.S grad or less	28.50%	White Collar	46.40%
Over 64	13.80%	Some college	27.00%	Sales and Service	35.40%
		College Degree, 4 yr	26.30%	Blue Collar	18.10%
Military		Post grad	18.30%	Government	11.10%
Veteran/ Active Duty	5.60%				

2020 Pres. Vote	Biden	265,393	(73%)	Trump	88,993	(24%)	
2016 Pres. Vote	Clinton	205,193	(69%)	Trump	67,956	(23%) Johnson	11,178 (4%)

Bellevue, Renton: The misty shores of Puget Sound have seen some of America's most vibrant economic growth over the past two decades. It has spread south and west from Seattle, over suburban territory to the outskirts of the once-industrial city of Tacoma. The subdivisions along the sound, which have some of the loveliest views in the U.S., tend to be high-income. But much of greater Seattle's prime industrial territory lies between the ridges that run north and south inland. In 2016, Weyerhaeuser, the world's largest private owner of softwood timber, moved its longtime headquarters in Federal Way to downtown Seattle. A host of smaller factories cluster near the rail lines that are the terminus from Minneapolis-St. Paul across the Great Plains to Puget Sound.

Boeing is a major presence in Renton, on the south end of Lake Washington. Its aircraft and electronic components plants have made it the nation's No. 1 exporter for many years. Renton manufactures 737 Max planes. In September 2018, the Seattle Times reported, the delayed delivery and assembly of many parts for the new 737s had resulted in workers putting in long overtime hours and "struggling to get planes finished" to meet the company's far-flung sales commitments. In the next six months, two of those Boeing-manufactured passenger planes crashed—in Indonesia and Ethiopia—resulting in large loss of lives and a worldwide shutdown of the Max that continued for nearly two years until explanations and solutions were found. With Boeing shutting down its 747 and 787 assembly lines in nearby Everett, there was speculation that assembly of the Max would shift from Renton to Everett. In November 2020, the Wall Street Journal reported that many earlier orders for the Max had been canceled due to the travel slowdown caused by the pandemic.

The 9th Congressional District of Washington covers much of this area. It includes Sea-Tac Airport and Renton, just south of Seattle, as well as Des Moines, and most of Kent and Federal Way. It includes the container port of Tacoma, though most of that city is in the 6th and 10th Districts. The 9th extends northward from the south Seattle suburbs, where it takes in the southeastern neighborhoods of Seattle proper. It also pushes into the eastern suburbs. As the city grew over the years, newcomers crossed the pontoon bridge across Mercer Island to Bellevue and made that area one of the most vibrant parts of metropolitan Seattle. Bellevue, where the population doubled from 1970 to 2010, is the fastest-growing neighborhood in Seattle, with many large residential and business projects underway. When Expedia abandoned its headquarters in Bellevue to move to Seattle's waterfront, Amazon made a deal to move more than 4,000 of its employees into the former Expedia headquarters in 2020. In September 2020, the Seattle Times reported that Amazon planned to locate 25,000 employees in Bellevue by 2025, which would be similar in size to its new headquarters in Arlington Virginia.

The Seattle and Tacoma ports have unified management in an alliance to compete more effectively with other ports. Their container cargo made the combined ports the fourth-largest in the United States, supporting 58,400 jobs statewide. Passenger traffic at Sea-Tac in 2019 was the eighth-busiest in the nation. A new international arrivals facility was scheduled to open in 2021. In late 2019, prior to the pandemic, local officials were weighing alternatives for additional airline capacity —either with an expansion at Sea-Tac or perhaps a second airport closer to Tacoma or Olympia.

More than 95 percent of the district is in King County. The 9th takes in much of Seattle's minority population and is the city's first majority-minority district. It is 24 percent Asian, 13 percent Hispanic, 12 percent African American. In 2020, Joe Biden led, 73%-24%.

Marilyn Strickland (D)

Elected 2020, 1st term, b. Sep 25, 1962; Seoul, South Korea; Tacoma Public Schools; University of WA, B.A.; Clark Atlanta University, M.B.A.; Not Known; Married (Pactrick Erwin); 2 stepchildren.

Elected Office: Member, Tacoma City Council, 2008-2009; Mayor, City of Tacoma, 2010-2017.

Professional Career: President/CEO, Seattle Metropolitan Chamber of Commerce, 2018-2020.

DC Office: 1004 LHOB 20515, 202-225-9740, strickland.house.gov

State Offices: Lacey, 360-459-8514; Lakewood, 253-533-8332.

Committees: *Armed Services*: Military Personnel; Readiness. *Transportation & Infrastructure*: Highways & Transit; Railroads, Pipelines & Hazardous Materials.

Election Results

Election	Name (Party)	Vote (%)		Cand. Spent	Ind. Exp. Support	Ind. Exp. Oppose
2020 General	Marilyn Strickland (D)..................	167,937	(49%)	$1,789,334	$151,758	$403,994
	Beth Doglio (D).................................	121,040	(36%)	$1,482,245	$668,643	
2020 Primary	Marilyn Strickland (D).....................	45,988	(20%)			
	Beth Doglio (D).................................	34,254	(15%)			
	Kristine Reeves (D)...........................	29,236	(13%)			

Democrat Marilyn Strickland won a runoff against another Democrat, a result of Washington's "top two" selection in its primary elections. She had wide experience in local politics and business. With the mixed demographics of her parents, she entered the House with two "firsts": the first African-American elected from her home state and the first Korean-American woman from anywhere in the nation, along with two first-term Republicans from California. She succeeded Democrat Denny Heck, who retired after four terms and was elected lieutenant governor.

Strickland was born in Seoul, South Korea. Her mother was a Korean native. Her father, an African American who served in World War II and the Korean War, was stationed there with the Army. In 1967, the family settled in Tacoma, where her father served at Fort Lewis, a large military base. Because of their mixed races, Strickland said, they earlier were denied legal residency in

Virginia. "My parents endured discrimination and hardships that I cannot imagine," she wrote in her campaign profile. She got her bachelor's degree from the University of Washington and a master's in business administration from Clark Atlanta University.

Strickland had multiple jobs in the private sector, including as manager of the online business of Starbucks and with an advertising agency to promote public broadband service for cable television in Tacoma. After two years on the Tacoma City Council, Strickland was elected mayor of the city from 2010 to 2018. In that position, she promoted foreign investment in Tacoma, including expansion of its large port facilities. The international visitors whom she hosted as mayor included China's President Xi Jinping. In "rebuilding an economy after an economic recession," she claimed credit for more than 40,000 new jobs in the Tacoma region.

After stepping down as mayor, Strickland became president of the Seattle Metropolitan Chamber of Commerce. In that position, she actively opposed proposals for businesses to pay a local "head tax," based on their number of employees and revenue. The Seattle City Council, responding to heated protests, repealed the tax shortly after it was enacted.

Following Heck's retirement announcement, 19 candidates entered the all-party primary for his seat. The top two, with 20 and 15 percent of the vote, were Strickland and Beth Doglio, a state representative and environmental activist who has focused on climate policy. Kristine Reeves, a state representative and adviser to international students, got 13 percent. Rian Ingrim, a military veteran who ran a fashion company, was the leading Republican; he finished fourth with 11 percent.

Doglio—who is openly bisexual, with a husband and two sons—was a leading opponent of controversial proposals for coal export terminals on the coast of Washington. She supported the Green New Deal and aggressive proposals to reach net-zero emissions in the electricity sector. Strickland, in supporting proposed projects in the Tacoma port that relied on natural gas, was opposed by environmental groups. In describing the contest, the Intercept, an activist news organization on the political left, wrote in September that the outcome "will say much about what kind of Democratic Party will be tackling climate change in the years ahead."

Doglio was backed by Sens. Bernie Sanders and Elizabeth Warren, plus labor and environmental groups. The political action committee of the Congressional Progressive Caucus, chaired by Rep. Pramila Jayapal of Washington, spent more than $400,000 on behalf of Doglio. Former Democratic Govs. Christine Gregoire and Gary Locke endorsed Strickland, as did the Congressional Black Caucus and three Democrats in the state's House delegation.

Strickland defeated Doglio, 49%-36%; write-in candidates got the remaining vote. Strickland won 52 percent in Tacoma-based Pierce County, which cast about three-fifths of the vote, and also led in the two smaller counties.

In the House, she got seats on Armed Services, and Transportation and Infrastructure—two committees where the Puget Sound region already is well-represented.

WA-10: Southwest Seattle Metro   Cook Partisan Voting Index: D+5

Population		Race and Ethnicity		Income	
Total	770,391	White	71.30%	Median Income	$75,114
Land area (sq. miles)	827	Black	6.40%	District Income Rank	129
Pop/ sq mi	931.92	Latino	12.60%	Poverty Rate	9.80%
Born in State	47.80%	Asian	7.30%	With health insurance	93.10%
		Two or more races	8.10%	Cash public assistance	3.30%
Age Groups		Other	6.80%	Food stamp/SNAP	12.20%
Under 18	22.60%				
18-34	24.40%	**Education**		**Work**	
35-64	37.90%	H.S grad or less	34.80%	White Collar	35.60%
Over 64	14.90%	Some college	37.20%	Sales and Service	38.40%
		College Degree, 4 yr	17.50%	Blue Collar	26.00%
Military		Post grad	10.40%	Government	21.50%
Veteran/ Active Duty	16.60%				

2020 Pres. Vote	Biden	216,800	(56%)	Trump	157,058	(40%)	Jorgensen	9,062	(2%)
2016 Pres. Vote	Johnson	17,003	(6%)	Stein	6,481	(2%)		

Tacoma Metro, Olympia: Beginning at Deception Pass, near present-day Mount Vernon and Anacortes, Puget Sound winds its way southward from the Strait of Juan de Fuca for more than 100 miles, through an intricate latticework of bays, straits and islands. At the far southern end of the sound, off Budd Inlet, is Olympia, the capital of Washington. In 1846, two New England natives, Lathrop Smith and Edmund Sylvester, hoping to take advantage of the location near the end of the Cowlitz Trail, platted a town in the New England style: a town square, carefully planned streets and land reserved for schools. They initially opted to name the town Smithster—a portmanteau of their surnames—but eventually opted for Olympia, after the mountains that are visible to the north on a clear day. It soon thereafter became the capital of Washington territory. As late as 1880, Olympia's population rivaled that of other major Washington cities. But the railroads passed it by, and other ports were developed in more advantageous positions closer to the mouth of Puget Sound. Olympia grew at a relatively slow but steady pace, sustained mostly by the lumber industry and state government. In 2018, the port supported 5,000 jobs and $300 million in business revenues in the area.

Today, the lumber industry is in decline in Olympia; the Georgia Pacific and St. Regis mills are long closed. Olympia is a relatively small city, with an economy that revolves mostly around government. The city has tried to diversify into tourism and as a hub for hydraulic fracturing, known as "fracking," a technique for extracting oil and natural gas. Environmentalists have protested shipments through the Olympia port of materials for fracking in the oil fields of North Dakota. Percival Landing, one of three waterfront parks in Olympia, features a mile-long boardwalk, restaurants, and piers for boats. Since 2000, Thurston County has grown 39 percent; fast-growing Lacey has grown almost as large as Olympia and has a higher median income.

Pierce County, which has grown 28 percent since 2000, has become a destination for homeowners who cannot afford the real-estate prices in Seattle and King County. In 2018, Pierce was second in the number of persons migrating within the area; Snohomish County, which is north of Seattle, ranked first. In Tacoma, where 40 percent of the population is minority, the city decided in 2017 not to expand its immigrant detention center, out of fear that it might facilitate round-ups and deportations by the Trump administration. The Puyallup tribe, one of the most urban Native American tribes in the nation, opened a huge casino in Tacoma in June 2020; it replaced a former bingo hall. Federal and state COVID regulations do not apply on reservations, though some federal economic relief has been provided to the tribes.

The 10th Congressional District centers around Olympia-based Thurston County and Tacoma-based Pierce County. A small fraction lives in Mason County, to the northwest. The district leans comfortably Democratic. Joe Biden won 56%-40%, an increase from Hillary Clinton's 50%-39% win in 2016; those figures were similar to the results in the adjacent 6th District.

WEST VIRGINIA

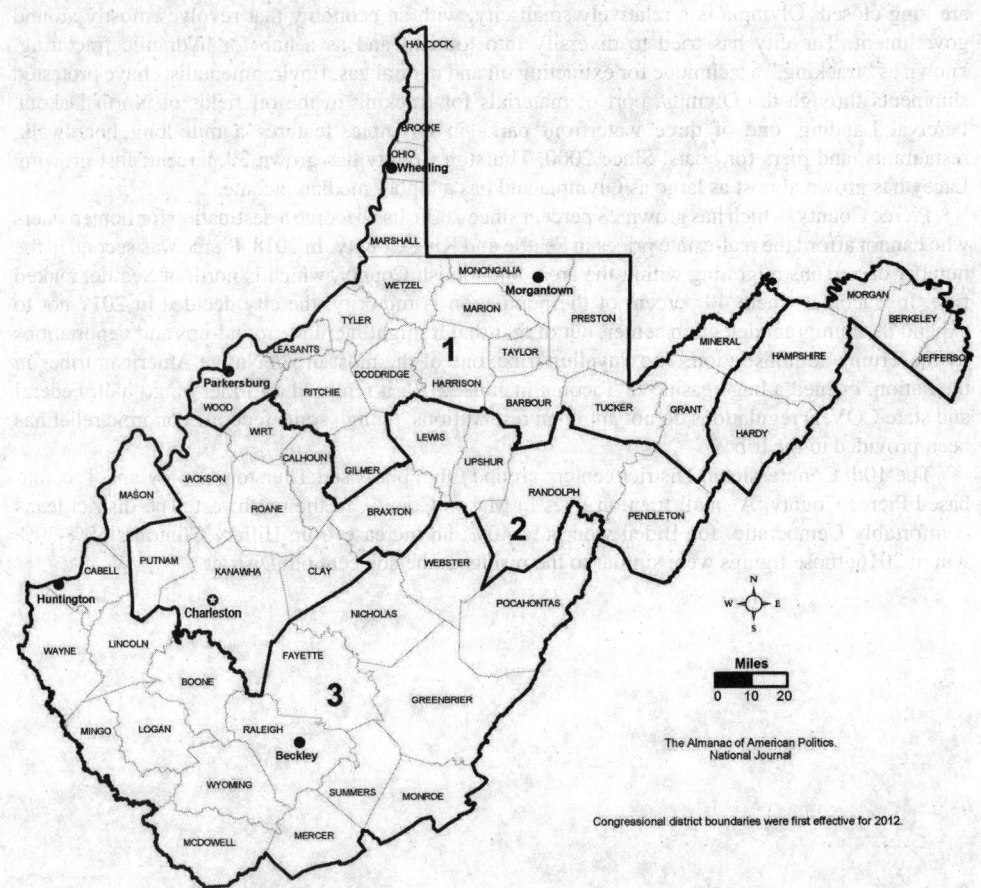

The Almanac of American Politics.
National Journal

Miles
0   10   20

Congressional district boundaries were first effective for 2012.

Few states have shifted more quickly, and more completely, from Democratic to Republican than West Virginia. Democratic presidential candidates haven't won the state since 1996, and none has won even a single county since 2008. In 2016, Donald Trump defeated Hillary Clinton, who was hobbled by an awkward comment that dramatized her view about putting coal miners out of work, by a 42-point margin. Four years later, Trump won West Virginia by a barely diminished 39 points. All this has occurred while the state has grappled with severe industrial decline and the resulting economic and social woes.

"Almost heaven" is what the song says about West Virginia, and there's something to it, at least in the minds of West Virginians who have never lost their affection for the state's hills and hollers. Yet the state has had more than its share of tragedy and heartbreak. It was first settled by Scots-Irish immigrants, fresh from internecine fighting and determined to stake out comfortable homesteads. The state slogan is Montani semper liberi: Mountaineers are always free. West Virginia was created as a separate state during the Civil War, when a Republican Congress admitted to the union 55 mountain counties from Virginia that had few slaves. In 2020, West Virginia's governor and lawmakers flipped the script and invited Virginia counties—thinking mainly of rural, conservative ones like Frederick County (Winchester) that were dismayed with the new Democratic control in Richmond—to join West Virginia instead.

West Virginia has long made a living from coal. The state flag features a farmer and a coal miner, and the state's hills and mountains are laced with the black mineral. There are coal seams in 53 of its counties; coal kept the sons of large mountaineer families from leaving the state for much of the 20th century, and it brought immigrants from odd corners of Europe. People also came from adjacent areas of the South, where the local farming economies were stagnant as West Virginia's coal economy was booming. West Virginia today is 93 percent White—trailing only Maine and Vermont—3.2 percent black and 1.4 percent Hispanic. In the mid-20th century, the availability of coal and local rock salt and brines led to the building of chemical plants in the Kanawha Valley around Charleston. Steel mills and glass factories went up in the Northern Panhandle and in the Monongahela River valley south of Pittsburgh; once there were 60 glass factories, but most are gone, save the Blenko Glass Co., which produces artisan-quality pieces in Milton.

The resource economy has been neither steady nor reliable. Demand for coal skyrocketed during World War II, and just after the war West Virginia coal production peaked at 179 million tons a year; not coincidentally, the state's population hit a record 2 million in the 1950 census. But demand for coal plunged as houses switched to oil for heat, and mechanization, especially in strip mines, reduced the demand for labor. To compensate, Democratic Sen. Robert Byrd leveraged his 50 years on the Senate Appropriations Committee to steer $1 billion of federal projects into the state, including the FBI's biggest division, with thousands of workers and contractors in Clarksburg. But coal remains a major industry in the state, and it maintains a sizable role in electricity generation. Where jobs still exist, miners can earn solid wages. However, the industry's decline has accelerated in recent years, as China has reduced its purchases, as U.S. natural gas production has expanded, and as production has shifted from the eastern United States to the West, where coal reserves have less sulfur and lie closer to the surface and thus can be removed more easily and cheaply. Trump's energetic support for the industry ended up not helping much, as numerous coal companies filed for bankruptcy during his presidency, including Murray Energy in 2019 and Rhino Resource Partners in 2020.

Despite safety improvements, work in the mines remains gritty and dangerous. In 2006, an underground explosion at the Sago mine killed 12; the mine had been cited for 208 violations. Then, in 2010, another explosion, at the Upper Big Branch mine, killed 29 miners, the worst coal-mining disaster in decades. After the latter tragedy, the company's CEO, Don Blankenship, was sentenced to a year in federal prison for conspiracy to willfully violate mine health and safety standards. Membership in the United Mine Workers has declined. In 2016, the Republican-controlled legislature passed a right-to-work law detested by labor unions, and it was upheld by the state Supreme Court in 2020. Miners have lobbied for federal and state laws to provide more generously for black lung disease, which recently hit a 25-year high for cases. "Throughout the 30 years that I've covered the statehouse, the specter of the decline of the coal industry has loomed over state government," the Charleston Gazette-Mail's Phil Kabler wrote. "But instead of working to build a post-coal economy, governors and legislatures—both Republican and Democratic—have devoted their efforts to propping up a dying industry."

West Virginia has some natural gas, too, in the Marcellus shale formation under several of the state's northern counties. This has helped ease the state's fiscal position, but "once the well is drilled, it doesn't take many people to manage that well," said John Deskins, director of WVU's Bureau of Business and Economic Research. The natural gas industry suffered a blow in 2020 when backers of the $8 billion West Virginia-to-North Carolina Atlantic Coast Pipeline scuttled the project, citing the "legal uncertainty that overhangs large-scale energy and industrial infrastructure development." A pattern has emerged from resource extraction in West Virginia: In the 1870s, the state legally separated land ownership from mineral rights, meaning that landowners didn't necessarily profit from underground deposits. "The big theme of West Virginia historically is our wealth and our income is not here—it's taken somewhere else," Sean O'Leary of the West Virginia Center on Budget and Policy told the New York Times.

West Virginia offers a litany of grim statistics. Its median household income ranks second from the bottom, exceeding only Mississippi's, and adjusting for inflation, it took until 2019 for the median income to climb back to its pre-Great Recession level. West Virginia's pre-pandemic poverty rate was 16.2 percent, fourth-highest in the country, with 20.8 percent of children in poverty, the seventh-worst of any state. West Virginia is neck and neck with Mississippi for the lowest labor force participation rate in the nation, and it ranks dead last in the percentage of residents with a bachelor's degree. On the environmental front, West Virginia ranked fifth-worst for the number of per capita violations by public water systems. The state continues to reel from the opioid epidemic, with the nation's highest overdose rate. Between 2007 and 2012, drug wholesalers shipped more than 780 million hydrocodone and oxycodone pills into the state, or 433 pain pills for every man, woman and child in West Virginia. The cycle of addiction has affected all corners of life; since 2013, the number of children taken into foster care in West Virginia has increased by two-thirds. Lawsuits against companies involved in opioids are proceeding on the state and federal level. Meanwhile, in 2019, the state narrowly escaped larger impacts from a cluster of HIV cases in Cabell County (Huntington) that were traced to shared needles. The following year, West Virginia struggled with the coronavirus pandemic but earned national praise for its speed in getting vaccines to seniors, thanks to close ties between mom-and-pop pharmacies and local residents. Securing broadband for remote schooling during the pandemic was difficult, however, due to fiscal shortcomings and the mountainous terrain. The legislature expanded school choice options in the 2021 session.

West Virginia has the dubious distinction of being the only state to have a smaller population today than it had in 1950. Since the 2010 census, West Virginia's population has fallen 3.2 percent, and impoverished coal counties have contracted even faster—12 percent in Mingo County and 20 percent in McDowell County. Part of this is age-related. West Virginia ranks third highest in the share of its population 65 and over, behind only Maine and Florida. The few growing areas of the state include Berkeley and Jefferson counties in the Eastern Panhandle, which are now effectively long-distance Washington D.C. suburbs; since 2010, they have grown 14 percent and 7 percent, respectively. Monongalia County, home to Morgantown and West Virginia University, has grown 9 percent. But even Kanawha County, home of the state capital, Charleston, has shrunk almost 8 percent. The population drain will cost West Virginia one of its three House seats.

West Virginia's political heritage from the Civil War days was Republican, though some counties tilted toward the Confederacy and Democrats. The United Mine Workers organized most of the West Virginia mines by 1902, and there were bloody strikes in 1912-13 and 1920-21. Under the UMW's John L. Lewis, coal country shifted toward New Deal Democrats, and for more than half a century, West Virginia was one of the nation's most Democratic states. In the 21st century, it has swung hard to the Republicans. A big reason was national Democrats' attitudes toward coal, as well as guns. In the 2000 presidential race, George W. Bush's strategist Karl Rove ignored precedent and targeted West Virginia; it paid off, as Bush won by six points. By 2008, the GOP presidential margin had expanded to 13 points, and in the 2012 Democratic presidential primary, 41 percent of registered Democrats voted for a convict instead of President Barack Obama.

The down-ballot dominoes started falling in 2014. The legislature, which had been Democratic since the 1930s, fell to the GOP; Republicans won all the state's House seats for the first time since

1921; and the GOP flipped the seat held by retiring Democratic Sen. John (Jay) Rockefeller. In 2016, businessman Jim Justice won the governorship as a Democrat but switched to the GOP less than a year later. In 2018, Democrat Joe Manchin narrowly won reelection, but by 2020, he became the last statewide elected Democrat, as the Democrats lost the state treasurer's post. In his 2020 reelection bid, Trump won Monongalia County by only about a point after winning it by 10 in 2016, and he saw his margins decrease in many of the state's more populated counties, including Kanawha, Cabell, Berkeley, Jefferson, and Ohio (Wheeling). But Trump still managed to win each of these five counties by 10 to 32 points, demonstrating that West Virginia has become some of the most solid Republican territory in the country.

Population		Race and Ethnicity		Income	
Total	1,792,147	White	93.10%	Median Income	48,850
Land area (sq. miles)	24,038	Black	3.70%	State Income Rank	49 out of 50
Pop/ sq mi	74.55	Latino	1.50%	Poverty Rate	16.00%
Born in state	68.50%	Asian	1.10%	With health insurance	93.30%
		Two or more races	1.80%	Cash public assistance	3.00%
Age Groups		Other	0.60%	Food stamp/SNAP	16.5%
Under 18	20.00%				
18-34	20.30%	**Education**		**Work**	
35-64	39.20%	H.S grad or less	53.10%	White Collar	33.30%
Over 64	20.50%	Some college	25.80%	Sales and Service	40.70%
		College Degree, 4 yr	12.60%	Blue Collar	26.10%
Military		Post grad	8.40%	Government	19.30%
Veteran/ Active Duty	8.70%				

Presidential Politics

2020 Primary (D)	Biden (D)	122,518(65%)	Sanders (D)	22,793(12%)			
2020 Pres. Vote	Trump (R)	545,382(69%)	Biden (D)	235,984(30%)			
2016 Pres. Vote	Trump (R)	489,371(69%)	Clinton (D)	188,794(26%)	Johnson (L)	23,004 (3%)	

From 1932 to 1996, the only Republicans who carried West Virginia were incumbents headed for landslide reelection victories—Dwight Eisenhower in 1956, Richard Nixon in 1972, and Ronald Reagan in 1984. But West Virginia has voted Republican in the last six presidential elections, and in 2020 was the second most Republican state in the country, with President Donald Trump defeating Joe Biden 69%-30%. That shift can be explained by two factors: culture and coal. West Virginia is the heart of Appalachia, the region of the country that has shifted the hardest against Democrats in the last two decades, as religious, socially conservative voters who resent the presumptions of coastal elites and blame Democrats for accelerating the coal industry's demise have moved to the GOP, especially as Republicans became a more populist, working-class party in the Trump era.

The Democratic decline began when George W. Bush targeted West Virginia. Bush's support of mountaintop mining and opposition to gun control helped him beat Al Gore 52%-46% in 2000 and John Kerry 56%-43% in 2004. In 2012, Mitt Romney carried the state 62%-36%, winning all 55 counties—the first nominee of either party to do so since the Civil War. Trump became the second, defeating Hillary Clinton 69%-27%, and he swept the state again in 2020. From 2008 to 2020, two of the three counties where the GOP saw its best county-level improvement in the country were in West Virginia, according to an NBC News analysis: Obama had carried both McDowell and Webster counties in 2008, but Trump won roughly 80 percent of their votes in 2020.

West Virginia's presidential primary, held in May, has not attracted much attention since 1960, when John F. Kennedy took on Hubert Humphrey and beat him with 61 percent of the vote, proving that a Catholic could succeed in a virtually all-Protestant state. In 2008, Clinton defeated Obama 67%-26%, her biggest margin except for Arkansas. In 2016, Vermont Sen. Bernie Sanders defeated Clinton, 51%-36%, carrying every county. Trump's opponents had already abandoned their bids when he won 77 percent of the vote. The state's 2020 primary was postponed to June because of the coronavirus, long after Biden had won the nomination; he defeated Sanders, 65%-12%.

Congressional Districts

117th Congress Lineup	3R	**116th Congress Lineup**	3R

West Virginia elected six members of the House in 1960 but only three in 1992. With the latest reapportionment, the delegation is shrinking to two. As recently as 1998, the state elected three Democrats. With voter hostility to the national party, Republicans have taken all three. With only two districts, the map-drawers have few options, even though Republicans have gained control of state government. They could split the state with a line that goes roughly east-west or one that goes north-south. In either case, the geographic realities appear to dictate one district that is Charleston-based and the other that hugs the Pennsylvania and Maryland state lines, with the remainder of the state split accordingly. When that happens, either two of the GOP incumbents will run against each other or one of them will bow out. It's not clear that any of the three has the personal influence to dictate the new map—though each will make a case for protection. Perhaps the most significant difference among the three is their age: Rep. Alex Mooney in the 2nd District will be 51 for the 2022 election and he reportedly has ambition to run for the Senate, perhaps in 2024. The other two are in their 70s and likely are serving in their final elected office. Potentially, that might lead Mooney to magnanimously defer in 2022 and take a long-term approach.

In 2011, Beltway Democratic strategists pressured West Virginia's legislators to be aggressive. Democratic state Sen. John Unger unveiled a proposal to keep untouched the district of Democrat Rep. Nick Rahall, who had held the southern 3rd District since 1976, and run the 1st and 2nd districts north-south rather than east-west, in effect pairing Republican Reps. Shelley Moore Capito and David McKinley and creating an open Eastern Panhandle seat. Furious Republicans pointed out that moving Mason County (population, 27,324) from the 2nd District to the 3rd District was all that was needed to equalize seats. The Unger plan earned tepid reception from Democrats, too. So, a few days later, the legislature passed and Democratic Gov. Earl Ray Tomblin signed the "Mason County flip" into law. Redistricting notwithstanding, in 2014, Rahall lost reelection and Republicans retained Capito's seat when she was elected to the Senate.

Jim Justice (R)

Elected 2016, term expires 2025, 2nd term; b. Apr. 27, 1951, Raleigh County; Marshall University, BA & MBA; Married (Cathy); 2 children.

Professional Career: Founder, Justice Family Farms, 1977; Developer, Stoney Brook Plantation; chief executive, Bluestone Industries and Bluestone Coal, 1993-2009.

Office: 1900 Kanawha Blvd., East Charleston, 25305; 304-558-2000; Fax: 304-342-7025
Atty. Gen: Patrick Morrisey (R) **Sec. of State:** Mac Warner (R)
State Legislature: Senate: 14D, 20R **House:** 41D, 59R

Election Results

Election	Name (Party)	Vote (%)
2020 General	Jim Justice (R)	497,944 (65%)
	Ben Salango (D)	297,024 (31%)
	Erika Koenich (L)	22,527 (3%)
2020 Primary	Jim Justice (R)	133,026 (63%)
	Woody Thrasher (R)	38,796 (18%)
	Mike Folk (R)	26,461 (12%)

Prior winning percentage: 2016 (49%)

Jim Justice, who has been a billionaire and often is described as West Virginia's richest man, has won two terms as governor, first as a Democrat and then as a Republican. During Justice's first campaign in 2016, many observers noted that he and Donald Trump shared key attributes, including their wealth, a range of controversies over their businesses, support for the coal industry, and a larger-than-life persona. Less than a year after winning the governorship, Justice joined Trump at a rally in the state and announced he was switching parties.

Justice was born in West Virginia and diversified his family's businesses. After earning a bachelor's and MBA at Marshall University, Justice started Bluestone Farms in 1977 and expanded it to cover 50,000 acres of corn, wheat and soybeans in West Virginia, Virginia, North Carolina and South Carolina. Following his father's death in 1993, Justice assumed control of Bluestone Industries Inc. and Bluestone Coal Corp. He proceeded to expand the company's operations in coal, Christmas tree farms, cotton gins, turfgrass, timber and golf courses. By the time he was elected governor, Justice was running approximately 100 companies. In 2009, he sold his coal company to the Russian firm Mechel OAO. But the new owner failed, and Justice purchased back his controlling interest in 2015 for a reported $5 million—less than 1 percent of what he'd sold it for. In the meantime, Justice had purchased the Greenbrier, the debt-plagued resort in White Sulphur Springs that was one of the nation's finest and most storied getaways, for $20.5 million in 2009. He added a casino and brought in such high-profile events as the PGA Tour and NFL and NBA training camps. He acquired other resorts and country clubs around the state. While running for governor, Justice had his daughter Jill run the Greenbrier while his son Jay oversaw the coal and agriculture businesses, though critics said Justice had not fully divested himself. (In March 2021, Forbes reported that Justice's wealth had fallen below $1 billion.)

Despite his wealth, Justice cultivated a down-home image. He has been involved with Little League baseball in Beckley for a quarter-century, and the six-foot-seven Justice has coached girls and boys basketball teams for more than 35 years; shortly after winning the governorship, he notched his 1,000th career win as a basketball coach. During major speeches, he has used hatchets and tackle boxes as props. He once rejected his Republican opponent's claim that he supported President Barack Obama as "complete dog snot" and, after winning the governorship, punctuated his veto of a budget passed by the Republican-controlled legislature by unveiling a copy of the budget topped by a pile of real-life bull feces.

Justice's business activities have been dogged by controversy. In 2014, NPR reported that his companies owed almost $2 million in unpaid fines. In 2015, Justice agreed to pay a $220,000 fine for failing to obtain Clean Water Act permits before building 20 dams at a hunting and fishing preserve. In September 2016, the Environmental Protection Agency announced a nearly $6 million agreement to settle thousands of pollution violations at coal facilities owned by Justice in West Virginia and other states, dating back to 2011. A follow-up to the NPR investigation in October 2016 concluded that Justice had become "the nation's top mine-safety delinquent," owing $15 million from operations in six states.

Justice got into politics by running to succeed retiring Gov. Earl Ray Tomblin, a culturally conservative Democrat. Justice did not have a clear path to the Democratic nomination, however: He faced a competitive three-way primary against former U.S. Attorney Booth Goodwin and state Senate Minority Leader Jeff Kessler. Goodwin touted his prosecution of cases stemming from one of the worst mine explosions in United States history, at West Virginia's Upper Big Branch mine that killed 29 men in 2010. Kessler, the candidate in the primary with the most extensive political experience, ran somewhat to the left of his rivals. But Justice, bolstered by his deep pockets and statewide familiarity, won the primary with 51 percent.

In the general election, Justice positioned himself as a conservative Democrat, almost an independent. He worked to put distance between himself and Hillary Clinton. He faced Republican state Senate President Bill Cole, who had attracted notice as a key player in state budget negotiations. But he preferred to emphasize his business background: He owned a car dealership and a share of a metal manufacturing plant in Tennessee. Cole offered a traditional conservative agenda that included tax and spending cuts, curbs on abortion, and charter schools. He also attacked Justice's business record. But Justice's ace in the hole was that he seemed to fit the national and state mood for an outsider willing to shake up politics-as-usual. Justice won, 49%-42%.

Inheriting a deficit of roughly $500 million, Justice proposed a toll hike on the West Virginia Turnpike for out-of-state motorists, a gasoline tax increase, a tax on sugary drinks and an increase in motor-vehicle fees. In April, the legislature approved a $4.1 billion budget, which prompted a veto and Justice's bull-feces display. He eventually let a budget become law without his signature. The legislature passed and Justice signed a bill legalizing medical marijuana. Justice often touted his personal relationship with Trump, and in August 2017, he joined the GOP. In January 2019, when it looked like Trump wouldn't be able to deliver his State of the Union address at the Capitol due to a federal shutdown, Justice invited him to give it in Charleston.

The biggest legislative battle of 2018 was prompted by a teacher strike in March. West Virginia teachers went on a nine-day strike and held rallies at the capitol. The walkout ended after Justice and the legislature agreed to raise salaries by 5 percent. Meanwhile, with the state struggling with the nation's highest rate of opioid overdoses, Justice signed limits on opioid prescriptions for most types of patients, even though most overdoses were the result of non-prescription drugs such as fentanyl and heroin. The second half of the year was dominated by revelations that justices on the state Supreme Court of Appeals had misused more than $1 million in funds when they renovated their offices. Amid impeachment efforts, three justices resigned, allowing Justice to appoint temporary replacements. All of Justice's appointees were ratified in special elections in November 2018.

In 2019 Justice pushed additional pay increases for teachers, but objected to Republican legislators' efforts to pair the pay hikes with expanded options for families such as charter schools. Ultimately he signed a bill, over the objections of teachers' unions, that paired teacher pay raises with a limited number of charter schools. Further school choice options were enacted in 2021.

Justice's switch on school choice came after he had taken fire from his party's right flank. The Republican executive committees of Kanawha County (Charleston) and Harrison County (Clarksburg) and the West Virginia Federation of College Republicans all approved motions of no confidence in Justice, and several key state senators expressed their disapproval as well. This dissatisfaction helped produce a competitive GOP primary field for Justice's reelection in 2020, including Woody Thrasher, an engineer who served as state commerce secretary until he was ousted by Justice, and Michael Folk, a former state delegate. He ended up winning the GOP primary with 63 percent, easily outpacing Thrasher with 18 percent and Folk with 13 percent.

Justice's initial handling of the coronavirus pandemic was somewhat rocky. Thanks to the state's isolation, it was the last state with no confirmed cases. But officials knew that high rates of underlying health conditions, from cancer to diabetes to smoking, portended a high risk of serious outbreaks. Justice ordered the closure of schools before neighboring Pennsylvania and Virginia did, and he banned travel and large meetings by state employees. His initial messaging was seen as confusing by some, but observers said Justice's handling of the virus improved with time. In July, he signed a mask order, saying "I know it's not the popular thing to do, but absolutely at this point in time it's the only right thing to do." And by February 2021, he was able to take a victory lap on national cable networks after West Virginia took an early lead in vaccinating its elderly population, an achievement the state credited to having opted out of a vaccine distribution program with national chain pharmacies in favor of working with trusted local drug stores.

Justice's high-profile role on the pandemic helped bolster his reelection prospects. On the Democratic side, Sen. Joe Manchin opted out of the race, leaving a contest largely between Ben Salango, a Kanawha County Commissioner; Stephen Smith, head of the WV Healthy Kids and Families Coalition; and physician and state Sen. Ron Stollings. Salango, the establishment choice, defeated Smith, the favorite of a resurgent Democratic left, 39%-34%, with Stollings taking 13%. In the general election, Salango hammered Justice over the controversies surrounding his business holdings, but Justice's reelection was never in doubt, and he prevailed, 65%-31%, winning every county.

In early 2021, Justice attracted notice for becoming virtually the only elected Republican in the country to not only support President Joe Biden's stimulus package but to say Biden should "go big or go home" with it, explaining that "we have tried to underspend and undersize what was really needed to get over the top of the mountain." But his plan to eliminate the state's income tax went down to defeat.

Joe Manchin (D)

Elected 2010, term expires 2024, 2nd full term, b. Aug 24, 1947; Farmington, WV; West Virginia University, B.S., 1970; Catholic; Married (Gayle Conelly); 3 children; 8 grandchildren.

Elected Office: WV House, 1982-1986; WV Senate, 1986-1996; WV Secretary Of State, 2000-2004; WV Governor, 2004-2010.

Professional Career: Co-owner, Manchin's Carpet & Tile, 1968-1982; Owner, Enersystems, 1989-2000.

DC Office: 306 HSOB 20510, 202-224-3954, Fax: 202-228-0002, manchin.senate.gov

State Offices: Charleston, 304-342-5855; Fairmont, 304-368-0567; Martinsburg, 304-264-4626.

Committees: Senate Democratic Policy and Communications Vice Chairman. *Appropriations*: Commerce, Justice, Science & Related Agencies; DOL, HHS & Education & Related Agencies; Financial Services & General Government; Military Construction & Veteran Affairs & Related Agencies; Transportation, HUD & Related Agencies. *Armed Services*: Airland; Cybersecurity (Chmn); Strategic Forces. *Energy & Natural Resources (Chmn)*: Ex Officio membership on all subcommittees. *Veterans' Affairs*.

Group Ratings

	ADA	ACLU	AFL-CIO	LCV	COC	HAFA	ACU	CFG	FRC
2020	-	23%	-	54%	-	37%	27%	-	-
2019	65%	C	94%	86%	87%	C	27%	28%	67%

Almanac Ratings 2019-2020

	Economy	Social	Foreign	Composite
Liberal	49%	49%	9%	36%
Conservative	51%	51%	91%	64%

Key Votes of the 116th Congress

1. EPA clean energy rules	N	5. Russia sanctions	Y	9. Barr as Atty. General	Y
2. U.S./Mex./Can. trade deal	Y	6. Troops in SYR, AFG	Y	10. Spending at the border	Y
3. Cut unemployment benefits	Y	7. Veto arms sales to Saudis	Y	11. Coney Barrett to Sup. Ct.	N
4. Shelton to Fed Reserve	N	8. Defense $$$, veto override	Y	12. Electoral College objections	N

Election Results

Election	Name (Party)	Vote (%)		Cand. Spent	Ind. Exp. Support	Ind. Exp. Oppose
2018 General	Joe Manchin III (D)	290,510	(50%)	$7,374,158	$6,736,278	$11,428,094
	Patrick Morrisey (R)	271,113	(46%)	$5,581,599	$2,903,392	$12,148,307
	Rusty Hollen (Lib)	24,411	(4%)			
2018 Primary	Joe Manchin III (D)	112,658	(70%)			
	Paula Jean Swearengin (D)	48,594	(30%)			

Prior winning percentages: 2018 (50%), 2012 (61%), 2010 special (53%); Governor: 2008 (70%), 2004 (64%)

The advent of a 50-50 Senate and Joe Biden's election have made Democrat Joe Manchin, West Virginia's senior senator, arguably the most influential lawmaker in Congress. Democrats needed Manchin's vote to pass Biden's coronavirus relief package by the narrowest of margins in early

2021, and Manchin continued to support filibuster, at least in some form, at a time when most of his Democratic colleagues would like to get rid of it.In June, he wrote in the Charleston Gazette-Mail that he opposed Democrats' election-reform bill and reasserted his opposition to steps to "weaken or eliminate the filibuster." That drew growing criticism—and alarms—from Democrats and their interest-group allies.

Manchin hails from a prominent political family. He grew up in Farmington, a few miles from the industrial city of Fairmont. Manchin took a semester off from college to help his father rebuild his carpet-and-furniture store after a fire. His grandfather and father both served as mayor of Farmington. His uncle, A. James Manchin, was elected to the West Virginia House of Delegates and served as the Mountain State's secretary of state and state treasurer. "As a child, Manchin never once left the state, and although he was recruited to play football by colleges across the country, there was never any doubt he'd go to West Virginia University," Jason Zengerle wrote in GQ. The idea of going farther was anathema to his father. "He's West Virginia," Manchin's sister Paula told Zengerle. "It's in his soul."

After graduating from WVU, Manchin went to work in the carpet-and-furniture business, helping send his four siblings to college. Then he started a coal-brokerage company and moved to Fairmont. (Manchin continues to hold shares worth between $1 million and $5 million in his old firm, according to disclosures.) Manchin was elected to the House of Delegates in 1982 and the state Senate in 1986. He ran for governor in 1996, only to lose in the Democratic primary to legislator Charlotte Pritt. When Secretary of State Ken Hechler ran for Congress in 2000, Manchin ran to succeed him, as did Pritt. This time, Manchin easily beat her in the primary and won the general election, too.

In 2003, Manchin announced that he would challenge Democratic Gov. Bob Wise in the 2004 primary. Later that month, Wise admitted that he'd had an extramarital affair and would not seek reelection. Manchin got support from both unions and businesses. His stands on cultural issues were impeccably conservative and in line with state preferences: He opposed abortion rights, gun control and same-sex marriage. Manchin won the Democratic primary with 53 percent of the vote, and he defeated Republican Monty Warner in the general election, 64% to 34%, carrying 52 of 55 counties.

Manchin had been in office for just one year when he gained renown as the public face of desperate attempts to rescue 13 trapped coal miners after the January 2006 explosion at the Sago Mine in central West Virginia. Manchin, whose uncle was killed in a 1968 mine accident that killed 78 people, gave numerous televised interviews from the mine site. He mistakenly announced "the miracle of all miracles"—that 12 of the miners had survived—when in fact they had died. The blunder could have been career-ending, but Manchin's standing skyrocketed in the polls, partly because West Virginia Republicans decided that invoking the disaster was a political line that they would not cross. In 2007, he signed legislation mandating certain ventilation practices and giving the state authority to temporarily shut down mines with violations. After two other deadly mining tragedies, Manchin ordered safety inspections at all mines in the state.

Manchin had success on other issues. In 2006, he signed into law eight health care bills, including giving low-income families' basic care at clinics and creating a catastrophic health care insurance program and a mental health commission. His tenure was marred by a controversy involving his daughter and politically potent institutions in the state. The Pittsburgh Post-Gazette reported that the governor's daughter, Heather Bresch, falsely claimed to have earned a master's degree in business in 1998 at West Virginia University. The school then gave her the degree in 2007, even though she had completed only about half the required 48 credit hours. Under pressure, several top university officials, including the school's president, resigned. Bresch—by then a high-level executive at Mylan, a maker of generic drugs that had donated heavily to the university and, through its top executives, to Manchin'scampaigns—never admitted wrongdoing. Manchin expressed support for Bresch. In 2008, he was reelected with 70 percent of the vote. In 2016, Bresch created new awkwardness for Manchin after Mylan began charging exorbitant sums for its EpiPen.

When Robert Byrd, West Virginia's senior senator, died in June 2010—after a record 51 years in the Senate plus six in the House—Manchin was considered Democrats' best hope for keeping the seat. Although he could have appointed himself to the Senate pending a special election, Manchin declined to do so. Instead, he appointed his former chief counsel, Carte Goodwin, as a placeholder. His GOP opponent was John Raese, a wealthy businessman whom Byrd had defeated four years earlier by nearly 2-1. But in a strong election cycle for the GOP, the deep-pocketed Raese had the wind at his back. He ran ads tying Manchin to President Barack Obama, and the National Republican Senatorial Committee launched its own ads portraying Manchin as a rubber stamp for Obama's agenda. Before long, the race was a toss-up. Manchin distanced himself from the president, even to the extent of flip-flopping. Early in 2010, he had supported Obama's health care overhaul; by October, Manchin was saying he would have voted against it had he been serving as a senator at the time. Manchin ran an ad in which he used a rifle to shoot a mock copy of the Democrats' cap-and-trade bill to curb carbon emissions, which was highly unpopular in coal country. Manchin hammered away at the steel and limestone magnate for owning a home in Palm Beach Florida that had a pink marble driveway. Although Manchin was outspent $6.3 million to $4.4 million, he won 53%-43%.

Taking office immediately after the election to begin serving the final two years of Byrd's term, Manchin voted to extend the Bush-era tax cuts except for taxpayers earning more than $1 million. He was the only Democrat to vote against a proposal repealing the ban on openly gay members in the military. Still, Manchin was roundly criticized at home for missing a final vote on repealing "don't ask, don't tell" as well as a major vote on a bill to give legal status to the children of some undocumented immigrants. The Charleston Gazette called him "absolutely gutless." Manchin apologized publicly, saying he missed the December votes to be with his grandchildren over the holidays. He further angered the newspaper in 2012 when he declined to say whether he would vote to reelect Obama. It refused to endorse him in that April's Democratic primary, but it hardly mattered: Manchin took 80 percent of the vote, setting up a rematch with Raese for a six-year term. Raese again said Manchin was an Obama rubber stamp, but the incumbent now had a voting record that demonstrated otherwise. Manchin won 61%-36%, even as GOP presidential nominee Mitt Romney took 62 percent of the vote.

In April 2013, after several months of taking colleagues out on his Washington-docked houseboat for evenings of beer and pizza, Manchin announced a proposed compromise on gun control with Republicans Mark Kirk of Illinois—his best friend in the chamber—and Pat Toomey of Pennsylvania. Its most significant feature was a proposal to expand background checks to gun purchases at gun shows and online. The measure did not go as far as Obama wanted, but it was the best chance to advance gun control legislation in years. Manchin had previously boasted of his "A" rating from the National Rifle Association, but the group now attacked him. In the end, the measure couldn't attract enough votes to overcome a GOP filibuster.

After the Democrats lost the Senate in the 2014 elections — a development Manchin called "a real ass-whuppin'" — he expressed deep frustration to The Washington Post about Obama and Senate Democratic Leader Harry Reid of Nevada, and he said he might not back Reid for party leader. But he recommitted to remaining with his party rather than switching to the GOP. Manchin toyed with leaving the chamber two years early in 2016 to run for governor, a job that would provide him with executive powers he had enjoyed before. But in early 2015, Manchin announced that he would remain in the Senate—a big boost for Democrats, who had few other options for winning a seat in increasingly Republican West Virginia.

The Republican-controlled Senate gave Manchin opportunities to work on legislation and display his differences with other Democrats. He was one of two Democrats who voted in 2015 to force a vote to prohibit federal funding of Planned Parenthood. In 2017, he joined the Appropriations Committee, where his in-state colleague, Shelley Moore Capito, already had a seat and Byrd had once reigned as chairman. In 2017, he was the only Democrat to vote to confirm GOP Sen. Jeff Sessions of Alabama to be Trump's first attorney general, prompting backlash from liberal activists. He also voted to confirm Scott Pruitt as head the EPA, but he voted against Wilbur Ross at Commerce, Tom Price at Health and Human Services, and Betsy DeVos at Education. In April 2017, Manchin joined Joe Donnelly of Indiana and Heidi Heitkamp of North Dakota as the only Democratic senators to vote to confirm Neil Gorsuch to the Supreme Court. Trump had nominated Gorsuch soon after taking office — after Senate republicans ignored Obama's nominee for the same seat for nearly a year.

Manchin rejected invitations to switch parties or join Trump's Cabinet and instead accepted a seat on the leadership team of Democratic Leader Chuck Schumer. He maintained a relationship —albeit rocky at times—with Trump, whom he praised for listening to him more thoroughly than Obama had. Manchin angered the White House by voting against the GOP-backed tax overhaul in 2017; he said the bill was too generous to the wealthy. In October 2018, he was the only Democrat to vote to confirm Trump's second nominee to the Supreme Court, Brett Kavanaugh. But not even this satisfied Republicans, who assailed Manchin for announcing his support only after GOP Sen. Susan Collins of Maine—another swing vote—had announced that she would vote yes, making Manchin's support unnecessary.

In 2018, Manchin easily prevailed over a primary challenger from his left, Paula Jean Swearengin, 70%-30%. But the GOP primary was a barnburner. The three main candidates were Rep. Evan Jenkins, state Attorney General Patrick Morrisey, and former coal magnate Don Blankenship. Some Republicans thought Jenkins would be best positioned to take on Manchin, although he had earlier in his career been a Democrat. Morrisey, meanwhile, had previously run for the House from New Jersey, opening him to criticism that he was a carpetbagger. The one thing most Republican officials were sure about is that they did not want Blankenship to be the nominee. A 2010 explosion at Blankenship's Upper Big Branch Mine had killed 29 workers, and in 2015, he was sentenced to a year in prison for conspiring to violate mine safety standards—a sentence that many West Virginians thought was too light. After his release, Blankenship channeled attempts at rehabilitation into a Senate bid, spending aggressively to portray himself both as a victim of government run amuck and as the ultimate political outsider. Facing concerted opposition from GOP Sen. Mitch McConnell, then the majority leader, Blankenship aired an ad attacking the Kentuckian as "Cocaine Mitch," based on an allegation that a shipping company owned by McConnell's father-in-law had once been connected to drug smuggling. In the end, the panic proved unnecessary; Morrisey won 35 percent of the vote, edging Jenkins with 29 percent and Blankenship with 20 percent.

The general election contest was competitive, but the GOP's momentum in West Virginia never quite matched what the party achieved in the other red-state contests that year. Trump aggressively touted Morrissey during rallies in the state, and the GOP framed Manchin as a tool of Democratic congressional leaders. But Manchin benefited from voter concern about health care. In a state that had experienced tangible gains from the Affordable Care Act, Manchin attacked Morrisey for signing on to a lawsuit designed to repeal the law, contrasting his own efforts to protect the law as Senate Republicans sought to overturn it. Manchin echoed his memorable ad on carbon emissions by airing one in which he fired on a copy of the lawsuit that Morrisey had helped draft. Manchin won 50%-46% —a far narrower margin than his 25-point edge six years earlier but far better than any other Democrat could have expected in the state.

After Manchin's victory, liberal activists objected when Schumer tapped him to be the top Democrat on the Energy and Natural Resources Committee, a crucial post for his state and one in which he could cause trouble for environmentalists. In April 2019, Manchin said he was again considering a run for governor in 2020, but he ultimately decided against it. Meanwhile, Manchin and Trump continued their on-again, off-again relationship. Manchin voted with the president more than any other Senate Democrat, but during Trump's first impeachment trial, Manchin voted to convict, dashing the president's hope that Manchin would provide a bipartisan sheen for acquittal. Trump called Manchin "weak& pathetic" and nicknamed him "Joe Munchkin," but despite it all, Manchin said Trump could be a "tremendous president."

In 2020, Manchin worked with Republican Sen. Lisa Murkowski of Alaska to pass a bipartisan energy package, eventually signed as part of an omnibus bill by Trump, that enacted a phase-out plan for climate-warming hydrofluorocarbons and promoted new technologies for reducing greenhouse gas emissions, including nuclear energy, carbon capture, and renewable energy. In April, in a move that was not foreordained, Manchin publicly endorsed Joe Biden for president. (Manchin later irked his fellow Senate Democrats when he offered a cross-party endorsement of Collins for reelection to the Senate in early 2019.) When Trump nominated Amy Coney Barrett to the Supreme Court in October 2020, Manchin—who had voted for Barrett's lower-court nomination, in addition to Trump's two prior nominees to the Supreme Court—voted no.

After Biden won and the Senate deadlocked 50-50, Manchin's already substantial leverage expanded further. In a Fox News interview, he sent a shot across the bow of the Democratic left, pledging to oppose expansion of the Supreme Court and saying he wouldn't back "Medicare for All" or the "Green New Deal." Manchin effectively killed the nomination of NeeraTanden to be director of the Office of Management and Budget, and he flexed his muscle in the crafting of Biden's relief package, first by voicing concerns about a national $15 hourly minimum wage (a hike that never made the final bill) and then by delaying the measure for hours over the scope of unemployment benefits. Most importantly, though, Manchin voted for the bill in the end. Looking ahead, Manchin urged spending up to $4 trillion on a new infrastructure bill, and as chairman of Energy and Natural Resources, he was poised to play a major role on any climate-change legislation moving through the chamber. Given the high degree of polarization, the passage of any legislation could depend on whether Manchin continues to support the filibuster. In March 2021, Manchin opened the door slightly to a filibuster overhaul, saying he'd consider adopting a "talking filibuster" that forced senators to talk on the floor in order to block action. "It really should be painful, and we've made it more comfortable over the years," Manchin said.Still, Democrats were struggling to find ways to accommodate him, while holding firm to Biden's agenda.

Shelley Moore Capito (R)

Elected 2014, term expires 2026, 2nd term, b. Nov 26, 1953; Glen Dale, WV; Duke University, B.S., 1975; University of Virginia, M.Ed., 1976; Presbyterian; Married (Dr. Charles Lewis Capito); 3 children; 4 grandchildren.

Elected Office: WV House, 1997-2001; US House, 2001-2015.

Professional Career: Career counselor, WV State College, 1976-1978; Director, Education Information Center, WV Board of Regents, 1978-1981.

DC Office: 172 RSOB 20510, 202-224-6472, Fax: 202-224-7665, capito.senate.gov

State Offices: Beckley, 304-347-5372; Charleston, 304-347-5372; Martinsburg, 304-262-9285; Morgantown, 304-292-2310.

Committees: *Appropriations*: Commerce, Justice, Science & Related Agencies; Department of Homeland Security (RMM); Department of the Interior, Environment & Related Agencies; DOL, HHS & Education & Related Agencies; Military Construction & Veteran Affairs & Related Agencies; Transportation, HUD & Related Agencies. *Commerce, Science & Transportation*: Aviation Safety, Operations & Innovations; Communications, Media & Broadband; Surface Transportation, Maritime Freight & Ports; Tourism, Trade & Export Promotion. *Environment & Public Works (RMM)*: Ex Officio membership on all subcommittees. *Rules & Administration*.

Group Ratings

	ADA	ACLU	AFL-CIO	LCV	COC	HAFA	ACU	CFG	FRC
2020	-	8%	-	15%	-	66%	68%	-	-
2019	5%	C	26%	29%	97%	C	68%	32%	100%

Almanac Ratings 2019-2020

	Economy	Social	Foreign	Composite
Liberal	0%	0%	2%	1%
Conservative	100%	100%	98%	99%

Key Votes of the 116th Congress

1. EPA clean energy rules	N	5. Russia sanctions	N	9. Barr as Atty. General	Y
2. U.S./Mex./Can. trade deal	Y	6. Troops in SYR, AFG	Y	10. Spending at the border	Y
3. Cut unemployment benefits	Y	7. Veto arms sales to Saudis	N	11. Coney Barrett to Sup. Ct.	Y
4. Shelton to Fed Reserve	Y	8. Defense $$$, veto override	Y	12. Electoral College objections	N

Election Results

Election	Name (Party)	Vote (%)		Cand. Spent	Ind. Exp. Support	Ind. Exp. Oppose
2020 General	Shelley Moore Capito (R)	547,454	(70%)	$3,318,796	$12,576	
	Paula Jean Swearengin (D)	210,309	(27%)	$1,981,834	$10	$320
	David Moran (L)	21,155	(3%)			
2020 Primary	Shelley Moore Capito (R)	173,847	(83%)			
	Allen Whitt (R)	20,075	(10%)			
	Larry Butcher (R)	14,717	(7%)			

Prior winning percentages: 2014 (62%), House: 2012 (70%), 2010 (69%), 2008 (57%), 2006 (57%), 2004 (48%), 2002 (60%), 2000 (48%)

Republican Shelley Moore Capito was elected West Virginia's junior senator in 2014 after serving seven terms in the House. The state's first Republican in the Senate since the 1950s and its first female senator, she is a well-liked moderate who is unwavering in her advocacy of West Virginia's coal industry. She got along well with Republican Leader Mitch McConnell, another senator from coal country, and joined his leadership team. Her policy focus has been largely tied to home-state interests and needs. She appears politically secure at home. In 2021, her position as the ranking Republican on the Environment and Public Works Committee, plus her deal-cutting instincts and

McConnell's trust, placed her potentially at the center of bipartisan negotiations on infrastructure legislation.

Capito grew up in northern West Virginia and the Washington D.C. area, where her father, Arch Moore, served in the House from 1957 to 1969. He was elected governor of West Virginia in 1968 and 1972, and then again in 1984. Capito graduated from Duke University with a degree in zoology and earned a master's degree in education from the University of Virginia. She worked for two years as a career counselor at West Virginia State University and then as director of the state's Educational Information Center from 1978 to 1981. She served two terms in the West Virginia House of Delegates.

Capito's opportunity to follow in her father's footsteps in the House came when Democratic Rep. Bob Wise ran for governor in 2000. She benefited from a divisive Democratic primary won by Jim Humphreys, a lawyer and former state senator. Capito, who supported abortion rights, started off as the underdog, but Humphreys proved to be a poor candidate despite spending $6 million of his own money in the general election. Capito won 48%-46%, becoming the first Cherry Blossom Princess elected to Congress. Capito has been the center of West Virginia's swing to the GOP. When she first ran for Congress in 2000, there were no Republicans in the delegation. By 2015, Sen. Joe Manchin —a longtime friend of Capito—was the only Democrat serving in federal office from West Virginia. A third generation of the family has emerged: Capito's son, Moore Capito, served in the House of Delegates.

In the House, Capito had a relatively moderate voting record; she was a member of the centrist Republican Main Street Partnership. She broke from conservatives to support programs important to her state, such as continued funding of rural air service and opposing drastic cutbacks in food stamps. In a rare encounter with controversy, in 2006, she dealt with the fallout from revelations of inappropriate sexual advances by GOP Rep. Mark Foley of Florida, which included contact with House pages. Capito, a member of the three-lawmaker board that oversaw the teenage page program, said she was unaware of the allegations until after the scandal became public.

Capito grew more partisan after the election of President Barack Obama, who was extremely unpopular in West Virginia. In 2011, she took over as chairwoman of the Financial Services Subcommittee on Financial Institutions and Consumer Credit. She focused on the regulatory burdens facing community banks and credit unions. Her husband, Charles, is a longtime banking executive, which raised eyebrows among watchdog groups. Capito said she makes her own decisions, telling Esquire magazine in 2010 that "no matter what your decisions are, no matter what your votes are, if you're not playing by the rules, you're taking a big risk."

After her reelection in 2012, Capito announced she would challenge Democratic Sen. Jay Rockefeller in 2014. Rockefeller, who was in his late 70s and had health problems, wanted no part of a tough race against Capito. During his 42 years as a statewide elected official, his only defeat came against her father in the 1972 contest for governor. Rockefeller announced his retirement after a poll showed her with a slight lead in a head-to-head matchup.

In the general, Capito faced Natalie Tennant, West Virginia's secretary of state and a former TV reporter. Tennant sought to make an issue of Capito and her spouse's close ties to banking interests, saying her own "West Virginia first" approach contrasted with Capito's record "working for Wall Street banks where her husband works." Capito ran a quietly effective campaign and was aided by Obama's deep unpopularity among West Virginians. Her move from the House to the Senate was such a certainty that by July, friends and colleagues reportedly began addressing her as "Senator." In November, she defeated Tennant 62%-35%.

Capito settled into the Senate with a seat on the Appropriations Committee, where she was the only freshman Republican tapped as a subcommittee chair. The assignment has outsize consequence for a state as poor as West Virginia. She took charge of the panel that funds congressional operations, a good way to make connections with Senate insiders. Since then, she has chaired the Financial Services and General Government Subcommittee and then the Homeland Security panel. She has been one of four senators to serve as counsel to McConnell, which could open the door down the road for her to move up as a leadership player. In a sensitive leadership assignment, Capito in 2018 worked with leaders of the Senate Rules and Administration Committee to craft a bipartisan plan to update the Senate's sexual harassment policy.

Capito joined two other panels of great importance to coal-producing West Virginia—the Energy and Natural Resources Committee and Environment and Public Works. On the latter, she chaired the Clean Air and Nuclear Safety Subcommittee. She was lead sponsor of the Affordable Reliable Energy Now Act, which sought to preempt the Obama administration's proposal to tackle climate change. "We're asking for a commonsense agreement that assures reliable and affordable energy, protects our economy and jobs and allows states to make their own decisions," she told reporters.

The measure won co-sponsorship of nearly three dozen senators, including one Democrat: Manchin. In 2021, she became the ranking Republican on the Environment committee.

The election of Donald Trump as president became a vital opportunity for Capito and her allies to reverse regulations and enforcement by the Environmental Protection Agency. In April 2018, she wrote that she was encouraged that "the war on coal is over." In subsequent committee reorganization, she took over as chairwoman of the Transportation and Infrastructure Subcommittee. She gave up her seat on the Energy panel to join Commerce, Science and Transportation, where her interests include expanded broadband coverage in rural areas. She claimed success of her "Capito connect" initiative to reduce the urban-rural digital divide.

On a related topic, she advocated for giving health care coverage to retired miners. McConnell spearheaded a related plan that was enacted as part of a government funding bill in 2017. Capito raised concerns about protecting her state's Medicaid funding amid GOP efforts to replace the Affordable Care Act. She joined three other GOP senators who wrote to McConnell about the need for "stability and certainty for individuals and families in Medicaid expansion programs or the necessary flexibility for states," including West Virginia. "I did not come to Washington to hurt people," she said during the health care debate. In the end, she supported the GOP's "skinny repeal" plan, though the Senate deadlocked.

Capito voted to acquit Trump in 2020 in his first impeachment trial, which came after he withheld from Ukraine congressionally approved military aid unless it interfered in the 2020 presidential election on his behalf. In early 2021, as Trump sought to undo his election loss and spread falsehoods about voter fraud, Capito voted against overturning the presidential election. A month later, she voted to acquit Trump in a second impeachment trial, which focused on his role in inciting that riot. She cited her belief that it is unconstitutional to impeach a former official. Minutes after the vote, she released a statement strongly critical of Trump: "What happened on January 6 threatened our foundational transfer of power and the actions were an embarrassment to our country and everything we stand for. The actions and reactions of President Trump were disgraceful, and history will judge him harshly."

She developed a good working relationship with President Joe Biden, who viewed her as a potentially vital bipartisan deal-maker on legislation to approve new highway and other infrastructure projects—one of his top priorities. As she quietly inserted herself into negotiations, she appeared to have the confidence of both parties plus the trust of Manchin.

As a House member, Capito was a founding member of the Congressional Women's Softball Team, a group that plays reporters in an annual faceoff. She eventually became a captain on the team and started at third base.

Capito coasted to reelection in 2020. She defeated Democrat Paula Jean Swearengin in a blowout, 70%-27%. While often criticized by the tea party pockets of the GOP, she is her own political force in West Virginia, thanks to her family's name recognition, her political skill and her state's conservative bent.

David McKinley (R)

Elected 2010, 6th term, b. Mar 28, 1947; Wheeling, WV; Purdue University, B.S., 1969; Episcopalian; Married (Mary McKinley); 4 children; 6 grandchildren.

Elected Office: WV House, 1980-1994.

Professional Career: Principal, McKinley & Association, 1981-2010; Chair, WV GOP, 1990-1994.

DC Office: 2239 RHOB 20515, 202-225-4172, Fax: 202-225-7564, mckinley.house.gov

State Offices: Morgantown, 304-284-8506; Parkersburg, 304-422-5972; Wheeling, 304-232-3801.

Committees: *Energy & Commerce*: Energy; Environment & Climate Change (RMM); Oversight & Investigations.

Group Ratings

	ADA	ACLU	AFL-CIO	LCV	COC	HAFA	ACU	CFG	FRC
2020	**	17%	**	29%	-	77%	63%	**	-
2019	5%	C	48%	7%	91%	C	63%	59%	95%

Almanac Ratings 2019-2020

	Economy	Social	Foreign	Composite
Liberal	25%	27%	27%	27%
Conservative	75%	73%	73%	73%

Key Votes of the 116th Congress

1. U.S./Mex./Can. trade deal	Y	5. Russia sanctions	Y	9. Firearms background checks N
2. First Coronavirus response	Y	6. Troops in Syria	Y	10. Spending at the border	Y
3. HEROES Act	N	7. Veto arms sales to Saudis	N	11. Marijuana liberalized rules	N
4. CASH Act	Y	8. Defense $$$, veto override	N	12. Electoral College objections N

Election Results

Election	Name (Party)	Vote (%)		Cand. Spent	Ind. Exp. Support	Ind. Exp. Oppose
2020 General	David McKinley (R)	180,488	(69%)	$841,057		$750
	Natalie Cline (D)	81,177	(31%)	$76,483		$371
2020 Primary	David McKinley (R)	64,789	(100%)			

Prior winning percentages: 2018 (65%), 2016 (69%), 2014 (64%), 2012 (62%), 2010 (50%)

Republican David McKinley, elected in 2010, is a coal-championing economic centrist. He has been an active legislator and has shown some independence from his party on big issues.

McKinley is a seventh-generation native of Wheeling. McKinley's great-grandfather ran for West Virginia governor as a Democrat in 1908. His father was a civil engineer who taught him to read blueprints when he was in third grade. He majored in civil engineering at Purdue University. After college, McKinley worked for several engineering and construction companies until he founded his own firm, McKinley & Associates, which restores historic properties and does other construction work. In West Virginia's House of Delegates, McKinley pushed for a bill to allow school and prison cafeterias to donate unused food to homeless shelters. He authored a law that prohibited insurance companies from canceling policies of people diagnosed with HIV. He ran for governor in 1996 but lost the primary to Cecil Underwood, who won the general election.

In his House bid in 2010, McKinley had the backing of national Republicans and won the primary with 35 percent of the vote. In the general election, he faced state Sen. Mike Oliverio, who had toppled 14-term Democratic Rep. Alan Mollohan in the primary as Mollohan faced a corruption scandal. McKinley emphasized his opposition to the Democrats' energy bill that would limit carbon emissions, arguing that it would hurt West Virginia's coal industry. Oliverio also opposed the bill. He charged that McKinley got rich from government contracts even as he criticized government spending, citing federal economic stimulus money that McKinley's architectural and engineering firm received to design a Marshall County school. McKinley eked out a victory of 1,440 votes, a split of 50.4%-49.6%. He hasn't faced serious opposition since in a district that has grown increasingly Republican over the past decade.

McKinley was one of a handful of Republicans in 2011 and 2012 to vote against Budget Committee Chairman Paul Ryan's budget blueprint, complaining that it did not adequately protect Medicare. He got a plum seat on the Energy and Commerce Committee and co-founded a Marcellus Shale Caucus to oppose restrictions on drilling in the oil-and-gas-rich area stretching along the Appalachians. In 2015, he took the lead for House Republicans in the enactment of tougher standards for energy efficiency. With Democratic Rep. Matt Cartwright of Pennsylvania, McKinley enacted a bill in 2016 that authorized the Bureau of Prisons to permit its officers to carry pepper spray for self-defense. He authored the bill after a federal correctional officer was murdered by an inmate. His 2017 bill to make it easier for corrections officers to carry firearms passed the House. In 2020, he was one of just 26 Republicans to support a Democratic bill to increase funding for the U.S. Postal Service and halt changes pushed by the Trump administration that critics said were disrupting service.

McKinley has been outspoken about the state's growing opioid epidemic. When pharmaceutical executives testified before Congress in 2018, McKinley exploded at them. "I just want you to feel shame about your roles, respectively, in all of this," McKinley told them. McKinley, who is hearing-impaired, has worked with the Veterans Affairs Department to help more veterans get cochlear implants, often at a lower rate than for non-military persons. "Society doesn't recognize when you have hearing loss," he told Roll Call. "They're not very patient with you."

McKinley has aggressively fought so-called coal-ash rules that affect industries such as concrete production and manufacturing of wallboard. He introduced a bill to create an enforceable minimum standard for the regulation of coal ash by the states, allowing its use in a manner that he said would protect jobs. It passed the House but stalled in the Senate. In February 2017, the House rescinded on a nearly party-line vote the coal-ash rule the Interior Department had written during the Obama administration; President Donald Trump signed the repeal measure.

McKinley cautioned that the coal industry would not be hiring nearly as many West Virginians as had worked in the mines a half-century ago, but he voiced hope that the industry would find new markets for exports. In 2018, he got an amendment added to the Interior Department's appropriations bill that would add $160 million to the EPA's Brownfields Program to clean up abandoned industrial sites for a new use. McKinley strongly supports the coal industry, while viewing climate change as a serious threat: In 2020, he and moderate Oregon Democratic Rep. Kurt Schrader partnered on a bill to address what they called "the greatest environmental and energy challenge of our time" in a joint op-ed. The plan called for increased government spending on clean energy technology innovation and infrastructure development, while opposing a carbon tax or limits on emissions.

McKinley has been reelected with at least 62 percent of the vote. In 2015 he ruled out a run for the open seat for governor. He was a vocal supporter of Trump and credited him with the coal resurgence in West Virginia, but was the only one of the state's three House members to vote to certify Joe Biden's election.

In 2016, the House Ethics Committee issued a letter of reproval—its mildest sanction—to McKinley because of his failure to remove his name from his engineering business after he had sold the company.

With West Virginia losing a House seat in 2020, it's unclear whether McKinley, age 74, will run again, though his district has lost less population than other parts of West Virginia. If he does and faces a House colleague, his quiet splits with Trump over the result of the 2020 election, as well as his cautious support for climate change legislation, could be problematic in a primary.

WV-1: Northern West Virginia   Cook Partisan Voting Index: R+22

Population		Race and Ethnicity		Income	
Total	601,811	White	93.60%	Median Income	$51,480
Land area (sq. miles)	6,276	Black	2.50%	District Income Rank	374
Pop/ sq mi	95.90	Latino	1.20%	Poverty Rate	14.80%
Born in State	67.80%	Asian	0.90%	With health insurance	94.00%
		Two or more races	1.80%	Cash public assistance	2.40%
Age Groups		Other	1.00%	Food stamp/SNAP	13.90%
Under 18	18.80%				
18-34	22.40%	**Education**		**Work**	
35-64	38.60%	H.S grad or less	49.70%	White Collar	34.60%
Over 64	20.20%	Some college	26.90%	Sales and Service	40.10%
		College Degree, 4 yr	13.50%	Blue Collar	25.30%
Military		Post grad	9.80%	Government	19.90%
Veteran/ Active Duty	8.40%				

2020 Pres. Vote	Trump	183,904	(68%)	Biden	81,849	(30%)		
2016 Pres. Vote	Trump	165,934	(68%)	Clinton	64,384	(26%)	Johnson	8,862	(4%)

Morgantown, Parkersburg: The northern part of West Virginia is in many ways an extension of the Pittsburgh metropolitan area. People here are Steelers and Pirates fans, they drink Iron City and Rolling Rock beer, they watch Pittsburgh television, and they live in the crevasses between hills cut by the Monongahela and Ohio rivers. This has been one of America's prime industrial areas. Northern West Virginia is part of the same coal-and-steel economy that made Pittsburgh one of the nation's largest cities and filled the narrow bottomlands along the rivers with steel and glass factories, foundries and coal yards.

As in Pennsylvania, these industries have been declining and they have become far less labor-intensive. Local jobs and population have declined. Since 1980, the 12,000 mining jobs in this part of West Virginia have dropped by more than two-thirds, with comparable fall-offs in manufacturing. The Weirton tin and steel mill (now called ArcelorMittal and owned by an integrated steel and mining company headquartered in Luxembourg) employed 14,000 workers in the mid-1970s but was down to 880 in 2019; Luxembourg-based ArcelorMittal sold the plant to Cleveland Cliffs in late 2020. Coal giant Murray Energy went into bankruptcy in 2020 and laid off hundreds in northern West Virginia. Service jobs have replaced some of these losses. Walmart has been West Virginia's second largest private employer since 1998, and the government has brought in thousands more jobs, compliments of the late Sen. Robert Byrd, the powerful Senate appropriator, whose legacy endures years after his death. One of the largest employers in Harrison County has been the Department of Justice, while the I-79 Technology Park in Fairmont houses offices for NASA, the National Oceanic and Atmospheric Association, the FBI and the Department of Homeland Security. Harrison County has become the state's leader in the Marcellus shale natural gas boom, with an influx of jobs and money that have resulted from more than 3,000 wells drilled in the state; in 2020 West Virginia Methanol said it would invest $350 million in a new natural gas plant in Pleasants County.

The 1st Congressional District of West Virginia includes 20 counties in the northern third of the state. On the Panhandle along the Ohio River is Wheeling, once one of the richest cities in the country with its steel and glass companies. South of Pittsburgh on the Monongahela River is Morgantown, with human capital from West Virginia University, the largest employer in the state. On the Ohio River is the former oil-refining and shipping center of Parkersburg, which has become a plastics and manufacturing hub. While much of the state has declined economically and lost population in recent decades, Morgantown's population grew from less than 27,000 in 2000 to almost 31,000 in 2019.

For most of the 20th century, much of the territory in the 1st District was solidly Democratic. But the decline of coal and dissatisfaction with the Clinton-Gore policies on mining and the environment helped Republican George W. Bush carry the district twice, and the local hostility accelerated with President Barack Obama's policies. Donald Trump won 68 percent of the district's vote in both 2016 and 2020.

Alex Mooney (R)

Elected 2014, 4th term, b. Jun 07, 1971; Washington, DC; Dartmouth College, A.B., 1993; Roman Catholic; Married (Grace Gonzalez); 3 children.

Elected Office: MD Senate, 1999-2010.

Professional Career: Aide, Rep. Roscoe Bartlett, 1993-1995; Executive, Council for National Policy Action, Inc, 1995-1998; Director, The National Journalism Center, 2005-2012; Chair, MD GOP, 2010-2013; Owner, consulting firm, 2011-2014.

DC Office: 2440 RHOB 20515, 202-225-2711, Fax: 202-225-7856, mooney.house.gov

State Offices: Charleston, 304-925-5964; Martinsburg, 304-264-8810.

Committees: *Financial Services*: Investor Protection, Entrepreneurship & Capital Markets; Oversight & Investigations.

Group Ratings

	ADA	ACLU	AFL-CIO	LCV	COC	HAFA	ACU	CFG	FRC
2020	**	26%	**	10%	–	95%	90%	**	–
2019	0%	C	24%	10%	80%	C	89%	90%	95%

Almanac Ratings 2019-2020

	Economy	Social	Foreign	Composite
Liberal	25%	8%	41%	25%
Conservative	75%	92%	59%	75%

Key Votes of the 116th Congress

1. U.S./Mex./Can. trade deal Y	5. Russia sanctions N	9. Firearms background checks N
2. First Coronavirus response N	6. Troops in Syria N	10. Spending at the border Y
3. HEROES Act N	7. Veto arms sales to Saudis Y	11. Marijuana liberalized rules N
4. CASH Act N	8. Defense $$$, veto override N	12. Electoral College objections Y

Election Results

Election	Name (Party)	Vote (%)	Cand. Spent	Ind. Exp. Support	Ind. Exp. Oppose
2020 General	Alex Mooney (R)..........................	172,195 (63%)	$832,414	$2,664	$863
	Cathy Kunkel (D)............................	100,799 (37%)	$614,200	$258	$445
2020 Primary	Alex Mooney (R)..........................	51,184 (72%)			
	Matt Hahn (R)...............................	20,186 (28%)			

Prior winning percentages: 2018 (54%), 2016 (58%), 2014 (47%)

Republican Alex Mooney, a former Maryland state senator who has run for office in three states, won a costly and contentious contest in 2014 in the sprawling 2nd District and has emerged as a fierce partisan in Congress.

Mooney was born in Washington D.C. to a Cuban refugee mother and a father from an Irish immigrant family who served in Vietnam. He graduated from Dartmouth College, where he was president of the Coalition for Life; during his time there, he ran for the New Hampshire House of Representatives but got just 8 percent of the vote and finished last of the seven candidates in the general election. After college, he was an aide to GOP Rep. Roscoe Bartlett of Maryland. Mooney won a Maryland state Senate seat in 1998 at age 27 and became Maryland GOP chairman after he lost reelection to the Senate in 2010. (His official bio deleted reference to his service in Annapolis.) He then set his sights on his former boss' House seat and started raising money for a potential run in 2012 after most assumed Bartlett would retire. But Mooney abandoned the effort after Bartlett announced he would run in what turned out to be a losing effort in a tougher district post-redistricting. Mooney kept the campaign cash, saying he would run in 2014, and went back to work for Bartlett part-time in 2012.

But Mooney had a change of plan and crossed the state line to West Virginia, where he entered a seven-way GOP primary after Rep. Shelley Moore Capito ran successfully for the Senate. He won with 36 percent of the vote to 22 percent for Ken Reed, a pharmacist. In the general election, Mooney campaigned on an anti-Obama platform, vowing to repeal the Affordable Care Act and pledging to fight government overreach. Nick Casey, a former Democratic state chairman, said he wanted to scrap some parts of the health care law, and argued that Washington needed more moderate voices.

The central fight was over whether geography or ideology mattered more. Casey, calling himself a "true West Virginian," branded Mooney a carpetbagger and opportunist. Mooney countered that he was a "West Virginian by choice," and therefore more committed to his adopted district's conservative values. He pointed out that his Maryland state Senate seat bordered West Virginia and that the two areas are similar. Each candidate spent about $2 million. Mooney benefited from more than $2.3 million in additional spending from Republican and conservative groups, compared with less than $900,000 that national Democrats delivered to Casey. The carpet bagging charge clearly hurt Mooney, but he held on in the conservative district for a 47%-44% victory.

In the House, Mooney has been a committed partisan. He joined the House Freedom Caucus and got a spot on the Budget Committee, where he supported the Republicans' spending plan and took credit for provisions that opposed funding of ozone standards by the Environmental Protection Agency and blocked regulations that would prohibit surface mining in West Virginia. On the Natural Resources Committee, he attacked Obama administration initiatives that were designed to limit the mining and use of coal, accusing Obama of being "intent on destroying coal as a domestic energy source." He bucked party leaders with his votes opposing trade promotion authority for Obama.

In 2017, Mooney moved to the Financial Services Committee, where he pursued his interest in community banking and housing issues. He introduced legislation to amend the Dodd-Frank banking law to repeal disclosures given to investors about the safety violations and worker deaths of publicly traded mining companies. In 2018, he filed a bill to end taxation of gold and silver coins and bars; he has voiced support for returning the United States to the gold standard.

Heading into the 2020 election, Mooney wrote in an op-ed that the Democratic Party had been hijacked by socialists who want the federal government to dictate everything "from the health care you receive to the car you drive." He strongly opposed proxy voting in the House, a temporary measure adopted because of the coronavirus. After Trump's election loss, Mooney vocally backed Trump's efforts to overturn the results. In December, he introduced a resolution to formally condemn any House Republicans who, in his view, had "prematurely" called on Trump to concede. He was one of 126 Republicans to join a lawsuit asking the Supreme Court to overturn the election, and when that failed, voted against certifying Joe Biden's victory on Jan. 6.

Mooney hasn't faced serious opposition since his first election. In 2016, when Democratic officials' preferred candidate lost to Charleston-area attorney and longtime state legislator Charles Hunt in the primary, they did little to help in the general election. Mooney won, 58%-42%.

In 2018, Talley Sergent, who served as Hillary Clinton's 2016 West Virginia state director, underscored her family's six-generation roots in the state. Sergent didn't mention her work for Clinton on her campaign bio and instead stressed her work for the State Department and former Democratic Sen. Jay Rockefeller. But Mooney played up those Clinton ties and his own support for Trump in an area where the president remained popular. Mooney won 54%-43%. In 2020, Democrats didn't bother to seriously contest the election; Mooney defeated energy analyst Cathy Kunkel, a member of the Democratic Socialists of America, 63%-37%.

With West Virginia losing a House seat, the 49-year-old Mooney's political future is uncertain. He could decide to prepare to run statewide in 2024, or potentially wage a primary battle to remain in the House, unless one of his septuagenarian House colleagues opts to retire.

WV-2: Central West Virginia   Cook Partisan Voting Index: R+20

Population		Race and Ethnicity		Income	
Total	623,039	White	91.80%	Median Income	$52,166
Land area (sq. miles)	8,017	Black	4.40%	District Income Rank	365
Pop/ sq mi	77.71	Latino	2.20%	Poverty Rate	15.00%
Born in State	61.00%	Asian	0.90%	With health insurance	92.90%
		Two or more races	2.30%	Cash public assistance	3.40%
Age Groups		Other	0.60%	Food stamp/SNAP	15.10%
Under 18	21.20%				
18-34	19.40%	**Education**		**Work**	
35-64	39.90%	H.S grad or less	51.10%	White Collar	32.90%
Over 64	19.50%	Some college	26.20%	Sales and Service	40.70%
		College Degree, 4 yr	13.60%	Blue Collar	26.50%
Military		Post grad	9.00%	Government	18.40%
Veteran/ Active Duty	9.60%				

2020 Pres. Vote	Trump	184,784	(65%)	Biden	92,623	(33%)		
2016 Pres. Vote	Trump	164,674	(66%)	Clinton	73,487	(29%)	Johnson	8,232	(3%)

Charleston, Martinsburg: Not all of West Virginia has been coal country, and not all its hills have been scarred by strip mining. Large parts of this naturally beautiful state look as verdant and unchanged as they must have when George Washington was speculating in land here. For miles, there are gentle hills and rugged mountains. Yet over another hill you might find, amid scenery primeval and rural, sudden evidence of industrialization: a pulp mill or charcoal factory in a clearing scraped out of the forest; a small factory town, built close to a river in a cleft bordered with hills; the entrance to an underground coal mine or a mountaintop blasted open to allow surface mining.

The 2nd Congressional District of West Virginia is a central slice of the state, from Berkeley Springs and Harpers Ferry in the Washington D.C. exurbs, more than 300 miles to beyond Charleston and the Ohio River town of Ravenswood. The district includes fast-growing parts of the state: the Eastern Panhandle counties, which are part of the extended Washington metropolitan area, and chemical-producing Putnam County, which is increasingly home to suburbanites commuting to Charleston. The Toyota engine and transmission plant in Buffalo just outside Charleston, which employed 1,600 people, celebrated its 20th anniversary in 2016 with plans for a $400 million expansion; by 2020, the company planned another $115.3 million investment to produce its first American-made hybrid transaxles. In Charleston, the state capitol sits on the banks of the Kanawha River, with a dome higher than that of the U.S. Capitol. When the city's two newspapers—The Charleston Gazette, which leans Democratic, and the Republican-tilting Charleston Daily Mail—

combined into the Charleston Gazette-Mail in 2015, it created one news staff and two separate editorial pages.

In the 1940s, the area produced all the nation's Lucite, polyethylene and nylon, as well as much of its artificial rubber and antifreeze. Today, the state boasts that it is home to more polymer producers than any other place on the planet; the chemical industry makes products used in the manufacturing of cosmetics, detergents, shampoo and other products. Those chemical plants employ thousands of workers in Kanawha and Putnam counties, but they can be hazardous. Charleston is West Virginia's professional center, with a few downtown office towers and some affluent residential areas. Politically, this ancestrally Democratic district has shifted in a big way to the GOP. Berkeley County, which has commuter rail to Washington, has grown over 50 percent since 2000 to become the second-largest county in the state. During that period, Kanawha County has dropped 7 percent, and Charleston is now the third-fastest shrinking city in the nation, with median home prices of just over $100,000; Charleston's population has shrunk by 10 percent in the past two decades, losing more than 5,000 people. Donald Trump won the district with 66 percent in 2016 and 65 percent in 2020.

Carol Miller (R)

Elected 2018, 2nd term, b. Nov 04, 1950; Columbus, OH; Columbia College, B.S., 1972; Baptist; Married (Matt Miller); 2 children.

Elected Office: WV State House, 2006-2018.

Professional Career: Bison Farmer; Real Estate Manager.

DC Office: 1605 LHOB 20515, 202-225-3452, miller.house.gov

State Offices: Beckley, 304-250-6177; Bluefield, 304-325-6800; Huntington, 304-522-2201.

Committees: *Select Committee on the Climate Crisis. Ways & Means*: Trade; Worker & Family Support.

Almanac Ratings 2019-2020

	Economy	Social	Foreign	Composite
Liberal	25%	26%	8%	20%
Conservative	75%	74%	92%	80%

Key Votes of the 116th Congress

1. U.S./Mex./Can. trade deal	Y	5. Russia sanctions	N	9. Firearms background checks	N	
2. First Coronavirus response	Y	6. Troops in Syria	N	10. Spending at the border	Y	
3. HEROES Act	N	7. Veto arms sales to Saudis	N	11. Marijuana liberalized rules	N	
4. CASH Act	N	8. Defense $$$, veto override	N	12. Electoral College objections	Y	

Election Results

Election	Name (Party)	Vote (%)		Cand. Spent	Ind. Exp. Support	Ind. Exp. Oppose
2020 General	Carol Miller (R)	161,585	(71%)	$489,738	$1,365	
	Hilary Turner (D)	64,927	(29%)	$93,560		$302
2020 Primary	Carol Miller (R)	40,226	(70%)			
	Russell Siegel (R)	17,024	(30%)			

Prior winning percentages: 2018 (56%)

Republican Carol Miller, elected in 2018, won competitive contests to take an open seat. She brought extensive political experience and embraced President Donald Trump, who was widely popular in her district. She faced Democrat Richard Ojeda, a feisty opponent who supported Trump in 2016 and distanced himself from his national party. Miller succeeded Rep. Evan Jenkins, who unsuccessfully sought the Republican nomination for the Senate in 2018 and later resigned to become a justice on the state Supreme Court. She was the only Republican in the large House freshman class of women.

Miller has a congressional pedigree, as the daughter of GOP Rep. Samuel Devine of Ohio. He served 22 years, including two years as chairman of the House Republican Conference, before he lost reelection in 1980. Miller graduated from Columbia College in South Carolina. She was a real-estate property manager and managed the Swann Ridge Bison Farm, where she raised and processed buffalo meat. She served 12 years in the state House of Delegates, where she was majority whip and chaired the Small Business Committee. Her husband, Matt Miller, was a prominent automobile dealer.

The opening created by Jenkins resulted in a wide-open Republican primary. Each of the four leading contenders served in the legislature or was a party official, and made clear their support for Trump. Miller ran ads that pledged "America First" principles. She gained backing from Rep. Susan Brooks of Indiana and Working for Women, a new group backing Republican women.

Miller won the primary with 24 percent of the vote. Rupie Phillips and Marty Gearhart, who both served with Miller in the House of Delegates, got 20 and 18 percent, respectively. Conrad Lucas, the former state party chairman who had support from the Republican Main Street Partnership, got 18 percent.

Ojeda, a state senator for two years, had an easier time in the Democratic primary, which he won with 52 percent against three opponents. A retired Army captain and ally of organized labor, he helped organize the strikes that led to higher teacher wages in the state. Ojeda's distinctiveness included reversal of his earlier support for Trump. "All he's done is shown that he's taking care of the daggone people he's supposed to be getting rid of," Ojeda told Politico. During a campaign appearance in Wheeling in September, Trump responded by calling Ojeda "a total wacko" and "stone-cold crazy." Miller said she welcomed Trump's support, though she would not have used those words.

Ojeda outspent Miller $2.8 million to $1.9 million, but the increasingly entrenched Republican lean of southern West Virginia helped Miller to a 56%-44% win, taking 16 of 18 counties, losing only Boone and Fayette, both in the Charleston suburbs. The 2020 election was a lot less interesting; Miller cruised to reelection 71%-29% over environmental activist Hilary Turner.

Miller stuck close to Trump in office, including supporting House Republicans' efforts to reject Joe Biden's electoral victory. But she's shown some bipartisan tendencies, partnering with Democratic House Oversight and Reform Committee Chairwoman Rep. Carolyn Maloney on a bill to expand parental leave policy for federal government employees and cofounding the bipartisan Congressional Energy Export Caucus.

Taking her House seat at age 68, Miller faced a potentially significant challenge, as the state loses one of its three districts as a result of the 2020 census and subsequent reapportionment. Because her district lacks the larger population centers of the other two districts and has lost a lot of population in the past decade, redistricting might leave her with less of a base than a potential competitor.

In early 2021, House GOP leaders appointed Miller to the powerful Ways and Means Committee, a signal—including to other Republicans—that they believe that the sophomore might be sticking around for a while.

WV-3: Southern West Virginia   Cook Partisan Voting Index: R+27

Population		Race and Ethnicity		Income	
Total	567,297	White	93.90%	Median Income	$42,553
Land area (sq. miles)	9,745	Black	4.10%	District Income Rank	426
Pop/ sq mi	58.21	Latino	1.00%	Poverty Rate	18.50%
Born in State	77.50%	Asian	0.50%	With health insurance	93.00%
		Two or more races	1.30%	Cash public assistance	3.20%
Age Groups		Other	0.10%	Food stamp/SNAP	22.00%
Under 18	20.00%				
18-34	19.00%	**Education**		**Work**	
35-64	39.20%	H.S grad or less	58.70%	White Collar	32.10%
Over 64	21.90%	Some college	24.30%	Sales and Service	41.50%
		College Degree, 4 yr	10.60%	Blue Collar	26.50%
Military		Post grad	6.40%	Government	19.90%
Veteran/ Active Duty	7.90%				

2020 Pres. Vote	Trump	176,694	(73%)	Biden	61,512	(25%)	
2016 Pres. Vote	Trump	158,763	(73%)	Clinton	50,923	(23%) Johnson	5,910 (3%)

Huntington, Beckley: Early in the 20th century, the coal fields of southern West Virginia were one of America's boom areas. Into rural farmland and hollows, inhabited by the same families that settled the mountains 100 years before, came coal company lawyers with mineral rights' leases to sign, coal company engineers to design and sink mineshafts, and men from other mountain counties to work the mines. Company houses were built, wages were low, work conditions were often dangerous and company stores were stocked with goods priced at whatever the company dictated. These conditions bred discontent, which ignited into the fire of industrial unionism. The Battle of Blair Mountain in Logan County, where 10,000 armed unionists faced off against 3,000 law enforcement officers and strikebreakers, presaged later efforts at organization by John L. Lewis, president of the United Mine Workers. During and after World War II, he called out his 300,000 coal miners on strikes, to the fury of Democratic Presidents Franklin Roosevelt and Harry Truman, who viewed the strikes as threatening to the war effort and postwar economic recovery.

Coal no longer is the dominant U.S. source of electricity. In 2020, it supplied 19 percent of the fuel to power utility plants, down from 39 percent as recently as 2014. Marion and Logan are the leading counties in this region for coal production, with at least 10 million tons each in 2017. Boone, Raleigh and Mingo counties, which were on that list a decade ago, have declined significantly in production. Production in the southern part of the state dropped from 116 million tons in 2008 to 46 million tons in 2017, which has become virtually the same total as in the northern counties. Statewide, the total of 14,000 jobs in the West Virginia mines in 2019 dropped from nearly 23,000 in 2011, and barely rebounded during the Trump administration. Mingo, McDowell and other nearby counties have suffered among the highest rates in the nation for opioid drug addiction and deaths.

The 3rd Congressional District of West Virginia includes most of the mountainous coal country in the southern part of the state, which for years was heavily Democratic. But the coal mining counties make up less than half the district. About a quarter of the population is in and around the industrial city of Huntington on the Ohio River, which includes Marshall University. Another quarter is to the east, in Beckley and the farming uplands. Also located there is the Greenbrier Resort, where the government built a massive secret fallout shelter, code-named "Project Greek Island," to house the entire Congress in the event of nuclear war. The district has shifted to Republicans in federal races the past two decades. Webster and McDowell counties were two of the three counties that moved hardest to the GOP in the entire country between 2008 and 2020; Obama carried both in 2008, while Trump won about four-fifths of the vote in both counties 12 years later. Trump won the district 73%-23% in 2016 and 73%-25% in 2020.

WISCONSIN

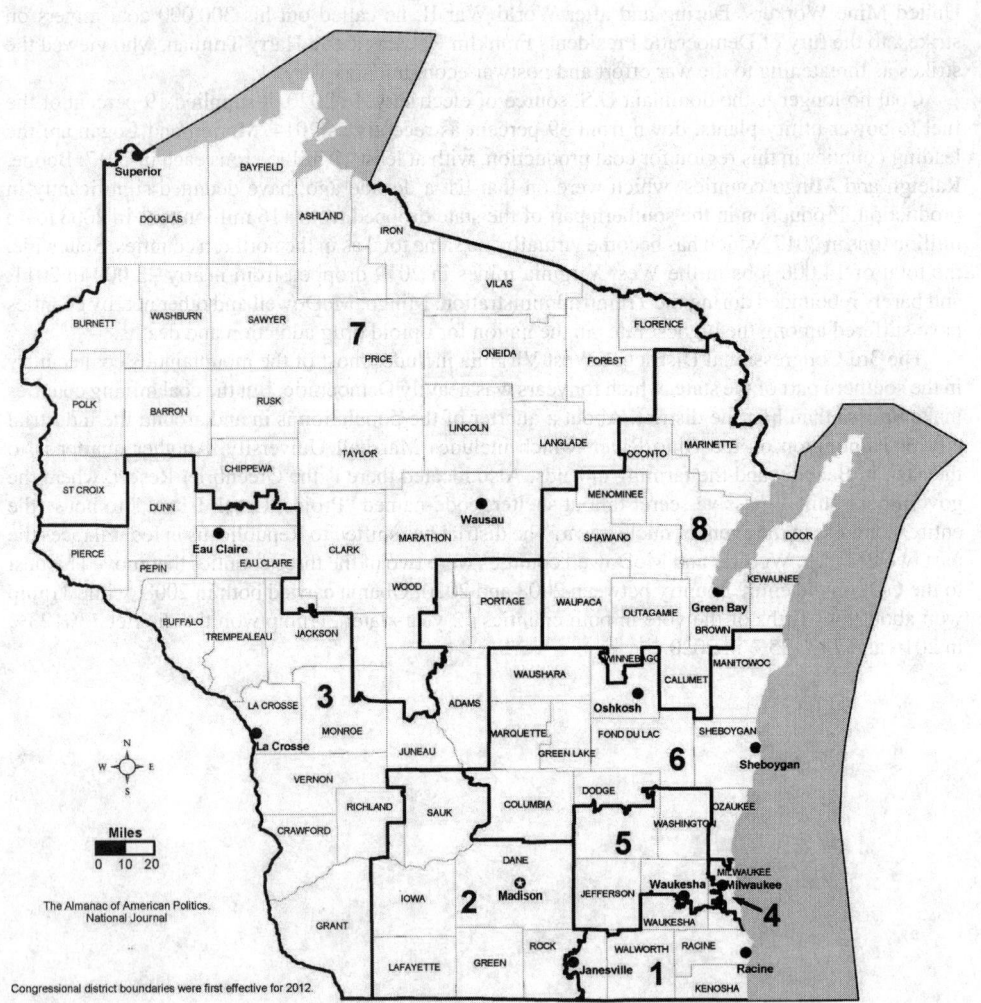

The Almanac of American Politics.
National Journal

Congressional district boundaries were first effective for 2012.

Wisconsin, as much as any state, was the focus of the 2020 presidential race. In 2016, Donald Trump won Wisconsin by fewer than 23,000 votes, securing his path to the White House. Four years later, Joe Biden reversed the script, winning the state by just under 21,000 votes. In 2020, it was the "tipping point" state in the Electoral College, the state whose electoral votes put the winner over the required 270.

Wisconsin has long been one of America's premier "laboratories of reform," in Justice Louis Brandeis' phrase—a state developing new public policies, debating them vigorously and even tumultuously, observing whether they worked, and serving as an example for other states. North of the dominant westward paths of migration, the state was sparsely settled, first by New England Yankees and then by waves of immigrants from Germany and Scandinavia. The German language is seldom heard now, but German place names and surnames are common in Wisconsin and, like the once plainly German beer and brat brands, now seem quintessentially American. On the rolling dairy land of Wisconsin and the orderly streets of Milwaukee, they built their own churches, kept their own language, and maintained old customs, from country weddings to Christmas trees to beer gardens— a source of friction in temperance-minded America. About half of Wisconsin residents, more than in any other state, reported in the 2010 census that they are of German descent, and Wisconsin still has an orderliness and steadiness that owes something to its Germanic heritage.

Wisconsin has been home to high-skill, precision instrument production at companies like Johnson Controls and Rockwell Automation. Madison, powered by the flagship campus of the University of Wisconsin, has become a technology hub. (A plan for an advanced manufacturing plant near Racine for Taiwan-based Fox conn has been less successful; originally driven with billions of dollars in subsidies, promised by Gov. Scott Walker and his fellow Republican legislators, the project's slow pace of building and hiring led Walker's Democratic successor, Tony Evers to hold back on state monies in 2020.) Wisconsin is also the nation's leading producer of paper, though the inexorable shift from printed to digital media has hobbled the industry. Agriculture remains a significant part of the economy, particularly dairy; Wisconsin ranks either first or second in the nation in most categories of milk and cheese production. However, improved productivity and competition from foreign countries, as well as California's giant agribusiness enterprises, has had an impact. Wisconsin lost 10 percent of its dairy farms in 2019 alone, the largest annual decline since 2004, when records were first kept. In 2020, farmers ignominiously had to dump large quantities of milk due to reduced demand from restaurants and schools during the coronavirus pandemic. Wisconsin, of course, is also a prime source of beer and sausage. Over time, Wisconsin's economy has ranked right around where the country is; its median income hovers just below the nation's.

Wisconsin's reputation for innovative public policy was established during the Progressive Era that began around 1900 and which owes its development to an extraordinary governor, Robert La Follette Sr., and the state's German heritage. Wisconsin is one of the two states that gave birth to the Republican Party in 1854 (the other is Michigan); Germans, then arriving in America in vast numbers, heavily favored the GOP. They opposed slavery and welcomed the free lands Republicans delivered in the Homestead Act, the educational opportunities provided by land grant colleges, and the transportation routes constructed by subsidized railroad builders. Wisconsin has also had a long history of labor activism. Milwaukee saw bloodshed on May 5, 1886, when 1,500 tradesmen and Polish immigrants demanding an eight-hour workday marched on the Rolling Mills iron plant in the city's Bay View neighborhood. Seven people, including a young boy, were killed; south of downtown Milwaukee, a memorial stands near where the blood was spilled.

From this seedbed sprouted the Progressive movement founded and symbolized by La Follette. At a time when Germany was the world's leader in graduate education and the application of science to government, La Follette had professors at the University of Wisconsin help develop the state workmen's compensation system and income tax. La Follette became a national figure, and after he died in 1925, liberal Democrats carried on his tradition—progressive at home and isolationist abroad. Meanwhile, Milwaukee developed its own distinct strain of governance on the left—the "sewer socialists" who occupied the Milwaukee mayor's office for much of the time between 1910 and 1960. Touting spending on public health, infrastructure, and parks, these officials "were known for their integrity, their tactical ingenuity and their relentless organizing," including "a volunteer army that could deliver the party's literature, in any of 12 languages, to every house in Milwaukee within 48 hours," Dan Kaufman wrote in the New York Times. Wisconsin became the first state to grant collective-bargaining rights to public employees, in 1959.

Starting in the 1990s, Wisconsin became a laboratory for conservative reforms driven by Republican Gov. Tommy Thompson, who beat a liberal Democrat in 1986 and was reelected three times. He cut taxes, sponsored a school choice program, and passed the nation's most sweeping welfare reforms that cut caseloads by equipping recipients to work. After a Democratic interregnum, the 2010 election produced another experiment in conservative reform as Republican Scott Walker, a former Milwaukee County executive, won the governorship and set off a firestorm with proposals to limit the power of public-sector unions. The effort was successful, and Walker turned back an energetic, labor-driven effort to recall him in 2012 before winning reelection in 2014. A University of Wisconsin study found that in the first eight years after passage of the anti-union measures, membership fell by almost 54 percent, more than double the national pace.

Wisconsin's population has grown, but at a modest rate, up 3.6 percent since the 2010 census. Both the city of Milwaukee and Milwaukee County have shrunk since the last census; the surrounding suburban counties of Waukesha, Ozaukee, and Washington, known as the "WOW" counties, have all grown between 3 and 4 percent during the same period. The state's fastest growth has occurred in Dane County (Madison), which has expanded by 11.7 percent since 2010, pushing growth to rural areas to the south and northeast. Other growth areas have included Outagamie County (Appleton) and Eau Claire County (Eau Claire), which have expanded by 6.2 and 5.7 percent, respectively, since the last census. The state remains primarily White, with a small, if rising, foreign-born population. Overall, Wisconsin is 6 percent Black, 7 percent Hispanic and 3 percent Asian. Racial tensions in Kenosha drew national attention in 2020 when police fired at Jacob Blake, a Black man, seven times in the back, paralyzing him. Daytime protests spiraled into clashes and arson at night, and Kyle Rittenhouse, a White teenager from Illinois aligned with militia members, was arrested for shooting three people, killing two of them.

The state's historical patterns for voting trace back to ethnic differences: Eastern Wisconsin is more German, and thus Republican, while western Wisconsin is more Scandinavian, making it more Democratic. But these leanings have been in flux in recent elections. The Fox River Valley, including the "BOW" counties of Brown, Outagamie, and Winnebago, have historically been Republican turf, though the midsized industrial cities they contain, such as Appleton, Oshkosh and Green Bay, have become a bit bluer in recent years. Western Wisconsin—areas along the Mississippi River, the small inland cities such as Wausau and Eau Claire and the counties along Lake Superior—have historically been more Democratic. But a seven-county portion of southwest Wisconsin known as the Driftless Area (for its geology) "boasts the nation's greatest concentration of Obama-Trump counties—places that voted for President Barack Obama in 2012 and Trump in 2016," the Milwaukee Journal Sentinel's Craig Gilbert has written. Many of those counties backed Evers for governor in 2018, but flipped back to Trump in 2020. Meanwhile, strong Republican support in the "WOW" counties has traditionally come close to canceling out Milwaukee's lopsided Democratic margins, though recently the suburban margins have narrowed somewhat. The most heavily Democratic region by far is around Madison. It has become ever more important for the party's electoral math: Dane County is both growing in population and turning leftward. Other pockets of historical Democratic strength include a belt of college cities—La Crosse and Eau Claire, each with University of Wisconsin campuses, and Rock County (Janesville), the home of Beloit College. With statewide races in Wisconsin often decided narrowly, a significant number of Wisconsinites are swing voters. Indeed, Wisconsin has elected and reelected both conservative Republican Ron Johnson and liberal Democrat Tammy Baldwin to the Senate.

Heading into the 2016 presidential election, some considered Wisconsin one of the Democrats' "blue wall" states—a supposed bulwark against Republicans in the Electoral College, because the state had not voted Republican for president since Ronald Reagan's 1984 landslide. But this ignored that the state's demographics, especially its above-average percentage of White, non-college-educated voters, favored the incipient Trump campaign. The full extent of Hillary Clinton's struggles in the state were hard to spot and were largely ignored by her campaign team. Her key weakness was in Wisconsin' rural areas and small towns, where Democrats had historically been competitive.

Ultimately, 23 of the state's 72 counties flipped in 2016, all from blue to red; a state Obama had won by seven points in 2012 ended up voting for Trump by less than a point.

The state remained swingy during Trump's presidency. Walker lost a tough battle for a third term to Evers; in 16 of Wisconsin's 20 least densely populated counties, Walker improved his performance, but he lost ground in the state's 35 densest counties, which on balance lost him the governorship. In an April 2019 judicial election, Wisconsin voters swung back to the right, but one year later, a liberal justice won a surprisingly strong victory, possibly aided by Democratic ire over the Republican legislature's refusal to allow Evers to expand mail voting amid the pandemic.

In 2020, both campaigns focused intently on Wisconsin. The Democratic National Convention was scheduled to be in Milwaukee, but party leaders took it virtual due to the pandemic. Biden held modest polling leads over Trump for most of the campaign, but when all the votes were counted, he won narrowly, by about six-tenths of a percentage point. Biden flipped two counties: Door County, on a Lake Michigan peninsula, and Sauk County (Baraboo). He also made incremental gains in a wide range of locales. He expanded the Democrats' winning margins by between one and six points in Milwaukee, Dane, La Crosse, Eau Claire, and Rock counties, and he narrowed Trump's winning margins by two to seven points in each of the WOW and BOW counties, as well as in St. Croix County, a Twin Cities exurb. But other counties, including a lot of mid-sized ones, showed little or no shift from 2016 to 2020, including Racine County (Racine), Marathon County (Wausau), Sheboygan County (Sheboygan), Fond du Lac County (Fond du Lac), and Walworth County (Lake Geneva). This suggested that large swaths of non-metropolitan Wisconsin have moved toward the GOP for the long term. "2016 was realigning," Gilbert wrote. "2020 was reinforcing." One of the few mid-sized counties to shift toward Trump in 2020 was Kenosha, by a bit less than three points, possibly an after-effect of the city's violent summer. The most pivotal shifts, however, were in Dane (which by itself provided enough net gains for Biden to erase Trump's 2016 margin) and the suburbs of Milwaukee County (which produced much of the rest of Biden's winning cushion, in locales like Wauwatosa, Fox Point, and Brown Deer). The statewide margin was close enough that Trump sought to pressure election officials to overturn his loss, but those efforts failed.

In April 2021, the candidate favored by Democrats won Wisconsin's nominally nonpartisan race for superintendent of public instruction with an impressive 58 percent of the vote. But as 2022 approached, Wisconsin voters looked forward to competitive races for governor and senator, and for the state to remain in the center of the nation's attention.

Population		Race and Ethnicity		Income	
Total	5,822,434	White	85.20%	Median Income	64,168
Land area (sq. miles)	54,158	Black	6.40%	State Income Rank	21 out of 50
Pop/ sq mi	107.51	Latino	7.10%	Poverty Rate	10.40%
Born in state	70.90%	Asian	3.50%	With health insurance	94.30%
		Two or more races	2.40%	Cash public assistance	1.60%
Age Groups		Other	3.10%	Food stamp/SNAP	12.1%
Under 18	21.70%				
18-34	21.90%	**Education**		**Work**	
35-64	38.80%	H.S grad or less	37.80%	White Collar	37.90%
Over 64	17.50%	Some college	30.90%	Sales and Service	35.70%
		College Degree, 4 yr	20.70%	Blue Collar	26.40%
Military		Post grad	10.70%	Government	12.30%
Veteran/ Active Duty	7.00%				

Presidential Politics

2020 Primary (D)	Biden (D)	581,463(63%)	Sanders (D)	293,441(32%)			
2020 Pres. Vote	Biden (D)	1,630,866(49%)	Trump (R)	1,610,184(49%)			
2016 Pres. Vote	Trump (R)	1,405,284(47%)	Clinton (D)	1,382,536(46%)	Johnson (L)	106,674 (4%)	

Wisconsin has seen some very close presidential elections. Since Lyndon Johnson's 1964 national landslide election, the only presidential candidate of either party to crack 55 percent of the vote was Barack Obama in 2008. Al Gore carried the state by 5,708 votes in 2000, John Kerry won it by 11,384 votes in 2004, and Donald Trump beat Hillary Clinton by 22,748 votes in 2016. In 2020, Joe Biden defeated Trump by 20,682 votes. Wisconsin was the tipping-point state that put him over the top in the Electoral College.

Trump won Wisconsin in 2016 because of a massive rightward swing in its rural and non-metropolitan (and largely White) territory, and a major dip in Democratic turnout across the state. Trump flipped 23 of the 35 counties Obama had carried in 2012, many of them in western Wisconsin; 34 counties saw a 10-percentage point decline in the Democratic share of the two-party presidential vote. Clinton netted 43,600 fewer votes from Milwaukee County than Obama did in 2012. She fared better in the conservative "WOW" counties of Washington, Ozaukee and Waukesha that make up much of suburban Milwaukee, cutting the GOP margin from 132,500 votes in 2012 to 104,500 votes for Trump in 2016. But it wasn't enough. Overall, turnout of eligible voters dipped to 70.5 percent, the lowest since 2000.

Much of the blame for Clinton's 2016 loss of a state that had voted Democratic in the previous seven presidential elections was laid on her absentee performance. Clinton never campaigned there during the general election and didn't air ads in the state until the final week. Veteran Democratic pollster Paul Maslin, who is based in Wisconsin, called that lack of attention "political malpractice."

Democrats weren't going to make the same mistake in 2020. They picked Milwaukee to host the Democratic National Convention, and the party and its affiliated super-PACs leaned hard into organizing the state. Milwaukee and Green Bay were among the top 10 media markets by total ads run in the 2020 campaign, according to the Wesleyan Media Project.

For the second consecutive presidential election, pollsters badly missed the mark in Wisconsin. Five Thirty Eight found Biden had an 8.4 point average polling lead heading into Election Day. But as returns started rolling in it became clear the election would be close. Trump initially led the state on election night, and prematurely declared victory. But Biden pulled ahead when a trove of mail ballots were tabulated Wednesday morning.

Trump protested, claiming widespread voter, but lost a number of court challenges and a recount actually slightly widened Biden's lead in the state. Biden's eventual margin of victory was 49.5%-48.9%, making Wisconsin the pivotal state that gave Biden enough Electoral College votes to win the White House.

Biden flipped back Wisconsin by improving just enough in the state's urban and suburban centers. He netted a whopping 181,000 votes in Madison's Dane County, 42,000 more than Clinton. That difference alone accounts for almost the entirety of the swing in the net margin from 2016 to 2020. Biden also netted 183,000 votes in Milwaukee County, 20,000 more than Clinton managed.

Trump won the "WOW" counties 62%-38%, with a 97,000-vote margin, down from 65%-30% in 2016. Biden flipped back Sauk County outside of Madison and Door County, a tourist and retiree haven up the Lake Michigan coast. The only other counties he carried were Ashland, Bayfield and Douglas, a trio of ancestrally Democratic Iron Range counties along Lake Superior in the North woods, and Menominee County, home of the Menominee Indian Reservation.

The only areas outside greater Milwaukee and Madison where Biden showed much significant improvement were in Eau Claire and La Crosse counties, which contain the eponymous large towns along the Mississippi. He actually dropped even further behind Clinton in parts of western Wisconsin and a handful of other more rural counties. Overall turnout jumped to 75.8 percent of the eligible population, putting Wisconsin behind only Colorado, Maine and Minnesota nationally.

Wisconsin once had one of the nation's most influential presidential primaries. It helped John Kennedy establish his lead over Hubert Humphrey in 1960, prompted Lyndon Johnson to withdraw as Eugene McCarthy was about to beat him there in 1968, gave George McGovern his first victory in 1972, gave Jimmy Carter a key victory in 1976 and chose "New Democrat" Gary Hart over Minnesota neighbor Walter Mondale in 1984. In 2016, the "never Trump" movement coalesced around Texas Sen. Ted Cruz before the April 5 GOP primary, with Republican Gov. Scott Walker leading the charge to give Cruz a 48%-35% victory. But Wisconsin would be the last primary or caucus that Trump would lose on his way to the GOP nomination. On the Democratic side, Vermont Sen. Bernie Sanders held multiple rallies across the state and outspent Clinton on television advertising, winning 56%-44%. In 2020, even as the coronavirus was surging, a half-dozen other states had postponed their primaries and numerous counties had shuttered most of their polling places, the vote went on. Biden won 58%-29%, and Bernie Sanders dropped out of the race two days later.

Congressional Districts

117th Congress Lineup	3D 5R	116th Congress Lineup	3D 5R

After Wisconsin lost a district in the 2000 census, the resulting consensus plan enabled all four Democrats and four Republicans running for reelection to win in 2002. The Green Bay-based 8th District has shifted twice since then and has returned to GOP control. Republican Sean Duffy picked up retiring Democrat David Obey's northwestern 7th District. In 2011, Republicans had total control over redistricting. With the state Senate under siege over a petition to oust six members in recall elections, Gov. Scott Walker quietly signed a pro-Republican map into law. The map shored up Duffy, giving him friendly St. Croix County in the Twin Cities exurbs and trading the liberal cities of Stevens Point and Wisconsin Rapids to 3rd District Democrat Ron Kind. It also boosted Republicans Paul Ryan in the 1st District and Tom Petri in the 6th District with an eye toward possible future open seats. In 2012, Republicans won 49 percent of all House votes but kept their 5-3 edge. Republican successors to Ryan and Petri later won with little difficulty.

In 2018, there were two significant developments. Democrat Tony Evers in November defeated Walker's bid for a third term as governor, thus breaking the Republican stranglehold on state governance. And after a three-judge federal panel found that the 2011 GOP plan was an unconstitutional "partisan gerrymander," the Supreme Court overturned that ruling and returned the case for further review. The Supreme Court's ruling in 2019 that alleged partisan gerrymanders in Maryland and North Carolina were not justiciable settled that conflict in Wisconsin.

Whatever the dynamics in the courts and in the legislature, Democrats surely will seek at least a fair fight for a fourth seat in the delegation, which could be based in the suburbs and exurbs north and south of Milwaukee. That could place the 1st or the 6th, or both, in play. The 5th District, which separates those two other districts, likely will remain safely Republican in the western suburbs. A new factor is the narrow reelection in 2020 of veteran Democratic Rep. Ron Kind in the western 3rd District. Perhaps a creative compromise would encourage two swing districts in the state.

Tony Evers (D)

Elected 2018, term expires 2023, 1st term; b. Nov. 05,1951, Plymouth, WA; University of Wisconsin, Madison, B.A.,1973, M.A., 1976, PhD, 1986; Unknown; Married (Kathy); 3 children.

Elected Office: WI Superintendent, 2009-2019.

Professional Career: Teacher.

Office: 115 E. Capitol Madison, 53702; 608-266-1212; Fax: 608-267-8983; Website: wisconsin.gov
Lt. Gov.: Mandela Barnes (D) **Atty. Gen:** Josh Kaul (D) **Sec. of State:** Doug La Follette (D)
State Legislature: Senate: 14D, 19R **House:** 36D, 63R

Election Results

Election	Name (Party)	Vote (%)
2018 General	Tony Evers (D)	1,324,307 (50%)
	Scott Walker (R)	1,295,080 (48%)
2018 Primary	Tony Evers (D)	225,082 (42%)
	Mahlon Mitchell (D)	87,926 (16%)
	Kelda Roys (D)	69,086 (13%)
	Kathleen Vinehout (D)	44,168 (8%)
	Michael McCabe (D)	39,885 (7%)
	Matthew Flynn (D)	31,580 (6%)
	Paul Soglin (D)	28,158 (5%)

Wisconsin's Tony Evers, low-key educator and administrator, ousted Republican Gov. Scott Walker in 2018, then spent much of the first two years of his term at loggerheads with the legislature and the state Supreme Court, both of which are in Republican hands.

Evers (it rhymes with "weavers") was born in Plymouth and met his wife, Kathy, there in kindergarten. His father practiced medicine at Rocky Knoll, a state tuberculosis sanitarium that also treated patients with silicosis, a disease often contracted by inhaling factory dust. His father would often testify on his patients' behalf. "It was about social justice," Evers told the New Yorker. "He could have gone into private practice, but he didn't. He decided to be a county employee and work with people who struggled." Evers earned a bachelor's, a master's and a Ph.D. from the University of Wisconsin-Madison and began his career in education as a science teacher in Baraboo, later becoming a principal in Tomah and running school districts in Oakfield and Verona. Eventually, Evers became deputy state superintendent of public instruction; during that time, he fought and beat esophageal cancer. In 2009 Evers was elected state superintendent, a nominally nonpartisan post, and was easily reelected in 2013 and 2017. After he won his third term, Evers began considering a run for governor.

Walker had spent two terms implementing a muscular conservative agenda, making him both a political celebrity and a target. He curbed collective bargaining for workers, tightened abortion restrictions, enacted tough voter ID rules, and eased limits on gun rights. He notched a 53%-46% victory in a 2012 recall, becoming the first governor anywhere to survive such a vote, then won a second term in 2014. By 2018, however, Democrats were energized against President Donald Trump, and Walker's bid for a third term became a titanic battle in a politically energized and narrowly divided state. The Democratic primary field was larger than any in state history, and it was not predestined that Evers would prevail. His rivals included Mahlon Mitchell, president of the Professional Fire Fighters Association of Wisconsin; former legislator Kelda Roys; state Sen. Kathleen Vinehout; former state Democratic chair Matt Flynn; Madison Mayor Paul Soglin; and activists Mike McCabe and Josh Pade. Mitchell and Roys received support from progressive groups (Roys aired an ad in which she breast-fed her baby) while Evers portrayed himself as a steady pragmatist. In the end, Evers ran away with it, winning 42 percent, ahead of Mitchell (16 percent) and Roys (13 percent).

Education became a major campaign issue. For years, Evers and Walker had frequently tussled over education budgets, higher education politics and legal issues. Walker portrayed himself as the "education governor" based on his efforts to expand school choice, but Evers painted the incumbent's record on school funding as a negative. A major issue in the contest was a deal Walker had negotiated in 2017, with President Donald Trump's backing, to subsidize the building of a new, 13,000-employee factory complex in Mt. Pleasant for Foxconn Technology Group, the Taiwanese-based manufacturing partner for such tech giants as Apple, Sony, Microsoft and Nintendo. Trump joined Walker in Wisconsin to break ground, but as time went on—and as Foxconn failed to live up to its promises of job creation—voters in the state became less enamored with the project. Walker and the legislature had approved some $4.5 billion in tax incentives to support the project, reportedly the nation's largest-ever subsidy for a foreign company. The nonpartisan Legislative Fiscal Bureau projected that a return on that investment might come as late as 2042.

Both candidates were charismatically challenged. Madison's newspaper, the Capital Times, called the race "bland vs. bland." But they differed sharply on policy. Evers backed driver's licenses and in-state tuition for undocumented immigrants, while Walker attacked Democratic-backed proposals for reforming the criminal justice system, saying in front of photographs of violent criminals, "I want to keep them in for their full terms." Evers, meanwhile, took Walker to task for supporting repeal of the Affordable Care Act. Several ex-Walker aides endorsed Evers, and national political figures from both parties flocked to campaign in the state.

The result was in doubt until late absentee returns from Milwaukee County sealed the contest for Evers, 49.5%-48.4%, a margin of just over 29,000 votes. Walker got 35,000 more votes than he had in 2014, but the Democratic nominee amassed more than 200,000 more votes than the nominee four years earlier. Crucially, Walker bled support in the Republican bastions of suburban Milwaukee. In Waukesha County, his 45-point margin in 2014 shrunk to 33 points in 2018; in Ozaukee County, his winning margin shrunk from 41 points to 27; and in Washington County, it shrunk from 53 points to 45. According to exit polls, Walker had won voters with college degrees by one point in 2014 but lost them by 13 points in 2018. The skirmishing didn't end on Election Day: To the outrage of the victorious Democrats, Republicans in a lame-duck session sought to tie Evers' hands as much as possible. Walker signed legislation that, among other things, hampered Evers' ability to modify the Walker-created Wisconsin Economic Development Corp.; made it harder for Evers and the newly elected Democratic attorney general, Josh Kaul, to withdraw from the anti-Affordable Care Act lawsuit; and placed tighter limits on early voting.

In 2019, the GOP-controlled legislature blocked Evers' proposed expansion of Medicaid under the Affordable Care Act, although lawmakers did approve a $1.6 billion increase in spending for Wisconsin's Department of Health Services. They also kept Evers from reversing part or all of Walker's restrictions on labor unions, and they steamrolled his efforts to tighten gun laws, taking just one minute to dispense with a special session the governor had called to address the matter. The legislature also ousted Evers' handpicked agriculture secretary, a historically rare move that Evers called "political B.S." Evers wasn't shy about blocking the legislature's priorities, either. He vetoed several anti-abortion bills, and he issued some 78 budget vetoes, nixing cuts to Milwaukee County's child welfare services, blocking initial funding to replace the Green Bay Correctional Institution, and reducing funding to enforce work requirements and drug screens for people who receive low-income assistance. A few notable bills did make it into law with bipartisan support, including changes to drug prescribing rules, a measure on hemp regulation, and an expansion of student loan forgiveness for minority teachers.

In 2020, Evers vetoed a GOP-backed tax cut, saying he wanted a mix of education spending and broad-based property tax relief instead. He also held back state subsidies for the Foxconn project after it became clear the project's scale was far smaller than initially promised. But three sometimes overlapping issues dominated the year: the coronavirus, race and elections. Evers repeatedly clashed with the legislature over such issues as stay-at-home orders and mask mandates, and at some points the governor was overruled by the state Supreme Court. One heated battle occurred in April, during the early weeks of the pandemic, as the state was preparing to hold a primary election. Evers called the legislature into special session, seeking to delay the election and conduct it by mail, a course some other states had taken by then. But legislators swiftly rebuffed him. Eventually, the court blocked an effort by Evers to implement the delay through an executive order. On Election Day, voters complained of long lines; in Milwaukee, the number of polling stations was cut from from 180 to five. But the Republicans' victory on the rules may have been pyrrhic; the battle seemed to energize Democrats, enabling them to flip a Supreme Court seat that was the most important contest on the ballot.

In August, police shot a Black resident of Kenosha, Jacob Blake, seven times in the back, paralyzing him. Some protests in Kenosha turned violent, and a 17-year-old aligned with armed militia members, Kyle Rittenhouse, was arrested for shooting three protesters, two fatally. By that time, Evers had called in the National Guard, but some saw his leadership as ineffectual. Evers again called the legislature into special session, this time to address policing and criminal justice, and once again GOP leaders gaveled it in and out almost instantaneously. On the right, the events in Kenosha, combined with Evers' policies on the coronavirus, helped sharpen calls for a recall election, but the effort fizzled.

Evers is expected to run for a second term in 2022, when he'll be 71 on Election Day. Walker has ruled out a run for his old office, but Wisconsin's GOP has a strong bench of possible contenders, including former White House Chief of Staff and former state GOP chair Reince Priebus, former Lt. Gov. Rebecca Kleefisch, former Senate candidate Kevin Nicholson, Rep. Mike Gallagher, former Rep. Sean Duffy, state Senate President Chris Kapenga, lobbyist Bill McCoshen, and Waukesha County Executive Paul Farrow.

Ron Johnson (R)

Elected 2010, term expires 2022, 2nd term, b. Apr 08, 1955; Mankato, MN; University of Minnesota, B.S., 1977; Lutheran; Married (Jane Johnson); 3 children; 2 grandchildren.

Professional Career: Owner, PACUR, LLC, 1979-2010; Accountant, Josten's.

DC Office: 328 HSOB 20510, 202-224-5323, Fax: 202-228-6965, ronjohnson.senate.gov

State Offices: Madison, 608-240-9629; Milwaukee, 414-276-7282; Oshkosh, 920-230-7250.

Committees: *Budget. Commerce, Science & Transportation*: Communications, Media & Broadband; Oceans, Fisheries, Climate Change & Manufacturing; Surface Transportation, Maritime Freight & Ports; Tourism, Trade & Export Promotion. *Foreign Relations*: East Asia, the Pacific & International Cybersecurity Policy; Europe & Regional Security Cooperation (RMM); State Dept & USAID Mngmnt, Internat'l Ops & Internat'l Dev. *Homeland Security & Government Affairs*: Government Operations & Border Management; Investigations (RMM).

Group Ratings

	ADA	ACLU	AFL-CIO	LCV	COC	HAFA	ACU	CFG	FRC
2020	-	8%	-	0%	-	92%	90%	-	-
2019	0%	C	11%	0%	77%	C	90%	62%	100%

Almanac Ratings 2019-2020

	Economy	Social	Foreign	Composite
Liberal	0%	0%	0%	0%
Conservative	100%	100%	100%	100%

Key Votes of the 116th Congress

1. EPA clean energy rules	N	5. Russia sanctions	N	9. Barr as Atty. General	Y
2. U.S./Mex./Can. trade deal	Y	6. Troops in SYR, AFG	Y	10. Spending at the border	Y
3. Cut unemployment benefits	Y	7. Veto arms sales to Saudis	N	11. Coney Barrett to Sup. Ct.	Y
4. Shelton to Fed Reserve	Y	8. Defense $$$, veto override	Y	12. Electoral College objections	N

Election Results

Election	Name (Party)	Vote (%)		Cand. Spent	Ind. Exp. Support	Ind. Exp. Oppose
2016 General	Ron Johnson (R)	1,479,471	(50%)	$27,590,817	$2,187,944	$8,418,011
	Russ Feingold (D)	1,380,335	(47%)	$25,190,356	$1,565,370	$16,527,845
	Phil Anderson (L)	87,531	(3%)			
2016 Primary	Ron Johnson (R)	Unopposed				

Prior winning percentages: 2016 (50%), 2010 (52%)

Republican Ron Johnson, Wisconsin's senior senator, has embraced a mix of conspiracy theories and misinformation in recent years that belied that he was the only GOP senator up for reelection in 2022 in a state President Donald Trump lost in 2020. Even before Trump's loss, Johnson used his position as chair of the Homeland Security and Governmental Affairs panel to propagate unsubstantiated claims about now-President Joe Biden's son Hunter and Ukraine. After January 6, 2021, Johnson downplayed the danger of the mob of Trump supporters who stormed the Capitol that day even though five people died and nearly 140 more were wounded, and he pushed false narratives about the COVID-19 pandemic and the vaccines for it. Although he said after a surprising win for a second term in 2016 that he wouldn't run again, he's left the door open and would be the Senate's most endangered Republican if he does.

Johnson grew up in Mankato Minnesota. He said he developed a strong work ethic at an early age, delivering newspapers, caddying at a golf course and baling hay on his uncle's dairy farm. He was a restaurant dishwasher at 15 and within a year won a promotion to night manager. Although Johnson didn't finish high school, he attended college, working full time and graduating with $7,000 in the bank. While working as an accountant, Johnson went to night school to earn an MBA. Just short of a degree in 1979, he decided to move to Oshkosh to start a plastics company, PACUR, with his brother-in-law. Their first customer was a company co-founded by his father-in-law. Since then, the business has become a major producer of specialty packaging for medical devices, employing about 120 workers. Johnson has said his political views have been influenced by Ayn Rand's 1957 novel "Atlas Shrugged," which argues that civilization cannot exist when people are slaves to society and government.

Johnson said that his motivation to run against Democrat Russ Feingold was the senator's support of Democrats' 2010 health care overhaul, which he called "the single greatest assault to our freedom in my lifetime." He entered the race in May, just days before the Republican State Convention. Three GOP candidates were already competing, including beer mogul and former state Commerce Secretary Dick Leinenkugel and Madison developer Terrence Wall. Johnson's ability to self-finance had an immediate effect. At the convention, Leinenkugel surprised everyone, including Johnson, by taking his turn at the lectern to drop out and endorse Johnson, saying, "It's not my time ... it's Ron Johnson's time." Wall reluctantly followed suit. Spending more than $4 million of his own money, Johnson went on to crush businessman Dave Westlake in the September primary.

The campaign between Johnson and Feingold—a liberal with a quirky, maverick streak was nasty. Without a legislative record to mine in Johnson's first bid for elected office, Feingold sought to concentrate on Johnson's record in business, attempting to depict him as someone more concerned about profits than people and "with a country club view of reality." Feingold also called Johnson a hypocrite for opposing federal economic stimulus funds and then allegedly seeking those funds for renovation of an opera house. Johnson fought back, noting in an ad that the Senate had 57 lawyers, including Feingold, but just one accountant and no manufacturers like himself. Johnson's GOP allies depicted the incumbent as an entrenched Washington insider who supported deficit spending. Feingold had $21 million to Johnson's $15 million, but it was not enough in a Republican wave year. Johnson won 52% to 47%.

In 2011, Johnson did not support Wisconsin Republican Rep. Paul Ryan's budget plan to slash the deficit and transform Medicare, arguing it did not cut spending enough. Johnson blocked a resolution to support military action in Libya as a way of calling attention to debt reduction, saying on the floor that the debt is "the single most important issue facing this nation."

Johnson has been blunt; one of his strategists, Brad Todd, has described him as "straight as a shot of uncut whiskey." He drew attention for grilling outgoing Secretary of State Hillary Clinton at a Foreign Relations Committee hearing in 2013 on the deadly terrorist attack at the U.S. consulate in Benghazi Libya. Johnson complained that lawmakers had been "misled" about the attack. When Clinton said it would have been inappropriate to contact diplomatic staff for details immediately afterward because the FBI was investigating, he replied, "I realize that's a good excuse." An exasperated Clinton retorted: "No, it's a fact. ... What difference, at this point, does it make?" The footage of her incensed answer was unspooled repeatedly by conservatives during the 2016 presidential campaign to remind voters of Clinton's biggest foreign policy blemish.

Johnson occasionally has drawn attention for emphasizing pragmatism over political purity. When he became chairman of the Homeland Security and Governmental Affairs Committee in 2015, he became more engaged with domestic security issues. He won Senate passage of the Integrated Public Alert and Warning System Modernization Act of 2015, and he distanced himself from the tea party. "I sprang out of the tea party movement, no question," he told National Journal, but he emphasized, "I've never joined any kind of tea party caucus or tea party group."

The rematch with Feingold became a marquee Senate race in 2016. The widespread assumption was Feingold would do better in a presidential election year than a low-turnout midterm year. Johnson regrouped in September with help from his older brother, Dean, a veteran television executive producer and host and a new team of consultants. They took the gloves off against Feingold, relentlessly attacking him as a creature of Washington and painting Johnson in softer hues; they highlighted Johnson's work with the Joseph Project, a faith-oriented jobs program. Johnson targeted small rural towns and worked to boost turnout in traditionally Republican areas that were lagging.

Johnson won 74,000 more votes than Trump did, and he defeated Feingold by 3 percentage points. Johnson's wider margin than Trump can be traced chiefly to the "WOW" counties in the Milwaukee suburbs—Washington, Ozaukee and Waukesha. These counties are historically Republican, but their relatively high education and income levels made them less fertile ground for Trump. In Ozaukee, Johnson won 65 percent of the vote; Trump took 57 percent. In Waukesha, Johnson nabbed 68 percent, while Trump won 61 percent. And in Washington County, Johnson garnered 72 percent, while Trump got 68 percent.

A significant ramification of Johnson's victory was his unhappiness that Senate Republicans —including Sen. Mitch McConnell of Kentucky, then the majority leader—had abandoned his campaign before his late comeback. "This has been a long-stewing simmer for him, and after they cut him loose, he was like, 'Screw them, I owe them nothing,'" the Daily Beast reported in June 2017, citing an anonymous Republican source. And if Johnson runs for reelection again in 2022, that same mindset may endure.

After the 2016 elections, Johnson urged leveraging the newly all-Republican-controlled federal government to enact a conservative agenda. He complained that McConnell and other GOP senators did not push more aggressively. "Let's face it, the vast majority of members of Congress, their primary motivation is getting elected and unfortunately it's about maintaining majorities. But to what end?" Johnson told the Washington Examiner in October 2017. "We need leadership on these big issues. ... We didn't get it with health care."

The Senate's failure to repeal the Affordable Care Act in 2017 was a sore spot for Johnson. He became a reluctant supporter of the limited repeal that McConnell presented to the Senate after extended closed-door negotiations in the Capitol. Johnson was especially unhappy that McConnell had bowed to pressure from other Republicans to defer cuts in Medicaid spending. During a meeting with business leaders in Green Bay in July 2017, Johnson said, "If our leader is basically saying, 'Don't worry about it, we've designed it so that these reforms will never take effect,' first of all, that's a pretty significant breach of trust," the Green Bay Press Gazette reported. He also complained about how McConnell crafted the alternative. "I kind of had to muscle my way into that core working group," he said. "I was shocked at the process. There was no information. Very little. It was the last step in the process. It doesn't surprise me that the result is far from what I'd like to see."

A few days later, when McConnell called for a Senate vote on his last-ditch alternative, the "skinny repeal," Johnson initially said that the plan would be "rather unsatisfying from my standpoint." Johnson subsequently had an unpleasant showdown with McConnell on the Senate floor before he reluctantly agreed to vote for the alternative. In the end, the opposition of three moderate Republicans torpedoed the deal.

Johnson continued his independence later in 2017 during debate of the Republican tax cuts. In the days before the Senate vote, he said he opposed the bill because it favored large companies over small businesses. He cited his own experience in the corporate world to complain that the Senate "doesn't understand numbers" in the tax bill, The Washington Post reported. Ultimately, Johnson said he would vote for the bill after he secured changes to adjust the tax breaks for businesses. "No major piece of legislation is ever perfect. But this bill is a significant improvement over our current tax system," Johnson said. He continued to take issue with the amount of spending during the Trump administration, telling the Post in December 2019, "It's depressing, isn't it?" The next year, with the economy reeling amid the coronavirus pandemic, Johnson opposed reauthorizing in June the popular Paycheck Protection Program, saying it needed to be more targeted. In December 2020, Johnson opposed additional $1,200 stimulus checks despite Trump's support for them. "When I first got here, I ran because we were mortgaging our kids' future," Johnson told Politico. "I'm not heartless. I want to help people. I voted to help people. I voted for the $2.2 trillion CARES Act, but I also am concerned about our children's future."

As chairman of the Homeland Security panel, Johnson or his committee aides "have derailed many of the most significant cybersecurity-related bills in the past four years," Politico reported in February 2019. His objections often resulted from his opposition to excessive government regulation of business. Johnson's committee "is the place where legislation goes to die on cybersecurity," a national security expert told Politico. Aides to Johnson defended his work as chairman, including approval of legislation on federal procurement and reorganization of the Homeland Security Department.

Johnson voiced repeated concerns about Trump's tariffs and said Congress should consider restricting his authority to take unilateral actions. Of the trade war resulting from the tariffs Trump had levied on Chinese imports, he said, "There's some real damage being done" to companies, including in Wisconsin, the Associated Press reported in July 2018.

But Johnson ended up being one of Trump's most consequential allies in the Senate, embracing many of the conspiracy theories the president perpetuated. Using his post on Homeland Security, Johnson pushed forward with an investigation into Hunter Biden's role with a Ukrainian gas company, which Trump had pressured the Ukrainian president to look into. That led to his 2019 impeachment by the House. Even after Trump was acquitted in the Senate during his first impeachment trial and as many Republicans wanted to drop the unsubstantiated allegations while the presidential race heated up, Johnson persisted. Along a party-line vote, the committee approved subpoenas for Blue Star Strategies, a Democratic public relations firm that did consulting work for Burisma, the Ukrainian energy company on whose board Hunter Biden sat.

Johnson denied he was doing this to help Trump's reelection chances, telling Politico, "I'm not doing anybody's bidding. I am doing this because I'm concerned about this democracy, and I'm concerned about what happened starting before the election, during the transition, and what continued certainly through the impeachment trial." Some Republicans defended Johnson, saying he was simply continuing an aggressive oversight role, but others were skeptical and believed the senator's efforts were playing into the hands of Russian propaganda; those critics included Richard Burr of North Carolina and Marco Rubio of Florida, who both chaired the Intelligence Committee during 2020. The panel's ranking Democrat at the time, Gary Peters of Michigan, told Politico, "We're in the middle of a pandemic, dealing with a whole host of threats to our national security. That's where we should be focused. Not on what basically looks like a political witch hunt."

As Johnson's investigation wore on, it appeared to become even more nakedly aimed at helping Trump. "What our investigations are uncovering, I think, will reveal that [Joe Biden] is not somebody that we should be electing president of the United States," Johnson told a Janesville radio station in September 2020. Republican Sen. Mitt Romney of Utah told the Milwaukee Journal Sentinel that Johnson's inquiry "had the earmarks of a political exercise, and I'm fearful that comments made in the media recently have only confirmed that perspective." The CIA also ignored Johnson's requests to brief the committee about any information pertinent to his investigation. Democratic congressional leaders accused Johnson of playing into Kremlin efforts to sow doubt into the American electoral process, writing in a letter to the FBI that didn't specifically mention the senator, though he was clearly referenced, that they were "gravely concerned, in particular, that Congress appears to be the target of a concerted foreign interference campaign, which seeks to launder and amplify disinformation in order to influence congressional activity, public debate and the presidential election in November."

After the 2020 elections, Johnson eventually recognized Biden as the legitimate winner, though in the lame-duck period he still used his committee perch to hold a hearing on election "irregularities" and "legitimate questions" about election administration in several swing states, including Wisconsin. "All I'm trying to do is hold a very upfront, straightforward hearing talking about what controls there are in place, what fraud does occur, what can we do to prevent fraud in the future," Johnson told the Journal Sentinel. The three-hour hearing gave a platform to Trump campaign lawyers who made accusations of widespread fraud in Nevada, Wisconsin and Pennsylvania, though many of their claims had already been disproved in court and others had no basis in fact. The hearing devolved into a bitter spat between Johnson and Peters. The GOP chairman summed up the hearing: "I can't sit by here and listen to this and say—this is not disinformation at this hearing today. We're not going to be able to just move on without bringing up these irregularities." Peters objected, but Johnson cut him off by telling the Democrat, "You lied." Peters retorted: "This is not about airing your grievances. I don't know what rabbit hole you're running down. This is terrible what you're doing to this committee."

Johnson wasn't among the few senators who objected to the electoral votes of Arizona and Pennsylvania on January 6, but in the aftermath of the attack on the Capitol, he began making befuddling claims about the severity of the attack that millions had watched unfold on TV in real time and the imminent risk members of Congress and Vice President Mike Pence faced. Johnson said he didn't believe it was an "armed insurrection" despite extensive evidence that rioters had weapons. In a March 2021 interview with the "Joe Pags Show," Johnson said he "never really felt threatened" by the mob of mostly white Trump supporters. "Now, had the tables been turned—Joe, this could get me in trouble—had the tables been turned, and President Trump won the election and those were tens of thousands of Black Lives Matter and Antifa protesters, I might have been a little concerned," Johnson told the radio program. The backlash was swift, but the senator claimed his opponents had "twisted" and "contorted" his words "into calling me a racist." "One of the reasons I'm being attacked is because I very honestly said I didn't feel threatened on January 6. I didn't," Johnson told a group of Wisconsin conservatives in March. "There was much more violence on the House side. There was no violence on the Senate side, in terms of the chamber." Johnson had also said he believed that liberal actors had infiltrated the crowd, though the FBI repeatedly debunked that claim.

Throughout 2020 and into 2021, Johnson also downplayed the coronavirus pandemic. He told The New York Times that while he supported the use of masks and vaccines, "We have grossly overreacted to this. We have not been smart. We should have isolated the sick, protected the vulnerable and then the rest of us carry on with our lives as safely as possible." But witnesses Johnson called before his committee in December 2020 countered his assertion that he still supported vaccines. One had pushed for the use of hydroxychloroquine, an anti-malarial drug Trump had also touted to treat COVID-19 but doctors said wasn't effective as such, and said she believed that vaccine mandates violated human rights. Another had claimed on Fox News that it was "settled science" that "social distancing doesn't work, quarantining doesn't work, masks don't work." And two others promoted the use of a drug used to fight lice and pinworms even though the National Institutes of Health had recommended against its use in COVID-19 patients. Peters, again, expressed his displeasure at Johnson's managing of the committee: "These fringe views run counter to what the Senate should be doing—working on a bipartisan basis to protect the American people and tackle this deadly pandemic." Johnson tested positive for the virus in October 2020 but appeared to draw the wrong conclusions when he didn't require treatment. In April 2021, Johnson again drew headlines when he downplayed the urgency to get a coronavirus vaccine. In an interview with conservative radio host Vicki McKenna, Johnson said he was skeptical of the government's "big push" to get everyone vaccinated. "From my standpoint, because it's not a fully approved vaccine, I think we probably should have limited the distribution to the vulnerable—to people that really aren't, you know, for the very young. I see no reason to be pushing vaccines on people," Johnson said. He also asked, "If you have a vaccine, quite honestly, what do you care if your neighbor has one or not? I mean, what is it to you?"

His controversies—from the Hunter Biden investigation to comments about the seriousness of the January 6 riot to downplaying coronavirus vaccines—further emboldened Democrats seeking to defeat Johnson in 2022. But while Johnson's focus hasn't been one typically of a senator aiming for reelection in a swing state, the Wisconsinite has always eschewed the norm, and even those close to him weren't sure whether he would run again. Either way, several Democrats made early moves toward the seat, including state Treasurer Sarah Godlewski, Milwaukee Bucks executive Alex Lasry and Outagamie County Executive Tom Nelson. Lt. Gov. Mandela Barnes could also run. If Johnson retires, Rep. Mike Gallagher is the Republican most likely to have the party coalesce around him.

Tammy Baldwin (D)

Elected 2012, term expires 2024, 2nd term, b. Feb 11, 1962; Madison, WI; Smith College, A.B., 1984; University of Wisconsin Law School, J.D., 1989; Religion not stated; Single.

Elected Office: Member, Madison City Council, 1986; Member, Dane County Board of Supervisors, 1986-1994; WI Assembly, 1992-1998; U.S. House, 1998-2012.

Professional Career: Practicing attorney, 1989-1992.

DC Office: 709 HSOB 20510, 202-224-5653, Fax: 202-224-9787, baldwin.senate.gov

State Offices: Ashland, 715-450-3754; Eau Claire, 715-832-8424; Green Bay, 920-498-2668; La Crosse, 608-796-0045; Madison, 608-264-5338; Milwaukee, 414-297-4451; Wausau, 715-261-2611.

Committees: Senate Democratic Conference Secretary. *Appropriations*: Agriculture, Rural Development, FDA & Related Agencies (Chmn); Department of Defense; Department of Homeland Security; DOL, HHS & Education & Related Agencies; Energy & Water Development; Military Construction & Veteran Affairs & Related Agencies. *Commerce, Science & Transportation*: Communications, Media & Broadband; Consumer Protection, Product Safety & Data Security; Oceans, Fisheries, Climate Change & Manufacturing (Chmn); Surface Transportation, Maritime Freight & Ports. *Health, Education, Labor & Pensions*: Employment & Workplace Safety; Primary Health & Retirement Security.

Group Ratings

	ADA	ACLU	AFL-CIO	LCV	COC	HAFA	ACU	CFG	FRC
2020	-	92%	-	92%	-	0%	2%	-	-
2019	100%	C	100%	100%	50%	C	2%	0%	0%

Almanac Ratings 2019-2020

	Economy	Social	Foreign	Composite
Liberal	93%	93%	86%	91%
Conservative	7%	7%	14%	9%

Key Votes of the 116th Congress

1. EPA clean energy rules	Y	5. Russia sanctions	Y	9. Barr as Atty. General	N
2. U.S./Mex./Can. trade deal	Y	6. Troops in SYR, AFG	N	10. Spending at the border	Y
3. Cut unemployment benefits	N	7. Veto arms sales to Saudis	Y	11. Coney Barrett to Sup. Ct.	N
4. Shelton to Fed Reserve	N	8. Defense $$$, veto override	Y	12. Electoral College objections	N

Election Results

Election	Name (Party)	Vote (%)	Cand. Spent	Ind. Exp. Support	Ind. Exp. Oppose
2018 General	Tammy Baldwin (D)........................ ... 1,472,914	(55%)	$29,105,509	$3,727,282	$8,728,234
	Leah Vukmir (R)............................. ... 1,184,885	(45%)	$5,594,610	$1,886,430	$3,553,187
2018 Primary	Tammy Baldwin (D)..................	(100%)			

Prior winning percentages: 2018 (55%), 2012 (51%); House: 2010 (62%), 2008 (69%), 2006 (63%), 2004 (63%), 2002 (66%), 2000 (51%), 1998 (53%)

Democrat Tammy Baldwin of Wisconsin is the first openly LGBTQ member of the Senate and the first woman elected to the chamber from Wisconsin. After her initial close election in 2012 over former Gov. Tommy Thompson, she was reelected easily in 2018—a notable accomplishment in her polarized home state. In the Senate, she has focused on issues dealing with LGBTQ rights, health, education and innovation and has had a strongly liberal voting record.

Baldwin grew up in Madison, where she was raised mostly by her maternal grandparents, a University of Wisconsin biochemist and the theater department's head costume designer. Her mother, who was 19 and a UW student when Baldwin was born, was "in the middle of a divorce and overwhelmed," Baldwin told the New York Times, adding that her mother had long battles with pain and addiction. "My grandparents were there, and I'm very, very grateful." Baldwin graduated first in her class at Madison West High School and went on to Smith College and UW law school. It was in college that it became "very clear" she was a lesbian.

Baldwin detailed her mother's health problems in 2018 for the first time, according to local news reports. Her mother had mental and physical illnesses, including pain for which she was prescribed narcotics. "At times in her life, she was addicted to the prescribed medication and she did not follow doctors' orders," the Appleton Post Crescent quoted Baldwin as saying in May 2018 after the senator participated in a roundtable about addiction. "She went through recovery and treatment multiple times." Her mother, Pamela Joan Bin-Rella, eventually got a master's degree and was a social worker. She died in August 2017 at 75. A week after the roundtable, Baldwin ran a campaign ad about her family history.

In 1986, at 24 and while in law school, Baldwin was elected to the Board of Supervisors of Dane County, which encompasses Madison. In 1992, she was elected to the Wisconsin State Assembly. Six years later, when moderate Republican Scott Klug honored his promise to serve only four terms in the House, Baldwin got into the race, along with three other Democrats and six Republicans. As a woman who favored abortion rights, she was supported by EMILY's List, which helped her raise about a quarter of her $1.5 million campaign chest. Baldwin won with 37 percent of the vote; then, in the general election, she beat former state Insurance Commissioner Jo Musser by nearly 6 percentage points. This made her the first openly gay non incumbent to win a seat in the House.

Baldwin's voting record was consistently one of the most liberal in the House. She secured a coveted seat on the Energy and Commerce Committee. In the minority for 10 of her 14 years in the House, her ability to accomplish many of her progressive goals was limited. She was sharply critical of many GOP proposals and policies, including the budget proposed by Wisconsin Rep. Paul Ryan and Gov. Scott Walker's move to limit collective bargaining rights for state workers, an effort that touched off a recall campaign against the GOP incumbent.

Baldwin's driving issue has been guaranteed health care for all Americans. The issue was personal: A serious illness, similar to spinal meningitis, kept her in the hospital for three months when she was a child, making her a patient with a pre-existing condition. Because she was living with her grandparents, they were unable to include her on their health insurance coverage and were forced to pay large costs for her medical care. Baldwin supported the Affordable Care Act even though it did not include a government-run "public option" to compete with private insurers, a provision she had favored.

Baldwin was a leading advocate for allowing same-sex marriages. In 2008, she and Massachusetts Democrat Barney Frank, another openly gay lawmaker, established the Congressional LGBT Equality Caucus. Baldwin told the New York Times that in the House, "I did a lot of sitting down with Republicans to talk about these bills. Often there was a real sort of intimacy in those conversations. People talked about gay brothers or a child who was gay, lesbian or transgender. I can't tell you how many of those stories I accumulated. I think I moved a number of my colleagues, and I think it at least caused a lot of internal conflict for those I didn't move." Baldwin is also one of a handful of lawmakers who haven't specified a religious affiliation. "They didn't let me put the phrase, 'It's complicated,' as Facebook might have," she told the Times.

Baldwin ran for the Senate in 2012 when Democrat Herb Kohl retired after four terms. She was unchallenged in the Democratic primary, giving her ample time to organize her campaign and raise money. Thompson, a popular former governor known as a pragmatic conservative, won the GOP primary against three more conservative candidates and started with a lead over Baldwin in the general election campaign. But Baldwin and her allies outspent Thompson and his backers by 3-1 in the weeks after the primary, and the race got ugly.

Baldwin ran a disciplined campaign, seeking to convince voters that she would be more attuned to the needs of Wisconsin than the 70-year-old Thompson, a former Health and Human Services secretary under George W. Bush who hadn't been a candidate for office in 14 years. Realizing it made little sense to attack Thompson's gubernatorial record, which many Wisconsinites of both parties remembered fondly, Baldwin instead blasted Thompson with negative television ads about his post-gubernatorial career, highlighting his work for a Washington D.C., lobbying firm. Meanwhile, Thompson and Republicans accused Baldwin of being a radical, but she downplayed her liberal views and highlighted her populist stands against China's trade policies and her efforts at bipartisanship. As the race neared its conclusion, Thompson veered to the right—he told a tea party group that he wanted to "do away with the Medicare and Medicaid," a stark departure from his previous positions —but the maneuver rang hollow with many swing voters. Baldwin won 51% to 46%.

In the Senate, Baldwin has continued to vote on a consistently liberal line, almost always taking the opposite stance from the state's senior senator, conservative Republican Ron Johnson. That has made Wisconsin one of the few remaining states with two senators of strongly divergent views. Craig Gilbert noted in the Milwaukee Journal Sentinel that they split over the Affordable Care Act, fast-track trade authority for the president, the Keystone XL pipeline, gun control, immigration, the minimum wage and a host of other issues. A rare point of unison, Gilbert found, was a shared vote in favor of ensuring same-sex spouses have access to Social Security and veterans' benefits.

Baldwin worked with fellow Rust Belt Democratic Sens. Sherrod Brown of Ohio and Bob Casey of Pennsylvania to insert a "Buy America" provision in a major water resources bill, and she introduced a measure to end the carried-interest tax loophole that benefits hedge fund managers. After the 2016 Pulse nightclub shooting in Orlando Florida, Baldwin worked to make sure that LGBTQ concerns related to the site were not overlooked in the rush to discuss gun violence and terrorism. "They needed someone on the floor to come and say, 'This is all of these things. Do not just sweep away the hate crime aspect of it—give these people's lives, give them a voice,'" she told Glamour magazine. Baldwin was among the leaders working to lift a longstanding Food and Drug Administration ban on men who've had sex with other men from donating blood. Language authored by Baldwin made it into the Comprehensive Addiction and Recovery Act signed by President Barack Obama in 2016. A strong supporter of Hillary Clinton in the 2016 Democratic presidential primary, Baldwin was reportedly among three dozen people considered for the vice presidential slot that eventually went to Virginia Sen. Tim Kaine.

Baldwin took an increased role in the health care debate. She co-sponsored in October 2017 the "Medicare for All" proposal filed by Sen. Bernie Sanders. "It would expand coverage to all the uninsured; make health care more affordable for working, middle-class families; and reduce growing prescription drug costs for taxpayers," she said. In 2019, along with Brown and Michigan Democratic Sen. Debbie Stabenow, Baldwin co-wrote a bill to give people between 50 and 64 the option of buying into Medicaid.

In 2017, Baldwin received an assignment in the Senate Democratic leadership: conference secretary. With a re-election campaign looming, she faced a balancing act between her party's drift to the left and her state's status as a linchpin of Donald Trump's presidential victory in 2016. She opposed more Trump nominees than most other Trump-state Democrats who were up for re-election in 2018. But back home, she emphasized more populist themes such as improving trade deals and lowering the cost of prescription drugs. Baldwin faced a competitive challenge in her politically polarized state.

As was the case during her 2012 election, Baldwin benefited from a hard-fought contest among Republicans that was not resolved until the August primary. The chief contenders were state Sen. Leah Vukmir and Kevin Nicholson, an Iraq veteran and a former president of College Democrats of America who evolved in his political views. Vukmir was backed by most Republican leaders in Wisconsin, including Walker. Nicholson had support from the Club for Growth and Steve Bannon, a former top aide to Trump. Vukmir won the primary 49%-43%, with three other candidates splitting the remainder. Meanwhile, conservative groups spent millions of dollars in ads attacking Baldwin. But she and her allies had even more money to respond and defend her record with key constituencies, including rural voters. She avoided discussing Trump.

In the general election, Baldwin had the wind at her back. The national mood favored Democrats, Vukmir was little-known beyond rank-and-file Republicans and the intense focus on Walker's bid for a third term worked in Baldwin's favor. Vukmir embraced Trump. In her closing ads, Baldwin highlighted Vukmir's record in the Legislature in which she repeatedly voted against health care services. Baldwin spent more than $31 million, while Vukmir spent less than $6 million for the entire campaign, including her primary.

Baldwin won 55%-45%. "Wisconsin voters went with Baldwin, a familiar figure who has been in public life for decades and has now built a personal brand that plays well around the state," the Journal Sentinel wrote. After her victory, she and fellow swing-state Democrat Casey gave a presentation during a Democratic Caucus meeting on how their colleagues could run and win in changing Rust Belt states.

Baldwin's ability to post impressive wins in such an evenly divided partisan state led to more chatter about her national prospects. In early 2019, an article in New York magazine called her perhaps the most "electable" potential Democratic nominee writing that there's "a strong case that the Democratic Party's most electable 2020 candidate is a proven progressive who would also give America the opportunity to elect its first female—and gay—president, simultaneously." But unlike a half-dozen of her Senate colleagues, Baldwin never appeared interested. She once again made it onto the short list of the nominee's potential vice presidential candidates, as she represented a critical swing state. "Tammy Baldwin is a person I respect very much because she doesn't make a lot of noise," Hawaii Sen. Mazie Hirono told Politico. "She just gets things done." After nominee Joe Biden picked California Sen. Kamala Harris, Baldwin told a local Fox affiliate, "I think I was on the short list, but not the short-short list. That's the best I can tell you."

Baldwin has, naturally, been a fervent voice for gay rights legislation. In 2019, she pushed for GOP Sen. Mitch McConnell of Kentucky, then the majority leader, to allow a floor vote on the Equality Act, which would bar discrimination against LGBTQ people. "Full equality has not been won," Baldwin told NBC News. "We can't confuse progress [on marriage equality] for victory." During the COVID-19 pandemic, Baldwin criticized Congress for failing to sufficiently fund hospital preparedness programs in the years before the novel coronavirus developed and spread. She also introduced a bill to require the federal government to collect and release detailed demographic data on coronavirus testing, treatment and deaths. And in a nod to perhaps one of the most important issues to Wisconsin voters, she proposed in 2019 the Go Pack Go Act, which would require all in-state cable, video and satellite providers give access to Green Bay Packers games.

There were some areas where Baldwin did find common ground with Republicans. In 2020, she supported the NAFTA replacement Trump had renegotiated, the U.S.-Mexico-Canada Agreement. Baldwin worked with one of the Senate's most conservative members, Josh Hawley of Missouri, to require the Federal Reserve to balance the country's trade deficit within five years or else allow them to impose a market access fee on foreign purchases of U.S. stocks, bonds, property and any other assets. "Foreign investors have driven up the American dollar, helping Wall Street profit but holding back stronger economic growth," Baldwin said. "We need reforms that create a competitive American dollar and an even playing field for manufacturers, farmers and workers." The two also asked the Federal Trade Commission to open an antitrust investigation into the meatpacking industry after many smaller family farms were overrun in the market by larger multinational firms. "The current COVID-19 crisis has exposed the vulnerabilities of American supply chains and the importance of ensuring that, when disaster strikes, America's food supplies are not in the hands of a few, mostly foreign-based firms," Baldwin and Hawley wrote.

Bryan Steil (R)

Elected 2018, 2nd term, b. Mar 03, 1981; Janesville, WI; Georgetown University, B.S., 2003; University of WI, J.D., 2007; Catholic; Single.

Professional Career: Congressional Staffer; Attorney

DC Office: 1408 LHOB 20515, 202-225-3031, steil.house.gov

State Offices: Janesville, 608-752-4050.

Committees: *Administration*: Elections (RMM). *Communications Standards Commission*.

Almanac Ratings 2019-2020

	Economy	Social	Foreign	Composite
Liberal	25%	33%	27%	29%
Conservative	75%	67%	73%	71%

Key Votes of the 116th Congress

1. U.S./Mex./Can. trade deal	Y	5. Russia sanctions	Y	9. Firearms background checks	N
2. First Coronavirus response	N	6. Troops in Syria	Y	10. Spending at the border	Y
3. HEROES Act	N	7. Veto arms sales to Saudis	N	11. Marijuana liberalized rules	N
4. CASH Act	N	8. Defense $$$, veto override	N	12. Electoral College objections	N

Election Results

Election	Name (Party)	Vote (%)		Cand. Spent	Ind. Exp. Support	Ind. Exp. Oppose
2020 General	Bryan Steil (R)	238,271	(59%)	$3,279,575		$750
	Roger Polack (D)	163,170	(41%)	$642,607	$10	
2020 Primary	Bryan Steil (R)	40,273	(100%)			

Prior winning percentages: 2018 (55%)

Republican Bryan Steil in 2018 won a contest that received more than the customary attention, largely because he sought to succeed Republican Rep. Paul Ryan, who retired following three years as House Speaker. Steil had extensive political experience, as both a protégé of Ryan and a member of the Board of Regents of the University of Wisconsin. Democratic opponent Randy Bryce, a blue-collar ironworker, became a nationwide fundraising sensation among progressives when he announced his challenge before Ryan had retired. Both were first-time candidates, though Bryce suffered from his inexperience.

Steil, like Ryan, was a native of Janesville, where their two families had close ties. He got his bachelor's degree from the business school at Georgetown University and a law degree from the University of Wisconsin. He was a legislative aide to Ryan in Washington. As an attorney with an expertise in business law, Steil worked for Regal Beloit Corp. and was general counsel for Wisconsin-based Charter NEX Films, which describes itself as "North America's leading independent producer of high-performance specialty polyethylene films used in flexible packaging." In 2016, Gov. Scott Walker appointed Steil to the Board of Regents, which had become controversial as it imposed major changes that Walker and his legislative allies made at the university, especially the Madison campus..

When Ryan announced his retirement in April 2018, several prominent Republicans turned down invitations to run for his seat—including former White House chief of staff Reince Priebus and Assembly Speaker Robin Vos, the Milwaukee Journal Sentinel reported. Steil stepped forward and described himself as "a problem solver," based on his nine years in manufacturing. Downplaying his close ties to Ryan and career politicians generally, he said he would take on "the chattering class in Washington."

Steil faced five other candidates in the Republican primary. They included Paul Nehlen, who echoed the harsh criticism that he voiced about Ryan on immigration and international trade when he challenged him in the 2016 primary; Ryan won that contest, 84%-16%. Nick Polce, who served in the Army Special Forces, said government had grown too large. Steil spent far more money than his opponents combined and won the primary with 52 percent of the vote; Polce was second, with 15 percent.

When Bryce initially took on Ryan, he unveiled a two-minute video that featured his blue-collar background, military service and success in battling cancer. He supported "Medicare for All," and an increase in the minimum wage to $15 per hour. His message to Ryan was: "You can come work the iron, and I'll go to D.C." With the resulting burst of attention, Bryce gained national media attention and raised more than $6 million prior to the Democratic primary. In a profile, the New Yorker reported that for many of his supporters, Bryce's "greatest appeal is that he is an ordinary worker, like them."

Other publications tracked down problems in Bryce's life, including his bankruptcy, delinquency in child-support payments to his ex-wife and nine arrests. Bryce's brother, a local police officer, criticized him and endorsed Steil. Bryce got 60 percent of the vote in the Democratic primary against Cathy Myers, a school-board member in Janesville.

During the closing weeks of the campaign, Steil largely drew the contrast with Bryce on their policy views, though outside groups ran ads that cited Bryce's personal problems. At local appearances with Ryan, Steil embraced his patron's easygoing demeanor and approach to the job. Despite tension between Ryan and President Donald Trump, Steil won 55%-42%, with big majorities in the Waukesha and Milwaukee parts of the district. Bryce spent $8.6 million, nearly four times Steil's total, though the winner got a boost from $2.7 million spent by Ryan's leadership PAC.

In the House, Steil won easy passage of two mostly uncontroversial bills: legislation to assist small businesses in finding investors, and a measure designed to expose the financing of human trafficking—with reports from the State Department about the actions of other governments. With his assignment to the Financial Services Committee, Steil said his objective was to "focus on helping families achieve financial stability."

Following the 2020 election, he joined Reps. Glenn Grothman and Mike Gallagher of Wisconsin in the minority of House Republicans who agreed to certify the results of the Electoral College count of the presidential vote. Steil was assigned to the House Administration Committee, where he became ranking Republican on the Elections Subcommittee—a sign that GOP leaders had confidence in him.

At home, he faced Democratic challenger Roger Polack, who worked several years for the Treasury Department's office of intelligence and analysis—including 20 months in Afghanistan, where he led an intelligence unit that focused on the financing of the Taliban. Polack spent $643,000; much of it went to social media, though none of it was spent for broadcast ads. He criticized Steil for his failure to wear a mask at campaign events during the pandemic, which placed "everyone that's around him at risk." Steil spent $3.3 million and criticized Polack for listing his home in Washington as his "principal residence." He had a comfortable 59%-41% victory.

WI-1: Southeast Wisconsin   Cook Partisan Voting Index: R+7

Population			Race and Ethnicity		Income	
Total	721,691		White	86.90%	Median Income	$68,695
Land area (sq. miles)	1,728		Black	6.00%	District Income Rank	180
Pop/ sq mi	417.66		Latino	10.10%	Poverty Rate	8.70%
Born in State	66.60%		Asian	2.20%	With health insurance	94.40%
			Two or more races	2.40%	Cash public assistance	1.90%
Age Groups			Other	2.50%	Food stamp/SNAP	10.00%
Under 18	22.50%					
18-34	19.60%		Education		Work	
35-64	40.60%		H.S grad or less	37.40%	White Collar	37.20%
Over 64	17.20%		Some college	32.00%	Sales and Service	36.10%
			College Degree, 4 yr	20.20%	Blue Collar	26.60%
Military			Post grad	10.40%	Government	11.00%
Veteran/ Active Duty	7.50%					

2020 Pres. Vote	Trump	220,668	(54%)	Biden	182,942	(45%)		
2016 Pres. Vote	Trump	187,372	(52%)	Clinton	150,436	(42%)	Johnson	12,926 (4%)

Janesville, Kenosha: The southern tier of Wisconsin, from Lake Michigan to the Rock River Valley, has been some of America's prime industrial country. Settled by Yankee and German farmers 170 years ago, it was once primarily dairy land. By the early 20th century, the steady habits and high skills of the local dairy farmers had made them a good labor pool for factories. There are still major plants here, including the headquarters of S.C. Johnson in Racine, with its Frank Lloyd Wright-designed tower. But the collapse of the domestic auto industry, including the closing of two large plants in the area, had a powerful impact on the local economy.

Local innovation remains alive. Kenosha, once primarily a factory town, has undergone a transformation, with some of the old smokestacks and shipyards along its lakefront replaced with museums, a marina, restaurants and boutiques that attract Chicagoans on weekends. Following a police shooting of a Black man who had a knife but no firearm in August 2020, Kenosha was rocked by street protests and demands for racial justice. Days later, the conflict took a troubling turn when a 17-year-old white male—a self-described militia supporter from the Chicago area—shot and killed two white men during the Kenosha protests, claiming self-defense.

In 2017, Foxconn Technology, the Chinese company that manufactures screens for Apple phones, said it was planning a $10 billion campus in Racine County, which initially was expected to hire 13,000 workers—a decision that was hailed by President Donald Trump and then-Gov. Scott Walker, who helped to secure $4 billion in state incentives. By the 2020 election, those hopes had largely collapsed, as Foxconn failed to deliver on its investment plans. Instead, the company planned a much smaller plant, reportedly for storage, and Gov. Tony Evers withdrew the tax benefits. In Kenosha County, German candy maker Haribo began work in 2020 on a $300 million plant in Pleasant Prairie to produce gummy bears—its first North American site. Some old lake resorts continue to thrive, most notably on Lake Geneva. In nearby Williams Bay is the University of Chicago's historic Yerkes Observatory, one of the nation's largest astronomy research centers.

The 1st Congressional District of Wisconsin runs from Lake Michigan west to Janesville in the eastern part of Rock County and encompasses all of Racine and Kenosha counties on Lake Michigan as well as parts of Walworth County, including Lake Geneva. Janesville is the home of former House Speaker Paul Ryan. The 1st takes in the southern Milwaukee County suburbs of Oak Creek and Greenfield and the southern tier of townships in suburban Waukesha County, including New Berlin. The district has been a competitive battleground. In 2008, Obama led, 51%-48%. Boosted a bit by Ryan's presence on the ticket, Mitt Romney in 2012 took the District, 52%-47%. President Donald Trump doubled that margin, with a 54%-45% win in 2020 in the 1st. Waukesha County is heavily Republican. Rock County gave Obama 61 percent of the vote in 2012. In 2020, Joe Biden won Rock with 55 percent. Kenosha, a swing county, supported Trump by 2,800 votes—the first presidential election since 1988 that it failed to support the winner. Though the overall change was significant in the 1st, each of the four districts to the north in Wisconsin had a larger shift toward the GOP in 2020.

Mark Pocan (D)

Elected 2012, 5th term, b. Aug 14, 1964; Kenosha, WI; University of WI - Madison, B.A., 1986; Married (Philip Frank).

Elected Office: Dane County Board of Supervisors, 1991-1996; WI Assembly, 1998-2012.

Professional Career: Owner, Budget Signs & Specialties, 1988-present; Public-relations specialist, WI Realtors Association, 1986-1988.

DC Office: 1421 LHOB 20515, 202-225-2906, Fax: 202-225-6942, pocan.house.gov

State Offices: Beloit, 608-365-8001; Madison, 608-258-9800.

Committees: *Appropriations*: Agriculture, Rural Development, FDA & Related Agencies; Financial Services & General Government; Labor, Health & Human Services, Education & Related Agencies. *Education & Labor*: Higher Education & Workforce Investment. *Joint Economic*.

Group Ratings

	ADA	ACLU	AFL-CIO	LCV	COC	HAFA	ACU	CFG	FRC
2020	**	88%	**	100%	-	0%	5%	**	-
2019	100%	C	90%	100%	43%	C	5%	17%	5%

Almanac Ratings 2019-2020

	Economy	Social	Foreign	Composite
Liberal	100%	56%	100%	86%
Conservative	0%	44%	0%	14%

Key Votes of the 116th Congress

1. U.S./Mex./Can. trade deal N	5. Russia sanctions Y	9. Firearms background checks Y
2. First Coronavirus response Y	6. Troops in Syria Y	10. Spending at the border N
3. HEROES Act Y	7. Veto arms sales to Saudis Y	11. Marijuana liberalized rules Y
4. CASH Act Y	8. Defense $$$, veto override N	12. Electoral College objections N

Election Results

Election	Name (Party)	Vote (%)	Cand. Spent	Ind. Exp. Support	Ind. Exp. Oppose
2020 General	Mark Pocan (D)............................318,523	(70%)	$671,987	$9,605	
	Peter Theron (R)...............................138,306	(30%)	$33,092		$113
2020 Primary	Mark Pocan (D)..................120,353	(100%)			

Prior winning percentages: 2016 (69%), 2014 (68%), 2012 (68%)

Democrat Mark Pocan, elected in 2012, has been a leader of the Progressive Caucus, where he has worked with others to demand action by party leaders. He also has shown insider skills as a member of the Appropriations Committee. Like his predecessor Tammy Baldwin, who was elected to the Senate, Pocan is openly gay. He has taken up many of her issues, plus her outspoken advocacy. Following the 2020 election, Pocan was a founder of the Labor Caucus and became a co-chair.

Pocan was born and raised in Kenosha, the child of two small-business owners. Pocan's father served on the Kenosha City Council, and as a kid Pocan campaigned with him. At the University of Wisconsin, Pocan said, "I started out as a poli-sci major until I took my first poli-sci class that talked about the Ottoman Empire and not political campaigns. So I decided to switch" to journalism. After graduating, he opened a Madison-based print shop. Around that time, Pocan dealt with personal trauma. After leaving a gay bar one night, he was physically assaulted by two men and needed stitches. "That was kind of a turning point because after that happened, that's when I got very active with a number of LGBT nonprofits," he said. Since gay marriage was not legal in Wisconsin in 2006, Pocan married in Canada.

In 1991, Pocan won a seat on the Dane County Board of Supervisors. He spent 14 years in the state Assembly, where he succeeded Baldwin for the first time. He co-chaired the influential Joint Finance Committee. Pocan helped expand health care coverage for children and extend domestic-partner benefits for gay couples. Milwaukee Magazine named him "best legislator" in 2009.

In an acrimonious contest for Baldwin's congressional seat, Pocan's chief rival was Kelda Helen Roys, also a Madison-area state representative. Pocan had support from unions and much of the party establishment, plus a roughly 2-to-1 fundraising advantage. Roys attacked him for compromising with Republicans and for taking money from political action committees. Pocan did not back away from his image as a strong progressive willing to work across the aisle. "There are those who scream and holler and put out a press release," he told the Wisconsin State Journal. "I decided I wanted to be the kind that gets things done." Pocan won 72%-22%. Since then, he has not been seriously challenged.

In the Republican-controlled House, Pocan sought opportunities for bipartisanship. He and conservative Republican Rep. Glenn Grothman of Wisconsin pursued steps to reduce student loan debt, including their bill to permit loan-holders to refinance at any time. His Almanac vote ratings have consistently ranked Pocan among the most liberal House members. In January 2017, he joined other gay House members in opposing the nomination of Betsy DeVos as secretary of Education, accusing her of supporting anti-gay causes. Also that month, he joined the Appropriations Committee, where his seniority has moved him close to a subcommittee chairmanship.

Pocan has pursued his liberal agenda at the Progressive Caucus. As co-chair, he sought new opportunities to expand the group's membership and influence after Democrats won the House majority. Asked by the Washington Post whether his group would be a Democratic version of the House Freedom Caucus, which often forced confrontations within the Republican majority, he responded: "The question comes up often. ... The difference is the tea party liked to say no and we like to say yes."

He added that caucus members have sought to assure that party leaders shared their ambition. Earlier, Pocan joined New York City Mayor Bill de Blasio and others to launch The Progressive Agenda to Combat Income Inequality, which Pocan said would "put meat on the bone of our progressive values."

In the weeks following the 2018 election, Pocan withheld his endorsement of Nancy Pelosi for House Speaker until she promised that progressives would have a prominent role in setting the House agenda. He included issues such as health care, the cost of prescription drugs, infrastructure projects and ethical standards, plus a proportional share of seats for progressives on key House committees. "We need to be big and bold and show people the path forward," he told the Wisconsin State Journal. In January 2020, Pocan endorsed Bernie Sanders for president and became chairman of his campaign in Wisconsin. Joe Biden won that contest by a 2-to-1 margin.

Pelosi gave Pocan a seat on the Select Committee on the Modernization of Congress. With Republican Rep. William Timmons, he proposed in October 2019 a change in the House schedule so members would work two full weeks in Washington, followed by two weeks in their district. The proposal failed to win broad support.

Following the 2020 election, Pocan was a co-founder with Democratic Rep. Donald Norcross of the Labor Caucus and became a co-chair. With Biden as president, Pocan said, "we must reaffirm our dedication to strengthening unions," including a minimum wage of $15 per hour, plus steps to encourage an increase in labor-union membership. Although he stepped down as a co-chair of the Progressive Caucus, he remained a co-chair of its political action committee.

WI-2: South-Central Wisconsin   **Cook Partisan Voting Index: D+18**

Population		Race and Ethnicity		Income	
Total	773,663	White	85.90%	Median Income	$72,036
Land area (sq. miles)	4,537	Black	4.40%	District Income Rank	149
Pop/ sq mi	170.53	Latino	6.80%	Poverty Rate	10.10%
Born in State	63.40%	Asian	4.50%	With health insurance	95.50%
		Two or more races	2.80%	Cash public assistance	1.40%
Age Groups		Other	2.40%	Food stamp/SNAP	6.70%
Under 18	20.90%				
18-34	26.00%	**Education**		**Work**	
35-64	37.70%	H.S grad or less	28.00%	White Collar	48.80%
Over 64	15.30%	Some college	27.00%	Sales and Service	32.50%
		College Degree, 4 yr	27.20%	Blue Collar	18.70%
Military		Post grad	17.70%	Government	18.50%
Veteran/ Active Duty	6.10%				

2020 Pres. Vote	Biden	323,807	(69%)	Trump	136,439	(29%)		
2016 Pres. Vote	Clinton	271,507	(65%)	Trump	119,608	(29%)	Johnson	14,385 (3%)

Madison: On a narrow isthmus between Lakes Mendota and Monona is the center of Madison, and in many ways, the center of Wisconsin. The state capitol rises at one end of State Street, and at the other end is the main campus of the University of Wisconsin, in a beautiful, park-like setting above Lake Mendota. For most of the 20th century, Wisconsin politics was dominated by the Madison-based LaFollettes and their liberal Democratic successors. University faculty were devoted to Robert LaFollette's "Wisconsin idea" of a supposedly apolitical bureaucracy and to his Wisconsin Tax Commission and workmen's compensation law—both firsts in the nation and conceived of by the former governor and senator.

Madison spawned an activist and sometimes violent student movement during the Vietnam War. The liberal campus opposed the welfare reform and school choice laws enacted while Republican Tommy Thompson was governor. The Madison community was the center of vocal opposition to Gov. Scott Walker's plan to end collective bargaining for most state workers and then led the unsuccessful recall effort to oust him in June 2012. Following his election to a second term, Walker took revenge of sorts with the 2015 enactment of a plan for the state to wield more control over the university, including faculty hiring, through its Board of Regents. Madison remains economically vibrant. The metropolitan area boasts one of the best-educated workforces in the country—51 percent of residents hold a college degree and 17 percent have a graduate degree. The growth industries include health care (Madison is home to American Family Insurance) and biotechnology startups tied to the university. In 2019, Madison trailed only Seattle, San Francisco and Washington D.C. with its share of the workforce that has a job in computer science or mathematics.

Madison is the center of Wisconsin's 2nd Congressional District, nearly half of which is urban and the remainder split between suburban and rural. It includes surrounding Dane County and dairy and alfalfa country to the north and south, as well as several rural dairy counties that have traditionally been Republican. Dodgeville, in Iowa County (not on the Iowa border), is the headquarters of Lands' End, the catalog retailer. Dane is about three-fourths of the district. In 2020, local Democratic state Sen. Fred Risser retired after 64 years, which is believed to be record legislative longevity in the United States.

The rural areas of Dane County, which had been open to Republicans as recently as the 1990s, have become bluer as Madison-area liberals move to the countryside, even as other parts of the state have become more crimson. The strongly Democratic lean of the county, plus its 50 percent population growth from 1990 to 2019 (while the population in the larger Milwaukee County has remained flat), has increased its voting power in the state. "Dane County is gradually altering the electoral math in Wisconsin," Craig Gilbert wrote in the Milwaukee Journal Sentinel in 2018. As governor, Walker understood the threat. "The last thing we need is more Madison in our lives," he tweeted. As of 2020, when its per capita income was nearly twice as high as the city of Milwaukee, its population was only 10 percent smaller. After Hillary Clinton won the district, 65%-29%, when she fell short statewide, Joe Biden took the district, 69%-29%—with a 17 percent increase in turnout.

Ron Kind (D)

Elected 1996, 13th term, b. Mar 16, 1963; La Crosse, WI; Harvard University, B.A., 1985; London School of Economics, M.A., 1987; University of MN, J.D., 1990; Lutheran; Married (Tawni Zappa Kind); 2 children.

Professional Career: Practicing attorney, 1990-1992; Assistant State Prosecutor, La Crosse County, 1992-1996.

DC Office: 1502 LHOB 20515, 202-225-5506, Fax: 202-225-5739, kind.house.gov

State Offices: Eau Claire, 715-831-9214; La Crosse, 608-782-2558.

Committees: *Ways & Means*: Health; Trade.

Group Ratings

	ADA	ACLU	AFL-CIO	LCV	COC	HAFA	ACU	CFG	FRC
2020	**	83%	**	90%	-	10%	12%	**	-
2019	90%	C	85%	97%	63%	C	12%	25%	0%

Almanac Ratings 2019-2020

	Economy	Social	Foreign	Composite
Liberal	100%	100%	50%	84%
Conservative	0%	0%	50%	16%

Key Votes of the 116th Congress

1. U.S./Mex./Can. trade deal Y	5. Russia sanctions Y	9. Firearms background checks Y
2. First Coronavirus response Y	6. Troops in Syria Y	10. Spending at the border Y
3. HEROES Act Y	7. Veto arms sales to Saudis Y	11. Marijuana liberalized rules Y
4. CASH Act Y	8. Defense $$$, veto override Y	12. Electoral College objections N

Election Results

Election	Name (Party)	Vote (%)		Cand. Spent	Ind. Exp. Support	Ind. Exp. Oppose
2020 General	Ron Kind (D)................................	199,870	(51%)	$4,182,277	$472,030	$1,607,124
	Derrick Van Orden (R)......................	189,524	(49%)	$1,972,239	$551,204	$638,712
2020 Primary	Ron Kind (D)................................	53,064	(81%)			
	Mark Neumann (D)............................	12,765	(19%)			

Prior winning percentages: 2018 (60%), 2016 (99%), 2014 (57%), 2012 (64%) 2010 (50%), 2008 (63%), 2006 (65%), 2004 (56%), 2002 (63%), 2000 (64%), 1998 (72%), 1996 (52%)

Ron Kind, a Democrat elected in 1996, is a moderate who has focused on health and agriculture issues and seeks bipartisanship on the Ways and Means Committee. In contrast to the dominant liberal core of Wisconsin Democrats, he has been a leader of the New Democrat Coalition, a business-oriented group that attempts to break through partisan gridlock. In 2015, Kind was the leading Democratic proponent in the bitter intraparty battle to give trade promotion authority to President Barack Obama. He has called for new Democratic leaders and voted against Nancy Pelosi as House Speaker. After his narrow reelection in 2020, Kind said he was looking at a Senate campaign in 2022.

Kind grew up in a large family in La Crosse, the son of a telephone repairman and a secretary in the local schools. He went to Harvard University on a scholarship and played quarterback. He was a summer intern for Democratic Sen. William Proxmire, doing research for Proxmire's Golden Fleece awards pointing out wasteful government spending. Kind attended the London School of Economics and the University of Minnesota's law school, practiced law in a large firm in Milwaukee, then returned home to La Crosse to work as an assistant prosecutor on rape and sexual abuse cases.

Kind ran for an open seat that had been Republican-held. Former state Sen. Jim Harsdorf won the Republican primary and made a case for a balanced budget and for Republican Gov. Tommy Thompson's "Wisconsin Works" welfare reform program. Kind presented his own balanced budget proposal and urged reform of campaign finance. He won, 52%-48%.Kind has taken a continuing interest in improving the health of the upper Mississippi River, which is vital to the well-being of his district. He has worked to restore the river, combat invasive species and ensure that it remains a resource for recreation and transportation.

Kind has focused heavily on agriculture issues that affect dairy farmers in his district. In 2007, he joined with conservative deficit hawks and suburban and urban Democrats in seeking to limit subsidies and provide more funds for land conservation and school nutrition. "For too long, we've had large taxpayer subsidies going to a few very large farming entities to the disadvantage of family farmers," Kind said. Democratic leaders were worried about angering farmers' groups in rural swing districts and refused to allow a House vote. Kind voted against the final version of the farm bill, calling it a "nightmare." In 2012, he complained in a letter to colleagues that the GOP-written farm bill "takes us backward in terms of budget-busting crop subsidies, unlimited insurance subsidies, and trade-distorting programs." He said that most producers he represents don't get huge subsidies because they're not large agribusinesses. He voted against the 2018 farm bill, which he called "status quo" legislation that continued huge subsidies to encourage over-production. "Too many of our family farmers in Wisconsin are just going out of business and declaring bankruptcy," he said.

In the health care debate in 2009, Kind cosponsored a bill to put greater emphasis on quality and coordination of care in reimbursing providers. He was one of three Democrats who joined committee Republicans in opposing the version that Ways and Means approved. After lengthy meetings that he and others held with Pelosi on containing the spiraling costs of Medicare, he agreed to support the legislation.

As a leader of House moderates, Kind has chaired the New Democrat Coalition. "We want to work hard to find that sensible center on policy and move the ball," he told The Hill newspaper. He was one of 15 Democrats who voted against Pelosi in the January 2019 House vote for Speaker. "I've been consistent in saying we're in desperate need of new leadership on both sides," Kind said.

On Obama's request in 2015 for trade promotion authority, Kind quietly assembled Democratic support. He faced fierce opposition from labor unions and many of his Democratic colleagues in his advocacy of Obama's top legislative priority of the year. Kind preserved cohesion among the depleted but still vital corps of 28 Democratic supporters of trade deals. He compared notes daily with White House officials. "Sometimes the phone rang and it was Obama himself," Roll Call reported. When President Donald Trump in 2017 withdrew the United States from the proposed Trans-Pacific

Partnership, Kind objected that the move "will cost us jobs in Wisconsin." In January 2019, Kind challenged Rep. Bill Pascrell of New Jersey for chairman of the Trade Subcommittee; the more-senior Rep. Earl Blumenauer of Oregon pre-empted both. Kind said Wisconsin's family farmers "are bearing the brunt of the president's trade war."

At home, Kind in 2004 had his first credible challenger, Republican state Sen. Dale Schultz, a moderate in the Wisconsin legislature. Schultz attacked Kind as a free trader who had sent jobs overseas. Kind affirmed his support for trade agreements, but criticized the Bush administration for supposedly failing to enforce their labor and environmental protection provisions. Kind won, 56%-43%. In 2010, Dan Kapanke, a Republican state senator, lambasted Kind for his support of the Affordable Care Act and Obama's economic agenda. Kind survived with a 50%-46% win. Until 2020, he had won comfortably with district lines more favorable for him.

In 2020, Kind faced Republican challenger Derrick Van Order, who spent 21 years as a Navy SEAL and wrote, *A Book of Man: A Navy SEAL's Guide to the Lost Art of Manhood.* He decided to challenge Kind in December 2019 when Kind voted to impeach Trump for what Van Orden called "purely political reasons." Kind outspent him, $4.2 million to $2 million. After Kind won, 51%-49%, capturing the three largest urban counties, Van Orden said he planned a rematch in 2022.

Kind, who has considered runs for statewide office in the past, said he might run for the Senate in 2022. He likely would face a primary with a liberal challenge.

WI-3: West-Central Wisconsin — Cook Partisan Voting Index: R+4

Population		Race and Ethnicity		Income	
Total	723,169	White	93.20%	Median Income	$59,426
Land area (sq. miles)	11,112	Black	1.50%	District Income Rank	275
Pop/ sq mi	65.08	Latino	2.90%	Poverty Rate	11.40%
Born in State	71.00%	Asian	2.50%	With health insurance	93.80%
		Two or more races	1.50%	Cash public assistance	2.20%
Age Groups		Other	1.40%	Food stamp/SNAP	8.60%
Under 18	20.50%				
18-34	24.30%	**Education**		**Work**	
35-64	36.90%	H.S grad or less	39.90%	White Collar	34.30%
Over 64	18.40%	Some college	33.10%	Sales and Service	36.30%
		College Degree, 4 yr	17.70%	Blue Collar	29.40%
Military		Post grad	9.30%	Government	13.80%
Veteran/ Active Duty	7.50%				

2020 Pres. Vote	Trump	202,659	(51%)	Biden	184,306	(47%)		
2016 Pres. Vote	Trump	177,172	(49%)	Clinton	160,999	(44%)	Johnson	14,511	(4%)

Eau Claire, La Crosse: On the rolling land of western Wisconsin, in the knobby hills just east of the Mississippi River, is some of the most beautiful river landscape in the country. This is where author Laura Ingalls Wilder's family built their little house in the big woods in the 1870s, before the first railroad came steaming up the narrow floodplain alongside the Mississippi River. Today, it is hard to imagine the big woods. The trees have long since been cut down, and the hillsides are covered with grass grazed by placid dairy cattle. Where the pioneers tried to scratch out diversified crops, later generations of farmers created America's premier dairy region, producing milk, butter and cheese. Some Amish communities from Pennsylvania have relocated here in recent years because land is cheaper than in the East. Since 1980, the dairy economy here has struggled. Numerous dairy farmers have gone out of business. Wisconsin also has had trouble competing against the European Union's subsidized cheese and butter, and more recently, with products from California's large-scale agribusiness. Cows have become more productive, and demand for milk has decreased. Former President Donald Trump's tariffs were unpopular in this area. With young people less willing to stay on the farms, immigrant workers have played a growing role in the local dairy industry, the La Crosse Tribune reported in 2017.

The 3rd Congressional District of Wisconsin follows the Mississippi from the border with Illinois north to Dunn County, covering the southern half of the western edge of the state. The district's two largest cities are La Crosse and Eau Claire, home to home-improvement giant Menards. Both cities have won recognition for their livability. Eau Claire has been rejuvenated by cleanup of the waterfront area and the opening of an arts center by the local campus of the University of Wisconsin.

The population of Eau Claire County was 105,000 in 2019—nearly double the total in 1950. The county has become a less expensive residential alternative for commuters from Minneapolis-St. Paul. The district stretches east to Democratic-leaning Portage County and Stevens Point, where the lakes, streams and trails make the area a recreational hotspot.

Settled largely by German and Scandinavian immigrants, the region once consistently voted for Wisconsin's LaFollette Progressives. In recent years, its voters have shown they cannot be taken for granted. Western Wisconsin was one of the few segments of rural America where President Barack Obama in 2012 ran even with historic Democratic percentages; his 55 percent of the vote was vital to his statewide victory. In the district's current lines, Obama did even better in 2008, when he took 59 percent and won every county. This area was a bulwark for Republican Gov. Scott Walker in his 2010 election and June 2012 recall, when he won every county in the district except La Crosse. That shift continued in 2020. Trump won the district, 51%-47%, a 12 percentage point drop in the Democratic vote in 12 years. Eau Claire, La Crosse and Portage counties all voted for Joe Biden, but narrowly. The rural counties went heavily for Trump.

Gwen Moore (D)

Elected 2004, 9th term, b. Apr 18, 1951; Racine, WI; Marquette University, B.A., 1978; Milwaukee Area Technical College, Att., 1983; Harvard University, Att., 2000; Baptist; Single; 3 children; 3 grandchildren.

Elected Office: WI Assembly, 1989-1992; WI Senate, 1992-2004, President pro tem, 1997-1998.

Professional Career: Housing & urban dev. specialist, 1985-1989.

DC Office: 2252 RHOB 20515, 202-225-4572, Fax: 202-225-8135, gwenmoore.house.gov

State Offices: Milwaukee, 414-297-1140.

Committees: *Science, Space & Technology*: Investigations & Oversight; Research & Technology. *Ways & Means*: Select Revenue Measures; Social Security; Worker & Family Support.

Group Ratings

	ADA	ACLU	AFL-CIO	LCV	COC	HAFA	ACU	CFG	FRC
2020	**	86%	**	100%	-	0%	3%	**	-
2019	95%	C	95%	97%	50%	C	3%	18%	0%

Almanac Ratings 2019-2020

	Economy	Social	Foreign	Composite
Liberal	100%	100%	83%	95%
Conservative	0%	0%	17%	5%

Key Votes of the 116th Congress

1. U.S./Mex./Can. trade deal	Y	5. Russia sanctions	Y
2. First Coronavirus response	Y	6. Troops in Syria	Y
3. HEROES Act	Y	7. Veto arms sales to Saudis	Y
4. CASH Act	Y	8. Defense $$$, veto override	Y

9. Firearms background checks	Y
10. Spending at the border	N
11. Marijuana liberalized rules	Y
12. Electoral College objections	N

Election Results

Election	Name (Party)	Vote (%)		Cand. Spent	Ind. Exp. Support	Ind. Exp. Oppose
2020 General	Gwen Moore (D)	232,668	(75%)	$970,844	$9,205	
	Tim Rogers (R)	70,769	(23%)			$113
	Robert Raymond (I)	7,911	(3%)			
2020 Primary	Gwen Moore (D)	68,898	(100%)			

Prior winning percentages: 2018 (76%), 2016 (77%), 2014 (70%), 2012 (72%), 2010 (69%), 2008 (88%), 2006 (71%), 2004 (70%)

Gwen Moore, a Democrat elected in 2004, has often recounted her personal struggles—in candid detail—as she has stood up for the poor, homeless and victims of domestic violence. As Wisconsin's first African-American member of Congress, she has highlighted her selection to the Ways and Means Committee. "Throughout my career as a public servant, I've learned that the only way to create change is to have a seat at the table," she told the House.

Moore was born in Racine, the eighth of nine children, and raised on the North Side of Milwaukee. As an 18-year-old college freshman, she became a single mother who relied on welfare to help support her daughter. She graduated from Marquette University and worked as a housing and urban development specialist. Moore said she got active in politics when a rent-to-own center repossessed her washer and dryer even though she had paid three times their value in interest. She led an effort to establish a community credit union. Elected to the state Assembly in 1989 and the Senate in 1992, she was the state's first Black woman senator. In 1990, she defeated Republican Scott Walker, who later served two terms as governor of Wisconsin.

In 2003, when blue-collar Democratic Rep. Gerald Kleczka announced he was retiring, Moore was the frontrunner. She was challenged in the primary by two political veterans, state Sen. Tim Carpenter and former state Democratic Chairman Matt Flynn, both White. Moore took advantage of the energized Black voter base and leveraged financial support from liberal women's organizations, teachers' unions, and other progressive groups. Flynn was endorsed by Kleczka. But he was damaged politically by his work as general counsel for the local Roman Catholic archdiocese in a priest sex abuse scandal. Carpenter was the only openly gay member of the Senate and had the support of national gay rights groups. Moore won 64 percent of the vote to 25 percent for Flynn and 10 percent for Carpenter. In the general election, Moore won easily, 70%-28%.

Moore has a staunchly liberal voting record, with Almanac vote ratings that have listed her in the top 5 percent of House progressives. She often has been harsh in her criticism of Republican policies. When House Republicans sought to defund Planned Parenthood during the 2011 budget debate, Moore drew on her own unwelcome experience of an unplanned pregnancy at age 18. "I just want to tell you a little bit about what it's like to not have Planned Parenthood," she said on the House floor. "You have to add water to the formula to make it stretch. You have to give your kids Ramen noodles at the end of the month to fill up their little bellies so they won't cry. You have to give them mayonnaise sandwiches."

In 2005, the House incorporated provisions of her Shield Act into the reauthorization of the Violence Against Women Act, to protect the identity of domestic-violence victims who receive homeless assistance. When the law came up in 2012, Moore stunned House colleagues by taking to the floor to graphically recount how a group of young men once discussed having sex with her. "The appointed boy, when he saw that I wasn't going to be so willing, completed a date rape and then took my underwear to display it to the rest of the boys. I mean, this is what American women are facing," she said.

Moore harshly criticized Donald Trump's views of women when she spoke to the Democratic convention in 2016. She was more temperate when the CBC met with Trump at the White House in March 2017. "It was important to sort of just clear the air," she said. "I don't think that our communities would be served well by our not engaging." Following Trump's response to the August 2017 White nationalist rally in Charlottesville Virginia, Moore said he should be impeached "to restore our national dignity." Prior to the 2020 election, she said he tried to use the street protests in Kenosha "as a prop for his vitriol, hatred (and) division."

Prompted by her selection as the second Wisconsin Democrat on Ways and Means—Ron Kind, a leader of centrist Democrats, has served on the committee for more than two decades—Moore said her recent treatments for small-cell lymphoma "quadrupled" her commitment to restore the individual mandate to the Affordable Care Act and expand government's role in health care. She told the Milwaukee Journal Sentinel that her cancer is in remission, and that it was "a cancer that I will live with for the rest of my life … not a cancer I will die from."

Moore remains firmly entrenched in her district. Former state Sen. Gary George challenged her in the Democratic primary three times and criticized her failure to use the "bully pulpit" to address crime and economic issues, though she won the nomination without opposition in 2020. That year, Moore was reelected with 75 percent of the vote.

WI-4: Milwaukee

Cook Partisan Voting Index: D+25

Population		Race and Ethnicity		Income	
Total	704,146	White	50.80%	Median Income	$47,421
Land area (sq. miles)	128	Black	33.70%	District Income Rank	404
Pop/ sq mi	5,486.14	Latino	17.60%	Poverty Rate	20.30%
Born in State	65.80%	Asian	4.00%	With health insurance	91.10%
		Two or more races	3.70%	Cash public assistance	2.40%
Age Groups		Other	7.80%	Food stamp/SNAP	21.30%
Under 18	24.90%				
18-34	28.20%	**Education**		**Work**	
35-64	34.90%	H.S grad or less	42.90%	White Collar	36.30%
Over 64	12.10%	Some college	27.80%	Sales and Service	39.80%
		College Degree, 4 yr	18.50%	Blue Collar	23.90%
Military		Post grad	10.80%	Government	11.30%
Veteran/ Active Duty	4.30%				

2020 Pres. Vote	Biden	242,263	(76%)	Trump	71,833	(22%)	
2016 Pres. Vote	Clinton	228,226	(73%)	Trump	67,287	(22%) Johnson 8,501 (3%)	

Milwaukee: Milwaukee is America's most German city, with an ethnic heritage noticeable not just in the names of its beers and its old German restaurants, but in the sturdiness of its houses and the orderliness of its streets. Until World War I inflamed sensitivities to all things German, the language was spoken on the streets and read in city newspapers; German beer was produced in dozens of breweries. A huge four-sided clock, nearly twice the size of London's Big Ben, rises above the Allen-Bradley factory, looking out over the industrial city. It is an apt symbol, a piece of precision engineering in this high-skill manufacturing town, with its skyline of smokestacks and church steeples —the closest thing in America to the German factory cities that inspired Milwaukee's early citizens. The city has led the nation in beer brewing, industrial control equipment, mining gear, cranes and independent foundries.

Downtown Milwaukee has seen major changes in the past few decades—with recent signs of an uptick. Many of the factories have shut down. It hemorrhaged population, with a drop from 740,000 in 1960 to 590,000. For the most part, the city has embraced Latinos. Many Hispanics have settled in the old immigrant neighborhoods of the city's South Side. The West Side and North Side are home to many of the city's African-American neighborhoods, such as Sherman Park and Bronzeville. Since 2000, its population has remained steady at 595,000, though it exceeded 600,000 in 2013. In July 2018, Vogue magazine profiled Milwaukee as "the Midwest's coolest (and most under-rated) city." Democrats had hoped to reinforce that theme when the city hosted their national convention in 2020 —but those plans were scrapped by the pandemic and the local factor became almost irrelevant.

That turnaround has been accompanied by a downtown building boom. New sites include Northwestern Mutual's office tower and apartment high-rise, the BMO Harris Financial Center office tower and the conversion of the Warner Grand Theater into the Milwaukee Symphony Orchestra's performance hall. Led by MillerCoors, the brewing industry continues to employ more than 7,000 in Milwaukee. The city has become a global hub for water technology and research, with many new tech start-ups. The University of Wisconsin-Milwaukee opened the first graduate school in the nation dedicated solely to the study of freshwater.

The 4th District of Wisconsin covers the entire city of Milwaukee and a few of its working-class suburbs—St. Francis, Cudahy and South Milwaukee on Lake Michigan, and West Milwaukee and part of West Allis. It includes to the north tonier suburbs along the lake, many with sizable Jewish populations—Shorewood, Whitefish Bay and Fox Point. These communities are politically competitive and closely attuned to state politics. About 30 percent of Milwaukee County voters reside in parts of three Republican-held districts in Wisconsin; that suggests potential redistricting options for Democrats. In the 4th, Blacks make up 34 percent of the population, while Hispanics comprise another 18 percent. It is easily Wisconsin's most Democratic district, with Joe Biden getting 76 percent of the vote here in 2020. Turnout in Milwaukee County grew by 28,000 voters from 2016. That increased Clinton's lead in the county by 20,000 votes. She lost statewide by fewer than 21,000 votes. President Donald Trump's claims of election fraud were largely debunked.

Scott Fitzgerald (R)

Elected 2020, 1st term, b. Nov 16, 1963; Chicago, IL; Army Command and General Staff College; University of WI - Oshkosh, B.S., 1985; Catholic; Married (Lisa Fitzgerald); 3 children.

Military Career: Lt. Colonel, U.S. Army Reserve, 1981-2009.

Elected Office: WI Senate, 1994-2021; Majority Leader, WI Senate, 2011-2021.

Professional Career: Owner/Associate Publisher, newspaper company.

DC Office: 1507 LHOB 20515, 202-225-5101, fitzgerald.house.gov

State Offices: Brookfield, 262-784-1111.

Committees: *Education & Labor*: Civil Rights & Human Services; Health, Employment, Labor & Pensions. *Judiciary*: Antitrust, Commercial & Administrative Law; Courts, Intellectual Property & Internet; Crime, Terrorism & Homeland Security. *Small Business*: Contracting & Infrastructure; Oversight, Investigations & Regulations.

Election Results

Election	Name (Party)	Vote (%)		Cand. Spent	Ind. Exp. Support	Ind. Exp. Oppose
2020 General	Scott Fitzgerald (R)	265,434	(60%)	$901,857	$6,100	
	Tom Palzewicz (D)	175,902	(40%)	$343,068		$43,590
2020 Primary	Scott Fitzgerald (R)	60,676	(77%)			
	Cliff DeTemple (R)	17,829	(23%)			

Republican Scott Fitzgerald, a longtime influential political leader in Wisconsin, was easily elected to fill an open House seat. He succeeded Jim Sensenbrenner, who served 42 years in Congress and was a powerful figure who chaired two House committees. Fitzgerald's partisan heft discouraged competition from a litany of potential contenders who were awaiting Sensenbrenner's retirement. Following his lengthy tenure as the GOP leader of the Wisconsin Senate, he could seek early opportunities for a leadership role in the House.

Fitzgerald, who was born in Chicago, has resided for most of his life in Dodge County, an exurban area north of Milwaukee. After getting his bachelor's degree from the University of Wisconsin (Oshkosh), he purchased in 1990 the Dodge County Independent News, based in Juneau. He sold the newspaper six years later, though he remained as associate publisher. With the Armor Division of the U.S. Army Reserve, Fitzgerald was a battalion commander and retired as a lieutenant colonel after 27 years.

He was first elected to the state Senate in 1994, when he won the Republican primary against an incumbent whom he criticized as "too moderate." He chaired the Corrections Committee and co-chaired the influential Finance Committee. In 2010, when Republicans took control of the state under Gov. Scott Walker, Fitzgerald became majority leader. He was instrumental in the sweeping changes the party made, which led to Democrats' unsuccessful effort in 2012 to recall Walker. The redistricting maps he helped craft that year helped assure GOP control of the legislature and congressional delegation for the next decade.

After Walker lost his bid for a third term to Democrat Tony Evers in 2018, Fitzgerald led legislative efforts to restrict the newcomer's influence—including proposals in 2020 to address the pandemic and the racial unrest that was centered in Kenosha.

In the state's polarized politics, Fitzgerald had strong critics. If elected, wrote John Nichols, associate editor of the (Madison) Capital Times, "he'll surely do his best to make a fractured and dysfunctional Congress more fractured and more dysfunctional." In a more sympathetic profile, Milwaukee Magazine wrote, "Fitzgerald has delivered on conservative policy ideas and, more recently, has helped maintain a substantial Republican majority in the legislature."

Republican embrace of Fitzgerald was evident when he breezed to victory for Sensenbrenner's seat. Clifford DeTemple, a small business owner with a graduate degree from the Naval War College, entered the GOP primary as a proponent of term limits and contended that he was more knowledgeable than his opponent about the federal government, though he had not held political office. Fitzgerald won 77%-23%.

Democratic opponent Tom Palcewicz, who owned a small business, said Fitzgerald had become an "obstructionist" in the legislature and criticized him in October for "not debating or holding town hall events" during their campaign. But he had no chance in this district. Fitzgerald spent a bit less than $1 million, a modest sum to win an open seat, and won 60 per cent of the vote. He won four of the six counties, trailing in Milwaukee and Walworth. Two years earlier, Sensenbrenner got 62 percent against Palcewicz—his lowest share of the vote since he was first elected.

Other members of the Fitzgerald family also have been politically influential. Scott's father, Steve Fitzgerald, was sheriff of Dodge County and a U.S. marshal before Walker appointed him as the top officer of the Wisconsin State Patrol. Jeff Fitzgerald, Scott's brother, served as speaker of the state Assembly for two years before he lost the Republican primary in 2012 for an open U.S. Senate seat for Wisconsin. He then became an influential lobbyist in his home state.

WI-5: East-Central Wisconsin   Cook Partisan Voting Index: R+11

Population		Race and Ethnicity		Income	
Total	733,314	White	90.50%	Median Income	$77,386
Land area (sq. miles)	1,891	Black	2.40%	District Income Rank	106
Pop/ sq mi	387.84	Latino	6.50%	Poverty Rate	6.40%
Born in State	76.40%	Asian	3.10%	With health insurance	96.40%
		Two or more races	2.20%	Cash public assistance	1.00%
Age Groups		Other	1.90%	Food stamp/SNAP	5.80%
Under 18	20.40%				
18-34	20.10%	**Education**		**Work**	
35-64	40.40%	H.S grad or less	31.40%	White Collar	43.20%
Over 64	19.10%	Some college	30.50%	Sales and Service	34.30%
		College Degree, 4 yr	26.00%	Blue Collar	22.60%
Military		Post grad	12.30%	Government	9.60%
Veteran/ Active Duty	6.90%				

2020 Pres. Vote	Trump	255,803	(57%)	Biden	187,851	(42%)		
2016 Pres. Vote	Trump	229,325	(57%)	Clinton	148,900	(37%)	Johnson	15,756	(4%)

Western Milwaukee Suburbs, Waukesha: For decades, the orderly, heavily German-American factory city of Milwaukee has spread, mostly west and north, into Wisconsin dairy country. There are high-income enclaves here, such as close-in Elm Grove and exurban Oconomowoc, halfway to Madison and tucked in around numerous lakes. There is office development in Brookfield, and subdivisions have spread to Menomonee Falls and farther, reaching small towns with roots in the 19th century. This is comfortable but not fancy territory, and the economy is still based heavily on skilled manufacturing. Not far from Milwaukee are West Bend, with West Bend kitchen appliances; and Pewaukee, with Harken sailboat hardware. Harley-Davidson began manufacturing on the city's West Side a century ago and has a payroll of about 1,000 employees who manufacture engines at the plant, now in Menomonee Falls. In July 2017, Harley announced local cutbacks, as it moved more of its production to Europe due to costly tariffs. Since then, Harley has further downsized its local workforce. During his final days of campaigning in late October 2020, Democratic challenger Joe Biden questioned the wisdom of President Donald Trump's trade war. "Harley-Davidson slashed 800 manufacturing jobs, repurchased stock ... and then shifted some of its production overseas. So much for helping," Biden said.

The 5th Congressional District of Wisconsin includes most of the western and northwestern suburbs of Milwaukee, spanning the Milwaukee County suburbs of Wauwatosa, Greenfield and West Allis; the northern half of Waukesha County, including New Berlin; and Jefferson County farther west. To the north, it includes all of Washington County and much of Dodge County. Nearly half the population is in Waukesha. For many years, this was the most Republican district in the state, and voters here tend to be better-off than Republicans elsewhere in Wisconsin. The median household income is $68,000, the highest of any district in the state, even the well-educated, Madison-based 2nd District.

Waukesha County, more than three-fourths of which is in the district, has been the conservative core of the state, providing the grassroots energy that fueled Gov. Scott Walker's victory during the June 2012 recall campaign. Waukesha gave Walker 72 percent of the vote in the recall and reported the second highest countywide turnout in the state. Trump under-performed in Waukesha. His victory margin in the county in 2016 was 63,000 votes with 61 percent of the vote, and 55,000 votes in 2020, compared with Mitt Romney's 84,000-vote lead and 67 percent in 2012 — even though Trump won and Romney lost statewide. In the outlying areas of Milwaukee County, some of which are in the 5th, Biden's victory margin of 37,000 votes was twice Clinton's lead in 2016, USA Today reported. Overall, the district voted 57 percent for Trump in November, which placed it behind the vote share in the two rural districts to the north that border Lake Superior.

Glenn Grothman (R)

Elected 2014, 4th term, b. Jul 03, 1955; Milwaukee, MI; University of WI - Madison, B.B.A., 1977; University of WI Law School, J.D., 1983; Lutheran; Single.

Elected Office: WI Assembly, 1994-2004; Assistant Minority Leader, WI Senate, 2012-2013; Assistant Majority Leader, WI Senate 2013; WI Senate, 2004-2014.

Professional Career: Attorney.

DC Office: 1427 LHOB 20515, 202-225-2476, Fax: 202-225-2356, grothman.house.gov

State Offices: Fond du Lac, 920-907-0624.

Committees: *Budget. Education & Labor*: Early Childhood, Elementary & Secondary Education; Higher Education & Workforce Investment. *Oversight & Reform*: National Security (RMM).

Group Ratings

	ADA	ACLU	AFL-CIO	LCV	COC	HAFA	ACU	CFG	FRC
2020	**	14%	**	5%	-	92%	92%	**	-
2019	0%	C	15%	10%	75%	C	94%	100%	95%

Almanac Ratings 2019-2020

	Economy	Social	Foreign	Composite
Liberal	25%	22%	30%	26%
Conservative	75%	78%	70%	74%

Key Votes of the 116th Congress

1. U.S./Mex./Can. trade deal	Y	5. Russia sanctions	N	9. Firearms background checks	N
2. First Coronavirus response	N	6. Troops in Syria	Y	10. Spending at the border	Y
3. HEROES Act	N	7. Veto arms sales to Saudis	N	11. Marijuana liberalized rules	N
4. CASH Act	N	8. Defense $$$, veto override	N	12. Electoral College objections	N

Election Results

Election	Name (Party)	Vote (%)		Cand. Spent	Ind. Exp. Support	Ind. Exp. Oppose
2020 General	Glenn Grothman (R)	238,874	(59%)	$1,785,317		$750
	Jessica King (D)	164,239	(41%)	$245,173	$10	
2020 Primary	Glenn Grothman (R)	52,247	(100%)			

Prior winning percentages: 2018 (56%), 2018 (55%), 2016 (57%), 2014 (57%)

Republican Glenn Grothman, elected in 2014, has been a staunch conservative with a lengthy record of provocative comments that raised national GOP concerns during his initial campaign. Since taking office, he has been relatively mainstream and has settled in with other Wisconsin Republicans.

Born in Milwaukee, Grothman earned his bachelor's and law degrees from the University of Wisconsin. He won a special election to the Wisconsin Assembly in 1993, then easily took the GOP nomination for a Senate seat in 2004, arguing that the incumbent was insufficiently conservative. He became assistant Republican leader in 2009 and was a vocal supporter of GOP Gov. Scott Walker's budget and policy changes.

In 2014, Grothman said he would challenge the moderate, low-profile Rep. Tom Petri. After 35 years in the House, Petri decided to retire in the face of what likely would have been a competitive contest. Grothman won the primary over state Sen. Joe Leibham by 219 votes, with 36 percent each. State Rep. Duey Stroebel finished third with 25 percent.

Both Grothman and Winnebago County Executive Mark Harris, the Democratic nominee, argued that the other was too extreme for the district. Harris said Grothman was weak on "women's issues," while Grothman in a fundraising email labeled Harris a "far-left politician." Harris cast himself as being more like Petri—a "thoughtful, quiet moderate." Grothman spent $1.2 million, more than four times as much as Harris. Grothman won 57%-41%. He took nine of the 11 counties; Harris narrowly won Columbia and Winnebago.

Grothman was a dream candidate for opposition researchers. In the legislature, he introduced a bill that would have required a state board to list single parenthood as a contributor to child abuse. He told the Capital Times that when he was in high school, "homosexuality was not on anybody's radar. And that's a good thing." He described welfare programs as "a bribe not to work that hard or a bribe not to marry someone with a full-time job."

Grothman initially attracted little attention in the House and kept busy with work on his committees. After his first two months, the Milwaukee Journal Sentinel reported, "we've hardly heard a word from him." He occasionally made provocative statements, but nothing sufficient to get him in trouble. At a meeting of the Oversight and Reform Committee in December 2019, Politico reported, "Grothman elicited some laughs—and groans" when he said that a lot of the research on the topic of the briefing was focused on females. "We get briefings on this, and everything's focused on the women, the women, the women," he said.

Grothman's candor extended to his dismissive comments about Donald Trump during the Wisconsin presidential primary in 2016. "You look at the way he behaves. If your 8-year-old child behaved that way, you'd wonder if there was something wrong with them," said Grothman, who had endorsed Ted Cruz. "So, he is not a human being who I think we want to emulate."

Following the 2020 presidential election, he showed little interest in defending Trump. During the formal count of the Electoral College results in January 2021, he opposed calls by other Republicans to review outcomes in two states. When a reporter for HuffPost asked Grothman whether he agreed with Trump's objections to the election count, he responded that "he hadn't watched the news."

With House Republicans in the minority, Grothman showed more interest in working with Democrats on legislation. In November 2019, he cosponsored with four Democrats a bill that capped annual charges at 36 percent for loans to members of the military and veterans. "Taking advantage of people who are either in desperate straits or more likely just plain financially illiterate is immoral," he said.

Despite his tight primary when he was first elected, no Republican has challenged him since. In 2016, Democratic challenger Sarah Lloyd was a dairy farmer who was on leave from a job at the Wisconsin Farmers Union. That rural background apparently did not strike a chord in this working-class district. Grothman won 57%-41%, nearly the same as his victory in 2014.

In 2018, the campaign financing escalated dramatically. Democrat Dan Kohl spent $3.4 million —of which $600,000 was self-financed—to $1.9 million for Grothman. Kohl, a nephew of former Democratic Sen. Herb Kohl, had been a lobbyist in Washington for an advocacy group on Israel and was an executive for his uncle's Milwaukee Bucks NBA basketball franchise. Kohl spotlighted "the stalemate and the dysfunction in Washington," and voiced concerns about Trump's trade war. Grothman's margin of victory narrowed to 55%-45%. Kohl led with 52 percent in Winnebago, which had the highest turnout. In 2020, Grothman faced Democrat Jessica King, a lawyer with a company that represents hospitals and patients against insurance companies. He outspent the challenger, $1.8 million to $245,000 and had his largest victory margin, 59%-41%. This time, he got 52 percent in Winnebago.

WI-6: East-Central Wisconsin

Cook Partisan Voting Index: R+10

Population		Race and Ethnicity		Income	
Total	715,828	White	91.60%	Median Income	$63,251
Land area (sq. miles)	4,918	Black	2.00%	District Income Rank	221
Pop/ sq mi	145.54	Latino	4.80%	Poverty Rate	8.00%
Born in State	77.90%	Asian	2.60%	With health insurance	95.40%
		Two or more races	1.90%	Cash public assistance	1.30%
Age Groups		Other	1.90%	Food stamp/SNAP	7.70%
Under 18	21.00%				
18-34	20.40%	**Education**		**Work**	
35-64	39.40%	H.S grad or less	40.50%	White Collar	33.50%
Over 64	19.00%	Some college	31.20%	Sales and Service	36.30%
		College Degree, 4 yr	19.40%	Blue Collar	30.20%
Military		Post grad	8.80%	Government	9.90%
Veteran/ Active Duty	7.50%				

2020 Pres. Vote	Trump	232,820	(57%)	Biden	170,457	(42%)		
2016 Pres. Vote	Trump	203,433	(55%)	Clinton	141,917	(38%)	Johnson	14,291 (4%)

Oshkosh, Sheboygan: Central Wisconsin is a producer of basic commodities—milk, butter, cheese, Kleenex, Mercury Marine outboard motors and military trucks. This is where the rolling hills and prairies of southern Wisconsin begin to give way to the pine and hardwood forests and glacial lakes of the Northwoods. First settled by Yankee Protestants, the 1850s brought the first large surge of German migration into the United States, and central Wisconsin was a favorite destination. They built the dairy farms and factory towns that seemed steadfastly prosperous, and they developed a manufacturing economy. Central Wisconsin was one of the birthplaces of the Republican Party, when a group of Whigs, Free Soilers and anti-slavery Democrats met in February 1854 in a small white schoolhouse in Ripon and proclaimed themselves Republicans. (A similar gathering took place in Jackson Michigan, which also claims to be the birthplace of the party.) The party grew rapidly, winning an effective majority in the House in that year's elections.

The German influence is still felt. Sheboygan is the Bratwurst Capital of the World. Johnsonville Foods, which began as a small family-owned company in 1945, employs more than 2,700 workers (including vendors), sells more sausage than any of its national competitors and remains privately owned. In 2017, the county had the lowest poverty rate in the nation. The city and surrounding county are home to more than 6,300 Hispanics and 6,000 Asians, mostly Hmong. Sheboygan, which hosts an annual Hmong summer festival, is the site of the Lao, Hmong and American Veterans Memorial, "to recognize and to honor the people who served and who died for the U.S. secret war." Oshkosh is no longer the place where children's clothing maker Oshkosh B'Gosh manufactures its products. It is home to the Oshkosh Corp., which produces everything from dump trucks to military vehicles. Also in Oshkosh, Alro Steel in May 2020 opened its new plant for distribution of metal, industrial supplies and plastics, with about 3,000 workers. The blue-collar town historically has been the center of numerous paper mills, several of which have closed in recent years. Kimberly-Clark, which employs 2,400 in the area, reversed plans in 2018 to shut down plants in Neenah and Fox Crossing; instead, with $24 million in tax incentives, the company spent $200 million to upgrade those sites. The bad news is that Wisconsin leads the nation in farm bankruptcies. In the past decade, about 40 percent of its dairy farms have shut down, though 7,500 remained, NPR reported in September 2019.

The 6th Congressional District is a slice of central Wisconsin from Lake Michigan to the Wisconsin River. It takes in the conservative, northern Milwaukee suburbs in Ozaukee County, including Port Washington. It includes Oshkosh-based Winnebago, the largest city and county in the district and the most Democratic-leaning; Sheboygan and Manitowoc on Lake Michigan; and Fond du Lac on the south shore of Lake Winnebago. The district includes four rural counties plus the Wisconsin Dells and its giant water park. Overall, the district has been Republican territory since that first meeting in Ripon. As with the 7th and 8th Districts to the north, Donald Trump twice won the 6th with nearly 10 percentage points more than Mitt Romney's victory in 2012. Barack Obama won each of the three districts in 2008.

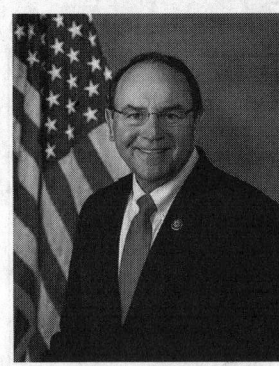

Tom Tiffany (R)

Elected 2020, 2nd term, b. Dec 30, 1957; Wabasha, MN; University of WI, River Falls, B.S., 1980; Not Known; Married (Christine Sully); 3 children.

Elected Office: Member, WI State Assembly, 2011-2013; WI Senate, 2013-2020.

Professional Career: Manager, petrolium and oil company; Town Supervisor, Town of Little Rice, WI.

DC Office: 1719 LHOB 20515, 202-225-3365, tiffany.house.gov

State Offices: Wausau, 715-298-9344.

Committees: *Judiciary*: Courts, Intellectual Property & Internet; Crime, Terrorism & Homeland Security; Immigration & Citizenship. *Natural Resources*: Energy & Mineral Resources; National Parks, Forests & Public Lands.

Election Results

Election	Name (Party)	Vote (%)		Cand. Spent	Ind. Exp. Support	Ind. Exp. Oppose
2020 General	Tom Tiffany (R)	252,048	(61%)	$2,604,786	$1,507,534	$99,258
	Tricia Zunker (D)	162,741	(39%)	$1,159,826	$55,842	$249,920
2020 Primary	Tom Tiffany (R)	62,142	(100%)			

Republican Tom Tiffany won a special election in May 2020. He had a lengthy record in Wisconsin politics and was supported by conservative groups. Tiffany succeeded Republican Sean Duffy, who resigned in September 2019 after five terms. Duffy switched control of the district that had been Democratic-held for four decades.

Tiffany grew up on a dairy farm near Elmwood Wisconsin and got a bachelor's degree in agricultural economics from the University of Wisconsin (River Falls). His business experience included ownership of a river cruise company in Wisconsin and management of a local oil company's petroleum distribution. He was town supervisor for four years of Little Rice (population, 306) in Oneida County and served 10 years in the state legislature, where he chaired the Sporting Heritage, Mining and Forestry Committee and was a member of the influential Joint Finance Committee.

When Duffy resigned, citing the medical problems of the ninth child that he and his wife were expecting, Tiffany faced a competitive primary with Jason Church, a first-time candidate. Church had been an aide to Sen. Ron Johnson of Wisconsin and served in Afghanistan, where he lost both his legs to an explosive device and retired as an Army captain. With few policy differences between them, Church drew a contrast: "I'm not trying to climb a [political] ladder.

Tiffany won the endorsements of Duffy and former Gov. Scott Walker and received extensive campaign support from the conservative Club for Growth and the House Freedom Caucus. He outspent Church, $1.5 million to $800,000 and won the primary, 57%-43%; of the 26 counties, he won all except for five in the southern part of the district.

Democratic nominee Tricia Zunker, a member of the school board of Wausau, was a lawyer who served on the board of directors of the American Civil Liberties Union in Wisconsin. She was a law professor and served as a judge of the Ho-Chunk Nation, a tribal group. Zunker supported "Medicare for All for those who want it" and was an advocate for the human rights of prisoners. During a campaign debate in May, Zunker rejected as "incredibly risky" Tiffany's call to reopen the Wisconsin economy to assist businesses that rely on tourism, which had been harmed by the pandemic shutdown.

Tiffany took 57 percent of the vote in the special election, winning all but three counties in the northwest corner of the district.

In the House, Tiffany filed a bill to support Taiwan and end the "One China Policy." Following violence in the streets of Madison and Kenosha during the summer of 2020, Tiffany criticized Gov. Tony Evers for having "ignored this crisis" and said that he should resign.

In a November rematch with Zunker, Tiffany won 61 percent of the vote. That was roughly the share Duffy received in his final three contests. Tiffany spent a total of about $2.5 million in the special and general elections combined, about $500,000 more than the total spent by his two opponents.

In 2021, he became the vice ranking member of the Natural Resources Subcommittee on National Parks, Forests and Public Lands.

WI-7: North-Central Wisconsin   Cook Partisan Voting Index: R+12

Population		Race and Ethnicity		Income	
Total	714,544	White	93.20%	Median Income	$60,706
Land area (sq. miles)	23,037	Black	0.80%	District Income Rank	252
Pop/ sq mi	31.02	Latino	2.60%	Poverty Rate	9.90%
Born in State	68.00%	Asian	1.70%	With health insurance	93.40%
		Two or more races	1.90%	Cash public assistance	1.50%
Age Groups		Other	2.50%	Food stamp/SNAP	9.20%
Under 18	21.30%				
18-34	17.10%	**Education**		**Work**	
35-64	40.50%	H.S grad or less	42.00%	White Collar	33.70%
Over 64	21.10%	Some college	33.60%	Sales and Service	34.60%
		College Degree, 4 yr	16.70%	Blue Collar	31.70%
Military		Post grad	7.70%	Government	13.10%
Veteran/ Active Duty	8.80%				

2020 Pres. Vote	Trump	248,822	(59%)	Biden	165,104	(39%)			
2016 Pres. Vote	Trump	213,467	(57%)	Clinton	137,874	(37%)	Johnson	12,613	(3%)

Wausau: In the late 19th century, thousands of migrants traveled the rail lines radiating northwest from Chicago and Milwaukee to settle the northern reaches of Wisconsin, the most thickly settled land this far north in the United States and east of the Mississippi. What attracted them was not cropland—there are no large wheat farms as in the Red River Valley of North Dakota—but trees, iron and cows. This was one of America's largest virgin timberlands, and the river towns are still dotted with paper mills. Farther north, iron brought Finns and Italians to the port of Superior, across St. Louis Bay from Duluth Minnesota, and to smaller towns on the chilly lake. The cleared forest lands became dairy farms. Dairy cattle, properly cared for, thrived in these northern uplands. Small cities grew, and some became home to big enterprises.

Those longstanding industries have encountered tough times. In Wausau, the city's eponymous paper industry has shrunk. The number of dairy farmers in the region is in sharp decline as the economics of their business have become less attractive. Prices have been low, as national consumption of milk has decreased. Cheese and butter consumption remained high, but those products are more costly to produce. Some farmers have turned to potatoes, vegetables and cranberries. Growing sales of high-quality ginseng in Marathon County were severely harmed by Trump's trade wars; sales that exceeded more than $40 million of the local crop, mostly with exports to China, were cut by more than half and prices had plunged. Wausau, which the 1980 census found to be the most ethnically homogeneous city in the nation, now has a sizable immigrant community. Many Hmong refugees moved there in the 1980s; as of 2019, 12 percent of the city's population was Asian.

This region makes up Wisconsin's 7th Congressional District. Its 21 counties stretch more than 200 miles from Lake Superior in the north to part of Monroe County, next to La Crosse. Commuter-oriented St. Croix County, part of the Minneapolis-St. Paul metro area, was the fastest-growing county in Wisconsin from 2000 to 2010, with its population now 91,000. In northern Iron County, after a resource firm abandoned in 2015 a proposal for an open-pit mine in an area rich with iron ore that environmentalists and Native American tribes had fought, other developers found opportunities. In 2017, the state lifted a moratorium on gold and silver mining in the area and also loosened restrictions on iron mining. In Ashland County, the Bad River Band of Lake Superior Chippewa tried to shut down an oil pipeline across its tribal reservation.

The politics of the 7th District have a rough-hewn quality, a lumberjack-populist flavor. Ancestrally Republican, the area favored the progressivism of Wisconsin's LaFollettes. Superior-based Douglas County has been the chief Democratic outpost, while Marathon, St. Croix and many of the smaller counties have leaned Republican. Barack Obama carried the new boundaries, 53%-45%, in 2008. There has been a remarkable transformation since then. President Donald Trump's 59%-39%

win made the 7th his best district in the state. Douglas and two small neighboring counties, Bayfield and Ashland, were the only ones that supported Joe Biden, with an increase of a couple of percentage points above their support for Hillary Clinton, though they total only 10 percent of the population of the district.

Mike Gallagher (R)

Elected 2016, 3rd term, b. Mar 03, 1984; Green Bay, WI; Princeton University Woodrow Wilson School of Public and International Affairs, B.A., 2006; National Intelligence University, M.S., 2010; Georgetown University, M.A., 2012; Georgetown University, M.A., 2013; Georgetown University, Ph.D., 2015; Catholic; Married.

Military Career: U.S. Marine Corps 2006-2013 (Iraq)

Professional Career: Staff, United States Senate Foreign Relations Committee, 2013-2016; Foreign Policy Advisor.

DC Office: 1230 LHOB 20515, 202-225-5665, Fax: 202-225-5729, gallagher.house.gov

State Offices: De Pere, 920-301-4500.

Committees: *Armed Services*: Cyber, Innovative Technologies & Information Systems; Military Personnel (RMM); Seapower & Projection Forces. *Transportation & Infrastructure*: Aviation; Coast Guard & Maritime Transportation; Highways & Transit.

Group Ratings

	ADA	ACLU	AFL-CIO	LCV	COC	HAFA	ACU	CFG	FRC
2020	**	20%	**	19%	-	94%	81%	**	-
2019	10%	C	24%	14%	83%	C	87%	85%	100%

Almanac Ratings 2019-2020

	Economy	Social	Foreign	Composite
Liberal	33%	31%	42%	36%
Conservative	67%	69%	58%	64%

Key Votes of the 116th Congress

1. U.S./Mex./Can. trade deal	Y	5. Russia sanctions	Y	9. Firearms background checks	N
2. First Coronavirus response	N	6. Troops in Syria	Y	10. Spending at the border	Y
3. HEROES Act	N	7. Veto arms sales to Saudis	Y	11. Marijuana liberalized rules	N
4. CASH Act	N	8. Defense $$$, veto override	Y	12. Electoral College objections	N

Election Results

Election	Name (Party)	Vote (%)		Cand. Spent	Ind. Exp. Support	Ind. Exp. Oppose
2020 General	Mike Gallagher (R)	268,173	(64%)	$2,670,209	$138,577	$750
	Amanda Stuck (D)	149,558	(36%)	$412,015	$1,107	
2020 Primary	Mike Gallagher (R)	50,176	(100%)			

Prior winning percentages: 2018 (64%), 2016 (63%)

Republican Mike Gallagher, elected in 2016 to an open seat in a district that has switched party control seven times since 1975, quickly established a reputation as a cerebral maverick who is eager to assert himself. A former Marine captain who worked in top-level intelligence circles, he played a prominent role in crafting extensive cybersecurity policy in the 2020 military spending bill. Gallagher has been easily reelected.

Gallagher was born in Green Bay. He moved with his mother to Costa Mesa California after his parents divorced when he was a toddler, though he spent summers with his father in Green Bay. He got his bachelor's from Princeton's School of Public and International Affairs and joined the Marine Corps the day he graduated. He served seven years on active duty as a human intelligence and counterintelligence officer, and as a regional affairs officer for the Middle East and North Africa. During that time, he learned to speak Arabic, served on Gen. David Petraeus's Central Command

Assessment Team in the Middle East and spent three years working in the intelligence community. During two tours in Iraq, he was deployed to Anbar Province and attempted to work with local Iraqis to identify both opportunities for action and threats to the safety of his Marine battalion. He later questioned the U.S. decisions both to invade Iraq and to remove troops from the region after it was pacified. "I do think it was an analytical failure and an intelligence failure," he told the Milwaukee Journal Sentinel. "The fact that we won the war and lost the peace I think is shameful."

Gallagher got a master's degree in strategic intelligence from the National Intelligence University, and another master's followed by a Ph.D in government from Georgetown University. After he left the Marines, Gallagher was a Republican aide for the Middle East, North Africa and counterterrorism on the Senate Foreign Relations Committee and later was the national security adviser for the presidential campaign of Wisconsin Gov. Scott Walker. He spent time in the private sector as the senior global market strategist at Breakthrough Fuel, a Green Bay-based energy and supply chain management company.

In the contest to replace retiring GOP Rep. Reid Ribble, Gallagher won the Republican primary with 75 percent of the vote against Frank Lasee, a two-term state senator, who got 20 percent. Democratic nominee Tom Nelson, the Outagamie county executive and a former state legislator, was a prime recruit for his party. Nelson said the limited time Gallagher had lived in Wisconsin combined with his support for international trade agreements showed he was out of touch with local voters. Each candidate ran attack ads about his opponent's positions on taxes and Social Security. The contest was a high-dollar affair. Gallagher outspent Nelson, $2.7 million to $1.8 million. Gallagher's unexpectedly wide 63%-37% win was part of a strong Republican performance in rural Wisconsin.

Gallagher quickly impressed many as a rising star in Congress. In April 2018, McClatchy News profiled his "unusually independent reputation in today's Republican Party." He filed with Democratic Rep. Ron Kind of Wisconsin a bill to reduce presidential authority to revise tariffs to achieve, he said, "a level and fair playing field for Wisconsin manufacturers and farmers." With Democratic Rep. Raja Krishnamoorthi of Illinois, he created the Middle-Class Jobs Caucus to encourage manufacturing and technical education. He worked with Democratic Rep. Seth Moulton of Massachusetts in the bipartisan "With Honor" group, to encourage military veterans to run for Congress.

With his seat on the Armed Services Committee, Gallagher hosted Republican Rep. Rob Wittman of Virginia on a tour of the Marinette Marine Shipyard, a Pentagon contractor and a vital employer in his district; Wittman chaired the Seapower and Projection Forces Subcommittee. At age 32 when he entered the House, he won in 2018 the annual three-mile race for members of Congress. He defeated Republican Sen. Tom Cotton of Arkansas, another national security hawk and fellow veteran, who had won the previous four years.

Gallagher wasn't afraid to challenge Trump. In an interview on Fox News in June 2018 about the "endless culture war," he criticized the president's penchant for "a side show distracting from real issues." Also that month, he told National Public Radio that he disagreed with Trump's unilateral decision to end joint military exercises with South Korea. With Rep. Liz Cheney in October 2019, he attacked the Chinese government's "appalling record of repression." In April 2020, he said Americans needed "a wake-up call … to increase defense investments in the Indo-Pacific."

In 2019-20, Gallagher co-chaired the bipartisan Cyberspace Solarium Commission, which prepared an extensive set of national security recommendations that were largely enacted in the annual Pentagon spending bill, including creation of a National Cyber Director. "We are attempting to galvanize the American public and spur a change in the status quo prior to that huge cyberattack," Gallagher told the New York Times.

With his professional and academic experiences, Gallagher offered insights on the problems with what he called the "broken Congress." In "How to Salvage Congress," a piece in The Atlantic in November 2018, Gallagher wrote: "It's much worse than you think." The problem, he said, is "a defective process and a power structure that, whichever party is in charge, funnels all power to leadership and stifles debate and initiative within the ranks." Congress is "no longer suited to making laws and providing oversight," he added. "It has instead become a theater used by both parties to stoke the outrage of their base." Among his recommendations—to strengthen House committees, chairmen should be selected by members of their committee rather than by leadership-dominated panels.

Prior to the January 2021 acceptance by Congress of the Electoral College vote, he led a small group of House Republicans who issued a statement criticizing " the reckless adoption of mail-in ballots and the lack of safeguards," but concluding that the job of Congress is "to count the electors submitted by the states, not to determine which electors the states should have sent."

WI-8: Northeast Wisconsin   **Cook Partisan Voting Index: R+10**

Population		Race and Ethnicity		Income	
Total	736,079	White	89.00%	Median Income	$65,346
Land area (sq. miles)	6,807	Black	1.70%	District Income Rank	209
Pop/ sq mi	108.14	Latino	5.60%	Poverty Rate	9.00%
Born in State	78.50%	Asian	2.50%	With health insurance	94.10%
		Two or more races	2.30%	Cash public assistance	1.50%
Age Groups		Other	4.50%	Food stamp/SNAP	6.90%
Under 18	22.20%				
18-34	20.40%	**Education**		**Work**	
35-64	39.70%	H.S grad or less	40.50%	White Collar	34.00%
Over 64	17.80%	Some college	32.20%	Sales and Service	36.50%
		College Degree, 4 yr	19.10%	Blue Collar	29.50%
Military		Post grad	8.10%	Government	10.60%
Veteran/ Active Duty	7.30%				

2020 Pres. Vote	Trump	241,140	(57%)	Biden	174,136	(41%)		
2016 Pres. Vote	Trump	207,620	(56%)	Clinton	142,677	(38%)	Johnson	13,691 (4%)

Green Bay, Appleton: In 1673, the French Catholic missionary and explorer Jacques Marquette sailed from the open waters of Lake Michigan into what is now the expansive Green Bay. He had hoped to find the Northwest Passage to the Pacific. Instead, he found the Fox River, which leads to Lake Winnebago and, after a not-too-difficult portage, the Wisconsin River, which flows into the Mississippi. Green Bay and the Fox River Valley remained mostly wilderness and Indian country for more than 150 years. But once settled by Europeans, they became, as Father Marquette would have liked, one of the most heavily Catholic parts of the United States. The area thrived economically, with paper mills, a busy port and high-skill manufacturing in Green Bay and Appleton. The number of jobs in the paper and pulp industry in the Fox River Valley dropped from 51,000 in the late 1990s to 30,000 in 2017.

A new paper mill opened in Green Bay in March 2021, following a $500 million overhaul of an aging mill; preserving 1,100 jobs, the facility is the first new paper plant in the United States in 20 years and the first in Wisconsin in more than 30 years. In Marinette County, located on the bay, the Marinette Marine shipyard has spurred an economic boomlet with a multibillion-dollar Navy contract to build new littoral combat ships, with a workforce of about 2,000. In 2018, the shipyard got a Navy contract for work on a next-generation guided-missile frigate. In a campaign-style visit to the shipyard in June 2020, President Donald Trump said the Navy was "bigger and stronger than before" under his leadership.

Green Bay is the home of professional football's Packers, the locally beloved franchise owned by 361,000 shareholders and unlikely ever to move. Under the team's quaint charter, if the Packers are sold, the proceeds would go to the local Sullivan-Wallen American Legion Post 11 "for the purposes of erecting a proper soldier's memorial." It might make for quite a memorial: the Packers are valued at more than $3 billion, according to Forbes. Individual shares cannot be traded and they pay no dividend. Thirty miles south is Appleton, which has produced famous, and infamous, Americans: novelist Edna Ferber, escape artist Harry Houdini and demagogue Sen. Joseph McCarthy, the central figure in the "red scare" of the 1950s and censured by the Senate. Green Bay's Latino community has increased from approximately 1,000 people in 1990 to 16,000 in 2019; the city is 16 percent Hispanic. Appleton officials said the city operates as a "sanctuary city" in terms of national immigration policy, though it did not officially adapt the designation.

The 8th Congressional District of Wisconsin includes Green Bay and the Fox River Valley south to Appleton. It also includes the inland dairy counties and the Northwoods, which has hundreds of pine-ringed lakes. The Door County peninsula, which extends from Green Bay into Lake Michigan, is a more upscale summer destination, with art galleries, boutiques and restaurants. Green Bay-based Brown County is one-third of the population; Appleton-based Outagamie is about one-fourth. With other non-urban parts of Wisconsin, the 8th has shifted dramatically in its politics. Barack Obama carried the district with 54 percent of the vote in 2008. By 2020, President Donald Trump took 57 percent. Tiny Menominee County, the site of an Indian reservation, was the only county Trump lost.

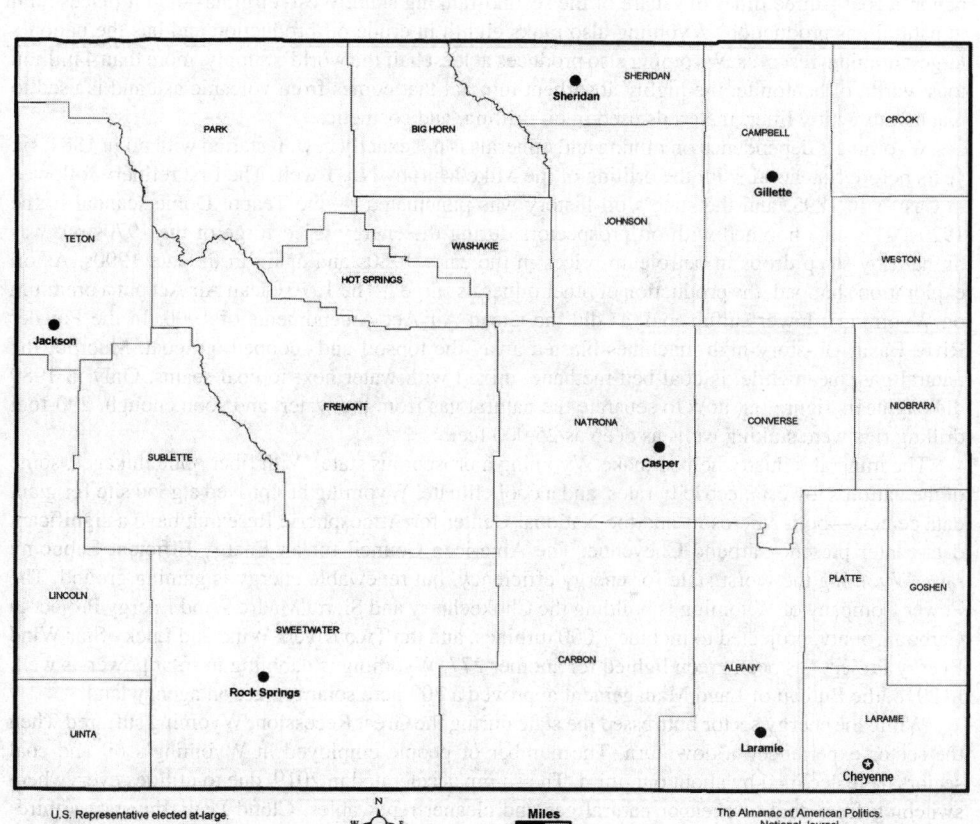

As one might expect of a state that's the nation's leading producer of coal, Joe Biden won a smaller percentage of Wyoming's presidential vote than he did in any state, duplicating Hillary Clinton's dubious achievement from four years earlier.

America's frontier disappeared in 1890, according to the Census Bureau and historian Frederick Jackson Turner, but some people in Wyoming defy that historical consensus. The state—symbolized by the cowboy astride a bucking bronco that graces its license plates—remains the most western of states in spirit. Largely unsettled even by the standards of its region, Wyoming's veneer of civilization stretches thinly across a forbidding and beautiful land. After the open range era, cattle ranches were made possible by the barbed wire that could fence in roaming herds and the steam locomotives that could carry cattle to markets in the East.

Wyoming is more than the land of the cowboy now. It produces almost 40 percent of the nation's coal—three times the share of the second-ranking state, West Virginia—and it places ninth in natural gas production. Wyoming also ranks eighth in crude oil production and has the nation's largest uranium reserves. Wyoming also produces at least half the world's supply, more than 4 million tons worth, of bentonite, the highly absorbent mineral that comes from volcanic ash and is used to manufacture kitty litter, materials used in oil drilling, and cosmetics.

Wyoming's dependence on mining and minerals is not exactly new. It started with oil in 1884, six years before statehood, with the drilling of the Mike Murphy No. 1 well. The first refinery followed in Casper in 1895, and the state's oil history was punctuated by the Teapot Dome scandal in the 1920s. The state boomed with oil prospectors during the energy price surge of the 1970s but was hit hard by steep drops in petroleum prices in the early 1980s and again in the late 1990s. As oil exploration slumped, the production of other minerals surged. The 1970 Clean Air Act put a premium on Wyoming's lower-sulfur coal, as did the Clean Air Act Amendments of 1990. In the Powder River Basin, 30-story-high machines blasted away the topsoil and scooped out coal. Much of the natural gas, meanwhile, is coal-bed methane, mixed with water next to coal seams. Only in 1989 did engineers figure out how to separate the natural gas from the water, and soon enough, 200-foot drilling rigs were sinking wells as deep as 25,000 feet.

The mineral industry helped make Wyoming a prosperous state. With fiber optic linkages, some of the nation's lowest electricity rates, and a cool climate, Wyoming has proved a good site for giant data centers—both Microsoft and the National Center for Atmospheric Research have a significant data-center presence around Cheyenne. The American Council for an Energy Efficient Economy rates Wyoming the worst state for energy efficiency, but renewable energy is gaining ground. The Power Company of Wyoming is building the Chokecherry and Sierra Madre Wind Energy Project in Carbon County, projected to include 1,000 turbines, and the Two Rivers Wind and Lucky Star Wind Energy Project has been green lighted for another 277. Wyoming is dabbling in solar power as well; in 2018, the Bureau of Land Management approved a 700-acre solar project on agency land.

While the energy sector buttressed the state during the Great Recession, Wyoming suffered when the sector experienced a downturn. The number of people employed in Wyoming's oil and coal sectors have declined by about one-third. The slump accelerated in 2019, due to utilities everywhere switching from coal to cheaper natural gas and cleaner renewables. Cloud Peak, the state's third-largest mining company, filed for bankruptcy, followed by Black jewel, the state's fourth-largest. In 2020, Peabody Energy and Navajo Transitional Energy Company announced layoffs numbering in the hundreds. Not only were jobs lost, but localities such as Campbell County found themselves short on millions in taxes owed by energy companies. Even the state's largest utility, PacifiCorp, announced that it would be accelerating the closure of several of its coal-fired plants. In the meantime, natural gas prices sagged due to the coronavirus pandemic and its resulting recession. "We need to truly diversify our economy," state Sen. Michael Von Flatern, an ex-coal miner, told High Country News. The state budget has been hit particularly hard; the energy and mining sector historically provided the treasury with about two-thirds of its revenue. Despite gains in tourism and technology—and a budding interest in crypto currency banking services—no other sector has produced enough revenue to fill in the gaps, and proposals to overhaul the state's tax structure have regularly languished.

Wyoming is the nation's least populous state—Washington D.C. is 22 percent bigger in population and 1,400 times smaller in area. Its population grew 14 percent in the decade ending in 2010, but only by an additional 2.3 percent in the next decade, buffeted by four straight years of population declines driven by the fall-off in energy and mining. Some counties, including Natrona (Casper), Campbell (Gillette), Sweetwater (Green River) and Fremont (Lander), expanded in population during the early part of the decade but shrank after the industry's downturn set in. Counties supported by other sectors have seen steadier growth of 7 to 10 percent since 2010— whether it's government (Laramie County, which includes the state capital of Cheyenne), higher education (Albany County, which includes Laramie, home of the University of Wyoming), or tourism (Teton County, which includes the resort area around Jackson Hole). Teton County, more than three times the size of Rhode Island, has benefited more than any, thanks to Wyoming's remarkable landscape. Yellowstone, established in 1872, was the nation's first national park; it has averaged about 4 million visitors annually in recent years, and Grand Teton National Park is a draw as well. Jackson Hole, just south of the parks, has become one of America's elite year-round resort areas since the early 1980s, as well as home to a large number of wealthy households.

The juxtaposition of civilization and wilderness has created some thorny issues, including management of elk, grizzly bear and gray wolf habitat, as well as policies on snowmobiles and snow coaches in Yellowstone and ice climbs on the Shoshone River. Then there's the sage grouse, which has a habitat that covers about a quarter of the state's land area, including regions eyed for drilling. In 2020, conservationists celebrated a victory as a federal court vacated some sales of oil and gas rights that could have affected grouse habitat.

The settled part of Wyoming consists of medium-sized towns, which are the state's largest cities. It is a small state, a single community really, where people remember who played what position, when and how well, and for what high school football team. Wyoming is 84 percent white, 10 percent Hispanic, and 1 percent Black. In 1969, 14 Black students at the University of Wyoming were kicked off the football team for seeking to wear armbands to protest racial injustice; the university apologized to the surviving players in 2021, more than half a century later. (One of the nation's most prominent Black artists, Kanye West, has chosen Cody—founded by showman Buffalo Bill Cody in 1901 and home to 10,000 residents—as the locus for his musical and entrepreneurial empire, though he was unable to make the Wyoming ballot in his brief 2020 presidential run.) When it was still a territory in 1869, Wyoming was the first to give women the vote. (The exception: New Jersey allowed women with property to vote between 1776 and 1807, but there weren't many women with property.) Wyoming also had the nation's first woman governor, Nellie Tayloe Ross, in the 1920s.

There was once a sharp economic and regional split reflected in its partisan politics. The big economic interests—cattle ranchers, organized in the Wyoming Stock Growers Association, and the Union Pacific Railroad management—favored Republicans, as did the wildcatters, independent producers and oil company geologists. The main Democratic constituency was made up of Union Pacific Railroad workers who built the first transcontinental line across southern Wyoming in the 1860s. (Cheyenne was established because it was the midpoint between the UP's operations in Omaha and Ogden Utah.) The southern tier of counties, from Cheyenne through Laramie to Evanston, once voted Democratic. But now the Democrats are strongest in Teton County, which has voted Democratic for president in every election starting in 2004, as well as in Albany County, home of Laramie and the University of Wyoming, which Obama carried in 2008 and Biden won in 2020. Wyoming hasn't elected a Democrat to the Senate since 1970 or to the House since 1976, though it has had Democratic governors during that time. Given how much the GOP has tightened its hold on rural America, it may be a while before the Democrats win the governorship—or any statewide office— again. Today, the Democratic legislative caucuses consist of two senators and seven House members.

Still, compared with other solidly Republican states where religious conservatives are dominant, Wyoming has historically had a libertarian, live-and-let-live ethos. In 1994, on the same Election Day when the GOP was winning a competitive gubernatorial race by a 3-2 margin (and rolling to big gains nationally), Wyoming voters rejected a tough anti-abortion ballot measure by an equivalent 3-2 margin. Wyoming attracted negative attention with the gruesome 1998 murder of Matthew Shepard, a gay college student, in Laramie. Since then, Laramie has approved an ordinance that banned discrimination on the basis of sexual orientation or gender identity, and in 2020, it was home to sizable racial justice protests that led to policing reforms. Wyoming's two most recent governors, Matt Mead and Mark Gordon, come from the GOP's establishment wing. But the Republican Party has increasingly pushed a socially conservative agenda in Wyoming, including anti-abortion legislation, with religious conservatives increasingly supplanting libertarian-oriented Republicans in primaries. Rural Weld County, in increasingly blue Colorado, has pursued the idea of attaching itself to more conservative Wyoming; in 2021, Gordon expressed his support, though carrying out the plan would require several difficult steps.

In the 2016 presidential election, Trump's winning margins in the state's biggest counties save Teton all expanded, typically by 7 to 14 points over 2012. The 2020 election edged the state closer to the Democrats on the presidential level, but only barely, as Biden narrowed Trump's winning statewide margin by about three points. In addition to flipping Albany County, Biden increased his winning margin in Teton County by 10 points. He also narrowed Trump's margin of victory by a couple of points in both Laramie and Natrona counties. Still, Trump won both easily, and the surge in turnout benefited Republicans down the ballot; Democrats lost several of the remaining legislative seats they had, with the combined Democratic caucus dropping to nine seats out of 90, the lowest in at least a century. "People just feel like the Democratic Party has forgotten people in rural states in the West," Stan Blake, a Sweetwater County state representative who lost to a Libertarian candidate in 2020, told the Washington Post. But as Wyoming remains solidly Republican, it remains to be seen what variety of Republicanism remains dominant. One of the top elected Republicans in the state, Rep. Liz Cheney, faced fierce attacks from allies of Trump after she voted for Trump's impeachment in 2021. She lost her position as chairwoman of the House Republican Conference and faced a strong challenge for renomination in the 2022 election.

Cook Partisan Voting Index: R+26

Population		Race and Ethnicity		Income	
Total	578,759	White	90.90%	Median Income	65,003
Land area (sq. miles)	97,093	Black	1.20%	State Income Rank	19 out of 50
Pop/ sq mi	5.96	Latino	10.10%	Poverty Rate	10.10%
Born in state	43.00%	Asian	1.50%	With health insurance	87.70%
		Two or more races	2.70%	Cash public assistance	1.80%
Age Groups		Other	4.40%	Food stamp/SNAP	5.8%
Under 18	23.20%				
18-34	22.60%	**Education**		**Work**	
35-64	37.00%	H.S grad or less	35.60%	White Collar	36.30%
Over 64	17.10%	Some college	35.30%	Sales and Service	36.60%
		College Degree, 4 yr	18.80%	Blue Collar	27.10%
Military		Post grad	10.40%	Government	21.70%
Veteran/ Active Duty	10.00%				

Presidential Politics

2020 Caucus (D)	Biden (D)	10,912(72%)	Sanders (D)	4,206(28%)			
2016 Caucus (D)	Sanders (D)	4,122(57%)	Clinton (D)	3,131(43%)			
2016 Conv. (R)	Cruz (R)	1,128(69%)	Rubio (R)	231(14%)	Trump (R)	112 (7%)	
2020 Pres. Vote	Trump (R)	193,559(70%)	Biden (D)	73,491(27%)			
2016 Pres. Vote	Trump (R)	174,419(68%)	Clinton (D)	55,973(22%)	Johnson (L)	13,287 (5%)	

Wyoming has long been one of the country's most Republican states. It was Donald Trump's best state in both 2016 and 2020, and was Romney's No. 2 state in 2012. No Democrat has topped 40 percent of the statewide vote since Lyndon Johnson won it in his 1964 landslide. Trump defeated Joe Biden, 70%-27%, after beating Hillary Clinton, 68%-22%. In 2020, he won 21 of the state's 23 counties. Biden carried Teton County, home to the ski town of Jackson, and Albany County, home to Laramie and the University of Wyoming.

In the state's April 2016 Democratic caucuses, Bernie Sanders won 57 percent of the state convention delegates. In Republicans' March 11 county conventions, Texas Sen. Ted Cruz out-organized his competitors and defeated Florida Sen. Marco Rubio, 66%-20%, with Trump a distant third. In 2020, Democrats delayed their April caucuses two weeks because of the coronavirus. Sanders suspended his campaign in the interim, and Biden won, 66%-24%.

Congressional Districts

117th Congress Lineup	1R	116th Congress Lineup	1R

Mark Gordon (R)

Elected 2018, term expires 2023, 1st term; b. Mar. 14, 1957, New York, NY; Middlebury College, B.A., 1979; Unknown; Married (Jennie) 4 children.

Elected Office: WI Treasurer, 2012-2019.

Professional Career: Rancher.

Office: 200 W. 24th St. Cheyenne, 82002-0010; 307-777-7434; Fax: 307-632-3909

Sec. of State: Edward Buchanan (R)

State Legislature: **Senate:** 3D, 27R **House:** 9D, 50R, 1V

Election Results

Election	Name (Party)	Vote (%)
2018 General	Mark Gordon (R)	136,412 (67%)
	Mary Throne (D)	55,965 (28%)
	Rex Rammell (CNP)	6,751 (3%)
2018 Primary	Mark Gordon (R)	38,951 (33%)
	Foster Friess (R)	29,842 (26%)
	Harriet Hageman (R)	25,052 (22%)
	Sam Galeotos (R)	14,554 (13%)
	Taylor Haynes (R)	6,511 (6%)

Mark Gordon easily won the general election for governor of Wyoming in 2018 after prevailing in a hard-fought, six-way Republican primary. Gordon, previously the state treasurer, was the establishment choice in the primary, and in office he has pursued a pragmatically conservative agenda.

Gordon grew up on a ranch near Kaycee and has continued to ranch throughout much of his career, running a cow-calf operation and growing hay with his wife, Jennie. He earned a bachelor's degree from Middlebury College and then ran several businesses in Buffalo and Sheridan, including two devoted to outdoor recreation and tourism. He also worked in the oil and gas industry. Gordon polished his financial skills as a member of the Board of the Federal Reserve Bank of Kansas City between 2008 and 2012; he also served as a board member of the Nature Conservancy of Wyoming. He was appointed state treasurer in 2012 following the death of the incumbent, Joseph Meyer. Gordon was elected to a term of his own in 2014.

Gordon entered a wide-open race to succeed outgoing, two-term Gov. Matt Mead. Mead, a Republican, had been elected in 2010 to succeed two-term Democratic Gov. Dave Freudenthal. Mead easily won a second term in 2014, though he grappled with declining revenues as the state's large energy sector experienced a downturn. In Wyoming, the Republican Party is so dominant that most of the ideological debate occurs within the party; Mead tended to be a pragmatist, and Gordon followed his model.

In the primary, Gordon faced Foster Friess, a prominent GOP donor who received President Donald Trump's endorsement; natural-resources attorney Harriet Hageman; businessman Sam

Galeotos; rancher Taylor Haynes; and businessman Bill Dahlin. Friess, running as an outsider and with a relatively small footprint in state politics, sought to leverage his wealth and national conservative connections, and he topped his rivals in spending on advertising. But Gordon, touting a message of fiscal responsibility, won key in-state endorsements and secured 33 percent of the vote. Friess was second with 26 percent. (Friess died in 2021)

The general election was anticlimactic. The Democrats nominated a respected former legislator, Mary Throne, who agreed with Gordon on some issues, such as promoting carbon sequestration, securing a role for coal and natural gas, and criminal-justice reform, but differed on others, including nondiscrimination laws for sexual orientation and gender identity. Throne supported Medicaid expansion; Gordon wouldn't go that far, but he said he'd back a waiver program for the state's Medicaid program. Meanwhile, Rex ("T-Rex") Rammell of the Constitution Party attacked Gordon from the right, calling climate change the "greatest hoax in human history," while Larry Streumpf, of the Libertarian Party, took a more middle-of-the-road approach, backing wind power and a property tax increase to improve the state's financial picture. In the end, Gordon defeated Throne, 67%-28%.

In office, Gordon signed a bill to improve data collection about missing or murdered indigenous people in the state and another to enact a statewide lodging tax to fund tourism promotion. He vetoed a measure that would have mandated life-saving efforts for infants born alive following an attempted abortion, arguing that the legislation was redundant and intrusive. However, Gordon approved legislation to bar the University of Wyoming's insurance plan from paying for abortions. Under Gordon, the state sued Washington state over its blockage of an export terminal used by Wyoming coal producers. Gordon urged measures to support the state's struggling coal industry, while championing technological research to curb coal's carbon emissions. "Wyoming has the solutions for our climate," Gordon told the University of Wyoming Board of Trustees, according to the Laramie Boomerang. "If you push as hard as you can to put a 100 percent renewable platform on this planet, you have done nothing to eliminate carbon dioxide in the atmosphere. We can take our coal products and we can make them part of the solutions."

During the coronavirus pandemic, Gordon walked a policy tightrope. In March 2020, he ordered the closure of bars, gyms, schools, and other public spaces, but he was one of the few governors in the nation not to impose a statewide stay-at-home order. In July, he became visibly angry as he urged residents to wear masks. "When somebody sends me a note that says, 'Well these people are gonna die anyway, they're just dying sooner,' I gotta say, 'I'm offended,'" Gordon told reporters. Coronavirus cases spiked in fall and winter, as they did in the rest of the nation, but fell to below-average levels by early 2021. The budget was one of the biggest casualties of the pandemic: The fossil fuel sector, a major contributor to the state's fiscal base, was already weak before the pandemic, and it suffered even more after the virus hit. The state faced a projected $1.5 billion shortfall over two years, and the state government laid off employees for the first time since the 1980s.

In his 2021 State of the State, Gordon committed Wyoming to net-zero CO2 emissions, continuing to stress the role of carbon capture as part of an all of the above energy strategy, including wind, solar, and hydrogen. In response to the Biden administration's moratorium on oil and gas leasing on federal land, Wyoming filed suit in federal District Court, alleging the president's executive order violated a number of laws applicable to leasing of federal lands .

By the time the legislature met in early 2021, the state's general fund revenues had somewhat stabilized. Still, the Legislature approved a supplemental budget with $430 million in cuts, But Wyoming's constitutionally mandated state funding of education faced significant shortfalls, with the Senate favoring larger cuts than the House and the House favoring some revenue increase. Gordon requested a 10 percent spending reduction from school districts .

John Barrasso (R)

Appointed 2007, term expires 2024, 2nd full term, b. Jul 21, 1952; Reading, PA; Georgetown University, B.S., 1974; Georgetown University School of Medicine, M.D., 1978; Presbyterian; Married (Bobbi Brown); 3 children (2 from previous marriage).

Elected Office: WY Senate, 2002-2007.

Professional Career: Orthopedic surgeon, 1983-2007; RNC Chairman, 1992-1996; Chief of staff, WY Medical Center, 2003-2005; Medical Director, WY Health Fairs.

DC Office: 307 DSOB 20510, 202-224-6441, Fax: 202-224-1724, barrasso.senate.gov

State Offices: Casper, 307-261-6413; Cheyenne, 307-772-2451; Riverton, 307-856-6642; Rock Springs, 307-362-5012; Sheridan, 307-672-6456.

Committees: Senate Republican Conference Chairman. *Energy & Natural Resources (RMM)*: Ex Officio membership on all subcommittees. *Finance*: Energy, Natural Resources & Infrastructure; Health Care; International Trade, Customs & Global Competitiveness. *Foreign Relations*: Africa & Global Health Policy; Europe & Regional Security Cooperation; Internat'l Dev Instit & Internat'l Econ, Energy & Environ Policy; West Hem Crime Civ Sec Dem Rights & Women's Issues.

Group Ratings

	ADA	ACLU	AFL-CIO	LCV	COC	HAFA	ACU	CFG	FRC
2020	-	8%	-	0%	-	74%	88%	-	-
2019	0%	C	16%	7%	73%	C	89%	59%	100%

Almanac Ratings 2019-2020

	Economy	Social	Foreign	Composite
Liberal	6%	6%	0%	4%
Conservative	94%	94%	100%	96%

Key Votes of the 116th Congress

1. EPA clean energy rules	N	5. Russia sanctions	N	9. Barr as Atty. General	Y
2. U.S./Mex./Can. trade deal	Y	6. Troops in SYR, AFG	Y	10. Spending at the border	Y
3. Cut unemployment benefits	Y	7. Veto arms sales to Saudis	N	11. Coney Barrett to Sup. Ct.	Y
4. Shelton to Fed Reserve	Y	8. Defense $$$, veto override	Y	12. Electoral College objections	N

Election Results

Election	Name (Party)	Vote (%)		Cand. Spent	Ind. Exp. Support	Ind. Exp. Oppose
2018 General	John Barrasso (R)	136,210	(67%)	$4,267,798		
	Gary Trauner (D)	61,227	(30%)	$895,349		
	Joe Porambo (Lib)	5,658	(3%)			
2018 Primary	John Barrasso (R)	74,292	(65%)			
	David Dodson (R)	32,647	(29%)			

Prior winning percentages: 2018 (67%), 2012 (76%), 2008 special (73%)

Since his appointment in June 2007 to fill a Senate vacancy, John Barrasso, now Wyoming's senior senator, has climbed the Republican leadership ranks. As chairman of the Republican Conference, he's become a top lieutenant to GOP Leader Mitch McConnell. He has used that clout to benefit Western states, including spearheading the enactment of a nationwide water resource bill in 2018. Unlike many of his regional colleagues, Barrasso has been willing to discuss the realities of climate change and how it could be addressed with emerging technologies.

Barrasso grew up in Reading Pennsylvania, the son of a World War II veteran who made a living as a cement finisher and who took his family to Washington every four years for presidential inaugurations. Barrasso earned his undergraduate and medical degrees from Georgetown University and moved to Wyoming in the 1980s to set up practice as an orthopedic surgeon in Casper. Barrasso made his name in local politics, serving as a Republican national committeeman and as state party treasurer. He was a local radio and television personality, dispensing practical medical advice on news programs and in public service announcements.

In 1996, a decade before his appointment to the Senate, Barrasso ran for an open seat when Republican Sen. Alan Simpson retired. He faced then-state Sen. Michael Enzi in a crowded GOP primary in which abortion played a key role. Running as a moderate, Barrasso favored abortion rights and had opposed a 1994 constitutional amendment to ban most abortions. Enzi, who had support from social conservatives, opposed abortion rights and edged out Barrasso 32%-30%. The two joined forces for the general election, with Barrasso serving as Enzi's finance chairman in the fall.

In 2002, Barrasso won election to the state Senate, where he worked on health care issues and chaired the Transportation, Highways, and Military Affairs Committee. He sponsored a bill to increase the criminal penalty for killing a pregnant woman, but Democratic Gov. Dave Freudenthal vetoed it. He occasionally crossed the political aisle to join with Democrats, backing a bill to exempt food from the state sales tax and supporting a ban on smoking in public buildings. He sponsored a law enabling physicians to talk freely with patients about medical complications without putting themselves at risk of the conversations being used against them in a lawsuit.

After Republican Sen. Craig Thomas died of leukemia in June 2007, Wyoming's Republican State Central Committee had 15 days to select three candidates to fill the vacancy; the governor was required to pick one of them. That triggered a scramble, as 31 candidates applied for consideration. Unlike in his Senate bid 11 years earlier, Barrasso emphasized his conservative credentials to the committee. "I believe in limited government, lower taxes, less spending, traditional family values, local control and a strong national defense," he told the committee. He noted that he had an "A" rating from the National Rifle Association, voted for prayer in public schools, sponsored legislation "to protect the sanctity of life" and opposed same-sex marriage.

The Republican committee named three finalists: Barrasso; Cynthia Lummis, who had served 14 years in the Legislature and two terms as state treasurer (and is now the state's junior senator); and Tom Sansonetti, who had been Thomas' chief of staff and an assistant attorney general in the Bush administration. Lummis was not on good terms with the governor, and Sansonetti had been a lobbyist for mining and ranching interests. Barrasso, by contrast, had worked with Freudenthal on health care issues. The governor tapped him for the seat. He ran in 2008 to fill out Thomas' term and was unopposed in the Republican primary. In the general election, he defeated Democratic lawyer Nick Carter, an underfunded political newcomer, 73%-27%. Wyoming has not elected a Democrat to the Senate since 1970.

Barrasso has shown wide-ranging interests, though they often have a local tilt. In 2009, he showed his early interest in health care and regional issues when he won approval of a provision to benefit rural doctors and hospitals. He broke with many conservatives—but joined many farm groups--in calling for lifting the U.S. ban on travel to Cuba, saying U.S. citizens should be free to visit relatives in the communist country. He proposed legislation to protect undeveloped areas of the Wyoming range from oil and gas development and to preserve 387 miles around the Snake River. It became law as part of a larger land management bill in 2009. As Indian Affairs Committee chairman in 2015, he worked with Montana Democrat Jon Tester, the committee's vice chairman, to reintroduce a bill to streamline federal reviews of Native American energy projects.

As a veteran member of the Energy and Natural Resources Committee and the Environment and Public Works Committee, Barrasso has reflected the views of constituents and local industries skeptical about federal regulation. In 2009, he said Democrats' cap-and-trade bill regulating carbon emissions would have unfairly punished his state's farmers and ranchers. In 2013, he lashed out at President Barack Obama's nominee to head the Environmental Protection Agency, Gina McCarthy, asserting that the agency was "making it impossible for our coal miners to feed their families." He filed legislation to bar the EPA from regulating greenhouse gases blamed for climate change.

He found some legislative success. Barrasso supported removing gray wolves from the Endangered Species List, telling The Associated Press: "This is a Wyoming concern that requires a Wyoming solution. It does not require interference from Washington." Barrasso loudly objected to a CIA center on climate change. The agency closed the center in 2012.

With Oklahoma Sen. Jim Inhofe term-limited as chairman of the Environment Committee, Barrasso took control in January 2017—the same month President Donald Trump brought radical change in resource policies and enforcement. Barrasso supported Scott Pruitt's nomination to lead the EPA in the Trump administration. Pruitt, a former attorney general of Oklahoma, "will be the strong leader the EPA needs," Barrasso said. As Pruitt ran into numerous ethical controversies, Barrasso stood by him—initially. But he agreed in June to Democratic demands to hold an oversight hearing to review conflicts of interest at Pruitt's EPA. Three weeks later, in the face of declining support from Republicans, Pruitt resigned, which Barrasso said was the right decision.

At a February 2017 hearing on proposals to "modernize" the Endangered Species Act, Barrasso said the law "is not working today" and he cited the many public officials and rural groups that have sought change. The law has not been reauthorized since 1992. In July 2018, he unveiled his proposal to revise the law by giving states greater authority to manage wildlife within their borders. A highlight was a provision to form federal-state teams to create conservation strategies for a listed species. "We must do more than just keep listed species on life support," Barrasso said. "We need to see them recovered." In 2020, he proposed requiring the Interior Department to monitor a species for five years after it was delisted from the endangered list.

Barrasso turned his attention to legislation to fund water infrastructure projects by the Army Corps of Engineers—including inland waterways, dams, irrigation and water storage. The bill received broad bipartisan backing and was signed by Trump in 2018. Included was modification of the Fontenelle Dam to permit increased storage along the Colorado River in Wyoming. With broad support, he won enactment of a bill in January 2019 that overhauled internal operations at the Nuclear Regulatory Commission.

Barrasso's attention as chairman turned to efforts during the Trump administration for a bipartisan infrastructure bill, working with ranking Democrat Tom Carper of Delaware. The committee unanimously passed a bill to spend $287 million on highway funding over five years, a 27 percent uptick from previous spending levels for roads, bridges and transit systems. "We surprised a few people today," Barrasso told the Casper Star-Tribune in July 2019. "We've been working on this all the way through behind-the-scenes, quietly—talking to other members, working things out to get to 21-nothing. This is a big, bipartisan show."

But there were still several roadblocks. First, there was disagreement with the Democratic-controlled House, which passed a $1.5 trillion plan. "The House basically took the 'Green New Deal' and changed the title to House infrastructure bill, so we didn't have any luck working with them," Barrasso told the Wall Street Journal. And Senate Finance Chairman Chuck Grassley of Iowa said in February 2020 that the Senate would have a "very difficult time finding the financing" for the legislation, Roll Call reported. Trump pitched his own $2 trillion idea in February 2020, but it never went anywhere, with the president's repeated "infrastructure weeks" usually falling apart, distracted by any number of ongoing controversies, so much so that they became a running joke in Washington. Barrasso pushed the infrastructure plan to be included in the July COVID-19 stimulus bill, but that too failed. Once Democrats took control of the White House and Congress in 2021, though, their infrastructure priorities changed. Barrasso blasted the Biden administration's $2 trillion proposal, which would give more money to electric cars and senior home care, as a "mere slush fund for liberal spending."

Barrasso's infrastructure bill, which unanimously passed the committee, notably acknowledged the existence of climate change, which many Republicans still deny, and provided funding to limit emissions from vehicles. Barrasso's thinking on the issue has evolved. Writing in a 2018 New York Times op-ed, he conceded that "the climate is changing and we, collectively, have a responsibility to do something about it." However, he opposed carbon taxes and higher energy costs to offset emissions. Instead, Barrasso pushed for further innovation to reverse warming trends, including new research into turning emissions into commodities and possible direct air capture of carbon dioxide in the atmosphere, a process being explored in Wyoming coal areas. Some progressives criticized that approach, while Barrasso called the "Green New Deal" pushed by progressives as a "socialist manifesto."

Barrasso gained a broader partisan platform, becoming a firm McConnell ally . In 2011, he took control of the Republican Policy Committee. In 2019, he moved up to become Republican Conference chairman, the No. 3 leadership position. At the same time, Rep. Liz Cheney of Wyoming chaired the House Republican Conference—an unusual mark for one state. Barrasso had largely been a loyal ally to Trump, but the senator broke with the former president in endorsing Cheney for reelection in 2022 after Trump had singled her out as his top target after she voted for his impeachment in the aftermath of the January 6 Capitol insurrection. "I support her," Barrasso said on NBC's "Meet the Press" in March 2021. "I disagree with her completely on the issue of impeachment. She voted one way, I voted the other." When Trump repeatedly attacked Dr. Anthony Fauci during the coronavirus pandemic, Barrasso came to his defense, calling the longtime head of the National Institute of Allergy and Infectious Diseases "one of the finest physicians and Americans you will ever meet."

In 2016, Barrasso chaired the Platform Committee of the Republican National Convention, where he worked with officials of the Trump campaign to find acceptable provisions. Barrasso occasionally offered mild critiques or warnings to Trump. Asked in an interview on CNN whether Trump should release his tax returns, Barrasso said, "I think it would be a good idea. I'm somebody who's in favor of transparency and openness." In response to Trump's travel ban on citizens from several Muslim-majority nations, which he issued a week after he took office, Barrasso said, "a religious test or ban is against everything our country stands for."

With Barrasso facing reelection in 2018, his comments caught the attention of some conservatives in Wyoming. Erik Prince, former head of the security contractor Blackwater USA, said that he was considering a challenge to Barrasso and had been encouraged by Steve Bannon, a former executive chairman of Breitbart and a onetime top Trump aide.

When Prince decided not to run, little-known businessman David Dodson self-financed nearly $2 million on a GOP primary challenge that sought to depict Barrasso as a Washington insider and advocated "a new way of doing business." Trump boosted Barrasso with a tweet that he was "absolutely outstanding in every way." Barrasso won the primary with 65 percent of the vote. In a November challenge from Democrat Gary Trauner, an executive at a medical center in Jackson Hole, Barrasso won 67%-30%. Trauner had run competitive campaigns for the House a decade earlier.

Barrasso was in line to chair the Energy committee. After Republicans lost Senate control in 2021, he became the ranking member instead.

Cynthia Lummis (R)

Elected 2020, term expires 2026, 1st term, b. Sep 10, 1954; Cheyenne, WY; University of Wyoming, B.S., 1976; University of Wyoming, B.S., 1978; University of Wyoming College of Law, J.D., 1985; Lutheran; Widow (Alvin Wiederspahn); 1 child ; 1 grandchild

Elected Office: WY House 1979-83, 1985-93; WY Senate, 1994-95; WY Treas., 1998-2006; U.S. House: 2009-17.

Professional Career: Attorney; Clerk, WY Supreme Court, 1985; General Counsel, Office of the Governor, 1995-1997; Interim Director, Office of State Lands and Investments, WY, 1997-1998; Operator, Sweetgrass Development; Owner, Lummis Ranch.

DC Office: 124 RSOB 20510, 202-224-3424, Fax: 202-228-0359, lummis.senate.gov

State Offices: Casper, 307-261-6572; Cheyenne, 307-772-2477; Cody, 307-527-9444.

Committees: *Banking, Housing & Urban Affairs*: Financial Institutions & Consumer Protection; Housing, Transportation & Community Development; Securities, Insurance & Investment. *Commerce, Science & Transportation*: Communications, Media & Broadband; Space & Science (RMM); Surface Transportation, Maritime Freight & Ports; Tourism, Trade & Export Promotion. *Environment & Public Works*: Clean Air & Nuclear Safety; Fisheries, Water, and Wildlife (RMM); Transportation & Infrastructure.

Election Results

Election	Name (Party)	Vote (%)		Cand. Spent	Ind. Exp. Support	Ind. Exp. Oppose
2020 General	Cynthia Lummis (R)	198,100	(73%)	$2,552,028	$780,707	
	Merav Ben-David (D)	72,766	(27%)	$563,690	$10	$66
2020 Primary	Cynthia Lummis (R)	63,511	(60%)			
	Robert Short (R)	13,473	(13%)			
	Bryan Miller (R)	10,946	(10%)			
	Donna Rice (R)	5,881	(6%)			

Republican Cynthia Lummis of Wyoming returned to Congress in 2021 after serving four terms in the House and stepping down in 2016. As a hard-line conservative and founding member of the House Freedom Caucus, Lummis won election to the Senate without facing a serious threat in the primary or general elections. Probably the turning point of her campaign was when Rep. Liz Cheney, who had succeeded Lummis in the House, said that she would not challenge her for the GOP nomination. That decision, which surprised many Republicans, averted what would likely have been a hard-fought and costly contest.

Born on a cattle ranch in Laramie County, Lummis earned bachelor's degrees in animal science and biology from the University of Wyoming. In college, she interned in the state Senate, an experience that opened the door to her career in public service. She started a cattle business, Lummis Livestock, which she later expanded.

In a lengthy 2011 report on her finances, WyoFile—an independent Wyoming news outlet supported by several foundations—wrote that Lummis was among the wealthiest members of Congress. Her career path and personal finances, according to the extensive report, "reveal an ambitious, intelligent woman from a wealthy family who gained political clout through her work on key state issues like tax revenue and the management of billions in state money."

With her two siblings, Lummis owned Sweet grass, a 2,350-acre development on the family's former ranchland. One of the largest ever in Cheyenne, the project was designed to include village shops, residential neighborhoods, trails and open space; plans for a $55 million hotel and convention center were announced in 2019.

At 24, Lummis became the youngest woman ever elected to the Wyoming Legislature. She served from 1979 to 1983 and again from 1985 to 1993. While serving in the state House, she earned a law degree from the University of Wyoming and then joined her family's law firm before returning to the political world. After winning election to the state Senate, she also became general counsel to Gov. Jim Geringer. He appointed her as interim director of the Office of State Lands and Investments.

In 1998, she was elected state treasurer in her first campaign for statewide office. In that office, where she served eight years, Lummis claimed credit for diversifying the state's investment portfolio by reducing its holdings in the mortgage giants Fannie Mae and Freddie Mac.

In 2008, when Republican Rep. Barbara Cubin announced her retirement from the House, Lummis ran for the seat and won the Republican primary with 46 percent of the vote against Mark Gordon, a rancher who out-spent her, 4 to 1. In the general election, she faced Democrat Gary Trauner, a businessman who lost to Cubin by 1,012 votes in 2006. Lummis won, 53%-43%, and consistently won reelection with at least 69 percent of the vote.

During her first term in the House, she won bipartisan approval of her bill for the Secretary of Interior to study the feasibility of adding the Heart Mountain Relocation Center to the National Park Service's portfolio. Subsequently, the center—which held thousands of Japanese Americans against their will during World War II—became a part of the National Park Service as a National Historic Landmark.

After the House GOP takeover in 2010, Lummis showed enough party loyalty to gain a seat on the Appropriations Committee. Two years later, after a dispute with Republican leadership over committee legislation, she took the unusual step of leaving the panel. That led to her positions as vice chair of the Natural Resources Committee and chair of the Oversight and Reform Subcommittee on Government Operations. She often was the only Republican woman serving on those committees. "It's pretty challenging within the conference for women, I've got to be honest," Lummis said.

Lummis co-chaired the Western Caucus, a 40-member group that frequently assailed Obama administration policies. "It's as if they sit around and try to out-do each other on how badly they can hurt Western economies and communities," she said after President Barack Obama released his proposed budget in 2013. She took a hard line against much of the federal land policy pursued by the Interior Department.

Lummis later said that she voted against the Obama administration more often than any other member of Congress. In 2016, she claimed credit for changes to the appropriations bill for the Interior Department that marked "a renewed effort to reinstate and reinforce state and local stewardship of our land, our water, our energy." She also passed that year the National Forest Systems Trail Stewardship Act, a bipartisan measure to maintain more than 157,000 miles of trails within the national forests.

As a proponent of firearms, Lummis filed multiple bills to prevent the State Department from interfering with imports of collectable firearms. She co-sponsored a successful proposal to permit gun owners to carry concealed weapons in federal parks.

She again ran into trouble with party leaders after she split with most Republicans in 2015 and voted against giving trade promotion authority to Obama. As a result, she was one of three Republicans whom Rep. Steve Scalise, then House majority whip, removed from his team. Publicly, at least, she voiced no hard feelings. A spokesman said Lummis understood that leadership members were expected to be team players, though more rebellious members were angered by the crackdown. With other Republicans in the Freedom Caucus, she worked on proposals to reduce federal spending and the deficit.

Lummis crossed the aisle to work with Democratic Rep. Carolyn Maloney of New York on a new push for an Equal Rights Amendment to the Constitution. Recalling that after graduating from college she was denied a job as a bank teller because of her gender, Lummis said, "When you face those kinds of reality in life, they stay with you."

After Donald Trump's election as president in 2016, Lummis served on his transition team and was interviewed to be secretary of the Interior. Instead, the House member from a neighboring state, Ryan Zinke of Montana, got that job. She was considered again in 2019, as a successor to Zinke.

When Republican Sen. Michael Enzi announced in May 2019 that he would not seek a fifth term, Lummis quickly made known her interest, citing the growing national debt as one reason she wanted to return to Congress. Lummis had retired in 2016 to tend to the family ranch after her husband's death two years earlier. Attention also turned to Cheney—if only because she had taken steps toward challenging Enzi in the GOP primary in 2014. Eventually, Cheney decided against that candidacy, she said, because of "serious health issues" in her family.

Cheney succeeded Lummis in the House in 2016, suggesting that the former vice president's daughter was prepared to take a longer route to the Senate. Instead, she issued a statement in January 2020 that she was committed to her position in the House leadership, where she chaired the Republican Conference. (In early 2021, Cheney lost her position after criticizing Trump's falsehoods about the 2020 election and his attempts to overturn its results.) That same day, the conservative Club for Growth endorsed Lummis for the Senate seat, with a statement that she was "a principled, pro-growth conservative who is a staunch advocate for limited government, liberty and economic freedom."

In a field of 10 candidates, Lummis won the Republican nomination with 60 percent of the vote, including all but one of the state's 23 counties. Robert Short, a former tech entrepreneur who was runner-up with 12 percent, won his home of Douglas-based Converse County.

In a state where three-term Sen. Gale McGee, who lost reelection in 1976, was the most recent Democrat who served in the Senate, the profile of the Democratic opponent of Lummis might have been her most notable feature: Merav Ben-David, a professor of zoology at the University of Wyoming, was born and raised in Israel. She moved to the United States to pursue her interest in wildlife ecology—with research that took her from Kenya to an ice-breaker in the Arctic Ocean. Ben-David, who focused her campaign on the need to address climate change, did not pose a serious threat. Lummis won her blow-out victory, 73%-27%, losing the Democratic island of Teton County. She spent $3 million throughout the race, including a $590,500 personal loan, while Ben-David spent just over $563,000. Lummis' win marked an important addition to the number of GOP women in the Senate, especially after both Georgia's Kelly Loeffler and Arizona's Martha McSally lost.

On January 6, 2021, after the Trump supporters stormed the Capitol during the Electoral College vote tally, Lummis joined six other Senate Republicans in objecting to the Pennsylvania results. (On an earlier vote on Arizona's votes, she had not objected.) In April 2021, Lummis told Politico that Trump's unsubstantiated claims of widespread voter fraud were "probably an overreaction." She added, "I do not believe the fraud, that did occur, would have changed the election."

In the Senate, Lummis was named to the Environment and Public Works Committee, a crucial one for Wyoming, especially after Sen. John Barrasso, the former chairman, had rotated off. She also got seats on the Commerce and Banking committees. She has been enthusiastic about crypto currency, telling Fox News, "I know there isn't much known about Bitcoin, especially in the Congress." In an interview with CNBC, she argued that Bitcoin was a better source of value because paper money has a finite supply. "That will not be the case with Bitcoin. Bitcoin provides a more stable value to people who are either saving now to live comfortably in the future but also people who are on fixed income or approaching fixed income now," she said, adding that it could be a "stabilizing mechanism for worldwide exchanges."

Liz Cheney (R)

Elected 2016, 3rd term, b. Jul 28, 1966; Madison, WI; CO College, B.A., 1988; University of Chicago Law School, J.D., 1996; Methodist; Married (Philip Perry); 5 children.

Professional Career: Staff, United States Agency for International Development, 1989-1992; Staff, United States Department of State, 1992; Attorney, International Finance Corporation, 199-2002; Deputy Assistant Secretary of State for Near Eastern Affairs, United States Department of State, 2002-2004; Presidential Campaign Staff, George W. Bush, 2004; Principal Deputy Assistant Secretary of State for Near Eastern Affairs, United States Department of State, 2005-2009; Non profit executive; Television commentator.

DC Office: 416 CHOB 20515, 202-225-2311, Fax: 202-225-3057, cheney.house.gov
State Offices: Casper, 307-261-6595; Cheyenne, 307-772-2595; Gillette, 307-414-1677; Riverton, 307-463-0482.

Committees: *Armed Services*: Intelligence & Special Operations; Strategic Forces.

Group Ratings

	ADA	ACLU	AFL-CIO	LCV	COC	HAFA	ACU	CFG	FRC
2020	**	10%	**	5%	-	82%	78%	**	-
2019	5%	C	30%	3%	79%	C	79%	65%	100%

Almanac Ratings 2019-2020

	Economy	Social	Foreign	Composite
Liberal	30%	4%	33%	23%
Conservative	70%	96%	67%	77%

Key Votes of the 116th Congress

1. U.S./Mex./Can. trade deal	Y	5. Russia sanctions	Y
2. First Coronavirus response	Y	6. Troops in Syria	Y
3. HEROES Act	N	7. Veto arms sales to Saudis	N
4. CASH Act	N	8. Defense $$$, veto override	Y

9. Firearms background checks	N
10. Spending at the border	Y
11. Marijuana liberalized rules	N
12. Electoral College objections	N

Election Results

Election	Name (Party)	Vote (%)		Cand. Spent	Ind. Exp. Support	Ind. Exp. Oppose
2020 General	Liz Cheney (R)	185,732	(69%)	$1,331,843	$1,620	
	Lynnette Grey Bull (D)	66,576	(25%)	$70,711	$10	
	Richard Brubaker (L)	10,154	(4%)			
	Jeff Haggit (C)	7,905	(3%)			
2020 Primary	Liz Cheney (R)	78,870	(73%)			
	Blake Stanley (R)	28,039	(26%)			

Prior winning percentages: 2018 (64%), 2016 (62%)

Liz Cheney of Wyoming was elected in 2016 to the seat that her father, Dick Cheney, held for a decade before he became secretary of Defense and, later, vice president. In November 2018, she was elected—without opposition—to chair the House Republican Conference. Cheney made a quick impression on other Republicans with her informed and often outspoken style. Despite earlier interest in running for the Senate, she decided not to seek in 2020 the open seat of retiring Sen. Mike Enzi.

Her increasing antagonism with President Donald Trump led her to cast one of 10 Republican votes for his impeachment in January 2021. That raised the ire of many conservatives among House Republicans. Although she easily survived a challenge to her Conference position weeks later, her future in GOP politics—both in Wyoming and in the House—seemed cloudy. When House GOP leaders turned against her, the Republican Conference ousted her in May—on a voice vote—and replaced her with Rep. Elise Stefanik of New York, who promised support of Trump. The move stirred both doubts about Cheney's reelection prospects in Wyoming and potential opportunities for leadership of the post-Trump party.

Growing up in the Cheney family, she resided chiefly in the Washington D.C. area and said she split her time in Casper Wyoming. She got her bachelor's from Colorado College and her law degree from the University of Chicago. Before law school, she worked with the State Department and the U.S. Agency for International Development, then joined the consulting firm of Richard Armitage. Cheney practiced international law in the private sector. In 2002, she was appointed deputy assistant secretary of State for Near Eastern Affairs and remained at the State Department until the end of the Bush presidency, except for a break to work on the Bush-Cheney reelection campaign. With the change in administration, she served as chair of Keep America Safe, a nonprofit organization, and assisted her father with his writing.

In 2013, Cheney mounted a challenge to Enzi , who was seeking his fourth term. She was criticized as an outsider who had spent little time living in the state. She was distracted by an unexpected intra-family split over same-sex marriage with her sister Mary, who is a lesbian. Trailing by more than 50 points in a poll, Cheney withdrew from the race in January 2014, citing health issues in her family. Enzi was easily reelected.

When Republican Rep. Cynthia Lummis announced that she would retire in 2016, Cheney ran for the open seat. She was endorsed by a wide range of national Republicans and conservative leaders. In the eight-candidate GOP primary, her chief challenger was state Sen. Leland Christensen, a leader of the "constitutionalist" movement; he was endorsed by Sen. Rand Paul, who frequently clashed with the Cheneys on national security issues. Christensen accused Cheney of repeatedly lying or misleading voters about her campaign and experience in Wyoming. Cheney spent $2.1 million for the cycle, more than three times as much as her top three GOP opponents combined. Cheney took 40 percent of the vote to 22 percent for Christensen.

In the general election, Democrat Ryan Greene was a political newcomer who worked for an oil-field services company. He called himself a "persuader" and said Cheney was "a bomb-thrower" and "long on political ambition but short on Wyoming experience." He spent $184,000 and was largely ignored by national Democrats and liberal groups. Cheney supported Donald Trump for president, though she described as "appalling" his comments about groping women that were publicized in October. Cheney won, 62%-30%.

In the House, Cheney got committee assignments that catered to her local and national interests, on Natural Resources and Armed Services. In February 2017, the House passed her bill to repeal the Bureau of Land Management's planning and management strategies, which were approved during the final days of the Obama administration. Trump signed the bill the following month. In November 2018, the Resources panel approved her bill to increase local input in enforcement of the Public Lands Act, including three wilderness areas of Wyoming that had been studied for four decades.

Revisiting an approach her father had pursued years earlier, Cheney urged Trump to restore enhanced interrogation techniques in the war on terror. Working on the annual defense spending bill in 2017, she added a provision to assure that at least 400 intercontinental ballistic missiles were retained at their site in Wyoming. With Republican Sen. Tom Cotton of Arkansas, she filed legislation that was designed to reduce Russia's advantage in tactical nuclear weapons. In December 2018, she said Trump had made a "serious strategic error" in calling for the withdrawal of U.S. troops from Syria, where they were supporting the fight against the ISIS caliphate. "American retreat will aid our adversaries, Russia and Iran, and hurt our allies, including Israel." Trump subsequently reversed himself and kept the troops in Syria.

Following the 2018 election in which Republicans lost House control, Cheney was elected without opposition to chair the House GOP Conference. Rep. Cathy McMorris Rodgers of Washington, who had held the position, decided not to seek another term. With direct criticism of her predecessor, Cheney wrote to other Republicans that the election results had shown that "our message isn't breaking through" and that "we must fundamentally overhaul and modernize our House GOP communications operation." In January 2019, she was an early proponent of the decision by Republican leaders to strip Rep. Steve King of Iowa of his committee assignments following his positive comments about "White supremacy."

With Enzi's May 2019 retirement announcement, Cheney was the initial favorite to succeed him. But the early decision by Lummis to seek the Senate seat led Cheney to hesitate. In January 2020, she decided not to run for the Senate. "I believe I can have the biggest impact for the people of Wyoming by remaining in leadership in the House of Representatives and working to take our Republican majority back," Cheney said. Her statement was viewed as a sign of interest, and confidence, in moving up the House leadership ladder. Meanwhile, she had growing clashes with Trump. In March 2020, she called for strong public actions to respond to what she called the "China virus." She told the House, "we must do all we can now to protect" Americans. When some Republicans, including in the Trump administration, criticized as alarmist Anthony Fauci, the government's chief expert on infectious diseases, Cheney tweeted that he was "one of the finest public servants we have ever had … [whose] only interest is saving lives." In foreign policy, when the administration reached an agreement with the Taliban to withdraw U.S. forces from Afghanistan, she demanded full details and said that she had "concerns."

Her independence raised growing concerns among Republicans that she was not voicing sufficient support for Trump. Some conservatives discussed the possibility of challenging her for another term as GOP Conference chair, Politico reported in October 2020, though none stepped forward. Still, she was outspoken about post-election claims of voter fraud by Trump and his lawyers. "If they have genuine evidence of this, they are obligated to present it immediately in court and to the American people," she said two weeks after the election. She was in the minority of House Republicans who voted to certify the Electoral College results in January 2021.

That same day, the breaking point for Cheney was the riot at the Capitol. In criticism that was among the harshest delivered that day, and which was cited admiringly by many Democrats, she said, "there is no question that the president formed the mob, the president incited the mob, the president addressed the mob. He lit the flame. This is what America is not." A week later, she voted for the impeachment charges. "The president could have immediately and forcefully intervened to stop the violence. He did not. There has never been a greater betrayal by a president of the United States of his office and his oath to the Constitution," she said.

Her independence stirred outrage among many conservatives in the House. At a rally outside the state capitol in Cheyenne, Rep. Matt Gaetz of Florida encouraged local Republicans to challenge her in the 2022 primary. But when other opponents forced a vote in the GOP Conference to strip Cheney of her chairmanship, their effort was overwhelmingly defeated—reportedly on a 145-61 vote. Minority Leader Kevin McCarthy spoke on her behalf, as did McMorris Rodgers. Subsequently, on most issues, Cheney remained an active GOP lieutenant.

At home, she has faced token Republican opposition in her two reelection campaigns. In the 2018 primary, two opponents each spent less than $5,000. She won with 68 percent of the vote. In 2020, she took 74 percent against another weakly funded GOP challenger.

Still, as more credible challengers stepped forward to challenge her in Wyoming in 2022, Trump's promised opposition to her reelection raised questions about her future. Her continuing outspoken criticism of Trump led McCarthy to decide that her role in House leadership was no longer tenable. After she gave up her post without a fight, Cheney stepped up her attacks of Trump and the need for the GOP to move beyond him.

THE INSULAR TERRITORIES

AMERICAN SAMOA

American Samoa, the only American territory south of the equator, remains almost as Polynesian today as it was when the United States took possession of it in 1900 at the request of tribal chiefs. These seven hot, rainy islands are 2,500 miles southwest of Hawaii, 1,700 miles northeast of New Zealand and have a land area slightly larger than the District of Columbia.

American Samoa has 55,000 people, the vast majority of them on the island of Tutuila. The islands' population had rapidly grown in recent decades, but has dipped from a peak of 58,000 amid economic struggles. Fear that outsiders would change the culture prompted demands for stricter immigration standards, though the population remained 89% Samoan as of 2010. A federal law in 1940 classified American Samoans as U.S. nationals but not as U.S. citizens; they can serve in the military, but not as officers. Many residents oppose automatic citizenship on grounds that it would impede longstanding traditions and cultural practices, such as communal land ownership for families. American Samoans living in the states, however, argue that obtaining citizenship is too onerous. A federal judge ruled in 2019 that the 14th amendment, which grants citizenship to anyone born in the U.S., applies to American Samoans. The federal government and the government of American Samoa have appealed the case.

The Interior Department has overseen administration of American Samoa since 1956 and operates a National Park based in northern Tutuila, which attracts close to 14,000 visitors per year. Due to local customs that prohibit selling the land on which the park sits, the U.S. government has leased it from local villages. American Samoa adopted its own constitution in 1967. Residents elect a governor and a two-house legislature known as the Fono. The secretary of the Interior appoints the chief justice and associate justice of the High Court. About 16 percent of American Samoans are Mormon. Many are bilingual. Close to 90 percent of the population speaks Samoan at home, but government is mostly conducted in English. Fono proceedings are in Samoan, and court sessions are conducted in English but translated into Samoan. Within this governmental framework, older Samoan traditions and politics survive. Local chiefs, or matai, oversee communal lands and kinship systems called aigas. The territory has had a non-voting delegate in Congress since 1981.

Pago Pago, the largest town in American Samoa, has one of the finest natural harbors in the Pacific. But the market economy has not made much progress here. American Samoa leans heavily on the federal government, which contributes more than half of its revenues. The territorial government employs almost 45 percent of the workforce. The tuna canning industry, the only real private sector work in the territory, has suffered in the past decade. Two big tuna canneries owned by StarKist and Chicken of the Sea once provided one-third of U.S. canned tuna and employed more than 5,000 workers. But dipping demand, international competition, regularly enforced minimum wage increases and regulatory issues decimated the industry and hurt the local economy. In 2020, things turned around for the industry: The coronavirus pandemic reignited demand for canned tuna due to its low cost. Producers had trouble meeting demand and some stores limited bulk purchasing. As of December 2020, American Samoa had not recorded a single case of COVID-19. The territory implemented a strict travel ban early in the pandemic, stranding some residents elsewhere and closing off the outside world entirely.

After the Bank of Hawaii, the only bank serving the territory, announced it was leaving in 2012, American Samoa responded by chartering its own bank, the first new U.S. public bank in almost a century. Its creation was approved by the Federal Reserve in 2018.

Wages have been a perpetual problem in the territory. Average household incomes in American Samoa hover around $22,000, less than half the national average. In 2007, Congress passed a law raising the minimum wage in American Samoa to $7.25 an hour by 2014, but federally mandated delays had frozen wages for cannery workers. As of 2019, it had risen to $5.56 an hour, making it hard for the territory to compete with nearby islands where workers make $1 an hour in canneries.

The territory has one of the highest obesity rates in the world. With obesity have come diabetes and heart disease. One in five babies born in American Samoa is overweight, and usually within a year most infants are obese, according to a Brown University study. One in three American Samoans suffer from diabetes. Still, American Samoans have developed a reputation for athleticism, most notably in American football. American Samoa has sent 30 players to the National Football League and more than 200 to colleges in the NCAA. Top coaches fly to the island to scout players.

American Samoa does not cast electoral votes for president, but it does send delegates to the major parties' national conventions. In 2020, the Democratic primary caucus produced a surprising result: former New York City mayor Michael Bloomberg won half of the popular vote and U.S. Representative Tulsi Gabbard, who was born in American Samoa, won nearly 30 percent. The contest was both candidates' best performances by far. Leading contenders Bernie Sanders and Joe Biden failed to secure any delegates.

Governor

Lemanu Palepoi Sialega "Peleti" Mauga ascended to the governorship in 2020 after eight years as American Samoa's lieutenant governor, succeeding term-limited Lolo Letalu Matalasi Moliga. A Democrat, Mauga previously served as a senator in the territory's legislature and in a number of military-related positions in the American Samoan government.

Mauga was born in the village of Nu'uuli and attended elementary school and some of high school in American Samoa, although he graduated high school in Hawaii. He obtained an associate's degree from American Samoa Community College, a bachelor's in political science at University of Hawaii-Manoa, and a master's in public administration from San Diego State University. Mauga spent 23 years in the military and was deployed during the Persian Gulf War and Operation Iraqi Freedom.

After leaving the military, Magua became the Director of Army Instructions in American Samoa's JROTC program and served as chief of the Office of Property Management. Later, he worked in the governor's office as a military liaison. After being elected to the territory's legislature in 2008, Magua served as chairman of the Budget and Appropriations Committee and the Homeland Security, Immigration, and Legal Affairs Committee. Lolo Letalu Matalasi Moliga selected Magua as his running mate in the 2012 gubernatorial election, which they won as independents with 53 percent of the vote. The pair ran again in 2016 and received 60 percent of the vote, this time affiliated with the Democratic Party.

During the 2020 gubernatorial race, which was non-partisan, Mauga and his running mate, former Attorney General Talauega Eleasalo Va'alele Ale, faced three other tickets. Mauga drew attention to climate change and said that American Samoa should conduct disaster preparedness training and build mitigation infrastructure. He also vowed to expand transportation options between the islands, noting that some areas lack government services or hospitals. Unlike other tickets, Mauga did not make a pledge against levying new taxes. His ticket won 60 percent of the vote, avoiding a runoff.

DELEGATE

Aumua Amata Coleman Radewagen (R)

Elected 2014, 4th term, b. Dec 29, 1947; Pago Pago, American Samoa; Sacred Hearts Academy; Loyola Marymount University; George Mason University; University of Guam, B.S., 1975; Roman Catholic; Married (Fred Radewagen); 3 children; 1 grandchild.

Professional Career: Journalist; Trainer; Staff, U.S. Rep. Philip Crane (IL), 1997-1999; Staff, U.S. Rep. J.C. Watts Jr. (OK), 1999-2003; White House Commissioner for Asian Americans & Pacific Islanders, 2001.

DC Office: 1339 LHOB 20515, 202-225-8577, Fax: 202-225-8757, radewagen.house.gov

Committees: *Natural Resources*: Indigenous Peoples of the United States, Water, Oceans & Wildlife. *Veterans' Affairs*: Health, Women Veterans Task Force.

Amata Catherine Coleman Radewagen, a Republican, became the first woman to represent American Samoa in Congress after defeating 13-term Democrat Eni F. H. Faleomavaega in 2014. A former Capitol Hill GOP leadership staffer and cancer survivor commonly known as Auma Amata, Radewagen grew up with 12 siblings and earned a degree from the University of Guam.

Her family has deep roots in Samoan politics. Peter Tali Coleman, her father, was the first Samoan appointed to serve as governor of the territory and its first popularly elected governor. He ruled from 1956 to 1993 and founded the territory's Republican Party. Radewagen has served on the Executive Council and Rules Committee of the Republican National Committee. She was a member of Donald Trump's transition in 2016 and supported him during his presidency. She backed Trump withdrawing the United States from the Trans-Pacific Partnership, his push for a United States-Mexico border wall and his pulling out of the Paris Climate Accords. She also agreed with him on reversing President Barack Obama's expansion of marine reserves in the Pacific Ocean.

In the House, Radewagen is a member of a Natural Resources panel responsible for insular affairs. She has had some legislative successes. In October 2016, Obama signed her bill raising the minimum wage in American Samoa 40 cents every three years until it aligned with the federal minimum. Obama signed another bill from Radewagen related to international fishery management agreements.

In 2015 and 2016, she supported decisions by federal courts not to grant birthright citizenship status to American Samoans, saying in a press release that the courts had reaffirmed "the bedrock principle that the American Samoan people, and not outside interest groups or federal courts, should have the final say in matters concerning their political status." In 2019, she introduced a bill that would make it easier for American Samoans to apply for citizenship.

Radewagen challenged Faleomavaega eight times before finally winning the seat in 2014. In 2014, Radewagen won 42 percent of the vote to Faleomavaega's 30 percent. Faleomavaega died in 2017. Radewagen has easily won all three of her reelection bids.

GUAM

Some 6,300 miles west of Los Angeles and 3,800 miles west of Hawaii, 17 hours of flying time from Washington D.C., is Guam, an American possession since 1898. Geographically, this island is in the center of the Marianas Islands, though Guam is legally separate. It was acquired from Spain after the Spanish-American War, while the United States permitted Germany to purchase the rest of the Mariana chain. It was ruled by Navy captains from 1898 to 1949, except for 31 months of Japanese occupation during World War II. In 1950, the Guam Organic Act made Guamanians U.S. citizens. Carlton Skinner, who as a captain integrated the crew of his Navy ship in 1943, became the first civilian governor in 1949 and helped write the territorial constitution. The local government is known as GovGuam, but Congress retains final power over the territory. It gave Guam a non-voting delegate to the House in 1972.

Guam is 36 miles long by four to nine miles wide, with 169,630 people as of mid-2020. Some 37 percent of the population is Chamorro (descendants of the original islanders) or from elsewhere in Micronesia; 26 percent is Filipino; 12 percent other Pacific Islander; 6 percent other Asian; and 10 percent white. The population is politically mixed and overwhelmingly Catholic, yet in 2015 Guam became the first U.S. territory to recognize same-sex marriage. The island's Catholic church has been wracked with scandal. Its previous archbishop was found to have sexually abused altar boys and was removed from office. The diocese filed for bankruptcy in 2019 to avoid payments in dozens of sexual abuse lawsuits.

The island's tropical environment can be dangerous. In August 1993, Guam experienced an earthquake measuring 8.2 on the Richter scale, comparable to San Francisco's in 1906. Guam has almost 300 invasive species, the most problematic of which is the brown tree snake. It has killed off nearly all of the island's bird population. In 2020, Guam received over $3 million in federal grants to control the species.

Guam is America's forward position in Asia, which some have used as a national security justification for statehood. Anderson Air Force Base is one of the busiest in the world and serves as the U.S. military's largest stockpile of bombs, missiles and bullets. The Air Force removed the last five B-52s from the island in 2020, the first time since 2004 that there have been no heavy bombers. Bases occupy one-third of the land, and an estimated 60 percent of the island's income is derived from the federal government. In 2013, the Pentagon announced plans to relocate 5,000 marines and

1,300 dependents from Okinawa to Guam by 2026, a move that defense officials predicted would add upwards of $37 million per year to Guam's economy. In 2017, the federal government announced that it will begin paying reparations to Guam residents who experienced wartime atrocities under Japan's occupation of the island during World War II.

Guam was at the center of a scandal early in the 2020 coronavirus pandemic. An outbreak on the USS Theodore Roosevelt forced the aircraft carrier to hospitalize and quarantine infected sailors in Guam's hotels and hospitals, upsetting many residents. The ship's commander, Captain Brett Crozier, was relieved from duty after his complaint about the Navy's lack of support for the aircraft carrier went public. Shortly after, acting Navy secretary Thomas Modly resigned over backlash to his speech calling Crozier "naïve or stupid" for thinking the complaint wouldn't leak As thanks for hosting the sick sailors, the military agreed to give some excess land to Guam.

Guam does not cast any electoral votes for president, but it elects delegates to national party conventions. In lieu of a general election, Guam began holding non-binding straw polls every four years starting in 1984. For the first time in its history, the straw poll in 2016 did not accurately predict the next president. About 72 percent of Guam voters chose Hillary Clinton over Donald Trump. Four years later the straw poll got it right again as Joe Biden prevailed over Trump with 55 percent of the vote.

Governor

Democrat Lou Leon Guerrero was elected Guam's governor in 2018, making her the first female governor in the island's history, the first Pacific Islander to serve as governor in any of the U.S. territories, and only the third Democrat to hold the office since the territory began voting for governor a half-century ago (the other six were Republicans). The election was a watershed moment in other ways: Her running mate, Joshua Tenorio, became Guam's first openly gay lieutenant governor, and the legislature became majority-female for the first time.

Guerrero, a former nurse, was a five-term territorial senator and president of the Bank of Guam. Her views matched mainland Democrats on many issues, something that's not always a given in the territories: She supported abortion rights and recreational marijuana, which became legal on the island in April 2019. Although abortion is legal in Guam, no doctors on the island are willing to perform them. She also campaigned on a pledge for more government investment to boost tourism and scrapping the island's sales tax, while supporting a task force to collect an estimated $200 million in unpaid taxes on the island. Guerrero won the race with 50.8 percent of the vote, barely avoiding a runoff.

Guerrero reacted quickly to the COVID-19 pandemic in 2020, closing schools and government offices just as the island caught its first cases. However, some residents were unhappy that she housed infected sailors from the USS Theodore Roosevelt in local hotels and hospitals.

DELEGATE

Michael San Nicolas (D)

Elected 2018, 2nd term, b. Jan 30, 1981; Talofofoam, Guam; University of Guam, B.A., 2004; Religion unknown; Married (Kathryn Santos Ko); 2 children.

DC Office: 1632 LHOB 20515, 202-225-1188, sannicolas.house.gov

Committees: *Financial Services*: Consumer Protection & Financial Institutions, Investor Protection, Entrepreneurship & Capital Markets, Nat'l Security, International Development & Monetary Policy, Task Force on Financial Technology. *Natural Resources*: Indigenous Peoples of the United States, National Parks, Forests & Public Lands.

Democrat Michael San Nicolas was elected to his second term as delegate in 2020, defeating former delegate Robert Underwood. He first won the seat in 2018 by beating incumbent Madeleine Bordallo in a primary.

San Nicolas, a former territorial senator, is a scion of a local political family: Both of his grandfathers were local legislators. Before entering politics he was a teacher, a financial adviser, and a vice president at the Bank of Guam.

Bordallo had been the territory's delegate in Congress since 2002 but was dogged by a House Ethics Committee investigation into whether she leased a home to the government of Japan and accepted free lodging at a beachfront hotel in Guam. San Nicolas narrowly defeated her in the 2018 Democratic primary. Once in Congress, San Nicolas joined the House Hispanic Caucus and Congressional Asian Pacific American Caucus. He landed seats on the Financial Services and Natural Resources Committees.

Underwood, who served as Guam's delegate from 1993 to 2003, challenged San Nicolas in the 2020 Democratic primary, which was eventually cancelled due to the coronavirus pandemic. He held San Nicolas to less than 50 percent of the vote in the all-candidate November general election. San Nicolas won the low-turnout runoff with 60 percent of the vote.

The House Ethics Committee announced in October 2019 that it would look into allegations that San Nicolas had affair with a staffer. He was also accused of using campaign funds for a personal trip with the woman. In June 2020, the Office of Congressional Ethics recommended an investigative subcommittee.

NORTHERN MARIANA ISLANDS

The Commonwealth of the Northern Mariana Islands, in American hands since 1944, is a chain of 14 islands, only three permanently inhabited, running north from Guam in the Western Pacific. The northern islands are volcanic and the southern islands are limestone and fringed with coral reefs. They are closer to mainland Asia than to the mainland United States, sitting roughly 2,100 miles southeast of Hong Kong and some 7,800 miles southwest of Los Angeles.

The Northern Marianas were first peopled by Micronesians three millennia ago and were visited by Magellan in 1521. Spanish Jesuits arrived in 1668, and the islands were a possession of Spain until the Spanish-American War in 1898. Over the centuries, they became depopulated, and then in the middle 19th century, began to be settled by Chamorros from Guam. In 1898, the United States acquired Guam as a coaling station but was content to see the Northern Marianas sold to Germany in 1899. They were seized by Japan in 1914 soon after it entered World War I, and the League of Nations gave Japan legal claim to them in 1920. They were occupied by U.S. forces in 1944, in the midst of World War II. In August 1945, the Enola Gay took off from Tinian on its mission to drop the atomic bomb on Hiroshima. That same year, the Northern Marianas were put in the custody of the new United Nations Security Council, and in 1947 they were declared part of the U.S. Trust Territory of the Pacific Islands.

While the other islands in time opted for independence, the Northern Marianas voted in 1975 to approve a covenant with the United States creating the Commonwealth of the Northern Mariana Islands, which went into effect in 1976. Under its terms, the CNMI was not subject to federal immigration or labor laws and not obliged to pay U.S. taxes, but it deferred entirely to the United States in foreign and military affairs. Foreign investors were limited to a 49 percent share of businesses or property, and land could be owned only by "persons of Northern Marianas descent." The CNMI government started operating after the 1977 elections.

In the early 1970s, the Northern Marianas had only 12,000 people. The airport had no modern runways and only one rickety flight a day from Guam. Then, in the mid-1980s, the CNMI government opened up the economy to foreign investment and rewrote its immigration laws to permit an influx of guest workers. This resulted in heavy investment in garment factories that imported workers, mostly female, from low-wage countries such as the Philippines, China and Vietnam. Products made here could be labeled "Made in U.S.A." and imported into the United States without being subject to textile import quotas. By the mid-1990s, there were 34 garment factories, employing 17,000 guest workers. Japanese investors also began building tourist destinations. The result was a population boom, and the CNMI grew to 69,000 people in 2000.

The tiny island chain has faced major swings in economic prosperity depending on seemingly minor shifts in its treatment by the United States or by nearby countries. In January 2005, a treaty that set quotas on textile imports into the U.S. expired. Suddenly the CNMI's exemption from those quotas became irrelevant, and Saipan was subject to lower-wage competition from Vietnam, Cambodia and China. By 2009, all of the islands' garment factories were shuttered. The second major blow occurred in October 2005 when Japan Airlines canceled its daily flights to Saipan, badly damaging the tourism industry. Gross domestic product dropped about 20 percent in 2009, and the CNMI's population decreased to less than 54,000 as of 2020.

The economy remains reliant on the growth of the tourism industry. Part of that growth came from an Imperial Pacific International mega-casino opened by Chinese investors. Its construction led to serious allegations of human rights and immigration violations, plus accusations of money laundering. The parent company's Saipan offices were raided by U.S. agents in early 2018, and its construction contractors reached a $13.9 million settlement with the Department of Labor for wages and damages for 2,400 workers. Although proponents of casino legalization argued that the Imperial Pacific International would be a source of government revenue, the company has reported a massive drop in profits in recent years. IPI went from paying $44 million in taxes throughout 2018 to less than $41,000 in the first half of the following year. Legislators have since eyed legalizing online gambling to supplement the drop in revenue. The islands are also a destination for "birth tourism," where hundreds of wealthy Chinese women go to Saipan annually to give birth to children who automatically receive U.S. birthright citizenship. In 2020, the Trump administration cracked down on birth tourism generally by tightening the tourism visa application process. However, the rule does not affect the CMNI, the only part of the U.S. that Chinese citizens can visit without a visa.

In October 2018, the islands were ravaged by Super Typhoon Yutu, one of the worst storms ever to hit U.S. soil. Much of Saipan and Titian lost power for months, more than 5,000 houses were destroyed or severely damaged, and more than a quarter of the islands' population was displaced. The storm ravaged tourism, with only 6,000 tourists visiting in the month after the storm, down from 49,000 the year before. The economy declined by 20 percent by the end of the year. Reconstruction was hampered when the Trump administration eliminated the Philippines from the list of countries whose citizens can receive temporary worker visas, limiting the pool of available construction workers. A year later, residents were still living in tent communities and waiting for schools to be rebuilt. Tourism fell even further as the coronavirus pandemic began to spread. In March 2020, Governor Ralph Torres warned of "the unequivocal and complete collapse of the foundations of our private sector on the islands."

In response to concerns about labor abuses and national security issues, Congress brought the CNMI under federal immigration law in 2008. The transition established a guest worker system to ensure an adequate labor supply to support the tourism and garment industries. Most CNMI politicians opposed the bill but had little power to stop it. It also gave the CNMI its first-ever delegate in Congress, replacing the territory's Resident Representative, a position funded by the CNMI that had been in place since 1978.

After the CIA closed its covert training base on Saipan in 1962, the U.S. military presence in the Northern Marianas became more limited than in nearby Guam. But the realignment of U.S. military operations in the Pacific could change that. The Marine Corps announced its intention to use the islands of Pagan and Tinian for live-fire amphibious training. Locals have hotly protested the plan, citing historical and environmental concerns. In September 2020, a federal court dismissed environmental groups' lawsuit challenging the training ranges.

Governor

Republican Ralph Torres became governor of the CNMI in December 2015, following the death of Gov. Eloy Inos, and was elected to a full term in 2018 with over 60 percent of the vote. Since then, Torres has been dogged by accusations that he accommodated the construction of a casino in exchange for millions of dollars in payments to his family.

Torres has been a vocal supporter of the growing casino tourism industry, helping to legalize gambling on the islands when he was in the state senate and defending the Chinese conglomerate that came in to build new casinos amid accusations of human rights abuses and violations of building regulations. Torres' opponents accused his family of receiving kickbacks, pointing out that Torres' brothers were on the Chinese company's payroll as attorneys for the deal and that the company bought a land lease from his sister-in-law for a massive profit.

In November 2019, the FBI searched both the company's and Torres' offices as part of an investigation into bribery, wire fraud, money laundering, and illegal campaign contributions. Torres has denied that his family received work in exchange for favors and called media reports on the investigation "irresponsible." As of March 2020, the investigation was continuing.

Torres was born in Saipan and attended high school and college in Idaho. He won election to the territory's legislature in 2008 and served as senate president from 2013 to 2015. In 2016, he drew national attention for his support of restricting ownership of some semi-automatic weapons. In the 2016 presidential race, Torres co-chaired the Asian-Pacific Advisory Committee for Donald Trump. In 2020, Torres supported Trump's reelection.

As governor, Torres has sought to boost tourism and grow the territory's workforce. He has also supported raising the cap on permits for foreign workers. He helped extend the Marianas' foreign guest worker program through 2029 and signed a bill authorizing recreational marijuana use.

DELEGATE

Gregorio Kilili Camacho Sablan (D)

Elected 2008, 7th term, b. Jan 19, 1955; Saipan, Northern Mariana Islands; University of Guam, Att.; University of HI, Manoa, Att., 1990; Roman Catholic; Married (Andrea C. Sablan); 6 children.

Elected Office: N. Marianas Islands Legislature, 1982-1986.

Professional Career: Gov.'s deputy chief admin. officer, CNMI Government, 1980-1981; Special Assistant for Management & budget, CNMI Government, 1994-1995; Executive Director, Commonwealth Election Commission, 1999-2008.

DC Office: 2411 RHOB 20515, 202-225-2646, Fax: 202-226-4249, sablan.house.gov

Committees: *Agriculture*: Subcommittee Nutrition, Oversight & Department Operations. *Education & Labor*: Early Childhood, Elementary & Secondary Education (Chmn). *Natural Resources*: National Parks, Forests & Public Lands. *Veterans' Affairs*: Health, Women Veterans Task Force.

Gregorio Kilili Camacho Sablan, the first delegate to the House from the Commonwealth of the Northern Mariana Islands, was elected in 2008. He is a senior Democrat on the Natural Resources Committee and had conflicts with the Trump administration on visas to the islands.

Sablan grew up in Saipan in an extended family involved in politics. His grandfather was the first elected mayor of Saipan, and his uncle was the city's longest-serving mayor. He attended the University of Guam and the University of California, Berkeley, but did not get a degree. He worked for Democratic Gov. Carlos Camacho, the CNMI's first elected governor, then served in the legislature from 1982 to 1986. Sablan worked for 18 months on the Washington staff of Democratic Sen. Daniel Inouye of Hawaii, who had a long interest in the Pacific territories. When he returned to Saipan, Sablan worked as special assistant for management and budget for Democratic Gov. Froilan Tenorio. Later, he was appointed executive director of the Commonwealth Election Commission.

After Congress voted in April 2008 to give the CNMI a non-voting delegate in Congress, Sablan joined a field of nine candidates seeking the seat. He ran as an independent rather than as a Democrat because he believed the local Democratic Party was poorly organized. Of 10,161 votes cast, Sablan led the field with 2,474 votes, edging Republican Pete A. Tenorio by 357 votes. In 2020, Sablan was not challenged.

Sablan has had some legislative successes, including enactment of a 2013 measure giving the CNMI ownership of submerged lands three miles out to sea and a December 2012 amendment to the defense authorization bill requiring that the flags of the CNMI and other territories be displayed whenever military units display all of the states' flags. In 2014, he helped to prolong a visa program that allows long-term foreign investors to reside on the islands. In 2016 and 2017, the House passed his bills increasing caps on foreign workers in the CNMI. The Trump administration reversed course on those visas, lowering the cap on foreign workers in 2018 and reducing it by more than half for

2019 to 4,999. Sablan worked with his rival, Republican Gov. Ralph Torres, as well as Sen. Lisa Murkowski of Alaska and Rep. Rob Bishop of Utah, both Republicans, to increase that cap and extend the program to 2029. In 2019-20, he worked with the Trump administration to establish permanent status for CNMI residents who were protected under Obama-era humanitarian parole. He unsuccessfully fought the Trump administration's decision to end Russian tourists' ability to come to the CNMI without visas. Sablan has called for extending U.S. voting rights protections to the territories and has supported increases in the minimum wage.

After years of trying to create a national park on the island of Rota, Sablan came a step closer in 2020 when a National Park Service study he requested declared that the area "is a special place with significant cultural and natural resources." The National Parks Service launched a series of virtual public forums on the report in September 2020.

PUERTO RICO

From Columbus' landing in 1493 until the Spanish-American War of 1898, Puerto Rico was a Spanish colony-and an important one in the three centuries when the port of San Juan was the gathering place for its annual convoy of gold and silver from the Americas to Spain. From the time it became an American territory in 1898 to the 1950s, it was considered "the poorhouse of the Caribbean," a sugar-producing island with a tiny elite. In the second half of the 20th century, it developed a recognizably first world economy and a solidly democratic-though sometimes turbulent-political system.

In the 21st century, however, Puerto Rico's forward momentum has ground to a halt. Its economic woes, financial instability and declining population created a tinderbox ready to explode. The match was struck in September 2017 when Hurricane Maria hit the island, causing thousands of deaths and widespread destruction. Puerto Rico faced further troubles in 2019 when Governor Ricardo Rosselló was forced out of office by massive protests. Despite these challenges, the island has had some bright moments recently: Puerto Rico had a relatively low death rate during the COVID-19 pandemic, has moved toward a resolution of its bankruptcy proceedings, and hit record tourism numbers before the pandemic.

Puerto Rico's economic crisis began when the federal government ended tax breaks that brought corporations and big businesses, particularly pharmaceutical companies, to the island. Spurred by the pharmaceutical manufacturing boom, the island's economy increased nearly 20% from 2000 to 2004. However, companies left as the tax breaks phased out. By the time Hurricane Maria hit, a decade of recession had erased the island's economic gains. Puerto Rico's poverty rate was around 45%, and it had half the per capita income of Mississippi, the poorest state in the union.

In the face of rapid economic decline and dwindling tax revenue, the government borrowed to make ends meet. By May 2017, the island had racked up $123 billion in bond debt and unfunded pension obligations, forcing it to take an unprecedented step toward insolvency. Although U.S. bankruptcy law prohibits Puerto Rico from restructuring its debt, Puerto Rico used a provision from a 2016 federal law to seek relief from its Wall Street creditors in a proceeding similar to bankruptcy. That law also established a seven-member oversight board to manage the territory's finances and debt restructuring. The broad powers granted to the board attracted criticism among Puerto Ricans, with some characterizing it as colonialism and calling the board a "junta." Population loss to the mainland tracked with Puerto Rico's economic and financial troubles. From 2004 to 2016, Puerto Rico's population dropped by 11%, from roughly 3.8 million to 3.4 million.

These struggles left Puerto Rico ill-prepared for Hurricane Maria, a Category 4 storm that hit on September 20, 2017. With its 155 mph winds, Maria caused around $100 billion in damage, fully destroying 70,000 homes and partially destroying another 300,000. Nearly 3,000 Puerto Ricans died from the storm, according to the official government estimate. It took one year to restore power to the entire island. With the island and its economy wrecked by the storm, even more Puerto Ricans headed to the mainland. Although accurate migration numbers are hard to come by, the Census Bureau estimated that nearly 130,000 people left in the following year, with many settling in central Florida. In 2019, the number of Puerto Ricans in central Florida returned to pre-Maria levels, suggesting some were returning to the island. Official estimates put the island population at less than 3.2 million in 2019.

The federal government's response to Maria was widely panned by Puerto Rican officials, who argued that the island received less aid than mainland areas struck by disasters in 2017. Indeed, a New York Times examination of FEMA data found that only 190 recovery projects had been approved in Puerto Rico compared to 3,700 mainland projects. President Donald Trump, however, called the response "an incredible, unsung success" and blamed corrupt government officials on the island for the slow recovery. The island needed further assistance after it was struck by earthquakes in January 2020 that caused over $100 million in damage. By late 2020, about $50 billion in federal assistance had been approved but most had not been dispersed. One official estimated that a full recovery could be 15 years away.

As they recover, Puerto Ricans say "Puerto Rico se levanta," which means "Puerto Rico is rising." The island's economy grew in 2019 as the tourism industry – which accounts for 6.5% of GDP – made a comeback and posted a record number of visitors. Tax revenue grew by 21% and economic indicators were pointing in the right direction. However, the tourism industry's success masked deeper issues in impoverished rural areas. As of August 2019, about 30,000 Puerto Ricans still had FEMA tarps as roofs on their homes.

Puerto Rico avoided another disaster in 2020 by clamping down early to stop the spread of COVID-19. Governor Wanda Vásquez, who replaced Rosselló after his resignation, swiftly imposed lockdowns at the beginning of the pandemic and added further restrictions whenever cases began to rise on the island. After initially barring cruise ships, Puerto Rico resumed tourism but with activity limits and testing requirements. As of December 2020, Puerto Rico had a lower death rate than all but seven mainland states. Still, the pandemic's effect on the island economy could be devastating.

The end of the island's bankruptcy is also in sight. The oversight board announced a plan in 2019 to reduce the island's debt from $129 billion to $86 billion. District Court Judge Laura Swain continued to oversee the restructuring and resolve disputes between the island and its creditors. The proceedings were expected to continue through 2021, at least.

Hurricane Maria and the financial crisis have given new life to the fundamental question of whether Puerto Rico should seek statehood, continue its current commonwealth status or, in what has traditionally been a minority view, declare independence. Puerto Rican statehood has increasingly been a focus of mainland partisan politics as Democrats see it as a solution to Republicans' advantage in the Senate. Pro-statehood Puerto Ricans, including former Governor Rosselló, say the island would be a swing state rather than solidly Democratic. Although a transition to statehood requires congressional approval, Puerto Ricans have voted on statehood six times and public opinion generally seems to be moving in favor of it. In the 1967 referendum, the commonwealth status prevailed over statehood, 60%-39%. In 1993, the commonwealth status won 48%-46%. In a 1998 referendum, the vote was 47% for statehood and 50% for "none of the above." In 2012, 52% voted against the current status; in a second question, statehood defeated independence and commonwealth status. In June 2017, 97% voted for statehood but anti-statehood parties boycotted the vote. All parties participated in a 2020 referendum and statehood received 52%.

Puerto Rico has elected a resident commissioner to Congress since 1900 with a four-year term, and residents of Puerto Rico have been American citizens since 1917. But they didn't elect their own governor until 1948. From the 1940s until the early 1960s, Puerto Rico was transformed by Gov. Luis Muñoz Marín and his Popular Democratic Party. Muñoz initiated "Operation Bootstrap" to lure businesses to Puerto Rico with promises of low-wage labor, government-built factories and tax exemptions. Muñoz also developed Puerto Rico's commonwealth form of government-in Spanish, Estado Libre Asociado, or, ELA, meaning Free Associated State-that was approved by referendum in 1952. Puerto Rico is part of the United States for purposes of international trade, foreign policy and war. But it has its own laws, taxes and representative government. It is not subject to federal income taxes and is not eligible for all federal benefits.

The island has developed its own political parties, most prominently Muñoz's Popular Democrats (the Spanish acronym is PPD) and the New Progressive Party (PNP), which favors statehood. PPD politicians have long been affiliated with the mainland Democratic Party, while PNP politicians have been split, with some favoring Democrats and some favoring Republicans. The most recent PNP governors exemplified this as Vásquez endorsed Trump in the 2020 election while Rosselló supported Democrats in the 2018 elections.

Rosselló, who was elected in 2016 on a pro-statehood platform, faced massive protests in July 2019 after leaked messages revealed insensitive remarks made by him and his advisors. He resigned and was replaced by Vásquez, his secretary of justice. In the 2020 PNP primary, Vásquez lost to former Resident Commissioner Pedro Pierluisi. With six candidates running in the low-turnout general election, Pierluisi won with just 33%. Three minor parties – the Puerto Rican Independence Party, the anti-colonial Citizen's Victory Movement, and the Christian democratic Project Dignity – won seats in the legislature, leaving neither major party with a clear governing mandate.

Governor

Pedro Pierluisi was elected as Puerto Rico's 14th governor in 2020 after a tumultuous year in the island's politics. Pierluisi, a veteran politician, defeated sitting Governor Wanda Vásquez in the Progressive New Party (PNP) primary. Vásquez became governor in 2019 after incumbent Ricardo Rosselló resigned in the face of mass protests.

Pierluisi was born in San Juan in 1959. He received his bachelor's from Tulane and a law degree from George Washington University. After law school, he worked as an aide to Resident Commissioner Baltasar Corrado del Rio and later joined a DC law firm. He returned to Puerto Rico in 1993 to become the secretary of justice under PNP Governor Pedro Rosselló, Ricardo's father. In 2008, he successfully ran for resident commissioner. Unlike previous PNP commissioners, he caucused with the Democratic Party in the House. He worked to extend the Affordable Care Act to Puerto Rico and pushed pro-statehood initiatives.

Pierluisi ran for governor in 2016 and faced Ricardo Rosselló in the PNP primary. Rosselló narrowly won the primary, 51%-49%, and prevailed in the general election against PPD candidate David Bernier. As governor, Rosselló dealt with the Hurricane Maria disaster and managed a volatile relationship with President Donald Trump. He also attempted to prevent a federal oversight board from imposing austerity measures to pay back the island's debts.

Rosselló faced a damaging scandal in July 2019 after a news outlet published leaked Telegram messages showing him and his advisors using profane language and conducting public business via a group chat. Remarks by some participants in the chat were highly offensive, including a joke about dead bodies during Hurricane Maria. Already angered by the island's financial situation and the response to the hurricane, TelegramGate led Puerto Ricans to protest en masse against Rosselló.

Rosselló announced he would resign, but his constitutionally-anointed successor, Secretary of State Luis Rivera Marín, was also ensnared in the scandal. Wanda Vásquez, the secretary of justice, was next in line, but protestors said she was too close to Rosselló. Thus, Rosselló had Marín resign and then appointed Pierluisi as secretary of state. However, the Puerto Rican Senate did not approve Pierluisi's appointment and challenged his ascension to the governorship. The Puerto Rico Supreme Court agreed with the Senate and Vásquez became governor after Pierluisi held the position for 5 days in early August.

As governor, Vásquez faced the difficult challenge of protecting the island's health and economy during the COVID-19 pandemic. With early shutdowns and limited tourism, Puerto Rico maintained a low death rate low throughout 2020 and avoided a public health disaster. Although she was initially uninterested in being governor and was dogged by scandals from her time as justice secretary, Vásquez ended up running for a full term and faced Pierluisi in the PNP primary. Despite Vásquez's aggressive campaign, Pierluisi won by nearly 20 percentage points.

The general election featured a fractured field and low turnout. Disillusioned by the PNP and PPD's governing failures, only about 51% of Puerto Ricans voted, down from 55% in 2016, and many turned to minor parties advocating for independence, decolonization, or Christian democracy. Pierluisi won with 33% of the vote, the lowest percentage for a successful candidate in recent history. Isabela Mayor Carlos Delgado, the PPD candidate, received about 32%. The minor parties also made gains in the legislature, leaving Pierluisi without a working majority.

RESIDENT COMMISSIONER

Jenniffer Gonzalez Colon (R)

Elected 2016, term expires 2024, 2nd term, b. Aug 05, 1976; San Juan, Puerto Rico; University of Puerto Rico, B.A.; Inter-American University of Puerto Rico, J.D.; Inter-American University of Puerto Rico, LL.M.; Single.

Elected Office: President, Puerto Rico Republian Party, 2004-2016; Vice President, New Progressive Party, 2008-2016; PR House, 2002-2016, Speaker, 2009-2012, Minority Leader, 2012-2016.

DC Office: 1609 LHOB 20515, 202-225-2615, Fax: 202-225-2154, gonzalez-colon.house.gov

Committees: *Natural Resources*: Water, Oceans & Wildlife. *Transportation & Infrastructure*: Economic Dev't, Public Buildings & Emergency Management, Highways & Transit, Water Resources & Environment.

Republican Jenniffer González-Colón, a member of Puerto Rico's pro-statehood New Progressive Party (PNP), was first elected in 2016. She was re-elected in 2020 and is a likely contender for governor down the line. She had a lukewarm relationship with President Donald Trump during her first term as she advocated for disaster relief following Hurricane Maria.

At 40 when she was elected, González-Colón is the youngest person to serve as resident commissioner and the first woman to hold the position. She had been a legislator in Puerto Rico since 2002 and became the island's youngest speaker of the house seven years later. She received a law degree from Puerto Rico's Inter American University and worked in San Juan as an attorney. In 2016, González-Colón succeeded two-term Resident Commissioner Pedro Pierluisi, a fellow PNP member who caucused with House Democrats. She defeated Popular Democratic Party candidate Hector Ferrer in the general election, 48.8%-47.2%. In 2019, she called for PNP Governor Ricardo Rosselló to resign when he faced mass protests over leaked Telegram messages. Although there was speculation she would replace Rosselló, she ran for re-election instead. With anti-establishment parties gaining traction on the island, she received just 41% of the vote in the five-candidate general election. It was the lowest percentage for a winning resident commissioner candidate since at least 1980.

González-Colón is active in Republican politics in Puerto Rico and on the mainland. In the 2016 presidential campaign, she backed former Gov. Jeb Bush and then Sen. Marco Rubio, both of Florida, for the Republican nomination. She was a fierce critic of Trump throughout the primary season, refusing to back him at the Republican National Convention because she didn't want to "validate the attack on the Latino community." She ended up supporting him in the general election. When Hurricane Maria devastated the island in 2017, González-Colón initially said she was "grateful" for the attention Trump paid to disaster response. But after Trump threatened to cut short disaster aid a few weeks later she called his remarks "shocking." Despite Trump's continued attacks on island officials, González-Colón participated in the group Latinos for Trump during the 2020 election and praised the president for approving additional disaster relief funds.

Aside from securing financial aid for the island, her primary legislative aim is Puerto Rican statehood. Although she caucuses with Republicans in the House, González-Colón frequently works on legislation with Democrats. This has been especially the case on statehood as Republican leaders have grown increasingly hostile to the idea, given its potential to shift the balance of power in the Senate. She serves on the Natural Resources and Transportation and Infrastructure committees.

VIRGIN ISLANDS

The U.S. Virgin Islands, acquired from Denmark in 1917, are near the northern end of the Antilles chain between the Caribbean Sea and the Atlantic Ocean. They were settled by the Dutch and Danish and had a polyglot colonial society, with one of the oldest Jewish communities in the Western Hemisphere. Their most famous son is Alexander Hamilton, who grew up on St. Croix but moved to New York and never returned. Almost all of the territory's 104,000 people live on the three main islands of St. Thomas, St. John and St. Croix. Since the 1990s, there has been little net change.

The Virgin Islands have lived primarily off tourism. St. Thomas has long been one of the top cruise ship destinations in the world and the islands together receive nearly 3 million visitors each year. Tourism accounts for approximately 60 percent of the territory's GDP and the government continues to incentivize travel to the islands, with increased airplane flights from the mainland. The Islands were devastated by two Category Five hurricanes, Irma and Maria, within two weeks in September 2017. Although tourism revived by September 2018, residents are still living with the effects; the lengthy rebuilding process has led to trauma and behavioral issues among children whose educations were disrupted. The 2020 coronavirus pandemic caused the tourism economy to falter again after the government banned leisure travelers from March to June and again from August to September.

Even with its reliable tourism industry, the Virgin Islands' economy was weakened after Hovensa, an oil refinery built on St. Croix by Hess Oil in 1966, was closed. Once one of the largest refineries in the world, it closed in 2012, with a loss of 2,200 jobs and $100 million in revenue to the territorial government. After nearly four years of inactivity, the Hovensa oil refinery was given a second chance in 2015 when the legislature approved a purchase agreement with Limetree Bay Holdings, a subsidiary of ArcLight Capital Partners. The reopening faced a number of obstacles: delays nearly cost the refinery its relationship with oil provider BP and the coronavirus pandemic lowered profits. It ultimately began operating in December 2020 after Limetree invested $2.7 billion.

Rum sales in the Virgin Islands are a staple of the economy and vital to local finances. Rum-producing U.S. territories have received $13.25 of the $13.50 per-gallon federal tax on rum since 1999. These payments have been used to incentivize rum producers to relocate to the Virgin Islands. In 2008, the Virgin Islands government made a deal with the British-based liquor company Diageo to move its Captain Morgan rum operations from Puerto Rico to a new $165 million distillery in the Virgin Islands. Puerto Rican politicians were unhappy with the plan to give a share of the revenue to Diageo and argued that it was illegitimate to use rum tax funds to lure a distillery operation from one territory to another. The rum tax rebate has been renewed since then, as criticism of the practice from fiscal hawks in Congress has grown louder.

More than one quarter of workers on the islands are employed by the government. In addition to a budget deficit, the islands have a crushing burden of $2.4 billion in bond debt. In February 2017, the territory's legislature passed the Revenue Enhancement and Economic Recovery Act, taxing alcohol, tobacco and carbonated beverages to generate new revenue. Following the hurricanes later that year, reconstruction was slowed, in part, by the delay of disaster funding by the Federal Emergency Management Agency. Bryan Jr. tried to sell $1 billion of its debt in exchange for the $250 million in excise taxes the territory receives every year, arguing that there not many options left. "If you don't have a better idea, then support this one," he said. The plan ultimately fell through due to lawsuits and amendments imposed by the state legislature.

Governor

Albert Bryan, a Democrat, was first elected in 2018. He defeated incumbent Kenneth Mapp, an independent, with 55 percent of the vote in a runoff after the pair advanced from a seven-candidate general election. Running on the "Change Course Now" theme, Bryan took advantage of many "self-inflicted wounds" by Mapp during his four years as governor, the Virgin Islands Consortium wrote. Bryan, who had wide experience in government on the Virgin Islands, styled himself as younger and more activist. Mapp was the third incumbent governor to lose a bid for a second term since 1974.

Bryan, a native of St. Thomas, got his bachelor's degree at Wittenberg University in Ohio and a Master of Business Administration from the University of the Virgin Islands. He had a lengthy career in the private sector, including executive positions with Hess Oil Corp. and Innovative Communications. In 2007, he was appointed as Commissioner of Labor for the Islands, a position that he held for eight years. After Mapp was elected governor, Bryan became chief executive of Aabra Group, a business consulting firm. His campaign in 2018 was his first bid for elected office. He won the Democratic primary with 39 percent of the vote against two opponents.

During his campaign, Bryan said that the Islands needed to establish "realistic and conservative budget practices" and that they could no longer spend more than available revenue. He opposed a congressional oversight board like that for Puerto Rico to deal with strained public finances. "If there are tough decisions to be made, we should be courageous enough to make them by and for ourselves," including steps to address the long-standing deficit, he told the St. Thomas Source on the eve of the election.

After taking office, Bryan moved quickly to deliver on a campaign promise to legalize marijuana for medical treatment, which Mapp had opposed. He also initiated steps to improve public-utility service and disaster preparedness in the wake of recent devastating hurricanes. Bryan has said that he wants the Islands to be a leader in the "resilience model" of climate change response, in which communities build infrastructure and preparedness initiatives before natural disasters strike. He also played a large role in establishing free tuition at the University of the Virgin Islands. In 2019, he signed an executive action declaring an emergency in access to mental health care on the island.

DELEGATE

Stacey Plaskett (D)

Elected 2014, 4th term, b. May 13, 1964; New York, NY; Georgetown University Foreign Service School, B.S., 1984; American University, WA College of Law, J.D., 1994; Lutheran; Married (Jeremy Buckney Small); 5 children.

Professional Career: Assistant District Attorney, Bronx; Consultant & legal counsel, Mitchel Madison Group; Practicing attorney; Staff, U.S. Department of Justice, 2002-2004; General counsel, Virgin Isl. econ. dev't. auth. 2007-2014.

DC Office: 2404 RHOB 20515, 202-225-1790, Fax: 202-225-5517, plaskett.house.gov

Committees: *Agriculture*: Biotechnology, Horticulture & Research (Chmn), Commodity Exchanges, Energy & Credit, Livestock & Foreign Agriculture. *Budget*. *Ways & Means*: Oversight.

Stacey Plaskett, a Democrat, was elected delegate from the Virgin Islands in 2014. She rose to national prominence for her role as an impeachment manager in the second Senate trial of President Donald Trump, the first nonvoting delegate to fill the position.

Plaskett grew up in Brooklyn, raised by parents who migrated to New York from the Virgin Islands in the 1950s. She attended Choate Rosemary Hall, a boarding school in Connecticut. She earned a degree in history and diplomacy from Georgetown University and a law degree from American University. Afterwards, she worked as an assistant district attorney in the Bronx and later as counsel to the House Ethics Committee. Before relocating to the Virgin Islands, Plaskett was a political appointee in the Department of Justice from 2002 to 2004 and served on the staff of Deputy Attorney General Larry Thompson. She switched parties and became a Democrat in late 2008.

Plaskett first ran for delegate in 2012 and lost to incumbent Donna Christensen in the Democratic primary, 57%-42%. In 2014, when Christensen ran unsuccessfully for governor, Plaskett ran again and won the general election with more than 90 percent of the vote. She has since been reelected easily.

In the House, Plaskett has been active on territorial issues, including advocating full citizenship for the insular territories. In 2015, Plaskett introduced legislation to increase the rebate the Virgin Islands receives from federal taxes on rum sales. The bill failed, but she continued to argue that the territory may be owed $100 million in revenues. Plaskett has also been active in national politics and endorsed former New York City Mayor Michael Bloomberg in the 2020 Democratic primaries.

Following the 2020 election, the Democratic Caucus approved Plaskett for a seat on the Ways and Means Committee. She was the first territorial representative to join the influential committee. Plaskett said that her priorities would be internal revenue measures to help the territory's economic development and including the Islands in infrastructure spending programs.

Plaskett asked Democratic leaders to name her a manager for Trump's first trial in 2019 but she was not selected. She got her chance during his second impeachment in early 2021, where she worked with Rep. Jamie Raskin, her former law professor. During the trial, Plaskett connected Trump's rhetoric to rioters' social media posts calling for violence against House Speaker Nancy Pelosi, Vice President Mike Pence, and other U.S. officials. She also presented security footage of a crowd searching the building for Pelosi.

LEADERSHIP

117th Congress
2021-2022

U.S. Senate
48D, 50R, 2I
Democrats

Majority Leader	Chuck Schumer (NY)
Majority Whip	Dick Durbin (IL)
Assistant Majority Leader	Patty Murray (WA)
President Pro Tempore	Patrick Leahy (VT)
Democratic Policy & Communications Committee Chairman	Debbie Stabenow (MI)
Democratic Conference Vice Chairman	E.Warren (MA), M. Warner (VA)
Democratic Steering Committee Chairman	Amy Klobuchar (MN)
Democratic Outreach Committee Chairman	Bernie Sanders (VT)
Democratic Outreach Vice Chair	Catherine Cortez Masto (NV)
Democratic Policy and Communications Vice Chairman	J.Manchin (WV), C. Booker (NJ)
Democratic Conference Secretary	Tammy Baldwin (WI)
Democratic Senatorial Campaign Committee Chairman	Gary Peters (MI)

Republicans

Republican Leader	Mitch McConnell (KY)
Republican Whip & Assistant Republican Leader	John Thune (SD)
Republican Conference Chairman	John Barrasso (WY)
Republican Conference Vice Chairman	Joni Ernst (IA)
Republican Policy Committee Chairman	Roy Blunt (MO)
National Republican Senatorial Committee Chairman	Rick Scott (FL)

U.S. House of Representatives
220D, 211R, 4 Vacant
Democrats

Democrats Speaker of the House	Nancy Pelosi (CA-12)
Majority Leader	Steny Hoyer (MD-5)
Majority Whip	James Clyburn (SC-6)
Assistant Speaker	Katherine Clark (MA-5)
Democratic Caucus Chairman	Hakeem Jeffries (NY-8)
Democratic Caucus Vice Chairman	Pete Aguilar (CA-31)
Democratic Steering and Policy Committee Co-Chair	Cheri Bustos (IL-17)
Democratic Steering and Policy Committee Co-Chair	Barbara Lee (CA-13)
Democratic Steering and Policy Committee Co-Chair	Eric Swalwell (CA-15)
Democratic Congressional Campaign Committee chairman	Sean Patrick Maloney (NY-18)

Republicans

Minority Leader	Kevin McCarthy (CA-23)
Minority Whip	Steve Scalise (LA-1)
Republican Conference Chairman	Elise Stefanik (NY-21)
Republican Policy Committee Chairman	Gary Palmer (AL-6)
Republican Chief Deputy Whip	Drew Ferguson (GA-3)
National Republican Congressional Committee Chairman	Tom Emmer (MN-6)
Republican Conference Vice Chairman	Mike Johnson (LA-4)
Republican Conference Secretary	Richard Hudson (NC-8)

SENATE SENIORITY

Senators are ranked by length of consecutive service in the Senate. If necessary, ties are broken based on previous public service and state population. The Senate seniority list was compiled from Senate Historical Office records. It is current as of Jun 24, 2021.

Senator (Party and State)	Start of Service	Senator (Party and State)	Start of Service
Patrick Leahy (D-VT)	Jan 03, 1975	Brian Schatz (D-HI)	Dec 27, 2012
Chuck Grassley (R-IA)	Jan 03, 1981	Tim Scott (R-SC)	Jan 02, 2013
Mitch McConnell (R-KY)	Jan 03, 1985	Tammy Baldwin (D-WI)	Jan 03, 2013
Richard Shelby (R-AL)	Jan 03, 1987	Chris Murphy (D-CT)	Jan 03, 2013
Dianne Feinstein (D-CA)	Nov 10, 1992	Mazie Hirono (D-HI)	Jan 03, 2013
Patty Murray (D-WA)	Jan 03, 1993	Martin Heinrich (D-NM)	Jan 03, 2013
Jim Inhofe (R-OK)	Nov 17, 1994	Angus King (I-ME)	Jan 03, 2013
Ron Wyden (D-OR)	Feb 06, 1996	Tim Kaine (D-VA)	Jan 03, 2013
Dick Durbin (D-IL)	Jan 03, 1997	Ted Cruz (R-TX)	Jan 03, 2013
Jack Reed (D-RI)	Jan 03, 1997	Elizabeth Warren (D-MA)	Jan 03, 2013
Susan Collins (R-ME)	Jan 03, 1997	Deb Fischer (R-NE)	Jan 03, 2013
Chuck Schumer (D-NY)	Jan 03, 1999	Ed Markey (D-MA)	Jul 16, 2013
Mike Crapo (R-ID)	Jan 03, 1999	Cory Booker (D-NJ)	Oct 31, 2013
Tom Carper (D-DE)	Jan 03, 2001	Shelley Moore Capito (R-WV)	Jan 03, 2015
Debbie Stabenow (D-MI)	Jan 03, 2001	Gary Peters (D-MI)	Jan 03, 2015
Maria Cantwell (D-WA)	Jan 03, 2001	Bill Cassidy (R-LA)	Jan 03, 2015
John Cornyn (R-TX)	Dec 01, 2002	James Lankford (R-OK)	Jan 03, 2015
Lisa Murkowski (R-AK)	Dec 20, 2002	Tom Cotton (R-AR)	Jan 03, 2015
Lindsey Graham (R-SC)	Jan 03, 2003	Steve Daines (R-MT)	Jan 03, 2015
Richard Burr (R-NC)	Jan 03, 2005	Mike Rounds (R-SD)	Jan 03, 2015
John Thune (R-SD)	Jan 03, 2005	Thom Tillis (R-NC)	Jan 03, 2015
Bob Menendez (D-NJ)	Jan 18, 2006	Joni Ernst (R-IA)	Jan 03, 2015
Ben Cardin (D-MD)	Jan 03, 2007	Ben Sasse (R-NE)	Jan 03, 2015
Bernie Sanders (I-VT)	Jan 03, 2007	Dan Sullivan (R-AK)	Jan 03, 2015
Sherrod Brown (D-OH)	Jan 03, 2007	Chris Van Hollen (D-MD)	Jan 03, 2017
Bob Casey (D-PA)	Jan 03, 2007	Todd Young (R-IN)	Jan 03, 2017
Amy Klobuchar (D-MN)	Jan 03, 2007	Tammy Duckworth (D-IL)	Jan 03, 2017
Sheldon Whitehouse (D-RI)	Jan 03, 2007	Maggie Hassan (D-NH)	Jan 03, 2017
Jon Tester (D-MT)	Jan 03, 2007	John Kennedy (R-LA)	Jan 03, 2017
John Barrasso (R-WY)	Jun 25, 2007	Catherine Cortez Masto (D-NV)	Jan 03, 2017
Roger Wicker (R-MS)	Dec 31, 2007	Tina Smith (D-MN)	Jan 03, 2018
Jeanne Shaheen (D-NH)	Jan 03, 2009	Cindy Hyde-Smith (R-MS)	Apr 02, 2018
Mark Warner (D-VA)	Jan 03, 2009	Marsha Blackburn (R-TN)	Jan 03, 2019
Jim Risch (R-ID)	Jan 03, 2009	Kyrsten Sinema (D-AZ)	Jan 03, 2019
Jeff Merkley (D-OR)	Jan 03, 2009	Kevin Cramer (R-ND)	Jan 03, 2019
Michael Bennet (D-CO)	Jan 21, 2009	Jacky Rosen (D-NV)	Jan 03, 2019
Kirsten Gillibrand (D-NY)	Jan 26, 2009	Mitt Romney (R-UT)	Jan 03, 2019
Joe Manchin (D-WV)	Nov 15, 2010	Mike Braun (R-IN)	Jan 03, 2019
Chris Coons (D-DE)	Nov 15, 2010	Josh Hawley (R-MO)	Jan 03, 2019
Roy Blunt (R-MO)	Jan 03, 2011	Rick Scott (R-FL)	Jan 08, 2019
Jerry Moran (R-KS)	Jan 03, 2011	Mark Kelly (D-AZ)	Dec 02, 2020
Rob Portman (R-OH)	Jan 03, 2011	Ben Ray Lujan (D-NM)	Jan 03, 2021
John Boozman (R-AR)	Jan 03, 2011	Cynthia Lummis (R-WY)	Jan 03, 2021
Pat Toomey (R-PA)	Jan 03, 2011	Roger Marshall (R-KS)	Jan 03, 2021
John Hoeven (R-ND)	Jan 03, 2011	John Hickenlooper (D-CO)	Jan 03, 2021
Marco Rubio (R-FL)	Jan 03, 2011	Bill Hagerty (R-TN)	Jan 03, 2021
Ron Johnson (R-WI)	Jan 03, 2011	Tommy Tuberville (R-AL)	Jan 03, 2021
Rand Paul (R-KY)	Jan 03, 2011	Alex Padilla (D-CA)	Jan 20, 2021
Richard Blumenthal (D-CT)	Jan 03, 2011	Jonathan Ossoff (D-GA)	Jan 20, 2021
Mike Lee (R-UT)	Jan 03, 2011	Raphael Warnock (D-GA)	Jan 20, 2021

HOUSE SENIORITY

Representatives are ranked by the total length of time served in the House. Members are given credit for prior service, and ties are broken alphabetically. The House seniority list was provided was compiled from information records and rules provided by the office of the Clerk of the House. It is current as of Jun 24, 2021.

Member (Party and State)	Start of Service	Member (Party and State)	Start of Service
Don Young (R-AK)	Mar 06, 1973	Sam Graves (R-MO)	Jan 03, 2001
Hal Rogers (R-KY)	Jan 03, 1981	Jim Langevin (D-RI)	Jan 03, 2001
Chris Smith (R-NJ)	Jan 03, 1981	Rick Larsen (D-WA)	Jan 03, 2001
Steny Hoyer (D-MD)	May 19, 1981	Betty McCollum (DFL-MN)	Jan 03, 2001
Marcy Kaptur (D-OH)	Jan 03, 1983	Adam Schiff (D-CA)	Jan 03, 2001
Peter DeFazio (D-OR)	Jan 03, 1987	Stephen Lynch (D-MA)	Oct 16, 2001
Fred Upton (R-MI)	Jan 03, 1987	Joe Wilson (R-SC)	Dec 18, 2001
Nancy Pelosi (D-CA)	Jun 02, 1987	Jim Cooper (D-TN)[2]	Jan 03, 2003
Frank Pallone (D-NJ)	Nov 08, 1988	Michael Burgess (R-TX)	Jan 03, 2003
Richard Neal (D-MA)	Jan 03, 1989	John Carter (R-TX)	Jan 03, 2003
Eleanor Holmes Norton (D-DC)	Jan 03, 1991	Tom Cole (R-OK)	Jan 03, 2003
Rosa DeLauro (D-CT)	Jan 03, 1991	Mario Diaz-Balart (R-FL)	Jan 03, 2003
Maxine Waters (D-CA)	Jan 03, 1991	Raul Grijalva (D-AZ)	Jan 03, 2003
Jerrold Nadler (D-NY)	Nov 03, 1992	Devin Nunes (R-CA)	Jan 03, 2003
Sanford Bishop (D-GA)	Jan 03, 1993	Mike Rogers (R-AL)	Jan 03, 2003
Ken Calvert (R-CA)	Jan 03, 1993	Dutch Ruppersberger (D-MD)	Jan 03, 2003
James Clyburn (D-SC)	Jan 03, 1993	Tim Ryan (D-OH)	Jan 03, 2003
Anna Eshoo (D-CA)	Jan 03, 1993	Linda Sánchez (D-CA)	Jan 03, 2003
Eddie Bernice Johnson (D-TX)	Jan 03, 1993	David Scott (D-GA)	Jan 03, 2003
Carolyn Maloney (D-NY)	Jan 03, 1993	Michael Turner (R-OH)	Jan 03, 2003
Lucille Roybal-Allard (D-CA)	Jan 03, 1993	G.K. Butterfield (D-NC)	Jul 20, 2004
Bobby Rush (D-IL)	Jan 03, 1993	Emanuel Cleaver (D-MO)	Jan 03, 2005
Bobby Scott (D-VA)	Jan 03, 1993	Jim Costa (D-CA)	Jan 03, 2005
Nydia Velázquez (D-NY)	Jan 03, 1993	Henry Cuellar (D-TX)	Jan 03, 2005
Bennie Thompson (D-MS)	Apr 13, 1993	Jeff Fortenberry (R-NE)	Jan 03, 2005
Frank Lucas (R-OK)	May 10, 1994	Virginia Foxx (R-NC)	Jan 03, 2005
Lloyd Doggett (D-TX)	Jan 03, 1995	Louie Gohmert (R-TX)	Jan 03, 2005
Mike Doyle (D-PA)	Jan 03, 1995	Al Green (D-TX)	Jan 03, 2005
Sheila Jackson Lee (D-TX)	Jan 03, 1995	Brian Higgins (D-NY)	Jan 03, 2005
Zoe Lofgren (D-CA)	Jan 03, 1995	Michael McCaul (R-TX)	Jan 03, 2005
Earl Blumenauer (D-OR)	May 21, 1996	Patrick McHenry (R-NC)	Jan 03, 2005
David Price (D-NC)[1]	Jan 03, 1997	Gwen Moore (D-WI)	Jan 03, 2005
Robert Aderholt (R-AL)	Jan 03, 1997	Cathy McMorris Rodgers (R-WA)	Jan 03, 2005
Kevin Brady (R-TX)	Jan 03, 1997	Debbie Wasserman Schultz (D-FL)	Jan 03, 2005
Danny Davis (D-IL)	Jan 03, 1997	Doris Matsui (D-CA)	Mar 08, 2005
Diana DeGette (D-CO)	Jan 03, 1997	Albio Sires (D-NJ)	Nov 07, 2006
Kay Granger (R-TX)	Jan 03, 1997	Gus Bilirakis (R-FL)	Jan 03, 2007
Ron Kind (D-WI)	Jan 03, 1997	Vern Buchanan (R-FL)	Jan 03, 2007
Jim McGovern (D-MA)	Jan 03, 1997	Kathy Castor (D-FL)	Jan 03, 2007
Bill Pascrell (D-NJ)	Jan 03, 1997	Yvette Clarke (D-NY)	Jan 03, 2007
Brad Sherman (D-CA)	Jan 03, 1997	Steve Cohen (D-TN)	Jan 03, 2007
Adam Smith (D-WA)	Jan 03, 1997	Joe Courtney (D-CT)	Jan 03, 2007
Gregory Meeks (D-NY)	Feb 03, 1998	Hank Johnson (D-GA)	Jan 03, 2007
Barbara Lee (D-CA)	Apr 07, 1998	Jim Jordan (R-OH)	Jan 03, 2007
John Larson (D-CT)	Jan 03, 1999	Doug Lamborn (R-CO)	Jan 03, 2007
Grace Napolitano (D-CA)	Jan 03, 1999	Kevin McCarthy (R-CA)	Jan 03, 2007
Jan Schakowsky (D-IL)	Jan 03, 1999	Jerry McNerney (D-CA)	Jan 03, 2007
Mike Simpson (R-ID)	Jan 03, 1999	Ed Perlmutter (D-CO)	Jan 03, 2007
Mike Thompson (D-CA)	Jan 03, 1999	John Sarbanes (D-MD)	Jan 03, 2007

Member (Party and State)	Start of Service	Member (Party and State)	Start of Service
Adrian Smith (R-NE)	Jan 03, 2007	Bill Foster (D-IL)[5]	Jan 03, 2013
Peter Welch (D-VT)	Jan 03, 2007	Dina Titus (D-NV)[6]	Jan 03, 2013
John Yarmuth (D-KY)	Jan 03, 2007	Andy Barr (R-KY)	Jan 03, 2013
Bob Latta (R-OH)	Dec 11, 2007	Joyce Beatty (D-OH)	Jan 03, 2013
Rob Wittman (R-VA)	Dec 11, 2007	Ami Bera (D-CA)	Jan 03, 2013
Andre Carson (D-IN)	Mar 11, 2008	Julia Brownley (D-CA)	Jan 03, 2013
Jackie Speier (D-CA)	Apr 08, 2008	Cheri Bustos (D-IL)	Jan 03, 2013
Steve Scalise (R-LA)	May 03, 2008	Tony Cárdenas (D-CA)	Jan 03, 2013
Gregorio Sablan (D-MP)	Nov 04, 2008	Matthew Cartwright (D-PA)	Jan 03, 2013
Gerald Connolly (D-VA)	Jan 03, 2009	Joaquin Castro (D-TX)	Jan 03, 2013
Brett Guthrie (R-KY)	Jan 03, 2009	Rodney Davis (R-IL)	Jan 03, 2013
Jim Himes (D-CT)	Jan 03, 2009	Lois Frankel (D-FL)	Jan 03, 2013
Blaine Luetkemeyer (R-MO)	Jan 03, 2009	Richard Hudson (R-NC)	Jan 03, 2013
Tom McClintock (R-CA)	Jan 03, 2009	Jared Huffman (D-CA)	Jan 03, 2013
Chellie Pingree (D-ME)	Jan 03, 2009	Hakeem Jeffries (D-NY)	Jan 03, 2013
Bill Posey (R-FL)	Jan 03, 2009	Dave Joyce (R-OH)	Jan 03, 2013
Kurt Schrader (D-OR)	Jan 03, 2009	Dan Kildee (D-MI)	Jan 03, 2013
Glenn Thompson (R-PA)	Jan 03, 2009	Derek Kilmer (D-WA)	Jan 03, 2013
Paul Tonko (D-NY)	Jan 03, 2009	Ann Kuster (D-NH)	Jan 03, 2013
Mike Quigley (D-IL)	Apr 07, 2009	Doug LaMalfa (R-CA)	Jan 03, 2013
Judy Chu (D-CA)	Jul 14, 2009	Alan Lowenthal (D-CA)	Jan 03, 2013
John Garamendi (D-CA)	Nov 03, 2009	Sean Maloney (D-NY)	Jan 03, 2013
Ted Deutch (D-FL)	Apr 13, 2010	Grace Meng (D-NY)	Jan 03, 2013
Tom Reed (R-NY)	Nov 02, 2010	Markwayne Mullin (R-OK)	Jan 03, 2013
Steve Chabot (R-OH)[3]	Jan 03, 2011	Scott Perry (R-PA)	Jan 03, 2013
Tim Walberg (R-MI)[4]	Jan 03, 2011	Scott Peters (D-CA)	Jan 03, 2013
Karen Bass (D-CA)	Jan 03, 2011	Mark Pocan (D-WI)	Jan 03, 2013
Mo Brooks (R-AL)	Jan 03, 2011	Tom Rice (R-SC)	Jan 03, 2013
Larry Bucshon (R-IN)	Jan 03, 2011	Raul Ruiz (D-CA)	Jan 03, 2013
David Cicilline (D-RI)	Jan 03, 2011	Chris Stewart (R-UT)	Jan 03, 2013
Rick Crawford (R-AR)	Jan 03, 2011	Eric Swalwell (D-CA)	Jan 03, 2013
Scott DesJarlais (R-TN)	Jan 03, 2011	Mark Takano (D-CA)	Jan 03, 2013
Jeff Duncan (R-SC)	Jan 03, 2011	Juan Vargas (D-CA)	Jan 03, 2013
Chuck Fleischmann (R-TN)	Jan 03, 2011	Marc Veasey (D-TX)	Jan 03, 2013
Bob Gibbs (R-OH)	Jan 03, 2011	Filemon Vela (D-TX)	Jan 03, 2013
Paul Gosar (R-AZ)	Jan 03, 2011	Ann Wagner (R-MO)	Jan 03, 2013
Morgan Griffith (R-VA)	Jan 03, 2011	Jackie Walorski (R-IN)	Jan 03, 2013
Andy Harris (R-MD)	Jan 03, 2011	Randy Weber (R-TX)	Jan 03, 2013
Vicky Hartzler (R-MO)	Jan 03, 2011	Brad Wenstrup (R-OH)	Jan 03, 2013
Jaime Herrera Beutler (R-WA)	Jan 03, 2011	Roger Williams (R-TX)	Jan 03, 2013
Bill Huizenga (R-MI)	Jan 03, 2011	Robin Kelly (D-IL)	Apr 09, 2013
Bill Johnson (R-OH)	Jan 03, 2011	Jason Smith (R-MO)	Jun 04, 2013
Bill Keating (D-MA)	Jan 03, 2011	Katherine Clark (D-MA)	Dec 10, 2013
Mike Kelly (R-PA)	Jan 03, 2011	Aumua Radewagen (R-AS)	Nov 04, 2014
Adam Kinzinger (R-IL)	Jan 03, 2011	Stacey Plaskett (D-VI)	Nov 04, 2014
Billy Long (R-MO)	Jan 03, 2011	Alma Adams (D-NC)	Nov 04, 2014
David McKinley (R-WV)	Jan 03, 2011	Donald Norcross (D-NJ)	Nov 04, 2014
Steven Palazzo (R-MS)	Jan 03, 2011	Pete Aguilar (D-CA)	Jan 03, 2015
David Schweikert (R-AZ)	Jan 03, 2011	Rick Allen (R-GA)	Jan 03, 2015
Austin Scott (R-GA)	Jan 03, 2011	Brian Babin (R-TX)	Jan 03, 2015
Terri Sewell (D-AL)	Jan 03, 2011	Don Beyer (D-VA)	Jan 03, 2015
Daniel Webster (R-FL)	Jan 03, 2011	Mike Bost (R-IL)	Jan 03, 2015
Frederica Wilson (D-FL)	Jan 03, 2011	Brendan Boyle (D-PA)	Jan 03, 2015
Steve Womack (R-AR)	Jan 03, 2011	Kenneth Buck (R-CO)	Jan 03, 2015
Mark Amodei (R-NV)	Sep 13, 2011	Buddy Carter (R-GA)	Jan 03, 2015
Suzanne Bonamici (D-OR)	Jan 31, 2012	Mark DeSaulnier (D-CA)	Jan 03, 2015
Suzan DelBene (D-WA)	Nov 06, 2012	Debbie Dingell (D-MI)	Jan 03, 2015
Thomas Massie (R-KY)	Nov 06, 2012	Thomas Emmer (R-MN)	Jan 03, 2015
Donald Payne (D-NJ)	Nov 06, 2012	Ruben Gallego (D-AZ)	Jan 03, 2015

Member (Party and State)	Start of Service	Member (Party and State)	Start of Service
Garret Graves (R-LA)	Jan 03, 2015	Stephanie Murphy (D-FL)	Jan 03, 2017
Glenn Grothman (R-WI)	Jan 03, 2015	Tom O'Halleran (D-AZ)	Jan 03, 2017
Jody Hice (R-GA)	Jan 03, 2015	Jimmy Panetta (D-CA)	Jan 03, 2017
French Hill (R-AR)	Jan 03, 2015	Jamie Raskin (D-MD)	Jan 03, 2017
John Katko (R-NY)	Jan 03, 2015	John Rutherford (R-FL)	Jan 03, 2017
Brenda Lawrence (D-MI)	Jan 03, 2015	Lloyd Smucker (R-PA)	Jan 03, 2017
Ted Lieu (D-CA)	Jan 03, 2015	Darren Soto (D-FL)	Jan 03, 2017
Barry Loudermilk (R-GA)	Jan 03, 2015	Thomas Suozzi (D-NY)	Jan 03, 2017
John Moolenaar (R-MI)	Jan 03, 2015	Ron Estes (R-KS)	Apr 11, 2017
Alex Mooney (R-WV)	Jan 03, 2015	Jimmy Gomez (D-CA)	Jun 06, 2017
Seth Moulton (D-MA)	Jan 03, 2015	Ralph Norman (R-SC)	Jun 20, 2017
Dan Newhouse (R-WA)	Jan 03, 2015	John Curtis (R-UT)	Nov 07, 2017
Gary Palmer (R-AL)	Jan 03, 2015	Conor Lamb (D-PA)	Mar 13, 2018
Kathleen Rice (D-NY)	Jan 03, 2015	Debbie Lesko (R-AZ)	Apr 24, 2018
David Rouzer (R-NC)	Jan 03, 2015	Michael Cloud (R-TX)	Jun 30, 2018
Elise Stefanik (R-NY)	Jan 03, 2015	Troy Balderson (R-OH)	Aug 07, 2018
Norma Torres (D-CA)	Jan 03, 2015	Michael San Nicolas (D-GU)	Nov 06, 2018
Bonnie Watson Coleman (D-NJ)	Jan 03, 2015	Kevin Hern (R-OK)	Nov 06, 2018
Bruce Westerman (R-AR)	Jan 03, 2015	Joseph Morelle (D-NY)	Nov 06, 2018
Lee Zeldin (R-NY)	Jan 03, 2015	Mary Gay Scanlon (D-PA)	Nov 06, 2018
Trent Kelly (R-MS)	Jun 02, 2015	Susan Wild (D-PA)	Nov 06, 2018
Darin LaHood (R-IL)	Sep 10, 2015	Ann Kirkpatrick (D-AZ)[7]	Jan 03, 2019
Warren Davidson (R-OH)	Jun 07, 2016	Ed Case (D-HI)[8]	Jan 03, 2019
Jenniffer González Colón (R-PR)	Nov 01, 2016	Steven Horsford (D-NV)[10]	Jan 03, 2019
James Comer (R-KY)	Nov 08, 2016	Colin Allred (D-TX)	Jan 03, 2019
Dwight Evans (D-PA)	Nov 08, 2016	Kelly Armstrong (R-ND)	Jan 03, 2019
Brad Schneider (D-IL)[9]	Jan 03, 2017	Cindy Axne (D-IA)	Jan 03, 2019
Jodey Arrington (R-TX)	Jan 03, 2017	Jim Baird (R-IN)	Jan 03, 2019
Don Bacon (R-NE)	Jan 03, 2017	Tim Burchett (R-TN)	Jan 03, 2019
Jim Banks (R-IN)	Jan 03, 2017	Sean Casten (D-IL)	Jan 03, 2019
Nanette Barragán (D-CA)	Jan 03, 2017	Benjamin Cline (R-VA)	Jan 03, 2019
John Bergman (R-MI)	Jan 03, 2017	Angie Craig (DFL-MN)	Jan 03, 2019
Andy Biggs (R-AZ)	Jan 03, 2017	Daniel Crenshaw (R-TX)	Jan 03, 2019
Lisa Blunt Rochester (D-DE)	Jan 03, 2017	Jason Crow (D-CO)	Jan 03, 2019
Anthony Brown (D-MD)	Jan 03, 2017	Sharice Davids (D-KS)	Jan 03, 2019
Ted Budd (R-NC)	Jan 03, 2017	Madeleine Dean (D-PA)	Jan 03, 2019
Salud Carbajal (D-CA)	Jan 03, 2017	Antonio Delgado (D-NY)	Jan 03, 2019
Liz Cheney (R-WY)	Jan 03, 2017	Veronica Escobar (D-TX)	Jan 03, 2019
Lou Correa (D-CA)	Jan 03, 2017	Lizzie Fletcher (D-TX)	Jan 03, 2019
Charlie Crist (D-FL)	Jan 03, 2017	Russ Fulcher (R-ID)	Jan 03, 2019
Val Demings (D-FL)	Jan 03, 2017	Chuy Garcia (D-IL)	Jan 03, 2019
Neal Dunn (R-FL)	Jan 03, 2017	Sylvia Garcia (D-TX)	Jan 03, 2019
Adriano Espaillat (D-NY)	Jan 03, 2017	Jared Golden (D-ME)	Jan 03, 2019
Drew Ferguson (R-GA)	Jan 03, 2017	Anthony Gonzalez (R-OH)	Jan 03, 2019
Brian Fitzpatrick (R-PA)	Jan 03, 2017	Lance Gooden (R-TX)	Jan 03, 2019
Matt Gaetz (R-FL)	Jan 03, 2017	Mark Green (R-TN)	Jan 03, 2019
Mike Gallagher (R-WI)	Jan 03, 2017	Michael Guest (R-MS)	Jan 03, 2019
Vicente Gonzalez (D-TX)	Jan 03, 2017	Jim Hagedorn (R-MN)	Jan 03, 2019
Josh Gottheimer (D-NJ)	Jan 03, 2017	Josh Harder (D-CA)	Jan 03, 2019
Clay Higgins (R-LA)	Jan 03, 2017	Jahana Hayes (D-CT)	Jan 03, 2019
Trey Hollingsworth (R-IN)	Jan 03, 2017	Chrissy Houlahan (D-PA)	Jan 03, 2019
Pramila Jayapal (D-WA)	Jan 03, 2017	Dusty Johnson (R-SD)	Jan 03, 2019
Mike Johnson (R-LA)	Jan 03, 2017	John Joyce (R-PA)	Jan 03, 2019
Ro Khanna (D-CA)	Jan 03, 2017	Andrew Kim (D-NJ)	Jan 03, 2019
Raja Krishnamoorthi (D-IL)	Jan 03, 2017	Susie Lee (D-NV)	Jan 03, 2019
David Kustoff (R-TN)	Jan 03, 2017	Andy Levin (D-MI)	Jan 03, 2019
Al Lawson (D-FL)	Jan 03, 2017	Mike Levin (D-CA)	Jan 03, 2019
Brian Mast (R-FL)	Jan 03, 2017	Elaine Luria (D-VA)	Jan 03, 2019
A. Donald McEachin (D-VA)	Jan 03, 2017		

Member (Party and State)	Start of Service	Member (Party and State)	Start of Service
Tom Malinowski (D-NJ)	Jan 03, 2019	Scott Franklin (R-FL)	Jan 03, 2021
Lucy McBath (D-GA)	Jan 03, 2019	Victoria Spartz (R-IN)	Jan 03, 2021
Daniel Meuser (R-PA)	Jan 03, 2019	Tracey Mann (R-KS)	Jan 03, 2021
Carol Miller (R-WV)	Jan 03, 2019	Ritchie Torres (D-NY)	Jan 03, 2021
Joe Neguse (D-CO)	Jan 03, 2019	Mondaire Jones (D-NY)	Jan 03, 2021
Alexandria Ocasio-Cortez (D-NY)	Jan 03, 2019	Ronny Jackson (R-TX)	Jan 03, 2021
Ilhan Omar (DFL-MN)	Jan 03, 2019	Troy Nehls (R-TX)	Jan 03, 2021
Chris Pappas (D-NH)	Jan 03, 2019	Kathy Manning (D-NC)	Jan 03, 2021
Greg Pence (R-IN)	Jan 03, 2019	Pat Fallon (R-TX)	Jan 03, 2021
Dean Phillips (DFL-MN)	Jan 03, 2019	Bob Good (R-VA)	Jan 03, 2021
Katie Porter (D-CA)	Jan 03, 2019	Michelle Fischbach (R-MN)	Jan 03, 2021
Ayanna Pressley (D-MA)	Jan 03, 2019	Madison Cawthorn (R-NC)	Jan 03, 2021
Guy Reschenthaler (R-PA)	Jan 03, 2019	Scott Fitzgerald (R-WI)	Jan 03, 2021
John Rose (R-TN)	Jan 03, 2019	Jake Auchincloss (D-MA)	Jan 03, 2021
Chip Roy (R-TX)	Jan 03, 2019	Jamaal Bowman (D-NY)	Jan 03, 2021
Kim Schrier (D-WA)	Jan 03, 2019	Andrew Garbarino (R-NY)	Jan 03, 2021
Mikie Sherrill (D-NJ)	Jan 03, 2019	Diana Harshbarger (R-TN)	Jan 03, 2021
Elissa Slotkin (D-MI)	Jan 03, 2019	Teresa Leger Fernandez (D-NM)	Jan 03, 2021
Abigail Spanberger (D-VA)	Jan 03, 2019	Matt Rosendale (R-MT)	Jan 03, 2021
Greg Stanton (D-AZ)	Jan 03, 2019	Nancy Mace (R-SC)	Jan 03, 2021
Pete Stauber (R-MN)	Jan 03, 2019	Young Kim (R-CA)	Jan 03, 2021
Bryan Steil (R-WI)	Jan 03, 2019	Yvette Herrell (R-NM)	Jan 03, 2021
Greg Steube (R-FL)	Jan 03, 2019	Lisa McClain (R-MI)	Jan 03, 2021
Haley Stevens (D-MI)	Jan 03, 2019	Peter Meijer (R-MI)	Jan 03, 2021
Van Taylor (R-TX)	Jan 03, 2019	Kaiali'i Kahele (D-HI)	Jan 03, 2021
William Timmons (R-SC)	Jan 03, 2019	Blake Moore (R-UT)	Jan 03, 2021
Rashida Tlaib (D-MI)	Jan 03, 2019	Mary Miller (R-IL)	Jan 03, 2021
Lori Trahan (D-MA)	Jan 03, 2019	Jerry Carl (R-AL)	Jan 03, 2021
David Trone (D-MD)	Jan 03, 2019	Cori Bush (D-MO)	Jan 03, 2021
Lauren Underwood (D-IL)	Jan 03, 2019	Maria Salazar (R-FL)	Jan 03, 2021
Jeff Van Drew (R-NJ)	Jan 03, 2019	Marjorie Greene (R-GA)	Jan 03, 2021
Michael Waltz (R-FL)	Jan 03, 2019	Burgess Owens (R-UT)	Jan 03, 2021
Jennifer Wexton (D-VA)	Jan 03, 2019	Carlos Gimenez (R-FL)	Jan 03, 2021
Fred Keller (R-PA)	May 21, 2019	Sara Jacobs (D-CA)	Jan 03, 2021
Dan Bishop (R-NC)	Sep 20, 2019	Marilyn Strickland (D-WA)	Jan 03, 2021
Gregory Murphy (R-NC)	Sep 20, 2019	Mariannette Miller-Meeks (R-IA)	Jan 03, 2021
Kweisi Mfume (D-MD)	Apr 28, 2020	Jake LaTurner (R-KS)	Jan 03, 2021
Mike Garcia (R-CA)	May 12, 2020	Pete Sessions (R-TX)	Jan 03, 2021
Tom Tiffany (R-WI)	May 12, 2020	Darrell Issa (R-CA)	Jan 03, 2021
Chris Jacobs (R-NY)	Jun 23, 2020	Kat Cammack (R-FL)	Jan 03, 2021
Barry Moore (R-AL)	Jan 03, 2021	David Valadao (R-CA)	Jan 03, 2021
Byron Donalds (R-FL)	Jan 03, 2021	Claudia Tenney (R-NY)	Jan 03, 2021
Carolyn Bourdeaux (D-GA)	Jan 03, 2021	Julia Letlow (R-LA)	Mar 20, 2021
Jay Obernolte (R-CA)	Jan 03, 2021	Troy Carter (D-LA)	Apr 24, 2021
Nikema Williams (D-GA)	Jan 03, 2021	Melanie Stansbury (D-NM)	Jun 14, 2021
Marie Newman (D-IL)	Jan 03, 2021		
Andrew Clyde (R-GA)	Jan 03, 2021		
Ashley Hinson (R-IA)	Jan 03, 2021		
Lauren Boebert (R-CO)	Jan 03, 2021		
Nicole Malliotakis (R-NY)	Jan 03, 2021		
Stephanie Bice (R-OK)	Jan 03, 2021		
Randy Feenstra (R-IA)	Jan 03, 2021		
Tony Gonzales (R-TX)	Jan 03, 2021		
August Pfluger (R-TX)	Jan 03, 2021		
Beth Van Duyne (R-TX)	Jan 03, 2021		
Frank Mrvan (D-IN)	Jan 03, 2021		
Deborah Ross (D-NC)	Jan 03, 2021		
Cliff Bentz (R-OR)	Jan 03, 2021		
Michelle Steel (R-CA)	Jan 03, 2021		

[1]Also served 1987-1995.
[2]Also served 1983-1995.
[3]Also served 1995-2009.
[4]Also served 2007-2009.
[5]Also served 2008-2011.
[6]Also served 2009-2011.
[7]Also served 2009-2011, 2013-2017.
[8]Also served 2002-2007.
[9]Also served 2013-2015.
[10]Also served 2013-2015.

SENATE COMMITTEES

Agriculture, Nutrition & Forestry
agriculture.senate.gov

328A RSOB
202-224-2035

Majority (D 11): Stabenow (MI), Chmn; Leahy (VT), Brown (OH), Klobuchar (MN), Bennet (CO), Gillibrand (NY), Smith (MN), Durbin (IL), Booker (NJ), Lujan (NM), Warnock (GA)
Minority (R 11): Boozman (AR), RMM; McConnell (KY), Hoeven (ND), Ernst (IA), Hyde-Smith (MS), Marshall (KS), Tuberville (AL), Grassley (IA), Thune (SD), Fischer (NE), Braun (IN)

SUBCOMMITTEES

Commodities, Risk Management & Trade

Majority (D 7): Warnock (GA), Chmn; Brown (OH), Durbin (IL), Smith (MN), Gillibrand (NY), Lujan (NM), Stabenow (MI)
Minority (R 6): Hoeven (ND), RMM; McConnell (KY), Hyde-Smith (MS), Tuberville (AL), Grassley (IA), Thune (SD)

Conservation, Climate, Forestry & Natural Resources

Majority (D 7): Bennet (CO), Chmn; Leahy (VT), Booker (NJ), Lujan (NM), Brown (OH), Klobuchar (MN), Stabenow (MI)
Minority (R 7): Marshall (KS), RMM; Hoeven (ND), Hyde-Smith (MS), Tuberville (AL), Thune (SD), Braun (IN), Boozman (AR)

Food & Nutrition, Specialty Crops, Organics & Research

Majority (D 7): Booker (NJ), Chmn; Leahy (VT), Klobuchar (MN), Gillibrand (NY), Warnock (GA), Bennet (CO), Stabenow (MI)
Minority (R 7): Braun (IN), RMM; McConnell (KY), Hoeven (ND), Ernst (IA), Marshall (KS), Fischer (NE), Boozman (AR)

Livestock, Dairy, Poultry, Local Food Sys & Food Safety & Sec

Majority (D 7): Gillibrand (NY), Chmn; Leahy (VT), Smith (MN), Durbin (IL), Booker (NJ), Warnock (GA), Stabenow (MI)
Minority (R 7): Hyde-Smith (MS), RMM; Ernst (IA), Marshall (KS), Grassley (IA), Fischer (NE), Thune (SD), Boozman (AR)

Rural Development & Energy

Majority (D 7): Smith (MN), Chmn; Klobuchar (MN), Lujan (NM), Brown (OH), Bennet (CO), Durbin (IL), Stabenow (MI)
Minority (R 7): Ernst (IA), RMM; McConnell (KY), Tuberville (AL), Grassley (IA), Fischer (NE), Braun (IN), Boozman (AR)

Appropriations
appropriations.senate.gov

220 HSOB
202-224-2981

Majority (D 15): Leahy (VT), Chmn; Murray (WA), Feinstein (CA), Durbin (IL), Reed (RI), Tester (MT), Shaheen (NH), Merkley (OR), Coons (DE), Schatz (HI), Baldwin (WI), Murphy (CT), Manchin (WV), Van Hollen (MD), Heinrich (NM)
Minority (R 15): Shelby (AL), RMM, McConnell (KY), Collins (ME), Murkowski (AK), Graham (SC), Blunt (MO), Moran (KS), Hoeven (ND), Boozman (AR), Capito (WV), Kennedy (LA), Hyde-Smith (MS), Braun (IN), Hagerty (TN), Rubio (FL)

SUBCOMMITTEES

Agriculture, Rural Development, FDA & Related Agencies

Majority (D 7): Baldwin (WI), Chmn; Merkley (OR), Feinstein (CA), Tester (MT), Leahy (VT), Schatz (HI), Heinrich (NM)
Minority (R 8): Hoeven (ND), RMM; McConnell (KY), Collins (ME), Blunt (MO), Moran (KS), Hyde-Smith (MS), Braun (IN), Shelby (AL)

Commerce, Justice, Science & Related Agencies
Majority (D 9): Shaheen (NH), Chmn; Leahy (VT), Feinstein (CA), Reed (RI), Coons (DE), Schatz (HI), Manchin (WV), Van Hollen (MD), Merkley (OR)
Minority (R 10): Moran (KS), RMM; Murkowski (AK), Collins (ME), Graham (SC), Boozman (AR), Capito (WV), Kennedy (LA), Hagerty (TN), Braun (IN), Shelby (AL)

Department of Defense
Majority (D 9): Tester (MT), Chmn; Durbin (IL), Leahy (VT), Feinstein (CA), Murray (WA), Reed (RI), Schatz (HI), Baldwin (WI), Shaheen (NH)
Minority (R 9): Shelby (AL), McConnell (KY), Collins (ME), Murkowski (AK), Graham (SC), Blunt (MO), Moran (KS), Hoeven (ND), Boozman (AR)

Department of Homeland Security
Majority (D 6): Murphy (CT), Chmn; Tester (MT), Shaheen (NH), Leahy (VT), Murray (WA), Baldwin (WI)
Minority (R 6): Capito (WV), RMM; Shelby (AL), Murkowski (AK), Hoeven (ND), Kennedy (LA), Hyde-Smith (MS)

Department of the Interior, Environment & Related Agencies
Majority (D 7): Merkley (OR), Chmn; Feinstein (CA), Leahy (VT), Reed (RI), Tester (MT), Van Hollen (MD), Heinrich (NM)
Minority (R 8): Murkowski (AK), RMM; Blunt (MO), McConnell (KY), Capito (WV), Hyde-Smith (MS), Hagerty (TN), Rubio (FL), Shelby (AL)

DOL, HHS & Education & Related Agencies
Majority (D 10): Murray (WA), Chmn; Durbin (IL), Reed (RI), Shaheen (NH), Merkley (OR), Schatz (HI), Baldwin (WI), Murphy (CT), Manchin (WV), Leahy (VT)
Minority (R 9): Blunt (MO), RMM; Shelby (AL), Graham (SC), Moran (KS), Capito (WV), Kennedy (LA), Hyde-Smith (MS), Braun (IN), Rubio (FL)

Energy & Water Development
Majority (D 10): Feinstein (CA), Chmn; Murray (WA), Tester (MT), Durbin (IL), Shaheen (NH), Merkley (OR), Coons (DE), Baldwin (WI), Heinrich (NM), Leahy (VT)
Minority (R 9): Kennedy (LA), RMM; McConnell (KY), Shelby (AL), Collins (ME), Murkowski (AK), Graham (SC), Hoeven (ND), Hyde-Smith (MS), Hagerty (TN)

Financial Services & General Government
Majority (D 5): Van Hollen (MD), Chmn; Coons (DE), Durbin (IL), Manchin (WV), Leahy (VT)
Minority (R 5): Hyde-Smith (MS), RMM; Moran (KS), Boozman (AR), Kennedy (LA), Shelby (AL)

Legislative Branch
Majority (D 4): Reed (RI), Chmn; Murphy (CT), Heinrich (NM), Leahy (VT)
Minority (R 3): Braun (IN), RMM; Shelby (AL), Rubio (FL)

Military Construction & Veteran Affairs & Related Agencies
Majority (D 9): Heinrich (NM), Chmn; Schatz (HI), Tester (MT), Murray (WA), Reed (RI), Baldwin (WI), Coons (DE), Manchin (WV), Leahy (VT)
Minority (R 9): Boozman (AR), RMM; McConnell (KY), Murkowski (AK), Hoeven (ND), Collins (ME), Capito (WV), Rubio (FL), Hagerty (TN), Shelby (AL)

State, Foreign Operations & Related Programs
Majority (D 7): Coons (DE), Chmn; Leahy (VT), Durbin (IL), Shaheen (NH), Merkley (OR), Murphy (CT), Van Hollen (MD)
Minority (R 8): Graham (SC), RMM; McConnell (KY), Blunt (MO), Boozman (AR), Moran (KS), Rubio (FL), Hagerty (TN), Shelby (AL)

Transportation, HUD & Related Agencies
Majority (D 10): Schatz (HI), Chmn; Reed (RI), Murray (WA), Durbin (IL), Feinstein (CA), Coons (DE), Murphy (CT), Manchin (WV), Van Hollen (MD), Leahy (VT)
Minority (R 9): Collins (ME), RMM; Shelby (AL), Blunt (MO), Boozman (AR), Capito (WV), Graham (SC), Hoeven (ND), Kennedy (LA), Braun (IN)

Armed Services	**228 RSOB**
armed-services.senate.gov	**202-224-3871**

Majority (D 13): Reed (RI), Chmn; Shaheen (NH), Gillibrand (NY), Blumenthal (CT), Hirono (HI), Kaine (VA), King (ME), Warren (MA), Peters (MI), Manchin (WV), Duckworth (IL), Rosen (NV), Kelly (AZ)

Minority (R 13): Rubio (FL), RMM; Burr (NC), Risch (ID), Collins (ME), Blunt (MO), Cotton (AR), Cornyn (TX), Sasse (NE), McConnell (KY), Inhofe (OK)

SUBCOMMITTEES

Airland
Majority (D 7): Duckworth (IL), Chmn; King (ME), Peters (MI), Manchin (WV), Kelly (AZ), Rosen (NV), Reed (RI)
Minority (R 7): Cotton (AR), RMM; Wicker (MS), Tillis (NC), Sullivan (AK), Scott (FL), Hawley (MO), Inhofe (OK)

Cybersecurity
Majority (D 5): Manchin (WV), Chmn; Gillibrand (NY), Blumenthal (CT), Rosen (NV), Reed (RI)
Minority (R 5): Rounds (SD), RMM; Wicker (MS), Ernst (IA), Blackburn (TN), Inhofe (OK)

Emerging Threats & Capabilities
Majority (D 7): Kelly (AZ), Chmn; Shaheen (NH), Kaine (VA), Warren (MA), Peters (MI), Gillibrand (NY), Reed (RI)
Minority (R 7): Ernst (IA), RMM; Fischer (NE), Cramer (ND), Scott (FL), Blackburn (TN), Tuberville (AL), Hawley (MO)

Personnel
Majority (D 4): Gillibrand (NY), Chmn; Hirono (HI), Warren (MA), Reed (RI)
Minority (R 4): Tillis (NC), RMM; Hawley (MO), Tuberville (AL), Inhofe (OK)

Readiness & Management Support
Majority (D 6): Kaine (VA), Chmn; Shaheen (NH), Blumenthal (CT), Hirono (HI), Duckworth (IL), Reed (RI)
Minority (R 6): Sullivan (AK), RMM; Fischer (NE), Rounds (SD), Ernst (IA), Blackburn (TN), Inhofe (OK)

Seapower
Majority (D 7): Hirono (HI), Chmn; Shaheen (NH), Blumenthal (CT), King (ME), Kaine (VA), Peters (MI), Reed (RI)
Minority (R 7): Cramer (ND), RMM; Wicker (MS), Cotton (AR), Tillis (NC), Scott (FL), Hawley (MO), Inhofe (OK)

Strategic Forces
Majority (D 7): King (ME), Chmn; Warren (MA), Manchin (WV), Duckworth (IL), Rosen (NV), Kelly (AZ), Reed (RI)
Minority (R 7): Fischer (NE), RMM; Cotton (AR), Rounds (SD), Sullivan (AK), Cramer (ND), Tuberville (AL), Inhofe (OK)

Banking, Housing & Urban Affairs
banking.senate.gov

534 DSOB
202-224-7391

Majority (D 12): Brown (OH), Chmn; Reed (RI), Menendez (NJ), Tester (MT), Warner (VA), Warren (MA), Van Hollen (MD), Cortez Masto (NV), Smith (MN), Sinema (AZ), Ossoff (GA), Warnock (GA)
Minority (R 12): Toomey (PA), RMM; Shelby (AL), Crapo (ID), Scott (SC), Rounds (SD), Tillis (NC), Kennedy (LA), Hagerty (TN), Lummis (WY), Moran (KS), Cramer (ND), Daines (MT)

SUBCOMMITTEES

Economic Policy
Majority (D 5): Warren (MA), Chmn; Reed (RI), Van Hollen (MD), Smith (MN), Ossoff (GA)
Minority (R 5): Kennedy (LA), RMM; Scott (SC), Tillis (NC), Cramer (ND), Daines (MT)

Financial Institutions & Consumer Protection
Majority (D 8): Warnock (GA), Chmn; Menendez (NJ), Tester (MT), Warner (VA), Warren (MA), Cortez Masto (NV), Van Hollen (MD), Sinema (AZ)
Minority (R 8): Tillis (NC), RMM; Shelby (AL), Scott (SC), Rounds (SD), Hagerty (TN), Lummis (WY), Moran (KS), Cramer (ND)

Housing, Transportation & Community Development
Majority (D 8): Smith (MN), Chmn; Reed (RI), Menendez (NJ), Tester (MT), Cortez Masto (NV), Van Hollen (MD), Ossoff (GA), Warnock (GA)
Minority (R 8): Rounds (SD), RMM; Shelby (AL), Crapo (ID), Hagerty (TN), Lummis (WY), Moran (KS), Cramer (ND), Daines (MT)

National Security & International Trade & Finance
Majority (D 4): Warner (VA), Chmn; Tester (MT), Sinema (AZ), Ossoff (GA)
Minority (R 4): Hagerty (TN), RMM; Crapo (ID), Kennedy (LA), Daines (MT)

Securities, Insurance & Investment
Majority (D 8): Menendez (NJ), Chmn; Reed (RI), Warner (VA), Warren (MA), Cortez Masto (NV), Smith (MN), Sinema (AZ), Warnock (GA)
Minority (R 8): Scott (SC), RMM; Shelby (AL), Crapo (ID), Rounds (SD), Tillis (NC), Kennedy (LA), Lummis (WY), Moran (KS)

Budget	**624 DSOB**
budget.senate.gov	**202-224-0642**

Majority (D 11): Sanders (VT), Chmn; Murray (WA), Wyden (OR), Stabenow (MI), Whitehouse (RI), Warner (VA), Merkley (OR), Kaine (VA), Van Hollen (MD), Lujan (NM), Padilla (CA)
Minority (R 11): Graham (SC), RMM; Grassley (IA), Crapo (ID), Toomey (PA), Johnson (WI), Braun (IN), Scott (FL), Sasse (NE), Romney (UT), Kennedy (LA), Cramer (ND)

Commerce, Science & Transportation	**512 DSOB**
commerce.senate.gov	**202-224-1251**

Majority (D 14): Cantwell (WA), Chmn; Klobuchar (MN), Blumenthal (CT), Schatz (HI), Markey (MA), Peters (MI), Baldwin (WI), Duckworth (IL), Tester (MT), Sinema (AZ), Rosen (NV), Lujan (NM), Hickenlooper (CO), Warnock (GA)
Minority (R 14): Wicker (MS), RMM; Thune (SD), Blunt (MO), Cruz (TX), Fischer (NE), Moran (KS), Sullivan (AK), Blackburn (TN), Young (IN), Lee (UT), Johnson (WI), Capito (WV), Scott (FL), Lummis (WY)

SUBCOMMITTEES

Aviation Safety, Operations & Innovations
Majority (D 7): Sinema (AZ), Chmn; Duckworth (IL), Tester (MT), Rosen (NV), Hickenlooper (CO), Warnock (GA), Cantwell (WA)
Minority (R 7): Cruz (TX), RMM; Thune (SD), Blunt (MO), Moran (KS), Lee (UT), Capito (WV), Wicker (MS)

Communications, Media & Broadband
Majority (D 14): Lujan (NM), Chmn; Klobuchar (MN), Blumenthal (CT), Schatz (HI), Markey (MA), Peters (MI), Baldwin (WI), Duckworth (IL), Tester (MT), Sinema (AZ), Rosen (NV), Hickenlooper (CO), Warnock (GA), Cantwell (WA)
Minority (R 14): Thune (SD), Blunt (MO), Cruz (TX), Fischer (NE), Moran (KS), Sullivan (AK), Blackburn (TN), Young (IN), Lee (UT), Johnson (WI), Capito (WV), Scott (FL), Lummis (WY), Wicker (MS)

Consumer Protection, Product Safety & Data Security
Majority (D 7): Blumenthal (CT), Chmn; Klobuchar (MN), Schatz (HI), Markey (MA), Baldwin (WI), Lujan (NM), Cantwell (WA)
Minority (R 7): Blackburn (TN), RMM; Thune (SD), Blunt (MO), Moran (KS), Lee (UT), Young (IN), Wicker (MS)

Oceans, Fisheries, Climate Change & Manufacturing
Majority (D 7): Baldwin (WI), Chmn; Blumenthal (CT), Schatz (HI), Markey (MA), Peters (MI), Lujan (NM), Cantwell (WA)
Minority (R 7): Sullivan (AK), RMM; Cruz (TX), Fischer (NE), Blackburn (TN), Johnson (WI), Young (IN), Wicker (MS)

Space & Science
Majority (D 8): Hickenlooper (CO), Chmn; Blumenthal (CT), Peters (MI), Sinema (AZ), Lujan (NM), Warnock (GA), Markey (MA), Cantwell (WA)
Minority (R 8): Lummis (WY), RMM; Cruz (TX), Fischer (NE), Young (IN), Lee (UT), Scott (FL), Moran (KS), Wicker (MS)

Surface Transportation, Maritime Freight & Ports
Majority (D 10): Peters (MI), Chmn; Klobuchar (MN), Blumenthal (CT), Schatz (HI), Markey (MA), Baldwin (WI), Duckworth (IL), Tester (MT), Warnock (GA), Cantwell (WA)
Minority (R 10): Fischer (NE), RMM; Thune (SD), Blunt (MO), Sullivan (AK), Young (IN), Johnson (WI), Capito (WV), Scott (FL), Lummis (WY), Wicker (MS)

Tourism, Trade & Export Promotion
Majority (D 7): Rosen (NV), Chmn; Klobuchar (MN), Duckworth (IL), Tester (MT), Sinema (AZ),
Hickenlooper (CO), Cantwell (WA)
Minority (R 7): Scott (FL), RMM; Sullivan (AK), Blackburn (TN), Johnson (WI), Capito (WV), Lummis
(WY), Wicker (MS)

Energy & Natural Resources   **304 DSOB**
energy.senate.gov   **202-224-4971**

Majority (D 10): Manchin (WV), Chmn; Wyden (OR), Cantwell (WA), Sanders (VT), Heinrich (NM), Hirono
(HI), King (ME), Cortez Masto (NV), Kelly (AZ), Hickenlooper (CO)
Minority (R 10): Barrasso (WY), RMM; Risch (ID), Lee (UT), Daines (MT), Murkowski (AK), Hoeven (ND),
Lankford (OK), Cassidy (LA), Hyde-Smith (MS), Marshall (KS)

SUBCOMMITTEES

Energy
Majority (D 8): Hirono (HI), Chmn; Wyden (OR), Sanders (VT), Heinrich (NM), King (ME), Cortez Masto
(NV), Hickenlooper (CO), Manchin (WV)
Minority (R 8): Hoeven (ND), RMM; Risch (ID), Murkowski (AK), Lankford (OK), Cassidy (LA), Hyde-
Smith (MS), Marshall (KS), Barrasso (WY)

National Parks
Majority (D 6): King (ME), Chmn; Sanders (VT), Heinrich (NM), Hirono (HI), Kelly (AZ), Manchin (WV)
Minority (R 6): Daines (MT), RMM; Lee (UT), Murkowski (AK), Hoeven (ND), Lankford (OK), Barrasso
(WY)

Public Lands, Forests & Mining
Majority (D 8): Cortez Masto (NV), Chmn; Wyden (OR), Heinrich (NM), Hirono (HI), King (ME), Kelly (AZ),
Hickenlooper (CO), Manchin (WV)
Minority (R 8): Lee (UT), RMM; Risch (ID), Daines (MT), Murkowski (AK), Lankford (OK), Cassidy (LA),
Hyde-Smith (MS), Barrasso (WY)

Water & Power
Majority (D 6): Wyden (OR), Chmn; Sanders (VT), Cortez Masto (NV), Kelly (AZ), Hickenlooper (CO),
Manchin (WV)
Minority (R 6): Hyde-Smith (MS), RMM; Risch (ID), Lee (UT), Hoeven (ND), Marshall (KS), Barrasso (WY)

Environment & Public Works   **410 DSOB**
epw.senate.gov   **202-224-8832**

Majority (D 10): Carper (DE), Chmn; Cardin (MD), Sanders (VT), Whitehouse (RI), Merkley (OR), Markey
(MA), Duckworth (IL), Stabenow (MI), Kelly (AZ), Padilla (CA)
Minority (R 10): Capito (WV), RMM; Inhofe (OK), Cramer (ND), Lummis (WY), Shelby (AL), Boozman
(AR), Wicker (MS), Sullivan (AK), Ernst (IA), Graham (SC)

SUBCOMMITTEES

Chem Safety, Waste Mngmnt, Enviro Justice & Reg Oversight
Majority (D 6): Merkley (OR), Chmn; Sanders (VT), Markey (MA), Kelly (AZ), Padilla (CA), Carper (DE)
Minority (R 6): Wicker (MS), RMM; Shelby (AL), Sullivan (AK), Ernst (IA), Graham (SC), Capito (WV)

Clean Air & Nuclear Safety
Majority (D 9): Markey (MA), Chmn; Cardin (MD), Sanders (VT), Whitehouse (RI), Merkley (OR),
Duckworth (IL), Stabenow (MI), Padilla (CA), Carper (DE)
Minority (R 9): Inhofe (OK), RMM; Cramer (ND), Lummis (WY), Shelby (AL), Boozman (AR), Wicker (MS),
Ernst (IA), Graham (SC), Capito (WV)

Fisheries, Water, and Wildlife
Majority (D 7): Duckworth (IL), Chmn; Cardin (MD), Whitehouse (RI), Markey (MA), Stabenow (MI), Kelly
(AZ), Carper (DE)
Minority (R 7): Lummis (WY), RMM; Inhofe (OK), Cramer (ND), Boozman (AR), Sullivan (AK), Ernst (IA),
Capito (WV)

Transportation & Infrastructure
Majority (D 9): Cardin (MD), Chmn; Sanders (VT), Whitehouse (RI), Merkley (OR), Duckworth (IL), Stabenow (MI), Kelly (AZ), Padilla (CA), Carper (DE)
Minority (R 9): Cramer (ND), RMM; Inhofe (OK), Lummis (WY), Shelby (AL), Boozman (AR), Wicker (MS), Sullivan (AK), Graham (SC), Capito (WV)

Finance	**219 DSOB**
finance.senate.gov	202-224-4515

Majority (D 14): Wyden (OR), Chmn; Stabenow (MI), Cantwell (WA), Menendez (NJ), Carper (DE), Cardin (MD), Brown (OH), Bennet (CO), Casey (PA), Warner (VA), Whitehouse (RI), Hassan (NH), Cortez Masto (NV), Warren (MA)
Minority (R 14): Crapo (ID), RMM; Grassley (IA), Cornyn (TX), Thune (SD), Burr (NC), Portman (OH), Toomey (PA), Scott (SC), Cassidy (LA), Lankford (OK), Daines (MT), Young (IN), Sasse (NE), Barrasso (WY)

SUBCOMMITTEES

Energy, Natural Resources & Infrastructure
Majority (D 5): Bennet (CO), Chmn; Carper (DE), Warner (VA), Whitehouse (RI), Hassan (NH)
Minority (R 5): Lankford (OK), RMM; Cornyn (TX), Scott (SC), Barrasso (WY), Daines (MT)

Fiscal Responsibility & Economic Growth
Majority (D 2): Warren (MA), Chmn; Wyden (OR)
Minority (R 2): Cassidy (LA), RMM; Burr (NC)

Health Care
Majority (D 10): Stabenow (MI), Chmn; Menendez (NJ), Carper (DE), Cardin (MD), Casey (PA), Warner (VA), Whitehouse (RI), Cortez Masto (NV), Hassan (NH), Warren (MA)
Minority (R 10): Daines (MT), RMM; Grassley (IA), Thune (SD), Burr (NC), Toomey (PA), Scott (SC), Cassidy (LA), Lankford (OK), Young (IN), Barrasso (WY)

International Trade, Customs & Global Competitiveness
Majority (D 10): Carper (DE), Chmn; Wyden (OR), Stabenow (MI), Menendez (NJ), Cardin (MD), Brown (OH), Bennet (CO), Casey (PA), Warner (VA), Cortez Masto (NV)
Minority (R 10): Cornyn (TX), RMM; Grassley (IA), Thune (SD), Portman (OH), Toomey (PA), Scott (SC), Daines (MT), Young (IN), Sasse (NE), Barrasso (WY)

Social Security, Pensions & Family Policy
Majority (D 5): Brown (OH), Chmn; Wyden (OR), Bennet (CO), Casey (PA), Hassan (NH)
Minority (R 5): Young (IN), RMM; Portman (OH), Cassidy (LA), Lankford (OK), Sasse (NE)

Taxation & IRS Oversight
Majority (D 7): Whitehouse (RI), Chmn; Stabenow (MI), Menendez (NJ), Cardin (MD), Brown (OH), Cortez Masto (NV), Warren (MA)
Minority (R 7): Thune (SD), RMM; Grassley (IA), Cornyn (TX), Burr (NC), Portman (OH), Toomey (PA), Sasse (NE)

Foreign Relations	**423 DSOB**
foreign.senate.gov	202-224-4651

Majority (D 11): Menendez (NJ), Chmn; Cardin (MD), Shaheen (NH), Coons (DE), Murphy (CT), Kaine (VA), Markey (MA), Merkley (OR), Booker (NJ), Schatz (HI), Van Hollen (MD)
Minority (R 11): Risch (ID), RMM; Rubio (FL), Johnson (WI), Romney (UT), Portman (OH), Paul (KY), Young (IN), Barrasso (WY), Cruz (TX), Rounds (SD), Hagerty (TN)

SUBCOMMITTEES

Africa & Global Health Policy
Majority (D 5): Van Hollen (MD), Chmn; Booker (NJ), Kaine (VA), Merkley (OR), Coons (DE)
Minority (R 5): Rounds (SD), RMM; Rubio (FL), Young (IN), Barrasso (WY), Paul (KY)

East Asia, the Pacific & International Cybersecurity Policy
Majority (D 5): Markey (MA), Chmn; Coons (DE), Murphy (CT), Schatz (HI), Merkley (OR)
Minority (R 5): Romney (UT), RMM; Cruz (TX), Johnson (WI), Rounds (SD), Hagerty (TN)

Europe & Regional Security Cooperation
Majority (D 5): Shaheen (NH), Chmn; Cardin (MD), Murphy (CT), Van Hollen (MD), Coons (DE)
Minority (R 5): Johnson (WI), RMM; Barrasso (WY), Romney (UT), Portman (OH), Young (IN)

Internat'l Dev Instit & Internat'l Econ, Energy & Environ Policy
Majority (D 5): Coons (DE), Chmn; Schatz (HI), Booker (NJ), Cardin (MD), Shaheen (NH)
Minority (R 5): Portman (OH), RMM; Young (IN), Paul (KY), Barrasso (WY), Rounds (SD)

Near East, South Asia, Central Asia & Counterterrorism
Majority (D 5): Murphy (CT), Chmn; Shaheen (NH), Markey (MA), Booker (NJ), Van Hollen (MD)
Minority (R 5): Young (IN), RMM; Paul (KY), Cruz (TX), Romney (UT), Hagerty (TN)

State Dept & USAID Mngmnt, Internat'l Ops & Internat'l Dev
Majority (D 5): Cardin (MD), Chmn; Kaine (VA), Schatz (HI), Murphy (CT), Markey (MA)
Minority (R 5): Hagerty (TN), RMM; Paul (KY), Cruz (TX), Johnson (WI), Rubio (FL)

West Hem Crime Civ Sec Dem Rights & Women's Issues
Majority (D 5): Kaine (VA), Chmn; Merkley (OR), Cardin (MD), Shaheen (NH), Markey (MA)
Minority (R 5): Rubio (FL), RMM; Portman (OH), Barrasso (WY), Hagerty (TN), Cruz (TX)

Health, Education, Labor & Pensions   **428 DSOB**
help.senate.gov   **202-224-0767**

Majority (D 11): Murray (WA), Chmn; Sanders (VT), Casey (PA), Baldwin (WI), Murphy (CT), Kaine (VA), Hassan (NH), Smith (MN), Rosen (NV), Lujan (NM), Hickenlooper (CO)
Minority (R 11): Burr (NC), RMM; Paul (KY), Collins (ME), Cassidy (LA), Murkowski (AK), Braun (IN), Marshall (KS), Scott (SC), Romney (UT), Tuberville (AL), Moran (KS)

SUBCOMMITTEES

Children & Families
Majority (D 8): Casey (PA), Chmn; Sanders (VT), Murphy (CT), Kaine (VA), Hassan (NH), Smith (MN), Hickenlooper (CO), Murray (WA)
Minority (R 8): Cassidy (LA), RMM; Romney (UT), Collins (ME), Murkowski (AK), Moran (KS), Marshall (KS), Tuberville (AL), Burr (NC)

Employment & Workplace Safety
Majority (D 6): Hickenlooper (CO), Chmn; Baldwin (WI), Smith (MN), Rosen (NV), Lujan (NM), Murray (WA)
Minority (R 6): Braun (IN), RMM; Tuberville (AL), Paul (KY), Scott (SC), Romney (UT), Burr (NC)

Primary Health & Retirement Security
Majority (D 9): Sanders (VT), Chmn; Casey (PA), Baldwin (WI), Murphy (CT), Kaine (VA), Hassan (NH), Rosen (NV), Lujan (NM), Murray (WA)
Minority (R 9): Collins (ME), RMM; Paul (KY), Murkowski (AK), Marshall (KS), Scott (SC), Moran (KS), Cassidy (LA), Braun (IN), Burr (NC)

Homeland Security & Government Affairs   **340 DSOB**
hsgac.senate.gov   **202-224-2627**

Majority (D 7): Peters (MI), Chmn; Carper (DE), Hassan (NH), Sinema (AZ), Rosen (NV), Padilla (CA), Ossoff (GA)
Minority (R 7): Portman (OH), RMM; Johnson (WI), Paul (KY), Lankford (OK), Romney (UT), Scott (FL), Hawley (MO)

SUBCOMMITTEES

Emerging Threats & Spending Oversight
Majority (D 5): Hassan (NH), Chmn; Sinema (AZ), Rosen (NV), Ossoff (GA), Peters (MI)
Minority (R 5): Paul (KY), RMM; Romney (UT), Scott (FL), Hawley (MO), Portman (OH)

Government Operations & Border Management
Majority (D 5): Sinema (AZ), Chmn; Carper (DE), Padilla (CA), Ossoff (GA), Peters (MI)
Minority (R 5): Lankford (OK), RMM; Johnson (WI), Romney (UT), Hawley (MO), Portman (OH)

Investigations
Majority (D 5): Ossoff (GA), Chmn; Carper (DE), Hassan (NH), Padilla (CA), Peters (MI)
Minority (R 5): Johnson (WI), RMM; Paul (KY), Lankford (OK), Scott (FL), Portman (OH)

Indian Affairs	**838 HSOB**
indian.senate.gov	**202-224-2251**

Majority (D 6): Schatz (HI), Chmn; Cantwell (WA), Tester (MT), Cortez Masto (NV), Smith (MN), Lujan (NM)
Minority (R 6): Murkowski (AK), Hoeven (ND), Lankford (OK), Daines (MT), Rounds (SD), Moran (KS)

Judiciary	**224 DSOB**
judiciary.senate.gov	**202-224-7703**

Majority (D 11): Durbin (IL), Chmn; Leahy (VT), Feinstein (CA), Whitehouse (RI), Klobuchar (MN), Coons (DE), Blumenthal (CT), Hirono (HI), Booker (NJ), Padilla (CA), Ossoff (GA)
Minority (R 11): Grassley (IA), RMM; Graham (SC), Cornyn (TX), Lee (UT), Cruz (TX), Sasse (NE), Hawley (MO), Cotton (AR), Kennedy (LA), Tillis (NC), Blackburn (TN)

SUBCOMMITTEES

Competition Policy, Antitrust & Consumer Rights
Majority (D 5): Klobuchar (MN), Chmn; Leahy (VT), Blumenthal (CT), Booker (NJ), Ossoff (GA)
Minority (R 5): Lee (UT), RMM; Hawley (MO), Cotton (AR), Blackburn (TN), Tillis (NC)

Constitution
Majority (D 4): Blumenthal (CT), Chmn; Feinstein (CA), Whitehouse (RI), Ossoff (GA)
Minority (R 4): Cruz (TX), RMM; Cornyn (TX), Lee (UT), Sasse (NE)

Criminal Justice & Counterterrorism
Majority (D 7): Booker (NJ), Chmn; Leahy (VT), Feinstein (CA), Whitehouse (RI), Klobuchar (MN), Padilla (CA), Ossoff (GA)
Minority (R 7): Cotton (AR), RMM; Graham (SC), Cornyn (TX), Lee (UT), Cruz (TX), Hawley (MO), Kennedy (LA)

Federal Courts, Oversight, Agency Action & Federal Rights
Majority (D 6): Whitehouse (RI), Chmn; Leahy (VT), Hirono (HI), Booker (NJ), Padilla (CA), Ossoff (GA)
Minority (R 6): Kennedy (LA), RMM; Graham (SC), Lee (UT), Cruz (TX), Sasse (NE), Tillis (NC)

Human Rights & the Law
Majority (D 3): Feinstein (CA), Chmn; Coons (DE), Blumenthal (CT)
Minority (R 3): Hawley (MO), RMM; Sasse (NE), Kennedy (LA)

Immigration, Citizenship & Border Security
Majority (D 7): Padilla (CA), Chmn; Feinstein (CA), Klobuchar (MN), Coons (DE), Blumenthal (CT), Hirono (HI), Booker (NJ)
Minority (R 7): Cornyn (TX), RMM; Graham (SC), Cruz (TX), Cotton (AR), Kennedy (LA), Tillis (NC), Blackburn (TN)

Privacy, Technology & the Law
Majority (D 5): Coons (DE), Chmn; Whitehouse (RI), Klobuchar (MN), Hirono (HI), Ossoff (GA)
Minority (R 5): Sasse (NE), RMM; Graham (SC), Hawley (MO), Kennedy (LA), Blackburn (TN)

Subcommittee on Intellectual Property
Majority (D 4): Leahy (VT), Chmn; Coons (DE), Hirono (HI), Padilla (CA)
Minority (R 4): Tillis (NC), RMM; Cornyn (TX), Cotton (AR), Blackburn (TN)

Rules & Administration	**305 RSOB**
rules.senate.gov	**202-224-6352**

Majority (D 9): Klobuchar (MN), Chmn; Feinstein (CA), Schumer (NY), Warner (VA), Leahy (VT), King (ME), Merkley (OR), Padilla (CA), Ossoff (GA)
Minority (R 9): Blunt (MO), RMM; McConnell (KY), Shelby (AL), Cruz (TX), Capito (WV), Wicker (MS), Fischer (NE), Hyde-Smith (MS), Hagerty (TN)

Small Business & Entrepreneurship	**428A RSOB**
sbc.senate.gov	**202-224-5175**

Majority (D 10): Cardin (MD), Chmn; Cantwell (WA), Shaheen (NH), Markey (MA), Booker (NJ), Coons (DE), Hirono (HI), Duckworth (IL), Rosen (NV), Hickenlooper (CO)
Minority (R 10): Paul (KY), RMM; Rubio (FL), Risch (ID), Scott (FL), Ernst (IA), Inhofe (OK), Young (IN), Kennedy (LA), Hawley (MO), Marshall (KS)

| **Veterans' Affairs** | **412 RSOB** |
| veterans.senate.gov | **202-224-9126** |

Majority (D 9): Tester (MT), Chmn; Murray (WA), Sanders (VT), Brown (OH), Blumenthal (CT), Hirono (HI), Manchin (WV), Sinema (AZ), Hassan (NH)
Minority (R 9): Moran (KS), RMM; Boozman (AR), Cassidy (LA), Rounds (SD), Tillis (NC), Sullivan (AK), Blackburn (TN), Cramer (ND), Tuberville (AL)

SPECIAL AND SELECT

| **Aging** | **G-41 DSOB** |
| aging.senate.gov | **202-224-0185** |

Majority (D 7): Casey (PA), Chmn; Gillibrand (NY), Blumenthal (CT), Warren (MA), Rosen (NV), Kelly (AZ), Warnock (GA)
Minority (R 7): Scott (SC), RMM; Collins (ME), Burr (NC), Rubio (FL), Braun (IN), Scott (FL), Lee (UT)

Ethics
ethics.senate.gov

Majority (D 3): Coons (DE), Chmn; Schatz (HI), Shaheen (NH)
Minority (R 3): Lankford (OK), Risch (ID), Fischer (NE)

| **Intelligence** | **211 HSOB** |
| intelligence.senate.gov | **202-224-1700** |

Majority (D 10): Warner (VA), Chmn; Feinstein (CA), Wyden (OR), Heinrich (NM), King (ME), Bennet (CO), Casey (PA), Gillibrand (NY), Schumer (NY), Reed (RI)
Minority (R 10): Rubio (FL), Burr (NC), Risch (ID), Collins (ME), Blunt (MO), Cotton (AR), Cornyn (TX), Sasse (NE), McConnell (KY), Inhofe (OK)

HOUSE COMMITTEES

Agriculture
agriculture.house.gov

1301 LHOB
202-225-2171

Majority (D 27): D. Scott (GA), Chmn; Adams (NC), Costa (CA), McGovern (MA), Vela (TX), Spanberger (VA), Hayes (CT), Delgado (NY), Rush (IL), Pingree (ME), Sablan (MP), Kuster (NH), Bustos (IL), Maloney (NY), Plaskett (VI), O'Halleran (AZ), Carbajal (CA), Khanna (CA), Lawson (FL), Correa (CA), Craig (MN), Harder (CA), Axne (IA), Schrier (WA), Panetta (CA), Kirkpatrick (AZ), S. Bishop (GA)
Minority (R 24): G. Thompson (PA), RMM; A. Scott (GA), Crawford (AR), DesJarlais (TN), Hartzler (MO), LaMalfa (CA), R. Davis (IL), Allen (GA), Rouzer (NC), T. Kelly (MS), Bacon (NE), D. Johnson (SD), Baird (IN), Hagedorn (MN), C. Jacobs (NY), Balderson (OH), Cloud (TX), Mann (KS), Feenstra (IA), M. Miller (IL), B. Moore (AL), Cammack (FL), Fischbach (MN), Letlow (LA)

SUBCOMMITTEES

Biotechnology, Horticulture & Research
Majority (D 12): Plaskett (VI), Chmn; Delgado (NY), Schrier (WA), Panetta (CA), Pingree (ME), S. Maloney (NY), Carbajal (CA), Lawson (FL), Harder (CA), Correa (CA), Kirkpatrick (AZ), D. Scott (GA)
Minority (R 10): Baird (IN), RMM; A. Scott (GA), Crawford (AR), R. Davis (IL), Bacon (NE), Hagedorn (MN), C. Jacobs (NY), Balderson (OH), Fischbach (MN), G. Thompson (PA)

Commodity Exchanges, Energy & Credit
Majority (D 10): Delgado (NY), Chmn; S. Maloney (NY), Plaskett (VI), Khanna (CA), Axne (IA), Rush (IL), Craig (MN), Kuster (NH), Bustos (IL), D. Scott (GA)
Minority (R 10): Fischbach (MN), RMM; A. Scott (GA), LaMalfa (CA), R. Davis (IL), C. Jacobs (NY), Balderson (OH), Cloud (TX), Feenstra (IA), Cammack (FL), G. Thompson (PA)

Conservation & Forestry
Majority (D 9): Spanberger (VA), Chmn; Vela (TX), Pingree (ME), Kuster (NH), O'Halleran (AZ), Panetta (CA), Correa (CA), Schrier (WA), D. Scott (GA)
Minority (R 8): LaMalfa (CA), RMM; DesJarlais (TN), Allen (GA), T. Kelly (MS), D. Johnson (SD), M. Miller (IL), B. Moore (AL), G. Thompson (PA)

General Farm Commodities & Risk Management
Majority (D 8): Bustos (IL), Chmn; Craig (MN), Vela (TX), Carbajal (CA), O'Halleran (AZ), Lawson (FL), S. Bishop (GA), D. Scott (GA)
Minority (R 7): A. Scott (GA), RMM; Crawford (AR), Allen (GA), Rouzer (NC), Mann (KS), M. Miller (IL), G. Thompson (PA)

Livestock & Foreign Agriculture
Majority (D 12): Costa (CA), Chmn; Spanberger (VA), Hayes (CT), Correa (CA), Harder (CA), Khanna (CA), Axne (IA), Rush (IL), Plaskett (VI), Craig (MN), S. Bishop (GA), D. Scott (GA)
Minority (R 10): Rouzer (NC), RMM; G. Thompson (PA), DesJarlais (TN), Hartzler (MO), T. Kelly (MS), Comer (KY), Bacon (NE), Baird (IN), Hagedorn (MN)

Subcommittee Nutrition, Oversight & Department Operations
Majority (D 11): Hayes (CT), Chmn; McGovern (MA), Adams (NC), Rush (IL), Sablan (MP), Carbajal (CA), Lawson (FL), Kuster (NH), Panetta (CA), S. Maloney (NY), D. Scott (GA)
Minority (R 9): Bacon (NE), RMM; Crawford (AR), DesJarlais (TN), Hartzler (MO), Baird (IN), C. Jacobs (NY), Cloud (TX), Cammack (FL), G. Thompson (PA)

Appropriations
appropriations.house.gov

H-307 The Capitol
202-225-2771

Majority (D 33): DeLauro (CT), Chmn; Lawrence (MI), Kaptur (OH), Price (NC), Roybal-Allard (CA), S. Bishop (GA), B. Lee (CA), McCollum (MN), Ryan (OH), Ruppersberger (MD), Wasserman Schultz (FL), Cuellar (TX), Pingree (ME), Quigley (IL), Kilmer (WA), Cartwright (PA), Meng (NY), Pocan (WI), Clark (MA), Aguilar (CA), Frankel (FL), Bustos (IL), Watson Coleman (NJ), N. Torres (CA), Crist (FL), Kirkpatrick (AZ), Case (HI), Espaillat (NY), Harder (CA), Wexton (VA), Trone (MD), Underwood (IL), S. Lee (NV)
Minority (R 26): Granger (TX), RMM; Cole (OK), H. Rogers (KY), Aderholt (AL), Simpson (ID), J. Carter (TX), Diaz-Balart (FL), Womack (AR), Fortenberry (NE), Fleischmann (TN), Herrera Beutler (WA), D. Joyce (OH), Calvert (CA), Harris (MD), Amodei (NV), Stewart (UT), Palazzo (MS), Valadao (CA), Newhouse

(WA), Moolenaar (MI), Rutherford (FL), Cline (VA), Reschenthaler (PA), M. Garcia (CA), Hinson (IA), Gonzales (TX)

SUBCOMMITTEES

Agriculture, Rural Development, FDA & Related Agencies
Majority (D 10): Bishop (GA), Chmn; Pingree (ME), Pocan (WI), Underwood (IL), Lee (CA), McCollum (MN), Wasserman Schultz (FL), Cuellar (TX), Meng (NY), DeLauro (CT)
Minority (R 7): Fortenberry (NE), RMM; Aderholt (AL), Harris (MD), Valadao (CA), Moolenaar (MI), Newhouse (WA), Granger (TX)

Commerce, Justice, Science & Related Agencies
Majority (D 8): Cartwright (PA), Chmn; Crist (FL), Meng (NY), Case (HI), Ruppersberger (MD), Lawrence (MI), Trone (MD), DeLauro (CT)
Minority (R 5): Aderholt (AL), RMM; Palazzo (MS), Cline (VA), M. Garcia (CA), Granger (TX)

Defense
Majority (D 11): McCollum (MN), Chmn; Ryan (OH), Ruppersberger (MD), Kaptur (OH), Cuellar (TX), Kilmer (WA), Aguilar (CA), Bustos (IL), Crist (FL), Kirkpatrick (AZ), DeLauro (CT)
Minority (R 8): Calvert (CA), RMM; H. Rogers (KY), Cole (OK), Aderholt (AL), J. Carter (TX), Womack (AR), Diaz-Balart (FL), Granger (TX)

Energy & Water Development & Related Agencies
Majority (D 10): Kaptur (OH), Chmn; Wasserman Schultz (FL), Kirkpatrick (AZ), S. Lee (NV), Ryan (OH), Kilmer (WA), Frankel (FL), Bustos (IL), Watson Coleman (NJ), DeLauro (CT)
Minority (R 7): Simpson (ID), RMM; Calvert (CA), Fleischmann (TN), Newhouse (WA), Herrera Beutler (WA), Reschenthaler (PA), Granger (TX)

Financial Services & General Government
Majority (D 8): Quigley (IL), Chmn; Cartwright (PA), S. Bishop (GA), Pocan (WI), Lawrence (MI), N. Torres (CA), Kirkpatrick (AZ), DeLauro (CT)
Minority (R 5): Womack (AR), RMM; Amodei (NV), Stewart (UT), D. Joyce (OH), Granger (TX)

Homeland Security
Majority (D 8): Roybal-Allard (CA), Chmn; Cuellar (TX), Underwood (IL), Price (NC), Ruppersberger (MD), Quigley (IL), Aguilar (CA), DeLauro (CT)
Minority (R 5): Fleischmann (TN), RMM; Palazzo (MS), Rutherford (FL), Hinson (IA), Granger (TX)

Interior, Environment & Related Agencies
Majority (D 8): Pingree (ME), Chmn; McCollum (MN), Kilmer (WA), Harder (CA), S. Lee (NV), Kaptur (OH), Cartwright (PA), DeLauro (CT)
Minority (R 5): D. Joyce (OH), RMM; Simpson (ID), Stewart (UT), Amodei (NV), Granger (TX)

Labor, Health & Human Services, Education & Related Agencies
Majority (D 10): DeLauro (CT), Chmn; Roybal-Allard (CA), B. Lee (CA), Pocan (WI), Clark (MA), Frankel (FL), Bustos (IL), Watson Coleman (NJ), Lawrence (MI), Harder (CA)
Minority (R 7): Cole (OK), RMM; Harris (MD), Fleischmann (TN), Herrera Beutler (WA), Moolenaar (MI), Cline (VA), Granger (TX)

Legislative Branch
Majority (D 6): Ryan (OH), Chmn; Clark (MA), Case (HI), Espaillat (NY), Wexton (VA), DeLauro (CT)
Minority (R 4): Herrera Beutler (WA), RMM; Amodei (NV), Newhouse (WA), Granger (TX)

Military Construction, Veterans Affairs & Related Agencies
Majority (D 8): Wasserman Schultz (FL), Chmn; S. Bishop (GA), Case (HI), Pingree (ME), Crist (FL), Trone (MD), S. Lee (NV), DeLauro (CT)
Minority (R 5): J. Carter (TX), RMM; Valadao (CA), Rutherford (FL), Gonzales (TX), Granger (TX)

State, Foreign Operations & Related Programs
Majority (D 8): B. Lee (CA), Chmn; Meng (NY), Price (NC), Frankel (FL), N. Torres (CA), Espaillat (NY), Wexton (VA), DeLauro (CT)
Minority (R 5): H. Rogers (KY), RMM; Diaz-Balart (FL), Fortenberry (NE), Reschenthaler (PA), Granger (TX)

Transportation, HUD & Related Agencies
Majority (D 10): Price (NC), Chmn; Quigley (IL), Clark (MA), Watson Coleman (NJ), N. Torres (CA), Aguilar (CA), Espaillat (NY), Wexton (VA), Trone (MD), DeLauro (CT)
Minority (R 7): Diaz-Balart (FL), RMM; Womack (AR), Rutherford (FL), M. Garcia (CA), Hinson (IA), Gonzales (TX), Granger (TX)

Armed Services   **2216 RHOB**
armedservices.house.gov   **202-225-4151**

Majority (D 31): A. Smith (WA), Chmn; Luria (VA), Langevin (RI), Larsen (WA), Cooper (TN), Courtney (CT), Garamendi (CA), Speier (CA), Norcross (NJ), Gallego (AZ), Moulton (MA), Carbajal (CA), Brown (MD), Khanna (CA), Keating (MA), Vela (TX), A. Kim (NJ), Houlahan (PA), Crow (CO), Slotkin (MI), Sherrill (NJ), Escobar (TX), Golden (ME), Morelle (NY), S. Jacobs (CA), Kahele (HI), Strickland (WA), Veasey (TX), Panetta (CA), S. Murphy (FL), Steven Horsford (NV)

Minority (R 28): M. Rogers (AL), RMM; Wittman (VA), J. Wilson (SC), Turner (OH), Hartzler (MO), A. Scott (GA), Brooks (AL), S. Graves (MO), Stefanik (NY), DesJarlais (TN), T. Kelly (MS), Gallagher (WI), Gaetz (FL), Bacon (NE), Banks (IN), Cheney (WY), Bergman (MI), Waltz (FL), M. Johnson (LA), M. Green (TN), Bice (OK), Franklin (FL), McClain (MI), Jackson (TX), Carl (AL), B. Moore (UT), Fallon (TX)

SUBCOMMITTEES

Cyber, Innovative Technologies & Information Systems
Majority (D 11): Langevin (RI), Chmn; Larsen (WA), Moulton (MA), Khanna (CA), Keating (MA), A. Kim (NJ), Houlahan (PA), Crow (CO), Slotkin (MI), Escobar (TX), Morelle (NY)

Minority (R 9): Banks (IN), RMM; Stefanik (NY), Brooks (AL), Gaetz (FL), M. Johnson (LA), Bice (OK), Franklin (FL), B. Moore (UT), Fallon (TX)

Intelligence & Special Operations
Majority (D 8): Gallego (AZ), Chmn; Larsen (WA), Cooper (TN), Keating (MA), Vela (TX), Sherrill (NJ), Panetta (CA), S. Murphy (FL)

Minority (R 7): T. Kelly (MS), RMM; A. Scott (GA), S. Graves (MO), Bacon (NE), Cheney (WY), Waltz (FL), Franklin (FL)

Military Personnel
Majority (D 7): Speier (CA), Chmn; A. Kim (NJ), Houlahan (PA), Escobar (TX), S. Jacobs (CA), Strickland (WA), Veasey (TX)

Minority (R 6): Gallagher (RI), RMM; Bice (OK), McClain (MI), Jackson (TX), Carl (AL), Fallon (TX)

Readiness
Majority (D 9): Garamendi (CA), Chmn; Courtney (CT), Speier (CA), Crow (CO), Slotkin (MI), Golden (ME), Luria (VA), Kahele (HI), Strickland (WA)

Minority (R 8): Lamborn (CO), RMM; J. Wilson (SC), A. Scott (GA), Bergman (MI), M. Johnson (LA), M. Green (TN), McClain (MI), B. Moore (UT)

Seapower & Projection Forces
Majority (D 9): Courtney (CT), Chmn; Langevin (RI), Cooper (TN), Norcross (NJ), Brown (MD), Vela (TX), Golden (ME), Luria (VA), S. Jacobs (CA)

Minority (R 8): Wittman (VA), RMM; Hartzler (MO), S. Graves (MO), T. Kelly (MS), Gallagher (WI), Banks (IN), Bergman (MI), Carl (AL)

Strategic Forces
Majority (D 9): Cooper (TN), Chmn; Langevin (RI), Garamendi (CA), Moulton (MA), Carbajal (CA), Khanna (CA), Morelle (NY), Panetta (CA), Horsford (NV)

Minority (R 8): Turner (OH), RMM; J. Wilson (SC), Lamborn (CO), Brooks (AL), Stefanik (NY), DesJarlais (TN), Cheney (WY), Waltz (FL)

Tactical Air & Land Forces
Majority (D 9): Norcross (NJ), Chmn; Gallego (AZ), Carbajal (CA), Brown (MD), Sherrill (NJ), Kahele (HI), Veasey (TX), S. Murphy (FL), Horsford (NV)

Minority (R 8): Hartzler (MO), RMM; Turner (OH), Wittman (VA), DesJarlais (TN), Gaetz (FL), Bacon (NE), M. Green (TN), Jackson (TX)

Budget   **204-E CHOB**
budget.house.gov   **202-226-7200**

Majority (D 21): Yarmuth (KY), Chmn; Jeffries (NY), B. Higgins (NY), Boyle (PA), Doggett (TX), Price (NC), Schakowsky (IL), Kildee (MI), Morelle (NY), Horsford (NV), B. Lee (CA), Chu (CA), Plaskett (VI), Wexton (VA), B. Scott (VA), Jackson Lee (TX), Cooper (TN), Sires (NJ), Peters (CA), Moulton (MA), Jayapal (WA)

Minority (R 15): J. Smith (MO), RMM; T. Kelly (MS), McClintock (CA), Grothman (WI), Burgess (TX), B. Carter (GA), Smucker (PA), C. Jacobs (NY), Cline (VA), Boebert (CO), Donalds (FL), Feenstra (IA), Good (VA), Hinson (IA), Obernolte (CA)

Education & Labor
edlabor.house.gov

2176 RHOB
202-225-3725

Majority (D 29): B. Scott (VA), Chmn; Bowman (NY), Grijalva (AZ), Courtney (CT), Sablan (MP), F. Wilson (FL), Bonamici (OR), Takano (CA), Adams (NC), DeSaulnier (CA), Norcross (NJ), Jayapal (WA), Morelle (NY), Wild (PA), McBath (GA), Hayes (CT), A. Levin (MI), Omar (MN), Stevens (MI), Leger Fernandez (NM), Jones (NY), Manning (NC), Mrvan (IN), Letlow (LA), Pocan (WI), Castro (TX), Sherrill (NJ), Yarmuth (KY), Espaillat (NY), Mfume (MD)
Minority (R 23): Foxx (NC), RMM; J. Wilson (SC), G. Thompson (PA), Walberg (MI), Grothman (WI), Stefanik (NY), Allen (GA), Banks (IN), Comer (KY), Fulcher (ID), Keller (PA), G. Murphy (NC), Miller-Meeks (IA), Owens (UT), Good (VA), McClain (MI), Harshbarger (TN), M. Miller (IL), Spartz (IN), Fitzgerald (WI), Cawthorn (NC), Steel (CA), Letlow (LA)

SUBCOMMITTEES

Civil Rights & Human Services
Majority (D 7): Bonamici (OR), Chmn; Adams (NC), Hayes (CT), Leger Fernandez (NM), Mrvan (IN), Bowman (NY), Mfume (MD)
Minority (R 5): Fulcher (ID), RMM; G. Thompson (PA), McClain (MI), Spartz (IN), Fitzgerald (WI)

Early Childhood, Elementary & Secondary Education
Majority (D 12): Sablan (MP), Chmn; Hayes (CT), Grijalva (AZ), Yarmuth (KY), F. Wilson (FL), DeSaulnier (CA), Morelle (NY), McBath (GA), A. Levin (MI), Manning (NC), Bowman (NY), B. Scott (VA)
Minority (R 8): Owens (UT), RMM; Grothman (WI), Allen (GA), Keller (PA), M. Miller (IL), Cawthorn (NC), Steel (CA), Letlow (LA)

Health, Employment, Labor & Pensions
Majority (D 9): DeSaulnier (CA), Chmn; Courtney (CT), Norcross (NJ), Morelle (NY), Wild (PA), McBath (GA), A. Levin (MI), Stevens (MI), Mrvan (IN)
Minority (R 7): Allen (GA), RMM; J. Wilson (SC), Walberg (MI), Banks (IN), Harshbarger (TN), M. Miller (IL), Fitzgerald (WI)

Higher Education & Workforce Investment
Majority (D 15): F. Wilson (FL), Chmn; Takano (CA), Jayapal (WA), Omar (MN), Leger Fernandez (NM), Jones (NY), Manning (NC), Bowman (NY), Pocan (WI), Castro (TX), Sherrill (NJ), Espaillat (NY), Grijalva (AZ), Courtney (CT), Bonamici (OR)
Minority (R 12): G. Murphy (NC), RMM; Grothman (WI), Stefanik (NY), Banks (IN), Comer (KY), Fulcher (ID), Miller-Meeks (IA), Good (VA), McClain (MI), Harshbarger (TN), Spartz (IN), Letlow (LA)

Workforce Protections
Majority (D 9): Adams (NC), Chmn; Takano (CA), Norcross (NJ), Jayapal (WA), Omar (MN), Stevens (MI), Jones (NY), Yarmuth (KY), B. Scott (VA)
Minority (R 7): Keller (PA), RMM; Stefanik (NY), Miller-Meeks (IA), Owens (UT), Good (VA), Cawthorn (NC), Steel (CA)

Energy & Commerce
energycommerce.house.gov

2125 RHOB
202-225-2927

Majority (D 32): Pallone (NJ), Chmn; R. Kelly (IL), Rush (IL), Eshoo (CA), DeGette (CO), Doyle (PA), Schakowsky (IL), Butterfield (NC), Matsui (CA), Castor (FL), Sarbanes (MD), McNerney (CA), Welch (VT), Tonko (NY), Clarke (NY), Schrader (OR), Cardenas (CA), Ruiz (CA), Peters (CA), Dingell (MI), Veasey (TX), Kuster (NH), Barragan (CA), McEachin (VA), Blunt Rochester (DE), Soto (FL), O'Halleran (AZ), K. Rice (NY), Craig (MN), Schrier (WA), Trahan (MA), Fletcher (TX)
Minority (R 26): McMorris Rodgers (WA), RMM; Upton (MI), Burgess (TX), Scalise (LA), Latta (OH), Guthrie (KY), McKinley (WV), Kinzinger (IL), Griffith (VA), Bilirakis (FL), B. Johnson (OH), Long (MO), Bucshon (IN), Mullin (OK), Hudson (NC), Walberg (MI), B. Carter (GA), Duncan (SC), Palmer (AL), Dunn (FL), Curtis (UT), Lesko (AZ), Pence (IN), Crenshaw (TX), J. Joyce (PA), Armstrong (ND)

SUBCOMMITTEES

Communications & Technology

Majority (D 18): Doyle (PA), Chmn; McNerney (CA), Clarke (NY), Veasey (TX), McEachin (VA), Soto (FL), O'Halleran (AZ), K. Rice (NY), Eshoo (CA), Butterfield (NC), Matsui (CA), Welch (VT), Schrader (OR), Cardenas (CA), R. Kelly (IL), Craig (MN), Fletcher (TX), Pallone (NJ)

Minority (R 14): Latta (OH), RMM; Scalise (LA), Guthrie (KY), Kinzinger (IL), Bilirakis (FL), B. Johnson (OH), Long (MO), Hudson (NC), Mullin (OK), Walberg (MI), B. Carter (GA), Duncan (SC), Curtis (UT), McMorris Rodgers (WA)

Consumer Protection & Commerce

Majority (D 14): Schakowsky (IL), Chmn; Rush (IL), Castor (FL), Trahan (MA), McNerney (CA), Clarke (NY), Cardenas (CA), Dingell (MI), R. Kelly (IL), Soto (FL), K. Rice (NY), Craig (MN), Fletcher (TX), Pallone (NJ)

Minority (R 10): Bilirakis (FL), RMM; Upton (MI), Latta (OH), Guthrie (KY), Bucshon (IN), Dunn (FL), Pence (IN), Lesko (AZ), Armstrong (ND), McMorris Rodgers (WA)

Energy

Majority (D 19): Rush (IL), Chmn; Peters (CA), Doyle (PA), McNerney (CA), Tonko (NY), Veasey (TX), Schrier (WA), DeGette (CO), Butterfield (NC), Matsui (CA), Castor (FL), Welch (VT), Schrader (OR), Kuster (NH), Barragan (CA), McEachin (VA), Blunt Rochester (DE), O'Halleran (AZ), Pallone (NJ)

Minority (R 15): Upton (MI), RMM; Burgess (TX), Latta (OH), McKinley (WV), Kinzinger (IL), Griffith (VA), B. Johnson (OH), Bucshon (IN), Walberg (MI), Duncan (SC), Palmer (AL), Lesko (AZ), Pence (IN), Armstrong (ND), McMorris Rodgers (WA)

Environment & Climate Change

Majority (D 14): Tonko (NY), Chmn; DeGette (CO), Schakowsky (IL), Sarbanes (MD), Clarke (NY), Ruiz (CA), Peters (CA), Dingell (MI), Barragan (CA), McEachin (VA), Blunt Rochester (DE), Soto (FL), O'Halleran (AZ), Pallone (NJ)

Minority (R 10): McKinley (WV), RMM; B. Johnson (OH), Mullin (OK), Hudson (NC), B. Carter (GA), Duncan (SC), Palmer (AL), Curtis (UT), Crenshaw (TX), McMorris Rodgers (WA)

Health

Majority (D 19): Eshoo (CA), Chmn; Sarbanes (MD), Butterfield (NC), Matsui (CA), Castor (FL), Welch (VT), Schrader (OR), Cardenas (CA), Ruiz (CA), Dingell (MI), Kuster (NH), R. Kelly (IL), Barragan (CA), Blunt Rochester (DE), Craig (MN), Schrier (WA), Trahan (MA), Fletcher (TX), Pallone (NJ)

Minority (R 15): Guthrie (KY), RMM; Upton (MI), Burgess (TX), Griffith (VA), Bilirakis (FL), Long (MO), Bucshon (IN), Mullin (OK), Hudson (NC), B. Carter (GA), Dunn (FL), Curtis (UT), Crenshaw (TX), J. Joyce (PA), McMorris Rodgers (WA)

Oversight & Investigations

Majority (D 11): DeGette (CO), Chmn; Kuster (NH), K. Rice (NY), Schakowsky (IL), Tonko (NY), Ruiz (CA), Peters (CA), Schrier (WA), Trahan (MA), O'Halleran (AZ), Pallone (NJ)

Minority (R 8): Griffith (VA), RMM; Burgess (TX), McKinley (WV), Long (MO), Dunn (FL), J. Joyce (PA), Palmer (AL), McMorris Rodgers (WA)

Ethics ethics.house.gov	**1015 LHOB** **202-225-7103**

Majority (D 5): Deutch (FL), Chmn; Wild (PA), Phillips (MN), Escobar (TX), Jones (NY)
Minority (R 5): Walorski (IN), RMM; Guest (MS), D. Joyce (OH), Rutherford (FL), Armstrong (ND)

Financial Services financialservices.house.gov	**2129 RHOB** **202-225-4247**

Majority (D 30): Waters (CA), Chmn; C. Maloney (NY), Velazquez (NY), Sherman (CA), Meeks (NY), D. Scott (GA), A. Green (TX), Cleaver (MO), Perlmutter (CO), Himes (CT), Foster (IL), Beatty (OH), Vargas (CA), Gottheimer (NJ), V. Gonzalez (TX), Lawson (FL), San Nicolas (GU), Axne (IA), Casten (IL), Pressley (MA), R. Torres (NY), Lynch (MA), Adams (NC), Tlaib (MI), Dean (PA), Ocasio-Cortez (NY), C. Garcia (IL), S. Garcia (TX), N. Williams (GA), Auchincloss (MA)

Minority (R 24): McHenry (NC), RMM; Wagner (MO), Lucas (OK), Posey (FL), Luetkemeyer (MO), Huizenga (MI), Stivers (OH), Barr (KY), R. Williams (TX), Hill (AR), Emmer (MN), Zeldin (NY), Loudermilk (GA), Mooney (WV), Davidson (OH), Budd (NC), Kustoff (TN), Hollingsworth (IN), A. Gonzalez (OH), Rose (TN), Steil (WI), Gooden (TX), Timmons (SC), Taylor (TX)

SUBCOMMITTEES

Consumer Protection & Financial Institutions
Majority (D 13): Perlmutter (CO), Chmn; Pressley (MA), Velazquez (NY), Meeks (NY), D. Scott (GA), Foster (IL), Lawson (FL), San Nicolas (GU), Casten (IL), R. Torres (NY), Sherman (CA), A. Green (TX), Vargas (CA)
Minority (R 10): Luetkemeyer (MO), RMM; Kustoff (TN), Lucas (OK), Posey (FL), Barr (KY), R. Williams (TX), Loudermilk (GA), Budd (NC), Rose (TN), Timmons (SC)

Diversity & Inclusion
Majority (D 8): Beatty (OH), Chmn; Pressley (MA), Dean (PA), S. Garcia (TX), N. Williams (GA), Lynch (MA), Tlaib (MI), Auchincloss (MA)
Minority (R 7): Wagner (MO), RMM; A. Gonzalez (OH), Lucas (OK), Budd (NC), Rose (TN), Gooden (TX), Timmons (SC)

Housing, Community Development & Insurance
Majority (D 11): Cleaver (MO), Chmn; Velazquez (NY), Lawson (FL), R. Torres (NY), C. Maloney (NY), Sherman (CA), A. Green (TX), Beatty (OH), Vargas (CA), V. Gonzalez (TX), Axne (IA)
Minority (R 9): Hill (AR), RMM; Steil (WI), Gooden (TX), Posey (FL), Huizenga (MI), Zeldin (NY), Hollingsworth (IN), Rose (TN), Taylor (TX)

Investor Protection, Entrepreneurship & Capital Markets
Majority (D 13): Sherman (CA), Chmn; C. Maloney (NY), Meeks (NY), D. Scott (GA), Foster (IL), Vargas (CA), V. Gonzalez (TX), San Nicolas (GU), Axne (IA), Casten (IL), Cleaver (MO), Himes (CT), Gottheimer (NJ)
Minority (R 10): Huizenga (MI), RMM; Hollingsworth (IN), Wagner (MO), Hill (AR), Emmer (MN), Mooney (WV), Davidson (OH), Steil (WI), A. Gonzalez (OH), Van Taylor (TX)

Nat'l Security, International Development & Monetary Policy
Majority (D 9): Himes (CT), Chmn; Gottheimer (NJ), San Nicolas (GU), R. Torres (NY), Lynch (MA), Ocasio-Cortez (NY), Auchincloss (MA), Dean (PA), C. Garcia (IL)
Minority (R 6): Barr (KY), RMM; Hill (AR), Zeldin (NY), R. Williams (TX), Davidson (OH), A. Gonzalez (OH)

Oversight & Investigations
Majority (D 7): A. Green (TX), Chmn; Cleaver (MO), Adams (NC), Tlaib (MI), C. Garcia (IL), S. Garcia (TX), N. Williams (GA)
Minority (R 5): Emmer (MO), RMM; Timmons (SC), Loudermilk (GA), Mooney (WV), Kustoff (TN)

Task Force on Artificial Intelligence
Majority (D 7): Foster (IL), Chmn; Sherman (CA), Casten (IL), Pressley (MA), Adams (NC), S. Garcia (TX), Auchincloss (MA)
Minority (R 5): A. Gonzalez (OH), RMM; Loudermilk (GA), Budd (NC), Hollingsworth (IN), Taylor (TX)

Task Force on Financial Technology
Majority (D 7): Lynch (MA), Chmn; Himes (CT), Gottheimer (NJ), Lawson (FL), San Nicolas (GU), R. Torres (NY), N. Williams (GA)
Minority (R 4): Davidson (OH), RMM; Luetkemeyer (MO), Emmer (MN), Steil (WI)

Foreign Affairs　　　　　　　　　　　　　　　　　　　　　　　　　　　　　　**2170 RHOB**
foreignaffairs.house.gov　　　　　　　　　　　　　　　　　　　　　　　　　**202-225-5021**

Majority (D 27): Meeks (NY), Chmn; Sherman (CA), Sires (NJ), Connolly (VA), Deutch (FL), Bass (CA), Keating (MA), Cicilline (RI), Bera (CA), Castro (TX), Titus (NV), Lieu (CA), Wild (PA), Phillips (MN), Omar (MN), Allred (TX), A. Levin (MI), Spanberger (VA), Houlahan (PA), Malinowski (NJ), A. Kim (NJ), S. Jacobs (CA), Manning (NC), Costa (CA), Vargas (CA), V. Gonzalez (TX), Schneider (IL)
Minority (R 24): McCaul (TX), RMM; Wagner (MO), C. Smith (NJ), Chabot (OH), J. Wilson (SC), Perry (PA), Issa (CA), Kinzinger (IL), Zeldin (NY), Mast (FL), Fitzpatrick (PA), Buck (CO), Burchett (TN), M. Green (TN), Barr (KY), Meuser (PA), Tenney (NY), Pfluger (TX), Steube (FL), Malliotakis (NY), Meijer (MI), Jackson (TX), Y. Kim (CA), Salazar (FL)

SUBCOMMITTEES

Europe, Energy, the Environment & Cyber
Majority (D 11): Keating (MA), Chmn; Wild (PA), Spanberger (VA), Sires (NJ), Deutch (FL), Cicilline (RI), Titus (NV), Phillips (MN), Costa (CA), V. Gonzalez (TX), Schneider (IL)
Minority (R 9): Fitzpatrick (PA), RMM; Wagner (MO), Kinzinger (IL), Mast (FL), Meuser (PA), Tenney (NY), Pfluger (TX), Malliotakis (NY), Meijer (MI)

Intern'l Dev't, Intern'l Orgs & Global Corporate Social Impact
Majority (D 6): Castro (TX), Chmn; Houlahan (PA), S. Jacobs (CA), Sherman (CA), Omar (MN), A. Kim (NJ)
Minority (R 4): Malliotakis (NY), RMM; Issa (CA), Zeldin (NY), Tenney (NY)

Middle East, North Africa & Global Counterterrorism
Majority (D 11): Deutch (FL), Chmn; Malinowski (NJ), Connolly (VA), Cicilline (RI), Lieu (CA), Allred (TX), Manning (NC), Keating (MA), Sherman (CA), Vargas (CA), Schneider (IL)
Minority (R 9): J. Wilson (SC), RMM; Perry (PA), Kinzinger (IL), Zeldin (NY), Mast (FL), Burchett (TN), Steube (FL), Jackson (TX), Salazar (FL)

West Hem, Civ Sec, Migration, & Intern'l Econ Policy
Majority (D 5): Sires (NJ), Chmn; Castro (TX), A. Levin (MI), V. Gonzalez (TX), Vargas (CA)
Minority (R 3): M. Green (TN), RMM; Pfluger (TX), Salazar (FL)

Africa, Global Health & Global Human Rights
Majority (D 8): Bass (CA), Chmn; Omar (MN), Phillips (MN), Bera (CA), Wild (PA), Malinowski (NJ), Jacobs (CA), Cicilline (RI)
Minority (R 6): Smith (NJ), RMM; Issa (CA), Steube (FL), Meuser (PA), Kim (CA), Jackson (TX)

Asia, the Pacific, Central Asia, Nonproliferation
Majority (D 10): Bera (CA), Chmn; Sherman (CA), Titus (NV), Levin (MI), Houlahan (PA), Kim (NJ), Connolly (VA), Lieu (CA), Spanberger (VA), Manning (NC)
Minority (R 8): Chabot (OH), RMM; Perry (PA), Wagner (MO), Buck (CO), Burchett (TN), Green (TN), Barr (KY), Kim (CA)

Homeland Security	**H2-176 FHOB**
homeland.house.gov	**202-226-2616**

Majority (D 19): B. Thompson (MS), Chmn; R. Torres (NY), Jackson Lee (TX), Langevin (RI), Payne (NJ), Correa (CA), Slotkin (MI), Cleaver (MO), A. Green (TX), Clarke (NY), Swalwell (CA), Titus (NV), Watson Coleman (NJ), K. Rice (NY), Demings (FL), Barragan (CA), Gottheimer (NJ), Luria (VA), Malinowski (NJ)
Minority (R 16): Katko (NY), RMM; McCaul (TX), C. Higgins (LA), Guest (MS), D. Bishop (NC), Van Drew (NJ), Norman (SC), Miller-Meeks (IA), Harshbarger (TN), Clyde (GA), Gimenez (FL), LaTurner (KS), Meijer (MI), Cammack (FL), Pfluger (TX), Garbarino (NY)

SUBCOMMITTEES

Border Security, Facilitation & Operations
Majority (D 6): Barragan (CA), Chmn; Correa (CA), Cleaver (MO), A. Green (TX), Clarke (NY), B. Thompson (MS)
Minority (R 5): C. Higgins (LA), RMM; Guest (MS), D. Bishop (NC), Clyde (GA), Katko (NY)

Cybersecurity, Infrastructure Protection & Innovation
Majority (D 7): Clarke (NY), Chmn; Jackson Lee (TX), Langevin (RI), Slotkin (MI), K. Rice (NY), R. Torres (NY), B. Thompson (MS)
Minority (R 6): Garbarino (NY), RMM; Norman (SC), Harshbarger (TN), Clyde (GA), LaTurner (KS), Katko (NY)

Emergency Preparedness, Response & Recovery
Majority (D 6): Demings (FL), Chmn; Jackson Lee (TX), Payne (NJ), A. Green (TX), Watson Coleman (NJ), B. Thompson (MS)
Minority (R 5): Cammack (FL), RMM; C. Higgins (LA), Miller-Meeks (IA), Garbarino (NY), Katko (NY)

Intelligence & Counterterrorism
Majority (D 7): Slotkin (MI), Chmn; Jackson Lee (TX), Langevin (RI), Swalwell (CA), Gottheimer (NJ), Malinowski (NJ), B. Thompson (MS)
Minority (R 6): Pfluger (TX), RMM; Guest (MS), Van Drew (NJ), LaTurner (KS), Meijer (MI), Katko (NY)

Oversight, Management & Accountability
Majority (D 5): Correa (CA), Chmn; Payne (NJ), Titus (NV), R. Torres (NY), B. Thompson (MS)
Minority (R 4): Meijer (MI), RMM; D. Bishop (NC), Harshbarger (TN), Katko (NY)

Transportation & Maritime Security
Majority (D 6): Watson Coleman (NJ), Chmn; Payne (NJ), Titus (NV), Gottheimer (NJ), Luria (VA), B. Thompson (MS)
Minority (R 5): Gimenez (FL), RMM; Van Drew (NJ), Norman (SC), Miller-Meeks (IA), Katko (NY)

House Administration
cha.house.gov

1309 LHOB
202-225-2061

Majority (D 6): Lofgren (CA), Chmn; Raskin (MD), Butterfield (NC), Aguilar (CA), Scanlon (PA), Leger Fernandez (NM)
Minority (R 3): R. Davis (IL), RMM; Loudermilk (GA), Steil (WI)

SUBCOMMITTEES

Elections
Majority (D 3): Butterfield (NC), Chmn; Aguilar (CA), Leger Fernandez (NM)
Minority (R 1): Steil (WI), RMM

Judiciary
judiciary.house.gov

2138 RHOB
202-225-3951

Majority (D 25): Nadler (NY), Chmn; Lofgren (CA), Jackson Lee (TX), Cohen (TN), H. Johnson (GA), Deutch (FL), Bass (CA), Jeffries (NY), Cicilline (RI), Swalwell (CA), Lieu (CA), Raskin (MD), Jayapal (WA), Demings (FL), Correa (CA), Scanlon (PA), S. Garcia (TX), Neguse (CO), McBath (GA), Stanton (AZ), Dean (PA), Escobar (TX), Jones (NY), Ross (NC), Bush (MO)
Minority (R 19): Jordan (OH), RMM; Chabot (OH), Gohmert (TX), Issa (CA), Buck (CO), Gaetz (FL), M. Johnson (LA), Biggs (AZ), McClintock (CA), Steube (FL), Tiffany (WI), Massie (KY), Roy (TX), D. Bishop (NC), Fischbach (MN), Spartz (IN), Fitzgerald (WI), Bentz (OR), Owens (UT)

SUBCOMMITTEES

Antitrust, Commercial & Administrative Law
Majority (D 13): Cicilline (RI), Chmn; Jayapal (WA), Neguse (CO), Swalwell (CA), Jones (NY), Deutch (FL), Jeffries (NY), Raskin (MD), Demings (FL), Scanlon (PA), McBath (GA), Dean (PA), H. Johnson (GA)
Minority (R 11): Buck (CO), RMM; Issa (CA), Gaetz (FL), M. Johnson (LA), Steube (FL), D. Bishop (NC), Fischbach (MN), Spartz (IN), Fitzgerald (WI), Bentz (OR), Owens (UT)

Constitution, Civil Rights & Civil Liberties
Majority (D 7): Cohen (TN), Chmn; Ross (NC), Raskin (MD), H. Johnson (GA), S. Garcia (TX), Jackson Lee (TX), Bush (MO)
Minority (R 5): M. Johnson (LA), RMM; McClintock (CA), Roy (TX), Fischbach (MN), Owens (UT)

Courts, Intellectual Property & Internet
Majority (D 12): H. Johnson (GA), Chmn; Jones (NY), Deutch (FL), Jeffries (NY), Lieu (CA), Stanton (AZ), Lofgren (CA), Cohen (TN), Bass (CA), Swalwell (CA), Ross (NC), Neguse (CO)
Minority (R 11): Issa (CA), RMM; Chabot (OH), Gohmert (TX), Gaetz (FL), M. Johnson (LA), Tiffany (WI), Massie (KY), D. Bishop (NC), Fischbach (MN), Fitzgerald (WI), Bentz (OR)

Crime, Terrorism & Homeland Security
Majority (D 12): Jackson Lee (TX), Chmn; Bush (MO), Bass (CA), Demings (FL), McBath (GA), Dean (PA), Scanlon (PA), Cicilline (RI), Lieu (CA), Correa (CA), Escobar (TX), Cohen (TN)
Minority (R 9): Biggs (AZ), RMM; Chabot (OH), Gohmert (TX), Steube (FL), Tiffany (WI), Massie (KY), Spartz (IN), Fitzgerald (WI), Owens (UT)

Immigration & Citizenship
Majority (D 8): Lofgren (CA), Chmn; Neguse (CO), Jayapal (WA), Correa (CA), S. Garcia (TX), Escobar (TX), Jackson Lee (TX), Scanlon (PA)
Minority (R 6): McClintock (CA), RMM; Buck (CO), Biggs (AZ), Tiffany (WI), Roy (TX), Spartz (IN)

Natural Resources
naturalresources.house.gov

1324 LHOB
202-225-6065

Majority (D 26): Grijalva (AZ), Chmn; C. Garcia (IL), Sablan (MP), Napolitano (CA), Costa (CA), Huffman (CA), Lowenthal (CA), Gallego (AZ), Neguse (CO), M. Levin (CA), Porter (CA), Leger Fernandez (NM), Velazquez (NY), DeGette (CO), Brownley (CA), Dingell (MI), McEachin (VA), Soto (FL), San Nicolas (GU), Case (HI), Cohen (TN), McCollum (MN), Tlaib (MI), Tonko (NY), Matsui (CA), Trahan (MA)
Minority (R 22): Westerman (AR) RMM; Young (AK), Gohmert (TX), Gonzalez-Colon (PR), Radewagen (AS), Lamborn (CO), Wittman (VA), McClintock (CA), Gosar (AZ), G. Graves (LA), Hice (GA), Webster

(FL), Fulcher (ID), Stauber (MN), Tiffany (WI), Carl (AL), Rosendale (MT), B. Moore (UT), Herrell (NM), Boebert (CO), Obernolte (CA), Bentz (OR)

SUBCOMMITTEES

Energy & Mineral Resources
Majority (D 9): Lowenthal (CA), Chmn; McEachin (VA), M. Levin (CA), Porter (CA), DeGette (CO), McCollum (MN), Huffman (CA), Dingell (MI), Grijalva (AZ)
Minority (R 7): Stauber (MN), RMM; Herrell (NM), Lamborn (CO), Gosar (AZ), G. Graves (LA), Tiffany (WI), Westerman (AR)

Indigenous Peoples of the United States
Majority (D 9): Leger Fernandez (NM), Chmn; Gallego (AZ), Soto (FL), McCollum (MN), San Nicolas (GU), Case (HI), Lowenthal (CA), C. Garcia (IL), Grijalva (AZ)
Minority (R 8): Young (AK), RMM; Obernolte (CA), Radewagen (AS), Carl (AL), Rosendale (MT), Boebert (CO), Bentz (OR), Westerman (AR)

National Parks, Forests & Public Lands
Majority (D 13): Neguse (CO), Chmn; Sablan (MP), DeGette (CO), Tonko (NY), Tlaib (MI), Trahan (MA), Gallego (AZ), Fernandez (NM), Dingell (MI), Case (HI), San Nicolas (GU), Porter (CA), Grijalva (AZ)
Minority (R 11): Fulcher (ID), RMM; Tiffany (WI), Gohmert (TX), Lamborn (CO), McClintock (CA), Hice (GA), Rosendale (MT), B. Moore (UT), Herrell (NM), Obernolte (CA), Westerman (AR)

Oversight & Investigations
Majority (D 6): Porter (CA), Chmn; Velazquez (NY), C. Garcia (IL), Cohen (TN), Huffman (CA), Grijalva (AZ)
Minority (R 5): Gosar (AZ), RMM; B. Moore (UT), Gohmert (TX), Hice (GA), Westerman (AR)

Water, Oceans & Wildlife
Majority (D 13): Huffman (CA), Chmn; Napolitano (CA), Costa (CA), M. Levin (CA), Brownley (CA), Dingell (MI), Case (HI), Matsui (CA), Lowenthal (CA), Cohen (TN), Soto (FL), Grijalva (AZ), Velazquez (NY)
Minority (R 12): Bentz (OR), RMM; Carl (AL), Young (AK), Wittman (VA), McClintock (CA), G. Graves (LA), Radewagen (AS), Webster (FL), Gonzalez-Colon (PR), Fulcher (ID), Boebert (CO), Westerman (AR)

Oversight & Reform
oversight.house.gov

2157 RHOB
202-225-5051

Majority (D 25): C. Maloney (NY), Chmn; Gomez (CA), Norton (DC), Lynch (MA), Cooper (TN), Connolly (VA), Krishnamoorthi (IL), Raskin (MD), Khanna (CA), Mfume (MD), Ocasio-Cortez (NY), Tlaib (MI), Porter (CA), Bush (MO), D. Davis (IL), Wasserman Schultz (FL), Welch (VT), H. Johnson (GA), Sarbanes (MD), Speier (CA), R. Kelly (IL), Lawrence (MI), DeSaulnier (CA), Pressley (MA), Quigley (IL)
Minority (R 20): Comer (KY), RMM; Jordan (OH), Gosar (AZ), Foxx (NC), Hice (GA), Grothman (WI), Cloud (TX), Gibbs (OH), C. Higgins (LA), Norman (SC), Sessions (TX), Keller (PA), Biggs (AZ), Clyde (GA), Mace (SC), Franklin (FL), LaTurner (KS), Fallon (TX), Herrell (NM), Donalds (FL)

SUBCOMMITTEES

National Security
Majority (D 7): Lynch (MA), Chmn; Mfume (MD), Welch (VT), H. Johnson (GA), DeSaulnier (CA), Wasserman Schultz (FL), Speier (CA)
Minority (R 5): Grothman (WI), RMM; Gosar (AZ), Foxx (NC), Gibbs (OH), C. Higgins (LA)

Select Investigative on the Coronavirus Crisis
Majority (D 7): Clyburn (SC), Chmn; Waters (CA), C. Maloney (NY), Velazquez (NY), Foster (IL), Raskin (MD), Krishnamoorthi (IL)
Minority (R 5): Scalise (LA), RMM; Jordan (OH), M. Green (TN), Malliotakis (NY), Miller-Meeks (IA)

Subcommittee on Civil Rights & Civil Liberties
Majority (D 9): Raskin (MD), Chmn; Ocasio-Cortez (NY), Mfume (MD), Wasserman Schultz (FL), R. Kelly (IL), Pressley (MA), Norton (DC), Tlaib (MI), D. Davis (IL)
Minority (R 7): Sessions (TX), RMM; Jordan (OH), Biggs (AZ), Mace (SC), Franklin (FL), Donalds (FL), C. Higgins (LA)

Subcommittee on Economic & Consumer Policy

Majority (D 7): Krishnamoorthi (IL), Chmn; Pressley (MA), Porter (CA), Bush (MO), Speier (CA), H. Johnson (GA), DeSaulnier (CA)

Minority (R 5): Cloud (TX), RMM; Keller (PA), Franklin (FL), Clyde (GA), Donalds (FL)

Subcommittee on Environment

Majority (D 7): Khanna (CA), Chmn; Tlaib (MI), Cooper (TN), Ocasio-Cortez (NY), Gomez (CA), Krishnamoorthi (IL), Bush (MO)

Minority (R 5): Norman (SC), RMM; Gosar (AZ), Gibbs (OH), Fallon (TX), Herrell (NM)

Government Operations

Majority (D 9): Connolly (VA), Chmn; Porter (CA), Norton (DC), Davis (IL), Sarbanes (MD), Lawrence (MI), Lynch (MA), Raskin (MD), Khanna (CA)

Minority (R 7): Hice (GA), RMM; Keller (PA), Clyde (GA), Biggs (AZ), Mace (SC), LaTurner (KS), Herrell (NM)

Rules	**H-312 The Capitol**
rules.house.gov	**202-225-9091**

Majority (D 9): McGovern (MA), Chmn; N. Torres (CA), Perlmutter (CO), Raskin (MD), Scanlon (PA), Morelle (NY), DeSaulnier (CA), Ross (NC), Joe Neguse (CO)

Minority (R 4): Cole (OK), RMM; Burgess (TX), Reschenthaler (PA), Fischbach (MN)

SUBCOMMITTEES

Expedited Procedures

Majority (D 5): Raskin (MD), Chmn; Ross (NC), N. Torres (CA), DeSaulnier (CA), McGovern (MA)

Minority (R 2): Fischbach (MN), RMM; Cole (OK)

Legislative & Budget Process

Majority (D 5): Morelle (NY), Scanlon (PA), Ross (NC), Neguse (CO), McGovern (MA)

Minority (R 2): Burgess (TX), RMM; Cole (OK)

Rules & Organization of the House

Majority (D 5): N. Torres (CA), Chmn; Perlmutter (CO), Scanlon (PA), Neguse (CO), McGovern (MA)

Minority (R 2): Reschenthaler (PA), RMM; Cole (OK)

Science, Space & Technology	**2321 RHOB**
science.house.gov	**202-225-6375**

Majority (D 22): E. Johnson (TX), Chmn; Lofgren (CA), Bonamici (OR), Bera (CA), Stevens (MI), Sherrill (NJ), Bowman (NY), Sherman (CA), Perlmutter (CO), McNerney (CA), Tonko (NY), Foster (IL), Norcross (NJ), Beyer (VA), Crist (FL), Casten (IL), Lamb (PA), Ross (NC), G. Moore (WI), Kildee (MI), Wild (PA), Fletcher (TX)

Minority (R 18): Lucas (OK), RMM; Brooks (AL), Posey (FL), Weber (TX), Babin (TX), A. Gonzalez (OH), Waltz (FL), Baird (IN), Sessions (TX), Webster (FL), M. Garcia (CA), Bice (OK), Y. Kim (CA), Feenstra (IA), LaTurner (KS), Gimenez (FL), Obernolte (CA), Meijer (MI)

SUBCOMMITTEES

Energy

Majority (D 8): Bowman (NY), Chmn; Bonamici (OR), Stevens (MI), McNerney (CA), Norcross (NJ), Casten (IL), Lamb (PA), Ross (NC)

Minority (R 6): Weber (TX), RMM; Baird (IN), M. Garcia (CA), Feenstra (IA), Gimenez (FL), Meijer (MI)

Environment

Majority (D 6): Sherrill (NJ), Chmn; Bonamici (OR), Kildee (MI), Fletcher (TX), Crist (FL), Casten (IL)

Minority (R 4): Bice (OK), RMM; A. Gonzalez (OH), Feenstra (IA), Gimenez (FL)

Investigations & Oversight

Majority (D 5): Foster (IL), Chmn; Perlmutter (CO), Bera (CA), G. Moore (WI), Casten (IL)

Minority (R 2): Obernolte (CA), RMM; Sessions (TX)

Research & Technology
Majority (D 8): Stevens (MI), Chmn; Tonko (NY), G. Moore (WI), Wild (PA), Foster (IL), Beyer (VA), Lamb (PA), Ross (NC)
Minority (R 6): Waltz (FL), RMM; A. Gonzalez (OH), Baird (IN), Sessions (TX), LaTurner (KS), Meijer (MI)

Space & Aeronautics
Majority (D 7): Beyer (VA), Chmn; Lofgren (CA), Bera (CA), Sherman (CA), Perlmutter (CO), Crist (FL), Norcross (NJ)
Minority (R 5): Babin (TX), RMM; Brooks (AL), Posey (FL), Webster (FL), Y. Kim (CA)

Select Committee on the Climate Crisis	**H2-359 FHOB**
climatecrisis.house.gov	**202-225-1106**

Majority (D 9): Castor (FL), Chmn; Bonamici (OR), Brownley (CA), Huffman (CA), McEachin (VA), M. Levin (CA), Casten (IL), Neguse (CO), Escobar (TX)
Minority (R 7): G. Graves (LA), RMM; Palmer (AL), B. Carter (GA), C. Miller (WV), Armstrong (ND), Crenshaw (TX), A. Gonzalez (OH)

Select Committee on the Modernization of Congress	**164 CHOB**
modernizecongress.house.gov	**202-225-1530**

Majority (D 6): Kilmer (WA), Chmn; Lofgren (CA), Cleaver (MO), Perlmutter (CO), Phillips (MN), N. Williams (GA)
Minority (R 6): Timmons (SC), R. Davis (IL), Latta (OH), D. Joyce (OH), Reschenthaler (PA), Van Duyne (TX)

Small Business	**2361 RHOB**
smallbusiness.house.gov	**202-225-4038**

Majority (D 15): Velazquez (NY), Chmn; Mfume (MD), Golden (ME), Crow (CO), Davids (KS), Phillips (MN), Newman (IL), Bourdeaux (GA), Chu (CA), Evans (PA), Delgado (NY), Houlahan (PA), A. Kim (NJ), Craig (MN), T. Carter (LA)
Minority (R 12): Luetkemeyer (MO), RMM; R. Williams (TX), Hagedorn (MN), Stauber (MN), Meuser (PA), Tenney (NY), Garbarino (NY), Y. Kim (CA), Van Duyne (TX), Donalds (FL), Salazar (FL), Fitzgerald (WI)

SUBCOMMITTEES

Contracting & Infrastructure
Majority (D 5): Mfume (MD), Chmn; Golden (ME), A. Kim (NJ), Newman (IL), T. Carter (LA)
Minority (R 5): Salazar (FL), RMM; Hagedorn (MN), Stauber (MN), Meuser (PA), Fitzgerald (WI)

Economic Growth, Tax & Capital Access
Majority (D 6): Davids (KS), Chmn; Newman (IL), Chu (CA), Evans (PA), A. Kim (NJ), Bourdeaux (GA)
Minority (R 5): Meuser (PA), RMM; Garbarino (NY), Y. Kim (CA), Van Duyne (TX), Donalds (FL)

Innovation, Entrepreneurship & Workforce Development
Majority (D 6): Crow (CO), Chmn; Bourdeaux (GA), Houlahan (PA), Davids (KS), Phillips (MN), Newman (IL)
Minority (R 5): Y. Kim (CA), RMM; R. Williams (TX), Tenney (NY), Garbarino (NY), Salazar (FL)

Oversight, Investigations & Regulations
Majority (D 6): Phillips (MN), Chmn; Craig (MN), Mfume (MD), Chu (CA), Evans (PA), Davids (KS)
Minority (R 5): Van Duyne (TX), RMM; Hagedorn (MN), Meuser (PA), Donalds (FL), Fitzgerald (WI)

Underserved, Agricultural & Rural Business Development
Majority (D 3): Golden (ME), Chmn; Delgado (NY), T. Carter (LA)
Minority (R 5): Hagedorn (MN), RMM; R. Williams (TX), Stauber (MN), Tenney (NY), Salazar (FL)

Transportation & Infrastructure	**2165 RHOB**
transportation.house.gov	**202-225-4472**

Majority (D 37): DeFazio (OR), Chmn; Davids (KS), Norton (DC), E. Johnson (TX), Larsen (WA), Napolitano (CA), Cohen (TN), Sires (NJ), Garamendi (CA), H. Johnson (GA), Carson (IN), Titus (NV), S. Maloney (NY), Huffman (CA), Brownley (CA), F. Wilson (FL), Payne (NJ), Lowenthal (CA), DeSaulnier (CA), Lynch (MA), Carbajal (CA), Brown (MD), Malinowski (NJ), Stanton (AZ), Allred (TX), C. Garcia (IL), Delgado (NY),

Pappas (NH), Lamb (PA), Moulton (MA), Auchincloss (MA), Bourdeaux (GA), Kahele (HI), Strickland (WA), N. Williams (GA), Newman (IL), T. Carter (LA)

Minority (R 32): S. Graves (MO), RMM; Young (AK), Crawford (AR), Gibbs (OH), Webster (FL), Massie (KY), Perry (PA), R. Davis (IL), Katko (NY), Babin (TX), G. Graves (LA), Rouzer (NC), Bost (IL), Weber (TX), LaMalfa (CA), Westerman (AR), Mast (FL), Gallagher (WI), Fitzpatrick (PA), Gonzalez-Colon (PR), Balderson (OH), Stauber (MN), Burchett (TN), D. Johnson (SD), Van Drew (NJ), Guest (MS), Nehls (TX), Mace (SC), Malliotakis (NY), Van Duyne (TX), Gimenez (FL), Steel (CA)

SUBCOMMITTEES

Coast Guard & Maritime Transportation
Majority (D 7): Carbajal (CA), Chmn; Larsen (WA), Auchincloss (MA), S. Maloney (NY), Lowenthal (CA), Brown (MD), Pappas (NH)

Minority (R 6): Gibbs (OH), RMM; Young (AK), Weber (TX), Gallagher (WI), Van Drew (NJ), Malliotakis (NY)

Economic Dev't, Public Buildings & Emergency Management
Majority (D 7): Titus (NV), Chmn; Norton (DC), Davids (KS), Pappas (NH), Napolitano (CA), Garamendi (CA), T. Carter (LA)

Minority (R 6): Webster (FL), RMM; Massie (KY), Gonzalez-Colon (PR), Guest (MS), Van Duyne (TX), Gimenez (FL)

Highways & Transit
Majority (D 30): Norton (DC), E. Johnson (TX), Sires (NJ), Garamendi (CA), H. Johnson (GA), S. Maloney (NY), Brownley (CA), F. Wilson (FL), Lowenthal (CA), DeSaulnier (CA), Lynch (MA), Brown (MD), Stanton (AZ), Allred (TX), C. Garcia (IL), Delgado (NY), Pappas (NH), Lamb (PA), Auchincloss (MA), Bourdeaux (GA), Strickland (WA), Napolitano (CA), Huffman (CA), Carbajal (CA), Davids (KS), Moulton (MA), Kahele (HI), N. Williams (GA), Newman (IL), Cohen (TN)

Minority (R 26): R. Davis (IL), RMM; Young (AK), Crawford (AR), Gibbs (OH), Massie (KY), Perry (PA), Katko (NY), Babin (TX), Rouzer (NC), Bost (IL), LaMalfa (CA), Westerman (AR), Gallagher (WI), Fitzpatrick (PA), Gonzalez-Colon (PR), Balderson (OH), Stauber (MN), Burchett (TN), D. Johnson (SD), Guest (MS), Nehls (TX), Mace (SC), Malliotakis (NY), Van Duyne (TX), Gimenez (FL), Steel (CA)

Railroads, Pipelines & Hazardous Materials
Majority (D 17): Payne (NJ), Chmn; Malinowski (NJ), Moulton (MA), Newman (IL), Cohen (TN), Sires (NJ), Carson (IN), F. Wilson (FL), C. Garcia (IL), Strickland (WA), Napolitano (CA), H. Johnson (GA), Titus (NV), Huffman (CA), Lynch (MA), Auchincloss (MA), T. Carter (LA)

Minority (R 14): Crawford (AR), RMM; Perry (PA), R. Davis (IL), Bost (IL), Weber (TX), LaMalfa (CA), Westerman (AR), Fitzpatrick (PA), Balderson (OH), Stauber (MN), Burchett (TN), D. Johnson (SD), Nehls (TX), Steel (CA)

Water Resources & Environment
Majority (D 14): Napolitano (CA), Chmn; Huffman (CA), E. Johnson (TX), Garamendi (CA), Lowenthal (CA), Malinowski (NJ), Delgado (NY), Pappas (NH), Bourdeaux (GA), F. Wilson (FL), Carbajal (CA), Stanton (AZ), Norton (DC), Cohen (TN)

Minority (R 12): Rouzer (NC), RMM; Webster (FL), Katko (NY), Babin (TX), G. Graves (LA), Bost (IL), Weber (TX), LaMalfa (CA), Westerman (AR), Mast (FL), Gonzalez-Colon (PR), Mace (SC)

Aviation
Majority (D 19): Carson (IN), Davids (KS), Kahele (HI), Williams (GA), Johnson (GA), Titus (NV), Maloney (NY), Brownley (CA), Payne (NJ), DeSaulnier (CA), Lynch (MA), Brown (MD), Stanton (AZ), Allred (TX), Lamb (PA), Norton (DC), Johnson (TX), Garamendi (CA), DeFazio (OR)

Minority (R 18): Graves (LA), RMM; Young (AK), Massie (KY), Perry (PA), Katko (NY), Mast (FL), Gallagher (WI), Fitzpatrick (PA), Balderson (OH), Stauber (MN), Burchett (TN), Van Drew (NJ), Nehls (TX), Mace (SC), Van Duyne (TX), Gimenez (FL), Steel (CA), Graves (MO)

Veterans' Affairs
veterans.house.gov

364 CHOB
202-225-9756

Majority (D 17): Takano (CA), Chmn; M. Levin (CA), Brownley (CA), Lamb (PA), Pappas (NH), Luria (VA), Mrvan (IN), Sablan (MP), Underwood (IL), Allred (TX), Brown (MD), Frankel (FL), Slotkin (MI), Trone (MD), Gallego (AZ), Ruiz (CA), Kaptur (OH)

Minority (R 13): Bost (IL), RMM; Radewagen (AS), Bergman (MI), Banks (IN), Roy (TX), G. Murphy (NC), Mann (KS), B. Moore (AL), Mace (SC), Cawthorn (NC), Nehls (TX), Rosendale (MT), Miller-Meeks (IA)

SUBCOMMITTEES

Disability Assistance & Memorial Affairs
Majority (D 5): Luria (VA), Chmn; Slotkin (MI), Kaptur (OH), Ruiz (CA), Trone (MD)
Minority (R 3): Nehls (TX), RMM; B. Moore (AL), Miller-Meeks (IA)

Economic Opportunity
Majority (D 5): M. Levin (CA), Chmn; Pappas (NH), Brown (MD), Trone (MD), Gallego (AZ)
Minority (R 4): B. Moore (AL), RMM; Mann (KS), Mace (SC), Cawthorn (NC)

Health
Majority (D 8): Brownley (CA), Chmn; Mrvan (IN), Lamb (PA), M. Levin (CA), Sablan (MP), Underwood (IL), Allred (TX), Frankel (FL)
Minority (R 6): Bergman (MI), RMM; Radewagen (AS), Roy (TX), G. Murphy (NC), Rosendale (MT), Miller-Meeks (IA)

Technology Modernization
Majority (D 3): Mrvan (IN), Chmn; Brown (MD), Takano (CA)
Minority (R 2): Rosendale (MT), RMM; Banks (IN)

Oversight & Investigations
Majority (D 4): Pappas (NH), Chmn; Lamb (PA), Luria (VA), Sablan (MP)
Minority (R 3): Mann (KS), RMM; Radewagen (AS), Bergman (MI)

Ways & Means   **1102 LHOB**
waysandmeans.house.gov   **202-225-3625**

Majority (D 25): Neal (MA), Chmn; DelBene (WA), Doggett (TX), M. Thompson (CA), Larson (CT), Blumenauer (OR), Kind (WI), Pascrell (NJ), D. Davis (IL), Sanchez (CA), B. Higgins (NY), Sewell (AL), Chu (CA), G. Moore (WI), Kildee (MI), Boyle (PA), Beyer (VA), Evans (PA), Schneider (IL), Suozzi (NY), Panetta (CA), S. Murphy (FL), Gomez (CA), Horsford (NV), Plaskett (VI)
Minority (R 18): Brady (TX), RMM; Nunes (CA), Buchanan (FL), A. Smith (NE), Reed (NY), M. Kelly (PA), J. Smith (MO), T. Rice (SC), Schweikert (AZ), Walorski (IN), LaHood (IL), Wenstrup (OH), Arrington (TX), Ferguson (GA), Estes (KS), Smucker (PA), Hern (OK), C. Miller (WV)

SUBCOMMITTEES

Health
Majority (D 11): Doggett (TX), Chmn; M. Thompson (CA), Kind (WI), Blumenauer (OR), B. Higgins (NY), Sewell (AL), Chu (CA), Evans (PA), Schneider (IL), Gomez (CA), Horsford (NV)
Minority (R 8): Nunes (CA), RMM; Buchanan (FL), A. Smith (NE), Reed (NY), M. Kelly (PA), J. Smith (MO), Schweikert (AZ), Wenstrup (OH)

Oversight
Majority (D 8): Pascrell (NJ), Chmn; Suozzi (NY), Chu (CA), Schneider (IL), Plaskett (VI), Doggett (TX), Evans (PA), Horsford (NV)
Minority (R 5): M. Kelly (PA), RMM; Walorski (IN), Wenstrup (OH), Ferguson (GA), Smucker (PA)

Social Security
Majority (D 8): Larson (CT), Chmn; Pascrell (NJ), Sanchez (CA), B. Higgins (NY), Horsford (NV), Blumenauer (OR), Sewell (AL), G. Moore (WI)
Minority (R 5): Reed (NY), RMM; T. Rice (SC), Arrington (TX), Estes (KS), Hern (OK)

Trade
Majority (D 11): Blumenauer (OR), Chmn; Kind (WI), D. Davis (IL), B. Higgins (NY), Kildee (MI), Panetta (CA), S. Murphy (FL), DelBene (WA), Beyer (VA), Sanchez (CA), Boyle (PA)
Minority (R 8): Buchanan (FL), RMM; Nunes (CA), T. Rice (SC), LaHood (IL), Arrington (TX), Ferguson (GA), Estes (KS), C. Miller (WV)

Worker & Family Support
Majority (D 8): D. Davis (IL), Chmn; Chu (CA), G. Moore (WI), Evans (PA), S. Murphy (FL), Gomez (CA), Kildee (MI), Panetta (CA)
Minority (R 5): Walorski (IN), RMM; Wenstrup (OH), Smucker (PA), Hern (OK), C. Miller (WV)

Select Revenue Measures
Majority (D 10): Thompson (CA), Chmn; Doggett (TX), Larson (CT), Sanchez (CA), DelBene (WA), Moore (WI), Boyle (PA), Suozzi (NY), Plaskett (VI), Sewell (AL)
Minority (R 8): Smith (NE), RMM; Rice (SC), Schweikert (AZ), LaHood (IL), Arrington (TX), Ferguson (GA), Hern (OK), Estes (KS)

OTHER COMMITTEES

Permanent Select on Intelligence   HVC-304 The Capitol Visitors Center
intelligence.house.gov   202-225-7690

Majority (D 12): Schiff (CA), Chmn; Himes (CT), Carson (IN), Speier (CA), Quigley (IL), Castro (TX), Welch (VT), Maloney (NY), Demings (FL), Krishnamoorthi (IL), Cooper (TN), Crow (CO)
Minority (R 10): Nunes (CA), RMM; Turner (OH), Wenstrup (OH), Stewart (UT), Crawford (AR), Stefanik (NY), Mullin (OK), Kelly (MS), LaHood (IL), Fitzpatrick (PA)

SUBCOMMITTEES

Counterterrorism, Counterintelligence & Counterproliferation
Majority (D 6): Carson (IN), Chmn; Speier (CA), Quigley (IL), Castro (TX), Welch (VT), Sean Maloney (NY)
Minority (R 4): Crawford (AR), RMM; Conaway (TX), Wenstrup (OH), Stewart (UT)

Defense Intelligence & Warfighter Support
Majority (D 6): Sewell (AL), Chmn; Himes (CT), Heck (WA), Welch (VT), Maloney (NY), Demings (FL)
Minority (R 4): Wenstrup (OH), RMM; Conaway (TX), Turner (OH), Hurd (TX)

Intelligence Modernization & Readiness
Majority (D 6): Swalwell (CA), Chmn; Sewell (AL), Speier (CA),Castro (TX), Demings (FL), Krishnamoorthi (IL)
Minority (R 4): Hurd (TX), RMM; Conaway (TX), Stefanik (NY), Ratcliffe (TX)

Strategic Technologies & Advanced Research
Majority (D 6): Himes (CT), Chmn; Carson (IN), Quigley (IL), Swalwell (CA), Heck (WA), Krishnamoorthi (IL)
Minority (R 4): Stewart (UT), RMM; Turner (OH), Stefanik (NY), Ratcliffe (TX)

Select Committee on the Climate Crisis   H2-359 FHOB
climatecrisis.house.gov   202-225-1106

Majority (D 9): Castor (FL), Chmn; Bonamici (OR), Brownley (CA), Huffman (CA), McEachin (VA), Levin (CA), Casten (IL), Neguse (CO), Escobar (TX)
Minority (R 7): Graves (LA), RMM; Palmer (AL), Carter (GA), Miller (WV), Armstrong (ND), Crenshaw (TX), Gonzalez (OH)

Select Committee on the Modernization of Congress   226 CHOB
modernizecongress.house.gov   202-225-1530

Majority (D 6): Kilmer (WA), Chmn; Lofgren (CA), Cleaver (MO), Perlmutter (CO), Phillips (MN), Williams (GA)
Minority (R 6): Timmons (SC), Davis (IL), Latta (OH), Joyce (OH), Reschenthaler (PA), Van Duyne (TX)

JOINT COMMITTEES

Joint Congressional Oversight Commission   ST-76 The Capitol
coc.senate.gov   202-224-5050

House (R 1): Hill (AR)
Senate (R 1): Toomey (PA)

Joint Congressional-Executive Commission on China
cecc.gov

House (R 1;D 1): McGovern (MA), Steel (CA)
Senate (D 1): Merkley (OR), Chmn

Joint Economic

jec.senate.gov

House (D 5;R 4): Beyer (VA), Chmn; Trone (MD), Beatty (OH), Peters (CA), Davids (KS), Schweikert (AZ), Herrera Beutler (WA), Estes (KS), Arrington (TX)
Senate (D 5;R 5): Heinrich (NM), VChmn; Klobuchar (MN), Hassan (NH), Kelly (AZ), Warnock (GA), Lee (UT), Cotton (AR), Portman (OH), Cassidy (LA), Cruz (TX)

Joint Library
cha.house.gov

House (D 3;R 2): Lofgren (CA), Ryan (OH), Butterfield (NC), Davis (IL), Loudermilk (GA)

Joint Printing
cha.house.gov

House (D 3;R 2): Lofgren (CA), Raskin (MD), Leger Fernandez (NM), Davis (IL), Loudermilk (GA)

Joint Security & Cooperation in Europe   **234 FHOB**
csce.gov   **202-225-1901**

House (D 4;R 4): Cleaver (MO), Cohen (TN), Moore (WI), Veasey (TX), Wilson (SC), Aderholt (AL), Fitzpatrick (PA), Hudson (NC)
Senate (D 5;R 4): Cardin (MD), Chmn; Blumenthal (CT), Shaheen (NH), Smith (MN), Whitehouse (RI), Wicker (MS), Boozman (AR), Rubio (FL), Tillis (NC)

Joint Taxation
jct.gov

House (D 3;R 2): Neal (MA), Chmn; Doggett (TX), Thompson (CA), Brady (TX), Nunes (CA)
Senate (D 3;R 2): Wyden (OR), VChmn; Stabenow (MI), Cantwell (WA), Crapo (ID), Grassley (IA)

2018 PRIMARY AND GENERAL ELECTION VOTES CAST FOR U.S. CONGRESS

The Federal Election Commission compiles every two years data on the total votes cast, by party, for all federal elections. This table shows the state-by-state turnout for each party in House contests—both primary and general elections—for 2016, which were the most recent results released by the FEC, as of June 2019.

This table is enhanced by a separate table on the following page that shows the total of citizen voting age population (CVAP), registered voters, plus voter turnout in each state in 2012, 2016 and 2018.

State	PRIMARY ELECTION			GENERAL ELECTION		
	Democratic	Republican	Other	Democratic	Republican	Other
AL	116,382	370,299		678,687	975,737	5,471
AK	40,551	70,105		131,199	149,779	1,188
AS				637	7,194	807
AZ	480,782	575,517	538	1,179,193	1,139,251	22,826
AR	40,344	107,097		312,978	556,339	19,981
CA	4,189,106	2,262,787	150,596	8,010,445	3,973,396	200,681
CO	580,796	436,182		1,343,211	1,079,772	90,923
CT	39,657	32,098		808,652	512,495	58,661
DE		36,932		227,353	125,384	1,077
DC	79,535	750	572	199,124	9,700	19,945
FL	1,092,027	707,749		3,307,228	3,675,417	38,831
GA	529,669	524,784		1,814,469	1,987,191	683
GU	24,321	2,854		19,193	15,398	399
HI	232,009	25,243	776	287,921	87,348	7,063
ID	55,070	171,476		207,303	367,993	20,428
IL	1,220,901	640,187	131	2,757,540	1,754,449	27,715
IN	292,879	491,801		1,000,104	1,247,978	8,067
IA	172,905	95,010	1,031	664,676	612,338	39,634
KS	149,706	306,652		464,380	563,190	22,752
KY	318,325	161,102		612,977	935,304	21,517
LA				553,184	835,715	71,694
ME	119,587	83,726		333,208	245,372	53,097
MD	582,934	183,386		1,493,047	737,906	55,331
MA	648,520	132,070		1,943,597	497,953	43,531
MI	1,094,386	842,150	1,058	2,344,333	1,853,459	151,904
MN	490,939	257,337		1,420,769	1,125,533	30,694
MS	81,996	186,634		398,770	471,162	68,971
MO	560,834	652,207	6,093	1,027,969	1,330,975	59,469
MT	111,915	136,406	1,538	233,284	256,661	14,476
NE	91,520	163,051		264,493	432,077	
NV	137,622	137,507		491,272	439,727	29,775
NH	121,041	93,326	994	311,242	248,986	10,516
NJ	410,695	225,893		1,856,819	1,198,664	43,260
NM	161,568	72,496	445	404,026	264,701	24,584
NY	343,322	21,472	1,282	3,899,563	1,726,318	578,502
NC	376,557	245,461	687	1,771,061	1,846,041	46,224
ND	33,801	66,465	71	114,377	193,568	13,587
MP					5,199	9,150
OH	604,956	755,554	246	2,084,854	2,295,373	32,341
OK	490,230	402,695		428,452	730,531	19,853
OR	390,482	257,546	12,926	1,061,412	702,531	83,703
PA	784,604	682,324		3,016,286	2,488,357	37,724
RI	105,870	25,065		242,575	129,838	867
SC	208,770	246,881		758,340	927,494	23,458
SD		100,711		121,033	202,695	12,237
TN	351,365	717,395		846,450	1,279,655	33,720
TX	1,213,819	1,553,347		3,852,752	4,135,359	214,597
UT	12,712	90,562		374,009	617,307	61,190
VT	66,744	24,579	382	188,547	70,705	13,199
VI				16,341		264
VA	185,891	108,240		1,867,061	1,408,701	37,449
WA	1,022,020	516,456	158,160	1,888,593	899,744	233,614
WV	153,313	114,524		234,568	337,146	6,277

WI	494,418	387,409	232	1,367,492	1,121,043	83,120
WY	16,959	111,013		59,903	127,963	13,379
Total:	**21,124,355**	**16,612,513**	**337,758**	**61,296,952**	**50,960,112**	**2,820,406**

Voter Registration and Turnout: 2016-2020

The voter registration table was compiled by Almanac staff from various sources to demonstrate trends in voter registration and turnout at the state level in federal elections from 2016-2020. Voter registration figures were retrieved from Secretary of State websites for each state and includes only individuals registered eligible to vote in the 2016 and 2020 federal elections respectively. Voter turnout for 2016 and 2019 elections "CVAP" indicates Civilian Age Voting Population. Citizen voting age population was retrieved from the U.S Census Bureau and is defined as citizens in the given geography that as U.S. citizens and meet all criteria to be eligible to vote.

Sources: U.S. Census Bureau, American Community Survey, 2016-19; Secretary of State websites, all states; The Almanac of American Politics, 2020.

State	2016 CVAP	2016 Total Registered	2016 Total Pres. Vote	2019 CVAP	2020 Total Registered	2020 Total Pres. Vote
Alabama	3,639,493	2,990,533	2,092,269	3,685,075	3,708,804	2,323,282
Alaska	527,811	361,000	298,566	530,995	598,107	359,530
Arizona	4,613,575	3,588,466	2,519,895	4,920,450	4,261,301	3,397,389
Arkansas	2,175,338	1,759,982	1,095,195	2,207,335	1,828,770	1,219,069
California	24,875,293	19,411,771	13,994,764	25,494,385	22,047,448	17,501,380
Colorado	3,824,440	3,292,062	2,685,475	4,063,875	4,261,765	3,256,980
Connecticut	2,582,883	2,357,733	1,619,463	2,605,410	2,505,076	1,824,456
Delaware	689,653	681,950	435,487	710,280	743,015	504,346
Florida	14,195,896	12,971,305	9,329,904	14,988,415	14,065,627	11,091,758
Georgia	7,063,804	6,637,939	4,092,373	7,356,560	7,600,000	4,999,960
Hawaii	1,006,727	749,917	424,429	1,018,390	832,466	574,469
Idaho	1,148,895	813,218	673,627	1,220,310	1,082,417	867,934
Illinois	9,003,481	6,665,000	5,446,340	9,049,960	8,364,099	6,049,500
Indiana	4,824,553	3,270,000	2,724,405	4,903,145	4,751,708	3,039,432
Iowa	2,295,040	2,171,165	1,513,838	2,321,085	2,243,758	1,690,871
Kansas	2,061,775	1,817,920	1,176,935	2,084,735	1,851,397	1,372,303
Kentucky	3,313,798	2,253,000	1,885,577	3,349,115	3,476,393	2,136,768
Louisiana	3,432,034	3,022,075	1,958,792	3,459,490	3,091,340	2,148,062
Maine	1,051,867	787,000	745,684	1,064,670	1,059,006	819,461
Maryland	4,212,263	3,900,090	2,700,702	4,280,945	4,109,762	3,037,030
Massachusetts	4,887,325	4,534,974	3,224,107	4,992,535	4,812,909	3,631,402
Michigan	7,408,626	5,620,000	4,720,518	7,495,885	7,151,051	5,547,186
Minnesota	3,980,474	3,269,260	2,804,041	4,069,675	4,118,462	3,277,171
Mississippi	2,217,764	1,725,000	1,185,845	2,232,330	1,985,928	1,313,759
Missouri	4,547,880	4,223,787	2,762,938	4,603,770	4,213,092	3,025,962
Montana	789,499	694,370	484,986	812,540	752,538	603,674
Nebraska	1,341,016	1,211,101	819,401	1,366,080	1,226,730	956,383
Nevada	1,902,282	1,679,254	1,088,702	2,018,930	1,822,166	1,405,376
New Hampshire	1,027,630	752,000	725,093	1,055,455	1,001,446	806,205
New Jersey	6,087,275	5,819,276	3,750,211	6,132,175	6,047,888	4,565,196
New Mexico	1,464,241	1,291,905	779,442	1,496,285	1,351,811	923,965
New York	13,605,854	12,493,250	7,552,299	13,723,455	13,555,547	8,632,255
North Carolina	7,203,790	6,918,150	4,682,073	7,514,970	7,359,798	5,524,804
North Dakota	555,691	424,000	331,986	564,480	581,379	361,819
Ohio	8,734,125	7,861,025	5,409,673	8,820,895	8,073,829	5,932,442
Oklahoma	2,787,654	2,157,450	1,452,992	2,837,290	2,152,571	1,560,699
Oregon	2,911,330	2,553,808	1,928,742	3,054,025	2,945,047	2,374,321
Pennsylvania	9,725,847	8,722,977	6,043,889	9,759,725	9,091,497	6,940,451
Rhode Island	780,248	552,000	447,814	792,920	809,821	517,757
South Carolina	3,620,829	3,153,521	2,059,966	3,785,355	3,513,225	2,513,329
South Dakota	627,070	544,428	366,029	639,670	578,655	422,609
Tennessee	4,876,605	4,110,318	2,464,017	5,019,115	3,931,248	3,053,851
Texas	17,177,623	15,101,087	8,846,407	18,181,330	16,955,519	11,313,626
Utah	1,903,497	1,576,494	1,109,205	2,029,030	1,857,861	1,505,931
Vermont	493,535	471,619	290,778	495,820	495,267	367,428
Virginia	5,998,907	5,619,151	3,869,190	6,140,255	5,975,717	4,460,524

Washington	5,008,035	4,284,936	3,125,344	5,257,900	4,892,871	4,087,631
West Virginia	1,453,212	1,274,887	701,169	1,434,260	1,269,219	794,731
Wisconsin	4,313,304	3,619,995	2,894,494	4,366,395	3,684,726	3,298,041
Wyoming	432,377	304,000	243,679	433,355	268,837	276,765

NBC Exit Polls: Vote by Party Candidate

The national exit polls, which have been conducted in recent presidential elections by several national news organizations, have been a gold mine of information about the voters and their choices. The data on the following four pages were compiled by NBC News from the results of the exit polls that were taken from 1992 to 2016, as voters exited polling booths on Election Day. In addition to voter preferences on the candidates, the data provide a unique demographic and ideological breakdown of the electorate.

NBC News generously provided the exit-poll data for the past seven presidential elections to the Almanac for the unique publication in this book. On close examination, the shifts during that time offer significant insight into the remarkable political changes in the nation since 1992. They also provide vital measures about the opportunities and hazards for each party in the 2020 presidential election. Many thanks to John Lapinski and his colleagues at NBC for their extensive assistance in preparing the data.

Source: NBC News Exit Polls

OVERALL		1996		2000		2004		2008		2012		2016		2020	
Exit Poll Topline	Clinton (D)	49	Gore (D)	48	Kerry (D)	48	Obama (D)	53	Obama (D)	50	Clinton (D)	48	Biden (D)	51
	Dole (R)	41	Bush (R)	48	Bush (R)	51	McCain (R)	45	Romney (R)	48	Trump (R)	46	Trump (R)	47
	Perot (I)	8	Ind.	2	Ind.	*	Ind.	--	Ind.	--	Ind.	4	Ind.	--
SEX		**1996**		**2000**		**2004**		**2008**		**2012**		**2016**		**2020**	
Men	Clinton (D)	43	Gore (D)	42	Kerry (D)	44	Obama (D)	49	Obama (D)	45	Clinton (D)	41	Biden (D)	45
	Dole (R)	44	Bush (R)	53	Bush (R)	55	McCain (R)	48	Romney (R)	52	Trump (R)	52	Trump (R)	53
	Perot (I)	10	Ind.	3	Ind.	*	Ind.	--	Ind.	--	Ind.	5	Ind.	--
Women	Clinton (D)	54	Gore (D)	54	Kerry (D)	51	Obama (D)	56	Obama (D)	55	Clinton (D)	54	Biden (D)	57
	Dole (R)	38	Bush (R)	43	Bush (R)	48	McCain (R)	43	Romney (R)	44	Trump (R)	41	Trump (R)	42
	Perot (I)	7	Ind.	2	Ind.	*	Ind.	--	Ind.	--	Ind.	4	Ind.	--
RACE & ETHNICITY		**1996**		**2000**		**2004**		**2008**		**2012**		**2016**		**2020**	
White	Clinton (D)	43	Gore (D)	42	Kerry (D)	41	Obama (D)	43	Obama (D)	39	Clinton (D)	37	Biden (D)	41
	Dole (R)	46	Bush (R)	54	Bush (R)	58	McCain (R)	55	Romney (R)	59	Trump (R)	57	Trump (R)	58
	Perot (I)	9	Ind.	3	Ind.	*	Ind.	--	Ind.	--	Ind.	5	Ind.	--
Black	Clinton (D)	84	Gore (D)	90	Kerry (D)	88	Obama (D)	95	Obama (D)	93	Clinton (D)	89	Biden (D)	87
	Dole (R)	12	Bush (R)	9	Bush (R)	11	McCain (R)	4	Romney (R)	6	Trump (R)	8	Trump (R)	12
	Perot (I)	4	Ind.	1	Ind.	*	Ind.	--	Ind.	--	Ind.	3	Ind.	--
Latino	Clinton (D)	72	Gore (D)	62	Kerry (D)	58	Obama (D)	67	Obama (D)	71	Clinton (D)	66	Biden (D)	65
	Dole (R)	21	Bush (R)	35	Bush (R)	40	McCain (R)	31	Romney (R)	27	Trump (R)	28	Trump (R)	32
	Perot (I)	6	Ind.	2	Ind.	0	Ind.	--	Ind.	--	Ind.	5	Ind.	--
Asian	Clinton (D)	43	Gore (D)	55	Kerry (D)	56	Obama (D)	62	Obama (D)	73	Clinton (D)	65	Biden (D)	61
	Dole (R)	48	Bush (R)	41	Bush (R)	44	McCain (R)	35	Romney (R)	26	Trump (R)	27	Trump (R)	34
	Perot (I)	8	Ind.	3	Ind.	0	Ind.	--	Ind.	--	Ind.	6	Ind.	--
AGE		**1996**		**2000**		**2004**		**2008**		**2012**		**2016**		**2020**	
18-29	Clinton (D)	53	Gore (D)	48	Kerry (D)	54	Obama (D)	66	Obama (D)	60	Clinton (D)	55	Biden (D)	60
	Dole (R)	34	Bush (R)	46	Bush (R)	45	McCain (R)	32	Romney (R)	37	Trump (R)	36	Trump (R)	36
	Perot (I)	10	Ind.	5	Ind.	*	Ind.	--	Ind.	--	Ind.	8	Ind.	--
30-44	Clinton (D)	48	Gore (D)	48	Kerry (D)	46	Obama (D)	52	Obama (D)	52	Clinton (D)	51	Biden (D)	52
	Dole (R)	41	Bush (R)	49	Bush (R)	53	McCain (R)	46	Romney (R)	45	Trump (R)	41	Trump (R)	46
	Perot (I)	9	Ind.	2	Ind.	1	Ind.	--	Ind.	--	Ind.	7	Ind.	--
45-59	Clinton (D)	48	Gore (D)	48	Kerry (D)	48	Obama (D)	49	Obama (D)	47	Clinton (D)	43	Biden (D)	49
	Dole (R)	41	Bush (R)	49	Bush (R)	51	McCain (R)	49	Romney (R)	52	Trump (R)	53	Trump (R)	50
	Perot (I)	9	Ind.	2	Ind.	*	Ind.	--	Ind.	--	Ind.	3	Ind.	--
60+	Clinton (D)	48	Gore (D)	51	Kerry (D)	46	Obama (D)	47	Obama (D)	46	Clinton (D)	46	Biden (D)	47
	Dole (R)	44	Bush (R)	47	Bush (R)	54	McCain (R)	51	Romney (R)	54	Trump (R)	51	Trump (R)	52
	Perot (I)	7	Ind.	2	Ind.	*	Ind.	--	Ind.	--	Ind.	3	Ind.	--
IDEOLOGY		**1996**		**2000**		**2004**		**2008**		**2012**		**2016**		**2020**	
Liberals	Clinton (D)	78	Gore (D)	80	Kerry (D)	85	Obama (D)	89	Obama (D)	86	Clinton (D)	84	Biden (D)	89
	Dole (R)	11	Bush (R)	13	Bush (R)	13	McCain (R)	10	Romney (R)	11	Trump (R)	10	Trump (R)	10
	Perot (I)	7	Ind.	6	Ind.	1	Ind.	--	Ind.	--	Ind.	5	Ind.	--

	1996		2000		2004		2008		2012		2016		2020	
Moderates	Clinton (D)	57	Gore (D)	52	Kerry (D)	54	Obama (D)	60	Obama (D)	56	Clinton (D)	52	Biden (D)	64
	Dole (R)	33	Bush (R)	44	Bush (R)	45	McCain (R)	39	Romney (R)	41	Trump (R)	40	Trump (R)	34
	Perot (I)	9	Ind.	2	Ind.	*	Ind.	--	Ind.	--	Ind.	6	Ind.	--
Conservatives	Clinton (D)	20	Gore (D)	17	Kerry (D)	15	Obama (D)	20	Obama (D)	17	Clinton (D)	16	Biden (D)	14
	Dole (R)	71	Bush (R)	81	Bush (R)	84	McCain (R)	78	Romney (R)	82	Trump (R)	81	Trump (R)	85
	Perot (I)	8	Ind.	1	Ind.	*	Ind.	--	Ind.	--	Ind.	2	Ind.	--

RELIGION	1996		2000		2004		2008		2012		2016		2020	
All Protestant / Other Christian	Clinton (D)	42	Gore (D)	42	Kerry (D)	40	Obama (D)	45	Obama (D)	42	Clinton (D)	39	Biden (D)	39
	Dole (R)	47	Bush (R)	56	Bush (R)	59	McCain (R)	54	Romney (R)	57	Trump (R)	56	Trump (R)	60
	Perot (I)	9	Ind.	2	Ind.	*	Ind.	--	Ind.	--	Ind.	3	Ind.	--
White Protestant	Clinton (D)	36	Gore (D)	34	Kerry (D)	32	Obama (D)	34	Obama (D)	30	Clinton (D)	26	Biden (D)	27
	Dole (R)	53	Bush (R)	63	Bush (R)	67	McCain (R)	65	Romney (R)	69	Trump (R)	69	Trump (R)	72
	Perot (I)	10	Ind.	2	Ind.	*	Ind.	--	Ind.	--	Ind.	3	Ind.	--
Catholic	Clinton (D)	53	Gore (D)	50	Kerry (D)	47	Obama (D)	54	Obama (D)	50	Clinton (D)	46	Biden (D)	52
	Dole (R)	37	Bush (R)	47	Bush (R)	52	McCain (R)	45	Romney (R)	48	Trump (R)	50	Trump (R)	47
	Perot (I)	9	Ind.	2	Ind.	*	Ind.	--	Ind.	--	Ind.	3	Ind.	--
Jewish	Clinton (D)	78	Gore (D)	79	Kerry (D)	74	Obama (D)	78	Obama (D)	69	Clinton (D)	71	Biden (D)	--
	Dole (R)	16	Bush (R)	19	Bush (R)	25	McCain (R)	21	Romney (R)	30	Trump (R)	23	Trump (R)	--
	Perot (I)	3	Ind.	1	Ind.	0	Ind.	--	Ind.	--	Ind.	6	Ind.	--
Mormon	Clinton (D)	n/a	Gore (D)	n/a	Kerry (D)	19	Obama (D)	24	Obama (D)	21	Clinton (D)	28	Biden (D)	n/a
	Dole (R)	n/a	Bush (R)	n/a	Bush (R)	80	McCain (R)	76	Romney (R)	78	Trump (R)	56	Trump (R)	n/a
	Perot (I)	n/a	Ind.	n/a	Ind.	1	Ind.	--	Ind.	--	Ind.	8	Ind.	n/a
None	Clinton (D)	59	Gore (D)	61	Kerry (D)	67	Obama (D)	75	Obama (D)	70	Clinton (D)	67	Biden (D)	65
	Dole (R)	23	Bush (R)	30	Bush (R)	31	McCain (R)	23	Romney (R)	26	Trump (R)	25	Trump (R)	31
	Perot (I)	13	Ind.	7	Ind.	1	Ind.	--	Ind.	5	Ind.	7	Ind.	--
Att. church at least once/week	Clinton (D)	n/a	Gore (D)	39	Kerry (D)	39	Obama (D)	43	Obama (D)	39	Clinton (D)	41	Biden (D)	n/a
	Dole (R)	n/a	Bush (R)	59	Bush (R)	61	McCain (R)	55	Romney (R)	59	Trump (R)	55	Trump (R)	n/a
	Perot (I)	n/a	Ind.	2	Ind.	*	Ind.	--	Ind.	--	Ind.	2	Ind.	n/a
White Evangelical	Clinton (D)	n/a	Gore (D)	n/a	Kerry (D)	21	Obama (D)	26	Obama (D)	20	Clinton (D)	16	Biden (D)	24
	Dole (R)	n/a	Bush (R)	n/a	Bush (R)	79	McCain (R)	73	Romney (R)	79	Trump (R)	80	Trump (R)	76
	Perot (I)	n/a	Ind.	n/a	Ind.	*	Ind.	--	Ind.	--	Ind.	2	Ind.	--

SIZE OF PLACE	1996		2000		2004		2008		2012		2016		2020	
Population over 500,000	Clinton (D)	68	Gore (D)	71	Kerry (D)	60	Obama (D)	70	Obama (D)	69	Clinton (D)	72	Biden (D)	64
	Dole (R)	25	Bush (R)	26	Bush (R)	39	McCain (R)	28	Romney (R)	29	Trump (R)	22	Trump (R)	33
	Perot (I)	6	Ind.	3	Ind.	0	Ind.	--	Ind.	--	Ind.	4	Ind.	--
Population 50,000-500,000	Clinton (D)	50	Gore (D)	57	Kerry (D)	49	Obama (D)	59	Obama (D)	58	Clinton (D)	53	Biden (D)	57
	Dole (R)	39	Bush (R)	40	Bush (R)	49	McCain (R)	39	Romney (R)	40	Trump (R)	41	Trump (R)	41
	Perot (I)	8	Ind.	2	Ind.	*	Ind.	--	Ind.	--	Ind.	5	Ind.	--
Suburbs	Clinton (D)	47	Gore (D)	47	Kerry (D)	47	Obama (D)	50	Obama (D)	48	Clinton (D)	45	Biden (D)	50
	Dole (R)	42	Bush (R)	49	Bush (R)	52	McCain (R)	48	Romney (R)	50	Trump (R)	49	Trump (R)	48
	Perot (I)	8	Ind.	3	Ind.	*	Ind.	--	Ind.	--	Ind.	4	Ind.	--
Population 10,000-50,000	Clinton (D)	48	Gore (D)	38	Kerry (D)	48	Obama (D)	45	Obama (D)	42	Clinton (D)	46	Biden (D)	54
	Dole (R)	41	Bush (R)	59	Bush (R)	50	McCain (R)	53	Romney (R)	56	Trump (R)	51	Trump (R)	45
	Perot (I)	9	Ind.	2	Ind.	1	Ind.	--	Ind.	--	Ind.	3	Ind.	--
Rural areas	Clinton (D)	44	Gore (D)	37	Kerry (D)	40	Obama (D)	45	Obama (D)	37	Clinton (D)	32	Biden (D)	39
	Dole (R)	46	Bush (R)	59	Bush (R)	59	McCain (R)	53	Romney (R)	61	Trump (R)	63	Trump (R)	60
	Perot (I)	10	Ind.	2	Ind.	1	Ind.	--	Ind.	--	Ind.	3	Ind.	--

FAMILY INCOME	1996		2000		2004		2008		2012		2016		2020	
Under $30,000	Clinton (D)	55	Gore (D)	55	Kerry (D)	59	Obama (D)	65	Obama (D)	63	Clinton (D)	53	Biden (D)	54
	Dole (R)	33	Bush (R)	40	Bush (R)	40	McCain (R)	33	Romney (R)	35	Trump (R)	40	Trump (R)	46
	Perot (I)	10	Ind.	4	Ind.	*	Ind.	--	Ind.	--	Ind.	--	Ind.	--
$30,000-$49,999	Clinton (D)	48	Gore (D)	49	Kerry (D)	50	Obama (D)	55	Obama (D)	57	Clinton (D)	52	Biden (D)	56
	Dole (R)	40	Bush (R)	48	Bush (R)	49	McCain (R)	43	Romney (R)	42	Trump (R)	41	Trump (R)	43
	Perot (I)	10	Ind.	2	Ind.	*	Ind.	--	Ind.	--	Ind.	5	Ind.	--
$50,000-$99,999	Clinton (D)	46	Gore (D)	46	Kerry (D)	44	Obama (D)	49	Obama (D)	46	Clinton (D)	46	Biden (D)	57
	Dole (R)	46	Bush (R)	51	Bush (R)	56	McCain (R)	49	Romney (R)	52	Trump (R)	49	Trump (R)	42

	1996		2000		2004		2008		2012		2016		2020	
	Perot (I)	7	Ind.	2	Ind.	*	Ind.	--	Ind.	--	Ind.	--	Ind.	--
$100,000 and over	Clinton (D)	38	Gore (D)	43	Kerry (D)	41	Obama (D)	49	Obama (D)	44	Clinton (D)	47	Biden (D)	42
	Dole (R)	54	Bush (R)	54	Bush (R)	58	McCain (R)	49	Romney (R)	54	Trump (R)	47	Trump (R)	54
	Perot (I)	6	Ind.	2	Ind.	1	Ind.	--	Ind.	--	Ind.	--	Ind.	4	Ind.	--

FAMILY'S FINANCIAL SITUATION

	1996		2000		2004		2008		2012		2016		2020	
Better today	Clinton (D)	66	Gore (D)	61	Kerry (D)	19	Obama (D)	37	Obama (D)	84	Clinton (D)	72	Biden (D)	26
	Dole (R)	26	Bush (R)	36	Bush (R)	80	McCain (R)	60	Romney (R)	15	Trump (R)	23	Trump (R)	72
	Perot (I)	6	Ind.	2	Ind.	*	Ind.	--	Ind.	--	Ind.	3	Ind.	--
About the same	Clinton (D)	46	Gore (D)	35	Kerry (D)	50	Obama (D)	45	Obama (D)	58	Clinton (D)	47	Biden (D)	65
	Dole (R)	45	Bush (R)	60	Bush (R)	49	McCain (R)	53	Romney (R)	40	Trump (R)	45	Trump (R)	34
	Perot (I)	8	Ind.	3	Ind.	1	Ind.	--	Ind.	--	Ind.	6	Ind.	--
Worse today	Clinton (D)	27	Gore (D)	33	Kerry (D)	79	Obama (D)	71	Obama (D)	18	Clinton (D)	19	Biden (D)	77
	Dole (R)	57	Bush (R)	63	Bush (R)	20	McCain (R)	28	Romney (R)	80	Trump (R)	77	Trump (R)	20
	Perot (I)	13	Ind.	4	Ind.	*	Ind.	--	Ind.	--	Ind.	3	Ind.	--

EDUCATION

	1996		2000		2004		2008		2012		2016		2020	
High school or less	Clinton (D)	53	Gore (D)	50	Kerry (D)	48	Obama (D)	54	Obama (D)	52	Clinton (D)	46	Biden (D)	46
	Dole (R)	34	Bush (R)	47	Bush (R)	52	McCain (R)	44	Romney (R)	46	Trump (R)	51	Trump (R)	54
	Perot (I)	12	Ind.	1	Ind.	*	Ind.	--	Ind.	--	Ind.	--	Ind.	--
Some college	Clinton (D)	48	Gore (D)	45	Kerry (D)	46	Obama (D)	51	Obama (D)	49	Clinton (D)	43	Biden (D)	47
	Dole (R)	40	Bush (R)	51	Bush (R)	54	McCain (R)	47	Romney (R)	48	Trump (R)	51	Trump (R)	50
	Perot (I)	10	Ind.	3	Ind.	*	Ind.	--	Ind.	--	Ind.	5	Ind.	--
College graduate or more	Clinton (D)	47	Gore (D)	48	Kerry (D)	49	Obama (D)	53	Obama (D)	50	Clinton (D)	52	Biden (D)	55
	Dole (R)	44	Bush (R)	48	Bush (R)	49	McCain (R)	45	Romney (R)	48	Trump (R)	42	Trump (R)	43
	Perot (I)	7	Ind.	3	Ind.	1	Ind.	--	Ind.	--	Ind.	4	Ind.	--
College graduate	Clinton (D)	44	Gore (D)	45	Kerry (D)	46	Obama (D)	50	Obama (D)	47	Clinton (D)	49	Biden (D)	51
	Dole (R)	46	Bush (R)	51	Bush (R)	52	McCain (R)	48	Romney (R)	51	Trump (R)	44	Trump (R)	47
	Perot (I)	8	Ind.	3	Ind.	1	Ind.	--	Ind.	--	Ind.	5	Ind.	--
Post graduate study	Clinton (D)	52	Gore (D)	52	Kerry (D)	55	Obama (D)	58	Obama (D)	55	Clinton (D)	58	Biden (D)	62
	Dole (R)	40	Bush (R)	44	Bush (R)	44	McCain (R)	40	Romney (R)	42	Trump (R)	37	Trump (R)	37
	Perot (I)	5	Ind.	3	Ind.	1	Ind.	--	Ind.	--	Ind.	4	Ind.	--

GENDER and RACE

	1996		2000		2004		2008		2012		2016		2020	
White men	Clinton (D)	38	Gore (D)	36	Kerry (D)	37	Obama (D)	41	Obama (D)	35	Clinton (D)	31	Biden (D)	38
	Dole (R)	49	Bush (R)	60	Bush (R)	62	McCain (R)	57	Romney (R)	62	Trump (R)	62	Trump (R)	61
	Perot (I)	11	Ind.	3	Ind.	*	Ind.	--	Ind.	--	Ind.	5	Ind.	--
White women	Clinton (D)	48	Gore (D)	48	Kerry (D)	44	Obama (D)	46	Obama (D)	42	Clinton (D)	43	Biden (D)	44
	Dole (R)	43	Bush (R)	49	Bush (R)	55	McCain (R)	53	Romney (R)	56	Trump (R)	52	Trump (R)	55
	Perot (I)	8	Ind.	2	Ind.	*	Ind.	--	Ind.	--	Ind.	4	Ind.	--
Black men	Clinton (D)	78	Gore (D)	85	Kerry (D)	86	Obama (D)	95	Obama (D)	87	Clinton (D)	82	Biden (D)	79
	Dole (R)	15	Bush (R)	12	Bush (R)	13	McCain (R)	5	Romney (R)	11	Trump (R)	13	Trump (R)	19
	Perot (I)	5	Ind.	1	Ind.	*	Ind.	--	Ind.	--	Ind.	5	Ind.	--
Black women	Clinton (D)	88	Gore (D)	94	Kerry (D)	90	Obama (D)	96	Obama (D)	96	Clinton (D)	94	Biden (D)	90
	Dole (R)	8	Bush (R)	6	Bush (R)	10	McCain (R)	3	Romney (R)	3	Trump (R)	4	Trump (R)	9
	Perot (I)	2	Ind.	*	Ind.	0	Ind.	--	Ind.	--	Ind.	1	Ind.	--
Latino men	Clinton (D)	65	Gore (D)	60	Kerry (D)	50	Obama (D)	64	Obama (D)	65	Clinton (D)	63	Biden (D)	59
	Dole (R)	25	Bush (R)	37	Bush (R)	47	McCain (R)	33	Romney (R)	33	Trump (R)	32	Trump (R)	36
	Perot (I)	8	Ind.	3	Ind.	2	Ind.	--	Ind.	--	Ind.	5	Ind.	--
Lation women	Clinton (D)	78	Gore (D)	63	Kerry (D)	57	Obama (D)	68	Obama (D)	76	Clinton (D)	69	Biden (D)	69
	Dole (R)	17	Bush (R)	34	Bush (R)	41	McCain (R)	30	Romney (R)	23	Trump (R)	25	Trump (R)	30
	Perot (I)	4	Ind.	2	Ind.	2	Ind.	--	Ind.	--	Ind.	5	Ind.	--

AGE by RACE

	1996		2000		2004		2008		2012		2016		2020	
Whites 18-29	Clinton (D)	45	Gore (D)	39	Kerry (D)	44	Obama (D)	54	Obama (D)	44	Clinton (D)	43	Biden (D)	44
	Dole (R)	41	Bush (R)	55	Bush (R)	55	McCain (R)	44	Romney (R)	51	Trump (R)	47	Trump (R)	53
	Perot (I)	11	Ind.	5	Ind.	*	Ind.	--	Ind.	--	Ind.		Ind.	--
Blacks 18-29	Clinton (D)	83	Gore (D)	91	Kerry (D)	88	Obama (D)	95	Obama (D)	91	Clinton (D)	85	Biden (D)	89
	Dole (R)	11	Bush (R)	8	Bush (R)	12	McCain (R)	4	Romney (R)	8	Trump (R)	9	Trump (R)	10

Group	1996	2000	2004	2008	2012	2016	2020
	Perot (I) 6	Ind. 1	Ind. *	Ind. --	Ind. --	Ind. 5	Ind. --
Whites 30-44	Clinton (D) 41	Gore (D) 41	Kerry (D) 37	Obama (D) 41	Obama (D) 38	Clinton (D) 37	Biden (D) 41
	Dole (R) 47	Bush (R) 56	Bush (R) 62	McCain (R) 57	Romney (R) 59	Trump (R) 54	Trump (R) 57
	Perot (I) 10	Ind. 2	Ind. 1	Ind. --	Ind. --	Ind. 7	Ind. --
Blacks 30-44	Clinton (D) 84	Gore (D) 91	Kerry (D) 88	Obama (D) 96	Obama (D) 94	Clinton (D) 89	Biden (D) 78
	Dole (R) 11	Bush (R) 7	Bush (R) 11	McCain (R) 4	Romney (R) 5	Trump (R) 7	Trump (R) 19
	Perot (I) 3	Ind. *	Ind. *	Ind. --	Ind. --	Ind. 3	Ind. --
Whites 45-59	Clinton (D) 43	Gore (D) 42	Kerry (D) 42	Obama (D) 42	Obama (D) 37	Clinton (D) 32	Biden (D) 38
	Dole (R) 46	Bush (R) 54	Bush (R) 58	McCain (R) 56	Romney (R) 62	Trump (R) 64	Trump (R) 61
	Perot (I) 9	Ind. 1	Ind. *	Ind. --	Ind. --	Ind. 3	Ind. --
Blacks 45-59	Clinton (D) 85	Gore (D) 89	Kerry (D) 88	Obama (D) 97	Obama (D) 93	Clinton (D) 89	Biden (D) 89
	Dole (R) 12	Bush (R) 9	Bush (R) 12	McCain (R) 3	Romney (R) 7	Trump (R) 9	Trump (R) 10
	Perot (I) 3	Ind. 1	Ind. *	Ind. --	Ind. --	Ind. 3	Ind. --
Whites 60 and older	Clinton (D) 45	Gore (D) 46	Kerry (D) 42	Obama (D) 41	Obama (D) 40	Clinton (D) 39	Biden (D) 42
	Dole (R) 47	Bush (R) 52	Bush (R) 58	McCain (R) 57	Romney (R) 59	Trump (R) 57	Trump (R) 57
	Perot (I) 7	Ind. 2	Ind. *	Ind. --	Ind. --	Ind. 3	Ind. --
Blacks 60 and older	Clinton (D) 82	Gore (D) 87	Kerry (D) 90	Obama (D) 95	Obama (D) 93	Clinton (D) 92	Biden (D) 92
	Dole (R) 16	Bush (R) 11	Bush (R) 9	McCain (R) 4	Romney (R) 7	Trump (R) 7	Trump (R) 7
	Perot (I) 1	Ind. 1	Ind. 0	Ind. --	Ind. --	Ind. 0	Ind. --

REGION	1996	2000	2004	2008	2012	2016	2020
From the East	Clinton (D) 55	Gore (D) 56	Kerry (D) 56	Obama (D) 59	Obama (D) 57	Clinton (D) 56	Biden (D) 58
	Dole (R) 34	Bush (R) 39	Bush (R) 43	McCain (R) 40	Romney (R) 42	Trump (R) 39	Trump (R) 41
	Perot (I) 9	Ind. 3	Ind. 1	Ind. --	Ind. --	Ind. 4	Ind. --
From the Midwest	Clinton (D) 48	Gore (D) 48	Kerry (D) 48	Obama (D) 54	Obama (D) 49	Clinton (D) 44	Biden (D) 47
	Dole (R) 41	Bush (R) 49	Bush (R) 51	McCain (R) 44	Romney (R) 49	Trump (R) 50	Trump (R) 51
	Perot (I) 10	Ind. 2	Ind. *	Ind. --	Ind. --	Ind. 5	Ind. --
From the South	Clinton (D) 46	Gore (D) 43	Kerry (D) 42	Obama (D) 45	Obama (D) 44	Clinton (D) 43	Biden (D) 46
	Dole (R) 46	Bush (R) 55	Bush (R) 58	McCain (R) 54	Romney (R) 54	Trump (R) 53	Trump (R) 53
	Perot (I) 7	Ind. 1	Ind. *	Ind. --	Ind. --	Ind. 4	Ind. --
From the West	Clinton (D) 48	Gore (D) 48	Kerry (D) 50	Obama (D) 57	Obama (D) 56	Clinton (D) 53	Biden (D) 57
	Dole (R) 40	Bush (R) 46	Bush (R) 49	McCain (R) 40	Romney (R) 42	Trump (R) 39	Trump (R) 41
	Perot (I) 8	Ind. 4	Ind. 1	Ind. --	Ind. --	Ind.	Ind. --

REGION and RACE	1996	2000	2004	2008	2012	2016	2020
Whites in the East	Clinton (D) 51	Gore (D) 52	Kerry (D) 50	Obama (D) 52	Obama (D) 46	Clinton (D) 45	Biden (D) 46
	Dole (R) 37	Bush (R) 44	Bush (R) 49	McCain (R) 47	Romney (R) 52	Trump (R) 49	Trump (R) 53
	Perot (I) 10	Ind. 4	Ind. *	Ind. --	Ind. --	Ind. 4	Ind. --
Blacks in the East	Clinton (D) 85	Gore (D) 90	Kerry (D) 86	Obama (D) 97	Obama (D) 94	Clinton (D) 93	Biden (D) 94
	Dole (R) 12	Bush (R) 9	Bush (R) 13	McCain (R) 2	Romney (R) 6	Trump (R) 5	Trump (R) 5
	Perot (I) 3	Ind. 1	Ind. *	Ind. --	Ind. --	Ind. 2	Ind. --
Whites in the Midwest	Clinton (D) 45	Gore (D) 44	Kerry (D) 43	Obama (D) 47	Obama (D) 41	Clinton (D) 37	Biden (D) 41
	Dole (R) 43	Bush (R) 53	Bush (R) 56	McCain (R) 51	Romney (R) 57	Trump (R) 57	Trump (R) 57
	Perot (I) 10	Ind. 2	Ind. *	Ind. --	Ind. --	Ind. 5	Ind. --
Blacks in the Midwest	Clinton (D) 79	Gore (D) 89	Kerry (D) 90	Obama (D) 96	Obama (D) 95	Clinton (D) 85	Biden (D) 81
	Dole (R) 16	Bush (R) 8	Bush (R) 10	McCain (R) 4	Romney (R) 5	Trump (R) 11	Trump (R) 19
	Perot (I) 4	Ind. 1	Ind. 0	Ind. --	Ind. --	Ind. 4	Ind. --
Whites in the South	Clinton (D) 36	Gore (D) 31	Kerry (D) 29	Obama (D) 30	Obama (D) 28	Clinton (D) 28	Biden (D) 32
	Dole (R) 56	Bush (R) 67	Bush (R) 70	McCain (R) 69	Romney (R) 70	Trump (R) 68	Trump (R) 67
	Perot (I) 8	Ind. 1	Ind. *	Ind. --	Ind. --	Ind. 4	Ind. --
Blacks in the South	Clinton (D) 87	Gore (D) 91	Kerry (D) 90	Obama (D) 95	Obama (D) 92	Clinton (D) 88	Biden (D) 88
	Dole (R) 10	Bush (R) 8	Bush (R) 9	McCain (R) 3	Romney (R) 8	Trump (R) 9	Trump (R) 11
	Perot (I) 3	Ind. *	Ind. *	Ind. --	Ind. --	Ind. 3	Ind. --
Whites in the West	Clinton (D) 43	Gore (D) 43	Kerry (D) 45	Obama (D) 49	Obama (D) 46	Clinton (D) 45	Biden (D) 50
	Dole (R) 44	Bush (R) 51	Bush (R) 54	McCain (R) 48	Romney (R) 51	Trump (R) 47	Trump (R) 49
	Perot (I) 9	Ind. 4	Ind. 1	Ind. --	Ind. --	Ind. 5	Ind. --
Blacks in the West	Clinton (D) 77	Gore (D) 85	Kerry (D) 80	Obama (D) 91	Obama (D) 89	Clinton (D) 90	Biden (D) 77
	Dole (R) 14	Bush (R) 11	Bush (R) 18	McCain (R) 8	Romney (R) 5	Trump (R) 7	Trump (R) 20
	Perot (I) 7	Ind. 1	Ind. 0	Ind. --	Ind. --	Ind. 3	Ind. --

Vital Statistics on Congress

Vital Statistics on Congress, first published in 1980, long ago became the go-to source of impartial data on the United States Congress. Vital Statistics' purpose is to collect and provide useful data on America's first branch of government, including data on the composition of its membership, its formal procedure (such as the use of the filibuster), informal norms, party structure, and staff. With some chapters of data dating back nearly 100 years, Vital Statistics also documents how Congress has changed over time, illustrating, for example, the increasing polarization of Congress and the diversifying demographics of those who are elected to serve.

Vital Statistics began as a joint effort undertaken by Thomas E. Mann of Brookings and Norman J. Ornstein of the American Enterprise Institute, in collaboration with Michael Malbin of the Campaign Finance Institute. The datasets were published in print until 2013 when the project migrated online for the first time. This year, Brookings' Molly E. Reynolds spearheaded Vital Statistics' most recent update.

The Almanac team obtained permission from the Brookings Institution to provide select tables of data relevant to Almanac readers. The following tables can be found in this section:

- 1-1 Apportionment of Congressional Seats, by Region and State, 1910-2010 (435 seats)
- 1-2 Democratic Party Strength in the House, by Region, 69th-117th Congresses, 1925-2021
- 1-3 Democratic and Republican Seats in the House, by Region, 69th-117th Congresses, 1925-2021
- 1-4 Democratic Party Strength in the Senate, by Region, 69th-117th Congresses, 1925-2021
- 1-5 Democratic and Republican Seats in the Senate, by Region, 69th-117th Congresses, 1925-2021
- 1-16 African Americans in Congress, 41st - 117th Congresses, 1869 - 2021
- 1-17 Asian Americans in Congress, 58th - 117th Congresses, 1903-2021
- 1-18 Hispanic Americans in Congress, 41st - 117th Congresses, 1869 - 2021
- 1-19 Women in Congress, 65th - 117th Congresses, 1917 - 2021
- 1-20 Political Parties of Senators and Representatives, 34th - 117th Congresses, 1855 - 2021

The full Vital Statistics on Congress report contains a great deal more data and information that Almanac readers may find useful. For more information, visit www.brookings.edu/multi-chapter-report/vital-statistics-on-congress.

Supplemental text, which includes any footnote definitions, is available for all tables on pages [2116 to 2118]

Table 1-1 Apportionment of Congressional Seats, by Region and State, 1910-2010 (435 seats)

Region and State	1910	1920	1930	1940	1950	1960	1970	1980	1990	2000	2010
South	104		102	105	106	106	108	116	125	131	138
Alabama	10		9	9	9	8	7	7	7	7	7
Arkansas	7		7	7	6	4	4	4	4	4	4
Florida	4		5	6	8	12	15	19	23	25	27
Georgia	12		10	10	10	10	10	10	11	13	14
Louisiana	8		8	8	8	8	8	8	7	7	6
Mississippi	8		7	7	6	5	5	5	5	4	4
North Carolina	10		11	12	12	11	11	11	12	13	13
South Carolina	7		6	6	6	6	6	6	6	6	7
Tennessee	10		9	10	9	9	8	9	9	9	9
Texas	18		21	21	22	23	24	27	30	32	36
Virginia	10		9	9	10	10	10	10	11	11	11
Border	47		43	42	38	36	35	34	32	31	30
Kentucky	11		9	9	8	7	7	7	6	6	6
Maryland	6		6	6	7	8	8	8	8	8	8
Missouri	16		13	13	11	10	10	9	9	9	8
Oklahoma	8		9	8	6	6	6	6	6	5	5
West Virginia	6		6	6	6	5	4	4	3	3	3
New England	32		29	28	28	25	25	24	23	22	21
Connecticut	5		6	6	6	6	6	6	6	5	5
Maine	4		3	3	3	2	2	2	2	2	2
Massachusetts	16		15	14	14	12	12	11	10	10	9
New Hampshire	2		2	2	2	2	2	2	2	2	2
Rhode Island	3		2	2	2	2	2	2	2	2	2
Vermont	2		1	1	1	1	1	1	1	1	1
Mid-Atlantic	92		94	93	88	84	80	72	66	62	58
Delaware	1		1	1	1	1	1	1	1	1	1
New Jersey	12		14	14	14	15	15	14	13	13	12
New York	43		45	45	43	41	39	34	31	29	27
Pennsylvania	36		34	33	30	27	25	23	21	19	18
Midwest	86		90	87	87	88	86	80	74	69	65
Illinois	27		27	26	25	24	24	22	20	19	18
Indiana	13		12	11	11	11	11	10	10	9	9
Michigan	13		17	17	18	19	19	18	16	15	14
Ohio	22		24	23	23	24	23	21	19	18	16
Wisconsin	11		10	10	10	10	9	9	9	8	8
Plains	41		34	31	31	27	25	24	22	22	21
Iowa	11		9	8	8	7	6	6	5	5	4
Kansas	8		7	6	6	5	5	5	4	4	4
Minnesota	10		9	9	9	8	8	8	8	8	8
Nebraska	6		5	4	4	3	3	3	3	3	3
North Dakota	3		2	2	2	2	1	1	1	1	1
South Dakota	3		2	2	2	2	2	1	1	1	1
Rocky Mountains	14		14	16	16	17	19	24	24	28	31
Arizona	1		1	2	2	3	4	5	6	8	9
Colorado	4		4	4	4	4	5	6	6	7	7
Idaho	2		2	2	2	2	2	2	2	2	2
Montana	2		2	2	2	2	2	2	1	1	1

Table 1-1 Apportionment of Congressional Seats, by Region and State, 1910-2010 (435 seats)

	1910	1920	1930	1940	1950	1960	1970	1980	1990	2000	2010
Nevada	1		1	1	1	1	1	2	2	3	4
New Mexico	1[a]		1	2	2	2	2	3	3	3	3
Utah	2		2	2	2	2	2	3	3	3	4
Wyoming	1		1	1	1	1	1	1	1	1	1
Pacific Coast	19		29	33	43	52	57	61	69	70	71
Alaska						1[b]	1	1	1	1	1
California	11		20	23	30	38	43	45	52	53	53
Hawaii						1[c]	2	2	2	2	2
Oregon	3		3	4	4	4	4	5	5	5	5
Washington	5		6	6	7	7	7	8	9	9	10

Table 1-2 Democratic Party Strength in the House, by Region, 69th-117th Congresses, 1925-2021

Region		69th (1925-1926)	75th (1937-1938)	81st (1949-1950)	87th (1961-1962)	93rd (1973-1974)	96th (1979-1980)	97th (1981-1982)	98th (1983-1984)	100th (1987-1988)	101st (1989-1990)	102nd (1991-1992)	103rd (1993-1994)	104th (1995-1996)	105th (1997-1998)	106th (1999-2000)	107th (2001-2002)
South	Percent	54.9	98.0	98.1	93.4	68.2	71.3	63.9	71.2	66.4	67.0	66.4	61.6	48.8	43.2	43.5	42.4
	Seats	101	101	105	106	107[c]	108	108	116	116	115[h]	116	125	125	125	124j	125
Border	Percent	14.7	95.2	88.1	84.2	77.1	77.1	68.6	76.4	67.6	67.6	67.6	65.6	50.0	40.6	40.6	37.5
	Seats	27	42	42	38	35	35	35	34	34	34	34	32	32	32	32	32
New England	Percent	2.2	44.8	39.3	50.0	60.0	72.0	64.0	66.6	62.5	58.3	66.7	60.9	60.9	78.3	78.3	73.9
	Seats	4	29	28	28	25	25	25	24	24	24	24	23	23	23	23	23
Mid-Atlantic	Percent	13.0	68.0	48.4	48.9	53.8	63.8	53.8	58.3	56.9	58.3	56.9	54.5	50.0	53.0	54.5	54.5
	Seats	24	94	93	88	80	80	80	72	72	72	72	66	66	66	66	66
Midwest	Percent	7.6	72.2	43.7	40.7	37.6	55.3	50.0	55.0	57.5	59.5	61.2	58.1	43.2	50.0	50.0	48.6
	Seats	14	90	87	86[a]	85[d]	85[f]	86	80	80	79[i]	80	74	74	74	74	74
Plains	Percent	3.3	38.2	16.1	19.4	36.0	40.0	36.0	54.2	45.8	50.0	54.2	54.5	36.4	36.4	40.9	36.4
	Seats	6	34	31	31	25	25	25	24	24	24	24	22	22	22	22	22
Rocky Mountains	Percent	2.2	93.3	75.0	68.8	42.1	47.4	36.8	33.3	37.5	37.5	45.8	45.8	25.0	20.8	20.8	25.0
	Seats	4	15	16	16	19	19	19	24	24	24	24	24	24	24	24	24
Pacific Coast	Percent	2.2	80.0	36.4	51.2	58.9	66.1	56.1	62.3	59.0	59.0	60.6	63.8	49.3	55.1	56.5	63.2
	Seats	4	30	33	43[b]	56[e]	56[g]	57	61	61	61	61	69	69	69	69	68[k]

Table 1-2 Democratic Party Strength in the House, by Region, 69th-117th Congresses, 1925-2021

Congress Region	108th (2003- 2004)	109th (2005- 2006)	110th (2007- 2008)	111th (2009- 2010)	112th (2011- 2012)	113th (2013- 2014)	114th (2015- 2016)	115th (2017- 2018)	116th (2019- 2020)	117th (2021- 2022)
South										
Percent	41.9	37.4	41.2	45	28.2	29	26.8	28	34.8	34.8
Seats	131	131	131	131	131	138	138	138	138	138
Border										
Percent	45.1	45.2	48.4	51.6	41.9	36.7	33.3	33.3	36.7	33.3
Seats	31	31	31	31	31	30	30	30	30	30
New England										
Percent	68.2	72.7	95.5	100	90.9	100	90.4	95.2	100.0	100.0
Seats	22	22	22	22	22	21	21	21	21	21
Mid-Atlantic										
Percent	53.2	54.8	66.1	74.2	59.7	56.9	51.7	53.4	72.4	67.2
Seats	62	62	62	62m	62	58	58	58	58	58
Midwest										
Percent	40.6	40.6	47.8	56.5	36.2	38.5	36.9	38.4	44.6	44.6
Seats	69	69	69	69n	69	65	65p	65	65	65
Plains										
Percent	31.8	36.4	54.5	50	31.8	33.3	33.3	28.5	42.9	28.6
Seats	22	22	22	22	22	21	21	21	21	21
Rocky Mountains										
Percent	25.0	28.6	39.3	60.7	35.7	41.9	32.3	38.7	51.6	45.2
Seats	28	28	28	28	28o	31	31	31	31	31
Pacific Coast										
Percent	64.3	63.8	65.7	65.7	64.3	70.4	71.8	71.8	83.1	77.5
Seats	70	69l	70	70	70	71	71	71	71	71

Table 1-3 Democratic and Republican Seats in the House, by Region, 69th-117th Congresses, 1925-2021

Congress	69th		75th		81st		87th		93rd		96th		97th		98th		101st		102nd		103rd	
Region	1925-1926		1937-1938		1949-1950		1961-1962		1973-1974		1979-1980		1981-1982		1983-1984		1989-1990		1991-1992		1993-1994	
	D	R	D	R	D	R	D	R	D	R	D	R	D	R	D	R	D	R	D	R	D	R
South																						
Percent	54.9	1.2	29.8	2.2	39.2	1.2	37.8	3.4	30.4	17.7	27.9	19.7	28.4	20.3	30.2	21.0	29.3	22.4	28.8	23.4	29.8	27.3
Seats	101	3	99	2	103	2	99	6	73	34	77	31	69	39	81	35	76	39	77	39	77	48
Border																						
Percent	14.7	7.8	12.0	2.2	14.1	2.9	12.2	3.4	11.3	4.2	9.8	5.1	9.9	5.7	9.7	4.8	8.9	6.3	8.6	6.6	8.1	6.3
Seats	27	19	40	2	37	5	32	6	27	8	27	8	24	11	26	8	23	11	23	11	21	11
New England																						
Percent	2.2	11.4	3.9	17.6	4.2	9.9	5.3	8.0	6.3	5.2	6.5	4.5	6.6	4.7	6.0	4.8	5.4	5.7	6.0	4.2	5.4	4.5
Seats	4	28	13	16	11	17	14	14	15	10	18	7	16	9	16	8	14	10	16	7	14	8
Mid-Atlantic																						
Percent	13.0	26.9	19.3	33.0	17.1	27.5	16.4	25.9	17.9	19.3	18.5	18.5	17.7	19.3	16.0	17.4	16.2	17.2	15.4	18.6	14.0	17.0
Seats	24	66	64	30	45	47	43	45	43	37	51	29	43	37	43	29	42	30	41	31	36	30
Midwest																						
Percent	7.6	28.2	19.6	19.8	14.4	28.7	13.4	29.3	13.3	27.6	17.0	24.2	17.7	22.4	16.4	21.6	18.1	18.4	18.4	18.6	16.7	17.6
Seats	14	69	65	18	38	49	35	51	32	53	47	38	43	43	44	36	47	32	49	31	43	31
Plains																						
Percent	3.3	13.5	3.9	17.6	1.9	15.2	2.3	14.4	3.8	8.3	3.6	9.6	3.7	8.3	4.5	7.2	4.6	6.9	4.9	6.6	4.7	5.7
Seats	6	33	13	16	5	26	6	25	9	16	10	15	9	16	12	12	12	12	13	11	12	10
Rocky Mountains																						
Percent	2.2	4.1	4.2	1.1	4.6	2.3	4.2	2.9	3.3	5.7	3.3	6.4	2.9	6.3	3.0	9.6	3.5	8.6	4.1	7.8	4.3	7.4
Seats	4	10	14	1	12	4	11	5	8	11	9	10	7	12	8	16	9	15	11	13	11	13
Pacific Coast																						
Percent	2.2	6.9	7.2	6.6	4.6	12.3	8.4	12.1	13.8	12.0	13.4	12.1	13.2	13.0	14.2	13.8	13.9	14.4	13.9	14.4	17.1	14.2
Seats	4	17	24	6	12	21	22	21	33	23	37	19	32	25	38	23	36	25	37	24	44	25
Total Seats	184	245	332	91	263	171	262	174	240	192	276	157	243	192	268	167	259	174	267	167	258	176

Table 1-3 Democratic and Republican Seats in the House, by Region, 69th-117th Congresses, 1925-2021

Congress	104th 1973-1974		105th 1997-1998		106th 1999-2000		107th 2001-2002		108th 2003-2004		109th 2005-2006		110th 2007-2008		111th 2009-2010		112th 2011-2012		113th 2013-2014		114th 2015-2016	
Region	D	R	D	R	D	R	D	R	D	R	D	R	D	R	D	R	D	R	D	R	D	R
South																						
Percent	29.9	27.8	26.1	31.3	25.6	31.5	25.1	32.3	26.8	33.2	24.4	35.3	23.2	38.1	23.0	40.4	19.2	38.8	20.0	41.6	19.7	40.9
Seats	61	64	54	71	54	70	53	71	55	76	49	82	54	77	59	72	37	94	40	97a	37	101
Border																						
Percent	7.8	7.0	6.3	8.4	6.2	8.6	5.7	9.1	6.8	7.4	7.0	7.3	6.4	7.9	6.3	8.4	6.7	7.4	5.5	8.2	5.3	8.1
Seats	16	16	13	19	13	19	12	20	14	17	14	17	15	16	16	15	13	18	11	19	10	20
New England																						
Percent	6.9	3.5	8.7	1.8	8.5	1.8	8.1	2.3	7.8	2.2	8.0	2.2	9.0	0.5	8.6	0.0	10.4	0.8	10.5	0.0	10.1	0.8
Seats	14	8	18	4	18	4	17	5	16	5	16	5	21	1	22	0	20	2	21	0	19	2
Mid-Atlantic																						
Percent	16.2	14.3	16.9	13.7	17.1	13.5	17.1	13.6	16.1	12.7	16.9	12.1	17.6	10.4	18.0	9.0	18.7	10.7	16.5	10.7	16.0	11.3
Seats	33	33	35	31	36	30	36	30	33	29	34	28	41	21	46	16	36	26	33	25	30	28
Midwest																						
Percent	15.7	18.3	17.9	16.3	17.5	16.7	17.5	16.8	13.7	17.9	13.9	17.7	14.2	17.8	15.2	16.3	13.0	18.2	12.4	16.7	12.8	16.6
Seats	32	42	37	37	37	37	37	37	28	41	28	41	33	36	39c	29	25	44	25b	39	24	41
Plains																						
Percent	3.9	6.1	3.9	6.2	4.3	5.9	3.8	6.4	3.4	6.6	4.0	6.0	5.2	5.0	4.3	6.2	3.6	6.2	3.5	6.0	3.7	5.7
Seats	8	14	8	14	9	13	8	14	7	15	8	14	12	10	11	11	7	15	7	14	7	14
Rocky Mountains																						
Percent	2.9	7.8	1.9	8.8	2.4	8.6	2.8	8.2	3.4	9.2	4.0	8.6	4.7	8.4	6.6	6.2	5.2	7.4	6.5	7.7	5.3	8.5
Seats	6	18	4	20	5	19	6	18	7	21	8	20	11	17	17	11	10	18	13	18	10	21
Pacific Coast																						
Percent	16.7	15.2	18.4	13.7	18.5	13.5	19.9	11.4	22.0	10.9	21.9	10.8	19.7	11.9	18.0	13.5	23.3	10.3	25.0	9.0	27.1	8.1
Seats	34	35	38	31	39	30	42	25	45	25	44	25	46	24	46	24	45	25	50	21	51	20
Total Seats	204	230	207	227	211	222	211	220	205	229	201	232	233	202	256	178	193	242	202	233	188	247

Table 1-3 Democratic and Republican Seats in the House, by Region, 69th-117th Congresses, 1925-2021

Congress	115th		116th		117th	
	2017–2018		2019–2020		2021–2022	
Region	D	R	D	R	D	R
South						
Percent	20.1	41.1	20.4	45.0	21.6	42.2
Seats	39	99	48	90	48	89
Border						
Percent	5.2	8.3	4.7	9.5	4.5	9.5
Seats	10	20	11	19	10	20
New England						
Percent	10.3	0.4	8.9	0.0	9.5	0.0
Seats	20	1	21	0	21	0
Mid-Atlantic						
Percent	16.0	11.2	17.9	8.0	17.6	8.5
Seats	31	27	42	16	39	18
Midwest						
Percent	12.9	16.6	12.3	18.0	13.1	17.1
Seats	25	40	29	36	29	36
Plains						
Percent	3.1	6.2	3.8	6.0	2.7	7.1
Seats	6	15	9	12	6	15
Rocky Mountains						
Percent	6.2	7.9	6.8	7.5	6.3	8.1
Seats	12	19	16	15	14	17
Pacific Coast						
Percent	26.3	8.3	25.1	6.0	24.8	7.6
Seats	51	20	59	12	55	16
Total Seats	194	241	235	199	222	211

Table 1-4 Democratic Party Strength in the Senate, by Region, 69th-117th Congresses, 1925-2021

Congress / Region	69th (1925-1926)	75th (1937-1938)	81st (1949-1950)	87th (1961-1962)	93rd (1973-1974)	96th (1979-1980)	97th (1981-1982)	98th (1983-1984)	100th (1987-1988)	101st (1989-1990)	102nd (1991-1992)	103rd (1993-1994)	104th (1995-1996)	105th (1997-1998)	106th (1999-2000)	107th (2001-2002)	108th (2003-2004)
South																	
Percent	100.0	100.0	100.0	100.0	63.6	50.0	54.4	50.0	72.7	68.2	68.2	59.1	36.4[a]	31.8	36.4	36.4	40.9
Seats	22	22	22	22	22	22	22	22	22	22	22	22	22	22	22	22	22
Border																	
Percent	50.0	100.0	80.0	60.0	50.0	70.0	70.0	70.0	60.0	60.0	60.0	60.0	50.0	50.0	40.0	50.0	40.0
Seats	10	10	10	10	10	10	10	10	10	10	10	10	10	10	10	10	10
New England																	
Percent	8.3	50.0	25.0	41.7	58.3	58.3	50.0	50.0	50.0	58.3	58.3	58.3	50.0	50.0	50.0	50.0	50.0
Seats	12	12	12	12	12	12	12	12	12	12	12	12	12	12	12	12	12
Mid-Atlantic																	
Percent	37.5	75.0	37.5	25.0	25.0	50.0	50.0	50.0	50.0	50.0	50.0	62.5	50.0	50.0	62.5	75.0	75.0
Seats	8	8	8	8	8	8	8	8	8	8	8	8	8	8	8	8	8
Midwest																	
Percent	10.0	80.0	20.0	70.0	60.0	80.0	60.0	60.0	70.0	70.0	70.0	80.0	60.0	60.0	50.0	60.0	60.0
Seats	10	10	10	10	10	10	10	10	10	10	10	10	10	10	10	10	10
Plains																	
Percent	0.0	50.0	16.7	25.0	58.3	41.7	25.0	25.0	50.0	50.0	58.3	58.3	58.3	58.3	58.3	66.7	58.3
Seats	12	12	12	12	12	12	12	12	12	12	12	12	12	12	12	12	12
Rocky Mountains																	
Percent	50.0	93.8	75.0	75.0	56.2	37.5	31.3	31.3	37.5	37.5	37.5	37.5	37.5	25.0	25.0	25.0	18.8
Seats	16	16	16	16	16	16	16	16	16	16	16	16	16	16	16	16	16
Pacific Coast																	
Percent	16.7	50.0	33.3	80.0	60.0	60.0	40.0	40.0	40.0	40.0	40.0	50.0	50.0	60.0	60.0	70.0	70.0
Seats	6	6	6	10	10	10	10	10	10	10	10	10	10	10	10	10	10

Table 1-4 Democratic Party Strength in the Senate, by Region, 69th-117th Congresses, 1925-2021

Congress Region	109th (2005- 2006)	110th (2007- 2008)	111th (2009- 2010)	112th (2011- 2012)	113th (2013- 2014)	114th (2015- 2016)	115th (2017- 2018)	116th (2019- 2020)	117th (2021- 2022)[b]
South									
Percent	18.2	22.7	31.8	27.3	27.3	13.6	13.6	13.6	18.2
Seats	22	22	22	22	22	22	22	22	22
Border									
Percent	40.0	50.0	50.0	50.0	50.0	40.0	40.0	30.00	30.00
Seats	10	10	10	10	10	10	10	10	10
New England									
Percent	50.0	50.0	58.3	50.0	66.7	66.6	75.0	75.0	75.0
Seats	12	12	12	12	12	12	12	12	12
Mid-Atlantic									
Percent	75.0	87.5	87.5	87.5	87.5	87.5	87.5	87.5	87.5
Seats	8	8	8	8	8	8	8	8	8
Midwest									
Percent	70.0	80.0	70.0	50.0	60.0	60.0	70.0	60.0	60.0
Seats	10	10	10	10	10	10	10	10	10
Plains									
Percent	50.0	50.0	50.0	50.0	41.7	25.0	25.0	16.7	16.7
Seats	12	12	12	12	12	12	12	12	12
Rocky Mountains									
Percent	25.0	31.3	43.8	43.8	43.8	31.3	31.3	43.8	56.3
Seats	16	16	16	16	16	16	16	16	16
Pacific Coast									
Percent	70.0	70.0	90.0	90.0	90.0	80.0	80.0	80.0	80.0
Seats	10	10	10	10	10	10	10	10	10

Table 1-5 Democratic and Republican Seats in the Senate, by Region, 69th-117th Congresses, 1925-2021

| Congress | | 69th 1925-1926 | | 75th 1937-1938 | | 81st 1949-1950 | | 87th 1961-1962 | | 93rd 1973-1974 | | 97th 1981-1982 | | 101st 1989-1990 | | 102nd 1991-1992 | | 103rd 1993-1994 | | 104th 1995-1996 | | 105th 1997-1998 | | 106th 1999-2000 | |
Region		D	R	D	R	D	R	D	R	D	R	D	R	D	R	D	R	D	R	D	R	D	R	D	R
South	Percent	53.7	0.0	28.9	0.0	40.7	0.0	33.8	0.0	25.0	16.7	23.9	18.9	27.3	15.6	26.8	15.9	22.8	20.9	19.1	24.5	15.6	27.3	17.8	25.5
	Seats	22	0	22	0	22	0	22	0	14	7	11	10	15	7	15	7	13	9	9	13a	7	15	8	14
Border	Percent	12.2	9.3	13.2	0.0	14.8	4.8	9.2	11.4	8.9	11.9	15.2	5.7	10.9	8.9	10.7	9.1	10.5	9.3	10.6	9.4	11.1	9.1	8.9	10.9
	Seats	5	5	10	0	8	2	6	4	5	5	7	3	6	4	6	4	6	4	5	5	5	5	4	6
New England	Percent	2.4	20.4	7.9	37.5	5.6	21.4	7.7	20.0	12.5	11.9	13.0	11.3	12.7	11.1	12.5	11.4	12.3	11.6	12.8	11.3	13.3	10.9	13.3	10.9
	Seats	1	11	6	6	3	9	5	7	7	5	6	6	7	5	7	5	7	5	6	6	6	6	6	6
Mid-Atlantic	Percent	7.3	9.3	7.9	12.5	5.6	11.9	3.1	17.1	3.6	11.9	8.7	7.5	7.3	8.9	7.1	9.1	8.8	7.0	8.5	7.5	8.9	7.3	11.1	5.5
	Seats	3	5	6	2	3	5	2	6	2	5	4	4	4	4	4	4	5	3	4	4	4	4	5	3
Midwest	Percent	2.4	16.7	10.5	6.3	3.7	19.0	10.8	8.6	10.7	9.5	13.0	7.5	12.7	6.7	12.5	6.8	14.0	4.7	12.8	7.5	13.3	7.3	11.1	9.1
	Seats	1	9	8	1	2	8	7	3	6	4	6	4	7	3	7	3	8	2	6	4	6	4	5	5
Plains	Percent	0.0	20.4	7.9	18.8	3.7	23.8	4.6	25.7	12.5	11.9	6.5	17.0	10.9	13.3	12.5	11.4	12.3	11.6	14.9	9.4	15.6	9.1	15.6	9.1
	Seats	0	11	6	3	2	10	3	9	7	5	3	9	6	6	7	5	7	5	7	5	7	5	7	5
Rocky Mountains	Percent	19.5	14.8	19.7	6.3	22.2	9.5	18.5	11.4	16.1	16.7	10.9	20.8	10.9	22.2	10.7	22.7	10.5	23.3	10.6	20.8	8.9	21.8	8.9	21.8
	Seats	8	8	15	1	12	4	12	4	9	7	5	11	6	10	6	10	6	10	5	11	4	12	4	12
Pacific Coast	Percent	2.4	9.3	3.9	18.8	3.7	9.5	12.3	5.7	10.7	9.5	10.9	11.3	7.3	13.3	7.1	13.6	8.8	11.6	10.6	9.4	13.3	7.3	13.3	7.3
	Seats	1	5	3	3	2	4	8	2	6	4	5	6	4	6	4	6	5	5	5	5	6	4	6	4
Total Seats		41	54	76	16	54	42	65	35	56	42	46	53	55	45	56	44	57	43	47	53	45	55	45	55

Table 1-5 Democratic and Republican Seats in the Senate, by Region, 69th-117th Congresses, 1925-2021

Region		107th 2001-2002 D	R	108th 2003-2004 D	R	109th 2005-2006 D	R	110th 2007-2008 D	R	111th 2009-2010 D	R	112th 2011-2012 D	R	113th 2013-2014 D	R	114th 2015-2016 D	R	115th 2017-2018 D	R	116th 2019-2020 D	R	117th[d] 2021-2022 D	R
South	Percent	16.0	28.0	18.8	25.5	9.1	32.7	10.2	34.7	12.7	36.6	11.8	34.0	11.3	35.55	6.81	35.2	6.5	36.5	6.7	35.8	8.3	36.0
	Seats	8	14	9	13	4	18	5	17	7	15	6	16	6	16	3	19	3	19	3	19	4	18
Border	Percent	10.0	10.0	8.3	11.8	9.1	10.9	10.2	10.2	9.1	12.2	9.8	10.6	9.43	11.11	9.09	11.1	8.7	11.5	6.7	13.2	6.3	14.0
	Seats	5	5	4	6	4	6	5	5	5	5	5	5	5	5	4	6	4	6	3	7	3	7
New England	Percent	12.0	12.0	12.5	9.8	13.6	9.1	12.2	8.2	12.7	7.3	11.8	8.5	15.1	4.4	18.2	3.70	19.5	1.9	20.0	1.9	18.8	2.0
	Seats	6	6	6	5	6	5	6	4	7	3	6	4	8	2	8	2	9	1	9	1	9	1
Mid-Atlantic	Percent	12.0	4.0	12.5	3.9	13.6	3.6	14.3	2.0	12.7	2.4	13.7	2.1	13.2	2.2	15.9	1.85	15.2	1.9	15.6	1.9	14.6	2.0
	Seats	6	2	6	2	6	2	7	1	7	1	7	1	7	1	7	1	7	1	7	1	7	1
Midwest	Percent	12.0	8.0	12.5	7.8	15.9	5.5	16.3	4.1	12.7	4.9	9.8	10.6	11.32	8.9	13.6	7.40	15	5.7	13.3	7.5	12.5	8.0
	Seats	6	4	6	4	7	3	8	2	7b	2	5	5	6	4	6	4	7	3	6	4	6	4
Plains	Percent	16.0	8.0	14.6	9.8	13.6	10.9	12.2	12.2	10.9	12.2	11.8	12.8	9.43	15.55	6.81	16.7	6.5	17.31	4.4	18.9	4.2	20.0
	Seats	8	4	7	5	6	6	6	6	6c	5	6	6	5	7	3	9	3	9	2	10	2	10
Rocky Mountains	Percent	8.0	24.0	6.3	25.5	9.1	21.8	10.2	22.4	12.7	22.0	13.7	19.1	13.2	20	11.4	20.4	10.87	21.15	15.6	17.0	18.8	14.0
	Seats	4	12	3	13	4	12	5	11	7	9	7	9	7	9	5	11	5	11	7	9	9	7
Pacific Coast	Percent	14.0	6.0	14.6	5.9	15.9	5.5	14.3	6.1	16.4	2.4	17.6	2.1	17.0	2.2	18.2	3.70	17.3	3.9	17.8	3.8	16.7	4.0
	Seats	7	3	7	3	7	3	7	3	9	1	9	1	9	1	8	2	8	2	8	2	8	2
Total Seats		50	50	48	51	44	55	49	49	55	41	51	47	53	45	44	54	46	52	45	53	48	50

Table 1-16 African Americans in Congress, 41st - 117th Congresses, 1869 - 2021

Congress		House D	House R	Senate D	Senate R	Congress		House D	House R	Senate D	Senate R
41st	(1869)		2		1	87th	(1961)	3			
42nd	(1871)		5			88th	(1963)	4			
43rd	(1873)		7			89th	(1965)	5			
44th	(1875)		7		1	90th	(1967)	5			1
45th	(1877)		3		1	91st	(1969)	9			1
46th	(1879)				1	92nd	(1971)	13			1
47th	(1881)		2			93rd	(1973)	16			1
48th	(1883)		2			94th	(1975)	16			1
49th	(1885)		2			95th	(1977)	15			1
50th	(1887)					96th	(1979)	15			
51st	(1889)		3			97th	(1981)	17			
52nd	(1891)		1			98th	(1983)	20			
53rd	(1893)		1			99th	(1985)	20			
54th	(1895)		1			100th	(1987)	22			
55th	(1897)		1			101st	(1989)	23			
56th	(1899)[a]		1			102nd	(1991)	25	1		
71st	(1929)		1			103rd	(1993)	38	1	1	
72nd	(1931)		1			104th	(1995)	37	2	1	
73rd	(1933)		1			105th	(1997)	36	1	1	
74th	(1935)	1				106th	(1999)	36	1		
75th	(1937)	1				107th	(2001)	35	1		
76th	(1939)	1				108th	(2003)	37			
77th	(1941)	1				109th	(2005)	40		1	
78th	(1943)	1				110th	(2007)	40		1	
79th	(1945)	2				111th[b]	(2009)	39			
80th	(1947)	2				112th	(2011)	40	2		
81st	(1949)	2				113th[c]	(2013)	41			1
82nd	(1951)	2				114th	(2015)	42	2	1	1
83rd	(1953)	2				115th	(2017)	45	2	2	1
84th	(1955)	3				116th	(2019)	52	1	2	1
85th	(1957)	3				117th[d]	(2021)	56	2	3	1
86th	(1959)	3									

Table 1-17 Asian Americans in Congress, 58th - 117th Congresses, 1903-2021

Congress		House D	House R	Senate D	Senate R	Congress		House D	House R	Senate D	Senate R
58th	(1903)					88th	(1963)	1		1	1
59th	(1905)					89th	(1965)	2		1	1
60th	(1907)					90th	(1967)	2		1	1
61st	(1909)					91st	(1969)	2		1	1
62nd	(1911)					92nd	(1971)	2		1	1
63rd	(1913)					93rd	(1973)	2		1	1
64th	(1915)					94th	(1975)	3		1	1
65th	(1917)					95th	(1977)	2		2	1
66th	(1919)					96th	(1979)	3		2	1
67th	(1921)					97th	(1981)	3		2	1
68th	(1923)					98th	(1983)	3		2	
69th	(1925)					99th	(1985)	3		2	
70th	(1927)					100th	(1987)	3	1	2	
71st	(1929)					101st	(1989)	3	1	3	
72nd	(1931)					102nd	(1991)	3		2	
73rd	(1933)					103rd	(1993)	4	1	2	
74th	(1935)					104th	(1995)	4	1	2	
75th	(1937)					105th	(1997)	4	1	2	
76th	(1939)					106th	(1999)	4		2	
77th	(1941)					107th	(2001)	5		2	
78th	(1943)					108th	(2003)	4		2	
79th	(1945)					109th	(2005)	4	1	2	
80th	(1947)					110th	(2007)	5	1	2	
81st	(1949)					111th	(2009)	4	1	2	
82nd	(1951)					112th	(2011)	7	1	2	
83rd	(1953)					113th	(2013)	10		1	
84th	(1955)					114th	(2015)	11		1	
85th	(1957)	1				115th	(2017)	13		3	
86th	(1959)	2		1		116th	(2019)	13		3	
87th	(1961)	2		1		117th[a]	(2021)	13	2	3	

Table 1-18 Hispanic Americans in Congress, 41st - 117th Congresses, 1869 - 2021

Congress		House		Senate		Congress		House		Senate	
		D	R	D	R			D	R	D	R
41st	(1869)					89th	(1965)	3		1	
42nd	(1871)					90th	(1967)	3		1	
43rd	(1873)					91st	(1969)	3	1	1	
63rd	(1913)	1				92nd	(1971)	4	1	1	
64th	(1915)	1	1			93rd	(1973)	4	1	1	
65th	(1917)	1				94th	(1975)	4	1	1	
66th	(1919)	1	1			95th	(1977)	4	1		
67th	(1921)	1	1			96th	(1979)	5	1		
68th	(1923)	1				97th	(1981)	6	1		
69th	(1925)	1				98th	(1983)	9	1		
70th	(1927)	1			1	99th	(1985)	10	1		
71st	(1929)					100th	(1987)	10	1		
72nd	(1931)	2				101st	(1989)	9	1		
73rd	(1933)	2				102nd	(1991)	10	1		
74th	(1935)	1		1		103rd	(1993)	14	3		
75th	(1937)	1		1		104th	(1995)	14	3		
76th	(1939)	1		1		105th	(1997)	14	3		
77th	(1941)			1		106th	(1999)	16	3		
78th	(1943)	1		1		107th	(2001)	16	3		
79th	(1945)	1		1		108th	(2003)	18	4		
80th	(1947)	1		1		109th	(2005)	19	4	1	1
81st	(1949)	1		1		110th	(2007)	20	3	2	1
82nd	(1951)	1		1		111th	(2009)	21	3	1	1
83rd	(1953)	1		1		112th	(2011)	19	8	1	1
84th	(1955)	1		1		113th	(2013)	23	5	1	2
85th	(1957)	1		1		114th	(2015)	23	9	1	2
86th	(1959)	1		1		115th*	(2017)	28	10	2	2
87th	(1961)	2		1		116th	(2019)	34	7	2	2
88th	(1963)	3		1		117th[1]	(2021)	32	12	3	2

Table 1-19 Women in Congress, 65th - 117th Congresses, 1917 - 2021

Congress		House D	House R	Senate D	Senate R	Congress		House D	House R	Senate D	Senate R
65th	(1917)		1			92nd	(1971)	10	3		1
66th	(1919)					93rd	(1973)	14	2	1	
67th	(1921)		2		1	94th	(1975)	14	5		
68th	(1923)		1			95th	(1977)	13	5		
69th	(1925)	1	2			96th	(1979)	11	5	1	1
70th	(1927)	2	3			97th	(1981)	10	9		2
71st	(1929)	4	5			98th	(1983)	13	9		2
72nd	(1931)	4	3	1		99th	(1985)	13	9		2
73rd	(1933)	4	3	1		100th	(1987)	12	11	1	1
74th	(1935)	4	2	2		101st	(1989)	14	11	1	1
75th	(1937)	4	1	2		102nd	(1991)	19	9	1	1
76th	(1939)	4	4	1		103rd	(1993)	36	12	5	1
77th	(1941)	4	5	1		104th	(1995)	31	17	5	3
78th	(1943)	2	6	1		105th	(1997)	35	16	6	3
79th	(1945)	6	5			106th	(1999)	40	16	6	3
80th	(1947)	3	4		1	107th	(2001)	41	18	10	3
81st	(1949)	5	4		1	108th	(2003)	38	21	9	5
82nd	(1951)	4	6		1	109th	(2005)	42	23	9	5
83rd	(1953)	5	7		1	110th	(2007)	50	21	11	5
84th	(1955)	10	7		1	111th	(2009)	57	17	13	4
85th	(1957)	9	6		1	112th	(2011)	52	24	12	5
86th	(1959)	9	8		1	113th	(2013)	56	20	16	4
87th	(1961)	11	7	1	1	114th	(2015)	62	22	14	6
88th	(1963)	6	6	1	1	115th	(2017)	62	21	16	5
89th	(1965)	7	4	1	1	116th	(2019)	89	13	17	8
90th	(1967)	5	5		1	117th[a]	(2021)	89	29	17	8
91st	(1969)	6	4		1						

Table 1-20 Political Parties of Senators and Representatives, 34th - 117th Congresses, 1855 - 2021

Congress		Senate					House of Representatives				
		# Senators	D	R	Other	Vacant	# Reps	D	R	Other	Vacant
34th	(1855 - 1857)	62	42	15	5		234	83	108	43	
35th	(1857 - 1859)	64	39	20	5		237	131	92	14	
36th	(1859 - 1861)	66	38	26	2		237	101	113	23	
37th	(1861 - 1863)	50	11	31	7	1	178	42	106	28	2
38th	(1863 - 1865)	51	12	39			183	80	103		
39th	(1865 - 1867)	52	10	42			191	46	145		
40th	(1867 - 1869)	53	11	42			193	49	143		1
41st	(1869 - 1871)	74	11	61		2	243	73	170		
42nd	(1871 - 1873)	74	17	57			243	104	139		
43rd	(1873 - 1875)	74	19	54		1	293	88	203		2
44th	(1875 - 1877)	76	29	46		1	293	181	107	3	2
45th	(1877 - 1879)	76	36	39	1		293	156	137		
46th	(1879 - 1881)	76	43	33			293	150	128	14	1
47th	(1881 - 1883)	76	37	37	2		293	130	152	11	
48th	(1883 - 1885)	76	36	40			325	200	119	6	
49th	(1885 - 1887)	76	34	41		1	325	182	140	2	1
50th	(1887 - 1889)	76	37	39			325	170	151	4	
51st	(1889 - 1891)	84	37	47			330	156	173	1	
52nd	(1891 - 1893)	88	39	47	2		333	231	88	14	
53rd	(1893 - 1895)	88	44	38	3	3	356	220	126	10	
54th	(1895 - 1897)	88	39	44	5		357	104	246	7	
55th	(1897 - 1899)	90	34	46	10		357	134	206	16	1
56th	(1899 - 1901)	90	26	53	11		357	163	185	9	
57th	(1901 - 1903)	90	29	56	3	2	357	153	198	5	1
58th	(1903 - 1905)	90	32	58			386	178	207		1
59th	(1905 - 1907)	90	32	58			386	136	250		
60th	(1907 - 1909)	92	29	61		2	386	164	222		
61st	(1909 - 1911)	92	32	59		1	391	172	219		
62nd	(1911 - 1913)	92	42	49		1	391	228	162	1	
63rd	(1913 - 1915)	96	51	44	1		435	290	127	18	
64th	(1915 - 1917)	96	56	39	1		435	231	193	8	3
65th	(1917 - 1919)	96	53	42	1		435	210[a]	216	9	
66th	(1919 - 1921)	96	47	48	1		435	191	237	7	
67th	(1921 - 1923)	96	37	59			435	132	300	1	2
68th	(1923 - 1925)	96	43	51	2		435	207	225	3	
69th	(1925 - 1927)	96	40	54	1	1	435	183	247	5	
70th	(1927 - 1929)	96	47	48	1		435	195	237	3	
71st	(1929 - 1931)	96	39	56	1		435	163	267	1	4
72nd	(1931 - 1933)	96	47	48	1		435	216[b]	218	1	
73rd	(1933 - 1935)	96	59	36	1		435	313	117	5	
74th	(1935 - 1937)	96	69	25	2		435	322	103	10	
75th	(1937 - 1939)	96	75	17	4		435	333	89	13	
76th	(1939 - 1941)	96	69	23	4		435	262	169	4	
77th	(1941 - 1943)	96	66	28	2		435	267	162	6	
78th	(1943 - 1945)	96	57	38	1		435	222	209	4	
79th	(1945 - 1947)	96	57	38	1		435	243	190	2	
80th	(1947 - 1949)	96	45	51			435	188	246	1	

Table 1-20 Political Parties of Senators and Representatives, 34th - 117th Congresses, 1855 - 2021

Congress		Senate				House of Representatives				
	# Senators	D	R	Other	Vacant	# Reps	D	R	Other	Vacant
81st (1949 - 1951)	96	54	42			435	263	171	1	
82nd (1951 - 1953)	96	48	47	1		435	234	199	2	
83rd (1953 - 1955)	96	46	48	2		435	213	221	1	
84th (1955 - 1957)	96	48	47	1		435	232	203		
85th (1957 - 1959)	96	49	47			435	234	201		
86th (1959 - 1961)	98	64	34			436[c]	283	153		
87th (1961 - 1963)	100	64	36			437[d]	262	175		
88th (1963 - 1965)	100	67	33			435	258	176		1
89th (1965 - 1967)	100	68	32			435	295	140		
90th (1967 - 1969)	100	64	36			435	246	187		2
91st (1969 - 1971)	100	58	42			435	243	192		
92nd (1971 - 1973)	100	54	44	2		435	255	180		
93rd (1973 - 1975)	100	56	42	2		435	239	192	1	3
94th (1975 - 1977)	100	61	37	2		435	291	144		
95th (1977 - 1979)	100	61	38	1		435	292	143		
96th (1979 - 1981)	100	58	41	1		435	276	157		2
97th (1981 - 1983)	100	46	53	1		435	243	192		
98th (1983 - 1985)	100	46	54			435	268	166	1	
99th (1985 - 1987)	100	47	53			435	252	182		1
100th (1987 - 1989)	100	55	45			435	258	177		
101st (1989 - 1991)	100	55	45			435	259	174		2
102nd (1991 - 1993)	100	56	44			435	267	167	1	
103rd (1993 - 1995)	100	57	43			435	258	176	1	
104th (1995 - 1997)	100	47	53			435	204	230	1	
105th (1997 - 1999)	100	45	55			435	207	227	1	
106th (1999 - 2001)	100	45	55			435	211	223	1	
107th (2001 - 2003)	100	50	50			435	211	221	2	1
108th (2003 - 2005)	100	48	51	1		435	205	229	1	
109th (2005 - 2007)	100	44	55	1		435	201	232	1	1
110th (2007 - 2009)	100	49	49	2		435	233	202		
111th (2009 - 2011)	100	55	41	2	1	435	256	178		1
112th (2011 - 2013)	100	51	47	2		435	193	242		
113th (2013 - 2015)	100	53	45	2		435	200	233		
114th (2015 - 2017)	100	44	54	2		435	188	247		
115th (2017 - 2019)	100	46	52	2		435	194	241		
116th (2019 - 2021)	100	45	53	2		434[e]	235	199		1
117th[f] (2021 - 2023)	100	48	50	2		433	222	211		2

Supplemental Text:

1-1 Apportionment of Congressional Seats, by Region and State, 1910-2010 (435 seats)

a. New Mexico became a state in 1912; in 1910 it had a nonvoting delegate in Congress.
b. Alaska became a state on January 3, 1959. In 1950 Alaska had a nonvoting delegate in Congress, making the total for that year 437; subsequent reapportionment reduced the total to 435.
c. Hawaii became a state on August 21, 1959. In 1950 Hawaii had a nonvoting delegate in Congress, making the total for that year 437; subsequent reapportionment reduced the total to 435.

Source: Congressional Quarterly's Guide to U.S. Elections (Washington, D.C.: Congressional Quarterly, various editions); Congressional Quarterly Weekly Report, various issues; U.S. Census data 2000, www.census.gov.

1-2 Democratic Party Strength in the House, by Region, 69th-117th Congresses, 1925-2021

Note: Figures represent the makeup of Congress on the first day of the session. Does not include independents. Seats is the total number of seats in each region, not the seats held by Democrats in each region.

a. J. Edward Roush (D-IN) was not sworn in until June 14, 1961 due to a disputed election result.
b. Alaska was admitted as a state in 1958 and Hawaii in 1959. There were 437 representatives elected in 1960, both included in the Pacific Coast row.
c. Hale Boggs (D-LA) was elected posthumously.
d. George Collins (D-IL) was elected in 1972 but died before being sworn into office.
e. Nicholas Begich (D-AK) was elected posthumously.
f. William Steiger (R-WI) was elected in 1978 but died before being sworn into office.
g. Leo Ryan (D-CA) was elected in 1978 but died before being sworn into office.
h. William Nichols (D-AL) was elected in 1988 but died before being sworn into office.
i. Daniel Coats (R-IN) won reelection in 1988 but was appointed to Dan Quayle's Senate seat on December 12, 1988.
j. Newt Gingrich (R-GA) was elected in 1998, but resigned from his seat before being sworn in.
k. Julian Dixon (D-CA) was elected in 2000 but died before being sworn into office.
l. Kirsten E. Gillibrand resigned to replace Hillary Clinton in the Senate on January 26, 2009, but was still present at the first session.
m. Rahm Emanuel resigned his seat to enter the Obama administration.
n. Nevada's Second District is vacant as August 21, 2012. It was formerly held by Dean Heller (R).
o. Ohio's Eighth District is vacant as of October 31, 2015. Vacancy due to the resignation of John A. Boehner (R).

Source: Congressional Directory, various editions; Congressional Quarterly Weekly Report, various issues; Clerk of the U.S. House of Representatives, http://clerk.house.gov; The Almanac of American Politics (Washington, D.C.: National Journal Group, various editions).

1-3 Democratic and Republican Seats in the House, by Region, 69th-117th Congresses, 1925-2021

Note: D indicates Democrats; R indicates Republicans. Third parties are omitted. Figures represent the makeup of Congress on the first day of the session.

a. Excludes South Carolina's 1st District - Tim Scott vacated the seat prior to the start of the 113th Congress after being appointed to the Senate and Mark Sanford did not assume office until May 7, 2013.
b. Excludes Illinois's 2nd District - Jesse Jackson Jr. resigned on November 21, 2012 and Robin Kelly did not assume office until April 11, 2013.
c. Excludes Illinois's 5th District - Rahm Emanuel resigned to become White House Chief of Staff and Mike Quigley did not assume office until April 7, 2009.

Source: Congressional Directory, various editions; Congressional Quarterly Weekly Report, various issues; Clerk of the U.S. House of Representatives, http://clerk.house.gov; The Almanac of American Politics (Washington, D.C.: National Journal Group, various editions).

1-4 Democratic Party Strength in the Senate, by Region, 69th-117th Congresses, 1925-2021

Note: Figures represent the makeup of Congress on the first day of the session. Third parties are omitted. Seats is the total number of seats in each region, not the seats held by Democrats in each region.

a. Excludes Richard Shelby (AL) who switched from the Democratic to the Republican Party on the day following the election and before the beginning of the 104th Congress (1995).
b. Vital Statistics collects information on member demographics as of the first day of the Congress. For the 117th Congress, we include both Jon Ossoff and Raphael Warnock, who were elected on January 5, 2021, and Kamala Harris, who did not resign from office until January 18th, 2021.

Source: Congressional Directory, various editions; Congressional Quarterly Weekly Report, various issues; US Senate, http://www.senate.gov; The Almanac of American Politics (Washington, D.C.: National Journal Group, various editions).

1-5 Democratic and Republican Seats in the Senate, by Region, 69th-117th Congresses, 1925-2021

Note: D indicates Democrats; R indicates Republicans. Third parties are omitted. Figures represent the makeup of Congress on the first day of the session.

a. Includes Richard Shelby (AL) who switched from the Democratic to the Republican Party on the day following the election and before the beginning of the 104th Congress.
b. Excludes Barack Obama (D-IL) who resigned from office prior to the beginning of the 111th Congress.
c. Excludes Al Franken (D-MN) who was not sworn in until July 7, 2009.
d. Vital Statistics collects information on member demographics as of the first day of the Congress. For the 117th Congress, we include both Jon Ossoff and Raphael Warnock, who were elected on January 5, 2021, and Kamala Harris, who did not resign from office until January 18th, 2021.

Source: Congresional Directory, various editions; Congressional Quarterly Weekly Report, various issues; US Senate, http://www.senate.gov; The Almanac of American Politics (Washington, D.C.: National Journal Group, various editions).

1-16 African Americans in Congress, 41st-117th Congresses, 1869-2021

Note: The data do not include nonvoting delegates or commissioners. Figures represent the makeup of Congress on the first day of the session.

a. After the 56th Congress, there were no African American members in either the House or Senate until the 71st Congress.
b. Roland Burris was not seated on the first day of the 111th session.
c. Tim Scott, who was appointed on December 17th to replace outgoing Senator Jim DeMint, is included in the Senate totals.
d. Vital Statistics collects information on member demographics as of the first day of the Congress. For the 117th Congress, we include both Jon Ossoff and Raphael Warnock, who were elected on January 5, 2021, and Kamala Harris, who did not resign from office until January 18th, 2021.

Source: Black Americans in Congress, 1870-1977, H. Doc. 95-258, 95th Cong., 1st sess., 1977; Congressional Quarterly Almanac (Washington, D.C.: Congressional Quarterly, various editions); Congressional Quarterly Weekly Report, various issues; Clerk of the U.S. House of Representatives, http://clerk.house.gov; "Membership of the 114th Congress: A Profile," Congressional Research Service

1-17 Asian Americans in Congress, 58th-117th Congresses, 1903-2021

Note: The data do not include nonvoting delegates or commissioners. Figures represent the makeup of Congress on the first day of the session.

a. Vital Statistics collects information on member demographics as of the first day of the Congress. For the 117th Congress, we include both Jon Ossoff and Raphael Warnock, who were elected on January 5, 2021, and Kamala Harris, who did not resign from office until January 18th, 2021.

Source: "Asian Pacific Americans in the United States Congress;" "Membership of the 114th Congress: A Profile", Congressional Research Service

1-18 Hispanic Americans in Congress, 41st-117th Congresses, 1869-2021

Note: The data do not include nonvoting delegates or commissioners. Figures represent the makeup of Congress on the first day of the session.

a. Vital Statistics collects information on member demographics as of the first day of the Congress. For the 117th Congress, we include both Jon Ossoff and Raphael Warnock, who were elected on January 5, 2021, and Kamala Harris, who did not resign from office until January 18th, 2021.

Source: Biographical Directory of the United States Congress 1774-1989; Congressional Quarterly Almanac (Washington, D.C.: Congressional Quarterly, various editions); Congressional Quarterly Weekly Report, various issues; Clerk of the U.S. House of Representatives, http://clerk.house.gov; http://www.senate.gov/galleries/daily/minority.htm; "Membership of the 114th Congress: A Profile", Congressional Research Service

1-19 Women in Congress, 65th-117th Congresses, 1917-2021

Note: The data include only women who were sworn in as members and served more than one day. Figures represent the makeup of Congress on the first day of the session.

a. Vital Statistics collects information on member demographics as of the first day of the Congress. For the 117th Congress, we include both Jon Ossoff and Raphael Warnock, who were elected on January 5, 2021, and Kamala Harris, who did not resign from office until January 18th, 2021.

Source: Women in Congress, H. Rept. 94-1732, 94th Cong., 2nd sess., 1976; Congressional Quarterly Almanac (Washington, D.C.: Congressional Quarterly, various editions); Congressional Quarterly Weekly Report, various issues; Clerk of the U.S. House of Representatives, http://clerk.house.gov; US Senate, http://www.senate.gov.; "Membership of the 114th Congress: A Profile", Congressional Research Service

1-20 Political Parties of Senators and Representatives, 34th-117th Congresses, 1855-2021

Note: Figures represent the makeup of Congress on the first day of the session.

a. Democrats organized House with help of other parties.
b. Democrats organized House because of Republican deaths.
c. Alaska was admitted as a state in 1958. The total figure includes the addition of Alaska's representative.
d. Alaska was admitted as a state in 1958 and Hawaii in 1959. The total figure includes the addition of Alaska's and Hawaii's representatives.
e. North Carolina's 9th District was not seated at the start of the 116th Congress as the election results had not been certified.
f. Vital Statistics collects information on member demographics as of the first day of the Congress. For the 117th Congress, we include both Jon Ossoff and Raphael Warnock, who were elected on January 5, 2021, and Kamala Harris, who did not resign from office until January 18th, 2021.

Source: Congressional Directory, various editions; Congressional Quarterly Weekly Report, various issues; Clerk of the U.S. House of Representatives, http://clerk.house.gov; US Senate, http://www.senate.gov; The Almanac of American Politics (Washington, D.C.: National Journal Group, various editions).

PROFILE LIST

Sires, Albio 1214-1217
Sisolak, Steve 1135-1137
Slotkin, Elissa 970-972
Smith, Adam 1968-1971
Smith, Adrian 1126-1129
Smith, Chris 1202-1205
Smith, Jason 1088-1090
Smith, Tina 1003-1006
Smucker, Lloyd 1584-1586
Soto, Darren 461-464
Spanberger, Abigail 1913-1916
Spartz, Victoria 695-697
Speier, Jackie 218-221
Stabenow, Debbie 941-945
Stansbury, Melanie 1241-1244
Stanton, Greg 130-131
Stauber, Pete 1026-1029
Steel, Michelle 320-322
Stefanik, Elise 1329-1332
Steil, Bryan 2012-2014
Steube, Greg 484-486
Stevens, Haley 977-980
Stewart, Chris 1854-1857
Stitt, Kevin 1485-1487
Stivers, Steve 1475-1477
Strickland, Marilyn 1971-1973
Sullivan, Daniel 87-90
Sununu, Chris 1161-1163
Suozzi, Thomas 1276-1278
Swalwell, Eric 221-224

T

Takano, Mark 300-302
Taylor, Van 1742-1745
Tenney, Claudia 1332-1334
Tester, Jon 1097-1101
Thompson, Bennie 1044-1047
Thompson, Glenn 1594-1596
Thompson, Mike 188-190
Thune, John 1672-1675
Tiffany, Tom 2028-2030
Tillis, Thom 1361-1365
Timmons, William 1653-1655
Titus, Dina 1144-1147
Tlaib, Rashida 983-986
Tonko, Paul 1326-1329
Toomey, Pat 1552-1556
Torres, Norma 283-286
Torres, Ritchie 1313-1315
Trahan, Lori 912-915
Trone, David 878-880
Tuberville, Tommy 54-56
Turner, Michael 1460-1463

U

Underwood, Lauren 658-660
Upton, Fred 963-967

V

Valadao, David 240-242
Van Drew, Jeff 1197-1200

Van Duyne, Beth 1800-1802
Van Hollen, Chris 857-861
Vargas, Juan 328-330
Veasey, Marc 1825-1828
Vela, Filemon 1828-1831
Velázquez, Nydia 1287-1290

W

Wagner, Ann 1070-1072
Walberg, Tim 967-969
Walorski, Jackie 686-689
Waltz, Michael 452-455
Walz, Tim 995-997
Warner, Mark 1889-1893
Warnock, Raphael 526-529
Warren, Elizabeth 895-900
Wasserman Schultz, Debbie
500-504
Waters, Maxine 306-309
Watson Coleman, Bonnie
1226-1228
Weber, Randy 1772-1775
Webster, Daniel 467-469
Welch, Peter 1879-1880
Wenstrup, Brad 1436-1439
Westerman, Bruce 154-156
Wexton, Jennifer 1922-1924
Whitehouse, Sheldon 1616-1620
Whitmer, Gretchen 939-941
Wicker, Roger 1036-1039
Wild, Susan 1574-1576
Williams, Nikema 539-542
Williams, Roger 1802-1805
Wilson, Frederica 504-507
Wilson, Joe 1647-1650
Wittman, Rob 1897-1900
Wolf, Thomas 1547-1549
Womack, Steve 151-153
Wyden, Ron 1516-1520

Y

Yarmuth, John 780-783
Young, Don 90-93
Young, Todd 677-681

Z

Zeldin, Lee 1271-1273